Abbreviations used in the text 本词典略语表 (详见 liv 页)

abbr	abbreviation	i e	which is to say	prep	preposition(al)
adj, adjj	adjective(s)	illus	illustration	pres p	present participle
adv, advv	adverb(s)	imper	imperative	pres t	present tense
adv part	adverbial particle	impers	impersonal	pron	pronoun
affirm	affirmative(ly)	indef art	indefinite article	pt	past tense
anom fin	anomalous finite	inf	infinitive	RC	Roman Catholic
attrib	attributive(ly)	int	interjection	reflex	reflexive
aux	auxiliary	interr	interrogative	rel	relative
[C]	countable noun	intrans	intransitive	sb	somebody
Cf, cf	compare	Lat	Latin	Scot	Scottish
collect	collective(ly)	Lc	length about	sing	singular
comp	comparative	masc	masculine	sth	something
conj	conjunction	n, nn	noun(s)	suff	suffix
def art	definite article	neg	negative(ly)	superl	superlative
demonstr	demonstrative	opp	opposite	trans	transitive
e g	for example	P	proprietary name	[U]	uncountable noun
esp	especially	part adj	participial adjective	US	America(n)
etc	and the others	pers	person	usu	usual(ly)
F	French	pers pron	personal pronoun	v, vv	verb(s)
fem	feminine	phr	phrase	[VP]	Verb Pattern
G	German	pl	plural	vi	verb intransitive
GB	British Britain	poss	possessive	vt	verb transitive
Gk	Greek	pp	past participle	⇨	look at
Hc	height about	pred	predicative(ly)	♂	male
I	Italian	pref	prefix	♀	female

Specialist English registers
专门名词

accounts
aerospace
algebra(alg)
anatomy(anat)
architecture(archit)
arithmetic(arith)
art
astronomy(astron)
ballet
biblical
biology(biol)
book-keeping
botany(bot)
business
chemistry(chem)
cinema
commerce(comm)
computers(comp)
cricket
ecclesiastical(eccles)
engineering(eng)
electricity(electr)
farming
finance(fin)
football
gambling
geology(geol)
geometry(geom)
grammar(gram)

history(hist)
journalism
legal
linguistics(ling)
mathematics(maths)
mechanics(mech)
medical(med)
meteorology(met)
military(mil)
music
mythology(myth)
nautical(naut)
pathology(path)
philosophy(phil)
phonetics(phon)
photography(photo)
physics(phys)
physiology(physiol)
politics(pol)
psychology(psych)
racing
radio telegraphy(radio)
rugby
science
sport
tennis
theatre
trigonometry(trig)
zoology(zool)

Stylistic values
字格标准

archaic
colloquial(colloq)
dated
derogatory(derog)
dialect(dial)
emotive(emot)
emphatic(emph)
euphemistic(euphem)
facetious(facet)
figurative(fig)
formal
humorous(hum)
ironical(ironic)
jocular(joc)
laudatory(laud)
literary(liter)
literally(lit)
modern use(mod use)
old use
pejorative(pej)
poetic(poet)
proverb(prov)
rare
rhetorical(rhet)
slang(sl)

牛津现代高级英汉双解词典

Oxford Advanced Learner's
English–Chinese Dictionary

第三版(简化汉字本)

Third Edition (Simplified Characters)

原 著

A S Hornby

Oxford University Press

Hong Kong

商务印书馆

北 京

English text originally published as *Oxford Advanced Learner's Dictionary of Current English* by Oxford University Press © Oxford University Press 1948, 1964, 1974, 1980.

Chinese text originally published (using Orthodox characters) as *Oxford Advanced Learner's Dictionary of Current English with Chinese Translation* by Oxford University Press © Oxford University Press 1970, 1984

Copyright in this dictionary © Oxford University Press 1988, 1989
First published 1988
Fourth impression 1990

英语版©牛津大学出版社 1948, 1964, 1974, 1980
英汉版(繁体字本)©牛津大学出版社 1970, 1984
英汉版(简化汉字本)©牛津大学出版社 1988
第一次印刷 1988
第四次印刷 1990

ISBN 0 19 583954 4 （paperback 平装版）
ISBN 0 19 583919 6 （hardback 精装版）

Oxford is a trade mark of Oxford University Press

Published by Oxford University Press, Warwick House, Quarry Bay, Hong Kong, and The Commercial Press, 36 Wang Fu Jing Street, Beijing. Distributed outside China by Oxford University Press, Hong Kong.

本词典由香港鲗鱼涌和域大厦牛津大学出版社暨北京王府井大街36号商务印书馆出版。香港牛津大学出版社并为中国以外总发行。

洛德加印刷公司（香港承印）
Printed in Hong Kong by Nordica Printing Company

Contents 目录

page 页码

Key to the phonetic symbols 音标例释   封面内页
Abbreviations used in the text 本词典略语表   封面内页
Key to the verb patterns 动词类型例释   封底内页
出版说明   iii
Contributors 编辑人员   v
Acknowledgements 志谢   v
General preface 总序   vi
Preface to the phonetic information 发音说明   vi
Key to the entries 词条例释   viii

Introduction 绪论
    Using the Dictionary 本词典用法说明   xii
    Finding words and meanings 查单词和词义   xiv
    Writing English 写英文   xx
    Speaking English 说英语   xxiii
    Grammar 语法   xxviii
    Style 字格   xxx

Verb patterns 动词类型   xxxiii
Anomalous verbs 变态动词   xlix
Strong and weak forms 强式和弱式   xlix
Contractions 缩写式   li
Key to the phonetic symbols 音标例释   liii
Abbreviations used in the text 本词典略语表   liv

THE DICTIONARY 本词典正文   1—1343

Appendices 附录
    1 Irregular verbs 不规则动词表   1344
    2 Common abbreviations 通用略语   1348
    3 Affixes (prefixes and suffixes) 词缀(前缀和后缀)   1353
    4 Numerical expressions 数字表达法   1358
    5 Weights and measures 度量衡表   1365
    6 Geographical names 地名   1369
    7 Common forenames 常见的名字   1385
    8 Shakespeare's works 莎士比亚的作品   1389
    9 Punctuation 标点使用法   1390
    10 Books of the Bible 圣经目录   1395

牛津现代高级英汉双解词典

（简化汉字本）

出 版 说 明

本书由 牛津大学出版社和商务印书馆 合作出版。原书由 牛津大学出版社提供，书名是《牛津现代高级英汉双解辞典》(Oxford Advanced Learner's Dictionary of Current English with Chinese Translation) (英文版第三版；英汉双解版 (繁体字本，1984 年)，主编张芳杰，编辑刘锡炳、林炳铮、滕以鲁、陈永昭、张先信。

该词典英文版自问世以来，曾先后三次修订，第三版不仅增加了大量语文方面的新词新义，还增收了若干科技方面的新词，为学习英语者所熟悉，风行世界，其英汉双解版备受读者欢迎。现将英汉版改用简体字出版，以便更加有助于海内外广大读者使用。

根据双方协议，商务印书馆对原书作了少量的修订：对某些词语作了删改，修改了某些科技名词、人地名等的汉译，或保留原译，增加了通用译法。

商务印书馆
1987 年 2 月

Contributors

General Editor
A S Hornby
with
A P Cowie

Pronunciation

Professor A C Gimson
Dr S M Ramsaran

Specialist Editors

Dr L Todd
S Murison-Bowie

Illustrations

Roger Gorringe
Carl James
Richard Lewington
Sean Milne
Colin Newman
Vyvyan Thomas
David Woodroffe

Acknowledgements

I continue to be indebted to correspondents in many parts of the world for calling attention to occasional misprints and errors, and for suggestions on possible additions. These suggestions have been carefully considered and acted on where I felt in agreement with them.

Professor V Gatenby and Mr H Wakefield shared the work of compiling the first edition (1942). The value of their contributions remains, although these were extensively revised and added to in the second edition (1963) and in this third edition.

I pay tribute to the editors of the English Language Teaching Department of the Oxford University Press, especially Christina Ruse and Jonathan Price, and to the staff of the computer type-setting section, for their work on the text of this edition.

A S HORNBY

General preface

This is a completely revised, up-dated and re-set impression of the third edition.

It combines the traditions of the Oxford Dictionaries with the language-teaching skills of A S Hornby. It provides the student or teacher of the English language with the most practically useful and comprehensive record of the language as it is spoken and written today.

There are four new features of this revised impression:

1 A simple but detailed *Introduction*, which not only explains what is in the Dictionary, but also suggests how the Dictionary can be used.

2 A phonetic interpretation and transcription by Professor A C Gimson, editor of the *English Pronouncing Dictionary*.

3 An Appendix on *Punctuation*, explaining how all the English punctuation marks are used.

4 A *Key to the verb patterns* inside the back cover, for constant easy reference.

Preface to the phonetic information

In this revised impression, the representation of pronunciation differs somewhat from that shown previously. The phonetic notation now conforms to that to be found in the majority of important English dictionaries used by non-native learners of English, and in particular to the latest (14th) edition of the *English Pronouncing Dictionary* (Dent, 1977). As a consequence, the length mark associated with certain vowels has been restored, though in strict phonological terms this mark may be considered redundant if the chosen vowel symbols distinguish qualitative differences. Nevertheless, the reactions of users of the Dictionary have suggested that an indication of length is widely held to be pedagogically useful, there being many occasions when quantitative as well as qualitative features provide significant cues to meaning. In addition, the simple vertical primary stress mark has been restored in place of the previous slanting mark, which was judged by many to be too readily suggestive of a specific tone.

The pronunciations recommended differ little from those shown previously. However, certain highly-elided forms have been replaced by others of a more careful style, judged to be more useful for even the advanced learner of English. Similarly, the marking of syllabic consonants in non-final positions has been abandoned, an expanded solution involving the insertion of a weak vowel being preferred.

The task of making these and other changes has been shared between my colleague Dr S M Ramsaran and myself.

A C GIMSON
University College London

志　谢

世界许多地区的读者，曾致书指出本词典偶有印刷错误和疏漏之处，并建议可能增添之处，谨此仍旧向他们表示谢意。他们的建议均经过审慎考虑，其中本人同意之处，均已按照建议处理。

盖登贝教授与威克斐尔德先生都曾分担第一版(1942)的编辑工作。本词典虽经第二版(1963)以及本版(第三版)大幅度的修订和增添，他俩宝贵的贡献依然存在。

为本版之问世，我很感谢牛津大学出版社英语教学部的编辑，特别是克丽丝蒂娜·露丝和詹纳桑·普莱斯以及电脑排版部的工作同仁。

郝恩贝

总　序

这是一部经完全修订后，最新的、重新排版过的第三版词典。本词典兼容牛津词典的传统及郝恩贝先生之语言教学技巧，可提供英语教学的学生或教师最实用的、综合性的今日英语说和写的记录。

本修订版本有四种特色：

一、简明而详尽的说明，不仅说明本词典的内容，并且指出其用途。

二、由"英语发音字典"编辑吉慕生教授作发音上的说明及注音。

三、附录标点使用法，说明所有英文标点符号之用途。

四、封底内页备有"动词类型例释"，以便易于经常参考。

发 音 说 明

本修订版中读音的表示与以往者略有不同。其发音符号与非以英语为母语的外国学习者使用的大多数重要英语词典一致，尤其符合最新版(十四版)的"英语发音字典"(Dent, 1977)。因此，我们又采用了与某些元音有关的长音符号，尽管就严格的语音学观点而言，如果这些元音符号辨别音质方面之不同时，此种长音符号可能被认为冗赘。虽然如此，本词典读者的反应建议中，曾提出长音符号在教学上普遍被认为是有用的，因为在许多情况中，音量和音质的特色表示对字义有不同的提示。此外，我们又恢复了简单的垂直重音符号，以代替以前使用的斜线重音符号，由于许多人觉得斜线重音符号极易被视作表示一特殊的音调。

本版采用的发音方法则无异于以往。虽然如此，鉴于对甚至高级的学习者都比较有用，某些常被省略元音或音节的形式已由经过更审慎处理后的形式代替。同样的，不是位于词尾的音节辅音符号亦被废除，整个的解决办法是插入一弱元音代替。

以上修订工作以及其他变更皆由我的同事罗慕兰博士和我共同担任。

吉姆逊
伦敦大学

Key to entries 词条例释

bal·lad /'bæləd/ *n* simple song or poem, esp one that tells an old story.

headword with pronunciation
词目及其发音

simple definition
简单的定义

both¹ /bəʊθ/ *adj* (of two things, person, etc) the two; the one and also the other; (*both* precedes the *def art.* demonstrative *adjj*, possessives, and other): *I want ~ books/the books/these books. I saw him on ~ occasions. Hold it in ~ (your) hands.*

examples of different uses of the headword
词目不同用法举例

can² /kən; *strong form*: kæn/ *anom fin* .... The strong forms are used): *What ˌcan he 'mean? What ˌcan we 'do about it? Where ˌcan they have 'got to?*

example sentences showing stress patterns
表示重音的例句

disc, disk /dɪsk/ *n* **1** [O] thin, flat, round plate, eg a coin, a gramophone record; round surface that ap-

alternative spelling of the headword
词目不同的拼法

faux pas /ˌfəʊ 'pɑː/ *n* (F) (*pl* unchanged) indiscreet action, remark, etc esp a social blunder.

borrowed foreign phrase, showing pronunciation
外来短语及其发音

gar·age /'gærɑːʒ US: gə'rɑːʒ/ *n* **1** building in which to keep a car or cars. **2** (US= *service station*)

American English pronunciation
美国英语发音

goose /guːs/ *n* (*pl* **geese** /giːs/) **1** water bird larger than a duck; female of this, ⇨ gander;

irregular plural, with pronunciation
不规则的复数及其发音

cross-reference to a related word
参看相关词

viii

hon·our² (US = honor) /'ɒnə(r)/ *vt* [VP6A]
1 respect highly, feel honour for; confer honour on:

American English spelling
美国英语拼法

---

lazy /'leɪzɪ/ *adj* (-ier, -iest) unwilling to work; doing little work; suitable for, causing, inducing, inactivity: *a ~ fellow; a ~ afternoon.* ⇨ idle. '~-bones *n* ~ person.
lazi·ly *adv* **lazi·ness** *n*

comparative and superlative forms of an adjective
形容词的比较级和最高级

compound, with stress pattern
复合词及其重音

---

leap /liːp/ *vi, vt* (*pt, pp* **leapt** /lept/ or **leaped** /liːpt/) **1** [VP2A, C, 3A] jump (*jump* is the usu word);

irregular form of a verb, with pronunciation
动词的不规则变化及其发音

---

li·able /'laɪəbl/ *adj* (usu *pred*) **1** ~ *for,* responsible according to law: *Is a man ~ for his wife's debts in your country?* **2** *be ~ to sth,* be subject to: *If you drive a car to the danger of the public, you make yourself ~ to a heavy fine, or even to imprisonment. He is ~ to seasickness.* **3** *be ~ to do sth,*

special uses of an adjective with a preposition
形容词接介词的特殊用法

---

mean·time /'miːntaɪm/ *adv, n* (*in the*) ~, meanwhile.

special grammatical way in which the headword is used
词目在语法上的特殊用法

---

pave·ment /'peɪvmənt/ *n* **1** (GB) paved way at the side of a street for people on foot (US = *sidewalk*).

where to divide the headword at the end of a line
词目在行尾时应如何分音节

different word used in American English
美国英语用语

ix

people /'piːpl/ *n* [U] (collective, with *pl* *v*. Note that for one human being, it is preferable to use *man*, *woman*, *boy*, *girl* and not *person*, which, although useful in definitions, may be derogatory or formal). **1** persons in general: *streets crowded with* — special note on problems of usage or grammar
用法或语法问题的特殊说明

pres·ent¹ /'preznt/ *adj* **1** being in the place in question: *the Smiths, and other people ~ (= who were ~). Were you ~ at the ceremony? ~ **company excepted**, (colloq) used to show that one's remarks do not apply to anyone who is ~. ⇨ **absent¹(1)**. **2** being discussed or dealt with; now being considered: *in the ~ case*, this case. **3** existing now: *the ~ government*. **4 ~ to**, felt, remembered by: *~ to the mind/ imagination*. **5** (archaic) ready at hand: '*a very ~ help in trouble*'. ☐ *n* **1 the ~**, the ~ time, the time now passing: *the past, the ~*,

— numbered headwords with the same spelling
以号码表示的拼法相同的词目

— stylistic value 字格标准

— cross-reference to a word of opposite meaning
参看反义词

— box to show a change in the part of speech
表示词类变化的方格
— part of speech 词类

pres·ent² /'preznt/ *n* gift: '*birthday ~s; I'm buying it for a ~ (= as a gift), so please wrap it up nicely*.

pre·sent³ /prɪ'zent/ *vt* **1** [VP14, 15A] ~ *sth* **to** *sb*; ~ *sb* **with** *sth*, give, offer; put forward; submit:

— verb patterns 动词类型

run² /rʌn/ *vi, vt* (*pl* **ran** /ræn/, *pp* **run**; **-nn-**) (For special uses and *adverbial particles* and *preps*, ⇨ **26** below; .... **26** [VP2O, 3A, 15B] (special uses with *adverbial particles* and *preps*):

— doubling of consonant 辅音重复

run across, pay a short informal visit: *run across to a neighbour's flat to borrow some sugar*. **run across sb/sth,** meet or find by chance: *I ran across my old friend Jean in Paris last week*.

run after sb/sth, (a) try to catch: *The dog was running after a rabbit*. (b) seek the society of; go after in order to get the attention of: *She runs after every good-looking man in the village*.

run against sb, compete with him by

— special uses of a verb with adverbial particles and prepositions
动词与副词性小品词及介词连用的特殊用法

running in a race; (esp US) compete with him (for an elected office).

shot[1] /ʃɒt/ n **1** [C] (sound of the) firing of a gun, etc; *hear~s in the distance*; ....

.... **a 'long ~,** an attempt to solve a problem, etc with little evidence, few facts to go on: *It's a long ~ but I think John must have known about the murder.* **,not by a 'long ~,** not even if circumstances were most favourable. **3** [C]

— idioms, showing stress patterns
成语及其重音类型

tibia / 'tɪbɪə / n (pl ~e/-briː/) (anat) shin-bone; inner and thicker of the two bones between the knee and the foot. ⇨ the illus at **skeleton**.

— specialist English usage
专门用语

— cross-reference to an illustration
参看插图

vi·ol·ate /'vaɪəleɪt/ vt [VP6A] **1** break (an oath, a treaty, etc); act contrary to (what one's conscience tells one to do, etc). **2** act towards (a sacred place, sb's seclusion, etc) without proper respect: *~ sb's privacy.* **3** rape. **vi·ol·ation** / ,vaɪə'leɪʃn / n [U] violating or being ~d: *act in violation of a treaty*; [C] instance of this: *violations of the rights of the citizens / the right of free speech,* etc.

— derivative, with pronunciation
派生词及其发音

— uncountable and countable uses of the noun
名词的可数与不可数用法

Using the Dictionary
本词典用法说明

This is a Dictionary that has been specially prepared for the learner of the English language. All its parts have been designed and put together to give the learner the most *practical* help in developing the three language skills: speaking, writing, and reading.

本词典特为学习英语者所编。各部分皆经设计和安排, 在培养说、写、读三种语言技能上, 给予学习者最实用的协助。

This is a Dictionary for the learner of English who has mastered the rules of English grammar and pronunciation, 'and has acquired a vocabulary that enables him to read and understand English of moderate difficulty. It is for the learner who wants to develop further his knowledge of how English words, compounds, and idiomatic expressions are used, what they mean, how they are pronounced, and how they are spelt.

使用本词典者应已熟谙英语语法和读法的规则, 并已掌握一部分词汇, 在阅读和了解英语方面不太感到困难。 本词典可供学习者进一步了解英语单词、复合词以及成语的用法、意义、读法和拼法。

The Introduction 绪论

The Introduction has 3 aspects. 绪论包括二方面。

1 It explains, in simple, clear language, all the different parts that go to make up the entries for the words in the Dictionary. It also contains examples of all these different parts of a dictionary entry.

以简易明晰的语言说明构成本词典所列各词目之不同部分, 并包含一个词目所有不同部分的例子。

2 It contains useful information about *spelling* (for example, how to spell the plurals of nouns), about *pronunciation* (for example, how to pronounce the inflections of nouns, verbs and adjectives), about *grammar* (for example, how to use a 'phrasal verb' like **take off**) and about *style* (for example, how to use idioms and proverbs).

包括拼法(如名词复数形式的拼法)、发音(如名词、动词及形容词语尾变化的读法)、语法(例如象 take off 等动词短语的用法)、以及字格(如成语和谚语的用法)等有用的说明。

3 It has 4 important lists, which the learner will find constantly useful: (i) Verb patterns (p xxxiii); (ii) The forms of the anomalous verbs (*eg can, could*) (p xlix); (iii) The strong and weak spoken forms of common words (*eg and, from*) (p xlix); (iv) The written and spoken forms of the common English contractions (*eg we're, wasn't*) (p li).

包括四种重要的表, 学习者随时都会发现它们很有用处: (i)动词类型(xxxiii页); (ii)变态动词(如 can, could)的形式(xlix页); (iii)常用词(如 and, from)的强弱读法(xlix页); (iv)常用英语缩写式(如 we're, wasn't)的写法和读法(li页)。

The Dictionary 本词典

This is a Dictionary of the English Language as it is written and spoken today by educated British men and women. It lists words, compound words and idiomatic expressions that the learner is likely to come across in everyday English speech, in official and informal writing, and in the literature of the 20th and 19th centuries. For all the listed items there is information on (i) spelling, (ii) pronunciation, (iii) grammatical use, (iv) meaning (or meanings). In addition, there are examples showing their use in current English. Guidance

is also given, wherever necessary or helpful, on difficult points of meaning, spelling and pronunciation. All special American English spellings and pronunciations are given.

本词典中的英语为今日英国受过教育的男女所写和说者。本词典所列之单词、复合词及成语,学习者很可能在日常的谈话,正式或非正式的写作以及二十世纪和十九世纪的文学作品中接触到。对于所列各词目,在拼法、发音、语法、意义等方面均有所说明。此外,尚有例句说明它们在当代英语中的用法。有必要或帮助时,凡是在词义、拼法和发音方面比较困难的地方也有所指引。 美国英语的待殊拼法和发音均一一列出。

The Illustrations 插图

There are a large number of illustrations, because a drawing is often a more useful way of showing a meaning than a written explanation. Many of these illustrations are found in groups, for example, *insects, wild cats* and *flowers*. Others are of systems that have many related parts, for example, *the respiratory system, the eye, the motor-car, football*. The learner is guided by a cross-reference from a word that is illustrated to the page where the illustration is found.

由于图画往往较文字解释更能表示一意义,本词典备有大量插图。 这些插图有很多是成类出现的,例如 insects, wild cats 及 flowers 的插图。有些插图表明具有许多相关部分的某些系统, 例如 the respiratory system, the eye, the motorcar, football 的插图。学习者可自一词之参看部分找出插图之所在。

The Appendices 附录

There are 10 Appendices at the end of the book, containing useful information for the learner of English. There are 3 that the learner is particularly recommended to use:

本词典末尾有十个附录, 供给学习英语者有用的知识。 其中有三个特别介绍给学习者使用:

Appendix 3 *Affixes*. These are the small items of the language that are used to build up many English words. They are divided into *prefixes*, which come at the beginning of a word (for example *ex-, extra-,* and *under-,* as in *ex-president, extra-thin,* and *underestimate*), and *suffixes,* which come at the end of a word (for example *-ee, -ish, -ize,* as in *employee, childish* and *criticize*). Notes on how these affixes are used to form words, their pronunciations, and examples of their use, are also given.

附录三词级。 词级是英语中形成许多英语单词的小项目,分作前级(例如 expresident, extra-thin 和 underestimate 中之 ex-, extra- 和 under-)及后级(例如 employee, childish 和 criticize 中之 -ee, -ish, -ize)。有关词级之构成单词,读音及用法举例均有注明。

Appendix 4 *Numerical Expressions*. This is a unique and comprehensive guide on how to use numbers and expressions that contain numbers. For example, there are sections on how to express *distance, temperature, sports scores, the time, the date, amounts of money* and *telephone numbers*. Notes on pronunciation, and many examples of usage, are also given.

附录四数字表达法。 本附录为一独特的综合性指南,说明如何表达数字和含有数字的词句。比方说, 本附录各部分分别说明如何表达距离、温度、运动分数、时间、日期、金钱数量以及电话号码等。读音与许多用法的实例也都列出来了。

Appendix 9 *Punctuation*. This is a detailed guide, with examples, on how to use all the English punctuation marks, for example *the comma, the colon, quotation marks, parentheses, the apostrophe*. There are also sections on the punctuation of *Abbreviations, Conversation, Quotations* and *Letters*.

附录九标点使用法。本附录对英语标点符号如逗点、冒号、引号、圆括弧、省略或所有格符号等的用法举实例详加说明。此外,尚有关于略语、会话、引句、书信等项目的标点用法的说明。

finding words and meanings

How is this Dictionary to be used?
本词典的用途

There are two chief ways in which the Dictionary can be used.

本词典有两种主要用途。

1 It can be used to help the learner *understand* the meanings of words, compounds and idioms, when he meets them for the first time in spoken or written English.

用以帮助学习者初次听到或看到某些单词、复合词及成语时了解它们的意思。

2 It can also help the learner to *use* words correctly in sentences of his own, (i) by giving their spelling and pronunciation, (ii) by showing their grammatical patterns and forms, (iii) by indicating (through examples) the contexts in which they are generally used.

也可帮助学习者造句时借下列三种方式正确运用字词: (i)表示拼法和读音,(ii)表明语法的型式,(iii)(以例句)表明字词在上下文中一般的用法。

If this *Introduction* is carefully studied, the user will come to understand the many different features of English words which are covered in the Dictionary. He will then be able to use the Dictionary regularly and successfully in reading, writing and speaking English.

使用者如能仔细阅读本绪论,将会了解本词典内英语词的许多不同特色,进而能在读、写、说英语方面经常和成功地使用本词典。

The user of the Dictionary should also work carfully through the companion Practice Book, *Use Your Dictionary*. By doing all the exercises in *Use Your Dictionary*, the learner will increase his understanding of what is contained in the Dictionary, and of how it can be fully used.

本词典的使用者亦应仔细阅读另一手册'利用你的词典'。在把'利用你的词典'中所有的练习做完后,将会进一步了解本词典的内容以及如何充分予以利用。

Finding words and meanings
查单词和词义

A headword 词目

How to find a word in the Dictionary
如何查单词

In the Dictionary the words explained are arranged in alphabetical order and printed in **bold** type. They are called *headwords*. The information explaining the meanings and uses of a headword is called an *entry*. Sometimes two or more headwords have the same spelling. These are numbered, for example **die¹, die²**. These headwords have the same spelling but they either have different meanings or they are different parts of speech.

本词典所解释的词均按照字母顺序排列,并以黑体字排印,这些词称作词目。 对词目的意义和用法所作的解释称作词条。有时两个或两个以上的词目拼法一样,它们均标有号码,例如die¹, die²。这些词目虽然拼法相同,但不是含义不同,便是属于不同的词类。

When you meet a word for the first time, in a book or paper, you will often find that its spelling is not the same as the headword to which it belongs, and which you need to refer to. This may be because it is the plural form of a *noun* (for example, *boxes, oxen, phenomena*). In the case of these three examples, the headword that you need to look up is the singular form of the nouns (**box, ox, phenomenon**) and you should refer to that. Note, however, that when a plural is very irregular (for example *brethren*), it will have an entry of its own.

当你在书籍或文件中初次遇到一词时,你时常会发现它的拼法与其所属而且是你需要参考的词目不同。这种情形可能因为它是一个名词的复数式(如 boxes, oxen, phenomena)。在上述三例中,你需要查阅的词目应是那些名词的单数式(box, ox, phenomenon)。但是要注意,当一复数式很不规则时(如 brethren),它会单独列为一个词条。

Sometimes, too, you will meet the irregular past tense or past participle

forms of *verbs* (for example *sprang, sprung,* or *bore, borne,* or *spoke, spoken*). In all these cases, the headwords are the infinitives (**spring, bear, speak**), and those are the words to look up. To help you, though, the Dictionary has special entries for all of the irregular forms *sprang, sprung,* etc and these refer you to the full entries for the verbs:

有时你也会遇到动词不规则的过去式或过去分词（例如 sprang, sprung, 或 bore, borne, 或 spoke, spoken）。在这种情况下，词目为不定式（spring, bear, speak），亦即需要查阅者。不过，为帮助学习者起见，本词典特地将 sprang, sprung 等不规则的动词形式列为词条，并说明应该参考的不定式词条：

sprang... *pt* of **spring**³.
sprung... *pp* of **spring**³.

Note, too, that if you meet the comparative (*faster*) or superlative (*fastest*) of an adjective (here, *fast*), it is the headword **fast** that you must refer to. Once again, irregular forms, such as *better* or *best*, have their own entries.

另外亦请注意，如果遇到形容词（如 fast）的比较级（faster）或最高级（fastest）时，则必须查词目 fast。此外如 better 或 best 等不规则形式，也都单独列为词条。

A derivative 派生词

A *derivative* is a word formed by adding an ending (called a *suffix*) to a headword, for example *-able, -ness, -ance, -ly, -ment,* as in *acceptable, dryness, acceptance, yearly, amazement.* Derivatives are printed in **bold** type, and are listed alphabetically at the end of an entry. Some may be written ~·**ness**, ~·**ly**, ~·**ment**, etc (where the tilde ~ represents the headword). Others are printed in full because the spelling has changed, for example **amazing, mag·nifi·cence**. (⇨ Appendix 3 for a list and explanation of endings such as *-able, -ness,* etc.)

派生词系由词目加后缀（suffix）而成，例如 acceptable, dryness, acceptance, yearly, amazement 中之 -able, -ness, -ance, -ly, -ment。所有的派生词均以黑体字排印，并按字母顺序排列，置于词条末尾。有些派生词印作 ~·ness，~·ly，~·ment 等（以波浪号 ~ 代表词目）。有些派生词由于拼法改变而整个字印出，例如 amazing, magnificence。（有关 -able, -ness 等词尾的说明，请参看附录三。）

Sometimes a derivative of a word has its own separate entry. This may be because its spelling is very different: compare **adhere** with its derivative **adhesion**. It may also be because its meaning is very different. For example, the derivative **scarcely** has a quite different meaning from that of its parent word **scarce**.

有时一个词的派生词会单独列为一个词条，这可能是因为拼法上有很大的差别：请比较 adhere 及其派生词 adhesion。也可能是因为词义上有很大的差别，譬如派生词 scarcely 与其母词 scarce 的意义就大不相同。

A compound 复合词

A *compound* is a word formed by adding another word to a headword. It is written as one word (**nightdress**), or as two words separated by a hyphen (**night-time**), or as two separate words (**night life**). The same compound may be found, in different books, newspapers, notices etc, written sometimes with a hyphen, sometimes as one word, sometimes as two words. Compare, for example, **head-master, headmaster, head master**. This indicates that there is no general agreement amongst the users of the language about how that compound is written. The form given in the Dictionary is the most common in modern British English usage. Compounds are printed in **bold** type, and are listed alphabetically at the end of an entry, but before derivatives. In the longer entries, they are placed at the end of the numbered sections to whose meanings they are most closely related.

复合词系以词目加另一词而成。有时写成一个词（nightdress）；有时写成两个词，中间以连字符分开（night-time）；有时单独写成两个词（night life）。在不同

的书、报纸、公告等中，同一复合词可能以不同形式出现：有时中间加有连字符，有时写成一个词，有时写成两个词（例如 head-master, headmaster, head master）。这表示英语的使用者对于该复合词的写法意见并不一致。本词典所列的形式为现代英国英语用法中最常见者。复合词系以黑体字印出，并按字母顺序排列于词条末尾，但在派生词之前。在较长的词条中，复合词则排在意义上与其关系最为密切那一项的末尾。

An idiom 成语

An *idiom* (also called an *idiomatic expression*) is a phrase or sentence of two or more words that has a special meaning of its own. Idioms are printed in ***bold italic*** type, and are listed alphabetically at the end of an entry, but before both compounds and derivatives. In the longer entries, they are placed at the end of the numbered sections to whose meanings they are most closely related. To find an idiom, look for it in the entry for the most important word in the phrase or sentence (usually a *noun, verb* or *adjective*). For example, ***pick holes in*** is found in the entry for **hole**; ***get hold of the wrong end of the stick*** is found in the entry for **stick**. (⇨ *Using idiomatic English* on page xxxi of this Introduction.)

成语(亦称惯用语)为本身有其特殊含义且由两个或两个以上的词构成的短语或句子。成语系以黑斜体字排印，依字母顺序排列于词条末尾，但在复合词与派生词之前。在较长的词条中，成语则排在意义上与其关系最密切那一项的末尾。查一个成语时，先找该短语或句子中最重要的一个词(通常为一名词，动词或形容词)，例如 pick holes in 可在 hole 的词条下查出; get hold of the wrong end of the stick 可在 stick 的词条下查出。(请参看本绪论 xxxi 页之'怎样用成语'。)

A verb with a particle or a preposition 与副词性小品词或介词连用的动词

English contains many phrases made up of a *verb* and an *adverbial particle,* for example ***go back, run away, take sth down,*** or of a *verb* and a *preposition,* for example, ***go through sth, run into sb, take after sb.*** Many of these phrases are idiomatic, and are printed and listed in the same way as other idioms.

英语中有许多短语是由动词与副词性小品词组成，如 go back, run away, take sth down,或由动词与介词组成，如 go through sth, run into sb, take after sb。这类短语有很多是习惯用法，它们排印和排列的方式与其他的成语相同。

   In the entries for the very common verbs like **go, make, put, take,** these verbal phrases are all gathered together in alphabetical order at the end of the verb's entry. They are called 'special uses with *adverbial particles* and *prepositions'.* For example, at the end of the entry for the verb **take** you will find ***take after sb, take sth apart, take (away) from sth, take sth back,*** etc. (⇨ *How to use a verb with the correct adverbial particle or preposition* on page xxix of this Introduction.)

在那些很常用的动词如 go, make, put, take 等的词条中，这类动词短语全按字母顺序集中排列在该动词词条的末尾，称作'与副词性小品词和介词连用的特殊用法'。例如在动词 take 这个词条的末尾，你会发现 take after sb, take sth apart, take (away) from sth, take sth back 等。(请参看本绪论 xxix 页之'怎样正确使用与副词性小品词或介词连用的动词'。)

   When you meet a *verb+particle* in speech or writing, it may take one of several forms. Compare *He took down the curtains; He took the curtains down; He took them down.* These are different ways of using ***take sth down*** and this is the phrase you should look up in the Dictionary. On the other hand, *go through John's pockets, go through them* are the two possible ways of using the *verb+preposition* ***go through sth,*** and that is the form which should be looked up.

当你在谈话或写作中遇到'动词＋副词性小品词'时，它可能以不同形式出现。比较 He took down the curtains; He took the curtains down; He took them down。这三个句子便是使用短语 take sth down 的不同方式，这也就是你在本词

典中应该查的短语。在另一方面，go through John's pockets, go through them 便是使用'动词＋介词' go through sth 的两种可能的方式，而 go through sth 就是你应该查的形式。

Definition numbers 定义的编号

How to find the meaning of a word 怎样查词义

Many entries are divided into sections numbered in bold type, i.e. **1, 2, 3, 4** etc. These numbers show the different meanings or usages that the headword has. For example, the verb **decorate** has three meanings: **1** to adorn, to make attractive. **2** to give a building paint, plaster, wallpaper, carpets, etc. **3** to award someone a medal. Definitions are listed in order of meanings from the most common or most simple to the most rare or most complicated.

有许多词条分成若干项，分别用黑体字 **1, 2, 3, 4,** 等予以编号。 这些号码表示词目所具有的各种意义或用法。譬如动词 decorate 有三种意义：**1** 装饰；美化。**2** 装修(房屋)；油漆(房屋)；(给房屋)涂灰泥，糊壁纸，铺地毯等。**3** 授勋；颁奖。各定义系按意义的顺序排列，从最常用或最简单的用法到最少用或最复杂的用法。

If you are faced with **decorate** used with one of these meanings you will want to have some way of deciding which of the numbered definitions is the right one. This is one of those occasions when the *example phrases and sentences* will prove of great value. Suppose that you have this sentence in front of you: *Two airmen were decorated for their heroism*. This will suggest that meaning **3** is the right one, as the sentence closely resembles the example provided in the entry: *Several soldiers were decorated for bravery*. It is by matching the sentence you have with the example sentences in the Dictionary entry that you are able to decide which definition is the right one.

当你碰到 decorate 一词用到其中的一种意义时，你会希望有某种方法来决定在那些编号的定义中，哪一个最合适。这正是本词典所收例句极具价值的时候。假若你面前有这样一个句子：Two airmen were decorated for their heroism, 这个句子将提醒你第 3 义最合适，因为它和词条中的例句 Several soldiers were decorated for bravery 很相近。唯有将你面前的句子和本词典词条中的例句相配，你才能够决定哪一个定义最合适。

Example phrases and sentences 例句

These form a very large and very important part of the Dictionary. They follow the definitions in *italic* type. They are included for 7 reasons.
本词典所收例句占很大篇幅，而且是很重要的一部分。例句都接在定义后面，以斜体排印。本词典所收例句，有七项理由：

1 They show how the headword, derivative, compound or idiomatic expression is used in different sentence patterns.
表示词目、派生词、复合词或成语如何用于不同的句型中。

2 They show the kinds of style or context in which the word or phrase is usually used. They include the words or sorts of words that the headword is usually used with. For example, at **sensational(2)** there is *a sensational writer/newspaper*; at **sense(4)** there is *have no sense of shame*; *a sense of one's own importance/responsibility*.
表明词或短语通常所用的各种文体或上下文。并且举出通常与词目用在一起的各类字词。例如，在 sensation 的第 2 义有 a sensational writer／newspaper 一例；在 sense 的第 4 义有 have no sense of shame; a sense of one's own importance／responsibility 等例。

3 They often include information on where to put the stress when using the headword in a phrase or sentence. For example, at **failure(3)** there is *'heart failure; 'engine failures*.
时常标明词目用在短语或句中时重音的所在，例如 failure 第 3 义中之 'heart failure; 'engine failures.

4 They teach the writing conventions of correct punctuation and the use of capital letters, because many of the examples are full, correctly written and

punctuated sentences.
教导如何使用正确标点和大写字母等写作常规，因为许多例句皆为完整且有正确标点的句子。

5 They help you to decide whether you have found the correct definition.
帮助读者决定是否已经找到正确的定义。

6 They help you to check that you have understood the meaning of the word or phrase.
帮助读者核对是否已经了解某词或短语的意义。

7 They help you to make your own sentences using the word or phrase.
帮助读者利用某词或短语造句。

The large box □
正方格

Many headwords can be used as more than one part of speech. For example, the word **picture** can be used as a *noun* or a *verb*; the word **welcome** as a *noun*, a *verb* or an *adjective*; the word **last**[1] as an *adjective*, an *adverb* or a *noun*. These different sections within an entry are divided from one another by a large box □.

许多词目可用作一种以上的词类，例如 picture 可用作名词或动词；welcome 可用作名词、动词或形容词；last[1] 可用作形容词、副词或名词。一词条下的不同词类系以正方格□彼此隔开。

The small box ▢
长方格

Sometimes a compound or a derivative of a headword can be used as more than one part of speech. For example, in the entry for **white**, the compound word **whitewash** can be used as a *noun* or a *verb*; in the entry for **alcohol**, the derivative **alcoholic** can be used as an *adjective* or a *noun*. These different sections, in the part of an entry that deals with compounds or derivatives, are divided from one another by the small box ▢.

一个词目的复合词或派生词有时可用作一种以上的词类，例如在 white 词条中，复合词 whitewash 可用作名词或动词；在 alcohol 词条中，派生词 alcoholic 可用作形容词或名词。复合词或派生词的不同词类系以长方格 ▢ 彼此隔开。

The tilde ~
波浪号

If a headword has more than three letters, to save space the symbol called the *tilde* ~ is used in place of the letters of the headword in example phrases and sentences, derivatives, compounds and idioms. For example, in the entry for **fresh**, you will find the example phrase ~ **paint**, the derivative ~**·en**, the compound '~·**water**, and the idiom **break ~ ground**. The tilde will be found useful for 2 reasons:

当词目的字母多于三个时，为了节省篇幅，在例句、派生词、复合词及成语中，用一个波浪号~代替词目的字母。例如在 fresh 词条中，你会发现例句 ~ paint, 派生词 ~·en, 复合词 '~·water, 以及成语 break ~ ground 等。有两种理由来说明波浪号的功用：

1 The tilde draws your attention immediately to how the word (or the derivative or compound formed from the word) is used in example phrases and sentences.
波浪号立即引你注意该词（其派生词或复合词）怎样用于例句中。

2 The tilde makes it easy for you to see how an ending is used to form a derivative. For example, at **dull** there is ~·**y**, at **star** there is ~**ry**, at **grit** there is ~**ty**. If the spelling of a headword is changed when forming a derivative, this is shown very clearly because the tilde is *not* used. For example, at **pretty** there is **prettily**.
波浪号可帮助你看出怎样用一个词尾形成一派生词，例如 dull 一词有 ~·y, star 一词有 ~ry, grit 一词有 ~ty。如果词目形成派生词拼法有所改变时，也有十分明显的表示，因为此种情况不用波浪号，而将派生词完全拼出来。例如 pretty 一词有 prettily。

The slant mark ╱
and brackets ( )

The slant mark ╱ is used in example phrases and sentences, compounds and idioms, to show an *alternative* word or phrase. For example, in **as mad as**

斜线和括弧

a March hare／as a hatter, the slant mark means that this idiom can be used in either of the forms *as mad as a March hare* or *as mad as a hatter*.

斜线／用于例句、复合词和成语中,表示另一可选择的词或短语。例如在 as mad as a March hare／as a hatter 中, 斜线表示该成语可作 as mad as a March hare, 亦可作 as mad as a hatter.

Brackets ( ) are used to show an *optional* word or phrase. For example, in *make* **(both)** *ends meet*, the brackets mean that this idiom can be used in either of the forms *make ends meet* or *make both ends meet*.

括弧( )用来表示一个可选择的词或短语。例如在 make (both) ends meet 中, 括弧表示这个成语可作 make ends meet 或 make both ends meet.

Sometimes both the slant and the brackets are used in the same phrase. For example, *on* **(an／the)** *average* means that the forms *on average*, *on an average* or *on the average* can be used.

斜线和括弧有时用于同一短语中。例如 on (an／the) average 则表示 on average, on an average, 或 on the average 皆可用。

When a slant mark or brackets are used in an idiom, it is important to notice that the alternative word shown by the slant, or the optional word shown by the brackets, is the *only* alternative or optional word that may be used in the idiom.

当斜线或括弧用在一个成语中时,千万要注意的是,斜线或括弧所表示的可选择的词,是唯一可用于该成语中另一可选择的词。

The use of the slant mark and of brackets in idioms is very important because it teaches the learner that many English idioms do not have fixed forms, and therefore that many idioms cannot be learnt by heart as one simple unit.

在成语中使用斜线和括弧是十分重要的,因为这可以让学习者知道,有许多英语成语并无固定的形式,故而不能当作一个单纯的单位去默记。

The abbreviations
sb and sth
缩写式 sb 与 sth

The abbreviations *sb* and *sth* are used in idioms. *sb* stands for 'someone', *sth* stands for 'something'. *sb* means that only a word that refers to a *person* can be used in that place in the idiom. *sth* means that only a word that refers to a *thing* (or an *animal*) can be used in that place. *sb／sth* means that a word that refers to either a person or a thing can be used.

缩写式 sb 和 sth 用于成语中。sb 代表 'Someone', sth 代表 'something'。sb 表示在该成语的那个位置只可用一个指人的词, sth 表示那个位置只能用一个指事物(或动物)的词。sb／sth 则表示指人或事物的词都可以用在那个位置。

Cross-references
前后参看

A cross-reference is an item in an entry using the sign ⇨. It is a way of guiding you from one part of the Dictionary to another. There are three sorts of cross-references:

在词条中前后参看系以符号⇨表示, 可引导你参考本词典的另一部分。 前后参看的方式有三种:

1 The first sort guides you to a word or phrase.

第一种是参看一个词或短语。

⇨ **finger** means 'look at the entry for the word **finger**'.

⇨ finger 表示 '参看 finger 词条'。

⇨ **fire¹(6)** means 'look at meaning number 6 in the entry for the word **fire¹**'.

⇨ fire¹(6) 表示 '参看 fire¹ 第 6 义'。

⇨ *first name* at **first¹(2)** means 'look at the compound *first name* at meaning number 2 in the entry for **first¹**'.

⇨ first name at first¹(2) 表示 '参看 first¹ 第 2 义中复合词 first name'。

2 The second sort guides you to an illustration.

第二种是参看一插图。

⇨ the illus at **mouth** means 'look at the illustration that appears with the entry for the word **mouth**'.

⇨ the illus at mouth 表示 '参看 mouth 之插图'。

3 The third sort guides you to one of the 10 Appendices at the back

of the book.

第三种是参看本词典后面十个附录之一。

⇨ **App 9** means 'look at Appendix number 9'.

⇨ **App 9** 表示'参看附录九'。

British and American English

英国与美国英语

Special British or American meanings, or comments on British or American usage, are given using the signs (GB) or (US). For example:

特殊的英国或美国词义，或是对英国或美国用法的说明，均以(英)或(美)表示之。

例如:

check[2]... **5** (US) cheque. (美)支票。

knock sb up, ... (GB colloq) waken or rouse him by knocking at his door. (英口)敲门唤醒某人。

sure ... **3** (colloq, esp US) certainly. (口,尤美)当然。

Writing English
写英文

How to check the spelling of a word
怎样查看一词的拼法

In order to learn how to spell a word you must find it in the Dictionary. It is important to know the alphabet well. You should be able to judge quickly whether any word comes before or after another one. Remember that if the first letters of two words are the same, you must look at the next letters to decide where to find the words in the Dictionary. In **care** and **cart** 'e' comes before 't' in the alphabet, so **care** comes before **cart** in the Dictionary.

为了学习一词的拼法，你必须查阅本词典。重要的是要熟悉字母，你应该能迅速判断某词是在另一词之前或后。 记住如果两个词的前几个字母相同，你必须看后面的字母来决定这两个词在本词典中的位置。 在 care 和 cart 两个词中，按字母顺序 e 在 t 之前，因此在本词典里 care 在 cart 之前。

How to find a word on any page of the Dictionary
怎样在本词典任何一页查单词

To help you quickly find a word in the Dictionary, the *first* and *last* headword are printed together in large bold type in the top left-hand or right-hand corner of that page. These two words are divided by a slant mark, for example **hold/home**. Suppose you want to check the spelling of the word **holiday**. Since it comes alphabetically between **hold** and **home**, immediately you see **hold/home** at the top of the page you know that that is the page where **holiday** is to be found.

为了帮助你在本词典中迅速地找到某词，在每一页的左上角或右上角均以大型黑体字印有该页的第一和最末一个词。 这两个词以斜线分开，例如 hold/home。 假若你要查 holiday 的拼法，由于依照字母顺序它在 hold 与 home 之间，在你一发现页上角的 hold/home，你便知道 holiday 就在这一页。

How to spell the plural of a noun
怎样拼名词的复数

The plural of a noun is formed by adding -*s* to the end of the noun. For example *boat*, plural *boats*; *apple*, plural *apples*; *idea*, plural *ideas*. But if the noun ends in -*s*, -*z*, -*x*, -*ch* or -*sh*, then the plural is formed by adding -*es* to the noun. For example *bus*, plural *buses*; *box*, plural *boxes*; *dish*, plural *dishes*.

名词的复数是由名词词尾加 -s 形成，例如 boat, boats; apple, apples; idea, ideas。 但是当一名词的词尾是 -s, -z, -x, -ch, 或 -sh 时，其复数则由该名词加 -es 而形成，例如 bus, buses; box, boxes; dish, dishes。

How to spell the plural of a noun ending in -y

Nouns ending in -*y*, if the -*y* is preceded by a consonant, form the plural by changing the -*y* into -*ies*. For example *city*, plural *cities*. If the -*y* is preceded by a vowel, the plural is -*ys*. For example *monkey*, plural *monkeys*. This spelling information is given in the Dictionary for all nouns ending in -*y*.

怎样把词尾为 -y 的 **名词拼成复数**	词尾为 -y 的名词, -y 前若为一辅音, 复数将 -y 变作 -ies, 例如 city, cities。-y 前若为元音, 复数为 -ys, 例如 monkey, monkeys。这种拼法用于本词典中所有词尾为 -y 的名词。

How to spell the **plural of a noun** **ending in -o** **怎样把词尾为 -o 的** **名词拼成复数**	Some nouns that end in -o add -s to form the plural. For example *piano*, plural *pianos*. Some add -es to form the plural. For example *tomato*, plural, *tomatoes*. Some add either -s or -es. For example *volcano*, plural *volcanos* or *volcanoes*. This spelling information is given in the Dictionary for all nouns ending in -o. 有些词尾为 -o 的名词, 其复数是加 -s, 例如 piano, pianos。有些加 -es 形成复数, 例如 tomato, tomatoes。还有一些则加 -s 或 -es 均可, 例如 volcano, volcanos 或 volcanoes。这种拼法用于本词典中所有词尾为 -o 的名词。

How to spell the **forms of a verb** **怎样拼动词**	The third person present singular of a verb is formed by adding -s to the end of the verb. For example *fit, it fits*; *write; she writes*; *see, he sees*. But if the verb ends in -s, -z, -x, -ch or -sh, then the third person present singular is formed by adding -es to the verb. For example *miss, she misses*; *mix, it mixes*; *touch, he touches*. 第三人称、现在式、单数的动词需加 -s, 例如 fit, it fits; write, she writes; see, he sees。但是在动词的词尾是 -s, -z, -x, -ch, 或 -sh 时, 第三人称、现在式、单数的动词需加 -es, 例如 miss, she misses; mix, it mixes; touch, he touches。 The past tense and the past participle of a verb are formed by adding -ed to the end of the verb. For example *pull, pulled*; *push, pushed*; *follow, followed*. But if the verb ends in -e or -ee, then the past tense and past participle are formed by adding -d to the end of the verb. For example *smile, smiled*; *agree, agreed*. 动词的过去式和过去分词是在词尾加 -ed 形成, 例如 pull, pulled; push, pushed; follow, followed。但当动词的词尾是 -e 或 -ee 时, 其过去式和过去分词则加 -d 即可, 例如 smile, smiled; agree, agreed。 The present participle of a verb is formed by adding -ing to the end of the verb. For example *think, thinking*; *go, going*; *be, being*; *see, seeing*. But if the verb ends in a 'silent' -e, then the present participle is formed by dropping this -e from the end of the verb and then adding -ing. For example *love, loving*; *owe, owing*; *tire, tiring*. 动词的现在分词是在词尾加 -ing 形成, 例如 think, thinking; go, going; be, being; see, seeing。但当动词词尾的 -e 不发音时, 其现在分词是将 -e 去掉后再加 -ing, 例如 love, loving; owe, owing; tire, tiring。

How to spell the **forms of a verb** **ending in -y** **怎样拼词尾为 -y** **的动词**	Verbs that end in -y form the past tense and the past participle by changing the -y into -ied. For example *carry*, past tense and past participle *carried*. This spelling information is given in the Dictionary for all verbs that end in -y. 词尾为 -y 的动词, 其过去式与过去分词是将 -y 变作 -ied, 例如 carry, 其过去式及过去分词为 carried。这种拼法用于本词典所有词尾为 -y 的动词。 The third person present singular of verbs ending in -y is formed by changing the -y to -ies. For example *you carry*, but *she carries*. 词尾是 -y 的动词, 其第三人称、现在式、单数系将 -y 变作 -ies, 例如 you carry, she carries。 The present participle of verbs ending in -y is formed by adding -ing to the end of the verb. For example *carry*, present participle *carrying*. 词尾为 -y 的动词, 其现在分词是加 -ing, 例如 carry, carrying。

Doubled **consonants** **重复辅音**	Many verbs that end with a single consonant have this letter repeated in the spelling for the present and past participles and the past tense. For example, *drop* has *dropping* and *dropped*. In the same way, some adjectives repeat the last consonant in the spelling for the comparative and superlative. For example, *hot* has *hotter* and *hottest*. If the consonant is doubled, the Dictionary

shows this by printing the repeated letter in brackets, for example, **drop (-pp-); hot (-tt-)**. (⇨ *How American English is written*, below.)

许多以单一辅音为词尾的动词，在形成现在和过去分词以及过去式时，需重复该一辅音，例如 drop, dropping, dropped。同样的，有些形容词的比较级和最高级亦需重复词尾的辅音，例如 hot, hotter, hottest。本词典内重复辅音处皆以括弧表示，例如 drop (-pp-); hot (-tt-)。（参看下列'怎样写美国英语'。）

How to divide a word when writing or typing 写作或打字时怎样断字

When writing or typing it is sometimes necessary to divide a word at the end of the line because there is not enough space for the complete word. This division is always shown by adding a hyphen(-) immediately after the first part of the divided word at the end of the line. Many people prefer not to divide words at all (especially when writing by hand), but if you do, here are three considerations to help you.

写作或打字时，由于行尾的篇幅不够容纳一个完整的词，有时需要断字。 这种断字总是在行尾断字的第一部份后面加一连字符(-)。许多人不愿意断字(尤其在手写时)，但假若你需要断字时，下列三点可供你参考。

1 By syllable 按照音节

This means dividing the word into syllables or units of sound. For example, the word **kind** has one syllable, **kind·ly** has two, **un·kind·ly** has three and **un·kind·li·ness** has four.

即依照音节或发音单位断字，例如 kind 有一个音节，kind·ly 有两个音节，un·kind·ly 有三个音节，un·kind·li·ness 有四个音节。

2 By structure 按照结构

This means dividing the word into the smaller units of meaning from which the word is built up. It may have a beginning (a prefix) such as *anti-, dis-, un-*, etc (as in **anti·sep·tic, dis·ap·pear, un·able**) or an ending (a suffix) such as *-age, -able, -fully* (as in **post·age, agree·able, grate·fully**).

即依照一个词结构上较小的意义单位来断字。一个词的开始可能是 anti-, dis-, un- 之类的前缀(如 anti·sep·tic, dis·ap·pear, un·able)，也可能是 -age, -able, -fully 之类的后缀(如 post·age, agree·able, grate·fully)。

3 By meaning 按照意义

This means deciding whether each part of the divided word can be understood or spoken so that the complete word is easily recognized from the two parts. For example, it may be a compound word made up of two different words, such as *spot* and *light* in **spot·light**.

即视断字后的每一部分是否代表一个意义或可以读出，以便从断字后的两部分容易地辨识全词，例如复合词 spot·light 一词系由二字组成，可分作 spot 和 light。

All three considerations must be used to decide whether and where you can divide a word. Here are six useful rules to help you:

以上三点可用来决定是否要断字、在何处断字，下面六项规则可以帮助你:

1 Never divide a word within a syllable.
不可在一个音节之内断字。

2 Never divide an ending (a suffix) of two syllables such as *-able, -ably, -fully*.
由两个音节组成的词尾，如 -able, -ably, -fully 等，不可断字。

3 With the exception of *-ly*, never divide a word so that an ending of two letters such as *-ed, -er, -ic* begins the next line.
除了 -ly 例外，不可以将两个字母的词尾如 -ed, -er, -ic 等置于下一行之首。

4 Never divide a word so that one of the parts is a single letter.
不可在断字之后让其中一部分只剩下一个字母。

5 Never divide a word of one syllable.
单音节的词不能断字。

6 Never divide a word of less than five letters.
未超过五个字母的词不能断字。

The bold dot.
黑点

The recommended places of word-division are given in the Dictionary for all headwords, derivatives and compounds. A bold dot (·) is printed where division is recommended, for example **sep·ar·ate**; **～·ly**. This means that these divisions are all possible:

本词典中所有的词目、派生词及复合词皆注明了断字之处,注明的方式是以一个黑点(·)分隔,例如 sep·ar·ate; ～·ly. 亦即说明下列各种情况皆可断字:

sep-	*separ-*	*separate-*
arate	*ate*	*ly*

How American
English is written
怎样写美国英文

When American spelling is different from British English, it is given in the Dictionary in brackets immediately after the headword, for example

当美国英语的拼法与英国不同时,本词典就把美国拼法放在括弧里,紧接在词目后面,例如

col·our (US=**color**), **py·ja·mas** (US=**pa·ja·mas**).

The main differences in spelling are:
英美拼法上主要的不同处如下:

British 英	**American** 美
-our (*honour*)	-or (*honor*)
-re (*centre*)	-er (*center*)
-ogue (*dialogue*)	-og (*dialog*)
-ence (*defence*)	-ense (*defense*)
-ize} (*realize*)	
-ise} (*realise*)	-ize (*realize*)
ae (*anaemia*)	e (*anemia*)

Sometimes American English spelling does not double the consonant at the end of a word, while British English spelling does, especially when the consonant is an 'l'. For example, *travel* has (GB) *travelling* and *traveller*, and (US) *traveling* and *traveler*. The Dictionary tells you these facts by putting (**-ll-; US -l-**) in the entry.

有时美国英语的拼法中不重复词尾的辅音,而英国则重复,尤其当辅音为 'l' 时,例如关于 travel 一字,英国拼法有 travelling 和 traveller, 美国则为 traveling 和 traveler。关于这方面的说明,本词典是在词条下以(-ll-; US -l-)列出。

Speaking English
说英语

How a word is
pronounced
怎样读一个词

In written English one letter can often be pronounced in different ways. For example, the letter *a* is pronounced differently in *hat, pass, came, water, dare, ago*. Phonetic spelling is a way of writing a word so that one symbol always represents only one sound. Two words may be spelt differently in ordinary spelling, but if they sound the same, then the phonetic spelling is the same. For example, *key* and *quay* have the same phonetic spelling /kiː/. Each headword and derivative has a phonetic spelling after the ordinary spelling. Inside the cover of the Dictionary there is a list of all the letters (*phonetic symbols*) used in the phonetic spelling.

英语中一个字母常作不同的发音。 譬如 a 这个字母在 hat, pass, came, water, dare, ago 等词中即有不同的读法。 音标中一个符号代表一个音。 在一般拼法中两个词虽然拼法不同, 但如果它们发音相同, 其音标是一样的, 例如 key 和 quay 这两个词的音标都是 /kiː/。 每一个词目和派生词在其一般拼法后都有一个音标。 在本词典封面内页有一个表, 说明音标中所用的全部字母(注音符号)。

Models of
pronunciation
读音的模式

A British English pronunciation is given for each word, and, in those cases where there is a marked difference, the American version is also shown. The British English form is that which has been called *Received Pronunciation* or *General British*. The forms recommended correspond to those given in the *English Pronouncing Dictionary* (Dent), but the pronunciation shown may not

always be that which appears first in *EPD*. Where there is a choice between several acceptable forms, that form is selected which is likely to be easiest for learners. The American pronunciation given is that which is widely acceptable in the United States and has been called *General American*.

本词典中每一个词所注的都是英国读音，但是在遇到英美读音有显著差别时，也加注了美国读音。英国读法即称作'公认的读法'或'一般的英国读法'。本词典所采用者与'英语发音字典(Dent)'一致，但是所注的读音并不一定总是采取'英语发音字典'中词目下第一个出现者。遇到有几种公认的读法可供选择时，我们总是选择学习者最容易读的一个。美国读音系采取美国普遍采用者，称作'一般的美国读法'。

In spoken British English an *r* at the end of a written word (either as the final letter or in an *re* ending as in *fire*) is not sounded unless another word that begins with a vowel sound follows in the same sentence. For example, the *r* is not heard in *His car was sold* but it is heard in *His car isn't old*. To show this, words which end in *r* or *re* have(r) at the end of the phonetic spelling in the dictionary, for example *car* /kɑː(r)/.

当一个词的词尾是 r（最后一个字母是 r 或者象 fire 中的 re），英国的读法是不将 r 音读出，除非句中其后接的词系以元音开始。 例如在 His car was sold 句中 r 即不发音，但在 His car isn't old 句中则发音。 本词典中系在音标的末尾以(r)表示词尾是 r 或 re 之词的发音，例如 car /kɑː(r)/。

How American English is pronounced 怎样读美国英语

Whenever Americans pronounce a word in a very different way from British speakers, the Dictionary gives the phonetic spelling of the American pronunciation after the British one, for example **half** /hɑːf *US:* hæf/; **address** /ə'dres *US:* 'ædres/. If only part of the pronunciation changes, only that part is given for the American pronunciation in order to save space, for example **attitude**/'ætɪtjuːd *US:* -tuːd/.

每当一个词的美国读法与英国读法差别很大时，本词典则在英国读法后面加注美国读法，例如 half /hɑːf *US:* hæf/; address /ə'dres *US:* 'ædres/。如果只有部分的读音改变，为节省篇幅起见，仅将该部分的美国读法注出，例如 attitude /'ætɪtjuːd *US:* -tuːd/。

American English forms are shown with the same phonetic symbols as are used for British English. However, particularly in the case of vowels, the same symbol will often mean somewhat different qualities in the British and American varieties. For example, in American English, the/ɒ/in *hot* is similar to the British English /ɑː/ sound, and the /ʌ/ of *cut* is similar to a stressed /ə/ sound.

美国英语是以英国所用的同样的音标注出。虽然如此，特别是元音，同一音标在英国和美国英语变化中往往表示略微不同的性质。例如美国英语 hot 之 /ɒ/ 音与英国的 /ɑː/ 音相似，cut 之 /ʌ/ 音与重读的 /ə/ 音相似。

There is one difference between British and American pronunciation that is *not* given in the Dictionary. This is the use of the /r/ sound in American English in words where British English does not use it, for example in the words **arm** and **poor**. The British pronunciations of these words are /ɑːm/ and /pʊə(r)/ (the symbol(r) is explained in *Models of Pronunciation* above); the American pronunciations are /ɑːrm/ and /pʊər/. The rule to follow in the case of the /r/ sound in American English is to sound the /r/ *whenever* it occurs in the spelling of a word.

英国和美国读音上有一点不同处本词典未加注明，就是关于/r/音的问题，美国读法发音，英国不发音，例如 arm 和 poor。这两个词英国读作/ɑːm/和/pʊə(r)/ ((r) 的用法在上列'读音的模式'中曾有说明)，美国读作 /ɑːrm/和/pʊər/。(r)音在美国英语中读法的规则就是每当它在拼字中出现时都发音。

Syllabic consonants 音节辅音

The consonants /n/ and /l/ often form a syllable by themselves, ie without a vowel, especially at the end of words. Thus, when *sudden, middle, nation, final*, for instance, are shown as /'sʌdn/, /'mɪdl/, /'neɪ∫n/, /'faɪnl/, this means that /n/ and /l/ are syllabic. But syllabic /n/ and /l/ may also occur before a vowel within a word. When this happens, /ən/ and /əl/ are usually

given in the Dictionary, representing an equally acceptable pronunciation which many learners may find easier. Thus we have *final* /'faɪnl/ and *finally* /'faɪnəlɪ/, where /-əl-/ may be said as a syllabic /l/ if preferred (so that in any case it is distinct from *finely* /'faɪnlɪ/).

/n/ 和 /l/ 这两个辅音在无元音的情况下，尤其是在词尾时，常单独形成一个音节。因此，当 sudden, middle, nation, final 注成 /'sʌdn/, /'mɪdl/, /'neɪʃn/, /'faɪnl/ 时，即表示 /n/ 和 /l/ 是自成音节的。但是自成音节的 /n/ 和/l/ 在词中也可能位于一个元音之前。遇到这种情形，本词典通常把它们注成 /ən/ 和 /əl/，这是一种同样公认的读音，也是学习者较易接受的读音。因此，我们把 final 注成 /'faɪnl/，把 finally 注成 /'faɪnəlɪ/；如果愿意的话，可以把此处的 /-əl-/ 称作自成音节的 /l/（以便在必要时能与 finely /'faɪnlɪ/ 有所不同）。

How a word is stressed
怎样读词的重音

When a word has more than one syllable, one of them is spoken with more force than the rest. This force is called *stress*, and the syllable which is stressed is shown with the stress-mark /'/ before it in the Dictionary. For example, *any* /'enɪ/ has a stress on the first syllable, *depend* /dɪ'pend/ has a stress on the second syllable.

当一个词有一个以上的音节时，其中一个音节读起来较其他的音节有力。这种力即称作重音，有重音的音节在本词典中是在它的前面加一重音符号 /'/ 来表示，例如 any/'enɪ/ 的重音在第一音节，depend/dɪ'pend/ 的重音在第二音节。

In some words, usually long ones, other syllables may also be spoken with more force than the rest, but with a stress that is not as strong as for those syllables marked /'/. The stress-mark /ˌ/ is used to show this.

在有些通常较长的词中，尚有其他的音节读起来又较其余者有力，但不若以/'/标示者有力，我们以/ˌ/表示这种音节。

So, /'/ is used to show the strongest or *primary* stress, and /ˌ/ is used to show the less strong or *secondary* stress, as in **pronunciation** /prəˌnʌnsɪ'eɪʃn/.

因此，/'/ 是用来表示最强的或主重音，/ˌ/ 则表示次重音，例如 pronunciation /prəˌnʌnsɪ'eɪʃn/。

How a two-word compound is stressed
怎样读两个词组成的复合词的重音

A compound that is made up of two separately written words, for example **national park**, is normally spoken with the strong stress in the second word: ˌnational 'park. If a compound does not have stress marks indicated, then it follows this normal pattern. Sometimes, however, a compound is spoken with the strong stress on the first word, for example 'post office. In this case, the stress mark is always shown.

由两个单词组成的复合词，例如 national park，其主重音通常是在第二个词: ˌnational 'park。未标出重音的复合词即遵照这种正常的方式去读。然而，有时复合词的主重音是在第一个词，例如 'post office, 此种情形重音总会标出。

How an idiom is stressed
怎样读成语的重音

One of the words in any idiom is always spoken with more force than the other words. Normally, this stressed word is the last 'important' word in that idiom, that is, the last word that is either a *noun*, a *verb*, an *adjective* or an *adverb*. For example, in the idiom *separate the sheep from the goats*, the word *goats* carries the strong stress, because it is the last important word (in this case a *noun*) in the idiom. In the idiom *play fast and loose with* the word *loose* carries the strong stress, because it is the last *adverb* in the idiom.

无论任何成语，其中总有一个词的读音较其他的词有力。通常有重音的词是成语中最后一个 '重要的' 词，这个词不是名词、动词、形容词就是副词。例如，在 separate the sheep from the goats 一成语中，重音在 goats 一词，因为它是该成语中最后一个重要的词(在此为一名词)。在 play fast and loose with 一成语中，重音在 loose，因为它是本成语最后一个副词。

In some idioms, however, a word that comes before the last important word in the idiom carries the strong stress. In this case, the word that is stressed is always shown with a stress mark. For example, *at 'any rate* and *for the 'most part*.

然而在有些成语中，重读的词是在最后一个重要的词之前。在此情形，重读的词

总标有重音, 例如 at 'any rate 和 for the 'most part.

How an inflection is pronounced 怎样读词尾变化

An *inflection* is the changed form a word takes when it is used in a particular grammatical way, for example, in the plural (*sky*, *skies*), in the past tense (*smile*, *smiled*), in the comparative (*wild*, *wilder*). Inflections are usually made by changing the ending of a word.

词形变化即是一个词在语法上有特殊用法时其形式上的变化, 例如用于复数 (sky, skies), 用于过去式(smile, smiled), 用于比较级(wild, wilder)。词形变化通常是由改变一个词的词尾而成。

The plural of nouns, and the third person singular present of verbs
名词的复数与动词的第三人称、单数、现在式

1 If the final sound of the noun's singular or the verb's infinitive is a *vowel* or /b, d, g, v, ð, m, n, ŋ, l/, the ending is formed by the addition of /-z/. For example *city* /'sɪtɪ/, *cities* /'sɪtɪz/; *ring* /rɪŋ/, *rings* /rɪŋz/.

名词的单数或动词的不定式的尾音若是元音或 /b, d, g, v, ð, m, n, ŋ, l/, 则接尾为/-z/。例如: city /'sɪtɪ/, cities /'sɪtɪz/; ring /rɪŋ/, rings /rɪŋz/。

2 If the final sound of the noun's singular or the verb's infinitive is /p, t, k, f, θ/, the ending is formed by the addition of /-s/. For example *work* /wɜːk/, *works* /wɜːks/.

名词的单数或动词的不定式的尾音若是 /p, t, k, f, θ/, 则接尾为/-s/。例如: work /wɜːk/, works /wɜːks/。

3 If the final sound of the noun's singular or the verb's infinitive is /s, z, ʃ, ʒ, tʃ, dʒ/, the ending is formed by the addition of /-ɪz/. For example *match* /mætʃ/, *matches* /'mætʃɪz/.

名词的单数或动词的不定式的尾音若是 /s, z, ʃ, ʒ, tʃ, dʒ/, 则接尾为/-ɪz/。例如: match /mætʃ/, matches /'mætʃɪz/。

The past tense and past participle of verbs
动词的过去式与过去分词

1 If the final sound of the verb's infinitive is a *vowel* or /b, g, v, ð, z, ʒ, dʒ, m, n, ŋ, l/, the past tense and the past participle are formed by the addition of /-d/. For example *hurry* /'hʌrɪ/, *hurried* /'hʌrɪd/; *judge* /dʒʌdʒ/, *judged* /dʒʌdʒd/.

动词的不定式的尾音若为元音或 /b, g, v, ð, z, ʒ, dʒ, m, n, ŋ, l/, 过去式和过去分词则加 /-d/。例如: hurry /'hʌrɪ/, hurried /'hʌrɪd/; judge /dʒʌdʒ/, judged /dʒʌdʒd/。

2 If the final sound of the verb's infinitive is /p, k, f, θ, s, ʃ, tʃ/, the past tense and the past participle are formed by the addition of /-t/. For example *stop* /stɒp/, *stopped* /stɒpt/.

动词的不定式的尾音为 /p, k, f, θ, s, ʃ, tʃ/, 过去式和过去分词则加 /-t/。例如: stop /stɒp/, stopped /stɒpt/。

3 If the final sound of the verb's infinitive is /t, d/, the past tense and the past participle are formed by the addition of /-ɪd/. For example *paint* /peɪnt/, *painted* /'peɪntɪd/.

动词的不定式的尾音为 /t, d/, 过去式和过去分词则加 /-ɪd/。例如: paint /peɪnt/, painted /'peɪntɪd/。

The comparative and superlative of adjectives
形容词的比较级与最高级

1 The comparative is formed by the addition of /-ə(r)/ to the final sound of the adjective. For example *high* /haɪ/, *higher* /'haɪə(r)/; *wild* /waɪld/, *wilder* /'waɪldə(r)/.

比较级是在形容词的尾音后面加 /-ə(r)/。例如: high /haɪ/, higher /'haɪə(r)/; wild /waɪld/, wilder /'waɪldə(r)/。

2 The superlative is formed by the addition of /-ɪst/ to the final sound of the adjective. For example low /ləʊ/, lowest /'ləʊɪst/; green /griːn/, greenest /'griːnɪst/.

最高级是在形容词的尾音后面加 /-ɪst/。例如: low /ləʊ/, lowest /'ləʊɪst/; green /griːn/, greenest /'griːnɪst/。

In the Dictionary, phonetic spelling is given for inflections only if the forms do not follow the ordinary rules, for example, the plural of **basis**: **bases** /'beɪsiːz/; the past tense of **read**: **read** /red/; the comparative of **young**: **younger** /'jʌŋɡə(r)/.

在本词典中, 如词尾变化的形式未遵照通常的规则, 则标示其注音, 例如 basis 的复数: bases /'beɪsiːz/; read 的过去式: read /red/; young 的比较级: younger /'jʌŋɡə(r)/。

How a derivative is pronounced
怎样读派生词

Most derivatives are formed by adding a *suffix* to the end of a word. The pronunciation of these suffixes is given in the special list of prefixes and suffixes found in Appendix 3, pages 1353—1357. These derivatives are pronounced simply by saying the suffix after the word. For example, the adverb **slowly** /'sləʊlɪ/ is made by joining the word **slow** /sləʊ/ to the suffix -ly /lɪ/.

大多数的派生词是在一词的末尾加一词尾而成。这些词尾的读音均列在本词典附录三前缀与后缀一表之中 (1353 — 1357 页)。这些派生词的读音只是将本词读出再将词尾读出即可, 例如副词 slowly /'sləʊlɪ/ 即由 slow /sləʊ/ 加上词尾 -ly /lɪ/ 而成。

However, whenever there is doubt about how a suffix or a derivative is pronounced, the phonetic spelling is given. For example **mouthful** /-fʊl/, **regretful** /-fl/. Also, if a change of stress is caused by adding a suffix to a word, then the pronunciation of the derivative is given in full, for example, **photograph** /'fəʊtəɡrɑːf/, but **photographer** /fə'tɒɡrəfə(r)/, **photographic** /ˌfəʊtə'ɡræfɪk/.

然而, 后缀与派生词在读法上有任何疑问时, 均加以注音。例如: mouthful /-fʊl/, regretful /-fl/。同时, 如一词由于加后缀而重音改变时, 则将该派生词的读音全部注出, 例如: photograph 读做 /'fəʊtəɡrɑːf/, 但是 photographer 则读做 /fə'tɒɡrəfə(r)/, photographic 则读做 /ˌfəʊtə'ɡræfɪk/。

How French words are pronounced in English
怎样用英语发音读法语

Some French words used in English are completely anglicized (ie no longer considered to be foreign words, and given a completely English pronunciation), for example *café* /'kæfeɪ/, *restaurant* /'restrɒnt/. There are other French words and phrases which are still regarded as foreign but which are normally given a completely English pronunciation, for example *à la carte* /ˌɑː lɑː 'kɑːt/, *table d'hôte* /ˌtɑːbl 'dəʊt/. A difficulty arises with the pronunciation of French nasalized vowels, as in *salon, en route*. Native speakers of English use different pronunciations in such cases, varying from total anglicization to a more or·less successful imitation of the French. This Dictionary gives the anglicized form, /'sælɒn/, /ˌɒn 'ruːt/.

英语中所用的法国字, 有些已完全英语化(即不再被认为是外国字, 并且完全照英语发音), 例如 café /'kæfeɪ/, restaurant /'restrɒnt/。虽然还有些法国词和短语 仍旧被当作外国语, 但它们通常完全注成英语发音, 例如 à la carte /ˌɑː lɑː 'kɑːt/, table d'hôte /ˌtɑːbl 'dəʊt/。困难发生在以鼻音发出的法语元音, 如 salon, en route 等中者。遇到这种情形, 英国人用不同的读音, 有的用完全英语化的读音, 有的相当成功地模仿法语读音。本词典所注的是英语化的读音, 如 /'sælɒn/, /ˌɒn 'ruːt/。

Grammar
语法

Irregular forms of nouns, verbs and adjectives

名词、动词和形容词的不规则形式

An *irregular* form of a word is one that is not made in the normal (or *regular*) way. For example, the normal way of forming the plural of an English noun in writing is to add -s or -es, and the normal way of forming a past tense or past participle of a verb is to add -d or -ed. Whenever a form is made in any other way, then this is given (together with the pronunciation if necessary), at the beginning of the entry. For example, **axis** /'æksɪs/ *n* (*pl* **axes** /'æksiːz/); **choose** /tʃuːz/ *vt, vi* (*pt* **chose**/tʃəuz/, *pp* **chosen**/'tʃəuzn/); **bad** /bæd/ *adj* (**worse, worst**).

一个词之不规则形式即不是以正常(或规则)的方式形成的词。譬如, 形成英语名词的复数的正常方式是加 -s 或 -es, 形成动词的过去式或过去分词的正常方式是加 -d 或 -ed。凡是以别的方式形成的形式, 本词典均在词条之首列出(必要时并加注音)。例如: axis /'æksɪs/ *n* (*pl* axes /'æksiːz/); choose /tʃuːz/ *vt, vi* (*pt* chose /tʃəuz/, *pp* chosen /'tʃəuzn/); bad /bæd/ *adj* (worse, worst)。

Comparative and superlative forms of adjectives

形容词的比较级和最高级

The comparative and superlatives forms of all adjectives of two or more syllables are made by using the words *more* and *most* before the adjective. For example, the comparative form of *interesting* is *more interesting*; the superlative form of *pleasant* is *most pleasant*.

所有两个或两个以上音节的形容词, 其比较级和最高级的形式是在前面加 more 和 most, 例如 interesting 的比较级是 more interesting, pleasant 的最高级是 most pleasant。

All adjectives of one syllable, and many adjectives of two syllables, make the comparative and superlative forms by adding -r, -st or -er, -est or -ier, -iest to the end of the adjective. For example, the comparative forms of *gentle, cold* and *happy* are *gentler, colder* and *happier*; the superlative forms are *gentlest, coldest* and *happiest*. In the Dictionary, an adjective that has a comparative and superlative form of this sort has (**-r, -st**) or (**-er, -est**) or (**-ier, -iest**) printed in the entry.

所有单音节和许多两个音节的形容词, 其比较级和最高级的形式是在形容词词尾加 -r, -st, 或 -er, -est, 或 -ier, -iest。例如 gentle, cold 和 happy 的比较级是 gentler, colder 和 happier; 最高级为 gentlest, coldest 和 happiest。在本词典中, 有此种比较级和最高级的形容词, 均在词条下加有 (-r, -st) 或 (-er, -est) 或 (-ier, -iest)。

Countable and uncountable nouns

可数与不可数的名词

The correct use of the *noun* is a very important but difficult skill to acquire when learning English. For example, some nouns can be used in the plural form, while others cannot. In addition, many nouns have several meanings, some of which may have a plural form, and some of which may not. This Dictionary gives the learner special help in this area, by the use of the symbols [C], [U] or [C, U] in an entry for a noun.

在学习英语过程中, 名词的正确用法是十分重要但也很难学到的技巧。例如有些名词可以用作复数, 有些则不可以。此外, 许多名词有好几种意义, 用作某些意义可作复数, 有些意义则不可以。关于这一方面, 本词典特别在名词词条下以[C], [U]或 [C, U] 等符号注明, 以帮助学习者。

[C] means that the noun has both a singular and a plural form. It can be used in the singular with *a, an, another* (*a bottle, an apple, another boy*), in the plural with *many* (*many bottles*) and in the singular or plural with numbers (*one apple, six apples*). Nouns that can be used in these ways are *countable*. [C] in the entry tells you this. When no information is given in a noun entry, it is an obvious countable noun.

[C] 表示一名词具有单数和复数形式, 单数时可与 a, an, another 连用(如 a bottle, an apple, another boy), 复数时可与 many 连用(如 many bottles), 此外

不论单复数均可与数字连用(如 one apple, six apples)。可以这样用的名词是'可数的',词条中的[C]即告诉你这一点。如果词条中没有注明,则表示它是个明显的可数名词。

[U] means that the noun does not have a plural form. It can be used in the singular with words like *some, enough, much, more* (*some information, enough money, much noise*). It cannot be used with *a, an, another,* or with *many,* or with numbers. Nouns that are used in this way are *uncountable*. [U] in the entry tells you this.

[U]表示一名词没有复数的形式。其单数形可与 some, enough, much, more 等连用(如 some information, enough money, much noise), 但不可与 a, an, another, many 或数字连用。象这样用的名词是'不可数的',词条中的[U]即告诉你这一点。

[C, U] means that the noun can be used either as countable or uncountable. For example, *coffee* is used as [C] in *Tow coffees, please,* and as [U] in *Have some more coffee*.

[C, U] 表示一名词可用作可数名词,也可用作不可数名词。例如 coffee 一词在 Two coffees, please 中是可数的, 在 Have some more coffee 中则是不可数的。

Some nouns (or some meanings of some nouns) are only used with the definite article *the,* or only with the indefinite article *a / an*. The Dictionary shows this by putting *the* or *a / an*+the noun in **bold** type at the beginning of the definition. For example **the sun, a sleep.**

有些名词(或有些名词中的某些意义)仅可与定冠词 the 连用, 或仅可与不定冠词 a 或 an 连用。这种情形, 本词典系在定义的开头以黑体排印的'the 或 a / an + 名词'表示之, 例如 **the sun, a sleep**。

How to use a verb with the correct adverbial particle or preposition
怎样用一个与正确的副词性小品词或介词连用的动词

Phrases like *__take off__* (a *verb* with an *adverbial particle*), *__go with__* (a *verb* with a *preposition*), and *__make up to__* (a *verb* with both an *adverbial particle* and a *preposition*) are very important in English because they are so common. They are treated with special care in the Dictionary. The correct particle or preposition is printed with the verb in ***bold italic*** type in the entry so that you can find it easily.

象 take off (动词与副词性小品词), go with (动词与介词), 和 make up to (动词与副词性小品词及介词)等短语, 由于十分普通, 在英语中是非常重要的。它们在本词典中均经过特别处理。正确的副词性小品词或介词和动词是以黑斜体排印, 以便读者易于查阅。

It is important to know why the dictionary uses the brackets ( ) and the slant / in providing this information. Brackets ( ) round a preposition or particle mean that the verb can be used with or without it. For example, *__prepare__* (***for***) can be used as in *prepare a meal,* or as in *prepare for an examination*. A slant / means that you can choose any of the words listed to make a sentence. For example, *__move / along / down / up__* shows that *move along the bus, move down the bus, move up the bus* are all correct.

要了解何以本词典在处理上述短语时使用括弧( )和斜线 / 是重要的。括弧表示动词可与括弧中的介词或副词性小品词连用, 也可以不与其连用。例如 prepare (for) 可用于 prepare a meal 或 prepare for an examination。斜线表示你可选择任何一个以斜线隔开的词来造句。例如 move along / down / up 表示 move along the bus, move down the bus, move up the bus 都是对的。

It is also important to know why and how the words *sb* (somebody) and *sth* (something) are used in these phrases.

要了解以及如何在这些短语中使用 sb (somebody) 和 sth (something) 也是重要的。

Consider the phrases *__take off__* (verb+particle). This is found in the dictionary in both the forms *__take off__* and *__take sth off__*. *__take off__* means that the phrase can be used without an object, for example *The aeroplane took off*. *__take sth off__* means that the phrase can be used with an object (in this case a thing), for example *She took her hat off* or *She took off her hat*.

试以 take off (动词+副词性小品词)一短语为例。在本词典内有 take off 和 take sth off 两种形式。take off 表示这个短语后面没有宾语, 例如 The aeroplane took off。take sth off 表示这个短语后面可接宾语(在此为物), 例如 She took her

hat off 或 She took off her hat。

Consider the phrase *go **with*** (*verb + preposition*). This is found in the dictionary only in the form ***go with*** sb/sth. This means that the phrase must be used with an object (in this case either a person or a thing) after the preposition, for example *Paul went with* (= accompanied) *Peter to Rome*, or *Your shirt doesn't go with* (= match) *your trousers.*

再以 go with (动词＋介词)为例，在本词典中有 go with sb/sth 的形式，意思是说这个短语必须在介词后接一宾语(在此为人或物皆可)，例如：Paul went with (= accompanied) Peter to Rome, 或 Your shirt doesn't go with (= match) your trousers。

You will notice that some verbs (*get, give, go,* etc) are used with a large number of prepositions and particles. Because many of these combinations (for example ***make up***) have a large number of meanings, you will find a section at the end of each of these verb entries called 'special uses with *adverbial particles* and *prepositions*'. In this section, these combinations are listed in bold italic type in alphabetical order (***make after, make at, make away, make for***, etc).

你会发现有些动词(get, give, go 等)与许多介词和副词性小品词连用。由于很多这种结成的短语(如 make up)有许多意义，你在这些动词词条的末尾会发现有一个项目，称作'与副词性小品词和介词连用的特殊用法'。在此项目下，这些短语是按照字母顺序(make after, make at, make away, make for 等)以黑斜体排印的。

How to use an adjective with the correct preposition **怎样用一个与正确的介词连用的形容词**	Many adjectives in English must, or may, be followed by a preposition, for example ***conversant with*** (where the preposition must be used), and ***distinct from*** (where *from* is optional). To help the learner to form correct sentences using these adjectives, the prepositions are included in bold print at the beginning of the entry. 英语中很多形容词必须或可能跟介词连用，例如 conversant with (此处必须跟介词 with) 和 distinct from (from 可用可不用)。为了帮助学习者用这些形容词造出正确的句子，这些介词是以黑斜体排印，列于词条之首，例如： **conversant...** *adj* ~ ***with,*** **distinct...** *adj* ~ (***from***). Note that brackets ( ) are used when the preposition is optional. 注意：括弧（ ）表示介词可用亦可不用。

Style
字格

How to choose the words that the headword usually combines with **怎样选择通常与词目连用的词**	Speaking and writing correct English is not only a matter of pronunciation, spelling or grammar. You must also know the kinds of context in which the headword is normally used. The example phrases and sentences are especially valuable in this respect, because they show the words (or kinds of words) that the headword often combines with. For example, at **regular**(1) there is *regular teeth/features*; at **regular**(2) there is *regular hours/habits*; at **regulate**(1) there is *regulate one's conduct/expenditure*; at **regulate**(2) there is *regulate a clock* and *regulate speed*. 说和写纯正的英语不仅是发音、拼法或语法方面的问题，你还得知道词目通常所用的种种上下文。在这方面本词典中的例句特别有价值，因为它们指出那些常与词目连用的词(或各种词)。例如在 regular 的第 1 义中有 regular teeth/features; 在 regular 的第2义中有 regular hours/habits; 在 regulate 的第1义中有 regulate one's conduct/expenditure; 在 regulate 的第2义中有 regulate a clock 和 regulate speed 等。

The learner wishing to make up sentences of his own will find examples containing the slant/particularly useful. For example, *inspired poets/artists* and *inspire sb with hope/enthusiasm/confidence.* He can compose different sentences using those alternatives; but they will also help him to guess other words that can be used. For example, *inspired musicians/dancers/painters*

and *inspire sb with new faith / passion / devotion.*

学习者在自己造句时会发现那些有斜线的例子特别有用，例如 inspired poets /
artists 与 inspire sb with hope / enthusiasm / confidence 等。他可以利用那些选
择造成不同的句子，而且它们也会帮助他去猜想其他可用的词，譬如 inspired
musicians / dancers / painters 与 inspire sb with new faith / passion /
devotion 等。

**How to use the
more usual or more
suitable word
怎样用较常用或
较适当的词**

You should also be confident that the kind or style of English you are using
is right in that particular context: that it is not too *formal* or *colloquial*, that
it will not offend the listener or reader, or that it is not *dated* (old-fashioned),
or *archaic* (no longer used). To help you, there is information in an entry
when the word is to be used only in a particular style or context. For example,
formal words are not used in everyday conversation, or in letters to friends
and relations; while colloquial words are not used in business letters, or in
conversation with a person whom you do not know well or who is your superior.
你也应该有把握，你所用的那种英语在某种特殊场合是正确的：它不会太正式或太
口语化，它不会冒犯听者或读者，它不是过时用语或古语。 为了帮助你，当一个词
要用在特殊标准或场合时，在词条下都有说明。 例如正式的词不用于日常谈话或
写给朋友亲戚的书信中，另方面口语用的词不用于商业信函或是对不熟悉的人或
尊长的谈话中。

Sometimes the Dictionary will warn you that a word is both a *dated* word
and a *slang* word (dated sl), or both a *modern* word and a *colloquial* word
(modern colloq).
有时本词典会警告你某一词既是过时用语也是俚语（过时俚语），或者既是现代
用语也是口语（现代口语）。

Sometimes the Dictionary will tell you what the more usual word is,
particularly in entries for *formal* or *dated* vocabulary.
有时本词典会告诉你哪些是较常用的词，尤其是在正式的或过时的词条中。

Remember that *slang* vocabulary is not popular for very long and that such
words should only be used if you are sure that they are not dated, that
they will sound quite natural when you use them, and that they will not cause
offence.
要记住俚语不会流行很久，只有在你确实知道它们并未过时，使用时听起来十分
自然，而且不会得罪人的情况下方可使用俚语。

**How to use
specialist
English words
怎样用
英语专门术语**

Some words are used only by a group of speakers or writers because of the
work they do, the way they live, the activity they are enjoying, the subject
they are studying, etc. These are 'specialist' areas such as *business, science, law,
sport, music, medicine*, etc. Trying to use specialist words outside the contexts
where they belong can make your English seem unnatural. To help you, the
Dictionary gives the specialist English area in brackets at the beginning of the
explanation of the meaning.
某一类说话者或作者由于工作关系、生活方式、喜爱的活动以及学习的科目等只用
到某些词。这些词都属于'专门的'领域，如商业、科学、法律、运动、音乐、医学等。
在不适当的场合用专门术语会使你的英语显得不自然。 为了帮助你，本词典特将
专门术语的领域置于括弧中，放在词义解释的前头。

**How to use
idiomatic English
怎样用成语**

An important sign of a person who has learnt English from a native-speaker
(or a person who has a native-speaker's command of the language) is his
knowledge of the meaning and correct use of expressions such as ***make up
one's mind, be all ears, with all one's heart***, etc. These are called *idioms*
or *idiomatic expressions*. They are groups of two or more words which must be
learnt as a whole because the meaning of the expression may be different from
the meanings of its parts. An example is ***hit the nail on the head***, which
means 'guess right'. In the Dictionary, these expressions are printed in ***bold
italic*** type.
一个已经从以英语为母语的人（或运用英语的能力相当于以英语为母语的人）那

里学会英语的人的重要征象是，他能够了解并且正确运用象 make up one's mind, be all ears, with all one's heart 之类的短语。这些短语称作成语或习惯用语。它们系由两个或两个以上的词组成，这些词必须当作一个整体来学，因为整个成语的意义可能和成语各部分的意义不同。例如 hit the nail on the head 这个成语的意思是'说中'。在本词典中，成语是用黑斜体排印。

Like the style for verbs with prepositions or particles (which are themselves types of idioms), brackets are used for words which can be omitted, as in **make (both) ends meet** and slants for alternatives as in **begin/start at the wrong end.** When there are no brackets or slants, the expression cannot be changed. For example, the idiom **have an ear to the ground** cannot be changed to *have a head to the ground* or *have an ear to the floor*. But the idiom **bear/keep something in mind** can be either *bear something in mind* or *keep something in mind*.

象处理动词与介词或副词性小品词连用的动词(它们本身即为成语类型)一样，可以省略的词都加有括弧，如 make (both) ends meet。可以选择的词都用斜线隔开，如 begin/start at the wrong end。如果没有括弧或斜线，则表示这个成语不可变更，例如 have an ear to the ground 不能改作 have a head to the ground 或 have an ear to the floor，但是 bear/keep something in mind 可作 bear something in mind 或 keep something in mind。

An exception to this is when *etc* is used after two or more words that are divided from one another by the slant mark. This means that *only words of a similar sort* to the words that are given (divided by the slant mark) may be used in the idiom. For example, the idiom **be pushing thirty/forty, etc,** means that only number words that express someone's age in years may be used in this idiom.

对上述者有一种例外的情况，即当 etc 用于以斜线隔开的两个或两个以上的词后面时。这表示'只有和列出的词(即斜线隔开者)相似的词'可用于该成语中。例如 be pushing thirty/forty, etc, 表示只有指年龄的数字可用在这个成语中。

When two or more idioms are divided from one another by a semicolon (;), this means that the idioms *have the same meaning*. For example, **take it from me** and **take my word for it**, which are listed together, separated only by a semicolon (;), in the entry for the verb **take,** have the same meaning, 'believe me when I say'.

当两个或两个以上的成语用分号(;)隔开时，这表示这些成语'意义相同'。例如 take it from me 和 take my word for it 并列在 take 词条下，用分号隔开，它们的意义相同，即'相信我的话'。

Native speakers use these expressions naturally and unconsciously. You will need to learn them before using them. The more you use them, the more they will become a natural part of your English. Unless you use them, your English will always be 'foreign'. But you must be very careful not to use the idioms you know too often, and not to use them one after another in the same sentence, or in sentence after sentence. An idiom must be used with care and thought, only when your meaning can best be expressed with the idiom's special 'strengh', 'flavour' or 'style'.

以英语为母语的人用这些成语时是自然的和不知不觉的。你则需要在运用以前先学习。你用得越多，它们便越会成为你的英语中自然的一部分。如果你不用它们，你的英语将永远是'外国的'。但是你必须很小心，不要太常使用你会用的成语，不要在同一句中一个接一个，或一句连一句的使用成语。运用成语必须小心和慎重，只有在以成语的特殊'力量'、'风味'或'文体'最能表达你的意思时，才去用它。

Proverbs
谚 语

You should note that *proverbs* are seldom used in ordinay speech or writing. Although the native speaker knows the meaning of most English proverbs, he will actually use one rarely, and then only when he is wanting to be humorous, or by referring to the proverb in an indirect way (for example by quoting only half of it), or by introducing it by saying something like 'You know what they say, . . .' or 'As the old saying goes, . . .' The reason is this. English proverbs are phrases or sentences containing advice, warning or truth.

Although they are expressed in striking language, in their meanings they are rather obvious remarks to make about human experience. They are thought of as the sort of remark that would be made by someone who is rather dull, someone who cannot express in his own words what he thinks or feels, but who has to borrow a proverb from the language to do this. A *proverb*, a *cliché*, a *truism*, a *hackneyed phrase*, and a *trite remark* are all the sorts of expressions that someone who wants to express himself clearly, carefully and honestly will try to avoid.

你应注意谚语很少用于一般谈话或写作中。虽然以英语为母语的人懂得大部分英语谚语的意思，但他极少去用一个谚语，即使是用也只有在他想要幽默，或间接提到某一谚语(譬如仅提及一半)，或者在说以前加上一种象 '你知道人们都这样说…' 或 '俗话说…' 等套语之后再用。原因是这样。英语谚语都是含有忠告、警告或真理的短语或句子。 虽然它们系由于人印象深刻的语言表达出来，但就其含义而言，它们都是些有关人世经验的颇为明显的话。 一般人认为用谚语的人头脑迟钝，不能以自己的话表达其思想或感受，而必须借用谚语。一个想清晰地，慎重地和真实地表达自己的人应避免用谚语、老套、老生常谈以及陈腔滥调。

The sign ⚠
标　号

Some words in the Dictionary are followed by the sign ⚠. These are *taboo* words. They are words used when the speaker wishes to swear, or be indecent, or be offensive. They are all words that are likely to cause embarrassment or anger if they are used in the wrong situation. The learner of English is strongly advised to avoid using them.

本词典中有些词后面有标号⚠。这些是应该避讳的词。想要咒骂或粗鄙无礼的人才用这些词。用在不当的情况它们多半会导致困窘或愤怒。学习英语的人最好尽量避免使用它们。

Verb patterns
动词类型

For anyone who is learning to speak or write correct English, the most important word in a sentence is the *verb*. For this reason the compilers of the Dictionary have paid particular attention to *verb patterns*. These show the learner how to use verbs to form correct sentences.

对于任何学着说或写正确英语的人而言，一个句子中最重要的一个词便是动词。因是之故，本词典的编辑们特别注意动词的类型。 这些动词类型告诉学习者怎样用动词造正确的句子。

A person learning English as a foreign language may be tempted to form sentences by *analogy*. For example, he hears or sees such sentences as *Please tell me the meaning* and *Please show me the way* (an indirect object followed by a direct object). By analogy he forms the incorrect sentence **Please explain me the meaning* (instead of *Please explain the meaning to me*). He hears or sees such sentences as *I intend to come, I propose to come*, and *I want to come*, and by analogy he forms the incorrect sentences as **I suggest to come* (instead of *I suggest that I should come*). He hears or sees such sentences as *I asked him to come, I told him to come*, and *I wanted him to come*, and by analogy he forms such incorrect sentences such as **I proposed him to come* and **I suggested him to come* (instead of *I proposed/suggested that he should come*). He notes that *He began to talk about the matter* means the same as *He began talking about the matter* and supposes, wrongly, that *He stopped to talk about the matter* means the same as *He stopped talking about the matter*.

把英语当作外国语去学习的人可能会受到诱惑，用 '类推' 的方式造句。 譬如他听到或看到 Please tell me the meaning 和 Please show me the way (间接宾语后跟直接宾语)这种句子，就会以此类推，造出 *Please explain me the meaning 这个错误的句子(正确者应为 Please explain the meaning to me)。他听到或看到 I intend to come, I propose to come, I want to come 等句子，就会以此类推，造出 *I suggest to come 这个错误的句子(正确者应为 I suggest that I should come)。他听到或看到 I asked him to come, I told him to come, 以及 I wanted him to

come 等句，就会以此类推，造出 *I proposed him to come 和 *I suggested him to come 等错误的句子(正确者应为 I proposed／suggested that he should come)。他注意到 He began to talk about the matter 与 He began talking about the matter 的意思一样，因而误以为 He stopped to talk about the matter 与 He stopped talking about the matter 的意义是相同的。

To help the learner to avoid such mistakes, the compilers of the Dictionary have provided a set of tables (on pages xxxiii-xlviii) in which various Verb Patterns are set out with examples. Each pattern has a numbered code (for example, [VP5], [VP6A], [VP21]), and this provides a link between the tables and the verb entries in the Dictionary, because every verb entry has its own code (or several codes if there are several meanings).

为了帮助学习者避免这种错误，本词典的编辑提供了一系列的表(xxxiii-xlviii 页)，列出各种动词类型和例句。每一类型都有一个标号(例如 [VP5], [VP6A], [VP 21])，由于动词条下也有类型标号(如有数种意义时就有数种标号)，这样可使本词典的动词类型表与动词词条之间互相连系。

A few examples will show how the learner can refer from the [VP] codes in entries to the [VP] tables in the Introduction. One of the patterns given in the Dictionary for **congratulate** is [VP14], and this verb is also used in one of the examples in the [VP] table for [VP14]: *We congratulated him on his success*. The pattern provided for the second meaning of **consider** is [VP6A]. If the learner turns to that table he will find several examples based on that pattern, for example *We all enjoyed the film*. This will help him to form a correct sentence with **consider** in [VP6A], for example *He considered the problem*.

举几个例可以说明学习者怎样从词条的标号去参考绪论中的动词类型表。譬如 congratulate 一词在本词典有[VP14]之标号，而在动词类型表[VP14]中亦有其例句：We congratulated him on his success。又如 consider 的第 2 义有[VP6A] 一型，如果学习者参看动词类型表，他会发现这一类型有几个例句，如 We all enjoyed the film 等，这会帮助他用 consider 根据[VP6A]造出一正确的句子，例如：He considered the problem。

Sometimes extra information is given in an entry to help the learner to learn the right pattern. For example, in the entry for **absolve**, he will find the verb + preposition ~ (*from*), placed after the codes [VP6A, 14]. This shows that the verb can be used as in *absolve a man from a vow*. In the entry for **accede** there are the codes [VP2A, 3A], followed by ~ (*to*), showing that the verb may be used as in *accede to a proposal*.

有时在词条中有额外的说明帮助学习者学得正确的句型。例如在 absolve 词条中，标号[VP6A, 14] 后有动词加介词 ~ (from) 之说明，这表示这个动词可以用于 absolve a man from a vow。在 accede 词条中，标号[VP2A, 3A] 后有 ~ (to) 之说明，表示这个动词可以用于 accede to a proposal。

It is important to note that the learner is not expected to memorize these verb patterns. They are a simple reference system, a practical tool to guide the learner who wants to form correct sentences. They are a way of helping the learner who will benefit from a list of the grammatical rules that underlie the different sorts of example sentences that are given in the entries for verbs.

要注意我们不是要学习者去熟记这些动词类型，这一点是重要的。它们是简单的参考系统，是引导想要造出正确句子的学习者一项实际的工具。它们是帮助学习者的一种方法，使他从动词词条下各种不同的例句所呈现的一系列语法规则当中获益。

A full treatment of these verb patterns is found in *Guide to Patterns and Usage in English*, by A S Hornby (Oxford University Press).

这些动词类型的详细说明见于郝恩贝所著‘英语句型及用法指南’一书(牛津大学出版社出版)。

Note: The use of the asterisk *indicates that the phrase or sentence is an example of *incorrect* usage.

注意：星号*表示该短语或句子为错误的用法。

[VP1]
动词 1 型

This pattern is for the verb *be*. The subject complement may be a noun, a pronoun, an adjective, an adjective phrase (eg a prepositional group). There may be an adverbial adjunct or an infinitive phrase.

此型使用于动词 be。主语补语可能是名词、代词、形容词、形容词短语（例如介词形成者），也可能是副词修饰语或不定式短语。

Subject + BE	subject complement／adjunct
1 *This is* 这是一本书。	*a book.*
2 *This suitcase is* 这个衣箱是我的。	*mine.*
3 *The children are* 孩子们睡着了。	*asleep.*
4 *This book is* 这本书是给你的。	*for you.*
5 *This is* 这就是我工作的地方。	*where I work.*

There are variations with introductory *there／it*.
there／it 用于句首时有变化。

There／It + BE	subject
1 *There was* 有一大群人。	*a large crowd.*
2 *It was impossible* 再走远些是不可能了。	*to go further.*
3 *It was a pity* 天气这样坏是遗憾的事。	*the weather was so bad.*

[VP2A]
动词 2 型 A 组

This pattern is for verbs which may be used without a complement. Such verbs are called complete intransitive verbs. Adjuncts are possible but not essential.

用作此类型的动词后面可以不接补语。此类动词称作完全不及物动词。可以与修饰语连用，但不是必须的。

Subject	vi
1 *We all* 我们都呼吸、饮水和吃东西。	*breathe, drink and eat.*
2 *The moon* 月亮升起了。	*rose.*
3 *A period of political unrest* 随后是一段政治不安时期。	*followed.*

There are variations with introductory *there／it*.
there／it 用于句首时有变化。

| 1 *There followed*
随后是很长一段政治不安时期。 | *a long period of political unrest.* |
| 2 *It doesn't matter*
我们现在或是晚些动身都没有关系。 | *whether we start now or later.* |

That-clauses are possible after *seem, appear, happen, chance* and *follow.*
在 seem, appear, happen, chance 和 follow 后可用 that 从句。

1 *It seemed* 那一天似乎永远也过不完。	*(that) the day would never end.*
2 *It so chanced／happened* 她来访时适逢我们不在家。	*(that) we were out when she called.*
3 *It doesn't follow* 这并不能断定他们是夫妻。	*(that) they are husband and wife.*

[VP2B]
动词 2 型 B 组

Verbs in this pattern are used with an adverbial adjunct of distance, duration, weight, cost, etc. *For* may occur before adverbials of distance and duration.

An indirect object may occur after *cost, last* and *take* (meaning 'require').

此型动词与表示距离、持续时间、重量、价值等的副词修饰语连用。在 cost, last 和 take (作'需要'解)后面可以用间接宾语。

Subject + *vi*	(*for*) + adverbial adjunct
1 *We walked* 我们步行了五英里。	(*for*) *five miles.*
2 *The meeting lasted* 会议开了两小时。	(*for*) *two hours.*
3 *The book cost (me)* 这本书花了(我)1.20镑。	£ *1.20.*
4 *This box weighs* 这个箱子重五公斤。	*five kilos.*

[VP2C]
动词 2 型 C 组

Many intransitive verbs are used with an adverbial adjunct (including an adverbial particle alone, or an adverbial particle followed by a preposition).

许多不及物动词与副词修饰语(单独副词性小品词或副词性小品词跟介词)连用。

Subject + *vi*	adverbial adjunct
1 *Go* 走开!	*away!*
2 *Please come* 请进来。	*in.*
3 *I'll soon catch* 我很快就会追上你。	*up with you.*
4 *It's getting* 快到半夜了。	*on for midnight.*
5 *It looks* 好象要下雨的样子。	*like rain／as if it were going to rain.*

[VP2D]
动词 2 型 D 组

Verbs in this pattern are followed by an adjective, a noun or, in the case of a reflexive verb, a pronoun. Inchoative verbs (eg *become, come, get*) and verbs of the senses (eg *smell, taste, feel*) are among the many verbs used in this pattern.

此型动词后接一形容词，名词或代词(如为反身动词时)。表始动词(如 become, come, get)，知觉动词(如 smell, taste, feel)，以及许多其他动词用于此型。

Subject + *vi*	adjective／noun／pronoun
1 *Her dreams have come* 她的梦想实现了。	*true.*
2 *The fire has burnt* 火势减弱了。	*low.*
3 *She married* 她早婚。	*young.*
4 *He died* 他死时为一百万富翁。	*a millionaire.*
5 *Later he became* 他后来成为一个卖艺人。	*an acrobat.*
6 *You're not looking* 你看来有点异样。	*yourself.*

[VP2E]
动词 2 型 E 组

In this pattern the predicative adjunct is a present participle.

在此型中表语的修饰语是现在分词。

Subject + *vi*	present participle
1 *She lay* 她躺着向我微笑。	*smiling at me.*
2 *Do you like to go* 你喜欢跳舞吗?	*dancing?*
3 *The children came*	*running to meet us.*

孩子们跑着过来接我们。

[VP3A]
动词 3 型 A 组

Verbs in this pattern are followed by a preposition and its object (which may be a noun, pronoun, gerund, phrase, or clause). The verb and preposition function as a unit.

用于此型的动词后跟一介词及其宾语(宾语可能是名词、代词、动名词、短语或从句)。动词和介词作为一个单位。

Subject + *vi*	preposition + noun /pronoun
1 *You may rely*	*on that man/his discretion/his being discreet.*
你可以信赖那个人(他的谨慎,他是谨慎的)。	
2 *Can I count*	*on your help?*
我能指望你的帮助吗?	
3 *What has happened*	*to them?*
他们怎么样了?	

An infinitive phrase may follow the noun/pronoun.
名词或代词后可接不定式短语。

1 *We're waiting*	*for our new car to be delivered.*
我们正等着我们的新车送来。	
2 *I rely*	*on you to be discreet.*
我信赖你的谨慎。	
3 *She pleaded*	*with the judge to have mercy.*
她向法官求情。	

[VP3B]
动词 3 型 B 组

The preposition is omitted before a *that*-clause, thus producing the same word order as in [VP9] (for transitive verbs).

介词在 that 从句前省略,故与动词 9 型(及物动词)的词序相同。

He insisted on his innocence. [VP3A]
He insisted that he was innocent. [VP3B]
Cf *He declared that he was innocent.* [VP9]

The preposition may be retained if its object is a dependent question, or if a preceding 'preposition + *it*' construction is used.

如遇宾语是一从属问句或前面有'介词 + *it*'之结构时,介词可以保留。

Subject + *vi*	(preposition (+ *it*))	clause
1 *I agree*		*that it was a mistake.*
我同意这是一项错误。		
2 *You must see,*	*(to it)*	*that this sort of thing never occurs again.*
你必须注意这一类的事情决不可以再发生。		
3 *I hesitated*	*(about)*	*whether to accept your offer.*
我对于是否接受你的提议犹豫不定。		
4 *Have you decided*	*(upon)*	*where you will go for your holidays?*
你决定了到哪里去度假吗?		
5 *Don't worry*	*(about)*	*how the money was lost.*
不要为了这笔钱是怎样遗失的而烦恼。		

[VP4A]
动词 4 型 A 组

In this pattern the verb is followed by a *to*-infinitive of purpose, outcome, or result.

此型动词后接一表示目的或结果的不定式。

Subject + *vi*	*to*-infinitive
1 *We stopped*	*to rest/to have a rest.*
我们停下来休息。	
2 *How did you come*	*to know her?*
你如何认识她的?	
3 *Will he live*	*to be ninety?*
他会活到九十岁吗?	
4 *Someone has called*	*to see you.*

有人来拜访你。

[VP4B]
动词 4 型 B 组

The infinitive may be equivalent to a co-ordinate clause.
不定式相当于对等从句。

Subject + *vi*	*to*-infinitive
1 *He awoke* 他醒来发现房子着火了。	*to find the house on fire.*
2 *The good old days have gone* 美好的往日已去,永不复回。	*never to return.*
3 *Electronic music has clearly come* 电子音乐显然已来临。	*to stay.*
4 *He looked round* 他回头观望,发现门慢慢打开了。	*to see the door slowly opening.*

[VP4C]
动词 4 型 C 组

The infinitive adjunct is used after some verbs which, in [VP3A], are used with prepositions.
有些动词后接不定式修饰语,这些动词用于动词 3 型 A 组时,是与介词连用。
Don't trouble / bother about that.
Don't trouble / bother to meet me.

Subject + *vi*	*to*-infinitive
1 *She hesitated* 她有些不愿告诉任何人。	*to tell anyone.*
2 *She was longing* 她渴望再见到她的家人。	*to see her family again.*
3 *He agreed* 他答应即刻就来。	*to come at once.*

[VP4D]
动词 4 型 D 组

The verbs *seem* and *appear* are used in this pattern. If the infinitive is *be* with an adjective or noun as complement, *to be* may be omitted (unless the adjective is one that is used only predicatively, as in [VP4E]).
动词 seem 和 appear 用于此型。如果不定式是 be,并以形容词或名词作补语,则 to be 可以省略(除非该形容词仅作表语用法,如动词 4 型 E 组)。

Subject + SEEM / APPEAR	(*to be*) + adjective / noun
1 *He seemed* 他似乎对这消息感到惊讶。	(*to be*) *surprised at the news.*
2 *This seems* 这似乎是一件严重的事。	(*to be*) *a serious matter.*
3 *I seem* 我好象玩得不快乐。	(*to be*) *unable to enjoy myself.*

There is a variation of this pattern with introductory *it*, when the subject is an infinitive or gerund, or a clause.
如遇 it 作句首,此型有一变化,主语为一不定式、动名词或从句。

It + SEEM / APPEAR	adjective / noun	subject
1 *It seemed* 再试一次似乎是合理的。	*reasonable*	*to try again.*
2 *It seems* 浪费掉所有那些食物似乎是一憾事。	*a pity*	*to waste all that food.*
3 *It doesn't seem* 继续下去好象没有什么用处。	*much use*	*going on.*
4 *It appears* 我们好象不大可能准时到达了。	*unlikely*	*that we'll arrive on time.*

[VP4E]
动词 4 型 E 组

If the adjective after *seem / appear* is used only predicatively (eg *awake, asleep, afraid*), *to be* is obligatory. *Happen* and *chance* are also used in this pattern.
如果 seem 和 appear 后面的形容词仅作表语用法(例如 awake, asleep, afraid),to be 则不可省略。happen 和 chance 也用于此型。

Subject + SEEM / APPEAR HAPPEN / CHANCE	to-infinitive
1 *The baby seems* 这婴儿好象睡着了。	*to be asleep / to be sleeping.*
2 *My enquiries seem* 我的质询似乎引起了怨恨。	*to have been resented.*
3 *She happened* 我往访时她凑巧不在家。	*to be out when I called.*
4 *We chanced* 我们在公园里偶遇。	*to meet in the park.*
5 *There seems* 好象有错误。	*to have been some mistake.*

[VP4F]
动词 4 型 F 组

The finites of *be* are used with a *to*-infinitive to convey a variety of meanings, ⇨*be*⁴(3)

限定动词 be 与不定式连用时可表达不同的意义(参看 be⁴ 第 3 义)。

Subject + BE	to-infinitive
1 *We're* 我们打算在五月里结婚。	*to be married in May.*
2 *At what time am I* 要我什么时候来?	*to come?*
3 *How am I* 我怎么可能偿还我的债务呢?	*to pay my debts?*

[VP5]
动词 5 型

In this pattern the auxiliary verbs or anomalous finites. *will / would, shall / should, can / could, must, dare, need* are followed by a bare infinitive (ie without *to*). The phrases *had better, had / would rather* and *would sooner* fit into this pattern.

此型中的助动词或变态限定动词 will / would, shall / should, can / could, must, dare, need 等后跟省去 to 的不定式。短语如 had better, had / would rather 和 would sooner 也适合此型。

Subject + anomalous finite	infinitive
1 *You may* 你现在可以走了。	*leave now.*
2 *You needn't* 你不必等。	*wait.*
3 *You'll* 你会在那个盒子里找到它。	*find it in that box.*
4 *I didn't dare* 我不敢告诉任何人。	*tell anyone.*
5 *You'd better* 你最好立刻动身。	*start at once.*

[VP6A]
动词 6 型 A 组

The verbs in this pattern have a noun or pronoun as direct object. Conversion to the passive voice is possible.

此型中的动词有一名词或代词作直接宾语。可能变成被动语态。

Subject + *vt*	noun / pronoun
1 *Did you enjoy* 你喜欢那部电影吗?	*the film?*
2 *We all had* 我们都玩得愉快。	*a good time.*
3 *Everyone likes* 每个人都喜欢她。	*her.*

[VP6B]
动词 6 型 B 组

The verbs in this pattern have a noun or pronoun as direct object, but conversion to the passive voice is not possible. *Have*, meaning 'possess / take / eat / drink', follows this pattern. Reflexive verbs, and verbs with cognate

objects, follow this pattern.

此型中的动词有一名词或代词作直接宾语， 但不可能变成被动语态。Have（作
'有, 吃, 饮' 解）用于此型。反身动词以及同源宾语的动词亦用于此型。

Subject + vt	noun/pronoun
1 *Have you had* 你吃过早饭了吗?	*breakfast yet?*
2 *She has* 她有绿色的眼睛。	*green eyes.*
3 *Have you hurt* 你伤了自己了吗?	*yourself?*
4 *She smiled* 她微笑以示谢意。	*her thanks.*
5 *He dreamed* 他做了一个非常怪的梦。	*a very odd dream.*

[VP6C]
动词 6 型 C 组

In this pattern the object is a gerund, not replaceable by a *to*-infinitive.

此型中的宾语是动名词, 不可用不定式代替。

Subject + vt	gerund
1 *She enjoys* 她喜爱打网球。	*playing tennis.*
2 *Have you finished* 你的话讲完没有?	*talking?*
3 *I resent* 我怨恨这般无礼地对我说话。	*being spoken to so rudely.*

[VP6D]
动词 6 型 D 组

In this pattern the object is a gerund. This may be replaced by a *to*-infinitive.
For the difference between *like swimming* and *like to swim*, see the notes on
[VP6D] in *Guide to Patterns and Usage*.

此型中的宾语为动名词, 也可用不定式代替。至于 like swimming 与 like to
swim 含义之不同, 请参阅 '英文句型及用法指南' 动词 6 型 D 组。

Subject + vt	gerund
1 *She loves* 她爱好看电影。	*going to the cinema.*
2 *I'll continue* 只要我健康良好, 我就要继续工作。	*working while my health is good.*
3 *He began* 他开始谈论他那些聪明的孩子。	*talking about his clever children.*

[VP6E]
动词 6 型 E 组

After *need*, *want* (=need) and *won't/wouldn't bear*, the gerund is equivalent
to a passive infinitive.

在 need, want (= need) 及 won't/wouldn't bear 后, 动名词相当于被动的不
定式。

Subject + NEED/WANT/BEAR gerund	
1 *He'll need* 他需要人照顾。	*looking after* (= to be looked after)
2 *My shoes want* 我的鞋子需要修补。	*mending* (= to be mended).
3 *His language wouldn't bear* 他的话不堪重述。	*repeating* (= was too bad to be repeated).

[VP7A]
动词 7 型 A 组

In this pattern the object of the verb is a *to*-infinitive. (For intransitive verbs
with the same word order, see [VP4].)

此型中动词的宾语为不定式。（关于用同样词序的不及物动词，请参看动词
4 型。）

Subject + vt	(*not*) + *to*-infinitive

1 *Do they want*	*to go?*
他们想去吗?	
2 *He pretended*	*not to see me.*
他假装没有看见我。	
3 *We hope / expect / intend*	*to climb Mount Qomolangma.*
我们希望(盼望,想要)攀登珠穆朗玛峰。	
4 *I forgot / remembered*	*to post your letters.*
我忘记(并未忘记)为你寄信。	

[VP7B]
动词 7 型 B 组

Ought, and the finites of *have* in this pattern indicate obligation. In colloquial style *have got to* is more usual than *have to.*

ought 和限定动词 have 用于此型,表示义务。在口语中 have got to 较 have to 常用。

Subject + HAVE/OUGHT	*(not)* + *to*-infinitive
1 *Do you often have*	*to work overtime?*
你时常必须加班工作吗?	
2 *You don't have*	*to leave yet, do you?*
你还不需要离开,对吗?	
3 *You ought*	*not to waste your money there.*
你不应该把你的钱浪费在那方面。	

[VP8]
动词 8 型

In this pattern the object of the verb is an interrogative pronoun or adverb (except *why* or *whether*), followed by a *to*-infinitive.

此型中动词的宾语为疑问代词或副词(why 或 whether 例外),后面跟不定式。

Subject + *vt*	interrogative pronoun / adverb + *to*-infinitive
1 *Do you know / see*	*how to do it?*
你知道怎样做了吗?	
2 *I couldn't decide*	*what to do next.*
我不能决定下一步做什么。	
3 *I've discovered*	*where to find him.*
我已发现到哪里可以找到他。	
4 *You must learn*	*when to give advice and when to be silent.*
你必须学会何时予人忠告以及何时保持沉默。	

[VP9]
动词 9 型

The object of the verb is a *that*-clause. *That* is often omitted, except after more formal verbs (eg *decide, intend*).

动词的宾语是一 that 从句。除非在较正式的动词(如 decide, intend)后,that 常被省略。

Subject + *vt*	*that*-clause
1 *I suppose*	*you'll be leaving soon.*
我认为你快要离开了。	
2 *I wish*	*you wouldn't interrupt.*
请你不要打岔。	
3 *Do you think*	*it'll rain?*
你想会下雨吗?	
4 *The workers decided*	*that they would go on strike.*
工人们决定继续罢工。	
5 *We intended*	*that John should be invited.*
我们打算邀请约翰。	

[VP10]
动词 10 型

In this pattern the object of the verb is a dependent clause or question. The clause is introduced by a relative adverb or pronoun, *what*, or *whether / if.*

此型中动词的宾语是一附属从句或问句。从句系由关系副词或代词、what 或 whether / if 所引导。

Subject + *vt*	dependent clause / question
1 *Does anyone know*	*how it happened?*

有人知道这事是怎样发生的吗?

2 *Come and see*   *what I've done!*
来看我做了些什么!

3 *I wonder*   *whether/if he'll come.*
我想知道他是否要来。

4 *She asked*   *why I was late.*
她问我为何迟到。

[**VP11**]
动词 11 型

The verb is followed by a noun or pronoun and a *that*-clause.
动词后跟一名词或代词和 that 从句。

Subject + *vt*	noun/pronoun	*that*-clause
1 *He warned*	*us*	*that the roads were icy.*
他警告我们那些道路是覆盖着冰的。		
2 *I convinced*	*the policeman*	*that I was innocent.*
我说服了警察我是无罪的。		
3 *We satisfied*	*ourselves*	*that the plan would work.*
我们确信计划可以实行。		

[**VP12A**]
动词 12 型 A 组

The verb is followed by an indirect object (IO) and a direct object (DO). The indirect object is equivalent to a prepositional object with *to*, as in [VP13A].
动词后跟一间接宾语(IO)与一直接宾语(DO)。间接宾语相当于介词 to 加宾语, 如动词 13 型 A 组所示。

Subject + *vt*	IO	DO
1 *Won't you lend*	*him*	*your car?*
你不愿意把你的汽车借给他吗?		
2 *He doesn't owe*	*me*	*anything.*
他什么东西也没有欠我。		
3 *He denied/grudged*	*her,*	*nothing.*
她要什么他便给她什么。		

[**VP12B**]
动词 12 型 B 组

In this pattern the indirect object is equivalent to a prepositional object with *for*, as in [VP13B].
此型中的间接宾语相当于介词 for 加宾语, 如动词 13 型 B 组所示。

Subject + *vt*	IO	DO
1 *She made*	*herself*	*a new dress.*
她为自己做了一件新装。		
2 *Will you do*	*me*	*a favour?*
你愿意帮我一个忙吗?		
3 *She cooked*	*her husband*	*some sausages.*
她为她的丈夫煎了些腊肠。		

[**VP12C**]
动词 12 型 C 组

Verbs in this pattern are rarely or never convertible to [VP13]. The labels IO and DO are not used.
此型中的动词极少或永不可变为 13 型。IO 和 DO 两个标示不用在此型。

Subject + *vt*	noun/pronoun	noun/pronoun
1 *Ask*	*him*	*his name.*
问他的姓名。		
2 *I envy*	*you*	*your fine garden.*
我羡慕你那座美好的花园。		
3 *He struck*	*the door*	*a heavy blow.*
他给了那门一个重击。		

[**VP13A**]
动词 13 型 A 组

In this pattern the verb is followed by a direct object, the preposition *to*, and the prepositional object. It is convertible to [VP12A].
此型动词后跟一直接宾语, 介词 to 及其宾语。此型可变为动词 12 型 A 组。

Subject + *vt*	DO	*to* + noun/pronoun

1 *She told*	*the news*	*to everyone in the village.*
她把这消息告诉了村子里的每一个人。		
2 *He sold*	*his old car*	*to one of his neighbours.*
他把他的旧汽车卖给了他的一个邻居。		
3 *I've sent*	*presents*	*to everyone in my family.*
我已给我每一位家人寄出了礼物。		

[VP13B]
动词 13 型 B 组

In this pattern the preposition is *for*. It is convertible to [VP12B]
此型中的介词是 for, 可变为动词 12 型 B 组。

Subject + vt	DO	for + noun / pronoun
1 *She made*	*a new dress*	*for her daughter.*
她为她的女儿做了一件新装。		
2 *Will you do*	*a favour*	*for a friend of mine?*
你愿意帮我朋友的忙吗?		
3 *Can you cash*	*this cheque*	*for me?*
你能为我将这张支票兑现吗?		

[VP14]
动词 14 型

In this pattern the verb is followed by a direct object and a preposition and its object. This pattern is not convertible to [VP12], as are [VP13A] and [VP13B], 'Give something to somebody' [VP12A] may be converted to 'Give somebody something' [VP13A]. 'Explain something to somebody' cannot be converted to '*Explain somebody something*'.
此型中的动词后跟一直接宾语与一介词及其宾语。 此型不象动词 13 型 A 和 B 组一样可以变为动词 12 型。 'Give something to somebody' (动词 12 型 A 组) 可以变作 'Give somebody something' (动词 13 型 A 组)。 'Explain something to somebody' 则不可以变作 '*Explain somebody something*'。

The preposition is linked to the verb and they must be learnt together, eg 'congratulate somebody *on* something', 'compare one thing *to / with* another'. In [VP15] however the prepositional phrase is variable, eg 'put something *on / under the table, in the drawer*'.
介词和动词相连接, 必须一起学习, 例如 'congratulate somebody *on* something'. 'compare one thing *to / with* another' 。 然而在动词 15 型 A 组中介词短语可以变化, 例如 'put something *on / under the table, in the drawer*' 。

Subject + vt	DO	prep	noun
1 *We congratulated*	*him*	*on*	*his success.*
我们向他祝贺他的成功。			
2 *Compare*	*the copy*	*with*	*the original.*
把这副本与原件比较一下。			
3 *He compared*	*the heart*	*to*	*a pump.*
他把心脏比作唧筒。			
4 *I explained*	*my difficulty*	*to*	*him.*
我把我的困难解释给他听。			

Variations are possible. If the DO is long, the prepositional phrase may precede it. Introductory *it* may be used when there is an infinitive phrase or a clause.
此型可以变化。 如果直接宾语很长, 介词短语可置于其前。 遇有不定式短语或从句时, 可用具有引导作用的 it。

Subject + vt	prep + noun	DO
1 *I explained*	*to him*	*the impossibility of granting his request.*
我把不可能答应他的请求解释给他听。		
2 *I must leave it*	*to your own judgement*	*to decide whether you should offer your resignation.*
我必须要你自己决定你是否应该提出辞职。		

Compare: 比较:	Subject + vt	DO	prep + noun
	1 *I explained*	*the problem*	*to him.*

我向他解释这问题。

2 *I must leave*   the decision   to you.

我应该让你来决定。

[VP15A]
动词 15 型 A 组

In [VP15A] the DO is followed by an adverbial phrase of place, duration, distance, etc which is obligatory. 'I read the book' [VP6] is a complete sentence, but '*I put the book' is not. *Put* needs an adjunct. eg 'I put the book *down/away/on the shelf*'. With verbs marked [VP15A] the adverbial is a prepositional phrase, which is variable (unlike [VP14]).

在动词 15 型 A 组中，直接宾语后面必须跟一表示地点、时间、距离等的副词短语。'I read the book'(动词 6 型)是一完整的句子，而 '*I put the book' 则否。put 需要一修饰语，例如 'I put the book *down/away/on the shelf*'。标号 15 型 A 组的动词后面的副词短语即介词短语，并可以变化(不似动词 14 型)。

Subject + vt	DO	adverbial phrase
1 *Don't let the child put*	*his head*	*out of the car window/into the plastic bag.*
不要让孩子把头伸出车窗外(伸入塑胶袋里)。		
2 *The secretary showed*	*me*	*to the door/into the reception room.*
秘书引我到门口(进入接待室)。		
3 *Please put*	*these papers*	*on that desk/in that file/in my briefcase.*
请把这些文件放在桌上(那个卷档里，我的手提箱里)。		

[VP15B]
动词 15 型 B 组

In this pattern adverbial particles are used. When the DO is a personal pronoun, the adverbial particle follows. When the DO is a noun or noun phrase, the adverbial particle may either follow or precede. If the DO is long, the adverbial particle usually precedes.

副词性小品词用于此型中。当直接宾语为一人称代词时，副词性小品词在其后。当直接宾语为一名词或名词短语时，副词性小品词在其前后均可。如果直接宾语很长，副词性小品词通常在其前。

Subject + vt	DO	adverbial particle
1 *Take*	*them/your shoes*	*off.*
把它们(你的鞋子)脱掉。		
2 *Don't throw*	*it/that old hat*	*away.*
不要把它(那顶旧帽子)丢掉。		
3 *Did you wind*	*it/the clock*	*up?*
你(给钟)上弦了吗?		

Subject + vt	adverbial particle	DO
1 *Lock*	*up*	*all your valuables.*
把你所有的贵重物品都锁起来。		
2 *She gave*	*away*	*all her old clothes.*
她把她所有的旧衣服都送给别人了。		
3 *Don't forget to switch*	*off*	*the lights in all the rooms downstairs.*
不要忘记关掉楼下所有房间里的灯。		

[VP16A]
动词 16 型 A 组

In this pattern there is an adverbial adjunct which is an infinitive phrase. This may be introduced by *in order to* or *so as to*. [VP16A] is to be distinguished from [VP17] (with the same word order).

此型中的副词修饰语为不定式短语，亦可由 in order to 或 so as to 引导。动词 16 型 A 组有别于动词 17 型(词序虽相同)。

Cf 参较: *I sent*   Tom   *to buy some fruit.* [VP16A]

我差汤姆去买些水果。(动词 16 型 A 组)

I want   Tom   *to buy some fruit.* [VP17]

我要汤姆去买些水果。(动词 17 型)

In [VP16A] the infinitive is one of purpose or intended result. In [VP17] the infinitive is part of the direct object.

动词 16 型 A 组中的不定式表示目的或意欲的结果, 动词 17 型中的不定式是直接宾语的一部分。

Subject + vt	DO	to-infinitive
1 *He brought*	*his brother*	*to see me.*
他带他兄弟来看我。		
2 *He opened*	*the door*	*to let the cat out.*
他打开门让猫出去。		
3 *They left*	*me*	*to do all the dirty work.*
他们让我做所有肮脏的工作。		

[VP16B]
动词 16 型 B 组

The DO is followed by a noun introduced by *as* or *like*, or a clause introduced by *as if or as though*.

直接宾语后跟一由 as 或 like 引导的名词, 或者由 as if 或 as though 引导的从句。

Subject + vt	DO	as / like + noun as if / though + clause
1 *I can't see*	*myself*	*as a pop singer.*
我无法想象自己做了流行歌曲歌手以后是什么样子。		
2 *Her parents spoilt*	*her*	*as a child.*
她的父母象小孩子般宠坏了她。		
3 *He carries*	*himself*	*like a soldier.*
他的举止象个军人。		
4 *You musn't treat*	*your wife*	*as if she were a servant.*
你不可以象对待仆人般对待你的妻子。		

[VP17]
动词 17 型

In this pattern the verb is followed by a noun or pronoun and a *to*-infinitive. The noun / pronoun + *to*-infinitive is the object of the verb.

此型中动词后跟一名词或代词及一不定式。 名词或代词及不定式为动词的宾语。

Subject + vt	noun / pronoun	(*not*) + *to*-infinitive
1 *He likes*	*his wife*	*to dress colourfully.*
他喜欢他的妻子衣着华丽。		
2 *They warned*	*us*	*not to be late.*
他们警告我们不要迟到。		
3 *Do you want / wish*	*me*	*to stay?*
你要(希望)我留下来吗?		

[VP18A]
动词 18 型 A 组

In this pattern the verb is used with a noun or pronoun and a bare infinitive. The verbs indicate physical perceptions. These verbs are also used in [VP19]. [VP18] indicates completed activity and [VP19] activity in progress.

此型中的动词与一名词或代词及一省去 to 的不定式连用。 这些动词表示身体上的感觉, 亦可用于动词 19 型。 动词 18 型表示完整的动作, 动词 19 型表示进行中的动作。

Subject + vt	noun / pronoun	infinitive
1 *Did you see / notice*	*anyone*	*leave the house?*
你看见(留意到)任何人离开那房屋吗?		
2 *We felt*	*the house*	*shake.*
我们觉得房子在摇动。		
3 *I once heard*	*her*	*sing the part of Aida.*
我一度听她唱过阿依达一角。		

[VP18B]
动词 18 型 B 组

A small number of verbs which do not indicate physical perceptions are used in this pattern. *Make* and *let* are examples. Compare *force / compel* and *allow / permit*, which are used in [VP17].

少数不表示身体上的感觉的动词用于此型。 make 和 let 即为其例。 比较用于动词 17 型的 force/compel 及 allow/permit:

Please let	*me*	*go.* [VP18B]
Please allow / permit	*me*	*to go.* [VP17]

Subject + *vt*	noun / pronoun	infinitive
1 *What makes*	*you*	*think so?*
什么使你这样想?		
2 *Let*	*me*	*go!*
让我走!		
3 *I've never known*	*him*	*behave so badly before.*
我从不知道他的行为这样坏。		

[VP18C]
动词 18 型 C 组

Have is used in this pattern when it means 'wish', 'experience' or 'cause'.
Have 表示'要', '经历' 或 '使' 时, 用于此型。

Subject + HAVE	noun / pronoun	infinitive
1 *What would you have*	*me*	*do?*
你要我做什么?		
2 *Have*	*the visitors*	*shown in, please.*
请把客人带进来。		
3 *I had*	*a frightening thing*	*happen to me yesterday.*
昨天我遭遇到一件可怕的事。		
4 *We often have*	*our friends*	*visit us on Sundays.*
我们时常让朋友在星期日来访。		

[VP19A]
动词 19 型 A 组

The verb is followed by a noun or pronoun and a present participle. The verbs indicate physical perceptions and are those used in [VP18A].
动词后跟一名词或代词及一现在分词。 这些动词表示身体上的感觉, 亦即用于动词 18 型 A 组中者。

Subject + *vt*	noun / pronoun	present participle
1 *Can you smell*	*something*	*burning?*
你能闻到有东西在燃烧吗?		
2 *She could feel*	*her heart*	*beating wildly.*
她可以感觉到她的心在猛跳。		
3 *Did you notice*	*anyone*	*standing at the gate?*
你注意到有人站在大门口吗?		
4 *Didn't you hear*	*me*	*knocking?*
你没有听见我敲门吗?		

[VP19B]
动词 19 型 B 组

This pattern is used for some verbs which do not indicate physical perceptions.
此型用于一些不表示身体感觉的动词。

Subject + *vt*	noun / pronoun	present participle
1 *I found*	*John*	*working at his desk.*
我发现约翰在书桌边工作。		
2 *They left*	*me*	*waiting outside.*
他们让我在外面等。		
3 *This set*	*me*	*thinking.*
此事使我思考。		
4 *Please start*	*the clock*	*going.*
请让钟走动。		
5 *He soon had*	*them all*	*laughing.*
他很快使得他们都大笑起来。		

[VP19C]
动词 19 型 C 组

In this pattern the noun or pronoun is followed by the *-ing* form of a verb, and this may be either the present participle or the gerund, depending upon whether it is preceded by a noun or pronoun, or a possessive. For fuller notes, see [VP19C] in *Guide to Patterns and Usage*.
此型中的名词或代词后跟一动词加 ing 的形式, 此一形式或为现在分词或为动名词, 要视其前为一名词或代词, 或一所有格而定。 较详细的说明请参看'英文句型

及用法指南'中'动词 19 型 C 组'。

Subject + *vt*	noun／pronoun／ possessive	*-ing* form of the verb
1 *I can't understand*	*him／his*	*behaving so foolishly.*
我不明白何以他的行为如此愚蠢。		
2 *Can you imagine*	*me／my*	*being so stupid?*
你能想象我是如此愚蠢吗?		
3 *Does this justify*	*you／your*	*taking legal action?*
这便是你要起诉的理由吗?		
4 *I can't remember*	*my parents／their*	*ever being unkind to me.*
我不记得我的父母(他们)曾对我不好。		
5 *I admire*	*Tom('s)／him／his*	*standing his ground.*
我钦佩汤姆(他,他的)坚持立场。		

[VP20]
动词 20 型

In this pattern the verb is followed by a noun or pronoun, an interrogative adverb (except *why*) or pronoun, and a *to*-infinitive. The pattern may be compared to [VP12A].
此型中的动词后跟一名词或代词,一疑问副词(why 除外)或代词,及一不定式。此型可与动词 12 型 A 组作比较。

Tell	*me*	*your name.* [VP12A]
Tell	*me*	*what to call you.* [VP20]

Subject + *vt*	noun／pronoun	interrogative + *to*-infinitive
1 *I showed*	*them*	*how to do it.*
我演示给他们看如何做这件事。		
2 *Tell*	*him*	*where to put it.*
告诉他把它放在哪里。		
3 *Ask*	*your teacher*	*how to pronounce the word.*
问你的老师怎样读这个词。		

[VP21]
动词 21 型

This pattern is similar to [VP20]. An interrogative clause follows the noun or pronoun.
此型与动词 20 型相似。疑问从句跟在名词或代词后。

Subject + *vt*	noun／pronoun	interrogative clause
1 *Tell*	*me*	*what your name is.*
告诉我你的姓名。		
2 *Ask*	*him*	*where he put it.*
问问他,他把它放在哪里。		
3 *Show*	*me*	*what you have in your* *pockets.*
把你口袋里的东西拿给我看。		

[VP22]
动词 22 型

The DO is followed by an adjective which indicates result or manner.
直接宾语后跟一表示结果或方式的形容词。

Subject + *vt*	DO	adjective
1 *We painted*	*the ceiling*	*green.*
我们把天花板漆成了绿色。		
2 *The sun keeps*	*us*	*warm.*
太阳保持我们温暖。		
3 *The mud made*	*walking*	*difficult.*
泥泞使行走困难。		

[VP23]
动词 23 型

The DO is followed by a noun (the object complement).
直接宾语后跟一名词(宾语补语)。

Subject + *vt*	DO	noun
1 *They made*	*Newton*	*President of the Royal Society.*
他们举牛顿为皇家学会主席。		
2 *They named*	*the baby*	*Richard.*

他们替那婴儿取名为理查。

3 *They usually call*		*him*	*Dick.*

他们平常叫他迪克。

[VP24A]
动词 24 型 A 组

The DO is followed by a past participle.
直接宾语后跟一过去分词。

Subject + *vt*	DO	past participle
1 *You must make*	*your views*	*known.*
你必须使你的意见让大家知道。		
2 *Have you ever heard*	*this opera*	*sung in Italian?*
你曾听过这歌剧用意大利语唱出吗？		
3 *We want*	*the work*	*finished by Saturday.*
我们要这工作在星期六以前完成。		

[VP24B]
动词 24 型 B 组

Have is used in this pattern to indicate what the subject of the sentence experiences, undergoes, or suffers (as in Nos 1 and 2), or what is held or possessed (as in No 3).
have 用于此型表示句中主语的经验或经历（如第 1, 2 句），或拥有之物（如第 3 句）。

Subject + HAVE	DO	past participle
1 *King Charles had*	*his head*	*cut off.*
查理王被人斩首。		
2 *I've recently had*	*my appendix*	*removed.*
我最近把阑尾割掉了。		
3 *They have*	*scarcely any money*	*saved for their old age.*
他们几乎没有储蓄什么钱以养老。		

[VP24C]
动词 24 型 C 组

Have and *get* are used in this pattern meaning 'cause to be'.
have 和 get 用于此型表示'使成为'。

Subject + HAVE/GET DO		past participle
1 *Can we have/get*	*the programme*	*changed?*
我们能将计划变更吗？		
2 *Please have/get*	*these letters*	*translated into English.*
请把这些信件译成英语。		
3 *I'll have/get*	*the matter*	*seen to.*
我会处理这件事。		

[VP25]
动词 25 型

The DO is followed by *to be* (often omitted) and an adjective or a noun. In spoken English [VP9] (ie with a *that*-clause) is preferred.
直接宾语后跟 to be（常被省略）与一形容词或名词。口语中则较常用动词 9 型（即与一 that 从句连用）。

Subject + *vt*	DO	(*to be*) + adjective/noun
1 *Most people considered*	*him*	(*to be*) *innocent.*
大多数人认为他是无罪的。		
2 *They all felt*	*the plan*	*to be unwise.*
他们都觉得这个计划不明智。		
3 *I've always found*	*Jonathan*	*friendly/a good friend.*
我一直觉得乔纳森很友善（是个好朋友）。		
4 *In Britain we presume*	*a man*	(*to be*) *innocent until he is proved guilty.*
在英国我们假定一个人在证实有罪以前是无罪的。		

For 1, *Most people considered that he was innocent* [VP9] is more usual. Introductory *it* is used if, instead of a noun, there is a clause, infinitive phrase, etc.
关于第 1 句, Most people considered that he was innocent（动词 9 型）较常用。遇有不是名词，而是从句，不定式短语等时，前面用 it。

Cf 参较: *Do you consider long hair for men strange?*
你认为男人留长发奇怪吗？

Do you consider it strange for men to let their hair grow long?
你认为男人把头发留得很长奇怪吗？

Anomalous verbs
变态动词

Some of the verbs in the Dictionary carry the description *anomalous verb* (abbreviated *anom v*) or *anomalous finite* (abbreviated *anom fin*). A verb is an *anomalous finite* if it forms its negative by adding the word *not* (or its contraction *-n't*) after the verb. For example, the negative of *must* is *must not* or *mustn't*. All the forms of the English anomalous verbs are set out in the table below.

本词典中有些动词附有 anomalous verb (变态动词, 略作 anom v) 或 anomalous finite (变态限定动词, 略作 anom fin) 的说明。如果一个动词的否定形式是在它的后面加 not (或缩写式 -n't)，此一动词便是变态限定动词，例如 must 的否定式是 must not 或 mustn't。兹将英语变态动词所有的形式列于下表。

Non-finite forms 非限定形式			Finite forms 限定形式	
Infinitive 不定式	Present Participle 现在分词	Past Participle 过去分词	Present Tense 现在式	Past Tense 过去式
be	*being*	*been*	*am, is, are*	*was, were*
have	*having*	*had*	*have, has*	*had*
do	*doing*	*done*	*do, does*	*did*
—	—	—	*shall*	*should*
—	—	—	*will*	*would*
—	—	—	*can*	*could*
—	—	—	*may*	*might*
—	—	—	*must*	—
—	—	—	*ought*	—
—	—	—	*need*	—
—	—	—	*dare*	—
—	—	—	—	*used*

Strong and weak forms
强式和弱式

The words listed below all have two or more different pronunciations: a *strong* form and one or more *weak* forms. It is the weak forms which occur most frequently in connected speech. For example, *from* is /frəm/ in *He ,comes from 'Spain.*

下列各词都有两种或两种以上不同的读法：一种强式读法及一种或一种以上弱式读法。弱式读法最常出现在连贯性的谈话中，例如在 He ,comes from 'Spain 一句中的 from 读作 /frəm/。

The strong form occurs when a word is said in isolation, or when it is given special emphasis in connected speech. For instance, *from* is /frɒm/ in *This ,present's not 'from John; it's 'for him.* In addition, when prepositions and auxiliary verbs come at the end of a clause they generally take their strong form, whether or not they are stressed. For example, *,Where do you 'come from? has* /frɒm/ (*not* /frəm/).

强式读法出现在一个词单独说出或在连贯性的谈话中特别被强调时。例如在 This ,present's not 'from John; it's 'for him 一句中的 from 读作 /frɒm/。此外，当介词和助动词位于一从句末尾时，不论是否重读，通常都是强式。例如 ,Where do you 'come from? 一句中的 from 读作 /frɒm/ (不是 /frəm/)。

The words below are very common in ordinary speech, and it is only by understanding the different forms and using them correctly that the learner will develop a mastery of natural, conversational English.

下列各词在一般谈话中很常用，学习者必须了解这些不同的形式而且正确地使用它们，方能精通自然的会话式的英语。

	STRONG FORM 强式	WEAK FORM 弱式	NOTES ON THE WEAK FORM 弱式的注解
DETERMINER 限定词			
a	/eɪ/	/ə/	
an	/æn/	/ən/	
his	/hɪz/	/ɪz/	Not used to begin a sentence 不用于句首
our	/ˈauə(r)/	/ɑː(r)/	
some	/sʌm/	/səm/	Used only when *some* means 'an undefined amount or number of' 仅用于当 some 表示 '未指明的量或数' 时
the	/ðiː/	/ðə/, /ðɪ/	/ðɪ/ before vowels 元音前读作 /ðɪ/
your	/jɔː(r)/	/jə(r)/	
CONJUNCTION 连接词			
and	/ænd/	/ən/	
as	/æz/	/əz/	
but	/bʌt/	/bət/	
than	/ðæn/	/ðən/	
that	/ðæt/	/ðət/	Also used when *that* is a relative pronoun 亦用于 that 作关系代词
PREPOSITION 介词			
at	/æt/	/ət/	
for	/fɔː(r)/	/fə(r)/, /fr/	/fr/ before vowels 元音前读作 /fr/
from	/frɒm/	/frəm/	
of	/ɒv/	/əv/	
to	/tuː/	/tə/	Not used before vowels 不用在元音前
PRONOUN 代词			
he	/hiː/	/iː/	Not used to begin a sentence 不用于句首
her	/hɜː(r)/	/ɜː(r)/, /ə(r)/	Not used to begin a sentence; /ə(r)/ in rapid speech 不用于句首; 说话急促时读作 /ə(r)/
him	/hɪm/	/ɪm/	
them	/ðem/	/ðəm/	
us	/ʌs/	/əs/	

1

STRONG FORM 强式	WEAK FORM 弱式	NOTES ON THE WEAK FORM 弱式的注解

VERB 动词

am	/æm/	/əm/	
are	/ɑː(r)/	/ə(r)/	
can	/kæn/	/kən/	
do	/duː/	/də/	Not used before vowels 不用于元音前
does	/dʌz/	/dəz/	
had	/hæd/	/həd/, /əd/	Auxiliary use only; /həd/ used to begin a sentence 仅用作助动词; /həd/用于句首
has	/hæz/	/həz/, /əz/, /z/, /s/	Auxiliary use only; /əz/ used after the consonants /s, z, ʃ, ʒ, tʃ, dʒ/; /həz/ used to begin a sentence 仅用作助动词; /əz/ 用在辅音 /s, z, ʃ, ʒ, tʃ dʒ/ 之后; /həz/ 用于句首
have	/hæv/	/həv/, /əv/	Auxiliary use only; /həv/ used to begin a sentence 仅用作助动词; /həv/ 用于句首
is	/ɪz/	/z/, /s/	Not used to begin or end a sentence 不用于句首或句尾
must	/mʌst/	/məst/	
shall	/ʃæl/	/ʃəl/	
was	/wɒz/	/wəz/	
were	/wɜː(r)/	/wə(r)/	
will	/wɪl/	/əl/	Not used to begin or end a sentence 不用于句首或句尾
would	/wʊd/	/əd/	Not used to begin or end a sentence 不用于句首或句尾

Contractions
缩写式

In English there are a number of contractions of words which are used in speech, and in writing which reproduces spoken language, for example drama, direct speech in novels and short stories, personal letters. It is important that the learner should learn and make use of these contracted forms if he wants his English to sound natural.

英语中有许多缩写的词在谈话里以及叙述谈话的写作中,例如戏剧、小说和短篇故事中的直接谈话、私人信件等。如果学习者想要他的英语听来自然,学习并运用这些缩写式是重要的。

When contractions are written, the two words are shortened by omitting one or two letters and joining the words together. The letters that are omitted are represented by an apostrophe(').

写缩写式时, 是将两个词省去一两个字母后连接起来。省略的字母用省略号(')来表示。

When contractions are spoken, the two words are shortened by omitting some sounds and pronouncing the two words as one.

说缩写式时, 是将两个词省略某些音后读作一个词。

PERSONAL PRONOUN + VERB

I'm	/aɪm/	I am	*she'll*	/ʃiːl/	she will
I've	/aɪv/	I have	*she'd*	/ʃiːd/	she would; she had
I'll	/aɪl/	I shall; I will			
I'd	/aɪd/	I would; I had	*it's*	/ɪts/	it is; it has
			it'll	/'ɪtl/	it will
you're	/jʊə(r)/	you are			
you've	/juːv/	you have	*we're*	/wɪə(r)/	we are
you'll	/juːl/	you will	*we've*	/wiːv/	we have
you'd	/juːd/	you would; you had	*we'll*	/wiːl/	we shall; we will
			we'd	/wiːd/	we would; we had
he's	/hiːz/	he is; he has			
he'll	/hiːl/	he will	*they're*	/'ðeɪə(r)/	they are
he'd	/hiːd/	he would; he had	*they've*	/ðeɪv/	they have
			they'll	/ðeɪl/	they will
she's	/ʃiːz/	she is; she has	*they'd*	/ðeɪd/	they would; they had

VERB + NOT

aren't	/ɑːnt/	are not	*mayn't*	/'meɪənt/	may not
can't	/kɑːnt/	cannot	*mightn't*	/'maɪtnt/	might not
couldn't	/'kʊdnt/	could not	*mustn't*	/'mʌsnt/	must not
daren't	/deənt/	dare not	*needn't*	/'niːdnt/	need not
didn't	/'dɪdnt/	did not	*oughtn't*	/'ɔːtnt/	ought not
doesn't	/'dʌznt/	does not	*shan't*	/ʃɑːnt/	shall not
don't	/dəʊnt/	do not	*shouldn't*	/'ʃʊdnt/	should not
hasn't	/'hæznt/	has not	*wasn't*	/'wɒznt/	was not
haven't	/'hævnt/	have not	*weren't*	/wɜːnt/	were not
hadn't	/'hædnt/	had not	*won't*	/wəʊnt/	will not
isn't	/'ɪznt/	is not	*wouldn't*	/'wʊdnt/	would not

OTHER COMMON CONTRACTIONS

here's	/hɪəz/	here is	*what's*	/wɒts/	what is?
how's	/haʊz/	how is?	*when's*	/wenz/	when is?
that'd	/'ðætəd/	that would	*where's*	/weəz/	where is?
that'll	/'ðætl/	that will	*who'd*	/huːd/	who would?
that's	/ðæts/	that is	*who'll*	/huːl/	who will?
there's	/ðeəz/	there is	*who's*	/huːz/	who is?
what'll	/'wɒtl/	what will			

Phonetic systems used
两种注音法

In the **Key to phonetic symbols** (facing page) two lists of symbols are provided. The first, headed 'Jones', represents the British English accent known as *Received Pronunciation* or *General British*; the second, headed 'Kenyon & Knott', represents the American English accent known as *General American*.
在下页的音标例释中, 列出两种注音法: 基于'公认的读法'或'一般的英国读法'的 Jones 音标、和基于'一般的美国读法'的 Kenyon & Knott 音标。

In the text of the dictionary, the first transcription given after each headword refers to the Jones system, and is followed by a semi-colon. The second refers to the Kenyon & Knott system.
本词典内词目所注的音标, 第一个是 Jones 音标, 第二个是 Kenyon & Knott 音标。

In cases where American pronunciation differs from British, the Jones system for British pronunciation is given first, followed by the American pronunciation in both the Jones and Kenyon & Knott systems.
若英式和美式读法有差别, 首先用 Jones 音标注出英式读法, 后面再加注 Jones 和 Kenyon & Knott 音标的美式读法。

Key to phonetic symbols   音标例释

Vowels and diphthongs   元音与双元音

Symbol 符号		Example 范例	Symbol 符号		Example 范例
Jones	Kenyon & Knott		Jones	Kenyon & Knott	
iː	i	see /siː; si/	ʌ	ʌ	cup /kʌp; kʌp/
ɪ	ɪ	sit /sɪt; sɪt/	ɜː	ɝ	fur /fɜː(r); fɝ/
e	ɛ	ten /ten; tɛn/	ə	ə	ago /əˈɡəʊ; əˈgo/
æ	æ	hat /hæt; hæt/	ɚ	ɚ	never /ˈnevə(r); ˈnɛvɚ/
ɑː	ɑr	arm /ɑːm; ɑrm/	eɪ	e	page /peɪdʒ; pedʒ/
	ɑ	palm /pɑːm; pɑm/	əʊ	o	home /həʊm; hom/
	æ	ask /ɑːsk; æsk/	aɪ	aɪ	five /faɪv; faɪv/
ɒ	ɑ	got /ɡɒt; gɑt/	aʊ	aʊ	now /naʊ; naʊ/
	ɔ	long /lɒŋ; lɔŋ/	ɔɪ	ɔɪ	join /dʒɔɪn; dʒɔɪn/
ɔː	ɔ	saw /sɔː; sɔ/	ɪə	ɪr	near /nɪə(r); nɪr/
	ɔr	born /bɔːn; bɔrn/	eə	ɛr	hair /heə(r); hɛr/
ʊ	ʊ	put /pʊt; pʊt/	ʊə	ʊr	pure /pjʊə(r); pjʊr/
uː	u	too /tuː; tu/			

Consonants   辅音

Symbol 符号		Example 范例	Symbol 符号		Example 范例
Jones	Kenyon & Knott		Jones	Kenyon & Knott	
p	p	pen /pen; pɛn/	s	s	so /səʊ; so/
b	b	bad /bæd; bæd/	z	z	zoo /zuː; zu/
t	t	tea /tiː; ti/	ʃ	ʃ	she /ʃiː; ʃi/
d	d	did /dɪd; dɪd/	ʒ	ʒ	vision /ˈvɪʒn; ˈvɪʒən/
k	k	cat /kæt; kæt/	h	h	how /haʊ; haʊ/
g	g	got /ɡɒt; gɑt/	m	m	man /mæn; mæn/
tʃ	tʃ	chin /tʃɪn; tʃɪn/	n	n	no /nəʊ; no/
dʒ	dʒ	June /dʒuːn; dʒun/	ŋ	ŋ	sing /sɪŋ; sɪŋ/
f	f	fall /fɔːl; fɔl/	l	l	leg /leg; lɛg/
v	v	voice /vɔɪs; vɔɪs/	r	r	red /red; rɛd/
θ	θ	thin /θɪn; θɪn/	j	j	yes /jes; jɛs/
ð	ð	then /ðen; ðɛn/	w	w	wet /wet; wɛt/
				hw	what /wɒt; hwɑt/

Abbreviations used in the text

/'/ or /ˈ/ represents *primary stress* as in **about** /əˈbaut; əˈbaʊt/

/'/ 代表 Jones 音标的重音, /ˈ/ 代表 K. K. 音标的重音, 如 about /əˈbaut; əˈbaʊt/ 中之重音。

/ˌ/ or /ˌ/ represents *secondary stress* as in **academic** /ˌækəˈdemɪk; ˌækəˈdɛmɪk/

/ˌ/ 代表 Jones 音标的次重音, /ˌ/ 代表 K. K. 音标的次重音, 如 academic /ˌækəˈdemɪk; ˌækəˈdɛmɪk/ 中之次重音。

(r) An 'r' in parentheses is heard in British pronunciation when it is immediately followed by a word, or a suffix, beginning with a vowel. Otherwise it is omitted. In American pronunciation no 'r' of the phonetic spelling or of the ordinary spelling is omitted.

在英式发音中, (r)后面紧跟的词或后缀以元音开始时, 则 r 音应该读出, 否则就省略。在美式发音中, 音标或普通拼字中的 r 音不能省略。

/-/ Hyphens preceding and/or following parts of a repeated transcription indicate that only the repeated part changes.

在部分之重复注音前面或后面所接的短划, 表示只有重复的部分有变化。

⇨ the Introduction for a full explanation of the phonetic information.

有关发音之详细说明, 请参看绪论。

Note that in the introductory pages of this dictionary, up to this page, for simplicity only the Jones phonetic system is used in the examples.

本页之前的绪论和其他解释, 只采用 Jones 音标于例子中, 以免混乱。

Abbreviations used in the text 本词典略语表

abbr	abbreviation	(略)	略语	neg	negative(ly)	(否定)	否定的(地)
adj, adjj	adjective(s)	(形)	形容词	opp	opposite	(相反)	相反的, 反义词
adv, advv	adverb(s)	(副)	副词				
adv part	adverbial particle	(副小品)	副词性小品词	P	proprietary name	(商标)	专利商标名
affirm	affirmative(ly)	(肯定)	肯定的(地)	*part adj*	participial adjective	(分形)	分词形容词
anom fin	anomalous finite	(变定)	变态限定动词	pers	person	(人称)	人称
attrib	attributive(ly)	(用作定语)	用作定语	*pers pron*	personal pronoun	(人称代)	人称代词
aux	auxiliary	(助)	助动词	phr	phrase	(短语)	短语
[C]	countable noun	(可数)	可数名词	*pl*	plural	(复)	复数(的)
Cf, cf	compare	(参较)	参较	*poss*	possessive	(所有)	所有格的
collect	collective(ly)	(集合用法)	集合用法	*pp*	past participle	(过去分词)	过去分词
comp	comparative	(比较级)	比较级	pred	predicative(ly)	(用作表语)	用作表语
conj	conjunction	(连)	连接词	*pref*	prefix	(前缀)	前缀
def art	definite article	(定冠)	定冠词	*prep*	preposition(al)	(介词)	介词, 介词的
demonstr	demonstrative	(指示)	指示词	*pres p*	present participle	(现在分词)	现在分词
e g	for example	(例如)	例如	*pres t*	present tense	(现在)	现在式
esp	especially	(尤指)	尤指	*pron*	pronoun	(代)	代词
etc	and the others	(等)	等等	*pt*	past tense	(过去)	过去式
F	French	(法)	法国的, 法语	RC	Roman Catholic	(天主教)	天主教
fem	feminine	(阴)	阴性的	*reflex*	reflexive	(反身)	反身的
G	German	(德)	德国的, 德语	*rel*	relative	(关系)	关系代词
GB	British/Britain	(英)	英国的, 英国用法	sb	somebody	(某人)	某人
				Scot	Scottish	(苏)	苏格兰的, 苏格兰语
Gk	Greek	(希)	希腊的, 希腊语				
				sing	singular	(单)	单数(的)
Hc	height about	(高约)	高度约为	sth	something	(某事物)	某物或某事
I	Italian	(意)	意大利的, 意大利语	*suff*	suffix	(后缀)	后缀
				superl	superlative	(最高)	最高级
i e	which is to say	(意即)	意即	trans	transitive	(及物)	及物的
illus	illustration	(插图)	插图	[U]	uncountable noun	(不可数)	不可数名词
imper	imperative	(祈使)	祈使语气	US	America(n)	(美)	美国(的)
impers	impersonal	(无人称)	无人称的用法	usu	usual(ly)	(通常)	通常的(地)
indef art	indefinite article	(不定冠)	不定冠词	*v, vv*	verb(s)	(动)	动词
inf	infinitive	(不定式)	不定式	[VP]	Verb Pattern	(动型)	动词类型
int	interjection	(感)	感叹词	*vi*	verb intransitive	(不及物动词)	不及物动词
interr	interrogative	(疑问)	疑问的				
intrans	intransitive	(不及物)	不及物的	*vt*	verb transitive	(及物动词)	及物动词
Lat	Latin	(拉)	拉丁语	⇨	look at	(参看)	参看
Lc	length about	(长约)	长度约为	♂	male	(男性)	男性(的)
masc	masculine	(阳)	阳性的	♀	female	(女性)	女性(的)
n, nn	noun(s)	(名)	名词				

Specialist English registers + abbreviations used 专门名词及其略语

accounts	帐目	history (hist)	历史(史)
aerospace	太空	journalism	新闻学
algebra (alg)	代数学(代数)	legal	法律
anatomy (anat)	解剖学(解剖)	linguistics (ling)	语言学(语言)
architecture (archit)	建筑学(建筑)	mathematics (maths)	数学(数学)
arithmetic (arith)	算术(算术)	mechanics (mech)	机械学(机械)
art	艺术	medical (med)	医学的(医)
astronomy (astron)	天文学(天文)	meteorology (met)	气象学(气象)
ballet	芭蕾舞	military (mil)	军语(军)
biblical	圣经的,圣经中的(圣经)	music	音乐
biology (biol)	生物学(生物)	mythology (myth)	神话
book-keeping	簿记	nautical (naut)	航海的(航海)
botany (bot)	植物学(植物)	pathology (path)	病理学(病理)
business	贸易(贸)	philosophy (phil)	哲学(哲)
chemistry (chem)	化学(化学)	phonetics (phon)	语音学(语音)
cinema	电影	photography (photo)	摄影术(摄影)
commerce (comm)	商业(商)	physics (phys)	物理学(物理)
computers (comp)	电子计算机(计算机)	physiology (physiol)	生理学(生理)
cricket	板球戏	politics (pol)	政治学(政治)
ecclesiastical (eccles)	教会的(教会)	psychology (psych)	心理学(心理)
engineering (eng)	工程学(工程)	racing	赛马,赛车
electricity (electr)	电学(电)	radio telegraphy (radio)	无线电报(无线电)
farming	农业	rugby	橄榄球
finance (fin)	财政学(财政)	science	科学
football	足球	sport	运动
gambling	赌博	tennis	网球
geology (geol)	地质学(地质)	theatre	戏剧
geometry (geom)	几何学(几何)	trigonometry (trig)	三角学(三角)
grammar (gram)	语法(语法)	zoology (zool)	动物学(动物)

Stylistic values　字格标准

archaic	古语(古)	laudatory (laud)	赞美语(赞)
colloquial (colloq)	口语、俗语(口)	literally (lit)	按照字面(字面)
dated	过时用语	literary (liter)	文学的(文)
derogatory (derog)	贬抑语(贬)	modern use (mod use)	现代用法
dialect (dial)	方言(方)	old use	旧用法
emotive (emot)	情感的(情感)	pejorative (pej)	轻蔑语(蔑)
emphatic (emph)	强势语	poetic (poet)	诗中用语(诗)
euphemistic (euphem)	委婉语	proverb (prov)	谚语(谚)
facetious (facet)	玩笑语	rare	罕用的(罕)
figurative (fig)	比喻用法(喻)	rhetorical (rhet)	修辞学的(修辞)
formal	正式用语	slang (sl)	俚语(俚)
humorous (hum)	诙谐语(谐)	vulgar (vulg)	粗鄙用语(鄙)
ironical (ironic)	反语的,反语用法(反语)	⚠ taboo	避讳语(讳)
jocular (joc)	戏谑语(谑)		

A a

A¹, a /eɪ; e/ (*pl* **A's, a's** /eɪz; ez/) the first letter of the English alphabet: 英文字母的第一个字母: *He knows the subject from A to Z*, knows it thoroughly. 他精通此一科目(从头到尾彻底了解)。 **A1** /ˌeɪ 'wʌn; ˌe'wʌn/ **(a)** (of ships) classified as first class. (指船舶)列为第一等的。 ⇨ **Lloyd's.** **(b)** (colloq) excellent: (口) 高级的; 头等的; 极佳的; *A1 dinner*; 头等餐; *feeling A1*, in excellent health. 感觉健康极佳。

a² /ə; ə; *strong form:* eɪ; e/, **an** /ən; ən; *strong form:* æn; æn/ *indef art* **1** one: 一个: *I said 'a train was coming, not 'the train.* 我是说'一辆火车'正驶来, 不是'那辆火车'. *I have a pen (pl some pens).* 我有一枝笔 (复数用 some pens)。 *Have you a pen (pl any pens)?* 你有一枝笔 (复数用 any pens) 吗? Cf 参较 **some, any, several, a few** with *pl nn.* **2** (used in the pattern *a + adj* or *pron* of number and quantity): (用于 a + adj 或 pron 的句型中, 表示数与量): *a lot of money*; 很多钱; *a great many friends*; 很多朋友; *a few books*; 几本书; *a little more.* 再多一点。 **3** (with possessives): (用于所有格名词或代词连用): *a friend of my father's*, one of my father's friends; 我父亲的一个朋友; *a book of John's*, one of John's books. 约翰的一本书。 **4** (used in the pattern *many / such / what + a*): (用于 many/such/what+a 的句型中): *Many a man would be glad of the opportunity / such an opportunity.* 许多人都会对有这机会(这样一个机会)感到高兴。 *What an opportunity you missed!* 你失去了多么好的机会呵! **5** (used in the pattern *half+a+n*): (用于 half+a+n 的句型中): *half a dozen*, 半打; *half an hour*; 半小时; (before 1971)*half a crown*, the sum of 2s 6d. (一九七一年以前) 半克朗 (等于二先令六便士之钱数)。 Cf 参较 *a half-crown*, former coin worth 2s 6d (=12½ p). 半克朗 (昔日面值二先令六便士的硬币)(=12½ 便士)。 **6** (used in the pattern *as/how/so/too+adj+a*): (用于 as/how/so/too+adj+a 的句型中): *He's not so big a fool as he looks.* 他并不是象他表面上看起来那样的一个大傻瓜。 *She's as clever a girl as you can wish to meet.* 她就是你希望遇见的那种聪明女孩子。 *It's too difficult a book for me.* 对我来说, 这是一本非常难的书。 **7** that which is called; any; every (no *article* in *pl*): 所谓的; 任何的; 每一(复数不用冠词): *A horse is an animal.* 马是动物。 Cf 参较 *Horses are animals.* **8** (When two objects, articles, are naturally go together and are thought of as a unit, the *indef art* is not repeated): (当两件物品等具有自然连带关系, 且被认为是一个单位时, 不须重复不定冠词): *a cup and saucer*; 一副杯碟; *a knife and fork.* 一副刀叉。 **9** (used with a person's name, and the title *Mr, Mrs*, etc to indicate that the person is perhaps unknown to the person addressed): (与人名及 Mr, Mrs 等称呼或头衔连用, 表示此人可能为对方所不认识): *A Mr White has called.* 有一位怀特先生来访过(或来过电话)。 *A Mrs Green is asking to see you.* 有一位格林太太要见你。 **10** one like: 象…的一个(人或物): *He thinks he's a Napoleon*, a man like Napoleon. 他认为他是一个象拿破仑似的人物。 **11** (in *at a*, (in some phrases) the same: (用于某些短语中) 相同的; 同一的): *They're all of a size.* 它们都是同样大小的(全是同号的)。 *Carry them three at a time.* 每次搬三件。 ***Birds of a feather flock together***, (prov) people of the same kind like to be together. (谚) 物以类聚; 人以群分。 **12** (used distributively): (作分配语用): *twice a month*, 每月两次; *20 p a pound*; 每磅二十便士; *50 p an hour*; 每小时五十便士; *sixty miles an hour.* 每小时六十英里。

aback /ə'bæk; ə'bæk/ *adv* backwards. 向后地; 后退地。 **be ˌtaken a'back**, be startled, disconcerted. 吃惊; 慌乱。

aba·cus /'æbəkəs; 'æbəkəs/ (*pl* **-cuses** /-kəsiz; -kə,siz/ or **-ci** /'æbəsaɪ; 'æbə,saɪ/) *n* frame with beads or balls sliding on rods, for teaching numbers to children, or (still in the East) for calculating; early form of digital computer. 算盘(木框内有珠或球可在细杆上滑动, 用以教儿童算术, 或仍用于东方作算具者); 早期的数字计算机。

an abacus

abaft /ə'bɑːft US: ə'bæft; ə'bæft/ *adv, prep* (naut) at, in, toward, the stern half of a ship; nearer the stern than; behind. (航海)在船艉; 向船尾; 较…更接近船尾; 在…之后。

aban·don¹ /ə'bændən; ə'bænden/ *vt* **1** [VP6A] go away from, not intending to return to; forsake: 抛弃; 遗弃: *The order was given to ～ ship* for all on board to leave the (sinking) ship. 下令弃船(命令船上所有的人员离开下沉中的船)。 *The cruel man ～ed his wife and child.* 那个狠心的男人遗弃了妻儿。 **2** [VP6A] give up: 放弃: *They ～ed the attempt*, stopped trying. 他们放弃尝试。 *They had ～ed all hope*, no longer had any hope. 他们已经放弃了一切希望(不再抱任何希望)。 *The new engine design had to be ～ed for lack of financial support.* 因缺乏资助, 不得不放弃新引擎的设计。 **3** [VP14] ～ **oneself to**, give oneself up completely to, eg passions, impulses: 纵情; 恣意; 耽溺: *He ～ed himself to despair.* 他陷于绝望。 **～ed** *part adj* **1** given up to bad ways; depraved; profligate: 耽于恶习的; 堕落的; 放纵的; 恣意的: *You ～ed wretch!* 你这个恶棍! **2** deserted; forsaken. 被遗弃的; 被抛弃的。 **～·ment** *n* [U]

aban·don² /ə'bændən; ə'bænden/ *n* [U] careless freedom, as when one gives way to impulses: 放任; 放纵; 纵情; 狂放: *waving their arms with ～.* 尽情挥舞着手臂。

abase /ə'beɪs; ə'bes/ *vt* [VP6B] ～ **oneself**, humiliate or degrade oneself; 屈辱; 自贬: ～ *oneself so far as to do sth.* lower oneself in dignity to the extent of doing sth. 自贬身份至做某事的地步。 **～·ment** *n* [U]

abash /ə'bæʃ; ə'bæʃ/ *vt* [VP6A] (passive only) cause to feel self-conscious or embarrassed: (仅用于被动语态)使感觉不自然; 使局促不安; 使困窘; 使感到尴尬: *The poor man stood/felt ～ed at this display of wealth*, was confused, not knowing what to do or say. 那个穷人面对着这番财富的炫耀, 感到惶恐不知所措。

abate /ə'beɪt; ə'bet/ *vt, vi* **1** [VP6A, 2A] (liter) (of winds, storms, floods, pain, etc) make or become less: (文)(指风, 暴风雨, 洪水, 疼痛等)减少; 减轻; 减退: *The ship sailed when the storm ～d.* 这船在暴风雨减弱时起航。 **2** [VP6A] (legal) bring to an end; abolish: (法律)废除; 停止: *We must ～ the smoke nuisance in our big cities.* 我们必须消除大城市里烟尘污染。 **～·ment** *n* [U] abating; decrease. 减少; 减小; 减退; 废除; 停止。

ab·at·toir /'æbətwɑː(r) US: ˌæbə'twɑːr; ˌæbə'twɑr/ *n* slaughter-house (for cattle, sheep, etc). (宰牛羊等

的)屠宰场。

abbé /'æbeɪ US: ˌæ'beɪ; 'æbeɪ/ n (courtesy title for a) French priest, esp one without official duties. 法国传教士(尤指无公务者);法国教士之尊称;神父。

ab·bess /'æbes; 'æbɪs/ n woman (*Mother Superior*) at the head of a convent or nunnery. 女修道院院长。

ab·bey /'æbɪ; 'æbɪ/ n (pl **-beys**) 1 building(s) in which men (*monks*) or women (*nuns*) live as a community in the service of God. 修道院(修士或修女修道之所)。2 the whole number of monks or nuns in an ∼. 修道院中全体修士或修女。3 church or house which was once an ∼ or part of an ∼. (曾为修道院或修道院之一部分的)大教堂或大宅第。the A∼, of that at Westminster A∼, London. (常用以指)伦敦威斯敏斯特大教堂;西敏寺。

ab·bot /'æbət; 'æbət/ n man (*Father Superior*) at the head of the monks in an abbey or monastery. 修道院院长;方丈;住持。

ab·bre·vi·ate /ə'briːvɪeɪt; ə'brivɪˌet/ vt [VP6A, 14] shorten (a word, title, etc): 将(词,头衔等)缩写: ∼ January to Jan. 将 January 缩写为 Jan。⇨ **abridge**. **ab·bre·vi·ation** /əˌbriːvɪ'eɪʃn; ə,brivɪ'eʃən/ n 1 [U] abbreviating or being ∼d. 缩写。2 [C] shortened form (esp of a word). (尤指词的)缩写式。⇨ App 2, 9. 参看附录二,九。

ABC /ˌeɪ biː 'siː; 'e'bi'si/ n 1 the letters A to Z of the (Roman) alphabet. 拉丁字母表。2 simplest facts of a subject, to be learnt first. (初学者必学的)基本知识;初步;入门。

ab·di·cate /'æbdɪkeɪt; 'æbdəˌket/ vt, vi 1 [VP6A] give up, renounce, a high office, authority or control, responsibility. 放弃(高职位,权柄或统治,职责)。2 [VP2A] give up the throne: 放弃王位;退位;逊位: *King Edward VIII* ∼ *d in 1936 and was created Duke of Windsor*. 英王爱德华八世于一九三六年放弃王位并受封为温莎公爵。**ab·di·ca·tion** /ˌæbdɪ'keɪʃn; ˌæbdə'keʃən/ n 1 [U] abdicating. 放弃权位、职责等;放弃王位;退位;逊位。2 [C] instance of this. 放弃权位、职责、王位等的实例。

ab·do·men /'æbdəmen; 'æbdəmən/ n 1 (colloq 口语 *belly*) part of the body that includes the stomach and bowels. 腹部(包括肠胃)。⇨ the illus at **trunk**. 看看 trunk 之插图。2 last of the three divisions of an insect, spider, etc. (昆虫,蜘蛛等之)腹部(即其身体三段中之最后一段)。⇨ the illus at **insect**. 参看 insect 之插图。

ab·domi·nal /æb'dɒmɪnl; æb'dɑmənl/ adj in, of, for, the abdomen: 腹部中的;腹部的: ∼ *pains;* 腹痛; *an* ∼ *operation*. 腹部手术。⇨ **intestinal**.

ab·duct /æb'dʌkt; æb'dʌkt/ vt [VP6A] take or lead (esp a woman or child) away unlawfully, by force or fraud. 绑架; 诱拐 (尤指妇女或小孩)。⇨ **kidnap**. **ab·duc·tion** /æb'dʌkʃn; æb'dʌkʃən/ n

abeam /ə'biːm; ə'bim/ adv (naut) on a line at a right angle to the length of a ship or aircraft: (航海)与船身(或航空器机身)成直角的;在正横; 横着: *The lighthouse was* ∼ *of the ship*. 灯塔正对着船的舷侧。

abed /ə'bed; ə'bɛd/ adv (old use) in bed. (旧用法)在床上。

ab·er·ra·tion /ˌæbə'reɪʃn; ˌæbə'reʃən/ n 1 [U] (usu fig) straying away from the right path, from what is normal: (通常作喻)偏离正道; 失常; 越轨: *stealing sth in a moment of* ∼. 一时反常偷了东西。2 [C] instance of this; defect: 失常之行为或实例; 过失: *The delay was caused by an* ∼ *in the computer*. 延搁系因电脑误差所致。**ab·er·rant** /æ'berənt; æb'ɛrənt/ adj straying away from what is normal, expected or usual; not true to type. 偏离正道的; 失常的; 越轨的; 差的。

abet /ə'bet; ə'bɛt/ vt (**-tt-**) [VP6A, 14] (legal) help (sb) (*in* doing wrong); encourage (vice, crime): (法律)帮助(某人)(为非作歹); 教唆; 唆使: ∼ *sb in a crime*. 教唆某人犯罪。*aid and* ∼ *sb*. (legal) be an accomplice

in his wrongdoing. (法律)与某人同谋共犯。

abey·ance /ə'beɪəns; ə'beəns/ n [U] (formal) condition of not being in force or in use for a time: (正式用语)暂时无效; 暂被使用: *The question is in* ∼, is suspended, eg until more information is obtained. 问题暂时搁置(例如,待获得较多资料时再行研究)。*fall / go into* ∼, (legal) (of a law, rule, custom, etc) be suspended; be no longer observed. (法律)(指法令,规则,习俗等)失效;不再为大家所遵行,中止。

ab·hor /əb'hɔː(r); əb'hɔr/ vt (**-rr-**) [VP6A] think of with hatred and disgust; detest: 憎恨; 厌恶: ∼ *cruelty to animals*. 憎恨虐待动物。**~·rence** /əb'hɒrəns US: -'hɔr-; əb'hɔrəns/ n [U] hatred and disgust: 憎恨; 厌恶: *hold sth in* ∼ *rence;* 憎恨某事物; *his* ∼ *rence of flattery*. 他对于谄媚之憎恶。**~·rent** /əb'hɒrənt US: -'hɔr-; əb'hɔrənt/ adj hateful; causing horror (to sb, to his feelings). 可恨的; 可恶的 (与 to 连用, 后接某人或某情)。

abide /ə'baɪd; ə'baɪd/ vt, vi (pt, pp (1, 2, 4) ∼d, (3) **abode** /ə'bəʊd; ə'bod/) 1 [VP3A] ∼ *by*, (formal) be faithful to; keep: (正式用语)忠于; 遵守: ∼ *by a promise/decision*. 遵守诺言(决定)。*I* ∼ *by* (colloq 'stick to') *what I said*. (等于俗语的 I stick to what I said) 我是言而有信的。*You'll have to* ∼ *by the consequences*, endure them. 你必将自食其果。(仅用于指不良之后果。) 2 [VP6A] (esp with *can't* or *couldn't*) endure; bear: (尤与 can't 或 couldn't 连用)忍耐; 忍受: *She can't* ∼ *that man*. 她无法忍受那个人。3 [VP2C] (in old or liter use) rest, remain, stay: (旧用法或文学用语)停留; 居留; 逗留: ∼ *at / in a place;* 居留于某处; ∼ *with sb*. 与某人同住。4 [VP 6 A] (liter) wait for: (文)等待: ∼ *the event;* 等待事件之发生; ∼ *sb's coming*. 等待某人来临。**abiding** adj (liter) never-ending; lasting. (文)永无终止的; 永恒的。

abil·ity /ə'bɪlətɪ; ə'bɪlətɪ/ n 1 [U] (potential) capacity or power (to do sth physical or mental): (从事体力或脑力活动的)能力; 潜力: *to the best of my* ∼, as well as I can. 尽我的能力。*I do not doubt your* ∼ *to do the work*. 我不怀疑你有能力胜任这项工作。2 [U] cleverness; intelligence: 聪明; 智慧; 才智: *a man of great* ∼. 极有才智的人。3 [C] (pl **-ties**) special natural power to do sth well; talent: 才能; 才干: *a man of many abilities*. 有多方面才能的人。

ab initio /ˌæb ɪ'nɪʃɪəʊ; 'æbɪ'nɪʃɪ,o/ adv (Lat) from the beginning. (拉)从头。

ab·ject /'æbdʒekt; 'æbdʒɛkt/ adj 1 (of conditions) wretched; miserable: (指境况)悲惨的; 可怜的: *living in* ∼ *poverty*. 生活赤贫。2 (of persons, their actions, behaviour) degraded; deserving contempt because cowardly or self-abasing: (指人,动作,行为)下流的; 下贱的; 卑鄙的; (因怯懦或自贬而)可鄙的: ∼ *behaviour;* 卑鄙的行为; *an* ∼ *apology*. 低声下气的道歉; 求饶。**~·ly** adv **ab·jec·tion** /æb'dʒekʃn; æb'dʒɛkʃən/ n

ab·jure /əb'dʒʊə(r); əb'dʒʊr/ vt [VP6A] (formal) promise or swear solemnly on oath or in public to give up, eg a belief, a right, evil ways: (正式用语)承诺或发誓放弃某种信仰、权利、恶习等: ∼ *one's religion*. 发誓放弃其宗教信仰。**ab·ju·ra·tion** /ˌæbdʒʊə'reɪʃn; ˌæbdʒʊ'reʃən/ n [U] abjuring; state of having been ∼d; [C] action of this: 誓弃; 誓绝; 发誓放弃之行为: *an abjuration of faith*. 放弃信仰。

ab·la·tive /'æblətɪv; 'æblətɪv/ adj, n (gram) name of a form in Latin nouns indicating an agent, instrument or cause. (语法)夺格(拉丁文名词表示动作者,工具或原因的格); 夺格的。the ∼ *case*, ⇨ case[1](3).

ab·laut /'æblaʊt; 'ablaʊt/ n (ling) systematic vowel changes in verb forms of Indo-European languages (as in *drive, drove, driven*). (语言)元音变换(印欧语系之语言中,动词有系统的变换,例如 drive, drove, driven 中各元音之变换)。

ablaze /ə'bleɪz; ə'blez/ pred adj, adv 1 on fire, in a

blaze: 着火; 燃烧; 炽燃: *set it* ~. 点燃。*The whole building was soon* ~. 整个建筑物不一会就全烧起来了。 **2** (fig) shining; bright; excited: (喻) 光辉明亮的; 激动 的: *The streets were* ~ *with lights*. 各街道灯火辉 煌。*Her face was* ~ *with anger*. 她怒容满面。

able /'eɪbl; 'ebl/ *adj* **1** *be* ~ *to do sth*, have the power, means or opportunity to do sth: 有能力,办法或 机会做某事; 能: *Shall/Will you be* ~ *to come?* 你能来 吗? *You are better* ~ *to do it than I am*. 你比我更 有能力担任此事。 ⇨ **can², could**. **2** (*-r, -st*) clever; capable; having or showing knowledge or skill: 聪明 的; 能干的; 有本事的: *an* ~ *lawyer*; 能干的律师; *an* ~ *speech*; 一篇精辟的演说; *The* ~*st/most* ~ *man I know*. 我所认识最有干劲的人。 ,~-'bodied /-'bɒdɪd; -'bɑdɪd/ *adj* physically strong. 身体强壮的。 ,~-'seaman, ,~-,bodied 'seaman *n* (GB abbr 英略 = AB) seaman trained and certified for all duties. (受 过训练并获证明能担承担各种任务的)一等水手; 二等水兵。 **ably** /'eɪblɪ; 'eblɪ/ *adv* in an ~ manner. 干练地; 能 干地。

ab·lu·tion /ə'bluːʃn; əb'luʃən/ *n* (usu *pl*) (formal) ceremonial washing of the hands or the body, esp as an act of religion: (通常用复数)(正式用语)洗手礼; 净体礼 (尤指宗教上者): *perform one's* ~*s*, (often joc or fac) wash oneself. (常作谑或玩笑语)沐浴。

ab·ne·ga·tion /ˌæbnɪ'ɡeɪʃn; ˌæbnɪ'ɡeʃən/ *n* [U] (formal) self-denial; (often 常作 ,**self-'**~) self-sacrifice. (正式用语)克制; 自我牺牲。

ab·nor·mal /æb'nɔːml; æb'nɔrml/ *adj* different, often in an undesirable way, from what is normal, ordinary or expected. 不正常的; 反常的; 变态的。 ~·**ly** *adv* ~·**ity** /ˌæbnɔː'mælɪtɪ; ˌæbnɔr'mælɪtɪ/ *n* [U] quality of being ~; [C] (*pl* **-ties**) sth that is ~. 不正 常; 反常; 变态(性)反常或变态的事物。

Abo /'æbəʊ; 'æbo/ *n* (*pl* Abos) △ (derog) (讳, 贬) = Aborigine.

aboard /ə'bɔːd; ə'bord/ *adv, prep* on (to) or in (to) a ship, aircraft, or (US) a train or motor-coach: 在 (向)船上, 飞机上, 或(美)火车或公共汽车上: *It's time to go* ~. 是上船(机、车等)的时候了。*All* ~! (eg as a come ~) 请各位上船(飞机等)! *Welcome* ~! (eg as a greeting by a stewardess on an aircraft.) 欢迎各位搭乘 本飞机(船等)! (例如女服务员对旅客的欢迎语。)

abode¹ /ə'bəʊd; ə'bod/ *n* **1** (old or liter use) house; dwelling-place: (旧用法或文学用语)房屋; 住所: *take up one's* ~ *with one's parents-in-law*, go and live with them. (男)与岳父母同住; (女)与翁姑同住。**2** (legal) (法 律) *place of* ~. domicile. 住所。*of/with no fixed* ~, having no fixed dwelling-place. 无固定住所。

abode² /ə'bəʊd; ə'bod/ *pt, pp* of **abide**.

abol·ish /ə'bɒlɪʃ; ə'bɑlɪʃ/ *vt* [VP6A] put an end to, do away with, eg war, slavery, an old custom. 废 止; 废除; 革除(例如战争, 奴役, 旧习俗)。**abol·ition** /ˌæbə'lɪʃn; ˌæbə'lɪʃən/ *n* [U] ~ing or being ~ed (esp used, in the 18 th and 19 th cc, of Negro slavery.) 废 止; 废除; (尤用以指十八之十九世纪之)黑奴制度的废除。 **abol·ition·ist** /ˌæbə'lɪʃənɪst; ˌæbə'lɪʃənɪst/ *n* (esp) person who wished to ~ Negro slavery. (尤指)主张废 除黑奴制度者。

A-bomb /'eɪ bɒm; 'e,bɑm/ *n* ⇨ **atomic**.

abom·in·able /ə'bɒmɪnəbl; ə'bɑmɪnəbl/ *adj* **1** causing hatred and disgust (*to* sb). 可憎恶的 (与 to 连用, 后接 某人)。**2** (colloq) unpleasant; bad: (口)令人不愉快的; 恶劣的: ~ *weather/food*. 恶劣的天气 (食物)。,~·'**snowman**, ~ yeti. **abom·in·ably** /-əblɪ; -əblɪ/ *adv*

abom·in·ate /ə'bɒmɪneɪt; ə'bɑmə,net/ *vt* [VP6A, C] detest; feel hatred and disgust for: (colloq) 憎恶; 厌恶; (口)不喜欢。**abom·in·ation** /ə,bɒmɪ'neɪʃn; ə,bɑmə'neʃən/ **1** [U] horror and disgust: 憎恶; 厌恶: *hold sth in abomination*. 憎恶某事物。**2** [C] sth that arouses horror and disgust (*to* sb). 令人憎恶之事物 (与 to 连用, 后接某人)。

abo·rig·in·al /ˌæbə'rɪdʒənl; ˌæbə'rɪdʒənl/ *adj* (of races of people, living creatures, etc) belonging to, existing in, a region from earliest times, or from the time when the region was first known. (指人类种族, 生 物等)从最早时就属于或存在于某一地区的; 当某一地区初 为人所知时就属于或存在于该地区的; 土著的。□ *n* ~ inhabitant, plant, etc of a region. (某地区之)土著; 土 人; 土产植物等。**abo·rig·ines** /ˌæbə'rɪdʒəniːz; ˌæbə-'rɪdʒə,niz/ *n pl* **the** ~, the ~ inhabitants. 土著; 土 人。**Abo·rig·ine** /ˌæbə'rɪdʒəni; ˌæbə'rɪdʒə,ni/ *n* Australian ~ person. 澳大利亚土人。

abort /ə'bɔːt; ə'bɔrt/ *vt, vi* [VP 6 A, 2 A] come to nothing; miscarry; terminate prematurely: (使)失败; (使)不能达到预期效果; 早期终止; 挫折; (使)流 产; 早产; 夭折: ~ *a space mission*, cancel it in space, eg because of mechanical trouble. 使一太空任务不能如 期完成(例如因机械故障而中止)。

abor·tion /ə'bɔːʃn; ə'bɔrʃən/ *n* **1** [U] (legal) expulsion of the foetus from the womb during the first 28 weeks of pregnancy; helping or causing this: (法律) 流产(于开始怀孕至二十八周中, 胎儿自子宫中排出); 小 产; 使流产; 堕胎: *A* ~ *was formerly a crime in Britain*. 以前在英国堕胎是一种犯罪行为。**2** [C] instance of this; miscarriage of birth: 流产之实例; 小产; 堕胎: *have/ procure an* ~. 流产; 堕胎。**3** [C] creature produced by ~; dwarfed or mis-shapen creature; (fig) plan, effort, etc that has failed to develop. 早产儿; 矮小或畸形之生 物; (喻)未能实现的计划、努力等。~·**ist** /-ɪst; -ɪst/ *n* person who brings about an ~; person who favours and supports legal ~. 给人打胎者; 赞成合法堕胎者。

abort·ive /ə'bɔːtɪv; ə'bɔrtɪv/ *adj* coming to nothing; unsuccessful; arrested in development. 成空的; 未成功 的; 失败的; 发育不全的; 进展受阻碍的; 挫折的: *plans that proved* ~; 半途而废的计划; *an* ~ *rebellion*. 一次 成空的叛变。~·**ly** *adv*

abound /ə'baʊnd; ə'baʊnd/ *vi* [VP3A] ~ *in/with*, have, exist, in great numbers or quantities: 大量存在; 富于: *The river* ~*s in fish*. 这条河中有大量的鱼。*Fish* ~ *in the river*. 鱼类大量地生存于这条河中。*The hut* ~*ed with vermin*. 这棚屋有极多的虫子(蚤、虱等)。*Vermin* ~*ed in the hut*. 虫子大量地生长在这棚屋中。

about¹ /ə'baʊt; ə'baʊt/ *adv of degree* (contrasted with *just* or *exactly*) a little more or less than; a little before or after: (与 just 或 exactly 相对) 比…稍多或稍 少; 在…的稍前或稍后; 大约; 前后; 左右: ~ *as high as that tree*; 大约象那棵树那样高; *for* ~ *three miles*; 大 约三英里; ~ *six o'clock*; 六点钟左右; *on or* ~ *the fifth of May*. 在五月五日或其前后。*I've had just* ~ *enough* (colloq understatement for 'quite enough'). 我已经差不 多够了(口, 是'十分够了'语气较轻的说法)。*It's* ~ *time you stopped being so rude* (colloq understatement for 'quite time'). 是你停止粗鲁行为的时候了(口, 是'现在 应该'语气较轻的说法)。*That's* ~ (*the size of*) *it*, (colloq) That is how I assess it, how I see it. (口) (大 小)差不多了; 大致如此(如我所估计或事实如此)。

about² /ə'baʊt; ə'baʊt/ *adv part* (may usu be replaced by *around* in 1, 2 and 3) (第1,2,3 义通常可用 around 代 替) **1** (with *vv* of movement) here and there, in no particular direction: (与表示动向的动词连用) 到处, 无 固定方向: *The children were rushing* ~. 小孩子们到处 乱闹。*The boys were climbing* ~ *on the rocks*. 男孩们在 岩石上乱爬。*Don't drop cigarette ash* ~. 勿乱弹烟灰。 *Don't leave waste paper and empty bottles* ~ *in the park*. 不要在公园中到处丢弃废纸及空瓶。*He's taking Jane* ~ *a lot these days*, eg to dances, cinemas, theatres. 他 近来带着珍妮到处去玩(例如参加舞会, 看电影, 看戏)。 **2** (with other *vv*, indicating position, etc): (与其他动 词连用, 表示位置等): *There were books lying* ~ *on the floor/people sitting* ~ *on the grass*. 有些书置放在地板 上(有些人坐在草地各处)。**3** (with *be*): (与 be 连用): *There was no one* ~, no one to be seen. 附近见不到一个 人。*There's a lot of influenza* ~, many people have it.

附近有很多人患流行性感冒。 **be (out and) ~**, be able to get out, work, etc after eg an illness. 能出外，工作等(例如病后复元)。 **be up and ~**, be out of bed and active. 起床走动。 **4 bring sth ~**, ⇨ **bring (6)**. **come ~**, ⇨**come (16)**. **5** facing round; in the opposite direction: 向后转；朝相反的方向: *It's the wrong way ~*. 方向错了，刚相反。 *A~ turn!* (GB)（英）, *A~ face!* (US)（美）, (mil commands) turn round to face the other way. (军，口令)向后转！ *~-'face vi* turn and face the other way. 向后转。 **6** (of two or more persons or groups) (指两个或两个以上的人，或指两组或多组) **take turns ~; (do sth) turn and turn ~,** ⇨ **turn¹(4)**.

about³ /ə'baut; ə'baut/ *prep* (may usu be replaced by *around* or *round* in **1, 2** and **3**)（第 1, 2, 3 义通常可用 around 或 round 代替）**1** (with *vv* of movement) here and there, in no particular direction: (与表示动向的动词连用)到处; 在…各处: *walking ~ the town*; 在市内到处走; *travelling ~ the world*. 环游世界。 **2** (with other *vv*, indicating position, state, etc): (与其他动词连用，表示位置、状况等): *idle men standing ~ on street corners*: 在街角上到处站立的闲人; *books and papers lying ~ the room*. 零乱散置于室内的书籍和文件。 *I haven't any money ~ me*, ie with me, in my pockets. 我身上没有带钱。 **3** near to: 在…近处; 在附近: *I dropped the key somewhere ~ here*. 我把钥匙掉在这附近某个地方了。 **4** concerning; regarding; in connection with: 关于; 有关: *He is careless ~ his personal appearance*. 他不关心他自己的仪表。 *What do you know ~ him?* 对于他，你知道些什么? *What is he so angry ~?* 他为何事如此发怒? *Tell me all ~ it*. 告诉我有关此事的一切。 *How/What ~ ...*, used to ask for information, to make a suggestion or to get sb's opinion: …怎么样(用以询问消息, 提供建议或征询意见): *What ~ his qualifications for the position?* 他对任此职的资格如何? *How ~ going to France for our holidays?* 我们到法国去度假如何? **5** concerned or occupied with: 从事; 忙于: *What are you ~?* (= colloq 'up to?'). 你在做什么么?(等于口语的 'up to?')。 *And while you're ~ it...*, while you're doing that. ... 在你做那事的时候…。 *Mind what you're ~*, Be careful what you do. 注意你所做的事; 小心。 **go/set ~ sth**, deal with it: 做某事; 从事: *Do you know how to go ~ it*, deal with the task? 你知道如何做这事吗? **6** round (which is now more usu preferred): 在周围; 围绕着 (现在比较常用 'round): *the fields ~ Oxford*. 在牛津四周的田野。 *She hung ~ his shoulders*. 她伏在他的肩膀上。 *He has his wits ~ him*, ⇨ **wit**. 他很机警。 **7 ~ to+inf**, on the point of (doing sth), just going to (do sth): 即将; 正要: *As I was ~ to say, when you interrupted me ...* 我正要说的时候, 你插嘴了。 *He was ~ to start*. 他即将动身。

above¹ /ə'bʌv; ə'bʌv/ *adv* (contrasted with *below¹*, *under¹*(1) and *underneath*) (与 below¹, under¹(1) 及 underneath 相对) **1** at a higher point; overhead; on high: 在较高处; 在头顶上空; 在上面; 在高处: *My bedroom is just ~*. 我的卧室就在上面。 *Seen from ~, the fields looked like a geometrical pattern*. 从高处看来, 那些田亩象是几何图案。 *A voice from ~ shouted a welcome*. 从上面传来大叫欢迎的声音。 **2** earlier (in a book, article, etc): (书籍, 文章等的)前文; 上文: *As was stated ~...*; 如上所述…; *See the statement ~/the ~ statement*, 见前文; 见上文。 **3** in Heaven: 天上; the *Powers ~*, the heavenly powers. 上天神明。 **'board** *adv* without deception or concealment; honourably. 无欺骗或蒙蔽; 光明正大地。 □ *pred adj* frank; open. 坦白的; 公开的; 磊落的。 □ **underhand**. **'mentioned**, **~-'named** *adjj* mentioned, named, ~ (or earlier) in this book, article, etc. (在本书, 本文等中)上述的; 前述的。

above² /ə'bʌv; ə'bʌv/ *prep* (contrasted with *below²*,

under² and *underneath*; ~ may sometimes be replaced by *over* or *beyond*) (与 below², under² 及 underneath 相对; above 有时可用 over 或 beyond 替换) **1** higher than: 高于; 在…上: *The sun rose ~ the horizon*. 太阳升到地平线之上。 *We were flying ~ the clouds*. 我们飞行在云层之上。 Cf 参较 We flew *over/across the Sahara*. 我们飞越过撒哈拉大沙漠。 *The water came ~ our knees*. 水深达膝部以上。 *A captain in the Navy ranks ~ a captain in the Army*. 海军的 captain (上校) 军阶高于陆军的 captain (上尉)。 **2** greater in number, price, weight, etc: (数目)大于; (价钱)高于; (重量)超过: *The temperature has been ~ the average recently*. 近来的气温一直比平均温度高。 *There is nothing in this shop ~/over fifty cents*. 这个店里没有一样东西价钱超过五角。 *It weighs ~/over ten tons*. 它的重量超过十吨。 *Applicants must be ~/over the age of 21*. 申请人年龄必须超过二十一岁。 **3** more than: 多于; 较…更为: *A soldier should value honour ~ life*. 军人应视荣誉重于生命。 **~ all**, more than anything else. 最重要者; 尤其。 **over and ~**, in addition to. 除…外。 **4** too great, good, difficult, etc for: (因太伟大, 太好, 太难等而)不做; 不为; 不屑; 对…太困难; 超过…之能力: *If you want to learn, you must not be ~ asking* (=not be too proud to ask) *questions*. 你如果要想学习, 就不要耻于发问。 *He is ~ meanness and deceit*, does not show meanness or practise deceit. 他不至于做卑鄙和欺骗的事情。 *This book is ~* (now more usu *beyond*) *me*, too difficult for me. 这本书对我是太难了(今比较常用 beyond 代替 above)。 **5** out of reach of (because too great, good, etc): (因太伟大, 奇佳等而)超越; 超出…的范围: *His heroism was ~/beyond all praise*. 他的英勇赞扬不尽。 *His conduct has always been ~ suspicion*. 他的行为一直无可置疑。 **6** (various uses): (其他各种用法): the *waterfall ~* (= up stream from) *the bridge*; 在桥上游的瀑布; *live ~/beyond one's means*, in a style too expensive for one's income. 生活奢侈, 所费超过其收入; *be ~ oneself*, in high spirits; 兴高采烈; *get ~ oneself*, become conceited, too self-satisfied and lacking in self-control. 得意忘形; 趾高气扬。 *She married ~ her station*, married sb from a higher social class. 她和一个社会等级比她高的男人结婚。

ab·ra·ca·dabra /ˌæbrəkə'dæbrə; ˌæbrəkə'dæbrə/ *n* [U] magic jargon; gibberish. 符咒; 咒语; 莫名其妙的话; 胡言乱语。

abrade /ə'breɪd; ə'bred/ *vt* [VP6A] rub or scrape off, wear away (skin, etc) by friction or hard rubbing. 擦掉; 磨损(表皮等); 刮除。

ab·ra·sion /ə'breɪʒn; ə'breʒən/ *n* [U] rubbing, scraping, or wearing off; [C] area where sth has been worn or scraped away: 擦掉; 擦伤; 磨损; 磨损, 磨伤之处; 擦伤之处: *an ~ of the skin*. 皮肤之擦伤处。

ab·ras·ive /ə'breɪsɪv; ə'bresɪv/ *n* [U] substance (eg emery) used for rubbing or grinding down surfaces; [C] particular type of ~. 磨料 (摩擦表面用的材料, 如金刚砂); 某种磨料。 □ *adj* causing abrasion; (fig) harsh, rough: (导致)擦伤的; (引起)磨损的; (喻)粗糙的: *an ~ voice/character*. 粗厉的声音(粗鲁的人)。

abreast /ə'brest; ə'brest/ *adv* (of persons, ships, etc) on a level, side by side, and facing the same way: (指人, 船等)并肩; 并排; 并列; 并驶: *walking three ~*; 三人并肩行走; *warships in line ~*. 成直线并驶编队的战舰。 **be/keep ~ (of/with)**, level with, not behind: 与…并进; 不落后: *You should read the newspapers to keep ~ of the times*, to be informed of the latest events, ideas, discoveries, etc. 你必须看报, 以便跟上时代(读报才能知道最新发生的事、新概念、新发现等)。

abridge /ə'brɪdʒ; ə'brɪdʒ/ *vt* [VP6A] make shorter, esp by using fewer words: 删节; 节略: *an ~d edition of 'David Copperfield';* 《大卫·科波菲尔》之节本; shorten (an interview, the time sth lasts). 缩短(会谈、某事物持续之时间)。 ⇨ **abbreviate**. **~·ment, abridg·ment** *n* [U] abridging; [C] sth, eg a book, that is ~d. 删节

节略;经删节的东西;(书等之)节本。

abroad /əˈbrɔːd; əˈbrɔd/ *adv* **1** in or to a foreign country or countries; away from one's own country: 在国外;到国外;出国: *be/go/live/travel* ~; 在外国(出国;旅居国外;在国外旅行); *visitors who have come from* ~. 从外国(或海外)来的游客。*Do you like it ~/being ~?* 你喜欢在外国生活吗? **2** far and wide; everywhere: 遍布;广布;到处: *There's a rumour ~ that ...*, People are saying that .... 谣言四播说是…。**3** (old use) out of doors: (旧用法)户外;室外: *You were ~ early this morning.* 你今天一大早就到户外去了。

ab·ro·gate /ˈæbrəgeɪt; ˈæbrə,get/ *vt* [VP6A] (formal) repeal or annul by authority. (正式用语)废止;废除。**ab·ro·ga·tion** /ˌæbrəˈgeɪʃn; ˌæbrəˈgeʃən/ *n*

abrupt /əˈbrʌpt; əˈbrʌpt/ *adj* **1** unexpectedly sudden: 突然的;意外的: *The road is full of ~ turns.* 这条路有很多急转弯。**2** (of speech, writing, behaviour) rough; brusque; disconnected: (指言语,写作,行为)粗鲁的;唐突的;不连贯的: *a man with an ~ manner*, ie rather impolite, gruff, blunt; 举止粗鲁的人; *an ~ style*, eg of speaking or writing. 不连贯的方式(如说话或写作)。**3** (of a slope) steep. (指斜坡)陡峭的。**~·ly** *adv* **~·ness** *n*

ab·scess /ˈæbses; ˈæb,sɛs/ *n* [C] collection of thick yellowish-white liquid (called *pus*) formed in a cavity in the body: 脓肿;脓疡: *~es on the gums.* 齿龈上的脓肿。

ab·scond /əbˈskɒnd; æbˈskɑnd/ *vi* [VP2A, 3A] ~ ***(with) (from)***, go away suddenly, secretly, and aware of having done wrong, esp to avoid arrest. 潜逃;逃亡。

ab·sence /ˈæbsəns; ˈæbsn̩s/ *n* **1** [U] being away *(from)*: 缺席;不在;离开(与 from 连用): *~ from school;* 旷课;缺课; *during his ~ in America*, while he was there. 在他离开此地到美国去的期间。*In the ~ of the Manager* (ie while he is away) *Mr X is in charge of the business.* 经理不在的期间,由某先生管理业务。***leave of ~***, ⇨ **leave²(1)**. **2** [C] occasion or time of being away: 一次缺席;不在的时间: *numerous ~s from school;* 无数次的旷课; *a long ~;* 离开很久; *after an ~ of three months.* 在离开了三个月之后。**3** [U] lack; non-existence: 缺乏;不存在: *in the ~ of definite information.* 在缺乏确定消息的情形下。*Cold is the ~ of heat.* 冷就是缺乏热。**4 ~ of mind,** absent-mindedness (⇨ below). 心不在焉;神不守舍(参看下条)。

ab·sent¹ /ˈæbsənt; ˈæbsn̩t/ *adj* **1 ~ *(from)***, not present (at): 缺…;旷…: *~ from school/work.* 旷课(旷工)。**2** lost in thought; abstracted: 迷茫于沉思中的;茫然的;恍惚的: *When I spoke to him he looked at me in an ~ way but did not answer.* 当我跟他说话时,他茫然地望着我而不答话。**~·ly** *adv* (rare) (罕) = ~-mindedly. **ˌ~-ˈminded** *adj* so deep or far away in thought that one is unaware of what one is doing, what is happening around one, etc. 心不在焉的;茫然的;恍惚的。**~-mind·ed·ly** *adv* **~-minded·ness** *n*

ab·sent² /əbˈsent; æbˈsɛnt/ *vt* [VP6B, 14] ***~ oneself (from)***, stay away (from): 离开;不在(与 from 连用): *Why did you ~ yourself (from school) yesterday?* 你昨天为什么不来(上学)?

ab·sen·tee /ˌæbsənˈtiː; ˌæbsn̩ˈti/ *n* person who is absent. 缺席者;旷课者;旷职者;不在者;在外者。**~ landlord,** land or house owner who habitually lives away from the place he owns. 不住在产权所在地的地主或房主;遥领地主。**~·ism** /-ɪzəm; -ˌɪzəm/ *n* [U] habitual failure to be present, eg the practice of being absent from work or regular duty frequently and without good reason. 时常的缺席(例如无缘无故的时常旷工或旷职)。

ab·sinthe, ab·sinth /ˈæbsɪnθ; ˈæbsɪnθ/ *n* [U] bitter, green alcoholic drink made with worm wood and other herbs. 苦艾酒。

ab·so·lute /ˈæbsəluːt; ˈæbsə,lut/ *adj* **1** complete; perfect: 完全的: *A child usually has ~ trust in its mother.* 小孩通常完全信任其母亲。*When giving evidence in a law court, we must tell the ~ truth.* 在法庭作证时,我们必须完全照实说。**2** unlimited; having complete or arbitrary power: 无限制的;有绝对权力的;有独裁权的;专制的: *An ~ ruler need not ask anyone for permission to do anything.* 一个有绝对权力的统治者做任何事都不必征得任何人的同意。**3** real; undoubted: 真实的;无疑的: *It is an ~ fact.* 那是绝对的事实。*He must not be punished unless you have ~ proof of his guilt.* 他不可受惩罚,除非你有确实的证据证明他有罪。**4** unconditional; unqualified: 无条件的: *An ~ promise must be kept whatever happens.* 无条件的诺言无论在任何情形下都必须遵守。**5** not relative; not dependent on or measured by other things. 非相对的;非基于他物或以他物来衡量的;绝对的。**~ zero,** lowest temperature theoretically possible, =−273.15°C. 绝对零度(理论上的最低温度,等于零下273.15摄氏度)。⇨ **App 5** 参看附录五。**~·ly** *adv* **1** completely: 完全地: *~ly impossible;* 绝对不可能; *~ly right.* 完全对。**2** unconditionally: 无条件地: *He refused ~ly.* 他说什么都不答应。**3** /ˌæbsəˈluːtlɪ; ˌæbsəˈlutlɪ/ (colloq, in answer to a question, or as a comment) quite so; certainly. (口,作为对一问题的回答或评语)十分对;对极了;当然。**ab·so·lut·ism** /ˈæbsəluːtɪzəm; ˈæbsəlut,ɪzəm/ *n* (pol) ~ (2) government; despotism. (政治)专制政治;专制主义。

ab·sol·ution /ˌæbsəˈluːʃn; ˌæbsəˈluʃən/ *n* [U] (RC Church) freeing (esp by a priest in the sacrament of penance) from the consequences of sin: (天主教)(尤指神父在告解中之)赦罪: *grant, pronounce ~ from sin.* 赦罪。⇨ **penance.**

ab·solve /əbˈzɒlv; æbˈsɑlv/ *vt* [VP6A, 14] **~ *(from)***, declare free (from sin, guilt, a promise, duty, etc): 宣布赦免(罪过);免除(履行诺言,责任等): *I ~ you from all blame/from your vows.* 我让你免受一切责难(我解除你的誓约)。

ab·sorb /əbˈsɔːb; əbˈsɔrb/ *vt* **1** [VP6A] take or suck in, eg a liquid; take in, eg heat, light, (fig) knowledge, etc: 吸收(如液体,热,光等);(喻)吸收(知识等): *Paper that ~s ink is called blotting-paper.* 吸收墨水的纸称为吸墨纸。*Dry sand ~s water.* 干沙吸收水份。*The clever boy ~ed all the knowledge his teachers could give him.* 那聪明的男孩把他老师所能教他的知识都吸收了。**2** [VP6A] use up much of the attention, interest or time of. 吸引…的注意力或兴趣;耗费…的时间;使全神贯注;使专心: *His business ~s him.* 他的业务使他全神贯注。*He is completely ~ed in his business.* 他完全专心于他的业务。*He was ~ed in a book.* 他全神贯注于一本书。**~·ent** /-ənt; -ənt/ *adj, n* (substance) capable of ~ing: 能吸收的(物质);有吸收力的(物质);吸水的(物质): *~ent cotton wool.* 吸水脱脂棉。**ab·sorp·tion** /əbˈsɔːpʃn; əbˈsɔrpʃən/ *n* [U] ~ing or being ~ed; engrossment: 吸收;专注: *Complete absorption in sport interfered with his studies.* 全心专注于运动妨碍了他的学业。

ab·stain /əbˈsteɪn; əbˈsten/ *vi* [VP3A, 2A] ~ ***(from)***, hold oneself back, refrain: 戒除;禁绝: *His doctor told him to ~ from beer and wine.* 他的医生告诉他要戒酒。*At the last election he ~ed (from voting).* 上次选举他弃权(没投票)。**~er** *n* person who ~s, esp *total ~er*, one who never takes alcoholic drinks. 戒除者;禁绝者;(尤指)绝对戒酒的人。

ab·stemi·ous /əbˈstiːmɪəs; æbˈstimɪəs/ *adj* sparing or moderate, esp in taking food and drink; frugal: (尤指在饮食方面)有节制的;节俭的: *~ habits;* 节制饮食的习惯; *an ~ meal.* 节俭的一餐。**~·ly** *adv* **~·ness** *n*

ab·sten·tion /əbˈstenʃn; æbˈstɛnʃən/ *n* [U] ~ ***(from)***, abstaining, esp not using one's vote at an election, etc; [C] instance of this: 戒除;(尤指选举投票等的)弃权,弃权的实例: *six votes for, three against and two ~s.* 六票赞成,三票反对,两票弃权。

ab·sti·nence /ˈæbstɪnəns; ˈæbstənəns/ *n* [U] ~

(from), abstaining, eg from food, enjoyment, esp alcoholic drink. (对食物, 享乐, 尤指饮酒之类) 禁戒; 戒除。 **,total '~**, refraining completely from alcoholic drink. 绝对戒酒。

ab·stract¹ /'æbstrækt; 'æbstrækt/ adj **1** separated from what is real or concrete; thought of separately from facts, objects or particular examples: 抽象的: A flower is beautiful, but beauty itself is ~. 花是美的, 但美的本身是抽象的。 **~ 'art**, art which does not represent objects, scenes, etc in an obvious way, but abstracts and isolates features of reality. 抽象艺术(不以显明的手法表现景物, 而只撷取实物特色的一种艺术)。 ⇨ **realism(1)**. **~ 'noun**, (gram) one that is the name of a quality or state, eg length, goodness, virtue. (语法)抽象名词(某一种性质或状态之名称, 例如长度、善良、美德)。 **2 in the ~**, regarded in an ideal or theoretical way. 从抽象的(即概念的或理论的)方面看; 观念上; 理论上。

ab·stract² /æb'strækt; æb'strækt/ vt [VP6A, 14] **~ (from)**, take out; separate: 提炼出; 取出; 抽出: ~ metal from ore; 从矿砂提炼金属; (colloq) steal: (口)窃取; 偷: ~ a wallet from sb's pocket. 从某人口袋中扒走皮夹。 **~ed** adj not paying attention; withdrawn in thought. 心不在焉的; 另有所思的; 出神的。 **~·ed·ly** adv in an absent-minded way. 心不在焉地; 出神地。

ab·stract³ /'æbstrækt; 'æbstrækt/ n [C] short account, eg of the chief points of a piece of writing a book, speech, etc: (文章, 书籍, 演说等的)摘要: an ~ of a sermon. 一篇布道词的摘要。

ab·strac·tion /æb'strækʃn; æb'strækʃən/ n **1** [U] abstracting or being abstracted. 提炼; 取出; 抽出。 **2** [U] absent-mindedness: 心不在焉; 出神: in a moment of ~; 一时心不在焉; with an air of ~. 带着心不在焉的神态。 **3** [C] visionary idea; idea of a quality apart from its material accompaniments: 幻想; 抽象的概念: Whiteness is an ~. 白是一种抽象的概念。 Don't lose yourself in ~s, ie keep a firm hold on reality. 不要沉迷于幻想中(意即要紧紧地把握住现实)。 **4** [U] formation of such an idea or ideas. 抽象概念之形成; 抽象。

ab·struse /æb'struːs; æb'strus/ adj whose meaning or answer is hidden or difficult to understand; profound. 深奥的; 难懂的。 **~·ly** adv **~·ness** n

ab·surd /æb'sɜːd; əb'sɚd/ adj unreasonable; foolish; ridiculous; 愚蠢的; 可笑的; 荒谬的: What an ~ suggestion! 多么荒谬的一个建议! Is was ~ of you to suggest such a thing. 你竟提议这样的一件事, 真可笑。 **~·ly** adv **~·ity** n (pl -ties) **1** [U] state of being ~; unreasonableness. 不合理; 愚蠢; 可笑; 荒谬。 **2** [C] ~ act or statement. 荒谬之行为或言词; 荒唐话。

abun·dance /ə'bʌndəns; ə'bʌndəns/ n **1** [U] great plenty: 丰富; 充裕: food and drink in ~; 丰富的饮食; live in ~, have plenty of those things that make life enjoyable. 过着丰衣足食的生活。 **2** (with indef art) quantity that is more than enough: (与不定冠词连用)丰富之量; 很多: an ~ of good things. 很多好东西。

abun·dant /ə'bʌndənt; ə'bʌndənt/ adj **1** more than enough; plentiful: 很多的; 丰富的; 充裕的: We have ~ proof of his guilt. 我们有充分的证据证明他有罪。 **2 ~ in**, rich in; well supplied with: 富于; 富有…; a land ~ in minerals with an abundance of or abounding in are more usu). 矿产丰富的土地 (较常用 with an abundance of 或 abounding in)。 **~·ly** adv: I've made my views ~ly clear. 我已充分说明了我的观点。

abuse¹ /ə'bjuːs; ə'bjus/ n **1** [U] ~ (of), wrong use; [C] instance of this: 滥用; 妄用; 滥用或妄用之实例: an ~ of trust. 辜负别人的信任。 **2** [C] unjust custom or practice that has become established: 不当习惯; 陋习; 弊端: remedy an ~; 矫正一项恶习; put an end to ~s. 废止不正当的习俗。 **3** [U] angry or violent attack in words; bad language; cursing: 辱骂; 痛骂; 咒骂: greet sb with a stream of ~; 一见某人就破口大骂; shower ~

on sb. 大骂某人。

abuse² /ə'bjuːz; ə'bjuz/ vt [VP6A] **1** make a bad or wrong use of: 滥用; 妄用; 误用: Don't ~ your authority/the confidence they have placed in you. 不要滥用你的威信(辜负他们对你的信任)。 **2** say severe, cruel or unjust things to sb or about sb. 辱骂; 诋毁; 讲(某人)的坏话。 **3** (old use) ill-treat. (旧用法)虐待。 **4** (old use, esp in the passive) deceive: (旧用法, 尤用于被动语态)欺骗: She has been much ~. 她老是受骗。

abus·ive /ə'bjuːsɪv; ə'bjusɪv/ adj using, containing, insults and curses: 辱骂的; 诅咒的: use ~ language to sb; 咒骂某人; become ~, begin to insult and curse. 开始骂。 **~·ly** adv

abut /ə'bʌt; ə'bʌt/ vi (-tt-) [VP3A] **~ on**, (of land) have a common boundary with; border on (指土地)与…接界; 与…毗连。 **~·ment** n (eng) structure that bears the weight of a bridge or an arch. (工程)桥台; 桥座(托架桥或拱的结构)。

abysm /ə'bɪzm; ə'bɪzəm/ n [C] (poet) abyss. (诗)深渊。

abys·mal /ə'bɪzml; ə'bɪzml/ adj (esp fig and colloq) bottomless; extreme: (尤用于喻及口)无底的; 极端的: ~ ignorance, (colloq) complete absence of knowledge. (口)极端的无知。 **~·ly** adv

abyss /ə'bɪs; ə'bɪs/ n hole so deep as to appear bottomless: 深渊; (fig)(喻) the ~ of despair. 绝望的深渊。 **the ~**, hell, or the lower world. 地狱; 阴间。

aca·cia /ə'keɪʃə; ə'keʃə/ n [C] **1** (sorts of) tree from which gum is obtained. 金合欢属; 相思树(属)(可从其提取树胶)。 **2** (false ~ or locust tree) (sorts of) similar tree grown as an ornament in parks and gardens. 洋槐(栽植于公园及花园中作装饰用)。

aca·demic /ˌækə'demɪk; ˌækə'dɛmɪk/ adj **1** of teaching, studying, of schools, colleges, etc; scholarly, literary or classical (contrasted with technical or scientific): 学术的; 学校的; 学者的; 文学的或古典作品的(与技术的或科学的相对): ~ subjects; 学校里的科目; the ~ year, (usu Oct to June in GB and US). 学年(在英国及美国, 通常是十月至次年六月)。 **~ freedom**, liberty to teach and to discuss problems without outside, eg Government, interference. 学术自由(教学及讨论问题而不受外力, 如政府等, 干扰之自由)。 **2** too much concerned with theory and logic; not sufficiently practical: 注重理论与逻辑的; 不够实际的: The question/issue is ~, is of no practical consequence. 此问题过于注重理论。 **3** of an academy: 学会学术的; 专科学校的: ~ rank / costume. 大专教师之等级(学位服)。 □ n [C] university teacher; professional scholar. 大学教师; 专业学者。 **aca·demi·cally** /-klɪ; -klɪ/ adv

aca·dem·icals /ˌækə'demɪklz; ˌækə'dɛməklz/ n pl academic costume (cap and gown), as worn on ceremonial occasions. 学位服(典礼时所穿戴的学位帽与学位袍)。

acad·emy /ə'kædəmɪ; ə'kædəmɪ/ n (pl -mies) **1** school for higher learning, usu for a special purpose: 高等学府; 专科学校: a 'naval / 'military ~; 海军(陆军)军官学校; an ~ of 'music; 音乐学院; a 'riding / 'fencing ~. 马术(击剑)学校。 **2** society of distinguished scholars; society for cultivating art, literature, etc, of which membership is an honour: 高等学术团体; 学会: The Royal A~ of Arts. (英国)皇家艺术学会。 **aca·dem·ician** /əˌkædə'mɪʃn US: ˌækəde'mɪʃn/ n member of an ~ (2), eg of the Royal A~ in GB or of the French A~. 学术团体之会员; 学会会员(例如英国皇家艺术学会或法兰西学院之会员); 院士。

ac·cede /æk'siːd; æk'sid/ vi [VP2A, 3A] **~ (to)**, (formal)(正式用法) **1** assent or agree, eg to a request or proposal. 允诺; 同意; 赞成(某一要求或建议)。 **2** take up or succeed to, eg an office, a post, a position of authority. 就职; 即位; 继承(王位)。

ac·cel·er·ando /æk,selə'rændəʊ; æk,selə'rændo/ n, adv, adj (music) (direction for) increasing speed gradually. (音乐)渐快速度; 逐渐加快速度地(的)。 ⇨

rallentando.

ac·cel·er·ate /ək'seləreɪt; æk'sɛlə,ret/ vt, vi 1 [VP 6A] increase the speed of; cause to move faster or happen earlier. 加快…之速度;使加速;催促。2 [VP2A] (of a motion or process)become faster. (指运动或程序)变快;加速。 **ac·cel·er·ation** /ək,selə'reɪʃn; æk,sɛlə'reʃən/ n [U] making or being made quicker; rate of increase of speed per unit of time: 加速;加速度;加速率: a car with good acceleration. 加速性能良好的汽车。

ac·cel·er·ator /ək'seləreɪtə(r); æk'sɛlə,retə/ n 1 device, eg the pedal in a car, for controlling speed. 加速装置 (例如汽车中之油门踏板);加速器。⇨ the illus at **motor**. 参看 motor 之插图。2 (phys) device for accelerating particles or nuclei, also called(colloq)an 'atom-smasher'. (物理)加速器(俗称'核粒子加速器')。

ac·cent /'æksənt US: 'æksɛnt; 'æksɛnt/ n [C] 1 prominence (by means of stress or intonation) given to a syllable: (借重读或音调所加于一音节上的)重音: In the word 'today' the ~ is on the second syllable. today — 字之重音在第二音节。2 mark or symbol, usn above a letter, used in writing and printing to indicate the quality of a vowel sound or syllabic stress. 重音符号 (通常标在字母上方,用于书写或印刷中,以表示元音性质或重音项)。⇨ **acute(5), circumflex and grave³**. 3 [sometimes 有时候为 U] individual, local or national way of pronouncing: (个人,地方民族的)口音; 腔调; 土腔: a Cockney ~, 伦敦东区的口音, speaking English with a foreign ~; 说英语带外国腔调; speak without an ~. 说话不带地方口音。4 (pl) way of speaking which indicates a particular quality, etc: (复)说话的语气; 声调; 语调: in the tender ~s of love. 以情意绵绵的语调。5 (colloq) emphasis given to some aspect of a display, performance, etc: (口)(加于展示,表演等某一方面的)强调; 着重; 重点: At this year's Motor Show the ~ is on sports cars. 今年的汽车展览会重点在跑车。□ vt /æk'sɛnt; 'æksɛnt/ [PV6A] pronounce with an ~; put emphasis on (a syllable or word); make prominent or conspicuous. 以重音读出; 重读(某一音节或词); 强调; 使显著。

ac·cen·tu·ate /ək'sɛntʃueɪt;æk'sɛntʃʊ,et/ vt [VP6A] give more force or prominence to; draw attention to. 加重; 强调。 **ac·cen·tu·ation** /ək,sɛntʃʊ'eɪʃn; æk,sɛntʃʊ'eʃən/ n

ac·cept /ək'sept; ək'sept/ vt, vi [VP6A, 9, 16B, 2A] 1 (consent to) receive (sth offered): 接受; 答应(别人所提供的事物): ~ a gift / an invitation. 接受礼物 (邀请)。 He asked her to marry him and she ~ed him / his proposal. 他请求她嫁给他, 她答应了他 (他的求婚)。I cannot ~ your apology. 我不能接受你的道歉。2 agree; recognize; regard with favour or approval: 同意; 认可; 赞同: I ~ that the change may take some time. 我同意改变颇费时日。It is an ~ed truth / fact, sth that everyone believes. 这是大家所公认的真理 (事实)。3 (comm) take responsibility for: (商)承受…的责任; 承兑: ~ a bill of exchange; 承兑汇票; ~ delivery of goods. 负责送货。 ~·able /-əbl; -əbl/ adj worth ~ing; welcome: 可接受的; 受欢迎的: if this proposal is ~able to you. 如果你觉得这个建议可以接受的话。 **ac·ceptabil·ity** /ək,septə'bɪlətɪ; ək,sɛptə'bɪlətɪ/ n **ac·ceptance** /-əns; -əns/ n [U] 1 ~ing or being ~ed. 接受; 答应; 同意; 认可。2 approval; favourable reception: 赞同; 嘉纳: The proposal met with / found general ~. 这建议得到普遍的赞同。3 (comm) agreement to pay; (legal) contract, bill of exchange, which has been offered and ~ed. (商)承兑; 认付; (法律)经提出且已接受的合约; 已认付的票据。 **ac·cep·ta·tion** /,æksep'teɪʃn; ,æksep'teʃən/ n generally ~ed meaning of a word or expression. 公认的词义。

ac·cess /'æksɛs; 'æksɛs/ n [U] 1 way (in) to a place: 通入之路; 通路: easy / difficult of ~; 易(难)进入的; 易(难)接近的; (attrib) (用作限定语) good ~ roads, roads giving good ~. 良好的通路。The only ~ to the farmhouse

is across the fields. 到达那农舍的唯一通路是穿过田间。 '~·road, (US) slip-road ⇨ **slip²**(8). (美)又道。2 ~ to, right, opportunity or means of reaching, using or approaching: 接触, 使用或接近的权利, 机会或方法: Students must have ~ to good books. 学生必须有机会读到好书。Only high officials had ~ to the Emperor. 只有高级官员可以接近皇帝。3 an ~ of, (old use) attack (of fever, etc); sudden attack, outburst (of anger, rage, despair, etc). (旧用法)(身体发烧等之)发作; (愤怒,绝望等之)突然发作; 爆发。 **~·ible** /ək'sɛsəbl; æk'sɛsəbl/ adj ~(to), able to be reached, used, visited, etc: 可接近的; 可进入的; 可用的; 可参观的: facts that are ~ible to all; 人人可得参考的事实资料; a collection of paintings not ~ible to the public; 公众无法看到的一批收藏的画; that can be influenced by: 可被…影响的: a man who is not ~ible to argument. 不为辩论所影响的人。 **ac·ces·si·bil·ity** /ək,sɛsə'bɪlətɪ; æk,sɛsə'bɪlətɪ/ n [U]

ac·ces·sary /ək'sɛsərɪ; æk'sɛsərɪ/ n (pl -ries), pred adj (= US 美 accessory(1).)(legal) person who helps in any act, esp a crime: (法律)帮手; (尤指)从犯; 帮凶的从犯; 从犯的: an ~ to a crime; 一件犯罪案的从犯; He was made ~ to the crime. 他被人利用, 成为这件犯罪案的从犯。 ~ before / after the fact, ⇨ **fact**(1)

ac·ces·sion /æk'sɛʃn; æk'sɛʃən/ n ~ to, 1 [U] reaching a rank, position or state: 达到某一地位或状态: the Queen's ~ to the throne; 女王之即位; on his ~ to the estate / to manhood. 在他承继产业(或达到成年)的时候。2 [U] addition; increase; [C] example of this: 增加; 添加; 增加之实例: recent ~s to the school library; 学校图书馆最近增添的数批新书; the ~ of new members to a political party. 某政党之增加新党员。

ac·ces·sory /ək'sɛsərɪ; æk'sɛsərɪ/ n(pl -ries) 1 = accessary. 2 sth extra, helpful, useful, but not an essential part of: 附件; 附属品: the accessories of a bicycle, eg the lamp, a pump; 脚踏车的附件(如车灯,打气筒); the accessories of a woman's dress, eg gloves, a handbag. 一件女装的配件(如手套,手提包)。

ac·ci·dence /'æksɪdəns; 'æksɪdəns/ n [U] (gram) that part of grammar which deals with meaningful differences in the form of a word, eg have, has, had; foot, feet, etc. The more usu term is now morphology. (语法)词法 (如 have, has, had; foot, feet 等。今较常用 morphology)。⇨ **syntax**.

ac·ci·dent /'æksɪdənt; 'æksɪdənt/ n 1 [C] sth that happens without a cause that can be seen at once, usu sth unfortunate and undesirable: 意外事件; 不测; 祸事; 偶发事件: There have been many railway ~s this year. 今年发生了许多次火车车祸。He was killed in a road / motoring ~. 他在一次车祸中死亡。There has been an ~ to ……. 发生过一次意外。 **A~s will happen**, (prov) Some unfortunate events must be accepted as inevitable. (谚)意外事故难免会发生。 meet with / have an ~, experience one: 遭遇意外事故: I had a slight ~ on the way to work this morning. 我今晨在上班途中遭遇一件小小的意外事故。 '~·prone, ⇨ **prone**, 2 [U] chance; fortune: 机遇; 命运: by ~ of birth. 生来就是; 由于出生的身世。 by ~, by chance: 偶然; 意外地: You might cut yourself by ~; you would not cut yourself on purpose. 你可能意外地割伤自己; 你不会故意割伤自己。 without ~, safely. 安全地; 无差地。 ~ insurance, against injury, damage or death which is the result of an ~. 事故保险。

ac·ci·den·tal /,æksɪ'dentl;,æksə'dɛntl/ adj happening unexpectedly and by chance: 偶然的; 意外的: an ~ meeting with a friend. 偶然遇到一位朋友。 ~·ly /-tl/ adv

ac·claim /ə'kleɪm; ə'klem/ vt 1 [VP6A,16B] welcome with shouts of approval; applaud loudly: 欢呼; 称赞: ~ the winner of a race; 向赛跑得胜者欢呼; ~ sb as a great actor. 喝彩称赞某人为伟大的演员。2 [VP23] make (sb) ruler, salute (sb) by ~ing: 欢呼以拥戴(某人)为统治者; 向(某人)欢呼致敬: They ~ed

him King. 他们欢呼拥戴他为国王。□ *n* [U] applause; approval: 欢呼; 喝彩; 赞同: *The play received great critical ~.* 该剧极获好评.

ac·cla·ma·tion /ˌækləˈmeɪʃn; ˌæklə'meʃən/ *n* 1 [U] loud and enthusiastic approval of a proposal, etc. (对提议等之) 高声而热烈的赞同: *elected/carried by ~, without voting.* (不经过投票表决而) 被全体一致以口头推选(通过). 2 (usu *pl*) shouts or applause of welcome, acceptance: (通常用复数) 欢呼; 喝彩: *the ~s of the crowd.* 群众的欢呼.

ac·cli·mate /'æklɪmɪt;æklə,met/ *vt, vi*=acclimatize.

ac·cli·ma·tion /ˌæklaɪˈmeɪʃn; æklə'meʃən/ *n*

ac·cli·ma·tize /əˈklaɪmətaɪz; ə'klaɪmə,taɪz/ *vt, vi* [VP 14, 2 A] ~ *(to),* get (oneself, animals, plants, etc) used to a new climate, or (fig) to a new environment, new conditions, etc. 使(自己, 动物, 植物等)习惯于新的气候;(使)服水土;(喻)(使)适应新环境: *You will soon get ~d.* 你很快就会适应的. **ac·cli·mat·iz·ation** /əˌklaɪmətaɪˈzeɪʃn US: -tɪ'z-; əˌklaɪmətə'zəʃən/ *n*

ac·cliv·ity /əˈklɪvətɪ; ə'klɪvətɪ/ *n* (*pl* -ties) [C] upward slope. 向上的斜坡. ⇨ declivity.

ac·col·ade /'ækəleɪd US: ˌækə'leɪd/ ˌækə'led/ *n* 1 bestowal of a knighthood by a tap on the shoulder with the flat of a sword. 爵位之授与(以剑面在肩上轻拍一下). 2 (fig) praise; approval: (喻) 赞颂; 赞成: *the ~s of the literary critics.* 文学批评家的赞美.

ac·com·mo·date / əˈkɒmədeɪt; ə'kɑmə,det/ *vt* [VP 6 A, 14] 1 have, provide, lodging for: 供给住宿: *This hotel can ~ 600 guests.* 这旅馆可供六百位客人住宿. 2 ~ *sb (with sth),* grant sth to sb; do sb a favour: 答应某人(某件事); 加惠于某人; 帮某人一个忙: *The bank will ~ you with a loan.* 银行将贷给你一笔款. 3 ~ *sth to,* change sth so that it fits with or is in harmony with (sth else): 使某事物配合(其他事物); 修改某事物使能自己一致; 使适应: *I will ~ my plans to yours.* 我将修改我的计划以配合你的计划. **ac·com·mo·dat·ing** *adj* willing to oblige others; easy to deal with. 乐于助人的; 随和的.

ac·com·mo·da·tion /əˌkɒməˈdeɪʃn; əˌkɑmə'deʃən/ *n* 1 [U] (GB) furnished, unfurnished room(s), eg in a flat, house, hostel or in a hotel, etc: (英)房间(泛指公寓, 一般房屋, 招待所或旅馆等中, 有或无家具设备的房间): *Wanted, ~ for a married couple with small child, in London,* eg as in a newspaper advertisement. 征租, 伦敦市内, 供夫妇及一小孩之房间(如报纸上之广告). *Hotel ~ was scarce during the Olympic Games.* 在奥林匹克运动会期间, 旅馆房间很难找. 2 (*pl,* US) lodgings; room(s) and food. (复,美) 住所; 膳宿. 3 [C] sth that helps; sth for convenience. 有益之物; 便利的设备. a *l'~ ladder,* (attrib) a portable one hung from the side of a ship. (用作定语) 舷梯(挂于船舷之可移动的梯子). 4 [U] (formal) compromise, settlement or adjustment (of one thing to another); [C] example of this: (正式用语)和解; 调解; 适应; 调节(与…连用); 调解或调节之实例: *come to an ~,* reach a compromise, eg in a dispute. 达成和解(如对某一争端). ⇨ agreement.

ac·com·pani·ment /əˈkʌmpənɪmənt/ *n* [C] 1 sth that naturally or often goes with another thing: 伴随物; 附属物: *Disease is often an ~ of famine.* 疾病常随饥馑而来. 2 (music) (usu) instrumental part to support a voice, choir or solo instrument: (音乐)(通常指对独唱, 合唱或独奏乐器之)伴奏: *a song with a piano ~.* 由钢琴伴奏之歌. **ac·com·pan·ist** /əˈkʌmpənɪst; ə'kʌmpənɪst/ *n* person who plays a musical ~. 伴奏者.

ac·com·pany /əˈkʌmpənɪ; ə'kʌmpənɪ/ *vt* (*pt, pp* -nied) [VP 6 A, 14] 1 go with: 伴随; 陪伴; 跟随: *Warships will ~ the convoy across the Atlantic.* 战舰将护送该船队过大西洋. *He was accompanied by his secretary.* 他有秘书随行. 2 attend; characterize: 带有; 以…为其特征: *fever accompanied with delirium;* 带昏语的发烧; *lightning accompanied with thunder.* 带雷的

闪电; 雷电交作. 3 occur or do at the same time as: 与…同时发生或做出: *~ one's words with blows.* 一边说一边动拳头. 4 (music) play an accompaniment to: (音乐)为…伴奏: *The singer was accompanied at the piano by Gerald Moore.* 该歌唱者由杰拉尔德·穆尔钢琴伴奏.

ac·com·plice /əˈkʌmplɪs US: ə'kʌm-; ə'kʌmplɪs/ *n* [C] helper or companion (in, esp, wrongdoing). 从犯; 帮凶; 同谋者(与 in 连用, 尤指做坏事).

ac·com·plish /əˈkʌmplɪʃ US: ə'kʌm-; ə'kʌmplɪʃ/ *vt* [VP 6 A] perform; succeed in doing; finish successfully: 实行; 完成; 成功地做完: ~ *a task:* 完成一件工作; *a man who will never ~ anything.* 永远一事无成的人. **an ~ed fact,** sth already done. 既成事实. **~ed** *adj* clever; skilled (*in*): 技巧的; 熟练的; 精于…的(后接 in): *an ~ed dancer;* 舞技高超的舞者; well trained or educated in such social arts as conversation, art and music: 在谈话, 绘画及音乐等社交艺术方面受过良好的训练或教育的; 善社交而多才多艺的: *an ~ed young lady.* 一位善社交而多才多艺的淑女. **~·ment** *n* 1 [U] completion; finishing: 完成: *the ~ment of their aims;* 他们目标之完成; *difficult of ~ment.* 难以完成. 2 [C] sth ~ed, esp sth well done. 完成之事; 成就; 技艺. 3 [C] skill in a social or domestic art: (社交或家事方面的)才艺; 教养; 技艺: *Among her ~ments were dancing, playing the piano, sewing and cooking.* 她的才艺包括跳舞, 弹钢琴, 缝纫及烹饪.

ac·cord[1] /əˈkɔːd; ə'kɔrd/ *n* 1 [U] **of one's own ~,** without being asked or forced; willingly. 主动地; 自动地. **in/out of ~ (with),** in/out of harmony with (with), agreeing/not agreeing with. (与…)(不)一致. **with one ~,** everybody consenting. 全体一致. 2 [C] treaty, agreement (*between* countries; *with* a country). (两国之间或与他国所订的)条约; 协定(与 between 或 with 连用).

ac·cord[2] /əˈkɔːd; ə'kɔrd/ *vi, vt* 1 [VP 2A, 2C, 3A] ~ *(with),* match, agree (with); be in agreement or harmony (with): (与…)相配合; 一致; 符合: *His behaviour and his principles do not ~ (well together).* 他的行为与他的原则不符合. *His behaviour does not ~ with his principles.* 他的行为不合他的原则. *What you say does not ~ with the previous evidence.* 你所说的与以前的证据不一致. 2 [VP 13A, 12A] (formal style) give; grant: (正式文体)给与; 赠与; 赐与: ~ *sb permission;* 允许某人; ~ *permission to sb.* 允许某人. *He was ~ed a warm welcome.* 他受到热烈的欢迎.

ac·cord·ance /əˈkɔːdns; ə'kɔrdn̩s/ *n* **in ~,** in agreement or conformity with: 依照; 根据: *in ~ with your wishes;* 根据你的愿望; *in ~ with custom/the regulations.* 依照惯例(规章).

ac·cord·ing /əˈkɔːdɪŋ; ə'kɔrdɪŋ/ 1 ~ *as,* conj in proportion as; in a manner that depends upon: 依照; 根据: *You will be praised or blamed ~ as your work is good or bad.* 你将依照你工作成绩的好坏而受到奖惩. 2 ~ *to,* prep (a) on the authority of: 根据: *A~ to the Bible, God created the world in six days.* 根据圣经所载, 上帝在六天之内创造了世界. (b) in a degree in proportion to: 视…而定: *He will be punished ~ to the seriousness of his crime.* 他所受的惩罚将视其犯罪的严重性而定. (c) in a manner consistent with: 按照; 依照: *The books are placed on the shelves ~ to authors.* 这些书按照作者的顺序摆在书架上. **~·ly** *adv* 1 for that reason; therefore. 因此; 所以; 于是. 2 as the (stated) circumstances suggest: 按照(所说的)情形: *I have told you the circumstances, so you must act ~ly.* 我已经告诉你这情况, 所以你必须按照我所说的办理.

ac·cord·ion /əˈkɔːdɪən; ə'kɔrdɪən/ *n* (also 亦作 **piano ~**) portable musical instrument with a bellows, metal reeds and a keyboard; (attrib) having narrow folds like the bellows of an ~: 手风琴(一种手提型乐器, 有风箱, 金属簧及键盘); (用作定语) 像手风琴其折箱般有细褶的: ~ *pleats in a skirt.* 裙子上像手风琴折箱般的细褶.

ac·cost /əˈkɒst US: əˈkɔːst; əˈkɒst/ vt [VP6A] go up to and speak to first, esp a stranger in a public place; (of a prostitute) solicit: 走上前与之(尤指与公共场所之陌生人)攀谈; (指妓女)勾搭; 拉客; 乞求: *I was ~ed by a beggar/a prostitute.* 一个乞丐(妓女)向我乞讨(勾搭)。

ac·couche·ment /əˈkuːʃmɒŋ; əˈkuʃmā/ n (F) lying in; confinement; childbirth. (法)分娩; 坐褥; 生产。 ⇨ *lie* in at *lie²(1)*.

ac·count¹ /əˈkaʊnt; əˈkaʊnt/ n 1 [C] (comm) statement of money (to be) paid or received (for goods, services, etc). (商)帐目; 帐; 帐户: *I have an ~ with the Midland Bank,* keep my money with that Bank, pay my debts, etc by means of cheques from that Bank, etc. 我在米德兰银行开有户头(存款于该银行, 开该行支票付款等)。 *open an ~; open a bank/post office, etc ~,* start to keep one's money at a bank, etc. 开户头; 开一银行(邮局等)户头(开始在银行, 邮局等中存款)。 *ask a shop/shopkeeper/store to put sth down to one's ~,* ask him to note the price of what is bought, for payment later. 请店铺(店东, 商店)将某货物记在自己的帐上。 *settle one's ~ (with),* pay what one owes (to a tradesman, etc); (fig) avenge oneself for an injury, etc). (向商人等)结清欠帐; 结帐; 清帐; (喻)报复; 报一箭之仇。 *send in/render an ~,* send a written statement of what is owed. 送帐单。 Hence, 由此产生, *,~ 'rendered,* an ~ previously sent in but not yet paid. 先行提出而尚未付清之帐单; 交验帐。 *balance/square ~s (with sb),* receive or pay the difference between debit and credit; (fig) remove moral grievances between people by giving or taking punishment. (与某人) 结清帐目; (喻) (与某人) 将恩怨怨怨消一了断。 *'budget ~,* (with a shop) one used for buying goods, paying bills, etc by making regular payments to the shop; (with a bank) special ~ with a bank which makes regular deductions for bills paid. 预算帐户(在一商店中所开的帐户, 以购买货物、付帐等, 定期付款给该商店; 或指在一银行中所开的特别帐户, 该银行定期从其存款中扣除已代付之费用)。 *'current ~, de'posit ~, 'joint ~, 'private ~, 'savings ~* ⇨ *current¹(3), deposit¹(1), joint¹, private(1)* and *save¹*. 2 (archaic) counting; calculation. (古)计算。 *money of ~,* used of sums of money, not of coins or banknotes. 计算货币; 虚位通货(指钱数, 不指硬币或钞票)。 ⇨ *guinea.* 3 (*sing* only) benefit; profit: (只用单数)利益: *invest one's money to good ~,* 将钱投资以获高利。 *turn/put sth to (good) ~,* use money, abilities, talent, etc profitably: 对某事物善加利用(如有利地利用金钱, 能力, 才能等): *He turned/put his knowledge of Spanish to good ~.* 他善加利用他对西班牙语文的知识。 *work on one's own ~,* for one's own purposes and profit, and at one's own risk. 为一己的目的及利益打算, 且自行负责。 4 [U] *call/bring sb to ~,* require him to justify or explain his conduct; state that he is answerable for sth. 叫某人解释其行为的理由; 责问; 质问。5 [U] *give a good ~ of oneself,* do well; act in a way that brings credit, eg by defeating opponents in contests. 大显身手(例如在比赛中击败对手)。6 [C] report; description; narrative: 报告; 叙述: *Don't always believe newspaper ~s of events.* 不要老是相信报纸的报导。 *by one's own ~,* according to what one oneself says. 据…自己说。 *by/from all ~s,* according to what everybody, all the papers, etc say. 人人(所有的报纸等)都如此说。7 [U] estimation: 估计; 价值; 考虑。 *be (reckoned) of some/small ~,* be (considered) of some/low value. (被认为)有相当价值(无甚价值)。 *take sth into ~; take ~ of sth,* note or consider it; pay attention to it. 对某事物加以考虑; 对某事物加以注意。 *leave sth out of ~; take no ~ of sth,* pay no attention to it. 对某事物不予注意; 对某事物不予考虑。8 [U] reason; cause. 理由; 原因。 *on ~ of,* because of. 因为。 *on this/that ~,* for this/that reason: 为了这个(那个)缘故: *He's angry on that ~.* 为

了那个缘故他很生气。 *Don't stay away on ~ of John/on John's ~.* 为了约翰, 不要离开。 *on no ~; not on any ~,* in no case; not for any reason. 决不; 切莫: *Don't on any ~ leave the baby alone in the house.* 切不可将婴儿独自留在家里。

ac·count² /əˈkaʊnt; əˈkaʊnt/ vt, vi [VP3A] *~ for,* serve as an explanation of; explain the cause of: 解释; 说明: *His illness ~s for his absence.* 他因为生病, 所以才缺席。 *Ah, that ~s for it!* 呵, 原来是这么一回事! *He has been asked to ~ for his conduct,* explain why he acted as he did. 他被要求解释他的行为(说明他何以如此)。 *There's no ~ing for tastes,* We cannot explain why people have different likes and dislikes. 人的好恶是无法解释的。 (b) give a reckoning of (money that has been entrusted to one): 报帐: *The boy has to ~ (to his parents) for the money they give him for school expenses.* 该男孩必须 (向他父母亲) 报帐, 说明他们所给他学杂费的支出细目。 (c) destroy; kill; capture: 摧毁; 杀死; 捕获: *We ~ed for a fine brace of partridges.* 我们猎获了一对很好的鹧鸪。2 [VP25] consider: 认为; 视为: *In English law a man is ~ed innocent until he is proved guilty.* 在英国法律上, 一个人未被证实有罪之前, 被视为清白的。 *~·able* /-əbl; -əbl/ adj *~able (to sb) (for sth),* responsible; expected to give an explanation: 对某人(某事)负责; 对…应加以说明: *I'll hold you ~able.* 我要唯你是问。 *A madman is not ~able for his actions.* 疯子对自己的行为没有责任。

ac·count·ancy /əˈkaʊntənsɪ; əˈkaʊntənsɪ/ n [U] profession of an accountant. 会计师或会计之职业。

ac·count·ant /əˈkaʊntənt; əˈkaʊntənt/ n [C] (in GB) person whose profession is to keep and examine business accounts¹. (英)会计师; 会计。 **chartered ~,** (abbr 略作 **CA**) ⇨ **charter** v(1) (US 美 = **certified public ~,** abbr 略作 **CPA**)。

ac·coutre·ments (US=**ec·cou·ter·ments**) /əˈkuːtəmənts; əˈkutəmənts/ n pl equipment; trappings; (mil) soldier's kit excluding clothes and weapons. 装备; 装饰物; (军)(军服及武器以外的)配备。

ac·credit /əˈkredɪt; əˈkredɪt/ vt [VP 14] (usu passive) (通常用被动语态) 1 appoint or send (sb) as an ambassador, with official letters of introduction: 委派 (某人)出任大使: *He was ~ed to/at Lisbon.* 他奉派出任驻里斯本大使。2 = **credit².** *~ed part adj* officially recognized (person); generally accepted (belief, opinion, etc); guaranteed to be of an approved quality. 官方认可的(人); 普遍接受的(信仰, 意见等); 保证品质良好的。

ac·cretion /əˈkriːʃn; əˈkriʃn/ n 1 [U] increase by organic addition or growth; the growing of separate things into one. 生长; 增大; 粘连; 长合。2 [C] sth added; sth resulting from ~. 增加物; 生长部份; 长合物。

ac·crue /əˈkruː; əˈkru/ vi [VP2A, 3A] *~ (to sb) (from sth),* come as a natural growth or development: 自然增长或产生: *If you keep your money in the Savings Bank, interest ~s.* 如果你把钱存在储蓄银行里, 就会自然生息。 *A~d interest is interest due, but not yet paid or received.* 应计利息是到期利息, 不过尚未付出或领取。

ac·cu·mu·late /əˈkjuːmjʊleɪt; əˈkjumjəˌlet/ vt, vi [VP6A, 2A] make or become greater in number or quantity; come or gather together; heap up: 累积; 积聚; 堆积: *By buying ten books every month, he soon ~d a library.* 他每月买十本书, 不久就积聚了一批藏书。 *Dust soon ~s if the rooms are not swept.* 房间如果不打扫, 灰尘不久就堆积起来了。 *By working hard you may ~ a fortune.* 努力工作你就可以积蓄一笔财产。

ac·cu·mu·la·tion /ə,kjuːmjʊˈleɪʃn; ə,kjumjəˈleʃən/ n 1 [U] accumulating; collection: 累积; 积聚; 收集: *the ~ of money/useful knowledge.* 金钱(有用知识)的积聚。2 [C] material, etc accumulated: 聚积物; 堆积物; 收集物: *an ~ of books/evidence/rubbish.* 收集的一批书籍 (一堆证据, 一堆垃圾)。 **ac·cu·mu·lat·ive** /əˈkjuːmjʊlətɪv US: -leɪtɪv; əˈkjumjəˌletɪv/ adj arising

from ~; growing by a succession of additions. 积聚起来的; 累积起来的。

ac·cu·mu·la·tor /ə'kjumjuleitə(r); ə'kjumjə,letə/ n [C] **1** (GB) storage battery, eg for a motor vehicle: (英)(汽车等的)蓄电池: *charge/discharge an ~*, cause a current to flow into/out of it. 使蓄电池充电(放电)。 **2** (in a computer) device which stores numbers and progressively adds numbers. (电脑中之)累积器(贮积及累计数字的装置)。

ac·cu·rate /'ækjərət; 'ækjərɪt/ adj **1** careful and exact: 精确的: *be ~ in one's work/in what one says*; 作事(说话)精确; *give ~ at figures*; 计算迅速而精确; *take ~ aim*. 瞄准精确。 **2** free from error: 正确无误的; 准确的: *~ scales*. 准确的秤。*Clocks in railway stations should be ~*. 火车站的钟应该准确。~·**ly** adv **ac·cu·racy** /'ækjərəsɪ; 'ækjərəsɪ/ n [U] exactness; correctness. 精确; 正确; 准确。

ac·cursed /ə'kɜːsɪd; ə'kɜːsɪd/, **ac·curst** /ə'kɜːst; ə'kɜːst/ adj (poetic) under a curse; detestable hateful. (诗)被诅咒的; 可憎的; 可恨的。

ac·cu·sa·tion /,ækju:'zeɪʃn; ,ækjə'zeʃən/ n **1** [U] accusing or being accused. 非难; 谴责; 控诉; 被控诉。 **2** [C] charge of doing wrong, of having broken the law: 控告: *bring an ~ of theft against sb*; 控告某人窃盗。*be under an ~ of theft.* 被控窃盗。

ac·cu·sa·tive /ə'kju:zətɪv; ə'kjuzətɪv/ adj, n (gram) (of the) form of a word when it is the direct object of a verb or preposition. (语法)宾格(用作动词或介词的直接宾语之词的一种形式); 宾格的, ⇨ case¹(3).

ac·cuse /ə'kju:z; ə'kjuz/ vt [VP6A, 14] ~ *sb (of sth)*, say that (sb) has done wrong, broken the law, is to be blamed: 控告某人(犯某项罪); 控诉; 告发; 非难; 谴责: ~ *sb of theft/cowardice*; 控告某人窃盗(责备某人怯懦); *be ~d of sth.* 被控犯某罪。*the ~d*, the person(s) charged in a criminal case. (刑案中的)被告。**ac·cuser** n **ac·cus·ing·ly** /ə'kju:zɪŋlɪ; adv in an accusing manner: 以控诉或谴责的态度: *He pointed accusingly at me.* 他以谴责的态度指着我。

ac·cus·tom /ə'kʌstəm; ə'kʌstəm/ vt [VP 14] ~ *(oneself) to*, make used to: 使习惯于: *When he became a soldier, he had to ~ himself to long marches.* 当他当兵的时候, 他不得不使自己习惯于长途行军。**become/be ~ed to**, become/be used to: 习惯于: *The boy soon became ~ed to hard work and poor food.* 那男孩不久就习惯于苦工及劣食了。*This is not the kind of treatment I am ~ed to*, not the kind I usually receive. 这不是我所习惯的那种待遇。~ed part adj usual; habitual: 通常的; 惯常的: *in his ~ed seat.* 坐在他通常的座位上。

ace /eɪs; es/ n [C] **1** the one on dice, on (playing-) cards or dominoes (⇨ these words); card so marked: (骰子, 纸牌或骨牌上)么点 (参看 dice, card, domino 各字); 么点牌: *the ~ of spades.* 黑桃牌之么点; 黑桃爱斯。**an ace in the hole**, (US sl, from the game of poker) sth held in reserve, likely to turn failure into success. (美俚, 源于扑克牌戏)保留着用以转败为胜之事物; 扭转乾坤之王牌。 **2** (colloq) person who is first-rate or expert at sth, esp an airman or a driver of racing cars. (俗)第一流人才或专家; (尤指)第一流飞行员或赛车驾驶员; 能手。 **3** *within an ace of*, failing, escaping, by a narrow margin: 差一点; 几乎: *within an ace of death/of being killed.* 死里逃生(险些丧命)。

acerb·ity /ə'sɜːbətɪ; ə'sɜːbətɪ/ n **1** [U] (formal) bitterness of speech, manner, temper. (正式用语)(言语, 态度, 性情之)刻薄; 尖刻。 **2** [C] (pl -ties) instance of this; bitter remark, etc. 刻薄之实例; 尖刻的言语; 刻薄话; 严厉的态度等。

acetic /ə'si:tɪk; ə'sitɪk/ adj of vinegar or ~ acid. 醋的; 醋酸的。~ **'acid**, the acid contained in vinegar. 醋酸。**acet·ate** /'æsɪteɪt; 'æsə,tet/ n salt of ~ acid: 醋酸盐: *acetate silk*, artificial silk made from cellulose acetate. 醋酸人造丝(醋酸纤维素制成之人造丝)。

acety·lene /ə'setəli:n; ə'sɛtl,in/ n [U] (chem) colourless gas (C_2H_2) which burns with a bright light, used in carbide lamps and for welding and cutting metal. (化学)乙炔(一种无色气体,分子式 C_2H_2, 燃烧时发出明亮的光, 用于电石气体及焊接或切断金属) ⇨ **oxyacetylene**.

ache /eɪk; ek/ n [C] (*sing*, with or without the *indef art*) dull continuous pain: (单数时可与不定冠词连用,不用不定冠词亦可)疼痛: *have ~s and pains all over.* 周身疼痛。(~ is only combined with *back, ear, head, heart, stomach, tummy* and *tooth*, as in *back~*. For other parts of the body a *pain/~ in my/his/the foot, etc* is used): (ache 仅与 back, ear, head, heart, stomach, tummy, tooth 等词结合, 如 backache; 身体其他部分之疼痛则用 pain 或 ache 表示, 例如 a pain (or ache) in my (his or the) foot): *have a 'head~*; 头痛; *suffer from 'back~s/from (the) 'tooth~.* 背(牙)痛。'**heart~**, ⇨ **heart**(7). □ vi **1** [VP2A] have a steady or continuous dull pain: 隐隐作痛; 持续地痛: *My head ~s/is aching.* 我头痛。*After climbing the mountain, he ~d all over.* 爬山以后,他浑身疼痛。*It makes my heart ~*, makes me sad. 它使我痛心。 **2** [VP3 A, 4A] ~ *(for)*, have a longing: 渴望: *His heart ~ed for her.* 他的心苦念着她。*He was aching for home.* 他渴望回家。*He ~d to be free.* 他渴望自由。

achieve /ə'tʃiːv; ə'tʃiv/ vt [VP6A] **1** complete; accomplish; get (sth) done: 完成; 达成; 成就: *He will never ~ anything*, will not do anything successfully. 他永不会有所成就。*I've ~d only half of what I hoped to do.* 我仅完成了我所希望的一半。 **2** gain or reach by effort: 借努力而获得或达到: ~ *one's purpose*; 达到目的; ~ *success/distinction in public life.* 为公家服务(或担任公职)获得成功(殊荣)。**achiev·able** /-əbl; -əbl/ adj that can be ~d: 可达到的; 可达成的: ~ *aims.* **achieve·ment** n **1** [U] achieving: 完成; 达成: *the ~ment of an undertaking/of one's aims;* 任务的完成(某人目标的达到); *impossible of ~ment;* 不可能完成的; ~ *ment test* (of skills, etc). (技巧等的)成就测验。 **2** [C] sth ~d; done successfully, with effort and skill: 成就; 成绩; 业; 功绩: *The inventor was rewarded by the Government for his scientific ~ments.* 该发明家由于他在科学上的成就受到政府的奖励。

Achilles /ə'kɪliːz; ə'kɪlɪz/ n **the heel of ~**, (fig) small but weak or vulnerable point, eg in sb's character: (喻)(某人之个性等中的)弱点: *Spelling is my ~' heel.* 拼字是我的弱点。

acid¹ /'æsɪd; 'æsɪd/ adj **1** sour; sharp to the taste: 酸的; 酸味的: *A lemon is an ~ fruit.* 柠檬是酸的水果。*Vinegar has an ~ taste.* 醋有酸味。~ **drops**, sweets of boiled sugar with an ~ flavour. 酸糖(一种用糖熬成而带酸味的糖果)。 **2** (fig) sharp; sarcastic: (喻)尖酸刻薄的; 讥讽的: *an ~ wit;* 讥讽的机智; ~ *remarks.* 刻薄话。

acid² /'æsɪd; 'æsɪd/ n **1** [U] (chem) substance that contains hydrogen, which may be replaced by a metal to form a salt: (化学)酸(所含之氢能被金属取代而成为盐类之物质): *Vinegar contains acetic ~.* 醋含有醋酸。H_2SO_4 *stands for sulphuric ~;* H_2SO_4 代表硫酸; [C] example of this: 酸类: *Some ~s burn holes in wool and cloth.* 有些酸类物质能在木料及布帛上烧成洞。~ **test** n (fig) test that gives conclusive proof of the value or worth of sth. 酸性试验; (喻)(足以证明某事物之价值的)决定性的考验。 **2** [U] (sl) (俚) = LSD. ⇨ **App 2**. ⇨ 看附录二。~·**ify** /ə'sɪdɪfaɪ; ə'sɪdə,faɪ/ vt, vi (pt, pp **-fied**) [VP6A, 2A] make or become ~. 使变酸; 变酸; 酸化。~·**ity** /ə'sɪdətɪ; ə'sɪdətɪ/ n [U] state or quality of being ~. 酸性; 酸味。**acid** /'æsɪdɪk; adj ~·**u·lated** /ə'sɪdjuleɪtɪd US: -dʒul-; ə'sɪdʒə,letɪd/ adj made slightly ~. 带酸味的; 微酸的。~·**u·lous** US: -dʒul-; ə'sɪdʒələs/ adj (lit or fig) somewhat sour in taste or manner; sharp; bitter: (字面或喻)微酸的; 坏脾气的; 乖戾的; 刻薄的: *an ~ulous drink/tone of*

voice. 微酸的酒 (尖刻的声调)。

ack-ack /ˌæk ˈæk; ˈækˌæk/ *n* (mil sl) anti-aircraft gun/fire, etc. (军俚) 高射炮 (炮火等)。

ac·knowl·edge /əkˈnɒlɪdʒ; əkˈnɑlɪdʒ/ *vt* 1 [VP6A, C, 9, 24A] confess; admit the truth, existence or reality of: 供认; 承认: *He refused to ~ defeat/that he was defeated.* 他拒绝承认失败 (被击败)。*He would not ~ his mistake.* 他不会认错。*He won't ~ himself beaten.* 他将不承认自己被打败。*He ~d having been frightened.* 他承认受惊。*Does he ~ the signature, agree or admit that it is his?* 他承认那是他的签字吗? [VP25] (liter style): (文言体): *We praise Thee, O God, we ~ Thee to be the Lord.* 我们赞美你, 呵上帝, 我们承认你是主。 [VP16B] *Stephen ~d Henry as his heir,* recognized his claim to be heir. 斯蒂芬认可亨利为他的继承人。 [VP25] *They all ~d him master,* agreed that he was their master. 他们一致承认他是主人。 2 [VP6A] report that one has received (sth): 说明已收到 (某物): *~ (receipt of) a letter.* 说明已收到一封来信。 [VP6A] express thanks for: 表示感谢; 为…致谢: *We must not fail to ~ his services to the town.* 我们必须感谢他对本市的贡献。 *We should always ~ gifts promptly.* 我们收到礼物应立即致谢。 4 [VP6A] indicate that one recognizes (sb) by giving a greeting, a smile, a nod of the head, etc: (以问候语, 微笑, 点头等) 表示认识 (某人), 向 (某人) 打招呼: *I passed her in the street but she didn't even ~ me when I smiled.* 我在街上遇到她, 可是当我向她微笑时, 她连招呼都没有向我打一下。**~·ment, ac·knowl·edg·ment** n 1 [U] act of acknowledging: 承认; 致谢; 感谢: *We are sending you a small sum of money in ~ment of your valuable help.* 兹奉上薄款对阁下之鼎力相助聊表谢意。 2 [C] sth given or done to ~ sth: 借以表示收到或感谢之物; 收悉通知或回报; 收条; 回帖: *We have had no ~ment of our letter,* no reply. 我们尚未收到回信。*This basket of fruit is a slight ~ment of your kindness.* 这一篮水果是用来对你的恩惠略表谢意。

acme /ˈækmɪ; ˈækmɪ/ *n* **the ~,** summit; highest point of development; point of perfection: 顶点; 极点; 极致: *the ~ of his desires/skill.* 他的欲望 (技艺) 的顶点。

acne /ˈæknɪ; ˈæknɪ/ *n* [U] disease (common among adolescents) in which there are pimples and blackheads on the face and neck. 痤疮; 粉刺 (青年人普遍的一种皮肤病, 在面部及颈部长丘疹及黑点粉刺)。

aco·lyte /ˈækəlaɪt; ˈækəˌlaɪt/ *n* person who helps a priest in some religious services, esp the celebration of Mass. 教士或僧侣在举行宗教仪式时 (尤指领弥撒时) 的助手。

ac·on·ite /ˈækənaɪt; ˈækəˌnaɪt/ *n* (bot) (sorts of) plant with blue or purple flowers; monkshood; drug from the dried poisonous root of one of these kinds, used to slow down the action of the heart. (植物) 附子; 乌头 (开蓝白紫花之一属植物); 乌头素 (由此属植物之毒根所提炼之药物, 用以减缓心脏的活动)。

acorn /ˈeɪkɔːn; ˈekən/ *n* seed or fruit of the oak tree. 橡子; 橡实。⇨ the illus at **tree.** 参看 tree 之插图。**'~-cup** cuplike holder of an ~. 橡实壳斗。

acous·tic /əˈkuːstɪk; əˈkustɪk/ *adj* of sound, the science of sound and the sense of hearing. 声音的; 声学的; 音响学的; 听觉的。□ *n* [C] studio, hall, etc from the consideration of its ~s (⇨ 2 below): 具有某种音响效果的录音室, 大厅等 (参看下列第 2 义): *Try recording the music in a better ~.* 试在传音性较好的厅里录该音乐。**acous·tics** *n* 1 (with *sing v*) the scientific study of sound. (用单数动词) 声学; 音响学。 2 (with *pl v*) the physical properties of sound; the properties of a hall, etc, that make it good, poor, etc for hearing music, speeches, etc: (用复数动词) 声的物理性质; (大厅等之) 传音性 (使演讲, 音乐演奏等的收听效果良好, 不良等): *The ~s of the new concert hall are excellent.* 这新音乐厅的传音性极佳。

ac·quaint /əˈkweɪnt; əˈkwent/ *vt* [VP 14] 1 **~ sb/**

---

oneself with, make familiar with, reveal to: 使某人 (自己) 熟悉于…, 使明白; 使通晓: *~ sb with the facts of the case;* 使某人知道该事件之详情; *~ oneself/become ~ed/make oneself ~ed with one's new duties.* 使自己明白自己的新职责。 2 **be ~ed (with sb),** have met (sb) personally: 与 (某人) 见过面; 认识; 熟识: *I am not ~ed with the lady.* 我不认识那位女士。*We are not ~ed.* 我们 (彼此) 不认识。

ac·quaint·ance /əˈkweɪntəns; əˈkwentəns/ *n* 1 [U] knowledge or information gained through experience: 从经验获得的知识; 习知: *He has some ~ with German, but does not speak it fluently.* 他略懂一点德文, 但说得不流利。**have a bowing/nodding ~ with,** have some ~ with (a person, a subject). 与 (某人) 为点头之交; 对 (某学科) 略知一二。**make sb's ~, make the ~ of sb,** get to know sb, eg by being introduced. 与某人结识 (如经过介绍)。**(up)on (further) ~,** when known for a (further) period of time. 经过 (较久) 一段时间的认识。 2 [C] person with whom one is acquainted; person whom one knows (less intimately than a friend): 相识的人 (不如朋友那样亲密): *He has a wide circle of ~s.* 他交际极广 (认识很多人)。 3 (older English, collective): (在旧式英语中用作集合名词): *He has a wide ~,* many ~s. 他交际广阔 (认识很多人)。**~·ship** /-ʃɪp; -ˌʃɪp/ *n* (circle of) ~s(2). 相识; 交际圈。

ac·quiesce /ˌækwɪˈes; ˌækwɪˈɛs/ *vi* 1 [VP2A] agree; accept silently or without protest. 同意; 默认; 默许; 顺从。 2 [VP3A] **~ in,** accept an arrangement, a conclusion, etc without protest: 不提抗议地接受 (安排, 结论等) 勉强同意: *Her parents will never ~ in such an unsuitable marriage.* 她的父母决不会同意这样不适宜的婚事。**ac·qui·es·cence** /ˌækwɪˈesns; ˌækwɪˈɛsns/ *n* [C] (act of) acquiescing. 同意; 默认; 默许; 顺从。**ac·qui·es·cent** /-ˈesnt; -ˈɛsnt/ *adj* disposed to ~. 同意的; 默认的; 默许的; 顺从的。

ac·quire /əˈkwaɪə(r); əˈkwaɪr/ *vt* [VP6A] gain by skill or ability, by one's own efforts or behaviour: (由技术, 能力, 努力或行为而) 获得; 得到: *~ a good knowledge of English/a reputation for dishonesty/a taste for brandy.* 熟谙英文 (蒙上不诚实之名; 养成喝白兰地酒的嗜好)。**an ~d taste,** one that comes when one has experimented with sth and, in the end, comes to like it: 后天的 (非天生的) 嗜好: *Retsina (=the resin-flavoured Gk wine) is an ~d taste for British people.* 英国人喝瑞星娜酒 (以树脂作香料的希腊葡萄酒) 是一种后天的嗜好。**~·ment** /- / n 1 [U] acquisition (now the more usu word). 获得; 得到 (今较常用 acquisition)。 2 [C] accomplishment(3) (now the more usu word). 才艺; 教养; 技艺 (今较常用 accomplishment)。

ac·qui·si·tion /ˌækwɪˈzɪʃn; ˌækwəˈzɪʃən/ *n* 1 [U] acquiring: 获得; 得到: *He devotes his time to the ~ of knowledge.* 他把时间都花在求知上。 2 [C] sth acquired: 获得物; 添加物: *my most recent ~s,* eg books I have bought recently. 我最近增添的东西 (例如新近才买的书籍)。*Mr A will be a valuable ~ to* (= a valuable new member of) *the teaching staff of our school.* A 先生将是本校教员阵容中的一支生力军。

ac·quis·itive /əˈkwɪzətɪv; əˈkwɪzətɪv/ *adj* fond of, in the habit of, acquiring: 贪求得的; 好获取的: *~ of new ideas.* 求求新知。**the ~ society,** that values the possession of more and more material things. 物欲横流的社会 (重视拥有更多更多的物质享受)。

ac·quit /əˈkwɪt; əˈkwɪt/ *vt* (-tt-) 1 [VP6A, 14] **~ sb (of/on sth),** give a legal decision that (sb) is not guilty, eg of an offence: 宣告某人无罪 (如对某一罪状): *He was ~ted of the crime/~ted on two of the charges.* 他被宣告无罪 (他被指控的罪状其中有两项被宣告无罪)。 2 [VP16B] conduct oneself: 持 (身); 行为: *He ~ted himself well/like a hero.* 他行为端正 (所作所为如英雄)。**~·tal** /əˈkwɪtl; əˈkwɪtl/ *n* [U] judgement that a person is not guilty: 无罪的判决: *a sentence of ~tal;* 判决无罪; [C] instance of this: 判决无罪的实例: *three*

convictions and two ~tals. 三人宜判有罪，两人判决无罪。

acre /'eɪkə(r); 'ekø/ *n* [C] measure of land, 4840 sq yds or about 4000 sq metres. 英亩 (= 4,840 平方码, 约 4,000 平方公尺)。 **God's ~,** churchyard (for burials). 教堂墓地。 **~·age** /'eɪkərɪdʒ; 'ekørɪdʒ/ *n* [U] area of land measured in ~s. 以英亩计算之土地面积; 英亩数; 亩数: *What is the ~age of the London parks?* 伦敦各公园共占地多少英亩?

ac·rid /'ækrɪd; 'ækrɪd/ *adj* (of smell or taste) sharp; biting: (指气味或味道)辛辣的; 难闻的; *the ~ smell of burning feathers;* 烧焦羽毛之难闻气味; (fig) bitter in temper or manner. (喻)(性情或态度)尖刻的。

ac·ri·mony /'ækrɪmənɪ US: -məʊnɪ; 'ækrə,monɪ/ *n* [U] (formal) bitterness of temper, manner, language. (正式用语)(性情, 态度, 言语的)尖刻; 刻薄。 **ac·ri·moni·ous** /ˌækrɪ'məʊnɪəs; ,ækrə'monɪəs/ *adj* (of arguments, quarrels, words) bitter. (指辩论, 争论, 言词)尖刻的; 刻薄的; 剧烈的。

ac·ro·bat /'ækrəbæt; 'ækrə,bæt/ *n* person who can perform difficult or unusual physical acts with skill, eg on a tightrope or trapeze. 杂技演员; 特技表演者; 走钢丝者; 走索者; 空中飞人。 **~ic** /ˌækrə'bætɪk;ækrə'bætɪk/ *adj* of or like an ~: 杂技的; 特技表演的: *~ic feats.* 杂技的技艺。 **~ics** *n pl* (used with *sing v*) ~ic tricks or feats: (用单数动词)杂技; 特技: *aircraft ~ics.* 飞行特技。

acrobats

ac·ro·nym /'ækrənɪm; 'ækrənɪm/ *n* [C] word formed from the initial letters of a name; eg **NASA** /'næsə; 'næsə/, National Aeronautics and Space Administration. 首字母缩略词 (由一名称之各词首字母所组成的字, 例如 NASA, 系由 National Aeronautics and Space Administration 各词首字母所组成)。 ⇨ **App2.** 参看附录二。

acrop·olis /ə'krɒpəlɪs; ə'krɑpəlɪs/ *n* fortified part of a Gk city in ancient times, esp **the A~,** that of Athens. 古希腊城市用以据守的城堡; 卫城; (尤指)雅典之卫城。

across¹ /ə'krɒs US: ə'krɔːs; ə'krɔs/ *adv* (used with *vv* in the senses of the *prep*): (与动词连用, 意义同介词): *Can you swim ~?* 你能游到对岸去吗? *Will you row me ~?* 我帮助那盲人走过街。 *I helped the blind man ~.* 我帮助那盲人走过街。 *Come ~ to my office this afternoon.* 今天下午我办公室来。 *The river is half a mile ~,* = wide. 这河面宽半英里。 **~ from,** (US) opposite: (美)在…的对面: *The bank is just ~ from the school.* 银行就在学校的对面。

across² /ə'krɒs US: ə'krɔːs; ə'krɔs/ *prep* 1 from one side to the other side of: 从…的一边到另一边; 横过: *walk ~ the street;* 走过街; *draw a line ~ a sheet of paper;* 在一张纸上画一条横线; *a bridge ~ the river;* 横跨河上的一座桥; *row sb ~ a lake.* 划船送某人过湖。 **~-the-'board,** including all groups, members, etc esp in an occupation or industry: (尤指在某一职业或产业中)包括各团体, 全体会员等; 全面的: *an ~-the-board wage increase.* 工资的全面提高。 **2** on the other side of:

在…的另一边: *My house is just ~ the street.* 我的房子就在街对面。 *We shall soon be ~ the Channel.* 我们不久即要渡过海峡了。 *He addressed me from ~ the room.* 他从房间的另一边向我讲话。 **3** so as to form a cross; so as to cross or intersect: 作十字形; 交叉: *He sat with his arms ~ his chest.* 他两臂交叉在胸前坐着。 *The two lines pass ~ each other at right angles.* 这两条线成直角相交。 **4** (with *vv*) ⇨ **come(16), drop²(13), get(17), put¹(11)** and **run²(26).**

acros·tic /ə'krɒstɪk US: -'krɔːs-; ə'krɔstɪk/ *n* word puzzle, word arrangement, in which the first, or the first and last, letters of the lines make a word or words. 离合字谜; 离合体诗(数行诗句之首字母, 或其首尾字母能联合成字者)。

acryl·ic /ə'krɪlɪk; ə'krɪlɪk/ *n* (comm) (商) ,~ 'fibre, (kinds of) synthetic fibre used for making dress materials, etc. 丙烯酸系纤维(用以制衣料等之数种合成纤维)。 ,~ 'resin, (kinds of) transparent colourless plastic widely used in industry, eg for plastic lenses, aircraft windows. 丙烯酸树脂(数种透明无色的树脂, 工业上使用极广, 如制镜片, 飞机窗等)。

act¹ /ækt; ækt/ *n* [C] **1** sth done: 行为; 举动: *To kick a cat is a cruel act.* 踢猫是残忍的行为。 *It is an act of kindness to help a blind man across the street.* 帮助盲人过街是慈善的行为。 **Acts (of the Apostles),** (NT) accounts of the missionary work of the Apostles. (新约)使徒行传。 **2** process of, instant of, doing; action. 行动; 行动之际。 **(catch sb) in the (very) act (of doing sth),** while performing the action: 正当其从事(某种行为)之际; 当场(抓住某人): *The thief was caught in the act of breaking into the house.* 那潜入房舍之际当场被捕获。 *In the act of* (= While) *picking up the ball, he slipped and fell.* 正当其拾球之际, 他失足跌倒。 **Act of God,** sth which is the result of uncontrollable natural forces, eg storms, floods, earthquakes. 天灾; 不可抗力(如风暴, 洪水, 地震)。 ⇨ also **grace(3). 3** law made by a legislative body: (立法机构所立的)法案: *an Act of Parliament;* (英国)议院的法案; *the Acts of Congress.* (美国)国会的法案。 **4** main division of a play: (戏剧的)一幕: *a play in five acts;* 一个五幕剧; *Hamlet, Act 1, Scene 3.* 哈姆雷特第一幕第三场。 ⇨ **scene(5). 5** one of a series of short performances in a programme: 节目单上之一项短的表演; 节目: *a circus/variety act.* 马戏表演(综艺表演)中的一项节目。 **6** (colloq) pretence: (口)伪装: *Don't take him seriously—it's just an ~.* 不要把他看得太认真——他只是假装那样而已。 **put on an act,** (colloq) pretend: behave in an affected way (to get one's own way, etc). (口)假装; 装模作样。

act² /ækt; ækt/ *vi, vt* **1** [VP2A, 3A] perform actions, do sth: 行动; 采取行动; 做某事: *The time for talking is past; we must act at once.* 空谈的时候已经过去了; 我们必须立刻行动。 *The girl's life was saved because the doctors acted so promptly.* 那女孩的生命由于医生们行动迅速而得以挽救。 *You have acted* (= behaved) *generously.* 你表现得很慷慨。 *act (up)on* (a suggestion / sb's advice / an order), do what is suggested, advised, etc. 按照(建议, 某人的忠告, 命令)行事。 **2** [VP2A, 3A] do what is required; function normally: 起作用; 操作正常: *The brakes wouldn't act, so there was an accident.* 煞车失灵, 故发生车祸。 *The pump is not acting well, not performing its proper function.* 泵(抽水机)不大灵光了。 *act (up) on,* have an effect (up)on: 对…起作用; 对…有功效: *This medicine acts on the heart / the bowels.* 这药品对心脏(肠)有功效。 **3** [VP 2A, C, 3A] perform in a professional or official capacity: (以专业人员或官员身分)执行职务: *The police refused to act,* would not interfere. 警方拒绝采取行动。 *act as,* be, perform, as an interpreter, mediator, etc. 充任; 担任(译员, 调解人等)。 *act for / on behalf of,* represent (sb) as a solicitor, barrister in a legal case: (如诉讼案件中的律师)代表; 代理: *A solicitor acts for his clients.* 律师代表他的当事人。 **4** [VP2A, C, 6A] take part in a play on the stage;

take the part of, eg a character in a play or cinema film, or in real life: 参加舞台剧演出; 演戏; 扮演(戏剧、电影, 或现实生活中的一个角色): *Who is acting (the part of) Hamlet?* 谁扮演哈姆雷特(这个角色)? *She acts well.* 她戏演得很好. *Don't act the fool/ass/idiot, don't behave foolishly.* 不要当傻瓜(愚人, 呆子). *Browning's plays won't act,* are not suitable for the stage. 布郎宁的戏剧不宜上演. *She's not really crying; she's only acting* (= pretending) *in order to gain your sympathy.* 她并非真哭; 她不过是假装哭以获得你的同情. [VP15B] **act sth out,** perform actions which represent, and may help to release, the fears, inhibitions, etc of a neurotic person. 动作化(指神经过敏者以动作表达或舒解内心的恐惧, 压抑等). **act up,** (colloq) behave badly so as to attract attention; cause pain, irritation, annoyance by functioning badly: (口)行为恶劣以引人注意; 因功能不良而引起疼痛, 不适, 烦恼;调皮;捣蛋: *My leg/car/TV, etc has been acting* (now more usu *playing*) *up all week.* 我的腿(车子, 电视机等)一个星期以来一直跟我捣蛋(今较常用 playing up).

act·ing /ˈæktɪŋ; ˈæktɪŋ/ *adj* doing the duties of another person for a time: 代理的; 代行的: *the A~ Manager/Headmaster;* 代经理(校长); *A~ Captain.* 代船长. □ *n* [U] (art of) performing in a play for the theatre, cinema, TV, etc: 演技; 演戏: *She did a lot of ~ while she was at college.* 她在大学时代演过很多次戏. **'~ copy,** (of a script) one for the use of an actor or actress. (指剧本原稿)演出脚本.

ac·tin·ism /ˈæktɪnɪzəm; ˈæktɪn,ɪzəm/ *n* [U] property of light rays that produces chemical activity and changes (as in photographic films). 光化性(光线的一种性质, 能引起化学作用及变化, 如对照相软片所发生的作用). **ac·tinic** /ækˈtɪnɪk; ækˈtɪnɪk/ *adj* of ~: 光化性的: *actinic rays,* component of the sun's radiation. (有)光化性射线(太阳辐射线的成分).

ac·tion /ˈækʃn; ˈækʃən/ *n* **1** [U] process of doing things; movement; (way of) using energy, influence, etc: 行动; 动作; 做法; 作用: *The time has come for ~, We must act now.* 行动的时候到了. *A man of ~ is not content just to talk.* 讲求行动的人不以空谈为满足. **bring/call sth into ~,** cause it to operate. 使起作用; 使生效;使操作. **put/set sth in ~,** cause it to start acting. 实行; 开动. **put sth out of ~,** stop it working; make it unfit for use. 使停止工作或活动;使不适用. **take ~,** begin to act. 开始行动;采取行动. **'~ painting,** form of abstract painting in which paint is splashed, dribbled, etc on to the canvas. 一种抽象画(作画时以喷、泼、滴等手法着颜料于画布上);泼墨画. **2** [C] thing done; act: 所作之事; 行为: *We shall judge you by your ~s, not by your promises.* 我们将凭你的作为, 而不以你的诺言来评判你. *She is impulsive in her ~s,* does things impulsively. 她做事很冲动. **A~s speak louder than words,** Doing sth is more convincing than talking about it. 行动比言论有力. **3** [C] **(a)** mechanism of a piano, gun or other instrument. (钢琴、枪炮或其他器械的)机械装置. **(b)** manner of bodily movement, eg of a horse when jumping, of an athlete. 姿势; 姿态(例如马跳跃时, 运动员的姿态). **4** [C] legal process. 诉讼. **bring an ~ against sb,** seek judgement against him in a law court. 向法院提起诉讼控告某人. **5** [U] fighting between bodies of troops, between warships, etc: (军队或兵舰等之间的)战斗行动: *go into ~,* start fighting: 开始战斗; *killed in ~,* 阵亡; [C] instance of this: 战斗行动的实例: *break off the ~,* stop fighting. 停止战斗. **'~ stations,** (mil) positions to which soldiers, etc go when fighting is expected to begin. (军) (即将开始作战时各士兵所应就的)作战岗位. **~·able** /-əbl; -əbl/ *adj* giving just cause for legal ~. 可控诉的.

ac·ti·vate /ˈæktɪveɪt; ˈæktə,vet/ *vt* [VP6A] make active; (chem) accelerate a reaction in, eg by heat (phys) cause radiation from. 使活泼; 使活动; (化学)加速…之反应(如借加热等); 活化; (物理)引起辐射; 赋与射能.

ac·ti·va·tion /ˌæktɪˈveɪʃn; ˌæktəˈveʃən/ *n*

ac·tive /ˈæktɪv; ˈæktɪv/ *adj* **1** doing things; able to do things; in the habit of doing things; energetic; characterized by activity: 做事的; 能做事的; 惯于做事的;精力充沛的;活动的;活跃的;灵活的;积极的: *He's over 90 and not very ~.* 他已九十多岁, 不太活动了. *A boy with an ~ brain will be more successful than a dull boy.* 头脑灵活的男孩将比迟钝的男孩有出息. *Mount Vesuvius is an ~ volcano,* is one that erupts. 维苏威山是一个活火山. *She has an ~* (= lively) *imagination.* 她有灵活的想像力. *He takes an ~ part in school affairs.* 他积极参加学校里的活动. **on ~ service,** (Navy, Army, Air Force) (GB) engaged in actual military service, esp in fighting during a war; (US) on full duty, not in the reserves. (海、陆、空军)(英)服现役; (尤指)战时参与战斗; (美)服现役. **under ~ consideration,** being considered or canvassed. 考虑中; 在彻底讨论中. **2** (gram) (语法) **the ~ (voice), (a)** form of a *v phrase* not containing be+ *pp,* as in: *He was driving,* Cf *He was being driven.* 主动语态(不含 be+pp 的动词短语形式, 如在 He was driving 句中, 动词短语 was driving 即是主动语态; 在 He was being driven 句中, was being driven 则为被动语态). ⇨ **passive. (b)** sentence containing a *vt* in which the n or pron preceding the v, and agreeing with it (the grammatical subject), refers to the doer of the action, ie the agent: *The children finished the cake* (active). Cf *The cake was finished by the children* (passive). 主动句(含一及物动词的句子, 句中的名词或代词位于动词之前, 数、人称等与动词一致, 为语法上之主语, 且为动作的做出者, 即行为者: 如 The children finished the cake 即是主动句; The cake was finished by the children 即是被动句). **~·ly** *adv*

ac·tiv·ist /ˈæktɪvɪst; ˈæktɪvɪst/ *n* [C] person taking an active part, eg in a political movement. 积极参与者(如参与政治运动者).

ac·tiv·ity /ækˈtɪvətɪ; ækˈtɪvətɪ/ *n* (*pl* **-ties**) **1** [U] being active or lively: 活动性; 活力: *When a man is over 70, his time of full ~ is usually past.* 当人活到七十以后, 他的充满活力的时期通常都已过去了. **2** [C] thing (to be) done; occupation: 所做或待做的事情; 活动: *Classroom activities are things done by pupils in the classroom; outdoor activities are things done outside.* 教室活动是学生们在教室里所作的事情; 户外活动是在室外所做的事情. *My numerous activities leave me little leisure.* 繁多的事务使我一点空闲也没有.

ac·tor /ˈæktə(r); ˈæktɚ/ *n* **1** man who acts on the stage, TV or in films. (舞台, 电视或电影)男演员. **2** person who takes part in a notable event, etc. 参加要事的角色.

ac·tress /ˈæktrɪs; ˈæktrɪs/ *n* woman actor(1). 女演员.

ac·tual /ˈæktʃʊəl; ˈæktʃʊəl/ *adj* existing in fact; real: 实在的; 真实的; 确实的; 实际的: *It's an ~ fact, I haven't invented or imagined it.* 这是真实的事实; 并不是我捏造或想像出来的. *Can you give me the ~ figures,* the real figures, not an estimate or a guess? 你能给我确实的数字吗 (不要单是估计或猜测)? *What is the ~ position of affairs?* 事情的实际情况如何? **~·ly** /-tʃʊlɪ; -tʃʊəlɪ/ *adv* in fact; really: 实际地; 实在地: *the political party ~ly in power.* 实际掌握政权的政党;执政党. *He looks honest, but ~ly he's a rogue.* 他外表忠厚, 但实际是个十足的流氓. **2** strange or surprising as it may seen: 居然;真地; *He ~ly expected me to do his work for him!* 他真地想要我替他做他的事! *He not only ran in the race; he ~ly won it!* 他不但参加了赛跑, 并且居然跑赢了. **~·ity** /ˌæktʃʊˈælətɪ; ˌæktʃʊˈælətɪ/ *n* (*pl* **-ties**) **1** [U] = existence; reality. 实际; 真实. **2** [C, usu *pl*] ~ conditions or facts; realities. (通常用复数)实际情况;真正的事实.

ac·tu·ary /ˈæktʃʊərɪ US: -tʃʊerɪ; ˈæktʃʊˌɛrɪ/ *n* (*pl* -ries) expert who calculates insurance premiums (by studying rates of mortality, frequency of fires, thefts, accidents, etc). 保险公司的统计员(负责研究死亡率, 火

灾、窃盗、意外事件等的出事率, 而统计保险费率者)。
ac·tu·ar·ial /ˌæktʃʊˈeərɪəl; ˌæktʃʊˈsrɪəl/ *adj* of an ~ or his work. 保险公司统计员的;保险统计的。

ac·tu·ate /ˈæktʃʊˌert; ˈæktʃʊˌet/ *vt* [VP6A] (formal) cause to act: (正式用语)使(活动); 使(行动): *A great statesman is ～d by love of his country, not by love of power.* 一个伟大政治家的行动系基于爱国,而非基于爱权。

acu·ity /əˈkjuːətɪ; əˈkjuətɪ/ *n* [U] (formal) acuteness. (正式用语)尖锐;锐利;敏锐。

acu·men /ˈækjʊmɪn; əˈkjumɪn/ *n* [U] sharpness and accuracy of judgement; ability to understand clearly: 敏锐及正确的判断力;清晰的了解力;聪明才智: *business ～.* 善理事务的才智;生意眼。

acu·punc·ture /ˈækjʊpʌŋktʃə(r); ˈækjuˌpʌŋktʃə/ *n* [U] (med) pricking or puncturing of the living tissues of the human body with fine needles to cure disease, to relieve pain and as a local anaesthetic. (医)针灸;针刺疗法;针术(用细针在人体生机组织上穿刺,借以治病,减除疼痛,并作局部麻醉)。

acute /əˈkjuːt; əˈkjut/ *adj* **1** (of the senses, sensations, intellect) keen, sharp, quick: (指五官,感觉,智力)深刻的;剧烈的;敏锐的: *Dogs have an ～ sense of smell.* 狗有敏锐的嗅觉。*Our anxiety became more ～.* 我们的焦虑越来越厉害。*He felt ～ remorse for his wrongdoing.* 他对于他所做的坏事深深地感到懊悔。*A bad tooth can cause ～ pain.* 一颗坏牙齿会引起剧痛。*He is an ～ observer.* 他是一个敏锐的观察者。**2** (of diseases) coming sharply to a crisis: (指疾病)急性的: *The patient has reached the ～ stage of the disease,* the brief period during which the disease is severe and at a turning point. 该患者已经到达了此病的急性期。*Pneumonia is an ～ disease,* one that comes quickly to a turning-point. 肺炎是一种急性病。⇨ **chronic. 3** (of sounds) high; shrill. (指声音)高音的;尖锐的。**4** ～ **angle,** angle of less than 90°. 锐角(小于90°之角)。⇨ the illus at **angle.** 参看 angle 之插图。**5** ～ **accent,** mark over a vowel (´), as over *e* in *café.* 尖音记号(标于元音上者,例如 café 中元音 e 上的 ´)。**～·ly** *adv* **～·ness** *n*

ad /æd; æd/ *n* [C] (colloq abbr for) advertisement: (口)广告(为 advertisement 之略): *'Want ads',* in newspapers, etc. (报纸等上的)'求才广告'。

ad·age /ˈædɪdʒ; ˈædɪdʒ/ *n* [C] old and wise saying; proverb. 谚语;格言。

adagio /əˈdɑːdʒɪəʊ; əˈdɑdʒo/ *n* (*pl* **-gios** /-dʒəʊz; -dʒoz/) *adj, adv* (music) (passage played) gracefully and in slow time. (音乐)慢板;慢板速度的乐章或乐曲;缓慢的(地)。

Adam /ˈædəm; ˈædəm/ *n* ~**'s 'apple,** part that projects in the front of the throat, esp in men, and moves up and down when one speaks. 喉结(尤指男人喉前面之突出部份,于说话时上下移动)。⇨ the illus at **head.** 参看 head 之插图。*the old ～,* (facet) the immoral, selfish side of human nature. (玩笑语)人性邪恶的一面;本性;私欲。*not know sb from ～,* not know him at all. 对某人全不了解;与某人素不相识。⇨ **know (2).**

ada·mant /ˈædəmənt; ˈædəˌmænt/ *n* [C] kind of stone that, it is said, cannot be cut or broken. 硬石(据说是一种不能被切割或敲碎的石头)。☐ *pred* unyielding; firm in purpose: 不让步的;固执的;坚定不移的: *He was ～ to their pleas.* 他毫不为他们的请求所动。*On this point I am ～,* Nothing can change my decision. 关于这一点,我是坚决的。*I only wish he were less ～.* 但愿他不那么固执。**ada·man·tine** /ˌædə-ˈmæntaɪn; ˌædəˈmæntɪn/ *adj* unyielding; inflexible. 不让步的;不屈不挠的;坚定不移的。

adapt /əˈdæpt; əˈdæpt/ *vt* [VP6A, 14] make suitable for a new use, need, situation, etc: 使适应; 使配合; 改编; 改写: *When you go to a new country, you must ～ yourself to new manners and customs.* 当你到了一个新的国家时,你必须使自己适应新的风俗习惯。*Difficult books are sometimes ～ed for use in schools.* 难的书

籍有时被改写, 以便适用于学校。*This book is ～ed to the needs of beginners/～ed for beginners.* 本书经过改写以适合初学者的需要。*The play has been ～ed from the French,* ie translated and changed to suit English audiences. 此剧系由法文本编译而成(以应英国观众的需要)。*Novels are often ～ed for the stage, television and radio.* 小说常被改编为舞台剧本,电视剧及广播剧脚本。**～·er, ～·or** /-tə(r); -tə/ *nn* person who ～s sth; device that enables sth to be used for a purpose, or in a way, different from that for which it was designed, eg a fitting for taking electric current from an outlet so that more than one piece of apparatus may be used. 适应某事物的人; 改造者; 改编者; 调节装物用于不同于原设计目的的装置,如多功能插座。**～·able** /-əbl; -əbl/ *adj* able to ～ oneself; able to be ～ed: 能适应的;可改编的: *an ～able man,* one who can ～ himself to circumstances, etc. 能适应环境的人。**～· a·bil·ity** /əˌdæptəˈbɪlətɪ; əˌdæptəˈbɪlətɪ/ *n* [U] power of ～ing or being ～ed. 适应性;适应力。**ad·ap·ta·tion** /ˌædæpˈteɪʃn; ˌædəpˈteʃən/ *n* ～**ation (of sth) (for/ to sth),** **1** [U] state of being ～ed; ～ing. 适应;改编;改作。**2** [C] sth made by ～ing: 改制物; 改编者; 改作: *an ～ation (of a novel) for the stage/for broadcasting.* (由小说)改编的舞台剧本(广播剧脚本)。

add /æd; æd/ *vt, vi* **1** [VP6A, 14] **add sth (to sth),** join, unite, put (one thing together with another): 加;增加; 加添: *If you add 5 and/to 5 you get 10.* 五加五得十。*The house has been added to from time to time,* new rooms, etc have been built on to it. 这栋房子曾经一再的扩建。*If the tea is too strong, add some hot water.* 如果茶太浓, 再加点开水。**'adding-machine** *n* machine for calculating mechanically. 计算器。**2** [VP6A, 9] say further; go on to say: 又说;继续说: *'and I hope you'll come early,' he added,* ie talked on. 他接着又说,'并且我希望你早点来。' *She added that ....* 她接着又说……。**3** [VP15B, 3A, 2C] (special uses with *adverbial particles* and *preps*): (与副词性小品词及介词连用的特殊用法): *add sth in,* include. 包括;将某事物算在内。
add to, increase: 增加: *This adds to our difficulties.* 这会增加我们的困难。
add sth together, combine two or more things. 将某些事物结合起来;凑合在一起。
add sth up, find the sum of: 合计; 加起来: *add up a column of figures;* 将一列数字加起来; *add up ten figures;* 将十个数目加起来; *add them up.* 求它们的总和。
add up (to), **(a)** give as a result, when joined: 加起来总和是: *The figures add up to 365.* 这些数目加起来总和是365。**(b)** (colloq) mean; indicate; amount to: (口)含义是;表示;等于;总而言之, *All that this adds up to is that you don't want to help, so why not say so at once?* 总而言之,你所不想帮忙,那么,为何不立即明说呢?**(c)** (colloq) make sense; be plausible; (口)有意义; 讲得通: *It just doesn't add up.* 这简直没有意义。

ad·den·dum /əˈdendəm; əˈdendəm/ *n* (*pl* **-da** /-də; -də/) thing (omitted) that is to be added. 补遗; 补编;附录。

ad·der /ˈædə(r); ˈædə/ *n* viper; any of several small poisonous snakes common in Europe, Africa (eg the *puff-~*) and Asia. 蝮蛇; 蝰蛇 (产于欧, 非, 亚洲的小毒蛇, 如产于非洲之鼓腹蝰蛇)。⇨ the illus at **snake.** 参看 snake 之插图。

ad·dict /əˈdɪkt; əˈdɪkt/ *vt* (usu passive) (通常用于被动语态) *be ～ed to,* be given to, habitually or compulsively: 耽溺于;嗜好: *He is ～ed to alcohol/ smoking/lying/study/drugs.* 他嗜好喝酒(抽烟,说谎,读书,麻醉药)。☐ *n* /ˈædɪkt; ˈædɪkt/ person who is ～ed, esp to sth harmful: 耽溺于某种(尤指危害身体)嗜好的人: *a 'drug ～.* 有毒瘾之人; 有药瘾者。**ad·dic·tion** /əˈdɪkʃn; əˈdɪkʃən/ *n* [U] being ～ed. 耽溺;瘾;癖好; 嗜好。**ad·dic·tive** /əˈdɪktɪv; əˈdɪktɪv/ *adj* causing ～ion: 引起嗜好的; 上瘾的: *～ive*

drugs. 引人上瘾的麻醉药。

ad·di·tion /ə'dɪʃn; ə'dɪʃən/ *n* 1 [U] process of adding: 加: *The sign* + *stands for* ~. + 号代表加。*in* ~ *(to)*, as well (as). 加之; 又; 除…之外; 并且。2 [C] sth added or joined: 增加物: *They've just had an* ~ *to the family*, another child. 他们家里刚又增加了一口。*He will be a useful* ~ *to the staff of the school*, a useful new teacher. 他将是该校教员中新增加的有用的一员。~al /-ʃənl; -ʃənl/ *adj* extra; added: 外加的; 附加的; 另加的: ~*al charges*. 外加的费用。~·ally /-ʃənəlɪ; -ʃənlɪ/ *adv*

ad·di·tive /'ædɪtɪv; 'ædətɪv/ *n* [C] substance added in small amounts for a special purpose: 为某一特殊目的而加入的少量物质; 添加剂: *food* ~*s*, eg to add colour; 食品添加剂; *petrol* ~*s*, eg to reduce engine knocking. 汽油添加剂(如减少引擎爆震者)。

addle /'ædl; 'ædl/ *adj* (usu in compounds) confused; muddled. (通常用于复合词中)糊涂的; 混淆不清的。'~-**brained**, '~-**pated** /-peɪtɪd; -'petɪd/ *adj* having confused ideas. 头脑不清的; 糊涂的。'~-**head**, *n* person with confused ideas. 头脑不清的人; 糊涂虫。□ *vt, vi* 1 [VP6A] confuse: 使糊涂; 搅昏: ~ *one's head/ brains*. 使某人的头脑昏乱。2 [VP2A] (of eggs) become rotten: (指蛋)变腐坏: ~*d eggs*. 坏蛋。

ad·dress¹ /ə'dres *US:* 'ædres; ə'drɛs/ *n* 1 details of where a person may be found and where letters, etc may be delivered: 通讯处; 住址: *What's your home/ business* ~? 你的住宅(办公)地址是什么? *Let me know if you change your* ~. 假若你变更通讯处, 请通知我。2 speech or talk (to an audience). (对听众的)演说; 谈话。**public** '~ **system**, system using microphones, loudspeakers, etc for amplifying speeches. 播讲系统; 扩音系统(利用麦克风, 扬声器等, 使演说的声音放大)。3 [U] (old use) manner or behaviour, esp in conversation: (旧用法)态度; 行为; (尤指)谈话风度: *a man of pleasing* ~. 谈吐风度优雅的人。4 ~, form of ~, style of written or spoken communication: 谈信或交谈中的称呼: *polite forms of* ~. 客气的称呼形式。5 *(pl)* (old use) polite attentions or courtship: (复)(旧用法)殷勤; 求爱: *pay one's* ~*es to a lady*, seek to win her hand in marriage; 追求一女子; *reject sb's* ~*es*, show that one does not welcome sb's wishes to be friendly. 不接受某人的殷勤。~**ee** /ˌædre'siː; ˌædrɛ'si/ *n*, person to whom sth is ~ed(2). 收件人。**A~·o·graph** /ə'dresoʊgrɑːf *US:* - græf; ə'drɛsoʊ,græf/ *n* (P) machine for printing ~es(1) on circulars, etc. (商标)姓名住址印刷机(用以印刷姓名住址于函件等)。

ad·dress² /ə'dres; ə'drɛs/ *vt* 1 [VP6A, 16B] make a speech to; speak to, using a title: 向…发表演说; 向…说话; 称呼: *Mr Green will now* ~ *the meeting*. 现在由格林先生向大会演说。*Don't* ~ *me as 'Colonel'; I'm only a major*. 不要称呼我为上校; 我只不过是少校。2 [VP6A] write a destination on (with the name of the person to whom sth is to be delivered): 在…上写收件人的姓名地址: *The letter was wrongly* ~*ed*. 这封信的地址写错了。3 [VP14] ~ *sth to*, send (a remark, complaint, etc) to: 向…提出(评论, 诉愿等): *Please* ~ *all enquiries to this office*. 一切查询请向本办公室提出。*Please* ~ *complaints to the manager*, not to me. 请把诉愿向经理提出, 不要向我提出。4 [VP14] ~ *oneself to*, (formal) (正式用语) work at, apply oneself to, be busy with (a task, etc): 从事于; 忙着做: *It's time we* ~*ed ourselves to the business in hand*, time we got busy with the business we are here for. 是动手做我们手上的事情的时候了。

ad·duce /ə'djuːs *US:* ə'duːs; ə'djus/ *vt* [VP6A] (formal) put forward (as proof, as an example): (正式用语) (作为证据或例子而)提出; 举出: ~ *reasons/ proof/authority*. 举出理由(证据, 根据)。

ad·en·oids /'ædɪnɔɪdz *US:* -den-; 'ædn̩,ɔɪdz/ *n pl* (anat) soft, sponge-like growth between the back of the nose and the throat, in some cases making breathing and

speech difficult: (解剖)腺样增殖体(生长于鼻腔与喉之间的海绵状柔软瘤肿, 有时可致呼吸及说话困难): *have one's* ~ *out*, ie by a surgical operation. 动手术把腺样增殖体割掉。*She's got* ~, (colloq) is suffering from inflammation of the ~. (口)她患了腺样增殖体炎。⇨ the illus at **head**. 参看 head 之插图。**ad·en·oidal** /ˌædɪ'nɔɪdl; ˌædn̩'ɔɪdl/ *adj* of the ~: 腺样增殖体的: *an adenoidal youth*, one suffering from diseased ~. 患腺样增殖的年轻人。

adept /'ædept; 'ædɛpt/ *adj* expert, skilled (*in* sth; *at* or *in* doing sth). 长于…的; 善于…的; 精于…的; (与 in 连用, 后接名词; 与 in 或 at 连用, 后接动名词)。□ *n* expert: 擅长者; 专家: *I'm not an* ~ *in photography*. 我并非摄影专家。

ad·equate /'ædɪkwət; 'ædəkwɪt/ *adj* satisfactory; sufficient; satisfying a requirement: 令人满意的; 适当的; 足够的; 符合要求的: £ *10 a week is not* ~ *to support a family*. 十镑一周不足以维持一个家庭。*Are you getting an* ~ *wage for the work you're doing?* 你目前工作的待遇是否令你满意? ~·ly *adv* **ad·equacy** /'ædɪkwəsɪ; 'ædəkwəsɪ/ *n* [U] state of being ~: 适当; 足够; 胜任: *He often doubts his adequacy as a husband and father*. 他常常怀疑自己是否是一个够格的丈夫及父亲。

ad·here /əd'hɪə(r); əd'hɪr/ *vi* [VP2A, 3A] ~ *(to)*, (formal) (正式用语) 1 stick fast (to): 粘着; 附着(与 to 连用): *Glue and paste are used to make one surface* ~ *to another*. 胶水和浆糊是用以粘合一个表面与另一表面的。2 remain faithful (to); support firmly: 忠于(与 to 连用); 坚持: ~ *to one's plans/to an opinion/to a political party/to a promise*. 坚持计划(坚持意见); 忠于政党; 坚守诺言。*We decided to* ~ *to the programme*. 我们决定坚持这项计划。(Cf 参较 *depart from*.) **ad·her·ence** /-rəns; -rəns/ *n*: *adherence to a plan*. 坚持计划。

ad·her·ent /əd'hɪərənt; əd'hɪrənt/ *n* supporter (of a party, etc, but not necessarily a member): 支持者; 拥护者(为政党之拥护者但不一定为其党员): *The proposal is gaining more and more* ~*s*. 该建议正得到越来越多的支持者。

ad·hesion /əd'hiːʒn; əd'hiʒən/ *n* 1 [U] adhering; being or becoming attached or united. 粘合; 粘附; 结合; 附着(力)。2 [U] support: 支持; 拥护: *give one's* ~ *to a plan*. 对某一项计划予以支持。3 [U] (path) joining together of tissues in the body, eg after an injury; [C] instance of this: (病理)体内组织之粘连(如于受伤后); 此种粘连的实例: *painful* ~ ~ *resulting from a wound that did not heal*. 因伤口未愈而引起的疼痛的粘连。

ad·hes·ive /əd'hiːsɪv; əd'hisɪv/ *adj* having the property of sticking: 带粘性的: ~ *tape/plaster*. 粘带; 胶布(绊创膏); 粘膏。□ *n* [C,U] substance, eg *gum*. 有粘着性之物(如树胶)。

ad hoc /ˌæd 'hɒk; 'æd'hɑk/ *adj, adv* (Lat) arranged for a particular purpose; not pre-arranged; informal: (拉)为某一目的而安排的; 特别的; 非预先安排的; 非正式的: *an* ~ *committee meeting*. 特别召开的委员会议。

adieu /ə'djuː *US:* ə'duː; ə'dju/ *n, int* (*pl* ~**s** or -**x** /ə'djuːz *US:* ə'duːz; ə'djuz/) (F) goodbye: (法)再会; 再见: *bid sb* ~; 向某人告别; *make one's* ~/~*s*, say goodbye. 告别; 辞行。

ad in·fi·ni·tum /ˌæd ˌɪnfɪ'naɪtəm; 'æd,ɪnfə'naɪtəm/ *adv* (Lat) without limit; for ever. (拉)无限地; 永恒地; 以至无穷。

ad inter·im /ˌæd 'ɪntərɪm; 'æd'ɪntərɪm/ *adj, adv* (Lat) in the meantime. (拉)其间; 在那个期间; 临时的; 过渡的。

adi·pose /'ædɪpəʊs; 'ædə,pos/ *adj* of animal fat; fatty: 脂肪的; 多脂肪的: ~ *tissue*. 脂肪组织。

ad·jac·ent /ə'dʒeɪsnt; ə'dʒesənt/ *adj* next (*to*), lying near (*to*) but not necessarily touching: 毗连的; 接近的; 邻近的(不一定相接触, 与 to 连用): ~ *rooms*: 相连的房间; ~ *angles*, ⇨ the illus at **angle**. 邻角(参看 angle 之插图)。*The house* ~ *to the church is the vicarage*. 那栋

毗邻教堂的房子是牧师住宅。

ad·jec·tive /'ædʒɪktɪv; 'ædʒɪktɪv/ n (gram) word that names a quality, or that defines or limits a noun. (语法)形容词。 **ad·jec·tiv·al** /ˌædʒɪk'taɪvl; ˌædʒɪk'taɪvl/ adj of or like an ~: 形容词的；似形容词的: an adjectival phrase/clause. 形容词短语(从句)。

ad·join /ə'dʒɔɪn; ə'dʒɔɪn/ vt, vi [VP6A,2A] ~ (to), be next or nearest to: 临近；邻近；接近；毗连: The playing-field ~s the school. 运动场临近学校。 The two houses ~. 这两栋房屋相毗连。 ~·ing part adj: ~ing bedrooms. 毗连的卧室。

ad·journ /ə'dʒɜːn; ə'dʒɜn/ vt, vi 1 [VP6A] break off, eg proceedings of a meeting, etc for a time: 使(会议等)停止一个时期；使休会: The meeting was ~ed for a week/until the following week. 会议休会一星期(下星期复会)。 2 [VP2C] (of a meeting, etc) be broken off in this way: (指会议等)休会: The meeting ~ed at five o'clock. 会议于五点钟休会。 3 [VP2A, C] (colloq, of person who have met together) (口，指聚在一起的人们) (a) break off proceedings and separate. 停止活动而分手。 (b) go to another place: 到另外一个地方去: When dinner was over they ~ed to the sitting-room. 当宴席完毕时，他们都到客厅里去了。 ~·ment n ~ing or being ~ed. 休会；散会。

ad·judge /ə'dʒʌdʒ; ə'dʒʌdʒ/ vt 1 [VP25,9] decide officially, by law: 宣判；判定: ~ sb (to be) guilty; 宣判某人有罪； ~ that a man is insane. 判定某人精神不正常。 2 [VP14] award: 判给；断与: ~ land and property to sb; 将土地及财产判与某人； ~ a prize/legal damages to sb. 将奖赏(法定损害赔偿)判归某人。

ad·ju·di·cate /ə'dʒuːdɪkeɪt; ə'dʒudɪˌket/ vt, vi 1 [VP6A, 14] (of a judge or court) give a judgement or decision upon: (指法官或法庭)判决；裁判: ~ a claim for damages. 裁定一项损害赔偿的要求。 2 [VP2A, 3A] sit in judgement in order to decide: 裁判；裁决: ~ (up)-on a question. 裁决一个问题。 3 [VP25] declare (sb to be): 宣布；宣判 (某人是): ~ sb bankrupt. 宣判某人破产。 **ad·ju·di·ca·tion** /əˌdʒuːdɪ'keɪʃn; əˌdʒudɪ'keʃən/ n **ad·ju·di·ca·tor** /-tə(r); -tɚ/ n (judge; member of a jury, eg in a musical competition. 审判官；裁判；评判员(如音乐比赛中者)。

ad·junct /'ædʒʌŋkt; 'ædʒʌŋkt/ n 1 sth extra but subordinate. 附加物；附属物。 2 (gram) word(s) or phrase added to qualify or define another word in a sentence. (语法)附加语；修饰语(加在句中用以修饰其他词者)。

ad·jure /ə'dʒʊə(r); ə'dʒʊr/ vt [VP17] (formal) ask (sb) earnestly or solemnly; require (sb) to do sth as though on oath or under penalty: (正式用语)恳求(某人)；以发誓的方式要求(某人)做某事: I ~ you to tell the truth. 我恳求你说实话。 **ad·jur·ation** /ˌædʒʊə'reɪʃn; ˌædʒʊ'reʃən/ n [U] adjuring; [C] earnest or solemn request. 恳求；诚恳或郑重的请求。

ad·just /ə'dʒʌst; ə'dʒʌst/ vt [VP6A,14] ~ oneself/sth (to), set right; put in order; regulate; make suitable or convenient for use: 调整；调节；使适用；使便于使用: The body ~s itself to changes in temperature. 身体能自行调节以适应气温变化。 You can't see well through a telescope unless it is ~ed correctly to your sight. 除非你把望远镜准确地调节到适合你的视力，否则你就看不清楚。 She will have to ~ herself to new conditions, change her ways of living, thinking, etc. 她将必须使自己能适应新的环境。 Please do not ~ your sets, warning on a TV screen that the controls need not be changed. 请不要调整你的电视机(电视荧光幕上的指示，请勿变换电视机的频道)。 You should ~ your expenditure to your income. 你必须量入为出(调节你的费用以配合你的收入)。 ‚well-'~ed, (psych) in harmonious relations with other persons: (心理)与他人保持和谐关系的；善于顺应的: a well-~ed child. 与他人和谐相处的小孩。 ~·able /-əbl; -əbl/ adj that can be ~ed. 可调节的；可调整的。 ~er n (comm) person from an

insurance company whose business it is to settle amounts due when claims are made, eg for loss. (商)保险公司调解员(其工作是，当投保人提出如损失赔偿要求时，由其出面协商决定适当的赔偿金额)。 ~·ment n 1 [U] adjusting; settling of, eg insurance, claims; [C] act of ~ing. 调节；调整；(保险、主张等之)调解。 2 [C] means of ~ing sth; part of an apparatus for ~ing sth. 调节器；调整器。

ad·ju·tant /'ædʒutənt; 'ædʒətənt/ n 1 (mil) army officer responsible for general administration and discipline in a battalion. (军)负责一营中之一般行政及风纪的陆军军官；副官。 2 (also 亦作 ~ **bird**) large Indian stork. (印度产之)大鹳。

ad lib /ˌæd 'lɪb; æd'lɪb/ adv (abbr of ad libitum) (colloq) freely; without restraint. (为 ad libitum 之略) (口)自由地；随意；无限制地。 **ad-lib** vi (-bb-) [VP2A] (colloq) improvise, eg by making additions to one's part in a play. (口)即席而作 (如在一剧中对其所扮演角色之台词予以增加)；临时穿插。 □ attrib adj made by ad-libbing: 即席而作的；临时穿插的: ad-lib comments. 即席而作的评论。

ad libitum /ˌæd 'lɪbɪtəm; 'æd'lɪbɪtəm/ adv (Lat; 拉) abbr 略作 ad lib) (music) (to be) performed with omissions as desired. (音乐)任意；听便。 ⇨ **obbligato (1)**.

ad·man /'æd mæn; 'ædˌmæn/ n (colloq) man who composes commercial advertisements. (口)制作商业广告的人。

ad·mass /'ædmæs; 'ædmæs/ n [U] that part of the public easily influenced by the mass media. 易受大众传播工具影响的民众。 ⇨ **media**.

ad·min·is·ter /əd'mɪnɪstə(r); əd'mɪnɪstɚ/ vt, vi 1 [VP6A] control, manage, look after business affairs, a household, etc: 管理；处理；照料；治理(商务，家务等): ~ a country, govern it. 治理国家。 2 [VP6A, 14] apply; put into operation; hand out; give: 执行；实施；给与；施与: ~ the law; 执法； ~ punishment to sb. 予某人以惩罚； ~ relief/help to people who are suffering from floods; 对水灾灾民施以救济(救助)； ~ a severe blow to the enemy; 予敌人严重的打击； ~ justice, do the work of a judge. 审判；执法。 3 [VP6A, 14] cause to take: 使作(誓言)；使接受: ~ the last sacraments, eg to a dying man. 行临终的圣餐礼(即使垂死之人领最后的圣餐)。 The oath was ~ed to him. 他受命宣誓。 4 ~ to, ⇨ **minister²**.

ad·min·is·tra·tion /ədˌmɪnɪ'streɪʃn; ədˌmɪnə'streʃən/ n 1 [U] management of affairs, etc, esp public affairs, government policy, etc. (事务等，尤指公共事务，国家政策等之)管理；经营。 2 [C] (often 常作 A~) (esp US) that part of the Government which manages public affairs: (尤美)政府的行政部门；政府；内阁: Successive A~s failed to solve the country's problems. 历届政府均未能解决该国的问题。 3 [U] the administering of justice, an oath, a sacrament, relief, a remedy, a punishment. 执法；宣誓；行圣餐礼；救济；用药；惩罚。 ⇨ **ministration**.

ad·min·is·tra·tive /əd'mɪnɪstrətɪv US: -streɪtɪv; əd'mɪnəˌstretɪv/ adj of the management of affairs; of an administration(2): 管理的；行政的: an ~ post; 行政的职位； lacking in ~ ability. 缺乏行政能力。

ad·min·is·tra·tor /əd'mɪnɪstreɪtə(r); əd'mɪnəˌstretɚ/ n person who administers; person with ability to organize; (legal) person officially appointed to manage the property of others, to take charge of an estate, etc. 管理者；具组织才能的人；(法律)(官方指定管理他人财产，或负责某一地产等的)财产管理人。

ad·mir·able /'ædmərəbl; 'ædmərəbl/ adj excellent; causing admiration 极佳的；令人钦佩的。 **ad·mir·ably** /-əbli; -əbli/ adv

ad·miral /'ædmərəl; 'ædmərəl/ n officer in command of a country's warships, or of a fleet or squadron; naval rank above vice-~ and below (GB) ~ of the fleet or (US) fleet ~. 舰(战)队司令；海军上将(海军军阶，在海军

·ty /'ædmərəltɪ; 'ædmərəltɪ/ *n* **1** office of ~. 海军上将或舰队司令之职务。**2** that branch of Government which controls the Navy. 海军部。**the A~ty**, (GB) headquarters of the naval administration. (英) 海军部之总司令令部 (指所在地)。**,Court of 'A~ty**, court for deciding law questions concerning shipping. 海事法庭。

ad·mir·ation /ˌædmə'reɪʃn; ˌædmə'reʃən/ *n* [U] **1** feeling of pleasure, satisfaction, respect or, formerly, wonder: 赞赏; 赞美; 钦佩; (昔时) 惊奇: *She speaks English so well that her friends are filled with* ~. 她英语说得好极了, 她的朋友皆赞美不已。*Everyone cried out in* ~. 人人皆惊呼赞叹。*We were lost in* ~ *of the scenery.* 我们沉醉在美丽的风景中。*My* ~ *for your skill is great.* 我对你的技巧非常钦佩。**2** (*sing* with *def art*) object that arouses ~. (单数与定冠词连用) 令人赞赏的对象。

ad·mire /əd'maɪə(r); əd'maɪr/ *vt* [VP6A] **1** look at with pleasure or satisfaction; have a high regard for: 赞赏; 钦佩; 羡慕: *Come and* ~ *the view!* 快来欣赏这风景! *Visitors to Britain usually* ~ *our policemen.* 来英国的游客通常钦佩我们的警察。**2** express admiration of: 表示赞美; 夸奖: *Don't forget to* ~ *the baby.* 不要忘记夸奖那婴儿。**ad·mirer** *n* person who ~s; man who finds a woman attractive: 赞美者; 羡慕者; 爱慕某一女子的男人: *Mary and her many* ~s. 玛莉和许多爱慕她的男人。**ad·mir·ing** *adj* showing or feeling admiration: 表示或感觉赞赏的; 赞美的; 羡慕的: *admiring glances,* (表示) 赞赏的目光; *an admiring crowd.* 赞赏的群众。**ad·mir·ing·ly** *adv*

ad·miss·ible /əd'mɪsəbl; əd'mɪsəbl/ *adj* **1** (legal) that can be allowed as judicial proof: (法律) 可被采纳为法庭之证据的: ~ *evidence.* 法庭可采纳的证据。**2** (formal) that can be allowed or is permitted: (正式用语) 可容许的; 可考虑的。**ad·missi·bil·ity** /əd,mɪsə'bɪlətɪ; əd,mɪsə'bɪlətɪ/ *n* [U]

ad·mis·sion /əd'mɪʃn; əd'mɪʃən/ *n* **1** [U] admitting, being admitted, to a society, a school, a building such as a theatre, a museum, etc; fee, charge or condition for this: (入会, 入学, 入场, 如戏院, 博物馆等的) 许可; 入会费; 门票: *A~ to the school is by examination only.* 就读该校必须通过考试。*Price of* ~, *10 p.* 门票价, 十便士。*A~ free.* 不收门票。**2** [C] statement admitting sth; confession or acknowledgement: 承认某事之陈述; 供认: *make an* ~ *of guilt;* 认罪; *an* ~ *that one has done wrong.* 承认做了错事。*To resign now would be an* ~ *of failure.* 现在辞职等于承认失败。*by/on his own* ~, as he himself admitted. 如他自己所承认的。

ad·mit /əd'mɪt; əd'mɪt/ *vt, vi* (-tt-) **1** [VP6A,14] ~ *sb/sth (into/in)*, allow (sb or sth) to enter; let in: 许可 (人或物) 进入; 让…进入: *The servant opened the door and* ~*ted me (into the house).* 仆人打开门让我进入 (到屋里去)。*Only one hundred boys are* ~*ted to the school each year.* 该校每年只收一百名男生。*I ordered that he was not to be* ~*ted.* 我下令不许他进来。*Children not* ~*ted.* 禁止儿童入场。*The windows are small and do not* ~ *enough light and air.* 窗户都很小, 不能使足够的光线和空气进入屋内。**2** [VP6A] (of enclosed spaces) have room enough for: (指范围之内的场所) 可容纳: *The harbour* ~*s large liners and cargo boats.* 该港口可停泊大型邮轮和货轮。*The theatre is small and* ~ *only 300 people.* 该戏院很小, 只能容纳三百人。**3** [VP6A] acknowledge, confess, accept, as true or valid: 采信; 认可; 认为有效: ~ *a claim/an assumption.* 认可一项权利 (采信某一假定)。**4** [VP6A, C, 9, 14, 25] acknowledge; confess: 承认; 供认: *The accused man* ~*ted his guilt.* 被告承认了他的罪行。*I* ~ *my mistake/that I was mistaken.* 我承认我的错误 (我错了)。*He* ~*ted having done wrong.* 他承认做了错事。*You must* ~ *the task to be difficult* (more *usu, that the task is difficult*). 你得承认这工作是困难的。*It is generally* ~*ted that ...,* 一般认为 ..., *Most people acknowledge or agree that ... .* 一般认为 ...。

5 [VP3A] ~ *of*, (formal) leave room for: (正式用语) 容许; 有…的余地: *The words* ~ *of* (= can have) *no other meaning.* 这些词句不容许有别的意义。*It* ~*s of no excuse,* There can be no excuse for it. 这是无容辩解的。~ *to*, make an acknowledgement; confess: 承认; 供认: *I must* ~ *to feeling ashamed of my conduct.* 我必须承认对自己的行为感到惭愧。~**·ted·ly** /əd'mɪtɪdlɪ; əd'mɪtɪdlɪ/ *adv* **1** without denial; by general admission: 无可否认地; 公认地: *He is* ~*tedly an atheist.* 他无可否认地是一个无神论者。**2** (usu in initial position) = 'I acknowledge, agree': (通常用于句首) 我承认; 我同意: *A~tedly I've never actually been there.* 我承认我从未实际到过那里。

ad·mit·tance /əd'mɪtns; əd'mɪtṇs/ *n* [U] act of admitting, being admitted (esp to a place that is not public); right of entry: 许可进入(尤指非公共场所); 进入的权利; 入场许可: *I called at his house but was refused* ~, was not allowed to enter. 我到他家去拜访他, 但被拒绝进门。*No* ~ *except on business.* 非公莫入; 闲人免进。

ad·mix /æd'mɪks; æd'mɪks/ *vt, vi* [VP6A, 2A] mix; become mixed; add as an ingredient. 混合; 混杂。**ad·mix·ture** /æd'mɪkstʃə(r); æd'mɪkstʃə/ *n* (formal) (正式用语) = mixture.

ad·mon·ish /əd'mɒnɪʃ; əd'mɑnɪʃ/ *vt* [VP6A, 14] (formal) give a mild warning or a gentle reproof to: (正式用语) 婉转警告; 劝告; 轻责; 训诫: *The teacher* ~*ed the boys for being lazy /* ~*ed them against smoking.* 老师训诫学生们不可懒惰 (抽烟)。**ad·mo·ni·tion** /ˌæd·mə'nɪʃn; ˌædmə'nɪʃən/ *n* [U] ~ing; warning; [C] instance of this. 劝告; 轻责; 训诫; 警告。**ad·moni·tory** /əd'mɒnɪtrɪ US: -tɔːrɪ; əd'mɑnə,torɪ/ *adj* containing admonition: 劝告的; 轻责的; 训诫的; 警告的: *an admonitory letter.* 训诫信。

ad nauseam /ˌæd 'nɔːzɪæm; 'æd 'nɔʃɪˌæm/ *adv* (Lat) to the point of being disgusted; (colloq) to a degree so as to cause annoyance, eg because of length or repetition. (拉) 令人厌烦地; (口) 令人厌烦的程度 (如因冗长或重复)。

ado /ə'duː; ə'du/ *n* [U] (archaic) fuss; trouble and excitement: (古) 无谓的纷扰; 兴狂: *Without more/much/further ado, he signed the agreement.* 他很干脆地签了约。

adobe /ə'dəʊbɪ; ə'dobɪ/ *n* [U] sun-dried brick (not fired in a kiln), of clay and straw: (未经窑中烧过的) 砖坯; 土坯: (attrib) (用作定语) *an* ~ *house.* 土坯屋。

adobe houses

ado·les·cence /ˌædə'lesns; ˌæd'lesṇs/ *n* [U] period of life between childhood and maturity; growth during this period. 青年期(介于孩童与成年之间的时期); 青年期的发育成长; 青春。**ado·les·cent** /-'lesnt; -l'esṇt/ *adj, n* (person) growing up from childhood (age 12 or 13 to 18). 青年; 少年; 青年期(十二、三岁至十八岁)的。

adopt /ə'dɒpt; ə'dɑpt/ *vt* [VP6A] **1** take (sb) into one's family as a relation, esp as a son or daughter, with legal guardianship: 以合法监护人的身份将(某人)收入家中为亲属; (尤指) 收养(某人)为养子或养女: *As they had no children of their own, they* ~*ed an orphan.* 他们没有亲生儿女, 就收养了一个孤儿。⇨ **foster. 2** take, eg an idea or custom, and use: 采取(意见, 风俗

等); 采用; *European dress has been ~ed by people in many parts of the world.* 欧洲服式为世界许多地方的人们所采用。**3** accept, eg a report or recommendation: 接受 (报告, 建议等): *Congress ~ed the new measures.* 国会通过了新的议案。**adop·tion** /ə'dɒpʃn; ə'dɑpʃən/ n ~ing or being ~ed: 收养; 采纳; 采取; 采用; 接受: *the country of his ~ion.* 他所归化的国家。**adop·tive** adj taken by ~ion: 收养的; 采取的: *his ~ive parents.* 他的养父及养母。

adore /ə'dɔ:(r); ə'dɔr/ vt **1** [VP6A] worship (God): love deeply and respect highly. 崇拜(上帝); 敬爱; 爱慕。**2** [VP6A, C] (colloq; not in progressive tenses) like very much: (口, 不用于进行式) 极为喜爱: *The baby ~s being tickled.* 那婴孩极喜欢被胳肢。**ador·able** /-əbl; -əbl/ adj lovable; delightful. 可爱的。**ador·ably** /-əblɪ; -əblɪ/ adv **ador·ation** /ˌædə'reɪʃn; ˌædə'reʃən/ n [U] worship; love: 崇拜; 敬爱: *his adoration for Jane.* 他对简的爱慕。**adorer** n person who ~s (sb). 崇拜者; 敬爱(某人)者; 爱慕者。**ador·ing** adj showing love: 表示爱慕的: *adoring looks.* 爱慕的神情。**ador·ing·ly** adv

adorn /ə'dɔ:n; ə'dɔrn/ vt [VP6A, 14] add beauty or ornament(s) to; decorate (oneself *with* jewels, etc); add distinction to. 装饰; 佩戴(珠宝等, 与 with 连用); 增加…的优美。**~·ment** n [U] ~ing; [C] sth used for ~ing; ornament; decoration. 装饰; 装饰物; 装饰品。

ad·renal /ə'dri:nl; æd'rinl/ adj (anat) of or near the kidneys: 肾上腺的; 肾旁的: ~ *glands.* 肾上腺。

ad·ren·alin /ə'drenəlɪn; æd'rɛnlɪn/ n [U] (med) hormones secreted by the adrenal glands, prepared as a substance used in the treatment of heart failure, etc. (医)肾上腺素; 副肾素(由肾上腺所分泌出的荷尔蒙, 经调制以用作治疗心脏衰弱等之药物)。

adrift /ə'drɪft; ə'drɪft/ adv, pred adj (of ships and boats) afloat, not under control and driven by wind and water; loose: (指船)失去控制而随风浪漂浮的); 漂流(的); 漂失(的): *cut a boat ~ from its moorings;* 切断系索使小船漂离系船处; (fig) at the mercy of circumstances: (喻)任由环境安排; 漂泊: *turn sb ~,* send him away, eg from home, without money or means of livelihood. 将某人(自家庭等)逐出使其过漂泊无依的生活。

adroit /ə'drɔɪt; ə'drɔɪt/ adj ~ (*at/in*), clever; skilful; ingenious or resourceful when dealing with; problems. 巧的; 熟练的; 机敏的; (处理问题时)能临机应变的。**~·ly** adv **~·ness** n

adu·la·tion /ˌædju'leɪʃn US: -dʒʊ'l-; ˌædʒə'leʃən/ n [U] (the giving of) excessive praise or respect, esp to win favour. 谄媚; 奉承; 逢迎; 拍马。

adult /'ædʌlt; ə'dʌlt/ adj grown to full size or strength; (of persons) intellectually and emotionally mature. 发育成熟的; (指人)智慧及感情上已发育成熟的; 成年的。□ n person or animal grown to full size and strength; (legal) person old enough to vote, marry, etc. 发育成熟的人或动物; (法律)成人(已到达投票, 结婚等年龄的成年人): *education for ~s;* 成人教育; *~ education.* 成人教育。**~·hood** /-hʊd; -hʊd/ n the state of being ~. 成年。

adul·ter·ate /ə'dʌltəreɪt; ə'dʌltə,ret/ vt [VP6A, 14] make impure, make poorer in quality, by adding sth of less value: 掺入劣质物于…; 以低级品掺进: ~d *milk,* milk with water added. 掺水牛奶。**adul·ter·ant** /ə'dʌltərənt; ə'dʌltərənt/ n sth used for adulterating. 用以掺杂的劣质物; 掺杂物。**adul·ter·ation** /əˌdʌltə'reɪʃn; ə,dʌltə'reʃən/ n

adul·tery /ə'dʌltərɪ; ə'dʌltərɪ/ n [U] voluntary sexual intercourse of a married person with sb who is not the person to whom he or she is married; [C] (pl **-ries**) instance of this. 通奸; 通奸之实例。**adul·terer** /ə'dʌltərə(r); ə'dʌltərɚ/ n man who commits ~. 犯通奸罪的男人; 奸夫。**adul·ter·ess** /ə'dʌltərɪs; ə'dʌltərɪs/ n woman who commits ~. 犯通奸罪的女人; 奸妇; 淫妇。

adul·ter·ous /ə'dʌltərəs; ə'dʌltərəs/ adj of ~. 通奸的。

ad·um·brate /'ædʌmbreɪt; æd'ʌmbret/ vt [VP6A] (formal) indicate vaguely or briefly; foreshadow (a coming event). (正式用语) 约略暗示; 预示。

ad valorem /ˌæd və'lɔ:rem; ˌædvə'lɔrəm/ adv (Lat) (of taxes) in proportion to the estimated value of the goods. (拉)(指税)从价课税; 按值计税; 照价。

ad·vance[1] /əd'vɑ:ns US: -'væns; əd'væns/ n **1** [U] forward movement; progress; [C] instance of this: 前进; 高升; 进步; 进步之实例: *With the ~ of old age, he could no longer do the work well.* 因为年事日高, 他已不能再把工作做得很好了。*Science has made great ~s during the last fifty years.* 科学在过去五十年内有很大的进步。*The country's industrial ~ has been remarkable.* 此国的工业进步是很惊人的。*Has there been an ~ in civilization during the 20 th century?* 在二十世纪里文明有进步吗? **in ~ (of),** before (hand): 事前; 在前; 预先: *Send your luggage in ~,* before you yourself leave. 将行李预先交寄(即在你动身之前)。*It's unwise to spend your income in ~.* 把你的收入预先花掉是不智之举。*Galileo's ideas were (well) in ~ of the age in which he lived.* 伽利略的思想(大为)超越了他生活的时代。**2** (attrib use) in ~: (用作定语)事前的; 预先的; 在前的: *an ~ copy of a new book,* one supplied before publication; (正式发行前所供给的)新书样本; *an ~ party,* party, eg of explorers, soldiers, sent in ~; (探险队, 军队等的)先头部队; 先遣部队; *have ~ notice,* eg of sb's arrival. 获得事先通知(如某人之抵达)。**3** [C] money paid before it is due, or for work only partially completed. 预付款。**~ 'booking,** reservation (of a room in a hotel, a seat in a theatre, etc) in ~ of the time when it is needed. (旅馆房间, 戏院座位等的)预定。

ad·vance[2] /əd'vɑ:ns US: -'væns; əd'væns/ vi, vt **1** [VP2A, B, 3A] come or go forward: 前进; *Our troops have ~d two miles.* 我们的部队已前进了两英里。*He ~d (up)on me in a threatening manner.* 他以威胁的姿态向我走来。*Has civilization ~d during this century?* 文明在本世纪里有所进步吗? *The forces of the enemy ~d against us.* 敌军向着我们推进。**2** [VP2A] (of costs, values, prices) rise: (指费用, 价值, 物价)上涨: *Stock market prices/Property values continue to ~.* 股票市场价格(不动产价值)继续上涨。**3** [VP6A, 14] move, put or help forward: 向前移; 提前; 提出; 提升; 促进: *The date of the meeting was ~d from the 10th to the 3 rd of June.* 会议日期由六月十日提前到六月三日。⇨ **postpone.** *May I ~ my opinion on the matter?* 我可以提出我对于这事的意见吗? *He worked so well that he was soon ~d (= promoted) to the position of manager.* 他工作非常努力, 所以不久就被提升到经理的职位上。*Such behaviour is not likely to ~ your interests.* 这种行为不会增进你的利益。**4** [VP6A] increase, raise (prices) (= colloq, 口, put up): 增加; 提高(物价): *The shopkeepers ~d their prices.* 店主们抬高物价。**5** [VP12A,13A] pay (money) before the due date: 预付(钱): *He asked his employer to ~ him a month's salary.* 他要求雇主先付他一个月的薪水。*The banks often ~ money to farmers for seed and fertilizer.* 银行常贷款给农民购买种子及肥料。**ad·vanced** part adj far on in life or progress, etc: 年高的; 程度高的; 高深的: ~d *in years,* very old; 年事已高的; 非常老的; ~d *courses of study.* 高级课程。*The professor is engaged in ~d studies.* 该教授正从事高深的学术研究。⇨ **elementary.** *He has ~d ideas,* ideas that are new and not generally accepted. 他有先进的思想(即尚未为一般人所接受的新思想)。**~d level** (abbr 略作 **A level**) (of examinations of the General Certificate of Education) securing admission, in GB, to a college or university. 高等(指普通教育文凭考试, 在英国可获得学院或大学之入学许可)。**~·ment** n [U] promotion; preferment; improvement: 擢升; 促进; 改进; 进步: *The aim of a university should be the ~ment of learning.* 大学的目标应该是促进学术的发展。

ad·van·tage /əd'vɑːntɪdʒ US: -'væn-; əd'væntɪdʒ/ *n* **1** [C] sth useful or helpful, sth likely to bring success, esp in competition: 益处; 便利; 优点; (尤指竞争中的)优势: *the ~s of a good education*. 良好教育的益处. *Living in a big town has many ~s, such as good schools, libraries and theatres*. 住在大都市里有许多优点, 例如好学校、图书馆及戏院. *have/gain/win an ~ (over); give sb an ~ (over)*, (have, give, etc) a better position or opportunity: 占(获得, 赢得, 给某人)优势(后接 over): *Tom's university education gave him an ~ over boys who had not been to a university*. 汤姆的大学教育使他较未上大学的男孩子占优势. *have the ~ of sb*, know sb or sth that he does not know. 较某人有利; 比某人强(知其所不知). **2** [U] benefit; profit: 利益: *He gained little ~ from his visit to London*. 他游历伦敦获益甚少. *take ~ of sb*, deceive him, play a trick on him. 欺骗某人; 捉弄某人. *take (full) ~ of sth*, use it profitably, for one's own benefit: (充分)利用某事物: *He always takes full ~ of the mistakes made by his rivals*. 他总是充分利用他的对手所犯的错误. *to ~*, in a way that enables sth to be seen, used, etc in the best way: 更加; 越发有效地: *The painting is seen to better ~ from a distance*. 这幅画从远处看更显眼. *You should lay out your money* (= decide how to spend or invest it) *to the best ~*. 你应该以最有效的方式来利用你的钱(决定如何花用或投资). *be/prove to sb's ~*, be profitable or helpful to him. 对某人有利; 有助于某人. *turn sth to ~*, make the most of it; use it profitably. 尽量利用某事物. **3** (tennis) the first point scored after deuce. (网球)平手以后所得到的第一分. □ *vt* [VP6A] benefit. 对…有利.

ad·van·tage·ous /ˌædvən'teɪdʒəs; ˌædvən'tedʒəs/ *adj* profitable; helpful. 有利的; 有益的. ~·ly *adv*

ad·vent /'ædvənt/ *n* **1** (usu *sing* with *def art*) coming or arrival (of an important development, season, etc): (通常单数与定冠词连用)来到; 来临(指重要发展、节期等): *Since the ~ of the atomic power, there have been great changes in industry*. 自从原子动力问世之后, 工业方面起了很大的改变. **2 A~**, (eccles) the coming of Christ; the season (with four Sundays) before Christmas Day. (教会)耶稣之降临; 降临节(圣诞节前包括四个星期日之时期). **3** the second coming of Christ at the Last Judgement. 最后审判耶稣之再临. **Ad·vent·ist** /'ædvəntɪst US: əd'ven-; 'ædvəntɪst/ *n* person who believes that Christ's second coming and the end of the world are near. 相信耶稣之再临及世界末日已近的人.

ad·ven·ti·tious /ˌædven'tɪʃəs; ˌædvən'tɪʃəs/ *adj* (formal) coming by chance; accidental: (正式用语)偶然的: ~ *aid*. 偶然的帮助.

ad·ven·ture /əd'ventʃə(r); əd'ventʃə/ *n* **1** [C] strange or unusual happening, esp an exciting or dangerous journey or activity: 奇遇; 冒险的经历: *A flight in an aeroplane used to be quite an ~*. 从前乘飞机飞行是相当冒险的事. *The explorer told the boys about his ~s in the Arctic*. 那探险家对他在北极的奇遇讲给那些男孩子听. **~ playground**, playground with large wooden, metal, etc materials and structures for children to play with, in or on. 儿童游乐场; 儿童乐园. **2** [U] risk; danger, eg in travel and exploration: 冒险; *fond of* ~; 喜爱冒险; *a story of* ~; 冒险故事; *Robin Hood lived a life of* ~. 罗宾汉过着冒险的生活. □ *vt* = venture (the usu word 通常用此字). **ad·ven·tur·er** *n* **1** person who seeks ~. 冒险者. **2** person who is ready to make a profit for himself by risky or unscrupulous methods. 冒险图利者; 投机者. **ad·ven·tur·ess** /-ɪs; -ɪs/ *n* woman ~r, esp one who is ready to use guile to obtain benefits. 女冒险者; (尤指)以诈欺手段冒险图利之女人; 女投机者. **ad·ven·tur·ous** /-əs; -əs/ *adj* **1** fond of, eager for, ~s. 喜冒险的. **2** full of danger and excitement: 充满危险和刺激的: *an adventurous voyage*. 惊险的航行. **~some** /-səm; -səm/ *adj* (rare or liter) (罕或文) = adventurous.

ad·verb /'ædvɜːb; 'ædvɜb/ *n* (gram) word that answers questions with *how, when, where* and modifies *vv, adjj* and other *advv*, etc, eg *soon, here, well, quickly*. (语法)副词(用以回答 how, when, where 之问句, 及修饰动词, 形容词及其他副词等之词, 如 soon, here, well, quickly). **ad·verb·ial** /əd'vɜːbɪəl; əd'vɜbɪəl/ *adj* of the nature of an ~. 副词性质的. □ *n* ~ or ~ial phrase. 副词; 副词(性质)的短语. **ad·verb·i·ally** /əd'vɜːbɪəlɪ; əd'vɜbɪəlɪ/ *adv*

ad·ver·sary /'ædvəsərɪ US: -serɪ; 'ædvɜˌsɛrɪ/ *n* (*pl* **-ries**) enemy; opponent (in any kind of contest). (任何比赛或竞争中的)敌手; 对手.

ad·verse /'ædvɜːs; əd'vɜs/ *adj* unfavourable; contrary or hostile (*to*): 不利的; 反对的; 敌对的(与 to 连用): ~ *weather conditions*; 恶劣的天候; ~ *winds*, eg for a sailing-ship; 逆风(例如对帆船而言者); *developments ~ to our interests*. 与我们利益相反的发展. **~·ly** *adv*

ad·ver·sity /əd'vɜːsətɪ; əd'vɜsətɪ/ *n* (*pl* **-ties**). **1** [U] condition of adverse fortune; trouble: 逆境; 厄运; 患难; 艰难: *be patient/cheerful in* ~. 在逆境中具坚忍(振奋)的精神; 逆来顺受. *A brave man smiles in the face of* ~. 勇敢的人临难不惧. **2** [C] misfortune; affliction. 不幸; 灾难; 祸患.

ad·vert¹ /əd'vɜːt; əd'vɜt/ *vi* [VP3A] (formal) (正式用语) ~ *to*, refer to (in speech or writing): (在谈话或写作中)论及; 谈到: ~ *to a problem*. 谈到一个问题.

ad·vert² /'ædvɜːt; 'ædvɜt/ *n* (GB colloq abbr for) advertisement(2). (英, 口)广告(为 advertisement 第2义之略).

ad·ver·tise /'ædvətaɪz; 'ædvɜˌtaɪz/ *vt, vi* [VP6A, 2A, 3A] make known to people (by printing notices in newspapers, etc or by other means, eg TV): 为…做广告; 登广告: ~ *one's goods*; 为其货品做广告; ~ *in all the newspapers*; 在所有的报纸上登广告; ~ *for an assistant in the local newspapers*, announce that one wishes to engage an assistant. 在本地报纸上登广告征求助手. **ad·ver·tiser** *n* person who ~s. 登广告者; 做广告者. **~·ment** /əd'vɜːtɪsmənt US: ˌædvər'taɪzmənt; ˌædvə'taɪzmənt/ *n* **1** [U] advertising. 做广告; 登广告: (attrib) (用作定语) *the ~ment manager*, eg of a newspaper. (如报社的)广告部经理. *A~ment helps to sell goods*. 登广告有助于销路. **2** [C] public announcement (in the press, TV, etc): 广告; 告白; 启事: *If you want to sell your piano, put an ~ in the newspaper*. 如果你要卖掉你的钢琴, 可在报纸上登一则广告. ⇨ **commercial** *n*

ad·vice /əd'vaɪs; əd'vaɪs/ *n* **1** [U] (informed) opinion about what to do, how to behave: 劝告; 忠告; 建议: *You won't get well unless you follow your doctor's ~*. 如果你不遵守医生的嘱咐, 你将不会痊愈. *If you take my ~ and study hard, you'll pass the examination*. 如果你听我的劝告用功读书, 你就会考及格. *You should take legal ~*, consult a lawyer. 你应该就教于律师. *act on sb's ~*, do what he suggests. 某人的建议去做; 依劝告行事. *(give sb) a piece/bit/word/few words of ~*, (give) an opinion about what to do, etc. (给某人)一项建议(一项劝告, 几句忠告). **2** [C] (comm) (usu *pl*) news from a distance, esp commercial: (商)(通常用复数)远来来的消息; (尤指)行情: ~s *from our Tokyo branch*. 从我们东京分公司来的消息. **'~-note, letter of ~**, (comm) formal notice of delivery of goods, a business call, etc. (商)正式通知(关于货物之寄运, 业务之接洽等).

ad·vis·able /əd'vaɪzəbl; əd'vaɪzəbl/ *adj* wise; sensible; to be advised or recommended: 明智的; 合理的; 适当的; 可行的: *Do you think it ~ to wait*? 你认为应该等候吗? **ad·visa·bil·ity** /əd,vaɪzə'bɪlətɪ; əd,vaɪzə'bɪlətɪ/ *n* [U]

ad·vise /əd'vaɪz; əd'vaɪz/ *vt, vi* [VP6A, C, 17, 20, 21, 14] give advice to; recommend: 劝告; 忠告; 建议: *The doctor ~d a complete rest*. 医生劝告要完全休息. *What do you ~ me to do*? 你看我该怎么办? *Please*

~ *me whether I should accept the offer.* 请你告诉我是否该接受此项提议。*We ~d an early start/their starting early/them to start early.* 我们建议早点开始(他们早点开始)。*Her father ~d her against marrying in haste.* 她的父亲劝告她不要匆匆结婚。*Who is the best man to ~ me on this question?* 关于这个问题,谁是我的最好顾问? **2** [VP6A, 21, 14] (comm) inform; notify: (商)通知: *Please ~ us when the goods are dispatched/~ us of the dispatch of the goods.* 货物交运时请通知我们(请将货物交运情形通知我们)。**3** [VP3A] **~ with (sb),** (old use) consult; take counsel with. (旧用法)就教于(某人);与(某人)商量。 **ad·viser** *n* person who gives advice, esp one who is habitually consulted: 顾问; 指导者: *~r to the Government.* 政府的顾问。 **ad·vised** *adj* (old use) considered; carefully thought out; deliberate. (旧用法)考虑过的; 仔细想出的; 故意的。 *ill ~d,* unwise; injudicious. 不智的; 欠考虑的。 *well ~d,* wise; judicious. 明智的; 考虑周到的。 **ad·vis·ed·ly** /əd'vaɪzɪdlɪ; əd-'vaɪzɪdlɪ/ *adv* after careful thought. 经仔细考虑后。 **ad·vis·ory** /əd'vaɪzərɪ; əd'vaɪzərɪ/ *adj* of advice; having the power to ~: 劝告的; 忠告的; 有权进言的; 供咨询的; 顾问的: *an advisory committee/council/panel.* 咨询委员会(顾问会议/顾问小组)。

ad·vo·cate /'ædvəkət; 'ædvəkɪt/ *n* **1** person who speaks in favour of sb or sth (esp a cause): 提倡者; 拥护者(尤指对某一主义或目标者): *an ~ of equal pay for men and women.* 提倡男女同酬者。 **2** (legal) person who does this professionally in a court of law in Scotland (= *barrister* in England and Wales). (法律)(苏格兰法庭上的)辩护士(相当于英格兰和威尔斯的barrister); 律师。 **the Faculty of A~s,** the Scots Bar. 苏格兰律师公会。 **Lord A~,** principal law officer in Scotland. (苏格兰的)检察长。 □ *vt* /'ædvəkeɪt; 'ædvə-ˌket/ [VP6A, C] support; speak publicly in support of: 提倡; 主张: *Do you ~ keeping all children at school till the age of sixteen?* 你主张将义务教育延长至十六岁吗? **ad·vo·cacy** /'ædvəkəsɪ; 'ædvəkəsɪ/ *n* [U] pleading in support (of a cause or sb). 主张; 支持; 提倡; 拥护(一主义或某人)。

adze, adz /ædz; ædz/ *n* carpenter's tool (with a blade at right angles to the handle) for cutting or shaping wood. 锛子; 横口斧(木工工具)。

aegis, egis /'iːdʒɪs; 'iːdʒɪs/ *n* protection; sponsorship. 保护; 支持。 *under the ~ of,* with the patronage or support of. 在…的保护或支持下。

aeon, eon /'iːən; 'iːən/ *n* [C] period of time too long to be measured. 永世; 亿万年(极长而无法计算的时期)。

aer·ate /'eəreɪt; 'eəˌret/ *vt* [VP6A] charge (a liquid) with air or gas; expose to the chemical purifying action of air: 充气于(液体); 暴露于空气净化作用中: 灌气: *the soil by digging.* 挖掘使土壤暴露于空气净化作用。 *Blood is ~d in the lungs.* 血液在肺部与氧结合。 **aer·ation** /eə'reɪʃn; ˌeə'reʃən/ *n*

aer·ial /'eərɪəl; 'erɪəl/ *adj* **1** existing in, moving through, the air: 存在空气中的; 由空中经过的; 空中的: *an ~ railway/ropeway,* a system of overhead suspension for transport. 高架铁道(架空索道)。 **2** (archaic) of or like air; immaterial. (古)空气的; 似空气的; 虚幻的; 无形的。 □ *n* that part of a radio or TV system which receives or sends out signals, usu a wire or rod, or number of wires or rods (US 美 = *antenna*). (无线电或电视的)天线。

aerie, aery, eyrie, eyry /'eərɪ; 'erɪ/ *n* eagle's nest; nest of other birds of prey which are built high up among rocks; eagle's brood. 鹰巢; (高筑于岩石中的)肉食鸟的鸟巢; 一窝鹰雏。

aero·bat·ics /ˌeərə'bætɪks; ˌerə'bætɪks/ *n* (sing v) [U] the performance of acrobatic feats by airmen, eg flying upside down. (用单数动词)(飞行员所表演的)特技飞行(例如翻身飞行)。

aero·drome /'eərədrəʊm; 'erəˌdrom/ *n* (US = *airdrome*) (dated) ground for the arrival and departure

and servicing of aircraft, with hangars, workshops, etc (*airfield* and *airport* are the more usu words). (过时用语)飞机场(今较常用 airfield 和 airport)。

aero·dy·nam·ics /ˌeərəʊdaɪ'næmɪks; ˌerodar'næ-mɪks/ *n pl* (*sing v*) [U] science dealing with the flow of air and the motion of aircraft, bullets, etc through air. (用单数动词)气体动力学。

aero·naut /'eərənɔːt; 'erəˌnɔt/ *n* person who pilots or travels in a balloon, airship or other aircraft. 轻气球、飞艇或其他航空器之驾驶员或乘客。

aero·naut·ics /ˌeərə'nɔːtɪks; ˌerə'nɔtɪks/ *n* (*sing v*) [U] science and practice of aviation (the more usu word). (用单数动词)航空学(较常用 aviation)。

aero·plane /'eərəpleɪn; 'erəˌplen/ *n* (US = *airplane*) heavier-than-air flying machine with one or more engines. 飞机。 ⇨ *aircraft, airliner* at **air**(7)。

aero·sol /'eərəsɒl US: -sɔːl; 'erəˌsɑl/ *n* [U] dispersion of fine solid or liquid particles, eg of scent, paint, insecticide, detergent, released (in a mist) by pressure from a container with compressed gas from a valve; [C] (P) the container itself. (香水, 油漆, 杀虫剂, 清洁剂等的)雾状喷酒; 喷雾; (商标)喷雾罐; 喷雾器。

aero·space /'eərəspeɪs; 'erəˌspes/ *n* the earth's atmosphere and the space beyond, considered as area available to air- or space-craft: 地球大气层及其外面的空间; 太空: *the ~ industry.* 太空工业。

aer·tex /'eəteks; 'erteks/ *n* (P) kind of loosely woven textile material (as used for underwear). (商标)一种松织的纺织品(用以制内衣等)。

aery /'eərɪ; 'erɪ/ *n* ⇨ aerie.

aes·thete, es·thete /'iːsθiːt US: 'esθiːt; 'esθit/ *n* person who has or claims to have great love of and understanding of what is beautiful, esp in the arts. 审美家(尤指精于艺术方面)。

aes·thetic, es·thetic /iːs'θetɪk US: es-; es'θetɪk/ *adj* of the appreciation of the beautiful, esp in the arts, (of persons) having such appreciation: (尤指有关艺术之)审美的; (指人)有审美能力的: *~ standards.* 审美标准。 □ *n* [U] particular set of ~ principles: 美学原理; 审美法: *the ~ to which he remained faithful.* 他仍然坚守的审美原则。 **aes·thet·ical, es·thet·ical** /-kl; -kl/ *adj* = aesthetic. **aes·thet·ically** /-klɪ; -klɪ/ *adv* **aes·thet·ics, es·thet·ics** *n* (*sing v*) [U] branch of philosophy which tries to make clear the laws and principles of beauty (contrasted with morality and utility). (用单数动词)审美学; 美学(哲学中的一门, 研究美之法则及原理; 与 morality 及 utility 相对)。

aether /'iːθə(r); 'iθər/ *n* ⇨ ether.

aeti·ol·ogy /ˌiːtɪ'ɒlədʒɪ; ˌitɪ'ɑlədʒɪ/ *n* ⇨ etiology.

afar /ə'fɑː(r); ə'fɑr/ *adv* (poet) far off or away. (诗)远; 遥遥地。 *from ~,* from a distance. 从远处。

af·fable /'æfəbl; 'æfəbl/ *adj* polite and friendly; pleasant and easy to talk to: 有礼而友善的; 和蔼可亲的; 友善而易与交谈的: *~ to everybody;* 对每个人都和蔼可亲; 谦逊的回答。 **af·fably** /-əblɪ; -əblɪ/ *adv* **affa·bil·ity** /ˌæfə'bɪlətɪ; ˌæfə'bɪlətɪ/ *n* quality of being ~ (*to* or *towards*). 和蔼可亲; 谦虚有礼(与 to 或 towards 连用)。

af·fair /ə'feə(r); ə'fer/ *n* [C] **1** concern; sth (to be) done; business: 事; 事务; 职务; 业务: *That's my ~, not yours.* 那是我的事, 不是你的事。 **2** (*pl*) business of any kind; day-to-day concerns of organization, etc: (复)任何种类的事务; (机关组织)业务: *A prime minister is kept busy with ~s of state,* the task of government. 首相为政务忙碌。 *When he asked me how much I earned, I told him to mind his own ~s,* not to ask questions about my business, etc. 当他问我赚多少钱的时候, 我告诉他少管闲事。 *We can't afford a holiday with ~s in their present state of ~s,* while things remain as they are now. 在目前的情形下, 我们无法去度假。 **Secretary of State for Foreign/Home/Welsh, etc A~s,** titles of Government Ministers in GB. (英国政府的)外交(内政, 威尔斯事务等)部

长。**3 have an ~ (with sb)**, have an emotional (and sexual) relationship with sb to whom one is not married: 与(某人,指非配偶)发生爱情(及性)关系; (与某人)私通: *The doctor, they say, is having an ~ with the rector's wife.* 据说那医生和校长夫人私通。**~ of honor,** duel. 决斗。**4** (colloq) occurrence; event; object: (口)事件; 东西; 物件: *The railway accident was a terrible ~.* 那次火车车祸是一件可怕事件。*Her hat was a wonderful ~.* 她的帽子是一件绝妙之物。*What a ramshackle ~ your old car is!* 你的老爷车破旧!

af·fect¹ /ə'fekt; ə'fɛkt/ *vt* [VP6A] **1** have an influence or impression on; act on: 影响: *The climate ~ed his health,* injured 气候影响(损害)了他的健康。*Some plants are quickly ~ed by cold.* 有些植物对寒冷敏感。*Will the changes in taxation ~ you personally,* Will you have to pay more (or less) in taxes? 税法的变更将会影响到你个人吗? *The rise in the price of bread will ~ us all.* 面包售价上涨, 我们大家都会受影响。**2** move the feelings of: 感动: *He was much ~ed by the sad news.* 这个凄怆的消息使他十分难过。*His death ~ed us deeply.* 他的死亡使我们深为感慨。**3** (of diseases) attack; cause a particular condition in: (指疾病) 侵袭: *The left lung is ~ed,* eg by cancer, tuberculosis. 左肺受到感染(如被癌症或结核病)。**4** *well/ill ~ed (towards),* well/ill disposed (the more usu word) or inclined (towards). (对…)有好(恶)感(较常用 disposed)。**~·ing** *adj* moving or touching (the feelings): 感人的; 动人的: *an ~ing sight.* 感人的情景。**~·ing·ly** *adv* tenderly; pathetically. 动人地; 哀惋地。

af·fect² /ə'fekt; ə'fɛkt/ *vt* **1** [VP6A, 7A] pretend to have or feel (ignorance, indifference); pretend (to do, etc): 假装; 佯为; 假装: *She ~s an American accent.* 她装出美国腔调。*He ~ed not to hear me.* 他假装没听见我。**2** [VP6A] have a liking for and use (esp for ostentation): 爱用; 爱穿; 爱好(尤指为了夸耀): *He ~s long and learned words,* uses them instead of short and simple words. 他爱用冗长而艰涩的词(不用短而简单的词)。*She ~s bright colours,* wears brightly coloured clothes, etc. 她爱穿颜色鲜艳的衣服。**~ed** *adj* pretended; not natural or genuine: 矫饰的; 造作的; 不自然的; 虚伪的: *an ~ed politeness;* 虚伪的礼貌; *~ed manners;* 矫揉造作的举止; *with an ~ed cheerfulness;* 强作高兴; *written in an ~ed style,* showing a liking for an artificial style. 以爱炫耀雕琢的文体写成的。

af·fec·ta·tion /ˌæfek'teɪʃn; ˌæfɪk'teʃən/ *n* **1** [U] behaviour that is not natural or genuine: 矫饰的行为; 不自然的行为; 虚伪的行为: *Keep clear of all ~,* Do not behave unnaturally; 请摒除一切矫饰; [C] instance of this: 行为矫饰或虚伪的实例: *Her little ~s annoyed me.* 她那些做作的小动作使我厌烦。**2** [U] pretence (made on purpose, for effect): (故意的, 为引人注意的) 假装; 虚饰; 做作: *an ~ of interest/indifference/ignorance.* 假装有兴趣(冷淡, 不知)。

af·fec·tion /ə'fekʃn; ə'fɛkʃən/ *n* **1** [U] kindly feeling; love: 亲爱; 爱: *Every mother has ~ for/feels ~ toward her children.* 每个母亲都爱她的孩子。*He is held in great ~,* is much loved. 他极为大家所爱戴。**2** [U or *pl*] *gain/win sb's ~(s),* win the love of. 获(赢)得某人的爱。**3** [C] (old use) disease; unhealthy condition: (旧用法)病; 疾病; 患病: *an ~ of the throat.* 喉咙痛。

af·fec·tion·ate /ə'fekʃənet; ə'fɛkʃənɪt/ *adj* loving; fond; showing love (to sb): 亲爱的; 挚爱的; 亲切的(与 to 连用, 后接某人): *an ~ wife:* 温柔体贴的妻子; *~ looks.* 表示亲爱的神情。**~·ly** *adv* *Yours ~ly,* used at the close of a letter, eg from a man to his sister. 书信末尾签名前的客气语(如一男人写给他姐姐或妹妹的信中所用者)。

af·fi·ance /ə'faɪəns; ə'faɪəns/ *vt* [VP6A] (usu passive; liter or old use) promise in marriage: (通常用被动语态)(文或旧用法)许诺婚约; 订婚; 定亲; 定聘: *be ~d to (sb),* be engaged to marry him/her. 与(某人)

订婚; 为某人之未婚妻(或未婚夫)。

af·fi·da·vit /ˌæfɪ'deɪvɪt; ˌæfə'devɪt/ *n* (legal) written statement, made on oath, (to be) used as legal proof or evidence: (法律) 宣誓书; 口供书(用作法定证据者): *swear/make/take an ~.* 立宣誓书。

af·fili·ate /ə'fɪlɪeɪt; ə'fɪlɪ,et/ *vt* [VP6A, 14, 2A] *~ (to/with),* (of a society or institution, or a member) enter into association: (指团体, 机构或会员)加盟; 入会: *The College is ~d to the University.* 该学院附属于该大学。*Is the Mineworkers' Union ~d with the TUC?* (英国)矿工工会是附属于劳工联合的吗?

af·fili·ation /əˌfɪlɪ'eɪʃn; ə,fɪlɪ'eʃən/ *n* [U] affiliating or being affiliated; [C] connection made by affiliating. 加盟; 入会; 加入; 联营。**'~ order,** (GB, legal) order made by a magistrate, determining the paternity of an illegitimate child and requiring the father to contribute towards its support. (英, 法律) 父子关系认定令(判定私生子之父, 以便要求其赡养)。

af·fin·ity /ə'fɪnətɪ; ə'fɪnətɪ/ *n* (*pl* **-ties**) *~ (between/to/for),* **1** [C] close connection, structural resemblance (between animals and plants, languages, etc) (or of one thing to/with another). 密切关系; 构造相似(与 between 连用, 指动植物, 语言等之间者; 与 to 或 with 连用, 指一物对另一物言); 类同。**2** [U] relationship; [C] relation (by marriage); similarity of character suggesting relationship. 关系; 姻亲关系; (显示可能有关系之)性格之相似。**3** [C] strong liking or attraction: 强烈的爱好或吸引力: *She feels a strong ~ to/for him.* 她感到他对她具有强烈的吸引力。**4** chemical or physical attraction: (化学或物理上的)亲和力: *the ~ of common salt for water.* 食盐与水之亲和力。

af·firm /ə'fɜːm; ə'fɝm/ *vt, vi* [VP6A,9,14] declare positively: 肯定; 断言: *~ the truth of a statement/~ that it is true;* 断言某项陈述的确实性; ~ *to sb that …* 向某人断言…。⇨ **deny. 2** [VP2A] (legal) (of a person who has conscientious objections to swearing on the Bible) declare solemnly but not on oath. (法律)(指宁可不本着良心不愿虔圣经发誓之人)郑重陈述。**~·ation** /ˌæfə'meɪʃn; ˌæfə'meʃən/ *n* **1** [U] ~ing. 肯定; 断言。**2** [C] sth ~ed; (legal) declaration made by ~ing(2). 证实之事; (法律)(本着良心不宣誓而作的)郑重陈述。**~·ative** /ə'fɜːmətɪv; ə'fɝmətɪv/ *adj, n* (answering) 'yes': 肯定的; 肯定; *an ~ative answer.* 肯定的回答。*The answer is the ~ative,* is 'Yes'. 回答是肯定的。⇨ **negative(1).**

af·fix¹ /ə'fɪks; ə'fɪks/ *vt* [VP6A, 14] *~ sth (to),* (formal) fix; fasten; attach: (正式用语)使固定; 结牢; 附加: *~ a seal/stamp to a document;* 在文件上加盖印信; add in writing: 加写; 添写: *~ your signature to an agreement.* 加添签字于合约上。

af·fix² /'æfɪks; 'æfɪks/ *n* suffix or prefix, eg *-ly, -able, un-, co-.* 词缀(接后缀或接前缀,例如 -ly, -able, un-, co-)。⇨ **App 3.** 参看附录三。

af·fla·tus /ə'fleɪtəs; ə'fletəs/ *n* [U] (formal) divine revelation; inspiration. (正式用语)神感; 灵感。

af·flict /ə'flɪkt; ə'flɪkt/ *vt* [VP6A, 14] cause bodily or mental trouble to: 使身体受痛苦; 使苦恼: *~ed with rheumatism;* 为风湿症所苦; *feel much ~ed at/by the news.* 为此消息感到很难过。

af·flic·tion /ə'flɪkʃn; ə'flɪkʃən/ *n* **1** [U] suffering; distress: 痛苦; 折磨: *help people in ~.* 帮助苦难的人们。**2** [C] cause or occasion of suffering: 痛苦之因; 痛苦之事: *the ~s of old age,* eg deafness, blindness. 老年之苦(如聋、盲等)。

af·flu·ence /'æfluəns; 'æfluəns/ *n* [U] wealth; abundance: 富裕; 丰富: *living in ~;* 生活富裕; *rise to ~,* become wealthy. 发财。

af·flu·ent¹ /'æfluənt; 'æfluənt/ *adj* wealthy; abundant: 富裕的; 丰富的: *in ~ circumstances.* 在富裕的环境中。**the ~ society,** society which is prosperous and whose members are concerned with material improvement. 富裕繁荣的社会(人们均关切物质享受的改善)。

af·flu·ent[2] /'æfluənt; 'æfluənt/ n [C] stream flowing into a larger one (*tributary* is the usu word). 支流(通常用 tributary)。

af·ford /ə'fɔːd; ə'fɔrd/ vt 1 [VP6A, 7A] (usu with *can/could, be able to*) spare or find enough time or money for: (通常与 can, could, be able to 连用)省出或找到足够的时间或金钱去(做某事); 力足以; …得起: *We can't ~ a holiday/can't ~ to go away this summer.* 今年夏天我们无法度假(抽不出时间去度假)。*Are you able to ~ the time for a holiday?* 你能抽出时间去度假吗？ 2 [VP7A] (with *can/could*) run a risk by doing sth: (与 can 或 could 连用)冒…之险: *I can't ~ to neglect my work.* 我不能疏忽我的工作。*She couldn't ~ to displease her boss.* 她得罪不起她的上司。 3 [VP12A, 13A, 6A] (formal) provide; give: (正式用语)供给; 给与: *The trees ~ a pleasant shade.* 这些树造成凉荫。*It will ~ me great pleasure to have dinner with you.* 与你共餐将是我的一大乐事。

af·for·est /æ'fɒrɪst; ə'fɔrɪst/ vt [VP6A] make into forest land. 使成为林地; 造林于。 **af·for·est·ation** / ə,fɒrɪ'steɪʃn US: ə,fɔr-; ə,fɑrɪs'teʃən/ n: *~ation projects*, projects for planting large areas with trees. 造林计划。

af·fran·chise /ə'fræntʃaɪz; ə'fræn,tʃaɪz/ vt [VP6A] free from servitude. 解除…之劳役; 恢复…之自由。

af·fray /ə'freɪ; ə'fre/ n [C] fight in a public place, causing or likely to cause a disturbance of the peace: 在公共场所打架滋扰安宁: *The men were charged with causing an ~.* 那些人被控滋扰公共安宁。

af·front /ə'frʌnt; ə'frʌnt/ vt [VP6A] insult on purpose; hurt sb's feelings or self-respect, esp in public: 故意侮辱; 当众使难堪: *feel ~ed at having one's word doubted.* 因自己的话受人怀疑而感到难堪。 □ n [C] public insult; deliberate show of disrespect: 公然侮辱; 故意表示不敬: *an ~ to his pride;* 对他自尊心的侮辱; *suffer an ~;* 受辱; *offer an ~ to sb.* 对某人加以侮辱。

afield /ə'fiːld; ə'fild/ adv far away from home; to or at a distance: 远离家乡地; 至远方; 在远处; 离乡背井: *Don't go too far ~.* 不要走得太远。

afire /ə'faɪə(r); ə'faɪr/ pred adj (poet) on fire. (诗)着火的。

aflame /ə'fleɪm; ə'flem/ pred adj (poet) in flames; burning; red as if burning: (诗)着火的; 燃烧中的; 红似火的; (fig) (喻) *~ with passion.* 怒火中烧; 热情如火。*The autumn woods were ~ with colour.* 那片秋林红似火。

afloat /ə'fləʊt; ə'flot/ pred adj 1 floating; borne up, carried along, on air or water: 飘浮在水中或空中的: *The ship stuck fast on the rocks and we couldn't get it ~ again.* 船牢牢地搁浅在礁石上, 我们无法使它再浮起来。 2 at sea; on board ship: 在海上的; 在船上的: *life ~,* the life of a sailor. 海上生涯; 水手生涯。 3 awash; flooded: 为海浪所冲打的; 为水所淹的。 4 (business) started; solvent: (贸)开张的; 新开的; 有偿付能力的: *get a new periodical ~,* launch it. 创办一种新期刊。 5 (of stories, rumours) current; in circulation. (指传说, 谣言)传播各处的; 流传的。

afoot /ə'fʊt; ə'fʊt/ pred adj 1 in progress or operation; being prepared: 在进行中的; 在准备中的: *There's mischief ~.* 有人在准备捣乱。*There's a scheme ~ to improve the roads.* 有人在计划改善道路。 2 (old use) on foot; walking. (旧用法)步行的。

afore /ə'fɔː(r); ə'fɔr/ adv, prep (naut) before. (航海)在前。*~ the mast,* as an unlicensed seaman with quarters in the forecastle. 在船桅前(如无照之船员居于船首甲板下之水手舱): *'~·said* pron, cdj (legal) (that has been) said or mentioned before. (法律)前述(的); 上述(的)。*'~·thought,* ⇨ **malice.**

a fortiori /,eɪ ,fɔːtɪ'ɔːraɪ; 'e,fɔrʃɪ'ɔraɪ/ adv (Lat) by a more convincing argument. (拉丁)更不用说; 何况; 更加。

afoul /ə'faʊl; ə'faʊl/ adv run/fall ~ of, (more usu run/fall foul of) come into collision with; get mixed up with. (较常用 run/fall foul of) 与…冲突; 与…纠缠在一起。

afraid /ə'freɪd; ə'fred/ pred adj 1 ~ (of), frightened (of): 害怕; 畏惧: *There's nothing to be ~ of.* 没有什么好害怕的。*Are you ~ of snakes?* 你怕蛇吗？ 2 ~ of ... gerund; ~ that, doubtful or anxious about consequences: 恐怕: *I was ~ of hurting his feelings/that I might hurt his feelings.* 我恐怕伤了他的感情。*She was ~ of waking her husband,* didn't want to wake him, perhaps because he was ill or in need of sleep. 她怕吵醒了她的丈夫(或因他丈夫生病, 或因他需要睡眠)。*She was ~ to wake her husband,* feared that he might be angry with her. 她不敢吵醒她的丈夫(怕他可能为此而生她的气)。*Don't be ~ (= Don't hesitate) to ask for my help.* 不要担心(尽管)向我求助。 4 ~ (that), (that usu omitted) (a polite formula used with a statement that may be unwelcome): (与 that 连用, 但通常省略掉; 要说的话可能不受欢迎时用的客套话): *I'm ~ (that) we shall be late.* 我恐怕我们行将会迟到。*We missed the last train, I'm ~.* 恐怕我们已经错过最后一班火车了。*I'm ~ I can't help.* 我恐怕不能相助。

afresh /ə'freʃ; ə'frɛʃ/ adv again; in a new way: 再; 重新: *Let's start ~.* 让我们重新开始。

Af·ri·can /'æfrɪkən; 'æfrɪkən/ n, adj (indigenous inhabitant) of Africa. 非洲的; 非洲人; 非洲人。

Af·ri·kaans /,æfrɪ'kɑːns; ,æfrɪ'kɑnz/ n language developed from Dutch, one of the two official European languages in the Republic of South Africa. 阿非利康士语(南非共和国所用的两种官方欧语之一, 系由荷兰语发展而成)。 □ adj of this language or the people who speak it. 阿非利康士语的; 说阿非利康士语之人的。**Afri·kaner** /-'kɑːnə(r); -'kɑnə/ n, adj (of) a native ~ speaker. 说阿非利康士语之人的(的)。

Afro- /'æfrəʊ; 'æfro/ pref (in compounds) of Africa or Africans: (用于复合词中)非洲的: *an A~·hairstyle.* 非洲式发型。,~·'Asian adj of Africa and Asia. 亚非的。,~·A'merican n American of African descent. 非裔美国人。,~·'wig n wig in the style of hairdressing of some African women. 非洲式假发(仿若干非洲女人所梳发型的假发)。

aft /ɑːft US: æft; æft/ adv (naut) at or near the stern of a ship, ⇨ the illus at **ship:** (航海)在船尾; 近船尾(参看船之插图): *go aft;* 到船尾去; *fore and aft,* ⇨ **fore.** 从船头到船尾。

after[1] /'ɑːftə(r) US: 'æf-; 'æftə/ adj (attrib only) (仅用作定语) 1 later; following: 以后的; 后面的; 随后的: *in ~ years.* 在往后的几年里。 2 (naut) toward the stern of a ship: (航海)向船尾的: *the '~ cabin;* 后舱; 较近船尾的舱; *the '~ mast.* 后桅。

after[2] /'ɑːftə(r) US: 'æf-; 'æftə/ adv later in time; behind in place: 以后; 后来; 在后: *He fell ill on Monday and died three days ~* (later is more usu). 他于星期一生病, 三天以后就死了(later 较常用)。*What comes ~?* 后来怎么样？*Soon ~* (afterwards is more usu), *he went to live in Wales.* 不久以后, 他就到威尔士去定居了(afterwards 较常用)。

after[3] /'ɑːftə(r) US: 'æf-; 'æftə/ conj at or during a time later than: (指时间)迟于: *I arrived ~ he (had) left.* 我在他离开以后到达。*I shall arrive ~ you leave/have left.* 我将在你离开以后到达。

after[4] /'ɑːftə(r) US: 'æf-; 'æftə/ prep 1 following in time; later than: (指时间)在…以后; 迟于: *~ dinner,* 餐后; *~ dark;* 天黑以后; *~ two o'clock,* 两点钟以后; *soon/shortly ~ six.* 刚过六点钟不久。Cf 参较 a little *before six.* ~ *that,* then; next; 然后; the *day ~ tomorrow;* 后天; *the week ~ next;* 下下礼拜; (US)(美) *half ~* (GB 英 = past) *seven.* 七时半。 2 next in order to; following: (指顺序)在…后面: *Put the direct object ~ the verb.* 把直接宾语放在动词后面。'*Against' comes*

~ 'again' in the dictionary. 在词典中 against 列于 again 之后。**3** behind: 在…后面: *Shut the door ~ you when you leave the room.* 你离开房间时，请随手关门。**4** in view of; as a result of: 鉴于；由于: *I shall never speak to him again ~ what he has said about me.* 由于他说了那些有关我的话，我将永远不再跟他说话。**5** ~ **all**, **(a)** in spite of all: 虽然；尽管: *A~ all my care, it wcs broken.* 虽然我已尽量小心；仍然把它打破了。**(b)** nevertheless: 依然: *He failed ~ all*, in spite of all that had been done, etc. 他毕竟还是失败了（虽然已尽了一切努力）。**6** (in the pattern: 用于 *n ~ n* 之句型中，indicating succession: 表示连续): *day ~ day*; 日复一日；一天一天地; *week ~ week*; 一星期一星期地; *time ~ time*; repeatedly, very often; 一次又一次地; 屡次; *shot ~ shot*. 一枪接一枪地。*one (damned) thing ~ another*, succession of unpleasant happenings, etc. 一连串不愉快的事件。**7** (indicating manner) in the style of; in imitation of: (指方式)有…之风; 仿照: *a painting ~ Rembrandt*; 一幅模仿伦勃兰特的画; *(do sth) ~ a fashion*; *a man ~ my own heart*, 搜寻, 询问): **fashion(1)**, **heart(2)**. **8** (with *vv*, indicating pursuit, search, inquiry): (与动词连用，表示追赶，搜寻，询问): *The policeman ran ~ the thief.* 警察追赶窃贼。*Did they inquire ~ me*, ask for news of me? 他们有没有问到我? *be/get ~ sb*, look for, in order to reprimand, punish, etc according to context: (为了给予申斥、处罚等而)寻找某人: *The po!ce are ~ him.* 警方正在捉拿他。*They'll be ~ you if you steal apples from this orchard.* 如果你从这果园里偷走苹果，他们将会到处抓你。*~ look ~, name sb ~, take ~, at* **look¹(7)**, **name²(1) and take(16)**. **9** (Irish usage) preceding a gerund, making an equivalent of a perfect tense: (爱尔兰用法)置于动名词前造成与完成式相等的结构: *He's ~ drinking*, has been drinking. 他一直在饮酒。

after- /ˈɑːftər/ *US:* /ˈæf-; ˈæftɚ/ *pref* second or later. 第二; 后来; 随后。'**~·care** *n* further treatment given to a person or class of persons, eg sb who has been ill or offenders discharged from prison. 后护法(对病人的病后照顾)，恢复期护养；(对犯人出狱后的)适应辅导; 就业辅导。'**~·damp** *n* poisonous mixture of gases after the explosion of firedamp in a coal-mine. 炸后浊气(煤矿坑内沼气爆炸后所形成之有毒混合气体)。'**~·effect** *n* effect that occurs afterwards, eg a delayed effect of a drug used medically. (药物等的)后作用; 后效。'**~·glow** *n* glow in the sky after sunset. (夕阳的)余晖，晚霞; 夕照。**(the)** '**~·life** *n* **(a)** the life believed to follow death. (有人相信的)死后的生活; 来世。**(b)** the later part of sb's lifetime (esp after a particular event). (尤指某一特殊事件后的)晚年; 余年; 后半辈子。'**~·math** /-mæθ; -mæθ/ *n* (of grass) crop from a second growth (after the hay harvest); (fig) outcome; consequence: (割取第二次长出的)再生草; (喻)结果; 后果; 余波: *Misery is usually the ~math of war.* 苦难通常是战后余殃。'**~·thought** *n* [U] reflection afterwards; [C] thought that comes afterwards. 回想; 反省; 事后才想起来的主意; 事后聪明。

after·noon /ˌɑːftəˈnuːn *US:* ˈæf-; ˌæftɚˈnuːn/ *n* [U, C] time between morning and evening: 下午: *in/during the ~*; *this/yesterday/tomorrow ~*; 今天(昨天, 明天)下午; *every ~*; 每天下午; *on Sunday ~*; 在星期日下午; *on the ~ of May 1st*; 在五月一日的下午; *one ~ last week*; 上星期的一个下午; *on several ~s*; 在几个下午; (attrib) (用作定语) *an ~ sleep/concert.* 午睡(午后演奏会)。

afters /ˈɑːftəz *US:* ˈæf-; ˈæftɚz/ *n pl* (colloq) last (usu sweet) course at a meal: (口)餐席的最后一道菜(通常为甜点): *What's for ~? Is it fruit and custard?* 最后一道菜是什么?是水果和乳蛋糕吗?

after·wards /ˈɑːftəwədz *US:* ˈæf-; ˈæftɚwɚdz/ *adv* after; later. 以后; 后来。

again /əˈɡen; əˈɡɛn/ *adv* **1** once more: 再一次; 再: *If you fail the first time, try ~.* 如果你第一次失败了，再试

一次。*Say it ~, please.* 请再说一遍。*Do you think she will marry ~*, remarry? 你认为她将会再婚吗? *You must type this letter ~*, retype it. 你必须把这封信重打一次。*~ now and ~*, occasionally. 偶尔; 间或。*~ and ~; time and (time) ~*, repeatedly; very often. 一再; 屡次地; 再三。**(the) same ~**, formula for re-ordering, eg a drink. 再来同样的(为再点酒类等的套语)。**2** (with *not*, *never*) any more: (与 not, never 连用)再: *This must never happen ~.* 这样的事情绝不可再度发生。*Don't do that ~.* 别再做那种事。**3** to or in the original condition, position, etc: 恢复原状: *You'll soon be well ~.* 你不久就会康复。*He was glad to be home ~.* 他能够再回到家里感到高兴。*You won't get the money back ~*, won't regain it. 你不会再回那笔钱。**be oneself ~**, be restored to a normal (physical or mental) condition. (指身体或精神)恢复常态。**4** *as many/much ~*, **(a)** the same number/quantity. 同样数目(分量)。**(b)** twice as many/much; the same in addition. 加一倍; 多一倍。*half as many/much/long, etc ~*, half as many/much, etc in addition. 加多(长等)一半。**5** (often preceded by *and* or *and then*) furthermore, besides: (常用于 and 或 and then 之后)再者; 此外; 而且: *Then ~, I feel doubtful whether …* 再者，我感到怀疑是否…

against /əˈɡenst; əˈɡɛnst/ *prep* **1** (indicating opposition): (表示相反): *Public opinion was ~ the proposal.* 舆论反对此建议。Cf 参较 *for, in favour of.* *We were rowing ~ the current.* 我们逆水划船。Cf 参较 *with.* *It was a race ~ time*, an attempt to finish before a certain time, before a possible happening, etc. 那是一项争取时间的努力(赶工，赶时间之意)。*She was married ~ her will.* 她违反本意而结婚。*Is there a law ~ spitting in the streets in this country?* 在这个国家里，有法律禁止在街上吐痰吗? *His appearance is ~ him*, is such that people are unlikely to favour or support him. 他的仪表于他不利。**2** (with *vv* indicating protest): (与动词连用，表示反对): *vote/cry out/write/raise one's voice ~ a proposal.* 投票(高呼，撰文，提高嗓音呼喊)反对一项提议。**3** (with *vv*, to indicate collision or impact): (与动词连用，表示冲突或碰撞): *The rain was beating ~ the windows.* 雨点拍打在窗户上。*He hit his head ~ the wall in the dark cellar.* 他的头在黑暗的地窖中撞到了。*run against at* **run¹(18)**. **4** in contrast to: 衬托; 相映; 对照: *The pine trees were black ~ the morning sky.* 在早晨天空的映照下，那些松树是黑的。**5** in preparation for; in anticipation of: 防备; 预防: *take precautions ~ fire*; 采取防火措施; *an injection ~ rabies*; 狂犬病预防针; *save money ~ a rainy day*, (prov) for a time of possible need. (谚)储蓄金钱，以备不时之需; 未雨绸缪。**6** (indicating support or close proximity): (表示支持或紧靠): *Place the ladder ~ the tree.* 把梯子靠在树上。*Put the piano with its back ~ the wall.* 把钢琴的后背紧靠墙放。*He wcs leaning ~ a post.* 他倚靠在一根柱子上。**7** *over ~*, **(a)** facing, opposite to. 面对; 相对。**(b)** (fig) in contrast with, in addition to. (喻)与…相比; 除…之外。

agape /əˈɡeɪp; əˈɡep/ *pred adj* (facet) with the mouth wide open (owing to wonder, surprise, or a yawn). (玩笑语)(因惊奇，惊愕或打呵欠而)大张着口; 目瞪口呆。

agar-agar /ˈeɪɡɑːr ˈeɪɡɑː(r) *US:* ˌɑːɡ- ˈɑːɡ-; ˈeɡɑr-ˈeɡɑr/ *n* [U] (jelly-like substance prepared from) seaweed. 石花菜; 洋菜(用石花菜制成的一种胶状食品)。

ag·ate /ˈæɡət; ˈæɡɪt/ *n* (sorts of) very hard stone, a form of silica, with bands or patches of colour. 玛瑙。

agave /əˈɡeɪvi; əˈɡevi/ *n* (bot) (kinds of) tropical fleshy-leaved plant (including *sisal*), cultivated for their fibres and as a source of intoxicating drinks, eg *pulque*. (植物)龙舌兰。

age¹ /eɪdʒ; edʒ/ *n* **1** [C] length of time a person has lived or a thing has existed: 年龄; 年纪; 年岁: *What's his age*, How old is he? *Their ages are 4, 7 and 9.* 他们的年龄是四岁，七岁和九岁。*At what age do children start school in your country?* 在你们国家，儿童

几岁开始上学? *What's the age of that old church?* 那座老教堂有多少年了? *When I was your age ....* 当我像你这样年纪时…. *I have a son your age,* a son the same age as you. 我有一个像你这样年纪的儿子。 *She ought to be earning her own living at her age,* She's old enough now to do this. 在她这样的年龄, 她应该自力谋生了。 *be/come of age,* be/become old enough to be responsible in law. 成年。 ⇨ *age of consent* at **consent. be of an age,** reach a stage in life when one ought to do sth: *He's of an age when he ought to be settling down,* eg get a good job, marry. 他已到了安定下来的年龄了(比如说成家立业) *over age,* having passed a certain age or age limit: 超过了某一年龄或某种年龄限制: *He won't be called up for military service;* *he's over age.* 他不会被征召入伍; 他已超过役龄。 ⇨ *age limit* at **limit¹. under age,** too young; not yet of age. 太年轻; 未达规定年龄; 未成年。 **'age-bracket** *n* period of life between two specified ages, eg between 20 and 30. 年龄分类; 年龄范围(例如二十岁至三十岁) **'age-group** *n* number of persons of the same age. 同龄的一群人。 **2** [U] later part of life (contrasted with *youth*): 老年; 晚年 (与 youth 相对): *His back was bent with age.* 他的背因年老而伛偻。 *If we could have the strength of youth and the wisdom of age, ...* 假使我们能够有青年的体力和老年的智慧, …。 **3** [C] great or long period of time, with special characteristics or events: (具有某特征或特殊事件的)时代: *the age of machinery;* 机器时代; *the atomic age;* 原子时代; *the Elizabethan Age,* the time of Queen Elizabeth I of England (1558—1603). 伊利莎白时代 (英国女王伊利莎白一世在位时期, 1558—1603)。 ⇨ *golden age, middle age,* the *Middle Ages,* the *Stone Age* at **golden(2), middle(3), stone(1). 4** [C] (colloq) very long time: (口)很长时间; 很久: *We've been waiting an age/for ages.* 我们已等侯很久了。

age² /eɪdʒ; edʒ/ *vt, vi* (*pres part* **ageing** or **aging,** *pp* **aged** /eɪdʒd; edʒd/) [VP6A, 2A, C] (cause to) grow old: (使)变老: *He's ag(e)ing fast.* 他老得很快。 *I found him greatly aged,* looking much older. 我发现他老得多了。 **aged** /eɪdʒd; edʒd/ *pred adj* of the age of: …岁的: *a boy aged ten.* 十岁的男孩。 □ *attrib adj* /'eɪdʒɪd; 'edʒɪd/ very old: 很老的; 年老的: *an aged man;* 老人; *the poor and the aged,* those who are poor and old. 贫者及老者。 **'aging, 'age-ing** *n* [U] process of growing old; changes that occur as the result of the passing of time. 变老的过程; 因时间过去而发生的变化。 **'age-less** *adj* eternal; always young; not affected by time. 永恒的; 永远年轻的; 不为时间所影响的。 **'age-long** *adj* lasting for centuries; handed down the ages. 延续几世纪的; 源远流长的。 **,age-'old** *adj* that has been known, practised, etc for a long time: 久为人所知, 所施行等的; 古老的: *age-old customs/ceremonies.* 古老的习俗 (礼仪)。

agency /'eɪdʒənsɪ; 'edʒənsɪ/ *n* (*pl* **-cies**) **1** business, place of business, of an agent(1): 经销处; 代理; 经销处: 代理处: *The Company has agencies in all parts of Africa.* 该公司在非洲各地均有代理店。 *He found a job through an employment ~.* 他经由职业介绍所找到一个工作。 *Not all travel agencies are reliable.* 并非所有旅行社都是可靠的。 **2** [U] **the ~ of,** the operation, action of: 动作; 作用; 工具; 力量: *Rocks are worn smooth through the ~ of water.* 岩石由于水的作用而变得光亮。 *He obtained a position in a government office through/by the ~* (= with the help or influence) *of friends.* 他借助于朋友的力量在政府机关里获得了一个职位。

agenda /ə'dʒendə; ə'dʒendə/ *n* [C] **1** (list of) things to be done, business to be discussed, eg by a committee: (委员会等的)待办事项或待讨论事务(表); 议程: *the next item on the ~;* 议程上的次一项目; *item No 5 on the ~.* 议程上的第五项。 **2** (comp) set of operations which form a procedure for solving a problem. (电脑)解决某一问题的一套作业程序。

agent /'eɪdʒənt; 'edʒənt/ *n* **1** person who acts for, or who manages the business affairs of, another or others: 代理人; 代理商; 代办人; 经纪人: a '*house-~,* one who buys, sells, lets and rents houses for the owners; 房产经纪人(代人买卖、租让房屋者); a '*literary ~,* one who helps authors to find a publisher; 著作经纪人 (帮助作家找出版商者); a '*shipping or 'forwarding ~,* one who sends goods by rail, sea, road, etc for merchants, manufacturers, etc. 货运商 (代商人、制造商等经由铁路、海运、公路等运送货品者)。 '*law~,* (in Scotland) lawyer. (苏格兰之)律师; 法律顾问。 ⇨ **free¹(3), secret(1). 2** person used to achieve sth, to get a result; (science) substance, natural phenomenon, etc producing an effect: 用以获得某事物或某一结果的人; 行为者; 动作者; 作用者; (科学)产生某种效果的物质; 自然力; 媒剂; 动因: *Rain and frost are natural ~s that wear away rocks.* 雨和霜都是磨蚀岩石的自然力。

agent pro·vo·ca·teur /ˌæʒɒn prəˌvɒkə'tɜː; ˌɑˈʒɑ-ˌproˌvoˌkaˈtɜːr/ *n* (*pl* **agents provocateurs,** pronunciation unchanged; (复数发音不变) (F) person employed to find suspected criminals or offenders by tempting them to commit an offence openly. (法)受雇诱使嫌疑犯公然犯罪以便加以逮捕之密探。

ag·glom·er·ate /ə'glɒməreɪt; ə'glɑmə,ret/ *vt, vi* [VP6A, 2A] gather, collect, into a mass. 聚结; 结块; 成团; 凝聚。 □ *adj* /ə'glɒmərət; ə'glɑmərɪt/ collected into, forming or growing into, a mass. 聚成成块的; 凝结成团的。 **ag·glom·er·ation** /əˌglɒmə'reɪʃn; ə,glɑmə-'reʃən/ *n* [U] action of agglomerating; [C] (esp untidy) heap or collection of ~d objects, eg a sprawl of untidy suburbs. 聚结; 结块; 成团; 凝聚; 聚集成的一堆 (尤指不整齐者, 例如大城市不规则向外延伸而造成的不整齐的郊区)。

ag·glu·tin·ate /ə'gluːtɪneɪt; ə'glutɪn,et/ *vt, vi* [VP 6A, 2A] join together as with glue; combine. (使)粘合; 胶合; 胶着; 结合。 **ag·glu·ti·nat·ive** /ə'gluːtɪnətɪv US: -tənertɪv; ə'glutn,etɪv/ *adj* (of languages) that combine simple words into compounds without change of form or loss of meaning. (指语言)胶着的(指某些语言可以由简单的词不变其形或义而连缀组成复杂之结合语的现象)。

ag·grand·ize /ə'grændaɪz; 'ægrən,daɪz/ *vt* [VP6A] (formal) increase (in power, rank, wealth, importance). (正式用语)增加(权力, 阶级, 财富, 重要性)。 **ag·grand-ize·ment** /ə'grændɪzmənt; ə'grændɪzmənt/ *n:* *a man bent on personal ~.* 专心致力于扩充个人权势财富的人。

ag·gra·vate /'ægrəveɪt; 'ægrə,vet/ *vt* [VP6A] **1** make worse or more serious: 使恶化; 使更严重: ~ *an illness/offence.* 加重病情(罪过)。 **2** (colloq) irritate: exasperate: (口)激怒; 惹: *He ~s her beyond endurance.* 他使她怒不可遏。 *How aggravating, annoying!* 多么可恼呵! **ag·gra·va·tion** /ˌægrə'veɪʃn; ˌægrə'veʃən/ *n* [U] aggravating or being ~; [C] sth that ~s. 增剧; 恶化; 使恶化之事物。

ag·gre·gate /'ægrɪgeɪt; 'ægrɪ,get/ *vt, vi* [VP6A, 2A] bring or come together in a mass. 聚集; 聚集成团; 凝结。 **2** [VP2E] amount to (specified total). 总计; 合计为(某一总数); 计达。 □ *n* /'ægrɪgət; 'ægrɪgɪt/ **1** total obtained by addition; mass or amount brought together. 合计; 总数; 总量; 聚合体。 *in the ~,* as a whole; collectively. 总计; 合计; 总共。 **2** materials (sand, gravel, etc) mixed with cement to make concrete. 骨材 (与水泥混合成混凝土的材料, 如沙, 砾石等)。 **ag·gre·ga·tion** /ˌægrɪ'geɪʃn; ˌægrɪ'geʃən/ *n* [U] number of separate things, materials, brought together into a mass or group. (由个别事物聚合而成的)集合体; 聚集; 集团。

ag·gres·sion /ə'greʃn; ə'greʃən/ *n* **1** [U] unprovoked hostility when beginning a quarrel or war: 侵略; 攻击: *It was difficult to decide which country was guilty of ~* (*on/upon the other*). 很难判定那一国犯侵略(他国)之罪。 **2** [C] instance of this. 侵略或攻击之实例。

ag·gres·sive /əˈgresɪv; əˈgrɛsɪv/ *adj* **1** quarrelsome; disposed to attack: 好与人争吵的;性好攻击的: *an ~ man;* 好与人争吵的人; *a man with an ~ disposition.* 性好攻击作风的人之人。 **2** offensive; of or for attack: 攻击性的; 侵略的: *~ weapons.* 攻击性的武器。 **3** pushing; not afraid of resistance: 有闯劲的;不怕阻力的: *A man who goes from door to door selling things has to be ~ if he wants to succeed.* 沿门兜售货物的人要想成功, 必须要有闯劲。 *~·ly adv ~·ness n* **ag·gres·sor** /-sə(r); -sɚ/ *n* person, country, making an ~ attack: 侵略者; 侵略国: (attrib) (用作定语) *the aggressor nation.* 侵略国。

ag·grieve /əˈgriːv; əˈgriv/ *vt* (usu passive) grieve: (通常用被动语态)使苦恼;使悲伤: *be ~d.* 感到痛心;悲伤。 *feel (oneself) much ~d (at/over sth),* feel that one has been treated unjustly; be hurt in one's feelings. (为了某事)觉得受了委屈;觉得感情受了伤害。

ag·gro /ˈægrəʊ; ˈægro/ *n* [U] (GB sl) aggression as shown by gangs of teenagers towards members, racial minorities, etc. (英俚) 少年帮派对其他帮派、少数种族等的挑衅行为。

aghast *US:* əˈgæst; əˈgæst/ *pred adj* filled with fear or surprise: 吃惊的;吓呆的: *He stood ~ at the terrible sight.* 他被那个可怕的景象吓呆了。

agile *US:* /ˈædʒaɪl; ˈædʒəl/ *adj* (of living things) quick-moving; active. (指有生命的东西)敏捷的; 灵活的; 活泼的。 *~·ly adv* **agil·ity** /əˈdʒɪlɪtɪ; əˈdʒɪlɪtɪ/ *n* [U].

agin /əˈgɪn; əˈgɪn/ *prep* (used jocularly for) against, (谑)反对,eg in: 例如: *~ the government.* 反对政府。

ag·ing *n* = ageing. ⇨ **age**[2].

agi·tate /ˈædʒɪteɪt; ˈædʒə,tet/ *vt, vi* **1** [VP6A] move or shake (a liquid); stir up (the surface of a liquid): 摇动(液体); 搅动(液体的表面)。 **2** [VP6A] disturb; cause anxiety to (a person, his mind or feelings): 扰乱;激动;使烦乱: *She was deeply ~d until she learnt that her husband was among the survivors.* 她十分焦急, 直到她听说她的丈夫在生还者之列, 她才放心。 *He was ~d about his wife's health.* 他为妻子的健康担忧。 **3** [VP3A] *~ for,* argue publicly in favour of, take part in a campaign for: 煽动; 鼓动; 鼓吹: *~ for the repeal of a law;* 鼓吹废止某项法律: *workers who ~d for higher wages.* 鼓动加薪的工人。 **agi·tated** *part adj* troubled; 烦恼的; 焦虑的。 **agi·tat·ing** *part adj* causing anxiety. 令人焦虑的。 **agi·ta·tion** /ˌædʒɪˈteɪʃn; ˌædʒəˈteʃən/ *n* **1** [U] moving or shaking (of a liquid). (对液体之) 摇动; 搅动。 **2** [U] excitement of the mind or feelings; anxiety: 激动; 烦乱; 心焦; 忧虑: *She was in a state of agitation.* 她处于激动的状态当中。 **3** [C, U] discussion or debate (for the purpose of bringing about a change); [U] social or political unrest or trouble caused by such discussion: (为改革而作的)讨论或辩论; 鼓吹(改革); 煽动; (因受鼓动而引起的社会或政治的)不安; 骚动: *Small shopkeepers carried on a long agitation against the big department stores.* 小本商人进行了很久的激辩, 反对大百货公司。 **agi·ta·tor** /-tə(r); -tɚ/ *n* person who ~s, esp politically. 鼓动者; (尤指政治方面的)煽动者。

aglow /əˈgləʊ; əˈglo/ *pred adj* **1** bright with colour; in a glow: 发光彩的; 发红光的: *The sky was ~ with the setting sun.* 天空因夕阳映照而发红光。 **2** (of persons) showing warmth from exercise or excitement: (指人)(因运动或兴奋而)发热的: *~ with pleasure;* 因高兴而发热; *shining:* 发光的: *a face ~ with health.* 因健康而红光满面。

ag·nail /ˈægneɪl; ˈæg,nel/ *n* [U] torn skin at the base of a finger nail. 逆剥; (指甲旁的)倒刺。

ag·nos·tic /ægˈnɒstɪk; ægˈnɑstɪk/ *n* person who believes that nothing can be known about God or of anything except material things. (对于神或物质以外的事物持)不可知论者。 □ *adj* of this belief. 不可知论的。 **ag·nos·ti·cism** /ægˈnɒstɪsɪzəm; ægˈnɑstə,sɪzəm/ *n* [U] this belief. 不可知论。

ago /əˈgəʊ; əˈgo/ *adv* (used to indicate time measured back to a point in the past; always placed after the word or words it modifies; used with the simple *pt*): (用以指从现在倒算到过去某一点之时间; 永远置于所修饰之字或词之后; 与简单过去式连用) …以前: *The train left a few minutes ago/not long ago.* 火车在几分钟(不久)以前开走了。 *That was many years ago/a long while ago.* 那是许多年(很久)以前的事了。 *How long ago is it that you last saw her?* 你上一次看见她是多久以前的事? *I met Mary no longer ago than* (= as recently as) *last Sunday.* 我就在上个星期天还遇见过玛莉。 *It was seven years ago that my brother died.* 我哥哥(弟弟)是七年以前死的。 Cf 参较 *It is seven years since my brother died.* 我哥哥(弟弟)去世于今已七年了。

agog /əˈgɒg; əˈgɑg/ *pred adj* eager; excited: 渴望的; 急切的; 兴奋的; 激动的: *~ for news;* 渴望听到消息; *~ to hear the news.* 急着要听那消息。 *The whole village was ~.* 全村的人都很兴奋。 *His unexpected return set the town ~,* eg was the cause of many rumours about the reasons for his return. 他意外的回来惊动了全镇的人(例如纷纷揣测他何以回来)。

ag·ony /ˈægənɪ; ˈægənɪ/ *n* (*pl* **-nies**) [U, C] great pain or suffering (of mind or body): (精神或肉体上的)极大的痛苦; *She looked on in ~ at her child's sufferings.* 她在旁痛苦地看着她的孩子受苦。 *I've suffered agonies/have been in agonies with toothache.* 我受到牙痛之苦。 *He was in an ~ of remorse.* 他处于悔恨的痛苦中。 **'~ column,** newspaper column with advertisements for news of missing friends, etc. (报纸上的)寻人广告栏(刊载寻友等之广告者)。 *pile on the ~,* (colloq) (口) ⇨ **pile**[2](1). **ag·on·ized** /ˈægənaɪzd; ˈægə,naɪzd/ *adj* expressing ~: 表示痛苦的: *agonized shrieks.* 痛苦的尖叫声。 **ag·on·iz·ing** /ˈægənaɪzɪŋ; ˈægə,naɪzɪŋ/ *adj* 引起痛苦的。

agora /ˈægərə; ˈægərə/ *n* (in ancient Greece) (place of) assembly; market-place. (古希腊之)民众大会 (场): 市场。 *~·phobia* /ˌægərəˈfəʊbɪə; ˌægərəˈfobɪə/ *n* [U] fear of (crossing) open spaces. 空旷恐怖; 广场恐怖; 空室恐怖。

agrar·ian /əˈgreərɪən; əˈgrɛrɪən/ *adj* of land (esp farmland) or land ownership: 土地的; (尤指)耕地的; 土地所有权的: *~ laws/problems/reforms/disputes.* 土地法(问题,改革,纠纷)。

agree /əˈgriː; əˈgri/ *vi, vt* **1** [VP2A, 3A, B] *~ (to),* say 'Yes'; consent: 同意;答应;允诺: *I asked him to help me and he ~d.* 我请他帮忙, 他答应了。 *Mary's father has ~d to her marrying John.* 玛莉的父亲已同意她嫁给约翰。 *He ~d to my proposal.* 他已同意我的提议。 **2** [VP3A, B, 4C, 7A] (also with an *inf* or a *that*-clause without a *prep*) be of the same opinion(s); be in harmony (*with sb on/about* sth, *as to* how to do sth, etc): (亦与不定词或 *that* 从句连用而不用介词)同意; 意见一致; (后接 *with* 某人, *on* 或 about 某事物, *as to* 如何做某事等): *We ~d to start early.* 我们同意早动身。 *I hope you will ~ with me that our teacher's advice is excellent.* 我希望你会同意我的意见, 认为我们的老师的劝告非常好。 *We all ~d on the terms.* 我们大家都同意这些条件。 *We ~d on an early start/on making an early start/that we should start early/to start early.* 我们同意早动身。 *We met at the ~d time,* at the time we had ~d on. 我们在约定的时间碰面了。 *We are* (= have) *all ~d on finding the accused man innocent.* 我们大家一致认为被告无罪。 *We are all ~d that the proposal is a good one.* 我们大家一致认为这是一项好的提议。 *We could not ~* (as to) *how it should be done.* 关于这事应如何做法, 我们大家意见不能一致。 *Have you ~d about the price yet?* 关于价钱你们的意见已经一致了吗? **3** [VP 2 A, C] (of two or more persons) be happy together; get on well with one another (without arguing, etc): (指两个以上的人)合得来; 和睦相处; 意气相投: *We shall never ~.* 我们将永不会合得来。 *Why can't you children ~ (together)?* 你们小孩子为什么不能在一起和谐相处呢? **4** [VP3A] *~*

(with), match, conform (with): 与…相配; 与…符合: *Your story ~s with what I had already heard.* 你所说的跟我所听到的相符。*This bill does not ~ with your original estimate, the two are different.* 这帐单与你原来的估计不符合。**5** [VP3A] **~ with,** suit, eg the health or constitution of: 适宜于…的健康或体质: *The climate doesn't ~ with me.* 这气候对我不相宜。*The mussels I had for lunch haven't ~d with me,* have upset my stomach. 我中餐所吃的淡菜不合我的胃口。**6** [VP3A] **~ with,** (gram) correspond in number, person, etc with: (语法)(在数, 人称等方面)与…一致: *The verb ~s with its subject in number and person.* 动词的数和人称与其主语一致。**7** [VP6A] (of figures, accounts, proposals, etc) accept or approve (as being correct): 认可(数字, 帐目, 提议等): *The Inspector of Taxes has ~d your return of income.* 税务稽查员已经认可你的所得税申报表。

agree·able /ə'griːəbl; ə'griəbl/ *adj* **1** pleasing; giving pleasure: 令人喜悦的; 令人愉快的; 宜人的: *She has an ~ voice.* 她的声音悦耳。**2** ready to agree: 准备同意的; 欣然同意的: *Are you ~ to the proposal?* 你能同意这提议吗? *I'm ~ to doing what you suggest.* 我同意照你的建议去做。**agree·ably** /-əbli; -əbli/ *adv:* 喜悦地; 愉快地: *I was agreeably surprised,* surprised and pleased. 我又惊又喜。

agree·ment /ə'griːmənt; ə'grimənt/ *n* **1** [U] having the same opinion(s); thinking in the same way: 同意; 意见一致: *We are in ~ on that point.* 关于那一点我们的意见一致。*I'm quite in ~ with what you say.* 我十分同意你所说的话。*There is no ~ upon/about what should be done.* 应该怎么办, 大家意见不一。**2** [C] arrangement or understanding (spoken or written) made by two or more persons; groups, business companies, governments, etc: (两个以上的人, 团体, 公司, 政府等所做口头或书面的)协议; 协定; 合同; 合约: *sign an ~;* 签订合约/ *~ to rent a house.* 租屋契约。**come to/arrive at/ make/reach an ~ (with sb),** reach an understanding. (与某人)达成协议; 商定。

ag·ri·cul·ture /'ægrɪkʌltʃə(r); 'ægrɪˌkʌltʃə/ *n* [U] science or practice of farming; cultivation of the soil. 农学; 农业; 农事; 农耕。**ag·ri·cul·tural** /ˌægrɪ'kʌltʃərəl; ˌægrɪ'kʌltʃərəl/ *adj* of ~: 农业的: *agricultural workers.* 农业工人; 农业工作者。

aground /ə'graʊnd; ə'graʊnd/ *adv, pred adj* (of ships) touching the bottom in shallow water: (指船)搁浅: *The ship went ~/was fast ~/ran ~.* 该船搁浅(不能动了)。

ague /'eɪgjuː; 'egju/ *n* [U, C] fever. 疟状发热。

ah /ɑː; ɑ/ *int* cry of surprise, pity, etc. 啊(表示惊愕, 怜悯等之感叹词)。

aha /ɑː'hɑː; ɑ'hɑ/ *int* cry of surprise, triumph, satisfaction, etc, according to context. 啊哈(表示惊愕, 胜利, 满足等之感叹词, 视上下文而定)。

ahead /ə'hed; ə'hed/ *adv ~ (of),* in front; in advance: 在前面; 在前头: *Tom was a quick walker and soon got ~ of the others.* 汤姆是一个健步者, 不久就走到别人前头去了。*He ran on ~.* 他跑在前面。*Standard time in Turkey is two hours ~ of Greenwich Mean Time.* 土耳其的标准时间, 比格林威治标准时间早两小时。*Full speed ~!* Go forward at full speed! 全速前进! **go ~,** **(a)** make progress: 进步; 进行: *Things are going ~.* 一切事情都在进行。**(b)** (colloq, also *do* *fire ~*) continue (with what you're about to say or do). (口)(指你正要说的话或正要做的事)继续下去。*in line ~,* (of warships) moving forward, anchored, in a column or file. (指军舰)成纵列前进或停泊。**look ~,** (fig) think of and prepare for future needs. (喻)为未来着想或打算; 未雨绸缪。

ahem /ə'hem; ə'hɛm/ *int* (usu spelling form of the) noise made when clearing the throat; noise made to give a slight warning or to call sb's attention. 啊哼(清喉咙的声音; 表示小小的警告或促使某人注意的声音)。

ahoy /ə'hɔɪ; ə'hɔɪ/ *int* greeting or warning cry used by seamen. 啊嗬; 喂(水手所用打招呼或警告的喊声)。

aid /eɪd; ed/ *vt* [VP6A, 17, 14] help: 帮助; 援助: *aid one another;* 彼此帮助; *aid sb to do sth;* 帮助某人做某事; *aid sb with money.* 以金钱帮助某人。□ *n* **1** [U] help: 帮助; 援助: *aid programmes,* those designed to give help, eg to developing countries. 援助计划(例如对发展中国家的援助)。*He came to my aid,* came to help me. 他来帮助我。*What is the collection in aid of,* What is the money to be used for? 所募集的款子将作何用途? ⇨ **first¹(2), legal. 2** [C] sth that helps. 有助之物。**visual aids,** pictures, films, film-strips, etc used in teaching. 视觉教具(如图片, 影片, 幻灯片等)。**'hearing-aid,** appliance that helps a deaf person to hear. (聋者所用的)助听器。

aide-de-camp /ˌeɪd də 'kɒm *US:* 'kæmp; ˌedde-'kæmp/ *n* (*pl* **aides-de-camp** pronunciation unchanged) naval or military officer who helps a superior by carrying orders, etc. (复数发音不变)副官; 侍从武官。

aide-mémoire /ˌeɪd mem'wɑː(r); ˌed,mem'wɑr/ *n* **1** (in diplomacy) memorandum. (外交)备忘录。**2** document, list etc to remind sb of sth. 备忘之文件、名单等。

aigrette, aigret /'eɪgret *US:* ˌeɪ'gret; 'egrɛt/ *n* tuft of feathers worn as an ornament on the head; spray of gems or jewels in imitation of this. 用做头饰的羽毛; 羽毛状珠宝首饰。

ail /eɪl; el/ *vt* **1** [VP6A] (old use) trouble: (旧用法)使烦恼; 使苦恼: *What ails him,* What's wrong with him, What's troubling him? 什么事使他烦恼? 他有什么烦恼? **2** [VP2A, B] be ill: 生病; 有病: *The children are always ailing,* always in poor health. 孩子们总是生病。

aileron /'eɪlərɒn; 'elə,rɑn/ *n* hinged part of the wing of an aircraft that helps to balance the aircraft and control ascent and descent. (飞机翼上帮助平衡飞机及控制升降的)副翼。⇨ the illus at **aircraft.** 参看 aircraft 之插图。

ail·ment /'eɪlmənt; 'elmənt/ *n* [C] illness. 疾病。

aim¹ /eɪm; em/ *vt, vi* **1** [VP6A, 14, 2A] *aim (at),* **(a)** point (a gun, etc) towards: 以(枪炮等)对准; 瞄准: *aim a gun at sb.* 以枪瞄准某人。*He aimed (his gun) at the lion, fired and missed.* 他瞄准那狮子, 放枪, 未打中。**(b)** send, direct, eg a blow, object (at sb or sth): 打击; 掷击(与 at 连用): *Tom got angry with his brother and aimed a heavy book at his head.* 汤姆对他的哥哥(弟弟)发怒, 拿起一本厚书向他的头掷去。(fig)(喻) *My remarks were not aimed at you.* 我的话不是针对你而发。**2** [VP3A, *aim at doing sth;* US 美 VP4A, *aim to do sth*] have as a plan or intention: 计划; 打算; 以…为目标: *Harry aims at becoming/to become a doctor.* 哈里立志要做医生。*What are you aiming at?* 你的意向如何?

aim² /eɪm; em/ *n* **1** [U] act of aiming, eg with a gun: (以枪等)对准; 瞄准: *Take careful aim at the target.* 仔细瞄准靶子。*He missed his aim,* did not hit the target. 他未击中标的。**2** [C] purpose; object: 目标; 目的: *What's your aim in life,* what do you want to do or be? 你的人生目标是什么? *He has only one aim in life—to be a millionaire.* 他只有一个人生目标——成为百万富翁。**aim·less** *adj* having no purpose: 无目标的; 无定向的: *an aimless life/task/journey.* 无目的的生活(工作, 旅行)。**aim·less·ly** *adv:* 无目的地: *wandering aimlessly about the town.* 在镇上无目的地游逛。

ain't /eɪnt; ent/ (vulg) contracted form of *are/is/am not,* and *have/has not:* (鄙)为 are not, is not, am not, have not, 及 has not 的缩写: *I ~ going.* 我不去。*We ~ got any.* 我们一点也没有。

air¹ /eə(r); ɛr/ *n* **1** [U] the mixture of gases that surrounds the earth and which we breathe: 空气: *Let's go out and have some fresh air.* 我们出去吸点新鲜空气

吧. *in the air*, (a) uncertain: 不定的; 未定的: *My plans are still quite in the air.* 我的计划还未定案. (b) (of opinions, etc) spreading about: (指意见等)传播的; 散布的: *There are rumours in the air that ....* 有谣言传说…. (c) (mil) uncovered, unprotected: 无掩蔽的; 无援护的: *Their left flank was left in the air.* 他们的左翼无掩护. *clear the air*, (a) make the air (in a room, etc) fresh again. 使(室内等之)空气恢复新鲜. (b) (fig) get rid of suspicion, doubt, etc by giving facts, etc. (喻)提出事实等以澄清疑虑. ⇨ also **castle, hot (8)**. 2 [U] the atmosphere as a place for aircraft to fly in; (attrib) of flying, aircraft, etc: 大气; (用作定语)飞行的; 飞机的; 航空的: *air freight／transport／travel.* 空运货物(航空运输, 乘飞机旅行). *by air*, in an aircraft: 乘飞机; 以空运: *travel by air*; 乘飞机旅行; *send goods by air.* 以航空空运货. 3 [U] (radio)(无线电) *on the air*, broadcasting: 广播: *Radio Lichtenburg is on the air 24 hours a day.* 利希滕堡广播电台全天二十四小时广播. *off the air*, not broadcasting. 停止广播. *come／go on the air*, start broadcasting. 开始广播. *come／go off the air*, stop broadcasting. 停止广播. *Why has that station gone off the air?* 那个电台为什么停止广播? 4 [C] (liter, naut) breeze, light wind. (文, 航海)微风. 5 [C] (old use) tune, melody. (旧用法)歌调; 曲调; 旋律. 6 [C] (a) appearance; manner: 容貌; 外表; 态度: *He has an air of importance*, seems to be, looks, important. 他有一种很了不起的样子. *The house has an air of comfort.* 这房子看起来象很舒适的样子. (b) (usu pl) (通常用复数) *give oneself／put on airs*, behave in an unnatural way in the hope of impressing people. 摆架子; 装腔作势. *airs and graces*, foolish, exaggerated ways of behaving. 装腔作势. 7 (compounds and attrib uses) (复合词及用作定语) **'air·bed** n mattress inflated with air. 气床垫. **'air-bladder** n (in animals and plants, esp seaweed) bladder filled with air. (动物及植物, 尤指海藻体内之)鳔; 气胞. **'air·borne** adj (a) transported by air. 空运的. (b) (of an aircraft) having taken off; in flight: (指飞机)已起飞的; 飞行中的: *We were soon airborne.* 我们不久就升空了. (c) (of troops) specially trained for air operations: (指军队)受特别训练以适于空中活动的; 空降的: *an airborne division.* 空降师. **'air·brake** n brake worked by compressed air. 气动制动器; (空)气煞车; 风闸. **Air (,Chief) 'Marshal, Air 'Commodore** nn highest ranks in the R A F. (英国皇家空军)空军大元帅; 空军准将. **'air-conditioned** adj (of a room, building, railway coach, etc) supplied with air that is purified and kept at a certain temperature and degree of humidity. (指房间, 建筑物, 火车车厢等)装有空气调节设备的; 有冷气设备的. **'air-conditioning** n this process. 冷气设备. **,air-'cooled** adj cooled by a current of air. 空气冷却的. **'air cover** n force of aircraft used to protect a military or naval operation, eg an invasion. 空中掩护 (掩护陆海军作战的空军掩护机群, 如在进攻时使用者). **'air·craft** n (sing or collective pl) aeroplane(s); airship(s). (单数或集合复数)航空器; 飞机; 飞艇; 飞船. ⇨ the illus at the end of **air**[1]. 参看 air[1] 末尾之插图. **'air·craft car·rier** n ship built to carry aircraft, with a long, wide deck for taking off and landing. 航空母舰. **'air·craft·man** /-men/ ;-men/ n lowest non-commissioned rank in the RAF. (英国皇家空军)空军兵. **'air·crew** n crew of an aircraft. 空勤人员 (一架飞机上的全体飞行人员). **'air cushion** n one inflated with air. 气垫; 气褥; 气枕. **'air-cushion vehicle** n vehicle or craft of the hovercraft type. 气垫式船或车. ⇨ the illus at **hover-craft**. 参看 hovercraft 之插图. **'air·drome** n (US) aerodrome. (美)飞机场. **'air drop** n dropping (of men, supplies) by parachutes from aircraft. (部队, 人员, 供应品之)空降; 空投. **'air duct** n device, eg in an aircraft or a ship's cabin, for directing a flow of air for the comfort of passengers. 通风设备(飞机, 船舱等中为旅客舒适而装置之通气管). **'air·field** n area of open,

level ground, with hangars, workshops, offices, etc for operations of (esp military) aircraft. 飞机场 (尤指军用机场). **'air·flow** n flow of air over the surfaces of an aircraft in flight. 气流(通过飞行中之飞机表面的空气之流动). **(an／the) 'air force** n (with sing or pl v) (与单数或复数动词连用) the part of a country's military forces that is organized for fighting in aircraft: 空军: (GB) (英) the *Royal Air Force (RAF)*. 皇家空军. **'air-frame** n complete structure of an aircraft without the engine(s). 飞机机架(不包括引擎). **'air gun** n gun in which compressed air is used to propel the charge. 气枪. **'air hostess** n stewardess in an airliner. (服务于客机中的)女服务员; 空中小姐. **'air letter** n sheet of light paper (to be) folded and sent, without an envelope, cheaply by airmail. 航空信; 航空邮简. **'air lift** n large-scale transport of persons or supplies by air, esp in an emergency. (尤指紧急时期之)人员或物资的大规模空运; 空中补给; 空运. **'air·line** n regular service of aircraft for public use. 航空公司. **'air·liner** n passenger-carrying aircraft. 航空公司的客机; 班机. **'air lock** n (a) (bubble of air in a pipe causing) stoppage in the flow of liquid. 使管中液体停止流动的气泡; 由此气泡引起的液体的停止流动; 气锁; 气塞. (b) compartment with air-tight doors at each end. 气密室; 不通空气的小室. **'air·mail** n [U] mail (to be) carried by air: 航空邮件: *'airmail edition*, (of newspapers, periodicals) printed on thin light paper for sending by airmail. (指报纸, 期刊)(用薄而轻之纸印刷以便航空寄之)航空版. **'air·man** /-men/ ;-men/ n man who flies in an aircraft as a member of the crew, esp a pilot; (RAF) man of any rank up to and including a Warrant Officer. 航空兵; 空勤组员; (尤指)飞行员; 驾驶员; (英国皇家空军)准尉或准尉以下任何一级的空军士兵. **,air-'minded** adj looking upon flying as a normal and necessary method of transport. 赞成航空运输的; 热心航空事业的. **'air pillow** n air cushion. 气垫; 气褥; 气枕. **'air·plane** n (US) aeroplane. (美)飞机. **'air pocket** n atmospheric condition (partial vacuum) causing an aircraft to drop some distance: 气穴; 气潭; 气阱(大气中的一种半真空状态, 可使飞机突然下降者): *We had a bumpy flight because of air pockets.* 我们的飞行甚为颠簸, 因为遇到了一些气穴. **'air·port** n public flying ground for commercial use by airliners. 民航飞机场; 航空站. **'air-pump** n pump for exhausting a vessel of its air. 气泵; 排气唧筒; 抽气机. **'air raid** n attack by aircraft that drop bombs; 空袭; (attrib, with hyphen): (用作定语, 加连字符): *air-raid warnings／precautions*; 空袭警报(预防措施); *air-raid warden*, person in charge of air-raid precautions. (应付空袭之)民防队长. **'air rifle** n = air gun. **'air·screw** n aircraft propeller. 飞机之推进器; 螺旋桨. ⇨ the illus at **screw**. 参看 screw 之插图. **,air-,sea 'rescue** n organization for, work of, rescuing airmen and passengers from the sea, eg by the use of motorboats or helicopters. 海空救护队; 海空救援 (在海上用汽艇或直升机等救助失事飞机的机员及乘客). **'air-shaft** n passage for air into a mine. (矿坑的)通风井. **'air·ship** n gas-filled flying-machine with engine(s). 飞艇; 飞船. ⇨ **balloon, dirigible**. **'air space** n part of the earth's atmosphere above a country: 空域; 领空: *violation of our air space by military aircraft.* 军机之侵犯我们的领空. **'air speed** n speed of an aircraft relative to the air through which it is moving. 空速(航空器经过空气之速度). **'air-strip** n strip of ground for the use of aircraft, esp one made for use in war or in an emergency. 航空短跑道; 飞机跑道(尤指战时或紧急时期所开辟的临时狭长跑道). **'air terminal** n terminus (in a town or city centre) to or from which passengers, etc travel to or from an airport. (城市中心区的)航空站(乘客往返于飞机场之间的集散处). **'air-tight** adj not allowing air to enter or escape. 不透气的; 气密的; 密闭的. **,air-to-'air** adj (of missiles) fired from one aircraft against another. (指导弹)空对空的. **,air-to-'ground**

LIGHT AIRCRAFT

COMBAT AIRCRAFT (jet-fighter and bomber)

aircraft

adj fired from an aircraft to hit a target on the ground. 空对地的. '**air umbrella** *n* = air cover. '**air·way** *n* route regularly followed by airliners; *(pl)* company operating a service of airliners: (民航班机所经常航行的)航空线; (复)航空公司: *British Airways*. 英国航空公司. '**air·woman** *n* (WRAF) woman of any rank up to and including a Warrant Officer. (英国皇家空军妇女队)准尉以下各级之空军女士兵. '**air·worthy** *adj* (of aircraft) fit to fly; in good working order. (指飞机)适航的; 适于飞行的; 机械运转情况良好的. '**air·worthiness** *n*

air² /eə(r); ɛr/ *vt* [VP 6 A] **1** put (clothing, bedding, etc) into the open air or into a warm place to make it quite dry: (将衣服、被褥等置于户外或热的处所)吹风; 晾干; 晒干: *The mattress needs to be aired.* 这个床垫需要拿出去晾一晾. **2** let air into (a room, etc). 让空气进入(房间等); 使通风. **3** cause others to know (one's opinions, a grievance, etc): 表示; 炫耀; 使人知道(自己的意见, 冤屈等): *He likes to air his knowledge, let people see how much he knows.* 他喜欢炫耀他的知识. **air·ing** /'eərɪŋ; 'ɛrɪŋ/ *n*: give sth an airing, expose it to the air or to a fire; 将某物晾晒或置于火旁烘烤; *go for an airing, take the children for an airing*, out in the fresh air. 到外面散步, 带小孩子们出去散散步. '**airing-cupboard** *n* warmed cupboard in which to keep bed-linen, towels, etc. (贮藏被褥、浴巾等之)暖橱.

Aire·dale /'eədeɪl; 'ɛr,del/ *n* large rough-coated terrier (kind of dog). 一种粗毛大狗.

air·less /'eəlɪs; 'ɛrlɪs/ *adj* **1** not having enough fresh air; stuffy: 无充分新鲜空气的; 空气不流通的; 通风不良的: *an ～ room.* 空气不流通的房间. **2** (of the weather) calm; still: (指天气)无风的; 平静的: *Isn't it ～ this evening!* 今天晚上的天气不是很平静吗!

airy /'eərɪ; 'ɛrɪ/ *adj* **1** having plenty of fresh air moving through it: 空气流通的: *a nice ～ room.* 一个空气流通的好房间. **2** of or like air, immaterial. 空气的; 似空气的; 无实质的. **3** not sincere; superficial: 不诚恳的; 表面的; 虚伪的: *～ promises,* unlikely to be kept;

虚伪的允诺; *an ～ manner,* careless and light-hearted. 无忧无虑而愉快的样子. **air·ily** /'eərəlɪ; 'ɛrəlɪ/ *adv*

aisle /aɪl; aɪl/ *n* **1** passage in a church, esp one that is divided by a row of columns from the nave; (in a small church) passage between rows of pews (= seats). 教堂中之走廊(尤指与正厅隔以柱列者); (小教堂中两排座位之间的)通道. ⇨ the illus at **church**. 参看 church 之插图. **2** (US) passage between any rows of seats, eg in a theatre or railway coach; any long and narrow passageway. (美)(两排座位之间的)通道(如戏院或火车车厢中者); 任何狭长的通道.

aitch /eɪtʃ; etʃ/ *n* the letter H. 英文字母 H. *drop one's ～s,* fail to utter the sound /h/ at the beginning of a word, eg by saying '*at for* hat. 未能发 /h/ 音(例如, 将 hat 发成 'at 音). '**～-bone** *n* (cut of beef over the) bone of the rump. 牛之臀骨; (指从牛之臀骨上切下之)臀部肉.

ajar /ə'dʒɑː(r); ə'dʒɑr/ *pred adj* (of doors) slightly open. (指门)半开; 微开.

akim·bo /ə'kɪmbəʊ; ə'kɪmbo/ *adv with arms ～,* with the hands on the hips and elbows bent outwards. 两手叉腰.

akin /ə'kɪn; ə'kɪn/ *pred adj ～ (to),* of similar character; like: 同性质的; 类似的: *Pity is often ～ to love.* 怜悯常近乎爱.

ala·bas·ter /'æləbɑːstə(r); 'ælə,bæstɚ/ US: -bæs-; 'ælə,bæstɚ/ *n* [U] soft, white stone like marble in appearance, used for ornaments. 雪花石膏(貌似大理石之软质白石, 用做装饰品). □ *adj* like *～* in smoothness and whiteness. 似雪花石膏的; 光滑白润的.

à la carte /ɑː lɑː 'kɑːt; ,ɑlə'kɑrt/ *adv* (F) (of meals) ordered from a list, course by course, not at a fixed price for the complete meal (as for *table d'hôte*). (法)(指在餐馆里吃饭)照菜单上点菜 (为客饭, 和菜或定餐之对).

alack /ə'læk; ə'læk/ *int* (old use) cry of regret or sorrow. (旧用法)表示惋惜或悲伤的感叹词.

alac·rity /ə'lækrətɪ; ə'lækrətɪ/ *n* [U] eager and

cheerful readiness. 欣然; 乐意; 敏捷.

à la mode /ˌɑː lɑːˈməʊd; ˌɑːləˈmoʊd/ *adv* (F) according to the latest fashion, ideas, etc; (US) served with ice-cream: (法)按照最时兴的样式、观念等; 时髦地; (美)(指甜点)加上冰淇淋: *apple pie* ~. 苹果饼加冰淇淋.

alarm /əˈlɑːm; əˈlɑrm/ *n* **1** [C] (sound or signal giving a) warning of danger; apparatus used to give such a warning: 警报; 警报之声音或讯号; 警报器: *a 'fire* ~. 火警警报. *give/raise/sound the* ~, ring a bell or in other ways send out a warning signal. 摇警报器; 发警报(如敲钟等). '~ (-clock) *n* clock that can be set to ring a bell or sound a buzzer at a fixed time to waken a sleeping person: 闹钟: *set the* ~(-clock) *for six o'clock.* 把闹钟拨在六点上。 **2** [U] fear and excitement caused by the expectation of danger: 惊慌; 恐慌: *He jumped up in* ~. 他惊慌地跳了起来. *I hope you didn't take/feel* ~ *at the news.* 我希望你没有因为听到那个消息而感到惊慌. □ *vt* [VP6A] give a warning or feeling of danger to; cause anxiety to: 警告; 使惊骇; 使恐慌; 使忧虑: *The noise of the shot* ~ed *hundreds of birds.* 枪声惊动了千百只鸟. *Everybody was* ~ed *at the news that war might break out.* 人人听到了战事可能爆发的消息都感到恐慌. ~**·ing** *part adj* causing ~. 惊人的; 吓人的. ~**·ist** /-ɪst; -ɪst/ *adj, n* (person) raising ~s with little cause. 大惊小怪的(人).

alas /əˈlæs; əˈlæs/ *int* cry of sorrow or regret. 唉; 哎呀(表示悲哀或惋惜的感叹词).

alb /ælb; ælb/ *n* white vestment reaching to the feet, worn by some Christian priests at ceremonies. (某些基督教牧师或天主教神父在典礼时所穿的长及足部之)白袍. ⇨ the illus at **vestment**. 参看 vestment 之插图.

al·ba·tross /ˈælbətrɒs; ˈælbəˌtrɔs/ *n* large, white, web-footed seabird, common in the Pacific and Southern Oceans. 信天翁(白色蹼足大海鸟, 常见于太平洋及南半球各海洋). ⇨ the illus at **water**. 参看 water 之插图.

al·beit /ˌɔːlˈbiːɪt; ɔlˈbiɪt/ *conj* (formal) though(1). (正式用语)虽然().

al·bino /ælˈbiːnəʊ US: -ˈbaɪ-; ælˈbaɪno/ *n* (*pl* ~s /-nəʊz; -noz/) animal or human being born without natural colouring matter in the skin and hair (which are white) and the eyes (which are pink). 白公; 白化动物者(生来其皮肤、毛发及眼睛即缺乏天然色素之动物或人, 肤发呈白色, 眼睛呈粉红色).

al·bum /ˈælbəm; ˈælbəm/ *n* **1** blank book in which a collection of photographs, autographs, postage stamps, etc can be kept. 相片簿; 签名纪念册; 集邮册(等). **2** holder for a set of discs; long-playing record with several pieces by the same musician(s), singer(s). (装一套唱片, 某音乐家之演奏专辑, 某歌星之歌辑之)唱片簿; 唱片集.

al·bu·men /ˈælbjuːmɪn; ælˈbjumən/ *n* [U] **1** white of egg. 蛋白。**2** substance as in white of egg, part of animal and vegetable matter. 蛋白质.

al·chem·ist /ˈælkɪmɪst; ˈælkəmɪst/ *n* person who studied or practised alchemy. 炼金术士.

al·chemy /ˈælkɪmɪ; ˈælkəmɪ/ *n* [U] chemistry of the Middle Ages, the chief aim of which was to discover how to change ordinary metals into gold. (中古时代企图将普通金属变成金的)炼金术.

al·co·hol /ˈælkəhɒl US: -hɔːl; ˈælkəˌhɔl/ *n* **1** [U] (pure, colourless liquid present in) such drinks as beer, wine, brandy, whisky. 酒精(存在于各种酒类, 如啤酒, 葡萄酒, 白兰地, 威士忌等中之纯净无色液体); 酒. **2** [U, C] (chem) large group of compounds of the same type as ~(1). (化学)(乙)醇类. ~**·ic** /ˌælkəˈhɒlɪk US: -ˈhɔːl-; ˌælkəˈhɔlɪk/ *adj* of or containing ~. 酒精的. □ *n* person addicted to ~ic drink. 酒精中毒者; 酗酒者. ~**·ism** /-ɪzəm; -ˌɪzəm/ *n* [U] addiction to ~ic drink; diseased condition caused by ~. 酗酒; 酒精中毒.

al·cove /ˈælkəʊv; ˈælkov/ *n* recess; partially enclosed extension of a room, often occupied by a bed or by seats; similar space within a garden enclosure. 壁凹(大房间内之凹形小室, 常置床或椅于此); (花园中)小亭.

al·der /ˈɔːldə(r); ˈɔldə/ *n* tree of the birch family, usu growing in marshy places. 赤杨 (桦树属, 通常生长于沼泽地带).

al·der·man /ˈɔːldəmən; ˈɔldəmən/ *n* (*pl* -**men** /-mən/) senior member of a city or borough council in England and Ireland, next in rank to a mayor, elected by fellow councillors. (英格兰及爱尔兰之)市议员 (地位次于市长, 由其他议员所选出者). ~**ic** /ˌɔːldəˈmænɪk; ˌɔldəˈmænɪk/ *adj*

ale /eɪl; el/ *n* [U] (GB) (kind of) beer; (英)(一种)啤酒; (old use) = beer. 麦酒 (旧用法). ⇨ also **ginger.** '**ale-house** *n* (old name for) public house. 酒馆 (public house 之旧名).

alee /əˈliː; əˈli/ *adv*, *pred adj* (naut) at, on, towards, the lee or sheltered side of a ship. (航海)在下风处; 向下风.

alert /əˈlɜːt; əˈlɜt/ *adj* watchful; fully awake; lively: 留心的; 警觉的; 清醒的; 机警的; 灵活的: ~ *in answering questions.* 留心回答问题. □ *n* **1** *on the* ~, on the look-out (*for* sth, *against* an attack, etc, *to do* sth). 注意; 提防; 小心(后接 for 某事物, against 攻击等或不定式). **2** [C] (period of) watchfulness under enemy attack, esp an air raid. 警戒; 警惕(尤指官兵警惕); 空袭警报期间. **3** [C] notice to stand ready: 促使准备妥当的通知: *They received the* ~ *at 10 am.* 他们上午十时接到通知, 要他们准备妥当。 □ *vt* [VP6A] put (troops, etc) on the ~. 命令(部队等)警戒. ~**·ly** *adv* ~**·ness** *n* being ~ or prompt (*in* doing sth). 机警; 机敏(与 in 连用, 指作某事时).

alex·an·drine /ˌælɪɡˈzændraɪn; ˌælɪɡˈzændrɪn/ *n* (of verse rhythm) iambic line of six feet or twelve syllables. (诗律)六音步或十二音节的抑扬格诗行; 亚历山大诗行.

alexia /əˈleksɪə; əˈleksɪə/ *n* [U] (path) disease in which cerebral lesions cause inability to read (popularly called 'word blindness'). (病理)失读症(由于脑损害所导致之不会认字, 俗称'字盲'). **alexic** /əˈleksɪk; əˈleksɪk/ *adj of* ~: 失读症的: *alexic children.* 患失读症的小孩.

al·falfa /ælˈfælfə; ælˈfælfə/ *n* [U] (US) (美) = **lucerne.**

al·fresco /ælˈfreskəʊ; ælˈfrɛsko/ *adj*, *adv* (of meals) in the open air; out of doors: (指餐食)露天的(地); 在户外(的): *an* ~ *lunch.* 露天午餐; *lunching* ~. 在户外吃午餐.

alga /ˈælɡə; ˈælɡə/ *n* (*pl* **algae** /ˈældʒiː; ˈældʒi/) (bot) water plant of very simple structure. (植物)海藻.

al·ge·bra /ˈældʒɪbrə; ˈældʒəbrə/ *n* branch of mathematics in which signs and letters are used to represent quantities. 代数学; 代数. ~**ic** /ˌældʒɪˈbreɪɪk; ˌældʒəˈbreɪ·ɪk/, ~**·ical** /-kl; -kəl/ *adj of* ~. 代数学的. ~**·ic·ally** /-klɪ; -klɪ/ *adv*

alias /ˈeɪlɪəs; ˈelɪəs/ *n* (*pl* ~**es** /-sɪz; -sɪz/) name by which a person is called on other occasions: 别名; 化名; 假名: *The criminal had several* ~es. 该罪犯有数个化名. □ *adv* also called. 亦称; 又名.

alibi /ˈælɪbaɪ; ˈæləˌbaɪ/ *n* (*pl* ~**s** /-baɪz; -baɪz/) **1** (legal) plea that one was in another place at the time of an alleged act, esp a crime: (法律)当时不在现场(尤指犯罪现场)之申辩: *The accused man was able to establish/prove an* ~. 该被告能够证明他当时不在现场. **2** (colloq) excuse (for failure, etc). (口)(失败等之)借口; 口实; 托词.

alien /ˈeɪlɪən; ˈeljən/ *n* (legal or official use) foreigner who is not a subject of the country in which he lives: (法律或官方用语)外侨; 外籍人: *An Englishman is an* ~ *in the United States.* 英国人在美国便是外国人. □ *adj* **1** foreign: 外国的: *an* ~ *environment.* 外国的环境. **2** ~ (*to*), differing in nature or character: 不同性质的;

These principles are ~ to our religion. 这些原则性质上与我们的宗教相异。**3** contrary or opposed (*to*): 相反的 (与 to 连用): *Cruelty was quite ~ to his nature.* 残忍与他的天性完全相反。

alien·ate /'eɪlɪəneɪt; 'eljən,et/ *vt* [VP6A, 14] **1** ~ *sb (from)*, estrange; cause (sb previously friendly) to become unfriendly or indifferent (by unpopular or distasteful actions): 离间; 使不和; 使疏远: *The Prime Minister's policy ~d many of his followers.* 首相的政策使许多拥护他的人疏远了他。*At various times artists have felt ~d from society,* felt shut out from society. 历代艺术家都与世隔离之感。**2** transfer ownership of (property): 转移(财产)的所有权; 让渡: *Enemy property is often ~d in time of war,* ie seized by the Government. 在战时敌产常被(政府)没收。**alien·ation** /,eɪlɪə'neɪʃn; ,eljən'eʃən/ *n* alienating or being ~d; estrangement; (theatre) critical detachment (of actors and audience) from, emotional non-involvement in, problems presented by a drama. 离间; 疏远; (所有权之)转移; 让渡; (戏剧)(演员与观众对问题所持之)超然态度。

alien·ist /'eɪlɪənɪst; 'eljənɪst/ *n* **1** (US) expert on the mental competence of witnesses in a law court. (美)鉴定出庭之证人其心智是否能适任作证之专家。**2** (old use) specialist in mental illness (now called a *psychiatrist*). (旧用法)精神病医生; 精神病学家(现称作 psychiatrist)。

alight¹ /ə'laɪt; ə'laɪt/ *pred adj* on fire; lighted up: 燃烧的; 发光亮的: *The sticks were damp and wouldn't catch ~.* 那些柴枝是潮湿的, 点燃不起来。(fig) (喻) *Their faces were ~* (= bright, cheerful) *with happiness.* 他们的脸焕发着喜悦的光彩。

alight² /ə'laɪt; ə'laɪt/ *vi* [VP2A, 3A] **1** get down (*from* a horse, bus, etc). 下(马, 公共汽车等, 与 from 连用)。**2** (of a bird) come down from the air and settle (*on* a branch, etc). (指鸟)落(于枝头等, 与 on 连用)。**3** ~ *on*, (formal) (fig) find by chance. (正式用语)(喻)偶然发现; 碰见。

align /ə'laɪn; ə'laɪn/ *vt, vi* **1** [VP6A, 2A] arrange in a line, bring into line (esp three or more points into a straight line); eg of soldiers, form in line: 排成一条直线; (尤指)使(三点或更多的点)成一直线; (士兵等)排成一行: *~ the sights of a rifle.* 将步枪瞄准。**2** [VP14, 3A] bring, come, into agreement, close co-operation, etc (*with*): 使一致; 与……一致; 使密切合作; 与……密切合作 (与 with 连用): *They ~ed themselves with us.* 他们已与我们密切合作。**~·ment** *n* [C, U] (an) arrangement in a straight line: 排成直线: *The desks are in/out of ~ment.* 桌子(没有)排成直行。*There was a new ~ment of European powers,* a new grouping (colloq, 俗称, line-up) of powers. 欧洲列强间有一新的联盟。

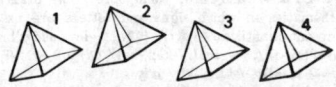

No 2 is out of alignment

alike /ə'laɪk; ə'laɪk/ *pred adj* similar; like one another: 相似的; 同样的: *The two sisters are very much ~.* 这两姐妹非常相象。*All music is ~ to him,* He has no ear for music, cannot distinguish one kind from other kinds. 所有的音乐对他都一样(他对音乐没有欣赏力, 对各种音乐不能加以辨别)。□ *adv* in the same way: 同样方式; 一样: *treat everybody ~;* 以同样方式对待每一个人; *the same:* 同样地: *summer and winter ~.* 夏季和冬季都一样。

ali·men·tary /,ælɪ'mentərɪ; ,ælə'mɛntərɪ/ *adj* of food and digestion. 食物及消化的。**the ~ canal,** parts of the body through which food passes (from the mouth to the anus. 消化管; 消化道(食物自口腔至肛门所经之管道)。

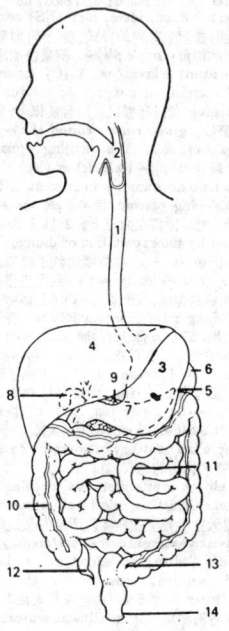

the alimentary canal

1 esophagus or gullet	8 gall bladder
2 pharynx	9 bile-ducts
3 stomach	10 colon or large intestine
4 liver	11 small intestine
5 pancreas	12 vermiform appendix
6 spleen	13 rectum
7 duodenum	14 anus

ali·mony /'ælɪmənɪ US: -məʊnɪ; 'ælə,monɪ/ *n* [U] money allowance (to be) paid by a man to his wife, or former wife, by a judge's order, after a legal separation or divorce. (经法院判决分居或离婚后男方对女方所付之)赡养费。

alive /ə'laɪv; ə'laɪv/ *pred adj* **1** living: 活着的; 在世的: *Who's the greatest man ~?* 当今最伟大的人物是谁? *You wouldn't like to be buried ~.* 你不会喜欢被活埋的。**2** in force; in existence: 有效力的; 实施中的; 存在的: *If a claim is kept ~, it is more likely to be recognised.* 如果把对于一项权利的要求持续下去, 它就更可能被承认。*An awareness of the dangers of air-pollution should be kept ~ by the press and TV.* 报纸及电视应经常提醒人们注意空气污染的危险。**3** ~ *to,* conscious or aware of: 觉察; 晓得: *He is fully ~ to the dangers of the situation/public opinion.* 他完全明白事态(舆论)的危险。**4** active; lively: 活泼的; 活动的: *He is very much ~.* 他非常活泼。*Look ~!* Hurry up! Get busy! 赶快! 加油! **5** ~ *with,* full of (living or moving things): 充满(活的或动的东西): *The lake was ~ with fish.* 湖中鱼多得很。

al·kali /'ælkəlaɪ; 'ælkə,laɪ/ *n* (*pl* ~s /-laɪz/, -laɪz/) (chem) one of a number of substances (such as soda, potash, ammonia) that combine with acids to form salts. (化) 碱(与酸化合成盐之物质, 如苏打, 钾, 氨)。**al·ka·line** /'ælkəlaɪn; 'ælkə,laɪn/ *adj* of ~s: 碱的; 碱性的: *soil of alkaline peat.* 碱性泥炭土。

all¹ /ɔːl; ɔl/ *adj* **1** (with *pl nn*) the whole number of;

(with *sing* material or abstract *nn*) the whole extent or amount of; (followed by the *def art*, demonstratives, possessives, and cardinal numbers): (与复数名词连用) 全数的; 所有的; (与单数的物质或抽象名词连用) 整个的; 全量的; (后接定冠词, 指示词, 所有格的词及基数): *All horses are animals but not all animals are horses.* 所有的马都是动物, 但并非所有的动物都是马。*All five men / All five of them are hard workers.* 他们五个人都是肯苦干的人。*All you boys need to work harder.* 你们所有的男孩都要多用功。*You've had all the fun and I've had all the hard work.* 所有的玩乐都归你享受了, 而所有的苦工都归我做了。*He has 'lived all his life in London.* 他一生都住在伦敦。*of 'all people,* specially; particularly: 特别地: *Of all people he should be the last to complain,* there is a strong reason why he shouldn't. 所有的人中, 他最不该发牢骚。*Why ask 'me to help,* of 'all people? I am the least likely person to be able to help, or the person to whom the speaker has the least right to apply for help. 天下那么多人, 为什么偏偏找我帮忙? (我是最帮不上忙或是最不应该帮忙的人。) *of all the idiots / nitwits,* an expression of annoyance with sb which has behaved foolishly. 大笨蛋(对行为愚蠢的人表示恼怒之词)。**on all fours,** ⇨ **four.** *all and every* (of) that year (= the whole of that year) in London. 他那一整年都消磨在伦敦。⇨ **whole(3). 3** (Cf *all* and *every.* *All* suggests the whole; *every* points to each member of a group individually): (参较 all 和 every。 all 指整个全体; every 个别地指一群中的每一个分子): *All (of) the boys enjoyed themselves.* 所有的男孩子都很快乐。Cf 参较 *Every one of the boys enjoyed himself.* 男孩子中每一个人都很快乐。**4 with all speed / haste,** the utmost possible. 尽速; 尽力; 尽可能; 尽快。**5** any: 任何: *beyond all doubt / argument / question,* there can't be any doubt, etc. 毫无疑问 (无可置辩; 毫无问题)。*He hates all* (= any) *criticism of his work.* 他不喜欢任何对于他的工作(著作)的批评。**6** ,All 'Fools' Day, 1 Apr; 愚人节; 万愚节(四月一日); ,All 'Hallows', ,All 'Saints' Day, 1 Nov; 万圣节 (十一月一日); ,All 'Souls' Day, 2 Nov. 万灵节(十一月二日)。

all² /ɔːl; ɔl/ *adv* **1** quite; entirely: 十分; 完全: *They were dressed all in black.* 他们全身穿着黑衣服。Cf 参较 *They were all dressed* (= All of them were dressed) *in black.* 他们大家都穿着黑衣服。*Your hands are all tar,* (colloq) covered with tar. (口) 你的双手满是柏油。*She was all* (colloq 口 = greatly) *excited.* 她非常兴奋。**be all about sth,** (colloq) be concerned with it. (口) 关心某事物。**all alone, (a)** not in the company of others. 独自一人。**(b)** without the help and company of other persons. 独力; 自力。**all along, (a)** for the whole length of: 沿着 … 的整个长度: *There are trees all along the road.* 整条路的两旁都种有树。**(b)** (colloq) all the time; from the start: (口) 自始至终; 从开始起一直: *But I knew that all along!* 但是我一开始就知道此事! **all clear,** ⇨ **clear¹(5), all for,** (colloq) strongly in favour of; anxious to have, etc: (口) 极其赞成; 急于要: *I'm all for accepting the offer.* 我极其赞成接受该项提议。**all the same,** yet, nevertheless. 仍然; 依然。**all the same to,** a matter not causing inconvenience to; a matter of indifference to: 对于 … 没有引起什么不便; 对 … 无所谓: *If it's all the same to you …;* 如果它对你没有什么不便的话 …; *It's all the same to me whether you go or stay.* 不论你是去还是留, 我都无所谓。**all in one, (a)** (colloq) exhausted: (口) 筋疲力竭的: *He was all in at the end of the race.* 赛跑结束时他已筋疲力竭。**(b)** *(all-in)* inclusive of everything: 包括一切的: *an all-in price;* 包括一切的价格; *all-in wrestling,* with no restrictions about methods or holds. 方法或抱、握等不加限制的角力。**all-out,** (colloq) using all possible strength, energy, etc: (口) 全力以赴的: *He was going all out / was making an all-out effort.* 他正全

力以赴。**all over, (a)** in every part of: 遍及 … 的每一部分: *He has travelled all over the world.* 他曾旅行全世界各地。**(b)** at an end. 结束; 完了。**all right,** (US) (美) **al·right (a)** satisfactory, satisfactorily; safe and sound; in good order: 满意的(地); 安然无恙的; 情况良好的: *Are you feeling all right?* 你觉得还好吗? **(b)** (as a response to a suggestion, etc) Yes, I consent. (作为对于建议等的回答)好的 (我同意)。**all there,** (colloq) having one's wits about one; mentally alert. (口) 精明的; 机敏的。**not all there,** (colloq) not quite sane; mentally deficient. (口) 头脑不很清楚的; 智力不健全的。**all told,** altogether; as the total: 一共; 合计: *There were six people all told* (= in all). 总共有六个人。**all up with,** at an end, over (with): 结束; 完了: *It's all up with him now,* He's likely to be ruined, to die, etc. 他现在一切都完了。**2 all the +** *comp adj,* much; so much: (用于 'all the + 比较级形容词' 之句型中)更加; 愈为: *You'll be all the better for a holiday.* 度一次假, 对你会更有好处。

all³ /ɔːl; ɔl/ *n* **my / his / their, etc** all, all that I / he / they, etc possess, value most, etc: 我 (他, 他们等)所有的, 所最宝贵的一切: *We must stake our all in this struggle.* 我们必须倾全力的一切于此一斗争之中。*He had lost his all.* 他已失去了所有的一切。

all⁴ /ɔːl; ɔl/ (in compounds) (用于复合词中) **1** (prefixed to many *adjj* and *pres participles*) in the highest degree; without limit: (接在许多形容词及现在分词的前端)极; 最; 无限的: ,all-'merciful; 极慈悲的; ,all-'powerful; 有无限权力的; 全能的; ,all-em'bracing. 包罗万象的; 包括一切的。**2** ,all-'mains *attrib adj* (of a radio receiver) adaptable to all voltages: (指收音机)可调节以适用于各种电压的: *an all-mains set.* 一架可调节以适用于各种电压的收音机。,**all-'round** *adj* having ability in many different ways: 多才多艺的; 门门皆通的: *an all-round sportsman,* good at many different games and sports. 擅长多种运动的运动家。Hence, 由此产生, ,all-'rounder *n* an ,all-star 'cast, (for a play, etc) one with star performers for all the chief parts. 大堆头明星阵容 (一出戏等的全部要角均由大牌明星担任的钻石阵容)。,all-time 'high / 'low *n* (colloq) highest / lowest figure, level, etc on record. (口) 空前最高(最低)记录; 记录上所列的最高(最低)数字, 水准等。,all-up 'weight, total weight of an aircraft, including crew, passengers, cargo, when in the air. (飞机在空中的)全重 (包括机上人员, 乘客, 货物等)。

all⁵ /ɔːl; ɔl/ *pron* **1** everything: 所有的一切: *He wanted all or nothing.* 他要么就全要, 要么就全不要。**2 all of,** every one, the whole: 每一个; 全体; 整个: *All of us want to go.* 我们全体都想去。*Take all of it.* 把所有的都拿去。**3** (used in apposition, in the same way as *both* and *each*): (用于同位, 与 both 和 each 之用法相同): *We all want to go.* 我们大家都想去。*Take it all.* 把整个都拿去。*They were all broken.* 它们全被打破了。**4** (followed by a relative clause, *that* being omitted): (后接关系从句, that 被省略): *All I want is peace and quiet.* 我所要的只是和平与安静。*He took all there was.* 他把所有的全拿去了。**5** (in prepositional phrases): (用于介词短语中): **above all,** ⇨ **above²(3). after all,** ⇨ **after¹(5). (not) at all,** /ə'tɔːl; e'tɔl/ (not) in any way, in the least degree: 根本(不); 全然(毫无); 最少程度(毫不): *if you are at all worried;* 如果你有任何焦虑的话; *not at all suitable for the post.* 完全不适于此一职位。**Not at all,** polite formula in answer to an expression of thanks. (回答对方表示感谢的客套语)别客气。Cf 参较 US (美): You're welcome. **for all** *(his wealth / great learning),* in spite of. 虽然; 尽管 (他极有钱; 学识渊博)。**for all I know / care, etc,** (used to show ignorance or indifference): (表示不知情或不关心)谁知道; 亦未可知 (我不很关心): *He may be dead for all I know.* 他可能死了, 也未可知。**in all,** ⇨ **in²(13). and all,** as well; including: 连同; 包括: *The dog ate the whole rabbit, head, bones and all.* 狗把整只兔子, 连头及

骨头，都吃掉了。*once (and) for all*, now and for the last or only time. 这是最后或唯一的一次；只此一次；决不再重复；断然。*It was all I/he, etc could do not to (laugh, etc)*, I/he, etc could hardly refrain from (laughing, etc). 已尽了最大努力忍住不(笑等)(意即我几乎忍不住要笑等)。*all in all*, of supreme or exclusive importance, interest, etc: 极其重要的；重于一切的；最关心的；最爱的: *They were all in all to each other*. 他们互相极为关切(亲爱)。*(taking it) all in all*, considering everything. 从各方面考虑；就整个而言。*not as/so + adj/adv + as all that*, to that extent; to that degree: 没有…到那个程度: *It's not so difficult as all that*, as is suggested, supposed, etc. 它并非困难到那种程度。*not all that + adj/adv*, (colloq or vulg): (口或鄙)并不算: *It isn't all that cheap*, not cheap if all things are considered. 并不便宜(如果仔细算算的话)。

Allah /'æle; 'ælə/ *n* name of God among Muslims. 阿拉(伊斯兰教的上帝)。

al·lay /ə'leɪ; ə'le/ *vt* (*pt, pp* -**layed**) [VP6A] make sth (eg pain, trouble, excitement, fears) less. 减轻；缓和(痛苦, 烦扰, 兴奋, 恐惧等)。

al·lege /ə'ledʒ; ə'ledʒ/ *vt* [VP6A, 9] declare; put forward, esp as a reason or excuse, in support of a claim or in denial of a charge: 宣称: (作为理由或托辞以支持一项主张或否认某一指控而)提出；供述: *In your statement you ~ that the accused man was seen at the scene of the crime*. 在你的口供中, 你供述曾经看到被告在犯罪现场。*The statement ~d to have been made by the accused is clearly untrue*. 那份被认为是被告所作的口供显然不确实。*An ~d thief*, person who is declared to be a thief. 被认为是窃贼的人; 盗窃嫌疑犯。**al·le·ga·tion** /,ælɪ'geɪʃn; ,ælə'geʃən/ *n* [U] alleging; [C] statement, esp one made without proof: 宣称; 声称; (尤指无证据的)供述; 空言; 辩解: *You have made serious allegations, but can you substantiate them?* 你已作将郑重的供述, 但你能证实吗? **al·leg·edly** /-ɪdlɪ; -ɪdlɪ/ *adv*

al·le·giance /ə'liːdʒəns; ə'lidʒəns/ *n* [U] duty, support, loyalty, due (to a ruler or government): (对统治者或政府之)忠诚; 忠贞; 忠顺; 效忠: *Members of Parliament took the oath of ~ to the Queen*. 国会议员们宣誓效忠女王。

al·le·gory /'ælɪgərɪ US: -gɔːrɪ; 'ælə,gorɪ/ *n* [C] (*pl* -**ries**) story, painting or description in which ideas such as patience, purity and truth are symbolized by persons who are characters in the story, eg Bunyan's *Pilgrim's Progress*. 讽喻; 寓言(以人物代表恶耐, 纯洁和真诚之类的观念, 如班扬的《天路历程》即是); 讽喻性的图画。**al·le·goric** /,ælɪ'gɒrɪk US: -'gɔːr-; ,ælə'gorɪk/, **al·le·gori·cal** /-kl; -kəl/ *adj*

al·le·gretto /,ælɪ'gretəʊ; ,ælə'grɛto/ *n, adj, adv* (I; music) (passage played) fast and lively, but not so brisk as allegro. (意; 音乐)稍快的(地); 稍快板; 小快板; 稍快的片段。

al·legro /ə'leɪgrəʊ; ə'lɛgro/ *n, adj, adv* (I; music) (passage played) in quick time; fast and lively. (意; 音乐)快速的(地); 快板; 快速的片段。

al·le·luia /,ælɪ'luːjə; ,ælə'lujə/ *int* = hallelujah.

al·lergy /'ælədʒɪ; 'ælədʒɪ/ *n* [C] (*pl* -**gies**) (med) (condition of) being unusually sensitive to particular foods, kinds of pollen, insect stings, etc (as in the case of a person who begins to suffer from asthma when he gets a certain kind of dust or pollen into his nose or month): (医)(对于某些食物、花粉、虫咬等之)过敏性反应; 过敏症(例如有人吸入某种灰尘或花粉即引起气喘); 变态反应性; 变应性。**al·ler·gen** /'ælədʒen; 'ælə,dʒɛn/ *n* (med, science) anything that causes an ~. (医, 科学)变应原(任何可引起变应性的东西)。**al·ler·gic** /ə'lɜːdʒɪk; ə'lɜːdʒɪk/ *adj* of ~. 过敏性的; 过敏性的; *allergic to*, having an ~ to (sth); (colloq) having a dislike of; unable to get on well with. 对(某物)有过敏性反应的; (口)厌恶的; 与…不能融洽相处。

al·levi·ate /ə'liːvɪeɪt; ə'livɪ,et/ *vt* [VP6A] make

(pain, suffering) less or easier to bear. 减轻(痛苦); 易于忍受; 使缓和。**al·levi·ation** /ə,liːvɪ'eɪʃn; ə,lɪvɪ'eʃən/ *n*

al·ley /'ælɪ; 'ælɪ/ *n* [C] (*pl* ~**s**) (also 亦作 '~·**way**) 1 narrow passage between houses or other buildings (often a narrow street). 小巷; 弄; 胡同(常为狭窄街道)。,**blind** '~, ~ closed at one end; (fig) occupation, eg that of an errand boy, that does not teach a trade or lead to a profession. 死巷; 死胡同; (喻)不能学得一种技能或导向专业的职业; 没有前途的职业(如差役)。2 path or walk in a garden or park. (花园或公园中的)小径。3 narrow enclosure for such games as bowls and skittles. 保龄球及九柱戏之球道或球场。

al·liance /ə'laɪəns; ə'laɪəns/ *n* 1 [U] association or connection. 联合。*in ~ (with)*, joined or united (with). (与…)联合。2 [C] union of persons, families, eg by marriage, or states (by treaty): 联结; 联姻; 联盟; 同盟: *enter into an ~ with a country*. 与某国结为同盟国。

al·lied /ə'laɪd; ə'laɪd/ ⇨ **ally**.

al·li·ga·tor /'ælɪgeɪtə(r); 'ælə,getɚ/ *n* reptile (like a crocodile but with a shorter snout) living in the lakes and rivers of southeastern US. ⇨ the illus at **reptile**; leather made from its skin. (一种产于美国东南部之河或湖中之)短吻鳄(参看 reptile 之插图); 短吻鳄之皮制成之革; 钝吻鳄。**~ pear**, avocado. 鳄梨(一种梨状热带果实)。

al·lit·er·ation /ə,lɪtə'reɪʃn; ə,lɪtə'reʃən/ *n* [U] repetition of the first sound or letter of a succession of words, eg *safe and sound*; *apt ~'s artful aid*. 头韵(即连续数字之起头音或字母之重复, 例如: safe and sound; apt ~'s artful aid). **al·lit·er·ative** /ə'lɪtrətɪv US: -təreɪtɪv; ə'lɪtə,retrɪv/ *adj* **al·lit·er·ative·ly** *adv*

al·lo·cate /'æləkeɪt; 'ælə,ket/ *vt* [VP6A, 14] ~ (**to/for**), give, put on one side, as a share or for a purpose: 分配; 配给; 拨出: ~ *duties to sb*; 分配职务给某人; ~ *a sum of money among several persons*; 把一笔款子分配给几个人; ~ *a sum of money to education*. 拨出一笔款子作为教育经费。**al·lo·ca·tion** /,ælə'keɪʃn; ,ælə'keʃən/ *n* 1 [U] allocating or distributing. 分配; 配给。2 [C] ~ (**to/for**), sth ~d or assigned (to or for a purpose, etc). 所分配之事物(与 to 或 for 连用, 后接目的, 等)。

al·lot /ə'lɒt; ə'lat/ *vt* (-**tt**-) [VP6A,12A, 13A, 14] ~ *sth (to)*, make a distribution of; decide a person's share of: 分配; 摊派: ~ *sth to sb for a purpose*; 为了某种目的而将某事物分配给某人; ~ *duties (to sb)*. 分配职务(给某人)。*Can we do the work within the time they have ~ed (to) us?* 我们能在他们所分配给我们的时间内把工作做完吗? *They were ~ted a house to live in*. 他们分配得一幢房子住。**~·ment** *n* 1 [U] division; distribution (of shares). 分配; 分配。2 [C] part or share. esp (in GB) small area of public land rented as a vegetable garden. 所配得的一份; (尤指英国)租来作为菜园用的一小块公地。

allow /ə'laʊ; ə'laʊ/ *vt, vi* 1 [VP6A, C, 17, 15B] permit: 允许; 许可: *Smoking is not ~ed here*. 此处禁止吸烟。*No dogs ~ed*, in this place (building, park, etc). 禁止携狗入内(指建筑物, 公园等)。*Please ~ me to carry your bag*. 请让我替你拿你的提包。*Please ~ the dog out after dark*. 破晚在天黑之后不准外出。2 [VP12A, 13A, 14] give, let (sb or sth) have; agree to give: 给; 让…得到; 同意给予: *How much money does your father ~ you for books?* 你的父亲给你多少钱买书? *He ~s his wife £100 a year for clothes*. 他每年给他妻子一百英镑购买衣服。*She ~ed her imagination full play*, did nothing to control it. 她让她的想象力尽量发挥。*The bank ~s 5 per cent interest on deposits*. 银行对存款给五厘(年)息。*We can ~* (= take off, deduct) *5 per cent for cash payment*. 付现款我们可以打九五折。3 [VP6A] (legal) agree that sth is right or just: (法律)同意其为正当: *The judge ~ed the claim*. 法官同意该项主张为正当。4 [VP25, 9] admit (now the more usu word): 承认(今较常用 admit): *We must ~*

him to be a genius. / ~ *that he is a genius.* 我们必须承认他是一个天才。**5**[VP3A]~ *for*, take into consideration: 考虑到; 顾虑到; 体谅; 连 ··· 算在内: *It will take thirty minutes to get to the station,* ~*ing for traffic delays.* 到车站去将需要三十分钟, 连路上交通的耽搁都算在内。~ *of*, admit of (now more usu): 容许(今较常用 admit of): *The situation* ~*s of no delay.* 情势不容许延误; 刻不容缓。 ~·able /-əbl/ ; -əbl/ *adj* that is or can be ~ed (by law, the rules, etc). (法律, 规则等)所许可的; 可承认的。

allow·ance /ə'lauəns; ə'lauəns / *n* **1** [C] sum of money, amount of sth, allowed to sb: 津贴; 特别经费; 所允许的分量: *a dress* ~ *of £70 a year.* 一年七十英镑的制装津贴。 *The Director has an entertainment* ~, money for entertaining important customers, etc. 董事有一笔交际费(招待重要主顾等)。 **2**[C] (comm, fin) deduction or discount. (商, 财政)折扣。 **3** (*sing* or *pl*) *make* ~(*s*) *for*, allow for, ➪ allow(5): (单或复) 考虑到; 顾虑到; 体谅: *We must make* ~(*s*) *for his youth,* remember that he is young, and not be too severe, etc. 我们必须体谅他年轻。

alloy /'æloɪ; 'æloɪ/ *n* [C, U] mixture of metals, esp a metal of low value mixed with a metal of higher value: 合金; 齐; (尤指)与贵重金属混合之其他金属; (used attrib) (用作定语) ~ *steel.* 合金钢(非纯钢)。 □ *vt* /ə'loɪ; ə'loɪ/ [VP6A] mix (one metal) with a metal or metals of lower value; (fig) spoil; impair. 熔合(金属); 使(金属)减低成色; (喻)使变质; 损害。

all·spice /'ɔːlspaɪs; 'ɔl,spaɪs/ *n* [U] spice made from the dried berries of a W Indian tree called the pimento. (西印度群岛所产之)甜胡椒; 甘椒。

allude /ə'luːd; ə'ljud / *vi* [VP3A] ~ *to*, refer (indirectly) to; mention (now the more usu word): 提及; 暗示; 说到 (今较常用 mention): *In your remarks you* ~ *to certain sinister developments.* 在你所说的话中你暗示若干不祥的发展。

allure /ə'luə(r); ə'lur / *vt* [VP6A, 14, 17] tempt; entice; lure (now the more usu word). 引诱; 吸引; 诱惑 (今较常用 lure)。 □ *n* [C, U] (liter) power to ~; fascination. (文)诱惑力; 魅力。 **allur·ing** *part adj* charming; fascinating. 迷人的; 诱惑人的。 ~**·ment** *n* [C, U] that which ~s; charm, attraction (now the more usu words). 有诱惑力之事物; 魅力; 吸引力(今较常用 charm 及 attraction)。

al·lu·sion /ə'luːʒn; ə'luʒən/ *n* [C] ~ (*to*), indirect reference to; passing 间接提及; 暗示; 暗指; 典故: *His speeches are full of classical* ~*s which few people understand.* 他的演说中用了很多鲜为人知的典故。 *That man has a glass eye but he doesn't like people to make any* ~ *to it.* 那个人有一只假眼, 但他不喜欢人以任何方式间接地提到它。 **al·lus·ive** /ə'luːsɪv; ə'lusɪv/ *adj* containing ~s. 含暗示的; 含典故的。

al·luv·ial /ə'luːvɪəl; ə'luvɪəl/ *adj* made of sand, earth, etc, left by rivers or floods: 冲积的; 淤积的: ~ *soil/deposits.* 冲积土(矿藏)

ally /ə'laɪ; ə'laɪ/ *vt* (*pt, pp* -**lied**) **1** [VP14] ~ (*oneself*) *with/to*, unite by treaty, marriage, etc: (使自己)与···联盟; 联姻: *Great Britain was allied with the United States in both World Wars;* 在两次世界大战中, 英国都与美国联盟; Hence: 由此产生: *the Allied* /'æleɪd; ə'laɪd/ *Powers.* 同盟国。 **2** *allied to*, (of things) connected with: (指事物)与···有关系; 与···同属一系; 与···相类似: *The English language is allied to the German language.* 英语与德语属于同一语系。 □ *n* /'ælaɪ; 'ælaɪ/ (*pl* -**lies**) person, state, etc, allied to another; person who gives help or support. 同盟者; 联盟者; 盟国; 盟邦; 盟友。

Alma Mater /ˌælmə 'mɑːtə(r); 'ælmə'metə/ *n* (Lat) name used for the university or school that a person attended; (US) school song or anthem. (拉)母校; (美)校歌。

al·ma·nac /'ɔːlmənæk; 'ɔlmə,næk/ *n* annual book or

calendar of months and days, with information about the sun, moon, tides, anniversaries, etc. 历书; 天文年历(内包括关于日, 月, 潮汐, 纪念日等之说明); 年鉴。

al·mighty /ɔːl'maɪtɪ; ɔl'maɪtɪ/ *adj* having all power; powerful beyond measure. 万能的; 全能的; 有无限权力的, esp 尤用于 *A~ God.* 全能的上帝。 □ *n the A~,* God. 全能者(上帝)。

almond /'ɑːmənd; 'ɑmənd/ *n* (nut inside the) hard seed (*stone-fruit*) of a tree allied to the peach and plum: 杏核; 杏仁: *ground* ~*s,* ~ nuts ground to powder; 杏仁粉; *shelled* ~*s,* ~ nuts removed from the shell or hard cover. 杏仁。 ~·'**eyed** *adj* having eyes that appear to slant upwards and become narrower. 杏眼的; 眼向上斜而呈狭长形的。

almoner /'ɑːmənə(r) US: 'ælm-; 'ælmənə/ *n* **1** (formerly) official who distributed money and help to the poor. (昔时)赈济员 (负责发救济金等给贫困者)。 **2** (GB) hospital official in charge of social service work for patients. (英)公立医院中为病人服务之社会工作员。

al·most /'ɔːlməust; ɔl'most/ *adv* **1** (with *vv, advv, adjj, nn*; replaceable by *nearly*): (与动词, 副词, 形容词, 名词连用; 可与 nearly 通用)几乎; 差一点就; 差不多: *He slipped and* ~ *fell.* 他滑了一下, 几乎跌倒。 *That's a mistake he* ~ *always makes.* 那是一个他几乎经常犯的错误。 *Dinner's* ~ *ready.* 晚餐差不多已经预备好了。 *It's* ~ *time to start.* 差不多是开始的时候了。 **2** (with *no, none, nothing, never,* not replaceable by *nearly*; often replaced by *hardly* or *scarcely* with *any*): (与 no, none, nothing, never 连用, 不与 nearly 通用; 常可与 hardly any 或 scarcely any 通用)几乎; 差不多: *A~ no one* = Hardly anyone) *believed her.* 几乎没有一个人相信她。 *The speaker said* ~ *nothing* (= scarcely anything) *worth listening to.* 那发言者所说的话几乎没有一句值得听的。

alms /ɑːmz; ɑmz/ *n* (*sing* or *pl*) money, clothes, food, etc given to the poor: (单或复)救济金; 救济品(衣服、食物等): *give* ~ *to sb;* 给予某人救济; *ask/beg (an)* ~ *of sb.* 向某人请求救济。 '~**-box** *n* 救济箱。 '~**-giving** *n* 施舍; 周济。 '~**-house** *n* (old use) house, founded by charity, in which poor people no longer able to earn money, may live without paying rent. (旧用法)救济院; 贫民院; 济贫院(为慈善机关所设, 收容穷困而无力谋生者)。

aloe /'æləu; 'ælo/ *n* **1** plant with thick, sharp-pointed leaves. (植物)芦荟。 **2** (also 亦作 **bitter** ~**s**) juice from this plant, used in medicine. 芦荟油(用于医药)。

aloft /ə'lɒft US: ə'lɔːft; ə'lɔft/ *adv* high up, esp a the masthead of a ship, or up in the rigging. 在高处; (尤指)在桅杆顶上; 在帆桅缆索上面。

alone /ə'ləun; ə'lon/ *pred adj, adv* ➪ **lonely**. **1** (= *by oneself/itself*) without the company or help of others or other things: 独自的(地); 孤独的(地); 独力的(地); 单独的(地): *He likes living* ~, by himself. 他喜欢孤独生活。 *The house stands on the hillside all* ~, with no other houses near it. 那房子孤零零地座落在山坡上。 *You can't lift the piano* ~, without help. 单凭你一人搬不动钢琴。 *His silence* ~ *is proof of his guilt.* 单是他的沉默就是他犯罪的证明。 **2** (following a *n* or *pron*) and no other: (跟于名词或代词之后)只有; 惟有; 没有别人: *Smith* ~ (= Smith and no one else) *knows what happened.* 只有史密斯知道发生了什么事。 *You* ~ (= You and no other person) *can help me in this task.* 只有你能帮助我做这件事。 **3** (in the *pred,* with *in*): (在表语中与 in 连用): *We are not* ~ *in thinking* (= not the only persons who think) *that* ..... 并非只有我们以为···。 **4** *let* ~, without referring to or considering: 且不论; 至于···更不必说: *He cannot find money for necessities, let* ~ *such luxuries as wine and tobacco.* 他连日常必需品都买不到嘛, 更不必说烟酒等奢侈品了。 *let/leave sb/ sth* ~, abstain from touching, moving, interfering with: 不动, 不碰或不干涉某人或某事物; 听其自然: *You had better leave that dog* ~; *it will bite you if you tease*

it. 你最好不要去惹那只狗；如果你捉弄它，它会咬你的。 *let well ~,* do not go further than what is already satisfactory. 不要画蛇添足。

along /ə'lɒŋ *US:* ə'lɔːŋ; ə'lɔŋ/ *adv* 1 (used with *vv* to indicate onward movement, often with the same sense as *on*): (与动词连用，表示向前移动，常与 *on* 同义): *Come ~!* 来吧！ *The dog was running ~ behind its master.* 那狗跟在它的主人后面跑着。*Move ~ please!* eg a request by a policeman to people who are holding up the movement of others. 请向前走动！(例如警察对阻碍他人前进的人所做的请求。) 2 (used, as are *over, across, up, down,* in informal requests): (用于非正式请求中，同 *over, across, up, down*) *Come ~ and see me some time.* 有空的时候过来看我。3 *all ~* ⇨ **all²(1).** *get ~,* ⇨ **get(17).** □ *prep* 1 from one end of to the other end of; through any part of the length of: 沿着；循: *We walked ~ the road.* 我们沿着路走。*There are trees all ~ the river banks.* 沿河两岸皆植有树木。*I ass ~ the bus please!* (a request that passengers should move on so as to leave the entrance clear). 请向车里面走！(对车上乘客的请求，使上下车的乘客不致于在入口处受阻)。2 *~ here,* in this direction. 朝这方向。**~·side** /ə,lɒŋ'saɪd; ə'lɔŋ'saɪd/ *adv, prep* close to, parallel with, the side of (a ship, pier, wharf). 傍靠；沿着或靠着(船，码头)的旁边。

aloof /ə'luːf; ə'luf/ *adv* apart. 远离地；分离地。*stand / hold / keep (oneself) ~ (from),* keep away from, take no part in sth: 站得远远的；不接近(某物)；不参与(某事): *Buyers are holding ~,* making no offers to buy. 购买者都裹足不前。□ *adj* cool; remote (by nature): 冷漠的; 疏远的: *I find him rather ~ character.* 我发现他颇为冷漠。*He's a very ~ character.* 他是个冷漠的怪人。**~·ness** *n*

aloud /ə'laʊd; ə'laʊd/ *adv* 1 in a voice loud enough to be heard, not in a whisper: 出声地: *Please read the story ~.* 请朗读这个故事。2 loudly, so as to be heard at a distance: 高声地: *He called ~ for help.* 他高声喊叫求救。

alp /ælp; ælp/ *n* 1 high mountain, esp one of those **(the Alps)** between France and Italy. 高山；高峰 (尤指属于法意边境之阿尔卑斯山脉者)。2 (in Switzerland) green pasture-land on a mountainside. (瑞士境内) 山坡上的牧场。

al·paca /æl'pækə; æl'pækə/ *n* 1 [C] sheep-like animal, kind of llama, of Peru. 羊驼(产于秘鲁)。2 [U] (cloth made from) its wool, often mixed with silk or cotton: 羊驼毛；羊驼毛织物(常混有丝或棉)；羊驼呢: *an ~ coat.* 羊驼呢外衣。

alpen·stock /'ælpenstɒk; 'ælpm,stak/ *n* long, iron-tipped stick used in climbing mountains. 登山手杖(长而有铁头者)。

al·pha /'ælfə; 'ælfə/ *n* the first letter (A, α) in the Gk alphabet: 希腊字母的第一个字母: *A~ and Omega,* the beginning and the end. 首尾；始终。**'~ particle,** helium nucleus given off by a radio-active substance. α 粒子； 阿尔伐质点 (放射性物质所放出的氢原子核)。**~ plus,** (of marks in an examination) very good indeed. (考试记分)甲上。

al·pha·bet /'ælfəbet; 'ælfə,bet/ *n* the letters used in writing a language, arranged in order: (用以拼写一种语言并按次序排列的全部)字母: *the Greek ~;* 希腊字母; *the ABC.* 基本知识；初步；入门。⇨ **App 4.** **~·i·cal** /,ælfə'betɪkl; ,ælfə'bɛtɪkl/ *adj* in the order of the ~: 按字母顺序的: *The words in a dictionary are in ~ical order.* 词典中的单词系按字母顺序排列的。**~·i·cally** /-klɪ; -klɪ/ *adv*

al·pine /'ælpaɪn; 'ælpaɪn/ *adj* of the Alps; of high mountains: 阿尔卑斯山脉的；高山的；高峰的: *~ plants;* 高山植物; *an ~ hut.* 高山茅舍。**al·pin·ist** /'ælpɪnɪst; 'ælpɪnɪst/ *n* ~ climber. 登阿尔卑斯山者；登高山者。

al·ready /ɔːl'redɪ; ɔl'rɛdɪ/ *adv* (nsu with *v*, but may be placed elsewhere for emphasis) (通常与动词连用，但

也可以放在别处以加强语气) 1 by this / that time: 已经；业已: *The postman has ~ been / has been ~.* 邮差已经来过了。*When I called, Tom was ~ dressed.* 当我去他家的时候，汤姆已经穿好衣服了。2 (Cf *yet* which usu replaces *already* in neg and interr sentences. In neg and interr sentences *already* is used to show surprise.): (参较 *yet*，在否定及疑问句中，通常以 *yet* 替换 *already*; 在否定及疑问句中用 *already* 是表示惊奇): *Have you had breakfast ~?* 你已经吃过早餐了吗? *Is it 10 o'clock ~?* 已经十点钟了吗? *You're not leaving us ~, are you?* 你不会这么早就要离开我们吧，是不是? 3 *previously; before now:* 早已; 曾经: *I've been there ~, so I don't want to go again.* 我早已去过那里了，所以我不想再去。

al·right /ɔːl'raɪt; ɔl'raɪt/ = all right, ⇨ **all²(1).**

Al·sa·tian /æl'seɪʃn; æl'seʃən/ *n* (US 美 = *German shepherd*) large breed of dog, like a wolf, often trained for police work. 一种大狼狗(常予以训练使担任警犬任务)。⇨ the illus at **dog.** 参看 dog 之插图。

also /'ɔːlsəʊ; 'ɔlso/ *adv* too; besides; as well. (In spoken English, *too* and *as well* are often preferred to *also*. *Also* in an affirm sentence is replaced by *either* in a neg sentence.): 也；亦；并且(在口语中，too 及 as well 常较 also 为佳。在肯定句中之 also，在否定句中换为 either): *Tom has been to Canada. Harry has ~ been to Canada.* 汤姆曾去过加拿大。哈里亦曾去过加拿大。*Cf* 参较 *Tom has not been to Brasil. Harry has not been to Brazil, either.* 汤姆没有去过巴西。哈里也没有去过巴西。*not only ... but ~,* both ... and: 不但...而且: *He not only read the book but ~ remembered what he had read.* 他不但读过此书，并且记得所读的内容。**'~-ran** *n* (racing) horse not among the first three at the winning post; (fig) unsuccessful person in a contest. (赛马)落选之马；(喻)(竞赛中)落选之人；败北者。

al·tar /'ɔːltə(r); 'ɔltə/ *n* 1 raised place (flat-topped table or platform) on which offerings are made to a god. (置祭品于神前的)祭坛。2 (in Christian churches) the Communion table, ⇨ the illus at **church.** (基督教中)圣餐桌；圣坛(参看 church 之插图)。*lead (a woman) to the ~,* marry her. 与(某女)结婚(指在教堂结婚)。**'~-piece** *n* painting or sculpture placed behind an ~. 祭坛后方所置之图画或雕刻。

al·ter /'ɔːltə(r); 'ɔltə/ *vt, vi* [VP6A, 2A] make or become different; change in character, appearance, etc: 改变；更改；变更；修改: *The ship ~ed course.* 该船改变航路。*That ~s matters / the case,* makes the situation different. 那就要使情势改观。*These clothes are too large; they must be ~ed.* 这些衣服太大，必须加以修改。*He has ~ed a great deal since I saw him a year ago.* 自从我去一年前见他以后，他已改变了很多。**~·able** /-əbl; -əbl/ *adj* that ~s or that can be ~ed. 可改变的；可修改的。**~·ation** /,ɔːltə'reɪʃn; ,ɔltə'reʃən/ *n* [U] ~ing; making a change; [C] act of changing; change that is the result of ~ing: 改变；更改；变更；修改: *There isn't much ~ation in the village; it's almost the same as it was twenty years ago.* 村中没有多少改变；它几乎和二十年前是一样的。*For making ~ations to a suit of clothes,* £1.20. 修改一套衣服，工资一英镑二十便士。

al·ter·ca·tion /,ɔːltə'keɪʃn; ,ɔltə'keʃən/ *n* (formal) [U] quarrelling; [C] quarrel; noisy argument. (正式用语)口角；争论；争辩；争吵。

al·ter ego /,æltər 'egəʊ *US:* 'iːgəʊ; 'æltə'igo/ *n* (Lat) one's other self; very intimate friend. (拉)他我；另一个我；密友；至交。

al·ter·nate¹ /ɔːl'tɜːnət; 'ɔltɜːnɪt/ *adj* 1 (of things of two kinds) by turns, first the one and then the other: (指两种事物)轮流的；交替的: *~ laughter and tears.* 时笑时哭；又哭又笑。*Tom and Harry do the work on ~ days,* eg Tom on Monday, Harry on Tuesday, Tom on Wednesday, etc. 汤姆与哈里隔日轮流做这工作。2 (of leaves along a stem) not opposite. (指沿茎之叶)互生的(并非对生的)。**~·ly** *adv*

al·ter·nate² /'ɔːltɜːneɪt; 'ɔltə,net/ *vt, vi* 1 [VP6A,

14] arrange or perform by turns; cause to take place, appear, one after the other: 轮流; 使交替发生或出现: *He ~d kindness with severity*, was kind, then severe, then kind again, etc. 他时而仁慈时而严厉(恩威并施)。 *Most farmers ~ crops*. 大多数的农民实行作物轮作。 ⇨ **rotation**(2). **2** [VP3A] **~ between**, pass from one state, etc to a second, then back to the first, etc: 一下子……一下子……: *He ~d between high spirits and low spirits*. 他一下子高兴一下子沮丧。 **~ with**, come one after the other, by turns: 轮流出现; 交互发生: *Wet days ~d with fine days*. 雨天与晴天交替更迭。 **‚alternating 'current**, current that reverses its direction at regular intervals, the cycle being repeated continuously, the number of complete cycles per second being known as the *frequency*. 交流; 交流电。 ⇨ direct[1](5). **al·ter·na·tion** /ˌɔːltəˈneɪʃn; ˌɔltəˈneʃən /n

al·ter·na·tive /ɔːlˈtɜːnətɪv; ɔlˈtɜːnətɪv/ *adj* (of two things) that may be had, used, etc in place of sth else: 二者任择其一的; 可选择的; 选择性的: *Either* 和 *or* are ~ conjunctions. Either 和 or 都是选择性的连接词。 *There are ~ answers to $x^2 = 16$* (ie x = +4 or x = −4). *'x* 的二次方等于十六' 有两个可能的答案(即 x 等于正 4 或负 4)。 □ *n* [C] **1** choice between two things: 二者择一; 二者之一; 变通办法; 选择余地: *You have the ~ of working hard and being successful or of working hard and being unsuccessful*. 你有两种选择: 努力工作而成功或不努力工作而失败。 *Is there no ~ to what you propose?* 你的提议没有变通的余地吗? **2** one of more than two possibilities. 数种可能之一。 ~**ly** *adv* as an ~: 作为一个代替的办法; 替换地: *a fine of £ 10 or ~ly six weeks imprisonment*. 罚锾十英镑或者易为六星期的徒刑。

altho /ɔːlˈðəʊ; ɔlˈðo/ (US spelling for) although. although 之美国拼法。

al·though /ɔːlˈðəʊ; ɔlˈðo/ *conj* ⇨ **though**.

al·tim·eter /ˈæltɪmiːtə(r) US: ælˈtɪmɪtər; ælˈtɪmətə/ *n* barometer, eg as used in aircraft, for showing height above sea-level. 高度测量器; 高度表 (如用于飞机中者)。

al·ti·tude /ˈæltɪtjuːd US: -tuːd; ˈæltəˌtjud/ *n* **1** (not of living things) height, esp above sea-level. (非生物之)高度; (尤指)海拔。 **2** (usu *pl*) place high above sea-level: (通常用复数)高处: 海拔甚高的地方: *It is difficult to breathe at these ~s*. 在这些高的地方呼吸感到困难。 **3** (astron) angular distance of a celestial object above the horizon. (天文)地平纬度(天体在地平上之角距)。

alto /ˈæltəʊ; ˈælto/ *n* (*pl* ~**s** /-təʊz; -toz/) **1** (musical part for, a person having a) male singing voice between tenor and treble; counter tenor; female voice of similar range *(contralto)*. 中音; 中音部; 唱中音者; 女低音。 **2** instrument with the same range: 中音乐器: ~*saxophone*. 中音萨克斯管。

al·to·gether /ˌɔːltəˈɡeðə(r); ˌɔltəˈɡɛðə/ *adv* **1** entirely; wholly: 完全地; 全部地: *I don't ~ agree with him*. 我不完全同意他。 *It's ~ out of the question*. 那是完全不可能的。 **2** (of a total quantity) taken as a whole: (指总数量)总计: *You owe me £ 3 ~*. 你一共欠我三英镑。 **3** (modifying a complete sentence) on the whole; considering everything: (修饰全句)从整体看来; 总而言之: *The weather was bad and the trains were crowded— ~, it wasn't a very satisfactory excursion*. 天气恶劣, 火车又挤——总之, 不是一次很满意的郊游。

al·tru·ism /ˈæltruːɪzəm; ˈæltruˌɪzəm/ *n* [U] principle of considering the well-being and happiness of others first; unselfishness; [C] instance of this. 利他主义; 利他; 利他的实例。 **al·tru·ist** /ˈæltruːɪst; ˈæltruɪst/ *n* / person who follows ~. 利他主义者。 **al·tru·is·tic** /ˌæltruːˈɪstɪk; ˌæltruˈɪstɪk/ *adj* **al·tru·is·ti·cally** /-klɪ; -klɪ/ *adv*

alum /ˈæləm; ˈæləm/ *n* [U] white mineral salt, used medically, in dyeing, etc. 明矾; 白矾 (用于医药, 染色等)。

alu·min·ium /ˌæljuˈmɪnɪəm; ˌæljəˈmɪnɪəm/ (US = **alu·mi·num** /əˈluːmɪnəm; əˈlumɪnəm/) *n* [U] light white metal (symbol **Al**) extracted chiefly from bauxite, used for making hard, light alloys for cooking utensils, electrical apparatus, etc. 铝(白色轻金属, 符号为 Al, 主要由铁铝氧石提炼而来, 用于制硬而轻的合金炊具, 电器等)。

alumna /əˈlʌmnə; əˈlʌmnə/ *n* (*pl* ~**e** /-niː; -ni/) (US) girl or woman who was a pupil or student of a school, college or university. (美)女校友; 女毕业生。

alum·nus /əˈlʌmnəs; əˈlʌmnəs/ *n* (*pl* -**ni** /-naɪ; -naɪ/) (US) boy or man who was a pupil or student of a school, college or university. (美)男校友; 男毕业生。

al·veolar /ælˈvɪələ(r); ælˈvɪələ/ *n*, *adj* (phon) (consonant) made by the tongue against the gum behind the upper front teeth, eg /t, d, s/. (语音)齿龈音(用舌顶住上齿龈而发出的辅音如 t, d, s 音); 齿龈的。

al·ways /ˈɔːlweɪz; ˈɔlwez/ *adv* **1** at all times; without exception: 永远地; 无例外地; 总是: *The sun ~ rises in the east*. 太阳总是在东方升起。 (*Always* may be modified by *almost*, *nearly* or *not*.) (Always 可以被 almost, nearly 或 not 修饰。) *He's nearly ~ at home in the evening*. 他晚上差不多总在家。 Cf 参较 *not ~* and *hardly ever*, *I'm not ~ at home on Sundays*, ie I'm occasionally away from home. 我星期日不一定总在家 (即偶然也会不在家)。 *I'm hardly ever* (= very seldom) *at home on Sundays*. 我星期日几乎从不(即极少)在家。 **2** (usu with the continuous tenses) again and again; repeatedly: (通常与进行时连用)再三地; 累次地; 总是: *He was ~ asking for money*. 他总是要钱。 *Why are you ~ finding fault?* 你为什么总是吹毛求疵?

am /*after 'I'*: m; *otherwise*: əm; əm; *strong form*: æm; æm/ ⇨ **be**[1].

amah /ˈɑːmə; ˈɑmə/ *n* (in the East) nursemaid; maidservant. (在东方各国)阿妈; 保姆; 奶妈; 女佣。

amain /əˈmeɪn/ *adv* (old use, or poet) (旧用法或诗) **1** violently. 猛烈地; 激烈地。 **2** in haste. 急忙地; 匆促地。

amal·gam /əˈmælɡəm; əˈmælɡəm/ *n* **1** alloy of mercury. 汞合金; 汞齐。 **2** soft mixture, eg one used for filling holes in decayed teeth. 任何软的混合物(如填补龋齿用的齿科汞合金)。

amal·ga·mate /əˈmælɡəmeɪt; əˈmælɡəˌmet/ *vt*, *vi* [VP6A, 2A] (of classes, societies, races of people, business companies) mix; combine; unite. (指部份, 社会, 民族, 公司)混合; 联合; 合并。 **amal·ga·ma·tion** /əˌmælɡəˈmeɪʃn; əˌmælɡəˈmeʃən/ *n* [U] mixing; combining. [C] combination; union. 混合; 联合; 合并。

am·anu·en·sis /əˌmænjuˈensɪs; əˌmænjuˈɛnsɪs/ *n* (*pl* -**ses** /-siːz; -siz/) person who writes from dictation or copies what sb else has written. 笔记者; 抄录者; 书记; 文书。

ama·ryl·lis /ˌæməˈrɪlɪs; ˌæməˈrɪlɪs/ *n* (kinds of) lily-like plant growing from a bulb. 孤挺花。 宫人草; 孤挺花。

amass /əˈmæs; əˈmæs/ *vt* [VP6A] pile or heap up; collect: 聚积: ~ *riches* / *a fortune*. 聚积财富(财产)。

ama·teur /ˈæmətə(r); ˈæmətʃur / *n* person who paints pictures, performs music, acts in plays, etc, for the love of it, not for money; person playing a game, taking part in sports, etc, without receiving payment: 业余爱好者(指由于爱好, 不是为了赚钱, 而从事绘画, 演奏音乐、演戏等的人): (attrib) (用作定语) *an ~ painter* / *photographer*. 业余画家(摄影家)。 ~ **professional**. ~**ish** /-rɪʃ; -rɪʃ/ *adj* inexpert; imperfect. 不熟练的; 不完善的。 ~**ism** /-rɪzəm; -rɪzm/ *n*

ama·tory /ˈæmətərɪ US: -tɔːrɪ; ˈæməˌtɔrɪ/ *adj* (formal) of or causing (esp sexual) love; of lovers of making love. (正式用语)爱情(尤指性爱)的; 色情的; 恋爱的; 性交的。

amaze /əˈmeɪz; əˈmez/ *vt* [VP6A] fill with great

surprise or wonder: 使大为惊异;使惊愕;使愕然: *You ~ me!* 你使我大为惊异! *I was ~d at the news/~d to hear that ....* 我听到这个消息(听到…)大为吃惊。 **amaz·ing** part *adj* **amaz·ing·ly** *adv*: *He's doing amazingly well.* 他做得非常(令人惊讶之)好。 **~ment** *n* [U]: *I heard with ~ment that ....* 我听到…大为吃惊。 *His ~ment at the news was immense.* 他听到这项消息极为吃惊。 *He looked at me in ~ment.* 他惊奇地望着我。

Ama·zon /ˈæməzən *US:* -zɒn; ˈæmə,zɑn/ *n* **1** (in old Gk stories) female warrior. (古希腊传说中之)女战士; 女勇士。 **2** (small *a*) tall, vigorous woman. (a 小写)高大强壮的女人。

am·bas·sa·dor / æmˈbæsədə(r); æmˈbæsədɚ / *n* **1** minister representing the Government of his country in a foreign country: (驻外国的)大使: *the British A~ to Greece.* 英国驻希腊大使。 **2** (often 常作 *A~ Extraordinary*) minister sent by the Government of one State to the Government of another on a special mission. 专使; 特使。 **3** authorized representative. 经授权指派的代表。 **am·bas·sa·dress** /æmˈbæsədrɪs; æmˈbæsədrɪs/ *n* female ~. 女大使; 女特使; 女代表。 **~·ial** /æm,bæsəˈdɔːrɪəl; æm,bæsəˈdɔrɪəl/ *adj* ⇨ **diplomat, embassy.**

am·ber /ˈæmbə(r); ˈæmbɚ/ *n* [U] hard, clear yellowish-brown gum used for making ornaments, etc; its colour (seen in traffic lights between red and green). 琥珀; 琥珀色(黄褐色)。

am·ber·gris /ˈæmbəɡriːs *US:* -ɡrɪs; ˈæmbɚˌɡrɪs/ *n* [U] wax-like substance present in the intestines of whales and found floating in tropical seas, used as a fixative in perfumes. 鲸蜡; 龙涎香(用做香水之固定剂)。

am·bi·dex·trous /ˌæmbɪˈdekstrəs; ˌæmbəˈdekstrəs/ *adj* able to use the left hand or the right equally well. 两手均可灵巧使用的。

am·bi·ence /ˈæmbɪəns; ˈæmbɪəns/ *n* environment; atmosphere. 环境; 四围的情况; 气氛。

am·bi·ent /ˈæmbɪənt; ˈæmbɪənt/ *adj* (formal) (of air, etc) on all sides; surrounding. (正式用语)(指空气等)环绕四周的; 周围的。

am·bi·guity /ˌæmbɪˈɡjuːɪtɪ; ˌæmbɪˈɡjuɪtɪ / *n* (*pl* -ties) **1** [U] state of being ambiguous. 意义含糊。 **2** [C] expression, etc that can have more than one meaning. 有两种以上意义的辞句; 意义含糊的话: *Let's clear up the ~ in this paragraph.* 让我们把这一段中意义含糊的辞句解说明白。

am·bigu·ous /æmˈbɪɡjʊəs; æmˈbɪɡjʊəs/ *adj* **1** having more than one meaning: 意义含糊的; 有两种以上之意义的: *'More' is in 'Ask me more difficult questions.'* 在 'Ask me more difficult questions' 一句中, 'more' 一词的意义含糊。 **2** of uncertain meaning or intention: 意向不明的; 暧昧的: *He gave me an ~ glance.* 他意图不明的看了我一眼。 **~·ly** *adv*

am·bit /ˈæmbɪt; ˈæmbɪt/ *n* (often *pl*) bounds; extent; range of power or authority. (常用复数)界限; 范围; 权力的范围。

am·bi·tion /æmˈbɪʃn; æmˈbɪʃən/ *n* **1** [U] strong desire (*to be or do sth, for sth*): 野心; 雄心(与不定式或 for 连用, 后接某事物): *A boy who is filled with ~ usually works hard.* 一个充满雄心的男孩通常很用功。 *His ~ to become prime minister is likely to be realized.* 他要做首相的雄心可能会实现。 **2** [C] particular desire of this kind: 某项特别的野心或志向; 抱负: *He has great ~s.* 他胸怀大志。 **3** [C] object of such a desire: 希望达到的目标; 抱负: *achieve one's ~(s).* 达到个人所希望的目标。

am·bi·tious /æmˈbɪʃəs; æmˈbɪʃəs/ *adj* **1** full of ambitions: 充满野心的; 雄心勃勃的: *an ~ boy;* 有野心的男孩子; *~ for fame;* 有成名之野心(热中功名)的; *~ for one's children;* 对儿女怀有热切的期望; *~ to succeed in life.* 立志要出人头地。 **2** showing or needing

ambition: 显示或需要雄心的; 抱负不凡的: *~ plans;* 显示出雄心的计划(野心很大的计划); *an ~ attempt.* 抱负不凡的尝试。 **~·ly** *adv*

am·biva·lent / æmˈbɪvələnt; æmˈbɪvələnt / *adj* having either or both of two contrary or similar values, meanings, etc. 具有两种相反或类似之价值、意义等的; 兼具两种互相冲突之感情的; 情绪矛盾的。 **am·biva·lence** /-ləns; -ləns/ *n*

amble /ˈæmbl; ˈæmbl/ *vi* [VP2A, C] (of a horse) move along without hurrying, lifting the two feet on one side together; (of a person) ride or walk at an easy pace. (指马)以缓步行走(同侧之两足同时举起); (指人)缓骑马或悠然缓缓而行。 □ *n* slow, easy, pace: 缓步; 慢步: *He was coming along at an ~.* 他以缓慢的步子走来。

am·bro·sia /æmˈbrəʊzɪə *US:* -əʊʒə; æmˈbroʒə/ *n* [U] (Gk myth) the food of the gods; anything that has a delightful taste or smell. (希神)神的食物; 美味佳肴。

am·bu·lance /ˈæmbjʊləns; ˈæmbjələns/ *n* closed vehicle for carrying people who are ill, wounded in war or hurt in accidents. 救护车(运送病人, 伤兵或灾祸受伤者之车)。

am·bus·cade /ˌæmbəˈskeɪd; ˌæmbəsˈked/ *n*, *vt* = **ambush.**

am·bush /ˈæmbʊʃ; ˈæmbʊʃ/ *n* [C, U] (the placing of) troops, etc, waiting to make a surprise attack: 埋伏(以备突击); 伏兵: *fall into an ~;* 中伏; 遭遇埋伏; *be attacked from (an) ~.* 遭伏兵狙击。 *lie/wait in ~ (for),* be hidden waiting to attack. 埋伏(以突击)。 □ *vt* [VP6A] attack from such a position. 埋伏并突击。

ameba /əˈmiːbə; əˈmibə/ *n* = **amoeba.**

ameer /əˈmɪə(r); əˈmɪr/ *n* = **amir.**

amel·ior·ate /əˈmiːlɪəreɪt; əˈmiljəˌret/ *vt*, *vi* [VP6A, 2A] (formal) (cause to) become better. (正式用语)改善; 改良; 变好。 **amel·ior·ation** /əˌmiːlɪəˈreɪʃn; əˌmiljəˈreʃən/ *n*

amen /ˌɑːˈmen *US:* ˌeɪˈmen; ˈeˈmɛn/ *int* (eccles) word used at the end of a prayer or hymn and meaning 'May it be so'. (教会)阿门(祈祷或颂诗终了时之语, 意为 '心愿如此')。

amen·able /əˈmiːnəbl; əˈminəbl/ *adj* **~ (to,** **1** (of persons) responsive; willing to be guided or controlled: (指人)易受感动的; 愿受指导或控制的; 服服从的: *~ to kindness/advice/reason.* 易受仁慈感动(愿接受劝告)通达情理的。 *Do you find your wife ~?* 你觉得你的妻子很顺从吗? **2**(legal) (of persons) responsible (*to*); in a position where one must do certain things or be punished for not doing them: (法律)(指人)有责任的; 应负责任的(与 to 连用); 有服从义务的: *We are all ~ to the law.* 我们都应该服从法律。 **3** (of cases, situations) able to be tested or dealt with: (指情形, 情势)可测验的; 可处理的; 可解决的: *The case is not ~ to ordinary rules.* 这情形不是按普通规则所能处理的。

amend /əˈmend; əˈmɛnd/ *vt, vi* **1** [VP6A, 2A] make or become better; improve; free from faults or errors: 改善; 改良; 改正: *He'll have to ~ his style of living.* 将必须改善生活方式。 **2** [VP6A] make changes in the wording of a rule, a proposed law, etc. 修正(规则, 提案等)。 **~·able** /-əbl; -əbl/ *adj* **~·ment** *n* [U] ~ing; [C] change proposed or made (*to* a rule, regulation, etc). 改善; 改良; 改正; 修正(与 to 连用, 后接某项规则, 条例等)。

amends /əˈmendz; əˈmɛndz/ *n pl* *make ~/all possible ~ (to sb) (for sth),* give compensation: (为某事)(对某人)赔偿; 补偿; 赔罪: *make ~ to sb for an injury.* 赔偿某人所受的伤害。

amen·ity /əˈmiːnətɪ; əˈmɛnətɪ/ *n* (*pl* -ties) **1** (*pl*) things, circumstances, surroundings, that make life easy or pleasant: (复)使人愉快的事物, 例如: *exchange of amenities, of courtesies polite expressions:* 寒暄; *a town with many amenities,* eg a park, a public

library, playing fields; 有许多休闲去处(如公园,公共图书馆,运动场)的城镇; *the amenities offered by a Bank*, eg the provision of travel cheques, payment of standing orders. 银行所提供便利客户之措施(例如旅行支票之准备、定期汇票之付款等). **2** (*sing*) pleasantness: (单)爽适;宜人: *the ~ of the climate*. 气候之宜人。

Amer·ica /ə'merɪkə; ə'mɛrɪkə/ n the United States of ~. 美国。

Amer·ican /ə'merɪkən; ə'mɛrɪkən/ adj in N or S America, esp the US. (北或南)美洲的; (尤指)美国的。 '~ **organ**, small organ with reeds but no pipes. 美国风琴(一种有簧无管之小型风琴)。 '~ **plan**, (at hotels) system of charges including room, all meals and service. 美国式旅馆计帐法(包括房间,三餐及服务费)。 □ n native or inhabitant of America; citizen of the US. 美国人; 美国居民; 美国公民。 ~**·ism** /-ɪzəm; -ɪzəm/ n [C] word or phrase typical of ~ English; [U] loyalty to the US or to things typically ~. 美国英语所特有之字词; 对于美国或美国所特有之事物的忠诚; 美国精神。

am·ethyst /'æmɪθɪst; 'æmɪθɪst/ n precious stone, purple or violet. 紫晶; 紫水晶。

ami·able /'eɪmɪəbl; 'emɪəbl/ adj good-tempered; kind-hearted; easy and pleasant to talk to: 好脾气的; 仁慈的; 友善的; 和蔼的; 亲切的: *I've always found him a most ~ fellow*. 我总觉得他是一位非常亲切的人。 **ami·a·bil·ity** /ˌeɪmɪə'bɪlətɪ; ˌemɪə'bɪlətɪ/ n 1 [U] friendliness. 友善; 和蔼; 亲切。 **2** (*pl*) (**-ties**) friendly remarks: 友善亲切的谈话: *after a few amiabilities*. 说过几句客套话之后。 **ami·ably** /-əblɪ; -əblɪ/ adv

amic·able /'æmɪkəbl; 'æmɪkəbl/ adj peaceable; done in a friendly way: 和平的; 温和的; 和善的; 友好的: *When countries cannot settle a dispute in an ~ way, they should settle it by arbitration*. 当国与国间不能和平解决一项争端时, 他们应由仲裁加以解决。 **amica·bil·ity** /ˌæmɪkə'bɪlətɪ; ˌæmɪkə'bɪlətɪ/ n **amic·ably** /-əblɪ; -əblɪ/ adv: *live together amicably, peacefully, in a friendly way*. 友好地生活在一起。

amid /ə'mɪd; ə'mɪd/, **amidst** /ə'mɪdst; ə'mɪdst/ preps (poet) among; in or into the middle of: (诗)在…之中; 在…之间。

amid·ships /ə'mɪdʃɪps; ə'mɪdʃɪps/ adv (naut) halfway between the bows and stern of a ship: (航海)在船之中部: *Our cabin is ~*. 我们的舱位在船的中腰。

amir, ameer, emir /ə'mɪə(r); ə'mɪr/ n title used by some Muslim rulers. 埃米尔; 穆斯林统治者。

amiss /ə'mɪs; ə'mɪs/ pred adj, adv wrong(ly); out of order: 误; 差错(地); 有毛病的: *There's not much ~ with it*. 它没有多大毛病。 *Nothing comes ~ to him*, (colloq) He's ready to welcome, is able to use, anything that comes to him. (口) 什么对他都是好的。 **take sth ~**, take offence at it, be hurt in one's feelings: (因为某事而)见怪; 生气: *Don't take it ~ if I point out your errors*. 假若我指出你的错误, 请勿见怪。

am·ity /'æmətɪ; 'æmətɪ/ n [U] friendship; friendly relations (between persons or countries): 友善; 和睦; 友好; (人与人或国与国间的)友好关系: *live in ~ with sb*; *a treaty of ~*. 友好条约。

am·me·ter /'æmɪtə(r); 'æm,mitə/ n meter that measures electric current in amperes. 安培计; 电表。

am·mo·nia /ə'məʊnɪə; ə'monɪə/ n [U] strong, colourless gas (**NH₃**) with a sharp smell, used in refrigeration and for the manufacture of explosives and fertilizers; solution of this gas in water. 阿摩尼亚; 氨(强烈无色气体, 符号为 NH₃, 味极臭, 用于冷却、制造炸药和肥料); 阿摩尼亚水; 氨水。 **am·mo·ni·ated** /ə'məʊnɪeɪtɪd; ə'monɪ,etɪd/ adj combined with ~. 与氨化合的。

am·mon·ite /'æmənaɪt; 'æmə,naɪt/ n coiled shell of an extinct mollusc. 菊石(已绝灭之鹦鹉螺的盘线形坚壳)。

am·mu·ni·tion /ˌæmjʊ'nɪʃn; ˌæmjə'nɪʃən/ n [U]

military stores, esp of explosives (shells, bombs, etc) to be used against the enemy. 军火; 弹药。

am·nesia /æm'niːzɪə US: -'niːʒə; æm'nɪʒɪə/ n [U] (path) partial or total loss of memory. (病理)记忆缺失; 健忘。

am·nesty /'æmnɪstɪ; 'æm,nɛstɪ/ n (pl **-ties**) [C] general pardon. esp for offences against the State: 大赦 (尤指对内乱罪犯而言): *The rebels returned home under an ~*. 叛徒们被特赦释放回家。

amoeba /ə'miːbə; ə'mibə/ n (pl **~s** or **~e** /-biː; -bi/, zool) simple microscopic form of living matter, found in water, soil and animal parasites, always changing shape and too small to be seen except with the help of a microscope. (动物)阿米巴; 变形虫(极微小之单细胞生物, 生存于水、土壤及寄生虫中, 随时改变形状, 除用显微镜外, 肉眼不能看见)。 **amoebic** /ə'miːbɪk; ə'mibɪk/ adj of, caused by, amoebae: 阿米巴的; 变形虫的: *amoebic dysentery*. 阿米巴痢疾; 变形虫痢疾。

amok /ə'mɒk; ə'mɑk/ adv (also 亦作 **amuck**) **run ~**, run about wildly and act violently. 杀气腾腾; 胡作非为。

among /ə'mʌŋ; ə'mʌŋ/, **amongst** /ə'mʌŋst; ə'mʌŋst/ preps **1** (showing position) surrounded by; in the middle of: (表示位置)被…所环绕; 在…中间: *a village ~ the hills*; 冈峦环绕的村庄; *sitting ~ her children*; 坐在她的孩子们的中间; *hiding ~ the bushes*. 隐藏在树丛中间。 (Note that the n or pron after among must be pl) (注意 among 后面的名词或代词必须是复数) Cf 参较 *Switzerland is situated between France, Italy, Austria and W Germany*. **2** (also with a pl n or pron, or a collective n, to show inclusion, association, connection): (亦与复数名词或代词, 或集合名词连用, 表示包括在内, 有连带关系)在…之中: *You are only one ~ many who need help*. 你不过是许多需要帮助的人中一个。 *A ~ those present were the Prime Minister, the Bishop of Barchester and Mrs Proudie*. 到场的人士中有首相、巴切斯特之主教及蒲劳迪夫人。 *I saw him ~ the crowd*. 我看见他在人群之中。 **3** (followed by a superl) one of: (后接最高级形容词)…之一: *Leeds is ~ the largest industrial towns in England*. 里兹是英国最大工业城市之一。 **4** (indicating division, distribution, possession or joint activity to, for or by more than two persons): (表示涉及二人以上之划分, 分配, 所有, 共同行为): *He divided his property ~ his sons*. 他把他的财产分给他的儿子们。 *You must settle the matter ~ yourselves*. 你们必须自行解决此事。 *They had less than £10 ~ them*. all of them together had less than £10. 他们的钱全部加起来不到十英镑。 ⇨ **between²(7). 5** (after a prep): (用于介词之后): *Choose one from ~ these*. 从这些中间选一个。

amoral /ˌeɪ'mɒrəl US: -'mɔːrəl; e'mɔrəl/ adj nonmoral; not concerned with morals. 非道德的; 与道德无关的。

am·or·ous /'æmərəs; 'æmərəs/ adj easily moved to love; showing love; of (esp sexual) love: 多情的; 爱情的; (尤指)性爱的; 色情的: ~ *looks*; 脉脉含情的表情; *an ~ young man*; 多情的青年; ~ *poetry*. 情诗。 ~**·ly** adv

amor·phous /ə'mɔːfəs; ə'mɔrfəs/ adj having no definite shape or form. 无定形的。

amor·tize /ə'mɔːtaɪz US: 'æmərt-; 'æmɚ,taɪz/ vt [VP6A] (legal) end (a debt) by setting aside money regularly for future payments. (法律)经常按时拨出一笔金钱借以逐渐分期清偿(债务); 摊还。 ⇨ *sinking fund* at **sinking**. **amor·ti·za·tion** /ə,mɔːtɪ'zeɪʃn US: ,æm-ərtɪ-; ,æmɚtɪ'zeʃən/ n

amount /ə'maʊnt; ə'maʊnt/ vi [VP3A] ~ **to**, add up to; be equal to: 总计; 等于: *His debts ~ to £ 5000*. 他的债务共达五千英镑。 *What he said ~ed to very little indeed*, didn't mean much, wasn't important. 他所说的话并不重要。 *Riding on a bus without paying the fare ~s to* (= is the same thing as) *cheating the bus company*. 乘公共汽车不付车资等于欺骗公共汽车公司。 *It*

~s to this, that ..., It means that .... 那就是说…。□ n 1 total; whole: 总额; 总数: He owed me £100 but could pay only half that ~, could only pay £50. 他欠我一百英镑, 但是只能偿还总数的一半(即五十英镑). 2 [C] quantity: 数量: A large ~ of money is spent on tobacco every year. 每年都要花费大量金钱在烟草上. There is still quite an ~ of prejudice against him. 人们对他尚有相当大的偏见. any ~ of, large quantity: 大量: He has any ~ of money, is very rich. 他的钱不可数计(极富有之意). in large/small, etc ~s, large/small, etc quantities at a time. 大量地; 大宗地; 大批地(小额地等).

amour /ə'muə(r); ə'mur/ n [C] (facet) love affair: (玩笑语) 恋爱: Don't bore us with accounts of your ~s. 不要老讲你的恋爱史来烦我们.

amour-propre /ˌæmuə 'prɔprə; ˌamur'propr/ n (F) self-respect; self-esteem. (法)自尊;自重;自负.

amp /æmp; æmp/ n (abbr) (略)=ampere.

am·pere /'æmpeə(r) US: 'æmpɪər; 'æmpɪər/ n unit for measuring electric current. 安培(计算电流之单位).

am·pheta·mine /æm'fetəmi:n; æm'fɛtəˌmin/ n [C, U] (med) (trade name 商标名 Benzedrine) (variety of) drug used medically, eg for slimming, and by drug addicts seeking euphoria. (医) 安非他明(用于减肥或有毒瘾者寻求精神欣快之药物).

am·phib·ian /æm'fɪbɪən; æm'fɪbɪən/ n 1 animal able to live both on land and in water, eg a frog. 两栖动物(如青蛙). 2 aircraft designed to take off from and

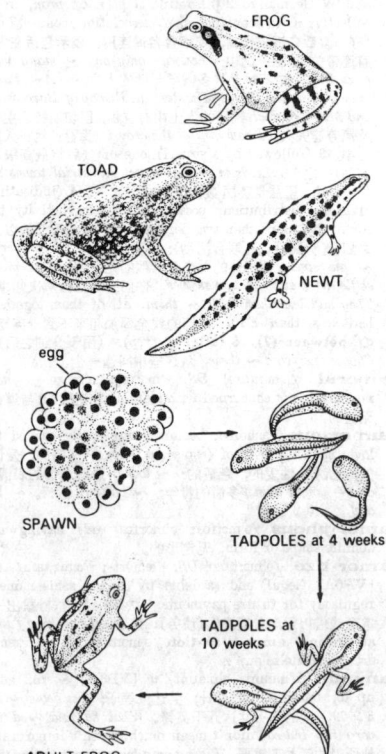

FROG

TOAD

NEWT

egg

SPAWN

TADPOLES at 4 weeks

TADPOLES at 10 weeks

ADULT FROG

amphibians

alight on either land or water. 两栖飞机; 水陆两用飞机. 3 flat-bottomed vehicle able to move in water and on land: 水陆两用之平底车辆: (attrib) (用作定语) ~ tank. 水陆两用战车.

am·phibi·ous /æm'fɪbɪəs; æm'fɪbɪəs/ adj adapted for both land and water: 水陆两栖的: ~ vehicles, vehicles that can cross rivers, etc as well as move on land; 两栖车辆; 水陆两用车辆; ~ operations, military operations in which land forces use ~ vehicles when making an invasion from the sea. (陆军部队使用两栖车辆自海上进攻的)两栖作战.

amphi·theatre (US = -ter) /'æmfɪθɪətə(r); 'æmfəˌθiətə/ n 1 round or oval unroofed building with rows of seats rising behind and above each other round an open space used for public games and amusements. (四周有阶梯式座位之) 露天圆形(或椭圆形) 竞技场或剧场. 2 (not US) rows of seats similarly arranged in a half-circle in a theatre. (不用于美)剧场中之半圆形阶梯式座位. 3 (natural ~) level space with hills rising on all sides. 四面被小山环绕之一块平地.

arena

an amphitheatre

am·phora /'æmfərə; 'æmfərə/ n (pl ~s or ~e /-ri:; -ˌri/) two-handled jar, used in ancient Greece and Rome for holding wine or oil. (古希腊和罗马用以盛酒或油的)双柄瓶; 双耳瓶.

ample /'æmpl; 'æmpl/ adj (-r, -st) 1 large-sized; with plenty of space: 大的; 广大的: This new car has an ~ boot. 这部新车有一很宽大的行李厢. There's ~ room for the children on the back seat. 后座很宽敞足以容纳孩子们. 2 plentiful; abundant: 丰富的: He has ~ resources, is wealthy. 他很富裕. 3 sufficient; quite enough: 足够的; 充足的: £5 will be ~ for my needs. 五英镑将足够应付我的需要了. **am·ply** /'æmplɪ; 'æmplɪ/ adv: amply supplied with money, having more than is needed; 有充足的经费(已超过需要); amply rewarded, well rewarded. 得到足够的报酬.

am·plify /'æmplɪˌfaɪ; 'æmpləˌfaɪ/ vt (pt, pp -fied) [VP6A] 1 make larger or fuller, esp give fuller information, more details, etc, about: 扩大; 放大; 扩充;详述: ~ a story/an account. 详述故事(将一项叙述作详细的陈述). 2 increase the strength of (voltage or current, etc). 增强(电压或电流等). **am·pli·fi·ca·tion** /ˌæmplɪfɪ'keɪʃn; ˌæmpləfə'keʃən/ n **am·pli·fier** /'æmplɪfaɪə(r); 'æmpləˌfaɪə/ n appliance for ~ing. 放大器; 扩音器;扩大器;增幅器.

am·pli·tude /'æmplɪtju:d US: -tu:d; 'æmpləˌtjud/ n [U] (formal) breadth; largeness; abundance. (正式用语)广阔;广大;丰富.

am·poule (US also **am·pule**) /'æmpu:l; 'æmpul/ n small container, esp for a hypodermic injection. 安瓿(装一次用量之皮下注射液的小玻璃管); 腹梅; 壶腹状玻管.

am·pu·tate /'æmpjuteɪt; 'æmpjəˌtet/ vt [VP6A] cut off, eg an arm, a leg, by surgery. (以外科手术)截断(臂, 腿等); 切除. **am·pu·ta·tion** /ˌæmpju'teɪʃn; ˌæmpjə'teʃən/ n

amuck /ə'mʌk; ə'mʌk/ adv ⇨ amok.

amu·let /'æmjulɪt; 'æmjəlɪt/ n sth worn in the belief or hope that it will protect the wearer (against evil, etc). 护身符; 驱邪物.

amuse /ə'mju:z; ə'mjuz/ vt [VP6A] 1 make time pass pleasantly for: 娱乐; 使快乐: The boys ~d

themselves (by) drawing caricatures of their teacher.
男孩子们画他们老师的漫画像以取笑。Keep the baby ~d
with these toys. 用这些玩具使婴儿高兴。2 make (sb)
laugh or smile: His foolish mistakes ~d
all of us. 他的愚笨的错误使我们都发笑。The children
were ~d at/by the storyteller's jokes. 小孩子们听了讲
故事者的笑话，觉得很好笑。We were ~d to learn
that …. 我们获悉…觉得好笑。amus·ing part adj
causing laughter or smiles: 好笑的；有趣的；引人发笑的:
an amusing story/storyteller. 好笑的故事（引人发笑的
讲故事者）。~·ment n 1 [U] state of being ~d: 娱
乐；快乐: She couldn't hide her ~ment at his foolish
mistake. 她看到他的愚笨的错误，隐藏不住想笑的心情。
To the great ~ment of everybody, the actor's beard fell
off. 使每个人都感到极其好笑的是那演员的胡须掉下来
了。He looked at me in ~ment. 他很感兴趣地望着我。
2 [C] sth that makes time pass pleasantly: 提供娱乐或
消遣的事物；娱乐品；游乐场所: There are plenty of
~ments here — cinemas, theatres, concerts, football
matches, and so on. 这里有很多娱乐—电影院,戏院,
音乐会,足球比赛等等。'~ment arcade, room or hall
containing pin-tables, gambling machines, etc, esp in
large towns, seaside resorts, etc. 游乐室；游乐厅（内设
弹球台，宾果机，赌博机等，尤指在大城镇，海滨胜地等
中者）。'~ment park/grounds, place with swings,
roundabouts, shooting galleries, and other means of
amusing oneself. 儿童乐园；游乐场（设有秋千,旋转木
马,打靶廊及其他游乐设备）。places of ~ment, cinemas,
theatres, etc. 娱乐场所（如电影院,戏院等）。do sth for
~ment, do it as a means of passing time pleasantly,
not for a serious purpose. 为消遣而做某事。
an¹ /æn; ən; strong form: æn; æn/ indef art ⇨ a².
an² /æn; æn/ conj (old use) if. (旧用法)假若; 倘使。
anach·ron·ism /ə'nækrənɪzm; ə'nækrə,nɪzəm/ n
[C] 1 mistake in dating sth; sth out of date now or in
a description of past events: 年代错误; 时代错误; 过时
之事物; 对过去事件之叙述中与当时的时代不符的事物:
In the sentence 'Julius Caesar looked at his wrist-watch
and lifted the telephone receiver' there are two ~s. 在‘凯
撒看看他的手表，拿起电话听筒’这句话中，有两项与时代
不符的事物。2 person, custom, attitude, etc regarded
(unfavourably) as out of date: 被视为过时（不合时宜）
的人,习俗,态度等: Most young people in Britain regard
Tory politicians who shoot grouse in Scotland as
dreadful ~s. 大多数的英国青年认为在苏格兰射猎松鸡
的保守党政客是不合时代要求的人。anach·ron·is·tic
/ə,nækrə'nɪstɪk; ə,nækrə'nɪstɪk/ adj
ana·conda /,ænə'kɒndə; ,ænə'kɑndə/ n large snake
of tropical S America, esp the kind that crushes its
prey. 南美洲的一种热带大蟒蛇（尤指能卷死其所捕获之
动物者）; 水蟒。
anae·mia (US = ane·mia) /ə'niːmɪə; ə'nimɪə/ n
[U] lack of enough blood; poor condition of the blood,
causing paleness. 贫血; 贫血症。anaemic(US=anemic)
/ə'niːmɪk; ə'nimɪk/ adj suffering from ~. 患贫血
症的。
an·aes·thesia (US = an·es·thesia) /,ænɪs'θiːzɪə
US: -'θiːʒə; ,ænəs'θiʒə/ n [U] state of being unable
to feel (pain, heat, cold, etc); branch of chemistry
concerned with substances producing this state. (对痛,
热,冷等之)感觉缺失; 麻木; 麻醉; 麻醉剂学(化
学中之一门)。an·aes·thetic (US = an·es·thetic)
/,ænɪs'θetɪk; ,ænəs'θɛtɪk/ n [C] substance (eg ether,
chloroform), technique, that produces ~: 麻醉药,麻醉
剂(如醚,氯仿); 麻醉术: under an anaesthetic. 在麻醉状
态中。general anaesthetic, one affecting the whole
body, usu administered in hospital. 全身麻醉药(通常在
医院中施用者)。local anaesthetic, one administered
by injection and affecting only part of the body, eg
into the gums by a dentist. 局部麻醉药(借注射使身
体局部麻醉,如牙医注射入齿龈中者)。an·aes·the·tize
(US = an·es·the·tize) /ə'niːsθətaɪz; ə'nɛsθə,taɪz/ vt

[VP6A] make insensible to pain, etc. 使麻醉; 施以麻
醉剂。an·aes·the·tist (US = an·es·the·tist) /ə'niː-
sθətɪst; ə'nɛsθətɪst/ n person trained to administer
anaesthetics. 麻醉师; 麻醉士。
ana·gram /'ænəgræm; 'ænəgræm/ n word made by
changing the order of the letters in another word (eg
plum-lump): 变位字 (经变动另一词中字母顺序而成之
词，例如 plum-lump): Let's play ~s, make words of
this kind. 我们来玩字谜游戏。
anal /'eɪnl; 'enl/ adj (anat) of the anus. (解剖)肛
门的。
ana·lects /'ænəlekts; 'ænə,lɛkts/ (also ana·lecta
/,ænə'lektə; ,ænə'lɛktə/) n pl collection of pieces of
literature: 文选; 语录; 选集: Confucian ~. 论语。
an·al·gesia /,ænæl'dʒiːzɪə US: -ʒə; ,ænæl'dʒiziə/ n
[U] (med) absence of, condition of not feeling, pain.
(医) 痛觉缺失; 无痛觉。an·al·gesic /,ænæl'dʒiːsɪk;
,ænæl'dʒizɪk/ n substance, eg an ointment which
relieves pain. 止痛药; 镇痛药(如止痛软膏)。
anal·og·ous /ə'næləgəs; ə'næləgəs/ adj ~ (with),
similar or parallel (to): 相似的; (与…)类似的: The two
processes are not ~ (with each other). 这两种过程(彼此)
不相似。~·ly adv
ana·logue (also -log) /'ænəlɒg US: -lɔːg; 'ænl,ɔg/
n 1 sth that is similar to another thing: 类似物: meat
~, artificial prepared substitute for meat (usu of soya
beans). 人造肉(通常以黄豆加工制成)。2 '~ computer
n one which can perform operations on numbers, the
numbers being represented by some physical quantity
or electrical signal. 模拟计算机。⇨ digital computer at
digit.
anal·ogy /ə'nælədʒɪ; ə'nælədʒɪ/ n (pl -gies) 1 [C]
partial likeness or agreement. 比喻; 相似; 类似。draw
an ~ between, describe the similarities: 在…之间作比
喻: The teacher drew an ~ between the human heart and
a pump. 教师打了一个比喻, 把人的心脏比做唧筒。2 [U]
by/from ~; on the ~ of, by a process of reasoning
between parallel cases: 用类推法; 根据…类推: argue by
~; 用类推法辩论: argument by/from ~. 用类推法所
作之议论。
ana·lyse (US = -lyze) /'ænəlaɪz; 'ænl,aɪz/ vt [VP6-
A] 1 examine (sth) in order to learn what it is made
up of: 分析(某事物)以发现其构造的成分: If we ~
water, we find that it is made up of two parts of
hydrogen and one part of oxygen. 如果我们分析水,
我们就会发现它是由二分氢一分氧构成的。2(gram) split
up (a sentence) into its grammatical parts. (语法) 分析
(句子)以寻出其语法成分。3 study or examine in order
to learn about: 分析研究: The leader tried to ~ the causes
of our failure. 领袖试图分析研究我们失败的原因。4 =
psycho~.
analy·sis /ə'næləsɪs; ə'næləsɪs/ n (pl -yses /-əsiːz;
-ə,siz/) 1 [U] (eg of a book, a character, a situation)
separation into parts possibly with comment and
judgement: (对某一部书,性格,情况等)分析(可能附带
评判): critical ~ of literary texts; 对文学作品本文的
批评分析: expert ~ of market trends, ie of how prices,
sales, etc are likely to go; 专家对市场趋势所作的分析;
[C] instance of this; statement of the result of doing
this. 分析的实例; 分析结果的说明。⇨ synthesis. 2 =
psycho~. ana·lytic /,ænə'lɪtɪk; ,ænl'ɪtɪk/, -i·cal
/-kl; -kl/ adj of ~; using ~. 分析的; 用分析法的。
ana·lyti·cally /-klɪ; -klɪ/ adv
ana·lyst /'ænəlɪst; 'ænlɪst/ n 1 person skilled in
making (esp chemical) analyses: 分析家; (尤指)化学分
析家: a food ~. 食物分析家。2 = psycho~.
ana·lyze /'ænə,laɪz/ = analyse.
ana·paest (US = -pest) /'ænəpiːst US: -pest; 'ænə-
,pɛst/ n (of verse rhythm) foot consisting of two
unaccented syllables followed by one accented syllable,
(⌣⌣-)as in eg 'I am 'mon/arch of 'all/I sur'vey'. (指
诗律) 抑抑扬格 (由两个轻音节后跟一个重音节组成之音

音步, 例如 'I am 'mon / arch of 'all / I sur'vey'). **ana·paes·tic**, (US = **-pestic**) /ˌænəˈpiːstɪk US: -ˈpest-; ˌænəˈpestɪk/ adj

an·archy /ˈænəkɪ; ˈænəkɪ/ n [U] absence of government or control; disorder; confusion. 无政府状态; 无秩序; 混乱。 **an·arch·ism** /-ɪzəm; -ɪzəm/ n [U] 无政府主义。 **an·arch·ist** /-ɪst; -ɪst/ n person who favours ~; person who wishes to overthrow all established governments. 无政府主义者。 **an·archic** /əˈnɑːkɪk; ænˈɑrkɪk/ adj **an·archi·cal·ly** /-klɪ; -klɪ/ adv

anath·ema /əˈnæθəmə; əˈnæθəmə/ n 1 (eccles) formal declaration of the Church, excommunicating sb or condemning sth as evil. (教会)教会的正式声明(将某人逐出教会或宣布某事物为邪恶者)。 2 sth that is detested. 极令人讨厌之事物。 ~·tize /əˈnæθəmətaɪz; əˈnæθəmə,taɪz/ vt, vi curse. 诅咒。

anat·omy /əˈnætəmɪ; əˈnætəmɪ/ n [U] science of the structure of animal bodies; study of their structures by separation into parts. 解剖学; 解剖。 **ana·tomi·cal** /ˌænəˈtɒmɪkl; ˌænəˈtɑmɪkl/ adj **anat·om·ist** /-ɪst; -ɪst/ n person who dissects corpses; person who studies or teaches ~. 解剖尸体者; 解剖学家。

an·ces·tor /ˈænsestə(r); ˈænsestɚ/ n any one of those persons from whom one is descended, esp one more remote than a grandparent: 祖先; 祖宗(尤指祖父母或比祖父母以上者)。 ~ worship, the worship of one's ~s as spirits or gods. 祭祖。 **an·ces·tress** /-trɪs; -trɪs/ n woman ~. 女祖宗; 女祖宗。 **an·ces·tral** /ænˈsestrəl; ænˈsestrəl/ adj belonging to, having come from, one's ~s: 祖先的; 祖宗传下的: his ancestral home. 他的祖居。 **an·ces·try** /ˈænsestrɪ; ˈænsestrɪ/ n (pl -ries) line of ~s. 祖先; 祖系。

an·chor /ˈæŋkə(r); ˈæŋkɚ/ n heavy piece of iron with a ring at one end, to which a cable is fastened, used for keeping a ship fast to the sea bottom or a balloon to the ground; anything that gives stability or security. (系船或汽球用的)锚; 予人稳定或安全感之事物; 借以支持或依靠之物。 let go/drop/cast the ~, lower it. 抛锚; 下锚。 weigh ~, raise it 起锚。 come to ~; bring (a ship) to ~, stop sailing and lower the ~. 锚泊; 下锚; 将(船只)停航并下锚。 lie/ride/be at ~, be made fast and held safe by the ~. 停泊妥当; 停泊着。 ~·man /-mən; -mən/, one who co-ordinates the work of a group of persons who work together, eg in a radio or TV studio. 协调员(协调一工作组之工作者); (广播电台或电视台新闻节目等中之)主播。 □ vt, vi [VP6A] make (a ship) secure with an ~; [VP2A] lower an ~. 下锚以使(船)停泊稳定; 下锚。 ~·age /-rɪdʒ; -rɪdʒ/ n place where ships may ~ safely. 船只可安全停泊之处所; 锚地; 泊地。

an·chor·ite /ˈæŋkəraɪt; ˈæŋkə,raɪt/ n hermit. 隐士; 隐居者。

an·chovy /ˈæntʃəvɪ; ˈæntʃəvɪ/ n (pl -vies) small fish of the herring family; it has a strong flavour and is used for sauces, etc. 鳀类鱼; 鳀鱼: (attrib) (用作定语) ~ paste/sauce. 鳀鱼酱(鳀鱼汁)。

ancient /ˈeɪnʃənt; ˈeɪnʃənt/ adj 1 belonging to times long past: 古代的; 远古的: ~ Rome and Greece; 古罗马及希腊; the ~s, the civilized people who lived long ago. 古人; 古代的文明人。 2 (often hum) very old: (常作诙谐用语)旧式的; 很旧的: an ~-looking hat. 一顶样子很旧的帽子。

an·cil·lary /ænˈsɪlərɪ US: ˈænsəlerɪ; ˈænsə,lɛrɪ/ adj 1 helping, providing a service to those carrying on the main business of an enterprise: 辅助的: The transport corps is ~ to the infantry. 运输队是步兵的辅助部队。 2 subordinate (to): 附属的: ~ roads/undertakings/industries. 附属道路(事业, 工业)。

and /usu forms: ən, ənd; ən, ənd; (after t, d, f, v, θ, ð, s, z, ʃ, ʒ) often n; n; strong form: ænd; ænd/ conj 1 (connecting words, clauses, sentences): (连接单词, 句子, 句子)和, 及; as: a table and four chairs; 一张

桌子和四把椅子; learning to read and write. 学习读和写。 (When two nn stand for things or persons closely connected, the determining word is not repeated before the second n): (当两个名词代表互有密切关系之物或人时, 第二个名词前之指定词不要重复): a knife and fork. 一副刀叉。 Cf 参较 a knife and a spoon; 一把刀及一把汤匙; my father and mother. 我的父母。 Cf 参较 my father and my uncle. 我的父亲和我的叔父。 2 (Note twenty-five and five and twenty, sometimes used in telling the time): (注意: twenty-five 亦可写成 five and twenty, 后者有时用以指钟点): five and twenty to six. 五点三十五分。 3 (In constructions replacing an if-clause): (用于代替‘假设’从句的构造中): Work hard and you will pass (= If you work hard, you will pass) the examination. 你若是用功读书, 就会考及格。 4 (indicating intensive repetition or continuation): (表示加强语意的重复或连续不断之意): for hours and hours; 许多许多小时; for miles and miles; 很多很多英里; better and better. 愈来愈好。 We knocked and knocked, continued to knock. 我们敲了又敲(继续不断地敲门)。 5 (colloq) to: (口) = to: Try and come early 尽量早来。 Go and buy one. 去买一个。

an·dante /ænˈdæntɪ; ænˈdæntɪ/ n, adj, adv (I; music) (piece of music to be played) in moderately slow time. (意; 音乐)以适度缓慢的拍子(来演奏的乐曲); 用中慢板的; 行板。

and·iron /ˈændaɪən; ˈænd,aɪɚn/ n iron support (usu one of a pair) for holding logs in a fireplace. 柴架(壁炉中用以支架木柴之铁架, 通常指一对柴架中之一只)。 Also called 亦称作 firedog.

an·ec·dote /ˈænɪkdəʊt; ˈænɪk,dot/ n short, usu amusing, story about some real person or event. 轶事; 趣闻(关于真人真事之小趣事)。

ane·mia, ane·mic ⇨ anaemia, anaemic.

anem·om·eter /ˌænɪˈmɒmɪtə(r); ˌænəˈmɑmɪtɚ/ n [C] (met) instrument for measuring the force and velocity of the wind. (气象)风速表; 风力计(测定风及风速之仪器)。

anem·one /əˈnemənɪ; əˈnɛmə,ni/ n 1 (bot) (also called 亦称 wind-flower) small star-shaped woodland flower; cultivated varieties of this flower. (植物)白头翁(生长于森林地带之星状小花); 秋牡丹(白头翁之园艺变种)。 2 'sea ~, popular name of a creature living in the sea, having a tube-like body with tentacles. 海葵(一种海生动物之通俗名称, 有带须之管状躯体)。

an anemone   a sea anemone

anent /əˈnent; əˈnɛnt/ prep (old use, or Scot) concerning; about. (旧用法, 或苏格兰语)关于。

an·er·oid /ˈænərɔɪd; ˈænə,rɔɪd/ adj, n ~ (barometer), one that measures air-pressure by the action of air on the elastic lid of a box partly exhausted of air. 不用液体的无液晴雨表; 空盒气压表。

an·es·thesia n ⇨ anaesthesia.

anew /əˈnjuː US: əˈnuː; əˈnju/ adv again; in a new or different way. 重新; 再一次; 以一种新的或不同的方式。

angel /ˈeɪndʒl; ˈendʒəl/ n 1 (esp in Christian belief)

messenger from God (usu shown in pictures as a human being in white with wings). (尤指基督教师所相信之)天使 (在图画中通常作人形, 穿白衣, 有翼)。**2** lovely or innocent person. 可爱或纯洁的人。**3** (as a compliment to sb who is kind, thoughtful, etc): (对仁慈, 体贴等之人的恭维语): *Thanks, you're an ~!* 谢谢, 你真是个大好人! **~·ic** /æn'dʒelɪk; æn'dʒɛlɪk/ *adj* of or like an ~. 天使的; 如天使的。**~i·cally** /-klɪ; -klɪ/ *adv*

an·gelica /æn'dʒelɪkə; æn'dʒɛlɪkə/ *n* [U] sweet-smelling plant, esp the kind used in cooking and medicine; its stem, boiled in sugar. 白芷; 白芷根之蜜钱。(一种有甜味之植物, 用于烹调及医药); 白芷根之蜜钱。

an·gelus /'ændʒɪləs; 'ændʒələs/ *n* (also 亦作 **A~**) (bell rung in RC churches at morning, noon and sunset to call people to recite) prayer to the Virgin Mary. (天主教在早晨, 中午及日落时所敲之)奉告祈祷钟; 奉告祈祷。

anger /'æŋɡər; 'æŋɡɚ/ *n* [U] the strong feeling that comes when one has been wronged or insulted, or when one sees cruelty or injustice; the feeling that makes people want to quarrel or fight: 怒; 忿怒: *filled with ~ at what he saw;* 对于他所见到的事感到愤怒; *speak in ~;* 忿怒地说话; *do sth in a moment of ~.* 在一时的忿怒之下做出某事。 □ *vt* [VP6A] fill (sb) with ~; make angry: 使(某人)发怒; 激怒: *He is easily ~ed.* 他容易被激怒。

an·gina pec·toris /æn,dʒaɪnə 'pektərɪs; æn'dʒaɪnə 'pektərɪs/ *n* (Lat) (path) heart disease marked by sharp pain in the chest. (拉)(病理)心绞痛; 胸气塞; 狭心症。

angle¹ /'æŋɡl; 'æŋɡl/ *n* **1** space between two lines or surfaces that meet. 角; 隅。**'~-dozer** /*n* mechanical scraper used for levelling roads or ground surfaces. (用以弄平路面或地面的)斜铲推土机。⇨ **bulldozer**. **'~-iron** *n* L-shaped length of iron or steel used to strengthen a framework. (用以加强构架之 L 形的)角铁。**'~-park** *vt, vi* park a vehicle at an angle to the side of the roadway, etc: 与马路等成斜地一角度停放汽车: *cars ~-parked as close as herringbones.* 停放在马路边侧彼此密接如鲱鱼骨般的汽车。**2** (fig) point of view: (喻) 观点; 看法; 角度: *Try looking at the affair from a different ~.* 试从不同的角度看这件事。*What ~ are you writing the story from?* 你是从何种观点来写这故事? □ *vt* [VP6A] *~ the news,* present it to the public in a particular way (usu to suit the bias of the writer or his employer). 从某一特殊观点报道新闻(通常为迎合报导者或其雇主之偏见); 歪曲报导新闻。

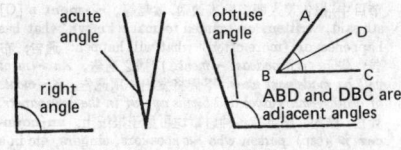

acute angle

obtuse angle

right angle

ABD and DBC are adjacent angles

angles

angle² /'æŋɡl; 'æŋɡl/ *vi* [VP2A, 3A] **1** fish (for trout, etc) with a rod, line, hook and bait. 钓(鱼)。**2** ~ **for,** (fig) use tricks, hints, etc in order to get sth: (喻)使用手腕, 暗示等以求获得某物; 引诱; 谋取: *~ for compliments;* 求取旁人的赞誉; *~ for an invitation to a party.* 设法让人邀请参加某宴会。**ang·ler** /'æŋɡlər; 'æŋɡlɚ/ *n* person who ~s. 钓(鱼)者。Cf 参较 *fisherman* using nets, etc. 渔夫(用网等捕鱼者)。**ang·ling** *n* [U] (art, sport of) fishing with a rod. 钓鱼; 钓鱼术; 垂钓。

Ang·li·can /'æŋɡlɪkən; 'æŋɡlɪkən/ *n, adj* (member) of the Church of England. 英国国教的; 英国国教徒。

ang·li·cize /'æŋɡlɪsaɪz; 'æŋɡləˌsaɪz/ *vt* [VP6A] make English or like English: 使成为英文; 英语化; 英国

化: *~ a French word.* 使一法文字成为英文字。**ang·li·cism** /'æŋɡlɪsɪzəm; 'æŋɡlɪˌsɪzəm/ *n* English way of saying sth. 英语语风; 英国人的说法。

Anglo- /'æŋɡloʊ; 'æŋɡlo/ *pref* English: 英国的: *~- French relations,* between GB and France. 英法关系。**,~-'Catholic** *n, adj* (member) of the party in the Anglican Church that insists upon its unbroken connection with the early Christian Church and that objects to being called Protestant. 英国国教高教会派(坚持其与早期基督教继续不断的关系, 并反对被称为新教派)的; 英国国教高教会派之教徒。**,~-'Indian** *n, adj* **(a)** (person) of British birth, living or having lived, in India. 英国出生而居于印度的(人)。**(b)** (person) of mixed British and Indian blood; Eurasian. 英印混血的(人)。**,~-'Saxon** *n, adj* (person) of English descent; one of the group of people who settled in England (from NW Europe) before the Norman Conquest; their language (also called *Old English*). 英国人(的); 盎格鲁撒克逊人(在诺尔曼人征服英国之前 自欧洲西北部移居英格兰者); 盎格鲁撒克逊语(亦称古英语)。

Anglo·mania /ˌæŋɡloʊ'meɪnɪə; ˌæŋɡlo'menɪə/ *n,* excessive love of and admiration for English customs, etc. 对于英国习俗之过份喜爱与赞赏; 英国狂。

Anglo·phile /'æŋɡloʊfaɪl; 'æŋɡloˌfaɪl/ (also **-phil** /-fɪl/ /-fɪl/) *n* person who loves England or English things. 亲英者; 醉心于英国事物者。

Anglo·phobe /'æŋɡloʊfoʊb; 'æŋɡloˌfob/ *n* person who hates or fears England or English things. 憎恶或恐惧英国或英国事物的人; 仇英者。

Anglo·phobia /ˌæŋɡloʊ'foʊbɪə; ˌæŋɡlo'fobɪə/ *n* excessive hatred or fear of England and of English things. 对英国及英国事物之过份憎恶; 仇英。

an·gora /æŋ'ɡɔːrə; æŋ'ɡorə/ *n* **1** [C] long-haired cat, goat or rabbit. 安哥拉猫; 安哥拉山羊; 安哥拉兔。**2** [U] material made from wool of ~ goats. (用安哥拉山羊毛织成之)安哥拉呢。

an·gos·tura /ˌæŋɡə'stjʊərə; ˌæŋɡəs'tjʊrə/ *n* [U] bitter liquid, used as a tonic, made from the bark of a S American tree. 安戈士拉苦味补剂 (用产于南美洲之一种树皮调制成的苦味液)。

angry /'æŋɡrɪ; 'æŋɡrɪ/ *adj* (**-ier, -iest**) **1** filled with anger (with sb, at what sb does or says, about sth): 忿怒的; 发怒的; 生气的 (后接 with 某人, at 某人之言行, about 某事): *He was ~ at being kept waiting.* 他因久候而生气。*He was ~ with himself for having made such a foolish mistake.* 他因犯如此愚蠢的错误而气恼自己。*He will be ~ to learn* (= when he learns) *that you have disobeyed his orders.* 他将知你违背他的命令, 会感生气的。**2** (of a cut, sore, wound) red; inflamed. (指刀伤, 疮, 伤口)发红的; 发炎的; 红肿的。**3** (of the sea, sky, clouds) stormy; threatening. (指海, 天, 云)狂风暴雨的; 狂烈的; 翻腾的。**ang·ri·ly** /-əlɪ; -əlɪ/ *adv*

angst /æŋst; ɑŋst/ *n* [U] (G) feeling of anxiety (eg caused by considering the state of world affairs). (德)焦虑; 恐怖(如因考虑世界局势所引起者)。

an·guish /'æŋɡwɪʃ; 'æŋɡwɪʃ/ *n* [U] severe suffering (esp of mind): (尤指心理上的)剧烈痛苦; 苦恼; 苦闷: *She was in ~ until she knew that her husband's life had been saved.* 她心里一直很痛苦, 直到她知道她丈夫的生命已经得救才放心。**~ed** *adj* expressing ~: 表现痛苦的; 显露苦恼的: *~ed looks.* 痛苦的表情。

angu·lar /'æŋɡjʊlər; 'æŋɡjələ/ *adj* **1** having angles or sharp corners. 有角的; 有尖角的。**2** (of persons) with the shape of the bones showing under the skin; (of a person's nature, etc) rather stiff and awkward: (指人)骨瘦如柴的; 瘦削的; (指人的性情等)拘执的; 不圆滑的; 不灵活的: *an ~ gait.* 僵挺的步态。**~·ity** /ˌæŋɡjʊ'lærɪtɪ; ˌæŋɡjə'lærətɪ/ *n* (*pl* **-ties**)。

ani·line /'ænɪliːn US: 'ænɪlɪn/ *n* substance obtained chemically from coal-tar, used in the manufacture of dyes, drugs, etc. 苯胺 (用化学方法自煤焦油中提出的物质, 用于制造染料、药品等)。

ani·mad·vert / ˌænɪmædˈvɜːt; ˌænəmædˈvɜt / *vi* [VP3A] ~ (*on*), (formal) make (esp critical) remarks (about sb's conduct). (正式用语)批评；指斥；非难. **ani·mad·version** /ˌænɪmædˈvɜːʃn US: -ʒn; ˌænəmædˈvɜʒən/ *n* criticism. 批评；指斥；非难.

ani·mal /ˈænɪml; ˈænəml/ *n* **1** living thing that can feel and move about. Men, dogs, birds, flies, fish and snakes are all ~s. 动物(如人, 狗, 鸟, 蝇, 鱼, 蛇等). **the '~ kingdom**, one of three divisions (the others being *vegetable* and *mineral*). 动物界(博物学上三种类别之一, 其他二界为植物界及矿物界). ⇨ the illus at **ape, bird, cat, dog, domestic, fish, insect, large, reptile, sea, small**. 参看 ape, bird, cat, dog, domestic, fish, insect, large, reptile, sea, small 之插图. **2** four-footed ~ (eg a dog or a horse): 兽; 四足动物(如狗, 马等): ~ *husbandry*, the breeding of cattle, sheep, horses, etc. 畜牧业(牛, 羊, 马等的饲养). **3** ~ other than man. 除人以外的动物. **4** (used attrib) of the physical, not spiritual, side of man: (用作定语)肉体(非精神)的: ~ *needs*, eg food; 肉体上的需要(如食物); ~ *desires*. 肉欲. ~ *spirits*, natural light-heartedness. 气乐; 天生的愉快精神. ~·**cule** /ˌænɪˈmælkjuːl; ˌænəˈmælkjul/ *n* microscopically small ~. 微生动物.

ani·mate /ˈænɪmeɪt; ˈænəmet/ *adj* living; lively. 有生命的; 活的; 生气勃勃的. □ *vt* /ˈænɪmeɪt; ˈænəmet/ [VP6A, 14] ~ *sb/sth* (*to/with sth*), give life to; make lively; inspire: 赋予生命; 鼓舞; 使活泼; 使生气: *A smile ~d her face.* 笑容使她的脸上平添无限生气. *There was an ~d discussion.* 有一场热烈的讨论. *The news ~d us to greater efforts/with greater enthusiasm.* 这消息鼓励我们作更大的努力(激起我们更大的狂热). *All his life this great man was ~d by a passion for truth and justice.* 这个伟人毕生热爱真理和正义. ~**d car'toon**, cinema film made by photographing a series of drawings. 卡通影片. **ani·ma·tion** /ˌænɪˈmeɪʃn; ˌænəˈmeʃən/ *n* [U] (esp) liveliness; ardour. (尤指)活泼; 有生气; 热心.

ani·mism /ˈænɪmɪzəm; ˈænəˌmɪzəm/ *n* [U] belief that all objects (trees, stones, the wind, etc) have souls. 万物(树, 石, 风等)有灵论; 泛灵信仰.

ani·mos·ity /ˌænɪˈmɒsɪtɪ; ˌænəˈmɑsətɪ/ *n* [U] ~ (*against/towards/between*), strong dislike, active enmity; [C] (*pl* -**ties**) instance of this. 憎恶; 仇恨; 敌意; 仇视; 此种情绪之实例.

ani·mus /ˈænɪməs; ˈænəməs/ *n* [U] animosity; (with *indef art*) instance of this: 憎恶; 仇恨; 敌意; 仇视; (与不定冠词连用)此种情绪之实例: *an ~ against me.* 对我的一种仇视.

an·ise /ˈænɪs; ˈænɪs/ *n* plant with sweet-smelling seeds. 大茴香. **ani·seed** /ˈænɪsiːd; ˈænɪˌsid/ *n* [U] seed of ~, used for flavouring. 大茴香子(调味用).

ankle /ˈæŋkl; ˈæŋkl/ *n* joint connecting the foot with the leg; thin part of the leg between this joint and the calf. 踝; 脚脖子. ⇨ the illus at **leg**. 参看 leg 之插图. '~ **socks**, short ones just covering the ~s. 仅盖住脚踝子的短袜. **ank·let** /ˈæŋklɪt; ˈæŋklɪt/ *n* ornament for the ~. 踝饰; 脚镯.

anna /ˈænə; ˈænə/ *n* former copper coin in Pakistan and in India, a sixteenth part of a rupee. 安那(巴基斯坦及印度往昔之一种铜币, 等于一卢比之十六分之一).

an·nals /ˈænlz; ˈænlz/ *n pl* story of events year by year; record of new knowledge or discoveries written year by year; yearly record of the work of a learned society. 编年史(新知识或新发现之)纪年表; 年鉴; (学会之)年报. **an·nal·ist** /ˈænəlɪst; ˈænlɪst/ *n* writer of ~. 编年史作者; 纪年表作者; 年报编撰人.

an·neal /əˈniːl; əˈnil/ *vt* [VP6A] cool (metals, glass, etc) very slowly after heating, in order to toughen and temper. 加热于(金属, 玻璃等)然后缓缓冷却, 使刚化; 退火.

an·nex¹ /əˈneks; əˈnɛks/ *vt* [VP6A, 14] **1** take possession of (territory, etc). 并吞; 霸占(领土等). **2** ~

(*to*), add or join (sth) (as an extra part *to* sth). 合并(某物)(作为另外某物之附属部份, 与它连用, 后接另外的某物). ~·**ation** /ˌæneksˈeɪʃn; ˌænɛksˈeʃən/ *n* [U] ~ing; [C] instance of this, that which is ~ed. 并吞; 合并; 并吞或合并之实例; 合并地; 附加物.

an·nex² /ˈæneks; ˈænɛks/ (also **an·nexe**) *n* [C] **1** smaller building added to, or situated near, a larger one: 增添之较小建筑; 附属建筑物; 扩建部份; 别馆: *an ~ to a hotel.* 旅馆之附属建筑物(或指扩建部份). **2** addition (*to* a document). (文件之)附件(与 to 连用).

an·ni·hi·late /əˈnaɪəleɪt; əˈnaɪəˌlet/ *vt* [VP6A] destroy completely; end the existence of (an army, a fleet): 彻底消灭; 毁灭; 歼灭; 摧毁(如军队, 舰队): *The invasion force was ~d.* 入侵的部队被歼灭了. (fig) (喻) *Radio communication has ~d space.* 无线电通讯已消除了空间的隔阂. **an·ni·hi·la·tion** /əˌnaɪəˈleɪʃn; əˌnaɪə-ˈleʃən/ *n* [U] complete destruction (of military or naval forces, etc). 彻底消灭; 歼灭; 摧毁(指陆海军等).

an·ni·ver·sary /ˌænɪˈvɜːsərɪ; ˌænəˈvɜsərɪ/ *n* [C] (*pl* -**ries**) yearly return of the date of an event; celebration of this: 周年纪念日; 周年纪念: *my wedding ~*; 我的结婚周年纪念; *the ~ of Shakespeare's birth*; 莎士比亚诞辰纪念日; *an ~ dinner*, one held to celebrate an ~. 周年纪念餐会.

Anno Domini /ˌænəʊ ˈdɒmɪnaɪ; ˈæno ˈdɑməˌnaɪ/ (Lat) (abbr form **AD** /ˌeɪ ˈdiː; ˈeˈdi/) in the year of our Lord: (拉)公元; 西元; 耶稣纪元后: *in AD 250*, 250 years after the birth of Jesus. 于公元250年. ⇨ *before Christ* (BC) at **before³**; ⇨ BC in **App 2.** 参看附录二之 BC.

an·no·tate /ˈænəteɪt; ˈænoˌtet/ *vt* [VP6A] add notes (to a book, etc) explaining difficulties, giving opinions, etc: 给(书等)作注释: *an ~d text/version.* 加有注释的本文(译本). **an·no·ta·tion** /ˌænəˈteɪʃn; ˌænoˈteʃən/ *n* [U] annotating; [C] note or comment. 注释; 注解.

an·nounce /əˈnaʊns; əˈnaʊns/ *vt* [VP6A, 9, 14] **1** make known: 宣布; 通告; 发表: *Mr Green ~d (to his friends)* his engagement to Miss White. 格林先生(向他的朋友们)宣布他与怀特小姐订婚. *Mr Green and Miss White will be married in May.* 格林先生与怀特小姐已宣布将于五月结婚. *The book was ~d as in preparation.* 根据预告该书正在印刷中. *The Government ~d that the danger was past.* 政府宣布危险业已过去. **2** make known the arrival of: 通报; 宣告…的来临: *The secretary ~d Mr and Mrs Brown*, spoke their names as they entered. 秘书通报布朗夫妇已到(即在他们进入时报出他们的姓名). **3** say that sb is about to speak, sing, etc (eg in a TV programme). (如在电视节目中)报告某人即将发表谈话, 歌唱等. ~·**ment** *n* [C] sth said, written, or printed to make known what has happened or (more often) what will happen: 通告; 布告; 告示: *a broadcast ~ment.* 广播之通告. *An ~ment will be made next week.* 下周将发出一项通告. *A~ments of deaths, marriages and births appear in the newspapers.* 死亡, 结婚, 出生等各种启事均可见于报纸上. **an·noun·cer** *n* (esp) person who ~s speakers, singers, etc in a radio or TV broadcast. 报告员; (尤指)广播员; 播音员; 无线电广播或电视之节目主持人.

an·noy /əˈnɔɪ; əˈnɔɪ/ *vt* [VP6A esp in passive] *be ~ed with sb/at sth/about sth*, irritate; make rather angry: (尤用于被动语态)打搅; 烦扰; 使烦恼; 使生气: *He was ~ed with his wife because the dinner was badly cooked.* 他对他的妻子感到生气, 因晚餐烹做得不好. *I felt ~ed when he refused to help.* 当他拒绝帮忙时, 我觉得有点生气. *Do stop ~ing your father!* 别再烦你父亲了! *He was ~ed to learn that the train would be delayed.* 他听说火车要误点, 心里感到烦恼. *He felt/got/was ~ed with the boy for being so stupid/was ~ed at the boy's stupidity.* 他对这孩子如此的愚笨所感到烦恼. ~·**ing** *part adj*: *It's ~ing to miss a train.* 赶不上火车是烦人的事. *How ~ing!* 真讨厌! 烦死人! *The ~ing thing about it is that …,* What causes trouble or

irritation is that ... . 讨厌的是···; 麻烦的是···。 ~·ance /-əns; -əns/ n 1 [U] vexation; being ~ed: 烦厌; 烦恼: *with a look of ~ance;* 带着烦恼的表情; *much to our ~ance;* 十分使我们讨厌地; *subject a person to ~ance,* worry him. 使某人受骚扰。 2 [C] sth that ~s: 可厌之事; 烦恼之事: *All these little ~ances did not spoil her sweet temper.* 这一切小小的烦扰并未损及她的好脾气。

an·nual /ˈænjʊəl; ˈænjʊəl/ adj 1 coming or happening every year. 一年一次的。 2 lasting for only one year or season. 一年生的; 仅持续一年或一季的。 3 of one year: 一年的: *his ~ income;* 他每年的收入; *the ~ production.* 年产量。 □ n 1 plant that lives for one year or season. 一年生植物; 一季生植物。 **,hardy** '~, (joc) event, etc which often recurs (and is considered tiresome or monotonous). (谑) 一再发生的事件(被认为是麻烦或单调没趣者)。 2 book, etc that appears under the same title but with new contents every year. 年鉴; 年刊; 年报。 ~·ly adv

an·nu·ity /əˈnjuːətɪ US: -ˈnuː-; əˈnuətɪ/ n [C] (pl -ties) fixed sum of money paid to sb yearly as income during his lifetime; form of insurance to provide such a regular, annual income. 年金; 养老金; 养老金保险。 **an·nui·tant** /əˈnjuːɪtənt US: -ˈnuː-; əˈnuətənt/ n person who receives an ~. 领年金者; 领养老金者。

an·nul /əˈnʌl; əˈnʌl/ vt (-ll-) [VP6A] put an end to, eg an agreement, a law, etc; declare (that sth, eg a marriage, is) invalid, of no effect. 废止(契约, 法律等); 取消(婚姻等); 宣告无效。 ~·ment n

an·nu·lar /ˈænjʊlə(r); ˈænjələ/ adj (rare) ringlike. (罕) 环状的; 如环的。

an·nun·ci·ate /əˈnʌnsɪeɪt; əˈnʌnʃɪet/ vt [VP6A] (formal) announce; proclaim. (正式用语)宣布; 宣告。 **an·nun·ci·ation** /ə,nʌnsɪˈeɪʃn; ə,nʌnsɪˈeʃən/ n **the A~,** (eccles) the announcement by the angel Gabriel to Mary that she was to be the mother of Jesus Christ; festival that commemorates this, 25 Mar. (教会)天使加百列向圣母马利亚报告她将生耶稣; 天使报喜; 天使报喜节(三月廿五日)。

an·ode /ˈænəʊd; ˈænod/ n (electr) (电) (US also called 美亦称 **plate**) 1 positively charged electrode (from which current enters). 阳极; 正极。 ⇨ **cathode.** 2 negative terminal of a battery. 电池的阴极接头。

ano·dyne /ˈænədaɪn; ˈænə,daɪn/ n, adj (medicine, drug) able to lessen pain; (sth) able to give comfort to the mind. 止痛的; 止痛药; 镇痛药; 能给予心灵以安慰的(事物)。

anoint /əˈnɔɪnt; əˈnɔɪnt/ vt [VP6A, 23, 14] apply oil or ointment to (esp as a religious ceremony): 涂油; 搽油; 涂膏(尤指作为一种宗教仪式而为者): ~ *sb with oil.* 将油涂在某人身上。 *The Lord ~ed thee King over Israel* (⇨ I Sam 15:17). 耶和华膏你作以色列的王(参看旧约圣经撒母耳记上第15章第17节)。 ~·ment n

anom·al·ous /əˈnɒmələs; əˈnɑmələs/ adj irregular; different in some way from what is normal. 不规则的; 变则的。 ~ **verb,** verb that forms its interr and neg without the helping verb do (eg must, ought). 不规则动词; 变态动词; 变则动词(指不用助动词 do 而能构成疑问式及否定式的动词, 如 must, ought)。 ~·ly adv **anomaly** /əˈnɒməlɪ; əˈnɑməlɪ/ n (pl -lies) ~ thing contrary to what is normal; irregularity. 异常之事物; 异例: *A bird that cannot fly is an anomaly.* 一只不会飞的鸟是一个异例。

anon [1] /əˈnɒn; əˈnɑn/ adv (old use) soon. (旧用法) 不久; 未几。 **ever and ~,** every now and then. 时时地; 不时地。

anon [2] /əˈnɒn; əˈnɑn/ (in footnotes, etc) short for *by an anonymous author.* (用于注脚等中)为未具名作家所作; 作者不详(为 by an anonymous author 之略)。

ano·nym·ity /,ænəˈnɪmətɪ; ,ænəˈnɪmətɪ/ n [U] state of being anonymous. 无名; 匿名; 作者不明。

anony·mous /əˈnɒnɪməs; əˈnɑnəməs/ adj without a name, or with a name that is not made known: 无名的; 不具名的; 匿名的: *an ~ letter,* not signed; *an*

~ *gift,* from sb whose name is not known; 由无名氏送的赠品; *an author who remains ~.* 一直不具名的作家。 ~·ly adv

anoph·eles /əˈnɒfɪliːz; əˈnɑfə,liz / n (kinds of) mosquito, esp the kinds that spread malaria. 蚊; (尤指)疟蚊; 斑翅蚊。 ⇨ the illus at **insect.** 参看 insect 之插图。

an·or·ak /ˈænəræk; ˈɑnə,rɑk/ n [C] jacket with a hood attached, worn as protection against rain, wind and cold; wind-cheater. (御雨、风、寒)带风帽的夹克。

an·other /əˈnʌðə(r); əˈnʌðə/ pron, adj ⇨ **other.** 1 an additional (one): 再一; 又一: *Will you have ~ cup of tea?* 你再喝一杯茶吗? *Where shall we be in ten years,* ten years from now? 再过十年我们的情况将变成什么样子? *I don't like this hat; please show me ~ (one).* 我不喜欢这顶帽子; 请再给我拿一顶看看。 2 a similar (one): 相似的(一个); 类似的(一个): *This young man is very clever; he may be ~ Edison,* an inventor as clever as Edison. 这个年轻人很聪明; 他可能成为另一个爱迪生(如爱迪生一样聪明的发明家)。 3 a different (one): 不同的(一个); 另一个: *We can do that ~ time.* 我们可以下一次再做。 *That's quite ~ matter.* 那完全是另一回事。 *Taking one thing/year, etc with ~,* on the whole, taking the average (of good and bad, etc). 大体而言; 平均看来。 **one ~,** ⇨ **one** [3] (3).

answer [1] /ˈɑːnsə(r) US: ˈæn-; ˈænsə/ n **(to),** 1 sth done in return; reply: (对···的)回答; 答复; 答辩: *Have you had an ~ to your letter?* 你的信是否已有回信? *She gave no ~,* said nothing in return. 她没有作答复。 *I have a complete ~ to the accusation,* can prove that it was wrongly made. 对于该项控告我能证明其为属于虚。 *in ~ (to),* as a reply (to): 作为对于···的回答; 应···之请求: *in ~ to your letter.* 应来函之请求。 *The doctor came at once in ~ to my telephone call.* 医生应我电话之请求而立即到来。 2 solution; result of working with figures, etc: 答案; 解答: *The ~ to 3 × 17 is 51. 3 × 17* 的答案是51。 **have/know all the ~s,** know, or believe one knows, a great deal about sth. 对某事物知之甚详。

answer [2] /ˈɑːnsə(r) US: ˈæn-; ˈænsə/ vt, vi 1 [VP6A, 9, 12A, 2A] say, write or do, sth in return (to): (用口说, 笔写或行动)答复; 回答: ~ *a question;* 回答一个问题; ~ *the teacher.* 回答老师。 *He ~ed nothing.* 他没有回答。 *What shall I ~?* 我将怎样回答呢? *Have you ~ed his letter?* 你回了他的信吗? *He ~ed that he knew nothing about it.* 他答复说关于此事他一无所知。 *No one ~ed.* 没有一个人回答。 *No one was able to ~ him a word* (⇨ Matt 22:46). 没有一个人能回答一言(参看新约圣经马太福音第22章第46节)。 *A~ me this question.* 回答我这个问题。 ~ *the door/the bell,* go to the door when sb has knocked or rung the bell. 应门(有人敲门或按门铃时前往开门)。 ~ *the telephone,* pick up the receiver and ~ the caller. 听电话; 接电话。 [VP2C, 15B] ~ *(sb) back,* impolitely, interrupt, esp when being corrected or scolded. (尤指在被纠正或受斥责时)回嘴; 还口。 2 [VP6A] fulfil; be suitable or satisfactory for: 符合; 适合: *Will this ~ your purpose?* 这将符合你的目的吗? 3 [VP2A] succeed; be satisfactory: 成功; 令人满意: *This plan has not ~ed; we must find a better one.* 这个计划未成功; 我们必须另立一个更好的计划。 4 [VP3A] ~ *to the name of,* (of a pet animal) have the name of: (指畜养以供玩赏的动物)名叫: *The dog ~s to the name of Spot.* 这狗名叫小花。 ~ *to a description,* correspond to it, be as described: 与所述相符: *He doesn't ~ to the description of the missing man that appeared in the newspapers.* 他与报纸上对于失踪之人的描述不相符。 5 [VP6A, 3A] ~ *(to) the helm,* (of a ship) change course when the helm is moved: (指船)随舵转向: *The ship no longer ~s the helm,* cannot be steered. 此船已不能随舵转向(即舵已失灵, 不能驾驶了)。 6 [VP3A] ~ *for,* be responsible for: 对···负责; 担保: *I can't ~ for his honesty,* cannot guarantee that he is honest. 我不能保证他诚实。 *I will ~ for it* (= promise)

that the next one will be better. 我可以保证下一个会好些。 *You will have to ~ for* (= suffer for) *your wrongdoing one day.* 你总有一天会因为做坏事而得到报应的。 *He has a lot to ~ for,* is responsible (*to* be blamed for, many things. 他有很多的事情要负责 (应受责备)。 **~·able** /-əbl; -əbl/ *adj* **1** that can be ~ed. 可回答的; 可答复的。 **2** (*pred* only) responsible (*to* sb *for* sth). (仅用作表语时)应负责的(与 to 连用, 后接某人; 与 for 连用, 后接某事)

ant /ænt; ænt/ *n* small insect, proverbial for industry, that lives in highly organized societies. 蚂蚁。 ⇨ the illus at **insect.** 参看 insect 之插图。 **'ant-eater** *n* name of various animals that live on ants. 食蚁兽。 **'ant-hill** *n* pile of earth, etc, over an underground nest of ants; cone-shaped nest of white ants. 蚁丘; 蚁垤; 蚁冢。 **,white 'ant** *n* white ant-like insect (termite) that destroys wood, etc by eating it. 白蚁(能毁坏木料等)。

an·tag·on·ism /æn'tægənɪzəm; æn'tægə,nɪzəm/ *n* [C, U] (instance of) active opposition: 对抗; 敌对; 对立: *the ~ between the two men;* 该二人之间的对立; *feel a strong ~ for/toward sb,* find oneself strongly opposed to him. 与某人相敌对。

an·tag·on·ist /æn'tægənɪst; æn'tægə,nɪst/ *n* person struggling against another; opponent. 敌对者; 对立者; 对手; 敌手。

an·tag·on·is·tic /æn,tægə'nɪstɪk; æn,tægə'nɪstɪk/ *adj* ~ (*to*), **1** hostile; opposed; contrary. 敌对的; 对立的; 相反的。 **2** (of forces) acting against each other. (指力量)互相对抗的; 互相抵制的。 **an·tag·on·is·ti·cally** /-klɪ; -klɪ/ *adv*

an·tag·on·ize /æn'tægənaɪz; æn'tægə,naɪz/ *vt* [VP 6A] make an enemy of (sb); irritate into conflict: 反对; 敌对; 与(某人)为敌; 激怒使起争执: *I advise you not to ~ him.* 我劝你别与他为敌。

ant·arc·tic /ænt'ɑːktɪk; ænt'ɑrktɪk/ *adj* of the south polar regions. 南极的。 **the ,A~ 'Circle,** the line of latitude 66¹/₂°S. 南极圈(即南纬 66 度半线)。

ante¹ /'æntɪ; 'æntɪ/ *n* stake in the game of poker that a player must put down after looking at his cards or before he can draw new cards. (赌扑克牌时, 看过手中牌后, 或尚未发新牌前所下的)赌注; 进牌金。 **raise the ~,** increase one's stake (or contribution to sth). 加大赌注; 增加捐献。

ante² /'æntɪ; 'æntɪ/ *pref* before: 在…之前: ~*nuptial,* before marriage. 在结婚之前的; 婚前的。

ante·ced·ent /,æntɪ'siːdnt; ,æntə'sidnt/ *adj* ~ (*to*), (formal) previous (to). (正式用语)在…之前的。 □ *n* **1** preceding event or circumstance. 前事; 前情。 **2** (*pl*) ancestors; past history of a person or persons. (复)祖先; 身世; 经历; 人之过去的历史。 **3** (*gram*) noun, clause or sentence, to which a following pronoun or adverb refers. (语法)先行词。 **ante·ced·ence** /-ns; -ns/ *n* priority. 在前; 占先。

ante·cham·ber /'æntɪtʃeɪmbə(r); 'æntɪ,tʃɛmbə/ *n* room leading into a large room or hall. (后连正厅之)前厅; 前堂(用作来宾接待室)。

ante·date /,æntɪ'deɪt; 'æntɪ,det/ *vt* [VP6A] **1** put a date on, eg a letter, document, etc, earlier than the true one; give an earlier than the true one to (an event). 在(信函, 文件等)上面填写较实际日期为早的日期; 以较实际发生日期为早之日期来记载(某事件)。 **2** come before in time: 发生前于: *This event ~s the arrival of Columbus by several centuries.* 这事件发生在哥伦布到达之前数世纪。

ante·di·luvian /,æntɪdɪ'luːvɪən; ,æntɪdɪ'ljuvɪən/ *adj* of, suitable for, the time before the Flood, (Genesis); old-fashioned; out of date. (创世纪所述之)洪水时代以前的; 太古的; 古式的; 过时的。 □ *n* old-fashioned person. 守旧之人。

ante·lope /'æntɪləʊp; 'æntl,op/ *n* deer-like, fast-running animal with thin legs. 羚羊。 ⇨ the illus at **large.** 参看 large 之插图。

ante mer·id·iem /,æntɪ mə'rɪdɪəm; 'æntɪmə'rɪdɪ,ɛm/ (Lat) (abbr 略作 **am**) time between midnight and noon: (拉)午前; 上午: *7.30 am.* 上午七时半。 ⇨ *pm* at **post meridiem;** ⇨ **App 4 (6).** 参看附录四之六。

ante·na·tal /,æntɪ'neɪtl; ,æntɪ'netl/ *adj* existing or occurring before birth; pre-natal: 存在或发生在出生以前的; 诞生前的; 产前的: ~ *clinics,* for pregnant women. 孕妇诊所; 产前诊所。

an·tenna /æn'tenə; æn'tɛnə/ *n* (*pl* ~**e** /-niː; -ni/) **1** jointed organ found in pairs on the heads of insects and crustaceans, used for feeling, etc. (昆虫及甲壳动物的)触角; 触须。 ⇨ the illus at **insect.** 参看 insect 之插图。 **2** (*pl* also 亦作 ~**s**) (esp US) (kind of) radio or TV aerial. (尤美)(无线电或电视的)天线。

ante·nup·tial /,æntɪ'nʌpʃl; ,æntɪ'nʌpʃəl/ *adj* before marriage: 婚前的: ~ *an ~ contract.* 婚约。

ante·pen·ul·ti·mate /,æntɪpɪ'nʌltmet; ,æntɪpɪ'nʌltəmɪt/ *adj* last but two: 倒数第三的: *the ~ syllable.* 倒数第三音节。

an·ter·ior /æn'tɪərɪə(r); æn'tɪrɪə/ *adj* (formal) coming before (in time or position). (正式用语)(时间或位置)在…前的。

ante·room /'æntɪrʊm US: -ruːm; 'æntɪ,rum/ *n* antechamber; waiting-room. 前厅; 前堂; 接待室。

an·them /'ænθəm; 'ænθəm/ *n* musical composition, usu for choir and organ, to be sung in churches. 教堂中合唱的歌曲(通常供唱诗班及风琴之用); 圣歌。 **,national '~,** song or hymn of a country, eg 'God Save the Queen'. 国歌(例如英国国歌'天佑吾王')。

an·ther /'ænθə(r); 'ænθə/ *n* (bot) part of the stamen containing pollen. (植物)雄蕊之花粉囊; 花药。 ⇨ the illus at **flower.** 参看 flower 之插图。

an·thol·ogy /æn'θɒlədʒɪ; æn'θɑlədʒɪ/ *n* [C] (*pl* **-gies**) collection of poems or pieces of prose, or of both, by different writers, or a selection from the work of one writer. 诗集; 文集; 诗文集; 文选; 诗选(作者为一人或多人均可)。

an·thra·cite /'ænθrəsaɪt; 'ænθrə,saɪt/ *n* [U] very hard form of coal that burns with little smoke or flame. 无烟煤。

an·thrax /'ænθræks; 'ænθræks/ *n* [U] infectious, often fatal, disease of sheep and cattle that may be transmitted to human beings. 痈; 炭疽; 脾脱疽。

an·thro·poid /'ænθrəpɔɪd; 'ænθrə,pɔɪd/ *adj* manlike. 似人类的。 □ *n* ~ animal, esp an ape, eg a gorilla. 似人类之动物; (尤指)猿类(如大猩猩)。

an·thro·pol·ogy /,ænθrə'pɒlədʒɪ; ,ænθrə'pɑlədʒɪ/ *n* [U] science of man, esp of the beginnings, development, customs and beliefs of mankind. 人类学(研究人类的起源、发展、习俗及信仰之科学)。 **an·thro·pol·ogist** /,ænθrə'pɒlədʒɪst; ,ænθrə'pɑlədʒɪst/ *n* expert in ~. 人类学家。 **an·thro·po·logi·cal** /,ænθrəpə'lɒdʒɪkl; ,ænθrəpə'lɑdʒɪkl/ *adj*

anti- /'æntɪ US: ,æntaɪ; 'æntɪ; ,æntaɪ/ *pref* against: 反对; 抵抗; 排斥: ~*-bal'listic;* 反弹道的; ~*-'clerical,* 反圣职的; 反对教士干预政治的; ~*-'christian,* opposed to Christianity. 反基督教的。

anti-air·craft /,æntɪ 'eəkrɑːft US: -kræft; ,æntɪ'ɛrkræft/ *adj* used against enemy aircraft: 用以对抗敌机的; 防空的; 对空的: ~ *guns.* 高射炮。

anti·biotic /,æntɪbaɪ'ɒtɪk; ,æntɪbaɪ'ɑtɪk/ *n, adj* (med) (substance, eg *penicillin*) produced by moulds and bacteria, capable of destroying or preventing the growth of bacteria. (医)抗生的; 抗生药; 抗生素(如盘尼西林)。

anti·body /'æntɪbɒdɪ; 'æntɪ,bɑdɪ/ *n* [C] (*pl* **-dies**) (physiol) (kinds of) substance formed in the blood tending to inhibit or destroy harmful bacteria, etc. (生理)抗体(血液中所形成之可抑制或消灭有害细菌等之各种物质)。

an·tic /'æntɪk; 'æntɪk/ *n* (usu *pl*) grotesque movement, step, attitude, intended to amuse, eg by a clown

at a circus; queer behaviour. (通常用复数)滑稽的动作、脚步或姿态(如马戏团小丑所作以娱乐宾者); 古怪的行为。

an·tici·pate /æn'tɪsɪpeɪt; æn'tɪsə,pet/ vt [VP6A, C, 9] 1 do, make use of, before the right or natural time: 过早做; 过早使用: *Don't ～ your income*, order goods, etc before you receive your income. 不要预先用掉你的收入 (如在未领得收入之前即先定购货物等)。 2 do sth before sb else does it: 在旁人未做之前先做某事; 先人一着; 占先: *It is said that Columbus discovered America, but he was probably ～d by sailors from Norway who reached Labrador 500 years earlier.* 大家都说哥伦布发现美洲, 但是在早他五百年前, 或许就有挪威航海者先他而到达了拉布拉多。 3 see what needs doing, what is likely to happen, etc and do what is necessary: 预见必须做或将发生之事, 并采取必要的措施; 事前处理; 预先准备: *He tries to ～ all my needs*, satisfy them before I mention them. 他设法将我所需的一切东西预为准备。 *A good general tries to ～ the enemy's movements.* 一个优秀的将领设法预知敌军的行动, 并加以应付。 4 expect (which is the more usu word): 盼望; 期望; 预期 (expect 较常用): *We don't ～ much trouble.* 我们不希望有太多的麻烦。 *The directors ～d a fall in demand/that demand would fall.* 董事们预期 (货物的) 需求会降低。 **an·tici·pa·tory** /æn,tɪsɪ'peɪtərɪ; æn'tɪsəpə,tɔrɪ/ adj

an·tici·pa·tion /æn,tɪsɪ'peɪʃn; æn,tɪsə'peʃən/ n [C, U] (in) ～ (of), action of anticipating; sth anticipated: 预料; 预测; 预期; 预期之事物; 事前行为: *We bought an extra supply of coal in ～ of a cold winter.* 我们多买了一些煤, 以防寒冬。 *Thanking you in ～*, in advance and expecting you to do what I have asked. 谨先致谢。

anti·cli·max /ˌæntɪ'klaɪmæks; ˌæntɪ'klaɪmæks/ n [C] sudden fall from sth noble, serious, important, sensible, etc; descent that contrasts with a previous rise. 高潮突降; 渐降。

anti·clock·wise /ˌæntɪ'klɒkwaɪz; ˌæntɪ'klɑkwaɪz/ adv in the direction opposite to the movements of the hands of a clock. 反时针方向地。

anti·cyc·lone /ˌæntɪ'saɪkləun; ˌæntɪ'saɪklon/ n [C] (met) area in which atmospheric pressure is high compared with that of surrounding areas, with an outward flow of air; the area is characterized by quiet, settled weather. (气象)反气旋, 逆旋风; 高气压圈。 ⇨ **depression** (4).

anti·dote /'æntɪdəut; 'æntɪ,dot/ n [C] medicine used against a poison, or to prevent a disease from having an effect: 解毒药; 抗毒药: *an ～ against/for/to snakebite.* 蛇咬解毒药。

anti·freeze /'æntɪfriːz; 'æntɪ'friz/ n [U] substance (usu a liquid) added to another liquid to lower its freezing point, eg as used in the radiator of a motor vehicle. 防冻剂 (通常为液体, 加于另一种液体中以减低其冰点, 例如加于汽车冷却器之中者)。

anti·hero /ˌæntɪ 'hɪərəu; 'æntɪ'hɪro/ n (pl ～es /-rəuz; -roz/) (in fiction and drama) protagonist lacking the traditional characteristics of a hero, such as courage and dignity. (小说与戏剧中之) 非英雄主角 (缺乏传统的英雄气质, 如勇气和威严)。

anti·knock /ˌæntɪ 'nɒk; 'æntɪ'nɑk/ n [U] substance added to the fuel in a motor-car engine to reduce noise. 防爆剂 (加于汽车引擎燃料中以防止爆音者)。 ⇨ **knock** [2] (3).

anti·log·ar·ithm /ˌæntɪ'lɒɡərɪðm US: -'lɔːɡ-; ˌæntɪ'lɔɡə,rɪðm/ n number to which a logarithm belongs: 反对数: *1000, 100 and 10 are the ～s of 3, 2 and 1.* 1000, 100, 10 是3, 2, 1 的反对数。

anti·ma·cas·sar /ˌæntɪmə'kæsə(r); ˌæntɪmə'kæsə/ n covering to protect the back or arm of a chair or sofa from grease-marks. (椅子或沙发之靠背或扶手以防油污用之)椅套。

anti·mony /'æntɪmənɪ US: -məunɪ; 'æntə,monɪ/ n [U] easily broken silvery white metal, (symbol Sb)

used in alloys, esp metal for type[1] (3). 锑 (易碎之银白色金属, 化学符号 Sb, 用于合金, 尤用以制铅字之合金)。

an·tipa·thy /æn'tɪpəθɪ; æn'tɪpəθɪ/ n ～ (to/towards/against) (between two persons). [U] strong and decided dislike; [C] (pl -thies) instance or object of this: 反感; 恶感; 憎恶; 反感之实例; 反感的对象; 讨厌的事物: *feel/show a strong/marked ～ to a place/against sb.* 对于某地 (某人) 有强烈 (显著) 的反感。 **anti·pa·thetic** /ˌæntɪpə'θetɪk; æn,tɪpə'θetɪk/ adj

anti·per·son·nel /ˌæntɪ ,pɜːsə'nel; ,æntɪ,pɜsə'nel/ adj (usu of mines)[2] (3) designed to kill or wound human beings (not to destroy vehicles). (通常指地雷) 用来杀伤人 (而非用来毁坏车辆) 的; 杀伤性的。

an·tipo·des /æn'tɪpədiːz; æn'tɪpə,diz/ n pl (usu 通常作 the ～) (two) place(s) on the opposite sides of the earth, esp the region opposite our own. 对跖之地点(地球上相反之地区); (尤指)与我们自己地区相反之地区。

anti·quar·ian /ˌæntɪ'kweərɪən; ˌæntɪ'kwerɪən/ adj connected with the study, collection or sale of antiquities: 研究、收藏或售卖古物的: *an ～ bookseller.* 售卖古书的商人。 □ n antiquary. 研究、收藏或售卖古物之人; 古物搜集家。

anti·quary /'æntɪkwərɪ US: -kwerɪ; 'æntɪ,kwɛrɪ/ n (pl -ries) person who studies, collects or sells, antiquities. 研究、收藏或售卖古物之人; 古物搜集家。

anti·quated /'æntɪkweɪtɪd; 'æntə,kwetɪd/ adj obsolete; out of date; (of persons) having old-fashioned ideas and ways. 已废弃的; 过时的; (指人) 有旧式思想或气派的。

an·tique /æn'tiːk; æn'tik/ adj belonging to the distant past; existing since old times; in the style of past times. 古代的; 自古即存在的; 古风的。 □ n [C] material (eg a piece of furniture, a work of art) of a past period (in GB at least 50 years old, in US 100 years). 古物; 古董; 古艺术品 (属于以往时代的东西, 如家具、艺术作品等。在英国, 至少为五十年以上者; 在美国, 一百年以上者)。 **the ～**, **～ style in art.** 古代艺术风格。 Cf 参较 second-hand, usu of things more recent. 旧的; 二手货的 (通常指比较近期的东西)。

an·tiquity /æn'tɪkwətɪ; æn'tɪkwətɪ/ n 1 [U] old times, esp before the Middle Ages; great age: 古代; 古老 (尤指中世纪以前者); 古远: *the heroes of ～;* 古代的英雄; *a city of great ～*, eg Athens; 古城 (如雅典); *in remote ～.* 在远古时代。 2 (pl -ties) buildings, ruins, works of art, remaining from ancient times: 古建筑物; 古废墟; 古艺术品; 古迹; 古物: *Greek and Roman antiquities.* 希腊罗马之古迹。

an·tir·rhi·num /ˌæntɪ'raɪnəm; ˌæntɪ'raɪnəm/ n (pl ～s) (bot) genus of plants; snapdragon. (植物)金鱼草。

anti·Sem·ite /ˌæntɪ 'siːmaɪt US: 'sem-; ˌæntɪ'sɛmaɪt/ n, adj (person) prejudiced against Jews, hating Jews. 对犹太人有有偏见或憎恨的(人); 反犹太的(人)。 **anti·Sem·itic** /ˌæntɪ sɪ'mɪtɪk; ˌæntɪsɪ'mɪtɪk/ adj **anti·Sem·itism** /ˌæntɪ'semɪtɪzəm; ˌæntɪ'semə,tɪzəm/ n 反犹太主义。

anti·sep·tic /ˌæntɪ'septɪk; ˌæntə'sɛptɪk/ n, adj (chemical substance) preventing a wound, etc from becoming septic, esp by destroying germs. 防腐剂; 消毒剂; 防腐的 n 有消毒力的物。

anti·social /ˌæntɪ'səuʃl; ˌæntɪ'soʃəl/ adj 1 opposed to social laws or to organized societies. 反对社会法律或有组织之社会的; 反社会的。 2 likely, tending, to interfere with or spoil public amenities: 想要, 倾向于扰乱或破坏公共游乐场所的; 违反公益的: *It is ～ to leave litter in public places/to play a transistor in public.* 在公共场所留下零乱杂物(在群众中收听晶体管收音机)是违反公益的。 3 not sociable. 不喜社交的。

anti·tank /ˌæntɪ'tæŋk; ˌæntɪ'tæŋk/ attrib adj for use against military tanks: 反坦克的; 防坦克的: *～ guns/ditches.* 反坦克炮(防坦克壕)。

an·tith·esis /æn'tɪθəsɪs; æn'tɪθəsɪs/ n (pl -ses /-siːz;

-siz/) **1** [U] direct opposite (of, to). 正相反（与の 或 to 连用）。**2** [U] opposition (of one thing to another, between two things); [C] instance of this; contrast of ideas vividly expressed, as in 'Give me liberty, or give me death'. 相反；反对；对照（后接の 一事物与另一事物, between 二事物）；(修辞学上の)反衬：对比(如 '不自由，毋宁死')。**anti·thetic** /ˌæntɪˈθetɪk; ˌæntɪˈθetɪk/, **anti·theti·cal** /-ɪkl; -ɪkl/ adj **anti·theti·cally** /-klɪ; -klɪ/ adv

anti·toxin /ˌæntɪˈtɒksɪn; ˌæntɪˈtaksɪn/ n substance (usu a serum) able to counteract a toxin or disease. 抗毒素；抗毒血清。

anti·trade /ˌæntɪˈtreɪd; ˈæntɪˌtred/ adj '~ **wind**, wind that blows in the opposite direction to a trade wind. 反贸易风；反信风。□ n (usu pl) ~ wind. (通常用复数)反贸易风；反信风。

ant·ler /ˈæntlə(r); ˈæntlə/ n branched horn; branch of a horn (of a stag or other deer). 分枝的兽角；鹿角。⇨ the illus at **large**. 参看 large 之插图。

an·to·nym /ˈæntənɪm; ˈæntəˌnɪm/ n [C] word that is contrary in meaning to another: 反义词: Hot is the ~ of cold. 热是冷的反义词。⇨ **synonym**.

anus /ˈeɪnəs; ˈenəs/ n (anat) opening at the end of the alimentary canal, through which waste matter passes out. (解剖)肛门。⇨ the illus at **alimentary**. 参看 alimentary 之插图。

an·vil /ˈænvɪl; ˈænvɪl/ n **1** large, heavy block of iron on which a smith hammers heated metal into shape. 铁砧。**2** (anat) bone in the ear. (解剖)砧骨。⇨ the illus at **ear**. 参看 ear 之插图。

anxiety /æŋˈzaɪətɪ; æŋˈzaɪətɪ/ n **1** [U] emotional condition in which there is fear and uncertainty about the future: 忧虑；焦虑；惶惶不安: We waited with ~ for news of her safe arrival. 我们焦虑地等待她安全到达的消息。Tom's foolish behaviour caused his parents great ~. 汤姆的愚蠢行为引起他的父母极大的不安。**2** [C] (pl -ties) instance of such a feeling: 忧虑或不安之实例: All these anxieties made him look pale and tired. 一切的忧虑使他面色苍白且有倦容。The Budget statement removed all anxieties about higher taxes. 预算案消除了一切关于增税的忧虑。**3** [U] keen desire: 渴望；切望: ~ for knowledge; 切望获得知识; his ~ to please his employers. 他急欲讨好雇主的切望。

anxious /ˈæŋkʃəs; ˈæŋkʃəs/ adj **1** ~ (about/for), feeling anxiety; troubled: 忧虑的；焦虑的；担心的；不安的: I am very ~ about my son's health. 我极为担心我儿子的健康。He is ~ for her safety/at her non-arrival. 他担心她的安全(因她未到达而忧虑)。**2** causing anxiety: 引起忧虑的；令人担心的: We have had an ~ time. 我们一直焦虑着。His illness has been a very ~ business, has caused us anxiety. 他的病是件极令人担心的事。**3** ~ to/for/about/that, strongly wishing: 渴望；切望: He was ~ to meet you, 他渴望会见你(渴望他的兄弟会见你). We were ~ that help should be sent promptly/~ for help to be sent. 我们渴望立刻派人救助。~**ly** adv

any[1] /ˈenɪ; ˈenɪ/ adj **1** ⇨ **some**[1](1). (in neg and interr sentences, and in clauses of condition, etc). (用于否定句、疑问句及条件从句等)。**2** (in affirm sentences, with negation implied, eg a v such as 'prevent', after the prep 'without', after such adv as 'hardly'): (用于肯定句中具有否定的含义，例如与动词 prevent 连用，在介词 without 之后，在副词 hardly 等之后): We did the work without any difficulty. 我们毫无困难地做了这工作。I have hardly any leisure nowadays. 我近些日子几乎毫无闲暇。Please try to prevent any loss while the goods are on the way. 货物在运送途中请尽量防止任何损失。**3** (usu stressed; usu in affirm sentences) no matter which: (通常重读；通常用于肯定句中)任何；无论哪一: Come any day you like. 随便哪一天来都可以。You will find me at my desk at any hour of the day, at all times. 你会发现一天之中的任何时刻我都在桌旁工作。We must find

an excuse, any excuse will do. 我们必须要找一个借口，任何借口都可以。**4** in 'any case, whatever happens, whatever the circumstances may be. 无论如何。at 'any rate, at least. 至少。**5** (colloq, used in affirm and neg sentences, with sing common nn for a(n) or one): (口; 用于肯定及否定句中，与单数普通名词连用，代替 a, an 或 one): This bucket is useless—it hasn't any handle. 这个桶没有用了—连个把手都没有。

any[2] /ˈenɪ; ˈenɪ/ adv of degree (used in neg, interr and conditional sentences, in contexts where negation or doubt is indicated or implied, and with comparatives. Cf the similar use of no and none.) (用于否定，疑问及条件句中，显示或暗示有否定或疑问意味上下文中，或与比较级词连用。参较 no 及 none 之类似用法。) at all; in any degree: 丝毫；任何程度: Is your father any better? 你父亲好些了吗? They were too tired to go any further. 他们疲倦得一点也不能再往前走了。The children didn't behave any too well, ie they behaved rather badly. 这些孩子的行为不太好。If it's any good/use, I'll buy it. 若是它有任何好处(用处)，我就买它。(not) any the better/the worse (for), (not) at all better/worse for: (丝毫没有)因…而好(坏)一点；(丝毫没有)受…的影响: He got well through in the rain yesterday but isn't any the worse for it, has not suffered in any way. 他昨天被雨淋湿透了，可是丝毫未受影响。

any[3] /ˈenɪ; ˈenɪ/ pron ⇨ **some**[2].

any·body /ˈenɪbɒdɪ; ˈenɪˌbɑdɪ/ n, pron **1** (in neg, interr, etc sentences: 用于否定、疑问句中: ⇨ **some·body, someone**). **2** (in affirm sentences) no matter who: (用于肯定句中) 无论谁；任何人: A~ will tell you where the bus stop is. 无论谁都会告诉你公共汽车站在哪里。A~ who saw the accident is asked to communicate with the police. 任何亲眼看见该祸事发生者，请与警方取得联络。That's ~'s guess, (colloq) is quite uncertain. (口)那是相当靠不住。⇨ **else, ⇨ else. 3** person of importance: 重要人物: You must work harder if you wish to be ~. 如果你想要成为重要人物，你必须更加努力。Was she ~ before her marriage, had she any social position? 她在结婚前有什么社会地位吗? He'll never be ~. 他永远不会成器的。

any·how /ˈenɪhaʊ; ˈenɪˌhaʊ/ adv **1** in any possible way; by any possible means: 以任何可能的方法；无论怎样: The house was empty and I couldn't get in ~. 屋子里没有人，我无论怎样都进不去。**2** carelessly; without order: 不仔细地；马马虎虎地；杂乱无章地: The work was done all ~. 这工作做得很马虎。**3** (adv or conj) in any case; at any rate: 无论如何；至少: A~, you can try, even if there's not much chance of success. 至少你可以试试(纵然没有多少成功的机会)。It's too late now, ~. 无论怎样，现在也已经太晚了。

any·one /ˈenɪwʌn; ˈenɪˌwʌn/ n, pron = **anybody**.

any·place /ˈenɪpleɪs; ˈenɪˌples/ adv (esp in US) (尤用于美国) = **anywhere**.

any·thing /ˈenɪθɪŋ; ˈenɪˌθɪŋ/ n, pron **1** (in neg, interr, etc sentences: 用于否定，疑问等句中: ⇨ **something**) (note the position of the adj): (注意形容词的位置): Has ~ unusual happened? 有什么不平常的事发生吗? **2** no matter what: 无论什么: I want something to eat; ~ will do. 我想要点东西吃；吃什么都可以。be ~ but, be definitely not: 绝对不: He's ~ but mad. 他一点也不生气。**3** (used adverbially, to intensify a meaning): (作副词用，加强某一意义): The thief ran like ~ when he saw the policeman. 那贼看见了警察跑得像什么似的。(as) easy as ~, (colloq) very easy. (口)容易得很。

any·way /ˈenɪweɪ; ˈenɪˌwe/ adv = **anyhow**(3).

any·where /ˈenɪweə(r); ˈenɪˌhwer/ adv **1** (in neg, interr, etc sentences: 用于否定，疑问句中: ⇨ **somewhere**) (note the use of ~ with post-adjuncts): (注意此字与后位附加语的连用法): I'll go ~ (that) you suggest. 你建议我到哪儿去，我就到哪儿去。Are we going ~ (in) particular? 我们要到什么特定的地方去吗? (意

即: 有没有一定的目标?) **2** (used as a *prep* object): (用
作介词之宾语): *That leaves me without ~ to keep all my
books*. 我，我连一点可以放这些书籍的地方也没有
了。**3** no matter where: 无论何处; 任何地方: *Put the
box down ~*. 把盒子放下来, 任何地方都可以。*We'll go
~ you like*. 你爱往哪儿去, 我们就往哪儿去。

aorta /eɪˈɔːtə; eˈɔrtə/ *n* chief blood-vessel through
which blood is carried from the left side of the heart.
大动脉。 ⇨ the illus at **respiratory**. 参看
respiratory 之插图。

apace /əˈpeɪs; əˈpes/ *adv* (old use, or liter) quickly:
(旧用法或文) 快地; 急速地: *Ill news spreads ~*. 坏消息
传得快(坏事传千里)。

apache /əˈpæʃ; əˈpaʃ/ *n* (in Paris) hooligan; rough.
(在巴黎)街头上的流氓或不良少年; 阿飞。

apa·nage (also **ap·pan·age**) /ˈæpənɪdʒ; ˈæpənɪdʒ/
n [U] **1** natural accompaniment; sth that necessarily
goes with sth else. 属性; 从属物。 **2** property, etc
coming to sb because of birth or office. 由世袭或职位所
得的财产等; 封地; 俸禄。

apart /əˈpɑːt; əˈpɑrt/ *adv* **1** distant: 远离地; 远隔地:
The two houses are 500 metres ~. 这两栋房子相距五百
米. *The negotiators are still miles ~*, show no signs of
agreeing. 谈判者之间仍有相当的距离(无协议的迹象)。
2 to or on one side: 向一边; 在一边: *He took me ~ in
order to speak to me alone*. 他把我拉到一边, 以便跟我单
独说话。*Why does she hold herself ~*, ie not mix with
other people? 她为什么落落寡合(与他人格格不入)?
joking/jesting ~, speaking seriously. 非开玩笑; 说正
经话。*set/put (sth/sb) ~ (from)*, put (it) on one
side; reserve it; make (sb) (appear) special: 储备; 保
留(某事物); 使(某人)(显得)特殊: *His far-sightedness
set him ~ from most of his contemporaries*. 他的远见使
他显得与其同辈的人迥然不同。**3** separate(ly): 分开; 分
离: *I can't get these two things ~*. 我分不开这两样东
西. *He was standing with his feet wide ~*. 他两足大开而
立。*~ from*, independently of; leaving on one side:
除开; 除…以外: *~ from these reasons*. 除了这些理由以

外. *tell/know two things or persons ~*, distinguish
one from the other. 能分辨两种东西或两个人。 ⇨
come(16), pull²(7), take¹(16).

apart·heid /əˈpɑːtheɪt; əˈpɑrthet/ *n* (S Africa)
(policy of) racial segregation; separate development of
Europeans and non-Europeans. (南非洲)种族隔离(政
策);欧洲人与非欧洲人之分别发展。

apart·ment /əˈpɑːtmənt; əˈpɑrtmənt/ *n* **1** single
room in a house. 房间。 **2** (*pl*) set of rooms, furnished
or unfurnished, either owned or rented by the week or
month, eg for a holiday at the seaside. (复)套房(指有
设备或无设备者, 或为私人产业或为按周或按月计租, 如
供海滨度假者)。**3** (US) set of rooms in a large building
(called *an* '~ *house*), usu on the same floor. (美)公寓
(称为apartment house的大楼中的一套房间, 通常在同一
层楼)。(US ~ = GB *flat*; US ~ *house* = GB *block
of flats*; US ~ *hotel* = GB *service flats*.) (美国的
apartment 等于英国的 flat; 美国的 apartment house 等
于英国的 block of flats; 美国的 apartment hotel 等于英
国的 service flats。) ⇨ **tenement**.

apa·thy /ˈæpəθɪ; ˈæpəθɪ/ *n* [U] absence of sympathy
or interest; indifference (*towards*). 不同情; 无兴趣; 冷
淡; 淡漠; 漠不关心(与 towards 连用)。 **apa·thetic**
/ˌæpəˈθetɪk; ˌæpəˈθetɪk/ *adj* showing or having ~. 不
同情的; 无兴趣的; 冷淡的; 淡漠的。**apa·theti·cally**
/-klɪ; -klɪ/ *adv*

ape /eɪp; ep/ *n* **1** tailless monkey (*gorilla, chimpanzee,
orang-outang, gibbon*). 猿(包括大猩猩, 黑猩猩; 长臂猿
等)。**2** person who mimics others: 模仿他人者: *play the
ape*, mimic. 模仿。**3** (colloq) clumsy, ill-bred person.
(口)笨拙而无教养的人; 粗野之人。 □ *vt* imitate (sb's
behaviour, etc). 模仿(某人之行为等)。

aperi·ent /əˈprɪərɪənt; əˈprɪrɪənt/ *n, adj* (formal)
laxative. (正式用语)通便的; 轻泻的; 通便剂; 轻泻药。

aperi·tif /əˈperətɪf US: əˌperiˈtiːf; aperiˈtif/ *n* [C]
alcoholic drink, (eg *vermouth*) taken before a meal. 饭
前酒;开胃酒(如 vermouth)。

ap·er·ture /ˈæpətʃə(r); ˈæpətʃɚ/ *n* opening, esp one

apes and monkeys

that admits light, eg to a camera lens. 孔；隙；洞(尤指通光线者,如照相机之光孔)。

apex /'eɪpeks; 'eɪpɛks/ n (pl ~es or **apices** /'eɪpɪsiːz; 'æpɪ,siz/) top or highest point: 顶点；最高点；峰；尖顶: the ~ of a triangle; 三角形之顶点; at the ~ of his career/fortunes. 他的事业(运气)的极盛时期。

apha·sia /ə'feɪzɪə US: -ʒə; ə'feʒə/ n [U] (path) loss of ability to use speech or to understand speech (as the result of brain injury). (由于脑部受伤害而致之)无运用或了解语言的能力；失语症。

aphid /'eɪfɪd; 'efɪd/ n = aphis.

aphis /'eɪfɪs; 'efɪs/ n (pl **aphides** /'eɪfɪdiːz; 'æfɪ,diz/) very small insect that lives by sucking juices from plants; plant louse. 蚜虫(靠吸取植物汁液而生存之小虫)。

aph·or·ism /'æfərɪzəm; 'æfə,rɪzəm/ n [C] short, wise saying; maxim. 格言；警句。

aph·ro·dis·iac /,æfrə'dɪzɪæk; ,æfrə'dɪzɪ,æk/ n, adj [C, U] (substance, drug) exciting sexual desire and activity. 催欲的；壮阳的；催欲剂；春药。

api·ary /'eɪpɪərɪ US: -ɪerɪ; 'epɪ,ɛrɪ/ n (pl -ries) place with a number of hives where bees are kept. 养蜂场；蜂房。 **api·ar·ist** /'eɪpɪərɪst; 'epɪərɪst/ n person who keeps bees. 养蜂者。 **api·cul·ture** /'eɪpɪkʌltʃə(r); 'epɪ,kʌltʃə/ n bee-keeping. 养蜂。

apiece /ə'piːs; ə'pis/ adv to, for or by, each one of a group: 每个；每件；每人: They cost a penny ~, each. 它们的价钱是每个一便士。

apish /'eɪpɪʃ; 'epɪʃ/ adj of or like an ape; foolishly imitative. 猿的；似猿的；愚蠢地模仿的。

aplomb /ə'plɒm; ə'plɑm/ n [U] self-confidence; assurance (in speech or behaviour): 自信；(言语或行为上的)沉着；镇定；泰然自若: He answered with perfect ~. 他沉着地回答。

apoca·lypse /ə'pɒkəlɪps; ə'pakə,lɪps/ n revelation (esp of knowledge from God). 启示；(尤指)天启。the A~, the last book in the Bible, recording the revelation to St John. 启示录(圣经之最后一卷,记载圣约翰所得之启示)。 ⇨ App 10. 参看附录十。 **apoca·lyp·tic** /ə,pɒkə'lɪptɪk; ə,pakə'lɪptɪk/ adj of or like an ~ or the A~. 启示的；天启的；似启示的；似天启的；启示录的。

Apoc·ry·pha /ə'pɒkrɪfə; ə'pakrəfə/ n pl (with sing v) those books of the Old Testament that are considered of doubtful authorship by the Jews and were excluded from the Bible at the time of the Reformation. (与单数动词连用)(旧约圣经中犹太人认为作者可疑,在宗教改革时被删除的)伪经。 ⇨ App 10. 参看附录十。 **apoc·ry·phal** /ə'pɒkrɪfl; ə'pakrɪfl/ adj of doubtful authority or authorship. 作者可疑的；真伪不明的。

apo·gee /'æpədʒiː; 'æpə,dʒi/ n 1 (astron) position (in the orbit of the moon or any planet) when it is at its greatest distance from the earth. (天文)远地点(月球或任何行星轨道上距离地球最远之点)。 2 (fig) highest point. (喻)最高点；极点。

apolo·getic /ə,pɒlə'dʒetɪk; ə,palə'dʒɛtɪk/ adj making an apology; expressing regret; excusing a fault or failure: 道歉的；表示歉意的；辩解过失的: He was ~ about/for arriving late. 他为迟到而表示抱歉。 He wrote an ~ letter. 他写了一封道歉信。 **apolo·geti·cally** /-klɪ; -klɪ/ adv **apolo·get·ics** n (usu with sing v) the art or practice of explaining or justifying a religious belief, political creed, etc. (宗教与单数动词连用)(对宗教信仰、政治信条等的)辩证术。 **apolo·gist** /ə'pɒlədʒɪst; ə'palədʒɪst/ n person who engages in ~. 辩护士；辩证者。

apolo·gize /ə'pɒlədʒaɪz; ə'palə,dʒaɪz/ vi [VP2A, 3A] ~ (to sb) (for sth), make an apology; say one is sorry: 道歉: You must ~ to your sister for being so rude. 你太无礼,必须向你姐姐(妹妹)道歉。

apol·ogy /ə'pɒlədʒɪ; ə'palədʒɪ/ n (pl -gies) 1 [C] ~ (to sb) (for sth), statement of regret (for doing

wrong, being impolite, hurting sb's feelings): 道歉；谢罪: offer/make/accept/refuse an ~; 表示(从事,接受,拒绝)道歉; make one's apologies (to sb), eg for being late, for not being able to come. (向某人)致歉意(如因迟到,因事不能来等)。 2 [C] explanation or defence (of beliefs, etc). (信仰等之)辩证;辩护。 ⇨ **apologetics. 3** an ~ for, a poor specimen of, eg a dinner/letter. 为…之勉强的代替物；为…之低劣的样品(如勉强算是一餐饭,勉强算是一封信);权充。

apo·phthegm, apo·thegm /'æpəθem; 'æpə,θɛm/ n [C] short, pointed or forceful, saying. 箴言；格言；警句。

apo·plexy /'æpəpleksɪ; 'æpə,plɛksɪ/ n [U] loss of power to feel, move, think, usu caused by injury to blood-vessels in the brain. 中风(因脑血管受伤而引起的昏迷状态)。 **apo·plec·tic** /,æpə'plektɪk; ,æpə'plɛktɪk/ adj connected with, causing ~; suffering from ~: 有关中风的；引起中风的；患中风的: an apoplectic stroke/fit; 中风发作; 中风; (colloq) red in the face; easily made angry. (口)红脸的；易怒的。

apos·tasy /ə'pɒstəsɪ; ə'pastəsɪ/ n [U] giving up one's beliefs or faith; turning away from one's religion; [C] (pl -sies) instance of this. 放弃信仰；背教；脱教；变节。 **apos·tate** /ə'pɒsteɪt; ə'pastet/ n, adj (person) guilty of ~. 叛教者；脱教者；叛教的；脱党的,变节的。

a pos·teri·ori /,eɪ ,pɒsterɪ'ɔːraɪ; 'epas,tɪrɪ'oraɪ/ adv, adj phrase (Lat) (reasoning) from effects to causes, eg saying, 'The boys are tired so they must have walked a long way'. (拉) 由结果推定其原因地(的)；归纳地(的)(例如说"孩子们很疲乏,所以他们一定走了很长的路")。 ⇨ **a priori.**

apostle /ə'pɒsl; ə'pasl/ n 1 one of the twelve men **(the Twelve A~s)** chosen by Jesus to spread his teaching; missionary of the early Christian Church, eg St Paul, the A~ to the Gentiles. 使徒(耶稣所选十二门徒中之一；早期基督教之传教士,如圣保罗即为在异教徒中传教之使徒)。 2 leader or teacher of reform, of a new faith or movement. 倡导改革,新教或新运动之人；倡导者；导师。 **apos·tolic** /,æpə'stɒlɪk; ,æpə'talɪk/ adj 1 of the ~s(1) or the times when they lived. 耶稣之使徒的；耶稣使徒时代的。 2 of the Pope. 教皇的；教宗的。

apos·trophe[1] /ə'pɒstrəfɪ; ə'pastrəfɪ/ n the sign, used to show omission of letter(s) or number(s), (as in can't, I'm, '05, for cannot, I am, 1905), for the possessive (as in boy's, boys'), and for the plurals of letters (as in There are two l's in Bell). 符号('): 用作省略号(表示字母或数字之省略, 如 can't = cannot, I'm = I am, '05 = 1905), 或用作所有格符号(如 boy's, boys'), 或用于构成字母的复数形(如 Bell 中有两个 l 字母,以 two l's 表示之)。 ⇨ App 9. 参看附录九。

apos·trophe[2] /ə'pɒstrəfɪ; ə'pastrəfɪ/ n passage in a public speech, in a poem, etc addressed to a particular person (who may be dead or absent). 演说或诗歌等中专对某已死亡或不在场之人(所说的一段话)顿呼语。 **apos·tro·phize** /ə'pɒstrəfaɪz; ə'pastrə,faɪz/ vt make an ~ to. 对…作顿呼语。

apoth·ecary /ə'pɒθɪkərɪ US: -kerɪ; ə'paθə,kerɪ/ n (pl -ries) (old use, but still in Scot) person who prepares and sells medicines and medical goods. (旧用法,但今仍用于苏格兰)卖药者；备药剂师。 **apothecaries' weight,** ⇨ App 5. 参看附录五。

apo·thegm ⇨ **apophthegm.**

apothe·osis /ə,pɒθɪ'əʊsɪs; ə,paθɪ'osɪs/ n (pl -ses -siːz; -sɪz/) 1 (of a human being) making or becoming a god or a saint: (指人)奉为神圣；成神；成圣；神圣化: the ~ of a Roman Emperor. 罗马皇帝之神圣化。 2 release from earthly life. 脱离我世的生命；解脱。 3 glorification; glorified ideal. 尊崇；颂赞；被颂赞的理想。

ap·pal (US also **ap·pall**) /ə'pɔːl; ə'pɔl/ vt (-ll-) [VP6A] fill with fear or terror; dismay; shock deeply: 惊吓; 使惊骇: *They were ~led at the news.* 他们被这消息吓坏了。 ~·ling adj: 骇人的; 可怕的: *When will this ~ling war end?* 这可怕的战争何时方可结束？ ~·ling·ly adv

ap·pa·nage ⇨ apanage.

ap·par·atus /ˌæpə'reɪtəs US: -'rætəs; ˌæpə'retəs/ n [C] (*pl* **~es**) (rarely *pl*; sometimes *a piece of ~*). (罕用复数; 有时用 a piece of ~). **1** set of instruments or other mechanical appliances put together for a purpose: 一套仪器; 一套器械; 装置: *a heating ~,* eg for supplying steam heat throughout a building. 暖气装置。 **2** bodily organs by which natural processes are carried on: (身体内之)器官: *Your digestive ~ takes the food you eat and changes it so that it can be used to build up the body.* 你的消化器官把你所吃的食物消化, 吸收, 用以增进身体的健康。

ap·parel /ə'pærəl; ə'pærəl/ n [U] (old use, or liter) dress; clothing. (旧日用法或文)衣服; 服装。 □ vt (-ll-; US -l-) dress; clothe. 穿以衣服; 穿着。

ap·par·ent /ə'pærənt; ə'pærənt/ adj **1** clearly seen or understood: 显然的; 明白的: *It was ~ to all of us ...,* We all saw clearly ... ; ... 这对我们大家是显而易见的; *as will soon become ~,* as you will soon see. 不久你即可明白。 **2** seeming; according to appearances: 外表的; 表面的: *in spite of her ~ indifference,* although she seemed to be indifferent. 尽管她表面上显得冷淡。~·ly adv

ap·par·ition /ˌæpə'rɪʃn; ˌæpə'rɪʃən/ n [C] the coming into view, esp of a ghost or the spirit of a dead person. 出现; (尤指)幽灵或鬼魂的出现。

ap·peal /ə'piːl; ə'pil/ vi [VP2A, 3A] ~ (to sb) (against/for/from sth), **1** make an earnest request: 恳求; 恳求: *The prisoner ~ed to the judge for mercy.* 囚犯恳求法官开恩。 *At Christmas people ~ to us to help the poor.* 圣诞节期间人们吁呼我们捐助贫穷的人们。 **2** (legal) take a question (to a higher court, etc) for rehearing and a new decision: (法律)(向上级法院)上诉: ~ *to another court;* 向另一法院上诉; ~ *against a decision,* 不服判决而上诉; ~ *from a judgement.* 不服裁判而上诉。 **3** go (to sb) for a decision: 请求(某人)决定; 听取(某人的)意见; 诉诸: (football, etc) (足球赛等中)~ *to the linesman;* 听取巡边员的意见; ~ *against the referee's decision;* 不服裁判的判决; (cricket) (板球) *The captain ~ed against the light,* said the light was too poor for further play. 队长对光线提出异议(认为光线太差不宜继续比赛)。 **4** attract; move the feelings of: 有吸引力; 引起兴趣: *Bright colours ~ to small children.* 鲜艳的色彩能吸引小小孩。 *Do these paintings ~ to you?* 你对这些画感兴趣吗? □ n **1** *an ~ for,* an earnest call for: 恳求; 呼吁: *make an ~ for help.* 恳求援助。 **2** [C] (legal) act of ~ing(2): (法律)上诉: *an ~ to a higher court;* 向上级法院上诉; *an ~ from a decision,* 不服判决而上诉; *to lodge an ~;* 提起上诉; [U] *to give notice of ~;* 经上诉后可于(获判无罪开释)。 **3** [C] (esp in sport) act of ~ing: (尤用于运动比赛中)请求决定; 听取意见: *an ~ to the referee.* 请求裁判员的裁决。 **4** [U] interest; (power of) attraction: 引起兴趣的力量; 吸引力: *That sort of music hasn't much ~ for me/has lost its ~.* 那种音乐引不起我多大兴趣(已经失去了它的吸引力)。 **5** [U] supplication: 乞求; 哀求: *with a look of ~ on her face,* asking for help or sympathy. 她的脸上带着乞求(帮助或同情)的表情。 ~·ing adj **1** moving; touching the feelings or sympathy. 感动人的; 哀求的。 **2** attractive. 动人的; 有吸引力的。 ~·ing·ly adv

ap·pear /ə'pɪə(r); ə'pɪr/ vi **1** [VP2A, C] come into view, become visible: 出现; 呈现: *When we reached the top of the hill, the town ~ed below us.* 当我们到达山顶时, 市镇就呈现在我们的脚下。 *The ship ~ed on the horizon.* 船出现在水平线上。 **2** [VP2A, C] arrive at; 到;

抵达: *He promised to be here at four but didn't ~ until six.* 他答应在四点钟来这里, 可是到六点钟才到达。 **3** [VP2A, C] **(a)** (of an actor, singer, lecturer, etc) come before the public: (指演员, 歌唱者, 演讲者)出场; 登台: *He has ~ed in every large concert hall in Europe.* 他曾在欧洲各大音乐厅演唱。 **(b)** (of a book) be published: (指书)出版; 发表: *When will your new novel ~?* 你的新小说将于何时出版? **(c)** (legal) present oneself publicly: (法律)到庭; 出庭: *The defendant failed to ~ before the court.* 被告未到庭。 **4** [VP2A, 4D, E] seem: 似乎; 显得; 好象: *Why does she ~ so sad?* 她为何显得如此悲伤? *He ~s to have many friends.* 他似乎有很多朋友。 *You don't want to ~ a fool,* to look like a fool. 你不要显得象个傻子似的。 *The house ~ed (to be) deserted.* 那房子看样子好象是没有人住的。 *It would ~ that his intention was/His intention ~ed to have been to arrive yesterday.* 他似乎原来打算昨天到达。 *There ~s to have been a mistake.* 看起来曾有错误。 *So it ~s.* 似乎是如此。 *It ~s not.* 看起来并非如此。 *It ~s to me that .../It begins to ~ that ...,* It looks as though ... . 在我看起来似乎…… (看起来似乎……)。

ap·pear·ance /ə'pɪərəns; ə'pɪrəns/ n [C] **1** act of appearing: 出现; 出场; 到场; 出庭: *make an ~;* 露面; 出庭; *make one's first ~,* (of an actor, singer, etc) appear in public for the first time. (指演员, 歌唱者等)初次登台。 *put in an ~,* show oneself, attend (a meeting, party, etc): 到场; 出席: *I don't want to go to the garden party but I'd better put in an ~.* 我本来不想参加那个园游会, 不过我最好还是去一下。 **2** that which shows or can be seen; what sth or sb appears to be: 外表; 外观; 容貌: *The child had the ~ of being (= looked as if it were) half starved.* 那孩子看起来似乎在半饥饿状态。 *She has a slightly foreign ~.* 她看起来有点象外国人。 *We mustn't judge by ~s,* by what can be seen outside, by outward looks. 我们不可以根据外貌判断; 不可以取以人。 *keep up ~s,* maintain an outward show (in order to hide what one does not wish people to see, eg by buying smart clothes and spending little on food, etc). 虚饰外表; 顾全面子; 撑场面; 打肿脸充胖子(例如购买华丽衣服而吃饭花钱很少等)。 *in ~,* so far as ~ is concerned; outwardly: 就外表而言; 外表上看起来: *In ~ it is a strong building.* 外表上看起来这建筑物很坚固。 *to/by/from all ~(s),* so far as can be seen: 就所能见及者而论; 显然: *He was to all ~(s) dead.* 他显然已死。

ap·pease /ə'piːz; ə'piz/ vt [VP6A] make quiet or calm: 使平息; 安抚: ~ *sb's anger;* 平息某人的怒气; ~ *sb's curiosity/hunger.* 满足某人之好奇心(充饥)。 ~·ment n [U] appeasing, eg by making concessions to potential enemies. 平息; 安抚; 绥靖(例如对可能之敌人作让步); 姑息。

ap·pel·lant /ə'pelənt; ə'pelənt/ adj (legal) concerned with appeals. (法律)上诉的。 □ n (legal) person who appeals to a higher court. (法律)上诉人。

ap·pel·la·tion /ˌæpə'leɪʃn; ˌæpə'leʃən/ n [C] (formal) name or title; system of names. (正式用语)名称; 称呼; 称号; 命名。

ap·pend /ə'pend; ə'pend/ vt [VP6A,14] ~ *sth (to),* (formal) add in writing or in print; add (sth) at the end: (正式用语)附加; 添加; 在后面增补: ~ *a clause to a treaty;* 在条约上附加一项条款; ~ *a seal or signature to a document.* 在文件上盖章或签署。

ap·pend·age /ə'pendɪdʒ; ə'pendɪdʒ/ n [C] sth added to, fastened to or forming a natural part of, a larger thing. 附加物; 附属物; 附属部分; 生成或固有的部分。

ap·pen·dix /ə'pendɪks; ə'pendɪks/ n **1** [C] (*pl* **-dices** /-dɪsiːz; -də,siz/) add added, esp at the end of a book. 附加物; (尤指书末之)附录。 **2** [C] (*pl* also 复数亦作 **~es**) small out-growth on the surface of a bodily organ, esp (**'vermiform ~**) a wormlike appendage of the large intestine. 盲肠(尤指阑尾)。 ⇨ the illus at

alimentary. 参看 alimentary 之插图。**ap·pen·di·ci·tis**
/ə,pendɪ'saɪtɪs; ə,pɛndə'saɪtɪs/ n [U] diseased condition
of the vermiform ~, requiring in many cases a
surgical operation. 阑尾炎(俗称盲肠炎)。**ap·pen·dec·
tomy** /,æpen'dektəmɪ/; ,æpən'dɛktəmɪ/ n (pl -mies)
removal by surgery of the vermiform ~. 阑尾切
除术。

ap·per·tain /,æpə'teɪn; ,æpə'ten/ vi [VP3A] ~ to,
(formal) belong to as a right; be appropriate: (正式用
语)作为一种权利而属于;专属: the duties ~ing to his
office. 他的职位所应尽的责任。

ap·pe·tite /'æprtaɪt; 'æpə,taɪt/ n [U] physical desire
(esp for food): 欲望; (尤指)食欲: She is suffering from
lack of ~. 她食欲不振。If you eat a lot of chocolate
before supper, it will spoil/take away your ~, prevent
you from enjoying your supper. 你如果在餐前吃很多巧
克力, 就会吃不下晚饭了。(fig) (喻) He had no ~ for
the fight. 他失去斗志。[C] instance of such a desire:
有食欲之实例: The long walk gave him a good ~. 长
时间的走路使他食欲旺盛。**ap·pe·tiz·er** /'æprtaɪzə(r)/;
'æpə,taɪzə/ n sth done (eg a walk) or served (eg olives,
a short alcoholic drink) in order to stimulate the ~.
增进食欲之事(如步行); 开胃的饮料或食物(如橄榄, 少许
的酒); 开胃品; 开胃药。**ap·pe·tiz·ing** adj pleasing to,
exciting, the ~: 引起欲望或食欲的; 促进食欲的; 开胃
的: an appetizing smell from the kitchen. 从厨房来的令
人垂涎的味道。

ap·plaud /ə'plɔːd; ə'plɒd/ vi, vt 1 [VP6A, 2A, B]
show approval (of) by clapping the hands: 鼓掌; 借鼓
掌表示赞许: The audience ~ed (the singer) for five
minutes. 听众(对歌唱者)鼓掌达五分钟。He was loudly
~ed. 他受到热烈的掌声。2 express approval of: 赞成;
赞许: I ~ your decision. 我赞成你的决定。

ap·plause /ə'plɔːz; ə'plɒz/ n [U] loud approval;
hand-clapping: 热烈赞许; 喝彩; 鼓掌: greeted with ~;
受到热烈的赞许; win the ~ of the audience. 赢得听众的
掌声。

apple /'æpl; 'æpl/ n (tree with) round fruit with
firm juicy flesh and skin that is green, red or yellow
when the fruit is ripe. 苹果;苹果树。⇨ the illus at
fruit. 参看 fruit 之插图。the ~ of one's eye, sb or sth
dearly loved. 极受珍爱之人或物; 掌上明珠。~ of
discord, cause of quarrel. 争吵的原因。upset the/
sb's '~-cart, spoil the/his plans. 破坏(某人之)计划。
in ~-,pie 'order, in perfect order, with everything in
the right place. 井然有序。'~-jack n (US) brandy
distilled from fermented cider. (美)苹果白兰地(由蒸馏
发酵的苹果汁而成)。~ 'sauce, (US = '~-,sauce) n
(a) sliced ~s stewed. 苹果酱。(b) (US colloq) nonsense;
insincere flattery. (美口) 胡说; 假意的恭维; 奉承。
Adam's ~. ⇨ Adam.

ap·pli·ance /ə'plaɪəns; ə'plaɪəns/ n [C] instrument
or apparatus: 工具;器械;用具: an ~ for rescuing
sailors from a wrecked ship, eg a rope that can be fired
from a gun; 拯救海上遇难船员之救生器具(如可自枪中
射出之绳索); household ~s, eg a washing-machine, a
food-mixer. 家庭用具(如洗衣机, 食物拌合器等)。

ap·pli·cable /'æplɪkəbl; 'æplɪkəbl/ adj ~ (to),
that can be applied; that is suitable and proper: 适用
的; 适当的; 合适的: Is the rule ~ to this case? 该规则适
用于这种情形吗?

ap·pli·cant /'æplɪkənt; 'æpləkənt/ n ~ (for),
person who applies (esp for a position): 申请人; 请
求者; (尤指)求职者: As the wages were low, there
were no ~s for the job. 因为工资低, 没有人申请这个
工作。

ap·pli·ca·tion /,æplɪ'keɪʃn; ,æplə'keʃən/ n 1 [U]
~ (to sb) (for sth), making of a request: 申请;请求
(向某人)(为某事): A list of new books may be had on ~
to the publishers; 新书目录可向出版者索取; [C] request (esp in writing):
申请书; 请求书: The manager received twenty ~s for the
position. 经理收到了二十件求职申请书。We made an ~

to the court for an enquiry. 我们曾请求法院调查。'~
form, form to be filled in when applying for sth. 申请
表格。2 [U] ~ (of sth) (to sth), putting one thing
on to another: 涂敷(某物于另一物体上): This oil is for
external ~ only, to be used only on the surface; 此油仅
供外敷用; [C] substance used: 涂敷物; 涂料; 涂药: The
doctor ordered an ~ of ice to the forehead. 医生吩咐额冰
于头上。Both cold and hot ~s are used to help people who
are in pain. 冷敷与热敷均用于减轻疼痛。3 [U] ~ (of
sth) (to sth), bringing a rule to bear on a case;
putting to practical use: 应用;运用: the ~ of the rule
to this case; 把该规则应用于此一情形; the ~ of a
discovery of a new process, etc to industry. 新发现(新方
法等)之应用于工业。4 [U] effort; attention: 努力;注
意: If you show ~ in your studies (= If you work
hard) you will succeed. 如果你在学业上努力, 你就会成
功。My work demands close ~, ie I have to concentrate
my thoughts on it. 我的工作需要聚精会神。

ap·plied ⇨ apply.

ap·pli·qué /æ'pliːkeɪ US: ,æplɪ'keɪ; ,æplɪ'ke/ n [U]
(esp in dress-making) ornamental work made of one
kind of material, or material of one colour, applied to
the surface of another. (尤指洋裁之)贴花(用不同的布
料或不同颜色的布料加于服装上的花饰)。□ vt ornament
in this way. 以贴花装饰。

ap·ply /ə'plaɪ; ə'plaɪ/ vt, vi (pt, pp -lied) 1 [VP2C,
3A] ~ (to sb) (for sth), (formally) ask for: (正式)
请求; 申请: ~ to the Consul for a visa. 你亲自或通信申
请均可。You may ~ in person or by letter. 你亲自或通信申
请均可。2 [VP6A, 14] lay one thing on to another;
cause (sth) to serve a purpose by doing this: 置一物于
另一物上; 敷用; 使用; 贴用; 敷涂: a plaster to a
cut; 贴膏药于割伤处; ~ the brakes (of a motor vehicle,
etc); 使用(汽车等之)刹车; (fig) (喻) We intend to ~
economic sanctions. 我们计划拟以经济制裁。3 [VP6A,
3A] ~ (to sth), (cause to) have a bearing (on);
concern: (使)与…有关系; 适用: The rule cannot be
applied in every case. 这规则并非适用于所有的情形。
What I have said does not ~ to you. 我所说的话与你无
关。4 [VP14] ~ oneself/one's mind/one's energies
(to sth/to doing sth), concentrate one's thoughts, etc
on a task, give all one's energy and attention to: 集中
精力(做某事); 全神贯注于: ~ your mind to your work.
专心于你的工作。We must ~ our energies to finding a
solution. 我们必须全力想出一个解决的办法。5 [VP14]
make practical use of (research, a discovery): 应用(研
究, 发现)作实际应用; 实际应用: We can ~ his findings
in new developments. 我们可将他的调查结果应用于新发
展中。**ap·plied** part adj put to practical use: 应用的;
实用的: applied mathematics, eg as used in engineering;
应用数学(如用于工程学中者); applied art, eg as used
in textile designs, for pottery, etc. 实用美术(如用于织
物图案, 陶器画等者)。

ap·point /ə'pɔɪnt; ə'pɔɪnt/ vt 1 [VP6A, 14, 16A] ~
sth (for sth), choose, decide, fix (a time/date, etc):
定; 决定; 指定(时间, 日期等): The time ~ed for the
meeting was 8.30 pm. 开会所定的时间是晚上八时三十
分。We must ~ a time/place for the next meeting. 我们必须定出一个时间再集会(定出下次的
会期)。2 [VP6A, 14, 16A, 23, 25] ~ sb (to sth),
choose for a post; set up by choosing members: 选
派, 指派, 委派, 任命(某人担任某职位); 选定会员以组成:
They ~ed White (to be) manager. 他们委派怀特为经理。
Smith was ~ed to the vacant post. 史密斯被派就那空缺。
The newly-~ed officials are all experts. 那些新派的官
员全是专家老手。We must ~ a committee. 我们必须选
派委员以组成一委员会。3 [VP9] (formal or older use)
give orders: (正式用语或旧用法)下令; 命令: ~ that sth
shall be done. 下令做某事。4 well/badly ~ed, well/
badly equipped. 设备好(坏)的。~ee /ə,pɔɪn'tiː; ə,pɔɪn'ti/
n person ~ed to an office or position. 被派任者; 被委派
者; 被指定人。

ap·point·ment /ə'pɔɪntmənt; ə'pɔɪntmənt/ n 1 [U] appointing: 约定；任用；委派: meet sb by ~, after fixing a time and place. 经约定时间地点而会见某人。 2 [C] arrangement to meet sb: 约会: make/fix an ~ with sb; 与某人约会; keep/break an ~. 践约(失约)。I have an ~ with my dentist at 3 pm. 我已约定下午三时去看牙医。 3 [C] position or office: 职务；职位: get a good ~ in a business firm: 在一商行获得一好职位; an ~ as manager. 担任经理的职位。4(pl) equipment; furniture· (复)设备；家具。

ap·por·tion /ə'pɔːʃn; ə'pɔrʃən/ vt [VP6A,12B,13B, 14] ~ (among/to), divide; distribute; give as a share: 分配；分配: I have ~ed you different duties each day of the week. 我已一周中每天的不同工作分派给你。This sum of money is to be ~ed among the six boys. 这笔钱将分配给这六个男孩子。

ap·po·site /'æpəzɪt; 'æpəzɪt/ adj strikingly appropriate for a purpose or occasion: 显然适当的；适切的: an ~ remark. 适当的言论。~·ly adj adv

ap·po·si·tion /ˌæpə'zɪʃn; ˌæpə'zɪʃən/ n [U] (gram) addition of one word or group of words to another as an explanation: (语法)同格: 同格: In the sentence, 'Herr Müller, our new teacher, is a German', teacher is in ~ to Müller; teacher and Müller are in ~. 在 Herr Müller, our new teacher, is a German (米勒先生，我们的新老师，是德国人)一句中，teacher 是 Müller 的同位语；teacher 和 Müller 同位。

ap·praise /ə'preɪz; ə'prez/ vt [VP6A] fix a price for; say what sth is worth: 估计；估价；评价；鉴定: the ability of one's pupils; 鉴定其学生之能力; property (at a certain sum) for taxation. 以财产之价值以为课税之依据。**ap·prai·sal** /ə'preɪzl; ə'prezl/ n valuation. 估计；估价；评价。

ap·preci·able /ə'priːʃəbl; ə'priʃəbl/ adj that can be seen, measured or felt: 可看见的；可测量的；可感到的: an ~ change in the temperature. 可感到的气温变化。 **ap·preci·ably** /-əblɪ; -əblɪ/ adv

ap·preci·ate /ə'priːʃɪeɪt; ə'priʃɪ,et/ vt, vi 1 [VP6A] judge rightly the value of; understand and enjoy: 正确地判断…的价值: 了解和欣赏; 鉴赏: You can't ~ English poetry unless you understand its rhythm. 你若不懂英诗的韵律，就不能欣赏英诗。We all ~ a holiday after a year of hard work. 经过一年之辛苦工作之后,我们大家都能领略假期的乐趣。 2 [VP6A] put a high value on: 重视; 宝贵；激赏: We greatly ~ all your help. 我们非常感激你的一切帮助。3[VP2B] rise in value, etc) increase in value: (指土地,货物等)价值增高；增值: The land has ~d greatly since the new railway was built. 自从新铁路筑成以后，这块地的价值大为增高。 4 [VP6A, 9, 10] realize and understand: 了解: I ~ your anxiety about your son's illness. 我了解你为儿子生病而忧虑的心情。

ap·preci·ation /əˌpriːʃɪ'eɪʃn; ə,priʃɪ'eʃən/ n 1 [C, U] (statement giving) judgement, valuation: 鉴识；判断；评价；欣赏；评论: Write an ~ of a new symphony. 写一篇评论一首新交响乐的文章。She showed little or no ~ of good music. 她对好音乐毫无欣赏的能力。 2 [U] proper understanding and recognition: 激赏; 感激: in sincere ~ of your valuable help. 对于你宝贵的帮助由衷感激。 3 [U] rise in value, eg of land, business shares. (如土地,股票等之)增值；涨价。**ap·preci·ative** /ə'priːʃɪətɪv; ə'priʃɪ,etɪv/ adj feeling or showing ~(2): 欣赏的；表现出欣赏能力的；赏识的；感激的: an appreciative audience; 有欣赏能力的听众; appreciative of kindness. 感激恩惠。**ap·preci·ative·ly** /ə'priː-ʃɪətɪvlɪ/ adv

ap·pre·hend /ˌæprɪ'hend; ˌæprɪ'hɛnd/ vt 1 [VP6A, 9] (old use) understand: (旧用法)了解；明了: You are, I ~, ready to ~. 我明了你已准备~。 2 [VP6A, 9] (formal) fear: (正式用语)忧虑恐惧: Do you ~ any difficulty/that there will be any difficulty? 你怕有困难吗？3 [VP6A] (legal) arrest, seize: (法律)逮捕: ~ a thief. 捕贼。**ap·pre·hen·sible** /ˌæprɪ'hensəbl;

ˌæprɪ'hɛnsəbl/ adj capable of being ~ed(1). 可了解的；可明了的。

ap·pre·hen·sion /ˌæprɪ'henʃn; ˌæprɪ'hɛnʃən/ n 1 [U] grasping (of ideas); understanding: 了解；明了: quick/slow of ~. 理解敏捷(迟钝)。 2 [C,U] fear; unhappy feeling about the future: 恐惧; 忧虑: feel ~ for sb's safety; 为某人之安全担忧; filled with ~; 内心充满忧虑; entertain an ~ of failure. 心中害怕失败。 3 (legal) seizing: (法律)逮捕: the ~ of a thief/deserter. 逮捕窃贼(逃亡者)。

ap·pre·hen·sive /ˌæprɪ'hensɪv; ˌæprɪ'hɛnsɪv/ adj uneasy; worried: 不安的；担心的；忧虑的: ~ of further defeats; 担心再失败; ~ for sb's safety; 为某人之安全担心; ~ that sb will be hurt. 担心某人会受到伤害。

ap·pren·tice /ə'prentɪs; ə'prɛntɪs/ n learner of a trade who has agreed to work for a number of years in return for being taught. 学徒；徒弟。□ vt [VP6A,14] ~ (to), bind as an ~: 使为学徒: The boy was ~d to a carpenter. 那孩子被送到木匠那里做学徒。~·ship /-tʃɪp; -tɪs,ʃɪp/ n (time of) being an ~: 做学徒；学艺；学徒身份;学徒期间: serve one's ~ship (with sb). (跟某人)当学徒。

ap·prise /ə'praɪz; ə'praɪz/ vt [VP14] ~ of, (formal) inform: (正式用语)通知: be ~d of sb's intentions: 获悉某人的意图; be ~d that ... . 已获悉…。

ap·pro /'æprəʊ; 'æpro/ n on ~, (comm sl) on approval: (商俚)看货后再做决定: goods on ~, to be returned if not satisfactory. 看货后再做决定之货物(如不满意可以退还)。

ap·proach /ə'prəʊtʃ; ə'protʃ/ vt, vi [VP6A, 2A] come near(er) (to): 走近；接近: A boy of eighteen is ~ing manhood. 十八岁的男孩快接近成年。As winter ~ed the weather became colder. 因为冬天渐近，天气变得冷些了。 (fig) (喻) Few writers can even ~ Shakespeare in greatness. 很少作家能与莎士比亚的伟大。2[VP6A] go to (sb) with a request or offer: 与(某人)接洽或交涉: When is the best time to ~ my employer about an increase in salary? 何时最适合与我的雇主交涉增加薪水? He is rather difficult to ~. It is not easy to get on friendly terms with him. 他是个不易接近的人。□ n 1 [U] act of ~ing: 渐近; The enemy ran away at our ~. 当我们渐近的时候，敌人就逃遁了。easy/difficult of ~, (a) (of a place) easy/difficult to get to. (指地方) 容易(不易)到达的。(b) (of a person) easy/difficult to meet and talk to. (指人)容易(不易)接近的。make ~es to sb, (a) try to obtain his interest, attract his attention. 设法博得某人的好感,或引起他的注意;亲近某人。(b) offer, try, to enter into personal relations with (eg of a man who wants intimate friendship with a girl or woman). (指欲与某女子建立亲密友谊之男人等)设法与 ~ 搭上关系。 2 [C] approximation: 近似; 接近: an ~ to perfection. 接近完善。 3 [C] way, path, road: 通路; 引道: All the ~es to the Palace were guarded by soldiers. 所有通至王宫的道路都有士兵防守。~·able /-əbl; -əbl/ adj (of a person or place) that can be ~ed; accessible. (指人)可亲近的; (指地方)可到达的。

ap·pro·ba·tion /ˌæprə'beɪʃn; ˌæprə'beʃən/ n [U] (formal) approval; sanction. (正式用语)许可; 批准; 赞许。

ap·pro·pri·ate¹ /ə'prəʊprɪət; ə'proprɪɪt/ adj ~ (for/to sth), suited to; in keeping with: (对某事物)适当的；适合于…的；与…一致的: Sports clothes are not ~ for a formal wedding. 运动衣不适合于正式婚礼。 Write in a style ~ to your subject. 以适合于你主题的文体来写。~·ly adv

ap·pro·pri·ate² /ə'prəʊprɪeɪt; ə'proprɪ,et/ vt [VP 6A, 14] 1 put on one side for a special purpose: 拨(款等)做某种特殊用途: £20000 has been ~d for the new school buildings. 已拨款两万英镑为建筑新校舍之用。

2 take and use as one's own: 擅用; 私用; 挪用; 窃用: *He often ~s my ideas.* 他时常剽窃我的见解. **ap·pro·pri·ation** /ə͵prəʊprɪ'eɪʃn; ə͵proprɪ'eʃən/ *n* **1** [U] appropriating or being ~d; [C] instance of this. 拨款; 拨用; 擅用; 挪用; 窃用; 剽窃. **2** [C] sth, esp a sum of money, that is ~d: 被拨用或擅用之物; (尤指)所拨之款: *make an appropriation for payment of debts;* 拨一笔款清偿债务; *Senate A~s Committee,* (US) one which deals with funds for salaries, welfare, etc. (美)参议院拨款委员会(负责防正, 福利等专款之划拨).

ap·prov·al /ə'pruːvl; ə'pruvl/ *n* [U] feeling, showing or saying, that one is satisfied, that sth is right, that one agrees to sth: 赞成; 认可; 同意; 批准: *Your plans have my ~.* 你的计划我赞成. *Does what I have done meet with your ~?* 我所做的你赞成吗? *She gave a nod of ~/nodded her ~.* 她点头表示同意. **goods on ~,** to be returned if not satisfactory. 不满意包换之货物.

ap·prove /ə'pruːv; ə'pruv/ *vt, vi* **1** [VP3A] *~ of sth/sb,* give one's approval of: 赞成; 同意; 认可; 批准: *Her father will never ~ of her marriage to you.* 她父亲永不会同意她和你结婚. *I cannot support a policy of which I have never ~d.* 我不能支持一项我所从未赞成的政策. **2** [VP6A] confirm; agree to: 同意; 认可; 通过: *The minutes (of the meeting) were read and ~d.* (会议)纪录经宣读通过. *The expenditure has been ~d.* 该笔费用已获通过. **'~d school,** (GB) boarding school for training and educating children under 17 who are sent there by magistrates for juvenile offences or because in need of care and protection. (US 美 = *reformatory, reform school*). (英)少年罪犯教养院; 少年感化院. **ap·prov·ing·ly** *adv*

ap·proxi·mate¹ /ə'prɒksɪmɪt; ə'prɑksəmɪt/ *adj ~ (to),* very nearly correct; about right: 极近于…的; 大约正确的; 大概的: *a sum of money ~ to what will be needed.* 一笔极接近所需数目的款子. *The ~ area of my land is half an acre.* 我的土地的面积大概为半英亩. **~·ly** *adv*

ap·proxi·mate² /ə'prɒksɪmeɪt; ə'prɑksə͵met/ *vi, vt* **1** [VP3A] *~ to,* come near to (esp in quality or number): 近; 接近(尤指在质或数方面): *His description of the event ~d to the truth but there were a few inaccuracies.* 他对于这件事的描述很接近于事实, 但仍有几处不正确的地方. **2** [VP6A, 3A] bring or come near to. 使接近; 接近. **ap·proxi·ma·tion** /ə͵prɒksɪ'meɪʃn; ə͵prɑksə'meʃən/ *n* [C] almost correct amount or estimate; [U] being or getting near (in number or quality). 差不多正确的量或估计; 概算; 接近; 近似值.

ap·pur·ten·ance /ə'pɜːtɪnəns; ə'pɝtnəns/ *n* (usu *pl*) (legal) sth that belongs to or usu goes with another thing: (通常用复数)(法律)附属物; 从属物; 从属权利: *the house and its ~s,* the lesser rights and privileges that go with ownership of the house. 房屋之所有权及其从属权利.

après-ski /͵æprɛ'skiː; ͵æprɛ'ski/ *attrib adj* of the evening period after skiing: 滑雪后之晚间的: *~ fun and games,* 滑雪后晚间之娱乐游戏; *~ clothes.* 滑雪后之晚装.

apri·cot /'eɪprɪkɒt; 'eprɪ͵kɑt/ *n* (tree with) round, orange-yellow or orange-red fruit with soft flesh and a hard stone-like seed; colour of this fruit when ripe. 杏; 杏树; 杏黄色.

April /'eɪprəl; 'eprəl/ *n* fourth month of the year. 四月. **~ 'fool,** person who is hoaxed on ͵All 'Fools' Day (1 April). 四月愚人(四月一日愚人节被人所愚弄的人).

a priori /͵eɪ praɪ'ɔːraɪ; 'eprɑɪ'orɑɪ/ *adv, adj* (Lat) (reasoning) from cause to effect, eg saying, 'The boys have walked a long way so they must be tired.' (拉丁)自原因推及结果地(的); 演绎地(的)(例如: '孩子们走了很多路, 所以他们一定累了.') ⪢ **a posteriori.**

apron /'eɪprən; 'eprən/ *n* **1** loose garment worn over the front part of the body to keep clothes clean; any similar covering. 围裙; 围腰布. *tied to his mother's/wife's '~-strings,* too long or too much under her control. 为母亲(妻子)所左右. **2** hard-surfaced (tarmac, concrete, etc) area on an air-field, used for manoeuvring and (un)loading aircraft. 停机坪(飞机场上用以调配飞机或装卸货物的一块铺有柏油或混凝土等的地方). **3** '~ stage, (in some theatres) part of the stage jutting out into the audience. 舞台前部. ⪢ **proscenium.**

apro·pos /͵æprə'pəʊ; ͵æprə'po/ *adv, pred adj* to the purpose; well suited (to what is being said or done): 与目的切合地(的); (与正在说的或做的)适当地(的): *His suggestion is very much ~.* 他的建议非常适当. *~ of* prep concerning, with reference to. 关于; 至于; 就…而论.

apse /æps; æps/ *n* semi-circular or many-sided recess, with an arched or domed roof, esp at the east end of a church. 建筑物之半圆形或多边形的凹室(顶为拱形或圆形, 尤指在教堂之东端者); 半圆形殿. ⪢ the illus at **church.** 参看 church 之插图.

apt /æpt; æpt/ *adj* (-er, -est) **1** *apt (at doing sth)* quick-witted: (做某事)聪明的; 敏捷的: *one of my aptest pupils;* 我的最聪明的学生之一; *very apt at picking up a new subject.* 极敏于学习新科目. **2** to the point; well suited: 切题的; 恰当的; 适当的: *an apt remark.* 适当的言论. **3** *apt to do sth,* having a tendency, likely to do sth: 有…的倾向的; 易于…的: *Cast iron is apt to break.* 生铁易于断折. *He's a clever boy but apt to get into mischief.* 他是个聪明的孩子, 但是好捣乱. **apt·ly** *adv* suitably, justly. 合适地; 适当地. **apt·ness** *n*

ap·ti·tude /'æptɪtjuːd; 'æptə͵tjud/ *n* [U] *~ (for),* natural or acquired talent: 资质; 才能: *He shows some ~ for languages.* 他表现出学习语言的才能. [C] particular talent: 某种才能: *He has a singular ~ for dealing with a crisis.* 他有处理危机的奇才. '*~ test,* test to discover and assess skills. 性向测验.

aqua·lung /'ækwəlʌŋ; 'ækwə͵lʌŋ/ *n* (P) breathing unit (face mask, valve unit and cylinder(s) of compressed air or oxygen) used for underwater swimming or diving. (商标)水肺(潜水者所用的面具, 活门及氧气筒). ⪢ the illus at **frogman.** 参看 frogman 之插图.

aqua·mar·ine /͵ækwəmə'riːn; ͵ækwəmə'rin/ *n* [C, U] bluish-green (jewel). 水蓝宝石; 蓝晶; 蓝绿色.

aqua·naut /'ækwənɔːt; 'ækwə͵nɔt/ *n* person trained to live for a long period, in a structure submerged in the sea, to study marine life, etc. 海底研究员(受过训练能长时间生活在置于海中之构造物中, 以研究海洋生物等).

aqua·plane /'ækwəpleɪn; 'ækwə͵plen/ *n* board on which a person stands while being pulled along by a fast motor-boat. 滑水板(由快艇牵引供人乘立之板, 系水上运动器具). □ *vi* ride on such a board. 乘滑水板作滑水运动.

aquar·ium /ə'kweərɪəm; ə'kwɛrɪəm/ *n* (*pl* -s, -ria /-rɪə; -rɪə/) (building with an) artificial pond or tank for keeping and showing living fish and water plants. 水族馆; 蓄鱼池; 养鱼缸.

Aquar·ius /ə'kweərɪəs; ə'kwɛrɪəs/ *n* the eleventh sign of the zodiac. 宝瓶宫(黄道十二宫中的第十一宫). ⪢ the illus at **zodiac.** 参看 zodiac 之插图.

aqua·tic /ə'kwætɪk; ə'kwætɪk/ *adj* **1** (of plants, animals, etc) growing or living in or near water. (指植物, 动物等)水生的; 生长或栖于水中(或水边)的. **2** (of sports) taking place on or in water, eg rowing, swimming. (指运动)水上的; 水中的(如划船, 游泳).

aqua·tint /'ækwətɪnt; 'ækwə͵tɪnt/ *n* [U] process of etching on copper, the picture being made by letting acid bite into a plate covered with a layer of resin dust; [O] picture made in this way. 凹版腐蚀制版法; 铜版蚀镂法(利用酸性腐蚀作用刻画于覆有一层树脂的铜版之方法); 以此种方法蚀镂之图画.

aqua·vit /'ækwəvɪt; 'ækwəvɪt/ n [U] strong Scandinavian liquor flavoured with caraway seed. 一种北欧烈酒(用葛缕子之子作为香料)。

aque·duct / ə'kwɪdʌkt; 'ækwɪ,dʌkt/ n artificial channel for supplying water, esp one built of stone or brick and higher than the surrounding land. 输水道;水道桥(人工水道,尤指用石或砖造成而高于周围陆地者)。

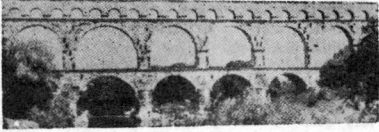

an aqueduct

aque·ous /'eɪkwɪəs; 'ekwɪəs/ adj of or like water: 水的;似水的: an ～ solution. 水溶液。

aqui·line /'ækwɪlaɪn; 'ækwə,laɪn/ adj of or like an eagle: 鹰的; 似鹰的: an ～ nose, hooked like an eagle's beak. 鹰钩鼻子。

Arab /'ærəb; 'ærəb/ n name applied to any of those Semitic people who speak Arabic and claim descent from the inhabitants of the Arabian Peninsula who, in the 7th c, were conquerors of N Africa, Syria and Mesopotamia: 阿拉伯人: the military conquests of the ～s; 阿拉伯人的军事征服地; the ～ League. 阿拉伯联盟。

ara·besque / ,ærə'besk; ,ærə'bɛsk/ n [C] (art) elaborate design of leaves, branches, scrolls, etc; (ballet) pose of a dancer on one leg, the other stretched backwards. (艺术)一种由叶,枝,涡卷等图形组成之精细的图案;阿拉伯花纹;(芭蕾)一种舞姿(单脚直立,另一脚向后伸直的姿势)。

Ara·bian /ə'reɪbɪən; ə'rebɪən/ n, adj (person) of (Saudi) Arabia or the Arabs. (沙特)阿拉伯的; (沙特)阿拉伯人(的)。 the ～ Nights, famous stories of the Arabs in ancient times. 天方夜谭(古代阿拉伯人的著名故事)。 the ～ camel, the dromedary. 阿拉伯骆驼; 单峰骆驼。

Ara·bic /'ærəbɪk; 'ærəbɪk/ adj of the Arabs. 阿拉伯人的。 ～ numerals, the signs 0, 1, 2, 3, etc. 阿拉伯数字。⇨ App 4. 参看附录四。□ n language of the Arabs. 阿拉伯语文。

Ara·bist /'ærəbɪst; 'ærəbɪst/ n student or specialist in Arabic culture, language, affairs, etc. 阿拉伯学者; 阿拉伯语专家(研究阿拉伯文化,语言,事务等)。

ar·able /'ærəbl; 'ærəbl/ adj (of land) suitable for ploughing; usually ploughed. (指土地)可耕的; 适于耕种的; 经常被耕作的。

arach·nid /ə'ræknɪd; ə'ræknɪd/ n (zool) member of the genus including spiders, scorpions and mites. (动物)蛛蜘类节肢动物(包括蜘蛛,蝎及小虱)。

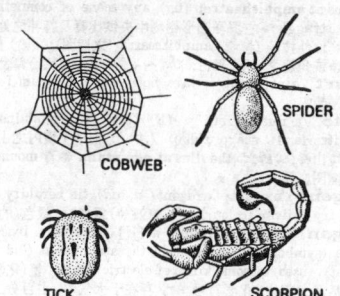

COBWEB   SPIDER

TICK   SCORPION

arachnids

ar·bi·ter /'ɑːbɪtə(r); 'ɑrbɪtə/ n 1 ～ (of), person with complete control (of sth): (对某事物)有完全控制力之人;主宰者;裁决者: the sole ～ of their destinies. 他们的命运的唯一主宰。 2 = arbitrator.

ar·bitra·ment /ɑː'bɪtrəmənt; ɑr'bɪtrəmənt/ n [U] (formal) deciding of a dispute by an arbiter; [C] decision made by an arbiter. (正式用语)仲裁; 调停; 仲裁人所作之决定。

ar·bit·rary /'ɑːbɪtrərɪ US: -trerɪ; 'ɑrbə,trerɪ/ adj 1 based on opinion or impulse only, not on reason. 恣意的; 任意的; 武断的。 2 dictatorial; using despotic power. 独裁的;专制的; 专横的。

ar·bi·trate /'ɑːbɪtreɪt; 'ɑrbə,tret/ vt, vi [VP6A,2A] ～ (between), decide by arbitration; judge between two parties to a dispute (usu at the request of the two parties): 由仲裁决定; 仲裁; 公断(通常系应争执中之双方之请求而作裁判): Mr X has been asked to ～ the dispute/to ～ between the employers and their workers. 某先生已被邀请仲裁,此项纠纷(仲裁雇主与工人之间的纷争)。 If countries would always ～ their quarrels, wars could be avoided. 假若各国都愿意由仲裁解决他们的纷争,战争就可以避免了。

ar·bi·tra·tion /,ɑːbɪ'treɪʃn; ,ɑrbə'treʃən/ n [U] (attempt at) settlement of a dispute by the decision of a person or persons chosen and accepted as judges or umpires: 仲裁; 公断: refer a wage dispute to ～; 将一项工资争执提请仲裁。 submit a claim for ～; 将一项争执提请仲裁; [C] instance of such a settlement. 仲裁之实例。 go to ～, arbitrate: 提请仲裁: The Union agreed to go to ～, ie for a settlement of their claims. 工会王国(指1706年英格兰与苏格兰的合并)同意提请仲裁解决。

ar·bi·tra·tor /'ɑːbɪtreɪtə(r); 'ɑrbə,tretə/ n (legal) arbiter; person appointed by two parties to settle a dispute. (法律)仲裁者; 公断人。

ar·bor ⇨ arbour.

ar·bor·eal /ɑː'bɔːrɪəl; ɑr'borɪəl/ adj (formal) of, living in, connected with trees: (正式用语)树的; 栖于树上的; 关于树的: ～ animals, eg squirrels, monkeys. 栖于树上的动物(如松鼠,猴等)。

ar·bour (US = ar·bor) /'ɑːbə(r); 'ɑrbə/ n shady place among trees, esp one made in a garden, with climbing plants growing over a framework. 树木中之荫处;花园中之藤架;凉亭。

arc /ɑːk; ɑrk/ n part of the circumference of a circle or other curved line. 弧(圆周或曲线之一部分)。⇨ the illus at circle. 参看 circle 之插图。 'arc-lamp, 'arc-light nm brilliant light produced by electric current flowing across a space between two carbon rods. 弧光灯;弧光(由电流通过两碳棒间之空处所产生之光亮)。

ar·cade /ɑː'keɪd; ɑr'ked/ n covered passage, usu with an arched roof, eg a passage with shops or market stalls along one or both sides; covered market. 骑楼; 连环拱廊(通常有拱形顶盖,尤指其一侧或两侧有商店或摊位之街道; 拱廊市场。 a'musement ～ ⇨ amusement.

Ar·cad·ian /ɑː'keɪdɪən; ɑr'kedɪən/ adj of an ideal rustic simplicity; simple and innocent. 一种理想乡村之简朴的; 淳朴的。□ n person with ～ tastes. 淳朴之人。

ar·cane /ɑː'keɪn; ɑr'ken/ adj secret; mysterious. 秘密的; 神秘的。

arch[1] /ɑːtʃ; ɑrtʃ/ n 1 curved structure supporting the weight of what is above it, as in bridges, aqueducts, gateways, etc. 拱(支持上面之重量的弓形构造,如见于桥梁,引水道,大门等者。⇨ the illus at aqueduct, church. 参看 aqueduct, church 之插图。 2 (also ar·ch '～·way) passageway under an ～, built as an ornament or gateway: 拱门;拱形牌坊: a triumphal ～. 凯旋门。 3 any curve in the shape of an ～, eg the curved under-part of the foot, ⇨ the illus at leg; a structure for supporting climbing roses, etc. 任何拱形之曲部(例如足穹,参看 leg 之插图);(用支以持攀缘之玫瑰

等之)拱梁。 □ vt, vi 1 [VP6A] form into an ~: 使弯
成拱形; The cat ~ed its back when it saw the dog. 猫见到
狗即拱其背。 Horses ~ their necks. 马拱其颈。 2 [VP
2C] be like an ~: 成拱状;成弓形: The trees ~ over the
river. 这些树的枝叶成弓形遮蔽河上。

arch² /ɑːtʃ/ attrib adj mischievous in an innocent
or playful way (esp of women and children): 顽皮的;
调皮的; 嬉戏的(尤指妇女及儿童): an ~ glance/smile.
调皮的一笑(一笑)。 ~·ly adv

arch- /ɑːtʃ/ pref chief; notable; extreme: 主要;
显著;极;首;大; ~-'enemy. 大敌;主敌。

ar·chae·ol·ogy (also **ar·che·ol-**) /ˌɑːkɪˈblɒdʒɪ/
ˌɑːkɪˈɒlədʒɪ/ n [U] study of ancient things, esp
remains of prehistoric times, eg tombs, buried cities.
考古学(研究古物,尤其是史前时代之遗物,如坟墓,湮灭之
古城等)。 **ar·chae·ologi·cal** /ˌɑːkɪəˈlɒdʒɪkl/, ˌɑːrkɪə-
ˈlɑːdʒɪkl/ adj of ~. 考古学的。 **ar·chae·ol·ogist**
/ˌɑːkɪˈbɒlədʒɪst/, ˌɑːrkɪˈɒlədʒɪst/ n expert in ~. 考古
学家。

ar·chaic /ɑːˈkeɪɪk/ ɑːrˈkeɪk/ adj 1 (of eg a word in a
language) not now used except for special purposes.
(指某一语言之某词等)除特殊情形外现已不用的;古的;已
不通用的。 2 of ancient times. 古代的。 **ar·cha·ism**
/ˈɑːkeɪɪzəm/ n [O] ~ word or expression;
[U] use or imitation of what is ~. 古词; 古语; 古词古
语之使用或模仿;古风;古体。

arch·angel /ˈɑːkeɪndʒl/ ˈɑːrkˈeɪndʒəl/ n angel of high
rank. 天使长;大天使。

arch·bishop /ˌɑːtʃˈbɪʃəp/ ˈɑːrtʃˈbɪʃəp/ n chief
bishop. 大主教。 **~·ric** n position or rank of an ~;
church district governed by an ~. 大主教之职衔; 大主
教之辖区。

arch·deacon /ˌɑːtʃˈdiːkən/, ˈɑːrtʃˈdiːkən/ n (in the C
of E) priest next below a bishop, superintending rural
deans. (英国国教) 副主教(负责监督乡村教会执事者)。
~ry n (pl **-ries**) position, rank, residence, of an ~.
副主教之职位,住宅。

arch·dio·cese /ˌɑːtʃˈdaɪəsɪs/ ˈɑːrtʃˈdaɪəˌsɪs/ n diocese
of an archbishop. 大主教教区。

arch·duke /ˌɑːtʃˈdjuːk/ US: -ˈduːk/ ˈɑːrtʃˈdjuːk/ n
(title given to) son or nephew of former Emperors of
Austria. 大公;大公爵(昔日奥国皇太子或皇侄之头衔)。

archer /ˈɑːtʃə(r)/ ˈɑːrtʃə/ n person who shoots with a
bow and arrows. 弓箭手。 **arch·ery** /ˈɑːtʃərɪ/ ˈɑːrtʃərɪ/
n [U] (art of) shooting with a bow and arrows. 射箭
术;射箭;箭艺。

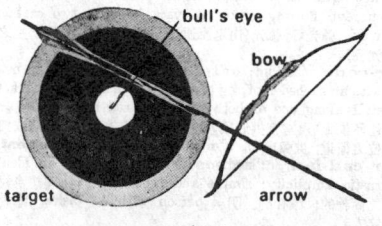

archery

arche·type /ˈɑːkɪtaɪp/ ˈɑːrkəˌtaɪp/ n prototype;
ideal form regarded as a pattern not to be changed. 原
型; 理想型。 **arche·typal** /ˌɑːkɪˈtaɪpl/ ˈɑːrkɪˈtaɪpl/ adj

archi·man·drite /ˌɑːkɪˈmændraɪt/, ˌɑːrkɪˈmændraɪt/
n head of a monastery in the Gk Orthodox Church. 希
腊正教之修道院长。

archi·pel·ago /ˌɑːkɪˈpeləgəʊ/ ˌɑːrkəˈpeləˌgo/ n (pl
~s, -es /-gəʊz/ -goz/) (sea with a) group of many
islands. 群岛;有群岛之海;多岛海。

archi·tect /ˈɑːkɪtekt/ ˈɑːrkɪtekt/ n person who
designs (and supervises the construction of) buildings,
etc. 建筑师。

archi·tec·ture /ˈɑːkɪtektʃə(r)/ ˈɑːrkəˌtektʃə/ n [U]
art and science of building; design or style of building(s).
建筑学; 建筑术; 建筑之设计或式样。 **archi·tec·tural**
/ˌɑːkɪˈtektʃərəl/, ˌɑːrkəˈtektʃərəl/ adj of ~: 建筑学(术)
的: the architectural beauties of a city. 某城中的设计优
美的建筑物。

ar·chives /ˈɑːkaɪvz/ ˈɑːrkaɪvz/ n pl (place for
keeping) public or government records; other historical
records. 档案;档案保管处;历史性的记录或文件。 **archi·
vist** /ˈɑːkɪvɪst/ ˈɑːrkəvɪst/ n person in charge of
~. 档案保管人。

arch·way /ˈɑːtʃweɪ/ ˈɑːrtʃˌweɪ/ n ⇨ **arch¹**(2).

arc·tic /ˈɑːktɪk/ ˈɑːrktɪk/ adj of the north polar
regions: 北极的: the A~ Ocean; 北冰洋; ~ weather,
very cold weather. 严寒的天气。 the ,A~ 'Circle,
the line of latitude 66¹/₂°N. 北极圈(即北纬六十六度
半线)。

ar·dent /ˈɑːdnt/ ˈɑːrdnt/ adj full of ardour. 热心的;
热情的: ~ supporters of the new movement. 新运动的热
烈拥护者。 **~·ly** adv

ar·dour (US = **-dor**) /ˈɑːdə(r)/ ˈɑːrdə/ n (for),
[C, U] warm emotion; enthusiasm. 热情;热心。

ar·du·ous /ˈɑːdjuəs US: -dʒʊ-/ ˈɑːrdʒʊəs/ adj 1 (of
work) needing and using up much energy. (指工作)费
力的; 艰巨的。 2 (of a road, etc) steep; hard to climb.
(指道路等)陡峭的;难登的。 **~·ly** adv

are¹ /ɑː(r)/ ; ə; strong form: ɑː(r); ɑː/ ⇨ **be¹**.

are² /ɑː(r)/ ; ɛr/ n metric unit of area, = 100 square
metres. 公亩(公制面积单位,等于一百平方公尺)。 ⇨ **App
5.** 参看附录五。

area /ˈeərɪə/ ˈɛrɪə/ n 1 [U] surface measure: 面积:
If a room measures 3×5 metres, its ~ is 15 square
metres/it is 15 square metres in ~. 假若一个房间是三
公尺宽五公尺长, 它的面积是十五平方公尺。 [C] in-
stance of this measurement. 面积之实例。 ⇨ **App 5.** 参
看附录五。 2 [C] region of the earth's surface: 地区:
desert ~s of North Africa; 北非洲的沙漠地区; the
postal ~s (more usu 较常用 districts) into which London
is divided. 伦敦所划分的邮递区。 3 [C] (fig) scope or
range of activity: (喻)活动的区域; 范围; 领域: the ~
of finance. 财政(金融)范围。 The ~s of disagreement
were clearly indicated at the Board Meeting. The subjects
on which members of the Board disagreed became clear.
在委员会的会议中意见不一致的地方变得很明显。 4 [C]
small courtyard giving light to the windows of basement
rooms, eg kitchen, scullery, in an old-fashioned town
house, usu with stone steps from the street pavement:
(英国旧式城市房屋) 地下室前的空地(厨房,下室采光、通
风,通常有石阶可通街上人行道的小天井): sitting on the
~ steps. 坐在地下室前的空地的石阶上。

areca /ˈærɪkə/ ˈærɪkə/ n kind of palm-tree from which
areca-nut (betel-nut) is obtained. 槟榔树。 ⇨ **betel.**

arena /əˈriːnə/ əˈriːnə/ n (pl **~s**) central part, for
games and plays, of a Roman amphitheatre, ⇨ the
illus at **amphitheatre**; (fig) any scene of competition
or struggle: 古罗马圆形剧场中央供比赛及打斗之处;比
武场; 竞技场 amphitheatre 之插图; (喻)任何
竞争或角逐之场所;舞台: the ~ of politics. 政治舞台。

aren't /ɑːnt/ ɑːrnt/ = are not: aren't I? = am I not?
不是吗?

arête /əˈreɪt/ æˈret/ n (F) (esp of mountains in
Switzerland) sharp ridge. (法)(尤指瑞士境内之山的)
险峻山脊; 峻岭。⇨ the illus at **mountain.** 参看 mountain
之插图。

ar·gent /ˈɑːdʒənt/ ˈɑːrdʒənt/ n, adj (in heraldry and
poetry) silver (colour). (纹章及诗)银(的);银色(的)。

ar·gon /ˈɑːɡɒn/ ˈɑːrɡɑːn/ n [U] chemically inactive
gas (symbol Ar), present in the atmosphere (0.8 per
cent), used in some kinds of electric lamps. 氩(化学性
不活泼之气体,化学符号 Ar, 存在于大气中,占百分之零
点八,用于某些电灯中)。

Ar·go·naut /ˈɑːɡənɔːt/ ˈɑːrɡəˌnɔt/ n (myth) one of

the heroes who sailed in the ship Argo /'ɑ:gəʊ; 'ɑrgo/ with Jason in search of the Golden Fleece. (神话)与 Jason 同乘 Argo 号船寻找金羊毛之英雄之一。

ar·go·sy /'ɑ:gəsɪ; 'ɑrgəsɪ/ n (pl **-sies**) (poet) large merchant ship, esp one with valuable cargo. (诗)大商 船(尤指载有贵重货物者)。

ar·got /'ɑ:gəʊ; 'ɑrgo/ n [U] jargon; slang. 隐语; 暗 语; 黑话; 俚语。

ar·gue /'ɑ:gju:; 'ɑrgjʊ/ vi, vt 1 [VP2A, C, 3A] ~ (with sb) (about/over sth), express disagreement; quarrel: 表示不同意; (与某人) 争论(某事); 争吵: Don't ~ with me; my decision is final. 不要跟我争论; 我的决定 是最后的了。Why are they always ~ing? 为什么他们总 是在争论? 2 [VP2A,3A,9] ~ (for/against/that...), maintain a case, give reasons (in support of, for, against, esp with the aim of persuading sb): 坚持; 提 出理由(以支持或反对, 尤指以说服某人为目的的); 争辩: He ~s soundly. 他争辩得很有道理。You can ~ either way, for or against. 你可以在正反两面择一辩护。He was arguing that poverty may be a blessing. 他主张贫 穷是福。3 [VP14] ~ sb into/out of doing sth, persuade by giving reasons: (提出理由以) 说服某人做 (不做)某事: They tried to ~ him into joining them. 他 们试图说服他参加他们。4 [VP6A] debate: 讨论; 辩论: The lawyers ~d the case for hours. 律师们辩论该案件达 数小时之久。**ar·gu·able** /'ɑ:gjʊəbl; 'ɑrgjʊəbl/ adj that can be ~d about. 可争论的; 可讨论的; 可辩论的。 **ar·gu·ably** /-əblɪ; -əblɪ/ adv

ar·gu·ment /'ɑ:gjʊmənt; 'ɑrgjəmənt/ n 1 [C] an ~ (with sb) (about/over sth), (perhaps heated) disagreement; quarrel: (与某人) (关于某事的)意见不 合; 争吵; 争吵: endless ~s about money; 有关金钱的永 远没完的争论; an ~ with the referee. 与裁判员之争论。 2 [U] reasoned discussion: 讨论; 辩论; 论据: It is beyond ~ that ... ; …是无可置辩的。[C] an ~ (for/against), instance of this: (赞成, 反对的)论据: an ~ for not gambling. 反对赌博的论据。I have no wish to engage in (an) ~ with you. 我不想跟你辩论。3 [C] summary of the subject matter of a book, etc. (一本书 等的)摘要; 概要。**ar·gu·men·ta·tive** /,ɑ:gju'mentətɪv; ,ɑrgjə'mentətɪv/ adj fond of arguing(1). 好争论的; 爱 辩论的。

ar·gu·men·ta·tion /,ɑ:gjumen'teɪʃn; ,ɑrgjəmen-'teʃən/ n [U] process of arguing; debate. 辩论法; 辩 论; 论争; 论证。

Ar·gus /'ɑ:gəs; 'ɑrgəs/ n (GK myth) monster with a hundred eyes. (希神)百眼巨人。~-'eyed adj observant; vigilant. 善于观察的; 机警的; 警醒的。

aria /'ɑ:rɪə; 'ɑrɪə/ n (pl ~s) song for a single voice (esp in 18th c operas and oratorios). (尤指十八世纪歌 剧及圣乐中之)独唱曲; 咏叹调; 抒情调。

arid /'ærɪd; 'ærɪd/ adj 1 (of soil, land) dry, barren; (of climate, regions) having not enough rainfall to support vegetation. (指土壤, 土地)干燥的; 不生草木 的; 不毛的; (指气候,地区)干旱的; 雨量稀少的。2 (fig) uninteresting. (喻)无趣味的; 枯燥的。**arid·ity** /ə'rɪdətɪ; ə'rɪdətɪ/ n [U] dryness. 干燥; 枯燥。

Aries /'eərɪːz; 'erɪz/ n the Ram, the first sign of the zodiac. 白羊宫(黄道带之第一宫)。⇨ the illus at **zodiac**. 参看 zodiac 之插图。

aright /ə'raɪt; ə'raɪt/ adv (archaic) rightly: (古)对; 不错; 正确地: if I heard ~. 假如我听得不错的话。 (Before a pp use rightly, as in to be rightly informed.) (在过去分词之前用 rightly, 如 to be rightly informed. 得到正确的消息。)

arise /ə'raɪz; ə'raɪz/ vi (pt arose /ə'rəʊz; ə'roz/, pp arisen /ə'rɪzn; ə'rɪzn/) 1[VP2A] come into existence; come to notice; present itself: 发生; 出现; 呈现; 起: A new difficulty has ~n. 一项新的困难发生了。If the need should ~ ... ; 假若有必要的话…; Before they could start a mist arose. 在他们出发之前, 起了雾。2 [VP3A] ~ from, result from: 产生: Serious obligations may ~

from the proposed clause. 由这项提议的条款可能产生一 些重大的责任。3 [VP2A] (old use) get up; stand up. (旧用法)起身; 起来; 起立。

ar·is·toc·racy /,ærɪ'stɒkrəsɪ; ,ærə'stɑkrəsɪ/ n (pl -cies) 1 [U] government by persons of the highest social rank; [C] country or state with such a govern- ment. 贵族政治; 实行贵族政治的国家。2 [C] ruling body of nobles; the social class from which these nobles come. 贵族统治集团; 贵族阶级。3 [C] best representa- tives in any class: (任何阶级之)最优秀代表; 第一流的人 物: an ~ of talent. 第一流的人才。

ar·is·to·crat /'ærɪstəkræt US: ə'rɪst-; ə'rɪstə,kræt/ n member of the class of nobles; person of noble birth. 贵族阶级之一员;出身贵族的人;贵族。~·ic /,ærɪstə'krætɪk US: ə,rɪstə-; ə,rɪstə'krætɪk/ adj of the aristocracy; having the ways and manners of an ~: 贵族的; 贵族政 治的; 有贵族气派的: with an ~ic bearing. 举止态度有贵 族气质的。~i·cally /-klɪ; -klɪ/ adv

arith·me·tic /ə'rɪθmətɪk; ə'rɪθmə,tɪk/ n [U] science of numbers; working with numbers. 算术; 计算。 **ar·ith·meti·cal** /,ærɪθ'metɪkl; ,ærɪθ'metɪkl/ adj of ~. 算术的。~al progression, series of numbers showing an increase, or decrease, by a quantity that is always the same, eg 1, 2, 3, etc, or 7, 5, 3, etc. 算术 级数; 等差级数。**arith·metician** /ə,rɪθmə'tɪʃn; ə,rɪθmə- 'tɪʃən/ n expert in ~. 精于算术的人; 算术家。

ark /ɑ:k; ɑrk/ n (in the Bible) (圣经) 1 covered ship in which Noah and his family were saved from the Flood. (世界大洪水时期挪亚及其家属乘借以保全性命 之有篷的) 方舟。2 **Ark of the Covenant**, wooden chest in which writings of Jewish law were kept. 圣约 柜(保藏犹太法刻文之木柜)。

arm[1] /ɑ:m; ɑrm/ n 1 either of the two upper limbs of the human body, from the shoulder to the hand: 臂: She was carrying a child in her arms. 她怀中抱着一个孩 子。He was carrying a book under his arm, between the arm and the body. 他腋下夹着一本书。She had a basket on her arm, with the handle supported on her arm. 她 手臂上挂着一个篮子。baby/child/infant in arms, child too young to walk. 怀抱中的婴儿; 尚不会走路的小 孩, 抱(即, carry sth) at arm's length, with the arm fully extended. 伸直手臂(执持某物)。keep sb at arm's length, (fig) avoid becoming familiar with him. (喻) 避免与某人亲近; 与某人保持距离。welcome sb/sth) with open arms, warmly, with enthusiasm. 热烈地; 热 情地(欢迎某人, 某事物)。walk ,arm-in-'arm, (of two persons) walk side by side, with the arm of one round

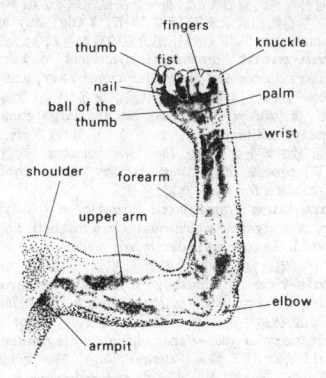

fingers
thumb
knuckle
fist
nail
palm
ball of the thumb
wrist
shoulder
forearm
upper arm
elbow
armpit

the arm and the hand

the arm of the other. (指二人)挽臂而行。 **'arm-band** n armlet. 袖带。 **'arm·chair** n chair with supports for the arms. 有扶手的椅子。 **'armchair critic,** person who offers criticism but is not actively involved. 安坐于扶手椅中的批评家(对所批评之作品措辞未深而提出批评意见者)。 **'arm-hole** n hole (in a shirt, jacket, etc) through which the arm is put. (衬衫,夹克等之)袖孔。 **'arm·let** /-lɪt; -lɪt/ n band (of cloth, etc) worn round the arm (on a sleeve). 袖带。 **'arm·pit** n hollow under the arm near the shoulder. 腋窝; 胳肢窝。 **2** sleeve: 袖子: The arms of this coat are too long. 这件外衣的袖子太长。 **3** large branch of a tree. (树的)大枝。 **4** sth shaped like or suggesting an arm: 形状似臂之物: an arm of the sea; 海湾; the arms of a chair. 椅子的扶手。 **5** (fig) (喻) **the (long) arm of the law,** the authority or power of the law. 法律之权威或力量; 法网恢恢。 **arm·ful** /'ɑːmfʊl; 'ɑrm,fʊl/ n as much as one arm, or both arms, can hold: (两臂或一臂)一抱之量: carrying in books by the armful. 抱进一抱的书。

arm² /ɑːm; ɑrm/ n branch or division of a country's armed forces: 兵种; 兵科: the infantry arm; 步兵; the air arm. 空军。

arm³ /ɑːm; ɑrm/ vt, vi [VP6A,14,2A] **arm (with),** supply, fit, weapons and armour; prepare for war: 供以或配备武器及甲胄; 装备; 备战: a warship armed with nuclear weapons; 有核武器装备的战舰; armed with a big stick; 持大棍作为武器; (fig) (喻) armed with patience/ with answers to all questions. 准备忍耐(回答一切问题)。 Their former enemy is arming again(= rearming). 他们往昔的敌人正在重整军备。 **the armed forces/services,** the army, navy and air force. 陆海空三军。 **armed neutrality,** policy of remaining neutral but prepared for defence against aggression. 武装中立。

ar·mada /ɑːˈmɑːdə; ɑrˈmɑdə/ n great fleet of warships, esp **the A~,** the fleet sent by King Philip II of Spain against England in 1588. 舰队; (尤指)无敌舰队(the Armada, 1588年西班牙国王菲力浦二世派征英国之舰队)。

ar·ma·dillo /ˌɑːməˈdɪləʊ; ˌɑrməˈdɪlo/ n (pl ~s /-ləʊz; -loz/) small burrowing animal of S America, with a body covered with a shell of bony plates, and the habit of rolling itself up into a ball when attacked. 犰狳(产于南美洲之穴居小动物; 身体覆有骨质坚甲,遇敌能缩成球状)。 ⇨ the illus at **small.** 参看 small 之插图。

Ar·ma·ged·don /ˌɑːməˈɡedn; ˌɑrməˈɡedn/ n **1** (biblical) (scene of) the last battle to be fought between the forces of good and evil, prophesied to happen at the end of time. (圣经)预言将在世界末日发生的善与恶的最后决战; 善与恶决战的战场。 ⇨ **Rev 16: 16.** 参看新约启示录第16章16节。 **2** (fig) any similar dramatic conflict. (喻)任何类似的戏剧性战争; 大决战。

ar·ma·ment /'ɑːməmənt; 'ɑrməmənt/ n **1** (usu pl) military forces and their equipment; navy, army, air force. (通常用复数)全体军队及其配备; 军备; 武备; 海陆空军。 **2** (usu pl) weapons, esp the large guns on a warship, military tank, etc: (通常用复数)武器; (尤指)战舰, 战车等上之)大炮: the '~s industry. 武器工业。 **3** [U] process of getting military forces equipped; preparation for war. 武装; 备战。

ar·ma·ture /'ɑːmətʃʊə(r); 'ɑrmətʃə/ n (electr) that part of a dynamo which rotates in a magnetic field and in which the current is developed; coil(s) of an electric motor. (电)(发电机中之)电动子; 电枢; 电动马达之线圈。

ar·mis·tice /'ɑːmɪstɪs; 'ɑrmɪstɪs/ n agreement during a war or battle to stop fighting for a time. 休战; 停战; 休战协定。 **'A~ Day,** 11 Nov, kept as the anniversary of the ~ that ended fighting in the First World War (US 美 = Veterans' Day). 第一次世界大战休战纪念日(十一月十一日)。 ⇨ **remembrance.**

ar·moire /'ɑːmwɑː(r) US: ɑːmˈwɑːr; ɑrˈmwɑr/ n [U] large cabinet or wardrobe. 大型的橱柜; 大衣橱; 大衣柜。

ar·mor ⇨ **armour.**

ar·mor·ial /ɑːˈmɔːriəl; ɑrˈmɔriəl/ adj of heraldry; of coats of arms. 纹章的; 盾徽的。 ⇨ **arms(2):** ~ bearings, a coat of arms. 盾形纹章; 盾徽。

ar·mour (US = **ar·mor**) /'ɑːmə(r); 'ɑrmə/ n [U] **1** defensive covering, usu metal, for the body, worn in fighting: 甲胄; 盔甲: a suit of ~. 一套盔甲。 **2** metal covering (steel plates, etc) for warships, tanks, motor vehicles, etc. (战舰,战车,汽车等之)装甲; 钢甲; 铁甲。 **3** (collective) tanks, motor vehicles, etc protected with ~. (集合用法)装甲车辆。 **'~-plate** n sheet of metal used as ~. 装甲钢板。 **~ed** part adj **1** covered or protected with ~: 装甲的: an ~ed cruiser/car. 装甲巡洋舰(汽车)。 **2** equipped with tanks, vehicles, guns, etc, that are protected with ~: 配有装甲车辆及武器的:

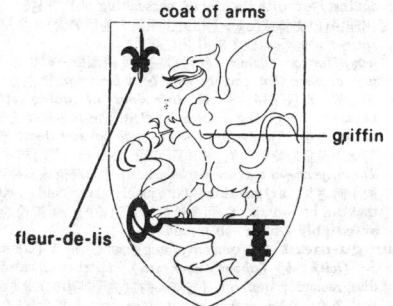

coat of arms

griffin

fleur-de-lis

escutcheon or shield

helmet
visor
cuirass
breastplate

gauntlet

greaves

chain-mail

armour

an ~*ed column/division, etc.* 装甲纵队(师等)。 ~**er** *n* **1** manufacturer or repairer of arms and ~. 制造或修理兵器及甲胄者。 **2** man in charge of fire-arms. 军械保管人。 ~**y** /'ɑːmərɪ; 'ɑrmərɪ/ *n* (*pl* -**ries**) place where arms are kept. 军械库。

arms /ɑːmz; ɑrmz/ *n pl* **1** weapons (note, *fire-arm*, used in the *sing* form): 武器;兵器(注意: fire-arm 用单数): (*in fire-definition*) *an* ~ *depot.* 军械库。*The soldiers had plenty of* ~ *and ammunition.* 士兵们有充足的武器和弹药。 **'~-race,** competition among nations on military strength. (各国间的)军备竞争。 **'fire-~,** those requiring explosives. 火器; 枪炮。 **'small** ~, fire-~ that can be carried by hand, eg revolvers, rifles, light machine-guns. 轻武器(指可用手携带者,如手枪,步枪,轻机枪)。 **lay down** (one's) ~, stop fighting. 放下武器, 停战。 **take up** ~; **rise up in** ~, (liter or fig) get ready to fight (*against*). (文或喻)拿起武器;武装起来; 准备作战(与 against 连用)。 **under** ~, provided with weapons and ready to fight. 配备武器并准备作战; 在备战状态。 **(be) up in** ~ (*about/over*), (usu fig) be protesting vigorously. (通常作比喻用法)激烈反抗; 强烈抗议。 **2** (heraldry) pictorial design used by a noble family, town, university, etc. (纹章)纹章; 徽章(代表贵族,城镇,大学等之图案徽志)。 **'coat of** '~, such a design, eg on a shield. 盾形纹章; 盾徽。 ⇨ the illus at **armour.** 参看 armour 之插图。

army /'ɑːmɪ; 'ɑrmɪ/ *n* (*pl* -**mies**) **1** (**an/the**) ~, (with *sing* or *pl v*) the part of a country's military forces that is organized for fighting on land: (与单数或复数动词连用)(一国之)陆军: *an* ~ *of 100,000 soldiers;* 十万陆军; *be in the* ~, be a soldier; 服兵役; 当兵; *go into/join the* ~, become a soldier. 入伍。 **'~ corps** *n* main subdivision of an ~. 军。 **'~ list** *n* official list of commissioned officers. 陆军现役军官名册。 **2** organized body of persons: 协会; 社; 团体: *the Salvation A~;* 救世军; large number: 大队; 大群: *an* ~ *of workmen/ officials/ants.* 大群工人(官员, 蚂蚁)。

ar·nica /'ɑːnɪkə; 'ɑrnɪkə/ *n* [U] medical substance (made from a plant) used for healing bruises and sprains. 山金车酊剂(用一种菊科植物山金车调制成的药酒,用以疗治疗疮伤及扭伤)。

aroma /ə'rəʊmə; ə'romə/ *n* **1** sweet smell, fragrance: 香味;香气;芬芳: *the* ~ *of a cigar.* 雪茄之芳香。 **2** (fig) quality or surrounding atmosphere considered typical: (喻)韵味; 情趣; 气氛; 气派: *the* ~ *of wealth.* 财富的气派。 **aro·matic** /ˌærə'mætɪk; ˌærə'mætɪk/ *adj* fragrant; spicy: 芳香的; 有香味的: *the* ~*tic bark of the cinnamon tree.* 肉桂树之芳香树皮。

arose /ə'rəʊz; ə'roz/ *pt* of **arise.**

around[1] /ə'raʊnd; ə'raʊnd/ *adv* **1** (**all**) ~, on every side; in every direction; here and there: 在四周; 在周围; 到处; 四方: *From all* ~ *we heard the laughter of children.* 我们到处都听见儿童的笑声。 *Don't leave your clothes lying* ~. 不要把你的衣服到处放。 **2** (colloq) not far away (in place or time): (口)(空间或时间)不远; 在近处; 不久: *I'll be seeing you* ~, *I expect.* 希望不久再见到你。 *I'll be seeing you* ~, *I expect.* 希望不久再见到你。 **have been** ~, have travelled widely, have had experience of life and the world: 曾四处旅游; 有生活和处世经验: *She's obviously been* ~ *a lot.* 她显然见过不少世面。 ⇨ **about**[2](1, 2, 3), **round**[2], **shop** *v*(1), **sleep**[2](1).

around[2] /ə'raʊnd; ə'raʊnd/ *prep* **1** (**all**) ~, throughout: 遍及: *He's been all* ~ *India.* 他走遍了印度。 **2** encircling (wholly or partly): 围绕; 环绕: *Take your arm from* ~ *my waist.* 把你围着我腰的手臂拿开。 *Go for a run* ~ *the clock.* 绕着街区跑一圈。 ⇨ **about**[3](1, 2, 3), **round**[4].

arouse /ə'raʊz; ə'raʊz/ *vt* [VP6A, 14] **1** awaken: 唤醒; 唤起; 引起: *behaviour that might* ~ *suspicion;* 可能引起嫌疑的行为; *sufferings that* ~ *our sympathy;* 引起我们同情的痛苦; ~ *sb from his sleep.* 将某人自睡梦中唤醒。 **2** cause (sb) to become active; stir (sb) up

from inactivity; stimulate sexually: 鼓动; 鼓舞; 激起; 激励; (性方面)刺激: *fully* ~*d.* 十分奋发的; 极度兴奋的。

ar·peg·gio /ɑː'pedʒɪəʊ; ɑr'pedʒɪˌo/ *n* (*pl* ~**s**) (I; music) the playing of the notes of a chord (2) in (usu upwards) succession. (意; 音乐)和音之急速的连续演奏; 琶音。

ar·que·bus /'ɑːkwɪbəs; 'ɑrkwɪbəs/ *n* early kind of portable gun, supported on a tripod or a forked rest, used before muskets were invented. 火绳枪(明时支于三脚架或叉架上, 在滑膛枪未发明之前所用者)。

ar·rack /'ærək; 'ærək/ *n* [U] strong alcoholic drink made in Eastern countries. (东方各国所酿造之)烧酒。

ar·raign /ə'reɪn; ə'ren/ *vt* [VP6A,14] (legal) bring a criminal charge against (sb); bring (sb) before a court for trial: (法律)控告(某人)犯某罪; 提讯; 传讯: ~*ed on charge of theft.* 因窃盗嫌疑被传讯。 ~**·ment** *n* ~ing or being ~ed. 控告; 讯问; 责难。

ar·range /ə'reɪndʒ; ə'rendʒ/ *vt, vi* **1** [VP6A] put in order: 安排; 排列; 布置; 整理: *She's good at arranging flowers.* 她擅长插花。 *I* ~*d the books on the shelves.* 我整理书架上的书籍。 *Before going away, he* ~*d his business affairs.* 在离开之前, 他把业务都安排好了。 **2** [VP6A, 15A, 3A] make plans in advance, see to the details of sth: 预做计划; 对某事之细节妥加注意; 筹备; 办妥: *A marriage has been* ~*d between Mr Brown and Miss White.* 布朗先生与怀特小姐的婚已经筹备好了。 *The Tourist Bureau* ~*d everything for our journey to Rome.* 观光局为我们到罗马去的旅行筹备一切。 *I have* ~*d to meet her at ten o'clock.* 我已约好于十点钟见她。 *I have* ~*d for a car to meet you at the airport.* 我已备妥一部车子到飞机场来接你。 *The Meeting* ~*d for tomorrow has been postponed.* 原定明天开的会业已延期, 改天再开。 *I can't* ~ *for everything.* 不能一切都靠我来办。 **3** [VP3A] ~ (**with sb**) (**for/about sth**), come to an agreement. 约定; 商定。 **4** [VP6A, 3A] ~ (**for**), adapt (a piece of music): 改写(乐曲): ~ *a piece of music for the violin.* 改写一首乐曲以适于小提琴演奏。 **5** [VP6A] settle, adjust (now the more usu words): 解决; 使协调(今较常用 settle 或 adjust): *Mrs White often has to* ~ *disputes/differences between the two boys.* 怀特太太时常得调解这两个孩子间的争论。

ar·range·ment /ə'reɪndʒmənt; ə'rendʒmənt/ *n* **1** [U] putting in order; arranging or being arranged: 安排; 排列; 布置; 整理: *The* ~ *of the furniture in our new house took a long time.* 在我们新房子里布置家具花了很长的时间。 **2** (*pl*) plans; preparations: (复)计划; 筹备: *Have you made* ~*s for your journey to Scotland?* 你已准备好了到苏格兰去旅行吗? *I'll make* ~*s for somebody to meet you/for you to be met at the airport.* 我将设法派个人到飞机场去接你。 **3** [U] agreement; settlement: 同意; 约定; 解决: *The price of the house is a matter for* ~, is a matter to be settled by discussion. 此屋的价钱可以商谈决定。 *We can come to some sort of* ~ *over expenses.* 关于费用, 我们可以获致某种程度的协议。 **4** [C] result or manner of arranging: 安排、排列、布置、整理的结果或方式: *an* ~ (eg of orchestral music) *for the piano.* (如由管弦乐)改写的钢琴曲。 *I have an* ~ *by which I can cash my cheques at banks everywhere in Britain.* 我有一种安排使我的支票可在英国各地银行兑到现金。

ar·rant /'ærənt; 'ærənt/ *adj* (always of sth or sb bad) in the highest degree: (总是指坏的事或人)绝顶的; 极端的; 最大的: *an* ~ *liar/knave/dunce/ hypocrite/rogue;* 第一号说谎者(骗子, 愚人, 伪君子, 恶徒); ~ *nonsense.* 荒谬绝伦的胡说。

ar·ras /'ærəs; 'ærəs/ *n* tapestry, esp the kind formerly hung on the walls of rooms. 花毡(尤指昔时装饰墙壁之挂毡)。

ar·ray /ə'reɪ; ə'reɪ/ *vt* [VP6A, 15A] (liter) (文) **1** place (esp armed forces, troops) in order for battle: 布署(军队等)以备作战; 列阵: *The Duke and his men* ~*ed*

themselves against the King, took up arms against the King. 公爵及其部属以武力反抗国王。**2** dress: 穿着; 盛装: *~ed in ceremonial robes;* 穿着礼服; *~ed like a queen.* 盛装如皇后。□ *n* (liter) (文) **1** order: 阵式: *troops in battle ~.* 列成战阵的军队。**2** clothes: 服装: *in holiday ~;* 穿着假日服装; *in bridal ~.* 穿着新娘礼服。**3** *~ (of),* display: (陈列之)一大批; 一系列: *a fine ~ of tools;* 一大批上选的工具; *an imposing ~ of statistics.* 一系列堂皇的统计数字。

ar·rears /əˈrɪəz; əˈrɪrz/ *n pl* **1** money that is owing and that ought to have been paid: 欠债; 应付而未付之款: *~ of rent/wages.* 欠租(工资)。***be in/fall into ~ (with),*** be late in paying. 拖欠。Cf 参较 *be behindhand with.* **2** work still waiting to be done: 尚待完成之工作: *~ of correspondence,* letters waiting to be answered. 待复之信件。

ar·rest /əˈrest; əˈrɛst/ *vt* [VP6A] **1** put a stop to (a process or movement): 阻止; 妨碍(一种进展或运动): *Poor food ~s the natural growth of children.* 粗劣食物妨碍儿童的自然生长。**2** catch (sb's attention): 吸引(某人的注意): *The bright colours of the flowers ~ed the child's attention.* 花卉之鲜艳颜色引起了那个小孩的注意。**3** seize (sb) by the authority of the law: 依法逮捕; 拘捕: *The police ~ed the thief and put him in prison.* 警察将该贼逮捕收押。□ *n* act of ~ing (a wrongdoer, etc): 逮捕; 拘捕: *The police made several ~s.* 警方逮捕数人。***under ~,*** held as a prisoner. 被拘禁。***be/place/put/under ~,*** be/be made a prisoner: 被收押; 被拘禁; 成为囚犯: *The officer was put under ~.* 该军官被拘禁起来了。**~er** *n* **ˈ~er hook,** device for reducing the speed of aircraft as they land on the deck of an aircraft carrier. 拦截钩(飞机降落航空母舰之甲板上时用以减低其速度之装置)。**~·ing** *adj* striking; likely to hold the attention. 显著的; 有趣的; 引人注目的。

ar·rière pensée /ˌærɪeə ˈpɒnseɪ *US:* pɒnˈseɪ; ˌa,rjɛr,pɑ̃ˋse/ *n* (F) ulterior motive; mental reservation. (法)隐秘未表明的动机; 隐而未宣的思想; 心事。

ar·ri·val /əˈraɪvl; əˈraɪvl̩/ *n* **1** [U] act of arriving: 到达; 抵达: *on ~ home;* 在到家的时候; *on his ~;* 在他到达的时候; *waiting for the ~ of news;* 等待消息到达; *to await ~,* (on a letter, parcel, etc) to be kept until the addressee arrives. (书于信封, 包裹等上面) 等待收信(件)人前来领取。**2** [C] sb or sth that arrives: 到达之人或物: *There are several new ~s at the hotel.* 旅馆里到了几个新客人。*The new ~* (colloq = The newborn child) *is a boy.* (口)新生儿是个男孩。

ar·rive /əˈraɪv; əˈraɪv/ *vi* [VP2A, C, 3A] **1** reach a place, esp the end of a journey: 到达; 抵达某地(尤指旅程的终点): *~ home;* 到家; *~ at a port;* 到达港口; *~ in harbour.* 抵达港内。**2** come: 到; 来: *At last the day ~d.* 那一天终于到了。*Her baby ~d* (= was born) *yesterday.* 她的婴儿昨天出生了。**3** *~ **at,*** reach (a decision, a price, the age of 40, manhood, etc). 达成(决议); 谈妥(价钱); 活到(四十岁); 到达(成年)等。**4** establish one's position or reputation. 成功; 成名。

ar·ro·gant /ˈærəgənt; ˈærəgənt/ *adj* behaving in a proud, superior manner; (of behaviour, etc) showing too much pride in oneself and too little consideration for others: 傲慢的; 自大的; (指行为等)目中无人的; 妄自尊大的: *speaking in an ~ tone.* 用傲慢的口吻说话。**~·ly** *adv* **ar·ro·gance** /-əns; -əns/ *n* [U]。

ar·ro·gate /ˈærəgeɪt; ˋærə,get/ *vt* [VP14] (formal) (正式用语) **1** *~ **to oneself,*** claim or take without right: 冒称; 妄称; 擅取: *He ~d to himself the dignity of a chair,* claimed to be a university professor (although he was only a lecturer). 他冒称自己为大学教授(虽然他不过是个讲师)。**2** attribute unjustly; ascribe: 无理地认为…是属于; 归因于: *Don't ~ evil motives to me.* 不要向我栽诬。

ar·row /ˈærəʊ; ˋæro/ *n* **1** thin, pointed stick (to be) shot from a bow. 箭; 矢。⇨ the illus at **archery.** 参看 archery 之插图。**2** mark or sign (→) used to show direction or position, eg on a map or as a road sign. 箭头记号(→)(用以指示方向或位置, 如地图上或作路标用者)。**ˈ~·head** *n* pointed end of an ~. 箭头; 镞。

ar·row·root /ˈærəʊruːt; ˋæro,rut/ *n* [U] starchy food made from the powdered root of a plant. 葛根粉所制之糊状食品。

arse /ɑːs; ɑrs/ (US = **ass** /æs; æs/) *n* (⚠, not in polite use) buttocks; anus. (讳, 不礼貌用语)臀部; 屁股; 肛门。***silly ~,*** fool. 傻瓜; 笨蛋。**ˈ~·hole** (US = **ˈass·hole**) *n* anus. 肛门。

ar·senal /ˈɑːsənl; ˋɑrsn̩əl/ *n* building(s) where weapons and ammunition are made or stored; (fig) reserve of strength. 兵工厂; 军火库; (喻)力量的贮存。

ar·senic /ˈɑːsnɪk; ˋɑrsn̩ɪk/ *n* [U] (chem) brittle, steel-grey crystalline chemical element (symbol **As**), used in glass-making, dyes, etc; white mineral compound of ~, a violent poison. (化)砷; 砒素(性脆, 钢灰色之结晶形化学元素, 化学符号 As, 用于制造玻璃, 染料等); 砒霜(砷之白色无机化合物, 有剧烈毒性)。

ar·son /ˈɑːsn; ˋɑrsn̩/ *n* [U] act of setting sth on fire intentionally and unlawfully, eg another person's property or one's own with the purpose of claiming under an insurance policy. 纵火; 放火(指非法有意之放火, 如对他人财物之放火, 或对自己财物之放火以领取保险金者)。

art¹ /ɑːt; ɑrt/ *n* **1** [U] the creation or expression of what is beautiful, esp in visual form; fine skill or aptitude in such expression: 美的事物(尤指肉眼可见者)的创造或表现; 艺术: *the art of the Renaissance;* 文艺复兴时期的艺术: *children's art;* 儿童艺术; *the art of landscape painting.* 风景画的艺术。*The story is developed with great art.* 那故事非常技巧地展开。**the ˌfine ˈarts,** drawing, painting, sculpture, architecture, music, ballet. 美术(包括绘画, 雕刻, 建筑, 音乐, 芭蕾舞)。**a ˌwork of ˈart,** a fine painting, piece of sculpture, etc. 美术品; 艺术品。**an ˈart gallery,** one for the display of works of art. 美术陈列馆; 艺术馆。**an ˈart school,** one at which the arts of painting, etc are taught. 艺术专科学校。**2** [C] sth in which imagination and personal taste are more important than exact measurement and calculation: 想象力及个人鉴赏力比精确计算更为重要的事情; 人文学科: *History and literature are among the arts/the arts subjects* (contrasted with science/science subjects). 历史及文学均属于人文科学(人文学科)(别于科学或科学学科)。*Teaching/Public speaking is an art.* 教学(演说)是人文学科。**ˌBachelor/ˌMaster of ˈArts,** (abbr 略作 **BA/MA**) person who has passed the examination and fulfilled other conditions for the award of a university degree in this branch of learning. 文科学士(硕士)。**3** [U] cunning; trickery; [C] trick: 诡计; 诈术; 手段; 巧计; 策术: *In spite of all her arts, the young man was not attracted to her.* 虽然她用尽了手段, 那青年仍不为她所动。**the black art,** magic (used for evil purposes). 魔术; 妖术(作邪恶之用途者)。**4** (attrib) relating to art(1); of artistic design: (用作定语)艺术的; 艺术设计的: *an ˈart historian/critic;* 艺术史家(批评家); *art needlework/pottery.* 艺术刺绣(陶器)。

art² /ɑːt; ɑrt/ *v* (*pres t* form of *be*) (archaic) used with *thou:* (古) be 的现在式, 与 thou 连用: *thou art,* you are. 你是。

ar·te·fact ⇨ **artifact.**

ar·ter·ial /ɑːˈtɪərɪəl; ɑrˈtɪrɪəl/ *adj* of or like an artery: 动脉的; 似动脉的: *~ blood;* 动脉血; *~ roads,* important main roads; 干道; 干线; *~ railways/traffic.* 铁路干线(交通干道)。

ar·terio·scler·osis /ɑːˌtɪərɪəʊskləˈrəʊsɪs; ɑrˈtɪrɪ-ˌosklɪˈrosɪs/ *n* [U] chronic disease with the hardening of the arteries, hindering blood circulation. 动脉硬化。

ar·tery /ˈɑːtərɪ; ˋɑrtərɪ/ *n* (*pl* **-ries**) **1** one of the tubes carrying blood from the heart to all parts of

59   **artesian/as**

the body. 动脉。 ⇨ the illus at **respiratory.** 参看 respiratory 之插图。 **2** main road or river; chief channel in a system of communications, etc: 主要道路或河流;干道;干线;主流: *arteries of traffic.* 交通干道。

ar·tesian /ɑːˈtiːzɪən *US:* -ɪʒn; ɑrˈtiʒən/ *adj* ~ **well,** perpendicular well producing a constant supply of water rising to the surface without pumping. 喷水井;自流井;钻井。

art·ful /ˈɑːtfl; ˈɑrtfəl/ *adj* cunning, deceitful; clever in getting what one wants. 狡猾的;诈骗的;诡计多端的。 ~**ly** /-fəlɪ; -fəlɪ/ *adv* ~**ness** *n*

ar·thri·tis /ɑːˈθraɪtɪs; ɑrˈθraɪtɪs/ *n* [U] inflammation of a joint or joints; gout. 关节炎。 **ar·thri·tic** /ɑːˈθrɪtɪk; ɑrˈθrɪtɪk/ *adj*

ar·ti·choke /ˈɑːtɪtʃəʊk; ˈɑrtɪˌtʃok/ *n* **1 globe** ~, plant like a large thistle, with a flowering head of thick, leaf-like scales used as a vegetable. 朝鲜蓟(花头可作蔬菜)。 ⇨ the illus at **vegetable.** 参看 vegetable 之插图。 **2 Jerusalem** ~, plant like a sunflower, with tuberous roots used as a vegetable. 菊芋(似向日葵,其块根可作蔬菜)。

ar·ticle /ˈɑːtɪkl; ˈɑrtɪkl/ *n* [C] **1** particular or separate thing: 物件;物品: ~*s of clothing,* eg shirts, coats; 衣物(如衬衫、外衣); *toilet* ~*s,* eg soap, toothpaste. 盥洗用的物品(如肥皂,牙膏)。 **2** piece of writing, complete in itself, in a newspaper or other periodical. (报纸或杂志上所刊载的)文章;论文;专论。 **,leading ˈ~,** (in a newspaper) ~ expressing the views of the editor(s). 报纸的社论。 **3** (legal) separate clause or item in an agreement: (法律)(契约的)条款;条目: ~*s of apprenticeship/employment.* 学徒(雇用)契约的条款。 **4** (gram) (语法) **definite** ~, 'the'. 定冠词(即 the)。 **indefinite** ~, 'a', 'an'. 不定冠词(即 a, an)。 □ *vt* bind, eg an apprentice by ~s(3): 使(学徒等)受协议条款约束: *an* ~*d clerk.* 受协议条款约束的职员。

ar·ticu·late¹ /ɑːˈtɪkjʊlət; ɑrˈtɪkjəlɪt/ *adj* **1** (of speech) in which the separate sounds and words are clear. (指言语)发音清晰的。 **2** (of a person) able to put thoughts and feelings into clear speech: (指人)能用清晰之言语表达思想感情的: *That man is not very* ~. 那人口齿不太伶俐。 **3** jointed. 有关节相连的; 连节的。 ~**ly** *adv*

ar·ticu·late² /ɑːˈtɪkjʊleɪt; ɑrˈtɪkjəˌlet/ *vt, vi* **1** [VP 6A, 2C] say (words) distinctly; speak (distinctly). 清楚地说(话); 说话清晰。 **2** [VP15A, 2C] connect by joints: 以关节连接: *bones that* ~ */are* ~*d with others.* 以关节与其他骨骼相连的骨骼。 **an** ~**d vehicle,** having parts joined in a flexible manner, eg a tractor flexibly joined to the part that carries the load. 曳引车; 挂接车(如一牵引机挂接一载货之车架所成者)。

ar·ticu·la·tion /ɑːˌtɪkjʊˈleɪʃn; ɑrˌtɪkjəˈleʃən/ *n* [U] **1** production of speech sounds: 发音;读音: *The speaker's ideas were good but his* ~ *was poor.* 这位演说者的思想很好, 但是发音很差。 **2** (connection by a) joint. 关节;由关节结合。

ar·ti·fact, ar·te·fact /ˈɑːtɪfækt; ˈɑrtɪˌfækt/ *n* [C] artificial product; something made by human being(s), esp a simple tool or weapon of archaeological interest. 人工制品(尤指由于考古兴趣的简单工具或武器)。

ar·ti·fice /ˈɑːtɪfɪs; ˈɑrtɪfɪs/ *n* **1** [C] skilful way of doing sth. 技术; 技巧。 **2** [U] cunning; ingenuity; trickery; [C] trick. 诡计; 巧计; 诈术; 手段; 策略。

ar·ti·fi·cer /ɑːˈtɪfɪsə(r); ɑrˈtɪfəsɚ/ *n* skilled workman. 技术工人;技工。 **engine-room** ~, (rank in the Navy of a) skilled machanic. (海军之)轮机室技工。

ar·ti·fi·cial /ˌɑːtɪˈfɪʃl; ˌɑrtəˈfɪʃəl/ *adj* not natural or real; made by the art of man: 非天然的;非真实的;人造的: ~ *flowers/teeth/light;* 人造花(假牙;人造光); ~ *silk,* (old name for) rayon; 人造丝(现称 rayon); ~ *manures,* chemical manures (not dung); 人造肥料;化

学肥料;人工堆肥(非粪尿); ~ *tears,* not caused by genuine sorrow; 假眼泪; ~ *manners,* affected, not natural manners. 做作的态度。 ~ *respiration,* method of forcing air into the lungs, eg to a man nearly drowned. 人工呼吸。 ⇨ also **insemination. ar·ti·fi·ci·ally** /-fəlɪ; -fəlɪ/ *adv*

ar·til·lery /ɑːˈtɪlərɪ; ɑrˈtɪlərɪ/ *n* [U] big guns (mounted on wheels, etc); branch of an army that uses these. 大炮;炮兵。

ar·ti·san /ˌɑːtɪˈzæn *US:* ˈɑːtɪzn; ˈɑrtəzn/ *n* skilled workman in industry or trade; mechanic. 工匠;技工。

art·ist /ˈɑːtɪst; ˈɑrtɪst/ *n* **1** person who practises one of the fine arts, esp painting. 艺术家; (尤指)画家。 **2** person who does sth with skill and good taste: 擅长做某事之人: *an* ~ *in words.* 擅长写作者。

art·iste /ɑːˈtiːst; ɑrˈtist/ *n* professional singer, actor, dancer, etc. 艺人(职业性的歌唱家,演员,舞蹈家等)。

ar·tis·tic /ɑːˈtɪstɪk; ɑrˈtɪstɪk/ *adj* **1** done with skill and good taste, esp in the arts; able to appreciate what is beautiful. 以在艺术方面的技巧与鉴赏力做成的; 有审美能力的。 **2** having or showing good taste. 高尚的, 具有美感的。 **3** of art or artists. 艺术的; 艺术家的。 **ar·tis·ti·cally** /-klɪ; -klɪ/ *adv*

art·istry /ˈɑːtɪstrɪ; ˈɑrtɪstrɪ/ *n* [U] artistic skill or work; qualities of taste and skill possessed by an artist. 艺术技巧;艺术工作;艺术家的修养与技巧。

art·less /ˈɑːtlɪs; ˈɑrtlɪs/ *adj* (contrasted with *artful*) natural; simple; innocent: (与 artful 相对)自然的; 单纯的; 天真烂漫的: *as* ~ *as a child of 5.* 天真似五岁的孩童。 ~**ly** *adv* ~**ness** *n*

arty /ˈɑːtɪ; ˈɑrtɪ/ *adj* (colloq) pretending or falsely claiming to be artistic. (口)假装具有艺术修养的;附庸风雅的。 ~**-crafty,** (colloq) of, using, making, handmade articles, esp in a way that is considered affected. (口)手工品(尤指冒牌货)的; 使用手工品的; 制造手工品的。

arum /ˈeərəm; ˈɛrəm/ *n* ~ **lily,** tall white lily. 白星海芋。

Aryan /ˈeərɪən; ˈɛrɪən/ *adj* of the family of languages called Indo-European, ie related to Sanskrit, Persian, Greek, Latin and the Germanic and Slavonic languages; of a race using an ~ language. 雅利安语系(即印欧语系, 包括梵文、波斯文、希腊文、拉丁文、日耳曼语系及斯拉夫语系)的; 雅利安人的。 □ *n* person whose mother tongue is one of the ~ languages; (popular sense, now discredited) person of Germanic or Scandinavian ancestry. 说雅利安语之一的人;雅利安人。

as¹ /əz; əz; *strong form:* æz; æz/ *adv* (followed by *as, conj*) in the same degree: (后接连接词 as) 一样;一般: *I'm as tall as you.* 我和你一般高。 *Is it as difficult as they say it is?* 那是不是象他们所说的一样困难? (In a neg sentence as is often replaced by *so*): (在否定句里, 常以 so 代替 as): *It's not so difficult as I expected.* 它并不如我所预料的那样难。

as² /əz; əz; *strong form:* æz; æz/ *conj* **1** when; while: 当...之时: *I saw him as he was getting off the bus.* 当他下公共汽车时,我看见了他。 *As he grew older he became less active.* 当他年老的时候,他变得不活泼了。 **2** (expressing reason) since; seeing that: (表示原因)由于;既然: *As he wasn't ready in time, we went without him.* 因他未及时准备好, 我们没有等他就先走了。 **3** (in comparisons of equality, in the patterns: 以下列型式用于平等的比较: *as+adj/adv+as; not as/so+adj/adv as*): *I want a box twice as large as this.* 我要一个有这个两倍大的箱子。 *It's not as/so big as you think it is.* 它并没有你所想象的那么大。 (Used in numerous proverbial phrases): (用于很多的谚语中): *as easy as ABC;* 极为容易; *as heavy as lead.* 象铅一样的重。 (Note the *pronouns* in these examples): (注意这些例句中的代词): *You hate him as much as I,* ie as much as I hate him; 你恨他象我恨他一样的深; *You hate him as much as me,* ie as much

as you hate me. 你恨他象恨我一样的深。(When there is no ambiguity, the object form of the *pronoun* is used in speech): (如果意义不会含混不明的话，在说话中用代词的宾语形式): *At your age, you can't expect to play football as/so well as me* (= as I do). 在你这样的年龄，不能期望足球踢得跟我一样好。**4** (introducing a concessive clause, usu replaceable by a construction with *although*): (引导让步从句，通常与 although 起首的从句通用): **(a)** (with an *adj* or *adv*): (与形容词或副词连用): *I know some of the family secrets, young as I am,* although I am young. 我虽然很小，可是我知道我家中的一些秘密。*Much as I like you* (= Although I like you much), *I will not marry you.* 我虽然很喜欢你，可是不愿与你结婚。**(b)** (with *vv*, esp *may, might, will, would*): (与动词连用，尤与 may, might, will, would 连用): *Try as he would* (= Although he tried, However hard he tried), *he could not lift the rock.* 他虽然尽了最大努力，仍旧搬不动那块石头。**5** (introducing adverbial clauses of manner) in the way in which; (引导表示状态的状语从句)如；象: *Do as I do.* 照我的样子做。*Do it as I do it.* 照我的样子做这件事。*Leave it as it is.* 保持原状，不要动它。**6** (introducing a complement of manner) like: (引导表示状态的补语)如；象；似: *Why is he dressed as a woman?* 他为什么打扮得象个女人？**7** (used to avoid repetition in the predicate): (用以避免谓语部分的重复): *Harry is unusually tall, as are his brothers, and his brothers are also unusually tall.* 哈里也象他的兄弟们一样，身材奇高。**8** in the capacity or character of: 作为…（某种身分）；当做；视为: *He was respected both as a judge and as a man.* 大家尊崇他是位好法官，同时也尊崇他是个好人。*Looking at Napoleon as a statesman, not as a soldier* .... 把拿破仑当做政治家，而不当做军人来看…。**9** (used in [VP16B] after *regard, view, represent, treat, acknowledge,* and *vv* similar in meaning but not after *consider,* to introduce a predicative): (用于 regard, view, represent, treat, acknowledge 及类似意义的动词之后，但不用于 consider 之后，引导一个用于表语中的名词或形容词): *Most people regarded him* (= looked upon him) *as a fool.* 大多数人认为他是个愚人。Cf 参较 Most people *considered him (to be) a fool.* 大多数人认为他是个愚人。*Do you treat all men as your equals?* 你是否把所有的人都当做与你平等的人看待？**10** (used to introduce illustrations or examples; usu preceded by *such;* replaceable by *for instance, for example* or *like*): (用以引述例证;通常跟在 such 后面;与 for instance, for example 或 like 通用): *Countries in the north of Europe, such as Finland, Norway, Sweden, ...* 北欧各国，如芬兰、挪威、瑞典…。**11** *as if; as though,* (introducing a clause of manner, with a *pt* in the clause): (引导表示状态的从句,从句内用过去式): *He talks as if he knew all about it.* 他说话的口气好象他全部都已经知道了。*He looks as if he had seen a ghost.* 他看起来好象看见了鬼似的。*It isn't as though he were poor.* 看起来他不象贫穷的样子。(followed by a *to*-infinitive): (后接带句的不定式): *He opened his lips as if to say something.* 他张开嘴好象要说什么。**12** *'as for,* with reference to (sometimes suggesting indifference or contempt): 至于（有时暗示不关心或轻视）: *As for you, I never want to see you here again.* 至于你，我再也不想在这里见到你。*'as to,* about; concerning (better avoided except when the words following *as to* are shifted to the beginning of a sentence for prominence): 关于;至于（最好避免用此语，除非将整个短语移至句首,以加强其语气）: *As to your brother, I will deal with him later;* 至于你哥哥(弟弟)，我以后再对付他; (with a *gerund*) *As to accepting their demand, ...* (与动名词连用)至于接受他们的要求，…。**13** (used as a *conj* to introduce relative clauses, chiefly after *same* and *such*): (用作连接词，引导关系从句，主要用于 same 及 such 之后): *Such women as knew Tom* (= Those women who knew him) *thought he was charming.* 认识汤姆的女人都认为他很有魅力。*Such women as Tom knew* (= Those women whom Tom knew)

thought he was charming. 汤姆所认识的女人都认为他很有魅力。*You must show my wife the same respect as you show me,* the respect that you show me. 你必须尊敬我的妻子，象你尊敬我一样。*We drove out of the town by the same road as we had entered by.* 我们沿着我们进城的同一道路开车出城。**14** (introducing a non-defining relative clause, the antecedent being inferred): (引导一个非限制性的关系从句，无显able先行词): *Cyprus, as* (= which fact) *you all know, is in the Mediterranean.* 塞浦路斯岛，你们大家都知道，是在地中海。*To shut your eyes to facts, as many of you do, is foolish.* 故意不去正视事实，如你们很多人所做的，乃是愚蠢的行为。**15** *'so as to,* **(a)** (introducing an infinitive of purpose): (引导表示目的的不定式)以便: *He stood up so as to* (= in order to) *see better.* 他站起来，以便看清楚些。**b** (introducing an infinitive of manner): (引导表示状态的不定式): *It is foolish to behave so as to annoy* (= in ways that annoy) *your neighbours.* 做出那种足以打扰你的邻居的行为乃是愚蠢的。**16** *as good as,* the same thing as: 象……一样; 几乎等于: *Will he be as good as his word? Will he do what he promised?* 他是否会言行一致（言而有信）？*He's as good as dead,* almost dead, sure to die soon. 他跟死了一样（很快就会死了）。**17** *as/so long as,* **(a)** on condition that: 只要: *You can go where you like so long as you get back before dark.* 你可以随意到那里去，只要你在天黑以前返回。**(b)** while: 在…的时候: *You shall never enter this house as long as I live in it.* 在我住在这里的时候，你永远不许进入这屋子。**18** *as much, so;* (what really amounts to) that: 如此; 实际和那个一样: *I thought as much.* 我本来就如此想。**19** *as far as,* ⇨ far²(2). *as such; such as,* ⇨ such pron. **20** (just) as soon; as soon as (not), ⇨ soon(3, 5). *as well (as),* ⇨ well²(8).

as·bes·tos /æz'bestɒs; æs'bɛstəs/ n [U] soft, fibrous, mineral substance that can be made into fire-proof fabrics or solid sheeting and used as a heat-insulating material. 石棉（可制成耐火织物及用作隔热材料）。

as·cend /ə'send; ə'sɛnd/ vt, vi 1 [VP6A, 2A, C] go or come up (a mountain, river, etc): 攀登(山); 往(河的)上(游)走; 登上; 上升: *We watched the mists ~ing from the valley.* 我们看着雾由山谷升起。*The path ~s here.* 路由此处转向上坡。**2** ~ *the throne,* become king or queen. 登王座; 即王位。

as·cend·ancy, -ency /ə'sendənsɪ; ə'sɛndənsɪ/ n [U] (position of) having power. 有权; 权势; 优势; 权势或优势之地位。*gain/have the ~ (over sb):* 获得(具有)超越某人的权势或优势: *He has the ~ over his rivals/his party.* 他获得压倒其敌手(其同伙)的优势。

as·cend·ant, -ent /ə'sendənt; ə'sɛndənt/ n *in the ~,* rising in power and influence. 权势的增长。

as·cen·sion /ə'senʃn; ə'sɛnʃən/ n act of ascending. 升高; 上升; 往上。*the A~,* the departure of Jesus from the earth, on the fortieth day after the Resurrection. 耶稣（复活后第四十日之）升天。

as·cent /ə'sent; ə'sɛnt/ n [U] act of ascending; way up; upward movement: 上升; 上行; 上坡路; 向上之运动: *The ~ of the mountain was not difficult.* 上这座山不难。*I have never made an ~* (= have never been up) *in a balloon.* 我从来没有乘过气球升空。*The last part of the ~ is steep.* 最后一段上坡路甚陡。

as·cer·tain /ˌæsə'teɪn; ˌæsɚ'ten/ vt [VP6A, 9, 8, 10, 17] find out (in order to be certain about); get to know: 探出真相; 确实知道; 探知: ~ *the facts;* 探知事实真相; ~ *that the news is true;* 确知消息属实; ~ *whether the train stops at X;* 探询清楚火车是否在某地停; ~ *what really happened.* 探查事情发生的真相。~**able** /-əbl; -əbl/ adj that can be ~ed. 可探知的; 可弄清楚的。

as·cetic /ə'setɪk; ə'sɛtɪk/ adj self-denying; austere; leading a life of severe self-discipline. 克己的; 苦行的; 过严格自律之生活的; 修道的。□ n person who (often

for religious reasons) leads a severely simple life without ordinary pleasures. 修道者; 苦行者. **as·ceti·cally** /-klɪ; -klɪ/ *adv* **as·ceti·cism** /ə'setɪsɪzəm; ə'sɛtə,sɪzəm/ *n*

as·cor·bic /ə'skɔːbɪk; ə'skɔrbɪk/ *adj* ~ **acid,** (also known as *vitamin C*) vitamin found in citrus fruits and vegetable products, used against scurvy. 抗坏血酸(即维他命 C).

as·cribe /ə'skraɪb; ə'skraɪb/ *vt* [VP14] ~ **to,** 1 consider to be the cause, origin, reason or author, of: 认为是…的原因, 根源, 理由或著作者; 归功于; 归咎于; 归因于: *He ~d his failure to bad luck.* 他把他的失败归咎于运气不好. *This play has been ~d to Shakespeare,* it has been said that Shakespeare was the author. 这个剧被认为是莎士比亚所作. 2 consider as belonging to: 认为…属于: ~ *a wrong meaning to a word.* 将一词诠释错误. **as·crib·able** /-bl; -əbl/ *adj* that can be ~d: 可归因于…的: *His quick recovery is ascribable to his sound constitution.* 他的迅速康复归功于他的健全体质. **as·crip·tion** /ə'skrɪpʃn; əs'krɪpʃən/ *n* ascribing: 归功; 归咎; 归因; 归与; 归属: *The ascription of this work to Schubert may be false.* 认为这乐曲是舒伯特的作品可能是错的.

as·dic /'æzdɪk; 'æzdɪk/ *n* device using reflected sound-waves, for detecting submarines, etc. 潜艇(等)探索器(利用声波反射的一种);反潜仪.

asep·tic /ˌeɪ'septɪk; ə'sɛptɪk/ *adj* (of wounds, dressings, etc) free from bacteria; surgically clean. (指伤口, 绷带等)无菌的; 外科手术上干净的. **asep·sis** /ˌeɪ'sepsɪs; ə'sɛpsɪs/ *n* [U] ~ condition. 无菌;无毒.

asex·ual /ˌeɪ'seksjʊəl; eɪ'sɛkʃʊəl/ *adj* 1 without sex or sex organs: 无性的; 非性的; 无性器官的: ~ *reproduction.* 无性生殖. 2 (of a person) showing no interest in sexual relations. (指人)缺乏性欲的. ~·ity /ˌeɪsekʃʊ'ælɪtɪ; e,sɛkʃʊ'ælətɪ/ *n*

ash[1] /æʃ; æʃ/ *n* forest-tree with silver-grey bark and hard, tough wood; [U] wood of this tree. 梣树; 梣木. **'ash-key** *n* winged seed of the ash. 梣皮树之翅果. ⇨ the illus as **tree.** 参看 tree 之插图.

ash[2] /æʃ; æʃ/ *n* [U or *pl,* but not with numerals] 1 powder that remains after sth has burnt: 灰烬;灰: *Don't drop cigarette ash on the carpet.* 不要让香烟灰落在地毯上. *Remove the ashes from the stove once a day.* 火炉里面的灰每天清除一次. *The house was burnt to ashes.* 房子烧成灰烬了. 2 (pl) the burnt (= cremated) remains of a human body. (复)骨灰. **Ash Wednesday,** first day of Lent. 灰星期三(四旬斋的第一日). **'ash-bin, 'ash-can** *nn* (esp US 尤美; = **dustbin**) large rigid receptacle for ashes, cinders, kitchen waste, etc. 垃圾箱. **'ash-pan** *n* tray (in a fireplace, stove, etc) into which ashes drop from a fire. (壁炉、火炉等下面之)盛灰盘. **'ash-tray** *n* small (metal, glass, etc) receptacle for tobacco ash. (金属, 玻璃等制之)烟灰盘; 烟灰碟; 烟灰缸.

ashamed /ə'ʃeɪmd; ə'ʃemd/ *pred adj* ~ (*of/that/ to do sth*), feeling shame: 感到羞耻的; 惭愧的: *You should be* ~ *of yourself/of what you have done.* 你应(对自己所做之事)感到惭愧. *He was/felt* ~ *to ask for help.* 他耻于向人求助. *He felt* ~ *that he had done/of having done so little.* 他因为做的事情太少而感到惭愧. *I feel* ~ *for you,* on your account, as if I were you. 我替你觉得可羞. **asham·ed·ly** /ə'ʃeɪmɪdlɪ; ə'ʃemɪdlɪ/ *adv*

ashen /'æʃn; 'æʃən/ *adj* of ashes; pale; ash-coloured: 灰烬的; 灰白的; 灰色的: *His face turned* ~ *at the news.* 他听到这消息脸就变成灰白.

ashore /ə'ʃɔː(r); ə'ʃor/ *adv* on, on to, the shore. 在岸上; 向岸上; 到岸上. **go** ~, (of a sailor, etc) leave a ship to go on land. (指水手等)登陆上岸; 登岸. **run/be driven** ~, (of a ship) be forced to the shore, eg by bad weather. (指船)如被恶劣天气迫向岸上; 被吹到岸

上; 搁浅.

ashy /'æʃɪ; 'æʃɪ/ *adj* of or like ashes; covered with ashes; ash-coloured; pale. 灰烬的;似灰的;覆盖着灰的; 灰色的;灰白的.

Asian /'eɪʃn US: 'eɪʒn; 'eʒən/ *n, adj* (native) of Asia. 亚洲的; 亚洲人.

Asi·atic /ˌeɪʃɪ'ætɪk US: -ʒɪ-; ,eʒɪ'ætɪk/ *n, adj* (native) of Asia (*Asian* is the preferred word). 亚洲的; 亚洲人 (Asian 为较常用词).

aside /ə'saɪd; ə'saɪd/ *adv* on or to one side: 在一边; 向一边: *He laid the book* ~, put it down and stopped reading it. 他丢开书(不读了). *We turned* ~ (= away) *from the main road.* 我们离开大路向旁边转弯. *The decision/verdict was set* ~, made of no effect. 决议(判决)被搁置(不生效). *Please put this* ~ *for me,* reserve it. 请把这个替我保留起来. *Joking* ~, ie speaking seriously, ... 并非开玩笑(说正经话)…. □ *n* [C] words spoken ~, esp (on the stage) words that other persons (on the stage) are supposed not to hear. 旁白 (只说给观众听, 而认为台上其他的人全不听见的台词).

as·in·ine /'æsɪnaɪn; 'æsn,aɪn/ *adj* 1 of asses. 驴的. 2 (colloq) stupid. (口)愚蠢的.

ask /ɑːsk US: æsk; æsk/ *vt, vi* (*pt, pp* **asked**) 1 [VP6A, 12C, 14 often with the indirect object omitted in 12C] call for an answer to; request information or service: (动词第十二型 C 中的间接宾语常被省略)问; 询问; 要求; 请求: *Did you ask the price?* 你问了价钱吗? *Ask (him) his name.* 问(他)他的名字. *May I ask (you) a question?* 我可以问(你)一个问题吗? *Have I asked too much of you/asked you for too much?* 我向你要求的太多吗? *You asked of me more than you asked of the others.* 你向我要求的比你向别人要求的为多. *He asked a favour of me.* 他请我帮个忙. *We must ask him about it.* 我们得问问他这件事. *He asked me for help.* 他请求我帮忙. [VP8, 20] *I will ask (him) how to get there.* 我将问问(他)怎样到达那里. *Did you ask (her) which to buy?* 你是否问过她买哪一个? [VP10, 21] *They asked (me) what my name was, where I came from, and why I had come.* 他们问(我)我的名字叫什么, 我从哪里来及我为何事而来. *Please ask (her) when she will be back.* 请去问问她将于何时回来. [VP3A] *ask after,* ask for information about: 问询; 问候: *He asked after you/your health.* 他问候你(身体好). 2 [VP6A,17,15B, 3A] invite: 邀请; 邀约: *We asked him to come again.* 我们邀请他再来. *I've been asked (out) to dinner.* 我已被请(外出)吃饭. *Mr Brown is at the door; shall I ask him in?* 布朗先生在门口; 我可以请他进来吗? *ask for trouble,* (colloq) (口) *ask for it,* behave in such a way that trouble is likely; invite trouble. 自找麻烦; 惹麻烦. 3 [VP7A, 9, 17, 10] request to be excused: 请求准许: *I must ask you to excuse me/ask to be excused.* 我必须请求你原谅我(请求原谅). *He asked permission to get up.* 他请求准许起床. *He asked to get up/that/if he might get up.* 他请求起床(他请求是否可以起床). 4 [VP6A, 12C, 14] demand as a price: 要价; 讨价: *He asked (me) £25 a month as rent for that house.* 那栋房子, 他(向我) 要二十五英镑一月的租金. *You're asking too much.* 你要价太高. *What are they asking for the house?* 那栋房子他们要价多少? 5 *ask the banns,* (old use; now use) *put up or publish*) publish them. (旧用法; 今通常用 put up 或 publish) 公布结婚预告.

askance /ə'skæns; ə'skæns/ *adv* (only in 只用于) *look* ~ *at sb/sth,* look with suspicion. 以猜疑的心情看(某人或某事物); 侧目而视.

askew /ə'skjuː; ə'skju/ *adv, pred adj* out of the straight or usual (level) position: 歪斜地; 歪斜的: *hang a picture* ~; 斜挂一幅画; 歪斜地挂画: *have one's hat on* ~; 歪戴帽; *cut a plank* ~, aslant. 斜劈一块木板.

ask·ing /'ɑːskɪŋ; 'æskɪŋ/ *n for the* ~, by requesting: 经索取; 经要求: *You may have it/It's yours for the* ~, You have only to ask for it and it will be given to you. 如经索取就会给你.

aslant /ə'slɑ:nt US: ə'slænt; ə'slænt/ adv, prep in a slanting direction (to): 斜地; 成斜角地(与 to 连用); 斜过: The wrecked coach lay ~ the railway track. 失事破毁的客车厢斜躺在铁轨上。

asleep /ə'sli:p; ə'slip/ adv, pred adj 1 sleeping: 睡; 睡着(的): He was fast ~. 他睡得很熟。He fell/dropped ~ during the sermon. 他在听讲道时睡着了。2 (of the arms or legs) without feeling (as when under pressure). (指四肢)麻木(的); 麻痹(的)(如受压迫时)。

asp[1] /æsp; æsp/ n = aspen.

asp[2] /æsp; æsp/ n (zool) small poisonous snake of Egypt and Libya. (动物)(产于埃及和利比亚之)小毒蛇。

as·par·a·gus /ə'spærəgəs; ə'spærəgəs/ n [U] plant whose young shoots are cooked and eaten as a vegetable; the shoots. 石刁柏; 芦笋。

as·pect /'æspekt; 'æspekt/ n 1 look or appearance (of a person or thing): 外貌; 外观; 容貌: a man of fierce ~; 面目狰狞之人; a man with a serious ~. 外貌严肃之人。2 front that faces a particular direction: (面对某一方向之)正面: a house with a southern ~. 面朝南的房子。3 (fig) particular part: (喻)特殊部分: study every ~ of a subject, study it thoroughly. 研究一个题目的每一方面; 彻底研究它。4 (gram) verb form which relates activity to passage of time. (语法)体; 态 (叙述活动与时间经过之关系的动词形式)。**as·pec·tual** /ə'spektʃuəl; æ'spektʃuəl/ adj: There is an ~ual difference between 'I saw him cross the road' and 'I saw him crossing the road'. 在 'I saw him cross the road' 与 'I saw him crossing the road' 两句中 cross 和 crossing 间有体的不同。

as·pen /'æspən; 'æspɪn/ n kind of poplar tree with leaves that move in the slightest wind. 白杨(其树叶在最轻微之风中即行飘舞)。

as·per·ity /æ'sperəti; æs'pɛrəti/ n (pl -ties) (formal) (正式用语) 1 [U] roughness, harshness (of manner); severity (of weather): 粗糙; (态度)粗暴; (气候)酷烈: speak with ~. 粗暴地说。2 (with pl) instance of one of these qualities: (用复数)此种性质之实例: the asperities of winter in Labrador; 拉布拉多冬天之严寒; an exchange of asperities, eg of hard or bitter words. 互以粗暴刻薄的言语相对。

as·perse /ə'spɜ:s; ə'spɜs/ vt [VP6A] (formal) slander; say false or unkind things about: (正式用语) 诽谤; 中伤; 破坏(名誉): ~ sb's good name/honour/reputation. 诽谤某人的好声誉(荣誉, 名誉)。**as·per·sion** /ə'spɜ:ʃn US: -ʒn; ə'spɜʒən/n (only in 只用于) cast aspersions (up)on sb/sb's honour, etc, slander him; say false things about him. 对某人(某人之名誉等)加以诽谤。

as·phalt /'æsfælt US: -fɔ:lt; 'æsfɔlt/ n [U] black, sticky substance like coal-tar used for making roofs, etc waterproof, and mixed with gravel or crushed rock, for making road surfaces. (地)沥青; 柏油(用以涂屋顶等以防漏, 并与碎石混合铺路)。□ vt [VP6A] surface (a road) with ~. 以沥青铺(路)。

as·pho·del /'æsfədel; 'æsfə,del/ n 1 sort of lily. 日光兰; 水仙花。2 (poet) immortal flower of the Gk Elysium (home of the dead) (诗)(希腊神话中极乐世界之)常春花。

as·phyxia /æs'fɪksɪə; æs'fɪksɪə/ n [U] condition caused by lack of enough air in the lungs; suffocation. 窒息状态; 窒息。**as·phyxi·ate** /æs'fɪksɪeɪt; æs'fɪksɪ,et/ vt [VP6A] make ill, cause the death of, through lack of sufficient air in the lungs: 使窒息; 闷死: The men in the coal-mine were ~ted by bad gas. 煤矿坑里的工人们为毒气所窒息。**as·phyxi·ation** /æs,fɪksɪ'eɪʃn; æs,fɪksɪ'eʃən/ n [U] = asphyxia; suffocation. 窒息。

as·pic /'æspɪk; 'æspɪk/ n [U] clear meat jelly: (肉类)冻子: chicken in ~. 鸡肉冻子。

as·pi·dis·tra /,æspɪ'dɪstrə; ,æspɪ'dɪstrə/ n (pl ~s) plant with broad, pointed leaves, usually grown as a

house plant. 蜘蛛抱蛋; 叶兰。

as·pir·ant /ə'spaɪərənt; ə'spaɪrənt/ n (to/after), person who is ambitious for fame, etc: 有抱负; 热望者; 希求者: an ~ to high office. 求高职者。

as·pir·ate[1] /'æspərət; 'æspərɪt/ n (phon) the sound of 'h'; sound with an 'h' in it: (语音) 'h' 音; 送气音: Mind your ~s, be careful to make the 'h' sounds where necessary. 注意你的 'h' 的发音。

as·pir·ate[2] /'æspəreɪt; 'æspə,ret/ vt (phon) say with an 'h' sound: (语音)带着 'h' 音说出; 把…发成送气音: The 'h' in 'honour' is not ~d. 'honour' 中之 'h' 不发音。

as·pir·ation /,æspə'reɪʃn; ,æspə'reʃən/ n [C, U] 1 — (for/after): ~ (to do/be), aspiring; desire: 愿望; 希望; 渴望; 热望: his ~s for fame; 他的求名之心愿; his ~ to be an actor; 他想做演员的愿望; the ~s of the developing countries. 发展中国家的愿望。2 aspirating. 发送气音。

as·pire /ə'spaɪə(r); ə'spaɪr/ vi [VP3A, 4A] be filled with high ambition: 有抱负; 有雄心; 立志; 热望: ~ after knowledge; 立志求知识; ~ to fame; 立志成名: ~ to become an author. 热望成为作家。

as·pirin /'æsprɪn US: -pər-; 'æspərɪn/ n [U] (P) medicine used to relieve pain and reduce fever; [C] tablet or measure of this: (商标)阿司匹林(止痛退烧药); 阿司匹林药片: Take two ~s for a headache. 吃两片阿司匹林治头痛。

ass[1] /æs; æs/ n 1 animal of the horse family with long ears and a tuft at the end of its tail; donkey; stupid person. 驴; 愚人; 傻瓜; 笨蛋。2 make an ass of oneself behave stupidly so that one is ridiculed. 行为愚蠢因而受人嘲弄; 弄出笑话来。

ass[2] /æs; æs/ n (US vulg) (美鄙) = arse.

as·sa·gai /'æsəgaɪ; 'æsə,gaɪ/ n = assegai.

as·sail /ə'seɪl; ə'sel/ vt [VP6A, 14] ~ (with), attack violently; pester: 猛击; 痛击; 困扰: ~ sb with questions/insults; 对某人加以质问 (侮辱); be ~ed with doubts. 为疑惑所困扰。~·able /-əbl; -əbl/ adj that can be attacked. 可攻击的。~·ant /-ənt; -ənt/ n attacker. 攻击者。

as·sas·sin /ə'sæsɪn US: -sn; ə'sæsɪn/ n person, often one hired by others, who assassinates. 暗杀者; 刺客(常为受人所雇者)。~·ate /ə'sæsɪneɪt US: -sən-; ə'sæsɪn,et/ vt [VP6A] kill sb (esp an important politician, ruler) violently and treacherously, for political reasons. 暗杀: 行刺(尤指政治要人, 统治者)。~·ation /ə,sæsɪ'neɪʃn US: ə,sæsən'eɪʃn; ə,sæsɪn'eʃən/ n [U] murder of this kind; [C] instance of this. 暗杀; 行刺。

as·sault /ə'sɔ:lt; ə'sɔlt/ n ~ (on/upon), violent and sudden attack: 猛烈而突然之攻击: They made an ~ on the enemy's positions. 他们突袭敌人的阵地。The sonic boom was an ~ on our nerves. 飞机的声爆是对我们神经的攻击。The enemy's positions were taken by ~, 敌人的阵地被攻陷。~ and battery, (legal) beating or hitting sb. (法律)殴打某人。'~ craft n portable boat with an outboard motor, used for making attacks across rivers, etc. 攻击舟(马达装于船外, 渡水攻敌用之轻便突击艇)。□ vt [VP6A] make an ~ on; attack (eg a fortress) by a sudden rush. 袭击; 突袭(堡垒等)。

as·say /ə'seɪ; ə'se/ n [C] ~ (of), test of the fineness. purity, or quality (of precious metals, ores, etc): (检验贵金属, 矿苗等之精度, 纯度或品质所作之)化验; 分析: make an ~ of an ore. 分析矿苗以测其含有矿度。□ vt 1 [VP6A] test, eg the purity of a metal, analyse, eg an ore, etc. 化验(金属之纯度); 分析(矿苗等)。2 ~ (to do sth), [VP6A,7A] (old use) attempt, eg test sth difficult. (旧用法)尝试(困难之事)。

as·se·gai /'æsəgaɪ; 'æsə,gaɪ/ n throwing-spear with a wooden haft, used by S African tribes. (南非洲部族所用之)木柄标枪。

as·sem·blage /ə'semblɪdʒ; ə'semblɪdʒ/ n 1 [U] bringing or coming together; assembly (now the usu word): 集合; 组合; 装置; 装配(现通常用 assembly): the

~ *of parts of a machine.* 机器零件的装配。**2** [C] collection of things or (joc) persons. 聚集之物;(谑)聚集的人群;会众。

as·sem·ble /ə'sembl; ə'sɛmbl/ *vt, vi* **1** [VP6A, 2A] gather together; collect: 集合;聚集: *The pupils ~d / were ~d in the school hall.* 学生们在学校礼堂中集合。**2** [VP6A] fit or put together (the parts of): 配合;装配(…之零件): ~ *a watch / clock.* 装配表(汽车)。

as·sem·bly /ə'semblɪ; ə'sɛmblɪ/ *n* (*pl* **-lies**) **1** [C] number of persons who have come together, esp a meeting of law-makers: 聚集的一群人;集会;(尤指立法者的)会议: *the Legislative A~;* 立法会议; *the school ~,* the daily ~ of pupils and staff. 学校集会(学生与教职员的每日集会)。'~ **room(s),** public hall in which meetings, balls, etc take place. 公共会堂(供集会、举行舞会等)。**2** '~ **hall,** one where a school meets for prayers, etc; workshop where parts of large machines, eg aircraft, are put together. 学校聚会堂(供祈祷等聚会用之场所);(装配大型机器,如飞机等之)装配场。'~ **line,** stage of mass production in which parts of a machine, vehicle, etc move along for progressive ~. 装配线(大量生产过程中将各部分零件逐步装配成为机器、车辆等之阶段)。**3** military call, by drum or bugle, for soldiers to assemble. (军中之)集合信号;集合号。

as·sent /ə'sent; ə'sɛnt/ *n* ~ **(to),** official agreement, eg to a proposal; (royal) agreement to a bill passed by Parliament. 官方同意(如某项建议);国王同意(议会所通过的法案);批准;认可。 *by common* ~, everybody agreeing. 一致赞成。 *with one* ~, unanimously; nobody opposing. 一致(通过)。无异议。 ⇨ **accord**[1](1), **dissent.** □ *vi* [VP2A, 3A] ~ *(to),* give agreement (eg to a proposal). 同意;赞成(如上,接一项建议等)。

as·sert /ə'sɜːt; ə'sɝt/ *vt* [VP6A] make a claim to, eg one's rights. 维护;辩护;要求(自己的权利等);主张。**2** [VP6A, 9, 25] declare: 宣称;断言: ~ *one's innocence / that one is innocent.* 声明自己的清白(自己是清白的); ~ *sth to be true.* 断言某事是真实的。 ~ *oneself,* display authority, self-confidence. 表现自己的权威与自信;自作主张;坚持己见。

as·ser·tion /ə'sɜːʃn; ə'sɝʃən/ *n* **1** [U] insisting upon the recognition of one's rights: 坚持要求承认自己的权利;断言: *self~.* 坚持己见。**2** [C] strong statement; claim: 强硬的声明;要求;主张: *make an* ~. 作强硬的要求。

as·ser·tive /ə'sɜːtɪv; ə'sɝtɪv/ *adj* having or showing positive assurance: 断然的;确然无疑的: *speaking in an* ~ *tone.* 以断然的口气说话。~·**ly** *adv*

as·sess /ə'ses; ə'sɛs/ *vt* [VP6A, 14] **1** decide or fix the amount of (eg a tax or a fine): 估定(税额或罚款)的数额: *Damages were ~ed at £100.* 损失赔偿计为一百英镑。**2** appraise; fix or decide the value of (eg property), the amount of (eg income), for purposes of taxation; (fig) test the value of: 估计; 估定(财产)之价值,(收入等)之数字(以作课税之根据); (喻)评定…的价值; 评估: ~ *a speech at its true worth.* 评定演说之真正价值。~·**ment** /-mənt/ *n* [U] ~ing; [C] amount ~ed. 估计; 评估; 所估计之数额。~·**or** /-sə(r); -sɚ/ *n* **1** person who ~es property, income, taxes, etc. (财产、收入、税款等之)估计员;估税员。**2** person who advises a judge, magistrate or official committee, etc on technical matters. (辅助法官,地方官,官厅委员会等解决技术问题之)顾问; 陪审推事。

as·set /'æset; 'æsɛt/ *n* **1** (usu *pl*) anything owned by a person, company, etc that has money value and that may be sold to pay debts. (通常用复)财产;资产。 ⇨ **liability. 2** valuable or useful quality or skill: 有价值的或有用的性质或技能: *Good health is a great* ~. 良好的健康极为可贵。

as·sev·er·ate /ə'sevəreɪt; ə'sɛvəˌret/ *vt* [VP6A, 9] (formal) assert solemnly: (正式用语)(郑重地)宣誓;声明: ~ *one's innocence / that one is innocent.* 郑重声明自己的清白(自己的). **as·sev·er·ation** /ə,sevə'reɪʃn/ *n*

as·si·du·ity /,æsɪ'djuːɪtɪ US: -'duː-; ,æsə'djuɛtɪ, -'duː-/ *n* **1** [U] constant and careful attention to what one is doing: 专心致志;勤勉不懈: *He plans everything with unfailing* ~. 他欢欢不倦地计划每一件事。**2** (*pl* **-ties**) constant attentions *(to).* 殷勤的照料;周到的关怀(与 to 连用)。

as·sidu·ous /ə'sɪdjuəs US: -dʒuəs; ə'sɪdʒuəs/ *adj* diligent; persevering: 勤勉的;努力的;有毅力的: ~ *in his duties.* 勤勉于他的职守。~·**ly** *adv*

as·sign /ə'saɪn; ə'saɪn/ *vt* [VP13A, 12A] ~ *sth (to sb / sth),* give for use or enjoyment, or as a share or part in a distribution, eg of work, duty: 分配;分派(工作、任务等给某人): *Those rooms have been ~ed to us.* 那些房间已经分配给我们。 *Your teacher ~s you work to be done at home.* 你的老师曾分配家庭作业给你。**2** [VP 13A, B] name, put forward as a time, place, reason, etc: 指定(时间、地点);提出(理由等): *Has a day been ~ed for the trial?* 审讯日期是否已定? *Can one* ~ *a cause to these events?* 谁能指出这些事件的起因吗? **3** [VP13B, 17] ~ *sb (to / to do),* appoint, name: 指派;选派: *A~ your best man to the job.* 选派你最好的人担任那工作。 *Two pupils were ~ed to sweep the classroom.* 两个学生被指派打扫教室。**4** [VP14] ~ *to,* (legal) transfer property, rights, etc. (法律)转让(财产、权利等);让与;过户给。~·**able** /-əbl; -əbl/ *adj* that can be attributed or ~ed: 可分派的;可能定的;可归因于…的: ~*able to several causes.* 可归于数种原因的。~·**ment** *n* [U] ~ing; [C] that which is ~ed. 分配;分派;所分派之事物。

as·sig·na·tion /,æsɪg'neɪʃn; ,æsɪg'neʃən/ *n* [C] appointment and fixing of a time and place for a furtive meeting between lovers. 约会;(情侣间秘密的)幽会。

as·simi·late /ə'sɪmɪleɪt; ə'sɪmlˌet/ *vt, vi* **1** [VP6A, 2A] absorb (food) into the body (after digestion); be thus absorbed: 将(消化后之食物)吸收于身体中;(消化后之食物)被吸收: *We ~ some kinds of food more easily than others.* 我们对于某些种类的食物比较容易吸收。 *Some kinds of food ~ easily.* 有些种类的食物易被吸收。 **2** [VP6A, 2A] (allow people to) become part of another social group or state: 同化: *The USA has ~d people from many countries,* has absorbed them, so that they are Americans. 美国同化了来自许多国家的人。 **3** [VP6A] absorb, eg ideas, knowledge. 吸收(观念,知识)。**4** [VP3A] ~ *to,* make or become like. 同化它;使变成一样;变成一样。**as·simi·la·tion** /ə,sɪmə'leɪʃn; ə,sɪml'eʃən/ *n* [U] assimilating or being ~d. 吸收;同化;吸收作用;同化作用。

as·sist /ə'sɪst; ə'sɪst/ *vt, vi* [VP6A,17,14,2A,3A] ~ *(sb) (with sth / in doing sth / to do sth),* (formal) help: (正式用语)帮助(某人)(做某事);援助: ~ *(sb) with the form-filling;* 帮助(某人)填表; ~ *sb to fill in the forms.* 帮助某人填写表格。 *Two men are ~ing the police in their enquiries,* are answering questions which may lead to the arrest of the criminal(s), or perhaps their own arrest as the criminals. 两个男人在答复警方的询问。~·**ance** /-ɔns; -ɔns/ *n* [U] help: 帮助;援助: *give / lend / render ~ance (to sb);* (对某人)予以援助; 施以援手; 给与~ance; 援助某人; 予以~ance *(to sb).* 帮助;援助(某人)。~·**ant** /-ɔnt; -ɔnt/ *n* helper: 助手;副手;助理: *an ~ant to the Manager;* 副经理;助理; *an assistant master,* in a school (学校中的)助教; a *'shop~ant,* one who serves customers. 店员。

as·size /ə'saɪz; ə'saɪz/ *n* **1** [U] trial by a judge and jury. 审讯; 审判。**2** (*pl*) (until 1971) sessions held periodically in every English County to try civil and criminal cases before High Court Judges: (复)(此制度一直施行到一九七一年止)(英国高等法院法官定期至各郡审判案件之)巡回审判庭期;巡回审判: (attrib, *sing*) 用作定语, 单数) *courts of* ~; 巡回审判法庭; *judges on* ~; 巡回审判法官; ~ *towns.* 巡回审判城市。 ⇨ *Crown Court* at **court**[1](1) for the new system.

as·so·ci·ate¹ /ə'səʊʃɪət; ə'soʃɪɪt/ *adj* joined in function or dignity: 伙同的; 副的: *an ~ judge*. 陪审推事. □ *n* person who has been joined with others *in work, business or crime*; person given certain limited rights in an association; companion. 同事; 同僚; 同人; 共犯;(会社之)准会员; 同伴; 伙伴.

as·so·ci·ate² /ə'səʊʃɪeɪt; ə'soʃɪ,et/ *vt, vi ~ with,* **1** [VP14] join or connect: 联合; 结交; 结交; 联系: *~ oneself with sb in a business undertaking;* 与某人合伙经商; *~ one thing with another.* 将一事(物)与另一事(物)联系在一起. *We ~ Egypt with the Nile.* 我们想起埃及就想起尼罗河. *I don't wish to ~ myself with what has been said*, don't want anyone to think that I have a part in it, or approve of it. 我不希望任何人以为我自己与所说的事有任何关联(或以为我赞成此事). **2** [VP3A] be often in the company of. 与…常在一起; 结交; 与…为友: *Don't ~ with dishonest boys.* 勿与不诚实的男孩为友.

as·so·ci·ation /ə,səʊsɪ'eɪʃn; ə,sosɪ'eʃən/ *n* **1** [U] ~ *(with),* associating; being associated; companionship: 联合; 结交; 结合: *I benefited much from my ~ with him/from our ~*. 我与他结交获益良多. *His English benefited through his long ~ with British children.* 由于他长期与英国儿童接触, 使他的英语得以长进. *in ~ (with),* together (with). 与…在一起; 与…联合; 结交或有关连. **2** [C] group of persons joined together for some common purpose: 协会; 社团; 会社: *the 'Automobile A~;* 汽车协会; *the 'Young Men's 'Christian A~.* 基督教青年会. **3**, **A~ 'football**, (common abbr 普通略作 *soccer*) game in which two teams of eleven players use a spherical ball that must not be touched with the hands except by the goalkeeper or when throwing in. 英式足球(每队十一人, 用圆球, 除门将或自边线发球外, 不可以手触球者). ⇨ the illus at **foot**. 参看 foot 之插图. **4** connection (of ideas). (观念的)联想.

as·son·ance /'æsənəns; 'æsənəns/ *n* agreement between stressed vowels in two words, but not in the following consonants, as in *sharper* and *garter.* 半韵; 半谐音(即两字间只有重读的母音相同, 而其后之辅音不相同, 如 sharper 与 garter 是).

as·sorted /ə'sɔːtɪd; ə'sɔrtɪd/ *part adj* **1** of various sorts; mixed: 各种各样的; 各色俱备的; 混合的; 什锦的: *a pound of ~ toffees,* toffees of different kinds, mixed together. 一磅什锦太妃糖. **2** matched, suited, one to another. 配合的; 合适的: *an ill-~ couple,* husband and wife who get on badly. 一对怨偶(相处不好的夫妻).

as·sort·ment /ə'sɔːtmənt; ə'sɔrtmənt/ *n* collection of different examples of one class or of several classes: 属于一类或数类的各色物品之集合: *This shop has a good assortment of goods to choose from.* 此店各色货物俱备, 任君选择.

as·suage /ə'sweɪdʒ; ə'swedʒ/ *vt* [VP6A] make (sth, eg pain, suffering, desire) less. 减轻(痛苦); 缓和(情绪或欲望); 镇定; 平息.

as·sume /ə'sjuːm US: ə'suːm; ə'sum/ *vt* **1** [VP6A, 9, 25] take as true before there is proof: (在未证实前)假定; 以为: *You ~ his innocence/him to be innocent/that he is innocent before hearing the evidence against him.* 在未听到对他不利的证言之前, 你假定他是无罪的. *You're not such a fool as you ~d* (= supposed) *him to be.* 他并非如你所以为的那样愚蠢. *Assuming this to be true* .... 假定这是真的…. ⇨ **presume(1).** **2** [VP6A] take up; undertake: 担任; 承当: *~ the direction of a business;* 负责主持一项业务; *~ office,* 就职; *~ the reins of government,* begin to govern. 开始执政. **3** [VP6A] take upon or for oneself sth not genuine or sincere: 假装; 伴作; 冒用: *~ a look of innocence;* 装作无辜的样子; *~ a new name.* 用新名字; 用化名.

as·sump·tion /ə'sʌmpʃn; ə'sʌmpʃən/ *n* **1** [C] sth taken for granted; sth supposed but not proved: 视为当然之事; 所假定而未经证实之事: *Their ~ that the war would end quickly was proved wrong.* 他们认为战争会迅

速结束的看法证明是错误的. *on the ~ that,* accepting it to be true that.... 承认…是真实的…. **2** [C] ~ *of,* the act of assuming(2): 担任; 承当: *his ~ of office /power /the presidency.* 他的就职 (当权, 就任大学校长). **3** [C] ~ *of,* the adopting of a manner, etc which is not genuine: 假装; 作态: *with an ~ of indifference,* pretending not to be interested. 装作冷淡的样子. **4 the A~,** reception into Heaven in bodily form of the Virgin Mary; Church feast commemorating this. 圣母升天, 圣母升天节.

as·sur·ance /ə'ʃʊərəns; ə'ʃʊrəns/ *n* **1** [U] (often 当作 *self-~*) confidence in oneself; belief and trust in one's own powers: 自信; 把握; 胸有成竹: *He answered all the questions with ~.* 他有把握地回答了所有的问题. *A businessman, to be successful, should act with perfect* (*self-*)*assurance.* 一个企业家要想成功, 做事应该有十足的自信心. **2** [C] promise; statement made to give confidence: 承诺; 担保; 保证: *He gave me a definite ~ that the repairs would be finished by Friday.* 他给我确切保证星期五以前修理好. **3** [U] (chiefly GB) insurance on sth that is certain: (主用于英国)(对于确知不可避免之事之)保险: *'life ~*, because death is certain. 人寿保险 (因为死亡是不可避免免的). ⇨ **insurance. 4** [U] impudence (the much more usu word). 厚颜; 无耻 (impudence 远较 assurance 常用). **5** ~ *(in),* [U] certainty; confidence (the much more usu word). 确信; 信心 (confidence 远较 assurance 常用)。*make ~ doubly sure,* remove all possible doubt. 扫除一切可能的疑虑; 做到万无一失.

as·sure /ə'ʃʊə(r); ə'ʃʊr/ *vt* **1** [VP11] say positively, with confidence: 断然地说; 有信心地说: *I ~ you (that) there's no danger.* 我向你保证没有危险. **2** [VP11, 14] cause (sb) to be sure, to feel certain: 使(某人)相信, 使确信: *We tried to ~ the nervous old lady that flying was safe.* 我们尽力说服那紧张的老妇人, 使她相信乘飞机是安全的. *He ~d me of his readiness to help.* 他使我相信他愿意帮忙. **3** [VP6A] ensure (the more usu word): 获得; 保证得到 (ensure 为较常用字): *Nothing can ~ permanent happiness.* 没有东西能担保永久的幸福. **4** [VP6A] insure, esp against the death of sb or oneself. 保险 (尤指人寿保险). **as·sured** *part adj* sure; confident. 确信的; 深信的. *rest ~d (that),* feel confident (that). (对…)放心. **as·sur·ed·ly** /ə'ʃʊərɪdlɪ; ə'ʃʊrɪdlɪ/ *adv* surely; confidently. 一定地; 深信地.

as·ter /'æstə(r); 'æstɚ/ *n* garden plant with flowers that have white, pink or purple petals round a yellow centre. 紫菀 (园艺植物, 花瓣为白色、粉红或紫色, 花心为黄色).

as·ter·isk /'æstərɪsk; 'æstə,rɪsk/ *n* the mark*, used to call attention to something, eg a footnote, or to show that letters are omitted, as in *Mr J***s,* for *Mr Jones*. 星号; 星标(用以指示应注意之事物, 如注脚, 或表示中有字母被省略, 如以 Mr J***s 代表 Mr Jones).

astern /ə'stɜːn; ə'stɝn/ *adv* **1** in or at the stern of a ship. 在船尾. ⇨ the illus at **ship**. 参看 ship 之插图. **2** backward: 向后: *Full speed ~!* 全速后退! **3** *fall ~ (of),* fall behind (another ship). 落于(另一船)之后.

as·ter·oid /'æstərɔɪd; 'æstə,rɔɪd/ *n* [C] any of many small planets between the orbits of Mars and Jupiter. 小行星(火星与木星轨道间之许多小行星之一). ⇨ the illus at **planet.** 参看 planet 之插图.

asthma /'æsmə US: 'æzmə; 'æzmə/ *n* [U] chronic chest disease marked by difficulty in breathing. 气喘; 气喘病. **asth·matic** /æs'mætɪk US: æz-; æz'mætɪk/ *adj* suffering from ~; of ~. 气喘的; 患气喘病的; 气喘病的.

astig·ma·tism /ə'stɪgmətɪzəm; ə'stɪgmə,tɪzəm/ *n* [U] defect in an eye or lens that prevents correct focusing. (指眼)乱视; 散光; (指透镜)像散性; 像散现象. **as·tig·matic** /,æstɪg'mætɪk; ,æstɪg'mætɪk/ *adj*

astir /ə'stɜː(r); ə'stɝ/ *adv, pred adj* **1** in motion; in a state of excitement: 在活动中; 在骚动状态中: *The whole*

village was ~ when news came that the Queen was coming. 听到女王要来的消息, 全村为之骚动。 **2** (dated) out of bed and about: (过时用语) 起床了还在走动: *You're ~ early this morning.* 你今天早晨起得很早。

as·ton·ish /ə'stɒnɪʃ; ə'stɑnɪʃ/ *vt* [VP6A] surprise greatly: 使大为惊异; 使惊骇; 使惊愕: *The news ~ed everybody.* 这消息令人感到惊愕。 *You look ~ed at the news.* 你对这消息似乎感到惊异。 *I was ~ed to see him there.* 我在那里见到他, 感到惊异。 *I am ~ed that he didn't come.* 他没有来, 使我感到惊异。 **~·ing** *part adj* very surprising: 非常惊人的; 极可惊的: *It is ~ing to me that he should be absent.* 他竟会缺席, 使我感到惊讶。 **~·ment** *n* [U] great surprise: 大惊异; 惊愕; 惊异: *I heard to my ~ment that ...;* 我听到…甚感惊愕; *He looked at me in ~ment.* 他惊异地望着我。

astound /ə'staʊnd; ə'staʊnd/ *vt* [VP6A] overcome with surprise, shock. 使大受惊骇; 震惊。

as·tra·khan /ˌæstrə'kæn US: 'æstrəkən; 'æstrəkən/ *n* [U] skin of young lambs with wool in tight little curls: 羔皮; 小羊皮(其毛卷成小圆者): (used attrib) (用作定语) *an ~ coat/cap.* 羔皮大衣(帽)。

as·tral /'æstrəl; 'æstrəl/ *adj* of or from the stars. 星的; 从星上来的。

astray /ə'streɪ; ə'stre/ *adv, pred adj* out of, off, the right path, esp (fig) into wrongdoing: 迷途; 离正路: (尤指, 喻入) 歧途: *The boy was led ~ by bad companions.* 那个男孩被坏同伴引入歧途。

astride /ə'straɪd; ə'straɪd/ *adv, pred adj, prep* with one leg on each side (of): 两腿分开(而骑); 跨骑: *riding ~;* 跨骑; *sitting ~ his father's knee.* 骑坐在他父亲的膝上。

as·trin·gent /ə'strɪndʒənt; ə'strɪndʒənt/ *n* (kind of) substance that shrinks soft tissues and contracts blood-vessels, thus checking the flow of blood. 收敛剂 (可收缩柔软之组织, 并可收缩血管以止血者)。 □ *adj* of or like an ~: (喻) harsh; severe. 收敛剂的; 似收敛剂的; 收敛性的; (喻) 严厉的; 严酷的。 **as·trin·gency** /ə'strɪndʒənsɪ; ə'strɪndʒənsɪ/ *n*

as·tro·dome /'æstrədəʊm; 'æstro,dom/ *n* small, transparent observation dome on the top of the fuselage of an aircraft, used by the navigator. 天文航行舱(机身顶部供领航员观测用的透明小圆顶)。

as·tro·labe /'æstrəleɪb; 'æstrə,leb/ *n* instrument used in the Middle Ages to determine the height of the sun, etc. 星盘(中古时期用以测定太阳等高度的一种观象仪)。 ⇨ **sextant**.

as·trol·ogy /ə'strɒlədʒɪ; ə'strɑlədʒɪ/ *n* [U] art of observing the positions of the stars in the belief that they influence human affairs. 占星术。 **as·trol·oger** /-ədʒə(r); -ədʒɚ/ *n* expert in ~. 占星家。 **as·tro·logi·cal** /ˌæstrə'lɒdʒɪkl; ˌæstrə'lɑdʒɪkl/ *adj*

as·tro·naut /'æstrənɔːt; 'æstrə,nɔt/ *n* person who travels in a spacecraft. 宇宙航行员; 太空人; 乘太空船旅行的人。 **~·ics** /ˌæstrə'nɔːtɪks; ˌæstrə'nɔtɪks/ *n* (sing v) (用单数动词) science and technology of travel through outer space. 宇宙航行学; 太空航行学。

as·tron·omy /ə'strɒnəmɪ; ə'strɑnəmɪ/ *n* [U] science of the sun, moon, stars and planets. 天文学。 **as·tron·omer** *n* student of, authority on, ~. 天文学者; 天文学家。 **as·tro·nomi·cal** /ˌæstrə'nɒmɪkl; ˌæstrə'nɑmɪkl/ *adj* of the study of ~; (colloq; of a quantity) very large: 天文学的; (口; 指数量)极大的: *an astronomical amount.* 极大的数量。

as·tro·phys·ics /ˌæstrəʊ'fɪzɪks; ˌæstro'fɪzɪks/ *n* (sing v) science of the chemical and physical conditions of the stars. (用单数动词)天体物理学。

as·tute /ə'stjuːt US: ə'stuːt; ə'stjut/ *adj* **1** quick at seeing how to gain an advantage. 敏于看出如何获得利益的; 狡黠的。 **2** shrewd; clever: 精明的; 聪明的; *an ~ lawyer/businessman.* 精明的律师(商人)。 **~·ly** *adv* **~·ness** *n*

asun·der /ə'sʌndə(r); ə'sʌndɚ/ *adv* (liter) (文) **1** (of

two or more things) apart: (指两件或两件以上之事物) 分开; 分离; 分散: *Parents and children were driven ~ (= separated) by the war.* 父母与子女因战事而分散。 **2** into pieces: 成碎片: *tear sth ~.* 将某物撕碎。

asy·lum /ə'saɪləm; ə'saɪləm/ *n* **1** [U] refuge; safety; protection from persecution, etc: 庇护; 安全; 避难: *ask for political ~;* 请求政治庇护; [C] place where this is found or given. 庇护所; 避难所。 **2** [C] (formerly) institution where mentally ill people were cared for, now called a *mental home/hospital/institution.* (昔时) 疯人院; 精神病院(现称 mental home, mental hospital 或 mental institution)。

at /ət; ət; *strong form:* æt; æt/ *prep* **1** (place and direction) (指地方与方向) (a) (indicating the place in or near which sth or sb was, is or will be): (指某人或某物所在之处, 或在其附近) *at his office;* 在他的办公室; *at my uncle's;* 在我叔父家; *at the station.* 在车站。 Cf 参较 *in* for countries and large towns, and places important to the speaker. 用于国家和大城市, 以及对说话者甚为重要的地方。 (b) (towards; in the direction of): (向; 朝着): *look at sth/sb;* 朝着某物(某人)看; *shoot/aim a gun at sth;* 对着某物射击 (以枪瞄准某物); *rush at the enemy;* 向敌人冲去; *laugh/growl at sb/sth;* 嘲笑某人或某事物(对着某人或某事物咆哮); *throw sth at sb;* ie intending to hit him; 对准某人投掷某物 (意欲击中他); ⇨ *throw to at* **throw¹**(1); *talk at sb,* ie make an indirect attack on him. ⇨ *talk to at* **talk²**(1)。 暗指某人而说; 暗讽(即间接攻击某人)。 (c) (indicating an attempt to get or reach sth, an uncompleted or imperfect action): (指试图得到或触及某物, 一种未完成或不完全的动作): *The drowning man clutched at the oar,* tried to seize it. 那溺水的人欲抓住浮木(但尚未抓住)。 *He had to guess at the meaning.* 他不得不猜测那意思。 (d) (indicating distance): (指距离): *hold sth at arm's length.* 与某物保持距离。 *It looks better at a distance.* 它在远处看起来更好。 (e) (indicating a point of entrance or exit) through; by: (指口入或出口处)经过; 经由: *What the teacher says often goes in (at) one ear and out (at) the other.* 老师所说的话常左耳进右耳出。 **2** (time and order) (指时间之顺序) (a) (indicating a point of time): (指时间之一点): *at 2 o'clock;* 在两点钟的时候; *at sunset;* 在日落的时候; *at any moment;* 在任何时刻; *at this (point),* when this happened. 当此事发生时。 (b) (of age): (指年龄): *He left school at (the age of) 15.* 他在十五岁时离开学校。 (c) (indicating order): (指顺序): *at the third attempt;* 第三次尝试的时候; *at first;* 首先; 起初; *at last.* 最后; 终于。 (d) (indicating frequency): (指次数多寡): *at (all) times,* 有时候(无论何时); 随时; 总是; *at regular intervals.* 在每隔一定时间。 **3** (activity, state, manner) (指活动, 情况, 状态, 方式) (a) (indicating occupation): (指所做之事): *at work,* 在工作; *at play.* 在游戏。 *What is he at now,* What is he doing? 他现在在做什么?; *hard 'at it,* working hard. 正在努力工作。 (b) (after *adjj*): (用于形容词之后): *busy at his tasks;* 忙着做他的事; *good at translation.* 擅长翻译。 (c) (state, condition): (指状态, 情况): *at war/peace;* 在战 (平) 时; *at leisure.* 在闲暇时。 (d) (manner): (指方式, 态度): *at a gallop;* 以奔驰的步子; *finish something at a sitting,* ie during one continuous period of activity. 一口气做完某事。 **4** (rate or degree, value, cost) (指速率或程度, 价值, 价钱) (a) (rate): (指速率): *at full speed;* 以全速; *at a snail's pace.* 以蜗牛的速度; 缓慢地。 (b) (value, cost, etc): (指价值, 价钱等): *at an immense cost;* 花极大的代价; *sell sth at a loss;* 亏本出售某物; *buy articles at 20p and sell them at 25p.* 以每件二十便士之价购入货品, 以每件二十五便士之价出售。 (c) (with *superl*): (与最高级形容词或副词连用): *at its/his/their, etc best;* 在它的(他的, 他们的等)最佳情况中; *at least;* 至少; 最少; *at (the) worst.* 在最坏到极点。 **5** (cause) (指原因) (a) (after *vv*): (用于动词之后): *The pupils marvelled at the extent of their teacher's knowledge.* 学生们对于其老师知

识范围之广感到惊奇。**(b)** (after *adjj* and *pp's*): (用于形容词及过去分词之后): *impatient at the delay*; 对于耽误的情形感到不耐烦; *delighted at the idea of going to England.* 一想到要去英国就感到高兴。 ⇨ also *n* entries for *at hand*, *at last*, *be in at the death* and others.

ata·brine /ˈætəbriːn; ˈætəbrin/ *n* [U] (P) bitter-tasting, anti-malarial drug. (商标) 疟涤平; 阿的平 (一种苦味的治疗疟疾的药)。

ata·vism /ˈætəvɪzəm; ˈætə͵vɪzəm/ *n* reappearance in a person of a characteristic or quality that has not shown itself for several or many generations. (人之特征或性格的) 隔代遗传; 祖型再现; 返祖遗传; 返祖性。 ⇨ **reversion, throwback. ata·vis·tic** /͵ætəˈvɪstɪk; ͵ætəˈvɪstɪk/ *adj*

ate /et *US*: eɪt; et/ *pt* of **eat**.

atel·ier /æˈteliːeɪ *US*: ͵ætlˈjeɪ; ˈætl͵je/ *n* (F)workshop; studio. (法) 工作室; 画室。

athe·ism /ˈeɪθɪɪzəm; ˈeθɪ͵ɪzəm/ *n* [U] belief that there is no God. 无神论。 **athe·ist** /ˈeɪθɪɪst; ˈeθɪɪst/ *n* person who believes that there is no God. 无神论者。 **athe·is·tic** /͵eɪθɪˈɪstɪk; ͵eθɪˈɪstɪk/ *adj* of ~ or atheists. 无神论(者)的。

athirst /əˈθɜːst; əˈθɜst/ *pred adj* ~ **(for)**, (liter) thirsty, eager (for news, etc). (文)渴的; 渴望的(与for连用,指after消息等)。

ath·lete /ˈæθliːt; ˈæθlit/ *n* person trained for competing in physical exercises and outdoor games, eg a person good at running, jumping, swimming, boxing. 运动选手; 运动员(如擅长跑,跳,游泳,拳击者)。

ath·letic /æθˈletɪk; æθˈlɛtɪk/ *adj* 1 of athletes. 运动员的。 **2** physically strong, with well-balanced proportions between the trunk and limbs: 体格健美的; 体格强健的: *an ~-looking young man.* 一个体格健美的年轻人。

ath·let·ics /æθˈletɪks; æθˈlɛtɪks/ *n pl* (usu with *sing v*) practice of physical exercises and sports, esp competitions in running, jumping, etc. (通常用单数动词)运动(各项体育运动之总称,尤指跑、跳等之竞赛); 竞技。

at-home /ətˈhəʊm; ətˈhom/ ⇨ **home¹(1)**.

athwart /əˈθwɔːt; əˈθwɔrt/ *adv*, *prep* ~ **(of)**, (naut) from one side to the other side. (航海)横越; 从(…之)一边至另一边。

atishoo /əˈtɪʃuː; əˈtɪʃu/ *int* (hum) spelling form used to indicate a sneeze. (谐)阿嚏(打打喷嚏)。

at·las /ˈætləs; ˈætləs/ *n* book of maps. 地图集; 地图。

at·mos·phere /ˈætməsfɪə(r); ˈætməs͵fɪr/ *n* **1** [U] esp 尤指 the ~, mixture of gases surrounding the earth. 大气; (绕于地球四周之)空气。 **2** [U] air in any place. (任何地方之)空气。 **3** [C] feeling, eg of good, evil, that the mind receives from a place, conditions, etc: 对于某一地方、情况等所得到的印象或感觉; 气氛: *There is an ~ of peace and calm in the country quite different from the ~ of a big city.* 在乡间有一种和平宁静之气氛,与大城市的气氛截然不同。

at·mos·pheric /͵ætməsˈferɪk; ͵ætməsˈfɛrɪk/ *adj* of, connected with, the atmosphere: 大气的; 关于大气的: ~ *conditions.* 大气的情况。 **,~ 'pressure,** pressure at a point due to the weight of the column of air above that point, about 14¹/₂ lb or 6.6 kg per square inch at sea level. 大气压力(在海平面,每平方英寸约 14¹/₂ 磅或 6.6 公斤)。 **at·mos·pher·ics** *n pl* electrical discharges that occur in the atmosphere and cause crackling sounds in radio receivers. (能收听收音机发生杂音之)天电。

atoll /ˈætɒl; ˈætɔl/ *n* ring-shaped coral reef(s) almost or entirely enclosing a lagoon. 环状珊瑚岛(几乎或完全围绕着一礁湖); 环礁。

atom /ˈætəm; ˈætəm/ *n* **1** smallest unit of an element that can take part in a chemical change: 原子(元素中能参加化学变化之最小单位): *A molecule of water* (H_2O) *is made up of two ~s of hydrogen and one ~ of oxygen.* 一分子的水是由二氢原子和一氧原子构成的。 ⇨ **electron,**

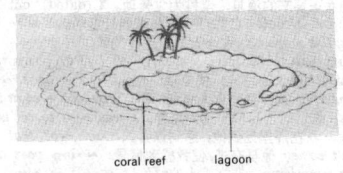

coral reef   lagoon

an atoll

neutron, nucleus, proton. **'~ bomb,** = atomic bomb. **2** very small bit: 微粒; 极小之物: *blow sth to ~s,* destroy it by explosion. 将某物炸得粉碎(借爆炸而毁掉它)。 *There's not an ~ of truth* (= no truth at all) *in what he said.* 他所说的话根本不是真的。

atomic /əˈtɒmɪk; əˈtɑmɪk/ *adj* of an atom, or atoms. 原子的。 **'~ bomb,** bomb of which the destructive power comes from the release of ~ energy in the shortest possible time. 原子弹。 **,~ 'energy,** energy obtained as the result of nuclear fission. 原子能。 **'pile,** ⇨ **reactor.** 原子炉。 **,~ 'weight,** weight of an atom of an element, expressed on a scale in which an atom of oxygen is 16. 原子量。 ⇨ **nuclear.**

at·om·ize /ˈætəmaɪz; ˈætəm͵aɪz/ *vt* reduce to atoms. 使成原子; 使成微粒如雾状。 **~r** *n* device for producing a fine spray, eg of perfume. 喷雾器(例如喷香水者)。

atonal /eɪˈtəʊnl; eˈtonl/ *adj* (music) not conforming to any system of key or mode. (音乐)无调的; 不合任何音调系统的。 **~ity** /͵eɪtəʊˈnælətɪ; ͵eto'næləti/ *n*

atone /əˈtəʊn; əˈton/ *vi* [VP2A, 3A] ~ **(for),** make repayment: 弥补; 补偿; 赎罪: ~ *(for) a fault by doing sth.* 借做某事以弥补过失。 *How can I ~ for hurting your feelings?* 我怎样才能补偿你伤你感情之过呢? *How can I ~?* 我如何能赎罪? **~·ment** *n* [U] atoning: 弥补; 补偿; 赎罪: *make ~ment for a fault.* 弥补过失。 **the A~ment,** the sufferings and death of Jesus. 耶稣为替世人赎罪所受之苦及死。

atop /əˈtɒp; əˈtɑp/ *adv* ~ **(of),** (US) on top of. (美)在(…之)顶上。

at·ra·bil·ious /͵ætrəˈbɪliəs; ͵ætrəˈbɪljəs/ *adj* (rare) melancholy; acrimonious. (罕)忧郁的; 坏脾气的; 刻薄的。

atro·cious /əˈtrəʊʃəs; əˈtroʃəs/ *adj* **1** very wicked or cruel: 极恶毒的; 凶暴的; 残忍的: *an ~ crime,* 凶暴的罪恶。 **2** (colloq) very bad: (口)极坏的; 极恶劣的: *an ~ dinner;* 极坏的一餐; ~ *weather.* 极恶劣的天气。 **~·ly** *adv*

atroc·ity /əˈtrɒsətɪ; əˈtrɑsətɪ/ *n* **1** [U] wickedness; [C] (*pl* **-ties**) wicked or cruel act: 恶毒; 残暴的行为: *the atrocities of which the enemy forces were guilty.* 敌军所犯的暴行。

atro·phy /ˈætrəfɪ; ˈætrəfɪ/ *n* [U] wasting away (of the body or part of it, or (fig) of a moral quality). (指身体或其一部)萎缩; (喻, 指道德)沦丧。 □ *vt*, *vi* [VP6A] cause ~ in; [VP2A, B] suffer ~. 使萎缩; 萎缩。

atta·boy /ˈætəbɔɪ; ˈætə͵bɔɪ/ *int* (US colloq) (expressing encouragement or admiration) Bravo! (美, 口) (表示鼓励或赞美)好极了! 好小子!

at·tach /əˈtætʃ; əˈtætʃ/ *vt*, *vi* **1** [VP14] ~ *sth* (*to sth*), fasten or join: 附上; 加上; 贴上; 系上: ~ *labels to the luggage;* 将标签系在行李上; ~ *a document to a letter;* 将文件附在信中; *the sample* ~*ed to the letter;* 函附送的样品; *a house with a garage* ~*ed.* 附有车房的房子。 *A*~*ed you will find/A*~*ed please find ...,* (business style) You will find, ~ed to this letter ... (商业函件形式)随函附上…,请查收。 **2** [VP14] ~ *one-self to,* join eg as a junior, and perhaps unwelcome, member: 参加; 加入(作一资浅或不受欢迎的会员等):

~ *oneself to a political party*／*to a travelling circus.* 加入某一政党(巡回马戏团)。 **3** *be* ~*ed to,* be bound to by love or affection: 为爱或感情所束缚; 爱慕; 依恋: *She is deeply* ~*ed to her young brother.* 她深爱她的幼弟。 *He is foolishly* ~*ed to old customs.* 他愚昧地执着于旧习俗。 **4** [VP14] ~ *sth to sth,* consider to have; connect with: 认为有; 使与…相关联: *Do you* ~ *much importance to what he says?* 你认为他所说的话有很大的重要性吗？ **5** [VP3A] ~ *to,* go with, be joined to: 伴随; (与…)相关联: *No suspicion*／*blame* ~*es to him,* he cannot be suspected／blamed. 他无可怀疑(责备)之处。 **6** [VP6A] (legal) seize by legal authority: (法律)依法扣留; 逮捕: 拘留; 查封: *Part of his salary was* ~*ed to,* (mil) appointed to whom he owed money. 他的一部分薪水被店主们依法扣下来偿付他所欠他们的债务。 **7** ~*ed to,* (mil) appointed to another unit for specialist duties: (军)被派遣至另一单位担任特定任务的; 配属的: *a gunnery officer* ~*ed to an infantry regiment.* 派遣至步兵团担任特定任务之射击军官。 ~·**ment** *n* **1** [U] act of ~*ing* or joining; being ~*ed.* 附着; 附属; 附带。 **2** [C] sth ~*ed,* esp an accessory ~*ed* to sth larger. 附属物; 附件。 **3** [C] affection; friendship: 情感; 深情; 友爱: *have an* ~*ment for sb.* 对某人有深情。 **4** legal seizing of goods, etc. (依法) 扣留; 查封(货物等)。 **5** *on* ~*ment to,* (temporarily) appointed to. (暂时)配属…。

at·**ta·ché** /ə'tæʃeɪ *US:* ˌætə'ʃeɪ; ˌætə'ʃe/ *n* person who is attached to the staff of an ambassador: (大使馆的) 随员; 馆员: *the naval*／*military*／*press* ~. 海军武官(陆军武官; 新闻参事)。 □ *case* /ə'tæʃɪ keɪs; ə'tæʃɪ kes/ *n* small, flat, rectangular box or holder for documents. 小型公文包。

at·**tack** /ə'tæk; ə'tæk/ *n* **1** [C] violent attempt to hurt, overcome, defeat: 攻击; 进攻; 攻打: *make an* ~ *upon the enemy.* 向敌人进攻。 [U] *The enemy came under* ~. 敌人受到攻击。 *A* ~ *is said to be the best form of defence.* 常言道, 攻击是最好的防御。 **2** [C] adverse criticism in speech or writing: (言语或文字的)攻击; 抨击: *a strong* ~ *against*／*on the Government's policy.* 对政府政策猛烈的抨击。 **3** [C] start, occurence, eg of disease: (疾病等之)发作; 侵袭: *an* ~ *of fever;* 发烧: *a 'liver* ~; 肝病突发; *a 'heart* ~, pain in the region of the heart, with irregular beating. 心脏病发作。 **4** [U] way of beginning an activity, eg playing the violin, playing a stroke in cricket. 着手的方式; 开始的手法(例如拉提琴, 在板球中之一击)。 □ *vt* [VP6A] make an ~ upon: 攻击; 进攻; 抨击; 侵袭: ~ *the enemy;* 攻击敌人; ~ *the Prime Minister's proposals;* 抨击首相的提议; *a disease that* ~*s children.* 侵袭儿童的疾病。 *Rust* ~*s metals.* 锈能侵蚀金属。 ~·**er** *n* person who ~*s.* 攻击者; 进攻者; 抨击者。

at·**tain** /ə'teɪn; ə'ten/ *vt, vi* **1** [VP6A] succeed in doing or getting: 达到; 成就; 实现; 遂(愿): *one's hopes*／*object*／*the end one has in view.* 实现其希望(达到其目的; 实现所抱的目标)。 **2** [VP3A] ~ *to,* reach, arrive at: 到达; 至; 得到: ~ *to perfection*／*power*／*prosperity;* 到达完美(权力、繁荣)的最高境界; ~ *to man's estate, reach manhood.* 到达成年。 ~·**able** /-əbl; -əbl/ *adj* that can be ~*ed:* 可达到的; 可得到的: *The goal is not yet* ~*able.* 该目标目前尚无法达到。 ~·**ment** *n* **1** [U] act of ~*ing:* 达到; 得到: *easy*／*difficult*／*impossible of* ~*ment,* easy, etc to ~: 容易(不易, 不可能)达到的; *for the* ~*ment of* (= in order to) his purpose. 为了达到他的目的。 **2** [C] (usu *pl*) sth ~*ed;* skill or accomplishment in some branch of knowledge, etc: (通常用复数)成就; 造诣: *legal*／*linguistic* ~*ments;* 法学(语言学)上的成就; *a scholar of the highest* ~*ments.* 造诣极高的学者。

at·**tain·der** /ə'teɪndə(r); ə'tendə/ *n* (legal) forfeiture of property and civil rights following sentence of death or outlawry. (法律)(宣判死刑或放逐后所致之)没收财产及褫夺公权。 **Bill of A**~, Parliamentary Bill imposing this penalty without trial. 褫夺公权之议案(强制此种刑

罚而不经受审之国会议案)。

at·**tar** /'ætə(r); 'ætə/ *n* [U] ~ *of roses,* perfume from rose petals. 玫瑰油(用玫瑰花瓣所制之香油); 玫瑰香水。

at·**tempt** /ə'tempt; ə'tεmpt/ *vt* **1** [VP7A, 6A] make a start at doing sth; try: 开始做; 试做; 尝试; 企图: *The prisoners tried to escape*／*an escape*／*but failed.* 囚犯们企图逃狱, 但是失败了。 *You have* ~*ed* (= made a start at performing) *a difficult task.* 你开始了一项艰难的工作。 *Don't* ~ *impossibilities,* Don't try to do impossible things. 不要试做不可能的事情。 **2** [VP6A] ~ *sb's life,* (old use) try to kill him. (旧用法)意图谋害某人的性命。 □ *n* [C] ~ *at doing sth,* ~ *at doing sth;* effort to do sth: 尝试做某事; 企图做某事: *They made no* ~ *to escape*／*at escaping.* 他们未曾企图脱逃。 *His first* ~ *at English composition was poor.* 他第一次作的英文作文很差。 *They failed in all their* ~*s to climb the mountain.* 他们攀登这山的一切尝试都失败了。 **2** ~ *at,* sth not very well done: 未做成功之事: *Her* ~ *at a Christmas cake had to be thrown away.* 她的圣诞蛋糕做得不好, 只好丢掉。 **3** ~ *on*／*upon,* attack on: 攻击; 袭击: *make an* ~ *on sb's life;* 谋害某人的性命; *an* ~ *on the world speed record.* 打破世界速度记录的尝试。

at·**tend** /ə'tend; ə'tεnd/ *vi, vt* **1** [VP3A, 2A] ~ *(to),* give care and thought (to): 注意; 用心; 照顾: ~ *to one's work;* 用心从事自己的工作; ~ *to what sb is saying,* listen carefully: 注意听某人的说话: ~ *to the wants of customers,* try to supply them. 顾及顾客的需要; 照顾生意。 *Are you being* ~*ed to?* (in a shop) Is anyone serving you? (在商店中) 有店员照应你吗？ *You're not* ~*ing, not listening,* not paying attention. 你没有在注意听。 **2** [VP6A, 3A] ~ *(on*／*upon),* wait on; serve; look after: 侍候; 看护; 照料: *Which doctor is* ~*ing you, giving you medical care?* 哪一个医生为你看病？ *The patient has three nurses* ~*ing (on) him.* 那病人有三位护士看护他。 *She has many servants* ~*ing upon her.* 她有许多仆人侍候她。 *He had the honour of* ~*ing upon the Prince.* 他有幸能侍候王子。 **3** [VP6A] go to; be present at: 到场; 出席; 参加; 上(学): ~ *school*／*church;* 上学(教堂); ~ *a meeting*／*lecture.* 参加会议(听演讲)。 *The lectures were well* ~*ed,* there were good audiences. 该项演讲听的人很多。 **4** [VP6A] (formal) accompany: (正式用语)伴随: *a method that is* ~*ed by some risk.* 带有相当冒险性的方法。 *Our plans were* ~*ed with great difficulties.* 我们的计划遇到很大的困难。 *May good luck* ~ *you!* (formal) May you have good luck! (正式用语)祝君幸运!

at·**tend·ance** /ə'tendəns; ə'tεndəns/ *n* **1** [U] *in* ~ *(on*／*upon),* act of attending(2): 侍候; 看护; 照料: *Major X was in* ~ *upon the Queen.* 某少校担任女王的侍卫。 *Now that the patient is out of danger, the doctor is no longer in* ~. 既然病人已经脱离险境, 医生就不再照料他了。 ⇨ **dance²(2).** **2** [C,U] (time of) being present, at school etc: 出席; 到校等之次数: *The boy was given a prize for regular* ~, for attending school regularly. 那男孩获颁全勤奖(从未缺课)。 *How many* ~*s has he made?* 他出席了几次？ *Is* ~ *at school compulsory?* 到校上课是硬性规定的吗？ **3** [C] (with *adj*) number of persons present: (与形容词连用)出席的人数: *There was a large* ~ *at church this morning.* 今天早上教堂中做礼拜的人很多。

at·**tend·ant** /ə'tendənt; ə'tεndənt/ *n* **1** servant or companion. 服务员; 仆役; 侍人。 **2** medical ~, doctor. 医生。 **3** (*pl*) persons who accompany an important person; (复)(要人的)随从人员: *the Prince and his* ~*s.* 王子及其随从人员。 □ *adj* **1** accompanying: 伴随的; 随之而来的: *famine and its* ~ *diseases,* the diseases that result from famine: 饥荒及随之而来的疾病; *old age and its* ~ *evils,* eg deafness. 老年及其伴随的疾患 (如耳聋)。 **2** waiting upon: 随侍的; 侍候的: *an* ~ *nurse.* 随侍护士。

at·**ten·tion** /ə'tenʃn; ə'tεnʃən/ *n* **1** [U] act of

directing one's thoughts to sth: 注意; 专心: *Pay ~ to what you're doing*, Don't let your thoughts wander. 注意你在做的事. *A teacher must know how to secure the ~ of his pupils.* 一个老师必须知道如何使学生专心上课. *No ~ was paid to my advice*, no one took it. 没有一个人听从我的劝告. *Give your whole ~ to what you are doing*, ie think of nothing else. 把全部注意力用于你所做的事. *He called/invited my ~ to some new evidence*, asked me to examine it. 他要我注意检查新的证据. *He shouted to attract ~*, to make people notice him. 他高声喊叫以引起别人的注意. *A~, Mr Roberts*, (in comm or official correspondence) This letter, memorandum, etc is to be dealt, with by Mr Roberts. (用于商业信件或公函中)本信件, 便函等由罗伯茨先生承办. **2** (often *pl*) kind or polite act: (常用复数)殷勤; 厚待: *They showed the old lady numerous little ~s*, were kind and helpful in numerous ways. 他们对那老太太殷勤款待, 无微不至. *A pretty girl usually receives more ~(s) than a plain girl*, finds men more willing to do things for her. 一个漂亮的女孩通常比一个不漂亮的女孩得到较多(男子所献)的殷勤. *pay one's ~s to a lady*, (dated) court her, be polite and kind in the hope of winning her affections. (过时用语)向某女士献殷勤; 追求某女士. **3** [U] (mil) drill position in which a man stands straight and still: (军)立正之姿势: *come to/stand at ~*; 立正; (as a military command): (用作军队之口令): *A~!* 立正! (shortened to 略作 *'shun* /ʃʌn; ʃʌn/).

at·tent·ive /əˈtentɪv; əˈtɛntɪv/ *adj ~ (to)*, giving or paying attention: 注意的; 留心的; 专心的; 殷勤的; 关怀的: *A speaker likes to have an ~ audience.* 演说者喜欢听众专心听. *Please be more ~ to your studies.* 请多用点心读书. *A good host is ~ to (the needs of) his guests.* 好主人留心客人的(需要). *She was always ~ to her young brother.* 她总是注意照料她的幼弟. ~·**ly** *adv*: *They listened ~ly to the teacher.* 他们专心听老师(讲话).

at·tenu·ate /əˈtenjʊeɪt; əˈtɛnjʊˌet/ *vt* [VP6A] (formal) make thin or slender; weaken; reduce. (正式用语)使变细; 使变弱; 使变薄; 减少.

at·test /əˈtest; əˈtɛst/ *vt, vi* **1** [VP6A] be or give clear proof of: 证明; 是…的明证: *The man's ability was ~ed by his rapid promotion*, His promotion was proof of his ability. 那人的能力由于他的迅速升迁而得到证明(他的迅速擢升是他能干的证明). *These papers ~ the fact that ...*. 这些文件证明了这个事实…. *~ a signature*, make it legal by witnessing it. 见证签字(签自己之名于另一签名之旁, 以证明签名属实而使生法律效力). ~**ed 'milk/'cattle**, certified free of disease, esp tuberculosis. 经检验合格的牛奶(经证明无病, 尤指无结核病的牛). **2** [VP6A] declare on oath; put (a person) on oath; cause (sb) to declare solemnly: 宣誓说出; 使发誓; 使郑重宣布: *I have said nothing that I am not ready to ~*, to say on oath. 我说的话句句属实, 皆可立誓为证. **3** [VP2A] enrol for military service (by taking the oath of allegiance). (宣誓)入伍; 从军. **4** [VP3A] ~ *to*, bear witness to: 为…作证: *feats which ~ to his strength of will.* 证明他坚强意志的功绩.

at·tic /ˈætɪk; ˈætɪk/ *n* space within the roof of a house: 屋顶下的小室; 顶楼; 阁楼: *two small rooms in the ~*. 顶楼的两个小房间.

At·tic /ˈætɪk; ˈætɪk/ *adj* of ancient Athens or Attica. 雅典的; 阿提喀(古希腊之一地区, 其首府为雅典)的.

at·tire /əˈtaɪə(r); əˈtaɪr/ *n* [U] (liter or poet) dress: (文或诗)服装: *in holiday ~*. 穿着假日的服装. □ *vt* [VP6A] (dated) dress: (过时用语)穿着: *~d in white/ satin*. 穿着白色的(缎制的)衣服.

at·ti·tude /ˈætɪtjuːd; ˈætəˌtjud/ *n* [C] **1** manner of placing or holding the body: 姿势; 姿态: *He stood there in a threatening ~*. 他以威胁的姿态站在那里. *strike an ~*, suddenly and dramatically take up an ~. 突然而戏剧性地摆出一种姿态. 装模作样. **2** way of feeling, thinking or behaving: 态度;意见;看法:

What is your ~ towards this question, What do you think about it, how do you propose to act? 你对这问题的态度如何? *We must maintain a firm ~*, not show signs of weakness. 我们应坚决的态度. **at·ti·tu·din·ize** /ˌætɪˈtjuːdɪnaɪz; US: -ˈtuːdən-, ˌætɪˈtjudnˌaɪz/ *vi* [VP2A] strike ~s; speak, write, behave in an affected way. 突然而戏剧性地做出一种姿态, 装模作样; 以娇饰的态度说话、写作或行动; 矫揉造作.

at·tor·ney /əˈtɜːnɪ; əˈtɝnɪ/ *n* (*pl ~s*) **1** person with legal authority to act for another in business or law: (在法律上有权代理他人办理业务或诉讼之)代理人; *letter/warrant of ~*, written authority by which a person appoints another to act for him; (委托他人代理之)委托书; *power of ~*, authority so given. 受委托代理之权;委托权. **2** *A~ 'General*, (a) legal officer with authority to act in all cases in which the State is a party, usu *district ~*. 首席检察官; 检察长(通常为地方检察官). (b) (US, in some States) public prosecutor. (美, 某州内的)检察官. **3** solicitor. 律师.

at·tract /əˈtrækt; əˈtrækt/ *vt* [VP6A] **1** pull towards (by unseen force): 吸引: *A magnet ~s steel.* 磁石吸引钢. **2** get the attention of; arouse interest or pleasure in: 引起…之注意或兴趣: *Bright colours ~ babies.* 鲜艳的颜色可引起婴孩的注意. *Bright lights ~ moths.* 亮光可招引灯蛾. *He shouted to ~ attention.* 他高声喊叫以引起别人注意. *Do you feel ~ed to her*, Do you like her? 你感到她对你有吸引力吗?

at·trac·tion /əˈtrækʃn; əˈtrækʃən/ *n* **1** [U] power of pulling towards: 吸引力: *The ~ of the moon for the earth causes the tides.* 月球对地球的吸引力造成潮汐. *He cannot resist the ~ of the sea on a hot day/of a pretty girl.* 他无法抗拒热天里海的(漂亮女郎的)吸引力. *The cinema has little ~ for some people.* 电影对某些人没有什么吸引力. **2** [C] that which attracts: 吸引人的事物: *the ~s of a big city*, eg theatres, concerts, cinemas, fine shops. 大城市之诱人之处(例如戏院, 音乐会, 电影院, 漂亮的商店).

at·trac·tive /əˈtræktɪv; əˈtræktɪv/ *adj* having the power to attract; pleasing: 有吸引力的; 动人的; 诱人的: *a most ~ girl*; 非常诱人的女郎; *goods offered at ~ prices*. 标价低廉诱人的货品. ~·**ly** *adv*

at·tribute[1] /əˈtrɪbjuːt; əˈtrɪbjʊt/ *vt* [VP14] ~ *to*, consider as a quality of, as being the result of, as coming from: 认为是…的属性; 是…的结果或来自…; 归于; 归因于: *He ~s wisdom to his teachers*, thinks they have wisdom. 他认为他的老师都很有智慧. *He ~s his success to hard work*, says that his success is the result of hard work. 他认为他的成功系由努力来的. *This comedy has been ~d to Shakespeare*, it has been said that Shakespeare was the author. 这个喜剧据说为莎士比亚所作. **at·tribu·table** /əˈtrɪbjʊtəbl; əˈtrɪbjʊtəbl/ *adj* that can be ~d (*to*). 可归(因于…的)(与 *to* 连用). **at·tri·bu·tion** /ˌætrɪˈbjuːʃn; ˌætrəˈbjuʃən/ *n* [U] **1** act of attributing (*to*); [C] that which is ~d. 归属; 归因; 所归属之事物.

at·tribute[2] /ˈætrɪbjuːt; ˈætrəˌbjut/ *n* [C] **1** quality looked upon as naturally or necessarily belonging to sb or sth: 性质; 属性: *Mercy is an ~ of God.* 宽恕是上帝的属性. *Politeness is an ~ of a gentleman.* 彬彬有礼是绅士的本色. **2** material object recognized as a symbol of a person or his position: (被认为代表某人或其地位的)象征: *The crown is an ~ of kingship.* 王冠是王位的象征.

at·tribu·tive /əˈtrɪbjuːtɪv; əˈtrɪbjətɪv/ *adj* ~ adjective, naming a quality and used with the noun as in 'old man', 'red hair', and contrasted with predicative. 定语形容词(指出一种性质, 并与名词连用, 如 old man, red hair 者, 与 predicative 相对). ~·**ly** *adv*

at·tri·tion /əˈtrɪʃn; əˈtrɪʃən/ *n* [U] wearing away by rubbing: 消耗; 消磨; 磨损: *war of ~*, war in which each side waits for the other to wear itself out. 消耗战.

at·tune /əˈtjuːn; *US*: əˈtuːn; əˈtjun/ *vt* [VP14] ~ *to*, bring into harmony or agreement with: 使协调; 使一致; 使适合: *hearts ~d to worship*; 适合礼拜之心情; *make used to*: 使习惯于: *ears ~d to the sound of gunfire*. 习惯于炮声的耳朵。

au·ber·gine /ˈəʊbəʒiːn; ˈobəˌʒin/ *n* [C] fruit of the eggplant, used as a vegetable. 茄子。 ⇨ the illus at **vegetable.** 参看 vegetable 之插图。

au·bri·e·tia /ɔːˈbriːʃə; ɔˈbriʃə/ *n* (kinds of) spring-flowering dwarf perennial grown on stone walls, rockeries, etc. 十字花科植物(春季开花之矮小的多年生植物, 生长于石墙, 假山等之上)。

au·burn /ˈɔːbən; ˈbən/ *adj* (usu of hair) reddish-brown. (通常指头发)赤褐色的; 赭色的。

auc·tion /ˈɔːkʃn; ˈɔkʃən/ *n* [C,U] public sale at which goods are sold to the persons making the highest bids or offers: 拍卖: *sale by ~*; 拍卖; *~-sale*; 拍卖; *sell goods by ~*; 拍卖货物; *put sth up to/for ~*; 将某物交付拍卖; *attend all the local ~s*; 本地所有各次拍卖全都到场; ~ *bridge*, ⇨ **bridge**[2]. □ *vt* [VP6A, 15B] *~ (off)*, sell by ~. 拍卖。*~·eer* /ˌɔːkʃəˈnɪə(r); ˌɔkʃənˈɪr/ *n* person who conducts an ~. 拍卖人。

aud·acious /ɔːˈdeɪʃəs; ɔˈdeʃəs/ *adj* 1 daring; bold. 大胆的; 勇敢的。 2 foolishly bold. 愚勇的。 3 impudent. 厚颜的; 无耻的。*~·ly* *adv* **aud·ac·ity** /ɔːˈdæsɪtɪ; ɔˈdæsəti/ *n*

aud·ible /ˈɔːdəbl; ˈɔdəbl/ *adj* loud enough to be heard: 可听见的; 听得见的: *in a scarcely ~ voice*. 以几乎听不见的声音。*The speaker was scarcely ~*, could be heard only with difficulty. 那演说者的声音小得几乎听不见。**aud·ibly** /-əblɪ; -əblɪ/ *adv* **audi·bil·ity** *n* /ˌɔːdəˈbɪlətɪ; ˌɔdəˈbɪləti/ *n* capacity for being heard. 可听见的程度; 能听度; 可闻度。

audi·ence /ˈɔːdɪəns; ˈɔdɪəns/ *n* 1 gathering of persons for the purpose of hearing a speaker, singer, etc: (集合在一起的)听众; 观众: *There was a large ~ in the theatre*. 剧院中的观众很多。*He has addressed large ~s all over England.* 他曾在英国各地向大群的听众演说。 2 persons within hearing, whether they are together or not: 在听得见的范围内的人(无论是否集合在一起): *A broadcaster may have an ~ of several million.* 广播演说者可能有几百万的听众。 3 (of a book) readers: (书的)读者: *His book has reached a wide ~.* 他的书已拥有广大的读者。 4 formal interview given by a ruler, the Pope, etc: (统治者, 教皇等所准许的)谒见; 觐见: *The Pope granted him an ~.* 教皇准许他谒见。*The Prime Minister was received in ~ by the Queen.* 首相被女王召见了。

audio- /ˈɔːdɪəʊ; ˈɔdɪˌo/ *pref* of hearing. 听。*~-visual* **'aids,** teaching aids such as record players and film projectors. 直观教具; 视听教具(如唱机及放映机等)。*,~-lingual* **'methods,** teaching methods making use of a language laboratory, tape recorders, etc. 耳听口说教学法(利用语言实验室, 录音机等)。*~* **'frequency,** (radio) frequency which, when converted into sound waves by a loudspeaker, can be heard. (无线电)成音频率; 音额。

au·dit /ˈɔːdɪt; ˈɔdɪt/ *n* official examination of accounts to see that they are in order. 审计; 帐目稽核; 查帐。□ *vt* [VP6A] examine, eg accounts, officially. 审计; 稽核(帐目等)。

aud·ition /ɔːˈdɪʃn; ɔˈdɪʃən/ *n* 1 [C] trial hearing to test the voice of a singer, speaker, etc who is applying for employment or of an actor wishing to take part in a play. (对于歌唱者, 演说者求职时或演员欲扮演剧中角色时的)试听。 2 [U] power of hearing; listening. 听力; 听。□ *vt* [VP6A] give an ~ to. 试听。

au·di·tor /ˈɔːdɪtə(r); ˈɔdɪtɚ/ *n* 1 listener to a speaker, etc. (演说者等的)听者。 2 person who audits. 查帐员。审计员; 稽核员。

au·di·tor·ium /ˌɔːdɪˈtɔːrɪəm; ˌɔdəˈtorɪəm/ *n* (*pl ~s*) building, or part of a building, in which an audience sits. 会堂; 礼堂; 演讲厅; 音乐厅。

au·di·tory /ˈɔːdɪtrɪ; ˈɔdəˌtɔrɪ/ *adj* of the sense of hearing: 听觉的: *the ~ nerve*. 听(觉)神经。⇨ the illus at **ear.** 参看 ear 之插图。

au fait /ˌəʊ ˈfeɪ; oˈfe/ *pred adj* (F) instructed: (法)熟谙; 精通: *put sb ~ of sth*, instruct him about it. 教某人使之精通某事。

au fond /ˌəʊ ˈfɒn; ˌoˈfɔ̃/ *adv* (F) basically. (法)基本上; 根本地。

au·ger /ˈɔːɡə(r); ˈɔɡɚ/ *n* carpenter's tool for boring large holes in wood, with a handle at right angles; instrument for boring in soil. (钻木或钻土用的)螺旋钻。⇨ the illus at **tool.** 参见 tool 之插图。

aught /ɔːt; ɔt/ *n* (archaic) anything: (古)任何事物: *for ~ I know/care*, used to indicate that the speaker does not know/care at all. 我根本不知道(在乎)。

aug·ment /ɔːɡˈment; ɔɡˈmɛnt/ *vt, vi* [VP6A, 2A] make or become greater; increase: 增大; 增加; *~ one's income by writing short stories.* 借写短篇小说而增加其收入。**aug·men·ta·tion** /ˌɔːɡmenˈteɪʃn; ˌɔɡmɛnˈteʃən/ *n* [U] ~ing or being ~ed; [C] sth added. 增大; 增加; 增加之物。

au·gur /ˈɔːɡə(r); ˈɔɡɚ/ *n* (in ancient Rome) religious official who claimed to foretell future events by omens from the entrails of birds, etc. (古罗马) 教会中之占兆官 (据称能根据鸟之内脏 等之征兆预卜吉凶)。□ *vi, vt* [VP6A, 2A] foretell, be a sign of: 预兆; 预示: *Does this news ~ war?* 这消息预示将有战争吗? *~ well/ill (for sb/sth),* be a good/bad sign for the future, for us. 预示(某人或某事之)吉(凶)兆。*~·y* /ˈɔːɡjʊrɪ; ˈɔɡjɚi/ *n* (*pl -ries*) [C] omen; sign. 征兆; 预兆。

au·gust /ɔːˈɡʌst; ɔˈɡʌst/ *adj* majestic; causing feelings of respect or awe. 威严的; 令人敬畏的。

Au·gust /ˈɔːɡəst; ˈɔɡəst/ *n* the eighth month. 八月。

Au·gust·an /ɔːˈɡʌstən; ɔˈɡʌstən/ *adj* of the best period of Latin literature; classical; of the period of English Literature including Dryden, Pope and Swift. 拉丁文学之全盛时期的; 古典的; 英国文学全盛时期(包括 Dryden, Pope 及 Swift 之时代)的。

auk /ɔːk; ɔk/ *n* northern seabird, with short wings used in swimming. 海雀 (北方海鸟, 有用以游水的短翅)。

auld lang syne /ˌɔːld læŋ ˈsaɪn; ˌɔld læŋ ˈsaɪn/ (Scot, name of song) good times long ago. (苏, 歌曲名) 美好的往事。

aunt /ɑːnt; *US*: ænt; ænt/ *n* sister of one's father or mother; wife of one's uncle. 姑母; 姨母; 婶母; 伯母; 舅母。*,A~* **'Sally,** wooden model of a woman's head, at which sticks are thrown, at fairs, etc; (fig) object, person, widely abused. 木人模型的女人头 (游乐场等中之一种娱乐游戏, 玩者以木棒向之投掷); (喻)众矢之的; 广受人指责的人或对象。**aun·tie, aun·ty** /ˈɑːntɪ; *US*: ˈæntɪ; ˈæntɪ/ *n* (familiar for) aunt. aunt之俗称。

au pair /ˌəʊ ˈpeə(r); oˈpɛr/ *n* (F) (in GB) girl from overseas who, in return for light household duties, receives board and lodging, and facilities for study. (法) (在英国) 作轻松家务以换得食宿及学习环境的海外女子。

aura /ˈɔːrə; ˈɔrə/ *n* atmosphere surrounding a person or object and thought to come from him or it: 人或物发出的气味; 气氛; 氛围; 气息: *There seemed to be an ~ of holiness around the Indian saint.* 在那印度圣人的四周似乎有一种神圣的气氛。

au·ral /ˈɔːrəl; ˈɔrəl/ *adj* of the organs of hearing: 听觉器官的; 耳的。*~·ly* *adv* 从耳科医生。

aure·ole /ˈɔːrɪəʊl; ˈɔrɪˌol/ *n* halo. 光轮; 光环。

au re·voir /ˌəʊ rəˈvwɑː(r); ˌorəˈvɔr/ *int* (F) till we meet again; goodbye. (法)再见; 再会。

aur·icle /ˈɔːrɪkl; ˈɔrɪkl/ *n* 1 the external part of the ear. 外耳; 耳廓。⇨ the illus at **ear.** 参看 ear 之插图。 2 either of the two upper cavities of the heart. 心耳 (心脏上方的两穴之一)。⇨ the illus at **respiratory.** 参看

respiratory 之插图。

aur·ic·u·lar /ɔːˈrɪkjʊlə(r); əˈrɪkjələ/ adj of or near the ear: 耳的; 近耳的: ~ confession, made privately in the ear, eg of a priest. 耳语招供; 秘密告解(对教士之私下供认)。

aur·if·er·ous /ɔːˈrɪfərəs; ɔˈrɪfərəs/ adj yielding gold. 含金的; 产金的。

aur·ora /ɔːˈrɔːrə; əˈrɔrə/ n 1 A~, Roman goddess of dawn. (罗马神话中的) 黎明女神。2 ~ bor·e·a·lis /ɔːˌrɔːrə ˌbɔːrɪˈeɪlɪs; əˈrɔrə ˌbɔrrˈælɪs/ n display of coloured light, in streamers and bands, mainly red and green, seen in the sky in the regions of the North Pole; also called Northern Lights. 北极光(北极区上空所见之带状彩色射光, 主要为红色和绿色); 亦称 Northern Lights). ~ aus·tra·lis /ɔːˌrɔːrə ɒˈstreɪlɪs; ˈɔrɔrə ɔsˈtrelɪs/ n similar display seen in the southern hemisphere. 南极光(南半球所见之类似射光)。

aus·pices /ˈɔːspɪsɪz; ˈɔspɪsɪz/ n pl under (the) ~ (of), helped and favoured by: 由…主办或赞助的: under favourable ~, with the omens in one's favour, with favourable prospects. 吉利地; 顺遂地。

aus·pi·cious /ɔːˈspɪʃəs; ɔˈspɪʃəs/ adj showing signs, giving promise, of future success; favourable; prosperous. 前途光明的; 吉利的; 兴隆的。 ~·ly adv

Aus·sie /ˈɒzɪ; ˈɔsɪ/ n (sl) Australian. (俚)澳大利亚人。

aus·tere /ɔːˈstɪə(r); ɔˈstɪr/ adj 1 (of a person, his behaviour) severely moral and strict. (指人或其行为) 严肃不苟的; 严峻的。2 (of a way of living, of places, styles) simple and plain; without ornament or comfort. (指生活方式、地方、文体)质朴的; 朴素无华的。 ~·ly adv **aus·ter·ity** /ɔːˈsterɪtɪ; ɔˈsterɪtɪ/ n (pl -ties) 1 [U] quality of being ~. 严肃; 严峻; 朴素; 质朴。2 (pl) practices, eg fasting, living in a cell, for religious reasons. (复)(为宗教理由的)苦修; 苦行(如斋戒; 居于密室等)。

aut·archy /ˈɔːtɑːkɪ; ˈɔtɑrkɪ/ n [C, U] (country under) absolute sovereignty. 独裁; 专制; 独裁或专制的国家。

aut·arky /ˈɔːtɑːkɪ; ˈɔtɑrkɪ/ n [U] self-sufficiency, esp of a State in its economy. (尤指一国)自给自足; 经济独立。

auth·en·tic /ɔːˈθentɪk; ɔˈθentɪk/ adj genuine; known to be true: 真实的; 可信的; 可靠的: ~ news; 可靠消息; an ~ signature. 真的签字。**auth·en·ti·cally** /-klɪ; -klɪ/ adv ~·ity /ˌɔːθenˈtɪsətɪ; ˌɔθenˈtɪsətɪ/ n [U] quality of being ~. 真实; 确实; 可靠: feel confident of the ~ity af a signature. 深信一个签名之真实。

auth·en·ti·cate /ɔːˈθentɪkeɪt; ɔˈθentɪˌket/ vt [VP 6A] prove to be genuine; prove beyond doubt the origin, authorship, etc of. 证明…为真; 证明…之来源、作者等为无讹; 鉴定。**auth·en·ti·ca·tion** /ɔːˌθentɪˈkeɪʃn; ɔˌθentɪˈkeʃən/ n [U] authenticating. 证明为真; 鉴定。

author /ˈɔːθə(r); ˈɔθə/ n 1 writer of a book, play, etc: (书、剧本等之)作者; 著作家: Dickens is his favourite. 狄更斯是他最喜爱的作家。2 person who creates or begins sth: 创造者; 创始者: God, the A~of our being. 上帝, 我们生命的创造者。~·ess /ˈɔːθərɪs; ˈɔθɪs/ n woman ~. 女作家。~·ship /-ʃɪp; -ʃɪp/ n [U] 1 occupation of an ~: 写作生涯; 著作业: It's risky to take to ~ship (= begin to write books) for a living. 靠写作为生是冒险的。2 origin of a book, etc: (书等的)来源, 作者等: Nothing is known of the ~ship of the book, about who wrote it. 此书作者为谁不得而知。

auth·ori·tar·ian /ɔːˌθɒrɪˈteərɪən; əˌθɔrəˈterɪən/ adj supporting or requiring obedience to authority, esp that of the State, contrasted with individual liberty. 主张或要求服从(尤指政府之)权力(与个人自由相对的); 权力主义的。□ n supporter of this principle. 权力主义者。~·ism /-ɪzəm/; -ˌɪzəm/ n

auth·ori·tat·ive /ɔːˈθɒrɪtətɪv US: -tertɪv; əˈθɔrə-ˌtetɪv/ adj 1 having, given with, authority: 有权力的; 赋有权力的; 有权威的: ~ orders. 必须服从的命令。2 having an air of authority; commanding: 有权威的一种权威之神态的; 命令式的: in an ~ manner, 以命令的方式; speaking in ~ tones. 命令式的口吻说。3 that can be trusted because from a reliable source: 权威的; 来源可靠的; 可信的: an ~ report; 可信的报告; ~ information; 可靠的消息; from an ~ source. 来自权威方面的。~·ly adv

auth·or·ity /ɔːˈθɒrɪtɪ; əˈθɔrətɪ/ n (pl -ties) 1 [U] power or right to give orders and make others obey: 权力; 权威; 权势; 威信: The problem of how to cope with ~, eg wrongdoers with the police, children with parents. 如何应付权威的问题(例如为非作歹者之应付警方, 孩子之应付父母亲)。An officer has/exercises ~ over the soldiers under him. 军官有(行使)权力指挥其属下士兵。Who is in ~ here? 谁是这里的主管? He has made his ~ felt, caused people to realize that he has power to make them obey. 他已使人们感到他的权威(使人们明白他有权使他们服从)。under the ~ of; under sb's ~, responsible(1) to: 归…负责; 受…管理: These boys are under the ~ of their teacher / under his ~. 这些男孩受他们的老师的(他的)管教。2 [U] ~ (for sth/to do sth), right given to sb: 赋予某人(做某事)之权: Only the treasurer has ~ to make payments. 只有出纳员才有权付款。He had the ~ of the Governor for what he did. 他所做之事曾得省主席(州长或总督)之授权。3 [U] person or (pl) group of persons having ~: 掌权之人; (复)掌权的一群人; 当局: the City, Municipal, County, etc authorities: 市(郡等)政府当局; 本地当局的: the health authorities; 卫生当局; the A,tomic 'Energy A~. 原子能管理委员会。4 [C, U] person with special knowledge; book, etc that supplies reliable information or evidence: 具有特殊知识之人; 提供可靠资料或证据的书籍等; 权威; 权威著作: He is a great ~ on phonetics. 他是语音学方面的权威。The 'Oxford English Dictionary is the best ~ on English words. '牛津英语大词典'是关于英文字的最高权威著作。What is your ~ for that statement? 你那句话有何根据? You should quote your authorities, give the titles of books, etc, names of persons, etc used as sources for facts. 你应该注明出处。

auth·or·ize /ˈɔːθəraɪz; ˈɔθəˌraɪz/ vt 1 [VP17] give authority to: 授权与; 委托代理: I have ~d him to act for me while I am abroad. 我已委托他在我出国期间代理我的业务。2 [VP6A] give authority for: 批准; 许可: The Finance Committee ~d the spending of £10000 on a new sports ground. 财政委员会批准用一万英镑建一个新运动场。This payment has not been ~d. 这笔付款尚未获批准。A~d 'Version, (common abbr 普通略作 AV) the English translation of the Bible, first published 1611. 圣经英译之钦定本(最初出版于1611年)。**auth·or·iz·ation** /ˌɔːθəraɪˈzeɪʃn US: -rɪ'z-; ˌɔθərəˈzeʃən/ n [U] authorizing; giving legal right (to do sth, for sth); the right given. 授权; 委托(与不定式或 for 连用, 后接某事物); 所授之权。

aut·ism /ˈɔːtɪzəm; ˈɔtɪzəm/ n [U] (psych) severe form of mental illness in children. (心理)孤独癖; 孤独性; 自闭(小孩的心理病态)。**aut·is·tic** /ɔːˈtɪstɪk; ɔˈtɪstɪk/ adj of ~: 孤独癖的; 孤独性的; 自闭的: autistic children. 孤独癖的小孩。

auto /ˈɔːtəʊ; ˈɔto/ n (US colloq abbr of) **automo·bile**. (美口)汽车(为 automobile 之略)。

auto- /ˈɔːtəʊ; ˈɔto/ pref (in compounds) self-, by oneself; independent(ly). 自己(用于复合词中)自己; 自身; 自行: ~intoxication, poisoning by substances produced within the body. 自身中毒; 自体中毒。'~changer, device (on a record-player) that plays a number of discs in succession without attention. (唱机上的)自动换片装置。

au·to·bahn /ˈɔːtəbɑːn; ˈɔtəˌbɑn/ n (pl ~s or (pl) ~en /-nən; -nən/) (G) (德) = **motorway**.

au·to·bi·ogra·phy /ˌɔːtəbaɪˈɒɡrəfɪ; ˌɔtəbaɪˈɑgrəfɪ/ *n* (*pl* **-phies**) 1 [C] story of a person's life written by himself. 自传. 2 [U] the art and practice of this sort of writing. 自传作法; 自传写作. **auto·bio·graphic** /ˌɔːtəbaɪəˈɡræfɪk; ˌɔtə,baɪəˈɡræfɪk/, **auto·bio·graphi·cal** /-ɪkl; -ɪkl/ *adjj* of, engaged in, ~. 自传的; 从事写作自传的.

au·toc·racy /ɔːˈtɒkrəsɪ; ɔˈtɑkrəsɪ/ *n* (*pl* **-cies**) 1 [U] government by a ruler who has unlimited power. 独裁政治; 专制政治. 2 [C] (country with a) government of this kind. 独裁政府; 独裁国家. **au·to·crat** /ˈɔːtəkræt; ˈɔtə,kræt/ *n* ruler with unlimited power; person who requires things to be done without considering the wishes of others. 独裁者; 专制者; 专横霸道的人. **~ic** /ˌɔːtəˈkrætɪk; ˌɔtəˈkrætɪk/ *adj* of or like an ~: 独裁者的; 专制的; 专横的: *Don't be so ~ic*, Don't behave as if you were an ~. 不要这样专横. **auto·crati·cally** /-klɪ; -klɪ/ *adv*

au·to·da·fé /ˌɔːtəʊ dɑː ˈfeɪ US: ˌautəu də; ˌɔtodə'fe/ *n* (*pl* **autos-da-fé** /ˌɔːtəʊz US: ˌautəuz; ˌɔtoz-/) trial and sentence of a heretic by the Inquisition; carrying out the sentence, esp by burning. 宗教法庭对异教徒之审判; 上述判决之执行(尤指将异教徒烧毙).

au·to·giro, -gyro /ˌɔːtəʊˈdʒaɪərəʊ; ˌɔtoˈdʒaɪro/ *n* (P) early form of helicopter with a propeller in front and rotors above. (商标)旋翼机(直升飞机之前身, 推进器在前方, 水平旋翼在上方).

au·to·graph /ˈɔːtəɡrɑːf US: -ɡræf; ˈɔtəˌɡræf/ *n* person's own handwriting, esp his signature: 亲笔; (尤指)亲笔签名: *~ book/album*, one in which signatures, eg of famous persons, are collected. 请人(如名人)签名留念的签名册. □ *vt* [VP6A] write one's name on or in: 签名于: *a book ~ed by the author*, 作者亲自签名的书; *an ~ed photograph*. 签名照片.

au·to·mat /ˈɔːtəmæt; ˈɔtə,mæt/ *n* (US) restaurant at which food and drink are obtained, by the customers themselves, from coin-operated closed compartments. (美)使用自动售卖机的餐馆; 自助餐厅.

au·to·mate /ˈɔːtəmeɪt; ˈɔtə,met/ *vt* (science, comm) convert to, control by, automation. (科学, 商)使自动化; 使自动操作; 使自动作业.

au·to·matic /ˌɔːtəˈmætɪk; ˌɔtəˈmætɪk/ *adj* 1 self-acting; self-moving; (of a machine) able to work or be worked without attention: 自动的; (指机器)不需人照料而能自行操作的: *an ~ pilot*, (on an aircraft) maintaining altitude, course, etc; (飞机上的)自动驾驶仪(保持高度, 航线等); *~ gear-change* (in a motor-vehicle); (汽车中的)自动变换排档; *~ weapons*, weapons that continue firing until pressure on the trigger is released. 自动武器(扣动扳机即继续发射的武器). 2 (of actions) done without thought; unconscious: (指动作)无意识的; 不自觉的: *Breathing is ~*. 呼吸是无意识的动作. □ *n* small ~ firearm. 小型自动武器. **au·to·mati·cally** /-klɪ; -klɪ/ *adv*

au·to·ma·tion /ˌɔːtəˈmeɪʃn; ˌɔtəˈmeʃən/ *n* [U] (use of) methods and machines to save human labour. 节省人力的方法与机器; 节省人力的方法与机器的使用; 自动化作业.

au·to·ma·ton /ɔːˈtɒmətən US: -tɒn; ɔˈtɑme,tɑn/ *n* (*pl* **~s**, **-ta** /-tə/; -tə/) person who appears to act involuntarily or without active intelligence; robot. 动作机械的人; 不善运用智力的人; 机器人.

au·to·mo·bile /ˈɔːtəməbiːl US: ˌɔːtəməˈbiːl; ˈɔtəmə-ˌbil/ *n* (esp US) motor-car. (尤美)汽车.

au·ton·omous /ɔːˈtɒnəməs; ɔˈtɑnəməs/ *adj* (of states) self-governing; free. (指州或那等)自治的; 自治权的; 自由的. **au·ton·omy** /ɔːˈtɒnəmɪ; ɔˈtɑnəmɪ/ *n* (*pl* **-mies**) [U, C] (right of) self-government; freedom. 自治; 自治权; 自由.

au·topsy /ˈɔːtɒpsɪ; ˈɔtɑpsɪ/ *n* (*pl* **-sies**) [C] (med) postmortem examination of a body (by cutting it open) to learn the cause of death. (医)尸体剖检(以追查死因).

⇨ **biopsy.**

au·to·strada /ˌautəʊˈstrɑːdə; ˌautoˈstrɑdə/ *n* (*pl* **~s**, (I) **-de** /-ˈstrɑːdeɪ; -ˈstrɑde/) (I) (意) = motorway.

au·tumn /ˈɔːtəm; ˈɔtəm/ *n* [C] (US 美 = *fall*) third season of the year, between summer and winter (Sept, Oct and Nov in the northern hemisphere): 秋; 秋天; 秋季: *in ~*; 在秋季; 秋天里; *in the ~ of 1980*; 在 1980 年之秋; *in (the) early/late ~*, 在初(晚)秋; (fig) (喻) *in the ~ of his life*; 在他的垂暮(开始衰老)之年; (attrib) (用作定语) *~ weather/fashions*. 秋天的天气(秋季的款式). **au·tum·nal** /ɔːˈtʌmnl; ɔˈtʌmnl/ *adj* of ~. 秋的; 秋天的; 秋季的.

aux·ili·ary /ɔːɡˈzɪlɪərɪ; ɔɡˈzɪljərɪ/ *adj* helping; supporting: 辅助的; 帮助的: *~ troops*, 辅助部队; *an ~ verb* (eg is in *He is working*; has in *He has gone*). 助动词(例如 He is working 中的 is, He has gone 中的 has, 均为助动词). □ *n* (*pl* **-ries**) 1 ~ verb. 助动词. 2 (usu *pl*) ~ troops (esp troops hired from a foreign or allied country, eg in the Roman Empire in ancient times). (通常用复数)辅助部队. (尤指昔日古罗马帝国所雇佣的)外籍辅助部队.

avail /əˈveɪl; əˈvel/ *vt, vi* 1 [VP14] ~ *oneself of*, make use of, profit by, take advantage of: 利用: *You should ~ yourself of every opportunity to practise speaking English*. 你应该利用每一个机会练习说英语. 2 [VP2A, 3A] (liter) be of value or help: (文)有价值; 有帮助; 有用: *Money does not ~ on a desert island*. 金钱在荒岛上没有用处. *Nothing ~ed against the storm*. 无一物可用以抵御暴风雨. □ *n of no/little ~*, not helpful; not effective: 无助的; 无效的; 无用的: *His intervention was of little ~*. 他的调停无效. *without ~*; *to no ~*, without result; unsuccessfully: 无结果; 无效; 不成功地: *We pulled him out of the river and tried to revive him, but to no ~*. 我们把他从河里拉出来, 并试图使他恢复知觉, 但是不成功. *Of what ~ is it to ...*, *What use is it to ...?* 有什么益处?

avail·able /əˈveɪləbl; əˈveləbl/ *adj* ~ (*for*) 1 (of objects) able to be used; that may be obtained: (指物) 可用的; 有效的; 可获得的: *These tickets are ~ for one month only*. 这些票的有效期仅为一个月. *The book you ordered is not ~*. 你订购的那本书没有货. 2 (of persons) able to be present: (指人)能出席的: *Are you ~ (for a meeting) tomorrow morning?* 你明天上午能出席(会议)吗? **avail·abil·ity** /əˌveɪləˈbɪlətɪ; ə,veləˈbɪlətɪ/ *n* [U]

ava·lanche /ˈævəlɑːnʃ US: -lænt; ˈævl,ænt/ *n* great mass of snow and ice at a high altitude, caused by its own weight to slide down a mountain side, often carrying with it thousands of tons of rock, and sometimes destroying forests, houses, etc in its path: 雪崩(大量冰雪因自身之重量自高山崩落, 常携带巨量岩石, 可毁坏森林、房舍等): (fig) (喻) *an ~ of words/letters/questions*. 滔滔不绝的言辞(如雪片飞来的信件); 一涌而至的问题.

avant-garde /ˌævɒn ˈɡɑːd; ˌɑvanˈɡard/ *n* (F) vanguard of an army; (fig) radical leader(s) of any movement (in art, drama, literature, etc): (法)先锋; 前锋; (喻)(艺术, 戏剧, 文学等之)激进派; 先驱; 前卫派; (attrib) (用作定语) *~ writers/artists*. 前卫派作家(艺术家).

av·ar·ice /ˈævərɪs; ˈævərɪs/ *n* [U] greed(for money or possessions); great eagerness to get or keep. 贪婪; 贪心. **av·ar·icious** /ˌævəˈrɪʃəs; ˌævəˈrɪʃəs/ *adj* ~ (*of*), greedy (of money, power, etc). 贪婪的; 贪心的; 贪求的. **av·ar·icious·ly** *adv*

avast /əˈvɑːst US: əˈvæst; əˈvæst/ *int* (naut) Stop! (航海)停住!

ava·tar /ˈævətɑː(r); ˌævəˈtar/ *n* (Hindu myth) (descent to earth of a) deity in human or animal form. (印度神话)(化身作凡人或动物之)天神; 天神下凡.

avaunt /əˈvɔːnt; əˈvɔnt/ *int* (old use) Begone; Go away! (旧用法)走开! 去!

avenge /ə'vendʒ; ə'vɛndʒ/ vt [VP6A, 14] get or take vengeance for: 为…报仇; 报复: ~ an insult; 为受辱而报复; ~ oneself/be ~d on an enemy (for an injury, etc). (为伤害等)向仇敌报复。He ~d his father's death upon the murderer, punished the murderer. 他报了杀父之仇(即已惩凶)。**aven·ger** n

av·enue /'ævənju US: -nu:; 'ævə,nu/ n 1 road with trees on each side, esp the private road going up to a large country house. 林荫道; 两侧有树的道路(尤指通往大庄园的私人道路)。2 wide street with buildings on one or both sides. (城市中一侧或两侧建筑物林立的)大街; 大马路。3 ~ (to), (fig) way (to some object or aim): (喻)(达到某种目的或目标的)方法; 途径: ~s to success/promotion. 成功(晋升)的途径。

aver /ə'vɜ:(r); ə'vʌs/ vt (-rr-) [VP6A, 9] ~ (that), (old use) state positively (that sth is true). (旧用法)断言; 确言(某事为真实)。

av·er·age /'ævərɪdʒ; 'ævərɪdʒ/ n 1 [C] result of adding several quantites together and dividing the total by the number of quantities: The ~ of 4, 5 and 9 is 6. 4, 5, 9 的平均数是 6。2 [U] standard or level regarded as ordinary or usnal: 一般的水准; 平均标准: Tom's work at school is above (the) ~, Harry's is below (the) ~ and Jim's is about up to (the) ~. 汤姆在校的功课在一般水准之上, 哈里的功课在一般水准之下, 吉姆的功课接近一般水准。on (an/the) ~, according to the ~: 根据平均标准; 平均而言: On (an/the) ~, there are twenty boys present every day. 平均说来, 每天有二十个男生出席。□ adj 1 found by making an ~: 平均的: The ~ age of the boys in this class is fifteen. 本班男生的平均年龄是十五岁。What's the ~ temperature in this town in August? 这市八月里的平均气温是多少? 2 of the ordinary or usual standard: 一般标准的; 普通的; 平常的: boys of ~ intelligence; 智力平常的男生; men of ~ ability. 能力普通的人。□ vt, vi 1 [VP6A] find the ~ of: 求…的平均数: If you ~ 7, 14 and 6, you get 9. 如果你求 7, 14 和 6 的平均数, 得 9。2 [VP2B] amount to an ~; do as an ~: 平均达到(数目); 平均做; 平均分配: ~ 200 miles a day during a journey. 旅程中平均每天行 200 英里。The rainfall ~s 36 inches a year. 雨量平均每年达 36 英寸。

averse /ə'vɜ:s; ə'vɜs/ adj ~ from/to, opposed, disinclined: 反对的; 嫌恶的; 不愿的: He is ~ to hard work. 他嫌恶繁重的工作。We are ~ from taking action. 我们不愿采取行动。

aver·sion /ə'vɜ:ʃn US: -ʒn; ə'vʒən/ n 1 [C, U] ~ to, strong dislike: 厌恶; 嫌恶: He has a strong ~ to getting up early. 他非常厌恶早起。He took an ~ to me. 他讨厌我。Do you feel any ~ to hard study? 你讨厌用功读书吗? 2 [C] sth or sb disliked. 讨厌之事物或人。pet ~, sth specially disliked. 特别讨厌的事物。

avert /ə'vɜ:t; ə'vɜt/ vt 1 [VP14] ~ (from), turn away (one's eyes, thoughts, etc): 转移 (目光, 思想等): ~ one's eyes/gaze from a terrible spectacle. 转移目光不看可怕的景象。2 [VP6A] prevent, avoid: 防止; 避免: ~ an accident; 避免灾祸; ~ suspicion; 避免嫌疑; ~ failure by hard work. 努力工作以免失败。

avi·ary /'eɪvɪərɪ US: -vɪerɪ; 'evi,ɛrɪ/ n (pl -ries) place for keeping birds, eg in a zoo. 大鸟笼; 鸟舍(如动物园中者)。

avi·ation /,eɪvɪ'eɪʃn; ,evi'eʃən/ n [U] (art and science of) flying in aircraft. 航空; 飞行; 航空术; 航空学。'~ spirit, high-octane motor spirit used in aircraft engines. 航空用酒精(含高辛烷, 用于飞机引擎者)。**avi·ator** /'eɪvɪeɪtə(r); 'evi,etə/ n airman (now usu pilot or captain) who controls an aircraft, airship or balloon. 航空员; 飞行员; (飞机、飞艇或气球之)驾驶员(今常用pilot或 captain)。

avid /'ævɪd; 'ævɪd/ adj ~ for, eager, greedy: 热望的; 贪求的; 贪图的: ~ for fame/applause. 热望名声(渴望受赞赏)的。~·ly adv ~·ity /ə'vɪdətɪ; ə'vɪdətɪ/ n [U] eagerness: 渴望; 热切: He accepted the offer with

~ity. 他热切地采纳了该项建议。

avo·cado /,ævə'kɑ:dəu; ,ævə'kɑdo/ n (pl ~s /-dəuz; -doz/) (also 亦作 alligator pear) pearshaped tropical fruit. 鳄梨(一种梨状之热带水果)。⇨ the illus at fruit. 参看 fruit 之插图。

avo·ca·tion /,ævə'keɪʃn; ,ævə'keʃən/ n (formal) occupation that is not a person's ordinary business. (正式用语)副业; 业余的爱好。

avoid /ə'vɔɪd; ə'vɔɪd/ vt [VP6A, C] keep or get away from; escape: 避免; 避开; 逃避: Try to ~ danger. 尽力避免危险。We only just ~ed an accident. 我们幸免于一场灾祸。You can hardly ~ meeting her if you both work in the same office. 如果你们两人在同一个办公室做事, 你几乎免不了要遇见她。~·able /-əbl; -əbl/ adj that can be ~ed. 可避免的。~·ance /-əns; -ns/ n [U] act of ~ing: 避免; 避开; 逃避: the ~ance of bad companions; 避免交坏朋友; ~ance of taxation, eg by not buying taxed goods such as tobacco and wine. 避税 (如不买有税的货物, 如烟酒)。

avoir·du·pois /,ævədə'pɔɪz; ,ævədə'pɔɪz/ n system of weights used, before metrication, in most English-speaking countries (1 pound = 16 ounces), used for all goods except precious metals and stones, and medicines. 常衡(改用十进制前大多数英语国家所用之衡制, 一磅等于十六盎司, 除贵金属、宝石、药品外, 一切货物均适用)。⇨ App 5. 参看附录五。

avouch /ə'vautʃ; ə'vautʃ/ vt, vi [VP6A, 9, 3A] (liter; now rare) assert; guarantee: (文; 今罕用) 确言; 担保; 保证; ~ (for) sth. 保证某事物。

avow /ə'vau; ə'vau/ vt [VP6A, 25 reflex VP25 用反身式] (formal) admit; declare openly: (正式用语) 承认; 公开宣布: ~ a fault. 承认错误。He ~ed himself (to be) a Christian. 他公开宣布他是基督教徒。~·al /-əl; -əl/ n [U] free and open confession; [C] instance of this: 坦白承认; [C]公开表示: make an ~al of one's sentiments. 公开表示自己的看法。~·ed·ly /ə'vauɪdlɪ; ə'vauɪdlɪ/ adv by confession; openly: 自认地; 公开地: He was ~edly in the wrong. 他自认错误。

avun·cu·lar /ə'vʌŋkjulə(r); ə'vʌŋkjələ/ adj (joc) of or like an uncle (esp a benevolent uncle). (谑)伯父或叔父之(尤指仁慈者)的; 如伯(叔)父的。

await /ə'weɪt; ə'wet/ vt [VP6A] 1 (of persons) wait for: (指人)等候: I ~ your instructions. 我等候你的指示。2 be in store for; be waiting for: 准备以待; 等待: A hearty welcome ~s you. 热烈的欢迎等待着你。Death ~s all men. 死亡等待着所有的人。

awake[1] /ə'weɪk; ə'wek/ vi (pt awoke /ə'wəuk; ə'wok/, pp (rare) (罕) awoken or ~d) 1 [VP2A] = wake. (awake is preferred for the fig uses, intrans, and awaken for the fig uses, trans.) (在比喻用法中, awake 以作 vi 较佳, awaken 以作 vt 较佳)。2 [VP3A] ~ to, become conscious of, realize: 觉醒; 醒悟; 觉悟; 明察; 领会: He awoke to his opportunities. 他觉察到他的机会。You must ~ to the fact (= You must realize) that failure will mean disgrace. 你必须觉悟到失败即是耻辱这一事实。When he awoke to his surroundings ..., realized where he was .... 当他明白了他所处的环境时 ...。[VP4B] He awoke to find himself famous, learnt, the next day, that he was famous. 他一觉醒来, 发现自己已经成名。

awake[2] /ə'weɪk; ə'wek/ pred adj roused from sleep: 被唤醒的; 醒着的: Is he ~ or asleep? 他是醒着还是睡着? ~ to, aware of: 知晓; 觉察: be ~ to what is going on/to a danger/to one's own interests. 了解正在进行中的事(危险, 自身的利益)。

awaken /ə'weɪkən; ə'wekən/ vt 1 [VP6A] =awake (awaken is preferred for fig uses, trans). (awaken 在比喻用法中以作 vt 较佳)。2 [VP14] ~ sb to sth, make sb aware of: 使某人知道; 唤起某人: ~ sb to a sense of his responsibility/to a sense of shame. 唤起某人的责任感(羞耻之心)。~·ing /ə'weɪknɪŋ; ə'wekənɪŋ/ n act of becoming aware, of realizing, esp sth unpleasant:

觉醒; 觉悟; 明白(尤指不愉快之事物): *It was a rude ~ing when he was told that he was to be dismissed for inefficiency.* 当他听说他将因工作效率低而被革职时, 他才猛然觉悟。

award /ə'wɔːd; ə'wɔrd/ vt [VP6A,12A,13A] give or grant (by official decision): 颁发; 授与; 赏给: *He was ~ed the first prize.* 他得到第一奖。 *The judge ~ed her £200 as damages.* 法官判给她二百英镑作为赔偿损失费。 *The gold medal was ~ed to Mr Brown for his fine show of vegetables.* 布朗先生因其优异的蔬菜展览而获得金质奖章。 □ n [C] **1** decision made by a judge or arbitrator. (法官,评判员或仲裁人所作的)决定; 决断。 **2** sth given as the result of such a decision, eg a prize in a competition: 经过决定而赠与之物(例如比赛之奖品): *His horse was given the highest ~ at the show.* 他的马在展览会中得到最高奖。 **3** money granted to a student at a university, etc. (给予大学生等的)助学金。

aware /ə'weə(r); ə'wer/ pred adj ~ of/that, having knowledge or realization: 知道的; 明白的; 觉察的; 意识到的: *Are you ~ that you're sitting on my hat?* 你可知道你坐在我的帽子上吗? *We are fully ~ of the gravity of the situation.* 我们十分明白情势的严重性。 *Without being ~ of it ....* 不曾觉察(留意)到它…。 *I was not ~ (of) how deeply he had felt the death of his mother.* 我不知道他对他母亲之去世多么伤感。 **~·ness** n [U]

awash /ə'wɒʃ; ə'wɑʃ/ pred adj washed over by, level with, the waves: 为海浪所冲打的; 与海浪平齐的: *rocks ~ at high tide.* 在涨潮时为海浪所冲打的岩石。 *The ship's deck was ~.* 此船的甲板与浪头平齐。

away /ə'wei; ə'we/ part **1** to or at a distance (from the place, person, etc in question): 向远处; 在远处(离开所说之地方、人等): *The sea is two miles ~.* 海离此地两英里远。 *The shops are only a few minutes' walk ~.* 商店离此只有几分钟的步行路程。 *Is our next football match at home or ~,* on our ground or on the ground of our opponents? 下一场足球赛是在我们的球场举行还是在对方的球场举行? *It's an ~ match.* 这是一场在对方球场举行的比赛。 *Take these things ~,* remove them. 不要让小孩走近火炉。 *Don't look ~* (ie in a different direction) *while I'm taking your photograph.* 在我给你拍照的时候, 不要看别处。 **2** ~ with...*, (used in verbless exclamations): (用于无动词的惊叹句): *A~ with them!* Take them ~! 把他们带走! **3** continuously; constantly: 继续不断地; 经常地: *He was working ~.* 他在不断地工作中。 *He was laughing/muttering/grumbling ~.* 他一直在笑(喃喃自语,发牢骚)。 ⇨ **grumble(1), laugh(2), mutter. 4** (used with vv to indicate loss, lessening, weakening, exhaustion): (与动词连用, 表示损失, 减少, 变弱, 耗尽): *The water has all boiled ~,* There is no water left. 水完全熬干了。 ⇨ **blaze²(4), boil²(4), die²(6), explain(2), melt(1). 5** (in phrases): (用于短语中): *far and ~,* very much: 远较; 大为: *This is far and ~ better.* 这个远好得多。 *out and ~,* beyond comparison: 无与伦比地; 超过其他地: *This is out and ~ the best.* 这个是最好的。 *right/straight ~,* at once, without delay. 立刻; 立即。

awe¹ /ɔː; ɔ/ n [U] respect combined with fear and reverence: 敬畏: *He had a feeling of awe as he was taken before the judge.* 当他被带到法官面前, 他有一种敬畏之感。 *Savages often live in awe of nature.* 未开化的人每对自然存敬畏之心。 *The lazy boy stood in awe of his stern teacher.* 那个懒惰的男孩畏惧他那位严厉的老师。 **'awe-inspiring** adj filling with awe: 令人敬畏的: *an awe-inspiring sight.* 令人敬畏的景象。 **'awe-stricken, 'awe-struck** adj suddenly filled with awe. 敬畏的; 畏惧的; 害怕的。 **'awe·some** adj, /-səm/ adj causing awe. 引起敬畏的; 令人畏惧的。

awe² /ɔː; ɔ/ vt [VP6A, 14] *awe (into),* strike with awe: 使敬畏; 使畏惧; 威吓; 吓倒: *I was awed by his solemn words.* 我被他的严肃之词吓住了。 *He awed them into obedience.* 他把他们吓得服从了。 *The*

children were awed into silence. 孩子们被吓得不敢做声了。

aweigh /ə'wei; ə'we/ adv (naut, of an anchor) hanging just clear of the sea bottom. (航海, 指锚)刚离海底而悬着地。

aw·ful /'ɔːfl; 'ɔfl/ adj **1** terrible; dreadful: 可怕的: *He died an ~ death.* 他死得可怕。 *His sufferings were ~ to behold.* 他的痛苦看起来令人可怕。 **2** (colloq, intensive) very bad; very great; extreme of its kind: (口, 强势语)极坏的; 极其的; 非常的; 极端的: *What an ~ nuisance!* 讨厌极了! *What ~ handwriting/weather!* 多么坏的书法(天气)! **~·ly** /'ɔːfli; 'ɔfli/ adv (chiefly colloq) very (much): (主用于口语)极为; 非常: *It has been ~ly not this week.* 这个礼拜天气一直很炎热。 *I'm ~ly sorry.* 我非常抱歉。 *Thanks ~ly.* 非常感谢。

awhile /ə'wail US: ə'hwail; ə'hwail/ adv for a short time: 一会儿; 片刻; 少顷: *Stay ~.* 请逗留片刻。

awk·ward /'ɔːkwəd; 'ɔkwəd/ adj **1** (of objects, places) not well designed for use; (of circumstances, etc) likely to cause inconvenience or difficulty: (指物件, 地方)设计不良而使用起来不方便的; (指环境等)可能引起不便或困难的: *This is an ~ staircase.* 这个楼梯不便上下。 *This is an ~ corner; there have been several road accidents here.* 这是一个不好转弯的拐角; 这里曾发生过几次车祸。 *The handle of this teapot has an ~ shape.* 这个茶壶柄的形状不好用。 *The meeting was at 9 o'clock, which was an ~ time for many people.* 会定在九点钟开, 这对于许多人是一个不方便的时间。 *It's ~ that Brown should be unable to play in our team this week.* 很糟糕, 布朗本星期不能参加我队比赛。 *an ~ customer,* (colloq) person or animal difficult or dangerous to deal with. (口)难以应付之人或动物; 危险之人或动物。 **2** (of living things) clumsy; having little skill: (指生物)笨拙的; 无技巧的; 不熟练的; 不灵活的: *The child is still ~ with his knife and fork.* 这小孩还不大会用刀叉。 *Some animals are ~ on land but able to move easily in the water.* 有些动物在陆地上不灵活, 但在水中却能活动自如。 **the '~ age,** years when adolescents are lacking in selfconfidence. 尴尬的年龄(缺乏自信心的青春初期)。 **3** embarrassed: 困窘的; 局促不安的: *an ~ silence/pause.* 困窘的寂静(停顿)。 **~·ly** adv **~·ness** n

awl /ɔːl; ɔl/ n small pointed tool for making holes, esp in leather or wood. 锥子(尤指用于皮革或木头上钻孔者)。 ⇨ the illus at **tool.** 参看 tool 之插图。

awn·ing /'ɔːnɪŋ; 'ɔnɪŋ/ n canvas covering (against rain or sun), eg over a ship's deck, over or before doors or windows. 帆布篷; 雨篷; 遮日篷; 遮阳(如用于轮船甲板或门窗之上者); 天遮。

awoke ⇨ **awake.**

awry /ə'rai; ə'rai/ adv, pred adj crooked(ly); wrong(ly): 扭; 曲; 斜; 歪; 错误: *Our plans have gone ~,* have gone wrong. 我们的计划出岔子了。

ax, axe /æks; æks/ n (pl **axes** /'æksiz; 'æksiz/) tool for felling trees or splitting wood, 斧(砍树、劈木的工具; 参看 tool 之插图): ⇨ the illus at **tool:** *apply the axe to public expenditure,* reduce its cost by economies, etc. (借省钱等)削减公家的经费。 *,have an 'axe to grind,* (fig) have private interests to serve. (喻)怀有私心; 别有企图。 *get the axe,* (colloq) be dismissed from one's job. (口)被革职; 被开除。 □ vt [VP6A] (colloq) reduce, eg costs, public services; dismiss: (口)减少; 削减(成本, 公共设施等); 开除: *He's just been axed,* ie to save money. 他刚被解雇(为了节省开支)。

ax·iom /'æksiəm; 'æksiəm/ n statement accepted as true without proof or argument. 公理(无须证明或无可辩论者)。 **axio·matic** /ˌæksiə'mætik; ˌæksiə'mætik/ adj of the nature of an ~; clear and evident without proof: 具有公理之性质的; 无须证明即可明白的: *It is ~atic that a whole is greater than any of its parts.* 整体大于其任何一部分, 是不待证明即可明白的。

axis /'æksis; 'æksis/ n (pl **axes** /'æksiːz; 'æksiz/)

1 line round which a turning object spins. (旋转物体所绕以旋转之)轴. **the earth's ~**, the imaginary line joining the North and South Poles through the centre of the earth, on which the earth rotates once in twenty-four hours. 地轴(通过地心连接南北两极之假想线, 地球以此为中心每二十四小时旋转一周). **2** line that divides a regular figure into two symmetrical parts, eg the diameter of a circle. 轴线(将一正的图形分为两个匀称部分之平分线, 如圆之直径). **3** political connection (not always an alliance) between two or more states: (两个或两个以上国家之)政治联合(不一定是联盟); 轴心: *the Berlin—Rome—Tokyo A~* (before 1939); (1939 年以前之)德、意、日轴心国; *A~ powers*. 轴心列强.

axle /'æksl; 'æksl/ *n* **1** rod upon or with which a wheel turns. 轮轴. **2** bar or rod that passes through the centres of a pair of wheels: (通过两轮中心之)车轴: *the back ~ of a bus*. 公共汽车之后车轴.

ayah /'aɪə; 'ɑjə/ *n* (In India and Pakistan) native nursemaid; lady's maid-servant. (在印度及巴基斯坦, 由本地人充任之)奶妈; 保姆; 女仆.

Aya·tol·lah /ˌaɪə'tɒlə; ˌaɪə'tɑlə/ *n* title of various senior Muslim leaders in Iran. 伊朗资深的穆斯林领袖之尊称. ⇨ **Imam.**

aye[1], ay /aɪ; aɪ/ *int, adv* (Scot and regional) yes; (naval) usual reply to an order: (苏格兰及方言)是的; 对; 不错; (海军)是(答复命令的通用语): *,Aye, 'aye, sir!* 是, 是, 长官! **2** *n* vote or person supporting a proposal: 赞成某一建议的票或人: *The ayes have it,* Those for it are in the majority. 赞成者占多数; 大多数通过.

aye[2] /eɪ; e/ *adv* (old use) always: (旧用法)永远; 永久; *for ~.* 永远地; 永久地.

aza·lea /ə'zeɪliə; ə'zeljə/ *n* (kinds of) flowering shrub of the rhododendron genus. 杜鹃花.

azi·muth /'æzɪməθ; 'æzəməθ/ *n* (astron) angular distance extending from the zenith to the horizon; (surveying) angle measured clockwise from the south or north. (天文)地平经度; (测量)方位角.

az·ure /'æʒə(r); 'æʒɚ/ *adj, n* (poet) bright blue: (诗)碧蓝(的); 蔚蓝(的): *an ~ sky.* 碧蓝的天空.

Bb

B, b /biː; bi/ (*pl* **B's**, b's/biːz; biz/) the second letter of the English alphabet. 英文字母的第二个字母。

baa /bɑː; bæ/ *n* cry of a sheep or lamb. 羊叫声; 咩。 □ *vi*. (baaing, baaed or baa'd /bɑːd; bæːd/) make this cry; bleat. (羊)叫。 '**~-lamb** *n* child's word for a sheep or lamb. (儿语)羊。

baas /bɑːs; bɑs/ *n* (S Africa) boss. (南非)主人; 老板。

babble /'bæbl; 'bæbl/ *vi, vt* **1** [VP2A, B, C] talk in a way that is difficult to understand; make sounds like a baby; (of streams, etc) murmur. 说话模糊不清; 发声如婴孩; 牙牙学语; (指流水等)作潺潺声。 '**~ (out)**, repeat foolishly; tell (a secret): 喋喋; 多嘴; 泄漏(秘密): *~ (out) nonsense/ secrets.* 胡说(泄漏秘密)。 □ *n* [U] **1** childish or foolish talk; confused talk not clearly to be understood (as when many people are talking at once). 无意义的话; 听不清的话(如许多人同时谈话)。 **2** gentle sound of water flowing over stones, etc. (流水经过石上所作的)潺潺之声。 **bab·bler** /'bæblə(r); 'bæblɚ/ *n* person who ~s, esp one who tells secrets. 唠叨者; 多嘴者; (专指)泄漏秘密者。

babe /beɪb; beb/ *n* **1** (liter) baby. (文)婴儿。 **2** inexperienced and easily deceived person. 无经验而易受欺骗之人。 **3** (US sl) girl or young woman. (美俚)女子; 少女; 小妞; 妮子。

babel /'beɪbl; 'bebl/ *n* **1** the **Tower of B~,** tower built to reach heaven. (Gen 11). 巴别塔(古代巴比伦建筑未成之通天塔, 见创世纪 11 章)。 **2** (*sing with indef art*) scene of noisy and confused talking: (单数与不定冠词连用)闹哄哄的情景; 人声嘈杂的地方: *What a ~!* 多么嘈杂呵! *A ~ of voices could be heard from the schoolroom.* 可以听见教室里一阵嘈杂的声音。

ba·boo, babu /'bɑːbuː; 'bɑbu/ *n* (as Hindu title) Mr; Hindu gentleman; Hindu clerk; (old use, pej) Hindu affecting English speech and manners. 先生(印度人对男子之尊称); 印度绅士; (会写英文之)印度书记; (旧用法, 蔑)爱用英语及英国习俗的印度人。

ba·boon /bə'buːn US: bæ-; bə'bun/ *n* large monkey (of Africa and southern Asia) with a dog-like face. 狒狒(一种大猴子, 产于非洲及亚洲南部, 面似狗)。⇨ the illus at **ape.** 参看 ape 之插图。

baby /'beɪbɪ; 'bebɪ/ *n* (*pl* -bies) **1** very young child: 婴儿; 婴孩; 小儿: *She has a ~/boy/ /girl.* 她有一个小男孩(女孩)。 *Which of you is the ~* (= the youngest member) *of the family?* 你们哪一个是全家最小的? *(be left) carrying/holding/to carry/to hold the ~,* (colloq) be left responsible for sth one does not wish to be responsible for (because of its difficulty or distastefulness). (口)做不愿做的事情(因其为困难或可厌之事)。 '**~ carriage,** (US) pram. (美)婴儿车。 '**~-faced,** looking much younger than one's age. 娃娃脸的。 '**~-farmer,** (often pej) woman who contracts to keep (esp unwanted) babies. (常为轻蔑语)受约看护婴孩(尤指不想要的婴孩)的女人; 代人育婴的女人。 '**~-minder,** woman paid to look after a ~ for long periods (eg while the mother is out working). 受雇长期照料婴儿的女人(例如当母亲外出工作时); 保姆。 '**~-sit·ter,** person paid to look after a ~ for a short time (eg while parents are at the cinema). 临时受雇照料婴儿的人(例如当父母去看电影时)。 Hence, 由此产生, '**~-sit** *vi,* '**~-sit·ting** *n* '**~-talk** *n* kind of speech used by or to babies with distorted vocabulary and syntax. 小儿语(婴儿所说或对婴儿说的言语, 其单词及句法均异于常型)。 **2** (used attrib) very small of its kind: (用作定语)特小的, 小型的: *a ~ car,* a small motor-car. 小型汽车。 *~ 'grand,* small grand piano. 小型平台钢琴。 **3** (sl) girl; sweetheart. (俚)女郎; 爱人。 □ *vt* [VP6A] (colloq) treat like a ~: (口)当婴儿看待: *Don't ~ the boy!* 别把那男孩当婴儿看待! '**~-hood** *n* state of being a ~; time when one is a ~. 婴儿期; 婴儿时代。 '**~-ish** *adj* of or like a ~: 婴儿的; 如婴儿的; 幼稚的: *~ish behaviour.* 幼稚的行为。

bac·ca·laur·eate /ˌbækə'lɔːrɪət; ˌbækə'lɔrɪt/ *n* [C] **1** last secondary school examination in France. 法国中学结业考试。 **2** university degree of Bachelor. 学士学位。

bac·ca·rat /'bækərɑː; ˌbækə'rɑ/ *n* [U] gambling game with playing cards. 一种纸牌赌博。

bac·cha·nal /'bækənl; 'bækənl/ *adj* **1** of or like Bacchus /'bækəs; 'bækəs/ (the GK god of wine) or his rites. 属于或象希腊酒神巴克斯或其崇拜仪式的。 **2** wild, excited, drunken: 狂欢暴饮的; 狂欢暴饮的: *a ~ feast.* 狂饮的宴会。 □ *n* **1** follower of Bacchus; drunken reveller. 酒神巴克斯之信徒; 狂饮作乐者。 **2** dance or song in honour of Bacchus; merrymaking. 酒神舞; 酒神歌; 作乐。 **bac·cha·na·lian** /ˌbækə'neɪliən; ˌbækə'nelɪən/ *adj* of ~s; noisy and drunken. 酒徒的; 发酒疯的; 狂饮作乐的。

baccy /'bækɪ; 'bækɪ/ *n* [U] (colloq) tobacco. (口)烟草。

bach·elor /'bætʃələ(r); 'bætʃələ/ *n* **1** unmarried man, ⇨ spinster; (用作定语)单身汉; (作定语)单身汉的; 适宜于单身汉的: *a ~* (= independent unmarried) *girl;* 自食

其力的未婚女子; ~ flats. 单身公寓. **2** (man or woman who has taken) first university degree: (大学毕业所得的)学士学位; 学士 (不分男女): B~ of Arts/ Science. 文(理)学士.

ba·cil·lus /bə'sɪləs; bə'sɪləs/ n (pl **-cilli** /-'sɪlaɪ; -'sɪlaɪ/) rod-shaped bacterium, esp one of the types that cause disease. 杆状细菌; (尤指能致病之)杆菌.

back[1] /bæk; bæk/ n **1** (of the human body) surface of the body from the neck to the buttocks; spine, ⇨ the illus at **skeleton**: (指人体)背部(自颈项至臀部之背付后部分);背脊(参看 skeleton 之插图): If you lie on your ~, you can look up at the sky. 如果你仰卧睡, 你就可以观天. He slipped and fell on his ~. 他仰天滑倒. **at the ~ of sb; at sb's ~**, giving him support or protection: 支持或保护某人: He knows that he has the head of the Department at his ~, and that the head is ready to support him. 他知道他有系主任支持他. Cf 参较 back sb up. **do/say sth behind sb's ~**, without his knowledge (always in connection with sth unpleasant, such as slander). 在某人背后做(说)某事物(总与不愉快之事有关, 如诽谤). **break one's ~**, fracture or dislocate one's spine; (fig) work (too) strenuously. 折断脊椎骨; (喻)拼命工作; 工作过于劳累. **break the ~ of sth** (eg a piece of work), finish the hardest or larger part of it. 完成某事物(如一件工作)最艰难的部分或其大部分. **get off sb's ~**, stop being a burden or hindrance. 不再为某人之累赘. **give sb a ~; make a ~ for sb**, bend down in the game of leapfrog, or to enable sb to climb on one's ~ in order to get over a wall, etc. (在跳蛙游戏中)弯下腰供人自背上跳越(或让人爬上其肩以翻越墙等). **be glad to see the ~ of sb**, feel pleased to see him go away. 因某人走开而高兴. **be with/have one's ~ to the wall**, be in a difficult position, forced to defend oneself. 处于困境; 被迫自卫. **be on one's ~**, (esp) be ill in bed. (尤指)卧病在床. **put one's ~ into sth**, work at it with all one's energy. 尽全力为之; 全力以赴. **put/get sb's ~ up**, make him angry.触怒某人; 使之生气. **turn one's ~ on sb**, turn away from him in an impolite way; avoid, shun, him. 掉头不理睬某人; 避开某人. **2** upper surface of an animal's body: 动物的背脊: Fasten the saddle on the horse's ~. 将鞍缚于马背上. **3** that part of a chair or seat on which a person's ~ rests. 椅或座位的靠背. **4** (contrasted with front) that surface of an object that is less used, less visible or important: (与front 相对)物体之较不常用、较不常见或较不重要之一面; 背面; 反面: the ~ of one's hand, with the nails and knuckles. 手背(有指甲及指节之面). You can't cut with the ~ of the knife. 你无法用刀背切割. You can't see the ~ of your head. 你看不见自己的后脑袋. You write the address on the front of an envelope, not on the ~. 你把地址写在信封的正面, 不写在信封的背面. **5** (contrasted with front) that part of a thing that is farthest from the front: (与front 相对)离前面最远之处; 后面: a room at the ~ of the house; 房屋内靠后面的一个房间; a garden at the ~ of a house. 房屋后面的花园; 后花园. **the B~s**, lawns and grounds (on the River Cam) of some Cambridge colleges. 剑桥大学之某些学院的草地和校园(在青河沿岸者). **6 break her ~**, (of a ship) break in two. (指船)断为两截. **7** ('full-~), ('half-)~, (football, etc) player whose position is between the half way line and the goal line. 足球等)(后)卫; (前)卫. ⇨ the illus at **football**. 参看 football 之插图.

back[2] /bæk; bæk/ adv part **1** (contrasted with forward) to or at the rear; away from the front or the centre: (与 forward 相对) 往后面; 在后面; 离开前面或中央: Stand ~, please! 请退后! The police held the crowd ~. 警察拦住群众不许向前. Fasten the curtains ~. 把窗帘拉开系下. Sit ~ in your chair and be comfortable. 舒舒着背靠背, 舒服舒服. The house stands ~ (ie at some distance) from the road. 那房子离大路有一段距离. **go ~ (up)on/from one's word**, fail to keep a promise. 食言; 不守信. **(in) ~ of**, (US colloq) behind. (美口)

在…后面: the houses ~ of the church. 教堂后面的房子. **2** in(to) an earlier position or condition: 在(至)先前的位置或情况: Put the dictionary ~ on the shelf. 把字典放回书架上. Throw the ball ~ to me. 把球掷还给我. Call that boy ~. 把那个男孩叫回来. We shall be ~ (= home again) before dark. 我们将在天黑以前回来. Shall we walk ~ or ride ~? 我们是步行回去呢? 还是坐车回去呢? How far is it there and ~? 到那里来回有多远? My brother is just ~ (ie has just returned home) from Paris. 我哥哥(弟弟)刚从巴黎回来. The company is now ~ on its feet, has re-established itself after a period of financial, etc difficulties. 该公司现在又稳定下来了(如经过一段时期的财务困难等). ~ and forth ⇨ **forth. 3** in return: 还报: If I hit you, would you hit me ~? 如果我打你, 你会不会还手? Don't answer ~, Don't retort or argue. 不要回嘴. When can you pay ~ (= repay) the money you borrowed? 你何时能归还你所借的钱? **have/ get one's own ~ (on sb)**, (colloq) have your revenge. (口)(向某人)报复. **4** (of time) ago; into the past: (时间)以前; 溯至过去: some few years ~; 好些年以前; far ~ in the Middle Ages. 远溯至中古时代.

back[3] /bæk; bæk/ vt, vi **1** [VP6A, 15A, 2A, C] go or cause to go ~ward(2):: 后退; 使后退: The horse ~ed suddenly. 马忽然向后退. He ~ed the car into/out of the garage. 他把汽车倒退着驶入(出)停车间. The wind ~ed, changed gradually in an anti-clockwise direction (eg from E through NE to N). 风向逐渐倒转(即循着反时针方向转, 例如自东风转为东北风, 再转为北风). ⇨ **veer**. ~ the oars; ~ water, use the oars to reverse a boat's forward motion. 划桨使船后退. **2** [VP6A, 15B] ~ (up), support: 支持; 拥护: ~ a friend in an argument or quarrel, in 在辩论或争论中支持朋友; ~ up an argument支持一论据. Hence, 由此产生, '~-up n (colloq) support; spare[1]. (口)支持; 备件. ~ a bill/note, endorse it as a promise to pay money if necessary. 背书(在票据背面签名, 表示承诺必要时即行付款). **3** [VP6A] bet money on (a horse, a greyhound): 下赌注于(某一匹马或某一条跑狗): The favourite was heavily ~ed, Much money was bet on its winning the race. 大家对那匹热门马下了重注(赌其将为得胜者). **4** [VP2C] ~ 'down (from), give up a claim. 放弃要求等: I see he has ~ed down from the position he took last week. 我看他已放弃了他上星期所采取的立场. Hence, 由此产生, '~-down n. ~ off, give up a claim. 放弃要求. ~ out (of), withdraw (from a promise or undertaking): 食言; 打退堂鼓: He promised to help and then ~ed out. 他答应帮忙, 后来却食言了. He's trying to ~ out of his bargain, escape from the agreement. 他在设法不履行合约规定. **5** [VP6A] put or be a lining to; put on as a surface at the ~: 加里衬于; 作为…的里衬; 加于…的背面: ~ed with sheet iron. 背面包上一层铁皮. **6** [VP6A, 3A] ~ (on) (to), be situated at the ~ of: 位于…的后面: Our garden ~s theirs. 我们花园在他们的花园后面. Their house ~s on (to) our garden. 他们的房子在我们花园的背后. ~er n **1** person who ~s a horse. 赛马中的下注者. **2** person who gives support or help (eg to a political movement); person who gives financial support to an undertaking. 支持者; 拥护者(如拥护某一政治运动); 赞助者(对某一事业予以财务上的赞助). ~ing n **1** [U] help; support; [C] body of supporters: 赞助; 支持; 支持者之集团; 赞助团; 后台: The new leader has a large ~ing. 此新领袖有大批的支持者. **2** [U] material used to form a thing's ~ or support. 用作某物之后背或支撑物的材料; 材料; 支材. **3** [U] (pop music) musical accompaniment to a singer: (流行音乐)流行歌曲的伴奏: vocal/instrumental ~ing. 声部(乐器)伴奏.

back[4] /bæk; bæk/ (used attrib, and in compounds, with references to the articles on the n, adv part and v above) (以上述名词、副词及动词各义用作定语, 并用于复合词中) **1** ⇨ **back**[1](1, 2). '~-ache n [U, C] ache or pain in the ~. 背痛. '~-band n strap over a horse's cart-saddle, supporting the shafts of a cart or carriage.

(马车鞍上的附搭于马背上用以支持车辕之)背带. '~·**bone**
n (a)line of bones down the middle of the ~, from the
skull to the hips; spine, spinal column, ⇨ the illus at
skeleton; (fig) chief support: 脊背; 脊柱(参看 skeleton
之插图); (喻)主要支持力; 主干; 中坚分子: Such men are
the ~bone of the country. 这种人才是国家的中坚分子.
(b) [U] (fig) strength; firmness: (喻) 刚强; 坚毅: He
hasn't enough ~bone, is weak in character. 他不够坚强.
(c) to the ~bone, (fig) completely; in every way: (喻)
彻头彻尾地; 道道地地: He's British to the ~bone. 他
是道道地地的英国人. '~·**break·ing** adj (of work)
exhausting. (指工作)费力的; 累人的. 2 ⇨ back¹(4, 5).
,~·'**hand(ed)** adj: ~hand blow/stroke, one that is
delivered with the ~ of the hand turned outwards, or
in a direction different from what is usual or expected.
(用手背)反掌或反向的打击;反手击. ⇨**forehand**. Hence,
由此产生, (fig) (喻): a ~handed compliment, one that
is ambiguous (eg suggesting sarcasm). 挖苦或含义不明
的恭维. '~·**scratcher** n (a) device with claws on a
long handle for scratching the ~ (when there is an
irritation, etc). 麻姑爪(长柄,一端有爪,背痒时用以抓背
的器具,有些地方叫'不求人'). (b) flatterer. 谄媚者.
⇨ **scratch** v(5). '~·**stroke** n (a) [U] swimming stroke
done on the ~, rotating the arms alternately. 仰泳.
(b) [C] ~handed stroke. 反掌或反向的打击; 反手击.
'~·**sword** n sword with only one cutting edge. 单刃
剑; 大砍刀. 3 ⇨ back¹(5) and back²(1). ,~·**to·'~**, (of
housing) of two rows of terrace houses, often separated
by a narrow alley, with the ~s facing. (指房屋)背靠
背的(指两排连栋式的房屋,通常由一小巷隔开,两排房屋
之后而均朝小巷). ,~·'**bench(er)** n (person occupying)
one of the seats in the House of Commons (or other
law-making body) used by those members, who, because
they do not or have not held office, are not entitled to
a front-bench seat. 在英国下议院或其他议会中之后排席
席; 在英国下议院或其他议会中, 坐于后排座位之议员(因
其非为, 或不曾为, 政府官员, 故无权坐于前排座位). ⇨
bench(1). '~·**blocks** n pl (in Australia) areas of land
a long way from a railway, river, the sea-coast, etc and
thinly populated. (澳大利亚)距离铁路、河道、海岸等均
甚远且人口稀少之地区; 偏僻地区. ,~·'**board** n movable
board at the ~ of a cart. (马车后面可以移动的)后板;
背板. '~·**cloth** n painted cloth hung at the ~ of a
stage in a theatre, as part of the scenery. (戏台后面所
挂的)背景幕; 天幕. ,~·'**door** n door at the ~ of a
house or other building; (attrib, fig) secret or indirect;
clandestine: 后门; (用作定语,喻)秘密的; 间接的; 幕后的;
暗中的: ~door influence. 幕后的势力. '~·**drop** n =
~cloth. '~·**ground** n (a) that part of a view, scene
(and, fig, a description) that serves as a setting for the
chief objects, persons, etc. 背景; (喻)衬托性叙述. ⇨
foreground. (b) person's past experiences, education,
environment. 个人的经历、学历与环境; 背景. (c)contem-
porary condition(s): 当时的情况; 时代背景: the social
and political ~ground; 当时社会及政治的情况; (comm)
details necessary to an understanding of company
business: (商) 了解公司业务所必需的细节: B~ground
information will be supplied at the Board meeting. 公司
业务的详细资料将于开董事会时提供. (d) (be/keep/
stay) in the ~ground, away from publicity; hidden.
在(保持在)幕后. (e) ~ground music/effects, etc,
music, etc that accompanies dialogue, action, etc (eg in
a radio or TV programme or a cinema film) but is not
essential to the story, etc. (无线电广播、电视节目或电影
中,配合对话、动作等,而非故事内容等所不可缺少的)配
乐(音响效果等). ~·**less** adj (of a dress), not covering
the ~; cut to the waist at the ~: (指女装)无背的; 露背
的; 背部裁到腰的: a ~less gown. 无背礼服. '~·**most**
adj farthest from the front. 最后面的. '~·**room** n
room at the ~ of a building: room in 建筑物后面的房间; 后
房: ~room boys, (colloq) scientists, engineers, research
workers in offices and laboratories. (口)办公室或实验

室中的科学家、工程师或研究工作人员. ,~·'**seat** n seat
at the ~. 后座. take a ~seat, (fig) behave as if one
were unimportant; humble oneself. (喻)谦逊; 自谦.
,~·**seat 'driver**, passenger (in a car) who corrects or
advises the driver. 后座驾驶员(坐在车中改正或劝告驾
驶员的乘客). '~·**side** n (colloq) buttocks: (口)臀部;
屁股: give sb a kick on the ~side. 踢某人屁股一下.
,~·'**stage** adv (a) behind the scenes (in a theatre): (戏
院中)在后台; 至后台: I was taken ~stage by the leading
actor. 我被主角带到后台去. (b) (attrib) (用作定语):
~stage life, of actors and actresses when not on
the stage. (演员的) 后台生活 (即非演戏时的私生活).
,~·'**stair** adj secret; underhand: 秘密的; 暗中的: ~stair
influence. 秘密势力; 暗中的影响力. ,~·'**stairs** n staircase
from servants' quarters: (通至仆人住处的) 后楼梯:
(attrib) ~stairs gossip, ie among servants. 仆人们的
闲话. '~·**stays** n pl (naut) set of ropes from
the mast-head to the sides of a ship, sloping towards
the stern. (航海) (自桅顶牵引至船侧并向船尾斜下之)后
拉索. '~·**wash** n movement of water going away
in waves, esp the rush of water behind a ship; (fig)
unpleasant after-effects of sth done. 向船后面移动
之波浪,尤指轮船等后面所搅起者;水之反溅;(喻)(完成某
事物后所留下不愉快的)反响; 余波. '~·**water** n (a) part
of a river not reached by its current, where the water
does not flow. 死水; 滞水(河流中水流不经过之处, 此
处之水不流动). (b) (fig) place, condition of mind,
untouched by events, progress, etc: (喻)穷乡僻壤; 思想
停滞: living in an intellectual ~water, untouched by
new ideas, etc. 生活于智力沉滞的状态之中. '~·**woods**
n pl uncleared forest land; (fig) culturally backward
area. 尚待开发的荒林地区; (喻)文化落后地区. '~·**woods-
man** /-men; -mən/ n (pl -men) man who lives in the
~woods; (fig) old-fashioned person. 居于偏僻的荒林
地区之人; (喻)守旧的人. ,~·'**yard** n (esp of terraced
houses) (usu paved) area at the ~ of a house: 后院(房
屋后面的空地,通常是加工铺过的,尤指一排房屋之后):
The dustbin is kept in the ~ yard. 垃圾箱是放在后院里.
4 ⇨ back²(2). to an earlier point in time; to a former
place. 至先前的时间; 至原先的位置. ,~·'**date** vt date
~ to a time in the past: 追溯至(过去某时): The wage
increases are to be ~dated to the first of January. 工资
的增加将追溯至元月一日. ,~·'**fire** n (sound caused by
the) too early explosion of gas in an internal combustion
engine, causing the piston to move in the wrong
direction. (内燃机气缸内爆发过早致使活塞倒行之)逆火;
逆火所引起的声响. □ vi produce, make the sound of, a
~ fire; (fig) produce an unexpected or undesired
result: 发出逆火声; 发出逆火的声响; (喻)产生意外或不良
的后果: The plot ~fired. 该秘密计划产生了不良的后果.
,~·**formation** n [U, C] (process of making a) word
that appears to be the root of a longer word (eg
televise, from television). 倒反构词; 反造词(根据一个
较长的词,反造出一个看来似乎为其词根之词, 例如根
据 television 造出 televise); 反造法. '~·**log** n accumulation of work or business (eg arrears of unfulfilled
orders) not yet attended to. 积压之待办事项(如订货之
迟未发出). ,~·**num·ber** n (a) issue of a periodical of
an earlier date, not now on sale. 过期的期刊(市面上
已不卖的); 旧杂志. (b) (fig, colloq) out-of-date or
old-fashioned method, thing, person, etc. (喻,口)过时
或旧式的方法,事物,人等; 老古董; 落伍的观念. '~·**pay/
rent/taxes, etc**, n pay, etc in arrears; pay, etc that
is overdue. 拖欠的款(房租,税等). ,~·'**pedal** vi (on
a bicycle, etc) pedal ~wards; (fig) retreat hurriedly
from sth stated or promised. (在脚踏车等上)倒踩脚踏
板; (喻)匆忙取消所说的或所答应的某事物. ,~·'**slide** vi
[VP2A] fall back from good ways into bad old ways of
living; lose interest in religious practice, morality, etc.
从良好的生活方式或习惯中返回以往的不良的方式; 对
于教规、道德等失去兴趣; 堕落; 退步. ,~·'**space** vi move
the carriage of a typewriter ~ one or more spaces by

pressing the key (called 称作 the '~*spacer key*) used for this purpose. 按退格键使打字机的滚筒倒退一格或数格。 5 ⇨ **back**²(3). in return; in reply. 还报; 回答。 '~**bite** *vt, vi* slander the reputation of (sb who is absent); speak slanderously about an absent person. 背后诋毁(某人)的名誉; 诽谤; 背后说人坏话; 中伤。 Hence, 由此产生, '~**biter** *n* person who ~bites. 背后说人坏话的人; 诽谤者。 '~**chat** *n* [U] (colloq) (exchange of) impertinent remarks: (口)恶言; 粗鲁的话; 恶言相向: *I want none of your ~chat.* 不可对我说这种粗鲁的话。 '~**lash** *n* [U] (a) excessive movement caused by loose connections between mechanical parts (often causing ~ward movement). 反撞; 齿隙(由于机器零件间连接的松弛而引起激烈运动, 常导致反向运动)。 (b) (fig) antagonistic reaction (esp in social or race relations). (喻)敌对反应 (尤指社会或种族关系中者)。 '~**talk** *n* [U] = ~chat. 恶言; 粗话; 恶言反驳。

back·gam·mon /'bæk'gæmən US: 'bæk-;'bæk,gæmən/ *n* [U] game for two players, played on a special double board with draughts and dice. 西洋双陆棋戏。

back·sheesh ⇨ **baksheesh.**

back·ward /'bækwəd; 'bækwəd/ *adj* 1 towards the back or the starting-point: 向后的; 倒着的: *a ~ glance / movement;* 向后的一看(动作); *a ~ flow of water.* 水之倒流。 2 having made, making, less than the usual or normal progress: 进步迟缓的; 落后的: *This part of the country is still ~; there are no railways or roads and no electricity.* 这个国家的这个地区仍甚落后; 没有铁道或公路, 也没有电力。 *Because of his long illness, Tom is ~ in his studies.* 汤姆因久病所以功课落后。 Cf 参较 *well up in.* Spring is ~ *this year.* 今年春天来得较迟。 3 shy; reluctant; hesitant: 羞怯的; 畏缩的; 迟疑的: *Although he is clever, he is ~ in giving his views.* 他虽然很聪明, 却不善发表他的意见。 □ *adv ~(s)* 1 away from one's front; towards the back. 向后; 向背后: *He looked ~(s) over his shoulder.* 他回头向后看。 2 with the back or the end first: 倒退着: *It's most easy to walk ~(s).* 倒退着走路不容易。 *Can you say the alphabet ~(s),* ie ZYXWV, etc? 你能倒念英语的二十六个字母吗? *know sth ~(s),* know it perfectly; be quite familiar with it. 熟记某事物; 熟谙某事物。 *~(s) and froward(s),* first in one direction and then in the other: 来回地; 往返地: *travelling ~(s) and forwards(s) between London and the south coast.* 往返于伦敦和南海岸之间。 Cf 参较 *back and forth: to and fro.*

bacon /'beɪkən; 'bekən/ *n* [U] salted or smoked meat from the back or sides of a pig. 腌的或熏的猪肉(系猪之脊肋部分)。 *bring home the ~,* (sl) succeed in one's undertaking. (俚)获得成功。 *save one's ~,* (colloq) escape death, injury, punishment. (口)死里逃生; 幸免于难; 免于受罚。

bac·ter·ium /bæk'tɪərɪəm; bæk'tɪrɪəm/ *n* (*pl* -**ria** /-rɪə; -rɪə/) (kinds of) simplest and smallest form of plant life, existing in air, water and soil, and in living and dead creatures and plants, essential to animal life and sometimes a cause of disease. 细菌。 **bac·ter·ial**

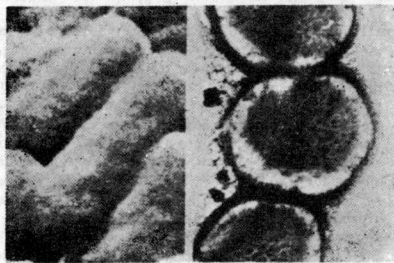

bacteria (seen through a microscope)

/-rɪəl; -rɪəl/ *adj* of bacteria: 细菌的: *bacterial contamination.* 细菌感染。 **bac·teri·ol·ogy** /bæk,tɪərɪ'ɒlədʒɪ 'bæk,tɪrɪ'ɑlədʒɪ/ *n* science or study of bacteria. 细菌学。 **bac·teri·ol·ogist** /-dʒɪst; -dʒɪst/ *n* student of, expert in, bacteriology. 细菌学者; 细菌学家。

bad¹ /bæd; bæd/ *adj* (**worse, worst**) 1 wicked, evil, immoral: 坏的; 邪恶的; 不道德的: *It is bad to steal.* 偷窃是坏事。 *He leads a bad life.* 他过着邪恶的生活。 *act in bad faith,* dishonestly, insincerely. 行为诡诈或不诚实。 *a bad egg / hat / lot,* (dated sl) morally unreliable person. (过时俚语)坏蛋。 *call sb bad names,* insult him. 辱骂某人。 *bad language,* swear-words; (the use of) obscene or profane words merely to insult or for emphasis. 诅咒; 粗话; 咒骂语; 咒骂语之使用。 *bad word,* swear-word: 咒骂语。 2 unpleasant; disagreeable; unwelcome: 令人不愉快的; 令人讨厌的; 不受欢迎的: *We've had some bad news.* 我们得到了一些坏消息。 *What bad weather we're having!* 多么可厌的天气呵! *There's a bad smell here.* 这里有股恶臭。 *The way he was sacked created a bad odour,* (fig) created unpleasant feelings. (喻)他被解雇的方式使他留下了不快之感。 3 (of things that are in themselves undesirable) notable; noticeable; serious: (指不好的事物)显著的; 严重的: *That was a bad mistake.* 那是一项大错。 *He's had a bad accident.* 他遭遇了一场严重的灾祸。 *There's been a bad falling-off in attendance.* 出席的人大为减少。 4 inferior; worthless; incorrect; of poor quality: 劣等的; 无价值的; 不正确的; 劣质的: *His pronunciation is bad.* 他的发音很差。 *He speaks bad English.* 他说的英语很差劲。 *What a bad drawing!* 多糟的画幅! *You can't take photographs if the light is bad.* 如果光线坏, 你就不能照相。 *be in a bad way,* be very ill or unfortunate; be in trouble or difficulty. 病重; 遭遇极大不幸; 在困境中。 *be in bad (with),* (US colloq) be in disfavour: (美口)失宠(于); 受(…的)轻视: *He's in bad with the boss.* 他失宠于其上司。 *go from bad to worse,* become seriously worse. 越来越坏; 每况愈下。 *with bad grace,* showing unwillingness. 不愿意地; 勉强地。 *not (so) bad,* (colloq understatement) quite good. (口, 含蓄说法)不坏; 不错。 *not half bad,* very good. 很好。 *a bad business / job,* (colloq) an unfortunate affair. (口)不幸的事。 *bad debt,* one unlikely to be paid. 不可能偿还的债务; 倒帐; 呆帐。 '*bad-lands* (US) barren, infertile regions. (美)贫瘠不毛地区。 *bad law,* one that cannot be sustained or held to be valid. 不能证明其为正确的定律; 错误的定律。 *bad shot,* (fig) wrong guess. (喻)误猜。 5 not able to be eaten; rotten: 不可食用的; 腐坏的: *bad eggs / meat.* 腐坏的蛋(肉)。 *go bad,* become unfit to eat: (食物)变坏: *Don't let that fish go bad—put it in the fridge.* 不要让那条鱼变坏了——把它放到冰箱里。 6 *bad for,* hurtful or injurious for; unsuitable for: 有害于; 不适宜于: *Smoking is bad for the health.* 吸烟有害健康。 *Very small print is bad for the eyes.* 印刷的字体太小对眼睛有害。 *It's bad for him to live alone.* 他不宜独居。 7 in ill health, diseased; 健康情况不佳的; 有病的: *a bad (= sore) finger;* 痛的手指; *a bad leg,* causing pain; 会痛的腿; (colloq) 它: *She feels bad today.* 她今天感觉不舒服。 *be taken bad,* (colloq) fall ill; become more ill: (口)生病; 病重: *She was taken bad during the night.* 她晚上病倒了。 8 (colloq) unfortunate: (口)不幸的: *It's too bad she's so ill.* 她病得这样厉害, 太不幸了。 9 (colloq) sorry; bothered: (口)抱憾的; 感到不安的: *I feel so bad about not being able to help you.* 未能相助极感不安。 **bad·ly** *adv* (**worse, worst**) (Cf 参较 *well, better, best.*) 1 in a bad manner; roughly; untidily, etc: 坏地; 粗陋地; 杂乱地; 不整齐地: *badly made / dressed / wounded.* 粗制滥造的(服装不整的); 伤得很厉害的。 2 by much: 大大地: *badly beaten at football;* 在足球赛中大败; *badly in need of repair.* 亟须修理。 3 (with *want, need*) very much: (与 *want, need* 连用)非常地: *She wants it badly* 她非常想要它。 4 *badly off,* poor. 穷的。 *badly off for,* in need of. 需要。 **bad·ness** *n* quality of being bad: 坏; 恶劣: *the badness of the weather / climate.* 天气

(气候)之恶劣。

bad² /bæd; bæd/ n [U] that which is bad: 坏的或恶劣的事物: *take the bad with the good*, take bad fortune with good fortune. 坏运与好运都要接受(逆来亦须顺受)。 *go to the bad*, become completely immoral; become ruined. 堕落; 自毁。 *to the bad*, (accounts) in loss: (帐目)亏损; 负债: *I am £50 to the bad*, have lost £50 as the result (of the deal, etc). 我亏损五十英镑(由于交易等的结果)。

bade /bæd; bæd/ ⇨ **bid**¹(4).

badge /bædʒ; bædʒ/ n 1 sth worn (usu a design on cloth or made of metal) to show a person's occupation, rank, etc or membership of a society. 徽章; 证章(通常为布或金属制成, 上有图案, 表示职业、等级等, 或会员身份)。 2 (fig) sth that shows a quality or condition: (喻) 象征; 代表: *Chains are a ~ of slavery.* 镣铐为奴隶之象征。

badger¹ /'bædʒə(r); 'bædʒɚ/ n small, grey animal living in holes in the earth and going about at night. 獾(灰色小动物, 居于地洞中, 夜出活动)。 ⇨ the illus at **small**. 参看 small 之插图。

badger² /'bædʒə(r); 'bædʒɚ/ vt [VP6A, 14, 16A] ~ *sb (with questions, etc) / (for sth) / (into doing sth)*, worry or tease: 烦扰; 阄着: *Tom has been ~ing his uncle to buy him a camera.* 汤姆一直阄着要他叔父给他买一架照相机。 *I was ~ed into doing what she wanted.* 我被阄得照着她所要求的做了。

ba·di·nage /'bædɪnɑːʒ US: ˌbædən'ɑːʒ; 'bædnɪdʒ /n [U] banter. 嘲弄; 戏谑; 打趣。

bad·min·ton /'bædmɪntən; 'bædmɪntən/ n game played with rackets and shuttlecocks across a high, narrow net. 羽毛球戏。

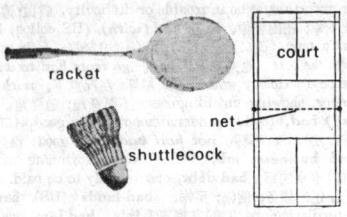

badminton

baffle¹ /'bæfl; 'bæfl/ vt [VP6A] puzzle; prevent (sb) from doing sth; be too difficult to do, understand, etc: 困惑; 阻止 (某人) 做某事; 难住; 难倒: *One of the examination questions ~d me completely.* 有道试题把我完全难住了。 *They were ~d in their attempt.* 他们的企图受挫。 *The scene ~d all description, could not be described.* 那情景笔墨难以形容。

baffle² /'bæfl; 'bæfl/ n plate, board, screen or other device, used to hinder or control the flow of a gas, a liquid or sound through an inlet or outlet. 阻碍或控制气体、液体或声音流进流出的)障板;阻板;折流板。

bag¹ /bæg; bæg/ n 1 container made of flexible material (paper, cloth, leather) with an opening at the top, used for carrying things from place to place: (纸、布、皮革所制之)袋子;提袋;提包: *'shopping-bag',* 购物袋; *'travelling-bag',* 旅行袋; *'handbag',* 女用手提包; *'kitbag',* (军人、水手或旅行者之)背包;背袋;行李袋; *'tool-bag',* 工具袋; *'mailbag',* (运送邮件用的)邮袋。 ⇨ these words; 参看各该词。 *bag and baggage*, with all one's belongings (used esp of sb who is expelled). 带着全部财产(尤指被驱逐之人)。 *a bag of bones*, a very thin person or animal. 很瘦的人或动物; 瘦皮猴。 *let the cat out of the bag*, tell a secret (without intending to do so). (无意中)泄露秘密。 *pack one's bags*, pack (for a journey). 整理行装(准备旅行)。 *the whole bag of tricks*, everything needed for a purpose; the whole lot. (口)为某一目的所需要的一切东西; 全部法宝。 2 (= *game-bag*)

all the birds, animals, etc shot or caught: 猎获的全部飞禽走兽: *They secured a good bag.* 他们猎获了很多鸟兽。 *be in the bag*, (colloq) (of results, outcomes, etc) be as desired: (口)(指结果、结局等)将如所愿; 稳操胜算; 十拿九稳;一定成功: *The election is in the bag.* 这场选举我们将稳操胜算。 3 *bags of*, (sl) plenty of: (俚)充足的; 很多的: *There's bags of room.* 空间很大。 *He has bags of money.* 他有很多钱。 4 *bags under the eyes*, (colloq) puffiness under the eyes (eg from lack of sleep). (口)肿眼泡; 眼睛下面的虚胀(例如因缺乏睡眠所致)。 5 *old bag*, (colloq) fussy, unattractive, boring woman. (口)爱挑剔,不漂亮,令人厌烦的女人。

bag² /bæg; bæg/ vt, vi (**-gg-**) 1 [VP6A, 15B] put into a bag or bags. 装入袋中: *to bag (up) wheat.* 把小麦装入袋中。 2 [VP6A] (of sportsmen) kill or catch: (指猎人)猎获: *They bagged nothing except a couple of rabbits.* 他们仅仅猎获两只兔子。 3 [VP6A] (colloq) take (sb else's property, etc without permission, but not intending to steal): (口)擅自取用(他人之物, 但非有心企图): *Who has bagged my matches?* 谁把我的火柴拿去了? *She bagged (= occupied, sat in) the most comfortable chair.* 她径自坐上最舒服的椅子。 *Try to bag an empty table,* secure one (eg in a crowded restaurant). 想办法弄一张空桌子(例如在拥挤的餐馆中)。 4 [VP2A, C] hang loosely, looking like a cloth bag: 松弛地悬垂(如布袋状): *trousers that bag at the knees.* 在膝盖处特别宽松的裤子。

baga·telle /ˌbægə'tel; ˌbægə'tɛl/ n 1 [U] kind of game like billiards, played on a board with holes instead of pockets. 一种弹子戏(台板上有洞而无袋者)。 2 [C] (often 常作 *a mere ~*) sth small and of no importance 小事物;不重要之事物。 3 [C] musical trifle. 音乐小品; 小曲。

bag·gage /'bægɪdʒ; 'bægɪdʒ/ n [U] 1 (more usu, except in US, *luggage*) all the bags, trunks, etc with which a person travels. (除美国外, 较常用 luggage) 行李 (旅行时所携带之全部袋、箱等)。 *'~ room,* (US) left luggage office. (美) 行李寄存处。 2 tents, bedding, equipment, etc, of an army: (军队之)辎重: *'~ animals,* *'~ train, etc,* animals, carts, trucks, etc, carrying ~. 运辎重的牲口、车辆等。 3 (dated) (playfully) saucy girl: (过时用语)(谑)调皮的女孩子: *You little ~!* 你这调皮的小丫头!

baggy /'bægɪ; 'bægɪ/ adj hanging in loose folds: 宽松而下垂的; 宽松如袋的: *trousers ~ at the knees;* 膝部特别宽松的裤子; *~ skin under the eyes.* 眼睛下面松弛的皮肤。

bagnio /'bɑːnɪəʊ; 'bænjo/ n (old use) (旧用法) 1 prison. 牢狱。 2 brothel. 妓院。

bag·pipe /'bægpaɪp; 'bægˌpaɪp/ n (often 常作 the ~s) musical instrument with air stored in a bag of wind held under one arm and pressed out through pipes in the 风笛(一种乐器, 吹奏者一只臂下的风袋中所贮藏的空气, 经由有簧的管中压出)。 ⇨ the illus at **kilt**. 参看 kilt 之插图。

bags /bægz; bægz/ n pl (colloq) trousers: (口)裤子: *Oxford;* 裤管宽松的裤子。 ⇨ **debag**.

bah /bɑː; bɑ/ int used as a sign of contempt. 呸(表示鄙视的感叹语)。

bail¹ /beɪl; bel/ n [U] sum of money demanded by a law court, paid by or for a person accused of wrongdoing, as security that he will appear for his trial, when time he is allowed to go free. (被告或替被告付与法院以保证按时到庭应讯之)保释金。 *go / put in / stand ~ (for sb),* pay money to secure his freedom in this way. (缴保释金)保释(某人)。 *(be) out on ~,* free after payment of ~. 在保释中。 *forfeit one's ~,* fail to appear for trial. 经保释在外而不按时到庭应讯。 *refuse ~,* (of a judge) refuse to accept ~ and give freedom to a prisoner. (指法官)不准保释。 *surrender to one's ~,* appear for trial after being out on ~. 经保释在外后如期到庭应讯。 □ vt [VP15B] *~ sb out,* obtain his freedom until trial by payment of ~. 把某人保释出

来。 **~ee** /ˌbeɪˈliː:; ˈbelˈiˈ/ n (legal) person to whom permission is given to have the goods of another (eg a laundry which accepts goods for washing or dry-cleaning). (法律)受托人(获准收取他人货物者, 例如接受衣物台水洗或干洗之洗衣店)。 **~·ment** n (legal) delivery of goods to a ~ee. (法律)托交(货物之托交给受托人)委托。 **~or** /ˈbeɪlɔː(r); ˌbelˈɔr/ n (legal) one who delivers goods to a ~ee. (法律)寄托人;委托人(将货物托交给受托人者)。

bail² /beɪl; bel/ n (cricket) either of the two cross pieces over the three stumps. (板球)门柱上之横木。 ⇨ the illus at **cricket**. 参看 cricket 之插图。

bail³ /beɪl; bel/ vt, vi 1 [VP6A, 15B, 2A, C] **~ (out)**, throw water out of a boat with buckets: etc: 用桶等将船内之水舀出: ~ing water (out); 将船内之水舀出; ~ing (out) the boat. 舀出船内之水。 2 (sometimes used for) **bale²**. (有时等于) bale²。

bailey /ˈbeɪlɪ; ˈbelɪ/ n outer wall of a castle; courtyard of a castle enclosed by strong walls. (中古城堡之)外墙; 城堡外庭(城堡中四周有坚堡围绕之庭院)。 **Old B~**, London Central Criminal Court. 伦敦中央刑事法庭。

Bailey bridge /ˈbeɪlɪ brɪdʒ; ˈbelɪ brɪdʒ/ n bridge (in prefabricated sections) designed for speedy assembly, used for spanning rivers, etc. 倍力桥(桥身各部预先铸好, 可迅速组合以供跨越河流等)。 ⇨ the illus at **bridge**. 参看 bridge 之插图。

bail·iff /ˈbeɪlɪf; ˈbelɪf/ n 1 law officer who helps a sheriff. 州县郡之副司法官。 2 landowner's agent or manager. 地主之代理人或管理人。

bairn /beən; bern/ n (Scot and N England) child. (用于苏格兰及英格兰北部)小孩。

bait¹ /beɪt; bet/ n 1 food, or sth made in imitation, put on a hook to catch fish, or in nets, traps, etc to attract prey: (挂于钓钩上以钓鱼或置于网中、陷阱等内以引诱猎物之)饵: The fish took/swallowed/rose to/nibbled at the ~. 鱼食(吞, 向上游至, 咬)饵。 **live ~**, small fish used as ~ to catch large fish. 活饵(作阴用的小鱼, 用以钓大鱼者)。 2 (fig) sth that allures or tempts. (喻)引诱物; 诱惑物; 饵。 **rise to the ~**, succumb to temptation. 受诱惑; 上钩。

bait² /beɪt; bet/ vt, vi 1 [VP6A] put food, real or imitation, (on a hook, etc) to catch fish, etc: 置饵于(钓等上)以捕鱼等): ~ a hook with a worm. 置蚯蚓于钩上以为饵。 2 [VP6A, 2A] give food to (horses on a journey; (of horses) take food. 在旅途中喂(马); (指马)吃草料。 3 [VP6A] worry (a chained animal) by making dogs attack it: 使狗骚扰 (被链锁住之动物): 'bear-~ing; 以狗逗熊戏; 'bull-~ing; 以狗逗牛戏; ~ a bear with dogs. 以狗逗熊。 4 [VP6A] torment (sb) by making cruel or insulting remarks. 以辱骂之语言折磨(某人); 奚落(某人)。

baize /beɪz; bez/ n [U] thick woollen cloth, usu green, used for covering (tables, etc): (做桌布等用, 通常为绿色之)厚毛呢: a '~-covered door; 以厚毛呢覆盖着的门; green ~ for the billiard-table. 铺绿子台用的绿色厚毛呢。

bake /beɪk; bek/ vt, vi [VP6A, 22, 2A, C] 1 cook, be cooked, by dry heat in an oven: (在炉中)烤; 烘; 焙: ~ bread/cakes; 烘面包(糕饼); ~d beans. 烘豆。 The bread is baking/being ~d. 面包在炉中烘着。 2 make or become hard by heating: 烤硬; 烧硬: The sun ~d the ground hard. 太阳将地晒得坚硬。 Bricks and earthenware articles are ~d in kilns. 砖及各种陶器是在窑中烧成的。 3 be warmed or tanned: 晒热; 晒黑: We are baking in the sun. 我们在晒太阳。 ,half-'~d adj (colloq) half-witted; lacking in experience or common sense: (口)愚蠢的; 缺乏经验或常识的; 未成熟的: half-~d ideas; 愚蠢的思想; a half-~d prophet. 缺乏经验的预言者。 'baking-'hot adj very hot: 炎热的; 极热的: a baking-hot day. 炎热的一日。 'baking-powder n mixture of powders used to make bubbles of gas in cakes, etc and so cause them to be light. (制糕饼等用以使其松软的)酸粉。 **baker** n person who ~s bread, etc. 烘制面包的人; 面包师傅。

~r's dozen, thirteen. 面包师之'打'(十三个, 较普通之'打'多一个)。 **bak·ery** /ˈbeɪkərɪ; ˈbekərɪ/ n (pl **-ries**) place where bread is ~d for many people. 面包厂; 面包店。

bake·lite /ˈbeɪkəlaɪt; ˈbekəˌlaɪt/ n [U] (P) synthetic resin compound as formerly used for old fountain pens, trays, telephones, etc. (商标)胶木; 电木(合成树脂化合物, 昔时用以制自来水笔, 托盘, 电话机等)。

bak·sheesh /ˈbækʃiːʃ; ˈbækʃɪf/ n [U] (in the Middle East) money given as a tip or as alms: (用于中东)小费; 小帐; 救济金: The porter expects ~ from you. 那脚夫期待你付小费。

bala·laika /ˌbæləˈlaɪkə; ˌbæləˈlaɪkə/ n (pl **~s**) guitar-like musical instrument (triangular, with three strings), popular in Russia and other countries in eastern Europe. 巴拉莱卡琴(流行于俄国及其他东欧国家之一种类似吉他的三角形的三弦琴)。 ⇨ the illus at **string**. 参看 string 之插图。

bal·ance¹ /ˈbæləns; ˈbæləns/ vt, vi 1 [VP6A, 14] weigh (a question, etc); compare (two objects, plans, etc) (in order to judge the relative weight, value, etc). 衡量(问题等); 权衡(二物品, 计划等)(以判定轻重、价值等)。 2 [VP6A, 15A] keep or put (sth, oneself) in a state of balance: 保持平衡; 使平衡: Can you ~ a stick on the end of your nose? 你能把一根棍子放在鼻尖上使之保持平衡吗? How long can you ~ (yourself) on one foot? 你用一只脚能站立多久? 3 [VP6A] (accounts compare debits and credits and record the sum needed to make them equal. (帐目)结帐; 平衡。 ~ the budget, arrange for income and expenditure to be equal. 平衡预算(使收支能相抵)。 [VP2A] (of the two sides of a balance-sheet) be equal: (指资产负债表上借贷双方)相抵; 平衡: My accounts ~. 我的帐收支相抵。 4 a ~d diet, one with the quantity and variety of food needed for good health. (维持健康所需的)包括各种食物及其正确数量的)均衡饮食。

bal·ance² /ˈbæləns; ˈbæləns/ n 1 apparatus for weighing, with a central pivot, beam and two scales or pans. 天平; 秤。 **be/hang in the ~**, (fig, of a result)

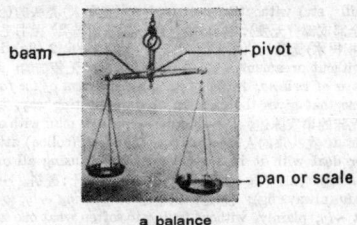

a balance

be still uncertain: (喻, 指结果)仍不一定; 尚未可知; 悬置未决: For a long time his fate was in the ~. 他的命运很久不能确定。 2 regulating apparatus of a watch or clock. (钟表内的)调整器; 平衡器。 '~-wheel n wheel, in a watch, that regulates the beat. (表内的)平衡轮; 摆轮。 3 [U] condition of being steady; condition that exists when two opposing forces are equal. 平衡状态; 均势状态。 **checks and ~s**, ⇨ check²(1). **hold the ~** have the power to decide. 有决定之权。 **in the ~**, undecided. 尚未决定的; 悬而未决的。 **keep one's ~**, keep steady, remain upright: 保持平衡; 保持直立: A small child has to learn to keep its ~ before it can walk far. 小孩在能走远以前, 必先学会保持平衡。 **Don't get excited; keep your ~**, (fig) keep calm. (喻)不要冲动; 保持冷静。 **lose one's ~**, become unsteady; fall; (fig) be upset mentally: 失去平衡; 倾倒; (喻) 心绪紊乱: He was surrounded by so many dangers that he lost his ~, became nervous and upset. 他为如此之多的危险所环绕, 故心绪甚为紊乱。 **throw sb off his ~**, upset him; cause him to fall. 使某人心情紊乱; 使某人跌倒。 **~ of power**,

condition in which no one country or group of countries is much stronger than another. (国际间的) 势力均衡状态. **4** [U] (in art) harmony of design and proportion: (艺术) 构图与比例之调和; 调谐: *a picture lacking in* ~. 构图与比例不调和的图画. **5** (accounts) difference between two columns of an account (money received and money paid out, etc). (帐目) 借贷双方的差额; 收支差额; 结余. **on** ~, taking everything into consideration. 将一切情形都考虑到. *strike a* ~ *(between…)*, find this difference; (fig) reach a solution or adjustment considered to be fair to all; (fig) compromise; find a middle course. 结算帐目; (喻) 寻出公平的解决办法; (喻) 采折衷办法; 取中庸之道. ~ **of payments**, statement (for a stated period) of the total payments to foreign countries (for imports, outflow of capital and gold) and the total receipts from foreign countries (for exports, inflow of capital and gold). 国际收支平衡表 (说明在某一段期间内为进口, 资本和黄金的外流而付给外国的及为出口, 资本和黄金的流入而收自外国的全部款项). ~ **of trade**, difference in value between exports and imports. 贸易差额. '~-**sheet**, written statement of this difference, with details, showing credit and debit. 借贷对照表; 资产负债表. **6** amount still owed after a part payment: (付过一部分款后之) 欠款; 余额; 尾款: ~ *to be paid within one week*. 应于一周内付清之尾款. **7 the** ~, (colloq) the remainder of anything; what is left. (口) 剩余.

bal·co·ny /'bælkənɪ; 'bælkənɪ/ *n* (*pl* -**nies**) **1** platform (with a wall or rail) built on an outside wall of a building, reached from an upstairs room. (筑于外墙, 与楼上一房间相通的) 阳台. **2** (in a theatre or concert hall) series of rows of seats above floor-level and (usu) rising one above the other. (US 美 = *gallery*). (戏院或音乐厅里的) 楼座 (通常其座椅一排比一排高). **bal·co·nied** *adj* having a ~ or balconies: 有阳台的: *a balconied house*. 有阳台的房子.

bald /bɔːld; bɔld/ *adj* (-**er**, -**est**) **1** (of men) having no or not much hair on the scalp; (of animals) hairless; (of birds) featherless; (of trees) leafless; (of land, hills, etc) without trees or bushes. (指男人) 秃头的 (头顶全部或部分无发); (指动物) 无毛的; (指鸟类) 无羽毛的; (指树木) 无叶的; (指土地, 山丘等) 无草木的. **2** (fig) dull; without ornament: (喻) 单调的; 枯燥的; 无装饰的: *a style of writing*; 单调的文体; *a* ~ *statement of the facts*, one that gives the facts in an uninteresting way. 枯燥无味的事实陈述. **3** '~-**head**, '~-**pate** *n* man with a ~ head. 秃头顶的人. *go at it* ,~-'**headed**, (colloq) attack or deal with it in a reckless manner, using all one's energy. (口) 不顾一切地全力去应付; 硬干; 硬拼. ~-**ly** *adv* (always *fig*): (总是作比喻用): *speaking* ~*ly; to put it* ~*ly*, plainly, without trying to soften what one says. 直言不讳地说. ~-**ness** *n*

bal·der·dash /'bɔːldədæʃ; 'bɔldə,dæʃ/ *n* [U] foolish or meaningless talk or writing. 胡言乱语; 无意义的话 (或文字).

bal·dric /'bɔːldrɪk; 'bɔldrɪk/ *n* belt (passing over the right shoulder to the left hip) for a sword, bugle, horn, etc. (经过右肩至左胯用以佩带剑、号角等之) 佩带; 肩带.

bale[1] /beɪl; bel/ *n* [C] heap of material pressed together and tied with rope or wire: 用绳索或铁丝紧扎在一起的一堆材料; 包; 捆: ~*s of cloth*, (usu packed in canvas); 布捆捆 (通常用帆布包装); ~*s of hay*, (tied in string). 干草捆 (用绳子扎者). □ *vt* [VP6A] make into, pack in, ~s: 使成捆; 包装成捆: *to* ~ *hay*. 捆干草.

bale[2] /beɪl; bel/ *vt* = **bail**[3] (2). ~ *out (of)*, (of an airman) jump with a parachute from a damaged aircraft or an aircraft out of control. (指飞行员) 自损坏或失灵之飞机中跳伞降落.

bale[3] /beɪl; bel/ *n* (old use, liter) evil. (旧用法, 文) 邪恶. ~-**ful** /-fʊl; -fəl/ *adj* evil, sinister, harmful: 邪恶的; 凶恶的; 有害的: ~*ful looks/influences*. 凶恶的面

容 (恶势力). ~-**fully** /-fʊlɪ; -fəlɪ/ *adv*

balk, baulk[1] /bɔːk; bɔk/ *n* **1** thick, roughly squared beam of wood. 方木材; 梁木. **2** hindrance; obstacle; cause of delay. 阻碍; 障碍; 妨碍; 迟延之原因.

balk, baulk[2] /bɔːk; bɔk/ *vt, vi* **1** [VP6A, 14] purposely get in the way of: 故意妨碍; 阻碍; 阻止: ~ *sb's plans*, prevent him from carrying them out; 阻止某人的计划 (使不能实现); ~ *sb of his prey*, prevent him from getting it; 故意妨碍某人使其捕不着猎物; *be* ~*ed in one's purpose*. 受到妨碍达不到目的. **2** [VP2A, 3A] ~ *(at)*, (eg of a horse) refuse to go forward; hesitate: (指马等) 拒绝向前走; 犹豫: *The horse* ~*ed at the high hedge*. 马在高树篱前面停蹄不前. *Her husband* ~*ed at the expense of the plans she had made*. 她丈夫对她的计划中所需要的经费感到犹豫.

ball[1] /bɔːl; bɔl/ *n* **1** any solid or hollow sphere as used in games ('*base-*, '*foot-*, '*tennis-*, '*cricket-*~, etc). (棒球、足球、网球、板球等游戏中之实心的或空心的) 球. ⇨ the illus at these *nn*. 参看各名词之插图. *be on the* ~, be alert, competent (in what one is doing). 小心谨慎、胜任愉快地从事 (正在做的事). *have the* ~ *at one's feet*, have a good chance of attaining success. 有成功的好机会. *keep the* ~ *rolling*, keep the conversation, etc going. 使谈话等持续不断. *play* ~, (colloq) cooperate: *The management refused to play* ~. 经理部拒绝合作. *start/set the* ~ *rolling*, start sth, esp conversation, going. 开始; (尤指) 开始谈话. *The* ~ *is in his, etc court/with him, etc*, The next move (in talks, etc) is his, etc. 在谈话等中下一个该轮到他 (等) 了. *three* ~*s*, pawnbroker's sign. 三球 (当铺标记). ,~-'**bearing(s)**, bearings (2) in which friction is lessened by the use of small steel ~s; (*sing*) one of these ~s. 球轴承; 滚珠轴承; (单) (滚珠轴承中之一粒) 钢珠. '~-**cock** *n* device which regulates the supply of water in a tank or cistern by means of a floating ~ which shuts or opens a valve as the water rises and falls. 球旋塞 (水箱中当水升降时借水面浮球关闭或开启活门以调节供水之装置). '~-**pen**, ,~-**point-'pen**, pen in which the ink flows round a ~-bearing that rotates on contact with the paper. 圆珠笔; 原子笔 (一种笔, 在写字时墨水沿着接触纸面之旋转小钢珠流出). **2** (cricket) single delivery of the ~ by the bowler. (板球) 投手所投之一球. *no* ~, delivery that breaks the rules; 犯规之投球; (baseball) any strike or throw: (棒球) 任何一击或一投: *a foul* ~; 界外球; (football) movement of the ~ by a player: (足球) 传球: *send over a high* ~. 传一个高吊球. **3** material gathered, rolled or wound, into a round mass: 聚成 (滚成或缠成) 球形之物: *a* ~ *of wool/string*; 一团毛线 (线球); *a 'snow* ~; 雪球; *a 'meat*~, (of minced meat. 用碎肉团成的) 肉丸子. **4** metal missile to be fired from a gun: 炮弹; 弹丸: '*cannon-*~, (old fashioned, cf *shell*). 炮弹 (旧式用语, 参较 shell). '~-**cartridge**, one containing a bullet (contrasted with *blank cartridge*). 实弹 (与 blank cartridge 相对). **5** round part: 圆形部份: *the* ~ *of the thumb*, near the palm, ⇨ the illus at **arm**; 大拇指之近手掌部份 (参看 arm 之插图); *the* ~ *of the foot*, near the base of the big toe, ⇨ the illus at **leg**. 脚掌近大拇趾根部份 (参看 leg 之插图). **6** △ (sl) testicle. (讳) (俚) 睾丸. □ *int* △ ~**s!** (sl) Nonsense! (讳) (俚) 胡说! □ *vi, vt* **1** form into a ~: 形成球形: *The snow* ~*ed under the horse's feet*. 雪在马蹄下凝成球形. **2** wind or squeeze into a ~. 缠绕或捏成球形. **3** ~*s sth up*, (sl) make a mess of it. (俚) 将某事物弄成一团糟. Hence, 由此产生, '~-**up** *n* mess. 杂乱.

ball[2] /bɔːl; bɔl/ *n* social gathering for dancing, with an organized programme, and (often) special entertainment. (节目事先安排好并常附有特别表演之) 舞会. ~-**dress**, woman's frock to be worn at ~s. 妇女于参加舞会时所穿之长礼服. '~-**room**, large room for ~s. 跳舞厅.

bal·lad /'bæləd; 'bæləd/ *n* simple song or poem, esp one that tells an old story. 民歌; 民谣; (尤指) 叙事歌.

bal·lade /bæ'lɑːd; bə'lɑd/ *n* [C] **1** poem of one

more stanzas, each with 7, 8 or 10 lines, each ending with the same refrain line, followed by an envoy. 联韵诗(通常为三节,每节七行、八行或十行,每节皆以同一重叠句收尾,最后为煞尾的短节). **2** musical composition of a romantic nature. 浪漫曲;叙事曲.

bal·last /'bæləst; 'bæləst/ n [U] **1** heavy material (eg rock, iron, sand) loaded into a ship to keep it steady. (船中所装用以保持平衡之)压舱物 (如石、铁、沙). in ~, carrying ~ only. 仅装压舱物的. **2** sand or other material carried in a balloon, to be thrown out to make the balloon go higher. (轻气球所携,在使气球升得更高时可以抛弃之沙或其他物质). **3** (fig) mental stability. (喻)心理之稳定. **4** gravel, crushed rock, etc used to make a foundation for a road, esp a railway. (铺路基,尤指铺铁道道床,所用的)碎石. □ vt [VP6A] supply with ~. 供应压舱物,压载物或碎石.

bal·ler·ina /ˌbæleˈriːnə; ˌbæleˈrinə/ n (pl ~s) (I) woman ballet-dancer, esp one who takes one of the chief classical roles. (意)芭蕾舞女演员;(尤指)芭蕾舞女主角.

bal·let /'bæleɪ; 'bæle/ n **1** [C] dramatic performance, without dialogue or singing, illustrating a story by a group of dancers. 芭蕾舞剧 (无对话,无歌唱,由一群舞者以动作叙述故事之表演). **2** [U] the dancers: 芭蕾舞剧演员之总称: a member of the ~. 芭蕾舞团之一演员. **3** [U] the ~, this kind of stage performance as an art. 芭蕾舞艺术. '~-dancer, person who dances in ~s. 跳芭蕾舞剧演员;舞剧演员. '~-skirt, short skirt worn by a ~-dancer. 芭蕾舞裙(跳芭蕾舞者所穿之短裙).

bal·lis·tic /bəˈlɪstɪk; bæˈlɪstɪk/ adj of projectiles: 抛射物的; 弹道的: intercontinental ~ missile (**ICBM**), long-range rocket for use in war. 洲际弹道导弹(略作 ICBM). **bal·lis·tics** n (usu with sing v) study, science, of projectiles. (通常与单数动词连用)弹道学;发射学.

bal·locks /'bɒlɒks; 'bɑlɒks/ n pl △ (vulg) (讳)(鄙)胡说. **1** testicles.睾丸. **2** nonsense. 屁话.

bal·loon /bəˈluːn; bəˈlun/ n **1** bag or envelope filled with air, or with gas lighter than air: 气球: captive ~, one moored to the ground. 固定在地上的气球;系留气球. '~ barrage, barrier of steel cables, supported by captive ~s, intended to give protection against low-flying enemy aircraft. 系留气球网(用气球支起于空中以对抗低飞敌机之钢丝障碍物). 'barrage ~, one of these captive ~s. 阻塞气球;障碍气球. hot-'air ~, apparatus for travel in the air with a basket or car (for the passengers, etc) suspended beneath a large bag of hot gas. 热气球(在充满热气体的大袋下悬挂一篮或座舱以供人乘坐的航空器). '~ tyre, low-pressure pneumatic tyre of great width. 宽型之低压充气轮胎. **2** (in a strip cartoon, etc) outline for

balloons

dialogue, exclamations, etc. (连环漫画等中供写出对话、呼喊等的) 气球状线圈. □ vi [VP2A, C] swell out like a ~. 膨胀如气球. ~·ist n person who goes up in ~s. 乘气球者.

bal·lot /'bælət; 'bælət/ n **1** [C] piece of paper (also 亦作 '~-paper), ticket or ball, used in secret voting; [U] secret voting; [C] instance of this. (秘密投票所用之)选举票(用纸制者,亦有用球者);秘密投票. take a ~, decide by voting. 投票决定. **2** votes so recorded. 投票总数. '~-box, box into which ~-papers are dropped by voters. 投票箱. □ vi [VP2A, 3A] ~ (for), give a vote; draw lots. 投票;投(……)票;抽签;拈阄.

bally /'bælɪ; 'bælɪ/ adj, adv (GB dated sl, euphem for bloody (3)) (used to show the speaker's strong feelings of like or dislike, etc): (英, 过时俚语, 为 bloody(3) 之委婉语) 甚; 很; 极 (用以表示说话者极度之喜爱或憎恶): What a ~ nuisance! 多么令人讨厌呀! 可厌透了!

bally·hoo /ˈbælɪhuː; US: 'bælɪhu; 'bælɪˌhu/ n [U] (colloq) (口) **1** noisy publicity or advertising; vulgar or misleading ways of attracting attention. 大吹大擂;大肆宣传. **2** uproar. 喧嚣;叫闹.

balm /bɑːm; bɑm/ n [U] **1** sweet-smelling oil or ointment obtained from certain kinds of trees, used for soothing pain or healing. (取自某些种树中,用以止痛或疗伤之)香油;香脂;香胶. **2** (fig) that which gives peace of mind; consolation. (喻)慰藉物;慰藉;安慰. ~·y adj **1** (of air) soft and warm. (指空气) 温暖的; 暖和的. **2** healing; fragrant. 能治疗的; 芳香的. **3** (sl) (俚) = barmy.

bal·oney /bəˈləʊnɪ; bəˈlonɪ/ n = boloney.

balsa /'bɔːlsə; 'bɔlsə/ n [C, U] (light-weight wood of a) tropical American tree; raft of floats fastened to a framework: 白塞树(产于热带美洲); 白塞木(白塞树的轻质木材);(用白塞木扎于架上而成的)筏: (attrib) (用作定语) a ~ raft. 白塞木筏.

bal·sam /'bɔːlsəm; 'bɔlsəm/ n **1** = balm(1). **2** tree yielding balm. 香油树; 香脂树; 香胶树. **3** flowering plant grown in gardens. 凤仙花.

bal·us·ter /'bæləstə(r); 'bæləstə/ n one of the upright posts supporting a handrail; (pl) banisters. 扶手栏杆的支柱;(复)楼梯外侧之扶手栏杆.

bal·us·trade /ˌbæləˈstreɪd; ˌbæləˈstred/ n row of balusters with the stonework or woodwork that joins them on top, round a balcony, terrace, flat roof, etc. (围绕于阳台、平台、平屋顶等之)栏杆.

bam·bino /bæmˈbiːnəʊ; bæmˈbino/ n (pl ~s) (I) (意) **1** baby. 婴孩; 婴儿. **2** representation in art of the infant Jesus. 耶稣幼时之像.

bam·boo /bæmˈbuː; bæmˈbu/ n [U] tall plant with hard, hollow, jointed stems, of the grass family; [C] (pl ~s) stem, used as a stick or support. 竹;竹竿;竹棍.

bam·boozle /bæmˈbuːzl; bæmˈbuzl/ vt (colloq) (口) [VP6A, 14] **1** mystify: 使困惑; 使迷惑: You can't ~ me. 你不能使我迷惑. **2** ~ sb (into/out of) (doing) (sth),trick, cheat him. 哄某人使(不)做某事;欺骗某人.

ban /bæn; bæn/ vt (-nn-) **1** [VP6A] order with authority that sth must not be done, said, etc: 下令禁止; 查禁: a ban-the-bomb demonstration, one calling for nuclear disarmament. 要求裁减核子武器之示威. The play was banned by the censor. 该剧本被新闻检查员查禁. **2** [VP6A, 14] ~ sb (from) (doing) (sth), order with authority that sb may not do sth: 禁止(某人做某事): He was ~ned from (attending) the meeting. 他被禁止出席该会议. □ n (also 亦作 '~ning-order)order that bans sth/sb: 禁令: under a ban, banned. 被查禁;被禁止.

ba·nal /bəˈnɑːl; US: 'beɪnl; 'benl/ adj commonplace; uninteresting: 平凡的;无趣味的: ~ remarks. 平凡的话. ~·ity /bəˈnælətɪ; bəˈnælətɪ/ n [U] quality of being ~; [C] (pl -ties) ~ remark, etc: 平凡; 无趣; 平凡的话等: conversation that was chiefly ~ities. 内容大半平凡的谈话.

ba·nana /bəˈnɑːnə US: bəˈnænə; bəˈnænə/ n [C] long, thick-skinned (yellow when ripe) fruit growing in bunches on the ~-tree in tropical and semi-tropical countries. 香蕉(产于热带及亚热带之长形水果,成串生长,果皮厚, 成熟时变黄色)。⇨ the illus at **fruit**. 参看 fruit 之插图。⇨ **plantain**¹.

band /bænd; bænd/ n **1** flat, thin strip of material, esp for fastening things together or for placing round an object to strengthen it: 带;箍: *iron ~s round a barrel;* 箍于桶外之铁箍; *papers kept together with a rubber ~.* 用橡皮圈束在一起之文件。'~**saw** n (eng) machine-driven saw consisting of an endless steel belt. (工程)带锯(机器推动的锯,由一条钢环带所组成)。 **2** flat, thin strip of material forming tne rest in an article of clothing: (构成衣服一部份之)扁平的薄条带: *Some shirts have a 'neck~ and two 'wrist~s.* 有些衬衫有一个领子和两个袖口。 **3** strip or line, different from tne rest in colour or design, on sth: (颜色或图案与其余部份不同之)条纹;条饰: *a white plate with a blue ~ round the edge.* 有一道蓝边的白盘。 **4** group of persons doing sth together under a leader and with a common purpose: 一队;一组;一伙;一帮: *a ~ of robbers / fugitives / revellers.* 一伙强盗(逃亡者,宴乐者)。 **5** group of persons who play music together, eg of wind-instrument performers (often 常作 *brass* ~): 乐队; 军乐队;管乐队; the *Regimental 'B~;* 团部军乐队; a *'dance ~;* 舞蹈之伴奏乐队; a *'jazz ~;* 爵士乐队; a *'steel ~.* 钢鼓乐队 (特立尼达等加勒比海地区特有之乐队,以截成各种高度之油桶为打击乐器)。'~·**master** /ˈbændmɑːstə(r); ˈbændˌmæstə/ n conductor of a ~. 乐队指挥。'~s·**man** /-mən; -mən/ n (pl **-men**) member of a ~. 乐队队员。'~·**stand** /ˈbændstænd; ˈbændˌstænd/ n raised platform usu roofed, for a ~ playing in the open air. (通常有顶之) 露天音乐演奏台。'~·**wagon** n wagon carrying the ~ heading a march or procession (esp of a political party). (为游行队伍开道的)乐队车 (尤指属于政党之游行队伍者)。 *climb / jump on / aboard the* ~**wagon,** join in what seems likely to be a successful enterprise. 加入大有成功希望之事业。 **6** (radio; short for *'wave-~*) range of frequencies that may be tuned in together: (无线电; wave-band 之简称) 频段; 波段: *the 19-metre* ~. 十九公尺之频带。 □ vt, vi **1** [VP6A] put a ~, strip or line on. 加带或条纹于…之上; 用带绑扎。 **2** [VP15B, 14, 2C] ~ *together,* unite, in a group: 结伙;结队;结合: ~ *people together;* 把人们结合起来; ~ *with others to do sth.* 伙同他人做某事。 *They* ~*ed together to protest.* 他们联合抗议。

ban·dage /ˈbændɪdʒ; ˈbændɪdʒ/ n strip of material for binding round a wound or injury, or for blindfolding sb. (包扎伤口之)绷带; 蒙眼巾。 □ vt [VP6A, 15B] ~ *(up),* tie up with a ~: 用绷带包扎; 缚以绷带: ~ *(up) a boy's leg;* 用绷带将一男孩之腿包扎起来; *a man with a* ~*d hand.* 一只手包了绷带的人。

band-aid /ˈbændeɪd; ˈbændeɪd/ n [C, U] (P) (US) type of plaster (3). (商标)(美)一种橡皮膏;一种绊创膏。

ban·danna /bænˈdænə; bænˈdænə/ n brightly coloured square of material with red or yellow spots, usn worn round the neck. (颜色鲜艳, 带红色或黄色斑点, 通常用以围脖子的)方巾; 丝巾。

band·box /ˈbændbɒks; ˈbændˌbɑks/ n light, cardboard box for millinery: (装女帽等之轻的)硬纸盒: *She looks as if she had just come out of a* ~, She looks extremely smart and neat. 她看起来极为整洁漂亮。

ban·deau /ˈbændəʊ US: -ˈdəʊ; bænˈdo/ n (pl **-deaux** /-dəʊz US: -ˈdəʊz; -ˈdoz/) band for keeping a woman's hair in place. (女用之)束发带。

ban·dit /ˈbændɪt; ˈbændɪt/ n robber, one of an armed band (eg of brigands attacking travellers in forests or mountains or towns, banks and offices). 土匪;强盗;劫匪。 ~**ry** n [U] activity of ~s. 匪盗之行为。

ban·do·leer, ban·do·lier /ˌbændəˈlɪə(r); ˌbændə-ˈlɪr/ n shoulder-belt with pockets for cartridges. (背于

肩上之)子弹带。

bandy¹ /ˈbændɪ; ˈbændɪ/ vt (pt, pp **-died**) [VP6A, 14, 15B] exchange (words, blows). 争吵; 互殴。 *have one's name bandied about,* be talked about in an unfavourable way, be a subject for gossip. 受人批评;遭人物议。 ~ *a story about,* pass it from person to person. 传播是非。 ~ *words with sb,* exchange remarks quickly, esp when quarrelling. 与某人争吵。

bandy² /ˈbændɪ; ˈbændɪ/ adj (of the legs) curving outwards at the knees. (指腿) 膝部向外弯曲的。'~·**legged** adj (of persons or animals) having ~ legs. (指人或动物)有膝部外弯之腿的。

bane /beɪn; ben/ n [U] **1** (only in compounds) poison: (仅用于复合词中) 毒药: *'rat's-~.* 毒鼠药; 杀鼠药。 **2** cause of ruin or trouble: 祸根; 祸害; 麻烦的起因; 累赘: *Drink was the ~ of his life.* 酒是毁他一生的祸根。 *He has been the ~ of my life,* caused me constant trouble and anxiety. 他是我一生的累赘。 ~·**ful** /-fʊl; -fəl/ adj evil: 不良的; 有害的: *a ~ful influence.* 不良的影响。 ~·**fully** /-fʊlɪ; -fəlɪ/ adv

bang¹ /bæŋ; bæŋ/ n violent blow; sudden, loud noise: 猛击; 猛撞; 碰撞的声音; 突然的巨响; 砰: *He fell and got a nasty ~ on the head.* 他跌了一跤, 头碰得很厉害。 *He always shuts the door with a ~.* 他关门总是砰然一声。 *The firework went off with a ~.* 烟火砰一声爆炸。 *go (off) with a ~,* (GB colloq) (英口); *go (over) with a ~,* (US colloq) (美口) (of a performance, etc) be successful, be greatly liked. (指表演等) 极为成功; 大受欢迎。 □ vt, vi **1** [VP6A, 15B, 2A, C] hit violently; give a ~ to; shut with a noise: 猛击; 砰然而击; 砰然关上: *He ~ed at the door.* 他砰砰地用力敲门。 *He was ~ing on the door with his fist.* 他用拳头猛敲门。 *He ~ed his fist on the table.* 他用拳头捶打桌子。 *She ~ed the keys of the piano.* 她用力敲钢琴键。 *The teacher tried to ~ grammar into the heads of his pupils.* 那老师想把语法硬塞入学生的脑中。 *Don't ~ the lid down.* 不要砰盖子砰然盖上。 *He ~ed the box down on the floor.* 他砰然一声把盒子摔在地上。 *A door was ~ing somewhere.* 什么地方有一扇门砰然作响。 *The door ~ed shut.* 门砰然一声关上。 **2** [VP2A, C] make a loud noise: 发巨响; 作嘭嘭声; 作隆隆声: *The fireworks ~ed away.* 烟火发出巨响。 *The guns ~ed away.* 枪炮不断地发出巨响。 *We were ~ing away (= firing continuously) at the enemy.* 我们砰砰地不断向敌人射击。 *Tell the children to stop ~ing about,* being noisy. 告诉孩子们不要到处弄出声响。 □ adv, int: *go ~,* burst with a loud noise; 发出碎裂或炭然一声巨响; *~ in the middle,* exactly in the middle; 恰恰在中间; 在正当中; *come ~ up (= violently) against sth.* 重重地碰撞在某物上。

bang² /bæŋ; bæŋ/ vt cut (the front hair) squarely across the forehead: 将(额前发) 剪成刘海式 (即横着剪齐): *She wears her hair ~ed.* 她的头发留有刘海式。 □ n [C] fringe of such hair. 刘海式之前额留发。

banger /ˈbæŋə(r); ˈbæŋə/ n (sl) (俚) **1** sausage. 腊肠; 香肠。 **2** noisy firework. (发巨响的)爆竹。 **3** old dilapidated car. 破烂的老爷车。

bangle /ˈbæŋgl; ˈbæŋgl/ n ornamental rigid band worn round the arm or ankle. 手镯; 脚镯。

ban·ian, ban·yan /ˈbænɪən; ˈbænjən/ n **1** Hindu trader. 印度商人。 **2** (also 亦作 '~**-tree**) Indian fig, whose branches come down to the ground and take root. 榕树(树枝垂至地上即可生根)。

ban·ish /ˈbænɪʃ; ˈbænɪʃ/ vt [VP6A, 14] **1** ~ *(from),* send away, esp out of the country, as a punishment: 放逐;充军;驱逐出境: *He was ~ed from the realm.* 他被驱逐出境。 **2** put away from, out of (the mind): (自脑中)驱除;排除;忘却: ~ *care.* 消除烦忧。 ~·**ment** n [U] state of being ~ed: 被放逐或驱除的状态: *go into* ~*ment.* 被驱逐出境; 被放逐。

ban·is·ter /ˈbænɪstə(r); ˈbænɪstə/ n post supporting the handrail of a staircase; (pl) posts and handrail together. 支撑楼梯扶手的支柱; (复)楼梯的扶手及栏杆。

banjo /'bændʒəʊ; 'bændʒo/ *n* (*pl* ~**s**, ~**es**) musical instrument played by plucking the strings with the fingers. 班卓琴. ⇨ the illus at **string**. 参看 string 之插图.

bank¹ /bæŋk; bæŋk/ *n* [C] **1** land along each side of a river or canal; ground near a river: 河岸: *A river flows between its ~s.* 河水在两岸之间流. *His house is on the south ~ of the river.* 他的房子是在河的南岸. **2** sloping land or earth, often forming a border or division: 斜坡; 土堤; 埂 (常构成一条界线或区分线): *low ~s of earth between rice-fields.* 稻田与稻田之间的低矮的田埂. *There were flowers growing on the ~s on each side of the country lanes.* 乡村小道两侧之斜坡上长有花. **3** (also 亦作 '**sand·~**) part of the sea-bed higher than its surroundings, but covered with enough water for ships except at low tide; (mining) coal-face. (海中的) 浅滩; 沙洲; (采矿) 煤层中的采掘面. **4** flat-topped mass of cloud, snow, etc esp one formed by the wind: 状似堤岸之云堆. 雪堆等: *The sun went down behind a ~ of clouds.* 太阳在云堤后面落下去了. **5** artificial slope made to enable a car to go round a curve with less risk. 公路上在弯路处便于汽车转弯所作之倾斜面.

bank² /bæŋk; bæŋk/ *vt, vi* **1** [VP6A, 15B, 2C] ~ *up*, (a) make or form into ~s, ~d bank: 形成堤状; (使) 堆积(参看上列第 4 义): *The snow has ~ed up.* 雪已堆成了雪堤. (b) stop water (of a river, etc) from flowing by making a ~ of earth, mud, etc. 筑堤防险 (河等之)水. (c) heap up (the fire in a fireplace or furnace) with coal-dust, etc so that the fire burns slowly for a long time. 以煤灰等堆在(炉火)上, 使其燃烧缓慢, 维持得久; 封(炉火). **2** [VP2A] (of a motor-car or aircraft) travel with one side higher than the other (eg when turning). (指汽车或飞机) 倾斜行进或飞行 (如在转弯时).

bank³ /bæŋk; bæŋk/ *n* **1** establishment for keeping money and valuables safely, the money being paid out on the customer's order (by means of cheques). 银行: **the B~**, the B~ of England, which is used by the British Government; 英国国家银行; 英格兰银行; *have money in the ~*, have savings; 银行中有存款; '~ *clerk*, clerk working in a ~. 银行办事员. '**~-bill** *n* bill drawn by one ~ upon another ~. 银行汇票. '**~-book** *n* (also 亦作 '*passbook*) book containing a record of a customer's account. 银行存折. '~ *draft*, = ~*bill*. '~ *holiday* *n* (GB) one of those days (not Sundays) on which ~s are closed by law, usu kept as general holidays (eg Good Friday, Easter Monday, Christmas Day); (US) any weekday on which ~s are closed . (英) (除星期日以外的)法定银行假日(如耶稣受难节, 复活节之次日, 圣诞节); (美)任何星期日以外的银行假日. '**~-note** *n* piece of paper money issued by a ~. (银行所发行的)钞票. '**~-rate** *n* rate at which the B~ of England (or other national ~) will discount bills, ⇨ bill³(5). 英国国家银行(或其他国家银行)之票据贴现率. '**~-roll** *n* roll of paper money. 钞票卷. **2** (gambling) sum of money held by the keeper of the gaming table, from which he pays his losses. (赌博)庄家的赌本. *break the ~*, (eg at Monte Carlo) win all this money. (例如在蒙特卡洛)赢得庄家的全部赌本. **3** (place for storing) reserve supplies. 储备之物品, 储备所; 库. '*blood·~* *n* place where blood or blood plasma is stored for use in hospitals, etc. 血库 (储备血液或血浆以供医院等使用的地方).

bank⁴ /bæŋk; bæŋk/ *vt, vi* **1** [VP6A] place (money) in a bank³(1): 存(款)于银行: *He ~s half his salary every month.* 他将每月薪水的一半存于银行. **2** [VP3A] ~ *(with)*, keep money in a bank: 在银行中有存款: *Who do you ~ with*, With what firm of bankers do you keep your money? *Where do you ~?* 你在何处(哪一家银行)存款? **3** [VP3A] ~ *on /upon*, base one's hopes on: 指望; 依靠: *I'm ~ing on* your help. 我指望着你的帮助. **~er** *n* person who owns, is a partner in, or is a governor or director of, a bank³(1); (gambling) keeper of a bank³(2). 银行家; 经营银行业务者; (赌场)庄家. '**~er's card**, card (issued by a bank) that guarantees the payment of a customer's cheque (up to a certain amount). 银行保证卡 (保证替顾客支付高达某一数额之支票). ,~**er's 'order**, = *standing order.* ⇨ **standing**(1). ~**·ing** *n* [U] the business of keeping a bank³(1): 银行业: *choose ~ing as a career;* 选择银行业为职业; ~*ing hours*, eg 10am to 3.30pm. 银行营业时间(如上午十时至下午三时半).

bank⁵ /bæŋk; bæŋk/ *n* **1** row of keys, switches, etc: 一排键; 键盘; 一排开关: *a three-~ / four-~ typewriter.* 一架三排键(四排键)之打字机. **2** bench for rowers in a galley(1). (古希腊罗马战舰中)划手坐的长凳. **3** row of cylinders (in an engine). (引擎中的)汽缸排列.

bank·rupt /'bæŋkrəpt; 'bæŋkrəpt/ *n* (legal) person judged by a law court to be unable to pay his debts in full, his property being distributed for the benefit of his creditors. (法律)(经法院宣告之)破产者(即无力偿清债务, 以其财产分配给债权人). □ *adj* **1** unable to pay one's debts. 无力还债的; 破产的. *go* ~, become ~, insolvent. 无力还债; 破产. **2** ~ *in /of*, completely without: 完全缺乏: *The newspapers accused the Government of being ~ in ideas.* 报纸指控政府完全缺乏主意. □ *vt* [VP6A] make ~. 使破产. ~**cy** /'bæŋkrəpsɪ; 'bæŋkrʌptsɪ/ *n* [U] ~ condition; [C] (*pl* **-cies**) instance of this: 破产; 倒闭: *There were ten ~cies in the town last year.* 本市去年有十家破产.

ban·ner /'bænə(r); 'bænə/ *n* **1** flag (now chiefly fig): 旗帜 (现主要作比喻用法): *the ~ of freedom.* 自由的旗帜. *under the ~ (of)*, belonging to, supporting (a particular faith or movement). 在…的旗帜下 (即属于或拥护某一信仰或运动). **2** flag or announcement, usu on two poles, carried in (eg religious or political) processions, making known principles, slogans, etc. 书有标语或口号之大旗 (通常用两根竿子举起, 执于宗教或政治游行的行列中). ~ *headline*, (in a newspaper) prominent headline in large type. (报纸中)大号字体的显著标题.

ban·is·ter *n* = **banister**.

ban·nock /'bænək; 'bænək/ *n* (Scot and N England) flat, oatmeal, home-made loaf. (苏格兰及北英格兰)用燕麦片自制的一种薄饼.

banns /bænz; bænz/ *n pl* public announcement in church that two persons are to be married: (教堂里的)结婚预告: *put up / publish the ~;* 公布结婚预告; *have one's ~ called.* 请求公布结婚预告. *forbid the ~*, declare opposition to a proposed marriage. 宣布反对所预告之婚姻.

ban·quet /'bæŋkwɪt; 'bæŋkwɪt/ *n* elaborate meal, usu for a special event, at which speeches are made: (通常为某一特殊事件所举行之)正式宴会 (会中并有演讲者): *a wedding ~.* 结婚喜宴. □ *vt, vi* [VP6A] give a ~ to (sb); [VP2A] take part in a ~; feast. 宴请(某人);参加宴会; 饮宴.

ban·shee /bæn'ʃiː US: 'bænʃiː; 'bænʃi/ *n* (Ireland and the Scottish Highlands) spirit whose cry is said to mean that there will be a death in the house where the cry is heard. (爱尔兰及苏格兰高地)(据说谁家听到其哭声就预示将有人死亡之)妖精.

bant /bænt; bænt/ *vi* [VP2A] (dated) adopt a diet designed to reduce weight (*slim* and *reduce* are the usu words). (过时用语)节食以减轻体重(通常用 slim 和 reduce). ~**·ing** *n* treatment of obesity by this means. 磐廷氏疗法; 节食减肥法.

ban·tam /'bæntəm; 'bæntəm/ *n* **1** small-sized kind of domestic fowl, esp the cock, which is a fighter. 一种矮小的鸡 (尤指公鸡, 被畜作斗鸡). **2** boxer between 112 and 118 lb. 最轻量级拳击手(体重自 112磅至 118 磅之间者).

ban·ter /'bæntə(r); 'bæntə/ *vt, vi* [VP6A, 2A] tease

in a playful way (by joking talk). 嘲弄；戏谑；开玩笑。 □ *n* [U] good-humoured teasing. 嘲弄；开玩笑。 ~·ing *adj* ~·ing·ly *adv*

Ban·tu /bæn'tu: US: 'bæn'tu/ *adj, n* (member) of a group of related Central and S African peoples; of their languages. 班图人(居于非洲中部及南部)；班图语；班图人的；班图语的。

ban·yan *n* = banian.

bao·bab /'beɪəbæb US: 'baʊbæb; 'beɔ,bæb/ *n* tree of tropical Africa with a trunk that grows to an enormous size. 猴面包(树)；猢狲面(产于热带非洲之一种巨树)。

bap·tism /'bæptɪzəm; 'bæptɪzəm/ *n* 1 [U] ceremony of sprinkling sb with, or immersing sb in, water, accepting him as a member of the Christian Church and (usu) giving him a name or names (in addition to the family name); [C] instance of this: 浸礼；洗礼(洒水于某人或将某人浸于水中，以示准许其为基督教徒，通常并授予名或教名)；浸礼或洗礼之实例: *There were six ~s at this church last week.* 此教堂于上周曾为六人施洗礼。2 (fig) first experience of a new kind of life: (喻)一种新生活的初次经验: *a soldier's ~ of fire,* his first experience of warfare. 一兵士初次临战之经验。**bap·tis·mal** /bæp'tɪz-mel; bæp'tɪzml/ *adj* of ~: 洗礼的；浸礼的: *~al name/water/font.* 洗礼名(水，盆)。

Bap·tist /'bæptɪst; 'bæptɪst/ *n, adj* (member) of the denomination of Christians who object to infant baptism and believe that baptism should be by immersion and at an age when a person is old enough to understand the meaning of the ceremony. 浸信会教友(反对婴儿受洗，认为洗礼应用浸水法施行，并且在一个人长大足以了解其意义时施行)；浸信会的。

bap·tize /bæp'taɪz; bæp'taɪz/ *vt* [VP6A, 23] give baptism to (sb): 给(某人)施洗礼: *He had been ~d a Roman Catholic.* 他曾受洗为天主教徒。

bar¹ /ba:(r); ba:r/ *n* 1 long piece of hard, stiff material (eg metal, wood, soap, chocolate). 棒；条(如金属、木、肥皂、巧克力糖)。2 rod or rail, rigid length of wood or metal, across a door, window or gate, or forming part of a grate (in a fireplace or furnace) or grid: 横杠；门窗之栓；(炉架或铁栅)上的) 铁条: *He was placed behind prison bars,* put into a prison cell. 他被关在监牢里。3 barrier (across a road) that could not be passed (in former times) until a sum of money (called a *toll*) was paid: (昔日横在道路上俟纳税后始准通行之) 障碍物；税卡门: *a toll bar.* 税卡门。4 bank or ridge of sand, etc across the mouth of a river or the entrance to a bay, deposited by currents or tides, often hindering navigation: (河口或海湾之入口处由于流水或潮汐所造成常妨碍航行的) 沙洲: *The ship crossed the bar safely.* 船安全地渡过沙洲。*We stuck fast on the bar.* 我们牢牢地搁浅在沙洲上。5 (fig) barrier or obstacle; sth that hinders or stops progress: (喻)障碍；阻碍物: *Poor health may be a bar to success in life.* 健康不佳可能成为一生中事业成功的障碍。*Poverty is not always a bar to happiness.* 贫穷不一定是幸福的障碍。6 narrow band (of colour, light, etc): 条；光等之) 带；条；纹: *As the sun went down, there was a bar of red across the western sky.* 日落时，西方天际有一道红晖。7 strip of metal across the ribbon of (esp a military) medal to indicate either award twice, 章或勋章之饰带上的金属横条，表示 (a) that the holder has received the same award twice, 佩带者两次获得同样的功勋, or (b) that he has served in a particular field of operations. 佩带者曾参与某一战区作战。8 (in music) vertical line across the stave marking divisions of equal value in time; one of these divisions and the notes in it: (音乐)(乐谱上划分各小节的) 小节线；小节: *the opening bars of the National Anthem.* 国歌开头的数小节。⇨ the illus at **notation.** 参看 notation 之插图。9 railing or barrier in a law court, separating the part where the business is carried on from the part for spectators: 法庭上将审讯场所与旁听席隔开的栏杆: *be tried at (the) Bar,* be tried in open court, where everyone may see and

hear, not secretly. 受公开审讯。*the prisoner at the bar,* the accused person. 被告。10 (in Parliament) railing dividing off the space to which non-members are admitted (eg for examination by members); similar place in the US Senate, House of Representatives and State Legislatures. 英国国会中区划非议员席之栏杆(即非议员席)；(美国参议院、众议院及州议会中的)非议员席。11 (fig) sth that can be compared to a judge or examiner: (喻)可比做法官或审问者之事物；制裁: *at the bar of public opinion,* 舆论的制裁; *the bar of conscience.* 良心的制裁。12 **the Bar,** the profession of barrister; all those who have the right to act as barristers. 律师业；律师界。*be called to the Bar,* be received as a member of the Bar. 被接受充当律师；获得律师资格。*read for the Bar,* study to become a barrister. 读法律；习法。13 (a) (in an inn or public house) room, counter, where drinks (such as beer and spirits) are served: (客栈或酒馆里的) 酒吧间；卖酒柜台；吧台；酒吧: *the Public Bar,* 大众酒吧间, *the Private Bar,* for different classes of users. 私用酒吧间(供不同等级使用者)。(b) (in a hotel, licensed restaurant or private house) room with such a counter. (旅馆、有执照之餐馆或私家之)酒吧间。'**bar·maid** *n* woman who serves drinks at a bar(13). 酒吧女侍者。'**bar·man** /-men; -mən/ *n* (*pl* **-men**) man who does this. 酒吧男侍者。'**bar·ten·der** *n* barmaid or barman. 酒吧招待；酒吧侍者。14 counter at which meals, etc are served and also eaten: 饮食贩卖部；简便饮食柜台: *a 'milk bar;* 牛奶贩卖部; *a quick-lunch bar.* 午间快餐柜台。

bar² /ba:(r); ba:r/ *vt* (-rr-) 1 [VP6A] fasten (a door, gate, etc) with a bar or bars¹(2). 闩(门等)。2 [VP15B] keep (sb) in or out: 把(某人)关在里面或外面: *He barred himself in,* fastened doors, windows, etc so that no one could enter the building. 他把自己关在房子里面(使外人不能入)。3 [VP6A] obstruct: 挡塞；阻碍: *bar a road/path.* 挡住路。*Soldiers barred the way and we couldn't go any farther.* 军队挡住路，我们不能再往前走。4 [VP6A, 14] *bar (from),* prohibit: 禁止: *bar sb from a competition,* order that he shall not take part. 禁止某人参加比赛。[VP6C] (colloq) (口): *She bars smoking in the drawing-room,* does not permit it. 她禁止在客厅里吸烟。*We bar playing cards for money.* 我们禁止玩纸牌赌钱。[VP12C] *I will bar no honest man my house,* will let any honest man visit my house. 我不阻止任何诚实的人到我家里来。5 [VP6A] (usu passive) mark with a stripe or stripes: (通常用被动语态)饰以条纹: *a sky barred with clouds.* 有条状云的天空。

bar³ /ba:(r); ba:r/, **bar·ring** /'ba:rɪŋ; 'ba:rɪŋ/ *prep* (colloq) except: (口) 除…以外；除非；若无: *We shall arrive at noon barring accidents,* unless there are accidents. 若无意外事件发生，我们将于中午到达。*bar none,* without exception. 无例外。*bar one,* except one. 有一例外。

bar⁴ /ba:(r); ba:r/ *n* large Mediterranean fish. 一种地中海大鱼。

barb /ba:b; ba:b/ *n* back-turning or back-curving point of an arrow, spear, fish-hook, etc. (箭、矛、鱼钩等上的)倒钩；倒钩。~ed *adj* having a ~ or. ~s. 有倒刺的；有倒钩的。~ed wire, wire with short, sharp points, used for fences, etc: 有铁蒺藜之铁丝: ~ed wire entanglements, for defensive purposes in war. (战争中作防卫用的)有铁蒺藜之铁丝网；有刺铁丝网。

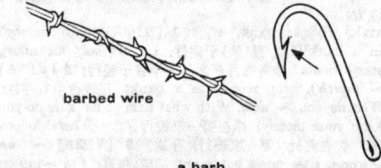

barbed wire

a barb

bar·bar·ian /bɑ:ˈbeəriən; bɑrˈbɛriən/ *adj, n* uncivilized or uncultured (person). 野蛮的; 未开化的; 野蛮人.

bar·baric /bɑ:ˈbærɪk; bɑrˈbærɪk/ *adj* of or like barbarians; uncultivated; rough and rude (esp in art and taste): 野蛮民族的; 未开化的; 粗陋的 (尤指在艺术与欣赏力方面): the ~ *splendour of Attila's court*. 阿提拉宫廷的粗俗华丽.

bar·bar·ism /ˈbɑ:bərɪzəm; ˈbɑrbə,rɪzəm/ *n* **1** [U] state of being uncivilized, ignorant, or rude: 未开化, 无知识或粗野的状态; 野蛮: *living in* ~. 生活于未开化状态的. **2** [C] instance of this; (esp) misuse of language by mixing foreign or vulgar words into talk or writing. 野蛮的实例; (尤指) 滥用文字 (于谈话或写作中搀入外国语或粗鄙字眼).

bar·bar·ity /bɑ:ˈbærəti; bɑrˈbærɪti/ *n* [U] savage cruelty; [C] (*pl* **-ties**) instance of this: 残忍; 残酷; 无人道: *the barbarities of modern warfare*, eg the bombing of towns, sinking of passenger liners. 现代战争之残酷 (如轰炸城市, 击沉客轮).

bar·bar·ize /ˈbɑ:bəraɪz; ˈbɑrbə,raɪz/ *vt* [VP6A] make barbarous. 使变粗野; 使变野蛮; 使言语荒杂.

bar·bar·ous /ˈbɑ:bərəs; ˈbɑrbərəs/ *adj* uncivilized; cruel; savage; unrefined in taste, conduct, or habits. 未开化的; 残忍的; 残酷的; 野蛮的; (趣味、行为或习惯) 粗俗的. □ **~·ly** *adv*

bar·be·cue /ˈbɑ:bɪkju:; ˈbɑrbɪ,kju/ *n* grill, iron framework, for cooking an animal whole; ox, pig, etc roasted whole; (outdoor) social occasion at which meat cooked over a charcoal fire is eaten. (炙烤整只动物的) 铁烤架; 炙烤的整只牛、猪等; (户外的) 烤肉野餐. □ *vt* roast (meat, etc) in this way. 烤 (肉等).

bar·bel /ˈbɑ:bl; ˈbɑrbl/ *n* large European fresh-water fish. 白鱼 (欧洲产之大淡水鱼).

bar·ber /ˈbɑ:bə(r); ˈbɑrbə/ *n* person whose trade is shaving and cutting men's hair (cf 参较 *hairdresser*, for both men and women). (给男人理发修面的) 理发师; 理发匠. **~'s pole**, pole painted in coloured spirals and used as a sign. 理发店招牌柱 (漆有彩色螺旋纹者). **'~'s shop**, (US 美 = '~ **shop**) place where a ~ does his work. 理发店; 理发厅.

bar·bi·can /ˈbɑ:bɪkən; ˈbɑrbɪkən/ *n* fortified building, esp a double tower over a gate or bridge, used in olden times as an outer defence to a city or castle. (古代城堡的) 外堡; 门首或桥头之望楼; 碉楼.

bar·bi·tone /ˈbɑ:bɪtəʊn; ˈbɑrbɪ,ton/ *n* [U] drug used to soothe the nerves and cause sleep; veronal. 巴比妥 (一种有镇定神经及安眠作用的药物).

bar·bitu·rate /bɑ:ˈbɪtjʊrət; ,bɑrˈbɪtjurət/ *n* [C, U] (chem) (kinds of) organic compound with a (possibly dangerous) soporific effect; pill for settling the nerves or inducing sleep. (化学) 巴比妥酸盐 (有机化合物, 具催眠之效, 可能导致危险); 巴比妥酸盐药片 (镇定剂或催眠剂).

bar·ca·role, bar·ca·rolle /ˈbɑ:kərəʊl; ˈbɑrkə,rol/ *n* song of Venetian gondoliers. 威尼斯船夫歌.

bard /bɑ:d; bɑrd/ *n* **1** (esp Celtic) minstrel. (尤指古代克尔特族之) 游唱诗人. **2** (liter) poet: (文) 诗人: *the* ~ *of Avon*, Shakespeare. 亚芬河河畔之诗人 (指莎士比亚). **bar·dic** *adj* of ~s or their songs. 游唱诗人或其诗歌的. **bar·dol·atry** /bɑ:ˈdɒlətrɪ; bɑrˈdɑlətrɪ/ *n* [U] enthusiastic admiration of Shakespeare. 对莎士比亚之狂热的崇拜.

bare[1] /beə(r); bɛr/ *adj* (**-r, -st**) **1** without clothing, covering, protection, or decoration: 无衣服的; 无遮盖的; 无保护的; 无装饰的: *fight with* ~ *hands*, without boxing gloves; 赤手 (未带拳击手套) 而战; ~ *to the waist*, clothed from the waist down; 腰际以上赤裸的; 裸露上身的; *with his head* ~, not wearing a hat; 头上未戴帽; 光着头; ~ *floors*, without carpets, rugs, etc; 光地板 (未铺地毯的地板); *a* ~ *hillside*, without shrubs or trees; 光秃的 (无树木的) 山坡; *hills* ~ *of vegetation*, 秃山; 草木不生的山峦; *trees that are already* ~, that have already

lost their leaves. 叶已落光的树木. *sleep on* ~ *boards* without a mattress, etc. 睡在硬木板上 (无褥垫等). *lay* ~, uncover, expose, make known (sth secret or hidden). 揭露; 揭发; 暴露 (隐秘之事物). *in one's* ~ *skin*, naked. 赤裸的. **'~·back** *adv* (of a horse) without a saddle: (指马) 无鞍地; 光背地: *ride* ~*back*. 骑无鞍之马. **'~·backed** *adj* having the back ~. 无鞍的; 光背的. □ *adv* = ~*back*. **'~·faced** *adj* insolent; shameless; undisguised: 傲慢的; 无耻的; 无掩饰的; 简直的; 公然的: *It's* ~*faced robbery to ask £15 for such an old bicycle!* 这架一辆旧脚踏车索价十五英镑, 这简直是抢劫! **~·faced·ly** *adv*. **'~·foot** *adv* without shoes and stockings: 赤足地; 光着脚地. **,~·'footed** *adj* with ~feet. 赤足的; 光着脚的. □ *adv* = **~foot**. 赤足地. **,~·'headed** *adj* with a ~ head; not wearing a hat. 光着头的; 未戴帽的. **,~·'legged** *adj* with the legs ~; not wearing stockings. 光着腿的; 未穿长袜的. **2** empty or almost empty: 空的; 几乎是空的: *a room* ~ *of furniture*; 几乎没有家具的房间; *a larder* ~ *of food*; 几乎没有食物的食物储藏室; ~ *shelves*. 几乎没有书的书架 (或几乎没有东西摆在上面的架子). *The garden looked* ~ *in winter*, had few or no flowers. 花园在冬天里几乎没有花草. **3** not more than; mere: 最起码的; 仅够的; 仅仅的: *the* ~ *necessities of life*, things needed merely to keep alive; 最起码的生活必需品; *earn a* ~ *living*, only just enough money to live on; 赚的钱仅足糊口; *approved by a* ~ *majority*, a very small one; 经勉勉强强的多数票通过; *a* ~ *possibility*, a mere or very slight one. 绝无仅有的可能性. **~·ly** *adv* **1** in a ~ way: 赤裸裸地; 空乏地: **~ly** *furnished rooms*, with little furniture. 几乎没有家具的房间. **2** just; scarcely: 仅仅; 仅只; 几乎不; 几乎没有: *We* ~ly *had time to catch the train*. 我们仅有勉强可以赶上火车的时间. *He can* ~ly *read and write*. 他仅粗通文字而已 (勉强能读能写). *I* ~ly *know her*. 我与她仅只认识而已. **~·ness** *n* state. 赤裸; 空乏; 无装饰.

bare[2] /beə(r); bɛr/ *vt* [VP6A] uncover; reveal: 揭露; 去除…的覆盖物: ~ *one's head*, take one's hat off; 脱下帽子; ~ *the end of a wire*, strip off the covering of rubber, etc (before making an electrical connection). (在连接电线之前) 剥去电线端上包覆之橡皮等. ~ *one's heart*, make known one's deepest feelings. 说出真心话; 表露真情. ~ *its teeth*, (of an animal) show its teeth in anger. (指动物愤怒时) 龇牙.

bar·gain /ˈbɑ:gɪn; ˈbɑrgɪn/ *n* **1** agreement to buy sell or exchange sth, made after discussion; (in industry) agreement between management and labour over wages, hours, etc; sth obtained as the result of such an agreement. (经过谈判以后所作买卖或交换之) 协议; (在工业中, 劳资双方有关工资、工时等的) 协议; 由此项协议所得之事物. *A* ~'s *a* ~, When an agreement has been made, it must be kept. 既经达成协议, 就必得遵守. *drive a hard* ~, try to force an agreement favourable to oneself. 试图使对方同意有利自己的协议. *a good/ bad* ~, one that favours/does not favour oneself. 占便宜的 (吃亏的) 交易. *into the* ~, as well; in addition; moreover. 另外; 此外; 加之. *make/strike a* ~ *(with sb)* *(over sth)*, reach agreement. 与某人 (就有关某事) 达成协议. **'~·ing position**, (in a debate, etc) state of affairs, arrangements, etc: (讨论等中之) 事态、安排等的情况; 协商境况: *The Foreign Secretary was in a good/ bad* ~*ing position in his dealings with his opposite number in France*, was in a favourable/unfavourable position when negotiating. 在与法国方面地位相当的官员 (指法国外交部长) 谈判中, 英国外相处于有利 (不利) 的协商地位. **2** sth offered, sold or bought cheap: 索价便宜、卖得便宜或买得便宜的货物: *a* ~ *sale*, sale of goods at reduced prices; 大减价; **'~·basement**, lowest floor of a shop, where goods are offered at reduced prices; 地下室廉价部; **'~·counter**, counter at which ~s are displayed or sold; 廉价品柜台 (展示并出售廉价品的柜台); **'~ price**, low price; 廉价; 特价; **'~·hunter**, person looking

for ~s. 寻找便宜货的人。□ vi, vt 1 [VP2A, 3A] ~ (with sb) (for sth), talk for the purpose of reaching an agreement (about buying or selling sth, doing a piece of work, etc): (与某人)(为某事物)讨价还价；讲价；谈条件；谈判：We ~ed with the farmer for a supply of milk and butter. 我们与那农民讲价，欲购买一批牛奶和黄油。 2 [VP3A] ~ about, = ~ over. ⇨ for, be ready or willing to accept or agree to: 愿意接受或同意；预料；期待：I didn't ~ for John arriving so soon, was surprised by this, didn't expect it. 我没有想到约翰会这么快到达。 get more than one ~s for, (colloq) be unpleasantly surprised at the consequences. (口)结果出乎预料之外(不愉快地感到惊奇)。 ~ over sth, ⇨ with sb for sth. 与人协议某事。 3 [VP9] make a condition: 提出条件：The men ~ed that they should not have to work on Saturday afternoons. 工人们提出条件他们不应于星期六下午还要工作。 4 [VP15B] ~ away, give up in return for sth; sacrifice: 放弃…以求获得另外的某物；牺牲；贱卖：~ away one's freedom, give it up in return for some advantage or other. 牺牲其自由(以求获得某种利益)。

barge[1] /bɑːdʒ; bɑrdʒ/ n 1 large flat-bottomed boat for carrying goods and people on rivers and canals, in harbours, etc with or without sails, towed by a tug or horse; similar boat with its own engine. 驳船(河上或港内载运货物的大平底船，或有帆或无帆，以拖船或马匹拖之)；本身装有引擎的类似的船。 2 warship's boat, for the use of the officers. 战舰上高级军官之座艇。 3 large rowing-boat for ceremonial occasions. 庆典用的大划艇。 '~-pole n long pole used for guiding a ~. 驳船之撑篙。 I wouldn't touch it with a ~-pole, I dislike or distrust it extremely. 我非常厌恶(不信任)它。

barge[2] /bɑːdʒ; bɑrdʒ/ vi (colloq) (口) 1 [VP3A] ~ into/against, rush or bump heavily into/against (sb or sth). 冲撞；碰撞(某人或某物)。 2 [VP2C, 3A] ~ about, move clumsily, without proper control of one's movements or without care (for persons or things). 笨拙地走动(对自己的动作没有适当的控制，或不顾其他之人或物)；乱碰乱闯。 ~ in/into, intrude; make one's way in, interrupt, rudely: 闯入；打扰；打断：Stop barging into our conversation. 不要打断我们的谈话。

bar·gee /bɑːˈdʒiː; ˌbɑrˈdʒi/ n master or member of the crew of a barge. 驳船的船主；驳船船夫。 swear like a ~, swear forcibly, and with a great variety of swear-words. 咒骂得很厉害；满口肮脏字眼。

bari·tone /ˈbærɪtəʊn; ˈbærəˌton/ n male voice between tenor and bass. 男中音。

bar·ium /ˈbeərɪəm; ˈbɛrɪəm/ n [U] 1 soft, silvery-white metal (symbol Ba) of which the compounds are used in industry. 钡(银白色软金属，化学符号 Ba，其化合物用于工业)。 2 chemical substance (~ sulphate) introduced into the intestines before an X-ray photograph of them is taken. 钡灌肠剂(硫酸钡，在 X 光照肠之前，引入肠内之化学物质)。

bark[1] /bɑːk; bɑrk/ n [U] outer covering or skin on the trunks, boughs and branches of trees. 树皮。 ⇨ the illus at tree. 参看 tree 之插图。 □ vt [VP6A] 1 take the ~ off (a tree). 剥去(树)的皮。 2 scrape the skin off (one's knuckles, shin, knee, etc) (by falling against sth, etc). (因跌跤等)擦破(指节、外胫、膝盖等)之皮。

bark[2] /bɑːk; bɑrk/ n the cry made by dogs and foxes; (fig) sound of gunfire, or of a cough. 狗及狐狸的叫声；吠声；(喻)炮火声；咳嗽声。 His ~ is worse than his bite, He is bad-tempered but not dangerous or (fig) malicious. 他的脾气很坏，但心地不恶。 □ vi, vt 1 [VP2A, C, 3A] (of dogs, etc) give a ~ or ~s: (指狗等)吠叫：The dog ~s at strangers. 狗对陌生人吠叫。 ~ up the wrong tree, (fig) direct one's complaint, accusation, etc wrongly. (喻)弄错了抱怨、控诉等的对象。 2 [VP6A, 15B] say (sth) in a sharp, commanding voice: 以严厉而威严的声音说出；咆哮着说出来：The officer ~ed out his orders. 军官严厉而威严的声音发出命令。'Come here!' he ~ed (out). '来这里！'他吼叫着。

bark[3], **barque** /bɑːk; bɑrk/ n 1 sailing-ship with 3 to 5 masts and sails. 三桅(四桅或五桅)帆船。 2 (poet) any ship or boat. (诗)船；小船。

barker /ˈbɑːkə(r); ˈbɑrkɚ/ n (colloq) (口) 1 person who stands outside a booth in a travelling show, or outside a shop, talking loudly to advertise the show, goods, etc. (杂耍戏棚外或店铺门外之)宣传员；招徕顾客者。 2 (sl) pistol. (俚)手枪。

bar·ley /ˈbɑːlɪ; ˈbɑrlɪ/ n [U] grass-like plant and its seed (called grain), used for food and for making beer and whisky. 大麦(用作食物，并酿造啤酒及威士忌酒)。 ⇨ the illus at cereal. 参看 cereal 之插图。 '~-corn n [U] grain of ~; (colloq) malt liquor. 大麦之实；大麦粒；(口)麦芽酒。 pearl ~ n ~ grain made smaller by grinding. 真珠麦(由大麦碾成之圆形颗粒)。 '~-sugar n [U] solid sweet substance, made from pure sugar. 麦芽糖；大麦糖(用纯糖所制之糖果)。 '~-water n [U] drink made by boiling pearl ~ in water and then straining it. 真珠麦汁(用水煮真珠麦，然后将真珠麦滤除而成之饮料)。

barm /bɑːm; bɑrm/ n [U] yeast. 酵母；酵素。

barmy /ˈbɑːmɪ; ˈbɑrmɪ/ adj (GB colloq) wrong in the head; foolish. (英口)精神不正常的；愚痴的。

barn /bɑːn; bɑrn/ n 1 covered building for storing hay, grain, etc on a farm. (农庄上储藏干草、谷物等的)谷仓。 '~ dance n kind of rustic dance. 谷仓舞(一种农村舞)。 '~-door n large door of a ~; (colloq fig) target too large to miss. 谷仓大门；(口，喻)过大而不会打不中的目标。 ~-door fowl n ordinary kind of fowl kept on farms. (农庄上所养的)普通家禽。 '~-storm vi (US) travel rapidly through the country making political speeches, presenting plays, etc. (美)旅行乡间作政治性演讲，演出戏剧等；在乡间作巡回演出。 Hence, 由此产生，'~·stormer n person who does this. 在乡间作旅行演说者；作巡回演出的艺人。 '~-yard n = farmyard. 2 (contemptuous) any large, plain building: (轻蔑语)大而简陋的房舍：What a ~ of a house! 这栋房屋简直象谷仓！ 3 (US) building for sheltering cattle or horses; depot for trams, buses, etc. (美)牛马房(电车、公共汽车等之)车库；停车场。

bar·nacle /ˈbɑːnəkl; ˈbɑrnəkl/ n small sea-animal that fastens itself to objects under water, rocks, the bottoms of ships, the timbers of wharves, etc. 藤壶(附于水面下之物体、岩石、船底、码头木柱等之小甲壳动物)。

ba·rom·eter /bəˈrɒmɪtə(r); bəˈrɑnətɚ/ n instrument for measuring the pressure of the atmosphere, used for forecasting the weather and measuring height above sea-level; (fig) something which forecasts changes or fluctuations (eg in public opinion, market prices). 气压计；晴雨表；海拔计；(喻)预言改变或波动之事物(例如在舆论、市价等方面)。 **baro·met·ric** /ˌbærəˈmetrɪk; ˌbærəˈmɛtrɪk/

bar·on /ˈbærən; ˈbærən/ n 1 (in GB) nobleman; lowest rank of Peer (called Lord —); holder of the non-British title (called Baron —). (在英国)贵族；男爵(称为 Lord —)；他国男爵爵位之持有者(称为 Baron —)。 2 (orig US) great industrial leader: (起源于美国)工业巨商：大王：oil ~s, 石油大王；beer ~s, 啤酒大王。 '~-age /-ɪdʒ; -ɪdʒ/ n the ~s collectively; book with a list of these Peers. 贵族(集合用法)；贵族名册。 ~·ess /ˈbærənɪs; ˈbærənɪs/ n a ~'s wife; woman holding the rank of a ~ in her own right. 男爵夫人；女男爵。 **bar·o·nial** /bəˈrəʊnɪəl; bəˈronɪəl/ adj; suitable for, ~s. 男爵的；适于男爵的。 **bar·ony** /ˈbærənɪ; ˈbærənɪ/ n rank of a ~: 男爵爵位：confer a ~y on sb, make him a ~. 将男爵爵位授与某人。

bar·onet /ˈbærənɪt; ˈbærənɪt/ n member of the lowest hereditary titled order, lower in rank than a baron but above a knight; shortened to Bart, added to the name, as Sir John Williams, Bart. 从男爵(最下级世袭爵位的贵族，等级在 baron 之下 knight 之上；简称 Bart，加在姓名之后，如 Sir John Williams, Bart)。 ~cy /ˈbærənɪtsɪ;

'bærənɪtsɪ/ n rank, title, of a ~. 从男爵之爵位及头衔.

ba·roque /bə'rɒk US: -əʊk; bə'rok/ n, adj (of the) florid or extravagant style in the arts (esp architecture) in Europe in the 17th and 18th cc. 巴洛克式 (十七及十八世纪欧洲艺术过份装饰之型式, 尤指建筑风格); 巴洛克式的.

ba·rouche /bə'ruːʃ; bə'ruʃ/ n four-wheeled carriage pulled by horses, with two seats facing each other and a folding top, for four occupants and a driver. 一种四轮大马车 (有两个对面座位及一可折叠之顶篷, 可供四客及一车夫乘坐).

barque /baːk; bark/ n ⇨ **bark**³.

bar·rack¹ /'bærək; 'bærɛk/ n 1 (usu pl with indef art and sing v) large building(s) for soldiers to live in: (常作复数, 与不定冠词和单数动词连用) 兵营; 营房: The ~s are/is quite new. 那 (些) 营房相当新. 2 any building of plain or ugly appearance. 外表简陋的房舍.

bar·rack² /'bærək; 'bærɛk/ vt, vi [VP6A, 2A] jeer at; make cries of protest against (eg slow play in a cricket match). 嘲笑; 叫嚣以示抗议 (如对板球比赛之缓慢动作等). ~·ing n slow clapping, etc. 喝倒彩 (如缓慢的拍掌等).

bar·ra·cuda /,bærə'kuːdə; ,bærə'kudə/ n large, fierce Caribbean sea-fish. 梭子鱼 (加勒比海产之凶猛大海鱼).

bar·rage /'bærɑːʒ US: bə'rɑːʒ; 'barɪdʒ, bə'raʒ/ n [C] 1 artificial obstacle built across a river (not across a valley) for storing water to be diverted into canals for irrigation (as on the Nile and the Indus). (拦河, 非拦谷, 所筑用以蓄水导入渠沟, 作灌溉用之) 堰坝 (如尼罗河及印度河上所筑者). ⇨ **dam**. 2 (mil) barrier made by heavy, continuous gunfire directed over a given area. (军) 弹幕 (针对某一地区不断发射猛烈炮火所造成的障碍). 3 balloon ~, ⇨ balloon, **balloon**. 系留气幕.

barred /baːd; bard/ pt, pp of **bar**².

bar·rel /'bærəl; 'bærɛl/ n 1 round container, made of wooden staves with bands or hoops, or of plastic; the amount that a ~ holds. (用木头或塑胶做的) 桶; 一桶之量. '~-roofed 'vault n (semi-) cylindrical roof. (半) 圆筒形屋顶. 2 metal tube of a rifle, revolver or pistol. 枪管; 炮筒. ⇨ the illus at **rifle**. 参看 rifle 之插图. 3 part of a fountain pen that holds the ink. (自来水笔中的) 储墨管. 4 '~-organ n instrument from which music is produced by turning a handle and so causing a cylinder to act mechanically on keys; usu played by a man who goes round the streets, playing it for money. 手风琴; 筒风琴 (摇动琴柄, 使滚筒转动, 打击琴键以发音; 奏者常在街头演奏, 以求赏钱). □ vt (-ll-) put in a ~ or ~s. 装入桶中. '~led part adj stored in a ~: 储于桶中的: ~led beer. 桶装的啤酒.

bar·ren /'bærən; 'bærən/ adj 1 (of land) not good enough to produce crops. (指土地) 贫瘠的; 不长五谷的.

2 (of plants, trees) not producing fruit or seeds. (指草木) 不结果的; 不结实的. 3 (of women, animals) unable to have young ones. (指妇人, 动物) 不生育的; 不孕的. 4 (fig) without value, interest, or result: (喻) 无价值, 趣味或结果的: a ~ subject/discussion; 无价值 (或无趣味) 的题目 (讨论); an attempt that was ~ of results. 无结果的尝试. ~·ness n

bar·ri·cade /,bærɪ'keɪd; ,bærə'ked/ n barrier of objects (eg trees, carts, overturned or burnt-out cars, barrels) placed across or in front of something as a defence. (利用树木、马车、倒翻或烧毁的汽车、木桶等横拦或置于某物之前, 作为防卫用的) 阻绝障碍物; 路障. □ vt [VP6A, 15B] ~ (in/off), block (a street, etc) with a ~: 以阻绝障碍物阻塞 (街道等): They ~d themselves in. 他们设置临时障碍物, 自己躲在里面.

bar·rier /'bærɪə(r); 'bærɪə/ n 1 sth (eg a wall, rail, fence, turnstile) that prevents, hinders or controls, progress or movement: 障碍物; 阻碍物; 控制进展或活动之物 (如墙、栅、篱、十字转门): The Sahara Desert is a natural ~ that separates North and Central Africa. 撒哈拉沙漠是北非洲与中非洲之间的天然屏障. Show your ticket at the ~, eg in a railway station. 在栅门口 (如在火车站者) 缴验你的票. ⇨ **crash**¹(1), **half**(3), **heat**¹(5) and **sound**²(3). 2 (fig) hindrance: (喻) 障碍; 阻碍: Poor health and lack of money may both be ~s to educational progress. 健康不佳和没有钱都可以成为教育进步的障碍.

bar·ring /'baːrɪŋ; 'barɪŋ/ prep excluding. 除…以外. ⇨ **bar**³.

bar·ris·ter /'bærɪstə(r); 'bærɪstə/ n (in England) lawyer who has the right to speak and argue as an advocate in higher law courts. (用于英国) (可在高等法院出庭的) 律师. ⇨ **advocate, solicitor, counsel**.

bar·row¹ /'bærəʊ; 'bæro/ n 1 = wheel-~. 2 (also 亦作 'hand-~, 'coster's ~) small cart with two wheels, pulled or pushed by hand. 两轮手推车. '~-boy/-man /-mæn; -mæn/ n costermonger. 沿街推车叫卖水果、蔬菜等之小贩. 3 (also 亦作 luggage-~) metal frame with two wheels used by porters for luggage (at railway-stations, in hotels, etc). (火车站、旅馆等内搬运工人所用之) 行李运送车.

bar·row² /'bærəʊ; 'bæro/ n mound, dating from prehistoric times, built over a burial ground. (史前时代的) 古冢; 古墓; 冢. ⇨ **tumulus**.

bar·ter /'baːtə(r); 'bartə/ vt, vi [VP15B, 14, 2A] ~ (with sb/for sth); ~ sth away, exchange (goods, property, etc) (for other goods, etc): (以货易货) 物物交换: ~ wheat for machinery; 以小麦交换机器; (fig) (喻) ~ away one's rights/honour/freedom. (为某种利益而) 出卖自己的权利/荣誉, 自由). □ n [U] exchange made in this way. 以货易货; 物物交换. ~·er n

ba·salt /'bæsɔːlt US: bə'sɔːlt; bə'sɔlt/ n [U] sorts of dark-coloured rock of volcanic origin. 玄武岩 (由火山岩

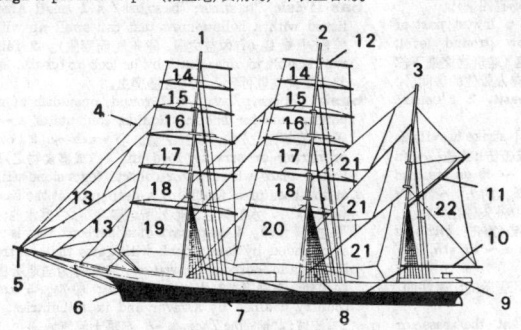

1 foremast	12 yard
2 mainmast	13 jibs
3 mizzenmast	14 skysails
4 stays	15 royals
5 bowsprit	16 topgallants
6 prow	17 upper topsails
7 hull	18 lower topsails
8 shrouds	19 foresail
9 poop	20 mainsail
10 boom	21 staysails
11 sprit	22 spanker

a barque

浆所形成之暗色岩石）.

bas·cule /'bæskjuːl; 'bæskjul/ n '~ **bridge,** (eng) kind of drawbridge of which the two halves can be raised and lowered with counter-weights. (工程) 跳开式吊桥; 活动桥(桥身之两半截可借平衡重量同时起落).

base¹ /beɪs; bes/ n **1** lowest part of anything, esp the part on which sth rests or is supported; 底; 根基; 基础: the ~ of a pillar, ⇨ the illus at column. 柱基(参看 column 之插图). '~·**board** n (US) skirting-board. (美)踢脚板; 壁脚板. **2** (geom) line or surface on which a figure stands or can stand: (几何)底边; 底面: BC is the ~ of the triangle ABC. BC 是三角形 ABC 之底边. ABCD is the ~ of the pyramid. ABCD 是角锥体的底面.

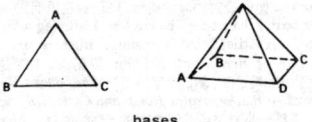

bases

3 (chem) substance capable of combining with an acid to form a salt; substance into which other things are mixed. (化学)盐基; 碱(可与酸化合成盐); (混合物之)主要成分. **4** place at which armed forces, expeditions, etc have their stores, hospitals, etc: (军队, 探险队等之) 基地; 根据地: a 'naval ~; 海军基地; an 'air ~; 空军基地; a ~ of operations; 作战根据地; a ~ camp, eg for a Qomolangma expedition. 基地营帐 (如珠穆朗玛峰探险队者. **5** (maths) the number (usu 10) which is the starting point for a logarithmic system. (数学)(对数之)底(通常为 10). **6** (~ball) one of four stations or positions. (棒球) 垒. **get to first ~,** (US); (fig) take a successful first step towards achieving sth. (美; 喻)迈向成功之路的第一步; 初步成功. ~ **hit** n hit on which a player gets to first ~. 一垒安打(击球者能上第一垒之一击). ~·**less** adj without cause or foundation: 无原因的; 无缘无故的; 无根据的: ~less fears. 无缘无故的恐惧.

base² /beɪs; bes/ vt [VP14] ~ sth on / upon, build or place; use as a basis for: 建于…之上; 以…为根据: Direct taxation is usually ~d upon income. 直接税通常以收入为根据. I ~ my hopes on the news we had yesterday. 我的希望是以我们昨天所得到的消息为根据.

base³ /beɪs; bes/ adj **1** (-r, -st) (of persons, their behaviour, thoughts, etc) dishonourable: (指人, 其行为、思想等)卑鄙的: acting from ~ motives. 动机卑鄙的行为. **2** ~ **metals,** non-precious metals. 贱金属. ~ **coin,** mixed with inferior metals. 搀有贱金属之硬币.

base·ball /'eɪsbɔːl; 'bes'bɔl/ n national game of the US, played with a bat and ball, by two teams of nine players each, on a field with our bases¹(6). 棒球戏; 棒球(美国之全国性运动, 两队各九人, 球场有四垒).

base·ment /'beɪsmənt; 'besmənt/ n lowest part of a building, partly or wholly below ground level; inhabited room(s) in this part. 地下室(建筑物之最下部分, 一部分或全部在地面之下); 地下层有人居住的房间.

bases 1 /'beɪsɪz; 'besɪz/ pl of **basis. 2** /'beɪsɪz; 'besɪz/ pl of **base¹.**

bash /bæʃ; bæʃ/ vt [VP6A, 15A, B] strike heavily so as to break or injure: 猛击(以致击破或击伤); 痛击: ~ in the lid of a box; 将盒盖子打陷进去; ~ sb on the head with a golf club; 用高尔夫球棍猛打某人的头; ~ one's head against sth in the dark. 黑暗中头碰在某物上. □ n violent blow or knock: 猛击; 痛击; 重击: give sb a ~ on the nose. 猛击某人的鼻子. **have a ~ at sth,** (sl) attempt it. (俚)尝试某事.

bash·ful /'bæʃfl; 'bæʃfəl/ adj shy. 害羞的; 羞怯的. ~**ly** /-fəlɪ; -fəlɪ/ adv

basic /'beɪsɪk; 'besɪk/ adj of or at the base or foundation; fundamental: 基础的; 基本的; 根本的:

the ~ processes of arithmetic, eg adding, subtraction, multiplying; 算术的基本方法 (如加法、减法、乘法); the ~ vocabulary of a language, the words that must be known. 一种语言的基本词汇 (即必须认识之词). **B~ English,** artificial, simplified form of English. 基本英语 (人为之简化英语). ~ **slag** n fertilizer containing phosphates. 含有磷酸盐之肥料; 碱性熔渣. **ba·si·cally** /-klɪ; -klɪ/ adv fundamentally. 基本上; 根本上.

□ base ● baseman

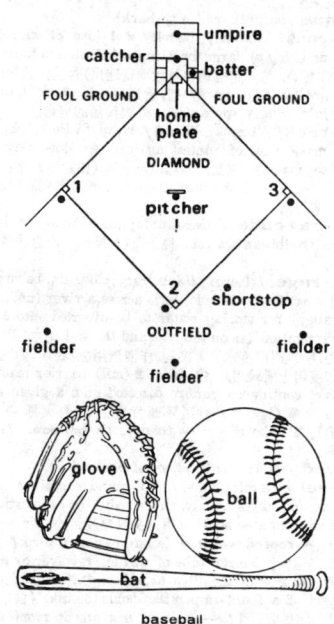

baseball

basil /'bæzl; 'bæzl/ n [U] sweet-smelling plant like mint, used in cooking. 罗勒; 紫苏 (味香如薄荷, 用于烹调).

ba·sil·ica /bə'zɪlɪkə; bə'sɪlɪkə/ n oblong hall with a double row of columns and an apse at one end (used in ancient Rome as a law court); building of this type used as a church: (古罗马作法庭之) 长方形会堂; 长方形教堂: the ~ of St Peter's in Rome. 罗马之圣彼得教堂.

basil·isk /'bæzɪlɪsk; 'bæsə,lɪsk/ n **1** small American lizard with a hollow crest that can swell up with air. 美洲小蜥蜴 (有中空之冠, 能充气而膨胀). **2** fabulous reptile able to cause death by its look or breath. 传说中其目光或气息可致人于死之怪爬虫.

basin /'beɪsn; 'besn/ n **1** round, open dish of metal, pottery, etc for holding liquids; contents of a ~. (金属、陶瓷等制之) 盆; 一盆之量. ⇨ wash-~. **2** bowl for preparing or serving food in. (煮或盛食物的) 碗. **3** hollow place where water collects (eg a stone structure at the base of a fountain, a deep pool at the base of a waterfall). 水汇聚之凹形处所 (喷泉下之) 盛水池; (瀑布下之) 深水潭. **4** deep part of a harbour that is almost surrounded by land; dock with gates that control the inflow and outflow of water. 港湾内为陆地所围绕之深水处; 有闸门控制水流出入之船坞; 船渠. **5** area of country drained by a river and its tributaries: (河流之) 流域; 盆地: the Thames ~. 泰晤士河流域.

basis /'beɪsɪs; 'besɪs/ n (pl **bases** /'beɪsiːz; 'besɪz/

1 substance into which others are mixed; most important part of a mixture. (混合物之) 主要成分. 2 foundation (usu fig): 基础 (通常作比喻用法): *the ~ of morality*: 道德的基础; *on a solid ~*; 在坚实的基础上; *arguments that have a firm ~*, that are founded in facts. 有事实为根据的论据. *On the ~ of our sales forecasts* (ie From what these indicate) *we may begin to make a profit next year*. 基于我们售货的预测, 我们明年将开始赚钱.

bask /bɑːsk US: bæsk; bæsk/ *vi* [VP2C] enjoy warmth and light: 享受温暖与阳光; 晒太阳: *sitting in the garden, ~ing in the sunshine*; 坐在花园里晒太阳; (fig) (喻)~*ing in her favour/approval*. 沐其恩泽(受其嘉许).

bas·ket /'bɑːskɪt US: 'bæskɪt; 'bæskɪt/ *n* 1 container, usu made of materials that bend and twist easily (eg osiers, canes, rushes) with or without a handle: (以柳条、藤子或葡萄等编制之)篮子; 筐子; 篓子: *a 'shopping ~*; 购物篮子; *a 'clothes ~*; 衣服筐子; *a waste-'paper ~*. 字纸篓. 2 as much as a ~ holds: 一篮(筐、篓)之量: *They ate a ~ of plums*. 他们吃了一篮李子. ~·**ball** /'bɑːskɪtbɔːl US: 'bæs-; 'bæskɪt,bɔl/ *n* game (resembling netball), played by two teams of five players who try to throw a large inflated ball into an open-ended net fixed 10 ft above the ground. 篮球戏; 篮球(似落网球戏, 球员分两队各五人, 竞相投球入球篮中, 篮高离地面十英尺). ⇨ **netball**.

basketball

bas-relief /ˌbæs rɪˈliːf; ˌbɑˌrɪˈlif/ *n* [U] (= *low relief*) form of art in which a flat surface of metal or stone is cut away so that a design or picture stands out as on a coin but often to a greater degree; [C] example of this. (于金属或石头的平面所作之)半浮雕; 浅浮雕 (如硬币上之图像, 但常更为突出). ⇨ the illus at **church**. 参看 church 之插图.

bass¹ /bæs; bæs/ *n* (*pl* unchanged) (zool) kinds of fish (perch) used as food, caught in rivers, lakes and in the sea. (复数不变)(动物) 鲈鱼类(可食, 在河、湖及海中均可捕得).

bass² /beɪs; bes/ *adj* deep-sounding; low in tone. 声音低沉的; 音调低的. □ *n* lowest part in music (voice and instruments); singer or instrument with lowest notes: 音乐 (人声及乐器) 之低音部; 低音歌手或低音乐器: ˌ~·clari'net; 低音竖笛; ˌ~ 'drum, ⇨ the illus at **percussion**; 低音鼓; 大鼓 (参看 percussion 之插图); ˌdouble-'~, ⇨ the illus at **string**; 低音提琴 (参看 string 之插图); ˌ~·'clef, ⇨ the illus at **notation**. 低音谱号 (参看 notation 之插图).

bass³ /bæs; bæs/ *n* [U] inner fibrous bark of the lime-tree, used for weaving baskets, mats, etc and for tying plants. 菩提树之纤维质的内皮 (用作编织篮、席等及捆绑植物).

Bass /bæs; bæs/ *n* (P) beer made by the brewers named Bass. (商标) 巴斯啤酒(由酿造者 Bass 而得名).

bas·si·net /ˌbæsɪˈnet; ˌbæsəˈnɛt/ *n* baby's cradle or carriage made of woven wicker, with a hood. (用柳条编制, 上有蓬盖的) 小儿摇篮或推车.

bas·soon /bəˈsuːn; bæˈsun/ *n* musical wind-instrument with double reeds, made of wood, giving very low notes. 低音管; 巴松管 (一种低音的双簧木管乐器). ⇨ the illus at **brass**. 参看 brass 之插图.

bast /bæst; bæst/ *n* [U] 1 = **bass³**. 2 other fibrous barks (eg raffia) used for tying and weaving. 用作缚结和编织之他种纤维质内皮 (例如拉菲亚棕榈树纤维); 韧皮.

bas·tard /'bɑːstəd US: 'bæs-; 'bæstəd/ *n* 1 illegitimate child: 私生子: (attrib)(用作定语) *a ~ child/daughter/son*. 私生子(女, 子). 2 △ (also as *int*) ruthless insensitive person (used as a term of abuse): (亦可用作感叹词) 残忍无情的人(用作责骂语): *You heartless ~! 你这无情的人! He's a real ~, leaving his wife in that way*; 他真狠心, 象那样离开了他的妻子; (also, not abusively, friendly colloq): (亦可作表示友善的口语, 无恶骂之含意): *Harry, you old ~! Fancy meeting you here!* 哈里, 你这老家伙! 想不到在这里遇见你! 3 △ unfortunate fellow: (诙)不幸的人: *Poor ~! He's been sacked and he won't find another job very easily*; 可怜的家伙! 他已经被解雇了, 而且很难再找到另一个工作; (also of an unfortunate incident, state, etc): (亦用以指不幸的事件, 情况等): *this ~ of a headache/essay*. 这讨厌的头痛(论文). 4 (usu attrib) (of things) not genuine or authentic; spurious. (通常用作定语)(指事物)赝的; 不真实的; 不可靠的; 假的; 伪造的. **~·ize** *vt* 1 prove to be, pronounce as a ~. 证实为私生子; 宣布为私生子; 认定为私生子. 2 make spurious: 使成为赝品; 使为伪造; 使不实: *a ~ized account of what happened*. 对所发生事故的不实报告. **~·y** *n* (legal) illegitimacy: (法律)私生: *a ~y order*, one (made by a magistrate) for the support of an illegitimate by its father (now called a *maintenance order*). 赡养令; 扶养令 (由法官的判令, 某私生子应由其父扶养, 今称为 maintenance order).

baste¹ /beɪst; best/ *vt* [VP6A, 15B] (in making clothes, etc) sew pieces together with long temporary stitches (so that adjustments are possible afterwards). (在制衣等中) 疏缝; 大缝; 绗缝(以长针脚将剪块暂时缝合, 以便以后修改).

baste² /beɪst; best/ *vt* [VP6A] *~ meat*, pour over it the fat, juices, etc which come from it during cooking. 煮肉时将肉所熬出的油脂、肉汁等浇于肉上.

baste³ /beɪst; best/ *vt* [VP6A] thrash; beat. 鞭打; 痛打.

bas·ti·nado /ˌbæstɪˈnɑːdəu; ˌbæstəˈnedo/ *n* (*pl* -**es**) caning on the soles of the feet. 跖刑(打脚掌的一种刑罚). □ *vt* [VP6A] punish by caning in this way. 施以跖刑.

bas·tion /'bæstɪən; 'bæstʃən/ *n* (often five-sided) part of a fortification that stands out from the rest; (fig) military stronghold near hostile territory; (fig) sth preserved from destruction or change. 棱堡 (防御工事之突出部分, 常有五面); 堡垒突角; (喻)临近敌境之军事据点; (喻)未被破坏或改变之物.

bat¹ /bæt; bæt/ *n* small mouse-like animal that flies at night and feeds on fruit and insects. 蝙蝠 (体小如鼠之动物, 于夜间飞翔, 食水果及昆虫). ⇨ the illus at **small**. 参看 small 之插图. **have bats in the belfry**, (sl) be eccentric, have queer ideas. (俚)古怪的; 思想古怪的. **as blind as a bat**, unable to see, not seeing, clearly. 半瞎的; 目力不行的.

bat² /bæt; bæt/ *n* 1 shaped wooden implement for striking the ball in games, esp cricket and baseball. (板球戏中所用的)球板; (棒球戏中所用的)棒球. ⇨ the illus at these entries. 参看 cricket 及 baseball 之插图. **carry one's bat**, (cricket) be 'not out' at the end of the innings (板球)在一局结束时未被判出局. **do sth off one's own bat**, (fig) do it without help. (喻)自己做 (不要人帮忙). 2 = batsman: 击球员: *He's a useful bat*. 他是个优异的击球员. □ *vi, vt* (-tt-) 1 [VP2A, B, C] use a bat: 使用球棒, 执棒: *Green batted (for) two hours*, was at the wicket for two hours. 格林执棒两小时. 2 [VP6A] hit (with a bat). (用棒)击; 打击. **batsman** /-smən; -smən/ *n* (*pl* -**men**) 1 (cricket) player who bats: (板球) 击球员: *He's a good batsman but no good as a bowler*. 他是个好击球员, 但不是个好投手. 2 (aviation) man who uses

a pair of bats (like those used in table-tennis) to guide an aircraft as and after it touches down (eg on the deck of an aircraft-carrier). (航空)(航空母舰船等上手持两板如乒乓球拍以)指挥飞机降落者.

bat³ / bæt; bæt/ *n go off at a terrific/rare bat*, (sl) at a fast rate. (俚)非常迅速地离去; 急速而行.

bat⁴ / bæt; bæt/ *vt* (**-tt-**) (sl) wink. (俚)霎(眼). *not bat an eyelid*, (**a**) not sleep at all. 未曾阖眼. (**b**) not show any surprise. 完全不露惊讶之色.

batch /bætʃ; bætʃ/ *n* **1** number of loaves, cakes, etc baked together: 一次所烘的若干个面包、糕饼等: *baked in ~es of twenty.* 每炉烘二十个. **2** number of persons or things receiving attention as a group: (人或物之)一批: *a ~ of letters to be answered;* 待回复之一批信件; *a ~ of recruits for the army.* 一批陆军的新兵.

bate / beɪt; bet/ *vt* = **abate**. *with ~d breath*, with the voice lowered to a whisper (in expectancy, anxiety, etc). 低声地; 屏息地(如在期望或焦虑时).

bath / bɑ:θ US: bæθ; bæθ/ *n* (*pl ~s* /bɑ:ðz US: bæðz; bæθz/) **1** washing of the body, esp by putting oneself completely in water: 沐浴; 洗澡: *I shall have a hot ~ and go to bed.* 我将洗个热水澡, 然后睡觉. *He takes a cold ~ every morning.* 他每天早晨洗冷水澡. '*~·robe n* loose-fitting robe worn before and after taking a ~. (沐浴前后所穿之)浴衣. **2** water for a ~: 洗澡水: *Your ~ is ready.* 你的洗澡水预备好了. '*~·tub n* (usu *bath* in GB except in trade use) large (usu oblong) vessel (of fibre-glass, porcelain or metal) in which ~s are taken. 浴盆; 澡盆; 浴缸(玻璃纤维、瓷质或金属制成), 供洗澡之长方形. 在英国, 除非商业用语, 通常称 bath). '*~·room n* room in which there is a ~tub (and usu a wash-hand-basin): 浴室(内有浴盆, 通常还有洗脸盆): *Every room in the hotel has a private ~room,* ie its own ~room. 这旅馆里的每一个房间都附有私用浴室. **3** (container for) liquid in which sth is washed or dipped (in chemical and industrial processes): (化学或工业程序中)用以浸洗某物之液体; 盛此液体之器皿; 浸缸: *an 'oil ~,* (for parts of a machine); (浸洗机器零件之)油池: *a 'hypo ~,* (photography). (洗相片用之)定影药液浸盆. **4** (*pl*) place where one can bath or swim: (复)澡堂; 游泳池: *public swimming ~s;* 公共游泳池; *the Turkish ~s.* 土耳其式的澡堂. □ *vt, vi* [VP6A, 2A] give a ~ to: 给…洗澡. *~ the baby;* 给婴儿洗澡; *take a bath:* 洗澡: *I ~ every night.* 我每天晚上洗澡. ⇨ also **sun**(4). **3** [VP2A] go into the sea, a river, lake, etc for sport, swimming, to get cool, etc. 到海里、河里或湖里做运动、游泳或泡水取凉等. □ *n* act of swimming in the sea, a river, lake, etc: (在海里、河里或湖里)游泳: *We had an enjoyable ~ before breakfast.* 我们在早餐前作了一次舒畅的游泳. *Let's go for a ~.* 我们游泳去吧. Cf 参较 *have/take a bath.* **bather** /'beɪðə(r); 'beðæ/ *n*

bath·ing /'beɪðɪŋ; 'beðɪŋ/ *n* act or practice of going into the sea, etc: 海(河、湖)水浴; 游泳: *The ~ here is safe,* It is safe to swim here. 在这里游泳是安全的. *He's fond of ~.* 他喜欢游泳. *There have been many fatal accidents here,* Many bathers have been drowned here. 这里曾有许多游水者遭灭顶之祸. '*~·cap n* cap to cover a woman's hair while in the water. (女用)游泳帽.

'*~-costume/suit n* garment worn for swimming (cf 较 *bikini, swimming-trunks*). 游泳衣. '*~-machine n* cabin on wheels, pulled down to the water's edge and (formerly)used by bathers for dressing and undressing. (昔时, 可以拖至水边的)游泳者更衣车.

bathos /'beɪθɒs; 'beθɑs/ *n* [U] (rhet) sudden change (in writing or speech) from what is deeply moving or sublime to what is foolish or unimportant. (修辞)(在写作或演说中由深刻动人或庄严突然转至诙谐或琐细的)突降法.

bathy·sphere /'bæθɪsfɪə(r); 'bæθɪ,sfɪr/ *n* large, strongly built, hollow sphere that can be lowered to great depths in the sea, for observation of marine life. (观察海洋生物之)深海潜水箱.

ba·tik /bə'ti:k; 'bætik/ *n* [U] method (originally in Java) of printing coloured designs on textiles by waxing the parts not to be dyed; [C] example of such a fabric. 蜡染法(创始于爪哇之一种印花布染印法, 将不欲染色之处, 以蜡涂之); 蜡染印花布料.

ba·tiste / bæ'ti:st; bæ'tist/ *n* [U] fine thin linen or cotton cloth. 上等细麻布或棉布.

bat·man /'bætmən; 'bætmən/ *n* (*pl* **-men** /-mən; -mən/) (GB mil) army officer's personal servant. (英军)勤务兵; 马弁.

baton /'bætən US: bə'tɒn; bæ'tɑn/ *n* **1** policeman's short, thick stick, used as a weapon: (警察用作武器的)警棍: *The police made a ~ charge,* drove the crowd back by using their ~s. 警察用警棍将群众驱退. **2** short, thin stick used by the conductor of a band or an orchestra. (乐队指挥所用的)指挥棒. **3** staff of office: 官杖; 司令权: *a Field-Marshal's ~.* 陆军元帅的司令杖.

bats / bæts; bæts/ *pred adj* (sl) mad; eccentric. (俚)疯癫的; 古怪的. ⇨ also **bat¹**.

bat·tal·ion /bə'tæliən; bə'tæljən/ *n* army unit made up of several companies and forming part of a regiment or brigade. (陆军之)营(由数连组成, 构成一团或一旅之一部分).

bat·ten¹ /'bætn; 'bætn/ *n* long board, esp one used to keep other boards in place, or to which other boards are nailed; (on a ship) strip of wood or metal used to fasten down covers or tarpaulins over a hatch. (固定木板所用之)板条; 夹板; 木条; 舱口压条(船舱上用以钉牢盖子或防水布之木条或金属条). □ *vt* [VP6A, 15B] *~ sth (down)*, make secure with ~s: 钉板条或压条以固定: 钉板条使坚固: *~ down the hatches.* 钉上舱口压条封闭舱口.

bat·ten² /'bætn; 'bætn/ *vi* [VP3A] *~ on/upon,* thrive, grow fat on (esp at the expense of others, or so as to injure others). 借…以成长或长肥(尤指损及他人者).

bat·ter¹ /'bætə(r); 'bætæ/ *vt, vi* [VP6A, 15A, B, 2C] strike hard and often; beat out of shape: 捣; 捶打; 击; 打得不成形: *The heavy waves ~ed the wrecked ship to pieces.* 巨浪将破船冲击成碎片. *Let's ~ the door down.* 我们把门击破吧. *Someone was ~ing (away) at the door.* 有人在用力敲门. *He was driving a badly ~ed old car and wearing a ~ed old hat.* 他驾着一辆旧破车, 戴着一顶旧破帽. '*~ing ram /-təm; -tərɪŋ/* (mil) big, heavy log with an iron head used in olden times for ~ing down walls. (昔)古代战争中用以击墙或破城门, 一端装有铁头之巨大圆木; 破城槌.

bat·ter² /'bætə(r); 'bætæ/ *n* [U] beaten mixture of flour, eggs, milk, etc for cooking. 面粉、蛋、牛奶等和成用以调制糕点之糊状物.

bat·tery /'bætərɪ; 'bætərɪ/ *n* (*pl* **-ries**) **1** army unit of big guns, with men and vehicles. 炮兵连(包括大炮, 人员及车辆). **2** group of big guns on a warship, or for coastal defence. 军舰上的炮组; 海岸上的防御炮台. **3** portable cell for supplying electricity: 电池; 电瓶: *a 'car ~.* 汽车用之电瓶. *This transistor has four small batteries.* 这部半导体收音机中有四个小电池. ⇨ **cell**(3). **4** set of similar utensils or instruments used together: (器皿或用具之)一套; 一组: *a ~ of lenses /*

ovens. 一套镜片 (一组烤炉). **5** *assault and* ~, (legal) attack upon or threatening touch (to sb). (法律)殴打. **6** series of boxes, etc in which hens are kept for laying eggs or for fattening. 养鸡房(用以放置母鸡或排小隔间, 以便让母鸡生蛋或将之养肥); 鸡屋; 鸡舍. .~ **'farm** n farm for hens kept in batteries. 养鸡场. **'~ hen** n hen kept in a ~. 养在养鸡房中的母鸡. ⇨ *free-range* at **free¹(3).**

bat·ting /'bætɪŋ; 'bætɪŋ/ n [U] cotton wool in flat wads. 棉絮.

battle /'bætl; 'bætl/ n **1** [C] fight, esp between organized and armed forces (armies, navies, aircraft); (fig) any struggle: (有组织的武装部队, 如陆、海或空军之间的)战争; 战役; 战斗; 交战; (喻)斗争; 奋斗: *the ~ of life.* 人生的奋斗. **2** [U] victory; success: 胜利; 成功: *The ~ is to the strong,* The strong are likely to win. 胜利属于强者. *Youth is half the ~,* Youthful strength brings likelihood of success. 年轻是成功的一半(青年的活力潜伏着成功的可能). **3** [U] *die in ~,* die fighting. 战死; 阵亡. *give/offer ~,* show readiness to fight. 挑战. *refuse ~,* refuse to fight. 拒绝应战. □ *vi* [VP3A] ~ *(with / against sth) (for sth),* struggle: (与某事物)作战; 奋斗: *battling against adversity.* 与逆境奋斗. *They ~d with the winds and waves.* 他们与风浪搏斗. **'~·axe** n **(a)** heavy axe with a long handle, formerly used as a weapon. (昔时用作武器的)战斧. **(b)** (colloq) domineering and assertive woman. (口)专横的女人. **'~-cruiser** n large fast cruiser with heavy guns and lighter armour than a ~ship. 战斗巡洋舰. **'~·dress** n soldier's uniform of belted blouse and trousers. 战地服装(军人制服, 衣裤旨用带子束起). **'~-field** n place where a ~ is or was fought. 战场. **'~·ground** n ~field. 战场. **'~·ship** n large kind of warship, with big guns and heavy armour. 主力舰; 战舰.

battle·dore /'bætldɔː(r); 'bætl,dor/ n bat or small racket used in the game called ~ and shuttlecock. (毽子戏中所用的)打毽板. ⇨ the illus at **badminton**. 参看 badminton 之插图.

battle·ments /'bætlments; 'bætl,ments/ n pl flat roof of a tower or castle enclosed by parapets with openings through which to shoot. (碉堡上的)城垛; 雉堞; 锯垛.

bat·tue /bæ'tuː; bæ'tu/ n [C] driving of game¹(6) (by beating bushes, etc) towards the sportsmen; occasion when this is done. 赶猎 (用打灌木树丛等方法, 将猎物驱赶向猎人); 赶猎时机.

batty /'bætɪ; 'bætɪ/ adj (sl) (of a person) crazy; slightly mad. (俚)(指人)疯狂的; 精神略微不正常的. ⇨ **bats.**

bauble /'bɔːbl; 'bɔbl/ n pretty, bright and pleasing ornament of little value. 美观而无价值之饰物.

baulk /bɔːk; bɔk/ ⇨ **balk.**

baux·ite /'bɔːksaɪt; 'bɔksaɪt/ n [U] clay-like substance from which aluminium is obtained. 铝土矿; 水矾土(提炼铝之原料).

baw·bee /bɔː'biː; 'bɔbi/ n (Scot) halfpenny. (苏)半便士.

bawd /bɔːd; bɔd/ n (old use) woman who keeps a brothel. (旧用法)开妓院的女人; 鸨母. **~y** adj (of talk, persons) vulgar; humorously coarse: (指谈话, 人)粗鄙的; 淫猥下流的; 猥亵的: ~y talk/stories; 淫猥下流的言语(猥亵的故事); a ~y old man. 粗鄙的老人. □ n ~y talk, etc. 淫猥粗俗的谈话; 猥亵话. **~·ily** adv

bawl /bɔːl; bɔl/ vt, vi [VP6A, 15A, 2C, 3A] shout or cry loudly: 大叫; 大喊: *He ~ed out a curse.* 他大声咒骂. *He ~ed to me across the street.* 他从街对街向我喊叫. *The frightened child ~ed for help.* 那受惊的小孩大叫求助. *~ sb out,* (US, sl) scold severely. (美, 俚)严厉责骂某人.

bay¹ /beɪ; be/ n **1** (also 亦作 *'bay-tree, 'bay laurel)* kind of tree or shrub with leaves that are used in cooking and are spicy when crushed. 月桂树 (叶捣烂作香料, 用于调味). **2** bays, **'bay-wreath,** laurel wreath given in olden times to poets and heroes, victors in war and athletic contests; (fig) honour; glory. 桂冠(古代用以奖饰诗人及英雄、战争或运动比赛之得胜者); (喻)荣誉; 光荣. **3** bay rum, hair lotion, made from the leaves of a W Indian tree. 贝兰发水 (用西印度群岛之一种树叶制成的头发香水).

bay² /beɪ; be/ n part of the sea or of a large lake, enclosed by a wide curve of the shore: 海湾; 大湖湾近似海湾之部分: *the Bay of Biscay;* 比斯开湾; *Hudson Bay.* 哈得孙湾.

bay³ /beɪ; be/ n **1** compartment between columns and pillars that divide a building into regular parts. (建筑物支柱与柱间的)间格. **2** extensions of a room beyond the line of one or two of its walls; recess. 房间向外凸出之部分; 壁凹. **,bay 'window,** window, usu with glass on three sides, built in such a recess. 凸窗(通常三面有玻璃, 建于墙壁之凸出部分). ⇨ the illus at **window.** 参看 window 之插图. **3** side-line and platform in a railway station, used as a starting-point and terminus for local trains, separate from the main lines. (火车站之与主线分开用作本地列车起站及终站的)侧线及月台. **4** compartment in the fuselage of an aircraft: (飞机机身中的)隔间; 隔室: *the 'bomb bay;* 飞机中的炸弹舱; part of a warship, college campus, etc for those who are ill or injured: (战舰、大学等供伤患疗养之)医务室; 医疗中心: *the 'sickbay;* 医务室; 医疗中心; compartment in a warehouse, barn etc for storing things: 仓库、谷仓等中之隔间; 仓房: *Put the equipment in No 3 bay.* 把装备放在第三号仓房.

bay⁴ /beɪ; be/ n deep bark, esp of hounds while hunting. (尤指出猎时的猎犬的)低沉的吠声. *at bay,* (of a hunted animal) forced to face its attackers and show defiance; (fig) in a desperate position, compelled, to struggle fiercely. (指被猎逐之兽)被迫作困兽之斗; (喻)处于绝望之境, 被迫作困兽之斗. *keep/hold sb at bay,* keep an enemy, etc at a distance; prevent him from coming too near. 阻止(敌人等)不使前进; 不让(敌人)接近. *bring (a stag, an enemy) to bay,* force (it him) to make a final resistance; come to close quarters so that escape is impossible. 围困(牡鹿, 敌人); 迫使做最后的抵抗; 迫近使之无法脱逃. □ vi [VP2A] (esp of large dogs, hounds) bark with a deep note, esp continuously, when hunting. (尤指大狗, 猎犬) 发出低沉的吠声(尤指狩猎时连续地发出).

bay⁵ /beɪ; be/ adj, n reddish-brown (horse): 红棕色的(马); 赤褐色的(马). *He was riding a dark bay.* 他骑着一匹深赤褐色的马.

bay·onet /'beɪənɪt; 'beənɪt/ n dagger-like blade that can be fixed to the muzzle of a rifle and used in hand-to-hand fighting. 刺刀(可装于步枪枪口上, 用于白刃战). □ vt [VP6A] stab with a ~. 用刺刀刺.

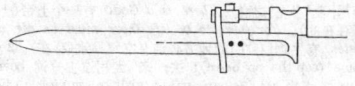

a bayonet

bayou /'baɪuː; 'baɪu/ n (in N America) marshy offshoot of a river. (北美洲境内河流之)多沼泽的支流.

ba·zaar /bə'zɑː(r); bə'zar/ n **1** (in Iran, India and other Eastern countries) street of workshops and shops; that part of a town where the markets and shopping streets are. (伊朗、印度及其他东方国家之)工场及商店集中之街道; (城市中的)市场及商业区. **2** (in GB, US) shop for the sale of cheap goods of great variety. (英国及美国之)廉价商店; 杂货店. **3** (place where there is a) sale of goods for charitable purposes: (为慈善目的而举行的)义卖; 慈善义卖场: *a church ~.* 由教堂主办的慈善义卖.

ba·zoo·ka /bə'zuːkə; bə'zukə/ n (pl ~s) portable

weapon for firing armour-piercing rockets. (轻便可携带,威力能穿甲之)火箭炮。

be[1] /biː; bi/ *vi* (*pres t* **am** /*after 'I':* m; m; *otherwise:* əm; əm; *strong form:* æm; æm/, **is** /z; z; *but* s; s *after* p, t, k, f, θ; *strong form:* ɪz; ɪz/, **are** /ə(r); ə; *strong form:* ɑː(r); ɑr/; *pt* **was** /wəz; wəz; *strong form:* wɒz; wɑz/, **were** /wə(r); wə; *strong form:* wɜː(r); wɜ/; contracted forms, **I'm** /aɪm; aɪm/, **he's** /hiːz; hiz/, **she's** /ʃiːz; ʃiz/, **it's** /ɪts; ɪts/, **we're** /wɪə(r); wɪr/, **you're** /jʊə(r); jʊr/, **they're** /ðeə(r); ðer/; neg **isn't** /ˈɪznt; ˈɪznt/, **aren't** /ɑːnt; ɑrnt/, **wasn't** /ˈwɒznt; ˈwɑznt/, **weren't** /wɜːnt; wɜnt/; *Am I not* is contracted to *aren't I* /ˈɑːnt; aɪ *US:* ˈænt; ɑrnt aɪ/; *pres p* **being** /ˈbiːɪŋ; ˈbiɪŋ/; *pp* **been** /biːn *US:* bɪn; bɪn/) [VP1] (linking *v* (or *copula*), between the subject and various complements) (连系动词),在主语与各种补语之间) **1** (with a *n* or *pron*, identifying or asking about the subject): (与名词或代词连用,示明或询及主语为何): *Today is Monday.* 今天是星期一。*Peter is a teacher / a Catholic.* 彼得是一个教师(天主教徒)。*Who is that?* (那)是谁? *It's me / him / her / the postman.* 是我(他,她,邮差)。**2** (with an *adj* or a *prep*, indicating a quality, an attribute): (与形容词或介词连用,表明性质或属性): *The world is round.* 地球是圆的。*He is ten years old.* 他十岁了。*Short skirts are in / out of fashion.* 短裙正流行(不流行了)。⇨ **fashionable, unfashionable. 3** (with a *prep* or *adverbial particle*, indicating a place): (与介词或副词性小品词连用,表示地方): *The lamp is on the table.* 那灯在桌上。*John's out in the garden.* 约翰在外头花园里。*Mary's upstairs.* 玛丽在楼上。*The station is a mile away.* 车站距此一英里远。**4** (with a *n* or a *prep*, indicating possession, actual or intended): (与名词或介词连用,表实际所有或意欲据有): *The money's not yours, it's John's.* 那笔钱不是你的,是约翰的。*The parcel is for you.* 那包裹是寄给你的。

be[2] /biː; bi/ *vi* ⇨ **be**[1] [VP1] (linking *v*, indicating a change from one quality, place, etc to another): (连系动词,表示从某种性质、某一地方等改变为另一性质、另一地方等): *He wants to be* (= become) *a fireman when he grows up.* 他长大时要当消防队队员。*Give me a pound, and the skirt is* (= will be) *yours.* 给我一英镑,那条裙子就是你的。*You can be* (= get) *there in five minutes.* 你于五分钟内就会到达该处。*Once more he was* (= again became) *the old John we used to know.* 他再一次变成我们所熟识的老约翰。*Suddenly his face was* (= became) *scarlet.* 突然间他的脸变红。

be[3] /biː; bi/ *vi* ⇨ **be**[1] [VP1] **1** (with introductory *there*): (与开端的 there 连用): *There's a bus-stop down the road.* 沿路下去有个公共汽车站。*There were six of us.* 我们共有六个人。*There are some stamps in that drawer.* 那个抽屉里有些邮票。*There's a letter for you,* A letter has come for you. 有一封给你的信。(Cf 参较 *One of the letters is for you.* 信件中有一封是给你的。) **2** (also with introductory *there*, meaning 'exist'): (亦与开端的 there 连用,表'存在'之意): *There is a God.* 有一个上帝(上帝是存在的)。*For there to be life there must be air and water.* 有生物(存在)的地方必定有空气和水(存在)。**3** go; come (esp the *pp* **been**); 去; 来 (尤用过去分词 been): *I've been to see* (= have paid a visit to) *my uncle.* 我去看过我的叔父了。*Have you ever been to Cairo?* 你到过开罗吗? *He has been to Paris.* 他曾到过巴黎。(Cf 参较 *He's gone to Paris,* ie is now either in Paris or on the way there. 他到巴黎去了(即现在巴黎,或在往巴黎的路上)。) *Has the postman been* (ie called) *yet?* 邮差已来过了吗? **4** ***the ˌbe-all and ˈend-all (of sth),*** the most important part (of it). (某事物之)最重要的部分。***been and ...*** , (vulg or hum) (used to indicate surprise, protest, etc): (鄙或谐) (用以表示惊异、抗议等): *You've been and bought a new hat!* 你竟买了一顶新帽子! *Who's been and taken my dictionary?* 谁把我的字典拿去了? ***for the time being,*** until some other arrangement. 暂时。⇨ also **being**. ***the ...-to-be,*** the future ...: 未来的…; 准…: *the bride / mother-to-be.* 未来的新娘; 准新娘。(未来的母亲)。**ˈwould-be** *adj* who wishes to be or imagines himself to be: 志愿做…的; 想象自己是…的; 自以为是…的: *a would-be poet.* 自以为是诗人的人; 有志为诗人的人。**might-have-been** *n* [C] past possibility. 已经过去的可能之事。

be[4] /biː; bi/ *aux v* ⇨ **be**[1] **1** (used with *pres p* to form the progressive or continuous tenses): (与现在分词连用,构成进行式): *They are / were reading.* 他们正在看书。*I shall be seeing him soon.* 我不久就可见到他了。*What have you been doing this week?* 你这个星期以来在干什么? **2** (used with a *pp* to form the passive voice): (与过去分词连用,构成被动语态): *He was killed in the war.* 他在战争中阵亡。*Where were they made?* 它们是在哪里制造的? *He is to be pitied.* 他是可怜悯的。**3** [VP4F] (used with a *to*-infinitive) (与带 to 的不定式连用)。**(a)** (equivalent to *must* or *ought*, to indicate duty, necessity, etc): (等于 must 或 ought, 表示责任或必要等): *I am to inform you* (= I have been told to inform you) *that ....* 我受托通知你…。*You are* (= ought, deserve) *to be congratulated.* 你该(值得)受祝贺。**(b)** intention: 意愿; 打算: *They are to be married in May.* 他们打算于五月里结婚。**(c)** possibility: 可能性: *The book was not to be* (= could not be) *found.* 那书根本找不到了。**(d)** a supposition or unreal condition: 假设; 非真实情况: *If I were to tell you / Were I to tell you ...;* 假使我告诉了你…; *If it were to rain* (=If it rained) *tomorrow....* 如果明天下雨…。**(e)** (chiefly *pt*) destiny: (主用过去式)命运: *He was never to see his wife and family again,* Although he did not know this at the time, he did not see them again. 他从那时起就再也见不到他的妻子儿女了(虽然他当时并不知道,但是以后没有再看见他们)。**(f)** mutual arrangement: 互相的约定: *We are to be married in May.* 我们定于五月里结婚。*Every member of the party was to pay his own expenses.* 参加餐会者各人须自付餐费。**(g)** the expressed wish of another person: 他人所表示的愿望: *At what time am I* (= do you want me) *to be there?* 我应于(你要我)何时到达那儿? **(h)** purpose: 目的: *The telegram was to say that she had been delayed.* 电报上要说的是她已因故延迟。

be- /bɪ-; bɪ-/ *pref* **1** all over; in every direction 全面; 到处; 遍 **(a)** (making *vv* from *vv*): (由动词构成动词): *besmear,* smear all over (with sth). 搽; 涂。**(b)** (making *vv* from *nn*): (由名词构成动词): *bedew,* cover with dew. 以露水沾湿。**2** (making an intransitive *v* transitive): (使不及物动词变为及物动词): *bemoan.* 悲悼; 恸哭。Cf 参较 *bemoan one's fate,* moan about one's fate. 自叹命苦。**3** (making *adjj* in *-ed* from *nn*) wearing: (由名词加 -ed 构成形容词) 戴…的: *bewigged;* 戴假发的; covered with: 盖以…的: *bejewelled.* 满饰珠宝的。**4** (intensifying): (加强语气): *begrudge;* 嫉妒; *belabour.* 殴打; 打击。

beach /biːtʃ; bitʃ/ *n* shore between high- and low-water mark, covered with sand or water-worn pebbles. 海滨; 海滩; 水滨。**ˈ~ ball** *n* very large lightweight one used for games on the ~. 海滩上玩游戏用的轻而大的球。**ˈ~ buggy** *n* small motorized vehicle, used for racing on waste ground, beaches, etc. 海滩车 (一种用来在荒地、海滩等上作比赛用之小汽车)。**ˈ~·comber** /-kəʊmə(r); -ˌkomə/ *n* **(a)** long wave rolling in from the sea. 由海上滚向海滨的长浪; 长卷浪。**(b)** man who makes a poor living on the waterfront in ports in the Pacific. 太平洋各港口码头区的贫苦谋生者。**ˈ~·head** *n* fortified position established on a ~ by an invading army. (登陆部队所建之)滩头阵地。⇨ **bridgehead. ˈ~·wear** *n* [U] clothes for sunbathing, swimming, playing games, etc on the ~. 在海滨日光浴、游泳、游戏等所穿之衣着; 海滩装。□ *vt* [VP6A] push or pull (a boat, a ship) up on to the shore or ~. 将(船)推或拖至岸边或海滩。

bea·con /ˈbiːkən; ˈbikən/ *n* **1** (old use 旧用法; also 亦作 **ˈ~-fire**) fire lit on a hill-top as a signal. (燃于山巅作为信号之)烽火。**2** light on a hill or mountain, or on the coast, on rocks, etc to give warning of danger or

for the guidance of ships, etc. (设于山上、海岸或岩石上等以警告有危险或引导船只航行的)信号灯。 **3** (also 亦作 '~-light) fixed lantern to warn or guide ships; flashing light to warn aircraft of high mountains, etc. (警告或引导航船之)陆上标灯(、(警告飞机该处有高山等之)信标光;灯标。 **4** (in GB) seven-foot high post with a lamp, used to indicate a street-crossing for pedestrians (在英国)指路灯(灯柱高七英尺,用以指示行人可于该处穿越马路): flashing ~ or Belisha /bə'li:ʃə; bə'liʃə/ ~, one with a light that flashes, to warn motorists that pedestrians have priority over wheeled traffic. 表示行人有权较车辆优先通过之闪光灯。 **5** (US) (美) = beam(4).

bead /bi:d; bid/ n **1** small ball of wood, glass, etc with a hole through it, for threading with others on a string or wire; (pl) necklace of ~s. (有孔可穿于线上之木质或玻璃质等的)小珠子; (复)珠子项链; 念珠。 **2** tell one's ~s, (old use) say one's prayers (while counting ~s on a rosary. (旧用法)(数念珠而)祷告。 **3** drop of liquid: 水珠; 滴: His face was covered with ~s of sweat. 他满脸汗珠。 ~-ing n wooden strip with a pattern of ~s, used for ornament; similar pattern on stonework; lace trimmings, etc with ~s. 有小珠花样的木条(用作装饰);石造物上类似的花样;串珠花边。

beadle /'bi:dl; 'bidl/ n (formerly) parish officer who helped the priest by keeping order in church, giving out money to the poor, etc. (昔时)教区助理员(负责协助牧师维持教堂秩序,发放赈款给贫民等)。

beady /'bi:dɪ; 'bidɪ/ adj (of eyes) small, round and bright. (指眼睛)小,圆而明亮的。

beagle /'bi:gl; 'bigl/ n small, short-legged hound used for hunting hares when those who take part are on foot, not on horse-back. 一种猎兔用的短腿小猎犬(猎者步行,非骑马)。 beag·ling /-glɪŋ; -glɪŋ/ n hunting hares with ~s. 带这种小猎犬猎兔。

beak[1] /bi:k; bik/ n **1** hard, horny part of bird's mouth, esp when curved. 鸟喙; 鸟嘴(指前端之坚硬角质部分,尤指弯曲者)。 ⇨ the illus at **prey**. 参看 prey 之插图。 **2** ram at the prow of a warship in ancient times. (古代战舰前端之)撞角; 铁嘴。

beak[2] /bi:k; bik/ n **1** (sl) magistrate: (俚)地方官: brought up before the ~. 被告到官厅里。 **2** (old use; sl) schoolmaster. (旧用法; 俚)校长; 教员。

beaker /'bi:kə(r); 'bikɚ/ n **1** open glass vessel with a lip (as used for chemical experiments, etc). 烧杯(如作化学实验等用)。 **2** (liter or archaic) large drinking vessel; goblet. (文或古)大酒杯。 **3** plastic vessel, shaped like and used as a drinking glass. 塑胶杯。

beam /bi:m; bim/ n **1** long horizontal piece of squared timber, or of steel, light alloy, concrete, supported at both ends, used to carry the weight of a building, etc. (建筑物中的)横梁; 桁(方木材,或为钢、轻合金、混凝土所制成)。 **2** horizontal cross-timber in a ship, joining the sides and supporting the deck(s); the greatest width of a ship, ⇨ the illus at **ship**. 船梁(船上连接两舷并支持甲板之横木); 船宽(参看 ship 之插图)。 **on/off the port/ starboard ~**, on/at a distance from either side. 在(远离)左(右)舷。 **on her/~'ends**, (of a ship) lying over to one side; almost capsizing. (指船)倾向一边; 几至倾覆。 **be on one's ~'ends**, (of a person) at the end of one's financial resources; destitute; (指人)经济拮据的; 穷困的。 **broad in the ~**, (colloq of a person) wide and stocky. (口,指人)矮胖而且臀部宽阔的。 **3 (a)** crosspiece of a balance, from which the scales hang. 天平的横杆。 ⇨ the illus at **balance**. 参看 balance 之插图。 **(b)** chief piece of timber in an old-style plough, to which the share is fastened. (旧式犁的)犁柄。 **4 (a)** ray or stream of light (eg from a lamp or lighthouse, the sun or moon); (fig) bright look or smile, showing happiness, etc: (发自灯、灯塔或日月等之)光柱; (喻)高兴的表情或微笑: with a ~ of delight. 带着一种高兴的表情。 **(b)** directed electromagnetic waves: 定向电磁波: the ~ system, by which short waves are directed to a specific

target. 无线电短波定向播送法(将短波向某一特定方向放送之方法)。 **(c)** radio signal used to direct an aircraft on its course. 指导飞机航道的无线电信号; 领航信号。 **on/off the ~**, (of an aircraft) following/not following the radio ~; (colloq) on the right/wrong track; behaving in a way likely/unlikely to be right. (指飞机)依从(未依从)航行信号; (口)在常轨上(入歧途); 行为(不)正当。 □ vt, vi **1** [VP2C] (of the sun, etc) send out light and warmth; (fig) smile happily and cheerfully: (指太阳等)发出光与热; 放射; (喻)高兴地微笑: ~ing with satisfaction. 满意地微笑着。 **2** [VP6A, 14] ~ sth (to), (telegraphy) broadcast (a message, radio programme, etc) in a particular direction: (电信)向某一特定方向播送(电信、广播节目等): ~ed from Britain to 8 America. 从英国向南美洲播送的。

bean /bi:n; bin/ n **1** (any of several plants bearing) seed in long pods (all used as vegetables): 豆子; 豆类(均用作蔬菜者):豆科植物: broad ~s, 蚕豆, 'kidney ~s, 菜豆, 'soya ~s. 大豆。 ⇨ the illus at **vegetable**. 参看 vegetable 之插图。 '~-stalk n stalk of tall-growing varieties of ~. 豆茎; 豆秆。 **2** seed similar in shape of other plants (esp 'coffee ~s, also called berries). 其他植物所产豆状之宝(尤指咖啡豆, 亦称 berries)。 **3** (sl used) (俚语用法) be without/not have a ~, be without any money. 身无分文; 一文不名。 full of ~s, lively; in high spirits or vigour. 有生气的; 活力充沛的; 愉快的; 高兴的。 **give sb ~s**, punish or scold him. 处罚某人; 责骂某人。 old ~, (dated sl, as a familiar form of address) old boy/fellow. (过时俚语, 用作亲密的称呼)老友; 老兄。 **spill the ~s**, give away information, esp sth not intended to be made known. 泄漏消息(尤指不欲人知的事); 泄漏秘密。 '~-feast; beano /'bi:nəʊ; 'bino/ nn (dated colloq) feast; celebration; jolly time. (过时口语)宴会; 庆祝; 欢乐时刻。

bear[1] /beə(r); bɛr/ n **1** large, heavy animal with thick fur. 熊。 ⇨ **cub, whelp**. '~-skin n tall military headdress of black fur (worn by the Brigade of Guards in Britain). (英国近卫旅士兵所戴之)黑色皮高帽。 **2** rough, clumsy ill-mannered person. 粗鲁之人; 卤莽之人。 **3 the Great/Little B~**, names of two constellations in the northern hemisphere. 大(小)熊星座。 **4** (stock exchange) person who sells stock for future delivery hoping before then to buy it cheap. (股票市场)空头业者(抛售股票, 希图于交割前再以低价补进者)。 ⇨ bull[1](3). ~ish adj rough; clumsy. 粗暴的; 笨拙的。

POLAR BEAR

GRIZZLY BEAR

bears

bear[2] /beə(r); bɛr/ vt, vi (pt bore /bɔ:(r); bor/, pp borne /bɔ:n; born/) **1** [VP6A, 15B] carry: 携带; 负荷; 负载; 一般而言 carry off. 负重。负重担。~ away, (now usu 今常用 carry off): ~ away the palm, excel in competition; ~ away (ie win) the prize. 得奖。 **2** [VP6A] have; show: 有; 显示: ~ the marks/signs/traces of blows/wounds/punishment; 有拳打(创伤, 处罚)的痕迹; a document that ~s your signature; 有你的签名的文件; ~ arms, be provided with weapons; 持有武器; 从军; ~

no/some/not much/little resemblance to sb or sth. 与某人或某事物没有（有点, 没有太多, 几乎没有）相似之处。
3 [VP6A] have; be known by: 有; 以…为人所知: ~ a good character; 有良好的品格; a family that bore an ancient and honoured name. 名门世家。 **4** [VP16B] ~ oneself, **(a)** carry oneself in a specified way: 举止: He ~s himself like a soldier, stands, walks, etc like one. 他举止(站立、步行等)似军人。 **(b)** behave; conduct oneself: 行为; 处己; 持身: He bore himself with dignity in these difficult circumstances. 他在这种困难的环境中表现出高尚的品格。 **5** [VP14, 12C] ~ (against/towards), have in the heart or mind: 心怀: ~ a grudge against sb; 对某人怀恨在心; ~ no malice towards sb; ~ sb no malice; 对某人毫无恶意; the love / hatred she bore him, felt towards him. 她对他所怀的爱(恨)。 **6** [VP6A, 14, 11] bring; provide. 带给; 供给。 ~ a hand, help. 帮助; 助一臂之力。 ~ witness (to sth), (fig) provide evidence; speak in support: (喻)提出证明; 做证: actions that ~ witness to his courage. 证明他有勇气的行为。 Will you ~ witness that I am innocent? 你愿为我做证证明我是无辜的吗? ~ false witness (against sb), give false evidence. 做(不利于某人的)伪证。 **7** [VP 6A, 2A] support; sustain: 支持; 负担: The ice is too thin to ~ your weight. 这冰太薄了, 支持不住你的重量。 The ice doesn't ~ yet. 这冰还支持不住。 Who will ~ the responsibility/expense? 谁将负担这个责任(费用)? **8** [VP 6A, 6D, 7A, 17] (usu with can/could, and esp in neg and interr) endure; tolerate; put up with: (通常与 can, could 连用, 尤用于否定或疑问句)忍耐; 忍受: I can't ~ (the sight of) that old man. 我不能忍受(看见)那老人。 The pain was almost more than he could ~. 那疼痛几乎使他受不了。 There's no ~ing (= It's impossible to ~) such rude fellows. 这种粗鲁的人令人无法忍受。 She couldn't ~ to see animals treated cruelly. 她不忍见动物受虐待。 She can't ~ to be laughed at / can't ~ being laughed at. 她不能忍受被取笑。 **9** [VP6E] be fit for: 适宜于; 堪: His language won't ~ repeating. 他的话不堪重述。 Your joke will ~ repeating, is amusing enough to be heard again. 你的笑话百听不厌。 **10** [VP6A, 12C] give birth to: 生产(孩子): ~ a child. 产一婴孩。 She has borne him six sons. 她已为他生了六个儿子。 Cf 参较 born: The eldest son was born in 1932. 长子生于一九三二年。 **11** [VP2C] ~ (to the), (of direction) turn, incline: (指方向)转; 倾斜: When you reach the top of the hill, ~ (to the) right. 当你到达山顶时, 向右转。 **12** [VP 15B, 2C, 3A] (with adverbial particles and preps): (与副词性小品词及介词连用):
bear down, overcome; defeat: 克服; 击败: ~ down the enemy; 击败敌人; ~ down all resistance. 克服一切阻力。 ~ **down on / upon**, (esp of a ship, car) move quickly towards. (尤指船、车)向…急速驶进; 逼近; 冲向。 **be borne 'in on / upon sb**, (of sb) be made to realize: 使(某人)了解; 完全认识: The terrible truth was borne in on him, he had to realize it. 他不得不相信这可怕的真相。 It was gradually borne in on me that..., The idea that...was one that I gradually had to accept. 我不得不渐渐相信…。
bear on / upon, have relation to, have influence on, be relevant to: 与…有关系; 对…有影响: How does this ~ upon the problem? 这个与该问题有何关系? These are matters that ~ upon the welfare of the community. 这些都是与社会福利有关的问题。 **bring to ~ on / upon**, make (sth) relate to, have influence on: 使(某事物)与…有关; 使对…有所影响; 将(某事物)施于…: bring all one's energies to ~ upon a task; 将全副精力用于一项工作; bring pressure to ~ on sb. 对某人施以压力。 ~ **hard / heavily / severely, etc on / upon**, be a burden on: 成为…之重担: Taxation ~s heavily on all classes in Britain. 捐税使英国各阶层均感受压迫。
bear (sth or sb) out, confirm (sth); support (sb): 证实(某事); 为(某人)作证: ~ out a statement. 证实一项陈述。 John will ~ me out / ~ out what I've said. 约翰将

会为我(我所说的话)作证。
bear up (against / under sth), be strong in the face of (sorrow, etc): (处于悲伤等之境)鼓起勇气; 坚强起来; 不颓丧: He bore up well against all these misfortunes. 他在这一切不幸之中表现得很坚强。 Tell her to ~ up, to have courage, not give way. 告诉她鼓起勇气吧。 **bear with sb**, treat him patiently or indulgently: 耐心对待; 宽纵对待; 忍受: If you will ~ with me (ie listen patiently to me) a little longer.... 如果你们再耐心地听我说一会儿…。
bear·able /'beərəbl; 'bɛrəbl/ adj (from 源自 bear²(8)) that can be borne or endured. 可忍受的; 忍得住的; 可容忍的。
beard¹ /bɪəd; bɪrd/ n **1** hair of the lower part of the face (excluding the moustache): 胡须; 髯(不包括髭): a man with a ~; 留胡子的人; a week's (growth of) ~ 一星期未剃的胡子; similar growth of hair on an animal: (动物的)胡子: a billy-goat's ~. 雄山羊的胡子。 **2** ~-like sheath on the grain of barley, oats, etc. (大麦、燕麦等的)芒。 ~**ed** adj having a ~. 有胡子的。 ~·**less** adj having no ~: 无胡须的: a ~less youth. 无胡须的青年。
beard² /bɪəd; bɪrd/ vt [VP6A] defy openly, oppose: 公然反抗; 反对: ~ the lion in his den, (fig) defy sb in his own stronghold. (喻)入虎穴取虎子; 进入某人的老窝与之对抗; 奋不顾身与其周旋。
bearer /'beərə(r); 'bɛrə/ n **1** person who brings a letter or message: 送信人; 信差: the ~ of good news; 传送好消息的人; the ~ of this letter. 持此信的人。 **2** person who helps to carry a coffin to a grave, who carries a stretcher, flag, etc. 抬棺者; 杠夫; 担架夫; 掌旗者。 **3** person employed to carry sth. 搬运夫; 挑夫。 **4** person who presents, at a bank, a cheque payable on demand. 即期支票持票人。 '~ **bonds** n pl bonds, interest on which is payable to the ~, the owner's name not being written on them. 不记名债券(利息付与持票人)。 ~ **s** (with adj) plant, tree, etc that produces fruit, crops, etc: (与形容词连用)结果实的植物、树木等: a good / poor ~. 结果实多(不多)的(树); 收获多(不多)的作物。
bear·ing /'beərɪŋ; 'bɛrɪŋ/ n **1** [U] way of behaving; way of standing, walking, etc: 行为之方式; 举止; 态度; (站立, 步行等)姿态: a man of noble / soldierly ~. 举止高贵(象军人)的人。 His kindly ~ caused all the children to like him. 他那种和蔼的态度使所有的孩子都喜欢他。 ⇨ **bear²(4)**. **2** [C, U] relation, aspect: 关系; 方面: We must consider the question in all its ~s. 我们必须从各方面考虑这个问题。 What he said has no / not much ~ on (ie is not connected with) the subject. 他所说的话与本题没有(没有多大)关系。 ⇨ **bear²(12)**. **3** [U] possibility of being endured; endurance: 可忍耐的限度; 忍耐: His conduct was beyond (all) ~. 他的行为令人忍无可忍。 ⇨ **bear²(8)**. **4** [C] direction in which a place, etc, lies (as measured, eg in degrees): (一个地方等所处之)方位; 方向(如用度数测量者): take a compass ~ on a lighthouse; 用罗盘测度灯塔之方位; (pl) relative position; direction. (复)相对的位置; 方向。 **get / take one's ~s**, find the direction of a ship's course; find one's position by looking round for landmarks, etc. 明辨船的航行方向; 环顾四周寻找陆标等以确定自己的位置。 **lose / be out of one's ~s**, be lost; (fig) be puzzled. 迷途; 迷失方向; 不知所措; 惶惑。 **5** (usu pl) (in a machine) device that supports moving parts and reduces friction: (通常用复数)(机器中之)轴承(承受各运转部分并减少摩擦): ball / roller ~s. 滚珠(滚子)轴承。 **6** [U] (of a tree, etc): (指树等): in full ~, producing fruit well. 盛产果实之际。 ⇨ **child-~**.
bear·ish /'beərɪʃ; 'bɛrɪʃ/ adj ⇨ **bear**¹.
beast /biːst; bist/ n **1** four-footed animal (animal is the usu word; beast is used in fables): 兽。 (animal 是常用词; beast 用于寓言中)。 **2** (farming) cow or bullock; animal for riding or driving. (农)牛; 供

骑乘或驱使的动物; 牲畜; 牛马。 **3** cruel or disgusting person. 残忍或令人厌恶的人; 凶恶的人。 **4** (reproachfully or playfully) person who behaves badly: (责备或戏谑语) 行为令人厌恶的人: *They hate that ~ of a foreman!* (eg of a foreman who is very strict). 他们恨那可恶的工头 (例如极严厉的工头)。 **~·ly** *adj* **1** like a ~ or its ways; unfit for human use. 似兽的; 兽性的; 不适宜于人类使用的。 **2** (colloq) nasty: (口) 可厌的; 恶劣的: *What ~ly weather!* 多么恶劣的天气! □ *adv* (colloq; used to intensify *adjj* and *advv* used in a bad sense) very; unpleasantly: (口; 用以加强恶意的形容词及副词) 非常; 极; 令人不快地: *He was ~ly drunk.* 他喝得烂醉。 ⇨ *jolly. It was ~ly cold.* 那天冷极了。 **~·li·ness** /-lɪnɪs; -lɪnɪs/ *n* [U]

beat¹ /biːt; bit/ *vt, vi* (*pt* beat, *pp* **~en** /'biːtn; 'bitn/) **1** [VP6A, 14, 2A, C] hit repeatedly (esp with a stick): (尤指用棍棒) 连续地击打: *She was ~ing the carpet/ ~ing the dust out of the carpet.* 她正在用棒子敲打地毯 (把地毯上的灰打落下来)。 *He was ~ing a drum.* 他正在打鼓。 *We heard the drums ~ing/being ~en.* 我们听见打鼓的声音。 *The boy was ~en until he was black and blue,* covered with bruises. 那男孩被打得青一块紫一块。 *The hunters had to ~ a way through the undergrowth,* make a path by forcing the branches, etc down. 猎人们不得不在灌木丛中开出一条路。 *Somebody was ~ing at/ upon the door.* 有人在敲门。 **~ one's brains,** ⇨ **brain** (4). **~ a retreat,** give the signal (by drum) to retreat; (fig) go back, retire. 鸣鼓撤退; 仓皇撤退; (喻) 打退堂鼓; 放弃。 **~ the woods,** go into them to drive out game (for sport, shooting). 入丛林中驱出猎物 (以为运动, 或以供猎射)。 **~·ing** *n* **(a)** continuous beating, esp by hitting repeatedly: 处罚; (尤指) 接连地打: *give sb/get a good ~ing.* 痛打某人 (挨一顿痛打)。 **(b)** (colloq) defeat: (口) 击败; 失败: *Our team got a sound ~ing.* 我们的队遭到惨败。 **2** [VP2C] (of the sun, rain, wind, etc) strike: (指太阳、雨、风等) 射; 打; 吹: *The rain was ~ing against the windows.* 雨打在窗户上。 **3** [VP6A, 14] mix thoroughly and let air into by using a fork or similar utensil: 搅拌; 打松: ~ *eggs;* 打蛋 (使蛋白蛋黄混合); ~ *cream* (to a froth); 搅乳脂 (使成泡沫); ~ *flour and eggs, etc,* (to a paste). 搅拌面粉及鸡蛋使成糊状。 ⇨ **whip²**(2). **4** [VP6A, 22, 15B] hammer, change the shape of by blows: 锤扣使变形: ~ *sth flat;* 将某物锤薄; ~ *out gold,* hammer it flat; 将金锤薄; ~ *the door in,* break in by hammering down the door. 破门而入。 **5** [VP6A, 14, 15A] defeat; do better than: 击败; 优于; 胜过: *Our army was ~en.* 我们的陆军被打败了。 *I'll ~ you to the top of that hill,* race you and get there first. 我们来比赛跑到山顶, 我将赢你。 *He ~ me at chess.* 他下棋赢了我。 ~ *the record,* break the record, make a new and better record. 打破纪录; 创新纪录。 **6** [VP6A] be too difficult for; perplex: 难倒; 使困惑: *That problem has ~en me.* 那个问题把我难倒了。 **7** [VP6A, 14, 2A, 3A] move up and down regularly: 拍(翅); 鼓(翼); 有规律地上下动: *The bird was ~ing its wings against the sides of the cage.* 那只鸟鼓动它的翅膀拍打笼子的侧边。 *His heart was still ~ing.* 他的心脏仍在跳动。 *Her heart was ~ing with joy.* 她的心因高兴而猛跳。 ~ *time,* measure time (in music) by making regular movements (with the hands, etc). (在音乐中, 用手等) 打拍子。 **8** (various uses): (各种用法): ~ *about the bush,* approach a subject without coming to the point. 兜圈子; 不直接谈正题。 *dead ~,* tired out. 疲惫极了。 ~ *it,* (sl) go away. (俚) 走开。 **9** [VP2C, 15B] (with *adverbial particles* and *preps*): (与副词性小品词及介词连用): *beat down* **(on),** 照射; 吹; 打: *The sun was ~ing down on our heads,* shining with great heat. 太阳直射在我们的头顶上。 *He wanted £800 for the car but I ~ him down* (= made him lower his price) *to £600.* 那车他索价八百英镑, 但我把他的价钱杀到六百英镑。 *I ~ down his price,* made him lower it. 我压低他的价钱。 *The wheat had been ~en down* (=

flattened) *by the rain.* 麦禾已被雨打倒了。 *beat sb/sth off,* 击退: *The attacker/attack was ~en off,* repulsed. 攻击者(攻势)被击退了。 *beat sth out,* 扑灭 (火); 敲出 (曲子): *The dry grass caught fire, but we ~ it out,* extinguished the fire by ~ing the burning grass. 干草着了火, 但是我们把它扑灭了。 *He ~ out* (= drummed) *a tune on a tin can.* 他在洋铁罐上敲出一首曲子。 *beat sb up,* 痛打; 毒打: *He was badly ~en up* (= beaten severely with cudgels, etc) *in a back alley.* 他在后巷里被人毒打了。 ~ *sth up (into/to),* mix thoroughly and let air into by using a fork or other utensil: 搅拌并打松些东西 (使成为…): ~ *the mixture up to a creamy consistency.* 将这混合物打松到象乳脂的浓度; ~ *the flour and eggs (up) to a paste.* 搅拌面粉及鸡蛋使成糊状。

beat² /biːt; bit/ *n* **1** regular repeated stroke, or sound of this: 有规律的敲击(声): *We heard the ~ of a drum.* 我们听见击鼓声。 *His heart ~s were getting weaker.* 他的心跳逐渐微弱。 **2** recurring emphasis marking rhythm in music or poetry. 音乐或诗中标明节奏之重复的强音; 节拍。 **3** route over which sb goes regularly; appointed course of a sentinel or policeman: 某人常走之路; 哨兵或警察之规定的巡逻路线: *The policeman was on his ~,* on the route he was ordered to patrol. 那警察在执行巡逻任务。 *be off/out of one's ~,* (fig) be doing sth with which one is not familiar, sth different from one's usual work, etc. (喻) 做自己不熟悉的事; 做非本行的工作。

beat³ /biːt; bit/ *attrib adj* of or like beatniks: (似) beatniks 的: *the ~ generation.* 反传统的一代。 □ *n* =beatnik.

beaten /'biːtn; 'bitn/ *adj* (esp) (尤指) **1** shaped by beating: 锤成的: ~ *silver.* 银箔。 **2** (of a path) worn hard by use: (指道路) 很多人走过的; 久经践踏的: *a well-~ path.* 很多人走过的路。 *go off/keep to the ~ track,* do sth/not do anything unusual. 做(不做任何) 越出常轨的事。

beater /'biːtə(r); 'bitə/ *n* **1** utensil used for beating, such as: 打或搅的器具, 如: '**carpet-~,** 打地毯的器具; '**egg-~,** 打蛋器; 搅蛋器。 **2** man employed to drive birds, etc to those waiting with guns to shoot them. 被雇用驱起鸟类等至猎人近处以便射击之人; 追猎夫。

bea·tif·ic /ˌbɪə'tɪfɪk; ˌbiə'tɪfɪk/ *adj* showing great happiness; making blessed. 极快乐的; 祝福的。

be·atify /bɪ'ætɪfaɪ; bɪ'ætə,faɪ/ *vt* [VP6A] (in the R C church) announce that a dead person is among the Blessed (ie those who will live for ever with God in a state of supreme happiness). (天主教) 为死者宣福; 宣布死者升天; 行宣福礼。 **be·ati·fi·ca·tion** /bɪˌætəfɪ'keɪʃn; bɪˌætəfə'keʃən/ *n* ~ing or being beatified; first step before canonization. 宣福; 封为圣徒之第一步。 ⇨ canonize.

be·ati·tude /bɪ'ætɪtjuːd *US:* -tuːd; bɪ'ætə,tjud / *n* [U] great happiness; blessedness. 至福; 天福。 **The B~s,** Christ's sermon on blessedness (in the Bible, Matt 5:3-11). 登山宝训 (耶稣论福所讲的福音, 在圣经中马太福音第 5 章第 3 至 11 节)。

beat·nik /'biːtnɪk; 'bitnɪk/ *n* (1950's) person adopting unconventional manners and dress as a defiant protest against current morality and as a means of self-expression. 比特尼克 (二十世纪五十年代以怪异之行为及服装公然反抗当时之道德, 借以表现自我之人)。 Cf 参较 hippy, a later word.

beau /bəʊ; bo/ *n* (*pl* **~x** /bəʊz; boz/) **1** (old use) rather old man who is greatly interested in the fashion of his clothes. (旧用法) 对衣着非常讲究衣着样式之男人。 **2** (now usu fac) man who pays great attention to women. (今常作玩笑语) 对女人献殷勤者。 **3** (now usu fac) girl's admirer or lover. (今常作玩笑语) 女子之爱者; 情郎; 爱人。 **4** ~ **ideal,** one's idea of what is most excellent or beautiful. 至善; 至美; 典型。 **the ~ monde** /ˌbəʊ 'mɔːnd; bo'mɑnd/ (F) fashionable society. (法) 上流社会。

Beau·jolais /'bəʊʒəleɪ US: ˌbəʊʒəˈleɪ/ ,boʒə'le/ n [U] (F) light wine (usu red) of Burgundy. (法) 法国中部 勃艮地所产的淡葡萄酒 (通常为红色)。

beau·te·ous /'bjuːtɪəs; 'bjutɪəs/ adj (poet) beautiful. (诗) 美丽的; 美丽的。

beau·tician /bjuːˈtɪʃn; bju'tɪʃən/ n person who runs a beauty-parlour. 经营美容院者。

beau·ti·ful /'bjuːtɪfl; 'bjutəfəl/ adj giving pleasure or delight to the mind or senses: 美的; 美丽的; 美观的; 令人生美感的: a ~ face / flower / voice; 美丽的面庞 (花朵、嗓音); ~ weather / music. 悦人的天气 (音乐)。 **~ly** /-flɪ; -fəlɪ/ adv in a ~ manner: 美地; 美好地: She sings ~ly. 她唱歌得得美极了。 That will do ~ly, will be most satisfactory. 那样好极了。 **beautify** /'bjuːtɪfaɪ; 'bjutə,faɪ/ vt [VP6A] make ~. 使美丽; 美化。

beauty /'bjuːtɪ; 'bjutɪ/ n 1 [U] combination of qualities that give pleasure to the senses (esp the eye and ear) or to the moral sense or the intellect: 美; 美好 (令视觉、听觉、或是非感或智力发生美感之各种性质之综合): Everyone must admire the ~ of a tropical sunset / a mother's love. 每个人必定会赞叹热带日落 (母爱) 之美。 B~ is only skin deep, (prov) We must not judge by outward appearance only. (谚) 美貌是肤浅的 (我们不可仅以貌取人)。 2 [C] (pl -ties) person, thing, specimen, feature, characteristic, that is beautiful or particularly good: 美丽或美好的人物、物、样品或特性: Isn't she a ~! 她真是个美人! Her smile is one of her beauties. 她的笑靥是她的美点之一。 Look at this rose—isn't it a ~! 请看这朵玫瑰花——它岂不是美的化身! I'm always finding new beauties in Shakespeare's poetry. 我经常在莎士比亚的诗中发现新的美点。 That's the ~ of it, the point that gives satisfaction. 那才是它真的所在 (令人满意之点)。 '~-parlour n establishment (now usu 今通常作 '~-salon) in which women receive treatment (of the skin, hair, etc) to increase their ~. (妇女) 美容院。 '~ queen n girl voted the most beautiful in a ~ contest. (选美会中经投票选出的) 后。 '~-salon, = ~-parlour. '~-sleep n sleep before midnight. 午夜前之睡眠。 '~-spot n 1 place with beautiful scenery. 名胜; 美景。 2 birthmark or artificial patch on the face, said to heighten ~. (脸上) 美人痣 (或为天生, 或由化妆而成)。

beaver1 /'biːvə(r); 'bivɚ/ n 1 fur-coated animal that lives both on land and in water, with strong teeth with which it cuts down trees and makes dams across rivers. 海狸 (一种水陆两栖的毛皮动物, 有坚齿, 可以啃倒树木, 并可以筑堤横过河流)。 ⇨ the illus at small. 参看 small 之插图。 2 [U] its fur. 海狸皮。 3 [U] heavy woollen cloth that looks like ~ fur. 似海狸皮之厚羊毛呢。 4 [C] high hat made of ~ fur, formerly worn by men. (昔日男人所戴之) 高顶海狸皮帽。

beaver2 /'biːvə(r); 'bivɚ/ n (on the helmet worn by soldiers in olden times) movable lower part that guarded the lips and chin. (昔时军人所戴连在头盔上之) 半面罩 (可移动, 用以遮脸之下部)。

beaver3 /'biːvə(r); 'bivɚ/ vi [VP2A, C] ~ away (at sth), (colloq) work hard. (口) 努力工作; 辛苦工作。

be·bop /'biːbɒp; 'bibɑp/ = bop.

be·calmed /bɪˈkɑːmd; bɪ'kɑmd/ pred adj (of a sailing-ship) stopped because there is no wind. (指帆船) 因无风而停止前进的。

be·came pt of become.

be·cause /bɪˈkɒz; bɪ'kɔz/ conj 1 for the reason that: 因为: I did it ~ they asked me to do it. 我做这事是因为他们要我做的。 Just ~ I don't complain, you mustn't suppose that I'm satisfied. 你不可只因为我不发怨言就以为我满意了。 (Note that when the reason is obvious, or is thought to be known, it is preferable to use as, or a construction with so: 注意: 如果理由是明显的, 或者被认为是已知的, 则以用 as 或有 so 的句法为佳: As it's raining, you'd better take a taxi. It's raining so you'd better take a taxi. 既然在下雨, 你最好乘计程车。 After

the noun reason, that is preferred to ~: 在名词 reason 的后面, 用 that 较用 because 为佳: The reason why we were late is that ... 我们迟到的原因是 ...) 2 ~ of, prep by reason of; on account of: 因为: B~ of his bad leg, he couldn't walk so fast as the others. 因为他的腿有毛病, 他不能跟别的人走得一样快。 I said nothing about it, ~ of his wife('s) being there. 因为他的妻子在那里, 我对这事一字未提。

beck1 /bek; bek/ n (N England) mountain stream or brook. (英格兰北部) 山涧; 山溪。

beck2 /bek; bek/ n movement of the head, hand or arm, as a signal or sign, used only in: 为作信号或示意的头或招手 (仅用于以下成语中): be at sb's ~ and call, be bound to obey his orders, to come and go, all the time. 听某人命令; 受某人指挥; 听某人差遣。 have sb at one's ~ and call, have sb always waiting to obey one's orders. 使某人随时听其命令或受其指挥。

beckon /'bekən; 'bɛkən/ vt, vi [VP6A, 15B, 16A, 2A] call sb's attention by a movement of the hand or arm, usu to show that he is to come nearer or to follow: 招手令他人走近或跟着来: He ~ed (to) me to follow. 他向我招手要我跟他去。 He ~ed me on / in. 他向我招手要我继续前进 (进去)。

be·come /bɪˈkʌm; bɪ'kʌm/ vi, vt (pt became /bɪˈkeɪm; bɪ'kem/, pp become) 1 [VP2D] come or grow to be; begin to be: 变为; 成为: He became a doctor. 他成为医生。 He has ~ a famous man. 因此他已成为名人。 The custom has now ~ a rule. 那习俗现已变为成规。 He has ~ accustomed to his new duties. 他对他的新职务已经习惯了。 It's becoming much more expensive to travel abroad. 现在出国旅行的费用贵得多了。 2 [VP3A] ~ of, happen to: (命运等) 降临; 使遭遇: What will ~ of the children if their father dies? 如果他们的父亲死了, 这些孩子的遭遇将怎样呢? I don't know what has ~ of him: 我不知道他的遭遇如何。 3 [VP6A] be well suited to: 适合: Her new hat ~s her. 她的新帽子她戴着很适合。 4 [VP6A] be right or fitting: befit: 与……相称; 适宜; 适于: He used language (eg insulting language) that does not ~ a man of his education. 他所用的字眼与一个受过他这样的教育的人不相称。 be·com·ing adj becoming (to), 1 (of dress, etc) well suited to the wearer: (指衣服等) 适于穿戴者的: a becoming hat / dress / style of hair-dressing. 合适的帽子 (服装、发型)。 2 suitable, appropriate: 合适的; 适宜的: with a modestly becoming to his low rank. 以一种适于其低微阶层的谦恭。 be·com·ing·ly adv

bed /bed; bed/ n 1 piece of furniture, or other arrangement, on which to sleep (Note omission and use of the articles): 床 (注意冠词的省略及使用): go to bed; 就寝; 睡觉; be in bed; 卧; 睡; get into / out of bed; 上 (起) 床; put the children to bed: 安置孩子们睡觉; sit on the bed; 坐在床上; find a bed for sb; 为某人安置床铺; (fig) love-making: (喻) 做爱: He thinks of nothing but bed. 他什么都不想, 只想到做爱。 single bed, for one person. 单人床。 double bed, for two persons: 双人床: I want a room with two single beds / a double bed. 我要一间有两张单人床 (一张双人床) 的房间。 twin beds, two exactly similar single beds. 两张形式大小完全相同的单人床。 spare bed(room), for a modestly bedroom for an occasional visitor. 留备偶然来访的客人住宿的空床; 客房。 bed and board, food and lodging; entertainment (at an inn, etc). 食宿; 款待 (在旅馆等)。 make the beds, put the bed-clothes (sheets, blankets, etc) in order, ready for use. 整理铺床; 铺床。 As you make your bed so you must lie on it, (prov) you must accept the consequences of your acts. (谚) 自作自受。 got out of bed on the wrong side, said of sb who is bad-tempered for the day. 他今天脾气不好。 take to / keep to one's bed, stay in bed because of illness. 卧病。 2 mattress: 床垫: a feather bed; 鸭 (鹅) 绒床垫; a spring-bed. 弹簧床垫。 3 flat base on which sth rests: 基座; 底座: The machine rests on a bed of concrete. 那机器

安装在水泥的基座上。 **4** bottom of the sea, a river, lake, etc; layer of rock, stone, etc, as a foundation for a road or railway; layer of clay, rock, etc, below the surface soil: 海底; 河床; 湖底; 公路或铁路之路基; (地面下之)地层: *If you dig here, you will find a bed of clay.* 如果你在这里挖掘, 你可以发现粘土层。 '**bed-rock**, solid rock below the soil, found at different depths in different places; (fig) ultimate facts or principles on wh. h a theory, etc, is based: (地面下之) 地盘岩; (喻)理论等所依据之基本事实或原理: *reach/get down to bed-rock.* 穷根究底。 **5** garden plot, piece of ground (for flowers, vegetables, etc): 花圃; 菜圃; 苗床: *'seed-bed; 苗床; 'onion-bed; 洋葱圃; 'flower bed.* 花圃。 **6** (compounds) (复合词) '**bed-bug** *n* wingless, blood-sucking insect. 臭虫。 '**bed-clothes** *n pl* sheets, blankets, etc for a bed. 床褥; 被褥; 铺盖(指被单、毯等)。 '**bed-fellow** *n* person with whom one shares a bed; (fig) companion. 同床者; 共床人; (喻)伙伴; 友伴。 '**bed-pan** *n* vessel for waste matter from the body, used by an invalid in bed. (病人在床上用的)便盆; 便器。 '**bed-post** *n* upright support of a bedstead (esp the old-fashioned sort). 床柱(尤指旧式者)。 '**bed-ridden** *adj* confined to bed by weakness or old age. 因体弱或年老而长久卧床的; 卧床不起的; 缠绵病榻的。 '**bed-roll** *n* portable roll of bedding (eg as used by campers). (如露营者留着用的可携带的) 铺盖卷。 '**bed-room** /*with -dr- as in 'dry'*, not separated as in '*head-room*' 本词中的 dr 应象 dry 中的 dr 那样读音, 不能象 head-room 中那样分开来读/ *n* room for sleeping in. 寝室; 卧室; 居房。 '**bed-side** *n* side of (esp a sick person's) bed: (尤指病人的)床侧: *Dr Green has a good bedside manner*, is tactful, knows how to fill his patients with confidence in himself; 格林医师很会对待病人(很机智, 知道如何使其病人信任医生); (attrib) (用作定语) *bedside table; 床侧小几; bedside books.* 置于床侧以便阅读的书籍。 **bed-'sit(ter)** (colloq for) **bed-'sitting-room** *n* room used (eg by students, single persons away from home) for both living in and sleeping in. (为bedsitting-room 的口语)(供离家的学生或单身者居住之)坐卧两用房间; 寝室、起居室两用之房间。 '**bed-sore** *n* sore on the back, etc of an invalid, caused by lying in bed for a long time. (因久卧病榻在背部等处所引起的)褥疮。 '**bed-spread** *n* covering spread over a bed during the day. 床罩。 '**bed-stead** *n* framework of wood and metal to support the mattress. 床架。 '**bed-time** *n* time for going to bed: 就寝时间: *His usual bedtime is eleven o'clock.* 他平常就寝的时间是十一点钟。

bed² /bed; bed/ *vt* (**-dd-**) [VP6A, 15A, B] **1 bed (in/out)**, plant (seedlings, etc): 种植 (幼苗等): *He was bedding out some young cabbage plants.* 他正在种植包心菜幼苗。 *He bedded the seedlings (in).* 他种植幼苗。 **2 bed (in)**, place or fix in a foundation: 置于基座中使固定; 置于基中: *Bricks and stones are bedded in mortar or concrete.* 砖石用灰泥或混凝土砌起来。 *The bullet bedded itself in* (= went deep into) *the wall.* 子弹深入于墙中。 *Heavy guns have to be bedded* (in) *before they will fire accurately.* 重炮必须安置稳固, 然后才会发射准确。 **3 bed down**, provide with a bed or bedding: 供以床或铺盖: *bed down a horse*, supply with straw, etc on which to rest; 为马铺稻草等供其休息; *bed down a soldier/traveller*, etc. 供应铺盖给战士兵(旅行者等)。 **-bed-ded**, having the specified type or number of beds: 有…床的: *a single-/double-/twin-bedded room.* 一个有一张单人床(一张双人床, 两张单人床)的房间。 '**bed-ding** *n* [U] **1** bed-clothes, eg blankets. 床褥; 被褥; 铺盖(毯子等)。 **2** straw, etc for animals to sleep on. 垫草(供牲畜睡卧的稻草等)。

be-daubed /br'dɔ:bd; br'dɔbd/ *pred adj* ~ **with**, smeared (with sth dirty, wet, sticky, etc). (被污秽、潮湿或粘性等之物)弄脏的; 污染的。

bed-ding /'bedɪŋ; 'bɛdɪŋ/ *n* [U] ⇨ **bed².**

be-decked /br'dekt; br'dɛkt/ *pred adj* ~ **with**, adorned, decorated (with flowers, jewels, etc). 以(花卉、

珠宝等)装饰或点缀的。

be-dev-il /br'devl; br'dɛvl/ *vt* (**-ll-**, US: **-l-**) (usu passive) confuse; complicate: (通常用被动语态)迷惑; 使复杂: *The issue is ~led by Smith's refusal to co-operate with us.* 该问题由于史密斯拒绝跟我们合作而变为复杂。 ~**ment** *n*

be-dewed /br'dju:d US: -'du:d; br'djud/ *pred adj* ~ **with**, (liter) sprinkled with, made wet with: (文)为…所沾湿的; 为…所洒湿的: *a face ~ with tears.* 泪泪沾湿的面庞。

be-dimmed /br'dɪmd; br'dɪmd/ *pred adj* ~ **with**, (liter) (of the eyes, mind) made dim: (文)(指眼, 心)模糊的; 朦胧的: (旧用法)朦胧的泪眼; 朦胧的目光; *a mind ~ with sorrow.* 因忧伤而心乱如麻。

bed-lam /'bedləm; 'bɛdləm/ *n* **1** (old use) asylum for mad people. (旧用法)疯人院。 **2** scene of noisy confusion: 闹哄哄的地方; 喧闹的地方: *When the teacher was called away the classroom was a regular ~.* 当老师被叫走的时候, 教室便呈现喧闹不堪。

Bed-ouin, Bed-uin /'beduɪn; 'beduɪn/ *n* (*pl* unchanged) nomadic Arab of the desert. (复数不变)游牧于沙漠中之阿拉伯人。

be-drag-gled /br'dræɡld; br'dræɡld/ *pred adj* (esp of clothing) made wet or dirty by rain, mud, etc. (尤指衣服)被雨, 泥等弄湿或弄脏的。

bee /bi:; bi/ *n* **1** small, four-winged, stinging insect that produces wax and honey after gathering nectar from flowers. 蜜蜂。 ⇨ the illus at **insect.** ⇨ see insect 之插图。 *have a bee in one's bonnet*, be obsessed by an idea. 老想着某一个念头。 *make a 'bee-line for*, go towards by the shortest way, go quickly towards. 取捷径前往; 迅速前往。 '**bee-hive** ⇨ **hive(1).** **2** (chiefly US) meeting for combined work and amusement (esp of neighbours and friends). (主用于美国)为了合力完成某事或举办娱乐活动所作之集会。 '**spelling bee**, competition in spelling. 拼字比赛。

beech /bi:tʃ; bitʃ/ *n* [C] forest tree with smooth bark and shiny dark-green leaves and small triangular nuts; [U] its wood. 山毛榉; 榉(树皮光滑, 叶深绿有光泽, 结三角形之小坚果); 其木材; 榉木。 '~ **mast** *n* [U] ~ **nuts.** 榉实; 榉子。

beef /bi:f; bif/ *n* **1** [U] flesh of an ox, bull or cow, used as meat. 牛肉(饲养以供食的牛)。 ~ **cattle**, bred and reared for ~. 肉牛(饲养以供肉食的牛)。 '**dairy cattle.** ~ **tea**, stewed juice from ~ (for people who are ill). (病人所吃的)牛肉汁。 '~**steak** *n* ⇨ **steak.** '~**eater** *n* yeoman of the guard; one of the warders of the Tower of London, dressed as in the days of the Tudor kings. 英王的卫士; 伦敦塔之狱吏(穿着都铎王朝时代服装)。 **2** [U] (in men) muscle: (男子之)肌肉; 膂力: *He's got plenty of ~.* 他的肌肉很结实(或膂力很足)。 **3** [U] (*pl* **beeves** /bi:vz; bivz/) fattened ox, considered as food. (养肥作为食用之)肉牛。 □ *vi* (sl) complain: (俚)发牢骚; 抱怨: *Stop ~ing so much!* 别再发这么多的牢骚! ~**y** *adj* (of a person) well covered with flesh; strong. (指人)结实的; 强壮的。

been ⇨ **be¹.**

beep /bi:p; bip/ *n* repeated signal (as during a phone conversation, indicating that it is being recorded). 哔哔声(如在电话通话中, 表示被记录之信号)。

beer /bɪə(r); bɪr/ *n* [U] alcoholic drink made from malt and flavoured with hops; other drinks made from roots, etc: 啤酒(用麦芽酿造, 加入蛇麻子使带苦味); 用植物之根等制成的其他饮料: *ginger-~*, 姜汁啤酒 (一种不含酒精之饮料), *'nettle-~.* 荨麻啤酒。 **small ~**, sth trifling and unimportant: 微不足道和不重要的事物: *He thinks no small ~ of himself*, has a high opinion of himself. 他自视甚高。 ~**y** *adj* like ~ in taste or smell; (eg of a person) smelling of ~. 味道或气味似啤酒的; (指人象)有啤酒味的。

bees-wax /'bi:zwæks; 'biz,wæks/ *n* [U] wax made by bees for honeycomb, used for polishing wood. 蜂蜡

(蜜蜂为筑蜂巢所制之蜡质物，可用为木材添加光泽)。□
vt polish with ~. 用蜂蜡打光。

beet /biːt/ bit/ *n* sorts of plant with a sweet root. 甜菜 (其根甜)。 '**red ~**, used as a vegetable, esp in salads. 红甜菜(作蔬菜用，尤用于拌生菜)。 '**white ~**, used for making sugar. 白甜菜 (用于制糖)。 ~ '**sugar**, sugar made from ~s, identical with cane sugar. 甜菜糖; 萝卜糖(与蔗糖完全相同)。 '~**·root** /'bitruːt; 'bit,rut *with* tr *as in* 'try' 本词中之 tr 读做 try 中之 tr/ *n* [C, U] root of ~; red ~. 甜菜根; 红甜菜。

beetle[1] /'biːtl; 'bitl/ *n* tool with a heavy head and handle, used for crushing, ramming and smoothing. 槌; 大槌。

beetle[2] /'biːtl; 'bitl/ *n* insect with hard, shiny wing-covers. 甲虫。 ⇨ the illus at **insect**. 参看 insect 之插图。

beetle[3] /'biːtl; 'bitl/ *vi* [VP2A] overhang; project: 突出; 凸出悬垂: *beetling cliffs.* 悬崖。 '~**-browed** *adj* having shaggy or projecting eyebrows. 眉毛粗浓或突出的。

beeves ⇨ **beef(3).**

be·fall /bɪ'fɔːl; bɪ'fɔl/ *vt, vi* (*pt* **befell** /bɪ'fel; bɪ'fel/ *pp* **befallen** /bɪ'fɔːlən; bɪ'fɔlən/ [VP6A, 2A] (used only in the 3rd person) (old use) happen (to): (仅用于第三人称)(旧用法)发生; 降临; 使遭遇: *What has ~en him?* 他发生了什么事?

be·fit /bɪ'fɪt; bɪ'fɪt/ *vt* (**-tt-**) [VP6A] (used only in 3rd person) (formal) be fitted for; be right and suitable for: (仅用于第三人称)(正式用语)适宜; 相当; 对于…是适当的: *It does not ~ a man in your position to....* 在你这样地位的人不应当…。 ~**·ting** *adj* right and proper. 适当的; 应当的。 ~**·ting·ly** *adv*

be·fogged /bɪ'fɒgd *US:* -'fɔːgd; bɪ'fɑgd/ *pred adj* (fig, of a person) puzzled; muddle-headed. (喻，指人)被弄糊涂的; 头脑不清的; 迷迷糊糊的。

be·fore[1] /bɪ'fɔː(r); bɪ'fɔr/ *adv* 1 (contrasted with *afterwards*) at an earlier time; in the past; already: (与 afterwards 相对)以前; 早些; 过去; 已经: *I've seen that film ~.* 我从前看过那部影片。 *It had been fine the day ~,* the previous day. (那天)前一天的天气很好。 *You should have told me so ~,* earlier. 你早就应该告诉我。 *That happened long ~,* a long time earlier. 那是很久以前发生的。 2 (of space or position): (指空间或位置): *They have gone on ~,* in advance. 他们走到前面去了。

be·fore[2] /bɪ'fɔː(r); bɪ'fɔr/ *conj* (contrasted with *after*) previous to the time when: (与 after 相对)在…以前(指时间): *I must finish my work ~ I go home.* 我在回家以前，必须把我的工作做完。 *Do it now ~ you forget.* 现在就做，免得忘记了。 *It will be five years ~ we meet again* (note the use of the present there). 再过五年以后我们才能再见(注意 meet 用现在式)。 Cf 参较 We shall not meet *again* until five years from now. 自现在起，五年内我们不能再见。

be·fore[3] /bɪ'fɔː(r); bɪ'fɔr/ *prep* 1 (contrasted with *after*) earlier than: (与 after 相对)在…以前(指时间): *the day ~ yesterday;* 前天; *the year ~ last;* 前年; *two days ~ Christmas;* 圣诞节前两天; *~ the holidays,* 在假日以前; *since ~ the war;* 从战前以来; *~ now /then;* 在此(那)以前; 不久以前。 不久。 ⇨ **Christ** (abbr 略作 **BC**): 公元前; 耶稣降生以前: *in 55 BC,* 55 years before the birth of Christ. 公元前五五年。 2 (contrasted with *after*) in front of (esp with reference to order or arrangement): (与 after 相对)在…之前(尤指顺序或排列): *B comes ~ C.* B 在 C 之前。 *Ladies ~ gentlemen,* ladies first; *Your name comes ~ mine on the list.* 名单上你的名字在我之前。 3 (contrasted with *behind*) in front of (with reference to position). (与 behind 相对)在…之前(指位置)。 (Except in a few phrases *in front of* is preferred to *before* in this sense, 除了在少数几个短语中外，用 in front of 表示此义较 before 为佳, eg 例如 There are some trees *in front of* the house. 房子的前面有一些树。) *carry all ~ one,* be successful in everything one attempts. 所谋无不成功; 万

事如意。 *sail ~ the mast,* as an ordinary seaman, not as an officer. 为普通水手，非为高级船员; 为水兵，非为军官。 *sail ~ the wind,* with the wind behind. 乘风而航; 顺风而行。 4 in the presence of; face to face with: 在…的面前; 与…面对面: *He was brought ~ the judge.* 他被带到法官面前。 *Don't hesitate to speak out ~ everyone* (ie in public) *about the way you've been treated.* 尽量向大家说出你所受待遇的情形。 5 rather than; in preference to: 宁…而不…; 而不: *Death ~ dishonour.* 宁死不受辱。

be·fore·hand /bɪ'fɔːhænd; bɪ'for,hænd/ *adv* earlier; before[1](1): 较早; 先前; 预先: *I knew what he would need, so I made preparations ~,* in advance, in readiness. 我早知道他需要什么，所以我预先做好了准备。 *Please let me know ~.* 请预先通知我。 *You ought to have told me ~.* 你早该在事前告诉我。 □ *pred adj (with),* early; in advance: 早的; 预先的: *When you go on a journey, it's a good thing to be ~ with your packing.* 你出门旅行的时候最好预先把行李包装好。 *She's always ~ with the rent,* pays it, or is ready to pay it, before it is due. 她的房租总是未到期就付好(或准备付)。

be·foul /bɪ'faul; bɪ'faul/ *vt* (liter) make dirty. (文)弄脏; 染污。

be·friend /bɪ'frend; bɪ'frɛnd/ *vt* [VP6A] make a friend of; be kind and helpful to (esp sb younger and needing help). 与…成为朋友; 扶助; 照顾(尤指对年轻需要帮助者)。

beg /beg; bɛg/ *vt, vi* (**-gg-**) 1 [VP6A, 2A, C, 3A, 14] **beg (for) (sth) (from /of sb),** ask for (food, money, clothes, etc); make a living by asking for money (in the streets, etc): 乞求(食物, 金钱, 衣服等); 在街上等)行乞; 乞讨: *He begged a meal.* 他乞讨一餐饭。 *He was so poor that he had to beg (for) his bread.* 他非常贫穷，所以不得不乞食。 *He made a living by begging from the rich.* 他依靠向富人行乞为生。 *a begging letter,* one that 'asks for help, esp money. 求援信(尤指金钱方面的资助)。 2 [VP6A, 7A, 17, 9, 2C. 14] ~ **(sth) (of sb),** ask earnestly, or with deep feeling: 恳求; 拜托: *beg a favour of sb,* ask him to help to do sth; 恳求某人帮忙; *beg (of) sb to do sth.* 恳求某人做某事。 *They begged us not to punish them.* 他们恳求我们不要处罚他们。 *I beg (of) you not to take any risks.* 我恳求你不要冒险。 *I begged (of) him to stay /that he would stay.* 我恳求他不要走。 *The children begged to come with us /that they might come with us.* 孩子们恳求要与我们同来。 *beg the question,* assume (usn unjustifiably) the truth of the matter that is in question. 以讨论中之问题为论据; 以未证实的假定为论据; 狡辩; 诡辩。 *go begging,* (of things) be unwanted: (指物)无人要的: *If these things are going begging* (= if nobody wants them), *I'll take them.* 如果这些东西没人要，我就要了。 *beg off,* ask to be excused: 恳求免除责罚或责任等: *He promised to come and help but has since begged off.* 他本来答应来帮忙，一却一直找借口，说是不能来。 *beg sb off,* ask that sb may be excused or forgiven. 为某人求情; 请求原谅某人。 ⇨ **pardon.** 3 [VP7A] take the liberty of (saying or doing sth): 冒昧; 失礼; 请原谅(说或做某事): *I beg to differ.* 对不起，本人有不同的意见。 *I beg to state /observe, etc that....* 敬启者(邮差以为)…。

be·gad /bɪ'gæd; bɪ'gæd/ *int* (old use) by God! (旧法)誓必!

be·gan ⇨ **begin.**

be·get /bɪ'get; bɪ'gɛt/ *vt* (**-tt-**) (*pt* **begot** /bɪ'gɒt; bɪ'gɑt/, old use **begat** /bɪ'gæt; bɪ'gæt/, *pp* **begotten** /bɪ'gɒtn; bɪ'gɑtn/ [VP6A] 1 (archaic) give existence to (as father): (古)(以父亲的身份)给予生命; 生(子): (Bible) (圣经) *Abraham begat Isaac.* 亚伯拉罕生以撒。 *The only begotten of the Father,* the only Son of God the Father. 圣父的独生子。 2 (liter) be the cause of: (文)为…之起因或根源: *War ~s misery and ruin.* 战争为贫困与毁灭的根源。 ~**ter** *n* one who ~s. 给予生命者; 父。

beg·gar /'begə(r); 'bɛgɚ/ *n* 1 (also 亦作 '~**-man,**

'**~woman**) person who lives by begging, eg for money, food; poor person. 乞丐; 穷人。 **B~s can't be choosers** must take whatever is offered them. 乞丐无选择(施者给什么, 他们就得拿什么)。 **2** person who begs for others, for charities, etc: (为他人或慈善机构等)劝募者: *He's a good ~,* successful in collecting money for charity, etc. 他是个善于劝募的人 (如替慈善机构劝募得钱)。 **3** (colloq; playful or friendly use) person; fellow: (口; 戏谑或友善用语)人; 家伙: *You lucky ~!* 你这幸运的家伙! □ vt **1** [VP6A] make poor, ruin: 使穷; 毁灭: *You'll ~ your family if you spend so much money on drink.* 如果你花这么多的钱喝酒, 你的家将陷于贫困。 **2** ~ *description,* make words seem poor and inadequate: 笔墨难以形容: *The scenery ~ed description.* 那风景之美笔墨难以形容。 **~·ly** adj very poor; mean; deserving contempt: 贫乏的; 少得可怜的; 卑贱的; 令人轻蔑的: *What a ~ly salary to offer me!* 给我的薪资实在少得可怜! **~·y** n [U] extreme poverty: 极端的穷困; 赤贫: *He complained that taxation was reducing him to ~.* 他抱怨说捐税使他陷于赤贫。

be·gin /bɪˈgɪn; bɪˈgɪn/ vt, vi (**-nn-**, pt **began** /bɪˈgæn; bɪˈgæn/, pp **begun** /bɪˈgʌn; bɪˈgʌn/) (For notes on the use of *begin* and *start,* ⇨ **start**.) (关于 begin 与 start 之用法, 参看 start。) **1** [VP6A, 2A, C] start: 开始: *When did you ~ English,* learn your first English words? 你什么时候开始学英语的? *It's time to ~ work.* 是开始工作的时候了。 *We shall ~ the meeting at seven o'clock.* 我们将于七点钟开始会议。 *The meeting will ~ at seven o'clock.* 会议将于七点钟开始。 *He has begun a new book,* is reading (or writing) the first few pages. 他已开始读(或写)一本新书。 ~ *(on),* [VP3A the *v* being understood 其后之动词可了解] *He has begun on (= is reading, writing) a new book.* 他已开始(读, 写)一本新书。 *Has he begun (on) another bottle,* begun to drink another bottle? 他已开始(喝)另一瓶酒了吗? **2** [VP7A, 6D] (used of activities and states that come into existence. The *inf* is preferred when the *pred* denotes a state of mind or a mental activity): (用于开始发生的动作和状态。 当表语所指心理状态或精神活动时, 以用不定式为佳): *She began to feel dizzy/afraid.* 她开始感觉眩晕(害怕)。 *I'm ~ning to understand.* 我渐渐懂得了。 *I began to think you were never coming.* 我渐开始觉得你永远不会来了。 (The *inf* is perferred when the grammatical subject is lifeless, not a person): (当语法上之主语为无生命之物而非人时, 用不定式为佳): *The plaster was ~ning to fall from the walls.* 墙上的灰泥开始脱落。 *The barometer began to fall.* 气压计开始下降。 *The water is ~ning to boil.* 水逐渐沸腾。 *The snow began to melt when the sun came out.* 太阳出来时, 雪就开始融化。 (Either the *inf* or the *gerund* is used when the grammatical subject is a person and when the *pred* indicates an activity or process, not a state. Alternatives are given in the examples. Note that if *begin* is used in one of the progressive tenses, an *inf* follows, not a *gerund):* (当语法上之主语是人, 表语所指是活动或过程, 而非某种状态时, 不定式或动名词均可用。 两种用法于例句中举出。 注意: 在进行时中, begin 之后用不定式, 不用动名词): *When did you begin learning/to learn German?* 你什么时候开始学德语的? *She began crying/to cry.* 她开始哭泣。 *It began raining/to rain.* (那时)开始下雨了。 *It is ~ning to rain (not ~ning raining).* 开始下雨了 (勿用 beginning raining)。 **3** ~ *at,* start from: 从…开始: *Today we ~ at page 30, line 12.* 今天我们从第 30 页第 12 行开始。 ~ *to with,* in the first place: 首先; 第一点: *We can't give Smith the position; to ~ with, he's too young; secondly,* I want my son to have the job. 我们不能给史密斯这个职位; 第一, 他太年轻; 其次, 我想要我的儿子担任这份工作。 ~ *life as,* start one's life of career as: 开始…的生涯: *He began life as a builder's labourer.* 他开始做建筑工人的生涯。 ~ *the world,* (old use; liter) start in life, enter upon one's career. (旧用法; 文)开始谋生; 踏入社会。 **~·ner** n (esp) person still learning

and without much experience. (尤指)初学者; 无经验者。 **~·ning** n starting point: 开始; 开端; 起点: *I've read the book from ~ning to end.* 我已把这书从头到尾读完了。 *When learning a foreign language, it's important to make a good ~ning.* 学外国语, 打一个良好的基础是重要的。 *Did democracy have its ~nings in Athens?* 民主制度是源于雅典吗?

be·gone /bɪˈgɒn US: -ˈgɔːn; bɪˈgɒn/ n (imper only) (liter) go away (stronger than 'Go!'): (仅用于祈使句)(文)走开!; 去你的!; 滚蛋(语气较 'Go!' 强): *B~!* 滚蛋! *B~, dull care!* 隐忧, 离去吧! ⇨ also **woe~**.

be·gonia /bɪˈgəʊnɪə; bɪˈgɒnjə/ n [C] garden plant with brightly coloured leaves and flowers. 秋海棠(叶与花的颜色鲜艳)。

be·gorra /bɪˈgɒrə; bɪˈgɒrə/ int (Irish form of) by God! by God! 上帝啊! 上帝啊! 之爱尔兰语用语!

be·got, be·got·ten ⇨ **beget.**

be·grimed /bɪˈgraɪmd; bɪˈgraɪmd/ pred adj made grimy: 污秽的; 被弄脏的: *hands ~ with oil and dirt.* 为油及污物弄脏的手。

be·grudge /bɪˈgrʌdʒ; bɪˈgrʌdʒ/ vt (intensive form of *grudge*) [VP13A, 12A, 6C] feel or show dissatisfaction or envy at: (为 grudge 之强语式)对…不满; 嫉妒; 妒恨; 羡慕: *No one ~s you your good fortune.* 没有人嫉妒你的好运气。 *We don't ~ your going to Italy.* 我们不羡慕你到意大利去。

be·guile /bɪˈgaɪl; bɪˈgaɪl/ vt **1** [VP6A, 14] ~ *sb (into),* cheat, deceive: 欺骗; 诱骗: *They were ~d into forming an unwise alliance.* 他们受骗而组成一不智的结盟。 **2** [VP6A, 14] ~ *(with),* cause (time, etc) to pass pleasantly: 使(时间等)过得愉快; 消遣; 消磨: *Our journey was ~d with pleasant talk.* 我们在旅行中, 以轻松的谈话为消遣。 **3** [VP6A, 14] ~ *(with),* amuse: 使娱乐: *We ~d the childern with fairy tales.* 我们讲童话故事以娱悦子们。

be·gum /ˈbeɪgəm; ˈbɪgəm/ n Muslim princess or lady of high rank. (摩斯林之)公主; 贵妇。

be·gun ⇨ **begin.**

be·half /bɪˈhɑːf US: -ˈhæf; bɪˈhæf/ n *in ~ of,* (US) in the interest of: (美)为了…的利益。 *on ~ of,* for, in the interest of, on account of, as the representative of. 为了…的缘故; 为了…的利益; 代表。 *on my/his/our/ John's, etc ~,* for me/him/us/John, etc: 代表(为了)我(他, 我们, 约翰等): *On ~ of my colleagues and myself,* speaking for them and me. 兹代表我的同事和我自己。 *Don't be uneasy on my ~,* about me. 不要为我担心。

be·have /bɪˈheɪv; bɪˈhev/ vi, reflex **1** [VP2A, C, 6B] act; conduct oneself: 行为; 举止: *He has ~d shamefully towards his wife,* has treated her in a shameful way. 他以可耻的态度对待他的妻子。 *Can't you make your little boy ~ (himself),* show good manners, be polite? 你不能教你的小孩学点礼貌 (或规矩些) 吗? *The troops ~d gallantly under fire.* 部队在炮火下表现得很英勇。 **2** [VP2A, C] (of machines, etc) work; function: (指机器等)工作; 运转; 开动: *How's your new car behaving?* 你的新车跑得如何? **be·haved** adj (in compounds) (用于复合词) *well-/,badly-'~d,* behaving well (badly): 行为良好(恶劣)的。 *What badly ~d children!* 多么顽劣的小孩啊!

be·hav·iour (US = **-ior**) /bɪˈheɪvɪə(r); bɪˈhevjə/ n [U] way of behaving; manners (good or bad); treatment shown towards others: 行为; 举止; 品行; 待人的态度: *His ~ towards me shows that he does not like me.* 他对我的态度显示他不喜欢我。 *Tom won a prize for good ~ at school.* 汤姆在学校里得到品行优良奖。 *be on one's best ~,* take great care to behave well. 非常小心以表现良好的行为; 行为检点; 很守规矩。 *put sb on his best ~,* advise or warn him to behave well. 劝导某人使表现良好的行为。 ~·**ism** /-ɪzəm; -ɪzəm/ n [U] (psych) doctrine that all human actions could, if full knowledge were available, be analysed into stimulus and response.

(心理)行为主义(认为一切人类的行为, 如果有充分的了解, 均可分析为刺激与反应)。~·ist /-ɪst; -ɪst/ n believer in this doctrine. 行为主义者。

be·head /bɪ'hed; bɪ'hɛd/ vt [VP6A] cut off the head of (as a punishment). 斩…之首; 砍…之头(作为一种刑罚)。

be·held ⇨ **behold**.

be·hest /bɪ'hest; bɪ'hɛst/ n (old use; only in) (旧用法; 仅用于) at sb's ~, on sb's orders: 受某人的指挥; 遵照某人的吩咐: at the King's ~. 听命于王。

be·hind¹ /bɪ'haɪnd; bɪ'haɪnd/ adv (contrasted with ahead or in front) (与 ahead 或 in front 相对) **1** in the rear: 在后: The dog was running ~. 狗跟在后面跑。The others are a long way ~. 其他的人落在后面很远。The enemy attacked us from ~. 敌人从后面向我们进攻。fall / lag ~, fail to keep up: 跟不上; 落后; 落伍: Keith was tired and fell ~. 基思疲倦了, 所以落后。stay / remain ~, stay after others have left. (别人都走了)留下来不走; 留在后面。**2** be ~ with / in, be in arrears with: 积压; 积欠: Are you ~ with your work / studies, etc, Have you done less than you ought to have done? 你有积压的(即该做而未做的)工作(功课等)吗? He was ~ in his payments, had not made payments (eg of rent) when they were due. 他未如期付出欠款(如欠租)。

be·hind² /bɪ'haɪnd; bɪ'haɪnd/ n (colloq) buttocks: (口)屁股; 臀部: He kicked the boy's ~. 他踢那男孩的屁股。He fell on his ~. 他摔了一个屁股墩儿(他向后跌倒, 屁股着地)。

be·hind³ /bɪ'haɪnd; bɪ'haɪnd/ prep **1** (contrasted with in front of) to the rear of: (与 in front of 相对)在…的后面: The boy was hiding ~ a tree. 那男孩躲在一棵树的后面。Come out from ~ the door. 从门后面出来。There is an orchard ~ the house. 房子的后面有一个果树园。The sun was ~ the clouds. 太阳被云遮住了。Walk close ~ me. 紧跟着我的后面走。He put the idea ~ him, (fig) refused to consider it. (喻)他对这主意不予考虑。⇨ also **back¹**(1), **scene**(6) and **leave¹**(3). **2** (contrasted with ahead of) not having made so much progress as: (与 ahead of 相对)较…落后; 不如: ~ other boys of his age; 不如同年龄的其他孩子了; a country far ~ its neighbours. 远比其邻国落后的一个国家。Mary is ~ the other girls in sewing. 玛莉在缝纫方面不如别的女孩子。**3** leave ~, leave remaining after: 留于身后; 走后留下: He left nothing but debts ~ him. 他除留下一堆债务外, 别无他物。The storm left a trail of destruction ~ it. 暴风雨所经过之处留下疮痍满目。**4** be ~ one, (of time) be in the past: (指时间)成为过去: My schooldays are far ~ me. 我的学生时代早已成为过去。~ time; ~ the time, ⇨ **time¹**(3, 10). **5** be / lie ~ sth, be the cause of, explanation for, it; 是…的原因; 是…的说明: What's ~ Guy's strange behaviour? 盖伊那种奇怪行为的原因是什么? B~ her harsh remarks lay a guilty and unhappy spirit. 她的厉声谈话说明了内心的愧疚和不快乐。

be·hind·hand /bɪ'haɪndhænd; bɪ'haɪnd,hænd/ pred adj **1** be / get ~ (with / in), be in arrears: 拖欠; 拖延: 延搁: be ~ with the rent; 欠租; get ~ in one's work. 拖延工作。**2** late; after others: 迟延; 落后: He did not want to be ~ in generosity, later than others in being generous. 他在慷慨方面不欲后人。

be·hold /bɪ'həʊld; bɪ'hold/ vt (pt, pp **beheld** /bɪ'held; bɪ'hɛld/) [VP6A] (old or liter use) take notice; see (esp sth unusual or striking). (旧用法或文学用语)注意; 看(尤指不寻常或可惊的事)。**lo and ~,** ⇨ **lo**. ~**er** n spectator. 观者; 看者。

be·holden /bɪ'həʊldən; bɪ'holdən/ pred adj ~ (to), under an obligation; owing thanks: (对…)感激的; 铭感的: We are much ~ to you for your help. 我们对于你的帮助深为感激。

be·hove /bɪ'həʊv; bɪ'hov/ (US = **be·hoove** /bɪ'huːv; bɪ'huv/) vt (impers) (无人称) it ~s one to do sth, (old formal use) it is right or necessary for one to do sth: (为旧时正式用语)某人做…是应当或必须的: It ~s

you to, It is your duty to, You ought to…. 你应当…。It does not ~ you to, You must not or ought not to…. 你不应当…。

beige /beɪʒ; beʒ/ n [U] colour of sandstone (brown, brownish grey or yellow); soft fabric of undyed and unbleached wool. 沙岩的颜色(即棕色, 棕灰色或灰黄色); (原毛未经染色及漂白织成的)本色软呢。

be·ing /'biːɪŋ; 'biɪŋ/ n **1** [U] existence. 存在; 生存。bring / call sth into ~, cause it to have reality or existence. 使产生; 实现。come into ~, begin to exist: 开始存在; 发生; 产生: We do not know when this world came into ~. 我们不知这个世界是何时开始存在的。in ~, existing. 现存的; 现有的。**2** [C] living creature. 生物。human ~, human creature: 人: Men, women and children are human ~s. 男人、女人和儿童都是人。**3 the Supreme B~,** God. 上帝。

be·jew·elled (US = **-eled**) /bɪ'dʒuːeld; bɪ'dʒuɛld/ part adj decorated, adorned, with jewels. 饰以珠宝的。

be·labour (US = **-bor**) /bɪ'leɪbə(r); bɪ'lebə/ vt [VP6A] (archaic) beat hard, give hard blows to: (古)痛打; 重击: The robbers ~ed him soundly. 强盗们把他毒打了一顿。

be·lated /bɪ'leɪtɪd; bɪ'letɪd/ adj **1** coming very late or too late: 来得太迟的; 误期的: a ~ apology / explanation. 过时的道歉(解释)。**2** (old use) overtaken by darkness: (旧用法)日暮时尚在途的: The ~ travellers lost their way in the forest. 日暮时尚在途中的旅客在森林中迷了路。~·ly adv

be·lay /bɪ'leɪ; bɪ'le/ vt [VP6A] (naut and mountaineering) make secure (a rope) round sth or sb. (航海与登山)用(绳)系绕于某物或某人之上。**be'lay·ing-pin** n fixed wooden or iron pin or cleat for ~ing. 系索栓(用以系绳之木桩或铁钉)。□ n turn of a rope in ~ing. (系绳于栓上时)绳索之一绕。

belch /beltʃ; bɛltʃ/ vt, vi **1** [VP6A, 15B] ~ (out), send, eg smoke, flames, out 喷出; 冒出(烟、火等): A volcano ~es out smoke and ashes. 火山喷出烟及灰烬。**2** [VP2A] send out gas from the stomach noisily through the mouth. 打嗝。□ n act or sound of ~ing; sth ~ed out (eg a burst of flame from a furnace). 喷出; 冒出; 打嗝(声); 喷出物; 冒出物(如由炉中冒出的火焰)。

bel·dam, bel·dame /'beldəm; 'bɛldəm/ n (old use) old, esp bad-tempered, woman. (旧用法)老太婆(尤指坏脾气的)。

be·leaguer /bɪ'liːgə(r); bɪ'ligə/ vt [VP6A] besiege. 围攻; 围困。

bel·fry /'belfrɪ; 'bɛlfrɪ/ n tower for bells; part of a church tower in which bells hang. 钟楼; (教堂里的)钟塔。⇨ the illus at **church**. 参看 church 之插图。bats in the ~, ⇨ **bat¹**.

be·lie /bɪ'laɪ; bɪ'laɪ/ vt [VP6A] **1** give a wrong or untrue idea of: 使人对于…得到一个错误或不实的观念; 掩饰; 使人误会; 给人错觉: His cheerful appearance ~d his feelings. 他愉快的外表掩饰了他的情绪。**2** fail to justify or be equal to (what is hoped for or promised). 使失望; 辜负。

be·lief /bɪ'liːf; bɪ'lif/ n **1** [U] ~ (in), the feeling that sth is real and true; trust; confidence: 相信; 信心; 信任; 信仰: I haven't much ~ in his honesty, cannot feel sure that he is honest. 我对他的诚实没有太大的信心。He had no great ~ in his doctor, had little confidence that his doctor could cure him. 他不太信任他的医生。He has lost his ~ in God. no longer accepts the existence of God as true. 他已不相信上帝(不相信上帝的存在)。It is my ~ that, I feel confident that…. in the very ~ that, feeling confident that: 相信: He came to me in the ~ that I could help him. 他到我这里来, 相信我能帮助他。to the best of my ~, in my genuine opinion. 我深信。**2** [C] sth accepted as true or real; sth taught as part of a religion; religion: 所相信的事物; 作为宗教的一部份而传授的东西; 信念; 信条; 教条: the ~s of the

Christian Church. 基督教之教条。

be·lieve /bɪ'liːv; bɪ'liv/ *vt, vi* 1 [VP6A, 9, 10, 25] feel sure of the truth of sth, that sb is telling the truth: be of the opinion (that): 相信 (事物的真实性, 人的诚实); 认为(可与名词从句连用): *I ~ that man.* 我相信那个人。*I ~ what that man says.* 我相信那个人所说的话。*People used to ~ (that) the world was flat.* 人们从前认为地球是扁平的。*They ~d him to be/~d (that) he was insane.* 他们认为他是疯了。*I ~ it to have been a mistake.* 我相信这是一个错误。*Nobody will ~ what difficulty there has been over this question/how difficult this question has been.* 没有人会相信这个问题曾经是那么困难。*Will they be ready tomorrow? Yes, I ~ so. No, I ~ not.* 他们明天会准备好吗?会的,我相信会。不会,我相信不会。*~ (you) me,* I assure you. 请(你)相信我; 我向你保证;不骗你。2 [VP3A] *~ in,* **(a)** have trust in: 相信; 信任; 信赖: *I ~ in that man.* 我信任那个人。**(b)** feel sure of the existence of: 相信…的存在: *~ in God.* 相信上帝的存在。 **(c)** feel sure of the value or worth of: 相信…之价值: *He ~s in getting plenty of exercise.* 他相信充分的运动必有益处。*He ~s in old-fashioned remedies.* 他相信旧式的药方有效。3 *make ~,* pretend: 假装; 假扮: *The boys made ~ that they were/made ~ to be explorers in the African forests.* 孩子们假装是非洲森林中的探险者。Hence, 由此产生, **'make-~** *n: Don't be frightened, it's all make-~,* all pretence. 不要害怕, 这全是假装的。**be·liever** *n* person who ~s, esp a person with religious faith. 相信者; (尤指) 信teacher者; 信徒。**be·liev·able** *adj* that can be ~d. 可信的。**be·liev·ing** *n seeing is believing,* you may ~ sth if you see it. 眼见是真(百闻不如一见)。

be·like /bɪ'laɪk; bɪ'laɪk/ *adv* (old use) possibly. (旧用法)可能地。

be·little /bɪ'lɪtl; bɪ'lɪtl/ *vt* [VP6A] cause to seem unimportant or of small value: 轻视; 藐视; 贬抑: *Don't ~ yourself,* be too modest about your abilities, etc. 不要小看你自己。

bell /bel; bɛl/ *n* 1 hollow vessel of cast metal, usu shaped like a cup, that makes a ringing sound when struck (usu by a tongue or clapper inside the ~ or, in an electric ~, by a small hammer). 钟; 铃; 电铃。*~, book and candle,* ecclesiastical curse of excommunication. 钟书烛(逐出教门的)的教会咒语。*as sound as a ~,* (fig) in first-rate condition. (喻)处于极佳情况。*ring a ~,* (colloq) recall to memory sth half forgotten. (口)令人回忆起一件几乎遗忘的事。2 (naut) time signal in the form of a bell rung from one to eight times every half hour, eg: (航海) 报时钟(每半小时敲一次, 每次敲一至八击): *eight ~s,* 12, 4 or 8 o'clock; 八击钟(十二时, 四时或八时); *four ~s,* 2, 6 or 10 o'clock. 四击钟(二时, 六时或十时)。3 **'~·boy, '~·hop** *n* (US) boy or man employed in a hotel to carry luggage, messages, etc. (美)(受雇于旅馆中为旅客搬送行李, 送信等的)男侍者; 服务生。⇨ **buttons(4)** (GB). **'~·bottomed** *adj* (of trousers) made very wide at the bottom of the leg (eg as worn by some sailors). (指裤子)裤管下部非常宽大的(如有些水手所穿者); 喇叭形的。**'~·bottoms** *n pl* trousers made this way. 喇叭裤。**'~·buoy** *n* buoy with a ~ that is made to ring by the movement of the waves. (利用波浪的力量当发铃声之)铃形浮标。**'~·flower** *n* any plant of the genus *campanula.* 山小菜属植物; 吊钟花。**'~·founder** *n* person whose trade is the casting of ~s. 铸钟者。**'~·foundry** *n* place where large ~s (for churches, etc) are cast. 教堂等所用之巨钟的铸造场。**'~·metal** *n* [U] alloy of copper and tin used for making ~s. 钟铜; 青铜 (用以铸钟之铜与锡之合金)。**'~·push** *n* button pressed to ring an electric ~. 电铃之按钮。**'~·ringer** *n* person who rings church ~s. 教堂之敲钟人。**'~·tent** *n* ~-shaped tent. 钟形帐篷。**'~·wether** *n* leading male sheep of a flock, with a ~ on its neck; (fig) ringleader. 颈间系铃以带领羊群之公羊; 铃羊; 带头羊; (喻)(暴乱等之)首领; 魁首。□ *vt* ~

the cat, (prov) do something dangerous in order to save others (from the fable of the mouse that suggested fastening a ~ round the cat's neck). (谚)冒险救人(源出伊索寓言, 老鼠建议在猫颈上系铃的故事)。

bella·donna /ˌbelə'dɒnə; ˌbɛlə'dɑnə/ *n* (drug prepared from) poisonous plant with red flowers and black berries. 颠茄; 莨菪(一种有毒植物, 开红花, 结黑浆果); 颠茄制剂。

belle /bel; bɛl/ *n* beautiful girl or woman: 美女; 美妇; 美人: *the ~ of the ball,* the most beautiful woman present. 舞会之花(舞会中最美的女人)。

belles-lettres /ˌbel'letrə; bɛl'lɛtrə/ *n pl* (with *sing v*) (F) literary studies and writings (contrasted with commercial, technical, scientific, etc). (法)纯文学; 纯文艺(以别于商业、专门技术、科学等之著作)。

bel·li·cose /'belɪkəʊs; 'bɛlə,kos/ *adj* (liter) inclined to fighting; anxious to fight. (文)好战的; 好打斗的。

-bel·lied /-belɪd; -belɪd/ ⇨ **belly.**

bel·liger·ency /bɪ'lɪdʒərənsɪ/ *n* [U] being warlike; state of being at war. 好战; 交战状态。

bel·liger·ent /bɪ'lɪdʒərənt; bə'lɪdʒərənt/ *adj, n* (person, nation, etc) waging war: 交战的 (人、国等): *the ~ Powers,* those that are waging war. 交战国。

bel·low /'beləʊ; 'bɛlo/ *vi, vt* 1 [VP2A] make a loud, deep noise (like a bull) ; roar; shout: (牛等)吼叫; 咆哮; 大叫: *He ~ed before the dentist had even started.* 牙医还未动手他就大叫起来。2 [VP6A, 15B] *~ (out),* utter loudly or angrily: 大声发出; 怒吼: *They ~ed out a drinking song.* 他们大声吼叫着唱饮酒歌。

bel·lows /'beləʊz; 'bɛloz/ *n pl a pair of ~,* sometimes有时作 *a ~* 1 apparatus for blowing air into a fire, eg in a forge. 风箱 (鼓风入火之器具, 如锻铁炉所用者)。2 apparatus for forcing air through the pipes of an organ, eg in a church. 风琴之风箱。

belly¹ /'belɪ; 'bɛlɪ/ *n* 1 (colloq) abdomen. (口)肚子; 腹部。**'~-flop** *n* (colloq) clumsy dive, landing in the water on the front of the body. (口)腹部先接触水面之笨拙跳水。**'~-laugh** *n* loud, coarse laugh. 粗鲁的高声大笑。□ *vi* give such a laugh.粗鲁地高声大笑。2 the stomach: 胃: *with an empty ~,* hungry. 空着肚子。**'~-ache** *n* (colloq) pain in the stomach or bowels. (口)胃痛; 腹痛。□ *vi* (colloq) grumble or complain bitterly, esp without good reason. (口)(尤指无理地)发怨言; 发牢骚。**~ button** *n* (colloq) navel. (口)肚脐。3 bulging part (concave or convex) of anything, eg the surface of a violin across which the strings pass. 任何东西的凹出(或凹入)如肚状的部份 (如提琴之腹板, 即支弦之部份)。**'~ landing** *n* landing made on the hull of an aircraft (when the under-carriage fails to operate). (当飞机起落架失灵时所作之) 机腹着陆降落。Hence, 由此产生, **'~-land** *vi -bellied adj:* 有…肚子的。*big-'bellied,* having a big ~. (有)大肚子的。**~·ful** /-fʊl; -fʊl/ *n* as much as one wants of anything: 所需要之量; 充分: *He's had his ~ful of fighting,* doesn't want any more. 他已打过瘾了(不想再打了)。

belly² /'belɪ; 'bɛlɪ/ *vi, vt* [VP6A, 15B, 2A, C] *~ (out),* (cause) to swell out: (使)鼓起; (使)张满: *The wind bellied (out) the sails.* 风使帆张满。*The sails bellied (out).* 帆张满。

be·long /bɪ'lɒŋ US: -'lɔːŋ; bə'lɔŋ/ *vi* 1[VP3A] *~ to,* **(a)** be the property of: 属于; 为…之财产: *These books ~ to me,* are mine. 这些书是我的。**(b)** be a member of, be connected with: 为…之一员; 已加入: *Which club do you ~ to?* 你是哪一个俱乐部的会员? 2 [VP2O] have as a right or proper place: 有一个适当的地位或位置; 应该在 (某处): *Do you ~ here,* live here? 你在这里居住吗? *Does this item of expenditure ~ under the head of office expenses,* is it rightly placed there? 此项开支是否该列在办公费项下? **~·ings** *n pl* movable possessions (not land, buildings, a business, etc): 动产; 财物 (非指土地、建筑物、企业等): *personal ~ings,* 个人所有的动

产; *I hope you've left none of your ~ings in the hotel.* 我希望你没有把你的财物遗忘在旅馆里。

be·loved /brˈlʌvd; brˈlʌvd/ *pp, pred adj* dearly loved: 深爱的; 钟爱的: ~ *by all;* 深受大家爱戴的; ~ *of all who knew her.* 被所有认识她的人所钟爱。 ~ *adj, n* /brˈlʌvɪd; brˈlʌvɪd/ (person) dearly loved; darling: 所深爱的(人); 爱人: *his ~ wife.* 他的爱妻。

be·low[1] /brˈləʊ; beˈlo/ *adv* (contrasted with *above*[1]; 与 *above*[1] 相对; also ⇨ **under**[1], **underneath**, **over**[1](2)) **1** (sometimes used after *from*, as if it were a *n*) at or to a lower level: (有时用于 *from* 之后, 似为名词)在较低之处; 向低处: *From the hilltop we saw the blue ocean ~.* 从山顶上我们看见了下面的蓝色海洋。 *The people in the rooms ~ are very noisy.* 楼下房间里的人非常吵。 *We heard voices from ~.* 我们听见有人声来自下面。 *be/go ~,* (in a ship) *be/go ~* deck in (to) a cabin, saloon, etc. 在舱内(下舱里去)。 **2** at the foot of a page, etc; later (in a book, article, etc): 在页底; 在(书籍、文章等之)较后部份: *see paragraph six ~.* 见下面第六段。 *Please affix your signature ~.* 请在下面签名。 **3** *down ~,* in the lower part of a building, in a ship's hold, etc (according to context). 在建筑物、船舱等的较低部份(视上下文而定); 在下面。 *here ~,* on earth. 在人世间。

be·low[2] /brˈləʊ; beˈlo/ *prep* (contrasted with *above*[2]; also ⇨ **under**[2], **over**[2](2)); *below* can sometimes, but not always, be replaced by *under;* when *under* is possible, it is given in the examples) (与 *above*[2] 相对; below 有时可与 under 通用, 但并非永远如此; 可与 under 通用时, 已在例句中标明) **1** lower than: 在…下面; 低于: *Skirts this year reach just ~ the knees.* 今年的裙子刚及膝盖下面。 *When the sun sets it goes ~ the horizon.* 太阳下山时就会落到地平线下面。 *Shall I write my name on, above or ~ the line?* 我应该把名字写在线上, 线的下方, 还是线的下面? *The temperature was five degrees ~ freezing-point.* 气温是冰点下五度。 *There is nothing ~ /under 50p,* costing less than this. 没有一样东西价钱在五十便士以下。 *The Dead Sea is ~ sea level.* 死海的海面低于海平面。 *A captain in the army ranks ~ a captain in the Navy.* 陆军的 captain (上尉)其军阶低于海军的 captain (上校)。 *Your work is ~ the average.* 你的工作(成绩)在一般水准之下。 *He can't be much ~ /under sixty,* is years of age. 他的年龄不可能比六十岁小很多。 ⇨ also **belt**(1), **mark**[1](8). **2** down stream from: 在…之下游: *a few yards ~ the bridge.* 在桥下游数码之处。 **3** (*speak*) *~ one's breath* (more usu 较常用 *under*), in a whisper. 低声地(说话)。 **4** (replaceable by *beneath*) unworthy of: (可与 beneath 通用)与…不相称; 不值得: ~ *one's dignity.* 有损其尊严。

belt /belt; belt/ *n* **1** adjustable band or strip of cloth, leather, etc worn round the waist or over one shoulder to support or keep in place clothes or weapons, or, like a corset, to support the abdomen: 带子; 布带; 皮带; 腰带; 肩带; 背带; 吊带; 腹带: *He ate so much that he had to loosen his ~ two holes.* 他吃得太多, 不得不把腰带放松两个洞。 *hit below the ~,* give an unfair blow, fight unfairly. 打击对方腰带以下的部份(按拳击规则系犯规行为); 做不公正的打击; 玩卑鄙手段。 *tighten one's ~,* ⇨ **tight**. **2** endless strap, used to connect wheels and so drive machinery. (连接机轮以带动机器之)皮带; 调革。 *'fan-belt,* in the engine of a car. (汽车引擎内的)风扇皮带。 **3** any wide strip or band, surrounding area, etc. 任何广阔之长条或周围地区等; 地带。 **the com'muter belt,** residential area outside a large town, eg London, from which people commute to and from work. 住宅区 (大城市, 如伦敦, 四周之住宅区, 居民每日往返上班工作)。 **the 'Cotton ~,** (US) area in which cotton is extensively grown. (美)棉花地带(广泛种植棉花之地区)。 *'green ~,* area of grassland, parks, etc, round a town. 绿色地带 (环绕一城市之草地、公园等地区)。 ☐ *vt, vi* **1** [VP6A, 15B] fasten with a ~: 以带系住: *The officer ~ed his sword on.* 那军官用带将剑佩上。 **2** [VP6A] thrash with a ~; (colloq) strike with the fist(s): 用皮带打; (口)拳打;

殴打; 揍: *If you don't shut up, I'll ~ you.* 你再不闭嘴, 我要揍你。 *~ ·ing n:* give the boy a good ~*ing,* thrash him well. 用皮带把那孩子狠打一顿。 **3** [VP2C, 3A] *~ along,* (colloq) move fast. (口)行动迅速。 **4** [VP15B] *~ out,* (colloq) sing loudly and forcefully: (口)大声用力唱: *No one can ~ out those old songs like she can.* 没有人能象她一样高声唱出老歌。 **5** [VP2C] *~ up,* (sl) stop talking. (俚)别讲话。

be·moan /brˈməʊn; brˈmon/ *vt* [VP6A] (poet) moan for; show great sorrow for: (诗)为…而悲痛或钦哭; 为…而表示极大之忧伤; 悲叹: ~ *one's sad fate;* 自叹命苦; ~*ing the loss of all her money.* 悲痛她全部钱财的损失。

be·mused /brˈmjuːzd; brˈmjuzd/ *pred adj* preoccupied; confused; bewildered. 恍惚的; 发呆的; 困惑的。

ben[1] /ben; ben/ *n* (Scot) inner room (usu of a two-roomed house). (苏)(通常指两间同房屋之)后房。

ben[2] /ben; ben/ *n* (Scot) mountain peak (used with names as *Ben Nevis*). (苏)山峰(通常与峰名连用, 例如 *Ben Nevis* 尼维斯山)。

bench /bentʃ; bentʃ/ *n* **1** long seat of wood or stone, eg in a public park, or across a rowing-boat; (in the House of Commons) seat occupied by certain classes of members: 长凳; 板凳; 石凳(如公园中或横置于划艇中者); (下议院中)某些议员的席位。 *'back-~es,* for members not entitled to a front ~. 后排席位(无资格坐前排席位之议员的席位)。 *'cross-~es,* for independent members who do not vote with either of the two main political parties. 横席位; 中立议员席位(投票时不附和两大政党之任何一方面的独立份子的席位)。 *'front-~es,* reserved for ministers or ex-ministers. 前排席位(为内阁大臣或前任内阁大臣所保留的席位)。 Hence, 由此产生, *back-/,cross-/,front-'bencher,* one of the above people. 后排席位(横席位, 前排席位)之人。 the *'Treasury B~,* for Ministers. 内阁大臣席; 国务大臣席。 *'~ seat,* (in a car) seat for 2 or 3 persons) extending the width of the car. (汽车中的)横排座位 (供二人或三人坐者)。 ⇨ **bucket seat.** **2** [U] (collective, with *def art,* often the **B~**) judges; magistrates; judge's seat or office; law court. (集合用法, 与定冠词连用, 常作 the Bench)法官; 行政司法官; 法官的席位或职位; 法院。 *be raised to the B~,* be made a judge or a bishop. 被升任为法官或主教。 **the ,King's /,Queen's 'B~ (Division),** of the High Court of Justice. (高等法院之)王座庭。 **3** worktable at which a shoemaker, carpenter, etc, works. (鞋匠、木匠等之)工作台。

bend[1] /bend; bend/ *vt, vi* (*pt, pp* **bent** /bent; bent/) **1** [VP6A, 15A, B] cause (sth rigid) to be out of a straight line or surface; force into a curve or angle: 使 (僵硬的东西)弯曲; 使成弧形或一角度: *It isn't easy to ~ a bar of iron.* 使铁棒弯曲不容易。 *He heated the iron rod and bent it into a right angle.* 他将铁杆烧热, 然后将之弯成直角。 *B~ the end of the wire up/down/back.* 将金属端端弯上来 (下去, 回来)。 *Rheumatism prevents him from ~ing his back.* 风湿痛使他不能弯腰。 *Her head was bent over her book.* 她埋头读书。 *~ the knee (to),* (rhet) bow, pray. (修辞)(向…)屈膝; 屈服; 祈祷; 恳求。 *on ~ed knees,* (liter) kneeling; in an attitude of prayer or entreaty. (文)屈膝的; 跪下的; 祈祷或恳求之态度。 *~ a rule,* (colloq) interpret it loosely (to suit the circumstances). (口)为适应情况)从宽解释一法令; 通权达变。 **2** [VP2A, C] become curved or angular; bow; stoop: 弯曲; 屈身: *The branches were ~ing (down) with the weight of the fruit.* 树枝被果实的重量压得弯曲 (下来)了。 *The branch bent but didn't break when the boy climbed on to it.* 当那男孩爬上树枝时, 树枝弯曲了, 但是没有断。 *Can you ~ down and touch your toes without ~ing your knees?* 你能够下腰, 不屈膝而触着你的足趾吗? *The tall man bent forward to listen to the little girl.* 那高个子弯下身来听那小女孩的话。 *Sit up straight: don't ~ over your desk.* 坐端正: 不要趴在桌子上。 *The river ~s* (= turns) *several times before reaching the sea.* 这

条河转了好几个弯才流入海中。*The road ~s to the left here.* 路在此向左弯。**3** [VP15A] direct: 使朝向: *It's time for us to ~ our steps homeward*, turn towards home. 是我们回去的时候了。*All eyes were bent on me*, Every one was looking at me. 大家都在看我。*She stood there with eyes bent on the ground*, looking down. 她站在那里，眼睛看着地。*He couldn't ~ his mind* (= give his attention) *to his studies.* 他不能够专心于他的功课。**4** [VP2C, 14] ~ *(sb) to*, compel to: 屈服; 顺从: ~ *to sb's will*; 顺从某人的意志; make (sb) submit: 使(某人)屈服或顺从: ~ *sb to one's will.* 使某人顺从其意志。**5** [VP6A] curve (a bow) in order to string it: 屈(弓)以上弦; 张(弓); 开(弓): *None of the suitors could ~ the bow of Odysseus.* 没有一个求婚者能拉得动奥德修斯的弓。**6 *be bent on***, have the mind set on, have as a fixed purpose: 专心致志于: *He is bent on mastering English*, determined to learn it thoroughly. 他专心致志于学通英文。*He is bent on mischief*, has plans to do sth mischievous. 他打算捣鬼。**bent** *pred adj* (sl) dishonest; corrupt; mad. (俚)不诚实的;不道德的:疯狂的。

bend² /bend/ *n* **1** curve or turn: 转弯; 弯: a *sharp ~ in the road.* 路上的一个急弯。***round the bend***, (sl) mad. (俚)发疯的。**2** sailor's knot (in a rope). (绳索之)水手结。**3 the ~s**, (colloq) pains in the joints, caused by working in compressed air, eg in a caisson(2). (口)潜水夫病(在压缩空气中工作所引起的关节痛)。

be·neath /bɪ'niːθ/ *prep, adv* **1** (old use, or liter) below, under (neath). (旧用法或文)在(…)下面; 在(…)底下。**2** not worthy of: 不值得; 与…不相称: *His accusations are ~ contempt /notice*, should be ignored. 他的指控不值一提。*It is ~ you to complain*, unworthy of you to do so. 你犯不上抱怨。

ben·edick /'benɪdɪk/ 'bedə,dɪk/ (US = **ben·e·dict** /'benɪdɪkt/; 'bene,dɪkt/ *n* recently married man, esp one who has been a bachelor for many years. 新婚的男人(尤指曾经过多年独身生活的男子)。

Bene·dic·tine /,benɪ'dɪktɪn/; ,bene'dɪktɪn/ *n, adj* **1** [C] (monk or nun) of the religious order founded in AD 529 by St Benedict. 班尼狄克教派的(该教派系由 St Benedict 创于公元 529 年); 班尼狄克教派之修士或修女。**2** [U] /-tiːn/; -tin/ liqueur made by monks of this order. 班尼狄克教派修士所酿造的一种甜酒。

bene·dic·tion /,benɪ'dɪkʃn/; ,bene'dɪkʃən/ *n* blessing (esp one given by a priest at the end of a church service): 祝福; 祝祷(尤指教士在礼拜结束时所作者): *pronounce the ~.* 祝祷。

bene·fac·tion /,benɪ'fækʃn/; ,bene'fækʃən/ *n* [U] doing good; [C] good deed (esp the giving of money for charity); charitable gift: 行善; 善行(尤指捐款给慈善事业); 为慈善目的所作之捐赠: *That man's ~s now amount to £10000.* 那个人的慈善捐款现已达一万英镑。

bene·fac·tor /'benɪfæktə(r)/; 'bene,fæktə/ *n* person who has given friendly help, esp financial help, to a school, hospital or charitable institution. 帮助者; 恩人: (尤指学校、医院或慈善机关的)捐助者。**bene·fac·tress** /'benɪfæktrɪs/; 'bene,fæktrɪs/ *n* woman ~. 女恩人; 女捐助者。

bene·fice /'benɪfɪs/; 'benefɪs/ *n* income-producing property (called 称作 a *church living*) held by a priest or clergyman (esp a vicar or rector). 神父或牧师(尤指教区牧师)所享有的教产; 圣俸。**bene·ficed** /-fɪst/; -,fɪst/ *adj* having a ~: 享有圣俸的: *a ~d clergyman.* 享有圣俸的牧师。

be·nefi·cence /bɪ'nefɪsns/; bə'nefəsns/ *n* [U] (formal) doing good; active kindness. (正式用语)行善; 善行; 善事; 善举。**be·nefi·cent** /bɪ'nefɪsnt/; bə'nefəsnt/ *adj* (formal) doing good; kind. (正式用语)行善的; 慈善的; 仁慈的。

bene·fi·cial /,benɪ'fɪʃl/; ,bene'fɪʃəl/ *adj* (formal) having a good effect; helpful: (正式用语)有益处的; 有帮助的: *Fresh air and good food are ~ to the health.* 新鲜空气和优良食物有益于健康。*I hope your holiday will be*

~, do you good. 我希望你的假期会对你有益。**~·ly** *adv*

bene·fi·ci·ary /,benɪ'fɪʃərɪ US: -'fɪʃɪerɪ; ,bene'fɪʃɪerɪ/ *n* [C] (*pl* **-ries**) person who receives a benefit, esp one who receives money, property, etc under a will (at sb's death). 受益人; 受惠人(尤指按死者遗嘱承受遗产者)。

bene·fit /'benɪfɪt; 'benefɪt/ *n* **1** [U] advantage; profit; help: 利益; 益处; 裨益; 帮助: *Did you get much ~ from your holiday*, did you feel better afterwards? 你的假期从度假中有很大的益处? *The book wasn't of much ~ to me*, didn't help me much. 这本书对我没有多大益处。*The money is to be used for the ~ of the poor*, to help poor people. 该款将用以救助贫困。*It was done for your ~*, to help you. 这事情是为了你的利益而做的。***give sb the ~ of the doubt***, assume that he is innocent because there is insufficient evidence that he is guilty. 因无充分的证据证明某人有罪而假定其无罪; 对某人之嫌疑作善意解释。~ *in kind*, ⇨ **kind²**(4). ! ~ **performance** /**concert** /**match**, theatrical performance /concert /cricket or football match, etc, money for which is for the ~ of a charity, a particular player, etc. (为慈善事业、某一演员、球员等等款的)义演(慈善音乐会, 义赛)。**2** [C] act of kindness; favour; advantage: 善行; 恩惠; 利益: *the ~s of a good education;* 良好教育的利益; *the ~s we receive from our parents and teachers.* 我们所受之于父母及师长的恩惠。**3** [C] allowance of money to which a person is entitled as a citizen or as a member of an insurance society, etc: (以公民或投保人有权享受而有资格领取之)救济金; 保险给付; 津贴: *medical, unemployment /sickness ~s.* 医疗(失业, 疾病)津贴。□ *vt, vi* **1** [VP6A] do good to: 有益于; 对…有益: *The new railway will ~ the district.* 新铁路将给该地区将有裨益。*The sea air will ~ you.* 海上的空气将对你有益。**2** [VP3A] ~ *from /by*, receive ~ from /by: 得益于; 自…获益: *You will ~ by a holiday.* 度假将有益于你。

bene·vol·ence /bɪ'nevələns; bə'nevələns/ *n* [U] wish to do good; activity in doing good: 仁慈; 善行; 善举: *His ~ made it possible for many poor boys to attend college.* 他的善行使许多贫苦的男孩能够上大学。

ben·ev·ol·ent /bɪ'nevələnt;bə'nevələnt/ *adj* ~ *to/ towards*, kind and helpful. 仁慈的; 慈善的; 乐善好施的。**~·ly** *adv*

be·nighted /bɪ'naɪtɪd; bɪ'naɪtɪd/ *part adj* **1** (liter or old use) without the light of knowledge; in moral darkness. (文或旧用法)愚昧无知的; 蒙昧的。**2** (old use, of travellers) overtaken by darkness. (旧用法, 指旅行者)天黑仍在赶路的。

be·nign /bɪ'naɪn; bɪ'naɪn/ *adj* **1** (of persons) kind and gentle. (指人) 和蔼可亲的; 慈祥的。**2** (of soil, climate) mild, favourable. (指土壤, 气候)温和的; 有利的。**3** (of a disease, tumour) not dangerous. (指病, 瘤)无危险的; 良性的。⇨ **malignant** (2). **~·ly** *adv*

be·nig·nant /bɪ'nɪgnənt; bɪ'nɪgnənt/ *adj* (formal) kind, gracious. (正式用语)仁慈的; 亲切的。**~·ly** *adv*

be·nig·nity /bɪ'nɪgnətɪ; bɪ'nɪgnətɪ/ *n* (formal) [U] kindness of heart; [C] kind act, favour. (正式用语)仁爱; 仁慈; 善行; 善举。

beni·son /'benɪzn; 'benɪzn/ *n* [C] (old use) blessing. (旧用法)幸福; 祝福; 神的恩典。

bent¹ /bent; bent/ *n* ~ *(for)*, inclination or aptitude; natural skill in and liking: (对…的)倾向; 爱好: *She has a ~ for sewing /music.* 她生性爱好缝纫(音乐)。*follow one's ~*, do what one is interested in and what one enjoys doing. 随自己之所好; 随心所欲。***to the top of one's ~***, to one's heart's desire. 尽心; 尽量; 尽情。

bent² ⇨ **bend¹** esp **(6)**.

be·numbed /bɪ'nʌmd; bɪ'nʌmd/ *pred adj* made numb; with all feelings taken away: 麻木的; 无感觉的; 僵的: *My fingers were ~ with cold.* 我的手指冻僵了。

Ben·ze·drine /'benzədriːn; 'benzədrin/ *n* (P) brand of amphetamine. (商标)氨基丙苯; 安非他明; 苯齐特林。

ben·zene /'benziːn; 'benzin/ *n* [U] colourless liquid (C₆H₆) obtained from petroleum and coal-tar, used in

the manufacture of numerous chemical products. 苯(无色液体, 分子式 C_6H_6, 自石油及煤溚中提出, 用以制造很多种的化学产品).

ben·zine /'benziːn; 'benzin/ n [U] colourless liquid (mixture of hydrocarbons) obtained from mineral oil, used for cleaning, etc. 轻油精; 石油精; 奔散油(无色液体, 为碳氢族混合物, 自矿物油中提出, 用作清洁剂等).

ben·zol /'benzɒl US: -zɔːl; 'benzol/ n [U] =benzene.

be·queath /bɪ'kwiːð; bɪ'kwiθ/ vt [VP6A, 12A, 13A] ~ (to), 1 arrange (by making a will) to give (property, etc. to sb) at death: (立遗嘱)赠与(财产等); 遗赠; 遗留: *He has ~ed me his gold watch.* 他已将他的金表遗赠给我. 2 (fig) hand down to those who come after. (喻)传给后代: *discoveries ~ed to us by the scientists of the last century.* 前一世纪的科学家传给我们的种种发现.

be·quest /bɪ'kwest; bɪ'kwest/ n 1 [U] bequeathing. 遗赠; 遗留; 传与. 2 [C] sth bequeathed: 遗产; 遗留物; 传给后代之物: *He left ~s of money to all his servants.* 他对所有的仆人都遗赠了一些金钱.

be·rate /bɪ'reɪt; bɪ'ret/ vt [VP6A] scold sharply. 严责; 痛骂.

be·reave /bɪ'riːv; bə'riv/ vt (pt, pp bereft /bɪ'reft; bə'rɛft/ or bereaved; usu bereft in (1) and bereaved in (2)) (过去式及过去分词为 bereft 或 bereaved, 通常第 1 义用 bereft, 第 2 义用 bereaved) [VP14] ~ of, 1 rob or dispossess (of sth immaterial): 夺去; 剥夺; 使丧失 (指无形物): *bereft of hope, without hope;* 失去希望; *bereft of reason, mad.* 失去理智(疯狂的). *Indignation bereft him of speech,* took away his power to speak. 他气愤得说不出话来. 2 (of death) leave sad by taking away (a relation, etc): (指死亡)使痛失 (亲属等): *the accident that ~d him of his wife and child;* 使他痛失妻儿的祸事; *the husband, the man whose wife had died.* 丧妻之人. ~**ment** n [U] being ~d; loss by death: 丧失亲人; 丧亲之痛: *We all sympathize with you in your ~ment;* 我们皆同情你的丧亲之痛; [C] instance of this: 亲人丧亡之实例: *Owing to a recent ~ment she did not attend the concert.* 因为她最近有亲人丧亡, 所以她没有参加音乐会.

be·reft ⇨ bereave.

be·ret /'bereɪ US: bə'reɪ; bə're/ n flat, round cap of felt or cloth, worn with sports and holiday clothes, and as military head-dress. 一种扁圆帽(为绒质或布质, 配运动衫或假日服装戴之, 亦作军帽).

berg /bɜːg; bɝg/ n =iceberg.

beri-beri /,berɪ 'berɪ; 'berɪ'berɪ/ n [U] disease, common in oriental and tropical countries, caused by lack of vitamins, etc. essential to health. (常见于东方及热带国家, 因缺乏维护健康所必需的维他命等而引起之)脚气病.

berry /'berɪ; 'berɪ/ n (pl -ries) 1 small seedy fruit: 浆果; 莓: *holly berries;* 冬青果; *straw~;* 草莓; *black-~;* 黑莓; *rasp~.* 蘼莓. ⇨ the illus at fruit. 参看 fruit 之插图. 2 coffee bean. 咖啡实; 咖啡豆.

ber·serk /bə'sɜːk; 'bɝsɝk/ pred adj be/go/send sb ~, be, go, cause sb to go uncontrollably wild: 发狂 (使某人发狂): *He suddenly went ~ with rage.* 他突然狂怒.

berth /bɜːθ; bɝθ/ n 1 sleeping-place in a train, a ship or an aircraft. (火车、轮船或飞机上的)铺位; 卧铺. 2 place at a wharf where a ship can be tied up; place for a ship to swing at anchor. (码头上供船只)停泊的地方; 可以有余地供船回转的停泊处. *give a wide ~ to,* (fig) keep well away from, at a safe distance from. (喻)避开; 远避(与…保持安全的距离). 3 (dated colloq) job. (过时口语)职业. *find a snug ~,* an easy or pleasant job. 找个轻松愉快的工作. □ vt, vi [VP15A, 2C] (naut) find, have, a sleeping-place (for): (航海) (为某人)安置铺位(上下连用); 给…停泊. *Six passengers can be ~ed amidships.* 在船中部有六个客人的铺位. 2 [VP6A] moor (a ship) in harbour, tie up (a ship) at a wharf, etc. 停泊(船只)于港口或码头.

beryl /'berəl; 'berəl/ n precious stone (usu green). 绿宝石; 绿玉.

be·seech /bɪ'siːtʃ; bɪ'sitʃ/ vt (pt, pp besought /bɪ'sɔːt; bɪ'sɔt/) [VP6A, 17 11 13B] (old use, or liter) ask earnestly or urgently: (旧用法或文)恳求; 祈求; 央求: *He besought an interview.* 他恳求面谈. *The prisoner besought the judge to be merciful/besought him for mercy.* 囚犯恳求法官宽赦. *Spare him, I ~ you.* 敕免他, 我恳求你. ~**-ing** adj (of a person's look, tone of voice, etc) entreating, appealing. (指人的表情、语调等)恳求的; 乞求的; 哀求的. ~**-ing·ly** adv

be·seem /bɪ'siːm; bɪ'sim/ vt (liter, old use) (only impers, in the 3rd person) be fitting or suitable: (文, 旧用法; 仅用于第三人称之无人称)适合; 宜宜: *It ill ~s you to refuse,* It is not fitting that you should refuse. 你不宜拒绝.

be·set /bɪ'set; bɪ'sɛt/ vt (-tt-, pt, pp beset) [VP6A] close in on all sides, have on all sides: 包围; 围困: *the temptations that ~ young people,* by which they are faced on all sides: 围绕在年轻人身旁的种种诱惑; *a problem ~ with difficulties;* 困难重重的问题; ~ by doubts, troubled by doubts. 为疑问所困扰. ~**ting** sin, sin that most frequently tempts a person: 易犯的罪恶: *His ~ting sin is laziness.* 他所易犯的毛病就是懒惰.

be·shrew /bɪ'ʃruː; bɪ'ʃru/ vt (archaic): (古) B~ me! May evil fall upon me! 愿灾祸降临在我身上!

be·side /bɪ'saɪd; bɪ'saɪd/ prep 1 at the side of; close to: 在…的旁边; 在…的近旁: *Come and sit ~ me.* 来坐在我的身边. *She would like to live ~ the sea,* at the sea-side. 她很愿住在海边. 2 compared with: 与…比较起来: *You're quite tall ~ your sister.* 与你姐妹(妹妹)相比, 你是相当高的了. *~ put against;* compare with: 与…相比: *There's no one to set ~ him as a general.* 作为一个将军, 他是无与伦比的. 3 ~ *the point/mark/question,* wide of, having nothing to do with (what is being discussed, etc). 离题; 与本题无关. 4 ~ *oneself,* at the end of one's self-control: 发狂; 忘形: *He was ~ himself with joy/anger.* 他高兴(愤怒)得发狂.

be·sides /bɪ'saɪdz; bɪ'saɪdz/ adv moreover; also: 再者; 加之; 而且: *I don't like that new dictionary; ~, it's too expensive.* 我不喜欢那本新词典; 而且, 它也太贵. *It's too late to go for a walk now; ~, it's beginning to rain.* 现在出去散步已经太晚; 再者, 天又下雨了. □ prep in addition to; as well as: 除…之外: *I have three other hats ~ this.* 除了这顶之外, 我还有三顶别的帽子. *There were five of us ~ John,* not including John. 除约翰之外, 我们还有五人. *He hadn't time to prepare his lecture, ~ which, he was unwell.* 他没有时间预备讲稿, 除此而外, 他的身体也不太舒服.

be·siege /bɪ'siːdʒ; bɪ'sidʒ/ vt 1 [VP6A] surround (a place) with armed forces and keep them there; attack from all sides: 围攻; 包围; 围困: *Troy was ~d by the Greeks for ten years.* 特洛伊城被希腊人围困达十年. 2 [VP14] ~ *with,* crowd round (with requests, etc): 拥集在…的周围; 纷纷向…提出(请求等): *The teacher was ~d with questions and requests from her pupils.* 学生们纷纷向那老师提出问题和请求. **be·sieger** n

be·smear /bɪ'smɪə(r); bɪ'smɪr/ vt ~ *with,* smear all over, eg with grease. 涂抹.

be·smirch /bɪ'smɜːtʃ; bɪ'smɝtʃ/ vt make dirty: 弄脏; 染污; (fig) (喻) *His reputation was ~ed.* 他的名誉受损.

be·som /'biːzəm; 'bizəm/ n broom made by tying a bundle of twigs to a long handle. 帚; 扫把.

be·sot·ted /bɪ'sɒtɪd; bɪ'sɑtɪd/ part adj ~ *by/with,* stupefied (by alcoholic drink, drugs, love, etc). (因饮酒、服药、沉溺于爱情等而)昏瞶糊涂的.

be·sought ⇨ beseech.

be·spangle /bɪ'spæŋgl; bɪ'spæŋgld/ pred adj ~ *with,* covered, decorated, with spangles. 饰以闪烁发光之小金属片等的.

be·spat·tered /bɪˈspætəd; bɪˋspætəd/ *pred adj* ~ ***with,*** covered with spots of mud, etc. 为(污泥等)所覆盖的; 溅污的。

be·speak /bɪˈspiːk; bɪˋspik/ *vt* (*pt* **bespoke** /bɪˈspəʊk; bɪˋspok/, *pp* **bespoke** or **bespoken** /bɪˈspəʊkən; bɪˋspokən/) **1** [VP6A] (old use) order in advance; engage or reserve (a table in a restaurant, a room in a hotel). (旧用法) 预约; 预定(餐馆座位、旅馆房间)。 **bespoke shoemaker/tailor,** one who makes goods to order (contrasted with a seller of ready-made shoes, etc). 专做定货的鞋匠(裁缝)(以别于卖现成之鞋、衣者)。 ⇨ *custom-built* at **custom(5)**. **2** [VP6A, 25] (formal) be evidence of: (正式用语) 显示; 表示: *His polite manners ~ the gentleman.* 他的彬彬有礼的态度显示他是个绅士。

best[1] /best; bɛst/ *adj* (independent *superl;* 独立最高级; ⇨ **good, better**) of the most excellent kind: 最好的; 最佳的; 最优的: *the ~ poetry/poets;* 最好的诗(最优秀的诗人); *the ~ dinner I have ever had;* 我所吃过的最好的一餐; *the ~* (= quickest, most convenient, etc) *way from London to Paris,* 由伦敦至巴黎最好的(即最快、最方便等的)走法。 ***the ˈ~ part of,*** most of; the greater part of: 大半的; 大部份的: *I've been waiting the ~ part of an hour.* 我已等候大半个钟头了。 ***the ~ thing to do,*** that which is most likely to bring about the desired result. 最好的办法; 最上策。 ***make the ~ use of one's time/gifts/opportunities, etc,*** use one's time, etc in the most useful way. 尽量善于利用自己的时间(天赋, 机会等)。 ***put one's ˈ~ foot forward,*** ⇨ **foot(1)**. ***with the ˈ~ will in the world,*** even making every effort to be fair, etc. 尽最大努力做到公平等。 ˌ**~ ˈman,** bridegroom's friend, supporting him at his wedding. 男傧相。

best[2] /best; bɛst/ *adv* (independent *superl;* 独立最高级; ⇨ **well, better**) **1** in the most excellent way: 最好; 最优; 最佳: *He works ~ in the morning.* 他在早晨工作成绩最好。 *She was the ~-dressed woman in the village.* 她是村中衣着最漂亮的女人。 ***as ~ one may/can,*** in the ~ way possible to one. 尽力。 ***think ~,*** judge to be the ~ way of acting: 认为最好: *Do as you think ~.* 你认为怎么好就怎么做。 **2** most: 最; 极: *He is the ~-hated man in the village.* 他是村中最为人所憎恨的人。 **ˈ~-ˈseller** *n* book that is sold in very large numbers: 畅销书: *His new novel is one of the season's ~-sellers.* 他的新小说是本季的畅销书之一。 **3** ***had ~,*** = had better. ⇨ **better**[2]**(2)**.

best[3] /best; bɛst/ *pron* (independent *superl;* 独立最高级; ⇨ **better**[3]) the outstanding person, thing, etc among several; the most excellent part, aspect, of sth: 杰出的人或物; 佼佼者; 最好的东西; (物之)最佳部份; 最好的一面: *He's the ~ of husbands,* is distinguished among husbands for good qualities. 他是一个杰出的丈夫。 *We're the ~ of friends,* very close friends. 我们都是非常要好的朋友。 ***be all for the ~,*** be good in the end (although not at first seeming to be good). 终归会是好的或幸运的(虽然最初似乎并非如此)。 ***do sth all for the ~,*** act with good intentions (although it may not seem so). 怀着善意做某事(虽在表面看起来也许并不如此)。 ***be/dress in one's (Sunday) ~,*** wear one's finest clothes: 穿着最漂亮的衣服; 盛装: *They were (dressed) in their ~ for the wedding.* 他们均盛装参加该婚礼。 ***All the ~!*** (used when parting from sb) With warmest wishes! (与某人分别时的祝语)一切顺利! 万事如意! ***the ˈ~ of it/the joke, etc,*** the amusing part (of what happened): (发生之事中的)有趣部份; 最佳处; 最妙处: *And the ~ of it/the ~ part of it was that ....* 最妙的是…。 ***at ~,*** taking the most hopeful view: 持最乐观的看法; 充其量: *We can't arrive before Friday at ~.* 即使作最乐观的估计, 我们也不能在星期五以前到达。 ***at its/their/his, etc ~,*** in the ~ condition: 处于最佳状态; 处于颠峰状态; 在全盛期中: *The garden is at its best this month,* looking most beautiful. 本月份那花园看起来最漂亮(百花盛开时期)。 *He was at his ~ yesterday evening and kept us all amused,* talked in his most amusing way. 他昨天晚上表现出最佳的谈吐, 使我们大家一直都很开心。 ***(even) at the ˈ~ of times,*** (even) when circumstances are most favourable. (甚至)在情势最有利的时候。 ***have/get the ~ of it/of the fight/quarrel/deal/bargain, etc,*** win; gain the advantage. (在打斗、争论等中)得胜; 赢; (在交易等中)获利。 ***have/get the ~ of everything,*** enjoy the ~ food, housing, etc. 享受最好的食物、居所等; 样样称心如意。 ***with the ~,*** as well as anyone: 不比任何人差; 不逊于他人: *Although he's nearly fifty, he can still play tennis with the ~.* 他虽然已近五十岁了, 打起网球来却不比任何人差。 ***with the ˈ~ of intentions,*** intending only to help. 好心好意地。 ***do one's ~/the ~ one can,*** do one's utmost. 尽全力; 尽量。 ***(do sth) to the ~ of one's ability/power,*** use all one's ability/power when doing it. 全力以赴。 ***make the ~ of a bad job/business,*** do what one can, in spite of failure, misfortune, etc. 尽自己之所能去应付失败或不幸等; 善处逆境。 ***make the ~ of one's way home,*** return home as quickly as possible, in spite of difficulties. 不顾一切困难, 以最快速度回家; 尽快回家。 ***make the ~ of things,*** be contented (although things are not satisfactory). 感觉满足(虽然事态并不令人满意)。 ***to the ~ of my knowledge/belief/recollection*** so far as I know/believe/recollect (though my knowledge, etc may be imperfect). 就我所知(相信, 记忆)。

best[4] /best; bɛst/ *vt* [VP6A] (colloq) get the better of; defeat. (口)胜过; 打败。

bes·tial /ˈbestɪəl; ˋbɛstʃəl/ *adj* of or like a beast; brutish; savage. 兽类的; 似兽类的; 兽性的; 残忍的; 野蛮的。 **~ly** *adv* **bes·ti·al·ity** /ˌbestɪˈælətɪ; ˌbɛstʃɪˋælətɪ/ *n* (*pl* **-ties**) [U] quality of being ~; [C] ~ or brutal act. 兽性; 残忍; 野蛮; 兽行; 残忍或野蛮之行为。

bes·ti·ary /ˈbestɪərɪ *US:* -tɪerɪ; ˋbɛstɪˌɛrɪ/ *n* medieval collection of moral stories about animals. 中世纪的动物寓言集。

be·stir /bɪˈstɜː(r); bɪˋstɝ/ *vt* (-rr-) [VP6A, 17] ~ ***oneself,*** (old use or joc) busy oneself, be active. (旧用法或谑)奋发; 振作。

be·stow /bɪˈstəʊ; bɪˋsto/ *vt* **1** [VP6A, 14] ***~ (on/upon),*** give as an offering: 给与; 授予; 赐赠: *~ an honour/a title on sb;* 给与某人一项荣誉(头衔); *the praise that has been ~ed upon him.* 他所受到的赞誉。 **2** [VP6A] (old use) put, place. (旧用法)放; 置。 **~al** *n* ~ing. 授予; 赠与; 放置。

be·strew /bɪˈstruː; bɪˋstru/ *vt* (*pt* **~ed,** *pp* **bestrewn** /-ˈstruːn; -ˋstrun/ or **~ed**) [VP6A, 14] ***~ (with),*** (poet) strew (a surface); scatter (things) about. (诗)(以…)撒布于(表面); 抛撒(某物)于各处。

be·stride /bɪˈstraɪd; bɪˋstraɪd/ *vt* (*pt* **bestrode** /bɪˈstrəʊd; bɪˋstrod/, *pp* **bestridden** /bɪˈstrɪdn; bɪˋstrɪdn/, **bestrid** /bɪˈstrɪd; bɪˋstrɪd/, **bestrode**) [VP6A] (formal) sit, stand, with one leg on each side of: (正式用语)跨; 跨坐; 跨立; 骑乘: *~ a horse/chair/bidet/ditch/fence* etc; 骑马(两腿分开跨坐椅上; 跨坐在坐浴桶上; 跨在沟上; 骑在墙上); (fig) dominate: (喻)统治: *Caesar bestrode the Roman Empire.* 凯撒统治罗马帝国。 ⇨ **astride.**

bet /bet; bɛt/ *vt, vi* (**-tt-**, *pt, pp* **bet** or **betted**) [VP9, 11, 12C, 2A, 3A] **1** ***bet on sth, bet (sb) that ....*** risk money on a race or on some other event of which the result is doubtful: 打赌(某事, 如赛马或其他结果不一定之事); 与(某人)打赌…; 赌: *He bet me a pound that Hyperion would win.* 他认为亥伯龙会赢, 与我赌一英镑。 *It's foolish to bet on horses.* 为赛马打赌是愚蠢的。 *Do you ever bet?* 你会与人打赌吗? **2** (colloq uses): (口语用法): *I bet,* I'm certain; 我敢打赌; 我有把握; 我确信; *you bet,* you may be certain. 的确; 当然。 □ *n* [C] agreement to risk money, etc on an event of which the result is doubtful; the money, etc offered: 赌; 打赌; 赌

金; 赌注: *make a bet*; 打赌: *win/lose a bet*; 赌赢(输); *accept/take up a bet*. 接受打赌; 同意与人打赌。

beta /'bi:tə US: 'beitə; 'betə/ *n* second letter (B, β) of the Greek alphabet. 希腊字母的第二个字母。 ⇨ **App 4.** 参看附录四。

be·take /bɪ'teɪk; bɪ'tek/ *vt* (*pt* **betook** /bɪ'tuk; bɪ'tuk/, *pp* **betaken** /bɪ'teɪkən; bɪ'tekən/) [VP14, reflex 与反身代词连用] ~ **oneself to**, (old use) go to, apply oneself to. (旧用法)赴; 去; 专心于; 致力于。

betel /'bi:tl; 'bitl/ *n* leaf which is wrapped round bits of areca-nut and used by some Indians for chewing. 蒌酱之叶(印度人用以包槟榔而嚼之)。'~ **nut**, areca-nut. 槟榔。

bète noire /,beɪt 'nwɑ:(r); 'bet'mwɑr/ *n* (F) thing or person one dislikes greatly. (法)为人所极其厌恶之事物或人。

bethel /'beθl; 'bɛθəl/ *n* nonconformist chapel; (esp US) chapel for seamen. 非英国国教徒之礼拜堂; (尤美)海员之礼拜堂。

be·think /bɪ'θɪŋk; bɪ'θɪŋk/ *vt* (*pt, pp* **bethought** /bɪ'θɔ:t; bɪ'θɔt/) [VP11, 14, 17, 20, 21] ~ **oneself (of)**, (old use) reflect, consider. (旧用法)思考; 考虑。

be·tide /bɪ'taɪd; bɪ'taɪd/ *vt* (only in) (仅用于) *woe* ~ *him/you, etc (if…)*, may misfortune come to him/you, etc (if…). (假使…)但愿他(你等)遭遇不幸。 愿天降灾于他(你等)。

be·times /bɪ'taɪmz; bɪ'taɪmz/ *adv* (old use) early; in good time. (旧用法)早; 及时: *We must be up ~ tomorrow.* 我们明天必须早起。

be·token /bɪ'təʊkən; bɪ'tokən/ *vt* [VP6A] (old use) indicate, suggest: (旧用法)指示; 表示; 预示: *Those black clouds ~ rain.* 那些乌云预示有雨。

be·took ⇨ **betake**.

be·tray /bɪ'treɪ; bɪ'tre/ *vt* 1 [VP6A] be disloyal to; act deceitfully towards: 不忠于; 背叛; 欺骗: *He ~ed his principles.* 他违背了他的原则。 2 [VP6A, 14] ~ **(to)**, give away or make known or sell treacherously: 出卖; 陷害: *Judas ~ed Jesus to his enemies.* 犹大将耶稣出卖给他的敌人。 3 [VP6A] allow (a secret) to become known, either by accident or on purpose. (无意或有意)泄露(秘密)。4[VP6A, 25]be or give a sign of, show: 暴露; 显示: *The boy's face ~ed the fact that he had been eating jam.* 那男孩的脸显示他吃过果酱。 *His accent at once ~ed the fact that he was/~ed him to be a foreigner.* 他的口音立刻显示出他是一个外国人。 ~ **oneself**, show what one really is, etc: 暴露出真实身份: *He had a good disguise, but as soon as he spoke he ~ed himself*, ie he was recognized by his voice. 他伪装很好, 但是他一说话就露出马脚了(他的声音使别人认出了他是谁)。~**al** /bɪ'treɪəl; bɪ'treəl/ *n* [U] ~ing or being ~ed; [C] instance of this. 背叛; 出卖; 陷害; 泄露; 暴露。~**er** *n*

be·troth /bɪ'trəʊð; bɪ'troð/ *vt* (old formal use) ~ **to**, [VP6A, 14] engage (a woman) in contract or marriage (usu in *pp*): (旧时正式用语)给(一女子)订亲; 许配(通常用过去分词): *His daughter was ~ed to a banker.* 他的女儿与一银行家订婚。~**ed** *n* person engaged to be married. 已订婚者。~**al** *n* engagement (the usual word) to be married. 订婚; 婚约(engagement 为常用词)。

bet·ter¹ /'betə(r); 'betə/ *adj* (independent *comp*; 独立比较级; ⇨ **good, best**) 1 *This is good but that is ~*. 这个很好, 但是那个更好。 *He's a ~ man than his brother.* 他的为人比他哥哥(弟弟)好。~ *than one's word*, more generous than one's promise. 所做的超过所说的; 比所许诺的更为慷慨。 *(do sth) against one's ~ judgement*, despite feeling that it may be unwise. 知其不可为(而为之)。 *no ~ than*, practically the same as: 实际等于; 简直是: *He's no ~ than a beggar*, is, in spite of appearances, etc, almost a beggar. (他虽然外表不似乞丐)他实际等于一个乞丐。 *be no ~ than she should be*, (old use) be a woman of low regard or easy virtue. (旧用法)是个不正经的女人。 ⇨ **virtue(2)**. *the ~ part of,*

the larger part of: 大部份的; 大半的: *Discretion is the ~ part of valour*, ⇨ **discretion(1)**. 慎重即勇过半矣。

see ~ days, be not so poor or unfortunate as at present: 不象目前之贫苦或潦倒; 享受过富裕的生活; 曾经富贵意过: *He has seen ~ days.* 他曾经富贵过(并非象现在这样贫穷或潦倒)。 *one's ~ feelings*, one's moral nature. 高尚的本性; 良心; 天良。 *his ~ half*, (colloq) his wife. (口)他的妻子。 2 (of health) recovering from illness (often contrasted with *ill* and related to *well*): (指健康)好些的; 情况较佳的; 康复的(常与 ill 相对, 与 well 有关): *The patient is ~ today but is still not well enough to get up.* 病人今天好些, 但仍不能起床。 *I'm quite ~ now*, am fully recovered. 我现在已完全康复了。

bet·ter² /'betə(r); 'betə/ *adv* (independent *comp*; 独立比较级; ⇨ **well, best**) 1 *The ~* (= The more) *I know her the more I admire her abilities.* 我对她认识愈深, 愈钦佩她的本领。 *You would write ~ if you had a good pen.* 假如你有一枝好笔, 你的字会写得更好些。 *You play tennis ~ than I do.* 你网球打得比我好。 *You'll like it ~* (= more) *when you understand it more.* 当你多了解一些, 你就会更喜欢它。 *be ~ off*, richer; more comfortable. 更富有; 更舒服。 *be ~ off without*, happier; more at ease: 若无…则为快乐; 无…更为舒适或安逸: *We'd be ~ off without all that din from the children's room.* 若是没有孩子房间里传来的嘈杂声, 我们会更为舒适。 *know ~*, **(a)** be wise or experienced enough not to do sth: 具有充分智慧或经验而不去做某事; 知道…是不对的: *You ought to know ~ than to go out without an overcoat on such a cold day.* 你不应糊涂到在这样的冷天出去不穿大衣。 **(b)** refuse to accept a statement (because one knows it is not true): 不相信某一句话(因为知其不实): *He says he didn't cheat, but I know ~*, feel sure that he did. 他说他没有欺骗, 但是我不相信(我确信他欺骗)。 *think (all) the ~ of sb*, have a higher opinion of him: 对某人更为钦服: *I shall think all the ~ of you after seeing how bravely you faced your misfortunes so bravely.* 看到你如此勇敢地忍受这些不幸事故, 我将对你更加钦佩。 *think ~ of sth/of doing sth*, decide, after thought, not to do it. 经再思而后决定作罢(不做某事)。 2 (used in 用于 [VP5]) *had ~*, would find it more suitable, more to your advantage, etc: 最好 (劝告或建议用语): *You had ~ mind your own business.* 你最好只管你自己的事(别管他人的事)。 *You'd ~ not say that*, I advise you not to say that. 你最好别提那件事。 *I had ~ begin by explaining . . .*, It will be useful if I begin by . . .; 我最好在开始的时候先解释…; *Hadn't you ~ take an umbrella?* 你不觉得带把伞比较好吗?

bet·ter³ /'betə(r); 'betə/ *n* one's (*elders and*) ~**s**, older, wiser, more experienced people: 自己的长辈; 比自己年长者; 比自己更明智或更有经验的人们; 胜于己者: *Don't ignore the advice of your elders and ~s.* 不要忽视长者的忠告。 Cf 参较 *superior*, as in: *He's my superior at chess.* 他的棋艺比我强。 *get the ~ of sb or sth*, overcome; defeat; win (an argument, etc): 克服(某事); 胜过; 打败(某人); 赢得(辩论等): *His shyness got the ~ of him*, he was overcome by shyness, was too shy to speak out. 他非常害羞; 他害羞得不敢说话。 *She always gets the ~ of these quarrels.* 在这种争吵中她总是赢过别人。 *for ~ (or) for worse*, in both good and bad fortune. 不论是好是歹; 好也罢, 歹也罢; 无论如何; Cf 参较 *for good or ill*.

bet·ter⁴ /'betə(r); 'betə/ *vt* 1 [VP6A] improve; do better than: 改善; 改良; 改进; 比…做得更好: *The Government hopes to ~ the conditions of the peasants.* 政府希望改善农民生活情况。 *Your work last year was good; I hope you will ~ it this year.* 你去年的成绩不错, 希望你今年能百尺竿头更进一步。 *get a ~ position, higher wages, etc.* 升调; 高升; 获得加薪。 ~**ment** *n* [U] making or becoming ~. 改善; 改良; 改进。

bet·ter⁵, **bet·tor** /'betə(r); 'betə/ *n* person who bets; punter (the more usu word). 打赌者; 下赌注的人 (punter 为较常用的词)。

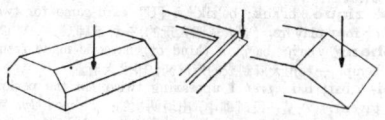

be·tween[1] /bɪˈtwiːn; bəˈtwin/ *adv* *(in)* ~, in(to) a place or time that is before the one (place or time) but after the other: 介于其间的地方或时间; 在其间: *We visited the Museum in the morning and the Art Gallery later, with a hurried lunch* ~. 我们上午参观博物馆, 后来又参观艺术馆, 中间匆匆地吃了一顿午餐; *far* ~, at wide intervals. 有很宽的间隔; 彼此相距很远。*few and far* ~, few and widely scattered or separate: 稀疏零落彼此相距很远: *In this part of Canada houses are few and far* ~. 在加拿大这一带, 房屋稀少而彼此相距甚远。

be·tween[2] /bɪˈtwiːn; bəˈtwin/ *prep* **1** (of place) (指地点) *The letter B comes* ~ *A and C*, ie after A but before C. 字母 B 在 A 与 C 之间(即在 A 之后但在 C 之前)。*The Mediterranean Sea is* ~ *Europe and Africa*. 地中海在欧洲与非洲之间。*A river flows* ~ *its banks*. 河在两岸之间流。(*Between* usu involves only two limits, but when boundaries are concerned, there may be more than two limits. Between 通常仅牵涉两个界限, 但当牵涉到边界时, 则可能有两个以上的界限。*Switzerland lies* ~ *France, Italy, Austria and Germany*. 瑞士位于法国、意大利、奥地利及德国之间。⇨ **among**.) **2** (of order, rank, etc): (指顺序、等级等): *An army major ranks* ~ *a captain and a colonel*. 陆军少校的军衔在上尉与中校之间。**3** (of time): (指时间): ~ *the two world wars*; 在两次世界大战之间; ~ *8 o'clock and 2 o'clock*; 在一点钟与两点钟之间; ~ *youth and middle age*. 在青年与中年之间。**4** (of distance, amount, etc): (指距离、数量等): ~ *five and six miles*; 在五英里与六英里之间; ~ *thirty and forty tons*; 在三十吨与四十吨之间; ~ *5p and 10p*; 在五便士与十便士之间; ~ *freezing-point and boiling-point*. 在冰点与沸点之间。**5** (of movement) to and fro: (指移动)来往于; 往返于: *This liner sails* ~ *Southampton and New York*. 这艘班轮来往航行于南安普敦与纽约之间。**6** (showing connection): (表示关联): *after all there has been* ~ *us*, in view of our past friendship, the experiences we have shared, etc. 鉴于过去我们之间的关系(指友谊或共同经历等)。*There is* **no 'love lost** ~ *them*, They dislike each other. 他们之间毫无爱情可言(互相憎恶)。*There's nothing to choose* ~ *them*, They are (both or all) alike. 它们之间无可选择(它们两个或全都一样)。**7** (to show sharing; used between two only): (表示分享; 仅用于二者): *Divide/Share the money* ~ *you*. 你们二人平分这钱。~ *ourselves*; ~ *you, me and the gatepost*; ~ *you and me*, in confidence. 当作秘密; 不得外传。**8** (to show combination, used of two, or more than two to show several and independent relationships): (表示连合, 用于二者或二者以上, 表示个别和独立的关系): *The first five batsmen scored 253 runs* ~ *them*. 头五个击球员共得 253 分。*We* (two or more) *saved up for a year and bought a secondhand car* ~ *us*. 我们(二人或更多人)积蓄了一年, 合伙买了一辆旧汽车。*B*~ *them* (ie as the result of their combined efforts) *they soon finished the work*. 他们大家一齐动手, 不久就把工作完成了。**9** ~ *sth and sth*, with these things combined: 由于…和…的原因: *B*~ *astonishment and despair she hardly knew what to do*. 在惊骇与绝望的双重打击下, 她简直不知怎么办。*My time is fully taken up* ~ *writing and relationship*. 我的时间全用在写作与演讲上面。**10** (showing relationship): (表示关系): *the relation* ~ *teacher and pupil*; 师生关系; *the distinction* ~ *right and wrong*; 是非的区别; *a comparison* ~ *two things*; 两件事物的比较; *quarrels/wars/ill-feeling/rivalries/friendships, etc* ~ *nations*. 国与国之间的不和(战争、恶感、竞争、友好等)。

be·twixt /bɪˈtwɪkst; bəˈtwɪkst/ *prep. adv* (old or liter use) (旧用法或文) =between. ~ *and between*, (colloq) in an intermediate state; neither one thing nor the other. (口)处于中间的状态; 既非此亦非彼。

bevel /ˈbevl; ˈbɛvl/ *n* sloping edge; surface with such a slope, eg at the side of a picture 'frame or a sheet of plate-glass. 有斜度的边缘; 斜面(如在镜框或玻璃板之边缘上者)。 ~ **gear**, either of a pair of gears with ~led

teeth surfaces. 斜齿轮。□ *vt* (-ll-, US = -l-) give a sloping edge to. 将…之边缘作成斜角向; 使有斜边。

bevels

bev·er·age /ˈbevərɪdʒ; ˈbɛvrɪdʒ/ *n* [C] (formal) any sort of drink except water, eg milk, tea, wine, beer. (正式用语)饮料(指除水以外之任何一种可饮用之液体, 例如牛奶、茶、酒、啤酒)。

bevy /ˈbevɪ; ˈbɛvɪ/ *n* **1** company or gathering. 一群。**2** flock (of birds, esp quail). 一群(鸟, 尤指鹌鹑, 与 of 连用)。

be·wail /bɪˈweɪl; bɪˈwel/ *vt* [VP6A] (poet) express sorrow over; mourn for. (诗)因…而悲伤; 哀痛; 哀悼。

be·ware /bɪˈweə(r); bɪˈwɛr/ *vi, vt* [VP2A, 3A, 10 in the imperative and infinitive only 仅用于祈使句及不定式] ~ *(of)*, be on guard, take care: 小心; 当心; 注意; 提防: *B*~ *of the dog!* 当心那只狗! *B*~ *of pickpockets!* 谨防扒手! *B*~ *(of) how you attempt it*. 小心注意你应该怎样去尝试它。*B*~, *sir*, *(of) what you do*. 先生, 请注意你自己的行为。

be·wil·der /bɪˈwɪldə(r); bɪˈwɪldɚ/ *vt* [VP6A] puzzle; confuse: 使迷惑; 使手足无措; 使着慌; 使昏乱; 使糊涂; 使发愣: *The old woman from the country was* ~*ed by the crowds and traffic in the big city*. 那乡下老婆子看到大城市里的人群及车辆就愣住了。*Tom was* ~*ed by the examination questions*. 汤姆被考试题目难住了。~**·ing** *adj* that ~s: 使迷惑的; 使手足无措的; 使发愣的: *find sth* ~*ing*. 发现某事很为难。~**·ment** *n* [U] state of being ~ed: 迷惑; 昏乱; 着慌; 发愣: *He looked at me in open-mouthed* ~*ment*. 他张大着嘴迷惑地看着我。

be·witch /bɪˈwɪtʃ; bɪˈwɪtʃ/ *vt* [VP6A] **1** work magic on; put a magic spell on: 对…施妖术; 蛊惑; 迷惑: *The old woman* ~*ed the cows so that they gave no milk*. 那老婆子对那些母牛施妖术, 使它们挤不出牛奶。**2** charm; delight very much: 迷(人); 使销魂; 使着迷; 使极为快乐: *She danced so well that she* ~*ed all the young men*. 她的舞姿极为美妙, 使所有在场的年轻小伙子都着了迷。~**·ing** *adj* that ~s: 迷人的; 销魂的: *a* ~*ing smile*. 迷人的微笑。~**·ing·ly** *adv*: 迷人地; 销魂地: *She smiled at him* ~*ingly*. 她迷人地对他微笑。

bey /beɪ; be/ *n* (Turkish word meaning) governor: (土耳其语)总督; 长官; 省长: *the Bey of Tunis*. 突尼斯总督。

be·yond[1] /bɪˈjɒnd; bɪˈjɑnd/ *adv* at or to a distance; farther on: 在远处; 在远处; 再往前去: *India and the lands* ~. 印度及印度那边的国家。*What is* ~? 再往前面是什么?

be·yond[2] /bɪˈjɒnd; bɪˈjɑnd/ *prep* **1** at, on or to, the farther side of: 在或向…的那一边; 越过: *The house is* ~ *the bridge*. 房屋在桥的那一边。*Don't go* ~ *the town boundary*. 不要走出市界。*We saw peak* ~ *peak*, a succession of peaks. 我们看见重重的山峰。**2** (of time) later than: (指时间)超过; 晚于: *Don't stay out* ~ *(after is the more usu word) 10 o'clock*. 不要在外面停留到十点钟以后还不回家(after 较常用)。*He never sees* ~ *the present*. 他从未看到将来。**3** surpassing, exceeding; out of reach of: 超出; 出乎…之外: *Your work is* ~ *all praise*, so good that it cannot be praised enough. 你的作品叫人赞扬不尽。*We succeeded* ~ *our hopes*, were more successful than we had hoped to be. 我们获得超乎之成功, 是我们始料所不及的。*That's going* ~ *a joke*, passes the limits of what is reasonable as a joke. 那样玩笑是太过火了。*He lives* ~ *his income*, spends more than he earns. 他的生活入不敷出。*It's quite* ~ *me*, is more than I can understand. 这我完全不懂。**4** (in neg

and interr) except: (用于否定及疑问句) 除…以外: *He has nothing ~ his pension.* 他除了养老金之外毫无积蓄。

be·zique /bɪˈziːk; bəˈzik/ *n* [U] card-game for two or four players. (二人或四人玩的)一种纸牌戏。

bhang /bæŋ; bæŋ/ *n* (kind of) narcotic made from hemp. 一种用大麻制成的麻醉药; 印度大麻。

bi- /ˌbaɪ; baɪ/ *pref* 1 appearing twice (in the period given): (在某一段时期中) 出现两次的: *ˌbi-ˈmonthly;* 每月两次的 (地); *bi-annual.* 每年两次的。2 lasting for two, appearing every two: 延续二…的; 每二…出现一次的; 每隔一…发生一次的: *biennial.* 二年生的; 两年一次的。3 having two: 有二…的; *bilateral;* 双边的; *bilingual;* 用两种文字写成的; 会说两种语言的(人); *biped;* 两足动物; *biplane.* 双翼飞机。4 in two ways; doubly: 以两种方式; 两面; 双: *bi-concave.* 双凹镜。

bias /ˈbaɪəs; ˈbaɪəs/ *n* 1 leaning of the mind towards or away from sth; predisposition: 偏见; 成见; 偏爱; 倾向; 癖性: *He has a ~ towards/against the plan,* is in favour of it/opposed to it without having full knowledge of it. 他对此计划有偏爱(有成见)。*He is without ~,* is impartial, unprejudiced. 他不偏不倚(公正, 无偏见)。2 cut on the ~, (dress-making, etc) cut across, slantingly. (裁缝等)斜裁。3 (esp of a ball in the game of bowls) tendency to swerve; the weighting causing this tendency. (尤指滚木球戏中的球)突然转向的趋势; 歪曲的球路; 造成歪曲球路的重力。□ *vt* (*pt, pp* **~ed** or **~sed**) [VP6A, 14] (towards/against), give a ~ to; influence (usu unfairly): 使有偏见; 以偏见影响: 使偏向一方: *The government used newspapers and the radio to ~ the opinions of the people.* 政府利用报纸及广播左右人民的舆论。*He is ~sed towards/against the plan,* is prejudiced. 他对该计划有偏爱(偏见)。*He's clearly ~sed,* 他显然有成见。

bib¹ /bɪb; bɪb/ *n* 1 piece of cloth tied under a child's chin. (系于婴儿下颔底下的)围嘴; 围脖。**bib and tucker,** ⇨ **tucker.** 2 upper part of an apron. 围裙的上部。

bib² /bɪb; bɪb/ *vi* (**-bb-**) drink too much or too often (rare except in *wine-bibbing, wine-bibber*). 喝得太多; 太常喝(罕用字, 除非用于复合词 wine-bibbing, wine-bibber 豪饮者)。

Bible /ˈbaɪbl; ˈbaɪbl/ *n* sacred writings of the Jews and the Christian Church. 圣经(犹太人及基督教的圣书)。**'~ puncher,** (colloq) evangelical preacher. (口)福音传道者; 牧师。**bib·li·cal** /ˈbɪblɪkl; ˈbɪblɪkl/ *adj* of, concerning, contained in, the ~: 圣经的; 有关圣经的; 圣经中的: *ˈbiblical style,* the style used in (esp the Authorized Version of) the ~. 圣经体裁(尤指钦定译本者)。

bib·li·og·ra·phy /ˌbɪblɪˈɒɡrəfɪ; ˌbɪblɪˈɑɡrəfɪ/ *n* 1 [C] (*pl* **-phies**) list of books and writings of one author or about one subject. 一(作家的)著作目录; (关于某一学科或题目的)书目。2 [U] study of the authorship, editions, etc of books. 目录学(研究书籍之作者、版本等)。**bib·li·og·ra·pher** /ˌbɪblɪˈɒɡrəfə(r); ˌbɪblɪˈɑɡrəfɚ/ *n* person who writes or studies bibliographies. 著作目录编纂者; 研究目录学者; 书志学者。

bib·lio·phile /ˈbɪblɪəfaɪl; ˈbɪblɪəˌfaɪl/ *n* person who loves and collects books. 珍藏书籍者。

bibu·lous /ˈbɪbjʊləs; ˈbɪbjələs/ *adj* (joc) fond of much alcoholic drink. (谑)嗜酒的; 好饮酒的。

bi·cam·eral /ˌbaɪˈkæmərəl; baɪˈkæmərəl/ *adj* (of a legislature) having two chambers, eg House of Commons, House of Lords. (指立法机关)有两个议院(例如下议院, 上议院); 两院制的。

bi·car·bon·ate /ˌbaɪˈkɑːbənət; baɪˈkɑrbənɪt/ *n* [U] acid salt of carbonic acid. 酸式碳酸盐。**~ of soda** (= *sodium ~*) **(NaHCO₃)**, used in cooking and in medicine. 碳酸氢钠; 小苏打(用于烹饪及医药)。

bi·cen·ten·ary /ˌbaɪsenˈtiːnərɪ US: -ˈsentənerɪ; baɪˈsentəˌnɛrɪ/ *n* (celebration of the) 200th anniversary of an event. 二百周年; 二百周年纪念。

bi·cen·ten·nial /ˌbaɪsenˈteniəl; ˌbaɪsenˈtɛnɪəl/ *adj* 1 happening once in 200 years. 每二百年一次的。2 lasting for 200 years. 延续二百年的。3 of a 200th anniversary. 二百周年的。□ *n* 200th anniversary. 二百周年。

bi·ceps /ˈbaɪseps; ˈbaɪseps/ *n* (*pl* unchanged) large muscle in the front part of the upper arm: (复数不变) (上臂前面之)二头肌: *His ~ is/are impressive.* 他的二头肌予人深刻的印象。

bicker /ˈbɪkə(r); ˈbɪkɚ/ *vi* [VP2A, C, 3A] **~ (with sb)** quarrel about sth unimportant: (与某人)(为某事)吵嘴; 争吵(有关琐细或不重要的小事): *Stop ~ing!* 别再吵嘴了!

bi·cycle /ˈbaɪsɪkl; ˈbaɪˌsɪkl/ *n* two-wheeled machine for riding on, propelled by using pedals. 脚踏车; 自行车。□ *vi* (usu shortened to 通常略作 **cycle** /ˈsaɪkl; ˈsaɪkl/) [VP2A, C] ride a ~. 骑脚踏车。

bid¹ /bɪd; bɪd/ *vt, vi* (**-dd-**) 1 (*pt, pp* **bid**) [VP6A, 14, 2A, 3A] **bid (for),** (at an auction sale) make an offer of money; offer (a certain price) for: (在拍卖场所)出价; 出(价): *Will anyone bid £5 for this painting?* 有人出五英镑买这幅画吗? *Mr X bid £20 for the horse so I bid £21.* 某先生出二十英镑买这匹马, 所以我出二十一英镑。*Is nobody else going to bid?* 再没有别人出价了吗? *What shall I bid?* 我要出多少价钱呢? *I hoped to get the house but a rich man was bidding against me,* offering higher prices. 我本来想买那栋房子, 可是一个有钱人出了更高的价。⇨ **outbid.** *The politicians are bidding for popular support,* making offers, eg of tax reductions, in order to get support from the public. 那些政客竞相发表动人的诺言(如减税), 以争取民众的支持。**bid up,** [VP15B] make the price higher by offering more money: 喊出高价借以提高价格; 哄抬…之价格: *The goods were bid up*

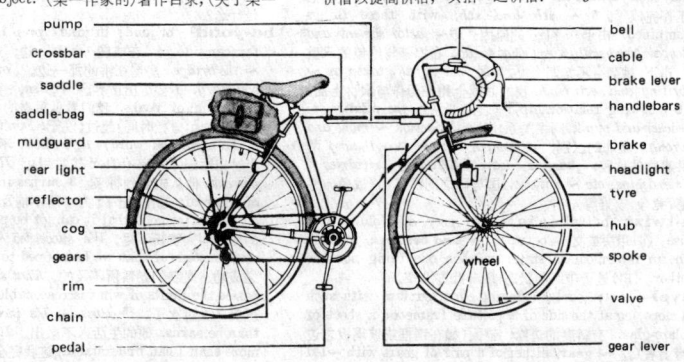

pump
crossbar
saddle
saddle-bag
mudguard
rear light
reflector
cog
gears
rim
chain
pedal

bell
cable
brake lever
handlebars
brake
headlight
tyre
hub
spoke
valve
gear lever

wheel

a bicycle

far beyond their real value. 这些货物的价格被哄高得远超出它们的实在价值。 **2** (*pt, pp* **bid**) [VP3A] **bid for,** (colloq) attempt to attain: 期望达到的; 寻求: *The army bid for power and succeeded.* 陆军希望增强实力并且如愿以偿。 **3** (*pt, pp* **bid**) [VP2A, 3A] **bid on,** (US) state a price for doing sth); put in a tender for: 提出价格 (承做某事); 投标: *The firm decided to bid on the new bridge.* 该商行决定投标承建这座新桥。 ⇨ **tender³. 4** (old use) (*pt* **bade** /bæd; bæd/, *pp* **bidden** /'brdn; 'brdṇ/, **bid**) [VP17, 18B] **(a)** command; tell: (旧用法) 命令; 吩咐: *He bade me (to) come in.* 他令我进来。 *Do as you are bid.* 照你所受到的吩咐做。 *Soldiers must do as they are bidden.* 军人必须服从命令。 *Bid him come in.* 叫他进来。 **(b)** invite: 邀请: *the bidden guests;* 所请之客人。 *bid sb to a wedding.* 邀请某人参加婚礼。 **(c)** [VP12A, 13A] say (as a greeting, etc): 说(问候的话等): *bid farewell* (= say goodbye) *to sb;* 向某人道别; *bid sb good morning.* 向某人问候早安。 **5 bid fair to,** seem likely to: 很有可能: *Our plan bids fair to succeed.* 我们的计划很有可能会成功。 **bid defiance to,** (old use) announce that one defies (the enemy, etc). (旧用法) 宣布对抗蔑视(敌人)等。 **6** (cards, bridge) make a bid: (牌戏, 桥牌戏) 叫牌: *bid 2 hearts.* 叫二红心。 ⇨ **bid²(4).** **'bid·dable** *adj* (colloq) docile; ready to obey. (口)温顺的; 顺从的; 听话的。 **bid·ding** *n* [U] **1** command. 命令。 *do sb's bidding,* do what he commands. 服从某人的命令; 照某人的吩咐做。 **2** act of offering a price at an auction sale: (在拍卖场所)出价: *Bidding was brisk,* There were many bids, quickly made. 出价很踊跃(即多而迅速)。 **3** (at cards) the making of bids(4). (纸牌戏) 叫牌。 **bid·der** *n* person who bids. 出价者; 投标人; 叫牌者。

bid² /brd; brd/ *n* **1** (at an auction sale) offer of a price: (在拍卖场所)出价: *Are there no bids for this very fine painting?* 没有人出价买这张极美的画吗? *Will no one make a higher / further bid?* 再没有人出更高的价吗? **2** (US) statement of price for a piece of work, etc: (美) 投标(承建工程等): *Bids were invited for the construction of a swimming-pool.* 招标建造游泳池。 ⇨ **tender³. 3 make a bid for,** (colloq) try to obtain: (口)力求获得; 争取: *make a bid for power / popular support.* 争取权力 (民众的支持)。 **4** (card games, esp bridge) statement of the number of tricks a player proposes to win: (纸牌戏, 尤指桥牌)叫牌: *a bid of 2 hearts / 3 no-trumps;* 叫二红心(三无王); *raise the bid.* 提高叫牌。

bide /baɪd; baɪd/ *vt* (liter; old use) abide. (文) 旧用法)等待。 (rare except in) (罕, 仅用于) **~ one's time,** wait for a favourable opportunity. 等待良机。

bidet /'biːdeɪ US: biːˈdeɪ; biˈde/ *n* (F) raised narrow bath (to be straddled) for washing the genitals and bottom. (法)(供跨坐以冲洗生殖器及臀部的)坐浴桶; 坐浴盆。

bi·en·nial /baɪˈenɪəl; baɪˈɛnɪəl/ *adj* lasting for two years; happening every alternate year. 持续二年的; 二年生的; 每隔一年发生的。 □ *n* plant that lives two years and has flowers and seeds in the second year. 二年生的植物。 **~·ly** *adv*

bier /bɪə(r); bɪr/ *n* movable wooden stand for a coffin or a dead body. 棺架; 尸架。

biff /bɪf; bɪf/ *n* (sl) sharp blow. (俚)猛击。 □ *vt* (sl) strike: (俚)打; 击: *~ sb on the nose.* 打某人的鼻子。

bi·focal /ˌbaɪˈfəʊkl; baɪˈfokl/ *adj* (esp of lenses in spectacles for the eyes) designed for both distant and near vision. (尤指眼镜片)视远景及近物两用的; 双焦点的; 双光的。 **bi·focals** *n pl* spectacles with ~ lenses. 双光眼镜。

bi·fur·cate /'baɪfəkeɪt; 'baɪfəˌket/ *vt, vi* [VP6A, 2A] (formal) (of roads, rivers, boughs of trees, etc) divide into two branches, etc; fork. (正式用语)(指道路、河流、树枝等)分为两支; 分叉。 □ *adj* (also 亦作 **~d**) forked. 分为两支的; 分叉的。 **bi·fur·ca·tion** /ˌbaɪfə·ˈkeɪʃn; ˌbaɪfəˈkeʃən/ *n*

big /bɪg; bɪg/ *adj* (**-gg-**) (antonym 反义词 *little;* cf 参较 *large,* and *small*) of large size, extent, capacity, importance, etc. 大的; 广大的; 容量大的; 重大的。 **get / grow too big for one's boots,** (colloq) become conceited. (口)自大; 自夸; 妄自尊大。 **have big ideas,** be ambitious. 有野心; 有抱负。 **talk big,** boast. 说大话; 自夸; 吹牛。 **'big bug** *n* (sl) (俚) ⇨ **bug(4). ,big 'business,** commerce on a ~ financial scale. 大企业。 **big game** *n,* **game¹(6). big end** *n* (eng) part of a connecting shaft that bears on a crankshaft. (工程)连轴之承接曲柄轴的部分。 **big noise** *n* (sl) (俚) ⇨ **noise. 'big shot** *n* (sl) (俚) ⇨ **shot¹(8).** **'big stick,** = ~ shot. **the 'big time,** (sl) highest level. (俚)最高标准; 第一流。 **'big·wig** *n* (sl) important person. (俚)要人; 大亨。

big·amy /'bɪgəmɪ; 'bɪgəmɪ/ *n* [U] having two wives or husbands living. 重婚(一夫二妻或一妻二夫)。 **'big·am·ous** /'bɪgəməs; 'bɪgəməs/ *adj* guilty of, involving, ~: 犯重婚罪的; 涉及重婚的: *a bigamous marriage.* 重婚的婚姻。 **'big·am·ist** /'bɪgəmɪst; 'bɪgəmɪst/ *n* person guilty of ~. 犯重婚罪者。

bight /baɪt; baɪt/ *n* **1** loop made in a rope. 绳子所绕成的圈; 绳圈。 **2** curve in a coast, larger than, or with not so much curve as, a bay. 湾浦(海岸线之弯曲部份, 较海湾宽大, 或其弯曲度不如海湾那样大)。

bigot /'bɪgət; 'bɪgət/ *n* person who holds strongly to an opinion or belief in defiance of reason or argument. (执着某一见解或信仰而不可理喻的)顽固者; 盲信者。 **~ed** /-ɪd; -ɪd/ *adj* intolerant and narrow-minded (in religion, etc). (对宗教等)顽固的; 偏执的。 **~ry** /-rɪ; -rɪ/ *n* [U] state of being ~ed; [C] act, etc, of a ~. 顽固; 固执; 固执之行为等。

bi·jou /'biːʒuː; 'biʒu/ *n* (F) jewel. (法)宝石。 □ *adj* small and elegant: 小巧玲珑的: *~ villas.* 小巧的别墅。

bike /baɪk; baɪk/ *n, vi* (colloq and common abbr for) bicycle. (口)脚踏车; 自行车(bicycle 之略)。

bi·kini /bɪˈkiːnɪ; bɪˈkinɪ/ *n* scanty two-piece garment (bra and briefs) worn by girls and women for swimming and sun-bathing: 比基尼装(一种既短又窄的两件式女泳装): ~ *top* (= bra); 比基尼上装; ~ *briefs,* ⇨ **briefs.** 比基尼短裤。

bi·lab·ial /ˌbaɪˈleɪbɪəl; barˈlebɪəl/ *adj, n* (phon) (consonant) pronounced with both lips, eg /b, p, m, w/. (语音)由双唇发出的; 双唇的; 双唇辅音(如 /b, p, m, w/ 等辅音)。

bi·lat·eral /ˌbaɪˈlætərəl; baɪˈlætərəl/ *adj* of, on, with two sides; (legal) (of an agreement, etc) made between two (persons, governments). 两边的; 在两边的; 有两边的; (法律)(指协定等)双边的; 由二人或两个政府所订立的。 **~·ly** *adv* **~·ism** /-ɪzəm; -ɪzəm/ *n* principle based upon ~ agreements, esp of trade and financial agreements between countries. (专指两国间之商务及金融协定)基于双边协议的原则;互惠主义。

bil·berry /'bɪlbərɪ US: -berɪ; 'bɪlˌbɛrɪ/ *n* (*pl* **-ries**) fruit of a dwarf hardy shrub growing on heaths, etc in N Europe (also called 亦称作 *blaeberry, whortleberry*). 覆盆子(一种浆果, 产于北欧)。

bile /baɪl; baɪl/ *n* [U] brownish-yellow bitter liquid produced by the liver to help in digesting food; (med) disorder of the ~; (fig) peevishness, bad temper. 胆汁; (医)胆病; (喻)脾气暴躁。 **'~-duct,** (anat) tube carrying ~ to the duodenum. (解剖)输胆管(将胆汁输往十二指肠之管道)。 ⇨ the illus at **alimentary.** 参看 **alimentary** 之插图。

bilge /bɪldʒ; bɪldʒ/ *n* [U] **1** almost flat part of a ship's bottom, inside or outside; (also 亦作 **'~-water**) the dirty water that collects in a ship's ~. 舱(船底内部或外部的平坦部分); 舱污水(积于船底的污水)。 **2** (sl) foolish or worthless talk or writing. (俚)无聊的谈话或文章。

bil·har·zia /ˌbɪlˈhɑːzɪə; bɪlˈhɑrzɪə/ *n* tropical disease caused by parasites, flatworms in the blood and

bladder. 血吸虫病 (由血液及膀胱中之寄生虫，条虫所引起的一种热带病)。

bi·lin·gual /baɪˈlɪŋgwəl; baɪˈlɪŋgwəl/ *adj* **1** speaking, using, two languages (esp when these are learnt together in childhood): 能说两种语言的 (尤指幼年时代同时学会者); 采用两种语言的: *a ~ country*, one in which two languages are used officially. 并用两种语言为官方语言的国家; 双语国家。**2** written, printed, in two languages: 用两种文字写成或印成的: *a ~ dictionary*. 两种文字对照的词典; 双解词典。□ *n ~* person. 能说两种语言的人。

bil·ious /ˈbɪlɪəs; ˈbɪljəs/ *adj* **1** caused by too much bile: 因胆汁过多而引起的: *a ~ complaint/headache/attack*; 胆汁过多症 (偏头痛; 胆病发作); suffering from such complaints: 患胆汁症的; 患胆病的: *~ patients*. 患胆汁症的病人。**2** peevish; taking a gloomy view of life. 性情乖戾的; 悲观的。**~·ness** *n*

bilk /bɪlk; bɪlk/ *vt* [VP6A, 14] *~ sb (out) of*, escape paying money to; cheat (esp by running away): 逃避付帐给; 欺骗 (尤指借逃走而达到欺骗目的者): *He ~ed us out of the money*. 他把我们的钱骗走了。

bill¹ /bɪl; bɪl/ *n* (also 亦作 *~·hook*) long-handled tool with a curved blade used for cutting off branches of trees. (砍断树枝用的) 长柄弯刃之刀; 钩刀。

bill² /bɪl; bɪl/ *n* horny part of the mouth of some birds. 鸟喙 (鸟嘴之角质部分)。 ⇨ the illus at **bird**. 参看 bird 之插图。□ *vi* (of doves) stroke ~ with ~. (指鸽子) 接嘴; 触嘴。 *~ and coo*, (fig) exchange caresses. (喻) 互相抚爱。

bill³ /bɪl; bɪl/ *n* **1** written statement of charges for goods delivered or services rendered: 帐单; 发票: *It's wrong to leave a hotel without paying all your ~s*. 未付清帐而离开旅社是不对的。*There are some ~s to pay/to be paid*. 有些帐要付。⇨ **estimate²**, **quotation(3)**. **foot the ~**, ⇨ **foot²**. **2** written or printed notice, poster, placard: 招贴; 广告; 海报; 通告: *a theatre/concert ~*, giving information about a play, concert etc. 戏院 (音乐会) 之节目单或海报。*fill/fit the ~*, be, do, all that is required or expected. 合乎要求; 做所期望的一切。*head/top the ~*, be advertised at the head of the list, in large type, etc. 领衔主演; 挂头牌。 *~ of fare*, list of dishes to be served at a hotel, restaurant, etc; menu. (旅馆、餐馆等的) 菜单。'*~·board* *n* (US) structure for the display of advertisements, eg at the roadside (GB 英 = *hoarding*). (美) (路旁等处张贴广告的) 广告牌。'*~·poster*, '*~·sticker* *nn* person who pastes up ~s or placards (on walls, hoardings, etc). 张贴广告、海报等者。**3** (legal) proposed law, to be discussed by a parliament (called an *Act* when passed). (法律) (向国会提出待讨论的) 议案 (通过后即称为法案 Act)。**4** (US) banknote: (美) 钞票: *a ten-dollar ~*. 一张十元的钞票。 *~·fold* *n* (US) wallet for banknotes. (美) 钱夹; 钞票夹; 皮夹子。**5 B~ of Exchange**, order to a bank to pay a sum of money on a given date. 票据; 汇票。 *~s payable*, *~s* of exchange due for payment by the holder. 应付票据。 *~s receivable*, such *~s* due for payment to the holder. 应收票据。**6** certificate. 证明书。 *~ of entry*, (comm) certificate from the Customs to indicate final clearance of imported goods. (商) 入港申报单(海关所发给, 表明进口货品各项手续均已办妥)。 *~ of health*, (naut) certificate regarding infectious disease in a ship's crew. (航海) 船员的检疫证书。 *clean ~ of health*, **(a)** one certifying that there is no such disease. 无疫情的检疫证书; **(b)** (fig) assurance of good health. (喻) 优良证明; 有利于某事物之报告。 *~ of lading*, ⇨ **lading**. *~ of quantities*, ⇨ **quantity(4)**. *~ of sale*, ⇨ **sale(1)**. □ *vt* **1** [VP6A] make known by means of *~s(2)* or placards; announce, put, in a programme: 贴传单以通告; 在节目单中宣布; 置于节目单中: *Olivier was ~ed to appear as Lear*, It was announced that he would play the part of Lear. 奥利弗经宣布将饰演李尔王。**2** [VP14] *~ sb for sth*,

submit a ~ (1) to: 为某事物送帐单给某人: *~ a client for services rendered*. 为所提供的服务送帐单给客户。

bil·let¹ /ˈbɪlɪt; ˈbɪlɪt/ *n* **1** place (usu a private house) where soldiers are boarded and lodged: 营舍 (军队食宿处, 常指民房): *The troops are in ~s*, in ordinary homes, not in camp or barracks. 军队住宿于民房中(非军营中)。**2** (colloq) appointment or situation; job: (口) 职业; 职位; 差事: *a soft/cushy ~*, one not needing much effort. 轻松的差事。□ *vt* [VP6A, 14] *~ (on)*, place (troops) in *~s*: 安置 (军队) 于住宿之处: *soldiers on sb/on a town/on the villagers*. 指定士兵住于某人之家 (镇上、村民的房屋中)。

bil·let² /ˈbɪlɪt; ˈbɪlɪt/ *n* thick piece of firewood. 粗木柴。

bil·let-doux /ˌbɪleɪ ˈduː; ˈbɪlɪˈdu/ *n* (*pl* **billets-doux**, pronunciation unchanged) (复数发音不变) (F) (joc) love-letter. (法) (谑) 情书。

bill·hook /ˈbɪlhʊk; ˈbɪlhʊk/ *n* ⇨ **bill¹**.

bil·liards /ˈbɪlɪədz; ˈbɪljədz/ *n* (with *sing v*) game played with small, hard, heavy balls and long tapering sticks (called *cues*) on an oblong, cloth-covered table: (用单数动词)弹子戏; 撞球戏(打弹子的球杆叫 cue): *play ~*; 打弹子; 敲杆。 *have a game of ~*. 打一杆弹子。 *B~ is played by women as well as by men*. 弹子戏男女都玩。'**billiard-player**/**-room**/**-table**/**-marker** *nn* (*sing* in compounds 在复合词中用单数)。打弹子者(弹子房; 弹子台; 弹子记分员)。

bil·lings·gate /ˈbɪlɪŋzgeɪt; ˈbɪlɪŋz,get/ *n* [U] (from the name of a London fish-market) abusive language full of swear-words. (源出于伦敦一鱼市名)下流话; 粗鄙语。

bil·lion /ˈbɪlɪən; ˈbɪljən/ *n* (GB) million millions or 10^{12}; (US) thousand millions or 10^9. (英)万亿; (美)十亿。⇨ **App 4**. 参看附录四。

bil·low /ˈbɪləʊ; ˈbɪlo/ *n* (liter) great wave; (*pl*, poet) the sea; (fig) anything that sweeps along like a great wave. (文)巨浪; (复, 诗)海; (喻)如巨浪般横滚而来之物。□ *vi* [VP2C] rise or roll like waves: 如巨浪般汹涌奔腾: *The flames ~ed over the prairie*. 大火象浪涛一般滚过原野。 *~y adj* rising or moving like *~s*. 汹涌奔腾如巨浪的。

billy /ˈbɪlɪ; ˈbɪlɪ/ *n* (*pl* **-lies**) (esp in Australia) tin can (sometimes called a *billy-can*) with a lid and a wire handle, used as a kettle or cooking pot, esp in camping out. (尤用于澳洲)烧水煮饭用的洋铁罐(尤指露营时所用者, 又称 billy-can)。

billy-goat /ˈbɪlɪ gəʊt; ˈbɪlɪ,got/ *n* male goat. 雄山羊。 ⇨ **nanny-goat**.

billy-(h)o /ˈbɪlɪ (h)əʊ; ˈbɪlɪ (h)o/ *n* (dated *sl*) (过时俚语) *like ~*, vigorously: 有力地; 强烈地; 猛烈地: *raining/fighting like ~*. 雨下得很大(猛烈战斗)。

bil·tong /ˈbɪltɒŋ; ˈbɪltɔŋ/ *n* [U] (in S Africa) sundried salted meat cut into strips. (在南非洲)干咸肉条。

bi·met·al·lism /ˌbaɪˈmetəlɪzəm; baɪˈmetl,ɪzəm/ *n* [U] system of having two metals, eg gold and silver, with a fixed ratio to each other as legal tender. 复本位币制(如金银二本位制, 二者之间保持一定之兑换率)。**bi·met·al·lic** /ˌbaɪmɪˈtælɪk; ˌbaɪməˈtælɪk/ *adj*

bin /bɪn; bɪn/ *n* large rigid container or enclosed space, usu with a lid, for storing coal, grain, flour, bread, etc: (贮藏煤、谷、面粉、面包等, 通常有盖之)箱或仓: '*dustbin*, bin for rubbish, ashes, etc; 垃圾箱; '*litter bin*. 杂物箱。

bi·nary /ˈbaɪnərɪ; ˈbaɪnərɪ/ *adj* of or involving a pair or pairs: 一双的; 一对的; 二; 双; 复: *a '~ system*, (astron) two stars revolving round a common centre or one round the other. (天文) 双星系统 (二星球绕一共同中心而转, 或一星球绕另一星球而转)。 *the ~ scale*, (maths) with two digits, 0 and 1, as the base of the notation: (数学) 二进位法 (用二个数字, 0 和 1, 作为记法之基础):

1	2	3	4	5	6	7	8	9	10
1	10	11	100	101	110	111	1000	1001	1010

bind /baɪnd; baɪnd/ *vt, vi* (*pt, pp* **bound** /baʊnd; baʊnd/) **1** [VP6A, 15B, 14] ~ (*to*); ~ (*together*) (*with*), tie or fasten, with rope, etc: (以绳等)束; 缚; 捆; 绑; 扎: *They bound his legs (together) so that he shouldn't escape.* 他们把他的两腿绑起来使他不能逃跑。*Joan of Arc was bound to the stake and burnt to death.* 圣女贞德被绑在火刑柱上烧死。*The prisoner was bound hand and foot,* His arms and legs were tied. 那囚犯手足都被绑起来。(fig) (喻): *Commerce ~s the two countries together.* 贸易把这两国连结起来(使关系密切)。*We are bound to him by gratitude/by a close friendship.* 我们对他有感激之情(有亲密的友情)。**2** [VP6A, 14] ~ (*with*), secure the edge of sth with tape, braid, etc: (用带子、花边等)绲(边); 镶(边): ~ *the edge of a carpet,* to prevent fraying; 给地毯绲边(以防磨损); ~ *the cuffs of a jacket with leather.* 在短外衣的袖口绲皮边。**3** [VP6A, 15B] ~ (*up*), tie or wind sth round: 包扎; ~ *up a wound.* 包扎伤口。*Before sweeping the house she bound up her hair in a large handkerchief.* 在打扫房屋之前，她把她的头发用一条大手帕包起来。**4** [VP6A, 15A, B] ~ (*up*), fasten (sheets of paper) into a cover: 装订: ~ *a book;* 装订一本书; *a well-bound book;* 一本装订优良的书; *bound in leather;* 皮面精装的; ~ *up two books into one volume.* 将两本书装订成一册。[VP2A in *progressive tenses* only 仅用于进行式] *The new impression is ~ing,* is being bound. 新版本正在装订中。**5** [VP6A, 15B, 2A] ~ (*up/together*), hold or stick together in a solid mass: (使)结成硬块; (使)凝固: *Frost ~s the soil.* 霜使土壤凝结。*The ground is frost-bound,* frozen hard. 地面被霜冻结了。*Clay ~s* (= becomes hard) *when it is baked.* 粘土被烘则行固结。*Stones bound together with cement make good roads.* 石头与水泥粘结在一起可以建造好道路。*Some kinds of food ~s the bowels/are ~ing,* cause constipation. 有些种类的食物会引起便秘。**6** [VP17A, 14, 15B, 16B] ~ *sb to sth/to sth,* hold (sb) (by legal agreement, a promise, or under penalty) to a certain course of action: (因契约、允诺或处以惩罚而)使(某人)负有义务; 使(某人): ~ *sb to pay a debt;* 使某人负偿债; ~ *sb to secrecy,* make him promise to keep sth secret. 使某人答应守密。~ *oneself to do sth,* promise, undertake, guarantee, to do it. 答应、许诺、保证做某事。~ *sb over* (to keep the peace, etc), order that he must appear before the judge again (if he fails to keep the peace, etc). 命某人具结必须再出庭(如果他妨碍治安等)。~ *sb over* (*as an apprentice*) (*to sb*), make an agreement that he shall be one: 立约使某人为(某人之)学徒: *The boy was bound over as an apprentice to a carpenter.* 那男孩经立约为一木匠之学徒。**7** [VP2A] (dated *sl*) complain; carp: (过时俚语)抱怨; 吹毛求疵: *Oh, do stop ~ing!* 哦, 别再埋怨了! **8 bound**[5] for special uses of the *pp.* 过去分词之特殊用法参看 bound[5]. **~er n 1** person who ~s, esp a '*book-~er* 包扎者; 捆绑东西的人; 绲边者; (尤指)装订书籍者. **2** thing that ties or holds things together, eg a machine, or part of a machine, that cuts and ~s grain; loose cover for unbound magazines; substance such as cement or bitumen for joining things. 用以绑或接合之物; 扎结器(如刈禾扎结机, 或刈禾机之刈禾并扎结成捆之部分); (尤指)杂志之页面封面; 起粘固作用之物质(如水泥或沥青). '~·ery *n* place where books are bound. 装订厂; 装订所. ~·ing *adj* be ~ing on/upon, ~ (6) or oblige sb to do sth: 有约束力的; 有束缚力的: *an agreement that is ~ing on/upon all parties.* 对于各方面均有拘束力的协定。⇔ also **bind**(5). □ *n* [C, U] (esp) (尤指) **1** book-cover. 书籍的封皮。**2** strip, braid, etc for protecting an edge or a seam (of a garment, etc). (保护衣边或衣缝等的)花边; 绲条.

bind·weed /'baɪndwiːd; 'baɪndˌwid/ *n* [U] kinds of wild convolvulus. 旋花属的野生植物.

bine /baɪn; baɪn/ *n* flexible stem of various kinds of climbing plants, eg hops. (攀缘植物，例如蛇麻草之软而弯曲的)蔓; 茎; 藤.

binge /bɪndʒ; bɪndʒ/ *n* (*sl*) *have a ~; go on the ~,* drink and make merry. (俚)纵酒作乐.

bingo /'bɪŋɡəʊ; 'bɪŋɡo/ *n* [U] popular gambling game, played with cards on which numbered squares are covered as the numbers are called at random: 宾果游戏: (*attrib*) (用作定语) ~ *halls.* 宾果厅(玩宾果游戏的大厅).

bin·nacle /'bɪnəkl; 'bɪnəkl/ *n* (*naut*) non-magnetic stand for a ship's compass (usu in front of the helm). (航海)罗盘架; 罗经箱(无磁性, 通常在舵轮的前方).

bin·ocu·lars /bɪ'nɒkjuləz; bɪ'nɑkjələz/ *n pl* field-glasses; instrument with lenses for both eyes, making distant objects seem nearer. 双筒望远镜.

lens

a pair of binoculars

bi·nomial /baɪ'nəʊmɪəl; baɪ'nomɪəl/ *adj* (maths) made up of two numbers or algebraic expressions joined by + or − (eg $a^2 - 3b$). (数学)二项的; 二项式的(例如 $a^2 - 3b$).

bio·chem·is·try /ˌbaɪəʊ'kemɪstrɪ; ˌbaɪə'kemɪstrɪ/ *n* [U] chemistry of living organisms. 生物化学.

bio·de·grad·able /ˌbaɪəʊdɪ'greɪdəbl; ˌbaɪədɪ'greɪdəbl/ *adj* (of substances) that can be broken down by bacteria: (指物质)可被细菌破坏的: *Are plastic bags indestructible or ~?* 塑胶袋是不可毁灭的或是可被细菌破坏的?

bi·ogra·phy /baɪ'ɒɡrəfɪ; baɪ'ɑɡrəfɪ/ *n* **1** [C] person's life-history written by another. 传记. **2** [U] branch of literature dealing with the lives of persons. 传记文学. **bi·ogra·pher** /baɪ'ɒɡrəfə(r); baɪ'ɑɡrəfə/ *n* person who writes a ~, 传记作者. **bio·graphic, -i·cal** /ˌbaɪə'ɡræfɪk, -ɪkl; ˌbaɪə'ɡræfɪk, -ɪkl/ *adj* of ~. 传记的.

bi·ol·ogy /baɪ'ɒlədʒɪ; baɪ'ɑlədʒɪ/ *n* [U] science of the physical life of animals (= *zoology*) and plants (= *botany*). 生物学. **bi·ol·ogist** /baɪ'ɒlədʒɪst; baɪ'ɑlədʒɪst/ *n* student of, expert in, ~. 生物学者; 生物学家. **bio·logi·cal** /ˌbaɪə'lɒdʒɪkl; ˌbaɪə'lɑdʒɪkl/ *adj* of ~: 生物学的: *a biological laboratory/experiment.* 生物实验室(实验). **bio·logical 'warfare,** deliberate use of bacteria to spread disease. 生物战; 细菌战.

bi·opsy /'baɪɒpsɪ; 'baɪɑpsɪ/ *n* (*pl* -**sies**) [C] (med) removal and examination of tissue or fluid from a living body. (医)活体检视; 活组织检查. ⇔ **autopsy.**

bio·scope /'baɪəskəʊp; 'baɪəˌskop/ *n* (S Africa) cinema. (南非)电影映机.

bi·par·ti·san /ˌbaɪpɑː'tɪzæn *US:* baɪ'pɑːrtɪzn; baɪ'pɑrtəzn/ *adj* of, supported by, consisting of, two otherwise opposed (esp political) parties: 两党的; 两党所支持的; 由两党所组成的: *a ~ foreign policy.* 两党同支持的外交政策.

bi·ped /'baɪped; 'baɪpɛd/ *n* animal with only two feet. 两足动物.

bi·plane /'baɪpleɪn; 'baɪˌplen/ *n* aircraft with two pairs of wings, one above the other. 双翼飞机.

birch /bɜːtʃ; bɜtʃ/ *n* **1** [C] (kinds of) forest tree growing in northern countries; it has smooth bark and slender branches. 桦树; 赤杨; 桦木树(产于北方国家, 皮光滑, 枝细长). **2** [U] its wood, eg as used for making canoes. 桦木. **3** [C] (also 亦作 '**~-rod**) bundle of ~ twigs tied together and used formerly for punishing schoolboys. (从前用以体罚学童的)桦树条. □ *vt* [VP6A]

punish with a ~-rod. 用桦树条体罚。

bird /bɜːd ; bɜːd/ n 1 feathered creature with two legs and two wings, usu able to fly. 鸟; 禽类。⇨ the illus below and at **fowl, prey, rare, water.** 参看附图以及 fowl, prey, rare, water 之插图。 *A ~ in the hand is worth two in the bush,* (prov) Sth which one has, though small, is better than sth larger, which one has not. (谚) 手中的一只鸟胜过枝头上的两只鸟 (实际所有 之物, 其值虽小, 犹胜无把 握获得 之价值较大之物)。 *(strictly) for the ~s,* (sl) bad; worthless. (俚) (毫)无 价值的; (毫)无用处的。 *get the ~,* (sl) be hissed, scorned or rejected. (俚)被人发嘘声; 被哄; 被蔑视; 被弃。 *give sb the ~,* (sl) hiss, scorn or reject him. (俚)对某 人发嘘声; 轻视或弃绝某人。 *kill two ~s with one stone,* achieve two aims at once. 一石二鸟; 一箭双 雕; 一举两得。 '~-**cage** n cage for a ~ or ~s. 鸟笼。 '~-**fancier** n person who knows about, collects, breeds or sells ~s. 懂鸟者; 养鸟者; 鸟商。 '~**lime** n sticky substance put on branches to catch ~s. (涂于树枝上以 捕鸟的)粘鸟胶。 ,~'s-'**eye** '**view** n wide view seen from high up; (fig) general survey of a subject. 鸟瞰; (喻) (某一科目之) 概览。 '~-**nesting** n hunting for birds' nests (to get the eggs). 猎鸟巢(以取蛋)。 '~-**watch** vi

[VP2A] study birds in their natural state; 研究鸟类之 自然状态; hence, 由此产生, '~-**watcher** n person who does this; 研究鸟类之自然状态者; hence, 由此产生, '~-**watching** n [U]. ⇨ also **feather**[1], **passage(1), prey. 2** (colloq) person: (口)人: *an odd/wise ~;* 一 个怪人(聪明人); *a cunning old ~.* 一个狡猾的老家伙。 **3** (GB sl) young woman. (英俚)年轻的女郎; 小妞。

bir·etta /brˈretə; beˈrstə/ n [C] (pl ~s) square cap worn by RC and some Anglican priests. (天主教及某些 英国国教僧侣所戴的)四角帽; 法冠。

biro /ˈbaɪərəu; ˈbaɪro/ n [C] (pl ~s) (P) (kind of) ball-pen. (商标)一种圆珠笔; 拜乐牌圆珠笔。

birth /bɜːθ; bɜːθ/ n 1 [U] (process of) being born, coming into the world; [C] instance of this: 出生; 诞 生; 诞生: *The baby weighed seven pounds at ~,* when it was born. 那婴儿生下来七磅重。*The boy has been delicate from (his) ~,* has been weak in health since he was born. 那男孩从生下来一直身体很弱。 *Cats sometimes have four or five young at a ~.* 猫有时一窝生四只或五 只小猫。 *There were 167 more ~s than deaths in the town last year.* 此镇去年出生者较死亡者多一百六十七人。 *give ~ to,* bring into the world; (fig) produce: 生产 (婴儿); (喻)产生; 造成: *give ~ to a child/a poem/a*

KINGFISHER

GREAT TIT

NIGHTINGALE

bill
feather — breast
tail
wing
leg
claw
SKYLARK
foot

SPARROW

ROBIN

SWIFT

SWALLOW

CROW

CUCKOO

PIGEON

small land birds

dispute. 生小孩(作出一首诗; 造成纷争). **2** [U] origin, descent: 起源; 血统; 出身: *She is Russian by ~ and British by marriage.* 她原来是俄国人, 但嫁给英国人(而成了英国人). **be of good ~**, (旧用法)出身高尚门第. '**~-control** *n* [U] (method of) preventing unwanted conception(2). 节制生育(法). '**~-day** *n* (anniversary of the day of one's ~. 生日;生日纪念. '**~-mark** *n* mark on the body at or from ~. 胎记; 胎痣. '**~-place** *n* house or district in which one was born. 出生的房子; 出生地; 诞生地. '**~-rate** *n* number of ~s in one year for every 1000 persons. 出生率(每年每一千人中之婴儿出生数目). '**~-right** *n* any of various rights, privileges and properties to which a person has a right as a member of his family, a citizen of his country, etc. (对于各种权利、特权和财产的)与生俱来的权利; 生为某家庭之一份子或某国之公民应享之权利; 生得权.

bis·cuit /'bɪskɪt; 'bɪskɪt/ *n* [C] **1** flat, thin, crisp cake of many kinds, sweetened or unsweetened. 饼干. **take the ~**, (sl) be the best/worst at something; be surprising. (俚) 成为前所未见或前所未闻之最好 (最坏) 事物; 令人惊讶. **2** (US) bread dough baked in small shapes (美小点心). **3** light-brown. 淡棕色; 浅褐色.

bi·sect /baɪ'sekt; baɪ'sɛkt/ *vt* [VP6A] cut or divide into two (usu equal) parts. 切或分为 (通常相等的) 两分. **bi·sec·tion** /baɪ'sekʃn; baɪ'sɛkʃən/ *n* [U] division into two (equal) parts. 分而为二; 二等分.

bi·sex·ual /ˌbaɪ'sekʃuəl/ *adj* of two sexes; having both male and female sexual organs; sexually attracted to either sex. 两性的; 兼具雌雄两性性器官的; 对男女两性均感兴趣的; 阴阳的. □ *n* individual showing one of these characteristics. 阴阳人; 两性体. **~·ity** /ˌbaɪseksʃu'ælɪtɪ; ˌbaɪseksʃu'ælɪtɪ/ *n* [U] condition of being ~. 兼具两性性; 雌雄同体.

bishop /'bɪʃəp; 'bɪʃəp/ *n* **1** Christian clergyman of high rank who organizes the work of the Church in a city or district. 主教(主管市或一教区之教务). ⇨ the illus at **vestment**. 参看 vestment 之插图. ⇨ **diocese. ~·ric** /-rɪk; -rɪk/ *n* office of a ~; district under a ~. 主教职; 主教辖区. **2** chess piece, ⇨ the illus at **chess**. 主教 (国际象棋中的一棋子, 参看 chess 之插图).

bis·muth /'bɪzməθ; 'bɪzməθ/ *n* [U] reddish-white metal (symbol **Bi**), used in alloys; compound of this used medically, eg for stomach troubles. 铋(带红之白色金属, 化学符号 Bi, 用于合金; 铋的化合物作医药用, 如治疗胃病).

bi·son /'baɪsn; 'baɪsn/ *n* (*pl* unchanged) (复数不变) European wild ox; American buffalo. 欧洲的野牛; 美洲野牛. ⇨ the illus at **large**. 参看 large 之插图.

bis·tro /'biːstrəʊ; 'bɪstro/ *n* [C] (*pl* ~s) small, cheap restaurant; (in France) small bar[13] or nightclub. 小餐馆; (法国之)小酒吧; 小型夜总会.

bit[1] /bɪt; bɪt/ *n* **1** mouth-piece (metal bar) forming part of a horse's bridle. 马嚼子; 马衔. ⇨ the illus at **harness**. 参看 harness 之插图. **take the bit between one's teeth**, (of a horse) run away out of control; (fig) apply oneself to sth difficult or risky or distasteful. 咬住马)脱缰逃跑; (喻)集中精力去做艰难、冒险或讨厌之事. **2** part of a tool that cuts or grips when twisted; tool for boring or drilling holes, fitted into a *drill* or a *brace*. 工具之切割或抓的部分; (钻子的)钻头; 锥. ⇨ the illus at **drill, brace.** 参看 drill, brace 之插图.

bit[2] /bɪt; bɪt/ *n* **1** small piece of anything: 一小块; 一点点: *He took some paper and a few bits of wood and soon made a fire.* 他拿了一些纸和几片木头, 不久就生了一堆火. *He ate every bit of* (= all) *his dinner.* 他把他的一份晚餐吃得精光. *He has saved a nice bit* (= a good sum) *of money.* 他已积蓄了相当数目的一笔钱. **bit by bit,** slowly, gradually. 一点一点地; 慢慢地; 逐渐地. **a bit at a time,** by degrees. 一步一步地; 逐渐地. **every bit as (good, etc)**, equally (good, etc). 同样地(好等).

do one's bit, perform one's share of a task; give as much help as is expected of one. 做分内之事; 尽力帮助. **wait a bit,** a short time. 等一会儿. **a bit,** rather: 相当地; 有点: *She's feeling a bit tired.* 她觉得有点疲倦. **a bit of a,** rather a: 相当地: *He's a bit of a coward.* 他是相当胆小的. **a bit of all right,** (GB sl) very fine. (英俚)很不错. **not a bit,** not at all; not in the least: 一点也不; 毫不: *He's not a bit better.* 他一点也没有好. *He doesn't care a bit.* 他一点也不在乎. *It's not a bit of use,* It's quite useless. 它一点用处也没有. *not a bit of it,* not at all (used as a strong denial): 一点也没有; 毫不(用作强烈的否认): *You'd think she'd be tired after such a long journey, but not a bit of it!* 你会以为在这样一次长途旅行之后她会疲倦, 可是一点也不(她一点也不会感到疲倦). **pull/cut/tear sth to bits,** into small pieces. 将某物扯 (切, 撕) 成碎块. **go/come to bits,** into small pieces. 成为碎块; 变成碎片. **2** (used colloq, like *piece*, with *news, advice, luck*): (口, 同 piece, 与 news, advice, luck 连用): *a bit of good advice.* 一个忠告. **3** (a) small coin: 小钱币: *threepenny bit,* (former) coin (GB) worth threepence. (昔时英国之) 三便士的钱币. (b) (US) 12½ cents. (美) 一角二分半. **4** (colloq, esp US) area common to a group of subjects, attitudes, etc: (口, 尤美) 一组题目, 看法等的共同领域: *She couldn't accept the whole drug-culture bit.* 她无法接受吸毒之风气.

bit[3] /bɪt; bɪt/ *n* (comp) unit of information expressed as a choice between two possibilities. (电脑)位元; 数元.

bit[4] /bɪt; bɪt/ ⇨ **bite**[1].

bitch /bɪtʃ; bɪtʃ/ *n* **1** female dog, fox, otter or wolf. 母狗; 母狐; 母獭; 母狼. **2** △ (derog sl) spiteful woman. (讳)(贬唾) 恶毒的女人; 坏女人; 泼妇. □ *vi* [VP2A] (colloq) complain in a sour way; speak spitefully to or about sb or sth. (口)尖刻地发牢骚; 不怀好意地搬弄是非. **~y** *adj* (colloq) spiteful. (口)恶意的.

bite[1] /baɪt; baɪt/ *vt, vi* (*pt* bit /bɪt; bɪt/, *pp* bitten /'bɪtn; 'bɪtn/). **1** [VP6A, 15B, 2A, 3A] ~ (*into*), cut into with the teeth: 咬: *The dog bit me in the leg.* 那狗咬了我的腿. *Does your dog ~, is it in the habit of biting people?* 你的狗咬人吗? *He bit into the peach.* 他咬取桃子. **~ at sth,** try to get it with the teeth; snap at. 用牙去咬某物(以图得到它). **~ off,** cut off with the teeth: 咬下来: *He bit off a large piece of the apple.* 他咬下一大块苹果. **~ off more than one can chew,** attempt too much. 贪多嚼不烂(从事太多的工作, 而无力完成). **(have) sth to ~ on,** sth to get one's teeth into; (fig) sth definite to do, examine, etc. (有)可咬的东西; (喻)(有)明确可为、可查考的事物; (有)可资把持之东西. **~ the dust,** (colloq) fall to the ground; be killed. (口)(喻)倒下; 被杀; 阵亡. **~ one's lips,** try to conceal one's anger or annoyance. 咬唇以图掩饰愤怒或厌恶. **once bitten twice shy,** (prov) a person who has been cheated, hurt, etc is likely to be cautious afterwards. (谚)一回上当二回乖; 上一次当学一次乖. **the biter bitten,** the person who intended to cheat was himself cheated. 欲骗人者反而被人骗; 害人反害己. **2** [VP6A] **(a)** (of fleas, mosquitoes, etc) sting: (指跳蚤、蚊子等)刺: *He was badly bitten by the mosquitoes.* 他被蚊子咬得很厉害. **(b)** (of fish) accept the bait: (指鱼)吃饵; 上钩: *The fish wouldn't ~.* 这些鱼不肯吃饵. *I tried to sell him my old car but he wouldn't ~,* (fig) would not consider the suggestion. (喻)我试图把我的旧车卖给他, 但他不肯上钩(不予考虑). **3** [VP6A, 2A, 3A] ~ (*into*), cause a smarting pain; to injure: 使感觉剧痛; 刺痛; 伤害: *His fingers were bitten by the frost/were frost-bitten.* 他的手指冻伤了. *Mustard and pepper ~ the tongue.* 芥末和胡椒粉刺痛舌头. *Strong acids ~ (into) metals,* make holes in them. 强酸能腐蚀金属. **4** [VP6A, 2A] take strong hold of; grip: 紧握; 抓紧: *The rails were covered with ice and the wheels did not ~.* 铁轨上面覆盖着冰, 车轮卡不住轨 (不能前行). **bit·ing** *adj* sharp; cutting: 尖刻的; 刺痛的: *a biting wind;* 刺骨

的寒风; *biting words.* 尖刻的话. **bit·ing·ly** *adv*

bite[2] /baɪt; baɪt/ *n* **1** act of biting: 咬: *eating sth at one* ~. 一口将某物吃下。 **2** injury resulting from a ~ or sting: 咬伤;叮: *His face was covered with insect* ~*s.* 他满脸都是蚊虫的咬伤。 **3** piece cut off by biting. 咬下的一块。 **4** (colloq) food to eat: (口) 食物: *I haven't had a* ~ *since morning,* have eaten nothing. 我从早晨到现在一口东西都未吃过。 **5** taking bait from a hook by fish: 鱼之吞饵;上钩: *He had been fishing all morning but hadn't had a* ~. 他钓了一上午的鱼, 但没有鱼上钩。 **6** [U] sharpness; sting: 尖刻;刺痛: *There's a* ~ *in the air this morning.* 今天早晨有点寒风刺骨。 **7** [U] grip; hold: 紧抓; 紧握: *a file/screw with plenty of* ~. 锐利的锉子(扭得牢的螺丝钉)。

bit·ten /ˈbɪtn; ˈbɪtn/ ⇨ **bite**[1].

bit·ter /ˈbɪtə(r); ˈbɪtə/ *adj* **1** tasting like beer or unsweetened coffee. 味道似啤酒或未加糖之咖啡的; 苦的。 ,~'**sweet** *adj* sweet but with a ~ taste at the end; (fig) pleasant but with a mixture of sth unpleasant. 甜的但最后带苦味的; 甜中带苦的; (喻) 乐中带苦的。 **2** unwelcome to the mind; hard to bear; causing sorrow: 难过的; 难以忍受的; 引起悲伤的; 痛苦的: ~ *hardships/ experiences.* 难以忍受的艰辛 (痛苦的经历)。 *His failure to pass the examination was a* ~ *disappointment.* 他考试失败是一件极令人失望的事。 *a* ~ *pill to swallow,* sth unpleasant to accept. 苦药丸; 勉强接受的苦事。 **3** filled with, showing, caused by, envy, hate, remorse, or disappointment: 充满或显示嫉妒、憎恨、懊悔或失望之情绪的; 由上述情绪所引起的: ~ *quarrels/words/ enemies/reproaches/tears.* 厉害的争吵(怨言; 死敌; 苛责/伤心泪)。 **4** piercingly cold: 寒冷刺骨的: *a* ~ *wind.* 刺骨的寒风。 **5** *to the* ~ *end,* until all that is possible has been done: (奋斗) 到底;拚命: *fight to the* ~ *end.* 战斗到底。 □ *n* **1** bitterness. 苦。 *take the* ~ *with the sweet,* accept misfortune as well as good fortune. 甘与苦都接受;不仅接受幸运, 也要接受不幸。 Cf 参较 *take the rough with the smooth,* which is more usu. 不快意的和快意的事同要接受 (为较常用之成语)。 **2** [U] ~ beer, ie heavily flavoured with hops: 苦啤酒: *a pint of* ~. 一品脱苦啤酒。 **3** (*pl*) liquor made from herbs, fruits, etc taken to help digestion or used to flavour gin, etc: (复) 苦味药酒 (用药草、果实等浸制成, 饮之能帮助消化, 或加于长松子酒以增添味): *orange* ~*s; bitter* ~*s; gin and* ~*s.* 杜松子药酒。 ~**·ly** *adv* ~**·ness** *n*

bit·tern /ˈbɪtən; ˈbɪtən/ *n* any of several kinds of wading birds that live on marshes, esp the kind known for its booming note. 麻鳽 (生活于沼泽地带之数种涉禽, 尤指能发低沉之鸣声者)。 ⇨ the illus at **water**. 参看 water 之插图。

bitu·men /ˈbɪtjʊmən; bɪˈtjumən/ *n* [U] black, sticky substance (from petroleum), used for making roads, etc; mineral pitch; asphalt. 沥青; 地沥青。 **bit·umi·nous** /bɪˈtjuːmɪnəs US: -ˈtuː-; bɪˈtjumənəs/ *adj* containing ~ or tar: 含沥青的; *bituminous coal,* burning with smoky yellow flames. 沥青炭; 沥青煤 (燃烧时发出含浓烟之黄色火焰)。

bi·valve /ˈbaɪvælv; ˈbaɪˌvælv/ *n* (zool) mollusc with a hinged double shell, eg an oyster, a mussel, a clam. (动物) 双壳贝类; 瓣鳃类 (如蚝、蛤贝、蛤等)。

biv·ouac /ˈbɪvuæk; ˈbɪvʊˌæk/ *n* soldiers' temporary camp without tents or other cover. (士兵之临时的) 野营 (无篷帐或其他遮盖); 露天营地。 □ *vi* (*pt, pp* **bivouacked**) [VP2A] make a ~; stay in a ~. 扎野营;露宿于野营中。

biz /bɪz; bɪz/ *n* (sl) (俚)=business: *Good biz!* Well done! 做得好! '**show·biz**, (sl) (providing and managing) popular entertainment. (俚) (筹备及安排) 一般之娱乐节目; 余兴节目。

bi·zarre /bɪˈzɑː(r); bɪˈzɑr/ *adj* grotesque; odd. 古怪的; 怪异的; 奇异的。

bi·zonal /ˌbaɪˈzəʊnl; ˈbaɪˌzonl/ *adj* of two zones. 两区的。

blab /blæb; blæb/ *vt, vi* (**-bb-**) [VP6A, 15B, 2A] (colloq) talk foolishly or indiscreetly: (口) 胡扯; 乱谈: *Don't* ~! 不要胡扯! ~ (*out*), tell (a secret): 泄漏(秘密): ~ *out a secret.* 泄漏秘密。

blab·ber /ˈblæbə(r); ˈblæbə/ *vt, vi*=**blab**. '~**-mouth** *n* person who ~s. 乱讲话的人; 泄密者。

black /blæk; blæk/ *adj* (**-er, -est**) **1** without light or almost without light; the colour of this printing-ink; opposite to white. 黑暗的; 黑色的; 黑的。 *be* ~ *and blue,* covered with bruises. 遍布青一块、紫一块的伤痕。 ~ *in the face,* dark red or purple (with anger or because of making great efforts). (因愤怒或使劲而) 脸色发红或发紫; 脸色发青。 *be in sb's* ~ *book(s),* ⇨ **book**[1](6). *look* ~ *at sb; give sb a* ~ *look,* look at him angrily. 怒视某人。 *not so* ~ *as one is painted,* not so bad as one is said to be. 不象传闻那么坏。 **2** (various uses, mostly to intensify the meaning of the *n*): (各种用法, 大都用以加强名词的意义): ~ *despair,* deep, dismal; 深深的绝望; ~ *tidings,* sad news, causing despair; 坏消息; 令人绝望的消息; ~ *deeds,* wicked; 黑心的事; *in one of his* ~ *moods,* silent and bad-tempered. 在他一阵默然不悦的心情中。 **3** (of work in a factory, shipyard, etc during a strike; of the materials, etc) not to be done, handled, etc: (指罢工期间工厂、船坞等中之工作; 指材料等) 不予完成、处理等的: *The strikers declared the work/cargo* ~. 罢工者宣布该工作不予完成 (船货不予处理)。 **4** (compounds, etc) (复合词等) ~ *and white,* ink drawing. 墨画。 (*have sth down*) *in* ~ *and white,* (have it) recorded in writing or print. (把某事) 记录下来; 写在纸上; 印出来。 ~ *art,* magic, used for evil purposes. 魔术; 妖术。 ~ *ball vt* prevent (sb) from being elected a member of a club by voting against him at a secret ballot. (在秘密投票中) 投反对票以阻止 (某人) 被选为会员。 '~**·beetle** *n* cockroach. 蟑螂。 '~**·berry** /ˈblækbəri US: -berɪ; ˈblækˌberɪ/ *n* (*pl* **-ries**) small berry, which when ripe, growing wild on bushes (called *brambles*): 黑莓 (一种小浆果, 成熟时呈黑色, 野生于称为悬钩子之灌木上): *go* ~*berrying* /-berɪŋ; -berɪŋ/, go out gathering ~berries. 出去采黑莓。 ⇨ the illus at **fruit**. 参看 fruit 之插图。 '~**·bird** *n* common European songbird. 山鸟类 (一种常见于欧洲之鸣禽)。 '~**·board** *n* board used in schools for writing and drawing on with chalk. 黑板。 ,~ '**box** *n* device for recording information about the performance of an aircraft. 黑盒 (记录飞机作业资料的装置)。 ,~ '**coffee** *n* coffee without milk, usu strong. 纯咖啡; 黑咖啡 (不加牛奶之咖啡, 通常很浓)。 ,~ '**comedy** *n* (theatre) comedy with a tragic element or basic pessimism, usu heavily ironical. (戏剧) 有悲剧或悲观成分的喜剧 (通常富于讽刺性)。 cf 参较 *sick joke.* the '**B**~ **Country,** the smoky, industrial area in Staffordshire and Warwickshire. 在斯塔福德郡及沃里克郡之烟雾弥漫的工厂区域。 ,~'**cur·rant** *n* kind of currant with ~ fruit. 黑醋栗。 ⇨ **currant**(2). the ,~ '**flag,** flag formerly

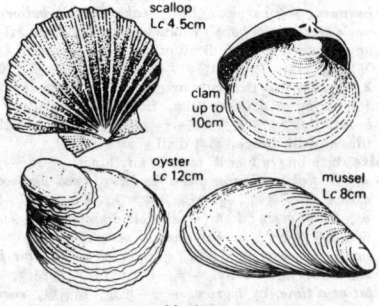

scallop
Lc 4.5cm

clam
up to
10cm

oyster
Lc 12cm

mussel
Lc 8cm

bivalves

used by pirates (sea-robbers); flag once used at prisons as a signal that a murderer had been executed by hanging. 黑旗(从前为海盗所用者,亦曾用于监狱,表示有杀人犯被处死刑). ,~ 'frost n hard frost without rime. 严霜; 严霜. '~·guard / 'blɑːgɑːd; 'blægəd/ n person who is quite without honour; scoundrel. 下流的人; 无赖; 流氓, 流氓. ⇨ vt call (sb) a ~ guard; use very bad language about or to (sb). 骂(某人)下流; 辱骂(某人). '~·guard·ly /'blægədlɪ/; 'blægədlɪ/ adj dishonest and immoral; like a ~guardly trick. 卑鄙的手段。 '~·head n (kind of) pimple on the skin, the top being ~. 尖头呈黑色之丘疹;黑头粉刺。 ,~ 'hole n (astron) region in space from which no matter or radiation (eg light) can escape. (天文)黑洞(太空中一区域,不会放出任何物质或辐射,如光等)。 ,~ 'ice n ice, esp on a road surface, which is almost invisible and dangerous to drive on. 黑冰(尤指路面上所结之几乎看不见的冰,驾车于其上有危险)。 ~·'lead n [U] soft, grey-black solid (plumbago, or graphite) used for lead pencils, polishing and as a lubricant. 石墨, 黑铅(用于制铅笔心, 打光及作润滑剂). ⇨ vt polish, eg a fireplace, with ~·lead. 用石墨打光(壁炉等)。 '~·leg n person who offers to work when the regular workers are on strike. 在正式工人罢工期间自求做工者; 不参加罢工的工人。 ⇨ vi, vt (-gg-) act as ~leg; betray (fellow workers) by doing this. 在罢工期间背叛(其他工人)而自行上工. '~·list n list of persons who are considered dangerous or who are to be punished. 黑名单(内列被认为系危险人物或应受惩罚者). ⇨ vt enter the name of (sb) on a ~list. 把(某人)列入黑名单。 ~ 'magic n witchcraft. 魔术; 妖术. '~·mail vt, n [U] (force sb to make a) payment of money for not making known sth discreditable about him. 敲诈; 勒索; 敲诈或勒索之款. Hence, 由此产生, '~·mailer n person who does this. 敲诈者; 勒索者. ⇨ Ma·ria /məˈraɪə; məˈraɪə/ n van for taking prisoners from and to jail. 囚车。 ,~ 'mark n (fig) mark(4) of bad conduct, failure, etc: (喻)行为不良、失败等之污点: Her continual lateness was a ~ mark against her promotion. 她不断的迟到是不利于她升职的一个污点。 '~·market n unlawful buying and selling of goods, currencies, etc that are officially controlled; place where such trading is carried on. 黑市交易(对于官方控制之货物、货币等之非法买卖); 黑市; 进行黑市交易之场所. ,~·marke'teer /ˌmɑːkɪˈtɪə(r);ˌmɑrkɪˈtɪr/ n person carrying on this trade. 经营黑市交易者;黑市商人. ,~ 'mass n worship of the RC Mass, performed for Satan instead of God. 黑弥撒(冒渎的模仿天主教之弥撒,所赞颂者是撒旦,而非上帝). '~·out n (a) (during wartime) the keeping of all buildings, etc, dark (by curtains, etc, in windows, by having no street-lighting, etc) in order to prevent any light being seen, esp from the air. (战时之)灯火管制(尤指为防空袭而实施者). (b) temporary complete failure of the memory or consciousness; (esp flying) temporary blindness caused by a sudden turn or a change in speed. 暂时的丧失记忆或知觉; (尤指)黑晕(飞行中因突然转向或改变速度所致的暂时性失明). (c) extinguishing of all lights on the stage of a theatre, eg for a change of scenery. 舞台上之熄灯(如为换布景). ⇨ ~ out vt, vi [VP15B, 2A] cause a ~out ((a) and (c) above); lose one's memory, etc, temporarily. 实施灯火管制; 熄去舞台上的全部灯光; 熄灯; 暂时失去记忆等. ,B~ 'Panther n (US, 1960's) member of a militant B~ Power group. 黑豹党党徒(美国黑人二十世纪六十年代黑权运动中之战斗份子). ,B~ 'Power n (US, 1960's) militant movement for civil rights for Negroes. 黑权运动(美国二十世纪六十年代争取黑人民权之战斗运动). ,~ 'pudding n sausage made of blood, suet, barley, etc. (用血、板油、大麦等制成的)黑香肠. B~ 'Sash n (S Africa) women's anti-apartheid organization. (南非)黑带组织(反对种族隔离制度之妇女组织). ,~ 'sheep n good-for-nothing person. 无用的人; 名誉很坏的人; 害群之马; 败家子.

'B~·shirt n member of the former Italian Fascist party. (昔之)意大利黑衫党(法西斯党)党员. '~·smith n man who makes and repairs things of iron, esp a shoer of horses. 铁匠; (尤指)马蹄铁匠. '~·spot n place (eg on a road) where accidents often happen. (道路等之)常发生意外之处. '~·thorn n thorny shrub which has white blossom before the leaves appear and purple fruit (sloe) like a small plum. 樱属的一种有刺灌木(在未发叶前开白花, 其果实称作 sloe, 呈紫色, 似小李子). ~·water 'fever n tropical disease with bloody urine. 黑水热; 黑尿热(带血尿之一种热带病). ⇨ n 1 [U] colour: 黑色: He was dressed in ~, in ~ clothes. 他穿着黑色衣服. 2 [U] = paint or dye. 黑色颜料或染料. 3 [C] particle of soot. 煤烟之微粒. 4 [C] Negro (formerly derog, but now widely used). 黑人(从前为贬抑语, 但今已广泛使用). 5 the ~, credit side of business accounts. (帐目之)贷方. be in/get into the ~, have/get assets that exceed liabilities. 有赢余. ⇨ red n(4). ⇨ vt [VP6A] 1 make ~, polish (boots, etc), with blacking. 使变黑: 用鞋油擦(靴等). 2 declare ~(3): 宣布…不予完成或处理: The strikers ~ed the ship/the cargo. 罢工者宣布不完成那艘船(不处理船货). ~ out, ⇨ ~out above

black·a·moor /'blækəmʊə(r); 'blækə,mʊr/ n (old use, hum or derog) black person. (旧用法, 谐或贬)黑人.

blacken /'blækən; 'blækən/ vt, vi 1 [VP6A, 2A] make or become black. 使黑; 变黑. 2 [VP6A] ~ (sb's name), speak evil of (sb's character). 说(某人)的坏话; 毁谤.

black·ing /'blækɪŋ; 'blækɪŋ/ n [U] black paste or liquid for polishing shoes (now usu 今通常作 shoe polish). 黑色鞋油.

blad·der /'blædə(r); 'blædə/ n 1 bag of skin in which urine collects in human and animal bodies. 膀胱. ⇨ the illus at kidney. 参看 kidney 之插图. 2 such a bag, or a bag of rubber, etc, that can be filled with air, eg the rubber ~ in a football. 可充气之囊袋或橡皮囊袋(如足球内之球胆).

blade /bleɪd; bled/ n 1 flattened cutting part of a knife, sword, chisel, etc: (刀、剑、凿等的)刃: a pocket-knife with two ~s; (可折合的)双刃小刀; a packet of five razor ~s. 一包五片的刮胡刀刀片. ⇨ the illus at razor. 参看 razor 之插图. 2 sword; swordsman. 剑; 剑术家; 剑手. 3 flat wide part of an oar (the part that goes into the water), bat, propeller, etc. 桨叶; (板球棒等的)击球板; 螺旋桨叶(等). 4 flat, long, narrow leaf, esp of grass and cereals (wheat, barley, etc). (扁平而狭长之)草叶; 叶片; 叶身; 叶尖; (小麦、大麦等之)叶片.

blae·ber·ry /'bleɪbərɪ US: -berɪ; 'blebərɪ/ n = bilberry.

blah /blɑː; blɑ/ n [U] (colloq) high-sounding but meaningless talk or writing. (口)浮夸而无意义的谈话或文章; 胡说.

blame /bleɪm; blem/ vt [VP6A, 14] ~ sb (for sth); ~ sth on sb, fix on sb the responsibility for sth done (badly or wrongly) or not done: 责备; 归咎(某事于某人): Bad workmen often ~ their tools. 拙劣的工人常常怪他们的工具不好. He ~d his teacher for his failure. 他把他的失败归咎于他的老师. He ~d his failure on his teacher. 他把他的失败归咎于他的老师. I have nothing to ~ myself for. 我没有什么可责备自己的. be to ~, deserve censure: 应受谴责;应负责任: Who is to ~ for starting the fire, Whom have we to find fault with? 火灾之引起应由谁负其咎? I am in no way to ~, and not in any way responsible. 怎么说我都不应负其责. ⇨ n [U] 1 responsibility for sth done (badly or wrongly) or not done: 对已做或未做事之责任的责任; 过失; 咎: Where does the ~ lie for our failure, Who or what is responsible; 我们的失败应归咎何人(或何事)? bear/take the ~ (for sth), take the responsibility. (将某事)负责; 负咎. put/lay the ~ on sb (for sth), make him responsible. (将某事)归咎于某人. 2 finding fault:

责难；非难；挑剔；指摘：*If you don't do the work well, you will incur ~*, people will find fault. 如果你不把工作做好, 你将会招人责难。~**·less** *adj* free from ~ or faults; innocent: 无可责备的; 无过失的: *I am ~less in this matter.* 在这件事中, 我是无过失的。~**·less·ly** *adv* ~**·worthy** /'bleɪmwɜːr; 'blem,wɜːrl/ *adj* deserving ~. 应受责备的。

blanch /blɑːntʃ US: blæntʃ; blæntʃ/ *vt, vi* [VP6A, 2A] make or become pale or white, eg by taking the skin off almonds, by not letting light get to plants make or become pale with fear, cold, etc. 使变白(如将杏仁皮剥去或不让光线射及植物); 变白; (因恐惧、寒冷等而)使变苍白; 变苍白。

blanc·mange /blə'mɒnʒ; blə'mɑnʒ/ *n* [C, U] jelly made in a mould with milk: 牛奶冻; 用牛奶在模型中制成的一种胶状点心: ~ *powder*, mixture of powdered milk, powdered gelatine, etc to make kinds of ~. 制此种点心之粉(系奶粉、胶粉等之混合物)。

bland /blænd/ *adj* 1 gentle or polite in manner or talk (usu in order to ingratiate oneself). (通常指为了人好印象而)态度或谈话温文有礼的。2 (of air, food, drink) mild; comforting. (指空气、食物、饮料)温和的; 使人舒适的。3 featureless; uninteresting. 无特色的; 枯燥无味的; 不动人的。~**·ly** *adv* ~**·ness** *n*

bland·ish·ment /'blændɪʃmənt; 'blændɪʃmənt/ *n* (usu *pl*) (formal) soft and gentle ways and speech intended to make sb do sth; flattery; coaxing. (通常用复数)(正式用语)为诱使某人做某事而表现的温和态度与言语; 谄媚; 哄诱。

blank /blæŋk; blæŋk/ *adj* 1 (of paper, parts of a document, etc) with nothing written, printed or drawn on it: (指纸, 部分文件等)空白的; 未写字、印字或画图的: *a ~ sheet of paper*, 一张白纸; *a ~ page/space* 空白的一页(一块空白)。~ **'bill**, Bill of Exchange on which the name of the person to be paid is not stated. 不记名汇票(受款人姓名未写明者)。,~ **'cheque**, one with the amount left for the payee to fill in. (金额由受款人自行填写的)空白支票。*give sb a ~ cheque*, (fig) full power to act as he thinks best. (喻)请某人全权处理。2 empty; without interest or expression: 茫然的; 空虚的; 无兴趣的; 无表情的: *There was a ~ look on his face*, He seemed not to be interested, not to understand, etc. 他的脸上毫无表情。*He looked ~*, puzzled. 他看起来似感困惑。*His future looks ~*, seems to be empty and dull. 他的前途似很黯淡。*My mind went ~*, I could not recall things, esp things I needed to be aware of. 我心中茫然(脑中一片空白, 什么都忘了)。,~ **'cartridge**, with a charge of powder, but no bullet. 空包弹(有火药而无弹丸的子弹)。~ **'verse**, (usu lines of ten syllables) without rhyme. 无韵诗(通常一行十个音节)。,~ **'wall**, one with no door, window or other opening. 无门窗或洞孔的墙。*come up against a ~ wall*, (fig) be unable to find support, information, etc. (喻)碰壁(未能觅得支援、资料等)。□ *n* 1 space left empty or to be filled (in sth printed or written): (表格等中的)空白处; 空格: *In a telegraph form there are ~s for the name and address, the message, etc.* 在电报纸上有填写姓名、住址、电文等的空白。*When Tom was doing his French translation, he left ~s for all the words he did not know.* 汤姆翻译法文时把所有不认识的字都空下来。2 lottery ticket that does not win a prize. 未中奖的奖券。*draw a ~*, get nothing (after hoping to win or find sth). 抽空签; 希望赢而未赢; 希望找到而未找到。3 empty surface; emptiness: 空白的表面; 空虚: *His mind/memory was a complete ~*, he could remember nothing. 他的记忆完全是一片空白(什么都记不得了)。*The death of her husband in the war left a big ~ in her life.* 她的丈夫在战争中死去了, 使她觉得一切均茫然空虚。4 [C, U] ~ cartridge: 空弹; 空包弹: *They fired twenty rounds of ~/twenty ~s.* 他们放了二十发空包弹。~**·ly** *adv*

blan·ket /'blæŋkɪt; 'blæŋkɪt/ *n* 1 thick, woollen covering used on beds, or for keeping a horse warm in

a stable, etc: 毛毯; 毡子: (fig) (喻) *a ~ of snow*. 一片白雪。*wet ~*, (colloq) person who, by being gloomy himself, prevents others from enjoying themselves. (口)自己不快活也不容别人快活的人; 扫兴的人。2 (used attrib) covering all cases or classes: (用作定语)包括一切情形或种类的; 综合的; 总括的: *a ~ (=comprehensive) insurance policy;* 统保保险单; 全险保单; *~ instructions,* intended to provide for everything. 总括的指示。□ *vt* [VP6A, 14] ~ *(in/with)*, cover thickly: 厚厚地盖着…; 浓密地弥漫着…: *The valley was ~ed with fog.* 浓雾弥漫着山谷。

blare /bleə(r); blɛr/ *n* [U] sound or noise (of trumpets or horns): (喇叭或号角之响声) *a ~ of a brass band.* 铜管乐队的奏鸣声。□ *vi, vt* 1 [VP2A, C] ~ *(out)*, make such sounds: 发出喇叭或号角之响声: *The trumpets ~d out.* 喇叭齐鸣。2 [VP15B] ~ *out*, produce with such sounds; utter loudly: 以喇叭或号角之响声发出; 高声地说: *The band ~d out a current hit.* 乐队响亮地奏出流行歌曲。*He ~d out a warning.* 他高声发出警告。

blar·ney /'blɑːnɪ; 'blɑrnɪ/ *n* [U] *vt, vi* (dated use) the kind of talk that flatters and deceives people: (过时用语)奉承的话; 甜言蜜语; 谄媚; 奉承: *Not so much of your ~!* 不要再奉承了!

blasé /'blɑːzeɪ US: blɑ'zeɪ; blɑ'ze/ *adj* ~ *(about)*, not showing signs of enjoying (sth) or being pleased (about sth): 对 (某事物) 不感兴趣的; 厌倦的: ~ *about her success.* 对她的成功不感兴趣。

blas·pheme /blæs'fiːm; blæs'fim/ *vi, vt* [VP2A, 6A] speak in an irreverent way about God and sacred things; use violent language about (sth): 对于神及神圣的事物说不恭敬的话; 亵渎(神祇); 辱骂; 谩骂(某人或某事物): ~ *the name of God.* 亵渎神的名。~**r** *n* person who ~s. 对神出言不敬者; 亵渎神祇者; 骂人者; 谩骂者。**blas·phem·ous** /'blæsfəməs; 'blæsfɪməs/ *adj* (of persons) using blasphemy; (of language) containing blasphemy. (指人)对神出言不敬的; (指语言)含有不敬神祇的话的。**blas·phem·ous·ly** *adv* **blas·phemy** /'blæsfəmɪ; 'blæsfɪmɪ/ *n* [U] contemptuous or irreverent talk about God and sacred things; [C] instance of this. 对神及神圣事物不敬的话; 亵渎神祇的话; 亵渎神祇。

blast /blɑːst US: blæst; blæst/ *n* 1 strong, sudden rush of wind: 一阵突然的强风: *A ~ of hot air came from the furnace.* 一股热气自火炉吹来。*When the window was opened an icy ~ came into the room.* 当窗子打开时, 一阵冰冷的风吹入房间。2 (often [U]) strong rush of air or gas spreading outwards from an explosion: (由爆炸而引起的)爆震: *Thousands of windows were broken by ~ during the air raids.* 在空袭期间, 成千算万的窗户都被爆炸所引起的爆震震破了。**'~-off**, ⇨ **blast** *v* (3). 3 stream of air used to intensify the heat in a furnace, etc. 向火炉等输送之风 (以增强火力)。*at full ~*, (colloq) with the maximum activity. (口)全力地; 全速地。*in/out of ~*, (of a furnace) working/not working (指火炉)正在输风而旺盛燃烧着/不在输风而停歇着。'~**-furnace** *n* furnace for melting iron ore by forcing into it a current of heated air. 鼓风炉; 熔铁炉。4 sound made by a wind-instrument: 管乐器奏出的声音: *The hunter blew a ~ on his horn.* 猎人吹出一阵号角声。*The ship sounded a prolonged ~ on the siren.* 轮船发出一阵长长的汽笛声。5 quantity of explosive (eg dynamite) used at one time (eg in a quarry). (如在采石场)爆炸一次所用之炸药量。□ *vt, vi* 1 [VP6A, 2A] blow up (rocks, etc) with explosives: (用炸药)炸破(岩石等); 炸裂; 炸开: *Danger! B~ing in progress!* 危险! 爆炸在进行中! 2 [VP6A] cause (sth) to come to nothing; shrivel; injure: 毁灭; 使枯萎; 损害: *blossom ~ed by frost.* 为霜所冻坏的花朵。*The tree had been ~ed by lightning.* 树为雷电所震毁。*His hopes were ~ed.* 他的一切希望都破灭了。3 [VP15B, 2C] ~ *of~*, (of spacecraft, etc) force, be forced, upwards by expanding

gases. (指太空船等)发射; 上升; 升空。Hence, 由此产生, '~-off n (time of) launching of such a spacecraft: (太空船等的)发射; 升空; 发射时间; 升空时间: the countdown to ~-off. 倒数秒数至发射的时刻。 4 [VP6A] (sl) reproach sb severely: (俚)严责; 苛责: be ~ed by one's boss: 被其上司严责: get a ~ing from sb. 为某人所严责。 5 (in curses, with May God understood) (用于咒骂语中, May God 二字省略)。B~ it/you! 该死! 活该! ~ed /'blɑːstɪd US: 'blæ-; blæstɪd/ attrib adj (in curses) damnable. (用于咒骂语中)可诅咒的; 该死的。

bla·tant /'bleɪtnt; 'bletnt/ adj noisy and rough; attracting attention in a vulgar and shameless way; too obvious: 喧哗的; 吵闹的; (指地方)荒凉的; 以粗俗而厚颜的方式引人注意的; 太明显的。 ~·ly adv

blather /'blæðə(r); 'blæðɚ/ n, v ⇨ **blether**.

blaze[1] /bleɪz; blez/ n [C] 1 bright flame or fire: 火焰; 火光: We could see the ~ of a cheerful fire through the window. 我们可以从窗户看见融融炉火的火焰。 I put some wood on the fire and it soon burst into a ~, began to burn brightly. 我放些木柴在火上, 它不久就发出火焰来了。 2 fire; burning building(s): 火灾; 燃烧中的建筑物: It took the firemen two hours to put the ~ out. 消防队员费了两小时才将火扑灭。 3 (pl) (sl) hell: (复) (俚)地狱: Go to ~s! 该死! He was working like ~s, working furiously. 他正在拼命地工作。 4 glow of colour; bright light: 光彩; 光辉; 光明; 明亮: The red tulips made a ~ of colour in the garden. 红色郁金香花在花园中呈现一片红光。The main street of the town is a ~ of light(s) in the evening. 城里的大街在晚间呈现一片辉煌的灯火。 5 violent outburst: 爆发; 突发: in a ~ of anger. 勃然大怒。

blaze[2] /bleɪz; blez/ vi, vt 1 [VP2A, C] burn with flame: 发出火焰而燃烧; 炽燃: There was a fire blazing on the hearth. 壁炉中的火正熊熊地燃烧着。When the firemen arrived the whole building was blazing. 救火人员到达的时候, 整座建筑物正炽烈地燃烧着。 ~ up, burst into flames. 突然燃起火焰。 2 [VP2A, C] be bright with colour; shine brightly or with warmth: 发光彩; 光耀地照耀; 和煦地照耀: The garden was blazing with colour. 花园中五彩缤纷。The sun ~d down on us. 阳光直射在我们身上。 3 [VP2A, C] burst out with strong feeling: 爆发出激烈的情绪; 发怒: He was blazing with anger/indignation. 他勃然大怒。 4 [VP2C, VP3A] ~ away, fire continuously with rifles, etc: (用步枪等)不断地射击: They ~d away at the enemy. 他们不断地向敌人射击。He ~d away all his ammunition. 他把他所有的弹药一口气打光了。 **blazing** adj: a blazing fire; 炽燃的火; (fig) conspicuous: (喻) 显然的: a blazing indiscretion; 明显的轻率; (foxhunting) (猎狐) a blazing (= very strong) scent. 强烈的臭味。

blaze[3] /bleɪz; blez/ n white mark on a horse's or an ox's face; mark on a tree by cutting the bark. 马或牛面部的白斑; 刻在树上的记号。 □ vt [VP6A] mark (a tree) by cutting off part of the bark. 在(树上)刻出记号。 ~ a trail, mark trees to show a path through a forest; (fig) do sth for the first time and show others how to do it. 在森林中的树上刻记号以指示路径; (喻)做预先锋; 领导。

blaze[4] /bleɪz; blez/ vt [VP6A, 15B] ~ (abroad), make known far and wide: 传播; 广布: ~ the news (abroad). 传播新闻。

blazer /'bleɪzə(r); 'blezɚ/ n loose-fitting jacket (sometimes in the colours of a school, club, team, etc) for informal wear. 宽松的外衣 (所用之颜色有时系代表某一学校、会社、球队等, 为非正式场合之服装)。

bla·zon /'bleɪzn; 'blezn/ n coat of arms, esp on a shield. 纹章(尤指盾形纹章上的)。☆ the illus at **armour**. 参看 armour 之插图。 □ vt = **blaze**[4]. ~**ry** n bright display. 夸示; 炫示。

bleach /bliːtʃ; blitʃ/ vt, vi [VP6A, 2A] make or become white (by chemical action or sunlight): (借化学作用或阳光) 漂白: 变白: ~ linen; 漂白麻布; bones of

animals ~ing on the desert sand. 在沙漠上变白的动物骨头。 '~ing-powder n (eg chloride of lime) substance used to remove colour from dyed materials. 漂白粉。 □ n chemical for ~ing and sterilizing: 漂白剂; 消毒剂: household ~. 家用漂白剂。

bleach·ers /'bliːtʃəz; 'blitʃɚz/ n pl (US) unroofed seats/planks at sports grounds. (美) 运动场的露天 (木板)看台。

bleak /bliːk; blik/ adj 1 (of the weather) cold and cheerless; (of a place) bare, swept by cold winds: (指天气)阴冷的; 寒冷的; (指地方)荒凉的; 空旷而萧瑟的; a ~ hillside. 荒凉的山坡。 2 (fig) dreary: (喻)阴郁的: 黯淡的; 凄凉的: ~ prospects. 黯淡的前途。 ~·ly adv

bleary /'blɪərɪ; 'blɪrɪ/ adj dim; blurred: 朦胧的; 模糊不清的。 ~-eyed /'blɪərɪ'aɪd; 'blɪrɪ'aɪd/ adj having ~ eyes: 眼睛朦胧的: He got out of bed all ~-eyed. 他睡眼惺忪的下了床。

bleat /bliːt; blit/ n cry of a sheep, goat or calf. 羊叫声; 小牛叫声。 □ vi, vt [VP2A] make a cry of this kind; [VP6A, 15B] ~ (out), speak, say (sth) feebly: 作羊或小牛叫声; 以微弱的声音说(话): He ~ed (out) a complaint. 他以微弱的声音申诉。

bleed /bliːd; blid/ vi, vt (pt, pp **bled** /bled; bled/) 1 [VP2A, C] lose, send out, blood: 流血; 失血: If you cut your finger it will ~. 如果你割破手指, 它会流血。He was slowly ~ing to death. 他正慢慢流血而死。 2 [VP2A, C, 3A simple tenses only 仅用简单时态] ~ (for), feel great distress: 悲痛; 伤心: Our hearts ~ for homeless people during this cold winter. 我们的心为在这严冬中无家可归的人而悲伤。 3 [VP6A] draw blood from: 抽血; 放血: Doctors used to ~ people when they were ill. 昔时人们病了, 医生常为他们放血。 4 [VP6A, 14] force (sb) to pay money unjustly: 勒索; 敲诈: The blackmailers bled him for £500. 敲诈者向他强索五百英镑。 5 [VP2A] (of a plant, tree, etc) lose sap or juice. (指植物、树木等)流浆汁; 流出树液。

bleep /bliːp; blip/ n high-pitched sound or signal sent out by radio, used eg as a summoning or warning device. 无线电所发送出的高音调的声音或信号(用以传唤或警告等)。 □ vi emit such sounds. 发出此种声响。

blem·ish /'blemɪʃ; 'blemɪʃ/ n [C, U] mark, etc that spoils the beauty or perfection of sb or sth; moral defect: 污点; 缺点; 瑕疵: without ~, faultless. 无瑕疵的。 □ vt [VP6A] spoil the perfection of. 损害…之完美。

blench /blentʃ; blentʃ/ vi [VP2A] make a quick movement of fear. 因恐惧而突然一动; 畏缩。

blend /blend; blend/ vt, vi (pt, pp ~ed or, liter, **blent** /blent; blent/) 1 [VP6A] mix together, esp sorts of tea, tobacco, spirits, etc, to get a certain quality: 混合(尤指混合各种茶、烟草、酒等以求得到某种品种): ~ed whisky. 混合威士忌。A grocer needs to know how to ~ tea. 杂货商以往都必须知道如何混合茶叶。Our coffees are carefully ~ed. 我们的各种咖啡都是经仔细地搀混制成的。 2 [VP2A, 3A] mix, form a mixture: 溶合; 成为混合物: Oil and water do not ~. 油与水不相溶合。Oil does not ~ with water. 油不溶于水。 3 [VP2A] go well together; have no sharp or unpleasant contrast: (esp of colours) pass by degrees into each other: 调和; (尤指颜色)溶合: These two colours ~ well. 这两种颜色色溶合得很好。How well their voices ~! 他们的声音配合得真好! □ n [C] mixture made of various sorts (of tea, tobacco, etc): 不同种类之(茶、烟草等的)混合物: This coffee is a ~ of Java and Brazil. 这咖啡是由爪哇咖啡和巴西咖啡混调成的。

blent ⇨ **blend**.

bless /bles; bles/ vt (pt, pp ~ed /blest; blest; and **blest**, as in (6) below) [VP6A] 1 ask God's favour for: 求神赐福于; 祝福: They brought the children to Jesus and he ~ed them. 他们把孩子带到耶稣的面前, 耶稣就求神赐福他们。The priest ~ed the people/the crops

牧师祝福人们(祝丰收). **2** wish happiness or favour to: 祝福: B~ *you, my boy!* 祝福你,我的孩子! **3** consecrate; make sacred or holy: 使化为神圣: *bread ~ed at the altar.* 奉献于祭坛之面包. **4** *be ~ed with,* be fortunate in having: 在…方面有福气; 很幸运地享有: *I am not greatly ~ed with worldly goods,* 我不是很多财产. 我没有很多财产. 愿你永远享有健康之福. **5** call (God) holy: 称(上帝)为神圣; 颂扬: *'We praise Thee, we ~ Thee.'* '我们赞美你,我们称你为圣'. *'We ~ Thy Holy Name'* 你的名为圣'. **6** (colloq, in exclamations, expressing surprise): (口,用于感叹句中表示惊奇): B~ *me!* 哎呀! B~ *my soul!* 哎呀! *Well, I'm blest!* 哎呀! *I'm blest if I know!* ie I don't know at all. 我一点也不知道呀! ~ed /'blesɪd/'blesɪd/ *adj* **1** holy, sacred. 神圣的. the **B~ed Virgin,** the mother of Jesus. 圣母(耶稣之母). the **B~ed Sacrament,** Holy Communion. 圣餐. **2**fortunate: 有福的; 幸福的; 幸运的: *B~ed are the poor in spirit.* 虚心的人有福了. **3** the **B~ed,** those who are with God in paradise. 与上帝同在天堂中的圣洁的人. **4** (sl, mild swearing) cursed: (俚,温和的咒骂语)受天罚的; 受诅咒的: *I've broken the whole ~ed lot.* 我把那鬼东西全打碎了. □ ~ed·ness /'blesɪdnɪs; 'blesɪdnɪs/ *n* [U] happiness. 幸福; 福祉. ~·ing *n* **1** the favour of God: prayer for God's favour; thanks to God before or after a meal: 神恩; 向神祈福的祷告; 餐前或餐后向神表示感谢的祈祷: *ask a ~ing.* 祈祷. ⇨ grace(5). **2** sth that one is glad of; sth that brings comfort or happiness: 可喜的事; 为人带来安适或幸福的事: *What a ~ing it is you didn't get caught in the storm yesterday!* 昨天你未受到暴风雨的袭击真是幸运! *a ~ing in disguise,* sth that seems unfortunate, but that is seen later to be fortunate. 起初似乎为不幸而后来转变为幸运之事; 塞翁失马.

blether /'bleðə(r); 'blɛðə/, **blather** /'blæðə(r); 'blæðə/ *n* [U] foolish talk. 愚蠢的谈话; 废话; 胡说乱道. □ *vi* [VP2A, C] talk nonsense. 说废话; 胡说; 胡扯.

blew /blu:; blu/ ⇨ **blow¹.**

blight /blaɪt; blaɪt/ *n* **1** [U] (sorts of) plant disease; mildew. 植物枯萎病; 霉; 黴. **2** [C] evil influence of obscure origin: (根源不明的)坏影响; 挫折: 打击: *a ~ upon his hopes.* 对于他的希望的一个打击. □ *vt* [VP6A] be a ~ on: 破坏; 挫折; 打击: *His hopes were ~ed.* 他的希望破灭了. *Her life was ~ed by constant illness* 她的一生因病魔的经常缠绕而摧残了. ~·er *n* (dated sl) (过时俚语) **1** annoying person. 可厌的人. **2** fellow: 人; 家伙: *You lucky ~er!* 你这个幸运儿!

Blighty /'blaɪtɪ; 'blaɪtɪ/ *n* (GB 1st world war sl) home (during service abroad). (第一次大战时英俚)(在国外服役期间所称的)老家; 英国本土. *a ~ wound,* one severe enough for a soldier to be returned to GB. 须送回英国本土治疗的重伤.

bli·mey /'blaɪmɪ; 'blaɪmɪ/ *int* (vulg) expressing surprise. (鄙)哎呀! 啧啧! (表示惊讶之词).

blimp /blɪmp; blɪmp/ *n* **1** small non-rigid airship. 软式小飞艇. **2** (**Colonel) B~,** pompous-looking reactionary person. 装模作样的顽固保守的人.

blind¹ /blaɪnd; blaɪnd/ *adj* **1** without the power to see: 盲目的; 瞎的: *Tom helped the ~ man across the road.* 汤姆帮助瞎子过街. *He is ~ in the right eye.* 他的右眼瞎了. *turn a/one's ~ eye to sth,* pretend not to see it. 装瞎未看见: 对…睁只眼闭只眼. *~ spot,* point on the retina insensible to light; (fig) inability to recognize, understand or sympathize with sth. 盲点(视网膜上对光线无感觉之点); (喻)不能认识、了解或同情某事物. **2** *~ (to),* unable to see effects, to judge or understand well: 缺乏眼光、判断力或了解力: *Mothers are sometimes ~ to the faults of their children.* 做母亲的有时不能觉察孩子们的过错. *A man would be ~ not to see that difficulty.* 连那个困难看不出来的人一定是瞎了眼. **3** reckless: thoughtless: 鲁莽的; 轻率的; 不顾后果的: *In his ~ haste he almost ran into the river.* 他匆匆忙忙地几乎跑到河里去了. **4** not ruled by purpose: 无目的的:

Some people think that the world is governed by ~ forces. 有些人认为这个世界受着无目的的力量所支配. **5** (sl) drunk (also 亦作 ~ **drunk.** (俚)醉酒的. **6** ~ **alley,** ⇨ **alley(1).** ~ **date,** ⇨ **date¹(4).** ~ **flying,** navigation, eg in cloud, fog, with the aid of instruments only. 盲目飞行(指在黑暗中或云雾中仅靠仪器飞行). ~ **turning,** (in a road) one that cannot easily be seen by drivers. 公路上为驾车者看清楚的转弯处. ~·**,man's 'buff** *n* game in which one player, who is blindfolded, tries to catch and identify one of the others who push him about. 捉迷藏游戏.

blind² /blaɪnd; blaɪnd/ *vt* [VP6A, 14] ~ *sb (to),* make ~; (fig) take away the power of judgement: 使盲; 使失明; 使瞎; (喻)使失去判断力: *a ~ing light.* 令人目眩的强光. *The soldier had been ~ed in the war.* 那兵士在战争中双目失明了. *His feelings for her ~ed him to her faults.* 他对她的感情使他看不见她的缺点. ~·**ers** *n pl* (US) (美) = blinkers. ~·**ly** *adv* ~·**ness** *n*

blind³ /blaɪnd; blaɪnd/ *n* **1** roll of cloth (usu strong linen) fixed on a roller and pulled down to cover a window (US 美 = *window-shade*): (布质卷轴式的)窗帘; 遮帘: *pull down/lower, draw up/raise the ~ s.* 拉下(放下,卷起,扯起)窗帘. **2** (fig) deception: (喻)欺骗; 欺瞒; 诡计: *It was only a ~,* sth intended to hide the reality. 它只是一种欺瞒的手法. **3** (US) hide¹ *n.* (美)(摄影者等用以观察野生动物,鸟类等之)隐藏处.

blind·fold /'blaɪndfəʊld; 'blaɪnd,fold/ *vt* [VP6A] cover the eyes of (sb) with a bandage so that he cannot see. 用一块布蒙住(某人)的眼睛使之不能见物; 使看不见. □ *n* [C] such a cover. 蒙眼布; 眼罩. □ *adj* with the eyes bandaged, covered with a handkerchief, etc. 眼睛被蒙住的.

blink /blɪŋk; blɪŋk/ *vi, vt* **1** [VP2A, C, 6A, 15B] shut and open the eyes quickly: 眨眼; 瞬目: *~ the eyes;* 眨眼睛; *~ away a tear.* 眨掉眼泪. **2** [VP6A] ~ *the fact that,* (fig) refuse to consider; ignore: (喻)不考虑…的事实; 忽视…的事实: *There's no ~ing the fact that… .* 我们不能忽视…之事实. **3** [VP2C] (of lights, esp when in the distance) come and go; shine in an unsteady way: (指灯光,尤指远处者)闪烁不定: *We saw the lights of a steamer ~ing on the horizon.* 我们看见一艘轮船上的灯光在地平线上闪烁着. □ *n* [C] instance of ~ing. 眨眼; 瞬目. 闪烁. ~·**ing** *adj* (colloq euphem for) bloody(3): (口,委婉语)极度的; 非常的: *It's a ~ing nuisance.* 那真是极度令人厌恶之事.

blink·ers /'blɪŋkəz; 'blɪŋkəz/ *n pl* (US 美=*blinders*) leather squares to prevent a horse from seeing sideways. 马眼罩(皮制方块, 置于马眼之两旁使不能看两侧). ⇨ the illus at **harness.** 参看 harness 之插图.

blip /blɪp; blɪp/ *n* spot of light on a radar screen. 雷达幕上的光点.

bliss /blɪs; blɪs/ *n* [U] perfect happiness; great joy. 福气; 极大的快乐. ~·**ful** /-ful; -fəl/ *adj* ~·**fully** /-fulɪ; -fəlɪ/ *adv*

blis·ter /'blɪstə(r); 'blɪstə/ *n* [C] **1** small bag-like swelling under the skin, filled with liquid (caused by rubbing, burning, etc): (皮肤因摩擦、灼烧等而起之)水泡: *If your shoes are too tight, you may get ~s on your feet.* 如果你的鞋太紧, (你的)脚上就可能起水泡. **2** similar swelling on the surface of metal, painted or varnished wood, a plant, etc. (金属表面、木器外表之油漆、植物表皮等所起之)浮泡. □ *vt, vi* [VP6A, 2A] cause, get, a ~ or ~s on: 起泡; 使起泡: *He is not used to manual work and his hands ~ easily.* 他不惯于体力工作, 他的手容易起泡. *The hot sun has ~ed the paint on the door.* 炎阳晒得门上的油漆都起了泡.

blithe·some /blaɪð, -səm; blaɪð, -səm/ *adj* (chiefly poet) gay and joyous. (主要用于诗中)快乐的; 快活的; 愉快的. ~·**ly** *adv*

blith·er·ing /'blɪðərɪŋ; 'blɪðərɪŋ/ *adj* (colloq) utter; contemptible (esp in): (口)完全的; 全然的; 卑劣的(尤用于): ~ *idiot.* 大傻瓜.

blitz /blɪts; blɪts/ n rapid, violent attack (esp from the air). 闪电式的猛烈袭击；闪击(尤指由空军从事者)。 □ vt [VP6A] damage or destroy in this way (esp in pp). 以闪击方式摧毁(尤用这方式分词)：~ed areas/towns, destroyed by bombing during air-raids. 在空袭中被炸毁的地区(市镇)。

bliz·zard /'blɪzəd; 'blɪzɚd/ n [C] violent and heavy snowstorm. 大风雪；暴风雪。

bloated /'bləʊtɪd; 'blotɪd/ adj swollen; fat and large in an unhealthy way: 肿胀的；过于肥胖的：a ~ face; 臃肿的脸；a fat, ugly man, ~ with over-eating, 一个肥胖丑陋男人，因吃得过多而臃肿不堪；(fig) (喻) ~ with pride, puffed up with pride. 骄气十足的。

bloater /'bləʊtə(r); 'blotɚ/ n kind of salted and smoked herring: 盐腌而又烟熏的鲱鱼：~ paste, paste made from ~s. 腌薰鲱鱼酱。⇨ **kipper**.

blob /blɒb; blɑb/ n drop of liquid, eg paint; small round mass, eg of wax; spot of colour. 一滴(如油漆)；一小圆块(如腊丸)；(颜色之)斑点。

bloc /blɒk; blɑk/ n combination of parties, groups, states, etc with a special interest: 为了某种特殊利益而结合的政党、团体、国家等之集团：the sterling ~, those countries with currencies related to sterling. 英镑集团(使用之货币与英镑有关之国家)。

block[1] /blɒk; blɑk/ n **1** large, solid piece of wood, stone, etc: (木、石等之)大块：A butcher cuts up his meat on a large ~ of wood. 屠夫在一个大木墩上切肉。The ~s of stone in the Pyramids are five or six feet high. 金字塔上的石块有五、六英尺高。The statue is to be carved out of a ~ of marble. 石像将由一大块大理石雕成。Children play with building ~s, cubes of wood put together to make toy houses, etc. 儿童们玩(堆砌玩具房子等的)积木。⇨ **chip**(1). **2** main part of a petrol engine, consisting of the cylinders and valves. 汽油机的主要部分 (包括汽缸及阀)。**3** the ~, (in olden times) large piece of wood on which a person put his neck to have his head cut off as a punishment. 古时死刑犯斩首时用以放头之大木块；断头台。**go/be sent to the ~**, to death in this way. 上(被送上)断头台；被处斩。**4** shaped piece of wood on which hats are moulded. 帽檀。**5** pulley, or system of pulleys, in a case (often ~ **and tackle**). 滑车；滑轮；(常作 block and tackle) 滑车组。**6** piece of wood or metal with designs, etc, cut (engraved) on it for printing. 木刻板；(金属制之)蚀刻版；印版。**7** mass of buildings (shops, offices, apartments, etc) joined together; (esp US) area of buildings bounded by four streets; the length of one side of such an area: 接连在一起的一片建筑物(如商店、办公室、公寓等)；四面临街的一片建筑物；街区；街区一边之长度(即两条街间的距离)：To reach the post-office, walk two ~s east and then turn left. 要到邮局去，请向东走两个街区，然后向左转。⇨ **-buster** /'blɒkˌbʌstə(r); 'blɑkˌbʌstɚ/ n powerful explosive to demolish buildings; (fig) forceful person or thing bringing about a sudden effect, eg in a dispute. 可摧毁建筑物的大型爆炸物；(喻)引起突然效果的人或物(例如在辩论中)。**8** division of seats in a theatre, concert hall, etc; large quantity of shares in a business. (戏院、音乐厅等)座位区；某一企业之大宗股份。**9** obstruction; sth that makes movement or flow difficult or impossible: 阻碍；障碍物；阻塞；阻塞物：There was a ~ in the pipe and the water couldn't flow away. 管子内有阻塞物，水不能流走。'**road** ~, barrier across a road at which documents, etc are checked. 路卡(横设于道路上之障碍物，用作检查证件等的关卡)。'**traffic** ~, (usu 通常作 traffic jam) large number of buses, cars, vans, trams, etc held up and unable to move on. 交通阻塞(大批的车辆被阻于途中不能前进道)。**10** '~ **grant**, fixed and non-recurring subsidy. 固定且不再发的补助金。'~ '**capitals**/'**letters**/'**writing**, with each letter separate and in capitals: 正楷大写字母；正楷大写字体：Write your name in ~ letters. 请用正楷大写字母写你的名字。**11** (cricket) spot on which a batsman rests his

bat before playing a ball. (板球)击球员在击球前置放球板之处。**12** (sl) (person's) head: (俚) (人的)头：I'll knock your ~ off! 我将把你摆平!

block[2] /blɒk; blɑk/ vt **1** [VP6A, 15B] ~ (**up**), make movement difficult or impossible in (by sth being in the way); obstruct; 阻碍；阻塞；堵塞：All roads were ~ed by the heavy snowfall. 所有道路均为大雪所阻塞。They ~ed up (=entirely covered) the entrance to the cave with big rocks. 他们用巨石将洞口全部堵塞起来。My cold gave me a ~ed-up nose. 伤风使我鼻塞。**2** [VP6A] obstruct (progress); make (action) difficult or impossible: 阻止(进行)；使(行动)困难或不可能：The general succeeded in ~ing the enemy's plans. 这位将军成功地阻挡住了敌军的企图。**3** [VP6A] (chiefly in pp) restrict the use or expenditure of (currency, assets, etc): (主要用过去分词)限制(通货、资产等)之使用或花费；封锁；冻结：~ed sterling. 冻结的英镑。**4** [VP6A] shape (eg hats) on a ~. (用木植)使(帽等)成形。⇨ **block**[1](4). **5** ~ **in/out**, make a rough sketch or plan of the general arrangement (of objects in a drawing, etc). 画略图；打草样。**6** (cricket) stop (the ball) with the bat (kept upright in front of the wicket). (板球)在三柱门前将球板举直以挡(球)。

block·ade /blɒ'keɪd; blɑ'ked/ n the enclosing or surrounding of a place, eg by armies or warships, to keep goods or people from entering or leaving. (使用陆军或海军)封锁(某一地区，使货物或人民不能出入)。**run the** ~, evade and get through the forces that are surrounding a place. 偷越封锁线；突破封锁；偷渡。**raise the** ~, end it. 解除封锁。'~**-runner** n ship, etc that gets through or past a ~. 偷越封锁线的船只等；偷渡者。 □ vt [VP6A] make a ~ around, eg a town, fort, etc. 封锁(城镇、要塞等)。

block·age /'blɒkɪdʒ; 'blɑkɪdʒ/ n [C] state of being blocked; sth that blocks: 被阻塞住之状态；阻塞；堵塞；阻塞物：There's a ~ in the drain-pipe. 排水管内有阻塞物。

block·head /'blɒkhed; 'blɑk,hed/ n slow and stupid person. 笨头笨脑的人；呆笨的人。

block·house /'blɒkhaʊs; 'blɑk,haʊs/ n military strongpoint with openings through which to shoot. 碉堡。

bloke /bləʊk; blok/ n (sl) man. (俚)男人；家伙。

blond /blɒnd; blɑnd/ n, adj (man) having fair[1](5) complexion and hair. 白肤金发的(男人)。

blonde /blɒnd; blɑnd/ n, adj (woman) blond. 白肤金发的(女人)。

blood[1] /blʌd; blʌd/ n [U] **1** red liquid flowing throughout the body of man and the higher animals: 血；血液：The soldiers shed their ~ (=died) for their country. 将士们为国捐躯。It was more than flesh and ~ (= human nature) could stand. 那是非血肉之躯(人性)所能忍受的。He gave his ~ to help his sister, gave ~ to be injected into his sister after a surgical operation or an accident. 他输血给他的姐姐(妹妹)以救助她(如手术过后或意外受伤后)。infuse new ~ (into sth), (fig) revive business, etc by introducing new talent. (喻)输入新血(引进新的人才以振兴事业等)；补充生力军。let ~, draw of ~ from a vein. (外科)放血。⇨ **7** below. 参看下列第 7 义。**2** passion; temper: 情绪；怒愁；脾气：His ~ is up, he is angry, filled with passion. 他发脾气了。His ~ ran cold, he was filled with terror or horror. 他吓得魂不附体。(**kill sb**) **in cold** ~, when one is not feeling angry or excited; deliberately. 非一时冲动地；蓄意地(杀死某人)。**make bad** ~ **between persons**, cause them to feel ill will towards one another. 在二人之间挑拨感情；挑拨离间。**make one's** '~ **boil**, make one very angry. 使人非常愤怒。**make one's** ~ **run cold**, fill one with fear or horror. 使其感到恐惧或恐怖。**3** relationships; family: 血缘；血亲；血统；血统：They are of the same ~, have ancestors in common. 他们是同宗。'**blue** '~ n aristocratic descent. 贵族血统；高

贵门第. *of the (royal)* ~, of royal family. 皇族的; 皇
家的. *one's (own) flesh and* ~, one's relations. 某人
之直系血亲; 亲属. *B~ is thicker than water,* (prov)
The ties of family relationship are real. (谚) 血浓于水;
疏不间亲 (亲属关系才是真的). '~ **feud** *n* deadly feud
between families. (两家族间不共戴天的) 夙仇; 世仇.
'~-**relation** *n* person related by ~, not by marriage.
血亲; 骨肉. **4** ~ *and iron,* (fig) relentless use of force.
(喻) 铁血政策; 滥用武力. **5** [C] (old colloq use) man of
fashion; rich, pleasure-loving young man. (旧口语用
法) 花花公子; 纨袴子. **6** ~ *and thunder attrib adj*
(of stories, dramas) melodramatic; full of exciting
incidents. (指小说、戏剧) 闹剧性的; 充满刺激性情节的.
7 (compounds) (复合词) '~ **bank** *n* ▷ **bank³(3).** '~-
bath *n* large-scale slaughter, eg in battle, or during a
revolution. (如战斗中或革命期中之) 大屠杀. '~ **brother,**
one who swears to treat another as a brother (perhaps
by the symbolic act of mixing his ~ with the other
person). 歃血盟誓的兄弟; 拜把兄弟. '~ **count** *n*
(counting of the) number of red and white corpuscles
in a certain volume of ~. 血球数 (某一定量血液中所含
之红血球及白血球之数目); 血球计数. '~-**curdling** *adj*
sending feelings of horror through the body. 使人毛
骨悚然的. '~-**donor** *n* person who gives ~ for ~
transfusions. 捐血者. '~-**group/type** *n* any of several
distinct classes of human ~. 血属; 血型. '~-**heat** *n*
the normal temperature of human ~ (about 98.5°F,
37°C). 人体的正常体温 (约为98.5华氏度, 37摄氏度).
'~-**hound** *n* large dog able to trace a person by scent.
一种大警犬 (能嗅嗅追踪人迹). ▷ the illus at **dog.** ▷
看狗之插图. '~-**letting** *n* surgical drawing off of some
of a patient's ~. 放血 (用外科手术放出病人若干血液).
'~-**lust,** desire for killing sb. 杀人欲. '~-**money** *n*
money obtained at the cost of a life, eg received by a
murderer for killing someone or as a reward for
betraying sb who is to be put to death. 血腥钱 (如受雇
杀人所得之钱, 或出卖他人使被处死刑所得之报酬). '~-
poisoning *n* condition that results when poisonous germs
enter the ~, esp through a cut or wound. 血中毒; 血毒
症. '~ **pressure** *n* the force exerted by ~ within the
arteries. 血压. '~ **red,** having the colour of ~. 血红
色的. '~-**shed** *n* killing or wounding of people; putting
to death: 流血; 杀伤: *There was great ~shed in
Paris during the years after the Revolution in 1789.* 在
一七八九年大革命后的几年中, 巴黎有很多的流血事件.
'~-**shot** *adj* (of the white of the eyes) red. (指眼白) 充血
的; 充满血丝的. '~-**sports** *n pl* outdoor sports in which
animals or birds are killed. 狩猎. '~-**stained** *adj* (a)
stained with ~: 血污的; 沾有血迹的: *a ~stained shirt.*
沾有血迹的衬衫. (b) disgraced by ~shed. 血腥的; 因杀
伤过人而不名誉的. '~-**stock** *n* (collective) thoroughbred
horses. (集合用法) 纯种马. '~-**sucker** *n* (a) creature
that sucks ~, esp a leech. 吸血虫; (尤指) 水蛭. (b)
(fig) person who unjustly forces another or others to
give him as much money as possible. (喻) 剥削他人之人;
吸血鬼. '~-**thirsty** *adj* cruel and eager to take life;
taking pleasure in killing. 残忍的; 嗜杀的. '~-**thirsti-
ness** *n* '~-**transfusion** *n* transfer of ~ (originally
taken) from the veins of one person to those of another.
输血 (将血液由一人之静脉抽出并输入另一人之静脉中).
'~-**vessel** *n* tube (vein or artery) through which ~
flows in the body. 血管. ▷ the illus at **respiratory.**
参看 respiratory 之插图. ~-**less** *adj* **1** without ~shed:
未发生流血事件的; 不流血的: *a ~less victory.* 不流血的
胜利. **2** pale; unfeeling and coldhearted. 无血色的; 苍
白的; 无情的; 冷酷的. ~-**less·ly** *adv*

blood² /blʌd/ *vt* [VP6A] allow the first taste
of ~ to (foxhounds, etc). 让 (猎狐犬等) 初次尝血的
味道.

bloody /'blʌdɪ; 'blʌdɪ/ *adj* **1** bleeding; covered with
blood: 流血的; 血污的: *a ~ nose.* 流血的鼻子. **2** with
much bloodshed: 伤亡很多的; 流血很多的: *a ~ battle.*

伤亡惨重的战役. **3** (vulg intensive): (鄙, 强势语):
What a ~ shame! 多么大的一项耻辱啊! (derog) (贬)
You're a ~ fool! 你这个大傻瓜! (land) (惯) *You're a
~ genius!* 你真是个鬼才! '~-**minded,** (sl) obstructive;
unwilling to co-operate. (俚) 存心阻挠的; 不愿合作的. □
adv (vulg sl): (鄙俚): *Not ~ likely!* (= not a tall
likely). 绝对不可能的! ~ **well,** (vulg sl) certainly. (鄙
俚) 无疑地; 确定地.

bloom /bluːm; blum/ *n* **1** [C] flower, esp of plants
admired chiefly for their flowers (eg roses, tulips,
chrysanthemums). 花 (尤指美其花而受人赞赏之植物的
花, 如玫瑰花, 郁金香, 菊花). *in* ~, (of plants)
flowering: (指花草) 在开花中: *The tulips are in full ~
now.* 郁金香现正盛开. Cf 参较 *in blossom* for shrubs
and trees. *in blossom* 用于灌木及树木. **2** [U] (time
of) greatest beauty or perfection: 青春; 茂盛(时期):
She was in the ~ of youth. 她正在青春时期. **3** [U]
covering of fine dust or powder on plums, grapes, etc
when they are at their best. 李子、葡萄等成熟时表面所
生的一层霜粉; 粉衣. *take the ~ off sth,* cause it to
seem stale. 使某物显得陈旧. □ *vi* [VP2A, C] **1** be in
flower; bear flowers: 开花: *The roses have been ~ing
all summer.* 这些玫瑰整个夏天一直都在开花. **2** (fig)
be in full beauty and perfection. (喻) 在青春美貌时期;
在完美时期; 在旺盛时期. ~-**ing** *adj* **1** (in the senses of
the *v*) 开花的; 青春美貌的; 完美的; 旺盛的. **2** /'blʌmɪŋ;
'blʌmɪŋ/ (colloq euphem for *bloody(3)*): (口, bloody
第3义之委婉语) 极端的; 非常: *You ~ing idiot!* 你这个
大白痴!

bloomer /'bluːmə(r); 'blumɚ/ *n* (sl) blunder: (俚)
错误; 谬误: *He made a tremendous ~.* 他犯了一次大错.

bloom·ers /'bluːməz; 'blumɚz/ *n pl* loose garment
covering each leg to the knee and hanging from the
waist, formerly worn by girls and women for games,
cycling, etc, with or without a skirt. (昔时妇女在运
动、骑车等时所穿长及膝部之) 灯笼裤 (有的带裙子, 有的
不带裙子).

blos·som /'blɒsəm; 'blɑsəm/ *n* [C] flower, esp of a
fruit-tree; [U] mass of flowers on a bush or tree. 花
(尤指果树的之花); (树上的)花丛; 花簇; 花团. ▷ the illus
at **flower.** 参看 flower 之插图. *in* ~, (of bushes and
trees) having flowers: (指树木) 在开花中的: *The apple-
trees are in ~.* 苹果树正在开花. ▷ **bloom(1).** □ *vi* **1**
[VP2A] open into flowers: 开花: *The cherry-trees will
~ next month.* 樱桃树将于下月开花. **2** [VP2C] ~ *out,*
develop: 发展: *He ~ed out as a first-rate athlete.* 他锻
练成为第一流的运动员.

blot /blɒt; blɑt/ *n* **1** mark caused by ink spilt on paper.
(墨水溅在纸上的) 污点; 墨水点. **2** fault; disgrace;
sth that takes away from the beauty or goodness of
sth: 缺点; 瑕疵: *a ~ on his character:* 他的品格上的一
个缺点: *a ~ on the landscape,* eg an ugly building or
advertisement. 破坏天然风景的一个景象 (如一座丑陋的
建筑物或广告). □ *vt* (-tt-) **1** [VP6A] make a ~ or
~s on (paper with ink). 在 (纸上) 弄上墨水点. ~ *one's
copy-book,* (colloq) do sth that spoils one's good record.
(口) 做有损声誉的事. **2** [VP6A] dry up (wet ink) with
~ting-paper. 用吸墨纸吸干(墨水). '~-**ting-paper** *n*
absorbent paper used to dry up wet ink quickly. (使墨
水快干之) 吸墨纸. **3** [VP15B] ~ *out,* (a) make a ~
over (words that have been written): 将(已写之字)涂
掉: *Several words in his letter had been ~ted out.* 他的
信中有几个字被涂掉了. (b) hide from view: 遮蔽: *The
mist came down and ~ted out the view.* 雾降下来把风景
遮住了. (c) destroy, exterminate (enemies, etc). 摧毁;
消灭 (敌人等). ~-**ter** *n* **1** book containing sheets of
writing-paper interleaved with sheets of ~ting-paper.
(每页附有吸墨纸的) 一本写字纸; 记事簿. **police-ter,**
(US) book in which the police enter records, eg of lost
and found articles, missing persons. (美) 警局记事
簿 (警察用以登记失物、被找到之物、失踪者等之记录簿).
2 piece or pad of ~ting-paper. 吸墨纸; 吸墨具.

blotch /blɒtʃ; blɑtʃ/ *n* large, discoloured mark, usu irregular in shape (eg on the skin, or of ink on paper). (皮肤上的)大块斑点; (纸上的)墨水污迹.

blotto /'blɒtəʊ; 'blɑto/ *pred adj* (sl) fuddled or intoxicated with alcoholic drink. (俚)酩酊大醉的.

blouse /blaʊz US: blaʊs; blaʊs/ *n* **1** outer garment from neck to waist, worn by women and girls (US 美 = *shirtwaist*). (妇女所穿从颈部到腰部之)短衫. **2** loose-fitting garment, often with a belt at the waist, worn by some workmen. (工人所穿腰部有束带之)宽松上衣. **3** tunic as worn by some sailors and soldiers. (水手, 士兵所穿之)紧身上衣; 军便服上衣.

blow¹ /bləʊ; blo/ *vi, vt* (*pt* **blew** /bluː; blu/, *pp* **blown** /bləʊn; blon/, or, (11) below, ~ed) **1** [VP2A, C] (with *air*, *wind*, or *it* as the subject) move along, flow as a current of air: (用 air, wind, 或 it 作主语) 吹; 刮; 吹动: *It was ~ing hard*, there was a strong wind. 风正刮得很厉害. *It was ~ing a gale/~ing great guns*, there was a (violent) gale. 正在刮大风(狂风). *The wind was ~ing round the street-corners*. 风正吹过街角. *It's ~ing up for rain*, the wind seems likely to bring rain soon. 似乎就要有雨(山雨欲来风满楼). **2** [VP15A, B] (of the wind) cause to move: (指风)刮走; 吹动: *The wind blew my hat off*. 风把我的帽子吹落了. *I. was almost ~n over by the wind*. 我几乎被风吹倒了. *The ship was ~n out of its course/on to the rocks*. 船被风吹离航线(吹上礁石). *The wind blew the papers out of my hand*. 风把我手里的文件吹走了. [VP12A] *It's an ill wind that ~s nobody any good*, ⇨ **ill**(2). **3** [VP2C, E] (of objects, etc) be moved or carried by the wind or other air current: (指物件等)被风或其他气流吹动; 被吹走: *My hat blew off*. 我的帽子被风吹掉了. *The door blew open*. 门被风吹开了. *The dust has ~n into the house*. 灰尘被风吹进房子里了. **4** [VP6A, 15B, 2C] send or force a strong current of air upon, into or through: 吹气于; 充气于: ~ *(on) one's food* (to cool it); 将食物吹凉; ~ *the dust off a book*; 将书上灰尘吹掉; ~ *(up) the fire*, make it burn better (eg by using a pair of bellows). (用风箱等)吹旺(火使燃烧旺盛). ~ *hot and cold*, (fig) vacillate. (喻)犹疑不决; 踌躇. ~ *one's nose*, in order to clear it. 擤鼻涕. **5** [VP6A] make by ~ing: 吹成; 吹出: ~ *bubbles*, by sending air through a pipe with soapy water, etc: 吹泡泡; shape by ~ing: 吹出(某种形状): ~ *glass*, by sending a current of air into molten glass. 吹制玻璃器皿. **6** [VP6A] use (sth) to produce a current of air: 使用(某物)以产生气流: ~ *bellows*, 扇风箱; work the bellows of: 操作…之风箱: ~ *an organ*. 操作风琴之风箱. **7** [VP6A, 2A] produce sound from (a trumpet, etc) by sending air into it; (of a wind-instrument, etc) produce sound: 吹奏(喇叭等); (指管乐器等)发出声音: *The referee blew his whistle*. 裁判鸣笛. *Stop work when the whistle ~s*. 汽笛一响就停止工作. *The huntsman blew his horn*. 猎人吹他的号角. *We heard the bugles ~ing*. 我们听见吹号. **8** [VP2A] breathe hard and quickly: 喘息; 喘气: *The old man was puffing and ~ing when he got to the top of the hill*. 那老人到达山顶时, 喘息著气. **9** [VP2A] force up a stream of air and water: (指鲸)喷起一股空气与水: *There she ~s! There is the fountain sent up by the whale!* 鲸鱼在那边喷水! **10** [VP2A, 2C, 6A, 15B] ~ *(out)*, (of a fuse)melt because the electric current is too strong; cause to do this: (指保险丝)为过强的电流所烧断; 烧断: *The fuse has ~n*. 保险丝烧断了. *The fuse blew out*. 保险丝烧了. *Don't* ~ *(out) the fuse*. 不要把保险丝烧断. **11** (sl uses) spend (money) recklessly or extravagantly: (俚)一掷千金; 挥(金)如土; 滥花(钱): ~ *£10 on a dinner with a girl friend*. 花十英镑同女友吃一顿饭. ⇨ **blue³**. *B~ the expense*, Don't worry about it. 尽量花钱吧(不要担心). *I'll be ~ed if.../B~ed if I will...*, I will certainly not... 我决不... ; 如果...我就不是人. *Well, I'm ~ed!* (indicating surprise). (表示惊愕之语)真该死! ~

one's top, lose one's temper; explode into angry words, etc. 发脾气; 发怒而骂人. **12** (compounds from the *v*) (由动词各义而形成之复合词) '~*-dry* *vt* [VP6A] dry (sth, esp hair) by passing a current of warm air over (it). (用热风)吹干(头发等). '~*-fly* *n* common meat fly. 大苍蝇; 琉璃蝇. '~*-hole* *n* **(a)** opening for air, smoke, etc, in a tunnel. (隧道中的)通风孔. **(b)** hole (in rocks, etc near the seashore) through which air and water are forced by rising tides. (海岸附近岩石等中的)气穴 (涨潮所驱迫的空气与水可从中通过者). '~*-lamp*, '~*-torch* *nn* lamp for directing an intensely hot flame on to a surface. 喷灯. '~*-pipe* *n* **(a)** tube for increasing the heat of a flame by forcing air into it. 吹风管; 吹管. **(b)** tube through which some primitive people ~ poisoned darts. (某些原始部族用以发射毒矢的)吹矢枪. **13** [VP2C,3A,15B] (special uses with *adverbial particles* and *preps*): (与副词及介词连用之特殊用法):
blow back, (of gas in a tube, etc) explode. (指导管中的煤气等)爆炸. Hence, 由此产生, '~*-back* *n* explosion of gas in a tube, etc. 煤气在导管中的爆炸. *blow in/into*, (colloq) arrive noisily, cheerfully, etc: (口)喧哗、高兴等地来临: *The door opened and John blew in/blew into the room*. 门一开约翰嘻嘻哈哈地进入房间里来.
blow off steam, release tension by arguing, being noisy, etc: 借辩论, 吵吵闹闹等以解除情绪的紧张: *Parents must let children ~ off steam sometimes*. 做父母的有时必须让孩子们吵吵闹闹, 发泄发泄.
blow out; ~ sth out, (be) put out by ~ing: 吹灭; 吹熄; 被吹熄: *The candle was ~n out by the wind*. 蜡烛被风吹灭了. *The flame blew out*. 火焰被吹熄了. ~ *itself out*, exhaust itself: 歇息; 停止: *The gale had ~n itself out*. 大风已经停止吹刮了. ~ *one's brains out*, kill oneself by shooting in the head. 以枪弹射入脑部自杀. '~*-out* *n* **(a)** sudden (often violent) escape of air, steam, etc; (esp) bursting of a tyre. 漏气; 喷气; (尤指) 轮胎爆裂. **(b)** ~ing out of an electric fuse. (电线保险丝)烧断. **(c)** (sl) abundant meal; feast. (俚)丰盛的餐食; 盛宴.
blow over, pass by; be forgotten: 过去; 被忘记; 平息: *The storm/scandal will soon ~ over*. 暴风雨(丑闻)不久就会平息.
blow up, **(a)** explode: 爆炸: *The barrel of gunpowder blew up*. 火药桶爆炸了. **(b)** arise: 起; 发生: *A storm is ~ing up*. 暴风雨就要起了. **(c)** lose one's temper; work up to a crisis: 发脾气; 逐渐接近危机: *I'm sorry I blew up at you*. 抱歉, 对你发了脾气. ~ *sb up*, (colloq) scold severely: (口)严厉责备某人: *The teacher blew John up for not doing his homework*. 老师严责约翰未做家庭作业. Hence, 由此产生, '~*-ing'up* *n* scolding. 骂; 责备. ~ *sth up*, **(a)** break or destroy by explosion: 炸毁; 炸断: *The soldiers blew up the bridge*. 士兵们炸断了那座桥. **(b)** inflate with air or gas: 使充气; 打气: ~ *up a tyre*. 给轮胎打气. **(c)** enlarge greatly: 大幅放大: ~ *up a photograph*. 大幅放大一张照片. Hence, 由此产生, '~*-up* *n* greatly enlarged photograph: 巨幅照片: *The men in the procession carried ~ups of their leader*. 游行队伍中的人们都举着他们领袖的巨幅照片. **(d)** exaggerate: 夸大: *His abilities have been greatly ~n up by the newspapers*. 报纸极力夸大了他的才能.

blow² /bləʊ; blo/ *n* blowing: 吹; 吹风: *Give your nose a good* ~, clear it thoroughly. 把你的鼻子擤干净. *have/go for a* ~, go outdoors for fresh air. 到户外去吹吹风(吸点新鲜空气).

blow³ /bləʊ; blo/ *n* **1** hard stroke (given with the hand, a stick, etc): (用拳、棒等之)打; 击; 捶打; 殴打: *He struck his enemy a heavy ~ on the head*. 他在他敌人的头上予以沉重的一击. *at one ~; at a (single) ~*, in a single effort: 一击; 一举; 一下子: *I killed six flies at a ~*. 我一下子打死了六只苍蝇. *come to ~s; exchange ~s*, fight. 打架; 互殴. *get a ~ in*, succeed in placing

a ~. 击中. **strike** a ~ **for**, perform a single act of support for, struggle for. 作支持或拥护…之举动; 为…而奋斗. **without striking** a ~, without having to fight. 不经战斗; 兵不血刃. a ~-**by-**~ **account**, a detailed account (eg of a boxing match). (拳击比赛等之)详细叙述; 详尽报导. **2** shock; disaster: 突然的打击; 灾祸; 不幸: *His wife's death was a great* ~ *to him.* 他的妻之死对他是一大打击. *It was a* ~ *to our hopes.* 这对我们的希望是一大打击.

blow⁴ /bləʊ; blo/ *vi* (*pp* ~**n** /bləʊn; blon/) (chiefly in *pp* as) (主用过去分词, 例如) *full-blown roses*, wide open, with petals about to fall. 盛开的玫瑰花 (花瓣即将掉落的). *She has a complexion like a new-blown rose*, a delicate pink complexion. 她的肤色象初开的玫瑰花 (淡粉红色).

blower /'bləʊə(r); 'bloɚ/ *n* **1** apparatus for forcing air, etc into or through sth. 吹风器; 鼓风器. **2** person who makes things by blowing (eg a *'glass-*~) or who pumps air into sth (eg an *'organ-*~). 吹制…者(如吹制玻璃器之工人); 充气于某物的人; 充气者 (如操作风琴风箱的人). **3** (colloq) speaking-tube; (GB sl) telephone: (口)通话管; (英俚)电话: *Get Jones on the* ~ *for me.* 请找琼斯来接我电话.

blown /bləʊn; blon/ *pp* of **blow¹**. ⇨ also **blow⁴**. □ *adj* breathless (as the result of effort). 喘息的; 喘不过气来的.

blowzy /'blaʊzɪ; 'blaʊzɪ/ *adj* (usu of a woman) red-faced, dirty-looking and untidily dressed. (通常指女人)红脸、脏兮兮、而且衣服不整的; 邋遢的.

blub·ber¹ /'blʌbə(r); 'blʌbɚ/ *n* [U] fat of whales and other sea-animals from which oil is obtained. 鲸脂; 其他海生动物之脂肪.

blub·ber² /'blʌbə(r); 'blʌbɚ/ *vi, vt* [VP2A] weep noisily; 吵闹大哭; [VP15B] ~ (**sth**) **out**, say with sobs. 哭泣着诉说(某事); 哭诉.

bludgeon /'blʌdʒən; 'blʌdʒən/ *n* short, thick stick with a heavy end, used as a weapon. 大头短棒(作武器用). □ *vt* [VP6A, 14] strike repeatedly with a ~: 用大头棒连打: *He had been* ~*ed to death.* 他被大头棒连打致死。~ *sb into doing sth*, (fig) compel him to do it. (喻)强迫某人做某事.

blue¹ /bluː; blu/ *adj* (**-r, -st**) coloured like the sky on a clear day or the deep sea when the sun is shining: 蓝色的; 蔚蓝的; 青色的: ~ *eyes.* 蓝色的眼睛. *His face was* ~ *with cold.* 他冻得脸发青. **,**~ **'blood(ed)** *adj, n* (of) aristocratic birth. 贵族出身的(的). **,**~ **'chips,** (fin) industrial shares considered valuable because of past records. (财政)(因以往业绩而被视为有价值的)优良股票. **,**~ **'film,** improper film. 猥亵的影片. **,**~ **'jokes,** improper jokes. 猥亵的笑话. **,B**~ **'Peter,** ~ flag with a white square in the centre, used to show that a ship is about to sail. 启航旗(中央有白色方块的蓝旗, 悬以表示船只即将出航). a ~ **'ribbon,** sign of great distinction: 蓝带; 荣誉之标志: *the* ~ *ribbon of the Atlantic*, held by the liner that has the record for the fastest crossing. 大西洋之蓝带奖(颁给保有横渡大西洋最快记录之班轮者之). *look* ~, (colloq) be sad or depressed. (口)面容沮丧; 面有忧色. **(Things are) looking** ~, depressing. (情势)不乐观. *once in a* ~ *moon*, very rarely. 非常少地.

blue² /bluː; blu/ *n* **1** ~ colour: 蓝色; 青色: *dressed in* ~; 穿着蓝色衣服; *Oxford* ~, dark ~; 深蓝色; *Cambridge* ~, light ~. 浅蓝色. **2** (the) sky. 青天; 蓝天. *appear/come out of the* ~, unexpectedly. 爆出冷门; 意外地出现. *a bolt from the* ~, sth quite unexpected. 晴天霹雳; 意外之事. **3** *win/get one's* ~ **(for sth),** (at Oxford or Cambridge University) gain the right to wear a ~ cap, scarf etc because one has represented the University in a sport: (在牛津或剑桥大学)因代表学校参加运动会等之学生所获戴蓝帽、围蓝围巾等之资格: *She got her* ~ *for tennis.* 她因为打网球而获得蓝色荣衔. Hence, 由此产生, person with this right: 获得蓝色荣衔之人: *He's a rowing* ~.

他是获得蓝色荣誉的划船队员. **4** (poet) (the) ~ (the) sea. (诗)海. **5** *a true* ~, a loyal member (of a political party, esp the Conservative). 忠实分子(指政党党员, 尤指保守党). **6** (*pl*) (dances, dance tunes, for) haunting jazz melodies originally of Negroes in the southern US. (复)布鲁斯(源出于美国南部黑人中之抑郁难忘的爵士曲调). 哀歌; 蓝调; 布鲁斯舞; 布鲁斯舞曲. **the** ~**s,** (colloq) condition of being sad, melancholy. (口)忧郁; 沮丧; 不乐. **7** (compounds) (复合词) **'**~**·bell** *n* (Scotland and N England) = harebell; (S England) wild hyacinth with ~ or white flowers growing in moist places and flowering in spring. (苏格兰及英格兰北部)山小菜; 蓝铃花 (= harebell); (英格兰南部) 野风信子(生长于潮湿地带, 春天开蓝花或白花). **'**~ **book** *n* book published by the Government containing a report. 蓝皮书 (政府所发表之报告书). **'**~**·bottle** *n* meat fly or blowfly. 青蝇; 大苍蝇; 琉璃蜗. **,**~**·'collar** *adj* of workers in factories, etc, who wear overalls (contrasted with *white-collar* workers). 蓝领的(用以指工厂等中穿着工作服之工人; 与白领相对), 蓝领阶级的. **'**~**·jacket** *n* seaman in the Navy. 海军战士; 水兵. **,**~**·'pencil** *vt* mark, censor, with a ~ pencil. 用蓝色铅笔作记号, 删改(稿件). **'**~**·print** *n* photographic print, white on ~ paper, usu for building plans; (fig) plan, scheme: (影印的白字蓝底, 通常为建筑设计用的)蓝图; 建筑蓝图; (喻)计划; 方案 (attrib) (用作定语) *the* ~*print stage.* 设计阶段; 筹划时期. **'**~**·stock·ing** *n* woman who is regarded as having superior literary tastes and intellectual interests. 女学究; 为人具有高度文学修养及知识趣味之女性; 女学者. **blu·ish** /'bluːɪʃ; 'bluɪʃ/ *adj* tending towards ~: 带蓝色的; 带蓝色的: *bluish green.* 蓝绿色.

blue³ /bluː; blu/ *vt* **1** make blue. 使成蓝色. **2** ~ *one's money*, (sl) spend it recklessly. (俚)乱用钱; 胡乱花钱.

bluff¹ /blʌf; blʌf/ *n* headland with a broad and very steep face. 伸入海中之悬崖绝壁. □ *adj* **1** (of headlands; cliffs, a ship's bows) with a broad, perpendicular front. (指悬崖绝壁、船首)陡峭的; 前面宽而垂直的. **2** (of a person, his manner, etc) abrupt; rough but honest and kind, simple and good-natured. (指人、其态度等)率直的; 坦诚的; 直爽的. ~**·ly** *adv* ~**·ness** *n*

bluff² /blʌf; blʌf/ *vt, vi* [VP6A, 14, 15B, 2A] deceive sb by pretending. 假装而骗(人); 虚张声势以吓(人); 诈骗. ~ *sb into doing sth*, lead sb to do sth or believe sth by deceiving him: 骗某人做(或相信)某事; 恫吓某人使做某事: *They were* ~*ed into supposing we were ill prepared.* 他们受骗以为我们没有好好准备. ~ *it out*, survive a difficult situation by pretence. 借假装以度过困境. ~ *one's way out of sth*, escape from a situation by pretence. 借假装以逃脱某种情况. □ *n* [U, C] deception of this kind: (the use of) threats that are intended to get results without being carried out. 诈骗; 虚张声势. *call sb's* ~, invite him to do what he threatened to do. 促使某人去做他所威胁着要做的事. ~**er** *n* person who tries to ~ people. 虚张声势以骗人者; 吓唬人者; 诈骗者.

blun·der /'blʌndə(r); 'blʌndɚ/ *vi, vt* **1** [VP2A, C, 3A] move about uncertainly, as if blind: 瞎闯; 乱闯: ~ *into a wall.* 瞎闯碰着了墙壁. **2** [VP2A] make foolish mistakes: 犯大错: *Our leaders have* ~*ed again.* 我们的领袖人又犯了大错. □ *n* [C] stupid or careless mistake. 大错; 愚笨或粗心的错误. ~**er** *n* person who commits a ~. 犯大错之人.

blun·der·buss /'blʌndəbʌs; 'blʌndɚˌbʌs/ *n* old-fashioned gun with a wide mouth, firing many bullets or small shot at once at short range. 老式大口径的短程散弹枪.

blunt /blʌnt; blʌnt/ *adj* (**-er, -est**) **1** without a point or sharp edge: 不尖的; 不利的; 钝的: *a* ~ *knife.* 钝刀. **2** (of a person, what he says) plain; not troubling to be polite: (指人、所说的话)直率的; 直言的; 不客气的: *He's a* ~ *man.* 他是个直率的人. *The* ~ *fact is that . . .* 不

可隐讳的事实是…. □ *vt* [VP6A] make ~: 使钝: *If you try to cut stone with a knife, you will ~ the edge.* 如果你试以刀砍石, 你就会把刀刃弄钝. **~ · ly** *adv: to speak ~ly,* plainly, without ceremony. 直率地说; 坦白地说; 不客气地说. **~ · ness** *n*

blur /blɜː(r); blɝ/ *n* **1** dirty spot or mark; smear of ink. 污点; 污迹; 墨水渍. **2** confused or indistinct effect: 模糊不清的现象; 一片模糊: *If, when you try to read small print, you see only a ~, you probably need glasses.* 如果你在看小字书印的时候, 你只看见一片模糊, 那么你很可能需要戴眼镜了. □ *vt, vi* (**-rr-**) [VP6A, 2A] make a dirty mark or smear on (sth); make or become unclear, confused in appearance: 弄污; 弄上污点; 使模糊不清; 变得模糊不清: *Tears ~red her eyes.* 泪水使她眼睛模糊. *Mists ~red the view.* 雾使风景模糊. *The writing was ~red.* 字迹被弄得模糊不清. *Rain ~red the windows of our car.* 雨水使我们的车窗模糊了.

blurb /blɜːb; blɝb/ *n* publisher's description of the contents of a book, printed on the paper jacket, etc. 出版商对书籍内容之说明(印在书的外封皮等处).

blurt /blɜːt; blɝt/ *vt* [VP15B] **~ sth out,** tell sth, eg a secret, suddenly, often thoughtlessly. 脱口说出某事 (如秘密).

blush /blʌʃ; blʌʃ/ *vi* **1** [VP2A, C, 3A] become red (in the face) from shame or confusion: (因羞愧或糊而)脸红; 赧颜: *She ~ed for/with shame.* 她因羞愧而脸红. *She ~ed at the thought of....* 她一想起…就脸红. *He ~ed as red as a peony.* 他的脸红得象一朵牡丹花. **2** [VP4B] (fig) be ashamed: (喻)羞于; 惭愧: **~ to confess that....** 羞于承认…. □ *n* **1** reddening of the face, eg from shame, etc: 脸红; 赧颜: *She turned away to hide her ~es.* 她转过身去掩饰她的脸红. **2** (old use) glimpse: (旧用法)一瞥: *at first ~,* at the first look. 初见; 乍看时. **~ · ing** *adj* **~ · ing · ly** *adv*

blus · ter /ˈblʌstə(r); ˈblʌstɚ/ *vi, vt* **1** [VP2A, C] (of the wind, waves, etc) storm; be rough or violent. (指风、浪等)猛袭; 狂作; 狂吹. **2** [VP2A] (of persons) act and speak in a forceful but rather unsteady, often rather boastful way. (指人)咆哮; 恫吓. **3** [VP15B] **~ out,** utter in this way: 咆哮着说出: *~ out threats.* 咆哮地说出恫吓的话. □ *n* [U] **1** noise of violent wind or waves. (狂风或大浪之)咆哮声; 吼啸声. **2** ~ing talk and behaviour; noisy threats. 咆哮之言行; 恫吓. **~ · y** *adj* (of the weather) rough and blowy. (指天气)刮大风; 狂风大作的.

bo(h) /bəʊ; bo/ *int* ⇨ **boo.**

boa /ˈbəʊə; ˈboə/ *n* **1** (also 亦作 **'boa-constrictor**) large non-poisonous snake that kills by crushing its prey. 蟒蛇(无毒之巨蛇, 能绞杀其捕获物以食之). ⇨ the illus at **snake.** 参看 snake 之插图. **2** (also 亦作 **'feather-boa**) feather stole (formerly) worn by women. (昔时)妇女所用之羽毛披肩.

boar /bɔː(r); bɔr/ *n* **1** wild male pig. 雄野猪. **2** uncastrated male domestic pig. 未阉的雄猪. ⇨ **hog, sow¹.**

board¹ /bɔːd; bɔrd/ *n* **1** long, thin, flat piece of wood with squared edges, used in building walls, floors, boats, ship's decks, etc. 木板(作墙壁、地板、船身、甲板等之)木板. **2** flat piece of wood or other material for a special purpose, sometimes bare, sometimes covered with cloth, leather, etc: (木质或其他材料, 作为某种特殊用途, 有时裸着, 有时覆盖布, 皮革等之)板子; 牌子: *'sign~;* 招牌; *'notice~;* 公告牌; a *'diving-~.* 跳水板. **3** flat surface with patterns, etc on which games, eg chess, are played. 做游戏用, 上有图案、格子等的平板; 棋盘. ⇨ the illus at **chess.** 参看 chess 之插图. **4** (from the ~s that form the stage of a theatre) (由舞台戏台之木板而来) **the ~s,** the theatre: 戏院; 剧场: *on the ~s,* employed as an actor; on the stage. 当演员; 在戏台上. **5** (from the ~s that form the deck of a ship) (由作甲板之木板而来) **on ~,** in a ship. 在船上. **go on ~,** go on to a ship or into an airliner (in US, also of trains).

上船; 上飞机; (在美国亦指)上火车. **go by the ~,** (of masts, etc) fall over the ship's side; (fig, of plans, hopes, etc) be given up or abandoned; fail completely. (指帆樯等)折断落到船外; (喻, 指计划, 希望的)被放弃; 完全失败. **6** (from the idea of *table,* used for gambling). (由作赌博之桌子而来) **above ~,** openly, without deception. 公开地; 无欺骗地. **sweep the ~,** win all the cards or the money staked; (fig) be completely successful. 赌博时赢了赌桌上所有的牌或赌注; (喻)完全成功. **7** (from the idea of *table*) council-table; councillors; committee; group of persons controlling a business, or a government department: (由桌子的意义而来)会议桌; 议员们; 委员会; 理事会; 董事会; 掌管一项事务或政府部门的一批人员: *the 'B~ of 'Governors,* eg of a school; (学校等的)董事会; *the ,B~ of 'Trade;* 贸易委员会; *Local 'Government B~;* 地方政府的官吏们; *'School B~,* (in England until 1902) controlling elementary schools known as *'b~-schools;* (英国在一九〇二年以前管理小学 board-schools 的)教育委员会; *a Se'lection B~,* one that selects from applicants or candidates. 选拔委员会. ,across-the-'~, ⇨ **across²(1).** **8** [U] food served at table, esp meals supplied by the week or month (eg at a lodging-house) or as part payment for service: 伙食; 膳食: *The hotel porter gets £40 a week and free ~.* 旅馆服务员每周工资四十英镑并供膳食. *B~ and lodging £45 weekly.* 膳食费每周四十五英镑. **9** thick, stiff paper, sometimes cloth-covered, used for book covers: 纸板(作封面用, 有时并包以布之)硬纸板: *bound in cloth ~s.* 布面精装的. ⇨ also **card~, paste~. 10** (compounds) (复合词) **'~-room** *n* room in which meetings of a B~ of Directors, etc) are held. (董事会之)会议室. **'~ walk** *n* (US) promenade, originally made of planks, esp along a beach. (美)(原为用木板做成的, 尤指沿着海滩的)散步道.

board² /bɔːd; bɔrd/ *vt, vi* [VP6A, 15B] make or cover with boards(1): 用木板做; 用木板覆盖: **~ up a window;** 将窗户用木板盖住; **~ (over) the stern of a boat,** cover it with boards to make a deck. 将船之尾部铺上木板(以便做成甲板). *The floor was ~ed.* 地板上加铺了木板. **2** (⇨ **board¹(8))** [VP6A, 3A, 2C] **~ (at sth/with sb),** get (from), supply (with); meals for a fixed weekly/monthly etc payment: (按周, 按月等)包饭; 搭伙; 寄食; 寄食: *Mrs Jones makes a living by ~ing students.* 琼斯太太靠给学生们包饭谋生. *Jim ~s at 'The Willows'/with Mrs Jones.* 吉姆在'柳屋'(琼斯太太)寄膳. **~ out,** take meals at a different place from that in which one lives. 不在住的地方吃饭. **3** [VP6A] get on or into (a ship, train, plane, bus, etc). 上(船、火车、飞机、公共汽车等). **~ing** *n* **1** person who ~s(2) with sb. 寄膳者; 搭伙者. **2** boy or girl at a ~ing-school (⇨ below). 寄宿学校的学生(男或女)(参看下列 board-ingschool). **~ · ing** *n* [U] **1** structure of ~s(1). 用木板建造之物. **2** providing or receiving of ~s(8). 供膳; 包饭; 寄膳. **'~-ing-card** *n* card allowing one to ~(3) (esp) a ship or plane. 乘船证; 登机证. **'~-ing-house** *n* private house that provides ~¹(8) and lodging 供给膳宿的私人房子; 给膳食之宿舍; 寄宿舍. **'~-ing-school** *n* school where pupils receive ~¹(8) and lodging as well as lessons. (供学生膳宿之)寄宿学校.

boast /bəʊst; bost/ *n* [C] **1** words used in praise of oneself, one's acts, belongings, etc: 自夸之词; 自负; 自吹自擂: *It was the enemy's ~ that they could never be defeated.* 敌人称他们永不打败仗, 系自夸之词. **2** cause for satisfaction; sth of which one may rightly be proud: 堪以自负、自豪或自傲之事: *It was his ~ that he had never failed in an examination.* 他考试从来不失败乃是他足以自傲之事. □ *vt, vi* [VP2A, 3A, B] **~ (of/about),** make a ~; say: 自夸; 自吹自擂: *He ~s of being/~s that he is the best tennis-player in the town.* 他自夸是全市最好的网球选手. *That's nothing to ~ of.* 那没有什么好夸耀的. *He often ~s to his neighbours about the successes of his children.* 他常常向邻人夸耀他

的孩子们的成就。**2** [VP6A] possess with pride: 很可自豪地拥有: *Our school ~s a fine swimming-pool.* 我们的学校很可自豪地拥有一个完善的游泳池。**~er** *n* person who ~s. 自专者; 自诩者; 大言者。**~•ful** /-fʊl; -fəl/ *adj* (of persons) fond of ~ing; (of words, etc) full of self-praise. (指人) 好自夸的; (指言辞等) 充满自夸的。**~•fully** /-fəlɪ; -folɪ/ *adv*

boat /bəʊt; bot/ *n* **1** small open vessel for travelling in on water, esp the kind moved with oars ('rowing ~'), sails ('sailing ~), or petrol or oil engines ('motor-~') also used of fishing-vessels and small steamers: 无篷的小船; (尤指) 用桨划之船; 帆船; (用汽油引擎之) 汽艇; (亦指) 渔船; 小汽船: *We crossed the river by ~/in a ~.* 我们乘船渡河。*B~s for hire—£2 an hour.* 游船出租——每小时两英镑。**be (all) in the same ~**, have the same dangers to face. (大家) 处于同一境遇 (尤指危险的境遇); 同舟共济。**burn one's ~s**, do sth that makes it impossible to retreat, to change one's plans, etc. 破釜沉舟; 断绝退路。**take to the ~s**, (of the crew and passengers of a ship) use ship's ~s to escape, eg when the ship is sinking. (指船上的船员与乘客在船遇难下沉时) 用救生艇逃生。**'~•hook** *n* long pole for fending off or holding a ~, eg at a landing-stage. (撑船用之一端有钩的) 钩篙。**'~•house** *n* shed in which ~s are stored. 船库 (存放船之棚子)。**'~•man** /-mən; -mən/ *n* (*pl* **-men**) man who rows or sails a small ~ for pay; man from whom rowing-~s may be hired. (划船上的) 船伕; 出租划船的人。**'~•race** *n* race between rowing-~s. 划船比赛。**'~•train** *n* train that takes people to or from a passenger ship, eg between London and Dover. 与邮船联运之火车 (如伦敦与多佛之间者)。⇨ **ferry, house[1] (7), life(14), mail[1](1).** **2** ~-shaped dish used at table for gravy or sauce. (餐桌上用以盛调味汁之) 船形碟子。□ *vi* [VP2A, C] travel in a ~, esp for pleasure: 乘船旅行; (尤指) 乘游艇游玩: *We ~ed down the river.* 我们乘船顺水而下。**go ~ing**, go out (esp in a rowing-~) for pleasure: 去划船 (玩乐)。

boater /'bəʊtə(r); 'botɚ/ *n* hard straw hat (formerly worn in summer for boating). (昔时在夏天划船时所戴之) 硬草帽。

boat•swain /'bəʊsn; 'bosn/ *n* senior seaman who controls the work of other seamen and is in charge of a ship's rigging, boats, anchors, etc. (船上的) 水手长; (管理其他水手之工作及素具、船上小艇、锚等之) 资深水手; 帆缆士官长。

bob[1] /bɒb; bab/ *vi* (**-bb-**) [VP2O] **1** move up and down: 上下地动: *The cork on his fishing-line was bobbing on the water.* 他的钓丝上的浮子在水面上下急动。**bob up**, (fig) carry on again; reappear: (喻)继续; (喻)再出现: *That fellow bobs up like a cork*, cannot be 'kept down', always becomes active again after being in trouble, etc. 那个人百折不回 (经过患难后总立刻又振作起来)。*That question often bobs up* (*crops up* is more usu), is often asked. 那个问题常被提起 (crops up 较常用)。**2 bob to sb**, also [VP6A] **bob a curtsy**, curtsy. 向某人行屈膝鞠躬礼。□ *n* quick up and down movement; curtsy. 上下来回的疾动; 屈膝鞠躬礼。

bob[2] /bɒb; bab/ *vt* (**-bb-**) (dated) cut (a woman's or girl's hair) so that it hangs loosely and short of the shoulders: (过时用语)将 (女人的头发) 剪短 (至耳根处): *She wears her hair bobbed.* 她留着短发。*I shall have my hair bobbed.* 我将要把我的头发剪短。□ *n* bobbed hair. 剪短之发型; 短发。

bob[3] /bɒb; bab/ *n* (*pl* unchanged; sl) former British coin, called 'shilling' (replaced by the 5p coin). (复数不变; 俚)昔时英国之一种硬币 (称为 "先令", 后为五便士之硬币所取代)。

bob•bin /'bɒbɪn; 'babɪn/ *n* small roller or spool for holding thread, yarn, wire, etc in a machine. 线轴; (缠绕钱丝等之)轴心。

bobby /'bɒbɪ; 'babɪ/ *n* (GB colloq) policeman. (英口) 警察。

bobby pin /'bɒbɪ pɪn; 'babɪ pɪn/ *n* (US) tight metal hair clip. (美)一种很紧的金属发夹。

bobby-socks, -sox /'bɒbɪ sɒks; 'babɪ,saks/ *n pl* (US, comm) girls' ankle socks. (美, 商)女短袜。

bobby-soxer /'bɒbɪ sɒksə(r); 'babɪ,saksɚ/ *n* (US sl during the 1940's) teenage or adolescent girl. (二十世纪四十年代之美国俚语)十几岁的姑娘; 少女。

bobo•link /'bɒbəlɪŋk; 'babl,ɪŋk/ *n* N American songbird. 食米鸟(北美产之鸣禽)。

bob•sled, bob•sleigh /'bɒbsled, -sleɪ; 'babsled, -sle/ *n* **1** sleigh made by joining two short sleighs, used in tobogganing. 连橇; 长橇。**2** large, long sleigh with brake and steering wheel, used for racing. (有制动器及方向盘, 供比赛用之)大连橇。

a racing bobsleigh

bob•tail /'bɒbteɪl; 'bab,tel/ *n* (horse or dog with a) docked tail. 尾巴剪短之马或狗; 剪短之尾巴。**the rag-tag and ~**, the rabble. 贱民。

bode /bəʊd; bod/ *vt, vi*, (old use or poet) (旧用法或诗) **1** [VP12B, 13B] be a sign of; foretell: 预兆; 预示: *This ~s us no good.* 这个对于我们不是吉兆。**2 ~ well/ill for**, be of good/bad promise for: 预示有好的 (不好的) 前途: *His idle habits ~ ill for his future*, suggest that his future career will be a failure. 他的懒惰习惯预示他将来不会有好的前途。**bod•ing** *n* feeling of coming evil. 对于将临之祸事的预感; 恶兆。

bod•ice /'bɒdɪs; 'badɪs/ *n* close-fitting part of a woman's dress or of an under-garment from the shoulders to the waist. 女装上半之紧身部分; 女人紧身胸衣。

-bodied /-bɒdɪd; -badɪd/ *adj* (with *adjj*): (与形容词连用): '*big-~*, '*strong-~*, having a big/strong body 身体魁梧的; 身体强壮的; *able-~*, ⇨ **able**

bod•ily /'bɒdɪlɪ; 'badlɪ/ *adj* of or in the human body or physical nature: 身体的; 肉体的: *supply a person's ~ wants* (eg food): 供给某人身体的需要(如食物); *~* (= physical) *assault*. 身体的攻击。□ *adv* **1** as a whole or mass; completely: 全部; 全体; 整个; 完全地: *The audience rose ~* (= everyone rose at the same moment) *to cheer the speaker.* 听众全体一致起立向演说者欢呼。*The building was transported ~* (= as a whole, without being pulled down) *one hundred yards down the street.* 那建筑物整座(未拆毁)被沿街移动了一百码。**2** in person; in the body. 亲自; 亲身。

bod•kin /'bɒdkɪn; 'badkɪn/ *n* blunt, thick needle with a large eye (used for drawing tape, etc through a hem). 不尖有大眼之粗针(用以拉带子等穿过衣边)。

body /'bɒdɪ; 'badɪ/ *n* (*pl* **-dies**) **1** The whole physical structure of a man or animal: (人或动物的)身体; 躯体; 肉体: *We wear clothes to keep our bodies warm.* 我们穿衣以保持身体温暖。⇨ the illus at **arm, head, leg, skeleton, trunk.** 参看 arm, head, leg, skeleton, trunk 之插图。⇨ **mind, soul, spirit. keep ~ and soul together**, remain alive: 维持生存; 活命; 苟延残喘: *He earns scarcely enough to keep ~ and soul together.* 他所赚的钱几乎不够维持温饱。**2** dead ~; corpse: 死尸; 尸体; 遗骸; 遗体: *His ~ was brought back to England for burial.* 他的遗体被运回英国埋葬。**3** main portion of a man or animal without the head, arms and legs: (人或动物的)躯干部; 躯体 (头和四肢除外): *He received one wound in the left leg and another in the ~.* 他左腿受了一

处伤，躯体也受了一处伤。4 main part of a structure: 建造物之主要部分: the ~ of a motor-car; 汽车的车身; the ~ of a concert hall, the central part where the seats are. 音乐会堂中座位所在的中央部分。5 group of persons who do sth together or who are united in some way: (共同从事某种工作之)团体; (为某种原因而结合在一起的)人群; 队伍: Large bodies of unemployed men marched through the streets demanding work. 一群群的失业者在街上游行要求工作。The affairs of the school are managed by the Governing B~. 学校的事务由行政部门处理。A legislative ~ is a group of persons who make laws. 立法团体就是一群制订法律的人。the ~ 'politic, ⇨ politic(3). in a ~, all together; as a whole: 全体; 全部; 整个: The staff resigned in a ~. 全体职员总辞职。6 (colloq) person; human being: (口)人: She's a nice old ~. 她是一个很好的老人。(in compounds): (用于复合词中): every~, any~, some~, no~. 每个人，任何人，某人，无人。7 mass, quantity, collection: 团; 量; 聚集: A lake is a ~ of water. 湖是一潭水。He has a large ~ of facts to prove his statements. 他搜集了很多事实以证明他的言论。8 distinct piece of matter: 物体: the heavenly bodies, the sun, moon and stars; 天体(即日、月、星辰); a foreign ~ (= a speck of dirt) in the eye. 眼中之异物。9 [U] (of wine, etc) full, strong quality: (指酒等)浓郁的品质: wine of good ~. 十分浓郁的酒。10 (compounds)(复合词) '~-guard n group of men (sometimes a single man) guarding an important person. (重要人物的)侍卫; 卫队; 保镖(有时指一人)。'~-language n interpreting the way sb sits, stands, moves etc as expressing his feelings. 身体语言(根据某人坐、站、行动等之方式来解释他所表达之感情)。'~-snatcher n (formerly) person who (illegally) dug up corpses and sold them for dissection. (昔时)掘墓盗尸(出售作解剖研究)者。'~-work n main outside structure of a motor vehicle. 汽车的外壳; 车身。

Boer /bɔ:(r); bɔr/ n (old use) South African of Dutch descent; Afrikaner. (旧用法) 荷裔南非人; 布尔人。□ adj (old use) of Dutch South Africa; Afrikaans. (旧用法)荷属南非洲的; 南非荷兰语的。~ war, between the ~s and the British (1899—1902). 布尔战争(1899年至1902年布尔人与英国人之间的战争)。

bof·fin /ˈbɒfɪn; ˈbɑfɪn/ n (sl) technician or scientist (esp one engaged in research). (俚) (尤指从事研究工作之)技师或科学家。

bog /bɒg; bɑg/ n 1 (area of) soft, wet, spongy ground (chiefly decayed or decaying vegetable matter). 沼泽; 沼泽区(地面主要为腐朽的植物)。2 (vulg sl) latrine. (鄙俚)厕所; 毛坑。□ vt, vi (-gg-) [VP15B, 2O] ~ down, (cause to) be stuck fast, unable to make progress: (使)陷于泥淖; (使)陷入困境: The tanks (got) ~ged down in the mud. 战车陷于泥淖中不能前进。Our discussions have ~ged down. 我们的讨论僵住了 (无法进展)。 **boggy** /ˈbɒgɪ; ˈbɑgɪ/ adj (of land) soft and wet. (指土地)软而湿的; 沼泽性的。

bo·gey¹ ⇨ bogy.

bo·gey² /ˈbəʊgɪ; ˈbogɪ/ n (golf) score that a good player makes for a hole (or the whole course) and that other players try to equal. (高尔夫球)(以高手为标准所定的)某一洞或全场的)标准杆数。⇨ par¹(2).

boggle /ˈbɒgl; ˈbɑgl/ vi [VP2A, 3A] ~ (at sth), be unwilling, hesitate; be alarmed, amazed: 对某事畏缩不前; 踌躇; 吃惊; 受惊: The mind/imagination ~s (at the idea). 心中(想象中)(对那种想法)感到吃惊。

bo·gie /ˈbəʊgɪ; ˈbogɪ/ n (also 亦作 **bogey, bogy**) 1 trolley. 台车。2 four-wheeled undercarriage fitted under (the end of) a railway engine or wagon to enable it to go round curves. 置于火车引擎或货车(的末端)底下用以帮助转弯之四轮车盘; 转向架。

bo·gus /ˈbəʊgəs; ˈbogəs/ adj sham; counterfeit. 假的; 伪造的; 赝造的。

bogy, bo·gey /ˈbəʊgɪ; ˈbogɪ/ n (pl -gies, -geys) evil spirit; sb or sth that causes fear. 妖怪; 使人害怕的

人或物; 怪物。

bo·he·mi·an /bəʊˈhi:mɪən; boˈhimɪən/ n, adj (person) not living in ways considered socially normal or conventional. 生活方式不正常或不合习俗的(人); 放荡不羁的(人)。

boil¹ /bɔɪl; bɔɪl/ n hard (usu red, often painful) poisoned swelling under the skin, which bursts when ripe. 疔疮; 疖子(皮下所生之硬肿毒, 通常呈红色, 常常很痛, 化脓时会溃裂)。

boil² /bɔɪl; bɔɪl/ vi, vt 1 [VP2A, B, C, D] (of water or other liquid, also of the vessel that contains it and of what is in the water) reach the temperature at which change to gas occurs; bubble up: (指水或其他液体, 亦指盛液体之器皿及水中之物)沸腾; (水)开: When water ~s it changes into steam. 水沸腾时就变成蒸汽。The kettle is ~ing. 壶里的水开了。The potatoes are ~ing. 马铃薯在煮着。Don't let the kettle ~ dry. 不要让壶里的水煮干了。Let the vegetables ~ gently. 把蔬菜用慢火煮着。**keep the pot ~ing**, (fig) earn or otherwise find enough money for food, etc. (喻)维持生活; 糊口。'~ing-point n temperature at which a liquid ~s. (液体的)沸点。**~ing hot**, (colloq) very hot: (口)极炎热的: a ~ing hot day. 极炎热的一日。2 [VP2A, C] (of the sea, of a person's feelings, etc) be agitated like ~ing water: (指海等)汹涌; (指感情等)激昂: The boat was swallowed up by the ~ing waves. 船被汹涌的浪涛吞没。He was ~ing (over) with indignation. 他怒气冲冲。Cruelty to animals makes her blood ~. 虐待动物使她极为愤怒。3 [VP6A, 22] cause water or other liquid to ~; cook in ~ing water: 使(水或其他液体)沸腾; 用开水煮: We ~ eggs, fish and vegetables. 我们烹煮蛋、鱼及蔬菜。Please ~ my egg for three minutes. 请把我的蛋煮三分钟。I like my eggs ~ed hard. 我喜欢吃煮老的蛋。My brother prefers soft-~ed eggs. 我的哥哥(弟弟)喜欢吃煮嫩一点的蛋。4 [VP2C, 15B] ~ away, (a) continue to ~: 继续沸腾: The kettle was ~ing away merrily on the fire. 壶里的水在火上沸腾着了。(b) ~ until nothing remains: 煮干; 烧干: The water had all ~ed away and the kettle was empty. 水完全烧干了, 壶也空了。~ down, be reduced in quantity: 在数量上减少: It all ~s down to this..., (colloq) The essence of the statement, proposal, etc) is.... (口)(指陈述、建议等)要点就是⋯。~ sth down, make less by ~ing: (fig) condense: 将某物煮沸; (喻)浓缩; 缩短; 摘要: ~ down a long article to two hundred words, make a précis of it. 将一篇长文压缩到二百个字。~ over, boil and flow over the side of a vessel: 沸腾而溢出: The milk had ~ed over. 牛奶已沸腾得溢出来了。□ n the ~, ~ing point: 沸点: be on the ~, be ~ing. 在沸点; 在沸腾中。**bring sth to the ~**, heat it until it ~s. 将某物煮至沸腾。**come to the ~**, begin to ~. 开始沸腾。

boiler /ˈbɔɪlə(r); ˈbɔɪlə/ n 1 metal container in which water, etc is heated, eg for producing steam in an engine; tank forming part of a kitchen range for supplying hot water; tank for heating water for a laundry. 锅炉; 汽锅; 热水器; 烧水壶。'~-suit n one-piece garment, overalls, for rough or dirty work. (做粗工或脏工作时所穿的)上衣连裤的工作服。2 person whose trade is boiling sth: 以煮物为业者: a 'soap-~. 制造肥皂者。

bois·ter·ous /ˈbɔɪstərəs; ˈbɔɪstərəs/ adj rough, violent: 狂暴的; 猛烈的: ~ weather; 狂风暴雨的天气; a ~ wind/sea; 暴风(波涛汹涌的海); (of a person, his behaviour) noisy and cheerful. (指人, 其行为)喧闹的; 闹嚷的。~·ly adv

bold /bəʊld; bold/ adj (-er, -est) 1 without, showing no, fear; enterprising. 无畏的; 大胆的; 有进取心的。be/make so ~ as to do sth, allow oneself to do it: 容许自己做某事; 不揣冒昧做某事: If I may be so ~ as to..., If I may venture or presume to... 我不揣冒昧⋯。**make ~ with sth**, (more usu 较常用 make free with) take the liberty of using it. 擅自使用(某

物)。a ~ **front,** ⇨ **front(4). 2** without feelings of shame; immodest. 无耻的; 无礼的。*as ~ as brass,* impudent. 厚颜的。**3** well marked; clear: 轮廓清楚的: *the ~ outline of a mountain;* 一座山之清晰轮廓; *a ~ headland; a painting made with a few ~* (=free and vigorous) *strokes of the brush.* 一幅由几笔劲道的笔触画成的画。**~·ly** adv ~ **·ness** n

bole /bəʊl; bol/ n trunk of a tree. 树干。

bol·ero /bə'leərəʊ; bo'lɛro/ n [C] (pl ~s) **1**(music for a) Spanish dance. 西班牙舞; 西班牙舞曲。**2** /'bɒlərəʊ; bo'lɛro/ short jacket with no front fastening. (前面不开扣的)短上衣。

boll /bəʊl; bol/ n round seed-vessel (of cotton and flax). (棉及亚麻之)圆蒴; 荚壳。⇨ the illus at **cotton.** 参看 cotton 之插图。,~ **'weevil** /'wiːvl; 'wivl/ n small destructive insect that infests cotton-plants. 棉虫(侵害棉禾之小昆虫)。

bol·lard /'bɒled; 'baləd/ n **1** upright post (usu of iron) on a quay or a ship's deck for making ropes secure. (码头上的)系船桩; (甲板上的)系缆桩。**2** protective post on a traffic island, or a roadway, sometimes with an arrow to direct traffic. (马路安全岛上或车道上的)保护桩(有时上有箭号以指示交通)。

bol·locks /'bɒleks; 'baləks/ n pl ⚠ (讳)=**ballocks.**

bo·loney /bə'leʊnɪ; bə'loni/ n [U] (US sl) nonsense; humbug. (美俚)胡说八道; 胡扯。

Bol·she·vik /'bɒlʃevɪk; 'balʃə,vɪk/ n 布尔什维克。

bol·shy /'bɒlʃɪ; 'balʃɪ/ adj (sl) rebellious; stubborn. (俚)反叛的; 反抗的; 顽强的。

bol·ster¹ /'bəʊlstə(r); 'bolstə/ n long under-pillow for the head of a bed. (床头上的)长枕垫。

bol·ster² /'bəʊlstə(r); 'bolstə/ vt [VP6A, 15B] ~ (up), support; give (greatly needed, often undeserved) support to, eg a cause, theory, etc, that would otherwise fail. 支持; 支援; 对于(不支持就会失败的运动、学说等)给予(极需要的, 常为不应得的)援助。

bolt¹ /bəʊlt; bolt/ n **1** metal fastening for a door or window, consisting of a sliding pin or rod and a staple into which it fits. (金属的)门闩; 窗闩。**2** metal pin with a head at one end and a thread (as on a screw) at the other, used with a nut for holding things together. 带帽的螺丝钉; 螺栓。**3** (old use) short heavy arrow shot

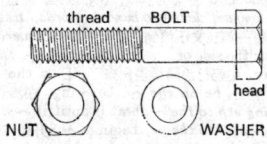

thread   BOLT

head

NUT   WASHER

a bolt

from a crossbow. (旧用法)粗短的箭; 矢。*shoot one's (last) ~,* make one's last effort. 尽其最后努力。**4** discharge of lightning. 闪电; 霹雳。⇨ **blue²(2); ~** *thunder ~* at **thunder(1). 5** (as a measure of cloth, canvas, etc) roll (as it comes from the loom). (做为布匹等织布机上取下时之度量)一匹, 一卷。口vt, vi [VP6A, 15B, 2A] fasten with a ~(1): 用闩闩住: *the doors and windows;* 将门窗闩住; ~ *sb in,* shut him in by ~ing the door(s); 把(某人)关在屋里; ~ *sb out,* keep him out by ~ing the door(s). 将某人关在门外。*The door ~s on the inside.* 这门要从里面闩。

bolt² /bəʊlt; bolt/ vi, vt [VP2A, C] run away quickly; (esp of a horse) run off out of control: 急逃: (尤指马)突跑; 狂奔: *As soon as I came downstairs the burglar ~ed through the back door.* 我一下楼来, 窃贼就从后门飞奔而逃。**2** [VP6A] swallow (food) quickly: 匆匆吞咽(食物): *We ~ed a few mouthfuls of food and hurried on.* 我们匆匆吞了几口食物, 就赶着继续前进。**3** [VP2A] (of plants) grow quickly upwards and go to

seed. (指植物)迅速成长并结实。口 n act of running away. 逃跑: 逃走。*make a ~ for it,* run off quickly (usu to escape from sth). 急忙逃走 (通常系逃避某某物)。'~**-hole** n hole or burrow into which to ~ for safety. 逃入以躲避危险之洞穴。

bolt³ /bəʊlt; bolt/ vt [VP6A] sift (flour). 筛(面粉)。

bolt⁴ /bəʊlt; bolt/ adv ~ **upright,** (of sb's posture) quite upright. (指某人的姿势)挺直的; 直立的。

bomb /bɒm; bam/ n hollow metal ball or shell filled either with explosive for causing destruction or with smoke, gas, or incendiary material, eg dropped from aircraft; (old use) hand-grenade. 炸弹 (中空之金属球或壳, 内充破坏性之爆炸物, 或产生烟雾、毒气或燃烧性之物质, 如从飞机上投下者); (旧用法)手榴弹。*go like a ~,* (sl) be very efficient, successful, etc: (俚)非常有效、成功等: *My new car goes like a ~.* 我的新车跑得棒极了。'~ **bay** n compartment (in an aircraft) for holding ~s. (飞机中的)炸弹舱。'~**-disposal squad,** squad for removing unexploded ~s and making them harmless. 炸弹处理小组(移除并销毁未爆炸之炸弹的小组)。'~**-proof** adj giving protection against exploding ~s: 不怕轰炸的; 炸不破的; 能防炸弹的: a ~*-proof shelter.* 防空避难室。'~**-shell** n (fig) sth that comes as a great surprise and shock. (喻)令人大为震惊的意外事件。'~**-sight** n device (in an aircraft) for aiming ~s. (飞机中的)轰炸瞄准器。'~**-site** n area (in a town) devastated by ~s: (城市中)被炸弹炸毁的地区: a *car park on a ~-site.* 被炸毁地区上的停车场。口 vt, vi **1** [VP6A, 15B] attack with ~s; drop ~s on. 轰炸。~ *out,* drive out (of buildings, etc) with ~s: 由于轰炸而被迫离开(建筑物等): ~*ed out families/factories.* 由于轰炸而被迫离开家庭(工厂)。**2** [VP15B, 2C] ~ *up,* load (an aircraft) with ~s. 装载炸弹于(飞机)中。装载炸弹。~*er* /'bɒmə(r); 'bamə/ n aircraft used for ~ing. ⇨ the illus at **aircraft.** (参看 aircraft 之插图)轰炸机。soldier trained in ~ing. 轰炸员。

bom·bard /bɒm'bɑːd; bam'bɑrd/ vt [VP6A, 14] ~ (with), attack with shells fired by big guns; (fig) worry with questions, requests, complaints, etc; (nuclear physics) send a stream of high-speed particles against (an atom, etc). 炮轰; (喻)(以问题、要求、指摘等)困扰; 质问; 轰击; (核物理学)(放出一股高速粒子)撞击(原子等)。~**·ment** n ~ing or being ~ed: 炮轰; 轰击: *after using a ~ment.* 经过长时间之轰击之后。

bom·bar·dier /,bɒmbə'dɪə(r); ,bambə'dɪr/ n (in an artillery regiment) non-commissioned officer below a sergeant. (炮兵团之)炮兵下士。

bom·bast /'bɒmbæst; 'bambæst/ n [U] insincere, high-sounding talk. 夸大之辞; 高调。**bom·bas·tic** /bɒm'bæstɪk; bam'bæstɪk/ adj (of a person, his talk, behaviour) promising much but not likely to do much; using fine high-sounding words. (指人、其言行)浮夸的; 口气大的; 唱高调的。**bom·bas·ti·cally** /-klɪ; -klɪ/ adv

bona fide /,bəʊnə 'faɪdɪ; 'bonə'faɪdɪ/ adj, adv (Lat) genuinely; sincerely; in good faith: (拉)真正的(地); 真诚的(地); 诚实的(地): (comm) (商) a ~ *buyer.* 老实的购买者。**bona fides** /,bəʊnə 'faɪdɪz; 'bonə'faɪdɪz / n (legal) honest intention; sincerity. (法律)诚意; 真诚。

bon·anza /bə'nænzə; bo'nænzə/ n [C] (pl ~s) (US) sth, eg a gold-mine, an oil-well, that is prospering greatly; (fig) bringing good luck and prosperity: (美)产量旺盛的金矿、油井等; 富矿源; 大为兴隆的事物; (用作定语)带来幸运及兴隆的: a ~ *year.* 幸运发财的一年。

bon·bon /'bɒnbɒn; 'ban,ban/ n sweet; sth made of sugar in a fancy shape, etc. 一种糖果。

bond /bɒnd; band/ n **1** agreement or engagement that a person is bound to observe, esp one that has force in law; document, signed and sealed, containing such an agreement. 契约; 合同; 票据; 保信; 此等文件: *enter into a ~ with sb,* agree to make a ~ with sb. 与某人订契

约. *His word is as good as his* ~, He is so honest that his spoken promise is as reliable as a written agreement. 他说的话有信用(与他的契约一样有效). **2** printed paper issued by a government or a corporation acknowledging that money has been lent to it and will be paid back with interest. (政府或公司发行的) 债票; 债券; 公债; 公司债券. '~**-holder** *n* person holding ~s. 债券持有人. **3** sth that joins or unites (usu fig): 连结物;束缚物(通常作比喻用): *the* ~(*s*) *of affection.* 感情的联系. *Common tastes form a* ~ *between the two men,* They are friends because they are interested in the same things. 共同的爱好使这两人结交为朋友. **4** the state of being joined; 连结; 结合: *Press the surfaces together to ensure a good, firm* ~. 将面与面紧压在一起伸使牢固粘合. **5** (*pl*) prisoner's chains: (复)镣铐;桎梏: *in* ~*s,* held as a prisoner or as a slave; 被囚禁;被奴役; *burst one's* ~*s,* win freedom. 挣脱枷锁;赢得自由. **6** (comm) (商) *in* ~, (of goods) in a Customs warehouse (until duties are paid). (指货物)被扣留在海关的堆栈中(待纳税后始可取出). *place goods in/take goods out of* ~. 将货物扣留在海关堆栈中以待纳税(纳税后自海关堆栈中取出货物). □ *vt* [VP6A] **1** put (goods) into a Customs warehouse. 海关扣留(货物)(置于堆栈中). ~*ed goods,* imported and placed in ~ until duty is paid. 被海关扣留的进口货. *a* ~*ed warehouse,* one in which goods are stored until duties are paid. 海关扣留货物所用的堆栈. **2** join securely (with glue, etc). (用胶等)粘合.
bond- /bɒnd-; band-/ *pref* in slavery, not free: 被奴役的; 不自由的: '~**man**, 'bonds-man /-mən; -mən/ 奴隶; 奴仆; '~**maid**; 女奴; '~**servant;** 奴仆; 奴隶; '~**slave.** 奴隶.
bond·age /'bɒndɪdʒ; 'bɑndɪdʒ/ *n* [U] slavery, servitude: 奴役; 束缚: *in hopeless* ~ *to his master.* 永为主人之奴隶(无获自由之希望).
bone /bəʊn; bon/ *n* **1** [C] one of the parts that make up the framework (ie skeleton) of an animal's body. (动物身体内的)骨;骨头. ⇨ the illus at **skeleton.** 参看 skeleton 之插图. *This fish has a lot of* ~*s in it.* 这种鱼骨头很多. *No* ~ *broken, I hope,* I hope you have not hurt yourself. 我希望你未受伤. ~ *of contention,* subject of dispute. 争论的题目. *feel in one's* ~*s that,* feel certain that. 确有把握. *have a* ' ~ *to pick with sb,* have sth to argue or complain about. 与某人有争执或抱怨. *make no* ~*s about (doing) sth,* not hesitate about it, do it without scruple; 毫不犹豫地做某事; 毫无顾忌地做某事: *They dismissed him and made no* ~*s about it.* 他们毫不犹豫地把他开除了. (*frozen*) *to the* ~, completely, in a penetrating way. (寒冻)入骨; 刺骨;彻骨. *will not make old* ~*s,* will not live long. 不会活得很久. **2** [U] hard substance of which ~s are made: 骨质的: *Buttons are sometimes made of* ~. 钮扣有时用骨质物制成. *He's all skin and* ~, is very thin. 他骨瘦如柴. **3** (*pl,* old use) castanets; dice. (复, 旧用法)响板;骰子. **4** (compounds). (复合词). ~, '**dry** *adj* quite dry. 极干燥的. (俚)愚蠢的;呆头呆脑的人;笨蛋. ~'**idle**/'**lazy** *adj* completely idle. 懒到极点的. '~**meal** *n* fertilizer of crushed and powdered ~s. 骨粉(肥料). '~**setter** *n* person who sets broken ~s. 接骨专家. '~**shaker** *n* (colloq) old bicycle without rubber tyres; old, shaky bus, car or cart. (口)无橡皮轮胎之老式脚踏车; 破旧颠簸的公共汽车、汽车或马车. ,**big**~/,**strong**~'**d** *adj* having big/strong ~s. 骨骼大(强壮)的. □ *vt* [VP6A] **1** take ~s out of (a chicken, a piece of meat, etc). 取出 (鸡、肉块等之)骨头; 去…之骨. **2** (old use) put ~s into (eg a corset). (旧用法)装骨架于(如妇女用的束腰). **3** (sl) steal. (俚)偷窃. ~ *up on (a subject),* (sl). study hard. (俚)钻研(一门学科).
boner /'bəʊnə(r); 'bonɚ/ *n* (US sl) blunder. (美俚)大错.
bon·fire /'bɒnfaɪə(r); 'bɑn,faɪr/ *n* large fire made outdoors either to celebrate some event or to burn up dead leaves, rubbish, etc: 在户外所举之火(或为庆祝某事, 或为焚毁枯叶、垃圾等); 祝火; 营火: *make a* ~ *of,* get rid of. 烧掉; 焚毁; 清除.
bongo /'bɒŋgəʊ; 'baŋgo/ *n* (*pl* ~**s**) '~ **(drum),** small drum played with the hands, usu one of a pair. 一种用手敲打之小鼓. ⇨ the illus at **percussion.** 参看 percussion 之插图.
bon·homie /'bɒnəmɪ; ,banə'mi/ *n* [U] (F) bluff, hearty pleasantness of manner. (法)坦诚;和善;亲切;温和;和蔼.
bo·nito /bə'niːtəʊ; bə'nito/ *n* large kinds of tunny of the Atlantic Ocean, esp the striped tunny. 鲣(产于大西洋, 尤指有条纹者).
bon·kers /'bɒŋkəz; 'baŋkɚz/ *pred adj* (*stark, raving*) ~, (sl) raving mad; completely insane. (俚)疯狂的.
bon mot /,bɒn 'məʊ; ,ban 'mo/ *n* (*pl* **bons mots** /'məʊz; 'moz/) witty saying or remark. 珠玑妙语; 隽语.
bon·net /'bɒnɪt; 'banɪt/ *n* **1** small, round head-dress without a hard brim, usu tied under the chin. (通常用带系于颔下之)无边小圆软帽. **2** soft, flat cap worn by men in Scotland and by soldiers in some regiments. (苏格兰男子及某些团的军人所戴之)扁平软帽. **3** protective cover of various sorts, eg over a chimney, or (US 美 = *hood*) over the engine of a motor-car. 各种保护性的覆盖物(如盖于烟囱上者或汽车引擎的盖子). ⇨ the illus at **motor.** 参看 motor 之插图.
bonny /'bɒnɪ; 'banɪ/ *adj* (Scot) (苏) **1** attractive, fine. 可爱的; 美好的. **2** healthy looking; with a glow of health: 健美的;容光焕发的: *a baby.* 健美的婴儿; *her* ~ *face.* 她那容光焕发的面庞. **bon·nily** *adv*
bo·nus /'bəʊnəs; 'bonəs/ *n* (*pl* ~**es**) payment in addition to what is usual, necessary or expected, eg an extra dividend to stockholders of a business company; (insurance) a share of profits to policy-holders, or an extra payment to workers: (分给股东的)额外利息; 红利;(保险)(分配给投保人的)余利;额外优给;(工资以外的)奖金; 津贴: *cost-of-living* ~, addition to wages or salaries because of rising prices. (因物价上涨所给薪资以外的)生活补助金. **no 'claims** ~, percentage reduction in an insurance premium (for a motor vehicle) if claims are not made. (汽车保险之)未要求赔偿之保险费之折扣优待.
bony /'bəʊnɪ; 'bonɪ/ *adj* (**-ier, -iest**) **1** full of bones: 多骨的: *a* ~ *fish,* eg a herring. 多骨的鱼(如鲱). **2** having big or prominent bones: 骨骼大的; 骨骼突出的: *a tall,* ~ *man.* 一个高而骨骼突出的人. **3** with little flesh: 肉少的; 瘦的: ~ *fingers.* 瘦的手指.
boo /buː; bu/ (also 亦作 **bo, boh** /bəʊ; bo/) *int* sound made to show disapproval or contempt; exclamation used to surprise or startle: 呸(表示不赞成或轻蔑之声); 吓人的声音: *He can't say boo to a goose,* is timid. 他胆子很小(对一只鹅也不敢叫 boo). □ *vt, vi* [VP6A, 15A, 2A] make such sounds: 发轻蔑之声; 发嘘声: *The speaker was booed off the platform.* 演说者被嘘下台来了. *The crowd booed and hooted.* 群众发出轻蔑的叫嚣声.
boob[1] *n* **1** = **booby. 2** (colloq) silly mistake. (口)愚蠢的错. □ *vi* (colloq) make a silly mistake. (口)犯愚蠢的错.
boob[2] /buːb; bub/ *n* (sl) woman's breast. (俚)(女人的)奶子.
booby /'buːbɪ; 'bubɪ/ *n* silly or stupid person. 傻瓜;呆子;笨蛋. '~ **prize** *n* prize given as a joke to the person who is last in a race or competition. (赛跑或竞赛之)末名奖(意在善意的开玩笑); 倒数第一奖. '~**trap** *n* sth balanced on the top of a door so that it will fall on the first person to pass through; (mil) apparently harmless object that will kill or injure sb when picked up or interfered with. 置于门顶让人开门经过即落于其头上之物; (军)诡雷(看似无害, 但一经捡拾或拨弄

即可杀伤人)。

boogie /'bu:gɪ US: 'bʊgɪ; 'bʊgɪ/ (also 亦作 **boogie-woogie** /-'wu:gɪ US: -'wʊgɪ; -'wʊgɪ/ n [C, U] (instance of) highly rhythmic variety of blues²(6). 布吉舞曲(一种极富节奏之布鲁斯舞曲);布吉舞。

book¹ /buk; bʊk/ n **1** number of sheets of paper, either printed or blank, fastened together in a cover; literary composition that would fill such a set of sheets; 书;书籍;薄本;文字着作: write a ~. 写一本书。 **2 the B~**, the Bible: 圣经: swear on the B~, take an oath. 对圣经发誓。 **3** main division of a large treatise or poem or the Bible: (大部著作之)卷; 篇: the B~ of Genesis. (圣经之)创世记篇。 **4** packet of similar items fastened together, eg postage stamps, bus tickets, matches. (邮票、车票等的)本; (火柴等的)包。 **5** record of bets. 赛马赌注纪录。 ⇨ ~**maker** in 8 below. 参看下列第 8 义之 bookmaker. make/keep a ~ (on), take bets, etc. 接受赌注; 下赌注; 打赌。 not suit one's ~, not be convenient. 对某人不方便; 某人不便。 **6** (pl) business accounts, records, etc: (复)商业帐册, 纪录等: The firm has full order ~s, orders for goods. 该商行有完善的订货记录。 be in sb's good/bad/black ~s, have/not have his favour or approval. 为某人所(不)宠信。 bring sb to ~ (for sth), require him to explain his conduct. 要求某人解释其行为; 斥责。 **7** libretto (of an opera): (歌剧之) 唱词脚本。 **8** (compounds): (复合词): '~·**case** n piece of furniture with shelves for ~s. 书架。 '~·**club** n organization that sells ~s at a discount to members who agree to buy a minimum number 读书会; 读书俱乐部(以折扣价格售书给会员, 而会员则需应每期最少应买若干书)。 '~·**ends** n pl pair of props used to keep ~s upright, eg on a table. (一对)书夹; 书挡; 书橱。 '~·**keeper** n person who keeps accounts, eg of a business, public office. 记帐员; 簿记员。'~·**keep·ing** n (art of) keeping (business) accounts. 簿记; 记帐。 '~·**maker** n person whose business is taking bets on horse-races. 以赌赛马为业者。 '~·**mark(er)** n sth placed between the pages of a ~ to mark the place. 书签。 '~·**mobile** /-məubi:l; -'məbl/ n (US) truck equipped as a mobile ~ store or lending library. (美)以货车装成的)流动书库; 流动图书馆。 '~·**seller** n person who sells ~s retail. 书店老板; 书商。 '~·**stall** n stall, kiosk, etc at which ~s, newspapers, etc are shown for sale outdoors, in a railway station, a hotel lobby, etc (US 美 = newsstand). (车站边、旅馆休息室等处之)书报摊。 '~·**token** n ⇨ token. '~·**worm** n small maggot that eats holes in ~s; (fig) person who is very fond of reading ~s. 书虫; 蠹鱼; (喻)书呆子;极爱读书者。

book² /buk; bʊk/ vt [VP6A] **1** write down (orders, etc) in a notebook; (of the police) record a charge against (sb): 记载(订货单等)于帐册中; (指警察)登记对(某人)之控告: be ~ed for exceeding the speed limit. 因超速驾车而被登记。 **2** give or receive an order for, eg seats at a theatre, tickets for a journey; engage (sb) as a speaker, entertainer, etc: 定(座)、定(票);接受定(座)或定(票);聘请(某人)为演讲者、表演者等: Seats (for the theatre) can be ~ed from 10 am to 6 pm. (戏院之)定座时间自上午十时起至下午六时止。 Have you ~ed your passage to New York, arranged for a cabin? 你到纽约去的船舱位定好了吗? Can I ~ (a ticket) through to Naples? 我可以买一张直达那不勒斯的票吗? **(fully)** ~**ed up**, (of a restaurant, theatre, etc) no more tables, seats, available; (of a lecturer, singer, etc) unable to accept further engagements. (指餐馆、戏院等)已满座; (指演说者、歌星等)演出时间已排满; 无空档; 无法再接节目。 '~·**ing clerk** n person who sells tickets, eg at a railway station. (火车站等之)售票员。 '~·**ing office** n office for the sale of tickets (for travel). (车站等之)售票处; 票房。'~·**able** /-əbl/ /-əbl] adj (of seats, etc) that can be reserved: (指座位等)可预定的: all seats ~able in advance. 可预定之所有座位。

bookie /'bukɪ; 'bʊkɪ/ n (colloq) bookmaker. (口)赌赛马为业者。 ⇨ book¹(8).

book·ish /'bukɪʃ; 'bʊkɪʃ/ adj of books and studies: 书的; 读书的: a ~ person, one who gives much time to reading: 花很多时间读书的人; 好读书的人; ~ expressions, found in books but not colloquial; 书中的(非口语的)词句; 迂腐的词句; a ~ style, literary, not colloquial. 文绉绉的(非口语的)文体。 ~·**ness** n

book·let /'buklɪt; 'bʊklɪt/ n thin book, usu in paper covers. 小册子(通常用纸面)。

boom¹ /bu:m; bum/ n **1** long spar used to keep the bottom of a sail stretched out. 帆之下桁。 ⇨ the illus at barque. 参看 barque 之插图。 **2** derrick ~, fastened to a derrick crane, used for (un-)loading cargo. (船上装卸货物起重用的)吊杆。 **3** heavy chain, mass of floating logs, etc held in position across a river or harbour entrance, eg as a defence in time of war, or to prevent logs from floating away. 横拦于河中或港口之大铁链或一道浮木(于战时御敌用, 或用以阻拦圆木漂走); 筏堰。 **4** long, movable arm for a microphone. (挂麦克风用)活动长杆(臂)。

boom² /bu:m; bum/ vt, vi **1** [VP2A, C] (of big guns, the wind, an organ) make deep, hollow, or resonant sounds. (指大炮、风、风琴)发出隆隆或轰轰的声音。 **2** ~ **out**, [VP15B] utter in a deep voice: 用低沉的声音说出: ~ing out Shakespearian verses. 用低沉的声音读出莎士比亚的诗句。 □ n deep, hollow sound: 低沉的声音: the ~ of the guns/surf; 大炮(海浪)的隆隆声; a sonic ~. 音爆(飞机飞行速度超过音速时所发生的爆炸声)。

boom³ /bu:m; bum/ n [C] sudden increase in trade activity, esp a time when money is being made quickly. 商业之突趋繁荣; (尤指)可以迅速发财的商业繁荣时期; 景气。 ⇨ slump. □ vi [VP2A, C] town showing sudden growth and prosperity. 高速成长繁荣的城市; 新兴城市。 □ vi [VP2A, C] have a ~; become well known and successful: 突趋繁荣; 声名大噪: Business is ~ing. 商业突趋繁荣。 Jones is ~ing as a novelist, becoming famous. 作为一个小说家, 琼斯的声誉日隆。

boom·er·ang /'bu:məræŋ; 'bumə,ræŋ/ n curved stick of hard wood (used by Australian Aborigines), which can be thrown so that, if it fails to hit anything, it returns to the thrower; (fig) argument or proposal that comes back and harms its author. (澳洲土人所用的)曲形硬木飞镖(此种飞镖若未击中目标, 即返回投掷者原处); (喻)损及原倡议人之辩论或提案。

boon¹ /bu:n; bun/ n **1** (liter) request; favour: (文)要求; 恩惠: ask a ~ of sb; 请求某人赐惠; grant a ~. 施恩; 施惠。 **2** advantage; blessing; comfort: 益处; 恩惠: Parks are a great ~ to people in big cities. 公园是大都市居民的恩物。 A vacuum cleaner is a tremendous ~ to busy housewives. 真空吸尘器是忙碌家庭主妇的方便之物。

boon² /bu:n; bun/ adj (only in) (仅用于) ~ **companion**, jolly, congenial, companion. 好朋友; 良伴。

boor /buə(r); bur/ n rough, ill-mannered person. 举止粗鲁的人。 ~·**ish** /-ɪʃ; -ɪʃ/ adj of or like a ~. 举止粗鲁的。 ~·**ish·ly** adv ~·**ish·ness** n

boost /bu:st; bust/ vt [VP6A] give (sb or sth) a push up; increase the value, reputation, etc of (sb or sth): 将(某人或某物)向上推; 推起; 举起; 为(某人或某事物)吹嘘; 捧: ~ed sales; 增进销售量; ~ed my morale. 看到他在那边提高了我的士气(使我精神振作)。 □ n [C] act of ~ing; being ~ed. (向上)推起; (被)举起; (被)捧起。~**er** n **1** thing that ~s: 帮助推起之物; 声援; 后援: His work got a welcome ~. 他的工作获得令人欣喜的后援。 '~**er rocket** n rocket used to give initial speed to a missile, after which it drops and leaves the missile to continue under its own power. (给予飞弹初速之)增力火箭(初速产生以后, 增力火箭脱落, 飞弹靠其本身之动力继续前进)。 **2** '~**er (injection)**, supplementary dose of vaccine to strengthen the effect of an earlier dose; extra dose of

morphine, etc (by drúg addícts). (加强前次疫苗注射效
力之)辅助注射; (毒瘾者之吗啡等的)额外剂量。
boot[1] /buːt/ *but*/ *n* **1** outer covering for the foot and
ankle, made of leather or rubber. 长靴; 皮靴; 胶套靴。
⇨ **shoe. high ～s**, reaching to the knee. (及膝的)长统
靴。**die with one's ～s on; die in one's ～s**, not in
bed; die while still working, etc. 横死; 暴毙; 死于非命;
在工作时死亡。**get the ～**, (sl) be dismissed, be kicked
out. (俚)被开除; 被解雇。**give sb the ～**, (sl) dismiss
him from his job. (俚)开除某人; 解雇某人。**lick sb's
～s**, behave in a servile way. 舐某人的靴; 巴结某人; 奉
承某人。**put the ～ in**, (sl) kick sb, eg in a brawl;
(fig) be ruthless. (俚)(在争吵等中)踢某人; (喻)残忍
的; 无情的。**'～lace** *n* string or leather strip for ～s.
皮靴带。**2** (GB) place for luggage in a coach or at the
back of a motor-car (US 美 = *trunk*). (英)(客车中或
小汽车之后部)放行李的地方。▫ *vt* [VP6A, 15A, B]
kick. 踢。**～ sb/sth out (of)**, (sl) get rid of (from);
dismiss, expel (from): (俚)除去; (俚)赶出: *He was
～ed out of the house.* 他被赶出屋外。**～ed** *adj* wearing
～s: 穿靴的: *～ed and spurred*, ready for a journey.
穿着靴子并装有马刺的(整装待发,准备好旅行的)。
boot[2] /buːt/ *but*/ *n to ～*, in addition, as well. 并且;
加之; 而且。
boot[3] /buːt/ *but*/ *vt* (old use, usu with *it*): (旧用法,
通常与 it 连用): *What ～s it to..., that...*, what use
is it to..., that...? (后接不定式或名词从句)…有何益?
It little ～s to; It ～s not to, It is of little/no avail
to. (后接不定式)…无益(毫无)益处。
bootee /buːˈtiː; buˈtiː/ *n* [C] (*pl* ～s) infant's knitted
wool boot; kind of warmly lined boot for women. 小儿
的毛线鞋; 女用暖靴。
booth /buːð US: buːθ; buθ/ *n* **1** shelter of boards,
canvas or other light materials, eg one where goods
are sold at a market or a fair. (木板,帆布或其他轻便材
料所搭成的)棚子; (专指市场或商展会之)摊棚; 摊位。**2**
enclosure for a public telephone. 公用电话亭。'**kiosk
3 'polling ～**, place for voting at elections. (选举时投票
所间隔起来的)投票处。'**listening ～**, (in a shop)
enclosure where customers may listen to records. (商店
中顾客试听唱片的)试听间。
boot·leg /ˈbuːtleg; ˈbutˌleg/ *vt* make, transport or
sell illicit alcoholic drinks: 酿造、偷运或贩卖私酒;
(attrib) (用作定语) ～ *liquor*. 私酒。**～·ger** /-legə(r);
-ˌlegə/ *n* person who does this. 酿造、偷运或贩卖私酒者。
boot·less /ˈbuːtlɪs; ˈbutləs/ *adj* (liter) useless;
unavailing. (文)无用的; 无益的。
booty /ˈbuːtɪ; ˈbutɪ/ *n* [U] things taken by robbers
or captured from the enemy in war (and usu to be
divided among those who take them). (强盗之)劫掠物;
赃物; (战争时自敌人手中所获之)掳获物; 战利品(通常分
给捕获者)。
booze /buːz; buz/ *vi* [VP2A, C] ～ **(up)**, (colloq)
drink alcoholic liquor, esp in excess. (口)饮酒; 狂饮; 暴
饮。Hence, 由此产生, '**～·up**, (colloq) occasion of heavy
drinking: 酒宴; 酒会: *go on/have a ～up.* 举行酒宴。
▫ *n* [U] (colloq) alcoholic drink. (口)酒。**go/be on
the ～**, start/be in a period of heavy drinking. 狂饮;
暴饮。**～·r** *n* one who ～s; (sl) pub. 饮酒者; 暴饮者; 酒
徒; (俚)酒馆。**boozy** *adj*
bop /bɒp; bɑp/ *n* (1940s) [U] style of jazz with a
strong beat; [U, C] dancing/dance to this. (二十世纪
四十年代之)巴卜(一种节拍强劲有力之爵士乐); (随着此
种爵士乐所跳之)巴卜舞。▫ *vi* [VP2A] dance to this.
跳巴卜舞。
bo·peep /ˌbəʊˈpiːp; boˈpip/ *n* [U] game of hiding
and suddenly showing oneself to a baby. 躲藏起来然后
突然出现以逗小孩之游戏; 躲猫猫游戏。
bor·acic /bəˈræsɪk; bəˈræsɪk/ *adj* of borax: 硼砂的:
～ *acid*, boric acid. ⇨ **boric**. 硼酸。
bor·age /ˈbɒrɪdʒ US: ˈbɔːrɪdʒ; ˈbɔrɪdʒ/ *n* [U] blue-
flowered, hairy-leaved plant of which the leaves are

used as a seasoning. 琉璃苣(蓝花毛叶植物, 其叶用作调
味料)。
borax /ˈbɔːræks; ˈbɔreks/ *n* white powder used to
make porcelain enamels, in glass manufacture and
other industries, and for cleaning. 硼砂(白色粉末, 用
于制窑釉、制玻璃及其他工业, 并可作清洁剂)。
Bor·deaux /bɔːˈdəʊ; bɔrˈdo/ *n* [U] (F) (often
attrib) wine from the ～ area of France; claret.
(法)(常用作定语)(法国波尔多地区产的)红葡萄酒。
bor·der /ˈbɔːdə(r); ˈbɔrdə/ *n* **1** edge; part near the
edge of sth: 边缘; 边际: *We camped on the ～ of a lake.*
我们在湖边扎营。*A woman's handkerchief may have a
lace ～.* 女人的手帕可能有花边。*There is a ～ of flowers
round the lawn.* 草坪的四周有花围绕。**2** (land near the)
line dividing two states or countries: 边界; 边境; 国界;
国境: *The criminal escaped over the ～.* 罪犯逃过了边
界。(attrib) (用作定语): *a ～ town*, 边境的市镇; ～
incidents, eg small fights between armed forces of two
neighbouring states. 两国间边界武装部队的小冲突; 边
界事件。**the B～**, (esp) that between England and
Scotland. (尤指英格兰与苏格兰之间的)边界。'**～·land**
/-lænd; -lænd/ *n* **(a)** district on either side of a ～ or
boundary. 边区; 边疆; 边境。**(b)** (*sing* with *def art*
and attrib) condition between: (单数与定冠词连用, 并
用作定语)介于二者之间的状态: *the ～land between
sleeping and waking*. 半醒半睡之混然状态。'**～·line** *n*
line that marks a ～. (两国等之间的)界线; 国境线。
～line case *n* one that is dubious, eg sb who may or
may not pass an examination. 难以确定的两可情形(例
如某人的考试可能及格也可能不及格)。▫ *vt, vi* **1**
[VP6A] put or be a ～ to: 加边界线于; 为…之边界线:
Our garden is ～ed by a stream. 我们的花园濒临一条小
河。**2** [VP3A] ～ **on/upon**, be next to: 毗连; 接界:
My land ～s (up)on yours. 我的土地与你的土地接界。
The park ～s on the shores of the lake. 公园毗连湖滨。**3**
[VP3A] ～ **on/upon**, resemble; be almost the same
as: 近似; 几乎是: *The proposal ～s upon the absurd.* 该
提议近乎可笑。**～er** *n* person living on or near a frontier, esp that between England and Scotland. 边境居民
(尤指居于英格兰与苏格兰之边境者)。
bore[1] /bɔː(r); bɔr/ *vt, vi* [VP6A, 14, 15A] make a
narrow, round deep hole in sth with a revolving tool;
make (a hole, one's way) by doing this or by digging
out soil, etc: 钻孔; 开凿; 掘地洞(或隧道)而前进: *a
hole in wood*; 于木中钻孔; ～ *a well*, 钻井; ～ *a tunnel
through a mountain*; 开凿隧道通过一座山; *animals* (eg
moles) *that ～ their way under the ground.* 在地下掘地
洞前进之动物(如鼹鼠)。▫ *n* **1** (also 亦作) '**～·hole**) hole
made by boring, eg to find water. 钻孔; 凿孔(如寻水等
在地下所凿者); 钻探孔。**2** hollow inside of a gun barrel;
its diameter. 枪膛; 枪炮的膛径或口径。**borer** *n* (kind
of) insect that ～s. 会钻孔的昆虫。
bore[2] /bɔː(r); bɔr/ *vt* [VP6A] make (sb) feel tired
by being dull or tedious: 令(人)厌烦: *I hope you're not
getting ～d listening to me.* 我希望你听我说话没觉厌烦。
*I've heard all that man's stories before; they ～ me/he
～s me.* 那个人所讲的事我都听过; 使我烦死了。～ *sb to
death/tears*, ～ him intensely. 烦死了某人。～(sb to)
person or thing that ～s 令人生厌之人或事物。**bor·ing**
adj: a boring evening. 一个百无聊赖的晚上。'**～·dom**
/-dəm; -dəm/ *n* [U] state of being bored. 厌烦; 厌倦。
bore[3] /bɔː(r); bɔr/ *n* [C] high tidal wave, often many
feet high, that advances up a narrow estuary. 海啸; 进
海口之高潮(常远很多英尺高之)。激潮。
bore[4] /bɔː(r); bɔr/ *pt* of **bear**.
boric /ˈbɔːrɪk; ˈbɔrɪk/ *adj* ～ *acid*, used as an antiseptic and a preservative. 硼酸(用作消毒及防腐剂)。
born /bɔːn; bɔrn/ one of the *pp's* of **bear**. bear 之过
去分词之一。**1 be ～**, come into the world by birth. 出
生; 出世。*born with a silver spoon in one's mouth*, ⇨
silver(1). **2** (with a complement) destined to be: (与
补语连用)生而为; 命中注定: *He was ～ a poet.* 他天生

是个诗人。 *He was ~ to be hanged.* 他命中注定要受绞刑。 **3** (attrib) by natural ability: (用作定语) 有天才的; 天生的: *a ~ orator.* 天才演说家。

borne /bɔːn; bɔrn/ *pp* of bear (except of birth). bear (除"出生"之义外)之过去分词。 ⇨ bear[2](10, 12).

boron /'bɔːrɒn; 'bɔrɑn/ *n* [U] non-metallic element (symbol **B**). 硼(非金属元素,化学符号 B)。

bor·ough /'bʌrə US: -rəʊ; 'bɝo/ *n* **1** (England) town, or part of a town, that sends one or more members to Parliament; town with a municipal corporation and rights of self-government conferred by royal charter. (英国)国会中有代表之市镇或市区; 享有皇授自治权之市镇。 **2** (US) any one of the five administrative units of New York City. (美)纽约市五个行政区中的一区。

bor·row /'bɒrəʊ; 'bɑro/ *vt* [VP6A, 14] ~ *(from)*, **1** get sth, or the use of sth, on the understanding that it is to be returned: 借来; 借入; (向某人)借; 借用: *May I ~ your pen?* 我可借用你的钢笔吗? *Don't ~ books from me — them from the library!* 不要向我借书 —— 去图书馆借吧! *He fell into the river and had to go home in ~ed clothes.* 他跌入河中, 所以不得不穿借来的衣服回家。 *Some people are good at ~ing but bad at giving back.* 有些人只晓得借, 不晓得还。 ⇨ **lend. 2** take and use as one's own: 擅自借用; 抄袭; 剽窃: ~ *sb's ideas/ methods.* 剽窃某人的见解(方法)。 ~**er** *n* person who ~s. 借入者; 借用者; 剽窃者。

borsch /bɔːʃ; bɔrʃ/ (US = **borscht** /bɔːʃt; bɔrʃt/) *n* [U] (kinds of) Eastern European soup, esp of beetroot. 罗宋汤(东欧之数种汤,尤指加甜菜根者)。

bor·stal /'bɔːstl; 'bɔrstəl/ *n* ~ (**institution**), place where young offenders live and receive training designed to reform them. 少年犯感化院或管训所。

bortsch /bɔːʃ; bɔrʃ/ *n* = borsch.

bor·zoi /'bɔːzɔɪ; 'bɔrzɔɪ/ *n* Russian wolf-hound. 俄国猎狼犬。

bosh /bɒʃ; baʃ/ *n, int* nonsense. 胡说; 无意义的话。

bosky /'bɒskɪ; 'baskɪ/ *adj* (of land) covered with trees and bushes. (文)(指土地)被草木所覆蔽的。

bo'sn /'bəʊsn; 'bosn/ ⇨ **boatswain**.

bosom /'bʊzəm; 'bʊzəm/ *n* [C] **1** (old use) person's chest; woman's breasts; part of dress covering this. (旧用法)胸; (女人的)乳房; (衣服的)胸部。 **2** centre or inmost part, where one feels joy or sorrow; 内心; 衷心; 胸怀; (attrib) (用作定语) *a ~ friend,* one who is dear and close. 知己的朋友; 心腹之交。 **3** midst: 中间: *in the ~ of one's family.* 在家属之中; 与家属在一起。

boss[1] /bɒs; bɔs/ *n* [C] (colloq) superior; person who controls or gives orders to workers: (口)上司; 老板; 工头: *Who's the ~ in this house,* Is the husband or the wife in control? 谁是这一家之主(是先生还是太太当家)? □ *vt* [VP6A, 15B] be the ~ of; give orders to: 指挥; 控制; 管: *He wants to ~ the show,* to make all the arrangements. 他想指挥一切。 ~ *sb about/around,* order sb here and there. 指挥某人使其团团转。 ~**y** *adj* (**-ier, -iest**) fond of ~ing, fond of giving orders. 爱管事的; 跋扈的; 专权的。

boss[2] /bɒs; bɔs/ *n* round metal knob or stud on a shield or as an ornament. 盾上的金属圆形突起物; 突起之圆形金属装饰。

boss[3] /bɒs; bɔs/ *n* (sl) (also 亦作 '**~ shot**) bad shot or guess; bungle: (俚)未中的射击; 未中的猜测; 拙劣的工作: *make a ~ shot at sth;* 尝试做某事而未成功; *make a ~ of sth.* 把某事弄得一团糟。 '**~-eyed** *adj* (sl) blind in one eye; cross-eyed. (俚)一只眼瞎的; 斜眼的。

bo'sun /'bəʊsn; 'bosn/ ⇨ **boatswain**.

bot·any /'bɒtənɪ; 'batṇɪ/ *n* [U] science of the structure of plants. 植物学。 **bot·an·ical** /bə'tænɪkl; bo'tænɪkl/ *adj* of ~. 植物学的。 **botanical gardens,** park where plants and trees are grown for scientific study 植物园。 **bot·an·ist** /' 植物学家。 **bot·an·ize** /'bɒtənaɪz; 'batṇ‚aɪz/ *vi* go out studying and collecting wild plants. 到野外研究并采集植物; 实地研究植物。

botch /bɒtʃ; batʃ/ *vt* [VP6A, 15B] ~ *sth (up)*, repair badly; spoil by poor, clumsy work: 修补得不好; 因技术拙劣而弄坏: *a ~ed piece of work.* 技术拙劣的工作。 □ *n* piece of clumsy, badly done work: 技术拙劣的工作: *make a ~ of sth;* 把某事搞得一团糟; clumsy patch[1](1). 笨拙的修补。 ~**er** *n* person who ~es work. 技术拙劣的工人。

both[1] /bəʊθ; boθ/ *adj* (of two things, persons, etc) the two; the one and also the other (*both* precedes the *def art,* demonstrative *adjj,* possessives, and other *adjj*): (指两件事物, 两个人等)二者…都; 两者…都 (both 用于定冠词, 指示形容词, 所有格的词及物主代词, 及其他形容词之前): *I want ~ books/the books/these books.* (这)两本书我都要。 *I saw him on ~ occasions.* 在那两个场合我都看到了他。 *Hold it in ~ (your) hands.* 用两只手拿着。 *B~ his younger brothers are in the army.* 他的两个弟弟均在服兵役。 *You can't have it ~ ways,* must decide on one or the other. 你不能鱼与熊掌两者得兼(必须决定其中之一)。 Cf 参较 *both* and *neither: B~ these books are useful.* 这两本书都有用处。 *Neither of these books is useful.* 这两本书都没有用处。 Cf 参较 *both* and *each: There are shops on ~ sides of the street.* 街的两边都有商店。 *There is a butcher's shop on each side of the street.* 街的每一边都有一家肉店。

both[2] /bəʊθ; boθ/ *adv* ~... *and,* not only... but also: 不但…而且: *Queen Anne is ~ dead and buried.* 安妮女王已经死了, 而且埋葬了。 *He is remarkable for ~ his intelligence and his skill.* 他不但智慧高, 而且技术好。 *He is ~ a soldier and a poet.* 他不但是个军人, 而且是个诗人。

both[3] /bəʊθ; boθ/ *pron* **1** the two; not only the one but also the other: 二者; 两者都: *B~ are good.* 二者都好。 *B~ of them are good.* 他们两人都好。 Cf 参较 *both* and *neither: B~ of us want to go.* 我们两人都想去。 *Neither of us wants to go.* 我们两人都不想去。 **2** (used in apposition, in the same way as *each* and *all*): (用于同位语, 与 each 及 all 用同法): *We ~ want to go.* 我们两人都想去。 *They are ~ useful.* 它们二者都有用。 *Take them ~.* 把二者都拿去。 *You must ~ work harder.* 你们二人都必须更用功些。

bother /'bɒðə(r); 'baðɚ/ *vt, vi* [VP6A, 14, 16A, 3A] cause or be cause trouble to; worry: 打扰; 搅扰; 烦扰: *Tell the children to stop ~ing their father.* 告诉孩子们不要再搅扰他们的父亲。 *Don't ~ me with foolish questions.* 不要拿傻问题来烦扰我。 *That man is always ~ing me to lend him money.* 那个人老是来闹着要我借钱给他。 ~ *(oneself/one's head) (about),* be/feel anxious about: 焦虑; 为…而操心或焦急: *It's not important; don't ~ your head about it.* 这是不重要的事; 不要为此心焦。 *We needn't ~ (about) when it happened.* 我们不必操心那是何时发生的。 **2** [VP3A, 4C, 2A] ~ *(about),* take trouble: 麻烦; *Don't ~ about getting/~ to get dinner for me today,* I'll eat out. 今天不要麻烦为我预备饭了; 我要在外头吃。 **3** (used as an exclamation of impatience or annoyance): (用作表示不耐烦或厌恶的感叹词): *Oh, ~ (it)! now,* 真讨厌! *B~ the flies!* 讨厌的苍蝇! *Oh, ~ you!* 呵, 讨厌你! □ *n* **1** [U] worry, trouble: 焦虑; 麻烦: *Did you have much ~ (in) finding the house?* 你是否费了很大麻烦才找到那房子? *It will be no ~ (to me),* won't involve much work or inconvenience. (对于我)它不会有什么麻烦(不会太费事或不方便)。 *We had quite a lot of ~ (in) getting here because of the fog.* 因为有雾, 所以我们曾了很大的事才找到这儿来。 *Don't put yourself to any ~,* inconvenience yourself. 不要跟自己找麻烦。 **2** [C] (with *indef art*) sb or sth that gives trouble: (与不定冠词连用)令人焦虑, 厌烦或引起麻烦的人或事物: *His lazy son is quite a ~ to him.* 他那个懒惰的儿子, 对他是个讨厌(使他伤脑筋)的事。 *This drawer won't shut; isn't it a ~!* 这个抽屉关不上; 岂不讨厌! ~**·ation** /‚bɒðə'reɪʃn; ‚baðə'reʃən/ *int* What a nuisance! 真讨

厌! **'~·some** /-səm; -səm/ adj causing ~; troublesome or annoying. 令人焦虑的; 麻烦的; 可厌的。

bottle /'bɒtl; 'bɑtl/ n container, usu made of glass and with a narrow neck, for milk, beer, wine, medicine, ink, etc; the contents of a ~: (盛牛奶、啤酒、酒、药水、墨水等, 通常为玻璃制的)瓶子; 瓶中所装之物; 一瓶之量: *Mary drinks two ~s of milk a day.* 玛丽每天喝两瓶牛奶。 **'~-fed; brought up on the ~,** (of a child) given milk from a feeding ~, not fed from its mother's breast. (指小儿)吃牛奶(非母奶)长大的。 *too fond of the ~,* of alcoholic drinks. 嗜酒如命。 **'~-'green** adj dark green. 深绿色的; 墨绿色的。 **'~-neck** n **(a)** narrow strip of road, between two wide parts, where traffic is slowed down or held up. 瓶颈路段(两段宽敞道路间的狭窄部分, 交通缓慢阻滞)。 **(b)** that part of a manufacturing process, etc, where production is slowed down (eg by shortage of materials). 瓶颈(工业生产过程中影响生产速率的部分, 如因缺乏原料等); 一瓶 vt [VP6A] put into, store in, ~s: 装于瓶中; 盛于瓶中; 瓶装: ~ *fruit.* 将水果装于瓶中。 ~ *up,* [VP15B] (fig) hold in, keep under control, eg anger. (喻)抑制; 控制(愤怒等)。

bot·tom /'bɒtəm; 'bɑtəm/ n **1** lowest part of anything, inside or outside: 底; 底部(内侧或外部): *There are some tea-leaves in the ~ of the cup.* 杯底有一些茶叶。 *He fell to the ~ of the well.* 他掉到井底去了。 *We were glad to reach the ~* (= foot) *of the mountain.* 我们很高兴到达了山脚下。 *Notes are sometimes printed at the ~* (= foot) *of the page.* 注解有时印在页底。 **2** part farthest from the front or more important part: 距离前端或较重要部分最远的部分; 后部; 尾部: *at the ~ of the garden;* 在花园的尽头; less honourable end of a table, class, etc: 末席; 末座; 末位: *The poor relations were seated at the ~ of the long table.* 穷亲戚们被排在长形餐桌的末座。 **3** bed of the sea, a lake, river, etc: 海底; 湖底; 河床: *The ship went to the ~,* sank. 船沉入水底了。 *The lake is deep and a swimmer cannot touch ~,* touch the bed of the lake with his toes. 湖水很深, 游泳者探不到底。 **4** seat (of a chair); part of the body on which a person sits; buttocks: (椅子)坐的部分; 屁股: *This chair needs a new ~.* 这张椅子的座面需要换新。 *She smacked the child's ~.* 她搧孩子的屁股。 **5** horizontal part of a ship near the keel: 船底: *The ship was found floating ~ upwards.* 该船被发现底朝天漂流着。 **6** foundation: 基础; 根基; 根源: *We must get to the ~ of this mystery,* find out how it began. 我们必须探查出这个谜的究竟。 *Who's at the ~ of this business,* Who's responsible? 到底谁是这个企业的主持人? **7** (fig uses); (比喻用法): *The ~ has fallen out of the market,* Trade has fallen to a very low level. 商业已落到极低的水准(景况不好)。 *at ~,* in essential character: 根本上; 基本上; 实际上: *He's a good fellow at ~.* 他本质上是个好人。 *from the ~ of my heart,* genuinely, deeply. 真诚地; 诚挚地; 衷心地。 *knock the ~ out of (an argument, etc)* prove that it is worthless. 打破(一论点等)的根基; 推翻(一论点等); 证明(一论点等)无价值。 **8** (attrib) lowest, last: (用作定语)最低的; 最后的: *Put the book on the ~ shelf.* 把书放在最低的架子上。 *What's your ~ price?* 你们的最低价是多少? *Who's the ~ boy of the class?* 该班的末名男生是谁? ⇨ also **gear(1), rock[1](6).** □ *vi ~ out,* (economics) reach a low level and remain there: (经济)降到并停留在最低标准: *The value of our oil shares on the Stock Market has now ~ed out,* ie from now on can only rise, not fall further. 在证券市场上我们的石油股票的价值已降到最低标准。 **~·less** adj very deep: 极深的; 无底的: *a ~less pit.* 无底的坑。

botu·lism /'bɒtjulɪzəm; 'bɑtʃə,lɪzəm/ n [U] type of food poisoning. 腊肠毒菌病(一种食物中毒)。

bou·doir /'buːdwɑː(r); buˈdwɑr/ n woman's private sitting-room or dressing-room. (妇人的)闺房。

bou·gain·vil·lea /ˌbuːgənˈvɪliə; ˌbugənˈvɪljə/ n tropical climbing shrub with tiny flowers surrounded by red, purple, etc bracts. 九重葛(一种热带灌木, 开小花, 花之四周围绕着红、紫等色之苞叶)。

bough /baʊ; baʊ/ n large branch coming from the trunk of a tree. 较粗大之树枝; 粗枝。 ⇨ the illus at **tree.** 参看 tree 之插图。

bought /bɔːt; bɔt/ pt, pp of **buy.**

bouil·lon /'buːjɒn; 'buljɑn/ n [U] (F) clear thin soup or broth. (法)稀薄的肉汤; 清燉肉汤。 ⇨ **stock[1](9).**

boul·der /'bəʊldə(r); 'boldɚ/ n large piece of rock, large stone, esp one that has been rounded by water or weather. 大石块(尤指因水或风雨的侵蚀而变圆者)。

boul·evard /'buːləvɑːd US: 'bʊl-; 'bʊlə,vɑrd/ n (F) wide city street, often with trees on each side. (法)大马路; 大道(两旁常植有树木)林荫大道。

bounce /baʊns; baʊns/ vi, vt **1** [VP2A, 6A] (of a ball, etc) (cause to) spring or jump back when sent against sth hard: (指球等)(使)遇坚硬物而回跳; 弹回: *A rubber ball ~s well.* 橡皮球的弹力好。 *The ball ~ed over the wall.* 球跳过墙去了。 *She was bouncing a ball.* 她在拍球。 ~ *back,* [VP2C] (fig) recover jauntily from a setback. (喻)得意地从挫折中扳回优势。 **2** [VP2C, 6A] (cause to) move up and down violently or noisily; rush noisily or speedily: (使)跳上跳下; 乱冲乱撞: *The boy was bouncing (up and down) on the bed.* 那男孩在床上蹦跳。 *He ~d into/out of the room.* 他猛然冲进(出)房间。 *She ~d out of her chair.* 她自椅子上跳了起来。 *The old car ~d along the bad roads.* 这辆旧车在坏路上颠簸而行。 **3** [VP2A] (colloq) (of a cheque) be returned by a bank as worthless: (口)(指支票)被银行退票: *Don't worry — my cheque won't ~.* 别担心——我的支票不会退票的。 □ n **1** [C] (of a ball) bouncing: (指球)跳动; 反弹: *catch the ball on the ~.* 在球跳起来的时候把它抓住。 **2** [U] (of a person) liveliness. (指人)活力。 **bouncer** n = chucker-out, ⇨ **chuck[1](1). bounc·ing** adj (colloq) (of a person) strong and healthy. (指人)健壮的。

bound[1] /baʊnd; baʊnd/ n (usu pl) limit: (通常用复数)范围; 界限; 止境: *It is beyond the ~s of human knowledge,* Man can know nothing about it. 那是超出人类知识范围以外的。 *There are no ~s to his ambition.* 他的野心是无止境的。 *Please keep within the ~s of reason,* do not say foolish things, attempt impracticable things. 请勿越出理智的范围(不要说愚蠢的话, 不要做不可能的事)。 *He sets no ~s to his desires.* 他放纵他的欲望。 *Is it within the ~s of probability?* 这件事是在可能的范围以内吗? *out of ~s,* outside the limits of areas that one is allowed to enter: 禁止入内: *Most of the bars had been placed out of ~s to troops.* 大多数的酒吧都已被列为禁止军人进入之地。 (US 美 = *off limits*).

bound[2] /baʊnd; baʊnd/ vt [VP6A, usu passive] limit (lit, fig); set bounds to; be the boundary of: (常用被动语态)限制(字面或喻); 定~之界限; 为~之界限: *England is ~ed on the north by Scotland.* 英格兰北界苏格兰。

bound[3] /baʊnd; baʊnd/ vi [VP2A, C, 4A] jump, spring, bounce; move or run in jumping movements: 跳; 弹回; 跳着跑; 跃进: *The ball struck the wall and ~ed back to me.* 球碰着墙又向我弹回来。 *His heart ~ed with joy.* 他内心欢喜若狂。 *His dog came ~ing to meet him.* 他的狗跳跃着来迎接他。 *Big rocks were ~ing down the hillside.* 巨石由山坡上滚滚而下。 □ n jumping movement upward or forward: 跳跃; 跃进: *at one ~;* 一跳; 一跃; *hit a ball on the ~* or *rebound* /'ri:baʊnd; 'ri,baʊnd/, after it has hit the ground and is in the air again. 在球跳起来的时候击之。 *by leaps and ~s,* (fig) very rapidly. (喻)极迅速地; 急速地。

bound[4] /baʊnd; baʊnd/ part adj ~ **(for),** ready to start, having started, in the direction of: 准备启程前往…; 在此…途中; 往…(的); Where are you ~ *(for),* Where are you going to? 你往哪里去? *The ship is ~ for Finland.* 此船系开往芬兰。 *If a British ship is going away from*

Britain, she is outward ~; *if she is returning to Britain, she is homeward* ~. 英国船如果离开英国他往,就是外航;如果是回英国,就是回航。

bound⁵ /baʊnd; baʊnd/ *pp* of **bind**. ~ *to do sth,* **(a)** certain to: 一定: *He hasn't got any money — so he's* ~ *to turn up sooner or later.* 他没有钱——所以,他迟早一定会出现的。**(b)** obliged to: 必须: *I'm* ~ *to visit my grandmother every week.* 我必须每个礼拜去看祖母。~ *'up in,* much interested in, very busy with: 埋头于; 专心于; 忙于: *He is* ~ *up in his work.* 他埋头于他的工作。~ ~ *'up with,* closely connected with: 与…有密切关系: *The welfare of the individual is* ~ *up with the welfare of the community.* 个人的福利与社会福利有密切的关系。

bound·ary /'baʊndrɪ; 'baʊndərɪ/ *n* (*pl* -**ries**) **1** line that marks a limit; dividing line: 分界线; 边界; 界限; 范围: *This stream forms a* ~ *between my land and his.* 这条小河构成我的地与他的地之间的分界线。*A* ~ *dispute is a quarrel about where a* ~ *is or ought to be.* 边界纠纷就是关于界线在何处或应在何处之纷争。*If something is beyond the* ~ *of human knowledge, man can know nothing about it.* 如果某事是超出人类之知识范围以外, 人类对它就一无所知。**2** (cricket) hit to or over the ~, scoring 4 or 6 runs. (板球) 击至(或击过)边线 (可获四分或六分)。

boun·den /'baʊndən; 'baʊndən/ *adj* (only in) (仅用于) *my* ~ *duty,* (archaic) what my conscience tells me I must do. (古) 我的良心要我必须做的事; 我的本分。

bounder /'baʊndə(r); 'baʊndə/ *n* (GB dated colloq) untrustworthy, ill-bred person. (英过时口语) 不足信赖的人; 不良好教养的人; 粗鲁的人。

bound·less /'baʊndlɪs; 'baʊndlɪs/ *adj* without limits: 无限的; 无穷的: *his* ~ *generosity.* 他的无限的慷慨。~·**ly** *adv*

boun·te·ous /'baʊntɪəs; 'baʊntɪəs/ *adj* (liter) generous; giving or given freely; abundant: (文) 慷慨的; 丰富的: *a* ~ *harvest.* 丰收。~·**ly** *adv*

boun·ti·ful /'baʊntɪfl; 'baʊntəfəl/ *adj* (liter) bounteous. (文) 慷慨的; 丰富的。'~·**ly** -fəlɪ; -flɪ/ *adv*

bounty /'baʊntɪ; 'baʊntɪ/ *n* (*pl* -**ties**) **1** [U] (formal) freedom in giving; generosity. (正式用语) 慷慨; 好施。**2** [C] (formal) sth given out of kindness (esp to the poor). (正式用语)(尤指对穷人之)施舍 (物); 施与。**3** [C] reward or payment offered (say by a government) to encourage sb to do sth (eg increase production of goods, kill dangerous wild animals). 奖金(通常由政府所提供以鼓励某人做某事者, 如增加货物生产, 捕杀危险野兽等)。

bou·quet /bʊ'keɪ; bu'ke/ *n* **1** bunch of flowers (to be) carried in the hand. (持于手中的)花束。**2** perfume of wine. 酒之香味。

bour·bon /'bɜːbən; 'bɜːbən/ *n* [U] kinds of whisky distilled (in the US) from maize and rye. (美) 波旁酒 (用玉蜀黍和裸麦酿造的一种威士忌酒)。

bour·geois /'bʊəʒwɑː *US:* ˌbʊər'ʒwɑː; bur'ʒwɑ/ *n, adj* (person) of the class that owns property or engages in trade; (pej) (person) concerned chiefly with material prosperity and social status. 资产阶级; (拥有资产或经商的)人; (蔑)热中于物质荣华及社会地位的(人)。**the** ~**ie** /ˌbʊəʒwɑː'ziː; ˌburʒwɑ'zi/ *n* persons of this class, collectively. (集合用法)资产阶级; 中产阶级。

bourn(e) /bʊən; bɔːn/ *n* (old use) stream. (旧用法) 小河; 小溪。

bourn(e) /bʊən; bɔːn/ *n* (old use) boundary; limit; goal. (旧用法) 界限; 终点; 目的地; 目标。

bourse /bʊəs; bʊrs/ *n* foreign stock exchange (esp that of Paris). 外国证券交易所; (尤指)巴黎证券交易所。⇨ **stock¹(5)**.

bout /baʊt; baʊt/ *n* **1** period of exercise, work or other activity: (运动、工作或其他活动之)一回; 一次; 一番: *a 'wrestling* ~. 摔角之一回合; *a* ~ *of fighting;* 一场战斗; *a 'drinking* ~. 一次饮食。**2** fit of (illness): (疾病的)发作: *a* ~ *of influenza;* 一次流行性感冒; *bad*

coughing ~*s.* 一阵阵的剧烈咳嗽。

bou·tique /buː'tiːk; bu'tik/ *n* small shop selling articles (clothes, cosmetics, hats, etc) of the latest fashion. 经售最新流行服饰(如服装、化妆品、帽子等)的小商店。

bov·ine /'bəʊvaɪn; 'bovaɪn/ *adj* of, like, an ox: 牛的; 如牛的: ~ *stupidity.* 象牛一样的愚笨。

bov·ril /'bɒvrɪl; 'bavrɪl/ *n* [U] (P) meat extract used like beef tea. (商标)保卫尔牛肉汁。

bow¹ /bəʊ; bo/ *n* **1** piece of wood curved by a tight string, used for shooting arrows. (射箭用的)弓。⇨ the illus at **archer**. 参看 archer 之插图。*have two strings to one's bow,* have more than one plan, more resources than one. 不止一个计划; 有几个办法。**2** rod of wood with horse-hair stretched from end to end, used for playing the violin, etc. (奏小提琴等用的)弓。⇨ the illus at **string**. 参看 string 之插图。**3** curve; rainbow; 弯形; 弓形; 虹。**4** knot made with a loop or loops; ribbon, etc, tied in this way: 蝴蝶结; 结成蝴蝶结之带子等: *Tie your shoelaces in a bow.* 把你的鞋带结成蝴蝶结。*She had a bow of pink ribbon in her hair.* 她的头发上有一个用粉红绸带打的蝴蝶结。ˌ**bow'legged** *adj* with the legs curved outwards at the knees; bandy. 腿之膝部向外弯曲的; 弓形腿的。ˌ**bow 'legs** *n pl* such legs. 弓形腿; 膝内翻。ˌ**bow 'tie** *n* necktie made into a bow. 蝶形领结。'**bow·man** /-mən; -mən/ *n* (*pl* -**men**) archer. 弓箭(射)手。□ *vt* use a bow on (a violin, etc). 用弓拉(小提琴等)。**bow·ing** *n: The violinist's bowing is excellent.* 这位小提琴家的弓法极佳。

bow² /baʊ; baʊ/ *vi, vt* **1** [VP2A, C, 6A, 3A] bend the head or body (as a sign of respect or as a greeting, or in submission, or to indicate assent); bend (the head or body): 鞠躬(表示尊敬、招呼、恭谦或应允); 俯(首); 弯(身): *I raised my hat to her and she bowed in return.* 我向她举帽示礼, 她鞠躬答礼。*They bowed down to the idol.* 他们向偶像鞠躬致敬。*They bowed their heads in prayer.* 他们低头祷告。*He bowed before the shrine.* 他在神龛前鞠躬示敬。*He bowed his thanks,* expressed his thanks by bowing. 他鞠躬致谢。[VP15B] *bow sb in,* receive a visitor with low bows. 鞠躬以迎某人入内。[VP15B] *bow sb out,* bow low to sb as he leaves. 鞠躬恭送客人。*bow oneself out,* bow as one goes out. 鞠躬告别(而出)。[VP2C, 15A, B] *bow (oneself) out (of),* dissociate, disengage: 脱离; 退出: *I'm bowing out of this scheme — I think it's a big mistake.* 我正要退出这个计划——我认为那是个大错误。*bow to sb's opinion, etc,* submit to it. 服从某人的意见(等)。*have a bowing acquaintance with,* ⇨ **acquaintance**. **2** [VP6A, 15B, usu passive] bend: (通常用被动语态) 弯曲: *His father is bowed with age.* 他的父亲因年高而驼腰驼背。*The branches were bowed down with the weight of the snow.* 树枝被积雪的重量压弯了。□ *n* bending of the head or body (in greeting, etc): 鞠躬; 颔首; 点头(表示招呼、表示礼节等): *He answered with a low bow.* 他深深一鞠躬表示尊敬。*He made his bow to the company and left the room.* 他向在座的人们鞠躬后离开房间。

bow³ /baʊ; baʊ/ *n* **1** (often *pl*) front or forward end of a boat or ship from where it begins to curve. (常用复数)船首; 船头(短高的部分); 艏。*on/off the (port, starboard) bow,* said of objects within 45° of the point right ahead. (指物体)在船首前面左右 45 度的弧内(在左舷的前方, 在右舷的前方)。⇨ the illus at **ship**. 参看 ship 之插图。**2** (in a rowing-boat) oarsman nearest the bow. (在划艇上)最靠近艏前之划桨者。⇨ **stroke**.

Bow Bells /ˌbəʊ 'belz; 'bo 'belz/ *n pl* the bells of Bow Church, London. 伦敦 Bow 教堂之钟。*born within the sound of* ~, (said of a true Cockney) born in the City of London. 出生于伦敦市区内(指真正的伦敦人而言)。

bowd·ler·ize /'baʊdləraɪz; 'baʊdlə,raɪz/ *vt* take out of (a book, etc) words, scenes, etc that might be considered improper, unsuitable for young readers,

etc. 删除（书等）不适宜于少年读者等之猥亵鄙俗的字句、场景等。

bowel /'baʊəl; 'baʊəl/ *n* **1** (usu *pl* except in medical use and when attrib) division of the food canal below the stomach; intestine: (除用于医学或用作形容词外通常用复数) 肠; 肠部: *a ~ complaint*. 肠部疾病; 泄泻。 *Keep your ~s open*, don't become constipated. 保持大便畅通。 ⇨ the illus at **alimentary**. 参看 alimentary 之插图。 **2** (always *pl*) innermost part: (总是用复数) 最内的部分; 中心; 核心: *in the ~s of the earth, deep underground*. 在地下之深处。

bower /'baʊə(r); 'baʊə/ *n* **1** summer-house in a garden, shady place under trees or climbing plants. 花园里的凉亭; 树荫处。 **2** (liter) boudoir. (文)(妇人的)闺房。

bowie knife /'baʊɪ naɪf; 'boʊɪ naɪf/ *n* long knife with a blade that is double-edged at the point, used as a weapon. 一种尖端两面有刃, 作武器用的长刀。

bowl¹ /baʊl; bol/ *n* **1** deep, round, hollow dish; contents of such a dish: 碗; 钵; 碗里所盛之物: *She ate three ~s of rice*; 她吃了三碗米饭; (compounds): (复合词): *'finger-~*, 洗指钵, *'salad-~*, 装生菜的碗, *'sugar-~*. 装糖的碗。 **2** sth shaped like a ~: 碗形物: *the ~ of a spoon*. 汤匙之盛汤部分。 *He filled the ~ of his pipe*, put tobacco into it. 他装满了烟斗。 *The electric light bulb is in an alabaster ~*. 这电灯泡装在一个雪花石膏似的灯罩里。 **3** (*esp US*) amphitheatre (for open-air concerts, etc): (尤美)(供露天音乐会等演出之)露天圆形剧场: *The Hollywood B~*. 好莱坞露天圆形剧场。

bowl² /baʊl; bol/ *n* **1** heavy, wooden or composition ball made so that it rolls with a bias. 滚木球戏用之沉重的木球(木质或合成物质做成, 滚动时球路略微弯曲)。 **2** (*pl*) game played with these balls: (复)滚木球戏; 保龄球: *have a game of ~s*; 玩一场滚木球戏; *play (at) ~s*. 玩滚木球戏。

bowl³ /baʊl; bol/ *vi, vt* **1** [VP2A] play bowls. 玩滚木球戏。 ⇨ **bowl²**(2). '**~-ing-green** *n* area of fine, smooth grass for playing bowls. 玩滚木球戏之草坪。 '**~-ing alley** *n* level area of wood, used for skittles, ninepins and tenpins. (撞柱戏、九柱戏及十柱戏中所用的木质的)球道。 **2** [VP2A, 6A] (cricket) send a ball to the batsman: (板球)投(球): *Smith ~ed ten overs*. 史密斯连投了十次球。 **over³** *~ (out)*, [VP6A, 15B] dismiss (a batsman) by hitting the wicket or knocking the bails off: 因击中三柱门或击落柱上横木而迫使(击球员)退场; 投杀: *The first two batsmen were ~ed (out)*. 头两个击球员被判出局了。 **3** *~ along*, [VP 2C] go quickly and smoothly on wheels: (车辆)轻快地行驶: *Our car ~ed along over the smooth roads*. 我们的车子在平滑的路上轻快地前行。 **4** *~ sb over*, [VP15B] (a) knock down. 击倒(某人)。 (b) make helpless, overcome: 使猥狈; 使所措; 使惊呆; 使崩溃: *He was ~ed over by the news*. 这消息使他不知所措。 *Her impudence ~ed me over*, left me speechless with surprise. 她的厚颜使我大为吃惊。

bowler¹ /'baʊlə(r); 'bolə/ *n* **1** person who plays bowls¹(2). 玩滚木球戏者。 **2** person who bowls in cricket. (板球戏之)投球手。

bowler² /'baʊlə(r); 'bolə/ *n* (also *亦作* *~ 'hat*) hard, rounded, usu black hat. 一种硬的圆质礼帽(通常为黑色)。

bow·line /'baʊlɪn; 'bolɪn/ *n* (also *亦作* '*~ knot*) simple but secure knot used by sailors, climbers, etc. 单结套(水手、攀登者等所用之一种简单而极牢固之索结)。 ⇨ the illus at **knot**. 参看 knot 之插图。

bowls /baʊlz; bolz/ *n* ⇨ **bowl²**(2).

bow·man /'baʊmən; 'bomən/ *n* (*pl* -**men**) archer. 弓箭射手。 ⇨ **bow¹**(1).

bow·sprit /'baʊsprɪt; 'baʊsprɪt/ *n* spar that extends from a ship's stem, to which ropes and supports sails, etc are fastened. 第一斜桅; 艏斜桅; 牙樯(自船材延伸用以拴帆'索之短木)。 ⇨ the illus at **barque**. 参看 barque 之插图。

bow win·dow /,baʊ 'wɪndəʊ; 'bo 'wɪndo/ *n* curved bay window. 弓形窗; 凸窗。 ⇨ the illus at **window**. 参看 window 之插图。

bow-wow /,baʊ 'waʊ; 'baʊ'waʊ/ *int* imitation of a dog's bark. 模拟之犬吠声。 □ *n* /'baʊ waʊ; 'baʊ'waʊ/ (young child's word for a) dog. (儿语)狗。

box¹ /bɒks; baks/ *n* **1** container, usu with a lid, made of wood, cardboard, plastic, metal, etc used for holding solids: 盒; 匣; 箱: *a box of matches*; 一盒火柴; *a 'tool-box*. 工具匣; 工具箱。 *Pack the books in a wooden box*. 把书籍装在木箱里。 '**box-kite** *n* kite made in the form of a box (or two boxes) of light material. 箱形风筝。 '**box-number** *n* number used in a newspaper advertisement as an address to which answers may be sent (and forwarded from the newspaper office). (报纸)广告号码 (为便于读者与登广告者通讯所用之代替住址的编号)。 **PO Box No** *n* number used as part of an address to which letters, etc may be directed. 邮政信箱号码。 ⇨ also **call-box, Christmas-box, letter-box, money-box, pillar-box**. **2** separate compartment, with seats for several persons, in a theatre, concert hall, etc. (戏院、音乐厅等之)包厢。 '**box-office** *n* office for booking seats in a theatre, concert hall, etc: (戏院、音乐厅等之)售票处; 票房: *The play was a box-office success*, a financial success. 该剧演出成功(指卖座好, 票房records高)。 **3** compartment in a law court for a special purpose: 法庭之特别席位: *'jury-box*; 陪审团席; *'witness-box*. 证人席。 **4** small hut or shelter, eg for a sentry or railway signalman. 小亭; 哨亭; (铁路上的)信号员亭。 **5** separate compartment in a stable or railway truck for a horse. 马厩或火车货车厢中一马所占之小间厩; 马栏。 **6** raised seat for the driver of a carriage(1) or coach(1). (马车上之)驭者座。 **box·ful** /-ful; -,ful/ *n* full box¹(1) (of sth). 一盒: 一盒(与……连用, 后接某物)。 □ *vt* [VP6A] put into a box. 装于盒中; 装箱。 **box sb/sth up**, [VP15B] shut up in a small space. 将某人关在(置某物于)一个小空间里; 幽禁某人。

box² /bɒks; baks/ *vt, vi* [VP6A, 2A, 3A] *box (with)*, fight (sb) with the fists, usu with thick gloves, for sport: 拳击; 与……拳击: *Do you box, Do you fight in this way?* 你会拳击吗? *box sb's ears*, give him a blow with the open hand on the ear. 打(某人)一个耳光; 揾。 '**box·ing-glove** *n* padded glove (one of a pair) for use in boxing. 拳击手套。 '**box·ing-match** *n* fight between two boxers. 拳击比赛。 □ *n* slap or blow with the open hand on the ear. 打耳光; 掌颊; 揾。 **boxer** /'bɒksə(r); 'baksə/ *n* **1** person who boxes. 拳击者; 拳击家; 拳手。 **2** breed of dog (like a bulldog). 拳师犬(象哈巴犬之一种猛犬)。 **box·ing** *n* [U] organised sport of fist fighting. 拳击。

box³ /bɒks; baks/ *n* [U] **1** (kinds of) small, evergreen shrub, used in garden borders. 黄杨(常绿小灌木, 用作花园的围篱)。 **2** (also *亦作* '**box·wood**) wood of this shrub. 黄杨木。

Box·ing Day /'bɒksɪŋ deɪ; 'baksɪŋ de/ *n* first week-day after Christmas Day. 圣诞节后的第一个周日。

boy /bɔɪ; bɔɪ/ *n* **1** male child up to the age of 17 or 18. (十七、八岁以下之)男孩; 男童。 '**boy·friend**, favoured male companion of a girl or young woman. 男朋友(女孩子或年轻妇女所喜欢的男伴)。 **2** son (colloq, of any age): 儿子(口, 不限年龄): *He has two boys and one girl*. 他有两个儿子一个女儿。 **3** *int* (US sl) expressing enthusiasm, relief, surprise, etc. (美俚)好家伙(表示热心、放心、惊讶等之感叹词)。 '**boy·hood** /-hʊd; -hʊd/ *n* [U] time when one is/was a boy. 男孩时代; 少年时代。

boy·ish *adj* of, for, like, a boy. 男孩的; 似男孩的。

boy·cott /'bɔɪkɒt; 'bɔɪkɑt/ *vt* [VP6A] (join with others and) refuse to have anything to do with, to trade with (a person, business firm, country, etc); refuse to handle (goods, etc). 抵制; 拒绝(与某人、公司、国家等)来往、通商; 拒绝买卖(货物等); 抵制; 杯葛。 □ *n* ~**ing**; treatment of this kind:

联合抵制 (货物等); 杯葛: *put sb/his shop/goods under a ~*; 联合抵制某人(其商店, 货物); *put a ~ on sb, etc*. 联合抵制某人。

bra /brɑ:; brɑ/ *n* (colloq abbr of) brassiere. (口)奶罩 (为 brassiere 之略)。

brace¹ /breɪs; bres/ *n* **1** sth used to clasp, tighten or support, eg the roof or walls of a building. 钩住、拉紧或支持(建筑物之顶或墙壁等)之物。 **2** revolving tool for holding another tool, eg a *bit* for boring holes, driving in screws, etc. (钻孔或螺丝起子之)曲柄。 **3** (*pl* unchanged) pair or couple (of dogs, game-birds): (复数不变)一对(狗、猎禽); 一双: *five ~ of partridge*. 五对鹧鸪。 **4** (*pl*) (US 美 = *suspenders*) straps passing over the shoulders, fastened to the front and back of trousers to keep them up. (复)吊裤带; 背带(搭过两肩之裤子背带)。 **5** (often *pl*) appliance of bands and wires fastened to the teeth to correct their alignment. (常用复数)齿列矫正器。 **6** (printing) (印刷) ⇨ **bracket (2)**.

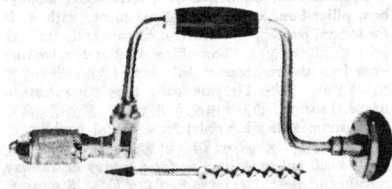

a brace and bit

brace² /breɪs; bres/ *vt* **1** [VP6A] support; give firmness to: 支持; 使坚固; 绷紧; 撑牢; 拉紧: *The struts are firmly ~d*. 那些支柱上得很牢靠。 **2** [VP6A, 15B, 16A] ~ (*up*), steady oneself; stand firm: 使自己稳定或沉着; 站稳; 奋起; 振作起来: *B~ up!* 打起精神来! 振作起来! *He ~d himself to meet the blow*. 他振奋起来以接受打击。 **3** (usu as *part adj* in *-ing*) enliven; stimulate: (通常作现在分词形容词用)使活泼; 使有生气; 激励; 鼓舞: *bracing air*; 令人精神爽快的空气; *a bracing climate*. 宜人的气候。

brace·let /ˈbreɪslɪt; ˈbreslɪt/ *n* ornamental band or chain for the wrist or arm. 手镯; 臂镯。

bracken /ˈbrækən; ˈbrækən/ *n* [U] large fern that grows on hillsides, waste land, etc; mass of such fern. 蕨; 羊齿(生于荒地及山坡等处); 此种植物之一丛。

bracket /ˈbrækɪt; ˈbrækɪt/ *n* **1** wood or metal support for a shelf; support on a wall for a gas or electric lamp. (钉于墙上之)托架; 撑架; (墙上所装的)煤气灯架或电灯座。 **2** (printing, writing) any one of the paired marks ( ) (*round ~s or parentheses*), [ ] (*square ~s*), { } (*braces*), used for enclosing words, figures etc to indicate separation from what precedes and follows. (印刷、书写)括弧(指圆括弧( ), 方括弧[ ], 或大括弧{ }之一任一)。 ⇨ **App 9**. **3** grouping; classification: 类别; 分类: *income ~*, eg of incomes from £3000 to £4500; 所得分类(例如所得自三千英镑至四千五百英镑之一类); *age ~*, eg 20 to 30 years of age. 年龄类别(例如二十至三十岁者)。 □ *vt* [VP6A, 15B] put inside, join with, ~s; put together to imply connection or equality: 置于括弧中; 以括弧连合; 放在一起(以表示关联或平等): *Jones and Smith were ~ed together at the top of the list*. 琼斯与史密斯并列第一。

brack·ish /ˈbrækɪʃ; ˈbrækɪʃ/ *adj* (of water) slightly salt; between salt and fresh water. (指水)略有盐味的; 介于咸水与淡水之间的。

bract /brækt; brækt/ *n* [C] leaf-like part of a plant, often highly coloured, situated below a flower or cluster of flowers (as in bougainvillea, poinsettia). (植物)苞; 苞叶(植物之生花或花丛下之似叶部分, 常呈鲜艳之颜色, 如九重葛, 圣诞红者是)。

brad /bræd; bræd/ *n* thin, flat nail with no head or a very small head. 无头钉(或头甚小者); 曲头钉; 土钉。

brad·awl /ˈbrædɔ:l; ˈbrædˌɒl/ *n* small tool for piercing holes for brads or screws. 小锥子(用以钻孔供上无头钉或螺旋钉者)。 ⇨ the illus at **tool**. 参看 tool 之插图。

brae /breɪ; bre/ *n* (Scot) slope; hillside. (苏)斜坡; 山坡。

brag /bræg; bræg/ *vi* (-gg-) ~ (*of/about*), [VP2A, 3A] boast: 自夸; 自吹; 夸耀: ~ *of what one has done*. 夸耀自己的作为。 **brag·ging** *n* [U] **brag·gart** /ˈbrægət; ˈbrægət/ *n* person who ~s. 自夸者; 大言者。

Brah·min /ˈbrɑːmɪn; ˈbrɑmɪn/ *n* member of the highest Hindu priestly caste. 婆罗门(印度四大阶级中之最高阶级)之一员。

braid /breɪd; bred/ *n* **1** [C] number of strands of hair woven together: 发辫; 辫子: *She wears her hair in ~s*. 她把她的头发编成辫子。 **2** [U] silk, linen, etc woven into a band, used for edging cloth or garments or (esp gold and silver ~) for decoration: (丝、亚麻等编成之)辫带; 穗带(用作衣布之花边); 金色银色者尤作装饰用): *The uniforms of the generals were covered with gold ~*. 将官的制服上装饰着金色穗带。 □ *vt* [VP6A] make into ~(s); trim with ~; put (hair) into ~s. 编成辫带; 饰以穗带; 将(头发)编成辫子。

braille /breɪl; brel/ *n* [U] system of writing and reading (using raised dots) for blind people, to enable them to read by touch. (利用浮凸点之排列)供盲人写作及阅读, 可以用手触摸之点字法。

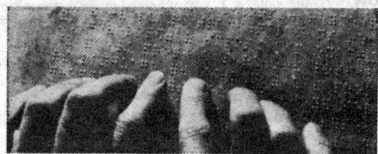

reading braille

brain /breɪn; bren/ *n* **1** (*sing*) (in man and animals) the mass of soft grey matter in the head, centre of the nervous system: (单数)(人类或动物的)脑(为神经系统的中枢): *The human ~ is a complex organ*. 人类的脑是一复杂的器官。 *The creature's ~ weighs a quarter of a kilo*. 这动物的脑重四分之一公斤。 ⇨ the illus at **head**. 参看 head 之插图。 **2** (colloq, usu *pl*) skull and brain(1) thought of together. (口, 通常用复数)头脑; 脑袋: *He fell and dashed his ~s out on the rocks*. 他摔在岩石上, 脑袋开了花。 *blow out one's ~s*, ⇨ **blow¹(13)**. **3** (*pl*) animal's ~s, eaten as food: (复)动物之脑的(作食物之动物的)脑: *calf's/sheep's ~s*. 牛(羊)脑。 **4** (colloq, usu *sing*) mind; intellect: (口, 通常用单数)心智; 智力; 智慧; 脑筋; 脑子: *have a good ~*; 有一副好脑筋; 很聪明; *use one's ~(s)*. 动脑筋; 运用智慧。 *beat/rack one's ~(s) (about sth)*, think very hard. (为某事)绞脑汁; 苦思。 *have sth* (eg money, sex) *on the ~*, think constantly about it. 经常想着某事(如金钱、性问题等)。 *tax one's ~*, set oneself/be set a difficult mental task. 绞尽脑汁。 *pick sb's ~(s)*, learn and use his ideas. 割窃或采用某人的思想。 **5** [C] clever, brilliant person: 聪明卓越的人: *He's the ~ of the school staff*. 他是学校教职员的智囊。 **6** (compounds) (复合词) '~-child *n* original idea, etc attributed to a person or group. (某人或某一群人的)脑力的产物(如创见等)。 '~ drain ⇨ **drain¹(2)**. '~-fag *n* (colloq) mental exhaustion: (口)神经衰弱; 脑筋疲劳: *suffering from ~fag*. 患神经衰弱。 '~-fever *n* inflammation of the ~ 脑膜炎。 '~-storm *n* mental upset with uncontrolled emotion, eg weeping, and violence. 脑猝变; 脑猝病(一种情绪不能控制, 如哭泣及行为暴烈的精神错乱)。 '~-teaser *n* difficult problem; puzzle. 困难的问题; 难题。 '**B~s Trust** *n* group of reputed experts giving advice, or answering questions put to them by members of an audience. (提供忠告, 或

答复听众或观众所提出的问题的)专家小组;智囊团。 '~-**washing** *n* process of forcing a person to reject old beliefs and accept new beliefs by use of extreme mental pressure, eg persistent questioning. 洗脑筋(使用极端的精神压迫,如长时间的审问,以达到迫使某人放弃门思想接受新思想之过程)。 '~-**wave** *n* (colloq) sudden inspiration or bright idea. (口)突然的灵感;灵机一动。 □ *vt* [VP6A] kill by a heavy blow on the head: 猛击头部以打死: ~ *an ox*. 击牛之头以毙之。~-**less** *adj* stupid. 无头脑的;愚笨的。~**y** *adj* (-**ier**, -**iest**) clever. 聪明的。

braise /breɪz; brez/ *vt* [VP6A] cook (meat, vegetables) slowly in a covered pan or pot: 燉(肉、蔬菜);煨;焖: ~*d beef/onions*. 燉牛肉(洋葱)。

brake[1] /breɪk; brek/ *n* device for reducing speed or stopping motion, eg of a bicycle, motor-car, train, etc: (脚踏车、汽车、火车等之)煞车;制动机: *put on/apply/* (colloq) (口) *slam on the ~s*; 使用煞车; 将车煞住; *act as a ~ upon (progress, initiative, etc)*, hamper it; control it. 阻碍(进展,发动等);控制。 ⇨ the illus at **motor** 参看 motor 之插图。 □ *vt, vi* [VP6A, 2A] put on the ~s: 煞车: *The driver ~d (his car) suddenly.* 驾驶者突然煞住(车子)。 '~-**man** /-mən; -mən/ *n* (*pl* -**men**) **guard**[1](5). (火车之)列车员;司闸员。

brake[2] /breɪk; brek/ *n* area or band of brushwood, thick undergrowth or bracken. 矮丛林区;丛林地带。

brake[3] /breɪk; brek/ *n* large wagon or open carriage pulled by one or more horses, and with facing side seats, formerly used for pleasure outings. 一种大马车(有篷或无篷,由一匹或数匹马牵曳,两边有对面座位,从前用以出外游玩)。 ⇨ **shooting-brake**.

bramble /'bræmbl; 'bræmbl/ *n* rough shrub with long prickly shoots; blackberry bush. 荆棘;悬钩子;黑莓灌木丛。

bran /bræn; bræn/ *n* [U] outer covering (husks) of grain (wheat, rye, etc) separated from flour by sifting. 糠;麦麸。

branch /brɑːntʃ US: bræntʃ; bræntʃ/ *n* **1** arm-like division of a tree, growing out from the trunk, or a bough, or another ~, ⇨ the illus at **tree**: 树枝(参看 tree 之插图): *He climbed up the tree and hid among the ~es.* 他爬上树藏到树枝中。 **2** (often attrib) division or subdivision of a river, road, railway, mountain range, etc; division or subdivision of a family, subject of knowledge, organization, etc: (常用作定语)(河流的)支流;(道路的)支路;(山脉的)支脉;(家族的)支系;(学术的)部门;(机构的)分支机构: *There is a ~ post office quite near.* 附近有一个邮局支局。 *The bank has ~es in all parts of the country.* 该银行在全国各地皆有分行。 *English is a ~ of the Germanic family of languages.* 英语是日耳曼语系中的一支。 *root and ~*, ⇨ **root**[1](1). □ *vi* [VP2A, C] send out, divide into, ~es: 长出枝子;分枝;分叉: *The trees ~ (out) over the river.* 那些树的枝子伸到河上去了。 *The road ~es here.* 路在此分叉。 ~ *off*, (of a car, road, train, etc) leave a main route and take a minor one. (指汽车、道路、火车等)离开干道进入支线;分叉;分歧。 ~ *out*, (of a person, business firm, etc) expand in a new direction, open new departments or lines of activities. (指人、商行等)向新的方向发展;创设新的部门或业务。 ~**y** *adj* with many ~es. 多枝的。

brand /brænd; brænd/ *n* **1** trademark (painted or printed on boxes, tins, packets, etc); particular kind of goods with such a mark: (印于盒子、罐头、包装等上的商标;牌子): *the best ~s of cigars*, 某种牌子的货物: 牌子极好的雪茄; *an excellent ~ of coffee*. 牌子极好的咖啡。 '~'**new** *adj* quite new (as if freshly stamped with a ~). 全新的 (好似刚盖上商标的);簇新的;崭新的。 **2** piece of burning wood: 燃烧中的木头: *a ~ from the burning*, person rescued from the consequences of sin; converted sinner. 从罪恶的渊薮中被救出的人;悔悟的罪人。 **3** (also 亦作 '~-**ing-iron**), iron used red-hot, for burning a mark into a surface; mark made in this way; (in olden times) mark burned on criminals, hence,

(fig) mark of guilt or disgrace: (烧红烙印用的)烙铁;烙印;(古时)罪犯身上的烙印;(喻)犯罪或不名誉的标记: *the ~ of Cain*, of a murderer. 谋杀者的标记;杀人罪。 **4** (poet) torch. (诗)火炬。 □ *vt* [VP6A, 16B] **1** mark (cattle, goods, etc) with a ~: 打烙印于 (牲畜等);印商标于 (货物): *On big farms cattle are usually ~ed.* 在大农场上,牲畜通常打有烙印。 *Criminals used to be ~ed.* 罪犯从前是打有烙印的。 (fig) (喻) *These frightful experiences are ~ed on his memory.* 这些可怕的经历深深印入他的记忆。 **2** give (sb) a bad name: 指(某人)为坏人;栽污: ~ *sb with infamy*; 破坏某人的名誉; ~ *sb (as) a heretic*. 指某人为异教徒。

bran·dish /'brændɪʃ; 'brændɪʃ/ *vt* [VP6A] wave about (to display, or before using): 炫耀地挥舞; (使用前)挥舞: ~*ing a sword*. 挥剑。

brandy /'brændɪ; 'brændɪ/ *n* [C, U] strong alcoholic drink distilled from wine of grapes: 白兰地酒: *two brandies and sodas*, two glasses of ~ mixed with soda water. 两杯搀苏打水的白兰地酒。 '~-**ball** *n* kind of sweet. 白兰地糖果(糖果之一种)。 '~-**snap** *n* kind of gingerbread wafer. 一种白兰地味道之姜饼。

bran-new /bræn 'njuː; 'bræn'nju/ *adj* = **brand-new**.

brash /bræʃ; bræʃ/ *adj* (colloq) (口) **1** saucy; cheeky. 莽撞的;无礼的。 **2** hasty; rash. 匆莽的;轻率的。

brass /brɑːs US: bræs; bræs/ *n* **1** [U] bright yellow metal made by mixing copper and zinc: (由铜和锌合成十分光亮的)黄铜 (扣子); ~ *rods/buttons*; 黄铜杆(扣子); *a ~ foundry*. 黄铜铸造厂。 *get down to ~ tacks*, begin to talk, discuss, etc in plain, straightforward terms. 直截了当说,讨论等;开门见山。 '**hat**, (army sl) high-ranking officer. (军里)高级军官。 ~ '**plate**, oblong plate of ~, on a door or gate, with the name, trade, occupation, etc, eg as used by doctors, lawyers, business firms. (医生、律师、商行等门外所悬挂刻有姓名、行业、职业等之长方形)铜牌。 *~***top** '~, (colloq, collective) high-ranking officers, managers, etc. (口, 集合用法)高级军官;经理。 **2** [U] (and *pl*) things made of ~, eg candlesticks, bowls, ornaments: (单数及复数均可)黄铜制品;黄铜器 (如烛台、碗、装饰物): *clean/do the ~/the ~es*. 擦黄铜器。 **3** the ~, (collective) (mus) musical instruments made of ~. (集合用法)(音乐)铜管乐器。 ~ '**band**, band of musicians with ~ instruments. 铜管乐队 (即军乐队)。 **4** [U] (GB sl) money. 美(俚)钱。 **5** [U] (sl) impudence. (俚)厚颜;无耻。 ⇨ **brazen**. ~**y** *adj* (-**ier**, -**iest**) **1** like ~ in colour or sound. 铜色的;声音似铜管乐器的。 ⇨ **3** above. 参看上列第 3 义。 **2** impudent. 厚颜的;无耻的。

bras·sard /'bræsɑːd; 'bræsard/ *n* (arm-band bearing a) badge worn on the sleeve. 臂章;袖章;臂铠。

brass·erie /'bræsərɪ; ,bræs'ri/ *n* beer-saloon or beer-garden (usu supplying food as well as drink). 啤酒店;啤酒园(通常并供应食物)。

brass·iere, ·ière /'bræsɪə(r) US: brəˈzɪər,; brəˈzɪr/ *n* (usu shortened to *bra*) woman's close-fitting support for the breasts. (通常略作 bra)(妇女用的)胸罩;奶罩。

brat /bræt; bræt/ *n* (derog) child. (贬)小儿;乳臭未干的小孩。

bra·vado /brəˈvɑːdəʊ; brəˈvado/ *n* **1** [U] display of boldness or daring: 故作勇武;虚张声势: *do sth out of ~*, in order to display one's courage. 为表现其勇武而做某事。 **2** [C] (*pl* ~**es**, ~**s**) instance of this. 故作勇武之实例。

brave /breɪv; brev/ *adj* (-**r**, -**st**) **1** ready to face danger, pain or suffering; having no fear: 勇敢的: 无畏的: *as ~ as a lion*. 勇如猛狮。 *Be ~!* 勇敢些! *It was ~ of him to enter the burning building*. 他敢进入那燃烧着的房屋,真是勇敢。 **2** needing courage: 需要勇气的: *a ~ act*. 英勇的行为。 **3** (old use) fine and splendid: (旧用法)绝丽的; 华丽的: *this ~ new world*. 这美好的新世界。 □ *n* (poet) American Indian warrior. (诗)北美印第安武士。 □ *vt* [VP6A] face, go into, meet, without showing fear: 勇敢地面对、进入、从事、应

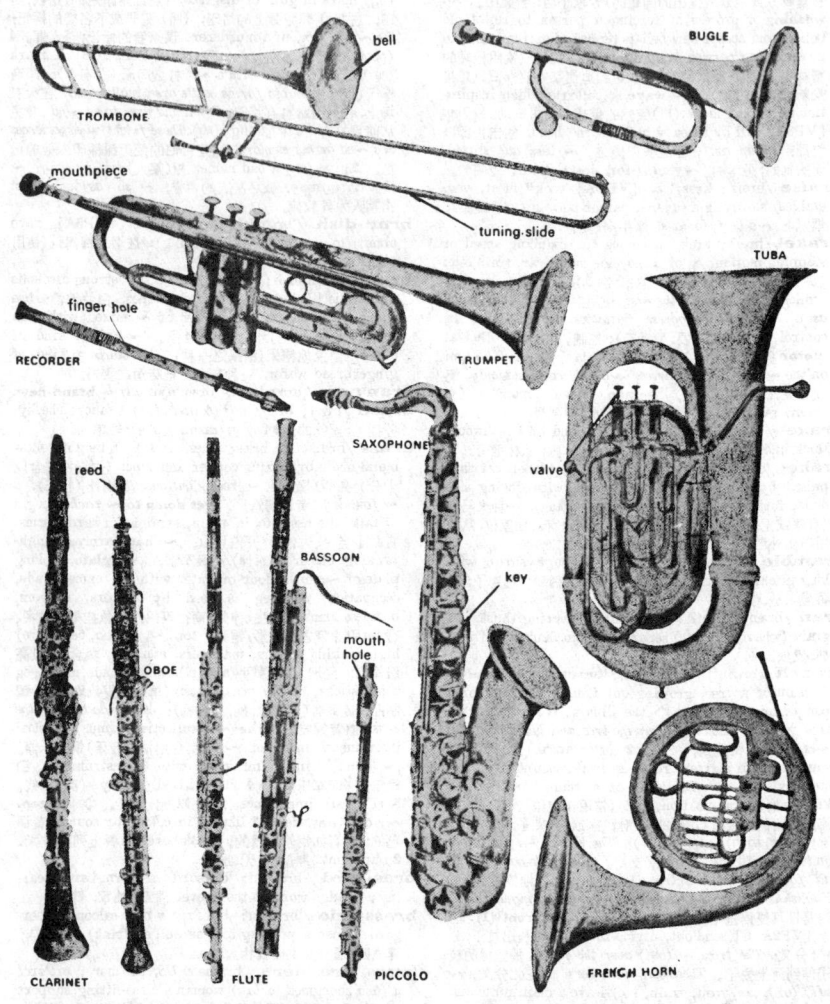

brass and woodwind instruments

付; 冒⋯⋯之危险: *He had ~d death a hundred times.* 他出生入死达百次之多。*We decided to ~ the storm,* to go out in spite of the storm. 我们决定冒暴风雨出去。 *~ it out,* [VP15B] disregard, defy, suspicion or blame. 不顾猜疑或责难; 硬干下去。 *~·ly adv* **brav·ery** /'breɪvərɪ; 'brevərɪ/ *n* [U] **1** courage; being ~. 英勇; 勇敢; 勇气。 **2** (old use) splendour (of dress, etc): (旧用法)(服装等的)华丽: *decked out in all their ~ry.* 穿着他们最华丽的衣服。

bravo /ˌbrɑː'vəʊ; 'brɑvo/ *n, int* (*pl* ~es, ~s) (cry of approval) Well done! Excellent! (喝彩声) 好极了! 要得!

brawl /brɔːl; brɔl/ *n* noisy quarrel or fight. 大声的争吵; 吵闹; 吵架。 □ *vi* [VP2A] quarrel noisily; take part in a ~; (of streams) flow noisily (over stones and rocks). 争吵; 吵闹; 吵架: (指溪流经过石上)淙淙而流。

~er n person who takes part in a ~. 争吵者; 吵闹者; 吵架者。

brawn /brɔːn; brɔn/ *n* [U] **1** muscle; strength. 肌肉; 体力。 **2** (not US) meat (esp pork) cut up, spiced and pickled, and compressed. (非美语)(经过切块及压缩的) 腌肉; (尤指) 腌猪肉。 *~y adj* (-ier, -iest) muscular: 肌肉多的; 有力的; 强壮的: *The miner has ~y arms.* 那矿工的胳臂很强壮。

bray /breɪ; bre/ *n* cry of an ass; sound of a trumpet. 驴叫声; 小喇叭声。 □ *vi* [VP2A] make a cry or sound of this kind. 发此种声音。

braze /breɪz; brez/ *vt* [VP6A] solder with an alloy of brass and zinc. 以铜锌合金焊接。

brazen /'breɪzn; 'brezn/ *adj* **1** made of brass; like brass: 黄铜制的; 如黄铜的: *a ~* (= hard-sounding) *voice;* 宏亮的声音; *the ~ notes of a trumpet.* 小喇叭之

响亮的声音。 **2** (often 常作 '**~-faced**) shameless. 厚颜的; 无耻的。 □ *vt* (only in) (仅用于) **~ it out**, behave, in spite of having done wrong, as if one has nothing to be ashamed of. (虽已做错仍)厚着脸皮干下去。

braz·ier /'breɪzɪə(r); 'breɪʒɚ/ *n* portable open metal framework (like a basket), usu on legs, for holding a charcoal or coal fire. (可移动, 通常有脚架的)金属炭盆; 火盆。

breach /briːtʃ; britʃ/ *n* **1** breaking or neglect (*of a rule, duty, agreement*, etc): 违犯; 怠忽; 破坏(与可约定用, 后接规则、职责、契约等): *a ~ of the peace*, unlawful fighting in a public place, eg the streets; 在公共场所(如街头)打架; 妨害治安; 骚动; *a ~ of contract* (in comm, etc); (商业上等之)违约 (违反契约上的规定); *a ~ of promise* (esp of a promise to marry); 背约; 毁约 (尤指婚约); *a ~ of faith*, act of disloyalty; 不忠的行为; *a ~ of confidence*; 泄密的行为; *a ~ of security*. 违反安全的行为。 **2** opening, esp one made in a defensive wall, etc by artillery, attacking forces, etc: 防御工事等为敌人炮火所穿之破洞; 突破口: *step into/fill the ~*, come forward to help; 上前帮助; *throw/fling oneself into the ~*, help those who are in trouble or danger; 救人于危难之境; 救人于水火之中; *stand in the ~*, bear the heaviest part of the attack; do most of the hard work. 承担最猛烈的攻击; 独当难局; 做大部分的困难工作; 挑重担。 **3** broken place; gap: 破洞; 缺口; 裂缝; 缝隙: *The sheep got out of the field where one of them had made a ~ in the hedge.* 一只羊在篱笆上弄了一个洞, 所有的羊都从牧地跑走了。 *The waves made a ~ in the sea wall.* 海浪在防波堤上冲出了一个缺口。 □ *vt* [VP6A] make a gap in, break through (a defensive wall, etc). 冲破; 突破(防御工事等)。

bread /bred; brɛd/ *n* [U] food made by mixing flour with water and yeast, kneading, and baking in an oven: 面包: *a loaf/slice/piece of ~*; 一条(片, 块)面包: (sl) money: (俚)钱: *I'm only doing it for the ~.* 我纯粹是为了钱才做那件事的。 **~ and butter** /ˌbred ən 'bʌtə(r); ˌbredṇ'bʌtɚ/, **(a)** slice(s) of ~ spread with butter. 涂有牛油的面包片。 **~-and-butter letter**, (colloq) of thanks for hospitality. 多谢款待的谢函。 **(b)** (colloq) means of living: (口)生计: *earn one's ~ and butter by writing.* 靠写作谋生。 **one's daily ~**, (共可通用)means of living. 谋生之道; 每日的生计; 每日的食粮。 *earn one's ~*, make enough money to live on. 糊口; 谋生。 *know which side one's ~ is buttered*, know where one may have advantages, where one's interest lies. 知道自己的利益所在; 知道如何于己有利。 *take the '~ out of sb's mouth*, take away his means of living, eg by business competition. 夺人之生计 (如借商业竞争); 抢人家的饭碗。 '**~·crumb** *n* [C] tiny bit of the inner part of a loaf, esp crumbled for use in cooking. 面包屑; 碎面包 (尤指弄碎而用于烹饪者)。 '**~·fruit** *n* tree with starchy fruit, grown in the South Sea Islands and W Africa. 面包树(果实含淀粉, 产于南太平洋诸岛及西非)。 '**~·line** *n* line of people waiting for food given as charity or relief: 领面包队伍; 领赈济食粮或救济品的队伍: (fig)(喻)*on the ~line*, very poor. 极贫穷的; 赤贫的。 '**~** in *pl* grain, flour. 制面包的原料(麦、面粉)。 '**~·win·ner** *n* person who works to support a family. 负担家庭生计者。

breadth /bredθ; brɛdθ/ *n* [U] ⇨ **broad¹**(2). **1** distance or measure from side to side: 宽度; 宽; 阔: *ten feet in ~*. 十英尺宽。 ⇨ **hair**(2). **2** largeness (of mind or view); boldness of effect (in music or art). 胸襟宽大; 气量宽宏; (音乐或艺术之)雄浑。 '**~·ways**, '**~·wise** *adv* so that the broad side is in front. 横(放); 横(置); 横着地。

break¹ /breɪk; brek/ *vt, vi* (*pt* **broke** /brəʊk; brok/ old Eng 古英语作 **brake** /breɪk; brek/, *pp* **broken** /'brəʊkən; 'brokən/) **1** [VP6A, 15B, 2A, C] (of a whole thing) (cause to) go or come into two or more separate parts as the result of force, a blow or strain (but not by cutting): (指完整的东西)打破; 击破; 打断;

破碎; 破裂; 断(但非由切割所致): *When she dropped the teapot it broke.* 她把茶壶掉在地上打碎了。 *The boy fell from the tree and broke his leg.* 那男孩从树上跌下, 跌断了腿。 *Glass ~s easily.* 玻璃容易破碎。 *If you pull too hard you will ~ the rope.* 你如果太用力拉, 就会把绳子拉断。 *The string broke.* 绳子断了。 **~ into pieces; ~ in two, etc,** (cause to) come or go into pieces, in two, etc parts: (使)成碎片; (使)破成两半: *He broke the box into pieces.* 他把匣子打成粉碎。 *When I hit the ball, my bat broke in two.* 当我击球时, 我的球棒断成两截。 **2** [VP 6A, 15B, 2A, C] (of a part or parts) (cause to) be separate or discontinuous because of force or strain: (部部分)(使)分离; (使)断folded; *He broke a branch from the tree.* 他从树上折下一枝树枝。 *The door-handle has broken off.* 门柄已经折断。 *A large part of it broke away, came off.* 它断了一大块。 **~ sb/oneself of a habit,** succeed in getting him/oneself to give it up. 使某人(自己)戒除一种习惯。 **3** [VP6A] make (sth) useless by injuring an essential part (of a machine, apparatus, etc): 损坏; 破坏(机器等): *~ a clock/a sewing-machine.* 损坏一座钟(一架缝纫机)。 **4** [VP 2D, 22] (with *adjj*): (与形容词连用): **~ 'even,** make neither a profit nor a loss. 不赚也不亏; 成和局; 不分胜负。 **~ 'loose (from),** get or become separate: 挣脱或脱离(锁链等): *The dog has broken loose*, got free from its chain. 狗挣脱锁链了。 *All hell has broken loose*, all the devils in hell have escaped; (fig) (used to describe a scene of confusion, eg a bombardment). 地狱里所有的恶魔都逃出来了; (喻)(用以描写混乱的情形, 例如炮轰)。 **~ sth open,** get it open by using force: 用力打开; 撬开: *~ open a safe/door/the lid of a desk.* 用力打开保险柜(门, 桌面)。 **5** [VP2A, C] (with various subjects): (与各种主语连用): *The abscess/blister/bubble broke*, burst. 脓疮(水泡, 气泡)破了。 *Day was beginning to ~*, daylight was beginning. 天开始亮了。 ⇨ **daybreak.** *His voice is beginning to ~*, change in quality as he reaches manhood. 他的声音开始变粗了(长大成人的现象)。 *She was filled with emotion and her voice broke*, She faltered, was unable to speak clearly because of emotion. 她激动得说不出话来。 *The storm broke*, began, burst into activity. 暴风雨骤然而来。 *The fine weather/The heat-wave/The frost broke*, The period of fine weather, etc ended after being settled. 好天气(热天气, 霜寒)(经过一段持续之后)突然转变。 Cf 参较 How long will the fine weather *hold*? 这好天气将会持续多久? *The clouds broke* = parted, showed an opening) *and the sun came through.* 云开出一条缝隙, 太阳就出来了。 *The waves were ~ing* (= curling and falling) *over/on/against the rocks.* 浪涛冲击着岩石。 *The sea was ~ing* (= sending waves that were ~ing) *on the beach/over the wrecked ship.* 海浪冲刷着海滩(破船的残骸)。 *The enemy broke* (= developed gaps in their lines, fell into confusion) *and fled.* 敌军败阵而逃。 *When the bank broke* (= was unable to carry on business because of lack of funds), *many people were ruined.* 当银行倒闭时, 许多人都跟着破产了。 *A good bowler can make the ball ~*, (in cricket) change from its course when it strikes the ground. (板球)好的球手能使球着地时改变方向。 **6** [VP6A] (with various objects): (与各种宾语连用): **~ sb's back/neck/nose, etc,** cause the bone(s) of the back, etc to be out of the right position. 击断某人的脊骨(颈项、鼻梁等)。 **~ back¹**(1). **~ the bank,** exhaust its funds: win all the money that the person managing a gambling game has. 把庄家所有的钱都赢来; 耗光庄家的赌本。 **~ bounds,** (mil)go out of bounds without permission or authority. (军)擅自进入禁止军人进入之场所。 **~ one's fall,** weaken its effect, make it less violent. 减弱其摔跌之力。 **~ the force of sth,** reduce its force by bearing part of it: 减弱某物的力量: *The tall hedge ~s the force of the wind.* 高的树篱能减弱风力。 ⇨ **windbreak. ~ fresh/new ground,** (fig) start work at sth new. (喻)

开辟新天地: 开创新事业。 ~ *sb's heart*, reduce him to despair. 令某人心碎; 令某人绝望。 ~ *a man*, ruin him; compel him to reveal a secret, etc. 使某人破产; 毁灭某人; 迫使其吐露秘密。 ~ *the news*, make it known. 泄漏消息。 ~ *the (bad) news (to sb)*, reveal the news in such a way that its effect is less of a shock. 用一点技巧(向某人)透露(坏)消息以便减轻听者所受的打击。 ~ *an officer*, dismiss him, take his commission from him. 开除一军官 (免去他的军职)。 ~ *a path/way*, make one by pushing or beating aside obstacles. (清除障碍) 开辟一条道路: 打出一条路来。 ~ *prison/gaol*, escape from, make one's way out of, prison. 越狱: 监狱。 ~ *ranks*, (of soldiers) leave the ranks without permission. (指士兵) (未获准而) 脱离队伍。 ~ *a (Commonwealth/Olympic/World, etc) record*, do better than it, make a new record. 打破(英联邦,奥运,世界等的)纪录; 创造新纪录。 ~ *a set of books/china, etc*, cause it to be incomplete by giving away or selling a part or parts of it. 拆散一套书籍(瓷器等)(如赠送或卖去一部分使之不能成套)。 ~ *the skin on one's elbow/knees/knuckles, etc*, graze it, so as to cause bleeding. 擦破手肘(膝盖、指节等)。 ~ *step*, (of soldiers) stop marching rhythmically in step, eg to avoid excessive vibration on a weak bridge. (指士兵) 改用便步走(例如在危桥上避免过分的震动)。 ~ *a strike*, end it by compelling the workers to submit. 迫使工人停止罢工。 ⇨ **strike breaker**. ~ *wind*, expel wind from the bowels or stomach. 放屁。 ⇨ also *code*(3), *cover*²(5), *ice*¹(1). **7** [VP6A, 15A, B] train or discipline; 训练: 驯养: ~ *a horse (in)*, bring it to a disciplined state; 驯马: a well-broken horse; 驯良的马; ~ *a horse to harness/to the rein*, accustom it to wearing harness, etc. 驯马使惯于戴马具(缰绳)。 **8** [VP6A, 15B] subdue, keep under, end by force: 压制; 制服; 控制: ~ *sb's spirit/will*; 瓦解某人的精神(意志); ~ (*down*) *the enemy's resistance*; 粉碎敌人的抵抗; ~ *the power of the rebel leader*. 消灭叛乱首领的势力。 **9** [VP6A] act in opposition to; infringe: 违犯; 违背; 违反; 侵犯; 侵害: ~ *the law/the rules/a regulation*; 违法 (规章); ~ *a contract/an agreement*; 违背契约(协定); ~ *the Sabbath*, do things on a Sunday that should not be done: 不守安息日 (在星期天做不应该做的事); ~ *one's word/a promise*, fail to keep a promise; 不守诺言; 食言; ~ *an appointment*, fail to keep it; 失约; 爽约; ~ *faith with sb*, betray or deceive him. 不忠于某人; 欺骗某人。 **10** [VP6A] interrupt or destroy the continuity of; end the operation or duration of; 使中止; 使中断; 停止: ~ (*the*) *silence*, end it, eg by speaking; 打破沉寂(如开始说话); ~ *one's journey (at a place)*; (在某地) 中止其旅行; ~ *the peace*, cause a disturbance; 破坏治安(引起骚动); ~ *one's fast*, (old use) take food after going without, ⇨ **breakfast**; (旧用法)开斋; 斋戒过后恢复进食; ~ *short (a conversation, etc)*, end it; 结束; 终止(谈话等): *a broken night's sleep*, one that is disturbed or interrupted. 一夜未能熟睡。 **11** [VP15B, 2C, 3A] (special uses with *adverbial particles* and *preps*): (与副词性小品词及介词连用之特殊用法):
break away (from), go away suddenly or abruptly; give up (habits, modes of thought or belief): 突然走开或转变方向; 挣脱; 脱逃; 革除(习惯、思想方式或信仰): *The prisoner broke away* (= escaped after a struggle) *from his guards*. 囚犯自看守者手中挣脱。 *Can't you ~ away from old habits?* 你不能戒除旧习惯吗? *About twenty members of the Conservative Party have broken away* (= seceded). 大约有二十名保守党党员脱党了。 *There has been a ~away from the Party*. 党中有人脱党。 *One of the provinces has broken away to form a new State.* 诸省中有一省已经脱离而独立成一新国家。
break 'down, (a) collapse: 崩溃; 瓦解: *His resistance will ~ down in time.* 他的抵抗终久是会瓦解的。 *Our plans have broken down.* 我们的计划已经失败了。 *Negotiations have broken down.* 谈判已破裂。 (b) become

disabled or useless: (指机器等)出毛病; 坏掉: *The car/engine/machinery broke down*, ie because of a mechanical fault. 汽车(发动机,机器)坏掉了。 *That old broken-down bus is not worth £5.* 那辆破旧的汽车值不了五英镑。 (c) suffer a physical or mental weakening: 身体或精神衰弱: *His health broke down*. 他的身体变衰弱了。 (d) be overcome by emotion, eg by bursting into tears: 情绪失去控制(如突然大哭): *She broke down when she heard the news, but quickly recovered.* 她听到那消息就哭了起来,但很快就恢复过来了。 ~ *sth down*, (a) get (a door, wall, etc) down by battering it. 将(门、墙等)捣毁。 (b) overthrow by force; suppress: 武力推翻; 镇压: ~ *down all resistance/opposition*. 镇压一切抵抗(反对)。 (c) divide, analyse, classify (statistical material): 分析; 分类(统计资料): ~ *down expenditure*, give details of how money is spent. 列出开支细目。 (d) change the chemical composition of: 分解…之化学成份: *Sugar and starch are broken down in the stomach.* 糖与淀粉在胃中被分解。 '~**down** *n* (a) failure in machinery, etc: (机器等)坏掉: 出毛病; *There was a ~down on the railway and trains were delayed.* 铁路出了毛病,列车误点了。 *The earthquake has caused a ~down of communications.* 地震造成了交通电讯的中断(交通与电讯设备的损坏)。 Hence, 由此产生, '~-**down gang**, men called to repair or remove a train, etc that has been derailed, smashed, etc. (修理或清除出轨、撞毁等之火车等的)抢修大队。 (b) collapse; weakening: 不支; 病倒; 衰弱: *He's suffering from a nervous ~down.* 他正患神经衰弱。 (c) statistical analysis: 统计分析; 析列: *a ~down of expenditure*. 支出析列。
break forth, (esp fig, of anger, indignation) burst out. (尤用于比喻,指怒气)爆发; 突发; 迸发。
break in, enter a building by force; 强行进入房屋: *Burglars had broken in while we were away on holiday.* 我们出外度假时,小偷闯入屋内行窃。 Hence, 由此产生, '~-**in** *n* The police are investigating a ~-in at the local bank. 警方正在调查一件闯入当地银行的窃案。 ~ *sb* (esp a horse) *in*, ⇨ **7** above; 参看上列第 7 义: train and discipline; accustom sb to a new routine. 使某人习惯于新的常规; 训练; (尤指)驯马。 ~ *in (up)on*, disturb; interrupt: 打扰; 打断: *Please don't ~ in on our conversation.* 请不要打断我们的谈话。
break into, (a) force one's way into (a buliding, etc): 强行进入; 闯入(建筑物等): *His house was broken into* (ie by burglars or thieves) *last week.* 他的房屋上星期曾有窃贼潜入。 (b) burst suddenly into: 突然开始: ~ (*out*) *into a loud laugh/into loud curses/into song/into praises of sb.* 突然发出大笑(大声诅咒, 唱起歌来,称赞某人)。 (c) change one's method of movement suddenly: 突然改变步法: ~ *into a run/trot/gallop*. 突然奔跑(疾走,飞奔)。 (d) occupy, take up, undesirably: 侵占: *Social duties ~ into my time/leisure.* 社交应酬侵占了我的时间(闲暇)。 (e) (of coins and notes): (指硬币及钞票): ~ *into a pound note*, use one to pay for sth costing less than this sum: 用一英镑的钞票支付不及一英镑之款额: *I can't pay you the 50p I owe you without ~ing into a £5 note.* 我要付你五十便士的欠款,就得兑散一张五英镑的钞票。 (f) open and draw upon emergency supplies: 打开并提取紧急补给品: *The garrison broke into their reserves of ammunition.* 卫戍部队启用储备的弹药。
break off, (a) stop speaking: 停止说话; 中断说话: *He broke off in the middle of a sentence.* 他一句话还未说完就中断了。 (b) pause; stop temporarily: 停顿; 暂时停止: *Let's ~ off for half an hour and have some tea.* 让我们小憩半小时喝点茶。 ~ (*sth*) *off*, (a) (cause to) separate (a part of sth): (使) 断折: *The mast broke off/was broken off.* 船桅断了。 (b) end abruptly: 突然断绝; 突然中止: ~ *off relations (with sb)*; (与某人) 绝交; ~ *off an engagement/conversation.* 解约(突然停止谈话)。
break out, ⇨ **outbreak**. (of fire, disease, war, rioting,

violence) appear, start, suddenly: (指火灾、疾病、战争、暴动、暴乱)突然发生: *A fire broke out during the night.* 夜间突然发生火警. *The quarrel broke out afresh.* 争吵再度爆发. *Riots and disorders have broken out.* 骚乱已经发生了. **～ out (of)**, escape: 逃脱: *Several prisoners broke out of the jail.* 有几个囚犯自狱中脱逃. **～ out in, (a)** suddenly become covered with: 突然布满: *His face broke out in pimples/a rash.* 他的脸突然间长出粉刺(红疹). *He broke out in a cold sweat, was struck with fear,* 他吓得浑身出冷汗. **(b)** show sudden violence in speech or behaviour: (言语或行为)突然激烈: *He broke out in a rage/in curses.* 他勃然大怒(破口大骂).

break through, make a way through (an enclosure, obstacles, etc): 突破(围墙、障碍物等): *The enemy's defences were strong but our soldiers broke through.* 敌人的防线很坚强, 但仍为我军所突破. *The sun broke through (the clouds).* 太阳钻出(云层)来了. **～ through sth**, overcome: 克服; 征服; 压倒: *～ through a man's reserve.* 打破某人含蓄缄默的态度. Hence, 由此产生, **'～·through** n **(a)** (mil) piercing (of the enemy's defences). (军) (敌人防线的)突破. **(b)** major achievement, eg in technology: (科学技术等方面的)主要成就; 突破: *～through in cancer research.* 癌症研究的突破.

break up, (a) come to pieces; disintegrate: 破碎; 碎裂; 瓦解: *The ship was ～ing up on the rocks.* 船在礁石上撞毁了. *The gathering broke up in disorder.* 集会一哄而散. **(b)** (fig, of persons) go to pieces; become weak: (喻,指人)身体衰弱; 变弱: *He broke up under the strain* 他累垮了. **(c)** (of a school, etc) separate at the end of term for holidays: (指学校等)学期结束; 放寒(暑)假: *When do you ～ 'up?* 你们(的学校)何时放寒(暑)假? **(d)** (of a couple, a relationship) come to an end: (指婚姻或关系)结束: *The marriage is ～ing up.* 该婚姻濒临破裂. **～ sth up, (a)** smash; demolish: 击碎; 捣毁: *～ up a box for firewood,* 拆箱子当柴烧: *～ up an old ship for scrap metal.* 拆毁旧船当废铁. **(b)** (cause to) split, or divide: (使)分开; 分成: *～ up a piece of work (among several persons).* 分配一件工作(由数人担任). **(c)** (cause to) disperse: (使)分散; 驱散: *The police broke up the crowd/meeting.* 警察驱散群众(集会的人). **(d)** bring to an end: 使结束; 终止: *They broke up the alliance.* 他们终止了联盟(或婚姻关系). Hence, 由此产生, **'～·up** n (end of a marriage, coalition, etc). (婚姻、联盟等的)结束. **(e)** (esp of a period of fine weather) change for the worse; end: (尤指经过一段时期的好天气之后)变坏; 终止: *The weather is ～ing up.* 天气变坏了.

break with, (a) end a friendship with: 与…绝交: *～ with an old friend.* 与老朋友绝交. **(b)** give up; make an end of: 放弃; 结束: *～ with old habits,* 革除旧习惯: *～ with old ties,* eg when leaving a district. 断绝旧关系(例如离开一个地区时).

break² /breɪk; brek/ n **1** breaking; broken place: 破裂; 破口; 断处: *a ～ in the water mains.* 总输水管之一破口. **2** [U] *～ of day (= day ～)*, dawn 天亮; 拂晓. **3** interval (in space of time): (一段时间中的)暂停; 间歇: *a ～ in the conversation,* 谈话中断的时间; *an hour's ～ for lunch;* 一小时的暂停以进午餐: *the 'tea-～*, eg in an office or factory; 饮茶时间 (如在办公室或工厂里); *during a ～ at school,* during an interval between lessons. 在学校的下课时间内. *without a ～*, continuously: 继续不断地; 不休息地: *He has been writing since 2 o'clock without a ～.* 他从两点钟起一直不断地在写. **4** change, disturbance: 改变; 变动: *a ～ in one's way of living;* 生活方式的改变: *a ～ in the weather.* 天气的变化. **5** change of course of a cricket or tennis ball on first striking the ground: (板球或网球初触地面时之)改向飞跳; 曲球: *a leg ～*, (cricket) one that breaks to the left. (板球)左曲球. **6** (billiards) continuous score: (弹子戏)连续得分: *make a ～ of 450.* 连续得450分. **7**

give sb a ～, (colloq) an opportunity (to make a new start or remedy an error). (口) 给予某人(改过自新的)机会. **8** (colloq) *a bad ～*, an unfortunate remark or ill-judged action; a piece of bad luck. (口) 失礼的话或不智的行动; 不幸; 倒霉. *a lucky ～*, a piece of good fortune. 幸运的事. **9** (=*break-out*) (attempt to) escape (esp from prison). 脱逃; (尤指)逃狱; 企图脱逃. (*make a*) *break for it*, escape. 逃跑; 逃走.

break³ /breɪk; brek/ n = **brake⁵**.

break·able /'breɪkəbl; 'brekəbl/ adj easily broken. 易破碎的. **break·ables** n pl = objects, eg glasses, cups and saucers. 易碎的物件(如玻璃杯、瓷杯、瓷碟).

break·age /'breɪkɪdʒ; 'brekɪdʒ/ n **1** act of breaking. 破坏; 破碎; 破损. **2** place in, part of, sth that has been broken. 破裂处; 裂开部分. **3** (usu pl) broken articles; loss by breaking: (通常用复数)破损的物件; 破碎的损失: *The hotel allows £150 a year for ～s,* for the cost of broken dishes, glasses, etc. 该旅社每年备有150英镑的杯盘等损失费.

breaker /'breɪkə(r); 'brekə/ n **1** large wave breaking into foam as it advances towards the shore; wave breaking against a rock, etc. 大浪冲岸后碎为泡沫之浪花; 冲击于礁石等上之碎浪. **2** person or thing that breaks. 击破者; 轧碎机. *'ice-～* n strongly built ship used to break up ice in harbours, etc. 破冰船(用以击破海港等内之冰). ⇨ **house~** and other similar compounds. 参看housebreaker及其他类似之复合词.

break·fast /'brekfəst; 'brɛkfəst/ n first meal of the day: 早餐; 早点: *Have a good ～.* 早餐吃饱(或好)一点. *He hasn't eaten much ～.* 他早餐没有吃多少. *They were having ～ when I arrived.* 我到达时, 他们正在吃早餐. □ vi have ～. 吃早餐.

break·neck /'breɪknek; 'brek,nɛk/ adj (usu) (通常作) *at (a) ～ speed*, at a dangerous speed. 以极危险的高速度.

break·water /'breɪkwɔːtə(r); 'brek,wɔtə/ n sth that breaks the force of waves, esp a structure built out into the sea to shelter (part of) a harbour. 减弱浪力之物; 挡浪板; (尤指港口的)防波堤.

a breakwater

bream /briːm; brim/ n (pl unchanged) (复数不变) **1** freshwater fish of the carp family. 鲷(一种鲤科之淡水鱼). **2** (also *'sea-～*) salt-water variety of this. 海鲷(一种咸水鱼, 系淡水鲷之变种).

breast /brest; brɛst/ n **1** either of the milk-producing parts of a woman: (女人之)乳房: *a child at the ～;* 正在吃奶的婴儿; *give a child the ～.* 哺乳婴儿. ⇨ **suckle.** *～·feed* vt feed a baby from the breast; suckle. 喂奶; 哺乳. *'～·fed* adj (of a baby) fed with milk from the ～. (指婴儿)人乳哺养的. Cf 参较 *bottle-fed.* **2** chest; upper front part of the human body, or of a garment covering this. (人体的)胸膛; 胸部; 衣服的胸部. *'～ pocket* n one in the ～ of a jacket, etc. 上衣胸前的口袋. *'～·stroke*, stroke (in swimming) in which both the arms are brought at the same time from in front of the head to the sides of the body. (游泳)俯泳 (两手同时自头前向身体两侧之划法). *,～·'high* adv high as the ～: 高与胸齐地; 与胸齐地: *The wheat was ～·high.* 麦禾高与胸齐. *,～·'deep* adv deep enough to reach the ～: 深及胸膛地: *In the 'middle of the stream the water was*

~-*deep*. 在溪流的中间，水深及胸。 '~-*plate* n piece of armour covering the ~. (盔甲之)护胸甲。 ⇨ the illus at **armour**. 参看 armour 之插图。 '~-*work* n low wall, eg of earth, sandbags, stones, put up as a temporary defence. 胸墙 (用泥土、沙袋、石头等临时构筑之高及胸部的防御工事). **3** (fig) feelings; thoughts: (喻)感情; 思想; 心情: *a troubled* ~. 心烦意乱。 *make a clean* ~ *of*, confess (wrong-doing, etc). 坦白承认 (过失等). **4** part of an animal corresponding to the human ~. (动物的)胸部。 □ vt [VP6A] present the ~(2) to, hence (fig), face, struggle with: 以胸抵抗; 挺胸以当; (由此产生)(喻)面对; 对付; 与…搏斗: ~ *the waves*. 与波涛搏斗。

breath /breθ; breθ/ n **1** [U] air taken into and sent out of the lungs; [C] single act of taking in and sending air out: 呼吸之空气; 气息; 一次呼吸: *take a deep* ~, fill the lungs with air. 作一次深呼吸。 *bad* ~, with an unpleasant smell. 带臭味的呼吸; 呼气很臭。 *catch/hold one's* ~, stop breathing for a moment (from fear, excitement, etc). (因恐惧、兴奋等而)屏息。 *get one's* ~ *(again/back)*, get back to the normal state. 恢复正常呼吸。 *in the same* ~, at the same moment: 在同一时刻: *They are not to be mentioned in the same* ~, cannot be compared. 他们不可同日而语。 *lose one's* ~, have difficulty in taking in ~, eg while running or working hard. (如因疾跑或工作辛苦而)喘不过气来; 喘息。 *out of* ~, unable to take in ~ quickly enough. 喘不过气来。 *speak/say sth below/under one's* ~, in a whisper. 低声地说某事。 *take* ~, get enough ~ (after exertion): (努力之后)喘喘气; 歇息一会儿: *Half-way up the mountain we stopped to take* ~. 爬到半山时，我们停下来喘喘气。 *take sb's '*~ *away*, startle or surprise him. 使某人大为吃惊。 Hence, 由此产生, '~-*taking*, adj exciting; causing awe. 紧张刺激的; 惊险的; 令人敬畏的。 *waste one's* ~, talk in vain 白费唇舌。 '~ *test* n test of the alcoholic contents of a person's ~'. 呼吸实验(试验人之呼吸中的酒精含量). **2** moving air; light breeze: 微风; 轻风: *There wasn't a* ~ *of air/wind*, The air was quite still. 一丝微风都没有。 **3** (fig) suggestion (*of*): (喻)—丝痕迹; 迹象: *not a* ~ *of suspicion/scandal*. 没有一丝疑心(闲言闲语). ~-*less* adj **1** out of ~; panting; likely to cause shortness of ~: 喘不过气来的; 喘息的; 可能引起喘息的: *in a* ~*less hurry*; 匆忙得喘不过气来; *listening with* ~*less atten-tion/in* ~*less expectation*, with the ~ held back (in concentration or excitement). 聚精会神地(抱着急切希望地)听。 **2** unstirred by wind: 无风的; 空气平静的: *a* ~*less* (=calm) *evening*. 无风的夜晚。 ~-*less·ly* adv

breath·a·lyse /'breθəlaɪz; 'brɛθəlaɪz/ vt [VP6A] (GB) measure the amount of alcohol in a person's breath. (英)呼吸试验(试验某人呼吸中的酒精含量). ~*r* n instrument for breathalysing sb (usu used by the police on the driver of a car). 呼吸试验器(警察通常用以试验汽车驾驶人呼吸中的酒精含量).

breathe /briːð; brɪð/ vi, vt **1** [VP2A, C, 6A, 15B] take air into the lungs and send it out again: 呼吸: ~ *in/out*. 吸入(呼出)吸(呼)气。 *He was breathing hard when he finished the race*. 他跑完赛跑时很费力地喘着气。 *We* ~ *air*. 我们呼吸空气。 *He* ~ *a sigh of relief*. 他放心地松了一口气。 *He's still breathing*, is still alive. 他还活着。 ~ *again/freely (again)*, be at ease, be relieved (after exertion, excitement, fear, etc). (在努力、兴奋、恐惧等之后)恢复常态; 恢复平静; 安心; 松一口气。 ~ *down sb's neck*, ⇨ **neck**. **2** [VP6A] utter; send out, eg a scent, feeling: 说出; 发出(气味、感情等): *Don't* ~ *a word of this*, keep it secret. 不要丝毫泄露这个消息。 **3** [VP6A] allow (a horse) to ~; gently and rest. 让(马)松一口气休息休息。 **breather** n **1** short pause for rest: 短时间的休息: *take/have a* ~. 松一口气休息休息。 **2** short period of exercise: 短时间的运动: *go for a* ~*r*. 去运动运动。 **breath·ing** n [U] **breath·ing-space** n time to ~; pause; rest. 喘气的工夫; 暂停; 休息。

bred pt, pp of **breed**.

breech /briːtʃ; britʃ/ n back part of a rifle or gun barrel, where the cartridge or shell is placed: (枪炮的)后膛(装子弹或炮弹的地方): *a* ,~-,*loading 'gun*, loaded at the ~, not through the muzzle. 由后膛装弹的枪炮。 '~-*block* n block of steel that closes the ~ of a gun. (枪炮之)闩体; 枪机闩。

breeches /'britʃɪz; 'britʃɪz/ n pl **1** 'knee-~, garment fitting round the waist and below the knees. 长及膝盖下之短裤。 '*riding-*~, garment covering the hips and thighs, buttoned below the knee, worn by men and women for riding on horseback. 马裤(男女骑装之短裤，膝下部分有钮扣). **2** (colloq) trousers; knickerbockers. (口)裤; 灯笼裤。 *wear the* ~, (said of a woman) rule her husband. (指女人)驾驭丈夫。 ~-*,buoy* /'britʃɪz-; 'britʃɪz-/ n pair of canvas ~ fastened to a lifebuoy, pulled along a rope, used for saving life at sea. 短裤型之救生具。

breed /briːd; brid/ vt, vi (pt, pp **bred** /bred; brɛd/) **1** [VP6A] keep (animals, etc) for the purpose of producing young, esp by selection of parents: 饲养(牲畜等); (尤指)选种繁殖: ~ *horses/cattle*. 养马(牛). **2** [VP2A] give birth to young; reproduce: 生育; 繁殖: *Rabbits* ~ *quickly*. 兔子繁殖迅速。 *Birds* ~ *in the spring*. 鸟类在春季繁殖。 **3** [VP6A] train, educate, bring up: 训练; 教育; 养育: *an Englishman born and bred*; 土生土长的英国人; *a well-bred boy*, one who has been trained to behave well. 一个教养良好的男孩子。 *What's bred in the bone will come out in the flesh*, (prov) Hereditary characteristics always show them-selves. (谚)遗传的特质总会显现出来的。 **4** [VP6A] be the cause of: 引起; 造成: *Dirt* ~*s disease*. 污秽引致疾病。 *War* ~*s misery and ruin*. 战争造成苦难与灾害。 ~*er* n **1** person who ~s animals. 畜养牲畜的人。 **2** apparatus (reactor) that produces more radio-active material than is put into it. (原子能)增殖反应堆; (放射物质)滋生反应器。 ~·*ing* n [U] **1** (in verbal senses): (照动词意义): *the* ~*ing of horses*; 养马; *the* ~*ing season for birds*. 鸟类的繁殖季节。 **2** knowledge of how to behave resulting from training: (所受的)教养: *a man of good* ~*ing*. 教养良好的人。 □ n [C] kind or variety (of animals, etc) with hereditary qualities: (牲畜等的)种: *a good* ~ *of cattle*. 良种牛。 ⇨ **cross-**~, *half-*~.

breeze[1] /briːz; briz/ n [C, U] wind, esp a soft, gentle wind: 和风; 微风: *a land/sea* ~, one blowing from the land/sea at certain hours; 在一定时刻由大陆(海上)吹来的风; 陆(海)风; *not much* ~; 很少的风; *not much of a* ~; 非常轻微的风; *spring* ~*s*. 春风。 □ vi [VP2C] (colloq) ~ *in/out*, come in/go out in high spirits, or without warning, unexpectedly. (口)飘然而来(去)(令人感到意外). **breezy** adj **1** exposed to windy ~'s. 迎风的; 当风的; 有风的。 **2** swept by ~s: 微风掠过的; 通风的: *a breezy corner*. 风凉的拐角处。 **3** (of persons) jovial; lively; good-humoured. (指人)喜谈笑的; 乐天的; 和气的。 **breez·ily** /'briːzɪlɪ; 'brɪzlɪ/ adv **breezi·ness** /'briː-zɪnɪs; 'brizɪnɪs/ n

breeze[2] /briːz; briz/ n [U] (not US) small coal cinders. (不用于美国)煤渣; 煤炭的余烬。 '~ *blocks*, light-weight concrete building blocks made of ~ and cement. (煤渣与水泥制成的)一种轻型水泥砖。

Bren /bren; brɛn/ n (also 亦作 '~-*gun*) light-weight, semiautomatic, light machine gun. 布朗式半自动轻机枪。 '~ *carrier* n small armoured vehicle that moves on tracks(5). 布朗式(履带)小战车。

breth·ren /'breðrən; 'brɛðrən/ n pl (old use) brothers. (旧用法)弟兄们。

breve /briːv; briv/ n (mus) note equal to two semibreves, now rarely used. (音乐)倍全音符; 二全音符(现已少用). ⇨ the illus at **notation**. 参看 notation 之插图。

bre·vet /'brevit *US:* brɪ'vɛt; brə'vɛt/ *n* document that gives sb higher rank without corresponding increase in pay or authority: 加衔之公文(使某人晋级而不予加薪或提高其职权): ~ *rank*, given by ~; 荣誉等级; 衔街等级; ~ *major*. 荣誉少校。

brevi·ary /'bri:vɪərɪ *US:* -ɪerɪ; 'brɪvɪˌɛrɪ/ *n* (*pl* -**ries**) book with prayers to be said daily by priests etc of the RC Church. (天主教神父等所用的)每日祈祷书。

brev·ity /'breviti; 'brɛvɪtɪ/ *n* [U] (formal) shortness (of statements, human life and other non-material things). (正式用语)简洁; 简短; 短暂(指言词、人生及其他非物质事物)。

brew /bru:; bru/ *vt, vi* **1** [VP6A] prepare (beer, tea, etc) by soaking or boiling grain, leaves, etc. [VP2A] make beer, etc. 酿(酒); 泡(茶); 调制; 酿酒; 调制饮料。 **2** [VP6A] (fig) bring about; [VP2A, C] gather, be forming: 造成; 图谋; 聚集; 形成; 酝酿: *Those boys are ~ing mischief*. 那些男孩子正图谋捣乱。 *A storm is ~ing*, gathering force. 风暴即将来临。*There's trouble ~ing between them*, They are likely to quarrel. 他们彼此之间正酝酿着不和。 □ *n* result of ~ing; liquid made by ~ing: 酿造物; 调制的饮料; 所酿的酒: *the best ~s of beer*; 酿得最好的啤酒; *a good, strong ~ of tea*. 上好的浓茶。 ~**er** *n* person who ~s beer. 酿啤酒者。 ~**·ery** /'bruːərɪ/ *n* (*pl* -**ries**) building in which ~ing of beer is carried on. 啤酒厂。

briar /'braɪə(r); 'braɪɚ/ *n* **1** [U] hard wood (root of a bush) used esp for making tobacco pipes. 石南根(见用于制烟斗)。 **2** [C] pipe made of this wood. 石南根烟斗。 **3** = **brier**.

bribe /braɪb; braɪb/ *n* [C] sth given, offered or promised to sb in order to influence or persuade him (often to do sth wrong) in favour of the giver: 贿赂: *offer/give/hand out/take ~s*. 行(受)贿。 □ *vt* [VP6A, 17, 15A] offer, give, a ~ to: 向…行贿; 贿赂: ~ *a judge/witness*. 贿赂法官(证人)。 *The child was ~d* to take the nasty medicine. 那小孩被哄着吃难吃的药。 *He had been ~d into silence*/*to say nothing*. 他受了贿赂保持缄默。 **bri·bable** /'braɪbəbl; 'braɪbəbl/ *adj* **bri·bery** /'braɪbərɪ; 'braɪbərɪ/ *n* [U] giving or taking of ~s. 贿赂; 行贿; 受贿。

bric-a-brac /'brɪk ə bræk; 'brɪkəˌbræk/ *n* [U] bits of old furniture, china, ornaments, etc, esp old and curious, of no great value. (不太值钱的)小古董; 小古玩。

brick /brɪk; brɪk/ *n* **1** [C] (usu rectangular block of) clay moulded and baked by fire or sun, used for building purposes: 砖: *a house made of red ~(s)*; 一所红砖造的房子; *a ~ wall*. 一道砖墙。 *drop a ~*, (colloq) do or say sth indiscreet. (口)失言; 失礼。 **make ~s without straw**, attempt a difficult and fruitless task. 做劳而无功的工作; 为无米之炊。 ~ *as a missile*: 碎砖; 砖块(尤指作为武器投掷用者): *The Minister collected a lot of ~bats*, (fig) much abuse. (喻)那部长备受各方的指责。 '~**field**, '~**kiln** *n* field, kiln, in which ~s are made. 砖场。砖窑; 砖窖。 '~**layer** *n* workman who builds with ~s. 砖匠; 泥水匠。 '~**work** *n* (part of a) structure made of ~. (建筑工程中的)砖工; 砖造部分。 **2** child's rectangular block (usu of wood) used for building toy houses, etc. 积木(儿童玩具)。 **3** ~-shaped block of sth, eg ice-cream. 形状似砖的一块东西(如冰淇淋砖)。 **4** (colloq) generous or kind-hearted person: (口)慷慨的人; 好心的人: *You've behaved like a ~*. 你的行为表现得象个好心的人。 □ *vt* [VP15B] ~ *up/in*, block (an opening) with ~s: 用砖堵住(洞口): ~ *up a window*. 用砖堵窗户堵住。

bri·dal /'braɪdl; 'braɪdl/ *n* wedding-feast; wedding; (attrib) of a bride or wedding: 结婚之酒宴; 婚礼; (用作定语) 新娘的; 婚礼的: *the '~ party*, the bride and her attendants and friends. 新娘及其伴娘和朋友。

bride /braɪd; braɪd/ *n* woman on her wedding-day; newly married woman. 新娘; 新婚妇人。 '~**·cake** *n* (old

name for) wedding-cake. 结婚蛋糕; 喜饼 (wedding-cake 之旧名)。

bride·groom /'braɪdgrum; 'braɪdˌgrum/ *n* man on his wedding-day; newly married man. 新郎; 新婚的男子。

brides·maid /'braɪdzmeɪd; 'braɪdzˌmed/ *n* girl or young unmarried woman (usu one of several) attending a bride at her wedding. 女傧相; 伴娘。 Cf 参较 *best man* for the bridegroom. 男傧相之男傧相。

bridge[1] /brɪdʒ; brɪdʒ/ *n* **1** structure of wood, stone, brickwork, steel, concrete, etc, providing a way across a river, canal, railway, etc. 桥; 桥梁。 '~**·head** *n* defensive post or area established on the enemy's side of a river, etc: (loosely) any military position occupied in the face of the enemy. (靠近敌人之)桥头阵地; 桥头堡。 ⇨ **beachhead**. **2** platform over and across the deck of a ship for the use of the captain and officers. 船桥; 舰桥(为船长及高级船员等发号施令之场所)。 **3** upper bony part of the nose. 鼻梁。 **4** movable part over which the strings of a violin, etc are stretched. (小提琴等等上绷弦的)琴马; 琴桥。 **5** device for keeping false teeth in place, fastened to natural teeth. 齿桥(装于真牙上以固定假牙的金属架子)。 □ *vt* [VP6A] join by means of a ~; build a ~ over: 以桥连接; 架桥于…上: *a 'bridging loan*, loan (esp from a bank) to cover a period of time, eg between the purchase of one house and the sale of another; 过渡贷款(尤指银行的贷款, 以过渡时期为限, 例如在购买新居与出售旧屋之间时的贷款); [VP15B] ~ *over*, (fig) overcome (obstacles, etc): (喻)克服(障碍等): ~ *over difficulties*. 渡过难关。

bridge[2] /brɪdʒ; brɪdʒ/ *n* [U] card game for four players in which one player looks on while his cards, placed face up on the table, are played by his partner. 桥牌戏(四人玩, 其中一人, 即梦家, 将牌摊于桌上, 交由其伙伴支配出牌, 自己则旁观)。 '**auction ~**, in which the right to name the trumps goes to the player who undertakes to make the highest score. (谁叫牌最高由谁决定王牌之)拍卖式桥牌戏。 '**contract ~**, variety of auction ~ with penalties for failure to make the score. 合约式桥牌戏(上述桥牌之一种, 若不能得到所叫之分数将受罚)。

bridle /'braɪdl; 'braɪdl/ *n* that part of a horse's harness that goes on its head, including the metal bit for the mouth, the straps and the reins. 马笼头(马具之套在马头上的部分, 包括口衔、嚼及缰)。 ⇨ the illus at **harness**. 参看 harness 之插图。 '~-**path**, '~-**road** *n* one fit for riders on horseback but not for cars, etc. 马径(适于骑马不宜行车者)。 □ *vt, vi* **1** [VP6A] put a ~ on (a horse), 套笼头于(马)。 **2** [VP6A] (fig) control, check: (喻)控制; 约束: *Try to ~ your passions*. 尽力控制你强烈的感情。 **3** [VP2A, C] throw back the head and draw in the chin (showing pride, contempt, vanity, etc): 仰头; 昂首(表示骄傲、轻视、自大等): ~ *with anger*; 怒气冲冲; ~ *up*; 昂首; ~ *at sb's remarks*. 轻视某人的言论。

brief[1] /bri:f; brif/ *adj* (-**er**, -**est**) (of time, events, writing, speaking) lasting only for a short time: (指时间、事件及言词、讲话)暂时的; 短的; 简短的; 简短的: *to be ~*, to speak shortly. 简而言之。 ⇨ **brevity**. *in ~*, in a few words. 简言之。 ~**·ly** *adv*

brief[2] /bri:f; brif/ *n* **1** [C] summary of the facts of a case, drawn up for a barrister: (提供给律师的)案情摘要: *have plenty of ~s*, (of a barrister) be busy with professional work. (指律师)业务兴旺, 忙于案件。 *hold a ~ for (sb)*, (fig) argue in support or favour of. (喻)为…辩护; 支持。 *hold no ~ for*, (fig) not be prepared to support. (喻)不准备支持。 ~**·case** *n* flat leather or plastic case, for documents, etc. (皮或塑胶制的供装公文等的)公事包。 **2** (also 亦作 '~-**ing**) information, instructions, advice, etc given in advance, eg to an aircraft crew before a combat mission. 简报; 任务提示 (如对一组空勤人员出发执行战斗任务前所作的)。 **3**

bridges

a pontoon bridge

an arch bridge

a trestle bridge

a suspension bridge

a Bailey bridge

a cantilever bridge

(comm) instructions: (商) 指示；说明: *My ~ did not include the buying of new materials.* 我的说明并不包括购买新材料。□ *vt* [VP6A] **1** instruct or employ (a barrister): 委托(律师)代理诉讼。**2** give a ~(2) to. 对…作任务提示。⇨ **debrief. 3** (comm) summarize the facts, eg of a business programme: (商) 摘要说明(例如有关业务计划方面者): *The Chairman will ~ the Board on the most recent developments.* 主席将向董事会摘要说明最近的发展。

briefs /bri:fs; brifs/ *n pl* close-fitting pants without legs, held in position by an elastic waistband. (无裤腿，用松紧腰带系牢的贴身)短裤。

brier, briar /'braɪə(r); 'braɪə/ *n* thorn-covered bush, esp the wild rose. 荆棘(尤指野蔷薇)。

brig /brɪg; brɪg/ *n* two-masted ship with square sails and an extra fore-and-aft sail on the mainmast. 一种双桅船(帆为方形，主桅上并另有纵帆)。⇨ the illus at **barque.** 参看 barque 之插图。

brig·ade /brɪ'geɪd; brɪ'ged/ *n* **1** army unit, usu of three battalions, forming part of an army division; corresponding armoured unit. 旅(陆军师的单位，通常包括三个营)；装甲兵旅。**2** organized body of persons in uniform with special duties (eg '**fire**-~). 身着制服担任特殊任务的团队(如消防队)。**Briga·dier** /,brɪgə'dɪə(r); ,brɪgə'dɪr/ *n* (formerly 昔作 ,Brigadier-'General, officer commanding a ~; army officer of rank between General and Colonel. 旅长；准将。

brig·and /'brɪgənd; 'brɪgənd/ *n* member of a band of robbers, esp a band that attacks travellers in forests or mountains. 强盗；土匪(尤指在山林中拦劫旅客为生者)。

brig·an·tine /'brɪgəntiːn; 'brɪgən,tin/ *n* = ~**brig.**

bright /braɪt; braɪt/ *adj* (-er, -est) **1** giving out or reflecting much light; shining: 光明的；发光的；明亮的: *Sunshine is* ~. 阳光是明亮的。*Polished steel is* ~. 磨光的钢是发亮的。*The leaves on the trees are* ~ *green in spring.* 春天里树上的叶子是翠绿的。**2** cheerful and happy; lit up with joy or hope: 愉快的；高兴的；乐观的: ~ *faces;* 高兴的面容; *a* ~ *smile;* 愉快的微笑; *see the*

~ *side of things.* 对事物抱乐观的态度。**3** quick-witted, clever: 聪明的；伶俐的: *A* ~ *boy learns quickly.* 聪明的孩子学得快。□ *adv* (chiefly with *shine*) (主要与 shine 连用) = ~*ly.* 光明地；光亮地。~**en** *vt, vi* [VP6A, 15B, 2A, C] ~*en up,* make or become ~er or lighter, more cheerful, etc: (使)更为光明; (使)更为愉快: *These flowers* ~*en the classroom.* 这些花朵使教室生辉。*The sky is* ~*ening.* 天正放晴。*His face* ~*ened up.* 他喜形于色。~**·ly** *adv* ~**·ness** *n*

brill /brɪl; brɪl/ *n* flat fish like a turbot. 一种鲽类之鱼。

bril·liant /'brɪlɪənt; 'brɪljənt/ *adj* very bright; sparkling; splendid, causing admiration: 极明亮的; 光辉灿烂的; 令人钦佩或赞赏的: *a week of* ~ *sunshine;* 天气晴朗的一周; *a* ~ *scientist;* 卓越的科学家; ~ *jewels.* 灿烂的珠宝。~**·ly** *adv* **bril·liance** /'brɪlɪəns; 'brɪljəns/, **bril·liancy** /'brɪlɪənsɪ; 'brɪljənsɪ/ *nn* (U) radiance, splendour, intelligence. 光辉灿烂; 显赫; 聪颖; 才气焕发。

bril·lian·tine /'brɪlɪəntiːn; 'brɪljən,tin/ *n* [U] cosmetic used to make the hair lie flat. (使头发柔顺的)美发油。

brim /brɪm; brɪm/ *n* **1** edge of a cup, bowl, glass, etc: (杯、碗等的)边: *full to the* ~, quite full. 满盈的。**2** out-turned part (rim) of a hat, that gives shade. (帽的)边。□ *vi* (-mm-) [VP2A, C] be full to the ~. 满盈。~ *over,* be so full that some spills over the ~: 溢出; (fig) (喻) ~*ming over with high spirits.* 兴高采烈。~**·full** /-ful/ /'brɪm,ful; 'brɪm'ful/ *adj* full to the ~: 盈满的; 充满的: *He is* ~*ful of new ideas.* 他有很多新的主意。

brim·stone /'brɪmstəʊn; 'brɪm,ston/ *n* [U] (old name for) sulphur. 硫黄石(硫黄之旧名)。

brindled /'brɪndld; 'brɪndld/ *adj* (esp of cows and cats) brown with streaks of another colour. (尤指牛及猫)棕色而有其他颜色之斑纹的。

brine /braɪn; braɪn/ *n* [U] salt water, esp for pickling. (尤指浸腌菜之)盐水。**briny** /'braɪnɪ; 'braɪnɪ/ *adj* salty. 盐的; 含盐的; 咸的。□ *n* **the briny,** (colloq)

the sea. (口) 海洋。

bring /brɪŋ; brɪŋ/ vt (pt, pp brought /brɔːt; brɔt/) (For uses with *adverbial particles and preps*, ⇨ **6** below.) (与副词性小品词及介词连用之各种用法，参看下列第 6 义。) **1** ⇨ **take** [VP 6A, 15B, 13A, B, 12A, B, C, 14] ~ *(with)*, come carrying sth or accompanying sb: 拿来; 取来; 带来(人或物): *Take this empty box away and* ~ *me a full one.* 把这个空盒子拿走，给我拿个满的来。*The soldiers came back* ~*ing ten prisoners (with them).* 士兵们带着十个俘虏回来了。B~ *Mary to the party with you.* 带玛丽一道来参加宴会。B~ *one for me.* 拿一个给我。B~ *me one.* 给我拿一个来。 **2** [VP 6A, 19B, 12C, 14] cause to come; cause to be: 使来; 带来; 引起: *Spring* ~*s warm weather and flowers.* 春天带来暖和的天气和百花。*The sad news brought tears to her eyes.* 噩耗使她不禁流泪。*His writings* ~ *him £5000 a year.* 他的著作每年可使他获得五千英镑。*A phone call brought him hurrying to Leeds.* 一通电话使他匆忙赶赴里兹。 **3** [VP17] ~ *sb/oneself to do sth*, persuade, induce, lead: 说服; 引诱; 引导: *They could not* ~ *themselves to believe the news.* 他们对这消息觉得难以置信。*She couldn't* ~ *herself to speak about the matter.* 她就不起勇气来谈这事。*I wish I could* ~ *you to see the situation from my point of view.* 我真希望能使你从我的观点来看这情况。 **4** [VP14] ~ *against*, (legal) start, put forward: (法律) 提起(诉讼): ~ *an action/charge/an accusation against sb.* 提起诉讼控告某人。 **5** (phrases) (短语) ~ *sb to book*, ⇨ **book**[1](8); ~ *sth to an end*, cause it to end; 使某事结束; 了结某事; ~ *sth home to sb*, ⇨ **home**[2](2); ~ *low*, reduce to a low condition; 使(健康情况、财富或地位等)低落; 降低; 贬抑; ~ *sth to light*, cause it to be visible or known; 使某事物可看得见; 发现; 发掘; 公布; ~ *sth to mind*; 忆起某事; ~ *sth to pass*, ⇨ **pass**[1](3); ~ *sth into line/play*, ⇨ **line**[1](11), **play**[1](8); ~ *sb to his senses*, ⇨ **sense**(2). **6** [VP15B] (special uses with *adverbial particles and preps*) (与副词性小品词及介词连用之特殊用法):

bring about, **(a)** cause to happen: 引起; 导致; 致使: ~ *about a war/reforms/sb's ruin.* 引起战争 (导致改革; 致使某人破产)。 **(b)** (naut) cause (a sailing-ship) to change direction: (航海) 使 (帆船) 改向: *The helmsman brought us about.* 舵手使船改向。

bring back, **(a)** return: 归还: *Please* ~ *back the book tomorrow.* 请于明天将书归还。(with *indirect object*): (与间接宾语连用): *If you're going to the market, please* ~ *me back ten eggs.* 如果你要上市场，请给我带十个蛋回来。 **(b)** call to mind; cause to remember: 使记起; 使回忆: *Your newsy letter brought back many memories.* 你那封带来许多消息的信唤起了许多回忆。 **(c)** restore; reintroduce: 使恢复; 再导入: *How many MP's favour* ~*ing back capital punishment?* 有多少国会议员赞成恢复死刑? ~ *sb back to*, restore to: 复归; 使恢复: *Her stay among the mountains brought her back to health.* 她在山里暂住使她恢复了健康。

bring down/sth down, **(a)** cause to fall; cause to come down: 使落下; 使跌下; 使倒下: ~ *down a hostile aircraft*, shoot it down; 打落一架敌机; ~ *down prices*, lower them; 削价; 减价: ~ (= overthrow) *a tyrant.* 打倒暴君。 **(b)** continue (records, etc) up to: 使(记录)延续到…: *a new history of Europe, brought down to modern times*, ie made up to date. 一直写到现代的一部新的欧洲史。 **(c)** kill or wound: 打死; 打伤; 打倒: *He aimed, fired, and brought down the antelope.* 他瞄准，射击，打倒了那只羚羊。 **(d)** (football) cause (an opponent) to fall by fouling; (Rugby) tackle. (足球) 犯规撞倒(对方); (橄榄球) 摛抱。 **(e)** (arith) transfer a digit from one part of a sum (from one column) to another: (算术) 进位; 退位: ~ *down the next two figures.* 将下两位数字进位。 ~ *the 'house down/* ~ *down the house*, ⇨ **house**(6). ~ *down sb's wrath/fury on one's head*, cause it to be aimed at oneself: 使某人的怒气发到自己头上来。

bring sth forth, produce (fruit); give birth to (young ones): 结 (果); 生产 (幼儿): *What will the future* ~ *forth?* 将来结果怎样?

bring sth forward, **(a)** cause to be seen, discussed, etc: 提出 (让人看见或讨论等): *Can you* ~ *forward* (= produce) *any proof of what you say?* 关于你所说的，你能提出证据吗? *Please* ~ *the matter forward at the next meeting.* 请将此一问题在下次会议提出讨论。 **(b)** advance: 提前: *The meeting has been brought forward from May 10 to May 3*, is to be a week earlier. 会期已自五月十日提前至五月三日。⇨ **postpone**. **(c)** (abbr 略作 **b/f**) (book-keeping) carry the total of a column of figures at the foot of one page to the top of the next page. (簿记) 承前(将页底一列数字之总和转至下一页之页顶)。

bring sth/sb in, **(a)** yield; (of capital, investments, etc) produce as profit: 产生; (指本金，投资等)生(息); 获(利): *His orchards* ~ (him) *in £200 a year.* 他的果园每年获利二百英镑。*He does odd jobs that* ~ *him in ten to twelve pounds a week.* 他做零工每周可赚十英镑至十二英镑。*This investment* ~*s (me) in 7½ per cent.* 此项投资(使我)可获百分之七点五的盈利。 **(b)** introduce: 介绍; 引进: ~ *in a new fashion/a new topic.* 引进新式样(提出新话题)。 **(c)** introduce (legislation): 提出(立法): ~ *in a Bill on road safety.* 提出道路安全法案。 **(d)** admit (as a partner, adviser, etc): 延聘(为伙伴，顾问等): *They've brought in experts to advise on the scheme.* 他们已延聘专家对该计划提供意见。 **(e)** (of the police) arrest; 带到派出所内: ~ *to a police station for questioning*, etc: (指警方) 逮捕; 带到派出所询问: *Two suspicious characters were brought in.* 两个可疑人物被拘捕。 **(f)** (of a jury) pronounce (a verdict): (指陪审团) 宣 (判): ~ *in a verdict of guilty.* 宣判有罪。

bring sth/sb off, **(a)** rescue (esp from a wrecked ship): 救助; 拯救(尤指遭遇船难者): *The passengers and crew were brought off by the Deal lifeboat.* 乘客及船员均经 Deal 救生艇救起。 **(b)** carry (an enterprise) to success; manage to do sth successfully: 经营成功; 将(某事)做得很成功: 完成任务: *It was a difficult task but we brought it off*, we succeeded. 那是一件困难的工作，但是我们终于完成任务。

bring sth/sb on, **(a)** lead to, (help to) produce: 引起; 导致; 促成: *He was out all day in the rain and this brought on a bad cold.* 他整天在外面淋雨，因此患了重感冒。 **(b)** cause to develop or advance: 使发展或进步: *The fine weather is* ~*ing the crops on nicely.* 好天气使农作物长得很好。 **(c)** help (a pupil, learner, etc) to develop: 帮助(学生、学习者等)发展; 教导; 指导: *The coach is* ~*ing on some youngsters in the reserve team.* 教练正在指导预备队的孩子们训练。

bring sth/sb out, **(a)** cause to appear, show clearly: 使显现; 阐释: ~ *out the meaning of a poem.* 阐明一首诗的意义。*The sunshine will* ~ *out the apple blossom*, cause it to open. 阳光将使苹果花开放。 **(b)** publish (a book, etc): 出版 (书籍等): *When are the publishers* ~*ing out his new book?* 出版商何时出版他的新书? **(c)** help to lose shyness or reserve: 帮助消除害羞心理或沉默寡言的态度: *She's a nice girl, but needs a lot of* ~*ing out.* 她是一个好女孩，但是需要多多劝导以消除害羞的心理。 **(d)** call forth (a quality): 产生并(使某一特质); 发挥: *Danger* ~*s out the best in him.* 危险使他发挥出最优的才能。 **(e)** cause to strike: 使罢工: *The shopstewards brought out the foundrymen.* 工会的工厂代表使铸造工人罢工。

bring sb over (to), (esp) convert (sb) (to a different way of thinking, to a cause, etc). 使 (某人) 改变; (尤指) 使改变思想、信仰等。

bring sb/sth round, **(a)** cause (sb) to regain consciousness after fainting: 使恢复知觉; 使苏醒: *Several girls fainted in the heat but they were soon brought round.* 有几个女孩子在炎热中昏倒，不过很快就被救醒了。 **(b)** convert to one's views, etc: 使改变观点等: *He wasn't*

keen on the plan, but we managed to ~ him round. 他本来对该计划没有兴趣，但我们终于使他改变过过来了。 **(c)** (naut) make a boat face the opposite way: (航海) 使船对着相反的航向: *B~ her* (ie the boat) *round into the wind.* 使船逆风而驶。 **~ sb/sth round to,** direct (discussion, etc) to sth new: 把 (讨论等) 转到新的话题上: *He brought the conversation round to his favourite subject.* 他把谈话转到他最喜欢的题目上。

bring sb through, save (sb who is ill): 挽救; 治愈 (病人): *He was very ill but good doctors and careful nursing brought him through,* restored him to health. 他的病很重，不过优良的医生和悉心的看护挽救了他(使他恢复健康)。

bring sb/sth to, (a) =~ round(a): 使复苏: *They brought the girl to with smelling salts.* 她们用嗅盐使那少女苏醒过来。 *They brought her to.* 她们使她恢复知觉。 **(b)** (naut) (cause to) stop: (航海) (使) 停止航行: *The ship was brought to,* eg by the firing of a gun across her bows. 那艘船被迫停航 (如开炮射过其船首)。 *The ship brought to,* came to a stop. 那艘船停止航行。

bring sb/sth under, (a) subdue; discipline: 制服; 降服; 控制: *The rebels were quickly brought under.* 叛徒们很快都被制服了。 **(b)** include (within a category): 归纳; 纳入(某一范畴): *The various points to be dealt with can be brought under three main heads.* 尚待处理的各点可以归纳为三大项目。

bring sb/sth up, (a) educate; rear: 教育; 养育: *She has brought up five children.* 她养育了五个孩子。 *If children are badly brought up they behave badly.* 如果孩子们的教养不好，他们的行为就不好。 **(b)** vomit: 呕吐: *~ up one's dinner.* 吃的饭都吐出来了。 **(c)** call attention to: 使注意到; 引述: *These are facts that can always be brought up against you,* used as evidence against you. 这些事实永远可以被引述做为不利于你的证据。 *These are matters that you can ~ up in committee.* 这些问题你可在委员会中提出。 **(d)** (mil) summon to the front line: (军) 调至前线: *We need to ~ up more tanks.* 我们需要调更多的战车来前线。 **(e)** ~ for trial: 审讯: *He was brought up on a charge of drunken driving.* 他因酒醉驾车而受审。 **(f)** cause to stop suddenly: 使突然停止: *His remarks brought me up short/sharp/with a jerk.* 他的话使我愣住了。 **~ up the rear,** come last (in a line): 排在(队伍的)最后一个; 殿后: *The cavalry brought up the rear of the column.* 纵队的最后面是骑兵。 **~ up at,** (old use, esp of a ship) end a journey: (旧用法，尤指船)结束旅程; 抵达终点: *The ship brought up at a port in Greece.* 该船抵达希腊某港。

brink /brɪŋk; brɪŋk/ *n* **1** upper edge of a steep place, a sharp slope, etc (place of water, esp when deep): 峭壁顶端的边缘; 濒临深水的陆地边缘: *He stood shivering on the ~,* hesitating to plunge into the water. 他站在岸边发抖(不敢跃入水中)。 **2** (fig) edge of sth unknown, dangerous or exciting: (喻) (未知的、危险的或刺激性事物的) 边缘: *on the ~ of war/ruin/an exciting discovery.* 在战争(毁灭，大发现)的边缘。 *on the ~ of the grave,* will die soon. 他已濒临坟墓的边缘(行将入土)。 **~·manship** /'brɪŋkmənʃɪp; 'brɪŋkmən,ʃɪp/ *n* pursuit of a dangerous policy to the limits of safety. 冒险政策的施行(一直推行危险政策直到安全的极限)。

briny ⇨ **brine.**

bri·oche /briː'əʊʃ; US: 'briːəʊʃ; 'briəʃ/ *n* (F) piece of pastry baked in a circular shape. (法) 奶油蛋卷。

bri·quette, bri·quet /brɪ'ket; brɪ'ket/ *n* block (brick- or egg-shaped) of compressed coal-dust. (用煤渣压制的) 煤砖; 煤块。

brisk /brɪsk; brɪsk/ *adj* (-er, -est) (of persons and movement) active; lively; quick-moving: (指人及动作) 活泼的; 活波的; 敏捷的; 轻快的: *a ~ walk;* 轻快的散步; *a ~ walker;* 走路轻快的人; *at a ~ pace;* 以轻快的步子; *a ~ demand for cotton goods.* 棉织品的畅销。 *Trade is ~.* 生意兴隆。 **~·ly** *adv*

bris·ket /'brɪskɪt; 'brɪskɪt/ *n* [U] breast of an animal, (sometimes eaten as a joint of meat). (兽类的) 胸部; (供作食用的) 胸肉。 ⇨ the illus at **dog.** 参看 **dog** 之插图。

bristle /'brɪsl; 'brɪsl/ *n* one of the short stiff hairs on an animal; one of the short stiff hairs in a brush: (动物身上的) 刚毛; 鬃; 刷子上的毛: *a toothbrush with stiff ~s.* 硬毛牙刷。 □ *vi* **1** [VP2A, C] ~ (up), (of hair) stand up, rise on end: (指毛发) 耸立; 竖起: *The dog was angry and ~d up, its hair ~d.* 那狗发脾气，毛都竖起来了。 **2** [VP2A, C] (fig) show rage, indignation, etc: (喻) 表示愤怒等: *~ with anger.* 怒发冲冠。 **3** ~ **with,** have in large numbers (sth difficult, sth suggesting ~s): (如荆棘) 丛生; (困难) 重重: *The battle-front ~d with bayonets.* 战线上刺刀林立。 *The problem ~s with difficulties* 这问题困难重重。 **brist·ly** /'brɪsli; 'brɪsli/ *adj* like ~; full of ~s; (of hair, etc) rough and coarse: 如刚毛的; 多硬毛的; 刚毛林立的; (指毛发等) 粗糙的: *She doesn't like his bristly moustache.* 她不喜欢他那刺人的胡髭。 *What a bristly, unshaven chin!* 没有修胡子的下巴多么刺人呵!

Brit·ain /'brɪtn; 'brɪtən/ *n* (also 亦作 **Great B~** 不列颠) England, Wales and Scotland; 不列颠 (包括英格兰、威尔士及苏格兰); *North B~,* Scotland. 北不列颠(即苏格兰)。 **Bri·tan·nic** /brɪ'tænɪk; brɪ'tænɪk/ *adj* of B~ 不列颠的 (chiefly in 主用于 *Her/His Britannic Majesty* 英(女)王陛下)。

Brit·ish /'brɪtɪʃ; 'brɪtɪʃ/ *adj* **1** of the ancient Britons. 古代不列颠人的。 **2** of Great Britain, the British Commonwealth or its inhabitants: 大不列颠的; 英国的; 英联邦的; 英国人的: *the B~,* B~ people; 英国人民 (总称); *B~ citizenship;* 英国公民资格; *a Jamaican with a B~ passport* 持有英国护照的牙买加人。 **~er** *n*

Briton /'brɪtn; 'brɪtn/ *n* **1** one of the native inhabitants of S Britain at the time of the Roman invasion about 2000 years ago. 古列颠人 (约两千年前罗马入人侵时的英国南部土人)。 **2** (liter) native of Britain. (文) 英国人。

brittle /'brɪtl; 'brɪtl/ *adj* hard but easily broken (eg coal, ice, glass): 脆的; 易碎的 (如煤、冰、玻璃); (fig) (喻) *He has a ~ temper,* quickly loses his temper. 他易发脾气。

broach[1] /brəʊtʃ; brɔtʃ/ *vt* [VP6A] make a hole in (a cask of liquor) and put in a tap in order to draw the wine, etc: (fig)begin discussion of (a topic). 凿孔于(酒桶)并插入活嘴以便汲酒; (喻)开始讨论(题目)。

broach[2] /brəʊtʃ; brɔtʃ/ *vi, vt* [VP2C, 15B] ~ **to,** (naut) veer or cause (a ship) to veer so that its side is presented to the wind and waves. (航海) 转动(船首) 使舷侧面向风浪。

broad[1] /brɔːd; brɔd/ *adj* (-er, -est) **1** wide, large across; 宽的; 阔的: *The river grows ~er as it nears the sea.* 河在愈接近海处愈宽。 *~ in the beam,* ⇨ **beam**(2). **2** (after a phrase indicating width) in breadth, from side to side: (用于指宽度的短语之后) 宽: *a river fifty feet ~.* 一条五十英尺宽的河。 **3** extending in various or all directions: 宽阔的; 广大的; 辽阔的: *the ~ ocean;* 无际的海洋; *~ lands.* 辽阔的陆地。 **4** full and complete. 充足的; 完全的。 *in ~ daylight,* when it is unmistakably light: 光天化日之下; 大白天里: *a bank raid in ~ daylight.* 光天化日之下的银行抢劫。 **5** general, not minute or detailed: 概略的; 粗略的; 大概的: *a ~ distinction.* 大概的区别。 *in ~ outline,* without details. 概略地; 粗枝大叶的。 **6**(of the mind and ideas) liberal; not kept within narrow limits: (指心理及思想) 胸襟开阔的; 宽宏大量的; 宽大的: *a man of ~ views,* a tolerant man. 对事宽大为怀的人。 **~'-minded** /-'maɪndɪd; -'maɪndɪd/ *adj* willing to listen sympathetically to the views of others even though one cannot agree with them; having a liberal and tolerant mind. 思想开明的; 胸襟开阔的; 气量宽宏的。 **7** (of speech) strongly marked, showing that the speaker is from a

definite part of the country: (指言语) 方音重的: ~ *Scots*; 方音很重的苏格兰人; *a ~ accent*. 方音很重的口音. **8** improper; coarse: 不适当的; 粗鄙的: *the ~ humour of Rabelais*. 拉伯雷的粗鄙的幽默. **9** (phrase) (短语) *It's as ~ as it is long*, It's all the same, however you view the problem. 横竖都一样; 怎么看那问题全都一样. **10** (compounds, etc) (复合词等) ~ **bean** *n* the common flattened variety, growing in large pods, 蚕豆. **B~ Church** *n* used of churchmen who do not insist upon dogma and doctrine. 不坚持教条的教派; 广教会派. **~·ly** *adv* **1** in a wide way. 广阔地; 广大地. **2** in a general way: 概略地; 大概地: *~ly speaking*, speaking in a general way, without going into detail. 总而言之; 概括地说. **~·ness** *n* = **breadth** (the usu word). (breadth 较常用). **~en** /'brɔːdn; 'brɔdn/ *vt, vi* (*pt, pp* broadcast **1** [VP6A] send out in all directions, esp by radio or TV: 广播; (尤指经由无线电或电视)播送: ~ *the news/a speech/a concert*. 广播 (或播送)新闻(演说,音乐演奏). **2** [VP2A] speak, sing, perform music, etc for ~ing: 发表广播 (或电视) 演说; 广播演唱(或演奏等);作电视演唱 (或演奏): *The Prime Minister will ~ this evening*. 首相将于今晚发表广播 (或作电视) 演说. **3** [VP6A, 2A] sow (seed) by scattering it, not by sowing it in drills, etc. 撒播(种子). □ *n* (often attrib) ~ing; sth ~: (常用作定语) 广播; 播送; 广播的内容: *today's ~*; 今天的广播节目; *a ~ of a football match*. 足球比赛之广播. ⊳ **telecast**. □ *adv* by ~ing: 用撒播的方式: *sow seed* ~. 撒种. ~·ing *n, adj*: *the British B~ing Corporation*, the B B C; 英国广播公司; *a ~ station*. 广播电台.

broad² /brɔːd/ *n* the ~ part (*of* sth): (某物之) 宽的部分(与 of 连用): *the ~ of the back*. 背部的宽处. **the B~s** *n pl* name used of wide stretches of water in Norfolk, used for boating holidays and barge traffic. 英国诺福克郡境内可供驾舟度假及航行平底驳船之大片的平静水面.

broad·cast /'brɔːdkɑːst US: -kæst; 'brɔːd,kæst/ *vt, vi* (*pt, pp* broadcast or ~ed) **1** [VP6A] send out in all directions, esp by radio or TV: 广播; (尤指经由无线电或电视)播送: ~ *the news/a speech/a concert*. 广播 (或播送)新闻(演说,音乐演奏). **2** [VP2A] speak, sing, perform music, etc for ~ing: 发表广播 (或电视) 演说; 广播演唱(或演奏等);作电视演唱 (或演奏): *The Prime Minister will ~ this evening*. 首相将于今晚发表广播 (或作电视) 演说. **3** [VP6A, 2A] sow (seed) by scattering it, not by sowing it in drills, etc. 撒播(种子). □ *n* (often attrib) ~ing; sth ~: (常用作定语) 广播; 播送; 广播的内容: *today's ~*; 今天的广播节目; *a ~ of a football match*. 足球比赛之广播. ⊳ **telecast**. □ *adv* by ~ing: 用撒播的方式: *sow seed* ~. 撒种. ~·ing *n, adj*: *the British B~ing Corporation*, the B B C; 英国广播公司; *a ~ station*. 广播电台.

broad·cloth /'brɔːdklɒθ US: -klɔːθ; 'brɔːd,klɔθ/ *n* [U] fine, smooth, double-width black cloth, formerly used for men's clothes. 一种双幅的黑色布料 (昔时用制男子服装).

broad·sheet /'brɔːdʃiːt; 'brɔːd,ʃit/ *n* popular ballad or tract printed on one side only of a large sheet of paper (as formerly sold in the streets). 印在大纸张上 (只印一面) 的通俗歌谣或劝善文字 (如昔时在街上出售者).

broad·side /'brɔːdsaɪd; 'brɔːd,saɪd/ *n* [C] **1** the whole of a ship's side above the water; (the firing on the same target of) all the guns on one side of a ship; (fig) strong attack of any kind made at one time against one person or group. 舷侧(吃水线以上之全部船侧);船舷一侧所有的炮;偏舷齐放(船舷一侧的所有各舷向同一目标齐发);(喻)对某一人或某团体所作之一次猛烈攻击. **2** ~ **on** (*to*), (of a ship) with one side presented to or facing: (指船) 以其一面对向: *a collision* ~ *on*, so that the ship's side collides with sth. 与舷侧发生的碰撞.

broad·ways, broad·wise /'brɔːdweɪz, -waɪz; 'brɔd,wez, -waɪz/ *adv* in the direction of the breadth. 横着; 横地.

bro·cade /brə'keɪd; bro'ked/ *n* [C, U] woven material richly ornamented with designs (eg in raised gold or silver thread). (用金、银线等织成)锦缎; 花缎. □ *vt* [VP6A] decorate (cloth) with raised patterns. 织成锦缎.

broc·coli /'brɒkəlɪ; 'brɑkəlɪ/ *n* [C] hardy kind of cauliflower with numerous white or purple sprouts (flower-heads), each like a small cauliflower. 一种花椰菜; 硬花甘蓝.

bro·chure /'brəʊʃə(r) US: brəʊ'ʃʊər; bro'ʃjʊr/ *n* short, usu descriptive, printed article in a paper cover; pamphlet: 小册子: *travel/holiday ~s*. 旅游 (度假) 手册.

brogue¹ /brəʊg; brog/ *n* strong, thick-soled, usu ornamented shoe for country wear. (通常为带有装饰性小孔在乡下穿的)结实的厚底皮鞋.

brogue² /brəʊg; brog/ *n* regional way of speaking, esp the Irish way of speaking English. 土腔(尤指爱尔兰人说英语之腔调).

broil /brɔɪl; brɔɪl/ *vt, vi* [VP6A, 2A] cook, be cooked, by direct contact with fire or on a gridiron; grill: (fig) be very hot: 烤; 烧; 炙; 在铁架上烤(肉类); (喻)很热; 炙热. ~*ing day*; 炎热的一日; *sit ~ing in the sun*. 坐着晒太阳. ~*er n* bird, eg a chicken, killed at the age of 10 to 12 weeks and suitable for being ~ed or roasted, esp one reared in a shed or concrete building (and contrasted with a *free-range* bird), ⊳ **battery (6)**. 适于烧烤的子鸡或嫩鸡(或指其他家禽,经饲养约十至十二星期,尤指养于鸡房中,而非养在空地上者).

broke /brəʊk; brok/ *attrib adj* (**stony/flat**) ~, (sl) penniless. (俚)身无分文; 一文不名.

bro·ken /'brəʊkən; 'brokən/ *pp* of break: *a ~ marriage*, one that has failed; 破裂的婚姻; *a ~ home*, one in which the parents have separated or are divorced, so that the children lack proper care, security, etc; 破裂的家庭(夫妻分居或离婚,因而孩子们缺少适当照顾); *~* (= imperfect) *English*; 不流利的英语; 蹩脚英语; *a ~ man*, a man reduced to despair; 绝望的人; 精神丧失的人; *~* (= uneven) *ground*; 崎岖不平的人; *~* (= disturbed, intermittent) *sleep*; 断续的睡眠; *~-hearted*, crushed by grief. 伤心的; 断肠的.

bro·ker /'brəʊkər; 'brokɚ/ *n* **1** person (eg *stock~*) who buys and sells (esp stocks and shares, bonds, etc) for others. (替人买卖股票、债券等之)掮客; 经纪人. **2** official licensed to sell the goods of sb unable to pay debts. 执行拍卖破产者财物之人员. ~·**age** /'brəʊkərɪdʒ; 'brokərɪdʒ/ *n* [U] ~'s commission for services. (掮客所收之)佣金; 经纪费.

brolly /'brɒlɪ; 'brɑlɪ/ *n* (colloq) umbrella. (口) 伞.

bro·mide /'brəʊmaɪd; 'bromaɪd/ *n* **1** [U] chemical compound of bromine, eg potassium ~, used in medicine to calm the nerves. 溴化物(如溴化钾,尤指用作镇静剂者). **2** [C] (colloq) trite remark; dull, tiresome or boring person. (口)庸俗或陈腐的话; 迟钝而令人厌倦的人.

bro·mine /'brəʊmiːn; 'bromin/ *n* [U] non-metallic element (symbol **Br**), compounds of which are used in photographic and other chemicals. 溴(非金属元素, 化学符号 Br, 溴化物用于制摄影及其他化学药品).

bron·chi /'brɒŋkaɪ; 'brɑŋkaɪ/ *n pl* (*sing* **bron·chus** /-kəs; -kəs/) two main branches into which the windpipe divides before entering the lungs, also called *bronchial tubes*. 支气管. ⊳ the illus at **respiratory**. 参看 respiratory 之插图. ~·**al** /-kɪəl; -kɪəl/ *adj* of or affecting the ~: 支气管的; 感染支气管的: *bronchial asthma*. 支气管性哮喘. **bronchi·tic** /brɒŋ'kɪtɪk; brɑŋ'kɪtɪk/ *adj* suffering from, prone to, bronchitis. 患支气管炎的; 易患支气管炎的. **bron·chi·tis** /brɒŋ'kaɪtɪs; brɑŋ'kaɪtɪs/ *n* inflammation of the mucous membrane of the ~. 支气管炎.

bronco /'brɒŋkəʊ; 'brɑŋko/ *n* (*pl* -**cos**) wild or half-tamed horse of Western N America. 北美西部之一种野马.

bronze /brɒnz; brɑnz/ *n* **1** [U] alloy of copper and tin: 青铜(铜与锡之合金): *a ~ statue*; 铜像; *a statue in ~*. 铜像. **the 'B~ Age**, period when men used tools and weapons made of ~(between the Stone Age and the Iron Age). 青铜器时代 (介于石器时代与铁器时代之间). **2** [U] colour of ~; reddish brown. 古铜色; 赤褐色. **3** [C] work of art, eg a vase, made of ~: 青铜器(作为艺术制品者,如花瓶): *a fine collection of ~s and*

ivories. 所收藏之一批精致的青铜器及象牙制品。 □ *vt, vi* [VP6A, 2A] make or become ~ colour: (使) 变成古铜色; (使) 变成赤褐色: *faces ~d by the sun and wind.* 饱经日晒风吹之赤褐色的面孔。

brooch /brəʊtʃ; brotʃ/ *n* ornamental pin for fastening or wearing on part of a woman's dress. (别于妇女服装上的) 花别针; 胸针。

brood /bruːd; brud/ *n* all the young birds hatched at one time in a nest; family of other egg-produced animals; (hum) young family of human beings. 一窝所孵的幼雏; 其他卵生动物之一窝; (谐) 一家里的孩子们。 '~-hen *n* hen for breeding. 孵雏的母鸡。 '~-mare *n* mare for breeding. 供繁殖之牝马; 传种母马。 □ *vi* 1 [VP2A, C] (of a bird) sit on eggs to hatch them. (指禽类) (坐于卵上) 孵雏; 孵蛋。 2 [VP3A] ~ (on/over), (fig) think about (troubles, etc) for a long time: (喻) 沉思: 思虑; 忧思: *She sat there ~ing on whether life was worth living.* 她坐在那里沉思人生是否值得活下去。 ~y *adj* (of hens) wanting to ~; (colloq, of women) feeling the desire to have children; (fig, of persons) moody; depressed. (指母鸡) 欲孵卵的; 要孵小鸡的; (口, 指女人) 有生孩子之欲的; (喻) 人忧郁的; 沮丧的。

brook[1] /brʊk; brʊk/ *n* small stream. 小河; 溪流。

brook[2] /brʊk; brʊk/ *vt* [VP6A, B] (formal) (usu in neg and interr) put up with; tolerate: (正式用语) (通常用于否定及疑问句中) 忍受; 容忍; 耐; 措: *He cannot ~ interference/being interfered with.* 他不能忍受他人的干涉。

broom[1] /bruːm; brum/ *n* [U] shrub with yellow or white flowers growing on sandy banks, etc. 金雀花 (生于沙岸等处)。

broom[2] /bruːm; brum/ *n* long-handled implement for sweeping floors, etc. 扫帚。 *a new ~,* (esp) a newly appointed official (who gets rid of old methods, traditions, etc): 新人; (尤指) 新上任的官员 (革除老法、旧传统等者); (prov) (谚) *A new ~ sweeps clean.* 新官上任三把火。 '~-stick *n* handle of a broom (on which witches were said to ride through the air). 扫帚柄 (传说巫婆乘之飞行于空中)。

Bros ⇨ **App 2.** 参看附录二。

broth /brɒθ; broθ/ *n* [U] water in which meat has been boiled; this, flavoured and thickened with vegetables, etc, served as soup. 煮肉的清汤; 肉汤 (再加入蔬菜及调味品煮浓后供食者)。

brothel /'brɒθl; 'broθəl/ *n* house at which prostitutes may be visited. 妓院。

brother /'brʌðə(r); 'brʌðɚ/ *n* 1 son of the same parents as another person: 兄弟: *my elder/younger ~;* 我的哥哥 (弟弟); *the ~s Smith, the Smith ~s;* the Smith 兄弟们; *Smith Brothers* or (com style) *Smith Bros.* 史密斯兄弟商店 (商业型式作 Smith Bros). '~-in-law /'brʌðər in lɔː; 'brʌðɚrin,lo/ *n* (*pl* ~s-in-law) ~ of one's husband or wife; husband of one's sister. 夫或妻的兄弟; 大伯; 小叔; 内兄; 内弟; 姐夫; 妹夫。 2 person united to others by membership of the same group, society, profession, etc; fellow member of a socialist organization, trade union, etc: 同道; 同人; 同行; 同业; 社会主义组织之一员; 公会会员 (等): (esp attrib) (尤用作定语) *a ~ doctor;* 加入公会的医生; ~*s in arms,* soldiers who are serving or have served together; (正在服役或已退役的) 军人; 袍泽; ~*officers,* in the same regiment. 同袍军官。 3 (*pl* **brethren** /'breðren; 'breðrin/) fellow member of a religious society. 同教会的教友。 **B~,** form of address: 称呼形式: *B~ Luke.* 卢克弟兄。 '~-hood /-hud; -,hʊd/ *n* 1 [U] feeling of ~ for. ~ 手足之情; 同胞之爱。 2 [C] (members of an) association of men with common interests and aims, esp a religious society or socialist organization. 具有共同兴趣及目的之团体 (尤指宗教性或社会主义组织); 同志会; 同道会; 公会 (等)。 ~ly *adj* of or like a ~('s): 兄弟的; 如兄弟的; 情同手足的: ~*ly affection.* 手足之情。

brougham /'bruːəm; 'bruəm/ *n* (19th c) four-wheeled closed carriage drawn by one horse. (十九世纪的) 单马有篷四轮马车。

brought *pt, pp* of bring.

brou·haha /'bruːhɑːhɑː; 'bruhɑhɑ/ *n* (dated colloq) fuss; excitement. (过时口语) 纷扰; 紧张; 兴奋。

brow /braʊ; braʊ/ *n* 1 (usu *pl*; 通常用复数; also 亦作 'eye-') ~s) arch of hair above the eye. 眉; 眉毛: *knit one's ~s,* frown. 皱眉头; 蹙额。 2 forehead. 额。 ⇨ *highbrow* at **high**[1](12); *lowbrow* at **low**[1](13). 3 top of a slope; steep slope; overhanging edge. 坡顶; 陡坡; 悬崖。

brow·beat /'braʊbiːt; 'braʊ,bit/ *vt* (*pt* **browbeat**, *pp* **browbeaten**) [VP6A, 14] ~ (into doing sth), intimidate by shouting or looking stern at; bully: (以声音或神情) 威吓 (使做某事): 吓唬: ~ *sb into doing sth;* 威吓某人做某事; *a poor, ~en little woman.* 一个可怜的、被吓制的小妇人。

brown /braʊn; braʊn/ *adj* (-er, -est), *n* colour of toasted bread, or coffee mixed with milk: 深黄色; 棕色; 褐色 (烤过的面包之色, 或咖啡加牛奶后之颜色): ~ *bread,* made with wholemeal flour; 黑面包 (以没有去麸的面粉制成者); ~ *paper,* coarse kind used for parcels, etc; 棕色包装纸; 牛皮纸; ~ *sugar,* half refined. 红糖。 *in a ~ study,* deep in thought; in a reverie. 在沉思冥想中。 '~-stone *n* [U] kinds of reddish-brown sandstone used for building. 一种赤褐色沙岩 (用于建筑)。 □ *vt, vi* [VP6A, 2A] make or become ~. (使) 变成褐色。 ~ed 'off, (sl) bored; fed up. (俚) 厌烦的; 忍受够了的。

brownie /'braʊnɪ; 'braʊnɪ/ *n* 1 small, good-natured fairy or elf. 善良的小精灵。 2 **B~** (**Guide**), (GB) junior member (age 8 to 11) of the Girl Guides. (英) 幼年女童军 (八至十一岁)。

browse /braʊz; braʊz/ *vi* [VP2A, C] 1 feed, as animals do (on grass, etc): (指动物) 食; 啮食 (草等): *cattle browsing in the fields.* 在田野中吃草的牛。 2 read (parts of a book or books) without any definite plan, for interest or enjoyment: 浏览 (书籍); 随便翻阅: *browsing among books in the public library.* 在公立图书馆中浏览各种书籍。 □ *n* (act, period, of) browsing: 浏览; (浏览的) 时间: *have a good ~.* 尽情浏览多时间。

bruin /'bruːɪn; 'bruɪn/ *n* (pop name, eg in fairy tales, for) bear. (在童话等中之) 熊的俗称。

bruise /bruːz; bruz/ *n* injury by a blow or knock to the body, or to a fruit, so that the skin is discoloured but not broken: (人体或水果由于打击或碰撞使皮肤或果皮变色但从未破裂之) 挫伤; 碰伤: 瘀伤 *covered with ~s after falling off his bicycle.* 因从脚踏车上跌下而满身受到挫伤。 □ *vt, vi* 1 [VP6A] cause a ~ or ~s to; batter, make dents in (wood or metal): 使受挫伤; 把 (木头或金属) 槌凹: *He fell and ~d his leg.* 他跌一跤挫伤了腿。 *Pack the peaches carefully so that they won't get ~d.* 小心包装桃子, 别让它们碰伤或压伤。 2 [VP2A] show the effects of a blow or knock: 显出挫伤或瘀伤的伤痕: *A child's flesh ~s easily.* 小孩的皮肉易显出挫伤的瘀痕。 **bruiser** *n* tough, brutal boxer. 粗野残酷的拳师。

bruit /bruːt; brut/ *vt* [VP15B] ~ *abroad,* (old use) spread (a rumour or report): (旧用法) 传布 (谣言或传闻等): *It ~ it abroad,* spread the news everywhere. 传遍各处。

brunch /brʌntʃ; brʌntʃ/ *n* (colloq) late morning meal instead of breakfast and lunch. (口) 早午餐 (代替早点及午餐者)。

bru·nette /bruː'net; bru'nɛt/ *n* European with dark skin and dark-brown or black hair. 皮肤深色、头发呈深褐色或黑色的欧洲人。 ⇨ **blond(e).**

brunt /brʌnt; brʌnt/ *n* chief stress or strain: 主要的压力或拉力; 中心力量: *bear the ~ of an attack.* 承受攻击的主力; 首当其冲。 *The main ~ of their criticism fell on us.* 他们批评的重点是针对着我们的。

brush /brʌʃ; brʌʃ/ *n* 1 implement of bristles, hair, wire, etc fastened in wood, bone, or other material,

used for scrubbing, sweeping, cleaning (eg *'tooth~*, *'nail~*), or tidying the hair (*'hair~*); tuft of hair, etc set in a handle, used by painters and artists: (用鬃、发、金属丝等制之)刷子(如牙刷、指甲刷、发刷); (画家的)画笔: *a 'paint-brush*. 画笔. **2** (act of) using a ~: 用刷子刷; 刷: *He gave his clothes a good ~*, used a ~ on them. 他把他的衣服好好地刷了一番. ⇨ also *'~-up* at **brush²(1)**. **3** fox's tail. 狐狸尾巴. **4** [U] rough low-growing bushes; undergrowth: 矮灌木丛: *a ~ fire*. 矮灌木丛之大火. ⇨ **bush(2)**. **5** short, sharp fight or encounter: 小战; 小冲突; 遭遇战: *a ~ with the enemy*. 与敌人之遭遇战. *'~·wood* n [U] = brush(4). *'~-work* n artist's style or way of using a paint-~. 画家的笔法.

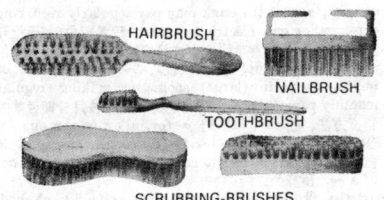

HAIRBRUSH
NAILBRUSH
TOOTHBRUSH
SCRUBBING-BRUSHES

brushes

brush² /brʌʃ; brʌʃ/ *vt, vi* **1** [VP6A, 15B, 22] use a brush on; clean, polish, make tidy or smooth: 用刷子刷; 使清洁整齐等; 刷清; 刷光; 挑拭: *~ your hat/clothes/shoes/hair/teeth*; 刷你的帽子(衣服, 鞋子, 头发, 牙齿); *~ sth clean*. 把某物刷干净. *~ sth away/off*, remove with a ~: 用刷子刷掉某物: *He ~ed away a fly from his nose*, used his hand to make the fly go away. 他用手赶走鼻子上的苍蝇. *She ~ed the crumbs off the tablecloth*. 她刷掉台布上的食品屑. *~ sth aside/away*, (fig) pay no or little attention to (difficulties, objections, etc). (喻)不理; 不顾(困难、反对等). *~ sb/sth off*, (colloq) reject, jilt; dismiss curtly: (口)拒绝; 抛弃; 唐突地摒除: *He tries to get the girl to go out with him, but she always ~es him off*. 他试图邀那女郎和他一起出去, 但总是被他拒绝. Hence, 由此产生, *'~-off* n (colloq) rejection or dismissal: (口)拒绝; 摒弃: *She gave him the ~-off*. 她拒绝了他. *~ sth up*, use a ~ on: 刷某物: *~ up the dust*; 把灰尘刷掉; (fig) study or practise (sth) in order to get back skill that has been lost: (喻)温习; 再练(俾能重获业已荒疏的技术): *If you're going to France you'd better ~ up your French*. 如果你要到法国去, 最好先温习你的法语. Hence, 由此产生, *'~-up* n: *Give your French a ~-up*. 把你的法语温习温习. **2** [VP2A, C, 6A] touch when passing: 擦过; 掠过: *He ~ed past/by/(up) against me in a rude way*. 他粗鲁地从我身边擦过. *The leaves of the trees ~ed my face as I ran through the forest*. 当我从树林中跑过时, 树叶在我的脸上擦过. **3** [VP2C] ~ *off*, come off as the result of being ~ed: 被刷掉: *The mud will ~ off when it dries*. 泥土干时可刷掉.

brusque /bruːsk; brʌsk/ *adj* (of speech or behaviour) rough and abrupt. (指语言或行为)粗鲁的; 唐突的. *~·ly adj ~·ness n*

Brus·sels /'brʌslz; 'brʌslz/ n (attrib) of or from ~ in Belgium: (用作定语)(比利时首都)布鲁塞尔的; 来自布鲁塞尔的: *~ lace/carpets*. 布鲁塞尔花边(地毯). *~ 'sprouts*, (plants with) buds growing thickly on the stem of a cabbage-like plant. 芽甘蓝. ⇨ the illus at **vegetable**. 参看 vegetable 之插图.

brutal /'bruːtl; 'brutl/ *adj* savage; cruel. 野蛮的; 残忍的. *~·ly* /-təlɪ; -tlɪ/ *adv* **bru·tal·ity** /bruː'tælɪtɪ; bru'tælətɪ/ *n* [U] cruelty; savagery; [C] cruel or savage act. 残忍; 野蛮; 残忍或野蛮的行为. *~·ize vt* [VP6A] make ~: 使变残忍; 使变野蛮: *Years of warfare*

had *~ized the troops*. 连年作战使得军队变得残忍.

brute /bruːt; brut/ *n* **1** animal (except man). 野兽. **2** stupid, animal-like or cruel person. 愚蠢的人; 兽面兽心的人; 残忍的人. **3** (attrib) animal-like; cruel and unthinking; unconscious or unreasoning; merely material: (用作定语)如野兽的; 残忍而无思想的; 无意识的; 无理性的; 仅仅是物质的: *~ force/strength*; 暴力(蛮力); *~ matter*. 无生命之物; 死物. **brut·ish** /'bruːtɪʃ; 'brʌtɪʃ/ *adj* of or like a ~: 野兽的; 如野兽的: *brutish appetites*. 兽欲. **brut·ish·ly** *adv*

bubble /'bʌbl; 'bʌbl/ *n* **1** (in air) floating ball formed of liquid and containing air or gas: (浮于空气中的)气泡; 泡: *soap ~s*; 肥皂泡; *blowing ~s*. 吹泡泡. **2** (in liquid) ball of air or gas that rises to the surface, eg in boiling water, in sparkling wines. (从液体中浮于水面的)气泡(如沸水、会冒泡的酒中者). **3** air-filled cavity in a solidified liquid, eg glass. 液体凝固后(如玻璃)内中存留的气泡. **4** (fig) visionary plan; idea, hope, etc that is not realized: (喻)幻想的计划; 无法实现的念念、希望等: *His ~ has burst*. 他的计划(或希望)已成泡影(破灭了). **5** *'~ car* n small car with a transparent dome as roof. 泡泡车(车顶为透明圆顶的小汽车). *'~ gum* n chewing gum which can be blown into bubbles on the lips. 泡泡糖(可以吹成泡的口香糖). □ *vi* [VP 2A, C] send up ~s; rise in ~s; make the sound of ~s: 发出气泡; 起泡; 发气泡声: *The water ~d up through the sand*. 水从沙中冒出气泡. *She was bubbling over with joy/high spirits/laughter*. 她得意洋洋(高兴, 咯咯地笑). **bubbly** /'bʌblɪ; 'bʌblɪ/ *adj* full of ~s. 充满泡沫的; 多泡的. □ *n* (hum) champagne. (谐)香槟酒.

bu·bonic /bjuː'bɒnɪk; bju'bɑnɪk/ *adj* ~ '**plague**, contagious disease that spreads quickly (spread by rats, and marked by chills, fevers and swelling in the armpits and groin). 淋巴腺鼠疫(一种蔓延迅速的传染病, 由老鼠传布, 症状为发冷发热, 腋窝及鼠蹊肿大).

buc·ca·neer /ˌbʌkə'nɪə(r); ˌbʌkə'nɪr/ *n* pirate; unscrupulous adventurer. 海盗; 无顾忌的冒险者.

buck¹ /bʌk; bʌk/ *n* **1** male of a deer, hare or rabbit. 牡鹿; 雄兔. ⇨ **doe**. *'~-skin* n [U] soft leather made from deerskin or goatskin, used for gloves, bags, etc. 鹿皮或羊皮所制成的柔软皮革(用制手套、皮包等). *'~-shot* n [U] large-size lead shot¹(4). 大型铅弹; 鹿弹. *'~-tooth* n (pl ~**teeth**) (usu upper) tooth that projects. (通常指上齿)獠牙; 突出齿. **2** (attrib) male. (用作定语)雄的.

buck² /bʌk; bʌk/ *vi, vt* **1** [VP2A] (of a horse) jump up with the four feet together and the back arched; [VP6A] throw (the rider) to the ground by doing this. (指马)四足离地拱背而跳跃; 由此种跳跃而将(骑者)摔于地上. **2** ~ *up*, [VP2C, esp in the *imperative* 尤用于祈使句] (colloq) hurry. (口)赶快. ~ *(sb) up*, [VP15B, 2C] make or become more vigorous or cheerful, ready for greater effort: (使)精神大振; 鼓励: *The good news ~ed us all up*. 这好消息使我们大为兴奋. *We were greatly ~ed up by the news*. 这消息令我们大为振奋.

buck³ /bʌk; bʌk/ *n* (US sl) US dollar. (美俚)美元.

buck⁴ /bʌk; bʌk/ *n pass the ~ (to sb)*, (sl) shift the responsibility (to). (俚)推诿责任(于某人). *The ~ stops here*, The responsibility cannot be shifted further. 该责任不能再推诿了.

bucket¹ /'bʌkɪt; 'bʌkɪt/ *n* **1** vessel of wood, metal, canvas, plastic, etc for holding or carrying water, milk, etc; (also 亦作 *'~-ful* /-fʊl; -fʊl/) the amount a ~ holds: (用木、金属、帆布、塑胶等制成以盛或提水、牛奶等之)水桶; 吊桶; 一桶之量: *The rain was coming down in ~s*, was very heavy. 大雨倾盆. **2** scoop of a dredging machine, grain-elevator, etc. (挖泥机、吊谷机等之)铲斗. *'~ seat* n (in a car or aircraft) seat with a rounded base for one person (contrasted with a *bench* seat). (汽车或飞机中之)单人圆背座位(与 bench seat 相对).

bucket² /'bʌkɪt; 'bʌkɪt/ vi ride a horse hard. 拚命策马飞奔; 骑马飞奔.

buckle /'bʌkl; 'bʌkl/ n 1 metal, plastic or bone fastener, with one or more spikes made to go through a hole in a strap, etc, to keep sth in place. (皮带等的)扣环. 2 ornamental clasp on a shoe. 鞋上的装饰性扣环. □ vt, vi 1 [VP6A,15B] ~ (on), fasten with a ~: 以扣环扣住: ~ a belt; 扣起带子; ~ on a sword / one's armour. 佩扣起扣环而佩带剑(穿上甲胄). 2 [VP2C] (of a shoe, belt, etc) fasten (in a certain way). (指鞋、带等)(以某种方式)结扎. 3 [VP2C] ~ to / down to (work, etc), begin (work) in earnest: 开始认真(工作等); 努力从事: ~ to a task. 努力从事一项工作. The sooner he ~s down to it, the better. 他越早认真开始做越好. 4 [VP2A] (of metal work, etc) bend, become twisted, crumple up from strain or heat. (指金属品等因受压力或热力而)弯曲; 扭曲; 卷曲.

buck·ler /'bʌklə(r); 'bʌklɚ/ n small round shield, usu held by a handle or worn on the arm. 小圆楯(通常有柄, 或戴在臂上).

buck·ram /'bʌkrəm; 'bʌkrəm/ n [U] stiff, rough cloth (esp as used for binding books). 硬粗布(尤指用于装订书籍者).

buck·shot /'bʌkʃɒt; 'bʌkˌʃɑt/ ⇨ **buck¹**(1).

buck·wheat /'bʌkwi:t US: -hwi:t; 'bʌkˌhwit/ n [U] (plant with) small triangular seed used for feeding horses and poultry. 荞麦(用作马及家禽饲料). '~ flour, flour made from this grain, used in US for breakfast cakes. 荞麦面粉(在美国用以制早餐糕饼).

bu·colic /bju:'kɒlɪk; bju'kɑlɪk/ adj of country life and farming, esp of shepherds: 农村生活的; 乡间的; 牧人的: ~ verse. 牧歌; 田园诗. **bu·col·ics** n pl pastoral poems. 田园诗.

bud /bʌd; bʌd/ n 1 leaf, flower or branch, at the beginning of its growth. (叶、花或枝初生时的)芽; 苞; 蓓蕾, **in bud**, having buds or sending out buds: 正在发芽; 含苞待放: The trees are in bud. 树正在发芽. **nip sth in the bud**, put an end to sth, eg a plot, while it is in the beginning stage. 趁某事尚未成熟即行消灭之. 2 partly opened flower. 初放的花. ⇨ the illus at **flower**. 参看 flower 之插图. □ vi (-dd-) put on buds. 发芽; 萌芽; 生芽. **bud·ding** adj beginning to develop: 发芽的; 开始发展的; 新进的: a budding lawyer / poet. 新进的律师(诗人).

Bud·dhism /'budɪzəm; 'budɪzəm/ n the religion founded by Gautama /'gautəmə; 'gɔtəmə/ or Siddhartha /sɪ'dɑ:tə; sɪ'dɑrtə/ Buddha /'budə; 'budə/ (= teacher) in N India, in about the 6th BC. 佛教(约于公元前六世纪, 佛陀创始于印度北部之宗教). **Bud·dhist** /'budɪst; 'budɪst/ n follower of Buddha. 佛教徒.

representations of Gautama Buddha

buddy /'bʌdɪ; 'bʌdɪ/ n (pl **-dies**) (sl, as a familiar form of address) chum; mate. (俚, 对熟朋友的称呼)老兄.

budge /bʌdʒ; bʌdʒ/ vt, vi [VP6A, usu in neg and with can, could; 通常用于否定句中, 与 can, could 连用; VP2A, C, usu in neg with won't, wouldn't 通常用于否

定句中, 与 won't, wouldn't 连用] (cause to) move very little, make the slightest movement; (fig) (cause to) change a position or attitude: (使)稍微移动; (喻)(使)改变位置或态度: I can't ~ it. 我无法使它移动分毫. It won't ~ an inch. 它一点也不动.

bud·geri·gar /'bʌdʒərɪgɑ:(r); 'bʌdʒərɪˌgɑr/ n Australian lovebird; kind of parakeet. 澳洲情鸟; 一种小鹦鹉. ⇨ the illus at **rare**. 参看 rare 之插图.

budget /'bʌdʒɪt; 'bʌdʒɪt/ n [C] estimate of probable future income and expenditure, esp that made by a Government; similar estimate made by a business company, society, private person, etc. 预算(对于未来可能收支之估计, 尤指政府之预算; 亦指工商公司、团体、私人等之预算). '~ account, account with a bank maintained by monthly transfers from a current account, so that the Bank may pay regularly recurring expenses, eg gas, electricity, rates. 预算帐户(在银行开立之帐户, 由甲种存款帐户中按月拨转款项, 使银行可代付经常开支费用, 如煤气、电费、税). '~ plan, system of buying goods in (large) shops by making regular monthly payments to them. (大)商店之按月分期付款的销货方法. □ vi [VP3A] ~ for, allow or arrange for (in a ~): 为…做预算: ~ for the coming year. 为明年做预算. ~·ary /'bʌdʒɪtərɪ US: -terɪ; 'bʌdʒɪˌterɪ/ adj of a ~. 预算的.

budgie /'bʌdʒɪ; 'bʌdʒɪ/ n (colloq abbr for a) budgerigar. (口)为 budgerigar 之略.

buff /bʌf; bʌf/ n [U] 1 thick, strong, soft leather. 厚而柔韧之皮革. 2 dull yellow colour. 暗黄色. 3 the bare skin, esp in: 不着衣饰的皮肤, 尤用于: stripped to the ~, without clothing. 赤裸的. 4 [US colloq) fan³, enthusiast. (美口)迷; 热中者. □ vt polish (metal) with ~(1). 用此种皮革擦(金属)使之光亮.

buf·falo /'bʌfələu; 'bʌfl̩o/ n (pl ~s, US also ~es) kinds of large, usu wild ox in India, Asia, Europe and Africa; N American bison: (产于印度、亚洲、欧洲及非洲的)水牛; (北美洲之)野牛: a herd of sixty ~s / ~es. 为数六十头之水牛群.

buf·fer¹ /'bʌfə(r); 'bʌfɚ/ n apparatus (either spring-loaded or hydraulic) for lessening the effect of a blow or collision, eg on a railway engine or van. (利用弹簧或水力以减轻撞击之)缓冲器(如装于火车头或货车上者). '~ state, state situated between two or more powerful states, lessening the risk of war between them. (介于两强国或数强国间以减少战争危险之)缓冲国.

buf·fer² /'bʌfə(r); 'bʌfɚ/ n (sl, usu 通常作 **old ~**) old-fashioned or foolish man. (俚)老古板; 愚人.

buf·fet¹ /'bufeɪ US: bə'feɪ; bʊ'fe/ n counter where food and drink may be bought and consumed, eg in a railway station or (GB, in the '~ car) on a train; sideboard or table from which food and drink are served, eg in a hotel: (火车站或英国火车餐车上之)饮食柜台; (旅馆等中之)食物台; 餐台: cold ~, (on a menu) cold cooked meat, etc; (菜单上)冷肉; ~ supper, meal served to guests who do not sit at a table. 自助(晚)餐.

buf·fet² /'bʌfɪt; 'bʌfɪt/ n blow, generally one given with the hand; (fig) misfortune; blow delivered by fate. (通常)打击; (喻)不幸; 命运的打击. □ vt, vi 1 [VP6A] give a ~ to sth; ~ sth to: 予以一击; 打击: flowers ~ed by rain and wind; 为风雨所摧残的花; ~ed by the waves / misfortunes. 受浪涛之打击. 2 [VP6A, 3A] (rare) contend (with): (罕)(与…)搏斗; 奋斗; 挣扎: ~ (with) the waves. 与浪涛搏斗.

buf·foon /bə'fu:n; bʌ'fun/ n clown; jester. 丑角; 滑稽演员. **play the ~**, do and say foolish things to amuse others. 扮演小丑; 做傻事说傻话以娱他人. ~·ery /-ərɪ; -ərɪ/ n [U] clowning; clown-like behaviour; (in pl) rough jokes and actions. 扮小丑; 小丑行为; (复数)粗俗的笑话和动作.

bug /bʌg; bʌg/ n 1 small, flat, ill-smelling, blood-sucking insect that infests dirty houses and beds. 臭虫(扁平吸血小虫, 出现在肮脏的房屋中及床上). ⇨ the

illus at **insect**. 参看 insect 之插图. **2** (esp US) any small insect ('*harvest bug*, '*mealy-bug*, etc). (尤美)任何小昆虫 (如秋虻,水蜡虫等). '**bug-hunter** *n* (colloq) entomologist. (口)昆虫学家. **3** (colloq) germ; virus infection: (口)细菌; 病菌; 滤过性病毒传染: *You've got the Asian 'flu bug*. 你染上了亚洲流行性感冒病毒. **4** (sl) *big bug*, important person. (俚)大人物; 要人. **5** (sl) defect; snag; (source of) malfunctioning, eg in a computer. (俚)缺点; 毛病; 障碍; (如计算机之)故障 (之根源). **6** small hidden microphone (for listening to conversations, etc). 小型的隐密扩音器(用以窃听谈话等); 窃听器. □ *vt* (**-gg-**) [VP6A] **1** (colloq) use electronic devices (in a room, etc) in order to listen secretly to conversations: (口)(在房间等中)使用电子装置以窃听谈话; 装置窃听器: '*bugging devices*. 窃听器. **2** (US colloq) cause to make mistakes. (美口) 使犯错. **3** (US sl) annoy: (美俚)打扰; 烦扰: *That man really bugs me*. 那个人真使我心烦.

buga·boo /'bʌgəbu:; 'bʌgə,bu/ *n* source of annoyance or fear. 烦扰或恐惧的来源; 令人烦扰或害怕的事物.

bug·bear /'bʌgbeə; 'bʌg,bɛr/ *n* sth feared or disliked, with or without good reason: (指有理由或无充分理由之)令人恐惧或讨厌的事物: *the ~ of rising prices*. 令人讨厌的高涨的物价.

bug·ger /'bʌgə(r); 'bʌgɚ/ *n* **1** (legal) sodomite. (法律)鸡奸者. **2** △ used as a vulgar term of abuse: (讳)(粗鄙的骂人语)畜生; 惠子: *You silly ~!* 你这傻崽子! □ *vt*, *vi* [VP6A] commit ~y with. 鸡奸; 犯鸡奸罪. **~** (*it*)*!* (int, used to express irritation, anger, etc.) (用以表示烦躁,愤怒等)该死! 畜生! **~ off**, (esp imper) go away. (尤用于祈使句中)走开. **~ sth up**, spoil, ruin it. 弄坏; 弄糟. Hence, 由此产生, '**bugg·ed** (*up*), spoilt, ruined. 弄坏的; 弄糟的. '**~-all** *n* nothing. 没什么. **~y** *n* sodomy. 鸡奸; 兽奸.

buggy /'bʌgɪ; 'bʌgɪ/ *n* (*pl* **-gies**) **1** light carriage, pulled by one horse, for one or two persons: 轻便马车 (一马拖拉,单座或双座): *the horse and ~ age*, period before motor vehicles came into use. (汽车问世前的)马车时代. **2** '*beach ~*, ⇨ beach. **3** (*baby*) *~*, (US) = pram. (美)婴儿车.

bugle /'bju:gl; 'bjugl/ *n* musical wind instrument of copper or brass (like a small trumpet but without keys or valves), used for military signals. 号角; 铜号; 军号. ⇨ the illus at **brass**. 参看 brass 之插图. **bugler** *n* ~ blower. 吹号者; 号手; 号兵.

buhl /bu:l; bul/ *n* [U] furniture decoration of inlaid brass, tortoise-shell and ivory. 镶有铜、龟壳及象牙的家具装饰: *a ~ cabinet*. 镶嵌着铜、龟壳及象牙的橱柜.

build¹ /bɪld; bɪld/ *vt*, *vi* (*pt*, *pp* **built** /bɪlt; bɪlt/) **1** [VP6A, 12B, 13B, 14] ~ *sth* (*of/out of*), make by putting parts, materials, etc together (with what is made as the direct object): (用…)构筑; 建造; 建筑(以建造物作直接宾语): ~ *a house/railway*. 建造房屋(铁路). *Some birds ~ nests out of twigs*. 有些鸟类用小枝筑巢. *The school is built of wood*. 该校校舍系木造. *Mr Green is making a garage for me/is ~ing me a garage*. 格林先生正替我造车房. **2** [VP14] ~ *sth into*, put parts together to form a whole (with the material as the direct object): 把 (某物) 建造成…(以材料作为直接宾语): *He has built these scraps of metal into a very strange-looking sculpture*. 他已将这些金属碎片造成一尊奇形怪状的雕塑品. **3** [VP15B, 14] ~ *in/into*, make (sth) form a firm and permanent part of sth larger: make (sth) a fixture: (在较大物体上)增建, 添建, 附加(固定而且永久之物): *Ask the carpenter to ~ in some cupboards/to ~ some cupboards into the walls*. 请木匠在墙上嵌加几个橱柜. Hence, 由此产生, **built-in**: *a bedroom with built-in wardrobes*; 带有嵌壁的卧室; *a radio with a built-in aerial*. 带有嵌入天线的收音机. **4** [VP15B, 2C] ~ *up*, (a) accumulate; form a block: 积累; 形成阻塞: *Traffic is ~ing up* (= The number of vehicles is increasing steadily) *along the roads to the coast*. 通往海边的道路上的车辆在不断增加. (b) come together (so as to increase or intensify): 结集; 聚集(借以增加或加强): *One day your books will ~ up into a library*. 有一天你的书籍将会聚集成一座图书馆. *Their pressure on the enemy is ~ing up*. 他们对敌人的压力正逐渐加强. ~ *sb/sth up*, (a) try to increase sb's reputation (through publicity, praise): 试图增加某人的信誉(如借宣扬或赞美): *Don't ~ me up too much—I may disappoint you*. 别把我捧上了天,我可能令你失望. (b) make, acquire, steadily and gradually: 逐渐造成; 逐渐获得; 建立: *He has built up a good business/a good reputation for his goods*. 他已经使他的生意兴隆起来(建立起货品优良的信誉). *He went on holiday and soon built up* (= strengthened) *his health*. 他去度一次假, 很快就增进了他的健康. (c) (passive and as *adj*) become covered with (buildings, etc): (用被动语态,并作形容词用)到处都是建筑物; 盖满了房屋: *The district has been built up since I was last there*. 该区自从我上次去过以后已经盖满房屋. Hence, 由此产生, '**built-up areas**. 到处建满房屋或其他建筑物之区域. (d) bring together (so as to increase or intensify): 集结(以增加或加强): *They are ~ing up their military forces*. 他们在集结他们的军队. Hence, 由此产生, '**~-up** *n* (a) increase: 增加; 加强: *a ~-up of forces/pressure*. 力量(压力)的增加. (b) accumulation: 聚集; 积累: *a ~-up of traffic*. 交通阻塞. (c) flattering publicity, etc. 宣扬; 赞扬; 捧场: *the ~-up of a politician's image*. 提高某政客在人们心目中的地位. *The press gave him a tremendous ~-up*. 报纸对他大大地捧了一番. **5** [VP15B, 3A] ~ *on/upon*, base (hopes, etc) on; rely on: 把(希望等)寄托于; 依靠; 依赖; 指望: *Don't ~ too many hopes upon his helping you*. 别指望他会给予你帮助. *Don't ~ on his promises*. 不要指望他的诺言. **6** (*pp* with *advv*): (过去分词, 与副词连用): *a well-built man*, a man whose body has good proportions; 体格匀称的人; *solidly built*, having a solid frame(work). 构造坚固的. ~**er** *n* person who ~s, esp a contractor for ~ing houses; (fig) person who creates: 建筑者; (有指)营造商; (喻)创造者: *a great empire ~er*. 大帝国创立者.

build² /bɪld; bɪld/ *n* general shape or structure; (of the human body) general characteristics of shape and proportion: 大体的形状或结构; (指人体)体格: *a man of powerful ~*. 体格强健的人. *We are of the same ~*. 我们的体格是属同一型的.

build·ing /'bɪldɪŋ; 'bɪldɪŋ/ *n* **1** [U] (art of) constructing houses, etc: 建筑: '~ *operations*; 建筑工作; '~ *materials*; 建筑材料; '~ *land*, (to be) used for houses, etc. (可供)建筑之土地; 建地. '~ *site*, an area of land on which an office-block, a house, etc is being built. (正在兴建办公大楼、房屋等的)工地. '~*society*, organization for making loans to members who wish to build or buy a house, using funds supplied by its members. 建屋互助协会; 建筑合作社. **2** [C] house or other structure: 房屋; 建筑物: *Houses, schools, churches, hotels factories and sheds are all ~s*. 住宅、学校、教堂、旅馆、工厂及棚屋均系建筑物.

bulb /bʌlb; bʌlb/ *n* **1** almost round, thick, underground stem, sending roots downwards and leaves upwards, of such plants as the lily, onion, tulip. (百合、洋葱、郁金香等植物之生于地面下的)球茎. **2** sth like a ~ in shape, esp an electric lamp or the swollen end of a glass tube,

  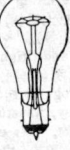

bulbs

eg in a thermometer. 状似植物球茎之物 (尤指电灯灯泡、气温表等玻璃管下端之球状部分). **bul·bous** /ˈbʌlbəs; ˈbʌlbəs/ *adj* of or having or like a ~; growing from a ~. 球茎的; 有球茎的; 似球茎生长出来的.

bul·bul /ˈbulbul; ˈbʊlbʊl/ *n* songbird of Asia and Africa. (亚洲及非洲的) 一种鸣鸟; 夜莺.

bulge /bʌldʒ; bʌldʒ/ *n* [C] irregular swelling; place where a swelling or curve shows; temporary increase in volume or numbers; (mil) salient. 不规则突起; 鼓起; 鼓起之处; 体积或数目暂时的增加; 膨胀; (军) 阵地之凸角: □ *vi, vt* [VP2A, C, 6A] (cause to) swell beyond the usual size; curve outwards: (使) 突起; 胀大; 膨胀; 鼓起. *He ~d his pockets with apples.* 他把口袋里装满苹果, 胀得鼓鼓的. *His pockets were bulging with apples.* 他的口袋里因装满苹果而胀得鼓鼓的. *He ~d his cheeks.* 他鼓起两颊.

bulk /bʌlk; bʌlk/ *n* [U] **quantity**, volume, esp when large. 量; 大量; 巨量; 巨大的体积. **in ~**, **(a)** in large amounts: 大量(地): *buy in ~*; *tankers to carry petroleum in ~.* 大量运输石油的油船. **(b)** loose, not packed in boxes, tins, etc. 散装的; 未装箱(罐等)的. **~ buying**, purchase at one time of a very large quantity of goods, eg by the state during a war. 大批购买; 整批购买. **the ~ of**, the greater part or number of: 大半; 大部: *He left the ~ of his property to his brother.* 他将大部财产遗留给他的胞弟. □ *vi* ~ *large.* appear large or important. 显得巨大或重要. **~y** *adj* taking up much space; clumsy to move or carry. 占地方的; 笨重而不易搬移的.

bulk·head /ˈbʌlkhed; ˈbʌlkˌhɛd/ *n* [C] water-tight division or dividing wall in a ship; similar division in a tunnel, etc. 船舱之不漏水的间隔或隔壁; 舱壁; 坑道等类似之隔壁; 分壁.

bull[1] /bul; bʊl/ *n* **1** uncastrated male of any animal of the ox family (⇨ **cow**): (未去势的) 公牛; 牡牛: *a man with a neck like a ~* (*a* '~-neck), with a thick neck. 一个粗脖子的人. *a ~ in a china shop,* person who is rough and clumsy where skill and care are needed. 动辄闯祸者; 笨手笨脚的人; 不能做精细工作者. **take the ~ by the horns,** meet a difficulty boldly instead of trying to escape from it. 不畏艰难; 毅然处断难局. '~-fight *n* fight between men and a ~ for public entertainment, as in Spain. 斗牛 (如风行于西班牙者). '~-fighter *n* '~-ring *n* arena for ~-fights. (圆形的) 斗牛场. '~-shit *n* ⚠ (vulg sl) nonsense: foolish and exaggerated talk. (伪) (鄙俚) 废话; 胡说. 多用于 **2** male of the whale, elephant and other large animals. 雄性的鲸、象和其他巨大动物. **3** (Stock Exchange; ⇨ **bear**[1] (4)) person who tries to raise prices with a view to selling at a profit: (股票市场) 多头业者 (抬高股价以图售出获利者): '~ *market*, with rising prices. 价格上涨的行情. **4** (compounds) (复合词) '~-dog *n* large, powerful breed of dog, with a short, thick neck, noted for its strong grip and its courage. 叭牛犬; 牛头犬 (一种身体大而结实, 颈粗短而善咬之猛犬). ⇨ the illus at dog. 参看 dog 之插图. '~-doze *vt* [VP6A, 14] **(a)** remove earth, flatten obstacles with a ~-dozer. 用推土机移土或铲平障碍物; 用推土机推平. **(b)** ~*doze sb into doing sth,* force sb to do sth by using one's strength or by intimidating him. 用强力或恐吓迫使某人做某事. ~-dozer /ˈbuldəuzə(r); ˈbʊlˌdozɚ/ *n* powerful tractor that pushes a broad steel blade or sheet in front, used for levelling land, shifting large quantities of earth, etc. 推土机 (前面装有一大块钢板, 用以推平地面或移动大量泥土等). '~-finch *n* small songbird with rounded beak and brightly coloured feathers. 照鸲 (一种小鸣禽, 圆喙, 羽色鲜丽). '~-frog *n* large American species of frog. 牛蛙 (美洲产之一种大青蛙). '~-headed *adj* clumsy, impetuous, obstinate. 笨拙的; 鲁莽的; 顽固的; 顽强的. '~-s-eye *n* centre of target (for archers, etc). 靶心; 鹄的. ⇨ the illus at archery. 参看 archery 之插图. '~-terrier *n* cross between a ~-dog and a terrier.

牛头犬与猃杂种所生之犬.

a bulldozer

bull[2] /bul; bʊl/ *n* official order or announcement from the Pope. 罗马教皇之勅令或训谕.

bull[3] /bul; bʊl/ *n* (also 亦作 **Irish ~**) foolish or amusing mistake in language, usu because there is a contradiction in terms 文字上的愚蠢或可笑的错误 (通常因为有逻辑上的矛盾) (eg 例如 'If you do not get this letter, please write and tell me' '如果你收不到这封信, 请你写信告诉我'): *It's a lot of ~*, nonsense. 胡说; 一派胡言.

bul·let /ˈbulɪt; ˈbʊlɪt/ *n* shaped piece of lead, usu coated with another metal, (to be) fired from a rifle or revolver. 子弹; 枪弹. Cf 参较 *shells* fired from guns. ⇨ the illus at **cartridge**. 参看 cartridge 之插图. '~-headed /-hedid/ *adj* having a small, round head. 有小圆头的. '~-proof *adj* able to stop ~s: 能防子弹穿入的; 防弹的: *a ~-proof jacket.* 防弹衣.

bul·le·tin /ˈbulɪtɪn; ˈbʊlɪtɪn/ *n* **1** official statement of news: 公报; 告示: *a ~ of news*; 新闻简报; a '*news ~.* 新闻快报. **2** printed sheet with official news or announcements. 通告; 公告.

bul·lion /ˈbulɪən; ˈbʊljən/ *n* [U] gold or silver in bulk or bars, before manufacture. 金条; 银条; 金块; 银块.

bul·lock /ˈbulək; ˈbʊlək/ *n* **1** young bull. 小公牛. **2** castrated bull. 阉牛.

bully[1] /ˈbulɪ; ˈbʊlɪ/ *n* (*pl* -lies) person who uses his strength or power to frighten or hurt those who are weaker. 恃强凌弱者. □ *vt* [VP6A, 14] ~ (*into doing sth*), use strength, etc in this way to persuade sb to do sth. 威胁某人 (做某事).

bully[2] /ˈbulɪ; ˈbʊlɪ/ *n* [U] (also 亦作 **~ beef**) tinned beef. 罐头牛肉.

bully[3] /ˈbulɪ; ˈbʊlɪ/ *adj* (sl) fine; excellent: (俚) 精美的; 特佳的: *B~ for you!* Well done! 妙极了! 棒透了! 干得好!

bully[4] /ˈbulɪ; ˈbʊlɪ/ *n* (hockey) way of putting the ball into play (beginning with two opposing players striking each others' sticks three times. (曲棍球) 开球 (开始时由敌对双方各一人互击球棍三次). □ *vi* [VP2C] ~ *off*, start to play in this way. (曲棍球) 开始打球.

bul·rush /ˈbulrʌʃ; ˈbʊlˌrʌʃ/ *n* [C] (kinds of) tall rush or reed with a thick velvety head. 蒲草属植物; 芦苇.

bul·wark /ˈbulwək; ˈbʊlwək/ *n* **1** wall, esp one built of earth, against attack; earthwork; (fig) sth that defends or protects: 壁垒; 堡垒; 防御工事; (喻) 保卫或保护之物; 屏藩; 保障: *Law is the ~ of society*, gives us security. 法律是社会的保障. **2** (usu *pl*) wall round (esp a sailing) ship's deck. (通常用复数) (尤指帆船) 船板上沿船壳之坚实围墙; 舷墙.

bum[1] /bʌm; bʌm/ *n* (colloq) part of the body on which one sits; buttocks. (口) 臀; 屁股.

bum[2] /bʌm; bʌm/ (sl) *n* habitual beggar or loafer. (俚) 职业乞丐; 流浪者; 无业游民. □ *adj* of poor quality; worthless. 劣质的; 无价值的. □ **1** *vi* (-mm-) [VP2C] ~ *around*, loaf, wander about doing nothing. 游荡; 游手好闲. **2** *vt* (-mm-) [VP6A, 14] ~ *sth* (*off /from sb*), succeed in getting sb to give (usu reluctantly) sth

to one: 乞讨; (向某人) 讨得 (某物): *He bummed a cigarette off me.* 他向我讨了一支香烟。

bumble-bee /'bʌmbl bi:; 'bʌmbl,bi/ n large kind of hairy bee with a loud hum. 大黄蜂; 土蜂(体多毛, 嗡声很大)。

bum·boat /'bʌmbəut; 'bʌm,bot /n (naut) small boat carrying fresh provisions to ships lying offshore. (航海) 运送新鲜食物至离岸停泊之船只的小舟; 贩卖舟。

bump /bʌmp; bʌmp/ *vt, vi* 1 [VP6A, 14, 3A] ~ *(against/into)*, come against with a blow or knock; 碰到; 撞到; 冲击: *The room was dark and I ~ed (my head) against the door.* 房间内很黑, 我 (我的头) 碰着门了。*The blind man ~ed into me.* 那瞎子撞了我个满怀。*The car ~ed against the kerb/~ed into the car in front.* 那汽车撞在街道的边石上(撞到了前面的车子)。~ *against/into*, hurt (one's head, etc) by striking it on sth. 碰伤(头等)。2 [VP2C] move with a jerky, jolting motion (like a cart on a bad road): 颠簸而行(如车子在坏路上走): *The heavy bus ~ed along the rough mountain road.* 那沉重的客车在崎岖的山路上颠簸而行。3 [VP15B] ~ *sb off*, (sl) murder him. (俚)谋杀某人。□ *adv* suddenly; violently: 突然地; 剧烈地: *Our bus ran ~ into the wall.* 我们的客车猛撞在墙上。□ *n* 1 blow or knock; dull sound made by a blow (as when two things come together with force). 碰撞; 碰撞声(如两物互相猛撞时所发出的声音)。2 swelling on the body caused by such a blow; natural bulge on the skull. 身体上因碰撞所成的肿块; 头骨上的天然隆起。⇨ **phrenology**. 3 swelling on any surface. 任何肿块或隆起。4 (jolt felt in an aircraft, caused by a) sudden change in air-pressure. 因气压突然改变在飞机中所感到的)颠簸; 气压之突然改变。~·y *(-ier, -iest) adj* with many ~s: 颠簸不堪的: *a ~y road/ride.* 颠簸不堪的道路(乘车旅行)。

bum·per¹ /'bʌmpə(r); 'bʌmpə/ n fender (usu a horizontal bar) on a bus, motor-car, etc (front and rear), to lessen the effect of a collision, ⇨ the illus at **motor**; (车辆前后通常为水平横杆的)保险杠(参看 motor 之插图); (US) (美)=**buffer¹**.

bum·per² /'bʌmpə(r); 'bʌmpə/ n 1 glass of wine, full to the brim. 满满的一杯酒。2 (attrib) sth unusually large or abundant: (用作定语)非常大或丰富之物: ~ *crops;* 结实累累的农作物; *a ~ harvest;* 丰收; *a ~ edition* (of a periodical). (期刊的)特大号。

bum·per³ /'bʌmpə(r); 'bʌmpə/ n (cricket) ball bowled that springs up high after striking the ground. (板球)反弹球。

bump·kin /'bʌmpkɪn; 'bʌmpkɪn/ n awkward person with unpolished manners, esp from the country: 乡下人; 粗人: *a country ~.* 乡巴佬。

bump·tious /'bʌmpʃəs; 'bʌmpʃəs/ adj conceited; self-important: 高傲的; 自大的: ~ *officials.* 高傲的官吏。~·**ly** *adv* ~·**ness** *n*

bun /bʌn; bʌn/ n 1 small, round, sweet cake, usu containing currants. 小而圆的甜面包(通常含有葡萄干)。2 *in a bun*, (of a woman's hair) twisted into a knot above the back of the neck. (指女人的头发)在脑后挽成一个髻。⇨ **chignon**.

bunch /bʌntʃ; bʌntʃ/ n 1 number of small, similar things naturally growing together: 串; 簇(自然地生长在一起的一些相同的小东西): *a ~ of grapes/bananas.* 一串葡萄(香蕉)。2 collection of things of the same sort placed or fastened together; 束; 捆(被放置或捆束在一起的同类物品): *a ~ of flowers/keys.* 一束花(一串钥匙)。3 (sl) mob; gang. (俚)暴民群众; 帮; 伙。4 *the best of the ~*, (colloq) the best or pick of the lot. (口)一批中之最好的; 精华。□ *vt, vi* [VP15B, 2A, C] ~ *(up/together)*, form into a ~ or ~es, or in folds: 形成一串; 聚成一簇; 捆成一束: *Don't ~ up,* ie cluster together. 不要聚在一起。

bundle /'bʌndl; 'bʌndl/ n number of articles fastened, tied, or wrapped together: 捆; 束; 扎; 包; 包

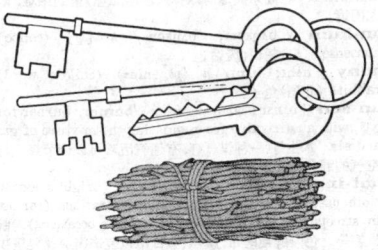

a bunch of keys

a bundle of sticks

裹: *a ~ of sticks/firewood;* 一捆棍子(柴); *a ~ of old rags.* 一捆破旧衣服。*The books were tied up in ~s of twenty.* 那些书被捆成二十本一捆。□ *vt, vi* 1 [VP15B] ~ *up/together*, make into a ~ or ~s: 捆扎; 包扎: *We ~d everything up.* 我们把每件东西都捆扎起来了。2 [VP15A] put together in a confused heap; put away without order: 乱堆在一起: *We ~d everything into a drawer.* 我们把所有的东西都塞在一个抽屉里。3 [VP15A, B, 2C] send or go in a hurry or without ceremony: 匆匆遣走; 匆匆离去: *They ~d him into a taxi.* 他们匆匆地把他推进一辆计程车。*His mother ~d him off to school.* 他母亲赶紧打发他去上学。*They ~d off/out/away.* 他们匆匆离去。

bung /bʌŋ; bʌŋ/ n large (usu wooden, rubber, cork or plastic) stopper for closing a hole in a cask or barrel. (通常为木、橡皮、软木、塑胶制成, 用以塞桶口之)塞子。□ *vt* [VP15B] ~ *(up)*, put a ~ into (the hole in a cask). 用塞子塞住(桶口)。'~-**hole** *n* hole for filling a cask. 桶口。~ *ed up*, (of the nose) stopped up with mucus; (of drains) clogged with dirt. (指鼻)为粘液塞住的; (指下水道)为污物塞住的。

bun·ga·low /'bʌŋgələu; 'bʌŋgə,lo/ n small house of only one storey; (in India) such a house surrounded by a large verandah. 单层屋; 平房; (在印度)四周围绕着大走廊的平房。**bun·ga·loid** /'bʌŋgəlɔid; 'bʌŋgə,lɔid/ adj of or like ~s: 平房的; 似平房的: *bungaloid growth,* area of unsightly building development with many ~s. 平房地区(不雅观地建着许多平房的建筑发展地区)。

bungle /'bʌŋgl; 'bʌŋgl/ *vt, vi* [VP6A, 2A] do (a piece of work) badly and clumsily; spoil (a task, etc) by lack of skill. 把(事情)做得一团糟; 由于技术拙劣而把(事情)做坏。□ *n* ~d piece of work. 拙劣的工作。**bung·ler** /'bʌŋglə(r); 'bʌŋglə/ n person who ~s. 工作拙劣的人。

bun·ion /'bʌnjən; 'bʌnjən/ n inflamed swelling, esp on the large joint of the big toe. 拇趾囊炎肿。

bunk¹ /bʌŋk; bʌŋk/ n narrow bed fixed on the wall, eg of a cabin in a ship or in a train; sleeping-berth. (船舱或火车等上, 固定于墙上的)床铺; 铺位。~ **beds**, pair of single beds, one fixed above the other, usu for children. 双层单人床(通常为小孩所睡者)。

bunk² /bʌŋk; bʌŋk/ *vi* (GB sl) run away; play truant. (英俚)逃走; 逃学。□ *n do a ~*, run away. 逃走。

bunk³ /bʌŋk; bʌŋk/ n [U] abbr for **bunkum**. bunkum 之略。

bunker /'bʌŋkə(r); 'bʌŋkə/ n 1 that part of a ship where coal or fuel oil is stored. (船上的)燃料储存处; 燃料舱。2 sandy hollow, made as an obstacle, on a golf-course. (高尔夫球场上人工造成作为障碍之)沙坑。3(mil) underground shelter, fortified point, of steel and concrete. (军)(钢筋混凝土构成的地下)重掩蔽体。□ *vt, vi* 1 [VP6A, 2A] fill a ship's ~ with fuel; (of a ship) obtain supplies of fuel. 装燃料于燃料舱; (指船)获得燃料补给。2 (usu passive) (通常用被动语态)

be ~*ed*, get one's ball into a ~ at golf; (fig) be in difficulties. 打高尔夫球时球掉入沙洼; (喻)遭遇困难; 陷入困境。

bun·kum /'bʌŋkəm; 'bʌŋkəm/ *n* [U] (colloq) nonsense. (口)胡说; 废话。

bunny /'bʌnɪ; 'bʌnɪ/ *n* (*pl* -nies) (child's word) rabbit. (儿语)兔子。

Bun·sen /'bʌnsn; 'bʌnsn/ *n*, ~ 'burner, burner for gas, with an air-valve for regulating the mixture of gas and air. 本生灯(一种煤气灯, 有通气活瓣可以调节煤气与空气的混合量)。

bunt·ing /'bʌntɪŋ; 'bʌntɪŋ/ *n* [U] (bright-coloured cloth used for making) flags and decorations (for use in streets and on buildings on festive occasions). 制旗帜等之色彩鲜艳的布; 旗帜(节日用以装饰街道及建筑物者)。

buoy /bɔɪ; bɔɪ/ *n* **1** floating object, anchored to the bottom, used to show a navigable channel or to indicate reefs, submerged wrecks, etc. (固定于海底而漂浮于海面上, 用以指示航道或礁石、海面下的沉船等之)浮标; 浮筒。 **2** (also 亦作 *life*-~) sth designed to keep a person afloat in the water, eg sth made of cork or sth that can be inflated with air. (用软木或可充气之材料制成的)救生圈。 ⇨ the illus at **life**. 参看 life 之插图。 □ *vt* **1** [VP6A] mark the position of with a ~: 以浮标指示: ~ *a wreck/channel.* 以浮标指示破船残骸(航道)。 **2** [VP15B] ~ *up*, keep afloat; (fig)keep up hopes, etc: 使漂浮; (喻)维持希望等; 振作; 鼓舞; 支持: ~*ed up with new hope.* 为新希望所鼓舞。

buoy·ancy /'bɔɪənsɪ; 'bɔɪənsɪ/ *n* [U] **1** power to float or keep things floating: 浮力: *Salt water has more* ~ *than fresh water.* 海水较淡水浮力为大。 **2** (fig) lightness of spirits; power to recuperate; (of the stock market) tendency of prices to rise. (喻)快活; 轻快的心情; 恢复力; (指股票市场)上涨的趋势; 看涨的行情。

buoy·ant /'bɔɪənt; 'bɔɪənt/ *adj* able to float or to keep things floating; (fig) light-hearted: 能漂浮的; 有浮力的; (喻)心情愉快的; 快活的: *a* ~ *disposition*; 乐天的性情; springy: 有弹性的: *with a* ~ *step*; 一跃; (of the stock market, etc) maintaining high prices. (指股票市场)维持高价的; 盘高的。 ~·ly *adv*

bur, burr /bɜː(r); bɜ/ *n* (plant with a) seed-case or flower-head that clings to the hair or fur of animals; (fig) sth or sb that sticks like a ~, esp a person who forces his company on others and is hard to shake off. 其芒刺易附着之毛上的种子壳或花头; 刺球; 芒刺; 有芒刺之植物; (喻)易附着之物或人; (尤指)强与人同处而不易摆脱之人。

burble /'bɜːbl; 'bɜbl/ *vi* make a gentle murmuring or bubbling sound: 作潺潺流水声或起泡声: *burbling with mirth.* 作欢笑声。

bur·den /'bɜːdn; 'bɜdn/ *n* **1** sth (to be) carried; load (esp one that is heavy); (lit and fig) sth difficult to bear: 负载; 负荷; (尤指)重担; 重负; (字面及比喻)难以担负的事物: *the* ~ *of taxation (up)on industry:* 工业所负担的重税; *a* ~ *of sorrow/grief.* 压在心头的悲伤。 *be a* ~ *to sb*, cause him expense and trouble: 是某人的负担(使某人花钱并惹麻烦): *He was always a* ~ *to his parents.* 他永远是他父母的负担(总是使父母花钱并惹麻烦)。 **beast of** ~, animal that carries packs on its back. 驮兽。 **2** [U] ship's carrying capacity, tonnage: 船的载重量; 吨位: *a ship of 3000 tons* ~. 载重三千吨的船。 **3** *the* ~ *of proof*, obligation to prove: 举证责任: *The* ~ *of proof rests with him.* He must prove the truth of his statement. 他必须拿出证据来。 **4** refrain or chorus (of a song); (with *def art*) chief theme of a statement, speech, etc: (歌曲的)叠句或合唱部分; 副歌; (与定冠词连用)(声明或演讲等的)主题; 主旨: *The* ~ *of his remarks was that ....* 他的言论的主旨乃是…。 □ *vt* ~ *sb/ oneself (with)*, [VP6A, 14] load; put a ~ on: 装载; 加负担于; 使负担: ~*oneself with a heavy overcoat:* 给自己加一件厚大衣; ~ *one's memory with useless facts:* 勉

强记一些无用的事实; ~*ed with taxation.* 为重税所累。 ~·**some** /-səm; -səm/ *adj* hard to bear; making (sb) tired; troublesome (*to* sb). 难以负担的; 沉重的; 累人的; 麻烦的(与 to 连用, 后接某人)。

bur·dock /'bɜːdɒk; 'bɜˌdɑk/ *n* wild plant with leaves like those of a dock and prickly flowerheads (burrs). 牛蒡(一种野生植物, 叶似酸模之叶, 花带芒刺)。

bureau /'bjʊərəʊ; 'bjʊro/ *n* (*pl* -reaux, /-rəʊz; -roz/) **1** (GB) writing desk with drawers. (英)有抽屉的写字桌; 写字台。 **2** government or municipal department or office: (政府机构)处; 局; 所: ˌInforˈmation B~; 新闻局; ˈTourist B~. 旅游局。 **3** (US)chest of drawers for clothes, etc, usu with a mirror. (美)五斗柜(通常附有镜子)。

bureau·cracy /bjʊəˈrɒkrəsɪ; bjuˈrɑkrəsɪ/ *n* [U] 官僚政治; 官僚的总称。

bureau·crat /'bjʊərəkræt; 'bjʊrəˌkræt/ *n* 官僚。 ~**ic** /ˌbjʊərəˈkrætɪk; ˌbjʊroˈkrætɪk/ *adj* of or like a ~; too much attached to rules; carried on according to official rules and habits. 官僚的; 官僚作风的; 繁文缛节的; 墨守成规的。 ~·**i·cally** /-ɪklɪ; -ɪklɪ/ *adv*

burette /bjʊˈret; bjuˈrɛt/ *n* graduated glass tube with a tap for measuring small quantities of liquid that are let out of it. 用以衡量少量液体的有刻度的玻璃管; 滴定管; 量管。

burg /bɜːg; bɜg/ *n* (US colloq) town; city. (美口)镇; 城; 市。

bur·geon /'bɜːdʒən; 'bɜdʒən/ *vi* (poet) put out leaves; begin to grow. (诗)发芽; 萌芽; 开始生长。

bur·ger /'bɜːgə(r); 'bɜgə/ *n* (colloq) (口) = hamburger.

burgh /'bʌrə; bʌg/ *n* borough in Scotland. (苏格兰之)市镇。

bur·gher /'bɜːgə(r); 'bɜgə/ *n* (old use) citizen (esp of a Dutch, Flemish or German town). (旧用法)(尤指荷兰、佛兰德或德国市镇之)市民; 公民。

bur·glar /'bɜːglə(r); 'bɜglə/ *n* person who breaks into a house in order to steal. (闯入屋内行窃的)窃贼。 **bur·glary** /'bɜːglərɪ; 'bɜglərɪ/ *n* [U] crime of breaking into a house to steal; [C] (*pl* -ries) instance of this: 窃盗罪; 窃案: *There have been numerous* ~*ies in this district recently.* 近来在这个区域内发生很多窃案。 '~*alarm* n device to give warning of ~s. 防盗铃。 '~*proof adj* made so that ~s cannot break in or into. 防盗的。 **burgle** /'bɜːgl; 'bɜgl/ *vt, vi* [VP6A] break into (a building) to commit ~y; [VP2A] commit ~y. 闯入 (建筑物) 行窃; 窃盗; 犯窃盗罪。 ~·**i·ous** /bɜːˈglɛərɪəs; bɜˈglɛrɪəs/ *adj* (legal) of ~y: (法律)窃盗的; 窃盗罪的: *guilty of a* ~*ious attempt.* 犯企图行窃罪。

burgo·mas·ter /'bɜːgəˌmɑːstə(r) US: -mæs-; 'bɜgəˌmæstə/ *n* mayor of a Dutch, Flemish or German town. (荷兰、佛兰德或德国市镇之)市长; 镇长。

Bur·gundy /'bɜːgəndɪ; 'bɜgəndɪ/ *n* [U] kinds of (usu red) wine of Burgundy (in Central France). 勃艮第葡萄酒(法国中部勃艮第所产葡萄酒, 通常为红色)。

burial /'berɪəl; 'bɛrɪəl/ *n* [U] burying; [C] instance of this. 埋葬。 '~*ground* n cemetery. 墓地。 'B~ Service, the religious ceremony at a funeral. (按宗教仪式所行的)葬礼。

burke /bɜːk; bɜk/ *vt* [VP6A] avoid: 避免: ~ *publicity/an issue;* 避免出风头或(避开一问题); suppress: 压制; 扣压: ~ *an inquiry.* 扣压一调查案件。

bur·lap /'bɜːlæp; 'bɜlæp/ *n* [U] coarse canvas (used for bags, wrappings, etc). 粗帆布(用以制袋、包布等)。

bur·lesque /bɜːˈlesk; bɜˈlɛsk/ *n* **1** [C] imitation, eg of a book, speech, person's behaviour, for the purpose of making fun of it or of amusing people. 模仿(书籍、演说、人的行为等)以达讽刺或娱悦他人的目的。 **2** [U] amusing imitation or parody. 滑稽的模仿; 游戏诗文。 **3** (US) variety entertainment. (美)杂耍表演; 综艺节目。 ⇨ **variety(5).** **4** (as *adj* or attrib) intended

as a ～. (作形容词或用作定语)意在讽刺或娱悦他人的。 □ *vt* [VP6A] make a ～ of; parody. 讽刺;滑稽地模仿。

burly /'bɜːlɪ; 'bɝlɪ/ *adj* (of a person) big and strong; solidly built. (指人)魁梧的;强壮的;结实的。

burn¹ /bɜːn; bɝn/ *n* (Scot) small stream. (苏)小溪;小河。

burn² /bɜːn; bɝn/ *vt, vi* (*pt, pp* **burnt** /bɜːnt; bɝnt/ or 或作 burned /bɜːnd; bɝnd/) (For uses with *adverbial particles* and *preps*, ⇨ **6** below.) 与副词性小品词及介词连用之用法,参看下列第 6 义。) **1** [VP6A] use for the purpose of lighting or heating: 燃烧(使发光或生热): *Most large steamships now ～ oil instead of coal.* 现在大多数的大轮船都烧油而不烧煤。*This lamp ～s oil.* 这盏灯烧油。*We have ～t all our logs.* 我们所有的木柴都烧光了。**2** [VP6A, 14] ～ (*to*), damage; hurt, destroy by fire, heat or the action of acid; 烧毁; 焚毁; 烧伤; 烫伤; (被酸类)灼伤; *Be careful not to ～ the meat.* 小心不要把肉烧焦了。*The coffee is very hot, don't ～ your mouth.* 咖啡非常热,不要烫着了你的嘴。*You've ～t my toast to a cinder!* so that it is hard and black. 你把我的面包烧焦了! *The child ～t itself/its fingers while playing with matches.* 那孩子玩火柴烧伤了自己(烧伤了自己的手指)。*Some acids are strong enough to ～ wood.* 有些酸类能酸性强得可以烧坏木头。～ **one's fingers**, ⇨ **finger**. '～**ing glass** *n* lens used to concentrate the sun's rays (to set fire to sth). (用以集中日光以取火的)凸透镜; 取火镜。**3** [VP2A, B, C] be on fire or alight; be capable of giving out light and heat: 燃烧; 灼热; 发光; 发亮; 能发出光和热: *Wood ～s easily.* 木头容易燃烧。*Stone won't ～.* 石头不会燃烧。*All the lights were ～ing.* 所有的灯都亮着。**4** [VP6A] make by heat; heat (a material) to make (sth): 烧制; 将(材料)加热以制成(某物): ～ *bricks/lime/charcoal;* (在窑中)烧砖(烧制石灰; 烧制木炭); ～ *clay to make bricks;* 烧粘土以制砖; ～ *a hole in a carpet,* eg by dropping a cigarette end. 把地毯烧一个洞(如因香烟头落于其上)。**5** [VP2A, C, 4A] be hurt or spoilt by fire or heat; scorch; be or feel warm or hot; (fig) be filled with strong feeling: 被烧坏; 被烧焦; 被晒黑; 被晒伤; 发烧; (喻)发火(怒); 感情激动: *The milk/sauce has ～t.* 牛奶(调味汁)已烧焦。*She has a skin that ～s easily,* is quickly hurt by the sun. 她的两颊因羞愧而发烧。*Her cheeks were ～ing with shame.* 她的两颊因羞愧而发烧。*They were ～ing to avenge the death of their leader.* 他们极为激动要为他们首领之死报仇。**6** [VP15B, 2C] (special uses with *adverbial particles* and *preps*): (与副词性小品词及介词连用之特殊用法):
burn (sth) away, (a) continue to ～ : 继续燃烧: *The fire was ～ing away cheerfully.* 炉火融融。(b) make, become less, by ～ing; destroy, be destroyed, by ～ing; 因燃烧而消耗;烧毁;烧尽;烧掉: *Half the candle had ～t away.* 蜡烛已烧掉了一半。*An area of skin on his hand was ～t away.* 他手上的一块皮肤被烧毁了。
burn (sth) down, be destroyed, destroy to the foundations, by fire: 烧毁; 焚毁; 烧光(到基础): *The house (was) ～t down.* 该房子整幢烧掉了。～ (*down*) (*low*), ～ less brightly as the material ～s or the fuel is used. 因物质燃烧或燃料消耗而不如原先那样明亮或旺盛: (灯烛等)烧残;(灯火)将烧尽;火力减弱。
burn (sth) out, (a) become extinguished: 熄灭; 烧完: *The fire ～t (itself) out.* 炉火烧灭了。(b) (of a rocket) use up its fuel. (指火箭)耗尽燃料;燃料用尽。(c)(of an electric motor, coil) stop working because high current has caused electrical ～ing. (指电动马达,线圈)因高电流而烧坏。(d) (usu passive) be destroyed, be reduced to a shell, by fire; be gutted: (通常用被动语态)被焚毁只剩下一个空壳; 内部被烧毁: ～ *out factories/tanks.* 内部被焚毁的工厂(战车)。～ *oneself out,* ruin one's health by overwork, dissipation, etc. 因过度工作、生活放荡等而毁了自己的健康。
burn (sth) up, (a) burst into flames, flare up: 迸出火

光;燃烧旺盛: *Put some wood on the fire and make it ～ up.* 加点柴在炉火上,使它烧旺一点。(b) consume, get rid of, by ～ing: 烧掉;焚化: *We ～t up all the garden rubbish.* 我们将花园中的垃圾全部焚化。(c)(of a rocket, etc, re-entering the atmosphere from space) catch fire and be destroyed. (指火箭等,从太空重返大气层时)着火烧毁。'～-**up** *n* (GB sl) high-speed race on a public road between young people on motorcycles. (英俚)青年人驾机车在公路上彼此快速竞逐。

burn³ /bɜːn; bɝn/ *n* **1** injury, mark, made by fire. heat or acid: (由火、热或酸类物造成之)烧伤;灼伤: *He died of the ～s he received in the fire.* 他死于火灾时所受到的灼伤。**2** (aerospace) one firing of a rocket: (太空)火箭的一次发射: *a two-minute ～ to correct course to the moon.* 为修正赴月球的航道所作之两分钟发射。

burner /'bɜːnə(r); 'bɝnɚ/ *n* **1** person who burns sth or makes sth by burning: 烧者; 烧制者: *a 'charcoal-burner.* 烧制木炭者。**2** that part of a lamp, stove, etc from which the light or flame comes: (灯、炉等之)灯头; 灯心: *a four-～ oil-stove.* 有四个炉心的油炉。

burn·ing /'bɜːnɪŋ; 'bɝnɪŋ/ *adj* **1** intense: 激烈的; 强烈的: *a ～ thirst / desire.* 极度的渴(强烈的欲望)。**2** exciting; hotly debated: 使人激动的;被热烈辩论的: *a ～ question.* 热烈辩论的问题。**3** notorious, scandalous: 不体面的;可耻的: *a ～ disgrace / shame.* 极为可耻之事。

bur·nish /'bɜːnɪʃ; 'bɝnɪʃ/ *vt, vi* [VP6A] polish (metal) by, or as if by, rubbing; [VP2A] take a polish: 擦亮(金属);磨光;使光亮;被擦亮: *material that ～es well.* 容易擦亮的物质。

bur·nouse /bɜː'nuːs; bɚ'nus/ *n* kind of cloak with a hood, worn by Arabs and Moors. (阿拉伯人和摩尔人所着之)连有兜帽之外衣。

burp /bɜːp; bɝp/ *n* [C] (colloq) belch. (口)打嗝。□ *vt, vi* [VP6A, 2A] (cause to) give a ～: (使)打嗝。～ *a baby.* 使婴儿打嗝。

burr¹ *n* ⇨ **bur.**

burr² /bɜː(r); bɝ/ *n* **1** whirring sound made by parts of machines that turn quickly. (机器各部急速运转所发的)辘辘声。'～-**drill** *n* one used by dentists. (牙医用的)钻孔器; 钻锥。**2** marked pronunciation of 'r'; marked (rural) accent: 显著的 r 音; 显著的(乡村)口音: *speak with a soft West-country ～.* 说话带些轻柔的西部乡村口音。

bur·row /'bʌrəʊ; 'bɝo/ *n* hole made in the ground (by foxes, rabbits, etc). (狐狸、兔子等在地下所掘的)洞穴。□ *vi, vt* [VP2A, C, 3A, 6A] ～ (*into sth*), dig (a ～); (fig) investigate (sth hidden). 掘(地洞); (喻)调查(隐藏的事物);探索;发掘。

bur·sar /'bɜːsə(r); 'bɝsɚ/ *n* **1** treasurer (esp of a college). (尤指大学内的)会计员。**2** (person holding a) scholarship at a university of Scotland, or a grant for continuation of studies: 苏格兰的大学奖学金或研究奖助金;此种奖学金或奖助金的享有人: *British Council ～s in Great Britain.* 英国文化协会在大不列颠所设的研究奖助金。～**y** *n* **1** college ～'s office. (大学里的)会计室。**2** scholarship; grant for continuation of studies. 奖学金;研究奖助金。

burst¹ /bɜːst; bɝst/ *vi, vt* (*pt, pp* **burst**) (For uses with *adverbial particles* and *preps*, ⇨ **5** below.) (与副词性小品词及介词连用之用法参看下列第 5 义。) **1** [VP2A] (of a bomb, shell. boiler, etc) fly or break violently apart from internal pressure; explode; (of river banks, a dam, an abscess, a boil) break outwards; (of a bubble) break; (of leaf and flower buds) open out. (指炸弹、炮弹、锅炉等)爆炸; (指河岸、堤坝、脓疮、疖疮)决口; 胀裂; 穿头; (指水泡)爆破; 指叶苞、花蕾)绽放。*be ～ing to,* be eager to: 急于: *He was ～ing to tell us the news.* 他极欲告诉我们那消息。**2** [VP6A, 22] cause to fly apart, explode, open suddenly, give way under pressure: 使爆破; 使爆裂; 使破口; 挤破; 胀裂: ～ *a tyre/balloon;* 使轮胎(汽球)爆破; *We had to ～ the door*

open. 我们不得不破门而入。*If you get much fatter you'll ~ your clothes*. 如果你再胖下去，你的衣服就要胀破了。*He ~ a blood-vessel*, suffered the ~ing of one: 他的一条血管破裂。*(fig) (喻) ~ one's sides with laughing*. 笑破肚子。**3 ~ (with)**, [VP2A, 3A] be full to overflowing; be able to contain with difficulty: 饱满，满盈，几乎装不下: *store-houses ~ing with grain*; 装满谷物的谷仓; *sacks ~ing with corn*. 装满玉蜀黍的大袋子。*They were ~ing with happiness/pride/excitement/impatience/health*. 他们乐不可支(满怀骄傲，兴奋，不耐烦，极为健康)。**4** [VP2C] make a way or entry suddenly or by force: 突然闯过; 强行进入: *He ~ into the room*. 他闯入室内。*The oil ~ (= gushed) out of the ground*. 油从地下冒出。*The sun ~ through the clouds, appeared through an opening in the clouds*. 太阳从云缝里钻出来。**5** [VP2C, 3A] (with *adverbial particles and preps*): (与副词性小品词及介词连用):
burst forth, ⇨ ~ *out*.
burst in (on, upon), **(a)** interrupt: 突然插嘴; 打断(谈话): *Stop him ~ing in*. 别让他打岔。*He ~ in upon our conversation*. 他打断我们的谈话。**(b)** appear or arrive suddenly: 突然出现或到达: *He'll be ~ing in on us at any moment*. 他随时会出现在我们的面前。
burst into, **(a)** send out suddenly; break out into: 突然发出; 猝发; 爆发成: *The oil-stove upset and ~ into flames*. 油炉翻倒，立刻燃烧起来。*~ into tears/laughter, etc*, suddenly begin to cry (laugh, etc): 突然大哭(大笑等); *~ into song*, begin to sing; 突然唱起歌来; *~ into angry speech*, begin to speak angrily. 大发雷霆。**(c)** *~ into bloom/blossom*, (of shrubs, trees) open out with blossom. (指灌木，树木)开花。**(d)** *~ into view/sight*, (of a scene, spectacle) suddenly become visible. (指景象、奇观)突然显现。
burst on/upon, come suddenly or unexpectedly to: 突然或意外地出现于: *The view ~ upon our sight*. 那景象突然出现于我们的眼前。*The truth ~ upon him*, he suddenly realized it. 他突然领悟那道理。*The cries of the mob ~ upon our ears*. 暴徒们的叫嚣突然传到我们的耳边。
burst out (into), exclaim; begin to speak: 大声地说: 咆哮地说: '*Why don't you behave?*' *he ~ out (= ~ forth)*. '你为什么不规矩些?'他大声地说。*He ~ out into threats*. 他突然大声威胁。*~ out laughing/crying*, suddenly begin to laugh/cry. 突然大笑(大哭)。
burst² /bɜːst; bɜst/ *n* **1** bursting explosion: 爆炸; 爆裂; 破裂: *the ~ of a shell/bomb*; 炮弹(炸弹)之爆炸; *a ~ in the water main*. 在输水总管上的一个裂口。**2** brief, violent effort: 短暂而猛烈的努力: *a ~ of energy/speed*; 一股劲/一阵高速); *work in sudden ~s*. 一阵一阵地努力工作。**3** outbreak: 爆发; 猝发: *a ~ of applause/anger/tears*; 一阵喝彩(发怒、眼泪); *a ~ of flame*. 一阵火焰。**4** short spurt: 一阵急射: *a ~ of gunfire*, eg from a machine-gun. 炮火(如机枪)之一阵射击。**5** ⇨ *bust²*.
bur·then /ˈbɜːðən; ˈbɜðən/ *n, v* (liter) (文) = burden.
bur·ton /ˈbɜːtn; ˈbɜtn/ *n* beer brewed at Burton-on-Trent, Derbyshire. 波顿啤酒(英格兰德贝郡，波顿城所酿制的啤酒)。*gone for a ~*, (GB sl) dead; missing. (英俚)死亡; 失踪。
bury /ˈberɪ; ˈbɛrɪ/ *vt* **1** [VP6A] place (a dead body) in the ground, in a grave or in the sea; (of a clergyman) perform the Burial Service over; (of relatives) lose by death: 埋葬(尸体); 土葬; 海葬; (指牧师)做~; 一举行葬礼; (指亲属)因~而丧失亲人: *William Shakespeare is buried in the church at Stratford on Avon*. 莎士比亚埋葬在亚芬河畔斯特拉福镇的教堂里。*He was buried at sea*. 他葬在海里。*Poor old Joe—he's dead and buried*. 可怜的老乔——他已死亡并且埋葬了。*She has buried five husbands*. 她曾五度丧夫。**2** [VP6A, 22, 15A] put underground; (over with earth, leaves, etc; cover up and forget; hide from view: 埋藏于地下; 以泥土、树叶等遮盖; 遮盖起来并且遗忘; 隐藏; 遮蔽; 隐匿:

buried treasure. 埋藏的财宝。*You wouldn't like to be buried alive*. 你不会喜欢被人活埋。*The dog buried the bone*. 狗将骨头埋藏起来。*The end of the post was buried in the ground*. 柱子的末端埋在地里。*The house was half buried under snow*. 那房屋半截被埋在雪里。*She buried (= hid) her face in her hands*. 她用双手蒙住她的脸。*~ oneself in the country*, go to a place in the country where one will meet few people. 蛰居于乡间; 隐居于乡间。*~ oneself in one's books/studies*, give all one's time and attention to them. 埋头读书(专心致力于研究)。*be buried in thoughts/memories of the past, etc*, be deep in thought, etc, paying no attention to other things. 沉思(缅怀往事等)。'*~ing-ground* *n* cemetery. 墓地; 坟场。
bus /bʌs; bʌs/ *n* **1** (= *omnibus* which is now dated) public conveyance that travels along a fixed route and takes up and sets down passengers at fixed points: (行驶一定路线并且在一定地点上下乘客之)公共汽车(昔称 *omnibus*): *Shall we walk or go by bus?* 我们是走路还是乘公共汽车? *miss the bus*, (colloq) be too late to use an opportunity. (口)坐失良机。'*bus·man* /-mən; -mən/ *n* bus-driver. 公共汽车驾驶人。*busman's holiday*, leisure time spent in the same kind of occupation as one's ordinary work. 应该休息而仍旧照常工作的假日。'*~ stop* *n* fixed stopping place for buses. 公共汽车(招呼)站。**2** (sl) aeroplane; motor-car. (俚)飞机; 汽车。□ *vi*, *vt* (**-ss-**) [VP2A, 6A] go, take, by bus; (esp US) transport children to their schools: 坐公共汽车去; 以公共汽车运送; (尤美)以公共汽车送孩子们上学: *the bussing of children to achieve racial integration*, eg by taking children from white areas to schools in black areas and vice versa. 以校车送孩子以达成种族融合之目的(例如将白人区的孩子送至黑人区的学校就读，或将黑人区的孩子送至白人区的学校就读)。
busby /ˈbʌzbɪ; ˈbʌzbɪ/ *n* (*pl* **-bies**) fur cap worn for ceremonial parades by soldiers of some British regiments. (英国某些部队于阅兵时所戴之)一种高顶皮军帽。
bush /bʊʃ; bʊʃ/ *n* **1** [C] low-growing plant with several or many woody stems coming up from the root. Cf *tree*, with a single trunk: 灌木(多枝而无主干的矮树)(参较 tree, 指有一主干的乔木): '*rose~*; 蔷薇树; 玫瑰树; '*fruit ~es*, eg currants, gooseberries. 灌木果树丛(如红醋栗、醋栗)。**2** [U] (often 常作 *the ~*) wild, uncultivated land, with or without trees or bushes, esp in Africa and Australia. (尤指非洲和澳大利亚的)未开垦的荒野。⇨ also *telegraph*. '*B~·man* /-mən; -mən/ *n* (*pl* **-men**) member of certain anciently settled tribes of West Southern Africa. 古代定居西南非洲的某些部落的土人。~*y* *adj* **1** covered with ~es. 灌木丛生的。**2** growing thickly; thick and rough: 密生的; 丛生的: ~*y eyebrows*; 浓眉; *a fox's ~y tail*. 狐狸的多毛的粗尾巴。
bushed /bʊʃt; bʊʃt/ *pred adj* (colloq) very tired. (口)疲惫不堪的。
bushel /ˈbʊʃl; ˈbʊʃəl/ *n* (before metrication) measure for grain and fruit (8 gallons). 蒲式耳(采用十进制前的谷物及水果量名，等于八加仑)。⇨ **App 5**. 参看附录五。*hide one's light under a ~*, be modest about one's abilities, good qualities, etc. 对于自己的能力、优点等持着谦逊态度; 不露锋芒。
busier, busiest, busily ⇨ **busy**.
busi·ness /ˈbɪznɪs; ˈbɪznɪs/ *n* **1** [U] buying and selling; commerce; trade: 买卖; 生意; 商业; 贸易: *We do not do much ~ with them*. 我们跟他们没有多少生意来往。*He's in the wool ~*, buys and sells wool. 他做羊毛生意。*He has set up in ~ as a bookseller*. 他在从事书籍的买卖。*He is in ~ for himself*, works on his own account, is not employed by others. 他自行经商(非受雇于他人)。*Which do you want to do, go into ~ or become a lawyer?* 你想干哪一行: 经商还是当律师? *on ~, for the purpose of doing ~*: 以办公事为目的; 因公; 有事: *Are you here on ~ or for pleasure?* 你在这里办公事还是

游玩？'~ **address**, address of one's shop, office, etc. 店铺、办公室等之地址；营业地址。Cf 参较 home address. '~ **hours**, hours during which ~ is done, eg 9am to 5pm. 营业时间(如上午九时至下午五时)。'~**-like** *adj* using, showing system, promptness, care, etc. 有系统的；迅速的；有条理的。'~**-man** /-mæn; -ˌmæn/ *n* (*pl* **-men**) man who is engaged in buying and selling, etc. 商人；生意人；实业家；工商业家。**2** [C] shop; commercial enterprise, etc: 商店；工商企业等: *He has a good ~ as a greengrocer.* 他开了一家很好的果菜商店。*He is the manager of three different ~es.* 他是三家商店的经理。*The newspapers advertise many small ~es for sale.* 报纸广告登出有许多小商店要出让。**3** [U] task, duty, concern; what has to be done: 任务；责任；事务: *It is a teacher's ~ to help his pupils.* 帮助学生是教师的责任。*I will make it my ~* (= will undertake) *to see that the money is paid promptly.* 我要负责督促迅速付款。*That's no ~ of yours*, is something about which you need not or should not trouble. 那事与你无关。**get down to** ~, start the work that must be done. 着手做必须做的事；言归正传。**mind one's own** ~, attend to one's own duties and not interfere with those of others. 管自己的事；少管闲事。**mean** ~, be in earnest. 当真；说正经的(不是开玩笑)。**send sb about his** ~, send him away and tell him not to interfere. 打发某人走开，叫他不要多管闲事。**4** [U] right: 权利: *You have no ~ to do that.* 你无权那样做。**5** (with *indef art*) difficult matter: (与不定冠词连用) 难事: *What a ~ it is getting the children off to school!* 打发孩子们上学是多难的事啊！**6** (often contemptuous) affair; subject; device: (常含轻蔑意味) 事情；题目；计策: *I'm sick of the whole ~*, tired of the affair. 我对这事情实在感到厌烦。**7** (colloq): (口): *the ~ end of a pin / a chisel, etc*, the sharp end, the end to be used. 针(凿子等)有尖(刃)的一端。**8** [U] (theatre) action, facial expression, etc of the actors in interpreting their parts (as distinct from the words they speak). (戏剧)演员的动作、表情等；做功(以别于台词,道白)。

busker /'bʌskə(r); 'bʌskɚ/ *n* person who entertains people informally for money in public places, eg by singing or dancing to queues outside cinemas. 为赚钱而在公共场所作非正式的表演，如在电影院外面向排队等候的人们唱歌或跳舞的)街头艺人。

bust[1] /bʌst; bʌst/ *n* **1** head and shoulders of a person cut in stone, or cast in bronze, gypsum, etc. (石雕、铜铸或石膏型的)半身像。**2** woman's bosom; measurement round the bosom and back. 女人的胸部；胸围尺寸。

bust[2] /bʌst; bʌst/ *vt, vi* (sl for **burst**) (burst之俚语) ~ *sth*, smash it. 击碎某物。**go** ~, fail; run out of money: 破产；缺钱: *The business went* ~. 这家商店破产了。□ *n* **have a** ~; **go on the** ~, a period of wild revelry. 纵情宴乐；纵饮。'~**-up** *n* (sl) quarrel. (俚)争吵。

bus·tard /'bʌstəd; 'bʌstɚd/ *n* large, swift-running bird. 鸨(一种体大善跑之鸟)。

bus·ter[1] /'bʌstə; 'bʌstɚ/ *n* (in compounds) bomb or shell that wrecks completely: (用于复合词中)有彻底摧毁力之炸弹或炮弹: 'dam-~; 能破坏水坝的炸弹; 'tank-~; 能击毁战车的炮弹; 'block-~, ie a bomb that may destroy a block of buildings. 能炸毁一街区建筑物的炸弹。

bus·ter[2] /'bʌstə(r); 'bʌstɚ/ *n* (US sl, as a form of address) fellow (= GB 英 mate[1] 1). (美俚, 称呼语)老兄；老友。

bustle[1] /'bʌsl; 'bʌsl/ *vi, vt* [VP2A, C, 15B] (cause to) move quickly and excitedly: (使)匆忙忙；慌忙: *Tell him to* ~, hurry. 叫他赶快。*Everyone was bustling about / in and out*, appearing to be very busy. 人人都在匆匆忙忙地来来去去(进进出出)。*She* ~d *the children off to school.* 她匆匆地把孩子们打发上学。□ *n* [U] excited activity: 兴奋的活动；匆忙；慌忙: *Everybody was in a* ~. 人人都很慌忙。*Why is there so much* ~? 为什

么这样忙乱？

bustle[2] /'bʌsl; 'bʌsl/ *n* frame formerly used to puff out a woman's skirt at the back. (昔时女裙臀部的)裙撑。

busy /'bɪzɪ; 'bɪzɪ/ *adj* (**busier, busiest**) **1** working; occupied; having much to do: 忙碌的；忙的: *The doctor is a ~ man.* 医生是一位忙碌的人。*He was ~ with / at / over his work.* 他忙于工作。**be ~ doing sth**, be in the process of doing it: 正忙于: *He was ~ getting ready for his journey.* 他正忙于准备旅行。**get** ~, start: 开始: *You'd better get ~ eating.* 你最好开始吃。'~**-body** *n* (*pl* **-bodies**) person who interferes in the affairs of other people, esp when his help is not wanted. 好管闲事的人；多事者。**2** full of activity: 充满活动的；繁忙的: *a ~ day*; 忙碌的一日; (of places) filled with active people, traffic, etc: (指地方)充满活动的人群、车辆等; 热闹的: *The shops are ~ before Christmas.* 商店在圣诞节前都很热闹。*This is one of the busiest underground stations in London.* 这是伦敦最热闹的地下车站之一。**3** (of a telephone line) in use. (指电话线路)通话中的。□ *vt* [VP14, 6A] ~ **oneself** (with); ~ **oneself** (by / in) **doing sth**, keep ~, occupy oneself with: 保持忙碌；使自己忙着: *He busied himself with all sorts of little tasks.* 他忙于做各种小事。*She busied herself by tidying up her desk.* 她忙于收拾她的书桌。**busi·ly** /'bɪzɪlɪ; 'bɪzɪlɪ/ *adv* in a ~ way: 忙碌地: *busily engaged in doing sth.* 忙于做某事。

but[1] /bʌt; bʌt/ *adv* only (now the usu word): 不过；只(此义今通常用 only): We can but try. 我们只有试一试。*He left but an hour ago.* 他不过一小时前才离去。*He's but a boy.* 他不过是一个孩子。**can not but** +*inf*, (formal) = can only + *inf*: (正式用语)不得不; 只好: *I cannot but think that ~*, am compelled to ...; 我不得不想...; *I could not but choose to go / I could not choose but go* (= had no alternative than to go). 我不得不去(我只好去)。*I cannot but admire* (= must admire, cannot help admiring) *your decision.* 我不得不钦佩你的决定。

but[2] /bət; bət; *strong form*: bʌt; bʌt/ (coordinating): (并列用法): *Tom was not there but his brother was.* 汤姆不在那儿，但是他的哥哥(弟弟)在那儿。*We tried to do it but couldn't.* 我们试着做，但是做不到。*He's a hardworking but not very intelligent boy.* 他是个用功但不很聪明的孩子。**2** (subordinating, with a neg implication): *I never go past my old school but I think* (= without thinking) *of Mr Wilkins, the headmaster.* 每当我走过我的母校时，我都想起校长长威尔金斯先生。*No man is so old but he may learn*, No man is too old to learn. 没有人因为太老而不能再学新的事物(活到老学到老)。*Never a month passes but she writes* (= in which she does not write) *to her old parents.* 她没有一个月不给她年老的双亲写信。

but[3] /bət; bət; *strong form*: bʌt; bʌt /*prep* (The uses of *but* as a *prep* and as a *conj* are not always clearly to be distinguished. The subject forms of the *pers pronouns* are often used after *but* meaning 'except', as if it were a *conj*. The object forms are also used, as if *but* were a *prep*). (but 作为介词及连接词的用法并非总能分得很清楚。在作 '除外' 解的 but 之后常用主格代词，这样使 but 好像是个连接词；也用宾格的，使 but 好似介词)。(With negatives, eg *no one, none, nothing,* and interrogatives, eg *who,* and such words as *all, every one*) except, excluding: (与 no one, none, nothing 等否定词连用; 又与 who 等疑问词连用; 也与 all, every one 等字连用)除...外: *Nothing but disaster would come from such a plan.* 除了招致灾祸，则无益处。*They're all wrong but me.* 除我以外，他们全错了。*None but the brave deserve the fair* (prov). (谚)只有英雄才配美人。*Who but Gloria would do such a thing?* 除了格洛里亚以外还有谁愿意干这种事？*first / next / last but one / two / three:* 第二(三, 四); 第三(四, 五); 倒数第二(三, 四): *Take the next turning but one* (= the second turning) *on your left.* 在你左方第二个转弯处转弯。*I*

live in the last house *but two* (= the third house from the end) *in this street.* 我住在这条街上倒数第三家。 *Smith was the last but one* (= second to last) *to arrive.* 史密斯是倒数第二个到达的。 '*but for*, except for, without: 若非; 要是: *But for your help we should not have finished in time.* 要不是你帮忙, 我们不会及时完工。 *But for the rain* (= If it had not rained) *we should have had a pleasant journey.* 要不是下雨, 我们那次旅行就惬意了。 '*but that*, except that: 要不是为了; 若非: *He would have helped us but that* (= if it had not been for the fact that) *he was short of money at the time.* 要不是他那时候没有钱, 他会帮助我们的。 *but then*, on the other hand: 不过; 在另一方面: *London is a noisy place, but then it's also the place where you get the best entertainment.* 伦敦是一个闹市, 不过另一方面它也是能给你最好娱乐的地方。

but[4] /bʌt/ *rel pron* (rare; formal) who/that do/does not: (罕; 正式用语)其人(或该物)不: *There is not one of us but wishes* (= not one of us who does not wish) *to help you.* 我们中间没有一人不愿意帮助你。 *There are few of us but* (= few of us who do not) *admire your determination.* 我们中间很少人不钦佩你的决心。

bu·tane /'bjuːteɪn; 'bjuten/ *n* [U] gas produced from petroleum supplied in metal containers for use in houses, etc, where there is no piped supply of gas (for cooking, heating, lighting, etc). (无煤气管设备之家庭烹调、取暖、照明等所用之)铁桶装的煤气; 钢瓶煤气。

butch /butʃ; bʌtʃ/ *adj* (colloq) (of a woman) having tendencies towards masculine behaviour and clothes; (of a man) exaggeratedly masculine. (口)(指女人)行为及服装倾向男性化的; (指男人)过于男子气的。 □ *n* such a person. 倾向于男性行为及服装的女人; 过于男子气的男人。

butcher /'butʃə(r); 'bʌtʃɚ/ *n* 1 person who kills, cuts up and sells animals for food. 屠夫; 肉商。 *~'s meat*, meat excluding poultry, game and bacon; 屠宰商所卖的肉; 鲜肉(不包括家禽、猎物及腌肉); *the ~'s*, the ~'s shop. 鲜肉店。 2 person who has caused unnecessary death, eg a general who wastes the lives of soldiers; person who kills savagely and needlessly. 造成不必要死亡的人(如无谓牺牲兵员之将领); 作野蛮及不必要屠杀的人; 刽子手。 □ *vt* [VP6A] kill violently, esp with a knife. (尤指用刀)残杀。 **~y** *n* [U] 1 (attrib) ~'s trade. (用作定语)屠宰业: *He's in the ~y business.* 他是干屠宰业的。 2 needless and cruel killing of people. 屠杀; 残杀(人类)。

but·ler /'bʌtlə(r); 'bʌtlɚ/ *n* head manservant (in charge of the wine-cellar, pantry, valuables, etc). 仆役长(管酒窖、食品室、贵重物品等)。

butt[1] /bʌt; bʌt/ *n* 1 large cask for wine or ale. 大酒桶。 2 large barrel for storing rainwater, eg from roofs. 盛装雨水(如自屋顶流下者)之大桶。

butt[2] /bʌt; bʌt/ *n* 1 thicker (usu wooden) end (esp of a fishing-rod or rifle). 较粗的一端(通常为木制); (尤指)钓鱼竿之柄。 (步枪之)枪托。 2 unburned end of a smoked cigar or cigarette, end of a used candle. (雪茄、香烟或用过之蜡烛之)未燃烧之一端。

butt[3] /bʌt; bʌt/ *n* 1 (usu *pl* with *def art*) shooting-range; the targets and the mound of earth behind them (used for practice in firing rifles). (通常用复数,并与定冠词连用)靶场; (供练习步枪射击用的)靶垛; 靶子。 2 person who is a target for ridicule, jokes, etc: 成为嘲笑对象的人: *He is the ~ of the whole school.* 他是全校的人所嘲笑的对象。

butt[4] /bʌt; bʌt/ *vt, vi* 1 [VP6A, 15A] push with the head (as a goat does): 以头抵(如山羊); 以头撞: *~ someone in the stomach.* 以头撞某人的腹部。 2 [VP2C] *~ in*, (colloq) force oneself into the conversation or company of others; interrupt sb: (口)插嘴; 介入; 闯入; 打扰: *May I ~ in?* 我可以打个岔吗? [VP3A] *~ into*, run into, head or front first. 以头或正面碰撞。

but·ter /'bʌtə(r); 'bʌtɚ/ *n* [U] 1 fatty food substance

made from cream by churning, used on bread, in cooking, etc: 奶油; 白脱油; 黄油: *~ will/would not melt in sb's mouth*, he has a demure and innocent appearance. 一本正经的样子。 '*~·bean*, large, dried haricot ~. 大的干扁豆。 '*~·cup* *n* wild plant with yellow flowers. 金凤花(开黄花的野生植物)。 '*~·fin·gers* *n* person unable to hold things well, esp one unable to catch a ball. 拿东西拿不稳的人; (尤指)常失球的选手。 '*~·milk* *n* liquid that remains after ~ has been separated from milk. 将奶油提出后的奶浆。 '*~·scotch* *n* [U] sweet substance made by boiling sugar and ~ together. (用奶油与糖熬成的)奶油糖果。 2 substance similar to ~, made from other materials: 人造奶油(用其他物质制成之类似奶油的东西): cocoa ~; 可脂; peanut ~. 花生酱。 □ *vt* 1 [VP6A] spread ~ on (esp bread); cook with ~. 涂奶油于(面包等); 用奶油烹调。 ⇨ also **bread**. 2 [VP15B] *~ sb up*, flatter. 阿谀; 谄媚。

but·ter·fly /'bʌtəflaɪ; 'bʌtɚ,flaɪ/ *n* (*pl* **-flies**) insect with four wings, often brightly coloured, and feelers. 蝴蝶。 '*~ (stroke)* *n* stroke used in swimming, both arms moving upward and outward at the same time as an up and down kick of the feet. 蝶泳(双脚上下踢动时, 双臂同时向上并向外划)。

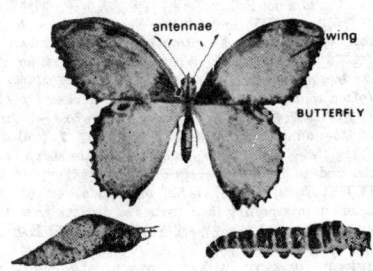

three stages in the life of a butterfly

but·tery /'bʌtərɪ; 'bʌtrɪ/ *n* (*pl* **-ries**) (in some GB universities) place where provisions (bread, butter, ale) are kept and from which they are served. (在某些英国大学里)放置及供应食物(面包、奶油及啤酒)的处所。

but·tock /'bʌtək; 'bʌtək/ *n* 1 either side of that part of the body on which a person sits: 臀(屁股之任一半): *an injection of penicillin in the left ~.* 在左臀注射一针盘尼西林。 2 (*pl*) (复) *the ~s*, the rump, the bottom: 臀部; 屁股: *a smack on the ~s.* 打在屁股上的一巴掌。 ⇨ the illus at **leg**. 参看 leg 之插图。

but·ton /'bʌtn; 'bʌtn/ *n* 1 small, usu round, bit of bone, metal, etc for fastening, on an article of clothing, or sewn on as an ornament. 钮扣。 '*~·hole* *n* hole through which a ~ is passed; flower worn in a ~hole (esp in the lapel of a jacket or coat). 钮扣孔; 插于钮扣孔上之花(如戴于男子外衣之翻领上面者)。 □ *vt* [VP6A] hold sb by the ~hole (to get his attention). 抓住某人的钮扣孔(以引起他的注意)。 '*~·hook* *n* hook for pulling a ~ into place through a ~hole. (牵引钮扣穿过扣孔之)钮扣钩; 绊钩。 '*~·wood* *n* tall tree with a ~-shaped fruit, related to the sycamore; its wood. 悬木属之植物(树干高, 果实如钮扣状); 篠悬木。 2 small, round ~-like object, esp one that, when pushed, makes an electrical contact, eg for a bell: 钮扣形之圆形小东西; 钮形物; (尤指开关电器之)按钮(如按电铃者): *press/push/touch the ~.* 按电钮。 3 small, unopened mushroom. 未张开的小蘑菇。 4 (*pl*) (colloq) boy wearing uniform, employed as a page in a club, hotel, etc. (复)(口)俱乐部、旅馆等处穿着制服的男侍役。

bell-hop. □ *vt, vi* [VP6A, 15B, 2A] ~ *(up/down)* fasten with a ~ or ~s: (以钮扣)扣上; 扣起; 扣紧: ~ *(up) one's coat;* 扣起外衣的钮扣; *a dress that* ~*s down the back.* 扣在背部扣钮扣的女装。*My collar won't* ~ *down,* I can't ~ it. 我的领子扣不起来。~ *up,* (colloq) complete safely, at last: (口)终于顺利完成: *That's that job* ~*ed up!* 也就是说, 那项工作终于顺利完成了! ,~*ed-up, adj* (colloq) (of a person) silent and reserved. (口)(指人)沉默寡言的。

but·tress /'bʌtrɪs; 'bʌtrɪs/ *n* support built against a wall, ⇨ the illus at **church**; (fig) prop; sth that supports: 撑墙; 拱壁(参看 church 之插图); (喻)支持物; 支柱: *the* ~*es of society/the constitution.* 社会(宪法)的支柱。□ *vt* [VP6A, 15B] ~ *(up),* strengthen, hold up (by building a ~); (fig) support, strengthen: (筑扶墙以)支撑; (喻)支持; 加强: ~ *up an argument.* 支持一论点。

buxom /'bʌksəm; 'bʌksəm/ *adj* (of women) good-looking healthy-looking and well covered with flesh. (指妇女)健美丰满的。

buy /baɪ; baɪ/ *vt, vi* (*pt, pp* bought /bɔːt; bɔt/) **1** [VP6A, 15B, 12B, 13B, 2A, U] get in return for money, get by paying a price: 购买: *Can money buy happiness?* 金钱能买幸福吗? *I bought this car from Chris.* 我从克里斯手中买得这辆汽车。*Buy one for me.* 给我买一个。*Buy me one.* 给我买一个。*I must buy myself a new shirt.* 我必须给我自己买件新衬衫。*He bought it for £2.* 他花了二英镑买它。*He bought them for / at 10p each.* 他以每个十便士的价钱买下它们。*Prices are low—buy now!* 廉价出售——快来买吧! **buy sth back;** 再买回来: *He sold his house and then bought it back again.* 他把他的房子卖掉, 然后又买回来了。**buy sth in, (a)** buy a stock of: 买一大批: *buy in coal for the winter.* 买一大批煤过冬。**(b)** (at an auction sale) bid for and obtain (one's own goods) by offering a higher price than the highest offered by others (when other bids are considered too low). 抬高自己的价钱买回(自己的货物)。**buy sth off,** get rid of (an unjust claim, a blackmailer) by making a payment. 付款摆脱(无理要求, 勒索者)。**buy sb out,** pay (sb) to give up a post, property, etc or a share in one's own business. 买通(某人)使放弃职位、财产等, 或自己公司的股份。贿赂(某人)。**buy sb over,** bribe or corrupt (sb). 贿赂(某人); 向…行贿。**buy sth up,** buy all or as much as possible of (sth). 全数买进; 尽量收购(某物)。**2** [VP6A] obtain at a sacrifice: 牺牲…以换得; 换得: *He bought fame at the expense of his health and happiness.* 他牺牲了健康和幸福换得名誉。*Victory was dearly bought.* 胜利是以很高的代价换得的。□ *n* (colloq) purchase: (口)购买; 买得: *a good buy,* a bargain. 便宜的买卖; 买得便宜的东西。**buyer** *n* person who buys. 购买者; 采购者; 买主。**buyers' market,** state of affairs when goods are plentiful and money scarce, so that low prices favour buyers. 购买者市场(市场货物充斥银根紧峭, 因而市价下跌有利于购买者的情况)。

buzz /bʌz; bʌz/ *vi, vt* **1** [VP2A, C] make a humming sound (as of bees or machinery in rapid motion). 作嗡嗡声(如蜜蜂); 作营营声(如疾速运转中的机器)。**2** [VP2C] move rapidly or excitedly: 急速或兴奋地活动: ~ *about/around,* 匆匆忙忙地来来去去; ~*ing along the road.* 沿路急急而行。~ *off,* (sl) go away. (俚)离去。**3** [VP2A] (of the ears) be filled with a noise: (指耳)充满嗡嗡之声; 鸣: *My ears began* ~*ing.* 我觉得耳鸣。**4** [VP6A] (of an aircraft) fly near to or low over (another plane) in a threatening manner: (指飞机, 以威胁的姿态)逼近或低飞掠过(另一架飞机): *Two fighters* ~*ed the airliner.* 两架战斗机掠过那架客机。□ *n* humming (of bees or other insects); sound of people talking, of whirling machinery, etc. (蜜蜂或其他昆虫的)嗡嗡声; (机器转动的)营营声。**give sb a** ~, make a telephone call to him. 给某人打电话。~*er n* electrical device that produces a ~ (eg to signal

time, a telephone call) when the current flows. 蜂音器 (一种通过电流后发出嗡嗡声的电铃, 用以报时、通知接电话等)。

buz·zard /'bʌzəd; 'bʌzəd/ *n* kind of hawk. 鵟; 鵟鹰。

by¹ /baɪ; baɪ/ *adv part* **1** near: 在近旁; 在附近: *He hid the money when nobody was by.* 当附近无人的时候, 他把钱藏起来。**standby,** ⇨ **stand²(10). 2** past: 从旁经过过: *He hurried by without a word.* 他匆匆经过未说一句话。*Fame passed him by.* 他失去了成名的机会。*I can't get by,* can't pass. 我不能通过。*The time has / is gone by* (= is past) *when ....* …的时代已经过去了。**3** *lay/ put/set sth by,* keep it, save it, for future use. 留作将来之用; 储藏起以备将来之需。**4** (in phrases) **by and by,** later on. 不久; 不一会儿。**by the by(e), by the way,** (used to introduce a new topic, or sth that has been forgotten). 且说; 对了; 顺便提起(用以提出一个新的话题, 或提起一件已经忘记的事)。**by and large,** on the whole; taking everything into consideration. 大体而言; 一般而论。

by² /baɪ; baɪ/ *prep* **1** near; at or to the side of; beside: 靠近; 在…近旁; 在…旁边; 向…旁边: *Come and sit by me/by my side.* 来坐在我的身边。*My house is by the river.* 我的家在河边。*We had a day by the sea.* 我们在海边过了一天。**by oneself,** alone: 独自地: *He went for a holiday (all) by himself.* 他独自一人去度假。⇨ **12** below. 参看下列第 12 义。**have sth by one,** have it handy, within easy reach: 手边有某物; 把某物放在伸手可及处: *It's useful to have a good dictionary by you when you're reading.* 当你在读书的时候, 手边放一本好词典是很有用的。**stand by sb,** support him. 支持某人。**2** (in reading the cardinal points) towards: (方位读法)偏向: *North by East,* one point towards the East from the North, ie between N and NNE; 正北偏东(即介于正北与北北东之间); *East by North,* one point North of East, ie between E and ENE. 正东偏北(即介于正东与东北东之间)。⇨ the illus at **compass.** 参看 compass 之插图。**3** (showing direction of movement) (= by way of) through, along, across, over: (表示移动的方向)通过; 沿; 横过; 越过: *We came by the fields, not by the roads.* 我们经由田间而来, 不是由大路而来。*Did you come by the nearest road?* 你是由最近的路来的吗? *We travelled to Paris by Dover and Calais.* 我们经由多佛与卡利斯而到巴黎。**4** past: 经过: *I go by* (= I pass) *the post office every morning on my way to work.* 我每天早晨上班都经过邮局。*He walked by me without speaking.* 他从我身旁走过没有说话。**5** (of time, esp to indicate conditions and circumstances) during: (指时间, 尤表示情况和环境)在…期间: *The enemy attacked by night.* 敌人乘夜间来袭。(emphasizing the circumstances — under cover of darkness, etc. 强调环境 — 在黑暗的掩护下。Cf 参较 Everything was quiet *during* the night. 在夜间一切都是宁静的)。*Do you prefer travelling by night or by day?* 你喜欢在夜间旅行, 还是白天旅行? *We went for a sail on the lake by moonlight.* 我们在月光下去湖上泛舟。*It's no use trying to escape by daylight.* 在白昼想逃跑是办不到的。**6** (of time) as soon as; not later than; when (the time indicated) comes: (指时间)一到; 不迟于; 当(某时候)时: *Can you finish the work by tomorrow?* 你能在明天以前把工作做完吗? *He ought to be here by this time/by now.* 此此刻(现在)应该已经来到这里了。*They were tired out by evening.* 他们至傍晚已疲倦极了。*By the time (that) you get there (that is almost always omitted) it will be dark.* 等到你到达那里的时候, 天会黑了(此种用法的那几乎总被省略)。**7** (to form adverbial phrases of time, length, weight, number): (形成时间、长度、重量、数目等之副词短语): *rent a house by the year;* 按年租屋; *hire a bicycle by the day,* eg £5 for one day's use; 按日租脚踏车(例如: 每日五英镑); *engage a clerk by the month;* 按月雇请办事员; *pay a labourer by the day/the hour;* 按日(按时)付工人工资; *sell cloth by the yard/coal by the ton/eggs by the dozen, etc;* 论码卖布(论吨卖煤; 论打卖蛋等): *freight*

charged by weight/volume; 按重量(体积)算运费的(装在车船上的)货物; a room 20 ft by 30 ft. 长二十英尺宽三十英尺的房间。 **8** through the agency, means, or instrumentality of: 由于…之作用,方法或工具;借着;由;被: *The streets are lighted by electricity.* 街道用电照明。 *This church was designed by Wren.* 这座教堂是雷恩设计的。 *He makes a living by teaching.* 他靠教书为生。 *He was shot by a sniper.* 他被狙击兵击毙。 *The man was killed by a falling tree/by lightning.* 那人被倒下来的树打死(被闪电死毙)。 (Note that by *lightning* is instrumentality, not instrument. 注意: '雷电'系一种作用,非工具。 Cf 参较 The rat was killed by Tom with a stick. 那只老鼠被汤姆用棍打死。 ⇨ **with (3)**.) **9** (indicating path or means of travel, transport, conveyance): (表示旅行、运输等之路线、工具或方法): *travel by land/sea/air*; 由陆路(水路、航空)旅行; *by bus/car/boat, etc* 乘公共汽车(汽车、船等); *send sth by post/hand.* 由邮局(专差)递送某物。 **10** (indicating a part of the body that is touched, etc): (表被接触等的身体之一部份): *take sb by the hand*; 拉他的手; *seize sb by the hair*; 抓住某人的头发; *grab sb by the scruff of his neck.* 抓住某人的颈背。 **11** *know/learn sth by heart*, so that one can repeat it from memory. 诸记某事; 牢记在心; 能背出。 *know sb by name/reputation/sight*, know only his name, etc but not know him personally. 只知道某人的姓名(名声,仅识某人之面)。 **12** (in adverbial phrases of manner) (用于表示方式或态度之副词短语中): *by accident/mistake*, accidentally, not on purpose or intentionally. 由于意外(错误);非有意。 *by chance/good fortune*, as the result of chance or good fortune. 由于机遇(幸运)。 *by oneself*, without help. 亲自;独自;无他人帮助。 ⇨ **1** above. 参看上列第1义。 **13** in accordance with; in agreement with: 根据;依照;依: *by request of my employer*; 由于我的雇主的请求; *by your leave*, with your permission; 如果你许可的话; 请原谅;恕我冒昧; *by (the terms of) Article 3 of the Treaty.* 根据条约之第3条(之条文)。 **14** according to: 根据;依据;按: *judging by appearances*; 就外表而论; *by rights*, rightly. 合理地; 正当地; 正确地. *By my watch it is 2 o'clock.* 按我的表, 现在是两点钟。 *That's nothing to go by,* One should not form judgements by that. 那是不(作为)根据遽下断语的。 **15** to the extent of: 至…之程度: *The bullet missed me by two inches.* 那枪弹差两英寸就击中我。 *It needs to be longer by two feet.* 它需要再长两英尺。 *He's too clever by half*, much too smart. 他实在太聪明了。 ⇨ **far² (2) 16** (in oaths) as surely as I believe in: (用于誓言中)如我对于…的信仰一样地确然; *I swear by Almighty God that....* 我对着全能的神发誓…。 *He swore by all that he held sacred that ....* 他对着他所崇奉为神圣的一切发誓…。 **17** (to express square or cubic measurement): (表示平方或立方的度量): *a carpet 30 metres by 20 metres.* 三十米乘二十米宽的地毯。 **18** (arith) (to express division, − *divided by*): (算术)(表示除): *15 by 3 is/equals 5.* 15除以3等于5.

bye /baɪ; baɪ/ *n* **1** sth subordinate or incidental: 附属

物;附带的东西: *by the bye.* 且说; 对了; 顺便提起。 ⇨ **by¹ (4)**. **2** (cricket) run scored on a ball that passes the batsman and the wicket-keeper. (板球)球越过击球手及守门员所得之分。

bye-bye /'baɪ-baɪ; 'baɪ,baɪ/ *n* (child's word for) sleep, bed: (儿语)睡觉; 床铺: *go to* ∼s 'baɪ baɪz; 'baɪ,baɪz/. 去睡觉。 □ *int* /,baɪ 'baɪ; 'baɪ'baɪ/ (colloq) goodbye. (口)再见。

by-elec·tion /'baɪ-ɪlekʃn; 'baɪɪˌlekʃən/ *n* election made necessary by the death or resignation of a member during the life of Parliament. (因国会议员任期未满而死亡或辞职而必须举行的)补选。 ⇨ **general election**.

by·gone /'baɪgɒn US: -gɔːn; 'baɪˌgɔn/ *adj* past: 过去的; 已往的: *in* ∼ *days*, in the time now past. 在已往的日子;在过去的时代。 □ *n* (*pl*) the past; past offences. (复)过去的事;过去的过错。 *Let* ∼*s be* ∼*s*, Forgive and forget the past. 过去的事让它过去吧; 既往不咎。

by-law, bye-law /'baɪlɔː; 'baɪ,lɔ/ *n* law or regulation made by a local, rather than a central, authority. 地方政府机关所制定的法规; 地方法。

by-pass /'baɪpɑːs US: -pæs; 'baɪ,pæs/ *n* new, wide road passing round a heavily populated urban area or village to take through traffic. (环绕人口稠密之市区或乡村借以畅通车辆交通之)新辟的宽路; 辅助道路。 □ *vt* [VP6A] **1** provide with a ∼: 在…外侧辟一条道路: ∼ *a village/falls on a river.* 在乡村外围(环绕河上之瀑布)辟一条辅助道路。 **2** make a detour round (a town, etc): 绕道而过(市镇等); (fig) (喻) *Let's* ∼ *that proposal*, ignore it. 我们别理该项提议吧。

by·path /'baɪpɑːθ US: -pæθ; 'baɪ,pæθ/ *n* less important or less direct path. 小道; 僻径。

by·play /'baɪpleɪ; 'baɪ,ple/ *n* [U] (theatre) action apart from that of the main story; dumb-show of minor characters. (戏剧)与剧情无关的动作; 配角的穿插动作。

by-prod·uct /'baɪprɒdʌkt; 'baɪ,prɑdəkt/ *n* [C] substance obtained during the manufacture of some other substance: (制造某物时的)副产品: *Ammonia, coal-tar and coke are valuable* ∼*s obtained in the manufacture of coal-gas.* 阿摩尼亚、煤炭油和焦炭都是制造煤气时的重要副产品。

by·road /'baɪrəʊd; 'baɪ,rod/ *n* side road; road that is not much used. 支路;街道;僻路。

by·stander /'baɪstændə(r); 'baɪ,stændə/ *n* person standing near but not taking part in an event or activity. 旁观者; 旁立而不参加活动之者。 *She was only an innocent* ∼. 她只是一个无辜的旁观者。

by·way /'baɪweɪ; 'baɪ,we/ *n* secondary or side road 偏僻小路; 旁道; (fig) (喻)∼*s of history/literature, etc*, less known departments of history, etc. 历史(文学等)的冷僻部门。

by·word /'baɪwɜːd; 'baɪ,wɜd/ *n* person, place, etc regarded and spoken of as a notable example: (通常因恶事而)为众人所谈论的人,地方等; 笑柄; 话柄: *She became the* ∼ *of the village.* 她成了村中的话柄。 *The place was a* ∼ *for iniquity.* 此地以多罪恶之事出名。

C c

C, c /siː; si/ (*pl* C's, c's /siːz; siz/) the third letter of the English alphabet, symbol for the Roman numeral 100, ⇨ **App 4**. 英文字母的第三个字母; 罗马数字表示100的符号(参看附录四)。

cab /kæb; kæb/ *n* **1** vehicle (now usu motorised, − *taxicab*) that may be hired for short journeys: 出租汽车; 计程车: *Shall we go by bus or take a cab?* 我们是乘公共汽车呢, 还是乘出租汽车呢? '**cab·man** /-mən; -men/, (*pl* -**men**) driver of a cab. 计程车司机。 '**cab-rank** *n* row of cabs waiting to be hired. 待租的出租汽车所排成

的行列。 '**cab·stand** *n* place where cabs are authorized to wait for customers. 经当局指定的出租汽车候客停车站。 ⇨ **hansom; taxi**. **2** part of a railway engine for the driver and fireman; part of a bus, lorry, etc for the driver. 火车机车内供司机及司炉所坐之处; (公共汽车、卡车等之)司机台。

ca·bal /kə'bæl; kə'bæl/ *n* (group of persons who carry on) secret intrigue (esp in politics). (尤指政治之)阴谋集团; 阴谋活动。

cab·aret /'kæbəreɪ US: ,kæbə'reɪ; 'kæbə,ret/ *n* (also

亦作 '~ **show**) entertainment (songs, dancing, etc) provided in a restaurant etc, while guests are at table. 餐馆等中的歌舞表演。

cab·bage /'kæbɪdʒ; 'kæbɪdʒ/ *n* [C] (kinds of) cultivated plant with a round head (often called the *heart*) of thick greenish-white or reddish-purple leaves, ⇨ the illus at **vegetable**; [U] these leaves cooked as a vegetable or eaten as salad, ⇨ **coleslaw**. 甘蓝(俗称包心菜或洋白菜)(参看 vegetable 之插图); (作为蔬菜烹煮吃的或作为生菜吃的)甘蓝菜叶。

cabby /'kæbɪ; 'kæbɪ/ *n* (colloq) driver of a cab. (口) 出租汽车司机。

ca·ber /'keɪbə(r); 'kebə/ *n* trunk of a roughly trimmed young fir-tree tossed in games (in the Highlands of Scotland) as a trial of strength and skill: (苏格兰高地竞技会中投掷以测验臂力及技巧的)小枞树干: *toss the ~.* 投掷枞树干; 投棒竞力。

cabin /'kæbɪn; 'kæbɪn/ *n* **1** room in a ship or aircraft, esp (in a ship) one for sleeping in. 船舱; 飞机舱; (尤指)船上可以睡觉的房舱。 '~ **cruiser** *n* large motor-boat with a ~ or ~s. 有舱房设备的大游艇。 **2** small, usu roughly made house (eg of logs); railway signal-box. (通常为简陋的)小屋; 木屋; (铁路的)信号房。

cabi·net /'kæbɪnɪt; 'kæbənɪt/ *n* **1** piece of furniture with drawers or shelves for storing or displaying things: 有抽屉或格架以储存或陈列物件之家具; 橱柜: a '*medicine* ~; 药柜; a '*filing* ~, for storing letters, documents; 文件档案柜; a '*china* ~, often with a glass front, for displaying ornamental china. 陈列装饰性瓷器之玻璃橱。 '~-**maker** *n* skilled workman who makes fine furniture. 家具木工; 细木工。 **2** plastic, wooden or metal container for radio or record-playing equipment. 收音机或唱机之塑胶、木质或金属外壳; 箱。 **3** group of men (chief ministers of state) chosen by the head of the government (the prime minister in GB) to be responsible for government administration and policy. (政府最高首长, 如英国的首相, 所任命负责行政事务及国策的) 内阁(包括各部会首长)。 '**C~ Minister**, one of these men. 内阁阁员。 **4** (old use) private room. (旧用法)私室。

cable /'keɪbl; 'kebl/ *n* **1** [C, U] (length of) thick, strong rope (of fibre or wire strands), used for making ships fast; rope or chain of an anchor. (一截)系船用的绳索或铁索; 锚索; 锚链。 **2** '~('s)-**length** *n* 100 fathoms one-tenth of a nautical mile. 索(长度单位=100 英寻, 或 ¹/₁₀ 海里)。 ⇨ **App 5.** 参看附录五。 **3** thick rope of wire strands for supporting a bridge, etc. (吊吊桥等的) 金属索; 缆。 '~-**car**, ' ~-**railway**, one up a steep hillside, worked by a ~ and a stationary engine; funicular railway. (攀登陡坡之) 缆车; 索车; 缆道车; 缆索铁路。 **4** protected bundle of insulated wires (laid underground or on the ocean bottom) for carrying messages by electric telegraph; message so carried (= ~gram). (用以通电报的) 地下电缆; 海底电缆; 电报(由地下电缆等所传送者)。 **5** insulated wires for conveying electric power overhead (⇨ the illus at **pylon**) or underground. (用以输送电力的架空或地下) 电缆(参看 pylon 之插图)。 □ *vt, vi* [VP6A, 2A] send (a message), communicate, inform (sb) by ~ (4). 打电报; 与(某人)通电报; 打电报通知(某人)。 '~-**gram** /'keɪblgræm; 'kebl,græm/ *n ~* and telegram. 海底电报; (有线)电报。

ca·boodle /kə'buːdl; kə'budl/ *n* (sl) *the whole* ~, (of persons or things) all; the lot. (俚)(指人或物)全体; 全部。

ca·boose /kə'buːs; kə'bus/ *n* **1** room on a ship's deck in which cooking is done. 甲板上的厨房。 **2** (US) small van at the end of a freight train for the use of the train men. (美)(铁路货车尾部供车上人员用的)守车。

ca'canny /kɑː'kænɪ; kɑ,kænɪ/ *n* workers' policy of restricting output (by working slowly). (工人限制生产量之)怠工政策。

ca·cao /kə'kɑːəʊ; kə'keo/ *n* **1** (also 亦作 '~-**bean**) seed of a tropical tree from which cocoa and chocolate

are made. 可可子 (一种热带树之种子, 可制可可及巧克力)。 **2** (also 亦作 '~-**tree**) the tree. 可可树。

cache /kæʃ; kæʃ/ *n* (hiding-place for) food and store left (eg by explorers) for later use. (探险者等)隐藏以供再来时用的食物及其他物品; 此种隐藏所。 □ *vt* place in a ~. 置于隐藏剖。

ca·chet /'kæʃeɪ US: kə'ʃeɪ; kæ'ʃe/ *n* distinguishing mark (to prove excellence, authenticity). (证明品质精良、真正无伪之)标记; 正字标记。

ca·chou /'kæʃuː US: kə'ʃuː; kə'ʃu/ *n* scented sweet formerly used by smokers to disguise the odour of tobacco in the breath. (从前吸烟者用以掩盖口中烟臭之)口香丸。

cackle /'kækl; 'kækl/ *n* [U] noise made by a hen after laying an egg; [C] loud laugh; [U] foolish talk. (母鸡生蛋后的)咯咯叫声; 大笑; 无意义的话。 □ *vi* (of a hen) make this noise; (of a person) talk or laugh noisily. (指母鸡)咯咯叫; (指人)高声谈笑。 **cack·ler** *n*

ca·coph·ony /kæ'kɒfənɪ; kæ'kɑfənɪ/ *n* loud, unpleasant mixture of sounds; discord (3). 不调和的声音; 刺耳的声音。 **ca·coph·onous** /-nəs; -nəs/ *adj*

cac·tus /'kæktəs; 'kæktəs/ *n* (*pl* ~**es, cacti** /'kæktaɪ; 'kæktaɪ/) (sorts of) plant from hot, dry climates with a thick, fleshy stem, usu with no leaves and covered with clusters of spines or prickles. 仙人掌; 仙人球。

cactuses

cad /kæd; kæd/ *n* person guilty of or capable of dishonourable behaviour. 行为下流的人; 可能做卑鄙事的人; 恶棍。 **cad·dish** /'kædɪʃ; 'kædɪʃ/ *adj* of or like a cad: 下流人的; 恶棍的; 卑鄙的: *a caddish trick.* 卑鄙的手段。

ca·daver /kə'deɪvə(r) US: kə'dævər; kə'dævə/ *n* corpse. 死尸。 **~·ous** /kə'dævərəs; kə'dævərəs/ *adj* looking like a corpse; deadly pale. 看来象死尸的; 面如死灰的; 苍白的。

caddy¹, caddie /'kædɪ; 'kædɪ/ *n* (*pl* -**dies**) person who is paid to carry a golfer's clubs for him round the course. 在高尔夫球场上受雇替人背球棒之人; 球童。

caddy² /'kædɪ; 'kædɪ/ *n* small box for holding the dried leaves used for making tea. 茶叶罐; 茶叶盒。

ca·dence /'keɪdns; 'kedns/ *n* rhythm in sound; the rise and fall of the voice in speaking; (music) sequence of sounds moving towards a pause or an end. 韵律; 节奏; 拍子; 说话时声调的抑扬顿挫; (音乐)终止。

ca·denza /kə'denzə; kə'denzə/ *n* ornamental passage to be played by the soloist, usu near the end of a movement, in an instrumental concerto. 装饰乐段(协奏曲中通常在近于一个乐章之尾部的技巧独奏部分)。

ca·det /kə'det; kə'det/ *n* **1** student at a naval, military or air force college. (陆、海、空军之)军校学员。 '~ **corps** *n* (at some GB schools) organization that gives military training to older boys. (某些英国中学之)学生军训队。 **2** young person under training for a profession: 受专业训练中的年轻人: '*police* ~*s*; 警察训练班的学员; *British Council* ~*s.* 在英国文化协会受专业训练的年轻人。

cadge /kædʒ; kædʒ/ *vt, vi* [VP6A, 2A] ~ (**from**), beg; (try to) get by begging: 乞求; 乞讨; 讨得: ~ *a meal from Auntie Ruby;* 向鲁比姑妈讨一顿饭吃; *be always cadging.* 总是讨着讨吃。 **cad·ger** *n* person who ~s, beggar. 乞讨者; 乞丐。

cad·mium /'kædmɪəm; 'kædmɪəm/ *n* [U] soft, silvery-white tin-like metal (symbol Cd). 镉(性软, 银白

色, 似锡之金属, 化学符号 Cd).

cadre /'kɑːdə(r); 'kædrɪ/ *n* **1** framework, 骨架; 支架; 骨干。 **2** (mil) permanent establishment of a regiment, that can be expanded when necessary; hence, small group of important persons. (军)(必要时可以扩充的)核心组织; (由此产生)重要干部。

Caesar /'siːzə(r); 'sizə/ *n* title of the Roman emperors from Augustus to Hadrian; any Roman emperor. 古罗马帝国 (自 Augustus 至 Hadrian) 皇帝之称号; 罗马皇帝。 **~·ian** /sɪ'zɛərɪən; sɪ'zɪrɪən/ ('section / 'birth') delivery of a child by cutting the walls of the abdomen and uterus. 剖腹取儿(术);帝王式切开术。

caesura /sɪ'zjʊərə US: -'ʒʊərə; sɪ'ʒʊrə/ *n* point at which a pause naturally occurs in a line of verse. 一行诗中自然停顿的地方。

café /'kæfeɪ US: kæ'feɪ; 'kɛfe/ *n* (in Europe) place where the public may buy and drink coffee, beer, wine, spirits, etc; (in GB) tea-shop, small restaurant at which meals (but not alcoholic drinks) may be bought. (在欧洲)咖啡馆; 酒店 (可以购饮咖啡、啤酒、葡萄酒、烈酒等的地方); (在英国)茶馆; 小餐馆 (但不供应酒类)。 **~-au-lait** /ˌkæfeɪ əʊ 'leɪ, ˌkæfɪ'le/ *n* (F) coffee with milk. (法)牛奶咖啡。

cafe·teria /ˌkæfɪ'tɪərɪə; ˌkæfə'tɪrɪə/ *n* restaurant at which customers collect their meals on trays at counters and carry them to tables. 自助餐厅。

caff /kæf; kæf/ *n* (GB sl) (英俚)=café.

caf·feine /'kæfiːn; 'kæfiɪn/ *n* [U] organic compound in tea leaves and coffee beans, used in medicine. 茶精(咖啡碱(茶叶与咖啡豆中所含的有机化合物, 用于医药)。

caf·tan /'kæftæn; 'kæftən/ *n* long tunic with a girdle at the waist, worn by men in the Near East; woman's loosely hanging long dress. 近东地区男人所穿之腰部束带的长袍; 长而松垂的女装。

cage /keɪdʒ; kedʒ/ *n* **1** framework, fixed or portable, with wires or bars, in which birds or animals may be kept. (畜养禽兽的)笼子; 鸟笼; 兽槛。 **2** camp for prisoners of war. 战俘营。 **3** framework in which containers are lowered or raised in the shaft of a mine. (矿坑中的)升降机。 □ *vt* [VP6A] put, keep, in a ~: 关入笼中: *a ~d bird.* 笼中鸟。

cagey /'keɪdʒɪ; 'kedʒɪ/ *adj* (colloq) cautious about sharing confidences; uncommunicative; secretive. (口)小心谨慎不泄露秘密的; 守口如瓶的。 **cag·ily** *adv*

ca·goule /kə'ɡuːl; kə'ɡul/ *n* light, waterproof garment with a hood and long sleeves, worn over clothes for protection against rain. 有帽的长袖雨衣。

ca·hoots /kə'huːts; kə'huts/ *n pl* **be in ~ (with)**, (US sl) be planning sth (esp sth disreputable), be in league. (美俚) 计划某事 (尤指不名誉之丑事); 与…共谋; 与…同伙。

cai·man, cay·man /'keɪmən; 'kemən/ *n* S American reptile resembling an alligator. 南美鳄鱼(似短吻鳄)。

cairn /keən; kɛrn/ *n* pyramid-shaped heap of rough stones set up as a landmark or a memorial. (作为界标或纪念碑之)角锥形石堆; 石标。

cais·son /'keɪsn; 'kesn/ *n* **1** chest or wagon for ammunition, usu attached to a big gun on wheels. (通常附于炮车后面的)弹药箱; 弹药车。 **2** large water-tight box or chamber in which men work under water (eg when building foundations): (工人在水面下工作, 如建筑桥基时, 所乘之大箱之)潜水箱; 沉箱: ⇨ *disease,* ⇨ **bend²(3).** 潜水工病。

cai·tiff /'keɪtɪf; 'ketɪf/ *n* (old use) despicable or cowardly person. (旧用法)可鄙或可怕之人; 懦夫。

ca·jole /kə'dʒəʊl; kə'dʒol/ *vt* [VP6A, 14] **~ sb (into / out of doing sth),** use flattery or deceit to persuade or soothe, or to get information, etc from sb. 以甜言蜜语哄骗 (某人做或不作某事); (向某人) 骗取 (消息等)。 **ca·jol·ery** *n*

cake /keɪk; kek/ *n* **1** [C, U] sweet mixture of flour, eggs, butter, etc baked in an oven: (面粉、鸡蛋、奶油等

调和烘焙而成之)蛋糕; 糕饼类: *an assortment of fancy ~s;* 形形色色漂亮的蛋糕; *a slice of ~,* ie of a large one that is cut into pieces. 一片蛋糕。 *a piece of ~,* (sl) sth very easy and pleasant. (俚)极其容易且使人愉快的事情。 **(both) have one's cake and eat it,** both preserve sth unchanged and allow it to change (ie an impossibility). 既想保有蛋糕, 又想把它吃掉; 想从事不可能的事情。 **~s and ale,** merry-making. 作乐; 行乐。 **(selling) like hot ~s,** very fast. (象刚出炉的蛋糕一样, 销售得)极快。 **take the ~,** (colloq) be the extreme example of sth. ⇨ **biscuit(1).** (口)成为极端的例子。 **2** [C] mixture of other kinds of food, usu compressed and cooked in a round or ornamental shape: 饼状食物: *'fish-~s;* 鱼饼; *'oat-~s.* 燕麦饼。 **3** [C] shaped piece of other materials or substances: (其他物质之成形的)一块: *a ~ of soap/tobacco.* 一块肥皂 (烟草)。 □ *vt, vi* [VP6A, 2A] coat thickly, become coated (with sth that becomes hard when dry); form into a thick hard mass: 覆以干硬的物质; 覆有干硬的物质; 结成厚厚的硬块: *His shoes were ~d with mud.* 他的鞋子粘着泥块。

cala·bash /'kæləbæʃ; 'kælə,bæʃ/ *n* (tree with) fruit or gourd of which the hard outer skin (or shell) is used as a container for liquids, grain, etc. 葫芦 (其坚硬之外壳可作液体、壳类等之盛器); 葫芦树。 ⇨ the illus at **gourd.** 参看 gourd 之插图。

ca·lam·ity /kə'læmətɪ; kə'læmətɪ/ *n* (*pl* **-ties**) great and serious misfortune or disaster (eg a big earthquake or flood, becoming blind, the loss of all one's money). 巨大而严重的不幸或灾祸(如大地震或洪水、眼睛失明、损失全部的钱财)。 **ca·lami·tous** /kə'læmɪtəs; kə'læmətəs/ *adj* marked by, causing, ~ *(to).* 遭受灾难的; 引起灾祸的(与to连用)。

cal·cify /'kælsɪfaɪ; 'kælsə,faɪ/ *vt, vi* [VP6A, 2A] change, be changed, into lime; harden by deposit of lime. (使)变成石灰; 因积存石灰质而硬化; 钙化。

cal·cine /'kælsaɪn; 'kælsaɪn/ *vt, vi* [VP6A, 2A] make, be made, into quicklime or powder by roasting or burning; burn to ashes. 烧成生石灰或石灰粉; 锻烧; 烧成灰。 **cal·ci·na·tion** /ˌkælsɪ'neɪʃn; ˌkælsɪ'neʃən/ *n* conversion of metals into their oxides by burning. 锻烧金属成氧化物; 锻烧; 锻。

cal·cium /'kælsɪəm; 'kælsɪəm/ *n* soft white metal (symbol Ca), the chemical basis of many compounds essential to life (occurs in bones and teeth, and forms part of limestone, marble and chalk). 钙(软性白色金属元素, 化学符号 Ca, 为生命所必需之许多化合物的主要化学成分; 存在于骨骼及牙齿中, 并构成石灰石、大理石及白垩之一部分成分)。 **~ 'carbide** *n* compound of ~ and carbon **(CaC₂),** used with water to make acetylene gas (C_2H_2). 碳化钙(加水可制乙炔即电石气)。 **~ hydroxide** /haɪ'drɒksaɪd; haɪ'drɑksaɪd/ *n* slaked lime. 氢氧化钙(熟石灰)。

cal·cu·lable /'kælkjʊləbl; 'kælkjələbl/ *adj* that may be measured, reckoned or relied upon. 可计算的; 可靠的。

cal·cu·late /'kælkjʊleɪt; 'kælkjə,let/ *vt, vi* **1** [VP6A, 9, 8, 10, 2A] find out by working with numbers: 计算; 算出: *~ the cost of a journey.* 计算旅行费用。 *Astronomers can ~ when there will be eclipses of the sun and moon.* 天文学家可以算出何时发生日蚀及月蚀。 **'calculating machine** *n* one that works with numbers automatically. 计算机。 **2 be ~d to,** be planned or designed to: 为…而计划或设计: *This advertisement is ~d to attract the attention of housewives.* 这个广告是为引起家庭主妇们的注意而设计的。 *a ~d insult,* said or done on purpose. 故意的侮辱。 **3** [VP3A] **~ on,** depend, bank (the usu words in GB) on: 依靠; 依赖; 指望 (英国通用 depend on 或 bank on): *We can't ~ on having fine weather for the sports meeting.* 我们不能指望有天气开运动会。 **4** [VP9] (US) suppose, believe. (美)认为; 觉得; 相信。 **5** [VP9] weigh reasons, etc and be confident (*that* sth will happen, etc); estimate. 经考

虑各种理由等而觉得有信心；确信(某事必然会发生等，后接由 that 引导之名词从句)；估计。**cal·cu·lat·ing** adj scheming; shrewd; crafty. 诡计多端的；精明的；狡猾的。**cal·cu·la·tion** /ˌkælkjuˈleɪʃən; ˌkælkjəˈleʃən/ n act of calculating; careful thought; [C] result of this: 计算；考虑；计算或考虑之结果: After much calculation, they decided to give Phil the position of manager. 经过慎重考虑后，他们决定给菲尔经理的职位。I'm out in my calculations, have made a mistake in them. 我计算(或考虑)错了。**cal·cu·lator** /-tə(r); -tɚ/ n person who ~s; calculating machine. 计算者；计算机。

cal·cu·lus /ˈkælkjuləs; ˈkælkjələs/ n (pl -li /-laɪ; -ˌlaɪ/ or -luses /-ləsɪz; -ləsɪz/) 1 branch of mathematics divided into two parts, (**differential** ~ and **integral** ~), that deals with variable quantities, used to solve many mathematical problems. 微积分(数学之一分支，分为微分与积分两部分，研究变量，用以解决许多数学问题)。 2 (med) stone in some part of the human body. (医)(人体内的)结石。

cal·dron /ˈkɔːldrən; ˈkɔldrən/ n = **cauldron**.

cal·en·dar /ˈkælɪndə(r); ˈkæləndɚ/ n 1 list of the days, weeks, months, of a particular year; list with dates that are important to certain groups of people. 日历；历书；(某些团体用的)行事历。 2 system by which time is divided into fixed periods, and marking the beginning and end of a year: 历法；年历法(分一年时间为若干固定单位之方法): the Muslim ~ 伊斯兰教历; the Gregorian ~ (with every fourth year a leap year of 366 days). 格雷戈里历法(定每第四年为闰年，即 366 日)。~ 'month n months as marked on the ~ (contrasted with a lunar month of 28 days). 历月(日历上所划分的月，与月球公转周期之 28 日的太阴月有别)。

cal·en·der /ˈkælɪndə(r); ˈkælɪndɚ/ n roller-machine for pressing and smoothing cloth or paper. (用以压光布与纸之)研光机；压光机；轮压机。□ vt [VP6A] put through a ~. 用研光机压光。

cal·ends, kal·ends /ˈkælɪndz; ˈkæləndz/ n pl first of the month in the ancient Roman calendar. 古罗马历之朔日；初一。on the Greek ~, never. 永远没有那一天；永不。

calf¹ /kɑːf US: kæf; kæf/ n 1 (pl calves /kɑːvz US: kævz; kævz/) young of the domestic cow, ⇨ the illus at **domestic**; young of the seal, whale and some other animals for the first year. 小牛; 犊 (参看 domestic 之插图); (一年以内的)小海豹，小鲸或其他幼小的动物。Cf 参较 bull, cow, heifer, ox, steer. cow in/with ~, pregnant cow. 怀孕的母牛。'~-love n childish love affair; love of a young or inexperienced person. (少年男女间的)幼稚的恋爱。 2 [U] (also 亦作 '~ skin) leather from the skin of a ~, esp as used in bookbinding and shoemaking. 小牛皮。(尤指用以装订书籍及制皮鞋者)。

calf² /kɑːf US: kæf; kæf/ n (pl calves /kɑːvz US: kævz; kævz/) fleshy part of the back of the human leg, between the knee and the ankle. 腓；小腿(小腿后部膝与踝之间之多肉部分)。⇨ the illus at **leg**. 参看 leg 之插图。

cali·brate /ˈkælɪbreɪt; ˈkæləˌbret/ vt [VP6A] determine or correct the calibre or scale of a thermometer. gauge or other graduated instrument. 测定或校准(温度计、计量器或其他有刻度之仪器)之口径或刻度。**cali·bra·tion** /ˌkælɪˈbreɪʃn; ˌkæləˈbreʃən/ n degree marks, etc on a measuring instrument. 计量器之度数记号等。

cal·ibre (US = **cali·ber**) /ˈkælɪbə(r); ˈkæləbɚ/ n 1 [C] inside diameter of a tube/gun/barrel, etc. (管子、枪炮、桶等之)口径；管径；圆管内径。 2 [U] quality of mind or character; (person's) standing or importance: 才能；才干；才具; (人之)地位或重要性: a woman of high ~. 很有才干的女人；很有地位的女人。

cal·ico /ˈkælɪkəʊ; ˈkæləˌko/ n [U] cotton cloth, esp plain white cloth used for bad sheets, or with coloured designs printed on it, used for shirts, dresses, etc. 白洋布(如做床单用者)；印花布(用做衬衫，女装等)。

cali·pers /ˈkælɪpəz; ˈkæləpɚz/ n pl (US) = **callipers**.

ca·liph, ca·lif /ˈkeɪlɪf; ˈkelɪf/ n title once used by rulers who were descendants and successors of Muhammad; chief civil and religious Muslim ruler: 旧伊斯兰教国国家世袭之统治者(即穆罕默德之后裔及继承者)的称号; 伊斯兰教国王兼教主: the C~ of Baghdad. 巴格达的国王兼教主。'~·ate /ˈkeɪlɪfeɪt; ˈkælɪˌfet/ n ~'s position and territory. 伊斯兰教国王兼教主的职位及辖区。

cal·is·then·ics /ˌkælɪsˈθenɪks; ˌkæləsˈθenɪks/ n pl (US) = **callisthenics**.

calk¹ /kɔːk; kɔk/ vt, n [VP6A] (provide with a) sharp iron plate in a horse-shoe or boot to prevent slipping. (附于马蹄铁或皮靴上防滑之)尖铁片；钉尖铁片。

calk² /kɔːk; kɔk/ vt = **caulk**.

call¹ /kɔːl; kɔl/ n 1 shout; cry: 呼喊; 喊叫: a ~ for help. 大呼求救。They came at my ~, when I shouted to them. 他们应我喊叫而来。within ~, within ~ing distance: 在呼喊听得及的范围内: Please remain within ~, close at hand. 请不要走远(留在可以听见呼唤的地方)。 2 characteristic cry of a bird; military signal (on a bugle, etc). 鸟的特殊叫声；(军队的)号音。 3 short visit (to sb's house, etc); short stop (at a place): 拜访；(在某地)小停: pay a ~ on a friend. 拜访朋友。I have several ~s to make. 我有几处朋友要去拜访。I must return their ~, visit them because they visited me. 我必须回拜他们。port of ~, one at which a ship stops for a short time. 船舶途中停靠之港口。 4 message; summons; invitation: 信息; 召唤; 邀请: telephone ~s. 电话。I'll give you a ~. 我会给你打电话。He felt the ~ of the sea, to be a sailor. 他想去当海员。'~-box n small cabin (in GB more usu called a 英国多称为 telephone kiosk) with a public telephone. 公用电话亭。'~-girl n prostitute hired by telephone. 应召女郎(以电话连络召唤之妓女)。 5 demand for money (esp unpaid capital from company shareholders); claim of any kind: 要求付款(尤指公司股东未付之资本); 任何要求: I have many ~s on my time. 我有许多事情需要时间去做。'~-loan; '~-money; money on ~; money payable at/on ~, money lent on condition that its return can be demanded without notice. 通知贷款; 通知存(付)款。 6 [U] (chiefly interr and neg) need; occasion: (主要用于疑问及否定句)需要; 理由: There's no ~ for you to worry. 你没有理由烦恼。 7 player's right or turn to make a bid at bridge²; bid thus made: (桥牌)叫牌权; 叫牌; 所叫的牌: Whose ~ is it? 轮到谁叫牌? Was the last ~ two spades? 刚叫的是二黑桃吗?

call² /kɔːl; kɔl/ vt, vi (For special uses with adverbial particles and preps, ⇨ below.) (与副词性小品词及介词连用的特殊用法，参看下列第9义。) 1 [VP2A, 3B, 3A] say sth in a loud voice; cry; speak or shout to attract attention: 大声说话；叫(引起注意); 招呼: Why doesn't my son come when I ~? 当我叫唤的时候，我的儿子为何不来? I thought I heard somebody ~ing. 我好象听见有人在叫。She ~ed to her father for help. 她向她的父亲喊叫求救。I've been ~ing (for) ten minutes. 我已叫了十分钟了。~ out, cry or shout when needing help, or from surprise, pain, etc. (因需要帮助，或因惊骇、疼痛等而)大叫。⇨ 9 below. 参看下列第9义。 2 [VP2A, C, 3A, 4A] ~ (on sb/at a place), pay a short visit; go to sb's house/office etc; stop at: 拜访；造访; 到…(停): ~ on Mr Green. 我拜访了格林先生。I ~ed at Mr Green's house. 我曾至格林先生府上拜访。I ~ed to see Mr Green. 我曾往访格林先生。Mr Green was out when I ~ed. 当我往访时，格林先生不在家。A man has ~ed to read the gas meter. 有人来抄煤气表。~ for, visit (a house, etc) to get sth, or to go somewhere with sb: 往人家等取某物或接某人同往某处: A man ~s every Monday for old newspapers. 有一个人每星期一来收旧报纸。I'll ~ for you at 6 o'clock. 我六点钟去接你。 ~ on/upon sb, visit: 造访; 来访者。 3 [VP23] name; describe as: 为…取名;把…称做: His name is Richard but we all ~ him

Dick. 他的名字是理查德，但是我们都称他迪克。 *What are you going to ~ the baby?* 你将替婴儿取什么名字？ *He ~s himself a colonel*, claims that he has the right to this title. 他自称为上校。 *You may ~ it what you like.* 你可以随意把它叫什么。 ⇨ also **spade(1)**. *~ sb names*, abuse or insult him. 骂驾某人。 *~ sth one's own*, claim as one's own property: 称某物为自己的财产: *We have nothing that we can ~ our own.* 我们没有一样东西可以说是我们自己的财产。 *~ it a day*, ⇨ **day (3)**. **4** [VP22, 23] consider; regard as: 认为；视为: *Do you ~ English an easy language?* 你认为英语是一种容易的语言吗？ *I ~ that a shame.* 我认为那是一种耻辱。 *I ~ that dishonest.* 我认为那是不诚实的。 *Shall we ~ it five quid*, (colloq) settle the price, sum, etc at five pounds? （口）我们就算作五英镑（指价钱、钱数等）好不好？ **5** [VP6A, 15B] summon; wake; send a message to: 召唤；请来；叫醒；传唤；传送信息: *Please ~ a doctor.* 请去请一位医生。 *Please ~ me* (= wake me up) *at 6 tomorrow morning.* 请在明天早晨六时叫醒我。 *The aircraft was ~ing* (ie sending radio signals to) *the control station at the airport.* 那飞机在（用无线电信号）呼叫飞机场的指挥台。 *This is London ~ing*, is the BBC, London. 这里是伦敦（英国广播公司）播音。 *The doctor was ~ed away to an accident.* 医生被请去救治意外灾害的受伤者。 *My brother ~ed me* (up) (= telephoned to me) *from Leeds last night.* 我的哥哥（弟弟）昨晚自里兹打电话给我。 [VP12B, 13B] (colloq): （口）: *Please ~ me a taxi/~ a taxi for me.* 请替我叫部计程车。 *be/feel ~ed to do sth*, be/feel it to be one's duty to do it: 想做；应该做: *~ed to be a doctor/to practise medicine.* 想做医生（行医）。 *~ing* in special duty; profession; occupation. 职业；行业。 **6** (special uses with *nouns*)（与名词连用之特殊用法） *~ sb's bluff*, ⇨ **bluff²**. *~ a halt (to)*, say that it is time to halt: 命令停止: *~ a halt to gambling*, forbid it. 命令禁止赌博。 *~ a meeting*, announce that one will be held and summon people to attend. 召集会议。 *~ the roll*, ⇨ **roll¹(4)**. *~ a strike*, order workers to come out on strike. 发动罢工。 **7** (card-games) bid or make a demand. (纸牌) 叫牌。 *call¹(7)*. **8** (phrases) (短语): *~ (sb) to account*, ⇨ **account¹(4)**. *~ attention to*, require (sb) to give his attention to. 要求（某人）注意…。 *~ the banns*, ⇨ **banns**. *be ~ed to the Bar*, ⇨ **bar¹(12)**. *~ sth in/into question*, declare that one has doubts about it. 宣称对某事怀疑；对某事提出质问。 *~ sb/a meeting to order*, ask for orderly behaviour, ask that attention should be paid to the rules. 请求某人（与会者）守秩序。 **9** [VP15B, 3A] (special uses with *adverbial particles and preps*): （与副词性小品词及介词连用之特殊用法）: *call by*, (colloq) visit briefly (usu when passing the house, etc). （口）短时间地拜访；(通常指)顺道拜访。 *call sb down*, (US sl) reprimand him severely. (美俚) 严厉斥责某人。 *~ sth down*, invoke, ask for it: 祈求；要求；请求: *~ down curses on his head.* 求神降祸于他。 *call for*, demand, require: 要求；需要: *You must take such steps as seem* (to be) *~ed for*, do what seems necessary. 你必须采取这些似乎必要的步骤。 *The occasion ~s for prompt action.* 情势所迫，必须立即采取行动。 *call sth forth*, **(a)** be the cause of: 引起; 招致: *His behaviour ~ed forth numerous protests.* 他的行为引起许多的抗议。 **(b)** produce and use: 鼓起；使发挥: *You will have to ~ forth all your energy.* 你必须全力以赴。 *call sth in*, order or request the return of: 下令收回; 请求收回: *The librarian has ~ed in all books.* 图书馆管理员已通知收回全部书籍。 *Gold coins were ~ed in by the Government.* 金币已被政府下令收回。 *He was so short of money that he had to ~ in the loans he had made.* 他非常缺钱，所以不得不收回他所借出的款子。 *call sth off*, **(a)** ~ away: 将…叫开: *Please ~ your dog off*, ~ to your dog so that it stops worrying me. 请把你的狗叫开。 **(b)** decide, give orders, to stop sth: 决定取消某事; 下令停止某事: *The strike/attack was ~ed off*,

was either not started or was stopped. 罢工(攻击)已取消(或已奉命停止)。 *You had better ~ the deal off*, not carry out what was agreed upon. 你最好取消这项交易。 ⇨ **2** above. 参看上列第2义。 *call on/upon sb*, **(a)** make a short visit to. 短暂地访问；拜访。 ⇨ **2** above. 参看上列第2义。 **(b)** *~ on/upon sb* (*to do sth*), appeal to, invite, require him: 恳求；请求；邀请；要求: *I ~ed on* (= appealed to) *him to keep his promise.* 我恳求他遵守诺言。 *I now ~ upon* (= invite) *Mr Grey to address the meeting.* 我现在请格雷先生向大会讲话。 *I feel ~ed upon* (= feel that I ought) *to warn you that ….* 我觉得我应该警告你…。 *call sb out*, **(a)** summon; esp to an emergency: 召唤(尤指应付紧急事件): *The fire brigade was ~ed out twice yesterday.* 昨天消防队被召唤两次。 *Troops had to be ~ed out.* (我们)不得不召来军队。 **(b)** instruct (workers) to come out on strike: 指示(工人)罢工: *The coal-miners were ~ed out by the Union officials.* 煤矿工人受工会职员指示而罢工。 *call sth over*, read (a list of names) to learn who is present. 点名；清点(名单)。 '*~-over n* (also 亦作 '*roll-~*) reading of a list of names (eg in school, the army). 点名(如学校中或军中)。 *call sb/sth up*, **(a)** telephone to: 打电话给: *I'll ~ you up this evening.* 我今晚将打电话给你。 **(b)** bring back to the mind: 唤起；使忆起: *~ up scenes of childhood.* 使回忆起童年时代的情景。 **(c)** summon for (military, etc) service: 征召…服兵役等: *If war breaks out, we shall be ~ed up at once.* 倘若战争爆发，我们将立即被征召服役。 Hence, 由此产生, '*~-up n*

cal·li·gra·phy /kəˈlɪɡrəfɪ; kəˈlɪɡrəfɪ/ n [U] (art of) beautiful handwriting. 书法; 美的字体。

cal·li·ope /kəˈlaɪəpɪ; kəˈlaɪəpɪ/ n steam-organ; musical instrument with steam whistles played by pressing keys. 蒸汽风琴（一种按键而由各种汽笛发音之乐器）。

cal·li·pers /ˈkælɪpəz; ˈkæləpəz/ n pl (pair of) ~, **1** instrument for measuring the diameter of round objects or the calibre of tubes, etc. (测量圆形物之直径或圆管等口径之)双脚规; 测径器。 **2** metal supports attached to the legs of a disabled person to enable him to walk. 装在残废者腿上助其行走的金属架。

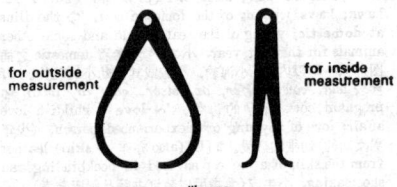

for outside measurement   for inside measurement

callipers

cal·lis·then·ics /ˌkælɪsˈθenɪks; ˌkæləsˈθenɪks/ n pl (usu with a *sing* v) exercises designed to develop strong and graceful bodies. (通常与单数动词连用) 柔软体操; 健身运动。

cal·los·ity /kæˈlɒsɪtɪ; kəˈlɑsɪtɪ/ n (*pl* -ties) area of hardened thick skin; callus. 皮肤硬化的部分; 胼胝。

cal·lous /ˈkæləs; ˈkæləs/ adj **1** (of the skin) made hard (by rough work, etc). (指皮肤因操劳等而)结有硬块的; 结茧的; 变硬的。 **2** ~ (*to*), (fig) unfeeling; indifferent: (喻)无情的; 无感觉的; 冷淡的: *~ to insults/his employees/the suffering of others.* 对侮辱无感觉(对雇员无情; 对别人的痛苦冷淡)。 *~·ness n*

cal·low /ˈkæləʊ; ˈkælo/ adj young; unfledged; inexperienced: 年幼的; 未生羽毛的; 无经验的: *a ~ youth.* 一个无经验的青年。 *~·ness n*

cal·lus /ˈkæləs; ˈkæləs/ n area of thick, hardened skin. 皮肤硬化的部分; 胼胝。

calm /kɑːm; kɑm/ adj (-er, -est) **1** (of the weather) quiet; not windy; (of the sea) still; without large waves. (指天气)平静的; 无风的; (指海)无风浪的。 **2** not excited;

untroubled; quiet: (心境)镇定的; 无忧虑的; 宁静的: *keep* ~. 保持镇定。 □ *n a* ~, a time when everything is quiet and peaceful. 安静太平的时候; 平静的时候; □ *vt, vi* [VP6A, 15B, 2C] ~ (**down**), make or become ~: 使平静; 平息; 静下来: *C~ yourself!* 请你安静(或镇定)下来! *The sea ~ed down.* 海上风浪平息下来了。 ~·**ly** *adv*
~·**ness** *n* ~ condition. 平静; 宁静; 安静。

calo·mel /'kæləmel; 'kæləml/ *n* [U] white, tasteless, insoluble substance used as a purgative. 甘汞; 氯化亚汞(白色无味的不溶性物质, 用作泻药)。

Calor gas /'kælə gæs; 'kælə gæs/ *n* [U] (P) butane. 商标(丁烷)。

cal·orie /'kælərɪ; 'kælərɪ/ *n* unit of heat; unit of energy supplied by food: 卡路里; 卡(热量单位; 食物所供给的能量单位): *An ounce of sugar supplies about 100* ~s. 一英两糖可供给约一百卡热。 **cal·or·ific** /ˌkælə'rɪfɪk; ˌkælə'rɪfɪk/ *adj* producing heat/energy: 生热的; 发热的; 生能的: *calorific value*, (of food or fuel) quantity of heat/energy produced by a given quantity. (食物或燃料之)热量; 能量。

cal·umny /'kæləmnɪ; 'kæləmnɪ/ *n* (*pl* -**nies**) (formal) [C] false statement about a person, made to damage his character; [U] slander. (正式用语) 中伤他人人格的谎话; 诽谤。 **ca·lum·ni·ate** /kə'lʌmnɪeɪt; kə'lʌmnɪ,et/ *vt* [VP6A] slander. 诽谤; 中伤。

Cal·vary /'kælvərɪ; 'kælvərɪ/ *n* hill outside Jerusalem where Jesus was crucified; carved representation of the Crucifixion. 髑髅地(耶路撒冷郊外的一座小丘, 耶稣在此被钉死在十字架上); (耶稣被钉死在十字架上的)受难像。

calve /kɑːv *US:* kæv; kæv/ *vi* give birth to a calf. 产小牛。

Cal·vin·ism /'kælvɪnɪzəm; 'kælvɪnɪzəm/ *n* religious teaching of the French Protestant, John Calvin. 法国宗教改革家卡尔文之教义。 **Cal·vin·ist** *n* follower of Calvin's teachings. 卡尔文教义之信徒; 卡尔文派教徒。

ca·lyp·so /kə'lɪpsəʊ; kə'lɪpso/ *n* (*pl* ~s /-səʊz; -soz/) improvised song, as composed by West Indians, on a subject of current interest. 以时下事件为主题所临时制作的歌曲(如西印度群岛土人所作者)。

ca·lyx /'keɪlɪks; 'kelɪks/ *n* (*pl* ~**es** or **calyces** /'keɪlɪsiːz; 'kelɪ,siz/) ring of leaves (called *sepals*) forming the outer support of the petals of an unopened flower-bud. 植物的花萼(花蕾的花瓣外层的一圈小叶, 称为 sepals 萼片)。 ⇨ the illus at **flower**. 参看 flower 之插图。

cam /kæm; kæm/ *n* projection on a wheel or shaft, designed to change circular motion into up-and-down or back-and-forth motion. 凸轮; 镜(轮或轮轴上的凸起设计; 用以改变圆周运动为上下或前后运动)。 **cam·shaft** /'kæmʃɑːft *US:* -ʃæft; 'kæm,ʃæft/ *n* (eg in a car) shaft to which cams are attached. (汽车等之)凸轮轴。

cama·rad·erie /ˌkæməˈrɑːdərɪ *US:* -ˈræd-; ˌkɑːmə'rɑːderɪ/ *n* (F) [U] friendliness and mutual trust of comrades. (法)同志的友爱及互信; 同志爱。

cam·ber /'kæmbə(r); 'kæmbə/ *n* upwards slope (eg of a road surface) of a curve. (路面等之)弯路的向上倾斜; 拱势; 侧倾; 翘曲; 弯度。 □ *vt, vi* (of a surface) have a ~; give a ~ to. (指表面)略为拱起; 使呈拱势或侧倾; (使)翘曲。

cam·bric /'keɪmbrɪk; 'kembrɪk/ *n* [U] fine, thin cloth of cotton or linen. 一种细而薄之棉布或麻布。

came *pt* of **come**.

camel /'kæml; 'kæml/ *n* long-necked animal, with either one (*dromedary*) or two humps on its back, used in desert countries for riding and for carrying goods. 骆驼(一种长颈动物, 背上有一或二驼峰, 沙漠国家用以骑乘或载运货物)。 ⇨ the illus at **large**. 参看 large 之插图。 '~-**hair** *n* fine hair for making the brushes used by artists; soft, heavy cloth of this hair: 驼毛(用以制画笔); 驼绒(驼毛织成之柔软的厚绒布): *a ~-hair coat.* 驼绒外衣。

ca·mel·lia /kə'miːlɪə; kə'melɪə/ *n* evergreen shrub

from China and Japan with shiny leaves and white, red or pink rose-like flowers; the flower. 山茶(原产于中国及日本之常青灌木, 叶有光泽, 开白、红、或粉红色玫瑰状花); 茶花。

Cam·em·bert /'kæməmbeə(r); 'kæməm,bɛr/ *n* (F) rich, soft cheese (of Normandy, France). (法)(产于诺曼底之)浓味软干酪。

cameo /'kæmɪəʊ; 'kæmɪ,o/ *n* (*pl* ~s /-əʊz; -oz/) **1** piece of hard stone with a raised design, often used as a jewel or ornament. 刻有不同颜色浮雕之硬石(用作宝石或装饰品)。 **2** short piece of writing or acting conveying the essential qualities of a person, place, event etc. (表现某人、某地、某事件等之特质之)短文; 短剧。

cam·era /'kæmərə; 'kæmərə/ *n* **1** apparatus for taking still photographs or ('**film**/'**movie** ~) moving pictures, or (**TV** ~) for receiving light images and transforming them for broadcasting live or for receiving on video tape. 照相机; 电影摄影机(film camera 或 movie camera); 电视摄象机 (TV camera)。 '~-**man** /-mæn; -mæn/ *n* (*pl* -**men**) person who operates a ~ for films or TV. 电影制片厂的摄影师; (电视广播台的)摄象机操作者。 **2** *in* ~, (Lat) in the judge's private room, not in court; privately. (拉)在法官的私室里(不在法庭上); 私下地; 秘密地。

EXPOSURE METER
TELEVISION CAMERA
FLASH LIGHT
view·finder
ground glass
mirror
spool
view·finder lens
film
lens
CINE·CAMERA
TWIN-LENS REFLEX CAMERA
35MM CAMERA

cameras

cam·ion /'kæmɪən; 'kæmɪən/ *n* (F) low, fourwheeled truck; lorry. (法)一种低的四轮货车; 卡车。

camo·mile, chamo·mile /'kæməmaɪl; 'kæmə,maɪl/ *n* [U] sweet-smelling plant with daisy-like flowers; the dried flowers and leaves used in medicine as

a tonic. 春黄菊属植物; 甘菊 (一种有香味的植物, 花状如雏菊); 晒干后之甘菊花及叶(医药上用作补剂)。

cam·ou·flage /'kæməfla:ʒ; 'kæmə,flɑʒ/ n [U] **1** that which makes it difficult to recognize the presence or real nature of sth: 掩饰; 掩护(使难以认出某物之存在或真实性质): *The white fur of the polar bear is a natural* ~, *because the bear is not easily seen in the snow*. 北极熊的白色毛皮是一种天然的掩护(因其在雪中不易被看见)。 **2** (in war) the use of paint, netting, boughs of trees, smoke-screens, etc to deceive the enemy by giving a false appearance to things. (战争中) (用涂料、网子、树枝、烟幕等) 伪装 (以欺骗敌人)。 □ vt [VP6A] try to conceal by means of ~. 掩护; 伪装。

camp¹ /kæmp; kæmp/ n **1** place where people (eg people on holiday, soldiers, boy scouts, explorers) live in tents or huts for a time: (度假者、军队、童子军、探险者等临时搭帐篷所住的)营地: *be in* ~; 在露营中; *pitch a* ~; 扎营 *strike/break up* ~, *pack up (the tents, etc)*. 拔营。 *,~·'bed/-·'chair/-·'stool* n one that can be folded and carried easily. (可折叠而便于携带的)行军床 (折椅; 折凳)。 *'~-fire* n one of logs, etc, made in the open air. (在野外燃烧木头等所做的)营火。 *'~-follower* n person (not a soldier) who follows an army to sell goods or services. 跟随军队贩卖货物或提供服务的人(非军人); 随营商贩。 ⇨ also **concentration** ~. **2** number of people with the same ideas (esp on politics or religion): (尤指政治或宗教观点相同的人所形成的)阵营; 阵线: *You and I belong to different political* ~s. 你我属于不同的政治阵营。 *We're in the same* ~, are in agreement, are working together. 我们是志同道合(共同工作)的。 □ vi [VP2A, C] ~ (*out*), (make, live in, a ~): 扎营; 宿营: *Where shall we* ~ *tonight?* 我们今晚将宿宫何地? *They* ~ed *out in the woods*. 他们在树林中宿营。 **go** ~**ing**, spend a holiday in tents, etc: 露营; 在野外搭帐篷住宿(一度度假方式): *The boys have decided to go* ~*ing next summer*. 男孩们已决定明年夏天去露营(参加明年的夏令营)。 ~er n ~·**ing** n (gerund) (动名词) [U] a ~*ing holiday*; 露营假日; *Do you like* ~*ing?* 你喜欢野营生活吗?

camp² /kæmp; kæmp/ adj (colloq) (口) exaggeratedly stylish: 过于时髦的: ~ *acting*; 过于时髦的表演; deliberately and amusingly old-fashioned: 过时而又有趣的: *those* ~ *old silent movies*; 那些过时而又有趣的老默片; affectedly effeminate: 故作女性化的; 矫揉造作的: *a* ~ *walk*. 矫揉造作的步态。 □ n exaggeration and affectation of this sort. 过于时髦; 矫揉造作。 □ vi, vt ~ (*it up*), behave in this way. 显得过于时髦; 显得矫揉造作。

cam·paign /kæm'peɪn; kæm'pen/ n [C] **1** group of military operations with a set purpose, usu in one area. 战役 (在某一地区所做一连串有固定目的的军事行动)。 **2** series of planned activities to gain a special object: 运动(为达到某一特殊目标所做的一连串有计划的活动): *a political* ~; 政治(竞选)运动; *an advertising* ~; 广告活动; *a* ~ *to raise funds*. 募捐运动。 □ vi [VP2A, 3A] take part in, go on, a ~. 参加某一战役; 参加运动; 从事活动。 ~er n person who ~s or who ~ed: 参与某一战役者; 参加运动者; 从事活动者: *He's an old* ~er, has much experience of adapting himself to circumstances. 他是一个老练的人(富有经验,能适应环境)。

cam·pa·nile /,kæmpə'ni:lɪ; ,kæmpə'nilɪ/ n bell tower, usu a separate building. 钟楼 (通常指独立建造者)。

cam·pan·ula /kəm'pænjulə; kæm'pænjulə/ n (kinds of) plant with bell-shaped flowers, usu blue or white. 风铃草属; 山小菜属; 风铃草(花如钟形,通常呈蓝或白色)。

cam·phor /'kæmfə(r); 'kæmfə/ n [U] strong-smelling white substance used medically and in the manufacture of celluloid. 樟脑(有强烈之白色物质,作药用,用以制赛璐珞)。 *'~ ball* n small ball of ~, used to keep moths, etc out of clothes. 樟脑丸 (用以驱除蛀蚀衣服之蠹等)。 ~·**ated** /'kæmfəreɪtɪd; 'kæmfə,retɪd/ adj containing

~: 含有樟脑的; ~ated *oil*. 樟脑油。

cam·pion /'kæmprən; 'kæmprən/ n [U] (kinds of) common flowering plant that grows wild on roadsides and in fields. 石竹科植物(常见之开花植物,长于路边及田间); 狗筋蔓。

cam·pus /'kæmpəs; 'kæmpəs/ n (pl ~es /-pəsɪz; -pəsɪz/) grounds of a school, college or university. (学校、学院或大学之)校区; 校园; 校苑。

can¹ /kæn; kæn/ n **1** metal container, usu with a lid, for liquids, etc: 金属容体,常带有盖子的金属罐: *'oil-can*, 油罐, *'milk-can*. 牛奶罐。 *carry the can (for sb)*, (sl) take the blame. (俚) (为某人)背黑锅; (代某人)受责。 *(be) in the can*, (of film, video-tape) exposed or recorded and stored ready for use. (影影片或电视录象带)已冲晒或录象完毕存以备用。 **2** (formerly US but now also GB) tin-plated airtight container for food, drink etc; contents of such a container: (从前用于美国,现在亦用于英国)不透空气的白铁罐; 罐头(用以装食物,饮料等); 罐头之内容: *a can of beer/peaches*. 一罐啤酒(桃子)。 ⇨ **tin**. **3** (US sl) prison. (美俚)监狱; 牢房。 □ vt (-nn-) [VP6A] preserve (food, etc) by putting in a can(2) which is then hermetically sealed: 装(食品等)于罐头(然后密封以便长时间保存): 罐装: *canned fish*; 鱼罐头; *canned music*, (sl) music recorded on discs, etc. (俚)录于唱片等上之音乐。 **canned** /kænd/ adj (US sl) drunk. (美俚)酒醉的。 **can·nery** /'kænərɪ; 'kænərɪ/ n place where food etc is canned. 罐头工厂; 装罐工厂。

can² /kən; kən; strong form: kæn; kæn/ anom fin (neg **cannot** /'kænɒt; 'kænɑt/ or **can't** /kɑ:nt US: kænt; kænt/, pt **could** /kəd; kəd; strong form: kud; kud/, neg **couldn't** /'kudnt; 'kudnt/) [VP5] **1** (indicating ability or capacity to do sth) be able to; know how to: (表示做某事之能力)能; 会: *Can you lift this box?* 你能抬起这个箱子吗? *I can't get the lid off*. 我打不开那盖子。 *She can speak French*. 她会说法语。 (*Could refers to ability or capacity in past time*): (could 用作过去时,指能力在过去能够): *She could read Latin and Greek when she was ten*. 当她十岁时就能读拉丁文及希腊文。 (*Could is used in if-clauses to indicate a condition, expressed or implied*): (could 用于假设从句中,表示明示或暗示的条件): *Could you lift that box (ie now, if you tried)?* (现在,如果你试一试)你能拿得起那只箱子吗? *Could you have lifted that box (ie if you had tried, eg yesterday)?* (如果你试过的话,譬如说昨天)你能拿得起那只箱子吗? (*Note that could is not used except in conditions, for an isolated achievement in past time. Instead, be able to, manage to or succeed in (doing sth) are preferred*): (注意:除非用于条件中,could 不可以用来指过去的某一次成就,宜用 be able to, manage to, 或 succeed in (doing sth)): *When the boat upset, they were able/managed to swim/succeeded in swimming to the bank* (not *they could swim to the bank* which is incorrect). 小船翻覆时,他们游泳抵达了岸上 (they could swim to the bank 是错误的)。 **2** (*Can is used with vv of perception in place of the simple tenses, which are less usual. Nothing is added to the meaning.*): (can 与感官动词连用,代替简单时,且较简单时常用。意义上无任何差异。): *I can see a sail on the horizon*. 我看到海平线上有一帆船。 *I can hear people talking in the next room*. 我听见隔壁房内有人谈话。 (*Could is used for past time*): (could 用以表明过去时): *We could hear someone singing in the bathroom*. 我们听到有人在浴室唱歌。 *She said she could smell something burning*. 她说她闻到有东西烧着的味道。 (*Can is used, colloquial style, to indicate permission. The use of may is more formal. In reported speech, could is used after a v in the pt. Could may also replace can in a tentative request in question form*): (can 用于口语中,表示许可。用 may 比较正式。在间接叙述句法中,could 用于过去之动词之后。在问句中可作试探性要求时,could 亦可代替 can): *You can (= may) go home now*. 你现在可以回家了。 *The children asked whether they*

could (=might) *go for a swim.* 孩子们问他们是否可以去游泳。*You can't travel first-class with a second-class ticket.* 你不可以拿二等票坐头等位子旅行。 *Put that cigarette out—you can't smoke near a petrol pump!* 把香烟熄掉——你不可以在靠近汽油泵(油帮浦)处抽烟! **4** (*Can/ could* are used to indicate what is possible or likely): (can 或 could 用以表示可能性): *One of the prisoners escaped yesterday—he can/could (= may) be anywhere by now.* 昨天有一个囚犯逃走了——他目前可能躲在什么地方。(*Can* has is used for past time): (can 可用以表示过去时间)。 *He's an hour late—he can have been delayed by fog, of course, that's a possibility.* 他迟到了一个钟头——当然,他可能是被雾所阻。**5** (*Can/could* in questions (and esp with *what(ever), where, how*) indicate surprise, bewilderment, impatience, etc, according to context. The strong forms are used): (can 或 could 在问句中,尤其与 what, whatever, where, how 连用时, 表示惊奇、困惑、不耐烦等, 视其上下文而定。can 或 could 应重读): *What ,can he 'mean?* 他能有什么用意? *What ,can we 'do about it?* 我们还能有什么办法? *Where ,can they have 'got to?* 他们还能上哪里去? *How ,can/,could you be so un'kind?* 你怎能那样无情? **6** (*Can/could* indicate what is considered characteristic, what sb or sth is considered capable of being or doing. Adverbials of frequency (eg *at times, sometimes*) often occur): (can 或 could 表示被视为特性者,某人或某事物之能为。常用表示次数之副词,如 at times, sometimes): *Children can sometimes be very trying.* 孩子们有时非常讨厌。*It can be very cold here, even in May.* 此时即使在五月里也可能非常冷。 *The Bay of Biscay can be very rough at times.* 比斯开海时常风浪汹涌。*When I first knew her she could be very sarcastic, but she's more tolerant now.* 当我第一次认识她时,她是非常尖刻的,不过现在她是较为宽容了。 **7** (*Could* is used to mean 'feel inclined to'): (could 用于指‘想要’之意): *I could smack your face!* 我真想掴你一巴掌! **8** (*Can* is used, colloquial style, with imperative force, meaning 'must'): (can 用于有命令意谓的口语中, 表示‘必须’): *Tell Mr Evans that he can come in now,* Tell him to come in. 叫埃文斯先生进来。 **9** (*Can/could* are used in polite requests): (=> **will**¹ **(3)**): (can, could 用于礼貌的请求): *Do you think I could leave now/Could I leave now, do you think?* Please may I leave now? 请问我可以走了吗? *Could you put out your cigarette, please?* Please put it out. 请把你的香烟熄掉好吗?

Ca·na·dian /kə'neɪdɪən; kə'nedɪən/ *n, adj* (native) of Canada. 加拿大人;加拿大的。

ca·nal /kə'næl; kə'næl/ *n* **1** channel cut through land for use of boats or ships (eg **the Suez**; 'suːɪz; 'suɛz; **C~**) or to carry water to fields for irrigation. (开辟地以供行船的)运河(如苏伊士运河); (引水灌溉田地的)渠;圳。 => the illus at **lock.** 参看 lock 之插图。'**~ boat** *n* long, narrow boat, some of which are pulled by horses, used on ~s. 行驶于运河的狭长形船(有些系用马拖)。 **2** tube or pipe (or system of these) in a plant or animal body for food, air, etc: 管(植物或动物体内输送食物、空气等的管道或一系列的通管): *the alimentary ~.* 消化管。=> the illus at **alimentary, ear.** 参见 alimentary 及 ear 之插图。**~·ize** /'kænəlaɪz; kə'nælaɪz/ *vt* [VP6A, 14] make (a river) into a ~ (by straightening, building locks, etc); (fig) direct; channel: 改造 (河道, 如改直河床、建设闸门等)使成为运河; (喻)指导;引导;导向某一方向前进: *~ize one's energies/efforts into charity work.* 致力于慈善事业。**~·iz·ation** /,kænəlaɪ'zeɪʃn US:-nəlɪ'z-; ,kænəlɪ'zeɪʃn/ *n*

can·apé /'kænəpeɪ US: ,kænə'peɪ; 'kænəpɪ/ *n* (F) thin piece of bread or toast spread with seasoned fish, cheese, etc. (法)加有经过调味的鱼、干酪等之薄面包片或烤面包片。

ca·nard /kæ'nɑːd; kə'nɑrd/ *n* (F) false report. (法)虚报;谣报。

ca·nary /kə'neərɪ; kə'nɛrɪ/ *n* (*pl* **-ries**) **1** (also 亦作 '**~-bird**) small, yellow-feathered song-bird, usu kept

in a cage; [U] its colour, light yellow. 金丝雀(黄羽毛小鸣禽,通常养于笼中); 金丝雀之毛色(浅黄色)。 **2** (also 亦作 '**~-wine**) sweet white wine from the C~ Islands. 加那利群岛所产之白色甜葡萄酒。

ca·nasta /kə'næstə; kə'næstə/ *n* card game for two to six players using two packs of cards. 卡纳斯塔(一种二至六人玩之纸牌戏,使用两副纸牌)。

can·can /'kænkæn; 'kænkæn/ *n* lively high-kicking dance performed by a group of women in long skirts. 康康舞(由一队穿长裙之女人所演之活泼的高踢腿舞)。

can·cel /'kænsl; 'kænsl/ *vt, vi* (**-ll-,** US **-l-**) **1** [VP6A] cross out, draw a line through (words or figures); make a mark on (sth, eg postage stamps, to prevent re-use): 删去;在(字或数字)的腰间画一线表示消去;勾掉;注销(某物,如邮票,以防再用): *~led stamps.* 已注销的邮票。 **2** [VP6A] say that sth already arranged or decided upon will not be done, will not take place, etc: 取消(已安排或决定的计划等): *He ~led his order for the goods,* said that he no longer wanted to receive them. 他取消货物定购单(不想再要)。*The sports meeting was ~led.* 运动会已取消。 **3** [VP2C, 15B] *~ out,* (arith) (of items from the numerator and denominator) equalize each other; (fig) neutralize, make up for, each other: (算术)(指分子及分母上的项目)使相等;消去;相消;(喻)互相抵消: *The arguments ~ (each other) out.* 议论(互相)对消。**~·la·tion** /,kænsə'leɪʃn; ,kænsl'eʃən/ *n* [U] ~ling or being ~led; [C] instance of this; mark used in, made by, ~ling (eg on postage stamps). 取消;删去;勾掉;注销;相消;注销记号(如加于邮票上者)。

can·cer /'kænsə(r); 'kænsə/ *n* [C, U] diseased growth in the body, often causing death: 癌(身体内的毒瘤,常可致死): *~ of the throat;* 喉癌; *'lung ~;* 肺癌; (fig) pernicious evil (eg in Society). (喻)(如社会之)害;罪恶。**~·ous** /'kænsərəs; 'kænsərəs/ *adj* of or like ~; having ~. 癌症的;似癌症的;患癌症的。

Can·cer /'kænsə(r); 'kænsə/ *n* **Tropic of ~,** the parallel of latitude 23¹/₂°N; fouth sign of the zodiac, => the illus at **zodiac.** 北回归线;夏至线; 巨蟹宫 (参看 zodiac 之插图)。

can·de·la·brum /,kændɪ'lɑːbrəm; ,kændə'lebrəm/ *n* (*pl* **-bra** /-brə; -brə/) ornamental holder, with branches, for candles. 装饰性的枝状大烛台。

can·did /'kændɪd; 'kændɪd/ *adj* **1** frank, straight-forward: 坦白的; 率直的: *I will be quite ~ with you: I think you acted foolishly.* 我要很坦白地对你说: 我认为你的行为愚蠢。 **2 ~ camera,** small camera for taking informal or unposed photographs of people. 一种小型相机(用以替人拍摄非正式或不必摆姿势之照片者)。 **~·ly** *adv*

can·di·date /'kændɪdət US: -deɪt; 'kændə,det/ *n* **1** person who wishes, or who is put forward by others, to take an office or position (eg for election to Parliament): 候选人(如竞选国会议员者): *The Labour ~ was elected.* 工党候选人当选。*He offered himself as a ~ for the post/job/position.* 他自荐为该职位的候选人。**2** person taking an examination. 参加考试者。 **can·di·da·ture** /'kændɪdətʃə(r); 'kændədetʃə/ *n* being a ~(1). 候选人资格。

can·died => **candy.**

candle /'kændl; 'kændl/ *n* round stick of wax, etc with a wick through it, which is lit to burn with a light-giving flame. 蜡烛。 *burn the ~ at both ends,* use up too much energy; work very early and very late. 消耗太多的精力; 清晨深夜都在工作; 日夜赶工操劳过度。 *can't/is not fit to hold a ~ to,* is not to be compared to, is not nearly so good as. 不能与…相比;比不上。 *The game is not worth the ~,* is not worth the trouble and expense than it is worth. 此事做起来得不偿失 (太麻烦, 花费太大)。'**~-light** *n* light of ~s: 烛光: *reading by ~ light.* 在烛光下看书; 乘烛夜读。'**~-power** *n* unit of light measurement: 烛光(量光度的单位): *a ten ~-power lamp.* 十烛光的灯。'**~-stick** *n* holder for (usu) a single ~.

烛台(通常指仅插一支蜡烛者)。

can·dour (US = **-dor**) /'kændə(r); 'kændɚ/ n [U] quality of being candid; saying freely what one thinks. 坦白; 直率.

candy /'kændɪ; 'kændɪ/ n 1 (also 亦作 **sugar-'~**) [U] sugar made hard by repeated boilings; [C] (pl **-dies**) piece of this. 冰糖; 冰糖块. 2 [C, U] (US only; GB = sweet(s)) (仅用于美国; 等于英国的 sweet(s)) shaped piece(s) of cooked and flavoured sugar, syrup, etc usu with fruit juices, milk, nuts, etc added. 糖果(用糖、糖浆等加入调味料制成, 形状不一, 通常并加入果汁、牛奶、果仁等). □ vt, vi 1 [VP6A] preserve (eg fruit) by boiling or cooking in sugar: 将(水果等)作成蜜饯: candied plums/lemon peel. 蜜饯李子(柠檬皮). 2 [VP2A] form into sugar crystals. 结晶成糖.

candy·tuft /'kændɪtʌft; 'kændɪˌtʌft/ n garden plant with flat tufts of white, pink or purple flowers. 蜀葵(园艺植物, 花成扁平簇; 呈白、粉红或紫色).

cane /keɪn; ken/ n 1 long, hollow, jointed stem of tall reeds and grass-like plants (eg bamboo, sugar-~), either [U] collectively and as material for making furniture, etc or [C] of one stem or a length of it (eg used for supporting plants, as a walking-stick): 长而有节的茎(如竹子, 甘蔗; 作不可数名词时为集合称, 并指做家具等的材料, 作可数名词时, 指一截竹子或甘蔗、藤条, 例如用以支持植物或作手杖者): a chair with a ~ seat; 有藤座的椅子; raspberry ~s. 覆盆子的新枝. '~sugar n sugar made from sugar-~, chemically the same as beet sugar. (甘蔗制成的)蔗糖(其化学成分与甜菜糖同). 2 length of ~ used as an instrument for punishing children by beating. (处罚儿童用的)藤鞭, 藤条: get the ~, be punished with a ~. 吃藤条; 挨打; 受处罚. □ vt [VP6A] punish with a ~(2). 用藤鞭责打.

ca·nine /'keɪnaɪn; 'kenaɪn/ adj of, as of, a dog or dogs. 狗的; 如狗的; 似犬的. '~ tooth n (in a human being) one of the four pointed teeth, one on each side of the four incisors, upper and lower. 犬齿(人的四颗尖齿之一, 长在上下门牙的两侧). ⇨ the illus at mouth. 参看 mouth 之插图.

can·is·ter /'kænɪstə(r); 'kænɪstɚ/ n 1 small box (usu metal) with a lid, used for holding tea, etc. 用以装茶叶等之有盖的小罐(通常为金属的); 茶罐; 茶筒. 2 cylinder which, when thrown, or fired from a gun, bursts and scatters its contents: 霰弹筒(手枪或以枪炮发射, 爆炸时其中破片等飞散): a 'tear-gas ~. 催泪毒气弹筒.

can·ker /'kæŋkə(r); 'kæŋkɚ/ n 1 [U] disease that destroys the wood of trees; disease that causes the formation of ulcers in the human mouth, in the ears of dogs and cats, etc. (伤害树木的)癌肿病; (生于人口里、猫狗等的耳朵里的)口疮; 溃疡. 2 (fig) evil influence or tendency that causes decay. (喻)造成腐败的恶劣影响或趋势; 积弊; 弊害; 弊病. □ vt destroy by ~; be a ~ to. 以此种植物病害摧残; 使溃烂; 使腐蚀; 为...腐败之因; 败坏. ~ous /-kərəs; -kɚəs/ adj of or like ~; causing ~. 此病害的; 象此种病的; 造成腐败的.

canna /'kænə; 'kænə/ n plant with large, dark leaves and bright yellow, red or orange flowers; the flower. 美人蕉属; 昙华(叶大而色深, 开鲜明的黄花、红花或橘黄色花); 昙华之花.

can·na·bis /'kænəbɪs; 'kænəbɪs/ n [U] Indian hemp, a drug also known as hashish and marijuana, smoked or chewed as an intoxicant. 印度大麻(药用, 亦称 hashish 及 marijuana, 抽吸或咀嚼的一种麻醉剂, 俗称大麻烟). ⇨ hemp.

canned, can·nery ⇨ can¹.

can·ni·bal /'kænɪbl; 'kænəbl/ n person who eats human flesh; animal that eats its own kind; (attrib) of or like ~s: 食人肉的野人; 食同类之肉的动物; (用作定语)(似)食人肉的; (似)食同类之肉的: a ~ feast. 食人肉的宴会. ~ism /'kænɪbəlɪzm; 'kænəbḷˌɪzəm/ n practice of eating the flesh of one's own kind. 食同类之肉的行为或

习俗; 食人俗. ~·is·tic /ˌkænɪ'bəlɪstɪk; ˌkænəbəl'ɪstɪk/ adj of or like ~s. (似)食人肉之野人的; 吃同类的. ~·ize /'kænɪbəlaɪz; 'kænəbəlˌaɪz/ vt use (one of a number of similar machines, engines, etc) to provide spare parts for others. 使用(若干相似之机器、引擎等之一)供给其他机器之备用零件; 拼修; 拼配.

can·non /'kænən; 'kænən/ n 1 (collective; sing often used instead of pl) large, heavy gun, fixed to the ground or to a guncarriage, esp the old kind that fired a solid ball of metal (called 称作 a '~ball). (Gun and shell are the words used for the modern weapons). (集合名词, 单数常用以代替复数)火炮(固定于地上或装于炮车上, 尤指旧式的发射实心金属弹丸者). (gun and shell 为现代用词). 2 heavy, automatic gun, firing explosive shells, used in modern aircraft in war. 空用炮; 机关炮 (现代飞机在战争中所使用之炮). '~-fodder n men regarded as expendable material in war. 在战争中被视为清耗品或牺牲品的兵员; 炮灰. ~·ade /ˌkænə'neɪd; ˌkænən'ed/ n continued firing of big guns. 大炮之连续轰击.

muzzle

a cannon

can·not /'kænət; 'kænɑt/ ⇨ can².

canny /'kænɪ; 'kænɪ/ adj (-ier, -iest) not prepared to take unknown risks; shrewd, esp about money matters. 不准备冒不可知之危险的; 谨慎的; 精明的(尤指关于金钱的事情). **can·nily** adv

ca·noe /kə'nuː; kə'nu/ n light boat moved by one or more paddles. 用一支或数支桨划的轻舟; 独木舟. □ vi [VP2A, C] travel by ~. 乘此种轻舟旅行. ~·ist /-ɪst/ n person who paddles a ~. 划独木舟者; 驾轻舟者.

paddle

canoeing

canon /'kænən; 'kænən/ n 1 ecclesiastical decree: 教会法规; ~ law, church law. 教会法规. 2 general standard or principle by which sth is judged: 标准; 准则: the ~s of conduct/good taste. 行为(高尚趣味)的准则. 3 body of writings accepted as genuine; those books of the Bible accepted as genuine by the Christian Church: 正经; 正典(基督教会所认为圣经中之真经部分): the ~ of Scripture; 圣经之真经; the Chaucer ~. 乔叟著作之真本. 4 official list. 正式名单. 正式名单. 5 priest (with the title 头衔为 the Rev Can) who is one of a group with duties in a cathedral. 在大教堂中担任职务的教士. ⇨ chapter(3). **ca·noni·cal** /kə'nɒnɪkl; kə'nɑnɪkḷ/ adj according to ~ law; authorized; regular: 依照教规的; 审定的; 正规的: ~ical books; 正经; 正典; ~ical dress

ie of priests. 法衣(即教士所着者)。

cañon /'kænjən; 'kænjən/ ⇨ **canyon**.

canon·ize /'kænənaɪz; 'kænənaɪz/ vt [VP6A] (RC Church) officially proclaim to be a saint(3); (colloq) authorize permanently. (天主教) 正式宣布为圣徒; (口) 永久认可。 **canon·iz·ation** /ˌkænənaɪ'zeɪʃn US: -nɪ'z-; ˌkænənəˈzeʃən/ n canonizing or being ~d. 正式宣布为圣徒; 永久认可。

can·opy /'kænəpɪ; 'kænəpɪ/ n (pl -pies) (usu cloth) covering above a bed, throne, etc or held (on poles) over a person; cover for the cockpit of an aircraft, ⇨ the illus at **air¹**; (fig) any overhanging covering: (通常为布制)床、王座等上面之罩篷(或架于支柱上遮盖在某人上空者); 华盖; 雨遮; 遮阳; 天篷; (飞机之)座舱罩(参看air¹之插图)。(喻)任何悬于上空的篷罩; 天幕: the ~ of the heavens, the sky; 苍穹; a ~ of leaves, eg in a forest. (森林等中)树叶所构成的天幕; 林冠。

cant¹ /kænt; kænt/ n [U] **1** insincere talk (esp implying false piety); hypocrisy. 虚伪之言(尤指假装的虔敬); 伪善。 **2** special talk, words, used by a class of people, a sect, etc; jargon: 某一阶层、宗派等所用的惯用语; 隐语; 术语; 切口: thieves' ~; 盗贼用的暗语; 黑话; (attrib)(用作定语) a ~ phrase. 隐语; 术语。

cant² /kænt; kænt/ n sloping or sideways surface or position. 倾斜; 倾斜面。 □ vt, vi [VP6A, 15B, 2A, C] give, have, a ~: (使)倾斜: ~ a boat for repairs. 使船倾斜以便修理。

can't /kɑːnt US: kænt; kænt/ = **cannot**, ⇨ **can²**.

Can·tab /'kæntæb; 'kæntæb/ adj of Cambridge University. 英国剑桥大学的。

can·ta·loup, -loupe /'kæntəluːp; 'kæntl,op/ n kind of melon. 一种香瓜; 甜瓜。

can·tank·er·ous /kæn'tæŋkərəs; kæn'tæŋkərəs/ adj bad-tempered; quarrelsome. 坏脾气的; 好争吵的。 **~·ly** adv

can·tata /kæn'tɑːtə; kæn'tɑtə/ n short musical work to be sung by soloists and a choir, usu a dramatic story, but not acted. 由独唱者及合唱团演唱的短篇乐曲(通常有一戏剧性的故事, 但无动作表演); 清唱剧。 ⇨ **oratorio, opera**.

can·teen /kæn'tiːn; kæn'tin/ n **1** place (esp in factories, offices, barracks) where food and drink are sold and meals bought and eaten. (尤指工厂、办公处、军营里的)饮食部。 **2** box or chest of table silver and cutlery (knives, forks, spoons): 餐具箱: a ~ of cutlery. 一箱餐具。 **3** soldier's eating and drinking utensils. 军人的饮食用具。

can·ter /'kæntə(r); 'kæntər/ n (of a horse) easy gallop: (指马)慢跑; 小跑: The horse won the race at a ~, win easily. 那匹马于比赛中轻易获胜。 □ vt, vi (cause to) gallop gently. (使)小跑; 慢跑。

can·ticle /'kæntɪkl; 'kæntɪkl/ n short hymn, esp one taken from the Bible. 短的颂歌(尤指取自圣经者)。

can·ti·lever /'kæntɪliːvə(r); 'kæntl,ivə/ n long, large, armlike bracket extending from a wall or base (eg to support a balcony). (自墙或基座伸出以支持阳台等之)悬臂; 肱梁。 '~ **bridge** one built on supports from which ~s extend and join. 悬臂桥(悬臂自处架伸出, 彼此相接而筑成的桥)。 ⇨ the illus at **bridge**. 参看 bridge之插图。

canto /'kæntəu; 'kænto/ n (pl ~s -təuz; -toz/) chief division of a long poem. 长诗中的篇章。

can·ton /'kæntən; 'kænton/ n subdivision of a country (esp of Switzerland). (尤指瑞士的)州; 郡。

can·ton·ment /kæn'tuːnmənt US: -'toun-; kæn'tanmənt/ n permanent military station; place where soldiers live. 军队驻扎地; 军营。

can·tor /'kæntɔː(r); 'kæntər/ n leader of the singing in a church or synagogue. (教堂或犹太教堂唱诗班之)领导者。

Ca·nuck /kə'nʌk; kə'nʌk/ n (US sl) French Canadian. (美俚)法裔加拿大人。

can·vas /'kænvəs; 'kænvəs/ n [U] strong, coarse cloth used for tents, sails, bags, etc and by artists for oil-paintings; [C] (piece of this for an) oil-painting. (用制帐篷、船帆、袋袋等之)帆布; 油画家所用的画布; 油画布; 油画。 **under ~, (a)** (of soldiers, scouts, etc) living in tents. (指军队、童子军等)住于帐篷中。 **(b)** (of a ship) with sails spread. (指船)张帆的。

can·vass /'kænvəs; 'kænvəs/ vt, vi **1** [VP2A, 3A] ~ **(for)**, go from person to person and ask for votes, orders for goods, subscriptions, etc or to learn about people's views on a question: 为了向人拉票、兜售货物、书报等或对某一问题征民意调查而奔走访问: He is ~ing for the Conservative candidate. 他正在替保守党候选人奔走拉票。 **2** [VP6A] discuss thoroughly; examine by discussion: 彻底讨论; 借讨论以探究: ~ views/opinions. 彻底讨论某些意见。 □ n ~ing. 奔走访问; 拉票; 兜揽生意; 调查; 讨论。

can·yon, cañon /'kænjən; 'kænjən/ n deep gorge (usu with a river flowing through it). 峡谷(通常有河流经过其中)。

cap /kæp; kæp/ n **1** soft head-covering worn by boys and men, by some sailors and soldiers, without a brim, but often with a peak; special cap awarded to members of football teams, etc or worn to show rank: (男孩、男人及某些海军及陆军所戴之无边但常有遮檐的)软帽; (足球队员等的)运动帽; (戴以表明等级的)制帽; 法帽: a cardinal's cap; 红衣主教法帽; academic head-dress with a flat top and a tassel: (平顶有帽缨的)学位帽; wearing his cap and gown. 穿戴他的学位服及学位帽。 ⇨ **mortarboard**. **2** indoor head-dress worn by nurses, and formerly by old women. 护士及从前老太婆在室内所戴的头饰。 **3** cap-like cover (eg on a milk bottle). 盖子(如牛奶瓶盖)。 **4** per'cussion cap, small quantity of gunpowder in a wrapper of paper, etc, used as a detonator. 雷管; 火帽(少量火药包于纸等之间, 用作起爆管)。 **5** (phrases) (短语) cap and bells, cap trimmed with bells, as formerly worn by jesters. 饰有小铃之帽子(如从前弄臣所戴者)。 if the cap fits, if a person feels that the remark applies to him. 如果某人觉得这话适用于他; 如果这话说得是恰当的。 cap in hand, humbly. 谦逊地; 谦恭地。 set one's cap at sb, (of a girl or woman) try to attract as a suitor. (指妇女)逗引(某人)使之向她求婚。 □ vt (-pp-) **1** put a cap on; cover the top of. 加帽于; 盖…之顶; 把…盖上盖子。 **2** do or say sth better than (what sb else has done or said). 做得或说得优于(别人所做或所说的); 胜过。 cap a story/joke, tell a more amusing one. 说一则更有趣的故事(笑话)。 **3** award (a player) a cap (as a member of a football team, etc): 授与(球员)队员帽(认可为某足球队有关队员): He's been capped 36 times for England. 他已经三十六次获授帽为英格兰足球队队员。 (Scottish universities) confer a degree on. (苏格兰之大学)授予学位。

ca·pa·bil·ity /ˌkeɪpə'bɪlətɪ; ˌkepə'bɪlətɪ/ n **1** [U] power (of doing things, to do things); fitness or capacity (for being improved, etc): 能力(指做某事的能力, 与 of 连用, 后接动名词, 亦可与不定式连用); 适宜或有可能(如有可能改进等, 与 for 连用, 后接动名词): nuclear ~, power, capacity, to wage nuclear war. 可发动核战争的能力。 **2** (pl) (-ties) undeveloped faculties; qualities, etc, that can be developed: (复)尚未发展出来的才能; 可以发展的性质等: The boy has great capabilities. 那男孩有很大的潜能。

ca·pable /'keɪpəbl; 'kepəbl/ adj **1** gifted; able: 有天才的; 有能力的; 能干的: a very ~ doctor/nurse/teacher. 极有能力的医生(护士、教员)。 **2** ~ of, **(a)** (of persons) having the power, ability or inclination: (指人)有某种能力或意向: Show your teacher what you are ~ of, Show him how well you can work. 向你的老师表现出你的才能。 He's quite ~ of neglecting his duty, is the sort of man who might do so. 他很可能会疏于职守。 He's ~ of any crime. 他能做得出任何犯罪的事。 **(b)** (of things, situations, etc) ready for; admitting of; open to: (指

事物、情况等) 可以…的; 容许 … 的; 易接受 … 的: *The situation is ~ of improvement.* 这情况可以改善。 **ca-pably** *adv*

ca·pa·cious /kə'peɪʃəs; kə'peʃəs/ *adj* able to hold much: 容量大的: *a ~ memory;* 能记忆很多事情的记忆力。 *~ pockets.* 容量大的口袋。 **-ness** *n*

ca·pac·ity /kə'pæsɪtɪ; kə'pæsətɪ/ *n* 1 [U] (and with *indef art*) ability to hold, contain, get hold of, learn things/qualities/ideas etc: (亦与不定冠词连用) 容纳力; 学习力; 理解力; 能量; 容量; 效能: *The hall has a seating ~ of 500,* has seats for 500 people. 此厅堂可坐五百人。 *The theatre was filled to ~,* was quite full. 戏院客满。 *He has a mind of great ~,* a mind well able to grasp ideas. 他的理解力极强。 *This book is within the ~ of* (= can be understood by) *young readers.* 这本书是少年读者可以了解的。 *Some persons have more ~ for happiness* (= a greater power of experiencing happiness) *than others.* 有些人比别人更善于体验幸福。 2 [C] (*pl* **-ties**) position; character. 地位; 身份; 资格。 *in one's ~ as,* in one's position as being: 以…的身份: *I am your friend, but in my ~ as an officer of the law I must take you into custody.* 我是你的朋友, 但是以执法人员的身份我必须逮捕你。

cap·à-pie /ˌkæp ə 'piː; ˌkæpə'pi/ *adv* armed ~, armed from head to foot, completely. 全副武装地。

ca·pari·son /kə'pærɪsn; kə'pærəsn/ *n* (often *pl*; old use) ornamental covering for a horse, or for a horse and the knight who rode it. (常用复数; 旧用法) 装饰性的马衣 (遮盖于马身上或连马带骑马武士一起遮盖着)。 *vt* put a ~ on (a horse). 以马衣盖于(马)的身上。

cape¹ /keɪp; kep/ *n* loose sleeveless garment, hanging from the shoulders. 披肩; 短披风; 短斗篷。

cape² /keɪp; kep/ *n* high point of land going out into the sea; headland. 伸入海中的尖形高地; 岬; 海角。 **the C~,** (S Africa) the C~ of Good Hope; C~ Province. (南非) 好望角; 角省。

ca·per¹ /'keɪpə(r); 'kepə/ *vi* jump about playfully. 跳跃嬉戏。 *n cut a ~/~s,* jump about merrily; act foolishly or fantastically. 跳跃嬉戏; 蹦蹦跳跳; 做出愚蠢或怪诞的行为。

ca·per² /'keɪpə(r); 'kepə/ *n* prickly shrub; (*pl*) pickled flower-buds of this shrub, used to make a sauce. 续随子(有刺灌木); (复)腌泡的续随子花蕾(用以制续随子酱)。

cap·il·lary /kə'pɪlərɪ US: 'kæpəlerɪ; 'kæpl,ɛrɪ/ *n* (*pl* **-ries**) tube with a hair-like diameter (eg joining the arteries and veins), ⇨ the illus at **respiratory**: 毛细管 (如连接动脉和静脉的微血管, 参看 respiratory 之插图): (attrib)(用作定语) *~ attraction,* attraction of the kind that causes blotting-paper to absorb ink, or oil to rise through the wick of an oil lamp. 毛细管作用; 毛管引力 (使吸墨纸能吸墨水, 或油能升上灯芯的作用)。

capi·tal¹ /'kæpɪtl; 'kæpətl/ *n* (often attrib) (常用作定语) 1 town or city where the government of a country, state or province is carried on: 国都; 首都; 首府(中央或地方政府所在地): *Toronto is the ~ of Ontario.* 多伦多是安大略省的首府。 *London, Paris and Rome are ~ cities.* 伦敦、巴黎和罗马都是国家首都。 2 (of letters of the alphabet) not small: (指字母)大写; 大写的: *The pronoun 'I' is written and printed with a ~ letter.* 代词 'I' 用大写字母写或印刷。 *Write your name in letters/in ~ s.* 用大写字母写你的名字。 3 head, top part, of a column. 柱头; 柱头。 ⇨ the illus at **column.** 参看 column 之插图。 *adj* 1 punishable by death: 处以死刑的: *~ offences.* 死罪。 2 (dated colloq) excellent, first-rate: (过时口语) 极好的; 上等的: *He made a ~ speech.* 他做了一次极好的演讲。 *What a ~ idea!* 真是一个妙主意!

capi·tal² /'kæpɪtl; 'kæpətl/ *n* [U] wealth/money/property that may be used for the production of more wealth; money with which a business, etc is started (eg for building or buying factories, buying machinery). 资本; 资金(可用以生产更多财富的财产;可以建立企业如

建造或购买厂房、机器的钱)。 ~ **expenditure,** money spent on equipment, building, etc. 资本支出(如购置设备、房屋等)。 ~ **gain,** profit made from the sale of investments or property. 资本利得(出售投资物或不动产所获之利得)。 ~ **goods,** goods used to produce other goods. 资本货物(用以从事生产的货品之物)。 ~ **levy,** taking by the State of a part of all the private wealth in the country. 资本课税; 资本特征(由国家征收国内全部私有财产的一部)。 '**fixed ~,** machinery, buildings, etc. 固定资本(指机器,建筑物等)。 '**floating ~,** ~ goods. 流动资本(= capital goods). *a ~ of,* ~ valued at. 值…的资本。 *make ~ of sth,* use it to one's own advantage. 利用。

capi·tal·ism /'kæpɪtəlɪzəm; 'kæpətl,ɪzəm/ *n* [U] 资本主义 ⇨ **socialism. capi·tal·ist** *n* 1 person who controls much capital². 资本家。 2 person who supports ~. 资本主义者。 *adj* of, supporting ~: 资本主义的: *a capitalist economy.* 资本主义经济制度。 **capi·tal·is·tic** /ˌkæpɪtə'lɪstɪk; ˌkæpɪtl'ɪstɪk/ *adj*

capi·tal·ize /'kæpɪtəlaɪz; 'kæpətl,aɪz/ *vt, vi* 1 [VP6A] write or print with a capital letter. 用大写字母书写或印刷。 2[VP6A] convert into, use as, capital². (fig) take advantage of; use to one's advantage or profit. 转作资本; 用作资本; 资本化; (喻)利用; 用以牟利。 3 [VP3A] ~ **on,** profit by; exploit: 由于 … 而获益; 利用: *~ on the errors of a rival firm.* 由于敌对公司的错误而获益。 **capi·tal·iz·ation** /ˌkæpɪtəlar'zeɪʃn US: -ɪ'zeɪʃn; ˌkæpətlə'zeʃən/ *n*

capi·ta·tion /ˌkæpɪ'teɪʃn; ˌkæpə'teʃən/ *n* (reckoning of) tax, fee, charge or grant of an equal sum per person. (计算)人头税; 丁税; 人口税; 按人均摊; 按人均分的补助费(每人数目相等)。

Capi·tol /'kæpɪtl; 'kæpətl/ *n* building in which the United States Congress meets. 美国国会大厦。

ca·pitu·late /kə'pɪtʃʊleɪt; kə'pɪtʃə,let/ *vi* [VP2A] surrender (on stated conditions). (按照提出的条件)投降。 **ca·pitu·la·tion** /kəˌpɪtʃʊ'leɪʃn; kəˌpɪtʃə'leʃən/ *n* [U] surrendering (on stated conditions). (有条件的)投降。

ca·pon /'keɪpən US: -pɒn; 'kepɑn/ *n* cock (male domestic fowl) castrated and fattened for eating. 阉鸡(养肥供食用者); 肉鸡。

ca·price /kə'priːs; kə'pris/ *n* 1 (often sudden) change of mind or behaviour that has no obvious cause; tendency to change suddenly without apparent cause. 反复无常; 多变(无明显理由而突然改变心意或行为); 善变。 2 piece of music in a lively, irregular style. (音乐)奇想曲; 随想曲; 异想曲。

ca·pri·cious /kə'prɪʃəs; kə'prɪʃəs/ *adj* often changing; irregular; unreliable; guided by caprice: 多变的; 不可靠的; 反复无常的; 无明显理由而突然改变心意或行为的: *a ~ breeze,* often or suddenly changing in direction. (指风)常或突然改变方向的)的多变的风。 **~·ly** *adv*

Cap·ri·corn /'kæprɪkɔːn; 'kæprɪ,kɔrn/ *n* **Tropic of ~,** the parallel of latitude $23\frac{1}{2}$° S; tenth sign of the zodiac, ⇨ the illus at **zodiac.** 南回归线; 摩羯座; 摩羯宫(十二宫中的第十宫,参看 zodiac 之插图)。

cap·si·cum /'kæpsɪkəm; 'kæpsɪkəm/ *n* kinds of plant with seed-pods containing hot-tasting seeds; such pods prepared for use in cooking, etc. 番椒属; 番椒(俗名辣椒或大椒)。 ⇨ **cayenne, pepper**(2)。

cap·size /kæp'saɪz; kæp'saɪz/ *vt, vi* [VP6A, 2A] (esp of a boat in the water) (cause to) overturn, upset. (尤指水中的船)(使)倾覆; 翻。

cap·stan /'kæpstən; 'kæpstən/ *n* upright barrel-like object turned (formerly) by men who walk round it pushing horizontal levers, or (more usu today) by steam, etc, power, used for raising anchors, sails, etc and for pulling a ship to a wharf, etc. 绞盘; 起锚机(从前由人绕四周走并推动水平杆以旋转之, 现今日更常见者, 以蒸汽等动力旋转之。用以起锚、张帆及拖船至码头等)。

cap·sule /'kæpsjuːl *US:* 'kæpsl; 'kæpsḷ/ *n* **1** seed-case that opens when the seeds are ripe. (植物的) 荚; 英(当种子成熟时即行裂开)。 **2** tiny container (eg for a dose of medicine, often soluble). (装一剂药物, 常会溶化的)胶囊。 **3** (recoverable or non-recoverable) receptacle (for scientific instruments, or an astronaut) which can be ejected from a spacecraft. (可从太空船弹射出的)太空舱(有的可收回, 有的不能收回, 内载科学仪器或太空人)。

a space-capsule

cap·tain /'kæptɪn; 'kæptɪn/ *n* **1** leader or chief commander: 队长; 官长: *the ~ of a ship / firebrigade / football or cricket team.* 船长; 舰长 (消防队长); 足球队或板球队长)。 **2** (in the army) officer (below a major and above a lieutenant) who commands a company; (in the navy) officer below an admiral and above a commander. 陆军上尉(在少校之下, 中尉之上, 统率一连); 海军上校(在将官之下, 中校之上)。 □ *vt* [VP6A] act as ~ of (a football team, etc). 担任(足球队等之)队长。

cap·tion /'kæpʃn; 'kæpʃən/ *n* short title or heading of an article in a periodical, etc; words printed with a photograph or illustration, etc; word(s) on a movie film to establish the scene of the story, etc (eg Dover 1940). (杂志等中文章的)标题; 题目; (附于照片、插图等上的)说明文字; (电影片上确立故事背景地等的)文字说明(例如: 多佛市 1940 年)。 Cf 参较 *sub-titles.*

cap·tious /'kæpʃəs; 'kæpʃəs/ *adj* (formal) (fond of) finding fault, making protests, etc esp about unimportant points. (正式用语)好找人之错的; 好吹毛求疵的; 好抗议的(尤其关于不重要的事情)。 ~·**ly** *adv*

cap·ti·vate /'kæptɪveɪt; 'kæptə,vet/ *vt* [VP6A] capture the fancy of; fascinate: 使迷惑; 使着迷: *He was ~d by Helen / ~d with her charm.* 他为海伦(为她的美色)所迷。

cap·tive /'kæptɪv; 'kæptɪv/ *n, adj* **1** (person, animal) taken prisoner, kept as a prisoner. 俘虏; 被俘虏的(人); 被捕获的(动物)。 *be taken / hold sb ~*, take or keep him prisoner. 被俘虏; 被捕获(俘虏某人)。 *, ~ bal'loon*, one that is held to the ground by a cable. 用绳索击于地面上的气球; 被拴住的气球。 **2** and **3** '**audience**, one that cannot get away easily and is, therefore, open to persuasion (eg school-children watching TV). 受制的听众; 受制的观众(无法轻易离开者, 故易受诱服, 如观看电视的学童)。 **cap·tiv·ity** /kæp'tɪvətɪ; kæp'tɪvətɪ/ *n* [U] state of being held ~: 被俘虏的状态; 囚禁: *Some birds will not sing in captivity.* 有的鸟被关住就不肯鸣叫。

cap·tor /'kæptə(r); 'kæptɚ/ *n* person who takes sb captive. 俘虏者; 捕获者。

cap·ture /'kæptʃə(r); 'kæptʃɚ/ *vt* [VP6A] make a prisoner of; take or obtain as a prize by force, trickery, skill, etc: 俘虏; 捕获; 斩获; 骗得; 巧取: *Our army ~d 500 of the enemy.* 我军俘虏敌军五百人。 *The police have not ~d the thief yet.* 警方尚未将该盗贼捕获。 *This advertisement will ~ the attention of readers everywhere.* 这个广告将可引起各处读者的注意。 □ *n* [U] act of capturing: 俘虏; 捕获; 斩获: *the ~ of a thief;* 一窃贼之捕获; [C] thing that is ~d. 被捕获之物; 战利品。

car /kɑː(r); kɑr/ *n* **1** motor-car. 汽车。 ⇨ the illus at **motor**. 参看 motor 之插图。 '**car-ferry** *n* ferry (sea or air) for taking cars (eg across the English Channel). 车辆渡船; 载汽车过渡之飞机(如渡英吉利海峡者)。 '**car-port** *n* open-sided shelter for a motor vehicle. (有顶无墙之)汽车棚。 **2** (on a railway train)(in GB) coach:

(英国)火车车厢; 客车: '*dining-car;* 餐车; '*sleeping-car;* 卧车; (in US also) wagon for goods: (美国亦指)货车: '*freight-car* (GB 英 = '*goods-wagon*). 货车。 **3** that part of a balloon, airship or lift (US 美 = *elevator*) used by passengers. (气球, 飞艇之载人的)座舱; (电梯的)座厢。 **4** (poet) wheeled vehicle; chariot: (诗)有轮的车子; 马车; 古代战车: *the car of the sun-god.* 日神的车子(指太阳)。

ca·rafe /kə'ræf; kə'ræf/ *n* water-bottle, or decanter for wine, for use at table. (餐桌上用的)水瓶; 酒瓶。

cara·mel /'kærəmel; 'kærəml/ *n* **1** [U] burnt sugar used for colouring and flavouring. 焦糖(用以着色和调味)。 **2** [C] samll, shaped piece of sticky boiled sugar; sweetmeat. 一种有粘性的糖果。

cara·pace /'kærəpeɪs; 'kærə,pes/ *n* shell on the back of a tortoise and crustaceans. (龟或其他甲壳动物的)甲壳。 ⇨ the illus at **crustacean, reptile**. 参看 crustacean 及 reptile 之插图。

carat /'kærət; 'kærət/ *n* **1** unit of weight (= 200 milligrams or about three and one-fifth grains) for precious stones. 克拉(宝石重量的单位, 等于 200 毫克或 3¹/₅ 喱左右)。 ⇨ **App 5**. 参看附录五。 **2** (US = *karat*) measure of the purity of gold, pure gold being 24 ~s: 开(金的纯度的度量名, 纯金为二十四开): *a gold ring of 20 ~s,* ie 20 parts gold, 4 parts alloy. 一只二十开的金戒指(即二十分金, 四分合金。

cara·van /'kærəvæn; 'kærə,væn/ *n* **1** company of persons (eg pilgrims, merchants) making a journey together for safety, usu across desert country. (朝圣者、经商者等经过沙漠时为安全计所组成的)旅行队; 商队。 **2** covered cart or wagon used for living in, eg by Gypsies or people on holiday, esp (today) the kind pulled behind a motor vehicle. 有盖顶可供居住的篷车(如吉普赛人或度假游客所住者); (尤指今日拖行于汽车后面的)拖车。 ⇨ also trailer at **trail**. ~·**ning** *n* (the practice of) taking holidays in a ~. 在篷车或拖车中度假。 ~·**sary**, ~·**serai** /,kærə'vænsərɪ, -sə,raɪ; ,kærə'vænsərɪ, -sə,raɪ/ *n* inn with a large inner courtyard where ~s put up in Eastern countries. (在

a caravan of camels

a gypsy caravan

a modern caravan

caravans

cara·way /'kærəweɪ; 'kærə,we/ n plant with spicy seeds used to flavour bread, cakes, etc. 黄蒿; 葛缕子(其子味香,用以为面包、糕饼等增味)。

car·bide /'kɑːbaɪd; 'kɑrbaɪd/ n compound of carbon. 碳化物。 ⇨ **calcium**.

car·bine /'kɑːbaɪn; 'kɑrbaɪn/ n short rifle (originally for soldiers on horseback). 卡宾枪(原为骑兵所用的短来福枪)。

carbo·hy·drate /,kɑːbəʊ'haɪdreɪt; ,kɑrbo'haɪdret/ n [C, U] (kinds of) organic compound including sugars and starches; (pl) starchy foods, considered to be fattening. 醣(有机化合物,包括糖与淀粉); 碳水化合物; (复)淀粉质食物(被认为是使人体发胖者)。

car·bolic acid /,kɑː'bɒlɪk 'æsɪd; kɑr'bɑlɪk 'æsɪd/ n [U] strong-smelling, powerful liquid used as an antiseptic and disinfectant. 石碳酸; 酚(味烈强力药水,用作防腐剂和消毒剂)。

car·bon /'kɑːbən; 'kɑrbən/ n 1 [U] non-metallic element (symbol C) that occurs in all living matter, in its pure form as diamonds and graphite and in an impure form in coal and charcoal. 碳(非金属元素, 化学符号 C, 存在于一切生物体内, 纯碳则如钻石及石墨, 不纯之碳存在于煤及木炭)。 '~ **black** n black powder obtained by partly burning oil, wood, etc. (部分燃烧油、木材等而得之)黑烟末。 '~ **dating**, method of dating prehistoric objects by measuring the decay of a radioactive isotope of ~. 碳鉴定法(测量碳的放射同位素之衰变以鉴定史前古物之年代的方法)。 2 [O] stick or pencil of ~ used in an electric arc-lamp. 碳精棒(用于电弧灯灯)。 3 [U, O] (also 亦作 ~**-paper**) (sheet of) thin paper coated with coloured matter, used between sheets of writing paper for taking copies. 复写纸。 4 [O] (also 亦作 ~ **copy**) copy made by the use of ~-paper. 复写本; 副本。 5 , ~ **di'oxide** n gas (CO_2) produced by animal bodies and breathed out from the lungs; synthetic version of this used in eg canned beers and soft drinks, to give fizz. 二氧化碳(动物体内所产生的气体, 自肺中呼出); 合成之二氧化碳(用于罐头啤酒及不含酒精的饮料等中, 使起泡及发嘶声)。 , ~ **mon'oxide** n poisonous gas (CO) produced when ~ burns, present in the exhaust gas of petrol engines and after explosions in coal mines. 一氧化碳(由碳燃烧所产生之有毒气体, 存在于用汽油的发动机所排出的废气中, 及发生爆炸后的煤矿坑中)。 ~**·ated** /'kɑːbəneɪtɪd; 'kɑrbə,netɪd/ adj containing ~ dioxide: 含二氧化碳的: ~ed beverages. 含二氧化碳的饮料。 ~**·if·er·ous** /ˌkɑːbə'nɪfərəs; ,kɑrbə'nɪfərəs/ adj (geol) producing coal: (地质)产煤的: 产炭的: ~iferous strata. 煤层。 ~**·ize** vt [VP6A] convert into ~ by burning. 烧成碳, 碳化。 ~**·iz·ation** /ˌkɑːbənaɪ'zeɪʃn US: -nɪ'z-; ,kɑrbənɪ'zeʃən/ n

car·bonic acid /kɑː'bɒnɪk 'æsɪd; kɑr'bɑnɪk 'æsɪd/ n [U] carbon dioxide dissolved in water (eg giving the sharp taste to soda water). 碳酸(溶解于水之二氧化碳, 如使汽水有辛辣味道者)。

car·bor·un·dum /ˌkɑːbə'rʌndəm; ,kɑrbə'rʌndəm/ n (P) hard compound of carbon and silicon, used for polishing and grinding. (商标)碳化硅; 金刚砂(用作磨擦材料)。

car·boy /'kɑːbɔɪ; 'kɑrbɔɪ/ n large, round glass or plastic bottle, usu enclosed in basketwork or a crate to protect it from being broken. 大而圆的玻璃瓶或塑胶瓶(通常套于柳条或木架中防破损)。

car·buncle /'kɑːbʌŋkl; 'kɑrbʌŋkl/ n 1 bright-red jewel. 鲜红玉; 红宝石。 2 red (usu painful) inflamed swelling under the skin. 痈(通常感到疼痛的皮下红色炎肿)。

car·bu·ret·tor (US = -**retor**) /ˌkɑːbju'retə(r) US: 'kɑːbərettər; 'kɑrbə,retə/ n that part of an internal combustion engine in which petrol and air are mixed to make an explosive mixture. (内燃机中的)汽化器(汽油与空气在其中混合以制成有爆炸性的混合物)。

car·cass, car·case /'kɑːkəs; 'kɑrkəs/ n 1 dead body of an animal (esp one prepared for cutting up as meat): 动物的尸体 (尤指其肉将被切开供食用者): ~ meat, meat from a ~ (contrasted with tinned or corned meat). 鲜肉 (以别于罐头肉或腌肉)。 2 (contemptuous) human body. (蔑)人类之尸体; 尸首。 3 = shell(2).

card¹ /kɑːd; kɑrd/ n 1 (usu small, oblong-shaped) piece of stiff paper or thin cardboard, as used for various purposes, (通常为长方形之小)卡片(用硬纸或薄纸板制成, 作各种用途), eg 例如 a 'visiting-~ (US 美 'calling ~), with a person's name, etc on it; 名片; 'Christmas / New 'Year / 'Birthday ~s, sent with greetings at Christmas, etc; 圣诞 (贺年, 生日)卡片; 'record ~, one for keeping records, notes, etc, and stored in a box or drawer; (装于箱匣或抽屉中之)纪录卡; ~ index, index on ~s. 卡片式索引。 ~**-carrying member** n registered member of a group, political party, trade union, etc. 已登记的会员(党员、工会会员等)。 '~ **vote** n vote taken at a trade union meeting at which each delegate has a ~ representing a certain number of workers. 卡片投票(工会的投票, 因每一代表有一卡片, 代表某一数目之工人, 故名)。 2 programme for a race meeting or game, with details, and space for marking results: 赛跑或比赛场合(印有详情介绍并留有空白以纪录结果)之节目单: a 'score ~, eg for cricket. 记分卡(如用于板球比赛者)。 3 (esp) one of the 52 cards (often 'playing-~) used for various games (canasta, bridge, poker, etc) and for telling fortunes. 纸牌; (尤指一副五十二张的)扑克牌(常作 playing-card, 可用以玩各种游戏, 如 canasta、桥牌、扑克等及算命)。 have a ~ up one's sleeve, have a secret plan in reserve. 暗中有密计; 有锦囊妙计。 hold/keep one's ~s close to one's chest, ⇨ chest(2). make a ~, take a trick (⇨ trick(5)) with it. 以一牌而赢一磴。 on the ~s, (from fortune-telling by ~s) likely or possible. (源于用纸牌算命)可能的。 one's best/strongest ~, one's strongest argument, best way of getting what one wants. 某人之王牌(即最有力的论据, 达到目的的最佳方法); 绝招; 妙策。 play one's ~s well, do one's business cleverly, with good judgement. 做事精明; 处理得当而有见地。 play a sure/safe/doubtful ~, use a plan or expedient that is sure, etc. 采用万全的(稳妥的, 靠不住的)办法。 put one's ~s on the table, make one's plans, intentions, etc, known. 摊牌(明白表示出其计划、意向等)。 '~**-sharper** n person who makes a living by swindling at ~ games. 以纸牌骗赌为生者; 打牌时经常作弊的人。 4 (hum) person who is queer or amusing. (谐)怪人; 有趣的人。

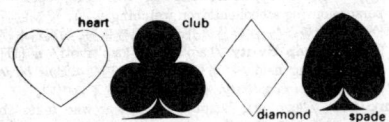

playing-card symbols

card² /kɑːd; kɑrd/ n toothed instrument, wire brush, for combing or cleaning wool, hemp etc. (梳理羊毛、大麻等的)梳子; 钢丝刷。 □ vt clean or comb with such an instrument. 用此种工具梳理。

car·da·mom /'kɑːdəməm; 'kɑrdəməm/ n [U] aromatic spice from seed-capsules of various East Indian plants. 小豆蔻(东印度群岛所产数种植物之种子荚所制的香料)。

card·board /'kɑːdbɔːd; 'kɑrd,bɔrd/ n [U] thick, stiff kind of paper or pasteboard, used for making boxes, binding books, etc. 厚硬纸板(用以制盒子、装订书籍等)。

car·diac /'kɑːdɪæk; 'kɑrdɪˌæk/ adj of the heart: 心

脏的: ~ *muscle*; 心肌; ~ *symptoms*, ie of heart disease. 心脏病症状。

car·di·gan /'kɑːdɪgən; 'kɑrdɪgən/ n knitted collarless woollen jacket that buttons up the front, made with sleeves. (胸前用钮扣开合的对襟长袖无领的) 羊毛衣; 羊毛衫。

car·di·nal /'kɑːdɪnl; 'kɑrdṇel/ adj chief; most important; on which sth depends: 主要的; 最重要的; 某事物所依赖的: *the ~ virtues*. 基本的美德。~ **numbers**, eg 5, 6, 7 (contrasted with *ordinal numbers*, eg 5th, 6th, 7th); 基数 (如五、六、七, 以别于序数第五、第六、第七); *the ~ points*, of the compass (N, S, E and W). 罗盘上的基本方位 (即北、南、东、西); 基点。⇨ the illus at **compass**. 参看 compass 之插图。□ n bishop in the RC Church who is able to participate in the election of a Pope. (天主教的) 红衣主教; 枢机主教 (有权选举教皇者)。

care¹ /keə(r); kɛr/ n 1 [U] serious attention or thought; watchfulness; pains: 审慎的注意或思索; 小心; 用心; 谨慎: *You should take more ~ over your work*. 你应当对你的工作更加用心。*This is made of glass, so handle it with ~! eg as a warning when goods are sent by rail*. 玻璃, 请小心! (如书于交铁路运输之货物箱上。) 警告语。*Take ~ (that) you don't get run over when you cross the street*. 当你穿越街道时, 小心不要被车子撞到。*Do your work with more ~*. 你要更加用心些。(Used with the *indef art*): (与不定冠词连用): *Have a ~* (= *Take ~*), be cautious. 小心; 注意。2 [U] protection; charge; responsibility: 保护; 照料; 管理; 责任: *The child was left in its sister's ~*. 这小孩留给他姐姐照料。*The library is under the ~ of Mr Grey*. 图书馆由格雷先生管理。*I will leave this in your ~*, leave you responsible for it. 我将把此事交由你负责。~ **of**, (often written 常写作 **c/o**) used in addresses before the name of the person(s) to whose house, office, etc a letter is sent. 由…转交 (书于信封等上被托请转信件人姓名之前)。**Child C~ officer** n (in GB but no longer current, now *social worker*) person appointed to look after children who are homeless or whose parents are neglectful, etc. 小孩保护官 (昔时英国之官员, 今称社会工作人员, 被指派照顾无家可归或父母疏于照料的孩童)。**take into ~**, (of such an officer) take (a child lacking proper ~) to an institution. (指上述之官员) 将 (缺乏适当照料的孩童) 送到孤儿院或教养院。**take ~ of**, (colloq) deal with, be responsible for. (口) 处理; 负责。'**~taker** n person paid to take ~ of a building during the owner's absence; (US 美 = *janitor*) person in charge of the upkeep of a public building such as a school or of a private building such as a block of flats. (房主不在时) 受雇替房主看管房屋之人; (公共建筑如学校或私人公寓等之) 管理员。**~taker Government**, administration that continues in office until a new one is formed to take over its work. 看守政府 (在新内阁未组成前继续执行政务之内阁)。3 [U] worry; anxiety; troubled state of mind caused by doubt or fear: 忧愁; 焦虑; 疑虑; 疑惧; 操心; 担忧: *free from ~*. 无忧无虑。*C~ had made him look ten years older*. 忧虑已使他显得老了十岁。'**~-free** adj showing no worry; cheerful. 无忧无虑的; 逍遥自在的; 快乐的。'**~laden**, '**~worn** adj showing worry; troubled. 忧心忡忡的; 操心劳碌的。4 [C] (usu pl) cause of sorrow and anxiety: (通常用复数) 忧愁之因: *Cares of every kind*. 各种各样的忧虑之事。*He was rich and free from ~s of every kind*. 他很富有, 又无任何可忧虑之事。*He was poor and troubled by the ~s of a large family*. 他贫穷又为众多的子女所累。

care² /keə(r); kɛr/ vi 1 [VP2A, 3A, B] (with *prep* usu omitted before a clause) (在从句前面, 通常省去介词) ~ (*about*), feel interest, anxiety or sorrow: (对…) 感到关切、操心或忧虑: *He failed in the examination but I don't think he ~s very much / he doesn't seem to ~*. 他虽然考试不及格; 但我认为他并不大在乎 (他似乎并不在

乎). *He doesn't ~ much (about) what happens to me*. 他不太关心我所发生的事。*He doesn't ~ what they say*. 他不管他们所怎么说。*I don't ~ who you are / how soon you leave*. 我不管你是谁 (我不在乎你多快离开)。*He doesn't ~ a damn*, is not in the least interested, worried, etc. 他一点也不在乎。*Who ~s?* 谁在乎? 2 [VP3A] ~ for, like (to have): 喜欢; 想要: *Would you ~ for a drink?* 你想喝一杯吗? *I shouldn't ~ for that man to be my doctor*. 我不要那个人替我看病。3 [VP3A] ~ for, have a taste for; like: 爱好; 喜爱: *Do you ~ for modern music?* 你爱听现代音乐吗? 4 [VP3A] ~ for, provide food, money, shelter, etc: 照顾; 养活: *Who will ~ for the children if their mother dies?* 如果这些孩子的母亲死了, 谁来照料他们? *The State must ~ for the families of soldiers killed in the war*. 国家必须照料阵亡军人家属的生活。5 [VP4O] like; be willing or desirous (inter and neg only): 想; 愿意; 欲望 (只用于疑问句及否定句): *Would you ~ to go for a walk?* 你想去散散步吗? *I don't ~ to be seen in his company*. 我不愿被人看见同他一起。

ca·reen /kə'riːn; kə'rin/ vt, vi 1 [VP6A] turn (a ship) on one side for cleaning, repairing, etc. 使(船)倾侧(以便清洁、修理等)。2 [VP6A, 2A] (cause to) tilt, lean over to one side. (使) 倾侧。

ca·reer /kə'rɪə(r); kə'rɪr/ n 1 [C] progress through life; development and progress of a party / principle etc: 一生的经历; (党派、主义等的) 发展和进步: *We can learn much by reading about the ~s of great men*. 阅读伟人一生经历的作品可获很多之心得。2 [C] way of making a living; profession: 谋生之道; 职业: *Should all ~s be open to women*, Should women be allowed to enter all occupations? 各行各业是否均应容许妇女参与? (attrib) professional: (用作定语) 职业性的; a ~ diplomat; 职业外交家; a '~ girl, (esp) one who prefers a ~ to marriage. 职业妇女 (尤指喜欢工作胜过结婚者)。3 [U] quick or violent forward movement: 飞跃; 猛进: *in full ~*, at full speed; 全速进行; *stop (sb) in mid ~*. 使 (某人) 中途停住。□ vi [VP2C, 3A] ~ along / past / through, etc, rush wildly. 飞奔; 急驰。**~·ist** n person whose chief interest is personal advancement in his profession. 追求名利的人。

care·ful /'keəfl; 'kɛrfel/ adj 1 (pred) (用作表语) be ~ (*about* / *of*), (of a person) taking care; cautious; thinking of, paying attention to, what one does, says, etc: (指人) 小心的; 当心的; 仔细的; 审慎的: *Be ~ not to break the eggs*. 小心不要打破鸡蛋。*Be ~ (about / of) what you do / what you say / where you go / how you carry it etc*. 对你所做的事 (所说的话, 到何处去, 怎样拿它等) 要小心。*Be more ~ with your work*. 对你的工作要更加注意。*Be ~ of your health*. 小心你的健康。2 done with, showing, care: 小心做出的; 显示小心或审慎的: ~ *guidance / a ~ guide*; 小心的指导 (审慎的向导); *a ~ piece of work*; 精细的作品; *a ~ examination of the facts*. 对于事实所作仔细的调查。~·**ly** /-fəli; -fɛlɪ/ adv ~**ness** n

care·less /'keəlɪs; 'kɛrlɪs/ adj 1 (of a person) not taking care; thoughtless: (指人) 不小心的; 不谨慎的; 粗心的: *He is ~ about leaving the door unlocked when he goes to bed*. 他粗心大意睡前忘记门闩。*A ~ driver is a danger to the public*. 粗心的驾驶员对于公众是一种危险。2 done or made without care: 不用心或不仔细做成的: *a ~ mistake*. 粗心的错误。3 (liter) light-hearted; gay: (文) 无忧无虑的; 快活的; ~ *little songbirds*. 快活的小鸣禽。4 ~ *of*, (liter) unconcerned about; uncomplainingly accepting: (文) 不在乎的; 不抱怨地接受的: *He is ~ of his reputation*. 他不在乎他的名声。*The soldiers were ~ of hardship*. 那些军人不在乎艰苦。~·**ly** adv ~·**ness** n: *a piece of ~ness*, a ~ act. 一次粗心的行为。

ca·ress /kə'res; kə'rɛs/ n [C] loving or affectionate touch or light stroke. 抚爱; 抚摸。□ vt [VP6A] give a ~ or ~s to. 抚爱; 抚摸。~·**ing** adj showing love.

示爱的。 **~·ing·ly** adv

caret /'kærət; 'kærət/ n mark (ʌ) used (eg in correcting proofs) to show, in writing or print, where sth is to be inserted. (如校对时用的)脱字记号; 加字记号(ʌ)。

cargo /'ka:gəʊ; 'kargo/ n (pl **~es**, US also **~s**/-gəʊz; -goz/) [C, U] goods carried in a ship, aircraft or other vehicle: 货物(船上、飞机或其他车辆所载的)的货物: a '~ ship / plane. 货轮(运输机)。Cf 参较 goods/freight train.

cari·bou /'kærɪbu:; 'kærə,bu/ n (pl **~s** or, collective pl 集合名词复数 **~**) N American reindeer. (北美洲产的)驯鹿。

cari·ca·ture /'kærɪkətjʊə(r); 'kærɪkətʃə/ n 1 [C] picture of sb or sth, imitation of a person's voice, behaviour etc, stressing certain features, to amuse or ridicule. 讽刺画; 漫画; 对某人之声音、行为等的模仿(借强调某些特征以引人发笑或予以嘲弄)。2 [C] art of doing this. 讽刺画之艺术; 讽刺性的滑稽模仿。□ vt [VP6A] make, give, a ~ of. 为…作讽刺画; 对…作讽刺性的滑稽模仿。**cari·ca·tur·ist** n expert in ~. 讽刺画家; 讽刺性的滑稽模仿者。

car·ies /'keəri:z; 'kɛriz/ n [U] (med) decay (of bones or teeth): (医)龋; 骨疡; 骨疽: dental ~. 龋齿。 **cari·ous** /'keərɪəs; 'kɛrɪəs/ adj (of bone) affected with ~. (指骨)患骨疽的。

car·il·lon /kə'rɪljən US: 'kærəlʊn; 'kærə,lɑn/ n set of bells in a tower on which tunes may be played by some kind of mechanism (eg a keyboard). (可用机械, 如键盘, 奏出曲调的)排钟; 钟琴。

Car·mel·ite /'ka:məlaɪt; 'karml,aɪt/ n, adj (friar or nun) of the religious order founded in 1155. (创始于1155年之)卡米尔教派的; 卡米尔教派之修道士或修女; 白袍苦行僧。

car·mine /'ka:maɪn; 'karmɪn/ n, adj deep red (colour or colouring matter). 深红(颜色, 色素); 洋红; 胭脂红。

car·nage /'ka:nɪdʒ; 'karnɪdʒ/ n [U] (liter) killing of many people (类): a scene of ~, 残杀(人类): eg a battlefield. 残杀的场所(如战场)。

car·nal /'ka:nl; 'karnəl/ adj (formal) of the body or flesh; sensual (opposite to spiritual): (正式用语)肉体的; 感官的(与 spiritual 之反义词): ~ desires. 肉欲。 **~·ly** adv

car·na·tion /ka:'neɪʃn; kar'neʃən/ n garden plant with sweet-smelling white, pink or red flowers; the flower. 红茂草(亦称作荷兰石竹, 园艺植物, 开白色、粉红色或红色的香花); 红茂草之花; 康乃馨。

car·ni·val /'ka:nɪvl; 'karnɪvl/ n [U] public merry-making and feasting, usu with processions of persons in fancy dress, esp in RC countries during the week before Lent; [C] festival of this kind. 公众饮宴作乐(通常并有化装游行, 尤指天主教国家在四旬斋前一周内之狂欢); 狂欢节; 嘉年华会。

car·ni·vore /'ka:nɪvɔ:(r); 'karnə,vor/ n flesh-eating animal. 食肉动物。 **car·ni·vor·ous** /ka:'nɪvərəs; kar'nɪvərəs/ adj flesh-eating. 食肉的。

carol /'kærəl; 'kærəl/ n song of joy or praise, esp a Christmas hymn: 欢乐或赞美之歌; (尤指)圣诞颂歌: '~ singers, singers who visit people's houses at Christmas to sing ~s (and usu to collect money for charity). (圣诞节挨户唱圣诞颂歌的)颂歌队队员(通常作为慈善募款)。□ vi, vt (-ll-, in US also -l-) sing joyfully; celebrate with ~s. 欢乐地唱; 唱颂歌以庆祝; 歌颂。 **~·ler** n

ca·rouse /kə'raʊz; kə'raʊz/ vi [VP2A] drink heavily and be merry (at a noisy meal, party etc). 在喧闹的宴会等)狂欢作乐。 **ca·rousal** /kə'raʊzl; kə'raʊzl/ n noisy drinking-party or revelry. 喧闹的饮宴或狂欢。

carp¹ /ka:p; karp/ n (pl unchanged) large freshwater fish that lives in lakes and ponds. (复数不变)鲤鱼(产于湖泊及养于池中之大淡水鱼)。

carp² /ka:p; karp/ vi [VP2A, 3A] **~ (at)**, make unnecessary complaints about small matters: 吹毛求疵; 找小错: 挑小毛病: a ~ing tongue; 爱找碴儿的嘴; ~ing

criticism. 吹毛求疵的批评。 She's always ~ing at her husband. 她老是挑拨丈夫的小毛病。

car·pal /'ka:pl; 'karpl/ adj (anat) of the wrist. (解剖)腕的。□ n (anat) bone in the wrist. ⟹ the illus at **skeleton**. (解剖)腕骨(参看 skeleton 之插图)。

car·pen·ter /'ka:pɪntə(r); 'karpəntə/ n workman who makes and repairs (esp) the wooden parts of buildings and other structures of wood. 木匠。⟹ **joiner**. **car·pen·try** /-trɪ; -trɪ/ n [U] work of a ~. 木工; 木作。

car·pet /'ka:pɪt; 'karpɪt/ n [C] 1 thick covering for floors or stairs, usu of wool, hair or synthetic fibres, often with a pattern or designs woven into it. 地毯(通常以羊毛、兽毛或合成纤维织成, 并常织有各种图案)。 **on the ~**, (colloq) being reprimanded. (口)受责罚; 受责备; 挨骂。 **sweep sth under the ~**, hide, ignore, sth, in order to delay action, escape blame, etc. 隐藏、不理某事物以期拖延行动、逃避受责等。 '**~-bag** n (old fashioned) travelling bag made of ~. (旧式之)毯制之旅行手提包。 '**~-bag·ger** n (US) person, during the American Civil War (1861—1865), from northern USA who went to the South to seek financial or political advantage. (美)一八六一年至一八六五年南北战争期中赴南方寻求金钱或政治利益的北方人。 '**~-knight** n soldier who has not seen active service, stay-at-home soldier; ladies' man. 未参加过实地作战之军人; 守在家里的军人; 喜与女人厮混的男人。 '**~-slippers** n pl (old-fashioned) kind of soft slippers with uppers of woollen cloth. 一种(旧式的)毛布为面的软拖鞋。 '**~-sweeper** n device with revolving brush(es) for sweeping ~s and rugs. (有旋转刷的)扫地器。 2 sth suggesting a ~: 毯状物; 象地毯般的覆盖物: a ~ of moss, eg in a garden. 一层(如地毯般的)青苔。□ vt [VP6A] 1 cover (as) with a ~: (如)以地毯覆盖: to ~ the stairs; 将楼梯铺上地毯; a lawn ~ed with fallen leaves. 盖着一层落叶的草地。 2 (sl) reprimand: (俚)申斥; 责骂: He's been ~ed. 他挨了骂。

car·riage /'kærɪdʒ; 'kærɪdʒ/ n 1 [C] vehicle, esp one with four wheels, pulled by a horse or horses, for carrying people: 车; (尤指一或数匹马拉的)载人的)四轮马车: a ~ and pair, one pulled by two horses 两匹马拉的马车。 ⟹ **coach¹**. '**~-way** n (part of a) road used by

a carriage

vehicles: 车道: Cars must not park on the ~way. 汽车不可停在车道上。 **dual** '**~-way**, road divided down the centre (by a barrier, a strip of pavement or grass) for traffic in each direction (US 美 = divided highway). 双车道公路(路之中央由栅栏、砌石或草坪分开, 两边车辆各向一方行驶)。 2 [C] wheeled vehicle for passengers on a railway train (US 美 = car): coach: (铁路列车的)客车厢; 客车: The first class ~s are in front. 头等车厢在前面。 3 [U] (cost of) carrying of goods from place to place. 货物运费; 货运。 **~ forward**, cost of ~ to be paid by the receiver 运费由收货人负担。 **~ free/paid**, ~ free to the receiver /paid by the sender. (收货人)免付运费; 运费已付。 4 [C] wheeled support on which a heavy object may move or be moved (eg a gun ~); moving part of a machine, changing the position of other parts (eg the roller of a typewriter). (可用以移动重物的)有轮支架(例如炮架); 轨运器(机器之活动的部分, 可以改变其他部分之位置者; 如打字机之滚筒)。 5 (sing only) manner of holding the head or the body (when

walking, etc): (仅用单数) 仪态: *She has a graceful* ~, She stands and walks gracefully. 她举止优雅。 ⇨ **carry (8).**

car·rier /'kærɪə(r); 'kærɪɚ/ *n* **1** person or company that carries goods or people for payment (eg a railway, shipping or aircraft company). 运货人; 货运公司(如铁路、轮船或航空公司), 运输业者。**2** support for luggage, etc fixed to a bicycle, motor-car, etc. (装于脚踏车、汽车等之)置物架; 行李架, 货架。**3** person, animal, etc that carries or transmits a disease without himself or itself suffering from it. 菌邮(携带或传染疾病而其本身不受感染之人或动物等); 带菌者。**4** vehicle, ship, etc used for the transport of troops, aircraft, tanks, etc. 运输军队、飞机、战车等之车辆、舰艇等。⇨ **aircraft-~, Bren-~, troop-~. 5** '~-**bag** *n* strong paper or plastic bag with hand grips for eg carrying away purchases from shops. 装货袋(如用以装购买自商店中带走的手提厚纸袋或塑胶袋)。 '~-**pigeon** *n* pigeon used to carry messages because it can find its way home from a distant place. 传信鸽。

car·rion /'kærɪən; 'kærɪən/ *n* [U] dead and decaying flesh. 腐肉。'~ **crow**, crow that lives on ~ and small animals. 食腐肉及小动物之乌鸦。

car·rot /'kærət; 'kærət/ *n* (plant with) yellow or orange-red root used as a vegetable, ⇨ the illus at **vegetable.** 胡萝卜(根部黄色或橘红色,作蔬菜食用); 参看 vegetable 之插图)。 *the stick and the* ~, threats and bribes. 威胁利诱。 *hold out/offer a* ~ *to sb*, entice by offering a reward or advantage. 许以报酬或利益以诱惑某人; 利诱某人。~-**y** *adj* (esp of hair) orange-red. (尤指头发)橘红色的。

carry[1] /'kærɪ; 'kærɪ/ *vt, vi* (*pt, pp* **carried**) (For uses with *adverbial particles* and *preps,* ⇨ **11** below.) (与副词性小品词及介词连用的用法,参看下列第 11 义。) **1** [VP 6A,15A,B] support the weight of and move from place to place; take a person, a message, etc from one place to another: 携带; 搬运; 传送; 将(人、信息等)由甲处送至乙地: *He was* ~*ing a box on his shoulder.* 他的肩上扛着一只箱子。 *She was* ~*ing the baby in her arms.* 她怀中抱着婴儿。 *Railways and ships* ~ *goods.* 铁路及船舶运输货物。 *He carried* (= went round and told) *the news to everyone in the village.* 他将消息传告村中每一个人。 *He ran off as fast as his legs could* ~ *him*, as fast as he could run. 他尽快飞奔而去。 *This bicycle has carried me 500 miles.* 这部脚踏车已载我跑了五百英里路。 *How far will five gallons of petrol* ~ *you?* 五加仑汽油可(载你)跑多少路? *Some kinds of seeds are carried by the wind for great distances.* 有些种类的种子借风力送到远的地方。 *The raft was carried by ocean currents to a small island.* 该筏被大洋的水流飘送至一小岛。 *A spy carries his life in his hands*, takes the risk of death. 间谍随时有死亡的危险。 '~-**cot** *n* light cot with handles (but no wheels) for ~ing a baby. (轻便有把手,但无轮子的)婴儿床。 **2** [VP6A,15A] have with one; wear; possess: 带着; 穿着; 有: *Do you always* ~ *an umbrella?* 你总是带伞吗? *Ought the police to be allowed to* ~ *fire-arms?* 警察应被准许携带武器吗? *I never* ~ *much money with me.* 我身边从来不带很多钱。 *Can you* ~ *all these figures in your head*, remember them without writing them down? 你能仅凭脑筋记得所有这些数字吗? *The wound left a scar that he will* ~ *with him to the grave*, that will remain for life. 那伤口给他留下了一个一辈子也去不掉的疤痕。 **3** [VP6A] support: 支持; 支撑: *These pillars* ~ *the weight of the roof.* 这些柱子支撑屋顶的重量。 *The girders are carried on trestles.* 这些大梁是由支架撑着。 **4** [VP6A] involve; entail; have as a result: 含有; 具有; 使负担; 有某种后果: *The loan carries* 3½% *interest.* 该贷款负担百分之三点五的利息。 *That argument does not* ~ *conviction*, is not convincing. 该论据不能令人折服。 *Power carries responsibility with it.* 权力本身带有责任的。 *His word/promise carries weight*, is influential. 他的话(承诺)具有分量(有影响力)。 **5** [VP6A, 15A] (of pipes, wires,

etc) conduct; take: (指管子、金属丝等)输送; 传导: *The oil is carried across the desert in pipe-lines.* 石油用管子送过沙漠。 *Copper carries electricity.* 铜能传电。**6** [VP15A] make longer; extend; take (to a specified point, in a specified direction, etc): 使延长; 伸展; 使延伸(至某一点、向某一方向等): ~ *a fence round a field*; 延伸篱笆围绕一块地; ~ *pipes under a street*; 将管子从街道下面延伸; ~ *a joke too far*, be no longer amusing. 把一则笑话说得太长(不再有趣)。 *Don't* ~ *modesty too far.* 不要谦逊得过分了。**7** [VP6A, 15A] win; capture; persuade; overcome: 赢得; 夺得; 说服; 克服: *The soldiers rushed forward and carried the enemy's position.* 士兵们冲上去夺得敌人的阵地。 *He carried his audience with him*, won their sympathy and agreement. 他博得了听众的赞同。 *The bill/motion/resolution was carried*, there were more votes for it than against it. 该提案(动议,决议)业经表决通过。 ~ *the day*, be victorious. 得胜; 胜利。 ~ *everything before one*, be completely successful. 万事如意; 完全成功。 ~ *one's point*, win approval for it. 意见获得赞同。**8** [VP6A, 15A, 16B] hold oneself/one's head/one's body in a specified way: (使自己、头部、身体)做出某种姿势或体态: *He carries himself like a soldier*, stands and walks like one. 他的举止行动象个军人。 *She carries herself badly*, eg by slouching or stooping. 她的体态欠佳(懒散或弯腰驼背)。**9** [VP2B, C] (of guns) send a shell, etc a certain distance; (of missiles, sounds, voices, etc) have the power to go to: (指枪炮)将(炮弹等)射至某一距离; (指发射物、声音、语音等)能达及; 能射至; 能传至: *Our guns do not* ~ *far enough.* 我们的炮射程不够远。 *The sound of the guns carried many miles.* 枪炮的声音传至多远处。 *The shot carried 200 metres.* 那子弹射至二百米远。 *A public speaker must have a voice that carries well.* 演说家必须有很远都能听到的(洪亮的)嗓音。**10** [VP6A] (of a newspaper, etc) print in its pages: (指报纸等)登载; 刊出: *a newspaper that carries several pages of advertisements.* 登载有数版广告的一份报纸。**11** [VP15B, 2C] (with *adverbial particles* and *preps*): (与副词性小品词及介词连用):

carry sb/sth away, (a) (usu passive) cause to lose self-control: (通常用被动语态) 使失去自我控制力; 使失去理智: *He was carried away by his enthusiasm*, was so enthusiastic that he was unable to judge calmly, etc. 他因太热情而失去理智。 (b) (naut) lose (masts, etc) by breaking: (航海)因折断而失去(桅等): *The ship's masts were carried away during the storm.* 该船的帆樯在暴风雨中全被折断。

carry sb back, take back in the memory: 使忆起: *an incident that carried me back to my school-days*, caused me to recall them. 一件使我忆起学生时代的偶然事件。

carry sth forward, (comm, book-keeping) transfer (a total of figures on a page) to the head of a new column or page. (商,簿记)(将一页的总数)转记于另一页或另一栏的开头; 延后; 结转; 过次。

carry sth off, win: 赢得: *Tom carried off all the school prizes.* 汤姆把学校里的奖品都得来了。 ~ *it/sth off (well)*, succeed in a difficult situation; cover a mistake, etc.在困难环境中获得成功; 将错误掩饰起来。

carry (sth) on, (a) conduct; manage: 进行; 经营: *Rising costs made it hard to* ~ *on the business.* 上涨的成本使生意难做。 *It's difficult to* ~ *on a conversation at a noisy party.* 在喧闹的宴会中谈话困难。 (b) talk volubly and complainingly; behave strangely or suspiciously: 滔滔不绝地带牢骚地谈话; 行为奇特或令人起疑: *How she does* ~ *on!* 她真是滔滔不绝,牢骚满腹! *Did you notice how they were* ~*ing on?* 你注意到他们的行为多奇怪吗? Hence, 由此产生, ~**ings-on**, *n pl*: *Such queer carryings-on next door*, such queer happenings! 隔壁邻家居然有这么奇怪的事情! ~ *on (with)*, continue (doing sth): 继续(做某事): C~ *on (with your work).* 继续做(你的工作)。 *They decided to* ~ *on in spite of the weather.* 不管天气如何他们决定继续做下去。 ~ *on (an affair) (with)*, (often suggesting disapproval) flirt with; have a love

affair with: (常表示不赞许)调情; 与…谈爱: *His wife is ~ing on with the postman.* 他的妻子正在和邮差调情. **(sth) to ~ on with,** (sth) (to do or use) for the time being: 暂时使用(某物); 凑合着用(某物): *I can't give you all you need, but here's £5 to ~ on／be ~ing on with.* 我不能给你所需的一切, 不过这里是五英镑供你暂时之用. **carry sth out, (a)** as required or specified: fulfil; complete: 实行; 完成: ~ *out a promise／threat／plan／instruction.* 实践诺言(实行威胁; 实现计划; 完成命令). **(b)** perform; conduct: 进行: ~ *out experiments／tests.* 进行试验. **carry sb／sth through, (a)** help (through difficulties, etc): 帮助(渡过难关等): *Their courage will ~ them through.* 他们的勇气将会使他们度过难关. **(b)** complete; fulfil: 完成: *Having made a promise, you must ~ it through.* 既已许下承诺, 你必须完成它(履行).

carry² /ˈkæri; ˈkærɪ /n **1** range of a gun, etc; distance that a shell, etc, goes. (枪炮等之)射程; 子弹等所能达到之距离. **2** portage; act of carrying boats, etc, from one river or lake to another; place where this must be done. 两水路间之陆上运送; 水陆联运; 将船只等自甲河(湖)运至乙河(湖); 此种联运地点.

cart /kɑːt; kɑrt /n two-wheeled vehicle pulled by a horse. 二轮单马车. ⇨ also **hand ~. be in the ~,** (sl) be in an awkward or losing position. (俚) 处于困厄或失利的地位. **put the ~ before the horse,** do or put things in the wrong order, take the effect for the cause (eg by saying 'I fail because I didn't study'). 做事本末倒置; 倒果为因(如说'我很懒惰因为我没有读书'). **turn '~-wheels,** turn somersaults sideways. 侧身翻斤斗. **'~-horse** n strong horse for heavy work. 担任重工作的壮马. **'~-load** n as much as a ~ holds: 一马车所载之量: *a ~-load of manure.* 一马车肥料. **'~-road／-track,** rough unmetalled road. 未铺碎石的不平道路. □ vt [VP6A, 15B] **1** carry in a ~: 用马车装运: ~*ing hay;* 用马车运干草; ~ *away the rubbish.* 用马车将垃圾运走. **2** (colloq) carry in the hands, etc: (口)用手等携带; 随身带: *Have you really got to ~ these parcels around for the rest of the day?* 在今天其余的时间里你真的非要把著这些包裹到处去拿吗? ~**age** / ˈkɑːtɪdʒ; ˈkɑrtɪdʒ/ n [U] (cost of) carting. 马车装运(费). ~**er** n man whose work is driving ~s; carrier (1). 马车伕; 运货人(货运公司)运输业者.

a cart

carte blanche /ˌkɑːt ˈblɒnʃ; ˈkɑrt ˈblɑnʃ/ n (F) full authority or freedom (to use one's own judgement about how to proceed, etc). (法)全权; 自由处理权(运用自己的判断力以决定如何进行等之权).

car·tel /kɑːˈtel;ˈkɑrtl/ n (comm) combination of traders, manufacturers, etc to control output, marketing, prices of goods, etc. (商)卡特尔; 同业联盟(工商业者之联合组织, 以便控制生产量、销售及货价等).

car·ti·lage /ˈkɑːtɪlɪdʒ; ˈkɑrtlɪdʒ/ n [C, U] (structure, part, of) tough, white tissue attached to the joints, in animal bodies; gristle. (动物体内连于关节上的)软骨; 软骨结构. **car·ti·lagi·nous** /ˌkɑːtɪˈlædʒɪnəs, ˌkɑrtlˈædʒənəs/ adj of or like ~. 软骨的; 如软骨的.

car·togra·pher / kɑːˈtɒgrəfə(r); kɑrˈtɑgrəfə/ n person who makes maps and charts. 绘制图表者; 绘图员. **car·togra·phy** / ˈkɑːtɒgrəfɪ; kɑrˈtɑgrəfɪ/ n [U] the drawing of maps and charts. 绘制图表; 制图法; 制图学.

car·ton /ˈkɑːtn; ˈkɑrtn/ n cardboard box for holding goods: (装货物的) 纸板盒: *a ~ of 200 cigarettes,* with 10 packets of 20. 一条香烟(共十包, 每包二十支).

car·toon /kɑːˈtuːn; kɑrˈtun/ n **1** drawing dealing with current (esp political) events in an amusing or satirical way. 卡通; 漫画(以时事, 尤指政治事件, 为题材所作之风趣或讽刺图画). **2** full-size preliminary drawing on paper, used as a model for a painting, a tapestry, a fresco, a mosaic, etc. 底图; 草图(作画、织锦、壁画、镶嵌细工等所用画于纸上的大样). **3** (= animated ~) cinema film made by photographing a series of drawings: 动画片;卡通影片(由拍摄一连串之图画所制成之活动影片): *a Walt Disney ~.* 一部沃尔特·迪斯尼制作的卡通影片. □ vt represent (a person). 以漫画画 (人物等). ~**·ist** n person who draws ~s(1). 漫画家.

car·tridge /ˈkɑːtrɪdʒ; ˈkɑrtrɪdʒ/ n **1** case (of metal, cardboard, etc) containing explosive (for blasting), or explosive with bullet or shot (for firing from a rifle or shot gun). 子弹(弹壳由金属或纸板等制成, 内装火药, 起爆炸作用); 弹筒(内装火药, 并带弹头, 自步枪或炮中发

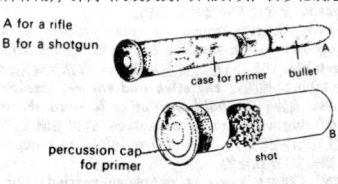

A for a rifle
B for a shotgun

case for primer   bullet

percussion cap for primer   shot

cartridges

射). ⇨ **blank** n (4). **'~-belt** n one with sockets for holding ~s. 子弹带. **'~-paper, (a)** paper for making ~ cases. 弹筒纸 (制弹筒用的厚纸板). **(b)** thick white paper for pencil and ink drawings. (铅笔画或墨水画用的)厚白纸. **2** detachable head of a pick-up (on a record-player), holding the stylus. (唱机之)唱头(装置唱针的部份). **3** (US)cassette. (美) 卡式录音带盒; 卡式胶卷盒.

carve /kɑːv; kɑrv/ vt, vi **1** [VP6A, 14, 15B] form (sth) by cutting away material from a piece of wood or stone: 雕刻;用木头或石头雕成(某物): ~ *a statue out of wood／a statue in oak;* 雕刻一座木(橡木)像; *a figure ~d from marble;* 大理石雕像; ~ *out a career for oneself,* (fig) achieve one by great effort. (喻)为自己创立一番事业. **2** [VP6A, 15A] inscribe by cutting on a surface: (在物之表面上)刻字; 铭刻: ~ *one's initials on a tree trunk;* 将其姓名之起首字母刻于树干上; ~ *an inscription on a bench.* 将字刻于长凳上. **3** [VP6A, 15B] cut up (cooked meat) into pieces or slices at or for the table: 将(煮熟的肉) 切成块或片以便食用: ~ *a leg of mutton／a turkey.* 将羊腿(火鸡)切开以便食用. **'carving-knife／-fork** n knife, fork, used for carving meat. (餐桌上用的)切肉刀、叉. **carver** n carving-knife; person who ~s; (pl)carving-knife and fork. 切肉刀; 切肉的人; (复)切肉刀叉. **carv·ing** n sth ~d in wood, etc. (木等之)雕刻品. ⇨ **sculptor, sculpture.**

cary·atid /ˌkærɪˈætɪd; ˌkærɪˈætɪd / n (archit) draped statue of a female figure used as a support (eg a pillar) in a building. (建筑)女像柱.

cas·cade /kæˈskeɪd; kæsˈked/ n waterfall; one section of a large, broken waterfall; wave-like fall of lace; cloth, etc. 瀑布; 大瀑布之一支; 分段瀑布; 花边、布等作波状之下垂; 波状花边. □ vi fall like a ~. 如瀑布落下.

case¹ /keɪs; kes/ n **1** instance or example of the occurrence of sth; actual state of affairs; circumstances or special conditions relating to a person or thing; (med) person suffering from a disease; instance of a diseased condition: 事例; 实情; 与某人或某事物有关的环境或特殊情况; (医)病人; 病例; 病案: *Is it the ~ (= Is it true)*

that you have lost all your money? 你的钱全部都损失了，是真的吗？ *No, that's not the* ～, is not true. 不，那不是事情的真相。 *If that's the* ～ (= If the situation is as stated or suggested)*, you'll have to work much harder.* 如果情形是那样的话，你将必须更加努力工作。 *I can't make an exception in your* ～, for you and not for others. *Such being the* ～ (= In view of, Because of, these facts, etc)*, you can't go away.* 既如此，你不能离开。 *It's a clear* ～ *of cheating,* is clear that cheating has taken place. 这显然是欺骗。 *There were five* ～*s of* (= five persons suffering from) *influenza.* 有五起患流行性感冒的病例。 *The worst* ～*s were sent to hospital.* 最严重的病人被送到医院去了。 *a* ～ *in point,* ⇨ *point¹ (9): (just) in* ～, if it should happen that; because of a possibility: 若；如果；万一: *It may rain—you'd better take an umbrella (just) in* ～. 可能会下雨——你最好带一把雨伞，以防万一。 *In* ～ *I forget, please remind me of my promise.* 如果我忘记了，请提醒我我的诺言。 *in* ～ *of,* in the event of: 若；如果：万一: *In* ～ *of fire, ring the alarm bell.* 万一失火的话，请按警铃。 *in 'any* ～, whatever happens or may have happened. 无论如何。 *in 'no* ～, in no circumstances. 决不。 *in 'this/'that* ～, if this/that happens, has happened, should happen. 若是这样（那样）的话。 '～-**book** *n* record kept by a professional man (eg a doctor) of ～ dealt with. (专业人员，如医生之)病历薄；个案纪录簿；事例集。'～**history** *n* record of the history of sb suffering from a disease, social or mental trouble, etc. (病人的)病历；个案历史。'～**work** *n* work involving personal study of individuals or families with social problems. (涉及社会问题之个人或家庭的)个案研究工作。 **2** (legal) question to be decided in a law court; the facts, arguments, etc, used on one side in a law court: (法律)案件；讼案；诉讼之一方所陈述之事实、理由等: *the* ～ *for the defendant,* the statement of facts, etc in his favour. 有利被告之事情的陈述。 *When will the* ～ *come before the Court?* 该案将于何时开庭审讯？ *State your* ～, Give the facts and arguments in your favour. 述说对你有利的事实和论点。 *He has a strong* ～. 他有充足的理由可为自己辩护。 **make out a** ～ (**for**) (sb, doing sth)**.** (为某人，为作某事) 提供有利的论点。 **make out one's** ～, prove that one is right. 证明自己有理。'～**law** *n* law based on decisions made by judges. 判例法。 **3** (gram) (change in the) form of a noun or pronoun that shows its relation to another word: (语法)格（名词或代词表示与他词之关系的形式或其变化）: *The first person singular personal pronoun in English has two forms:* 'I' *(subject* ～)*, and* 'me' *(object* ～). 英语里的第一人称单数代词有两个格的形式: 'I'(主格)和 me(宾格)。

case² /keɪs/ *kes* *n* **1** box, bag, covering, container: 盒；袋；套；箱: *'packing-*～, large box in which goods are packed; 货物包装箱; *glass* ～, for the display of specimens, etc(eg in a museum): 玻璃匣、橱等(如博物馆中展览标本等者); *a 'watch* ～; 表壳; *a 'jewel* ～, lined with velvet for keeping jewels in; (有丝绒衬里的)珠宝盒子; *a 'seed* ～, on a plant, in which the seeds ripen; (植物的)种子荚; *a 'pillow-*～, of cloth for covering a pillow; 枕头套; *a 'dressing-*～, a bag for hairbrushes, combs, razors, etc. (装发刷、梳子、刮胡刀等之)梳妆盒; 化妆袋。 ⇨ also *suit*～, *book*～. '～**hardened** *adj*(fig) made callous by experience. (喻)由于经验多而变得硬心肠或无感情的; 老于世故而冷酷无情的。 **2** (printing): (印刷): *upper* ～, capital letters; 大写字母; *lower* ～, small letters 小写字母。 □ *vt* [VP6A] enclose in a ～ or casing; encase. 置于箱或匣中; 装盒; 装箱。

casein /'keɪsiːn; 'kesɪn/ *n* [U] body-building food (protein) present in milk and forming the basis of cheese. 酪蛋白; 酪素。

case·ment /'keɪsmənt; 'kesmənt/ *n* window that opens outwards or inwards like a door, not up or down or from side to side. ⇨ **sash window** and the illus at **window**; (poet) window. (象门一样向外或向内开之)门

式窗(非上下推或左右拉者,参看 window 之插图); (诗)窗。

cash /kæʃ; kæʃ/ *n* [U] **1** money in coin or notes: 现款; 现金; 现钞: *I have no* ～ *with me—may I pay by cheque?* 我没有带现款——我可以付支票吗? *We sell goods for* ～ *only—we don't give credit.* 我们售货只收现金——不予赊帐。 '～ **crops** *n* crops (eg coffee, sisal) to be sold for ～ (contrasted with *subsistence crops* such as millet, beans, grown for use by the growers). 售现农作物 (为出售换得现金而种的农作物, 例如咖啡、西沙尔麻, 与subsistence crops 相对) '～ **desk,** desk or counter (in a shop, etc) where payments (by ～ or cheque) are made. 柜台(商店等中付帐之处)。'～ **dispenser,** machine(outside some banks) which, by the use of a personal coded card, dispenses ～. (有些银行外面所陈设的利用个人号码卡而取钱的)自动付款机。 ～ **down,** ～ **on delivery,** payment on delivery of the goods. 交货收款; 货到付款。 ⇨ **credit¹**(1). '～ **price** *n* price for immediate payment. 现金售价。 ～ **register** *n* ～ box with a device for recording and storing ～ received. 现金收入纪录机; 收银机。 ～ **and 'carry store** *n* one where goods are sold (usu at lower prices)for ～ payment if the buyer takes them away with him. 现实现带购现金付现款即带走所购货物的商店, 通常价格较廉)。 **2** money in any form: 钱; 款子: *be short of* ～; 缺钱; *be rolling in* ～; 极为富有; *pay in* ～, without money. 没钱。 □ *vt, vi* **1** [VP6A, 12B, 13B] give or get ～ for: 兑现; 兑付; 付现: ～ *a cheque.* 兑现一张支票。 *Can you* ～ *this cheque for me/* ～ *me a cheque?* 你能将这张支票兑换现金给我吗? **2** [VP2C] ～ *in (on),* take advantage (of); benefit (from): 利用; 从…中获利: *shopkeepers who* ～ *in on shortages by putting up prices.* 因货量不足而借提高价钱以获利的店主们。 ～**able** /-əbl; -əbl/ *adj* that can be ～ed. 可兑现的; 可兑换现金的。

a cash register

ca·shew /'kæʃuː; kə'ʃu/ *n* (tropical American tree with) small kidney-shaped nut. 槚如树 (一种热带美洲树); 都咸子(此树之肾状小坚果)。

cash·ier¹ /kæ'ʃɪə(r); kæ'ʃɪr/ *n* person who receives and pays out money in a bank, store, hotel, restaurant, etc. (银行、商店、旅馆、餐厅等中之)出纳员。

cash·ier² /kæ'ʃɪə(r); kæ'ʃɪr/ *vt* [VP6A] dismiss (eg an officer) with dishonour and disgrace. 革除(军官等)之职; 撤职。

cash·mere /kæʃ'mɪə(r); 'kæʃmɪr/ *n* [U] fine soft wool of Kashmir goats of Asia: 开士米 (亚洲克什米尔山羊之细软羊毛): *a* ～ *shawl.* 开士米围巾。

cas·ing /'keɪsɪŋ; 'kesɪŋ/ *n* covering; protective wrapping: 匣; 套; 鞘; 封壳; 盒: 保护性的外罩: *copper wire with a* ～ *of rubber:* 包有胶皮的铜丝; ～*s for sausages.* 制香肠的肠衣。

ca·sino /kə'siːnəʊ; kə'sino/ *n* (*pl* ～**s**) public room or building for gambling and other amusements. (供赌博及其他娱乐之)娱乐场; 俱乐部。

cask /kɑːsk *US:* kæsk; kæsk/ *n* barrel for liquids: (装液体之) 桶: *a* ～ *of cider.* 一桶苹果酒; amount that a ～ holds. 一桶所装之量。

cas·ket /'kɑːskɪt *US:* 'kæskɪt; 'kæskɪt/ *n* **1** small box to hold letters, jewels, cremated ashes, etc. (收藏信件、珠宝、骨灰等之)小箱。 **2** (US) coffin. (美)棺; 柩。

cas·sava /kə'sɑːvə; kə'savə/ *n* [U] tropical plant with starchy roots from which tapioca is extracted. 参茨(热

带植物，根含淀粉质）；木薯。⇨ the illus at **vegetable**. 参看 vegetable 之插图。

cas·ser·ole /ˈkæsərəul; ˈkæsə‚rol/ n covered and heat-proof dish in which food is cooked and then served at table; food so cooked: 烤锅（有盖的耐热浅锅，食品置于其中烤煮，然后连锅端上餐桌）；砂锅；焙盘；用炒锅等所做之食物：a ~ of lamb. 羊肉砂锅。

cas·sette /kəˈset; kəˈsɛt/ n [C] (US 美 = cartridge) container for magnetic tape (for use with a ~ tape-recorder) or for photographic film (to be fitted into a camera). 卡式录音带盒（配合卡式录音机用者）；卡式胶卷盒（装于摄像机中用者）。⇨ the illus at **tape**. 参看 tape 之插图。

cas·sock /ˈkæsək; ˈkæsək/ n long, close-fitting outer garment, worn by some priests. （某些教士所穿之）紧身长外衣；法衣。⇨ the illus at **vestment**. 参看 vestment 之插图。

cas·so·wary /ˈkæsəweərɪ; ˈkæsə‚wɛrɪ/ n (pl -ries) large bird of SE Asia, unable to fly, similar to, but smaller than, an emu. 食火鸡（一种东南亚产之大鸟，不能飞，似鸸鹋，但较小）。⇨ the illus at **rare**. 参看 rare 之插图。

cast¹ /kɑːst US: kæst; kæst/ vt, vi (pt, pp **cast**) 1 [VP6A, 15A, B] throw; allow to fall or drop: 投；掷；抛；脱落：The fisherman ~ his net into the water. 渔夫撒网于水中。Snakes ~ their skins. 蛇蜕皮。His horse ~ a shoe, one of its shoes came off. 他的马脱落了一只蹄铁。~ anchor, lower it. 下锚。be ~ down, be depressed, unhappy. 沮丧；不乐。⇨ downcast. ~ lots; ~ in one's lot with, ⇨ lot² (1, 3). ~ a vote, give a vote. 投票。~·ing vote n one given (eg by the chairman) to decide a question when votes on each side are equal. 决定票（例如当双方票数相等时由主席所投之一票）。~ sth in sb's teeth, ⇨ tooth(1). 2 [VP6A, 15A, 2C] turn or send in a particular direction: 转向或送至某一特定方向；投射：~ one's eye over sth, look at, examine, it; 看看（某物）。~ a gloom/shadow on sth, make it seem gloomy, depressing; 在某件事上投下一片阴影（使其看起来令人愁闷、沮丧）；~ a new light on a problem, etc, make it clearer, easier to understand; 使某一问题容易明白，更易于了解；~ a rather wary glance at sb, look at him warily; 机警地看着某人一眼；~ a slur on someone's reputation, say things to damage it. 中伤某人的名誉。~ about for, (anxiously) look for, try to find (eg allies, excuses). 焦急地寻找（盟友，借口等）。3 [VP6A] pour (liquid metal) into a mould; make (eg a statue in bronze, etc) in this way: 浇（液化金属）于模中；铸造（铜像等，与此连用）：a figure ~ in bronze. 青铜铸成的人像。~ iron n iron in a hard, brittle form, made by shaping in moulds after melting the ore in a blast furnace, and usually converted into wrought iron or steel before being used. 生铁；铸铁（铁砂在鼓风炉中熔化后经注于模中所形成之坚而脆之铁块，在使用前通常再炼成锻铁或钢）。Hence, 由此产生, '~-iron adj (a)made of ~ iron. 铸铁造的。(b) (fig)hard; unbending; unyielding: (喻)坚强的，不懈的；不屈不挠的：a man with a ~-iron will/constitution. 意志坚强(体格强壮)的人。4 [VP6A, 15B] ~ up, add, calculate (more usu add up or tot up): 加起；计算（较常用 add up 或 tot up）：~ up a column of figures. 加起一栏数字。5 [VP15B, 2C] ~ (sb/sth) aside, (=cast off, (b)) abandon; throw away as useless or unwanted. 抛弃；因其无用或不需要而丢弃某物。~ (sth) off, (a) unloose (a boat) and let go. 解缆；放（船）。(b) (fig)abandon; throw away as unwanted. (喻)抛弃；丢弃。Hence, 由此产生, '~-off 'clothes; '~-offs n pl clothes that the owner will not wear again. 不要的衣服；不再穿的衣服；被丢弃的衣服。~ off, (knitting) remove the last row of stitches from the needles. （编织）收针。~ on, (knitting) make the first row of stitches. （编织）起针。6[VP6A] give(an actor) a part in a play: 派(演员)担任戏中角色：He was ~ for the part of Hamlet. 他被派扮演哈姆雷特的角色。

shaped by being poured in a mould (eg a wheel or axle), ⇨ 3 above. 铸造之物(如车轮或车轴)；铸件；铸品（参看上列第 3 义）。

cast² /kɑːst US: kæst; kæst/ n 1 act of throwing (eg a net or fishing line): 投；掷；抛 (如渔网或钓丝)：stake everything on a single ~ of the dice. 孤注一掷。2 sth made by casting (3) or by pressing soft material into a mould: 铸造物；模造物：His leg was in a plaster ~. 他的腿打了石膏。3 mould where metal is poured or where soft material is pressed. (铸金属之)模子；内型；(压制软质物之)模型。4 set of actors in a play; the distribution of the parts among these actors: (一出戏的)演员阵容；演员角色分配：a play with an all-star ~. 全由名角演出的一出戏。5 type or quality: 类型；特质：~ of features; 面貌；~ of mind. 性情；脾气。6 (of the eyes) slight squint. (指眼)斜视。

cas·ta·nets /‚kæstəˈnets; ‚kæstəˈnɛts/ n pl instruments of hardwood or ivory used in pairs on the fingers to make rattling sounds as a rhythm for dancing. 响板(用硬木或象牙制之二片板，系于手指上，互击而发出咯咯声，作为舞蹈的节奏)。⇨ the illus at **cash**. 参看 cash 之插图。

castanets

cast·away /ˈkɑːstəwər US: ˈkæst-; ˈkæstə‚we/ n shipwrecked person, esp one reaching a strange country or lonely island. 乘船遇难之人 (尤指漂流至异乡或孤岛者)。

caste /kɑːst US: kæst; kæst/ n one of the Hindu hereditary social classes; any exclusive social class: [U] this system. 印度之世袭的社会等级之一；任何排他的社会等级；此种等级制度。lose ~ with/among, lose the right to be respected; come down in social rank. 失去被尊敬的社会地位；等级地位降低。

cas·tel·lated /ˈkæstəletrd; ˈkæstə‚letɪd/ adj having turrets or battlements (like a castle). (似城堡之)有角楼或城垛的；有雉堞的。

cas·ti·gate /ˈkæstɪgert; ˈkæstə‚get/ vt [VP6A] punish severely with blows or by criticizing. 痛殴；苛评。**cas·ti·ga·tion** /‚kæstɪˈgeɪʃn; ‚kæstəˈgeʃən/ n [C, U] (instance of) severe punishment. 严惩；严惩之实例。

castle /ˈkɑːsl US: ˈkæsl; ˈkæsl/ n large building or group of buildings fortified against attack, esp as in olden times; house that was once such a fortified building; piece (also called 亦称 rook) used in the game of chess, ⇨ the illus at **chess**. 城堡；堡全；古堡；原为城堡之房舍；(国际象棋中之)城形棋子(参看 chess 之插图)。~s in the air; ~s in Spain, day-dreams; plans or hopes that are unlikely to be realized. 白日梦；不可能实现的计划或希望；空中楼阁。an Englishman's house is his ~, his place of refuge and safety. 一个英国人的住宅是他的避难所。□ vi (chess) move the king side-ways two squares towards the ~ and place the ~ on the square the king moved across. (国际象棋) 将王向着城堡横移二格，并将城堡放于王所移越过的空格中。

cas·tor, cas·ter /ˈkɑːstə(r) US: ˈkæs-; ˈkæstə/ n 1 wheel (on a swivel) fixed to each leg of a piece of furniture (so that it may be turned and moved easily). 脚轮(装于家具腿部旋转座上，以便于转动及移动者)。2 bottle or metal pot, with holes in the top, for sugar, salt, etc. 装糖、盐等顶端有孔之小瓶；调味瓶。'~ sugar n white, finely powdered sugar. 细白糖。

cas·tor oil /ˌkɑːstə 'ɔɪl US: 'kæstər ɔɪl; 'kæstə ɔɪl/ n [U] thick, yellowish oil, made from beans of the ~ plant, used as a purgative. 蓖麻油(带黄色之浓汁, 自蓖麻子取出, 用作泻剂)。

cas·trate /kæ'streɪt US: 'kæstreɪt; 'kæstret/ vt [VP6A] remove the sex glands of (a male animal); make (a male animal) useless for breeding purposes. 割去(雄性动物)之性腺; 阉割; 去势(使不能生殖)。 **cas·tra·tion** /kæ'streɪʃn; kæs'treʃən/ n castrating. 阉割; 去势。

cas·ual /'kæʒʊəl; 'kæʒʊəl/ adj 1 happening by chance; 偶然的; 不意的: a ~ meeting. 偶然的相会。 2 careless; undesigned; unmethodical; informal: 不小心的; 无心的; 马虎的; 疏忽的; 随便的: a ~ glance; 不经心的一瞥; clothes for ~ wear, for informal occasions, holidays, etc. 便服; 便装。 She's a very ~ person, eg is careless and thoughtless about the convenience of others. 她是一个极疏忽(如不顾他人方便)的人。 3 irregular; not continued: 非经常的; 非长期的: earn a living by ~ labour; 靠做短工为生; ~ labourers, not permanently engaged by one employer. 零工; 短工(非由一主人永久雇用者)。 ~·ly adv

casu·alty /'kæʒʊəltɪ; 'kæʒʊəltɪ/ n [C] 1 accident, esp one involving loss of life. 意外; (尤指有人死亡的)灾祸。 2 soldier or sailor who is killed, wounded or missing; person killed or seriously injured in an accident: 伤亡或失踪的陆海军战士; 意外灾祸中的伤亡者; 伤亡: The enemy suffered heavy casualties. 敌人伤亡惨重。 C~ lists were published the day after the train accident. 伤亡名单在火车意外事件发生后的第二天就公布了。 'C~ Ward/Department n part of a hospital to which persons injured, eg in road accidents, are taken for urgent treatment. 猝伤病室; 急诊室(医院中的一个部门, 收容并急诊伤害车祸等中之伤者)。

casu·ist /'kæzjʊɪst; 'kæʒʊɪst/ n expert in ~ry. 诡辩家。 ~·ry /-rɪ; -rɪ/ n [U] judgement of right and wrong by reference to theories, social conventions, etc, (often with false but clever reasoning); [C] false but clever argument used in this way. (引述理论、社会习俗惯例所作之似是而非的)诡辩; 曲解。 **casu·is·tic, -ti·cal** /ˌkæzjʊ'ɪstɪk, -tɪkl; ˌkæʒʊ'ɪstɪk, -tɪkl/ adj of or like ~ry. 诡辩的; 曲解的。

casus belli /ˌkeɪsəs 'belaɪ; ˌkesəs 'belaɪ/ n (Lat) act that is held to justify war. (拉)开战理由。

cat /kæt; kæt/ n 1 small, domestic, fur-covered animal often kept as a pet, to catch mice, etc; (= 'wild cat) any animal of the group that includes tigers, lions, panthers and leopards. 猫(家庭养驯之小毛皮动物, 常养作宠物、养以捕鼠等); 猫科动物(包括虎、狮、美洲豹及豹)。

bell the cat, ⇨ bell vt. let the cat out of the bag, ⇨ bag¹(1). like a cat on hot bricks, very nervous or jumpy. 似热砖上的猫; 似热锅上的蚂蚁; 紧张而激动的。 put/set the cat among the pigeons, cause alarm and confusion. 制造紧张及混乱。 wait for the cat to jump; see which way the cat jumps, refuse to give advice, make plans, etc, until one sees what other people are thinking and doing. 观望形势 (在未获悉别人的想法和做法之前拒作忠告、计划等)。 ˌcat-and-'dog life, one full of quarrels. 经常吵闹的生活。 2 (short for 系下词之略) ˌcat-o'-'nine-tails n whip with many knotted cords, formerly used for punishing wrong-doers. 九尾鞭(从前用以惩罚犯罪者)。 room to swing a cat in, just enough space. 刚好够的空间。 3 (compounds, etc) (复合词等) 'cat burglar n one who enters a building by climbing up walls, rainpipes, etc. (攀窗墙、檐水管等而潜入屋内的)窃贼。 'cat·call n, v (make a) loud, shrill whistle expressing disapproval (eg at a political meeting). (发出) 响亮而尖锐的口哨声(表示不赞成, 如在政治集会场合所发出者)。 'cat·fish n large fish without scales, with feelers around the mouth. 蛤鱼(无鳞大鱼, 口之周围有触须)。 'cat-nap, 'cat-sleep n short sleep (in a chair, etc, not in bed). (在椅等之中而非在床上之)小睡; 假寐。 ˌcat's 'cradle n children's game with a length of string looped over the fingers of both hands and transferred between the fingers of two players. 翻绳戏; 挑绷子游戏; 翻绞绞; 编花篮 (二人玩之儿童游戏, 用一根线套于两手之手指间, 玩者彼此互翻套换)。 'cat's eye n reflector stud placed in roadways to guide traffic in darkness or on the rear of a vehicle (eg a bicycle). (装于路上以便于黑暗中指示交通或装于车辆如脚踏车等后部的)反光钮。 'cat's paw n person who is used as a tool by another. 被他人利用为工具之人。 'cat suit n woman's or child's close-fitting one-piece garment for the whole body. (女人或儿童之上下身连成一片的)紧身衣。 'cat-walk n narrow footway along a bridge, or through a mass of machinery, engines, etc. 沿桥梁之步行小道; 机器、引擎等中间的甬道。

cata·clysm /'kætəklɪzəm; 'kætəˌklɪzəm/ n [C] sudden and violent change (eg a flood, an earthquake, a great war, a political or social revolution). 突然而剧烈的变动 (如洪水、地震、大战、政治的或社会的革命)。 **cata·clys·mic** /ˌkætə'klɪzmɪk; ˌkætə'klɪzmɪk/ adj

cata·combs /'kætəkuːmz; 'kætəˌkomz/ n pl series of underground galleries with openings along the sides for the burial of the dead (as in ancient Rome). (如古罗马之)地下墓穴; 陵寝。

cata·falque /'kætəfælk; 'kætəˌfælk/ n decorated stand or stage for a coffin at a funeral. 灵柩台 (葬礼时

some wild cats

用以置棺材者）。

cata·lepsy /ˈkætəlepsɪ; ˈkætəˌlɛpsɪ/ n [U] disease in which the sufferer has periods when he loses consciousness and sensation and his muscles become rigid. 强直性昏厥；类痫症(患者时而有一阵失去知觉，肌肉亦变得僵硬）。 **cata·lep·tic** /ˌkætəˈleptɪk; ˌkætəˈlɛptɪk/ adj of, having, ~. 类痫症的；患类痫症的。 □ n person who has ~. 类痫症患者。

cata·logue (US also **catalog**) /ˈkætəlɒg US: -lɔːg; ˈkætlˌɔg/ n list of names / places / goods etc, in a special order: (人名、地名、货物等之)目录；概览；一览表: a library ~. 图书馆之图书目录。 □ vt [VP6A] make a ~ of; put in a ~. 编列目录；列入目录。

ca·talpa /kəˈtælpə; kəˈtælpə/ n (kinds of) tree with heart-shaped leaves and trumpet-shaped flowers. 梓树属；黄金树(叶如心状，开喇叭状花)。

cata·ly·sis /kəˈtæləsɪs; kəˈtæləsɪs/ n the process of aiding or speeding up a chemical process by a substance that does not itself undergo any change. 触媒作用；催化作用；接触反应(一种本身不起变化的物质所帮助或促进化学变化之程序)。 **cata·lyst** /ˈkætəlɪst; ˈkætlɪst/ n [C] substance that causes ~; (fig) sb or sth that helps to bring about a change. 触媒；催化剂；(喻)促使改变之人或事物。 **cata·lyt·ic** /ˌkætəˈlɪtɪk; ˌkætlˈɪtɪk/ adj of ~; causing ~. 触媒的；有触媒作用的；催化的。

cata·maran /ˌkætəməˈræn; ˌkætəməˈræn/ n boat with twin hulls; two boats or canoes fastened side by side (as used in the South Seas). 一种双船身的小艇；(两只船并侧而系结在一起之)双身船(如用于南洋者)。

hulls

a catamaran

cat·a·pult /ˈkætəpʌlt; ˈkætəˌpʌlt/ n 1 Y-shaped stick with a piece of elastic, for shooting stones, etc from; (in ancient times) machine for throwing heavy stones in war. 弹弓(由一根叉木及一条橡皮制成，用以发射石子等)；弹弩(古代战争中用以投掷大石头之机械)。 2 apparatus for launching aircraft without a runway (eg from the deck of a carrier). (不需跑道而发射飞机起飞之)飞机弹射器(如于航空母舰甲板上所用者)。 □ vt launch (aircraft) with a ~; shoot (as) from a ~. 用弹射器弹射(飞机)升空；(如用弹弓发射)弹射。

cata·ract /ˈkætərækt; ˈkætəˌrækt/ n [C] 1 large, steep waterfall. 大而陡峭的瀑布。 2 (path) disease of the eye, in which the lens slowly clouds over, obscuring sight. (病理)白内障(水晶体生翳而遮蔽视线之眼疾)。 ⇨ the illus at **eye**. 参看 eye 之插图。

ca·tarrh /kəˈtɑː(r); kəˈtɑr/ n [U] inflamation of the mucous membrane, esp of the nose and throat, causing flow of liquid, as when one has a cold; this liquid. 卡他；粘膜炎(尤指鼻喉之粘膜炎，可引致流出液体，如伤风时之现象)；卡他液。

ca·tas·trophe /kəˈtæstrəfɪ; kəˈtæstrəfɪ/ n [C] sudden happening that causes great suffering and destruction (eg a flood, earthquake, fire). 突如其来的成极大苦难及毁灭之)大灾害；异常的灾祸(如洪水、地震、火灾等)。 **cata·strophic** /ˌkætəˈstrɒfɪk; ˌkætəˈstrɑfɪk/ adj

catch¹ /kætʃ; kætʃ/ vt, vi (pt, pp **caught** /kɔːt; kɔt/) 1 [VP6A] stop (sth that is in motion) (eg by getting

hold of it with the hands, by holding out sth into which it may come): 捕捉(运动中的物体)；(用手等)抓住；(用袋状物等)捕住: I threw the ball to him and he caught it. 我将球抛给他，他接住了。 The dog caught the bit of meat in its mouth. 那狗用嘴接住了那块肉。 [VP15B] ~ sb out, (cricket) dismiss a batsman by ~ing the ball he has struck before it touches the ground. (板球)在球触地之前捕住球而迫使(击球员)出场；接杀出局。 ⇨ also 3 below. 亦参看下列第 3 义。 2 [VP6A] capture; seize; intercept; (catch sth wrong): 逮获；捉住；攫取；拦截: ~ a rat in a trap; 用捕鼠机捕住一只鼠； ~ a thief. 捉住一个贼。 How many fish did you ~? 你捕到了几条鱼？ Cats ~ mice. 猫捕鼠。 I caught him (= met him and stopped him) just as he was leaving the house. 我在他正要出门的时候拦住了他。 3 [VP6A, 19B, 14, 15B, 22] come unexpectedly upon (sb) doing sth(esp sth wrong); surprise or detect: 撞见(某人)做某事(尤指坏事)；当场破获；发觉: I caught the boys stealing apples from my garden. 我撞见那些孩子们偷我园中的苹果。 You won't ~ me (= There's no likelihood of my being discovered) doing that again! 你将不会再发现我做那事! ~ sb at sth; ~ sb in the act (of doing sth), come upon him while he is actually doing it: 当场抓住；撞见某人做某事: Just let me ~ you at it again (— then there'll be trouble)! 你要是再让我逮到的话(——就有你好看了)! ~ sb out, detect him making a mistake. 发现某人做错事(犯过)。 ~ sb napping, ⇨ nap¹. 4 [VP6A] be in time for: 及时赶到；赶上: ~ a train / the bus, etc; 赶上火车(公共汽车等)；~ the post, post letters before the box is emptied by the postman. 赶上邮局的一班收信时刻(在邮差从邮筒取信之前投递)。 5 [VP15B, 2C] ~ sb up; ~ up (with sb), (a) come up to sb who is going in the same direction; overtake: 赶上向同一方向行进之人；赶上某人: Go on in front, I'll soon ~ you up / ~ up (with you). 你在前面走，我一会儿就会赶上你。 (b) do all the work that has not yet been done: 赶做未做完的工作；赶工: Tom was away from school for a month so now he's got to work hard to ~ up with the rest of the class. 汤姆有一个月未到校上课，所以他现在必须努力用功，好赶上班里其他的同学。 6 [VP6A, 2A, 3A, 14, 15A] ~ (in / on), (cause to) become fixed or prevented from moving; (cause to) be entangled: (使)绊住；(使)缠住；挂住: The nail caught her dress. 钉子钩住了她的衣服。 Her dress caught on a nail. 她的衣服被钉子钩住了。 I caught my fingers in the door, trapped them between the door and the doorpost. 我的手指被夹在门缝中了(门与门柱的中间)。 This bolt doesn't ~, cannot be fastened. 这个门闩闩不住了。 The latch has caught, stuck fast. 这门闩拨不出来了。 The car was caught between two lorries. 那部汽车被两辆货车夹在中间。 He caught his foot on a tree root and stumbled. 他的一只脚被树根绊住，因而跌倒。 7 [VP6A] get (the meaning of sth); hear (the sound of sth); receive (punishment, etc): 懂得；了解(某事物的意义)；听见(某物的声音)；受到(处罚等): I don't quite ~ your meaning. 我不十分懂得你的意思。 I didn't ~ the end of the sentence. 我未听见那句话的末尾。 I don't quite ~ (= fully understand) the idea. 我不十分明白那意思。 [VP2C] ~ on (to sth), understand. 明白。 ~ it, be scolded, punished, hit, etc: 挨骂；受罚；被打中: You'll ~ it if you're not careful! 你若是不小心就会挨骂的! He caught it (= was hit) right in the eye. 他的眼睛被打个正着。 ~ sb's attention / fancy, succeed in getting it. 引起某人的注意(迎合某人的心意)。 ~ sb's eye, look at him to attract his attention when he looks in your direction. 注视某人以引起他的注意。 Hence, 由此产生, 'eye-~ing adj ⇨ eye¹(3). ~ sight / a glimpse of, see for a short time. 一瞥；瞥见；一看。 8 [VP6A] become infected with: 染患；罹患: ~ a disease / a fever; 患病(发烧); ~ a cold. 患感冒；伤风。 9 [VP3A] ~ at, try to grasp: 试图抓住；想把捉住: A drowning man will ~ at a straw. 快要溺死的人连一根稻草也要设法抓住。 He will ~ at (=take eagerly) any opportunity of practising his English. 他会

把握住任何机会练习他的英语。⇨ clutch¹. [VP15B] ~ up, grasp; seize: 把握; 抓; 抢: ~ up a loose end of rope. 抓住绳子未系牢的一端。They were caught up (fig, carried away) in the wave of enthusiasm. (喻)他们被热情的浪潮冲昏了头。 [VP15A] ~ hold of, seize, grab. 握住; 攫取。 10 ~ (fire), begin to burn: 着火; 烧着: The wood soon caught (fire). 那木头不一会儿就烧着了。 11 [VP6A, 12C, 15A] hit: 打; 击: ~ sb a blow. 打某人一拳。She caught him one (= gave him a blow) on the cheek. 她打了他一记耳光。 12 ~ one's breath, fail to breathe regularly for a moment (from surprise, etc). (因吃惊等)暂时不能规律地呼吸; 屏息。 '~-crop n quick-growing crop (eg lettuce) grown between rows of other crops. (种植于其他作物行间生长迅速的)间作作物 (如莴苣菜)。 '~-penny adj designed or intended merely to get sales: 仅为赚钱而设计的; 以赚钱为目的的: a book with a ~penny title. 其书名仅为赚钱而设计的一本书。 '~·word n 1 word placed so as to draw attention to an article, eg the subject of a paragraph; first or last word of a page in a dictionary, printed above the columns. 眉题; 标字(用以引起注意一篇文章, 如一段文章的主题; 印于词典之每一栏上方的每一页的首词及末词)。 2 phrase or slogan in frequent current use. 流行的口号; 标语。~er n (baseball) player who stands behind the batter to ~ the ball thrown by the pitcher. (棒球)立于打击手之后以接投手投来之球的)捕手。~·ing adj (esp of diseases) infectious. (尤指疾病)传染性的。~y adj 1 (of a tune, etc) easily remembered. (指曲调等)容易记忆的。 2 tricky, deceptive, 骗人的; 引人上当的。

catch² /kætʃ; kætʃ/ n 1 act of catching (esp a ball): 捕捉(尤指球): That was a difficult ~. 那是一个难接的球(但已接住)。 2 that which is caught or worth ~ing: 所捕获或值得捕获之物: a fine ~ of fish. 捕获的鱼很多。He's a good ~ for some young woman, is a good man to get as a husband. 他是少女结婚的好对象。 3 sth intended to trick or deceive; cunning question or device: 引人上当的事物; 使人受骗的问题; 诡计: There's a ~ in it somewhere. 这里面有诡诈。Does the teacher ever include ~ questions in examination papers? 老师在试卷中出过令人迷惑的问题吗? 4 device for fastening or securing a lock, door, etc. (使锁、门等牢固的)搭扣; 锁环; 挂钩; 弹簧栓。⇨ the illus at latch. 参看 latch 之插图。 5 song for a number of voices starting one after another. 轮唱曲。

catch·ment /'kætʃmənt; 'kætʃmənt/ n '~(-area) land from which a river or reservoir draws its rainfall (also '~-basin). (fig) area(s) from which central body draws its members, eg a school its pupils, a hospital its patients; [U] amount of rainfall, etc caught. 集水区域; 集水盆地; (喻)人员集结区(如学区, 医疗区); 集聚之雨量。

catch·up /'kætʃəp; 'kætʃəp/ n = ketchup.

cat·echism /'kætɪkɪzəm; 'kætə,kɪzəm/ n [U] instruction (esp about religion) by question and answer; [C] number, succession of questions and answers designed for this purpose: 问答教学法(尤指教义之传授); 为达此目的而设计的一连串的问答; 教义问答教本: put a person through his ~, question him closely. 详细诘问某人。

cat·echize /'kætɪkaɪz; 'kætə,kaɪz/ vt [VP6A] teach or examine by asking many questions. 用问答法教学或考试。

cat·egori·cal /,kætɪ'gɒrɪkl US: -gɔːr-; ,kætə'gɔrɪkl/ adj (of a statement) unconditional; absolute; detailed; explicit. (指陈述)无条件的; 绝对的; 详细的; 明显的。~ly /-ɪklɪ; -ɪklɪ/ adv

cat·egory /'kætɪgərɪ US: -gɔːrɪ; 'kætə,gɔrɪ/ n (pl -ries) division or class in a complete system or grouping. (整个系统或组合中的)部门; 种类; 范畴。cat·egor·ize /'kætɪgəraɪz; 'kætəgə,raɪz/ vt, [VP6A] place in a ~. 置于某一部门中; 分门别类。

cater /'keɪtə(r); 'ketə /vi 1 [VP3A] ~ for, provide

food: 备办食物: Weddings and parties ~ed for, The advertiser will supply food for weddings, etc. 包办婚礼及宴会酒席 (广告文字)。 2 [VP3A] ~ for/to, make provision for, supply what is desired or required to; pander to: 提供; 迎合: TV programmes usually ~ for all tastes. 电视通常提供各种不同趣味的娱乐节目。Some tabloid newspapers ~ to low tastes. 有些小型报纸迎合低级趣味。~er n person who provides meals, etc brought from outside, to clubs, homes, etc; owner or manager of restaurant, etc. 旅馆、餐馆等之老板或经理。

cat·er·pil·lar /'kætəpɪlə(r); 'kætə,pɪlə/ n 1 larva of a butterfly or moth, ⇨ the illus at butterfly. 蝎; 蝶或蛾的幼虫; 毛虫 (参看 butterfly 之插图)。 2 endless belt passing over toothed wheels, used to give vehicles, tanks, etc, a good grip on soft or uneven surfaces: (装于带齿车轮上以便在软地或不平之地行走, 如战车等之)环带; 履带; 防滑带: ~ tractor, one fitted with such belts. 环形牵引车 (农场用)。

cat·er·waul /'kætəwɔːl; 'kætə,wɔl/ vi, n (make a) cat's howling cry. (发出)猫叫春的声音。

cat·gut /'kætgʌt; 'kæt,gʌt/ n [U] material used for the strings of violins, tennis rackets, etc (made by twisting the intestines of sheep and other animals). (用以做小提琴弦、网球拍等之)羊肠筋; 肠线(用羊肠或其他动物之肠绞成)。

ca·thar·sis /kə'θɑːsɪs; kə'θɑrsɪs/ n (pl -arses /-siːz; -sɪz/) 1 [C, U] (med) emptying of the bowels. (医) 导泻; 通便。 2 outlet for strong emotion (eg as given by the drama, or by a willing account of deep feelings given to another person). 强烈情绪的发抒; 净化作用(由观剧或向他人叙述自己的深刻感思, 而使自己的感情得到发抒)。 ca·thar·tic /kə'θɑːtɪk; kə'θɑrtɪk/ n (med), adj (substance) giving ~. (医)缓泻剂的; 通便的; 导泻的; 发抒感情的。

ca·the·dral /kə'θiːdrəl; kə'θidrəl/ n chief church in a diocese, in which is the bishop's throne, under the charge of a dean. (内设主教圣座而由首席牧师主持的)总教堂; 大教堂; 主教座堂。

cath·ode /'kæθəʊd; 'kæθod/ n 1 negative electrode in the form of a filament which, when hot, releases negative electrons which are attracted towards the (positive) anode. 阴电极 (灯丝形, 受热时, 放出为阳电极所吸引的阴电子)。 2 negative terminal of a battery. (电池之)阴极。~ 'ray n invisible stream of electrons from the ~ in a vacuum tube (as used in radar, television, etc), called a ~ 'ray tube. 阴极射线(真空管中由阴极放出肉眼不能见的电子流, 此种真空管用于雷达、电视等, 称为阴极射线管)。

cath·olic /'kæθəlɪk; 'kæθəlɪk/ adj 1 liberal; general; including many or most things: 宽大的; 普遍的; 广泛的: a man with ~ tastes and interests; 兴趣广泛的人; 他的同情心。 2 the C~ Church, the whole body of Christians. 基督教徒之总称。Roman C~, n, adj (member) of the Church that has the Pope as its chief bishop. 天主教的; 天主教徒(的)。⇨ Pope, Protestant, Roman(3). Ca·tholicism /kə'θɒləsɪzəm; kə'θalə,sɪzəm / n teaching, beliefs, etc, of the Roman Catholic Church. 天主教之教义、信仰等。cath·ol·ic·ity /,kæθə'lɪsətɪ; ,kæθə'lɪsətɪ/ n [U] quality of being ~ (1). 普遍性; 广泛性; 宽大。

cat·kin /'kætkɪn; 'kætkɪn/ n [C] tuft of soft, downy flowers hanging down from twigs of such trees as willows and birches. (垂于柳树及桦树枝头之)软毛花穗; 荑荑花序; 柳絮。

cat·sup /'kætsəp; 'kætsəp/ n = ketchup.

cat·tish, cat·ty /'kætɪ; 'kætɪ/, /'kætɪʃ; 'kætɪ/ adj (esp) sly and spiteful. (尤指)狡滑的; 恶意的。cat·ti·ness n

cattle /'kætl; 'kætl/ n pl oxen (bulls, bullocks, cows) 牛的总称: twenty head of ~. 二十头牛。C~ were allowed to graze on the village common. 牛被允许在村中的公

地上吃草。'~-cake n [U] food fed to ~, made from various materials. 牛饼(用各种材料制成的牛的饲料)。

Cau·casian /kɔːˈkeɪzɪən US: kɔːˈkeɪʒn; kɔˈkeʒən/ n, adj (member) of the Indo-European group of people. 高加索人;白种人;高加索人的;白种人的。

cau·cus /ˈkɔːkəs; ˈkɔkəs/ n (meeting of the) organization committee of a political party (making plans, decisions, etc). (政党中负责设计、决策等之)组织委员会 (或其会议)。

caught /kɔːt; kɔt/ pt, pp of **catch**.

caul /kɔːl; kɔl/ n (physiol) thin skin enclosing a foetus, part of which, when covering a baby's head, was once thought to be a charm against drowning. (生理)胎膜(昔时认为覆于初生婴儿头上之部分俾防止溺毙)。

caul·dron /ˈkɔːldrən; ˈkɔldrən/ n large, deep, open pot in which things are boiled. 大而深的敞口锅。

cauli·flower /ˈkɒlɪflaʊə(r) US: ˈkɔːlɪ-; ˈkɑlɪˌflaʊɚ/ n [C, U] (cabbage-like plant with a) large, white flower-head, used as a vegetable. 花椰菜; 菜花。⇨ the illus at **vegetable**. 参看 vegetable 之插图。

caulk /kɔːk; kɔk/ vt [VP6A] make (joins between planks, etc) tight with fibre or a sticky substance. (用纤维或粘性物) 使 (木板等之间的连接处) 严密不透水; 填隙。

causal /ˈkɔːzl; ˈkɔzl/ adj of cause and effect; of, expressing, cause. 因果的;原因的;表示原因的。~·ity /kɔːˈzælɪtɪ; kɔˈzælɪtɪ/ n [U] relation of cause and effect; the principle that nothing can happen without a cause: 因果关系;事必有因之原理;因果律:the law of ~ity, eg cause always precedes effect. 因果律 (如先因后果)。**cau·sa·tion** /kɔːˈzeɪʃn; kɔˈzeʃən/ n [U] ~ity; causing or being caused. 因果关系; 起因; 造因。**cau·sa·tive** /ˈkɔːzətɪv; ˈkɔzətɪv/ adj acting as, expressing, cause. 为…之起因的; 表示原因的。

cause /kɔːz; kɔz/ n 1 [C, U] that which produces an effect; thing, event, person, etc, that makes sth happen: 原因; 导致某事发生之事物、人、人等;起因: The ~ of the fire was carelessness. 起火的原因是不谨慎。We can't get rid of war until we get rid of the ~s of war. 我们不能消灭战争,除非我们先消灭战争的起因。2 [U] reason: 理由: There is no ~ for anxiety. 没有理由要焦虑。You have no ~ for complaint/no ~ to complain. 你没有理由抱怨。Don't stay away without good ~. 不要无故缺席或离开。3 [C] purpose for which efforts are being made: 努力的目的; 目标; 道: work in/for a good ~; 为崇高的目标而工作; fight in the ~ of justice. 为正义而战。make common ~ with sb, help and support him (in a political, social, etc movement). (在政治、社会等运动中)帮助并支持某人。□ vt [VP6A, 17, 12A, 13A] be the ~ of; make happen: 引起; 致命; 使发生; 为…之/因: What ~s the tides? 潮汐的原因为何? What ~d his death? 他的死因为何? You've ~d trouble to all of us. 你给我们大家都惹来了麻烦。This has ~d us much anxiety. 这事使我们极为担心。What ~d the plants to die? 那些植物系死于何种原因? (What made them die 较常用。) He ~d the prisoners to be put to death. (He had them put to death is more usual.) 他使囚犯们被处死。(He had them put to death 较常用。) ~·less adj without any natural or known ~. 无缘无故的;无自然或已知之理由的。

caus·erie /ˈkəʊzəri; ˌkozəˈri/ n informal discussion. 非正式的讨论;闲谈;漫谈;随笔。

cause·way /ˈkɔːzweɪ; ˈkɔzˌwe/ n raised road or footpath, esp across wet land or swamp. (尤指湿地或沼泽中的) 堤道; 砌道。

caus·tic /ˈkɔːstɪk; ˈkɔstɪk/ adj 1 able to burn or destroy by chemical action. 腐蚀性的; 苛性的。~ **soda** n (Sodium Hydroxide /haɪˈdrɒksaɪd; haɪˈdrɑksaɪd/ **NaOH**) corrosive chemical substance used in the manufacture of soap. 烧碱(以制肥皂之)苛性钠。2 (fig) biting; sarcastic: (喻)刻薄的;讥讽的: ~ remarks; 刻薄话。a ~ manner. 讥讽的态度。**caus·ti·cally** /-klɪ;

-klɪ/ adv

cau·ter·ize /ˈkɔːtəraɪz, ˈkotəˌraɪz /vt [VP6A] burn (eg a poisoned wound, a snake-bite) with a caustic substance or with a hot iron (to destroy infection). (用腐蚀性物质或烙铁) 炙烧; 烧灼 (如中毒伤口、蛇咬) 以消毒; 烙。

cau·tion /ˈkɔːʃn; ˈkɔʃən/ n 1 [U] taking care; paying attention (to avoid danger or making mistakes): 小心; 谨慎(以免危险或犯错): When crossing a busy street we must use ~. 穿越热闹的街道时, 我们必须小心。2 [O] warning words: 警告; 提醒注意的话: A sign with 'DANGER!' on it is a ~. 书有'危险'的牌子就是一个警告。The judge gave the prisoner a ~ and set him free. 法官警告那犯人一番就把他释放了。3 (sing with indef art) (sl) person whose appearance, behaviour or conversation causes amusement. (单数与不定冠词连用) (俚)外貌、行动或谈话使人发噱的人。□ vt [VP6A, 17, 14] ~ (against), give a ~ to: 予以警告: I ~ed him against being late. 我曾警告他不要迟到。We were ~ed not to drive fast. 我们曾受警告勿开快车。The judge ~ed the prisoner, warned and reproved him. 法官警告并责备那犯人。~·ary /ˈkɔːʃnrɪ US: ˈkɔːʃənerɪ; ˈkɔʃənˌɛri/ adj conveying advice or warning: 表达忠告或警告的: ~ary tales. 警世的故事。

cau·tious /ˈkɔːʃəs; ˈkɔʃəs/ adj having or showing caution: 小心的; 谨慎的: ~ about/of giving offence; 慎防得罪人; ~ not to give offence. 小心不得罪人。~·ly adv

cav·al·cade /ˌkævlˈkeɪd, ˌkævlˈked/ n [C] company or procession of persons on horseback or in carriages. 一队骑马或坐马车的人;一队人马; 马车行列。

cava·lier /ˌkævəˈlɪə(r); ˌkævəˈlɪr/ n 1 (old use) horseman or knight. (旧用法) 骑士; 武士。2 (in the Civil War, England, 17th c) supporter of Charles I. (十七世纪英国内战中)拥护查理一世者; 保王党人。□ adj (of a person) without due seriousness; off-hand; discourteous. (指人)随便的; 不礼貌的。~·ly adv

cav·alry /ˈkævlrɪ; ˈkævlrɪ/ n (usu with pl v, collective) soldiers who fight on horseback: (通常与复数动词连用, 集合名词)骑兵; 骑兵部队: (attrib)(用作定语) ~ soldier/officer. 骑兵 (骑兵军官)。

cave /keɪv; kev/ n hollow place in the side of a cliff or hill; large natural hollow under the ground. (山崖边的) 穴洞; (地下的) 天然大穴洞。'~-dweller n person living in a ~, esp in prehistoric times. (尤指史前时代之)穴居者。'~-man /-mæn; -mæn/ n (pl -men) dweller; (colloq) man of primitive instincts and behaviour. 穴居者; (口)有原始人本能及行为之人; 野蛮人; 粗野的人。□ vi, vt [VP2C, 15B] ~ in, (cause to) fall in, give way to pressure: (使)凹陷;塌陷; 陷落: The roof of the tunnel ~d in. 隧道的顶端陷了。Hence, 由此产生, '~-in n

ca·veat /ˈkeɪvɪæt; ˈkevɪˌæt/ n 1 (legal) process to suspend proceedings. (法律)中止诉讼程序之申请。2 (formal) qualification; proviso: (正式用语)条件; 限制: put in/enter a ~ (against). 申请中止(对…之)诉讼。

cav·ern /ˈkævən; ˈkævən/ n (liter) cave. (文)洞穴。~·ous adj like a ~; full of ~s; (of a person's eyes) deepset. 如洞穴的;多洞穴的;(指人的眼睛)深陷的。

caviar, cavi·are /ˈkævɪɑː; ˌkævɪˈɑr/ n [U] pickled roe (eggs) of the sturgeon or certain other large fish. (鳝鱼或某些其他大鱼鱼子所做的) 鱼子酱。~ **to the general**, too fine or delicate to be appreciated by ordinary people. 过于高雅因而不能为一般人所欣赏; 曲高和寡; 阳春白雪。

cavil /ˈkævl; ˈkævl/ vi (-ll-, US also -l-) [VP2A, 3A] ~ (at), (formal) make unnecessary complaints against, find fault with. (正式用语)无端苛摘; (对…)吹毛求疵。

cav·ity /ˈkævətɪ; ˈkævətɪ/ n (pl -ties) empty space; small hole, within a solid body: 固体物中的)洞; 腔; 窝: a ~ in a tooth; 齿腔; 龋齿或蛀牙所造之洞; ~ walls;

hollow, to provide insulation. 空壁(起绝缘作用的中空的墙壁).

ca·vort /kə'vɔːt; kə'vɔrt/ vi (colloq) prance or jump about like an excited horse. (口)(象一匹受刺激的马般地)跳跃;腾跃.

caw /kɔː; kɔ/ n cry of a raven, rook or crow. 乌鸦的叫声. □ vi, vt **1** [VP2A] make this cry. (乌鸦)叫; 发出乌鸦的叫声;哇哇地叫. **2** [VP15B] caw out, utter in a cawing tone. 用似乌鸦叫的声调说出; 哇哇地说出.

cay·enne /keɪ'en; kaɪ'ɛn/ n (also 亦作 ~ /'keɪen; 'kaɪɛn/ **'pepper**) [U] very hot kind of red pepper. 一种极辣的红辣椒.

cay·man ⇨ caiman.

cease /siːs; sis/ vt, vi [VP6A, D, 7A, 2A, 3A] ~ **(from)**, (formal) come or bring to an end; stop (the more usual word): (正式用语)停止; 中止 (stop 较常用): C~ fire (= stop shooting)! 停止射击! The old German Empire ~d to exist in 1918. 旧德意志帝国于一九一八年灭亡. The factory has ~d making bicycles. 该工厂已停止制造脚踏车. Since he ~d (from) working, ... 他既然已停止不再工作,.... ~·fire n signal to stop firing (guns); truce. 停火(战)信号; 休战. □ n (only in) (仅用于) without ~, incessantly. 不断地; 不停地. ~·less adj never ending. 永不休止的. ~·less·ly adv

cedar /'siːdə(r); 'sidə/ n [C] evergreen tree with hard, red, sweet-smelling wood used for making boxes, pencils, fences, etc; [U] the wood: 雪松; 西洋杉; 香柏(一种暗绿树, 木质甚坚, 红色, 有香味, 用制盒子, 铅笔, 篱笆等);香柏木: a ~ cigar box. 香柏木雪茄烟盒.

cede /siːd; sid/ vt [VP6A, 14] ~ **(to)**, give up (rights, land, etc to another state, etc). 割让; 让(权利, 土地等)给(另一国家等).

ce·dilla /sɪ'dɪlə; sɪ'dɪlə/ n mark put under the c (ç) in the spelling of some French, Spanish and Portuguese words (as in façade) to show that the sound is /s/. (某些法文、西班牙文及葡萄牙文字中)字母 c 下面的一撇 (ç) (如 façade, 以表示该字母 c 读作 /s/).

ceil·ing /'siːlɪŋ; 'silɪŋ/ n **1** top inner surface of a room. 天花板; 平顶. **2** cloud level; highest (practicable) level (to be) reached by an aircraft: 云幕高度; 一架飞机所(能)飞的最高限度; 升限: an aircraft with a ~ of 20000 ft. 一架能飞两万英尺高的飞机. **3** maximum height, limit or level: 最高限度; 最高度: price ~s; 最高的限价; wage ~s 最高的工资.

cel·an·dine /'selandaɪn; 'selən,daɪn/ n small, wild plant with yellow flowers. 白屈菜 (小野生菜, 开黄花).

cel·ebrant /'selɪbrənt; 'seləbrənt/ n priest who leads the service of the Mass. 天主教主领弥撒之神父.

cel·ebrate /'selɪbreɪt; 'selə,bret/ vt [VP6A, but with the direct object sometimes to be understood) (属动词 6A 型, 但直接宾语有时省略) **1** do sth to show that a day or an event is important, or an occasion for rejoicing: 庆祝;祝贺: ~ Christmas/one's birthday/a wedding anniversary/a victory; 庆祝圣诞节(某人的生日, 结婚纪念日, 胜利); ~ Mass, lead the ceremony of the Eucharist. 主领弥撒. It's your birthday tomorrow, so we must celebrate (it). 明天是你的生日, 所以我们必须庆祝(它). **2** praise and honour: 褒扬; 赞扬; 称颂: The names of many heroes are ~d by the poets. 许多英雄的名字为诗人所歌颂. **cel·ebrated** (pp as adj) famous: (过去分词作形容词用)著名的: a ~d painter; 一位著名的画家; ~d for its hot springs; 以其温泉著名的; ~d as a hot spring resort. 以温泉胜地著称. **cel·ebra·tion** /ˌselɪ'breɪʃn; ˌselə'breʃən/ n [U, U] (the act of, an occasion of) celebrating. 庆祝(之活动或场合); 庆祝会; 庆典. **ce·leb·rity** /sɪ'lebrɪtɪ; sə'lɛbrətɪ/ n **1** [U] being ~d; fame and honour. 著名; 名望; 名声. **2** [C] (pl -ties) ~d person: 名人; 闻人: all the celebrities of the London theatre, all the famous actors and actresses performing in London. 伦敦戏剧界所有的名人 (指在伦敦演戏之所有著名的男女演员).

ce·ler·ity /sɪ'lerɪtɪ; sə'lɛrətɪ/ n [U] (formal)

quickness. (正式用语)敏捷; 迅速.

cel·ery /'selərɪ; 'sɛlərɪ/ n [U] garden plant of which the stems are eaten raw as salad or cooked as a vegetable: 芹菜 (茎可生吃或熟吃): a bunch/stick/head of ~; 一束(一根、一棵)芹菜; ~ soup. 芹菜汤.

ce·les·tial /sɪ'lestɪəl US: -tʃl; sə'lɛstʃəl/ adj **1** of the sky; of heaven: 天空的; 天上的: ~ bodies, eg the sun and the stars; 天体 (如太阳及星辰); ~ joys. 天堂之乐. **2** divinely good or beautiful. 极美的;极佳的.

cel·ibacy /'selɪbəsɪ; 'sɛləbəsɪ/ n [U] state of living unmarried, esp as a religious obligation. 独身; 独身状态; 独身生活 (尤指出于宗教上之承诺者). **celi·bate** /'selɪbət; 'sɛləbɪt/ n [C] unmarried person (as a priest who has taken a vow not to marry). 独身者 (尤指发誓不结婚的神父).

cell /sel; sɛl/ n **1** small room for one person (esp in a prison or a monastery). 供一人住的小室; (尤指监狱里的)小囚房; (修道院里的)密室. **2** compartment in a larger structure, esp in a honeycomb. 较大结构物中的小间隔; (尤指蜂巢中的)小蜂窝. ⇨ the illus at honeycomb. 参看 honeycomb 之插图. **3** unit of an apparatus for producing electric current by chemical action, eg of metal plates in acid, often part of a battery. 电池 (通常以金属片置于酸中, 借化学作用产生电流的装置,通常为battery 之一部分). **4** microscopic unit of living matter enclosing a nucleus with self-producing genes. (生物的)细胞 (包含一细胞核, 带有自生能力的遗传因子). **5** (of persons) centre or nucleus of (usu revolutionary) political activity: (指人)(通常指革命的)政治活动小组: communist ~s in an industrial town. 共产党在一工业城中的活动小组.

cel·lar /'selə(r); 'sɛlə/ n underground room for storing coal, wine, etc; (person's) store of wine. 贮藏煤、酒等的地下室; 地窖; (某人)所贮藏的酒. **~·age** /'selərɪdʒ; 'sɛlərɪdʒ/ n amount of ~ space; charge for storing sth in a ~. 地窖的容积; 藏物于地窖中的贮藏费.

cello /'tʃeləʊ; 'tʃɛlo/ n (pl ~s) bass violin, held between the player's knees. ⇨ the illus at string. 大提琴; 低音提琴 (参看 string 之插图). **cel·list** /'tʃelɪst; 'tʃɛlɪst/ n ~ player. 大提琴手.

cel·lo·phane /'seləfeɪn; 'sɛlə,fen/ n [U] (P) thin, moisture-proof, transparent material used for wrapping and packing. (商标) (包装用之薄而防湿的透明的) 玻璃纸.

cel·lu·lar /'seljʊlə(r); 'sɛljələ/ adj **1** consisting of cells (名): 由细胞组成的: ~ tissue. 细胞组织. **2** (of textile materials) loosely woven: (指织物)松织的: ~ shirts. 纱织布料做成的衬衫.

cel·lu·loid /'seljʊlɔɪd; 'sɛljə,lɔɪd/ n [U] (P) flammable plastic substance used for making toys, toilet articles, etc (and formerly for photographic film). (商标)赛璐珞 (一种易着火的可塑物质, 用以制玩具、化妆用具等,昔时用以制照相底片).

cel·lu·lose /'seljʊləʊs; 'sɛljə,los/ n [U] **1** structural tissue that forms the chief part of all plants and trees, and hence of paper and many textile fibres; wood fibre. 细胞膜质 (构成一切花草、树木以及纸和织物纤维之主要部分的结构组织); 纤维素; 纤维质. **2** (popularly, for ~ 'acetate) plastic substance used for many industrial purposes (eg explosives, ornaments, toughened glass). (cellulose acetate 的俗称)醋酸纤维素 (作许多工业用途的可塑物质, 如制炸药、装饰品、韧玻璃).

Celsius /'selsɪəs; 'sɛlsɪəs/ n (of thermometers) (指温度计) = centigrade.

Celt /kelt US: selt; sɛlt/ n member of the last group of immigrants to settle in Britain before the coming of the Anglo-Saxons; (loosely) one of the Irish, Welsh, Gaelic or Breton people today. 克尔特人 (亦译作塞尔特人;在盎格鲁撒克逊人来到之前, 最后一批移民而定居于英国的人;广义指现今之爱尔兰人, 威尔士人, 盖尔人或不列塔尼人). ~·ic n, adj (language) of the ~s. 克尔特人的; 克尔特语.

ce·ment /sɪ'ment; sə'mɛnt/ n [U] **1** grey powder (made by burning lime and clay) which, after being wetted, becomes hard like stone and is used for building, etc. 水门汀；水泥(用石灰及粘土烧制成之灰色粉末，加水即变坚硬如石，用以盖房子等)。 ⇨ **concrete**. '**~-mixer** n revolving drum in which ~ is mixed with other material to make concrete. 水泥搅拌机(旋转的鼓形容器，水泥在其中与其他物质拌合而成混凝土)。 **2** any similar soft substance that sets firm, used for filling holes (eg in the teeth), or for joining things. 用以填洞，如填于牙齿中，或粘接物件之任何能凝固之类似水泥的软物质；坚；接合剂。 □ vt [VP6A, 15B] put ~ on or in; joint with ~; (fig) strengthen; unite firmly: 加水泥于；用坚填填；用接合剂粘着；(喻)加强；团结；使强固。 ~ a friendship. 巩固友谊。

cem·etery /'semetrɪ US: 'semətɛrɪ; 'sɛmə,tɛrɪ/ n (pl -ries) area of land, not a churchyard, used for burials. 墓地(非指毗连教堂者)；公墓。

ceno·taph /'senətɑːf US: -tæf; 'sɛnə,tæf/ n monument put up in memory of a person or persons buried elsewhere. (为葬于别处之死者所立之)纪念碑。

cen·ser /'sensə(r); 'sɛnsə/ n vessel in which incense is burnt in churches. (教堂中之)香炉。

cen·sor /'sensə(r); 'sɛnsə/ n **1** official with authority to examine letters, books, periodicals, plays, films, etc and to cut out anything regarded as immoral or in other ways undesirable, or, in time of war, helpful to the enemy. 新闻检查员(有权检查信件、书籍、期刊、剧本、影片等并删去其中被认为不道德或在其他方面不当，或在战时有利于敌方之部分)。 **2** (ancient Rome) officer who prepared a register or census of citizens and supervised public morals. (古罗马之)监察官(负责登记及调查市民并监督公众道德行为者)。 □ vt [VP6A] examine, cut out, parts of (a book, etc); act as a ~. 检查并删剪(书籍等)之部分。 ~·ship /-ʃɪp; -,ʃɪp/ n function or duties of a ~. 新闻检查员的职责；新闻书刊等之检查。

cen·sori·ous /sen'sɔːrɪəs; sɛn'sorɪəs/ adj faultfinding; severely critical: 吹毛求疵的；严苛批评的: ~ of one's neighbours. 严苛批评邻居的。

cen·sure /'senʃə(r); 'sɛnʃə/ vt [VP6A, 14] ~ sb (for), criticize unfavourably for: (为某事)批评某人；责难；非难；责备。 ~ sb for being lazy. 责备某人懒惰。 □ n [U] rebuke; disapproval: 谴责；责难；非难；不赞成: pass a vote of ~ (on sb) 通过(对某人的)不信任投票；lay oneself open to public ~; 给人以责难的口实；[C] expression of disapproval: 非难的言词: a review containing unfair ~s of a new book. 对某一新书肆意攻讦的一篇评论。

cen·sus /'senses; 'sɛnsəs/ n (pl ~es) official counting of the population. (官方的)人口统计；人口调查；户口调查。

cent /sent; sɛnt/ n the 100th part of a US dollar and many other metric units of currency; metal coin of this value. 一分钱(美金一元或其他十进制货币单位之百分之一)；价值一分钱的硬币。 per ~, (%) in, by or for, every 100. 百分率; 百分之…。 (agree, etc) one hundred per ~, completely. 百分之百地(赞成，同意等)；完全地。

cen·taur /'sentɔː(r); 'sɛntɔr/ n (Gk myth) fabulous creature, half man and half horse. (希神) 半人半马怪物。 ⇨ the illus at **Minotaur**. 参看 Minotaur 之插图。

cen·ten·ar·ian /,sentɪ'neərɪən; ,sɛntɛ'nɛrɪən/ n, adj (person who is) 100 or more years old. 一百岁或百岁以上(老人)；人瑞。

cen·ten·ary /sen'tiːnərɪ US: 'sentəneərɪ; 'sɛntə,nɛrɪ/ adj, n (pl -ries) (having to do with a) period of 100 years; 100th anniversary. 一百年(的)；百年纪念。

cen·ten·nial /sen'tenɪəl; sɛn'tɛnɪəl/ adj, n = **centenary**. ~·ly /-ɪ; -nɪəlɪ/ adv

cen·ter /'sentə(r); 'sɛntə/ n (US) = **centre**.

centi- /'sentɪ; 'sɛntɪ/ pref one-hundredth part of: 表 "百分之一"之义: ~gram, 厘克 (百分之一克), ~metre. 公分,厘米(百分之一米)。 ⇨ **App 5**. 参看附录五。

cen·ti·grade /'sentɪgreɪd; 'sɛntə,gred/ adj in or of the temperature scale that has 100 degrees between the freezing-point and the boiling-point of water: 摄氏寒暑表(自水之冰点至沸点为100度)的: the ~ thermometer; 摄氏寒暑表；摄氏温度计; 100° ~ (100°C). 100 摄氏度。 ⇨ **Fahrenheit** and **App 5**. 参看 Fahrenheit 及附录5。

cen·time /'sɒntiːm; 'sɑntim/ n the 100th part of a franc. 生丁(一法郎之百分之一)。

cen·ti·pede /'sentɪpiːd; 'sɛntə,pid/ n small insectlike crawling creature with a long, thin body, numerous joints, and a pair of feet at each joint. 蜈蚣(似昆虫之爬行小动物,体细长, 多节, 每节有足一对)。

cen·tral /'sentrəl; 'sɛntrəl / adj at, from or near, the centre: 中央的；中心的；在中心的；自中心的；近中心的: My house is very ~, is in or near the middle of the town. 我的家非常近市中心区。 ~ heating, method of warming a building by steam, hot air or water in pipes from a ~ source. 中央系统供暖 (大建筑物内用管将蒸汽、热空气或热水自中心处输至各部分之供暖方法)；中央系统暖气设备。 **2** chief; most important: 主要的; 最重要的: the ~ idea of an argument; 一项议论的主要思想; the ~ figures (=the chief persons) in a novel. 小说的中心人物。 the ~ government n that of the whole country. (全国的)中央政府。 □ n (US) telephone exchange. (美)电话总机。 ~·ly /'sentrəlɪ; 'sɛntrəlɪ/ adv

cen·tral·ize /'sentrəlaɪz; 'sɛntrəl,aɪz/ vt, vi[VP6A, 2A] bring to the centre; come, put, bring, under central control: 集于中央; 由中央统一管理; 实行中央集权: ~ the administration of the coal mines. 统一管理所有煤矿。 **cen·tral·iz·ation** /,sentrəlaɪ'zeɪʃn US: -lɪ'z-; ,sɛntrələ'zeʃən/ n

centre (US = **center**) /'sentə(r); 'sɛntə/ n **1** middle part or point: 中心；中央；中心点: the ~ of London; 伦敦市的中心; the ~ of a circle. 圆心。 ⇨ the illus at **circle**. 参看 circle 之插图。 ~ of gravity, that point in an object about which the weight is evenly balanced in any position. (物体的)重心。 '~-bit, tool for boring holes in wood. 三叉钻头。 '~ brace. '~-board, movable board that can be raised or lowered through a slot in the keel of a sailing-boat to prevent drifting to leeward. 垂板龙骨; 船中板(帆船中可穿过龙骨上的槽而上升或放下之活动船板, 以防船向下风漂流)。 '~-piece, ornament for the ~ of a table, ceiling, etc; (fig) most important part. (餐桌、天花板等的)中心装饰; (喻) 最重要部分。 **2** place of great activity, esp one to which people are attracted from surrounding districts or from which they go out: 活动极其繁多之地方; (尤指很多人来往的) 中心区: the 'shopping ~ of a town; 一城市的购物中心区; a ~ of commerce. 商业中心。 **3** person or thing that attracts interest, attention etc: 引人兴趣、注意的中心人物或事物: She loves to be the ~ of interest. 她喜欢成为引人注意的中心人物。 **4** that which occupies a middle position, eg in politics, persons with moderate views, between two extremes. (政治上的)中立派; (两极端之间的)中间派。 □ vt, vi **1** [VP6A, 15A] place in, pass to, come to, be at, the ~: 置于中央; 传至中央; 集中; 在中央: The defender ~d the ball. 守卫者将球传至中央。 **2** [VP3A, 14] ~ on /upon, focus, fix, on: 集中于; 专注于: Our thoughts ~ upon / are ~d upon one idea. 我们的思想集中于一个观念。

cen·tri·fu·gal /,sen'trɪfjʊgl; 'sɛn'trɪfjʊgl / adj moving, tending to move, away from the centre or axis: 离心的: ~ force, the force which causes a body spinning round a centre to tend to fly off. 离心力 (使绕一中心旋转之物体有飞散之势的力量)。 **cen·tri·fuge** /'sentrɪfjuːdʒ; 'sɛntrə,fjudʒ/ n (mech) ~ machine, eg for separating small solid particles in a liquid by rotating motion. (机械)离心分离机(例如借旋转使液体中之小固体粒子分离之机器)。

cen·tri·pe·tal /,sen'trɪpɪtl; sɛn'trɪpɛtl/ adj tending towards the centre or axis. 向心的; 向轴心的。

cen·tur·ion /sen'tʃʊərɪən US: -'tʊər-; sɛn'tʃjʊrɪən/ n (in ancient Rome) leader of a unit of 100 soldiers. (古

罗马的)百人队队长(一队一百名士兵的队长)。

cen·tury /'sentʃərɪ; 'sɛntʃərɪ/ n [C] (pl -ries) **1** 100 years. 一百年。 **2** one of the periods of 100 years before or since the birth of Jesus Christ: 世纪 (指耶稣基督出生前或后每一百年之期间): in the 20th ~, A.D. 1900—1999. 在二十世纪中(即自公元一九〇〇年至一九九九年)。 **3** (cricket) 100 runs made by a batsman in one innings: (板球)(击球员在一局所得的)百分: make/score a ~. 得百分。

ce·ramic /sɪ'ræmɪk; sə'ræmɪk/ adj of the art of pottery. 制陶术的。 **ce·ram·ics** n **1** (sing v) art of making and decorating pottery. (用单数动词)陶器制法; 制陶术; 陶艺。 **2** (pl v) articles made of porcelain, clay, etc. (用复数动词)陶瓷制品。

cer·eal /'sɪərɪəl; 'sɪrɪəl/ n (usu pl) any kind of grain used for food: (通常用复数) 作食物用的任何谷物: ~ grasses; eg wheat, rye, barley; 谷类禾本植物(如小麦、裸麦、大麦); food prepared from ~s: 用谷类调制成的食物: 'breakfast ~s. 作为早餐的麦粥。

cer·ebral US: /sə'riːbrəl; 'sɛrəbrəl/ adj **1** of the brain: 大脑的; 脑的: ~ haemorrhage; 脑出血; 脑溢血; ~ palsy. 脑麻痹; 大脑性瘫痪。 ⇨ **spastic**. **2** intellectual; excluding the emotions. 智力的; 智慧的; 理智的。

cer·ebra·tion /ˌserɪ'breɪʃn; ˌsɛrə'breʃən/ n [U] (formal) working of the brain; thinking. (正式用语) 大脑活动; 思想; 思考。

cer·emo·nial /ˌserɪ'məʊnɪəl; ˌsɛrə'monɪəl/ adj formal; as used for ceremonies: 正式的; 用于典礼或仪式的: ~ dress. 礼服。 □ n [C, U] special order of ceremony, formality, for a special event, etc: 特殊的礼仪: the ~s of religion. 宗教礼仪。 **·ly** adv

cer·emo·ni·ous /ˌserɪ'məʊnɪəs; ˌsɛrə'monɪəs/ adj fond of, marked by, ceremony or formality. 好礼的; 讲究礼节的; 显示礼仪的; 隆重的。 **~·ly** adv

cer·emo·ny /'serɪmənɪ US: -məʊnɪ; 'sɛrə,monɪ/ n (pl -nies) **1** [C] special act(s), religious service, etc on an occasion such as a wedding, funeral, the opening of a new public building, etc. 典礼; 仪式(如为结婚、送葬、新公共建筑物开幕等场合所举行者)。 Master of 'Ceremonies n person in charge of such formal proceedings. 典礼官; 司仪。 **2** [U] behaviour required by social customs, esp among officials, people of a special group, etc: (社会风俗所要求的)礼节; 礼貌(尤指行于官员、特殊团体人士等之间者): There's no need for ~ between friends. 朋友之间不必拘礼。 There's too much ~ on official occasions. 在正式的场合礼节太多。 stand on ~, pay attention to rules of behaviour: 极注意礼节; 拘于礼节: Please don't stand on ~, please be natural and easy. 请勿拘礼; 请不要客气。

ce·rise /sə'riːz US: -iːs; sə'riz/ adj, n (of a) light, clear red. 鲜红色(的)。

cert /sɜːt; sɝt/ n (sl) sth looked upon as certain to happen or that certainly has happened: (俚) 被认为一定会发生之事; 确已发生之事: a dead ~, an absolute certainty. 绝对确实的事情。

cer·tain /'sɜːtn; 'sɝtn/ adj **1** (pred only) settled; of which there is no doubt: (仅作表语)确定的; 无疑的; It is ~ that two and two make four. 二加二等于四是确定无疑的。 **2** (pred only) (仅用作表语) ~ (that...); ~ (of/about); ~ to do sth, convinced; having no doubt; confident: 确信的; 无疑惑的; 深信的: I'm ~ (that) he saw me. 我确信他看见了我。 I'm not ~ (of) who he is/where he went, etc. 我不敢确知他是谁(他到哪里去了, 等)。 You can be ~ of success. 你一定会成功。 Are you ~ of/about that? 你对那事确信无疑吗? He is ~ to come, there is no doubt that he will come. 他一定会来。 for ~, without doubt: 无疑地; 确定地: I cannot say for ~ (= with complete confidence) when he will arrive. 我不敢确定地说他将于何时到达。 I don't know for ~, have no definite knowledge. 我不确切知道。 make ~, (a) inquire in order to be ~: 弄清楚; 弄明白: I think there's a train at 8.20 but you ought to make ~. 我想在八点二十分有一班火车, 不过你应该问清楚。 (b) do sth in order to be assured: 采取行动以便确有把握: I'll go to the theatre and make ~ of our seats, eg by reserving them in advance. 我要到戏院去把我们的座位订好(以便有把握到开演时有座位)。 **3** assured; reliable; sure to come or happen: 有把握的; 可靠的; 一定会来到或发生的: There is no ~ cure for this disease. 此病没有可靠的治疗药物。 The soldier faced ~ death. 那名士兵勇敢地面对必然来临的死亡。 **4** (attrib only) not named, stated or described, although it is possible to do so: (仅用作定语)(虽可指明或说明而)未指明的; 未说明的; 某: for a ~ reason; 为了某种理由; on ~ conditions; 附带某些条件; a ~ person I met yesterday; 我昨天遇到的某一个人; a person of a ~ age (usu = middle-aged). 某一年龄的人(通常指中年人)。 **5** (attrib only) some, but not much: (仅用作定语)一些; 一点; 少许; 多少: There was a ~ coldness in her attitude towards me. 她对我的态度有一点冷淡。 There is a ~ pleasure in pointing out other people's errors. 指出他人的错误多少有点乐趣。 **~·ly** adv **1** without doubt: 无疑地; 确定地: He will ~ly die if he doesn't get a doctor. 如果你请不到医生, 他一定会死的。 ⇨ **surely**. **2** (in answer to questions) yes: (用于回答问题)当然可以; 好的: Will you pass me the towel, please? C~ly! 请把毛巾递给我可以吗? 当然可以! Will you lend me your toothbrush? C~ly not (= No)! 把你的牙刷借给我可以吗? 当然不可以! **~·ty** n (pl -ties) **1** [C] sth that is ~: 确定的事情: Prices have gone up—that's a ~ty. 物价已上涨——那是确定的事情。 for a ~ty, for ~, without doubt: 确定地; 无疑地: I know for a ~ty that.... 我确实知道.... **2** [U] state of being ~; freedom from doubt: 确知; 确信; 确实; 必然: I can't say with any ~ty where I shall be next week. 我不能确说我下星期将在何处。 We can have no ~ty of success. 我们对于成功没有把握。 Would the ~ty of punishment deter criminals? 犯罪必然能阻止犯罪吗?

cer·ti·fi·able /ˌsɜːtɪ'faɪəbl; 'sɝtɪ,faɪəbl/ adj that can be certified: 可证明的: a ~ lunatic, a person who can be certified by a doctor as insane. 可由医生出具证明之精神错乱者。

cer·ti·fi·cate /sə'tɪfɪkət; sɚ'tɪfəkɪt/ n written or

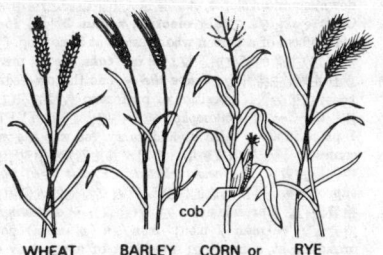

cereals

WHEAT   BARLEY   CORN or   RYE
                      MAIZE

cob

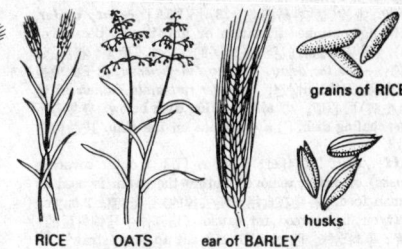

grains of RICE

husks

RICE   OATS   ear of BARLEY

printed statement, made by sb in authority, that may be used as proof or evidence of sth: (由有关方面所出具的) 证明书: *a 'birth/'marriage ~*; 出生(结婚)证书; *a 'health ~*, from a doctor; (医生所开出的)健康证明书. *~ of origin*, (comm) document stating the country or origin of imported goods. (商)(进口货品之)原产地证明书. □ *vt* provide with a ~. 授证书于…. **cer·ti·fi·cated** /-keɪtɪd/ *adj* having the right or authority to do sth as the result of obtaining a ~: 领有证书的; 合格的: *~d teachers*, who have obtained teaching diplomas (now called 今称作 *qualified teachers*). 检定合格教员. **cer·ti·fi·ca·tion** /ˌsɜːtɪfɪˈkeɪʃn /ˌsɜːtəfəˈkeʃən/ *n* [U] act of certifying; state of being certified; [C] that which certifies. 证明; 被证明; 证明书.

cer·tify /'sɜːtɪfaɪ/ 'sɜːtəˌfaɪ/ *vt, vi* 1 [VP6A, 9, 16B, 25] declare (by giving a certificate) that one is certain of sth, that sth is true, correct, in order: (通常以出具证明书)证明(某事物是真实、正确、合格的): *I ~ (that) this is a true copy of …*. 兹证明本件确系…之副本. *I ~ this as /to be a true copy of …*. 兹证明本件确系…之副本. *He was certified (as) insane*, The doctor(s) wrote a certificate declaring that he was insane. 他已由医生出具证明书证明他是精神错乱. *The accounts were certified (as) correct*. 帐目业经查核证明无误. **certified cheque**, cheque the value of which is guaranteed by the bank. 保付支票 (款额由银行担保之支票). 2 [VP3A] *~ to sth*, attest it: 证明或保证某事物: *~ to sb's character*, declare that one is satisfied that it is reliable, etc. 证明某人之品格良好.

cer·ti·tude /'sɜːtɪtjuːd US: -tuːd/ *n* [U] (formal) certainty (the more usu word). (正式用语) 确知; 确信; 确实; 必然 (certainty 为较常用词).

ceru·lean /sɪˈruːlɪən; səˈruːlɪən/ *adj* (formal) sky-blue. (正式用语)天蓝色的; 蔚蓝色的.

cer·vix /'sɜːvɪks; 'sɜːvɪks/ *n* (*pl* **cervices** /'sɜːvɪsiːz; səˈvaɪsiz/ or *-es*) (anat) narrow part of the womb. (解剖)子宫颈. ⇨ the illus at **reproduce**. 参看 reproduce 之插图. **cer·vi·cal** /'sɜːvaɪkl US: 'sɜːvɪkl; 'sɜːvɪkl/ *adj* of the ~: 子宫颈的: *cervical smear*, smear taken from the ~, to test for cancer. 子宫颈涂片 (取自子宫颈之涂片, 用以检验子宫癌者).

Cesar·ean =Caesarean.

ces·sa·tion /seˈseɪʃn; seˈseʃən/ *n* [U] (formal) ceasing: (正式用语)停止; 中止; 中断: *the ~ of hostilities*. 战争的停止.

ces·sion /'seʃn; 'seʃən/ *n* [U] act of ceding (giving up lands, rights, etc by agreement); [C] sth ceded. 让与; 割让土地; 放弃权利; 让与或放弃之事物.

cess·pit /'sespɪt; 'sespɪt/, **cess·pool** /'sespuːl; 'sespul/ *nn* (usu covered) hole, pit or underground tank into which drains (esp for sewage) empty; (fig) filthy place. (通常有盖之)容纳污水的洞、坑或地下池; 污水池; 污水坑; 粪坑; 化粪池; (喻)肮脏的地方; 污秽的场所.

chafe /tʃeɪf; tʃef/ *vi, vt* 1 [VP6A] rub (the skin, one's hands) to get warmth. 摩擦(皮肤、手)以获得温暖. 2 [VP2A, 6A] make or become rough or sore by rubbing: 由于摩擦而(使)变粗糙或感疼痛: *A stiff collar may ~ your neck*. 硬领可能擦痛你的颈子. *Her skin ~s easily*. 她的皮肤容易擦伤. 3 [VP3A] *~ at/under*, feel long-continued irritation or impatience (because of sth): (因某事物而)感受长时间的恼怒或不耐烦; 被激怒: 发怒: *~ at the delay/hold-up/inefficiency*; 由于此项拖延(停顿, 无能)而恼怒; *~ under restraints/illness*. 因受制(生病)而心烦. ⇨ also **chafing dish** below. 参看下列之 chafing dish. □ *n* ~d place on the skin. 皮肤擦伤之处.

chaff[1] /tʃɑːf US: tʃæf; tʃæf/ *n* [U] 1 outer covering (husks) of grain, removed before the grain is used as human food. (谷物在食用前所去掉的)谷壳; 糠. 2 hay or straw cut up as food for cattle. (切碎作牛马饲料用的)干草; 草料; 秣. □ *vt* [VP6A] cut up (hay, straw). 切(干草, 稻草).

chaff[2] /tʃɑːf US: tʃæf; tʃæf/ *n* [U] good-humoured teasing or joking. 打趣; 开玩笑. □ *vt, vi* [VP2A, C, 6A, 15A] make good-humoured fun (of): 打趣; 开玩笑: *~ sb about sth*. 为某事开某人的玩笑.

chaf·finch /'tʃæfɪntʃ; 'tʃæfɪntʃ/ *n* small European song-bird. 鹨类; 碛鹨(欧洲产小鸣鸟); 苍头燕雀.

chaf·ing dish /'tʃeɪfɪŋ dɪʃ; 'tʃefɪŋ dɪʃ/ *n* vessel with a heater under it, used at table for cooking food or keeping it warm. (餐桌上所用, 下面附有火炉, 用以煮或保持食物温热的)火锅.

chag·rin /'ʃæɡrɪn US: ʃəˈɡriːn; ʃəˈɡrɪn/ *n* [U] feeling of disappointment or annoyance (at having failed, made a mistake, etc): (因失败、犯错等所生)失望或厌烦之感; 恼怒; 懊恼: *Much to his ~, he did not win the race*. 他在赛跑中未能得胜使他大为懊恼. □ *vt* [VP6A] (usu passive) affect with ~: (通常用被动语态)使懊恼; 使恼怒: *be/feel ~ed at/by*. 因…而感懊恼.

chain /tʃeɪn; tʃen/ *n* 1 flexible line of connected rings or links for connecting, continuing, restraining, ornamenting, etc, ⇨ the illus at **bicycle**; (*pl*) fetters of this kind, used for prisoners. (由若干圈环连接而成之可弯曲的)链子; 链条; (用以连接、接续、限制、装饰等)锁; ⇨ the illus at bicycle 之插图; (复)(用于囚犯的)镣铐. *in ~s*, kept as a prisoner or slave. 被囚禁; 为奴隶. 2 number of connected things, events, etc - a series: 一连串(事物、事件等): *a ~ of mountains/ideas/events/proof*. 山脉(一系列的观念; 一连串的事件; 一系列的证据). 3 measure of length (66 ft). 测链 (长度单位, 等于 66 公尺). ⇨ **App 5.** 参看附录五. 4 (compounds) (复合词) '*~-armour*, -mail, armour made of metal rings linked together. 用金属圈连接成的甲胄; 链子甲. ⇨ the illus at armour. 参看 armour 之插图. '*~-gang*, gang of convicts fastened together with ~s while at work outside their prison. 用铁链系在一起在监狱外面做工的一群囚犯. '*~-letter*, letter of which the recipient is asked to make copies to be sent to other persons, who will do the same. 连锁书信 (要求收信人照抄若干分转寄他人, 而他人又同样抄寄他人者). '*~ reaction*, chemical change forming products that themselves cause more changes so that the process is repeated again and again (as in the atomic bomb). 连锁反应 (变化之产物能引起更多变化之一连串化学反应, 如原子弹中者). '*~-smoker*, person who smokes cigarettes in continuous succession. 一支接一支地吸香烟的人. '*~-stitch*, kind of sewing in which each stitch makes a loop through which the next stitch is taken. (每一针针脚打一个圈由次一针脚穿入之)链形缝法; 连锁针脚. '*~-store*, one of many retail shops owned and controlled by the same company. 连锁商店 (由同一公司所经营管理的许多零售商店之一). □ *vt* [VP6A, 15A, B] make fast with a ~ or ~s: 用铁链锁住: *The prisoners were ~ed to the wall*. 囚犯们被铁链锁在墙上. *C~ up your dog*. 把你的狗用链子拴起来.

chair /tʃeə(r); tʃɛr/ *n* 1 separate movable seat for one person, usu with a back and in some cases with arms (*arm~*): 椅子 (通常有靠背, 有时并有扶手, 即 armchair): *Won't you take a ~, sit down?* 你不坐吗? '*~-lift n* aerial ropeway with seats for carrying persons at and down mountain slopes, etc. (送送人上下山坡之)空中吊椅. Cf 参较 ski-lift. ⇨ also electric, sedan. 2 [U] *the ~* seat, office, of a person who presides at a meeting. (主持会议之)主席的座位或职位: *be in/take the ~*, preside. 就任主席; 主持开会. *leave the ~*, end the proceedings. 闭会; 结束会议. 3 position of professor: 教授的职位; 讲座: *the C~ of Philosophy*. 哲学讲座. □ *vt* [VP6A] 1 place in a ~, raise up and carry (sb who has won a contest): 置于椅中或轿中, 举起, 并抬着走 (指对于比赛中的得胜者): *The newly elected MP was ~ed by his supporters*. 那新当选的国会议员被支持他的人们用椅子抬着游行. 2 preside over: 主持(会议): *~ a meeting*. 主持会议. '*~-man* /-mən; -mən/ *n* (*pl -men*) person presiding at a meeting; president of a company or a committee: (主持开会的)主席; (公司之)董事长; (委员

会之) 主任委员: ~*man's report*, annual report of a company, signed by the ~man and presented at the annual general meeting. (公司于年会中由董事长签名提出之)年度报告。

chaise /ʃeɪz; ʃez/ n low, two- or four-wheeled horse-carriage (formerly) used by people driving for pleasure. 一种二轮或四轮的低马车(昔时供人驾驶以为娱乐者)。 ~ 'longue /lɒŋ US: lɔːŋ; lɔŋ/ n (pl ~s longues, pronunciation unchanged 复数发音不变) (F) kind of long, low chair, with an arm at one side only, for lying on. (法)(一侧有扶手的)躺椅。

chalet /'ʃæleɪ; ʃæ'le/ n Swiss mountain hut built of wood and with sharply sloping and overhanging roof; summer cottage built in the same style; small hut in a holiday camp, etc. 瑞士山中屋顶极为倾斜而悬垂之木屋;同形式的夏季别墅;假期营地之小屋等。

chal·ice /'tʃælɪs; 'tʃælɪs/ n wine-cup, esp that used for the Eucharist. 酒杯; (尤指)圣餐杯。

chalices

chalk /tʃɔːk; tʃɔk/ n 1 [U] soft, white, natural substance (a kind of limestone) used for making lime. 白垩(软性白色天然物质,系石灰石之一种,用以制石灰)。 '~·pit n one from which ~ is dug. 白垩坑(挖掘白垩的坑洞)。 2 [C, U] this material, or a material similar in texture, white or coloured, made into sticks for writing and drawing. (用白垩或类似物质制成之白色或彩色的)粉笔。 ▷ **blackboard. 3** as different as ~ and cheese; as like as ~ (is) to cheese, essentially unlike. 根本不同;实质不同。 by a 'long ~, by far, by much. (差得)很远;…得多。 □ vt write, draw, mark, with ~; whiten with ~. 用白垩或粉笔写、画、作记号; 用白垩涂白。 [VP15B] ~ sth up, write a score or record. 记分; 记录; 记下。 ~y adj of, containing, like, ~. 白垩的; 含白垩的; 似白垩的。

chal·lenge /'tʃælɪndʒ; 'tʃælɪndʒ/ n 1 invitation or call to play a game, run a race, have a fight, etc to see who is better, stronger, etc. 邀请比赛(以较量高低); 挑战(以定强弱等)。 2 order given by a sentry to stop and explain who one is: (哨兵令人止步并说明身份的)口令: 'Who goes there?' is the ~. '什么人?' 便是哨兵的口令。 □ vt [VP6A, 17, 14] ~ (to), give, send, be, a ~ to; ask for facts (to support a statement, etc): 向…挑战; 要求提出事实(以证明一项陈述等); 提出异议; 质问: ~ sb to a duel; 向某人要求决斗; ~ sb to fight; 向某人挑战; ~ sb's right to do sth; 对某人作某事的权利提出异议; ~ a juryman, (legal) object to his being a member of the jury. (法律)对一陪审员的身份提出异议(反对其为陪审员)。 **chal·lenger** n one who ~s. 挑战者; 质问者; 诘难者。

cham·ber /'tʃeɪmbə(r); 'tʃembə/ n 1 (old use) room, esp a bedroom. (旧用法)房间; 室; (尤指)卧室。 '~ concert, concert of ~ music. 室内乐演奏会。 ~ of 'horrors, place where gruesome objects are displayed. 展示恐怖物品的房间。 ~·maid, housemaid who keeps bedrooms in order (now chiefly in hotels). 清理卧室的女仆; (今主用以指旅馆的)清理房间的女服务员。 ~ music, music for a small number of players (eg a string quartet). 室内乐(由少数人演奏的音乐,例如弦乐四重奏)。 ~·pot, vessel for urine, used in a bedroom. (卧室中所用之)尿壶;

夜壶。 2 (pl) judge's room for hearing cases that need not be taken into court; (not US) set of rooms in a large building to live in or to use as offices. (复) 法官办公室; 内庭 (法官审讯不须上法庭之案件的小室); (不用于美国) 大厦中供居住或办公的一套房间。 3 (hall used by a) group of legislators (eg in US, the Senate and the House of Representatives), often distinguished as the 'Upper C~ and the 'Lower C~. 国会中的议院 (常分为上议院及下议院,如美国之参议院及众议院); 议院中的全体议员。 4 offices of barristers, etc esp in the Inns of Court. 律师事务室(尤指伦敦之四法学会中者)。 5 group of persons organized for purposes of trade: 为贸易目的所组织的团体。 a C~ of Commerce. 商会。 6 enclosed or walled space in the body of an animal or plant: (动植物体内的) 窝; 穴; 室: a ~ of the heart, ▷ auricle, ventricle; 心腔; similar cavity in some kinds of machinery; enclosed space in a gun (where a shell or cartridge is laid). (某些机器内部之)室; (枪炮之)药室; 弹膛。

cham·ber·lain /'tʃeɪmbəlɪn; 'tʃembəlɪn/ n (old use) officer who manages the household of a king, noble, etc. (旧用法)(国王或贵族家中的)管家。

cha·me·leon /kə'miːlɪən; kə'miliən/ n small longtongued lizard whose colour changes according to its background, ▷ the illus at reptile; person who changes his voice, manner, etc to match his surroundings. 变色蜥蜴; 避役(能随背景而变色的长舌小蜥蜴)(参看 reptile 之插图); 能配合环境而改变声音、态度等的人; 善变的人。

chammy-leather /'ʃæmɪ leðə(r); 'ʃæmɪ 'leðɚ/ n = chamois-leather.

cham·ois /'ʃæmwɑː US: 'ʃæmɪ; 'ʃæmɪ/ n small goat-like animal that lives in the high mountains of Europe and SW Asia. 臆羚 (欧洲及亚洲西南部高山所产之小羚羊)。 ~·leather /'ʃæmɪ leðə(r); 'ʃæmɪ 'leðɚ/ n soft leather from the skin of goats and sheep. 雪米皮; 麂皮; 油鞣革(用山羊及绵羊皮所制的软皮革)。

chamo·mile n (US) = camomile.

champ¹ /tʃæmp; tʃæmp/ vt, vi [VP6A, 2A, C, 4A] 1 (of horses) bite (food, the bit) noisily. (指马) 大声地嚼(食物, 衔铁)。 2 (fig) show impatience: (喻) 表示不耐烦: ~ with rage. 大发雷霆; 因愤怒而显示忍无可忍之状。 The boys were ~ing to start/~ing at the bit. 孩子们急于要出发(极不愿受拘束)。

champ² /tʃæmp; tʃæmp/ n (colloq abbr of) champion (2). (口) 冠军(champion 之略)。

cham·pagne /ʃæm'peɪn; ʃæm'pen/ n (kinds of) white sparkling (because charged with gas) French wine. 香槟酒(法国产之因充有气体而起泡的白色葡萄酒)。

cham·pion /'tʃæmpɪən; 'tʃæmpɪən/ n 1 person who fights, argues or speaks in support of another or of a cause: 为支持他人或某项运动而奋斗、辩论或演说的人; 支持者; 赞助者; 拥护者; 提倡者; 斗士: a ~ of free speech/ of woman's rights. 为言论自由(女权)而奋斗的人。 2 person, team, animal, etc taking the first place in a competition: 冠军 (比赛中获得第一名之个人、团体或动物); a boxing/swimming/tennis, etc ~. 拳击(游泳、网球等)冠军; (attrib) (用作定语) the ~ team; 冠军队; the ~ horse. (赛马中获得冠军之)头马。 □ adj, adv (colloq) splendid(ly): (口)极好的(地): That's ~! 好极了! □ vt [VP6A] support; defend. 支持; 卫护。 ~·ship /-ʃɪp; -ʃɪp/ n [U] act of ~ing; [C] position of being, or competition to decide, a ~: 拥护; 支持; 卫护; 优胜; 冠军的地位; 冠军赛; 锦标赛: to win a world swimming ~·ship. 赢得世界游泳冠军。

chance¹ /tʃɑːns US: tʃæns; tʃæns/ n 1 [U] the happening of events without any cause that can be seen or understood; the way things happen; fortune or luck: 事件之发生无可见或可了解之原因; 机会; 幸运; 运气; 偶然发生的事: Let's leave it to ~. 我们就让它听其自然(听凭机会)吧。 Let ~ decide. 听凭机会决定吧。 by ~, by accident, not by design or on purpose. 偶然地; 非预谋或故意地。 game of ~, one that is decided by luck, not by skill. 凭机会而不凭本领之游戏。 take one's ~, trust to luck,

take whatever happens to come. 碰运气; 冒险。 2 [C, U] possibility: 可能性: *He has no ~ /not much ~ /a poor ~ of winning:* 他没有可能(没有多少可能, 只有微小的可能)会赢。 *I've had no ~ to get away of getting away.* 我一直没有机会脱身。 *What of success is there?* 成功的可能性如何? *What is our ~ /are our ~s of succeeding?* 我们成功的可能性如何? *What are the ~ s that we shall succeed?* 我们成功的可能性如何? *The ~s are a hundred to one against you,* It's most unlikely that you will succeed. 你只有百分之一成功的可能。 *If, by any ~, ..., If, by some ~ or other...,* If it so happens that.... 如果凑巧...; 万一...。 *on the (off) ~ that /of doing sth,* in view of the possibility, in the hope: 也许能够(做到某事); 希望能够(做某事): 指望: *I'll call at his office on the ~ that I'll see /of seeing him before he leaves.* 我将到办公室去访他, 希望能在他下班前见到他。 3[C] opportunity; occasion when success seems very probable: 机会; 成功可能性极大的机遇: *This was the ~ he had been waiting for.* 那正是他一直等待的机会。 *It's the ~ of a lifetime,* a favourable opportunity that is unlikely ever to come again. 这是一生中难得再遇到的机会。 **stand a good /fair ~ (of...),** have a fair prospect (of sth). 大(颇)有...希望。 **the ,main '~** opportunity of making money: 赚钱的机会: *He always has an eye to the main ~,* sees where money can be made. 他总在注意赚钱的机会。 4 (attrib) coming or happening by ~ (1): (用作定语)偶然的: *a ~ meeting;* 偶然的相遇; *a ~ companion.* 萍水相逢的友伴。

chance[2] /tʃɑːns *US:* tʃæns; tʃæns/ *vi, vt* 1 [VP3A] *~ on /upon,* find or meet by chance. 偶然发现; 偶然遇到。 [VP4E, 2A, after it 用于 it 之后] happen by chance: 偶然发生; 恰巧: *I ~d to be there.* 我恰巧在那里。 *It ~d that I was out /I ~d to be out when he called.* 他来访时适逢我不在家。 2 [VP6A, C] take a risk, 冒险, esp (尤用于) *~ it;* ~ *one's arm,* (colloq) take a chance of success although failure is probable. (口)虽极可能失败而仍然试图获得成功; 冒险一试。

chan·cel /tʃɑːnsl *US:* tʃænsl; tʃænsl/ *n* eastern part of a church, round the altar, used by the priest(s) and choir. 圣台 (教堂中靠东端绕着圣坛的部分, 为神父或牧师及唱诗班所在的地方)。 ⇨ the illus at **church.** 参看 church 之插图。

chan·cel·lery /tʃɑːnsəlrɪ *US:* tʃæns-; tʃænsələrɪ/ *n* (*pl* -**ries**) 1 chancellor's position, department or residence. 大臣的职位、部、府或官邸。 2 place of business of an embassy, legation or consulate. 大使馆、公使馆或领事馆的办公处。

chan·cel·lor /tʃɑːnsələ(r) *US:* tʃæns-; tʃænsələ/ *n* 1 (in some countries, eg W Germany) chief minister of state. (某些国家, 如西德)总理; 首相。 2 (of some universities) titular head or president (the duties being performed by the Vice-C~) (某些大学的)名义上的校长 (其职务由副校长负责)。 3 (GB) chief secretary of an embassy. (英)(大使馆的)一等秘书。 4 State or law official of various kinds: 大臣; 法官: *the Lord C~ of England, the Lord High C~,* the highest judge (and chairman of the House of Lords); 英国的大法官(最高之法官, 兼上议院议长); *the C~ of the Exchequer.* 财政大臣。

chan·cery /tʃɑːnsərɪ *US:* tʃæns-; tʃænsərɪ/ *n* (*pl* -**ries**) 1 (GB) Lord Chancellor's division of the High Court of Justice. (英)大法官法厅(高等法院中之一部分)。 **ward in ~,** person (usu a *minor(n)*) whose affairs are in the charge of the Lord Chancellor (eg because of the death of the ward's parents). 受大法官监护的人 (如未成年孤儿儿)。 2 (US) court of equity for those cases with no remedy in common law. (美) 衡平法院 (处理习惯法中无解决之案件)。 3 office of public records. 档案处。 4 ⇨ **chancellery(2).**

chancy /tʃɑːnsɪ *US:* tʃænsɪ; tʃænsɪ/ *adj* (colloq) risky; uncertain. (口)冒险的; 不可靠的。

chan·de·lier /ˌʃændə'lɪə(r); ʃændl'ɪr/ *n* ornamental branched holder (usu hanging from the ceiling) for a number of lights. 装饰性的灯架 (有分枝, 通常悬于天花板上, 可装数枝灯者); 枝形吊灯架。

chan·dler /tʃɑːndlə(r) *US:* tʃænd-; tʃændlə/ *n* 1 person who makes or sells candles, oil, soap, paint, etc. 制造或贩卖蜡烛、油类、肥皂、漆等之商人。 2 **ship's ~,** dealer in canvas, ropes and other supplies for ships. 贩卖船上用具(如帆布、索具等)之商人。

change[1] /tʃeɪndʒ; tʃendʒ/ *vt, vi* 1 [VP6A, 14, 2A] *~ (from /out of) (to /into); ~ (for),* leave one place and go to, enter, another; take off sth and put sth else on: 换(掉); 换(上); 更换; 更 (衣); 改换: *I must ~ these trousers—they've got oil on them.* 我必须换条裤子——裤子上沾了油。 *It won't take me five minutes to ~,* to put on different clothes. 我换衣服不需要五分钟。 *He ~d out of his overalls (and into a suit).* 他换掉了工作裤(换上了一套西服)。 *He ~d his overalls (for a suit).* 他脱下工作裤(换上一套西服)。 *We seldom ~ for dinner,* eg seldom ~ into formal evening dress. 我们很少为了进晚餐而换上晚礼服。 *I've ~d my address,* moved to a different house, flat, etc. 我的住址改变了, *The house has ~d hands several times,* has been bought and sold several times. 此屋曾数度易手(易主)。 *~ (trains),* leave one train and get into another during a journey: 换火车 (在旅程中由甲车转至乙车): *~ (trains) at Crewe for Stockport.* 在克鲁换火车前往斯托克波特。 *Where do we ~?* 我们在哪里换车? *All ~!* (a cry heard at stations when a train is going no further). 所有旅客一律换车! (在火车站当一列车不再前进时所听到的报告声)。 *~ up /down,* (motoring) change to a higher /lower gear. (汽车驾驶)改为高(低)挡。 2 [VP6A, 14] *~ sth (for /into sth else),* give and receive in return: 兑换; 互换; 付出(某物)并换回(他物): *Can you ~ this five-pound note,* give me notes and /or coins of smaller denominations? 你能兑换这张五英镑的钞票 (换成小额钞票或硬币) 吗? *He ~d his Italian money before leaving Rome.* 他在离开罗马前已经意大利钱币兑换掉了。 *Shall we ~ seats?* 我们换座位好不好? *I ~d places with her.* 我与她互换位置。 *He ~d his car for a foreign make.* 他换了一部外国厂牌的车。 3 [VP6A, 14, 2A, C] *~ (from) (into /to),* make or become different; 改变(成不同的); 改变; 变化: *That has ~d my ideas.* 那使我改变了主意。 *My plans have ~d.* 我的计划已经改变了。 *Caterpillars ~ into butterflies or moths.* 毛虫会变成蝴蝶或蛾。 *The traffic lights ~d from red to green.* 那交通指示灯从红色变成绿色。 *You've ~d since I last saw you.* 自从我上次见你以后你已变了。 *~ over (from) (to),* abandon an old system and take up a new one: 从 (旧的) 变成(新的): *the country has ~ed over from military to democratic rule.* 该国已从军政变为民主治理。 Hence, 由此产生, *'~-over n. ~ one's mind,* decide on a new plan, have a new opinion, etc. 改变主意。 *~ one's note /tune,* become more humble, sad, etc. 改变态度 (变得更为谦卑、忧愁等)。 *~ step,* (when marching with a group) march so that the other foot is keeping time (eg with the beat of a drum). (在团体中行军时)换步(以便使另一足合着节拍, 如踏着鼓音)。 *~able* *adj* likely to alter; often altering; able to be ~d: 易变的; 常变的; 能被改变的: *~able weather;* 多变的天气; *a ~able sort of person,* one whose moods often ~. 喜怒无常的人; 善变的人。 *~able·ness* *n*

change[2] /tʃeɪndʒ; tʃendʒ/ *n* 1 [C] changed or different condition(s); sth used in place of another or others; move from one place to another: 变化后的情况; 不同的情况; 代替物; 从一地移至另一地; 换车: *a welcome ~ from town to country life.* 令人舒畅的从城市生活改变到乡村生活的情况。 *We have a new house—it's a great ~ for the better.* 我们有了一栋新房子——一切变得好多了。 *Take a ~ of clothes with you,* extra clothes to ~ into. 带一套换洗的衣服。 *He had to make a quick ~* (ie of trains) *at Crewe.* 他不得不在克鲁匆忙换车 (如换另一列车)。 *a ~ of air /climate,* eg a holiday away from home. 换换空气(气候)(例如离家度假)。 *ring the ~s,* ⇨ **ring**[2](11). 2 [U] money in small(er) units; money that is the

difference between the price or cost of sth and the sum offered in payment: (较) 小额货币; 零钱; (购物付款后) 找回的钱: *Can you give me ~ for a one-pound note?* 你能替我找一英镑零钱吗? *I have no small ~,* no coins of small value. 我没有零钱. *Don't leave your ~ on the shop counter!* 不要把你找回的钱遗忘在店中的柜台上! **get no ~ out of (sb),** (colloq) get no help, information or advantage from. (口)从(某人)处得不到帮助或消息; 无法从其得到好处; 在…身上无利可图; 拿(他)没办法. **3**[C, U] alteration; changing: change; 变化; 改变: *C~ is not necessarily a good thing in itself.* 改变, 其本身并不一定都是好的。*We shall have to make a ~ in the programme.* 我们势必将节目内容变动一下。*Let's hope there will be a ~ in the weather.* 但愿天气会变好。**for a ~,** for the sake of variety; to be different from one's routine: 为求变化起见; 为了与日常生活有所不同: *I usually have breakfast at 7:30, but during the holidays I'm having it at 8:30 for a ~.* 我通常七点半吃早餐, 但在假期中我八时半吃早餐。**~ of life, =** menopause. **'~·ful** /-ful; -fəl/ *adj* continually changing; likely to change 不断改变的; 易变的; 多变的. **'~·less** *adj* unchanging. 不变的.

change·ling /ˈtʃeɪndʒlɪŋ; ˈtʃendʒlɪm/ *n* child secretly substituted for another in infancy, esp (in old stories) a strange, ugly or stupid child left by fairies in place of one they have stolen. 调包儿(被秘密换入的婴儿, 尤指旧传说中由神仙在偷走一个小孩后所留下的一个又怪又丑又笨的孩子).

chan·nel /ˈtʃænl; ˈtʃænl/ *n* **1** stretch of water joining two seas: (连接两海的) 海峡: *the English C~,* between France and England. 英吉利海峡 (在法国与英国之间). **2** natural or artificial bed of a stream of water; passage along which a liquid may flow. (天然或人工的) 河床; 水道; 沟渠; 槽. **3** deeper part of a waterway: 水道之较深处; 航道: *The ~ is marked by buoys.* 航道有浮标标示。*Keep to the ~—the river is shallow at the sides.* 照着航道走—河面的两旁水浅。**4** (fig) any way by which news, ideas, etc may travel: (喻)(消息、意见等传播的)途径; 路线; 方法: *He has secret ~s of information.* 他有秘密的消息来源。**through the usual ~s,** by the usual means of communication (between persons, groups, etc): 经由通常的途径(指经由人与人间、团体与团体间等通常的沟通): *A debate on this question can be arranged through the usual ~s,* eg, in Parliament, through the leaders of political parties. 对此问题的辩论可循通常的途径予以安排(例如在国会中, 经由各政党的领袖). **5** (radio, TV) band of frequencies within which signals from a transmitter must be kept (to prevent interference from other transmitters). (无线电、电视)波段; 波道; 频道(自发射台所发出的电波为了避免受其他发射台的干扰所必须遵守的频率带). □ *vt* (**-ll-,** US also **-l-**) [VP 6 A, 14] **1** form a ~ or ~s in, cut out (a way): 形成河床; 冲出 (一条路): *The river had ~led its way through the soft rock.* 河水已在松软的岩石中冲成一条水道. **2** cause to go through a ~ or ~s. 使经过某种路线前进; 引导.

chant /tʃɑːnt *US*: tʃænt; tʃænt/ *n* [C] often-repeated tune to which psalms and canticles are fitted; several syllables or words to one note. (赞美诗及颂歌中所用之) 常重复的曲调; 用同一首调唱出的几个音节或词句. □ **hymn.** □ *vi, vt* [VP2A, 6 A] sing; sing a ~; use a singing note (eg for a prayer in Church): 唱歌; 重复地唱; 用唱歌的调子 (如教堂做祷告者): ~ *sb's praises,* (fig) praise constantly. (喻)不断地称赞; 歌颂.

chantey, chanty /ˈʃænti; ˈʃænti/ *n* (US)**=shanty**[2].

chaos /ˈkeɪɒs; ˈkeas/ *n* [U] complete absence of order or shape; confusion: 完全无秩序或无整齐; 纷乱; 混乱; 一团糟: *The room was in a state of ~ when the burglars had left.* 窃贼离去后, 室内杂乱不堪. **cha·ot·ic** /keɪˈɒtɪk; keˈatɪk/ *adj* in a state of ~; confused. 无秩序的; 混乱的; 乱七八糟的. **cha·ot·i·cal·ly** /keɪˈɒtɪklɪ; keˈatɪklɪ/ *adv*

chap[1] /tʃæp; tʃæp/ *vt, vi* (**-pp-**) **1** [VP2A] (of the skin) become sore, rough, cracked: (指皮肤) 发痛; 变粗糙; 破裂: *My skin soon ~s in cold weather.* 我的皮肤在冷天里很快就会破裂. **2** [VP 6 A] cause to become cracked or rough: 使致裂或变粗糙: *hands and face ~ped by the cold.* 因寒冻而致裂的手和脸. □ *n* crack, esp in the skin. (尤指皮肤上的)裂口.

chap[2] /tʃæp; tʃæp/ *n* (also 亦作 *chop*) (*pl*) jaws, esp of animals; cheeks. (复)(动物的)颚; 颊. **'~·fallen** *adj* dispirited, dejected. 沮丧的; 失望的.

chap[3] /tʃæp; tʃæp/ *n* (colloq) man; boy; fellow. (口)人; 小伙子; 家伙.

chapel /ˈtʃæpl; ˈtʃæpl/ *n* **1** place (not a parish church) used for Christian worship, eg in a large private house, school, prison, etc. (大私宅、学校、监狱等处所附属的)基督教礼拜堂 (非教区教堂). **2** small place within a Christian church, used for private prayer, with an altar, and usually named (eg a '*Lady C~,* one dedicated to Mary, the mother of Jesus). (大教堂里的) 小礼拜堂 (用作个人礼拜之所, 有祭坛, 通常另有名称, 如 '圣母礼拜堂' 系奉献给圣母玛利亚者). 参看 church 之插图. **3** (GB; obsolescent use) place of worship used by those who do not belong to the established (Anglican) Church of England: (英; 逐渐废用) 非国教教徒之礼拜堂; 自由教堂: *the Methodist ~.* 美以美会礼拜堂. *Are you church or ~,* Do you belong to the Church of England or to one of the Free Churches? 你是国教徒还是自由教徒? ⇨ **free**[1] (3). **'~·goer** /-gəʊə(r); -gɔʒ/ *n* nonconformist (contrasted with a member of the Church of England). 自由教徒(与英国国教相对); 非国教徒. **4** [U] service held in a ~ (1, 3): 基督教礼拜堂或自由教堂的礼拜式: *go to ~.* 到自由教堂做礼拜.

chap·er·on /ˈʃæpərəʊn; ˈʃæpə,ron/ *n* married or elderly person (usu a woman) in charge of a girl or young unmarried woman on social occasions. 陪未婚少女上社交场所之已婚或较年长的人(通常为妇人); 女伴; 陪伴. □ *vt* [VP6A] act as a ~ to. 作…之陪伴; 陪伴.

chap·fallen /ˈtʃæpfɔːlən; ˈtʃæp,fɔlən/ *adj* ⇨ **chap**[2].

chap·lain /ˈtʃæplɪn; ˈtʃæplɪn/ *n* priest or clergyman, esp in the navy, army or air force, or officiating in a chapel(1). 海、陆、空军之随营牧师; 军中传教士; 主持非教区教堂之礼拜的牧师. ⇨ **padre.** **'~·cy** /-sɪ; -sɪ/ *n* function, area or house of a ~. 随营牧师等之职责、辖区或住宅.

chap·let /ˈtʃæplɪt; ˈtʃæplɪt/ *n* wreath of leaves, flowers, jewels, etc) for the head; string of beads (a short rosary) for counting prayers. 用枝叶、花、珠宝等编成戴在头上的花环; 花冠; 祈祷时计数用的念珠(短念珠).

chap·man /ˈtʃæpmən; ˈtʃæpmən/ *n* (*pl* **-men**) (old use) pedlar. (旧用法)贩夫; 小贩.

chap·ter /ˈtʃæptə(r); ˈtʃæptə/ *n* **1** (usu numbered) main division of a book. (书的)章; 篇(通常有编号). *~ of accidents,* number of misfortunes closely following one another. 接踵而来的灾祸。*~ and verse,* exact reference to a passage, etc or authority (for a statement, etc) for. (一段话等之)确实的出处; 精确引证; 典故(for 连用). **2** period; epoch: 时期; 时代: *the most brilliant ~ in the history of the French court.* 法国王朝史上最光辉的时代. **3** (general meeting of the) whole number of canons of a cathedral church, or the members of a monastery or convent. 大教堂的全体教士(大会); 修道院或女修道院的全体修士(大会). **'~·house** *n* building used for such meetings. 教士或修士大会会堂.

char[1] /tʃɑː(r); tʃɑr/ *vt, vi* (**-rr-**) [VP6A, 2A] (of a surface) make or become black by burning: (指表面)烧焦; 烧黑: ~*red wood.* 木炭.

char[2] /tʃɑː(r); tʃɑr/ *vi* (**-rr-**) do the cleaning of offices, houses, etc with payment by the hour or the day: 替办公室、私宅等做清洁之临时工(按小时或按日计酬): *go out ~ring.* 出去做打扫清洁之零工. □ *n* = woman. 替人打扫清洁之女工. **'~·lady, '~·woman** *nn* woman who earns money by ~ring, paid by the hour or the day. (按小时或按日计酬)替人打扫清洁之女工.

char³ /tʃɑː(r); tʃɑr/ n [U] (GB sl) tea: (英俚) 茶: *a cup of ~*. 一杯茶.

char-à-banc, char·a·banc / ˈʃærəbæŋ; ˈʃærə-ˌbæŋk/ n (not US)(now usu called 现通常称做 *coach*) single-decked motor-coach with all seats facing forward, used for pleasure trips. (不用于美国)(座位一律向前之) 单层游览汽车.

char·ac·ter /ˈkærəktə(r); ˈkærɪktər/ n **1** [U] (of a person, community, race, etc) mental or moral nature; mental or moral qualities that make one person, race, etc different from others: (指个人、社会、民族等之) 天性; 性情; 性格; 特质; 个性: *a woman of fine/strong/noble, etc ~*; 性情很好/个性坚强, 气质高贵等)之女人; *the ~ of Julius Cæsar/of the French*. 朱利阿斯·恺撒(法国民族)的性格. *in/out of ~*, appropriate/inappropriate to the actions, etc known to be in accord with a person's ~. (指行为等)合(不合)于个性. **2** [U] moral strength: 道德的力量; 品格: *a man of ~*. 有品格的人. *Should ~ building be the chief aim of education?* 品格的培养应该是教育的主要目的吗? **3** [U] all those qualities that make a thing, place, etc what it is and different from others: (事物、地方等与其他不同之)特点; 特质; 特征: *the ~ of the desert areas of N Africa*. 北非洲沙漠地区之特质. **4** [C] person who is well known: 出名的人; 闻人: *a public ~*; 社会知名人士; person in a novel, play, etc: (小说、戏剧等中的)角色; 人物: *the ~s in the novels of Charles Dickens*; 狄更斯小说中的人物; person who is in some ways unusual: 某些方面不平常的人: *He's quite a ~*, has peculiarities of his own, is not an average or typical sort of person. 他是个很特殊的人物. *'~ actor* n one who specialises in portraying unusual or eccentric people. 性格演员 (善于饰演奇特人物之演员). **5** [C] (old use) description of a person's abilities and qualities, esp in a letter by an employer, that may be used when applying for a job(*testimonial* is now the usu word). (旧用法)雇主对于雇员之能力及品行所出的证明信(可用以另外求职者; 现通常用 *testimonial*). **6** [C] reputation: 名誉: *He has gained the ~ of a miser*. 他博得了一个守财奴之名. **7** [C] letter, sign, mark, etc used in a system of writing or printing: 文字; 字母: *Greek/Chinese, etc ~s*. 希腊字母 (汉字等). **~·is·tic** /ˌkærəktəˈrɪstɪk; ˌkærɪktəˈrɪstɪk/ adj forming part of, showing, the ~ of: 构成…的性格之一部分的; 表明…的性格的; 性格中所特有的; 特别的: *with his ~istic enthusiasm*. 以他所特有的热心. *It's ~istic of him*, It's what people would expect to do, because of his ~. 那是他的特殊作风. □ n [C] special mark or quality: 特点; 特质; 特性; 特色; 特征: *What are the ~istics that distinguish the Chinese from the Japanese?* 中国人与日本人不同的特质是什么? **~·is·ti·cal·ly** /ˌkærəktəˈrɪstɪklɪ; ˌkærɪktəˈrɪstɪklɪ/ adv '~·ize v [VP6A] show the ~ of; give to; mark in a special way: 显示…之特征; 赋予…特征; 以特别的方式标明: *Your work is ~ized by lack of attention to detail*. 你的工作的特点是不注意细节. *The camel is ~ized by the ability to go for long periods without water*. 骆驼的特点是能够长期行走而不喝水. **~·less** adj without ~; undistinguished; ordinary. 无特点的; 无特色的; 不出众的; 平常的.

cha·rade US: -ˈreɪd; ʃəˈreɪd/ n [C] episode in a game in which a word is guessed by the onlookers after the word itself, and each syllable of it in turn, have been suggested by acting a little play; (pl, with sing v) this game; (fig) action of no or sham significance; pretence. 比手画脚猜字游戏的谜面(借短短的表演暗示一每一音节然后令观者猜着的字); (复)(与单数动词连用)比手画脚猜字游戏; (喻)无意义的行为; 虚伪的行为; 假装.

char·coal /ˈtʃɑːkəʊl; ˈtʃɑrˌkol/ n [U] black substance, used as fuel, as a filtering material and for drawing, made by burning wood slowly in an oven with little air: 木炭 (将木材置于炉中闷烧而成之黑色物质, 用作燃料、过滤材料及作画): *a bale/stick/piece, etc of ~*. 一

捆(根, 块等)木炭. **'~-burner** n person who makes stove, etc in which ~ is used as the fuel. 烧制木炭者; 木炭炉.

chard /tʃɑːd; tʃɑrd/ n (often 常作 *Swiss ~*) variety of beet of which the leaves are used as a vegetable. 其叶可当作蔬菜食用之一种甜菜.

charge¹ /tʃɑːdʒ; tʃɑrdʒ/ n **1** accusation; statement that a person has done wrong, esp that he has broken a law: 指控; 控告 (尤指控告某人犯法者): *arrested on a ~ of theft*. 因偷窃的罪名而被逮捕. *bring a ~ (of sth) against sb*, accuse him (of a crime, etc). 控告某人(犯某种罪等). *face a ~ (of sth)*, have to answer it in court: 必须出庭应付答辩: *He faces serious ~s*. 他必须到庭应付严重的控告. *lay sth to sb's ~*, bring an accusation of sth against him. 为某事控告某人. *'~-account* n (US) credit account. (美) 赊帐. **2** sudden and violent attack at high speed(by soldiers, wild animals, a football player, etc). (指军队、野兽、足球队队员等所做之)迅速突袭; 突袭; 猛攻; 冲锋. **3** price asked for goods or services: 索取之价钱(指货价); (因服务而采取的)费用: *hotel ~s*. 旅馆费用. **'~-account** n (US) credit account. (美) 赊帐. **4** amount of powder, etc (to be) used in a gun or for causing an explosion; amount of electricity (to be) put into an accumulator, contained in a substance, etc: 枪炮发一弹或爆炸一次所用的火药量; 储于蓄电池内或某物质等中所含的电量; 电荷; 充电: *a positive/negative ~*. 阳电荷/阴电荷(负电荷/阴电荷). **5** [C] work given to sb as a duty; thing or person given or entrusted to sb to be taken care of; [U]responsibility; trust: 交与某人的工作责任; 托付某人照料的事务或人; 责任; 委托: *This ward of the hospital is in/under the ~ of Dr Green*. 本医院的这间病房是由格林医生负责. *I hope you'll never become a ~ on the public*, ie become a pauper, to be supported at public expense. 我希望你永远不会变成受公众照料的人(变成贫穷而须由公家赡济). *put sb/be in ~ (of)*, be (put) in a position of responsibility (for): (使) 负责管理: *Mary was (put) in ~ of the baby*. 玛丽负责照料这个婴儿. *Who's in ~ here?* 这里是谁负责? *put sb/be in sb's ~*, be(put)in his care: (使)由…负责管理: *The baby was (put) in Mary's ~*. 这个婴儿是由玛丽负责照料. *give sb in ~*, give him up to the police. 将某人交付警方. *take ~ of*, become responsible for. 负责管理. **6** directions; instructions: 命令; 指示: *the judge's ~ to the jury*, instructions concerning their duty (in reaching a verdict). 法官对于陪审团(裁决案件)的职责所作的指示.

charge² /tʃɑːdʒ; tʃɑrdʒ/ vt, vi **1** [VP6A, 14] ~ *sb (with)*, accuse; bring a charge(1) against: 指控; 控告 (某人做某事): *He was ~d with murder*. 他被控告谋杀. *He ~d me with neglecting my duty*. 他指控我疏忽职责. **2** [VP6A, 2A, C] make a charge(2) against; rush forward and attack: 突袭; 猛攻; 冲锋; 向前冲进并攻击: *Our soldiers ~d the enemy*. 我军向敌军猛攻. *One of our strikers* (ie in a game of football) *was violently ~d by the defender*. (指足球赛中)我们的前锋之一受到(对方)后卫的猛袭. *The wounded lion suddenly ~d at me*. 那只被击伤的狮子突然向我冲袭. **3** [VP2B, 14] ~ *(for)*, ask as a price; ask in payment: 索价; 要价: *He ~d me fifty pence (for it)*. (这件东西)他(向我)索价五十便士. *How much do you ~ for mending a pair of shoes?* 你补一双鞋要多少钱? **4** [VP14, 15A, B] ~ *to; ~ up; ~ up to*, make a record of (as a debt): 记帐: *Please ~ these purchases to my account*. 请将这些购货价款记在我的帐上. **5** [VP6A, 2A] load (a gun); fill, put a charge(4) into: 装弹药于(枪炮); 充电于: ~ *an accumulator*. 充电于蓄电池. *Electrons are negatively ~d with electricity; protons are positively ~d*. 电子是带负(阴)电荷; 质子是带正(阳)电荷. **6** [VP14] ~ *with*, give as a task or duty; give into sb's care: 交付责任; 交…负责照料: *He was ~d with an important mission*. 他被交付重要使命. *He ~d himself with* (= undertook) *the task of keeping*

the club's accounts in order. 他负起替协会管帐的责任.
7 [VP6A, 17] (esp of a judge, or person in authority) command; instruct: (尤指法官或主管)命令; 指示; 训令: *I ~ you not to fcrget what I have said.* 我命令你不要忘记我所说的话. *The judge ~d the jury, gave them directions about how to perform their duty.* 法官训示陪审团(指示他们如何执行职务).

charge·able /'tʃɑːdʒəbl; 'tʃɑrdʒəbl/ *adj* **1** that can be, is liable to be, charged: 可被控告的; 可能遭受控告的: *If you steal, you are ~ with theft.* 如果你偷窃, 你就会被控盗窃罪. **2 ~ on/to** (comm) that may be added (to an account): (商)可记在(帐上)的: *sums ~ to a reserve;* 可记入准备金项下的款项; *that may be made an expense:* 可报帐的: *Costs of repairs are ~ on the owner of the building.* 修缮费可向房东报帐.

chargé d'affaires /ˌʃɑːʒeɪ dæˈfeə(r); ˌʃɑrˈʒedæˈfɛr/ *n* (*pl* chargés d'affaires, pronunciation unchanged 复数读音不变) official who takes the place of an ambassador or minister when the ambassador, etc is absent from his post. 代办(大使或公使公出时的代理者).

charger[1] /'tʃɑːdʒə(r); 'tʃɑrdʒɚ/ *n* (old use) army officer's horse. (旧用法)(陆军军官的)战马.

charger[2] /'tʃɑːdʒə(r); 'tʃɑrdʒɚ/ *n* (old use) large, flat dish; platter. (旧用法)大浅盘.

char·iot /'tʃærɪət; 'tʃærɪət/ *n* open, two-wheeled, horse-drawn carriage, used in ancient times in fighting and racing. (古代作战和比赛用的)两轮无篷马车. **char·io·teer** /ˌtʃærɪəˈtɪə(r); ˌtʃærɪətˈɪr/ *n* driver of a ~. 驾驶此种马车者.

cha·ris·ma /kəˈrɪzmə; kəˈrɪzmə/ *n* **1** (theology) spiritual grace. (神学)上帝的恩赐(如治病的能力等). **2** capacity to inspire devotion and enthusiasm. 激励忠诚及热情的才能. **char·is·matic** /ˌkærɪˈmætɪk; ˌkærɪzˈmætɪk/ *adj*

chari·table /'tʃærɪtəbl; 'tʃærətəbl/ *adj* showing, having, charity (*to*); for charity: 表示慈善的; 有慈善心的 (与 to 连用); 为慈善的: *~ institutions,* 慈善机关(救济贫困及受难者); *~ to all men.* 对所有的人表示慈悲. **'chari·tably** /-blɪ; -blɪ/ *adv*

char·ity /'tʃærətɪ; 'tʃærɪtɪ/ *n* **1** [U] willingness to judge other persons with kindness; neighbourly love: 宽厚; 仁恕; 博爱; 慈悲: *judge other people with ~.* 宽厚待人; 仁恕待人. *C~ begins at home,* (prov) A person's first duty is to help the members of his own family. (谚) 慈善始于家庭(意谓一个人的首要责任是照顾自己的家属). **2** (kindness in giving) help to the poor; money, food, etc so given. 慈善; 施与; 赒济; 救济金; 赒济品; 施舍之食物等. *live on/off ~,* live by accepting money etc from others. 靠别人济过日子. **3** [C](*pl -ties*) society or organization for serving those in need: 慈善团体: *He left all his money to charities,* to charitable institutions. 他把所有的钱都捐给了慈善团体.

chari·vari /ˌʃɑːrɪˈvɑːrɪ US: /ˌʃɪvəˈriː/; /ʃəˌrɪvəˈri/ *n* [U] hubbub; medley of noises and voices. 喧杂; 喧嚣; 骚闹.

char·lady /'tʃɑːleɪdɪ; 'tʃɑrˌledɪ/ *n* (*pl* -**ladies**) char-woman. 做零工的女佣. ⇨ char[2]

char·la·tan /'ʃɑːlətən; 'ʃɑrlətn/ *n* person who claims to have more skill, knowledge or ability than he really has, esp one who pretends to have medical knowledge. 冒充内行者; (尤指)冒充医生者; 庸医; 江湖医生.

Charles·ton /'tʃɑːlstən; 'tʃɑrlstən/ *n* fast dance with side kicks from the knee(popular in the 1920's). 查尔斯顿舞(一种快速的舞蹈, 膝向外侧踢, 流行于二十世纪二十年代).

char·lock /'tʃɑːlɒk; 'tʃɑrlək/ *n* wild mustard, a weed with yellow flowers. 野茶菜(一种开黄花之野草).

charm /tʃɑːm; tʃɑrm/ *n* **1** [U] attractiveness; power to give pleasure; [C] pleasing quality or feature: 吸引力; 给人快感之能力; 可爱的性质或特点; 魅力; 魔力: *Her ~ of manner made her very popular.* 她的风度之优雅使她

极受大家欢迎. *He fell a victim to her ~s,* her beauty, her attractive ways, etc. 他为她的姿色所倾倒. **2** [C] sth believed to have magic power, good or bad: 被认为是具有(善或恶)魔力之物; 符咒: *under a ~,* influenced in a magic way; 着魔的; *~s against evil spirits;* 能驱除恶魔之符咒; *a ~ to bring good luck,* eg a trinket worn on the body. 可带来福气之物(如戴于身上的小饰物); 吉祥物. *work like a ~,* with complete success. 完全成功的工作(或作品). □ *vt, vi* **1** [VP6A, 2A] attract; give pleasure to: 吸引; 给与快感; 使陶醉; 使欣赏; 讨人喜欢: *Does goodness ~ more than beauty?* 善良是否较美色更能使人欣赏? *We were ~ed with the scenery.* 我们陶醉在风景中. *I'm ~ed (pleased* is more usu 较常用 *pleased) to meet you* (used as a polite formula). 幸会; 幸会(客套语). **2** [VP6A, 15A] use magic on; influence or protect as if by magic: 施魔术于; 似以魔力影响或保护: *He's had a ~ed life,* has escaped dangers, as if protected by magic. 他的性命似有神力保护; 他有吉星高照(使他得以避开危险). *She ~ed away his sorrow,* caused him to forget his troubles. 她驱走了他的悲伤. **~·ing** *adj* delightful: 娇媚的; 迷人的: *a ~ing young lady.* 娇媚的少女. **~·ing·ly** *adv ~er n* (usu joc) young man or woman with ~. (通常为谑)迷人的青年男子或女子. **'snake ~er** *n* person able to ~ (2) snakes. 玩蛇者; 弄蛇者.

char·nel house /'tʃɑːnl haʊs; 'tʃɑrnl haʊs/ *n* place where dead human bodies or bones are stored. 存放死人尸体或骸骨之所; 藏骸所; 积骨堂.

chart /tʃɑːt; tʃɑrt/ *n* **1** map used by sailors, showing the coasts, depth of the sea, position of rocks, lighthouses, etc. (水手所用, 标示海岸线、海洋深度、礁石、灯塔等之位置的)航海图. **2** sheet of paper with information, in the form of curves, diagrams, etc (about such things as the weather, prices, business conditions, etc): (以曲线、图解等表示气象、物价、商情等资料之)图表: *a 'weather/'temperature ~.* 气象(温度)图表. □ *vt* [VP6A] make a ~ of; show on a ~. 制成图表; 以图表表示.

char·ter /'tʃɑːtə(r); 'tʃɑrtɚ/ *n* **1** (written or printed statement of) rights, permission to do sth, esp from a ruler or government (eg to a town, city or university). (由统治者或政府发给城镇或大学等的)特许状; 营业执照; 特权; 特许, 宪章. **2** hiring or engagement (of an aircraft, a ship, etc): 包租(飞机、船等); 包船: *a '~ flight.* 包机. 油轮的包租可以按时间计费或按航程计费. for the voyage. □ *vt* [VP6A] **1** give a ~ to; grant a privilege to. 发给特许状; 给与特权. **~ed ac'countant,** (in GB) member of the Institute of Accountants(which has a royal ~). (英)会计师(获有皇家特许状, 为会计师协会之会员). **2** hire or engage a ship, an aircraft, etc for an agreed time, purpose and payment: (议定时间、用途及价款)包租(船、飞机等): *travel in a ~ed aircraft.* 乘包机旅行. **'~-party** *n* (comm) agreement between a shipowner and merchant for the use of a ship. (商)包船租约(商人向船主租船所订的租约); 租船契约.

Chart·ism /'tʃɑːtɪzəm; 'tʃɑrtɪzəm/ *n* early 19th c working-class movement for social and industrial reform. 宪章运动. (十九世纪早期致力于社会和工业改革的)民权运动. **Chart·ist** /-ɪst; -ɪst/ *n*

char·treuse /ʃɑːˈtrɜːz US: -'truːz; ʃɑrˈtrɜːz/ *n* (kinds of) liqueur (green, yellow) made by Carthusian /kɑːˈθjuːzɪən US:-'θuːʒn; kɑrˈθjuʒən/ monks (of an austere monastic order founded in S France in 1086). 荨麻酒 (一○八六年 创于法国南部之卡尔特苦行修道团的僧侣所造之绿色或黄色酒).

char·woman /'tʃɑːwʊmən; 'tʃɑrˌwʊmən/ *n* ⇨ char[2].

chary /'tʃeərɪ; 'tʃɛrɪ/ *adj* **~ (of),** cautious, wary, careful: 小心的; 谨慎的; 注意的: *~ of catching cold;* 当心受凉; *a teacher who is ~ of giving praise,* who seldom praises his pupils. 不轻易称赞学生的教师. **char·ily** *adv*

Cha·ryb·dis /kəˈrɪbdɪs; kəˈrɪbdɪs/ *n* ⇨ **Scylla.**

chase[1] /tʃeɪs; tʃes/ *vt, vi* **1** [VP6A, 3A, 15A, B] ~

(after), run after in order to capture, kill, overtake or drive away: 追捕；追急；追赶；驱逐: *Dogs like to ~ rabbits.* 狗喜欢追逐兔子. *C~ that dog out of the garden.* 把那条狗赶出花园去. *The letter had been chasing after him for weeks,* eg had been following him from place to place during his travels. 此信已追踪他数星期 (如当他在旅行中由甲地追至乙地，又由乙地追至丙地等). *This'll ~ away the blues!* 这将把忧郁驱散! **2** [VP2C] (colloq) hurry; rush: (口)赶快；急跑: *The children all ~d off after the procession.* 孩子们纷纷追去跟随游行的队伍. □ *n* act of chasing: 追赶；追逐: *After a long ~, we caught the thief.* 经过很久的追逐，我们终于捉住了那个小偷. *give ~ (to),* run after; start in pursuit (of). 追逐；追赶；追击. *in ~ of sb/sth,* pursuing, running after. 追逐和追赶某人 (某物). *(go on) a ,wild 'goose ~,* (embark on)a search, expedition, etc that can have no success. (从事)不会成功的搜索，探险等; (从事)劳而无功的事. **chaser** *n* (in compounds) person or thing that ~s; (colloq) drink taken after another, eg a mild chaser to a strong: (用于复合词中) 追踪或追击之人或物; (口)酒后所饮之酒或饮料 (例如烈性酒饮过后再饮淡性酒): *whisky with beer ~rs.* 威士忌之后再饮啤酒.

chase² /tʃeɪs; tʃes/ *vt* [VP6A] cut patterns or designs on (metal or other hard material); engrave: 刻图于 (金属或其他硬材料); 雕镂: *~d silver.* 雕花银器.

chasm /'kæzəm; 'kæzəm/ *n* deep opening or crack in the ground; abyss; gorge; (fig) wide difference (of feeling or interests, *between* persons, groups, nations, etc). (地上的)深坑或裂缝; 罅隙; 深渊; 峡; (喻)(个人、团体或国家等之间感情或利害的)分歧; 冲突; 裂痕 (与 between 连用).

chas·sis /'ʃæsɪ; 'ʃæsɪ/ *n* (*pl* spelling unchanged, but pronounced 复数拼法不变, 但读作 /'ʃæsɪz; 'ʃæsɪz/) base framework of a motor-vehicle, radio or TV, on which the body and working parts are mounted. (汽车、收音机或电视机的)底盘.

chaste /tʃeɪst; tʃest/ *adj* **1** virtuous in word, thought and deed; (esp) abstaining from promiscuous or all sexual intercourse.(言语、思想及行为)有德行的; 纯洁的; (尤指)不乱交的; 贞洁的. **2** (of style, taste) simple; without ornament; pure. (指风格、嗜好)简单的; 朴实无华的; 纯朴的. **~·ly** *adv*

chas·ten /'tʃeɪsn; 'tʃesn/ *vt* [VP6A] **1** punish in order to correct; discipline. 惩戒; 磨炼. **2** make chaste (2). 使纯朴.

chas·tise /tʃæ'staɪz; tʃæs'taɪz/ *vt* [VP6A] punish severely. 严惩; 责罚. **~·ment** *n* [U] punishment. 惩戒; 惩罚.

chas·tity /'tʃæstətɪ; 'tʃæstətɪ/ *n* [U] state of being chaste. 纯洁; 贞节; 纯朴.

chas·uble /'tʃæzjʊbl; 'tʃæzjʊbl/ *n* (eccles) loose, sleeveless garment worn over all other vestments by a priest at the Eucharist. (教会) 十字褡 (神父行圣餐礼时所着，罩于其他衣服之外的宽松无袖长袍). ➪ the illus at vestment. 参看 vestment 之插图.

chat /tʃæt; tʃæt/ *n* [C] friendly talk (usu about unimportant things): 闲谈; 聊天: *I had a long ~ with him.* 我与他闲谈了半天. □ *vi, vt* (-tt-) **1** [VP2A, C] have a ~: 闲谈; 聊天: *They were ~ting (away) in the corner.* 他们在屋角里闲聊. **2** [VP15B] *~ sb up,* (colloq) ~ to in order to win friendship, or for fun (口) (为获得友谊或欢乐)与某人聊天: *~ up a pretty barmaid.* 与可爱的酒吧女侍聊天. **~·ty** *adj* fond of ~ting. 喜好闲谈的.

châ·teau /'ʃætəʊ; ʃæ'to/ *n* (*pl* ~x /-təʊz; -toz/) castle or large country house in France. (法国的)古堡; 乡间大庄园; 别墅.

chat·el·aine /'ʃætəleɪn; 'ʃætl,en/ *n* (old use) set of short chains fastened to a woman's belt for carrying keys, etc; mistress of a large country house or castle. (旧用法)系于妇人腰带上以悬挂钥匙等之短链子; 大别墅或古堡的女主人.

a château

chat·tel /'tʃætl; 'tʃætl/ *n* (legal) article of personal movable property (eg a chair, a motor-car, a horse): (法律)动产(如椅子、汽车、马匹): *a person's goods and ~s.* 一个人所有的杂物用品.

chat·ter /'tʃætə(r); 'tʃæts/ *vi* [VP2A, C] **1** (of a person) talk quickly or foolishly; talk too much. (指人)唠叨, 喋喋不休. **2** (of the cries of monkeys and some birds, of typewriter keys, of a person's upper and lower teeth striking together from cold or fear) make quick, indistinct sounds. (指猴子和某些鸟类的叫声, 打字机的按键, 人的牙齿因寒冷或恐惧而碰击在一起)发出迅速而不清晰的声响; 格格作响. □ *n* [U] sounds of the kind noted above: 上述的各种声音: *the ~ of sparrows/children.* 麻雀的喞喞声 (儿童的)的喋喋活声. '**~·box,** person who ~s, esp a small child. 话匣子; 碎嘴子; 喋喋不休之人(尤指小儿).

chauf·feur /'ʃəʊfə(r) US: ʃəʊ'fɜːr; 'ʃofɚ/ *n* man paid to drive a privately-owned motor-car. 受雇驾驶私人汽车之司机. **chauf·feuse** /'ʃəʊfəːz US: ʃəʊ'fɜːz; ,ʃo'fsz/ *n* woman ~. 受雇驾驶私人汽车的女司机.

chau·vin·ism /'ʃəʊvɪnɪzəm; 'ʃovɪn,ɪzəm/ *n* [U] unreasoning enthusiasm for (esp) the glory of one's own country. 沙文主义; (尤指)本国至上主义. **chau·vin·ist** /-ɪst; -ɪst/ *n* person with such enthusiasm. 沙文主义者; 本国至上主义者. **male chauvinist; chauvinist male** (mod use) man who believes that men are superior to women and acts accordingly. (形容用法) 相信男子比女子优越并有所行动者: 大男子主义者. **chau·vin·is·tic** /,ʃəʊvɪ'nɪstɪk; ,ʃovɪ'nɪstɪk/ *adj* of ~ or chauvinists. 沙文主义的.

chaw /tʃɔː; tʃo/ *n, vt* (vulg) chew. (鄙)咀嚼. '**~-bacon** *n* ignorant bumpkin. 无知的乡巴佬.

cheap /tʃiːp; tʃip/ *adj* (-er, -est) **1** low in price; costing little money: 价低的; 价廉的; 花费少的: *the ~est seats in a theatre,* 戏院中票价低廉的座位; *travel by the ~est route,* 采取花钱最少的路线旅行; *~ tickets/trips,* at specially reduced fares: 特价票(旅行); (used as *adv*): (用items副词): *buy/sell/get sth ~,* ie for a low price. 廉价买得(卖出, 取得)某物. *go ~,* be offered or bought for a low price: 廉价出售; 便宜卖出: *Cauliflowers going ~ — only 10p each!* 菜花便宜卖——十便士一棵! *on the ~,* (colloq) for a low price: (口)廉价地: *buy/sell/get sth on the ~.* 廉价买得(卖出, 取得)某物. **2** worth more than the cost; of good value for the money. 便宜的; 花钱少而货色好的; 合算的. **3** of poor quality: 品质低劣的: *~ and nasty,* 品质恶劣的. '**~-jack** *adj* ~ and shoddy. 质劣而冒充好货的. **4** shallow; insincere: 肤浅的; 不真诚的: *~ emotion;* 虚伪的感情; *~ flattery.* 拍马奉承. **5** *feel ~,* (colloq) feel ashamed. 口 感觉惭愧. *hold sth ~,* put a low value on it, despise it. 认为某事物无甚价值; 轻视某事物. *make oneself ~,* behave so that one's reputation goes down. 做出自贬身份之行为. *~ gibe n* unkind taunt. 辱骂. **~·ly** *adv* for a low price: 价廉地: *buy/sell/get sth ~ly.* 廉价买得 (卖出, 取得)某物. **~·ness** *n*

cheapen /'tʃiːpən; 'tʃipən/ *vt, vi* [VP6A, 2A] make or become cheap; lower the price of: 贬损价值; 降低…的价格; 减价: *You mustn't ~ yourself,* behave so that you lower your reputation. 你不可自贬身价.

cheat /tʃiːt; tʃit/ *vi, vt* [VP6A, 2A, C, 14] ~ *sb (out of sth); ~(in/at sth)*, act in a dishonest way to win an advantage or profit: 欺骗; 骗取(利益等): ~ *the customs*, 不(如不报应完税之货物); ~ *sb out of his money*, 骗某人的钱; ~ *at cards*; 玩纸牌时作弊; ~ *in an examination*. 在考试中作弊. □ *n* person who ~s; dishonest trick. 骗子; 骗徒; 欺骗; 欺诈; 欺骗手段.

check¹ /tʃek; tʃɛk/ *vt, vi* 1 [VP6A, 15B, 2C] examine in order to learn whether sth is correct: 检查; 查证; 核对 (以查明是否正确): ~ *a bill;* 核对帐单; ~ *sb's statements.* 查证某人的陈述. *Will you please* ~ *these figures?* 请检查这些数字可有无错误? ~ *sth off,* mark it as having been found correct. 做记号于某物上表示已核对无误. ~ *sth up; ~ up on sth,* (US 美 = ~ *sth out*) examine or compare to learn whether it is correct. 检查或核对某物(以查明是否正确). ~ *up on sb,* examine his credentials to see whether he is what he claims to be. 检查某人的各种证明文件(以核证其所声称各项是否属实). 2 [VP6A] hold back; restrain; cause to go slow or stop: 抑止; 控制; 阻止; 阻滞: *We have* ~*ed the enemy's advance.* 我们业已挡住敌军的前进。 *He couldn't* ~ *his anger.* 他未能抑制他的愤怒。 *This extravagant spending must be* ~*ed.* 这种奢侈的花费必须停止。 3 [VP6A] (chess) put in ~²(4). (下棋)攻王棋; 将军. 2 [VP2C] ~ *in (at)*, arrive and register at a hotel/a factory etc. 到达登记(指到达旅馆、工厂等). ~ *out (from)*, pay one's bill and leave (a hotel, supermarket etc): 付帐离开(旅馆、超级市场等): '~-*out time,* time at which a room must be vacated. 结帐迁出时间(过时则要多算一天房钱). '~-*out n* (esp) (paying (e in a supermarket) where one pays the bill, wraps one's goods and leaves. (尤指超级市场等之)付帐、包装所购货物并离开的地方; (付款处。 5 (US) [VP6A] get a ticket, a piece of wood, metal, etc that shows a right to sth (eg hat and coat at a theatre, luggage sent by train or left at a railway station): (美) 寄存; 托运(在戏院寄存外套, 在火车站托运或寄存行李等, 并取得一个代表取物权的卡片、木牌或金属制的号牌等): *Have you* ~*ed (=got a* ~²(3) *for) all your baggage?* 你所有的行李都已寄存了吗? □ *n* person who ~s stores, orders, etc. 查查存货、定货单等之人.

check² /tʃek; tʃɛk/ *n* [U] 1 control; person or thing that checks or restrains: 控制; 起控制、制止或阻止作用的人或物: *Wind acts as a* ~ *upon speed.* 风对于速度是一种阻力. *Our forces have met with a* ~, Their advance has been stopped, they have suffered a reverse. 我军遭遇了阻遏. *We are keeping/holding the enemy in* ~, are preventing their advance. 我们正阻挡着敌人(使不能前进). *I advise you to keep a* ~ *on* (=control) *your temper.* 我劝你要控制你的脾气. '~*s and* *'balances* *n pl* (methods of) control or supervision by Government, or other authorities, to guard against misuse of power. 为预防滥用权力, 政府或其他当局所施之控制或督导(的方法). 2 examination to make certain of accuracy; mark or tick (usu written√) to show that sth has been examined and proved to be correct: 查查; 查核; 核对; 表示业经检查正确无误之记号(通常写作√): *If we both add up the figures, your result will be a* ~ *on mine.* 如果我们两人都加算这些数字, 你的得数就可以跟我的核对. '~-*list* *n* list of items, titles, etc, used in checking sth. 供核对用的清单或名册. '~-*out n* ⇨ check¹(4). '~-*point* *n* (esp) place where traffic is halted for inspection. 检查站(尤指停车以供检查的地方). '~-*up n* (esp a medical) examination made to certify sb/sth. 为证明某人或某事物所作的检查; (尤指)身体检查; 体格检查. 3 receipt (bit of paper, piece of wood or metal with a number on it, etc) given in return for sth handed over to sb (eg a hat and coat at a theatre, luggage sent by train). (在戏院寄存外套, 交火车运送行李等所取得之纸制、木制、或金属制之)号牌票; 行李票. '~-*room,* (US) left-luggage office. (美)行李寄存室. 4 *in* ~, (chess) position of an opponent's king when it is

exposed to direct attack. (下棋)敌方王棋受攻击之位置; 将军. ⇨ **checkmate**. 5(US)=**cheque**. '~-*book*, (US) = **chequebook**. 6 (US) (美) = **bill²**(1): *I'll ask the waiter for my* ~. 我要叫服务员拿帐单来.

check³ /tʃek; tʃɛk/ *n* 1 pattern of crossed lines forming squares (often of different shades or colours); cloth with such a pattern: (明暗或颜色不同之)方格花式或布料: *Which do you want for your new dress, a stripe or a* ~? 你要哪一种布做你的新衣, 条子布还是方格布? 2 (attrib) (用作定语) *a tablecloth* 方格花式的. ~ *pattern.* 方格花式. **checked** /tʃekt; tʃɛkt/ *adj* with a ~ pattern: ~*ed material.* 方格花布料.

checker /'tʃekə(r);'tʃɛkɚ/ *vt* (US) = **chequer**.

check·ers /'tʃekəz; 'tʃɛkəz/ *n* (US) (美)= **draughts**.

check·mate /'tʃekmeɪt; 'tʃɛkˌmet/ *vt* [VP6A] 1 (chess) make a move that prevents the opponent's king from being moved away from a direct attack (and so win the game). (下棋) 进攻敌方之王棋使无路可走因而获胜; 将死. ⇨ **check²(4)**. 2 obstruct and defeat (a person, his plans). 阻止并击败(某人, 其计划). □ *n* complete defeat. 完全击败.

Ched·dar /'tʃedə(r);'tʃɛdɚ/ *n* [U] kind of hard yellow cheese. 一种黄色硬干酪.

cheek /tʃiːk; tʃik/ *n* 1 either side of the face below the eye. 颊. ⇨ the illus at **head**. 参看 head 之插图. ~ *by jowl*, close together. 紧靠在一起. *turn the other* ~, respond to violence with non-violence. 忍受暴力; 忍受侮辱. ⇨ Matt 5. 39. 参看马太福音第5章第39节. '~-*bone* the bone below the eye. 颧骨. ⇨ **tongue-in-**~ ⇨ **tongue**. 2 [U] impudence; saucy talk or behaviour: 厚颜; 失礼的话或行为: *He had the* ~ *to ask me to do his work for him!* 他居然有脸要我替他做他的工作! *No more of your* ~! 不要再这样厚皮了! □ *vt* [VP6A] be impudent to: 对…无礼: *Stop* ~*ing your mother!* 不要再顶撞你的母亲! -**cheeked** *suffix* (with an *adj*): (与形容词连用): *,rosy-,*~*ed 'boys*, boys with rosy ~s. 脸颊红润的男孩子们. '~*y adj* saucy; impudent. 失礼的; 厚颜的. '~*·ily adv*

cheep /tʃiːp; tʃip/ *vi, n* [VP2A, C] (make a) weak, shrill note (as young birds do). (发) 轻微而尖锐的声音(如雏鸟之唧唧声或吱喳声).

cheer¹ /tʃɪə(r); tʃɪr/ *vt, vi* 1 [VP6A, 15B] ~ *sb (up)* fill with gladness, hope, high spirits; comfort: 使…充满欢喜、希望、高兴; 鼓舞; 安慰: *Your visit has* ~*ed (up) the sick man.* 你的访问(探病)使病人高兴. *Everyone was* ~*ed by the good news.* 每个人皆为此好消息而高兴. ~*·ing adj: That's* ~*ing news.* 那是令人兴奋的消息. 2 [VP2C] ~ *up*, take comfort, become happy: 高兴起来: *He* ~*ed up at once when I promised to help him.* 当我答应帮他的忙时, 他立刻高兴起来. 3 [VP6A, 15B, 2A, C] ~ *(on)*, give shouts of joy, approval or encouragement to: 欢呼; 喝彩; 高声加油: *The speaker was loudly* ~*ed.* 演说者受到高声的欢呼. *Everyone* ~*ed the news that the war was over.* 人人为战争结束的消息而欢呼. *The boys* ~*ed their football team.* 男孩子们为他们的足球队加油. ~*·ing n* [U] : *The* ~*ing could be heard half a mile away.* 欢呼之声半英里以外都可听得到.

cheer² /tʃɪə(r); tʃɪr/ *n* 1 [U] (old use) state of hope, gladness: (旧用法) 振奋; 高兴; 喜悦: *words of* ~, of encouragement. 鼓励的话. 2 [U] *good* ~, (old use) good food and drink.(旧用法)佳肴美酒. 3 [C] shout of joy or encouragement: 欢呼; 喝彩: *give three* ~*s for,* cry or shout 'Hurrah!' three times. 向…欢呼三声. '~-*leader n* (US) one who leads organised cheering by a group or crowd. (美)啦啦队队长. 4 (old use) (旧用法) *What* ~? How do you feel? 你好吗? 5 **C~s!** Word used when one drinks to sb's health, etc. 祝福! 祝健康! 干杯 (当举杯祝某人健康等时的用词)

cheer·ful /'tʃɪəfl; 'tʃɪrfl/ *adj* 1 bringing or suggesting happiness: 令人高兴的; 快乐的; 愉快的: *a day/room/smile;* 令人高兴的日子(房间, 微笑); ~ *conversation.* 愉快的谈话. 2 happy and contented;

willing: 高兴的; 乐意的: ~ *workers*. 高兴的工人们.
~·**ly** /-fəlɪ; -felɪ/ *adv* ~·**ness** *n*

cheer·io /ˌtʃɪərɪˈəʊ; ˌtʃɪrɪˌo/ *int* (colloq) (口) **1** (at parting) goodbye. (分手时)再见; 再会. **2** (not US; dated) (in drinking) To your health! (不用于美国; 过时用语)(敬酒时)祝你健康!

cheer·less /ˈtʃɪəlɪs; ˈtʃɪrləs/ *adj* without comfort; gloomy; miserable: 无欢笑的; 无慰藉的; 阴郁的; 凄凉的: *a wet and ~ day*; 阴雨天; *a damp, cold and ~ room*. 潮湿, 寒冷而阴森的房间. ~·**ly** *adv* ~·**ness** *n*

cheery /ˈtʃɪərɪ; ˈtʃɪrɪ/ *adj* lively; genial; merry: 活泼的; 欢乐的; 愉快的: *a ~ smile/greeting*. 愉快的笑(欢迎). **cheer·ily** /ˈtʃɪərəlɪ; ˈtʃɪrəlɪ/ *adv*

cheese /tʃiːz; tʃiz/ *n* [U] solid food made from milk curds; [C] shaped and wrapped portion or ball of this: (由凝乳制成的)干酪; 乳酪; 干酪块; 干酪团: *two cream ~s*. 两块干酪. '~·**cake**, *n* (a) tart filled with a sweet cream of curd, eggs, etc. 以凝乳、蛋等混合为馅之甜饼. (b) (sl) displays of a shapely female body (in a photograph, advertisement, etc). (俚)(照片、广告等中)女性身段美之展示; 半裸美女照. ⇨ *pin-up* at *pin²(1)*. '~·**cloth**, thin cotton cloth (gauze) put round some kinds of ~; similar (thicker) cloth used to make shirts, etc. 包某些干酪用的纱布; 一种类似而较厚的棉布(用以制衬衫等). '~·**paring**, excessive carefulness in the spending of money: 用钱过于谨慎(的); 极为节俭(的): 吝啬(的): *~-paring economies*. 过于谨慎的节俭.

chee·tah /ˈtʃiːtə; ˈtʃitə/ *n* kind of wild cat of Africa, resembling a leopard, which can be trained to hunt deer. (一种非洲产, 可以训练来猎鹿的)猎豹.

chef /ʃef; ʃef/ *n* head cook in a hotel, restaurant, etc. (旅馆、餐厅等)厨师之领班; 主厨.

chef-d'œuvre /ˌʃeɪ ˈdɜːvrə; ˌʃeˈdœvrə/ *n* (*pl* **chefs-d'œuvre**, pronunciation unchanged 复数读音不变) (F) (person's) masterpiece. (法)(某人之)杰作; 名著.

chemi·cal /ˈkemɪkl; ˈkemɪkl/ *adj* of, made by, chemistry: 化学的; 经化学程序制成的: ~ *warfare*, using poison gas, smoke, incendiary bombs, etc. 化学战 (使用毒气、烟幕、燃烧弹等). □ *n* (often *pl*) substance used in, or obtained by, chemistry. (常用复数)化学药品; 化学产品(用于化学或以化学方法制成之物质). ~·**ly** /-klɪ; -klɪ/ *adv*

che·mise /ʃəˈmiːz; ʃəˈmiz/ *n* loose, long undergarment formerly worn by women and girls; loose beltless dress. 昔时妇女所穿之宽松内衣; 无腰带的宽松女衣.

chem·ist /ˈkemɪst; ˈkemɪst/ *n* **1** person trained or expert in chemistry. 化学家. **2** (US 美 = *druggist*) pharmacist; person who prepares medicines (from prescriptions) and sells medical goods, toilet articles, etc: 药剂师; 药商(根据药方配药并贩卖药品、化妆用品等): ~'s *shop*, pharmacy. 药店; 药房.

chem·is·try /ˈkemɪstrɪ; ˈkemɪstrɪ/ *n* [U] branch of science that deals with how substances are made up, how they (their elements) combine, how they act under different conditions. 化学(科学的一部门, 研究物质之构成及其元素, 其化合及其在不同情况下之作用).

chemo·ther·apy /ˌkeməʊˈθerəpɪ; ˌkemoˈθerəpɪ/ *n* [U] treatment of disease by drugs that attack microbes. 化学疗法(指使用药物杀灭病菌的疗法).

che·nille /ʃəˈniːl; ʃəˈnil/ *n* velvety cord used for trimming dresses and furniture. (用以装饰衣服及家具之)丝绒线.

cheque /tʃek; tʃek/ *n* (US = **check**) written order (usu on a printed form)to a bank to pay money: 支票 (开向银行取款之单据, 通常为印好的固定形式): *a ~ for £10*; 一张十英镑的支票; *pay by ~*. 以支票付款. Cf 参较 *pay in cash*. 付现款. '~·**book** *n* number of blank ~s bound together. 支票簿. '~ **card**, = *banker's card*. ⇨ **bank⁴**.

chequer /ˈtʃekə(r); ˈtʃekɚ/ *vt* (US = **checker**) (usu passive) mark with a pattern of squares or patches of different colours or shades; (fig) mark by changes of

good and bad fortune, etc: (通常用被动语态)使具有不同色彩或色度的方格花式; (喻)使交替遭遇好运与恶运等: *a lawn ~ed with sunlight and shade*; 阳光与树荫交错的草坪; *a ~ed career*, full of ups and downs of fortune, with variety of incident. 饱经沧桑的一生; 盛衰多变的一生.

cher·ish /ˈtʃerɪʃ; ˈtʃerɪʃ/ *vt* [VP6A] **1** care for tenderly. 珍爱; 抚爱. **2** keep alive (hope, ambition, feelings, etc) in one's heart: 心中怀着(希望、志愿、感情等): *For years she ~ed the hope that her husband might still be alive*. 许多年来, 她一直怀着她的丈夫可能仍活在人世的希望. *Don't ~ the illusion that your father will always pay your debts*. 不要心存你父亲会永远替你偿债的幻想.

che·root /ʃəˈruːt; ʃəˈrut/ *n* cigar with both ends open. 方头的雪茄烟(即无尖头者).

cherry /ˈtʃerɪ; ˈtʃerɪ/ *n* (*pl* **-ries**) (tree with)soft, small, round fruit, red, yellow or black when ripe and with a stone-like seed in the middle, 樱桃(一种有软的小圆果, 成熟时呈红、黄或黑色, 中心有坚硬果核; 参看 *fruit* 之插图); [U] the wood of this tree. 樱桃木; 樱桃之木. □ *adj* red: 红色的: ~ *lips*. 樱唇.

cherub /ˈtʃerəb; ˈtʃerəb/ *n* **1** (*pl* ~**s**) small beautiful child; (in art)such a child with wings. 美丽的孩童; (艺术中)有翼的小天使. **2** (*pl* ~**im** /ˈtʃerəbɪm; ˈtʃerjəbɪm/) (biblical) one of the second highest order of angels. (圣经)二级天使. ⇨ **seraph**. **che·ru·bic** /tʃɪˈruːbɪk; tʃəˈrubɪk/ *adj* (esp) sweet and innocent looking; roundfaced. (尤指)甜美而天真无邪的; 圆脸的.

cher·vil /ˈtʃɜːvɪl; ˈtʃɜvɪl/ *n* [U] garden herb used to flavour soups, salads, etc. 山萝卜(其嫩叶用于汤、沙拉等之调味).

chess /tʃes; tʃes/ *n* [U] game for two players with sixteen pieces each (each called a '~·**man** /-mæn; -mæn/, on a board with sixty-four squares (called a '~·**board**). 国际象棋(二人对弈, 每人十六子, 称为棋子, 置于有六十四方格之盘上, 称为棋盘).

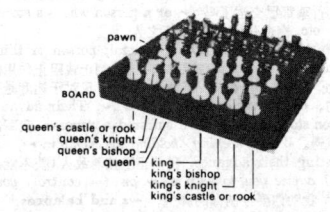

pawn
BOARD
queen's castle or rook
queen's knight
queen's bishop
queen
king
king's bishop
king's knight
king's castle or rook

chess

chest /tʃest; tʃest/ *n* **1** large, strong (usu wooden) box with a lid for storing, eg clothes, tools, money, medicine, tea, etc. (大而坚固, 通常系木制之有盖的)箱: 大木箱(用以存放衣服、工具、钱财、医药、茶等). ~ **of drawers**, large ~ with drawers for clothes. (制衣服的)五屉柜; 衣柜. **2** (anat) upper front part of the body, enclosed by the ribs, containing the heart and lungs. (解剖)(人体的)胸部(外为肋骨, 内含心脏及肺). ⇨ t'us illus at **trunk**. 参看 trunk 之插图. *get sth off one's ~*, (colloq) say sth one is anxious to say. (口) 倾吐胸中积闷; 说出所要说的话. *hold/keep one's cards close to one's/the ~*, be secretive. 善于保守秘密; 秘而不宣的. **3** (US) (funds of the) treasury of a public institution: (美)(公家机构的)金库; 经费; 基金: *the community ~*, for charitable purposes. (用于慈善事业的)社会基金.

ches·ter·field /ˈtʃestəfiːld; ˈtʃestɚˌfild/ *n* **1** single-breasted overcoat with a flap that covers the buttonholes. 单排扣并有盖遮住扣眼之外衣. **2** long padded couch with sides and a back. 有扶手及靠背之长沙发.

chest·nut /'tʃesnʌt; 'tʃesnət/ n 1 [C, U] (sorts of, wood of) tree with smooth, bright reddish-brown nut; the nut of this tree (those of the Spanish or sweet ~ being edible). 栗树(所结之栗子光滑而呈鲜明之红褐色); 栗木; 栗子(西班牙栗树或甜栗树所结可食之栗子)。⇨ the illus at **tree**; 参看 tree 之插图; ⇨ **horse(4)**. 2 colour of the nut. 栗子色; 枣红色。 **3** reddish-brown colour. 栗色马; 枣红色马。 **4** (colloq) story or joke that is too old or well known to be amusing. (口) 已不能再引起人兴趣的陈腐的故事或笑话。

cheval glass /ʃə'væl glɑːs US: -glæs; ʃə'væl,glæs/ n full-length mirror mounted on upright supports on which it can be tilted. 装于直立的架上可以倾斜的全身镜; 穿衣镜。

chev·ron /'ʃevrən; 'ʃevrən/ n bent line or stripe (V or Λ) worn on the sleeve by soldiers, policemen, etc to show rank, etc. 军人、警察等佩于袖上以代表等级等的臂章; (作 V 或 Λ 形的)袖章。

chew /tʃuː; tʃu/ vt, vi 1 [VP6A, 15B, 2A, C] ~ (up), work (food, etc) about between the teeth in order to crush it: 咀嚼(食物等): C~ your food well before you swallow it. 食物在吞咽前要仔细咀嚼。 '~ing-gum n [U] sticky substance sweetened and flavoured for ~ing. 橡皮糖; 口香糖。⇨also **bite¹(1)** and **cud**. 2 [VP15B, 3A] ~ sth over; ~ (up)on sth, (colloq) think over, consider. (口) 考虑; 思量 (某事)。 ~ the rag, (dated sl) discuss matters (esp old grievances). (过时俚语)讨论事情 (尤指旧日的苦情); 发牢骚。 ~ the cud of ~ing; sth (to be) ~ed: 咀嚼; 所(要)嚼之物: a ~ of tobacco. 一次所嚼之烟草; 一块烟烟。

Chi·anti /kɪ'æntɪ; kɪ'æntɪ/ n [U] dry red or white Italian wine. 一种无甜味的红色或白色意大利葡萄酒。

chi·aro·scuro /kɪ,ɑːrə'skʊərəu; kɪ,ɑrə'skjʊro/ n (I) distribution of light and shade (esp in a painting). (意) (尤指图画中)明暗之配合; 明暗对照法。

chic /ʃiːk; ʃik/ n [U] (of clothes, their wearer) style that gives an air of sophisticated elegance. 使衣服或穿衣者)高雅的风格或款式。 □ adj stylish. 有高雅之风格的; 漂亮的; 时髦的; 潇洒的。

chi·can·ery /ʃɪ'keɪnərɪ; ʃɪ'kenərɪ/ n [U] (use of) legal trickery; [C] (pl -ries) false argument. 法律上的狡计; 奸诈手段; 诡辩; 狡辩。

chi·chi /'ʃiːʃiː; 'ʃiʃi/ adj (colloq) pretentious; affected; vulgar. (口)自命不凡的; 娇饰的; 鄙俗的。

chick /tʃɪk; tʃɪk/ n 1 young bird just before or after hatching, esp a young chicken. 即将孵出或刚孵出的小鸟; 幼雏; (尤指)小鸡。 '~·pea n [C] (plant with) edible yellow pea-like seeds. 雏豆 (结黄色可食似豆的子); 埃及豆。 '~·weed n [U] common small weed whose leaves and seeds are eaten by birds. 繁缕(常见之小野草, 其叶及种子为鸟之食物)。 2 small child; (sl) girl. 婴孩; 小孩; (俚)女孩儿。

chicken /'tʃɪkɪn; 'tʃɪkɪn/ n 1 young bird, esp a young hen: 幼鸟; 幼雏; (尤指)小母鸡: She's no ~, (fig sl) is no longer young. (喻,俚)她年纪不轻了。 ⇨ the illus at **fowl**. 参看 fowl 之插图。 (Don't) count one's ~s before they are hatched, (Don't) be too hopeful of one's chances of success, etc. (不要)蛋尚未孵出先数鸡; (不要)对于成功等的可能性过于乐观。 '~·feed n (fig, sl) sth of relatively small value. (喻,俚)价值极少的东西; 微不足道的东西。 ,~·'hearted /-hɑːtɪd; -'hɑrtɪd/ adj lacking in courage. 无勇气的; 胆小的; 怯懦的。 '~·pox n [U] disease (esp of children) accompanied by red spots on the skin. (尤指多为儿童之)水痘。 '~·run n fenced-in area for ~s to run in. 鸡栏(四周设围供养鸡的地方)。 2 [U] its flesh as food. 小鸡肉; 嫩鸡肉。 □ pred adj (sl) cowardly. (俚)胆小的; 怯懦的。

chicle /'tʃɪkl; 'tʃɪkl/ n [U] chief ingredient of chewing-gum. 奇可树液(制口香糖的主要原料)。

chic·ory /'tʃɪkərɪ; 'tʃɪkərɪ/ n [U] plant used as a vegetable and for salad, the root of which is roasted and made into a powder (used with or instead of coffee).

菊苣(可作蔬菜并可凉拌食之, 其根经烘焙并制成粉, 可与咖啡同用, 或做咖啡之代用品)。⇨ the illus at **vegetable**. 参看 vegetable 之插图。

chide /tʃaɪd; tʃaɪd/ vt, vi (pt chided /'tʃaɪdɪd; 'tʃaɪdɪd/ or chid /tʃɪd; tʃɪd/, pp chided, chid or chidden /'tʃɪdn; 'tʃɪdn/ [VP6A, 14] ~ sb (for), (liter) scold; rebuke. (文)责骂; 斥责。

chief /tʃiːf; tʃif/ n 1 leader or ruler: 首领; 酋长; 头目: the ~ of the tribe. 该部族之酋长。 2 head of a department; highest official. 机关首长。 C~ of Staff, senior staff officer. 参谋长。 in ~, most of all, especially: 主要地; 尤其: for many reasons, and this one in ~. 为了许多理由, 尤其这一点。 -in-', supreme: 最高的: the Commander-in-~. 统帅; 总司令。 □ adj (attrib only; no comp or superl) (仅用作定语; 无比较级或最高级) 1 principal; most important: 主要的; 最重要的: the ~ rivers of India; 印度之主要的河流; the ~ thing to remember. 要记住的最重要事情。 2 first in rank: 等级最高的: the C~ Justice; 审判长官; the ~ priest. 祭司长。 ~·ly adv 1 above all; first of all. 尤要者; 首要者。 2 mostly; mainly: 大半; 主要: It is ~ly composed of.... 它主要系由…构成。

chief·tain /'tʃiːftən; 'tʃiftən/ n leader of a clan or tribe; chief. 族长; 部落酋长; 首长; 首领。 ~·cy /'tʃiːf-tənsɪ; 'tʃiftnsɪ/n position or rank of a ~. 族长或首长等的地位或等级。

chif·fon /'ʃɪfɒn US: ʃɪ'fɒn; ʃɪ'fɑn/ n [U] thin, transparent silk material used for scarves, veils, etc. 一种透明的丝绸薄纱(用以制围巾、面纱等)。

chif·fon·ier /ˌʃɪfə'nɪə(r),ˌʃɪfə'nɪr/ n 1 (GB) movable low cupboard with a flat top used as a table. (英)一种可移动的矮橱 (其平顶可用作桌子)。 2 (US) high chest of drawers (GB 英 = tallboy). (美)高衣橱。

chignon /'ʃiːnjɒn; 'ʃinjɑn/ n (F) knot or roll of hair worn at the back of the head by women. (法)妇人梳于头后之发髻。

chil·blain /'tʃɪlblein; 'tʃɪl,blen/ n [C] painful swelling, esp on the hand or foot, caused by exposure to cold. (尤指手或脚上的)冻疮。 ~ed /-eɪnd; -end/ adj having ~s. 有冻疮的; 生冻疮的。

child /tʃaɪld; tʃaɪld/ n (pl children /'tʃɪldrən; 'tʃɪl-drən/) unborn or newly born human being; boy or girl; son or daughter (of any age). 婴儿; 小孩(男或女); 孩子(子或女,不限年龄)。 '~'s play, sth very easily done 极易做之事。 be with ~, (archaic) be pregnant. (古)怀孕。 '~-bearing n [U] giving birth to children: 生产小孩: Ten years of ~-bearing exhausted her strength. 生产小孩十年耗尽了她的体力。 '~-birth n [U] the process of giving birth to a ~: 分娩; 生产(小孩): She died in ~-birth. 她因生产而死。 '~-hood /-hʊd/ -,hʊd/ n [U] state of being a ~; time during which one is a ~: 儿童期; 童年时代: have a happy ~hood. 有快乐的童年。 second ~hood, dotage (in extreme old age). 老耄; 衰老。 ~·ish adj of, behaving like, suitable for, a ~; not suited to an adult: 像小孩的; 行为如儿童的; 适合于儿童的; 幼稚的; 不适合成年人的: ~ish games /arguments. 小儿玩的游戏 (幼稚的论点)。 ~·less adj having no child(ren): 无子女的: a ~less couple. 无子女的夫妇。 '~·like adj simple, innocent, frank. 率直的; 纯真的; 天真无邪的。

chile, chili, chili /'tʃɪlɪ; 'tʃɪlɪ/ n (US) = **chilli**.

chill /tʃɪl; tʃɪl/ n 1 (sing only) unpleasant feeling of coldness: (仅用单数) 由寒冷所引起不舒服的感觉; 寒意: There's quite a ~ in the air this morning. 今天早晨的空气颇有寒意。 Take the ~ off the water, warm it a little. 将这水热一热。 2 (fig) (sing only) depressing influence; sth that causes a downhearted feeling: (喻)(仅用单数)扫兴; 沮丧; 使人沮丧或扫兴之事: The bad news cast a ~ over the gathering. 这个坏消息使聚会的人感到扫兴。 3 [C] illness caused by cold and damp, with shivering of the body: 由寒冷与潮湿所引起之疾病(身体有抖现象): 寒栗; 寒战; 感冒: catch a ~. 受寒。 □ adj unpleasantly

cold: 冷得使人不舒服的; 寒冷的; 冷酷的: *a ~ breeze.* 带寒意的微风; *a ~ welcome.* 冷淡的欢迎。 □ *vt, vi* [VP6A, 2A, C] make or become cold or cool: 使寒冷; 变为寒冷: *He was ~ed to the bone.* 他觉得寒冷彻骨。 *Don't ~ their enthusiasm.* 不要向他们的热心泼冷水。 **~ed beef**, beef preserved in cold storage at a moderately low temperature but not frozen. 冷藏牛肉(仅保持适当的低温度,但未冰冻)。 **~y** *adj* (**-ier, -iest**) **1** rather cold: 颇冷的; 相当冷的; 寒冷的:*a ~y room;* 寒冷的房间; *feel ~y.* 觉得冷。 *It's rather ~y this morning.* 今天早晨相当冷。 **2** (fig) unfriendly: (喻)不友善的; 冷淡的: *a ~y welcome;* 冷淡的欢迎; *~y politeness.* 冷淡的礼貌。

chilli, chilly, chile, chili /'tʃɪlɪ; 'tʃɪlɪ/ *n* (*pl* **-ies**) dried pod of red pepper (capsicum), often made into powder and used to give a hot flavour to sauces, etc. 干辣椒(常磨成粉用以为调味汁等添加辣味)。

chime /tʃaɪm; tʃaɪm/ *n* (series of notes sounded by a) tuned set of bells: 钟乐(一组乐音); 管钟: 钟琴所发出的乐音: *a ~ of bells;* 一组钟琴; *ring the ~s;* 击奏钟琴; *listen to ~s.* 听钟琴之乐声。 □ *vi, vt* **1** [VP6A, 15A,2A, C] (of bells, a clock) make (bells) ring; ring (~s) on bells; show (the hour) by ringing: (指乐钟、时钟)鸣响; 发钟声; 鸣钟报(时): *The bells / The ringers ~d out a tune.* 乐钟(鸣钟者)奏出曲调。 *The bells are chiming.* 乐钟在响。 *The church clock ~d midnight.* 教堂里的时钟敲出午夜的时间。 **2** [VP2C] **~ in**, break in on the talk of others, usu to express agreement: 当别人谈话时突然插嘴(通常表示同意): *'Of course,' he ~d in.* '当然,' 他突然插嘴说。 **~ (in) with**, be in agreement with; suit: 与…一致; 适合: *I think your plans will ~ in with mine.* 我想你的计划会与我的一致。

chim·era, chim·aera /kaɪˈmɪərə; kəˈmɪrə/ *n* **1** (Gk myth) monster with a lion's head, a goat's body, and a serpent's tail. (希腊神话)凯米拉(狮头、羊身、蛇尾之怪物)。 **2** horrible creature of the imagination. 想象中的可怕的怪物。 **3** (fig) wild or impossible idea or fancy. (喻)幻想; 妄想; 狂想。 **chim·eri·cal** / kaɪˈmerɪkl; kəˈmɪrɪkl / *adj* unreal; visionary 非真实的; 幻想的: *chimerical ideas / schemes.* 幻想的念头(计谋)。

chim·ney /'tʃɪmnɪ; 'tʃɪmnɪ/ *n* **1** structure through which smoke from a fire is carried away through the wall or roof of a building. 烟囱; 烟筒。 **'~-breast** *n* projecting wall in a room that contains the ~. 烟囱凸肚墙(室内凸出的墙,里面有烟囱)。 **'~ corner**, seat in an old-fashioned fireplace. 旧式壁炉边的座位。 **'~-piece** *n* =mantel. **'~-pot** *n* pipe(earthenware or metal) fitted to the top of a ~. 陶制或金属制的烟囱顶管。 **'~-stack** *n* group of ~ tops. (包括数个烟道的)总烟囱。

chimneys

'~-sweep(er) *n* man who sweeps soot from ~s. 扫烟囱的人。 **2** glass tube that protects the flame of an oil-lamp from draughts. (油灯用以遮风的)玻璃灯罩。 **3** (mountaineering) narrow cleft or opening by which a cliff face may be climbed. (爬山术)悬崖表面可供爬山者攀登之窄狭的裂缝或缺口。⇨ the illus at **mountain.** 参看 mountain 之插图。

chimp /tʃɪmp; tʃɪmp/ *n* (colloq abbr of) chimpanzee. (口)为chimpanzee之略。

chim·pan·zee /,tʃɪmpænˈziː; ,tʃɪmpænˈzi/ *n* African ape, smaller than a gorilla. 非洲人猿; 黑猩猩(较gorilla为小)。⇨ the illus at **ape.** 参看 ape 之插图。

chin /tʃɪn; tʃɪn/ *n* part of the face below the mouth;

front of the lower jaw. 下巴; 下颌(面部之在嘴以下之部分, 下颚之前端)。⇨ the illus at **head.** 参看 head 之插图。 **keep one's '~ up**, (colloq) show determination to face trouble without betraying fear or sorrow. (口)表示决心应付困难而无畏。 **'~-strap** *n* strap(on a helmet) held on the ~. (头盔上)套住下巴的皮带。 **'~-wagging** *n* (colloq) talking, gossiping. (口)闲谈; 聊天。

china /'tʃaɪnə; 'tʃaɪnə/ *n* [U] baked and glazed fine white clay; (collective) articles (eg cups, saucers, plates) made from this. 陶瓷; (集合名词)瓷器(如杯、碟、盘)。 **'~-closet** *n* cupboard in which ~ is kept or displayed. 放置或展示瓷器皿的橱柜。 **'~-ware** *n* [U] dishes, ornaments, etc made of ~ clay. 瓷器(如盘碟、装饰品等)。

chin·chil·la /tʃɪnˈtʃɪlə; tʃɪnˈtʃɪlə / *n* [C] small S American animal that looks sth like a squirrel; [U] its soft grey fur. 南美洲产之栗鼠类(类似松鼠); 栗鼠之柔软的灰色毛皮。

chine /tʃaɪn; tʃaɪn/ *n* animal's backbone or part of it as a joint of meat. 动物的脊椎骨; 脊肉; 排骨肉。

chink[1] /tʃɪŋk; tʃɪŋk/ *n* narrow opening or crack (eg between boards in the wall of a shed, through which the wind blows or through which one may peep). 缝隙; 裂缝(如棚屋之墙板中间, 风可以吹入, 或可用以窥视者)。

chink[2] /tʃɪŋk; tʃɪŋk/ *vi, vt* [VP6A, 15B, 2A, C] make the sound of coins, glasses, etc striking together; cause (coins, etc) to make such sounds. 发出硬币、玻璃制品等碰击时之叮当声; 使(硬币、玻璃制品等)发叮当声。 □ *n* **a / the ~ (of)**, this sound: 碰击硬币、玻璃制品等所发出之)叮当声: *I heard the ~ of coins.* 我听见钱币碰击的声音。

chintz /tʃɪnts; tʃɪnts/ *n* [U] kind of cotton cloth (usu glazed) with printed designs in colours, used for curtains, furniture covers, etc. 印花棉布 (通常表面光滑,用制帷幔、家具套等)。

chip /tʃɪp; tʃɪp/ *n* **1** small piece cut or broken off (from wood, stone, china, glass, etc). (木、石、瓷、玻璃等之)细片; 碎片; 渣; 屑。 **~·board** *n* building material made from compressed ~s of waste wood, sawdust, etc and glue. 木渣板(用木屑、锯屑等废材连同胶紧压而成的建材)。 **~ off the old block**, son who is very like his father. 酷似其父之子。 **have a '~ on one's shoulder**, have a defiant air, as if expecting and ready to accept a challenge; resent prejudice against oneself as (often incorrectly) perceived in other people. 象要跟人打架的样子; 气势汹汹; 愤恨别人对自己(常为不正确地)怀有偏见。 **2** strip cut from an apple, a potato, etc: (自苹果、马铃薯等)切下的细长的)条: *fish and ~s,* fried fish and potato ~s. 油炸的鱼和马铃薯条。 **3** place (eg in a cup) from which a ~ has gone. (如茶杯之)缺口。 **4** thin strip cut from wood, palmleaf, etc, used in making baskets, hats, etc: (编篮子、帽子等所用之)薄木片条、棕叶片条等 (usu attrib) (通常用作定语)薄木条: *~ bonnets;* 用上述材料所编之无边女帽; *~ baskets.* 用上述材料所编之篮子。 **5** flat plastic counter used as a money token (esp in gambling). (尤指赌钱用的塑胶制的)筹码。 **have had one's ~s**, (sl) one's last chance. (俚)再也没有机会了。 **(when) the ~s are down**, (when) a crisis point is reached. (当)危急关头来临。 □ *vt, vi* (**-pp-**) **1** [VP6A, 15A, 15B] **~ off/from**, cut or break a piece: 切下切去破一片: *~ a piece off (the edge of a cup);* (在杯子的边上)打破一块; *~ old paint from the side of a ship.* 自船侧铲去旧油漆。 *All the plates have ~ped edges.* 所有的盘子边上都有破损。 **2** [VP6A] make sth ~s(2): 切成细条; 切成薄片: *~ped potatoes.* 把马铃薯切成细长条。 **3** [VP2A] (of things) be easily broken at the edge: (指物件)边缘容易破损: *These cups ~ if you are not careful.* 这些杯子,如果你不小心, 边缘容易破损。 **4** [VP2C] **~ in**, (colloq) (口) **(a)** interrupt; join in (a conversation). 插嘴; 加入(谈话)。 **(b)** contribute money (to a fund). 捐献金钱(给某一基金)。 **5** [VP6A] shape (sth) by cutting the edge or surface (with an axe or a chisel). (用斧或

凿)劈凿（某物）的边缘或表面使成某种形状. '**~·pings** n pl bits of stone, marble, etc made by ~ping: 劈凿下来的碎石等; 碎屑; 碎片: '*road ~pings,* for making a road surface. 铺路用的碎石.

chip·munk /'tʃɪpmʌŋk; 'tʃɪpmʌŋk/ n small, striped N American squirrel-like rodent 金花鼠（北美洲所产有条纹似松鼠的啮齿小动物）.

Chip·pen·dale /'tʃɪpəndeɪl; 'tʃɪpən,del/ n light style of drawing-room furniture (18th c in England): 齐本德耳式家具（十八世纪英国之客厅家具的轻巧款式）: ~ chairs. 齐本德耳式椅.

chi·rop·odist /kɪ'rɒpədɪst; kaɪ'rɑpədɪst/ n person who is expert in the treatment of troubles of the feet and toenails. 足科医生（专医足及足趾甲之疾患）. **chi·rop·ody** /kɪ'rɒpədɪ; kaɪ'rɑpədɪ/ n [U] work of a ~. 足病的治疗.

chiro·prac·tor /'kaɪərəʊpræktə(r); 'kaɪrə,præktə/ n person who treats diseases by manipulating the joints (esp the spinal column). 按摩关节(尤指脊椎)以治病者; 按摩术士.

chirp /tʃɜːp; tʃɝp/ vi, vt, n [VP2A, C, 6A] (make) short, sharp note(s) or sound(s) (as of small birds or insects); utter in this way: (发) 唧唧声 (如小鸟之鸣声) 或吱唧声(如昆虫鸣声), 以此种声音说话: *the ~s of the sparrows / cicadas;* 麻雀之吱喳声(蝉之吱唧声;) *grasshoppers ~ing all day.* 终日唧唧叫鸣的蚱蜢.

chirpy /'tʃɜːpɪ; 'tʃɝpɪ/ adj (colloq) lively, cheerful. (口) 活泼的; 高兴的. **chirp·ily** /'tʃɜːpɪlɪ; 'tʃɝpɪlɪ/ adv **chirpi·ness** n

chir·rup /'tʃɪrəp; 'tʃɪrəp/ vt, vi, n (make a) series of chirps. (发)连续的吱喳鸣声.

chisel /'tʃɪzl; 'tʃɪzl/ n steel tool with a bevelled edge for shaping wood, stone or metal. 凿子(修凿木、石或金属之有斜刃的钢制工具). ⇨ the illus at **tool**. 参看 tool 之插图. □ vt (-ll-, also -l- in US) [VP6A, 15B, 14] 1 cut or shape with a ~: 用凿子凿成某种形状; 凿刻: *~led features,* (of a person's appearance) clear cut; well modelled. (指人的容貌) 轮廓鲜明的五官. 2 (colloq) cheat; swindle. (口) 欺骗; 诈骗. **~·ler** /'tʃɪzələ(r); 'tʃɪzlɚ/ n person who ~s(2). 骗子; 骗徒.

chit[1] /tʃɪt; tʃɪt/ n young child; young, small, slender woman (often used rather contemptuously): 幼儿; 瘦小的少女(常含轻蔑之意): *a mere '~ of a child;* 不过是一个小毛头; *only a '~ of a woman.* 只不过是一个黄毛丫头.

chit[2] /tʃɪt; tʃɪt/ n short note or letter; note of sum of money owed (eg for drinks, etc at a hotel). 短信; 便条; 欠款之单据; 挂帐之单据(如旅馆之酒帐等).

chit-chat /'tʃɪt tʃæt; 'tʃɪt,tʃæt/ n [U] light, informal conversation. 闲谈; 聊天.

chiv·al·ry /'ʃɪvlrɪ; 'ʃɪvlrɪ/ n [U] laws and customs (religious, moral and social) of the knights in the Middle Ages; the qualities that knights were expected to have (courage, honour, courtesy, loyalty, devotion to the weak and helpless, to the service of women). (中世纪的) 武士制度 (一种宗教的、道德的和社会的法律及习俗); 骑士道; 武士精神(包括勇敢、荣誉心、礼貌、忠贞、热心帮助弱者及妇女). **chival·rous** /'ʃɪvlrəs; 'ʃɪvlrəs/ adj of, as of, the age of ~; of, as of, the knights of the Middle Ages; honourable; courteous. 武士时代的; 中世纪之武士的; 侠义的; 可敬的; 有礼貌的.

chive /tʃaɪv; tʃaɪv/ n [U] small plant of the onion family, of which the slender leaves are used as a seasoning (in salads, etc). 细香葱; 虾夷葱 (葱属小植物, 其细长的叶子可用以调味, 用于沙拉等).

chivy, chivvy /'tʃɪvɪ; 'tʃɪvɪ/ vt [VP15B] (colloq) ~ *sb about / along / up,* pester; chase; harass. (口) 使某人苦恼; 对追逐某人; 烦扰.

chlor·ide /'klɔːraɪd; 'klɔraɪd/ n [U] (chem) compound of chlorine: (化)氯化物: ~ *of lime / soda / potash.* 漂白粉(氯化钠)(氯化钾).

chlor·ine /'klɔːriːn; 'klɔrin/ n [U] (chem) greenish-yellow, bad-smelling poisonous gas(symbol **Cl**), obtained

from common salt (= *sodium chloride*), used as a sterilizing agent and in industry (化)氯(黄绿色有臭味毒气, 化学符号 Cl, 自普通盐即氯化钠中提出, 用作消毒剂及用于工业中). **chlor·in·ate** /'klɔːrɪneɪt; 'klɔrɪ,net/ vt treat, sterilize, with ~: 以氯处理或消毒: *chlorinated water,* water purified from disease germs by this treatment. 以氯消毒过的水. **chlori·na·tion** /,klɔːrɪ'neɪʃn; ,klɔrɪ'neʃən/ n

chloro·form /'klɒrəfɔːm US: 'klɔːr-; 'klɔrə,form/ n [U] thin, colourless liquid formerly given, in the form of vapour, to make a person unconscious during a surgical operation. 氯仿; 哥罗仿; 三氯甲烷 (稀薄无色液体, 昔时经汽化用于外科手术作麻醉剂).

chloro·phyll /'klɒrəfɪl US: 'klɔːr-; 'klɔrə,fɪl/ n [U] (bot) green colouring matter in the leaves of plants. (植)叶绿素.

chock /tʃɒk; tʃɑk/ n block or wedge of wood used to prevent sth (eg a wheel, barrel, door) from moving. (防止某物如轮子、桶、门等移动所用之)垫木; 轮档. □ vt [VP6A, 15B] ~ *(up),* 1 make fast with, support on, a ~ or ~s. 用楔子支持. 2 (colloq) (口): *a room ~ed up with furniture,* filled up with far too much furniture. 为家具所拥塞不堪的房间. '**~-full (of),** /'~-a-'block (with); ~-a-,block 'full (of),** adjj (pred) filled to the limit. (用作表语)充满的; 塞满的.

choc·olate /'tʃɒklət; 'tʃɔkəlɪt/ n 1 [U] substance (powder or slab) made from the crushed seeds of the cacao tree; drink made by mixing this with hot water or milk; [C, U] (colloq abbr 俗略作 **choc** /tʃɒk; tʃɑk/) sweet substance made from this, usu sweetened and often flavoured: 巧克力(自磨碎之可可子中提取之物质, 粉状或块状); 由巧克力与热水或牛奶混合的饮料; (由巧克力制制成的) 巧克力糖 (通常加糖且常加香料): *a bar of ~;* 一块巧克力糖; *a box of ~s;* 一盒巧克力糖; (attrib)用作定语) ~ *biscuit,* covered with ~; 覆有巧克力的饼干; ~ *cream,* sweet paste covered with ~. 奶油夹心巧克力. 2 the colour of this substance, dark brown. 巧克力色; 深褐色. **choc-ice** /'tʃɒkaɪs; 'tʃɑk aɪs/ n (colloq) slab of ice-cream coated with ~. (口)外加一层巧克力的雪糕; 巧克力雪糕.

choice /tʃɔɪs; tʃɔɪs/ n 1 act of choosing: 选择; 挑选: *make a careful ~;* 细心选择; *be careful in your ~;* 仔细从事选择; *take your ~.* 随你选择. 2 [U] right or possibility of choosing: 选择的权利或可能: *I have no ~ in the matter,* cannot choose, must act in this way. 在这件事中我没有选择的余地(必须这样做). *for ~,* by preference; if one must select: 凭着喜爱; 如果必须选择: *I should take this one for ~.* 要选我就选这个. *Hobson's ~,* no ~ at all because there is only one thing to take or do. 没有选择的余地(因为只有一样事物可取或可做). 3 variety from which to choose: 备选的种类: *This shop has a large ~ of clothes;* 此店有甚多种类的衣服可供挑选. 4 person or thing chosen: 所选择的人或物: *This is my ~.* 这就是我所选的. □ adj carefully chosen; uncommonly good: 精选的; 上等的: ~ *fruit.* 上选的水果.

choir /'kwaɪə(r); kwaɪr/ n 1 company of persons trained to sing together, esp to lead the singing in church. 合唱团; (尤指教堂里领导众人唱诗的) 唱诗班; 圣乐队. 2 part of a church building for the ~. 教堂里唱诗班的席位. ⇨ the illus at **church**. 参看 church 之插图. '**~-school** n grammar school (attached to or connected with a cathedral) for '**~-boys.** 大教堂为唱诗班的男童所附设的中学.

choke[1] /tʃəʊk; tʃok/ vi, vt 1 [VP2A, 3A] be unable to breathe because of sth in the windpipe, or because of emotion: 因某物塞住气管或因感情激动而不能呼吸: 窒息; 有物哽于喉中: ~ *over one's food;* 喉为食物所塞; ~ *with anger;* 怒气哽喉; ~ *to death.* 哽死. 2 [VP6A, 14] ~ *(with),* stop the breathing of, by pressing the windpipe from outside or blocking it up inside, or (of smoke, etc) by being unfit to breathe: 由外扼住或由内

塞住气管使不能呼吸;(指烟)因不适宜于呼吸而使人窒息;使闷气: *~ the life out of sb.* 将某人扼毙。*The smoke almost ~d me.* 这烟几乎使我窒息。*Her voice was ~d with sobs.* 她因啜泣而不能成声。*Anger ~d his words.* 他因发怒而说不出话来。*He swallowed a plum-stone and was almost ~d,* ie to death. 他吞下了一个梅核几乎哽死。**3** [VP3A, 6A, 15B] ***~(up) (with),*** fill, partly or completely, a passage, space, etc that is usually clear: 堵塞; 阻塞; 充塞(通道, 空间等): *a chimney/ drain ~d (up) with dirt.* 为污物所堵塞的烟囱(排水管)。*The garden is ~d with weeds.* 花园中野草丛生。*Weeds have ~ed (up) the garden.* 野草长满了花园。*The room was ~d up with useless old furniture.* 此房充塞着无用的旧家具。**4** [VP15B] ***~ sth back/down,*** hold or keep back/down: 忍住; 抑制: *~ back one's tears/indignation;* 忍住眼泪(怒火); *~ down one's anger.* 抑制住愤怒。***~ sb off,*** (colloq) discourage him (from doing sth); reprimand him for doing sth wrong: (口)劝阻某人做某事;申斥某人做错事: *He got ~d off for being late.* 他因迟到而被申斥。**'~-damp,** carbon dioxide gas, left after an explosion in a coal-mine. 矿坑中爆炸后所留下的二氧化碳气体。

choke[2] /tʃəʊk; tʃok /*n* valve in a petrol engine to control the intake of air: 汽油发动机内控制空气进入的活门; 阻流瓣; 抗流器: *pull out the ~,* ie the ~ control. 拉阻流瓣。

choker /ˈtʃəʊkə(r); ˋtʃokɚ / *n* **1** (hum) stiff, high collar; clerical collar. (谐)硬高领; 神父的衣领。**2** close-fitting necklace (eg of pearls) or scarf. 紧围在脖子上的(珠宝)项链或围巾。

chokey, choky /ˈtʃəʊkɪ; ˋtʃokɪ/ *n* (GB; dated sl) prison. (英;过时俚语)监牢;牢房。

choler /ˈkɒlə(r);ˋkɑlɚ/ *n* (old use, or poet, liter) anger. (旧用法或诗, 文) 愤怒。**~ic** /ˈkɒlərɪk; ˋkɑlərɪk/ *adj* easily made angry; often angry. 易激怒的; 常发怒的。

chol·era /ˈkɒlərə; ˋkɑlərə/ *n* [U] infectious and often fatal disease, common in hot countries, with vomiting and continual emptying of the bowels. 霍乱(一种传染性且常为致命的疾病, 常发生于热带国家, 病状为上吐下泻)。

choose /tʃu:z; tʃuz/ *vt, vi (pt* **chose** /tʃəʊz; tʃoz/, *pp* **chosen** /ˈtʃəʊzn; ˋtʃozn̩/) **1** [VP6A, 16A, B, 23, 2A, C, 3A] ***~(from/out of/between),*** pick out from a greater number; show what or which one wants by taking: (从多数中)选择; 挑选; 选取: *She took a long time to ~ her new hat.* 她花了很久的时间挑选她的新帽子。*The greedy boy chose the largest apple in the dish.* 那贪心的孩子挑选了盘中最大的一只苹果。*There are only five to ~ from.* 只有五个可供选择。*C~ your friends carefully.* 审慎择友。*You have chosen well.* 你选得好。*They chose me as their leader/to be their leader.* 他们选了我做他们的领袖。*I was chosen (as) leader.* 我被选为领袖。*He had to ~ between death and dishonour.* 他不得不在死亡和屈辱之间做一选择。***There is nothing/not much/little to ~ between (two or more people or things),*** They are about equal, are equally good/bad, etc. 二者之间没有什么可选择的余地(意谓二者或二者以上的人或事物差不多相等, 同样地好或坏等)。**2** [VP7A, 2A] decide; be pleased or determined: 决定; 愿意; 下决心: *I do not ~ to be a candidate.* 我不愿意竞选。*He chose to stay where he was.* 他决定停留在他原来的地方。*Do just as you ~,* whatever pleases you. 你愿意怎么做就怎么做。***cannot ~ but,*** (liter) must, have to: (文)不得不; 必须: *He cannot ~ but obey.* 他不得不服从。

choosy, choosey /ˈtʃu:zɪ; ˋtʃuzɪ/ *adj* **(-ier, -iest)** (colloq, of persons) careful and cautious in choosing; difficult to please. (口, 指人)小心挑选的; 挑三拣四的; 难以取悦的; 好挑剔的。

chop[1] /tʃɒp; tʃɑp/ *vt, vi* **(-pp-)** [VP6A, 15A, B] ***~ (up) (into),*** cut (into pieces) by blow(s) with an axe or other edged tool: (用斧或其他有刃的工具)砍; 劈; 剁: *He was ~ping wood,* cutting wood into sticks. 他在劈柴。*Meat is often ~ped up into cubes before being cooked.* 肉在烹煮之前常切成小块。*He ~ped a branch off the tree.* 他从树上砍下一树枝。*I'm going to ~ that tree down.* 我要把那棵树砍倒。*We had to ~ a way* (= make a path by ~ping) *through the undergrowth.* 我们必须在矮树林中砍伐出一条路来。[VP3A] ***~ at sth,*** aim a cutting blow at. 向某物砍去。

chop[2] /tʃɒp; tʃɑp/ *n* **1** chopping blow. 砍; 劈。**2** thick slice of meat with bone in it, (to be) cooked for one person. 供一人吃的一块连骨的肉;一块排骨肉。**'~-house** *n* (now usu 今通常称 *steakhouse*) restaurant serving chops and steaks. 供应排骨肉及牛排的餐馆; 牛排馆。**3** ***be for/get the ~,*** be about to be/be killed or sacked[2]. 即将被杀或解雇; 被杀或解雇。**4** (boxing) short downward blow. (拳击)向下的短击。

chop[3] /tʃɒp; tʃɑp/ *n* official seal or stamp; trademark; brand of goods; (colloq) quality. 官印; 图章; 商标; 货物的牌子;(口)品质。

chop[4] / tʃɒp; tʃɑp / *vi* **(-pp-) 1** [VP2A] ***~ and change,*** (emphatic for *change)* be inconsistent: (change 之加强语)多变; 善变: *He's always ~ping and changing,* always changing his opinions, plans, etc. 他总是朝秦暮楚(总是改变意见、计划等)。**2** [VP2C] ***~ about,*** (of the wind) change direction. (指风) 改变方向。

chop[5] /tʃɒp; tʃɑp/ *n* ⇨ **chap**[2].

chop·chop /ˌtʃɒp ˈtʃɒp; ˋtʃɑpˋtʃɑp/ *adv* (sl) quickly. (俚)快; 迅速地。

chop·per[1] / ˈtʃɒpə(r); ˋtʃɑpɚ / *n* heavy tool with a sharp edge for chopping meat, wood, etc. (砍肉、柴等之)刀或斧。⇨ the illus at **tool.** 参看 tool 之插图。

chop·per[2] / ˈtʃɒpə(r) ; ˋtʃɑpɚ/ *n* (colloq) helicopter. (口)直升飞机。

choppy /ˈtʃɒpɪ; ˋtʃɑpɪ/ *adj* **(-ier, -iest)** (of the sea) moving in short, broken irregular waves; (of the wind) continually changing. (指海)波涛汹涌的; (指风)不断改变方向的。

chop·sticks / ˈtʃɒpstɪks; ˋtʃɑpˌstɪks/ *n pl* pair of tapering sticks (wood, ivory, etc) used by the Chinese and Japanese for lifting food (placed on the thinnest ends) to the mouth. 筷子(木、象牙等制, 为中国人及日本人进食的餐具, 指一双)。

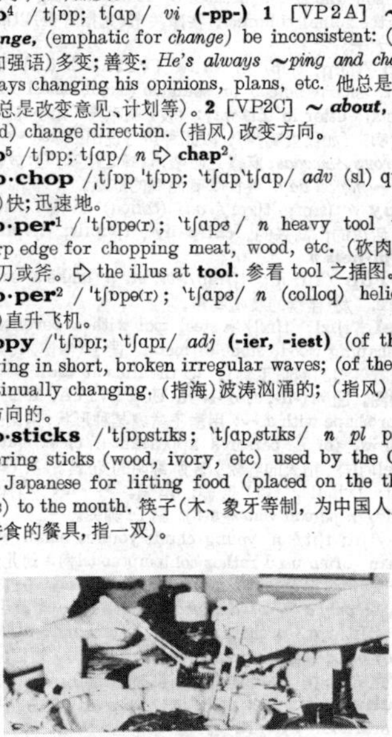

chopsticks

chop suey /ˌtʃɒp ˈsu:ɪ; ˋtʃɑpˋsuɪ/ *n* [U] dish of meat or chicken served with rice, onions, etc (as in a Chinese restaurant). 一盘附带米饭、洋葱等之肉或鸡肉(如中国餐馆所供应者); 杂碎。

choral /ˈkɔ:rəl; ˋkorəl/ *adj* of, for, sung by or together with, a choir: 唱诗班的; 合唱的; 唱诗班所唱的; 与唱诗班合唱的: *a '~ society;* 合唱会; *a ~ service;* 唱诗礼拜; *Beethoven's ~ symphony.* 贝多芬的合唱交响曲。

chorale /kəˈrɑ:l; koˋrɑl/ *n* simple hymn tune, usu sung by the choir and congregation together. 通常由会众与唱诗班合唱之简单圣歌调。

chord /kɔ:d; kord/ *n* **1** straight line that joins two points on the circumference of a circle or the ends of an arc. 弦 (连接圆周上任意两点或一弧之两端的直线)。⇨ the illus at **circle.** 参看 circle 之插图。**2** (music) combination of three or more notes sounded together in harmony. (音乐)和弦; 和(谐)音。⇨ **discord** and also the illus at **notation.** 参看 notation 之插图。**3** (now usu spelt 现常拼作 *cord*) (anat) string-like structure, as in the throat *(the vocal ~s)* or the back *(the spinal ~).* (解剖)带(身体内的带状组织, 如喉部之 vocal chords 声带, 背

部之 spinal chord 脊髓。 ⇨ the illus at **head**. 参看 head 之插图。 **4** string (of a harp, etc): (竖琴等的)弦: *touch the right* ~, (fig) appeal cleverly to emotion. (喻) 巧妙地触动情绪; 扣人心弦。

chore /tʃɔː(r); tʃor/ n small duty or piece of work, esp an ordinary everyday task (in the home, on a farm, etc); unpleasant or tiring task. (家庭中、农场上等处之)杂务; 杂事; 零星的事务; (尤指)日常之普通工作; 不愉快的工作; 令人疲劳的工作。 Cf 参较 *char*.

chor·eogra·phy /ˌkɒrɪˈɒɡrəfɪ US: ˌkɔːr-; ˌkɔrɪˈɑɡrəfɪ/ n [U] art of designing and specifying the steps of ballet. 芭蕾舞设计术。 **chor·eogra·pher** n

chor·is·ter /ˈkɒrɪstə(r) US: ˈkɔːr-; ˈkɔrɪstə/ n member of a choir, esp a choir-boy. 合唱团员(尤指男童团员); 唱诗班中的男童歌手。

chortle /ˈtʃɔːtl; ˈtʃɔrtl/ vi, n (give a) loud chuckle of glee. (发)咯咯笑声; 欢笑。

chorus /ˈkɔːrəs; ˈkɔrəs/ n **1** (music for a) group of singers. 合唱团; 合唱曲。 '~-girl n one of a group of girls who sing and dance in a musical play. 歌剧中担任歌舞之女演员; 歌舞团女团员。 **2** (part of a) song for all to sing (after solo verses): (歌曲独唱部分之后的)合唱部份: *Bill sang the verses and everybody joined in the* ~. 比尔唱独唱部份, 然后大家一起唱合唱部分。 **3** sth said or cried by many people together: 由许多人一起说出或喊出的话; 异口同声: *The proposal was greeted with a* ~ *of approval.* 该项提议获得大家异口同声的赞成。 *in* ~, all together: 大家一起; 共同: *sing/answer in* ~. 齐声歌唱 (回答)。 ⇨ **unison**. **4** (in old Gk drama) band of singers and dancers whose words and actions are a commentary on the events of the play. (古希腊戏剧中的)合唱歌舞队(其唱词及舞姿对剧情 提供 一种解释)。 **5** (eg in Shakespeare's plays) actor who recites the prologue and epilogue. (如在莎士比亚的戏剧中)朗诵序诗及收场诗的演员。 □ vt sing, speak, in ~. 齐声唱; 齐声说。

chose, chosen ⇨ **choose**.

chow /tʃaʊ; tʃaʊ/ n **1** dog of a Chinese breed. 一种中国狗。 **2** (sl) food. (俚)食物。

chow·der /ˈtʃaʊdə(r); ˈtʃaʊdə/ n (US) thick soup or stew of fish or clams with vegetables. (美) (鱼或蛤与蔬菜同煮之)浓汤或炖菜。

Christ /kraɪst; kraɪst/ n title (= *anointed one*) given to Jesus, now used as part of (ie *Jesus* ~) or as an alternative to his name. 基督(加于耶稣的头衔, 意谓"受膏者", 现与其名连用或互用)。 '~-like adj or like a ~, showing the spirit of a ~. 基督的; 似基督的, 表示出基督精神的。

christen /ˈkrɪsn; ˈkrɪsn/ vt [VP6A, 23] **1** receive into the Christian church by baptism; give a name to at the baptism. 施洗礼使成为基督徒; 在施洗礼时为…取教名。 *The child was* ~*ed Mary.* 此孩取教名玛丽。 **2** give a name to (eg to a new ship when it is launched): 予以命名(例如当新船行下水礼时)。 '~-ing n ceremony of baptizing or naming: 洗礼; 命名典礼: *There were ten* ~*ings at this church last month.* 本教堂在上月之内曾为十个婴孩施洗礼。

Christen·dom /ˈkrɪsndəm; ˈkrɪsndəm/ n all Christian people and Christian countries. 所有信基督教的人们及国家; 基督教世界。

Chris·tian /ˈkrɪstʃən; ˈkrɪstʃən/ adj of Jesus and his teaching: of the religion, beliefs, church, etc based on this teaching. 耶稣基督及其教训的; 基督教及其信仰、教会等的。 ~ **era**, time reckoned from the birth of Jesus. 耶稣纪元(自耶稣降生算起); 公元。 '~ **name**, name given at baptism. (在施洗礼时所取的)教名。 Cf 参较 *family name*. ~ **'Science**, church and religious system of healing through spiritual means. 基督教信仰医疗法(借精神信仰的疗病法)。 □ n person believing in the ~ religion. 基督教徒。 **Chris·ti·an·ity** /ˌkrɪstɪˈænɪtɪ; ˌkrɪstʃɪˈænɪtɪ/ n [U] the ~ faith or religion; being a ~; ~ character. 基督教; 基督教的教义; 做基督教徒者; 信基督教; 基督教徒的性格。

Christ·mas /ˈkrɪsməs; ˈkrɪsməs/ n (also 亦作 ~ 'Day) yearly celebration of the birth of Jesus Christ, 25 Dec; the week beginning on 24 Dec: 耶稣诞生之纪念日, 即十二月廿五日; 圣诞节期(自十二月廿四日圣诞前夕起算之一周间): (attrib) (用作定语) *the* ~ *holidays.* 圣诞节假期。 '~-box n (not US) money given for services during the year. (不用于美国) 圣诞节时酬谢终年辛劳之赏金。 '~ **card**, sent to friends at ~ to wish them 'A Merry ~ and a Happy New Year', etc. 圣诞卡。 ⇨ **Father** '~, traditional figure who is supposed to give children gifts at ~ (= *Santa Claus*). 圣诞老人。 '~-tide/-time, the ~ season. 圣诞节期。 '~-tree n small evergreen tree set up at ~ and decorated with tinsel, candles, presents, etc. 圣诞树(竖立并装饰着闪光之金属丝片、蜡烛、礼物等之小常绿树)。

chro·matic /krəʊˈmætɪk; kroˈmætɪk/ adj **1** of, in, colour(s): 颜色的; 彩色的; 五彩的: ~ *printing.* 彩色印刷。 **2** (music) of, having notes of the ~ scale, that is, the succession of semitones, twelve to the octave, normal in Western music. (音乐)半音的; 半音音阶(由连续的十二个半音组成)的。

chrome /krəʊm; krom/ n yellow pigment, colouring matter, obtained from chromium salts, used in paints, rubber, ceramics, etc. 铬黄(取自铬盐之黄色颜料, 用于油漆、橡皮、陶器等中)。 '~ **steel** n alloy of steel and chromium. 铬钢(钢与铬的合金)。

chro·mium /ˈkrəʊmɪəm; ˈkromɪəm/ n [U] element (symbol **Cr**) used for plating taps, hardware, motor-car fittings, etc and in steel alloys (including stainless steel): 铬(元素之一, 化学符号 Cr, 用于电镀龙头、五金器具、汽车配件等, 及用于钢合金, 包括不锈钢): ~ *plating*, 镀铬; ~*-plated 'fittings.* 镀铬的配件。

chro·mo·some /ˈkrəʊməsəʊm; ˈkroməˌsom/ n [C] (biol) one of the minute threads in every nucleus in animal and plant cells, carrying genes. (生物) 染色体 (每一动植物细胞核中所含的带有遗传因子的细丝之一)。

chronic /ˈkrɒnɪk; ˈkrɑnɪk/ adj **1** (of a disease or condition) continual, lasting for a long time: (指疾病或情况)延续性久的; 缠绵甚久的; 慢性的: ~ *rheumatism;* 慢性的风湿症; *a* ~ *invalid,* a person with a ~ illness. 慢性病患者。 ⇨ **acute**(2). **2** (sl) intense; severe. (俚)紧张的; 严重的; 剧烈的。 **chro·ni·cally** /-klɪ; -klɪ/ adv

chron·icle /ˈkrɒnɪkl; ˈkrɑnɪkl/ n [C] record of events in the order of their happening. 编年史。 □ vt [VP6A] make a ~ of; record in a ~. 将…编为编年史; 载入编年史。

chro·no·logi·cal /ˌkrɒnəˈlɒdʒɪkl; ˌkrɑnəˈlɑdʒɪkl/ adj in order of time: 按时间顺序的; 按年代先后的: *Shakespeare's plays in* ~ *order,* in the order in which they were written. 按著作年代先后次序编辑的莎士比亚戏剧集。 ~**ly** /-klɪ; -klɪ/ adv

chro·no·logy /krəˈnɒlədʒɪ; krəˈnɑlədʒɪ/ n [U] science of fixing dates; [C] (pl -gies) arrangement of events with dates; list or table showing this. 编年学; 年代学; 年代纪; 年代表。

chro·no·meter /krəˈnɒmɪtə(r); krəˈnɑmətə/ n kind of watch that keeps very accurate time, esp as used for fixing longitude at sea. 精密时计(尤指用于海上测量经度者); 天文钟; 船钟; 经线仪。

chry·sa·lis /ˈkrɪsəlɪs; ˈkrɪslɪs/ n (pl -lises /-lɪsɪz; -lɪsɪz/) form taken by an insect during the torpid stage of its life (ie between the time when it creeps or crawls as a larva and the time when it flies as a moth, butterfly, etc); the sheath that covers it during this time. 金蛹(昆虫生活史的第二阶段, 如蛾、蝶等之介于幼虫爬行期与成虫飞行期的阶段); 茧(蛹之外壳)。 ⇨ the illus at **butterfly**. 参看 butterfly 之插图。

chry·san·the·mum /krɪˈsænθəməm; krɪˈsænθə-məm/ n (flower of) garden plant blooming in autumn and early winter. 菊; 菊花(于秋季及初冬开花)。

chubby /ˈtʃʌbɪ; ˈtʃʌbɪ/ adj (-ier, -iest) plump: 丰满的; 圆胖的: ~ *cheeks.* 丰满的两颊; round-faced: 圆脸

的: *a ~ child.* 圆脸的小孩。

chuck[1] /tʃʌk; tʃʌk/ *vt* (colloq) (口) **1** [VP15A, B, 12A, 13A] throw: 投; 抛; 掷: ~ *away rubbish;* 抛弃垃圾; ~ *a drunken man out of a pub.* 把一个醉汉从酒店中推出去。 '~er-'out *n* (sl) person whose duty it is to throw out troublesome people (from public-houses, political meetings, etc). (俚) 负责驱逐在酒店、政治会议等中捣乱者之人; 打手; 保镖。 **2** [VP6A, 15B] ~ (**up**), abandon, give up (in disgust): 抛弃; (因厌恶而) 放弃: ~ *up one's job;* 放弃其职业; ~ *work.* 抛弃工作。 *C~ it,* (sl) Stop doing that! (俚) 停止! 住手! **3** ~ *sb under the chin,* touch him or her playfully with the back of the fist under the chin. 用拳背触弄某人的下巴。 □ *n the ~,* (sl) dismissal from one's job: (俚) 解雇; 革职: *get the ~,* be dismissed; 被解雇; *give sb the ~,* dismiss him. 解雇某人。

chuck[2] /tʃʌk; tʃʌk/ *n* that part of a lathe which grips the work to be operated on or which grips the bit on a drill. 车床上能夹紧工件以待操作或夹紧钻头的部份; 夹头; 卡盘; 拍子; 钻轧头。 ⇨ the illus at **lathe**. 参看 lathe 之插图。

chuckle /'tʃʌkl; 'tʃʌkl/ *n* low, quiet laugh with closed mouth (indicating satisfaction or amusement). 抿着嘴的轻笑 (表示满意或觉得有趣)。 *vi* laugh in this way: 抿着嘴轻笑: *He was chuckling to himself over what he was reading.* 他读到有趣的地方就自个儿很着嘴笑。

chuffed /tʃʌft; tʃʌft/ *pred adj* (GB colloq) very pleased: (英口) 非常高兴的: *be/feel/look ~.* 觉得 (显得) 非常高兴。

chug /tʃʌg; tʃʌg/ *vi* (**-gg-**) [VP2C] make the muffled explosive sound (of an oil-engine or small petrol-engine running slowly): 发出 (重油发动机或汽油发动机缓动时之) 突突声; 噗噗作响; 轧轧地响: *The boat ~ged along.* 船发着突突声而行进。 □ *n* this sound. 突突声; 噗噗声; 轧轧声。

chuk·ker /'tʃʌkə(r); 'tʃʌkɚ/ *n* (polo) one of the periods into which the game is divided. (马球) 一巡。

chum /tʃʌm; tʃʌm/ *n* close friend (esp among boys): 密友; 至友 (尤指男孩之间者): (Australia) (澳) *new ~,* new arrival; recent immigrant; 新到的人; 新移民; (US) room-mate. (美) 同寝室者; 室友。 □ *vi* (**-mm-**) [VP2C] ~ *up* (*with sb*), form a friendship (with). (与某人) 结为密友。 ~**my** *adj* friendly; like a ~. 友善的; 亲切的; 如密友的。

chump /tʃʌmp; tʃʌmp/ *n* **1** short, thick block of wood. 短而厚的木块。 **2** thick piece of meat: 一块厚厚的肉: *a ~ chop.* 一块厚厚的排骨肉。 **3** (sl) fool; blockhead. (俚) 愚人; 笨蛋; 蠢货。 **4** (sl) head. (俚) 头。 *off one's ~,* crazy. 发疯的; 发狂的。

chunk /tʃʌŋk; tʃʌŋk/ *n* thick, solid piece or lump cut off a loaf, a piece of meat/cheese etc. (自面包、一块肉、干酪等切下的) 厚而密实的一块; 厚块; 大块。 ~**y** *adj* (**-ier, -iest**) short and thick. 短而厚的; 粗短的。

church /tʃɜːtʃ; tʃɜtʃ/ *n* **1** building for public Christian worship. 教堂。 ⇨ **chapel.** ,~ 'register *n* records of births, marriages and deaths in a parish. 教堂记录 (登记教区中之出生、婚姻及死亡之记录)。 '~·yard *n* burial ground round a ~. 教堂墓地 (教堂四周的墓地)。 ⇨ **cemetery.** **2** [U] service in such a building: 在教堂中

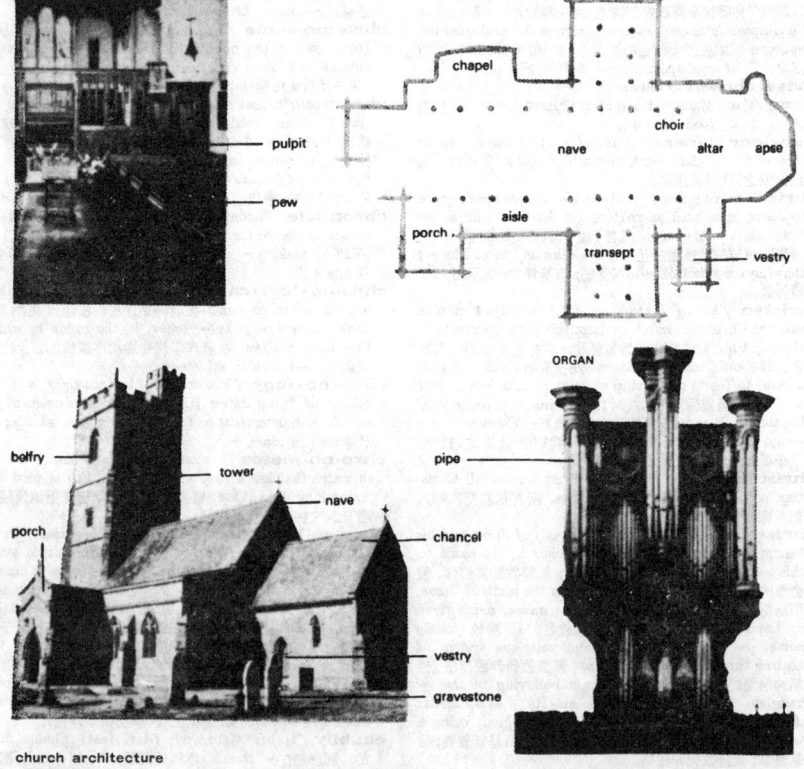

church architecture

的礼拜仪式: *What time does ~ begin?* 礼拜何时开始?
They're in/at ~, attending a service. 他们在教堂中做
礼拜。Cf 参较 *They're in the ~*, inside the building. 他
们在教堂里面。*How often do you go to ~?* 你多久去教
堂做一次礼拜? '**~·goer**/ -gəʊə(r); -ˌɡoʊ/ *n* person who
attends ~ services regularly. 经常上教堂做礼拜的人。
3 [U] *the C~ (of Christ)*, the whole body of Christians. 全体基督教徒。*the C~ of England*, England's
official Protestant ~, founded in the 16th century by
King Henry VIII. 英国国教 (十六世纪英王亨利八世所
创之新教); 英格兰教会。*enter the C~*, become a
minister[1] (3) or monk/nun. 做牧师; 做修道士; 做修
女。**~·war·den** *n* elected representative of a C~ of
England parish, not a priest, who helps to manage the
business, funds, etc of a ~. 英国国教每教区所选举出的
教会执事(非牧师,其职司为协助管理教会事务、经费等)。
churl /tʃɜːl; tʃɝl/ *n* bad-tempered person. 坏脾气的
人。**~·ish** *adj* bad-tempered; ill-bred. 坏脾气的; 无教
养的。**~·ish·ly** *adv*
churn /tʃɜːn; tʃɝn/ *n* **1** tub in which cream is shaken
or beaten to make butter. 在其中搅动乳脂以制成奶油之
桶; 搅乳器。**2** (not US) very large can in which milk is
carried from the farm. (不用于美国)自农场装运牛奶之
大罐。□ *vt, vi* **1** [VP6A] make (butter), beat and
shake (cream) in a ~. 在搅乳器制(奶油); 搅(乳脂)。**2**
[VP6A, 15B, 2A, C] *~ (up)*, stir or move about
violently; 剧烈地搅动: *The ship's propellers ~ed the
waves to foam/~ed up the waves.* 轮船的推进器将海
浪搅起泡沫。(fig) agitate the emotions. (喻) 激动感情。
~ out, produce in a mass: 大量生产: *~ out silly romantic*

novels. 大量生产可笑的浪漫小说。
chute /ʃuːt; ʃut/ *n* **1** long, narrow, steep slope down
which things may slide (eg for coal, barrels, etc into a
cellar, logs down a hillside, letters, refuse, etc from the
upper storeys of a high building). 狭长而陡峭, 物件可
以在上面滑下之斜槽。(例如将煤、酒桶等滑至地窖者,将
圆木材滑至山坡下者,信件、垃圾等自高楼中滑下之管道);
滑运道; 导槽; 滑槽。**2** smooth, rapid fall of water over
a slope. 斜坡上之平滑的急流。**3** (colloq abbr of)
parachute. (口)降落伞 (为 parachute 之略)。
chut·ney /'tʃʌtnɪ; 'tʃʌtnɪ/ *n* [U] hot-tasting mixture
of fruit, peppers, etc eaten with curry, cold meat, etc.
水果辣椒等混合制成的辣酱 (与咖哩,冷肉等合食)。
cic·ada /sɪˈkɑːdə; sɪˈkedə/ *n* winged insect with
transparent wings, the male of which chirps shrilly in
hot, dry weather. 蝉(翅翼透明之昆虫, 雄者在干燥的暑
天发出尖锐的鸣声)。⇨ the illus at **insect**. 参看 insect
之插图。
ci·cala /sɪˈkɑːlə; sɪˈkɑːlə/ *n* = cicada.
cica·trice /'sɪkətrɪs; 'sɪkətrɪs/, **cica·trix** /'sɪkətrɪks;
'sɪkətrɪks/ *n* (*pl* **-trices** /-'traɪsiːz; -'traɪsɪz/) scar left
by a healed wound. 伤疤; 伤痕。
cice·rone /ˌtʃɪtʃəˈrəʊnɪ; ˌsɪsəˈroʊnɪ/ *n* (*pl* **-ni** /-niː;
-niː/) (I) guide who understands and describes to
sightseers places and objects of interest. (意)向游客指点
名胜古迹之向导; 导游。
cider /'saɪdə(r); 'saɪdə/ *n* [U] fermented apple juice.
发酵的苹果汁; 苹果酒。'**~·press** *n* machine for pressing
juice from apples. 苹果榨汁机。
cigar /sɪˈɡɑː(r); sɪˈɡɑr/ *n* tight roll of tobacco leaves

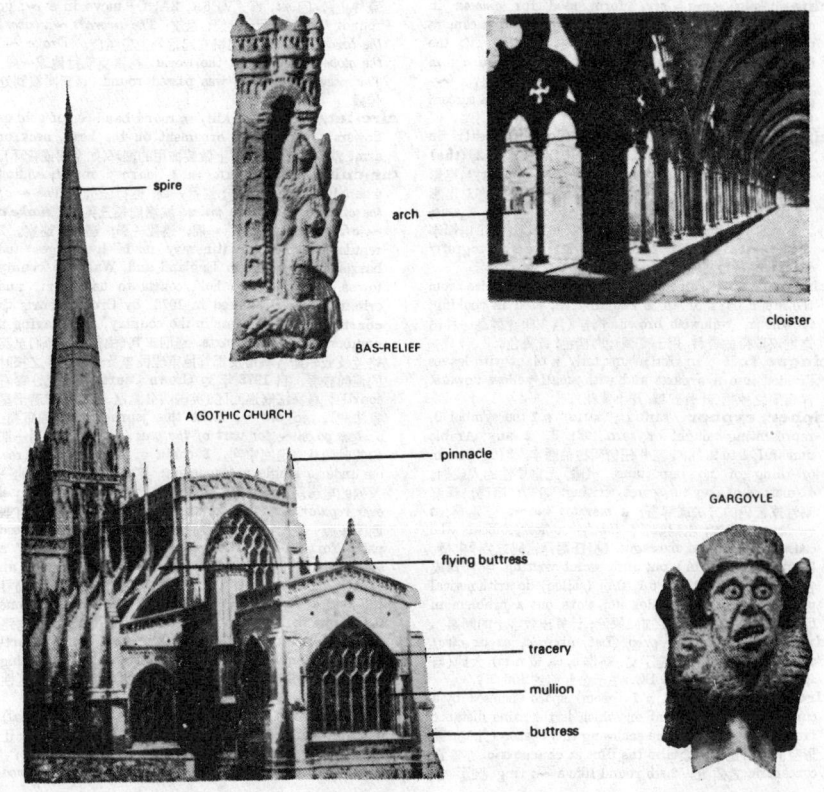

spire

arch

cloister

BAS-RELIEF

A GOTHIC CHURCH

pinnacle

GARGOYLE

flying buttress

tracery

mullion

buttress

with pointed end(s) for smoking. 雪茄烟(用烟叶卷紧, 两端或一端作尖形以便吸食之烟卷)。 '**~-shaped**, shaped like a cylinder with pointed ends. 两头尖的棒形的; 雪茄烟形的。

ciga·rette /ˌsɪgəˈret US: ˈsɪgəret, ˌsɪgəˈret, ˈsɪgəˌret/ n roll of shredded tobacco enclosed in thin paper for smoking. 香烟; 纸烟(将烟丝卷于薄纸中供吸食之烟卷)。 '**~-case** n one in which a supply of ~s may be carried in the pocket or handbag. 香烟盒(装香烟以便带于口袋或手提包中)。 '**~-holder** n tube in which a ~ may be put for smoking. 烟嘴。 '**~-paper**, that used to make ~s. (卷香烟用的)烟纸。

cinch /sɪntʃ; sɪntʃ/ n (US sl) something that is certain; something easy and sure. (美俚)有把握之事; 易做而有把握之事。

cin·chona /sɪŋˈkəʊnə; sɪnˈkonə/ n tree from whose bark quinine is obtained. 金鸡纳树(自其树皮可提取奎宁)。

cinc·ture /ˈsɪŋktʃə(r); ˈsɪŋktʃə/ n (liter) belt or girdle. (文)带; 环带。

cin·der /ˈsɪndə(r); ˈsɪndə/ n small piece of coal, wood, etc partly burned, no longer flaming, and not yet ash. 经部份燃烧, 已无火焰但尚未成灰之煤渣、焦木块等; 余烬。 **burnt to a ~**, (of a cake, etc) cooked so that it is hard and black. (指糕饼等)被烤焦; 被烧焦; 被烧糊。 '**~-track** n running track made with fine ~s. 用细煤渣铺的跑道。

Cin·de·rella /ˌsɪndəˈrelə; ˌsɪndəˈrelə/ n girl or woman whose attraction, merits, etc have not been recognized; (fig) sth long neglected. 魅力、优点等尚未为人所识的女子; (喻)长期为人所疏忽的事物。

cine- /ˈsɪnɪ; ˈsɪnɪ/ pref form used for cinema in compounds. 电影(用于复合词中)。 '**~-cam·era** n camera used for taking pictures. 电影摄影机。 参看 illus at **camera**. 参看 camera 之插图。 '**~-film** n film used in ~-cameras. 拍摄电影用的软片; 电影胶片。 '**~-pro·jec·tor** n machine for showing ~-films on a screen. 电影放映机。

cin·ema /ˈsɪnəmə; ˈsɪnəmə/ n 1 (not US) theatre in which films are shown. (不用于美国)电影院。 **2 (the) ~**, motion pictures as an art-form or an industry: 电影艺术; 电影事业: Are you interested in (the) ~? 你对电影(艺术)有兴趣吗? Of 参较 (the) drama. 参看 drama。 '**~-tic** /ˌsɪnɪˈmætɪk, ˌsɪnɪˈmætɪk/ adj of ~(2). 电影艺术的; 电影事业的。 **~·to·graphy** /ˌsɪnɪmˈtɒgrəfɪ; ˌsɪnɪməˈtɑgrəfɪ/ n [U] ~(2). 电影摄影术; 电影事业。

cin·na·mon /ˈsɪnəmən; ˈsɪnəmən/ n [U] spice from the inner bark of an E Indian tree, used in cooking; its colour, yellowish brown. 肉桂(自东印度群岛一种树之内皮取得的香料, 用于烹调); 肉桂色; 黄褐色。

cinque·foil /ˈsɪŋkfɔɪl; ˈsɪŋkˌfɔɪl/ n plant with leaves divided into five parts and with small yellow flowers. 洋莓属之植物(叶分五瓣, 开小黄花)。

cipher, cypher /ˈsaɪfə(r); ˈsaɪfə/ n **1** the symbol 0, representing nought or zero. 零; 0。 **2** any Arabic numeral, 1 to 9. 自 1 至 9 任何阿拉伯数字。 **3** (fig) person or thing of no importance. (喻)无重要性的人或物。 **4** (method of, key to) secret writing: 暗号; 暗码: a message in ~; 密码信; a ~ key; 密码本; 密码解答; the '~ officer, officer who codes and decodes messages. 译电员。 □ vt, vi **1** [VP6A] put into secret writing. 将⋯译成密码; 用密码写。 **2** [VP6A, 2A] (colloq) do arithmetical problems; add up, divide, etc; work out a problem in figures. (口)做算术题; 加减乘除; 计算出数字上的问题。

circa /ˈsɜːkə; ˈsɜːkə/ prep (Lat, abbr c, ca or circ) about (with dates): (拉丁文, 略作 c, ca 或 circ) 大约(与年代连用): born ~150 BC. 生于公元前约 150 年。

circle /ˈsɜːkl; ˈsɜːkl/ n **1** (geom) space enclosed by a curved line, every point on which is the same distance from the centre; the line enclosing this space. (几何) 圆形空间; 圆; 圆周。 ⇨ also the illus at **concentric**. 亦参看 concentric 之插图。 **2** sth round like a ~; ring: 圆形物

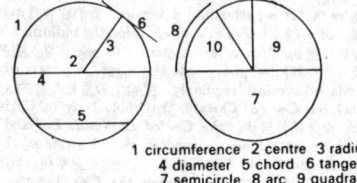

1 circumference　2 centre　3 radius
4 diameter　5 chord　6 tangent
7 semicircle　8 arc　9 quadrant
10 sector

parts of a circle

圈; 环: a ~ of trees/hills; 一圈树木(山丘); standing in a ~. 站成一个圆圈。 **a vicious ~**, ⇨ **vicious**. **3** block of seats in curved rows, one above the other, between the highest part (the gallery) and the floor (the stalls) of a theatre or hall. 电影院、剧院或音乐厅中的中楼座(介于最高楼座与地面座位之间, 座位排成弧形, 一排比一排高)。 **4** number of persons bound together by having the same or similar interests: 同道或同好的集团; (社会上的)⋯界; 圈子: in theatrical ~s, among actors, etc; 在戏剧界(在演员等的圈子里); moving in fashionable ~s, among those in fashionable society; 在上流社会中走动; business ~s. 工商界。 He has a large ~ of friends. 他的交游极广。 They are newcomers to our ~. 他们是我们这一圈中的新进者。 **5** complete series: 循环; 周而复始: the ~ of the seasons, the four seasons in succession. 四季的循环。 **come full ~**, end at the starting-point. 绕行一周(在起点终止)。 □ vt, vi [VP6A, 2A, C] move in a ~; go round: 环绕; 绕行; 盘绕; 盘旋: The aircraft ~d (over) the landing-field. 该飞机在起落场上空盘旋。 ~ed the globe, sailed round the world. 德雷克航行地球一周。 The news ~d round, was passed round. 该新闻被到处传播。

circ·let /ˈsɜːklɪt; ˈsɜːklɪt/ n round band (eg of gold or flowers) worn as an ornament on the head, neck or arm. 戴在头、颈或手臂上做装饰用的圈环(如金圈或花环)。

cir·cuit /ˈsɜːkɪt; ˈsɜːkɪt/ n **1** journey round, ending where one began: 周游; 巡行一周; 巡行; 巡回: The ~ of the city walls is three miles. 城墙周长三英里。 **make a ~ of**, go round. 环行一周; 巡视一周; 巡回; 巡察。 **2** regular journey or itinerary made by judges and barristers to towns in England and Wales to county towns (~ towns) to hold courts to hear civil and criminal cases, replaced in 1972 by Crown Courts ⇨ **court**[1]. One of six areas in the country, each having a number of Crown Courts. 巡回审判(法官与律师们至英格兰及威尔斯各城市及郡首邑审理民事及刑事案件之按时的巡回旅程, 自 1972 年为 Crown Courts 所取代; 参看 court[1]); 皇家法庭巡回区(英国共分六区, 每区均有若干皇家法庭)。 **go on ~**, make this journey: 作巡回审判: Judges go on ~ for part of the year. 法官们每年用一部份的时间从事巡回审判。 **3** chain of cinemas, theatres, etc under a single management: 某一企业下所经营的一系列的电影院、剧院等: Some theatrical companies travel over regular ~s, visit certain towns in succession. 有些剧团按照一定的路线前往某些市镇作巡回演出。 **4** closed path for an electrical current; apparatus with a sequence of conductors, transistors, etc for carrying an electric current: 电路(电流的通路, 或装设着一系列导体、电晶体等以传导电流之全部装置): ~ diagram, one that shows the connections in such an apparatus. 电路图。 **closed ~ (TV)**, ⇨ **close**[4](2). **short ~**, ⇨ **short**[1]. **5** regional group of Methodist churches sharing preachers. 聘有共同传道士之若干美以美会教堂的地区性集团。

cir·cu·itous /sɜːˈkjuːɪtəs; sɜˈkjuɪtəs/ adj (formal) indirect; going a long way round: (正式用语)间接的; 迂回的: a ~ route. 迂回的路线; 绕圈子的路。

cir·cu·lar /ˈsɜːkjʊlə(r); ˈsɜːkjələ/ adj round or curved

in shape; moving round: 圆形的; 弧形的; 环绕而行的: a ~ building; 一座圆形的建筑物; the North C~ Road, round the North of London, for through traffic; 伦敦北端的环伺马路(供经过伦敦中途不停之车辆行驶者); a ~ tour/trip, ending at the starting-point without visiting a place more than once. 环游各地的旅行。 ~ **letter** n one sent out to many persons. 寄与许多人传阅的函件。 ~ **saw** n disc-shaped saw that revolves by machinery. (由机件旋转的)圆形锯。 □ n printed letter, advertisement, announcement, etc of which many copies are made and distributed. 同式而印发许多份之函件、广告、通告等; 传阅之文件; 传单。 ~ **·ize** /'sɜːkjʊləraɪz/ vt [VP6A] send ~s to. 将传阅文件送给; 寄传单给。

cir·cu·late /'sɜːkjuleɪt; 'sɝkjə,let/ vi, vt 1 [VP2A, C] go round continuously; move from place to place freely: 流通; 循环; 传播: Blood ~s through the body. 血在人体内循环。 In many buildings hot water ~s through pipes to keep rooms warm. 在许多建筑物中, 用热水在管中循环的方法保存室内的温暖。 Bad news ~s quickly. 坏消息传播迅速。 In times of prosperity money ~s quickly; during a depression it ~s slowly. 在商业景气的时期, 钱流通得快; 在商业萧条的时期, 钱流通得慢。 **circulating library,** one from which books may be borrowed, usu on payment of a subscription. 书籍可以借出的图书馆(通常要付租书费);流通图书馆。 2 [VP6A] cause to ~: 传播; 散布: People who ~ false news are to be blamed. 散布流言者该受谴责。

cir·cu·la·tion /,sɜːkju'leɪʃn; ,sɝkjə'leʃən/ n 1 [U,C] circulating or being circulated, esp the movement of the blood from and to the heart: 循环(尤指血液从从心脏之运行): He has (a) good/bad ~. 他的血液循环很好(不良)。 The ~ of rumours is common in wartime. 在战时谣言的流传是常事。 2 [U] state of being circulated: 流通;流动;发行: Are there many forged banknotes in ~? 有许多假钞票在流通吗? That book has been withdrawn from ~, cannot now be obtained. 该书业已停止发行(现在买不到了)。 When were the decimal coins put into ~? 十进制硬币何时发行的? 3 [C] number of copies of a newspaper or other periodical sold to the public: (报纸、期刊等的)发行数额: a newspaper with a (daily) ~ of more than one million. (每日)发行额超过一百万份的报纸。

cir·cum·cise /'sɜːkəmsaɪz; 'sɝkəm,saɪz/ vt remove the foreskin of (a male) or the clitoris of (a female). 环割(男性)的包皮; 割除(女性)的阴蒂。 **circum·cision** /,sɜːkəm'sɪʒn; ,sɝkəm'sɪʒən/ n circumcising, esp (of males) as a religious rite among Jews and Muslims. 环割术; 包皮环割; (尤指)割礼(犹太人及回教徒之割包皮, 作为一种宗教仪式)。

cir·cum·fer·ence /sə'kʌmfərəns; sɚ'kʌmfərəns/ n (geom) line that marks out a circle or other curved figure; distance round sth: (几何)圆周; 周围长度: The ~ of the earth is almost 25000 miles. 地球的周围长度约为二万五千英里。 ⇨ the illus at circle. 参看 circle 之插图。

cir·cum·flex /'sɜːkəmfleks; 'sɝkəm,flɛks/ n (also 亦作 ~ **accent**) mark placed over a vowel to indicate how it is to be sounded (as in French rôle). 置于元音上指示发音方法的符号(如法文 rôle 中之 ^)。

cir·cum·lo·cu·tion /,sɜːkəmlə'kjuːʃn; ,sɝkəmlo-'kjuʃən/ n [C,U] (instance of) saying in many words what may be said in few words. 迂回说法; 累赘冗法; 累赘的句子。

cir·cum·navi·gate /,sɜːkəm'nævɪgeɪt; ,sɝkəm-'nævə,get/ vt [VP6A] (formal) sail round (esp the world). (正式用语)环航(尤指世界)一周。 **cir·cum·navi·ga·tion** /,sɜːkəm nævɪ'geɪʃn; ,sɝkəm,nævə'geʃən/ n

cir·cum·scribe /'sɜːkəmskraɪb; ,sɝkəm'skraɪb/ vt [VP6A] (formal) draw a line round; mark the limits of; narrow down, restrict: (正式用语) 在周围画一条线; 标出…的范围或界限; 限制: ~ one's interests 限制

某人的爱好。 **cir·cum·scrip·tion** /,sɜːkəm'skrɪpʃn; ,sɝkəm'skrɪpʃən/ n 1 [U] circumscribing or being ~d. 划界限; 限制。 2 [C] words inscribed round a coin. 钱币周围所刻的字。

cir·cum·spect /'sɜːkəmspekt; 'sɝkəm,spɛkt/ adj paying careful attention to everything before taking action; cautious. 在采取行动之前考虑周详的; 慎审的。 ~**·ly** adv **cir·cum·spec·tion** /,sɜːkəm'spekʃn; ,sɝkəm-'spɛkʃən/ n [U] prudence; care. 谨慎; 小心。

cir·cum·stance /'sɜːkəmstəns; 'sɝkəm,stæns/ n 1 (usu pl) conditions, facts, etc connected with an event or person: (通常用复数)与某事件或某人有关的情况、事实等; 环境; 情势: Don't judge the crime until you know the ~s. 在你未了解一切情况之前, 勿对此罪行下断决。 C~s alter cases, (prov) What may be good, wise, praiseworthy, etc in some ~s may be bad, foolish or blameworthy in other ~s. (谚)情势改变事态; 人的行为须因时地制宜(在某种情势下是好的、明智的、值到称赞的, 在别的情势下也许是坏的、愚蠢的或该受责备的)。 in/under the ~s, the ~s being so; such being the state of affairs. 在此种情形下; 情形既然如此。 in/under no ~s, never; whatever may happen. 决不; 无论在何种情况下均不可。 2 fact or detail: 详情; 细节: There is one important ~ you have not mentioned. 还有一件重要的事实你没有提到。 He has plenty of money, which is a fortunate ~. 他有充足的钱, 这是一件幸运的事。 3 (pl) financial condition: (复)经济情形; 境况: in easy/good/flourishing ~s. having enough or plenty of money; 在富裕的生活环境中; in reduced/straitened ~s, poor. 经济拮据; 贫困。 4 (sing) (used only in) (与下列连用) pomp and ~, show and ceremony. 铺张; 排场。

cir·cum·stan·tial /,sɜːkəm'stænʃl; ,sɝkəm'stænʃəl/ adj 1 (of a description) giving full details. (指描写)周详的; 详尽的。 2 (of evidence) based on, consisting of details that strongly suggest sth but do not provide direct proof. (指证据) 根据情况的; 间接的; 旁(证); 佐(证)。 ~**·ly** /-ʃəlɪ; -ʃɔlɪ/ adv

cir·cum·vent /,sɜːkəm'vent; ,sɝkəm'vɛnt/ vt [VP6A] (formal) prevent (a plan) from being carried out; find a way to get round (a law, rule, difficulty, etc). (正式用语)阻遏(计划)实现; 设法规避(法律、规则、困难等)。 **cir·cum·ven·tion** /,sɜːkəm'venʃn; ,sɝkəm'vɛnʃən/ n

cir·cus /'sɜːkəs; 'sɝkəs/ n 1 (in ancient Rome) round or oval place with seats on all sides for public games. (古罗马)四周有座位之圆形(或椭圆形)竞技场。 2 (in modern times) a travelling show, usu given in a large tent (called the big top) of performing animals, clever horse-riding, etc; persons and animals giving such a show. (现代)马戏表演(通常在大帐篷'the big top'内表演);马戏团。 3 (esp in proper names) open space where a number of streets converge: (尤用于专有名词中) 数条街道会集的广场: Piccadilly C~, in London. (伦敦的)比加得力广场。

cir·rho·sis /sɪ'rəusɪs; sɪ'rosɪs/ n [U] chronic (and often fatal) disease of the liver. 肝硬化(慢性且常为致命的肝病)。

cir·rus /'sɪrəs; 'sɪrəs/ n type of cloud, high in the sky, delicate and feathery in appearance. (高空中纤细如羽毛状的)卷云。

cissy /'sɪsɪ; 'sɪsɪ/ adj, n=sissy.

cis·tern /'sɪstən; 'sɪstɚn/ n water tank, eg as above the bowl of a WC, or for storing water in a building, with pipes to taps on lower storeys. 储水箱(如水马桶的水箱; (有水管通往低层楼之龙头的)贮水桶; 贮水池; 水塔。

cita·del /'sɪtədel; 'sɪtədl/ n fortress for protecting a town; (fig) place of refuge or safety. 护城碉堡; 城砦; 城堡; (喻)避难所; 安全地点。

cite /saɪt; saɪt/ vt [VP6A] 1 give or mention as an example (esp by quoting from a book, to support an argument, etc). 引述; 引证; 引用(某书中之字句, 以证明论点等)。 2 (US) mention for bravery in war: (美)因英勇作战而予以褒扬: ~d in dispatches. 在公报中被褒扬。 3

(legal) summon at law: (法律)传唤至法庭; 传讯: *be* ~*d in divorce proceedings.* 因离婚案被传讯. **ci·ta·tion** /saɪˈteɪʃn; saɪˈteʃən/ *n* [U] citing; [C] sth, esp a statement, that is ~d; (US) mention in an official record (eg for a brave act in war). 引述; 引证; 条文; 引用文; (美)(在公报中)褒扬; 表扬 (如为作战英勇事迹); 奖状.

citi·zen /ˈsɪtɪzn; ˈsɪtəzn/ *n* **1** person who lives in a town, not in the country: (城市中的)市民: *the* ~*s of Paris.* 巴黎市民. **2** person who has full rights in a State, either by birth or by gaining such rights: (一国中享有完全权利之)公民 (或因出生在该国, 或因取得此项权利): *immigrants who have become* ~*s of the United States,* 已成为美国公民之外来移民, Cf 参较 **British subject;** 英国的臣民; ~ *of the world,* cosmopolitan person. 世界之公民; 无国家偏见之人. '~·**ship** /-ʃɪp; -ˌʃɪp/ *n* being a ~; rights and duties of a ~. 公民资格; 公民之权利和义务.

cit·ric /ˈsɪtrɪk; ˈsɪtrɪk/ *adj* ~ **acid** *n* (chem) acid from such fruits as lemons and limes. (化学)(由柠檬和宜母子等酸味水果中提取之)柠檬酸.

cit·ron /ˈsɪtrən; ˈsɪtrən/ *n* (tree with) pale yellow fruit like a lemon but larger, less acid, and thicker skinned. 枸橼; 香橼 (浅黄色水果, 似柠檬但较大, 较不酸, 皮亦较厚); 香橼树.

cit·rous /ˈsɪtrəs; ˈsɪtrəs/ *adj* of the citrus fruits. 柑橘属水果的.

cit·rus /ˈsɪtrəs; ˈsɪtrəs/ *n* (bot) genus of trees that includes the lemon, lime, citron, orange and grapefruit: (植物)柑橘属 (包括柠檬, 宜母子, 香橼, 柑橘及柚子等); (用作定语)柑橘属的: ~ *fruit.* 柑橘属水果.

city /ˈsɪtɪ; ˈsɪtɪ/ *n* (*pl* -**ties**) **1** large and important town; town given special rights in self-government (in GB by royal charter, in US by a charter from the State). 都市; 城市; 享有特别自治权之城市 (在英国由皇家特许状所赋予, 在美国由州的特许状所赋予). **the C**~, the oldest part of London, now the commercial and financial centre. 伦敦市之最古老的部份, 现为商业及金融中心. **2** people living in a ~. 全市居民. **3** (attrib): (用作定语): ~ '**centre,** central area of a city; 市中心区; ~ '**editor,** (GB) one who deals with financial news; (US) one in charge of local news; (英)财经新闻编辑; (美)地方新闻编辑; 采访主任; ~ '**hall,** building for transaction of the official business of a ~; 市政厅; 市政府; a 'C~ **man,** engaged in commerce or finance; 经营商业或金融业的人; ~ **state,** city that is also an independent sovereign state (eg Athens in ancient times). 城邦 (既为城市, 亦为独立自主之国家, 如古代之雅典).

civet /ˈsɪvɪt; ˈsɪvɪt/ *n* **1** (also 亦作 '~**-cat**) small spotted cat-like animal of Africa, Asia and Europe. 麝猫; 灵猫; 香猫 (体内有斑点似猫之动物, 产于非、亚、欧洲). **2** [U] strong-smelling substance from certain glands of this animal. 麝猫香 (自麝猫之某种腺体中取出之极香的物质).

civic /ˈsɪvɪk; ˈsɪvɪk/ *adj* of the official life and affairs of a town or a citizen: 市政的; 市民的; 公民的: ~ *duties;* 公民的义务; ~ *pride;* 公民的自豪; a ~ *centre,* where the official buildings, eg the town hall, library, hospitals, etc, are grouped together. 市政中心(如市政府、图书馆、医院等集中之地). **civ·ics** *n pl* (*sing v*) study of city government, the rights and duties of citizens, etc. (用单数动词)公民学(研究市政、公民权利与义务等的课程).

civ·ies /ˈsɪvɪz; ˈsɪvɪz/ *n pl* (GB sl) civilian clothes. (英俚)普通人民穿的衣服.

civil /ˈsɪvl; ˈsɪvl/ *adj* **1** of human society; of people living together: 人类社会的; 群居之人们的; 公民的: *We all have* ~ *rights and* ~ *duties.* 我们都有公民的权利和义务. ~ **diso'bedience,** organized refusal to obey the laws (esp as part of a political campaign). 人民之集体的拒绝遵守法律(尤指作为一项政治运动之一部份者); 非暴力抵

抗. ~ **engi'neering,** the design and building of roads, railways, canals, docks, etc. 土木工程(设计及建筑道路、铁路、运河、码头等). ~ **'law,** law dealing with private rights of citizens, not with crime. 民法(处理公民私有权利而非处理犯罪之法律). ~ **'marriage,** without religious ceremony but recognized by law. 未经宗教仪式但为法律所认可之婚姻. ~ **'rights,** rights of a citizen to political, racial, legal, social freedom or equality. 公民权(公民享有之对政治、种族、法律、社会之自由或平等之权利). ~ **'rights movement,** organized movement aiming to secure for all citizens the enjoyment of constitutional rights. 公民权运动(为所有公民争取享有宪法上所制定的权利的有组织运动). ~ **'war,** war between two sides in the same country, eg in the US 1861—1865, in Spain 1936—1939. 内战(同一国内两派间之战争, 例如一八六一至一八六五美国之南北战争及一九三六至一九三九西班牙之内战). **2** not of the armed forces. 平民的 (对军人而言); 非军人的. ,**C~ De'fence Corps,** organization to deal with results of attack (esp from the air). 民防队; 民众防护团(尤指处理空袭善后者). ~ **'servant,** official in the C~ Service. (政府里的)文官; 公务员. **tha ,C~ 'Service** all government departments except the Navy, Army and Air Force. 政府的文职机关 (即除海、陆、空军以外者). **3** politely helpful: 文明的; 有礼貌的: *The boy gave me a* ~ *answer.* 那男孩给我一个有礼貌的回答. *Can't you be* ~? 你不能有点礼貌吗? *It was* ~ *of them to offer to help us.* 他们肯招待我们真令我人钦佩. **4** '~ **list,** (GB) allowance of money made by Parliament for the royal household and royal pensions. (英)国会拨给皇室作为皇室年俸之专款; 王室年金. ~·ly /ˈsɪvɪlɪ; adv politely. 有礼貌地. **ci·vil·ity** /sɪˈvɪlətɪ; səˈvɪlətɪ/ *n* [U] politeness (*to*); (*pl*; -**ties**) polite acts. (对人)有礼貌(与之连用); 有礼的举动.

ci·vil·ian /sɪˈvɪlɪən; səˈvɪljən/ *n, adj* (person) not serving with the armed forces: 未在军中服役的; 平民的; 平民: *I asked the soldier what he was in* ~ *life.* 我问那军人他做平民时是干什么的. *He left the army and returned to* ~ *life.* 他离开军队恢复平民生活. *In modern wars* ~*s as well as soldiers are killed.* 在现代战争中, 平民和军人一样地丧命.

civi·li·za·tion /ˌsɪvɪlaɪˈzeɪʃn US: -əlɪˈz-; ˌsɪvləˈzeʃən/ *n* **1** [U] civilizing or being civilized; state of being civilized: 教化; 开化; 教导: *The* ~ *of mankind has taken thousands of years.* 人类的开化已经有几千年. **2** [C] system, stage of, social development: 文化; 文明 (达到化的方式或阶段): *the* ~*s of ancient Egypt, Babylon and Persia.* 古埃及、巴比伦和波斯的文化. **3** [U] civilized States collectively: (集合用法)文明世界; 文明国家: *acts that horrified* ~. 令文明国家震惊的行为.

civi·lize /ˈsɪvəlaɪz; ˈsɪvlˌaɪz/ *vt* [VP6A] **1** bring from a savage or ignorant condition to a higher one (by giving education in methods of government, moral teaching, etc). (借教以治理方法、道德训示等)使自野蛮或无知的状态进入较高等的阶段; 教化; 开化. **2** improve and educate; refine the manners of: 使之进步并教育; 教导: *Many a rough man has been* ~*d by his wife.* 许多粗野的男人都被妻子教好了.

civ·vies /ˈsɪvɪz; ˈsɪvɪz/ *n pl* = **civies.**

Civvy Street /ˈsɪvɪ striːt; ˈsɪvɪ ˈstrɪt/ *n* (GB sl) civilian life. (英俚)平民生活.

clack /klæk; klæk/ *vi, n* (make the) short, sharp sound of objects struck together: (发出)短而尖锐的碰撞声: *the* ~ *of her knitting needles;* 她手中的针的卡嗒声; 短促音; ~*ing typewriters;* 噼哩啪啦响的打字机; ~*ing tongues at the Women's Institute.* 妇女会馆里哇吱吱喳喳的说话声.

clad /klæd; klæd/ *old pp* of **clothe:** clothe 的旧式过去分词: *poorly* ~, dressed in poor clothes: 衣着粗劣的; (poet): *hills* ~ *in verdure.* 覆满葱绿树木的丘陵; (in compounds): (用于复合词中): *'steel-*~; 钢面的; *'iron-*~. 包着铁皮的.

claim [1] /kleɪm; klem/ *vt, vi* [VP6A, 7A, 9, 2A] **1**

demand recognition that one is, or owns, or has a right to (sth): 要求承认某人之身份、所有权或对(某物)享有某种权利: *Does anyone ~ this umbrella?* 有没有人认领这把伞? *Every citizen in a democratic country may ~ the protection of the law.* 一民主国家的每一个公民都可以要求法律的保护。*He ~ed to be the owner of/~ed that he owned the land.* 他要求承认为该土地之所有人。*Have you ~ed yet,* eg made a ~ *under an insurance policy?* 你提出要求了吗(如按保险单上的约定提出某项要求)? □ *damages,* (legal) (法律) ⇨ **damage.** ⇨ also **bonus. 2** assert; say that sth is a fact: 声言; 宣称; 说某事为事实: *He ~ed to have/~ed that he had done the work without help.* 他声言未得到帮助而完成了此工作。*He ~ed to be the best tennis player in the school.* 他自称是全校最佳的网球手。**3** (of things) need; deserve: (指事物)需要; 值得: *There are several matters that ~ my attention.* 有数桩事值得我注意。

claim² /kleɪm; klem/ *n* **1** [C] assertion of a right; act of ~ing¹(1): 要求承认其所有权或某种权利: *Does anyone make a ~ to* (but more usu *Does anyone ~*) *this purse,* say that it is his? 有没有人认领这个钱包? (但较常用 Does anyone claim this purse.) *His ~ to own the house is invalid.* 他对该房产所有权的要求是无效的。**lay ~ to** demand (sth) as one's due: 宣称 (某物) 应归其所有: *If the land really belongs to you, why don't you lay ~ to it,* say so and try to get it? 假若这块土地真是属于你的, 你何不请求归还产权? **2** [C] sum of money demanded under an insurance agreement (for loss, damage, etc): 根据保险合同所要求的赔款(如因损失、损坏等): *make/put in a ~ (for sth).* (因某物之损坏) 提出赔偿要求。**3** [U, C] right to ask for: 债权: *You have no ~ on my sympathies.* 你无权求我同情。**4** [C] sth that is ~ed; piece of land (esp in a gold-bearing region) allotted to a miner: 所要求之物; (尤指产金矿的地区)分配给矿工之一块地: *stake out a ~,* mark boundaries to assert ownership. 标出地界以维护所有权。'**~·ant** /'kleɪmənt; 'klemənt/ *n* person who makes a ~, esp in law. 要求者(尤指提出法律要求者)。

clair·voy·ance /kleə'vɔɪəns; klɛr'vɔɪəns/ *n* [U] power of perceiving what is not present to the senses; exceptional insight. 对于非眼前事物的觉察力; 超人的洞察力。 ⇨ **telepathy. clair·voy·ant** /kleə'vɔɪənt; klɛr'vɔɪənt/ *n* person with such power. 有超人洞察力的人。

clam /klæm; klæm/ *n* large shell-fish, with a shell in two halves, used for food. 蛤; 蚌(壳分两半之大贝类, 用作食物)。 ⇨ the illus at **bivalve.** 参看 bivalve 之插图。~·**bake** /'klæmbeɪk; 'klæm,bek/ *n* (US) seashore picnic at which ~s and other foods are baked. (美)海滨蚌野餐(在海滩上烤蚌壳类及其他食物的野餐)。 □ *vi* (**-mm**) **1** [VP2A] dig for, go out for, ~s. 掘蚌; 抬蚌。 **2** [VP2C] ~ **up,** (colloq) (suddenly) become silent; refuse to speak. (口)(突然)变为沉默; 拒绝说话。

clam·ber /'klæmbə(r); 'klæmbɚ/ *vi* [VP2C] climb with some difficulty, using the hands and feet: 攀爬; 爬上; 攀登: ~ *up/over a wall.* 爬上/过墙。 □ *n* awkward or difficult climb. 麻烦的或艰难的攀登。

clammy /'klæmɪ; 'klæmɪ/ *adj* (**-ier, -iest**) damp; moist; cold and sticky to the touch: 潮湿的; 冷而粘的: ~ *hands;* 又冷又粘的手; *a face ~ with sweat.* 汗湿的脸。**clam·mi·ly** *adv*

clam·our (US = **clam·or**) /'klæmə(r); 'klæmɚ/ *n* [C, U] loud confused noise or shout, esp of people complaining angrily or making a demand. 喧闹; 叫嚣; (尤指)群众之愤怒或有所要求的呼喊。 □ *vi, vi* [VP2A, C, 4A] make a ~: 喧闹; 叫嚣; 大声呼喊: *The foolish people were* ~*ing for war.* 愚昧的人们叫嚣着要求打仗。*The newspapers are* ~*ing against the government's policy.* 报纸大声疾呼反对政府的政策。*The troops were* ~*ing to go home.* 军队大声喊着要回国。**clam·or·ous** /'klæmərəs; 'klæmərəs/ *adj* noisy: 吵闹的; 叫嚷的: *a clamorous mob.* 喧嚷的暴民。

clamp /klæmp; klæmp/ *n* **1** appliance for holding things together tightly by means of a screw. 夹钳。**2** band of iron, etc for strengthening or tightening. 钉夹; 铁箍; 夹板; 铁马钉。 □ *vt, vi* **1** [VP6A, 15B] put a ~ or ~s on; put in a ~. 用螺丝钳夹; 置于螺丝钳中; 加铁箍或置于铁箍中。**2** [VP2C] ~ **down (on),** (colloq) put pressure on; exert pressure against (in order to stop sth): (口)施加压力于; 用力制止; 箝制: *They* ~*ed down on the newspapers.* 他们施加压力制止报纸报导。Hence, 由此产生, '**~-down** *n*

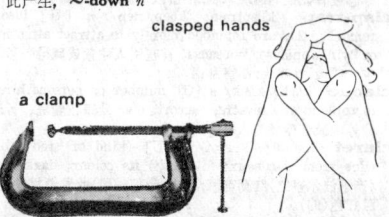

clasped hands

a clamp

clan /klæn; klæn/ *n* large family group, as found in tribal communities, esp Scottish Highlanders with a common ancestor: 大家族; 宗族; 氏族(或见于部落社会者); (尤指)同一祖宗的苏格兰高地人: *the Campbell ~.* 坎贝尔氏宗族。

clan·des·tine /klæn'destɪn; klæn'dɛstɪn/ *adj* (formal) secret; done secretly; kept secret: (正式用语)秘密的; 秘密而做的; 被保密的: *a ~ marriage.* 秘密的结婚。

clang /klæŋ; klæŋ/ *vt, vi,* [VP6A, 2A] (make a) loud ringing sound (eg a hammer striking an anvil): (使)(发出)叮璫声; 璫琅声(如铁锤击铁钻之声): *The tramdriver* ~*ed his bell.* 电车司机踏铃。~ *er* (sl) (俚) **drop a** ~*er,* say sth indiscreet or embarrassing. 说出不得体或令人困窘的话。

clang·our (US = **clangor**) /'klæŋə(r); 'klæŋɚ/ *n* continued clanging noise; series of clangs. 连续的叮璫声。**clangor·ous** /'klæŋərəs; 'klæŋərəs/ *adj*

clank /klæŋk; klæŋk/ *vt, vi, n* [VP6A, 2A] (make a) dull metallic sound (not so loud as a clang) (eg chains or knives striking together): (使)(发出)叮璫声(较 clang 声为小, 如铁链或刀相击之声): *prisoners* ~*ing their chains.* 使镣铐琅璫作声的囚犯。

clan·nish /'klænɪʃ; 'klænɪʃ/ *adj* showing clan feeling; (of people) in the habit of supporting one another against outsiders. 表现宗族感情的; (指人们)习惯于团结排外的。~·**ly** *adv*

clans·man /'klænzmən; 'klænzmən/ *n* (*pl* **-men**) member of a clan. 同一宗族的人; 族人。

clap¹ /klæp; klæp/ *vt, vi* (**-pp-**) **1** [VP6A, 2A, B] show approval, applaud, by striking (often) the front part of the hands together: 鼓掌(表示赞成、赞许); 拍(手): *When the violinist finished the audience* ~*ped for five minutes.* 当小提琴手演奏完时, 听众鼓掌达五分钟。*The baby* ~*ped its hands.* 那婴孩在拍手。**2** [VP14] strike or slap lightly with the open hand, usu in a friendly way: (用手掌)轻拍(通常以友善的方式): ~ *sb on the back.* 拍拍某人的背。**3** [VP15A, B] put quickly or energetically: 迅速而有力地放置: ~ *sb in prison;* 把某人投入狱中; ~ *one's hat on;* 迅速用力地将帽戴上; ~ *on sail,* spread more sail. 张多一点帆。~ **eyes on sb,** (colloq, esp in neg) catch sight of: (口, 或用于否定句中)看见; 见到: *I haven't* ~*ped eyes on him since 1960.* 我从一九六〇年以后就没有见到过他。 □ *n* **1** loud explosive noise (eg of thunder). 大的爆发声; 轰隆声(例如雷声)。 **2** sound of the front of the hands brought together. (*Clapping* is the usu word for applause, not *claps*). 击掌声; 拍手声。(指鼓掌喝彩通常用 clapping, 非 claps)。

clap² /klæp; klæp/ *n* [U] (**the**) ~, (sl) venereal disease; (esp) gonorrhea. (俚)性病; (尤指)淋病。

clap·board /'klæpbɔ:d US: 'klæbə:rd; 'klæbəd/ n weather-board. (房屋外面的）墙面板；护墙板；鱼鳞板；檐板。

clap·per /'klæpə(r); 'klæpə/ n tongue or striker of a bell; noisy hand rattle (used, for example, to scare birds from crops)., (钟铃之）击锤；铃（钟）舌；手摇之鸣响器(如用以吓走田中之鸟者)。 '~·board n (filming) divided, hinged and marked board which is sharply closed to mark the start of filming. (电影)场记板(刻有标志装有铰链的两块木板，拍击以示摄影开始)。

clap·trap /'klæptræp; 'klæp.træp/ n [U] ideas, remarks, that are intended merely to attract attention or win applause; nonsense. 旨在引人注意或赢得喝彩的主意或谈话；噱头；胡言乱语。

claque /klæk; klæk/ n [C] number of persons hired to applaud in a theatre, concert, etc. 受雇在剧院、音乐会等中鼓掌捧场的人群。

claret /'klærət; 'klærət/ n (U) (kind of) red table wine from Bordeaux; (also adj) its colour, dark red. (产于波尔多之)红葡萄酒；(亦作形容词用)此酒之颜色；深红色(的)。

clar·ify /'klærɪfaɪ; 'klærə,faɪ/ vt, vi [VP6A, 2A] make or become clear; make (a liquid, etc) free from impurities. 澄清；使明白；使(液体等)清洁(不含杂质)。 **clari·fi·ca·tion** /,klærɪfɪ'keɪʃn; ,klærəfə'keʃən/ n [U] ~ing or being clarified. 澄清；阐明。

clari·net /,klærɪ'net; ,klærə'nɛt/ n musical woodwind instrument, with finger holes and keys. 单簧管；竖笛。 ⇨ the illus at **brass**. 参看 brass 之插图。 **~·ist**, **~·tist** n person who plays the ~. 吹奏单簧者；竖笛手。

clar·ion /'klærɪən; 'klærɪən/ n loud, shrill call made to rouse and excite; (attrib) loud and clear: (有唤起或激励作用的）号角声；(用作定语)响亮清晰的：a ~ call; 响亮的号角声。 a ~ voice. 响亮的嗓音。

clar·ity /'klærətɪ; 'klærətɪ/ n [U] clearness. 清楚；清彻；透明。

clash /klæʃ; klæʃ/ vi, vt 1 [VP6A, 15B, 2A, C] make a loud, broken, confused noise (as when metal objects strike together): (使)发撞击声(如金属物体互撞而发者)；发铿锵之声：Their swords ~ed. 他们的剑互击而发响声之声。She ~ed the pans down on the stone floor. 她把炒锅哐啷一声掉在石地上。The cymbals ~ed. 铙钹鸣声而发响亮之声。2 [VP2A, C] come suddenly together; meet in conflict: 互撞；互碰：The two armies ~ed outside the town. 两军在城外交锋。3 [VP2A, C] (of events) interfere with each other because they are (to be) at the same time on the same date: (指事件)时间冲突 (即在同一日期的同一时刻)：It's a pity the two concerts ~, I want to go to both. 可惜两个音乐会时间冲突，我两个都想去听。4 [VP3A, 2A, C] ~ (with), be in disagreement or at variance: (与…)不合；不一致：I ~ed with him/ We ~ed at the last meeting of the Council. 在上一次议会的集会中我与他(我们)的意见不合。The colour of the curtains ~es with the colour of the carpet. 窗帘的颜色与地毯的颜色不调和。The date of your party ~es with another engagement. 你的宴会的日期与另一约会相抵触。□ n 1 ~ing noise: 撞击声；碰击声：the ~ of weapons/ of pots falling/ of cymbals. 武器互击(锅跌落，铜钹)的响声。2 disagreement; conflict: 不合；不调和；冲突；抵触：a ~ of views/opinions/colours. 见解(意见, 色彩)不合。

clasp /klɑːsp US: klæsp; klæsp/ n 1 device with two parts that fasten, used to keep together two things or two parts of one thing (eg the ends of a necklace or belt). (扣于用的）钩扣；扣钩；扣环(如用以扣住项链或腰带的两端者)。 '~·knife, folding knife with a ~ for fixing the blade when open. (打开时有扣环可以固定刀刃的)折迭式小刀。2 bar of silver, etc on a medal-ribbon (with the name of the battle, campaign, etc at which the person to whom the medal was awarded was present). 勋表附饰；勋标(勋章饰带上刻着受勋者所曾参加之战役等名称之银质或其他颜料扣杆)。3 firm hold (with the fingers or arm); handshake; embrace. (用手指或臂膀)紧握；握

手；拥抱。□ vt, vi 1 [VP6A, 15A] hold tightly or closely: 紧握；紧抱：~ed in each other's arms; 互相紧紧拥抱；~ sb by the hand. 紧握住某人的手r The thief was ~ing a knife in his hand. 窃贼手中紧握着一把刀。~ hands, shake hands with sb (showing more emotion than in the usual handshake). 紧紧地握手 (比普通的握手表示较多的感情)。~ one's hands, press them together with the fingers interlaced: 将两手手指互相交叉而握着：with hands ~ed in prayer; 在祷告时交叉屈指合掌；with his hands ~ed behind him. 将两手交叉屈于背后。2 [VP6A,15A] fasten with a clasp(1): 用钩环扣住：~ a bracelet round one's wrist. 将手镯扣戴在手腕上。3 [VP2A] This bracelet won't ~, cannot be ~ed. 这只手镯扣不住。

class /klɑːs US: klæs; klæs/ n 1 group having qualities of the same kind; kind, sort or division: 种；类；门类；类别；等级：There used to be first-~, second-~ and third-~ carriages on the trains in Britain. 英国火车从前分为头等、二等、三等车厢。The second highest division of the animal or vegetable kingdom is a ~. 动植物的第二高类别叫纲。⇨ **family, genus, order**[1](15), **phylum, species**. As an actor A is not in the same ~ with B, is not so good as B. 作为一个演员而论，甲不如乙。2 [U] system of ranks in society; caste system: (社会的)阶级；阶级制度：It will be difficult to abolish ~ 要废除社会阶级制度是很难的；(used attrib): (用作定语)：~ conflicts; 社会阶级间的冲突；the '~ struggle. 阶级斗争。'~-conscious, realizing one's ~ in society and the differences between social ~es 有阶级觉悟的。'~-feeling, feeling of envy, etc of one ~ for another. 阶级感 (阶级间互相嫉妒等之感觉)。~·'warfare, struggle, enmity, between ~es. 阶级斗争。3 [C] all persons in one of these ranks: 所有同一阶级的人：Society may be divided into upper, middle and lower ~es. 社会可分为上层、中层和下层等级。4 group of persons taught together; their course of teaching. (学生的)班；级；课。'~-fellow/-mate, pupil or past member of the same ~. 同班同学：Jim and I were ~-mates last term. 吉姆和我上学期同班。'~·room, room where a ~ is taught. 教室。5 (US) group of pupils or students who enter school or college in the same year and leave together: (美)同年入学同年毕业之一班学生；级：the ~ of 1973, those who finished their school course in that year 1973 级 (此年毕业之一班学生)。6 all those men conscripted for service in the armed forces in a year: 同年征召入伍的士兵：the 1970 ~. 1970 年次的役男。7 (not US) grade or merit after examination: (不用于美国)考试成绩之等第：take a first/second-~ degree. 考取第一(第二)等。'~-list, honours list issued by examiners. (由主试者公布的)成绩优秀学生名单。8 (colloq; often attrib) distinction; excellence; style: (口）常用作定语)优秀；特优；卓越；风度；气质：He's a ~ tennis player. 他是一个优秀的网球选手。There's not much ~ about her. 她没有什么气质。□ vt [VP6A, 14] place in a ~(1): 分入某类；归类：a ship ~ed A 1; 列为 A 级的船；to ~ one thing with another. 将甲物与乙物归入一类。~·less adj without distinctions of ~(2): 无阶级的：Is a ~less society possible? 一个无阶级的社会是可能的吗？

clas·sic /'klæsɪk; 'klæsɪk/ adj 1 of the highest quality; having a value or position recognized and unquestioned. 最佳的；最高等的；第一流的；具有公认而无可争议之价值或地位的。2 of the standard of ancient Greek and Latin literature, art and culture. 古代希腊及罗马文学、艺术和文化之标准的；古典的。3 with qualities like those of ~(2) art, ie simple, harmonious and restrained. 有古典艺术风格的 (即朴素的、调和的和严谨的)。4 famous because of a long history: 因历史悠久而著名的：a ~ event, eg the Oxford and Cambridge boat race or the Derby. 历史悠久而著名的大赛会(如牛津大学与剑桥大学的划船赛或英国大赛马)。5 (of style in costume, etc) traditional; not new. (指服装等的式样)传统的；非新式的。□ n 1 writer, artist, book, etc of the highest

class: 第一流的作家、艺术家、著作家: *Milton is a ~*. 弥尔顿是第一流的作家. *'Robinson Crusoe' is a ~*. 《鲁滨逊漂流记》是一部名著. **2** ancient Greek or Latin writer. 古希腊或罗马的作家; 古典作家. **3 the ~s,** (literature of the) ancient languages of Greece and Rome. 古希腊、罗马的文学或语文; 古典文学; 古典语文. **C~s,** university course in these subjects: (大学课程中的)古典文学或古典语文: *He read ~s at Oxford.* 他在牛津大学攻读古典文学. **4 ~** event, ⇨ the *adj* **4** above. 历史悠久的大事; 传统悠久的大赛会(参看上列形容词第 4 义).

clas·si·cal /'klæsɪkl; 'klæsɪkl/ *adj* **1** in, of ancient Gk and Roman art and literature: 古希腊、罗马之文学艺术的; ~ *studies;* 古典文学艺术研究; *a '~ education;* 古典文学艺术的教育; *a '~ scholar.* 精通古典文学艺术的学者. **2** of proved value because of having passed the test of time: 经过时间的考验被证明为有价值的: ~ *music,* usually taking traditional, well-defined form as a concerto, symphony, etc, eg of Haydn and Mozart. 古典音乐(通常为协奏曲、交响曲等传统曲式, 如海顿及莫扎特的作品). **3** simple and restrained; not over-ornamented. 古典式的; 有古典之风格的(即朴实、严谨而无华的). ~**·ly** /-kəlɪ; -klɪ/ *adv*

clas·si·cist /'klæsɪsɪst; 'klæsəsɪst/ *n* follower of classic style; classical scholar: 崇尚古典风格者; 古典主义者; 古典学者: *Milton was a ~.* 弥尔顿是一位古典派作家.

clas·si·fi·ca·tion /ˌklæsɪfɪ'keɪʃn; ˌklæsəfə'keʃən/ *n* [U] classifying or being classified; [C] group into which sth is put. 分类; 归类; (某物所归入的)类别; 门类; 种类.

clas·sify /'klæsɪfaɪ; 'klæsə,faɪ/ *vt* [VP6A] arrange in classes or groups; put into a class(1): 分类; 归类: *In a library books are usually classified by subjects.* 在图书馆里, 书籍通常是按科目分类的. **clas·sified** *adj* arranged in classes(1): 按种类分列的; 分类的; 类别的: *classified advertisements* (also, colloq, *classified ads*): 分类广告 (口语亦作 *classified ads*); *classified directory,* one in which the entries (eg of business firms) are entered in classes (eg builders, electricians, plumbers): 分类电话簿(这类电话簿由各项目分类, 如建筑商、电工、铅管工等); (US) put in a group that is officially secret: (美)归入官方机密的: *classified information.* 机密的资料. **clas·si·fi·able** /'klæsɪfaɪəbl; 'klæsə,faɪəbl/ *adj* that can be classified. 可分类的; 可归类的.

classy /'klɑːsɪ US: 'klæsɪ; 'klæsɪ/ *adj* **(-ier, -iest)** (colloq) stylish; superior; upper-class. (口) 漂亮的; 时髦的; 优良的; 上等的.

clat·ter /'klætə(r); 'klætɚ/ *n* (*sing* only) (仅用单数) **1** long, continuous, resounding noise (as of hard things falling or knocking together): 长而连续的回响声 (如坚硬物体落地或互相碰撞的声音): *the ~ of a horse's hoofs on a hard road;* 马蹄在硬路上行走的踢踏声; *the ~ of machinery;* 机器的辘辘声; *the ~ of cutlery.* 刀、剑的碰击声. **2** noisy talk: 喧嚷的谈话: *The boys stopped their ~ when the teacher came into the classroom.* 当老师走进教室时, 男生们停止喧哗. □ *vi, vt* [VP6A, 2A, C] make a ~(1): (使)发出长而连续的回响声: *Pots and pans were ~ing in the kitchen.* 盆子锅子在厨房里碰击作响. *Don't ~ your knives and forks.* 不要让你的刀叉碰击出声. *Some of the dishes ~ed down during the earthquake.* 有些盘子在地震的时候哗啦啦地落在地上.

clause /klɔːz; klɔz/ *n* **1** (gram) component of a (complex) sentence, with its own subject and predicate, esp one doing the work of a noun, adjective or adverb: (语法) 从句(构成(复杂)句子的一个成分, 自有其主语和谓语, 尤指其功用属名词、形容词或副词者): *dependent / subordinate ~.* 从句. **2** (legal) complete paragraph in an agreement, legal document, etc. (法律)(契约、法律文件等的)完整的一款.

claus·tro·pho·bia /ˌklɔːstrə'fəʊbɪə; ˌklɔstrə'fobɪə/ *n* [U] morbid fear of confined places (eg a lift, cave or coal-mine). 幽闭恐怖(对于狭窄幽闭处所如电梯、洞穴或煤矿坑等的恐惧症).

clavi·chord /'klævɪkɔːd; 'klævɪˌkɔrd/ *n* stringed

instrument with a keyboard, predecessor of the piano. 古钢琴(有键盘之弦乐器, 为钢琴之前身).

clav·icle /'klævɪkl; 'klævəkl/ *n* (anat) collar-bone. (解剖) 锁骨. ⇨ the illus at **skeleton** 参看 skeleton 之插图.

claw /klɔː; klɔ/ *n* **1** one of the pointed nails on the feet of some animals, reptiles and birds; foot with such nails. (某些兽类、爬虫类及鸟类足上的)爪; 有爪之足. ⇨ the illus at **bird**. 参看 bird 之插图. **2** pincers of a shell-fish (eg a lobster). (甲壳类如龙虾的)螯. ⇨ the illus at **crustacean**. 参看 crustacean 之插图. **3** instrument or device like a ~ (eg a steel hook on a machine for lifting things). 似爪之工具(如吊物机之钢抓钩). '~-**hammer** *n* hammer with one end of the head bent and divided for pulling nails out of wood. (一端略弯中间有缝可自木中拔钉之)羊角锤; 拔钉锤. □ *vi, vt* [VP3A, 6A, 15B] ~ *at;* ~ *(back),* (try to) get hold of, pull, scratch, with ~s or hands. (用爪或手)抓; 撕; 扯; 搔. Hence, 由此产生, '~-**back** *n* (colloq) regaining sth with effort and persistence. (口) 努力复得某事物.

clay /kleɪ; kle/ *n* [U] stiff, sticky earth that becomes hard when baked; material from which bricks, pots, earthenware, etc are made: 粘土; 陶土 (经烘焙即变硬, 为制砖、钵、陶器等之材料): (attrib) (用作定语) ~ *soil.* 粘质土壤; *a ~ pipe,* tobacco pipe made of white ~. 白粘土制的烟斗; 陶制烟斗. ~**ey** /'kleɪ; 'kle·ɪ/ *adj* of, like, containing, covered with, ~. 粘土的; 似粘土的; 内含或覆盖着粘土的.

clean[1] /kliːn; klin/ *adj* **(-er, -est) 1** free from dirt: 清洁的; 无污垢的: ~ *hands;* 清洁的手; 白白; ~ *air,* free from smoke; 清洁(无烟)的空气; *a ~ bomb,* atomic or hydrogen bomb that, it is claimed, explodes without fall-out. 净弹(据称爆炸后无原子尘之原子弹或氢弹). ⇨ **fall**[2] **(14).** *Keep the classroom ~.* 保持教室清洁. *Wash it ~.* 把它洗干净. **2** not yet used; fresh: 尚未用过的; 新鲜的; 干净的: *Put some ~* (eg after having been washed) *sheets on the bed.* 铺一些干净的(如刚洗过的)褥单在床上. *Give me a ~ sheet of paper.* 给我一张没有用过的纸. **3** pure; innocent; free from wrong-doing or indecency: 纯洁的; 清白的; 无犯过或下流行为的; 无邪料的: *a ~ joke.* 一则干净(不下流)的笑话. *You must lead a ~ life.* 你必须过纯洁的生活. *He has a ~ record,* is not known to have done wrong. 他的记录清白(从无犯罪行为). *Keep the party ~,* (colloq) Don't use bad language or tell improper stories. (口)不要说下流的话或不道德的故事. **4** well-formed; of good shape: 整齐的; 好看的; 形式美观的: *a motorcar / ship with ~ lines.* 外貌美观的汽车(船). '~-'**limbed** *adj* having well-shaped limbs. 四肢的样子好看的; 姿态优美的; 手足匀称的. **5** even; regular; with a smooth edge or surface: 匀称的; 规则的; 边缘或表面光滑的: *A sharp knife makes a ~ cut.* 快刀切得干净俐落. *C~ timber has no knots in it.* 光洁的木料没有节疤. **6** skilful; smart: 技术熟练的; 干净俐落的: *a ~ boxer,* 技术熟练的拳击手; (cricket) (板球) ~ *fielding;* 技巧的接球; *a ~ stroke / blow.* 干净俐落的一击. **7** having ~ habits: 有清洁习惯的; 爱清洁的: *a ~ cat.* 爱清洁的猫. **8** fit for food: 可食的; ~ */un~ animals,* those that are / are not considered fit for food (by religious custom). (按宗教习俗)被认为可食(不可食)的动物. **9** thorough, complete. 彻底的; 完全的. *make a ~ sweep of,* ⇨ **sweep**[1](1). ⇨ also **breast** and **slate**(2). □ *adv* completely; entirely: 完全地; 全然: *I ~ forgot about it.* 我完全忘记它了. *The bullet went ~ through his shoulder.* 枪弹同穿过他的肩膀. *come ~,* make a full confession. 全部供认. ˌ~-'**bowled** *adj* (cricket) bowled with no possibility of doubt. (板球) 毫无疑问地被投出场的. ˌ~-'**cut** *adj* sharply and pleasingly outlined: 轮廓鲜明可爱的: ~-*cut features.* 轮廓鲜明可爱的脸庞. ˌ~-'**living** *adj* chaste. 纯洁的. ˌ~-'**shaven** *adj* with the hair of the face shaved off; not having a moustache or beard. 脸面修得干净的; 不留胡髭的.

clean² /kli:n; klin/ *vt, vi* **1** [VP6A] make clean (of dirt, etc): 弄干净; 使清洁 (使无污垢等): *Wash your hands and ~ your nails.* 洗你的手并把指甲弄干净。*I must have this suit ~ed,* sent to the dry-cleaner's. 我必须把这套衣服送去(干洗店)干洗。⇨ **dry¹(12).** *C~ your shoes before you come into the house,* ie remove the mud, etc. 在进入屋内以前请把鞋子弄干净。⇨ **brush, polish. 2** [VP2A] *A porcelain sink ~s easily,* is easy to ~. 瓷水槽容易弄清洁。**3** [VP15B, 2C] (special uses with *adverbial particles* and *preps*): (与副词性小品词及介词连用之特殊用法): **~ *sth down,*** ~ by brushing or wiping: 清扫; 刷干净; 擦干净: *~ down the walls.* 把墙上的尘土扫下。**~ *sb out,*** win or take all the money from ~: 赢得或取去~的全部金钱: *They really ~ed me out at Las Vegas,* I lost all my money gambling there. 我在拉斯韦加斯把所有的钱全输光了。**~ *sth out,*** ~ the inside of, remove dirt, dust, etc from: 打扫某物之内部; 扫除某物上之尘土等: *It's time you ~ed out your bedroom.* 现在该是你打扫卧室的时候了。**be ~ed out,** (colloq) have no money left. (口)一文不名。**~ *up,*** make clean or tidy; put in order: 打扫清洁或收拾整齐; 整理: *You should always ~ up after a picnic,* burn wastepaper, collect litter, empty bottles, etc. 野餐过后你一定要收拾干净(烧掉废纸, 收拾杂物, 空瓶等)。**~ *sth up,* (a)** get rid of criminal and immoral elements, etc: 清除罪犯和不道德的份子等; 整顿(某事物): *The mayor has decided to ~ up the city,* end corruption, etc. 市长已决定要整顿市政(清除贪污等)。**(b)** (colloq) make money (as gain or profit). (口)赚(钱); 获(利)。**'~-up** *n* (esp) (process of) ending or reducing crime, corruption, etc. (尤指)清除或减少犯罪、腐化作等; 整顿。□ *n* ~ing: *Give it a good ~,* ~ it well. 把它好好地清洁清洁。**~er** *n* person or thing that ~s; tool, machine, etc for ~ing; substance that removes dirt, stains, grease, etc: 做清洁工作的人或物; 打扫清洁的工具、机器等; 洗濯污垢、污渍、油渍等之物质; 清洁器; 吸尘器; 清洁剂; 洗涤剂: *send/take a suit to the (dry) ~'s,* 把一套衣服送去(干洗)洗衣店去; *'window-~er;* 擦窗门的工人; *'vacuum-~er.* 真空吸尘器。

cleanly¹ /'klenlɪ; 'klɛnlɪ/ *adj* **(-ier,-iest)** habitually clean; having clean habits: 经常干净的; 有清洁习惯的; 爱清洁的: *Are cats ~ animals?* 猫是爱清洁的动物吗? **clean·li·ness** /'klenlɪnəs; 'klɛnlɪnəs/ *n* [U] being clean. 干净; 清洁。

cleanly² /'kli:nlɪ; 'klinlɪ/ *adv* exactly; sharply; neatly: 正确地; 清清楚楚地; 干净利落地; 整洁地: *This knife doesn't cut ~.* 这把刀子切起来不利落。*He caught the ball ~,* without fumbling. 他干净俐落地接住了那个球。

cleanse /klenz; klɛnz/ *vt* [VP6A] (formal or archaic) make thoroughly clean; make pure (正式用语或古语)彻底清洁; 使纯洁; 涤净: *~ of/from sin.* 清除…的罪。**~r** *n* [C, U] substance that ~s: 使彻底清洁的东西(如合成的清洁剂): *a synthetic detergent.* 洗涤剂。

clear¹ /klɪə(r); klɪr/ *adj* **1** easy to see through: 清澈的; 清澈的; 容易看穿的: *~ glass;* 透明的玻璃; *the ~ water of a mountain lake;* 清澈的高山湖水; free from cloud: 无云的; 晴朗的: *a ~ sky;* 晴朗无云的天空; bright, pure: 光明的; 纯净的: *a ~ light;* 亮光; *a ~ fire,* burning without much smoke; 明亮的火(没有很多烟); distinct; easily seen: 清晰的; 容易看清楚的: *a ~ outline ~ in the morning sky;* 衬托在清晨天空中清晰可见的一排山峦; *a ~ photograph;* 照得很清楚的相片; *a ~ reflection in the water.* 映在水中清楚的倒影。**2** free from guilt or blame: 无愧疚的; 清白的: *a ~ conscience,* knowledge that one is innocent. 清白的良心; 问心无愧。**3** (of sounds, etc) easily heard; distinct; pure: (指声音等)清晰可闻的; 响亮的; 清纯的: *a ~ voice;* 嘹亮的嗓音; *the ~ note of a bell;* 清晰的钟声; *speak so that one's words are ~.* 咬字清楚地说。**4** ~ (about), (of or to the mind) free from doubt or difficulty: (指心智和对于心智)明白无疑的; 不难懂的: *a ~ thinker/statement.* 条理清晰的思想家(陈

述). *My memory is not ~ about/on that point.* 关于此点我的记忆已不清楚了。*It was ~ (to everyone) that the war would not end quickly.* 人人都明白战争不会很快结束。**make oneself/one's meaning ~,** make oneself understood: 使自己(自己的意思)让人明白: *Now, do I make myself ~?* 现在, (你们)明白我了吗? **,~-'headed,** having good understanding. 头脑清楚的; 理解力强的。**,~-'sighted,** able to see, think, understand well. 目力好的; 有眼光的; 有见识的。**5 ~ (of),** easy or safe to pass along; free from obstacles, dangers, etc: 通行容易或安全的; 无障碍、危险等的: *Is the road ~?* 这条路畅通吗? *The coast is ~,* (fig) There is no one about (so one can escape, etc). (喻)毫无阻碍(可以逃走等); 可放心而为; 是行动的好机会。*Is the sea ~ of ice yet?* 海上的浮冰消失了吗? *The signal 'All ~' was sounded,* eg after an air raid, to inform people that the raiders had left. '解除'警报响过了(如在空袭过后通知人民敌机已去)。**'~-way** *n* (in GB) section of the public highway on which vehicles must not stop or park. (在英国)畅通道(公路车道上禁止行车停止或停放的一段道路)。**6 ~ (about),** confident; certain: 有把握的; 确知的: *I want to be quite ~ on this point.* 关于这一点我要完全弄清楚。*I am not ~ as to what you expect me to do.* 我不明白你期望我做什么。**7 ~ (of),** free from debt, suspicion, a charge): 偿务已清偿的; 嫌疑已释除的; 已证明无所控之罪的: *I wish I were ~ of debt.* 但愿我的债已还清。*You are now ~ of suspicion.* 现在你的嫌疑已澄清。**8** complete: 完全的; 整个的: *for three ~ days;* 整整三天; without limitations; with nothing (to be) deducted: 无限制的; 不折不扣的; 净得的; 十足的: *a ~ profit of £5;* 五英镑之净利; *passed by a ~ majority of ten.* 以足足超过十票之多数通过。□ *n in the ~,* free from suspicion, danger, etc. 无嫌疑、危险等的。**~ness** *n* [U] state of being ~; clarity: 明显; 明晰; 清晰度; 清澈: *~ness of the atmosphere;* 大气之清晰度; *~ness of vision.* 视力清楚; 视力敏锐。

clear² /klɪə(r); klɪr/ *adv* **1** distinctly: 清楚地; 明白地: *speak loud and ~.* 说话声音响亮而清楚。**,~-'cut** *adv* well defined; distinct; having ~ outlines: 措词清楚的; 明显的; 轮廓清晰的: *~-cut ideas/plans.* 清楚的观念(计划)。**2** quite; completely: 十分地; 完全地: *The prisoner got ~ away.* 该囚犯逃得无踪无影。**3 ~ (of),** without touching; at or to a distance: 分离地; 不接触地; 有距离地: *He jumped three inches ~ of the bar.* 他以超过三英寸的高度跳过竿去。*Stand ~ of the gates of the lift.* 要与电梯门离开一些站着。**keep/stay ~ of,** avoid; have nothing to do with: 避开; 不与…来往: *You should keep ~ of that fellow.* 你不应与那家伙来往。*You should keep ~ of alcohol if you're driving.* 驾车时不应饮酒。

clear³ /klɪə(r); klɪr/ *vt, vi* **1** [VP6A, 14] **~ *sth (of/ from),*** remove, get rid of, what is unwanted or unwelcome: 清除; 清理: *~ the streets of snow/~ snow from the streets;* 清除街上的积雪; *~ a canal of obstructions/~ obstructions from a canal;* 清除运河中的障碍物; *~ a desk,* of papers, etc; 清理书桌(把文件等收拾整齐起来); *~ the table,* after a meal; 收拾餐桌(指餐后收拾餐桌上的餐具); *~ land of trees,* esp before cultivation; (尤指耕种前之)砍去树木开拓土地; *~ one's mind of doubt;* 释除心中的疑虑; *~ oneself (of a charge),* prove one's innocence. 证明自己无所控之罪嫌。**~ the air,** ⇨ **air¹(1).** **~ the decks (for action),** get a ship ready for a fight; (fig) make ready for any kind of struggle or activity. 清戒备战(清除甲板上的障碍物以备作战); (喻)准备奋斗; (为任何活动)作准备。**~ one's throat,** eg by coughing. 清嗓子(如借轻咳)。**2** [VP6A] get past or over without touching: 通过或越过而未触及; *The winner ~ed six feet,* jumped this without touching the bar. 得胜者剧落地跃过六英尺(高的横杆)。*Can your horse ~ that hedge?* 你的马能例落地跃过那树篱吗? *Our car only just ~ed the gatepost.* 我们的汽车差一点就碰着门柱了。*Jack up that wheel until it ~s* (= no longer

rests on) *the ground*. 用千斤顶把那个轮子顶起，直到它完全离地为止。**3** [VP6A] make as a net gain or profit: 净赚; 获净利: ~ *£50;* 净赚五十英镑; ~ *expenses,* make enough money to cover them. 赚的钱足够开销。**4** [VP6A] get (a ship or its cargo) free by doing what is necessary (signing papers, paying dues, etc) on entering or leaving a port: 为(船或船货)办清手续(如签署文件、缴纳关税等): ~ *goods through customs,* deal with requirements of the customs ('eg by paying any necessary duties) 为货物办清通过海关的手续(如按照海关规定，如缴税等); leave (a port) after doing this. 手续办清驶离(港口)。办清结完手续出(港)。**5** [VP6A] pass a cheque／bill of exchange etc through a clearing-house. 使支票(票据等)通过票据交换所。**6** [VP15B, 2C] (special uses with *adverbial particles* and *preps*): (与副词连用之特殊用法):

clear away, pass away: 消散; 消失: *The clouds have* ~*ed away.* 云已消散。~ *sth away,* take away, get rid of: 拿去; 收起; 清除: ~ *away the tea-things.* 把茶具收起。**4** *clear off,* (colloq, of a person) go away; get rid of:(口,指人)离去; 除去: *they* ~*ed off／we* ~*ed them off fast.* 他们离开了(我们迅速把他们打发了)。~ *sth off,* get rid of, make an end of: 除去; 清除; 结束: ~ *off a debt;* 清偿债务; ~ *off arrears of work.* 做完积压的工作。

clear out, (colloq) go away; leave: (口)离去; 走开; 溜走: *The police are after you, you'd better* ~ *out!* 警察在追踪你, 你最好溜吧! ~ *sth out,* empty, make clear by taking out the contents of: 使空; 清除内含之物: ~ *out a drain／a cupboard.* 清除水沟(食橱)中的污物。*All these hospital expenses have* ~*ed me out,* (colloq) have left me without money. (口)所有这些医院费用花掉了我所有的钱。*clear up,* become clear: (天气)变晴: *The weather／The sky is* ~*ing up.* 天气变晴了(天空朗了)。~ *sth up,* **(a)** put in order, make tidy: 清理某事物; 整理: *C*~ *up your desk before you leave the office.* 在离开办公室以前, 请把你的桌子整理一下。*Who's going to* ~ *up the mess?* 谁来负责清理这些乱七八糟的东西? **(b)** make clear; solve (a mystery, etc): 说明; 解决; 解明(神秘之事物等): ~ *up a difficulty／misunderstanding.* 解决困难(澄清误会)。

clear·ance /'klɪərəns; 'klɪrəns/ *n* **1** clearing up, removing, making tidy: 清理; 清洁; 清除: *a* ~ *sale,* a sale to clear out unwanted or superfluous stocks of goods. 出清存货大减价。*You've made a tremendous* ~ *in the flat,* made it tidy, etc by getting rid of what was unwanted. 你已把这公寓做了一番大扫除。**2** [C, U] free space; space between, for moving past: 余地; (某物经过另一物时两者之间的)间隙; 空间: *a* ~ *of only two feet,* eg for a ship moving through a canal. 仅有二英尺的余地(如通过运河之船两侧之余地)。*There is not much／not enough* ~ *for large lorries passing under this bridge.* 没有足够的空间供大卡车在此桥下通过。**3** (certificate of) clearing a ship, ⇨ **clear³ (4).** (指进出港口船只之) 结关手续; 结关单; 结关证书; 出(入)港船照。

clear·ing /'klɪərɪŋ; 'klɪrɪŋ/ *n* open space from which trees have been cleared in a forest. 森林中伐去一片树木所成之空地。'~**-house,** office at which banks exchange chiques, etc and settle accounts, the balance being paid in cash. 票据交换所(各银行在此交换支票等, 结算帐目, 差额付现)。

clear·ly /'klɪəlɪ; 'klɪrlɪ/ *adv* **1** distinctly: 清楚地; 明白地: *speak* ~; 说话清楚; *state one's facts* ~. 把事实说明白。*It is too dark to see* ~. 天太黑看不清楚。**2** obviously; undoubtedly: 显然地; 无疑地: *'Was he mistaken?' 'C*~.' '他错了吗?' '他显然无疑问。'

cleat /kliːt; klit/ *n* **1** strip of wood, etc fastened to a gangway, etc to prevent slipping. 钉于梯口等上以防滑倒之木条等。**2** piece of wood, metal, etc bolted on to sth, on which ropes may be fastened (by winding). 固定某物上可以栓绳之木桩(或金属等制之桩); 系绳栓; 系索扣。**3** piece of material fastened to the underside of a shoe or boot (eg for football) to prevent slipping. (贴于

鞋或靴底上, 如足球鞋鞋底上的)防滑片。**4** V-shaped wedge. 楔子; 三角木。

cleav·age /'kliːvɪdʒ; 'klivɪdʒ/ *n* split or division; direction in which sth tends to split or divide; place where there is a split or cleft; (colloq) the cleft between a woman's breasts as seen above a low neckline of a dress. 劈开; 劈裂; 分裂; 趋于劈裂的方向; 裂开之处; 裂痕; (口)(女人两乳房之间的)乳沟(穿低领女装时所见者)。

cleave¹ /kliːv; kliv/ *vt, vi* (*pt* **clove** /kləʊv; klov/, **cleft** /kleft; kleft/ or **cleaved** /kliːvd; klivd/, *pp* **cloven** /'kləʊvn; 'kloven/, **cleft** or **cleaved**) **1** [VP 6A, 22, 15A, B] cut into two (with a blow from a heavy axe, etc); split: 用大斧等)劈成两半: ~ *a block of wood in two;* 将一木头劈成两半; ~ *a man's head open with a sword.* 一剑劈开人头。**2** [VP2A] come apart; split: 裂开; 分裂: *This wood* ~*s easily.* 这种木材容易裂缝。**3** [VP6A, 14] ~ **(through),** make by cutting: 劈出; 砍成: ~ *one's way through the crowd;* 在人群中辟开一条路而前进; ~ *a path through the jungle.* 在丛林中砍伐出一条路。*in a cleft stick,* (fig) in a tight place where neither advance nor retreat is possible. (喻) 处于进退两难之境。'**cleft 'palate** a malformation in the roof of the mouth because the two sides of the palate did not join before birth. 裂腭(上腭分为两半, 系由先天发育不全而形成的一种口腔畸形)。**cloven 'hoof** a divided hoof of an ox, a sheep, a goat (and a devil). 分趾蹄; 偶蹄(如牛、羊、恶魔之蹄)。

cleave² /kliːv; kliv/ *vi* (*pt* ~**d** or, old use, 旧用法, **clave** /kleɪv; klev/ *pp* ~**d**) [VP3A] ~ *to,* stick fast to; (fig) be faithful to. 固守; (喻)忠于。

cleaver /'kliːvə(r); 'klivɚ/ *n* heavy knife used by a butcher for chopping up meat. 屠夫用以切肉的大砍刀。

clef /klef; klɛf/ *n* (music) symbol placed at the beginning of a stave to show the pitch of the notes. (音乐)(置于谱表之首的)谱号; 音部记号。⇨ the illus at **notation.** 参看 notation 之插图。

cleft¹ /kleft; kleft/ *n* crack or split (eg in the ground or in rock); opening made by a cleavage. 裂痕; 裂缝(例如地上或岩石中者); 裂开; 裂口。

cleft² /kleft; kleft/ *pt, pp* of **cleave¹.**

cle·ma·tis /'klemətɪs; 'klɛmətɪs/ *n* [U] (kinds of) climbing plant with white, yellow or purple flowers. 铁线莲; 女萝属(攀缘类植物, 开白、黄或紫色花); 铁线莲。

clem·ency /'klemənsɪ; 'klɛmənsɪ/ *n* [U] (formal) mercy; mildness (of temper or weather). (正式用语)仁慈; 温和(指性情或天气)。

clem·ent /'klemənt; 'klɛmənt/ *adj* (formal) showing mercy; (of the weather, a person's temper) mild. (正式用语)仁慈的; (指天气或人的脾气)温和的。

clench /klentʃ; klɛntʃ/ *vt* **1** [VP6A] press firmly together, close tightly: 紧握; 紧闭: ~ *one's teeth／jaws;* 咬紧牙关; ~ *one's fingers／fist;* 紧握拳头; ~ *ed-fist* salute. 握拳敬礼。**2** [VP14] grasp firmly: 抓紧; 抓牢: ~ *sth in／with one's hand(s).* 用手抓紧某物。**3** = **clinch.**

clere·story /'klɪəstɔːrɪ; 'klɪr,stɔrɪ/ *n* (*pl* **-ries**) upper part of a wall in a large church, with windows in it above the aisle roofs. (大教堂内高于侧廊之顶的)高窗(为墙之连窗的上部)。⇨ the illus at **church.** 参看 church 之插图。

clergy /'klɜːdʒɪ; 'klɝdʒɪ/ *n* (collective *n* with *pl v*) persons ordained as priests or ministers of the Christian Church: (集合名词, 用复数动词) 基督教会正式任命的神父或牧师; 教士; 圣职人员: *Thirty of the* ~ *were present at the ceremony.* 牧师有三十人参加典礼。*The* ~ *are opposed to the plan.* 牧师们反对该计划。'~**-man／-men;** **-men/** *n* (*pl* **-men**) (not used of a bishop) ordained minister, esp of the Church of England. (不用以指主教)正式任命的牧师(尤指英国国教者)。

cleric /'klerɪk; 'klɛrɪk/ *n* clergyman. 牧师; 神父; 教士; 圣职人员。

cleri·cal /'klerɪkl; 'klɛrɪkl/ *adj* **1** of the clergy: 牧师

的; 神父的; 教士的; 圣职人员的: ~ *dress;* 牧师服; *a ~ collar.* 神父的硬领。 **2** of, for, made by, a clerk or clerks(1): 办事员的; 书记的: *'~ work;* 办事员的工作; *a ~ error,* one made in copying or writing. 抄写的错误; 笔误。

cleri·hew /'klerɪhjuː; 'klɛrəhju/ n witty or nonsensical piece of verse, usu two rhyming couplets of varying length. 诙谐的或无意义的短诗(通常为四行时, 每两行押韵, 每行长短不一)。

clerk /klɑːk *US:* klɜːrk; kləːk/ n **1** person employed in a bank, office, shop, etc to keep records and accounts, copy letters, etc: 银行、办公室、商店等所雇用的)办事员; 书记(保管案卷、帐册、抄写信件等): *a 'bank ~;* 银行办事员; *a ,corre'spondence ~.* 管来往信件的办事员。 **2** officer in charge of records, etc: 负责管理档案等之官员: *the Town C~;* 市政府秘书; *the C~ to the Council,* (usu a lawyer); 议会秘书(通常为律师); *~ of the works,* having charge of materials, etc for building done by contract. 工程管理员(掌管包工之建筑材料者)。 **3** (US) shop-assistant; salesman or saleswoman. (美)商店的店员。 **4** (formal or legal): (正式或法律用语): ~ *in holy orders,* clergyman. 牧师; 教士。 **5** lay officer of the church with various duties: 教会中非僧职的执事(管理杂务者): *the parish ~.* 教区执事。 **6** (old use) person who can read and write: (旧用法)能识字写字的人: *I'm no great ~,* am not much good at writing. 我不大会写字。 □ vi (US only) work as a ~ (3). (仅用于美国)做店员。

clever /'klevə(r); 'klɛvə/ adj **(-er, -est) 1** quick in learning and understanding things; skilful: 聪明的; 敏于学习和了解的; 伶俐的; 有技巧的: *He's a ~* at arithmetic /at making excuses. 他在算术(找借口)方面很聪明。 *How ~ of you to do that!* 你会做那个可真聪明啊! *He's a ~* workman. 他是个有技巧的工人。 **2** (of things done) showing ability and skill: (指做成之事物)显示能力和技巧的: *a ~ speech /book.* 巧妙的演说(书)。 **3** nimble: 灵活的; 敏捷的: ~ *fingers.* 灵活的手指。 **4** smart: 机敏的; 精明的: *He was too ~ for us,* he outwitted us. 他太精明了, 我们斗不过他。 ~**·ly** adv ~**·ness** n

clew /kluː; klu/ n (naut) metal loop attached to the lower corner of a sail; loop holding the strings of a hammock. (航海)附连于船帆下角的金属环; 吊床上穿绳用的金属环。 □ vt (also *clue*) (naut) haul (a sail) up or down. (航海)扯(帆); 上(帆); 下(帆)。

cliché /'kliːʃeɪ *US:* kliːʃeɪ; kliʃe/ n [C] idea or expression that has been too much used and is now out-dated; stereotyped phrase: 陈腔滥调; 陈腐的话; 老套: *a ~-ridden newspaper article.* 满篇陈腔滥调的报纸文章。

click¹ /klɪk; klɪk/ vi, vt, n [VP6A, 2A] (make, or cause to make, a) short, sharp sound (like that of a key turning in a lock): (发, 使发)喀搭声; 滴答声(似钥匙开锁之声): *The door ~ed shut.* 门喀搭一声关上。 *The soldier ~ed his heels and saluted.* 那兵两足跟喀搭一声立正敬礼。 *Some African languages contain several ~s,* ~ing sounds. 有些非洲语言含满喀嘭之音。

click² /klɪk; klɪk/ vi [VP2A] (sl; not US) strike up an acquaintance, become friends, at once. (俚; 不用于美国)刚一认识就成了朋友; 很易如故。

cli·ent /'klaɪənt; 'klaɪənt/ n **1** person who gets help or advice from a lawyer or any professional man: (律师或专门职业的)当事人; 委托人: *a successful lawyer with hundreds of ~s.* 一个生意兴隆、拥有数以百计委托人的律师。 **2** customer (at a shop). (商店的)顾客。 **cli·en·tele** /,kliːən'tel *US:* ,klaɪən-; ,klaɪən'tɛl/ n (collective) customers; patrons of a restaurant, theatre, etc. (集合名词)顾客; 餐馆、戏院等之老主顾。

cliff /klɪf; klɪf/ n steep face of rock, esp at the edge of the sea. 悬崖; 峭壁; 绝壁(尤指海边者)。 '~**-hanger** n episode in a story or contest of which the end is uncertain, so that the reader or spectator is held in suspense. 吊人胃口的故事情节或比赛(因结局不明而令读者或观众疑虑悬者); 悬疑。

cli·mac·ter·ic /klaɪ'mæktərɪk; klaɪˈmæktɪrɪk/ n critical turning-point in (the body's) physical development. 更年期; 断经期。

cli·mac·tic /klaɪ'mæktɪk; klaɪ'mæktɪk/ adj forming a climax. 形成高潮的。

cli·mate /'klaɪmɪt; 'klaɪmɪt/ n **1** weather conditions of a place or area; conditions of temperature, rainfall, wind, etc. 气候(某一地区之天气状况)温度、雨量、风等之状况)。 **2** area or region with certain weather conditions: 具有某种气候之区域: *A drier ~ would be good for her health.* 气候较干爽的地区会对她的健康有益。 **3** prevailing condition: 普遍的情形; 一般的趋势: *the political ~;* 政坛上的一般情况; ~ *of opinion,* general attitude of people to an aspect of life, policy, etc. 民意趋向(一般人民对于生活之某一方面、政策等之态度)。 **cli·mat·ic** /klaɪ'mætɪk; klaɪ'mætɪk/ adj of ~. 气候的; 具有某种气候之地区的。 **cli·mati·cally** /-klɪ, -klɪ/ adv **cli·ma·tol·ogy** /,klaɪmə'tɒlədʒɪ; ,klaɪmə'tɑlədʒi/ n [U] science of ~. 气候学。

cli·max /'klaɪmæks; 'klaɪmæks/ n event, point, of greatest interest or intensity (eg in a story or drama): 顶点; 极点; 高潮(如故事或戏剧中最有趣或最紧张的地方): *bring matters to a ~;* 使事态发展到高潮; *work up to a ~;* 逐渐发展到顶点; *as a ~ to the day's entertainment.* 作为一天游艺活动之高潮。 □ vt, vi bring or come to a ~. (使)达到顶点或高潮。

climb /klaɪm; klaɪm/ vt, vi [VP6A, 2A, C] go or get up (a tree, wall, rope, mountain, etc) or down; (of aircraft) go higher, gain height; (of plants) grow upwards by turning round a support, or with the support of tendrils, etc; rise by effort in social rank, position, etc: 攀登; 攀爬; 爬上(树、墙、绳索、山等)或爬下; (指飞机)爬升; 升高; (指植物)盘绕支架向上生长或借卷须攀升生长; 因努力而在社会等级、职位等方面高升: ~ *a tree;* 爬树; ~ *up/down a tree;* 爬上(下)树; ~ *a wall;* 爬墙; ~ *over a wall.* 爬过墙。 *Monkeys ~ well.* 猴子善于攀爬。 ~ *down,* (fig) admit that one has been mistaken, unreasonable, boastful, etc. (喻)自认错误、无理、夸大等; 屈服; 认输; 让步。 Hence, 由此产生, '~**-down** n such an admission. 认错; 认输; 屈服; 让步。 '~**ing irons** n spikes (to be) fastened to the boots for ~ing trees, ice-slopes, etc. 系于鞋底以便爬树、爬冰坡等之铁钉; 攀树器。 □ n ~ing; place (to be) ~ed: 攀登; 攀登之地; 被攀登之地: *a hard ~.* 艰难的攀登。 *Have you done that ~?* 你已攀登过那个地方吗? ~**er** n person who tries to advance socially; ~ing plant. 攀登者; 爬山者; 在社会中努力求高升者; 钻求更高社会地位的人; 攀缘植物。

clime /klaɪm; klaɪm/ n (poet) climate(2). (诗)具有某种气候之地区。

clinch /klɪntʃ; klɪntʃ/ vt, vi **1** [VP6A] make (a nail or rivet) fast by hammering sideways the end that protrudes. 横着锤击突出在外的钉头以使(钉子)牢固; 将钉头弯曲或敲平以使(钉子)牢固。 **2** [VP6A] settle (a bargain, an argument) conclusively: 确定地解决或成功(交易、议论): *That ~es the argument,* ends all doubt. 那就澄清了这项议论(结束了一切疑问)。 **3** [VP2A] (boxing) come to grips, with one or both arms round the opponent's body: (拳击)(以一臂或两臂搂抱对方身体)扭在一起; 互相扭住: *The boxers ~ed and the referee intervened.* 拳击者互扭在一起, 裁判即以阻止。 □ n (boxing) the act, an instance, of ~ing: (拳击)互相扭抱: *get into a ~;* 互相扭抱在一起; *break a ~;* 摆脱扭抱; 将互扭在一起的两人分开; (colloq) embrace. (口)拥抱。 ~**er** n (colloq) ~ing argument. (口)颠扑不破的论据。

cline /klaɪn; klaɪn/ n graded sequence of differences. 分类差异序列; 族群相。 ⇨ **continuum**。

cling /klɪŋ; klɪŋ/ vi(pt, pp clung /klʌŋ; klʌŋ/) [VP2C, 3A] ~ *to/together,* hold tight; resist separation: 坚守; 固执; 抱紧; 抓紧; 坚拒分开: ~ *to one's possessions;* 坚守自己的财产不肯放弃; ~ *to a hope of*

being rescued. 坚定地抱着获救的希望。*They clung together when the time came to part.* 分离的时候到了，他们紧抱着不肯分开。*The ship clung to* (= did not go far from) *the coast.* 这船紧靠着海岸航行。*The child clung to its mother's skirt/garments.* 那孩子紧紧地抓着他妈妈的裙子(衣服)。*She's the ~ing sort,* is prone to depend upon others. 她是缠人不放那一类型的女人(易于依附他人者)。'~**·ing clothes** *n* showing the shape or outline of the body or limbs. 紧箍在身上的衣服;曲线毕露的衣服。

cli·nic /'klɪnɪk; 'klɪnɪk/ *n* **1** (part of a) hospital or institution where medical advice and treatment are given and where students are taught through observation of cases; teaching so given; class of students taught in this way. (供学生作临床观察的)教学医院或医疗机构; 临床教学; 接受临床教学的一班学生。**2** medical establishment for a specified purpose: 诊所; 门诊所: *a 'birth-control ~;* 节制生育诊所; *an ˌante-'natal ~;* 产前诊所; *an a'bortion ~.* 流产诊所。

cli·ni·cal /'klɪnɪkl; 'klɪnɪkl/ *adj* **1** (of medical teaching given) at the hospital bedside: (指医科教学)临床的; 临床教学的: *~ thermometer,* one for measuring the temperature of the body. 体温计。**2** objective(2); uninvolved: 客观的; 未牵扯在内的: *~ judgement.* 客观的判断。

clink[1] /klɪŋk; klɪŋk/ *vi, vt, n* [VP6A, 2A, C] (make, or cause to make) sound of small bits of metal, glass, etc knocking together: (发出, 使发出)小片金属、玻璃等互相碰撞之声音; 叮玲声: *the ~ of keys/glasses.* 钥匙(玻璃杯)碰击之叮玲声。*They ~ed glasses,* brought their glasses together before drinking each other's health. 他们碰杯互祝健康。

clink[2] /klɪŋk; klɪŋk/ *n* (sl) prison: (俚)监牢: *be in ~;* 坐牢; *be put in ~;* 被关入狱; *go to ~.* 入狱。

clinker /'klɪŋkə(r); 'klɪŋkɚ/ *n* [C, U] (piece of the) mass of rough, hard, slag-like material left in a stove, furnace, etc after coal has been burned. (煤在火炉、熔炉等中燃烧后所留下的)渣滓; 熔渣; 熔块。

clinker-built /'klɪŋkə bɪlt; 'klɪŋkɚˌbɪlt/ *adj* (of boats) made with the outside planks or metal plates overlapping downwards. (指船)外侧之木板或金属板向下迭接的; 鱼鳞迭接的。

clip[1] /klɪp; klɪp/ *n* [C] **1** wire or metal device for holding things (eg papers) together. 金属丝或金属所制夹物之具(例如夹纸者); 夹子; 回形针; 两脚针。**2** holder (with loops) for cartridges (to be used in a magazine rifle). (带有圈套的)弹夹(用于装弹夹之步枪中)。□ *vt, vi* (**-pp-**) [VP6A, 15B, 2C] put or keep together with a ~ or ~s: 用夹子夹在一起: ~ *papers together;* 把文件夹在一起; ~ *one paper to another.* 把一件文件跟另一件文件夹在一起。'**~-on** *adj* (attrib) that can be attached with a ~: (用作定语)用夹子夹住的: *a ~-on tie/brooch.* 可用夹子夹戴的领带(花别针)。

clips

clip[2] /klɪp; klɪp/ *vt* (**-pp-**) **1** [VP6A, 22, 15A, B] cut with scissors or shears; make short or neat; cut off wool from (a sheep, etc): 用剪刀剪; 剪短; 剪整齐; 修剪; 自(绵羊等身上)剪下羊毛: ~ *a hedge;* 修剪树篱; ~ *a bird's wings;* 剪短鸟翼; ~ *sb's wings,* (fig) prevent him from doing what he is ambitious to do. (喻)阻止某人实现其野心; 断其双翼。~ *sth out (of),* remove by ~ping:(自…)剪下某物: ~ *an article out of a newspaper.* 自报纸上剪下一篇文章; 剪报。'**~-joint** *n* (US sl) club that overcharges; business that defrauds. (美俚)敲竹杠的俱乐部或夜总会; 欺骗顾客的场所。**2** [VP6A] omit or

abbreviate (esp the end of) sounds of (words). 省略或简略(字)中之音(尤指尾音)。**3** [VP6A] punch a hole in (a bus, tram or train ticket). 在(公共汽车、电车或火车票)上剪洞。**4** (sl) hit or punch sharply: (俚)猛击; 猛打: ~ *sb's ear;* 打某人的耳光; ~ *sb on the jaw.* 打某人的下巴。□ *n* **1** operation of shearing. 剪羊毛的作业。**2** amount of wool cut from (a flock of) sheep at one time. 一次自(一群)绵羊身上所剪下羊毛之量。**3** smart blow: 痛击: *a ~ on the jaw.* 对下巴之一击。**4** (US) fast speed. (美)高速。'**~·ping** *n* (in verbal senses) (esp) sth ~ped off or out: (具有动词之各种意义)(尤指)剪下之物: *newspaper ~pings.* 报纸之剪辑; 剪报。

clip·per /'klɪpə(r); 'klɪpɚ/ *n* **1** (*pair of*) *~s,* instrument for clipping: 修剪之工具; 剪取器; 剪刀: *'hair-~s;* 理发剪; *'nail-~s.* 指甲刀。**2** sailing ship built for speed and used formerly esp in the tea-trade, ⇨ the illus at **barque;** (before jet aircraft) propeller-driven air-liner. (从前用于做茶叶生意之特建的)快速帆船(参看 barque 之插图); (喷气式飞机问世前之)螺旋桨推进的客机。

clique /kliːk; klik/ *n* group of persons united by common interests (esp in literature or art), members of which support each other and shut out others from their company. 由志同道合者(尤指文学艺术方面)所组成彼此辅助而排斥外人之派别; 私党; 朋党; 派系; 门阀。**cliquish** /'kliːkɪʃ; 'klikɪʃ/ *adj* of or like a ~; tending to form a ~. 派别的; 似派别的; 有形成派别之趋向的。

clit·oris /'klɪtərɪs; 'klaɪtərɪs/ *n* (anat) erectile organ at the upper end of the vulva, analogous to the penis. (解剖)阴蒂; 阴核(女阴上端能勃起之器官, 类似男人之阴茎)。

cloak /kləʊk; klok/ *n* loose outer garment, without sleeves; (fig) sth used to hide or keep secret: 披风; 斗篷; (喻)遮盖物; 掩饰物; 掩护物: *use business as a ~ for espionage;* 利用商业作为间谍活动的掩饰; *under the ~ of darkness.* 在黑暗的掩护下。~ *and dagger,* (used attrib) in the style of, concerning, espionage, melodramatic intrigue, etc. (用作定语)具有间谍、闹剧式密谋等之风格的; 有关间谍、闹剧式密谋等的。'**~-room** *n* place where hats, coats, parcels, etc may be left for a short time (eg in a theatre or a railway station); (euphem) lavatory. (戏院或火车站临时寄存衣帽、小包等之)衣帽间; 寄物处; (婉)厕所。□ *vt* [VP6A] (chiefly fig) conceal (thoughts, purposes, etc). (主用作喻)掩藏(思想、目的等)。

clob·ber[1] /'klɒbə(r); 'klɑbɚ/ *vt* [VP6A] (sl) (俚) **1** strike violently and repeatedly; hurt badly: 连续猛击; 痛击; 严重伤害: ~ *the taxpayer,* by heavy taxation. (以苛税)整惨纳税人。**2** defeat thoroughly; 彻底打败; 打垮: *Our team got ~ed on Saturday.* 星期六我们的球队惨败了。

clob·ber[2] /'klɒbə(r); 'klɑbɚ/ *n* (GB sl) clothing; equipment. (英俚)衣服; 装备。

cloche /klɒʃ; kloʃ/ *n* [C] **1** glass or clear plastic protection, placed in long rows over tender plants; (older use) bell-shaped glass cover for a plant. (成长排置于幼嫩植物之上借以发生保护作用之)园艺玻璃罩或透明塑胶罩; (旧用法)(用于一棵植物之)钟形玻璃罩。**2** woman's close-fitting hat. (紧套于头上之)女帽。

clock[1] /klɒk; klɑk/ *n* instrument (not carried or worn like a watch) for measuring and showing the time. 钟; 时钟; 时计(非挂表或手表)。*put the '~ back,* (**a**) move the hands of the ~ back (eg when Summer Time ends). 将时钟拨回(如于夏令时间终止时将时钟拨回标准时间)。(**b**) (fig) take reactionary measures. (喻)开倒车。*work against the ~,* work fast to finish before a certain time. 加速工作以争取时间。(*work*) *round the ~,* (work) all day and night. 日夜工作。Hence, 由此产生, ˌ**round-the-'~,** (used attrib) (用作定语): *a round-the-~ watch/guard on sth,* all day and night. 不分昼夜的监视(看守某人)。'**~-face/-dial,** surface of a ~ showing figures marking the hours, etc. (标明钟点数字

的)钟面。 **~-'golf,** game in which a golfball is putted on greens arranged in a circle. 草地高尔夫（在圆形之草地上，轻击高尔夫球之一种球戏)。 **'~-tower,** tall structure (forming part of a building, eg a church) with a ~ high up on an outside wall. 钟楼(形成建筑物之一部份，如教堂上者，其外墙上高悬一时钟)。 **'~-watching,** practice (of some workers) of thinking constantly of how soon work will end. (指某些工作者)经常挂念着何时可以下班的习气。 **'~-wise /,anti-'~wise** adj, adv moving in a curve in the same direction as/in the direction opposite to that taken by the hands of a ~. 顺时针(反时针)方向(旋转)的(地)。 **~-work,** (often attrib) mechanism with wheels and springs like a ~: (常用作定语) 有似时钟之齿轮与发条的机械： ~work toys; 有发条与齿轮的玩具； a ~work driven train; 以发条推动的玩具火车； with ~work precision; 如钟表之精确地； like ~work, smoothly, without trouble. 顺利地；无毛病地。 □ vt, vi 1 [VP6A] measure the time of; do sth (eg run a race) in a measured period of time: 计…之时; 在一段计时的时间内做某事(如赛跑): He ~ed 9.6 seconds for the 100 metres. 他一百米跑了九秒六。 2 [VP2C, 15B] ~ (sb) in/out; ~ (sb) on/off, record/ have recorded the time of (eg arrival/departure): 记录…之时间 (如到达或离去的时间): Workers in this factory, are required to ~ in and out. 这个工厂里的工人规定必须记录其到离厂(上下班)的时间。 3 [VP6A] (GB sl) strike; hit: (英俚)打;击;揍: If you don't shut up, I'll ~ you one. 如果你不闭嘴，我可要揍你一顿。

clock[2] /klɒk; klɑk/ n design sewn or woven on the side of a sock or stocking, at the ankle. 在袜子侧面的踝部所织的图案；绣花。

clod /klɒd; klɑd/ n lump (of earth, clay, etc). (泥土、粘土等之)块。 **'~-hop·per** /-hɒpə(r); -,hɑpɚ/ n (derog) clumsy, heavy-footed person, esp a rough farm worker. (贬)笨拙而脚步沉重的人；(尤指)庄稼汉；乡下佬。

clog[1] /klɒg; klɑg/ n 1 shoe with a wooden sole; shoe carved out of a block of wood. 木底鞋；木屐。 **'~-dance** n dance in which the dancer wears ~s or wooden-soled shoes. 木屐舞(舞者穿着木屐)。 2 block of wood fastened to the leg of an animal to prevent its straying: (dg) encumbrance: 缚于动物之腿部以防其走失之木块；(喻)障碍物；累赘: a ~ on his movements. 加于他的行动的一种障碍。

clogs

clog[2] /klɒg; klɑg/ vt, vi (-gg-) [VP6A, 15B, 2A, C] ~ (up), 1 (cause to) be or become blocked with waste matter, dirt, grease, etc so that movement, flow of liquid, etc is difficult or prevented: (使)被废物、污物、油腻等塞住以致活动、液体流动等困难或受阻;阻碍;妨碍; 阻塞: pipes ~ged with dirt; 为污物所阻塞之管子; machinery ~ged (up) with grease. 因为油脂太多而运转不灵的机器。 2 encumber; burden: 塞满; 堆满: Don't ~ (up) your memory with useless facts. 不要使你的记忆中堆满无益的事情。 ~gy adj (-ier, -iest) lumpy; sticky. 多块的; 粘腻的。

cloi·sonné /klwɑː'zɒneɪ US: ˌklɔɪzə'neɪ; ˌklɔɪzə'ne/ n [U] enamel ware, in which the colours of the design are kept apart by thin metal strips. 景泰蓝(一种搪瓷器,其图案中之各种颜色系由细金属条分开)。

clois·ter /'klɔɪstə(r); 'klɔɪstɚ/ n 1 covered walk, usu on the sides of an open court or quadrangle, with a wall on the outer side and columns or arches on the inner side, esp within a convent, cathedral or college building. (修道院、大教堂或大学建筑物之)回廊(通常围绕着一个开放之院子,庙之外侧有墙,内侧有一排柱子或拱门);游廊。 ⇨ the illus at church. 看看 church 之插图。 2 (life in a) convent or monastery. 修道院; 修道院之生活; 寺院;僧侣之生活。 the ~ n the seclusion of a convent, etc. 修道院之隐居生活。 □ vt [VP6A] put in, live in, a (~): 置于修道院或寺院中; 过修道院生活: live a ~ed life, a life of seclusion. 过隐居生活。

clone /kləʊn; klon/ n (biol) (member of a) group of organisms or plants produced non-sexually from one ancestor. (生物)无性繁殖系 (由一母体经无性生殖而繁殖的一群生物或植物)。

close[1] /kləʊs; klos/ adj (-r, -st) 1 near (in space or time): 近的(指时间或时间): fire at ~ range; 在近距离射击; in ~ combat; 白刃战; 肉搏; in ~ proximity, almost touching. 极为接近。 a ~ call/thing, almost an accident, disaster or failure. 险些儿造成意外、灾祸或失败的事。 a ~ shave, (fig) a narrow escape from collision or accident. (喻)间不容发的危险遭遇; 幸免于难; 仅以身免。 '~-up n (a) photograph, esp as shown on a cinema or television screen, taken at ~ range and showing the subject on a large scale. 电影或电视在近距离所拍摄的放大镜头; 特写镜头。 (b) close view. 精密的观察。 2 with little or no space in between: 紧密的;密集的: ~ writing; 写得很密的文字; material of ~ texture, eg woven with the threads ~ together. 质地紧密的布料。 The soldiers advanced in ~ order, with little space between them. 士兵们成密集队形前进。 3 strict; severe; rigorous: 严格的; 严密的; 严厉的: a ~ blockade/siege; 严密的封锁(包围); in ~ confinement; 被严密监禁; be (kept) under ~ arrest. 被严密拘留。 keep a ~ watch on sb, watch him carefully. 严密看守某人。 4 detailed; leaving no gaps or weak points; showing each step clearly: 详尽的; 精密的; 无懈可击的; 精细的: a ~ argument; 周密(无懈可击)的论点; ~ reasoning 精密的推理; a ~ reasoner. 精密的推理者。 5 thorough; concentrated: 彻底的; 集中心思的; 专心的; 用心的: after ~ consideration; 经过彻底的考虑以后; on ~ examination. 经过进一步的考查。 You must give me your ~ attention. 你必须对我特别注意(你必须特别用心听我所说的话)。 Please make a ~ (= faithful and exact) translation. 请作精确的翻译。 6 intimate: 亲密的; 亲近的: a ~ friend/friendship. 亲密的朋友(友谊)。 7 restricted; limited: 有限制的: a ~ scholarship, open only to a restricted category of candidates. 限于给某类候选人之奖学金。 8 (of competitions, games, their results) in which the competitors are almost equal: (指比赛、游戏或其结果)势均力敌的; 几乎平手的: a ~ contest/match/election/finish. 势均力敌的比赛 (比赛, 竞选,结局)。 9 (phonetics; of vowels) made with the tongue and the roof of the mouth fairly close together: (语音学; 指元音)合口的 (舌与上颚相当接近的): The English vowels /iː/ and /uː/ are ~. 英语中的元音 /iː/ 和 /uː/ 是合口的。 10 (also 亦作 ,~-'fisted) stingy; niggardly. 吝啬的;手紧的。 11 '~ season, time (the breeding season) during which the killing of certain wild birds and animals, and the catching of certain fish, is illegal. (禁止猎猎某些鸟兽或鱼类的)禁猎期(即其繁殖时期)。 12 (of the weather) stifling; (of a room, etc) unventilated; having little fresh air; (of the air) difficult to breathe because heavy: (指天气) 沉闷的;(指房间等)空气不流通的; 新鲜空气少的;(指空气)闷得叫人呼吸的;室闷的: Open the windows—this room/the air here is too ~. 把窗户打开——这房间(这里的空气)太闷了。 13 concealed; secret; not in the habit of talking about one's affairs: 隐藏的; 秘密的; 不好谈论自己的事情的: keep/lie ~ for a while, keep one's whereabouts secret, not show oneself; 躲藏一些时候(将自己的行踪保守秘密,不露面); keep sth ~, say nothing about it, keep it secret; 将某事保守秘密; be ~ (= secretive) about sth, 对某事保守秘

密, Cf 参较 *keep sth to oneself*. **~·ly** adv in a ~ manner; 接近地; 紧密地; 严密地; 密切地: *listen ~ly*; 细心地听; *follow an argument ~ly*; 注意聆听一项议论; *a ~ly contested election*. 旗鼓相当的竞选. *She ~ly resembles her mother*. 她非常像她的母亲. **~·ness** n being ~: 接近; 紧密; 严密; 精密: *the ~ness of a resemblance/friendship/translation/pursuit*. 相似之极 (友谊之亲密; 翻译之精确; 追赶之接近).

close² /kləʊs; klos /adv in a close manner; near together; tightly: 接近地; 紧密地; 紧紧地: *follow ~ behind sb*; 紧跟在某人的后面; *stand / sit ~ against the wall*; 紧靠着墙壁而立(坐); *come ~r together*; 更靠近一点; ~ *shut*. 密闭的. ~ *at hand*, not far away. 在旁边; 在眼前. ~ *by (sth)*; ~ *to sth*, near (it): 在…的近旁: *He lives ~ by (the church)*. 他住在附近(在教堂的附近). *There's a bus-stop ~ to the school*. 在学校近旁有一公共汽车站. *The ship kept ~ to the coast*. 该船靠近海岸航行. ~ *up (to sb/sth)*, very near in space (to him/it): 靠近; 贴鲁: *Snuggle as ~ up to me as you can*. 尽量挨近我. ~ *on/upon*, almost; very near to: 差不多; 极靠近: *He is ~ upon sixty*. 他年近六十. *It was ~ upon midnight*. 那时已将近午夜. **sail ~ to the wind**, sail almost against the wind; (fig) almost break a law or a moral principle. 抢风(几乎逆风)行驶; (喻)几乎犯法或违反道德准则. ~·'**cropped**/'**cut** adj (of hair, grass, etc) cut very short. (指头发、草等)剪得很短的. ~·'**fitting** adj fitting ~ (to the body, etc): 紧贴(身体等)的; 紧身的: *a ~fitting dress*. 一套紧身的女装. ~·'**grained** adj (esp of wood) having a grain in which the lines in the pattern made by growth are ~ together (eg mahogany). (尤指木材)纹理细密的(如桃花心木). ~·'**hauled** adj (of a sailing-ship) with the sails set for sailing as nearly as possible in the direction from which the wind is blowing. (指帆船)迎风的; 逆风的; 抢风的(帆)风驶的. ~·'**set** adj set, placed, ~ together: 紧靠在一起的: *~-set eyes/teeth*. 紧靠在一起的眼睛(牙齿).

close³ /kləʊs; klos/ n 1 grounds round a cathedral, abbey or school, usu with its buildings (houses of the clergy, etc) round it. 大教堂、寺院或学校周围的场地(通常其周围有教士的住宅等). 2 cul-de-sac. 死巷.

close⁴ /kləʊz; kloz/ vt, vi 1 [VP6A, 2A] shut; 关; 合起: *If you ~ your eyes, you can't see*. 如果你闭起眼, 你就看不见了. *Did you ~ all the doors and windows?* 所有的门窗都关了吗? *This box/The lid of this box doesn't ~ properly*, The lid does not fit properly. 这箱子(这箱子的盖子)关不拢. *Many flowers open in the morning and ~ at night*. 有许多花早晨开放晚上合起. *~d book*, (fig) subject about which one knows nothing: (喻)完全不懂的学科: *Nuclear physics is a ~d book to most of us*. 核物理学是我们大多数的人完全不懂的一门学科. 2 [VP6A, 2A] be, declare, be declared, not open: 封闭; 宣布关闭; 不开: *This road is ~d to heavy motor traffic*. 此路禁止重型车辆通行. *The theatres have ~d for the summer*. 戏院已关闭歇暑. *It's Sunday, so the shops are ~d*. 今天是星期天, 店铺皆不开门. *Wednesday is early-closing day here*, the day on which shops ~ for a half-holiday. 星期三是这里的店铺提早停止营业(休息半日)的日子. *When is 'closing time*, the time at which shops, etc, stop doing business? 什么时间关门(如店铺停止营业)? *The inquiry was held behind/with ~d doors*, the public being excluded. 那次质询会系秘密进行(拒绝旁听). ~d '**circuit** n (in TV) circuit by which the current from the camera to the screen has its path along wires all the way (instead of being transmitted through the air): (电视)闭路(电流自电视摄影机至荧光屏经由电线传送而非经由空中传送之电路): (attrib) (用作定语), ~d-*circuit 'television*. 闭路电视. ~d '**shop** n trade or profession, workshop, factory, establishment, etc in which employment is open only to members of an approved trade union. 只雇用工会会员之行业、工厂、企业等. 3 [VP6A, 2A] bring or come to an end: 结束; 终结: ~ *a discussion*; 结束讨论; *the*

closing days of the year; 年终的日子; *the closing* (= last, final) *day for applications*. 申请(报名)截止之日. *The chairman declared the discussion ~d*. 主席宣布讨论结束. *I want to ~ my account*, settle it by paying or receiving money that is due. 我想结帐(结清应付或应收之款). ~ *a deal*, complete it, by agreeing to the terms, etc. 完成一项交易; 成交. '**closing prices**, (comm) prices of shares quoted at a Stock-Exchange at the end of a day's business. (商)(股票交易所之某一天的)收盘股价. 4 [VP6A, 2C] bring or come together by making less space or fewer spaces between: (使)靠紧; (使)靠拢 (以减少其间距离): ~ *the ranks*; 使行列靠拢; ~ *up*, (of soldiers, etc) ~ r together in line or lines. (指士兵等)互相靠紧; 排队集合. 5 [VP15B, 2A, 3A] (special uses with *adverbial particles* and *preps*): (与副词性小品词及介词连用的特殊用法):

close down, (a) (of a factory, business, etc) stop production, shut completely: (指工厂、商行等)关门; 停业: *The factory (was) ~d down because of a lack of orders*. 该工厂因无人定货而关闭. (b) (of a broadcasting station) stop transmitting: (指广播电台)结束一次的广播节目; 停止播送: *It is midnight and we are now closing down*. 时间已到午夜, 我们今天的各项广播节目到此结束. Hence, 由此产生, '**~-down** n

close in, The days are closing in, getting shorter. 白昼逐渐变短. ~ *in on / upon*, (a) envelop: 包围: *Darkness ~d in on us*. 暮色笼罩着我们(暮色四合). (b) come near(er) and attack: 迫近并攻击: *The enemy ~d in upon us*. 敌军迫近并攻击我们.

close with, (a) come within striking distance of (an enemy, etc). 与(敌军等)短兵相接. (b) accept (an offer); make a bargain with. 接受(建议、提供); 与…达成协议或交易.

close⁵ /kləʊz; kloz/ n (sing only) end (of a period of time); conclusion (of an activity, etc): (仅用单数)(一段时间的)末尾; (活动等之)结束: *towards the ~ of the 17th century*; 将近十七世纪末叶; *(at) (the) ~ of play*, (cricket) (at the) end of play for the day. (板球)(在)当天比赛结束的时候. *The day had reached its ~*. 天已黑. **draw/bring sth to a ~**, end. 结束(某事物).

closet /'klɒzɪt; 'klɑzɪt/ n 1 (now chiefly US) small room for storing things. (现主美)储藏物品之小房间; 储藏室. ⇨ **cupboard**, **storeroom**. 2 (old use) small room for private interviews. (旧用法)秘密会谈之小房间. 3 (old use) watercloset. (旧用法)便所; 厕所. ⇨ **water¹** (7). □ *attrib* adj (colloq) acting only in private; not publicly known: (口)私下活动的; 秘密的: *I suspect he's a ~ fascist*. 我猜想他是个秘密活动的法西斯党员. □ vt (usu passive) (通常用被动语态) *be ~ed with sb/ together*, have a private meeting with: 与…密谈; 在一起密谈: *He was ~ed with the manager/They were ~ed together for two hours*. 他与经理密谈(他们在一起密谈)了二小时.

clo·sure /'kləʊʒə(r); 'kloʒɚ/ n 1 (US =cloture) [C, U] (in Parliament) device to end debate by taking a vote on a question: (议会用)用投票表决问题以终止辩论的策略: *apply the ~ to a debate*; 用投票表决法终止辩论; *move the ~*. 提议停止辩论付诸投票表决. ⇨ **guillotine**. 2 [C] act of closing: 关闭; 停业; 终止: *pit ~s*, eg of coal-mines which are no longer economic. 矿井关闭(如采矿井亏损不再有经济价值的矿坑(如煤矿)).

clot /klɒt; klɑt/ n [C] 1 half-solid lump formed from liquid, esp blood. (液体, 尤指血液所结的)凝块; 血块. 2 (dated schoolboy sl) idiot, fool. (过时学童俚语)白痴; 呆子. □ vt, vi (-tt-) [VP6A, 2A] form into ~s: 结块; 凝结成块: *~ted cream*, made by scalding it; 凝结的乳脂(将乳脂加热煮沸而成); *~ted hair*, stuck together by dirt or blood, etc. 被污垢或血液粘结成团的头发.

cloth /klɒθ US: klɔːθ; klɔθ/ n (pl ~s /klɒθs US: klɔːðz/ klɔθs/) 1 [U] material made by weaving (cotton, wool, silk, linen, etc): (棉、羊毛、丝、麻等织的)

布;布料;毛料、丝绸;麻布: *three yards of* ~; 三码布; *a book with a* ~ *binding.* 布面精装的书。**2** [C] piece of this material for special purpose: 作某种特殊用途的一块布: *a 'floor*~; 擦地板布; *a 'dish*~. 洗碟布。**3** [U] profession as shown by the clothes worn: 以某种服装所代表的行业: *the respect due to his* ~. 对他的职业应有的尊敬。**the** ~, the clergy. 传教士。

clothe /kləʊð; kloʊð/ vt (*pt*, *pp* **clothed** /kləʊðd; kloʊðd / , old style **clad** /klæd; klæd/) [VP6A] **1** wear clothes; put clothes on, supply clothes for: 穿衣服; 给…衣服: *warmly* ~*d*; 穿得暖的; ~*d in wool.* 穿着毛料衣服的。*He has to work hard in order to* ~ *his family*, earn money for their clothes. 他必须辛苦工作赚钱替家里的人买衣服。**2** (fig) express: (喻)表示;表达: *His sentiments were* ~*d in suitable language.* 他的感情借适当的语言表达出来了。

clothes /kləʊðz *US*: kleʊz; kloz/ n *pl* (no *sing*; not used with numerals) (无单数形,不与数字连用) **1** coverings for a person's body; dress: 衣服;服装: *a baby in long* ~; 在襁褓中的婴孩; *a '*~-brush. 衣刷。**2 'bed**~, sheets, blankets, etc, for or on a bed. (床上的)被褥;被单、毯等。**'**~**-basket**, one for ~ which are to be, or have been, washed. (装待洗或已洗之衣服的)衣篮。**'**~**-horse**, frame for airing ~ that have been washed and dried. 晾衣架 (用以晾已洗净并已经干之衣服者)。**'**~**-line**, rope (stretched between posts) on which ~ are hung to be dried after being washed. 晒衣绳(索引于两柱间,用以挂晒洗净之衣服者)。**'**~**-peg** /-**pin**, one used for fastening ~ to a ~-line. (用于晒衣绳上夹衣服的)衣夹。⇨ the illus at **peg.** 参看 peg 之插图。

cloth·ier /'kləʊðɪə(r); 'kloʊðjɚ/ n dealer in cloth or clothes. 做布匹或衣服生意的人;布商;服装商。

cloth·ing /'kləʊðɪŋ; 'kloʊðɪŋ/ n [U] (collective) clothes: (集合名词)衣服; *articles of* ~. 衣物。

clo·ture /'kləʊtʃə(r); 'kloʊtʃɚ/ n (*US*)=**closure(1).**

cloud /klaʊd; klaʊd/ n **1** [C,U] (separate mass of) visible water vapour floating above the earth: 云;云团: *The top of the mountain was covered with/hidden under* ~. 山顶为云所覆盖。*Large, black* ~*s announced a coming storm.* 大堆的乌云预示着将临的暴风雨。**'**~-**bank** n thick mass of low ~. 云堤(低而密的云团)。**'**~-**burst** n sudden and violent rainstorm. (突然的)暴雨;骤雨。**'**~-**capped** adj (eg of mountains) having the top enveloped in ~. 顶部为云所笼罩的(如高山)。**'**~-'**cuckoo-land** n imaginary and ridiculously ideal place. 想像中的荒谬的理想地方。**2** mass of things in the air moving together: 飞掠而过的一大群东西: *a* ~ *of arrows/insects/horsemen, etc.* 一阵密集的箭(一大群飞虫,骑兵等)。**3** mass (of smoke, dust, sand, etc) in the air. 飞扬于空中之一阵(烟、尘、沙等,与of连用)。**4** vague patch on or in a liquid or a transparent object. (液体或透明体中的)混浊的一点;污斑。**5** something that causes unhappiness or fear: 引起不愉快或恐惧之事物: *the* ~*s of war*; 战云; *a* ~ *of gloom.* 愁云。**under a** ~, out of favour, under suspicion, in disgrace. 失宠;受到怀疑;失体面。**6** (*pl*) (复) **(have one's head) in the** ~**s**, (fig) with one's thoughts far away, not paying attention to one's surroundings, etc. (喻)心不在焉;沉入冥想;茫然。□ vi, vt [VP2A, C, 3A, 6A] ~ **(over)**, become, make, indistinct (as) through ~ : (使)变得不清楚(如为云所蔽);(使)变模糊: *The sky* ~*ed over.* 天空布满了云。*Her eyes were* ~*ed (over) with tears.* 她泪眼朦胧(因两眼蒙上一层泪水)。*All these troubles have* ~*ed his mind*, have affected his reason. 所有这些困难已使他理智不清。~·**less** adj free from ~*s*; clear: 无云的;晴朗的: *a* ~*less sky.* 晴朗的天空。~·**y** adj (-**ier**, -**iest**) **1** covered with ~s: 为云所遮蔽的;有云的;阴的: *a* ~*y sky.* 阴天。**2** (esp of liquids) not clear. (尤指液体)不清的;混浊的。

clout /klaʊt; klaʊt/ n **1** (colloq) blow or knock (on the head, etc, given with the hand). (口)(用手)敲;打

(头等)。**2** (archaic) piece of old cloth used for housework, etc: (古)家庭中用以擦拭物件的一块旧布;抹布: *a 'dish-*~. 洗碟布;洗碗布。**3** (archaic) article of clothing. (古)一件衣服。□ vt (colloq) hit: (口)打;敲: ~ *sb on the head.* 打某人的头。

clove[1] ⇨ **cleave**[1].

clove[2] /kləʊv; klov/ n dried, unopened flower-bud of a tropical tree, used as a spice. 丁香(一种热带树)的干花蕾(用作香料或调味品)。**oil of** ~**s**, oil extracted from ~s and used in medicine. 丁香花油(作药物用)。

clove[3] /kləʊv; klov/ n one of the small, separate sections of a compound bulb: (复合球茎之)一瓣;一片: *a* ~ *of garlic.* 一瓣蒜。

clove hitch /'kləʊv hɪtʃ; 'klov hɪtʃ/ n knot for fastening a rope round a pole, etc. 丁香结;卷结(用以缚绳于竿柱等之结成法)。⇨ the illus at **knots.** 参看 knots 之插图。

clo·ven ⇨ **cleave**[1].

clo·ver /'kləʊvə(r); 'klovɚ/ n [U] low-growing plant with (usu) three leaves on each stalk, and purple, pink or white flowers, grown as food for cattle, etc. 三叶草;苜蓿(一种低矮植物,每一叶柄上通常有三片叶子,开紫、粉红或白花,用作牛等之饲料)。**be/live in** ~, enjoy a great comfort and luxury. 生活安逸奢侈。**'**~-**leaf**, highway intersection with flyovers, etc forming the pattern of a four-leaved ~. 四叶苜蓿形交流道(有天桥等交叉呈四叶苜蓿形的公路交叉点)。**,four-leaf '**~, rare variety with four-leaved stalk, the finding of which is considered to be a good omen. 四叶苜蓿;幸运草(极稀少,如发现它认为是好预兆)。

clown /klaʊn; klaʊn/ n person (esp in a circus or pantomime) who makes a living by performing amusing or foolish tricks and antics; person acting like a ~; rude, clumsy man. (马戏团或哑剧中靠玩笑把戏及滑稽动作为生的)丑角;小丑; 行动似小丑的人;粗鲁、笨拙的人。□ vi [VP2A] behave like a ~: 扮演丑角; 做出如小丑之行为: *Stop all this* ~*ing.* 不要再耍小丑了。~·**ish** adj of or like a ~. 小丑的;丑角的;似小丑的。

cloy /klɔɪ; klɔɪ/ vt, vi [VP6A, 2A] make or become distasteful by excess, sweetness, richness (of food, pleasure, etc); satiate. (对于食物、玩乐等)(使)因享受得过多,或因味太甜、太浓而生厌;吃腻;玩腻;厌腻: ~*ed with pleasure*; 玩乐腻了; ~ *the appetite by eating too much sweet food.* 因吃太多甜食而致食欲不佳。

club[1] /klʌb; klʌb/ n **1** heavy stick with one thick end, used as a weapon. (一端较粗,用作武器之)棍;棒。**2** stick with a curved head for hitting the ball in golf and hockey. (一端有弯曲之头的)高尔夫球棒; 曲棍球棒。□ vt(-**bb**-) [VP6A, 14] hit with a ~: 用棍棒打击: *He had been* ~*bed to death.* 他被棍棒打死。*They* ~*bed him with their rifles.* 他们用枪托打他。~**,'foot** n foot that is (from birth) thick and badly formed. 天生特厚之畸形足。Hence, 由此产生, ~,'**footed** adj

club[3] /klʌb; klʌb/ n one of the thirteen playing-cards with a black three-leaf design printed on it: 印有黑梅花(即一黑色三叶状图案)之纸牌: *the ace/ten of* ~*s*; 梅花牌之十点;梅花 A (10); *play a small* ~; 打小点之梅花牌; ~*s are trumps.* 梅花是王牌。⇨ the illus at **card.** 参看 card 之插图。

club[2] /klʌb; klʌb/ n society of persons who subscribe money to provide themselves with sport, social entertainment, or any other shared activity, sometimes in their own grounds, buildings, etc where meals and bedrooms are available; the rooms or building(s) used by such a society (also called a '~**house**). 会社; 社团;俱乐部(各人自费供作体育运动或社交娱乐等,其会所并备有餐食及宿舍,有时也供作此项活动的地方);俱乐部所用的房屋;会所(亦作 clubhouse)。□ vi (-**bb**-) [VP2C] ~ **together,** join or act (together, with others) for a common purpose: 为共同目的而结合或共同行动;联合行动: *The villagers* ~*bed together to help the old pensioners whose house had been burnt down.* 全村的人联合起来

救助那些房子被烧毁的退休老人。'**~·bable** /'klʌbəbl; 'klʌbəbl/ adj fit for membership of a ~; sociable. 有资格加入会社为会员的；好交际的。

cluck /klʌk; klʌk/ n [VP2A] (make the) noise made by a hen, eg when calling her chickens. (作)母鸡的咯咯声(如唤小鸡时所发出者); 咯咯叫.

clue /klu:; klu/ n fact, idea, etc that suggests a possible answer to a problem: 线索; 端倪(即对一问题提示可能之答案的事实、想法等): get/find a ~ to a mystery. 获得有关某事的线索—条线索. **not have a ~,** (colloq) be completely ignorant of, unable to understand or explain (what is in question). (口)(对当前讨论的问题)毫无头绪；一无所知；完全不懂。

clump[1] /klʌmp; klʌmp/ n group or cluster (of trees, shrubs or plants): (树、灌木或花草之)丛；薮: growing in ~s. □ vt plant in ~s. 成丛地种植。

clump[2] /klʌmp; klʌmp/ vi [VP2A, C] tread heavily: 重踏脚步而行: ~ about, walk about putting the feet down heavily. 重踏实的脚步到处行走。

clumsy /'klʌmzi; 'klʌmzɪ/ adj (-ier, -iest) 1 heavy and ungraceful in movement or construction; not well designed for its purpose: (行动或构造)笨拙的；笨重的；设计与用途不很符合的: The ~ workman put his elbow through the window and broke it. 那笨拙的工人把肘拐伸入窗子，把它弄破了. An axe would be a ~ tool to open a tin of jam with. 斧头用来开果酱罐头是一种不合用的工具. 2 tactless; unskilful: 不圆滑的；缺乏技巧的: a ~ apology/forgery/. 笨拙的辩解(伪造); ~ praise. 不得体的赞扬. **clum·sily** /-zəli; -zəlɪ/ adv **clum·si·ness** n

clung /klʌŋ; klʌŋ/ pt, pp of **cling.**

clunk /klʌŋk; klʌŋk/ vi, n (make the) dull sound of heavy metals etc striking together. (发出)金属等之沉浊碰击声。

clus·ter /'klʌstə(r); 'klʌstɚ/ n 1 number of things of the same kind growing closely together: (指紧密地生长在一起的同类东西)丛；簇；束；串；团: a ~ of flowers/berries/curls; 一簇花(浆果、鬈发); hair growing in thick ~s. 成丛生长的毛发. 2 number of persons, animals, objects etc in a small, close group: (指人、动物、物件等)小群: a ~ of bees/spectators/islands; 一小群蜜蜂(观众，岛屿); consonant ~s (in phonetics, eg str in strong;) 辅音群(语音学术语，如 strong 中之 str); houses here and there in ~s. 到处成簇集结的房屋. □ vi [VP2A, C, 3A] ~ (together) (round), be in, form, a close group round: 绕着…结集成群；绕着…丛生；围集在…的周围: roses ~ing (round) round the window. 绕着窗户丛生的玫瑰花. The village ~s round the church. 村子的房屋围集在教堂的四周。

clutch[1] /klʌtʃ; klʌtʃ/ vt, vi [VP2A, 3A, 15A] ~ **(at),** seize; take hold of tightly with the hand(s); attempt to seize: 用手抓住；攫取；试图抓住；捕捉: He ~ed (at) the rope we threw to him. 他抓住了(或试图抓住)我们抛给他的绳索. A drowning man will ~ at a straw, will make a last, desperate but hopeless attempt to be saved. 将要溺死的人会一根草也要抓紧. Mary ~ed her doll to her breast. 玛丽把她的玩偶紧抱在怀里. □ n 1 the act of ~ing: 抓; 捕; 握: make a ~ at sth. 向某物抓去. 2 (esp in pl) control; power. (尤用复数)控制；掌握. **be in/out of the ~es of; get into/out of the ~es of,** eg of moneylenders. 在(不在)…的控制中；陷入(摆脱)…(如放债者的)掌握. 3 device, eg a pedal, in a machine or engine for connecting and disconnecting working parts: (机器或引擎中使工作机件接合或分离的), 离合器, 离合器踏板; 啮合子: let in/disengage/withdraw the ~; 接合(分离, 退离)离合器; put the ~ in/out. 接合(分离)离合器. The ~ is in/out. 离合器是接合的(分离的). ⊂ the illus at **motor.** 参看 motor 之插图。

clutch[2] /klʌtʃ; klʌtʃ/ n set of eggs placed under a hen to hatch at one time; number of young chickens hatched from these. 母鸡一次所孵之鸡蛋；一窝小鸡.

clut·ter /'klʌtə(r); 'klʌtɚ/ vt [VP6A, 15B] ~ **(up),** make untidy or confused by crowding: 使散乱；乱堆；乱

塞: a desk ~ed up with papers; 堆满散乱文件的写字桌; ~ up a room with unnecessary furniture. 将房间里塞满了不必要的家具. □ n [C, U] untidy or confused state: 杂乱; 零乱: in a ~, in disorder or confusion. 乱作一团; 乱七八糟. Get rid of all this ~! 快把这些乱糟糟的东西弄走!

co- /kou; ko/ pref together with (another or others): 与(他人)共同: co-author; 合著者; co-heir; 共同继承人; co-exist; 共存; co-belligerents. 共同参战国。

coach[1] /koutʃ; kotʃ/ n 1 four-wheeled carriage pulled by four or more horses, used to carry passengers and mail before railways were built ('stage-~ and 'mail-~ for public use; 'state-~ used by a head of state on ceremonial occasions). 由四匹(或四匹以上)马拉的四轮马车 (在铁路筑成以前用以载客和邮件, stage-coach 及 mail-coach 供一般用, state-coach 供国家元首在典礼时用). **drive a ~ and horses through (sth),** defeat the intention of (a regulation, etc) by finding serious faults in its wording. 挑剔其文字上的严重错误以打击(某一法规等)的意图. 2 (US 美 =car) railway carriage, often divided into compartments. 铁路客车厢(常划分为若干小间). 3 ('motor-~) long-distance, single-decked motorbus: 长途单层客运汽车: travel by ~; 乘长途汽车旅行; a ~-tour of Europe; 乘长途汽车旅行欧洲; leave by ~ for Edinburgh. 乘长途汽车往爱丁堡. '~-builder n craftsman who builds the body-work of motor vehicles. 打造汽车车身的工匠。

a state-coach

coach[2] /koutʃ; kotʃ/ n teacher, esp one who gives private lessons to prepare students for a public examination; person who trains athletes for contests: (为学生准备参加考试之)私人补习教师; (训练运动员参加比赛的)教练: a 'baseball ~. 棒球教练. □ vt, vi [VP6A, 14, 2A] teach or train: 教授; 训练: ~ sb for an exam; 指导某人准备参加考试; ~ the crew for the boat race. 训练船员划船比赛。

co·agu·late /kou'ægjuleit; ko'ægjə,let/ vt, vi [VP 6A, 2A] (of liquids) change to a thick and solid state, as blood does in air. (指液体)凝结; 凝固(如血液在空气中凝结). **co·agu·lation** /kou,ægju'leiʃn; ko,ægjə'leʃən/ n

coal /koul; kol/ n [U] black mineral that burns and supplies heat, and from which ~-gas is made; [C] piece of this material, esp (a live ~) one that is burning: 煤(能燃烧生热并可制煤气之黑色矿物);煤块(尤指正燃烧中者, 称为 a live coal): A hot ~ fell from the fire and burnt a hole in the carpet. 火炉中掉出来一块煤, 把地毯烧了一个洞. **carry ~s to Newcastle,** take goods to a place where they are already plentiful. 运煤至产煤地; 多此一举. **heap ~s of fire on sb's head,** return good for evil and so induce remorse. 以德报怨而使人懊悔. '~-face n part of a seam from which ~ is being cut. 煤层中的采掘面. '~-field n district in which ~ is mined. 煤矿区; 煤田. '~-gas n the mixture of gases made by treating ~, used for lighting and heating. 煤气(用煤制成的混合气体, 用以发光或加热). '~-hole n cellar for storing ~. 贮藏煤的地下室; 地下煤库. '~-house n shed for storing ~. 储煤的简陋小屋; 煤库. '~-mine/-pit nn mine from which ~ is dug. 煤矿(坑). '~-scuttle n container for a supply of ~ near a

fireside.(壁炉边的)煤斗; 煤桶。 '**~-seam** n underground layer of ~. (地下的)煤层。 '**~-tar** n [U] (sometimes 有时作 '*gas-tar*) thick, black, sticky substance produced when gas is made from ~. 煤馏; 柏油; 煤焦油(自煤中提取煤气时所得之浓厚,黑色,粘性物质)。 □ *vt, vi* [VP6A, 2A] put ~ (into a ship, etc); take in ~: 装煤; 加煤: *The ship called at Gibraltar to ~*. 该船停靠直布罗陀加煤。 *Coaling (a ship) is a dirty job*. 加煤(于船)是一件肮脏的工作。 '**~-ing-station** n port where ships can obtain supplies of ~. 轮船可以加煤的港口;加煤站。

co·alesce /ˌkəʊəˈles; ˌkoəˈles/ *vi* come together and unite into one substance, group, etc. 联合; 合并; 结合。 **co·ales·cence** /ˌkəʊəˈlesns; ˌkoəˈlesns/ n

co·ali·tion /ˌkəʊəˈlɪʃn; ˌkoəˈlɪʃən/ n [U] uniting; [C] union of political parties for a special purpose: 联合; 各政党为某一特殊目的所组的联盟: *a ~ government*; 联合政府; *the left-wing ~*; 左翼联盟; *form a ~*. 组织联盟。

coam·ing /ˈkəʊmɪŋ; ˈkomɪŋ /n raised rim round a ship's hatches to keep water out. 舱口缘围(船舱口周围防水流入之凸起边缘)。

coarse /kɔːs; kɔrs/ *adj* (-r, -st) **1** (of material) not fine and small; rough and lumpy: (指质料)粗糙的; 粗的: ~ *sand/sugar*; 粗沙(糖); having a rough surface or texture: 表面或织地粗糙的: *a dress made of ~ cloth*; 粗布做的衣服; *a ~ skin/complexion*. 粗糙的皮肤(颜面)。 **2** (of food) common; inferior: (指食物)普通的; 粗劣的: ~ *fish*; ~ 肉粗的鱼; ~ *fishing*, eg for coarse fish, pike. 捕粗肉鱼 (如诸子鲭,斜齿鳊,梭子鱼)。 **3** vulgar; not delicate or refined: 粗鲁的; 粗俗的; 不高雅的: ~ *manners/language/words/laughter/jokes/tastes*; 粗鲁的举止(言语,话语,笑声,笑话,嗜好); ~ *of speech*. 说话粗鲁的。 **coarsen** /ˈkɔːsn; ˈkɔrsn/ *vt, vi* [VP6A, 2A] make or become ~. (使)变粗糙; (使)变粗劣; (使)变粗俗。 **~·ly** *adv* **~·ness** n

coast¹ /kəʊst; kost/ n [C] land bordering the sea; seashore and land near it: 海岸; 海滨: *The ship was wrecked on the Kent ~*. 该船在肯特海岸触礁。 *There are numerous islands off the ~*. 在这海岸外有无数的岛屿。 *The village is on the south ~*. 该村在南海岸。 '**~·guard** n officer on police duty on the ~ (to prevent or detect smuggling, report passing ships, etc). 海岸巡逻队; 水上警察 (防止或缉查走私, 报告经过的船只等)。 '**~·line** n shoreline, esp with regard to its shape: 海岸线(尤指其形状): *a rugged ~line*. 崎岖的海岸线。 **~al** /ˈkəʊstl; ˈkostl/ *adj* ~*al navigation*. 沿海岸的航行。 '**~·wise** *adj, adv* along the ~. 沿海岸的(地)。

coast² /kəʊst; kost/ *vi, vt* [VP2A, C, 3A, 6A] **1** ~ (*along*), go in, sail, a ship along the coast. 乘船沿海岸而航行。 **2** ride or slide down a hill or slope without using power (eg along a road on a bicycle). 不用动力而自斜坡向下滑行(如沿脚踏车道路滑下)。 ~**er** n **1** ship that sails from port to port along the coast. (来往于沿海各港埠之)沿海船; 近海船。 **2** small mat, etc (for a drinking-glass, etc)to protect a polished table, etc from drips or moisture. 茶杯垫子(垫于茶杯等下面以防滴水或水气污损桌面油漆等)。

coat /kəʊt; kot/ n **1** long outer garment with sleeves, buttoned in the front. (在前面扣合的有袖的)长外衣。 ⇨ **over-~**; *rain-~* at **rain¹**(1). *turn one's ~*, change one's side or principles, desert one army or party and join the other. 改变立场或主义; 背叛甲军或甲党而加入乙军或乙党; 变节; 改宗。 ~ *of 'arms*, ⇨ **arms**. ~ *of 'mail*, piece of armour of metal rings or plate for the upper part of the body. (金属圈或片制成保护上身的)甲胄。 ⇨ the illus at **armour**. 参看 armour 之插图。 '**~-tails** n *pl* divided tapering part of a *tail-~*, ⇨ **tail**(2). 燕尾服之尾。 **2** jacket (1). 夹克。 **3** any covering that can be compared to a garment, eg an animal's hair or wool. 被比做衣服之任何覆盖物(如动物之毛或羊毛)。 **4** layer of paint or other substance put on a surface at one time: 一层(一次涂于表面的油漆或其他物质): *The*

woodwork has had its final ~ of paint. 木造部份已经涂过了最后一层油漆。 □ *vt* [VP6A, 14] cover with a ~ or layer: 外加一层; 覆以一层: *furniture ~ed with dust*; 上面覆一层灰尘的家具; ~ *pills with sugar*. 将药丸加上一层糖衣。 *Tinplate is made by ~ing sheets of iron with tin*. 洋铁皮是在铁皮上镀一层锡制成的。 '**~·ing** n **1** thin layer or covering: 薄层; 覆盖一层物: *two ~ings of wax*. 两层薄蜡。 **2** [U] cloth for ~s(1, 2). 外衣料; 夹克料。

coatee /kəʊˈtiː; ˈkotˈi/ n short coat. 短外衣。

coax /kəʊks; koks/ *vt, vi* [VP6A, 17, 15B, 14, 2A] ~ (*from/into/out of*), get sb or sth to do sth by kindness or patience: 以和善或耐性使某人或某物做某事; 哄诱; 劝诱: ~ *a child to take his medicine*; 哄小孩吃药; ~ *a fire to burn*; 耐心使火燃烧起来; 引火; ~ (*up*) *he fire*; 耐心地设法使炉火烧旺(起来); ~ *sb into/out of doing sth*; 哄某人做(不做)某事; ~ *a smile from the baby*. 逗婴孩一笑。 ~·**ing** n [U, C] being ~ed: (受)哄诱。 (受)劝诱: *give sb a ~ing*. 劝诱某人。 *He took a lot of ~ing before he agreed to take her to the theatre*. 经过很久的劝诱之后,他才答应带她去看戏。 '**~·ing·ly** *adv*

cob /kɒb; kɑb/ n **1** male swan. 雄天鹅。 **2** strong short-legged horse for riding. 供骑乘之强壮而腿短的马。 **3** (also 亦作 '**cob-nut**) large kind of hazelnut. 大榛实。 **4** (also 亦作 '**corn-cob**) central part of an ear of maize on which the grain grows: 玉蜀黍的穗轴; 玉米轴: *corn on the cob*. 尚未自穗轴上剥下的玉蜀黍。 ⇨ the illus at **cereal**. 参看 cereal 之插图。

co·balt /ˈkəʊbɔːlt; ˈkobɔlt/ n hard silvery-white metal (symbol **Co**) used in many alloys; deep blue colouring matter made from its compounds, used to colour glass and ceramics. 钴(坚硬的银白金属, 化学符号 Co, 用于许多种合金); 用钴化合物所制的深蓝色颜料(用以加颜色于玻璃及陶器); 钴蓝。

cob·ber /ˈkɒbə(r); ˈkɑbə/ n (Australia; colloq) fellow. (澳; 口)同伴; 伙伴。

cobble¹ /ˈkɒbl; ˈkɑbl/ n (also 亦作 '**~-stone**) stone worn round and smooth by water and used for paving. 由水冲磨成圆而光滑的石头(用以铺路); 大砾石; 鹅卵石。 □ *vt* pave with these stones: 用圆石头铺(路): ~*d streets*. 用圆石头铺成的街道。

cobble² /ˈkɒbl; ˈkɑbl/ *vt* [VP6A] mend, patch (esp shoes), or put together roughly. 补缀(尤指鞋); 粗劣地修补。

cob·bler /ˈkɒblə(r); ˈkɑblə/ n **1** mender of shoes. ('shoe-repairer is now the usu word). 补鞋匠(现在通常用 shoe-repairer)。 **2** clumsy workman. 笨拙的工人。 **3** (US) type of pie. (美)一种馅饼。 *a load of (old) ~s*, (GB sl) nonsense. (英俚)胡说; 废话。

co·bra /ˈkəʊbrə; ˈkobrə/ n poisonous snake of Asia and Africa. 眼镜蛇(亚洲及非洲产之毒蛇)。 ⇨ the illus at **snake**. 参看 snake 之插图。

cob·web /ˈkɒbweb; ˈkɑbˌwɛb/ n [C] fine network or single thread made by a spider. 蜘蛛网; 蛛丝。 ⇨ the illus at **arachnid**. 参看 arachnid 之插图。

Coca-Cola /ˌkəʊkə ˈkəʊlə; ˌkokəˈkolə/ n (P) popular non-alcoholic carbonated drink. (商标)可口可乐(流行的非酒类充碳酸气的饮料)。

co·caine /kəʊˈkeɪn; koˈken/ n [U] product (from a shrub) used by doctors as a local anaesthetic, and also used as a stimulant by drug addicts. 古柯碱(由一种灌木中提取的产物, 医师们用之作局部麻醉剂, 药瘾者用之作兴奋剂)。

cochi·neal /ˌkɒtʃɪˈniːl; ˌkɑtʃəˈnil/ n [U] bright red colouring-matter made from the dried bodies of certain insects. 用某些昆虫干骸所制的鲜红颜料; 洋红; 胭脂红。

coch·lea /ˈkɒklɪə; ˈkɑklɪə /n spiral-shaped part of the inner ear. 耳蜗(内耳之螺旋形部份)。 ⇨ the illus at **ear**. 参看 ear 之插图。

cock¹ /kɒk; kɑk/ n **1** (used alone) adult male bird of the domestic or farmyard fowl (US 美=**rooster**) ⇨ the illus at **fowl**. (单独用)公鸡; 雄鸡 (参看 fowl 之插图)。

'**~-crow** n early dawn. 天刚亮；黎明；破晓；拂晓。 **'~-a-hoop** adj, adv with boastful crowing; exultant(ly). 得意洋洋的(地)；狂喜的(地)。 **~-a-doodle-doo** /ˌkɒk ə ˌduːl ˈduː/: 'kɑkə,dud]'du / n the crow of the ~(1). 雄鸡的啼声；喔喔；(儿语之)雄鸡。 **'~-and'bull story**, foolish story that one should not believe. 无稽之谈。 ⇨ **game**[1](6). 斗鸡游戏(以供玩赏者)。 **live like 'fighting-~s**, live on the best possible food. 享受最佳的食物；过奢侈生活。 **~ of the walk**, person who dominates others. 某行业的首领；头子；头目。 **2** (in compounds) male of other kinds of bird: (用于复合词中)别种鸟类的雄者: '**pea~**; 雄孔雀; **,~-'sparrow**; 雄知更鸟。 '**~-'robin**. 雄知更鸟。

cock² /kɒk; kɑk/ n **1** tap and spout for controlling the flow of a liquid or a gas, eg from a pipe, barrel. (控制管、桶等中液体或气体流出之)龙头；活栓。 **2** lever in a gun; position of this lever when it is raised and ready to be released by the trigger. (枪上的)击铁；击铁张开的位置(待扣扳机射击)。 **at half / full ~**, half ready / quite ready to be fired. 击铁半(全)张；半(全)准备射击。 **go off at half ~**, of schemes, ceremonies, etc, begin before the arrangements are complete. (指计划、典礼等)尚未全部安排就绪即行开始。 **3** △ (vulg sl) penis. (讳)(鄙俚)阴茎；鸡巴。

cock³ /kɒk; kɑk/ vt [VP6A, 15B] **~ (up)**, **1** turn upwards, cause to be erect (showing attention, inquiry, defiance, etc): 向上翘起；竖起；使直立(表示注意、询问、轻蔑等): The horse ~ed its ears. 马竖起耳朵。 The horse stopped with its ears ~ed up. 马停下来，耳朵竖着。 He ~ed his eye at me, glanced or winked at me knowingly, or raised his eyebrow. 他对我使眼色。 ,~ed 'hat n triangular hat, pointed front and back, worn with some uniforms. 前后尖突形的三角帽(配合某种制服戴者)。 **knock sb / sth into a ~ed hat**, knock shapeless, or so that recognition is impossible; beat thoroughly. 将(某人或某物)打得不成样子；将…弄得面目全非；彻底打败。 **2** [VP6A] raise the cock of (a gun) ready for firing. 扳起(枪)的击铁准备发射。 ⇨ **cock²**(2). **3 ~ up**, (sl) make a mess of; upset: (俚)将…弄得一团糟；扰乱: They completely ~ed up the arrangements for our holiday. 他们把我们度假的计划完全搞乱了。 Hence, 因此， '**~-up** n

cock⁴ /kɒk; kɑk/ n small, cone-shaped pile of straw or hay. 小的圆锥形干草堆。 □ vt pile (hay) in ~s. 将(干草)堆成小的圆锥形堆。

cock·ade /kɒ'keɪd; kɑk'ed/ n knot of ribbon worn on a hat as a badge. 结在帽上作为徽章之带结；帽章。

cocka·too /ˌkɒkə'tuː; kɑke'tu/ n crested parrot. 美冠鹦鹉；白鹦。 ⇨ the illus at **rare**. 参看 rare 之插图。

cock·chafer /'kɒktʃeɪfə(r); 'kɑk,tʃefɚ/ n large beetle that flies with a loud whirring sound and is destructive to vegetation. 金龟子(飞起来带响闹的嗡嗡声之大甲虫，对植物有害)。

cocker /'kɒkə(r); 'kɑkɚ/ n breed of spaniel. 一种长毛垂耳之犬。

cock·erel /'kɒkərəl; 'kɑkərəl/ n young cock¹(1), not more than one year old. (未满一年的)小公鸡。

cock-eyed /'kɒkaɪd; 'kɑk,ɑrd/ adj (sl) (俚) **1** squinting; crooked; turned or twisted to one side. 斜视的；弯曲的；向一边歪扭的。 **2** wild, ill-judged: 轻率而未予妥善判断的: a ~ scheme. 轻率的计划。

cock·horse /,kɒk'hɔːs; 'kɑk'hɔrs/ n ride a ~, (children's word) ride on horseback or on a rocking-horse. (小儿语)骑马；骑摇动木马。 ⇨ **rock²**.

cockle /'kɒkl; 'kɑkl/ n **1** edible shellfish; (also 亦作 '**~-shell**) its shell. 乌蛤；海扇(一种可食的贝类)；海扇壳。 **2** small, shallow boat. 浅的小船；小舟。 **3** (warm, delight, etc) the ~s of one's heart, one's feelings. (使)某人的情绪(振奋，愉快等)。

cock·ney /'kɒknɪ; 'kɑknɪ/ adj, n (characteristic of a) native of the East End of London: 伦敦东区人；伦敦

东区人的个性: a ~ accent: 伦敦 东区人的口音: ~ humour. 伦敦东区人的幽默。

cock·pit /'kɒkpɪt; 'kɑk,pɪt/ n **1** enclosed space where game-cocks fought, ⇨ cock-fighting at **cock¹**(1); (fig) area where battles have often been fought: 斗鸡场；(喻)屡经战役的战场: Belgium, the ~ of Europe. 比利时，欧洲的战场。 **2** compartment in a small aircraft for the pilot. 小型飞机的驾驶舱；座舱。 Cf 参较 flight deck of an airliner, (客机的)驾驶室；diver's seat in a racing-car. (赛车的)驾驶座。 ⇨ the illus at **air¹**. 参看 air¹ 之插图。

cock·roach /'kɒkrəʊtʃ; 'kɑk,rotʃ/ n large, darkbrown insect that comes out at night in kitchens and places where food is kept. 蟑螂(深褐色的大昆虫，夜间外出，在厨房及置食物处觅食)。 ⇨ the illus at **insect**. 参看 insect 之插图。

cocks·comb /'kɒkskəʊm; 'kɑks,kom/ n **1** red crest of a cock¹(1). (雄鸡的)鸡冠。 ⇨ the illus at **fowl**. 参看 fowl 之插图。 **2** jester's cap. 丑角所戴的鸡冠帽。 **3** plant with clusters of red or yellow feather-like flowers. 鸡冠花(开密集之红色或黄色羽状花之植物)。

cock·sure /,kɒk'ʃʊə(r); 'kɑk'ʃʊr/ adj presumptuously or offensively sure (of or about sth); confident. 自信得令人厌恶的；过于自信的(与 of 或 about 连用，后接某事)；确信的。

cock·tail /'kɒkteɪl; 'kɑk,tel/ n [C] **1** mixed alcoholic drink, esp one taken before a meal, eg gin and vermouth. 鸡尾酒(各种混合之酒，尤指饭前所饮者，如杜松子酒与苦艾酒混合者)。 **2** mixture of fruit juices, or spiced tomato juice, served in a glass as an appetizer; quantity of crab meat or shrimps, similarly served. 混合果汁或加有香料之蕃茄汁(以杯进食，作为开胃品)；(作为开胃品的)蟹肉或虾肉。 **3** mixed fruit salad served in a glass. (置于杯中进食之)什锦水果沙拉。

cocky /'kɒkɪ; 'kɑkɪ/ adj (-ier, -iest) (colloq) cocksure; pert; conceited. (口)过于自信的；无礼的；自负的。

coco /'kəʊkəʊ; 'koko/ n (also 亦作 '**~-palm**, '**~-nut palm**) tropical seaside palm-tree. (生于热带海滨之)椰子树。 **~-nut** /'kəʊkənʌt; 'kokənɑt/ n large hardshelled seed of this palm-tree, filled with milky juice and a solid white eatable lining from which oil is extracted; 椰子(外有硬壳，内有乳状汁，壳内有一层白色可食的物质，即榨子肉，可制椰子油)。 ⇨ **copra**. 参看 illus at **palm**. 参看 palm 之插图。 '**~-nut 'matting**, made from the tough fibre of the ~nut's outer covering. (用椰子壳之坚韧的纤维制成之)棕席。

co·coa /'kəʊkəʊ; 'koko/ n [U] powder of crushed cacao seeds; hot drink made from this with water or milk. 可可(可可磨成的)可可粉；用可可粉与水或牛奶所制成的热饮料。

co·coon /kə'kuːn; kə'kun/ n silky covering made by a caterpillar to protect itself while it is a chrysalis, esp that of the silkworm. 茧(毛虫在作蛹时期结丝以保护自己的外壳)；(尤指)蚕茧。 ⇨ the illus at **butterfly, silk**. 参看 butterfly 及 silk 之插图。 □ vt [VP6A] protect by covering completely. 完全盖住以保护；封存。

co·cotte /kɒ'kɒt; ko'kɑt/ n (F) (dated) fashionable prostitute. (法)(过时用语)上流社会的娼妓；高级妓女。

cod¹ /kɒd; kɑd/ n **1** [C] (pl unchanged) (复数不变) (also 亦作 '**cod·fish**) large sea fish. 鳕。 **2** [U] its flesh as food. 鳕鱼肉(作为食物者)。 '**~-liver oil** /,kɒd 'lɪvər ɔɪl; ,kɑdlɪrvɚ'ɔɪl/ n [U] used as a medicine. 鱼肝油(作药物用)。

cod² /kɒd; kɑd/ vt, vi (-dd-) [VP6A, 2A] (dated colloq) hoax; make a fool of: (过时口语)欺骗；愚弄: You're codding (me)! 你在骗我(骗我)!

coda /'kəʊdə; 'kodə/ n passage (often elaborate in style) that completes a piece of music. (乐曲的)尾声(常为加意雕琢之作)。

coddle /'kɒdl; 'kɑdl/ vt [VP6A] **1** (also 亦作 '**molly-~**) treat with great care and tenderness; pamper: 娇

养；溺爱；宠爱；纵容: ~ *a child because it is in poor health.* 娇养一个孩子因其体弱。**2** cook, eg eggs, in water just below boiling-point. 以仅低于沸点的温度在水中煮(蛋等)；软煮。

code /kəʊd; kod/ n [C] **1** collection of laws arranged in a system. 法典；法规；章程；规程。**2** system of rules and principles that has been accepted by society or a class or group of people: (社会或某阶层所遵守的)礼法；规约；惯例；道德律: *a high moral ~*; 崇高的道德准则; *a ~ of honour.* 社交礼法；绅士淑女之道。*You must live up to the ~ of the school,* accept its unwritten rules of honour and conduct. 你必须遵守学校的传统规约。**3** (also 亦作 [U]) system of signs used for secrecy or brevity, eg in wartime, or for economy in sending cables, or for a computer: 密码(如在战时用以保守机密者)；(打电报或电脑中所用以节时省字的)电码: *send a message in ~*; 用密码发送消息; *a 'telegraph ~;* (电报之) 电码; *a ~ telegram;* 密码电报; 电码电报; *a ,five-'letter ~,* eg one in which BXYMA stands for a phrase or sentence. 五字母密码(如 BXYMA 即代表一短语或句子)。*break a ~,* discover how to interpret a secret ~. 解密码。**the 'Morse ~,** using dots and dashes for letters and numerals. 摩尔斯电码(用点及长划代表字母和数字)。□ vt (also 亦作 **en~** /en'kəʊd; en'kod/) put in a ~(3). ⇨ **decode.** 编成密码；译成电码。

co·deine /'kəʊdiːn; 'kodiˌin/ n [U] narcotic derived from opium. 可待因(自鸦片提制成的一种麻醉药)。

co·dex /'kəʊdeks; 'kodɛks/ n (pl codices /'kəʊdɪsiːz; 'kodəˌsiz/) manuscript volume (esp of ancient texts). (尤指古代典籍之)抄本。

codger /'kɒdʒə(r); 'kɑdʒɚ/ n (colloq) queer old person; fellow. (口)古怪的老人；老怪物；家伙。

codi·ces ⇨ **codex.**

codi·cil /'kəʊdɪsl US: 'kɒdəsl; 'kɑdəsl/ n appendix to a will, esp sth modifying or revoking part of it. 遗嘱的附录(尤指修改或取消遗嘱之部分内容者)；遗嘱更改;

codi·fy /'kəʊdɪfaɪ US: 'kɒdəfaɪ; 'kɑdəˌfaɪ/ vt [VP6A] put into the form of a code(1): 编成法典; 编纂: *~ the laws.* 编纂法典。**codi·fi·ca·tion** /ˌkəʊdɪfɪ'keɪʃn US: ˌkɒd-; ˌkɑdəfə'keʃən/ n

cod·ling /'kɒdlɪŋ; 'kɑdlɪŋ/ n young codfish. 幼鳕。

cod·piece /'kɒdpiːs; 'kɑd,pis/ n (15th and 16th cc) bag or flap concealing the opening in the front of a man's close-fitting hose²(2). (十五及十六世纪男人紧身裤前面开口之)遮裆袋或遮裆。

co-ed /ˌkəʊ ed; 'ko'ɛd/ n (US colloq) (girl or woman at a) co-educational school or college. (美口)男女同校的学校；男女同校中的女生。

co-edu·ca·tion /ˌkəʊ ˌedʒʊ'keɪʃn; ˌkosdʒə'keʃən/ n [U] education of boys and girls together. 男女同校的教育;男女同校。**~al** /-'keɪʃənl; -'keʃənl/ adj

co-ef·fi·cient /ˌkəʊɪ'fɪʃnt; ˌkoɪ'fɪʃənt/ n **1** (maths) number or symbol placed before and multiplying another quantity, known or unknown. (数学)系数(置于已知或未知数之前表示相乘之数或符号)。(In 3xy, 3 is the ~ of xy). (在 3xy 中，3 是 xy 的系数)。**2** (phys) multiplier that measures some property. (物理)率；系数。

co·erce /kəʊ'ɜːs; ko'ɝs/ vt [VP6A, 14] ~ *sb (into doing sth),* use force to make sb obedient, etc; compel sb to a course of action. 强迫某人(服从等)；强迫某人(做某事)。**co·ercion** /kəʊ'ɜːʃn US: -ʒn; ko'ɝʃən/ n [U] coercing or being ~d; government by force: 强迫；被迫；强制；压制: *He paid the money under coercion.* 他被迫付钱。**co·ercive** /kəʊ'ɜːsɪv; ko'ɝsɪv/ adj of coercion; using coercion: 用强迫力量的: *coercive methods/measures.* 压制方法(手段)。

co·eval /ˌkəʊ'iːvl; ko'ivl/ adj, n ~ *(with),* (person) of the same age; (person, things) existing at, lasting for, the same period of time. (与…)同年龄的(人)；同时期的(人、事物)。

co·exist /ˌkəʊɪg'zɪst; ˌko·ɪg'zɪst/ vi [VP2A, 3A] ~ *(with),* exist at the same time. (与…)同时存在；共存。**~·ence** /-təns; -təns/ n [U] (esp) peaceful existence side by side of states with opposed political systems. (尤指政治制度相反的各国间之)和平共存。

cof·fee /'kɒfɪ US: 'kɔːfɪ; 'kɔfɪ/ n [U] bush or shrub with berries containing seeds (called *beans*) which, when roasted and ground to powder, are used by infusing with boiling water for making·a drink; the seeds; the powder; [C, U] the drink: 咖啡树(所结浆果内的子，称咖啡豆，经焙炒磨成粉，加开水用以调制饮料)；咖啡豆；咖啡子；咖啡粉；咖啡饮料；咖啡: *three black ~s,* three cups of ~ without milk; 三杯不加牛奶的咖啡; *white ~,* with milk. 加牛奶的咖啡。**'~ bar** n small café serving ~ beverages and light refreshments. (供应咖啡饮料及小点心的)小咖啡馆。**'~-house** n (formerly, in England) place frequented by literary men as a sort of club. (昔时英国)文人常去聚谈的似俱乐部的地方；咖啡馆。**'~-mill** n device for grinding roasted ~-beans. 磨咖啡机。**'~-stall** n movable stand selling hot ~ and food in the streets (esp at night). 街头的流动咖啡摊 (卖热咖啡及食物，尤指于夜间)。

cof·fer /'kɒfə(r); 'kɔfɚ/ n **1** large, strong box, esp one for holding money or other valuables; (pl) place for storing valuables: 大而坚固之箱；保险箱；(复)储藏贵重物品的地方；金库；宝库: *the ~s of a bank.* 银行的金库。**2** ornamental panel in a ceiling, etc. (天花板等之)饰板；镶板。**3** (also 亦作 '**~·dam**) caisson (2). 潜水箱。

cof·fin /'kɒfɪn; 'kɔfɪn/ n box or case for a dead person to be placed in and then buried. (安置和埋葬死人的)棺材；柩。*drive a nail into sb's ~,* do sth that will bring his death or ruin nearer. 做某事使某人提早死亡或使其事业提早崩溃。

cog /kɒg; kɑg/ n one of a series of teeth on the rim of a wheel which transfers motion by locking into the teeth of a similar wheel. 轮齿；钝齿(与相似的轮之轮齿扣合，可以传递动力)。⇨ the illus at **bicycle, gear.** 参看 bicycle, gear 之插图。*be a cog in the machine,* (fig) an unimportant part of a large enterprise. (喻)为大企业中不重要的部分。'**cogwheel** n toothed wheel. 镶齿轮；嵌齿轮。

co·gent /'kəʊdʒənt; 'kodʒənt/ adj (of arguments) strong and convincing. (指论据)有说服力的。**co·gency** /'kəʊdʒənsɪ; 'kodʒənsɪ/ n [U] force or strength (of arguments). (论据之)力量；说服力。

cogi·tate /'kɒdʒɪteɪt; 'kɑdʒə,tet/ vi, vt [VP2A, 3A, 6A, 14] (formal or facet) meditate; think deeply: (正式用语或玩笑用语)沉思；思考: ~ *upon sth.* 慎思某事；~ *mischief against sb.* 想坏主意害人。**cogita·tion** /ˌkɒdʒɪ'teɪʃn; ˌkɑdʒə'teʃən/ n **1** [U] cogitating: 慎思；沉思；思考: *after much cogitation.* 经过长久的思考之后。**2** (pl) thoughts; reflections. (复)想法；看法。

cognac /'kɒnjæk; 'konjæk/ n [U] fine French brandy. 上等的法国白兰地酒。

cog·nate /'kɒgneɪt; 'kɑgnet/ adj **1** ~ *(with),* having the same source of origin: (与…)同根源的: *English, Dutch and German are ~ languages.* 英语，荷兰语和德语是同源语言。**2** related; having much in common: 有关系的；有关联的；有很多共同点的: *Physics and astronomy are ~.* 物理学和天文学是互有关联的科学。□ n [C] word, etc that is ~ with another. 同词源的词；同源词。

cog·ni·tion /kɒg'nɪʃn; kɑg'nɪʃən/ n [U] (phil) knowing; awareness (including sensation but excluding emotion). (哲学)认识；认知(包括感觉，但不包括感情)。

cog·ni·zance /'kɒgnɪzns; 'kɑgnəzəns/ n [U] **1** (legal) being aware, having conscious knowledge (of sth). (法律)察觉；认识；知道。*take ~ of,* become officially aware of. 正式获知。**2** (right of) dealing with a matter legally or judicially. 依法审理；审理权；管辖权。*fall within / go beyond one's ~,* be sth one can /

cannot deal with. 归(不归)某人处理; 在(不在)某人的管辖之内。 **cog·ni·zant** /'kɒɡnɪzənt; 'kɑɡnəzənt/ *adj* ~ **of**, (phil, legal) having knowledge, being fully aware of. (哲学, 法律)认识的; 知道的; 知晓的。

cog·no·men /kɒɡ'nəumen; kɑɡ'nomən/ *n* [C] (formal) (正式用语) **1** surname. 姓。 **2** descriptive nickname, eg *Rusty* or *Shorty*. (描绘某人特征的)绰号 (例如 Rusty 或 Shorty)

co·habit /kəu'hæbɪt; ko'hæbɪt/ *vi* (formal) (usu of an unmarried couple) live together. (正式用语)(通常指一对未婚的情侣) 共同生活; 同居。 **co·habi·tation** /,kəuhæbɪ'teɪʃn; ko,hæbə'teʃən/ *n*

co·here /kəu'hɪə(r); ko'hɪr/ *vi* [VP2A] (formal) stick together; be or remain united; (of arguments, etc) be consistent, (正式用语)粘在一起; 粘着; 连结在一起; 凝结; (指论据等)连贯; 前后一致。 **co·her·ence** /,kəu'hɪərəns; ko'hɪrəns/ *n* **co·her·en·cy** /-rənsɪ; -rənsɪ/ *n* **co·her·ent** /-rənt; -rənt/ *adj* **1** sticking together. 粘在一起的; 结合在一起的。 **2** consistent; (esp of speech, thought, ideas, reasoning) clear; easy to understand. 一致的; 连贯的; (尤指言词、思想、观念、推理)清晰的; 易懂的。 **co·her·ent·ly** *adv*

co·he·sion /kəu'hiːʒn; ko'hiʒən/ *n* cohering; tendency to stick together; force with which molecules cohere. 附着; 粘着; 附着力; 结合力; (分子的)内聚性; 内聚力。 **co·he·sive** /kəu'hiːsɪv; ko'hisɪv/ *adj* having the power of cohering; tending to cohere. 有附着力的; 有内聚力的。

co·hort /'kəuhɔːt; 'kohort/ *n* **1** (in the ancient Roman armies) tenth part of a legion. (古罗马军队)军团的十分之一; 大队。 **2** number of persons banded together. 一队(人)。

coif /kɔɪf; kɔɪf/ *n* (old use) close-fitting cap covering the top, back and sides of the head. (旧用法)一种复盖着头顶、头后及两侧之紧帽。

coif·feur /kwɑː'fɜː(r); ,kwɑ'fɚ/ *n* (F) hairdresser. (法)(为妇女理发的)理发师。 **coif·fure** /kwɑː'fjuə(r); kwɑ'fjur/ *n* style of hairdressing. 妇女的发式; 发型。

coign /kɔɪn; kɔɪn/ *n* ~ **of 'vantage** (formal, usu fig) place from which one has a good view of sth. (正式用语, 通常用作喻)对于某事物能作仔细观察的地方; 有利的地位。

coil /kɔɪl; kɔɪl/ *vt, vi* [VP6A, 15A, B, 2A, C] wind or twist into a continuous circular or spiral shape; curl round and round: 绕成状状; 盘绕; 缠绕; 一圈一圈地卷起: ~ *a rope*. 卷起绳索。 *The snake ~ed (itself) round the branch* / ~ed *itself up*. 那蛇盘绕在树枝上 (把身体盘绕起来)。 □ *n* **1** sth ~ed; a single turn of sth ~ed: 盘绕之物; 所盘绕之一圈: *the thick ~s of a python*. 蟒蛇所盘绕之厚粗的圈圈。 ⇨ the illus at **snake**. 参看 snake 之插图。 **2** length of wire wound in a spiral to conduct electric current. (用金属丝所绕成以传导电流的)线圈。 **3** (colloq) an intra-uterine contraceptive device in the shape of a ~. (口)(置于子宫中的)圈形避孕器。

coin /kɔɪn; kɔɪn/ *n* [C, U] (piece of) metal money: (一枚)铸币; 硬币: *a small heap of ~s*; 一小堆硬币; *gold and silver ~s*; 金币和银币; *false ~*, imitation ~ in metal of low value. 用贱金属所制的假钱; 伪造的钱币。 *the other side of the ~*, (fig) other aspect of the matter. (喻)事情的另一方面。 *pay a man back in the same/his own ~*, treat him as he has treated you. 他曾怎样对待你, 你也怎样对待他; 以其人之道还治其人之身。 □ *vt* [VP6A] make (metal) into ~s; invent (esp a new word). 用(金属)铸造钱币; 创造; 杜撰(尤指新词)。 *be '~ing money*, be making money fast, be making large profits. 迅速地发财; 暴富; 赚大钱。 *to ~ a phrase*, (ironic) to use a very well established idiom as if it were a new one. (反语)将一盛行已久的惯用语当作新鲜成语使用。 **~·age** /kɔɪnɪdʒ; 'kɔɪnɪdʒ/ *n* **1** [U] making ~s; the ~s made; [U] system of ~s in use: 铸造钱币; 所铸之钱币; 通用的货币制度: *a decimal ~age*. 十进货币制度。 **2** [U] inventing (of a new word);

[C] newly invented word. (新词的)创造; 新创造的词。 **~·er** *n* maker of counterfeit ~s. 伪造钱币者。

co·incide /,kəuɪn'saɪd; ,ko·ɪn'saɪd/ *vi* [VP2A, 3A] ~ **(with)**, **1** (of two or more objects) correspond in area and outline. (指两个或更多的物件)在面积与轮廓上相符合。 **2** (of events) happen at the same time; occupy the same period of time: (指事件)同时发生; 占同一时期; 巧合: *They could not go to the theatre together because his free time never ~d with hers*. 他们无法一同去看戏, 因为他们的闲暇从来凑不到一起。 **3** (of ideas, etc) be in harmony or agreement: (指意见等)一致; 协调: *The judges did not ~ in opinion*. 裁判们的意见不一致。 *His tastes and habits ~ with those of his wife*. 他的嗜好和习惯与他妻子的恰好一致。

co·inci·dence /kəu'ɪnsɪdəns; ko'ɪnsədəns/ *n* [U] the condition of coinciding; [C] instance of this, happening by chance: 符合; 巧合; 巧合之事情: *by a curious ~*. 刚好; 凑巧; 碰巧。 *What a ~!* How curious, etc that these two events should come together! 多么凑巧的事情啊! (这两件事发生在同一时, 多么巧啊!) **co·inci·dent** /-dənt; -dənt/ *adj* coinciding. 同时发生的; 一致的; 巧合的。 **co·inci·dental** /kəu,ɪnsɪ'dentl; ko,ɪnsə'dentl/ *adj* of the nature of a, exhibiting ~. 巧合性的; 巧合的。

coir /'kɔɪə(r); kɔɪr/ *n* fibre from coconut shells, used for making ropes, matting, etc. 椰子壳之纤维(用以制绳、席等)。

co·ition /kəu'ɪʃn; ko'ɪʃən/ *n*=**coitus**.

co·itus /'kəuɪtəs; 'ko·ɪtəs/ *n* [U] (formal) sexual intercourse to the point of (mutual) orgasm between two human beings; the insertion of the penis into the vagina. (正式用语)(双方)达性欲高潮的性交; 性交; 交媾。

coke¹ /kəuk; kok/ *n* [U] rough, light substance that remains when gas has been taken out of coal by heating it in an oven, used as a fuel in stoves and furnaces (将煤置于炉中加热去掉煤气后所剩余的)焦炭; 焦煤(作为火炉或熔炉之燃料)。 □ *vt* turn (coal) into ~. 将(煤)制成焦煤。

coke² /kəuk; kok/ *n* (P) (colloq abbr of) Coca-Cola. (商标)(口)可口可乐(Coca-Cola 之略)。

coke³ /kəuk; kok/ *n* (sl) cocaine. (俚)古柯碱。

coker·nut /'kəukənʌt; 'kokə,nʌt/ *n*=**coconut**.

col /kɒl; kɑl/ *n* depression or pass in a mountain range. (山脉中的)峡口; 峡路; 隘口。 ⇨ the illus at **mountain**. 参看 mountain 之插图。

cola /'kəulə; 'kolə/ *n*=**kola**.

col·an·der, cul·len·der /'kʌləndə(r); 'kʌləndə/ *n* bowl-shaped vessel or dish with many small holes, used to drain off water from vegetables, etc in cooking. 滤锅; 滤盆(有许多小孔, 烹调时用以漏去蔬菜等中之水)。

cold¹ /kəuld; kold/ *adj* **1** of low temperature, esp when compared with the human body: 气温低的; 寒冷的; 冷的(尤指与人的体温相比而言): ~ *weather*; 寒冷的天气; *a ~ wind*; 寒风; 冷风; 冷~; 感觉冷; *a hotel with hot and ~ water in every bedroom*. 每间房间都有冷热水设备的旅馆。 *give sb the ~ shoulder*, (fig) snub him; show distaste for his company. (喻)以冷淡态度对待某人; 表示不欢迎某人。 Hence, 由此产生, *,~·'shoulder vt* [VP6A] snub. 冷落; 轻待。 *have ~ feet*, feel afraid or reluctant (to do sth involving risk or danger). 感觉害怕或迟疑(指不敢做冒险或危险的事)。 *leave one ~*, leave one unmoved, unimpressed. 未能打动某人的心; 没使其留下深刻印象。 *(kill sb) in ~ blood; make one's 'blood run ~*, a blood¹. *pour/throw water on, '~ water¹(1)*. '~ **chisel**, one for cutting soft metals while they are ~. 冷錾(用以切割冷却之软金属的錾子)。 '~ **comfort**, poor consolation. 令人寒心的事。 '~ **cream**, ointment for cleansing and softening the skin. 冷霜(清洁并滋润皮肤的油膏)。 '~, **'front**, ⇨ **front(7)**. ,~ **'meat**, meat that has been

cooked and cooled: (煮熟的)冷肉: ~ *meat for supper.* 晚餐吃的冷肉。 **,~ 'steel,** [U] cutting or stabbing weapon (eg a sword or bayonet contrasted with firearms). 砍或刺戳的武器 (如剑或刺刀, 以别于枪炮)。 **,~ 'turkey, ~ turkey, ~ 'war,** struggle for superiority waged by hostile propaganda, economic measures, etc without actual fighting. 冷战 (借宣传、经济措施等, 而非借实际战斗以获得优势)。 **,~-'blooded** /-'blʌdɪd; -'blʌdɪd/ *adj* **(a)** having blood that varies with the temperature (eg fish, reptiles). 冷血的; 血液能随温度而改变的(如鱼、爬虫类)。 **(b)** (fig of persons, their actions) without feeling; pitiless. (喻)指人, 人之行为)无情的; 无怜悯心的; 冷酷的。 **,~-'hearted** /-'hɑːtɪd; -'hɑrtɪd/ *adj* without sympathy; indifferent. 无同情心的; 冷漠的。 **2** (fig) (喻) **(a)** unkind; unfriendly: 冷淡的; 不亲热的: *a ~ greeting/welcome, etc.* 冷淡的招呼 (欢迎等)。 **(b)** sexually unresponsive. 性方面无反应的; 性冷感的。 **3** (of colours) suggesting ~, eg grey and blue. (指颜色)令人感觉凉爽的 (如灰色和蓝色)。 **~·ly** *adv* **~·ness** *n* [U] state of being ~: 冷; 寒冷: *Because of the ~ness of the weather, we stayed indoors.* 因为天气寒冷, 所以我们呆在室内。

cold² /kəʊld; kold/ *n* **1** [U] **(the) ~,** relative absence of heat; low temperature (esp in the atmosphere): 冷; 寒冷; 低温度(尤指气温): *He was shivering with ~.* 他冷得直发抖。 *He disliked both the heat of summer and the ~ of winter.* 他既不喜欢夏天之热, 也不喜欢冬天之冷。 *Don't stay outside in the ~, come indoors by the fire.* 不要呆在外面受寒, 到室内火炉边来。 **(be left) out in the ~,** (fig) (be) ignored or neglected. (喻)(被)冷落。 **2** [U] (phys) freezing-point of water or below. (物理)(水之)冰点或冰点以下: *five degrees of ~.* 冰点以下五度。 **3** [C, U] inflammation of the mucous membrane of the nose or throat: 伤风; 感冒: *have a ~;* 患伤风; 感冒; *catch (a) ~.* 受凉。 *Half the boys in the school were absent with ~s.* 半数的男生均因患感冒而缺席。

cole·slaw /'kəʊlslɔː; 'kol,slɔ/ *n* [U] finely shredded dressed raw cabbage (as a salad). 切丝生拌的包心菜(作生菜食用)。

colic /'kɒlɪk; 'kɑlɪk/ *n* [U] severe pain in the stomach and bowels without diarrhoea. 腹部绞痛 (但无腹泻); 疼痛。

co·li·tis /kə'laɪtɪs; ko'laɪtɪs/ *n* [U] (med) inflammation of the mucous membrane of the colon. (医)结肠炎(结肠粘膜发炎)。

col·lab·or·ate /kə'læbəreɪt; kə'læbə,ret/ *vi* **1** [VP2A, 3A] ~ (on sth) (with sb), work in partnership, esp in literature or art: (尤指文学或艺术方面)(与某人)合著; 合作(某作品): *~ on a biography with a friend.* 与一朋友合著一部传记。 **2** [VP3A] ~ with, work treasonably, esp with enemy forces occupying one's country. 做叛国的工作(尤指与占领的敌军合作); 勾结(敌人); 通敌。 **col·lab·or·ator** /kə'læbəreɪtə(r); kə'læbə,retɚ/ *n* person who ~s (1, 2). 合著者; 合作者; 通敌者。 **col·lab·or·ation** /kə,læbə'reɪʃn; kə,læbə'reʃən/ *n* [U] collaborating: 合著; 合作; 通敌: *working in collaboration with others.* 与别人合作。 **col·lab·or·ation·ist** /kə,læbə'reɪʃənɪst; kə,læbə'reʃənɪst/ *n* person who ~s (2). 通敌者。

col·lage /'kɒlɑːʒ US: kə'lɑːʒ; kə'lɑʒ/ *n* [U, C] (art) (picture made by an) unusual combination of bits of paper, cloth, photographs, metal etc. (艺术)(用纸片、碎布、照片、金属等的)美术拼贴; 拼贴画。

col·lapse /kə'læps; kə'læps/ *vi* [VP2A] **1** fall down or in; come or break to pieces suddenly: 倒塌; 塌陷: *The weight of the snow on the roof caused the shed to ~.* 棚顶积雪的重量使得小棚倒塌。 *The roof ~d under the weight of the snow.* 屋顶因积雪的重压而倒塌。 *If you cut the ropes of a tent, it will ~.* 如果你割断帐篷的绳索, 它就会倒塌。 **2** lose physical strength, courage, mental powers, etc; break down: 失去体力、勇气、心智能力等; 病倒; 颓丧; 崩溃; 瓦解: *If you work too hard*

you/your health may ~. 如果你工作过度, 你会病倒。 *Our plans will ~ unless we get more help.* 我们的计划将会瓦解, 除非我们能得到更多的帮助。 *The price of copper ~d,* dropped to a low level. 铜的价钱暴跌。 **3** (of apparatus) close or fold up. (指器械)折叠。 **4** *vt* [VP6A] cause to ~: 使倒塌; 使崩溃; 使折叠: *~ a canvas chair.* 将一帆布椅折起。 □ *n* collapsing: 倒塌; 崩溃; 病倒; (价格之)暴跌: *the ~ of a table/tent/tower, etc;* 桌子(帐篷, 塔等)的倒塌; (fig): (喻): *the ~ of their plans/hopes;* 他们的计划(希望)的破灭; *suffer a nervous ~.* 精神崩溃。 **col·laps·ible, -able** /-səbl; -səbl/ *adj* that can be ~d (4) (for packing, etc): 可折叠(以便包装等)的: *a collapsible boat/chair.* 可折迭的小船(椅子)。

col·lar /'kɒlə(r); 'kɑlɚ/ *n* **1** part of a garment that fits round the neck; turned-over neckband of a shirt, dress, etc: 衣领; 领: *The wind was so cold that he turned his coat ~ up.* 风太冷了, 所以他把外套的领子翻起来。 **'blue/'white ~ workers,** ▷ blue, white. **2** separate article of clothing (linen, lace, etc) worn round the neck and fastened to a shirt or blouse. (可与衬衫或短上衣扣合, 用亚麻布、花边等做成的)假领; 领饰。 **'~ stud** *n* small button-like device for fastening a ~ to a shirt. 领扣(用以将衣领与衬衫扣合)。 **3** band of leather, etc put round the neck of a dog, horse or other animal. (狗、马或其他动物颈间所系, 用皮革等做的)项圈。 ▷ the illus at **harness.** 参看 harness 之插图。 **4** metal band joining two pipes, rods or shafts, eg in a machine. (连结两管、两杆或机械之轴之)环管; 轴环。 **5 '~-bone** *n* bone joining the shoulder and the breast-bone. (连接肩与胸骨的)锁骨。 ▷ the illus at **skeleton.** 参看 skeleton 之插图。 □ *vt* [VP6A] **1** seize (sb) by the ~; take hold of roughly: 扭住(某人的)领子; 抓住: *The policeman ~ed the thief.* 警察抓住那窃贼。 **2** (dated colloq) take without permission: (过时口语)未得许可而拿走; 擅取: *Who's ~ed my pen?* 谁把我的钢笔拿去了?

col·late /kə'leɪt; kə'let/ *vt* [VP6A] make a careful comparison between (copies of texts, manuscripts, books, etc) to learn the differences between them: 详细比较(若干本正文、原稿、书籍等)以寻出其间差别; 对照; 校勘: *~ a new edition with an earlier edition.* 将新版本与旧版本作详细比较。

col·lat·eral /kə'lætərəl; kə'lætərəl/ *adj* **1** secondary or subordinate but from the same source: 次要的; 附属的; 附带的(但系同一来源): *~ evidence;* 附属证据; *~ security,* property, eg stocks or bonds, pledged as security for repayment of a loan. (保证归还借款之)抵押品(如股票或债券)。 **2** descended from a common ancestor but in a different line, ie through different sons or daughters. (指亲属) 旁系的 (如兄弟姐妹之子女)。 □ *n* [U] (-) security. 抵押品。

col·la·tion /kə'leɪʃn; kɑ'leʃən/ *n* [C] (formal) light meal, (usu 通常作 *cold* ~), often one served at a time different from usual meal times. (正式用语)(常指正餐时间以外所备的)便餐。

col·league /'kɒliːg; 'kɑlig/ *n* one of two or more persons working together and (usu) having similar rank and duties: (在一起工作, 通常并有同等地位和职务的)同事; 同僚: *the Prime Minister and his ~s,* the other members of the Cabinet. 首相及其同僚 (即其内阁之阁员)。

col·lect¹ /kə'lekt; kə'lekt/ *vt, vi* **1** [VP6A, 15B] ~ (up/together), bring or gather together; get from a number of persons or places: 收集; 搜集; 募集: *The teacher told the boys to ~ (up/together) all the waste paper lying about and then burn it.* 那老师告诉男学生们, 在野餐以后把四处散置的废纸捡集起来烧掉。 *If he could ~ all the money people owe him, he would be a rich man.* 他要能够把所有别人久欠他的钱都要回来, 他就会成为一位富翁了。 *A man who ~s taxes is called a tax-or.* 收税的人叫税务员。 **2** [VP6A] obtain specimens of (books, stamps, etc), eg as a hobby or in order to study sth: 搜集(书籍、邮票等)之样品(例如作为

癖好或为了研究）：~ *foreign stamps / old china.* 搜集外国邮票（古瓷器）。**3** [VP2A, C] ~ *(together)*, come together: 聚集；聚积：*A crowd soon ~s (together) when there's a street accident.* 当街头发生意外事件的时候，立刻就有一群人聚集起来。**4** [VP6A] fetch: 拿来；接来：~ *a child from school.* 自校中接回小孩。**5** [VP6A] gather together, recover control of (one's thoughts, energies, oneself): 使（思想、精力）集中；使（心神）镇定：*Before you begin to make a speech, you should ~ your thoughts and ideas.* 在你开始发表演说之前，你应当集中思想和意念。☐ *adj, adv* (US comm) paid for on delivery: （美商）收到时即付款的（地）；由收件人付款的（地）：*a ~ telegram.* 收报人付款的电报。*I'll pay for the goods* ~, when they are delivered. 我收到货时即会付款。~**ed** *adj* (esp of a person) calm; not distracted. （尤指人）镇静的；心思不乱的。~**ed·ly** *adv*

col·lect² /'kɒlekt; 'kɑlɛkt/ *n* short prayer of the Church of Rome or the Church of England, to be read on certain appointed days. （天主教或英国国教之在某些指定的日子所念的）短祈祷文。

col·lec·tion /kə'lekʃn; kə'lɛkʃən/ *n* **1** [U] collecting; [C] instance of this: 收集；收取：*How many ~s of letters are there every day,* How often does the postman empty the boxes? 邮差每天收几次信？**2** [C] group of objects that have been collected and that belong together: 搜集品；收藏品（所收藏的同类物品）：*a fine ~ of old swords / paintings / postage stamps.* 所收藏的一批珍贵的古剑（图画，邮票）。**3** heap of materials or objects that have come together: 聚集在一起的东西；聚积物：*a ~ of dust / rubbish.* 一堆灰尘（垃圾）。**4** [C] money collected at a meeting, a Church service, etc. （集会、礼拜等时候）所募集的捐款。*take (up) / make a ~: The ~ will be taken (up) / made after the sermon.* 在讲道之后将作捐献。

col·lec·tive /kə'lektɪv; kə'lɛktɪv/ *adj* **1** of a group or society (of persons, nations, etc) as a whole: 群体的；社会的；共有的；集体的(指人、国家等)：~ *leadership,* (emphasis on) government by a group rather than an individual. 集体领导(强调由一群人而非一个人所领导的政治)；~ *ownership of the land / of means of production, etc,* by all citizens for the benefit of all; 土地(生产工具等)之集体所有权(为全体公民所有并享用)；~ *security,* security of a State or States against aggression by means of common military, etc preparedness. 集体安全(一国或数国为抵抗侵略在军事等方面所作之共同的防御措施)。~ *farm,* (eg in a Socialist State) one owned by the State and run by the workers for the benefit of all the citizens, 集体农场(如在社会主义国家中者，农场为国家所有，为工人所经营，利益归全民所享)。**2** ~ *noun,* (gram) one that is singular in form but stands for many individuals, as *cattle, crowd, audience:* (语法)集合名词(形式上是单数但实际上代表许多个体之名词，如 cattle, crowd, audience)：*In 'to catch fish', fish is a ~ noun.* In to catch fish 中，fish 是集合名词。**col·lec·tiv·ize** /kə'lektɪvaɪz; kə'lɛktɪ,vaɪz/ *vt* [VP6A] change, eg farm lands, from private ownership to a system of State control. 变私有(如耕地)为国有；使集体化。**col·lec·tiv·iz·ation** /kə,lektɪvaɪ'zeɪʃn US: -vɪ'z-; kə,lɛktəvə'zeʃən/ *n*

col·lec·tor /kə'lektə(r); kə'lɛktɚ/ *n* person who collects: 收集者；搜集者；收藏者：*a 'stamp~;* 集邮者；*a 'tax~;* 收税人；税务员；*a 'ticket~,* eg at a railway station. (火车站等之)收票员。~**'s item / piece,** article sought by ~s, eg a book, a piece of china or furniture, because of its beauty, rarity, etc. 收藏家所寻求之物(如珍贵的书籍、瓷器或家具)。

col·leen /'kɒliːn; 'kɑlin/ *n* (Irish) young girl. (爱尔兰语)少女。

col·lege /'kɒlɪdʒ; 'kɑlɪdʒ/ *n* **1** [C, U] school for higher or professional education; body of teachers and students forming part of a university; their building(s): 高等教育机关；专科学校；学院(为大学之一部分，亦可指其

师生全体，亦可指其建筑物)：*go to ~；*读大学；上大学；*be at ~,* 在大学求学；*a C~ of Agriculture / Pharmacy, etc;* 农(药)等学院；*the Oxford and Cambridge ~s;* 牛津及剑桥诸学院；*Heads of C~s,* ⇨ for their titles **Master¹(9), President, Principal, Provost, Rector, Warden.** 大学之首长(其正式头衔参看 Master¹(9), President, Principal, Provost, Rector, Warden)。**2** [C] union of persons with common purposes and privileges: (有共同目的和特权的)学会；社团：*the C~ of Surgeons;* 外科医师学会；*the C~ of Cardinals,* who elect and advise the Pope. 红衣主教团(可选举教皇并为其顾问)。**col·le·giate** /kə'liːdʒɪət; kə'lidʒɪɪt/ *adj* of or like a ~ or student: 学会的；学院的；大学的；大学生的：*collegiate life,* life in ~s and universities. 大学生活。

col·lide /kə'laɪd; kə'laɪd/ *vi* [VP2A, C, 3A] ~ *(with),* **1** come together violently; meet and strike: 互撞；碰撞：*As the bus came round the corner, it ~d with a van.* 公共汽车在转过街角时与一辆敞车互撞。*The bus and the van ~d.* 公共汽车与敞车互撞。*The ships ~d in the fog.* 船在浓雾中互撞。**2** be opposed; be in conflict: 相反；冲突：*If the aims of two countries ~, there may be war.* 如果两国的目标冲突，就可能发生战争。

col·lie /'kɒlɪ; 'kɑlɪ/ *n* Scottish sheep-dog with shaggy hair. 苏格兰产之粗毛牧羊犬。⇨ the illus at **dog.** 参看 dog 之插图。

col·lier /'kɒlɪə(r); 'kɑljɚ/ *n* **1** coal-miner. 煤矿工人。**2** ship that carries coal as cargo. 运煤船。

col·liery /'kɒljərɪ; 'kɑljərɪ/ *n* (*pl* **-ries**) coal-mine (and the buildings, etc connected with it). 煤矿场(包括附属建筑物)。

col·li·sion /kə'lɪʒn; kə'lɪʒən/ *n* [U] colliding; [C] instance of this: 互撞；猛烈碰撞；互撞之实例；冲突；抵触：*a head-on ~ between two buses;* 两辆公共汽车迎面互撞；*a railway ~;* 火车撞车事件；*on (a) ~ course,* likely to collide. 可能互撞。*be in / come into ~ (with),* have collided / collide (with)：(与…)互撞：*The liner is reported to have been in ~ with an oil-tanker.* 据报导该客船与一油轮互撞。*The two ships were in / came into ~.* 两船互撞。*People with anarchic ideas may find themselves in ~ with the forces of the law,* get into trouble with the police. 抱有无政府主义思想的人可能和执法的人发生冲突。

col·lo·cate /'kɒlekeɪt; 'kɑlo,ket/ *vi* [VP2A, 3A] ~ *(with),* (of words) combine in a way characteristic of language: (按习惯用法)连用；连用：'Weak' ~s with 'tea' but 'feeble' does not. weak 与 tea 连用而 feeble 则不能。**col·lo·ca·tion** /,kɒle'keɪʃn; ,kɑlo'keʃən/ *n* [C, U] coming together; collocating of words: (词之)配置；搭配；连用：'Strong tea' and 'heavy drinker' are English collocations; so are 'by accident' and 'so as to'. strong tea 与 heavy drinker 都是英语中习惯上的搭配；by accident 及 so as to 也是。

col·loquial /kə'ləʊkwɪəl; kə'lokwɪəl/ *adj* (of words, phrases, style) belonging to, suitable for, ordinary conversation; not formal or literary. (指词)、短语、风格)属于或适于日常会话的；非正式的；非文学性的；通俗的；口语的。~**·ly** *adv* ~**·ism** *n* [C] ~ word or phrase. 俗字；俗语；口语说法。

col·lo·quy /'kɒlekwɪ; 'kɑlekwɪ/ *n* (*pl* **-quies**) [C, U] (formal) conversation: (正式用语)谈话；会谈：*engage in ~ with sb.* 某某人会谈。

col·lu·sion /kə'luːʒn; kə'luʒən/ *n* [U] secret agreement or understanding for a deceitful or fraudulent purpose: 暗中串通；勾结；共谋(以骗人)：*act in ~ with sb;* 与某人暗中串通；~ *between persons who appear to be opposed to each other.* 二人表面相敌对而实实际暗中勾结。**col·lus·ive** /kə'luːsɪv; kə'lusɪv/ *adj*

colly·wobbles /'kɒlɪwɒblz; 'kɑlɪ,wɑblz/ *n* (colloq) stomach-ache; slight feeling of fear (with nausea). (口)肚子痛；(有恶心的)轻微的害怕。

co·lon¹ /'kəʊlən; 'kolən/ *n* lower and greater part of

the large intestine. 结肠(大肠下端之较大的部分)。 ⇨ the illus at **alimentary**. 参看 alimentary 之插图。

co·lon² /'kəʊlən; 'kolən/ n punctuation mark (:) used in writing and printing (to direct special attention to what follows). 冒号(书写及印刷中的标点符号,即(:),以指示特别注意下列者)。 ⇨ **App 9**. 参看附录九。

colo·nel /'kɜːnl; 'kɝnl/ n army officer above a lieutenant-~ and (in US) commanding a regiment; (abbr for) lieutenant-~. 陆军上校(在中校之上,在美国统率一团军队); 陆军中校 (lieutenant-colonel 之略称)。

co·lo·nial /kə'ləʊnɪəl; kə'lonɪəl/ adj 1 of a colony or colonies (1). 殖民地的。 '**C~ Office**, (GB) former State department in charge of colonies. (英)(昔日之)殖民部(专司殖民地事务)。 **2** (esp US) in the style of architecture in the British colonies in N America before and during the Revolution. (美)(在美国革命前或期中)北美洲英国殖民地之建筑式的。 □ n inhabitant of a colony (1), esp a descendant of those who colonized it. 殖民地居民; (尤指)殖民地开拓者后裔。 ~·ism n [U] policy of having colonies(1) and keeping them dependent. 殖民政策; 殖民主义。 ~·ist n supporter of ~ism; one who favours the retention of colonies(1). 支持殖民政策者; 殖民主义者。

col·on·ist /'kɒlənɪst; 'kɑlənɪst/ n pioneer settler in a colony (1). 新殖民地开拓者。

col·on·ize /'kɒlənaɪz; 'kɑlə,naɪz/ vt [VP6A] establish a colony in; establish as a colony: 开拓殖民地于; 殖民于: The ancient Greeks ~d many parts of the Mediterranean. 古代希腊人在地中海区域开拓了许多殖民地。 **col·on·iz·ation** /ˌkɒlənaɪ'zeɪʃn US: -nɪ'z-; ˌkɑlənɪ'zeʃən/ n [U] colonizing 殖民; 拓殖; 殖民: the colonization of N America by the British, Dutch and French. 英国人, 荷兰人和法国人对北美洲之拓殖。 **col·on·izer** n one who helps to establish a colony (1). 帮助建立殖民地的人; 殖民地开拓者。

col·on·nade /ˌkɒlə'neɪd; ˌkɑlə'ned/ n row of columns(1) set (usu) at equal distances. (通常为)距离相等的一列柱子; 柱廊。 ⇨the illus at **column**. 参看 column 之插图。 **col·on·naded** /ˌkɒlə'neɪdɪd; ˌkɑlə'nedɪd / adj ~. 有柱廊的。

col·ony /'kɒlənɪ; 'kɑlənɪ/ n (pl -nies) **1** country or territory settled by migrants from another country, and controlled by it. 殖民地(由某国移民所定居的国家或领土, 且为该国所控制者)。 **2** group of people from another country, or of people with the same trade, profession or occupation, living together: 来自他国并生活在一起的一批人民; 侨民; 同行业并生活在一起的一群人: the American ~ in Paris; 在巴黎的美国侨民; a ~ of artists, group of people famous for its scenic beauty. 一群艺术家 (如居于著名的风景优美之地者)。 **3** (biol) number of animals or plants, living or growing together: (生物)群居或生长在一起的若干动物或植物; 群体: a ~ of ants. 一窝蚂蚁。

color (US) =colour.

col·ora·tura /ˌkɒlərə'tʊərə; ˌkʌlərə'tjʊrə/ n [U] flowery or ornamental passages in vocal music; 歌曲中的花腔部分; 花腔; (attrib)(用作定语): a ~ soprano. 花腔歌手; 花腔女高音。

co·los·sal /kə'lɒsl; kə'lɑsl/ adj immense. 巨大的。

co·los·sus /kə'lɒsəs; kə'lɑsəs/ n (pl -lossi /-'lɒsaɪ; -'lɑsaɪ/, ~es /-'lɒsəsɪz; -'lɑsəsɪz/) immense statue (esp of a man, much greater than life-size); immense person or personification of sth. 巨大的雕像(尤指大于真人的人像); 巨人; 某物之巨大的拟人像。

col·our¹ (US=color) /'kʌlə(r); 'kʌlɚ/ n **1** [U] sensation produced in the eye by rays of decomposed light; [C] effect produced by a ray of light of a particular wavelength, or by a mixture of these: 颜色; 色彩(白光分解以后之各种光线在眼中所产生的感觉; 具有某种特定波长的光线或混合光线所产生的效果): ~ films; 彩色影片; 彩色电影片; ~ TV. 彩色电视(机)。 Red, blue and yellow are ~s. 红、蓝和黄都是颜色。 There isn't

enough ~ in the picture. 这幅画中的色彩不够。 '~-**blind** adj unable to distinguish between certain ~s, or to see certain ~s. 色盲的(不能分辨或看不见某些颜色的)。 '~ **scheme** n scheme for combination of ~s in a design (eg for the furnishing and decoration of a room, the planting of a flower garden). 色彩设计(如房间内部装潢的设计, 花园中花卉种植的设计)。 '~-**wash** n coloured distemper. 彩色涂料。 **2** [U] redness of the face: 面部的红润之色; 血色: She has very little ~, has a pale face. 她面上几无血色(面色苍白)。 change, grow paler or redder than usual. 面部变色 (变白或变红)。 **have a high ~**, have a red complexion. 面部绯红。 **lose ~**, become pale. 脸色变白; 失色。 **be/feel/look off ~**, (colloq) be/seem unwell, in low spirits. (口)气色不好; 神情沮丧。 **3** (pl) materials used by artists; paint: (复)(画家用的)颜料: 'water-~s; 水彩颜料; 'oil-~s; 油画颜料; ⇨ **oil, water**; appearance produced by their use: 由于使用色彩所产生的外观: paint sth in bright/dark ~s, (fig) make it appear favourable/unfavourable. (喻) 对某事物加以粉饰(贬抑); 强调其光明(黑暗)面。 **(see sth/appear) in its true ~s**, as it really is. 看清某事物的真相(原形毕露)。 **4** [U] (of events, descriptions) appearance of reality or truth; pretext. (指事件、描写)表面的真实性; 托辞。 **give/lend ~ to**, give an appearance of probability to: 使有某种迹象; 使看起来有可信: His torn clothing gave ~ to his story that he had been attacked and robbed. 他被撕破的衣服使他所说被袭击和抢劫的事显得可信。 **give false ~ to**, give a wrong character or tone to: 曲解; 歪曲(事真相): Newspapers often give false ~ to the news they report, twist the meaning to suit their aims. 报纸常常对其所报导的新闻加以曲解(以求配合其目的)。 **5** local ~, (in literature) use of details to make a description of a place, scene or time realistic. (文学中的)地方色彩(利用细节使对某一地方、场面或时间的描写有真实感)。 **6** (in music) [U] timbre, quality; variety of expression. (音乐)音质; 音色; 表现法之变化。 **7** (pl) ribbon, dress, cap, etc, worn as a symbol of a party, a club, a school, etc, or to show ownership of a race-horse, etc: (复)徽章; (代表党派、会社、学校等之)有颜色的丝带、帽子、帽等; (代表赛跑马匹之主人等的)色彩识别: The owner of a horse is always glad to see his ~s get to the winning-post first, to see his horse win a race. 马主永远高兴看到戴着他的识别的马最先到达终点。 **get/win one's ~s**, (at college, etc) be awarded a place in a sports team. (在大学等)被选为某运动队的队员。 **8** (pl) flag (of a regiment); ensign or standard of a regiment: (复)船旗; 队旗; 军旗: salute the ~s; 向军旗敬礼; serve with/join the ~s, the Navy, Army or Air Force. (在海军、陆军或空军)服兵役(从军)。 **come through/off with flying ~s**, make a great success of sth. 凯旋; 奏凯歌; 大为成功。 **lower one's ~s**, give up one's demands or position; surrender: 放弃要求或立场; 让步; 投降。 **nail one's ~s to the mast**, make a decision, announce it, and show strong determination not to change it. 做了一项决定, 宣布出去, 并且显示坚强的决心, 决不加以更改; 宣扬永不改变的决心。 **sail under false ~s**, be a hypocrite or impostor. 打着假招牌骗人。 **show one's true ~s**, show what one really is. 露出真面目。 **stick to one's ~s**, refuse to change one's opinion or party. 坚持自己的主张; 不改其志; 忠于其党。 **9** [U] racial characteristic of skin ~. 代表种族特征的肤色。 '~-**bar**, legal and/or social distinction between different races. 肤色隔阂(不同人种之间在法律上和社会上的差别地位)。 ~-**ful** /-fl; -fəl/ adj full of ~; bright; gay; exciting; vivid, etc: 富有色彩的; 鲜艳的; 多彩多姿的; 生动的: a ~ful scene; 多彩多姿的景象; a ~ful style of writing; 多彩的文体; 生动的文体; lead a ~ful life. 过一种多彩多姿(富于刺激性)的生活。 ~-**less** adj without ~; pale; (fig) lacking in interest, character, vividness: 无色的; 苍白的; (喻)无趣味的; 无特色的; 不生动的: a ~less style; 不生动的文体; leading a ~less existence. 过着平淡的生活。

col·our² (US=**color**) /ˈkʌlə(r); ˋkʌlɚ/ *vt, vi* **1** [VP6A, 22] give colour to; put colour on: 染色；着色；涂颜色于：*~ a wall green*. 将墙壁涂为绿色。**2** [VP2A, C] *~ (up)*, take on colour; blush: 变为有色；变色；变红：*The leaves have begun to ~*, to take on their autumn colours of yellow, brown, etc. 树叶已开始变色(变成秋天的黄、褐等色)。*The girl is so shy that she ~s (up) whenever a man speaks to her*. 那女孩非常害羞，每当一个男人跟她讲话时，她就脸红。**3** [VP6A] change or misrepresent in some way: 渲染；歪曲：*News is often ~ed*, changed to suit the views of those who supply it or those who will read it. 新闻常被歪曲报导(以符合报导者或读者的观点)。*Travellers' tales are often highly ~ed*, exaggerated. 旅行者的故事常是极为夸大的。**~ed** *adj* **1** (in compounds) having the colour specified: (用于复合词中)有某种颜色的：*ˈcream-~ed*; 奶油色的；*ˈflesh-~ed*. 肉色的。**2** (of persons) partly of European descent; (esp) of the Negro race. (指人)具有部分欧洲人血统的；有色人种的；(尤指)黑种的。**(Cape) C~ed** *n* South African person of mixed race. 南非的混血种人。**~·ing** *n* [U] sth that produces colour; face colour style in which sth is ~ed; style in which an artist uses colour. 颜料；面色；着色的格调；(艺术家)用色的风格；着色法；色调。

colt¹ /kəult; kolt/ *n* young horse (male) up to the age of 4 or 5, ⇨ **filly**; (四、五年以下的)雄驹；(fig) young man with little experience. (喻)无经验的年青人。**~·ish** /ˈkəultɪʃ; ˋkoltɪʃ/ *adj* like a ~; frisky. 似小马的；蹦蹦跳跳的；活泼的。

colt² /kəult; kolt/ *n* (P) (US) early type of revolver or pistol. (商标)(美)卡尔特式手枪(一种早期的左轮或手枪)。

col·ter /ˈkəultə(r); ˋkoltɚ/ (US) =**coulter.**

col·um·bine /ˈkɒləmbaɪn; ˋkɑləm,baɪn/ *n* garden plant with spur-shaped flowers and petals. 耧斗菜(花及花瓣形似刺马钉)。

col·umn /ˈkɒləm; ˋkɑləm/ *n* **1** tall, upright pillar, usu of stone, either supporting or decorating part of a building, or standing alone as a monument. 柱；圆柱；石柱(或用以支持屋顶，或用以装饰建筑物的一部分，或独立作为纪念碑)。**2** sth shaped like or suggesting a ~: 柱状物：*a ~ of smoke* (rising straight up); 向上直升的烟柱；*the spinal ~*, the backbone; 脊椎骨；脊柱；*a ~ of mercury* (in a thermometer); (寒暑表中的)水银柱；*a refining ~*, one in which oil, heated to vapour, is refined into fuel oil, petrol, etc. 精炼柱(原油在其中加热蒸发，以提炼成燃油、汽油等)。**3** vertical division of a printed page (eg of this page); or of a newspaper, occupied regularly by one subject: 直栏(如本页中者)；(报纸上经常为一主题所占用的)专栏；栏：*the correspondence ~s of 'The Times'*; '泰晤士报'上的通讯栏；*the advertising ~s*. 广告栏。**4** series of numbers arranged under one another: 直式排列的一列数字；纵行：*add up a long ~ of figures*. 加起一长列的数字。**5** line of ships following one another; deep arrangement of soldiers in short ranks, one behind the other. (舰队的)纵队柱；行；(军队的)纵队(横排很短而纵深顺次配置的队形)。**fifth ~**, ⇨ **fifth. col·um·nist** /ˈkɒləmnɪst; ˋkɑləmɪst/ *n* journalist who regularly writes a ~ of miscellaneous news, political comment, etc for a newspaper. (为报纸经常写新闻杂拾、政治评论等的)专栏作家。

coma /ˈkəumə; ˋkomə/ *n* unnatural deep sleep usu from injury or illness. (通常因伤或病)昏迷；昏厥；昏睡。*be in a ~; go into a ~*, be in, pass into such a sleep. 陷于昏迷状态。**~·tose** /ˈkəumətəus; ˋkɑmə,tos/ *adj* in a ~; unconscious. 在昏迷状态中；不省人事的。

comb /kəum; kom/ *n* **1** piece of metal, rubber, plastic, etc with teeth for cleaning the hair, making it tidy, keeping it in place, etc or as an ornament. 梳子(由金属、橡皮、塑胶等制成，有齿可以梳理头发使之整齐而不蓬乱，亦可作为装饰品)。**2** part of a machine with a ~-like look or purpose, esp for tidying and straightening wool, cotton, etc for manufacture. 梳直羊毛、棉花等之机件中的梳状部分；梳齿。**3** wax structure made by bees for honey. 蜂房；蜂巢(蜜蜂为产蜜而作的蜡质结构体)。⇨ **honey ~**. **4** red fleshy crest of fowl. 鸡冠。⇨ **cocks ~**. **5** crest of a large wave. (大浪的)浪头；浪峰。□*vt, vi* [VP6A, 15B] **1** use a ~ on (the hair). (用梳子)梳(头发)。**2** prepare (wool, flax, etc) with ~s for manufacture. 精梳(羊毛、亚麻等)以供纺织。**3** search thoroughly: 彻底搜查：*The police ~ed the whole city in their efforts to find the murderer*. 警方搜遍全市，以求找到凶手。**4** *~ out*, (fig) take out (unwanted things, persons) from a group: (喻)(自团体中)去除(不需要的东西、人)：*~ out a government department*, get rid of officials who are not really needed, who are inefficient, etc. 裁汰政府一部门中的冗员、无能者等。Hence, 由此产生，**ˈ~-out** *n* act of getting rid of (unnecessary officials, etc). 淘汰；裁汰(冗员或无能者等)。**5** [VP2C, 3A] *~ over*, (of a wave) break, curl: (指浪)涌起浪花；滚腾：*waves ~ing over the ship*. 溅至船上的海浪。

com·bat /ˈkɒmbæt; ˋkɑmbæt/ *n* fight; struggle: 战斗；斗争；搏斗；奋斗；打斗：(attrib)(用作定语) *a ~ mission*. 战斗任务。**single ~**, fight between two persons only. 一对一的打斗。□ *vt, vi* [VP6A, 3A] *~ (against/with)*, fight; struggle: 战斗；斗争；搏斗；奋斗；打斗：*~ the enemy*; 与敌人搏斗；*~ error*; 努力改正错误；*a ship ~ing with the wind and waves*. 与风浪搏斗的船。**~·ant** /ˈkɒmbətənt; ˋkɑmbətənt/ *adj* fighting. 战斗的；搏斗的；奋斗的。□ *n* one who fights: 战斗人员：*In modern wars both ~ants and non-~ants are killed in air attacks*. 在现代战争中，战斗员与非战斗

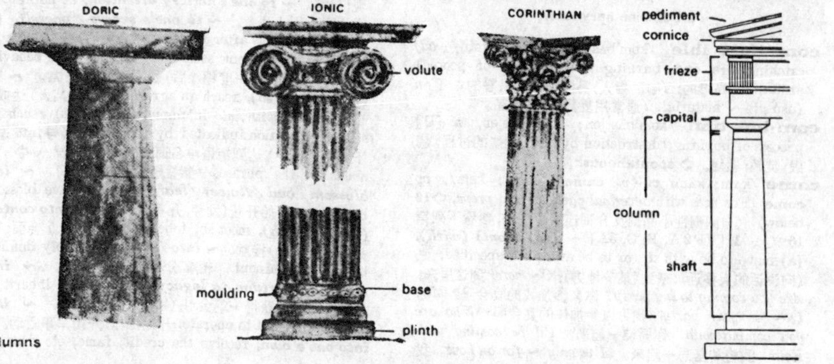
DORIC
IONIC
volute
moulding
base
plinth
CORINTHIAN
pediment
cornice
frieze
capital
column
shaft
columns

员均有可能死于空袭中。 ~·ive /'kɒmbətɪv; kəm'bætɪv/ *adj* fond of fighting; ready to fight. 好战的; 好斗的。 ~·ive·ly *adv*

com·bi·na·tion /ˌkɒmbɪ'neɪʃn; ˌkɑmbə'neʃən/ *n* **1** [U] joining or putting together; state of being joined: 联合; 结合; 化合; 合并; 组合: *in ~ with*; 与…联合在一起; *enter into ~ with*; 与…结合在一起; *every possible ~ and permutation*, every possible arrangement. 每一可能的组合及排列。 **2** [C] number of persons or things that are joined: 结合在一起的若干人或物; 团体; 组合: *The college is supported by a ~ of income from endowments and fees from students.* 该学院的经费系由捐款收入及学生所缴的学费联合支付的。 '~ **room**, (at Cambridge) common-room. (剑桥大学之) 教授休息室; 学生交谊厅。 ⇨ **common**¹(1). **3** [C] motor-bike with sidecar attached. 带侧车的机器脚踏车。 **4**(*pl*) one-piece undergarment covering body and legs. (复)衫裤连在一起的内衣。 **5** [C] formula, complicated arrangement, for the lock (= '~-lock) of a safe, strong-room, etc: 保险柜、保险室等之保险锁所用的暗码: *How did the thieves learn the ~ used to open the safe?* 窃贼们如何晓得用以开保险柜的暗码?

com·bine¹ /kəm'baɪn; kəm'baɪn/ *vt, vi* [VP6A, 14, 2A, 3A, 4A] ~ *(with)*, (cause to) join together; possess at the same time: (使)联合; 连接; 结合; 兼有: *We can't always ~ work with pleasure.* 我们不能永远在工作中享受到乐趣。*Hydrogen and oxygen ~/Hydrogen ~s with oxygen to form water.* 氢与氧化合成水。*Some films ~ education with recreation.* 有些影片使教育与娱乐融合在一起。*Everything ~d against him*, Circumstances, etc made his task difficult or impossible. 一切情势均对他不利。~*d operations/exercises*, in which air, sea and land forces work together. 陆、海、空军联合作战(演习)。

com·bine² /'kɒmbaɪn; 'kɑmbaɪn/ *n* **1** group of persons, trading companies, etc joined for a purpose (such as controlling prices). (个人、贸易公司等为某一目的, 如控制物价, 所组织的)团体; 组合; 联营组织。 **2** (also 亦作, ~ 'harvester) machine that both reaps and threshes (grain). (兼具收割及打谷功能的)联合收获机。

a combine harvester

com·bust·ible /kəm'bʌstəbl; kəm'bʌstəbl/ *adj* catching fire and burning easily; (fig, of people) excitable. 易燃的, (喻; 指人)易激动的; 易怒的。 □ *n* (usu *pl*) ~ material. (通常用复数)易燃物品。

com·bus·tion /kəm'bʌstʃən; kəm'bʌstʃən/ *n* [U] process of burning; destruction by fire. 燃烧的过程; 烧毁; 焚毁; 燃烧。 ⇨ **spontaneous.**

come /kʌm; kʌm/ *vi* (*pt* **came** /keɪm; kem/, *pp* **come**) (For uses with *adverbial particles* and *preps*, ⇨**16** below.) (与副词性小品词及介词连用之用法, 参看下列第 16 义。) **1** [VP2A, B, C, 3A] ~ *(to/from) (with)*, **(a)** move to be with sb, or to a place specified: 来 (向说话的人移近); 来到(某一地方): *C~ here!* 到这里来! *Are you coming to my party?* 你来参加我的宴会吗? *May I ~ to your party?* 我可以参加你的宴会吗? *Who are you coming with?* 你同谁一起来? *I'll be coming with Keith.* 我将和基思一起来。*I've only ~ for an hour.* 我

才来了一小时。 **(b)** arrive: 到达: *Help has ~.* 援助来了。*They came to a river.* 他们来到了河边。*He's just ~ from Leeds.* 他刚从里兹来。 **(c)** [VP4A with infinitive of purpose, 与表示目的之不定式连用, 3A] ~ *here to work.* 他来此工作。*They've ~ all the way from London to look for a book.* 他们老远从伦敦来找这件。*He's ~ to get/~ for his book.* 他已来取他的书。*They've ~ for* (= to get) *me!* 他们为为我而来(他们来找我的, 来找我的)。*C~ to see what I've done* (colloq 口 *C~ and see what I've done,* ⇨ **and**(5)). 过来看看做了些什么。 **(d)** [VP2E] (with a *pres p* to indicate two activities or states that occur together): (与现在分词连用, 表示发生在一起的两个活动或情况): *The children came running* (= ran) *to meet us.* 孩子们跑着来迎接我们。*He came hurrying* (= hurried) *to her bedside as soon as he heard she was ill.* 一听到她生病了, 他就赶着来到她的床边。*She came smiling/crying up to me.* 她笑着(哭着)来到我面前。 **2** [VP2C, E] ~ *(into/onto/in/on, etc)*, move into, etc the place where the speaker is: 进入(说话者的地方); 来到(…地方): *C~ into the hallway out of the rain.* 到走廊里来避雨。*The train came puffing into the station.* 火车喷着烟驶入车站。*Can you ~ out with me for a walk?* 你能跟我出来散散步吗? *He came back to have a word with me.* 他回来跟我谈谈。*The sunshine came streaming through the windows.* 阳光自窗户射入。 **3** [VP3A] **(a)** ~ *to sth*, reach; rise to; fall to (a particular level, figure, point): 到达; 升至; 落到; 落到(某一水准、数字、点): *Your bill ~s to £20.* 你的帐单计达二十英镑。*His earnings ~ to more than £5000 a year.* 他一年所赚的钱超过五千英镑。~ *to much/ little/nothing*, amount to much, etc: 很有(无甚、没有)结果或作为: *All his plans came to nothing*, had no result, no success. 他所有的计划都归失败。*He will never ~ to much*, will never be successful, etc. 他将来绝不会很有作为。~ *to this/that, etc*, reach the state of affairs indicated, or a particular state of affairs: 达到上下文所暗示的某种地步; 达到某种情况: *What you say ~s to this*, means this. 你所说的话就是这个意思。*When it ~s to helping his wife with the housework, John never grumbles.* 临到约翰帮忙他太太做家务时, 他从不会出怨言。*If it ~s to that…,* If that is the state of affairs…. 如果事已至此…。 **(b)** (in fixed phrases) reach the state or condition indicated by the *nouns* for which there is often an equivalent *verb*. (用于固定短语中)达到短语中名词所表明的情况。 ⇨ the noun entries. 参看以下各短语之名词。~ *to an agreement*, agree. 达成协议。~ *to blows (with)*, start fighting. 开始打架; (与…)互殴。~ *to a decision*, decide. 决定。~ *to an end*, end, finish. 终止; 结束。~ *to fruition*, ripen, mature. 成熟。~ *to a halt/ standstill*, stop. 停止; 静止。~ *to light*, become known; be revealed or discovered. 被知晓; 被揭露; 被发现; 显露。~ *to one's notice/attention*, be noticed. 被人注意; 引人注意。~ *to one's senses/oneself*, **(a)** become conscious after fainting. (昏厥后)恢复知觉; 苏醒; 复苏。 **(b)** become sensible or normal after behaving foolishly. (行为一度糊涂后)恢复明智或正常。~ *to terms (with sb)*, reach an agreement. (与某人)达成协议。 **4** (used with *into* in numerous phrases) reach the state or condition indicated by the *nouns*. (与 into 连用于许多短语中)达到短语中名词所表明的情况。 ⇨ the nouns in the phrases. 参看短语中的各名词。~ *into blossom/bud/flower/leaf*, begin to have blossom, buds, etc. 开始开花(发芽, 开花, 发叶)。~ *into contact (with sb/sth)*, meet sb, touch sth. (与某人)会面; 接头; (与某事物)接触。~ *into focus*, be sharply defined; become prominent. 轮廓分明; 变为明显。~ *into money/a fortune/a legacy, etc*, receive, inherit it. 接受、承继或获得一笔金钱(财产, 遗产等)。~ *into operation*, start to operate. 开始操作; 开始军事行动。~ *into one's own*, receive the credit, fame, etc that one

deserves, what rightly belongs to one, etc. 得到其所应得(如荣誉、名誉等或属其所有之物)。 **~ into power**, (of a political party, etc) form the Government. (指政党等)取得政权;组织政府。 Cf 参较 go into Opposition. 成为反对党(在野党)。 **~ into sight/view**, appear. 出现;显现。 ⇨ also **collision**, **effect**(1), *existence* at **exist**, **fashion**(2), **force**[1](5), **line**[1](11), **open** (*n*), **play**[1](8), **possession**(1), *prominence* at **prominent**, **question**[1](2), **use**[1](1). **5 ~ to sb (from sb)**, be left, willed, to sb (by Will and Testament, on death): (某人死时经由遗嘱)遗留或遗赠给某人: *He has a lot of money coming to him*, will receive it, eg when sb dies. 他将获得一大笔遗赠的钱(例如当他去世后)。 *The farm came to him on his father's death.* 他父亲去世时遗留给他那农场。 **6 ~ to sb**, occur to, strike sb; befall sb: 发生在某人身上;使某人想起;降临于某人: *The idea came* (= occurred) *to him in his bath.* 他在洗澡时想起那主意。 *No harm will ~ to you if you're careful.* 只要你小心,你不会遭遇损害的。 *He had it coming to him*, (colloq) used only of unpleasant events) what happened was fated, and probably deserved. (俚,仅用以指不愉快的事件,极可能是其应得的)他活该有此遭遇。 **7** [VP4A] reach a point where one sees, understands, etc: 到达了明白、了解等之点: *He came to realize that he was mistaken.* 他终于明白他错了。 *He had ~ to see the problem in a new light.* 他终于对此问题获得新的认识。 *I have ~ to believe that...,* I now believe that.... 我现在相信...了。 *When we ~ to know them better....* 等我们同他们认识清清楚楚的时候.... **8** [VP4A] (usu with *how*) asking for an explanation or reason: (通常与 how 连用)要求解释或说明理由: *How did you ~* (archaic 古: *How came you) to find out where she's living?* 你如何打听到她住在哪里? *How did you ~ to be so foolish?* 你为什么如此愚蠢? *(Now that I) ~* (= happen) *to think of it....* (既然我)想到了它...。 **How ~ (that)**, (sl) How does/did sth happen: (俚)...是如何发生的;...是怎么回事: *How ~ (that) you just sat there doing nothing?* 你只坐在那里什么事也没做,是怎么回事? **9** [VP2C] occur; be found; have as its place: 发生;出现;在: *May ~s between April and June.* 五月在四月与六月之间。 *On what page does it ~?* 它在哪一页? *His resignation came as a surprise/It came as a surprise when he resigned.* 他的辞职令人惊异。 **10** [VP2C, D] be; become; prove to be: 成为;证实为: *Your dream will one day ~ true*, be realized. 你的梦想将有一天会实现。 *It ~s easily with practice.* 一经练习,就很容易。 *The handle has ~ loose.* 把柄松了。 *It ~s cheaper if you buy things in bulk.* 大批购物会便宜些。 *Everything will ~ (all) right in the end.* 一切问题终会解决;一切困难终会过去。 *That sort of thing ~s naturally to her*, she does it without having to learn or make an effort. 那种事情她不学自会。 **be as clever/stupid, etc as they ~**, be very clever/stupid, etc. 非常聪明(愚蠢等)。 **11** [VP2D] (with *part adjj* prefixed with *un-*, denoting undesirable conditions, etc) become: (与带前缀 un- 之分词形容词连用,表示不良的情况)成为;变成: *My shoelaces have ~ undone.* 我的鞋带松开了。 *The seam came unstitched.* 衣缝绽线了。 *The flap of the envelope has ~ unstuck.* 信封口的粘胶不粘了。 ⇨ **unstuck** for a colloq use. 参看 unstuck 的口语用法。 **12** [VP2D] (with a *n* or *adj*, usu with the *def art*, used adverbially as the nominal part of the predicate) (colloq) play the part of; behave, talk, etc as if one were (often with the suggestion of overdoing sth): (与通常加定冠词之名词或形容词连用,作为谓语的名词部分)(口)担任...之角色;行为、谈话等宛如(常暗示'做得过火'): *Don't ~ the bully/the high and mighty over me*, don't (try to) bully me. 不要恃强凌弱我。 *He tried to ~ the artful/virtuous over me*, impress me by being artful/virtuous. 他想对我耍手段(在我面前故作善良)。 *That's coming it a bit strong*, is making an extravagant claim or assertion. 那做(要求或说)得太过火了一点。 ⇨ also the **noun** entry for the *heavy swell*. **13** (as a *to-inf*, used as a

pred adj) future: (以不定式形式,用作表语形容词)将来的;未来的: *in years to ~;* 在未来的年岁里; *books to ~*, forthcoming books; 行将出版的书籍; *the life to ~*, life in the next world; 来生; *for some time to ~*, for a period of time in the future. 在将来的一段时期。 **14** (colloq uses): (口语用法): *two years ~ Christmas*, two years including the time from now to Christmas. 从过去的某时算起到下一个圣诞节的两年间(包括从现在至圣诞节之一段期间)。 *She will be 21 ~ May*, when May comes, ie next May. 她将于(明年或今年)五月满二十一岁。 *Mary is coming ten*, is in her tenth year, will be ten on her next birthday. 玛丽快十岁了(到了她生日的那一天就满十岁)。 **15** [VP2A] (colloq) reach orgasm. (口)达到性交高潮。 **16** [VP2C, 3A] (special uses with *adverbial particles* and *preps*): (与副词性小品词及介词连用的特殊用法):

come about, happen: 发生: *It came about in this way.* 它就是这样发生的。 *How does it ~ about that...?* ...是怎样发生的? ⇨ **8** above. 参看上列第 8 义。

come across sb/sth, (a) find or meet by chance: 偶然发现或遇见某人(某物): *I came across this old brooch in a curio shop.* 我在一家古玩店里偶然发现了这枚古老的扣花。 **(b)** occur to: 出现于...中: *The thought came across my mind that...*, occurred to me.... ...的想法出现于我的脑海中; 我忽然想到.... Cf 参较 *It crossed my mind that ... ~ across (with),* (sl) pay (money owing); agree to give information. (俚)偿付(欠款); 同意提供消息或情报; 同意说出。

come after sb, follow in pursuit of: 跟随; 追踪; 追捕: *The farmer came after the intruders with a big stick.* 那农民拿着一根大棍子追捕侵入者。

come along, (a) (imper) try harder; make more effort: (祈使)再努力点; 加紧努力: *C~ along, now—someone must know the answer!* 再想想着——一定有人知道答案的! **(b)** progress: 进步: *The garden is coming along quite nicely.* 那花园越来越美。 **(c)** appear; arrive: 出现; 到达: *When the right opportunity ~s along, he'll take it.* 当良机到来时, 他会抓住的。 **(d)** (imper) hurry up; make haste: (祈使)快一点, 赶快: *C~ along—we'll be late for the theatre!* 赶快——我们看戏要迟了! **come apart, ~**, fall, to pieces. 破掉; 碎掉: *The teapot just came apart in my hands.* 那茶壶就在我手中碎了。

come at sb/sth, (a) reach; get access to: 达到; 接近; 得到: *The truth is often difficult to ~ at* (*get at* is more usu). 事实真相常常难获知(较常用 get at)。 **(b)** attack: 攻击; 袭击: *The man came at me with a big stick.* 那人手持粗棍向我打来。 Hence, 由此产生, **~-at-able** /ˌkʌmˈætəbl/ kʌmˈætəbl/ *adj* (colloq) accessible (*get-at-able* is more usu). (口)可接近的; 可获得的(较常用 get-at-able)。

come away (from), become detached: (从...)脱落; 掉下: *The light switch came away from the wall.* 电灯开关从墙上掉下来了。

come back, return; (of fashions) become popular again: 回来; 返回; (时尚样)再度流行? *Will ruffs ~ back?* 宽硬的绉领会再度流行吗? **~ back at**, retort; retaliate: 反驳; 报复: *He came back at the speaker with some sharp questions.* 他以一些尖刻的问题反驳演说者。 **~ back (to one)**, return to the memory: 重现于(某人)的记忆中: *Their names are all coming back to me now, I'm beginning to remember them.* 他们的名字, 我现在都渐渐想起来了。 Hence, 由此产生, '**~-back** *n* **(a)** (eg of actors, politicians, sportsmen, etc) successful return to, reinstatement in, a former position: (如演员、从政者、运动员等的)恢复先前的地位: 东山再起: *Can he stage a ~-back?* 他能够东山再起吗? **(b)** retort; repartee. 反驳; 反击。 **(c)** redress; recompense (for a loss, etc): 补偿; 赔偿(损失等): *If you're uninsured and you're burgled, you'll have no ~-back.* 如果你未投保而被窃偷光顾, 你将得不到赔偿。

come before sb/sth, (a) be dealt with by: 被...讨论: *The complaint will ~ before the United Nations Assembly*

next week. 该项控诉将于下周提交联合国大会讨论。 **(b)** have precedence over: 地位高于: *Baronets ~ before knights.* 从男爵的地位高于爵士。

come between, (a) interfere with a relationship: 干预; 扰乱: *It is not advisable to ~ between a man and his wife.* 干预别人夫妻间之事是不智的。 **(b)** prevent sb from having sth: 阻挠某人有某物或使某事; 阻碍; 阻止: *He never lets anything ~ between him and his evening paper.* 他从不让任何事阻碍他看晚报。

come by sth, (a) obtain by effort; become possessed of: 努力获得; 获有: *Was the money honestly ~ by?* 那钱的来路正当吗? *Jobs were hard to ~ by.* 工作难求。 **(b)** receive by accident or chance: 由于意外事件或偶然地受到: *How did you ~ by that cut on your wrist?* 你手腕上的割伤是怎么来的?

come down, (a) collapse: 塌陷; 崩溃: *The ceiling came down on our heads.* 天花板塌下来掉在我们的头上。 **(b)** (of rain, snow, hail) fall: (指雨、雪、雹)落下: *The rain came down in bucketfuls.* 大雨倾盆。 **(c)** (of prices, temperature, etc) fall. (指物价、气温等)跌落; 下落; 下降。 **(d)** ~ from a city or large town to a smaller locality: (从城市或大镇)到较小的地方; 下乡: *She came down from Glasgow last year and settled in the village.* 她于去年从格拉斯哥下乡来并定居在该村中。 **(e)** (colloq) pay money: (口)付钱;出手: *My rich uncle came down generously, made a generous gift of money.* 我那有钱的叔父出手大方(给了相当多的钱)。 **~ down (from),** leave university (esp Oxford or Cambridge): 大学毕业或肄业(尤指自牛津或剑桥大学): *His son has just ~ down from Oxford.* 他儿子刚自牛津大学毕业。 **~ 'down in the world,** lose social position; become poor. 失去社会地位; 失势; 变穷; 败落。 Hence, 由此产生, **'~-down** *n* fall in social position; humiliation: (社会地位或声望)衰落; 低落; 败落; 贬抑; 屈辱: *He has had to sell his house and furniture—what a ~down for him!* 他不得不卖掉房屋及家具—对他该是多大的屈辱! **~ down in favour of sb/sth; ~ down on the side of sb/sth,** decide to support: 决定支持; 决心拥护: *He came down on the side of a more flexible trade policy.* 他决定支持比较有弹性的贸易政策。 **~ down on sb,** (colloq) rebuke severely: (口)严责: *The headmaster came down on the boy like a ton of bricks.* 校长凶猛地对那男孩严加斥责。 **~ down on sb for sth,** demand payment of money owing: 向某人索还钱等: *Tradesmen came down on him for prompt settlement of his accounts.* 商人们要他迅速结帐。 **~ down to,** (a) reach to: 到达; 垂及: *Her hair ~ down to her waist.* 她的头发下垂到腰部。 **(b)** reduce to: 减少或降低至: *Your choices in the matter ~ down to these.* 有关此事你的选择只限于这些。 **(c)** (of traditions, etc) be handed down: (指传统等)传下; 世代相传: *legends that have ~ down to us,* ie from our ancestors. 古代相传至今的传说。 **~ down to doing sth,** be forced, eg by poverty, to do sth humiliating: (如因穷困等)被迫做屈辱的事: *He had ~ down to begging.* 他已沦为乞丐。 **~ down to earth,** return to reality: 回到现实: *Now that his money has all been spent, he's had to ~ down to earth.* 既然他的钱已全部花掉了, 他不得不回到现实的(生活)里来。 **~ down to it,** examine the meaning, the essentials. 审查含义或要点。 **~ down with,** (colloq) contribute: (口)捐献: *I had to ~ down with £10 to her favourite charity.* 我不得不捐十英镑来给她所喜欢的慈善事业。

come forward, (a) offer or present oneself: 自告奋勇; 自愿效劳: *Will no one ~ forward as a candidate?* 无人出来竞选吗? *No witness of the accident has ~ forward.* 没有人出来做那意外事件的见证人。 **(b)** (comm) become available: (商)可供销售; 可资运用: *the number of cattle coming forward for slaughter,* brought to market to be sold. 可供宰杀的肉牛数目。

come from, (a) (not with progressive tenses) have as a birthplace, place of origin, etc: (不用进行时)出生于; 来自; 源自: *He ~s from Kent.* 他是肯特郡人。 *Much of the butter eaten in England ~s from New Zealand.* 英格

兰境内所食用的黄油有很多来自新西兰。**(b)** = ~ of (b).

come home to, ⇨ home[2](2).

come in, (a) (of the tide) rise: (指潮水)涨: *The tide is coming in.* 潮涨了。 **(b)** become seasonable: 当令; 应时正在上涨。 **(b)** become seasonable: 当令; 应时: *When do oysters ~ in?* 蚝何时上市? **(c)** become fashionable: 开始流行: *When did women's trousers ~ in?* 妇女的长裤何时开始流行? **(d)** (of a batsman in cricket) take his stand at the wicket: (指板球戏中的击球手)就其在三柱门旁之位置; 上场: *When the next man came in, ...* 当下一个击球手上场的时候。 **(e)** take a place in the result of a race: 在赛跑中得名次: *Which horse came in first?* 哪一匹马跑第一名? **(f)** be elected; ~ into power: 当选; 当权;执政;上台: *If the Democrats ~ in, ...* 假若民主党上台的话, …。 **(g)** be received as income, etc: 作为收入等而被收到: *There's not much money coming in at present.* 目前没有多少钱收入。 **(h)** have a part to play: 担任职务: *Here is the plan of attack, and this is where you ~ in.* 这是攻击计划, 此处是你的任务岗位。 *Where do I ~ in,* (according to context) What is my share, How do I benefit, etc? (根据上下文)我的职务是什么, 我的好处在哪里等? **~ in handy/useful (for sth),** happen to be useful, serve a purpose: 偶然会有; 可能有用: *Don't throw it away—it may, ~ in handy one day.* 不要把它丢掉—它有一天也许会有用处。 **~ 'in for, (a)** receive (as an inheritance, a share, etc): 得到 (遗产、一份等): *She has ~ in for a fortune.* 她得到了一笔财产。 **(b)** attract; be the object of: 吸引; 为…之对象; 招致: *Their handling of the case has ~ in for a great deal of criticism.* 他们对该案件的处理已经招致了许多的批评。 **~ in on,** join; take part in: 加入; 参加: *If you want to ~ in on the scheme, you must decide now.* 如果你要参加此计划, 你必须现在就作决定。

come into sth, ⇨ **4** above. 参看上列第4义。

come of, (a) be descended from: 为…之后裔; 出身于: *She ~s of an interesting family.* 她出身于有趣的家庭。 **(b)** be the result of: 为…之结果: *He promised his help, but I don't think anything will ~ of it.* 他答应帮忙, 但我不认为他的帮忙会有任何结果。 *No harm can ~ of trying.* 试试无妨(不会有害)。 **~ of age,** ⇨ age[1](1).

come off, (a) take place: 发生; 举行: *The match didn't ~ off.* 比赛未举行。 *Did the proposed visit to Rome ever ~ off?* 所提访之罗马之行实现了吗? **(b)** (of plans, attempts) succeed: (指计划、企图)成功: *The experiment did not ~ off.* 这项实验未成功。 *The film doesn't quite ~ off.* 该影片不大成功。 **(c)** (of persons) fare; prosper; acquit oneself: (指人)进展; 成就; 行为; 表现: *They came off well/badly.* 他们表现得很好(坏); 他们做得很成功(失败)。 *Who came off best, who won?* 谁获胜? 谁赢得? **~ off (sth), (a)** become detached or separated (from): (从某物上)脱落; 分离; 掉下: *A button has ~ off my coat.* 我的外衣掉了一颗扣子。 *Please use lipstick that doesn't ~ off on the wineglasses.* 请用不会印在酒杯上的口红。 *When we came off the gold standard...,* abandoned it ... 当我们废弃金本位制时…。 **(b)** fall (from): (自…)跌下: *~ off a horse/bicycle.* 自马(脚踏车)上跌下。 *Don't ~ off!* 不要摔下来! **(c)** get down (from): (自…)下来: *C~ off that wall before you fall off (it).* 快下来, 免得从墙上摔下来。 ⇨ also **perch**[2](2). **(d) ~ off it,** (colloq, imper) stop pretending, or talking nonsense: (口, 祈使)别装八道; 住口: *Oh, ~ off it! What do you know about horseracing?* 唉, 别吹了! 关于赛马你懂什么?

come on, (a) follow: 跟随: *You go first, I'll ~ on later.* 你先去, 我随后跟来。 Hence, 由此产生, **'~-on** (sl) lure; seductive action. (俚)诱惑; 引诱。 **(b)** (as a challenge): (作为挑战语): *C~ on! Let's race to the bottom of the hill.* 来吧! 我们赛跑到山脚下。 **(c)** make progress; develop: 进步; 发展; 发育: *How's your garden coming on?* 你的花园发展的情形如何? *The baby is coming on well.* 婴儿的发育情形良好。 **(d)** (of rain, the seasons, night, illness, etc) start; arrive: (指雨、季、夜、

病等)开始;来到: *Night/Darkness came on.* 夜色(黑暗)降临。 *The rain came on again worse than ever.* 雨又下了,较前更为加剧。 *He said he felt a cold coming on, was beginning to suffer from a cold.* 他说他感到有患感冒的迹象。 **(e)** (of questions, lawsuits) arise for discussion: (指问题、讼案)被提出讨论: *When does the case ~ on for trial,* When will the court deal with it? 该案何时开庭审讯? **(f)** (cricket, of a bowler) begin to bowl. (板球戏,指投手)开始投球。 **(g)** (of an actor) appear on the stage; (of a play) be performed: (指演员)登场; 上场; (指剧本)上演: *'Macbeth' is coming on again next month.* '麦克佩斯'下月将再度上演。 **~ on to** + *inf,* begin to: 开始: *It came on to rain.* 开始下雨。

come out, (a) appear; become visible: 出现; 显现: *The sun/stars come out.* 太阳(星星)出来了。 *The buds/flowers are coming out,* are opening. 蓓蕾(花)绽放。 **(b)** become known: (消息)传出;(真相)大白: *When the news came out ...* .当消息传出的时候···。 *If the truth ever ~s out ...* .如果事实真相终久得出···。 **(c)** be published: 出版: *When will his new book ~ out?* 他的新著将于何时出版? **(d)** (of workmen) strike: (指工人)罢工: *The car workers have all ~ out again.* 汽车工人再度全体罢工。 **(e)** (of details, etc in a photograph; of qualities) appear: (指相片上的细微处; 指品质)显现; 表露: *You have ~ out well in that photograph,* It is a good likeness. 你的那张相片照得很好。 *His arrogance ~s out in every speech he makes.* 他的骄气表露于他每一次的演讲中。 **(f)** (of stains, etc) be removed: (指污迹等)被除去: *These ink stains won't ~ out.* 这些墨迹洗不掉。 **(g)** (of dyes, etc) fade; disappear: (指染料等)褪色;消失: *Will the colour ~ out if the material is washed?* 这料子经洗涤后会褪色吗? **(h)** (of problems) be solved: (指问题)被解决: *I can't make this sum/equation ~ out,* can't solve it. 我算不出这个算术题(方程式)。 **(i)** make a debut; (colloq) begin to live publicly as sth. 初入社交场合; (口)出头。 **(j)** (of meaning, sense) become clear: (指意思, 意义)变明白: *The meaning of the passage ~s out clearly in his interpretation.* 这一段文字的意义经他的解释后就明白了。 **~ out at,** (of totals, averages, etc) amount to: (指总数、平均数等)合计为: *The total ~s out at 756,* is 756. 总数达到756。 **~ out first/last, etc,** (in examinations) have a certain position: (在考试中)得第一名(最后一名等): *Tom came out first.* 汤姆(考试成绩)名列第一。 **~ out in,** be partially covered in (pimples, a rash, etc): 部分覆盖着(粉刺、疹等): *She's ~ out in spots!* 她身上出痧子了! **~ out with,** utter; say: 说出; 道出: *He came out with a most extraordinary story/a string of oaths.* 他说出了一个非常惊人的故事(一连串的咒骂语)。

come over, (a) ~ from a distance: 从远处来: *Won't you ~ over to England for a holiday?* 你不来英国度假吗? **(b)** change sides or opinion: 改变立场或见解: *He will never ~ over to our side.* 他决不会改变立场参加我们这一边。 **~ over sb,** (of feelings, influences) take possession of: (指感情、影响)掌握住某人; 占据: *What has ~ over you,* Why have you changed in this way? 你为什么会变成这个样子? *A fit of dizziness came over her,* She suddenly felt dizzy. 她突然感到晕眩。 **~ over queer/funny/dizzy,** (colloq) suffer a feeling of faintness/sickness/dizziness. (口)感到头晕(不适、晕眩)。

come round, (a) ~ by a circuitous route: 由迂回的路线而来; 走弯路: *The road was blocked so we had to ~ round by the fields.* 道路阻塞了, 所以我们不得不绕道而来。 **(b)** pay an informal visit to: (非正式地)访问: *Won't you ~ round and see me some time?* 什么时候来看我好吗? **(c)** recur: 再现; 再来; 再临: *Christmas will soon ~ round,* be here again. 圣诞节不久又要来临了。 **(d)** change views, etc: 改变观念、见解: *He will never ~ round to our way of thinking,* share his views and adopt ours. 他决不会放弃他的观点而采取我们的。 *He has ~ round,* has accepted/agreed. 他已接受(同

意)。 **(e)** regain consciousness: 恢复知觉; 苏醒: *Pour a jug of water on his face—he'll soon ~ round.* 浇一罐水在他的脸上, 他马上就会苏醒。 **(f)** recover from ill temper, etc: 从坏脾气等恢复过来: *Don't scold the boy; he'll ~ round in time.* 不要责骂那个男孩; 他的坏脾气终会过去的。

come through, (a) recover from a serious illness, from risk of injury: (从重病中)复元; (从遭遇受伤危险中)度过; 脱险: *With such a weak heart, he was lucky to ~ through.* 他的心脏如此衰弱, 竟能复元是幸运。 *How did you manage to ~ through without even a scratch,* to escape even a slight injury? 你用什么方法能够丝毫未受伤(安然脱险)? **(b)** arrive (by telephone, radio, etc): (经由电话、无线电等)到达; 打通: *Listen—a message is just coming through.* 听——电讯刚接通。 **(c)** pass through official channels: 获得官方批准: *Your posting has just ~ through: it's Hong Kong!* 你的派令刚下来: 地点是香港! **~ through sth,** survive: 经历···之后仍然活着: *He has ~ through two world wars,* has lived safely through them. 他身经两次世界大战。

come 'to, (a) recover consciousness; ⇨ **come round(e).** 恢复知觉(苏醒)。 **(b)** ~ **to sth,** ⇨ **3** above. 参看上列第3义。

come under sth, (a) be classed among; be in (a certain category, etc): 归入(某一类等): *What heading does this ~ under?* 这个应归入哪一项? **(b)** be subjected to: 受到: *~ under sb's notice/influence.* 受到某人的注意(影响)。

come up, (a) (of seed, herbaceous plants, etc) show above the ground: (指种子、草本植物等)长出地面: *The seeds/snowdrops haven't ~ up yet.* 种子(雪花草)尚未发出芽来。 **(b)** arise; be put forward: 发生; 被提出: *The question hasn't ~ up yet,* has not been raised or discussed. 问题尚未被提出来讨论。 *Her divorce case ~s up next month,* will be dealt with then. 她的离婚案件将于下月讨论。 **(c)** (colloq) be drawn (in a lottery): (口) (在抽奖中)中签: *My sweepstake ticket came up; I won £100.* 我的马票中奖了(号码被抽出); 我中了一百英镑。 **(d)** occur; arise: 发生; 出现: *We shall write to you if a vacancy ~s up.* 如果出缺我们会与你结信。 **(e)** rise in social position: 社会地位升高; 出头: *He came up the hard way,* succeeded through his own, unaided efforts. 他靠自己的努力而出人头地。 **~ up against,** meet (difficulties, opposition). 对付; 应付(困难、反对)。 **~ up to, (a)** reach: 达到; 及于: *The water came up to my waist.* 水深及于我的腰部。 **(b)** equal: 等于; 达到: *Your work has not ~ up to my expectations/to the required standards.* 你的工作没有达到我的期望(要求的标准)。 **~ up with, (a)** draw level with: 与···并行; 赶上: *We came up with a party of hikers.* 我们赶上了一队远足者。 **(b)** produce; find (a solution, an answer). 产生; 发现(解决办法, 答案)。

come upon sb/sth, (a) attack by surprise; strike: 突袭; 突临: *the disaster that came upon them.* 突然降临于他们的灾祸。 *Fear came upon us.* 我们突然感到害怕。 **(b)** = come across (a).

com·edian /kə'miːdiən; kə'midiən/ *n* actor who plays comic parts in plays, broadcasts and TV; person who behaves in a comic way and who cannot be taken seriously. 戏剧、广播或电视中担任滑稽角色的演员; 喜剧演员; 行动滑稽的人; 丑角。 **com·edienne** /kə,miːdi'en/ kə,midɪ'ɛn/ *n female.* 喜剧中的女演员; 女丑角。

com·edy /'kɒmədɪ; 'kɑmədɪ/ *n* **1** [U] branch of drama that deals with everyday life and humorous events: 喜剧 (戏剧的一分支, 描写日常生活及可笑的事件): *He prefers ~ to tragedy;* 他比较喜欢喜剧而不大喜欢悲剧; [C] (*pl* **-dies**) play for the theatre, of a light, amusing kind. 轻松滑稽的舞台剧; 喜剧。 **,musical '~,** such a play, with music, songs and dancing. 滑稽歌舞剧; 喜歌喜剧。 **2** [C, U] amusing activity or incident in real life: 真实人生中有趣的事情; 趣事; 趣闻: *There's not much ~ in modern war.* 现代战争并不是好玩的事。

come·ly /'kʌmlɪ; 'kʌmlɪ/ adj (-ier, -iest) (old use, usu of a person) pleasant to look at. (旧用法,通常指人) 漂亮的;好看的。 **come·li·ness** n

comer /'kʌmə(r); 'kʌmə/ n (chiefly in compounds) one who comes: (主用于复合词中) 来的人;来者;到者: the first ~; 最先到达者; the late-~s; 迟到者; 晚来的人; all ~s. 全体来到者。

com·est·ible /kə'mestəbl; kə'mestəbl/ n (formal, usu pl) thing to eat. (正式用语,通常用复数)食物;食品。

comet /'kɒmɪt; 'kɒmɪt/ n heavenly body (looking like a star with a bright centre and a less bright tail) that moves round the sun in an eccentric orbit. 彗星(为一天体,看来象星,中心明亮而有较暗之尾,循离心轨道绕太阳旋转)。

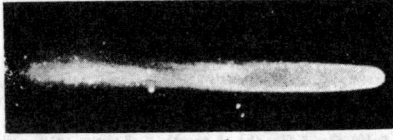

a comet

come·up·pance /kʌm'ʌpəns; kʌm'ʌpəns/ n deserved punishment or misfortune: 应得的惩罚或灾祸: The tyrant President got his ~ when his country was invaded and conquered. 当他的国家被攻克时,那位暴虐的总统得到了他应得的惩罚。

com·fit /'kʌmfɪt; 'kʌmfɪt/ n (old use) sweetmeat; fruit (eg a plum) preserved in sugar. (旧用法)糖果;蜜饯(如梅子)。

com·fort /'kʌmfət; 'kʌmfət/ n 1 [U] state of being free from suffering, anxiety, pain, etc; contentment; physical well-being; 舒服(身体无痛无虑无苦的状态);满足;(身体的)安逸: become fond of ~ as one grows old; 人年纪大了就变得喜欢安逸; living in great ~. 生活极为舒适。 **2** [U] help or kindness to sb who is suffering: (对受痛苦者的)安慰; 慰藉: a few words of ~; 几句安慰的话; news that brought ~ to all of us. 令我们大家都感到安慰的消息。 ~ cold ~, not much consolation. 无关痛痒的安慰。 **3** [C] person or thing that brings relief or help: 带来安慰的人或事物: Your letters have been a great ~ to me. 你的来信给我很大的安慰。 It's a ~ to know that she is safe. 知道她平安无事,是一项安慰。 The hotel has every modern ~/all modern ~s. 这旅馆中有各种现代设备。 '~ station, (US) public lavatory. (美)公共厕所。 □ vt [VP6A] give ~ to: 安慰;鼓舞: ~ those who are in trouble. 安慰处于困难的人。 The child ran to its mother to be ~ed. 那孩子跑到妈妈身边偎得到安慰。 ~·less adj without ~: 不舒适的: a ~less room. 不舒适的房间。

com·fort·able /'kʌmftəbl; 'kʌmfətəbl/ adj 1 giving comfort to the body: (使身体)舒适的;安逸的: a ~ chair/bed. 舒适的椅子(床)。 **2** having or providing comfort: 享有或供给舒适的: a ~ life/income. 舒适的生活(相当丰富的收入)。 **3** at ease; free from (excessive) pain, anxiety, etc: 舒畅的; 无(过度)痛苦,忧虑等的: to be/feel ~. 感到舒适。 Make yourself ~! 别客气! **com·fort·ably** /-təblɪ; -təblɪ/ adv in a ~ manner: 舒适地; 安逸地; 舒服地: a car that holds six people comfortably. 能够舒舒服服地供六人坐的汽车。 **be comfortably off**, have enough money to live in comfort. 生活富裕。

com·forter /'kʌmfətə(r); 'kʌmfətɚ/ n 1 person who comforts. 安慰者。 **the C~**, (= strengthener) the Holy Spirit. 保惠师(圣灵)。 **2** (GB) warm woollen scarf, worn round the neck. (英)绕在颈的羊毛围巾。 **3** (GB) teat of a baby's dummy 美 US ~ = pacifier). (英)奶嘴。 **4** (US) quilt. (美)棉被。

com·frey /'kʌmfrɪ; 'kʌmfrɪ/ n [U] tall wild plant with rough leaves and purple or white flowers. 紫草科植物(高茎野生植物,叶粗糙,开紫或白花)。

comfy /'kʌmfɪ; 'kʌmfɪ/ adj (-ier, -iest) (colloq) comfortable. 〈口〉舒适的;安逸的;舒服的。

comic /'kɒmɪk; 'kɑmɪk/ adj 1 causing people to laugh: 使人发笑的; 滑稽的: a ~ song; 滑稽歌曲; intended to amuse: 娱乐性的: ~ strips, strips of humorous drawings, as printed in newspapers, etc. (如报纸上所刊载的)连环漫画。 **2** of comedy: 喜剧的; opera. 喜歌剧。 □ n 1 music-hall comedian. 杂耍戏院里的滑稽演员。 **2** (US 美 = '~ book) book or magazine containing stories etc in the form of drawings. 附有连环漫画的书或杂志;连环图画。

comi·cal /'kɒmɪkl; 'kɑmɪkl/ adj amusing; odd: 有趣的; 奇特的; 古怪的: a ~ old hat. 古怪的旧帽。 ~·ly /-klɪ; -klɪ/ adv

coming /'kʌmɪŋ; 'kʌmɪŋ/ n arrival: 来到; 到达; 抵达: He believes in the Second C~, the return of Jesus Christ when the world ends. 他相信世界末日时耶稣基督的再临。 □ adj which will come: 未来的; 将来的: in the ~ years; 在未来的年岁里; the ~ generation. 下一代。 **a ~ man**, a man who is likely to be important, famous, etc. 一个前程似锦的人(将成为重要人物或将成名等)。

com·ity /'kɒmɪtɪ; 'kɑmətɪ/ n [U] (formal) harmonious friendliness; courtesy. (正式用语)和睦, 礼让; 礼貌。 ~ **of nations**, friendly recognition, shown by one nation, of the laws, customs, etc of other nations. 国际间对于彼此之法律、风俗等的互相尊重;国际礼让。

comma /'kɒmə; 'kɑmə/ n punctuation mark (,) to indicate a slight pause or break between parts of a sentence. 逗点 (,) (用以表示句中各部分间之一略微的停顿)。 **in,verted '~s**, the marks (" ") or (' '). 引号 ("" 或 ''). ⇨ App 9. 参看附录九。

com·mand[1] /kə'mɑːnd US: -'mænd; kə'mænd/ vt, vi 1 [VP6A, 17, 9, 2A] order (usu with the right to be obeyed): 命令(通常有使对方必须服从之权): Do as I (you). 照我的命令去做。 The officer ~ed his men to fire. 那军官命令其部下开火。 The pirate chief ~ed that the prisoners should be shot. 海盗首领下令将俘虏枪杀。 The officer ~s and man obeys. 军官命令,士兵服从。 **2** [VP6A, 2A] have authority over; be in control of: 统率; 指挥: The captain of a ship ~s all the officers and men. 舰长统率舰及全体官兵。 Who ~s the army? 谁指挥陆军? Who ~s here? 这里由谁指挥? **3** [VP6A] restrain; hold back; control (the more usu word): 抑制; 克制; 控制(较常用control): ~ oneself/one's temper/one's passions. 克制自己(自己的脾气,自己的情感)。 **4** [VP6A] be in a position to use; have at one's service: 可以使用; 能够支配: He ~s great sums of money, is able to use them if he so wishes. 他可以支配大笔的款子。 A Minister of State ~s the services of many officials. 国务大臣可以支配许多官员。 **5** [VP6A] deserve and get: 应该得到并且得到; 博得: Great men ~ our respect. 伟人受我们尊敬。 He ~s the sympathy of all who have heard the story of his sufferings. 他的苦难遭遇博得所有听众的同情。 **6** [VP6A] (of a place) be in a position that overlooks (and may control): (指地点)俯视(也可以控制): The fort ~ed the entrance to the valley. 该碉堡俯视(控制)山谷的入口。 The hill ~s a fine view, a fine view can be obtained from the top. 此山俯览一片美景。 ~·ing adj that ~s: 命令的; 指挥的: the ~ing officer; 司令官; 指挥官; in a ~ing tone; 以命令的口吻; in a ~ing position. 居于指挥的地位。

com·mand[2] /kə'mɑːnd US: -'mænd; kə'mænd/ n 1 [C] order: 命令: His ~s were quickly obeyed. 他的命令很快就执行了。 Give your ~s in a loud, confident voice. 以响亮自信的声调发布你的命令。 **at the word of ~**, (mil) when the ~ is given. (军)命令一发; 当命令发出时。 **2** [U] authority; power (to control): 权力; 统率权; 指挥权: General X is in ~ of the army. 某军由将军统率陆军。 The army is under the ~ of General X. 陆军由某将军统率。 He has twenty men under his ~. 他有二十人由他指挥。 **have/take ~ of**, have/take authority: 指

挥: *When the major was killed, the senior captain took ~ of the company.* 当少校阵亡时, 全连由资深的上尉指挥。 **do sth at/by sb's ~,** on his authority: 奉某人之命做某事: *It was done by the Queen's ~.* 此事系奉女王之命而行。 **be at sb's ~,** ready to obey: 愿某人的指挥; 听某人的吩咐: *I am at your ~,* ready to obey you. 我愿受你的指挥; 我随时听候你的吩咐。'**~ module,** part of a spacecraft carrying the crew and control equipment. 指挥舱(太空船装载人员及控制装备部分)。 **performance,** (at a theatre) one given at the request of a head of State. (戏院中) 应国家元首之请求而举行的特别表演; 御前表演。 **3** [C] part of an army, air force, etc under separate ~: 由单独指挥系统所辖的部分陆军、空军等; 指挥部; 部队: *Western C~;* 西方部队; *Bomber C~.* 轰炸指挥部。 **4** [U] possession and mastery: 有并能自由使用; 支配: *He has a good ~ of the English language,* is able to use it well. 他精通英语。 *He has no ~ over himself,* cannot control his feelings, temper, etc. 他不能克制自己(如情感、脾气等)。 *He offered me all the money at his ~,* all the money he controlled. 他把所有由他支配的钱都给我了。

com·man·dant /ˌkɒmən'dænt; ˌkɑmən'dænt/ *n* commanding officer. 指挥官。

com·man·deer /ˌkɒmən'dɪə(r); ˌkɑmən'dɪr/ *vt* [VP6A] seize (horses, stores, buildings, etc) for military purposes under martial law. 在戒严令下征用 (马匹、物资、建筑物等) 作为军用。

com·mander /kə'mɑːndə(r) US: -'mæn-; kə'mændɚ/ *n* person in command: 司令官; 指挥官; 部队长; 队长: *the ~ of the expedition;* 探险队队长; *C~, Lieutenant-'C~,* naval officers (above lieutenant and below captain); 海军中校; 海军少校; *Wing-C~,* rank in the RAF; 英国空军中校; *~-in-'chief,* one of all the military forces of a State. (统率全国所有陆、海、空军之) 总司令。

com·mand·ment /kə'mɑːndmənt US: -'mænd-; kə'mændmənt/ *n* divine command. 神的戒律; 圣诫。 **the Ten C~s,** the ten laws given by God to Moses. ▷ **Exod 20:1-17.** 十诫(上帝授予摩西的十条戒律; 参看旧约圣经出埃及记第 20 章第 1 至 17 节)。

com·mando /kə'mɑːndəʊ US: -'mæn-; kə'mændo/ *n* (pl ~s or ~es) (member of a) body of men specially picked and trained for carrying out raids and making assaults. (特别挑选并加以训练担任突击任务的) 突击队 (员)。

com·mem·or·ate /kə'meməreɪt; kə'meməˌret/ *vt* [VP6A] keep or honour the memory of (a person or event); (of things) be in memory of: 纪念 (人或事件); (指事物) 作为对于…之纪念; 庆祝: *Christmas ~s the birth of Christ.* 圣诞节纪念基督的降生。 *A monument was built to ~ the victory.* 立一纪念碑以纪念胜利。 **com·mem·or·ative** /kə'memərətɪv US: -'meməret-; kə'meməˌretɪv/ *adj* serving to ~: 作为纪念的, 纪念的: *commemorative stamps/medals.* 纪念邮票(章)。

com·mem·or·ation /kəˌmemə'reɪʃn; kəˌmeməˈreʃən/ *n* [U] act of commemorating: 纪念; 庆祝: *in ~ of;* 纪念; 庆祝; [C] (part of a) service in memory of a person or event. 纪念仪式; 庆祝活动。

com·mence /kə'mens; kə'mɛns/ *vt, vi* [VP6A, C, 2A, 3A] (formal) begin; start (the more usu words). (正式用语) 开始 (begin 和 start 为较常用词)。 **~·ment** *n* **1** beginning. 开始。 **2** (in US universities, and at Cambridge and Dublin) ceremony at which degrees are conferred. (美国各大学、英国剑桥大学及爱尔兰都柏林大学) 学位授予典礼; 毕业典礼。

com·mend /kə'mend; kə'mɛnd/ *vt* **1** [VP6A, 14] ~ *sb (on/upon sth),* praise; speak favourably of: 称赞; 赞扬: *~ someone upon his good manners;* 称赞某人有礼貌; *~ a man to his employers.* 向某人之雇主称赞某人。 *His work was highly ~ed.* 他的工作极受赞扬。 **2** [VP14] ~ *sth to,* entrust for safekeeping to: 将某事物付托给…; 信托; 托; 保管: *~ one's soul to God.* 将灵魂付托上帝。 **3** [VP14] ~

oneself/itself to, be to the liking of; be acceptable to: 投…之所好; 受…的欢迎; 使感兴趣: *This book does not ~ itself to me.* 我对这本书不感兴趣。 *Will the proposal ~ itself to the public?* 这建议会受大众的欢迎吗? ~·**able** *adj* worthy of praise. 可称赞的; 值得赞扬的。 **com·men·da·tion** /ˌkɒmen'deɪʃn, ˌkɑmənˈdeʃən/ *n* [U] praise; approval. 称赞; 赞扬; 赞成。

com·men·sur·able /kə'menʃərəbl; kə'mɛnʃərəbl/ *adj* ~ (to/with), that can be measured by the same standard (as): 可以用同一标准衡量的; 有公度的; 有公比量的; 相称的; 相当的: *Their achievements are not ~.* 他们的成就是不相称的。

com·men·sur·ate /kə'menʃərət; kə'mɛnʃərɪt/ *adj* ~ (to/with), in the right proportion (to): (与…) 相当的; 相称的; 成适当比例的: *Was the pay you received ~ with the work you did?* 你所得的薪资与你所作的工作相称吗?

com·ment /'kɒment; 'kɑmɛnt/ *n* [C, U] opinion given briefly in speech or writing about an event, or in explanation or criticism of sth: (对某事件用言语或文字所作简短的) 评论; (对某事) 说明; 解释; 批评: *Have you any ~(s) to make upon my story?* 你对于我的故事有没有什么意见? *Her strange behaviour caused a good deal of ~,* of talk, gossip, etc. 她奇怪的行为引起了诸多议论。 *No ~!* I've nothing to say on this subject. 无可奉告(对于此问题我没有什么好说的)! □ *vi* [VP2A, 3A] ~ *(on/upon),* make ~s (on); give opinions. 发表(有关…的)意见或议论; 批评。

com·men·tary /'kɒməntri US: -teri; 'kɑmənˌtɛri/ *n* (pl -ries) **1** collection of comments, eg on a book: 集注; 注释(如关于某书者): *a Bible ~.* 圣经集注。 **2** series of continuous comments (on an event): (关于某事件的) 连续的评论或报导: *a broadcast ~ on a football match.* 一场足球赛的广播报导。 *a running ~,* number of remarks following one another continuously while an event is taking place: (某一事件发生中的) 现场转播: *He kept up a running ~ on the race.* 他不断地转播比赛的况况。 **com·men·tate** /'kɒmenteɪt; 'kɑmənˌtet/ *vi* [VP3A] **commentate on,** give a ~ on. 对…加以注释, 评论或报导。 **com·men·ta·tor** /'kɒmenteɪtə(r); 'kɑmənˌtetɚ/ *n* eyewitness who gives a broadcast ~ on an event, eg a horse-race or football match; writer of a ~(1). 实况广播(如赛马或足球比赛)并兼作评论者; 广播评论家; 撰写评注者; 评注家。

com·merce /'kɒmɜːs; 'kɑmɚs/ *n* [U] trade (esp between countries); the exchange and distribution of goods: 贸易; (尤指) 国际贸易; 商业; 商务: *a Chamber of C~.* 商会。

com·mer·cial /kə'mɜːʃl; kə'mɚʃəl/ *adj* of or for commerce: 商业的; 商务的: *~ education;* 商业教育; *a ~ attitude.* 商业态度。 **~ traveller,** person who travels with samples of goods to obtain orders. (携带货样至各地的) 旅行推销员。 **~ TV/radio,** financed by charges made for ~ advertising in programmes. 靠商业广告维持的电视(无线电广播)事业。 **~ vehicles,** vans, lorries, etc, for the transport of goods. 商用车辆; 货车(供搬运货物用的有篷货车、卡车等)。 □ *n* [C] advertisement inserted in a TV or radio programme. 电视或无线电广播节目中插入的广告。 **~·ly** /-ʃəli; -ʃəli/ *adv* **~·ize** /kə'mɜːʃəlaɪz; kə'mɚʃəlˌaɪz/ *vt* [VP6A] (try to) make money out of: 使商业化; (企图) 从…当中赚钱: *Is it wise to ~ize sport?* 将运动商业化是明智的吗?

com·mi·na·tion /ˌkɒmɪ'neɪʃn; ˌkɑməˈneʃən/ *n* [C, U] (formal) threatening of divine vengeance. (正式用语) 天谴的威胁; 神罚的威吓。 **com·mina·tory** /'kɒmɪnətri US: -tɔːri; 'kɑmənəˌtori/ *adj* threatening. 威胁的; 恐吓的。

com·mingle /kə'mɪŋgl; kə'mɪŋgl/ *vt, vi* [VP6A, 2A] mingle together. 混合; 掺合; 混杂。

com·mis·er·ate /kə'mɪzəreɪt; kə'mɪzəˌret/ *vi* [VP3A] ~ *with,* feel, say that one feels, pity for: 感觉怜悯或同情; 表示怜悯或同情: *~ with a friend on his*

misfortunes. 对朋友的不幸表示同情。 **com·mis·er·ation** /kə,mızə'reıʃn; kə,mızə'reʃən/ n [C, U] (expression of) pity or sympathy (*for sb*). 怜悯或同情(的表示)(与 for 连用,后接某人。)

com·mis·sar /'kɒmɪsɑː(r); ‚kɑme'sɑr/ n 1 (formerly) head of a major Government Department of the USSR. (昔时苏联政府主要部门之)首长; 人民委员。 2 (formerly) political officer in the army of the USSR. (昔日苏联军队中之)政委。

com·mis·sar·iat /‚kɒmɪ'seərɪət; ‚kɑme'serɪət/ n 1 (formerly) major Government Department of the USSR. (昔时苏联政府的)人民委员会。 2 (formerly) department that supplied food and other stores to troops. (昔时)军需部(供应粮食及其他补给品给军队者)。 3 food supply. 粮食补给。

com·mis·sary /'kɒmɪsərɪ US: -serɪ; 'kɑmə,serɪ/ n (pl -ries) 1 (formal) deputy, delegate. (正式用语)代表。 2 (formerly) officer responsible for supplying food to troops. (昔时)军需官(负责军中之粮食补给者)。 ,~ 'general, head of a commissariat(2). 军需部部长。

com·mis·sion /kə'mɪʃn; kə'mɪʃən/ n 1 [U] the giving of authority to sb to act for another; [C] instance of this; [C] action or piece of business that is done: 授权某人代办; 委托; 所办之事: *He has secured two ~s to design buildings for a local authority.* 他已承包两起为当地政府设计建筑物的业务。 2 [U] performance or committing (*of crime*). 犯(罪)。 3 [C] [U] payment to sb for selling goods, etc, rising in proportion to the results gained: (请人销售货物等,按获利比例所付的)佣金; 酬劳金; 回扣: *He receives a ~ of 10 per cent on sales, as well as a salary.* 他按销售数量处取百分之十的佣金, 另外还有一份薪水。 *on ~*, drawing a percentage of the receipts: 抽佣金: *to sell goods on ~.* 按抽佣金办法售货。 4 [C] official paper (called a *warrant*) giving authority; (esp) (in GB) warrant signed by the Sovereign appointing an officer in the armed services: 任官令; 委任状; (尤指英国由君主签署的)军职任命状: *get/resign one's ~.* 获得(辞去)军职。 5 [C] body of persons given the duty of making an inquiry and writing a report: 考察团; 调查团(由若干人组成受命调查某事并写成报告之团体); 委员会: *a Royal C~ to report on betting and gambling.* 由英王委派的调查赌博的委员会。 6 group of people legally authorized to discharge a task. 合法受权执行某一任务的一群人。 ‚C~ of the 'Peace, Justices of the Peace collectively. (集合用法)保安官; 治安法官。 7 *in ~*, (eg of a ship) with crew and supplies complete; ready for sea. (指船只等)人员及供应品均齐备的; 已准备好即可出海的。 *out of ~*, kept in reserve; not in working order; (fig) not working, not available. 保留的; 后备的; 损坏了的; (喻)不能用的。 □ vt [VP6A, 17] give a ~(1) to: 委托; 请托: *~ an artist to paint a portrait;* 请画家画一张肖像; *be ~ed to buy books for a friend.* 受托替友人买书。 **com·mis·sioned** adj (of officers) holding rank by ~(4). (指军官)经过委任保有官阶的; 受委任的。 ⇨ **non-~ed.**

com·mis·sion·aire /kə,mɪʃə'neə(r); kə,mɪʃən'er/ n uniformed porter at the entrance to a cinema, theatre, hotel, large shop, etc. (电影院、戏院、旅馆、大商店等大门口)穿制服的侍者。

com·mis·sioner /kə'mɪʃənə(r); kə'mɪʃənə/ n 1 member of a commission (5, 6), esp one with particular duties: (尤指负有特殊任务之委员会、调查团或考察团的)委员: *the C~s of* Inland Revenue, who control Income Tax; 国内税收监督官(管理所得税者); *the Civil Service C~s,* who conduct the Civil Service examinations. 文官考试委员。 2 person who has been given a commission (1): 受委托负某种责任的人: *a C~ for Oaths,* solicitor (given commission by the Lord Chancellor) before whom documents are sworn on oath. 宣誓公证人(受英国大法官之委托负责监视签署文件者宣誓)。 3 representative of high rank: 高级代表: *the High C~ for Canada,* eg representing the Canadian Government in

London; 加拿大高级代表(如代表加拿大政府驻伦敦者): *the British High C~ in Accra.* 驻阿克拉的英国高级代表。

com·mit /kə'mɪt; kə'mɪt/ vt (-tt-) 1 [VP6A] perform (a crime, foolish act, etc): 犯(罪、错等): *murder/suicide/an offence.* 犯谋杀罪(自杀; 犯罪)。 2 [VP14] ~ *sb/sth to,* entrust, give up, hand over to, for safe keeping or treatment: 交托; 交付; 移交(为保管或处理): *~ a man to prison;* 将某人交付监禁; *~ a patient to a mental hospital;* 将病人交付精神病院; *~ sth to paper/to writing,* write it down. 将某事写下来。 *The body was ~ted to the flame,* was cremated. 尸体被火化。 *~ to memory,* learn by heart. 牢记。 *~ a prisoner for trial, ~* him to prison for trial later. 将囚犯收押候审。 3 [VP6A, 14, 16A] *~ oneself (to ...),* make oneself responsible; undertake: 承诺; 答应负责; 使自己负有责任: *He has ~ted himself to support his brother's children.* 他已答应负责养育他的侄子。 *He refused to ~ himself by talking about the crime,* refused to say anything because it might get him into trouble. 他对此犯罪案拒绝表示任何意见, 以免自己受牵累。 4 [VP6A, 14] (often reflex) pledge; bind (oneself): 保证; 束缚(自己)使(自己)受约束: *I won't ~ myself to that course of action.* 我决不承诺采取彼项行动。 ⇨ **uncommitted.** **~·ment** n [U] being ~ted (2, 3, 4); sth to which one has ~ted(3) oneself; promise; pledge; undertaking: 委托; 所承诺之事; 许诺; 保证; 承约: *If you have agreed to give a number of lectures, help to pay your brother's school expenses and give your sister £100 a year for clothes, you have quite a lot of ~ments.* 假如你已答应作些若干次演讲, 又补助你弟弟的学费, 又给你妹妹一年一百英镑的置装费, 那么你就作了相当多的承诺。

com·mit·tee /kə'mɪtɪ; kə'mɪtɪ/ n group of persons appointed (usu by a larger group) to attend to special business: (通常由较大的团体所委派以处理特殊事务的)委员会: *to attend a '~ meeting;* 参加委员会会议; *to be/sit on the ~;* 为委员会之委员; *a Parliamentary C~,* one appointed by the House of Commons (or Lords) to examine a Bill. 英国国会中的调查委员会(由下议院或上议院指派组织, 负责研究议案)。 *~-man,* functioning as (a member of) a ~. 执行委员会之职权; 担任委员。

com·mode /kə'məʊd; kə'mod/ n 1 chest of drawers. 五斗橱; 衣柜。 2 piece of bedroom furniture to hold a chamber-pot. 便桶。

com·modi·ous /kə'məʊdɪəs; kə'modɪəs/ adj having plenty of space for what is needed: 宽敞的; 有充分的空间足供需要的: *a ~ house/cupboard.* 宽敞的房子(食橱)。

com·mod·ity /kə'mɒdətɪ; kə'mɑdətɪ/ n (pl -ties) [C] useful thing, esp an article of trade: 有用的物品; (尤指)商品; *household commodities,* eg pots and pans. 家庭用品(如锅、盆)。

com·mo·dore /'kɒmədɔː(r); 'kɑmə,dor/ n naval officer having rank above a captain and below a rear-admiral; president of a yacht club; senior captain of a shipping line: 海军准将(在上校之上少将之下); 游艇俱乐部主席; 轮船公司的资深船长: *the ~ of the Cunard Line;* 丘纳德轮船公司的资深船长; *Air C~,* officer in the Air Force. 空军准将。

com·mon¹ /'kɒmən; 'kɑmən/ adj 1 belonging to, used by, coming from, done by, affecting, all or nearly all members of a group or society: (为团体或社会所有)共有的; 公用的; 共为的; 共有的; 共为的; 共用的; 共为的: *The husband is French, the wife German, and the lodger Italian, but they have English as a ~ language,* they can all use English. 丈夫是法国人, 妻子是德国人, 房客是意大利人, 但是英语是他们的共同语言。 *It is to the ~ advantage* (= to everyone's advantage) *that street traffic should be well controlled.* 街市上的交通应善加管理, 这是为了大家的利益。 *~ ground,* (fig) basis for argument accepted by persons in a dispute, etc. (喻)(辩论等之双方所承认

的)共同立论基础。 **~ knowledge,** what is known to most persons, esp in a group: (尤指某一团体内)大多数人所知道之事: *It was ~ knowledge among bankers that....* ...是银行界人所共知之事。Cf 参较 *general knowledge.* **'~ land,** land that belongs to, or may be used by, the community, esp in a village. (为全社区,尤指村,所共有或可共同使用的)公地。⇨ **common²(1). ~ factor / multiple,** (maths) belonging to two or more quantities. (数学)公因子(公倍数)。 **~ law,** (in England) unwritten law developed from old customs, eg in Saxon and Danish times, and decisions made by judges. (英国由古代,如撒克逊和丹麦的习惯及法官判例所发展成的)不成文法;习惯法。⇨ *statute law* at **statute,** and *case-law* at **case¹(2). ~-law wife,** woman with whom a man lives, as if she were his wife, but without marrying her. 非正式太太(与男人同居,却未办正式婚姻手续的女人)。 **the C~ Market** n (officially *the European Economic Community*), economic, social and political association, established in 1958, of Belgium, France, Italy, Luxembourg, the Netherlands and West Germany, since enlarged in 1973 by the inclusion of Britain, Ireland and Denmark, with associate membership (for economic preferences) by other countries. 欧洲共同市场 (正式名称为 the European Economic Community 欧洲经济共同体,于1958年由比利时、法国、意大利、卢森堡、荷兰及西德所组成之经济、社会及政治的联盟,此后由于1973年英国、爱尔兰共和国及丹麦之纳入组织而扩大,尚有其他以经济利益为优先的准会员国家)。 **~ noun,** (gram) name that can be used for any member of a class, eg *book* or *knife.* (语法)普通名词(可用以指同类事物之任何一个之名称,如 book 或 knife)。 **a ~ nuisance,** an offence that is harmful to the community and for which there is legal remedy. 妨害治安的行为(有害于社会,法律并订有制裁办法者)。⇨ also **cause** and **prayer. '~-room,** room for use of the teachers or students at a school, college, etc. (中小学、大学等之)教师室;教授室;学生室。 **2** usual and ordinary; happening or found often and in many places: 普通的;常见的;常常发生的;到处可见的: *a ~ flower;* 常见的花; *a ~ experience.* 普通的经验。*Pine-trees are ~ in many parts of the world.* 松树在世界上许多地方都很常见。*Is this word in ~ use?* 这个词常用吗? **the ~ man/people,** the ordinary or average citizen(s): 常人;普通人;老百姓: *The ~ man in every country wants peace.* 每一个国家的老百姓都想要和平。 **~ metre,** hymn stanza of 4 lines, with 8, 6, 8, 6 syllables. 普通韵律(赞美诗用之,四行成一节,各行音节数目为 8, 6, 8, 6)。 **~ sense,** practical good sense gained by experience of life, not by special study. 常识(由生活经验得来,而非由特别研究得来的实用判断力)。 **~ time/measure,** two or four beats in a bar. (音乐)普通拍子(每小节两拍或四拍)。 **3** (colloq) (of persons, their behaviour and possessions) vulgar; of inferior quality or taste: (口)(指人,其行为及所有物)粗鄙的;劣等的;低级的: *manners;* 粗鄙的举止; *speak with a ~ accent;* 以粗俗的口音说话; *a girl who looks ~/who wears ~ clothes.* 貌不美(穿粗俗衣服)的女子。 **~·ly** adv **1** usually: 通常地: *That very ~ly happens.* 那事极常发生。*Thomas, ~ly called Tom.* 托马斯,通常呼为汤姆。 **2** in a ~(3) way: 粗鄙地;粗劣地: *~ly dressed.* 衣着不整洁的。

com·mon² /'kɒmən; 'kɑmən/ n **1** [C] area (usu in or near a village) of unfenced grassland for all to use: (通常在村内或附近,不围篱的)公用草地;村公园: *Saturday afternoon cricket on the village ~.* 星期六下午在村公园举行的板球比赛。 **2** *in ~,* for or by all (of a group). (团体)共同的;公有的。 **have in ~ (with),** share (with): (与…)共有: *They have nothing in ~ with one another,* have no similar interests, etc. 他们彼此毫无共同之点(没有同样的兴趣等)。 **in ~ with,** together with: 与…一起; 与…一样: *In ~ with (= Like) many people he prefers meat to fish.* 象许多人一样,他喜欢肉而不喜欢鱼。 **out of the ~,** unusual. 不平常的。

com·mon·alty /'kɒmənəltɪ; 'kɑmənltɪ/ n **the ~,** the common people (contrasted with the upper classes). 普通人民;平民(与高阶层人士相对)。

com·moner /'kɒmənə(r); 'kɑmənɚ/ n one of the common people, not a member of the nobility. (一个)平民(非贵族)。

com·mon·place /'kɒmənpleɪs; 'kɑmən,ples/ adj ordinary or usual: 平常的;平凡的;平庸的: *a ~ kind of man.* 一种平凡的人。 □ n remark, event, etc that is ordinary or usual: 老生常谈;平常的事: *conversation full of mere ~s.* 充满老生常谈的谈话。*Travel by air is now a ~.* 航空旅行现在是一件平常的事。

com·mons /'kɒmənz; 'kɑmənz/ n pl **1** the ~, (old use) the common people. (旧用法)平民。⇨ aristocracy, nobility. **the ,House of C~,** assembly of those elected by the common people; lower house of the British Parliament. (英国的)下议院(议员系由平民所选)。 **2** provisions shared in common. 公用的食物。 **be on short ~,** not have enough to eat. 缺乏食物。

com·mon·wealth /'kɒmənwelθ; 'kɑmən,welθ/ n **1** State; group of States (eg *the C~ of Australia*) associating politically for their common good. 国家;(为共同利益所组织的)联邦(例如澳大利亚联邦)。 **2 the C~** a free association of sovereign independent states (formerly colonies and dominions of GB) with their dependencies. 英联邦(若干昔为英国殖民地及自治领而现为独立自主国家及其属地的自由结合)。

com·mo·tion /kə'məʊʃn; kə'moʃən/ n [U] noisy confusion; excitement; [C] instance of this; violent uprising or disturbance: 骚动;骚扰;暴动;暴乱: *You're making a great ~ about nothing.* 你简直是在无理取闹。

com·mu·nal /'kɒmjʊnl; 'kɑmjunl/ adj **1** of or for a community: 社会的;公有的: *~ disturbances,* eg in countries where there are antagonisms between people of different races and religions. 社会的动荡不安(例如在某些国家人民间有种族和宗教的敌视)。 **2** for common use; shared: 公用的;共用的: *~ land/kitchens.* 公用的土地(共用的厨房)。

com·mune¹ /kə'mjuːn; kə'mjun/ vi [VP2C, 3A] (together) ~ (with), feel at one with; feel, be in close touch with; talk with in an intimate way: (与…)感觉一致; (感觉)与…很亲近;与…亲密地交谈: *~ with nature/one's friends/God in prayer;* 在祷告中与上帝作灵的沟通; (与朋友亲密交谈;在祷告中与上帝作灵的沟通) *friends communing together.* 在一起亲密交谈的朋友。

com·mune² /'kɒmjuːn; 'kɑmjun/ n **1** (in France, Belgium, Italy, Spain) smallest territorial district for purposes of administration, with a mayor and council. (在法国、比利时、意大利、西班牙)最小的地方行政区(设市长及议会)。 **2** organized group of people promoting local interests. 为促进地方福利而组成的人民团体;福利社。 **3** group of people living together and sharing property and responsibilities. 生活在一起,共有财产、分担职责的一群人;公社。

com·mu·ni·cable /kə'mjuːnɪkəbl; kə'mjunɪkəbl/ adj (of ideas, illness, etc) that can be communicated or imparted. (指观念、疾病等)可沟通的;传染性的。

com·mu·ni·cant /kə'mjuːnɪkənt; kə'mjunɪkənt/ n **1** one who (regularly) receives Holy Communion. (按时)领受圣餐者。 **2** informer (the more usu word). 报信者;通报者 (informer 为较常用词)。

com·mu·ni·cate /kə'mjuːnɪkeɪt; kə'mjunə,ket/ vt, vi **1** [VP6A, 14] ~ *sth (to),* pass on (news, information, feelings, heat, motion, an illness, etc). 传达(新闻、消息、感情); 传播(热力); 传递(运动); 传染(疾病)。 **2** [VP3A] ~ *with,* share or exchange (news, etc): 共有或交换(消息等): 通信;通讯: *We can ~ with people in most parts of the world by telephone.* 我们可以借电话与世界上大多数地区的人通讯。*Young people sometimes complain of not being able to ~ with their parents.* 年轻人有时抱怨无法与父母沟通思想。 **3** [VP2A, 3A] ~ *(with),* (of rooms, gardens, roads, etc) be connected:

(指房间、花园、道路等)互通；通连: *My garden ~s with the garden next door by means of a gate*. 我的花园与隔壁的花园有门相通。*We asked the hotel to let us have communicating rooms*, rooms with a connecting door. 我们向旅馆要有门互通的房间。

com·mu·ni·ca·tion /kə,mjuːnɪˈkeɪʃn; kə,mjunəˈke-ʃən/ *n* 1 [U] the act of communicating: 传达；传播；传递；传染；通信: *Among the deaf and dumb ~ may be carried on by means of the finger alphabet*. 聋哑的人可以借手语传达意思。*Spitting in public places may lead to the ~ of disease*. 在公共场所吐痰可能导致疾病的传染。*I'm in/I must get into ~ with him on this subject*. 关于这问题，我正(必须)与他交换意见。2 [C] that which is communicated (eg news): 被传播之事(如新闻)；信息；消息: *This ~ is confidential*. 这消息是机密的。3 [C, U] means of communicating: roads, railways, telephone or telegraph lines connecting places, radio and TV: 交通或通讯设施；(联络各地的)公路、铁路、电话或电报线；无线电；电视: *a world ~s network*; 世界性通讯网; *~ satellites*; 通讯人造卫星; *mass ~s media*. 大众通讯媒介。*Telegraphic ~/~s between Amman and Baghdad has/have been restored*. 安曼与巴格达之间的电报通讯业已恢复。*All ~ with the north has been stopped by snowstorms*. 与北部的一切交通均为风雪所阻。'~ **cord**, cord that passes along the length of a train inside the coaches, to be pulled (to stop the train) in an emergency. 火车厢内顺着乘客所装，在发生紧急事件时拉之以通知刹车之警铃线。

com·mu·ni·cat·ive /kəˈmjuːnɪkətɪv US: -keɪtɪv; kəˈmjunəˌketɪv/ *adj* ready and willing to talk and give information. 好说话的；直言的；不隐讳的。 ⇨ *reserved* at **reserve²**.

com·mu·nion /kəˈmjuːnɪən; kəˈmjunjən/ *n* 1 [U] sharing in common; participation (*with*). 共有；同享；参与(与 with 连用)。2 [U] exchange of thought and feelings; intercourse. (思想感情的)交流。*hold '~ with oneself*, think deeply (esp about moral or religious problems). 深思；独自思考(尤指关于道德或宗教的问题)。*self-~*, thinking about oneself. 自省；独自深思。3 [C] group of persons with the same religious beliefs: 由同一宗教信仰的人所构成的团体；教会；教派: *We belong to the same ~*. 我们属于同一教会。4 (**Holy**) **C~**, (in the Christian Church) celebration of the Lord's Supper. 圣餐(基督教会纪念耶稣最后晚餐的仪式)。*go to C~*, (a) attend church for this celebration. 参加圣餐礼。(b) receive the Eucharist. 领圣餐。

com·mu·ni·qué /kəˈmjuːnɪkeɪ; kəˌmjunəˈke/ *n* official announcement, eg as issued to the press. 公报；官报。

com·mu·nism /ˈkɒmjunɪzm; ˈkamjuˌnɪzəm/ *n* [U] 共产主义。**com·mu·nist** /ˈkɒmjunɪst; ˈkamjunɪst/ *n* 共产主义者；共产党员。 □ *adj* of ~. 共产主义的；共产主义者的。

com·mun·ity /kəˈmjuːnətɪ; kəˈmjunətɪ/ *n* (*pl* **-ties**) 1 **the ~**, the people living in one place, district or country, considered as a whole: (由同住于一地、一地区或一国的人所构成的)社会；社区: *work for the good of the ~*. 为社会利益而工作。'~ **centre**, building(s), etc where people meet for adult education classes, amateur dramatics, informal social intercourse, etc. 社区活动中心(民众可以在此共同参加成人教育班、业余戏剧公演、非正式社交活动等)；公共会堂。 **~ chest**, (US) welfare fund for helping people in distress. (美)社区(救济穷困者的)福利基金。2 [C] group of persons having the same religion, race, occupation, etc or with common interests: 由同宗教、同种族、同职业或共同利益的人所构成的团体: *a ~ of monks*; 一群和尚; *the Jewish ~ in London*; 在伦敦的犹太侨民团体; *the European ~ in Karachi*. 住在卡拉奇的欧洲侨民团体。3 [U] condition of sharing, having things in common, being alike in some way: 共享；共有；相同: *~ of race/religion/interests*. 种族(宗教、利益)的相同: *a ~ spirit*,

shared feeling of membership. 团队精神。*in ~, together*. 一起；共同。'**~ singing**, organized singing in which all present take part. (所有在场的人一齐参加的)大合唱。

com·mut·able /kəˈmjuːtəbl; kəˈmjutəbl/ *adj* that can be exchanged or converted (*into/for*). 可交换的；可改变的(与 into 及 for 连用)。

com·mu·ta·tion /ˌkɒmjuːˈteɪʃn; ˌkamjuˈteʃən/ *n* 1 [U] commuting; making one kind of payment instead of another, eg money instead of service. 折算；折合偿付；代偿(如以金钱代偿劳役)。2 [C] payment made in this way. 代偿金。3 [C] reduced punishment: 减刑: *a ~ of the death sentence to life imprisonment*. 由死刑改为无期徒刑的减刑。4 **~ ticket**, (US) season ticket. (美)月季票。

com·mu·ta·tor /ˈkɒmjuːteɪtə(r); ˈkamjuˌtetə/ *n* device for altering the direction of an electric current. (改换电流方向的)换向器；整流器。

com·mute /kəˈmjuːt; kəˈmjut/ *vt, vi* 1 [VP6A, 14] **~ (into/for)**, exchange one thing (esp one kind of payment) for another: 改换某物(为另一物)；折合(以一物代替另一物，尤指其偿付方式): *~ one's pension*; 改换养老金的偿付方式; *~ an annuity into/for a lump sum*. 将年金合算为一总数，一次付清。2 [VP6A, 14] **~ (to)**, reduce the severity of a punishment: 减(刑): *a death sentence (to one of life imprisonment)*. 将死刑减刑(为无期徒刑)。3 [VP2A] travel regularly, eg by train or car, between one's work in a town and one's home in the country or suburbs. 经常来往；通勤(如搭乘火车或汽车，经常往返于市区工作地点与乡村或郊区住家之间)。**com·muter** *n* person who ~s(3). 经常往来于某两地间的人；通勤者。

com·pact¹ /ˈkɒmpækt; ˈkampækt/ *n* agreement between parties; contract; covenant. 合同；合约；契约；协定。

com·pact² /kəmˈpækt; kəmˈpækt/ *adj* closely packed together; neatly fitted; (of literary style) condensed. 包扎紧密的；压紧的；致密的；恰好合适的；(指文体)简洁的。 □ *vt* (usu passive) join firmly together. (通常用被动语态)紧密结合。**~·ly** *adv* **~·ness** *n*

com·pact³ /ˈkɒmpækt; ˈkampækt/ *n* small, flat container for face-powder (and often with a mirror), made for carrying in a woman's handbag. (妇女手提包中所带的)粉盒(常附有镜子)。

com·pan·ion¹ /kəmˈpænɪən; kəmˈpænjən/ *n* 1 person who goes with, is often or always with, another: 同伴；同行者；伴侣 (时常或总是跟另一个人在一起者): *my ~s on the journey*. 我的旅伴。2 person who shares in the work, pleasures, misfortunes, etc of another: 与另一人同工作、共享乐或共患难等的人: *~s in arms*, fellow soldiers; 军中同僚; 战友; *~s in misfortune*, associated in it; 患难朋友; *a faithful ~ of 50 years*, eg said by a man speaking of his wife. 五十年的忠实伴侣(如夫指其妻而言)。3 person with similar tastes, interests, etc: 好者；志趣相投者: *He's an excellent ~*. 他是一个极合得来的人。*His brother is not much of a ~ for him*. 他哥哥(弟弟)与他志趣不甚相投。4 one of two or more things that go together; thing that matches another or is one of a pair: 成套物件之一；成对物件之一: *Here's the glove for my left hand, but where's the ~?* 我左手的手套在这里，可是右手的在哪里？(also attrib): (亦用作定语): *the ~ volume(s)*. 上册或下册；成套书的一卷。5 person paid to keep another (usu old or ill) person company. 受雇陪伴老人或病人等的人。6 handbook or reference book: 手册；参考书；指南: *the Gardener's C~*. 园艺指南。7 **C~**, member of some Orders: 有某种勋位者: *C~ of the Bath*. 有巴斯勋位者。 ⇨ **order¹**(9). **~·able** *adj* friendly; sociable. 和善的；友爱的；友善的。**~·ship** /-ʃɪp; -ˌʃɪp/ *n* state of being ~s: 伴同；同伴之谊: *enjoy sb's ~*; 乐与某人为友; *a ~ship of many years*. 多年之交谊。

com·pan·ion² /kəmˈpænɪən; kəmˈpænjən/ *n* (usu

通常作 **,~·way**) staircase from the deck of a ship to the saloon or cabins. 舱梯(由甲板通至交谊厅或船舱的梯子）。

com·pany /ˈkʌmpəni; ˈkʌmpəni/ n 1 [U] being together with another or others: 伴随; 陪伴; 与他人在一起: I shall be glad of your ~ (= to have you with me) on the journey. 我将很高兴与你同行。 **be good/poor/bad/excellent, etc ~**, be a good, etc, companion (3). 与人很(不良, 极等)合得来的同伴。 **for ~**, to provide companionship: 作为同伴; 陪伴: I'll go with you as far as the station for ~. 我将陪伴你到车站。 **in ~ (with)**, together (with): (与…)一起: He came in ~ with a group of boys. 他与一群男孩子同来。 We went in ~. 我们一起去的。 **keep sb ~; keep ~ with sb**, be or go with him: 陪伴某人: He stayed at home to keep his wife ~. 他留在家里陪伴他的妻子。 **part ~ (with sb)**, ⇨ part²(1). 2 [U] group of persons; number of guests: 人群; 一群客人: We're expecting ~ (= guests, visitors) next week. 我们下星期将有客人来访。 He's not well enough to receive a great deal of ~, many visitors. 他的健康尚未十分恢复, 不能接见很多访客。 **sin in good ~**, better men have done the same. 人非至贤, 孰能无过。 3 [U] persons with whom one spends one's time: 同伴; 伙伴; 友伴: You may know a man by the ~ he keeps, judge his character by his friends. 看他与什么人来往, 你就可以知道他是个什么样的人。 **Don't get into/keep bad ~**, Don't become friendly with/mix with bad persons. 勿与坏人交往。 4 (often 常作 C~, abbr 略作 Co) [C] (pl -nies) number of persons united for business or commerce: (由若干人组成经营商业的)公司: a steamship ~. 轮船公司。 **a ,Limited ,Lia'bility C~**, C~ whose partners are not included in the title: 有限责任公司; 商号上不列合伙人姓名的公司: ,T ,S 'Smith & Co. 史密斯公司(及其合伙人)。 5 number of persons working together: 一队(在一起工作的人): a ~ of players, actors who perform plays together: 一队在一起演戏的演员; a theatrical ~; 剧团; 剧社; 戏班; the ship's ~, the crew. 船上的全体船员。 6 subdivision of an infantry battalion, commanded by a captain or major. 连(步兵营以下之单位, 由上尉或少校指挥)。

com·par·able /ˈkɒmpərəbl; ˈkɑmpərəbl/ adj (~ /with), that can be compared: 可与相比的; 可与比拟的: The sets of figures are not ~. 这两组(或这几组)数字是不能相比的。 His achievements are ~ with the best. 他的成就可与最优者相比。

com·para·tive /kəmˈpærətɪv; kəmˈpærətɪv/ adj 1 having to do with comparison or comparing: 比较性的; 与比较有关的: the ~ method of studying, ie by finding out what is similar and different in two or more branches of knowledge; 比较研究法(借寻出二或多门学问间之异同, 以从事研究之方法); ~ religion; 比较宗教; ~ linguistics. 比较语言学。 2 measured or judged by comparing: 比较而言的; 相当的: living in ~ comfort, eg comfortably compared with others, or with one's own life at an earlier period. 生活比较舒适的(与他人或自己早期的生活比较起来算是舒适)。 3 (gram) of or related to the form of adjectives and adverbs expressing 'more', (语法)(形容词和副词之)比较级的, as in 如 worse, harder, more difficult, more prettily. □ n ~ degree: 比较级: 'Better' is the ~ of 'good'. better 是 good 的比较级。 **~·ly** adv

com·pare /kəmˈpeə(r); kəmˈper/ vt, vi 1 [VP6A, 14] ~ (with), examine, judge to what extent persons or things are similar or not similar: 比较(研究、评判人与人或事物与事物之间相同或相异之程度): ~ two translations; 比较两种译文; ~ your translation with the model translation on the blackboard. 将你的译文与黑板上的模范译文加以比较。交换意见; 商量。 2 [VP14] ~ to, point out the likeness or relation between: 喻为; 比拟(指出其间的相似或关系): Poets have ~d sleep to death. 诗人一直把睡眠比作死亡。 Mine cannot be ~d to yours,

is quite different. 我的与你的极不相同。 3 [VP3A] ~ with, be ~ed with; bear comparison with: 与…比较; 匹敌: He cannot ~ with Shakespeare as a writer of tragedies, is nearly so great. 作为一个悲剧作家, 他无法与莎士比亚相比。 This cannot ~ with that, no comparison is possible because they are so different. 这个与那个无法比较(因其完全不同)。 4 (gram) form the comparative and superlative degrees (of adjectives and adverbs). (语法) 构成(形容词和副词的)比较级和最高级。 □ n (poet) comparison (but only in) (诗)比较(但仅用于) **beyond/past/without ~**, 无可比拟的; 无匹敌的; 无双的: She is lovely beyond ~, so lovely that none can be ~d to her. 她的可爱是无与伦比的。

com·pari·son /kəmˈpærɪsn; kəmˈpærəsn/ n 1 [U] by/in ~ (with), when compared (with): (与…)比较起来; 相较; 较之: This one costs more but is cheaper by/in ~, is plainly better value when you compare them and examine the quality, etc. 这件东西价钱贵一点, 但是比较起来(比较其质料等)还是便宜。 The tallest buildings in London are small in ~ with those of New York. 伦敦最高的建筑物与纽约的比较起来, 仍然很小。 **the ~ of X and/with Y**, the act of comparing X with Y. X 与 Y 的比较; 相比。 2 [C] (make) a ~ between X and Y/of X to Y, (perform) an act of comparing; an instance of this: (X 与 Y 间之)比较; 比拟(这种比较的实例); 比喻: It is often useful to make a ~ between two things. 比较两件事物常是有用的。 The ~ of the heart to a pump/between the heart and a pump has often been made. 常有人将心脏比作帮浦。 There's no ~ between them, They cannot be compared, one being clearly much better than the other. 两者不可同日而语(因其相差悬殊)。 **~s are odious**, in this case it is unfair to make any ~. 在此情况下作比较是不公平的。 3 **bear/stand ~ with**, be able to be compared favourably with: 比得上; 不亚于: That's a good dictionary, but it won't/can't stand ~ with this. 那是一部好词典, 但是还比不上这一本。 4 **degrees of ~**, (gram) positive, comparative and superlative (of adjectives and adverbs), eg good, better, best. (语法)比较级(指形容词和副词之原级、比较级及最高级, 例如 good, better, best)。

com·part·ment /kəmˈpɑːtmənt; kəmˈpɑrtmənt/ n one of several separate divisions of a structure, esp of a railway carriage or coach: (构造物之)隔间; (尤指铁路客车等中的)小间; 车室: The first-class ~s are in front. 头等房间在前端。 The ship's hold is built in watertight ~s. 船舱建造成许多水密舱区。 **com·part·men·tal·ize** /ˌkɒmpɑːtˈmentəlaɪz; ˌkɑmpɑrtˈmentl̩ˌaɪz/ vt divide into ~s or categories. 分成隔间或部门; 区划。

com·pass¹ /ˈkʌmpəs; ˈkʌmpəs/ n 1 (mag'netic) ~, device with a needle that points to the magnetic north: 指南针; 罗盘; 罗经: the points of the ~ (N, NE, E, SE,

the points of the compass

S, SW, W, NW, etc); 罗经上的方位(北、东北、东、东南、南、西南、西、西北等); similar device, eg 类似的装置, 例 如 *a radio* ~, for determining direction. (用以指定方位的)电子罗经. **2** (old use 旧用法 pair of ~es) ~(es), V-shaped instrument with two arms joined by a hinge, used for drawing circles, measuring distances on a map or chart, etc. 两脚规; 圆规(一种 V 字形仪器, 用以画圆、量地图或图表上的距离等). ⇨ the illus at **dividers**. 参看 dividers 之插图. **3** extent; range: 范围: *beyond the* ~ *of the human mind;* 超出人类智力的范围; *outside the* ~ (= range) *of her voice.* 超出她的音域.

com·pass² /'kʌmpəs; 'kʌmpəs/ vt encompass (the more usu word). 围绕; 包围(encompass 为较常用词).

com·pas·sion /kəm'pæʃn; kəm'pæʃən/ n [U] pity; feeling for the sufferings of others, prompting one to give help: 怜悯; 同情: *have/take* ~ *on sufferers;* 同情受苦者: *be filled with* ~ *for the refugees;* 对于难民们充满了怜悯; *look at someone in/with* ~; 以怜悯的目光看某人; *give a man money out of* ~. 由于同情心而给人钱. ~·**ate** /kəm'pæʃənət; kəm'pæʃənət/ adj showing or feeling ~: 显示同情心的; 感觉怜悯的: *The soldier was granted* ~ate *leave,* given leave²(2), eg because personal affairs made necessary his presence at home. 该士兵请事假回家获得准许.

com·pat·ible /kəm'pætəbl; kəm'pætəbl/ adj ~ (**with**), (cf ideas, arguments, principles, etc) suited (to), in accord (with), able to exist together (with): (指观念、议论、原则等)适宜(于…)的; (与…)符合的; 能共存的; 相容的: *pleasure* ~ *with duty;* 与职责不背的行乐; *driving a car at a speed* ~ *with safety.* 以兼顾安全的速度驾车. **com·pat·ibly** /-əblɪ; -əblɪ/ adv **com·pati·bil·ity** /kəm,pætə'bɪlətɪ; kəm,pætə'bɪlətɪ/ n [U] the state of being ~. 相合; 相容; 一致; 可合性; 不矛盾.

com·patriot /kəm'pætrɪət US: -'peɪt-; kəm'peɪtrɪət/ n person born in, or citizen of, the same country as another; fellow-countryman. 同国人; 同胞(生于同国或为同一国家公民的人).

com·peer /'kʌmpɪə(r); kəm'pɪr/ n person equal in rank or capacity. (地位或能力)相等的人; 同伴.

com·pel /kəm'pel; kəm'pel/ vt (-ll-) **1** [VP17] ~ *sb/sth to do sth,* force (sb or sth to do sth); get, bring about, by force: 强迫; 迫使(某人或某物做某事); 强取; 强致: *His conscience* ~led *him to confess.* 他的良心迫使他承认. *He was* ~led *by illness to resign.* 他因病被迫辞职. **2**[VP14, 6A] ~ (**from**), obtain by pressure: 施压力以获得: *Can they* ~ *obedience from us,* force us to obey? 他们能强迫我们服从吗?

com·pen·di·ous /kəm'pendɪəs; kəm'pendɪəs/ adj (of authors, books, etc) giving much information briefly. (指作家、书籍等)简要的; 精简的.

com·pen·dium /kəm'pendɪəm; kəm'pendɪəm/ n concise and comprehensive account; summary. 简明而广泛的叙述; 摘要; 撮要; 概要.

com·pen·sate /'kʌmpenseɪt; 'kɑmpən,set/ vt, vi [VP6A, 14, 3A] ~ (**sb**) (**for sth**), make a suitable payment, give something to make up (for loss, injury, etc): 赔偿; 补偿(损失、伤害等): *Do employers in your country* ~ *workers for injuries suffered at their work?* 贵国工人在工作时受伤, 雇主是否予以赔偿? *Nothing can* ~ *for the loss of one's health.* 失去健康是无可补偿的事. **com·pen·sa·tory** /kəm'pensətərɪ US: -tɔːrɪ; kəm'pensə,tɔrɪ/ adj compensating. 赔偿的; 补偿的; 报答的.

com·pen·sa·tion /,kʌmpen'seɪʃn; ,kɑmpən'seʃən/ n [U] compensating; [C] sth given to compensate: 赔偿; 补偿; 赔偿物: *He received £5000 in* ~/*by way of* ~/*as a* ~ *for the loss of his right hand.* 他失去右手, 获得五千英镑的赔偿.

com·père /'kʌmpeə(r); 'kɑmper/ n (F) organizer of a cabaret or broadcast entertainment who introduces the performers, speakers, etc. (法) (餐馆歌舞表演或广播综艺节目的)安排并报告节目者; 节目主持人(介绍演员、演讲

者等). □ vt act as ~ for. 为…担任安排并报告节目者; 担任…之主持人.

com·pete /kəm'piːt; kəm'pit/ vi [VP2A, 3A] take part in a race, contest, examination, etc: (参加赛跑、比赛、考试等)竞争; 比赛: *to* ~ *in a race* (*against/with others,* for a prize, etc): 参加赛跑, (同别人, 为奖品, 为得第一名等)竞争; *to* ~ *against/with other countries in trade.* 与别的国家在贸易上竞争.

com·pet·ence /'kʌmpɪtəns; 'kɑmpɪtəns/ n 1 [U] being competent; ability: 称职; 胜任; 能力: *his* ~ *in handling money/to handle money.* 他的理财(处理金钱)的能力. **2** (usu 常作 **a** ~) income large enough for a person to live on in comfort: 足以使人过舒适生活的收入: *have/enjoy a small* ~. 有一笔足以过舒适生活的小收入. **3** [U] (of a court, a magistrate) legal capacity: (指法庭、地方法官)管辖权; 权限: *business that is within/beyond the* ~ *of the court.* 在法院管辖权以内(以外)的业务.

com·pet·ent /'kʌmpɪtənt; 'kɑmpətənt/ adj **1** (of persons) having ability, power, authority, skill, knowledge, etc (to do what is needed): (指人)有能力、权力、权威、技能、知识等(去做必须做之事)的; 能干的; 胜任的: *Is Miss X* ~ *in her work/* ~ *as a teacher/* ~ *to teach French?* 某小姐能胜任她的工作(能任教员, 能教法语)吗? **2**(of qualities) sufficient, adequate: (指性质)足够的; 适当的: *Has she a* ~ *knowledge of French?* 她的法语知识够用吗? ~·**ly** adv

com·pe·ti·tion /,kʌmpə'tɪʃn; ,kɑmpə'tɪʃən/ n **1** [U] competing; activity in which persons compete: 竞争; 竞赛; 角逐; 竞争的活动: *trade* ~ *between countries;* 国际间的贸易竞争; *keen* ~ *for a job.* 求职的激烈竞争. *At the Olympic Games our representatives were in* ~ (= were competing) *with the best swimmers from all parts of the world.* 在奥运会上, 我们的代表会与世界各地的最佳游泳选手角逐. **2** [C] instance of competing; contest; meeting(s) at which skill, strength, knowledge, etc is tested: 比赛; (比赛技巧、体力、知识等的)赛会: *boxing/chess* ~s. 拳击(国际象棋等)比赛.

com·peti·tive /kəm'petətɪv; kəm'pɛtətɪv/ adj in or for which there is competition: 竞争性的; 比赛性的: ~ *examinations for government posts.* 公职甄选考试. *Our firm offers you* ~ *prices,* prices that compare favourably with those of other firms. 本店向你提出竞争性的价格(比其他商店公道的价格).

com·peti·tor /kəm'petɪtə(r); kəm'pɛtətə/ n person who competes. 竞争者; 敌手.

com·pile /kəm'paɪl; kəm'paɪl/ vt [VP6A] collect (information) and arrange (in a book, list, report, etc): 搜集(资料)并编辑(成书、表、报告等): 编纂; 编辑: ~ *a dictionary/a guide-book/an index.* 编辑词典(旅行指南, 索引). **com·piler** n person who ~s. 编纂者; 编辑. **com·pi·la·tion** /,kʌmpɪ'leɪʃn; ,kʌmpr'leʃən/ n [U] compiling; [C] thing that is ~d. 编辑; 编纂; 编制; 编纂物.

com·pla·cence /kəm'pleɪsns; kəm'plesns/ n [U] self-satisfaction; quiet contentment. 自满; 得意; 暗自满足. **com·pla·cency** /-'pleɪsnsɪ; -'plesnsɪ/ n

com·pla·cent /kəm'pleɪsnt; kəm'plesnt/ adj self-satisfied: 自满的; 得意的: *with a* ~ *smile/air.* 带着得意的微笑(神情). ~·**ly** adv

com·plain /kəm'pleɪn; kəm'plen/ vi [VP2A, 3A, B] ~ (**to sb**) (**about/of sth**), say that one is not satisfied, that sth is wrong, that one is suffering: 抱怨; 不满; 发牢骚; 诉苦: *She* ~ed *to me of his rudeness/that he had been rude to her.* 她向我诉说他的粗鲁(他曾对她有粗鲁的行为). *We have nothing to* ~ *of/about.* 我们没有什么可抱怨的. *He never* ~s *about the pain/about being in pain.* 他从来不为那痛苦抱怨. ~·**ing·ly** adv

com·plain·ant /kəm'pleɪnənt; kəm'plenənt/ n (legal) plaintiff. (法律)原告.

com·plaint /kəm'pleɪnt; kəm'plent/ n **1** [U] complaining; [C] statement of, grounds for, dissatisfaction:

抱怨; 不满; 抱怨的话; 不满的理由; 控诉: *You have no cause / grounds of / for ~*. 你没有理由抱怨。 *Have you any ~s to make?* 你有什么苦要诉吗? *Some children are full of ~s about their food.* 有些孩子满口抱怨他们的食物不好。 *Why don't you lodge a ~ against your noisy neighbours?* 你为何不控告你的喧嚣的邻居? **2** [C] illness; disease: 疾病: *a heart / liver ~;* 心脏(肝)病; *childish ~s*, illnesses common among children. 小儿常患的疾病。

com·plais·ance /kəmˈpleɪzns; kəmˈplezns/ *n* [U] easy-going habit of mind; readiness and willingness to do what pleases others: 随遇而安的心理; 乐于做出使旁人高兴之事的意愿; 殷勤; 顺从: *do sth out of ~*. 为献殷勤而做某事。 **com·plais·ant** / -zent; -znt/ *adj* obliging; disposed to please: 殷勤的; 顺从的: *a complaisant husband*. 顺从的丈夫。

com·ple·ment /ˈkɒmplɪment; ˈkɑmpləment/ *n* **1** that which makes sth complete; the full number or quantity needed: 补充物; 补充物; 所需要的全数或量; 足数; 足量: *the ship's ~*, the full number of officers and men. 船上的编制员额。 **2** (gram) word(s esp *adjj* and *nn*, used after *vv* such as *be* and *become* and qualifying the subject: (语法)补语; (尤指形容词及名词, 用于 be 及 become 等动词之后以形容主语): *In the sentence 'I'm tired' tired is the ~*. 在 'I'm tired' 句中, tired 是补语。 **~·ary** /ˌkɒmplɪˈmentri; ˌkɑmpləˈmentəri/ *adj* forming a ~. 补足的; 补充的。 □ *vt* [VP6A] complete; form the ~ to. 补足; 补充; 为…的补足物。

com·plete¹ /kəmˈpliːt; kəmˈplit/ *adj* **1** having all its parts; whole: 完整的; 完全的; 全部的; 整个的: *a ~ edition of Shakespeare's plays*. 莎士比亚戏剧全集。 **2** finished; ended: 完成的; 结束的: *When will the work be ~?* 这项工作将于何时完成? **3** thorough; in every way: 彻底的; 完完全全的: *He's a ~ stranger to me*. 对我来说他完全是个陌生人。 *It was a ~ surprise to me*, I wasn't expecting it and hadn't even thought of it. 它对我完全是件意外的事 (我未预料到它, 甚至未曾想到它)。 **~·ly** *adv* wholly; in every way: 完全地; 彻底地: *~ly successful*. 完全成功。 **~·ness** *n*

com·plete² /kəmˈpliːt; kəmˈplit/ *vt* [VP6A] finish; bring to an end; make perfect: 完成; 使完善: *The railway is not ~d yet*. 铁路尚未完工。 *I need one volume to ~ my set of Dickens*. 我只差一本书就可有全套狄更斯作品了。

com·ple·tion /kəmˈpliːʃn; kəmˈpliʃən/ *n* [U] act of completing; state of being complete: 完成; 完工; 完满; 完结; 完全: *You may occupy the house on ~ of contract*, when the contract of sale has been completed. 买卖契约手续完成时, 你就可以住进此屋。

com·plex¹ /ˈkɒmpleks *US*: kəmˈpleks; kɑmˈpleks/ *adj* made up of closely connected parts; difficult to understand or explain: 由许多密切联系的部分合成的; 难以了解或解释的; 复杂的: *a ~ argument / proposal / situation*; 复杂的论据 (提议, 情况); *a ~ system of government*; 复杂的行政制度; *a ~ sentence*, (gram) one containing subordinate clauses. (语法)复合句(包含从句的句子)。 **~·ity** /kəmˈpleksəti; kəmˈpleksəti/ *n* [U] state of being ~; [C] (*pl* **-ties**) sth that is ~. 复杂的状态; 复杂之物。

com·plex² /ˈkɒmpleks; ˈkɑmpleks/ *n* [C] **1** complex whole; number of dissimilar parts intricately related: 复合体; 复杂相关的一群相异的部分: *a building ~*. 综合建筑。 **2** (psych) (abnormal) mental state which is the result of past experiences or suppressed tendencies; (colloq) obsessive concern or fear: (心理学)由于过去的经验或被压抑的性向所造成的(不正常)心理状态; 情结; (口)萦绕于心的忧虑或恐惧: *He has a ~ about his weight*. 他过分关心他的本重。 ⇨ *inferiority* at **inferior**, *superiority* at **superior**.

com·plexion /kəmˈplekʃn; kəmˈplekʃən/ *n* [C] **1** natural colour, appearance, etc of the skin, esp of the face: (天然的)肤色; 面色; 面貌: *a good / dark / fair ~*.

妖好的(棕黑的; 白皙的)肤色。 **2** general character or aspect (of conduct, affairs, etc): (指行为、事情等)一般表征; 一般形势; 外观: *This victory changed the ~ of the war*, made the probable outcome different, gave hope of an early end, etc. 这一场胜仗使使大战形势为之改观 (使可能的结果发生变化, 使之可望早日结束等)。

com·pli·ance /kəmˈplaɪəns; kəmˈplaɪəns/ *n* [U] **1** action of complying: 顺从; 听从; 依从: *in ~ with your wishes*, as you wish(ed) us to do). 顺从你的愿望; 依你所愿; 遵嘱。 **2** tendency to give way to others; unworthy submission. 顺从他人的意向; 屈从。

com·pli·ant /kəmˈplaɪənt; kəmˈplaɪənt/ *adj* ready or disposed to comply. 愿意顺从的; 听从的。

com·pli·cate /ˈkɒmplɪkeɪt; ˈkɑmpləˌket/ *vt* [VP6A] make complex; make (sth) difficult to do or understand: 使复杂; 使(某事物)难做或难懂: *This ~s matters*. 这把事情弄复杂了。 **com·pli·cated** *adj* made up of many parts; difficult to do or understand: 复杂的; 难做的; 难懂的: *a ~d machine*; 复杂的机器; *a ~d business deals*. 复杂的商业交易。

com·pli·ca·tion /ˌkɒmplɪˈkeɪʃn; ˌkɑmpləˈkeʃən/ *n* [C] **1** state of being complex, confused, difficult; sth that adds new difficulties: 复杂的状态; 混乱; 困难; 增加新困难的事物: *Here are further ~s to worry us*. 这里还有更多的复杂的事情困扰我们。 **2** (med) new illness, or new development of an illness. that makes treatment more difficult: (医)(增加治疗困难的)新发病症或病情之新的发展; 并发症: *influenza with ~s*; 流行性感冒带并发症; *if no ~s set in*. 如果不发生并发症的话。

com·plic·ity /kəmˈplɪsəti; kəmˈplɪsəti/ *n* [U] ~ *(in)*, taking part with another person (in crime). (与另一人)共谋; 串通。

com·pli·ment /ˈkɒmplɪmənt; ˈkɑmpləmənt/ *n* [C] **1** expression of admiration, approval, etc, either in words or by action, eg by asking sb for his advice or opinions, or by imitating him. (以言语或行动表示的)恭维之表示; 敬意; 赞扬(例如向某人请教或效法他)。 *pay sb a ~ / pay a ~ to sb (on sth)*: (为某事物)恭维某人: *They paid me a well-deserved ~*. 他们给了我极应得的赞扬。 **2** (*pl*) (formal) greetings: (复)(正式用语)问候; 致意; 道贺: *My ~s to your wife*, Please give her a greeting from me. 请代我向尊夫人致意。 *With the ~s of the season*, phrase used at Christmas and the New Year. 恭贺圣诞, 并贺年禧(圣诞节及新年期间的致意话)。 *With the author's / publisher's ~s*, phrase used when an author / publisher sends a gift of a book newly issued. 作者(出版者)敬赠(作者或出版者赠送新出版之书与他人时的客套)。 □ *vt* /ˈkɒmplɪment; ˈkɑmpləˌment/ [VP6A, 14] ~ *sb (on sth)*, pay a ~: 恭维; 称赞: *I ~ed him on his skill*. 我称赞他的技术。

com·pli·men·tary /ˌkɒmplɪˈmentri; ˌkɑmpləˈmentəri/ *adj* **1** expressing admiration, praise, etc. 恭维的; 表示钦佩、赞美等的。 **2** given free, out of courtesy or kindness: (因礼貌或客气而)免费赠送的: *a ~ ticket / copy of a book, etc*. 赠送的票(一册书等)。

com·plin, com·pline /ˈkɒmplɪn; ˈkɑmplɪn/ *n* (in RC and Anglo-Catholic ritual) last (church) service of the day. (天主教或英国国教高教会仪式)一日中的最后崇拜; 晚祷。

com·ply /kəmˈplaɪ; kəmˈplaɪ/ *vi* [VP2A, 3A] ~ *(with)*, act in accordance (with a request, command, sb's wishes, etc): 依从; 顺从; 听从; 服从(请求、命令、某人的愿望等): *You must ~ with ~* (= obey) *the rules*. 你必须遵守规则。 *He refused to ~*. 他拒绝服从。

com·po·nent /kəmˈpəʊnənt; kəmˈponənt/ *adj* helping to form (a complete thing): 组成的; 构成(全物)的的: ~ *parts*. 组成的各部分; 组成件。 □ *n* ~ part: 成分: *the ~s of a camera lens*. 组成照相机镜头的各部分。

com·port /kəmˈpɔːt; kəmˈport/ *vt*, *vi* (formal) (正式用语) **1** [VP15A] (*usu reflex*) behave; conduct: (通常用反身式)行为; 持(己); 举止: ~ *oneself with dignity*. 举止庄重。 **2** [VP3A] ~ *with*, suit, be in harmony

with: 适合；相称；一致: *His conduct did not ~ with his position.* 他的举止与他的地位不相称。 ~**ment** n.

com·pose /kəm'pəʊz; kəm'poz/ vt, vi 1 [VP6A] (of elements) make up, form: (指要素)组成；构成: *the parts that ~ the whole;* 组成全体的各部分; (usu in the passive) *be ~d of,* be made up of: (通常用被动语态) 由…组成: *Water (H₂O) is ~d of hydrogen and oxygen.* 水由氢与氧化合而成。 *Our party was ~d of teachers, pupils and their parents.* 我们这一伙由教员、学生及学生的父母组成。 2 [VP6A, 2A] put together (words, ideas, musical notes, etc) in literary, musical, etc, form: 著作；作(曲等): ~ *a poem/a song/an opera/ a speech.* 作诗(歌、歌剧、演讲稿)。 *He teaches music and also ~s,* writes music. 他教音乐，并且作曲。 3 [VP6A] (printing) set up (type) to form words, paragraphs, pages, etc. (印刷) 排 (活字) 成词、段、页等。 ⇨ **compositor.** 4 [VP6A, 16A] get under control; calm: 控制；使镇定；使安静: ~ *one's thoughts/passions.* 镇定思绪(情绪)。 *She ~d herself to answer the letter.* 她镇静下来回信。 *Try to ~ your features,* make yourself look calm. 尽量保持镇静的神色。 **com·posed** adj calm; with feelings under control. 镇静的；神情泰然的。 **com·pos·ed·ly** /kəm'pəʊzɪdlɪ; kəm'pozɪdlɪ/ adv in a ~d manner. 镇静地；泰然地。

com·poser /kəm'pəʊzə(r); kəm'pozɚ/ n (esp) person who composes music. (尤指)作曲家。

com·pos·ite /'kɒmpəzɪt; kəm'pɑzɪt/ adj made up of different parts or materials: 由各种不同的部分或材料组成的；集成的；拼成的；综合的: *a ~ illustration,* made by putting together two or more drawings, etc. 综合图说(集合若干图片等而成的说明)。

com·po·si·tion /ˌkɒmpə'zɪʃn; ˌkɑmpə'zɪʃən/ n 1 [U] act or art of composing, eg a piece of writing or music, type for printing, objects that will be included in a painting: 著作；作曲；排字；构图: *He played a piano sonata of his own ~,* that he himself had composed. 他弹奏了一首自作的钢琴奏鸣曲。 2 [C] that which is composed, eg a poem, a book, a piece of music, an arrangement of objects to be painted or photographed; (esp) exercise in writing by one who is learning a language. 著作物；制作物(如诗、书、乐曲、绘画或照相的构图)；(尤指学习语文者为练习写作所作的)作文。 3 [U] the parts of which sth is made up: (组成某物的)成分: *Scientists study the ~ of the soil.* 科学家研究土壤的成分。 *He has a touch of madness in his ~,* There is an element of madness in him. 他生来就有点疯疯癫癫。 4 [C] substance composed of more than one material, esp an artificial substance: (由多种材料尤指人造物质)合成之物；混合物；人造物: ~ *floors.* 合成地板。

com·po·si·tor /kəm'pɒzɪtə(r); kəm'pɑzɪtɚ/ n skilled person who composes type for printing. 排字工人。

compos mentis /ˌkɒmpəs 'mentɪs; ˌkampəs'mentɪs/ adj (Lat) (colloq) sane: (拉丁)(口)心理健全的；神智清楚的: *He's not quite ~,* is a little mad. 他的精神不十分健全(有点疯狂)。

com·post /'kɒmpɒst; 'kampost/ n [U] prepared mixture, esp of rotted organic matter, manure, etc, for use in horticulture. (由腐烂的有机物、粪便等混成用于园艺的)混合肥料；堆肥。 □ vt [VP6A] make into ~; treat with ~. 制成堆肥；施以堆肥。

com·po·sure /kəm'pəʊʒə(r); kəm'poʒɚ/ n [U] condition of being composed in mind; calmness (of mind or behaviour): 心神镇静；态度沉着；泰然自若: *behave with great ~.* 态度极为镇定。

com·pote /'kɒmpɒt; 'kampot/ n [C, U] (dish of) fruit cooked with sugar and water. 一道蜜钱水果。

com·pound¹ /'kɒmpaʊnd; 'kampaund/ n, adj 1 (sth) made up of two or more combined parts: 复合的；结合的；合成的；复合物；化合物: *Common salt is a ~ of sodium and chlorine.* 食盐是钠和氯的化合物。 2 (gram) item composed of two or more parts, (written as one or two words, or joined by a hyphen), themselves usu words, (语法)复合词(由两个或更多的部分合成，这些部分本身通常都是词，复合词写作一字或二字，或由一连字符相连)，eg (of) 'bus conductor. ,~ 'sentence, one containing two or more co-ordinate clauses (linked by *and, but,* etc). 并列句(含两个或更多对等从句的句子，各从句间用 and, but 等连接)。 3 ,~ 'interest, interest on capital and on accumulated interest. 复利(本金利息加累积利息的利息)。 ,~ 'fracture, breaking of a bone complicated by an open wound in the skin. 哆开骨折；穿破骨折；复杂骨折。

com·pound² /'kɒmpaʊnd; 'kampaʊnd/ vt, vi 1 [VP6A] mix together (to make sth new or different): 混合(以制新物或不同之物)；掺合；调合: ~ *a medicine;* 配药; *a cake ~ed of the best ingredients.* 用各种最好的材料调制成的糕饼。 2 [VP6A, 2A, 3A] ~ *(with sb) (for sth),* settle (a quarrel, a debt) by mutual concession; come to terms: (与人互作让步而)和解；解决(争端、债务)；达成协议；谈妥: *He ~ed with his creditors for a remission of what he owed.* 他与债权人谈妥豁免余其债务。 3 [VP6A] add to, increase (an offence or injury) by causing another: (由于引起另一罪行或伤害而)加重(罪行或伤害): *That simply ~s the offence.* 那只会加重罪过。

com·pound³ /'kɒmpaʊnd; 'kampaʊnd/ n enclosed area with buildings, etc, eg a number of houses, a commercial or trading centre. 围地(场内有建筑物，如房屋等)；商业或贸易中心。

com·pre·hend /ˌkɒmprɪ'hend; ˌkamprɪ'hend/ vt [VP6A] 1 understand fully. 充分了解；领悟。 2 include. 包括；包含。

com·pre·hen·sible /ˌkɒmprɪ'hensəbl; ˌkamprɪ'hen·səbl/ adj that can be understood fully: 可充分了解的: *a book that is ~ only to specialists.* 只有专家才可以了解的一本书。 **com·pre·hen·si·bil·ity** /ˌkɒmprɪˌhen·sə'bɪlətɪ; ˌkamprɪ,hensə'bɪlətɪ/ n.

com·pre·hen·sion /ˌkɒmprɪ'henʃn; ˌkamprɪ'hen·ʃən/ n 1 [U, C] mind's act or power of understanding: 理解；领会；理解力: *The problem is above/beyond my ~.* 这问题超出我的理解力以外。 2 exercise aimed at improving or testing one's understanding of a language (written or spoken). (对某种语言的文字或口语的)理解力练习；理解力测验；阅读测验；听力测验。 3 power of including: 包含力；含蓄力: *a term of wide ~,* eg a word that includes many meanings, uses, etc. 含义广泛的名词(例如一含义和用法甚多的词)。

com·pre·hen·sive /ˌkɒmprɪ'hensɪv; ˌkamprɪ'hen·sɪv/ adj that comprehends (2) much: 包罗广泛的；综合性的: *a ~ description/review of the term's work, etc;* 综合性的描述(全学期功课的温习等); *a man with a ~ mind/grasp of ideas.* 富有理解力(对于各种观念有广泛之了解力)的人。 '~ (school), large school that combines all types of secondary education, ie academic and technical. 综合中学(一种包含学术及技能教育的大型中学)。 ~·ly adv ~·ness n

com·press¹ /kəm'pres; kəm'prɛs/ vt [VP6A, 14] 1 press together; get into a small(er) space: 紧压；压缩(以便置于较小之空间): ~ed air, 压缩空气; ~ cotton into bales. 将棉花压紧打包。 2 put (ideas, etc) into fewer words; condense. 扼要叙述；摘要叙述(要点等)。

com·press² /'kɒmpres; 'kamprɛs/ n pad or cloth pressed on to a part of the body (to stop bleeding, reduce fever, etc): 贴在身上某部分(以止血、退热等)之压布; 敷布: *a cold/hot ~.* 冷(热)敷布。

com·pres·sion /kəm'preʃn; kəm'prɛʃən/ n [U] compressing; being compressed: 压紧；压缩: ~ *of ideas.* 言简意赅。

com·prise /kəm'praɪz; kəm'praɪz/ vt [VP6A] be composed of; have as parts or members: 由…组成；包括；包含: *The committee is ~ men of widely different views.* 委员会中包括意见极不相同的分子。 *The force ~d two battalions and a battery.* 该部队包含两个步兵营及一个炮兵连。

com·pro·mise /ˈkɒmprəmaɪz; ˈkɑmprə‚maɪz/ n [U] settlement of a dispute by which each side gives up sth it has asked for and neither side gets all it has asked for; [C] instance of this; settlement reached in this way: 由于彼此让步而解决争端; 和解; 妥协; 折衷(每一方面放弃一部分要求, 两方面都不能得到全部所要求的); 折衷处理; 折衷办法: *The strike was not ended until they resorted to ~.* 罢工到双方互相让步才终止。*A ~ agreement was at last arrived at.* 一个折衷的协议终于达成。*Can we effect a ~?* 我们能想出一个折衷办法吗? □ *vt, vi* 1 [VP6A, 2A] settle a dispute, etc, by making a ~: 以折衷办法解决争端等: *if they agree to ~.* 如果他们同意折衷的话。2 bring (sb, sth, oneself) under suspicion by unwise behaviour, etc: 由于不智的行为等致使(某人、某事物、自己)受牵连; 损害: *You will ~ yourself/your reputation if you spend all your time gambling.* 如果你终日赌博, 你就会损害自己(你的名声)。3 imperil the safety of (by folly or rashness, etc): (由于愚昧或鲁莽等而)危及…的安全: *The position of the army was ~d by the general's poor judgement.* 这支军队的阵地由于将军不智的判断而受危害。

comp·trol·ler /kənˈtrəʊlə(r); kənˈtrolə/ n (in some titles) controller: (在某些职衔中)主任; 长; 主计长; 会计主任; 审计长: ~ *of accounts.* 审计长; 审计官。

com·pul·sion /kəmˈpʌlʃn; kəmˈpʌlʃən/ n [U] compelling or being compelled. 强迫; 被迫, *under ~,* because one must: 被迫; 不得已: *A defeated country usually signs a treaty of peace under ~.* 战败国通常被迫签订和约。

com·pul·sive /kəmˈpʌlsɪv; kəmˈpʌlsɪv/ adj having a tendency or the power to compel; caused by an obsession: 强迫性的; 强制的; 由于成见或顽念所引起的: *a ~ eater /TV viewer,* one who feels compelled to eat/watch TV; 强迫性食者(看电视者)(被萦绕心中的固执偏见所驱使而去吃东西或看电视者); *a ~ liar,* one who lies repeatedly. 一再说谎者。~·**ly** *adv*

com·pul·sory /kəmˈpʌlsərɪ; kəmˈpʌlsərɪ/ adj that must be done; required: 必须做的; 必修的; 规定的; 强迫的; *Is military service ~ in your country?* 在贵国, 服兵役是义务的吗? *Is English a ~ subject?* 英语是必修科吗? **com·pul·sor·ily** /kəmˈpʌlsərəlɪ; kəmˈpʌlsərəlɪ/ adv

com·punc·tion /kəmˈpʌŋkʃn; kəmˈpʌŋkʃən/ n [U] uneasiness of conscience; feeling of regret for one's action: 良心的不安(对于自己行为的)懊悔; 后悔; 抱歉: *She kept me waiting without the slightest ~.* 她使我久候而丝毫没有歉意。

com·pu·ta·tion /‚kɒmpjuˈteɪʃn; ‚kɑmpjəˈteʃən/ n [U] computing; [C] result of computing; calculation: 计算; 计算的结果; 估计: *It will cost £5000 at the lowest ~.* 根据最低的估计, 它将值五千英镑。*He has wealth beyond ~.* 他的财富无法估计。*Addition and division are forms of ~.* 加法和除法都是计算的方法。

com·pute /kəmˈpjuːt; kəmˈpjut/ vt, vi [VP6A, 14, 2A] ~ (at), reckon; calculate: 计算; 估计: *He ~d his losses at £50.* 他估计他的损失在五十英镑。*What is the ~d horse-power of the engine?* 这引擎的估计马力是多少?

com·puter /kəmˈpjuːtə(r); kəmˈpjutə/ n electronic device which stores information on eg magnetic tape, analyses it and produces information as required from the data on the tapes. 电子计算机; 电脑(储存资料于磁带上等, 将之加以分析, 并能应需要提供所存有之资料的电子装置)。~·**ize** *vt* [VP6A] store (information) with or in a ~ or system of ~s; supply with a ~ or ~s. 用电子计算机储存(资料); 将(资料)存入电脑中; 供以计算机; 以电脑配备。

com·rade /ˈkɒmreɪd US: -ræd; ˈkɑmræd/ n 1 trusted companion; loyal friend: 同志; 可靠的友伴; 忠实的朋友: ~*s in arms,* fellow soldiers; 战友; ~*s in exile,* those who are exiled together. 同被放逐者。2 fellow member of a trade union, a (left-wing) political party, etc. 工会的同人, (左翼政党等)同志。~·**ly** /ˈkɒmreɪdlɪ;

ˈkɑmrædlɪ/ adv ~·**ship** /ˈkɒmreɪdʃɪp; ˈkɑmræd‚ʃɪp/ n

con¹ /kɒn; kɑn/ adv pro and con, for and against: 正反两面地: *argue pro and con for hours.* 正反两面辩论数小时。□ *the pros and cons,* the arguments for and against. 辩论的正反两面理由。

con² /kɒn; kɑn/ (sl) short for confidence, in attrib uses: (俚)(confidence 之略)(用作定语): *a con man;* 骗子; the *con game.* 骗术。⇨ **confidence**(3). □ *vt* (-nn-) [VP 6A, 14] con *sb (into doing sth),* (colloq) swindle him to do sth in this way. (口)取得某人信赖后再欺骗; 骗某人(作某事)。

con·cat·ena·tion /kɒn‚kætɪˈneɪʃn; ‚kɑnkætnˈeʃən/ n [U] linking together; [C] series of things or events linked together. 连锁; 一连串的东西或事件。

con·cave /ˈkɒnkeɪv; kɑnˈkev/ adj (of an outline or surface) curved inwards like the inner surface of a sphere or ball. (指轮廓或表面)凹的 (如圆球之内面)。⇨ the illus at convex. 参看 convex 之插图。**con·cav·ity** /kɒnˈkævətɪ; kɑnˈkævətɪ/ n [U] ~ condition; [C] (pl -ties) ~ surface. 凹性; 凹状; 凹面。

con·ceal /kənˈsiːl; kənˈsil/ vt [VP6A, 14] ~ (from), hide; keep secret: 隐藏; 隐匿; 隐瞒: ~ *sth from sb.* 向某人隐瞒某事物。*He tried to ~ the fact that....* 他企图隐瞒…之事实。*C~ed turning,* (as a road sign) warning that a turning into a road is hidden from view, eg by bushes or trees. 荫蔽弯路 (公路标志, 警告前面弯路为树林等所遮蔽)。~·**ment** n [U] act of ~ing; state of being ~ed: 隐藏; 隐匿; 躲藏; 隐藏: *to stay in ~ment until the danger has passed.* 躲藏起来直到危险过去。

con·cede /kənˈsiːd; kənˈsid/ vt [VP6A, 9, 13A, 12A] admit; grant; allow: 承认; 让与; 容许: ~ *a point in an argument.* 在辩论中承认某点正确。*He ~d ten points to his opponent / ~d him ten points,* ie in a game. (在比赛中)他让他的对手十分。*They have ~d us the right to cross their land.* 他们已容许我们经过他们的土地。*You must ~ that I have tried hard.* 你必须承认我已尽力为之。*We cannot ~ any of our territory,* allow another country to have it. 我们不能放弃一寸国土。

con·ceit /kənˈsiːt; kənˈsit/ n 1 [U] over-high opinion of, too much pride in, oneself or one's powers, abilities, etc: 对于自己或自己的能力等之过高的评价; 自大; 自负; 自豪: *He's full of ~.* 他极其自负。*in one's own ~,* (old use) in one's own judgement. (旧用法)自认为。*out of ~ with,* (old use) no longer pleased with. (旧用法)对…不再欢喜。2 [C] humorous or witty thought or expression. 诙谐或机智的思想或词句。~·**ed** adj full of ~. 极其自负的。~·**ed·ly** /-ɪdlɪ; -ɪdlɪ/ adv

con·ceive /kənˈsiːv; kənˈsiv/ vt, vi 1 [VP6A, 10, 3 A, 9, 14] ~ (of), form (an idea, plan, etc) in the mind: 想出 (一个主意、计划等); 构思; 想象: *Who first ~d the idea of filling bags with gas to make balloons?* 谁最先想到充气体于袋中以制成气球的? *I can't ~ why you allowed / can't ~ of your allowing the child to travel alone.* 我想不通你为什么让那孩子独自旅行。*I ~d that there must be some difficulties.* 我料想到一定有些困难。*Why have you ~d such a dislike for me?* 你为什么对我感到这样厌恶? 2 [VP2A, 6 A] (of a woman) become pregnant: (指女人)受孕; 怀孕: ~ *a child.* 怀孕。**con·ceiv·able** adj that can be ~d or believed: 可想象的; 可相信的: *It is hardly conceivable (that) to me) that....* (我)简直难以想象…。**con·ceiv·ably** /-əblɪ; -əblɪ/ adv

con·cen·trate /ˈkɒnsntreɪt; ˈkɑnsn‚tret/ vt, vi 1 [VP6A, 14, 2A] bring or come together at one point: 集中 (于一点); 集合: *to ~ soldiers in a town.* 将军队集中于城内。*The troops were ordered to scatter and then ~ twenty miles to the south.* 这军队奉命解散, 然后在南方二十英里处集合。2 [VP14, 3A, 2A] ~ (on /upon), focus one's attention on: 集中注意力于; 专心于; 注意: *You should ~ (your attention) on your work.* 你应该专心(集中你的注意力)于你的工作。*You'll solve the problem if you ~ upon it,* give all your attention to it. 如果你全神贯注, 你会解决这问题。*I can't ~!* 我的注意力无法集

中! **3** [VP6A] increase the strength of (a solution) by reducing its volume (eg by boiling it). (用蒸发方法)浓缩(溶液). □ *n* product made by concentrating(3). 浓缩物; 浓缩液. **con·cen·trated** *adj* 1 intense; 加强的: ~*d hate*; 强烈的仇恨; ~*d fire*, the firing of guns all aimed at one point. 集中一点而发射的炮火; 集中射击. **2** increased in strength or value by evaporation of liquid: 浓缩 (借蒸发液体而增强其力量或价值) 的: a ~*d solution*; 浓缩溶液; ~*d food*. 浓缩食物.

con·cen·tra·tion /ˌkɒnsn'treɪʃn; ˌkɑnsṇ'treʃən/ *n* **1** [C] that which is concentrated: 集中物; 集结物: ~*s of enemy troops*. 敌军在数处之集结. **2** [U] concentrating or being concentrated on: 集合; 集中: *a book that requires great* ~; 需要全神贯注才能读得懂的书; *a child with little power of* ~. 注意力不能集中的小孩. '~ **camp**, place where civilian political prisoners or internees are brought together and confined. 集中营(集中监禁政治犯或被拘留者的地方).

con·cen·tric /kən'sentrɪk; kən'sɛntrɪk/ *adj* ~ (**with**), (of circles) having a common centre. (指数个圆)同中心的; (与另一圆)同心的.

concentric circles

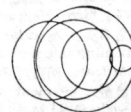
circles not concentric

con·cept /'kɒnsept; 'kɑnsɛpt/ *n* [C] idea underlying a class of things; general notion. 一类事物的基本观念; 概念.

con·cep·tion /kən'sepʃn; kən'sɛpʃən/ *n* **1** [U] conceiving of an idea or plan; [C] idea or plan that takes shape in the mind: 构思; 构想; 想象; 想出的意念或计划: *A good novelist needs great powers of* ~. 一个好的小说家需要极大的构想力. *I have no* ~ *of what you mean*. 我想不出你的意思是什么. *An actor must have a clear* ~ *of the part he is to play*. 一个演员对他所要演的角色, 必须要有一个清楚的了解. **2** [U, C] conceiving(2); becoming pregnant. 怀孕; 妊娠. '~ **control**, more precise, but less common, term for *birth-control*. 节制怀孕 (为 birth-control 之较精确名词, 但较不普遍).

con·cern[1] /kən'sɜːn; kən'sɜːn/ *vt* **1** [VP6A] have relation to; affect; be of importance to: 与…有关系; 影响; 对…有重要性: *Does this* ~ *me*? 这个与我有关系吗? *Don't trouble about things that don't* ~ *you*. 不要操心与你无关的事. *He is said to have been* ~*ed in the crime*, to have had some connection with it. 据说他与此犯罪案有关连. *So/As far as I'm* ~*ed*..., so far as the matter is important to me, or affects me.... 就(此事)与我个人(的关系)而言…. *Where the children are* ~*ed*..., in matters where it is necessary to think of them.... 在与孩子们有关的事情方面…. *as* ~*s*, regarding. 关于. **2** [VP14] ~ *oneself with/in/about*, be busy with, interest oneself in. 忙于; 从事; 关心; 关切. **3** [VP6A] (esp in the passive 尤用于被动语态 *be* ~*ed about/for sb/sth*) worry; trouble; bother: 使担忧; 使烦恼; 使操心: *Don't let my illness* ~ *you*. 不要为我的病担忧. *Please don't be* ~*ed about her safety*. 请不要为她的安全担忧. *We are all* ~*ed for/about her safety*. 我们大家都担心着她的安全. ~·**ing** *prep* about. 关于.

con·cern[2] /kən'sɜːn; kən'sɜːn/ *n* **1** [C] relation or connection; sth in which one is interested or which is important to one: 关系; 关连; 关心之事; (对某人)关系重大之事: *It's no* ~ *of mine*, I have nothing to do with it. 这事与我无关. *Mind your own* ~*s* (*business is more usu*), *Don't interfere in other people's affairs*. 管你自己的事 (不要管别人的事情); (business 较常用). *What* ~ *is it of yours*, Why do you take an interest in it? 此事与你何干? (你为何要介入)? **2** [C] business or undertaking: 营

业; 事务; 业务: *The shop has now become a paying* ~, is making profits. 这商店现在已可赚钱了. *a going* ~, one that is active and in operation, not merely planned. 已开始营业(活动等)(非仅计划中之事而已). **3** [C] share: 股份: *He has a* ~ *in the business*, is a part-owner. 他在这企业中有一股份(为股东之一). **4** [U] anxiety: 忧虑; 担心: *filled with* ~; 满怀忧虑; *look at sb in* ~. 担心地看着某人. *There is some cause for* ~ *but no need for alarm*. 是有点令人忧虑, 但不必惊慌. ~·**ed** /-'sɜːnd; -'sɜːnd/ *adj* anxious: 焦虑的; 担心的: *with a* ~*ed look*. 焦虑的神情. ~·**edly** /-'sɜːnɪdlɪ; -'sɜːnɪdlɪ/ *adv*

con·cert[1] /'kɒnsət; 'kɑnsət/ *n* **1** [C] musical entertainment, esp one given in a public hall by players or singers. (在公共厅堂中由演奏者或歌唱者所举行的)音乐会. ~ **grand**, grand piano of the largest size, for ~s, (音乐会用的)大型平台钢琴. '~-**hall**, hall for ~s. 音乐会堂; 音乐厅. ⇨ **music-hall**. *at* ,~ '**pitch**, (fig) in a state of full efficiency or readiness. (喻)在效率极高或准备极佳的状态. ⇨ *keyed up* at **key[2]**. **2** [U] *in* ~, combination of voices or sounds: 齐声: *voices raised in* ~. 一起提高的声音. **3** [U] agreement; harmony. 一致; 协调. *in* ~ (*with*), together (with): (与…)一起: *working in* ~ *with his colleagues*. 与其同事协力工作.

con·cert[2] /kən'sɜːt; kən'sɜːt/ *vt* arrange with others. 与他人共同安排. Chiefly in 主用于 ~**ed** *adj* planned, performed, designed (by two or more) together: (由二人或更多的人)共同计划、表演、设计的; 一致的: *to take* ~*ed action*; 采取一致行动; *to make a* ~*ed attack*. 联合攻击.

con·cer·tina /ˌkɒnsə'tiːnə; ˌkɑnsə'tinə/ *n* musical wind instrument consisting of a pair of bellows, held in the hands and played by pressing keys at each end. 六角形手风琴(由一对风箱构成, 捧于手中, 按两端之键而奏的一种手风琴).

a concertina

con·certo /kən'tʃeətəʊ; kən'tʃɛrto/ *n* (*pl* ~s) musical composition for one or more solo instruments supported by an orchestra: 协奏曲(供一件或数件乐器独奏而由管弦乐队配合之乐曲): *a* '*piano* ~; 钢琴协奏曲; *a* ~ *for two violins*. 双小提琴协奏曲.

con·ces·sion /kən'seʃn; kən'sɛʃən/ *n* **1** [U] conceding; [C] that which is conceded, esp after discussion, a difference of opinion, an argument, etc: 让步; 妥协; (尤指)经过讨论、异议、辩论等之后所作的让步: *As a* ~ *to the public outcry, the Government reduced the tax on petrol*. 政府减低汽油税作为对民众反对的让步. **2** [C] (esp) right given by owner(s) of land, or by a Government, to do sth (eg take minerals from land): (尤指)所有者或政府许可的特权(如土地中的矿物开采权); 转让; 租让: *oil/mining* ~*s*. 石油开采权(采矿权). **con·ces·sive** /kən'sesɪv; kən'sɛsɪv/ *adj* (gram) expressing ~: (语法)让步的: *a concessive clause*, eg introduced by *as* or *although*, implying a contrast between circumstances, etc. 让步从句 (以 as 或 although 等所引的以句, 表示前后的情况等之差异). ~·**aire** /kənˌseʃə'neə(r); kənˌsɛʃən'ɛr/ *n* holder of a ~(2). 特许权所有人.

conch /kɒntʃ; kɑŋk/ *n* shellfish with a large spiral shell. 海螺(有大螺旋贝壳). ⇨ the illus at **mollusc**. 参看 **mollusc** 之插图. **con·chol·ogy** /kɒŋ'kɒlədʒɪ;

kɒn'kɒlədʒɪ / n [U] study of shells and shellfish. 贝类学.

con·ci·erge /ˌkɒnsɪ'eəʒ US: ˌkɒnsɪ'eərʒ; ˌkɑnsɪ'ɛrʒ/ n (F) (in France, etc) door-keeper, porter (of a block of flats, etc). (法) (法国等地之公寓等的)看门人.

con·cili·ate /kən'sɪlɪeɪt; kən'sɪlɪˌet/ vt [VP6A] win the support, goodwill or friendly feelings of; calm the anger of; soothe. 赢得…的支持、善意或友情; 与…和解; 平息…的怒气; 安慰; 抚慰. con·cili·atory /kən'sɪlɪətərɪ US: -tɔːrɪ; kən'sɪlɪəˌtɔrɪ/ adj intending to or likely to ~: 有助于或可能促进和解的: a conciliatory act / gesture / spirit. 和解的行动(姿态, 精神).

con·cili·ation /kənˌsɪlɪ'eɪʃn; kənˌsɪlɪ'eʃən/ n [U] conciliating or being conciliated: 和解; 安慰; 调解: The dispute in the engineering industry is being dealt with by a ~ board, a group of persons who arbitrate, etc. 工程业的纠纷现由一调解委员会处理中.

con·cise /kən'saɪs; kən'saɪs/ adj (of a person's speech or style of writing, etc) brief; giving much information in few words. (指某人的语言或文体等) 简洁的; 简明的; 用少数词传达多量意思的. ~·ly adv ~·ness n

con·clave /'kɒnkleɪv; 'kɑnklev/ n [C] private or secret meeting (eg of cardinals to elect a Pope). 秘密会议(如红衣主教所开选举教皇者). sit in ~, hold a secret meeting. 举行秘密会议.

con·clude /kən'kluːd; kən'klud/ vt, vi 1 [VP6A, 14, 2A, 3A] come or bring to an end; 结束: to ~ a speech / a lecture. 结束演说(学术演讲). 他结束时说… The meeting ~d at 8 o'clock. 会议在八点钟结束. The concert ~d with the National Anthem. 音乐会最后演奏国歌而结束. 2 [VP6A, 14] ~ sth (with sb), arrange; bring about: 安排; 订立; 使成立: Wales ~ed a treaty with Scotland. 威尔斯与苏格兰订立条约. 3 [VP9] arrive at a belief or opinion: 作结论: The jury ~d, from the evidence, that the accused man was not guilty. 陪审团依据证据作出结论, 认定被告无罪. 4 [VP7A] (esp US) decide, resolve (after discussion): (尤用于美国)(经讨论后)决定; 决心: We ~d not to go. 我们(经讨论后)决定不去.

con·clusion /kən'kluːʒn; kən'kluʒən/ n [C] 1 end: 结束; 终结: at the ~ of his speech; 在他演说结束时; bring a matter to a speedy ~. 使事情迅速结束. in ~, lastly. 最后地. 2 arranging; deciding; settling (of): 安排; 订立; 决定; 解决(与 of 连用): the ~ of a peace treaty. 和约的订立. 3 belief or opinion which is the result of reasoning: 结论; 论语; 由推理所得到的结论或意见: come to / reach the ~ that…; 得到以下的结论…; to draw a ~ (from evidence, etc). (由证据等)获得结论. a foregone ~, something settled or decided in advance, not to be doubted. 早已确定的结论; 必然的结论; 毫无疑问的事. 4 try ~s with, have a trial of skill with. 与…较量高低; 与…一决胜负.

con·clus·ive /kən'kluːsɪv; kən'klusɪv/ adj (of facts, evidence, etc) convincing; ending doubt: (指事实、证据等)令人确信的; 确定的; 决定性的; 释除疑问的: ~ evidence / proof of his guilt. 关于他的罪行的决定性的证据. ~·ly adv

con·coct /kən'kɒkt; kɑn'kɑkt/ vt [VP6A] 1 prepare by mixing together: 混合调制; 配合: to ~ a new kind of soup. 调制一种新汤. 2 invent (a story, an excuse, a plot for a novel, etc). 虚构(故事、口实、小说情节等). con·coc·tion /kən'kɒkʃn; kɑn'kɑkʃən/ n [U] ~ing; [C] sth that is ~ed. 配合; 调制; 虚构; 调配之物; 杜撰或捏造之事.

con·comi·tant /kən'kɒmɪtənt; kɑn'kɑmətənt/ adj (formal) accompanying: (正式用语)伴随的; 随…而至的: ~ circumstances. 伴随情况. n (usu pl) accompanying thing: (通常用复数)伴随物: the infirmities that are the ~s of old age. 随老年而至的虚弱.

con·cord /'kɒŋkɔːd; 'kɑŋkɔd/ n 1 [U] agreement or harmony (between persons or things): (人与人或事物与事物之间的)一致; 协调; 和谐; 和睦: live in ~ (with…);

(与…)和睦相处; [C] instance of this. 和睦之实例. 2 (gram) [U] agreement between words in number, etc, eg between a verb and its subject in the present tense. (语法) (词与词之间单复数等的)一致(例如现在时中动词与主语的一致).

con·cord·ance /kən'kɔːdəns; kən'kɔrdns/ n 1 [U] agreement. 一致; 协调; 和谐. 2 [C] arrangement in ABC order of the important words used by an author or in a book: 著作家或书籍中所用之重要语词索引(按字母顺序排列): a 'Bible ~; 圣经语词索引; a 'Shakespeare ~. 莎士比亚语词索引.

con·cord·ant /kən'kɔːdənt; kən'kɔrdnt/ adj ~ (with), agreeing, harmonious. (与…)一致的; 协调的; 和谐的.

con·cordat /kən'kɔːdæt; kɑn'kɔrdæt/ n agreement, eg between a State and the Church, for settlement of ecclesiastical affairs. 协定; 协约(例如教会与政府间为解决宗教事务所订者).

con·course /'kɒnkɔːs; 'kɑnkɔrs/ n 1 coming or moving together of things, persons, etc: (事物、人等的)汇聚; 聚集; 会合: an unforeseen ~ of circumstances. 不能预见的各种情况的凑合. 2 place (usu not enclosed) where crowds come together; (esp US) large hall of a railway station. 群众聚集的场所(通常为空地); (尤美)火车站的大厅.

con·crete¹ /'kɒnkriːt; 'kɑnkrit/ adj 1 of material things; existing in material form; that can be touched, felt, etc: 实物的; 具体存在的; 有形的; 可触摸、感觉等的: A lamp is a ~ but its brightness is abstract. 灯是具体的, 但其光亮是抽象的. ~ music, composed of re-arranged recorded natural sounds. 实体音乐(将录好之自然音响重新组合而成). ~ noun, name of a thing, not of a quality. 具体名词(非指性质之名词). 2 definite; positive; 明确的; 确定的; 无问题的; 无可非议的: ~ proposals / evidence / proof. 确切的建议(证据, 证明). □ n 1 [U] building material made by mixing cement with sand, gravel, etc: 混凝土; 三合土 (水泥与沙、碎石等混合成的建筑材料): roads surfaced with ~; 混凝土路面的道路; a ~ wall; 混凝土墙; a '~ mixer (usu a revolving drum). 混凝土搅拌器 (通常为旋转的圆筒形容器). □ vt [VP6A] cover with ~; 铺以混凝土: ~ a road. 以混凝土铺路. ~·ly adv

con·crete² /'kɒnkriːt; kɑn'krit/ vi [VP2A] form into a mass; solidify. 固结; 凝固; 凝结. con·cretion /kən'kriːʃn; kɑn'kriʃən/ n [U] process of forming into a mass; [C] mass formed in this way. 凝固; 凝结物.

con·cu·bine /'kɒŋkjubaɪn; 'kɑŋkjʊˌbaɪn/ n 1 (old use) woman who lives with a man as if she were his wife, without being lawfully married to him. (旧用法)姘妇(与男人同居, 过夫妇生活, 却未正式结婚之女人). 2 (in some countries, where polygamy is legal) lesser wife. (在某些容许一夫多妻的国家)妾; 小老婆; 姨太太.

con·cu·pis·cence /kɒn'kjuːpɪsns; kɑn'kjupəsns/ n [U] (formal) sexual desire; lust. (正式用语)性欲; 色欲.

con·cur /kən'kɜː(r); kən'kɝ/ vi (rr-) 1 [VP2A, 3A] ~ (with sb) (in sth), agree in opinion: (与某人)(在某事上)意见一致; 同意: I ~ with the speaker in condemning what has been done. 我同意发言者对所做之事加以谴责. 2 [VP4A] (of circumstances, etc) happen together: (指周围的情况等)同时发生: Everything ~red to produce a successful result. 一切情况凑合起来产生一个圆满的结果. ~·rence /kən'kʌrəns; kən'kɝəns/ n [U, C] agreement; coming together: 同意; 一致; 协力; 齐来; 俱发: a ~rence of ideas; 意见一致; ~rence in helping to find homes for refugees. 协力帮忙寻求安置难民的处所.

con·cur·rent /kən'kʌrənt; kən'kɝənt/ adj concurring; existing together; co-operating. 同意的; 一致的; 同在的; 合作的; 协力的. ~·ly adv

con·cuss /kən'kʌs; kən'kʌs/ vt [VP6A] injure (the

brain) by concussion. 使(脑)受震荡而伤害。

con·cus·sion /kənˈkʌʃn; kənˈkʌʃən/ n [C, U] (an) injury (to the brain); (a) violent shaking or shock (as caused by a blow, knock or fall). (对脑部的)伤害; 脑震荡; (由打击或捧跌所造成的)剧烈震荡。

con·demn /kənˈdem; kənˈdɛm/ vt 1 [VP6A, 14, 16 B] ～ (for), say that sb is, or has done, wrong or that sth is wrong, faulty or unfit for use: 责备; 责难; 谴责; 指摘; 指责; 不当: We all ～ cruelty to children. 我们大家一致谴责虐待儿童。Everyone ～ed his foolish behaviour. 每个人都责备他的愚昧行为。The newspapers ～ed the Prime Minister for.... 各报纸因为...而责难首相。The meat was ～ed as unfit for human consumption. 此肉被指为不宜于人类食用。This old bridge is unsafe; it should be ～ed. 这旧桥不安全, 应予宣告不适用。2 [VP6A, 14] ～ sb (to), (legal) give judgement against: (法律)判罪; 处刑: ～ a murderer to life imprisonment. 判凶手无期徒刑。～ed cell, cell where a person ～ed to death is kept, 幽禁死刑犯之小室。3 [VP6A, 14, 17] ～ sb (to sth/to do sth), doom, send, appoint to sth unwelcome or painful): 注定, 差遣, 派遣 (做或面对不愉快的或痛苦的事): an unhappy housewife, ～ed to spend hours at the kitchen sink. 注定要花很多时间做乏味家务的不快乐的主妇。He got well again, although the doctors had ～ed him, said that he would not recover. 虽然医生们曾经宣布他的病已绝望, 可又康复了, 虽然医生们曾经宣布他的病已绝望。4 [VP6A] declare (smuggled goods, property, etc) to be forfeited: 宣告没收; 充公 (走私的货物、财产等): Merchant ships captured in war were often ～ed, taken from the owners without compensation. 在战时所截获的商船常被没收。5 [VP6A] show conviction of guilt: 显示有罪: His looks ～ed him. 他的神情显示他有罪。**con·dem·na·tion** /ˌkɒndemˈneɪʃn; ˌkɑndɛmˈneʃən/ n [U] ～ing or being ～ed. 责难谴责; 判罪; 注定; 没收。

con·den·sa·tion /ˌkɒndenˈseɪʃn; ˌkɑndɛnˈseʃən/ n [U] condensing or being condensed: 浓缩; 凝结; 冷凝: The ～ of milk, by taking out most of the water; 牛乳之浓缩 (去除其中大部分水分); the ～ of steam to water, 蒸气之凝结为水; [C, U] (mass of) drops of liquid sormed when vapour condenses: (由水蒸气凝结成的)水滴; 凝块: A cloud is a ～ of vapour. 云就是水蒸气凝结成的。

con·dense /kənˈdens; kənˈdɛns/ vt, vi 1 [VP6A, 14, 2A, 3A] (of a liquid) (cause to) increase in density or strength, to become thicker: (指液体)(使)浓缩; 凝结: to ～ milk; 浓缩牛乳; ～ed milk; 浓缩之牛乳; 炼乳; (of a gas or vapour) (cause to) change to a liquid: (指气体或水蒸气)(使)凝结成液体: Steam ～s/is ～d to water when it touches a cold surface; 水蒸气触及冷的表面即凝结成水; (of light) focus, concentrate (by passing through a lens). (指光线)集中; 使(经过透镜而)集中。2 [VP6A, 14] put into fewer words: 缩短(文章); 摘要: 精简; 压缩: a ～d account of an event. 对某事件之简要的叙述。

con·den·ser /kənˈdensə(r); kənˈdɛnsə/ n apparatus for cooling vapour and condensing it to liquid; apparatus for receiving and accumulating static electricity; mirror or lens that concentrates light, eg in a film projector. (使水蒸汽凝结成水之)冷凝器; (收受并蓄存静电的)电容器; (如用于电影放映机之)聚光器; 聚光器。

con·de·scend /ˌkɒndɪˈsend; ˌkɑndɪˈsɛnd/ vi [VP2 A, 3A, 4A] ～ to sb/sth; ～ to do sth, 1 (in a good sense) do sth, accept a position, etc that one's rank, merits, abilities, etc do not require one to do. (好的意思)屈尊; 俯就 (做些照自己的地位、功名、能力等所不需要做的事)。2 (in a bad sense) stoop, lower oneself: (坏的意思)屈尊; 卑躬; 降低身份: He occasionally ～ed to trickery (of taking bribes). 他偶尔也自贬身价从事欺诈 (接受贿赂)。3 behave graciously, but in a way that shows one's feeling of superiority: 态度虽亲切却又显出自己的优越感: Mr Pigge sometimes ～s to help his wife with the housework. 皮基先生有时以屈尊的姿态帮他的妻子做家务。Mrs Drudge doesn't like being ～ed to. 德拉基太

不喜欢旁人以屈尊的姿态对待她。～ing adj ～ing·ly adv **con·de·scen·sion** /ˌkɒndɪˈsenʃn; ˌkɑndɪˈsɛnʃən/ n [U] ～ing (all senses); [C] instance of this. 屈尊; 俯就; 屈身; 卑躬; 优越感。

con·dign /kənˈdaɪn; kənˈdaɪn/ adj (formal) (of punishment, vengeance) severe and well deserved. (正式用语)(指惩罚、复仇)严厉而应得的; 适当的。

con·di·ment /ˈkɒndɪmənt; ˈkɑndəmənt/ n [C, U] sth used to give flavour and relish to food, eg pepper, salt, spices. 调味品; 佐料 (如胡椒、盐、香料)。

con·di·tion¹ /kənˈdɪʃn; kənˈdɪʃən/ n 1 sth needed before sth else is possible; sth on which another thing depends: (在别的事物实现之前必需的)条件; 要素: Ability is one of the ～s of success in life. 能力是人生中成功的条件之一。Her parents allowed her to go, but made it a ～ that she should get home before midnight. 她的父母准许她去, 但是有一个条件, 就是她要在午夜以前回家。on ～ (that), only if; provided (that): 只有在...的条件下; You can go swimming on ～ (that) you don't go too far from the river bank. 你只有在不远离河岸的条件下才可以去游泳。on 'this/'that/'no/'what ～: 在这种(那种, 没有的, 什么)情形下: You must on no ～ tell him what has happened, whatever he may say, do, ask, etc. 你无论在什么情形下都不可告诉他所发生的事。On what ～ will you agree, What is necessary before you agree? 你要在什么条件下才答应? 2 the present state of things; nature, quality, character of sth or sb: 目前的情况: (事物或人的)状况; 状态: The ～ of my health prevents me from working. 我的健康情况不容许我工作。The ship is not in a ～ to make a long voyage. 此船的情况不宜于长程航行。in good, etc ～, unspoiled, undamaged, etc: 情况良好等: Everything arrived in good ～, undamaged, fit for use. 一切均安全到达(毫未受损)。in no ～ (to), unable to because ill, cold, etc: 不能(作某事): He's in no ～ to travel, is not well or strong enough. 他的健康情况不宜于旅行。in/out of ～, in good/poor health; physically (un)fit: 健康良好(不佳); 体况适合(不适合): I can't go climbing this summer: I'm out of ～. 今年夏天我不能去爬山——我的健康不佳。3 (pl) circumstances: (复)环境; 情形: under existing/favourable ～s. 在现有的(有利的)情形下。4 position in society: 社会地位: persons of every ～/of all ～s. 社会各阶层的人。5 state of ill-health: 健康不良: a heart/liver ～. 心脏(肝脏)不良。

con·di·tion² /kənˈdɪʃn; kənˈdɪʃən/ vt [VP6A] 1 determine; govern; regulate: 决定; 支配; 限制: My expenditure is ～ed by my income. 我的支出受我的收入限制。2 bring into a desired state or condition: 使达到所要求的情况: We'll never ～ Jackson to a willing acceptance of lower wages. 我们永不能使杰克逊心甘情愿接受较低的工资。ˌill-/ˌwell-'～ed; 情况不佳(良好); bring (dogs, horses, etc) into good physical condition: 使(狗,马等)肥壮: ～ing powders, for this purpose. 壮狗(马)粉。**con·di·tioned** part adj subject to certain provisions or conditions; having a specified condition: 受某种条件限制的; 有某种情况的: air-～ed cinemas. 装有空气调节设备的电影院。～ed reflex, reflex action (one done normally in answer to a stimulus) that is a response, through practice or training, to a different stimulus not naturally connected with it. 条件反射; 制约反射(经由练习或训练的结果, 使对于非自然关联的刺激产生某种反应的作用)。

con·di·tional /kənˈdɪʃənl; kənˈdɪʃənl/ adj ～ (on/upon), depending upon, containing, a condition: 依赖条件的; 含有条件的: a ～ clause, beginning with 'if' or 'unless'. 条件从句 (以 if 或 unless 起首的从句)。My promise to help you is ～ on your good behaviour. 我答应帮助你, 要以你的品行优良为条件。～·ly /-ʃənlɪ; -ʃənlɪ/ adv

con·dole /kənˈdəʊl; kənˈdol/ vi [VP3A] ～ with sb (on/upon sth), express sympathy, regret, at a loss, misfortune, etc. (为损失、不幸等)表示同情、惋惜或悲悼(

con·dol·ence /kən'dəuləns; kən'doləns/ n (often pl) expression of sympathy: (常用复数) 慰问的话; 吊词: Please accept my condolences. 谨致慰问之意。

con·dom /'kɒndəm; 'kandəm/ n protective sheath, ⇨ sheath(2). 保险套。

con·do·min·ium /ˌkɒndə'mɪnɪəm; ˌkandə'mɪnɪəm/ n joint control of a State's affairs by two or more other States. (两个或更多的国家对于另一国家之事务的) 共同管辖(权)。

con·done /kən'dəun; kən'don/ vt [VP6A, C] (of a person) overlook or forgive (an offence): (指人) 宽恕; 原谅; 宥恕 (旁人对不起他的事): ~ a husband's infidelity; 宥恕丈夫的不忠: (of an act) atone for; make up for: (指行为) 补偿; 弥补: good qualities that ~ his many shortcomings. 足够补他的许多缺点的优点。**con·do·na·tion** /ˌkɒndəu'neɪʃn; ˌkandə'neʃən/ n

con·dor /'kɒndɔ:(r); 'kandə/ n large kind of vulture (in S America). (南美洲产之) 神鹰; 大兀鹰。

con·duce /kən'dju:s US: -'du:s; kən'djus/ vi [VP3A] ~ to/towards, (formal) contribute to; help to produce: (正式用语) 有助于; 导致: Does temperance ~ to good health? 节制有助于健康吗? **con·duc·ive** /kən'dju:sɪv US: -'du:s-; kən'djusɪv/ adj conducive to, helping to produce: 有助于…的; 有益于…的: Good health is conducive to happiness. 健康有助于幸福。

con·duct¹ /'kɒndʌkt; 'kandʌkt/ n [U] 1 behaviour (esp moral): 行为; (尤指道德方面的) 品行; 操行: good or bad ~; 好的或坏的行为; the rules of ~. 行为的守则。 2 manner of directing or managing affairs: 督导或处理事务的方式: People were not at all satisfied with the ~ of the war, the way in which the leaders were directing it. 人民完全不满当局的作战方式。

con·duct² /kən'dʌkt; kən'dʌkt/ vt, vi 1 [VP6A, 14, 15A, B] lead or guide: 领导; 指导; 引导: The Curator ~ed the visitors round the museum. 馆长领着游客们在博物馆中参观。Do you prefer ~ed tours or independent travel? 你比较喜欢有向导的游览抑或独自旅行? The secretary ~ed me in/out. 秘书领我进去 (出来)。C~ her to the door! 领她到门口吧! 2 [VP6A] control; direct; manage: 管理; 指挥; 处理: to ~ a meeting/negotiations; 主持会议 (谈判); If he ~s his business affairs in the careless way he ~s his private affairs, they must be in confusion. 如果他处理公事也象他处理私事一样的粗心, 那些事情一定会素乱。Who is ~ing (the orchestra) this evening? 今晚由谁指挥 (管弦乐队)? 3 [VP6A, 15A, 16A] (reflex, with adv) behave: (反身式, 与副词连用) 持 (身) 行为: He ~s himself well. 他行为端正。 4 [VP6A, 2A] (of substances) transmit; allow (heat, electric current) to pass along or through: (指物质) 传导; 容许 (热, 电流) 通过: Copper ~s electricity better than other materials. 铜传电比较其他物质为优。**con·duc·tion** /kən'dʌkʃn; kən'dʌkʃən/ n [U] transmission of or ~ing, eg of electric current along wires, of liquids through pipes, of heat by contact. 传导 (如电流经过电线); 输送 (如液体经过管子); 传播 (如热由接触传播)。**con·duc·tive** /kən'dʌktɪv; kən'dʌktɪv/ adj able to ~ (heat, electric current, etc). 能传 (热、电流) 的; 有传导性的。**con·duc·tiv·ity** /ˌkɒndʌk'tɪvətɪ; ˌkandʌk'tɪvətɪ/ n (pl -ties) property or power of ~ing. 传导性; 传导力。

con·duc·tor /kən'dʌktə(r); kən'dʌktə/ n 1 person who conducts esp one who conducts a group of singers, a band, an orchestra. 领导者; 指导者: (尤指合唱团、管乐队、管弦乐队的) 指挥。 2 person who collects fares on a bus or tram; (US) person in charge of passengers on a train. (公共汽车或电车上的) 售票员, (美) (火车上的) 列车员。⇨ guard (GB). 3 substance that conducts heat or electric current: (传导热或电流的) 导体: ~ rail, rail (laid parallel to tracks) from which a locomotive picks up electric current. 输电轨条 (与轨道平行安设, 火车头可由此接电)。**con·duc·tress** /kən'dʌktrɪs; kən'dʌktrɪs/ n woman ~ (on a bus, etc). (公共汽车等之) 女售票员。

con·duit /'kɒndɪt US: -du:ɪt; 'kandɪt/ n large pipe or waterway; tube enclosing insulated electric wires. 大管道; 水道导管; (绝缘电线由其中通过的) 线管。

cone /kəun; kon/ n 1 solid body which narrows to a point from a round, flat base. 圆锥体 (尖顶圆底之实体)。 2 sth of this shape whether solid or hollow. eg a ~-shaped basket hoisted as a storm signal, as an indication of road repairs, or an edible container for ice-cream. 圆锥形之物 (无论实体或中空, 如高悬作风暴信号或修路标记之锥形篮、用以温示之锥形的圆锥形蛋卷)。 3 fruit of certain evergreen trees (fir, pine, cedar). 某些常绿树 (如枞、松、西洋杉) 的球果。⇨ the illus at tree. 参看 tree 之插图。□ vt [VP15 B] ~ off, mark off with ~s: 用锥形信标标明: ~ off a section of the motorway during repairs. 用锥形信标标明在修理中的一段快车道。

 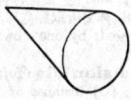

cones

co·ney n = cony.

con·fab /'kɒnfæb; 'kanfæb/ n, vi (-bb-) (colloq) abbr of confabulation or confabulate. (口, 为 confabulate 或 confabulation 之略)。

con·fabu·late /kən'fæbjuleɪt; kən'fæbjə,let/ vi [VP2A, 3A] ~ (with), have a confabulation. (与…) 谈话; 闲谈; 会谈。**can·fabu·la·tion** /kənˌfæbju'leɪʃn; kənˌfæbjə'leʃən/ n [C] friendly and private conversation. 友善的私下的谈话; 会谈。

con·fec·tion /kən'fekʃn; kən'fekʃən/ n 1 [C] mixture of sweet things; sweet cake. 糖果; 甜点。 2 [U] mixing; compounding. 混合; 调和。 3 [C] (dress-making trade) stylish or fancy ready-made article of dress (usu for a woman). (制衣业) 时髦或别致的成衣 (通常指女装)。~er n person who makes and sells pastry, pies, cakes, etc. 制卖糖果、糕饼、点心等的商人。~ery n /kən'fekʃənərɪ US: -ʃənerɪ; kən'fekʃən,erɪ/ n [U] sweets, chocolates, cakes, pies, pastry, etc; [C] (pl -ries) (place of) business of a ~er. 糖果、糕饼等; 糖果糕饼业 (店)。

con·fed·er·acy /kən'fedərəsɪ; kən'fedərəsɪ/ n (pl -cies) union of states, parties or persons: (州、党或人的) 联盟; 同盟: the Southern C~, the eleven States that separated from the Union (US, 1860—61) and brought about the Civil War. 美国南部邦联 (一八六○至一八六一年间退出美利坚合众国, 因而导致美国内战之南部第十一州)。

con·fed·er·ate¹ /kən'fedərət; kən'fedərɪt/ adj joined together by an agreement or treaty: 联盟的; 同盟的; 邦联的: the C~ States of America. 美国南部同盟。□ above. 参看上条。□ n [C] 1 person or State joined with another or others. 与他人或他国结合的人或国; 盟友; 盟邦。 2 accomplice (in a plot, etc). (阴谋等的) 共谋者; 共犯; 党羽。

con·fed·er·ate² /kən'fedəreɪt; kən'fedə,ret/ vt, vi [VP6A, 14, 2A, 3A] ~ (with), bring or come into alliance. (使) 联盟; (使) 结成同盟。**con·fed·er·ation** /kənˌfedə'reɪʃn; kənˌfedə'reʃən/ n [U] confederating or being confederated; [C] alliance; league. 组织同盟; 同盟; 联盟。

con·fer /kən'fɜ:(r); kən'fɜ/ vt, vi (-rr-) 1 [VP14] ~ sth on/upon, give or grant (a degree, title, favour): 授予 (学位, 头衔, 恩惠): The Queen ~red knighthoods on several distinguished men. 女王将爵士头衔授予数位杰出人士。 2 [VP2A, 3A] ~ (with sb) (on/about sth), consult or discuss: (与某人) 商谈 (有关某事); 商议; 讨论: ~ with one's lawyer. 与律师商谈。~·ment n

con·fer·ence /'kɒnfərəns; 'kanfərəns/ n [C, U]

meeting for) discussion; exchange of views: 会谈; 商谈; 谈判; 会议: *The Director is in ~ now.* 主任现在正在开会. *Many international ~s have been held in Geneva.* 许多国际会议曾在日内瓦举行.

con·fess /kənˈfes; kənˈfɛs/ *vt, vi* 1 [VP6A, 9, 14, 2A, 3A, 3B, 25] ~ *(to),* say or admit (that one has done wrong); acknowledge: 认错; 招供; 承认; 供认: *He ~ed that he had stolen the money.* 他承认他偷了那笔钱. *The prisoner refused to ~ (his crime/to his crime).* 犯人拒绝招供. *She ~ed herself (to be) guilty.* 她承认自己有罪. *She ~ed to (having) a dread of spiders,* admitted that she was afraid of them. 她承认她害怕蜘蛛. **2** [VP 6A, 2A, 3A] ~ *(to),* (esp in the RC Church) make known one's sins to a priest; (of a priest) listen to sb doing this: (尤指天主教)向神父认罪忏悔; 告解; (指神父)听某人告解. ~ *one's sins.* 认罪; 悔罪. *The criminal ~ed to the priest.* 犯罪者向神父告解. *The priest ~ed the criminal.* 神父听取那犯罪者告解. ~**ed·ly** /-ɪdlɪ; -ɪdlɪ/ *adv* as ~ed; by one's own confession. 承认地; 自认地; 自白地.

con·fes·sion /kənˈfeʃn; kənˈfɛʃən/ *n* 1 [U] confessing; [C] instance of this: 承认; 自认; 自白; 招供; 供认; (天主教)告解; 忏悔: *The accused man made a full ~.* 被告已全部供认. *On his own ~ he had taken part in the robbery.* 据他自己供认, 他曾参与此抢案. *She is a Catholic and goes to ~ regularly.* 她是个天主教徒, 经常去告解. *The priest is ready to hear ~s in Italian, French or English.* 那神父可以接受以意语、法语或英语告解. ⇨ **absolution, penance. 2** [C] declaration (of religious beliefs, or of principles of conduct, etc): 声明; 表白(指宗教信仰或行为准则等): *a ~ of faith.* 宗教信仰之声明.

con·fes·sional /kənˈfeʃənl; kənˈfɛʃənl/ *n* private place *(stall(4))* in a church where a priest sits to hear confessions: 忏悔室; 告解所 (教会中神父接受告解的秘室): *the secrets of the ~.* 在告解所中所吐露的隐情.

con·fes·sor /kənˈfesə(r); kənˈfɛsə/ *n* priest who has authority to hear confessions. 有权听取告解的神父.

con·fetti /kənˈfetɪ; kənˈfɛtɪ/ *n (pl; sing v)* small bits of coloured paper showered on people at weddings and carnivals. (复) 用单数动词(婚礼及狂欢节撒掷在人身上的)五彩碎纸; 纸米.

con·fi·dant /ˌkɒnfɪˈdænt; ˌkɑnfəˈdænt/ *n* person who is trusted with private affairs or secrets (esp about love affairs). (可以倾诉衷肠, 尤其是恋爱方面之秘密的)密友; 知己.

con·fide /kənˈfaɪd; kənˈfaɪd/ *vt, vi* 1 [VP14] ~ *to,* tell (a secret) to sb; give to be looked after; give (a task or duty) to sb: 向某人倾诉(秘密); 交托给(某人)加以照料; 交托(工作或职责)于某人: *He ~d his troubles to a friend.* 他向朋友倾诉烦恼事. *We ~d the boys to the care of the ship's captain.* 孩子们被交托船长监护. *She ~d to me that....* 她私密告诉我…. **2** [VP3A] ~ *in,* have trust or faith in: 信赖; 信任: *Can I ~ in his honesty?* 我能信任他的诚实吗? *There's no one here I can ~ in.* 这里没有一个人可以信赖的人. **con·fid·ing** *adj* truthful; trusting: 诚实的; 易信赖的: *The girl is of a confiding nature,* ready to trust others, unsuspicious. 这女孩天生易信赖他人. **con·fid·ing·ly** *adv*

con·fi·dence /ˈkɒnfɪdəns; ˈkɑnfədəns/ *n* 1 [U] (act of) confiding in or to. 信赖; 信任. *in strict ~,* expecting sth to be kept secret: 期待对某事保密: *I'm telling you this in strict ~,* I am confiding... 我告诉你此事系绝对对秘密(请你守密). *take sb into one's ~,* tell sb one's secrets, etc. 告诉某人一己之秘密. **2** [C] secret which is confided to sb: 向知己倾诉的秘密: 知心话: *The two girls sat in a corner exchanging ~s about the young men they knew.* 那两个女孩坐在角落里互相秘密谈论她们所认识的青年男子. **3** [U] belief in oneself or others or in what is said, reported, etc; belief that one is right or that one is able to do sth: 信心(对自己或别人, 或对所说、所报告的); 相信(自己是对的或自己能做某事); 自信: *to have/lose ~ in*

sb; 对某人有(失去)信心; *to put little/complete/no ~ in sb/sth;* 对某人(某事)无甚(完全地, 毫无)信心; *Don't put too much ~ in what the newspapers say.* 不要过份相信报纸上所说的. *There is a lack of ~ in the government,* People do not feel that its policies are wise. 人民对政府缺乏信心. *I hope he will justify my ~ in him/my ~ that he will do well.* 我希望他将会证明我对于他(对于他会做得好)的信心是对的. *The prisoner answered the questions with ~.* 那囚犯很有自信地回答问题. '~ *trick,* persuasion of a foolish person to entrust valuables to sb as a sign of ~(3). 信用欺骗(说服愚人以贵重物品相托, 作为信任之表示, 借以骗财). '~ *man/trickster* (also 亦作 '**con-man**), one who swindles people in this way. 骗子.

con·fi·dent /ˈkɒnfɪdənt; ˈkɑnfədənt/ *adj* ~ *(of/that),* feeling or showing confidence; certain: 感觉有信心的; 显示信任的; 有把握的: *He feels ~ of passing/that he will pass the examination.* 他自信能考及格. *The little girl gave her mother a ~ smile.* 那小女孩向她母亲作信赖的微笑. *We are ~ of success.* 我们有信心能成功. ~**·ly** *adv*

con·fi·den·tial /ˌkɒnfɪˈdenʃl; ˌkɑnfəˈdɛnʃəl/ *adj* 1 (to be kept) secret; given in confidence: 机密的; 应被守密的: ~ *information.* 机密消息. **2** having the confidence of another or others: 获他人信任的: *a ~ clerk/secretary.* 机要书记(秘书). **3** (of persons) inclined to give confidences: (指人) 易于信任他人的: *Don't become too ~ with strangers.* 不要太信任陌生人. ~**·ity** /ˌkɒnfɪˌdenʃɪˈælətɪ; ˌkɑnfəˌdɛnʃɪˈælɪtɪ/ *n* ~**·ly** /-ʃəlɪ/ *adv* -ʃəlɪ/ *adv*

con·fig·ur·ation /kənˌfɪgjʊˈreɪʃn; kənˌfɪgjəˈreʃən/ *n* [C] shape or outline; method of arrangement: 形状; 外貌; 轮廓; 形相; 排列方法: *the ~ of the earth's surface.* 地球表面的形状.

con·fine /kənˈfaɪn; kənˈfaɪn/ *vt* 1 [VP 14] ~ *to,* keep or hold, restrict, within limits: 限制; 限于范围内: *I wish the speaker would ~ himself to the subject.* 我希望演说者不要离题. *Please ~ your remarks to the subject we are discussing.* 请你发言不要离开你所讨论的题目. **2** [VP6A, 14] keep shut up: 关起来; 禁闭: *Is it cruel to ~ a lark in a cage?* 将云雀关在笼子里是残忍的吗? *He is ~d to the house by illness.* 他受疾病的限制不能出门. *I should hate to be ~d within the four walls of an office all day.* 我讨厌终日被关在办公室里. **3** *be ~d,* (passive only) (old use) be in bed to give birth to a child: (仅用于被动语态)(旧用法)分娩: *She expects to be ~d next month.* 她预期下月分娩. **con·fined** *adj* (of space) limited; narrow; restricted: (指空间)有限的; 狭窄的: ~**·ment** *n* 1 [U] being ~d; imprisonment: 限制; 监禁; 禁闭; 拘禁: *He was placed in ~ment,* in prison, in a mental hospital, etc. 他被监禁(关在精神病院等). *The prisoner was sentenced to three months' solitary ~ment.* 那囚犯被判处三个月的单独监禁. **2** [U] giving birth to a child; [C] instance of this: 分娩; 分娩的实例: *Dr Spock has attended six ~ments this week.* 斯波克医生这一星期接了六次生. *When does she expect her ~ment?* 她预期何时分娩?

con·fines /ˈkɒnfaɪnz; ˈkɑnfaɪnz/ *n pl* limits; borders; boundaries: 界限; 境界; 范围; 疆界: *beyond the ~ of human knowledge;* 超出人类知识的范围; *within the ~ of this valley.* 在此山谷的范围内.

con·firm /kənˈfɜːm; kənˈfɜrm/ *vt* [VP6A, 9] **1** make (power, ownership, opinions, feelings, etc) firmer or stronger: 使(权力, 所有权, 意见、权利、感情等)更巩固或坚强; 证实: *Please ~ your telephone message by letter,* send a letter repeating the message. 请来信证实一下你在电话里所说的话. *The report of an earthquake in Greece has now been ~ed,* We now know that the report was true. 希腊发生地震的报导现在已经证实. *What you tell me ~s my suspicions.* 你告诉我的话证实了我的怀疑. **2** ratify; agree definitely to (a treaty, an appointment, etc). 批准; 认可 (条约、任命等). **3** admit to full

membership of the Christian Church: (教会) 施坚振礼 (使成为正式教徒); 施坚信礼: *She was baptized when she was a month old and ~ed when she was thirteen.* 她在一个月大时受洗礼, 在十三岁时受坚振礼。**con·firmed** *part adj* (esp) unlikely to change or be changed: (尤指)确定的; 证实的; 不会改变的: *a ~ed invalid,* one who is unlikely to be well again; 终身不会康复的病人; 患痼疾的病人; *a ~ed drunkard,* one who cannot be cured of drunken habits; 饮酒成癖 (永不能戒除) 的人; *a ~ed report,* one that can be trusted. 可靠的报导。

con·fir·ma·tion /ˌkɒnfəˈmeɪʃn; ˌkɑnfəˈmeʃən/ *n* [C, U] ~ (of), confirming or being confirmed (all senses): 巩固; 强化; 证实; 批准; 认可; (教会的)坚振信礼: *We are waiting for ~ of the news.* 我们正在等该消息的证实。*Evidence in ~ of his statements is lacking.* 缺乏证据证实他的声明。*C~ admits persons to full membership of the Church.* 坚振礼许可人成为教会的正式教徒。

con·fis·cate /ˈkɒnfɪskeɪt; ˈkɑnfɪsˌket/ *vt* [VP6A] (as punishment or in enforcing authority) take possession of (private property) without compensation or payment: (作为惩罚或执行权力)充公; 没收(私有财产): *If you try to smuggle goods into the country, they may be ~d by the Customs authorities.* 如果你企图走私货物进入国内, 货物可能被海关当局没收。**con·fis·ca·tion** /ˌkɒnfɪˈskeɪʃn; ˌkɑnfɪsˈkeʃən/ *n* [U] confiscating or being ~d; [C] instance of this: 充公; 没收; 充公或没收的实例: *numerous confiscations of obscene books.* 多次的没收淫书。

con·fla·gra·tion /ˌkɒnfləˈɡreɪʃn; ˌkɑnfləˈɡreʃən/ *n* [C] great and destructive fire, esp one that destroys buildings or forests. (尤指毁灭房屋或森林的)大火灾。

con·flict¹ /ˈkɒnflɪkt; ˈkɑnflɪkt/ *n* 1 [C] fight; struggle; quarrel: 战斗; 斗争; 争执: *a wordy ~,* a bitter argument; 舌战; *a long-drawn-out ~ between employers and workers.* 劳资之间拖延甚久的争执。2 [C, U] (of opinions, desires, etc) opposition; difference: (指意见, 欲望等)相左; 冲突; 抵触: *the ~ between duty and desire;* 责任与欲望的冲突; *a ~ of evidence;* 证据之互相抵触; *be in ~ (with),* not agree(with): (与…)相冲突; *a statement that is in ~ with other evidence.* 与其他证据相冲突的陈述。

con·flict² /kənˈflɪkt; kənˈflɪkt/ *vi* [VP2A, 3A] ~ (with), be in opposition or disagreement (with): (与…)相反; 抵触; 冲突: *Our accounts ~.* 我们的报导不一致。*Their account of the causes of the war ~s with ours.* 他们对于战争起因的报导与我们的相反。~**ing** *adj*: ~*ing views / passions / evidence.* 相反的意见(情欲, 证据)。

con·flu·ence /ˈkɒnfluəns; ˈkɑnfluəns/ *n* flowing together, esp a place where two rivers unite. 汇流; 合流; (尤指)两条河的合流点。**con·flu·ent** /ˈkɒnfluənt; ˈkɑnfluənt/ *adj* flowing together; uniting. 汇流的; 会合的。

con·form /kənˈfɔːm; kənˈfɔrm/ *vi, vt* [VP2A, 3A] ~ (to), be in agreement with, comply with (generally accepted rules, standards, etc): 符合; 顺从; 遵守(一般所接受的规则, 准则等): *You should ~ to the rules / to the wishes of others / to the usages of society / to the usages of the Established Church.* 你应该遵守规则(顺从他人的愿望, 遵从社会习惯, 遵守国教的习俗)。2 [VP14] ~ to, make similar to; adapt oneself to: 使相似; 适应: ~ *one's life to certain principles.* 使自己的生活符合某些准则。~**able** *adj* obedient; submissive; in agreement. 服从的; 顺从的; 一致的; 符合的。

con·for·ma·tion /ˌkɒnfɔːˈmeɪʃn; ˌkɑnfɔrˈmeʃən/ *n* way in which sth is formed; structure. 构造; 结构; 组成。

con·form·ist /kənˈfɔːmɪst; kənˈfɔrmɪst/ *n* person who conforms; conventional person; (hist) person who followed the practices of the Church of England. 遵奉者; 顺从习俗者; (史) 信奉英国国教者。⇨ *dissenter* at **dissent²**, *nonconformist* at **non-**.

con·form·ity /kənˈfɔːmətɪ; kənˈfɔrmətɪ/ *n* [U] 1 ~ (to), action, behaviour, in agreement with what is usual, accepted or required by custom, etc: 遵守; 顺从(社会习俗等)的行为: *C~ to fashion* (=Having things of the latest fashions) *is not essential to the happiness of all women.* 顺应时髦并非对于所有妇女的幸福都是必要的。2 *in ~ with,* in agreement with: 与…一致; 符合: *in ~ with your request.* 按照你的要求。*Was his action in ~ with the law?* 他的行动是否合法?

con·found /kənˈfaʊnd; kənˈfaʊnd/ *vt* 1 [VP6A] fill with, throw into, perplexity or confusion: 使困惑; 使迷惑; 使糊涂: *His behaviour amazed and ~ed her.* 他的行为使她感到惊愕而困惑。*I was ~ed by the news.* 我听到…感到大惑不解。2 [VP6A, 14] ~ (with), mix up, confuse (ideas, etc): 混淆; 分不清(意念等): *Don't ~ the means with the ends.* 不要使手段与目的混淆不清。3 [VP6A] (liter) defeat; overthrow (enemies, plans, etc). (文)击败; 推翻(敌人, 计划等)。4 [VP6A] (dated) used to express annoyance or anger: (过时用语)用以表示厌恶或怨怒: *C~ it!* 讨厌! 该死! *C~ you!* 天哪你! 混蛋! ~**ed** *part adj* (from 4 above; dated): (由上列第 4 义转成; 过时用语)讨厌的: *You're a ~ed nuisance!* 你真是个可厌的东西! ~**edly** /-ɪdlɪ; -ɪdlɪ/ *adv* very: 非常; 极: ~*edly hot.* 极热的。

con·frère /ˈkɒnfreə(r); ˈkɑnfrɛr/ *n* (F) fellow member of a profession, learned society, etc. (法)同仁; 同志; (同一学术社团的)会员; 成员。

con·front /kənˈfrʌnt; kənˈfrʌnt/ *vt* 1 [VP14] ~ *sb with,* bring face to face: 使面对: *The prisoner was ~ed with his accusers.* 那犯人被传与起诉者对质。*When ~ed with the evidence of his guilt, he confessed at once.* 当面对着他的犯罪证据的时候, 他立即认罪。2 [VP6A] be or come face to face with: 面对; 面临: *The difficulties that ~ us seem insuperable.* 我们所面临的困难似乎是不可克服的。*A soldier has to ~ danger.* 军人须面对危险。3 [VP6A] be opposite to: 与…相对: *My house ~s his.* 我的家与他的相对。

con·fron·ta·tion /ˌkɒnfrʌnˈteɪʃn; ˌkɑnfrʌnˈteʃən/ *n* [C, U] (instance of) defiant opposition, of being face to face: 公然反对; 对峙; 敌对: *the ~ between Israel and the Arab world.* 以色列与阿拉伯世界之间的敌对。

Con·fu·cian /kənˈfjuːʃn; kənˈfjuʃən/ *adj, n* (follower) of Confucius. 孔子的; 孔子的门徒。

con·fuse /kənˈfjuːz; kənˈfjuz/ *vt* [VP6A, 14] ~ (with), 1 put into disorder; mix up in the mind: 使混乱; 使糊涂: *They asked so many questions that they ~d me / I got ~d.* 他们问了许许多多的问题, 把我弄糊涂了。2 mistake one thing for another: 误甲为乙; 弄混淆: *Don't ~ Austria with / and Australia.* 不要把奥地利跟澳大利亚弄混淆了。**con·fus·ed·ly** /-ɪdlɪ; -ɪdlɪ/ *adv* in a ~d manner. 混乱地; 混淆地。

con·fusion /kənˈfjuːʒn; kənˈfjuʒən/ *n* [U] being confused; disorder: 混乱; 纷乱; 混淆; 无秩序: *He remained calm in the ~ of battle.* 他在战事的混乱中保持镇静。*His unexpected arrival threw me into ~.* 他的突然光临使我手忙脚乱。*Everything was in ~.* 一切都在混乱中。*There has been some ~ of names.* 有人把名字弄混了。

con·fute /kənˈfjuːt; kənˈfjut/ *vt* [VP6A] prove (a person) to be wrong; show (an argument) to be false. 证明(某人或论点)是错误的; 推翻; 驳倒。**con·fu·ta·tion** /ˌkɒnfjuˈteɪʃn; ˌkɑnfjuˈteʃən/ *n*

con·gé /ˈkɒŋʒeɪ; ˈkɑnʒe/ *n* 1 formal permission to depart: 正式许可离去: *give sb his ~.* 允许某人离去。2 abrupt and unceremonious dismissal. (突然而不客气的)革退; 罢黜; 撤职。

con·geal /kənˈdʒiːl; kənˈdʒil/ *vt, vi* [VP6A, 2A] make or become stiff or solid (esp as the effect of cold, or of the air on blood); thicken as if frozen: (使)凝固; 凝结(尤指冷冻的结果或空气对于血液之作用); 变浓(如冻结): *His blood was ~ed,* (fig) eg through fear. 他的血液都凝结起来了(喻, 犹言被吓呆了)。

con·gen·ial /kənˈdʒiːnɪəl; kənˈdʒinjəl/ adj 1 (of persons) having the same or a similar nature, common interests, etc: (指人) 有相同或相似的性情或兴趣的; 志趣相投的: *In this small village he found few persons ~ to him.* 在这小村中他发现很少人跟他志趣相投。2 (of things, occupations, etc) in agreement with one's tastes, nature: (指事物,职业等) 与某人的趣味、天性相合的; 适意的; 合意的: *a ~ climate;* 适意的气候; *~ work.* 合意的工作。 **~·ly** /-ɪəlɪ; -jəlɪ/ adv

con·geni·tal /kənˈdʒenɪtl; kənˈdʒenətl/ adj (of diseases, etc) present, belonging to one, from or before birth: (指疾病等) 与生俱来的; 先天的; 天生的: *~ idiocy.* 先天性白痴。

con·ger /ˈkɒŋɡə(r); ˈkɑŋɡɚ/ n (also 亦作 ,~ˈeel) ocean eel of large size. 海鳗 (海生大鳗)。 ⇨ the illus at **sea.** 参看 sea 之插图。

con·gested /kənˈdʒestɪd; kənˈdʒɛstɪd/ part adj 1 too full; overcrowded: 过分充满的; 拥塞的; 充塞的: *streets ~ with traffic;* 交通拥挤的街道; *~ areas of a large town.* 大城市中拥塞的区域。2 (of parts of the body, eg the brain, the lungs) having an abnormal accumulation of blood. (指身体的,如脑,肺) 充血的。

con·ges·tion /kənˈdʒestʃən; kənˈdʒɛstʃən/ n [U] being congested: 充满; 拥塞; 充塞; 充血: *~ of the lungs;* 肺充血; *delayed by the ~ of traffic in town.* 为城市中拥挤的交通所耽误。

con·glom·er·ate[1] /kənˈɡlɒmərət; kənˈɡlɑmərɪt/ adj, n (made up of a) number of things or parts come together in a mass (eg rock made up of small stones held together); (fig; comm) large corporation made up of many different firms. 由许多东西或部分聚成的; 一团; 一块(如由小石头聚结成的大石块); 砾岩(的); (喻; 商)由许多公司组成的大公司; 企业集团。

con·glom·er·ate[2] /kənˈɡlɒmərɪt; kənˈɡlɑmɪret/ vt, vi [VP6A, 2A] collect into a mass. (使) 聚结成一团或一块。

con·glom·er·ation /kənˌɡlɒməˈreɪʃn; kənˌɡlɑmɚˈreʃən/ n [U] conglomerating or being conglomerated; [C] mass of conglomerated things. 聚结; 团; 块。

con·gratu·late /kənˈɡrætʃʊleɪt; kənˈɡrætʃəˌlet/ vt [VP6A, 14] ~ *sb (on/upon sth),* 1 tell sb that one is pleased about sth happy or fortunate that has come to him: (为某事) 向(某人) 道贺; 祝贺; 庆贺: *~ sb on his marriage.* 向某人祝贺结婚。2 (reflex) consider oneself fortunate: (反身式) 自庆; 私自庆幸: *I ~d myself on my escape/on having escaped unhurt.* 我能安然逃脱,深自庆幸。 **con·gratu·la·tory** US: -tɔːrɪ; kənˈɡrætʃələˌtɔrɪ/ adj that ~s: 祝贺的; 庆贺的: *a congratulatory letter/telegram.* 祝贺信(电报); 贺函; 贺电。

con·gratu·la·tion /kənˌɡrætʃʊˈleɪʃn; kənˌɡrætʃəˈleʃən/ n (often pl) words that congratulate: (常用复数) 祝贺词: *offer a friend one's ~ s on/upon his success.* 向朋友祝贺成功。

con·gre·gate /ˈkɒŋɡrɪɡeɪt; ˈkɑŋɡrɪˌget/ vi, vt [VP 6A, 2A, C] come or bring together: 集合; 聚集: *People quickly ~d round the speaker.* 人们迅速地围拢在演说者的四周。

con·gre·ga·tion /ˌkɒŋɡrɪˈɡeɪʃn; ˌkɑŋɡrɪˈɡeʃən/ n [U] congregating; [C] gathering of people; (esp) body of people (usu except the minister and choir) taking part in religious worship. 集合; 人群; (尤指) 参加宗教礼拜式(通常除牧师及唱诗班外)的会众。 **~al** adj of a ~. 群众的; 会众的。 **C~al** adj of the Union of Free Churches in which individual churches manage their own affairs. 公理会(为独立教会之联盟,各教会自行处理其事务)的。

con·gress /ˈkɒŋɡres; ˈkɑŋɡrəs/ n 1 [C] meeting, series of meetings, of representatives (of societies, etc) for discussion: (学术团体等的) 代表会议; 讨论会: *a medical ~;* 医学会议; *the Church C~.* 教会代表会议。2 **C~,** law-making body eg of US; political party in India. 国会(例如美国国会); 国大党(印度的政

党)。 **'C~·man** /-mən; -mən/ n (pl -men) /~·woman n (pl -women) member of US C~. (美国)国会议员; 国会议员。 Cf 参较 **senator. con·gres·sional** /kənˈɡreʃənl; kənˈɡreʃənl/ adj of a ~: 会议的; 国会的: *~ional debates.* 大会中的辩论。

con·gru·ent /ˈkɒŋɡruənt; ˈkɑŋɡruənt/ adj 1 ~ *(with),* suitable; agreeing (with). 适合的; (与…) 一致的。2 (geom) having the same size and shape: (几何) 全等的: *~ triangles.* 全等三角形。

con·gru·ous /ˈkɒŋɡruəs; ˈkɑŋɡruəs/ adj ~ *(with),* (formal) fitting; proper; harmonious. (正式用语)适合的; 适当的; 协调的。

conic /ˈkɒnɪk; ˈkɑnɪk/ adj of a cone: 圆锥体的; ~ *sections.* 圆锥曲线; 锥线。 **coni·cal** /ˈkɒnɪkl; ˈkɑnɪkl/ adj cone-shaped. 圆锥形的。 ⇨ the illus at **projection.** 参看 projection 之插图。

coni·fer /ˈkɒnɪfə(r); ˈkɑnəfɚ/ n tree of the kind (eg pine, fir) that bears cones. 针叶树 (结球果之树, 如松、枞)。 **co·nif·er·ous** /kəˈnɪfərəs; kəˈnɪfərəs/ adj (of kinds of trees) that bear cones. 针叶树的; 结球果的。

con·jec·ture /kənˈdʒektʃə(r); kənˈdʒektʃɚ/ vi, vt [VP6A, 9, 2A, 25] guess; put forward an opinion formed without facts as proof: 猜测; 推测; 臆测; 推想; 发表无事实为证的意见: *It was just as I ~d.* 它正如我所猜测的。 *May we ~ that…?* 我们可以推想…吗? □ n [C, U] guess; guessing: 猜测; 臆测; 猜想: *I was right in my ~.* 我的猜想对了。 *We had no facts, so were reduced to ~.* 我们没有事实为资料,所以只好猜测。 **con·jec·tural** /kənˈdʒektʃərəl; kənˈdʒektʃərəl/ adj involving ~; inclined to ~. 猜测的; 好猜测的。

con·join /kənˈdʒɔɪn; kənˈdʒɔɪn/ vt, vi [VP6A, 2A] (formal) join together; unite. (正式用语)结合; 连接; 联合。 **~t** /kənˈdʒɔɪnt; kənˈdʒɔɪnt/ adj united; associated. 结合的; 联合的。 **~t·ly** adv

con·ju·gal /ˈkɒndʒʊɡl; ˈkɑndʒʊɡl/ adj of marriage and wedded life; of husband and wife: 婚姻的; 婚姻生活的(夫妇之爱); 夫妻间的: *~ happiness/affection/infidelity.* 婚姻之乐(夫妇之爱; 对配偶不忠)。 **~·ly** /-ɡlɪ; -ɡlɪ/ adv

con·ju·gate /ˈkɒndʒʊɡeɪt; ˈkɑndʒəˌget/ vt, vi 1 [VP6A] give the forms of (a verb) for number, tense, etc. 列举(动词)数、时态等的变形。2 [VP2A] (of a verb) have these forms. (指动词) 有各种变形; 变化。 **con·ju·ga·tion** /ˌkɒndʒʊˈɡeɪʃn; ˌkɑndʒəˈɡeʃən/ n [C, U] scheme or system of verb forms; [C] class of verbs ~d alike. 动词变化的系统; 动词活用表; 变形方式相同的一类动词。

con·junc·tion /kənˈdʒʌŋkʃn; kənˈdʒʌŋkʃən/ n 1 [C] (gram) word that joins other words, clauses, etc, eg *and, but, or.* (语法) 连接词(连接词、从句等的词, 例如 and, but, or 等)。2 [U] joining; state of being joined: 连接; 连结; 连接在一起: *the ~ of skill and imagination in planning a garden.* 计划一座花园之技术与想象力的结合。 *in ~ with,* together with. 连同。3 [C] combination of events, etc): (指事件等) 凑合; 结合: *an unusual ~ of circumstances.* 各种情况之非常的巧合。

con·junc·tiva /ˌkɒndʒʌŋkˈtaɪvə; ˌkɑndʒʌŋkˈtaɪvə/ n (anat) thin transparent membrane connecting the upper and lower inner eyelids, covering the cornea. (解剖) 结膜。 ⇨ the illus at **eye.** 参看 eye 之插图。 **con·junc·ti·vitis** /kənˌdʒʌŋktɪˈvaɪtɪs; kənˌdʒʌŋktəˈvaɪtɪs/ n [U] inflammation of the ~. 结膜炎。

con·junc·tive /kənˈdʒʌŋktɪv; kənˈdʒʌŋktɪv/ adj serving to join; connective. 有连接作用的; 连接性的。 □ n ~ word. 连接词。

con·junc·ture /kənˈdʒʌŋktʃə(r); kənˈdʒʌŋktʃɚ/ n [C] combination of events or circumstances. 事件或情况的凑合; 局面; 时机。

con·jur·ation /ˌkɒndʒʊˈreɪʃn; ˌkɑndʒʊˈreʃən/ n [C] (formal) solemn appeal, incantation. (正式用语)祈求; 咒语; 咒文。

con·jure /ˈkʌndʒə(r); ˈkʌndʒɚ/ vt, vi 1 [VP2A, 15A] do clever tricks which appear magical, esp by quick

movements of the hands: 玩魔术; (尤指以敏捷的手法)变戏法; 用戏法变出: *a conjuring trick*; 魔术; ~ *a rabbit out of a hat*. 从帽子里变出一只兔子来. **a name to ~ with**, sb of great importance / influence. 极重要之人; 极有影响力之人. **2** [VP15B] ~ **up**, cause to appear as if from nothing, or as a picture in the mind: 使从虚无中显现; 使在脑中显现如画画; 想象; 追忆: ~ *up visions of the past*; 回忆过去的景象; compel (a spirit) to appear by invocation: 念咒召 (鬼魂): ~ *up the spirits of the dead*; 念咒召唤死者的灵魂; ~ *up a meal*, produce it quickly. 象变魔术似地很快做出一顿饭菜. **3** /kən'dʒʊə(r); kən'dʒʊr/ [VP17] (formal) appeal solemnly to: (正式用语) 恳求; 祈求: *I ~ you not to betray me*. 我恳求你不要背弃我. **con·jurer, con·juror** /'kʌndʒərə(r); 'kʌndʒərə/ n person who performs conjuring tricks. 魔术师. ⇨ **1** above. 参看上列第 1 义.

conk¹ /kɒŋk; kɑŋk/ n (GB sl) nose. (英俚) 鼻.

conk² /kɒŋk; kɑŋk/ vi ~ **out**, (colloq) (of a machine) fail or give signs of failing: (口) (指机器) 失灵; 发生故障; 有发生故障的迹象: *The engine's ~ing out*. 引擎快要发生故障了.

conker /'kɒŋkə(r); 'kɑŋkə/ n (colloq) horse chestnut. (口) 七叶树; 七叶树之实.

con-man /'kɒn mæn; 'kɑn ˌmæn/ n ⇨ **confidence** (3).

con·nect /kə'nekt; kə'nɛkt/ vt, vi **1** [VP6A, 15A, B, 14, 2A, 2C, 3A] ~ **(up) (to / with)**, join; be joined (materially, by personal relationships, etc): 连接; 连结 (在物质上, 人事关系上等): ~ *telephone subscribers*; 为电话用户接线; ~ *up the cells of a battery / to / with one another*). 连接电池组的各个电池. *The two towns are ~ed by a railway*. 这两市镇有铁路相连. *A railway ~s Oxford and Reading / ~s Oxford to / with Reading*. 牛津和雷丁间有一铁路相连. *Where does the cooker ~ with the gas-pipe*? 煤气炉在何处与煤气管衔接? *Mr Y has been ~ed with this firm since 1950*. Y 先生从一九五〇年起就一直在此公司做事. *He is ~ed with the Smiths / He and the Smiths are ~ed by marriage*, ie his wife is a member of the Smith family. 他与史密斯家联姻 (娶史家小姐为妻). *The 9.00am train from London ~s with the 12.05pm train at Crewe*, ie arrives at Crewe so as to enable passengers to continue their journeys by the 12.05 pm train. 上午九时自伦敦开出的列车在克鲁与下午十二点五分的列车相衔接 (长途乘客可在此换车). **well ~ed**, with relatives who are high in society, or who hold important positions, etc. 有优越的社会关系 (有亲属或亲戚在社会上居高位或要职). **2** [VP14] ~ **(with)**, think of (different things or persons) as being related to each other: 联想 (在思想中使之间的事物或人联系起来): *to ~ Malaya with rubber and tin*. 提到马来亚就联想到橡胶和锡.

con·nec·tion /kə'nekʃn; kə'nɛkʃən/ n **1** [C, U] connecting or being connected; point where two things are connected; thing which connects: 连接; 连结; 连接点; 连接物: *a bicycle pump ~*. 脚踏车打气筒的接头. *How long will the ~ of the new telephone take*, How long will it take to connect the house by telephone to the exchange? 新装的电话机与总机接线需要多久的时间? *What is the ~ between the two ideas*? 这两个意念之间有何关联? **in this / that ~**, with reference to this / that. 关于这 (彼) 点. **in ~ with**, with reference to: 与…相连; 关于: *The meeting is in ~ with a proposal to construct a new swimming-pool*. 该集会与建一个新的游泳池有关. **2** [C] train, boat, etc timed to leave a station, port, etc soon after the arrival of another, enabling passengers to change from one to the other: (与另一到达的交通工具在时间上相连接以便旅客换乘的) 联运列车、船舶: *The train was late and I missed my ~*. 火车误点了, 我没赶上联运车 (船). **3** [C] (collective noun) number of customers, clients. etc: (集合名词) 商店的主顾; 医生的病家; 律师的委托人; 一批顾客: *He set up in business and soon had a good ~*. 他开设营业经商, 很快就有相当多的顾客. *This dressmaker has good ~s among the well-to-do women of the town*. 这个女裁缝

在本镇富家妇女之中拥有相当多的顾客. **4** [C] number of people united in a religious organization: 结合于一宗教组织中的人 (教派): *the Methodist ~*. 美以美教派.

con·nect·ive /kə'nektɪv; kə'nɛktɪv/ adj serving to connect. 有连接作用的. □ n (esp) word that connects (eg a conjunction). (尤指) 起连接作用的词 (如连接词).

con·nex·ion /kə'nekʃn; kə'nɛkʃən/ occasional GB spelling for *connection*. 偶尔使用的 connection 的英国拼法.

con·ning tower /'kɒnɪŋ taʊə(r); 'kɑnɪŋ ˌtaʊə/ n (on a warship) superstructure from which steering, etc is directed (esp of a submarine on or near the surface). (战舰上的) 指挥塔 (尤指潜艇在水面上或近水面时的驾驶台或瞭望塔).

con·nive /kə'naɪv; kə'naɪv/ vi [VP3A] ~ **at**, take no notice of (what is wrong, what ought to be opposed) (suggesting that tacit consent or approval is given): 假装不见 (应纠正或反对之事); 默许; 纵容: ~ *at an escape from prison*. 故纵逃狱. **con·niv·ance** /kə'naɪvəns; kə'naɪvəns/ n [U] conniving (at / in a crime): 默许; 纵容: *done with the connivance of / in connivance with....* 得到…的默许而做的.

con·nois·seur /ˌkɒnə'sɜ:(r); ˌkɑnə'sɝ/ n person with good judgement on matters in which taste (5) is involved: 鉴赏家; 鉴定家; 内行: *a ~ of painting / old porcelain / antique furniture / wine*. 名画 (古瓷, 古老家具, 葡萄酒) 鉴定家.

con·note /kə'nəut; kə'not/ vt [VP6A] (of words) suggest in addition to the fundamental meaning: (指词) (除本义外) 含有…的意义; 有…的含意: *The word 'Tropics' means the area enclosed between about 23° N and 23° S; it ~s heat*. *Tropics* 一词本义指约自北纬 23 度至南纬 23 度之间的地区; 它含有炎热的意义. **con·no·ta·tion** /ˌkɒnə'teɪʃn; ˌkɑnə'teʃən/ n [C] that which is ~d. 含着的意义; 含意; 内涵; 包蕴.

con·nu·bial /kə'nju:bɪəl US: -'nu:-; kə'nubɪəl/ adj (formal) of marriage; of husband and wife. (正式用语) 婚姻的; 夫妇的.

con·quer /'kɒŋkə(r); 'kɑŋkə/ vt [VP6A] **1** defeat or overcome enemies / bad habits, etc. 击败 (敌人); 克服 (恶习等). **2** take possession of by force: 借武力占领: ~ *a country*. 征服一国. **con·or** /'kɒŋkərə(r); 'kɑŋkərə/ n one who ~s: 征服者; 战胜者: *William the C~or*, King William I of England. 征服者威廉 (英王威廉一世的称号).

con·quest /'kɒŋkwest; 'kɑŋkwɛst/ n **1** [U] conquering (eg a country and its people): 征服 (如一国及其人民): *the (Norman) C~*, of England by the Normans in 1066. 诺曼第人之征服英国 (时为一〇六六年). **2** [C] sth got by conquering: 由征服所得之物; 斩获品; 战利品: *the Roman ~s in Africa*. 罗马人在非洲的征服所得物. **make a ~ (of)**, win the affections (of). 赢得 (…的) 爱情.

con·quista·dor /kɒn'kwɪstədɔ:(r); kɑn'kwɪstəˌdɔr/ n (16th c) one of the Spanish conquerors of Mexico and Peru. (十六世纪) 西班牙征服者 (征服墨西哥与秘鲁之西班牙人).

con·san·guin·ity /ˌkɒnsæŋ'gwɪnətɪ; ˌkɑnsæn'gwɪnətɪ/ n [U] (formal) relationship by blood or birth: (正式用语) 血亲关系; 血缘; 血亲: *united by ties of ~*. 为血缘关系所系.

con·science /'kɒnʃəns; 'kɑnʃəns/ n [C, U] the consciousness within oneself of the choice one ought to make between right and wrong: 良心; 天良; 良知; 道德心; 是非心: *have a clear / guilty ~*. 问心无 (有) 愧. **have no ~**, be as ready to do wrong as right. 没有良心; 失去良知. **(have sth) on one's ~**, (feel) troubled about sth one has done, or failed to do. (因做了某事未能做某事而感到) 内疚; 受良心谴责. **'~ money**, money paid to rectify sth and ease one's ~ (esp when no other person knows that it is owing). 良心上不安所付的钱 (尤指所欠为他人所不知者). **'~-smitten** /-smɪtn; -ˌsmɪtn/ adj filled with remorse. 良心不安的; 受良心谴责的. **for '~' sake**,

to satisfy one's ~. 为求心之所安. *in all* ~, (forms of emphatic declaration) surely; (colloq) by all that is fair: (加强语气之宣言的套语)当然; 一定; 确实地; (口)凭良心; 公道地; 公正地: *I cannot in all* ~ *agree.* 凭良心我不能赞成. *make sth / be a matter of* ~, make sth / be a question which one's ~ must decide. 使某事成为良心必须决定的问题; 是有关良心的事.

con·scien·tious /ˌkɒnʃɪˈenʃəs; ˌkɑnʃɪˈenʃəs/ *adj* **1** (of persons) guided by one's sense of duty: (指人)有责任心的; 负责的; 尽责的: *a '~ worker.* 尽责的工作者. **objector,** person who objects to doing sth (esp serving in the armed forces) because he thinks it is morally wrong. 因觉违背道德而反对做某事(尤指服兵役)的人; 基于道德理由的拒绝者. **2** (of actions) done carefully and honestly: (指行为)谨慎的; 本良心做的: ~ *work.* 本良心做的工作. ~**·ly** *adv* ~**·ness** *n*

con·scious /ˈkɒnʃəs; ˈkɑnʃəs/ *adj* **1** ~ (*of / that*), (pred use) awake; aware; knowing things because one is using the bodily senses and mental powers: (用作表语)清醒的; 明白的; 察觉的; (因用感官和脑力而)知道的: *They were* ~ *of being / that they were being watched.* 他们知道有人在监视他们. *He was* ~ *of his guilt.* 他自知有罪. *Are you* ~ *(of) how people will regard such behaviour?* 你可知道人们对此此种行为作何观感? *A healthy man is not* ~ *of his breathing.* 健康的人对自己的呼吸无所感觉. *The old man was* ~ *to the last,* aware of what was happening round him until the moment he died. 那老人临终仍甚清醒. **2** (of actions, feelings, etc) realized by oneself: (指行动、感情等)自觉的: *He spoke / acted with* ~ *superiority.* 他说话(举止)带着自觉的优越感. ~**·ly** *adv*

con·scious·ness /ˈkɒnʃəsnɪs; ˈkɑnʃəsnɪs/ *n* [U] **1** being conscious; 知觉: *We have no* ~ *during sleep.* 我们在睡眠时没有知觉. *The blow caused him to lose* ~ . 那一击使他失去知觉. *He did not recover / regain* ~ *until two hours after the accident.* 他在祸事发生以后两个小时才恢复知觉. **2** all the ideas, thoughts, feelings, wishes, intentions, recollections, of a person or persons: 意识(指一人或众人之所有的观念、思想、感情、愿望、意向、记忆): *the moral* ~ *of a political party.* 一政党之道德意识.

con·script /kənˈskrɪpt; kənˈskrɪpt/ *vt* [VP 6 A, 14] ~ (*into*), compel (sb) by law to serve in the armed forces; summon for such service: 征召(某人)服兵役; 召集(服役): ~*ed into the army.* 被征召入陆军服役. ⇨ **draft²(2).** □ *n* /ˈkɒnskrɪpt; ˈkɑnskrɪpt/ person who is ~ed; 被征召者的; (attrib)(用作定语) ~ *soldiers.* 征召的士兵; 应征部队入. **con·scrip·tion** /kənˈskrɪpʃn; kənˈskrɪpʃən/ *n* [U] ~ing (of men into the armed forces); taxation or confiscation of property (as a penalty or for war needs). 征兵; (作为处罚或因战时需要)对于私有财产之课税或征用; 征用制度.

con·se·crate /ˈkɒnsɪkreɪt; ˈkɑnsɪˌkret/ *vt* [VP6A, 14, 23] ~ (*to*), set apart as sacred or for a special purpose; make sacred: 奉为神圣; 供献(作为特殊用途); 奉献; 使成为神圣: *to* ~ *one's life to the service of God / to the relief of suffering.* 奉献自己的生命为神服务(从事解除世人的苦难). *The new church was* ~*ed by the Bishop of Chester.* 新教堂的奉献礼系由切斯特的主教主持. *He was* ~*ed Archbishop last year.* 他于去年被奉为大主教(任大主教之圣职).

con·se·cra·tion /ˌkɒnsɪˈkreɪʃn; ˌkɑnsɪˈkreʃən/ *n* [U] consecrating or being consecrated; [C] instance of this: 供献; 奉献; 神圣化; 供献或奉献之实例: *the* ~ *of a church;* 教堂的奉献; *the* ~ *of a bishop,* the ceremony at which a priest is made a bishop. 主教授职礼(由神父升任主教之典礼).

con·secu·tive /kənˈsekjʊtɪv; kənˈsekjətɪv/ *adj* following without interruption; coming one after the other in regular order: 连续不断的; 接连而来的: *on five* ~ *days.* 连续五天. ~**·ly** *adv*

con·sen·sus /kənˈsensəs; kənˈsɛnsəs/ *n* [C, U] general

agreement (*of opinion, etc*); collective opinion. (意见等的)共同一致; 舆论. ~ **politics,** the practice of basing policies on what will gain wide support. 舆论政治(以能够获得大众支持之事物为施政方针之依据).

con·sent /kənˈsent; kənˈsɛnt/ *vi* [VP2A, 3A, 4C] ~ (*to*), give agreement or permission: 同意; 答应; 应允: *He* ~*ed to the proposal.* 他同意这提议. *Anne's father would not* ~ *to her marrying a foreigner.* 安妮的父亲不会答应她嫁给外国人. □ *n* [U] ~ (*to*), agreement; permission: 同意; 答应; 许可: *He was chosen leader by general* ~, when everyone agreed. 他为大家一致赞同选为领袖. *Her parents refused their* ~ *to the marriage.* 她的父母不答应此桩婚事. *Silence gives* ~, If no one objects, it seems that ~ is given. 沉默即是同意. *with one* ~, unanimously. 全体一致地. *age of '*~, age at which the law recognizes a person's responsibility for agreeing to sexual intercourse, a person's right to ~ to marry, etc. 承诺年龄(法律上许可一人有权同意与人发生性关系、婚姻有自主权等的年龄).

con·se·quence /ˈkɒnsɪkwens US: -kwens; ˈkɑnsəˌkwens/ *n* **1** [C] that which follows or is brought about as the result or effect of sth: (某事的)后果; 影响: *If you behave so foolishly you must be ready to take the* ~*s,* accept what happens as a result. 你要是这样愚蠢下去, 你必须准备自食其果. *in* ~ (*of*), as a result (of). 结果; 因…而. **2** [U] importance: 重要性: *It's of no* ~. 它无重要性. *Is it of any / much* ~? 它有任何(大的)重要性吗? *He may be a man of* ~ (= an important man, or a man of high rank) *in his own village, but he's nobody here.* 他在他自己的村中也许算是个要人, 但在此地微不足道.

con·se·quent /ˈkɒnsɪkwent; ˈkɑnsəˌkwɛnt/ *adj* ~ *on / upon,* (formal) following as a consequence: (正式用语)随之发生的; 由…而起的: *the rise in prices* ~ *upon the failure of the crops.* 由于农作物歉收而引起的物价上涨. ~**·ly** *adv*

conse·quen·tial /ˌkɒnsɪˈkwenʃl; ˌkɑnsəˈkwɛnʃəl/ *adj* **1**=**consequent.** **2** (of a person) self-important. (指人)自大的; 自傲的; 自以为了不起的. ~**·ly** /-ʃəlɪ; -ʃəlɪ/ *adv*

con·ser·vancy /kənˈsɜːvənsɪ; kənˈsɜrvənsɪ/ *n* (*pl* -cies) **1** [C] commission controlling a port, river, etc: (港口、河道等)管理委员会: *the Thames C*~: 泰晤士河管理委员会; *the Nature C*~. 自然资源管理委员会. **2** [U] official conservation (of forests, etc). 政府(对于森林等)的保护.

con·ser·va·tion /ˌkɒnsəˈveɪʃn; ˌkɑnsəˈveʃən/ *n* [U] preservation; prevention of loss, waste, damage, etc: 保护; 保存(以免损失、浪费、损坏等): *the* ~ *of forests / waterpower etc;* 对于森林(水力等)的保护; *the* ~ *of energy,* the principle that the total quantity of energy in the universe never varies. 能量守恒; 能量不灭律(宇宙间能源总是和永远不变之定律).

con·ser·va·tism /kənˈsɜːvətɪzm; kənˈsɜrvəˌtɪzm/ *n* [U] tendency to maintain a state of affairs (esp in politics) without great or sudden change; the principles of the Conservative Party in British politics. (尤指政治上主张维持现状而不作大幅度或突然之改革的)保守性; 保守主义; 英国政界保守党的政策.

con·ser·va·tive /kənˈsɜːvətɪv; kənˈsɜrvətɪv/ *adj* **1** opposed to (great or sudden) change: 反对(大幅度或突然)改革的; 保守的; 守旧的: *Old people are usually more* ~ *than young people.* 老年人通常较青年人为保守. **2** *the* '**C~ Party,** one of the main political parties in Great Britain. 保守党(英国之一政党). ⇨ *Labour* at **labour(3),** *Liberal* at **liberal(4),** *Socialist* at **socialism. 3** cautious; moderate: 谨慎的; 审中庸之道的: *a* ~ *estimate of one's future income.* 对于自己将来收入的保守的估计. □ *n* ~ person; member of the C~ Party. 守旧的人; 保守者; 保守党党员. ~**·ly** *adv*

con·ser·va·toire /kənˈsɜːvətwɑː(r); kənˈsɜrvəˈtwɑr/ *n* (F) (esp in Europe) public school of music, drama etc.

(法)(尤用于欧洲)音乐学校; 戏剧学校等。

con·ser·va·tory /kənˈsɜːvətrɪ US: -tɔːrɪ; kənˈsɜːvə-ˌtɔrɪ/ n (pl -ries) 1 building, or part of a building, with glass walls and roof in which plants are protected from cold. 温室; 花房(保护植物使免受寒冻的玻璃房子)。 2 = conservatoire.

con·serve /kənˈsɜːv; kənˈsɜːv/ vt [VP6A] keep from change, loss or destruction: 保存; 保全 (以免变质或损毁): ~ one's strength /energies /health; 保持实力(精力), 健康; ~ fruit, eg by making it into jam. 保藏水果使不变坏(例如用水果制成果酱)。□ n (usu pl) fruit preserved in sugar; jam. (通常用复数)蜜饯; 果酱。

con·sider /kənˈsɪdə(r); kənˈsɪdə/ vt 1 [VP6A, C, 8, 10] think about: 考虑; 思考: Please ~ my suggestion. 请考虑我的建议。We are ~ing going to Canada. 我们正考虑赴加拿大。Have you ~ed how to get /how you could get there? 你曾考虑过如何能到达那里吗? Have you ever ~ed the fact that your pension will be inadequate? 你曾经考虑过你的养老金将会不够(生活)吗? one's ~ed opinion, one's opinion arrived at after some thought: (某人之)经过考虑后所得到的意见: It's my ~ed opinion that you should resign. 经过考虑后我的意见是你应该辞职。2 [VP6A] take into account; make allowances for: 顾虑; 顾及; 体谅: We must ~ the feelings of other people. 我们必须顾及他人的感情。You should ~ his youth. 你应当体谅他的年轻。all things ~ed, taking into account, thinking of, all the events, possibilities, etc. 综合各项情势而观; 把一切情形、可能等都考虑到。3 [VP25, 9] be of the opinion; regard as: 认为; 以为; 觉得: They ~ed themselves very important. 他们自以为是非常重要的。Do you ~ it wise to interfere? 你觉得干预是明智的吗? He will be ~ed a weak leader. 他会被认为是个能力不足的领袖。C~ yourself (= You are) under arrest. 你是在拘禁中(别想逃走)。We ~ that you are not to blame. 我们认为你不应受责(不是你的错)。

con·sider·able /kənˈsɪdərəbl; kənˈsɪdərəbl/ adj great; much; important: 相当大的; 相当多的; 相当重要的: a ~ income /distance; 相当可观的收入(相当远的距离); bought at a ~ expense; 花相当多的钱购买的; a ~ man in local affairs. 地方事务上相当重要的人物。 ~·ably /-əblɪ; -əblɪ/ adv much; a great deal: 相当地; 十分地: It's considerably colder this morning. 今天早晨冷得多。

con·sider·ate /kənˈsɪdərət; kənˈsɪdrɪt/ adj ~ (of), thoughtful (of the needs, etc, of others): 考虑他人之需要者; 为着他人着想的; 体谅的; 体贴的; 考虑周到的: It was ~ of you not to play the piano while I was having a sleep. 在我睡觉的时候你不弹钢琴, 真是考虑得周到。 ~·ly adv ~·ness n

con·sider·ation /kənˌsɪdəˈreɪʃn; kənˌsɪdəˈreʃən/ n 1 [U] act of considering, thinking about: 考虑; 思考: Please give the matter your careful ~. 请对此事细加思考。The proposals are still under ~. 那些提议仍在考虑中。leave sth out of ~, neglect or fail to consider it: 对某事未加考虑: There is one important fact that has been left out of ~. 有一重要事实未曾考虑到。take sth into ~, (esp) make allowances for: 考虑到某事; (尤)顾及(体谅); 原谅; 考虑到: When marking Tom's examination papers, the teacher took Tom's long illness into ~. 在评阅到汤姆的考卷时, 老师考虑到汤姆患了很久的病。2 [U] ~ (for), quality of being considerate; thoughtful attention to the wishes, feelings, etc, of others: 体谅; 考虑; 顾及他人的愿望、感情等: He has never shown much ~ for his wife's feelings. 他从来不大顾及他妻子的情绪。in ~ of; out of ~ for, considering(2). 体谅; 顾及。3 [C] sth which must be thought about; fact, thing, etc thought of as a reason: 必须考虑的事; 被当做理由的事实、事物等; 因素: Time is an important ~ in this case. 在这件事中, 时间是一个重要的因素。Several ~s have influenced me in coming to a decision. 好几个因素影响我作出决定。on no ~, in no circumstances; in no case. 无论如何决不。 4 [C] reward; payment: 报酬; 酬资: He's the sort of

man who would do anything for a ~, if he were paid to do it. 他是只要能获取报酬, 什么事都做得出来的那种人。5 [U] (rare use) importance: (罕用)重要性: It's of no ~ at all. 它一点也不重要。

con·sider·ing /kənˈsɪdərɪŋ; kənˈsɪdərɪŋ/ prep, adv in view of; having regard to: 鉴于…而论: She's very active, ~ her age. 就她的年龄而论, 她真是非常活跃的。You've done very well, ~, ie in view of the circumstances, etc. 就目前情况而言, 你做得很好。

con·sign /kənˈsaɪn; kənˈsaɪn/ vt ~ (to), 1 [VP6A, 14] send (goods, etc) for delivery: 寄递; 运送(货物等): The goods have been ~ed by rail. 货物已交由铁路运送。2 [VP14] hand over, give up: 移交; 交付: ~ a child to its uncle's care; 将小孩交其叔父照顾; ~ one's soul to God. 把心灵交给上帝; 归主。 ~ee /ˌkɒnsaɪˈniː; ˌkɑnsaɪˈni/ n person to whom sth is ~ed. 收件人; 受付托者。 ~er, ~or /-nə(r); -nə/ nn person who ~s goods. 寄件人; 发货人。 ~·ment n [U] ~ing; ~ed. 运送; 委托; 所递送的货物; 委托物。 on ~ment, with payment for goods to be made after they have been sold by the receiver: 以委托方式 (待货品售出后方付款给货主); 以寄售方式: take /send /ship goods on ~ment. 以寄售方式接受(寄出, 运送)货品。 '~ment note, one sent with a ~ment of goods. 发货通知书。

con·sist /kənˈsɪst; kənˈsɪst/ vi [VP3A] 1 ~ of, (not in the progressive tenses) be made up of: (不用进行时)由…组成: The committee ~s of ten members. 委员会由十人组成。2 ~ in, have as the chief or only element: 在于; 以…为主要或唯一因素: The happiness of a country ~s in the freedom of its citizens. 一国之幸福以其全民之自由为首要。

con·sist·ence /kənˈsɪstəns; kənˈsɪstəns/ n = consistency.

con·sist·ency /kənˈsɪstənsɪ; kənˈsɪstənsɪ/ n 1 [U] the state of always being the same in thought, behaviour, etc; keeping to the same principles: (思想, 行动等的永远)一致; 一贯; 固守同样的原则: His actions lack ~. 他的行动缺乏一贯性。2 [C, U] (pl -cies) degree of thickness, firmness or solidity (esp of a thick liquid, or of sth made by mixing with a liquid): 浓度; 坚度; 硬度; 稠度(尤指浓稠液体或与液体混合物的浓度等): mix flour and milk to the right ~; 混合面粉和牛奶至适当的浓度; mixtures of various consistencies. 各种不同浓度的混合物。

con·sist·ent /kənˈsɪstənt; kənˈsɪstənt/ adj 1 (of a person, his behaviour, principles, etc) conforming to a regular pattern or style; regular: (指人, 其行为、立身之道等)一致的; 经常的; 一贯的: He's been a ~ friend to me. 他是我历久不渝的朋友。The ideas in his various speeches are not ~. 他在各项演说中所持的观念不一致。2 ~ (with), in agreement: (与…)一致: What you say now is not ~ with what you said last week. 你现在所说的话与你上星期所说的话不相符合。 ~·ly adv

con·sis·tory /kənˈsɪstərɪ; kənˈsɪstərɪ/ n (pl -ries) C~(Court), court of clergymen to deal with church business. (由教士组成以处理教会事务的)宗教法庭。

con·so·la·tion /ˌkɒnsəˈleɪʃn; ˌkɑnsəˈleʃən/ n 1 [U] consoling or being consoled; sth that consoles: 安慰; 慰藉; 安慰物: a few words of ~; 几句安慰的话; a letter of ~. 慰问信。'~ prize, given to a competitor who has just missed success or come last. (给予参加比赛未获名次或得末名者的)精神奖; 安慰奖。2 [C] circumstances or person that consoles: 令人安慰的情势或人: That's one ~. 那是一件可以告慰的事。Your company has been a great ~ to me. 你能陪伴我真是件极可安慰的事。

con·sola·tory /kənˈsɒlətrɪ US: -tɔːrɪ; kənˈsɑlətˌtɔrɪ/ adj comforting; intended to console: 安慰的; 旨在安慰人的: a ~ letter. 慰问信。

con·sole¹ /kənˈsəʊl; kənˈsol/ vt [VP6A, 14] give comfort or sympathy to (sb who is unhappy, disappointed, etc): 给予(愁苦者, 失望者等)安慰或同情; 慰问: ~ sb for a loss; 安慰遭受损失的人; ~ oneself

with the thought that it might have been worse. 以情形没有变得更坏而告慰自己. **con·sol·able** adj that can be ~d. 可安慰的.

con·sole² /'kɒnsəul; 'kɑnsol/ n 1 bracket to support a shelf. 板架的支架. '~ **table**, narrow table held up by a bracket or brackets fixed to a wall. 用三角支架装在墙壁上的狭台. 2 frame containing the keyboards, stops, etc of an organ. 风琴的操作部分 (包括键盘, 音栓等). 3 radio or TV cabinet made to stand on the floor (not a table model). 落地式收音机或电视机的支架. 4 panel for the controls of electronic or mechanical equipment. (电子或机械装置的) 控制盘.

con·soli·date /kən'sɒlɪdeɪt; kən'sɑlə,det/ vt, vi 1 [VP6A, 2A] make or become solid or strong: (使) 巩固; (使) 坚强: ~ one's position/influence. 巩固其地位 (势力). 2 [VP6A] unite or combine into one: 团结; 联合; 合并; 统一: ~ debts/business companies/banks. 合并债务 (商行, 银行). ~d **annuities**, (also 亦称 **consols** /'kɒnsɒlz; 'kɑnsalz/) Government securities of Great Britain, ~d in 1751 into a single stock. 英国政府 (一七五一年发行的) 统一公债. **C~d Fund** n fund from taxation, used for payment of interest on the national debt. 由税收拨出的公债利息基金.

con·soli·da·tion /kən,sɒlɪ'deɪʃn; kən,sɑlə'deʃən/ n [U] consolidating or being consolidated; [C] instance of this: 巩固; 团结; 联合; 合并; 统一: successive ~s of the national debt. 公债之历次的合并.

con·sols /'kɒnsɒlz; 'kɑnsalz/ n pl consolidated annuities. 英国政府之统一公债. ⇨ consolidate(2).

con·sommé US: /kən'sɒmeɪ US: ,kɑnsə'me/ n (F) clear, meat soup. (法) 清炖肉汤.

con·son·ance /'kɒnsənəns; 'kɑnsənəns/ n [U] 1 agreement. 一致. 2 harmony. 协调, 和谐.

con·son·ant¹ /'kɒnsənənt; 'kɑnsənənt/ n [C] speech sound produced by a complete or partial stoppage of the breath; letter of the alphabet or symbol (eg phonetic) for such a sound: b, c, d, f, etc. 辅音(由完全阻塞或不完全阻塞呼气所发的语音); 辅音字母 (如 b, c, d, f 等); 辅音符号(如辅音音标).

con·son·ant² /'kɒnsənənt; 'kɑnsənənt/ adj(formal) ~ **with**, harmonious: (正式用语) (与～) 协调的; 和谐的: actions ~ with his beliefs; 与其信仰一致的行动; a position in the service ~ with your rank. 与你的军阶相符合的军职. ~ **to**, agreeable: 一致的; 符合的: ~ to reason. 合理的人.

con·sort¹ /'kɒnsɔːt; 'kɑnsɔrt/ n 1 husband or wife, esp a ruler: 配偶; 夫或妻 (尤指君王之夫或妻): the queen ~, the king's wife; 王后; the prince ~, the reigning queen's husband. 女王的丈夫; 王夫. 2 ship sailing with another (esp for safety during a war). (尤指战时为安全而)结伴航行的船只.

con·sort² /kən'sɔːt; kən'sɔrt/ vi [VP3A, 2C] ~ **with**, 1 pass time on the company of: 陪伴; 结交; 交往: ~ with criminals/one's equals. 与犯罪者(平辈)交往. 2 be in harmony, go well: 协调; 一致; 符合: His practice does not ~ with his preaching, He behaves in one way, but talks in another way. 他的言行不符.

con·sor·tium /kən'sɔːtɪəm US: -'sɔːrʃɪəm; kən'sɔrʃəm/ n (pl -tia /-tɪə US: -ʃɪə; -ʃɪə/) temporary co-operation of a number of powers, companies, banks, etc for a common purpose: (若干强国、大公司、银行等为一共同目的而临时合作组成的)国际财团; 国际银行团; 协会; 联营; 协营: the ~ of Upper Clyde shipbuilders. 上克莱德造船公司协营.

con·spec·tus /kən'spektəs; kən'spektəs/ n (pl ~es /-ɪz; -ɪz/) general view of a subject, scene, etc; synopsis (eg in the form of tables). (对于某一学科, 地点等的)概览; 概要; 大纲(如列成图表者).

con·spicu·ous /kən'spɪkjuəs; kən'spɪkjuəs/ adj easily seen; attracting attention; remarkable: 显而易见的; 显著的; 引人注目的; 值得注意的; 特出的; 出众的: ~ for his bravery. 以其英勇而受人注意. Traffic signs

should be ~. 交通标志应该显明. **make oneself** ~, attract attention by unusual behaviour; wearing unusual clothes, etc. 借不寻常的行为、穿着不寻常的衣服等而引人注目; 标新立异出风头. ~·**ly** adv ~·**ness** n

con·spir·acy /kən'spɪrəsɪ; kən'spɪrəsɪ/ n [U] act of conspiring; [C] (pl -cies) plan made by conspiring: 阴谋; 共谋; 谋反: a ~ to overthrow the Government; 推翻政府的阴谋; a ~ of silence, an agreement not to talk publicly about sth. 缄默协定(同意不公开讨论某事).

con·spire /kən'spaɪə(r); kən'spaɪr/ vi, vt 1 [VP2A, 3A, 4A] ~ (with)(against), make secret plans (with others, esp to do sth wrong): 阴谋; 密谋; 密商: ~ against the Government. 阴谋反对政府. His enemies ~d to ruin him. 他的仇人阴谋毁灭他. 2 [VP6A] plot: 阴谋; 密谋: ~ sb's ruin. 阴谋毁灭某人. 3 [VP4A] (of events) act together; combine: (指事件)合作; 联合; 凑合: events that ~d to bring about his downfall. 凑合起来使他垮台的各项事件. **con·spira·tor** /kən'spɪrətə(r); kən'spɪrətə/ n person who ~s. 阴谋者; 共谋者; 谋叛者. **con·spira·tor·ial** /kən,spɪrə'tɔːrɪəl; kən,spɪrə'tɔrɪəl/ adj of conspirators or a conspiracy: 阴谋(者)的; 共谋(者)的; 谋反(者)的: with a conspiratorial air. 带着一种密谋的神情.

con·stable /'kʌnstəbl US: 'kɒn-; 'kɑnstəbl/ n 1(GB) **(po'lice)** ~, policeman or policewoman of basic grade. (英)(等级最低之)警察; 女警. **Chief C~**, head of the police force of a county, etc. (郡等的)警察局长. **special** ~, person who acts as a ~ on special occasions or for special duty. (在特殊场合或负有特殊任务的)临时警察; 特种警察. 2 (hist) principal officer of a royal household; governor of a royal castle, etc. (史)宫廷长官; 皇家侍卫长; 皇家城堡等的总管. **con·sta·bu·lary** /kən'stæbjuləri US: -leri; kən'stæbjə,leri/ n (pl -ries) organized body of police ~s; police force. 警察队; 保安队.

con·stancy /'kɒnstənsɪ; 'kɑnstənsɪ/ n [U] quality of being firm, unchanging: 坚定不移; 恒久不变: ~ of purpose. 志向不变.

con·stant /'kɒnstənt; 'kɑnstənt/ adj 1 going on all the time; frequently recurring: 经常的; 永恒的; 屡见不断的: ~ complaints. 不断的抱怨. 2 firm; faithful; unchanging: 坚定的; 忠实的; 不变的: a ~ friend. 忠实的朋友. He has been ~ in his devotion to scientific studies. 他坚毅地致力于科学的研究. □ n (maths, phys) number or quantity that does not vary. (数学, 物理)常数; 恒量; 恒定. ~·**ly** adv continuously; frequently. 经常地; 不断地; 时常地.

con·stel·la·tion /,kɒnstə'leɪʃn; ,kɑnstə'leʃən/ n named group of fixed stars (eg the Great Bear); (fig) group. 业经命名的恒星群; 星座(如大熊星座); (喻)群体.

con·ster·na·tion /,kɒnstə'neɪʃn; ,kɑnstə'neʃən/ n [U] surprise and fear; dismay. 惊愕; 惊恐; 惊慌: filled with ~; 充满惊恐之情; looking back in ~. 惊愕地向后张望.

con·sti·pate /'kɒnstɪpeɪt; 'kɑnstə,pet/ vt [VP6A] cause constipation: 使便秘: to find some kinds of food constipating. 发现某些食物会引起便秘.

con·sti·pated /'kɒnstɪpeɪtɪd; 'kɑnstə,petɪd/ part adj having bowels that can be emptied infrequently or only with difficulty. 便秘的.

con·sti·pa·tion /,kɒnstɪ'peɪʃn; ,kɑnstə'peʃən/ n [U] difficult or infrequent emptying of the bowels. 便秘.

con·sti·tu·ency /kən'stɪtjuənsɪ; kən'stɪtjuənsɪ/ n (pl -cies) [C] (body of voters living in a) town or district that sends a representative to Parliament. 英国国会议员选区; 居于一选举区之议员的选民.

con·sti·tu·ent /kən'stɪtjuənt; kən'stɪtjuənt/ adj 1 having the power or right to make or alter a political constitution: 有权制定或修改宪法的: a ~ assembly. 立宪议会; 国民代表大会. 2 forming or helping to make a whole: 组成的; 构成的: a ~ part. 组成的成分. □ n 1

member of a constituency. 英国国会议员选举区之选民。 **2** component part: 成分; 组分; 组成物: *the ~s of happiness.* 幸福的要素。

con·sti·tute /'kɒnstɪtjuːt US: -tuːt; 'kɑnstə,tjut/ *vt* **1** [VP23] give (sb) authority to hold (a position, etc): 任命 (某人) 担任 (某项职位等): *They ~d him chief adviser.* 他们委任他为首席顾问。*What right have you to ~ yourself a judge of my conduct?* 你有何权自命为我的行为的评判人? **2** [VP6A] establish; give legal authority to (a committee, etc). 成立; 授合法之权与(委员会等)。 **3** [VP6A] make up (a whole); amount to; be the components of: 组成 (整体); 构成; 为…之成分: *Twelve months ~ a year.* 十二个月构成一年。*He is so ~d* (= His nature is such) *that he can accept unjust criticism without getting angry.* 他的性情天生如此, 能受不公正的批评而不动怒。

con·sti·tu·tion /,kɒnstɪ'tjuːʃn US: -'tuːʃn/ ,kɑnstə'tjuʃən/ *n* **1** [C] system of government; laws and principles according to which a state is governed: 政治制度; 宪法 (治理一国所依据的法规): *Great Britain has an unwritten ~; the United States has a written ~.* 英国的宪法是不成文的; 美国的宪法是成文的。 **2** [C] general physical structure and condition of a person's body: 体格; 体质: *Only people with strong ~s should climb in the Himalayas.* 只有体格强健的人才可以攀登喜马拉雅山。 **3** [C, U] general structure of a thing; act or manner of constituting: 物的一般构造; 组织; 任命、成立、授权或构成的行为或方式: *the ~ of the solar spectrum;* 太阳光谱的构成; *the ~ of one's mind and character.* 某人之心理和性格的素质。

con·sti·tu·tional /,kɒnstɪ'tjuːʃənl US: -'tuː-; ,kɑnstə'tjuʃənl/ *adj* **1** of a constitution(1): 宪法的; 立宪的: ~ *government;* 立宪政体; *a ~ ruler,* controlled or limited by a constitution (受宪法控制或限制的君主); ⇨ *reform.* 宪法修改。 ⇨ **absolute,** *autocratic* at **autocrat. 2** of a person's constitution (2): 体格的; 体质的: *a ~ weakness* 体格的虚弱。□ *n* (dated colloq) short walk for the health's sake: (过时口语) 为健康 (运动) 而散步: *go for/take a ~.* 散散步; 作散步健行。~·**ly** /-ʃənlɪ; -ʃənlɪ/ *adv* ~·**ism** /-'iz/ *n* [U] (belief in) ~ government or ~ principles. 立宪政体; 立宪主义。 ~·**ist** *n* supporter of ~ principles. 立宪主义者。 ~·**ize** /-ʃənlaɪz; -ʃənlaɪz/ *vt* make ~. 使文施立宪政体。

con·sti·tut·ive /kən'stɪtjutɪv; 'kɑnstə,tjutɪv/ *adj* constructive, formative; essential. 构成的; 组成的; 基本的; 必要的。

con·strain /kən'streɪn; kən'stren/ *vt* [VP6A, 17] make (sb) do sth by using force or strong persuasion; (of conscience, inner forces) compel: 强迫 (某人) 做某事; (指良心、内在力量) 驱使: *I feel ~ed to write and ask for your forgiveness.* 我不得不写信请你原谅。 ~**ed** *part adj* (of voice, manner, etc) forced; uneasy; unnatural. (指声音、态度等) 勉强的; 不自然的; 做作的。 ~·**ed·ly** /-ɪdlɪ; -ɪdlɪ/ *adv*

con·straint /kən'streɪnt; kən'strent/ *n* [U] constraining or being constrained: 强迫; 逼迫; 迫使; 勉强; 拘束: *to act under ~,* because one is forced to do so; 受逼迫而行动; *to feel/show ~ in a person's presence,* to hold back one's natural feelings. 在某人面前感觉 (表现) 拘束。

con·strict /kən'strɪkt; kən'strɪkt/ *vt* [VP6A] make tight or smaller; cause (a vein or muscle) to become tight or narrow: 使紧或变小; 使 (静脉或肌肉) 收缩; 压缩; 收紧; (fig) (喻) a ~*ed outlook,* one that is narrow or limited. 狭隘的看法。**con·stric·tion** /kən'strɪkʃən; kən'strɪkʃən/ *n* [U] ~ing; [C] feeling of being ~ed: 压紧; 收缩; 压迫的感觉: *a ~ in the chest;* 胸部感到压迫; [C] sth that ~s. 能压紧或收缩之物。

con·struct /kən'strʌkt; kən'strʌkt/ *vt* [VP6A] build; put or fit together: 建筑; 建造; 建立; 构筑: ~ *a factory/an aircraft/a sentence/a theory;* 建工厂 (造飞机; 造句子; 建立理论) *a well-~ed novel.* 结构很完善

的小说。~**or** /-tə(r); -tɚ/ *n* person who ~s things: 建筑者; 建造者: *motor-car body ~ors.* 车体承造商。

con·struc·tion /kən'strʌkʃn; kən'strʌkʃən/ *n* **1** [U] act or manner of constructing; being constructed: 施工; 构筑; 修筑; 建造: *the ~ of new roads.* 新道路的修筑。*The new railway is still under ~/in the course of ~.* 新的铁路尚在修筑中。*The new factory is of very solid ~.* 那新工厂造得很坚固。 **2** [C] sth constructed; structure; building. 建筑物; 构造物。 **3** [U] meaning; sense in which words, statements, acts, etc are taken: 意义; (个人对于词、句、行为等的) 解释: *Please do not put a wrong ~ on his action,* misunderstand its purpose. 请不要误会他的行动的用意。*The sentence does not bear such a ~,* cannot be understood in that way. 这句话并不含有那样的意思 (不能那样解释)。⇨**construe. 4** [C] arrangement and relationships of words in a sentence: 词在句中的安排及词与词之间的关系; 句法结构: *This dictionary gives the meanings of words and also illustrates their ~s.* 本词典解释词义, 并且举例说明词在句中的构造法。

con·struc·tive /kən'strʌktɪv; kən'strʌktɪv/ *adj* helping to construct; giving helpful suggestions: 建设性的; 有裨益的; 积极的: ~ *criticism/proposals.* 建设性的批评 (提议)。 ~·**ly** *adv*

con·strue /kən'struː; kən'stru/ *vt, vi* **1** [VP6A, 2A] translate or explain the meaning of words, sentences, acts; 译注; 解释; 铨释 (词、句、行为): ~ *a passage from Homer.* 注释荷马史诗中的一段文字。*His remarks were wrongly ~d,* were misunderstood. 他的话被误解了。 **2** [VP6A] analyse (a sentence); combine (words with words) grammatically. 分析 (句子); 按语法连 (字) 造句。 **3** [VP2A] be capable of being analysed: 可被分析: *This sentence won't ~.* 这个句子不可分析。

con·sub·stan·ti·ation /,kɒnsəb,stænʃɪ'eɪʃn; ,kɑnsəb,stænʃɪ'eʃən/ *n* [U] doctrine that the body and blood of Christ co-exist with the bread and wine in the Eucharist. 合体共在论 (基督之圣体和圣血与圣餐中之面包和葡萄酒共在的教义)。

con·sul /'kɒnsl; 'kɑnsl/ *n* **1** State's agent living in a foreign town to help and protect his countrymen there. (派驻外国协助和保护侨民的) 领事。 **2** (in ancient Rome) either of the two Heads of the State before Rome became an Empire. (古罗马变成帝国之前的) 两执政官之一。 **3** any one of the three chief magistrates of the French Republic, 1799—1804. 一七九五至一八〇四年法兰西共和国三个主要执政官之一。 ~·**ship** /-ʃɪp; -ʃɪp/ *n* position of a ~; period of time during which a ~ holds his position. 领事或执政官的职位或任期。

con·su·lar /'kɒnsjulə(r) US: -səl-; 'kɑnslə/ *adj* of a consul or his work. 领事的; 执政官的; 领事或执政官的职务的。

con·su·late /'kɒnsjulət US: -səl-; 'kɑnslɪt/ *n* consul's position; offices of a consul(1); period of consular government in France. 领事或执政官的职位; 领事馆; 法国的执政统治时期。

con·sult /kən'sʌlt; kən'sʌlt/ *vt, vi* **1** [VP6A, 14] go to a person, a book, etc for information, advice, opinion, etc: 向(人)求教; 查阅 (书籍等) 以便寻得资料、参考意见等: *to ~ one's lawyer/a map/the dictionary;* 就教律师 (查阅地图; 查字典); *a ~ing engineer,* one with special knowledge of one or more branches of engineering. 工程顾问; 顾问工程师 (具有一门或数门工程方面之特殊知识)。 **2** [VP6A] (old use; *consider* is now preferred) take into consideration or account: (旧用法; 今人喜用 consider) 考虑; 顾及: *We must ~ his convenience,* cause him as little inconvenience as possible. 我们必须顾及他的方便。 **3** [VP3A] ~ *with,* discuss with: 商量; 商议: ~ *with one's partners.* 与合伙人商量。

con·sul·tant /kən'sʌltənt; kən'sʌltənt/ *n* person who gives expert advice (eg in medicine, surgery, business): 提供专家意见的人 (如有关医药、外科、商业等方面者): 顾问: (attrib) (用作定语) *a ~ surgeon;* 外科顾问医师 (不应

诊只提供专家意见的外科医生); *a firm of* ~*s.* 顾问公司 (供应专家作顾问的公司)。

con·sul·ta·tion /ˌkɒnsl'teɪʃn; ˌkɑnslˈteʃən/ *n* **1** [U] consulting or being consulted: 请教；就教；咨询；商议: *in* ~ *with the director.* 与主任商议。 **2** [C] meeting for consulting: 商量的会议；协议会: *The doctors held a* ~ *to decide whether an operation was necessary.* 医生们会诊以决定是否需要动手术。

con·sult·ative /kənˈsʌltətɪv; kənˈsʌltətɪv/ *adj* of for the purpose of, consulting: 供咨询的；顾问的: *a* ~ *committee.* 顾问委员会。

con·sume /kənˈsjuːm US: -ˈsuːm; kənˈsum/ *vt, vi* **1** [VP6A] eat or drink. 食；饮。 **2** [VP6A] use up; get to the end of; destroy by fire or wastefulness: 用尽；耗尽；被火或因浪费而毁灭；荡尽: ~ *all one's energies.* 耗尽其所有的精力。*The flames quickly* ~*d the wooden huts.* 火焰很快地吞灭了那些简陋的木屋。*He soon* ~*d his fortune,* spent the money wastefully. 他不久就把他的财产挥霍殆尽。*He was* ~*d* (=filled) *with envy/hatred/ greed.* 他心中充满着嫉妒 (仇恨, 贪婪)。*This is time-consuming work,* work that takes up a lot of time. 这是一项费时的工作。 **3** ~ *away,* waste away. 丧失体力与健康；消瘦；憔悴。**con·sum·ing** *part adj* possessing or dominating: 占有的；控制的；支配的: *consuming ambition.* 占有的野心；支配的野心。

con·sumer /kənˈsjuːmə(r) US: -ˈsuː-; kənˈsumə/ *n* (opp to *producer*) person who uses goods. (为 producer 之反义词)消费者；用户。~ **goods,** those which directly satisfy human needs and desires (eg food and clothing) (opp to *capital goods,* eg factory equipment). 消费品(直接满足人类需要及欲望的货品, 如食品和衣服, 与 capital goods 相对, 如工厂设备): 生活资料。~ **research,** market research, ⇨ **market¹(4).** 消费者调查；市场调查。~ **sales resistance,** unwillingness of people to buy a product. 消费者销货阻力；消费抵制。~**·ism** /-ɪzəm/ -ɪzəm/ *n* [U] protection of ~*s'* interests. 消费者利益之保护。

con·sum·mate¹ /kənˈsʌmət; kənˈsʌmɪt/ *adj* supremely skilled; perfect: 高度技巧的；完全的；完美的: ~ *skill/taste.* 高超的技术(鉴赏力)。

con·sum·mate² /ˈkɒnsəmeɪt; ˈkɑnsəˌmet/ *vt* [VP 6A] **1** accomplish; make perfect: 完成；使圆满；使完善: *Her happiness was* ~*d when her father took her to Paris.* 当她父亲带她到巴黎时，她的快乐达到了极点。 **2** make complete (esp marriage by sexual intercourse). 使完全。(尤指)完婚；圆房。

con·sum·ma·tion /ˌkɒnsəˈmeɪʃn; ˌkɑnsəˈmeʃən/ *n* [C, U] action or point of completing, perfecting, or fulfilling: 完成；圆满成功；成就: *the* ~ *of a life's work/ one's ambitions/a marriage.* 毕生事业(志愿, 婚姻)的完成。

con·sump·tion /kənˈsʌmpʃn; kənˈsʌmpʃən/ *n* [U] **1** using up, consuming (of food, energy, materials, etc); the quantity consumed: 消费(指食物、精力、物资等)；消耗量: *The* ~ *of beer did not go down when the tax was raised.* 啤酒税增高时, 啤酒的消耗量并未降低。 **2**(popular name for) pulmonary tuberculosis. 痨病 (肺结核的通俗名称)；肺病。

con·sump·tive /kənˈsʌmptɪv; kənˈsʌmptɪv/ *adj* suffering from, having a tendency to, consumption(2). 患肺病的；有肺病之倾向的。□ *n* person. 肺病患者。

con·tact /ˈkɒntækt; ˈkɑntækt/ *n* **1** [U] (state of) touching or communication; (process of) coming together, esp in: 接触；传达；交换意见；接触或传达的状态；接触的过程: (尤用于): **be in/out of** ~ (**with**)**; come/ bring into** ~ **(with):**(与...)在接触中(停止接触)；接触及(使接触到)；(使)与...交往: *Our troops are in* ~ *with the enemy.* 我们的部队已与敌军接触。*The opposing forces are now in/out of* ~ *(with each other).* 敌对的两军现正接触中(现已停止接触)。*A steel cable came into* ~ *with an electric power line.* 一条钢索触到了电线。*We can learn much by being brought into* ~ *with other minds/*

opposing opinions, etc. 由于与他人交换意见 (听取反对意见等)，我们可以学到很 多东西。**make** ~ **(with),** come into ~ (with), esp after searching, striving, etc: (尤指经过搜寻、努力等之后, 与...)接触；接近；交往: *I finally made* ~ *with him in Paris.* 我终于在巴黎与他联络上了。 *We never really succeeded in making* ~. 我们从未真正地结识。 *They made* ~ *by radio / made radio* ~ *with headquarters.* 他们用无线电与总部互通信息 (与总部作无线电接触)。**make/break** ~, complete / interrupt an electric circuit. 接通 (阻断) 电路。**'**~ **lens,** one of thin plastic material made to fit closely over and in ~ with the eyeball to improve vision. 隐形眼镜 (薄的塑胶制成的镜片, 附在眼球上, 与眼球接触, 借以增进视力)。 **2** [C] meeting with a person; person one has met or will meet: 与人接触或会晤；所接触或将会晤的人: *He made many useful social* ~*s while he was in Canada,* met people who could be useful to him. 他在加拿大期间, 曾结识了许多对他有益的社会人士。*Do you have any* ~*s in Rangoon?* 你在仰光有要会晤的人吗？ **3** [C] connection (for electric current); device for effecting this. (电流的)接触；接触器。 **4** [C] (med) person recently exposed to a contagious disease. (医) 接触者 (最近与传染病接触过的人)。□ *vt* [VP6A] get in ~ with (sb); reach (sb) (by message, telephone, etc): 与(某人)接触；与(某人)会晤；(以讯息、电话等)与(某人)联系: *Where can I* ~ *Jeff's wife?* 我在何处可以会晤杰夫的太太？

con·tagion /kənˈteɪdʒən; kənˈtedʒən/ *n* [U] the spreading of disease by contact or close association; [C] disease that can be spread by contact;(fig)the spreading of ideas, false rumours, feelings, etc; [C] influence, etc that spreads: (疾病的)接触传染；触染；接触传染病(可借接触而传布的疾病)；触染病；(喻)(思想、谣言、情绪等的)传布；蔓延；散播的影响力等: *A* ~ *of fear swept through the crowd.* 一种恐惧的感觉侵袭群众。

con·tagious /kənˈteɪdʒəs; kənˈtedʒəs/ *adj* **1** (of disease) spreading by contact: (指疾病)传染性的；由接触而传染的；触染的: *Scarlet fever is* ~. 猩红热是传染性的。 **2** (of a person) in such a condition that he may spread disease. (指人) 患传染病的；可能传染疾病的。 **3** (fig)spreading easily by example: (喻)容易引起同感的；有感染性的: ~ *laughter / enthusiasm.* 使人感觉之笑声 (能激起热心之热心)；有感染力的笑声 (热情)。*Yawning is* ~. 打呵欠是有感染性的。~**·ly** *adv*

con·tain /kənˈteɪn/ *vt* [VP6A] (not in the progressive tenses) (不用进行时) **1** have or hold within itself: 包含；含有: *The atlas* ~*s forty maps, including three of Great Britain.* 这地图集含有四幅地图, 包括三幅英国地图在内。*Whisky* ~*s a large percentage of alcohol.* 威士忌酒含有酒精的百分比甚高。 **2** be equal to: 等于: *A gallon* ~*s eight pints.* 一加仑等于八品脱。 **3** be capable of holding: 能容纳；可盛；可装: *How much does this bottle* ~? 这瓶子能装多少？ **4** keep feelings, enemy forces, etc under control, within limits: 控制 (情绪,敌军等)；围堵；牵制: *Can't you* ~ *your enthusiasm?* 你不能控制你的热情吗？ *He couldn't* ~ *himself for joy,* was so happy that his feelings burst out. 他抑制不住他的欢乐之情。*He couldn't* ~ *his wine,* was sick, became drunk, etc. 他不能控制他的酒量(病了, 醉了等)。 *Has the cholera outbreak been* ~*ed,* prevented from spreading? 霍乱的发生已经被控制住 (不再蔓延) 了吗？ **5** (geom) form the boundary of: (几何)构成...的边界；围；夹: *The angle* ~*ed by the lines AB and AC in the triangle ABC is a right angle.* 在三角形 *ABC* 中为 *AB* 和 *AC* 两边所夹的角是直角。 **6** (maths) be divisible by, without a remainder: (数学)可除尽；可整除: 除 12 =3, 4 和 6. 12 可被 2, 3, 4 和 6 除尽。~**·er** *n* **1** box, bottle, etc designed to ~ sth. 容器(箱、匣、瓶等)。 **2** large metal box or other

scaled ~er for transport of goods by road, rail, sea or air: 集装箱 (公路、铁路、海上或空中货运用的大型金属箱或其他密闭式的容器): '~er crane, large crane mounted on a gantry, used on quays, etc to move ~ers(2). 集装箱起重机 (码头等处装于桥形台架上用以装卸集装箱的大型起重机). '~er train / liner, one designed such ~ers; 集装箱列车 (货运班机);' ~er traffic; 集装箱交通; '~er depot, eg where ~ers are loaded and unloaded. 集装箱站 (装卸集装箱的地点). ~·ment n [U] policy of preventing a State from extending its sphere of influence. (阻止一国家延伸其势力范围的)封锁政策; 遏制政策。

con·tami·nate /kən'tæmɪnet; kən'tæmə,net/ vt [VP6A] make dirty, impure or diseased (by touching, or adding sth impure): (由于接触或加入污物而)染污; 弄脏; 污损。(例如为毒气或放射性物质所)染污的衣服。 *Flies ~ food.* 苍蝇会染污食物。*His morals have been ~d by bad companions.* 他的品行已为不良的友伴所败坏。

con·tami·na·tion /kən,tæmɪ'neɪʃn; kən,tæmə'neʃən/ n 1 [U] contaminating or being contaminated: 染污; 弄脏; 沾染; 污损: ~ of the water supply. 给水之污染。 2 [C] that which contaminates. 污秽之物; 可染污他物之物。

con·temn /kən'tem; kən'tɛm/ vt [VP6A] (liter) despise; disregard. (文)轻侮; 蔑视。

con·tem·plate /'kɒntempleɪt; 'kɑntəm,plet/ vt, vi 2 [VP6A] look at (with the eyes, or in the mind): 注视; 熟视; 沉思: *She stood contemplating her figure / herself in the mirror.* 她站着注视她(自己)镜中的身影。 2 [VP6A, C, 19C] have in view as a purpose, intention or possibility: 打算 (作为一种目的, 意愿或可能): *She was contemplating a visit to London.* 她正打算赴伦敦观光。 *I hope your mother does not ~ coming to stay with us.* 我希望你的母亲不打算来与我们同住。 *I do not ~ any opposition from him,* do not think this is likely or possible. 我猜他不至于反对。3 [VP2A, 6A] meditate (esp as a religious practice). 冥思(尤指宗教习惯上的)。

con·tem·pla·tion /,kɒntem'pleɪʃn; ,kɑntəm-'pleʃən/ n [U] contemplating; deep thought; intention; expectation: 注视; 默察; 沉思; 打算; 希望; 期待: *He sat there deep in ~.* 他坐在那儿沉思默想。

con·tem·pla·tive /kən'templətɪv; 'kɑntəm,pletɪv/ adj thoughtful; fond of contemplation; given up to religious contemplation. 多思想的; 好深思的; 专注于宗教思想的。

con·tem·por·aneous /kən,tempə'reɪnɪəs; kən-,tɛmpə'renɪəs/ adj ~ (with), originating, existing, happening, during the same period of time: 起源、存在或发生于同一时期的; 同期的; 同时代的: ~ events. 同时代的事件。 ~·ly adv

con·tem·por·ary /kən'tempərərɪ US: -ərerɪ; kən-'tɛmpə,rɛrɪ/ adj of the time or period to which reference is being made; belonging to the same time: 同时的; 同时代的; 属于同一时期的: *a ~ record of events,* one made by persons living at that time; 该时代的人对该时代的事所作的记载; *furniture in ~ style,* of the present time (contrasted with period(2) furniture). 目前流行的式样的家具(与 period furniture 相对)。 *Dickens was ~ with Thackeray.* 狄更斯与萨克雷属于同一时代。 □ n (pl -ries) person ~ with another: 同时的人; 同时代的人: *Jack and I were contemporaries at college.* 杰克与我同时读大学。

con·tempt /kən'tempt; kən'tɛmpt/ n [U] 1 condition of being looked down upon or despised: 被轻视; 被蔑视; 被鄙视: *to fall into ~ by foolish or bad behaviour.* 由于愚昧或不良的行为而被鄙视。 *Such behaviour will bring you into ~.* 这种行为将使你遭受鄙视。 *A man who is cruel to his children should be held in ~.* 虐待自己孩子的人应受鄙视。 2 mental attitude of despising: 轻视;

蔑视; 鄙视: *We feel ~ for liars.* 我们对于说谎者有鄙视的心理。 *beneath ~:* Such an accusation is beneath ~, not worth despising (because it is so ridiculous, etc). 这种控告不值得一顾。 3 disregard or disrespect; total disregard: 藐视; 不尊敬; 完全不理: *in ~ of all rules and regulations.* 藐视一切规章。 *He rushed forward in ~ of danger.* 他完全不顾危险地往前冲。 *He showed his ~ of death by rushing at the enemy.* 他冲向敌人表现出不怕死的精神。 *Familiarity breeds ~,* (prov) (谚) ⇨ familiarity(1). ,~ of 'court, disobedience to an order made by a court, disrespect shown to a judge. 不服从法庭的命令; 轻蔑法官; 藐视法庭。

con·tempt·ible /kən'temptəbl; kən'tɛmptəbl/ adj deserving or provoking contempt. 可鄙的; 可轻蔑的。

con·temptu·ous /kən'temptʃʊəs; kən'tɛmptʃʊəs/ adj showing contempt: 显示轻蔑的: ~ of public opinion. 藐视舆论。 ~·ly adv

con·tend /kən'tend; kən'tɛnd/ vi, vt 1 [VP3A] ~ with / against / for, struggle, be in rivalry or competition: 奋斗; 斗争; 竞争: ~ing with difficulties; 与困苦奋斗; ~ing for a prize; 争取奖品; ~ing passions, strong feelings of different kinds (eg pity, a sense of justice) that make decision difficult. 使人难做决定的矛盾的心情(如怜悯与正义感)。 2 [VP9] argue, assert: 主张; 力辩; 断言: ~ that the universe is expanding. 断言宇宙正在扩展中。 ~·er n competitor, rival, eg one who challenges the holder of a boxing title. 竞争者; 敌手(如拳击卫冕赛的挑战者)。

con·tent¹ /kən'tent; kən'tɛnt/ adj (not used attrib; ⇨ contented below) (不用作定语; 参看下列 contented) 1 ~ (with), not wanting more; satisfied with what one has: 满足的; 满意的; 不再想要更多的: *Are you ~ with your present salary?* 你对于你现在的薪水感觉满意吗? *She is ~ with very little.* 她很容易满足。 2 ~ to do sth, willing or ready (to do sth): 愿意做某事: *I am ~ to remain where I am now.* 我愿意保持现状。 *I should be well ~* (= quite pleased) *to do so.* 我很高兴这样做。 □ n [U] condition of being satisfied: 满意的状态; 满足: *living in peace and ~.* 生活平静满足。 *to one's heart's ~,* to the extent that brings satisfaction. 心满意足; 尽情; 尽兴。 □ vt [VP6A, 14] ~ sb / oneself (with), make ~; satisfy: 使满意; 使满足: *There's no ~ing some people,* It's impossible to please or satisfy them. 欲使某些人满意是不可能的。 *As there's no butter we must ~ ourselves* (= be satisfied) *with dry bread.* 既然没有黄油, 我们只好吃干面包了。 ~ed adj satisfied; showing or feeling ~: 满意的; 显示或感到满意的: *with a ~ed look / smile.* 带满意的表情(微笑)。 ~·ed·ly adv ~·ment n [U] state of being ~. 满意; 满足。

con·tent² /'kɒntent; 'kɑntɛnt/ n 1 (pl) that which is contained in sth: (复)内容; 内部所有之物: *the ~s of a room / a book / a schoolboy's pockets, etc.* 房间内部的东西(书的内容; 学童衣袋里面的东西等)。 *table of ~s,* list of the matter in a book, periodical, etc. (书籍、杂志等的)目录; 目次。 2 (sing or pl; with sing v) the amount which a vessel will hold; capacity: (单或复)与单数动词连用)(容器的)容量; 容积: *the ~(s) of a barrel or cask.* 一桶的容积。 3 (sing) substance; essential meaning (of a book, speech, etc as opposed to its form): (单)(书籍、演说等的)内容; 要义(与其形式相对): *Do you approve of the ~ of the article / speech?* 你赞同此文(演说)的内容吗? 4 ~ (of sth), (sing; preceded by a measure) amount (of it): (单; 前有一名词)(该名词的)成分; 含量: *a high fat ~;* 高度脂肪含量; *the silver ~ of a coin,* 一硬币中银的成分; *the sugar ~ of milk.* 牛奶中糖的成分。

con·ten·tion /kən'tenʃn; kən'tɛnʃən/ n 1 [U] contending(2); quarrelling or disputing: 争辩; 争论: *This is not a time for ~.* 此时不是争论的时候。 ⇨ bone. 2 [C] argument used in contending: 争辩中所持的论点: *My ~ is that....* 我的论点是…。

con·ten·tious /kən'tenʃəs; kən'tɛnʃəs/ adj quarrelsome; likely to cause contention: 好争论的; 可能引起争

论的:*a ~ clause in a treaty.* 条约中可引起争论的条款。

con·ter·mi·nous /kɒnˈtɜːmɪnəs; kənˈtɜːmənəs/ *adj* = coterminous.

con·test /kənˈtest; kənˈtɛst/ *vt, vi* **1** [VP6A, 9] argue; debate; dispute 争辩; 争论; 辩论; 反驳: *~ a statement / point,* try to show that it is wrong; 反驳某陈述(论点); *~ sb's right / that sb has a right to do sth.* 对某人做某事之权表示异议。 **2** [VP3A] contend (1). 奋斗;斗争;竞争。 **3** [VP6A] fight or compete for; try to win: 竞争以夺取; 争取: *~ a seat in Parliament.* 争取国会席次。 *The enemy ~ed every inch of the ground,* fought with determination not to retreat. 敌人寸土必争。 □ *n* /ˈkɒntest; ˈkɒntɛst/ [C] struggle; fight; competition: 斗争;竞争;比赛: *a keen ~ for the prize;* 对于奖品之激烈的竞争; *a ~ of skill;* 技能竞赛; *a 'speed ~;* 速度竞赛; (boxing) (拳击)*a three-round feather-weight ~.* 三回合之次轻级比赛。 ▷ **ant** /kənˈtestənt; kənˈtɛstənt/ *n* one who ~s. 奋斗者;竞争者;比赛者。

con·text /ˈkɒntekst; ˈkɑrtɛkst/ *n* [C, U] **1** what comes before and after a word, phrase, statement, etc helping to fix the meaning: (词、短语、句子等的前后可帮助确定其意义的)上下文: *Can't you guess the meaning of the word from the ~?* 你不能从上下文猜出此词的意义吗? *Don't quote my words out of ~,* eg so as to give a false impression of what I mean. 别把我所说的话断章取义(曲解我的意思)。 **2** circumstances in which an event occurs. (某一事件发生的)环境;背景。 **con·tex·tual** /kɒnˈtekstʃʊəl; kənˈtɛkstʃʊəl/ *adj* according to the ~. 依照上下文的;由上下文而定的。

con·ti·guity /ˌkɒntɪˈgjuːətɪ; ˌkɑntɪˈgjuətɪ/ *n* [U] the state of being contiguous. 接触;相邻;近近。

con·tigu·ous /kənˈtɪgjʊəs; kənˈtɪgjʊəs/ *adj ~ to,* (formal) touching; neighbouring; near. (正式用语)接触的;相邻的;接近的。 ~·**ly** *adv*

con·ti·nence /ˈkɒntɪnəns; ˈkɑntənəns/ *n* [U] self-control; self-restraint (esp of passions and desires). 自制;自律;节制(尤指激情及欲望)。

con·ti·nent [1] /ˈkɒntɪnənt; ˈkɑntənənt/ *n* one of the main land masses (Europe, Asia, Africa, etc). (欧、亚、非等)大洲之一;洲;大陆。 **the C~,** (as used by people in GB) the mainland of Europe. (英国人所指的)欧洲大陆。 **con·ti·nen·tal** /ˌkɒntɪˈnentl; ˌkɑntəˈnɛntl/ *adj* **1** belonging to, typical of, a ~: 属于大陆的;大陆性的: *a ~al climate.* 大陆性气候。 **2** of the mainland of Europe: 欧洲大陆的: *~al wars / alliances.* 欧洲大陆的战争(联盟)。 ~**al breakfast,** one of coffee and bread only. 仅含咖啡和面包的早餐。 ~**al Sunday,** as in Europe (with wider freedom for theatrical and other entertainments, sport, etc than formerly in GB). 欧洲大陆式的星期日(人们在享受文艺表演、娱乐活动方面比从前在英国国内享有较广泛的自由)。 □ *n* inhabitant of the mainland of Europe. 欧洲大陆人。

con·ti·nent [2] /ˈkɒntɪnənt; ˈkɑntənənt/ *adj* (formal) self-controlled; having control of one's feelings and (esp sexual) desires; (med) able to retain excretion voluntarily. (正式用语)自制的;自律的(指守制情感与欲望,尤指性欲);禁欲的;(医)能自动抑制排泄物的。

con·tin·gency /kənˈtɪndʒənsɪ; kənˈtɪndʒənsɪ/ *n* [U] uncertainty of occurrence; [C] (*pl -cies*) uncertain event; event that happens by chance; sth that may happen if sth else happens: 偶发性;偶发性事;偶发事件;意外事件;偶然事故;可能附带发生之事: *to be prepared for all contingencies;* 准备应付一切偶发事件; *a result that depends upon contingencies;* 依赖临时情形方可决定的结果; (attrib) (用作定语) ~ *arrangements / plans.* 为(预防发生)临时事故而作的安排(计划)。

con·tin·gent [1] /kənˈtɪndʒənt; kənˈtɪndʒənt/ *adj* **1** uncertain; accidental: 偶然的; 意外的; 偶发的: *a ~ advantage.* 偶然的获益。 **2** ~ **upon,** dependent upon (sth that may or may not happen). 视(可能发生或可能不发生之某事)而定的; 视当时情形而定的; 不一定的, 靠不住的。

con·tin·gent [2] /kənˈtɪndʒənt; kənˈtɪndʒənt/ *n* [C] body of troops, number of ships, lent or supplied to form part of a larger force; group of persons forming part of a larger group. (借调或派遣加入大军的)分遣队; 分遣舰队,构成较大集团之一部分的一批人。

con·tin·ual /kənˈtɪnjʊəl; kənˈtɪnjʊəl/ *adj* going on all the time without stopping, or with only short breaks: 连续不断的(或仅有短暂之间歇的); 不停的: *Aren't you tired of this ~ rain?* 你对于这不停的雨不觉得厌烦吗? ~·**ly** *adv* again and again; without stopping. 屡次地; 再三地; 不断地。

con·tin·uance /kənˈtɪnjʊəns; kənˈtɪnjʊəns/ *n* (*sing* only) (仅用单数) **1** time for which sth continues; duration (the more usu word): 继续的期间; 持续时间(duration 为较常用词): *during the ~ of the war.* 在战争持续期间。 **2** remaining; staying: 停留; 保持; 持续: *a ~ of prosperity.* 繁荣的持续。

con·tinu·ation /kənˌtɪnjʊˈeɪʃn; kənˌtɪnjʊˈeʃən/ *n* ~ (*of*), **1** [U] continuing; starting again after a stop: 继续; 连续; (停一段时间后的)再继续: *C~ of study after the holidays was difficult at first.* 假期过后再继续读书在起初是困难的。 **2** [C] part, etc by which sth is continued: 连续的部分: *The May number of the magazine will contain a ~ of the story.* 本杂志五月号将刊载该故事的续篇。

con·tinue /kənˈtɪnjuː; kənˈtɪnju/ *vi, vt* **1** [VP2A, B, D, E, 6A, D, 7A] go farther; go on (being); go on (doing); stay at / in; remain at / in: 延伸; 延续; 继续; 仍旧: *The desert ~d as far as the eye could reach.* 沙漠向前延伸至视线的尽处。 *How far does this road ~?* 这条路全长多少? 通至何处? *I hope this wet weather will not ~.* 我希望这种雨天不会连续下去。 *He hopes to ~ at school for another year.* 他希望再继续求学一年。 *The weather ~d calm.* 天气仍然平静。 *He is to live with his parents after his marriage.* 他结婚后仍旧与其双亲同住。 *How long will you ~ working?* 你将继续工作多久? *You must ~ your study of French.* 你必须继续读你的法语。 **2** [VP6A, 2A] start again after stopping: (停顿后)再继续; 恢复: *The story will be ~d in next month's issue.* 这故事将于下月号续刊。 *'Well,' he ~d, 'when we arrived...'* '后来,' 他接着说, '当我们到达的时候...' **3** [VP14] retain (sb in office, etc): 使留任; 挽留(某人): *The Colonial Secretary was ~d in office.* 殖民大臣留任。

con·ti·nu·ity /ˌkɒntɪˈnjuːətɪ US: -ˈnuː-; ˌkɑntəˈnuətɪ/ *n* [U] **1** the state of being continuous: 连续; 继续; 连续性: *There is no ~ of subject in a dictionary.* 词典没有主题的连续性。 **2** (cinema, TV) scenario; arrangement of the parts of a story: (电影, 电视)脚本; 分景剧本; 电影或电视故事之各部分的排列: *Films and TV programmes are often made out of ~,* eg a scene in the middle may be filmed before a scene near the beginning. 电影或电视节目的拍摄常不按照先后的次序(例如中段的一景也许较在前段的一景先行拍摄)。 **3** connecting comments, announcements, etc, made between the parts of a broadcast programme. 广播节目各部分之间的插白; 节目说明。

con·tinu·ous /kənˈtɪnjʊəs; kənˈtɪnjʊəs/ *adj* going on without a break: 连续不断的; 不停歇的: *~ performance, 1.00 pm to 11.30 pm,* eg at a cinema. 连续表演; 循环表演: 下午一时至十一时三十分。 ▷ **tense, ⇨progressive** (1). ~·**ly** *adv*

con·tin·uum /kənˈtɪnjʊəm; kənˈtɪnjʊəm/ *n* (*pl -uums or -ua* /-ʊə; -ʊə/) **1** sth that is continuous. 连续之事物。 **2** graded sequence of differences. 分类差异序列; 族群相。 ▷ **cline.**

con·tort /kənˈtɔːt; kənˈtɔrt/ *vt* [VP6A, 14] force or twist out of the usual shape or appearance: 扭歪; 使扭曲: *使成奇形怪状: a face ~ed with pain;* 因痛苦而扭曲的面孔; (fig) (喻) *~ a word out of its ordinary meaning.* 曲解词义(不照其通常的意义解释)。

con·tor·tion /kənˈtɔːʃn; kənˈtɔrʃən/ *n* [U] contorting or being contorted (esp of the face or body);

[C] instance of this; contorted condition: 扭曲; 扭曲 (尤指使面部或身体变成异样); 扭歪或扭曲的状况: *the ~s of an acrobat.* 杂技演员所做的软功。**~·ist** /-fənɪst; -fənɪst/ *n* acrobat clever at contorting his body. 擅长软功的杂技演员。

con·tour /'kɒntʊə(r); 'kɑntur/ *n* [C] outline (of a coast, mountain range, etc); (on a map, design, etc) line separating differently coloured parts. (海岸、山脉等的) 轮廓; 周线; 围线; (地图、图案等) 各着色区域间的区分线。'**~ line**, line (on a map) showing all points at the same height above sea-level. (地图上表示所有海拔相同各点之) 等高线。'**~ map**, one with ~ lines at fixed intervals (eg of 25 metres). 等高线地图 (按固定间隔, 如 25 米, 以等高线绘出者)。'**~ ploughing**, ploughing in which furrows follow ~ lines (on a hillside, etc) to prevent soil erosion. 循等高线耕犁法 (用于山坡上等处, 以防雨水冲蚀土壤)。□ *vt* [VP6A] mark with ~ lines; make(a road) round the ~ of a hill. 绘以等高线; 以等高线标明; 顺着山之起伏开辟 (道路)。

contra- /'kɒntrə-; 'kɑntrə-/ *pref* against. 反对。

contra·band /'kɒntrəbænd; 'kɑntrə,bænd/ *n* [U] bringing into, taking out of, a country goods contrary to the law; (trade in) goods so brought in or taken out. 走私 (将货物违法的运入或运出一国); (买卖) 私货; 违禁品。**~ of war**, goods (eg ammunition) supplied by neutral countries to countries that are at war, which can be seized by any of the countries at war. 战时违禁品 (中立国运往交战国并可由任一交战国没收的禁运品, 如军火)。(attrib)(用作定语) **~ goods**; 私货; 禁运品; *trade.* 私货之买卖; 走私。

contra·bass /'kɒntrəbeɪs; 'kɑntrə,bes/ *n* =**double-bass.**

contra·cep·tion /,kɒntrə'sepʃn; ,kɑntrə'sepʃən/ *n* [U] practice, method, of preventing or planning conception(2). 避孕; 避孕法; 计划生育。**contra·cep·tive** /,kɒntrə'septɪv; ,kɑntrə'septɪv/ *n* [C] device or drug intended to prevent conception (2). 避孕器; 避孕药; 避孕剂。□ *adj* preventing conception: 避孕的: *contraceptive pills/devices.* 避孕丸(器)。

con·tract¹ /'kɒntrækt; 'kɑntrækt/ *n* 1 [C] binding agreement (between persons, groups, states); agreement to supply goods, do work, etc at a fixed price. (个人、团体、国家间的) 合约; 合同; (按固定价格供应货物或做工的) 契约。**enter into / make a ~ (with sb) (for sth)**, make such an agreement. (与某人) (为某事) 订立合约。**exchange ~s**, eg for the purchase of a house. (如购买房屋成交时之) 交换合约。**sign a ~**, eg for the sale of land or buildings. 签订合约 (如房地产买卖)。[U] (phrases in which no article is used): (不用冠词之短语): **bind oneself by ~**; 立约保证; **work to be done by private ~**; 需包给私人做的工作; **work on ~**; 做包工; **breach of ~**; 违约; **conditions of ~**; 合约的条件; (attrib use) (用作定语) **~ price / date**, price, date, agreed to. 合约价格 (日期)。2 **'~ 'bridge**, kind of bridge² in which only tricks bid¹(6) and won count towards game¹(4). 合约桥牌 (只有所叫并赢得的墩数才计入每局所获得的分数)。

con·tract² /kən'trækt; kən'trækt/ *vt, vi* 1 [VP6A, 14, 4A] **~ (with)(for)**, make a contract or agreement: (与某人) (为某事或做某事而) 订立合约; 订契约; 承包; 承建; 承购; **~ a marriage**; 缔结婚姻; 订结婚约; **~ to build a bridge**; 立约承建桥梁; **~ with a firm for 1000 tons of cement**; 向某公司立约承购一千吨水泥; **~ an alliance with another country.** 与另一国成立联盟。[VP2C] **~ out (of)**, withdraw from an agreement: 废弃合约的条件: **~ out of an agreement / alliance.** 废弃合约(联盟条约); 退出。2[VP6A] **~ debts**, become liable for them. 负债。3 [VP6A] catch (an illness); form; acquire (eg bad habits). 染患 (疾病); 形成; 获得; 染上 (恶习等)。**~or** /-tə(r); -ər/ *n* person, company, firm, that enters into ~s: 立契约的人或商店: 包工; 承包商: *engineering ~ors*; 工程承包商; 营造商; *army ~ors.* 军需品承包商。

con·trac·tual /kən'træktʃʊəl; kən'træktʃʊəl/ *adj* or (the nature of) a ~. 契约(性质)的。

con·tract³ /kən'trækt; kən'trækt/ *vt, vi* [VP6A, 14, 2A, C] 1 make or become smaller or shorter: 收缩; 缩小; 缩短: *Metals ~ as they become cool.* 金属冷则收缩。'*I will ~ed to 'I'll'.* I will 缩写成为 I'll。2 make or become tighter or narrower: 缩紧; 缩窄: *to ~ a muscle*: 收缩肌肉; *to ~ the brows / forehead.* 皱眉头 (前额)。*The valley ~s as one goes up it.* 当人循山谷上行时, 山谷渐狭。**~·ible** *adj* that can be ~ed. 可收缩的; 可缩小的。**con·trac·tile** /kən'træktaɪl US: -tl; kən'træktl/ *adj* that can ~ or be ~ed: 可收缩的: *~ile wings*, eg of an insect, that can be folded over the body. (昆虫等) 可收折于背上的翅翼。

con·trac·tion /kən'trækʃn; kən'trækʃən/ *n* 1 [U] contracting or being contracted: 收缩; 缩小: *the ~ of a muscle*; 肌肉的收缩; *the ~ of the mercury in a thermometer.* 水银在寒暑中中的收缩。2 [C] sth contracted; shortened form, as *can't* for *cannot.* 收缩之物; 缩写式 (如 can't 为 cannot 的缩写式)。

con·tra·dict /,kɒntrə'dɪkt; ,kɑntrə'dɪkt/ *vt* [VP6A] 1 deny the truth of (sth said or written); deny (the words of a person): 否定 (所说或所写之事物) 之真实性; 否定 (某人所说的话); 反驳; 驳斥: *to ~ a statement.* 反斥一项声明。*Don't ~ me.* 不要反驳我。2 (of facts, statements, etc) be contrary to: (指事实、陈述等) 与…相矛盾、相抵触、相反: *The reports ~ each other.* 这些报告互相矛盾。**con·tra·dic·tion** /,kɒntrə'dɪkʃn; ,kɑntrə'dɪkʃən/ *n* 1 [U] ~ing; [C] instance of this. 反驳; 驳斥。2 [U] absence of agreement. 不一致; 矛盾。**be in ~ion with, =~**; 否定…的真实性; 与…相矛盾: *Your statements today are in ~ion with (ie they ~) what you said yesterday.* 你今天的声明和你昨天所说的话互相矛盾。[C] instance of this. 否定的实例; 相矛盾的实例。*a ~ion in terms*, statement that includes words that ~ each other (eg *a generous miser*). 语词矛盾的说法 (在一陈述中使用互相矛盾之词, 如慷慨的守财奴)。**con·tra·dic·tory** /,kɒntrə'dɪktərɪ; ,kɑntrə'dɪktərɪ/ *adj* ~ing: 互相矛盾的: *~ory statements / reports.* 互相矛盾的陈述 (报告)。

contra·dis·tinc·tion /,kɒntrədɪ'stɪŋkʃn; ,kɑntrədɪ'stɪŋkʃən/ *n* (formal) distinction by contrast: (正式用语) 对比起来的不同; 对照的区别: *the crossing of the Atlantic by air in a few hours, in ~ to the longer journey by sea.* 乘飞机只要数小时即可横渡大西洋, 与乘船之漫长的航程不可同日而语。

contra·dis·tin·guish /,kɒntrədɪ'stɪŋwɪʃ; ,kɑntrə-dɪ'stɪŋwɪʃ/ *vt* [VP14] **~ from**, distinguish by contrast. 以对比的方式区别。

con·tralto /kən'træltəʊ; kən'trælto/ (*pl* **~s** -təʊz; -toz/) *n* lowest female voice; woman with, musical part to be sung by, such a voice. 女低音; 女低音歌唱家; 乐曲之女低音部份。

con·trap·tion /kən'træpʃn; kən'træpʃən/ *n* (colloq) strange-looking apparatus or device. (口) 奇异的器械或装置; 稀奇的玩意儿。

contra·pun·tal /,kɒntrə'pʌntl; ,kɑntrə'pʌntl/ *adj* of or in counterpoint. (音乐) 对位法的; 对位的。

contra·riety /,kɒntrə'raɪətɪ; ,kɑntrə'raɪətɪ/ *n* (formal) [U] opposition or antagonism (in nature, quality or action); [C] (*pl* **-ties**) sth that is inconsistent or contrary: (正式用语) (本质、性质或行为的) 相反; 对立; 不一致或相反的事物: *contrarieties in nature.* 本质相反的事物。

con·trari·wise /'kɒntrəraɪwaɪz; 'kɑntrərɪ,waɪz/ *adv* 1 on the contrary. 相反地。2 in the opposite way. 在相反的方面; 以相反的方式行之。3 /kɒn'treərɪwaɪz; kən-'trɛrɪwaɪz/perversely; in a manner showing opposition. 倔强地; 态度上表示反对地。

con·trary¹ /'kɒntrərɪ US: -treri; 'kɑntrɛrɪ/ *adj* 1 opposite in nature or tendency: (在性质或倾向上) 相反的: *'Hot' and 'cold' are ~ terms.* 热与冷系相反之词。

2 (of the wind and weather) unfavourable (for sailing): (指风向和天气)不利(于航行)的: *The ship was delayed by ~ winds.* 此船为逆风所阻而延误。**3** (/kən'trɛəri; kən-'trɛri/) obstinate; self-willed. 顽固的; 倔强的。**4 ~ to,** (compound *prep*) in opposition to; against; (复合介词)反对; 违反: *to act ~ to the rules;* 违规行事; *events that went ~ to my interests.* 与我不利的事件。*What you have done is ~ to the doctor's orders.* 你所做的与医生的指示相反。*The result was ~ to expectation.* 结果与期望相反。**con·trar·ily** /ˈkɒntrərəli US: -trɛrəli; ˈkɑntrɛrəli/ *adv* in a ~ manner. 相反地; 不利地; 固执地; 倔强地。**con·trari·ness** /-nɪs; -nɪs/ *n* being ~. 相反; 不利; 固执; 倔强。

con·trary[2] /ˈkɒntrəri US: -trɛri; ˈkɑntrɛri/ *n* (*pl* **-ries**) **1** [U] **the ~,** opposite: 反面; 反义词: *The ~ of 'wet' is 'dry'.* '湿'的反义词是'干'。**on the ~,** phrase used to make a denial or contradiction more emphatic: 相反地 (强调否定或反驳之词): *'You've nothing to do now, I suppose.' — 'On the ~, I have piles of work.'* '我想你现在没有事可做了。'——'恰好相反, 我有成堆的工作。' *to the ~,* to the opposite effect: 有相反的意思; 相反的(地): *I will come on Monday unless you write to the ~, telling me not to come.* 我将于星期一来, 除非你写信叫我不要来。*I shall continue to believe it until I get proof to the ~,* proof that it is not true. 在我未得到相反的证据之前, 我将继续相信它。**2** [C] **by contraries, (a)** ~ to expectation: 与预期相违: *Many things in our lives go by contraries.* 我们一生之中有很多事情与愿望相违。**(b)** by way of opposition: 表相反之意; 有相反之情形: *She said that dreams go by contraries,* eg that a dream about bad fortune may foretell good fortune. 她说梦境预兆相反的事(如梦见恶运可能预兆好运)。

con·trast[1] /kən'trɑːst US: -'træst; kən'træst/ *vt, vi* **1** [VP6A, 14] ~ **(with /and),** compare so that differences are made clear: 比较 (某物与另一物) 以明其相异之点; 对比; 比一比 (…与…): *C~ these imported goods with /and the domestic product.* 把这些进口货与国货比比看 (就知道它们的差别了)。*It is interesting to ~ the two speakers.* 把那两位演说者比一比, 真是有趣。**2** [VP2C, 3A] ~ **(with),** show a difference when compared: 比较起来显示出差别; 成对照: *His actions ~ sharply with his promises.* 他的言行相差太远(行动与许诺太不相符)。*His actions and his promises ~ sharply.* 他的言行相差太远。

con·trast[2] /ˈkɒntrɑːst US: -træst; ˈkɑntræst/ *n* **1** [U] the act of contrasting: 比较; 对比; 对照: *C~ may make something appear more beautiful than it is when seen alone.* 对比可使某物显得比单独看时更美。**2 ~ (to/ with); ~ (between/ of),** [C, U] difference which is clearly seen when unlike things are put together; sth showing such a difference: (不同之物摆在一起所现出的) 明显的差别; 显示明显差别之物: *There is a remarkable ~ between toe two brothers.* 这两兄弟间有极显著的差别。*The white walls make a ~ to/with the black carpet.* 白墙与黑毯构成了显著的对比。*The ~ of light and shade is important in photography.* 明暗的对比在摄影术上是很重要的。**by/in ~ (with); in ~ (to),** when a ~ is made (to/with): (与…相比): *His white hair was in sharp ~ to his dark skin.* 他的白头发与他的黑皮肤构成鲜明的对比。*Tom's marks (eg 90 per cent) by ~ with Harry's marks* (eg 35 per cent) *were excellent.* 汤姆的分数 (例如 90 分) 与哈里的分数 (例如 35 分) 比起来算是上乘的。

con·tra·vene /ˌkɒntrə'viːn; ˌkɑntrə'vin/ *vt* [VP6A] **1** act in opposition to; go against (a law, a custom). 违反; 违犯 (法律, 习俗)。**2** dispute, attack (a statement, a principle). 反驳; 攻击 (陈述、原则)。**3** (of things) conflict with; be out of harmony with. (指事物) 抵触; 与…冲突; 与…不协调。**con·tra·ven·tion** /ˌkɒntrə'venʃn; ˌkɑntrə'venʃən/ *n* [C, U] act of contravening (a law, etc). 违反; 违犯 (法律等)。*in ~ of sth,* so as to break or violate it. 违犯规则。

contre·temps /ˈkɒntrətɒm; kɔ̃trə'tɑ̃/ *n* (*pl* unchanged) (复数不变) (F) unfortunate happening; unexpected hitch; setback. (法) 不幸的事件; 阻碍; 挫折。

con·trib·ute /kən'trɪbjuːt; kən'trɪbjʊt/ *vt, vi* ~ **(to), 1** [VP6A, 14, 2A, 3A] join with others in giving help, money, etc (to a common cause, for a purpose); give ideas, suggestions, etc. (指出力、出钱等)捐赠; 捐助 (与 to 连用, 后接某种公益事业; 与 for 连用, 后接目的); 贡献 (意见、建议等): ~ *food and clothing for the refugees;* 捐赠食物和衣服给难民; ~ *to the Red Cross;* 捐助红十字会; ~ *new information on a scientific problem.* 对于一项科学问题贡献新的知识。**2** [VP3A] have a share in; help to bring about: 有助于; 促成: *Drink ~d to his ruin.* 饮酒促成他的毁灭。**3** [VP14, 3A] write articles, etc) and send in: (为…写) 写 (文章等); 投稿: *Mr Green has ~d (poems) to the 'London Magazine' for several years.* 格林先生向《伦敦杂志》投 (诗) 稿已有几年了。**con·tribu·tor** /-tə(r); -tə/ *n* person who ~s (money to a fund, articles to a periodical, etc). 捐助人; 捐款者; 投稿人(与 to 连用)。

con·tri·bu·tion /ˌkɒntrɪ'bjuːʃn; ˌkɑntrə'bjuʃən/ *n* **1** [U] act of contributing; [C] sth contributed (捐助; 捐赠); 贡献; 促成; 投稿; 捐助或贡献之物; 捐款; 捐赠物; 稿件: ~*s to the relief fund.* 捐给救济基金的捐款。*Do you consider ~s to the village funds a duty or a pleasure?* 你认为捐款给村庄基金是义务还是乐事? *The editor is short of ~s for the May issue.* 编者缺乏稿件编五月号的杂志。**2** [C, U] compulsory payment. 强收的税款。*lay under ~,* require ~s from. 向…强收税款。

con·tribu·tory /kən'trɪbjutri US: -tɔːri; kən'trɪbjə,tɔri/ *adj* **1** helping to bring about: 有助于…的; 促成…的: ~ *negligence,* eg that helped to cause an accident. 造成意外事件的疏忽。**2** for which contributions are to be made: 待捐助的; 靠捐助的: *a ~ 'pension scheme.* 靠捐助的年金方案。

con·trite /ˈkɒntraɪt; ˈkɑntraɪt/ *adj* filled with, showing, deep sorrow for wrongdoing: 对做错的事深表懊悔的; 痛悔前非的; 悔罪的: *a ~ heart.* 悔罪的心。~**·ly** *adv*

con·trition /kən'trɪʃn; kən'trɪʃən/ *n* [U] deep sorrow (for sins, wrongdoing); repentance. (对于罪行、过失的)悔恨; 痛悔; 忏悔。

con·triv·ance /kən'traɪvəns; kən'traɪvəns/ *n* **1** [U] act or manner of contriving: 发明; 设计; 设法: *the ~ by which botanists fertilize flowers to obtain hybrids.* 植物学家使花受粉而得到杂种的发明。**2** [U] capacity to invent: 发明的才能: *Some things are beyond human ~.* 有些东西是人类发明不出来的。**3** [C] sth contrived; deceitful practice; invention or mechanical device: 想出的办法; 骗术; 发明物; 机械装置: *a ~ to record both sides of a telephone conversation on magnetic tape.* 一种将电话中双方的谈话录于磁带上的机械装置。

con·trive /kən'traɪv; kən'traɪv/ *vt, vi* **1** [VP6A, 7A] invent; design; find a way of doing (sth), of causing (sth to happen): 发明; 设计; 想办法; 动脑筋: *to ~ a means of escape from prison;* 设法逃狱; *to ~ to live on a small income.* 设法靠着微薄的收入过活。*He ~d to make matters worse,* made them worse by his efforts, even though this was not his intention. 他想的办法把事情弄得更糟了(虽然这并非他的意图)。*Can you ~ (= manage) to be here early?* 你能设法早一点儿到这里吗? **2** [VP 2A] (liter) manage successfully: (文)设法应付; 设法完成: *She finds it difficult to ~ (= manage her housekeeping economically) now that prices are rising every month.* 因为物价每月上涨, 使她觉得难以料理家务。**con·triver** /kən'traɪvə(r); kən'traɪvə/ *n* (liter) one who ~s, esp one who manages household affairs: 设计者; 发明者; (尤指)料理家务者: *His wife is a good ~r.* 他的妻子善理家务。

con·trol[1] /kən'trəʊl; kən'trol/ *n* **1** [U] power or authority to direct, order, or restrain: 指挥、命令或控制的权力; 管理; 管束; 监督; 支配; 控制; 克制; 抑制: *children who lack parental ~,* who are not kept in order

by parents. 缺乏父母管束的孩子们. *be in ~ (of)*, be in command, in charge. 握有(对…的)控制力; 控制. *be/come/bring/get under ~*, be, become, cause to be, under authority, under restraint, in working properly: 在(变成或使在, 置于)控制之下; (使)操作情况良好: *get flood waters under ~*. 使泛滥的洪水受到控制. *be/get out of ~*, in a state where authority, etc is lost: 失去控制(不受控制); 不能(不受)操纵: *The children are/have got out of ~*. 孩子们不听管教. *have/get/keep ~ (over/of)*, have, get, keep authority, power, etc: (对…)有(得到, 保有)权威、权力等; 能控制: *a teacher who has no ~ over his class*; 不能维持教室秩序的教师; *get ~ over a horse*, make it obey. 能驾驭一匹马; 驯服一匹马. *lose ~ (of)*, be unable to manage or contain: 不能驾驭或控制; 失去对…的控制: *lose ~ of one's temper.* 不能抑制自己的脾气. *take ~ (of)*, take authority. 操持; 管理; 控制: *We must find someone to take overall ~ of this project.* 我们必须找个人来总揽这个计划. **2** [U] management; guidance: 管制; 指导: *~ of traffic/traffic ~*; 交通管制; *~ of foreign exchange.* 外汇管制. **'birth-~** n planning of the number of births, eg by the use of contraceptives. (借使用避孕器或避孕药等的)节育. **3** [C] means of regulating, restraining, keeping in order; check: 管理、限制、控制的手段: *Government ~s on trade and industry.* 政府对工商业的控制. *The chairman's power to veto a proposal is a ~ over what the committee may do.* 主席对于提议的否决权, 是限制委员会权力的一种手段. **4** [C] standard of comparison for results of an experiment: (鉴定实验结果的)比较标准: *The tests were given to three groups, Group Two being used as a ~.* 受测验者有三组, 以第二组为比较标准. *We must make more ~ experiments.* 我们必须多做有比较标准的实验. **5** (usu *pl*) means by which a machine, etc is operated or regulated: (通常用复数)(机器等的)操纵装置: *the ~s of an aircraft*, for direction, altitude, etc; 飞机的操纵装置(借以控制方向、高度等); *a car with dual ~s/a dual-~ car*; 一部双操纵装置的车子; *the ~s of a transistor radio*, eg the volume ~, regulating the volume of sound; 半导体收音机的各种控制器(如音量控制器); *the '~ tower of an airport*, for regulating air traffic. (航空站指挥飞机活动的)指挥塔. 塔台. **6** [C] station at which cars taking part in a race may stop for overhaul, etc. (参加赛车的汽车可以停车接受检修等的)检修站. **7** [C] (spiritualism) spirit actuating a medium(4). (招魂术)驱使灵媒的精灵.

con·trol² /kən'trəʊl; kən'trol/ *vt* (**-ll-**) [VP6A] **1** have restraint, authority, power over: 控制; 管理; 支配; 抑制; 指挥: *to ~ one's temper/expenditure/a horse/oneself*, for regulating one's own 控制己身的脾气(开支, 马, 自己). **~ling interest** n (fn) holding of enough stock(5) of a company to ~ policy. (财政)拥有足以控制公司政策的股票; 控制股权. **2** regulate (prices, etc). 节制(物价等). **3** check; verify: 检查; 查验: *to ~ the accounts.* 查帐. **~lable** adj that cat be ~led. 可控制的.

con·trol·ler /kən'trəʊlə(r); kən'trolə/ n **1** (also 亦作 **comptroller**) person who controls expenditure and accounts. 会计长; 审计官; 主计员(管理开支及帐册的人). **2** person who controls or directs a department or division of a large organization: (大机关里的)组、处主任: *~ of BBC Radio.* 英国广播公司无线电组主任.

con·tro·ver·sial /ˌkɒntrə'vɜːʃl; ˌkɑntrə'vɝʃəl/ adj likely to cause controversy: 可能引起争论的: *a ~ speech*. 可能引起争论的演说; (of persons) fond of controversy. (指人)好争论的. **~·ly** /-ʃəli; -ʃəlɪ/ adv **~·ist** n person who is fond of or good at controversy. 喜争论者; 善于争论者.

con·tro·versy /'kɒntrəvɜːsɪ; 'kɑntrə,vɝsɪ/ n (pl **-sies**) [C, U] prolonged argument, esp over social, moral or political matters: 长期的争论: (尤指关于社会、道德或政治问题的)论战: *engage in a ~ with/against sb (on or about sth)*; 与某人(关于某事)进行论战; *a question that has given rise to much ~*; 曾经引起很多

争论的问题; *facts that are beyond ~*, that cannot be argued about. 无可置辩的事实.

con·tro·vert /ˌkɒntrə'vɜːt; 'kɑntrə,vɝt/ vt [VP6A] (formal) dispute about; deny; oppose. (正式用语)辩驳; 否认; 反对.

con·tu·ma·cious /ˌkɒntjuː'meɪʃəs; ˌkɑntju'meʃəs/ adj (formal) stubborn and rebellious; obstinate and disobedient. (正式用语) 顽强的; 拒不服从的. **~·ly** adv

con·tu·macy /'kɒntjuməsɪ US: kən'tuːməsɪ; 'kɑntjuməsɪ/ n [U] (formal) obstinate resistance; stubborn disobedience; [C] (pl **-cies**) instance of this. (正式用语)顽强; 顽抗; 拒不服从.

con·tu·melious /ˌkɒntjuː'miːlɪəs US: -tə'm-; ˌkɑntju'mɪlɪəs/ adj (formal) insolent; opprobrious. (正式用语)侮慢的; 无礼的.

con·tu·mely /'kɒntjuːmlɪ US: kən'tuːməlɪ; 'kɑntju,mɪlɪ/ n [U] (formal) abusive language or treatment; [C] instance of this; humiliating insult. (正式用语)侮辱的言语或态度; 侮辱.

con·tuse /kən'tjuːz US: -'tuːz; kən'tjuz/ vt [VP6A] (med) bruise; injure (part of the body) by a blow, without breaking the skin. (医)挫伤; 打伤; 撞伤; 打青(而不破皮). **con·tusion** /kən'tjuːʒn US: -'tuː-; kən'tjuʒən/ n [C] bruise. 挫伤; 打伤; 撞伤; 青肿.

co·nun·drum /kə'nʌndrəm; kə'nʌndrəm/ n [C] puzzling question, esp one asked for fun; riddle. 难答的问题; 难题(尤指为好玩而问者); 谜语.

con·ur·ba·tion /ˌkɒnɜː'beɪʃn; ˌkɑnɚ'beʃən/ n [C] area of large urban communities where towns, etc have spread and become joined beyond their administrative boundaries. 集合城市 (由数市镇等扩展连接而成的大都市区).

con·va·lesce /ˌkɒnvə'les; ˌkɑnvə'lɛs/ vi [VP2A] regain health and strength after an illness: 病后康复: *She is convalescing after a long illness.* 她在久病之后正康复中. **con·va·les·cent** /ˌkɒnvə'lesnt; ˌkɑnvə'lɛsnt/ n, adj (person who is) recovering from illness: 康复中的(病人): *a ~nt hospital*, one for ~nts. 疗养院. **con·va·les·cence** /ˌkɒnvə'lesns; ˌkɑnvə'lɛsns/ n [U] gradual recovery of health and strength. 逐渐康复.

con·vec·tion /kən'vekʃn; kən'vɛkʃən/ n [U] the conveying of heat from one part of a liquid or gas to another by the movement of heated substances. 热的对流(借受热物质之运动作用, 热从液体或气体之一部传至他之现象).

con·vec·tor /kən'vektə(r); kən'vɛktɚ/ n apparatus (for heating a room, etc) by which air is warmed as it passes over hot surfaces. 环流机(一种使房间等温暖之设备, 能使空气经过热的表面而变热); 换流器.

con·vene /kən'viːn; kən'vin/ vt, vi **1** [VP6A] summon (persons) to come together; form (a meeting, etc): 召集(人们); 召开(会议等): *~ the people/the meeting.* 召集人们(召开会议). **2** [VP2A] come together (for a meeting, council, etc). 集合(开会等). **con·vener** n member (of a society, etc) whose duty it is to ~ meetings. (社团等的)会议召集人.

con·veni·ence /kən'viːnɪəns; kən'vinjəns/ n **1** [U] the quality of being convenient or suitable; freedom from difficulty or worry: 方便; 合适; 无困难; 无忧虑: *I keep my reference books near my desk for ~.* 我把我的参考书籍放在我的写字桌近旁以求方便. *The house was planned for ~, not for display*, ie planned so as to be easy to live and work in. 那房屋的设计是为了方便, 而非为了排场. *Please send the goods at your earliest ~*, at the earliest time that does not give you trouble. 请将货品尽速寄下. *Please do the work at your own ~*, how and when it best suits you. 这工作如何做, 何时做, 悉听尊便. *It was a marriage of ~*, one in which material advantage was the chief consideration. 那是一项着眼于实利的婚姻. **2** [C] appliance, device, arrangement, etc that is useful, helpful or convenient: 有用的、有益

的或方便的用具、装置、安排等: *It was a great ~ to have the doctor living near us.* 有医生住在我们附近，极为方便。*The house has all modern ~s,* eg central heating, hot water supply, points for electric current. 此屋具有所有现代化的设备(如暖气、热水供应、电源插座)。*The nearest public ~s* (= WC's, lavatories) *are in West Street.* 最近的公共厕所在西街。***make a ~ of sb,*** use his services unreasonably; take too much advantage of his good nature. 过份利用某人(利用他的热心服务或善良忠厚); 欺负老实人。***flag of ~,*** ⇨ **flag**[1]. **'~ food** *n* [U, C] food (eg sold in a tin, packet, etc) that needs very little preparation. 方便食品。

con·veni·ent /kən'viːnɪənt; kən'vinjənt/ *adj* ~ ***(for),*** suitable; handy; serving to avoid trouble or difficulty; easy to get to or at: 合适的; 方便的; 使免麻烦或困难的; 容易接近的: *Will it be ~ for you to start work tomorrow?* 明天开始工作对你方便吗? *This is a ~ tool for the job.* 这对那工作是一种合适的工具。*Will the 3.50 train be ~ for you?* 三点五十分的火车对你方便吗? *We must arrange a ~ time and place for the meeting.* 我们必须安排一个合适的时间和地点开会。**~·ly** *adv* in a ~ manner: 方便地: *My house is ~ly near the bus stop.* 我的家离公共汽车站近，实在方便。

con·vent /'kɒnvənt *US:* -vent; 'kanvɛnt/ *n* **1** society of women (called 称作 *nuns*) living apart from others in the service of God. (与尘世隔绝以侍奉上帝的)女修道会; 修女会。⇨ **monastery.** **~ (school)** *n* one run by nuns. 修女会所办的学校。**2** building(s) in which nuns live and work: 女修道院: *enter a ~,* become a nun. 当修女。

con·ven·ticle /kən'ventɪkl; kən'vɛntɪkḷ/ *n* (building used for) secret religious meetings. 秘密的宗教性集会; 秘密的宗教性集会所。

con·ven·tion /kən'venʃn; kən'vɛnʃən/ *n* **1** [C] conference of members of a society, political party, etc devoted to a particular purpose (eg election of candidates); conference of persons in business, commerce, etc: (社团、政党等为某一特殊目的，如选举候选人，所召开的)大会; (商业界等人士所开的)会议; 年会: *the Democratic Party C~.* 民主党大会。Cf 参较 *conference* in GB. **2** [C] agreement between States, rulers, etc (less formal than a treaty): (国家、君王等之间的)协约; 协定(不及条约正式): *the Geneva C~s,* about the treatment of prsioners of war, etc. (关于战俘之待遇等的)日内瓦公约。**3** [U] general (usu tacit) consent (esp about forms of behaviour); [C] practice or custom based on general consent: 公认的标准(通常指大众所默认者，尤指关于行为者); 惯例; 常规; 习俗: *When men wore hats, ~ required them to raise them when they met a woman they knew.* 当男人戴着帽时，社会的习俗要求他们在遇到他们所认识的女子时要举帽示礼。*It is silly to be a slave to ~/to social ~s.* 做传统习俗(社会习俗)的奴隶是不智的。**4** [C] (in various card and board games, esp bridge) practice that is generally followed in bidding, leading cards, making an opening move in chess, etc. (在各种牌戏及下棋，尤指桥牌中，叫牌、出牌、下第一步棋等的)一般常规。

con·ven·tional /kən'venʃənl; kən'vɛnʃənḷ/ *adj* **1** based on convention(3, 4): 根据惯例的: *~ greetings;* 惯用的问候语; *a few ~ remarks.* 几句老生常谈的话。**2** following what has been customary; traditional: 习俗的; 传统的: *a ~ design for a carpet;* 地毯上用的老式花样; *~ art;* 传统的艺术; *~ weapons,* ie excluding atomic bombs, etc; 传统武器(不包括原子弹等); *a ~ power station,* using coal or oil as fuel (contrasted with heat from a nuclear reactor). 传统发电厂 (使用煤或油作燃料者， 为利用核反应炉生热为动力之核发电厂之对)。**~·ly** /-ʃənəlɪ; -ʃnəlɪ/ *adv*

con·ven·tion·al·ity /kən,venʃə'nælətɪ; kən,vɛnʃən-'ælətɪ/ *n* **1** [U] conventional quality or character: 习俗性; 传统性; 因袭; 老式: *the ~ of the paintings at the Academy Exhibition.* 在英国皇家艺术学会所举行之一年一度的美术展览会上所展出之绘画的传统性。**2** [C, U] (*pl* **-ties**) convention(3). 习俗; 惯例。

con·verge /kən'vɜːdʒ; kən'vɝdʒ/ *vi* [VP2A, 2C, 3A] ***~ (at/on/upon)*** (of lines, moving objects, opinions) come towards each other and meet at a point; tend to do this: (指线条、运动的物体、意见)自四面八方向一点汇合; 收敛; 辐辏; 聚集: *armies converging on the capital.* 自各方面向首都进发的大军。*Parallel lines ~ at infinity.* 平行线永远不会相交。**con·ver·gence** /kən'vɜːdʒəns; kən'vɝdʒəns/ *n* **con·ver·gent** *adj*

con·ver·sant /kən'vɜːsnt; 'kanvəsṇt/ *adj* **~ *with,*** having a knowledge of: 具有关于…的知识; 通达; 懂得; 熟谙: *~ with all the rules.* 熟谙所有的规则。

con·ver·sa·tion /,kɒnvə'seɪʃn; 'kanvə'seʃən/ *n* [U] talking; [C] talk: 谈话; 会话; 会谈; 交谈: *I saw him in ~ with a friend.* 我看见他与朋友谈话。*No ~ while I'm playing the piano, please.* 我在弹钢琴的时候，请勿谈话。*I've had several ~s with him.* 我已经和他谈过几次了。**~al** /-ʃənl; -ʃənḷ/ *adj* (of words, etc) used in, characteristic of, ~; colloquial. (指词等)用于谈话的; 会话性质的; 口语的; 通俗的。

con·verse[1] /kən'vɜːs; kən'vɝs/ *vi* [VP2A, C, 3A] **~ *(with sb) (about/on sth),*** (formal) talk. (正式用语)谈话; 谈论。

con·verse[2] /'kɒnvɜːs; 'kanvɝs/ *n, adj* **1** (idea, statement which is) opposite (to another). 相反的(观念、陈述); 反; 逆。**2** (logic) form of words produced by transposing some of the words of another: (逻辑)倒转命题(调换一命题中数字所成之相反命题); 反转句; 反转语: *'He is happy but not rich' is the ~ of 'He is rich but not happy'.* '他乐而不富'是'他富而不乐'的反转句。**~·ly** *adv*

con·verse[3] /'kɒnvɜːs; 'kanvɝs/ *n* [U] (old use) conversation. (旧用法)谈话; 谈论; 交谈。

con·ver·sion /kən'vɜːʃn *US:* -ʒn; kən'vɝʃən/ *n* [U] converting or being converted: 转变; 改变; 转化: *the ~ of cream into butter/of forest land into arable land/of pagans to Christianity;* 乳脂之变为奶油(林地之变为耕地; 异教徒之变为基督教徒); *the improper ~ of public funds to one's own use,* eg by a government official; 公款之非法移作私用(如政府官吏所为者); [C] instance of ~: 转变的实例: *many ~s to Buddhism;* 许多人的皈依佛教; *building firms which specialize in house ~s,* eg of large houses into flats. 专门改建房屋的建筑公司(如将大房屋改建成公寓者)。

con·vert[1] /kən'vɜːt; kən'vɝt/ *vt* [VP6A, 14] **1 ~ *sth (from sth)(to/into sth),*** change (from one form, use, etc into another): 使(自一种形式、用途等)转变(为另一种): *to ~ rags into paper/securities into cash/pounds into francs;* 将破布变成纸(证券变成现款，英镑换成法郎); *~ club funds to one's own use,* use them unlawfully. 挪用会社基金。**2 ~ *sb (from sth) (to sth),*** cause him to change his beliefs, etc: 使人改变信仰等: *to ~ a man from atheism to Christianity.* 使某人由无神论改信基督教。**3** (Rugby football) complete (a try) by kicking a goal. (橄榄球)将球踢入球门而完成(进球)。**~ed** *part adj* that has been ~ed: 改建的; 改造的: *a ~ed mews,* stable(s). rebuilt, decorated, etc for use as a residence. 由马厩改建成的住宅。

con·vert[2] /'kɒnvɜːt; 'kanvɝt/ *n* person converted, esp to a different religion (or from no religion), or to different principles: 改教者; 改宗者; 由不信教改为信教者; 皈依者; 改变信仰者: *a ~ to socialism.* 改信社会主义者。

con·vert·ible /kən'vɜːtəbl; kən'vɝtəbḷ/ *adj* that can be converted: 可变换的; 可改变的: *Banknotes are not usually ~ into gold nowadays.* 现今纸币通常不能兑换为黄金了。□ *n* (esp US) touring car with a folding or detachable roof. (尤美)车篷可折迭起来或拆卸的旅行车。**con·verti·bil·ity** /kən,vɜːtə'bɪlətɪ; kən,vɝtə'bɪlətɪ/ *n*

con·vex /'kɒnveks; 'kanvɛks/ *adj* with the surface curved like the outside of a ball: 表面弯曲如球的外侧

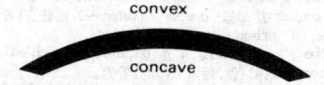

的; 凸起的: *a ~ lens*. 凸透镜. ⇨ **concave**. ~·**ly** *adv*
~·**ity** /kɒnˈveksətɪ; kənˈvɛksətɪ/ *n* state of being ~.
凸; 凸状。

convex
concave

con·vey /kənˈveɪ; kənˈve/ *vt* [VP6A, 14] **1** ~
(from)(to), take, carry: 运输; 运送: *Pipes ~ hot water
from this boiler to every part of the building.* 水管将热
水自此烧水器输送至大楼的每一部分. *This train ~s both
passengers and goods.* 这班列车客货均载. **2** ~ **(to sb)**,
make known ideas, views, feelings, etc to another
person: 传达(意思、见解、感情等): *Words fail to ~ my
meaning.* 言语不能表达我的意思. *This picture will ~ to
you some idea of the beauty of the scenery.* 这幅画可将那
处风景的美丽向你传达一二. **3** ~ **to**, (legal) give full
legal rights (in land or property): (法律) (将土地或产
业经合法手续) 让与; 转让: *The land was ~ed to his
brother.* 此地已让与他的兄弟. ~·**er**, **~or** / -veɪə(r);
-'veɪ/ *n* person or thing that ~s: 运送者; 运输装置; 运
送机: *a 'coal ~er*. 运煤装置; 运煤设备. '~**-er-belt**, (eg in
a factory) flexible band or chain moving over wheels
for ~ing packages, etc. (如工厂中的) 运输带 (装于轮子
上转动以运送包裹等的带或链).
con·vey·ance /kənˈveɪəns; kənˈveəns/ *n* **1** [U]
conveying. 运输; 运送. **2** [C] sth which conveys;
carriage or other vehicle. 运输工具; 车辆. **3** [C, U]
(legal) (document) conveying property. (法律) 财产让与
(证书). **con·vey·ancer** *n* lawyer who prepares ~s.
办理财产让与的律师。
con·vict¹ /kənˈvɪkt; kənˈvɪkt/ *vt* [VP6A, 14] ~ *sb*
(of sth), **1** cause (sb) to be certain that he has done
wrong, made a mistake: 使(某人)确信自己有罪或有错:
to ~ sb of his errors; 使某人相信他自己所犯之错; *to be
~ed of sin.* 确信有罪. ⇨ **convince**. **2** (of a jury or
a judge) declare in a law court that (sb) is guilty (*of*
crime): (指陪审团或法官) 宣告 (某人) 有罪 (与 *of* 连用,
后接罪行): *He was ~ed of murder.* 他被判谋杀罪.
con·vict² /ˈkɒnvɪkt; ˈkɑnvɪkt/ *n* person convicted of
crime and undergoing punishment. (已定罪并在服刑中
的) 囚犯; 监犯。
con·vic·tion /kənˈvɪkʃn; kənˈvɪkʃən/ *n* **1** [U] the
convicting of a person for a crime; [C] instance of this:
定罪; [C] *The ~ of the accused man surprised us.* 被告
被判定有罪我们吃惊. *There were five acquittals
and six ~s.* 有五人宣判无罪, 六人宣判有罪. **2** [U] the
act of convincing, of bringing certainty to the mind.
使信服; 使确信. **(not) carry ~**, (not) be convincing.
(不能) 令人相信. **be open to ~**, be ready to listen to
evidence, etc that may convince one. 愿意听取可作之证
据等; 服理. **3** [C, U] firm or assured belief: 坚信; 确
信; 深信: *I speak in the full ~ that...*, firmly convinced
that.... 我深深相信.... *Do you always act up to your
~s*, do what you are convinced is right, just, etc? 你
是否永远行动与信仰一致(照你认为对的,正当的去做)?
con·vince /kənˈvɪns; kənˈvɪns/ *vt* [VP6A, 11, 14]
~ *sb* **(of sth/that...)**, make (sb) feel certain; cause
(sb) to realize: 使(某人)信服; 使(某人)明白: *I am ~d
of his honesty / that he is honest.* 我深信他的诚实 (他是
诚实的). *We couldn't ~ him of his mistake.* 我们无法使
他明白他的错. **con·vinc·ing** *adj* that ~s: 令人信服的:
a convincing speaker / argument. 有说服力的演说家(论
据). **con·vinc·ing·ly** *adv*: *to speak convincingly.* 说话
能令人信服. **con·vinc·ible** /kənˈvɪnsəbl; kənˈvɪnsəbl/
adj willing, ready, to be ~d. 愿被说服的; 易服理的。
con·viv·ial /kənˈvɪvɪəl; kənˈvɪvɪəl/ *adj* **1** gay; fond
of chatting, merry-making, drinking, etc: 欢乐的; 好
闲谈、饮酒作乐等的: ~ *companions.* 酒肉朋友. **2** marked
by merry-making, etc: 有作乐之事的: *a ~ evening.* 作

乐的一晚. ~·**ly** /-ɪəlɪ; -ɪəlɪ/ *adv* ~·**ity** /kənˌvɪvɪ-
ˈælətɪ; kənˌvɪvɪˈælətɪ/ *n* (*pl* **-ties**) [C, U] merry-
making; being ~. 饮宴作乐; 欢乐。
con·vo·ca·tion /ˌkɒnvəˈkeɪʃn; ˌkɑnvəˈkeʃən/ *n* **1**
[U] convoking; calling together. 召集; 召集会议. **2**
[C] legislative assembly of the Church of England, of
graduates of some universities. (英国教会或某些大学毕
业生的) 评论会。
con·voke /kənˈvəʊk; kənˈvok/ *vt* [VP6A] (formal)
call together, summon (a meeting): (正式用语) 召集;
召开(会议): *to ~ Parliament.* 召开国会。
con·vo·luted /ˈkɒnvəluːtɪd; ˈkɑnvəˌljutɪd/ *part adj*
(zool, biol) coiled; twisted (eg a ram's horn); (fig)
complicated and difficult: (动物,生物的) 盘绕的; 回旋状的
(如公羊角); (喻) 复杂困难的: *a ~ argument.* 复杂错综
的争论。
con·vo·lution /ˌkɒnvəˈluːʃn; ˌkɑnvəˈluʃən/ *n* [C]
coil; twist: 盘旋; 缠绕: *the ~s of a snake.* 蛇所盘绕的
圈圈。
con·vol·vu·lus /kənˈvɒlvjʊləs; kənˈvɑlvjələs/ *n*(*pl*
~**es** -ləsɪz; -ləsɪz/) kinds of twining plant including
bindweed and morning-glory (with white, pink or blue
flowers). 旋花植物(包括野生旋花植物及牵牛花, 开白、粉
红或蓝花)。
con·voy¹ /ˈkɒnvɔɪ; kənˈvɔɪ/ *vt* [VP6A] (esp of a
warship) go with, escort (other ships) to protect (them):
(尤指战舰)护送(其他船只); 护卫; 护航: *The troopships
were ~ed across the Atlantic.* 运兵的船只被护送渡过大
西洋。
con·voy² /ˈkɒnvɔɪ; ˈkɑnvɔɪ/ *n* **1** [U] convoying or
being convoyed; protection: 护送; 护卫; 护航: *The supply
ships sailed under ~.* 补给船在护送之下航行. **2** [C]
protecting force (of warships, troops, etc). 护航舰队;
护送部队. **3** [C] ship, number of ships, under escort;
supplies, etc under escort: 被护送之船只或者船; 被护
送之船只等: *The ~ was attacked by submarines.* 被护送之船只受到
潜水艇的攻击。
con·vulse /kənˈvʌls; kənˈvʌls/ *vt* [VP6A] (usu in
passive) cause violent movements or disturbances: (通常
作被动语态) 使剧烈震动; 震撼; 摇动; 使起骚动; 使不安:
~*d with laughter / anger / toothache;* 笑得前仰后合(愤
怒; 牙齿剧痛); *a country that has often been ~d by
earthquakes / civil war.* 常为地震(内战)所苦的国家。
con·vul·sion /kənˈvʌlʃn; kənˈvʌlʃən/ *n* **1** [C]
violent disturbance: 剧烈震动; 震撼; 动乱; 骚动: *a ~ of
nature*, eg an earthquake; 自然的动乱; 天灾 (如地震);
civil ~, riots, etc; 内乱; 人祸 (如暴动等); *a political ~.*
政治的骚动. **2** (usu *pl*) violent irregular movement of
a limb or limbs, or of the body, caused by contraction
of muscles: (通常用复数) (由肌肉收缩所造成四肢或身体
的) 痉挛; 抽搐: *The child's ~s filled us with fear.* 那孩子
的抽筋使我们害怕极了. **3** (*pl*) violent fit of laughter:
(复) 狂笑; 大笑: *The story was so funny that we were all
in ~s.* 那故事有趣极了, 使我们大家都捧腹大笑。
con·vul·sive /kənˈvʌlsɪv; kənˈvʌlsɪv/ *adj* violently
disturbing; having or producing convulsions: 剧烈震动
的; 摇撼的; 抽搐的; 痉挛的: ~ *movements.* 抽动。
cony, coney /ˈkəʊnɪ; ˈhonɪ/ *n* (*pl* **conies, coneys**)
1 (US) rabbit. (美) 家兔. **2** rabbit-skin, esp when dyed
and prepared so as to resemble the fur of some other
animal. 兔的毛皮 (尤指经过染色及处理与其他动物之毛
皮相似者)。
coo /kuː; ku/ *vi, vt, n* (*pt, pp* **cooed** /kuːd; kud/,
pres p **cooing**) [VP2A] (make a) soft, murmuring
sound (as of doves); [VP6A] say in a soft manner: (发)
(作)咕咕声(如鸽子); 低声说话; 喁喁而言: *to coo one's
words.* 低声说话. ⇨ **bill²**.
cook /kʊk; kʊk/ *vt, vi* **1** [VP6A, 2A, 12B, 13B]
prepare (food) by heating (eg boiling, baking, roasting,
frying). 烹调 (如煮、焙、烤、炸); 做饭; 烧菜. ~ *sb's
goose*, ⇨ **goose**. **2** [VP2A] undergo ~ing: 受煮; 经
煮: *These apples ~ well.* 这种苹果适于烹煮. '~**ing**

apple, pear, etc, suitable for ~ing. 适于烹煮的苹果，梨等。Cf 参较 *dessert / eating apples.* 3 [VP15B] ~ **up,** concoct, invent (a story, tale, etc): 编造；虚构；杜撰 (故事、小说等): *Don't give me some ~ed-up yarn!* 不要说编造的故事给我听！4 [VP6A] tamper with; prepare fraudulently: 窜改；伪造: ~ *the books / the accounts,* falsify them. 窜改书籍(帐目)。□ *n* person who ~s food. 厨师。'~**book** *n* =**cookery-book.** '~**-house** *n* detached or outdoor kitchen (eg in a camp); ship's galley. 厨房；露天厨房(如露营时)；船上的厨房。~**·ing** *n* [U] '~ing lessons. 烹饪课。

cooker /'kʊkə(r); 'kʊkɚ/ *n* 1 (esp in compounds, as '*oil-~,* '*gas-~*) apparatus, stove, for cooking food. 烹饪做菜用的炊具；炉 (尤用于复合词中，如油炉、煤气炉)。2 kind of fruit, etc (esp apples, pears, plums) grown for cooking: 为烹食而种植的果物(尤指苹果、梨、李子): *These apples are good ~s.* 这些苹果适于煮食。Cf 参较 *dessert apples,* to be eaten uncooked. 点心苹果(不经烹煮而食者)。

cook·ery /'kʊkərɪ; 'kʊkɚɪ/ *n* [U] art and practice of cooking. 烹调术；烹饪术；烹饪法。'~**-book,** one that deals with ~; book of cooking recipes. 烹饪书；食谱。

cooky, cookie /'kʊkɪ; 'kʊkɪ/ *n* (*pl* -**kies**) (Scot) small, flat, thin, sweet cake (esp home-made) (苏) 小甜饼(尤指自制者)；(美) 饼干。

cool[1] /kuːl; kul/ *adj* 1 between warm and cold: 凉的；微凉的；不热的: ~ *autumn weather.* 秋凉天气。*Let's sit in the shade and keep ~.* 我们坐到树荫下去凉爽凉爽吧。*The coffee's not ~ enough to drink.* 咖啡还未凉得能喝。2 providing or allowing a feeling between warm and cold: 凉爽的；凉快的; *a ~ room / dress.* 凉爽的房间(衣服)。3 calm; unexcited: 冷静的; 镇定的: *Keep ~!* 保持镇定。*He was always ~ in the face of danger.* 他面临危险时总能保持镇定。*He has a ~ head,* doesn't get agitated. 他冷静的头脑(不激动，不慌张)。Hence, 由此产生, **~-'headed** *adj* 4 impudent in a calm way; without shame: 厚颜；无耻的: *What ~ behaviour—taking my lawn-mower without asking my permission!* 我得到我的许可就拿走我的刈草机——这是多么可耻的行为呵！5 (of behaviour) not showing interest or enthusiasm: (指行为)冷淡的；不感兴趣的: *They gave the prime minister a ~ reception.* 他们很冷淡地接待那位首相。**play it ~,** (colloq) deal calmly with a situation; be relaxed. (口)冷静应付；放轻松。6 (of sums of money, distances, etc) putting emphasis on the figure, and perhaps suggesting complacency:(指钱的数目、距离等)整整的；不折不扣的: *My new car cost me a ~ thousand.* 我的新车整整花了我一千(英镑)。*He suggested that we should walk a ~ twenty miles farther.* 他建议我们至少再向前行二十英里。7 (US sl) pleasant; fine. (美俚)适意的；好的。□ *n* 1 (usu 通常作 **the ~**) ~ air or place; ~ness: 凉爽的空气或地方；凉爽: *in the ~ of the evening;* 在傍晚凉爽的空气中; *the ~ of the forest.* 林中的凉快处。2 [U] (colloq) composure. (口)镇静；沉着；冷静。**keep one's ~,** remain calm, unworried. 保持镇静；不慌。~**·ly** /'kuːllɪ; 'kullɪ/ *adv* ~**·ness** *n*

cool[2] /kuːl; kul/ *vt, vi* [VP6A, 2A] make or become cool: (使)变凉；平息: *The rain has ~ed the air.* 雨已使空气变凉。*Has his anger ~ed yet?* 他的怒气平息了吗？[VP2C] ~ **down / off,** (esp fig) become calm, less excited or enthusiastic: (尤用于比喻) 变冷静；变冷淡: *Her passion for me has ~ed down.* 她对我的热情已渐冷淡。~**·ing 'off period,** (in industrial disputes, etc) a compulsory delay (to ~ tempers) before a threatened strike. (劳资争执中，在可能发生罢工前强制实行了)冷静期(让情绪平静下来)。~ **one's heels,** be kept waiting: 等候；久候: *Let him ~ his heels in the outer office— that will teach him to be more polite.* 让他在外面的办公室等等候——那将给他以后要有礼貌。~**·ing-tower** *n* large container used in industry to ~ hot water before re-using it. 冷却塔(工业中用以冷却热水以备再度使用的大型容器)。

cool·ant /'kuːlənt; 'kulənt/ *n* [C, U] (kind of) fluid used for cooling (eg in nuclear reactors). 冷却剂(液态，如核子反应炉中者)。

cooler /'kuːlə(r); 'kulɚ/ *n* container in which things are cooled: 冷却器: *a wine / butter ~;* 葡萄酒(黄油)冷却器; (sl) prison cell. (俚)监房；囚房。

coolie /'kuːlɪ; 'kulɪ/ *n* △ (sl, derog) unskilled Asian labourer. (讳)(俚，贬)(亚洲的)苦力。

coon /kuːn; kun/ *n* 1 raccoon. 浣熊。2 △ (sl, derog) Negro. (讳)(俚，贬)黑人。

coop /kuːp; kup/ *n* cage, esp for hens with small chickens. 笼; (尤指为带着小鸡的母鸡而设置的)鸡笼; 鸡舍。□ *vt* [VP6A] ~ **up,** put in a cage; confine (a person): 关入笼中; 拘禁(人): *How long are we going to stay ~ed up in here?* 我们要被困在此地多久？

co-op /'kəʊ ɒp; ko'ɑp/ *n* (the ~, (colloq) the cooperative society (shop, store): (口) 合作社: *She does all her shopping at the ~.* 她一切东西都在合作社购买。

cooper /'kuːpə(r); 'kupɚ/ *n* maker of tubs, barrels, casks, etc. 制桶工人；桶匠。

co·op·er·ate /kəʊ'ɒpəreɪt; ko'ɑpə,ret/ *vi* [VP2A, 3A, 4A] ~ **(with sb) (in doing / to do sth),** work or act together in order to bring about a result: 合作; 协力; 相配合: ~ *with friends in starting a social club.* 与友人合作创立一交谊会。*Everything ~d to make our holiday a success.* 一切凑合起来使我们的假期圆满过去。**co-op·er·ator** /-tə(r); -tɚ/ *n*

co·op·er·ation /kəʊ,ɒpə'reɪʃn; ko,ɑpə'reʃən/ *n* [U] working or acting together for a common purpose. (为一共同目的而)合作; 协力。**in ~ with; with the ~ of,** together with: 与…合作: *The workers, in ~ with the management, have increased output by 10 per cent.* 工人们与厂方合作已使生产量增加了百分之十。

co·op·er·ative /kəʊ'ɒpərətɪv; ko'ɑpə,retɪv/ *adj* of co-operation; willing to co-operate. 合作的; 协作的。a ~ **society** *n* group of persons who cooperate, eg to buy machines and services for all to share, or to produce, buy and sell goods among themselves for mutual benefit, or to save and lend money. 合作社; 信用合作社 (如共同购买机器或雇工，或自行生产互相买卖共同获利，或办理储蓄及贷款)。~ (shop of a) ~ society; ~ group: 合作社; 合作商店; 合作机构: *agricultural ~s in India.* 印度的农业合作社。

co-opt /kəʊ'ɒpt; ko'ɑpt/ *vt* [VP6A, 14] (of a committee) add (a person) as a member by the votes of those who are already members: (委员会)(由原有委员)投票选举而增添(新委员): *a new member on to the committee.* 投票增选该委员会的一名新委员。

co·or·di·nate[1] /kəʊ 'ɔːdɪnət; ko'ɔrdɪnɪt/ *adj* equal in importance. (重要性)平等的; 同等的; 并列的。~ **clause,** (gram) clause in a compound sentence, equal in rank to, and often joined by a conjunction to, the other clause(s) in that sentence. (语法)并列从句(并列句中，与其他从句地位相等，且常由连接词相连者)。⇨ **subordinate.** □ *n* ~ thing or person. 同等之物或人。~**·ly** *adv*

co·or·di·nate[2] /kəʊ 'ɔːdɪneɪt; ko'ɔrdn,et/ *vt* [VP6A] make co-ordinate; bring or put into proper relation: 使平等; 使同等; 使成适当关系; 使协调: to ~ *ideas;* 调和各项意见; *to ~ one's movements when swimming / ~ the movements of the arms and legs.* 游泳时协调各部的动作(协调臂与腿的动作)。**co·or·di·na·tor** /-neɪtə(r); -netɚ/ *n* person who co-ordinates. ~ 协调人; 调和者。

co·or·di·na·tion /kəʊ ,ɔːdɪ'neɪʃn; ko,ɔrdn'eʃən/ *n* the act of co-ordinating; the state of being coordinate. 平等; 同等; 协调; 调和; 调整。

coot /kuːt; kut/ *n* name of several kinds of swimming and diving birds. 大鹬(水鸟)。'**bald ~,** one with a white spot on the forehead. 秃头大鹬(前额有白斑)。Hence, 由此产生, **as bald as a ~,** very bald. 头顶光秃的。

cop[1] /kɒp; kɑp/ *n* (sl) policeman. (俚)警察。

cop² /kɒp; kɑp/ *vt, vi* (**-pp-**) (sl) (俚) **1 cop it**, be punished. 受罚。 **2** [VP2C] *cop out (of)*, abandon (an attempt, responsibility, etc). 放弃 (尝试、责任 等)。 Hence, 由此产生, '**cop-out** *n* act of or excuse for copping out. 放弃尝试或责任; 放弃尝试; 责任等之借口。 □ *n* (sl) (俚) **1** capture. 捕获。 *it's a fair cop*, I have/ He has, etc been caught and arrested in the act of committing the offence. 我 (他等) 被当场逮捕。 **2** *not much cop*, nothing to value highly. 没有什么值得珍视; 无甚价值。

co-part·ner /keʊ 'pɑːtnə(r); koʊˈpɑrtnə/ *n* partner, eg an employee, who has a share in the profits of a business, etc in addition to his salary or wages. 合伙人 (如职工股东, 除其薪资外并可分红者)。 ~ **·ship** /-ʃɪp; -ˌʃɪp/ *n* system, practice, of having a ~ in business or industry. (工商企业之) 职工股东制度; 劳资合伙。

cope¹ /keʊp; kop/ *n* long, loose cloak worn by clergy on some special occasions. 某些教士主礼时所穿之长而宽大的披风。 ⇨ the illus at **vestment**. 参看 vestment 之插图。

cope² /keʊp; kop/ *vi* [VP2A, 3A] ~ (**with**), manage successfully; be equal to: (成功地) 应付; 对付; 对抗: ~ *with difficulties*. 应付困难。

co·peck /'keʊpek; 'kopek/ *n* (Russian coin worth) one-hundredth part of a rouble. 一卢布之百分之一; 戈比 (苏联辅币名; 一百戈比等于一卢布)。

Co·per·ni·can /keʊˈpɜːnɪkən; koʊˈpɜrnɪkən/ *adj* **the ~ system/theory**, of Copernicus, a Polish astronomer, that the planets, including the earth, move round the sun. 哥白尼系 (学说) (哥白尼, 波兰天文学家, 认为行星, 包括地球, 绕太阳旋转)。

cop·ing /'keʊpɪŋ; 'kopɪŋ/ *n* (archit) line of (sometimes overhanging) stonework or brickwork on top of a wall. (建筑) 压顶; 墙顶(墙上端有时作悬突状的石工或砖工线)。 '~**-stone** *n* (fig) final act, crowning, of a piece of work. (喻)一项工作之最后的润色; 完成一项工作之最后的行为。

copi·ous /'keʊpɪəs; 'kopɪəs/ *adj* plentiful: 丰富的:a ~ *supply*; 丰富的贮藏; ~ *tears*; 很多的眼泪; (of a writer) writing much. (指作家)多产的。 ~**·ly** *adv*

cop·per¹ /'kɒpə(r); 'kɑpə/ *n* **1** [U] common reddish-brown metal (symbol Cu): 铜 (化学符号 Cu): (attrib) (用作定语) ~ *wire/cable/alloy*. 铜线(缆, 合金)。 **2** [C] coin made of ~ or a ~ alloy. 铜币(用铜或其合金铸成的硬币)。 **3** [C] large vessel made of metal, espo one in which clothes are boiled. 金属锅(尤指煮衣用者)。 ⇨ **boiler**(1)。 **4** ~ **beech** *n* kind of beech-tree with ~-coloured leaves. 铜掬(一种掬树, 叶呈铜色)。 ,~-'**bottomed** *adj* (**a**) (of a ship) having the bottom plated with copper (and therefore seaworthy). (指船) 铜皮包底的(因此是建造良好适于航行的)。 (**b**) (fig) safe in every way: (喻) 各方面均安全的; 扎实的; 可靠的: ~-*bottomed guarantees*. 牢靠的抵押品。 '~**·head** *n* poisonous snake of the US. 铜头蛇 (产于美国的一种毒蛇)。 ~**·'plate** *n* polished ~ plate on which designs, etc, are engraved: (刻有图案 等 以便印刷的) 铜版: ~**-plate (hand)·writing** *n* clear, neat and clear. 铜版字(清晰的草体字)。 '~**-smith** *n* one who works in ~. 铜匠。 □ *vt* (also 亦作 ,~-'**bottom**) sheathe (a ship's bottom, etc) with ~. 以铜皮包 (船底等)。

cop·per² / 'kɒpə(r); 'kɑpə/ *n* (sl) policeman. (俚) 警察。

cop·pice /'kɒpɪs; 'kɑpɪs/ *n* [C] small woodland area of undergrowth and small trees (grown for periodical cutting, eg for bean and pea sticks). 一小片矮树丛 (可定期砍伐以作豆荚等而种植者)。 矮林。

copra /'kɒprə; 'koprə/ *n* [U] dried kernels of coconuts, from which oil is extracted for making soap, etc. 干椰子肉(可从其中榨油以制肥皂等)。

copse /kɒps; kɑps/ *n* = **coppice**.

Copt /kɒpt; kɑpt/ *n* one of the direct descendants of the ancient Egyptians (about one-tenth of the population

of modern Egypt). 科普特人(古埃及人的嫡系后裔, 占今埃及人口的十分之一)。 **Cop·tic** /'kɒptɪk; 'kɑptɪk/ *n* language used in the liturgy of the ~ic Church of Egypt and Ethiopia. 科普特语(埃及与埃塞俄比亚境内, 科普特教会礼拜式所用的语文)。 □ *adj* of the ~s. 科普特人的。

cop·ula /'kɒpjʊlə; 'kɑpjələ/ *n* (gram) verb form (eg the finites of *be* and *become*) that connects a subject and the complement. (语法) 连系动词 (连接主语与补语的动词词形, 例如 be 和 become 之限定形式)。

copu·late /'kɒpjʊleɪt; 'kɑpjəˌlet/ *vi* [VP2A, 3A] ~ (**with**), (esp of animals) unite in sexual intercourse. (尤指动物) 交配; 交合; 性交。 **copu·la·tion** /ˌkɒpjʊˈleɪʃn; ˌkɑpjəˈleʃən/ *n* act or process of copulating. 交配; 交媾; 性交。 **copu·lat·ive** /'kɒpjʊlətɪv; 'kɑpjəˌletɪv/ *adj* (formal) serving to connect. (正式用语) 有连系作用的。 □ *n* (gram) word that connects (and which implies combination). (语法) 连系连接词。

copy¹ /'kɒpɪ; 'kɑpɪ/ *n* (*pl* -**pies**) **1** thing made to be like another; reproduction of a letter, picture, etc: 复制品; 抄本; 复本; 誊本; (信件的)副本; 加印之图片; (影片之)拷贝: *Make three carbon copies of the letter.* 将此信打三份复写本。 **rough** ~, the first (often imperfect) outline or draft of sth written or drawn. (写作或绘画的)草稿; 草图。 **fair** ~, the final form of sth written or drawn. 誊清之稿。 '~**·book** *n* exercise book containing models of handwriting for learners to imitate: 习字帖; 习字簿: ~*book maxims*, commonplace maxims (as formerly found in ~books). 陈腐的格言 (从前常见于习字帖中)。 ▷ also **blot**. '~**·cat** *n* (colloq) slavish imitator. (口) 毫无创造性的模仿者; 文抄公。 **2** one example of a book, newspaper, etc of which many have been made: (书籍, 报纸等印刷物之)一本; 一份: *If you can't afford a new ~ of the book, perhaps you can find a secondhand ~.* 如果你买不起新的, 你或许可以找得到一本旧的。 **3** [U] material to be sent to a printer: (送印刷厂的) 原稿; 底稿; 稿子: *The printers are waiting for more ~.* 印刷厂正等着更多的稿子。 *The fall of the Cabinet will make good ~*, will make exciting news for the journalists to write about. 内阁的垮台将成为大新闻。 '~ **desk** *n* (US) desk in a newspaper office where ~ is edited and prepared for printing. (美) 报馆里编辑稿件以备付印的办公桌。 '~**-writer** *n* person who writes advertising or publicity ~. 撰写广告文字者。

copy² /'kɒpɪ; 'kɑpɪ/ *vt, vi* **1** [VP6A, 15A, B] make a copy of: 抄写; 誊写; 复写; 制一份⋯的副本: ~ *notes (out of a book, etc) into a notebook*; 抄录(某书之要点于笔记簿中; ~ *out a letter*, make a complete copy of it; 将信誊抄一副本。 ~ *sth down (from the blackboard)*. 将⋯(自黑板上) 抄下来。 **2** [VP6A] do, try to do, the same as; imitate: 摹仿; 仿效: *You should ~ his good points, not his bad points.* 你应当仿效他的优点, 不要仿效他的缺点。 **3** [VP2A] cheat by looking at a neighbour's paper, etc: 在考试中作弊, 抄袭座的答案等: *He was punished for ~ing during the examination.* 他因考试时抄邻座答案而被罚。 ~**·ist** /'kɒpɪɪst; 'kɑpɪɪst/ *n* person who copies or transcribes (eg old documents); imitator. (古旧文件等之)誊写者; 抄写者; 摹仿者。

copy·hold /'kɒpɪhəʊld; 'kɑpɪˌhold/ *n* [U] (GB) the holding of land on conditions that were laid down in records of the manor; land held in this way. (英) 根据领从册籍中的条件享有的土地权; 凭券管业; 如此所享有的土地。 ~**er** *n* person holding land in this way. 凭券管业者。

copy·right /'kɒpɪraɪt; 'kɑpɪˌraɪt/ *n* [U] sole legal right, held for a certain number of years, by the author or composer of a work, or by someone delegated by him, to print, publish, sell, broadcast, perform, film or record his work or any part of it; (attrib) protected by ~. 著作权; 版权(著作家或作曲家, 对其所委托的代表, 在一定年限以内对其著作物所独享的法定权益, 如印刷、出版、销售、广播、上演、拍片或录音); (用作定

语) 受版权保护的; 有著作权的. □ vt secure ~ for (a book, etc). 取得(书等)的版权.

co·quetry /'kɒkɪtrɪ; 'kokɪtrɪ/ n [U] flirting; [C] (pl -ries) instance of this; flirtatious act. (女子的) 卖弄风情; 调情; 调情行为.

co·quette /kɒ'ket; ko'kɛt/ n girl or woman who flirts. 卖弄风情的女子. **co·quet·tish** /kɒ'ketɪʃ; ko'kɛtɪʃ/ adj of or like a ~:卖弄风情的: coquettish smiles. 卖弄风情的微笑. **co·quet·tish·ly** adv

cor·acle /'kɒrəkl; 'korəkl/ n small, light boat made of wicker, covered with watertight material, used by fishermen on Welsh and Irish rivers and lakes. 一种用枝条编成外覆防水布等的轻便小舟(威尔士及爱尔兰渔民用于河川湖泽之上).

coral /'kɒrəl US: 'kɔːrəl; 'karəl/ n 1 [U] hard, red, pink or white substance built on the sea bed by small creatures (polyps). 珊瑚(质坚呈红、粉红或白色的物质, 产于海底, 由小生物水螅所造成). ~ 'island, one formed by the growth of ~. 珊瑚岛. '~-reef, accumulation of ~. (由珊瑚累积成的)珊瑚礁. ⇨ the illus at atoll. 参看 atoll 之插图. 2 [C] sea organism that makes this substance. (造成珊瑚的)珊瑚虫. □ adj like ~ in colour; red or pink: 珊瑚色的; 红的; 粉红的: ~ lips. 粉红色的唇.

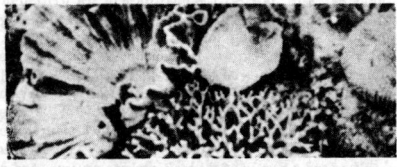

coral

cor an·glais /ˌkɔːr ˈɒŋglei US: ˈɔːŋglei, ˌkɒrəŋˈgleɪ/ n (music) woodwind instrument (tenor oboe). 英国管(一种双簧木管乐器, 又称次中音木管). ⇨ the illus at brass. 参看 brass 之插图.

cor·bel /'kɔːbl; 'kɔrbl/ n (archit) stone or timber projection from a wall to support sth (eg a cornice, an arch). (建筑)(自墙上伸出作支撑用的石质或木质)承材 (如飞檐, 拱顶); 枕梁; 牛腿. ⇨ the illus at window. 参看 window 之插图.

cord /kɔːd; kɔrd/ n 1 [C, U] (length of) twisted strands, thicker than string, thinner than rope. (一截)粗线; 细绳; 索; 带. 2 [C] part of the body like a ~: 身体上的带状部位: the spinal ~; 脊髓; the vocal ~s. 声带. ⇨ chord(3). 3 [C] measure of wood cut for fuel (usu 128 cubic ft). 量柴堆的体积单位 (通常为128立方英尺). □ vt put a ~ or ~s(1) round. 以绳索捆扎. **cord·age** /'kɔːdɪdʒ; 'kɔrdɪdʒ/ n [U] cords, ropes, etc, esp the rigging of a ship. 绳索的总称; (尤指)船的缆索.

cor·dial /'kɔːdɪəl US: 'kɔːrdʒəl; 'kɔrdʒəl/ adj warm and sincere (in feeling, behaviour): (在感情或行为上)热诚的; 恳挚的; 诚恳的: a ~ smile/welcome/handshake; 热诚的微笑/欢迎/握手; strongly felt: 深切感到的: ~ dislike. 深深的厌恶. □ n sweetened, invigorating liquor: 提神的甜酒: lime juice ~. 莱姆汁酒. ~·ly /-dɪəlɪ US: -dʒəlɪ; -dʒəlɪ/ adv ~·ity /ˌkɔːdɪˈælətɪ US: ˌkɔːrdʒɪˈælətɪ; ˌkɔrdʒɪˈælətɪ/ n [U] quality of being ~; [C] (pl -ties) expression of ~ feeling. 热诚; 恳挚; 热诚的表示.

cor·dite /'kɔːdaɪt; 'kɔrdaɪt/ n [U] smokeless explosive substance. 无烟火药; 抛射药.

cor·don /'kɔːdn; 'kɔrdn/ n [C] 1 line, ring, of police, soldiers, military posts, etc acting as guards: 由警察、士兵、哨岗等所构成的警戒线: a sanitary ~, a guarded line separating infected and uninfected districts. 卫生警戒线(隔绝传染区与非传染区的界线); 防疫线. 2 fruit-tree with all its branches pruned back so

that it grows as a single stem (usu against a wall or along wires). 剪去一切分枝仅留主干的果树(通常靠墙或沿金属线生长者). 3 ornamental ribbon of an Order[1](9) (usu worn across the shoulder). 代表职位的饰带(通常斜披于肩上); 绶带. ~ bleu /ˌkɔːdɒn ˈblɜː; korˈdɔ̃ˈblœ/, (F) award to a cook or restaurant for high quality cooking. (法)(为其高超的烹饪手艺而颁给厨师或餐馆的)优异奖. □ vt [VP15B] ~ off, separate, keep at a distance, by means of a ~(1): 以警戒线隔离或阻拦: The crowds were ~ed off by the police. 群众为警察的警戒线所阻拦.

cords /kɔːdz; kɔrdz/ n pl (colloq abbr) corduroy trousers. (口)灯芯绒裤子; 棱纹布裤子(为 corduroy trousers 之略).

cor·du·roy /'kɔːdərɔɪ; ˌkɔrdəˈrɔɪ/ n 1 [U] thick coarse, strong cotton cloth with raised lines on it. 有棱纹之厚粗棉布; 灯芯绒. 2 (pl) trousers made of this cloth. (复)灯芯绒裤子; 棱纹布裤子. 3 ~ road, one made of tree trunks laid across swampy land. (以树干置于低湿之地所筑成的)木排路; 木杆道.

core /kɔː(r); kor/ n 1 (usu hard) centre, with seeds, of such fruits as the apple and pear. (苹果及梨等的)果心(通常坚硬, 并含籽). ⇨ the illus at fruit. 参看 fruit 之插图. 2 central or most important part of anything: 任何物之中心或最重要的部份: 核心部份: the ~ of an electro-magnet (a bar of soft iron); 电磁铁心(即构成电磁铁之核心的一条软铁); to get to the ~ of a subject. 触及论题的核心. to the ~, right to the centre; 直至中心; 透心: rotten to the ~, (lit or fig) completely bad. (字面或喻)烂透了的; 坏透了的. He is English to the ~, completely English in manner, speech, dress, etc. 他是个道道地地的英国人(态度、说话、服装等是英国式的). □ vt [VP6A] take out the ~ of: 去…的核心: to ~ an apple. 去苹果的核心.

co·re·ligion·ist /ˌkəʊ rɪˈlɪdʒənɪst; ˌko·rɪˈlɪdʒənɪst/ n one of two or more persons who adhere to the same religion. 信奉同一宗教的人.

co·re·spon·dent /ˌkəʊ rɪˈspɒndənt; ˌko·rɪˈspandənt/ n (legal) person charged with adultery with the spouse (husband or wife) of the respondent (petitioner or plaintiff) in a divorce suit. (法律)在离婚案件中被控与原告之夫或妻通奸者; 共同被告.

corgi /'kɔːgɪ; 'kɔrgɪ/ n breed of small Welsh dog. 威尔士产的一种小狗.

Co·rin·thian /kəˈrɪnθɪən; kəˈrɪnθɪən/ n, adj 1 (native) of Corinth /'kɒrɪnθ; 'kɔrɪnθ/. 科林斯的; 科林斯人. 2 (archit) of the most ornate of the three types of column (1) in ancient Greek architecture, with a decoration of leaves on the capital[1](3), 科林斯式的柱子(古希腊建筑最华丽的三种柱式之一, 柱冠饰有叶形雕花). ⇨ the illus at column. 参看 column 之插图.

cork /kɔːk; kɔrk/ n 1 [U] light, elastic, tough substance, the thick outer bark of the tree called the ~-oak; (attrib) made of this material: 木栓层; 软木 (轻、有弹性、坚韧, 为软木橡树的外层树皮); (用作定语)软木制的: a ~ jacket. 软木制的背心(救生衣). 2 [C] round piece of this material used as a stopper for a bottle: 软木制的瓶塞; (软木制)塞子: to draw/pull out the ~. 拔开软木塞. '~-screw n tool for drawing ~s from bottles. 起软木塞的螺丝起子; 瓶塞钻. □ vt[VP6A, 15B] ~ (up), stop with, or as with, a ~: 以…(似)用软木塞塞住: to ~ a bottle; 用软木塞将瓶口塞住; (fig): (喻): to ~ up one's feelings. 抑制感情. **corked** adj (of wine) contaminated by decayed ~ or a bad ~: (指酒)被腐坏软木塞败坏的; 被腐坏软木塞败坏的红葡萄酒.

cork·age /'kɔːkɪdʒ; 'kɔrkɪdʒ/ n [U] charge made by a restaurant for serving wine not supplied by itself. (饭店对于非由其店中供应之酒所收取之)开瓶费.

corker /'kɔːkə(r); 'kɔrkə/ n (dated sl) (过时俚语) 1 sth remarkable or astonishing. 不平常或惊人的事物. 2 unanswerable argument. 无法辩驳的论点.

corm /kɔːm; kɔrm/ n (bot) bulb-like swelling on the

underground stem of a plant (eg a crocus or a gladiolus), from the top of which buds sprout. (植物) (植物如蕃红花或郁金兰之生长于地下的) 球茎。Cf 参较 *bulb* which has scales. 有鳞苞的球茎。

cor·mor·ant / ˈkɔːmərənt; ˈkɔrmərənt / n large, long-necked seabird with a pouch under its beak for holding the fish it catches. 鸬鹚 (大的长颈水鸟, 喙下有囊可存所捕之鱼)。⇨ the illus at **water**. 参看 water 之插图。

corn[1] /kɔːn; kɔrn/ n 1 [U] (collective) (seed of) any of various grain plants, chiefly wheat, oats, rye and (esp US) maize; such plants while growing: (集合名词) 谷类; 五谷 (主指小麦、大麦、燕麦、裸麦, 在美国尤指玉蜀黍); 谷禾: *a field of* ~; 一片谷类作物; *a '*~*-field*; 谷田; *a sheaf of* ~. 一捆谷禾。⇨ the illus at **cereal**. 参看 cereal 之插图。'~**-cob**, thick, cylindrical part of an ear of maize, on which the grains 'grow. 玉蜀黍穗轴。~ **on the cob**, maize cooked and eaten in this form. 带轴烹煮并食用的玉蜀黍。'~·**crake** / -kreɪk; -krek/, common European bird, the male of which has a loud, harsh cry. 秧鸡 (欧洲常见之鸟, 雄者鸣声粗宏)。'~**-exchange**, place where dealers in ~ do business. 粮食市场 (粮食贩做生意的地方)。'~·**flakes** n pl cereal of toasted maize flakes. 烘过的玉蜀黍片 (用作食物)。'~·**flour** (US 美/'~·**starch**), flour made from maize, rice or other grains. 玉蜀黍、米或其它谷物所磨成的粉。'~·**flower**, name of various flowers growing wild in ~-fields, esp a blue-flowered kind (also grown in gardens). 矢车菊 (野生于谷田中, 尤指开蓝花者, 亦种于花园中)。'**C**~ **Laws**, (esp) laws in GB, repealed in 1846, regulating trade in ~. (尤指英国于一八四六年所废除的) 谷物法。'~ **pone** /-pəʊn; -pon/, (US) baked or fried maize bread. (美) 烤或煎的玉蜀黍粉制成的面包。'~·**starch**, (US) ⇨ flour. (美) 玉蜀黍、米或其它谷物所磨成的粉。2 [C] single grain (of wheat, pepper, etc). 谷粒; 辣椒子。

corn[2] /kɔːn; kɔrn/ n small area of hardened skin on the foot, esp on a toe, often with a painful centre and root. 鸡眼 (一小块硬化的皮肤, 生于足部, 尤指足趾上, 常有疼痛的中心及根)。*tread on sb's* ~s, (fig) hurt his feelings. (喻) 触及某人的伤心处; 令某人伤心。

corn[3] /kɔːn; kɔrn/ vt preserve (meat) in salt: 用盐腌 (肉): ~*ed beef*. 腌牛肉。

cor·nea /ˈkɔːnɪə; ˈkɔrnɪə/ n (anat) tough transparent part of the eyeball, covering the pupil and iris. (解剖) 角膜 (眼球的坚韧透明外膜, 覆盖着瞳孔及虹彩)。⇨ the illus at **eye**. 参看 eye 之插图。~**l** adj of the ~: 角膜的: *a* ~*l graft*. 角膜移植片。

cor·nel·ian /kɔːˈniːlɪən; kɔrˈniljən/ n semi-precious stone, reddish, reddish-brown or white. 红玉髓 (次等宝石, 红色、红褐色或白色)。

cor·ner /ˈkɔːnə(r); ˈkɔrnər/ n 1 position (exterior or interior) of the angle where two lines, sides, edges or surfaces meet; angle enclosed by two walls, sides, etc that meet: 角; 隅角, 边或面相交之外部或内部之位置; 或指两墙、边等所围成之角落: *standing at a street* ~. 站在街角上; *a shop situated on/at the corner*; 位于街角的商店; *just round the* ~, (colloq) very near; (口) 十分弯近; 是附近; *sitting in the* ~ *of the room*. 坐在屋内的一隅。*cut off a* ~, go across, not round, it; take a short cut. 走直路, 走近路 (不绕过转角处)。*cut* ~s, of (the driver of a motor vehicle) go across, not round them when travelling fast; (fig) simplify proceedings, ignore regulations, etc to get work done quickly: (指驾驶汽车者) 小转弯; 斜切 (当开快车时不绕角而斜切而行); (喻) 简化过程、忽视规则等使工作速成: *We've had to cut a few* ~s *to get your visa ready in time*. 我们必须简化手续使你的护照签证及时弄好。*drive sb into a* ~, (fig) put him in a difficult situation from which escape is difficult. (喻) 迫人入困境。*turn the* ~, (fig) pass a critical point in an illness, a period of difficulty, etc. (喻) (在病中、困境中) 度过危险期; 脱险; 度过难关。*be in*

a tight ~, in an awkward or difficult situation. 处于困境中。'~·**stone** n **(a)** stone that forms a ~ of the foundation of a building (often laid in position at a ceremony). 建筑物的基石 (常在奠基礼中下土)。**(b)** (fig) foundation: (喻) 基础: *Hard work was the* ~*stone of his success*. 努力工作是他成功的基础。2 hidden, secret, or out-of-the-way place: 隐密处; 偏僻处: *money hidden in odd* ~s; 藏在隐密难寻之处的钱; *hole-and-* ~ *methods/transactions*, secret and underhand. 秘密而狡诈的方法 (交易)。3 region; quarter: 地区; 区域: *to the four* ~s *of the earth*. 至世界各地; 遍及四面八方。4 (comm) the buying up of all or as much as possible of the supply of an article of trade, a commodity, a stock, etc in order to secure a monopoly and control the price. (商) 垄断市场 (买尽或尽量买进某项商品、货物、股票等, 以图独家垄断而控制价格)。囤积居奇。*make a* ~ *in sth*, (comm) the buying of wheat). 垄断某物 (如收购小麦) 之市场。5 (Assoc football) (also 亦作 '~**-kick**) kick from the ~ of the field, allowed when the ball has been kicked by an opponent over his own goal-line. (英式足球) 角球 (自场角所罚之球, 因对方球员将球自其球门线踢出场外所罚之)。□ vt, vi 1 [VP6A] force into a ~; put into a difficult position: 迫入角隅; 逼入困境: *The escaped prisoner was* ~*ed at last*. 那逃犯终被逼入绝境, 无法逃脱。*That question* ~*ed me*. 那问题把我难倒了。2 [VP 6A] make a ~ (4) in (wheat, etc): 垄断 (小麦等) 市场: ~ *the market*. 垄断市场。3 [VP2A] (of a vehicle, its driver) turn a ~ (on a road, etc): (指车辆、其驾驶人) (在路上等处) 转弯; 拐角: *My new car* ~s *well*, remains stable when going round ~s. 我的新车转弯时车行很稳。~**ed** adj (in compounds) having ~s: (用于复合词中) 有角的: *a three-*~*ed hat*. 三角帽。

cor·net[1] /ˈkɔːnɪt; ˈkɔrnɪt/ n 1 small musical instrument of brass, like a trumpet. 短号; 短喇叭。2 piece of paper twisted into the shape of a cone, to hold sweets; cone-shaped container for ice-cream. 锥形纸袋 (用以装糖果); 盛冰淇淋的锥形杯。

cor·net[2] /ˈkɔːnɪt; ˈkɔrnɪt/ n (in former times) officer in a troop of cavalry who carried the colours[8](8). (从前) 骑兵队的旗手。

cor·nice /ˈkɔːnɪs; ˈkɔrnɪs/ n (archit) projecting part, above the frieze, above a column. ⇨ the illus at **column**; ornamental moulding (eg in plaster) round the walls of a room, just below the ceiling; horizontal strip of carved wood or stone along an outside wall; overhanging mass of snow above a precipice. (建筑) 柱顶壁缘 上方的突出部分; 柱带 (参看 column 之插图); 室内沿墙与天花板之间装饰性的嵌线 (如用灰泥做成者); 壁带; 沿外墙之雕木或刻石飞檐; 雪檐 (冻结于悬崖上的悬垂的雪块)。

cor·nu·co·pia /ˌkɔːnjuˈkəʊpɪə; ˌkɔrnəˈkopɪə/ n ornamental horn shown in art as overflowing with flowers, fruit and corn; (myth) horn of plenty; (fig) abundant supply. 艺术品中所示装满花果和玉蜀黍之装饰性的羊角; (神话) 希腊神话中哺乳 Zeus 神的山羊角 (= horn of plenty); (喻) 丰富; 丰饶。

corny /ˈkɔːnɪ; ˈkɔrnɪ/ adj (-ier, -iest) (sl) hackneyed; often heard or repeated: (俚) 陈腐的; 陈旧的; 老生常谈的: ~ *jokes/music*. 陈旧的笑话 (音乐)。

co·rolla /kəˈrɒlə; kəˈrɑlə/ n (bot) ring of petals forming the cup of a flower. (植物) 花冠。⇨ the illus at **flower**. 参看 flower 之插图。

co·rol·lary /kəˈrɒlərɪ US: ˈkɒrələrɪ; ˈkɔrə,lɛrɪ/ n (pl -ries) [C] natural sequence or outcome of sth; sth self-evident after sth else has been proved. 自然的结果; (由已证明之事物所得的) 推论; 系定理。

co·rona /kəˈrəʊnə; kəˈronə/ n (pl ~s /-nəz; -nəz/, ~e /-niː; -ni/) ring of light seen round the sun or moon, eg during an eclipse. 日月周围的光环 (如日月蚀时所现者); 日冕; 日华; 月华。⇨ the illus at **eclipse**. 参看 eclipse 之插图。

cor·on·ary /ˈkɒrənrɪ US: ˈkɔːrənerɪ; ˈkɔrə,nɛrɪ/ adj

(anat) of arteries supplying blood to the heart: (解剖) 冠状动脉的: ∼ *thrombosis*, formation of a clot in a ∼ artery. 冠状动脉血栓的形成. □ *n* (*pl* -ries)(colloq) attack of ∼ thrombosis. (口)冠状动脉血栓塞之发作; 冠状动脉血栓之发作。

cor·on·ation /ˌkɒrəˈneɪʃn *US:* ˈkɔːr-; ˌkɑrəˈneʃən/ *n* ceremony of crowning a king, queen or other sovereign ruler: (王、女王或其他君主的) 加冕礼: (attrib) (用作定语) *the queen's* ∼ *robes*. 女王的加冕袍。

cor·oner /ˈkɒrənə(r) *US:* ˈkɔːr-; ˈkɔrənə/ *n* official who inquires into the cause of any death thought to be from violent or unnatural causes: (调查死因的)验尸官; 法医: ∼*'s inquest*, such an inquiry (held with a jury). 验尸(会同陪审团)。

cor·onet /ˈkɒrənet *US:* ˈkɔːr-; ˈkɔrənɪt/ *n* small crown worn by a peer or peeress; band of precious materials worn as (part of) a woman's head-dress; garland of flowers. (贵族所戴的)小冠冕; (作为妇女头饰的)珠宝带; 花环。

cor·poral¹ /ˈkɔːpərəl; ˈkɔrpərəl/ *adj* (formal) of the human body. (正式用语)人体的; 身体的; 肉体的。 **punishment**, eg whipping, beating. 体罚(如鞭打)。

cor·poral² /ˈkɔːpərəl; ˈkɔrpərəl/ *n* (army) non-commissioned officer (below a sergeant); (陆军)下士(军阶低于中士); (navy): (海军): *ship's* ∼, one with police duties. 舰上下士(执行警卫任务的下士)。

cor·por·ate /ˈkɔːpərət; ˈkɔrpərɪt/ *adj* 1 of or belonging to a corporation: 法人的; 团体的; 社团的; 公司的; 市自治体的; 市政当局的: ∼ *property*; 社团财产; ∼ *bonds*, (Stock Exchange term for) bonds held by a group or company. 法人债券; 公司债券(由一团体或公司所持有之债券)。 2 of, shared by, members of a group of persons: 全体的; 共同的: ∼ *responsibility/action*. 共同责任(行动)。 3 united in one group: 结合成为一个团体的: *a* ∼ *body*. 法人团体。

cor·por·ation /ˌkɔːpəˈreɪʃn; ˌkɔrpəˈreʃən/ *n* 1 group of persons elected to govern a town: 被选为主持市政的一批人; 市政当局: *the Mayor and* ∼; 市长及全体市政当局; *the municipal* ∼; 市自治机关; 市行政机关; (attrib) (用作定语) *the* ∼ *tramways*. 市营电车。 2 group of persons authorized to act as an individual, eg for business purposes: 法人(团体行动如一人者, 如以贸易为目的的团体); 公司; 社团: *In Great Britain the Electricity Authority and the National Coal Board are public* ∼*s*. 在英国, 电力管理处和国家煤矿管理处都是公法人。 3 (US) limited liability company. (美)有限责任公司。 4 (colloq) large belly. (口)大肚子; 大腹便便。

cor·por·eal /kɔːˈpɔːrɪəl; kɔrˈpɔrɪəl/ *adj* (formal) (正式用语) 1 of or for the body: 身体的: ∼ *needs*, eg food and drink. 身体的需要(如食物和饮料)。 2 physical (contrasted with *spiritual*). 肉体的(与 spiritual 相对)。

corps /kɔː(r); kɔr/ *n* (*pl* **corps** /kɔːz; kɔrz/) 1 one of the technical branches of an army: 陆军中的特种部队: *the Royal Army Medical C*∼. 英国皇家陆军医疗队。 2 military force made up of two or more divisions. 军(由两师或两师以上之兵力组成)。 3 ∼ **de ballet** /kɔː də ˈbæleɪ; ˌkɔrdə bæˈle/ (F) company of dancers in a ballet. (法)芭蕾舞团。 *the Diplomatic C*∼; **the C∼ Diplomatique** /kɔː ˌdɪpləməˈtiːk; kɔrˌdɪpləˌmæˈtik/ (F) all the ambassadors, ministers and attachés of foreign states at a capital or Court. (法)(驻于一国首都或宫廷的)各国外交使团。

corpse /kɔːps; kɔrps/ *n* dead body (esp of a human being). 尸体(尤指人体的)。 ⇔ **carcass**.

cor·pu·lent /ˈkɔːpjʊlənt; ˈkɔrpjələnt/ *adj* (of a person or his body) fat and heavy. (指人或其身体)肥胖的。 **cor·pu·lence** /ˈkɔːpjʊləns; ˈkɔrpjələns/ *n*

cor·pus /ˈkɔːpəs; ˈkɔrpəs/ *n* (*pl* **corpora** /ˈkɔːpərə; ˈkɔrpərə/) body, collection, esp of writings on a specified subject or of material for study (eg for linguists, a collection of examples of spoken and written usages): 身体; 集体; (尤指某专题著作之)文集; 全集; 研究资料之集成(如语言学者所收集之口语及文字用法实例大全)。

cor·puscle /ˈkɔːpʌsl; ˈkɔrpəsl/ *n* one of the red or white cells in the blood. 血球(红血球或白血球之一)。

cor·ral /kəˈrɑːl *US:* -ˈræl; kəˈræl/ *n* 1 enclosure for horses and cattle or the capture of wild animals. (关牛马或捕野兽的)畜栏; 兽栏。 2 =**laager**. □ *vt* (-ll-) [VP6A] drive (cattle, etc) into, shut up in, a ∼; form (wagons) into a ∼. 驱(牛马)入栏; 关入畜栏; 布(篷车)成阵阵。

cor·rect¹ /kəˈrekt; kəˈrekt/ *adj* 1 true; right: 正确的; 对的: *a* ∼ *answer*; 正确的答案; *the* ∼ *time*; 正确的时刻; ∼ *in every particular*. 每一细节均极正确。 2 (of conduct, manners, dress, etc) proper; in accord with good taste or convention: (指行为、礼貌、服装等)合适的; 高尚的; 合礼仪的: *the* ∼ *dress for a ceremony*; 典礼时应穿的礼服; *a very* ∼ *young lady*. 仪态非常端庄的年轻女士。 ∼·**ly** *adv* ∼·**ness** *n*

cor·rect² /kəˈrekt; kəˈrekt/ *vt* [VP6A, 14] 1 make right; take out mistakes from: 改正; 修正; 修改: *I* ∼*ed my watch by the time signal*. 我照报时信号校正我的表。 *Please* ∼ *my pronunciation*. 请改正我的发音。 2 point out the faults of; punish: 告诫; 惩戒: ∼ *a child for disobedience*. 惩戒小孩不听话。

cor·rec·tion /kəˈrekʃn; kəˈrekʃən/ *n* 1 [U] correcting: 校正; 修改; 矫正: *the* ∼ *of schoolchildren's work*. 学童作业的批改。 **speak under** ∼, speak while knowing that one may need to be corrected. 自知所说不一定对而发言。 **house of** ∼, (old name for a) prison. 监狱(旧称)。 2 [C] sth put in place of what is wrong: 所修改之处; 改正的东西: *a written exercise with* ∼*s in red ink*. 有红墨水修改的笔写练习。

cor·rec·ti·tude /kəˈrektɪtjuːd *US:* -tuːd; kəˈrektəˌtjud/ *n* [U] (formal) correctness (esp of conduct, eg in diplomacy). (正式用语)端正(尤指外交方面等的行为)。

cor·rect·ive /kəˈrektɪv; kəˈrektɪv/ *n*, *adj* (sth) serving to correct: 有矫正作用的(事物): ∼ *training*, eg for juvenile delinquents. 感化教育(如施于少年罪犯者)。

cor·re·late /ˈkɒrəleɪt *US:* ˈkɔːr-; ˈkɔrəˌlet/ *vt*, *vi* [VP6A, 14, 2A, 3A] ∼ (**with**), have a mutual relation, bring (one thing) into such a relation: (与…)有相互关系; 使(一物)(与另一物)发生联系: *Results in the natural sciences seldom* ∼ *with those in history or art*. 自然科学的结果很少与历史或艺术的结果有相互关系。 *Research workers find it hard to* ∼ *the two sets of figures / to* ∼ *one set with the other*. 从事研究工作者发现很难使两组数字发生相互关系。

cor·re·la·tion /ˌkɒrəˈleɪʃn *US:* ˌkɔːr-; ˌkɔrəˈleʃən/ *n* mutual relationship: 相互关系; 关连; 相关: *the* ∼ *between climate and vegetation*. 气候与植物的相互关系。

cor·rela·tive /kəˈrelətɪv; kəˈrelətɪv/ *n*, *adj* (word or thing) having a mutual relation: 有相互关系的(字或物): *'Either' and 'or' are* ∼ *conjunctions*. Either 和 or 是相关连接词。

cor·re·spond /ˌkɒrɪˈspɒnd *US:* ˌkɔːr-; ˌkɔrəˈspɑnd/ *vi* [VP2A, 3A] 1 ∼ (**with**), be in harmony: (与…)调和; 符合: *The house exactly* ∼*s with my needs*. 这房子恰好符合我的需要。 *His actions do not* ∼ *with his words*. 他的言行不符。 2 ∼ (**to**), be equal; be similar (in position, etc): 相等(于); (地位等)相似; 相称; 相当; 相配: *His expenses do not* ∼ *to his income*. 他的花费与他的收入不相称。 *The American Congress* ∼*s to the British Parliament*. 美国的国会相当于英国的议会。 3 ∼ (**with**), exchange letters. (与…)通信。 ∼·**ing** *adj* that ∼(s): 相当的; 相应的: *Imports for 1—10 July this year are larger by 10 per cent than for the* ∼*ing period last year*. 今年七月一日至十日的输入量较去年同一期间超出百分之二。 ∼·**ing·ly** *adv*

cor·re·spon·dence /ˌkɒrɪˈspɒndəns *US:* ˌkɔːr-; ˌkɔrəˈspɑndəns/ *n* 1 [C, U] agreement; similarity: 相

符; 一致; 相似: *There is not much ~ between their ideals and ours.* 他们的理想与我们的理想之间没有多少相似之处。 **2** [U] letter-writing; letters: 通信; 信件; 书信: *I have been in ~ with him about the problem.* 关于这问题, 我与他一直有书信往来。 *Is commercial ~ taught in the school?* 学校中是否教授商业尺牍? *He has a great deal of ~ to deal with.* 他有大批信件需要处理。 **'~ course,** course of academic study by posting essays, etc to one's tutor. 函授课程。

cor·re·spon·dent /ˌkɒrɪ'spɒndənt US· ˌkɔːr-; ˌkɑrə'spandənt / n **1** person with whom one exchanges letters: 通信者: *He's a good ~/bad ~,* writes regularly/seldom. 他是个勤(懒)于写信的人。 **2** person regularly contributing local news or special articles to a newspaper: 报纸通讯员; 通讯记者(经常为报纸报导地方新闻或撰写特稿的人): *our Hong Kong ~;* 我们派驻香港的通讯员; *a foreign/war ~,* person writing reports from a foreign country / a war. 国外(战地)通讯记者。 **3** (comm) person, firm, bank, etc which has regular business relations with another (esp in a foreign country). (商)(尤指与国外)有商务关系之个人、公司、银行等; 客户。

cor·ri·dor /'kɒrɪdɔː(r) US· 'kɔːr- ; 'kɔrədə/ n long narrow passages from which doors open into rooms or compartments. 有门通至各房间的狭长通道; 走廊。 **~s of power,** places where influence is unofficially exerted. 势力走廊。 **'~ train,** one with coaches having ~s which open into compartments. 首尾有走廊相通的列车。

cor·rie /'kɒrɪ US· 'kɔːrɪ; 'kɔrɪ/ n [C] (Scot) round hollow in a hillside. (苏)山边的圆形洼地。

corri·gen·dum /ˌkɒrɪ'dʒendəm US· ˌkɔːr-; ˌkɔrɪ-'dʒendəm/ n(pl **-da** /-də; -də/) thing to be corrected (esp in a printed book). (尤指出版之书籍中)需要改正之处。

cor·ri·gible /'kɒrɪdʒəbl US· 'kɔːr-; 'kɔrədʒəbl/ adj (formal) capable of being corrected; (of persons) submitting to correction. (正式用语)可改正的; (指人)尚可教药的。

cor·rob·or·ate /kə'rɒbəreɪt; kə'rɑbə,ret/ vt [VP 6A] give support or certainty to (a statement, belief, theory, etc). 支持; 证实(陈述、信仰、理论等)。 **cor·rob·or·at·ive** /kə'rɒbərətɪv US· -reɪtɪv; kə'rɑbə,retɪv/ adj tending to ~. 可确证的; 可证实的。 **cor·rob·or·ation** /kəˌrɒbə'reɪʃn; kə,rɑbə'reʃən/ n [U] support or strengthening by further evidence; additional evidence: (以进一步的证据)确证; 证实; 进一步的证据: *in ~ (of),* giving further support (of). 为(⋯之)确证。

cor·rode /kə'rəʊd; kə'rod/ vt, vi [VP6A, 2A] wear away, destroy slowly by chemical action or disease; be worn away thus: (由于化学作用或疾病而)腐蚀;侵蚀;受损害; 受损伤的: *Rust ~s iron.* 锈能蚀铁。 *Iron ~s easily.* 铁易锈蚀。 **cor·rosion** /kə'rəʊʒn; kə'roʒən/ n [U] corroding or being ~d. 腐蚀;侵蚀;损害;受损。

cor·ros·ive /kə'rəʊsɪv; kə'rosɪv/ adj, n (substance) that corrodes: 腐蚀性的(物质): *Rust and acids are ~.* 锈及酸类系腐蚀性的物质。

cor·ru·gate /'kɒrəgeɪt US· 'kɔːr-; 'kɔrəget/ vt, vi [VP6A, 2A] make into folds, wrinkles or furrows: (使)起皱纹; 成波状; 使起褶: *~ the forehead;* 皱额头; *~d cardboard,* used for packing fragile goods; 波状纸板(用以包装容易破碎之货物); *~d roads in tropical countries,* with a furrowed surface caused by weather and use. 热带国家因天气及使用关系所造成的起伏不平的波状道路。 **,~d 'iron,** sheet iron made into folds, used for roofs, fences, etc. 波状铁皮(用作屋顶、藩篱等)。 **cor·ru·ga·tion** /ˌkɒrə'geɪʃn; ,kɔrə'geʃən/ n [C, U] fold(s); wrinkle(s). 皱纹; 波纹; 沟纹; 波形; 皱折。

cor·rupt¹ /kə'rʌpt; kə'rʌpt/ adj **1** (of persons, their actions) immoral; depraved; dishonest (esp through taking bribes): (指人、其行动)不道德的; 腐化的; 不诚实的(尤指贪污受贿的): *~ practices,* (esp) the offering and

accepting of bribes. 舞弊; (尤指)贿赂; 行贿; 受贿。 **2** impure: 不纯洁的: *~ air / blood.* 不纯洁的空气(血)。 **3** (of languages, texts, etc) debased by errors or alterations: (指语文、原文等)(因讹误或涂改而)贬值的; 败坏的; 转讹的: *a ~ form of Latin.* 不标准的拉丁文。 **~·ly** adv **~·ness** n

cor·rupt² /kə'rʌpt; kə'rʌpt/ vt, vi [VP6A, 2A] make or become corrupt: (使)腐败; 败坏; 贿赂: *young persons whose morals have been ~ed;* 其品行已经败坏的年轻人; *to ~ the electorate,* ie try to win their votes by bribing them. 向选民行贿(以图拉票)。 *Does pornography ~?* 色情文学会使人腐化吗? **~ible** adj that can be ~ed: 可败坏的; 可贿赂的: *~ible government officials.* 可贿赂的政府官吏。 **~·i·bil·ity** /kəˌrʌptə'bɪlətɪ; kə,rʌptə'bɪlətɪ/ n

cor·rup·tion /kə'rʌpʃn; kə'rʌpʃən/ n [U] corrupting or being corrupt; decay: 腐败; 腐烂; 腐化; 败坏: *the ~ of the body after death;* 死后身体的腐烂; *the ~ of a language;* 语文之被误用; *officials who are proof against ~,* who cannot be bribed. 不贪污腐化的官吏。

cor·sage /kɔː'sɑːʒ; kɔr'sɑʒ / n upper part of a woman's dress (round the bust); (US) small bouquet of flowers to be worn on this part of the dress or at the waist. 女服的胸部; (美)饰于女服胸部或腰部的花束。

cor·sair /'kɔːseə(r); 'kɔrsɛr/ n (hist) pirate or pirate ship, esp of N Africa, attacking ships of European countries. (史)海盗; 海盗船(尤指北非骚扰欧洲各国船只者)。

corse /kɔːs; kɔrs/ n (archaic or poet) corpse. (古或诗)尸体。

corse·let, cors·let /'kɔːslɪt; 'kɔrslɪt/ n coat of armour, esp one covering the trunk only. 甲胄(尤指体甲)。

cor·set /'kɔːsɪt; 'kɔrsɪt/ n close-fitting reinforced undergarment confining the waist and hips, to shape the body to the current style (often named, in trade, a *foundation,* or *foundation garment*). 女用紧身胸衣(以保持腰及臀部之曲线者;商用名称常作 foundation 或 foundation garment)。

cor·tege, cor·tège /kɔː'teɪʒ; kɔr'teʒ / n(F)train of attendants; procession, eg at the funeral of a king or president. (法)侍从队伍; 扈从; 行列(例如为国王或总统送葬者)。

cor·tex /'kɔːteks; 'kɔrteks/ n (pl **cortices** /'kɔːtɪsiːz; 'kɔrtɪ,siz/) outer shell or covering (eg the bark of a tree); outer layer of grey matter of the brain. 外壳; 表皮层(如树皮); (脑的)外层灰质; 皮质。 **cor·ti·cal** /'kɔːtɪkl; 'kɔrtɪkl/ adj of the ~. 外壳的; 皮层的; 皮质的。

cor·ti·sone /'kɔːtɪzəʊn; 'kɔrtɪ,son/ n (P) [U] substance (a hormone from the adrenal gland) used medically in the treatment of arthritis and some allergies. (商标)可的松; 可体松(取自肾上腺的一种荷尔蒙, 医学上用以治疗关节炎及某些过敏症)。

co·run·dum /kə'rʌndəm; kə'rʌndəm/ n hard crystallized mineral used chiefly in abrasive, in powder form (for polishing). 刚石(旧称刚玉, 一种坚硬的结晶矿石, 主用于作磨料, 呈粉状, 起磨光作用)。

cor·us·cate /'kɒrəskeɪt US· 'kɔːr-; 'kɔrəs,ket / vi [VP2A] flash, sparkle: 闪光; 闪烁: *coruscating wit.* 焕发的机智。 **cor·us·ca·tion** /ˌkɒrə'skeɪʃn US· ˌkɔːr-; ,kɔrə'keʃən/ n

cor·vée /'kɔːveɪ; kɔr've/ n [C] (F)(in feudal times) day's unpaid work which had to be done by French peasants; (modern use) hard task or duty unwillingly performed. (法)(封建时代)法国农双一天的强迫劳役; 徭役; (现代用法)强迫劳役。

cor·vette /kɔː'vet; kɔr'vet/ n (old use) warship with sails and one tier of guns; (modern use) small fast warship designed for escorting merchant ships. (旧用法)装单排炮位的帆舰; (现代用法)小型快速战舰(为担任商船护航而设计者)。

cos[1] /kɒs; kɑs/ *n* (kind of) long-leaved lettuce. (一种)长叶莴苣。

cos[2] /kɒs; kɑs/ *n* (abbr of) cosine. (三角学)余弦(cosine 之略)。

cos[3] /kəz; kəz/ *conj* (colloq abbr or) because. (口)因为;为了(because 之略)。

cosh /kɒʃ; kɑʃ/ *vt, n* (GB sl) (strike with a) length of lead pipe rubber tubing filled with metal, etc. (英俚)一截铅管或内充金属等的橡皮管;短棍;用此种短棍打。

cosher /ˈkəʊʃə(r); ˈkɑʃə/ *adj, n* = **kosher.**

co-signa·tory /ˌkəʊ ˈsɪgnətərɪ *US:* -tɔːrɪ; koˈsɪgnəˌtorɪ/ *adj, n* (*pl* **-ries**) (person) signing jointly with others. 共同签字的(人);连署(者)。

co·sine /ˈkəʊsaɪn; ˈkosaɪn/ *n* (trig; abbr **cos**) sine of the complement of a given angle. (三角学; 略作 cos) 余弦(某角之余角的正弦)。

cos·metic /kɒzˈmetɪk; kɑzˈmɛtɪk/ *adj, n* [C] (preparation, substance, esp one that adds colour) designed to make the skin or hair beautiful, eg *face-cream, lipstick*. 化妆用的;化妆品(尤指上色的,如面霜、口红)。**~ surgery,** to restore or correct outward appearance. 整型外科手术。**cos·me·tician** /ˌkɒzməˈtɪʃn; ˌkɑzməˈtɪʃən/ *n* person employed in the preparation or sale of **~**s. 化妆品制作人;化妆品贩卖商。

cos·mic /ˈkɒzmɪk; ˈkɑzmɪk/ *adj* of the whole universe or cosmos: 宇宙的: **~ rays,** radiations that reach the earth from outer space. 宇宙射线(自外太空射至地球的辐射线)。

cos·mog·ony /kɒzˈmɒgənɪ; kɑzˈmɑgənɪ/ *n* (*pl* **-nies**) (theory of) the origin, creation and evolution of the universe. 宇宙的起源及进化; 宇宙起源论; 宇宙进化论。

cos·mo·naut /ˈkɒzmənɔːt; ˈkɑzməˌnɔt/ *n* = **astronaut.**

cos·mo·poli·tan /ˌkɒzməˈpɒlɪtən; ˌkɑzməˈpɑlətn̩/ *adj* **1** of or from all, or many different parts of, the world: 属于(或来自)全世界各地的; 世界性的: *the ~ gatherings at the United Nations Assembly*. 联合国大会之各种世界性集会。**2** free from national prejudices because of wide experience of the world: 无国家偏见的;有四海一家之观念的; 世界主义的: *a statesman with a ~ outlook*. 有四海一家之胸襟的政治家。□ *n* **~**(2) person. 无国家偏见者;世界主义者。

cos·mos[1] /ˈkɒzmɒs; ˈkɑzməs/ *n* the universe, all space, considered as a well-ordered system (contrasted with *chaos*). 宇宙(被认为系井然有序的整个空间, 与 chaos 相对)。

cos·mos[2] /ˈkɒzmɒs; ˈkɑzməs/ *n* garden plant with white, pink or purple flowers. 大波斯菊(园艺植物,开白、粉红或紫花)。

cos·set /ˈkɒsɪt; ˈkɑsɪt/ *vt* pamper. 溺爱;纵容。

cost[1] /kɒst *US:* kɔːst; kɔst/ *vi* (*pt, pp* **cost**) [VP2B] (the adverbial adjunct indicating price, etc may be preceded by an indirect object; not used in the passive voice). (表示价钱等的副词修饰语之前可置间接宾语; 不用于被动语态)。**1** be obtainable at the price of; require the payment of: 价值(若干); 花(多少钱): *The house ~ him £15 000*. 此屋花了他一万五千英镑。*It ~s them £500 a year to run a car*. 使用一部小汽车每年花他们五百英镑。*It ~s too much*. 它的价钱太贵。*Compiling a dictionary ~s much time and patience*. 编一部词典花很多时间和耐性。**2** result in the loss of: 丧失; 牺牲: *Careless driving may ~ you your life*. 粗心大意的驾车可能使你丧命。**3** bring (injury or disadvantage): 使受损害;引起麻烦: *The boy's bad behaviour ~ his mother many sleepless nights*. 那孩子的不良行为使他的母亲许多夜睡不着。**4** *vt* [VP6A] (*pt, pp* **~ed**) (industry and comm) estimate the price to be charged for an article based on the expense of producing it. (工商业)按生产成本估计货品应售价格。**~·ing** *n* [U] (industry) fixing of prices: (工业)作价;成本计算: *the ~ing department*. 成本计算部门。

cost[2] /kɒst *US:* kɔːst; kɔst/ *n* **1** [C, U] price (to be) paid for a thing: 价钱;成本;费用: *the ~ of living;* 生活费用; *living ~s,* the general level of prices; 生活费用(物价的一般水准); *the ~-of-living index,* 生活费指数, ⇨ **index(3);** *the ~ price of an article,* the **~** of producing it or the price at which it may be bought wholesale, ⇨ **retail;** 货品的成本价格; 批发价(格); *to sell sth at ~,* ie at **~** price; 按批发价售卖某物; 照成本卖。*He built his house without regard to ~,* without considering how much money would be needed. 他不计花钱多寡盖房子。ˈ**~ accountant/clerk,** one who keeps a record of every item of expense in a business, etc. (工商企业的) 成本会计员。ˌ**cost-efˈfective** *adj* economical compared with money spent; 划算的; hence, 由此产生, ˌ**cost-efˈfectiveness** *n* [U]. **2** [C, U *sing* only] that which is used, needed or given to obtain sth: (欲获得某物所付的)代价: *The battle was won at (a) great ~ in human lives,* only after many soldiers had been killed. 牺牲了许多士兵的性命才换来这场战役的胜利。***at ˈall ~s,*** whatever the **~** may be. 不惜任何代价; 无论如何。***at the ~ of,*** at the loss or expense of: 丧失; 牺牲: *He saved his son from drowning, but only at the ~ of his own life*. 他救了他儿子的命免于溺死,但却牺牲了他自己的生命。***count the ~,*** consider the risks, possible losses, etc before doing sth. 事前详细盘算得失等。***to one's ~,*** to one's loss or disadvantage: 使某人遭受损失或不便: *Wasps' stings are serious, as I know to my ~,* as I know because of personal suffering from them. 我知道被黄蜂螫了是严重的事情, 因为我曾身受其害。**3** *(pl)* (legal) expense of having sth settled in a law court: (复)(法律) 诉讼费用: *pay a £25 fine and £7 ~s*. 缴二十五英镑罚金和七英镑诉讼费。

co-star /ˌkəʊ ˈstɑː(r); ˈkoˈstɑr/ *vi, vt* (**-rr-**) (journalism) (新闻) **1** [VP6A] present (one star(4)) as having equal status with another or others: 合演;联合主演; 使(一明星)与另一明星或其他明星联合主演: *The film ~red Robert Redford*. 该影片由罗伯特·雷德福与其他明星联合主演。**2** [VP3A] **~ with,** (of an actor or actress) appear as a star(4) with: (指演员) 与…联合主演: *Laurence Olivier ~s with Maggie Smith in this production*. 劳伦斯·奥利弗与马吉·史密斯在本剧中联合主演。□ *n* /ˈkəʊstɑː(r); ˈkostɑr/ person who **~**s. 合演者;联合主演者。

cos·ter·monger /ˈkɒstəmʌŋgə(r); ˈkɑstəˌmʌŋgə/ *n* person who sells fruit, vegetables, etc from a barrow in the street. 沿街推车叫卖水果、蔬菜等的小贩。

cos·tive /ˈkɒstɪv; ˈkɑstɪv/ *adj* (liter) constipated. (文)便秘的。

costly /ˈkɒstlɪ *US:* ˈkɔːst-; ˈkɔstlɪ/ *adj* (**-ier, -iest**) of great value; costing much: 贵重的; 昂贵的; 造成严重损失的: *a ~ mistake,* one involving great loss or sacrifice. 造成重大损失或牺牲的错误。**cost·li·ness** *n*

cos·tume /ˈkɒstjuːm *US:* -tuːm; ˈkɑstjum/ *n* **1** [U, C] style of dress: 服装的式样: *actors wearing historical ~,* clothes in the style of a period in the past; 穿着古装的演员: *Scotsmen in Highland ~,* wearing the kilt, etc; 穿着苏格兰高地服装(如褶叠短裙等)的苏格兰男子; *a* ˈ*~ piece/play,* one in which the actors wear historical **~**. 古装剧。ˈ**~ jewellery,** artificial jewellery. 戏装用的珠宝; 假珠宝。**2** [C] (dated) woman's suit (short coat and skirt of the same material). (过时用语) 女装;女服(西装式短上衣及裙子,上下系同一布料)。⇨**bathing.**

cos·tumier /kɒˈstjuːmɪə(r) *US:* -ˈstuː-; kɑsˈtjumɪə/ *n* maker of, dealer in, **~**s. 女装商人(制作或贩卖女装者)。

cosy[1] /ˈkəʊzɪ; ˈkozɪ/ *adj* (**-ier, -iest**) warm and comfortable: 温暖而舒适的;安逸的: *a ~ little room*. 温暖而舒适的小房间。**cosi·ly** *adv* **cosi·ness** *n*

cosy[2] /ˈkəʊzɪ; ˈkozɪ/ *n* covering for a teapot, or an egg in an egg-cup. (茶壶或盛煮蛋的蛋杯的)暖盖。

cot[1] /kɒt; kɑt/ *n* **1** small, narrow, easily moved bed; bed for a young child (usu with sides to prevent the

child from falling out) (US 美 = *crib*). 狭小而容易移
动的床；小儿床 (通常设有栏杆以防小儿跌出)。**2** (US)
camp bed; bunk bed on board ship. (美) (可折叠而便于
携带的) 行军床，(船上的) 床铺。

cot[2] /kɒt; kɑt/ n **1** small building for sheltering
animals: (牲畜的) 小棚；圈: *a sheep-cot*. 羊圈。**2** (poet)
cottage. (诗) 茅舍；小屋。

cote /kəʊt; kot/ n shed or shelter for domestic animals
or birds: (牲畜及家禽的) 棚；圈；栏: *a 'dove-~; 鸽棚；
a 'sheep-~*. 羊圈。

co-ten·ant /ˌkəʊ 'tenənt; ko'tɛnənt/ n joint tenant.
共同租地人；共同佃户；合租人。

co·te·rie /'kəʊtərɪ; 'kotərɪ/ n group of persons
associated by common interests, tastes, etc, one
that tends to be exclusive: 由于共同兴趣、嗜好等所形成
的小集团 (尤指有排他性者): *a literary ~*. 文人之小
集团。

co·ter·mi·nous /ˌkəʊ'tɜːmɪnəs; ko'tɜmənəs/ adj
having a common terminus or boundary. 共终点的；共
边界的；毗连的；邻接的。

co·til·lion, co·til·ion /kə'tɪljən; ko'tɪljən/ n
name of several kinds of lively French dance originated
in the 18th c; music for these. 高替洋舞 (源于十八世纪
的数种活泼的法国舞)；高替洋舞曲。

cot·tage /'kɒtɪdʒ; 'kɑtɪdʒ/ n small house, esp in the
country: 茅舍；村舍；农舍: *farm labourers' ~s*; 农舍;
house at a summer resort. (避暑胜地的) 别墅。~
cheese, soft, white kind, made from curds. (由凝乳制
成的) 松软白干酪。~ **industry**, one that can be carried
on in ~s, eg knitting, pottery, some kinds of weaving.
乡村工艺 (可在农舍里做的手工,如编织、制陶器、某些种纺
织)。

cot·tar, cot·ter /'kɒtə(r); 'kɑtə/ n (Scot) man
living in a cottage on a farm and working on the farm.
(苏) 农事工人或佃农 (住在农舍里,在农场上工作)。

cot·ton /'kɒtn; 'kɑtn/ n [U] **1** soft, white fibrous
substance round the seeds of the '~-plant, used for
making thread, cloth, etc: 棉花 (棉花子周围之柔软的白
色纤维物质,用以纺纱织布等): (attrib) (用作定语)~
yarn; 棉纱; ~ *cloth*; 棉布; ~ *goods*. 棉织品。**2** thread
spun from ~ yarn: 棉线: *a ,needle and '~*. 一根穿有棉
线的针。'~ **batting** n(US) cotton-wool. (美) 棉花; 脱脂
棉。'~-**cake**, cattle food made by pressing out oil from
seeds of the ~-plant. 棉子饼 (由棉子榨出其中之油压成
之,作牲畜饲料)。~ **seed 'oil**, oil obtained from ~
seed. 棉子油 (由棉子中提取之油)。'~-**tail** n (US)rabbit.
(美)家兔。~-**wool**, (GB) cleaned raw ~ or natural ~;
absorbent ~ as used for padding, bandaging, etc. (英)
棉花;原棉;生棉;脱脂棉 (用作填料、敷料等)。□ vi ~ **up
(to)**, (dated sl) make friendly advances (to). (过时俚
语,用...) 亲近;巴结。~ **on (to)**, (sl) understand. (俚)
懂得。

a cotton-plant

coty·ledon /ˌkɒtɪ'liːdn; ˌkɑtl'idn/ n (bot) first leaf
growing from a seed. (植物) 子叶 (最初自种子中长出的
叶)。

couch[1] /kautʃ; kautʃ/ n **1** (liter) bed: (文)床; 榻: *retire
to one's ~*. 就寝。**2** long bed-like seat for sitting on or
lying on during the day: 长沙发 (供昼间坐卧,似床之长
椅): *studio-~*. 可以拉开来成为整张床的长沙发。

couch[2] /kautʃ; kautʃ/ vt, vi **1** [VP6A, 14] ~ **(in)**,
(formal) put (a thought, etc, in words): (正式用语) 措
辞; (以话语或文字) 表达 (思想等): *The reply was ~ed in
insolent terms*. 回答措辞蛮横。**2** [VP2A] (of animals)
lie flat (either in hiding, or ready for a jump forward):
(指动物) 俯卧; 蹲伏 (或为躲藏,或准备向前跳): *a deer
~ed on a grassy bank*. 蹲伏在草堆上的一只鹿。**3** [VP6
A] lower (a spear or lance) to the position for attack.
平执; 平握 (枪矛等,作攻击姿势)。**4** (pp only; liter or
poet) reclining (as if) on a couch[1]: (仅用过去分词,文或
诗) 俯卧的: ~ed in slumber. 俯卧而眠。

couch[3], **couch-grass** /kautʃ; (grɑːs US: græs);
'kautʃ(græs)/ n [U] kind of grass with long creeping
roots. 茅草 (生蔓延的长根)。

couch·ant /'kautʃənt; 'kautʃənt/ adj (heraldry, of
animals in a coat of arms, etc) lying with the body
resting on the legs and the head raised. (纹章,指盾形徽
章等上之动物图形) 身体卧于四肢上而头抬起的; 昂首蹲
伏的。

cou·chette /kuː'ʃet; kau'ʃɛt/ n (F) sleeping berth
(in a railway compartment). (法) (火车上的)卧铺。

cou·gar /'kuːgə(r); 'kugə/ n large wild cat, also
called a *puma*. 美洲豹 (亦称作 puma)。⇨ the illus at
cat. 参看 cat 之插图。

cough[1] /kɒf US: kɔːf; kɔf/ vi, vt [VP2A, 15B] send
out air from the lungs violently and noisily. 咳嗽。~
sb down, (of an audience) prevent him by ~ing, from
being heard. (指听众) 以咳嗽的方式使演说者的话不被听
到。~ *sth up*, get it out of the throat by ~ing; (fig,
sl) say, produce (it) reluctantly. 咳出; (喻,俚)勉强说
出某事; 勉强交出或提出某物。

cough[2] /kɒf US: kɔːf; kɔf/ n **1** act or sound of
coughing: 咳嗽; 咳嗽声: *He gave me a warning ~*. 他以
咳嗽警告我。**2** condition, illness, that causes a person
to cough often: 咳嗽病: *to have a bad ~*; 咳嗽得很厉
害; '~-*drop*, '~-*lozenge*, taken to relieve a ~. 止咳
药片。

could /kud; kud /, weak form /kəd; kəd/ neg 变态否定
式 couldn't /'kudnt; 'kudnt/ anom fin 变态限定动词
pt of can, used in indirect speech in place of *can* if the
main verb is *pt*; to express conditions, and to express
occasional occurrence and inclination. can 之过去式,用
于间接引用语中以代替 can, 假如其主要动词为过去式;
亦可表示条件,以及偶然发生的事情和意向。⇨ **can**.

couldst /kudst; kudst/ old form of *could*, used with
thou. could 之古体,与 thou 连用。

coul·ter (US = **col·ter**) /'kəʊltə(r); 'koltə/ n iron
blade fixed vertically in front of a plough share (to cut
the soil before it is lifted and turned by the share). 犁
头铁;犁刀 (垂直装于犁之前端以切入泥土而翻转之)。

coun·cil /'kaunsl; 'kaunsl/ n group of persons
appointed, elected or chosen to give advice, make rules,
and carry out plans, manage affairs, etc, esp of
government: 议会; 政务会 (由委派或选举之议员组成,其
任务为提供意见、制定规章、实行计划、处理公务等);会议:
a city/county ~; 市(郡)议会; *the municipal ~*; 市议会;
to be/to meet in ~; 举行议会; *the C~ of the Republic*,
upper house in the French legislature; 法国议会中的上
议院; *a ~ of war*, assembly of officers called by the
Commander-in-Chief, etc; (由总司令等所召集的)军事会
议; 作战会议; *the Privy C~*. 英国枢密院。'~-**board**,
table at which members of a ~ sit. 会议桌。'~-**chamber**, in which a ~ meets. 会议室。'~ **estate**, housing
estate built by a city, county, etc ~. 市(郡等)议会所
建的房产。⇨ **housing**. '~ **flat/house**, flat/house in
a ~ estate. 议会所建的公寓(房屋)。

coun·cil·lor (US also **coun·cil·or**) /'kaunslə(r);
'kaunslə/ n member of a council. 议会议员。

coun·sel[1] /'kaunsl; 'kaunsl/ n **1** [U] (formal) advice;
consultation; opinions; suggestions. (正式用语)劝告;忠
告;意见;建议。*keep one's own ~*, keep one's views,
plans, etc secret. 对于自己的意见、计划等保守秘密。

hold/take ~ with sb, consult him. 听取某人的意见；与…商量。**2** *take ~ together*, consult together. 共同商议。**2** (with *indef art* or in *pl* but not with numerals): (与不定冠词连用或用复数，但不与数字连用): *a ~/~s of perfection*, excellent advice that cannot be followed. 不能实现的理想建议。**3** (*pl* unchanged) barrister, or group of barristers, giving advice in a law case: (复数不变) 辩护律师；法律顾问: *when the jury had heard ~ on both sides*, the barristers for the prosecution and the defence. 当陪审团听完了原告及被告双方律师之辩护以后，**Queen's / King's 'C~**, (abbr to 略作 **QC / KC**) barrister appointed to act for the State, higher in authority than other barristers. 王室律师(权位高于其他律师)。

coun·sel² /'kaʊnsl; 'kaʊnsl/ *vt* (**-ll-**, US also **-l-**) [VP 6A, D, 17] advise; give counsel to: 劝告；向…建议: *to ~ an early start*; 建议早开始; *to ~ patience*. 劝告多忍耐。*Would you ~ our giving up/~ us to give up the plan?* 你会建议我们放弃这计划吗？

coun·sel·lor (US also **coun·sel·or**) /'kaʊnsələ(r); 'kaʊnslɚ/ *n* adviser; (in Ireland and US) lawyer. 顾问；参事；(在爱尔兰及美国) 律师。

count¹ /kaʊnt; kaʊnt/ *vt, vi* **1** [VP2A, C, 3A] ~ (*from*) (*to*), say or name (eg the numerals) in order: 按顺序数(数目等): *to ~ from 1 to 20*. 从一数到二十。*He can't ~ yet*. 他还不会数数目。~-**able** *adj* that can be ~ed. 可数的；可计数的。**2** [VP6A] find the total of: 数一数(以便知其总数); 计数: *Don't forget to ~ your change*. 不要忘记这一数时核对你的零钱。*Have the votes been ~ed yet?* 选票计数了没有？'~-**ing-house** *n* building or room where accounts are kept (eg in a bank). 会计室；帐房(例如银行中者)。**3** [VP6A, 14, 2A, C] include, be included, in the reckoning: (被)计算在内，在考虑之列: *fifty people, not ~ing the children*. 五十人，儿童不算。*That doesn't ~*, need not be considered or reckoned. 那个不必考虑。**4** [VP25, 16B] consider (sth or sb) to be: 认(某物或某人)为；视为: *I ~ myself fortunate in being here*. 我能在这里实在很幸运。*I ~ it a great honour to serve you*. 我认为为你服务是很大的光荣。*I'm afraid we must ~ him as dead*. 恐怕我们得算他死了。**5** [VP14, 15B, 3A, 2C] (special uses with *adverbial particles and prepositions*): (与副词性小品词及介词连用之特殊用法):

count against sb; ~ sth against sb, be regarded, consider, to the disadvantage of: 认为(某事物)不利于某人；因(某事物)而低估某人: *His past record ~s against him*. 以往的纪录对他不利。*He is young and inexperienced, but please do not ~ that against him*. 他年轻而无经验，但请不要因此而低估他。

count among sb; sth; ~ sb/sth among sb/sth, be regarded, regard, as one of: 被认为(视为)…之一: *You ~/You are ~ed among my best friends*. 你可算是我的好朋友之一。*I no longer ~ him among my friends*. 我不再认为他是我的朋友。

count down, ~ seconds backwards (eg 10, 9, 8, 7…) as when launching a rocket, etc into space. (如发射火箭等进入太空时) 倒数秒 (例如十、九、八、七…)。Hence, 由此产生, '~-**down** *n*

(not) count for anything/nothing/much/little, (not) be of any/no etc worth or importance: 没有(无甚) 价值或重要性: *Knowledge without common sense ~s for little*. 有知识而无常识则无甚价值。*Such men do not ~ for anything*. 这种人无足轻重。

count sb/sth in, include: 包括；计及: *Go and see how many plates we have but don't ~ in the cracked ones*. 去看看我们有多少个盘子──但不要算有裂纹的。*If you're all going to the pub for a drink, you can ~ me in*, I will certainly be one of the party. 如果你们全都要去酒馆喝酒，把我算在内(我一定也要参加)。

count on/upon sb/sth, expect with confidence; rely upon: 指望；仰赖；依赖: *We ~ on your help/~ on you to help*. 我们仰赖你的帮助。*You had better not ~ on an*

increase in your salary this year. 你今年最好不要指望加薪。

count sb/sth out, (a) ~ things (slowly), one by one: (慢慢地) 一个一个地数东西: *The old lady ~ed out fifteen pence and passed it to the salesgirl*. 那老太婆慢吞吞地一个一个地数了十五便士然后交给女店员。(b) ~ up to ten over a boxer who has been knocked out: 在被击倒的拳击者上面从一数到十；判…被技术击倒: *The referee ~ed him out in the first round*. 裁判判他在第一回合被技术击倒。(c) not include: 不包括；不计及: *If it's going to be a rowdy party, ~ me out*, I shall certainly not be there. 如果那是一个吵闹的聚会，别把我算在内(我不会去)。*the House out*, (GB, House of Commons) ~ the members present and declare that, because enough members are not present, there must be an adjournment. (英国下议院) 因清点出席人数不足而宣布休会。

count sth up, find the total of: 算出总数: *Just you ~ up the number of times he has failed to keep a promise!* 你算算看他总共失信多少次了！

count² /kaʊnt; kaʊnt/ *n* **1** [C] act of counting; number got by counting: 计算；计数；得数: *Four ~s were necessary before we were certain of the total*. 要计算四次，我们对于总和才有把握。*keep/lose ~ (of)*, be aware/fail to know how many there are (of): 晓得(不晓得) 有多少? *I've bought so many new books this year that I've lost ~ of them*. 今年买的新书多得算不清。*take the ~; be out for the ~*, (boxing) be counted out. (拳击) 被判被技术击倒；被判失败。⇨ **count¹**(5). **2** [U] account(7); notice (the more usn words): 重视；注意: 顾虑 (account 及 notice 较常用): *to take no/some/any/not much, etc ~ of what people say*. 不(有一点，不太等) 顾虑别人说什么。**3** [C] (legal) one of a number of things of which a person has been accused: (法律) 被控告的各点之一; 被控事项: *He was found guilty on all ~s*. 他被控各点均经认定有罪。

count³ /kaʊnt; kaʊnt/ *n* title of nobility in France, Italy, etc (but not in GB). 伯爵 (贵族的头衔，用于法、意等国，但不用于英国)。⇨ **countess, earl**.

coun·ten·ance¹ /'kaʊntɪnəns; 'kaʊntənəns/ *n* (formal) (正式用语) **1** face, including its appearance and expression: 面容；面色: *a woman with a fierce ~*; 面目狰狞的女人; *to change ~*, change one's expression because of emotion. (因为情绪的关系而) 改变面色。*keep one's ~*, maintain one's composure (esp by not laughing). 保持镇静；不动声色(尤指忍住不笑)。*put/stare sb out of ~*, disconcert him, cause him to feel troubled or at fault (by looking at him steadily). 藐视某人) 使局促不安；使感到苦恼或茫然。**2** [U] support; approval: 支持；赞成；鼓励: *to give ~ to a person/a plan*. 支持某人(计划)。

coun·ten·ance² /'kaʊntɪnəns; 'kaʊntənəns/ *vt* [VP 6A] give support or approval to: 支持；赞助；鼓励: *to ~ a fraud*. 鼓励欺骗。*We can never ~ a war of aggression*. 我们决不可鼓励侵略战争。

counter¹ /'kaʊntə(r); 'kaʊntɚ/ *n* table or flat surface on which goods are shown, customers served, in a shop or bank. (商店、银行的) 柜台。*under the ~*, (of goods in shops) bought or sold surreptitiously, eg when they are scarce and difficult to obtain. (指商店中的货物) 暗中买卖的(如当缺货不易购得时)。

counter² /'kaʊntə(r); 'kaʊntɚ/ *n* **1** small (usu round) flat piece of metal, plastic, etc used for keeping count in games, etc; piece used in draughts(6), etc. 游戏、牌戏等中用以记分的筹码 (通常为扁平之小圆形物，用金属、塑胶等制成)；(国际象棋中所用的) 棋子。**2** (in compounds) device for keeping count (in machinery, etc): (用于复合词中) 机器等中的计算器；计数器: *'speed-~*; 计速器; *,revo'lution-~*. 转数器。

counter³ /'kaʊntə(r); 'kaʊntɚ/ *adv* ~ *to*, contrary; in the opposite direction; in opposition: (与…) 相反; (与…) 方向相反; 反对: *to act ~ to a person's wishes*; 违背某人的意愿而行事; *requirements that run/go ~ to one's*

inclinations. 与某人意见不合的要求。

counter¹ /'kauntər/; 'kauntə/ *vt, vi* [VP6A, 14, 2A, 3A] ~ *(with)*, oppose; meet an attack (with a return attack): 反驳; 反击; 还击: *They ~ed our proposal with one of their own.* 他们提出一项建议以对抗我们的建议。 *The champion ~ed with the right,* (boxing) parried a blow and returned it with a right-handed blow. (拳击) 卫冕者闪过一拳并还以右拳。

counter- /ˌkauntər/; ˌkauntə/ *pref* **1** opposite in direction: 方向相反: ~*-attraction*; 反引力; ~*-productive.* 反生产的。 **2** made in answer to: 反还: '~*-attack*; 反攻; 反击; 还击; ,~*-'espionage /-in'*telligence. 反间谍(情报)。 **3** corresponding: 对应的: '~*-part.* 互相对应的人或物; 对手。

counter·act /ˌkauntər'ækt; ˌkauntə'ækt/ *vt* [VP 6A] act against and make (action, force) of less or no effect: 抵消; 抵抗; 减少或消解(作用、力量): ~ *(the effects of) a poison/sb's bad influence.* 抵消毒物的作用 (某人之恶劣影响)。 **counter·action** /ˌkauntər'ækʃn; ˌkauntə'ækʃən/ *n* ~ing. 抵消; 消解; 反作用。

counter·at·tack /'kauntər ətæk; 'kauntərə,tæk/ *n* attack made in reply to an attack by the enemy. 反攻; 反击: □ *vt, vi* make a ~ (on). 反攻; 反击。

counter·at·trac·tion /'kauntər ə'trækʃn; ,kauntərə'trækʃən/ *n* [C] rival attraction. 反引力。

counter·bal·ance /'kauntə,bæləns; 'kauntə,bæləns/ *n* [C] weight, force, equal to another and balancing it. (与另一重物或力量相等而与之平衡的) 衡重体; 平衡锤; 平衡力。 □ *vt* /ˌkauntə'bæləns; ˌkauntə'bæləns/ [VP 6A] act as a ~ to. 与…平衡; 使平衡。

counter·blast /'kauntəblɑːst US: -blæst; 'kauntə,blæst/ *n* [C] violent reply. 猛烈的反击; 强硬的反驳。

counter·claim /'kauntəkleɪm; 'kauntə,klem/ *n* claim made in opposition to another claim: 反要求; 反诉: *a ~ for damages,* by a defendant in a lawsuit. (讼案中之被告) 反诉要求赔偿损失。

counter·clock·wise /ˌkauntə'klɒkwaɪz; ,kauntə-'klɑk,waɪz/ *adv*=**anti-clockwise** (the more usu word). (anti-clockwise 较常用)。

counter·espion·age /ˌkauntər'espɪənɑːʒ; ,kauntə-'espɪonɪʒ/ *n* [U] spying directed against the enemy's spying. 反间谍活动。

counter·feit /'kauntəfɪt; 'kauntəfɪt/ *n, adj* (sth) made or done in imitation of another thing in order to deceive: 伪造的; 仿造的; 假装取的; 假装悲伤的: ~ *money/jewels/grief.* 伪造钱币(仿造珠宝; 假装悲伤)。 *This ten-dollar bill is a ~.* 这张十元券是伪钞。 □ *vt* [VP6A] copy, imitate (coins, handwriting, etc) in order to deceive. 伪造 (钱币、笔迹等)。 ~*er n* person who ~s. 伪造者; 仿造者。

counter·foil /'kauntəfɔɪl; 'kauntə,fɔɪl/ *n* section of a cheque, receipt, etc kept by the sender as a record. (支票, 收据等的) 存根。 ⇨ **stub(2).**

counter·in·tel·li·gence /ˌkauntər ɪn'telɪdʒəns; ,kauntərɪn'telədʒəns/ *n* [U] =**counter-espionage.**

counter·ir·ri·tant /ˌkauntər'ɪrɪtənt; ,kauntə'ɪrə-tənt/ *n* sth used to produce a surface irritation and in this way relieve a more deeply seated pain, eg rheumatism. 对抗制激剂(用以产生表层刺激之药物, 以减轻剧部位较深之痛楚, 如风湿痛)。

counter·mand /ˌkauntə'mɑːnd US: -'mænd; ,kauntə'mænd/ *vt* [VP6A] take back, cancel, a command already given. 撤回或取消(已发出之命令)。

counter·mine /'kauntəmaɪn; 'kauntə,maɪn/ *n* (in war) mine (on land or sea) to counteract one of the enemy's; (fig) counterplot. (战争中) (布于陆上或水中以使敌方所布者先行爆发之) 反雷; 诱发地雷; 诱发水雷; (喻) 反计; 对抗策略。 □ *vt, vi* oppose by ~s; make a ~. 以反布雷抵消; 反布雷。

counter·offer /'kauntərɒfə(r); 'kauntə,ɑfə/ *n* offer made in reply to an offer made by sb else. 反报价; 还价。

counter·pane /'kauntəpeɪn; 'kauntə,pen/ *n* covering for a bed; bedspread. 床罩; 床单。

counter·part /'kauntəpɑːt; 'kauntə,pɑrt/ *n* person or thing exactly like, or closely corresponding to, another. 与另一个完全相似或极为相当的人或物; 互相对应的人或物; 配对物; 对方; 相对物。

counter·plot /'kauntəplɒt; 'kauntə,plɑt/ *n* plot made to defeat another plot. 反计(用以对付另一计谋之计谋); 对抗策略。 □ *vt, vi* (-tt-) make a ~ (against). 用反计(对抗); 将计就计。

counter·point /'kauntəpɔɪnt; 'kauntə,pɔɪnt/ *n* (music) (音乐)**1** [C] melody added as an accompaniment to another melody. 对位; 配合另一旋律之旋律。 **2** [U] art or method of adding melodies as accompaniment according to fixed rules. 对位法; 旋律配合法。

counter·poise /'kauntəpɔɪz; 'kauntə,pɔɪz/ *n* **1** [C] weight used to balance another weight; force, power or influence that counterbalances another. 用以平衡另一重物之重物; 秤锤; 砝码; 平衡力; 均衡力。 **2** [U] the condition of being in balance; equilibrium. 平衡; 均衡。 □ *vt* bring into balance, keep in equilibrium. 使平衡; 保持平衡。

counter-rev·ol·ution /ˌkauntə,revə'luːʃn; ,kauntə-,revə'luʃən/ *n* [U, C] political movement directed against a revolution. 反革命(对抗一项革命的政治运动)。 ~*ary* /-'luːʃənərɪ US: -nerɪ; -'luʃən,ɛrɪ/ *adj* characteristic of a ~. 反革命的。 □ *n* (*pl* -**ries**) person engaged in ~(s). 从事反革命的人; 反革命分子; 反动分子。

counter·sign /'kauntəsaɪn; 'kauntə,saɪn/ *n* password; secret word(s) to be given, on demand, to a sentry before he allows sb to pass: 口令; 答令(对哨兵以便通过之暗语): *'Advance and give the ~'.* '向前来说出口令'。 □ *vt* [VP6A] add another signature to (a document) to give it authority. 加另一签字于(文件)上以加强其效力; 连署; 副署; 会签。

counter·sink /'kauntəsɪŋk; 'kauntə,sɪŋk/ *vt* (*pt* -**sank** /-sæŋk; -,sæŋk/, *pp* -**sunk** /-sʌŋk; -,sʌŋk/) **1** enlarge the top of (a hole) so that the head of a screw or bolt fits in level with or below the surface. 锪孔; 加大(孔洞)的顶端以便螺丝钉或螺栓头旋入而与表面平齐或低于表面; 钻大(孔口)。 **2** sink the head of a screw or bolt) in such an enlarged hole. 将(螺丝钉或螺栓头)旋入此种加大之孔中。

counter·tenor /ˌkauntə'tenə(r); ,kauntə'tenə/ *n* (music) (part for an) (adult person with a) male voice higher than tenor; male alto. (音乐)上次中音(成人男声之最高者); 乐谱中的上次中音部;唱上次中音者。

counter·vail /'kauntəveɪl; ,kauntə'vel/ *vt, vi* **1** [VP6A] counterbalance. 使平衡。 **2** [VP2A] have equal or compensating power against: 抵销: ~*ing duties*(3), to be paid (as part of a tariff) on imports on which a subsidy is paid in the exporting country. (对有出口津贴的进口货所征收的) 抵销关税。

count·ess /'kauntɪs; 'kauntɪs/ *n* wife or widow of a count or earl; woman to whom an earldom has descended. 伯爵夫人; 女伯爵。

count·less /'kauntlɪs; 'kauntlɪs/ *adj* that cannot be counted (because too numerous). (因太多而) 不能数的; 无数的; 数不清的。

coun·tri·fied /'kʌntrɪfaɪd; 'kʌntrɪ,faɪd/ *adj* rural; rustic; having the unsophisticated ways, habits, outlook, etc, of those who live in the country(4), not of towns. 乡村的; 有乡村特色的; 有乡下人之单纯方式、习惯、见解等的; 纯朴的; 土气的。

coun·try /'kʌntrɪ; 'kʌntrɪ/ *n* (*pl* -**ries**) **1** [C] land occupied by a nation: 国家; 国土: *European countries.* 欧洲国家。 **2** [C] land of a person's birth or citizenship: 故乡; 祖国: *to return to one's own ~.* 返回故乡。 **3** the ~, the people of a ~(1); the nation as a whole: 一国的人民; 全国: *Does the ~ want war?* 全体国人都要战争吗? *go to the ~,* (GB) appeal to the public by a

general election for the right to form a government(3). (英)举行大选(要求全民普选以决定组阁之权)。**4 the ~**, land used for farming, land consisting of open spaces, etc; the contrary of town and suburb: 乡间;田野;乡间 (与城市及城郊相对): *to live in the ~*; 居住于乡间; *to spend a day in the ~*. 在乡间度过一日。**5** (used attrib) of or in the **~**(4): (用作定语) 乡间的; 乡下的: *~ life*. 乡间生活; *~ roads*. 乡下的路。**~ club**, club in the **~** or suburbs, where members may enjoy outdoor sports, etc. 乡村俱乐部(会员可在此享受户外运动等)。**~ cousin**, (colloq) person who is unaccustomed to town life and ways, (口) 不惯城市生活的人; 乡巴佬; 乡下佬。**~ dance**, (esp GB) one in which couples are face to face in two long lines or face inwards from four sides. (尤指英国的) 土风舞(由男女面对面排成两长排或面向内排成四边形而舞之)。**~ gentleman**, man who owns land in the **~** and has a house there. 乡绅(在乡间拥有田地房产之人)。**~-house**, **~-seat**, house of a **~** gentleman. 乡绅的住宅; 庄园。**'~ party**, political party supporting agricultural interests (against manufacturing interests). 农民党(支持农民利益以对抗实业利益的政党)。**6** [U] (with attrib *adj*) area of land (esp considered with reference to its physical or geographical features): (与定语形容词连用) (带有某种地形或地理特点的) 旷野; 地域; 地带: *We passed through miles of densely wooded ~*. 我们经过了许多英里茂密的森林地带。*This is unknown ~ to me*, I have not been through it before(or, fig, This is a branch of learning, etc with which I am unfamiliar). 这地方我未曾到过。(或作喻) 这门学问我不懂。

coun·try·man /ˈkʌntrɪmən; ˈkʌntrɪmən/, **coun·try·woman** /ˈkʌntrɪwʊmən; ˈkʌntrɪˌwʊmən/ *n* (*pl* **-men, -women**) **1** person living in the country(4). 乡下人;乡下女人。**2** person of one's own (or a specified) country(1). 同国人;同胞;某国人。

coun·try·side /ˈkʌntrɪsaɪd; ˈkʌntrɪˌsaɪd/ *n* [U] rural area(s) (contrasted with urban areas): 乡村地区; 乡间(与市区相对): *The English ~ looks its best in May and June*. 英国的乡村在五、六月间最美。*The preservation of the ~ is important*. 乡村地区的保护是重要的。

county /ˈkaʊntɪ; ˈkaʊntɪ/ *n* **1** [C] division of GB, the largest unit of local government: 郡; 州(英国的最大地方行政区域): *the ~ of Kent*. 肯特郡。**~ borough**, town having the right to send one or more representatives to Parliament and administrative powers similar to those of a **~** council. 行政自治市(有权自行选出一位或更多国会议员之城市,其行政权同郡议会)。**~ council**, body of persons elected to govern a **~** family. 郡议会。**~ court**, local court for certain legal matters, eg recovery of debt. 郡法院(审判某些法律案件的地方法院,如债务)。**~ family**, family that has lived in a **~** for many generations and has an ancestral home in it. 郡中世家 (许多代居于某郡内并有祖居在该郡的家族)。**~ town**, (US 美 = **~ seat**) chief town of a **~**, where administration is carried on. 郡之首府(郡政府所在地)。**the home counties**, those round London. 伦敦四周的郡都。**the ~**, (with *sing* or *pl v*) all the **~** families. (用单数或复数形词) 所有的郡中世家。**2** (in US and other countries) subdivision of a State. (美国及其他国家之) 郡; 县 (州之下的行政区分)。**3** (GB; pred use) of a **~** family: (英) 用作表语) 郡中世家的: *Are you ~?* 你世代都居于郡中吗?

coup /kuː; kuː/ *n* (*pl* **~s** /kuːz; kuːz/) (F) sudden action taken to get power, obtain a desired result, etc: (法) (为获得权力、达到欲求的目的所采取的) 突然行动; 猝然一击; 奇袭妙计: *He pulled off / made a great ~*, succeeded in what he attempted. 他大为(一举)成功。**d'état** /kuː deɪˈtɑː; ˈkudeˈtɑ/, violent or unconstitutional change in government. 政变(以暴力或不合宪法方式改变政权)。**~ de grâce** /kuːdəˈɡrɑːs US: ˈɡrɑːs; kudeˈɡrɑːs/, finishing stroke. 最后(致命的)一击。

coupé /ˈkuːpeɪ US: kuːˈpeɪ; kuˈpe/ *n* (*pl* **~s** /-peɪz;

-ˈpez/) **1** closed horse-drawn carriage with one inside seat for two people and an outside seat for the driver. 一种有篷的二人座位(车篷内一个座位可坐两人,篷外有车夫座)。**2** (US **coupe** /kuːp; kup/) two-door motor-car for two people. (可容两人之) 双门小轿车。

couple[1] /ˈkʌpl; ˈkʌpl/ *n* two persons or things, seen together or associated: 一对; 一双(在一起或互有关系的两个人或物): *married ~s*; 夫妇; *courting ~s*. 对对情侣。*Ten ~s took the floor*, went out into the middle of the room to dance. 有十对下池跳舞。*He went out shooting and came back with a ~ of rabbits*. 他出去打猎,猎获几只兔子回来。

couple[2] /ˈkʌpl; ˈkʌpl/ *vt, vi* **1** [VP6A, 14] fasten, join (two things) together: 连合或连接(二物): *to ~ two railway coaches*. 连接二节火车客车厢。*The dining-car was ~d on at Crewe*. 餐车是在克鲁挂上的。*We ~ the name of Oxford with the idea of learning*. 我们将牛津之名与学术的观念联在一起。**2** [VP6A, 2A] marry; [VP 2A] (of animals) unite sexually; [VP2A] (of things) come together; unite. (和…) 结婚; (指动物) 交配; (指事物) 联合; 关系; 联合。

coup·let /ˈkʌplɪt; ˈkʌplɪt/ *n* two successive lines of verse, equal in length and with rhyme: 相连、同长度并押韵的两行诗句; 对句: *a heroic ~*, one with five feet*(6) and ten syllables. 英雄双行体(每行各五音步十音节)。

coup·ling /ˈkʌplɪŋ; ˈkʌplɪŋ/ *n* [U] act of joining; [C] link, etc that joins two parts, esp two railway coaches or other vehicles. 连合; 结合; 接连; 联接器; 耦合 (尤指火车车厢或其他车辆的) 挂钩; 车钩。

cou·pon /ˈkuːpɒn; ˈkupɑn/ *n* ticket, part of a document, paper, bond, etc, which gives the holder the right to receive sth or do sth, eg a voucher given with a purchase to be exchanged for goods; entry form for a competition: 证明持有人有某种权利的卡片、条子、票、券等(例如购物时所附赠以交换赠品的礼券);参与竞争的登记单: *fill in the football ~s*, by forecasting results of matches. 填写足球赛门票的附单(以预测比赛的结果)。

cour·age /ˈkʌrɪdʒ; ˈkɜːrɪdʒ/ *n* [U] bravery; quality that enables a person to control fear in the face of danger, pain, misfortune, etc. 勇敢; 勇气(使人能在危险、痛苦、不幸等之中有克制恐惧的精神力量): *have the ~ of one's convictions*, be brave enough to do what one feels to be right. 有勇气去做自己认为对的事。*not have the ~ (to do sth)*, not be brave enough. 没勇气…。*lose ~*, become less brave. 失去勇气。*take / pluck up / master up / summon up ~*, be brave. 鼓起勇气。*take one's ~ in both hands*, summon up one's ~ for sth needing to be done. 鼓起勇气(做必须做的事)。

cou·rageous /kəˈreɪdʒəs; kəˈredʒəs/ *adj* brave; fearless; 勇敢的; 无畏的; 不怕的: *He was ~ of him to oppose his chief*. 他敢反对他的上司,真是勇敢。**~·ly** *adv*

cour·gette /kʊəˈʒet; kʊrˈʒet/ *n* (US 美 = *zucchini*) small green marrow(3) eaten as a vegetable. 小胡瓜(作蔬菜食用的一种小而绿色的葫芦科植物); 一种菜瓜。⇔ the illus at **vegetable**. 参看 vegetable 之插图。

cour·ier /ˈkʊrɪə(r); ˈkʊrɪə/ *n* **1** person who is paid to attend to details of travel (eg buying tickets, arranging for hotels, etc) and (sometimes) accompanying travellers. (受雇照料旅行事务如买票、订旅馆等, 有时并陪伴旅客的)旅游服务员。**2** messenger carrying news or important government papers. 递送新闻或重要官署文件的信差。

course[1] /kɔːs; kɔrs/ *n* **1** [U] forward movement in space or time: (空间或时间的) 前进; 进行: *the ~ of life from the cradle to the grave*; 人生自摇篮至墓穴的旅程; 从出生到死亡的人生旅程; *a river in its ~ to the sea*; 流向大海的河; *the ~ of events*. 世事的发展。*in ~ of*, in process of: 在…过程中: *The railway is in ~ of construction*, being built. 铁路正在修筑中。*in due ~*, in the natural order; at the normal time: 照自然的顺序; 到适

当的时候: *Sow the seed now and in due ~ you will have the flowers.* 现在就播种，到时候你就会有花。 **in the ~ of**, during: 在…期间: *in the ~ of the discussion;* 在讨论期间; *in the ~ of conversation, while we were talking;* 在谈话中; *in the ~ of centuries, as the centuries pass.* 经过数百年的期间。 **in the (ordinary) ~ of nature/events/things**, normally; as part of the normal or expected sequence of events. 照正常的情形; 依自然发展的常理。 **in (the) ~ of time**, at length; finally; when (enough) time has passed. 终于; 最后; 总有一天。 **2** [C] direction taken by sth; line along which sth moves; line of action: (某事物的)进行方向; 所经之路; 行动方针: *a map that shows the ~s of the chief rivers;* 示明主要河流所经过之区域的地图; (liter) (文) *the stars in their ~s.* 沿着轨道运行的星辰。 *Our ~ was due north.* 我们的路线是向正北。 *The ~ of the argument suddenly changed, went in a different direction.* 辩论的方向忽然改变了。 *What are the ~s open to us,* the ways in which we may proceed to act? 我们有些什么路可走(即有些什么办法可以采取)? *He took to evil ~s,* formed bad ways of living. 他自甘堕落(耽于放荡的生活)。 **run/take its ~**, develop as is normal; proceed to the usual end: 听其自然发展; 进行到通常的结局为止: *The disease must run its ~.* 这病一定要完全发作过后才会好。 *The law must take its ~,* the lawyers cannot save you from punishment. 法律必循其道(律师也无法教你使你免于受罚)。 *We can do nothing except let matters run/take their ~.* 我们除了一切听其自然之外别无办法。 **(as) a matter of ~,** (in)a way that one would expect to be or happen, for which no effort is needed: 当然之事; 自然之事(如所预料必然发生而不需费力的事): *You needn't ask him to come; he'll come as a matter of ~.* 你不需要请求他来; 他自然会来。 *Some people take my help as a matter of ~,* expect to get it without asking for it (or even thanking me for it). 有些人把我对他们的帮助视为当然之事(认为不必要求我也应该帮助他们, 甚至连谢也不谢)。 **of ~,** naturally; certainly: 自然; 当然: *'Do you study hard?' 'Of ~ I do'.* '你用功读书吗?' '我当然用功'。 **on/off ~,** in the right/wrong direction: 在正确(不正确)方向: *Our ship was blown off ~.* 我们的船被(风)吹离航道。 **3** [C] ground for golf: 高尔夫球场: *a 'golf-~;* 高尔夫球场; place for horse-races: 跑马场: *a 'race-~.* 跑马场。 **stay the ~,** (lit, fig) continue going until the end; not give up. (字面,喻)继续进行至结局为止; 贯彻到底; 不放弃。 **4** [C] series of talks, treatments, etc: (谈话、治疗等的)一连串; 连续; 疗程: *a ~ of lectures/study/instuction;* 连续的讲演(一门课程; 一门教程); *a ~ of X-ray treatment/pills;* X 光治疗(药丸治疗)疗程; *the highschool ~.* 中学学程。 **5** [C] continuous layer of brick, stone, etc in a wall: (墙壁中砖、石等之连续的)层: *a 'damp~,* layer of slate or other material to prevent damp rising from the ground. (由一层石板或其他材料砌成以防止地上潮气上升的)防湿层。 **6** [C] one of the several parts of a meal, eg soup, fish, dessert: 一道菜或点心: *a dinner of five ~s/a five-~ dinner;* 五道菜的正餐; *the main ~.* 主菜。 **7** (naut) sail fastened to the lowest yard of a mast. (航海)大横帆(系于最低帆桁者)。

course² /kɔːs; kɔrs/ *vt, vi* **1** [VP6A, 2A] chase (esp hares) with dogs (greyhounds). 用猎犬追猎(尤指野兔)。 **2** [VP2C] move quickly; (of liquids) run: 急行; (指液体)流动: *The blood ~d through his veins.* 血在他的血管中奔流。 *Tears ~d down her cheeks.* 眼泪从她的两颊流下。 **cours·ing** /ˈkɔːsɪŋ; ˈkɔrsɪŋ/ *n* sport of chasing hares with greyhounds (by sight, not scent). 用猎犬借视觉而不借嗅觉追捕野兔。

courser /ˈkɔːsə(r); ˈkɔrsə/ *n* (poet) swift horse. (诗)骏马。

court¹ /kɔːt; kɔrt/ *n* **1** [C] place where law-cases are held; the judges, magistrates, and other officers who administer justice: 法院; 法庭; 执法者(指法官及其他执法官员): *a ~ of 'law/a 'law ~;* 法院; *a '~-room;*

法庭; *a ~ of justice;* 法院; *a po'lice-~;* 警务法庭; *a (military or naval) ~ of inquiry,* one that deals with cases of indiscipline, etc. (陆军或海军的)侦讯法庭; 调查庭 (处理违纪等案件)。 *The prisoner was brought to ~ for trial.* 那囚犯被提上法庭受审。 *The judge ordered the ~ to be cleared,* ordered members of the public to leave. 法官令旁听的群众离开法庭。 *The case was settled out of ~,* a settlement was reached that made it unnecessary for the case to be decided in ~. 该案在庭外和解(不必再由法庭裁判)。 **be ruled/put out of ~; put oneself out of ~,** do or say sth so that one is not entitled to be heard in ~. 诉讼不被受理; 遭驳回。 **~ of assize;** (C) **quarter sessions,** ~s in England and Wales before 1971. 一九七一年以前的英格兰及威尔士法庭。 **Crown C~,** (since 1971) one that may sit anywhere in England and Wales for all cases above magistrates' level (replacing the former assize and quarter sessions). 直辖法院(一九七一年以后取代以上述的 ~ of assize 及 ~ of quarter sessions, 可在英格兰及威尔士之任何地方开庭审判一切案件, 权力在地方法院之上)。 **2** [U] residence of a sovereign; his family and officials, councillors, etc: 朝廷; 宫廷: *The C~ of St James's,* the ~ of the British sovereign. 英国宫廷。 *The C~ went into mourning when the Queen's uncle died.* 当女王的叔父逝世时, 王宫服丧。 **be presented at ~,** make one's first appearance at a state reception at the sovereign's ~. 初次入朝觐见帝王; 初次受帝王接见。 **hold ~,** = hold†(12). 1~card, playing card with a king, queen or knave. 绘有王、后或侍卫的纸牌(即扑克牌中的 K, Q 或 J)。 **3** [C] space marked out for certain games: 某些游戏的场地: *a 'tennis-~.* 网球场。 *Do you prefer grass ~s or hard ~s?* 你比较喜欢草地球场还是硬地球场? ⇨ the illus at **tennis.** 参看 tennis 之插图。 **4** (also 亦作 '~·yard) unroofed space with walls or buildings round it, eg in a college at Cambridge, in a castle or an old inn; the buildings round such a space. (四周由墙壁或建筑物围 ' 成的)庭院; 大天井(如剑桥大学之学院内、古堡内或古客栈内者); 天井周围的建筑物。 Cf 参较 *quadrangle* at Oxford. ⇨ **close³.** **5** [C] small enclosed part of a house, usu opening off a street. 与街道相通的小院。 **6** [U] *pay ~ to (a woman),* (formal) try to win her affections. (正式用语)向女人献殷勤求爱。

court² /kɔːt; kɔrt/ *vt, vi* **1** [VP6A, 2A] try to win the affections of, with a view to marriage: 向…求爱; 追求: *He had been ~ing Jane for six months.* 他追求简已六个月之久。 *There were several ~ing couples in the park.* 公园中有几对谈情说爱的男女。 **2** [VP6A] try to win or obtain: 设法赢得; 设法获得; 恳求; 乞求: *to ~ sb's approval/support;* 求某人赞成(支持); *to ~ applause.* 设法赢得喝彩或称赞。 **3** [VP6A] act in such a way that one may meet or receive (sth disagreeable): 招惹; 招致(不愉快之事): *to ~ defeat/danger/disaster.* 招致失败(危险, 灾祸)。

cour·te·ous /ˈkɜːtɪəs; ˈkɜrtɪəs/ *adj* having, showing, good manners; polite and kind (to). 彬彬有礼的; 谦恭的; 客气的(与 to 连用)。 ~·ly *adv*

court·esan /ˌkɔːtɪˈzæn US: ˈkɔːtɪzn; ˈkɔrtəzn/ *n* (in former times, esp in court(2) circles) refined or highplaced prostitute who (because of her beauty, wit, success) could limit the number of men to whom she gave herself. (昔时, 尤指王公贵族中之)高雅或高等妓女(因其美色、才智或成就, 仅接待少数男人)。

cour·tesy /ˈkɜːtəsɪ; ˈkɜrtəsɪ/ *n* **1** [U] courteous behaviour. 礼貌; 谦恭的态度。 **2** [C] (pl -sies) courteous act. 谦恭的行为。 **3** '~ title, (GB) title of nobility having no legal validity. (英)礼貌上的贵族衔称(实际上被称呼者并未拥有此头衔)。 **by ~ of,** by favour or permission, usu free of charge: 由于…的好意或许可(通常免费): *a radio programme presented by ~ of ...* 由…所提供的广播节目。

court·ier /ˈkɔːtɪə(r); ˈkɔrtɪr/ *n* person in attendance at the court of a sovereign: 朝臣(朝廷中的侍臣): *the*

King and his ～s. 国王及其朝臣。

court·ly /'kɔːtlɪ; 'kɔrtlɪ/ *adj* (**-ier, -iest**) polite and dignified. 谦和而威严的。 **court·li·ness** *n*

court-mar·tial /ˌkɔːt'mɑːʃl; 'kɔrtmɑrʃəl/ *n* (*pl* **courts-martial**) court for trying offences against military law; trial by ～. 军事法庭 (审讯违犯军法案件);军法审判。 □ *vt* [VP6A] try (sb) in a court of this kind. 在军事法庭审讯(某人);以军法审判。

court·ship /'kɔːtʃɪp; 'kɔrtʃɪp/ *n* courting(1); [C] period during which this lasts: 求爱; 追求; 追求期间: *after a year's ～;* 经过了一年的追求; *after a brief ～.* 经过短时间的追求。

court·yard /'kɔːtjɑːd; 'kɔrtˌjɑrd/ *n* = **court**[1](4).

cousin /'kʌzn; 'kʌzn/ *n* **first ～,** child of one's uncle or aunt. 堂兄弟; 堂姐妹; 表兄弟; 表姐妹。 **second ～,** child of one's parent's first ～. 远房堂(表)兄弟姐妹。 **～·ly** *adj* of, suitable for, ～: (适合于)堂(表)兄弟姐妹的: *～ly affection.* 堂(表)兄弟姐妹之亲情。

cove[1] /kəʊv; kov/ *n* small bay[2]. 小海湾。

a cove

cove[2] /kəʊv; kov/ *n* (GB, dated *sl*) person. (英,过时俚语)人。

coven /'kʌvn; 'kʌvən/ *n* assembly of witches. (女巫们的)集会。

cov·en·ant /'kʌvənənt; 'kʌvənənt/ *n* 1 (legal) formal agreement that is legally binding. (法律)(有法律约束力的正式)合约;契约;盟约。 **deed of '～,** written, signed and sealed agreement, usu concerning property. (经签字并盖章,通常为有关房地产的)契据; 契约书。2 undertaking to make regular payments to a charity, trust, etc. (为慈善事业、信托财产等而定期付款的)承诺。□ *vt, vi* [VP6A, 7A, 9, 14, 3A] ～ **(with sb) (for sth),** make a ～. 订立契约。

Cov·en·try /'kɒvntrɪ; 'kʌvəntrɪ/ *n* town in Warwickshire, GB. 考文垂(英国沃里克郡之一镇)。 **send a person to ～,** refuse to associate with him (esp by not speaking to him). 拒绝与某人交往 (尤指不与其交谈)。

cover[1] /'kʌvə(r); 'kʌvə/ *vt* [VP6A, 15A, B] 1 place (one substance or thing) over or in front of (another); hide or protect (sth) in this way; lie or extend over; occupy the surface of: 用东西盖住 | 加盖以藏匿或保护; 遮盖; 遮蔽…的表面: *C～ the table with a cloth.* 在桌上铺一块台布。 *Pull your skirt down and ～ your knees.* 把你的裙子拉下一点, 遮住你的膝盖。 *We shall ～ the seat of this old chair with chintz.* 我们将用印花布罩住这旧椅子的椅面。 *Snow ～ed the ground.* 雪盖住地面。 *The floods ～ed large areas on both banks of the river.* 洪水淹没了河两岸很大的区域。 *She ～ed her face in/with her hands.* 她以双手掩面。 *He laughed to ～ (= hide) his nervousness.* 他大笑以掩饰其紧张的心情。 **～ in,** complete the ～ing of: 完全盖上: *The grave was quickly ～ed in,* filled with earth. 墓穴很快就被泥土盖满。 **～ over,** spread sth over: 盖住; 覆盖: *to ～ over a hole in a roof.* 盖住屋顶漏洞。 **～ up,** wrap up, hide: 包裹; 隐藏: *C～ yourself up well.* On warm clothes, etc. 衣服穿暖一点。 *How can we ～ up our tracks/our mistakes?* 我们如何能掩藏住我们的踪迹(错误)? Hence, 由此产生

～-up *n* (fig, colloq) way of hiding: (喻, 口)掩饰或隐藏的方法: *a ～-up for her shyness.* 掩饰她害羞的方法。 **～ed wagon** *n* (US) large wagon with an arched canvas roof, used by pioneers for travel across the prairies. (美) 大篷车 (昔时拓荒者用以旅行于大草原之上的有弧形遮篷的大车)。 2 **be ～ed with, (a)** have a great number or amount of: 有很多的:*trees ～ed with blossom / fruit;* 开满花(结满果实)的树; *roses ～ed with greenfly.* 生满绿蚜虫的玫瑰。 **(b)** have as a natural coat: 天然生有(毛皮):*Cats are ～ed with fur and dogs are ～ed with hair.* 猫长着一身绒毛,狗长着一身粗毛。 **(c)** (of non-material things) be overcome by: (指精神或心灵) 为…所克服: *～ed with shame / confusion.* 不胜羞愧(惶惑)。3 sprinkle or strew with: 溅; 洒; 撒布: *A taxi went by and ～ed us with mud.* 一辆计程车驶过去, 溅了我们一身泥。 *The wind blew from the desert and ～ed everything with sand.* 风从沙漠里吹过来, 使一切东西都覆盖着一层沙。 4 (reflex) bring upon oneself: (反身)使自身满载或蒙受: *～ oneself with glory / honour / disgrace.* 使自身感到光荣(获得荣誉、蒙受耻辱)。5 protect: 保护; 掩护; 庇护: *He ～ed his wife from the man's blows with his own body.* 他以自己的身体掩护他的妻子, 使不致受到那人的殴打。 *Warships ～ed the landing of the invading army,* fired their guns to keep the enemy at a distance, etc. 战舰炮火掩护攻击部队登陆。 *Are you ～ed* (= insured) *against fire and theft?* 你们是否已保火险及窃盗险? 6 travel (a certain distance): 走(一段路程): *By sunset we had ～ed thirty miles.* 日落的时候, 我们已走了三十英里。7 (of guns, fortresses, etc) command(6); dominate: (指大炮、堡垒等)炮火能及; 射程能达到; 能控制: *Our heavy artillery ～ed every possible approach to the town.* 我们的重炮炮火控制了通达镇上的每一条路。8 keep a gun aimed at sb (so that he cannot shoot or escape): 以枪炮瞄准着某人 (使其不能射击或逃走): *C～ your man!* 瞄准你的敌人! *Keep them ～ed!* 举枪对着他们瞄准(不要中止)! 9 (of money) be enough for: (指钱)够用; 足敷: *£10 will ～ my needs for the journey.* 十英镑即足够我的旅行费用。 *We have only just ～ed our expenses,* made enough for our expenses, but no profit. 我们的收入仅够开支而已(无盈余)。10 include; extend over; be adequate for: 包括; 包罗; 涵盖; 适用于: *Professor A's lectures ～ed the subject thoroughly.* A 教授的演讲将这题目讲得很透彻。 *His researches ～ed a wide field.* 他的研究范围很广。 *This book does not fully ～ the subject,* does not deal with all aspects of it. 这本书对于这题目阐述不够详尽。 *Do the rules ～ (= Are they adequate for) all possible cases?* 这些规则是否适用于所有可能的情形? 11 (in games such as cricket and baseball) stand behind (a player) to stop balls that he may miss: (板球及棒球戏)立于 (球手) 后方以捕捉所失之球: *The short-stop ～ed second base.* 游击手立于第二垒之后守球。12 (of a journalist) report (what is said and done at meetings, on public occasions, etc): (指新闻记者)采访; 报道(会议、公众场合等之新闻): *～ the Labour Party's annual conference.* 采访工党年会新闻。 **～·ing** *n* sth that ～s: 遮盖物: *a leafy ～ing,* the trees. 树木;树荫。 □ *part adj* ～**ing letter,** one sent with a document, or with goods, etc.公文,货物等的附函。

cover[2] /'kʌvə(r); 'kʌvə/ *n* 1 thing that covers: 遮盖物; 盖子; 套子: *When the water boils, take the ～* (= lid) *from the pan.* 当水开了的时候, 将锅盖揭开。 *Some chairs are fitted with loose ～s.* 有些椅子装着可以随意取下和套上的套子。2 binding of a book, magazine, etc; either half of this: (书籍、杂志等的)封面; 壳面: *The book needs a new ～.* 这书需要装个新封面。 *from ～ to ～,* from beginning to end: 从头到尾: *The child read the book from ～ to ～.* 那孩子将书从头读到尾。 **～ girl,** girl who poses for photographs to be used on the cover of a magazine. (杂志的)封面女郎。3 wrapper or envelope. 封套; 封皮。 *under plain ～,* in a parcel or envelope which has no indication of the firm, the contents, etc: 在未写明商号、内容等的包裹或信封中: *The book of*

photographs of girls in the nude is being sent under plain ~. 那本裸体女郎照片的书是用未写明寄件者商号及内容的信封邮寄的。**under separate ~,** (comm) in a separate parcel or envelope: (商)在另一包裹或信封中; 另行封寄: *We are sending the goods under separate ~.* 货品我们将另行封寄。**4** [U] place or area giving shelter or protection: 可以隐蔽的地方; 躲避处; 庇护所: *The land was flat and treeless and provided no ~ for the troops.* 该地平坦且无树木, 军队无法隐蔽。**take ~,** place oneself where one is protected or concealed: 利用掩护物将自己隐藏起来; 掩蔽: *There was nowhere where we could take ~,* eg from rain. 没有一个我们可以躲避的地方(如避雨)。**under ~,** sheltered. 在遮蔽之下; 在保护之下。**5** [U] woods or undergrowth protecting animals, etc.(隐藏动物等的)丛林。**break ~,** (eg of a fox) come out of the undergrowth, etc. (指狐狸等)自所隐藏的树丛中出来。**6** [U] **under ~ of,** with a pretence of: 以…之名义; 在…的伪装下; 以…为借口; 假托…之名: *under ~ of friendship / religion;* 借友谊 (宗教) 之名: *murders committed under ~ of patriotism.* 假借爱国之口实所犯的谋杀罪行。**7** [U] protection from attack: 保护(以免受攻击); 掩护: *give ~.* 给予掩护。**8** place laid at table for a meal: 餐桌上所布置的席位: *C~ s were laid for six.* 布置了六个席位。'**~ charge** n (in a restaurant) charge in addition to the cost of the food and drink. (餐馆中饮食费用以外之)附加费; 服务费。**9** [U] (comm) money deposited to meet a liability or possible loss.(商)保证金; 负债或亏损准备金。**10** [U] insurance against loss, damage, etc: 损坏保险: *Does your policy provide adequate ~ against fire?* 你的保险单是否提供适当的火险? '**~ note,** document from an insurance company to provide temporary ~ between the acceptance and issue of a policy. 临时保单(保险公司所发给之文件, 提供在接受投保至发给保单之期间的临时保单)。

cover·age /'kʌvərɪdʒ; 'kʌvərɪdʒ/ n [U] covering of events, etc: 采访新闻; 新闻报道: *TV ~ of the election campaign,* eg by televising political meetings, interviews with candidates and voters. 竞选活动的电视报道(如转播政党大会实况, 访问侯选人及投票人等)。⇨ **cover¹(12).**

cover·let /'kʌvəlɪt; 'kʌvəlɪt/ n bedspread. 床单; 床罩。

cov·ert¹ /'kʌvət; 'kʌvət/ adj (half-) hidden; disguised: (半)隐藏的; 掩饰的; 暗地的: ~ *glances / threats.* 偷偷的瞥视(暗地的威胁)。~**·ly** adv ⇨ **overt.**

cov·ert² /'kʌvət; 'kʌvət/ n area of thick undergrowth in which animals hide. 动物所隐藏的树丛。*draw a ~,* search it (for foxes, etc). 搜索树丛(找寻狐狸等)。⇨ **cover²(5).**

coveo /'kʌvɪt; 'kʌvɪt/ vt [VP6A] desire eagerly (esp sth that belongs to sb else). 垂涎; 贪图(尤指属于他人的东西)。

covet·ous /'kʌvɪtəs; 'kʌvətəs/ adj ~ **(of),** eagerly desirous (esp of things belonging to sb else). 垂涎的; 贪图(尤指他人之物)的。~**·ly** adv ~**·ness** n

covey /'kʌvɪ; 'kʌvɪ/ n (pl ~**s**) brood, small flock of partridges. 一窝或一小群鹧鸪。

cow¹ /kau; kau/ n fully grown female of any animal of the ox family, esp the domestic kind kept by farmers for producing milk, ⇨ the illus at **domestic;** also female elephant, rhinoceros, whale, etc. 母牛; 牝牛; (尤指饲养以取其乳之)乳牛(参看 domestic 之插图); (亦指)母象; 母犀牛; 母鲸 (等)。⇨ **bull¹(1), calf¹(1), heifer, steer¹.** '**cowbell,** bell hung round a cow's neck to indicate her whereabouts. 牛铃(系于牛颈上的铃, 用以指示其所在)。'**cow·boy,** man (usu on horseback) who looks after cattle in the western parts of the US. 美国西部的牧人(通常骑于马上照料牛群)。'**cowcatcher,** metal frame fastened to the front of a railway engine to push obstacles off the track. (火车机车前的)排障装置。'**cow·hand, 'cow·herd,** person who looks after cattle at pasture. 牧牛者; 牧人; 牧童。'**cow·hide,** leather (or a strip of leather as a whip) made from a

cow's hide. 牛皮所制的皮革; 牛皮鞭。'**cow·house, 'cow·shed,** building in which cows are kept when not at pasture, or to which they are taken to be milked. 牛舍(在未放牧时关牛的房舍, 或挤牛奶的地方)。'**cow·man** /-mon; -mən/ (pl -**men**), man responsible for milking cows. 挤牛奶的工人。**cow·skin,** (leather from the) skin of a cow. 牛皮; 牛皮革。

cow² /kau; kau/ vt [VP6A] frighten (sb) into submission: 恐吓(某人)使屈服: *The child had a cowed look,* looked frightened because of threats of violence, etc. 那孩子(因受恐吓等而)显出畏惧的样子。

cow·ard /'kauəd; 'kauəd/ n person unable to control his fear; person who runs away from danger. 胆小的人; 胆怯者; 懦夫。*turn ~,* become a ~. 变成懦夫。~**·ly** adj **1** not brave. 胆小的; 怯懦的。**2** contemptible; of or like a ~: 可鄙的; 懦夫的: *a ~ly lie;* 可鄙的谎言; ~*ly behaviour.* 懦夫的行为。

cow·ard·ice /'kauədɪs; 'kauədɪs/ n [U] feeling, way of behaviour, of a coward; faint-heartedness. 胆小; 怯懦; 卑怯。

cower /'kauə(r); 'kauə/ vi [VP2A, C] lower the body; crouch; shrink back from cold, misery, fear, shame: 屈缩身体; 畏缩; 退缩(因寒冷、痛苦、恐惧或羞耻): *The dog ~ed under the table when its master raised the whip.* 那条狗在主人扬起鞭子时缩到桌子下面去了。

cowl /kaul; kaul/ n **1** long, loose gown (as worn by monks) with a hood that can be pulled over the head; the hood itself. (僧人等所穿)连带头巾的宽松长袍; 头巾。**2** metal cap for a chimney, ventilating pipe, etc, often made so as to revolve with the wind and improve the draught (1). 装于烟囱、通风管等顶上可以随风旋转以利通风的罩子; 通风帽。~**·ing** n removable metal covering for an (aircraft) engine. 发动机整流罩(飞机等引擎的活动金属罩)。

cow·pox /'kaupɒks; 'kau,paks/ n contagious disease of cattle, caused by a virus which, when isolated, is the source of vaccine for smallpox. 牛痘(由于病毒所引起的一种牛的传染病, 此种病毒经过分离后即为牛痘苗之来源)。

cow·rie /'kaurɪ; 'kaurɪ/ n (pl ~**s**) small shell formerly used as money in parts of Africa and Asia. 子安贝(从前为非洲及亚洲某些地区用作钱币)。

cow·slip /'kauslɪp; 'kau,slɪp/ n small plant with yellow flowers, growing wild in temperate countries. 黄花九轮草; 立金花; 野樱草(开黄花, 野生于温带国家)。

cox /kɒks; kɑks/ n (colloq abbr of) coxswain. (口)舵手(coxswain 之略)。□ vt, vi [VP6A, 2A] act as coxswain (of a rowing-boat): 做(划船的)舵手; 掌舵: *The Oxford boat was coxed by....* 牛津大学的赛艇由…人掌舵。

cox·comb /'kɒkskəum; 'kɑks,kom/ n **1** vain, foolish person, esp one who pays too much attention to his clothes. 爱虚荣而糊涂的人; (尤指)特别注意衣着的人; 花花公子。**2** = **cockscomb(2).**

cox·swain /'kɒksn; 'kaksṇ/ n person who steers a rowing-boat, esp in races, person in charge of a ship's boat and crew. 掌(尤指赛船之)舵的人; 舵手; 轮船上管理小艇及其水手的人; 小艇长。⇨ the illus at **eight.** 参看 eight 之插图。

coy /kɔɪ; kɔɪ/ adj (-er, -est) (esp of a girl) shy, modest; pretending to be shy; seeming more modest than one really is. (尤指女孩)害羞的; 娇羞的; 假装害羞的; 忸怩的。**coy·ly** adv **coy·ness** n

coy·ote /kɔɪ'əut; kaɪ'ot/ n prairie wolf of western N America. (北美洲西部大草原的)山狗; 郊狼。

coypu /'kɔɪpu:; 'kɔɪpu/ n S American rodent with webbed hind feet, bred for its fur (*nutria* fur). 河鼠(产于南美洲之啮齿动物, 后足有蹼, 畜养以取其毛皮)。⇨ **nutria.**

cozen /'kʌzn; 'kʌzn/ vt [VP6A, 14] ~ **sb (out) of sth,** (liter) defraud him of sth. (文)欺骗; 诈骗; 哄骗某人取得某物。~ **sb into doing sth,** (liter) beguile him

into it. (文)哄骗某人做某事。

cozy /ˈkəʊzɪ; ˈkozɪ/ adj (US) (美) = **cosy.**

crab[1] /kræb; kræb/ n [C] ten-legged shellfish; [U] its meat as food. 蟹; 蟹肉(作为食物者)。 ⇨ the illus at **crustacean.** 参看 crustacean 之插图。 **catch a ~,** (rowing) make a faulty stroke with one's oar. (划船)划错一桨。

crab[2] /kræb; kræb/ n (also 亦作 '**~-apple**) wild apple-tree; its hard, sour fruit. 野苹果(树); 山楂(子树)。

crab[3] /kræb; kræb/ vi, vt (-bb-) (colloq) complain; grumble; criticize. 抱怨; 批评。

crab·bed /ˈkræbɪd; ˈkræbɪd/ adj 1 bad-tempered; easily irritated. 脾气乖戾的; 易怒的。 2 (of handwriting) difficult to read; (of writings, authors) difficult to understand. (指字迹)难辨认的; (指作品、作家)难懂的。

crack[1] /kræk; kræk/ n 1 (a) line of division where sth is broken, but not into separate parts: 罅裂; 裂缝: a cup with bad ~s in it. 裂得很厉害的茶杯。 Don't go skating today—there are dangerous ~s in the ice. 今天不要去溜冰, 冰上有危险的裂缝。 (b) narrow opening. 窄缝; 小缝。 **open sth a ~,** open it very slightly. 将某物打开一点点。 **the ~ of dawn,** (colloq) daybreak. (口) 破晓; 黎明。 2 sudden, sharp noise (as of a rifle or whip, or sth breaking): 噼啪声(如放枪、抽鞭或物件破碎的声音): the ~ of a pistol shot; 手枪的射击声; a ~ of thunder. 雷声。 the ~ of doom, the peal of thunder on the Day of Judgement. 世界末日的霹雳声。 3 sharp blow which can be heard: 听得见响声的重击: give sb/get a ~ on the head. 对准某人头部一击(头上挨了一击)。 4 (sl) (=wise~) lively, forceful, or cutting comment or retort, esp one that causes laughter. (俚)俏皮话; 幽默的讽刺或反驳语。 5 (sl) attempt. (俚)试图; 尝试。 **have a ~ at sth,** try to do sth which is difficult. 尝试做某件困难事。 6 (attrib use) first-rate; very clever or expert: (用作定语)第一流的; 技艺高超的: a ~ polo-player; 第一流的马球选手; a ~ regiment. 精锐的团; 劲旅。 He's a ~ shot expert at using a rifle. 他是一位神枪手。 7 '**~-brained** adj crazy; foolish: 疯狂的; 狂妄的; 愚蠢的: a ~-brained scheme. 愚蠢的计谋。

crack[2] /kræk; kræk/ vt, vi 1 [VP6A, 14, 2A, C] get or make a crack or cracks(1) in: 打裂; 击裂; 破裂: I can ~ it, but I can't break it. 我能打裂它, 但不能打碎它。 You've ~ed the window. 你把窗户打裂了。 The glass will ~ if you pour boiling water into it. 这杯滚烫水一倒滚开水进去就会破裂。 He fell out of the window and ~ed his skull. 他自窗户上跌出去, 把头盖骨跌裂了。 2 [VP6A, 2A] make, cause to make, a crack or cracks(2): (使)发噼啪声: to ~ a whip/the joints of the fingers. 抽鞭子(屈指节)使发响声。 The hunter's rifle ~ed and the deer fell dead. 猎人的枪一响, 鹿即倒地而死。 We heard a ~ing noise among the trees. 我们听见树林中有噼啪声。 ~ open, open with a ~ing sound: 啪的一声打开了: to ~ open a safe. 啪的一声打开了保险箱。 3 [VP2A] (of the voice) become harsh; (of a boy's voice when he is reaching puberty) undergo a change and become dissonant (break is more usu). (指嗓音)变沙哑; (指男孩初达青春期)变声; 变嗓(break 较常用)。 4 [VP6A] decompose (petroleum) by using heat and pressure so as to change thick oils into thinner oils. 将(石油)加热加压, 使自重油变成较轻油, 裂化; 裂解。 Hence, 由此产生, ~ing plant. 裂解工厂。 5 (colloq and sl uses) (俚口用法) ~ down on sb/sth, take disciplinary action against: 处罚(某人, 某事): ~ down on gambling. 处罚赌博。 Hence, 由此产生, '~-down n. ~ sb/sth up (to be sth), [VP15B] praise highly, or in an exaggerated way: (夸大地)赞扬; 颂扬(某人或某事): He's not so clever as he's ~ed up to be. 他并不如人们所赞扬的那样聪明。 ~ up, (a) [VP2C] lose strength (in old age); suffer a mental collapse. (老年)体力衰退; 精神崩溃。Hence, 由此产生, '~-up n failure; breakdown. 失败; 崩溃。 (b) [VP2C, 15B] (of a vehicle) (cause to) suffer damage, crash. (指车辆)(使)毁坏; 撞毁。 ~ a

bottle, open one and drink the contents. 打开(酒)瓶喝(酒)。 ~ a joke, make one. 说笑话。 ⇨ **crack**[1](4). **get ~ing,** get busy (with work waiting to be done). 赶工。

cracker /ˈkrækə(r); ˈkrækɚ/ n 1 thin, flaky, dry biscuit (as eaten with cheese). 薄脆的饼干(如与干酪同食者)。 2 firework that makes cracking noises when set of. 爆竹; 鞭炮。 '**Christmas ~,** one made of brightly coloured paper, which explodes harmlessly when the ends are pulled. 用五彩花纸做成, 两端一拉即可爆炸(但不伤人)的纸炮。 3 (pl, 复, also 亦作 '**nut-~s**) instrument for cracking nuts. 轧果壳钳; 胡桃钳。

crackers /ˈkrækəz; ˈkrækɚz/ pred adj (GB sl) mad; crazy. (英俚)疯狂的。

crackle /ˈkrækḷ; ˈkrækḷ/ vi [VP2A, C] make a series of small cracking sounds, as when one treads on dry twigs, or when dry sticks burn: 发连续不断的细碎响声(如践踏干树枝或干柴燃烧时所发出者): a crackling camp-fire. 哔哔啪啪响的营火。 A cheerful wood fire was crackling in the sitting-room. 熊熊的柴火在起居室炉中哔啪作响。 □ n [U] 1 small cracking sounds, as described above: 细碎的声音; 哔啪声: the distant ~ of machine-gun fire. 远处的机枪声。 2 (also 亦作 '**~-china**/**~-ware**) china, etc covered with a network of what appear to be tiny cracks. 表面饰有细碎裂纹图案的瓷器。

crack·ling /ˈkræklɪŋ; ˈkræklɪŋ/ n [U] 1 ⇨ crackle(1). 2 crisp, well-cooked skin of roast pork. (烤猪肉的)脆皮。

crack·pot /ˈkrækpɒt; ˈkrækˌpɑt/ n eccentric person with strange ideas: 有怪念头的怪人; 狂想者: (attrib) (用作定语) ~ ideas. 怪念头; 怪主意。

cracks·man /ˈkræksmən; ˈkræksmən/ n (pl -men) burglar. 窃贼; 夜贼。

cradle /ˈkreɪdl; ˈkredl/ n 1 small, low bed sometimes mounted on rockers, for a newborn baby: (新生婴儿用的)摇篮; 摇床: from/in the ~, from/during infancy; 自(在)幼小时期; from the ~ to the grave, from birth to death. 从生到死。 2 (fig) place where sth is born or begins: (喻)发源地; 发祥地: Greece, the ~ of Western culture. 希腊, 西方文化的发源地。 3 framework resembling a ~ or which is used like a ~, eg a structure on which a ship is supported while being built or repaired; platform that can be moved up and down an outside wall by means of ropes and pulleys, used by workmen; part of a telephone apparatus on which the receiver rests. 形似摇篮之架架; (造船或修船时)船台; (工人用绳索及滑轮操纵, 可沿外墙)升降的平台; 电话机的听筒支架。 □ vt [VP6A, 14] place, hold, in or as in a ~: (把)置于摇篮中: ~ a child in one's arms; 将婴孩抱于臂膀中; ~ the telephone receiver, put it down. 放下电话听筒。

craft /krɑːft US: kræft; kræft/ n 1 [C] occupation, esp one in which skill in the use of the hands is needed; such a skill or technique: 职业; (尤指)手工业; 手艺; 工艺: the potter's ~; 陶器业; to learn the ~ of the woodcarver; 学习木雕的工艺; a school for arts and ~s. 工艺学校。 Used in many compounds, 用于许多复合词中, 如如 '**needle-~, 'wood-~, 'handi-~, 'stage-~.** 2 (collective) those engaged in such an occupation, organized in a guild or union: (集合用法)同业; 公会: the ~ of masons; 泥瓦匠工会; the C~, brotherhood of Freemasons. 互助会(之全体会员)。 3 (pl unchanged) boat(s), ship(s): (复数不变)船; 艇; 舰: a handy and useful little ~. 轻便小艇。 The harbour was full of all kinds of ~/~ of all kinds. 港内泊满了各式各样的船只。 ⇨ air~ at **air**[1](7), space~ at **space.** 4 [U] cunning; trickery; skill in deceiving: 狡猾; 诡计多端; 欺骗的伎俩: Be careful when you do business with that man: he's full of ~. 与那人做生意你得小心, 他诡计多端。 He got it from me by ~. 他用诡计从我这里得到它的。 ~y adj (-ier, -iest) full of ~(4): 诡计多端的; 狡猾的: a ~y politician; 狡猾的政客; as ~y as a fox. 狡猾如狐狸。 ~·ily adv ~·i·ness n

crafts·man /'krɑːftsmən US: 'kræfts-; 'kræftsmən/ *n* (*pl* **-men**) skilled workman who practises a craft. 技工；工匠；精于一门工艺的匠人。 **~·ship** /-ʃɪp; -,ʃɪp/ *n* skilled workmanship. 精巧的技艺；手艺。

crag /kræg; kræg/ *n* [C] high, steep, sharp or rugged mass of rock. 峭壁；危岩。 **~ged** /'krægɪd; 'krægɪd/ (poet) (诗)，**~gy** (**-ier, -iest**) *adjj* having many ~s. 多峭壁的；嶙峋的。 '**crags·man** /-mən; -mən/ *n* (*pl* **-men**) one who is clever at climbing ~s. 善于攀登陡崖峭壁者。

crake /kreɪk; krek/ *n* kinds of bird. 秧鸡。 ⇨ **corncrake** at **corn¹(1)**.

cram /kræm; kræm/ *vt, vi* (**-mm-**) [VP6A, 14, 15B, 2A] 1 ~ (*into*); ~ *up*) (*with*), make too full; put, push, very much or too much into: 填塞；勉强塞入: *to* ~ *food into one's mouth* / ~ *up one's mouth with food;* 将食物塞入口中; *to* ~ *papers into a drawer;* 将文件塞入抽屉内; *an essay* ~*med with quotations.* 充满引用句的文章。 2 fill the head with facts (for an examination): (为考试而)做填鸭式的教学: *to* ~ *pupils;* 以填鸭的方式教学生; *to* ~ *up a subject,* commit facts to memory (without serious study). 强记一门功课(而不求甚解)。 **,~'-full** *adj, adv* as full as ~ming can make it. 填饱; 塞满。 **~·mer** *n* special school where students are ~med; teacher paid to ~ students for examinations; textbook designed for ~ming; student who ~s for examinations. 为应付考试而实施填鸭式教学的补习学校; 为应付考试而聘请的补习教师; 为应付考试而编的教科书; 强记功课以应付考试的学生。

cramp¹ /kræmp; kræmp/ *n* [U] sudden and painful tightening of the muscles, usu caused by cold or overwork, making movement difficult: 抽筋; 痉挛(通常由寒冷或过劳而起, 使活动困难): *writer's* ~, of the finger muscles. 书写痉挛。 *The swimmer was seized with* ~ *and had to be helped out of the water.* 游泳者忽然抽筋, 因而不得不由他人救助出水。

cramp² /kræmp; kræmp/ *vt* [VP6A] 1 keep in a narrow space; hinder or prevent the movement or growth of: 限制 (于狭窄的空间); 阻碍活动或生长: *All these difficulties* ~*ed his progress.* 所有这些困难阻碍了他的进步。 *be* ~*ed for room* / *space etc,* be without enough room etc. 没有足够的空间等。 ~ *one's style,* (colloq) prevent one from doing sth as well as one could do it in more favourable circumstances. (口)使某人不能发挥其才能。 2 cause to have, afflict with, cramp¹. (使抽筋)。 3 fasten with a cramp³: 以铁箍扣紧: ~ *a beam.* 用铁箍将梁紧扣。 **cramped** *part adj* (of handwriting) with small letters close together and for this reason difficult to read. (指字迹)字母小而紧密的; (因此而)难辨认的。

cramp³ /kræmp; kræmp/ *n* 1 (also 亦作 '**~-iron**) metal bar with the ends bent, used for holding together masonry or timbers. 铁箍; 铁搭; 钢筋 (用以固结石造物或木材)。 2 = **clamp¹**.

cram·pon /'kræmpɒn; 'kræmpən/ *n* (usu *pl*) iron plate with spikes, worn on shoes for walking or climbing on ice, rock etc. (通常用复数)(固定在鞋底上用以在冰上行走或攀爬岩石等)的尖铁钉。

cran·berry /'krænberɪ US: -berɪ; 'kræn,berɪ/ *n* (*pl* **-ries**) small, red, tart berry of a dwarf shrub, used for making jelly and sauce. 大果越桔; 蔓越橘(一种矮小灌木所结之小红酸莓, 用以制果冻及果酱)。

crane¹ /kreɪn; kren/ *n* 1 large wading bird with long legs and neck. 鹤(长腿长颈之大涉水鸟)。 ⇨ the illus at **water**. 参看 water 之插图。 2 machine with a long arm that can be swung round, used for lifting and moving heavy weights. 起重机(有可以转动之长臂, 用以吊起及移动重物); 吊车。

crane² /kreɪn; kren/ *vt, vi* [VP6A, 16A, 2A, C] stretch (the neck); stretch the neck like a crane¹(1): 引(颈); (象鹤一样)伸长脖子: *to* ~ *forward;* 将头向前伸出; *to* ~ *one's neck to see sth.* 伸长脖子看东西。

crane-fly /'kreɪn flaɪ; 'kren flaɪ/ *n* (*pl* **-flies**) kind of fly with very long legs; daddy-long-legs. 大蚊; 一种长足之蝇; 蚊蚊。

cran·ial /'kreɪnɪəl; 'kreɪnɪəl/ *adj* (anat) of the skull. (解剖)头盖骨的。

cran·ium /'kreɪnɪəm; 'kreɪnɪəm/ *n* (anat) bony part of the head enclosing the brain; skull. (解剖)头盖骨; 颅。 ⇨ the illus at **head**. 参看 head 之插图。

crank¹ /kræŋk; kræŋk/ *n* L-shaped arm and handle for transmitting rotary motion. (用以传送旋转动作的)曲柄。 **'~·shaft** *n* shaft that turns or is turned by a ~. (转动或由曲柄转动的)机轴; 曲轴。 □ *vt* [VP6A, 15B] ~ (*up*), (of an engine) start, cause to start, by turning a ~. (指引擎)转动曲柄以发动。

crank² /kræŋk; kræŋk/ *n* person with fixed (and often strange) ideas, esp on one matter: (尤指对某一事)有怪诞成见的人; 思想怪异的人: *a fresh air* ~, one who insists on having windows open, however cold, stormy, etc, it may be. 对于新鲜空气有怪诞成见之人 (不管天气多冷或是狂风暴雨仍坚持开窗)。 **~·y** *adj* (**-ier -iest**) (of people) odd; eccentric; (of machines, etc) unsteady; unreliable. (指人)古怪的; 任性的; (指机器等)不稳固的; 不可靠的。

cranny /'krænɪ; 'krænɪ/ *n* (*pl* **-nies**) small crack or opening, eg in a wall. (墙壁等上的)缝隙; 小孔。 **cran-nied** *adj* full of crannies. 多缝隙的。

crap /kræp; kræp/ *vi* (**-pp-**) △ defecate. (讳)排便; 拉屎。 *n* △ (讳) 1 [U] excrement. 粪; 屎; 排泄物。 2 [C] act of defecating: 排便; 拉屎: *have a* ~. 大便; 拉屎。 3 [U] (sl) nonsense; sth unpleasant or unwanted. (俚)笨话; 愚行; 不愉快之事; 无用之物。 **~·py** *adj* (sl) bad; worthless; unpleasant. (俚)不好的; 无用的; 不愉快的。

crape /kreɪp; krep/ *n* [U] black silk or cotton material with a wrinkled surface (formerly used for mourning). 黑绉绸或绉纱(昔时用以表示哀悼)。 ⇨ **crêpe.**

craps /kræps; kræps/ *n* (also 亦作 '**crap-shooting**) [U] (US) gambling game played with two dice. (美)掷两颗骰子的赌博。 *shoot* ~, play this game. 掷两颗骰子(赌博)。

crash¹ /kræʃ; kræʃ/ *n* 1 (noise made by a) violent fall, blow or breaking: 猛烈的坠落、打击或破裂(所发的)响声: *The tree fell with a great* ~. 那树哗啦一声倒下来。 *His words were drowned in a* ~ *of thunder.* 他的话为一声响雷所淹盖。 *He was killed in an* 'air ~. 他于飞机失事中丧生。 '~ **barrier**, fence, rail, wall, etc designed to keep people, vehicles, etc apart where there is danger (eg one in the centre of a motorway). 防撞栅栏 (设置于快车道中央等危险地带, 以隔开行人、车辆等)。 '~**-dive** *n* sudden dive made by a submarine, eg to escape attack. 潜水艇所作的紧急下沉(如逃避攻击)。 □ *vi* dive in this way. 紧急下沉。 **,~-'land** *vi, vt* (of aircraft) land, be landed, partly or wholly out of control, with a ~. (指飞机)(因部分或完全失去控制而)紧急降落; 强迫着陆。 Hence, 由此产生, **,crash-'landing** *n* '**~-helmet**, padded helmet worn to protect the head in case of a ~, eg by a motorcyclist. (骑摩托车等的人

cranes

jib

所戴之)安全帽;护头盔. '~ pad, (sl) place to sleep in an emergency. (俚)紧急时睡觉之处. '~ programme, one made with intensive efforts to achieve quick results. 全力以赴伸求速成的计划; 应急计划. 2 ruin; collapse (eg in trade, finance): (贸易, 财政等之)毁灭; 败亡; 破产; 崩溃: The great ~ on Wall Street in 1929 ruined international trade. 一九二九年华尔街的股市暴跌使国际间的贸易大为萧条. □ adv with a ~. 哗啦一声地.

crash² /kræʃ; kræʃ/ vt, vi 1 [VP2A, C, 6A] fall or strike suddenly, violently, and noisily (esp of things that break): 猛跌或撞击并带破碎声; 撞碎; 撞坏; 坠毁: The bus ~ed into a tree. 公共汽车猛撞在一棵树上. The tree ~ed through the window. 树哗啦一声倒入窗内. The dishes ~ed to the floor. 那些盘子哗啦一声掉在地上. The aircraft ~ed. 那飞机坠毁了. 2 [VP2A, C] force or break through violently; 冲入; 闯进: ~ through a barrier; 冲过障碍物; [VP6A] (sl)(俚)= gatecrash. ⇨ gate. 3 [VP2A] (of a business company, government, etc) come to ruin; meet disaster: (指商业公司、政府等)破产; 垮台: His great financial scheme ~ed. 他的大财政计划失败了. 4 [VP6A] cause to ~: 使毁碎; 毁坏: to ~ a plane. 使飞机撞毁.

crash³ /kræʃ; kræʃ/ n [U] coarse linen cloth (as used for towels, etc). (作毛巾等的)粗麻布.

crass /kræs; kræs/ adj (of such qualities as ignorance, stupidity, etc) complete; very great. (指无知、愚笨等)完全的; 非常的.

crate /kreɪt; kret/ n 1 large framework of light boards or basketwork for goods in transport. (运货用的)大板条箱; 枝条编成的篓或篮. 2 (sl) old, worn-out motor-car or aircraft. (俚)用坏而破烂的汽车或飞机; 老爷车; 老爷机. □ vt put in a ~. 装于板条箱中.

cra·ter /'kreɪtə(r); 'kretə/ n mouth of a volcano; hole in the ground made by the explosion of a bomb, shell, etc. 火山口; (炸弹、炮弹等在地上所炸成的)弹坑. ~ lake, lake in the ~ of an extinct volcano. 火山湖(在死火山口内所形成的湖泊).

cra·vat /krə'væt; krə'væt/ n piece of linen, lace, etc loosely folded and worn as a necktie. 松折而系于颈上作为领带的麻布等制的饰巾; 旧式领带.

crave /kreɪv; krev/ vt, vi [VP6A, 3A] ~ (for), ask earnestly for, have a strong desire for: 恳求; 渴望: to ~ (for) mercy/forgiveness; 恳求宽恕(原谅); to ~ for a drink. 极欲饮水. **crav·ing** /'kreɪvɪŋ; 'krevɪŋ/ n [C] strong desire: 渴望; 热望: a craving for strong drink. 极欲喝烈酒.

cra·ven /'kreɪvn; 'krevən/ n, adj (person who is) cowardly. 怯懦的; 懦夫.

craw·fish /'krɔːfɪʃ; 'krɔ,fɪʃ/ n = **crayfish**.

crawl /krɔːl; krɔl/ vi [VP2A, C] 1 move slowly, pulling the body along the ground or other surface (as worms and snakes do); (of human beings) move in this way, or on the hands and knees: 爬; 爬行(如虫类和蛇所为); (指人)匍匐而行; 爬行: The wounded soldier ~ed into a shell-hole. 那受伤的兵爬入一炮弹坑. to **sb**, (colloq) try to bring oneself into his favour. (口)向某人拍马屁; 巴结. 2 go very slowly: 徐缓而行: Our train ~ed over the damaged bridge. 我们的列车缓慢地开过受损的桥. 3 be full of, covered with, things that ~: 充满或覆满爬行的东西: The ground was ~ing with ants. 地上爬满了蚂蚁. The child's hair was ~ing with vermin. 那孩子的头发生满了虱子. 4 (of the flesh) feel as if covered with ~ing things: (指肌肤)起鸡皮疙瘩: She says that the sight of snakes makes her flesh ~. 她说她看见蛇就起鸡皮疙瘩. □ n 1 a ~, ~ing movement: 爬行; 缓慢行进: Traffic in Oxford St was reduced to a ~ during the rush hours. 牛津街上的车辆和行人在上下班拥挤时则慢得成了缓慢的蠕动. '**pub-~** vi, n visit(ing) and drink(ing) at several pubs in succession: 在数家酒馆连续饮酒: go pub-~ing; 在酒馆喝酒; go on a pub-~. 连续在几家酒馆喝酒. 2 (**the**), high-speed swimming stroke with alternate circular arm movements and rapid leg kicks.

自由式游泳(以双臂呈圆形交替的动作与急速的两腿踢动形成的快速游泳法). ~er n person or thing that ~s; (pl) overall garment made for a baby to ~ about in. 爬行之人或物; (复)幼儿所穿可以到处爬行的全身罩服.

cray·fish /'kreɪfɪʃ; 'kre,fɪʃ/ n freshwater lobster-like chellfish. (淡水中的)螯虾; 小龙虾.

crayon /'kreɪən; 'kreən/ n stick or pencil of soft coloured chalk, wax or charcoal. 有色的粉笔; 蜡笔; 炭笔. □ vt draw with ~s. 用蜡笔或炭笔画.

craze /kreɪz; krez/ n enthusiastic interest that may last for a comparatively short time; the object of such interest: 为时短暂的浓厚兴趣; 一时的狂热; 此种狂热的对象: schoolboy ~s, eg the making of paper darts as weapons; 学童们流行一时的狂热兴趣(如折纸镖); the modern ~ for bingo. 现今对宾果游戏的狂热.

crazed /kreɪzd; krezd/ adj (also 亦作 **half-~**) wildly excited; mad: 极度兴奋的; 疯狂的: a ~ look/expression; 疯狂的神情(表情); a half-~ prophet. 疯狂的预言者.

crazy /'kreɪzɪ; 'krezɪ/ adj (-ier, -iest) 1 ~ (about), (colloq) wildly excited or enthusiastic: (口)狂热的; 醉心的: He is ~ about skiing. 他酷心于滑雪. I'm ~ about you, darling. 亲爱的, 我爱你我爱得发狂. 2 suffering from mental disorder; foolish: 癫狂的; 糊涂的: You were ~ to lend that man your money. 你把钱借给那个人, 真糊涂. It was ~ of you to let such a young girl drive your car. 你让这样年轻的女孩驾你的车, 真糊涂. 3 (of buildings, etc) unsafe; likely to collapse. (指建筑物等)不安全的; 可能坍塌的. 4 (of quilts, pavements, etc) made up of irregularly shaped pieces fitted together: (指棉被、人行道等)由形状不规则的块子拼凑成的: ~ paving. 不规则的石块拼凑成的人行道. **craz·ily** adv **crazi·ness** n

creak /kriːk; krik/ n, vi [VP2A] (make a) sound like that of an unoiled door-hinge, or badly-fitting floorboards when trodden on. (发)咯吱吱声; 叽喳声(如铰链未上油的门铰链或踏在松脱的地板上). ~y adj (-ier, -iest) making ~ing sounds: 咯吱作响的: ~y stairs. 咯吱吱响的楼梯. ~ily adv

cream /kriːm; krim/ n [U] 1 fatty or oily part of milk which rises to the surface and can be made into butter. 乳脂; 乳皮; 奶酥 (可制奶油). 2 kind of food containing or resembling ~: 含乳脂或似乳脂的食品: ~ cheese; 干乳酪; ice-~; 冰淇淋; ~ ices; 冰淇淋; chocolate ~; 巧克力奶油; ~ buns. 奶油小面包. 3 substance like ~ in appearance or consistency, used for polishing, as a cosmetic, etc: (似乳脂之物, 用以擦亮或作化妆品用的)膏; 霜: 'furniture ~; 家具油; 'shoe-~; 鞋油; 'face-~; 面霜; 'cold-~. 冷霜. 4 part of a liquid that gathers at the top: 液体之浮于面上的部分: ~ of tartar / lime. 酒石(英)(石灰乳). 5 best part of anything: 精华; 精粹: the ~ of the crop; 收成的精华; the ~ of the story, the most amusing part, the point of it. 故事的精采处. 6 (attrib) yellowish-white: (用作定语)乳脂色; 乳白色; 淡黄色; 米色: ~laid / ~wove paper, smooth ~coloured writing-paper. 光滑的淡黄色写字纸. □ vt take ~ from (milk); make ~y; add ~ to: 撇去(牛奶)的乳脂; 使成乳脂状; 加乳脂于: ~ed potatoes, cooked so that they have the consistency of ~. 乳脂马铃薯(加乳脂煮熟的马铃薯). ~y adj (-ier, -iest) smooth and rich like ~; containing much ~. 滑腻似乳脂的; 含有多量乳脂的. ~ery n (pl ~ries) place where milk, ~, butter, cheese, etc are sold. 卖乳品的商店. 2 butter and cheese factory. 奶油及干酪工厂.

crease /kriːs; kris/ n 1 line made (on cloth, paper, etc) by crushing, folding or pressing: (由搓揉、折迭、或压紧而在布、纸等上所造成的)折痕; 皱折: ~-resistant cloth, which does not easily form into ~s. 不皱布料. 2 (cricket) white line on the ground to mark the positions of certain players (bowlers, batsmen). (板球)地上标识某些球员(投球者、击球者)位置的白线. ⇨ the illus at cricket. 参看 cricket 之插图. □ vt, vi [VP6A, 2A] make a ~ or ~s in; fall into ~s; get ~s in: (使)起折痕; 起皱: Pack the dresses so that they won't ~. 把衣服装

起来，免得弄皱了。 *This material ~s easily.* 这种料子容易皱。

cre·ate /kriː'eɪt/ kriː'et/ *vt* **1** [VP6A] cause sth to exist; make (sth new or original): 创作；创造: *God ~d the world.* 上帝创造世界。 *Dickens ~d many wonderful characters in his novels.* 狄更斯在他的小说中创造了许多奇妙的人物。 ⇨ **a part,** (of an actor) be the first to play it. (指演员)为某个角色的最初扮演者。 **2** [VP6A] give rise to; produce: 产生；制造: *His behaviour ~d a bad impression.* 他的行为给人恶劣的印象。 *Her appearance ~d a sensation.* 她的出现曾轰动一时。 **3** [VP23, 6A] invest (sb) with a rank: 封(某人)爵位；任命: *He was ~d Baron of Bunthorp.* 他被封为班纳浦男爵。 *Eight new peers were ~d.* 新封了八个贵族。

cre·ation /kriː'eɪʃn/ kriː'eʃən/ *n* **1** [U] the act of creating: 创造: *the ~ of great works of art.* 伟大艺术作品的创造。 *Economic conditions may be responsible for the ~ of social unrest.* 经济状况可能是产生社会不安的根源。 *Is the ~ of new peers desirable?* 加封新的贵族是否必要？ **2** [U] all created things: 一切被创造之物；万物: *man, the lord of ~.* 人，万物的主宰。 **(the) C~,** (theology) the world or universe as created by God. (神学)(上帝所创造的)世界或宇宙。 **3** [C] production of the human intelligence, esp one in which imagination has a part: 人类智慧的产物；(尤指)想象的产物: *the ~s of poets, artists, composers and dramatists.* 诗人、艺术家、作曲家及剧作家的作品。 *The women were wearing the newest ~s of the Paris dressmakers.* 妇女们穿着巴黎裁缝师的最新制作的服装。

cre·ative /kriː'eɪtɪv/ kriː'etɪv/ *adj* having power to create; of creation: 有创造力的；创造的: *useful and ~ work,* ie requiring intelligence and imagination, not merely mechanical skill. 有用的和创造性的工作(即需要智慧与想象，而不仅是呆板的技术)。 **~·ly** *adv* **~·ness** *n*

cre·ator /kriː'eɪtə(r)/ kriː'etɚ/ *n* one who creates. 创造者。 **the C~,** God. 上帝。

crea·ture /'kriːtʃə(r)/ 'kriːtʃɚ/ *n* **1** living animal: 动物: *dumb ~s,* animals. 不能说话的下等动物；畜牲。 **2** (with an *adj*) living person: (与形容词连用)人: *a lovely ~,* a beautiful person. 美丽的人; *a poor ~,* a contemptible person, or a person who is to be pitied; 可鄙的人；可怜的人; *a good ~,* a kindhearted person. 善心人; 好心人。 **~ comforts,** material needs such as food and drink. 物质的需要(如饮食)。 **3** person who owes his position to another, esp one who is content to carry out another person's wishes without question: 依人为生者；唯命是听者；走狗: *mere ~s of the dictator.* 独裁者的走狗。

crèche /kreɪʃ US: kreʃ/ kreʃ/ *n* **1** (GB) public nursery where babies are looked after while their mothers are at work. (英)(为职业妇女所设的)托儿所。 **2** (US) (美) = crib¹(3).

cre·dence /'kriːdns/ 'kriːdns/ *n* [U] *give/attach ~ to,* (formal) believe (gossip, what is said, etc). (正式用语) 相信(闲话、传言等)。 *letter of ~,* letter of introduction. 介绍信。

cre·den·tials /krɪ'denʃlz; krɪ'denʃəlz/ *n pl* letters or papers showing that a person is what he claims to be: 证明身份、学历、经历等的信件或文件: *His ~ were so satisfactory that he was given the post of manager.* 他的各项证件令人极为满意，因此给他经理的职位。

cred·ible /'kredəbl; 'kredəbl/ *adj* that can be believed: 可信的；可靠的: *~ witnesses.* 可信的证人。 *It hardly seems ~,* seems almost impossible to believe. 它似乎是难以置信的。 **cred·ibly** *adv* in a ~ manner: 可信地; 确实地: *We are credibly informed that....* 我们获得可靠的消息。 **credi·bil·ity** /ˌkredɪ'bɪlɪtɪ; ˌkredə'bɪlətɪ/ *n* [U] the ability to be believed in. 确实性; 可信性。 **credi'bility gap,** the difference between what sb says and what is considered to be true. 可信度(某人所说的话及其真实性之间的差异)。

credit¹ /'kredɪt; 'kredɪt/ *n* **1** [U] belief of others that a person, business company, etc can pay debts, or will keep a promise to pay: (个人、公司等对于偿债方面的)信用; 信誉: *No ~ is given at this shop,* payment must be in cash. 这家商店概不赊欠。 *His ~ is good for only £50.* 他的信用仅限于五十英镑。 *If you're very rich, you can probably get unlimited ~.* 如果你是个很富有的人，你或许能获得无限的信用。 *buy/sell on ~,* buy/sell goods, payment being made later. 赊买(卖)货物。 **'~ account,** (US 美 = charge account) account with a shop, store, etc under an agreement for payments at a later date (eg monthly or quarterly). 赊帐; 欠帐(商店等记载顾客定期按月或按季付款赊购货物的帐目)。 **'~ card, (a)** card issued by a business firm enabling the holder to obtain credit and services on ~. 信用卡(由一公司行号所发行，持卡人可记帐先取得货物或享受服务)。 **(b)** card issued by a bank, allowing the holder to draw money from its branches and use its cheques in payment for goods and services, with a maximum for each occasion. 信用卡(银行所行，持卡之客户可在各分行提款，且使用该行支票偿付货款及工资，但每笔款有一定的限额)。 **'~ note,** (comm) one that gives ~ to a customer for goods returned or for overcharged goods. (商)信用票据。 **'~ sales,** sales for which payment is made, by agreement, later. 赊售; 赊卖(经同意先交货后收款)。 Cf 参较 *cash sales.* **,letter of ~,** letter from a bank to its agent(s) giving authority for credit to the holder. 信用状(银行发给其代理银行，授权对持有人予以信任的函件)。 **'~-worthy** *adj* accepted by tradesmen, hire-purchase companies, etc as safe for ~. 信用可靠的(其信用安全为商店、分期付款公司等所接受的)。 Hence, 由此产生, **'~-worthiness** *n* **2** [U] money shown as owned by a person, company, etc in a bank account: (银行帐户中的)存款: *How much have I standing to my ~?* 我的存款尚有多少？ *You have a ~ balance of £250.* 你的存款余额为二百五十英镑。 **3** [C] sum of money advanced or loaned (by a bank, etc): (银行等对客户的)预付款; 垫款: *The bank refused further ~s to the company.* 银行拒绝再贷款给该公司。 **'~ squeeze,** (government) policy of making it difficult to borrow money (eg by raising interest rates), as part of a policy against inflation. 紧缩贷款(如借提高利率增加借款的困难，为抵制通货膨胀的一部分)。 **4** (bookkeeping) record of payments received: (簿记)贷方: *Does this item go among the ~s or the debits?* 这笔帐应记入贷方抑或借方？ **'~-side,** right-hand side of an account for recording payment received. 贷方。 ⇨ **debit. 5** [C] (US) entry on a record to show that a course of study has been completed: (美)(表示某一学科业已修毕的)学分登记: *~s in history and geography;* 历史与地理的学分; *a '~ course,* university course depending upon the number of grades and ~s received. 学分学科(根据所获之等级及学分数目的大学学分)。 **6** [U] honour, approval, good name or reputation: 光荣; 荣誉; 赞许; 好名声; 名誉; 名望; 名气: *a man of the highest ~.* 极有名望的人。 *get/take ~ (for sth),* get/take recognition, honour etc: 得到赏识; 获得荣誉; (为…)而获得声誉: *Candidates will get additional ~* (ie marks) *for clearly labelled diagrams.* 参加考试者若有清晰标明的图解将获得额外的学分。 *It is dishonest to take ~ for work done by others.* 拿他人所完成的工作以谋个人的荣誉，是不诚实的。 *give ~ (to sb) (for sth),* give recognition, praise, approval: (为某事)认可、称赞或赞许(某人): *He's cleverer than I gave him ~ for,* than I thought. 他的聪明伶俐超过我所料想的。 *I gave you ~ for being more sensible,* You are less sensible than I thought. 我未料到你会如此不懂事。 *One must give ~ where it is due.* 该赞许的就得赞许。 **7** *do sb ~; do ~ to sb; be/stand to sb's ~; reflect ~ on sb,* add to his reputation: 增加某人的声誉; 成为某人的光荣; 使某人大有面子: *The work does you ~.* 这项工作他英俊的仪表使他的裁缝师的技艺益为生色。 *His smart appearance does ~ to his tailors.* *It is/stands greatly to your ~ that you have passed such a*

difficult examination. 这样难的考试你都考及格了，是你莫大的光荣。*His fluency in Arabic reflects great ~ on/is greatly to the ~ of his teacher.* 他说得一口流利的阿拉伯语，为他的老师增光不少。*be a ~ to sb/sth,* add to the good name of sb/sth: 增加某人(某事物)的声誉: *The pupils are a ~ to their teacher/school.* 学生们为他们的老师(学校)增光。*~s; '~ titles,* names, shown on a cinema or TV screen, of persons responsible for the acting, direction, production, etc. (电影银幕或电视屏幕上所显示的)演员、导演、制作人等的名单。**8** [U] belief; trust; confidence: 相信；信托；信任: *The rumour is gaining ~.* 那谣言已渐为人所相信。*lend ~ to,* strengthen belief in: 加强对…之信任: *The latest news lends ~ to the earlier reports.* 最新的消息可证实早先的报导是可靠的。

credit² /'kredɪt; 'krɛdɪt/ vt [VP6A, 14] ~ *sb/sth (with sth); ~ sth (to sb/sth),* **(a)** believe that he/it has sth: 相信…具有…；信赖: *Until now I've always ~ed you with more sense.* 到现在为止，我一直都相信你不至如此糊涂。*The relics are ~ed with miraculous powers.* 这些遗骸被认为是具有神奇的力量。*Miraculous powers are ~ed to the relics.* 人们认为这些遗骸具有神奇力量。**(b)** enter on the ~ side of an account: 记入贷方: *a customer with £8;* 在客户的贷方记入八英镑; *~ £8 to a customer/an account.* 在客户(帐目)的贷方记入八英镑。⇨ **credit¹(4).**

credi·table /'kredɪtəbl; 'krɛdɪtəbl/ adj ~ *(to),* that brings credit(6, 7, 8): 可称赞的; 增加声誉的; 可信的: *a ~ attempt;* 可称赞的努力; *conduct that was very ~ to him.* 他的极可称赞的品行。**credi·tably** /'kredɪtəblɪ; 'krɛdɪtəblɪ/ adv

credi·tor /'kredɪtə(r); 'krɛdɪtɚ/ n person to whom one owes money: 债主；债权人: *run away from one's ~s.* 躲避债主。

credo /'kri:dəu; 'krido/ n (pl ~s /-dəuz; -doz/) creed. 信条。

cre·du·lity /krɪ'dju:lətɪ US: -'du:-; krɪ'dulətɪ/ n (pl -ties) [U, C] too great a readiness to believe things. 易信；轻信。

credu·lous /'kredjuləs US: -dʒʊ-; 'krɛdʒələs/ adj (too) ready to believe things: 易信的; 轻信的:~ *people who accept all the promises of the politicians.* 易受政客们的许诺哄骗的人们。~**·ly** adv

creed /kri:d; krid/ n [C] (system of) beliefs or opinions, esp on religious doctrine. (尤指宗教的)信条; 教条。the C~, short summary of Christian doctrine. 使徒的信条(基督教信条的精义)。

creek /kri:k; krik/ n **1** (GB) narrow inlet of water on the sea-shore or in a river-bank. (英)海岸的小湾; 河边的小溪。**2**(N America) small river. (北美洲)小河; 溪流。*be up the ~,* (sl) be in difficulties. (俚)在困难中; 在困境。

creel /kri:l; kril/ n angler's wicker basket for carrying the fish he catches. 渔人用的柳条鱼篓。

creep /kri:p; krip/ vi (pt, pp **crept** /krept; krept/) [VP2A, B, C] **1** move along with the body close to the ground or floor; move slowly, quietly or secretly: 爬行(以身体紧贴地面移动); 缓慢地、无声地或暗暗地移动; 偷偷; 蹑动: *The cat crept silently towards the bird.* 那只猫一声不响地爬向那只鸟。*The thief crept along the corridor.* 那贼偷偷地在走廊上潜行。**2** (of time, age, etc) come on gradually: (指时间、年龄等)不知不觉而来: *Old age ~s upon one unawares.* 不知不觉间老年就来临了。*A feeling of drowsiness crept over him.* 一种昏昏欲睡的感觉逐渐袭着他。**3** (of plants, etc) grow along the ground, over the surface of a wall, etc: (指植物等)沿地面、墙壁的表面等而蔓延; 攀爬: *Ivy had crept over the ruined castle walls.* 常春藤已爬满了那荒堡残垣。**4** (of the flesh) have the feeling that things are ~ing over it (as the result of fear, repugnance, etc); (指肌肤) 有虫爬的感觉(如由于恐惧、嫌恶等之结果); 起鸡皮疙瘩: *The sight of the cold, damp prison cell, with rats running*

about, made her flesh ~. 看见那又冷又湿的牢房,还有老鼠在里面跑来跑去,使她起鸡皮疙瘩。⇨ **crawl(4).** □ n **1** (sl) despicable person who tries to win favour by doing small favours, snooping, etc. (俚)(借施小惠,打小报告等以求取宠的)卑鄙小人。**2** *give sb the ~s,* (colloq) cause the flesh to ~(4); cause distaste in sb. (口)使某人皮肤感觉有如虫爬(不寒而栗); 使人厌恶。

creeper /'kri:pə(r); 'kripɚ/ n insect, bird, etc that creeps; plant that creeps along the ground, over rocks, walls, etc. 爬行的昆虫、鸟等; 蔓延于地上、岩石上、墙上等处的植物; 爬藤。

creepy /'kri:pɪ; 'kripɪ/ adj (**-ier, -iest**) (colloq) having or causing a creeping of the flesh, 爬的; **creep(4):** (口)令人感觉皮肤上有虫爬似的; 令人毛骨悚然的: *a ~ story.* 令人毛骨悚然的故事。

creepy-crawly /,kri:pɪ'krɔːlɪ; ,kripɪ'krɔlɪ/ n (pl -ies) (colloq) creeping or crawling insect etc. (口)爬行的昆虫。

cre·mate /krɪ'meɪt; 'krimet/ vt [VP6A] burn (a corpse) to ashes: 火葬; 烧(尸)成灰: *He says he wants to be ~d, not buried.* 他说他(死后)要火葬,不要土葬。**cre·ma·tion** /krɪ'meɪʃn; krɪ'meʃən/ n [U] cremating; [C] instance of this. 火葬。**cre·ma·tor·ium** /,kremə'tɔːrɪəm; ,kremə'torɪəm/ n furnace, building, place, for the cremating of corpses. 焚尸炉; 火葬场。**cre·ma·tory** /'kremətərɪ US: -tɔːrɪ; 'krimə,torɪ/ n (pl -ries) = crematorium.

crème de menthe /,krem də 'mɒnθ; krɛmdə'mãt/ n [U] sweet, thick, green liqueur flavoured with peppermint. (法)一种带薄荷味的甜、浓、绿酒。

cren·el·lated (US=**-el·ated**) /'krenəleɪtɪd; 'krɛnḷ,etɪd/ adj having battlements. 有城垛的; 有雉堞的; 有枪眼的; 有炮门的。

Cre·ole /'kri:əʊl; 'kriol/ n, adj **1** (person) of pure European or mixed European and African descent in the West Indies, Spanish America or the old French or Spanish states of the Southern US. 生于西印度群岛、西班牙美洲、或昔时美国南部法国或西班牙所属各州的欧洲人或欧非混血儿(的); 克里奥尔人(的)。**2** (of a) dialect of French, Spanish or English spoken by persons of mixed European and African descent in N and S America and the W Indies. 南北美洲和西印度群岛之欧非混血人种所说的法国、西班牙或英国方言(的); 克里奥尔语(的)。

creo·sote /'krɪəsəʊt; 'krɪə,sot/ n [U] **1** thick, brown, oily liquid obtained from coal-tar, used to preserve wood. 杂酚油(褐色浓油,取自煤溚,用以防护木料)。**2** antiseptic obtained from wood-tar. (取自木溚之)防腐油。

crêpe, crepe /kreɪp; krep/ n [U] **1** any crape that is not black. 绉绸; 绉纱(非指黑纱)。⇨ **crape. 2** ~ **rubber,** raw rubber pressed into blocks. It has a wrinkled surface and is used for the soles of shoes, etc. 绉纹胶(一种压成块状的生胶, 可做鞋底等用); 绉(橡)胶。**3** ~ **paper,** thin paper with a wavy or wrinkled surface. 绉纹纸。

crepi·tate /'krepɪteɪt; 'krɛpə,tet/ vi [VP2A] make a series of sharp, crackling sounds. 作一连串之小爆裂声。**crepi·ta·tion** /,krepɪ'teɪʃn; ,krɛpə'teʃən/ n crepitating (sound). 此种爆裂(声)。

crept ⇨ **creep.**

cre·pus·cu·lar /krɪ'pʌskjulə(r); krɪ'pʌskjolɚ/ adj (formal) of, seen, heard or active during twilight. (正式用语)晨昏之际(可见,可闻或活动)的。

cres·cendo /krɪ'ʃendəʊ; krɪ'ʃɛndo/ n (pl ~s /-dəuz; -doz/), adv, adj (passage of music to be played, sth heard) with, of, increasing loudness; (fig) progress towards a climax. 音量渐强的(一节乐曲或声音); (喻)渐趋高潮。⇨ **diminuendo.**

cres·cent /'kresnt; 'krɛsṇt/ n **1** (sth shaped like) the curve of the moon in the first quarter, ⇨ the illus at **phase;** row of houses in the form of a ~. 弦月; 新月;

弦月状之物;(参看 phase 之插图); 弦月状之一排房屋。**2 the C~**, (fig) faith and religion of Islam: (喻)伊斯兰教: *the Cross* (Christianity) *and the C~*. 基督教与伊斯兰教。**3** (attrib)~-shaped; increasing in size: (用作定语)弦月状的;渐大的:*a ~ moon.* 弦月; 蛾眉月。

a crescent

cress /kres; krɛs/ n [U] name of various plants, esp the kind with hot-tasting leaves (used in salads and sandwiches). 水芹; 水董(指叶味辣者,用于沙拉、三明治)。

crest /krest; krɛst/ n **1** tuft of feathers on a bird's head; cock's comb. 鸟冠; 鸡冠。⇨ the illus at **fowl, water**. 参看 fowl, water 之插图。**'~-fallen,** (fig) dejected, disappointed (at failure, etc). (喻)(因失败等)沮丧的; 垂头丧气的; 受挫折的。**2** ~-like decoration formerly worn on the top of a helmet; (poet) helmet. 昔时头盔顶上所戴之鸡冠状装饰物; (诗)盔。**3** design over the shield of a coat of arms, or used separately (eg on a seal, or on notepaper): 盾形纹章上端之饰章; 单独使用之饰章 (例如用于印信或便笺上者): *the family ~,* one used by a family. 家族饰章。**4** top of a slope or hill; white top of a large wave. 斜坡或小山的顶; 浪头; 浪峰。*on the ~ of a wave,* (fig) at the most favourable moment of one's fortunes. (喻)在某人最得意的时刻。~ed adj having a ~(3): 有饰章的; ~ed note-paper; 有饰章的信笺; (in compounds, as names of birds) *the golden-~ed wren.* (用于复合词中,作为鸟类名称)金冠鹪鹩。□ vt, vi reach, form into, a ~ of a hill / wave. 达到(山,浪)之顶;形成顶。

cre·ta·ceous /krɪ'teɪʃəs; krɪ'teʃəs/ adj (geol) of (the nature of) chalk: (地质)白垩(质)的: *the ~ age,* when chalk-rocks were formed. 白垩纪。

cre·tin /'kretɪn US: 'kri:tn; 'kritn/ n deformed and mentally undeveloped person (diseased because of weakness of the thyroid gland). 畸形而低能者(因甲状腺功能太弱而引起者); 白痴; 矮呆子。~·ous /'kretɪnəs US: 'kri:t-; 'kritnəs/ adj

cre·tonne /'kretɒn; krɪ'tɑn/ n [U] cotton cloth with printed designs, used for curtains, furniture covers, etc. (做窗帘、家具套等之)印花棉布。

cre·vasse /krɪ'væs; krə'væs/ n deep, open crack, esp

in ice on a glacier. (冰河等的)裂缝; 破口。⇨ the illus at **mountain**. 参看 mountain 之插图。

crev·ice /'krevɪs; 'krɛvɪs/ n narrow opening or crack (in a rock, wall, etc). (岩石、墙等的)裂缝; 罅隙。

crew[1] /kru:; kru/ n **1** (collective noun) all the persons working on a ship, aircraft, train, etc (集合名词)船上, 飞机或火车上全体工作人员。**'ground ~,** mechanics who service an aircraft on the ground. 地勤组(在地面维护飞机的机械士)。**2** group of persons working together; gang. 一群共同工作的人; 帮; 群。**'~-cut** n closely cropped style of hair-cut for men. 小平头(男人的一种发式)。**'~-neck** n style of round, close-fitting collar. 圆式紧衣领。□ vi act as ~ on a boat: 做赛艇工作人员: *Will you ~ for me in tomorrow's race?* 明天赛艇时你做我的助手好吗?

crew[2] /kru:; kru/ pt of **crow**[2].

crib[1] /krɪb; krɪb/ n **1** wooden framework from which animals can pull out fodder; manger. (牲畜用的)秣糟; 刍糟; 食槽。**2** (US) bin or box for storing maize, salt, etc. (美)贮藏玉蜀黍、盐等的箱或盒。**3** (US 美 = crèche) representation (eg in a church at Christmas) of the nativity. 耶稣诞生的图画或演示(例如圣诞节教堂内展出者)。**4** bed for a newborn baby. 婴儿睡的小床。□ vt (-bb-) shut up in a small space. 关闭在狭小的地方。

crib[2] /krɪb; krɪb/ n **1** sth copied dishonestly from the work of another. 抄袭他人的作品; 剽窃之物。**2** word-for-word translation of a foreign text used by students of the language. (外语学生用的)逐字翻译本。□ vt, vi (-bb-) use a ~(2); copy (another pupil's written work) dishonestly. 使用直译本; 抄袭(另一学生的作业)。

crib·bage /'krɪbɪdʒ; 'krɪbɪdʒ/ n [U] card-game for two, three or four persons, who use pegs and a board ('~-board) with peg-holes in it for keeping the score. 一种纸牌戏(二人、三人或四人游戏,用木钉及有孔的木板记分)。

crick /krɪk; krɪk/ n (usu 常作 **a ~**) stiff condition of the muscles of the neck, or the back causing sudden, sharp pain: 颈或背部肌肉的痉挛(会引起剧痛): *to have / get a ~ in the neck.* 颈部发生痉挛; 感觉颈项不能转动。□ vt produce a ~ in: 引起痉挛: *to ~ one's neck / back.* 引起颈项(背部)痉挛。

cricket[1] /'krɪkɪt; 'krɪkɪt/ n small, brown jumping insect which makes a shrill noise by rubbing its front wings together: 蟋蟀(一种能跳跃的褐色小昆虫,摩擦其翅可发出尖锐的叫声): *the chirping of ~s.* 蟋蟀的唧唧鸣声。⇨ the illus at **insect**. 参看 insect 之插图。

cricket[2] /'krɪkɪt; 'krɪkɪt/ n [U] ball game played on a grass field by two teams of eleven players each, with bats and wickets. 板球; 板球戏(两队各十一人,以板及三

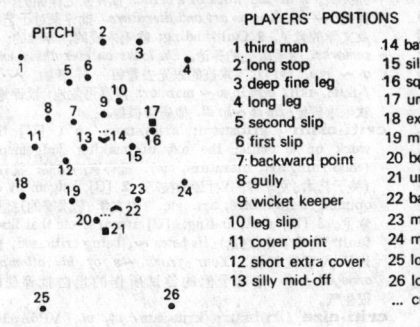

PITCH

PLAYERS' POSITIONS

1 third man	14 batsman
2 long stop	15 silly mid-on
3 deep fine leg	16 square leg
4 long leg	17 umpire
5 second slip	18 extra cover
6 first slip	19 mid-off
7 backward point	20 bowler
8 gully	21 umpire
9 wicket keeper	22 batsman
10 leg slip	23 mid-on
11 cover point	24 mid-wicket
12 short extra cover	25 long-off
13 silly mid-off	26 long-on
	... crease

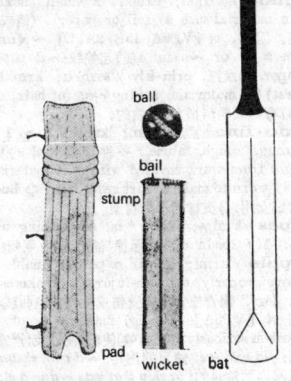

ball

bail

stump

pad   wicket   bat

Note   Although in fact only eleven men in addition to the batsmen and umpires are on the field at one time, they can be placed in any of these positions

cricket

柱门在草地上比赛)。***not* ~,** (colloq) unfair; unsportsmanlike. (口)不公平的; 不合运动精神的。**~er** *n* **~ player.** 板球选手, 玩板球者。

cried /kraɪd; kraɪd/ ⇨ **cry**[1].

crier /ˈkraɪə(r); ˋkraɪə/ *n* **1** officer who makes public announcements in a court of law. (法庭上的)传令员。**ˌtown-ˈ~,** (old use) man who goes round the streets to make proclamations and announcements. (旧用法) 沿街向市民传告政令的人。**2** person (esp a young child) who cries(2) a lot. 好哭的人(尤指婴儿)。

cries /kraɪz; kraɪz/ *prest* of **cry**[1]; *pl* of **cry**[2].

cri·key /ˈkraɪkɪ; ˋkraɪkɪ/ *int* (colloq) exclamation of surprise. (口)嗳呀(表示惊讶的叫声)。

crime /kraɪm; kraɪm/ *n* **1** [C] offence for which there is severe punishment by law; [U] such offences collectively; serious law-breaking: 为法律所严惩的罪; 犯罪行为; 严重的犯法: *to commit a serious ~;* 犯重罪; *the ~s of which he was proved guilty.* 他所犯的业已证明的罪行。*It is the business of the police to prevent and detect ~ and of the law courts to punish ~.* 防止及侦察犯罪是警察的职务而惩罚犯罪是法庭的责任。**ˈ~ fiction,** novels in which the detection of ~ is the chief interest. 描写侦察犯罪为主的小说; 侦探小说。**2** foolish or wrong act, not necessarily an offence against the law: 愚昧或错误的行为(不一定是犯法的行为): *It would be a ~ to send the boy out on such a cold, wet night.* 在这样寒冷的雨夜把孩子遣出是不对的。**3** (in the army) serious breaking of the regulations (not necessarily an offence against civil law). (军中)严重违犯军纪; 犯大过(不一定触犯民法)。**ˈ~ sheet,** record of a soldier's offences. 犯军纪的记录。□ *vt* charge (a man) with, convict (a man) of, a military offence. 告或判(某人)违犯军纪。

crimi·nal /ˈkrɪmɪnl; ˋkrɪmənl/ *adj* of crime: 犯罪的; 犯法的: *a ~ act;* 犯罪的行为; *a ~ offender;* 犯刑事罪者; *~ law.* 刑法。⇨ *civil law* at **civil(1).** □ *n* person who commits a crime or crimes. 犯罪者; 罪犯。**~·ly** /-əlɪ; -lɪ/ *adv*

crimi·nol·ogy /ˌkrɪmɪˈnɒlədʒɪ; ˌkrɪməˋnɑlədʒɪ/ *n* [U] the study of crime. 犯罪学。

crimp /krɪmp; krɪmp/ *vt* make (eg hair) wavy or curly (as with a hot iron). 使(发等)卷曲(如用热铁棒)。

crim·son /ˈkrɪmzn; ˋkrɪmzn/ *adj, n* deep red. 深红色(的)。□ *vt, vi* make or become ~. (使)变成深红色。

cringe /krɪndʒ; krɪndʒ/ *vi* [VP2A, C] **1** **~ *(at),*** move (the body) back or down in fear: (因恐惧而)退缩; 畏缩: *The dog ~d at the sight of the whip.* 那狗看见鞭子就畏缩。**2** behave (towards a superior) in a way that shows lack of self-respect; be too humble: (对长上)表现卑躬屈膝的样子; 过分谦卑: *a cringing beggar;* 卑躬的乞丐; *to ~ to/before a policeman.* 对警察卑躬屈膝。

crinkle /ˈkrɪŋkl; ˋkrɪŋkl/ *n* small, narrow wrinkle (in material such as foil or paper). (箔或纸上的)小褶绉。□ *vt, vi* [VP6A, 15B, 2A, C] **~ *(up),*** make or get a ~ or ~s in: (使)起绉纹: *~d paper,* eg crêpe paper. 绉纹纸。**crin·kly** /ˈkrɪŋklɪ; ˋkrɪŋklɪ/ *adj* **(-ier, -iest)** (of materials) having ~s; (of hair) curly. (指材料)有绉纹的; (指发)卷曲的。

crino·line /ˈkrɪnəlɪn; ˋkrɪnlɪn/ *n* **1** [U] stiff, strong, rough fabric. 一种硬而坚牢的粗布。**2** [C] light framework covered with stiff material, as formerly worn to make a skirt swell out; ⇨ **hoop**[1]**(1).** (从前妇女用以)支撑裙子的衬架。

cripes /kraɪps; kraɪps/ *int* (expressing astonishment, etc) My Goodness! (表示惊异等)天啊! 啊呀!

cripple /ˈkrɪpl; ˋkrɪpl/ *n* person unable to walk or move properly, through injury or weakness in the spine or legs. 因脊椎骨或腿受伤或发育不良而跛者; 残废者。□ *vt* [VP6A] (lit, fig) make a ~ of, damage or weaken seriously: (字面, 喻)使跛; 使残废; 严重地损坏或削弱: *~d soldiers;* 跛足的伤兵; *~d with rheumatism;* 因患风湿症而跛足的; *a ship that was ~d in a storm;* 在暴风雨中受到严重损坏的船; *activities ~d by lack of money.* 因缺乏经费而停顿的活动。

cri·sis /ˈkraɪsɪs; ˋkraɪsɪs/ *n* (*pl* **crises** /-siːz; -siz/) turning-point in illness, life, history, etc; time of difficulty danger or anxiety about the future: (疾病、生命、历史等之)转捩点; 艰苦危难的时期; 危机; 紧要关头: *a financial ~.* 财政的危机。*Things are coming to/drawing to/reaching a ~.* 事情渐近紧要关头。*We must bring things to a ~,* do sth to reach the state when a definite decision must be taken. 我们必须采取步骤促使事情达于决定阶段。

crisp /krɪsp; krɪsp/ *adj* **1** (esp of food) hard, dry and easily broken: (尤指食物)脆的; 酥的: *~ toast/biscuits.* 脆的烤面包(饼干)。*The snow was ~ underfoot.* 脚底下的雪踩起来是脆的。**2** (of the air, the weather) frosty, cold and dry: (指空气, 天气)有霜气的; 寒冷而干燥的: *the ~ air of an autumn morning.* 秋晨的霜气。**3** (of hair) tightly curled. (指毛发)卷得紧的。**4** (of style, manners) quick, precise and decided; showing no doubts or hesitation: (指风度、态度)干脆的; 明快的; 斩钉截铁的: *a man with a ~ manner of speaking.* 说话态度爽快的人。□ *n* (US 美 = *chip*) (also 亦作 **poˌtato ˈ~**) thin slice of potato, fried and dried (usu sold in bulk in packets). 炸马铃薯片(通常装于小袋中售卖)。□ *vt, vi* make or become ~. (使)变酥脆; (使)变寒冻; (使)变卷紧; (使)变明快。**~·ly** *adv* **~·ness** *n*

criss·cross /ˈkrɪskrɒs *US:* -krɔːs; ˋkrɪsˌkrɔs/ *adj* with crossed lines: 线条互相交叉作十字状的: *a ~ pattern/design.* 十字形图案。□ *adv* crosswise. 互相交叉地。□ *vt, vi* move crosswise; mark with lines that cross. 交叉而行; 以十字线标示。

cri·terion /kraɪˈtɪərɪən; kraɪˋtɪrɪən/ *n* (*pl* **-ria** /-rɪə; -rɪə/ or ~s) standard of judgement; principle by which sth is measured for value: 判断的标准; 衡量某事物之价值的准则: *Success in money-making is not always a good ~ of real success in life.* 在赚钱方面的成功, 不一定是人生事业真正成功的一个好的准则。

critic /ˈkrɪtɪk; ˋkrɪtɪk/ *n* **1** person who forms and gives judgements, esp about literature, art, music, etc: (文学、艺术、音乐等的)批评家: *music(al)/drama(tic)/literary, etc ~s.* 音乐(戏剧, 文学等)批评家。**2** person who finds fault, points out mistakes, etc: 吹毛求疵者; 非难者: *I am my own most severe ~.* 我对自己要求非常严格。

criti·cal /ˈkrɪtɪkl; ˋkrɪtɪkl/ *adj* **1** of or at a crisis: 在危机期中的; 紧要关头的; 转捩点的: *We are at a ~ time in our history.* 我们正处于我们的历史的危急时期。*The patient's condition is ~,* He is dangerously ill. 病人的情况甚危。*This is a ~ moment,* eg one when there will be a change for the better or the worse. 这是生死存亡的关头。**2** of the work of a critic: 批评家之作品的; 批评的: *~ opinions on art and literature.* 批评家对于艺术及文学的意见。**3** fault-finding: 吹毛求疵的; 非难的: *~ remarks.* 吹毛求疵的评论。*She looks on everything with a ~ eye.* 她以吹毛求疵的眼光去看每一样事物。**~·ly** /-ɪklɪ; -ɪklɪ/ *adv* in a ~ manner: 岌岌可危地; 批评地; 吹毛求疵地: *He is ~ly ill.* 他病得很重。

criti·cism /ˈkrɪtɪsɪzəm; ˋkrɪtəˌsɪzəm/ *n* **1** [U] the work of a critic; the art of making judgements (concerning art, literature, etc). 批评家的作品; 批评; (关于艺术、文学等的)批评的技巧。**2** [C] judgement or opinion on literature, art, etc. (对文学、艺术等的)批评意见。**3** [U] fault-finding; [C] remark, etc that finds fault: 吹毛求疵(之论): *He hates ~,* being criticized. 他讨厌人家批评他。*Your frank ~s of his attempts annoyed him.* 你对于他的尝试所作的坦白批评使他很生气。

criti·cize /ˈkrɪtɪsaɪz; ˋkrɪtəˌsaɪz/ *vt, vi* [VP6A, 14, 2A] **~ *(for),*** form and give a judgement of; find fault with: 批评; 非难; 吹毛求疵: *~ sb's work;* 批评某人的作品; *~ sb for doing/not doing sth.* 责备某人(未)做某事。

cri·tique /krɪˈtiːk; krɪˋtik/ *n* [C] critical essay or review. 批评的文章; 评论。

croak /krəʊk; krok/ n deep, hoarse sound (as made by frogs or ravens). 蛙或乌鸦的叫声; 深沉的嘎声。□ vt, vi 1 [VP2A, 6A, 15B] ~ (out), make this kind of sound; say (sth) in a ~ing voice; foretell (evil); express dismal views about the future. 发此种声音; 说话声音如乌鸦叫; 以粗厉的声音说(某事); 预言(凶事); 对于未来表示悲观的看法。2 [VP2A] (sl) die². (俚)死亡。

cro·chet /ˈkrəʊʃeɪ US: krəʊˈʃeɪ; kroˈʃe/ vt, vi [VP 6A, 2A] make (needlework, eg a shawl) with a thread looped over others with the help of a small hooked needle (called a '~-hook). 用钩针(crochet-hook)编织(披肩等)。□ n [U] material (eg lace) made or being made in this way. 用钩针编织的织物(如花边)。

crock¹ /krɒk; krɑk/ n pot or jar made of baked earth, eg for containing water; broken piece of such a pot: (装水等的)瓦罐, 瓦罐碎片: Fill the bottom of the flower-pot with ~s for drainage. 在花钵的底部填以瓦罐碎片以便排水。

crock² /krɒk; krɑk/ n (colloq) horse that has become old, weak and useless; person who cannot work well because of bad health, lameness, etc; very old motor vehicle, etc. (口)老弱无用的马; 因健康不佳, 跛足等而不能工作的人; 极破旧的车辆等。□ vi, vt [VP2C, 15B] ~ up, become, cause to become, a ~: (使)变为无用; (使)变衰弱: This attack of influenza has ~ed me up. 这一场流行性感冒使我衰弱得无法工作。The poor man is ~ing up. 那可怜的人渐渐无用了。

crock·ery /ˈkrɒkərɪ; ˈkrɑkərɪ/ n [U] pots, plates, cups, dishes and other utensils (made of baked clay). 瓦器; 陶器(如罐、盘、杯、碟等)。

croco·dile /ˈkrɒkədaɪl; ˈkrɑkə͵daɪl/ n 1 large river reptile with a long body and tail, covered with a hard skin. 鳄鱼(河产爬虫, 体及尾甚长, 皮甚坚硬)。⇨ the illus at reptile. 参看 reptile 之插图。'~ tears n pl insincere sorrow. 假悲伤。2 (GB colloq) school children walking in procession, two by two. (英口)成双列排队而行的学童。

cro·cus /ˈkrəʊkəs; ˈkrokəs/ n (pl ~es /-sɪz; -sɪz/) (kind of) small plant growing from a corm, with coloured flowers early in spring. 番红花(自球茎长出之小植物, 花色不一, 初春时开放)。

Croe·sus /ˈkriːsəs; ˈkrisəs/ n (6th c BC) wealthy king in Asia Minor. 克里萨斯(公元前六世纪小亚细亚一富有之王)。a ~, very wealthy person. 大富翁。

croft /krɒft US: krɔːft; krɔft/ n (GB) small, enclosed field; small farm. (英)围起来的小块地; 小农场。~er n person who rents or owns a small farm, esp a joint tenant of a divided farm in Scotland. 小农场佃户或场主; (尤指)苏格兰之小农场佃农。

crom·lech /ˈkrɒmlek; ˈkrɑmlɛk/ n prehistoric structure of large flat stones laid horizontally on upright stones. (史前时代以扁平巨石平置于竖立石块上之)大石碑坊。

crone /krəʊn; kron/ n withered old woman. 干瘪的老太婆。

crony /ˈkrəʊnɪ; ˈkronɪ/ n close friend; companion; close associate. 密友; 同伴; 亲密的伙伴。

crook /krʊk; krʊk/ n 1 stick or staff with a rounded hook at one end, esp such a stick used by a shepherd. 一端有弯钩的棍杖(尤指牧羊人用者)。⇨ hook. 2 bend or curve, eg in a river or path. (河道或道路等的)弯处; 弯子。'~-back(ed), hunchback(ed). 驼背(的)。3 (colloq) person who makes a living by dishonest or criminal means. (口)骗子; 恶棍; 流氓。4 on the ~, (sl) dishonest(ly). (俚)狡诈的(地); 诡诈的(地)。□ vt, vi [VP6A, 2A] bend into the shape of a ~: 使弯曲: to ~ one's finger/arm. 屈指(臂)。

crooked /ˈkrʊkɪd; ˈkrʊkɪd/ adj 1 not straight or level; twisted; bent: 不平直的; 扭曲的; 弯曲的: a ~ lane. 弯曲的小巷。You've got your hat on ~. 你把帽子戴歪了。2 (of a person or his actions) dishonest; not straightforward. (指人或其行动)不诚实的; 欺骗的; 狡诈的。

~·ly adv ~·ness n

croon /kruːn; krun/ vt, vi [VP6A, 13A, 15A, 2C] hum or sing gently in a narrow range of notes: 轻哼; 低唱: ~ to oneself; 独自轻声低唱; ~ a lullaby; 轻唱摇篮曲; ~ the baby to sleep. 轻唱以使婴儿入睡。~er n (1930's and 1940's) person who ~s, esp a public entertainer who sings sentimental songs with a microphone held at the lips. (二十世纪三·十年代及二十世纪四十年代)轻唱歌手(尤指对着扩音器唱感伤歌曲以娱听众者)。

crop¹ /krɒp; krɑp/ n [C] 1 yearly (or season's) produce of grain, grass, fruit, etc; (pl)agricultural plants in the fields: (谷物、蔬果类等)一年或一季的收获; (复)田中的农作物: the 'potato ~; 马铃薯的产量; a good ~ of rice. 稻谷的丰收; to get the ~s in: 收割田中的谷物; (attrib) (用作定语)农作物的: ~ failures. 谷物收成不好。The land is in/under ~, being cultivated. 这块土地种有作物。The land is out of ~, not being cultivated. 这块土地未种作物。~-dusting, dusting (eg from low-flying aircraft) of growing ~s with insecticide or fertiliser. (自低飞的飞机等)对农作物喷撒杀虫剂或肥料。2 group of persons or things, amount of something, appearing or produced together: 一大堆(同时出现或产生的人、物、数量): The Prime Minister's statement produced a ~ of questions. 首相的声明引起了一大堆问题。

crop² /krɒp; krɑp/ n [C] 1 bag-like part of a bird's throat where food is broken up for digestion before passing into the stomach. 鸟的嗉囊(食物在进入胃以前在此磨碎以便消化)。neck and ~ ⇨ neck. 2 handle of a whip; (also 亦作 'hunting-~) whip-handle with a loop instead of a lash. 鞭柄; 作环的圈而无皮条的鞭柄。3 very short hair-cut: 剪得极短的发式; 平头: You look as if you've had a prison ~, had your hair cut very short, like men in prison. 你的头发看来剪得象牢里的犯人一样短。

crop³ /krɒp; krɑp/ vt, vi (-pp-) 1 [VP6A, 22] (of animals) bite off the tops of (grass, plants, etc); graze: (指牲畜)吃去(青草、植物等)的尖端; 吃青草: The sheep had ~ped the grass short. 羊群已将青草吃短。2 [VP 6A, 22] cut short (a person's hair, a horse's tail or ears). 剪短(人的头发, 马的尾巴或耳朵)。3 [VP6A, 14] ~ (with), sow or plant: 播种; 种植: to ~ ten acres with wheat. 种植十英亩地的小麦。4 [VP2A] bear a crop: 收获: The beans ~ped well this year. 豆子今年丰收。⇨ crop¹(1). 5 [VP2C] ~ up/out, (of rock, minerals) show up above the earth's surface. (指岩石, 矿物)露出地面之上。⇨ outcrop. 6 [VP2C] ~ up, appear or arise (esp unexpectedly): 出现或发生(尤指意外地): All sorts of difficulties ~ped up. 各种各样的困难一齐都来了。The subject ~ped up in the course of conversation. 谈话时无意中谈到了这个题目。

crop·per /ˈkrɒpə(r); ˈkrɑpɚ/ n 1 good/bad/heavy/light ~, plant yielding a good etc crop: 结实或收成好(坏, 多, 少)的植物: These peas are good ~s. 这些豆子结实甚丰。2 person or thing that crops. 收割者; 收割机。⇨ share-cropper at share¹(1). 3 come a ~, (colloq) have a fall; meet with failure (eg in an examination). (口)跌倒; 失败 (如考试不及格)。

cro·quet /ˈkrəʊkeɪ US: krəʊˈkeɪ; kroˈke/ n [U] game played on short grass with wooden balls which are knocked with wooden mallets through hoops. 槌球游戏 (在短草地上玩, 以木槌击木球钻小圈)。

cro·quette /krəʊˈket; kroˈkɛt/ n [C] ball of minced meat, fish, potato etc, coated with bread-crumbs and cooked in fat. (以碎的肉, 鱼或马铃薯等外粘面包屑而炸成之)炸肉丸; 炸鱼丸; 炸马铃薯丸。

crore /krɔː(r); kror/ n (India and Pakistan) ten millions; one hundred lakhs (of rupees). (印度及巴基斯坦)一千万(卢比等)。

cro·sier, cro·zier /ˈkrəʊzɪə(r) US: -ʒər; ˈkroʒɚ/ n bishop's staff, usu shaped like a shepherd's crook. 主教的权杖(通常作牧羊人的牧杖形)。⇨ the illus at

vestment. 参看 vestment 之插图。

cross[1] /krɒs US: krɔ:s; krɔs/ *n* **1** mark made by drawing one line across another, thus: ×, +: 十字形或叉形记号: *The place is marked on the map with a ~.* 该地在地图上以十字记号标出。 *make one's ~,* put a ~ on a document instead of one's signature (as in former times by illiterate persons). 画押; 画十字(如昔时文盲在文件上画十字以代替签名者)。 **2** line or stroke forming part of a letter (eg the horizontal stroke on a 't'). 字母(例如 t) 上的一横。 **3** stake or post with another piece of wood across it like **T**, † or **X**, as used in ancient times for crucifixion, esp **the C~,** that on which Christ died; model of this as a religious emblem; sth (esp a monument) in the form of a ~ (eg one in stone set up in the market-place of a village or town, called a **'market-~**); sign of a ~ made with the right hand as a religious act. 在木柱上另钉一块横木构成的十字架(如古代用作刑具者); (尤指)钉死耶稣的十字架; 作为宗教标志的十字架模型; 十字形石碑(如立于村镇市场者,称为 market-cross); 用右手所画的十字(系宗教行为)。 **4** (fig) suffering; affliction; burden of sorrow: (喻)苦难; 痛苦; 磨难; 忧患: *to bear one's ~;* 忍受苦难; *to take up one's ~,* be ready to bear affliction or suffering. 准备忍受苦难。 **5** emblem, in the form of a ~ or a star, (to be) worn by an order of knighthood; decoration for personal valour; (某等级爵士所戴的)十字徽章; (纪念英勇行为的)十字勋章: *the Victoria C~;* 维多利亚十字勋章; *the Distinguished Service C~.* 服务优异十字勋章。 **6** (place of) crossing. 交叉(处)。 *cut on the ~,* (dress-making) cut diagonally: (裁缝)斜地剪裁: *This skirt material was cut on the ~,* on the bias. 这裙子料是斜裁的。 **7** offspring of animals or plants of different sorts or breeds: 异种动物或植物杂交所产生的混合种: *A mule is a ~ between a horse and an ass.* 骡系马与驴配所生的混合种。

Greek   Latin   Maltese   Cross of
                              Lorraine

crosses

cross[2] /krɒs US: krɔ:s; krɔs/ *vt, vi* **1** [VP6A, 2A, C] **~ (from) (to),** go across; pass from one side to the other side (of): 横过; 越过; 渡过: *to ~ a road/river/bridge/the sea/the Sahara, etc;* 横越道路(河流, 桥梁, 海, 撒哈拉沙漠等); *to ~ from Dover to Calais.* 自多佛海峡渡海至加来。 *~ a person's path,* meet him: 遇见某人: *I hope I shall never ~ that man's path again.* 我希望我永不再遇见那个人。 *~ one's mind,* (of ideas, etc) occur to one: (指念头等)出现于脑中: *The idea has just ~ed my mind that....* 我刚才想到…。 **2** [VP6A, 15A, B] *~ (off/out/through),* draw a line or lines across or through (to cancel): 画横线于(以删除): *Two of the words had been ~ed out.* 其中有两个字被划去了。 *I ~ed his name off the list.* 我把他的名字从名单中删除了。 *~ a cheque,* draw two lines across it so that payment can be made only through a bank. 画两条线于支票(表示仅能经由银行兑现)。 *~ed 'cheque n* one that must be paid into a bank account, and cannot be cashed unless made out to 'self' or 'cash'. 画线支票(必须存入户头, 如未标明 'self' 或 'cash' 字样不可兑现)。 *~ one's t's and dot one's i's,* (fig) be careful and exact. (喻)谨慎而严正。 **3** [VP6A, 14] put or place across or over: 交叉: *to ~ one's legs;* 交叉两腿; *to ~ one's arms on one's chest.* 交叉两臂于胸前。 *~ sb's palm with silver,* give a coin to him (esp to a fortune-teller). 拿一枚铜钱给某人(尤指给算命者)。 *~ swords with sb,* fight or argue with him. 与某人交锋; 与某人辩论。 *keep one's fingers ~ed,* (fig) hope for the best, that

nothing will happen to upset one's plans, etc. (喻)求神保佑一切顺利; 希望不要有意外事情妨碍计划等。 **4 ~ oneself,** make the sign of the cross on or over oneself as a religious act, to invoke God's protection, or as a sign of awe. 用右手在胸前画十字(系宗教行为); 意为求上帝保护或表示敬畏)。 **5** [VP6A, 2A] (of persons travelling, letters in the post) meet and pass: (指行路的人, 邮递中的信件)互相在路上错过: *We ~ed each other on the way.* 我们两人在路上错过去了。 *Our letters ~ed in the post.* 我们的信件在邮局错过。 *Your letter ~ed mine in the post.* 你的信跟我的信在邮局中错过。 *~ed line,* interruption by mistake into a telephone connection. 电话岔线。 **6** [VP6A] oppose or obstruct (sb, his plans, wishes, etc): 反对或阻碍(某人, 其计划、意愿等): *He was angry at having his plans ~ed.* 他因计划受阻而怨怒。 *He ~es me in everything.* 他处处与我作对。 *He has been ~ed in love,* has failed to win the love of the woman he was in love with. 他在爱情上曾受挫折(未获所爱之女人的垂青)。 **7** [VP2A, 6A, 14] *~ (with),* produce a cross(7) by mixing breeds; (cause to) interbreed; crossfertilize (plants, etc). 使杂种交配以产生混合种; 使杂交; 杂配(植物等)。 ⇨ **crossbreed.**

cross[3] /krɒs US: krɔ:s; krɔs/ *adj* **1** (colloq) bad-tempered; easily or quickly showing anger: (口)脾气坏的; 易怒的: *Don't be ~ with the child for being late.* 不要对那迟到的孩子发脾气。 *I've never heard a ~ word from her lips.* 我从未听到她说过一句发脾气的话。 *Don't pull the dog's tail, you'll make him ~.* 不要拉狗的尾巴, 你会使它发脾气的。 *as ~ as two sticks,* (colloq) very bad-tempered. (口)脾气乖戾的。 **2** (of winds) contrary; opposed: (指风)相反的; 逆的: *Strong ~ winds made it difficult for the yachts to leave harbour.* 强烈的逆风使那些小艇不易出港。 **~·ly** *adv* **~·ness** *n*

cross·bar /'krɒsbɑ:(r) US: 'krɔ:s-; 'krɔs,bɑr/ *n* bar going across, eg the bar joining the two upright posts of the goal (in football, etc) or the front and rear ends of a bicycle frame. 横木; 横杠(例如足球门两之横木或脚踏车之横杠)。 ⇨ the illus at **bicycle.** 参看 bicycle 之插图。

cross·beam /'krɒsbi:m US: 'krɔ:s-; 'krɔs,bim/ *n* beam placed across, esp one that supports parts of a structure; girder. 房屋的横梁; 横桁; 大梁。

cross·benches /'krɒsbentʃɪz US: 'krɔ:s-; 'krɔs,bentʃɪz/ *n pl* those benches in the House of Commons used by members who do not vote regularly with either the Government or the Opposition. 英国下议院不固定投政府票或反对票的)中立议员席。 Hence, 由此产生, **crossbencher** *n* ⇨ **bench.**

cross·bones /'krɒsbəʊnz US: 'krɔ:s-; 'krɔs,bonz/ *n pl* (design of) two thigh bones laid across each other, usu under a skull, as an emblem of death (used as a warning of danger, and on the black flag once used by pirates). 通常置于头盖骨下面象征死亡的两条交叉股骨; 此种图形(用作危险的警告, 昔时海盗亦用于黑旗上)。

cross·bow /'krɒsbəʊ US: 'krɔ:s-; 'krɔs,bo/ *n* old kind of bow placed across a grooved wooden support, used for shooting arrows, bolts, stones, etc. 十字弓; 弩(一种旧式弓, 横置于有沟的木架上, 以发射箭、矢、石等)。

cross·bred /'krɒsbred US: 'krɔ:s-; 'krɔs,bred/ *adj* produced by crossing breeds: 由杂交所产生的; 杂种的: *~ sheep.* 杂种绵羊。

cross·breed /'krɒsbri:d US: 'krɔ:s-; 'krɔs,brid/ *n* (in farming, etc) animal, plant, etc, produced by crossing different kinds. (在畜牧, 农业等中)由杂交所产生的杂种(动物, 植物等)。 □ *vi, vt* [VP2A, 6A] produce in this way. (使)杂交; (使)异种繁配。

cross-check /'krɒs 'tʃek US: 'krɔ:s-; ,krɔs 'tʃek/ *vt, vi* [VP6A, 2A] verify, eg a method, calculation, by using a different method, etc: (以不同方法)查核; 核对(采用不同方法加以查核对): *We ~ed the results twice.* 我们将结果核对了两次。 □ *n* verification of this sort: 以不同方法查核; 核对: *We'd better do a ~ on these*

figures. 我们最好核对一下这些数字。

cross·country /ˌkrɒsˈkʌntrɪ US: ˌkrɔːs-; ˈkrɔs,kʌntrɪ/ *adj, adv* across the country or fields, not along roads: 越野的(地): a ~ *race.* 越野赛跑。

cross·cur·rent /ˈkrɒs kʌrənt US: ˈkrɔːs; ˈkrɔs,kɤrənt/ *n* current flowing across another; (fig) body of opinion contrary to that of the majority (on sth of public interest). 交叉的水流; (喻)(对有关公益事件)与大多数人相反的意见。

cross·cut /ˈkrɒskʌt US: ˈkrɔːs; ˈkrɔs,kʌt/ *adj* (of a saw) with teeth designed for cutting across the grain of wood. (指锯)有特种锯齿而能横木纹而锯的; 横切的。□ *n* diagonal cut or path; short cut. 对角线切; 斜路; 捷径。

cross-division /ˌkrɒs dɪˈvɪʒn US: ˌkrɔːs; ˈkrɔsdə'vɪʒn/ *n* [U] division of a group according to more than one factor at the same time so that sub-divisions interrelate; [C] instance of this. 横式区分(同时根据几个因素划分一团体, 俾使再分成的部分有相互关系); 此种区分的实例。

crosse /krɒs US: krɔːs; krɔs/ *n* kind of long-handled racquet used in lacrosse. 曲棍球棒。

cross-exam·ine /ˌkrɒs ɪgˈzæmɪn US: ˌkrɔːs; ˈkrɔsɪg'zæmɪn/ *vt* [VP6A] question closely, esp to test answers already given to someone else, as in a law court, by counsel, etc. 严密询问; (尤指在法庭等中由辩护律师等就某人对他人所作之回答进行)盘问/盘诘。**cross-exam·iner** /-mɪnə(r); -mɪnɚ/ *n* **cross-exam·in·ation** /ˌkrɒs ɪgˌzæmɪˈneɪʃn US: ˌkrɔːs; ˈkrɔsɪg,zæmə'neʃən/ *n*.

cross·eyed /ˈkrɒsaɪd US: ˈkrɔːs; ˈkrɔs'aɪd/ *adj* with one or both eyeballs turned towards the nose. 一眼球或二眼球向鼻子斜的; 内斜视的; 斗鸡眼的。

cross-fer·ti·lize /ˌkrɒs ˈfɜːtəlaɪz US: ˌkrɔːs; ˈkrɔs'fɜtl,aɪz/ *vt* (bot) carry pollen from the stamens of one plant to the pistil of another plant to produce hybrids. (植物)使异花受精(将异种雄蕊之花粉送至雌蕊受精以产生杂种)。**cross-fer·ti·li·za·tion** /ˌkrɒs,fɜːtəlaɪˈzeɪʃn US: ˌkrɔːs; ˈkrɔs,fɜtl'ɔ'zeʃən/ *n*.

cross·fire /ˈkrɒsfaɪə(r) US: ˈkrɔːs-; ˈkrɔs,faɪr/ *n* [U, C] (mil) firing of guns from two or more points so that the lines of fire cross; (fig) situation in which questions are put to sb from different persons. (军)交叉射击(自两处或多处向同一目标射去, 以致炮火交错); (喻)(自不同人士对某人发出的)交相质问。

cross-grained /ˌkrɒs ˈgreɪnd US: ˌkrɔːs; ˈkrɔs'grend/ *adj* 1 (of wood) with the grain in crossing directions. (指木材)纹理交错的。2 (fig) perverse; difficult to please or get on with. (喻)执拗的; 难以取悦或相处的。

cross-head(·ing) /ˈkrɒs hed(ɪŋ) US: ˈkrɔːs-; ˈkrɔs,hed(ɪŋ)/ *n* (in a newspaper, etc) heading within an article, dividing a column. (报纸等之)小标题(插在各段落之间); 子题。

cross-index /ˌkrɒsˈɪndeks US: ˌkrɔːs; ˈkrɔs'ɪndeks/ *n, vt* [VP6A] (supply with) cross-reference. (供以)前后参看。

cross·ing /ˈkrɒsɪŋ US: ˈkrɔːs; ˈkrɔsɪŋ/ *n* 1 [U, C] the act of going across, esp by sea: 横越; (尤指渡海)渡海: *We had a rough ~ from Dover to Calais.* 我们由多佛渡海至加来时, 风浪很大。2 [C] place where two roads, two railways, or (esp) a road and a railway cross. 十字路口; 两铁道交叉处; (尤指)(铁路与公路交叉处的)平交道。,**level** '~, one without a bridge (US 美 = *grade* ~). 平交道。3 *pe,destrian* /ˌzebra* '~, place on a street where pedestrians are requested to cross (often marked by studs or white lines and sometimes by traffic lights operated by pedestrians) (US 美 = *crosswalk*). 人行横道; 行人穿越道(常以饰钉或白线表示, 有时由行人操纵交通灯控制); 斑马线。

cross·keys /ˈkrɒsˈkiːz US: ˈkrɔːs-; ˈkrɔs'kiz/ *n pl* (design of) crossed keys as Papal arms, and as an inn sign. 交叉钥匙(图形)(如教皇纹章或旅馆招牌上的标记)。

cross-legged /ˌkrɒs ˈlegd US: ˌkrɔːs; ˈkrɔs'legɪd, -'legd/ *adv* (of a person sitting) with one leg placed across the other. (指坐着的人)两腿交叉地。

cross·patch /ˈkrɒspætʃ US: ˈkrɔːs; ˈkrɔs,pætʃ/ *n* (colloq) cross, bad-tempered person. (口)脾气乖戾的人。

cross·piece /ˈkrɒs piːs US: ˈkrɔːs; ˈkrɔs,pis/ *n* piece (of a structure) lying across another piece. (指构造物中)置于他物上的横放物; 横档。

cross·pur·poses /ˌkrɒs ˈpɜːpəsɪz US: ˌkrɔːs; 'pɤpəsɪz/ *n pl be at ~*, (of two persons or groups) misunderstand one another; have different and conflicting purposes. (指二人或团体)互相误解; 持有不同而且冲突的目的。

cross-question /ˌkrɒs ˈkwestʃən US: ˌkrɔːs; ˈkrɔs-'kwestʃən/ *vt* = **cross-examine.**

cross-ref·er·ence /ˌkrɒs ˈrefrəns US: ˌkrɔːs-; ˈkrɔs-'refərəns/ *n* [C] reference from one part of a book, index, file, etc to another, for further information. 书中前后互相参看之处。

cross·road /ˈkrɒsrəʊd US: ˈkrɔːs-; ˈkrɔs,rod/ *n* 1 road that crosses another. 交叉路。2 **a/the ~s,** (used with *sing v*) place where two roads meet and cross: (用单数动词)十字路口: *We came to a ~s.* 我们走到一个十字路口。3 *at the ~s,* (fig) at a critical turning-point (in life, etc). (喻)处于(人生等的)转折点。

cross-sec·tion /ˌkrɒs ˈsekʃn US: ˌkrɔːs; ˈkrɔs'sekʃən/ *n* [C] (drawing of a) piece or slice made by cutting across, eg a tree trunk; (fig) typical or representative sample of the whole: 横切面(例如树干者); 横切面之图; (喻)可以代表全体的样品; 抽样: *a ~ of the electors/the middle classes.* 选举人(中产阶级)的代表。

cross-stitch /ˈkrɒs stɪtʃ US: ˈkrɔːs; ˈkrɔs,stɪtʃ/ *n* [C] stitch formed of two stitches that cross; [U] needlework in which this stitch is used. 十字针法; 用十字针法编织的织物。

cross-talk /ˈkrɒs tɔːk US: ˈkrɔːs; ˈkrɔs,tɔk/ *n* [U] (GB, colloq) rapid exchange of remarks, eg by comedians in a variety entertainment or in a quarrel; talk in which conversation is garbled, eg by crossed telephone lines. (英, 口)斗嘴(例如杂技团中滑稽角色之插科与吵架时之对骂); (电话中因线路交错而由他处传来的)片断对话。

cross·trees /ˈkrɒstriːz US: ˈkrɔːs-; ˈkrɔs,triz/ *n pl* two horizontal timbers bolted to a lower mast to support the mast above and to support ropes, etc. 桅顶横木(二平行木材, 闩于较低之桅顶以支持上端较高之桅及缆索等)。

cross·walk /ˈkrɒswɔːk US: ˈkrɔːs-; ˈkrɔs,wɔk/ *n* ⇨ **crossing (3).**

cross·wind /ˈkrɒswɪnd US: ˈkrɔːs-; ˈkrɔswɪnd/ *n* [C] wind blowing at right angles, eg to an aircraft's line of flight or to traffic on a motorway. 侧风(例如成直角吹向一飞机的航线或在高速公路上行驶的车辆者)。

cross·wise /ˈkrɒs waɪz US: ˈkrɔːs; ˈkrɔs,waɪz/ *adv* across; diagonally; in the form of a cross. 横地; 斜地; 作十字状地。

cross·word /ˈkrɒswɜːd US: ˈkrɔːs; ˈkrɔs,wɝd/ *n* (also 亦作 '~ *puzzle*) puzzle in which words have to be written (from numbered clues) vertically (= clues *down*) and horizontally (= clues *across*) in spaces on a chequered square or oblong. 纵横字谜(依号码排列的提示, 在一块方阵或长方阵之许多小方格内, 按纵横方向填字的一种游戏)。

crotch /krɒtʃ; krɑtʃ/ *n* 1 place where a branch forks from a tree: 树的枝桠; 树叉: *The child was sitting in a ~ of a tree.* 那孩子坐在一个树叉上。2 place where a pair of trousers or a person's legs fork from the trunk. (裤子的)裤裆; (人体的)胯部。

crotchet /ˈkrɒtʃɪt; ˈkrɑtʃɪt/ *n* 1 (music) (US 美 = *quarter note*) black-headed note with stem (♩), half of a minim. (音乐)四分音符。⇨ the illus at **notation.** 参

看 notation 之插图。**2** strange, unreasonable idea. 不合理的奇怪想法；~**y** adj full of ~s(2); bad-tempered. 充满奇思怪想的；脾气坏的。

crouch /krautʃ; krautʃ/ vi [VP2A, C, 4A] ~ **(down)**, lower the body with the limbs together (in fear or to hide, or, of animals, ready to spring). 蹲伏（四肢收缩，身体低下，因恐惧或欲隐藏，或指动物预备猛扑的姿势）。□ n ~ing position. 蹲伏的姿势。

croup¹ /kru:p; krup/ n [U] children's disease in which there is inflammation of the windpipe, with coughing and difficulty in breathing. 格鲁布性喉头炎；哮吼（儿童疾病，气管发炎，有咳嗽及呼吸困难现象）。

croup² /kru:p; krup/ n rump or buttocks of certain animals. （某些动物之）臀部。⇨ the illus of horse at **domestic.** 参看 domestic 项下 horse 之插图。

crou·pier /'kru:pɪeɪ US: -pɪər; 'krupɪə/ n person who rakes in the money at a gaming table and pays out winnings. 赌桌上收取及偿付赌注的人。

crow¹ /krəʊ; kro/ n (kinds of) large, black bird with a harsh cry. 乌鸦。⇨ the illus at **bird.** 参看 bird 之插图。⇨ also **carrion, jackdaw, raven, rook¹. as the '~ flies,** in a straight line. 成直线地。**'~'s-nest,** protected look-out platform fixed at the mast-head of a ship (eg a whaling ship) for the look-out man. 桅楼；瞭望台（例如捕鲸船桅尖顶供瞭望者所用者）。**'~'s-feet** n pl network of little lines on the skin near the outer corners of a person's eyes. 鱼尾纹（成人眼角外侧附近皮肤上的皱纹）。

crow² /krəʊ; kro/ vi (pl **crowed** or (archaic) (古) **crew** /kru:; kru/, pp **crowed** [VP2A, 3A] **1** (of a cock) make a loud, shrill cry. （指公鸡）啼；叫；喔喔。**2** (of a baby) make sounds showing happiness. (指婴儿）发笑声。**3** ~ **(over)**, (of persons) express gleeful triumph: （指人）表示得意洋洋：to ~ over an unsuccessful rival. 面对失败的敌手而得意洋洋。□ n ~ing sound. 公鸡的啼声；婴儿笑声。

crow·bar /'krəʊbɑː(r); 'kro,bɑr/ n straight iron bar, often with a forked end, used as a lever for moving heavy objects. 作为杠杆移动重物的铁棍；铁撬；铁梃；撬棍。

crowd /kraʊd; kraʊd/ n [C] **1** large number of people together, but without order or organization: 人群；群众：There were large ~s of people in the streets on New Year's Eve. 除夕的街上有大批的人群。He pushed his way through the ~. 他从人群中挤过去。**(would) pass in a ~,** is not obviously unsatisfactory or defective. 还过得去；还不坏。**2 the ~,** the masses; people in general. 民众；大众。**follow / move with the ~,** be content to do what most people do. 从众；跟大家一样。**3** (colloq) company of persons associated in some way; set or clique of persons: （口）一伙；一班；一帮：I can't afford to go about with that ~; they're too extravagant. 我没有财力同那伙人打交道；他们太奢侈了。**4** large number (of things, usu without order): 一大批(指东西，通常是杂乱的)：a desk covered with a ~ of books and papers. 杂乱地堆满书籍和文件的写字桌。□ vi, vt **1** [VP2B, C, 6A, 14, 15A, B] come together in a ~; fill (a space) with people: 群聚；拥挤；使挤满：~ a beach / square / hall. 群聚于海滨(广场, 大厅)。Now, don't all ~ together! 不要统挤在一起呀！~ round, form a circle (round): 围拢；聚拢：People quickly ~ round when there is a street accident. 街上发生意外事故时，人们很快地就围了起来。The pupils ~ed round the teacher to ask questions. 学生们围着老师问问题。~ through / in/into, etc; ~ (sth) with, (cause to) move through, etc in a ~; fill with: (使)挤进(挤入等)；(使)充塞：They ~ed through the gates into the stadium. 他们挤过大门，进入运动场。They ~ed the buses with passengers; ~ed people into the buses. 他们使公共汽车挤满了乘客（使人们挤进公共汽车）。Let's not ~ the room with furniture. 我们不要在这房间里摆设太多的家具吧。Memories ~ed in upon me, came thick and fast into my mind. 往事一

齐涌入我的脑海。~ **sb / sth out (of)**, keep out by ~ing: 将某人（某物）挤到（…的）外面：There was an overflow meeting for those who were ~ed out, unable to obtain admission. 为被挤在外面的人(无法进入者)另外举行了一个会。Your contribution to the magazine was ~ed out, There was no space for it. 你为那杂志所写的稿件因稿挤而未被刊登。**2** (naut) ~ **on sail,** hoist many sails (so as to increase speed). (航海)扬起许多帆(以增船速)。**3** [VP6A] (colloq) put pressure on: （口）施以压力；逼迫：Don't ~ me; give me time to think! 不要逼我；给我时间让我想想！~**ed** part adj having large numbers of people: 挤满人群的：~ed cities / trains / buses. 拥挤的城市(火车, 公共汽车)。

crown¹ /kraʊn; kraʊn/ n **1** ornamental headdress of gold, jewels, etc worn by a sovereign ruler; royal power: 王冕；皇冠(君主所戴以黄金、珠宝等制成者)；王权；君权：to wear the ~, rule as a sovereign; 即王位；为王；succeed to the ~, become the sovereign ruler; 继承王位；为王；an officer of the ~, a State official; 国家的官吏；a minister of the ~, a Cabinet Minister; 内阁阁员；a ~ appointment, one made by the sovereign. 国王任命的差事。**C~ Colony,** one governed completely by Great Britain. 英国直辖殖民地。~**-land,** land that belongs to the C~. 属于君主的土地；王室领地。~ **prince,** next in succession to the throne. 皇太子(王位继承人)。~ **princess,** wife of a ~ prince. 皇太子之妃。~**witness,** witness for the Prosecution in a criminal case. (刑事)原告方面的证人。**2** circle or wreath of flowers or leaves worn on the head, esp as a sign of victory, or as a reward: 荣冠；花冠(尤指象征胜利或作为奖赏者)：a martyr's ~. 烈士的花冠。**3** British coin worth 25p, formerly 5 shillings. 英国硬币(值25便士，昔时值五先令)。**half a ~; a half ~,** (until 1971) British coin worth 12¹/₂p. (一九七一年以前)英国硬币(值12¹/₂便士)。**4** top of the head or of a hat; part of a tooth that shows; (fig) perfection, completion: 头顶；帽顶；齿冠(牙齿露于顶外的部分)；(喻)完美；完满：the ~ of one's labours; 某人劳力之完满成果(功成名就)；the ~ of the year, the autumn, season of harvests. 秋季；收获的季节。**5** ~-shaped ornament (eg a crest or badge). 冠状饰物(例如饰章或徽章)。

crown² /kraʊn; kraʊn/ vt [VP6A, 23] put a crown on (a king or queen): 为(王或女王)加冕：They ~ed the heads (= kings and queens) of Europe. 欧洲的帝王和女王。They ~ed him king. 他们为他加冕(立之为王)。**2** [VP 6A, 14] ~ **(with),** reward with a crown; give honour to; reward: 赏以荣冠；褒奖；赏赐：to be ~ed with victory; 获得胜利的荣誉；efforts that were ~ed with success. 如愿以偿的努力。**3** [VP6A, 14] ~ **(with),** be or have at the top of: 位于…之顶；顶上有：The hill is ~ed with a wood. 山顶上有森林。**4** [VP6A] put a happy finishing touch to: 对…作圆满的润饰：to open a bottle of wine to ~ a feast. 开一瓶葡萄酒使宴会圆满结束。**to ~ (it) all,** to complete good / bad fortune, etc: 更妙(糟糕)的是；加之；尤其是：It was raining, we had no umbrellas, and, to ~ all, we missed the last bus and had to walk home. 下雨了，我们没有带伞，更糟糕的是我们误了最后一班公共汽车，于是不得不步行回家。**5** [VP6A] put an artificial cover on a broken tooth. 镶(牙)。⇨ **crown¹**(4). ~**ing** part adj (attrib only) (仅作定语) completing; making perfect: 使完善的；使圆满的：the ~ing touch to the evening's entertainment. 使晚会圆满的一项行动。Her ~ing glory is her hair. 她最美的地方是她的头发。

cro·zier /'krəʊzɪə(r) US: -ʒər; 'kroʒə/ n = crosier.

cru·cial /'kru:ʃl; 'kruʃəl/ adj decisive; critical: 决定性的；关系重大的：the ~ test / question; 决定性的测验(问题)；at the ~ moment. 在重要的关头。~**ly** /-ʃəlɪ; -ʃəlɪ/ adv

cru·cible /'kru:sɪbl; 'krusəbl/ n pot in which metals are melted; (fig) severe test or trial. (可熔金属的)坩埚；(喻)严厉的考验。

cru·ci·fix /'kru:sɪfɪks; 'krusə,fɪks/ n model of the Cross with the figure of Jesus on it. 有耶穌像的十字架模型；耶穌受難像。

cru·ci·fixion /ˌkru:sɪ'fɪkʃn; ˌkrusə'fɪkʃən/ n [U] putting to death, being put to death, on a cross(3); [C] instance of this. (被)釘死于十字架上。**the C~**, that of Jesus. 耶穌之被釘死于十字架。

cru·ci·form /'kru:sɪfɔ:m; 'krusə,fɔrm/ adj cross-shaped. 十字形的。

cru·ci·fy /'kru:sɪfaɪ; 'krusə,faɪ/ vt put to death by nailing or binding to a cross(3). 釘于十字架或綁于十字架以处死。

crud /krʌd; krʌd/ n (GB sl) unpleasant person. (英俚)讨厌的人。**~dy** adj unpleasant. 讨厌的；使人不愉快的。

crude /kru:d; krud/ adj 1 (of materials) in a natural state; not refined or manufactured: (指物质)原状的；未提炼的；未加工制造的；粗糙的；生的： ~ oil, petroleum; 原油(石油)； ~ sugar; 粗糖； ~ ore. 原矿石。2 not having grace, taste or refinement: 粗鄙的；粗劣的； ~ manners. 粗鲁的举止。3 nct finished properly; badly worked out: 制制温差的； 不完善的： ~ schemes / methods / ideas; 不完善的计划(方法，思想)； ~ paintings, showing lack of skill; 技巧拙劣的绘画； ~ facts, presented in an undisguised way, with no attempt to make them less unpleasant; 赤裸裸(未加掩饰)的事实； a ~ log cabin. 简陋的木屋。**~·ly** adv

crud·ity /'kru:dɪtɪ; 'krudɪtɪ/ n [U] the state or quality of being crude; [C] (pl **-ties**) instance cf this; crude act, remark, etc. 粗糙；粗野；粗鲁；粗暴的行为，言辞等。

cruel /'kruəl; 'kruəl/ adj (**-ller, -llest**) 1 (of persons) taking pleasure in the suffering of others; ready to give pain to others: (指人)残忍的；残暴的；以他人受苦为乐的；好虐待的： a ~ master; 残暴的主人； a man who is ~ to animals. 虐待动物的人。It was ~ of him to make the donkey carry such a heavy load. 他让那驴子驮这样重的东西，真是残忍。2 causing pain or suffering; showing indifference to the sufferings of others: 残酷的；无情的： a ~ blow / punishment / disease / war; 残酷的打击(惩罚，疾病，战争)； in a ~ (= distressing) predicament. 在痛苦的折磨中。**~·ly** /'kruəlɪ; 'kruəlɪ/ adv

cruelty /'kruəltɪ; 'kruəltɪ/ n 1 [U] readiness to give pain or cause suffering to others; delight in this; cruel nature: 残忍；残暴；残酷；残忍的天性；C~ to animals is severely punished in England. 虐待动物在英国处罚很重。2 [C] (pl **-ties**) cruel act 残暴的行为。

cruet /'kru:ɪt; 'kruɪt/ n 1 small glass bottle for vinegar or oil for use at table. 餐桌上用的装醋或油类的小玻璃瓶；调味瓶。2 (also 亦作 **'~-stand**) stand for oil and vinegar ~s, and for mustard, chutney, etc. 置放油瓶，醋瓶，芥子酱瓶，调味酱瓶等的瓶架；五味瓶架；调味瓶架。

cruise /kru:z; kruz/ vi [VP2A, C] 1 sail abcut, either for pleasure, or, in war, looking for enemy ships. 乘船巡游(或为游乐，或为搜寻敌舰)；巡航。2 (of cars, aircraft) travel at the speed (and of aircraft at the altitude) most economical of fuel, less than the top speed: (指汽车，飞机)以最省燃料的速度或高度(但不及最高速度)行进：The car has a cruising speed of 50 miles an hour. 该汽车之省油速度为每小时五十英里。□ n cruising voyage: 乘船巡游：巡航：to go on / for a ~. 乘船巡游。The liner is making a round-the-world ~ this year, a pleasure voyage. 这艘客轮今年正在作环球航行。**cruiser** /'kru:zə(r); 'kruzɚ/ n 1 fast warship. 巡洋舰。2 **'cabin-~r,** motor-boat (with sleeping accommodation, etc) designed for pleasure ~s. 游览汽艇(供睡眠设备等)。

crumb /krʌm; krʌm/ n 1 [C] very small piece of dry food, esp a bit of bread or cake rubbed off or dropped from a large piece: 干食品的屑末；(尤指)面包屑或糕饼屑：sweep up the ~s; 扫去食品屑；[U] soft,

inner part of a loaf of bread. 面包心。⇨ **crust(1).** 2 (fig) small amount: (喻)少许；少量：a few ~s of information / comfort. 少许的消息(安慰)。

crumble /'krʌmbl; 'krʌmbl/ vt, vi [VP6A, 2A, C] break, rub or fall into very small pieces: 弄碎；碎为细屑：to ~ one's bread, rub it into crumbs; 将面包弄成碎屑；crumbling walls, that are falling into ruin; 崩塌中的墙壁； great empires that have ~d (= decayed) and fallen; 已崩溃衰落的一些大帝国； (fig) (喻) hopes that ~d to dust, came to nothing. 成为泡影的希望。

crum·bly /'krʌmblɪ; 'krʌmblɪ/ adj easy to crumble. 易粉碎的。

crummy /'krʌmɪ; 'krʌmɪ/ adj (sl) bad; worthless; unpleasant. (俚)不好的；无用的；不愉快的：a ~ party; 不愉快的聚会；feel ~, ill. 觉得不舒服。

crum·pet /'krʌmpɪt; 'krʌmpɪt/ n (GB) (英) 1 flat, round, soft, unsweetened cake, usu toasted and eaten hot with butter spread on it. 一种松脆无甜味的圆饼(通常烤后趁热涂奶油食之)。2 (sl) head. (俚)头。3 (sl) sexually attractive girl or woman. (俚)性感的女郎或妇人。

crumple /'krʌmpl; 'krʌmpl/ vt, vi [VP6A, 15B, 2A, C] 1 press or crush into folds or creases: 压皱；挤皱：to ~ one's clothes, eg by packing them carelessly. 把衣服压皱(如因装理不小心所致)。2 become full of folds or creases: 变得有许多折皱：Some kinds of material ~ more easily than others. 有些料子比其他的料子易皱。Do nylon sheets ~? 尼龙床单会起皱吗？3 ~ up, (lit, fig) crush; collapse: (字面，喻)压碎；崩溃：to ~ up a sheet of paper into a ball; 将一张纸揉做一团；to ~ up an opposing army. 击溃敌军。The wings of the aircraft ~d up. 飞机的两翼撞坏了。

crunch /krʌntʃ; krʌntʃ/ vt, vi [VP6A, 2A, C] 1 crush noisily with the teeth when eating: 进食时用牙咬碎嘎扎作响：The dog was ~ing a bone. 那狗在啃一块骨头。People who ~ peanuts in the cinema can be very annoying. 在电影院里剥食花生的人十分讨厌。2 crush, be crushed, noisily under one's feet, under wheels, etc: (被)踩碎或(被)碾碎而发碎裂声：The frozen snow ~ed under the wheels of our car. 冻结了的雪在我们的汽车轮下发出碎裂声。Our feet ~ed the gravel. 我们的脚踏在碎石上沙沙作响。□ n the act of ~ing; noise made by ~ing. 踩碎(声)；碾碎(声)。**when it comes to the ~; when the ~ comes,** (colloq) the moment of crisis or decision is reached. (口)当紧要关头来临时。

crup·per /'krʌpə(r); 'krʌpɚ/ n leather strap fastened to the back of a saddle or harness and looped under the horse's tail; hindquarters of a horse. 连在马鞍或挽具后边兜住马尾下的皮带；马的臀部。⇨ the illus at **harness.** 参看 harness 之插图。

cru·sade /kru:'seɪd; kru'sed/ n 1 any one of the military expeditions made by the Christian rulers and people of Europe during the Middle Ages to recover the Holy Land from the Muslims. 十字军(中世纪由基督教君主及欧洲人民组成向伊斯兰教地区进攻以图夺回圣地的远征军)。2 any struggle or movement in support of sth believed to be good or against sth believed to be bad: 任何赞助善事或反对恶事的奋斗或运动：a ~ against bribery. 反对授受贿赂运动。□ vi [VP2A, 3A] ~ (**for / against**), take part in a ~. 参加某种运动(以赞助或反对)。**cru·sader** n person taking part in a ~. 参加某种运动的人；十字军战士。

crush[1] /krʌʃ; krʌʃ/ vt, vi 1 [VP6A, 15A, B] press, be pressed, so that there is breaking or injury: (被)压碎；(被)压破；压伤；使挤入：Don't ~ this box; it has flowers in it. 不要把这个盒子压破了；里面装的有花。Wine is made by ~ing grapes. 葡萄酒是压榨葡萄制成的。Several people were ~ed to death as they tried to escape from the burning theatre. 有几个人欲自失火燃烧中的戏院里逃出而被压死了。We can't ~ any more people into the hall; it's crowded already. 我们再也不能让任何人进入大厅了；里面已经很挤了。~ **up,** make into

powder by ∼ing. 压为粉末. ∼ **out (of)**, force out by ∼ing: 压出; 榨出: *to ∼ out the juice from oranges*. 榨出橙汁. **2** [VP6A, 15A, B, 2A, C] (cause to) become full of creases or irregular folds; lose shape: (使) 起皱; (使) 变形: *Her dresses were badly ∼ed when she took them out of the suitcase*. 她把衣服从箱中取出时, 衣服被压皱得一塌糊涂. *Some of the new synthetic dress materials do not ∼*. 有些新式的人造衣料不会皱. **3** [VP 6A] subdue; overwhelm: 镇服; 制服; 压倒: *He was not satisfied until he had ∼ed his enemies*. 他直到完全制服敌人后方才满足. *Our hopes have been ∼ed*. 我们的希望已破灭. *He smiled at her, but she ∼ed him* (= made him feel abashed) *with a haughty look*. 他向她微笑, 但她却摆出一副傲慢神情使他难堪. **4** [VP2C] (of persons) ∼ **in/into/through/past, etc**, press or push in, etc: (挤入)挤入(过等): *They all tried to ∼ into the front seats*. 他们大家都想挤到前排的座位去. [VP15A, B] (With cognate object) (与同源宾语连用) *We had to ∼ our way through the crowd*. 我们不得不由人群中挤过去. ∼**ing** *adj* overwhelming: 压倒的: *a ∼ing defeat*; 大败; in a manner intended to subdue or disconcert: 意欲降服对方或使对方不知所措的: *a ∼ing reply*. 使无言以对的回答; 使旦瞠口呆的回答. ∼**ing·ly** *adv*

crush² /krʌʃ; krʌʃ/ *n* **1 a/the ∼**, crowd of people pressed together: 拥挤的人群: *There was a violent ∼ at the gate into the stadium*. 运动场的大门口人群拥挤不堪. '∼ **barrier**, one erected to keep back crowds (eg along a pavement when crowds of people are expected): 阻拦人群的障碍物(例如置于预料有人群的人行道上者). **2** (colloq) crowded social gathering. (口)拥挤的社交集会. **3** (sl) (俚) **get/have a ∼ on sb**, (usu of a young person) be, imagine oneself to be, in love with him. (通常指年轻人)迷恋; 对…自作多情. **4** [U] fruit drink made by pressing out juice (eg from oranges). 果汁饮料(例如橙汁).

crust /krʌst; krʌst/ *n* **1** [C, U] (piece of the) hard-baked surface of a loaf; outer covering (pastry) of a pie or tart. (一片)面包皮; 糕饼的面制外壳. **2** [C, U] hard surface: 硬壳: *a thin ∼ of ice/frozen snow*; 一层薄冰(冻结的雪); *the earth's ∼*, the outer portion. 地壳. **3** hard deposit on the inside of a bottle of wine. 酒瓶内沉淀的渣. □ *vt, vi* [VP6A, 2A, C] ∼ *(over)*, cover, become covered, with a ∼; form into a ∼: 以硬壳覆盖; 为硬壳覆盖; 结一层硬壳: *The snow ∼ed over* (= froze hard on top) *during the night*. 雪在夜里结了一层冰.

crus·ta·cean /krʌˈsteɪʃn; krʌsˈteʃən/ *n* any of a numerous class of animals, mostly living in water (and popularly called *shellfish*) with a hard shell (eg *crabs, lobsters*). 甲壳类动物(大半生活于水中, 俗称贝类, 例如蟹、龙虾).

crustaceans

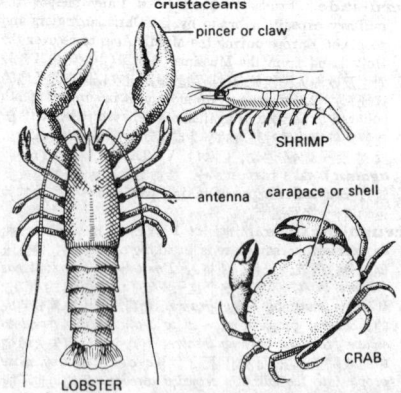

pincer or claw

SHRIMP

antenna   carapace or shell

LOBSTER

CRAB

crusted /'krʌstɪd; 'krʌstɪd/ *adj* **1** having a crust. 有外壳的; 有硬壳的. **2** ancient; venerable. 古老的; 因古老而可敬的. **3** fixed; engrained: 根深蒂固的; 确立的: *∼ prejudices/habits*. 根深蒂固的偏见(习惯).

crusty /'krʌstɪ; 'krʌstɪ/ *adj* (**-ier, -iest**) **1** having a crust; hard like a crust: 有硬壳的; 硬如壳的: *∼ bread*. 硬面包. **2** (of persons, their behaviour) curt, harsh; quick to show irritation, etc. (指人, 其行为)厉声厉色的; 脾气暴躁的.

crutch /krʌtʃ; krʌtʃ/ *n* **1** support used under the arm to help a lame person to walk: (跛足者腋下用的)拐杖: *a pair of ∼es*; 一对拐杖; *to go about on ∼es*. 靠拐杖行动. **2** support that is like a ∼ in shape or use; (fig) any moral support. 似拐杖之支持物; (喻)任何精神上的支持. **3** crotch(2). 裤裆; 胯部.

crux /krʌks; krʌks/ *n* (*pl* **∼es**) part of a problem that is the most difficult to solve: 问题的关键; 最难解决之处: *The ∼ of the matter is this*. 问题的关键在此.

cry¹ /kraɪ; kraɪ/ *vi, vt* (*pt, pp* **cried**) **1 cry (out)**, [VP2A, B, C, 3A, 4A] (of persons, animals, birds) make (usu loud) sounds that express feelings (eg pain, fear) but not ideas, thoughts, etc: (指人、兽、禽)喊叫; 号叫; 鸣叫(如因痛楚、恐惧所发出者, 仅表感情而不表思想等): *A baby can cry as soon as it is born*. 婴儿一生下来就会哭. *The child cried with pain when the dentist pulled the tooth out*. 当牙医为他拔牙时他痛得叫了起来. **2** [VP 2A, B, C, 3A, 6A, 15B] (of persons) weep; shed tears (with or without sounds): (指人)哭泣; 啜泣: *The boy was crying because he had lost his money*. 那男孩因丢了钱而哭. *She was crying over her misfortunes*. 她为她的不幸遭遇而哭. *She was crying for joy, because she was happy*. 她喜极而泣. *The child was crying for* (= because he wanted) *his mother*. 那孩子哭着要妈妈. *The boy was crying with pain/hunger*. 那男孩痛(饿)得哭起来. *She cried hot tears*. 她热泪直下. **cry one's 'eyes/'heart out**, weep very bitterly. 痛哭. **cry oneself to sleep**, cry until one falls asleep. 哭到睡着了. **give sb sth to cry for/about**, punish him for crying without a good or obvious cause. 处罚某人无缘无故的哭. **3** [VP 6A, 14, 9, 2C, 3A, 4A] exclaim; call out loudly in words: 高声喊叫; 大声说: '*Help! Help!*' *he cried*. '救命啊! 救命啊!' 他高声叫喊. *The starving people cried to their chief for bread*. 那些饥饿的人向他们的首领高声要面包. *He cried for mercy*. 他喊着求饶. **cry for the moon**, demand sth impossible. 要求不可能的事物. ⇨ **shame** (3). **4** [VP6A, 15A, B] announce for sale; make known by calling out: 叫卖; 以叫喊使大家知道: 高声传报: *to cry one's wares*; 叫卖货物; *to cry the news all over the town*. 将新闻向镇上高声传报. **5 cry sth down**, suggest that it is worth little. 轻视某事物. **cry off**, withdraw from sth that one has undertaken: 打退堂鼓; 打消原意: *I had promised to go, but had to cry off at the last moment*. 我本来答应要去, 但最后不得不打消去意. **cry sth up**, praise it highly. 极力赞扬某事物.

cry² /kraɪ; kraɪ/ *n* (*pl* **cries**) **1** loud sound of fear, pain, grief, etc; loud, excited utterance of words: (因恐惧、痛苦、悲伤等)号叫; 哭号; 大叫; 高喊: *a cry for help*; 求救的呼声; *the cry of an animal in pain*; 动物痛楚的叫声; *a cry of triumph*; 胜利的欢呼; *angry cries from the mob*. 暴民愤怒的叫嚣. *They set up/raised a cry of 'Traitor!'* 他们高喊'卖国贼!' **a far/long cry from**, a long way from; very different from: 遥远的路途; 极大的差别: *Being a junior clerk is a far cry from being one of the Directors*. 做小职员与做董事差别甚大. **in full cry**, (cf a pack of hounds) barking together as they pursue or hunt (an animal); (fig) eagerly attacking (sb). (指一群猎犬)一齐嗥叫着紧追(动物); (喻)猛烈攻击(某人). **much cry and little wool**, (prov) much fuss with little result. (谚)大事纷扰而无甚结果; 雷声大而雨点小. **within cry (of)**, within hearing; near enough to hear a call. 在可听得到呼声的地方. ⇨ **hue²**. **2** words spoken loudly to give information: 大声传报的

消息: *the cry of the night watchman;* 守夜人的叫声; call announcing sth for sale (by a person in the street): (街上小贩的)叫卖声: *the old (street) cries of London, eg 'Fresh Herrings'.* 伦敦街上旧有的叫卖声, 例如'鲜鲱'。⇨ **crier(1)**. **3** watchword or phrase, used for a principle or cause: (代表主义或运动的)口号: *a 'war-cry;* (作战时的)喊杀声; (政党等的)口号; *a 'battle-cry.* (作战时的)呐喊; 标语; 口号。*'Asia for the Asians' was their cry.* '亚洲人的亚洲'是他们的口号。**4** fit of weeping: 一阵哭泣: *have a good cry,* find emotional relief by shedding tears. 尽情哭一场(以抒发郁积的感情)。*Let her have her cry out,* let her weep until she becomes calm again. 让她哭个痛快吧。**'cry-baby,** child who cries often or easily without good or apparent cause. 好哭的婴儿(常无故而哭)。

cry·ing /'kraɪɪŋ; 'kraɪɪŋ/ *attrib adj* (esp of evils) demanding attention: (尤指恶事)需要注意的: *a ~ shame/evil/need.* 奇耻大辱(急待矫正的弊病); 迫切的需要)。

crypt /krɪpt; krɪpt/ *n* underground room, esp of a church. (尤指教堂的)地下室。

a church crypt

cryp·tic /'krɪptɪk; 'krɪptɪk/ *adj* secret; with a hidden meaning, or a meaning not easily seen: 秘密的; 含有隐藏之意义的; 意义深远的: *a ~ remark.* 含义深远的评语。**cryp·ti·cally** /-klɪ; -klɪ/ *adv*

crypto- /'krɪptəʊ; 'krɪpto/ (in combination) hidden, secret: (用于复合词)隐藏的; 秘密的: *a ~-'fascist,* person who has fascist sympathies but does not make them public. 秘密同情法西斯党的人。

crypto·gram /'krɪptəʊgræm; 'krɪptə‚græm/ *n* [C] sth written in a secret code. 密码文件。

crys·tal /'krɪstl; 'krɪstl/ *n* **1** [U] transparent, natural substance like quartz; [C] piece of this as an ornament: 水晶石; 水晶制的装饰品: *a necklace of ~s;* 水晶珠项链; (attrib)(用作定语) *~ ornaments;* 水晶制的装饰品; *~ detector,* type used in early radio sets (called a '~ **set**). 晶体检波器(用于早期无线电收音机'crystal set')。*~ clear,* entirely clear; (fig) completely understood. 完全透明的; (喻)极其明白的; 十分清楚的。*'~-gazing,* looking into a ~ ball in an attempt to see future events pictured there. 水晶球占卜术(向水晶球里窥视以期借里面所呈现的图形窥知未来的事情)。**2** [U] glassware of best quality, made into bowls, vases, vessels, etc: 品质最好的玻璃器皿(如碗、瓶、盘碟等): *The diningtable shone with silver and ~.* 餐桌上摆设的银器和玻璃器琳琅满目。**3** [C] (science) definite and regular shape taken naturally by the molecules of certain substances: (科学)(某些物质的分子自然形成的)结晶体: *sugar and salt ~s;* 糖和盐的结晶体; *snow and ice ~s.* 雪和冰的结晶体。**4** (US) glass over the face of a watch. (美)表面玻璃。

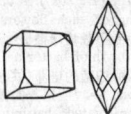

crystals

diamonds

crys·tal·line /'krɪstəlaɪn; 'krɪstl̩ɪn/ *adj* made of crystal(s); like crystal; very clear. 水晶制的; 似水晶的; 结晶质的; 透明的。

crys·tal·lize /'krɪstəlaɪz; 'krɪstl̩‚aɪz/ *vt, vi* **1** [VP6A, 2A] form, cause to form, into crystals. 形成结晶体; 使结晶。**2** [VP6A] cover (fruit, etc) with sugar-crystals: 将糖的结晶体覆于(水果等)上: *~d ginger.* 蜜饯的姜。**3** [VP6A, 2A] (fig, of ideas, plans) become, cause to be, clear and definite: (喻; 指思想, 计划)(使)变得明确: *His vague ideas ~d into a definite plan.* 他那些模糊的概念变成一个明确的计划。**crys·tal·li·za·tion** /‚krɪstəlaɪ'zeɪʃn US: -lɪ'z-; ‚krɪstl̩ə'zeʃən/ *n*

cub /kʌb; kʌb/ *n* **1** young lion, bear, fox, tiger. 幼狮、熊、狐、虎。**cub reporter,** young and inexperienced newspaper reporter. 年轻无经验的记者。**Cub (Scout),** member of the junior branch of the Scout Association. 幼年童子军。**2** ill-mannered young man. 不懂规矩的年轻人。

cubby-hole /'kʌbɪ həʊl; 'kʌbɪ‚hol/ *n* small enclosed space; snug place. 围起来的小天地; 舒适的地方。

cube /kjuːb; kjub/ *n* **1** solid body having six equal square sides; block of something so shaped or similarly shaped. 正六面体; 立方体; 立方形物(块)。**2** (maths) product of a number multiplied by itself twice: (数学)立方(某数的三乘幂或自乘两次的积): *The ~ of 5 (5^3) is $5×5×5 (=125)$.* 5的立方就是$5×5×5 (=125)$。*The ~ root of 64 ($\sqrt[3]{64}$) is 4 ($4×4×4=64$).* 64的立方根是4。□ *vt* [VP6A] multiply a number by itself twice: 以某数自乘二次; 求立方: *10 ~d is 1000.* 10的立方为1000。

cu·bic /'kjuːbɪk; 'kjubɪk/ *adj* having the shape of a cube; of a cube: 立方形的; 立方体的: *one ~ metre,* volume of a cube whose edge is one metre; 一立方公尺(每边各一公尺之立方体积); *~ content,* volume expressed in cubic measurement; 体积; 容积; *a motor vehicle with a 2000cc capacity,* ie 2000 ~ centimetres. 一部排气量为两千立方公分的汽车。

cu·bi·cal /'kjuːbɪkl; 'kjubɪkl/ *adj* = **cubic.**

cu·bicle /'kjuːbɪkl; 'kjubɪkl/ *n* small division of a larger room, walled or curtained to make a separate compartment, eg for sleeping in, or for (un)dressing at a swimming-pool. 大房间内以墙或幕隔成的小室(例如小寝室或游泳池内更衣室)。

cub·ism /'kjuːbɪzəm; 'kjubɪzəm/ *n* [U] style in art in which objects are represented so that they appear to be largely of geometrical shapes. 立体主义; 立体派(所作绘画中的物体似大半由几何图形构成)。**cub·ist** /'kjuːbɪst; 'kjubɪst/ *n* artist who practises ~. 立体派艺术家。

cu·bit /'kjuːbɪt; 'kjubɪt/ *n* old measure of length (18 to 22 inches or 45 to 56 centimetres). 腕尺(旧长度单位, 约18至22英寸或45至56公分)。

cuck·old /'kʌkəʊld; 'kakld/ *n* (archaic) man whose wife has committed adultery. (古)妻子与人私通的男人; 戴绿帽子的男人。□ *vt* [VP6A] (of a man) make (another man) a ~ by seducing his wife; (of a woman) make (her husband) a ~. (指男人)勾引人妻使(他人)戴绿帽子; (指女人)与人私通(使其)戴绿帽子。

cuckoo /'kuku:; 'kuku/ *n* bird whose call is like its name, a migratory bird which reaches the British Isles in spring and lays its eggs in the nests of small birds. 布谷鸟; 杜鹃(候鸟, 春天到英国, 产卵于小鸟之巢)。⇨ the illus at **bird.** 参看 bird 之插图。**'~-clock,** one that strikes the hours with notes like the call of a ~. 报时似布谷鸟叫的时钟。

cu·cum·ber /'kju:kʌmbə(r); 'kjukʌmbə/ *n* [C, U] (creeping plant with) long, green-skinned fleshy fruit, usu sliced and eaten in salads, or made into pickle. 胡瓜; 黄瓜(藤类植物, 长形, 绿皮, 通常切片做生菜食之, 或制腌菜)。⇨ the illus at **vegetable.** 参看 vegetable 之插图。*as cool as a ~,* unexcited; self-possessed. 冷静的; 沉着的; 不激动的。

cud /kʌd; kʌd/ n [U] food which oxen, etc bring back from the first stomach and chew again. (牛等从第一胃吐出之)反刍之食物. **chew the cud,** (fig) reflect; ponder. (喻)反省; 细思.

cuddle /'kʌdl; 'kʌdl/ vt, vi [VP6A, 15B, 2C] 1 hold close and lovingly in one's arms: 抚爱地紧抱; 搂抱: *The baby doesn't like being ~d herself, but she likes to ~ her doll.* 那婴孩自己不喜欢被人搂抱, 但她却喜欢搂抱她的洋娃娃. 2 ~ up (to/together), lie close and comfortably: 贴身而睡; 蜷曲着身子: *They ~d up (together) under the blankets.* 他们拥睡在毯子下面. *She ~d up to him to get warm.* 她依偎着他以获得温暖. □ n act of cuddling; hug. 拥抱; 搂抱. ~**some** /-səm; -səm/, **cuddly** /'kʌdlɪ; 'kʌdlɪ/ adjj suitable for, inviting, cuddling: 适于搂抱的; 令人欲搂抱的: *a nice cuddly teddy bear.* 可爱的令人欲搂抱的玩具熊.

cud·gel /'kʌdʒəl; 'kʌdʒəl/ vt, n (-ll-; US also -l-) [VP6A] (hit with a) short, thick stick or club. 短棒; 用短棒打击. **take up the ~s for,** (rhet) fight for; support strongly. (修辞)为…而奋斗; 极力支持. ~ **one's brains,** think hard on a difficult problem; try to think of sth one has forgotten. 苦思一难题; 竭力回想已经忘记的事.

cue[1] /kjuː; kju/ n [C] 1 sth (eg the last words of an actor's speech) which shows when sb else is to do or say sth. 提示(例如演员台词的最后一句, 暗示其他演员出台或接话者). 2 hint about how to behave, what to do, etc: (关于如何行动或做什么的)暗示: *take one's cue from sb,* observe what he does as a guide to one's own action. 看某人怎么做就怎样做.

cue[2] /kjuː; kju/ n billiard-player's long, tapering, leather-tipped rod, for striking the ball. (撞球戏)球杆(尖端有皮革).

cuff[1] /kʌf; kʌf/ n 1 end of a shirt or coat sleeve at the wrist. (衬衫或外衣的)袖口. **play it off the ~,** (colloq) use one's wits in a situation for which one is unprepared. (口)临时利用机智. '~-**links,** used for fastening ~s. 衬衫袖口的链扣. 2 (US) turned-up fold at the bottom of a leg of a pair of trousers. (GB 英 = turn-up). (美)西装裤脚的反褶部分. 3 (pl, colloq) handcuffs. (复,口)手铐.

cuff[2] /kʌf; kʌf/ vt, n [VP6A] (give sb a) light blow with the open hand. 以手轻拍或轻推(某人).

cuir·ass /kwɪˈræs; kwɪˈræs/ n piece of armour to protect the body, breastplate and plate for the back, fastened together. 胸甲(保护前胸后背的甲胄). ⇨ the illus at **armour.** 参看 armour 之插图. **cuir·as·sier** /ˌkwɪrəˈsɪə(r); ˌkwɪrəˈsɪr/ n horse-soldier wearing a ~. 着胸甲的骑兵.

cui·sine /kwiˈziːn; kwɪˈzin/ n [U] (F) (style of) cooking: (法)烹调(的方式): *French ~;* 法国式烹调; *a hotel where the ~ is excellent.* 菜肴特佳的旅馆.

cul-de-sac /ˈkʌl də sæk; ˈkʌldəˌsæk/ n(F) street with an opening at one end only; blind alley. (法)仅有一端与外间相通的街道; 死巷.

cu·li·nary /ˈkʌlɪnərɪ; ˈkjuləˌnɛrɪ/ adj of cooking or a kitchen: 烹调的; 厨房的: *a ~ triumph,* a superbly cooked dish or meal; 烹调极佳的一道菜或一餐; ~ *plants,* suitable for cooking. 适于烹调的植物; 蔬菜.

cull /kʌl; kʌl/ vt [VP6A] pick (a flower); select: 采摘(花); 拣选: *extracts ~ed from the best authors.* 名家著作精选. □ n sth that is ~ed (eg a hen that no longer lays well, picked out and killed for food). 剔除之物(例如不大生蛋而被挑出杀来宰的母鸡).

cul·len·der /ˈkʌləndə(r); ˈkʌləndə/ n = colander.

cul·mi·nate /ˈkʌlmɪneɪt; ˈkʌlməˌnet/ vi [VP3A] ~ in, (of efforts, hopes. careers, etc) reach the highest point: (指努力、希望、事业等)达于极点: *misfortunes that ~d in bankruptcy.* 终于导致破产的种种不幸. **cul·mi·na·tion** /ˌkʌlmɪˈneɪʃn; ˌkʌlməˈneʃən/ n highest point: 顶点; 极点: *the culmination of his career.* 他的事业的顶点.

culp·able /ˈkʌlpəbl; ˈkʌlpəbl/ adj (legal) blame-worthy; deserving punishment: (法律)该受责备的; 应受惩罚的: *hold a person ~;* 认为某人该受责备; *dismissed for~ negligence,* wrongly neglecting to do sth. 因重大疏忽而被解雇. **culp·ably** /ˈkʌlpəblɪ; ˈkʌlpəblɪ/ adv **cul·pa·bil·ity** /ˌkʌlpəˈbɪlətɪ; ˌkʌlpəˈbɪlətɪ/ n

cul·prit /ˈkʌlprɪt; ˈkʌlprɪt/ n person who has done wrong; offender. 犯过者; 犯罪者.

cult /kʌlt; kʌlt/ n [C] 1 system of religious worship. 礼拜(仪式); 崇拜. 2 devotion to a person (esp a single deity) or practice: 对某人(尤指对一个神)或风尚的崇拜: *the ~ of archery;* 崇尚箭术; *the ~ of Browning.* 对布朗宁的崇拜. 3 (group of persons devoted to a) popular fashion or craze: 时尚; 崇拜某一时尚的一群人: (attrib) (用作定语) a '~ *word,* one used because it is fashionable among members of such a group. 时髦的用语(崇拜某一时尚的人们所流行的用语).

cul·ti·vable /ˈkʌltɪvəbl; ˈkʌltəvəbl/ adj that can be cultivated. 可耕种的; 可培养的.

cul·ti·vate /ˈkʌltɪveɪt; ˈkʌltəˌvet/ vt [VP6A] 1 prepare (land) for crops by ploughing, etc; help (crops) to grow (eg by breaking up the soil around them, destroying weeds, etc). 耕种(田地); 培植(禾物)(如翻土、除草等). 2 give care, thought, time, etc to develop or develop sth: 培养; 修养; 花费心思、时间等以发展某事物: *to ~ the mind/sb's friendship.* 修养心性(培养与某人的友谊). *He ~s (= tries to win the good will of) the sort of people who can be useful to him in his business.* 他培养对于他事业有用的人. **cul·ti·vated** adj (of a person) having good manners and education. (指人)举止文雅的; 有教养的.

cul·ti·va·tion /ˌkʌltɪˈveɪʃn; ˌkʌltəˈveʃən/ n [U] cultivating or being cultivated: 耕种; 耕耘; 开垦; 培养; 修养: *the ~ of the soil;* 耕地; 犁地; *land that is under ~;* 耕种中的土地; *to bring land into ~;* 开垦荒地; *to allow land to go out of ~.* 让地荒芜.

cul·ti·va·tor /ˈkʌltɪveɪtə(r); ˈkʌltəˌvetə/ n person who cultivates: machine for breaking up ground, destroying weeds, etc. 耕种者; 耕耘机.

cul·tural /ˈkʌltʃərəl; ˈkʌltʃərəl/ adj having to do with culture: 文化的; 文明的: ~ *studies,* eg art, literature; 与文化有关的学科(例如艺术、文学); *a ~ institute.* 文化研究所.

cul·ture /ˈkʌltʃə(r); ˈkʌltʃə/ n 1 [U] advanced development of the human powers; development of the body, mind and spirit by training and experience: 人类能力的高度发展; 借训练与经验而促成的身心的发展; (身体的)锻炼; (心性与精神的)修养: *Physical ~ is important, but we must not neglect the ~ of the mind.* 体格的锻炼是重要的, 但是我们不可忽略心性的修养. 2 [U] evidence of intellectual development (of arts, science, etc) in human society: 人类社会智力发展(指人文、科学等)的证据; 文明; 文化: *He is a man of considerable ~.* 他是个文化修养很高的人. *Universities should be centres of ~.* 大学应该是文化的中心. 3 [U] state of intellectual development among a people; [C] particular form of intellectual development: 一个民族的智力发展状况; 某一特定形式的文化: *We owe much to Greek ~.* 我们得益于希腊文化之处甚多. *He has studied the ~s of Oriental countries.* 他曾研究东方各国的文化. 4 [U] all the arts, beliefs, social institutions, etc characteristic of a community, race, etc: 某一社会、种族等特有的文艺、信仰、风俗等: *the ~ of the Eskimos.* 爱斯基摩人的文化. 5 [U] cultivating; the rearing of bees, silkworms, etc: 培养; 种植; 栽培; (蜂、蚕等的)饲养: *He has five acres devoted to bulb ~,* to the growing of such flowers as daffodils and tulips. 他用五英亩地专事栽培球根植物(如水仙花、郁金香). 6 [C] (biol) growth of bacteria (for medical or scientific study): (生物)细菌的培养(供医学或科学研究): *a ~ of cholera germs.* 一次所培养的霍乱菌. **cul·tured** adj (of persons) cultivated; having ~ of the mind; (of tastes, interests, etc) refined. (指人)

文雅的; 有修养的; (指嗜好、兴趣等)高尚的; 优雅的。 '~d **pearl**, pearl produced in an oyster shell into which a piece of grit has been introduced. 养珠(经人工将砂粒 置于耗壳内培养出来的珍珠)。

cul·vert /'kʌlvət; 'kʌlvət/ n sewer or drain that crosses under a road, railway or embankment; channel for electrical cables under the ground. (穿过道路、铁路 或路堤的)下水道或阴沟;地下电缆道。

cum·ber /'kʌmbə(r); 'kʌmbə/ vt [VP6A, 14] ~ **(with)**, hamper; burden: 阻碍; 拖累: ~ *oneself with an overcoat on a warm day*; 在暖和的日子穿大衣是个累赘; ~ed *with parcels*. 被一些小包裹所拖累。

cum·ber·some /'kʌmbəsəm; 'kʌmbəsəm/ adj burdensome; heavy and awkward to carry: 沉重的; 笨 重而不便携带的: *A soldier today would find old-fashioned armour very* ~. 现代的士兵会觉得旧式的甲胄非常 笨重。

cum·brous /'kʌmbrəs; 'kʌmbrəs/ adj = cumbersome.

cum·mer·bund /'kʌməband; 'kʌmə,bʌnd/ n sash worn round the waist. 围腰之巾;腰巾。

cumu·lat·ive /'kju:mjulətɪv US: -leɪtɪv; 'kjumje,letɪv/ adj increasing in amount by one addition after another. 累积的。

cumu·lus /'kju:mjuləs; 'kjumjeləs/ n (pl -li /-laɪ; -,laɪ/), adj (cloud) made up of rounded masses on a flat base. 积云(由圆形云团所形成而且底部水平的云层); 由圆形云团形成的。

cunei·form /'kju:nɪfɔ:m US: kju:'nɪəfɔ:rm; kju'nɪe,fɔrm/ adj wedge-shaped: 楔形的: ~ *characters*, as used in old Persian and Assyrian writing. 楔形文字(如古代 波斯和亚述文团中所用者)。

cuneiform characters

cun·ning¹ /'kʌnɪŋ; 'kʌnɪŋ/ adj 1 clever at deceiving; showing this kind of cleverness: 善于欺骗的; 狡猾的; 奸 诈的: *a* ~ *old fox*; 狡猾的老狐狸; *a* ~ *trick*. 诡计; 奸计。 2 (old use) skilful: (旧用法)技术熟练的: *a* ~ *workman*. 技术熟练的工人。 3 (US) attractive; cute: (美)吸引人的; 可爱的; 动人的: *a* ~ *smile/baby/kitten*. 可爱的微笑(婴儿,小猫)。 ~·**ly** adv

cun·ning² /'kʌnɪŋ; 'kʌnɪŋ/ n [U] quality of being cunning: 狡猾; 奸诈: *The boy showed a great deal of* ~ *in getting what he wanted*. 那孩子在取得他所需要的东 西的过程中,表现得极为狡猾。 2 (old use) skill: (旧用 法)技巧: *My hand has lost its* ~. 我的手不灵活。

cunt /kʌnt; kʌnt/ n (讳) 1 vagina. 阴道。 2 female pudenda. 女性生殖器官之外部; (讳) 4 (by transference) woman or girl, regarded as a sexual object. (鄙; 俚)(转为)女人或女郎(视为性欲对象)。 4 (vulg; derog sl) despicable person. (鄙)卑鄙的人。

cup¹ /kʌp; kʌp/ n 1 small porcelain bowl, usu with a handle, used with a saucer, for tea, coffee etc; contents of a cup: (通常有柄, 用时带碟的)瓷杯(用以装茶、咖啡 等); 杯中所盛之物: *a teacup*; 茶杯; *a ,cup and 'saucer*; 一套杯碟; *a ,cup of 'coffee*; 一杯咖啡; *two cups of flour* (used as a measure in cooking). 两杯面粉(烹调时用作量 器)。 *not my cup of tea*, (colloq) not what I like, not what suits me. (口)不是我所喜欢的; 不适合于我。 2 = **chalice**. 3 (fig) that which comes to a person; experience: (喻)命运; 经历; 遭遇: *His cup of happiness was full*. 他享 尽幸福。 4 vessel (usu of gold or silver) given as a prize in competitions. (比赛时赠为奖品的)金杯; 银杯。 ~,**cup-'final**, (football) final match to decide a competition. (足球)优胜杯决赛。 '**cup-tie**, (football) match to eliminate teams competing for a cup. (足球)优胜杯淘汰 赛。 5 (from '*wine cup*) wine. (由酒杯而来)酒。 *in his*

cups, partly or wholly intoxicated. 醉酒(半醉或全醉)。 '**cup-bearer**, official of a royal or nobleman's household who serves wine at banquets. (宫廷或贵族宅第宴会上 的)司酒官; 上酒者。 6 sth shaped like a cup: 杯形物: *the cup of a flower*; 花萼; *an 'egg-cup*; 盛一个煮蛋的小杯; *'acorn-cups*: 橡实壳斗; *the cups of a bra*. 胸罩之罩杯。 7 iced drink of wine, etc, usu flavoured: 加冰的酒等 饮料(通常加有调味料): *'claret-cup*; 加冰的红葡萄酒; *'cider-cup*. 加冰的苹果汁。 **cup·ful** /'kʌpful; 'kʌp,ful/ n (pl **cupfuls**) as much as a cup will hold. 一杯之量。

cup² /kʌp; kʌp/ vt (-pp-) [VP6A] 1 put into the shape of a cup: 做成杯状: *to cup one's hands*, eg to catch a ball; 两手做捧物状 (例如接球时); put round or over the cup: 置于其四周或上方作杯状: *with her chin cupped in her hand*. 她以手捧着她的下巴。 2 (archaic) perform the operation of cupping on (a person). (古)为(某人) 作杯吸手术。 ⇨ **cupping** below. 参看下列之 cupping.

cup·board /'kʌbəd; 'kʌbəd/ n set of shelves with doors, either built into a room as a fixture, or a separate piece of furniture, used for dishes, provisions, clothes, etc: (嵌于室内墙壁上或自成一件家具之)橱; 碗 橱;食橱; 衣橱: *a ,kitchen-'~*; 碗橱或食橱; *a 'hanging-~*, one in which dresses, suits, etc may be hung on coat-hangers. 挂衣橱(其中之衣服可挂于衣架上者)。 Cf US 参较美 china-closet, linen-closet. '~-**love**, affection that is shown in the hope of getting sth by it (eg a child hoping for cake). 为企图得到某物所表示的亲爱(例如小 儿想吃糕饼时所表现者)。

Cu·pid /'kju:pɪd; 'kjupɪd/ n Roman god of love; (picture or statue of a) beautiful boy (with wings and a bow and arrows) as symbol of love. 邱比特(罗马的爱 神); (有双翼,手持弓箭,视为爱的象征的)美童; 美童的像 片或雕像。

cu·pid·ity /kju:'pɪdətɪ; kju'pɪdətɪ/ n [U] greed, esp for money or property. 贪婪; (尤指)贪财。

cu·pola /'kju:pələ; 'kjupələ/ n small dome forming (part of) a roof; ceiling of a dome. 圆屋顶; 圆屋顶的内 面;穹窿天花板。

cuppa /'kʌpə; 'kʌpə/ n (GB sl) cup of tea: (英俚)一 杯茶: *What about a* ~? 来杯茶如何?

cup·ping /'kʌpɪŋ; 'kʌpɪŋ/ n [U] (archaic) operation of drawing blood to or through the skin by creating a partial vacuum over the area by means of a glass cup (called a '~-**glass**). (古)借玻璃吸杯 (cupping-glass) 在 皮肤上造成局部真空以吸藏或吸取血液的手术; (医)拔火 罐;杯术;吸罐放血法。

cu·pric /'kju:prɪk; 'kjuprɪk/ adj containing copper. 含铜的。

cu·pro-nickel /ˌkju:prəʊ'nɪkl; ˌkjupro'nɪkl/ n [U] alloy of copper and nickel used for making coins. 铜镍 合金(用以制硬币)。

cur /kɜ:(r); kɜ/ n bad-tempered or worthless dog (esp low-bred); cowardly or badly behaved man. 脾气坏或 无用之狗(尤指品种低贱者);懦夫;行为卑劣者。

cur·able /'kjuərəbl; 'kjuəbl/ adj that can be cured. 可治疗的; 可矫正的。 **cura·bil·ity** /ˌkjuərə'bɪlətɪ; ˌkjurə'bɪlətɪ/

cura·çao, -çoa /ˌkjuərə'səʊ US: -'saʊ; ˌkjurə'so/ n liqueur (sweet and syrupy) flavoured with peel of bitter oranges. (加苦橙皮味的)柑香酒。

cur·acy /'kjuərəsɪ; 'kjurəsɪ/ n (pl -cies) office or work of a curate. 副牧师的职位或职务。

curate /'kjuərət; 'kjurɪt/ n clergyman who helps a parish priest. 副牧师;助理牧师。

cura·tive /'kjuərətɪv; 'kjurətɪv/ adj helping to, able to, cure (disease or ill health): 帮助治疗的; 能治病的; 医疗的: *the* ~ *value of sunshine and sea air*. 阳光与海边 的空气的医疗价值。

cu·ra·tor /kjuə'reɪtə(r); kju'retə/ n official in charge (esp of a museum or art gallery). (尤指博物馆或艺术馆 之)馆长。

curb /kɜ:b; kɜb/ n 1 chain or leather strap passing

under a horse's jaw, used to control it. 马勒；马衔索(兜于马嘴下面以控制马的链或皮带)。⇨ the illus at **harness.** 参看 harness 之插图。**2** (fig) sth that holds one back or restrains: 抑制的东西: *put/keep a ~ on one's anger/passions.* 抑制自己的怒气(激情)。**3** = **kerb.** □ *vt* [VP6A] **1** control (a horse) by means of a ~. 借马衔以控制(马)。**2** keep (feelings, etc) under control: 抑制(感情等): *to ~ one's impatience.* 抑制自己的不耐烦。

curd /kɜːd/ *n* (often *pl*) thick, soft substance, almost solid, formed when milk turns sour, used to make cheese. (常用复数)凝乳(牛乳变酸时所凝结的物质,可用以制乳酪)。**2** [U] (in compounds) substance resembling ~: (用于复合词中)似凝乳的物质: *lemon-'~,* made from eggs, butter and sugar, flavoured with lemon. 柠檬乳糕(用鸡蛋、奶油和糖制成,加有柠檬味)。

curdle /'kɜːdl; 'kɝdl/ *vi, vt* [VP6A, 2A] form, cause to form, into curds; become curd-like: (使)结成凝乳;变成凝乳状: *The milk has ~d.* 牛奶已凝结。(fig uses): (比喻用法): *What a blood-curdling* (= horrifying) *yell!* 多么令人心惊胆战的喊叫! *His blood ~d at the sight,* He was filled with horror. 他看见这景象就吓呆了。

cure[1] /kjʊə(r); kjʊr/ *n* [C] **1** curing or being ~d(1): 治疗；治愈: *The doctor cannot guarantee a ~.* 医生不能保证治愈。*His ~ took six weeks.* 他花了六个星期才治好。**2** substance or treatment which ~s(1): 治疗的药物；治疗法: *Is there a certain ~ for cancer yet?* 迄今对癌症有无有效的治疗方法?*He has tried all sorts of ~s, but is still ill.* 他已试过各种药物,但病仍未愈。*You need a 'rest-~,* a holiday from your work. 你需要休假疗养。**3** spiritual charge(5): 圣职; 传教的职务: *to obtain/resign a ~,* a position as a priest. 就任(辞去)牧师的职务。

cure[2] /kjʊə(r); kjʊr/ *vt, vi* [VP6A, 14] **1** ~ *sb (of sth); ~ sth,* bring (a person) back to health; provide and use successfully a remedy for a disease, ill health, suffering; get rid of (an evil): 使(人)恢复健康; 治愈: 治疗(疾病, 病患, 痛苦); 除祛(恶害): *to ~ a man of a disease;* 治愈某人的病; *to ~ an illness;* 治病; *to ~ poverty/drunkenness;* 消除贫困(矫正酒癖); *to ~ a child of bad habits;* 纠正孩童的恶习; *to try to ~ social discontent at home by making war abroad.* 向外发动战争以安抚国内社会的不满。**'~-all** *n* sth which, it is claimed, ~s all ills. 万灵丹; 万应药。**2** treat meat, fish, skin, tobacco, etc in order to keep it in good condition by salting, smoking, drying, etc: (用盐腌、烟熏、干燥等法)保存(肉、鱼、皮革、烟草等): *well-~d bacon.* 腌得好的腌肉。

curé /'kjʊəreɪ US: kjʊ'reɪ; kjʊ're/ *n* parish priest in France. 法国的教区牧师。

cur·few /'kɜːfjuː; 'kɝfju/ *n* **1** (old use) ringing of a bell as a signal for lights to be put out and fires covered; bell for this; hour at which the bell was rung. (旧用法)晚间令人熄灭灯火的钟声; 为此所用的钟; 晚钟; 鸣晚钟的时刻。**2** (modern use) time or signal (under martial law) for people to remain indoors: (现代用法)(实施戒严期间)禁止外出的时间或信号; 宵禁: *to impose a ~ on a town;* 在镇上实施宵禁; *to lift/end the ~.* 解除宵禁。

curio /'kjʊərɪəʊ; 'kjʊrɪ,o/ *n* (*pl* ~**s**) work of art of a strange or unusual character and valued for this reason. 古玩; 古玩; 珍品。

curi·os·ity /ˌkjʊərɪ'ɒsɪtɪ; ˌkjʊrɪ'asɪtɪ/ *n* **1** [U] being curious (1, 2): 好奇心; 求知欲; 好管闲事: *about/~ to learn about distant lands;* 对于远方异地的好奇心(求知欲); *to be dying of/burning with ~ to know what was happening.* 极欲(渴望)知道发生了什么事。*He yielded to ~ and opened the letter addressed to his sister.* 他因好奇心的驱使,拆开了别人写给他姐姐(妹妹)的信。**2** [C] (*pl* -**ties**) curious(3) thing; strange or rare object. 珍奇的事物; 珍品。

curi·ous /'kjʊərɪəs; 'kjʊrɪəs/ *adj* **1** ~ (*to do sth*);

~ (*about sth*), (in a good sense) eager (to learn/know, etc); interested (in sth): (用在好的意义上)好奇的; 渴望知道的; 对(某事)有兴趣的: ~ *about the origin of mankind.* 对人类的起源有兴趣的。*I'm ~ to know what he said.* 我极想知道他说了什么。*If a boy is ~, he is always asking questions.* 一个男孩是好奇的, 就会经常发问。**2** ~ (*about sth*), meddlesome; having or showing too much interest in the affairs of others: 爱管闲事的; 对他人之事过分感兴趣的: ~ *neighbours.* 爱管闲事的邻居。*Don't ask so many ~ questions.* 不要问这么多关于别人的问题。*Hide it where ~ eyes won't see it.* 把它藏在好奇者的眼睛看不见的地方。*What is he so ~ about?* 他要打听什么的闲事? **3** strange; unusual; hard to understand: 古怪的; 不寻常的; 难懂的: *What a ~ mistake!* 多么奇怪的错误! *There was a ~ silence.* 有一种出乎寻常的沉默。*Isn't he a ~-looking little man!* 他岂不是一个相貌奇特的矮人! **4** (rather old use) showing the result of care and attention: (颇旧用法)精细的; 精工的: *a jewel of ~ workmanship.* 精工琢磨的珠宝。**~·ly** *adv*

curl[1] /kɜːl; kɝl/ *n* **1** [C] sth naturally like or twisted into a shape like a spiral or the thread of a screw, esp a lock of hair of this shape: 天然或扭曲似螺纹之物; (尤指)卷发: ~*s (of hair) falling over her shoulders;* 垂在她肩上的卷发; *hair falling in ~s over her forehead;* 垂于前上的卷发; *a ~ of smoke rising from a cigarette.* 自香烟升起的一缕轻烟; *the ~ of a wave;* 浪头; *a ~ of the lips,* expressing scorn. 撇嘴(表示轻蔑)。**2** [U] the state of being curly: 卷曲的状态: *How do you keep your hair in ~?* 你怎样使头发保持卷曲的?

curl[2] /kɜːl; kɝl/ *vt, vi* [VP6A, 15A, B, 2A, C] ~ (*up*), make into curls; twist; grow or be in curls: 使卷曲; 扭曲; 长成卷曲状: *She has ~ed her hair.* 她已卷过她的头发。*Does her hair ~ naturally?* 她的头发是天然卷曲的吗? *The smoke from the camp fire ~ed upwards.* 烟自营火缭绕上升。*The frost made the young leaves ~ (up)/~ed up the young leaves.* 严霜使嫩叶卷缩。*The dog ~ed (itself) up on the rug.* 狗蜷着身子卧在地毯上。~ (*sb*) *up,* (cause to) collapse: (使)崩溃; (使)倒下: *The cricket ball hit him on the head and he ~ed up* (= fell to the ground) *at once.* 板球击中他的头部, 他立即倒在地堆上。*She ~ed up* (with laughter) *at his joke.* 他的笑话使她笑弯了腰。*The blow ~ed him up completely.* 那一击使他完全倒下。**'~er,** small cylindrical object round which warmed or wet hair is wound to create a ~. (卷发用的圆筒形)卷发器。**'~ing-tongs/-irons,** instruments (heated before use) for ~ing or straightening the hair. (使用前加热的)烫发钳; 卷发钳。**'~ing-pins,** clips (used cold) for ~ing the hair. (不加热的)卷发夹子。

cur·lew /'kɜːljuː; 'kɝlu/ *n* wading bird with a long, slender, down-curved bill. 麻鹬(一种嘴细长且下弯的涉禽)。⇨ the illus at **water.** 参看 water 之插图。

curl·ing /'kɜːlɪŋ; 'kɝlɪŋ/ *n* [U] Scottish game played on ice with heavy, flat-bottomed stones ('~**-stones**) with handles, sent along the ice towards a mark. 一种苏格兰的游戏,在冰上将有柄、沉重而且平底的石头(curling-stones)滑向某一目标。

curly /'kɜːlɪ; 'kɝlɪ/ *adj* (-**ier**, -**iest**) having curls; arranged in curls: 有卷发的; 卷曲的: ~ *hair;* 鬈发; *a '~-headed girl.* 头发卷曲的女孩。

cur·mudgeon /kɜː'mʌdʒən; kɝ'mʌdʒən/ *n* (colloq) bad-tempered or miserly person. (口)脾气坏或吝啬的人。

cur·rant /'kʌrənt; 'kɝənt/ *n* **1** small, sweet, dried seedless grape (grown in Greece and neighbouring countries) used in buns, cakes, puddings, etc. 一种小的甜葡萄干(产于希腊及其邻近各国,用以制小圆面包、糕饼、布丁等)。**2** (cultivated bush with) small black red or white juicy fruit growing in clusters. 红醋栗(黑、红或白色的多汁小果,簇生); 红醋栗树(灌木)。

cur·rency /'kʌrənsɪ; 'kɝənsɪ/ *n* **1** [U] the state of being in common or general use: 流行; 通用; 流通:

Many slang words have short ~, soon go out of use. 许多俚语流行不久就不再用了。The rumour soon gained ~, was repeated until many people were aware of it. 谣言不久就传开了。**give ~ to,** make current(1); spread: 使流行; 传播: Do not give ~ to idle gossip. 不要传播闲言。2 [C,U] (pl -cies) money that is actually in use in a country: (一国中实际通用的)货币: a gold/paper ~; 金(纸)币; foreign currencies; 外币; a decimal ~. 十进制货币。

cur·rent¹ /'kʌrənt; 'kɝənt/ adj 1 in common or general use; generally accepted: 通用的; 流行的; 通行的; 公认的: ~ coin/money; 通货; ~ opinions/beliefs; 许多人持有的意见(信仰); words that are no longer ~. 已不通行的词。2 now passing; of the present time: 现行的; 现时的; 现今的: ~ expenses/prices; 经常费(时价); the ~ issue of a magazine; 杂志之最近的一期; the ~ year, this year; 今年; a newsreel showing ~ events. 报导时事的新闻影片。3 ~ account, (with a bank) one from which money may be drawn without previous notice. (在银行的)活期存款(不需事先通知即可提款)。 ⇨ deposit account at deposit²(1), savings account at save¹. ~ assets, (comm) assets which are not fixed but which change in the course of business (eg amounts owing). (商)流动资产(非固定的资产, 商业过程中可变动者, 例如负债)。~·ly adv in a ~(1, 2) manner: 通行地; 流行地; 现今地; 最近地: It is ~ly reported that.... 据最近报导…。

cur·rent² /'kʌrənt; 'kɝənt/ n 1 stream of water, air, gas, esp one flowing through slower moving or still water, etc: 流; 水流; 气流; (尤指缓流或静水中之)激流: A cold ~ of air came in when the door was opened. 门打开时进来了一股冷风。Although he was a strong swimmer he was swept away by the ~ and was drowned. 虽然他的游泳术高强, 但是他被激流卷走淹死了。The warm ~s in the Atlantic influence the climate of Great Britain. 大西洋中的暖流影响英国的气候。2 flow of electricity through sth or along a wire or cable. (通过物体或沿线缆的)电流。⇨ alternate²(2), direct¹(5). 3 course or movement (of events, opinions, thoughts, etc): (事件, 意见, 思想等的)动向; 趋势; 潮流: Nothing disturbs the peaceful ~ of her life. 在她平静的生活中, 没有任何的骚扰。The government used the radio to influence the ~ of thought. 政府利用无线电广播影响思想的趋向。

cur·ricu·lum /kə'rɪkjuləm; kə'rɪkjələm/ n (pl ~s or -la /-lə; -lə/) course of study in a school, college, etc. (学校, 学院等所开的)课程。~ vitae /'viːtaɪ; 'vaɪti/ (Lat) brief written account of one's past history (eg education, employment), used when applying for a job, etc (US ⇨ résumé). (拉)履历(求职等时所写个人之学历, 经历等)。

cur·rish /'kɜːrɪʃ; 'kɝɪʃ/ adj like a cur. 脾气坏的; 下贱的; 卑怯的。~·ly adv

curry¹ /'kʌrɪ; 'kɝɪ/ n (pl -ries) [C, U] (dish of) meat, fish, eggs, etc cooked with hot-tasting spices: 用咖喱调制的肉, 鱼, 蛋等; 一道咖喱菜: a chicken ~; 咖喱鸡; Madras curries; 马德拉斯咖喱菜; to eat too much ~. 吃太多咖喱调制的菜。'~-powder, mixture of spices for a ~ ground or beaten to a powder. 咖喱粉。□ vt prepare (food) with hot-tasting spices; flavour (food) with ~-powder: 用咖喱烹调(食物); 加咖喱粉于(食物): curried chicken. 咖喱鸡。

curry² /'kʌrɪ; 'kɝɪ/ vt [VP6A] rub down and clean (a horse); prepare (tanned leather) by soaking, scraping, etc. 刷洗(马); (用泡, 刮等方法)制(革); 硝(皮)。~ favour (with sb), try to win favour or approval (by using flattery, etc). (借谄媚等)求恩宠; 曲意逢迎。

curse¹ /kɜːs; kɝs/ n 1 word, phrase or sentence calling for the punishment, injury or destruction of sth or sb. 诅咒(祈天惩罚, 伤害或毁灭某物或某人)。be under a ~, suffer as the result of a ~. 因被诅咒而受灾祸。call down ~s (from Heaven) upon sb, ask God or Heaven to punish sb. 祈天降祸于某人。lay sb under a ~,

make him suffer as the result of a ~. 使因被诅咒而受灾祸。2 cause of misfortune or ruin: 祸因; 祸源; 为祸之物: Gambling is often a ~. 赌博常是祸因。The rabbits are a ~ (ie do a lot of damage to crops, etc) in this part of the country. 兔子在这一带农村是一种祸害(即损坏农作物等)。His wealth proved a ~ to him. 他的财富成为他的祸因。3 word or words used in violent language expressing anger. 怒骂之词。4 the ~, (colloq) menses. (口)月经。

curse² /kɜːs; kɝs/ vt, vi 1 [VP6A] use a curse against; use violent language against. 诅咒; 咒骂; 詈骂。2 [VP2A, 3A] ~ (at), utter curses: 口出恶言; 咒骂: to ~ and swear; 口出恶言; to ~ at fate. 诅咒命运。3 be ~d with, suffer misfortune, trouble, etc because of: 因…而受害: to be ~d with idle daughters/a violent temper. 受了懒惰女儿(暴躁脾气)的害。

cursed /'kɜːsɪd; 'kɝsɪd/ adj dammable; hateful (often used colloq merely to show annoyance): 该死的; 可恨的; (口)可厌的: This work is a ~ nuisance. 这工作极为讨厌。~·ly adv

cur·sive /'kɜːsɪv; 'kɝsɪv/ adj (of handwriting) with the letters rounded and joined together. (指书法)草书的; 草体的。⇨ script.

cur·sory /'kɜːsərɪ; 'kɝsərɪ/ adj (of work, reading, etc) quick; hurried; done without attention to details: (指工作, 阅读等)匆促的; 粗略的; 不精细的; 不注意细节的: a ~ glance/inspection. 匆匆的一瞥(检查)。**cur·sor·ily** /'kɜːsərəlɪ; 'kɝsərəlɪ/ adv

curst /kɜːst; kɝst/ adj = cursed.

curt /kɜːt; kɝt/ adj (of a speaker, his manner, what he says) short-spoken; hardly polite: (指说话者, 其态度, 所说的话)简短的; 礼貌不周的; 唐突的: to give sb a ~ answer; 给某人一简短的回答; a ~ way of speaking. 说话唐突。~·ly adv ~·ness n

cur·tail /kɜː'teɪl; kɝ'tel/ vt [VP6A] make shorter than was at first planned; cut off a part of: (较最初计划)缩短; 减省; 提早结束: to ~ a speech/one's holidays; 提早结束演说(休假); to ~ the allowance one has been making to sb, give him less money. 减少给予某人的津贴。~·ment n [U, C] act or result of ~ing. 缩短; 缩减; 减少。

cur·tain /'kɜːtn; 'kɝtn/ n 1 piece of cloth or lace hung up at a window or door or (in former times) round a bed: 窗帘; 门帘; (昔时围于床四周的)帐帷: Please draw the ~s, pull them across the window(s). 请将窗帘拉上。draw a ~ over sth, (fig) say no more about it. (喻)停止讲某事; 不再提某事。'~-lecture, (old use) wife's scolding of her husband in private (originally in bed after the bed-~s were drawn). (旧用法)妻子在私下对丈夫的责备(原指在床帷拉上的时候)。2 sheet of heavy material to draw or lower across the front of the stage in a theatre before and after each scene of a play: (戏台上在一景戏演出前后所启闭的)幕: The ~ rises/is raised, The play/act begins. 幕启(戏开演)。The ~ falls, The play/act ends. 幕落(戏演完)。'~-call, call (given by the audience) to an actor or actress to appear before the ~ for applause. (观众)要求演员出场谢幕(接受鼓掌)的呼声。'~-raiser, short piece performed before the chief play. 开场戏(正戏前的短戏)。'safety-~, one that is fire-proof. 安全幕(防火者)。3 (various senses indicating cover or protection): (各种表示遮蔽或保护的意义): A ~ of mist hid the view. 一层薄雾遮住视线。The troops went forward behind a ~ of fire (gun-fire from their artillery). 军队在炮火掩护下前进。□ vt 1 [VP6A] furnish or cover with ~s: 装以帘幕; 以帘幕遮盖: ~ed windows, 有窗帘的窗户; enough material to ~ all the windows. 足够为所有窗子装窗帘的布料。2 [VP15B] ~ off, separate or divide with a ~ or ~s: 用帘幕分隔: to ~ off part of a room. 用帘幕隔出房间的一部分。

curt·sey, curtsy /'kɜːtsɪ; 'kɝtsɪ/ n (pl ~s, -sies) gesture of respect (bending the knees) made by women

and girls (eg to a queen): 妇女所行的屈膝礼(如对女王所行者): *to make/drop/bob a ~ (to sb)*. (向某人)行屈膝礼. □ *vi (pt, pp ~ed, curtsied)* make a *~ (to)*. 行屈膝礼(与……连用).

cur·va·ture /ˈkɜːvətʃə(r) *US*: -tʃʊər; ˈkɝvətʃə/ *n* [U] curving; the state of being curved: 弯曲; 屈曲; 曲度: *to suffer from ~ of the spine*; 患脊椎骨弯曲症; *the ~ of the earth's surface*. 地球表面的曲度.

curve /kɜːv; kɝv/ *n* line of which no part is straight and which changes direction without angles: 曲线; 弧线; 弯曲处: *a ~ in the road*. 弯路. *The driver of a car should not go round/take ~s at high speed*. 汽车驾驶人不应在高速上下转弯. □ *vt, vi* ~: (使)成弯形: *The river ~s round the town*. 河水环绕市镇.

cushion /ˈkʊʃn; ˈkʊʃən/ *n* 1 small bag filled with feathers or other soft material (eg foam rubber), to make a seat more comfortable, or to kneel on, etc; sth soft and like a ~ in shape or function: 软垫子; 坐垫; 垫(内装羽毛或其他柔软物质, 如泡沫橡胶, 以垫座位或跪时垫于膝下等); 形式或功用似软垫之物. *a ~ of moss*; 一层青苔; *a 'pin-~*; (裁缝插针用的)针垫. *a ~ of air*, as for a hovercraft. 气垫(如气垫船之喷射引擎向下喷出之气体所形成者). 2 soft, resilient lining on the inner sides of a billiardtable where the balls hit. 撞球台边缘内侧碰球的有弹性的里衬. □ *vt* [VP6A, 14] supply with ~s; protect from shock with ~s: 装垫子; 用垫子保护(以免碰撞): *~ed seats*; 有垫子的座位; (fig)protect from harmful changes: (喻)保护(以免受变动之害): *farmers who are ~ed against falls in prices*, eg by subsidies. 受保护(例如政府津贴)以免受物价下跌影响之农民.

cushy /ˈkʊʃɪ; ˈkʊʃɪ/ *adj* (-ier, -iest) (sl) (of a job, etc) not requiring much effort: (俚)(指工作等)轻松的; 不费力的: *get a ~ job in the Civil Service*. 在文职机关获一轻松的工作.

cusp /kʌsp; kʌsp/ *n* pointed end (esp of a leaf). 尖点; (尤指)叶的尖端.

cus·pi·dor /ˈkʌspɪdɔː(r); ˈkʌspəˌdɔr/ *n* (US) spittoon. (美)痰盂.

cuss /kʌs; kʌs/ *n* (sl) (俚) 1 curse. 诅咒. *not give/care a ~*, be quite unworried. 一点不在乎. *not worth a tinker's ~*, quite worthless. 一文不值的. 2 person: 人: *a queer old ~*. 老怪物.

cussed /ˈkʌsɪd; ˈkʌsɪd/ *adj* (colloq) perverse; obstinate. (口)刚愎的; 固执的. *~·ly adv ~·ness n*

cus·tard /ˈkʌstəd; ˈkʌstəd/ *n* [C, U] (egg-) ~, (dish of) mixture of eggs and milk, sweetened and flavoured, baked or boiled; mixture of powdered eggs, etc (**'~powder**) prepared by adding sugar and milk to flavoured cornflour, eaten with fruit, pastry, etc. 牛奶蛋糊; 乳蛋糕(亦作 egg-custard, 鸡蛋和牛奶混合加糖及味料经烘焙或烹煮制成的食品)以一道乳蛋糕; 蛋粉糊(亦作 custard-powder, 以糖和牛奶加含有味料的玉蜀黍粉制成, 与水果、糕饼等共食).

cus·to·dian /kʌˈstəʊdɪən; kʌsˈtodɪən/ *n* person who has custody of sth or sb; caretaker of a public building. 保管人; 监护人; (公共建筑物的)管理员.

cus·tody /ˈkʌstədɪ; ˈkʌstədɪ/ *n* [U] 1 (duty of) caring for, guarding: 照顾; 监护(的责任): *A father has the ~ of his children while they are young*. 孩子幼时, 父亲有监护之责. *When Mary's parents died, she was placed in the ~ of her aunt*. 玛丽的父母去世以后, 她就交由她的姑母照顾. *If you are going away for a long time you should leave your jewellery in safe ~*, eg with your bank. 如果你将离家很久, 你应将珠宝饰物交付(银行等)保管. 2 imprisonment. 监禁. *(be) in ~*, in prison (eg awaiting trial). 在羁押中(如候审). *give sb into ~*, hand him over to the police. 将某人交给警察. *take sb into ~*, arrest him. 逮捕某人.

cus·tom /ˈkʌstəm; ˈkʌstəm/ *n* 1 [U] usual and generally accepted behaviour among members of a social group: 风俗; 习俗(某一社会团体各份子间通常一般公认的行为方式): *Don't be a slave to ~*, Do not do things merely because most people do them and have always done them. 不要做习俗的奴隶(仅因大多数人如此做或经常如此做而亦如此做). *It has become the ~ (= has become usual) for our family to go to the seaside in summer*. 我们家在夏季常去海滨. 2 [C] particular way of behaving which, because it has been long established, is observed by individuals and social groups: (个人的)习惯; (社会的)习俗; 惯例: *Social ~s vary in different countries*. 社会风俗各国不同. *It was Tom's ~ to get up early and go for a walk before breakfast*. 汤姆的习惯是很早起床, 并于早餐以前散步. (Cf 参较 *habit*, a word that means sth that a person does regularly, and that he cannot easily give up. 指个人经常所做之事而不容易放弃者.) 3 [U] regular support given to a tradesman by those who buy his goods: (由于经常购买其货物而给予经商者的)照顾; 惠顾: *We should very much like to have your ~*, should like to buy our goods. 我们竭诚欢迎你来光顾. *I shall withdraw my ~ from that shop*, not buy goods there in future. 我将不再照顾那家商店(即不再购买他们的货物). 4 (*pl*) taxes due to the government on goods imported into a country; import duties; department of government (*the C~s*) that collects such duties: (复)(由政府所征收的)货物进口税; 关税; 海关(作 the Customs): *How long will it take us to pass (= get through) the C~s?* 通过海关检查要花我们多少时间? *The C~s formalities are simple*. 海关检查的手续很简单. *'~ house*, office (esp at a port) where ~s are collected. (尤指港口的)海关办公处. *'~s union*, agreement by States on a common policy on tariffs. 关税同盟(国际间对征课关税之共同协定). 5 (attrib use only) made to order. (仅作定语)定制的. *~·'built*, as specified by the buyer. 定制的; 买主特定的. *~·'made adj* (of clothes) made-to-measure; making things to order: (指衣服)定做的; 专做定货的: *~ tailors/shoemakers*. 专做定货的裁缝(鞋匠). ⇨ *be spoke* at **bespeak**; *tailor-made* at **tailor**.

cus·tom·ary /ˈkʌstəmərɪ *US*: -merɪ; ˈkʌstəmˌɛrɪ/ *adj* in agreement with, according to, custom (1, 2): 合于风俗或习惯的; 根据风俗或习惯的: *Is it ~ for guests at hotels in your country to tip the waiters?* 在贵国住旅馆的客人依惯例是否给侍者小费? *There was the ~ vote of thanks to the chairman*. 依照惯例向主席致谢. **cus·tom·ar·ily** /ˈkʌstəmərəlɪ *US*: ˌkʌstəˈmerəlɪ; ˈkʌstəmˌɛrəlɪ/ *adv*

cus·tomer /ˈkʌstəmə(r); ˈkʌstəmə/ *n* 1 person who buys things, esp one who gives his custom (3) to a shop: 顾客; 顾主; (尤指)经常照顾某商店者: *Mr X has lost some of his best ~s*. X先生已丧失一部分最好的老顾客. 2 (colloq) person or fellow, esp in: (口)人; 家伙; 汉子(尤用于): *a queer ~*; 怪人; *an awkward ~*, person who is difficult to deal with. 难缠的家伙.

cut[1] /kʌt; kʌt/ *vt, vi* (-tt-) (*pt, pp cut*) (For uses with *adverbial particles* and *preps* ⇨ 10 below; for uses with *adj* ⇨ 7 below; for use with *nouns* or *pronouns* ⇨ 6 below.) (与副词性小品词和介词连用参看下列第 10 义; 与形容词连用参看下列第7义; 与名词或代词连用参看下列第 6 义.) 1 [VP6A, 12B, 13B, 15A, 2A] make an opening, incision (with a sharpedged instrument), eg a knife, a pair of scissors, or other edged tool): (用有刃的器具如刀, 剪刀子等)切, 割, 剪, 刺(a) make a mark, wound, in sth: 割伤: *He cut his face/himself while shaving*. 他在刮胡子的时候把脸割伤了. ⇨ *cut into sth* in 10 below. 参看下列第 10 义之 cut into sth. (b) sever; reap: 切断; 收割: *Don't pluck the flowers; it's better to cut them*. 不要用手采花; 最好用剪刀剪. *Has the wheat been cut (= harvested, reaped) yet?* 小麦已经收割了吗? (c) shorten: 剪短: *to cut one's nails*; 剪指甲; *to cut a hedge*; 修剪树篱; *to have one's hair cut*. 理发. Hence, 由此产生, **'hair-cut n** ⇨ also *cut sth short* in 7 below. 亦参看下列第 7 义之 cut sth short. (d) separate; remove from sth

larger: 使分开；自较大部分切下：*Please cut a slice of cake for me / cut me a slice of cake.* 请给一块蛋糕给我。*Cut yourself some pineapple.* 你自己切些凤梨吃吧。*Cut some pineapple for your sister.* 给你姐姐(妹妹)切些凤梨。*Two scenes / episodes were cut by the censor.* 两个镜头(情节)被检查员删除了。⇨ also *cut off* and *cut out* in 10 below. 亦参看下列第 10 义之 cut off 及 cut out。(e) reduce sth by removing part: 减少：*Was your salary cut?* 你的薪水减少了吗？*The new jet service cuts the travelling time by half.* 新喷气客机减少了一半旅行的时间。⇨ *cut down* in 10 below. 参看下列第 10 义之 cut down。(f) divide into smaller pieces: 分成小块：*Will you cut the cake?* ie into pieces. 请你切蛋糕好吗？*If you'll cut the bread (ie into slices), we'll make toast.* 如果你切面包，我们就来烤面包。⇨ *cut up* in 10 below. 参看下列第 10 义之 cut up。(g) divide, separate into two: 分割为二：*Don't cut the string, untie the knots.* 不要剪断那绳子，把绳结打开。*The Minister cut the tape to open a new section of motorway.* 部长为一段新完工的高速公路剪彩。(h) make, fashion, by removing material with tools, machines, etc that use: 制成；切成；挖成；雕成：*to cut steps in the ice;* 在冰上挖出踏脚之处；*to cut a tunnel through a hill;* 穿山挖一条隧道；*to cut a road up a hillside;* 沿一条路至山坡上；*to cut an inscription / one's initials.* 刻牍文(自己名字的为首字母)。⇨ *cut out* in 10 below. 参看下列第 10 义之 cut out。**2** [VP2A, C] **(a)** (of a sharp tool, instrument, etc) be suitable to use: (指锋利的工具等)适于使用：*This knife does not cut well.* 这把刀切起来不利。**(b)** (of a material) be capable of being cut: (指原料)可被切，割，剪等：*Sandstone cuts easily.* 沙岩很容易切开。*This cloth is too narrow to cut well,* is narrow and difficult to cut into the shapes needed. 这块布料太窄，不易裁成所需式样。**3** [VP6A] (colloq) stay away from, be absent from (sth one ought to attend): (口)缺席；不出席(应出席之场所)：*to cut a class / a lecture.* 逃学；逃课。**4** [VP6A] (of lines) cross: (指线条)相交：*Let the point where AB cuts CD be called E.* 假设 AB 线与 CD 线相交之点为 E。**5** [VP6A] (sport, esp cricket, tennis, billiards) strike (a ball) so that it spins or is deflected; hit the edge of (a ball). (尤指板球，网球，撞球等)击(球)使其回旋；斜击(一球)；削(球)。**6** [VP6A] (used with *nouns* or *pronouns*) (与名词或代词连用) *cut the cards / pack,* lift part of a pack of playing-cards lying face downwards and turn it up to decide sth (eg who is to deal, who are to be partners). 翻牌决定(自一副面向下的纸牌拿起一部分并翻转以决定谁发牌或与谁同伙)。*cut one's coat according to one's cloth,* suit one's expenditure to one's income; not be too ambitious in one's plans. 量入为出；不存奢望；不抱太大野心。*cut (off) a corner,* go across, not round it. 走直路；走近路(不经过转角处)。*take a short-cut.* (喻)抄捷径。*cut a disc / record,* record music, etc on to a gramophone record. 将音乐等录于唱片上。*cut the ground from under sb / from under sb's feet,* leave him in a weak or illogical position; destroy the foundation of his plan, argument, etc. 拆某人的台；破坏某人的计划、论据等的基础。*cut no / not much ice (with sb),* have little or no effect or influence (on him): (对某人)无作用或影响力。*cut one's losses,* abandon a scheme that has caused financial losses before one loses too much. 及早放弃造成经济损失的计划以免遭受更大的损失。*cut a tooth,* have a new tooth just begin to show itself above the gum. 长牙；生新牙(刚自牙肉中生出)。*cut one's teeth on sth,* learn, gain experience, from: 自…获取经验：*There's a job for you to cut your teeth on.* 有一个使你增加经验的工作。*cut both ways,* (of an action or argument) have an effect both for and against. (指行动或论据)骑墙；两面顾。⇨ also *caper¹*, *dash¹(6)*, *figure(5)*, *Gordian*. **7** [VP22] (with an *adj* as complement) (与补语作形容词连用) *cut sb dead,* pretend not to have seen; treat as a complete stranger: 佯装未见某人；完全把某人当做陌生人看待：*She cut me*

dead in the street, ignored me completely. 她在街上把我视若路人。*cut it fine,* (colloq) leave oneself only the minimum of what is needed (esp time): (口)只剩下最低限度；扣得很紧(尤指时间)：*He cut it rather fine,* eg by reaching the station half a minute before his train was due to leave. 他把时间扣得太紧了(例如在火车开行前半分钟才到达车站)。*cut sb / sth free (from),* make or get free by cutting: 割断绳索等以解脱：*He cut himself free from the ropes with which they had bound him.* 他割断他们用以绑他的绳索而逃脱了。*cut sth / sb loose (from),* make loose or separate by cutting: 割断(绳索等)以解脱：*cut loose a boat / cut a boat loose;* 割断绳索以放开船；*cut oneself loose from one's family,* live an independent life. 离家自立谋生。*cut sth open,* make an opening or split in: 切破；使裂：*He fell and cut his head open.* 他摔了一跤跌破了头。*cut sth short,* make shorter: 缩短；删节：*to cut a long story short;* 把长的故事截短；长话短说；*to cut short a person's remarks;* 打断某人的话；*a career cut short by illness.* 因病半途而废的事业。**8 C~!** (cinema; imper) Stop (shooting a scene)! (电影；祈使) 停止(拍摄一镜头)！**9** (uses with the *pp*) (过去分词的用法) *cut and dried,* (of opinions, etc) already formed and unlikely to be changed. (意见等)已决定的；不大会改变的。*cut 'flowers,* flowers cut for decoration (contrasted with flowers growing in the garden, in pots, etc). (为装饰用而)剪下的花(与园中，盆中等长的花相对)。*cut 'glass,* glass with patterns and designs cut on it. 雕花玻璃。*cut-'price attrib adj* at a reduced price, and below those of rivals or those recommended by the manufacturers, etc. 削价的(低于同业或厂商所定的价格的)。*cut-'rate attrib adj = cut-price.* *cut to'bacco,* shredded (contrasted with *cake tobacco*). 烟丝(与 cake tobacco 相对)。*cut·ting part adj* **(a)** sharp; piercing: 锐利的；刺人的：*a cutting wind.* 刺骨的风。**(b)** sarcastic; wounding: 讥刺的；伤害的：*cutting remark.* 伤感情的话。**10** [VP3A, 15B, A, 2C] (uses with *adverbial particles* and *preps*): (与副词性小品词及介词连用的用法)：

cut across sth, **(a)** take a shorter route across (a field, etc). 取捷径穿过(田地等)。**(b)** be contrary to: 与…相反：*Opinion on preserving the environment cut clean across normal political loyalties.* 保护环境的意见与政治上普遍的忠诚完全相反。

cut at sb / sth, aim a sharp blow at (eg with a sword or whip): (用刀剑或鞭等)对准…而猛击：*cut at a hedge / a group of nettles with a stick.* 用棍棒对着树篱(一簇荨麻)猛击。

cut sth away, remove by cutting: 割掉；砍去：*We cut away all the dead wood from the tree.* 我们把树上所有的枯枝都砍去了。*The yacht was in danger of sinking until they cut away the broken mast and rigging.* 那游艇有沉没的危险，后来他们砍去那断桅及缆索，危险方告消除。

cut sth back, **(a)** (of shrubs, bushes, etc) prune close to the stem. (指矮树，灌木等)剪短(其枝叶)。**(b)** reduce: 减少；减低：*cut back production.* 减低生产。Hence, 由此产生，*'cut·back n* **(a)** reduction: 减少；减低：*a cutback in expenditure.* 减少开销。**(b)** flashback. (电影)倒叙。

cut sth / sb down, **(a)** cause to fall by cutting: 砍倒：*cut down a tree.* 砍倒一树。**(b)** kill or injure by striking with a sword or other edged weapon: (用刀剑或其他有刃武器)砍杀；杀伤：*He cut down his enemy.* 他杀伤了他的敌人。**(c)** deprive of life or health (by disease, etc): (为疾病等)夺去生命或健康；病死；病倒：*He was cut down in the prime of manhood.* 他在壮年时期病故了。**(d)** reduce in quantity, amount, etc: 减少(数量等)：*cut down expenses.* 减低费用。*I won't have a cigarette, thanks—I'm trying to cut down,* reduce the number of cigarettes I smoke. 谢谢，我不要抽烟——我正在设法减少抽烟量。**(e)** persuade (sb) to reduce a price, charge, etc: 说服(某人)减价等：*We managed to cut him down by £30.* 我们总算说服他把价钱减低了三十英镑。**(f)** reduce the length of: 减短：*cut down a pair of trousers,* eg for

sb who is shorter. 改短裤脚(给矮者穿). *cut down an article to make it fit the space available*, in a periodical, etc. 删节一篇文章使适合杂志中所留的篇幅. *cut 'down on*, reduce one's consumption of: 减少对…之消耗量: *He's trying to cut down on cigarettes and beer.* 他在设法减少吸香烟和饮啤酒的量. *cut sb down to size*, (colloq) show him that he is not so important as he thinks he is: (口)告诉某人他并不象他自己所想的那样重要: *Some of these so-called experts really need cutting down to size.* 这些所谓专家当中有些真需要让他们知道他们并不象他们自己所想的那样重要.

cut in (on), (of the driver of a motor vehicle, etc, who has overtaken another vehicle) return too soon to his own side of the road (with possibility of collision, etc): (指汽车等驾驶者, 超车后)驶入原车道过急(可能与他车相撞等): *Accidents are often caused by drivers who cut in (on other cars).* 车祸常常因驾驶者超车过急而造成. *cut sb in*, (colloq) include sb in a (profitable)venture: (口)让某人加入(赚钱的)冒险事业: *If you'll contribute £500 we'll cut you in.* 如果你愿意拿出五百英镑, 我们就让你入伙. *cut in (on)/into*, interrupt (a conversation etc): 打断(谈话等): 插嘴: *Don't cut into the story/in on the conversation/in so rudely—let her finish.* 不要打断这故事(打断谈话, 那样鲁莽地插嘴)——让她说完. *cut in half/two/three, etc; cut into halves/quarters/thirds, etc*, divide: 切为两half(二, 三, 四等块): 分割: *The submarine was cut in half by a destroyer.* 那潜艇被一驱逐舰击成两half. *Cut the cable in two.* 将此缆载成两段. *Cut the apples into halves.* 将这些苹果各切为两half.

cut into sth, (a) make a cut in: 切开(某物): *Mary cut into her birthday cake and everybody clapped.* 玛丽切开她的生日蛋糕, 大家鼓掌庆贺. (b) interfere with: 妨碍: *All this extra homework cuts into his weekends, leaves him less free time.* 所有这些额外的课外作业使他在周末都没有多少空闲.

cut sb/sth off (from), (a) remove (esp sth at an extremity) by cutting: 切去(尤指尖端部分): *Don't cut your fingers off!* 不要切你的手指切断了! *Cut the chicken's head off.* 把鸡头砍掉. *He cut off a metre of cloth from the roll.* 他自那卷布上剪下一米. (b) stop; interrupt; isolate: 停止; 打断; 使孤立: *be cut off while talking by telephone*; 正在打电话时线路被切断; *cut off the gas/electricity supply*, eg because of unpaid accounts: 切断煤气(电力)供应(如因未缴清欠款); *cut off an army from its base*, by getting in between: 切断军队与基地的连络; *cut off stragglers*, separate them from the main body and so capture them; 截住掉队者(以便捕捉之); *be cut off from all possibility of help*; 被切断一切受援助的可能; *towns cut off* (= isolated) *by floods*; 为洪水所围困的市镇; *cut off by the tide*, isolated on a rock, sandbank, etc by the incoming tide; 为涨潮所困(如被孤立在岩石, 沙滩等上); *cut off sb's supplies/a son's allowance*, no longer allow him to receive them; 切断某人的供应来源(不再给儿子零用钱); *cut off sb with a shilling*, disinherit him (eg a son who has behaved badly) except for a small sum (to show that the act is deliberate). 留一先令剥夺某人之继承权(例如儿子品行不良, 仅留给他很少的一点钱, 表示此举是故意的). *cut (off) a corner*, ⇨ 6 above. 参见上列第 6 义.

cut out, stop functioning: 停止作用: *One of the aircraft's engines cut out.* 那架飞机的一个引擎失去作用. *cut sth out*, (a) remove by cutting (eg from a periodical): (自刊物等)剪下; 切去: *That's an interesting article—I'll cut it out.* 那是篇有趣的文章—我要把它剪下来. (b) make by cutting: 剪成; 砍成: *cut out a path through the jungle.* 在丛林中砍出一条路. (c) shape (a garment) by cutting the outlines of the parts on cloth: 剪裁(衣服): *cut out a dress.* 剪裁一件衣服. (d) (colloq) leave out; omit: (口)删去: *Let's cut out unimportant details.* 我们删去不重要的细节. 干脆吧. (e) (colloq) stop doing or using (sth): (口)戒除; 不用: *My doctor told me I must cut out tobacco, stop smoking.* 我的医生说我必须戒烟. *cut sb*

out, defeat, eliminate (a rival, esp in competition for sth): 击败(对手, 尤指在竞争中): *cut out all rivals for a girl's affections.* 击败所有情敌而赢得某女郎的爱情. *cut it/that out*, (colloq, imper) stop fighting, squabbling, etc: (口, 祈使)停止打斗、争吵等: *Now just cut it out, you two!* 你两个现在不要再吵(打)了! *cut out (the) dead wood*, (colloq) remove unnecessary or unproductive parts: (口)除去不必要或不能生产部分: *There's a lot of dead wood to be cut out if the industry is to be efficient.* 如欲提高工业的效率, 许多不必要之处应予除掉. *(not) be cut out for*, (not) have the qualities and abilities needed for: (无)有…所需要的才能: *He's not cut out for that sort of work.* 他没有担任那种工作的才能. *have one's work cut out (for one)*, be faced with as much work as one can manage: 对着尽已占用某人全部时间和精力的工作: *It's a big job; he'll have his work cut out for him to meet the dead-line.* 这是桩艰巨的工作; 他得全力以赴, 始能如期完成. *'cut-out n* (a) design, figure, etc (to be) cut out from paper, cardboard, etc. 由纸, 纸板等剪下的图案, 图形等. (b) (electr) device that interrupts or disconnects a circuit (eg to avoid too heavy a load). (电)断流器(如避免过重负荷, 截断电流之设计); 保险开关.

cut sb to the heart / quick, cause him pain or suffering: 使某人痛苦: *His ingratitude cut her to the heart.* 他的忘恩负义使她伤心. *cut sb/sth to pieces*, destroy by cutting, by gunfire, etc: 切碎; 打坏: 炮火等)摧毁: *The enemy were cut to pieces.* 敌人被炮火摧毁.

cut sth/sb up, (a) cut into pieces: 切碎: 剪碎: *cut up one's meat.* 将肉切碎. (b) destroy: 摧毁; 粉碎: *cut up the enemy's forces.* 摧毁敌人军力. (c) (colloq, usu passive) cause mental suffering to: (口, 通常用被动语态)使伤心; 使悲痛: *He was badly cut up by the news of his son's death.* 他得知儿子的死讯, 极为悲伤. *Don't be so cut up about it.* 不要为此过于悲伤. (d) criticize adversely; point out the faults of: 苛评; 严评: *His latest novel has been cut up by the reviewers.* 他最近的小说被评论家批评得体无完肤. *cut up (into)*, be capable of being cut up (into): 能被切成; 能被切成: *This piece of cloth will cut up into* (= has enough material in it for) *three suits.* 这块布将可裁制三套衣服. *cut up (for)*, (colloq) be worth: (口)有价值: *The old man cut up for ten thousand*, left £10 000 to be divided among his heirs. 那老人死后留下一万英镑(供给承者去分). *cut up rough*, (sl) behave aggressively; be violent and aggressive: (俚)大发脾气; 大动大闹: *He'll cut up rough if you don't give him what he asked for.* 你要是不给他所要求的, 他会大吵大闹.

cut² /kʌt/ *kʌt/ n* **1** act of cutting; stroke with a sword, whip, etc; result of such a stroke; opening made by a knife or other sharp-edged tool, etc: 切; 割; 刻; 鞭打; 砍; 砍伤: 用刀或其他利器所割的破口: *give a horse a cut across the flanks*; 在马的侧腹抽一鞭子; *a deep cut in the leg*; 腿上深入的割伤; *cuts on the face*, eg after shaving. 脸上的伤口(例如刮脸后). *cut and thrust*, (usu fig) vigorous argument, etc: (常喻)激烈的争论等: *the cut and thrust of debate.* 辩论的激烈. **2** reduction in size, amount, length, etc: 减少; 减低; 减短: *a cut in prices/salaries*: 减价(薪); *a cut in expenditure/production*; 减低开支(生产); *a power cut*, a reduction in the strength of electrical current, or a period for which current is cut off. 电力减弱; 停电期间. **3** a cutting out; part that is cut out: 剪去; 剪去的部分: *There were several cuts in the film*, Parts of it had been cut out (eg by the film censors). 该影片有数处被剪去(如为影片检查员所剪). *Where can we make a cut in this long article?* 我们能在什么地方把这篇长文删掉一些吗? **4** sth obtained by cutting: 切下或割之物: *a nice cut of beef*; 一块上好牛肉; *a cut off the joint*, a slice from a cooked joint of meat; 自煮调好的一大块腿肉上切下的一块; *this year's cut of wool*, the wool sheared from the sheep. 今年所剪的羊毛(总量). **5**

style in which clothes, etc are made by cutting: 衣服等剪裁的式样: *I don't like the cut of his trousers.* 我不喜欢他的裤子的式样。 ⇨ **jib**[1](1). **6** (cricket, tennis) quick, sharp stroke: (板球, 网球)快速而使球旋转的一击; 搓球; 削球: *a cut to the boundary.* 削到边线的一球。 **7** remark, etc that wounds a person's feelings: 伤人感情的话: *That remark was a cut at me,* was directed at me. 那句话是对我而发的。 **8** refusal to recognize a person: 装做未见某人; 佯装不识: *give sb a cut,* 毫不理睬某人。 ⇨ *cut so dead* at **cut**[1](7). **9** short cut, way across (from one place to another) that shortens the distance. 近路; 捷径。 **10** *a cut above,* (colloq) rather superior to: (口)颇优于; 胜过; 超过: *She's a cut above the other girls in the office,* is better educated, has wider interests, etc. 她在办公室中较其他的女职员为强(教育程度较高, 兴趣范围较广 等). *That's a cut above me,* above my range of interests, my abilities, etc. 那非我的兴趣(能力等)所及。 **11** railway cutting; canal. 低于地面开凿的铁道路基; 运河河道。 ⇨ **cutting**(1). **12** block or plate on which a design, illustration, etc has been cut; picture, etc, made from such a block. 图版; 刻版; 版画。 ⇨ *woodcut* at **wood**(4).

cute /kjuːt; kjut/ *adj* (-r, -st) **1** sharp-witted; quick-thinking. 机敏的; 聪颖的。 **2** (US colloq) attractive; pretty and charming. (美口)吸引人的; 美丽而逗人喜爱的。 ~ **ly** *adv* ~ **ness** *n*

cu·ticle /'kjuːtɪkl; 'kjutɪkl/ *n* outer layer of hardened skin (esp at the base of a finger-nail or toe-nail). 表皮; 外皮(尤指手指甲或脚指甲根部者)。

cut·lass /'kʌtləs; 'kʌtləs/ *n* **1** (hist) sailor's short, one-edged sword with a slightly curved blade. (史)(水手所用)刀锋略弯的单刃短刀。 **2** cutting tool (= *machete*) used by cacao-growers and copra-growers. 种植可可及干椰子者所用的刀子。

cut·ler /'kʌtlə(r); 'kʌtlə/ *n* man who makes and repairs knives and other cutting tools and instruments. 刀匠 (制造及修理各种刀具的人). ~**s** *n* [U] trade of a ~; implements used at table (knives, forks, spoons, esp if made of stainless steel); things made or sold by ~s. 刀剑制造业; 餐具(刀、叉、匙、尤指不锈钢制成者); 刀剑等利器。

cut·let /'kʌtlɪt; 'kʌtlɪt/ *n* slice of meat or fish for one person: (一人份)肉片或鱼片: *a veal ~.* (一人份的)一块小牛肉。

cut·purse /'kʌtpɜːs; 'kʌt,pɜrs/ *n* (hist) pickpocket. (史)扒手。

cut·ter /'kʌtə(r); 'kʌtə/ *n* **1** person or thing that cuts: 切割者; 裁剪器; 削切器: *a tailor's ~,* who cuts out cloth; 成衣店的裁剪师; a *'wire-~.* 剪金属线的器具。 **2** sailing-vessel with one mast; ship's boat, for use between ship and shore. 独桅帆船; 属于大船而用于船岸之间的小艇。

cut-throat /'kʌtθrəʊt; 'kʌt,θrot/ *n* **1** murderer. 凶手; 刺客。 **2** (attrib uses) ruthless, cruel: (用作定语)凶狠的; 残忍的: ~ *competition,* likely to ruin the weaker competitors. 拼命的竞争; 抑嗌竞争(较弱之一方可能毁灭的竞争)。 ~ **razor,** one with no guard on the long blade. 无安全设备的剃刀。 ⇨ the illus at **razor.** 参看 razor 之插图。

cut·ting /'kʌtɪŋ; 'kʌtɪŋ/ *n* **1** unroofed passage dug through the ground for a road, railway, canal, etc. 自山丘或地面开凿出来的道路, 铁路, 运河河床等; 路堑。 **2** sth cut from a newspaper, etc and kept for reference: 自报纸等中剪下的参考资料; 剪报: *'press ~s.* 剪报。Cf 较 US 美 **clipping.** **3** short piece of a plant, to be used for growing a new plant: 插枝(自植物剪下供分栽的小枝): *chrysanthemum ~s;* 菊花插枝; *to take a ~.* 剪枝(供插栽)。 **4** [U] process of editing films, tape recordings, etc, by cutting out unwanted parts. 剪辑(电影片、录音带等剪去不需要部分的剪接工作)。Hence, 由此产生, '~-**room,** room where this is done. 剪辑室。 *part adj* (of words, etc) wounding the feelings, etc: (指言语等)伤感情的: ~ *remarks.* 伤感情的话。

cut·tle·fish /'kʌtlfɪʃ; 'kʌt,fɪʃ/ *n* sea-water animal with long arms (tentacles), which sends out a black liquid when attacked. 墨鱼; 乌贼(海产动物, 有长触手, 受攻击时能放出黑色液体). ⇨ the illus at **mollusc.** 参看 mollusc 之插图。

cut·worm /'kʌtwɜːm; 'kʌt,wɜrm/ *n* caterpillar that eats through the stems of young plants level with the ground. 夜盗虫; 糖蛾的幼虫(能沿地面咬断初生植物)。

cy·an·ide /'saɪənaɪd; 'saɪə,naɪd/ *n* [U] poisonous compound substance: 氰化物(有毒的化合物): *potassium ~;* 氰化钾; *sodium ~.* 氰化钠。

cy·ber·net·ics /ˌsaɪbə'netɪks; ˌsaɪbə'nɛtɪks/ *n* (*sing v*) the science of communication and control in machines and animals (including man). (单用数动词)控制论; 神经机械学(研究机械和动物(包含人类)之资讯传送及控制之科学). **cy·ber·netic** *adj*

cyc·la·men /'sɪkləmən *US:* 'saɪk-; 'sɪkləmən/ *n* kinds of plant, wild and cultivated, of the primrose family, with delicate, small flowers. 樱草属植物(野生及栽培之有美丽小花)。

cycle /'saɪkl; 'saɪkl/ *n* **1** series of events taking place in a regularly repeated order: 按一定规律重复发生的一连串事情; 循环; 周期; 周期: *the ~ of the seasons.* 四季的循环。 **2** complete set or series: 全集; 全套; 全本: *a song ~,* eg by Schubert: 联篇歌曲(联合若干短篇为一题的歌集, 如舒伯特所作的): *the Arthurian /ɑː'θjʊərɪən US: -'θʊər-; ɑr'θjʊrɪən/ ~,* the stories of King Arthur and his knights. 亚瑟王和他的武士们的全套故事。 **3** (short for) bicycle or motor-cycle. 两轮之机器脚踏车(的简称)。 □ *vi* [VP2A, B, C] ride a bicycle. 骑脚踏车。

cyc·lic /'saɪklɪk; 'saɪklɪk/ *adj* recurring in cycles. 循环的; 有周期性的。

cyc·li·cal /'saɪklɪkl; 'saɪklɪkl/ *adj* = **cyclic.**

cyc·list /'saɪklɪst; 'saɪklɪst/ *n* person who rides a cycle. 骑脚踏车或机车者。

cyc·lone /'saɪkləʊn; 'saɪklon/ *n* violent wind rotating round a calm central area; violent windstorm. 气旋(风中心平静而四周猛烈的风); 暴风; 旋风。 **cy·clonic** /saɪ'klɒnɪk; saɪ'klɑnɪk/ *adj* of or like a ~. 气旋(式)的; (似)暴风的。

cyclo·pae·dia /ˌsaɪklə'piːdɪə; ˌsaɪklə'pidɪə/ *n* = **encyclopaedia.**

Cyclo·pean /saɪ'kləʊpɪən; ˌsaɪklə'piən/ *adj* of or like a Cyclops /'saɪklɒps; 'saɪklɑps/ (a one-eyed giant in Greek myth); huge; immense. (似)(希腊神话独眼巨人)塞克拉普斯的; 巨大的。

cyclo·style /'saɪkləstaɪl; 'saɪklə,staɪl/ *n* apparatus for printing copies from a stencil. 一种油印机。 □ *vt* reproduce (copies) with this. 用此种油印机印刷(文件)。

cyclo·tron /'saɪklətrɒn; 'saɪklə,trɑn/ *n* apparatus used for producing heavy electric particles moving at high speed, used experimentally in nuclear research work. 回旋加速器(用以产生高速运动之带电重粒子, 用于核研究实验)。

cyder /'saɪdə(r); 'saɪdə/ *n* = **cider.**

cyg·net /'sɪgnɪt; 'sɪgnɪt/ *n* young swan. 小天鹅。

cyl·in·der /'sɪlɪndə(r); 'sɪlɪndə/ *n* **1** solid or hollow body with equal, circular ends and regular, curving sides. 柱; 圆筒; 滚筒(实心或空心)。 ⇨ the illus here and

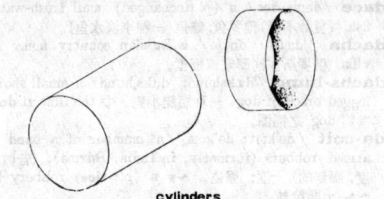

cylinders

at **projection**. 参看本条与 projection 之插图。**2 ~**-shaped chamber (in an engine) in which gas or steam works a piston: 汽缸(引擎内汽油或蒸汽推动活塞之一圆形筒): *a six-~ engine / motor-car*. 有六个汽缸的引擎(汽车). **(working) on all ~s**, (colloq) with the maximum power or effort. (口)尽全力(工作); 倾全力.
cy·lin·dri·cal /sɪ'lɪmdrɪkl; sɪ'lɪmdrɪkl/ *adj* ~-shaped. 圆筒状的.
cym·bal /'sɪmbl; 'sɪmbl/ *n* one of a pair of round brass plates struck together to make clanging sounds. 铜钹; 铙钹(一对互击可以发响亮之声音的圆盘形铜乐器之一). ⇨ the illus at **percussion**. 参看 percussion 之插图.
cynic /'sɪnɪk; 'sɪnɪk/ *n* person who sees little or no good in anything and who has no belief in human progress; person who shows this by sneering and being sarcastic. 愤世嫉俗者(对世间一切都看不顺眼, 不相信人类的进步); 讽刺者. **cyni·cism** /'sɪnɪsɪzm; 'sɪnə,sɪzəm/ *n* [U] ~'s opinions or attitude of mind; [C] expression of this attitude. 愤世嫉俗的意见或态度; 此种态度的表现; 犬儒主义.
cyni·cal /'sɪnɪkl; 'sɪnɪkl/ *adj* of or like a cynic; sneering or contemptuous: 愤世嫉俗的; 嘲骂的; 讥刺的; ~·ly /-klɪ; -klɪ/ *adv*

a ~ smile / remark. 嘲讽的笑容; 冷笑(讥刺的话). ~·ly /-klɪ; -klɪ/ *adv*
cyno·sure /'sɪnə'zjʊə(r) US: 'samʊʃʊər; 'samə,ʃʊr/ *n* sth or sb that draws everyone's attention; centre of attraction. 引起众人注视的事物或人; 吸引人的地方.
cy·pher /'saɪfə(r); 'saɪfə/ *n* = **cipher**.
cy·press /'saɪprəs; 'saɪprəs/ *n* (kinds of) tall, thin, cone-bearing evergreen tree with dark leaves and hard wood. 柏树(高而细的常绿树, 叶深色, 木坚, 生球果).
Cyril·lic /sɪ'rɪlɪk; sɪ'rɪlɪk/ *adj* the ~ **alphabet**, that used for Slavonic languages (eg Russian). 斯拉夫语(如俄语)用的字母.
cyst /sɪst; sɪst/ *n* enclosed hollow organ in the body containing liquid matter. (身体内含有液体物质的)胞; 囊.
czar /zɑ:(r); zɑr/ *n* (also 亦作 **tsar**) emperor of Russia (before 1917). 沙皇(一九一七年以前俄国皇帝的称号).
czar·ina /zɑ:'ri:nə; zɑ'rinə/ *n* Russian empress. 俄国的皇后或女王.
Czech /tʃek; tʃek/ *n* member of a branch of the Slavs; their language. 捷克人(斯拉夫民族之一支); 捷克语.

Dd

D, d /di:; di/ (*pl* **D's, d's** /di:z; diz/) the fourth letter of the English alphabet; Roman numeral for 500. 英文字母的第四个字母; 罗马数字的 500. **'d**, used for *had* or *would* (esp after *I, we, you, he, she, they, who*). 尤在 I, we, you, he, she, they, who 各字之后, 'd 以代替 had 或 would.
dab[1] /dæb; dæb/ *vt, vi* (-bb-) [VP6A, 14, 15A, B, 2C, 3A] ~ **(at)**, touch, put on, lightly and gently: 轻拍; 轻触; 轻柔地涂敷: *dab one's eyes with a handkerchief*: 用手帕轻拭眼睛; *dab paint on a picture*, suggesting light, quick strokes of the brush. 以轻快的笔法作画. *She was dabbing (at) her cheeks with a powder-puff*. 她以粉扑搽她的脸颊. □ *n* [C] **1** small quantity (of paint, etc) dabbed on. 轻轻涂上的少量(颜料等). **2** slight tap; brief application of sth to a surface (without rubbing): 轻拍; 轻触(而不揉擦): *A dab with a sponge won't remove the dirt, you'll have to rub it*. 用海绵轻轻地吸, 去不掉那污物, 你必须用力擦.
dab[2] /dæb; dæb/ *n* kind of flat-fish. 孙鲽(比目鱼之一种).
dab[3] /dæb; dæb/ *n* ~ **(hand)**, (colloq) expert (at games, etc, at doing things): (口)(运动的)健将; (做事的)能手: *She's a dab hand at tennis*. 她是网球健将.
dabble /'dæbl; 'dæbl/ *vt, vi* **1** [VP6A, 15A, B, 2C] splash (the hands, feet, etc) about in water; put in and out of water. 用(手,足等)溅水; 玩水; 戏水; 使出入水中. **2** [VP3A] ~ **at / in** (art, politics, etc), engage in, study, as a hobby, not professionally. 业余性地研究(艺术, 政治等); 涉猎. **dab·bler** /'dæblə(r); 'dæbləʳ/
da capo /ˌdɑː 'kɑːpəʊ; dɑ'kɑ:po/ (I, music) (as a direction) repeat from the beginning. (意, 音乐)从头再奏(作为指引).
dace /deɪs; des/ *n* (*pl* unchanged) small fresh-water fish. (复数不变)雅罗鱼; 鲦鱼(一种小淡水鱼).
dacha /'dætʃə; 'dɑtʃə/ *n* Russian country house or villa. 俄罗斯乡间邸宅或别墅.
dachs·hund /'dækshʊnd; 'dɑks,hʊnd/ *n* small short-legged breed of dog. 一种短腿小狗。⇨ the illus at **dog**. 参看 dog 之插图.
da·coit /də'kɔɪt; də'kɔɪt/ *n* member of a band of armed robbers (formerly, in India, Burma). (昔时印度、缅甸的)土匪; 强盗。~**y** *n* (*pl* -**ties**) robbery by ~**s**. 土匪抢劫.

dac·tyl /'dæktl; 'dæktl/ *n* (prosody) metrical foot of one accented syllable followed by two unaccented syllables (韵律学) 扬抑抑格(即一重音节后跟两轻音节之音步). (~eg 如 *'tenderly*), as in: 又如: *'under the / 'blossom that / hangs on the / 'bough*. ~**ic** /dæk'tɪlɪk; dæk'tɪlɪk/ *adj*
dad /dæd; dæd/ *n* (colloq) father. (口)爸爸.
daddy /'dædɪ; 'dædɪ/ *n* (*pl* -**dies**) child's word for 'father'. (儿语)爹爹; 爸爸。~-'**long-legs** *n* (popular name for the) crane-fly (a long-legged flying insect). 蚊蛛(一种长腿会飞的昆虫, 为 crane-fly 的俗称).
dado /'deɪdəʊ; 'dedo/ *n* (*pl* ~**s**, US ~**es** /-dəʊz; -doz/) lower part of a wall in a room, when this is different from the upper part in colour or material. 墙裙; 墙壁之底部(颜色或质料与墙壁上部者不同); 护墙.
dae·mon /'di:mən; 'dimən/ *n* =**demon**.
daf·fo·dil /'dæfədɪl; 'dæfədɪl/ *n* yellow flower with long narrow leaves growing from a bulb. 黄水仙(花黄色, 叶狭长, 自球茎生出)。⇨ the illus at **flower**. 参看 flower 之插图.
daft /dɑːft US: dæft; dæft/ *adj* (-er, -est) (colloq) silly; foolish; reckless. (口)傻的; 笨的; 卤莽的。~·ly *adv*
dag·ger /'dægə(r); 'dægəʳ/ *n* **1** short, pointed, two-edged knife used as a weapon. 短剑; 匕首(短而尖的双刃刀, 用作武器). *at ~s drawn (with sb)*, about to fight. 剑拔弩张; (与某人)即将打起来。*look ~s at sb*, look with an expression of hatred and enmity. 对某人怒目而视. **2** (printing) mark of reference(†) (印刷)剑号(即†, 表示附注之记号).
dago /'deɪgəʊ; 'dego/ *n* (*pl* ~**s** /-gəʊz; -goz/) ⚠ (sl, term of contempt for an) Italian, Spaniard or Portuguese. (讳)(俚, 含轻蔑之意)意大利人; 西班牙人; 葡萄牙人.
da·guerreo·type /də'gerətaɪp; də'gerə,taɪp/ *n* photograph taken by an early photographic process. 用早期照像术所制的像.
dah·lia /'deɪlɪə US: 'dæljə; 'dæljə/ *n* garden plant with brightly coloured flowers, growing from tuberous roots. 天竺牡丹; 大丽花(园艺植物, 花色鲜艳, 自块茎长出).
Dail Eire·ann /ˌdɔɪl 'eərən; 'dɔɪl'erən/ *n* legislative assembly of the Republic of Ireland. 爱尔兰共和国之下议院.

daily /'deɪlɪ; 'delɪ/ *adj, adv* happening, done, appearing, every day (or every weekday): 每日的(地); 每周日的(地): *Most newspapers appear ~.* 大多数的报纸每日出版. *Thousands of people cross this bridge ~.* 每日有数以千计的人通过此桥. **~ dozen,** one's usual physical exercises. 每天都做的运动. **one's ~ bread,** one's necessary food, etc. 人必需的粮食; 生计. □ **n 1** newspaper published every weekday. 每周日出版的报纸; 日报. **2** (colloq) person who is paid to do housework every weekday. (口)每周日来做家务的工人.

dainty[1] /'deɪntɪ; 'dentɪ/ *adj* (**-ier, -iest**) **1** (of persons) pretty, neat and delicate (**1, 3**) in appearance and tastes: (指人)娇美的; 俏丽的; 优雅的. *a ~ little lady.* 小巧玲珑的女子. **2** (of persons and animals) rather difficult to please because of delicate tastes: (指人及动物)因嗜好甚高而难以取悦的; 讲究的; 挑剔的: *She's ~ about her food.* 她对于饮食甚为讲究. *My cat is a ~ feeder.* 我的猫对于食物很挑剔. **3** (of things) pretty; delicate(3), easily injured or broken: (指物) 美丽的; 漂亮的; 娇嫩而易破损的: *~ cups and saucers.* 漂亮的杯盘; *~ spring flowers.* 娇艳的春花. **4** (of food) delicate(8) and delicious. (指食物)味美的. **dain·ti·ly** *adv* in a manner: 优雅地; 好看地; 娇艳地; 讲究地: *a daintily dressed young lady.* 衣着高雅的少女. **dainti·ness** *n*

dainty[2] /'deɪntɪ; 'dentɪ/ *n* (*pl* **-ties**) (usu *pl*) dainty morsel or dish of food: (通常作复数)美味的(少量)食物; 珍肴: *There were dainties of every kind in the picnic basket.* 野餐篮里有各种美味的食品.

dairy /'deərɪ; 'derɪ/ *n* (*pl* **-ries**) **1** (part of a) building where milk is kept and milk products are made. 牛奶场; 奶品场. **'~-farm,** that produces milk and butter. 奶品农场. **~·ing, '~-farming,** the business of a ~-farm. 奶品制造业. **'~ cattle,** cows raised to produce milk, not meat. 乳牛(为产奶而非为产肉所饲养者). **'~-maid,** woman who works in a ~. 奶品厂的女工. **2** shop where milk, butter, eggs, etc, are sold. 售牛奶、奶油、鸡蛋等的商店. **'~-man** /-mən; -mən/ (*pl* **-men**) dealer in milk, etc. 牛奶商; 奶品商.

dais /'deɪɪs; 'de·ɪs/ *n* (*pl* **-es** /-sɪz; -sɪz/) platform (esp at the end of a hall) for a table, lectern etc. 讲台 (尤指设于大厅之一端者, 其上可置放桌子, 讲桌等).

daisy /'deɪzɪ; 'dezɪ/ *n* (*pl* **-sies**) small white flower with a yellow centre, commonly growing wild; similar garden flower; other plants of various sorts (*Michaelmas ~*, etc) resembling it or of the same species. 雏菊; 延命菊(菊之一种小白花, 通常野生); 家园艺菊花卉; 其他各种大小类似或同属的花 (如紫菀等). *push up the daisies,* ⇨ push[2](9).

dale /deɪl; del/ *n* (esp in N England and in poetry) valley. (尤用于英格兰北部及诗中)山谷. **dales·man** /'deɪlzmən; 'delzmən/ *n* (*pl* **-men**) person who lives in the ~s (in N England). (英格兰北部)山谷中的居民.

dally /'dælɪ; 'dælɪ/ *vi* **1** [VP2A, 3A] **~ (with),** trifle; think idly about: 玩弄; 戏弄; 不慎重考虑; 玩忽: *~ with an idea or proposal;* 不慎重考虑一项意见或建议; *~ with a woman's affections,* flirt with her. 玩弄女人的爱情(调戏她). **2** [VP2A, 3A] **~ (over),** waste time: 浪费时间: *Don't ~ over your work.* 不要浪费你工作的时间.

dal·ma·tian /ˌdælˈmeɪʃn; ˌdælˈmeɪʃn/ *n* large, short-haired dog, white with dark spots. 一种短毛大狗 (毛色白, 带有黑色斑点).

dam[1] /dæm; dæm/ *n* **1** barrier built to keep back water and raise its level (eg to form a reservoir, or for hydroelectric power). 闸 (挡住流水的去路以升高其水面, 如构成蓄水库或用作水力发电). ⇨ 参较 *barrage,* a barrier across a river, usu for irrigation purposes. 作灌溉用之水堰.) **2** reservoir formed by such a barrier. 水坝围成的水库. □ *vt* (**-mm-**) [VP6A, 15B] **~ (up),** make a dam across (a narrow valley,

etc); hold back by means of a dam; (fig) hold back: 拦 (峡谷等)修筑水坝; 借水坝拦阻; (喻)拦阻; 抑制: *to dam up one's feelings/sb's eloquence.* 抑制其感情(阻止某人的雄辩).

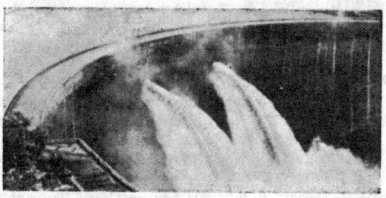

a dam

dam[2] /dæm; dæm/ *n* mother (of four-footed animals). (四足动物的)母兽. ⇨ **sire**(3).

dam·age /'dæmɪdʒ; 'dæmɪdʒ/ *n* **1** [U] **~ (to),** harm or injury that causes loss of value: 损害; 损毁 (使失去价值): *The storm did great ~ to the crops.* 那次暴风雨对农作物造成极大的损害. *The insurance company will pay for the ~ to my car.* 保险公司将赔偿我的汽车所受的损害. **2** (*pl*) (legal) money claimed from or paid by a person causing loss or injury: (复)(法律)损害赔偿金 (向造成损害者索取或由其所付的赔偿费): *He claimed £5000 ~s from his employers for the loss of his right arm while at work.* 他为在工作时所丧失的右臂向雇主要求五千英镑的赔偿费. **3** *What's the ~?* (colloq) What's the cost? (口)值多少钱? □ *vt* [VP6A] cause ~(1) to: 使受损毁; 损坏: *furniture ~d by fire.* 为火所损坏的家具.

dam·as·cene /'dæməsiːn; 'dæməˌsin/ *adj* of damask 锦缎的; 大马士钢的. □ *vt* work into damask steel. 制成大马色钢.

dam·ask /'dæməsk; 'dæməsk/ *n* [U] **1** silk or linen material with designs shown up by reflection of light: (由反光而显示图案的)花缎; 锦缎; 织花麻布; (attrib)(用作定语) ~ table-cloths; 织花桌布; ~ silk. 锦缎. **2** steel with a pattern of wavy lines or with inlaid gold or silver: 大马色钢(带波纹图案或镶有金银); (attrib)(用作定语) (or *damascene*) steel. 大马色钢. **3** '~ rose, variety originally brought from Damascus; its colour (bright pink). 粉红色蔷薇(原产于大马士革); 粉红蔷薇色.

dame /deɪm; dem/ *n* **1** (old use) woman, esp a married woman. (旧用法)妇女(尤指已婚者). **2** (title of a) woman who has been awarded the highest grade of an order[1](9): 英国获有爵位的妇女; 此种头衔: *D~ Ellen Terry.* 埃伦·特里夫人. (Cf 参较 the title *Lady*.) **3** title as used eg in 作为头衔用于 D~ Nature, D~ Fortune, nature, fortune, personified. '自然', '幸运' 的人格化. **4** (US, sl) woman. (美, 俚)女人.

damn /dæm; dæm/ *vt* [VP6A] **1** (of God) condemn to everlasting torment. (指上帝)使永远受折磨; 使永远受罚; 使下地狱. **2** condemn; say that sth or sb is worthless, bad, etc: 谴责; 指斥; 说某事物或某人无价值、坏等: *The book was ~ed by the critics.* 此书遭批评家指责. **3** (colloq) (esp as *int*) used to express anger, annoyance, impatience, etc: (口)(尤用作感叹词)用以表示愤怒、厌烦、急躁等: *D~!* 该死! *I'll be ~ed if I'll go,* I refuse to go. 我要是去就不是人(我绝不去). *D~ it all!* 该死的! *D~ you / your impudence!* 混帐! □ *n* (colloq) *not give / care a ~,* not care at all. (口)一点也不在乎. *not (be) worth a ~,* (be) worthless. 无价值. □ *adj, adv* (colloq) (intensive): (口, 强势语)非常的(地): *Don't be ~ silly / a ~ fool.* 不要那么傻(不要做个大傻瓜). **~ well,** certainly. 必然; 当然.

dam·nable /'dæmnəbl; 'dæmnəbl/ *adj* hateful; deserving to be damned; (colloq) very bad: 可恨的; 可恶的; 该受天罚的; (口)极坏的: *~ weather.* 极恶劣的天气. **dam·nab·ly** /'dæmnəblɪ; 'dæmnəblɪ/ *adv*

dam·na·tion /dæm'neɪʃn; dæm'neʃən/ *n* [U] being damned; ruin: 遭天罚; 毁灭: *to suffer eternal ~.* 受到永远的惩罚。

damned /dæmd; dæmd/ *adj* **1** the ~, souls in hell. 在地狱中受罚的灵魂。**2** (colloq) damnable: (口) 该遭天罚的; 该死的: *You ~ fool!* 你这该死的傻瓜! □ *adv* (colloq) extremely: (口) 极: ~ *hot / funny.* 极热 (可笑) 的。

Damocles /'dæməkliːz; 'dæmə,kliːz/ *n sword of* ~, threatened danger in the midst of prosperity (from the old Greek story of a man who feasted while a sword hung by a thread over him). 达摩克里斯之剑 (喻幸福中所隐伏的危机; 源出于古希腊故事, 谓有人被置于以一线悬吊之剑下而作饮宴之乐)。

damp¹ /dæmp; dæmp/ *adj* (-r, -est) not thoroughly dry; having some moisture (in or on): 不完全干燥的; 潮湿的; 有湿气的: ~ *clothes*; 湿衣服; *to wipe a window with a* ~ *cloth.* 用湿布擦窗户。*Don't sleep between* ~ *sheets.* 不要睡在潮湿的被褥中。⇨ **squib.** ⇨ **squib.** □ *n* [U] **1** state of being ~; ~ atmosphere; moisture on the surface of, or existing throughout, sth: 潮湿; 湿气; 某物之表面或内部所含的水分: *The* ~ *rising from the ground caused the walls to stain badly.* 自地面上升的湿气使墙壁沾上严重的污迹。*Don't stay outside in the* ~. 不要停留在外面的潮湿空气中。⇨ ~*-course* at **course¹(5).** **2** cast / strike a ~ over, (fig) cause dejection or unhappiness: (喻) 使沮丧或不快乐: *Their mother's illness cast a* ~ *over the celebrations.* 他们母亲的病使他们在那些庆典中闷闷不乐。**3** (also *as* ~ *'fire.*~) dangerous gas which may collect in coal-mines. 瓦斯 (可能在煤矿内聚集的) 一种危险气体; 坑气; 沼气; 甲烷。~*·ish adj* rather ~. 相当潮湿的。~*·ly adv* ~*·ness n*

damp² /dæmp; dæmp/ *vt, vi* **1** [VP6A] make damp(1): 使潮湿: *to* ~ *clothes before ironing them.* 在烫衣服前将衣服打湿。**2** [VP6A] (also *as* ~ '**dampen**) make sad or dull: 使沮丧; 使忧戚; 使扫兴: *Nothing could* ~ *his spirits.* 任何事都不能败他的兴。**3** [VP15B] ~ *down*, make (a fire) burn more slowly (eg by heaping ashes on it, or by controlling the draught of air entering a stove, etc). 减弱 (火势) (如堆灰于其上, 或控制通入炉中之中的气流)。**4** [VP2C] ~ *off*, (of young plants) rot and die because of excessive damp(1). (指幼苗) 因水分过多而烂死。

dampen /'dæmpən; 'dæmpən/ *vt*=**damp²(2).**

damper /'dæmpə(r); 'dæmpə/ *n* **1** movable metal plate that regulates the flow of air into a fire in a stove or furnace. 风挡; 气流调节器; 炉喉调节闸 (火炉或锅炉中用以控制通风量的金属板)。气闸。**2** person or thing that checks or discourages. 控制或扫兴的人或物。**damp¹(2).**

dam·sel /'dæmzl; 'dæmzl/ *n* (old use) girl; young unmarried woman. (旧用法) 闺女; 未婚少女。

dam·son /'dæmzn; 'dæmzn/ *n* (tree producing) small dark-purple plum; dark-purple. 布拉斯李 (树); 西洋李子 (树) (结深紫色小李子); 深紫色。

dance¹ /dɑːns US: dæns; dæns; dæns/ *n* [C] **1** (series of) movements and steps in time with music; special form (eg a *waltz*), tune, piece of music, for such movements and steps: 跳舞; 舞蹈; 舞步 (伴音乐而有节奏的步法); 某种形式的舞蹈 (如华尔兹舞); 舞曲; 舞乐: *May I have the next* ~, Will you be my partner in the next ~? 下一支曲子可否请你与我共舞? *Shall we join the* ~, go out among the dancers? 我们与大家齐舞好吗? *lead sb a (pretty)* ~, cause him a lot of trouble, make him follow from place to place. 使某人遭受许多麻烦; 使某人到处跟踪。**2** social gathering for dancing: 社交舞会: *to give a* ~, arrange for and invite persons to such a gathering. 举行舞会。**3** (attrib): (用作定语): '~*-rhythm.* 舞步的节拍。'~*-band* / *-orchestra nn* providing music for dancing. 奏舞曲的乐队。'~*-hall n* hall for public ~s, with a charge for admission. (收取门票的) 公共舞

厅。⇨ *ballroom* at **ball².**

dance² /dɑːns US: dæns; dæns/ *vi, vt* **1** [VP2A, C] move along in rhythmical steps, usu with music, either alone, or with a partner, or in a group: 跳舞; 舞蹈 (按照有节奏的步法移动, 通常伴随音乐, 或个人舞, 或与舞伴共舞, 或团体共舞): *Will you* ~ *with me?* 你愿和我共舞吗? *They went on dancing until after midnight.* 他们跳舞一直跳到午夜以后。**2** [VP6A] perform (a named kind of such movements or the named (style of) music for it): 跳 (某一种舞): *to* ~ *a waltz / a ballet / Swan Lake.* 跳华尔兹 (芭蕾舞, 天鹅湖)。*Is the polka often* ~*d nowadays?* 波尔卡舞现在还常有人跳吗? ⇨ *attendance upon sb*, follow him about, pay great attention to his wishes, etc. 小心侍候某人; 亦步亦趋地奉承某人; 迎合某人的心意。~ *to sb's tune*, obey him. 服从某人。**3** [VP2A, C] move in a lively way, quickly, up and down, etc: 跳跃; 雀跃: *The leaves were dancing in the wind.* 树叶随风飘舞。*She* ~*d for joy.* 她因快乐而跳跃。*The sudden pain made him* ~ *up and down.* 突然的疼痛使他蹦跳不已。*Look at that boat dancing on the waves.* 看那只随波飘荡的船。**4** [VP6A, 15A] cause to ~(3): 使跳跃: *to* ~ *a baby on one's knee.* 使婴儿在膝上跳跃。**dancer** *n* person who ~s: 舞蹈者; 舞者: *a clever* ~; 灵巧的舞者; person who ~s in public for pay. 职业舞者。⇨ **ballerina, ballet-~r. danc·ing** *part adj* who or that ~s: 跳舞的; 跳跃的: *a dancing 'dervish.* 崇拜时身体回旋舞动的伊斯兰教托钵僧。□ *n* (gerund) (动名词) [U] **1**(attrib)(stress on the first element): (用作定语) (在下列词语中重音在动名词): '*dancing-master*, professional teacher of dancing; 职业舞蹈教师; '*dancing-partner*, person with whom one (usu) ~s: (惯常的) 舞伴; '*dancing-shoes*, light shoes for dancing. 舞鞋。**2** (stress on the first element): (重音在前一词): '*ballet-dancing*; 芭蕾舞; '*tap-dancing.* 踢踏舞。

dan·de·lion /'dændɪlaɪən; 'dændl,aɪən/ *n* small wild plant with bright yellow flowers and deeply notched leaves. 蒲公英 (小野生植物, 开鲜黄色花, 叶边有深的缺口)。

dan·der /'dændə(r); 'dændə/ *n* (colloq, only in) (口, 仅用于) *get sb's* ~ *up*, make him angry. 激怒某人; 触怒某人。*get one's* ~ *up*, become angry. 发怒; 发脾气。

dandle /'dændl; 'dændl/ *vt* [VP6A, 15A, B] move (eg a child) up and down on one's knee(s) or in the arms. 在膝上或怀抱中将 (婴儿等) 举上跳下以逗弄之。

dan·druff /'dændrʌf; 'dændrəf/ *n* [U] dead skin in small scales among the hair of the scalp; scurf. 头发间的头皮屑; 皮垢。

dandy¹ /'dændɪ; 'dændɪ/ *n* man who pays too much care to his clothes and personal appearance. 过份注意衣着和外表的男人; 花花公子。**dan·di·fied** /'dændɪfaɪd; 'dændɪ,faɪd/ *adj* dressed up, etc like a ~: 衣着等似花花公子的: *a dandified appearance.* 油头粉面; 花花公子的外表。

dandy² /'dændɪ; 'dændɪ/ *adj* (sl) excellent; first-rate: (俚) 极棒的; 第一流的; 头等的: *fine and* ~. 极好的。

Dane /deɪn; den/ *n* native of Denmark. 丹麦人。

dan·ger /'deɪndʒə(r); 'dendʒə/ *n* **1** [U] chance of suffering, liability to suffer, injury or loss of life: 危险 (受害的机会); 受害、受伤或丧命的可能): *D~* ~ *thin ice!* 危险! ——薄冰! *Is there any* ~ *of fire!* 有遭火灾的危险吗? *In war a soldier's life is full of* ~. 在战争中, 士兵的生命是充满危险的。*at* ~: *The signal* (on a railway line) *was at* ~, in the position giving a warning of ~. (铁路线上的) 信号标志指在警告有危险的位置上。*in* ~ (*of*): *His life was in* ~. 他有生命的危险。*He was in* ~ *of losing his life.* 他有丧命的危险。*out of* ~: *He has been very ill, but the doctors say that he is now out of* ~, not likely to die. 他的病一直很严重, 但是医生们说他现已脱离险境。'~ *money*, extra pay for dangerous work. 危险工作的额外工资。**2** [C] sth or sb that may cause ~: 可能引起危险的物或人: *He looked round carefully for hidden* ~s. 他四周仔细观察看有

无隐伏的危险。*The wreck is a ~ to shipping.* 那艘遇难的船舶对于航运是个危险的东西。*That man is a ~ to society.* 那个人对于社会是个危险人物。

dan·ger·ous /'deɪndʒərəs; 'dendʒərəs/ *adj ~ (to/for),* likely to cause danger or be a danger: 可能引起危险的; (对…)有危险的: *a ~ bridge/journey/illness.* 危险的桥梁(旅程,疾病)。*The river is ~ for bathers.* 在这河里游泳有危险。*That dog looks ~,* looks as though it might attack people. 那只狗看来有危险(看来有咬人的可能)。**~·ly** *adv*

dangle /'dæŋgl; 'dæŋgl/ *vi, vt* 1 [VP2A, C, 6A, 15A] hang or swing loosely; carry (sth) so that it hangs or swings loosely: 悬吊着或摆动不定; 携带(某物)使悬吊着或摆动不定: *a bunch of keys dangling at the end of a chain;* 在链子的一端悬吊着的一串钥匙; *to ~ a toy in front of a baby;* 将玩具在婴儿的面前摇摆; (fig)(喻) *to ~ bright prospects* (eg of wealth, a well-paid position) *before a man.* 用光明的远景(如财富,高薪的职位)引诱某人。2 [VP2C] *~ round/about,* remain near (sb or sth) (as an admirer) hoping to obtain sth: 追随(某人或某物) 希望获得某物: *She always has half a dozen men dangling round her.* 她总有五六个男人追求她。

Dan·iel /'dænjəl; 'dænjəl/ *n* upright judge, ⇨ **Dan 1 to 6;** 正直的法官 (参看旧约但以理书1至6章); person of great wisdom, ⇨ **Mer of Ven, 4:1.** 智慧极高的人(参看《威尼斯商人》第四幕第一场)。

Dan·ish /'deɪnɪʃ; 'denɪʃ/ *n, adj* (language) of Denmark or the Danes. 丹麦的; 丹麦人的; 丹麦语。

dank /dæŋk; dæŋk/ *adj* (-er, -est) damp in an unpleasant or unhealthy way: 阴湿的 (因而令人感觉不愉快或影响健康): *the ~ undergrowth of a forest.* 森林中阴湿的下层林丛; *a ~ and chilly cave.* 阴冷的洞穴。

daphne /'dæfnɪ; 'dæfnɪ/ *n* kinds of flowering shrub. 瑞香; 月桂树(数种开花的灌木)。

dap·per /'dæpə(r); 'dæpɚ/ *adj* (usu of a small person) neat and smart in appearance; active in movement: (通常指矮小的人)整洁漂亮的; 行动迅速的: *Isn't he a little man!* 他岂不是一个短小而行动矫健的人!

dapple /'dæpl; 'dæpl/ *vt* [VP6A] (usu in *pp*) mark, become marked, with rounded patches of different colour or shades of colour, esp of an animal, or of sunlight and shadow: (通常用过去分词)使成斑点, 或变成有各种不同颜色或颜色深浅不同之圆形斑点(尤指动物, 或指阳光与阴影): *~d deer,* 有圆形斑点之鹿; *a ~d horse,* 有圆形斑点之马; *~d shade,* as when sunlight comes through the leaves of trees. (阳光通过树叶间在树下所形成)有点点阳光的树荫。*~·grey adj, n* (horse) of grey with darker patches. 灰色而带深灰色斑点的(马)。

Darby and Joan /'dɑːbɪ ən 'dʒəʊn; 'dɑrbɪ ən 'dʒon/ *n* old and loving married couple: 恩爱老夫妻: *a ~ club,* one for old couples. 老夫妻俱乐部。

dare¹ /deə(r); dɛr/ *anom fin* (*pt* **dared** /deəd; dɛrd/ or, less often, **durst** /dɜːst; dɜst/) (*dare not* is abbr to *daren't* /deənt; dɛrnt/, *3rd pers sing* is *dare,* not *dares*) (Used with an inf without *to,* chiefly in neg sentences, including those with *hardly, never* and *no one, nobody,* and in interr and conditional sentences, and in sentences to indicate doubt.) (dare not 缩写为 daren't, 第三人称单数不加 s) (与不带 to 的不定式连用, 主要用于否定句, 包括有 hardly, never, no one, nobody 的句子, 此外尚用于疑问, 条件和表示怀疑的句中) [VP5] have the courage, impudence or effrontery to: 敢; 敢于; 胆敢: *Don't (you) ~ do that again!* 不要再这样胆大妄为! *I ~n't/don't ~ speak to him.* 我不敢和他谈话。*I wonder whether he ~ try.* 我不知他是否敢于一试。*No one/Nobody ~ ask him about his intentions.* 无人敢问他的意思是什么。*He will hardly/never ~ go there again.* 他几乎不(永不)敢再去那儿了。*How ~ he say such rude things about me!* 他怎敢说出这样对我不礼貌的话! *I ~ say,* it seems to me likely or possible: 我觉得很可能; 我敢说: *I ~ say he'll come later.* 我敢说他过些时候会来的。

dare² /deə(r); dɛr/ *vt, vi* 1 [VP5, 4A] (with or without *to*) be brave enough to: (用或不用 to) 敢; 敢于: *He didn't ~ (to) go.* 他不敢去。*I wonder how he ~s (to) say such things.* 我奇怪他怎么敢说这些话。*I've never ~d (to) ask him.* 我一直不敢问他。*They wouldn't ~ (to be so rude)!* 他们不敢(这样不礼貌)! 2 [VP6A] take the risk of; face: 敢冒(危险); 面对; 不惧: *He will ~ any danger.* 他敢冒任何危险。3 [VP6A, 17] *~ sb (to do sth),* challenge; suggest that sb has not the courage or ability to do sth: 挑战; 暗示某人无勇气或能力没某事: *I ~ you to say that again!* 我谅你不敢再说那话! *He ~d me to jump from the bridge into the river.* 他挑激我, 说我不敢自桥上跳下河。*Go on, insult me! I ~ you!* 好, 你侮辱我吧! 我谅你也不敢! *'~-devil n* (often attrib) person who is foolishly bold or reckless: 蛮勇的人; 冒失鬼; 胆大鬼: *You ~-devil!* 你这个冒失鬼! *What a ~-devil fellow he is!* 他真是个冒失的家伙! □ *n* challenge. 挑激。*do sth for a ~,* do sth because one is ~d(3) to do it. 因受挑激而做某事。

dar·ing /'deərɪŋ; 'dɛrɪŋ/ *n* [U] adventurous courage; audacity: 冒险精神; 勇敢; 勇气: *the ~ of the paratroops,* 伞兵部队的冒险犯难精神, *lose one's ~.* 失去勇气。□ *adj* brave; audacious: 勇敢的; 大胆的, *a ~ robbery.* 大胆的抢劫。*What a ~ thing to do!* 这真是件有胆量的才敢做的事! **~·ly** *adv*

dark¹ /dɑːk; dɑrk/ *n* [U] 1 absence of light: 黑暗; 无光: *All the lights went out and we were left in the ~.* 所有的灯都熄了, 我们陷入黑暗中。*Some children are afraid of the ~.* 有些小孩怕黑暗。*Don't leave me alone in the ~.* 不要留下我一个人在黑暗中。*before/after ~,* before/after the sun goes down: 日落天黑以前(后): *Try to get home before ~.* 尽量在天黑以前回家。*The place is so dangerous that we don't often go out after ~.* 这地方很危险, 所以我们在天黑以后就不常出门。2 (fig) ignorance. (喻)愚昧; 无知。*keep sb/be in the ~ (about sth),* keep sb/be in ignorance: 把某人蒙在鼓里; 不让某人知道(某事): (对某事)毫不知情: *We were completely in the ~ about his movements.* 我们丝毫不知道他的行动。

dark² /dɑːk; dɑrk/ *adj* (-er, -est) 1 with no or very little light: 黑暗的: *a ~, moonless night;* 一个黑暗的, 无月光的夜晚; *a ~ corner of the room.* 房间里黑暗的角落。*It's getting too ~ to take photographs.* 天色太晚, 不能照相。*'~ lantern,* one that can have its light covered. 有遮光装置的灯笼。*'~-room,* one that can be made ~ for photographic work. (冲洗相片用的)暗房。2 (of colour) not reflecting much light; nearer black than white: (颜色)深色的; 暗色的: *a ~ dress/suit;* 深色的衣服(西装); *a ~ blue/green/brown;* 深蓝(绿, 褐)色; *~-brown eyes.* 深褐色的眼睛。3 (of the skin) not fair: (指皮肤)棕黑的: *a ~ complexion.* 棕黑的肤色。4 (fig) hidden, mysterious: (喻)隐藏的; 神秘的: *a ~ secret,* one that is closely guarded. 严守的秘密。*keep it ~,* keep a secret. 保守秘密。*the D~ Continent,* (pej) Africa (used of the time when most of it was unexplored and mysterious). (蔑)黑暗大陆; 非洲(指非洲在从前大部分未开发因而带神秘性的时代)。*a ~ horse,* race-horse with unexpected or unknown capabilities, (fig) person whose capabilities may be greater than they are known to be. 黑马 (赛马会中出人意料之外得胜的马); (喻)能力可能出人意外高强的人。5 hopeless; sad; cheerless: 无希望的; 悲伤的; 无精打采的: *Don't look on the ~ side of things.* 不要抱悲观的态度观察事物。6 unenlightened (morally or intellectually). (道德或智力)未启蒙的; 未发展的。*the D~ Ages,* (in European history) from the 6th to the 12th cc; (also) between the end of the Roman Empire (AD 476) and the close of the 10th c. 欧洲中世纪; (欧洲历史上的)黑暗时代(自六世纪至十二世纪; 亦指自罗马帝国衰亡, 即公元476年, 至十世纪末)。7 not clear to or in the mind: 意义不明的; 不易了解的; 暧昧的: *a ~ saying,* one that is obscure. 意义不明的话。**~·ly** *adv* **·ness** *n* [U] the state of

being ~: 黑暗; 晦暗: *The room was in complete ~ness* 室内一片漆黑。

darken /'dɑ:kən; 'darkən/ *vt, vi* [VP6A, 2A] make or become dark. (使)变黑暗等。 ~ *sb's door,* (facet) visit him. (玩笑语)拜访某人。

Darkey, Darkie, Darky /'dɑ:kɪ; 'darkɪ/ *n* △ (colloq) (offensive term for a) Negro or Negress. (诽) (口)黑鬼(对黑人无礼貌的称呼)。

dar·ling /'dɑ:lɪŋ; 'darlɪŋ/ *n* **1** person or object very much loved: 亲爱的人; 极可爱的人; 宠爱之物: *She's a little ~,* 她是个极可爱的小孩; *My ~!* 亲爱的! **2**(attrib, colloq) charming; delightful: (口, 用作定语)迷人的; 可爱的; 宜人的: *What a ~ little cottage!* 多么宜人的小村舍!

darn[1] /dɑ:n; dɑrn/ *vt, vi* [VP6A, 2A] mend (esp sth knitted, eg a sock) by passing thread in and out and in two directions: 织补(编织物, 如袜子): *My socks have been ~ed again and again.* 我的袜子已经一补再补。 □ *n* place mended by ~ing. 织补之处。 '~·ing *n* (esp) things needing to be ~ed. (尤指)需织补之物。 '~ing-needle, large sewing needle used for ~ing. 织补用的大针。

darn[2] /dɑ:n; dɑrn/ *vt* [VP6A] (sl) damn(3): (俚)用以表示愤怒, 厌烦, 急躁等: *Well, I'll be ~ed.* 唉, 我真要烦死了。

dart[1] /dɑ:t; dɑrt/ *n* [C] **1** quick, sudden, forward movement: 急速而突然的向前冲; 急进; 飞奔: *The child made a sudden ~ across the road.* 那小孩突然冲出马路。 **2** small, sharp missile (feathered and pointed), to be thrown at a target (marked with numbers for scoring) in the game called ~s. 飞镖(小而尖锐的投掷物,尾端有羽毛, 向目标投掷,标盘上有计分的数字,此种游戏即称为 darts)。

dart[2] /dɑ:t; dɑrt/ *vi, vt* [VP2A, C, 6A, 15A, B] (cause to) move forward suddenly and quickly; send suddenly and quickly: (使)突然而急促地向前冲; 飞奔; 投掷; 投射: *The deer ~ed away when it saw us.* 鹿看见我们就飞奔而逃。 *The snake ~ed out its tongue.* 蛇吐出舌头。 *She ~ed an angry look at him.* 她向他投以愤怒的一瞥。 *Swallows were ~ing through the air.* 燕子飞镖似地穿过空中。 *She ~ed into the shop.* 她冲进店中。

dash[1] /dæʃ; dæʃ/ *n* **1** [C] sudden rush; violent movement: 急奔; 猛冲; 突击: *to make a ~ for shelter / freedom;* 急奔以寻求隐蔽(自由); *to make a ~ at the enemy.* 向敌人突袭。 *a ~,* quickly and smartly: 迅速而利落地: *The cavalry rode off at a ~.* 骑兵队急驰而去。 **2** (usu 通常作 **a** / **the ~ of**) (sound of) liquid striking sth or being thrown or struck: 冲击或溅洒之液体(的声音): *the ~ of the waves on the rocks;* 海浪在岩石上的冲击声; *the ~ of oars striking the water.* 摇桨击水的声音。 *A ~ of cold water will revive a person who has fainted.* 泼溅冷水可使昏厥的人复苏。 **2** [C] small amount of sth added or mixed: (加入或混合的)少许; 少量: *a ~ of pepper in the soup;* 加入汤中的少许胡椒; *water with a ~ of whisky in it;* 加入少许威士忌的水; *red with a ~ of blue.* 略带蓝色的红色。 **4** [C] stroke of the pen or a mark (—) used in printing. 破折号。 ⇨ **App 9.** 参看附录九。 **5 the ~,** short race, sprint: 短跑; 短距离赛跑: *the 100-metres ~.* 一百米短跑。 **6** [U] (capacity for) vigorous action; energy: 活力; 精力; 干劲: *an officer famous for his skill and ~.* 以干练与干劲闻名的军官。 *cut a ~,* make a brilliant show (in appearance and behaviour). (在外表及行为上)大出风头。 '~·board, (a) screen on the front part of a horse-drawn cart, wagon, etc to protect from mud splashed up from the road. (马车等前部的)遮泥板(挡住自路上溅起的泥)。 **(b)** panel beneath the windscreen of a motor-car, with speedometer, various controls, etc. (汽车挡风玻璃下面, 装置速率表, 各种控制器等的)仪表板。 ⇨ the illus at **motor.** 参看 motor 之插图。

dash[2] /dæʃ; dæʃ/ *vt, vi* **1** [VP6A, 15A, B, 2C] send or throw violently; move or be moved violently: 猛掷;

猛撞; 猛击; 猛冲: *The boat was ~ed against the rocks.* 那船猛撞在礁石上。 *The huge waves ~ed over the rocks.* 掀天大浪冲击在岩石上。 *The elephants ~ed through the undergrowth.* 那些大象急速冲过下层林丛。 *D~ a bucketful of water over this muddy floor.* 拿一桶水把这泥污的地板冲洗一下。 *A motor-car ~ed past us ~ed mud all over us as it passed.* 一辆汽车自我们身边飞驰而过(飞驰而过时, 溅了我们满身泥)。 ~ *sth off,* write or draw sth quickly: 匆匆而写或画: *I must ~ off a few letters before I go out.* 我在出去以前必须赶写几封信。 **2** [VP6A] ~ *sb's hopes,* destroy, discourage, them. 使某人的希望破灭。 **3** [VP6A] (colloq, used as a mild substitute for) Damn!: (口)可恶! (咒骂语, 较 Damn 语气稍弱) *D~ it!* 可恶! ~'ing *adj* impetuous; lively; full of, showing, energy: 猛烈的; 有生气的; 精力充沛的: *a ~ing cavalry charge;* 骑兵的猛攻; *a ~ing rider,* eg one who rides a horse boldly. 勇猛的骑马者。 ~·ing·ly *adv*

das·tard /'dæstəd; 'dæstərd/ *n* (old use) bully; coward who is brutal when there is no risk to himself. (旧用法)欺软怕硬的懦夫(在无危险时却很凶)。 ~·ly *adj* of or like a ~. 怯懦的; 欺软怕硬的。

data /'deɪtə; 'deɪtə/ *n pl (pl of Lat datum)* (拉丁文 datum 的复数形) **1** facts; things certainly known (and from which conclusions may be drawn): 数据; 事实资料; 可据以下断语的材料: *unless sufficient ~ are available.* 除非有充分的事实资料可以利用。 **2** (usu with *sing v*) information prepared for and operated on a computer programme: (通常与单数动词连用)供电脑程式使用的资料: *The ~ is ready for processing.* 资料已齐备, 等待处理。 ~ **bank,** centre with a comprehensive file of computer ~. 数据库; 资料库(有包罗广泛的电脑资料卷档)。 ~ **'processing,** the performing of operations on ~ to obtain information, solutions to problems, etc. 数据处理; 资料处理(电脑对资料的操作, 以获取情报, 问题的答案等)。

date[1] /deɪt; det/ *n* **1** statement of the time, day, month, year, one or all three of these, when sth happened or is to happen: (某事在过去发生或将来发生的)日期; 年代: 年月日: *D~ of birth, 20 April 1974:* 出生日期. 1974 年 4 月 20 日; *the ~ of the discovery of America by Columbus (1492).* 哥伦布发现美洲的年代(1492)。 *What's the ~ today?* 今天是几月几日? *Has the ~ for the meeting been fixed?* 开会的日期决定了吗? '~-line, (a) (*International ~-line*) meridian 180° from Greenwich, east and west of which at any given time the calendar ~s differ by one day. 日界线; 国际换日线(即距格林威治 180度之子午线,在此线以东及以西的地区,日历上的日期永远相差一日)。 **(b)** phrase giving the ~ and place of origin of an article in a periodical. 期刊中载明一篇文章出版日期和出处的文字。 **2** [U] period of time, eg one to which antiquities belong: (古物等所属的)时代: *Many ruins of Roman ~ (= of the time of ancient Rome) are to be seen in the south of France.* 许多古罗马时代的遗迹可以在法国南部看到。 **3** (phrases) (短语) *be / go, out of '~,* be / become not modern: 过时的; 陈旧的: *will denim jeans ever go out of ~?* 斜纹粗棉布牛仔裤会过时吗? Hence, 由此产生, *out-of- adj: out-of-~ clothes / ideas / slang.* 过时的衣服(陈旧的观念; 已废的俚语)。 *be / bring sth ,up to '~,* **(a)** be / make it modern. (使)时新的; (使)合于现代标准的。 **(b)** be / bring it up to the present time: (使)直到现在: *bring a catalogue up to ~.* 增订目录使包括最近的资料。 ⇨ **update.** Hence, 由此产生, **'up-to-~** *adj:* 时新的; 现代的; 直到现在的: *up-to-~ styles / methods / books.* 最新的式样(方法, 书)。 *to ~,* so far; until now: 到目前为止: *There's no news to ~.* 到目前为止还没有消息。 **4**(colloq) social meeting arranged with sb at a certain time and place; appointment: (口)(与某人定好时间和地点的)约会: *I've got a ~ with her tonight.* 我今天晚上和她有约会。 ,**blind '~,** arrangement to meet sb socially, having not met him before. 与从未晤面的人作

社交约会。 **5** (by extension; colloq) companion of the other sex with whom ~s (4) are arranged. (引伸之义; 口) 约会的异性友伴。 ~·**less** *adj* endless; immemorial. 无尽的; 古老至人所不能记忆的。

date² /deɪt; det/ *vt, vi* **1** [VP6A] have or put a date(1) on: 加日期于: *Don't forget to ~ your letters.* 不要忘记在你的信上加日期。 *The letter is ~d from London, 24 May.* 此信系五月二十四日寄自伦敦。 **2** [VP6A] give a date(2) to: 鉴定(古物等)的时代: *to ~ old coins / sth found in an excavation.* 鉴定古币(发掘物)的时代。 *That suit ~s you, shows your age (because it is old-fashioned).* 那套衣服显示出你的年纪(因其老式的样子)。 ⇨ **4** below. 参看下列第 4 义。 **3** [VP2C, 3A] ~ **from / back to,** have existed since: 自…时代存在至今: *The castle ~s back to the 14th century,* was built then. 此堡建于十四世纪。 *The prosperity of the family ~s from the war,* They became rich (eg by making munitions) during the war. 这家人的发迹始于大战时期 (如借战时制造军火)。 **4** [VP2A] show signs of becoming out-of-date: 逐渐过时或变陈旧; *Isn't this textbook beginning to ~?* 这本教科书已开始陈旧了吗? **5** [VP6A] make a date(4) with. 与…作社交约会。 **dated** *adj* out of fashion; (of words and phrases) used in the past but not now current. 陈旧的; (指词和短语) 现已不再采用的。 **dat·able** *adj* that can be dated(2). 可鉴定时代的。

date³ /deɪt; det/ *n* small, brown, sweet, edible fruit of the date-palm, common in N Africa and SW Asia. (椰枣树所结的) 枣子(常见于北非及西南亚)。 ⇨ the illus at **palm.** 参看 palm 之插图。

dat·ive /'deɪtɪv; 'detɪv/ *n, adj* (gram) (in Latin and other inflected languages) (of the) form of a word showing that it is an indirect object of the verb; (in English, loosely used for) indirect object (eg *me* in 'Tell me your name'). (语法) 与格; 间接宾格(拉丁语及其他曲折语言中的一种词形变化, 表示其为动词的间接宾语); (英语中非严谨用法) 间接宾语(如 Tell me your name 中的 me 即是)。 ⇨ **case**¹(3)

datum /'deɪtəm; 'detəm/ *n* fact. 事实资料; 数据。 ⇨ **data.**

daub /dɔːb; dɔb/ *vt, vi* **1** [VP6A, 14, 15A, B] put paint, clay, plaster, etc roughly on a surface: 在表面涂抹(油漆, 泥, 灰泥等): *to ~ plaster on a wall;* 涂灰泥于墙上; *to ~ a wall with paint.* 油漆墙壁。 *Don't ~ the paint on too thickly.* 不要把油漆涂得太厚。 **2** [VP6A, 2A] paint (pictures) without skill or artistry. 涂鸦式地绘(画)。 **3** [VP6A, 14] make dirty: 弄脏: *trousers ~ed with paint.* 沾有油漆的裤子。 □ *n* [C,U] (covering of) soft, sticky material, eg clay. 软而黏的涂料(如黏土); 涂抹。 **2** [C] badly painted picture. 拙劣的画; 涂鸦的作品。 ~**er** *n* person who paints unskilfully. 拙劣的画者。

daugh·ter /'dɔːtə(r); 'dɔtə/ *n* one's female child. 女儿。 ~**-in-law** /'dɔːtər ɪn lɔː; 'dɔtərɪn,lɔ/ (*pl* **s~-in-law** /'dɔːtəz ɪn lɔː; 'dɔtəzɪn,lɔ/) wife of one's son. 儿媳。 ~**·ly** *adj* befitting a ~: 适于女儿的: ~*ly affection.* 女儿对父母之爱。

daunt /dɔːnt; dɔnt/ *vt* [VP6A] discourage: 挫折; 使气馁: *nothing ~ed,* not at all discouraged. 毫无惧色; 毫不气馁。

daunt·less /'dɔːntlɪs; 'dɔntlɪs/ *adj* not daunted; persevering. 勇敢的; 无畏的; 勇往直前的。 ~**·ly** *adv*

dau·phin /'dɔːfɪn; 'dɔfɪn/ *n* title of the King of France's eldest son (from 1349 to 1830). (自一三四九至一八三〇年间)法国皇太子的称号。

dav·en·port /'dævənpɔːt; 'dævən,port/ *n* **1** (GB) piece of furniture with drawers and a hinged flap that opens so that it can be used as a writing-desk. (英) 一种有抽屉并带一块木板以铰链相连可以垂下或升起用做写字台的家具; 活动书桌。 **2** (US) long seat for two or three persons, with arms and a back. (美)有扶手及靠背的长沙发。 ⇨ **settee.**

davit /'dævɪt; 'dævɪt/ *n* one of a pair of small cranes(2), curved at the top, for supporting, lowering and raising a ship's boat. 吊艇架; 轮船上悬小艇的吊柱(顶端弯曲, 可将小艇放下和拉起)。

daw /dɔː; dɔ/ *n* = **jackdaw.**

dawdle /'dɔːdl; 'dɔdl/ *vi, vt* [VP2A, C, 15B] ~ **(away),** be slow; waste time: 行动迟缓; 虚耗时光; 闲荡: *Stop dawdling and do something useful!* 不要闲荡了, 做点有益的事吧! *Don't ~ away your time!* 不要虚耗光阴! *He's always dawdling.* 他老是闲着不做事。 **daw·dler** /'dɔːdlə(r); 'dɔdlə/ *n* person who ~s. 闲荡不做事者。

dawn¹ /dɔːn; dɔn/ *n* **1** [U, C] first light of day; daybreak: 天初亮; 黎明; 破晓: *We must start at ~.* 我们必须天一亮即动身。 *He works from ~ till dark.* 他自天亮工作到天黑。 *It's almost ~.* 天差不多要亮了。 **2** [U, C] (fig) beginning; birth: (喻)开始; 发端; 诞生: *the ~ of intelligence / love / civilization.* 智力(爱情, 文明)的萌芽。 *The war ended and we looked forward to the ~ of happier days.* 大战结束了, 我们盼望较幸福日子的来临。

dawn² /dɔːn; dɔn/ *vi* **1** [VP2A] begin to grow light: 破晓; (天)初亮: *The day was just ~ing.* 天才开始亮。 **2** [VP2A, 3A] ~ **(on / upon sb),** begin to appear; grow clear (to the mind): 开始现出; 变得(为人所)明白: *The truth began to ~ upon him.* 他开始明白那道理。 *It has just ~ed on me that ...,* I have just begun to realize that .... 我刚刚才明白....

day /deɪ; de/ *n* **1** [U] time between sunrise and sunset: 白昼; 日间 (自日出至日落); 白天: *He has been working all day.* 他已工作了一整天。 *We travelled day and night / night and day without stopping.* 我们日夜不停的旅行。 *before day,* before daylight comes. 在天亮以前。 *by day,* during daylight: 昼间; 日间; 白天里: *We travelled by day and stayed at hotels every night.* 我们白天旅行, 每晚住旅馆。 *pass the time of day (with sb),* exchange greetings (eg by saying 'Good morning'). 与某人)互道安好(如说'早安')。 **2** [C] period of twenty-four hours (from midnight): 一日; 一昼夜(自午夜起至十四小时): *There are seven days in a week.* 一周有七日。 *I saw Tom three days ago.* 我在三天前看见汤姆。 *I shall see Mary in a few days' time,* a few days from now. 我再过几天就要见到玛丽了。 *What day of the week is it?* It's Monday. 今天星期几? 今天星期一。 *the day after tomorrow: If today is Wednesday, the day after tomorrow will be Friday.* 假若今天是星期三, 后天就是星期五。 *the day before yesterday: If today is Wednesday, the day before yesterday was Monday.* 假若今天是星期三, 前天就是星期一。 *this day week: If today is 1 May, this day week will be 8 May.* 假若今天是五月一日, 下星期的今天就是五月八日。 *this day fortnight: If today is 1 May, this day fortnight will be 15 May.* 假若今天是五月一日, 两星期后的今天就是五月十五日。 *day after day; every day,* for many days together. 日复一日; 一天又一天; 每日; 一连许多天。 *day in, day out,* continuously. 一天又一天; 连续不断地。 *from day to day; from one day to the next:* No one can be certain about what will happen from day to day. 没有人能确知逐日会发生什么事。 *one day,* on a day (past or future). (过去) 某一天; (将来) 有一天。 *the other day,* a few days ago. 前几天; 数天前。 *some day,* on some day in the future. 将来有一天; 他日。 *one of these days,* (used in making a promise or a prophecy) before long. (用于许诺或预言) 不久; 过不了几天。 *one of those days,* day of much misfortune. 不幸的日子。 *that'll be the day,* (ironic) that will never happen. (反语)那永远不会发生。 *if he's a day,* (of age) at least: (指年龄) 至少: *He's eighty if he's a day!* 他至少八十岁了! *not be one's day,* day when things go badly for one. 倒霉的一天; 不如意的一天。 *to a / the day,* exactly: 恰好; 刚好: *three years ago to the day.* 三年前不差一天。 Note the omission of relatives after day: 注意 day 后面关系代词的省略: *the day (on which)*

I met you. 我遇到你的那一天。*We shall have many days (on which) to talk things over.* 我们将有很多的日子可以讨论一切。**3** the hours of the day given to work: 每日工作的小时数: *I've done a good day's work.* 我已做了足足一日的工作。*His working day is eight hours.* 他每天的工作时数是八小时。*They want a six-hour day and a five-day week.* 他们要求每日工作六小时，每周工作五日。*Most workers are paid weekly, but some are paid by the day.* 大多数的工人都是按周计酬，但也有一些按日计酬。**call it a day,** decide that we have done enough (work) for one day: 认为一日的工作量已够: *Let't call it a day,* stop. 这一天的工作够了，停工吧。**all in a / the day's work,** all part of the normal routine. 每日所应做的事。**at the end of the day,** when the work, etc is completed. 工作等完成时。**early / late in the day,** (too) early / late. (太)早(迟)。**day 'off,** holiday. 假日。**day release,** permission for a worker to attend a college during a working day. 准许工人于工作日进大学进修。**4** (often *pl*) time; period: (常用复数)时代; 时期: *in my schooldays;* 在我的学生时代; *in his boyhood days;* 在他的幼年时代; *in the day of Queen Victoria,* 维多利亚女王时代; *in days of old / in olden days,* in former times; 在昔日; 昔时; *in days to come,* in future times; 在未来的时代; *the men of other days,* of past times. 昔人; 古人。**better days,** times when one was, or will be, richer, more prosperous, etc: (过去或未来) 生活更富裕繁荣的日子: *Let's hope we'll soon see better days.* 希望我们不久能过好日子。**fall on evil days,** suffer misfortune. 遭遇不幸。**the present day,** the time we are now living in. 现代。Hence, 由此产生, **'present-day** *attrib adj: present-day,* (= modern) *writers.* 现代作家。**(in) these days,** nowadays. 如今; 目下。**in those days,** then. 在当时。**in this day and age,** (cliché) in this present period. (陈辞)在今天这个时代。**5** (*sing* preceded by *his, her, their,* etc) lifetime; period of success, prosperity, power, etc: (单数, 前用 his, her, their 等) 一生; 鼎盛时期: *Colonialism has had its day.* 殖民主义曾盛极一时。*She was a beauty in her day,* before she grew old. 她年轻的时候是个美人。*Every dog has its day,* (prov) We all have good luck or a period of success at some time or other. (谚) 人人都有一段走运的时期。*those were the days,* (cliché) ie better times. (陈辞)那是在好时期; 那才是好年头。**6 the day,** contest: 竞赛: *We've won / carried the day.* 我们获胜了。*The day is ours.* 我们赢了。*We're lost the day.* 我们比赛失败了。**7** (used attrib, and in compounds) (用作定语, 并用于复合词中) **'day bed,** bed or couch for daytime sleep or rest. 白天睡觉或休息的床; 睡椅。**'day-book,** (comm) book for record of sales as they take place, for transfer to a ledger. (商)流水帐; 日记帐 (买卖东西随时的记录，将来转至总帐)。**'day-boy / girl,** one who attends school daily but sleeps at home. 走读生 (每日到校上课，晚上回家睡觉)。**day 'care** *n* [U] care for small children, away from home, during the day: 托儿(白天替人照顾幼儿): *a 'day-care center.* 托儿所。**'day-dream** *n, vi* [VP2A](think) pleasant thoughts. (作)白日梦。**'day-labourer,** one who is hired by the day. 按日计酬的雇工。**'day-long** *adj, adv* (lasting) for the whole day. 终日的 (地)。**'day nursery,** place where small children may be left during the day. 日托儿所。**'day re'lease** *n* [U] system of allowing employees off work (eg for one day per week) for educational purposes. (员工每周一日的)休假进修。**'day-return** *n* [C] return ticket (often at a reduced rate) available both ways on one day only. 限当天有效的来回票(通常票价较低)。**'day-school,** used as the opp of *boarding-school, evening school,* and *Sunday school.* 日校(用为寄宿学校，夜校及主日学校之对)。**'day shift,** (workers working a) period during the day, esp in a mine. (尤指矿场)白天工作的一段时间; 日班; 日班工人。**'day-spring,** (poet) dawn. (诗)拂晓; 黎明。**'day-time,** day(1), 白昼; 日间; 白天; 尤用于: *in the*

day-time. 在日间; 在白昼。

day·light /'deɪlaɪt; 'de,laɪt/ *n* [U] **1** light of day: 日光; 日光: *Can we reach our destination in* ~, before it gets dark? 我们能在天黑以前到达目的地吗? ~ **robbery** *n* [U] **(a)**open cheating. 公开的欺骗。**(b)** high, unfair price(s). 过高的价钱。~ **saving** *n* [U] putting the hands of the clock forward so that darkness falls later. 日光节约 (夏天 将时钟的针向前拨以使天晚一点黑)。⇨ *summer time* at **summer.** **2** dawn: 破晓; 黎明: *leave / arrive before* ~. 在天亮以前启程(到达)。

daze /deɪz; dez/ *vt* [VP6A] make (sb) feel stupid or unable to think clearly: 使(某人)茫然或晕眩: *If someone gave you a heavy blow on the head, you would probably feel* ~*d.* 假使有人在你头上猛敲一记, 你就可能会感觉晕眩。*He looked* ~*d with drugs/ was in a* ~*d state.* 他看样子似因服药物而致晕眩(在晕眩中)。□ *n in a* ~. in a bewildered condition. 在恍惚之中; 不知所措。**dazed·ly** /'deɪzɪdlɪ; 'dezɪdlɪ/ *adv* in a ~d manner. 恍惚地; 迷迷糊糊地。

dazzle /'dæzl; 'dæzl/ *vt* [VP6A] make (sb) unable to see clearly or act normally because of too much light, brilliance, splendour, etc: 使(某人)因强光, 绚烂, 壮丽等而看不清楚或行动失常; 使眼花; 使目眩: ~*d by bright lights;* 因强光而目眩; *dazzling sunshine / diamonds.* 眩目的阳光(钻石)。□ *n* [U] glitter. 闪光; 辉曜。

D-day /'di: deɪ; 'di,de/ *n* (code name for the) day (6 June 1944) on which British and American forces landed in N France, during the Second World War; unnamed day on which important work is to start. 大规模进攻开始日(二次世界大战时英美盟军在法国北部登陆的日子)(一九四四年六月六日); 该日的秘密代号; 重大工作开始之日。

dea·con /'di:kən; 'dikən/ *n* minister or officer who has various duties in certan Christian churches (eg in the Church of England, below a bishop or priest; in nonconformist churches, a layman attending to secular affairs). 基督教会中的执事牧师或职员(如英国国教中, 位于主教或牧师之下者; 在独立教会中职司非宗教事务之非正职人员)。~·**ess** /'di:kənɪs; dikənɪs/ *n* woman with duties similiar to a ~'s. 基督教会中的女执事或女职员。

dead /ded; dɛd/ *adj* **1** (of plants, animals, persons) no longer living: (指植物, 动物, 人) 已死的, 凋谢的: ~ *flowers / leaves.* 凋谢的花(叶)。*The hunter fired and the tiger fell* ~. 猎人开枪, 老虎倒地而亡。*D~ men tell no tales,* (prov, used as an argument for killing sb whose knowledge of a secret may cause one loss or trouble). (谚)死人泄露不了秘密(用作杀人灭口的理由)。*wait for a* ~ *man's shoes,* wait for sb to die in order to step into his position. 等着某人死去以便接替他的职位。*the* ~, all those who have died or been killed: 死者(之全体): *to rise from the* ~; 死后复活; *the* ~ *and the wounded.* 死者及伤者。~ **march,** piece of slow, solemn music for a funeral. 哀乐; 送葬进行曲; 悼丧进行曲。**2** never having had life: 无生命的: ~ *matter,* eg rock. 无生命的物质 (如岩石)。**3** without movement or activity: 无活动的: *in the* ~ *hours of the night,* when everything is quiet; 夜阑人静的时刻; (as *n*)(用作名词)*in the* ~ *of winter,* when there is no growth of vegetation, when the weather makes outdoor activity difficult, etc. 在隆冬时期(一切草木皆已死亡, 因为气候关系户外活动亦甚困难等)。~ **end** *n* cul-de-sac. 死巷。*be at / come to / reach a* ~ *end,* (fig) the stage from which further progress appears impossible. 到达似乎不可能再有所进步的阶段; 陷入僵局; 面临绝境。⇨ **9** below. 参看下列第9义。**4** (of ·languages, customs, etc) no longer used or observed. (指语言, 习俗等) 不通用或废行的。~ **language,** eg ancient Greek. 死的语言 (如古希腊语)。~ **letter, (a)** regulation to which attention is no longer paid. 已成具文的规章; 不再受人重视的规章。**(b)** letter kept by the postoffice because the person to whom it is addressed has not claimed it and neither he nor the

sender can be found. 死信 (邮局所保存无法投递的信件)。 **5** (of the hands, etc) numbed, eg by cold; unable to feel anything: (指手等) 麻木的 (例如受冻); 无感觉的: ~ *fingers.* 被冻僵的手指。 ~ **to,** unconscious of, hardened against: 对于…无感觉; 感觉已麻木。: ~ *to all feelings of shame;* 对于羞耻全无感觉; 不知羞耻; ~ *to the world,* (fig) fast asleep. (喻) 酣睡。 **6** complete, abrupt; exact: 全然的; 突然的; 精确的: *to come to a ~ stop;* 完全停顿下来; *runners on a ~ level,* running side by side; 并肩而跑者; *a ~ calm,* not even a breath of wind. 连一丝风也没有的平静状态; 死寂。 **go into/be in a ~ faint,** complete unconsciousness. 全然失去知觉。 ~ **heat,** a race in which two or more runners reach the winning-post together. 胜负不分的赛跑 (有两个或更多个赛跑选手同时到达终点的比赛)。 ~ **loss,** a complete loss, with no compensation; (sl, of a person) one who is of no help or use to anyone. 无可补偿的损失; (俚, 指人) 无用的人。 **the ~ centre,** the exact centre. 正中心。 ~ **shot,** person who hits the target without fail; shot that goes to the exact point aimed at. 非常准确的射手或射击。 ~ **silence,** complete silence. 十分寂静。 ~ **sleep,** a deep sleep (as if ~). 熟睡 (睡得象死人一样)。 **7** that can no longer be used: 已不可再用的: *a ~ match,* one that has been struck; 已擦过的火柴; *a ~ wire,* one through which electric current on longer passes. 不再通电的电线。 *The telephone went ~,* did not transmit sounds. 电话没有声音了。 **8** (of sound) dull, heavy; (of colours) lacking brilliance; (cricket, tennis, etc) (of the surface of the ground) such that balls move solwly: (指声音) 沉闷的; (指色彩) 不鲜明的; (板球, 网球等) (指地面) 崎岖不平的; 使球在上面滚动缓慢的: *a ~ pitch;* (板球) 三柱门之间球滚动缓慢的场地; (of the ball, in various games) out of play. (各种游戏中的球) 不合规则的; 死(球)。 **9** (various uses) (各种用法) ~·**line** n fixed limit of time for finishing a piece of work: 截止的期限: *meet a ~line,* do, finish sth by the time assigned for it. 在截止期限内做完某事。 ~·**pan** adj (of a person's face, looks) showing no emotion. (口) (指人的面孔, 样子) 不动声色的; 无表情的。 ~**weight** n **1** (with *indef art*) heavy inert mass. (与不定冠词连用) 沉重的物体。 **2** (comm) ship's loaded weight, including fuel and cargo. (商) 船之总载重量 (包括燃料和货物)。 □ adv completely; absolutely; thoroughly: 完全地; 绝对地; 彻底地: ~ *'beat/'tired;* 疲惫已极; ~ *'certain/'sure;* 绝对相信; 确信; ~ *'drunk,* so drunk as to be incapable; 烂醉如泥; ~ *slow,* as slowly as possible; 尽可能的慢; 极为缓慢; ~ *ahead,* directly ahead. 正前方。 *The wind was ~ against us.* 风正对我们迎面吹来。 *You're ~ right!* 你对极了! **cut sb ~,** ⇒ cut¹(7).

deaden /'dedn; 'dɛdn̩/ vt [VP6A] take away, deprive of, force, feeling, brightness: 除去; 消除 (力量, 感情, 亮度): *drugs to ~ the pain;* 止痛药; *thick walls that ~ street noises;* 隔绝市街闹声的厚墙; *thick clothing that ~ed the force of the blow.* 减轻了所受打击力的厚衣服。

dead·lock /'dedlɒk; 'dɛd͵lɑk/ n [C, U] complete failure to reach agreement, to settle a quarrel or grievance: 处于僵局 (完全不能达成协议, 解决争端或诉愿的局面): *to reach ~;* 造成僵持状态: *to be at/come to a total ~.* 处于僵持状态。 **break the ~,** cause change in the blocked state. 打破僵局。

dead·ly /'dedlɪ; 'dɛdlɪ/ adj (-ier, -iest) **1** causing, likely to cause, death: (可能) 致死的; 致命的: *weapons/poison.* 致命的武器 (毒药)。 *Fog is one of the sailor's deadliest enemies.* 雾是水手的死敌之一。 **2** filled with hate: 充满仇恨的: ~ *enemies.* 深仇死敌。 **3** that may result in damnation: 可遭天罚的: *the seven ~ sins.* 七项可遭天罚的大罪。 **4** that of death: 如死一般的: *a ~ paleness.* 如死人般的苍白。 **5** (colloq) excessive. (口) 过度的: ~ *determination.* 过份坚决。 □ adv like that of death: 如死一般地: ~ *pale;* 死人般地苍白; (colloq) excessively: (口) 过度地: ~ *serious.* 非常严重。

deaf /def; dɛf/ adj **1** unable to hear at all; unable to

hear well: 聋的; 听力不佳的: *to become ~;* 变聋; *the ~ and dumb alphabet,* one in which signs made with the hands are used for letters or words; 聋哑人用的字母 (以手势代替文字者); 手语; *to be ~ in one ear.* 一只耳聋。 '~-**aid** n hearing aid; small device, usu electronic, that helps a ~ person to hear. 助听器 (装有电子设备以助听觉的小器具)。 ~ **'mute** n person who is ~ and dumb. 聋哑人。 **2** unwilling to listen: 不愿意听的: ~ *to all advice/entreaty.* 不听一切劝告 (恳求)。 *He turned a ~ ear to* (=refused to listen to) *our requests for help.* 他对我们的请求援助置之不理。 ~·**ness** n

deafen /'defn; 'dɛfən/ vt [VP6A] make so much noise that hearing is difficult or impossible: 震耳欲聋; 闹声太大使不易听得清楚: *We were almost ~ed by the uproar.* 喧嚣之声使我们什么也听不清。 *There were ~ing cheers when the speaker finished.* 当演说者讲完时, 欢呼之声震耳欲聋。

deal¹ /diːl; dil/ n (board of) fir or pine wood: 枞木或松木 (板); 杉板: (chiefly attrib) (主要用作定语) ~ *furniture;* 枞木家具; *a ~ table;* 枞木桌; *made of white ~.* 白枞木制的。

deal² /diːl; dil/ n *a (good/great) ~ (of sth),* much; many: 大量; 许多: *spend a good ~ of money;* 花很大一笔钱; *take a great ~ of trouble;* 费尽心力; *cause sb a ~ of anxiety;* 使某人非常忧虑; *have a great ~ of friends;* 有很多朋友; *be a good ~ better;* 好得多了; *see sb a great ~,* often. 常常见到某人。

deal³ /diːl; dil/ vt, vi (pt, pp **dealt** /delt; dɛlt/) **1** [VP6A, 15B, 2A, 12A, 13A] ~ **(out),** give out to a number of persons: 分配; 配发 (给若干人): *The money must be ~t out fairly.* 这笔钱必须公平分配。 *Whose ~ the cards?* 谁发的牌? *He had been ~t four aces.* 他被分到四张么点牌。 *It is the duty of a judge to ~ out justice.* 公正执法是法官的职责。 ~ *sb a blow;* ~ *a blow at/to sb,* (a) hit or strike him: 予某人打击: *He ~t me a hard blow on the chin.* 他对准我的下巴用力一击。 (b) (fig) hurt; upset: (喻) 使心绪烦乱: *The news ~t me a severe blow.* 那消息使我心绪烦乱。 **2** [VP3A] ~ **in sth,** stock, sell: 经营; 买卖: *a shop that ~s in goods of all sorts;* 经营各种货物的商店; spend time on: 消磨时间于: *to ~ in gossip and slander.* 把时间用于论人是非和散布谣言。 **3** [VP3A] ~ **with sb/at a place,** do business: 与…有生意往来: *Do you ~ with Smith, the butcher?* 你与肉商史密斯有生意来往吗? *I've stopped ~ing at that shop—their prices are too high.* 我已不在那店铺购物; 他们的价钱太贵。 **4** [VP3A] ~ **with, (a)** have relations with: 与…往来; 与…相处: *That man is easy/difficult/impossible to ~ with.* 那人容易 (不易, 极难) 相处。 **(b)** behave towards; treat: 对待; 对付: *How would you ~ with an armed burglar?* 遇到持有武器的窃盗, 你将如何对付? *What is the best way of ~ing with young criminals,* How can we make best use of good citizens? 对付少年犯最好的办法是什么 (如何使他们变成好公民)? **(c)** (of affairs) manage; attend to: (指事务) 处理。 *How shall we ~ with this problem?* 我们将如何处理这问题? **(d)** be about; be concerned with: 关于; 有关: *a book ~ing with West Africa.* 关于西非的一本书。 **5** ~ *well/badly by sb,* treat him well/badly (usu in passive): 善 (虐) 待某人 (通常用于被动语态): *He has always ~t well by me.* 他一直对我很好。 *You've been badly ~t by.* 你受到了虐待。

deal⁴ /diːl; dil/ n [C] **1** (in games) distribution of playing cards: (游戏) 发纸牌: *It's your ~,* your turn to deal out the cards. 轮到你发牌。 *a new ~,* (originally 原指 *the New D~*) programme of social and economic reform (in US); any new plan that is thought to be just or fair. 新政 (美国社会经济的改革计划); 任何被视为公正或公平的新计划。 **2** business transaction or agreement; (colloq) bargain: 成交; (口) 交易: *Well, it's a ~,* I agree to do business with you on those terms. 好的, 这样就算成交了。 *I'll do a ~ with you,* make a bargain. 我愿与你做一项交易。 *a fair/square ~,* fair

treatment. 公平的对待. *a raw / rough ~*, harsh or unjust treatment. 粗暴或不公平的对待.

dealer /'di:lər/; 'dilə/ *n* **1** person who deals out playing-cards. 发牌者. **2** trader: 商人; 贩子: *a ~ 'horse-~*; 贩马商; *a ~ in* (=person who buys and sells) *stolen goods*; 买卖赃物者; *a 'car ~*. 汽车商. Cf 参较 *a coal merchant*.

deal·ing /'di:lɪŋ; 'dilɪŋ/ *n* **1** [U] dealing out or distributing; behaviour towards others: 分配; 分发; 对待他人的态度: *He is well known for fair ~*. 他以公平待人著名. **2** (*pl*) business relations: (复)交易; 来往: *I've always found him honest in his ~s with me*. 在他与我的交易中, 我一直觉得他很诚实. *I advise you to have no ~s with that fellow*. 我劝你不要跟那个人来往.

dealt /delt; delt/ *pt, pp* of **deal**[3].

dean /di:n; din/ *n* **1** clergyman at the head of a cathedral chapter. 大教堂全体教士的主持; 主持牧师. **2** rural ~, clergyman who, under an archdeacon, is responsible for a number of parishes. 在副主教之下负责若干教区的牧师; 乡区牧师. **3** (in some universities) person with authority to maintain discipline; head of a department of studies. (某些大学的)教务长; 系主任. **4** = **doyen**. ~·**ery** /'di:nərɪ; 'dinərɪ/ *n* (*pl* -**ries**) office, house, of a ~. 大教堂主持牧师的办公室或宅邸; *group of parishes under a rural ~*. 受乡区牧师管辖的诸教区.

dear /dɪə(r); dɪr/ *adj* (-er, -est) **1** ~ (*to*), loved (by); lovable: 亲爱的; 可爱的; *Your mother is ~ to you*. 你的母亲是你所爱的. *What a ~ little child!* 多么可爱的小孩! *hold sth / sb ~*, (formal) love very much. (正式用语)挚爱某物或某人. **2** used as a form of address (polite or ironical) in speech, and at the beginning of letters: 用作称谓之词(表示客气或讽刺, 用于说话及信函的开端): *My ~ Jones*; 亲爱的琼斯; *D~ Madam / Sir*; 女士(先生)大鉴; 敬启者; *D~ Mr Green*. 格林先生阁下. **3** high in price; (of a shop) asking high prices: 索价昂贵的; *Everything is getting ~er*. 一切都涨价了. *That's a ~ shop*. 那是个索价高的商店. '*~ money*, (when loans are difficult to obtain) on which a high rate of interest must be paid. (贷款不易时)付高利借来的钱. **4** ~ (*to*), precious (to); greatly valued: (对…)贵重的; 珍贵的: *He lost everything that was ~ to him*. 他失去了所珍贵的一切. □ *adv* at a high cost: 高价地; 昂贵的: *If you want to make money, you must buy cheap and sell ~*. 如果你想要赚钱, 你必须贱买贵卖. □ *n* **1** lovable person: 可爱的人; *Isn't she a ~!* 她岂不是个可爱的人儿! *Aren't they ~s!* 他们不是很可爱吗! **2** (also 亦作 ~·**est**) (used to address a person): (用作对人的称呼): *'Come, my ~est.' 'Yes, ~'*; '来吧, 亲爱的.' '来啊, 亲爱的'; (used with *indef art*, esp when coaxing sb): (与不定冠词连用, 尤用于哄骗人): *'Drink your milk up, Anne, there's a ~.'* '把你的牛奶喝完, 安妮, 这样才是个乖宝宝.' □ *int* used to express surprise, impatience, wonder, dismay, etc: 作感叹词用, 表示惊愕、不耐烦、奇怪、惊愕等: *Oh ~!* 天啊! *D~ me!* 我的天啊! ~·**ly** *adv* **1** very much: 极; 非常: *He would ~ly* (=earnestly) *love to see his mother again*. 他极想再见到他的母亲. *He loves his mother ~ly*. 他极爱他的母亲. **2** at great cost: 付出很大的代价; 高价地: *Victory was ~ly bought*, eg when hundreds of soldiers were killed. 胜利的代价很高 (如牺牲了数以百计的士兵的生命). ~·**ness** *n* being ~; great cost. 亲爱; 昂贵.

dearth /dɜ:θ; dɜθ/ *n* ~ (*of*), (*sing* only) scarcity; too small a supply: (仅用单数)稀少; 缺乏: *in time of ~*; 在缺乏(粮食)时; *a ~ of food*. 缺乏粮食. ⇨ **shortage**, a much commoner word. shortage 远比 dearth 常用.

deary, dearie /'dɪərɪ; 'dɪrɪ/ *n* (colloq) dear one; darling (used esp by an older person to a younger person, eg by a mother to a child). (口语)可爱的人; 亲爱; 小宝贝 (尤指长辈对晚辈, 如母亲对孩儿的称呼).

death /deθ; deθ/ *n* [C, U] (as shown in the examples)

(如例句所示) **1** dying; ending of life: 死亡; 毙命; 逝世: *There have been several ~s from drowning here this summer*. 今夏这里曾有数起溺毙的事件. *His mother's ~ was a great blow to him*. 他母亲的去世对他是一大打击. *at ~'s door*, dying; in danger of ~. 在死亡的边缘; 有死亡的危险. *to ~*, so that dying occurs: 致死: *Two children were burnt to ~ in the fire*. 大火中有两个小孩被烧死. *Don't work yourself to ~*, work so hard that you become ill and die. 不要工作得把你自己累死了. *bore sb to ~*, bore him extremely. 使某人非常厌烦. *sick to ~ of sb / sth*, extremely tired, bored, etc. 对某人或某事物厌烦了. '*~-bed*, bed on which one dies: 临死所卧之床: *The criminal made a ~-bed confession*, confessed his crimes while dying. 那罪犯临死才忏悔. '*~-duties*, taxes (to be) paid on a person's property before it passes to his heir(s). 遗产税(对死者遗产未遗留给继承人前所征的税). '*~'s head*, human skull (as an emblem of ~). 骷髅; 骷髅像(用作死亡的象征). '*~-rate*, yearly number of ~s per 1000 of population. 死亡率(每年一千人中死亡的人数). '*~ rattle* *n* unusual rattling sound in the throat of a dying person. 临终前喉间发出的急促而不清楚的声音. **2** killing or being killed: 杀死; 处死: *The murderer was sentenced to ~*, to be executed. 凶手被判死刑. *be in at the ~*, (fox-hunting) see the fox killed; (fig) see the end of an enterprise, etc. (猎狐)亲见狐被射死; (喻)亲见企业等衰落. *put sb to ~*, kill him; execute him. 将某人处死. *stone sb to ~*, kill him by throwing stones at him. 用石头将某人砸死. '*~-roll*, list of persons killed (in war, in an earthquake, etc). (战争, 地震等的)死亡名单. '*~-trap*, place where persons are likely to be killed (eg one where many fatal traffic accidents occur); place, set of circumstances, where people lose their lives (eg a burning building with no means of escape). 有生命危险的处所(如曾经发生多次车祸的地方); 使人遭难的场所(如无逃生设备的燃烧中的大楼). '*~-warrant*, official paper giving authority for the execution of a criminal, traitor, etc; (fig) sth which destroys prospects of life or happiness, ends an old custom, etc. (对罪犯, 卖国贼等)死刑执行令; (喻)毁灭人生前途或幸福, 或破除旧习俗等的事物. **3** [U] state of being dead: 死亡的状态: *eyes closed in ~*; 死后紧闭的两眼; *united in ~*, eg of husband and wife in the same grave. 死后合葬(如夫妇同葬一墓). *D~ comes to all men*. 人皆有死. (*a fate*) *worse than ~*, to be greatly dreaded. 比死亡更可怕的(命运). '*~-mask*, cast taken of a dead person's face. 照死者面孔所制的面型. ⇨ the illus at **mask**. 参看 mask 之插图. **4** *be the ~ of sb*, be the cause of sb's ~: 为某人的死因: *That old motor-bike will be the ~ of you one of these days*, you will have a fatal accident. 总有来年一天, 你的命会断送在那辆旧摩托车上. *Don't make me laugh so much*; *you'll be the ~ of me*, make me die of laughing. 不要使我笑得这么厉害; 你会使我笑死的. *catch one's ~ (of cold)*, (colloq) catch a cold that will be fatal. (口)患感冒甚重, 可能致死. '*~-blow*, blow that causes ~; (fig) shock from which recovery is impossible: 致命的一击; (喻)致命的打击: *a ~-blow to his hopes of success*. 对于他成功的希望之致命打击. *the Black 'D~*, pestilence in Europe in the 14 th c. 黑死病(欧洲十四世纪所流行的瘟疫). **5** (fig) destruction; end: (喻)毁灭; 消灭: *the ~ of one's hopes / plans*. 希望(计划)的破灭.

death·less /'deθlɪs; 'dɛθlɪs/ *adj* never dying or forgotten; immortal: 不死的; 不朽的; 永恒的: ~ *fame / glory*. 不朽的盛名(光荣).

death·like /'deθlaɪk; 'dɛθ͵laɪk/ *adj* like that of death: 像死一般的: *a ~ silence*. 死一般的沉寂.

death·ly /'deθlɪ; 'dɛθlɪ/ *adj* like death: 死一般的: *a ~ stillness*. 一片死寂. □ *adv* like death: 如死一般地: *~ pale*. 死人般地苍白.

deb /deb; dɛb/ *n* (abbr of) **débutante**. 为 débutante 之略.

dé·bâcle /deɪˈbɑːkl; deˈbɑkl/ *n* (F) confused rush or stampede; sudden and great disaster; downfall. (法)大混乱; 突然的大灾难; 崩溃.

de·bag /ˌdiːˈbæg; diˈbæg/ *vt* (**-gg-**) [VP6A] forcibly take off the trousers from. 用力脱下…的裤子.

de·bar /dɪˈbɑː(r); dɪˈbɑr/ *vt* (**-rr-**) [VP14] ~ *sb from*, shut out; prevent (sb) by a regulation (from doing or having sth): 排除; 按法令褫夺(某人)的行为权利或权利: ~ *persons who have been convicted of crime from voting at elections.* 褫夺被判罪者的选举投票权.

de·bark /dɪˈbɑːk; dɪˈbɑrk/ *vt, vi* **de·bark·ation** /ˌdiːbɑːˈkeɪʃn; ˌdibɑrˈkeʃən/ *n* =**disembark**

de·base /dɪˈbeɪs; dɪˈbes/ *vt* [VP6A] make lower in value, poorer in quality, character, etc: 贬低 (价值, 品质, 品格等): *to* ~ *the coinage,* eg by reducing the percentage of silver. 减低铸币的成色(如减低其含银的百分率). ~**·ment** *n*

de·bat·able /dɪˈbeɪtəbl; dɪˈbetəbl/ *adj* that can be debated or disputed; open to question: 可争辩的; 成问题的: ~ *ground.* 有争议的土地; 可争议之处.

de·bate /dɪˈbeɪt; dɪˈbet/ *n* [C, U] formal discussion, eg at a public meeting or in Parliament; contest between two speakers, or two groups of speakers, to show skill and ability in arguing: 正式讨论(如公共集会或国会中者); 辩论; 辩论会(二人或二团体间, 以示辩论的技巧和能力): *After a long* ~ *the bill was passed by the House of Commons and sent to the House of Lords.* 经过长久讨论后, 该议案在下议院中通过, 并经送达上议院. *After much* ~ *Harry was chosen captain of the football team.* 经过许多讨论后, 哈里被选为足球队长. *Who opened the* ~, *was the* first *to speak?* 谁最先发言(开始辩论)? *The question under* ~ *was* .... 在争辩中的问题是…. □ *vt, vi* [VP6A, 8, 10, 2A, C] have a ~ about; take part in a ~; think over in order to decide: 正式讨论; 辩论; 参加辩论; 考虑以便决定: *to* ~ *a question with sb;* 与某人辩论一问题; *to* ~ *about sth;* 辩论某事; *a debating society.* 辩论社. *We were debating whether to go to the mountains or to the seaside.* 我们正在辩论到底是去山上还是去海边. **de·bater** *n* one who ~s. 辩论者.

de·bauch /dɪˈbɔːtʃ; dɪˈbɔtʃ/ *vt* [VP6A] cause (sb) to lose virtue, to act immorally; turn (sb) away from good taste or judgement. 使(某人)失去美德或道德败坏; 使(某人)陷于低级趣味. □ *n* [C] occasion of excessive drinking, immoral behaviour, usu in company: a *drunken* ~. 纵饮及行为放荡的场合(通常指与同伴在一起): *a drunken* ~. 纵饮作乐. ~**·ery** /dɪˈbɔːtʃərɪ; dɪˈbɔtʃərɪ/ *n* [U] intemperance and indulgence in sensual pleasures: 放纵及沉溺于声色的享乐: *a life of* ~*ery;* 放荡的生活; (*pl* **-ries**) instances or periods of this. 放荡的实例或时期. ~**ee** /dɪˌbɔːˈtʃiː; ˌdebɔˈtʃi/ *n* ~*ed* person. 放荡者.

de·ben·ture /dɪˈbentʃə(r); dɪˈbentʃər/ *n* [C] (fin) certificate given by a business corporation, etc as a receipt for money lent at a fixed rate of interest until the principal(4) is repaid. (财政)债券(企业公司等发行, 言明一定的利息至本金还回时为止).

de·bili·tate /dɪˈbɪlɪteɪt; dɪˈbɪlə͵tet/ *vt* [VP6A] make (a person, his constitution) weak: 使 (人, 其体格)衰弱: *a debilitating climate.* 不宜人的气候.

de·bil·ity /dɪˈbɪlətɪ; dɪˈbɪlətɪ/ *n* [U] weakness (of health, purpose): (健康, 决心的)衰弱; 虚弱; 软弱: *After her long illness she is suffering from general* ~. 久病之后, 她现在全身虚弱.

debit /ˈdebɪt; ˈdɛbɪt/ *n* (book-keeping) entry (in an account) of a sum owing. (簿记)(帐簿中所记)负债的项目; 借方金额. '~**-side,** lefthand side of an account, on which such entries are made. 借方(帐簿中左方记载借方金额之处). ⇨ **credit**¹(4). □ *vt* [VP6A, 14] ~ *sth* (*against / to sb*), put money on the ~ side of (sb's account): 将 (一笔钱) 记入 (某人帐户的) 借方: ~ *£5 against my account,* 在我的帐户的借方记入五英镑; ~*£5 to me.* 在我的帐户的借方记入五英镑. ~ *sb* (*with sth*),

give him a ~ (of money): 在某人的借方记入(一笔钱): ~ *sb / sb's account with £5.* 在某人(某人帐户)的借方记入五英镑.

deb·on·air /ˌdebəˈneə(r); ͵dɛbəˈnɛr/ *adj* cheerful; bright and light-hearted. 高兴的; 心情愉快的.

de·bouch /dɪˈbaʊtʃ; dɪˈbautʃ/ *vt, vi* [VP6A, 2A] (cause to) emerge or issue. (使)出现或发出.

de·brief /ˌdiːˈbriːf; diˈbrif/ *vt* [VP6A] question, examine, eg persons who have returned from a mission, etc, to obtain information. 向(任务完毕归来人员等)询问以获取情报. ⇨ **brief**².

de·bris, dé·bris /ˈdeɪbriː; dəˈbri:; deˈbri/ *n* [U] scattered broken pieces; wreckage: 散乱的碎片; 残骸: *searching among the* ~ *after the explosion.* 爆炸后在碎片中搜寻.

debt /det; dɛt/ *n* [C, U] payment which must be, but has not yet been, paid to sb; obligation: 必须付出而尚未付出的钱款; 债; 债务; 人情债: *If I pay all my* ~*s I shall have no money left.* 如果我偿清了所有的债, 我就一文钱不剩了. *I owe him a* ~ *of gratitude for all he has done for me.* 我欠他一笔人情债因为他曾帮我的忙. **be in / out of** ~, owe / not owe money, 欠(不欠)债. **get into / out of** ~, reach a point where one owes / does not owe money: 欠(偿)债: *It's much easier to get into* ~ *than to get out of* ~. 欠债容易偿债难. **National D**~ *n* money owed by the State to those who have lent it money. 公债 (国家对人民所负的债). ⇨ **bad**¹(4), **honour**¹(2). ~**or** /-tə(r); -tɚ/ *n* person who is in ~ to another. 负债者; 债务人.

de·bug /ˌdiːˈbʌg; diˈbʌg/ *vt* (**-gg-**) [VP6A] (colloq) search for and remove (possible causes of trouble, faults, errors, eg from a computer programme, engines on a production line). (口)寻找并除去(可能导致例如自电脑作业或生产线之引擎中的麻烦, 错误等的原因).

de·bunk /ˌdiːˈbʌŋk; diˈbʌŋk/ *vt* [VP6A] reveal the truth about (a person, idea, institution) by stripping away false sentiments, traditions, etc. 揭开虚伪的感情, 传统等以露出关于(人, 观念, 习尚等)的真相.

debut, début /ˈdeɪbjuː; dɪˈbju:; drˈbju/ *n* (esp of a young woman) first appearance at adult parties and other social events; (of an actor, musician, etc) first appearance on a public stage: (尤指年轻女子)初次参加成人的宴会及其他社交场合; (指演员, 音乐家等)初次登台: *to make one's* ~. 初次登台; 初次参加社交活动.

debu·tante, déb~ /ˈdebjuːtɑːnt; ͵dɛbjuˈtɑnt / *n* young woman making her debut in high society. 初次参加上流社交场合的少女.

deca- /ˈdekə; ˈdɛkə/ *pref* ten (in the metric system). (米制中)十.

dec·ade /ˈdekeɪd; ˈdɛked/ *n* period of ten years: 十年的期间: *the* first ~ *of the* 20*th century,* ie 1900—1909. 二十世纪的最初十年(一九〇〇至一九〇九年).

deca·dence /ˈdekədəns; ˈdɛkədns/ *n* [U] falling to a lower level (in morals, art, literature, etc esp after a period at a high level). (道德, 艺术, 文学等经过极盛时期以后的)衰颓; 衰微; 颓废.

deca·dent /ˈdekədənt; ˈdɛkədənt/ *adj* in a state of decadence. 衰落的; 衰微的; 堕落的. □ *n* person in this state. 堕落者; 颓废者.

Deca·logue /ˈdekəlɒg; ˈdɛkə͵lɔg/ *n* **the** ~, the Ten Commandments of Moses. 摩西的十诫. ⇨ **commandment**; ⇨ **Exod 20: 1—17.** 参看旧约圣经出埃及记第 20 章 1 至 17 节.

de·camp /dɪˈkæmp; dɪˈkæmp/ *vi* [VP2A, 3A] (*with*), go away suddenly (and often secretly). 突然(且时常秘密地)离开; 逃亡.

de·cant /dɪˈkænt; dɪˈkænt/ *vt* [VP6A] pour (wine, etc) from a bottle into another vessel slowly so as not to disturb the sediment. 慢慢地自瓶中将(酒等)倒于另一盛器中, 使不致搅动瓶中的沉淀物. ~**er** *n* vessel, usu of decorated glass with a stopper, into which liquor is ~ed. 玻璃酒瓶(通常有塞子, 用以盛去沉淀的酒等).

decanters

de·capi·tate /dɪˈkæpɪteɪt; dɪˈkæpəˌtet/ vt [VP6A] behead (esp as a legal punishment). 斩首; 杀头(尤指作为刑罚者). **de·capi·ta·tion** /dɪˌkæpɪˈteɪʃn; dɪˌkæpəˈteʃən/ n

de·car·bon·ize /ˌdiːˈkɑːbənaɪz; diˈkɑrbənˌaɪz/ vt remove carbon from, esp an internal combustion engine. 除去(内燃机等)的碳.

deca·syl·lable /ˈdekəsɪləbl; ˈdekəˌsɪləbl/ n deca·syl·labic /ˌdekəsɪˈlæbɪk; ˌdekəsɪˈlæbɪk/ adj (line) of ten syllables. 含十个音节的(一行诗).

de·cay /dɪˈkeɪ; dɪˈke/ vi [VP2A] go bad; lose power, health: 变坏; 腐败; 衰落; 衰败; 衰弱: ~ing teeth / vegetables. 龋齿(腐烂的蔬菜). Our powers ~ in old age. 我们的体力在老年时衰退. What caused the Roman Empire to ~? 罗马帝国衰亡的原因何在? □ n [U] decaying: 变坏, 腐败; 衰落; 衰败; 衰弱: the ~ of the teeth. 牙齿的腐损. The house is in ~. 这房子已腐朽. Old civilizations may fall into ~, lose strength. 古老的文化可能衰落.

de·cease /dɪˈsiːs; dɪˈsis/ n [U] (formal, legal) (a person's) death. (正式用语, 法律)(人的)死亡. □ vi die. 死亡. the ~d, (formal, legal) person who has, persons who have, recently died. (正式用语, 法律)死者; 最近去世者.

de·ceit /dɪˈsiːt; dɪˈsit/ n 1 [U] deceiving; causing a person to accept as true or genuine sth that is false: 欺骗; 蒙骗: She is incapable of ~, would never tell lies, etc. 她是绝不会欺骗的. 2 [C] lie; dishonest trick. 谎言; 骗术.

de·ceit·ful /dɪˈsiːtfl; dɪˈsitfəl/ adj 1 in the habit of deceiving: 惯于欺骗的: No one can admire a ~ boy. 没有人会赏识爱骗人的男孩. 2 intended to deceive; misleading in appearance, etc: 用以骗人的; 外表等使人发生错误想法的: ~ words / behaviour. 骗人的话(行为). ~·ly /-fʊlɪ; -fəlɪ/ adv ~·ness n

de·ceive /dɪˈsiːv; dɪˈsiv/ vt [VP6A, 14] ~ (in / into), cause (sb) to believe sth that is false; play a trick on; mislead (on purpose): 使(某人)相信不真实的事; 欺骗; 诈骗; (故意)使人有错误的想法: You can't pass the examination without working hard, so don't ~ yourself. 你不用功就不能考及格, 所以不要自欺. I've been ~d in you, have found that you were not what I thought you were. 我对你感到失望(发觉你并非如我原来所想象的那样). We were ~d into the belief / ~d into believing that ... 我们被骗得相信 …. **de·ceiver** /-və(r); -vɚ/ n person who ~s. 骗者; 骗子; 欺骗的人. **de·ceiv·ing·ly** adv

de·celer·ate /ˌdiːˈseləreɪt; diˈseləˌret/ vt, vi (cause to) diminish speed. (使)减速. ⇨ **accelerate**.

De·cem·ber /dɪˈsembə(r); dɪˈsembɚ/ n twelfth month of the year. 十二月.

de·cency /ˈdiːsnsɪ; ˈdisnsɪ/ n 1 [U] (the quality of) being decent; (regard for the) general opinion as to what is decent; 正派; 适合; 可敬; (合乎)一般人对于规矩和礼貌的看法: an offence against ~, eg appearing naked in public. 违犯社会行为标准的事; 可羞的事(如当众裸体). 2 (pl) (复) the decencies, requirements of respectable behaviour in society: 社会所要求的可敬的行为或标准; 礼貌; 规矩: We must observe the decencies. 我们必须遵守社会行为标准.

de·cent /ˈdiːsnt; ˈdisnt/ adj 1 right and suitable; respectful: 正当而合适的; 可敬的: Put on some ~ clothes before you call on the Smiths. 去拜访史密斯家人的时候, 应穿适当的衣服. Poor people cannot always live in ~ conditions. 穷人生活不能经常保持体面. 2 modest; not likely to shock or embarrass others (the only sense for which indecent is the opposite): 文雅的; 优雅的; 不致使别人感觉可羞的(这是唯一一与indecent相反的意义): ~ language and behaviour. 高雅的谈吐和行为. Never tell stories that are not ~. 切勿讲不雅的故事. 3 (colloq) likeable; satisfactory: (口)尚可的: He's a very ~ fellow. 他是个很规矩的人. He gave us quite a ~ dinner. 他请我们吃了一顿很不错的饭. ~·ly adv in a ~ (1, 2) manner: 尚佳地; 合规矩地; 高雅地: ~ly dressed; 穿着体面; behave ~ly; 行为规矩; (colloq): (口): He's doing very ~ly, eg making a good income. 他的境况尚佳(如收入不错).

de·cen·tra·lize /ˌdiːˈsentrəlaɪz; diˈsentrəˌlaɪz/ [VP6A] give greater powers (for self-government, etc) to (places, branches, etc away from the centre). 分权(给予各地方, 分支机构等较大的自治权等). **de·cen·tra·liz·ation** /ˌdiːˌsentrəlaɪˈzeɪʃn US: -lɪˈz-; dɪˌsentrələˈzeʃən/ n

de·cep·tion /dɪˈsepʃn; dɪˈsepʃən/ n 1 [U] deceiving; being deceived: 欺骗; 诈骗; 受骗: to practise ~ on the public. 欺骗公众耳目. 2 [C] trick intended to deceive: 诈术; 骗术; 诡计: a gross ~. 粗鄙的骗术.

de·cep·tive /dɪˈseptɪv; dɪˈseptɪv/ adj deceiving: 欺骗的; 不实的: Appearances are often ~. Things are not always what they seem to be. 外表常是靠不住的. ~·ly adv

deci- /ˈdesɪ; ˈdesɪ/ pref one-tenth (in the metric system). (米制中)十分之一.

deci·bel /ˈdesɪbel; ˈdesəˌbel/ n unit for measuring the relative loudness of sounds. 分贝(测音量大小的单位).

de·cide /dɪˈsaɪd; dɪˈsaɪd/ vt, vi 1 [VP6A, 14, 2A, 3A] settle a question (or a doubt); give a judgement (between, for, in favour of, against): 解决(问题或疑惑); 判断(与between, for, in favour of, against连用): We ~d the question by experiment. 我们用实验解决此问题. The judge ~d the case. 法官对这个案子已做了判决. It's difficult to ~ between the two. 很难在这二者之间做一取舍; 很难判定这二人的曲直. The judge ~d for / in favour of / against the plaintiff. 那法官的判决有利(有利, 不利)于原告. 2 [VP6A, 7A, 8, 9, 10, 3A] ~ (on / against), think about and come to a conclusion; make up one's mind; resolve: 考虑并下一结论; 下决心; 决定: The boy ~d not to / ~d that he would not become a sailor. 那男子决定将来不做海员. It has been ~d that the exhibition shall not be open on Sundays. 经决定展览会星期日不开放. He could not ~ what to do / what he should do next. 他不能决定该怎么办(下一步该怎么办). In the end she ~d on (buying) / ~d to buy the green hat. 最后她决定(决定买)那绿色的帽子. We ~d against (going for) / ~d not to go for a holiday in Wales. 我们决定不要去威尔士度假. 3 [VP17] cause to ~ (2): 使决定: What ~d you to give up your job? 什么使你决定放弃你的职业? **de·cided** part adj 1 clear; definite: 清楚的; 明确的; 显然的: There is a ~d difference between them. 他们之间有显然的不同. He's a man of ~d opinions. 他是个很有主见的人. 2 (of persons) having firm opinions; determined: (指人)有坚定之意见的; 坚决的: He's very ~d about it. 关于此事他的态度十分坚决. **de·cid·ed·ly** adv definitely; undoubtedly: 明确地; 无疑地: answer ~dly; 明确地答复; behave ~dly. 行事明确. 显然极佳.

de·cidu·ous /dɪˈsɪdjuəs; dɪˈsɪdʒuəs/ adj (of trees) losing their leaves annually (esp in autumn). (指树)每年(尤指秋季)落叶的.

deci·mal /ˈdesɪml; ˈdesəml/ adj of tens or one-tenths:

十进的: *the* '~ *system*, for money, weights, etc; 十进制 (指货币, 重量等); *a* ~ *fraction*, eg 0.091; 小数 (如 0.091); *the* ~ *point*, the point in eg 15.61. 小数点(如 15.61 中之小数点). ~**·ize** *vt* [VP6A] express as a ~ fraction: 以小数表示: 1¹/₂ ~*ised is* 1.5; 1¹/₂ 以小数表示为 1.5; change to a ~ system: 改为十进制: ~*ize the currency*. 改货币为十进制。 ~**·iz·ation** /ˌdesɪməlaɪˈzeɪʃn US: -lˈz-; ˌdesəməlɪˈzeɪʃən/ *n*

deci·mate /ˈdesɪmeɪt; ˈdɛsə,met/ *vt* [VP6A] kill or destroy a larger part of: 杀死或毁灭…的大部分: *a population ~d by disease*. 因病死亡占大部分的人口。

de·cipher /dɪˈsaɪfə(r); dɪˈsaɪfə/ *vt* [VP6A] find the meaning of (sth written in cipher, bad handwriting, sth puzzling or difficult to understand). 解释 (密码文字, 潦草的笔迹, 难懂的事物)。 ~**·able** /dɪˈsaɪfrəbl; dɪˈsaɪfərəbl/ *adj* that can be ~ed. 可解释的。 明的。

de·ci·sion /dɪˈsɪʒn; dɪˈsɪʒən/ *n* 1 [U] deciding; judging; [C] result of this; settlement of a question: 决定; 判断; 问题的解决: *give a ~ on a case*. 判决一案件。 *Have they reached/come to/arrived at/taken/made a ~ yet?* 他们是否已有所决定? *His ~ to retire surprised all of us*. 他决定退休使我们大家都为之一惊。 2 [U] ability to decide and act accordingly; the quality of being decided(2): 决定及照此决定行动的能力; 坚定; 决心; 决断: *A man who lacks ~* (=who hesitates, cannot decide questions) *cannot hold a position of responsibility*. 缺乏决断力的人不能担负重任。

de·cis·ive /dɪˈsaɪsɪv; dɪˈsaɪsɪv/ *adj* 1 having a decided or definite outcome or result: 决定性的; 有明确的结果的: *a ~ battle*, deciding which side wins the war. 一次决定性的战役 (决定那一方在整个战争中获胜者)。 2 showing decision(2); definite: 表示决心的; 决定的; 确定的: *He gave a ~ answer*. 他给了一个确定的回答。 ~**·ly** *adv*

deck¹ /dek; dɛk/ *n* 1 any of the floors of a ship, usu of wooden planks, in or above the bull: 船的甲板 (通常系木板造, 在船身的内部或上层): *My cabin is on E ~*. 我的舱位在 E 甲板。 *Shall we go up on ~*, up (from a cabin, saloon, etc) on to the main (or promenade) ~? 我们 (从舱中、大厅等) 到主甲板 (或散步甲板) 上去好吗? ⇨ the illus at **ship**. 参看 ship 之插图。 *clear the ~s*, ⇨ **clear³**(1). '~ **cabin**, one on an open ~, one that is below the main ~. 甲板舱 (主甲板以上的房舱)。 '~ **chair**, collapsible chair of canvas, on a wooden or metal frame, used out of doors, eg in parks, the sea front, and on the ~s of ships. 用于户外可折叠的帆布椅 (有木或金属架, 例如用于公园, 海滨, 及轮船甲板上者)。 '~ **hand**, member of a ship's crew who works on ~. 甲板上工作的海员。 '~ **officers**, the captain and mates (contrasted with the engineers). 舱面船员 (指船长及大副, 二副等, 以别于轮机员)。 '~ **passenger**, one who does not use a cabin or the public rooms, but eats and sleeps on ~. 舱面乘客 (不使用舱位或厅房而食宿均在甲板上者)。 '~ **quoits** /kɔɪts; kwɔɪts/, game played on a ~(1) in which a ring (*quoit*) is thrown. 甲板上玩的掷环套桩游戏。 2 any similar surface, eg the floor of a bus: 任何似甲板的一层 (例如公共汽车车厢): *the top ~ of a London bus*. 伦敦公共汽车的上层。 3 (chiefly US) pack of playing-cards; (comm) collection of punched cards from a particular file. 3 (美) 纸牌; (商) 钉存文件中的一组卡片。 ~**er** *n* (in compounds) having a specified number of ~s: (用于复合词中) 有特定数目之甲板或层数的: 3 层甲板的船; *a single-/double-/triple-~er bus*: 单 (双) 层公共汽车; *a double-/triple-~er sandwich*, one with three/four layers of bread. 三 (四) 层三明治。

deck² /dek; dɛk/ *vt* [VP6A, 14, 15A] 1 ~ (*with/out in*), decorate: 装饰; 点缀: *streets ~ed with flags*. 挂满旗帜的街道。 *She was ~ed out in her finest clothes*. 她穿着盛装。 2 cover, provide (a boat, ship) with a deck. 为(船)装甲板。

deckle-edged /ˌdekl ˈedʒd; ˈdɛkl'sdʒd/ *adj* (of some kinds of paper, eg hand-made notepaper) having untrimmed edges. (指某些纸, 如手工制的信纸) 毛边的。

de·claim /dɪˈkleɪm; dɪˈklem/ *vi, vt* 1 [VP2A, 3A] ~ (*against*), speak with strong feeling; attack in words. 谴责; 以言辞攻击。 2 [VP6A, 2A] speak in the manner of addressing an audience or reciting poetry; recite, eg a poem, rhetorically. 如演说或朗诵诗般说话; 朗诵 (诗歌等)。

dec·la·ma·tion /ˌdekləˈmeɪʃn; ˌdɛkləˈmeʃən/ *n* [U] declaiming; [C] speech full of strong feeling; formal speech. 谴责; 以言辞攻击; 激昂的言辞; 正式演说。 **de·clama·tory** /dɪˈklæmətrɪ US: -tɔːrɪ; dɪˈklæmə,tɔrɪ/ *adj* of ~. 谴责的; 演说的。

dec·lar·ation /ˌdekləˈreɪʃn; ˌdɛkləˈreʃən/ *n* [U] declaring; [C] that which is declared: 宣布; 宣言: *a ~ of war*; 宣战; *the D~ of Independence*, that made by the N American colonies of Great Britain, on 4 July 1776, that they were politically independent, 独立宣言 (发表于一七七六年七月四日, 英国的北美洲殖民地宣布独立); *a ~ of income*, one (to be) made to the Inspector of Taxes. (向税务稽查员所提出的) 所得申报。

de·clare /dɪˈkleə(r); dɪˈklɛr/ *vt, vi* 1 [VP6A, 14, 25] make known clearly or formally; announce: 宣布; 公告: *to ~ the results of an election*. 公告选举结果。 *I ~ this meeting closed*. 我宣告散会。 ~ (*an innings closed*), (cricket) (of the captain of the team) announce that the team will not continue batting although the innings is not finished: (板球) (指队长) 宣布球队将不继续击球 (虽然赛局未结束): *Australia ~d when the score reached 500*. 当积分达 500 分时, 澳洲队宣布不再继续击球。 ~ *trumps*, (in bridge²) say which suit(5) will be played as trumps. (桥牌) 宣布王牌。 ~ *war* (*on/against*), announce that a state of war exists. (对…) 宣战。 2 [VP9, 25] say solemnly; say in order to show that one has no doubt: 郑重地说; 断言; 声称: *The accused man ~d that he was not guilty/~d himself innocent*. 被告人声言他无罪 (声言他本人无罪)。 3 [VP3A] ~ *for/against*, say that one is/is not in favour of. 赞成(反对)。 4 [VP6A] make a statement (to customs officials) of dutiable goods brought into a country, (or to a Tax Inspector) of one's income: (向海关官员) 申报进口应纳税的货物; (向税务员) 申报其收入额: *Have you anything to ~?* 你是否带有应该报税的东西? 5 (*int*) expressing surprise: (感叹词) 表示惊愕: *Well, I ~!* 真奇怪! **de·clar·able** /dɪˈkleərəbl; dɪˈklɛrəbl/ *adj* that must be ~d(4). 必须申报纳税的。

de·class·ify /ˌdiːˈklæsɪfaɪ; dɪˈklæsə,faɪ/ *vt* [VP6A] remove from a special class (esp sth hitherto secret): 公开 (原属秘密性的资料): ~ *information concerning nuclear fission*. 公开原子分裂的秘密资料。 **de·class·ifi·ca·tion** /ˌdiːˌklæsɪfɪˈkeɪʃn; ˈdɪˌklæsəfɪˈkeʃən/ *n*

de·clen·sion /dɪˈklenʃn; dɪˈklenʃən/ *n* (gram) [U] varying the endings of *nouns*, *pronouns*, and *adjectives*, according to their use in a sentence (eg in Latin). ⇨ **case¹**(3), **decline**(4); [C] class of words whose endings for different cases are alike. (语法) 名词, 代词及形容词因其在句中 (如拉丁文) 之用法而生的词尾变化; 各种词尾同形的一类词。

de·cli·na·tion /ˌdeklɪˈneɪʃn; ˌdɛkləˈneʃən/ *n* deviation of the needle of a compass, E or W from the true north. 罗盘指针的偏差 (即偏东或偏西而非指正北); 磁偏角。

de·cline¹ /dɪˈklaɪn; dɪˈklaɪn/ *vt, vi* 1 [VP6A, 7A, 2A] say 'No' (to); refuse (sth offered): 辞谢; 婉拒(邀请等); 谢绝: *to ~ an invitation to dinner*. 辞谢吃饭的邀请。 *He ~d to discuss his plans with the newspaper men*. 他谢绝与新闻记者讨论他的计划。 2 [VP2A, C] continue to become smaller, weaker, lower: 继续变小, 变弱, 变低: *a declining birthrate*, 在下降中的出生率; *declining sales*. 销售不景气。 *His strength slowly ~d*. 他的体力渐衰。 *He spent his declining years* (= the years

when, in old age, he was losing strength) *in the country.*
他在乡间度过他的晚年。**3** [VP2A] (of the sun) go
down. (指太阳)落下。**4** [VP6A] (gram) give the cases
(ie the *declension*) of a word. (语法)列述(某词)之各种
格位的词尾变化。⇨ **case¹(3)**, **inflect(1)**.

de·cline² /dɪ'klaɪn; dɪ'klaɪn/ *n* [C] declining; gradual and continued loss of strength: 逐渐衰弱；衰落；
衰败: the ~ of the Roman Empire; 罗马帝国的衰亡; a
~ in prices / prosperity. 物价的跌落(繁荣的逐渐衰
退)。**fall into a ~**, lose strength. 衰弱。**on the ~**,
declining. 衰落中；衰退中。

de·cliv·ity /dɪ'klɪvətɪ; dɪ'klɪvətɪ/ n [C] (pl **-ties**)
downward slope. 下倾的斜面。⇨ **acclivity**.

de·clutch /ˌdiː'klʌtʃ; di'klʌtʃ/ vi [VP2A] discon-
nect the clutch (of a motor vehicle) in readiness for
changing gear. 使(汽车)离合器分离以备更换排档；放
空档。

de·code /ˌdiː'kəʊd; di'kod/ vt [VP6A] decipher
(sth written in code). 译解(密码文字)。⇨ **encode**.
de·coder n (esp) device for translating data from one
code to another. (尤指)翻译密码器(将一种密码译成另一
种密码的机器)。

de·coke /ˌdiː'kəʊk; di'kok/ vt (colloq) (口) = **de-
carbonize**.

dé·colleté /ˌdeɪ'kɒlteɪ US: -kɒl'teɪ; ˌdekal'te/ adj
(F) (of a gown, etc) leaving the neck and shoulders
uncovered; (of a woman) wearing such a gown. (法)
(指女子长服等)露出颈及肩部的；(指女人)穿着此种衣服
的。

de·col·on·ize /ˌdiː'kɒlənaɪz; di'kɑlə,naɪz/ vt [VP6A]
change from colonial to independent status. 使非殖民
化;使脱离殖民地的地位。**de·col·on·iz·ation** /ˌdiː,kɒlə-
naɪ'zeɪʃn US: -nɪ'z-; ˌdi,kɑlənə'zeʃən/ n

de·com·pose /ˌdiː'kəm'pəʊz; ˌdikəm'poz/ vt, vi **1**
[VP6A] separate (a substance, light, etc) into its
parts: 分解(物质, 光线等)的成分: A prism ~s light. 三
棱镜可以分解光线。**2** [VP6A, 2A] (cause to) become
bad or rotten; decay. (使)腐烂。**de·com·po·si·tion**
/ˌdiː'kɒmpə'zɪʃn; ˌdikɑmpə'zɪʃən/ n

de·com·press /ˌdiː'kəm'pres; ˌdikəm'prɛs/ vt [VP6A]
bring back (sb in compressed air, eg in a diving suit)
to normal pressure; reduce compression in (sth). 解除
(在压缩空气中, 如潜水衣中, 之人的)压力; 减低(某物)之
压力。**de·com·pression** /ˌdiː'kəm'preʃn; ˌdikəm'prɛʃən/
n: a ~ion chamber. 减压室。

de·con·tami·nate /ˌdiː'kən'tæmɪneɪt; ˌdikən'tæmə-
ˌnet/ vt [VP6A] remove contamination from (eg what
has been affected by poison-gas or radioactivity). 净化；
消毒(如感染毒气或放射现象者)。**de·con·tami·na·tion**
/ˌdiː'kən,tæmɪ'neɪʃn; ˌdikən,tæmə'neʃən/ n

de·con·trol /ˌdiː'kən'trəʊl; ˌdikən'trol/vt (-ll-) [VP6A]
release from control (eg of trade by the Government
during a war). 解除管制(如战时政府对贸易的管制)。

dé·cor /'deɪkɔː(r) US: deɪ'kɔːr; de'kor/ n all that
makes up the general appearance, eg of a room or the
stage of a theatre. 全部陈设(例如室内);(舞台的)全套
布景。

dec·or·ate /'dekəreɪt; 'dekə,ret/ vt [VP6A, 14] **1**
~ (with), put ornaments on; make (more) beautiful
by placing adornments on or in: 装饰;加装饰品于…使
之(更加)美丽: to ~ a street with flags / the house with
holly at Christmas. 以旗帜装饰街道(在圣诞节以冬青装
饰屋子)。**2** paint, plaster, etc the outside of (a
building); put paint, wallpaper, etc on the inside
rooms of (a building). 涂油漆, 灰泥等于(房屋)之外侧;
粉刷(房屋);油漆或糊纸于(室内墙壁);装修(房屋)。**3** ~
(for), give (sb) a mark of distinction (eg a medal, an
order): 授予(某人)荣誉(如奖章, 勋位): Several soldiers
were ~d for bravery. 数名士兵因英勇而获奖。**dec·or-
ator** /-tə(r); -tə/ n workman who ~s(2): 装饰工人或油
工人;装潢工人: interior decorators. 室内装潢设计师。

dec·ora·tion /ˌdekə'reɪʃn; ˌdekə'reʃən/ n **1** [U]

decorating or being decorated. 装饰。**2** [C] sth used for
decorating: 装饰品: Christmas ~s. 圣诞节用的装饰物
品。**3** [C] medal, ribbon, etc given and worn as an
honour or award. (代表荣誉或奖励的)奖章, 勋绶等。

dec·or·ative /'dekərətɪv US: 'dekərətɪv; 'dekə,retɪv/
adj suitable for decorating(1): 适于作装饰品的; 装饰用
的: Holly, with its bright red berries, is very ~. 冬青因
有鲜红的果子, 极适于用作装饰品。

dec·or·ous /'dekərəs; 'dekərəs/ adj polite; decent.
有礼貌的;高雅的。**~·ly** adv

de·corum /dɪ'kɔːrəm; dɪ'korəm/ n **1** [U] right and
proper behaviour, as required by social custom. 社会习
俗所要求的正当而合礼的行为; 礼貌。**2** (pl) requirements
of polite society. (复)上流社会的礼节或惯例。

de·coy /'diːkɔɪ; dɪ'kɔɪ/ n **1** (real or imitation) bird
(eg a duck) or animal used to attract others so that
they may be shot or caught; place designed for this
purpose (eg a sheet of water with nets in which birds
are trapped). 用以引诱别的鸟兽以便射杀或捕捉的真鸟
或假鸟(如野鸭), 或真动物或假动物; 鸟媒; 囮子; 饵鸟; 诱
捕鸟兽之预定场所(如设有捕禽鸟之网的水面)。**2** (fig)
person or thing used to tempt sb into a position
of danger. (喻)引诱某人使陷入险境的人或物。□ vt
/dɪ'kɔɪ; dɪ'kɔɪ/ [VP6A, 14] trick (sb or sth) into a
place of danger by means of a ~: 以诡计引诱(某人或
某物)使陷于危险的境地: He had been ~ed across the
frontier and arrested as a spy. 他被引诱越过边界, 然后
当做间谍被捕。

de·crease /dɪ'kriːs; dɪ'kris/ vt, vi [VP6A, 2A] (cause
to) become shorter, smaller, less: (使)缩短, 变小, 减
少: Your hunger ~s as you eat. 你吃过东西以后就不
饿了。The population of the village has ~d by 150
to 500. 该村的人口已减少150, 只剩下 500 人。□ n
/'diːkriːs; 'dikris/ [U] decreasing; [C] amount by
which sth ~s: 减少;减少之量:There has been a ~ in our
imports this year. 我们今年的输入物品减少了。**on the
~**, decreasing: 在减少中: Is crime on the ~? 犯罪案件
是否在减少中?

de·cree /dɪ'kriː; dɪ'kri/ n [C] **1** order given by a
ruler or authority and having the force of a law: 君主
或政府所下的具有法律效力的命令;法令: issue a ~; 下
令; rule by ~. 以法令统治。**2** judgement or decision of
some law courts: 法院的判决: a ~ of divorce. 离婚判
决。~ **nisi** /dɪ'kriː 'naɪsaɪ; dɪ'kri 'naɪsaɪ/ n order
for a divorce unless cause to the contrary is shown
within a fixed period. 离婚之假判决; 有条件的离婚判决
(经一固定期间无异议方予执行)。□ vt [VP6A, 9] issue
a ~; order by ~: 下令; 发布命令: It had been ~d
that . . . ~d 下令…。Fate ~d a surprise. 命运注定一
突然或意外之事。

de·crepit /dɪ'krepɪt; dɪ'krɛpɪt/ adj made weak by old
age or hard use: 衰老的;衰老的: a ~ horse. 衰老的马。

de·crepi·tude /dɪ'krepɪtjuːd US: -tuːd; dɪ'krɛprtjud/ n
[U] the state of being ~. 老弱; 衰老。

de·cry /dɪ'kraɪ; dɪ'kraɪ/ vt [VP6A] try, by speaking
against sth, to make it seem less valuable, useful, etc;
disapprove of. 责难; 谴责; 指出某事物的缺点以贬低其价
值, 效用等。不赞成。

dedi·cate /'dedɪkeɪt; 'dedə,ket/ vt [VP6A, 14] ~
(to), **1** give up, devote (one's time, energy, etc, to a
noble cause or purpose): 奉献(如时间, 精力等以从事崇
高的事业或目的): He ~d his life to the service
of his country. 他献身为国服务。**2** devote with solemn
ceremonies (to God, to a sacred use). 举行庄严的仪式
奉献(给神, 作神圣的用途)。**3** (of an author) write (or
print) a person's name at the beginning of a book (to
show gratitude or friendship to). (指作者)将(人名)写在
书之首页(以表示感谢或友谊)。**dedi·ca·tion**
/ˌdedɪ'keɪʃn; ˌdedə'keʃən/ n [U] dedicating: 奉献; 贡
献: the dedication of a church; 教堂的奉献; [C] words
used in dedicating a book. 将一本书题献某人所用的字
句;题献辞。

de·duce /dɪ'djuːs US: dɪ'duːs; dɪ'djus/ vt [VP6A, 14, 9] ~ *(from)*, arrive at (knowledge, a theory, etc) by reasoning; reach a conclusion: (根据事实)推理; 推想; 演绎出(知识, 学说等); 获致结论: *If you saw a doctor leaving a house, you might ~ the fact that someone in the house was ill.* 假如你看见一个医生离开一个人家, 你就可以推想那家里有人生病。

de·duct /dɪ'dʌkt; dɪ'dʌkt/ vt [VP6A, 14] take away (an amount or part). 扣除; 减除(一个数量或部分)。 ⇨ **subtract** for numbers. (数字的减算用 subtract)。 ~·**ible** /dɪ'dʌktəbl; dɪ'dʌktəbl/ adj that may be ~ed. 可扣除的; 可减除的。

de·duc·tion /dɪ'dʌkʃn; dɪ'dʌkʃn/ n 1 [U] deducting; [C] amount deducted: 扣除; 扣除之量: ~*s from pay for insurance and pension.* 自薪金中所扣除的保险费及退休金。 2 [U] deducing; [C] conclusion reached by reasoning from general laws to a particular case. 推论; 演绎法; 由一般法则推演到特殊事例所获的结论。 **de·duct·ive** /dɪ'dʌktɪv; dɪ'dʌktɪv/ adj of, using, reasoning by, ~(2). 推论的; 推断的; 用演绎法的。

deed /diːd; did/ n 1 sth done; act: 所做的事; 行为; 行动: *be rewarded for one's good* ~s. 因所做的善事而得到报酬。 *D~s are better than words when people are in need of help.* 当有人需要救助的时候, 行动胜于言语。 2 (legal) written or printed signed agreement, esp about ownership or rights. (法律)(证明所有权或其他权力的)证书; 契据。 '~ *of* '**covenant,** ⇨ **covenant**(1). '~·**box** n one in which legal ~s are stored. 契据箱。 '~·**poll** n legal ~ made by one person only. 一人立的契据。

deem /diːm; dim/ vt [VP9, 25] (formal) believe; consider: (正式用语)相信; 认为: *He thought that it was/ ~ed it his duty to help.* 他认为助人是他的责任。

deep¹ /diːp; dip/ adj 1 going a long way down from the top: 深的: *a ~ well / river.* 深井(河)。 ⇨ **shallow.** '~·**sea,** '~·**water,** attrib adjj, of the deeper parts of the sea, away from the coastal water: 深海; 远离海岸的: ~*-sea fishing.* 深海捕鱼。 ⇨ **end¹**(1). *in* ~ *water(s),* (fig) in great difficulties, etc. (喻)在困境中。 2 going a long way from the surface or edge: 深长的: *a ~ shelf;* 深的搁架; *a wound;* 深的伤口; *a huge, ~-chested wrestler.* 一个高大而且胸部肥厚的摔交家。 3 placed or extending down, back or in (with words to indicate extent): 置于深处的; 纵深的(与表示程度的词连用): *a hole two feet ~;* 两英尺深的洞; *with his hands ~ in his pockets;* 两手深藏在口袋里; *water six feet ~;* 六英尺深的水; *ankle-~ in mud;* 泥深至踝; *to be ~ in debt;* 深陷于债务中; 债台高筑; *a plot of land 100 feet ~,* ie going back this distance from a street, road or other frontage. 纵深达一百英尺的一块土地(即自街道, 马路或其他前沿算起)。 *The people were standing twenty ~ to see the Queen go past.* 民众一层层站立共达二十层以观看女王经过。 4 (of sounds) low: (指声音)低沉的: *a ~ voice;* 以低沉的声调; *the ~ notes of a cello.* 大提琴之低沉的音调。 5 (of sleep) profound: (睡眠)酣: *in a ~ sleep,* from which one is not easily awakened. 在酣睡中。 6 (of colours) strong; intense: (指颜色)深浓的: *a ~ red.* 深红色。 7 brought from far down: 自深处发出来的: *a ~ sigh;* 深长的叹息; strongly felt; coming from the heart: 强烈地感到的; 来自内心的: ~ *sorrow / feelings / sympathy.* 内心深处所感到的哀伤(感情, 同情)。 8 ~ *in,* absorbed in; having all one's attention centred on: 专心的; 全神贯注的: ~ *in thought / study / a book.* 专心于思想(研究, 一本书)。 9 (fig) difficult to understand or learn about: (喻)深奥的; 难懂的; 难了解的: *a ~ mystery;* 难了解的神秘事物; *a ~ secret;* 难了解的秘密; (of a person) artful; concealing his real feelings, motives, etc: (指人)诡计多端的; 不使感情, 动机等表露于外的: *He's a ~ one.* 他是个诡计多端的人。 10 (fig) going far; not superficial: (喻)深入的; 不肤浅的: ~ *learning;* 深奥的学问; *a man with ~ insight.* 具有深远之见解的人; *a ~ thinker.* 深入的思想家。 ~·**en** /'diːpən;

'dipən/ vt, vi make or become ~. (使)变深。 ~·**ly** adv far; profoundly; intensely: 深远地; 深入地; 深刻地; 深厚地: *to bite ~ly;* 咬得很深; *He is ~ly interested in the subject.* 他对此门学科有浓厚的兴趣。 *She felt her mother's death ~ly.* 她对她母亲的去世内心深感悲伤。 ~·**ness** n

deep² /diːp; dip/ adv far down or in: 深深地: *We had to dig ~ to find water.* 我们必须挖得很深才能发现水。 *He went on studying ~ into the night.* 他继续读到深夜。 *Still waters run ~,* (prov) said of a person whose real feelings, ideas, etc are not openly displayed. (谚)静水流深; 大智若愚; 沉默者深谋(指感情, 学识等不露于外的人)。 ~·'**freeze** vt freeze (food) quickly in order to preserve it for long periods: 迅速冷冻(食物)以便长期保藏之; 冷藏: ~*-frozen fish.* 冷藏的鱼。 □ n special type of refrigerator (or a special part of an ordinary refrigerator) used for this purpose: 特别用于冷藏的电冰箱; 普通电冰箱中之冷藏室: *put surplus fruit and vegetables in the ~-freeze.* 将剩余的水果和蔬菜放在冷藏室中。 ~·'**laid,** (of schemes, etc) secretly and carefully planned. (指方案等)秘密而仔细计划的。 ~·'**mined,** (of coal) from ordinary coal-mines (contrasted with open-cast; ⇨ **open¹**(11)). (指煤)自普通煤矿矿坑中开采出来的(与 open-cast 相对)。 ~·'**rooted,** not easily removed: 根深蒂固的; 不易除去的: *his ~-rooted dislike of hard work.* 他对根难工作根深蒂固的厌恶。 ~·'**seated,** firmly established: 基础巩固的; 根源深的: *The causes of the trouble are ~-seated.* 这毛病的根源很深。

deep³ /diːp; dip/ n (poet) (诗) the ~, the sea. 海。

deer /dɪə(r); dɪr/ n (pl unchanged) (kinds of) graceful, quick-running animal, the male of which has horns. (复数不变)鹿(外形优雅, 善跑, 雄者有角)。 ⇨ the illus at **large.** 参看 large 之插图。 '~·**skin,** (leather made of) ~'s skin. 鹿皮(革)。 '~·**stalker, (a)** sportsman who stalks ~. 以埋伏或偷袭法猎鹿者。 **(b)** cloth cap with two peaks, one in front and the other behind. 有两个遮檐(一在前, 一在后)的布帽。 '~·**stalking,** sport of hunting ~ by approaching them stealthily or from concealment. 埋伏或偷袭猎鹿法。

de·esca·late /di:'eskəleɪt; di'eskə‚let/ vt [VP6A] decrease the area or intensity of, eg a war. 减少(战争等)之区域或强度。 **de·esca·la·tion** /dɪ‚eskə'leɪʃn; di‚eskə'leʃən/ n

de·face /dɪ'feɪs; dɪ'fes/ vt [VP6A] spoil the appearance of (by marking or damaging the surface of); make engraved lettering (eg on a tombstone) illegible. 污损或毁伤...的外表; 使(墓碑等的)碑文不易辨认。 ~·**ment** n [U] defacing or being ~d; [C] sth that ~s. (被)毁损外表; 毁损外表之物。

de facto /‚deɪ 'fæktəʊ; dɪ'fækto/ adj, adv (Lat) in fact, whether by right *(de jure)* or not: (拉丁)事实上(的); 实际上(不论合法与否)(的): *the ~ king.* 实际的国王。

de·fal·ca·tion /‚di:fæl'keɪʃn; ‚difæl'keʃən/ n [U] (legal) misappropriation of money entrusted to one; [C] instance of this; amount of money misappropriated. (法律)挪用公款或委托金; 所挪用的钱数。

de·fame /dɪ'feɪm; dɪ'fem/ vt [VP6A] attack the good reputation of; say evil things about. 诽谤; 诋毁; 中伤。 **defa·ma·tion** /‚defə'meɪʃn; ‚defə'meʃən/ n [U] defaming or being ~d; harm done to sb's reputation. 诽谤中伤; 某人名誉所受的伤害。 **de·fama·tory** /dɪ'fæmətrɪ US: -tɔːrɪ; dɪ'fæmə‚tɔrɪ/ adj intended to ~; 诽谤的; 意在诽谤的: *defamatory statements.* 诽谤他人名誉的话。

de·fault¹ /dɪ'fɔːlt; dɪ'fɔlt/ n [U] failure to act: 不负责; 不到场; 拖欠: *to win a case / a game by ~,* because the other party / team / player does not appear. 因对方不到庭而胜诉(不到场而赢得比赛)。 *in ~ of,* in the absence of; if (sth) is not to be obtained, does not take place, etc. 因为没有或缺乏...; 倘若(某物)未获得, 未发生等。

de·fault² /dɪ'fɔːlt; dɪ'fɔlt/ vi [VP2A] fail to perform

a duty, or to appear (eg in a law court) when required to do so, or to pay a debt. 不负责; 不到场; 不到法庭应讯; 拖欠。 **~er** n **1** person who ~s. 不负责, 不到场或不还债者。 **2** soldier guilty of a military offence. 触犯军纪的军人。

de·feat /dɪˈfiːt; dɪˈfit/ vt [VP6A] **1** overcome; win a victory over: 击败; 胜过: *They were ~ed in their attempt to reach the top of the mountain.* 他们达到山巅的企图未成功。 **2** bring to nothing; make useless; cause to fail: 使归于失败; 使无用; 使失败: *Our hopes were ~ed.* 我们的希望幻灭了。 □ n [U] ~ing or being ~ed: 击败; 失败: *a baseball team that has not yet suffered a ~;* 还没有输过的棒球队; [C] instance of this: 失败的实例: *six victories and two ~s.* 六胜二败。 **~·ism** /-ɪzəm/, -ɪzəm/ n [U] attitude, conduct, use of arguments, based on expectations of ~; 失败论; 失败主义(预期前途将失败的态度, 行为, 言论)。 **~·ist** n person with such an attitude, etc. 失败论者; 失败主义者。

de·fe·cate /ˈdefəkeɪt; ˈdefəˌket/ vi [VP2A] (med) empty the bowels. (医)通便。 **def·eca·tion** /ˌdefəˈkeɪʃn; ˌdefəˈkeʃən/ n

de·fect¹ /ˈdiːfekt; dɪˈfɛkt/ n [C] fault; imperfection; shortcoming; sth lacking in completeness or perfection: 缺点; 短处; 美中不足: *~s in a system of education.* 教育制度上的缺点。

de·fect² /dɪˈfekt; dɪˈfɛkt/ vi [VP2A, C, 3A] **~ (from) (to)**, desert one's country, one's allegiance, etc: 背叛; 变节: *the soldier who ~ed from Ruritania to Lilliput,* eg by asking for political asylum. 从理想国投奔小人国的士兵(例如以求政治庇护)。 **de·fec·tor** /-tə(r); -tɚ/ n person who ~s: 背叛者; 变节者: *~ors from the Republican Party.* 背叛共和党者。

de·fec·tion /dɪˈfekʃn; dɪˈfɛkʃən/ n [U] falling away from loyalty to a political party (or its leader), religion or duty; [C] instance of this: 背叛政党(或政党领袖); 脱党; 叛教; 变节: *~s from the Socialist Party.* 自社会党脱党的事例。

de·fec·tive /dɪˈfektɪv; dɪˈfɛktɪv/ adj having a defect or defects; imperfect: 有缺点的; 不完善的: *~ in workmanship / moral sense;* 技艺(道德感)不高的; *mentally ~,* mentally subnormal; 低能的: *a ~ verb,* eg *must.* 不完全变化词(例如 must)。 **~·ly** adv **~·ness** n

de·fence (US = **de·fense**) /dɪˈfens; dɪˈfɛns/ n **1** [U] defending from attack; fighting against attack: 防御; 防卫; 保卫战: *money needed for national ~;* 国防所需要的经费; *to fight in ~ of one's country;* 为保卫祖国而战; *weapons of offence and ~.* 攻击与防卫的武器。 *I never fight except in self-~.* 我除了自卫以外决不言战。 **2** [C] sth used for defending or protecting; means of defending: 防御物; 防御设备: *coastal ~s,* against attacks from the sea. 沿海防御工事。 *People used to build strong walls round their towns as a ~ against enemies.* 人们从前在城镇四周筑坚固城墙以抵御敌人。 *A thick overcoat is a good ~ against the cold.* 一件厚大衣足以御寒。 **3** [C, U] (legal) argument(s) used to contest an accusation; the lawyer(s) acting for an accused person: (法律)被告人的答辩; 被告人的辩护律师: *The accused man made no ~.* 被告未作答辩。 *Counsel for the ~ put in a plea for mercy.* 被告人的辩护律师递状请求从轻处刑。 *Counsel worked out a very convincing ~.* 辩护律师完成一甚有说服力的答辩。 **~·less** adj having no ~; unable to defend oneself. 无防卫的; 未设防的; 不能自卫的。 **~·less·ly** adv **~·less·ness** n

de·fend /dɪˈfend; dɪˈfɛnd/ vt [VP6A, 14] **1 ~ (against / from)**, guard; protect; make safe: 保护; 防御; 保卫: *to ~ one's country against enemies;* 保卫祖国抵御敌人; *to ~ sb from harm.* 保护某人使不受伤害。 *When the dog attacked me, I ~ed myself with a stick.* 那狗向我攻击时, 我以手杖自卫。 **2** speak or write in support of: 以言语或文字替…辩护: *~ a claim* (= uphold) *a claim;* 支持一要求; *~ a lawsuit* (= contest) *a lawsuit.* 为一诉讼辩护。 *He made a long speech ~ing his ideas.* 他发表一长

篇的演说为他的见解辩护。 *You will need lawyers to ~ you.* 你将需要律师为你辩护。 **~er** n **1** person who ~s. 辩护者; 保卫者。 Note legal term at **defence(3)**. 注意 defence(3) 的法律名词。 **2** (in sport, eg football) player who guards his goal area against attacks from the other side. (足球等运动)守门; 防守者。

de·fend·ant /dɪˈfendənt; dɪˈfɛndənt/ n person against whom a legal action is brought. 被告; 被告人。 ⇨ **plaintiff**.

de·fense /dɪˈfens; dɪˈfɛns/ (US) ⇨ **defence**.

de·fens·ible /dɪˈfensəbl; dɪˈfɛnsəbl/ adj able to be defended. 可保卫的; 可防御的; 可辩护的。

de·fens·ive /dɪˈfensɪv; dɪˈfɛnsɪv/ adj used for, intended for, defending: 防卫用的; 防御性的: *~ warfare / measures.* 防御战(措施)。 *Whether a gun is a ~ or an offensive weapon may depend upon whether you're behind it or in front of it.* 大炮是防御性武器还是攻击性武器, 可以根据你是在它的后面, 还是在它的前面而定。 □ n (usu without the) *be / act on the ~,* be in a state / act from a position of defence. 处于防御的状态; 采取守势。 **~·ly** adv

de·fer¹ /dɪˈfɜː(r); dɪˈfɝ/ vt (-rr-) [VP6A, C] put off to a later time; postpone: 延缓; 展期: *a ~red telegram,* one sent later at a cheaper rate; 迟发电报(费用较低者); *a ~red annuity;* 缓发的年金; *to ~ one's departure for a week;* 延缓一星期离开了; *to ~ making a decision;* 暂缓作决定; *payment on ~red terms,* ie by instalments after purchase. 分期付款。 ⇨ **on hire-purchase** at **hire**. **~·ment** n

de·fer² /dɪˈfɜː(r); dɪˈfɝ/ vi (-rr-) [VP3A] **~ to**, give way; yield (often to show respect): 服从; 顺从(常表示尊敬): *to ~ to one's elders / to sb's opinions.* 顺从长上(某人的意见)。

de·fer·ence /ˈdefərəns; ˈdefərəns/ n [U] giving way to the wishes, accepting the opinions or judgements, of another or others; respect: 顺从他人的意愿; 接受他人的意见或判断; 尊重: *to treat one's elders with ~;* 以恭顺的态度对待长上; *to show ~ to a judge.* 对法官表示尊重。 *in ~ to,* out of respect for. 尊重。 **de·fer·en·tial** /ˌdefəˈrenʃl; ˌdefəˈrɛnʃəl/ adj showing ~. 表示顺从或尊重的。 **de·fer·en·tially** /-ʃəlɪ; -ʃəlɪ/ adv

de·fiance /dɪˈfaɪəns; dɪˈfaɪəns/ n [U] open disobedience or resistance; refusal to recognize authority; defying. 公然反抗; 蔑视权威; 不顾; 不尊重。 *in ~ of,* showing contempt of or indifference to: 表示蔑视或不顾的: *to act in ~ of orders,* do sth one has been ordered not to do. 行动违抗命令。 *He went swimming in the sea in ~ of the warning sign telling him not to.* 他不顾警告标志而到那海中游泳。 *bid ~ to,* challenge, offer to fight. 向…挑战。 *set sth at ~,* treat with contempt; challenge: 蔑视; 挑战: *If you set the law / public opinion at ~,* you'll get into trouble. 如果你蔑视法律(舆论), 你将招致麻烦。

de·fiant /dɪˈfaɪənt; dɪˈfaɪənt/ adj showing defiance; openly disobedient. 表示违抗的; 公然不服从的。 **~·ly** adv

de·fi·ciency /dɪˈfɪʃnsɪ; dɪˈfɪʃənsɪ/ n (pl -cies) **1** [U] the state of being short of, less than, what is correct or needed; [C] instance of this: 缺乏; 不足(正确或所需之数): *suffering from a ~ of food;* 受到食物不足的痛苦; *~ diseases,* caused by a ~ of sth, eg vitamins, in diet. 营养缺乏症; 因食物中缺乏维他命等所引起的病症。 **2** [C] amount by which sth is short of what is correct or needed: 不足之数量与正确或所需之数量间的差额: *a ~ of £5.* 短少五英镑。 **3** [C] sth imperfect: 缺点; 不完美之处; 缺陷: *Cosmetics do not always cover up the deficiencies of nature.* 化妆品有时亦不能遮盖天生的缺陷。

de·fi·cient /dɪˈfɪʃnt; dɪˈfɪʃənt/ adj not having enough of: 没有足够的; 缺乏的: *~ in courage;* 缺乏勇气的; *a mentally ~ person,* one who is mentally subnormal. 低能的人。

defi·cit /'defɪsɪt/; 'dɛfəsɪt/ n [C] amount by which sth, esp a sum of money, is too small; amount by which payments exceed receipts. (尤指钱款之)不足额；收支不平衡之数；亏绌；赤字。⇨ **surplus.**

de·file¹ /dɪ'faɪl/; dɪ'faɪl/ vt [VP6A] make dirty or impure: 弄脏；使不纯洁: *rivers ~d by waste from factories.* 被工厂废物所污染的河流。 ~·**ment** n [U] defiling or being ~d; pollution. 污染；玷污；(使)不洁。

de·file² /'dɪ'faɪl/; dɪ'faɪl/ n narrow way, gorge, through mountains. □ vi /dɪ'faɪl/; dɪ'faɪl/ (of troops) march in a single file or a narrow column. (指军队)成单行或纵队行进。

de·fine /dɪ'faɪn/; dɪ'faɪn/ vt [VP6A] **1** state precisely the meaning of (eg words): 精确地解释(词等)的意义；下定义。 **2** state or show clearly: 叙述明白；详明说明；示明: *Please listen while I ~ your duties.* 请听我详细说明你的职务。*The powers of a judge are ~d by law.* 法官的权力法律有明文规定。*When boundaries between countries are not clearly ~d, there is usually trouble.* 国与国间的国界未明白划定时，通常会发生纠纷。*The mountain was clearly ~d against the eastern sky.* 那山在东方天际的衬托下显得轮廓分明。**de·fin·able** /-əbl; -əbl/ adj that can be ~d. 可释明其意义的；可下定义的；可详细说明的。

defi·nite /'defɪnət/; 'dɛfənɪt/ adj clear; not doubtful or uncertain: 明白的；确定的；无疑的: *I want a ~ answer: 'Yes' or 'No'.* 我要一个明确的回答：'是'或'否'。*I want an appointment for a ~ time and place.* 我要一个有确定的时间和地点的约会。~ **'article** n the word 'the'. 定冠词 (即the)。~·**ly** /'defɪnətlɪ; 'dɛfənɪtlɪ/ adv **1** in a ~ manner. 明确地；确切地。**2** (colloq, in answer to a question) yes, certainly. (口, 用于回答问题)是的，一点不错。

defi·ni·tion /,defɪ'nɪʃn; ,dɛfə'nɪʃən/ n **1** [U]defining; [C] statement that defines: 阐明；定义；解说: *To give a ~ of a word is more difficult than to give an illustration of its uses.* 给一个词下定义，较之给例说明它的用法为难。**2** [U] clearness of outline; making or being distinct in outline; power of a lens (in a camera or telescope) to show clear outlines. 轮廓清楚；(使)轮廓鲜明；(照相机或望远镜中)透镜之清晰度。

de·fini·tive /dɪ'fɪnətɪv; dɪ'fɪnətɪv/ adj final; to be looked upon as decisive and without the need for, or possibility of, change or addition: 最后的；被认为决定性的(而不需要或不可能加以改变或增添的): *a ~ offer/answer/edition of sb's poetry.* 最后的提议(明确的回答；某人之诗集的确定的版本)。

de·flate /dɪ'fleɪt; dɪ'fleɪt/ vt [VP6A] **1** make (a tyre, balloon, etc) smaller by letting out air or gas; (fig) lessen the conceit of: 放出(轮胎,气球等)中的空气或气体；(喻)挫…之傲气: ~ *a pompous politician.* 挫一自大的政客的傲气。**2** /,dɪ'fleɪt; dɪ'fleɪt/ take action to reduce the amount of money in circulation in order to lower or keep steady the prices of salable goods. 采取行动紧缩通货以降低或稳定物价。**de·fla·tion** /dɪ'fleɪʃn; -eʃən/ n [U] the action of deflating. 放出空气；紧缩通货以稳定物价。**de·fla·tion·ary** /,dɪ'fleɪʃnərɪ US: -nerɪ; dɪ'fleʃən,ɛrɪ/ adj produced, designed or intended to produce monetary deflation: 用以紧缩通货以降低或稳定物价的: *deflationary measures applied by the Chancellor.* 首相所采取的紧缩通货以稳定物价的措施。⇨ **inflate.**

de·flect /dɪ'flekt; dɪ'flekt/ vt, vi [VP6A, 14, 2A, 3A] ~ *(from),* (cause to) turn aside (from): (使)偏斜；(使)转向: *The bullet struck a wall and was ~ed from its course.* 那枪弹击中墙壁，因而偏斜了。**de·flec·tion** /dɪ'flekʃn; dɪ'flekʃən/ n

de·flower /di:'flaʊə(r); di:'flauə/ vt (liter or old use) deprive of virginity; ravage; spoil. (文或旧用法)夺去…的童贞；蹂躏；糟蹋。

de·foli·ate /,di:'fəʊlɪeɪt; di:'foʊlɪ,et/ vt [VP6A] destroy the leaves of: 毁去…的叶: *forests ~d by chemical means.* 用化学方法除去树叶的森林。**de·foli·ation** /,di:'fəʊlɪ'eɪʃn;

dɪ,foʊlɪ'eʃən/ n **de·foli·ant** /,di:'fəʊlɪənt; di:'foʊlɪənt/ n chemical used, eg by spraying, on vegetation to destroy the leaves. 用以毁去草木之叶的化学药品(例如喷射剂)。

de·for·est /,di:'fɒrɪst US: -'fɔːr-; di:'fɔrɪst/ vt (esp US) (尤美) = **disafforest.**

de·form /dɪ'fɔːm; dɪ'fɔrm/ vt [VP6A] spoil the form or appearance of; put out of shape. 破坏…的外形或外表；使不成形；使成畸形。**de·formed** part adj (of the body, or a part of it; fig, of the mind) badly shaped; unnaturally shaped: (指身体或其一部；喻, 指心理)畸形的；形状不自然的；不正常的: *The boy has a ~ed foot and cannot play games.* 那孩子有一只脚畸形，不能玩游戏。**de·form·ity** /dɪ'fɔːmətɪ; dɪ'fɔrmɪtɪ/ n [U] being deformed; [C] (pl -ties) deformed part (esp of the body). 畸形；(尤指身体的)畸形部分。

de·fraud /dɪ'frɔːd; dɪ'frɔd/ vt [VP6A, 14] ~ *(of),* trick (sb) out of what is rightly his; get by fraud: 骗取(某人)的所有物；以骗术得到: ~ *an author of his royalties by ignoring copyright.* 由漠视版权而骗得作者的版税。

de·fray /dɪ'freɪ; dɪ'fre/ vt [VP6A] supply the money needed for sth, pay (the cost or expenses of sth). 供给为某事物所需要的钱；付给；支付(某事物的费用)。~·**al** /dɪ'freɪəl; dɪ'freəl/ n ~·**ment** n

de·frock /dɪ'frɒk; dɪ'frɑk/ vt = **unfrock.**

de·frost /,di:'frɒst US: ,di:'frɔːst; di:'frɔst/ vt [VP6A] remove, get rid of, ice or frost (eg in a refrigerator, on the windscreen of a motorcar). 除去(电冰箱中的，或汽车挡风玻璃上的)冰霜；除霜。~·**er** n device that ~s. 除霜器；除霜装置。

deft /deft; deft/ adj quick and clever (esp with the fingers). (尤指用手指)敏捷的；灵巧的。~·**ly** adv ~·**ness** n

de·funct /dɪ'fʌŋkt; dɪ'fʌŋkt/ adj (of persons) dead; (of things, eg laws) extinct. (指人)死的；(指事物, 如法律)废绝的。**the ~,** (legal) the dead person (who is being discussed). (法律)(被讨论中的)死者。

de·fuse /,di:'fjuːz; di:'fjuz/ vt [VP6A] remove or render useless the fuse of, eg an unexploded bomb or shell; (fig) make calm; reduce the tension in: 拆除或毁去(未爆炸的炸弹或炮弹的)信管；(喻)使镇定；减除紧张或不安: ~ *a situation/crisis.* 减少一局势(危机)之紧张。

defy /dɪ'faɪ; dɪ'faɪ/ vt (pt, pp -**fied**) **1** [VP6A] resist openly; say that one is ready to fight. 公然反抗；声言不惜以武力相对。**2** [VP6A] refuse to obey or show respect to: 不服从；不尊重；违抗: ~ *ing one's superiors.* 违抗长上。*If you ~ the law, you may find yourself in prison.* 如果你不服从法律，你就可能会坐牢。**3** [VP6A] offer difficulties that cannot be overcome: 有无法克服的困难: *The problem defied solution,* could not be solved. 这问题不能解决。*The door defied all attempts to open it.* 这门无论如何打不开。**4** [VP17] ~ *sb to do sth,* call on sb to do sth that one believes he cannot or will not do: 挑激某人做某事(即相信他做不到或不愿做): *I ~ you to prove that I have cheated.* 我敢说你不能证明我曾欺骗。⇨ **defiance.**

de·gauss /,di:'gaʊs; di:'gaus/ vt [VP6A] neutralize the magnetic field of, eg a TV screen. 中和…之磁场(例如电视之荧光幕)。

de·gen·er·ate /dɪ'dʒenəreɪt; dɪ'dʒɛnə,ret/ vi [VP2A, 3A] ~ *(into),* pass from a state of goodness to a lower state by losing qualities which are considered normal and desirable: (由于失去被认为是正常和优良的特质而)退步；堕落；腐化；恶化: *Thrift is desirable, but do not let it ~ into avarice.* 节俭是好的，但不要使它变成贪财。*He denied that the young men of today were degenerating,* eg that they were becoming less hard-working, less intelligent, less honest, than those of earlier times. 他否认这一代的年轻人不如上一代(例如不如他们上一代努力,聪明,诚实)。□ adj /dɪ'dʒenərət; dɪ'dʒɛnərɪt/ having lost qualities (physical, moral or mental) that are considered normal and desirable: 失去原有正常和良好

之特质的(指身体、道德或心理上的);退步的;堕落的;腐化的: *He didn't let riches and luxury make him ~.* 他并没有让财富及奢侈使他堕落。□ *in/dʒɪˈdʒenərət; dɪˈdʒenərɪt/ ~* person or animal. 退步的人; 退化的动物。 **de·gen·er·acy** /dɪˈdʒenərəsɪ; dɪˈdʒenərəsɪ/ *n* [U] state or condition of being ~; process of degenerating. 退化; 堕落; 退步的过程。 **de·gen·er·ation** /dɪˌdʒenəˈreɪʃn; dɪˌdʒenəˈreʃən/ *n* [U] degenerating; the state of being ~d. 退化;堕落;腐化;恶化。

de·grade /dɪˈɡreɪd; dɪˈɡred/ *vt* [VP6A] **1** reduce in rank or status. 降…的阶级或职位。 **2** cause (sb) to be less moral or less deserving of respect: 使(某人)道德堕落或不值得尊敬: *to ~ oneself by cheating and telling lies.* 因欺骗说谎而自甘堕落。 **degra·da·tion** /ˌdeɡrəˈdeɪʃn; ˌdeɡrəˈdeʃən/ *n* [U] degrading or being ~d: 降级; 堕落: *a family living in degradation,* eg one that lives in slum conditions. 生活潦倒的家庭(如生活于贫苦的环境中者)。

de·gree /dɪˈɡriː; dɪˈɡri/ *n* **1** unit of measurement for angles: 度(角的单位): *an angle of ninety ~s,* (90°) a right angle; 90 度的角(即直角); *a ~ of latitude,* about 69 miles. 纬度的一度(约 69 英里)。 **2** unit of measurement for temperature: 度(温度的单位): *Water freezes at 32 ~s Fahrenheit* (32°F) *or zero (= nought ~s) Centigrade* (0°C). 水在华氏 32度或摄氏零度结冰。 **3** [C, U] step or stage in a scale or process: 阶段;程度: *The boys show various ~s of skill in their use of carpentry tools.* 孩子们对于木工用具的使用能力各有不同。 *His work has reached a high ~ of excellence.* 他的作品已达炉火纯青之境。 *He was not in the slightest ~ interested,* was completely uninterested. 他丝毫不感觉兴趣。 *by ~s,* step by step; gradually: 一步一步地; 逐渐地: *Their friendship by ~s grew into love.* 他们的友谊逐渐成长为爱情。 *to a ~,* (colloq) = to the highest ~: (口)非常: *He is scrupulous to a ~.* 他非常谨慎。 **to a high/the highest ~,** intensively; exceedingly: 非常;极: *He is vain to a high ~.* 他虚荣心极大。 **to what ~,** to what extent; how much: 达于何种程度;如何: *To what ~ are you interested in botany?* 你对于植物学的兴趣达到何种程度? *first ~,* stage of seriousness: 严重阶段: *first ~ burns;* 一度烧伤; *first ~ murder.* 一级谋杀。 **third ~,** severe and long examination (eg by the police) of an accused man to get information or a confession: 为让犯人供出所作严厉而长时间的审问; 刑讯逼供; 拷问: *Are third-~ methods used in your country?* 贵国使用刑讯吗? **4** [U] position in society: 社会地位: *persons of high ~.* 社会地位高的人。 **5** academic title; rank or grade given by a university to one who has passed an examination: (大学授予通过考试者的)学位: *studying for a ~;* 读学位; *the ~ of Master of Arts* (MA). 文学硕士。 ⇨ **graduate, undergraduate. 6** (music) interval from one note to another on a stave. (音乐)音阶;度。 **7** (gram) one of the three forms of comparison of an *adj* or *adv*: (语法)形容词或副词比较的三种级之一: *~s of comparison.* 表示比较的各种级。 *'Good', 'better' and 'best' are the positive, comparative and superlative ~s of 'good'.* good, better 及 best 是 good 的原级, 比较级及最高级。 *'Rich', 'richer' and 'richest' are the positive, comparative and superlative ~s of 'rich'.* rich, richer 及 richest 是 rich 的原级, 比较级及最高级。

de-horn /ˌdiː ˈhɔːn; diˈhɔrn/ *vt* [VP6A] remove the horns from (cattle). 除去(牛)的角。

de·hu·man·ize /ˌdiːˈhjuːmənaɪz; diˈhjuməˌnaɪz/ *vt* [VP6A] take away human qualities from. 使失去人性。

de·hy·drate /ˌdiːˈhaɪdreɪt; diˈhaɪdret/ *vt* [VP6A] deprive (a substance) of water or moisture: 去掉(物质)中的水份; 使脱水: *~d vegetables/eggs,* often in powdered form. 脱水蔬菜(鸡蛋)(通常系粉状)。

de-ice /ˌdiː ˈaɪs; diˈaɪs/ *vt* [VP6A]free, eg the surfaces of an aircraft, from ice. 防止(如飞机的表面)结冰;除去…的冰。

de·ify /ˈdiːɪfaɪ; ˈdiəˌfaɪ/ *vt (pt, pp* **-fied**) [VP6A] make a god of; worship as a god. 使成神;奉为神。 **de·ifi·ca·tion** /ˌdiːɪfɪˈkeɪʃn; ˌdiəfəˈkeʃən/ *n* [U] ~ing or being deified: (被)奉为神; 神化: *the deification of a Roman emperor.* 罗马皇帝之被奉为神。

deign /deɪn; den/ *vi* [VP4A] ~ **to do sth,** condescend; be kind or gracious enough to: 屈尊; 俯就: *He passed by without ~ing to look at me.* 他走过时不屑看我一眼。

de·ism /ˈdiːɪzəm; ˈdiɪzəm/ *n* belief in the existence of a Divine Being, but without acceptance of revelation or religious dogma. 自然神论; 理神论(相信有神存在,但不相信神能对人有所启示或宗教教条)。 **de·ist** /ˈdiːɪst; ˈdiɪst/ *n* supporter of ~. 自然神论者; 理神论者。 ⇨ **theism.**

de·ity /ˈdiːɪtɪ; ˈdiɪtɪ/ *n* **1** [U] divine quality or nature; state of being a god or goddess. 神性。 **2** [C] *(pl* **-ties**) god or goddess: 神; 女神: *Roman deities,* eg Neptune, Minerva. 罗马诸神(如海神,司智慧等之女神)。 **the D~,** God. 神;上帝。

déjà vu /ˌdeɪʒɑː ˈvjuː; deʒa ˈvju/ *n* [U] (F) feeling that one remembers an event or scene that one has not experienced or seen before; (colloq) feeling that one has experienced sth too often. (法)记忆错觉; (口)对某事经历次数太多的感觉。

de·ject /dɪˈdʒekt; dɪˈdʒɛkt/ *vt* (usu in *pp*) make sad or gloomy: (通常用过去分词)使悲伤;使沮丧: *Why is she looking so ~ed,* in such low spirits? 她为什么神情如此沮丧? **de·ject·ed·ly** *adv* **de·jec·tion** /dɪˈdʒekʃn; dɪˈdʒɛkʃən/ *n* [U] ~ed state; low spirits: 忧戚; 沮丧: *He left in ~.* 他快怏而去。

de jure /ˌdeɪ ˈdʒʊərɪ; diˈdʒʊrɪ/ *adj, adv* (Lat) by right; according to law: (拉)合法的; 有权的; 依法: *the ~ king;* 合法的王; *king ~.* 合法的王。 ⇨ **de facto.**

dekko /ˈdekəʊ; ˈdeko/ *n* (sl) (俚) **have a ~,** have a look (at sth). (对某物)看一眼。

de·lay /dɪˈleɪ; dɪˈle/ *vt, vi* **1** [VP6A, 2A, B] make or be slow or late: 延迟; 延缓: *Don't ~.* 不要拖延。 *The train was ~ed (for) two hours.* 火车迟延两小时。 *I was ~ed by the traffic.* 我因交通拥挤而迟到。 **~ed-action** *adj,* n operating after a lapse of time: 经过一段时期后始起作用(的): *a ~ed-action bomb,* with a device causing it to explode after a pre-determined interval. 定时炸弹。 **2** [VP6A, C] put off until later: 展期: *We must ~ our journey until the weather improves.* 我们必须延缓旅行, 等天气好转后再说。 *Why have they ~ed opening the new school?* 他们为什么迟迟不让那新学校开学? □ *n* **1** [U] ~ing or being ~ed: 迟延; 延后; 延期: *We must leave without ~.* 我们必须立即离开。 **2** [C] instance of this; time of being ~ed: 耽误;迟延的时间; *after several ~s;* 经过数次延搁以后; *after a ~ of three hours.* 经过三小时的耽误以后。

de·lec·table /dɪˈlektəbl; dɪˈlɛktəbl/ *adj* (liter) delightful; pleasant. (文)宜人的; 令人愉快的。

de·lec·ta·tion /ˌdiːlekˈteɪʃn; ˌdilɛkˈteʃən/ *n* [U] (liter, ironic) enjoyment; entertainment: (文, 反语)享受; 娱乐: *TV programmes suitable for the ~ of half-educated people.* 投合未受很多教育者所好的电视节目。

del·egacy /ˈdeləɡəsɪ; ˈdɛlɪɡəsɪ/ *n (pl* **-cies**) system of delegating; body of delegates. 代表制度;代表团。

del·egate¹ /ˈdeləɡət; ˈdɛlɪˌget/ *n* person to whom sth is delegated (eg an elected representative sent to a conference or convention). (被选派参加会议等的)代表; 受托者。

del·egate² /ˈdeləɡeɪt; ˈdɛləˌget/ *vt* [VP17, 14] **(to),** appoint and send (sb) as a representative to a meeting; entrust (duties, rights, etc to sb): 派遣(某人)为代表(参加某会); 付托(责任, 权利等于某人): *to ~ sb to perform a task;* 请某人代表执行任务; *to ~ rights to a deputy.* 付托权利予代理人。 **del·ega·tion** /ˌdeləˈɡeɪʃn; ˌdɛləˈɡeʃən/ *n* **1** [U] delegating or being delegated. 派代表; 被派为代表。 **2** [C] group of delegates. 代表团。

de·lete /dɪ'liːt; dɪ'lit/ vt [VP6A, 14] ~ *(from)*, strike or take out (sth written or printed): 消去; 删除 (稿件或印刷物中的词句): *Several words had been ~d from the letter by the censor.* 那封信中有好几个字被新闻检查员删去了. **de·le·tion** /dɪ'liːʃn; dɪ'liʃən/ n [U] deleting; sth deleted. 删除; 删除之词句.

del·eteri·ous /ˌdelɪ'tɪəriəs; ˌdelɪ'tɪrɪəs/ adj (formal) harmful (to mind or body). (正式用语) 有害 (于身心)的.

delft /delft; delft/, (also 亦作 **delf** /delf; delf/, or 或作 '**~·ware**) n [U] kind of glazed earthenware, usu with blue designs or decorations. 一种上釉的陶器(通常带蓝色图案或花纹).

de·lib·er·ate¹ /dɪ'lɪbərət; dɪ'lɪbərɪt/ adj 1 done on purpose; intentional: 故意的; 存心的: *a ~ lie/insult.* 存心的谎言(侮辱). 2 slow and cautious (in action, speech, etc): (行动,言谈等)从容而谨慎的: *a ~ speech.* 从容而谨慎的演说. *He entered the room with ~ steps.* 他从容不迫地走进室内. **~·ly** adv

de·lib·er·ate² /dɪ'lɪbəreɪt; dɪ'lɪbə,ret/ vt, vi [VP6A, 8, 10, 2A, 3A] ~ *(over/on/upon)*, consider, talk about, carefully: 仔细考虑; 研讨; 商讨: *We were deliberating what to do/how it might be done/whether to buy a new motor-car.* 我们在商讨怎么办(如何是好,是否买一部新汽车). *They're still deliberating upon/upon the question.* 他们仍然在慎重考虑这问题. **de·lib·er·ative** /dɪ'lɪbərətɪv US: -reɪtɪv; dɪ'lɪbə,retɪv/ adj for the purpose of deliberating: 以商讨为目的的: *a deliberative assembly.* 讨论会.

de·lib·er·ation /dɪˌlɪbə'reɪʃn; dɪˌlɪbə'reʃən/ n 1 [C, U] careful consideration and discussion; debate: 慎重考虑; 商讨; 辩论: *After long ~, they decided ....* 经过很久的商讨以后, 他们决定···. *What was the result of your ~(s)?* 你(们)考虑的结果如何? 2 [U] being deliberate(2); slowness of movement: 从容不迫; 不慌不忙: *to speak/take aim/walk into a room with great ~.* 目前的政治情势是极微妙的(需要小心处理). **de·li·ca·tessen** /ˌdelɪkə'tesn; ˌdelɪkə'tɛsn/ n [C, U] (shop selling) prepared foods ready for serving (esp cooked meat, smoked fish, pickles): 做熟售卖的菜肴(尤指煮熟的肉,熏鱼,腌菜); 熟食店: *The ~ (shop) closes at 5:30.* 熟食店五点半停止营业.

deli·cacy /'delɪkəsɪ; 'dɛləkəsɪ/ n (pl -cies) 1 [U] quality of being delicate (all senses): 精美; 细致; 纤弱; 微妙; 优美; (颜色)柔和; (感官)灵敏; (仪器)精密; 体贴; 美味: *Everyone admired the ~ of her features, their fineness and tenderness.* 人人都欣赏她的花容月貌. *Because of the ~ of her skin* (= Because it is easily hurt by the sun), *she never sunbathes.* 因为她的皮肤极为细嫩 (易受阳光晒坏), 所以她从不作日光浴. *The girl's ~* (= The fact that she is delicate in health) *has always worried her parents.* 那女孩之纤弱的体质一直使她的父母心焦. *The political situation is one of great ~, requires careful handling.* 目前的政治情势是极微妙的(需要小心处理). *The violinist played with great ~, with a very fine touch.* 那小提琴家以极其优美的手法演奏. 2 [C] delicate(8) kind of food: 珍馐; 美味: *all the delicacies of the season.* 一切应时的珍馐美味.

deli·cate /'delɪkət; 'dɛləkət/ adj 1 soft; tender; of fine or thin material: 软软的; 细嫩的; 纤细的: *as ~ as silk;* 柔滑如绸; *the ~ skin of a young girl.* 女孩子的柔细的皮肤. 2 fine; exquisite: 精致的; 细腻的: *jewellery of ~ workmanship.* 精工镶嵌的珠宝饰物. 3 easily injured; needing great care: 易损的; 身体脆弱的; 需要小心照料的: *~ china/plants;* 精致而易损坏的瓷器 (需要小心照料的植物); *a ~-looking child;* 看起来瘦弱的小孩; *in ~ health.* 身体娇弱的. 4 requiring careful treatment or skilful handling: 需要小心或技巧处理的: *a ~ surgical operation,* 动 on sb's eyes. 精密的外科手术(如施于眼部者). *The international situation is very ~ at present.* 目前的国际局势极其微妙. 5 (of colours) soft; not strong: (颜色)柔和的; 淡的; 浅的: *a ~ shade of pink.* 淡粉红色. 6 (of the senses, of instruments) able to appreciate or indicate very small changes or differences: 灵敏的; 敏感的; 精密的: *a ~ sense of smell/touch;* 灵敏的嗅(触)觉; *the ~ instruments needed* *by scientists,* eg for weighing or measuring. 科学家所需要的精密仪器 (如用以称量或度量者). 7 taking great care not to be immodest, not to hurt the feelings of others: 极其小心不使自己失礼, 不伤人感情的; 贤淑的; 体贴的: *a ~ speech.* 得体的演说. 8 (of food, its flavour) pleasing to the taste and not strongly flavoured: (指食物, 其味)美味的; 清淡可口的: *Chicken is more ~ than beef.* 鸡肉比牛肉味美. *When people are ill they need ~ food.* 当人生病的时候, 他们需要清淡可口的食物. *Some kinds of fish have a more ~ flavour than others.* 某些种类的鱼, 其味较他种鱼类为佳. **~·ly** adv

de·li·cious /dɪ'lɪʃəs; dɪ'lɪʃəs/ adj giving delight (esp to the senses of taste and smell, and to the sense of humour): 美味的; 有香味的; 堪玩味的(尤指使人在味觉, 嗅觉与幽默感方面发生乐趣的): *a ~ cake.* 美味的糕饼. *Doesn't it smell ~!* 其味岂不美哉! *What a ~ joke!* 多么有趣的笑话! **~·ly** adv

de·light¹ /dɪ'laɪt; dɪ'laɪt/ n 1 [U] great pleasure; joy: 欣喜; 乐趣; 高兴; 愉快: *to give ~ to sb.* 给予娱乐; 使某人高兴. *To his great ~ his novel was accepted for publication.* 他的小说被接受出版, 使他极为高兴. **take ~ in,** find pleasure in: 喜好; 以···为乐: *The naughty boy takes great ~ in pulling the cat's tail.* 那顽皮的男孩以拉猫的尾巴为乐. 2 [C] cause or source of great pleasure: 赏心乐事; 嗜好: *Dancing is her chief ~.* 跳舞是她主要的嗜好. *He often thinks of the ~s of life in the country.* 他时常怀念乡村生活的乐趣. **~·ful** /-fl; -fəl/ adj giving ~ (to): 令人愉快的; 可爱的(可与to连用): *a ~ful holiday.* 愉快的假日. **~·fully** /-fəlɪ; -fəlɪ/ adv

de·light² /dɪ'laɪt; dɪ'laɪt/ vt, vi 1 [VP6A] give great pleasure to; please greatly: 给予乐趣; 使极为喜悦; 使非常高兴: *Her singing ~ed everyone.* 她的歌唱使人人欢喜. 2 (passive): (被动态态): *be ~ed,* be greatly pleased. 极为高兴. *I was ~ed to hear the news of your success/~ed at the news.../~ed that you were successful.* 我听到你成功的消息甚为高兴. 3 [VP3A, 4C] ~ *(in),* take or find great pleasure: 引以为乐; 喜欢: *He ~s in teasing his young sister.* 他以逗弄他的小妹妹为乐. *He ~s to prove his brother wrong.* 他很喜欢证明他的哥哥(弟弟)错误.

de·limit /dɪ'lɪmɪt; dɪ'lɪmɪt/, **de·limi·tate** /dɪ-'lɪmɪteɪt; dɪ'lɪmə,tet/ vt [VP6A] determine the limits or boundaries of. 定···的界线; 划界线. **de·limi·ta·tion** /dɪˌlɪmɪ'teɪʃn; dɪ,lɪmə'teʃən/ n [C, U].

de·lin·eate /dɪ'lɪnɪeɪt; dɪ'lɪnɪ,et/ vt [VP6A] (formal) show by drawing or by describing; portray. (正式用语) 描画; 描绘; 描写. **de·lin·ea·tion** /dɪˌlɪnɪ'eɪʃn; dɪ,lɪnɪ'eʃən/ n [C, U].

de·lin·quency /dɪ'lɪŋkwənsɪ; dɪ'lɪŋkwənsɪ/ n 1 [U] wrong-doing; neglect of duty: 过失; 失职; 违法; 犯罪: *the problem of juvenile ~,* wrong-doing by young persons. 少年犯罪问题. 2 [C] (pl -cies) instance of this; misdeed. 罪行; 恶行.

de·lin·quent /dɪ'lɪŋkwənt; dɪ'lɪŋkwənt/ n, adj (person) doing wrong, failing to perform a duty. 犯过的(人); 犯法的(人); 失职的(人).

deli·ques·cent /ˌdelɪ'kwesnt; ˌdɛlə'kwɛsnt/ adj (chem) becoming liquid in air (by absorbing moisture). (化学)潮解的(在空气中吸收水分而溶解的).

de·lir·i·ous /dɪ'lɪrɪəs; dɪ'lɪrɪəs/ adj 1 suffering from delirium; wildly excited: 精神错乱的; 谵妄的; 极激动的; 发狂的: *The patient's temperature went up and he became ~.* 那病人的体温升高, 变得胡言乱语. *The children were ~ with joy.* 孩子们欣喜若狂. 2 showing the effects of delirium: 显示精神错乱的: *a ~ speech.* 狂语; 谵语. **~·ly** adv

de·lirium /dɪ'lɪrɪəm; dɪ'lɪrɪəm/ n [U] violent mental

disturbance caused by illness, often accompanied by wild talk, esp during feverish illness; wild excitement. 谵妄(精神错乱, 常伴随胡言乱语, 尤指在发烧的病症中); 发狂。 ~ 'tremens /'tri:menz; 'trimənz/ (usu used as d t(s) /,di: 'ti:(z) ; di'ti(z)/), ~ caused by extreme alcoholism. 震颤性谵妄(因极度酗酒中毒引起者); 酒狂。

de·liv·er /dɪ'lɪvə(r); dɪ'lɪvə/ vt 1 [VP6A] take (letters, parcels, goods, etc) to houses, to the person(s) to whom they are addressed, to the buyer(s): 递送(信件、包裹、货物等)至收件处, 收件人或购货人; 交付: A postman is a man employed to ~ letters and parcels. 邮差就是雇来投递信件及包裹的人。 Did you ~ my message to your father? 你已将我的信交给你父亲了吗? ~ the goods, (fig) do what is wanted. (喻)实践诺言; 不负所望。 2 [VP14] ~ from, (old use) rescue, save, set free: (旧用法)拯救; 解救; 释放: May God ~ us from all evil. 愿上帝使我们脱离一切邪恶(宗教用语)。 3 [VP6A] give forth in words: 发言; 陈述; 发表(演说): to ~ a sermon/a course of lectures; 讲道(讲授一门功课); to ~ oneself of an opinion. 发表意见。 4 [VP6A] (of a medical attendant, a midwife) help (a woman) in childbirth: (指医护人员, 如助产士)助产: to be ~ed of a child, give birth to one. 产一小孩。 5 [VP6A, 15B] ~ (up/over)(to), surrender; give up; hand over: 交出; 放弃; 移交: to ~ up stolen goods; 交出赃物; to ~ over one's property to one's son; 将财产交付与儿子; to ~ (up) a fortress to the enemy. 将一要塞放弃给敌人。 6 [VP6A] launch; aim; send against: 冲击; 予以: (fig) (喻) to ~ a blow in the cause of freedom. 予自由运动出头一棒。 ~er n one who ~s; rescuer; saviour. 递送者; 交付者; 拯救者; 解救者; 发言者; 陈述者; 演讲者。

de·liv·er·ance /dɪ'lɪvərəns; dɪ'lɪvərəns/ n 1 [U] ~ from, delivering(2); rescue; being set free. 拯救; 救助; 被释放。 2 [C] formal or emphatic statement of opinion. 正式的或强调的意见声明; 意见。

de·liv·ery /dɪ'lɪvərɪ; dɪ'lɪvərɪ/ n 1 [U] delivering (of letters, goods, etc); [C] (pl -ries) periodical performance of this: 递送(信, 货等); 按时递送; We guarantee prompt ~ of goods. 我们担保送货迅速。 How many deliveries are there in your town (= How often does the postman deliver letters) every week? 你们的城里每周送几次信? on ~, at the time of ~. 送达时; 交货时。 take ~ of, receive: 收到: When can you take ~ of the new car? 你何时能收到新车? '~ note n note, usu in duplicate, sent with goods, to be signed by the recipient. 交货单(通常有副本, 由收货人签名)。 '~ truck n (US) goods van. (美)货车。 2 (sing only) manner of speaking (in lectures, etc): (仅用单数)(演讲等的)说话方式; 演讲的技术: His speech was good, but his ~ was poor. 他的演讲内容很好, 可是表达的技巧很差。

dell /del; del/ n small valley, usu with trees on its sides. 小山谷(通常两侧有树木); 幽谷。

de·louse /ˌdi:'laus; di'laus/ vt rid (sb or sth) of lice. 除去(某人或某物)身上的虱子。

Del·phic /'delfɪk; 'delfɪk/ adj of the oracle of Apollo /ə'pɒləu; ə'palo/ at Delphi (in ancient Greece); obscure; ambiguous. 阿波罗神庙(古希腊)神之神谕的; 含义不明的; 意义模棱两可的。

del·phin·ium /del'fɪnɪəm; del'fɪnɪəm/ n (kinds of) garden plant, usu with tall spikes of usu blue flowers. 飞燕草(数种园艺植物, 通常生高大的穗状花)。

delta /'deltə; 'deltə/ n Greek letter d, ⇨ App 4; land (with alluvial deposits) in the shape of a capital ~ (Δ) at the mouth of a river between two or more branches: 希腊字母的第四个字母(Δ, δ)(参看附录四); 在河口由数条支流冲积成的三角洲: the Nile D~: 尼罗河三角洲; ,~-'winged, (of aircraft) having ~-shaped wings. (指飞机)有三角翼的之。

de·lude /dɪ'lu:d; dɪ'lud/ vt [VP6A, 14] ~ sb with sth/into doing sth, deceive; mislead (on purpose): 欺骗; (故意)使人有错误想法: to ~ sb with promises one does not intend to keep; 以不打算实现的诺言欺骗某人;

to ~ oneself with false hopes; 以虚幻的希望自欺; to ~ sb/oneself into believing that …. 欺骗某人(自己)使相信…。

del·uge /'delju:dʒ; 'dɛljudʒ/ n [C] 1 great flood; heavy rush of water; violent rainfall. 洪水; 大水灾; 暴雨。 the D~, the flood at the time of Noah /'nəuə; 'noə/ ⇨ Gen 7. 诺亚时代的大洪水(参看旧约圣经创世纪第7章)。 2 anything coming in a heavy rush: 如洪水涌至的事物: a ~ of words/questions/protests. 一连串的话(问题, 抗议)。 □ vt [VP6A, 14] ~ (with), flood; come down on (sb or sth) like a ~: 泛滥; 如洪水涌上(某人或某物): He was ~d with questions. 他为大堆的问题所困。

de·lusion /dɪ'lu:ʒn; dɪ'luʒən/ n [U] deluding or being deluded; [C] false opinion or belief, esp one that may be a symptom of madness: 欺骗; 被欺; 幻念; 幻想(尤指可能为癫狂之病症者): to be under a ~/under the ~ that …; 处于幻觉中(误以为…); to suffer from ~s. 患妄想症。

de·lus·ive /dɪ'lu:sɪv; dɪ'lusɪv/ adj not real; deceptive. 非真实的; 虚幻的; 令人发生错觉的。 ~·ly adv

de luxe /dɪ 'lʌks; dɪ'lʌks/ adj (F) of very high quality, high standards of comfort, etc: (法)品质高超的; 精美的; 极舒适的; 豪华的: a ~ edition of a book. 一书之精装本。

delve /delv; delv/ vt, vi 1 [VP6A, 2A] (old use) dig. (旧用法)挖掘。 2 [VP3A] ~ into, make researches into: 钻研; 深入研究: to ~ for information into old books; 在古书中搜求资料; to ~ into sb's past. 深入调查某人的过去。

de·mag·net·ize /ˌdi:'mægnɪtaɪz; di'mægnə,taɪz/ vt [VP6A] deprive of magnetic properties. 除去磁性。 **de·mag·net·iz·ation** /ˌdi:ˌmægnɪtaɪ'zeɪʃn US: -tɪ'z-; ˌdimægnətə'zeʃən/ n

dema·gogue /'deməgɒg US: -gɔ:g; 'dɛmə,gɔg/ n political leader who tries, by speeches appealing to the feelings instead of to reason, to stir up the people. 用诉诸感情而非理智的演说以煽动民众的政治领袖; 煽动家。 **dema·gogy** /'deməgɒgɪ; 'dɛmə,godʒɪ/ n [U] principles and practices of a ~. 煽动; 煽动性; 煽动行为。 **dema·gogic** /ˌdemə'gɒgɪk; ˌdɛmə'gadʒɪk/ adj of or like a ~. 煽动家的; 似煽动家的。

de·mand¹ /dɪ'mɑ:nd US: -'mænd; dɪ'mænd/ n ~ (for), 1 [C] act of demanding(1); sth demanded(1): 要求; 所要求之物: The workers' ~s (eg for higher pay) were refused by the employers. 工人们的要求(如要求加薪)为雇主所拒。 It is impossible to satisfy all ~s. 不可能满足所有的要求。 I have/People make many ~s on my time, I am expected to do many things, etc. 我有许多事情要做。 There have been ~s for the prime minister to resign/for his resignation/that he should resign. 已有人要求首相辞职。 on ~, when demanded: 即期(应付)支票。 '~ (note), note that demands payment, eg of income tax. 缴款(如缴所得税)通知。 2 [U] (or with an indef art and adj) desire, by people ready to buy, employ, etc (for goods, services, etc): (或与不定冠词及形容词连用)(社会对于货物、人才等的)需求; 需要: There is a great ~ for typists but a poor ~/not much ~ for clerks. (目前社会上)极需要打字员, 而不大需要书记员。 There is little ~ for these goods. 这些货物的需要量极小。 The ~ for fish this month exceeds the supply. 本月的鱼市供不应求。 in ~, wanted; popular: 需要的; 受欢迎的: His records are always in ~/are in constant ~. 他的唱片一直很畅销。

de·mand² /dɪ'mɑ:nd US: -'mænd; dɪ'mænd/ vt 1 [VP6A, 7A, 9] ask for (sth) as if ordering, or as if one has a right to: 要求(某事物): ~ an apology from sb. 要求某人道歉。 The gatekeeper ~ed my business, asked what I wanted. 守门人问我有何事。 The policeman ~ed his name and address/~ed to know where he lived. 警察要求他说出姓名和住址(要求他说出住在何处)。 He

came to my house and ~ed help / ~ed that I should help him. 他来到我家来并要求我帮助。He ~s that I shall tell him everything / ~s to be told everything. 他要求我告诉他一切。**2** [VP6A] need; require: 需要; 需求: This sort of work ~s great patience. 这种工作需要极大的耐性。Does the letter ~ an immediate answer, Must it be answered at once? 此信需要立即答复吗?

de·mar·cate /'di:mɑːkeɪt; dɪˈmɑrket/ vt [VP6A] mark or fix the limits of, eg a frontier. 划范围; 划界线 (如边界)。

de·mar·ca·tion /ˌdiːmɑːˈkeɪʃn; ˌdimɑrˈkeʃən/ n [U] marking of a boundary or limit; separation: 划界线; 区分; 划分: a line of ~; 分界线; ~ problems in industry, eg settling the kind of work to be done by workers in different trades. 工业上各部门工作范围的划分问题。

dé·marche /'deɪmɑːʃ; deˈmɑrʃ/ n (F) political step or proceeding; diplomatic representation (to a foreign government). (法) 政治上的步骤或手段; (驻外) 外交代表。

de·mean /dɪˈmiːn; dɪˈmin/ vt [VP6A] ~ oneself, lower oneself in dignity, social esteem. 自贬身份。

de·mean·our (US = -or) /dɪˈmiːnə(r); dɪˈminɚ/ n [U] way of behaving: 行为; 举止; 态度; 风度: I dislike his supercilious ~. 我不喜欢他傲慢的态度。

de·mented /dɪˈmentɪd; dɪˈmɛntɪd/ adj mad; (colloq) wild with worry: 疯狂的; (口) 因忧虑而发狂的; 精神错乱的: a poor, ~ creature. 可怜的, 精神错乱的人。She'll become ~ if you don't stop asking silly questions. 假若你再不停止问傻问题, 她会发疯的。~·ly adv

deme·rara /ˌdeməˈreərə; ˌdeməˈrerə/ n [U] ~ sugar, light brown raw cane sugar (from Guyana). (圭亚那所产的) 淡褐色蔗糖。

de·merit /'di:merɪt; dɪˈmɛrɪt/ n [C] fault; defect. 过失; 缺点。

de·mesne /dɪˈmeɪn; dɪˈmen/ n [U] (legal) the holding of land as one's own property: (法律) 土地的占有 (作为私产): land held in ~; 占有的地产; [C] landed estate held in this way, not let to tenants. 领有供自用 (而非租给佃户) 的地产。

demi·god /'demigɒd; ˈdeməˌgɑd/ n one who is partly divine and partly human; (in GK myth, etc) the son of a god and a mortal woman, eg Hercules /'hɜːkjuːliz; ˈhɝkjəˌliz/. 半神半人; (在希腊神话等中) 天神与凡女所生之子 (如海克力斯)。

demi·john /'demidʒɒn; ˈdemɪˌdʒɑn/ n large narrow-necked bottle, usu encased in wicker-work. 一种细颈大坛 (通常套于柳条编的套中)。

de·mili·tar·ize /ˌdiːˈmɪlɪtəraɪz; diˈmɪlətəˌraɪz/ vt [VP6A] (of a country, or part of it) require, by treaty or agreement, to have no military forces or installation in: (指国或国之一部) (按照条约或协定) 解除武装; 非军事化。a ~d zone. 非军事区。

demi·monde /ˌdemiˈmɔːnd; ˈdemɪˌmɑnd/ n the ~, (F) (class of society made up of) people on the fringe of respectable society. (法) 名声不好的女人; 妓女; 娼妓界。**demi·mon·daine** /ˌdemimɔːnˈdeɪn; ˌdɛmmɑnˈden/ n woman of this class. 妓女; 交际花。

de·mise /dɪˈmaɪz; dɪˈmaɪz/ n (legal) death. (法律) 死亡。

de·mist /ˌdiːˈmɪst; dɪˈmɪst/ vt remove the mist from, eg the windscreen of a motor vehicle. 擦去 (汽车之挡风玻璃等) 的雾水。~er /-stə(r); -stɚ/ n device that ~s. 除雾器。

demo /'deməʊ; ˈdemo/ n [C] (colloq abbr for) demonstration (2). (口) 示威 (为 demonstration 之略)。

de·mob /ˌdiːˈmɒb; diˈmɑb/ vt (-bb-) and n (GB colloq abbr for) demobilize and demobilization. (英口) 遣散; (使) 复员 (为 demobilize 与 demobilization 之略): When do you get ~bed / your ~? 你何时可获遣散?

de·mo·bil·ize /ˌdiːˈməʊbəlaɪz; diˈmobl̩ˌaɪz/ vt [VP6A] release from military service. 遣散 (兵员); 使 (军

队) 复员。**de·mo·bil·iz·ation** /dɪˌməʊbəlaɪˈzeɪʃn US: -lɪˈz-; ˌdimobl̩əˈzeʃən/ n

democ·racy /dɪˈmɒkrəsɪ; dəˈmɑkrəsɪ/ n (pl -cies) **1** [C, U] (country with principles of) government in which all adult citizens share through their elected representatives. 民主政治 (由全体成年公民通过其所选举的代表共同参与施政的政治制度); 实行民主政治的国家。**2** [C, U] (country with) government which encourages and allows rights of citizenship such as freedom of speech, religion, opinion and association, the assertion of the rule of law, majority rule, accompanied by respect for the rights of minorities. 民主政体 (准许公民享有各种公民权如言论、信仰、意见及集会结社之自由, 主张法治, 服从多数同时并尊重少数者之权利); 拥有民主政体的国家。**3** [C, U] (society in which there is) treatment of each other by citizens as equals and with absence of class feeling: 公民互相平等待遇 (的社会): Is there more ~ in Australia than in Great Britain? 在澳大利亚是否比英国更为自由平等?

demo·crat /'deməkræt; ˈdeməˌkræt/ n **1** person who favours or supports democracy. 赞成或支持民主政治的人。**2** D~, (US) member of the Democratic Party. (美)民主党员。

demo·cratic /ˌdeməˈkrætɪk; ˌdeməˈkrætɪk/ adj **1** of, like, supporting, democracy(1, 2). 民主政治的; 民主政体的; 民主国家的; 类似或支持民主政治的。**2** (esp) of, supporting, democracy(3); paying no or little attention to class divisions based on birth or wealth. (尤指)赞成人人平等的; 不分贵贱的, 不分贫富的。**3 the 'D~ Party**, (US) one of the two main political parties. (美)民主党 (美国两大政党之一)。⇨ Republican. **demo·crati·cally** /-klɪ; -klɪ/ adv

de·moc·ra·tize /dɪˈmɒkrətaɪz; dəˈmɑkrəˌtaɪz/ vt [VP6A] make democratic. 民主化; 平民化。**de·moc·ra·tiz·ation** /dɪˌmɒkrətaɪˈzeɪʃn US: -tɪˈz-; dɪˌmɑkrətɪˈzeʃən/ n

dé·modé /'deɪˈməʊdeɪ US: ˌdeɪməʊˈdeɪ; ˌdemoˈde/ adj (F) outmoded; out of fashion. (法)过时的; 已不流行的; 老式的。

de·mog·ra·phy /dɪˈmɒɡrəfɪ; dɪˈmɑɡrəfɪ/ n [U] (study of) statistics of births, marriages, diseases, etc to show the condition of a community. 人口统计 (包括出生、死亡、疾病等的统计, 以示明社区状况); 人口统计学。**demo·graphic** /ˌdeməˈɡræfɪk; ˌdiməˈɡræfɪk/ adj

de·mol·ish /dɪˈmɒlɪʃ; dɪˈmɑlɪʃ/ vt [VP6A] pull or tear down, eg old buildings; destroy, eg sb's argument; make an end of. 拆除 (旧建筑物等); 推翻 (某人的论据等); 毁坏; 破坏。**demo·li·tion** /ˌdeməˈlɪʃn; ˌdeməˈlɪʃən/ n [U] ~ing or being ~ed; [C] instance of this. 拆除; 推翻; 毁坏; 破坏。

de·mon /'diːmən; ˈdimən/ n evil, wicked or cruel supernatural being or spirit; (colloq) fierce or energetic person: 恶魔; 魔鬼; (口) 凶恶的或精力充沛的人: a ~ bowler, (cricket) very fast bowler. (板球) 凶猛的投手。He's a ~ for work, (colloq) works with great energy. (口)他做起事来精力过人。~ic /diːˈmɒnɪk; dɪˈmɑnɪk/ adj

de·monet·ize /ˌdiːˈmʌnɪtaɪz; diˈmɑnəˌtaɪz/ vt deprive (a metal) of its value as currency; withdraw (a metal) from use as currency. 废止 (金属) 充作货币之价值; 停止 (金属) 充作货币。**de·monet·iz·ation** /dɪˌmʌnɪtaɪˈzeɪʃn US: -tɪˈz-; dɪˌmɑnətɪˈzeʃən/ n

de·mon·iac /dɪˈməʊnɪæk; dɪˈmonɪˌæk/ n, adj (person who is) devilish, frenzied, fiercely energetic. 邪恶的(人); 狂乱的(人); 精力充沛的(人)。~al /ˌdiːməˈnaɪəkl; ˌdiməˈnaɪəkl/ adj; ~·ally /ˌdiːməˈnaɪəklɪ; ˌdiməˈnaɪəklɪ/ adv

de·mon·strable /'demənstrəbl; ˈdɛmənstrəbl/ adj that can be demonstrated or logically proved. 可用证据或逻辑证明的。**de·mon·strably** /-blɪ; -blɪ/ adv **de·mon·stra·bil·ity** /ˌdemənstrəˈbɪlɪtɪ; ˌdɛmənstrəˈbɪlətɪ/ n

dem·on·strate /'demənstreɪt; 'dɛmən͵stret/ vt, vi
1 [VP6A, 9] show clearly by giving proof(s) or
example(s): 拿出证据或举例证明; 演示: How would you
~ that the world is round? 你如何证明世界是圆的? The
salesman ~d the new washing-machine, showed how it
was used. 那售货员演示如何使用新式洗衣机。2 [VP2A,
3A] take part in a demonstration(2): 示威; 参加示威运
动: The workers marched through the streets with flags
and banners to ~ against the rising cost of living. 工人
们在街上游行, 手执旗帜示威抗议生活费用的高涨。

dem·on·stra·tion /͵demən'streɪʃn; ͵dɛmən'streʃən/
n [C, U] 1 demonstrating(1): 证明; 演示; 示范: to
teach sth by ~; 示范教学; by way of affection, eg when a
child puts its arms round its mother's neck; 亲爱的表
示(如小孩用两臂搂着母亲的脖子); ~ of a new car,
to show how it works. 示范新式汽车的使用。2 public
and organised display of opinion by a group, eg of
workers, students. (工人, 学生等之)示威运动。

de·mon·stra·tive /dɪ'mɒnstrətɪv; dɪ'mɑnstrətɪv/
adj 1 (of persons) showing the feelings: (指人)表露出
感情的: Some children are more ~ than others, readier
to show affection, etc. 有些小孩比其他的小孩容易表露
感情。2 marked by open expression of feelings: 将感情
公然表露出来的: ~ behaviour. 将感情表露出来的行为。
3 serving to point out; indicate; esp (gram) (尤指语法
上的) ,~ 'pronoun, 指示代词 (this, these, that, those).
~·ly adv

dem·on·stra·tor /'demənstreɪtə(r); 'dɛmən͵stretɚ/
n 1 person who demonstrates(2): 游行示威者: The ~s
were dispersed by the police. 游行示威者为警察所驱散。
2 person who teaches or explains by demonstrating(1).
用演示法教学或示范者。

de·moral·ize /dɪ'mɒrəlaɪz US: -'mɔːr-; dɪ'mɔrəl͵aɪz/
vt [VP6A] 1 hurt or weaken the morals of: 败坏···的
道德: a boy who was ~d by bad companions. 与坏
人为友而道德被败坏的孩子。2 weaken the courage,
confidence, self-discipline, etc of, eg an army. 消弱(军
队等)的勇气, 自信, 纪律等; 使士气沮丧。⇨ morale.
de·moral·iz·ation /dɪ͵mɒrəlaɪ'zeɪʃn US: -͵mɔːrəlɪ'z-;
dɪ͵mɔrələ'zeɪʃn/ n

de·mote /͵diː'məʊt; dɪ'mot/ vt [VP6A] reduce to a
lower rank or grade. 使降级。⇨ promote. demotion
/͵diː'məʊʃn/ n

de·motic /dɪ'mɒtɪk; dɪ'mɑtɪk/ adj of, used by, the
common people: 民众(用)的; 通俗的: ~ Greek, the
colloquial form of modern Greek. 通俗的希腊语。

de·mur /dɪ'mɜː(r); dɪ'mɝ/ vi (-rr-) [VP2A, 3A] ~
(at/to), (formal) raise a doubt or an objection: (正
式用语)提出异议; 反对: to ~ to a demand; 反对某项要求
提出异议; to ~ at working on Sundays. 反对星期日上
班。□ n [U] hesitation or objection: 踌躇; 犹豫; 异议:
(chiefly in) without ~. 无异议。

de·mure /dɪ'mjʊə(r); dɪ'mjʊr/ adj quiet and serious:
娴静的; 严肃的; 端庄的: a ~ young lady; 娴静的少女;
pretending to be, suggesting that one is, ~: 佯作或显
示娴静严肃的: She gave him a ~ smile. 她向他故作端庄
(佯作娴静)的一笑。~·ly adv ~·ness n

den /den; den/ n 1 animal's hidden home, eg a cave.
兽穴(如山洞)。2 secret resort: 秘密之所; 窟: an opium
den; 鸦片烟窟; a den of thieves. 贼窝。3 (colloq) room
in which a person works and studies without being
disturbed. (口)私人的工作室或研究室。

den·ary /'diːnərɪ; 'dɛnərɪ/ adj = decimal.

de·nation·al·ize /͵diː'næʃənəlaɪz; di'næʃənl͵aɪz/ vt
[VP6A] transfer (a nationalized industry, etc) to
private ownership again. 使(国营工业等)复归民营;
解除国有化。⇨ nationalize. **de·nation·al·iz·ation**
/͵diː͵næʃənəlaɪ'zeɪʃn US: -lɪ'z-; di͵næʃənl͵aɪ'zeɪʃn/ n

de·natured /͵diː'neɪtʃəd; di'netʃəd/ adj that has been
made unfit for eating and drinking (but may still be
used for other purposes): 被变成不适于饮食用的(但仍
可作其他用途): ~ alcohol; 变性酒精; having lost

natural qualities: 已失去自然本质的: ~ rubber, no
longer elastic. 失去弹性的橡皮。

de·ni·able /dɪ'naɪəbl; dɪ'naɪəbl/ adj that one can
deny. 可否认的; 可拒绝的; 可反对的。

de·nial /dɪ'naɪəl; dɪ'naɪəl/ n ~ (of), 1 [U] denying
(2, 3); [C] instance of this: 否认; 拒绝一项要求: the
~ of justice/a request for help. 不予公平处理或待遇
(拒绝他人之求助)。2 [C] statement that sth is not true:
否认某事为事实的声明: the prisoner's repeated ~ of
the charge brought against him. 该囚犯对于被指控的罪
名之再三的否认。⇨ self-~ at self-

den·ier /'denɪə(r); 'dɛnɪr/ n unit of fineness for rayon,
nylon and silk yarns: 但尼尔(一种测量人造丝, 尼龙和丝
线细度的单位): 30-~ stockings. 细度为三十但尼尔的
长袜。

deni·grate /'denɪɡreɪt; 'dɛnə͵gret/ vt [VP6A] defame.
毁坏名誉。**deni·gra·tion** /͵denɪ'greɪʃn; ͵dɛnə'greʃən/ n

denim /'denɪm; 'dɛnəm/ n 1 [U] twilled cotton cloth
(used for jeans, overalls, etc). 一种斜纹棉布(用以制牛
仔裤, 工作服等)。2 (pl) (colloq) jeans made from ~.
(复)(口)此种斜纹布制的牛仔裤。

deni·zen /'denɪzn; 'dɛnəzn/ n person, kind of animal
or plant, living or growing permanently in the district,
etc mentioned: 永远定居于某地区的人或动物; 永远生长
在某地区的植物: ~s of the Arctic. 恒生于北极地区的人
或生物。

de·nomi·nate /dɪ'nɒmɪneɪt; dɪ'nɑmə͵net/ vt [VP23]
give a name to; call. 命名; 取名。

de·nomi·na·tion /dɪ͵nɒmɪ'neɪʃn; dɪ͵nɑmə'neʃən/ n
[C] 1 name, esp one given to a class or religious group
or sect: (尤指给予阶级或教派的)名称: The Protestant
~s include the Methodists, Presbyterians and Baptists.
新教会包括美以美会, 长老会和浸信会。2 class or unit
(in weight, length, numbers, money, etc): (重量,长
度,数目,货币等之)单位或类别: The US coin of the lowest
~ is the cent. 美国钱币的最低单位是分。We can reduce
fractions to the same ~, eg 1/2, 5/8=8/16, 10/16. 我们
可把分数化成同一分母(例如 1/2, 5/8=8/16, 10/16)。~·al
/-'neɪʃnl; -'neʃənl/ adj of ~s(1): 各教派的: ~al
schools. 各教派的学校。

de·nomi·na·tor /dɪ'nɒmɪneɪtə(r); dɪ'nɑmə͵netɚ/ n
number or quantity below the line in a fraction, eg 4
in 3/4. 分母(分数线下的数目, 例如 3/4 中的 4)。

de·note /dɪ'nəʊt; dɪ'not/ vt 1 [VP6A] be the sign or
symbol of; be the name of: 为···之符号; 为···之名
称; 代表; 指: In algebra the sign x usually ~s an
unknown quantity. 在代数学中, 符号 x 通常代表一未知
数。2 [VP6A, 9] indicate: 指示; 指出: The mark (ʌ)
~s a place of omission/~s that something has been
omitted. 记号 (ʌ) 指示有脱漏的地方。

dé·noue·ment /͵deɪ'nuːmɒŋ US: ͵demuˈmɒŋ;
de'numã/ n (F) final stage, where everything is made
clear, in the development of the plot of a story, play,
etc. (法)(小说, 戏剧等)情节发展的最后阶段; 结局; 收场。

de·nounce /dɪ'naʊns; dɪ'naʊns/ vt 1 [VP6A, 16B]
speak publicly against; give information against: 公开
指摘; 揭发; 告发: to ~ a heresy; 公开指摘异端邪说; to
~ sb as a spy. 指某人为奸细。2 [VP6A] give notice
that one intends to end (a treaty or agreement). 通知废
止(条约或协定)。

dense /dens; dɛns/ adj (-r, -st) 1 (of liquids, vapour)
not easily seen through: (指液体, 蒸气)不易透视的; 浓密
的: a ~ fog; 浓雾; ~ smoke. 浓烟。2 (of people and
things) crowded together in great numbers: (指人和物)
密集的; 稠密的: a ~ crowd; 拥挤的人群; a ~ forest.
茂密的森林。3 (colloq) stupid; having a mind that
ideas can penetrate only with difficulty. (口)愚钝的; 不
易受教的。~·ly adv: 浓密地: a ~ly populated country;
人口稠密的国家; ~ly wooded, covered with trees
growing close together. 林木茂密的。~·ness n

den·sity /'densɪtɪ; 'dɛnsətɪ/ n 1 [U] the quality of
being dense: 浓密; 稠密; 密集: the ~ of a forest/the

fog / the population. 森林的茂密(雾的浓密; 人口的稠密)。 **2** [C, U] (*pl* **-ties**) (phys) relation of weight to volume. (物理)密度(重量与体积的关系)。

dent /dent/ n hollow, depression, in a hard surface made by a blow or by pressure; (fig, colloq): (坚硬的表面上因受打击或压力所形成的)凹痕; 凹陷; (喻, 口): *a ~ in one's pride.* 自尊心受到的创痕。 □ *vt, vi* **1** [VP6A] make a ~ or ~s in: 使凹陷; 造成凹痕于: *a motor-car badly ~ed in a collision.* 在撞车中受撞凹得厉害的汽车。 **2** [VP2A] get ~s in: 被撞凹: *metal that ~s easily.* 易被撞凹的金属。

den·tal /'dentl; 'dɛntl/ adj **1** of or for the teeth: 牙齿的; 适于牙齿的: *a ~ plate*, a denture; 一副假牙; *a ~ surgeon.* 口腔外科医师。 **2** (phon) with the tip of the tongue near or touching the upper front teeth: (语音)齿音的(以舌尖靠近或接触上门牙): *~ sounds*, eg /θ, ð/. 齿音(例如 /θ, ð/)。

den·ti·frice /'dentɪfrɪs; 'dɛntə‚frɪs/ n [U] tooth-powder or toothpaste (the usu words). 牙粉; 牙膏 (toothpowder 及 toothpaste 的通常用语)。

den·tist /'dentɪst; 'dɛntɪst/ n person whose work is filling, cleaning, taking out teeth and fitting artificial teeth. 牙医(其业务为补牙、洗牙、拔牙及装假牙)。 **~ry** /'dentɪstrɪ; 'dɛntɪstrɪ/ n [U] work of a ~. 牙医术。

den·ture /'dentʃə(r); 'dɛntʃə/ n [C] plate (fitted on the gums) of artificial teeth. (装于齿龈上的)假牙。

de·nude /dɪ'njuːd US: -'nuːd; dɪ'njud/ vt [VP6A, 14] ~ (*of*), **1** make bare; take away covering: 使裸露; 取去其覆盖物: *trees ~d of leaves.* 叶子落尽的秃树; *hillsides ~d of trees.* 无树木的秃山坡。 **2** deprive: 剥夺: *~d by his creditors of every penny he had.* 被债权人剥得分文不留。 **de·nud·ation** /‚diːnjuː'deɪʃn US: -nuː-; ‚dinju'deʃən/ n

de·nunci·ation /dɪ‚nʌnsɪ'eɪʃn; dɪ‚nʌnsɪ'eʃən/ n [C, U] denouncing: 公开指摘; 揭发; 通知废止: *the ~ of a traitor.* 揭发某人为奸逆。

deny /dɪ'naɪ; dɪ'naɪ/ vt **1** [VP6A, C, 9, 25] say that (sth) is not true: 否认(某事); 不承认: *The accused man denied the charge.* 被告人不承认所控之罪。 *I ~ that the statement is true.* 我不承认这说法是真的。 *He denied this to be the case.* 他不承认情形是如此。 *He denied knowing anything about / denied any knowledge of their plans.* 他否认知悉他们的计划。 *It cannot be denied that … / There is no ~ing the fact that …*, Everyone must admit that …. 不可否认的是…(我们必须承认…)。 ⇨ **affirm.** **2** [VP6A] say that one knows nothing about; disown; refuse to acknowledge: 否认知情; 拒认: *He denied the signature*, said that it was not his. 他否认这是他的签字。 *Peter denied Christ.* 彼得不认基督。 **3** [VP12A, 13A] say 'no' to a request; refuse to give (sth asked for or needed): 拒绝; 不给(所请求或需要之物): *He denies himself / his wife nothing.* 他对自己(妻子)有求必应。 *He gave to his friends what he denied to his family.* 他尽量赠朋友不与家人。 *She was angry at being denied admittance.* 她因被拒进入而发怒。

deo·dar /'diːədɑː(r); 'die‚dɑr/ n Himalayan cedar. 雪松。

de·odor·ant /diː'əʊdərənt; di'odərənt/ n substance that disguises or absorbs (esp body) odours. 防臭剂; 除臭剂(尤指除体臭者)。

de·odor·ize /diː'əʊdəraɪz; di'odə‚raɪz/ vt [VP6A] remove odour (esp bad smells) from. 除去…之气味(尤指臭气); 防臭。

de·part /dɪ'pɑːt; dɪ'pɑrt/ vi **1** [VP2A, 3A] ~ (*from*), go away; leave (esp in timetables, abbr **dep**): 离开; 出发; 开出(尤用于行车时刻表中, 略作 dep): *dep Leeds 4. 30 pm.* 下午四时三十分自里兹开出。 ⇨ **arrive. 2** [VP3A] ~ *from*, behave in a way that differs from: 不按照, 不遵守: *~ from routine / the usual procedure / old customs*; 不按照常规(通常手续, 旧风俗)行事; *~ from the truth.* 违背真理。 **3** ~ (*from*) *this life*, (archaic) die; 逝世。 (古)亡故; 逝世。 *~ed* part adj bygone:

过去的; 逝去的: *thinking of ~ed glories.* 怀念过去的光荣。 □ **the ~ed**, (*sing*) person who has recently died; (*pl*) those who have died: (单)最近亡故的人; (复)死者: *pray for the souls of the ~ed.* 为死者的灵魂祈祷。

de·part·ment /dɪ'pɑːtmənt; dɪ'pɑrtmənt/ n **1** one of several divisions of a government, business, shop, university, etc: (政府或商业机构中的)部门; (大学中的)系科: *the Education D~/D~ of Education*; 教育部 (系); *the shipping ~* (of a business firm); (商业公司的)装运部; *the men's clothing ~* (in a large shop); (大商店中的)男装部; *a '~ store*, a large shop where many kinds of goods are sold in different ~s. (货物分门别类的)百货公司。 **2** (F) administrative district. (法)行政区。 **~al** /‚diːpɑːt'mentl; dɪ‚pɑrt'mɛntl/ adj of a ~ (contrasted with the whole): 一个部门的(与整体相对): *~al duties / administration.* 各部门的职责(行政)。

de·par·ture /dɪ'pɑːtʃə(r); dɪ'pɑrtʃə/ n ~ (*from*), **1** [U] departing; going away; [C] instance of this: 离开; 离去; 出发: *His ~ was unexpected.* 他离去出人意外。 *There are notices showing arrivals and ~s of trains near the booking-office.* 在售票处附近有公告说明火车到站及开出的时刻。 *Which is the ~ platform, from which the train leaves?* 哪一个月台是开车月台? **2** [C, U] turning away or aside; changing: 背驰; 转变; 改变: *a ~ from old custom*; 不照旧俗行事; *a new ~ in physics*, the discovery of nuclear fission. 物理学上的新起点(如核裂变之发现)。

de·pend /dɪ'pend; dɪ'pɛnd/ vt [VP3A] ~ *on/upon*, **1** (not in the progressive tenses) need, rely on (the support, etc of) in order to exist or to be true or to succeed: (不用于进行时)依赖; 依靠(…的支持及可存在, 成为事实或成功): *Children ~ on their parents for food and clothing.* 小孩依赖他们的父母供给衣食。 *Good health ~s upon good food, exercise and getting enough sleep.* 良好的健康仰赖良好的食物, 运动和充足的睡眠。 *He ~s on his pen for a living*, makes a living by writing. 他靠笔杆(写作)为生。 *that ~s; it (all) ~s*, (alone, or at the beginning of a sentence) the result ~s on sth else: 视情形而定(单独使用或置于句首): *It ~s how you tackle the problem.* 那要看你如何应付这问题。 **2** trust; be certain about: 信赖; 相信: *you can always ~ upon John to be there when he is needed.* 当你需要约翰的时候, 你可永远相信他一定在那儿。 *You may ~ upon his coming / ~ upon it that he will want to come.* 你可相信(我敢说)他会来。 *Can I ~ upon this railway guide or is it an old one?* 这火车时刻手册是可靠的, 还是旧的? ~ *upon it*, (at the beginning or end of a sentence) you can be quite certain: (用于句首或句尾)你可以完全相信; 我敢说: *The strike will ruin the country, ~ upon it.* 这次罢工将使国家遭受严重损失, 我敢说。 ~·**able** adj that may be ~ed upon. 可信赖的; 可靠的。

de·pend·ant /dɪ'pendənt (also -ent) /dɪ'pendənt; dɪ'pɛndənt/ n sb who depends upon another or others for a home, food, etc; servant. 依赖他人生活者; 眷属; 仆从。 ⇨ **dependent** adj.

de·pend·ence /dɪ'pendəns; dɪ'pɛndəns/ n ~ *on/upon*, [U] **1** the state of depending; being supported by others: 依赖; 依靠: *Why don't you find a job and end this ~ upon your parents?* 你为何不找个职业, 不要再依靠你的父母? **2** confident trust; reliance: 信赖; 信任: *He's not a man you can put much ~ on*, you can't rely on him. 他不是个可靠的人。 **3** the state of being determined or conditioned by: 视…而定的状态; 受到限制的状态: *the ~ of the crops upon the weather*; 作物之视天气状况而定; *drug ~.* 药瘾。

de·pend·ency /dɪ'pendənsɪ; dɪ'pɛndənsɪ/ n (*pl* **-cies**) country governed or controlled by another: 属地; 附庸地: *The Hawaiian Islands are no longer a ~ of the USA.* 夏威夷群岛不再是美国的属地。

de·pend·ent /dɪ'pendənt; dɪ'pɛndənt/ n = **dependant.** □ adj ~ *on/upon*, depending: 依赖的; 依靠的: *The man was out of work and ~ on his son's earnings.*

那人失业了，依赖其子之收入过活。 *Promotion is ~ upon your record of success.* 晋级依据优良的考绩。

de·pict /dɪˈpɪkt; dɪˈpɪkt/ *vt* [VP6A] show in the form of a picture; describe in words: 描绘; 描写: *biblical scenes ~ed in tapestry.* 绣帷上所绣的圣经故事。 **de·pic·tion** /dɪˈpɪkʃn; dɪˈpɪkʃən/ *n*

de·pila·tory /dɪˈpɪlətrɪ US: -tɔːrɪ; dɪˈpɪlə,tɔrɪ/ *adj*, *n* (liquid, cream, etc) able to remove superfluous hair. 能除去多余毛发的; 脱毛的; 脱毛剂。

de·plane /diˈpleɪn; diˈplen/ *vi* (usu of troops, etc) disembark from an aircraft. (通常指军队等)下飞机。

de·plete /dɪˈpliːt; dɪˈplit/ *vt* [VP6A, 14] ~ (of), use up, empty until little or none remains; 用尽; 使竭尽: *to ~ a lake of fish;* 将湖中之鱼捕尽; *~d supplies.* 用尽的必需品。 **de·pletion** /dɪˈpliːʃn; dɪˈpliʃən/ *n* [U] depleting or being ~d. 取尽; 用尽。

de·plore /dɪˈplɔː(r); dɪˈplor/ *vt* [VP6A] show, say, that one is filled with sorrow or regret for; condemn. 表示为…而悲痛或懊悔; 指责。 **de·plor·able** /dɪˈplɔːrəbl; dɪˈplorəbl/ *adj* that is, or should be, ~d: 可悲的; 可怜的; 不幸的: *deplorable conduct;* 可悲的行为; *a deplorable accident.* 悲惨的意外祸事。 **de·plor·ably** /-əblɪ; -əblɪ/ *adv*

de·ploy /dɪˈplɔɪ; dɪˈplɔɪ/ *vt, vi* [VP6A, 2A] (mil, of troops etc) (cause to) spread out, eg into line of battle; (fig) bring into action: (军, 指部队等)(使)展开 (成战斗队形等); (喻)使开始活动或工作: ~ *arguments.* 展开辩论。 ~**·ment** *n*

de·pon·ent /dɪˈpəʊnənt; dɪˈponənt/ *n* (legal) person who gives written testimony for use in a law court. (法律)作书面证词供法院使用的人; 作证者。

de·popu·late /ˌdiːˈpɒpjuleɪt; diˈpɑpjə,let/ *vt* [VP6A] lessen the number of people living in a place: 减少(居住某地之)人口: *a country ~d by war/famine.* 因战争(饥荒)而人口减少的国家。 **de·popu·la·tion** /ˌdiːˌpɒpjuˈleɪʃn; ,dipɑpjəˈleʃən/ *n*

de·port¹ /dɪˈpɔːt; dɪˈport/ *vt* [VP6A] expel (an unwanted person) from a country: 驱逐(不受欢迎者)出境: *The spy was imprisoned for two years and then ~ed.* 那间谍经监禁两年后被驱逐出境。 **de·port·ation** /ˌdiːpɔːˈteɪʃn; ,dɪporˈteʃən/ *n* ~*ing or being* ~*ed:* 驱逐出境; 被放逐: *Years ago criminals in England could be sentenced to ~ation to Australia.* 许多年前, 英国的罪犯可能被判放逐至澳洲。 ~**ee** /ˌdiːpɔːˈtiː; ˌdɪporˈti/ *n* ~*ed person.* 被放逐者。

de·port² /dɪˈpɔːt; dɪˈport/ *vt* [VP6A, 16B] (reflex, formal) behave: (用反身式, 正式用语)行为; 持身; 处己: *to ~ oneself with dignity.* 举止庄重。 ~**·ment** *n* [U] behaviour; way of holding oneself in standing and walking: 行为; 举止: *Young ladies used to have lessons in ~ment.* 少女们以前从师学习举止行动的规范。

de·pose /dɪˈpəʊz; dɪˈpoz/ *vt, vi* 1 [VP6A] remove, esp a ruler such as a king, from a position of authority; dethrone. 迫使(君王等)下台; 废除(王位等)。 2 [VP3A, 9] ~ (*to* + *gerund*), (legal) bear witness, give evidence, esp on oath in a law court: (法律)(尤指在法庭宣誓)作证: *to ~ that one saw ...;* 宣誓证实曾亲见…; *to ~ to having seen ....* 宣誓作证曾亲见…。 ⇨ **deposition.**

de·posit¹ /dɪˈpɒzɪt; dɪˈpɑzɪt/ *vt* [VP6A] 1 lay or put down: 置; 放下: *He ~ed the books on the desk.* 他将书籍放在写字桌上。 *Some insects ~ their eggs in the ground.* 有些昆虫产卵于土中。 2 put or store for safe-keeping: 存放; 贮存; 交与～保管: *to ~ money in a bank/papers with one's lawyer.* 将钱存于银行(将文件交与律师保管)。 3 make part payment of money that is or will be owed: 付定金; 先付一部分: *We should like you to ~ a quarter of the price of the house.* 我们希望您能先付房价的四分之一。 4 (esp of a liquid, a river) leave (a layer of matter on): (尤指液体, 河流)沉淀; 淤积: *When the Nile rises it ~s a layer of mud on the land.* 尼罗河涨水时在地上淤积一层泥。

de·posit² /dɪˈpɒzɪt; dɪˈpɑzɪt/ *n* [C] 1 money that is deposited(2, 3): 存款; 定金; 定钱: *The shopkeeper promised to keep the goods for me if I left/paid/made a ~.* 店主答应, 如果我付一点定钱, 他就可将货物替我保留下来。 '~ **account,** money deposited in a bank, not to be withdrawn without notice, on which interest is payable. (需预先通知方可提取而且可以拿利息的)存款帐户。 ⇨ *current account* at **current¹(3).** *money on* ~, money deposited in this way. 存款。 '~ **safe,** safe in the strong-room of a bank, rented for the custody of valuables. 银行保险库内之保险箱(可租用置放贵重物品者)。 2 layer of matter deposited(4): 沉淀物; 淤积物: *A thick ~ of mud covered the fields after the floods went down.* 洪水过后, 田地上盖着一层厚厚的淤泥。 3 layer of solid matter left behind (often buried in the earth) after having been naturally accumulated: (天然积聚而成, 通常埋藏于地下的)矿床; 矿层: *Valuable new ~s of tin have been found in Bolivia.* 宝贵的新锡矿床已在玻利维亚发现。

de·posi·tion /ˌdepəˈzɪʃn; ˌdepəˈzɪʃən/ *n* 1 [U] deposing from office; dethronement. 革职; 废王位。 2 [C] (legal) statement made on oath. (法律)经宣誓所作的证言。 3 [U] depositing, eg of mud. (泥等的)淤积; 沉淀。

de·posi·tor /dɪˈpɒzɪtə(r); dɪˈpɑzɪtə/ *n* person who deposits, eg money in a bank. 寄托者; (存款于银行等中的)存款者。

de·posi·tory /dɪˈpɒzɪtrɪ US: -tɔːrɪ; dɪˈpɑzə,tɔrɪ/ *n* (*pl* -ries) place where goods are deposited; store-house. 存放物的地方; 仓库。

de·pot /ˈdepəʊ US: ˈdiːpəʊ; ˈdipo/ *n* 1 storehouse, esp for military supplies; warehouse; place for storing vehicles (eg buses). 军需库; 仓库; 库房; (公共汽车等之)车库。 2 (US) railway or bus station. (美)火车站; 公共汽车站。

de·prave /dɪˈpreɪv; dɪˈprev/ *vt* [VP6A] make morally bad; corrupt (usu in *pp*): 使道德败坏; 使腐败(通常用过去分词): ~*d persons;* 堕落的人; ~*d* (= vicious or perverted) *tastes.* 邪恶的嗜好。

de·prav·ity /dɪˈprævətɪ; dɪˈprævətɪ/ *n* [U] depraved state; viciousness: 堕落; 邪恶; 腐败: *sunk in* ~; 沉沦; 堕落; [U] (*pl* -ties) vicious act. 邪恶的行为。

dep·re·cate /ˈdeprɪkeɪt; ˈdeprɪ,ket/ *vt* [VP6A, C] (formal) feel and express disapproval of: (正式用语)表示不赞成; 反对: *Hasty action is to be ~d.* 草率行事应予反对。 *He ~s changing the rules at present.* 他不赞成在目前改变规章。 **dep·reca·tion** /ˌdeprəˈkeɪʃn; ˌdeprəˈkeʃən/ *n*

de·pre·ci·ate /dɪˈpriːʃɪeɪt; dɪˈpriʃɪ,et/ *vt, vi* [VP6A, 2A] make or become less in value; say that (sth) has little value: (使)减低价值; (使)贬值; 轻视; 贬抑: *Shares in this company have ~d.* 这家公司的股票已贬值了。 *Don't ~ my efforts to help.* 不要轻视我为了帮忙所作的努力。 **de·pre·ci·atory** /dɪˈpriːʃətrɪ US: -tɔːrɪ; dɪˈpriʃɪə,tɔrɪ/ *adj* tending to ~: 贬值的; 轻视的; 贬抑的: *depreciatory remarks about my work.* 对我的工作有所贬抑的话。 **de·pre·ci·ation** /dɪˌpriːʃɪˈeɪʃn; dɪˌpriʃɪˈeʃən/ *n* [U] lessening of value or estimation. 贬值; 折旧; 轻视。

dep·re·da·tion /ˌdeprɪˈdeɪʃn; ˌdeprɪˈdeʃən/ *n* (usu *pl*) (formal) destruction or pillaging of property. (通常用复数)(正式用语)毁坏或劫掠财产。

de·press /dɪˈpres; dɪˈprɛs/ *vt* [VP6A] 1 press, push or pull down: 压下; 推下; 拉下: *to ~ a lever/the keys of a piano.* 压下杠杆(钢琴键)。 ~*ed* '**classes,** classes of people who are prevented from rising, or unable to rise, socially or economically, eg by a rigid caste system. 受压迫的阶级; 下层阶级之人民(社会或经济地位不能提高之人, 如因受严格的阶级制度所阻碍者)。 2 make sad, low in spirits: 使悲愁; 使沮丧: *Wet weather always ~es her.* 雨天总使她愁苦。 *The newspapers are full of ~ing news nowadays,* eg of war, crime, natural disasters, rising prices. 报纸如今充满了令人忧愁的消息

(例如战争, 犯罪, 天灾, 物价上涨). **3** make less active; cause (prices) to be lower: 使不活泼; 使跌价; 使萧条: *When business is ~ed there is usually an increase in unemployment.* 当商业萧条时, 通常失业就会增加. **,~ed 'area**, part of a country where industry is ~ed (with consequent poverty and unemployment). 工商业萧条(结果造成贫穷和失业)的地区.

de·press·ion /dɪ'preʃn; dɪ'prɛʃən/ *n* **1** [U] being depressed(2); low spirits: 愁苦; 沮丧; 抑郁: *He commited suicide during a fit of ~.* 他一时想不开自杀了. **2** [C] hollow, sunk place, in the surface of sth, esp the ground: 表面(尤指地面)凹陷之处; 洼穴; 坑: *It rained heavily and every ~ in the bad road was soon filled with water.* 雨下得很大, 不久那坏路上的每一坑凹都积满了水. *The soldiers hid from the enemy in a slight ~.* 士兵们藏在一个浅坑里躲过了敌人的视线. **3** [C] time when business is depressed(3). 商业萧条的时期. **4** [C] lowering of atmospheric pressure; (esp) area of low barometric pressure; the system of winds round it: 气压降低; 低气压; (尤指)低气压区域; 低气压区域周围的风: *a ~ over Iceland.* 冰岛上空的低气压.

de·press·ive /dɪ'presɪv; dɪ'prɛsɪv/ *adj* tending to depress; of depression(1): 压抑的; 压下的; 不景气的; 沮丧的; 抑郁的: *~ financial measures;* 平抑物价的金融措施; *a ~ fit.* 一阵沮丧. □ *n* person tending to suffer from depression(1). 沮丧者; 抑郁者.

de·prive /dɪ'praɪv; dɪ'praɪv/ *vt* [VP14] *~ of*, take away from; prevent from using or enjoying: 取走; 剥夺; 使丧失; 使不能使用或享受: *trees that ~ a house of light.* 遮住房中光线的树木. *What would a student do if he were ~d of his books?* 一个学生倘若没了书籍, 将怎么办? **de·prived** *adj* = **underprivileged**. **depri·va·tion** /,depri'veɪʃn; ,dɛprɪ'veʃən/ *n* [U] depriving or being ~d: 剥夺; 夺去: *deprivation of one's rights as a citizen;* 某人公民权之被剥夺; [C] sth of which one is ~d. 被夺之物.

depth /depθ; dɛpθ/ *n* **1** [C, U] being deep; distance from the top down, from the front to the back, from the surface inwards: 深; 深度(自顶端而下, 自前至后, 自表面向内的距离): *What is the ~ of the well?* 此井深度若干? *Water was found at a ~ of 30 feet.* 水在三十英尺深处被发现. *At what ~ is the wreck lying?* 破船残骸在多深的水中? *The snow is three feet in ~.* 雪积三英尺深. *in ~*, thoroughly: 彻底的(地): *explore a subject in ~;* 彻底研究一题目; *a study in ~.* 彻底的研究. *be/go/get out of one's ~*, (a) be in/enter water too deep to stand in: 入水至不能立稳(即触不到底或过顶)的深度: *If you can't swim, don't go out of your ~.* 你如果不会游泳, 不要到水太深的地方去. (b) (fig) attempt the study of sth that is too difficult: (喻)企图研究过于难懂的事物: *When people start talking about nuclear physics I'm out of my ~.* 当人们谈起核物理学, 我就茫无所知了. *'~-bomb /-charge*, bomb used against a submarine, for explosion under water. 深水炸弹(在水中爆炸, 以攻击潜艇者). **2** [C, U] deep learning, thought, feeling, etc: 深奥的学问, 思想, 感情等: *a book that shows scholarship and ~ of thought.* 显示出学术及思想之深度的书. *She showed a ~ of feeling that surprised us.* 她表现出的强烈的感情令我们吃惊. **3** the *~(s)*, deepest or most central part(s): 最深之处; 最内部: *in the ~ of one's heart;* 在心的深处; *in the ~ of winter;* 在隆冬; *in the ~s of despair;* 在极度绝望中; *in the ~ of the country,* a long way from any town. 在穷乡僻壤.

depu·ta·tion /,depju'teɪʃn; ,dɛpjə'teʃən/ *n* group of representatives; number of persons given the right to act or speak for others. 代表团(被授权代表他人行为或发言的若干人).

de·pute /dɪ'pjuːt; dɪ'pjut/ *vt* [VP14, 17] *~ sth to sb/sb to do sth*, give (one's work, authority, etc) to a substitute; give (another person) authority to act as one's representative. 将(工作, 职权等)交与代理人; 给予

(某人)代表行事之权.

depu·tize /'depjutaɪz; 'dɛpjə,taɪz/ *vi* [VP2A, 3A] *~ (for sb)*, act as deputy. (为某人之)代理.

dep·uty /'depjutɪ; 'dɛpjətɪ/ *n* (*pl* -ties) **1** person to whom work, authority, etc is deputed: 受托代理工作, 职权等的人; 代表; 代理人: *I must find someone to act as (a) ~ for me during my absence.* 我必须找一个人, 在我离开期间代理我的职务. **2** (in some countries, eg France) member of a legislative assembly. (在某些国家, 例如法国)议员.

de·rail /dɪ'reɪl; di'rel/ *vt* [VP6A] cause (a train, etc) to run off the rails: 使(火车等)出轨: *The engine was ~ed.* 火车头出轨了. **~·ment** *n*

de·range /dɪ'reɪndʒ; dɪ'rendʒ/ *vt* [VP6A] put out of working order; put into confusion; disturb: 使失去正常的作用或功能; 使混乱; 搅乱: *He is mentally ~d,* insane. 他精神错乱了. **~·ment** *n*

de·rate /,diː'reɪt; di'ret/ *vt* [VP6A] (GB) relieve (industries, etc) from a proportion of the local rates(3): (英)减低(工业等)的房地产税: *the Derating Act, 1929.* 一九二九年所制定的减低房地产税法案.

derby¹ /'dɑːbɪ *US*: 'dɝbɪ; 'dɝbɪ/ *n* **1** The D~, annual horserace at Epsom, England. 在英国埃普瑟姆所举行一年一度的大赛马. **'D~ Day**, day of the race (in June). 举行此项大赛马的日子(在六月). **2** (US) any of several annual horseraces. (美)任何每年举行的赛马会. **3** sporting contest. 运动比赛. **local ~**, one between local teams. 本地队间的赛马比赛.

derby² /'dɑːrbɪ; 'dɝbɪ/ *n* (US) bowler hat. (美)圆顶礼帽.

der·el·ict /'derelɪkt; 'dɛrə,lɪkt/ *adj* abandoned; deserted and left to fall into ruin: 被弃的; 被遗弃的: *a ~ house;* 被弃的房屋; *a ~ ship;* 弃船; *~ areas,* eg those made squalid by open-cast mining, gravel digging. 被弃地区(例如因地上开采矿物, 掘砂砾石而被弃置的污秽地区). **der·el·ic·tion** /,derə'lɪkʃn; ,dɛrə'lɪkʃən/ *n* **1** making ~. 放弃. *the dereliction caused by a war.* 战争造成的废墟. **2** (wilful) neglect of duty. (故意的)怠忽职责.

de·requi·si·tion /,diː,rekwɪ'zɪʃn; di,rɛkwə'zɪʃən/ *vt* [VP6A] free (requisitioned property, etc). 退还(被征用的财产等).

de·re·strict /,diːrɪ'strɪkt; ,dirɪ'strɪkt/ *vt* [VP6A] cancel a restriction upon: 解除限制: *a ~ road,* remove a speed limit from it. 解除某路之行车速率限制.

de·ride /dɪ'raɪd; dɪ'raɪd/ *vt* [VP6A, 16B] mock; laugh scornfully at: 嘲弄; 嘲笑: *They ~d his efforts as childish.* 他们嘲笑他的努力为幼稚.

de rigueur /də rɪ'gɜː(r); dərɪˈgœr/ *pred adj* (F) required by etiquette or custom: (法)礼节或风俗上所需要的: *Evening dress is ~ at the Casino.* 晚礼服在娱乐场是礼节上所需要的.

de·ri·sion /dɪ'rɪʒn; dɪ'rɪʒən/ *n* [U] deriding or being derided; ridicule, mockery: 嘲弄; 嘲笑; 被嘲笑的事物; 笑柄: *hold sb/sth in ~,* 嘲笑某人(某事物); [U] *become an object of ~;* 成为嘲笑的对象; *make sb/sth an object of ~.* 使某人(某事物)成为笑柄.

de·ris·ive /dɪ'raɪsɪv; dɪ'raɪsɪv/ *adj* showing or deserving derision: 嘲笑的; 嘲弄的; 可笑的: *~ laughter;* 嘲弄的笑声; *a ~ offer,* eg £100 for a car that is worth £1000. 可笑的出价(如出一百英镑欲买价值一千英镑的汽车).

de·ris·ory /dɪ'raɪsərɪ; dɪ'raɪsərɪ/ *adj* = **derisive**.

deri·va·tion /,derɪ'veɪʃn; ,dɛrə'veʃən/ *n* **1** [U] deriving or being derived; origin; descent: 引出; 导出; 根源; 由来: *the ~ of words from Latin;* 源于拉丁文的词的由来; *a word of Latin ~.* 源出于拉丁文的词. **2** [C] first form and meaning of a word; statement of how a word was formed and how it changed: 词的最初的形式; 词的起源及变化的说明: *to study the ~s of words.* 研究词的起源及变化.

de·riva·tive /də'rɪvətɪv; də'rɪvətɪv/ *adj, n* [C] (thing,

word, substance) derived from another; not original or primitive: 由他物而来的(物件, 物质); 由他词而来的(词);非本来的; 非原始的; 转来的; 衍生物; 派生词: *'Assertion' is a ~ of 'assert'.* assertion 一字由 assert 转化而来。

de·rive /dɪ'raɪv; dɪ'raɪv/ *vt, vi* **1** [VP14] ~ **from,** (formal) get: (正式用语)得来; 得到: *to ~ great pleasure from one's studies; 自读书研究获得极大的乐趣; medicine from which she has ~d little benefit.* 使她得益很少的药物。**2** [VP14, 3A] ~ **from,** take/have as a starting-point, source or origin: 源出; 起源: *Thousands of English words ~ are ~d from Latin.* 英语有成千上万的词源出于拉丁语。

der·ma·tol·ogy /,dɜːmə'tɒlədʒɪ; ,dɜːmə'tɑlədʒɪ/ *n* [U] medical study of the skin, its diseases, etc. 皮肤(病)学。**der·ma·tol·ogist** /,dɜːmə'tɒlədʒɪst; ,dɜːmə'tɑlədʒɪst/ *n* expert in ~. 皮肤(病)学家。

dero·gate /'derəgeɪt; 'dɛrə,get/ *vi* [VP3A] ~ **from,** (formal) take away (a merit, good quality, right). (正式用语)取去: 除去(功绩、良好的品质、权利)。**dero·ga·tion** /,derə'geɪʃn; ,dɛrə'geʃən/ *n* [U] lessening (of authority, dignity, reputation, etc). 减低(权威、尊严、名誉等, 与 of 连用)。

de·roga·tory /dɪ'rɒgətrɪ *US:* -tɔːrɪ; dɪ'rɑgə,tɔrɪ/ *adj* (abbr *derog* used in this dictionary) (本词典中略作 derog) ~ **(to),** tending to damage or take away from (one's credit, etc); insulting: 损毁或减低(人之荣誉等)的; 侮蔑的; 贬抑的: *remarks that are ~ to my reputation.* 有损我名誉的言论。*Is the slang word 'cop' as ~ as 'pig' for 'policeman',* Are policemen likely to object to it as being insulting? 用俚语 cop 称警察和用 pig 称他们一样会引起反感(会使警察因受辱而反对)吗?

der·rick /'derɪk; 'dɛrɪk/ *n* **1** ~ **crane,** large crane for moving or lifting heavy weights, esp on a ship. (尤指船上的)起重机。**2** (also 亦作 *oil-rig*) framework over an oil-well or bore-hole, to hold the drilling machinery, etc. (在油井或其他钻孔上用以支持钻具等的)铁架塔。

    derrick cranes   **an oil derrick**

der·ring-do /,derɪŋ 'duː; 'dɛrɪŋ'du/ *n* [U] (old use) desperate courage: (旧用法)不顾危险的勇敢: *deeds of ~.* 不顾死活的勇敢行为。

derv /dɜːv; dɜv/ *n* [U] fuel oil for diesel engines (from *diesel engined road* vehicle). 柴油机所用的燃料油; 柴油(原名由 *diesel engined road* vehicle 四字为首字母拼成)。

der·vish /'dɜːvɪʃ; 'dɜvɪʃ/ *n* member of an order of Muslim religious enthusiasts: (伊斯兰教之)苦修僧人: *dancing ~es,* who engage in whirling dances; 崇拜时身体回旋舞动的苦修僧人; *howling ~es,* who shout loudly. 高声吼叫的苦修僧人。

de·sali·nate /,diː'sælɪneɪt; di'sælə,net/ *vt* [VP6A] = desalinize. **de·sali·na·tion** /,diː,sælɪ'neɪʃn; ,disælə'neʃən/ *n*

de·sali·nize /,diː'sælɪnaɪz; di'sælɪ,naɪz/ *vt* [VP6A] remove salt from (sea water or saline water). 除去(海水或盐水中的)盐分。**de·salin·iz·ation** /,diː,sælɪnaɪ'zeɪʃn *US:* -nɪ'z-; ,disælɪ,naɪ'zeʃən/ *n*

de·salt /,diː'sɔːlt; di'sɒlt/ *vt* = desalinize.

de·scale /,diː'skeɪl; di'skel/ *vt* [VP6A] remove the scale from, eg the inside of boiler tubes. 除去(汽锅管内等)的锅垢或锈皮。

des·cant /'deskænt; 'dɛskænt/ *n* (music) additional independent accompaniment (often improvised) to a melody. (音乐)附加的独立伴奏或伴唱旋律(常是即与而作的)。□ *vi* /dɪ'skænt; dɛs'kænt/ [VP3A] ~ **on/upon, (a)** (music) sing or play a ~ on. (音乐)为…唱或演奏独立伴奏曲。**(b)** comment on, enlarge upon (a topic). 评论; 详论(一题目)。

de·scend /dɪ'send; dɪ'sɛnd/ *vi, vt* **1** [VP2A, C, 6A] (formal) come or go down: (正式用语)下来; 下去: *On turning the corner, we saw that the road ~ed steeply.* 在转弯的时候, 我们看见路陡然下斜。*The balloon ~ed in Poland.* 汽球落于波兰境内。*He ~ed the stairs.* 他下楼。**2** *be ~ed from,* have as ancestors: 为…的后裔: *According to the Bible, we are all ~ed from Adam.* 根据圣经, 我们都是亚当的后裔。**3** [VP2C] (of property, qualities, rights) pass (from father to son) by inheritance; come from earlier times. (指财产,气质,权利)遗传; 传代; 由较早的时代传下来。**4** [VP3A] ~ **on/upon,** attack suddenly; (colloq) visit unexpectedly: 突击; (口)出其不意地拜访: *The bandits ~ed upon the defenceless village.* 匪徒突击无防御的村庄。**5** [VP3A] ~ **to,** lower oneself to: 自贬身份; 流于: *You would never ~ to fraud/cheating.* 你绝不至沦于欺骗。**6** ~ **to particulars,** pass on (in an argument, etc) to details, eg after a general introduction to a subject. (在辩论等中介绍过题目的概要过后)进入详细讨论阶段。~**ant** /-ənt; -ɛnt/ *n* person who is ~ed from (the person or persons named): 后裔; 后代; 子孙: the ~*ants of Queen Victoria.* 维多利亚女王的后裔。

de·scent /dɪ'sent; dɪ'sɛnt/ *n* **1** [C, U] coming or going down: 下来; 下去: *The land slopes to the sea by a gradual ~,* slopes gradually. 陆地逐渐向海倾斜下去。*The ~ of the mountain took two hours.* 下山花了两个小时。**2** [U] ancestry: 世系; 祖籍: *of French ~,* having French ancestors; 祖籍法国; *Darwin's 'D~ of Man',* ie his theory of evolution. 达尔文的'进化论'。*He traces his ~ from the Queen of Sheba.* 他追溯他的世系出于希巴女王。**3** [C] ~ **on/upon,** sudden attack on; (colloq) unexpected visit to: 突袭; (口)出其不意的拜访: *The Danes made numerous ~s upon the English coast during the 10th century.* 在第 10 世纪中, 丹麦人曾对英国沿海作无数次的突袭。**4** [U] handing down, eg of property, titles, qualities, etc by inheritance. (财产, 名位, 特质等)世代相传。

de·scribe /dɪ'skraɪb; dɪ'skraɪb/ *vt* **1** [VP6A, 14, 10, 16B] ~ **(to/for),** say what (sb or sth) is like; give a picture of in words: 描写; (用语言文字)描绘; 描述: *Words cannot ~ the beauty of the scene.* 此景之美非笔墨所能形容。*Can you ~ it to/for me?* 你能把它描述给我听吗? *Please ~ what you saw.* 请叙述所见。**2** [VP16B] ~ **as,** qualify; say that (sb or sth) has certain qualities: 形容; 说(某人或某事物)有某种性质: *I hesitate to ~ him as really clever.* 我不愿说他是真正的聪明。*He ~s himself as a doctor.* 他自称系医生。**3** [VP6A] mark out, draw (esp a geometrical figure): 作图; 画(尤指几何图形): *It is easy to ~ a circle if you have a pair of compasses.* 如果你有一副圆规, 很容易画一个圆。

de·scrip·tion /dɪ'skrɪpʃn; dɪ'skrɪpʃən/ *n* **1** [U] describing; [C] picture in words: 描写; 描述; 形容: *He's not very good at ~.* 他不太会描写。*The scenery was beautiful beyond ~.* 这风景美得难以形容。*Can you give me a ~ of the thief,* 你能为我描述一下那个贼的模样吗? ⇨ **answer²(4). 2** [C] (colloq) sort: (口)种类; 式样: *The harbour was crowded with vessels of every ~.* 那港内充满各式各样的船只。

de·scrip·tive /dɪ'skrɪptɪv; dɪ'skrɪptɪv/ *adj* serving to describe; fond of describing: 描写的; 喜欢描写的: *There is some excellent ~ writing* (eg descriptions of scenery) *in Hardy's novels.* 在哈代的小说中, 有些极美

的描写(如描写风景)。

des·cry /dɪ'skraɪ; dɪ'skraɪ/ vt [VP6A] (formal) catch sight of; see (esp sth a long way off). (正式用语) 察觉;看见(尤指远处之物)。

des·ecrate /'desɪkreɪt; 'dɛsɪ,kret/ vt [VP6A] use (a sacred thing or place) in an unworthy or wicked way. 把(圣物或圣地)作俗用或恶用。**des·ecra·tion** /,desɪ'kreɪʃn; ,dɛsɪ'kreʃən/ n [U] desecrating or being ~d. 亵渎;污辱(圣物或圣地)。

de·seg·re·gate /,diː'segrɪgeɪt; di'sɛgrəget/ vt [VP6A] abolish (esp racial) segregation in: 废除(尤指种族)隔离: ~ schools in Alabama. 消除亚拉巴马州学校内的种族隔离。**de·seg·re·ga·tion** /,diː,segrɪ'geɪʃn; di,sɛgrɪ'geʃən/ n

de·sen·si·tize /,diː'sensɪtaɪz; di'sɛnsə,taɪz/ vt [VP6A] render insensitive or less sensitive, eg to light or pain. 使无感觉;使较不敏感(如对光线或苦痛)。**de·sen·si·tiz·ation** /,diː,sensɪtaɪ'zeɪʃn US: -tɪ'z-; ,disɛnsəta-'zeʃən/ n

de·sert¹ /dɪ'zɜːt; dɪ'zɝt/ vt, vi 1 [VP6A] leave; go away from: 离开;放弃;抛弃: The village had been hurriedly ~ed, perhaps because bandits were in the district. 全村的人都匆匆逃走了，或许因为有土匪到达该地区。The streets were ~ed, no people were to be seen. 街上行人绝迹。We sheltered from the storm in a ~ed hut, one that had been abandoned. 我们住在一个空无人住的茅屋里躲暴风雨。2 [VP6A] leave without help or support, esp in a wrong or cruel way: 背弃; 遗弃不顾(尤指以不当或残忍的方法): He ~ed his wife and children and went abroad. 他遗弃妻子儿女不予顾，出国去了。He has become so rude that his friends are ~ing him. 他变得粗暴无礼，所以朋友们都不和他来往了。3 [VP6A, 2A] run away from; leave (esp service in a ship, the armed forces) without authority or permission: 潜逃;未经准假而离开(尤指船上,军中的职守); 逃亡; 开小差: A soldier who ~s his post in time of war is punished severely. 在战时逃兵的处罚很重。4 [VP6A] fail: 使失败;使失望: His courage/presence of mind ~ed him. 他的勇气(镇静功夫)尽失。~er n person who ~s(3). 背弃者; 潜逃者; (尤指)逃兵。**de·ser·tion** /dɪ'zɜːʃn; dɪ'zɝʃən/ n [C, U] (instance of) ~ing or being ~ed. 离开;放弃;背弃;遗弃;逃亡。

des·ert² /'dezət; 'dɛzɚt/ n [C, U] (large area of) barren land, waterless and treeless, often sandcovered; 沙漠(无水,无树,常为沙覆盖的一大片不毛之地); 荒地: the Sahara D~. 撒哈拉沙漠。□ adj 1 barren; uncultivated: 荒凉的;不毛的: the ~ areas of N Africa. 北非洲的荒漠地区。2 uninhabited: 无人居住的: wrecked on a ~ island. 在一荒岛触礁失事。

de·serts /dɪ'zɜːts; dɪ'zɝts/ n (pl) what sb deserves: (复)某人应得的赏罚: to be rewarded/punished according to one's ~, 受到应得的奖赏(惩罚); to get/meet with one's ~. 得到应得的赏罚。

de·serve /dɪ'zɜːv; dɪ'zɝv/ vt, vi (not used in the progressive tenses; 不用于进行时; ⇨ **deserving**.) 1 [VP6A, 7A] be entitled to (because of actions, conduct, qualities); merit: (因为行为,品行,才干而)应该得到;值得: Good work ~s good pay. 好的工作应得到的报酬。He certainly ~s to be sent to prison. 他的确应该送去坐监牢。These people ~ our help. 这些人值得我们帮助。2 to ~ well/ill of, to ~ to be well/badly treated by: 应该受到…之优(虐)待: He ~s well of his country. 他应得国家的优待。**de·served** adj that ought to be given; just: 应得的: ~d punishment/reward/praise. 应得的惩罚(报酬,赞美)。His promotion wasn't ~d. 他的升迁是不应得的。**de·serv·ed·ly** /dɪ'zɜːvɪdlɪ; dɪ'zɝvɪdlɪ/ adv according to what is ~d; justly; rightly: 按功过应得地;当然应该地: to be ~dly punished. 罚得应该。

de·serv·ing /dɪ'zɜːvɪŋ; dɪ'zɝvɪŋ/ adj ~ (of), having merit; worthy of: 值得的: to give money to a ~ cause; 捐款给有价值的事业; 值得同情的: a ~ case, a person who, because of his

circumstances, etc, deserves interest, sympathy, help, etc. 因其环境等值得关心,同情或帮助的人。

dés·habillé /,deɪzæ'biːeɪ; dezabi'je/ (F) (法) = **dishabille.**

des·ic·cant /'desɪkənt; 'dɛsəkənt/ n (US) substance used to absorb moisture. (美)干燥剂。

des·ic·cate /'desɪkeɪt; 'dɛsɪket/ vt [VP6A] dry out all the moisture from, esp solid food, to preserve it: 除去(固体食物等)的水份以保存之; 干燥: ~d fruit/coconut. 水果(椰子)干。

de·sid·er·atum /dɪ,zɪdə'rɑːtəm; dɪ,sɪdə'retəm/ n (pl -rata /-'rɑːtə; -'retə/) sth felt to be lacking and needed. 感到缺乏或需要的东西。

de·sign /dɪ'zaɪn; dɪ'zaɪn/ n 1 [C] drawing or outline from which sth may be made: 图样; 设计图样: ~s for a dress/garden; 服装(花园)的设计图样; [U] art of making such drawings, etc: 设计制图术: a school of ~. 设计制图学校。2 [U] general arrangement or planning (of a picture, book, building, machine, etc): (图画,书籍,建筑物,机器等的)设计; 布局; 配置: The building seats 2000 people, but is poor in ~. 这建筑物有二千人的座位,但设计很差。A machine of faulty ~ will not sell well. 设计不良的机器销路不会好。3 [U] pattern; arrangement of lines, shapes, details, as ornament, eg on a bowl or carpet: 图案(线条,图形,枝节的安排,作为装饰,如碗上或地毯上者): a vase with a ~ of flowers on it. 有花形图案的花瓶。4 [C, U] purpose; intention; mental plan: 目的; 意向; 计划: Whether by accident or ~, he arrived too late to help us. 无论是意外或故意,他到得太迟了,帮不上我们的忙。Was the world made by ~ or did it come into existence by chance? 宇宙是按照计划造成的,还是偶然产生的? have ~s on/against, intend (selfishly or evilly) to get possession of: (自私或不轨地)图谋占有或夺取: That man has ~s on your money/your life; 那人图谋你的钱财(性命); (colloq) (口) He has ~s on that young girl, wants to be intimate with her. 他想打那个年轻女郎的主意。□ vt, vi 1 [VP6A] prepare a plan, sketch, etc (of sth to be made): 为…画图样: ~ a dress/garden. 为服装(花园)画图样。2 [VP2A, C] make ~s(1) from which sth will be made: 设计图案: He ~s for a large firm of carpet manufacturers. 他为一织绒造地毯的大公司设计图案。3 [VP14, 16A, B] ~ for, set apart, intend, plan: 留作某种用途;打算;计划: This course of study is ~ed to help those wishing to teach abroad. 这门课程是为帮助欲至国外教书的人而开的。This room was ~ed for the children/~d as a children's playroom. 这个房间预定留给孩子们用(留作孩子们的游戏室)。~ed·ly /-ɪdlɪ; -ɪdlɪ/ adv by ~(4); on purpose. 故意地;存心地。

des·ig·nate¹ /'dezɪgneɪt; 'dɛzɪgnɪt/ adj (placed after the n) appointed to an office (but not yet installed): (置于名词之后)已受命(而尚未就职的): the bishop ~. 已受命而尚未就职的主教。

des·ig·nate² /'dezɪgneɪt; 'dɛzɪg,net/ vt 1 [VP6A] mark or point out clearly; give a name or title to: 标明;指明;命名: to ~ boundaries. 标明界限。2 [VP6A, 17, 16B] appoint to a position or office: 任命;指派: He ~d Smith as his successor. 他指定史密斯为他的继任人。

des·ig·na·tion /,dezɪg'neɪʃn; ,dɛzɪg'neʃən/ n [U] appointing to an office; [C] name, title or description. 任命;委派;名义;头衔。

de·sign·er /dɪ'zaɪnə(r); dɪ'zaɪnɚ/ n person who designs, eg machinery, dresses. (机器,服装等的)设计人; 制图样者。

de·sign·ing /dɪ'zaɪnɪŋ; dɪ'zaɪnɪŋ/ adj artful and cunning; fond of intrigue. 狡猾的; 诡谲的; 喜好阴谋的。□ n [U] art of making designs (for machinery, etc). (机器等的)设计术。

de·sir·able /dɪ'zaɪərəbl; dɪ'zaɪrəbl/ adj to be desired; causing desire; worth having: 想要的;令人想望的; 值得有的: This ~ property to be sold or let, as in a

house-agent's advertisement. 优良房产出售或出租(房产经纪人的广告). *It is most ~ that he should attend the conference*. 他能参加此项会议, 是最好不过了. **de·sir·abil·ity** /dɪˌzaɪərə'bɪlətɪ; dɪˌzaɪrə'bɪlətɪ/ n

de·sire[1] /dɪ'zaɪə(r); dɪ'zaɪr/ n 1 [U] strong longing; strong sexual attraction; [C] instance of this; earnest wish: 欲望; 殷望; 渴望; 情欲: *He has no / not much ~ for wealth*. 他对于财富无(无大)欲望. *He works hard from a ~ to become rich*. 他因渴望致富而努力工作. *He spoke about his country's ~ for friendly relations / that friendly relations should be established*. 他说明他的国家欲建立友好关系的愿望. *It is impossible to satisfy all their ~s*. 使他们所有的欲望都得到满足是不可能的. **2** (sing) request: (单)请求: *at the ~ of Her Majesty*. 根据女王的请求. **3** [C] thing that is wished for: 所渴望得到之物: *I hope you will get all your heart's ~s*, all you wish for. 我希望你想得到的东西都能得到.

de·sire[2] /dɪ'zaɪə(r); dɪ'zaɪr/ vt [VP6A, 7A, 17, 9] **1** (formal) long for; wish; have a desire(1) for: (正式用语)渴望; 愿望; 欲得到: *We all ~ happiness and health*. 我们都想得到幸福和健康. *Our rooms at the hotel were all that could be ~d*, were quite satisfactory. 我们在旅馆中所住的房间令我们满意极了. *What do you ~ me to do?* 你想要我做什么? **2** (official style) request: (官方文体)请求: *It is ~d that this rule shall be brought to the attention of the staff*. 请转告全体工作人员注意本条规章.

de·sir·ous /dɪ'zaɪərəs; dɪ'zaɪrəs/ adj ~ (of), (formal, official) feeling desire: (正式及官方用语)想望的; 渴望的: *~ of peace*; 想望和平的; *~ to do sth*; 渴望做某事; *~ that ....* 渴望….

de·sist /dɪ'zɪst; dɪ'zɪst/ vi [VP2A, 3A] ~ (from), (formal) cease: (正式用语)停止; *~ from gossiping*. 停止谈闲话.

desk /desk; desk/ n 1 piece of furniture (not a table) with a flat or sloping top and drawers at which to read, write or do business, eg one for office or school use. 读书写字桌; 书桌; 办公桌. **2** reception desk, ⟹ reception(1): 接待处; 服务桌: *leave a message at the ~ (of the hotel)*. 留信于(旅馆之)服务台. '~ clerk n (US) reception clerk. (美)接待人员.

deso·late /'desələt; 'deslɪt/ adj 1 (of a place) in a ruined, neglected state; (of land or a country) unlived in; unfit to live in; barren: (指地方)荒废的; 荒芜的; (指土地或国家)无人烟的; 不适于居住的, 不毛的: *a ~, wind-swept moorland area*. 荒凉又多风的荒地. **2** friendless; wretched; lonely and sad: 孤独的; 可怜的; 凄凉的: *a ~-looking child*; 其状堪怜的孩童; *a ~ life*. 凄凉的一生. **~·ly** adv □ vt /'desəleɪt; 'desl,et/ [VP6A] make ~. 使荒凉; 使成废墟;使凄惨. **deso·la·tion** /,desə'leɪʃn; ,desl'eʃən/ n [U] making or being ~: 荒凉; 荒芜: *the desolation caused by war*. 战争所造成的荒凉.

des·pair[1] /dɪ'speə(r); dɪ'spɛr/ n [U] **1** the state of having lost all hope: 一切希望断绝的情况; 绝望: *Your stupidity will drive me to ~*. 你的愚笨将会使我绝望. *He gave up the attempt in ~*. 绝望之余, 他放弃尝试. *He was filled with ~ when he read the examination questions*. 他一看到考试题目, 就感到绝望了. *The refugee's ~ of ever seeing his family again filled us with pity*. 那难民对于再也见不到他的家人所抱的绝望心情, 令我们感到怜悯. **2** be the ~ of, be sb or sth that causes loss of hope to: 成为令人绝望的事物: *This boy is the ~ of all his teachers*, They no longer hope to teach him anything. 这孩子使他所有的老师都对他感到绝望. *He is the ~ of all other pianists*, plays so well that they cannot hope to rival him. 他使所有其他的钢琴家感到绝望(因其演奏技巧使他们望尘莫及).

des·pair[2] /dɪ'speə(r); dɪ'spɛr/ vi [VP2A, 3A] ~ (of), be in ~ about: 绝望: *to ~ of success / of ever succeeding*. 毫无成功希望. *His life was ~ed of*, All hope that he would live was lost. 已经完全没有救活他的希望了. **~·ing·ly** adv

des·patch /dɪ'spætʃ; dɪ'spætʃ/ n, vt = dispatch

des·per·ado /,despə'rɑːdəu; ,despə'redo/ n (pl ~es; US also ~s /-dəuz; -doz/) person ready to do any reckless or criminal act. 亡命之徒; 暴徒.

des·per·ate /'despərət; 'despərɪt/ adj **1** (of a person) filled with despair and ready to do anything, regardless of danger: (指人)因绝望而不惜冒险的: *The prisoners became ~ in their attempts to escape*. 那些囚犯拚命企图逃亡. **2** lawless; violent: 不法的; 凶暴的: *~ criminals*. 凶暴的罪犯. **3** extremely serious or dangerous: 极严重或危险的: *The state of the country is ~*. 该国的情况极为严重. **4** giving little hope of success; tried when all else has failed: 甚少成功希望的; 在甚少成功希望的补救方法. **~·ly** adv **des·per·ation** /,despə'reɪʃn; ,despə'reʃən/ n [U] the state of being ~(1): 不顾一切的冒险; 拚命: *The wretched people rose in desperation against their rulers*. 可怜的人们不顾一切起来反抗他们的统治者. *You'll drive me to desperation*, (colloq) fill me with despair, make me ready to do sth. (口)你将使我绝望而走极端.

des·pic·able /dɪ'spɪkəbl; 'despɪkəbl/ adj deserving to be despised; contemptible. 可鄙的; 卑劣的. **des·pic·ably** /-əblɪ; -əblɪ/ adv

des·pise /dɪ'spaɪz; dɪ'spaɪz/ vt [VP6A] feel contempt for; consider worthless: 鄙视; 轻视; 瞧不起: *Strike-breakers are ~d by their workmates*. 破坏罢工者为同事者所鄙视. *A dish of strawberries and cream is not to be ~d*, is very good and should not be refused. 一盘草莓和乳酪不算很差.

des·pite /dɪ'spaɪt; dɪ'spaɪt/ prep in spite of: 不管; 不顾: *~ what she says ....* 不论她怎么说…. □ n (obsolescent) ~ of; in ~ of, in spite of (which is now the usu phrase). (过时用语)不管; 不顾(如今通常用in spite of). **~·ful** /-ful; -fəl/ adj (archaic) spiteful. (古)怀有恶意的. **~·fully** /-fəlɪ; -fəlɪ/ adv

de·spoil /dɪ'spɔɪl; dɪ'spɔɪl/ vt [VP6A, 14] ~ sb (of), (liter) rob, plunder. (文)夺取; 掠夺;抢夺.

de·spon·dency /dɪ'spɒndənsɪ; dɪ'spɑndənsɪ/ n [U] loss of hope; melancholy: 失望; 沮丧; 意气消沉: *to fall into ~*. 变得沮丧. **de·spon·dent** /dɪ'spɒndənt; dɪ'spɑndənt/ adj having or showing loss of hope: 感到失望的;沮丧的;消沉的: *Don't become despondent*. 不要灰心. **de·spon·dent·ly** adv

des·pot /'despɒt; 'despət/ n ruler with unlimited powers, esp one who uses these powers wrongly or cruelly; tyrant. 拥有无限权力的专制统治者;暴君. **~·ic** /dɪ'spɒtɪk; dɪ'spɑtɪk/ adj of or like a ~ or tyrant. 暴君(似)的. **~·ism** /'despɒtɪzəm; 'despət,ɪzəm/ n [U] the rule of a ~; tyranny; [C] country ruled by a ~. 专制; 暴政; 专制国家.

des·sert /dɪ'zɜːt; dɪ'zɜt/ n **1** course of fruit, etc, at the end of a meal: 正餐后的水果等: (attrib) (用作定语) *a ~ apple*. 一个餐后食用的苹果. '~-spoon, medium-sized spoon. 中匙(吃餐后食品用者). '~-spoon·ful /-ful; -,ful/ n as much as a ~spoon will hold. 一中匙(之量). ⟹ teaspoon at **tea**, tablespoon at **table**. **2** (US) any sweet dish, eg pie, pudding, ice-cream, served at the end of a meal (GB 英 = *sweet, pudding*). (美)正餐后的甜点心(如水果饼,布丁,冰淇淋).

des·ti·na·tion /,destɪ'neɪʃn; ,destə'neʃən/ n place to which sb or sth is going or is being sent. (某人或某物所去的或被运送的)目的地.

des·tine /'destɪn; 'destɪn/ vt [VP17, 14] (usu passive) ~ (for), set apart, decide or ordain in advance: (通常用被动语态)命中注定; 预定: *He was a soldier's son and was ~d from birth for the army*, His father had decided, when the boy was born, that he should become a soldier. 他是军人之子, 并且从生下来就注定(为其父所决定)要做军人. *They were ~d never to meet again*, Fate had determined that they should never meet again. 他们命中注定将永不能再见. *His hopes were ~d to be realized*, His hopes came true. 他的希望后来

都实现了。

des·tiny /'destɪnɪ; 'dɛstənɪ/ n 1 [U] power believed to control events: 命运(被相信为主宰人事的力量): *the tricks played on human beings by ~.* 命运之神对人类的戏弄。2 [C] (pl **-nies**) that which happens to sb, thought of as determined in advance by fate: 定数；天命(认为系命运所定的遭遇): *It was his ~ to die in a foreign country, far from his family.* 天命要他死在异邦，远离其家人。

des·ti·tute /'destɪtjuːt US: -tuːt; 'dɛstə,tjut/ adj 1 without food, clothes and other things necessary for life: 缺乏衣，食及其他必需品的；穷困的: *When Mr Hill died, his wife and children were left ~.* 当希尔先生去世的时候，他的妻子儿女皆陷于穷困。2 **~ of,** not having: 缺乏；没有: *officials who are ~ of ordinary human feelings.* 缺乏同情心的官史。**des·ti·tu·tion** /,destɪ'tjuːʃn US: -'tuːʃn; ,dɛstə'tjuʃən/ n [U] being ~ (1): 匮乏；穷困: *a war that brought desolation and destitution;* 带来荒凉与穷困的战争; *reduced to destitution,* to complete poverty. 陷于赤贫之境。

de·stroy /dɪ'strɔɪ; dɪ'strɔɪ/ vt [VP6A] break to pieces; make useless; put an end to: 毁灭；摧毁；毁坏；破坏: *Don't ~ that box — it may be useful.* 不要把那个盒子毁掉——它也许有用。*The forest was ~ed by fire.* 森林为大火所毁。*All his hopes were ~ed.* 他的一切希望都破灭了。**~er** n 1 person or thing that ~s, 毁灭者。2 small, fast warship for protecting larger warships or convoys of merchantships. (保护较大战舰或商船队的)驱逐舰。

de·struc·ible /dɪ'strʌktəbl; dɪ'strʌktəbl/ adj that can be destroyed. 可破坏的；可毁灭的。**de·struc·tibil·ity** /dɪ,strʌktə'bɪlətɪ; dɪ,strʌktə'bɪlətɪ/ n

de·struc·tion /dɪ'strʌkʃn; dɪ'strʌkʃən/ n [U] destroying or being destroyed: 破坏；毁坏；毁灭: *the ~ of a town by an earthquake;* 地震所毁之市镇; *that which ruins or destroys:* 毁灭之根源: *Gambling was his ~.* 赌博是他毁灭的根源。

de·struc·tive /dɪ'strʌktɪv; dɪ'strʌktɪv/ adj causing destruction; fond of, in the habit of, destroying: 毁灭性的；喜好或习惯于破坏的: *a ~ storm;* 造成损害的暴风雨; *~ criticism.* 破坏性的批评。*Are all small children ~?* 所有的小孩子都喜好破坏吗？ **~·ly** adv **~·ness** n

desue·tude /'dɪsjuːrtjuːd US: -tuːd; 'dɛswɪ,tjud/ n [U] (formal, esp in) (正式用语，尤用于) *fall into ~,* pass out of use: 已不用；废止: *customs/fashions/words that have fallen into ~.* 已废的习俗(时尚，词)。

des·ul·tory /'desltrɪ US: -tɔːrɪ; 'dɛsl,tɔrɪ/ adj without system, purpose; not continuous: 无系统或目的的；不连贯的: *~ reading.* 散漫的阅读。

de·tach /dɪ'tætʃ; dɪ'tætʃ/ vt 1 [VP6A, 14] **~ (from),** unfasten and take apart; separate: 解开；拆开；使分离: *to ~ a link from a chain/a coach from a train.* 将一环自一链条上取下(将车厢自一列车上分离)。 ⇨ **attach.** 2 [VP6A, 16A] (armed forces) send (a party of men, ships, etc) away from the main body: (部队)派遣；分遣(兵员，船舰等): *A number of men were ~ed to guard the right flank.* 若干士兵被派遣保卫右翼。**de·tached** part adj 1 (of the mind, opinions, etc) impartial; not influenced by others; (colloq) unemotional: (指心理，意见等)超然的；不受他人影响的；客观的；(口)冷静的: *to take a ~ed view of an event.* 对某事件持超然的看法。2 (of a house) not joined to another on either side. (指房屋)左右与其他房屋相连的；独立的。 ⇨ *semi-~ed* at semi-. **~·able** /-əbl; -əbl/ adj that can be ~ed: 可分开的；可分遣的: *a ~able lining in a coat.* 外衣内可取下的衬里。

de·tach·ment /dɪ'tætʃmənt; dɪ'tætʃmənt/ n 1 [U] detaching or being detached: 分开；分离: *the ~ of a key from a key-ring.* 钥匙之自钥匙环取下。2 [U] the state of being detached; being uninfluenced by surroundings, the opinions of others, etc; being indifferent and uninterested: 独立；超然；不受环境或他人意

见的影响；不偏不倚: *He answered with an air of ~.* 他以超然的神态回答。3 [C] group of men, ships, etc, detached(2) from a larger number (for a special duty, etc). 分遣队(分遣担任特殊任务的部队或舰队等)。

de·tail[1] /'diːteɪl US: dɪ'teɪl; 'ditel/ n 1 [C] small, particular fact or item: 细节；琐碎的事: *Please give me all the ~s.* 请让我知道所有的细节。*Don't omit a single ~.* 不要遗漏一点细节。*Every ~ of her dress was perfect.* 她衣服上的每个小地方都很完美。2 [U] collection of such small facts or items. 细目；详情。**go/enter into ~s; explain sth in ~,** to give the facts, item by item. 详细说明。3 [U] (in art) the smaller or less important parts considered as a whole: (艺术)枝节部分: *The composition of the picture is good but there is too much ~.* 这幅画的构图不错，但是枝节太多。4 [C] = **detachment**(3).

de·tail[2] /'diːteɪl US: dɪ'teɪl; dɪ'tel/ vt 1 [VP6A, 14] **~ (to/for),** describe fully; give full ~s of: 详细描写或说明: *a ~ed description,* given with every detail; 详细的描写; *The characteristics of the machine are fully ~ed in our brochure.* 这机器的性能在我们的小册子内有详细说明。2 [VP6A, 16A] appoint for special duty: 派遣担任特殊任务: *Three soldiers were ~ed to guard the bridge.* 三个兵被派去守卫那桥。 ⇨ **detail**[1](4).

de·tain /dɪ'teɪn; dɪ'ten/ vt [VP6A, 16A] keep waiting; keep back; prevent from leaving or going forward: 使等候；使延迟；阻止；耽搁；拘留: *He told his wife that he had been ~ed in the office by unexpected callers.* 他告诉他妻子他因为临时有人来访而留在办公室里。*This question need not ~ us long,* can be settled quickly. 这个问题不需要很久的时间解决(可以很快地解决)。*The police ~ed the man to make further inquiries.* 警局拘留那人以便进一步调查。**~ee** /,diːteɪ'niː; dɪ,te'ni/ n person who is ~ed (esp by the authorities, as one who is suspected of wrongdoing, political agitation, etc). 被拘留者(尤指因涉嫌犯罪，政治煽动等被当局拘留者)。

de·tect /dɪ'tekt; dɪ'tɛkt/ vt [VP6A] discover (the existence or presence of sb or sth, the identity of sb guilty of wrongdoing): 查明；查出(某人或某物之存在或在场，犯罪者的姓名等): *The dentist could ~ no sign of decay in her teeth.* 牙医在她的牙齿上找不出腐蚀的迹象。*Can you ~ an escape of gas in this corner of the room?* 你能觉察出这屋角有煤气漏出来吗？**~·able** /-əbl; -əbl/ adj that can be ~ed: 可找出的；可发出的。**~·or** /-tə(r); -tɚ/ n device for ~ing, eg changes of pressure, temperature or a radio signal. 探查器(例如测压器，测温器，检波器等)。**'lie-~or,** ⇨ **lie**[1].

de·tec·tion /dɪ'tekʃn; dɪ'tɛkʃən/ n [U] detecting; discovering: 查明；查出；发现: *the ~ of crime.* 犯罪之查明。*He tried to escape ~ by disguising himself as an old man.* 他乔装成一老人，企图逃过侦查者的耳目。

de·tec·tive /dɪ'tektɪv; dɪ'tɛktɪv/ n person whose business it is to detect criminals. 侦探(以侦察犯罪者为职业的人)。**'~ story/novel,** one in which the main interest is a puzzling crime and the process of solving it. 侦探小说(以一离奇的犯罪案件及其侦破经过为主题的小说)。

dé·tente /,deɪ'tɑːnt; de'tãt/ n [U] (F) easing of strained relations, esp between countries. (法)国际间紧张关系之缓和。

de·ten·tion /dɪ'tenʃn; dɪ'tɛnʃən/ n [U] detaining or being detained; (eg a pupil in school after ordinary hours, as a punishment; a prisoner without a trial). 阻止；延迟；留置；拘留(例如令学生放学以后不得回家以为处罚；审判前拘留的犯人)。

de·ter /dɪ'tɜː(r); dɪ'tɝ/ vt (-rr-) [VP6A, 14] **~ (from),** discourage, hinder (sb from doing sth): 使灰心；阻碍(某人做某事)使... 不敢去做; *turn him from trying again.* 失败并未使他灰心不再尝试。**~·rent** /dɪ'terənt US: -'tɜː-; dɪ'tɝrənt/ adj, n (thing) tending to, intended to, ~: 阻止性或用来阻止的(事物)；防止的(物): *Do you believe that the hydrogen bomb is a ~rent,* that it will ~

countries from making war? 你相信氢弹能够防止战争吗?

de·ter·gent /dɪˈtɜːdʒənt; dɪˈtɚdʒənt/ *adj, n* (substance) that removes dirt, esp from the surface of things: 洗涤(剂); 清洁(剂): *Most synthetic ~s are in the form of powder or liquid.* 大多数合成清洁剂都是制成粉状或液状。

de·terio·rate /dɪˈtɪərɪəreɪt; dɪˈtɪrɪəˌret/ *vt, vi* [VP 6A, 2A] make or become of less value, or worse in quality: (使)变坏; (使)变质: *Leather quickly ~s in a hot, damp climate.* 皮革在热而湿的气候中极易变坏。
de·terio·ra·tion /dɪˌtɪərɪəˈreɪʃn; dɪˌtɪrɪəˈreʃən/ *n*

de·ter·mi·nant /dɪˈtɜːmɪnənt; dɪˈtɚmɪnənt/ *adj, n* determining or deciding (agent, factor, element, etc). 决定性的(人,事物,要素等)。

de·ter·mi·nate /dɪˈtɜːmɪnət; dɪˈtɚmɪnɪt/ *adj* limited; definite; fixed. 有限的; 确定的; 固定的。

de·ter·mi·na·tion /dɪˌtɜːmɪˈneɪʃn; dɪˌtɚməˈneʃən/ *n* [U] **1** ~ *of*, determining or being determined; deciding: 决定: *The ~ of the meaning of a word is often difficult without a context.* 没有上下文, 决定一个词的意义常常是件难事。 **2** ~ *of*, calculation or finding out (of an amount, etc): 计算; 测定(数量等): *the ~ of the amount of metal in a specimen of ore.* 矿砂样品中所含金属量的测定。 **3** ~ (**to do sth**), firmness of purpose; resolution: 决心(做某事); 决意; 坚决: *his ~ to learn English;* 他要学英语的决心; *to carry out a plan with ~;* 坚决地实现一项计划; *with an air of ~,* with a purposeful look. 带有坚决的表情。

de·ter·mi·nat·ive /dɪˈtɜːmɪnətɪv US: -neɪtɪv; dɪˈtɚmə,netɪv/ *n, adj* (thing) having the power to direct, determine, limit; (gram) determiner. 有指示、决定或限制制力的(事物); (语法)指定或限定其后之名词的词; 限定词。

de·ter·mine /dɪˈtɜːmɪn; dɪˈtɚmɪn/ *vt, vi* **1** [VP6A, 10] decide; fix precisely: 决定; 确定: *to ~ the meaning of a word;* 决定一词的意义; *to ~ a date for a meeting.* 确定开会的日期。 **2** [VP6A] calculate; find out precisely: 测定; 明确地找出: *to ~ the speed of light, the height of a mountain by trigonometry.* 测定光速(用三角学测定一山之高度)。 **3** [VP6A, 7A, 9, 8, 10, 3A] ~ *to do sth;* ~ *on/upon sth,* decide firmly, resolve, make up one's mind: 下决心: *He ~d to learn Greek.* 他决心学希腊语。 *We ~d to start early/~d on an early start.* 我们决定早些动身。 *He has ~d on proving/~d to prove his friend's innocence.* 他决心为他的朋友洗清罪名。 *Have they ~d where the new school will be built?* 他们决定了新学校的校址吗? *He has ~d that nothing shall / will prevent him.* 他已决心不顾一切的阻碍。 *His future has not yet been ~d,* but he may study medicine. 他的未来尚未决定, 不过他可能读医科。 **4** [VP17, 14] ~ *sb to do sth/against sth,* cause to decide: 使决定: *What ~d you to accept the offer?* 什么原因使你决定接受此项提议? *The news ~d him against further delay.* 此项消息使他决定不再拖延。 **5** [VP6A] be the fact that ~s: 作为决定性的事实; 决定: *The size of your feet ~s the size of your shoes.* 你的脚的大小决定你的鞋子的大小。 *Do heredity and environment ~ a man's character?* 遗传与环境决定人的个性吗? **de·ter·min·able** /-əbl; -əbl/ *adj* that can be ~d. 可决定的。

de·ter·miner /dɪˈtɜːmɪnə(r); dɪˈtɚmɪnɚ/ *n* [C] (gram) word that determines or limits the noun that follows. (语法)指定或限定其后之名词的词; 限定词; 指定词。

de·ter·rent ⇨ **deter.**

de·test /dɪˈtest; dɪˈtest/ *vt* [VP6A, C] hate strongly: 深恨; 深恶; 憎恶; 极讨厌: *to ~ dogs;* 极讨厌狗; *to ~ having to get up early.* 极讨厌不得不早起。 **~·able** *adj* hateful; deserving to be hated. 可恨的; 可厌恶的。 **~·ably** /-əbli; -əbli/ *adv* **de·tes·ta·tion** /ˌdiːteˈsteɪʃn; ˌdits·teʃən/ *n* [U] strong hatred; [C] sth that is strongly hated. 深恨; 极厌恶; 极可厌之事物。

de·throne /ˌdiːˈθrəʊn; dɪˈθron/ *vt* [VP6A] remove (a ruler) from the throne, or (fig, a person) from a position of authority or influence. 迫使(君王)去位; (喻)使(当权者)下野或垮台。 **~·ment** *n*

det·on·ate /ˈdetəneɪt; ˈdetə,net/ *vt, vi* [VP6A, 2A] (cause to) explode with a loud noise. (使)轰然爆炸; 起爆。 **det·on·ator** /ˈdetəneɪtə(r); ˈdetə,netɚ/ *n* part of a bomb or shell that explodes first. causing the substance in the bomb, etc to explode. (炸弹或炮弹中的)起爆管; 雷管。 **det·on·ation** /ˌdetəˈneɪʃn; ˌdetəˈneʃən/ *n* explosion; noise of an explosion. 爆炸(声)。

de·tour /ˈdiːtʊə(r) US: dɪˈtʊər; ˈditʊr/ *n* roundabout way, eg a way used when the main road is blocked; diversion: 迂回路(如当干道堵塞时所用者); 转向: *to make a ~.* 迂回; 绕道而行。 □ *vt* [VP6A] make a ~. 迂回; 绕道而行。

de·tract /dɪˈtrækt; dɪˈtrækt/ *vi* [VP3A] ~ *from,* take away (from the credit, value, etc, of): 减损(…之功绩、价值等): *to ~ from sb's merit,* make it less. 减损某人的功绩。 **de·trac·tor** /-tə(r); -tɚ/ *n* person who ~s; person who tries to make sb's reputation, etc, smaller. 损毁某人之名誉者; 贬抑者。 **de·trac·tion** /dɪˈtrækʃn; dɪˈtrækʃən/ *n* ~ing; disparagement. 减损; 贬抑。

de·train /ˌdiːˈtreɪn; dɪˈtren/ *vt, vi* [VP6A, 2A] (of troops, etc) (cause to) get out of a train. (指军队等)(使)下火车。

de·tribal·ize /ˌdiːˈtraɪbəlaɪz; dɪˈtraɪbḷ,aɪz/ *vt* [VP 6A] render (a person) no longer a member of a tribe; destroy the tribal customs of. 使(某人)脱离某部族; 除去…的部族习俗。 **de·tribal·iz·ation** /ˌdiːtraɪbəlaɪˈzeɪʃn US: -lɪˈz-; dɪˌtraɪbəlɪˈzeʃən/ *n*

det·ri·ment /ˈdetrɪmənt; ˈdetrəmənt/ *n* [U] damage; harm: 损害; 伤害: *I know nothing to his ~,* nothing against him. 我一点也不知道对他不利的事。 *to the ~ of,* harming: 有害于: *He works long hours to the ~ of his health.* 他工作的时间过久, 有害于他的健康。 **det·ri·men·tal** /ˌdetrɪˈmentl; ˌdetrəˈmentḷ/ *adj* ~ (*to*), harmful: 有害的; 有损的: *activities that would be ~al to our interests.* 会损及我们利益的活动。 **det·ri·men·tally** /-təli; -tḷɪ/ *adv*

de·tri·tus /dɪˈtraɪtəs; dɪˈtraɪtəs/ *n* [U] matter, eg sand, silt, gravel, produced by wearing away (from rock, etc). 岩屑(自岩石等脱落的碎砂石)。

de trop /də ˈtrəʊ; dəˈtro/ *pred adj* (F) in the way; not wanted; unwelcome. (法)挡路的; 碍事的; 不需要的; 不受欢迎的。

deuce[1] /djuːs US: duːs; djus/ *n* **1** the two on playing cards or dice. (纸牌或骰子上的)二点。 **2** (tennis) the score of 40 all, or five games each, after which either side must gain two successive points (or games) to win the match (or set). (网球)平手(两方各获 40 分或各胜五局, 然后任何一方必须连获二分方为胜)。

deuce[2] /djuːs; djus/ *n* (**the**) ~, (dated colloq, in exclamations of annoyance) the devil, bad luck. (过时口语, 表烦恼的感叹词)鬼; 倒霉; 晦气。 **deuced** /ˈdjuːst US: ˈduːst; djust/ *adj* very great. 极大的; 非常的。 **deuced·ly** /ˈdjuːsɪdlɪ US: ˈduː-; ˈdjusɪdlɪ/ *adv* very. 非常地。

de·value /ˌdiːˈvæljuː; diˈvæljʊ/ (US also **de·val·u·ate** /ˌdiːˈvæljʊeɪt; diˈvæljʊˌet/) *vt* [VP6A] make the value of a currency less (esp in terms of gold): 使(货币价值)贬值(尤指以金计算): *to ~ the dollar/pound.* 使美元(英镑)贬值。 **de·val·u·ation** /ˌdiːˌvæljʊˈeɪʃn; ˌdiˌvæljʊˈeʃən/ *n* [U, C] (of currency) change to a new, lower fixed value. (指货币)贬值。

dev·as·tate /ˈdevəsteɪt; ˈdevəs,tet/ *vt* [VP6A] ruin; make desolate: 毁坏; 破坏; 使荒凉; 使成废墟: *towns ~d by fire/floods/war.* 为火(洪水, 战争)所毁坏的城镇。 **dev·as·ta·tion** /ˌdevəˈsteɪʃn; ˌdevəsˈteʃən/ *n* devastating or being ~d. 毁坏; 破坏; 成为废墟。

de·vel·op /dɪˈveləp; dɪˈvɛləp/ *vt, vi* **1** [VP6A, 2A, 3A] ~ (*from*) (*into*), (cause to) grow larger, fuller

or more mature, organized; (cause to) unfold: (使)成长; (使)发育; 发展; 开发: *Plants ~ from seeds.* 植物由种子发育而成. *A chicken ~s in the egg.* 鸡在卵中孕育. *We must ~ the natural resources of our country,* make the minerals, forests, etc available for use. 我们必须开发我们国家的天然资源(如使矿产,森林等成为有用之物). *The plot of the new novel gradually ~ed in the author's mind.* 那新小说的布局在作者的头脑中逐渐形成. *,~ing 'country,* one which is advancing to a higher (economic) state. 发展中国家(经济情况进步中的国家). **2** [VP6A, 2A, C] (of sth not at first active or visible) come or bring into a state in which it is active or visible: (指起初不活动或看不见的东西)发展成为活动性的或看得见的; 出现; 发生: *Symptoms of malaria ~ed,* appeared. 疟疾的征候出现了. *He ~ed a cough.* 他咳嗽起来了. **3** [VP6A, 2A] (photo) treat (an exposed film or plate) with chemicals so that the picture can be seen. (照相)冲洗; 显影(用化学药品处理已曝光的底片使影像显出). **4** use (an area of land) for the building of houses (or shops, factories, etc) and so increase its value. (一块土地)上建筑房屋,商店,工厂等以增高其价值; 利用(土地). **~er** *n* person who, authority which, ~s land, etc; substance used to ~ films and plates. 开发或利用土地的人或当局; (冲洗底片用的)显影剂.

de·vel·op·ment /dɪ'veləpmənt; dɪ'vɛləpmənt/ *n* **1** [U] developing or being developed (all senses): 成长; 发育; 发展; 开发; 出现; 发生; (照相)冲洗; 显影; (土地之)利用: *He is engaged in the ~ of his business.* 他正从事于发展业务. *Which is more important, moral ~ or physical ~?* 道德修养与体格的培养哪一样较重要? *The ~ of photographic films requires a dark-room.* 冲洗照相底片需要暗房. *This land is ripe for ~,* for being developed(4). 这块土地已达可以利用的成熟阶段. **'~ area,** one to which new industries are directed as a means of increasing employment. 新社区(被建立起新工业以增加就业机会之地区). **2** [C] new stage which is the result of developing: stage; the latest ~s in foreign affairs. 外交上最近的发展. *We must await further ~s.* 我们必须等待进一步的发展.

de·vi·ant /'di:vɪənt/ *n, adj* (person who is) different in moral and social standards from what is normal or customary. 道德与社会标准观念不合常轨或惯例的(人).

de·vi·ate /'di:vɪeɪt/ *vi* [VP3A] ~ *from,* turn away, leave (what is usual, customary, right, etc): 离(常轨, 惯例, 正道等); 不符合; 背离: *to ~ from the truth/a rule/one's custom.* 与事实(规则,人的习惯)不符合.

de·vi·a·tion /ˌdi:vɪ'eɪʃn; ͵dɪvɪ'eʃən/ *n* [U] ~ *(from),* turning aside or away; difference: 逸出常轨; 不符合; 离正道; 偏差: *~ from the rules;* 与规则不合; [C] instance or amount or degree of this: 偏差或不合的事例或程度: *slight ~s of the magnetic needle,* in a compass; (罗盘上)磁针之略微的偏差; *~s from the rules of syntax.* 不合进句规则之处. **~·ist** *n* person who deviates, esp from the principles of a social or political system. (背离某种社会或政治制度之原则的)异端分子; 偏差分子. /ˌ ͵ɪzm/ 和 /ˌ ͵ɪzən/ *n*

de·vice /dɪ'vaɪs; dɪ'vaɪs/ *n* [C] **1** plan; scheme; trick: 计划; 策略; 诡计: *a ~ to put the police off the scent.* 引诱警察追查方向的诡计. *leave sb to his own ~s,* let him do as he wishes, without help or advice. 让某人自行设法(不予帮助或建议). **2** sth thought out, invented or adapted, for a special purpose: 为某种特殊用途而设计, 发明或改制的东西; 装置物: *a ~ for catching flies;* 捕捉苍蝇的装置; *a nuclear ~,* eg an atomic or hydrogen bomb. 核装置(如原子弹或氢弹). **3** sign, symbol or figure used in a decoration, eg a crest on a shield. 用于装饰品上的图案(如盾形徽章上端的饰章).

devil¹ /'devl; 'dɛvl/ *n* **1** the spirit of evil; wicked spirit; cruel or mischievous person. 恶魔; 魔鬼; 残暴的

人; 恶人. *between the ~ and the deep (blue) sea,* in a dilemma. 进退两难; 进退维谷. *give the ~ his due,* be just, even to one who does not deserve much or who is unfriendly. 即使对于恶人亦宜待以公平; 一视同仁. *go to the ~!* go away! 走开! 滚开! *play the ~ with,* harm, ruin. 伤害; 毁坏. **the D~,** the supreme spirit of evil, Satan. 魔王; 撒旦. **~'s advocate,** sb who points out the faults of sb or sth so that there can be a full discussion. 指出某人或某事物之缺点而引起辩论的人; 唱反调的人. **2** (usu 通常作 *poor ~*)wretched or unfortunate person. 可怜或不幸的人. **printer's ~,** (old use) errand-boy in a printing-office. (旧用法)印刷所的童仆或学徒. **3** (colloq) used to give emphasis: (口)(用以加强语气): *what/who/why/where the ~ ...?* 到底什么(谁,为何,何处)...? *He has the ~ of a time,* ie according to context, a difficult, exciting, amusing, etc time. (意义视上下文而定)他处于极端(困难, 兴奋, 欢娱等)之境. *He was working/running like the ~,* very hard. 他拼命工作(跑). *There will be the ~ to pay,* trouble to be faced (as the result of sth done or said). (由于做某事或说某话)后果不堪设想. **~·may-'care** *adj* reckless. 不要命的; 不顾一切的.

devil² /'devl; 'dɛvl/ *vt, vi* (-ll-, US -l-) **1** [VP6A] grill with hot condiments: 加辛辣调味品烧烤: *~led kidneys/ham.* 加辛辣调味品的烤腰子(火腿). **2** [VP2A, 3A] ~ *for,* work (for a barrister). 做(律师的)助手; 代(律师)工作.

devil·ish /'devlɪʃ; 'dɛvlɪʃ/ *adj* wicked; cruel: 恶毒的; 残忍的: *a ~ plot.* 恶毒的阴谋. □ *adv* (colloq) very: (口)极; 非常: *~ hot.* 极热的.

devil·ment /'devlmənt; 'dɛvlmənt/, **dev·ilry** /'devlrɪ; 'dɛvlrɪ/ *nn* **1** [C] mischief: 恶作剧: *She's up to some ~ or other.* 她正忙于某种恶作剧. **2** [U] high spirits: 高兴: *full of ~.* 兴高采烈.

de·vi·ous /'di:vɪəs; 'divɪəs/ *adj* winding; roundabout; not straightforward: 弯曲的; 迂回的; 不直的: *to take a ~ route to avoid busy streets;* 绕道而行以免经过闹街; *to get rich by ~* (= cunning, underhand) *ways.* 以不正道致富. **~·ly** *adv* **·~·ness** *n*

de·vise /dɪ'vaɪz; dɪ'vaɪz/ *vt* [VP6A, 8] think out; plan: 想出; 计划; 设计; 发明: *to ~ a scheme for making money;* 想办法赚钱; *to ~ how to do sth.* 计划如何进行某事. **~ device.** **2** [VP14] ~ *to,* (legal) leave (property) by will. (法律)遗嘱将(财产)赠予.

de·vital·ize /ˌdi:'vaɪtəlaɪz; dɪ'vaɪtḷ͵aɪz/ *vt* [VP6A] take away strength and vigour from. 使失去活力. **de·vital·iz·ation** /ˌdi:͵vaɪtəlaɪ'zeɪʃn US: -lɪ'z-; dɪ͵vaɪtḷə'zeʃən/ *n*

de·void /dɪ'vɔɪd; dɪ'vɔɪd/ *adj* ~ *of,* without; empty of: 没有; 空虚的; 无: *~ of shame/sense.* 无耻(无见识).

de·vol·ution /ˌdi:və'lu:ʃn US: ͵dev-; ͵dɛvə'luʃən/ *n* [U] deputing or delegating (of power or authority); decentralization. (权或权力之)转移; 移交; 授予权力; 地方分权.

de·volve /dɪ'vɒlv; dɪ'vɑlv/ *vi, vt* **1** [VP3A] ~ *on/upon,* (of work, duties) be transferred or passed to: (指工作或职务)被转移或移交: *When the President is ill, his duties ~ upon the Vice-President.* 当总统生病时, 其职务交由副总统代理. **2** [VP6A, 14] ~ *(to/upon),* pass, transfer (work, duties, to sb). 传递; 转移; 移交(工作, 职务给某人).

de·vote /dɪ'vəʊt; dɪ'vot/ *vt* [VP14] ~ *oneself/sth to,* give up (oneself, one's time, energy, etc) to: 奉献(自己, 时间, 精力等); 致力于; 专门; 献身于: *to ~ oneself to the cure of cancer/one's spare time to sport.* 致力于癌症的治疗(以空闲的时间从事运动). **de·voted** *adj* very loving or loyal: 热爱的; 非常忠实的: *a ~ friend.* 忠实的朋友. *She is ~d to her children.* 她热爱她的子女. **de·vot·ed·ly** *adv*

devo·tee /ˌdevə'ti:; ͵dɛvə'ti/ *n* ~ *(of),* person who is devoted to sth: 专心的人; 热心者: *a ~ of sport/music;* 热心运动(音乐)的人; zealous supporter (of a

sect, etc). (对教派等)热心支持者。 ⇨ **votary**.

de·vo·tion /dɪ'vəʊʃn; dɪ'voʃən/ n 1 [U] ~ *(for)*, deep, strong love: 深爱；挚爱；热爱: *the ~ of a mother for her children.* 母亲对子女的挚爱。 2 [U] ~ *(to)*, devoting or being devoted to: 忠实；专心；热心: ~ *to duty;* 忠于职守; *a teacher's ~ to the cause of education.* 教师对于教育事业的热心。 3 *(pl)* prayers: (复)祈祷: *The priest was at his ~s.* 祭司在祈祷。 ~**al** /-'vəʊʃənl; -'voʃənl/ *adj* of ~; used in ~s(3): 忠诚的; 用于祈祷的: ~*al literature,* for use in worship. 祈祷文献。

de·vour /dɪ'vaʊə(r); dɪ'vaʊr/ vt [VP6A] 1 eat hungrily or greedily: 贪婪地吃；吞食: *The hungry boy ~ed his dinner.* 那饥饿的孩子狼吞虎咽地吃饭。 (fig) (喻) *She ~ed the new detective story.* 她一口气看完了那本新的侦探小说。 *The fire ~ed twenty square miles of forest.* 那场大火吞噬了二十平方英里的森林。 2 *be ~ed by* (curiosity, anxiety, etc), be filled with, have all one's attention taken up by. 心中充满(好奇, 忧虑等); 全部注意力为…所吸引。

de·vout /dɪ'vaʊt; dɪ'vaʊt/ *adj* 1 paying serious attention to religious duties: (对宗教)虔诚的；虔敬的: *a ~ old lady.* 虔诚的老太太。 2 (of prayers, wishes, etc) deepfelt; sincere: (指祈祷, 愿望等)衷心的；热诚的: *a ~ supporter;* 热诚的支持者; ~ *wishes for your success.* 衷心祝你成功。 ~**ly** *adv* eagerly; sincerely. 热心地; 热诚地。 ~**·ness** n

dew /djuː US: duː/ n [U] tiny drops of moisture condensed on cool surfaces between evening and morning from water vapour in the air: 露；露水(空中的水蒸气于夜间在凉冷的物体表面上所凝结的水珠): *The grass was wet with dew.* 草为露水沾湿。'**dew drop** n small drop of dew. 露珠。 **dewy** *adj* wet with dew. 为露水沾湿的; 带露水的。

dew·lap /'djuːlæp US: 'duː-; 'djuːlæp/ n fold of loose skin hanging down from the neck of an animal such as a cow or ox. (牛等)自喉部垂下的松皮; 喉袋。

dex·ter·ity /dek'sterɪtɪ; deks'terɪtɪ/ n [U] skill, esp in handling things. 技巧; (尤指用手做事的)灵巧; 灵活。

dex·ter·ous, dex·trous /'dekstrəs; 'dekstərəs/ *adj* clever, skilful with the hands. 两手灵巧的; 善于用手的。 ~**·ly** *adv*

dex·trose /'dekstrəʊz US: -əʊs; 'dekstros/ n [U] form of glucose. 葡萄糖(右旋糖。

dho·ti /'dəʊtɪ; 'dotɪ/ n loin-cloth as customarily worn by male Hindus. 印度男子习惯缠的腰布。

dhow /daʊ; daʊ/ n single-masted ship, esp as used by Arab sailors for coastal voyages. 单桅帆船(尤指阿拉伯水手用于沿海航行者)。

dia·betes /,daɪə'biːtɪz; ,daɪə'bitɪs/ n [U] disease of the pancreas in which sugar and starchy foods cannot be properly absorbed. 糖尿病(对糖及淀粉食物不能适当吸收的胰脏病症)。

dia·betic /,daɪə'betɪk; ,daɪə'betɪk/ *adj* of diabetes. 糖尿病的。 □ n person suffering from diabetes. 糖尿病患者。

dia·bolic /,daɪə'bɒlɪk; ,daɪə'balɪk/ *adj* of or like a devil; very cruel or wicked. 恶魔(似)的; 极残忍或恶毒的。 ~**al** /-kl; -kl/ *adj* **dia·boli·cally** /-klɪ; -klɪ/ *adv*

dia·critic /,daɪə'krɪtɪk; ,daɪə'krɪtɪk/ *adj, n* (of a) mark (eg '⌒'·), used in writing and printing to indicate different sounds of a letter. 加于字母上的变音符号(在印刷中用以表示字母之不同发音的记号, 例如: '⌒'·)的。 ~**al** /-kl; -kl/ *adj* ~.

dia·dem /'daɪədem; 'daɪə,dem/ n crown, worn as a sign of royal power; wreath of flowers or leaves worn round the head. (象征王权的)王冠; 冕; 戴于头上的花冠或叶冠。

di·aer·esis, di·er·esis /daɪ'erɪsɪs; daɪ'erəsɪs/ n *(pl -eses /-əsiːz; -əsiz/)* mark (as in *naïve*) placed over a vowel to show that it is sounded separately from a preceding vowel. 分音符(置于元音之上, 以示其与前一

元音分开发音, 如 naïve 中之 ¨)。

di·ag·nose /'daɪəgnəʊz US: -əʊs; ,daɪəg'nos/ vt [VP6A, 16B] determine the nature of (esp a disease) from observation of symptoms: 诊断(由观察征候而断定疾病等的性质): *The doctor ~d the illness as diphtheria.* 医生诊断该病为白喉。

di·ag·nosis /,daɪəg'nəʊsɪs; ,daɪəg'nosɪs/ n *(pl -noses* /-'nəʊsiːz; -'nosɪz/ [U] diagnosing; [C] (statement of the) result of this. 诊断; 诊断的结果; 诊断书。

di·ag·nos·tic /,daɪəg'nɒstɪk; ,daɪəg'nɑstɪk/ *adj* of diagnosis: 诊断的: *symptoms that were of little ~ value,* that were not very useful in determining the disease. 无甚诊断价值(无助于诊断)的征候。

di·ag·onal /daɪ'ægənl; daɪ'ægənl/ n, *adj* (straight line) going across a straight-sided figure, eg an oblong, from corner to corner; slanting; crossed by slanting lines. 直边形(如长方形)的对角线; 连接对角的; 斜的; 为斜线所交叉的。 ⇨ the illus at **quadrilateral**. 参看 quadrilateral 之插图。 ~**·ly** /-nəlɪ; -nəlɪ/ *adv*

dia·gram /'daɪəgræm; 'daɪə,græm/ n drawing, design or plan to explain or illustrate something: 图解(作解释或说明的图表): *a ~ of a gear-box.* 齿轮箱的图解。 ~**·matic** /,daɪəgrə'mætɪk; ,daɪəgrə'mætɪk/, ~**·mati·cal** /-kl; -kl/ *adjj* ~**·mati·cally** /-klɪ; -klɪ/ *adv*

dial /'daɪəl; 'daɪəl/ n 1 face (of a clock or watch). 钟面；表面。 2 marked face or flat plate with a pointer for measuring (weight, volume, pressure, consumption of gas, etc). 各种仪表(如计量重量, 容量, 压力, 耗油等)的标度盘; 针面; 盘面。 3 plate, disc, etc on a radio set with names or numbers, showing wavelengths of broadcasting stations. 刻度盘(收音机上标示周率或电台波长的盘面)。 4 part of an automatic telephone, with numbers and/or letters, used to make a connection. 自动电话机的拨号盘。 □ vt (**-ll-;** US **l-**) [VP6A] call by means of a telephone ~: 拨号码打电话: *to ~ 01-2301212.* 拨 01-2301212。 '~**ling code,** code of numbers for a telephone exchange to be ~ed before the number of the person to whom the call is to be made: 电话区域号码(交换地区号码): *The ~ling code for the London area is 01.* 伦敦地区的电话区号是01。 '~**ling tone,** the sound showing that one may proceed to ~ the number wanted. 拨号音; 表示可以拨号打电话的嗡嗡声音。

A TELEPHONE DIAL   **A CLOCK DIAL**

dia·lect /'daɪəlekt; 'daɪə,lekt/ n [C, U] form of a language (grammar, vocabulary and pronunciation) used in a part of a country or by a class of people: 方言；土话；某一阶级之人说话的方式: *the Yorkshire ~;* 约克郡的方言; *a play written in ~;* 用方言写的剧本; (attrib)(用作定语) ~ *words/pronunciations.* 方言用词(发音)。 ~**al** /,daɪə'lektl; ,daɪə'lektl/ *adj* of a ~ or ~s: 方言的; 土话的: ~*al differences between two counties.* 两郡间方言的差异。

dia·lec·tic /,daɪə'lektɪk; ,daɪə'lektɪk/ n *(also pl with sing v)* critical analysis of mental processes; art of logical disputation. (亦作复数, 用单数动词)思维方法的评判分析; 论理辩证法; 辩证法。 **dia·lec·ti·cal** /-kl; -kl/ *adj* of ~: 论理辩证法的; 辩证法的: *the ~al conflict* (= the logical dispute) *between innovators and conser-*

vatives. 革新者与保守人士间理论上的争辩。 **,~al ma·'terialism,** 辩证唯物主义 ⇨ **Marxist. dia·lec·tician** /ˌdaɪəlek'tɪʃn; ˌdaɪəlek'tɪʃən/ *n* person skilled in ~. 论理学家; 辩证学者。

dia·logue (US also **dia·log**) /'daɪəlɒg *US*: -lɔːg; 'daɪəˌlɔg/ *n* **1** [U] (writing in the form of a) conversation or talk: 对话; 用对话体写的作品: *Plays are written in* ~. 戏剧用对话体写。 *There is some good descriptive writing in the novel, but the* ~ *is poor.* 这小说里有些很好的描写, 但对话很差。 **2** [C] exchange of views (between leaders, etc): (领导人物等间之)交换意见: *a* ~ *between the two Prime Ministers.* 两位首相间之交换意见。 **3** [C] talk: 谈话: *a* ~ *between two comedians.* 两位喜剧演员间之冗长的对话。

di·am·eter /daɪ'æmɪtə(r); daɪ'æmɪtɚ/ *n* measurement across any geometrical figure or body; (length of a) straight line drawn from side to side through the centre, esp of a circular, spherical or cylindrical form: 直径(横过任何几何图形或物体的度量); 穿过圆心、球心, 或圆柱中心、两端及于周边之直线或其长度); 对径; 径; 倍: *the* ~ *of a tree-trunk;* 树干的直径; *a lens that magnifies* 20 ~*s,* that makes an object look 20 times longer, wider, etc than it is, ⇨ the illus at **circle.** 放大二十倍的透镜(参看 circle 之插图)。

dia·metri·cally /ˌdaɪə'metrɪklɪ, ˌdaɪə'metrɪklɪ/ *adv* completely; entirely: 完全地; 全然地: ~ *opposed views.* 完全相反的意见。

dia·mond /'daɪəmənd; 'daɪəmənd/ *n* **1** brilliant precious stone of pure carbon in crystallized form, the hardest substance known: 金钢钻; 钻石(由纯碳结晶而成之最烂宝石, 系已知中之最坚硬的物质): *a ring with a* ~ *in it;* 钻石戒指; (attrib)(用作定语) *a* ~ *ring / necklace.* 钻石戒指(项链)。 ⇨ the illus at **crystal.** 参看 crystal 之插图。 ~ **wedding** *n* sixtieth anniversary of a wedding. 钻石婚 (结婚六十周年纪念)。 **rough** ~, person with rough manners but a kind heart. 行动粗鲁而心肠好的人。 **2** piece of this substance (often artificially made) as used in industry, or as a stylus for playing gramophone records. 工业用的金钢钻(常系人造品); 唱机用的钻石唱针。 **3** figure with four equal sides whose angles are not right angles; this shape (as printed in red on playing-cards): 菱形(等边而非直角的四边形); 纸牌上的红方块: *the ten of* ~*s.* 方块牌的十点。 ⇨ the illus at **card.** 参看 card 之插图。 **4** (baseball) the space inside the lines that connect the bases. (棒球)内场(四垒连线之内的场地)。 ⇨ the illus at **baseball.** 参看 baseball 之插图。

dia·per /'daɪəpə(r); 'daɪəpɚ/ *n* **1** (linen fabric with) geometric pattern of lines crossing to make diamond shapes which are shown up by reflection of light. 接连的菱形图案(图案由反光而显出); 有菱形图案的格子麻布。 **2** (US) napkin(2) for a baby. 婴儿的尿布。

dia·pha·nous /daɪ'æfənəs; daɪ'æfənəs/ *adj* (of material for veils, dresses, etc) transparent; translucent. (指制面料、女服等的布料)透明的; 半透明的。

dia·phragm /'daɪəfræm; 'daɪəˌfræm/ *n* **1** internal wall of muscle between the chest and the abdomen. (胸腔与腹腔间的)膈; 横膈膜。 ⇨ the illus at **respiratory.** 参看 respiratory 之插图。 **2** arrangement of thin plates that control the inlet of light, eg through a camera lens. 光圈; 照相机镜头上的光圈。 **3** vibrating disc or cone in some instruments, eg a telephone receiver, a loud-speaker, producing sound-waves. (电话机受话器等扩音机等中产生声波的)膜片。

di·ar·chy /'daɪɑːkɪ; 'daɪɑrkɪ/ *n* (*pl* **-chies**) government shared by two joint authorities or rulers. 两头政治(由两个独立的当政者或权力机构统治)。

di·ar·rhoea (also **di·ar·rhea**) /ˌdaɪə'rɪə; ˌdaɪə'riə/ *n* [U] too frequent and too watery emptying of the bowels. 腹泻; 泻肚子。

diary /'daɪərɪ; 'daɪərɪ/ *n* (*pl* **-ries**) (book for) daily record of events, thoughts, etc: 日记(对事件, 思想

等每日的记载); 日记簿: *keep a* ~. 写日记。 **dia·rist** /'daɪərɪst; 'daɪərɪst/ *n* person who keeps a diary. 写日记的人。

Di·as·pora /daɪ'æspərə; daɪ'æspərə/ *n* **the D~,** the dispersion of the Jews among the Gentiles after their period of exile (538 BC): (纪元前 538年)犹太人被放逐后之散居世界各地非犹太人中: *People from every country of the* ~ *now live in Israel.* 散居世界各国的犹太人现在都住在以色列。

dia·tonic /ˌdaɪə'tɒnɪk; ˌdaɪə'tɑnɪk/ *adj* (mus) of a key¹(9). (音乐)全音阶的。 ~ **scale** *n* = **key¹**(9).

dia·tribe /'daɪətraɪb; 'daɪəˌtraɪb/ *n* [C] ~ (**against**), bitter and violent attack in words. 怒骂; 猛烈的抨击。

dibble /'dɪbl; 'dɪbl/ *n* (also 亦作 **dib·ber** /'dɪbə(r); 'dɪbɚ/) short wooden tool with a pointed end for making holes in the ground (for tubers, young plants, etc). (在地上挖洞以种植块茎植物、幼苗等用的一端尖的)短木杵; 点播器。 □ *vt* [VP15B] put (plants, etc, *in*) with a ~. 用短木杵或点播器挖洞栽种(幼苗等)(与 in 连用)。

dice /daɪs; daɪs/ *n pl* (*sing* (formal) **die** or (colloq) **dice**) (其单数形式在正式用法中为 die, 在口语中仍为 dice) small cubes of wood, bone, etc marked with 1—6 spots, used in games of chance: 骰子(木质或骨质小六面体, 每面刻有 1—6 个点数, 用作赌具): *to play* ~. 掷骰子。 *The die is cast,* (prov) One's course is determined and cannot now be changed. (谚)已做决定, 不能更改。 (Note: except in this prov, *die* is rarely used. 'One of the dice' is preferred to 'a die.') (注意: 除此谚语外, die 现多半少用。用 one of the dice 较为妥当)。 '~**-box** *n* deep, narrow box in which ~ are shaken and from which they are thrown. (摇掷骰子用的)骰子筒。 □ *vi*, *vt* **1** [VP2A] play ~. 掷骰子。 ~ **with death,** (colloq) act dangerously and at the risk of death. (口)冒死的危险。 **2** [VP6A] cut (food, eg carrots) into small cubes like ~. 将(胡萝卜等)切成似似骰子的小方块; 将…切丁。

dice　　　　　　printer's dies

dicey /'daɪsɪ; 'daɪsɪ/ *adj* (colloq) risky; uncertain. (口)冒险的; 不确定的。

di·chot·omy /daɪ'kɒtəmɪ; daɪ'kɑtəmɪ/ *n* (*pl* **-mies**) division into two (usu contradictory classes or mutually exclusive pairs): 两分(通常指将互相矛盾的类别或互不相容的两种东西分为二): *the* ~ *of truth and falsehood.* 真理与谎言的划分。

dick·ens /'dɪkɪnz; 'dɪkɪnz/ *n* (colloq) used like **devil** and **deuce:** (口)(与 devil 和 deuce 用法相同): '*Who / What / Where the* ~...?' 到底是谁(什么, 何处)…?'

dicker /'dɪkə(r); 'dɪkɚ/ *vi* (colloq) [VP2A, 3A] bargain or haggle (*with* sb, *for* sth). (口)谈生意; 讲价钱; (与 with 连用后接某人, 与 for 连用后接某事物)。

dicky¹, dickey /'dɪkɪ; 'dɪkɪ/ *n* (colloq) (口) **1** (also 亦作 '~**-seat**) small, extra folding seat at the back of a two-seater motor-car. 供二人乘坐的汽车后部备用的折叠小椅。 **2** false shirt-front. 假衬胸(衬衫的假胸)。 **3** '~**-bird,** child's word for a bird. (儿语)鸟。

dicky² /'dɪkɪ; 'dɪkɪ/ *adj* (sl) unsound; weak: (俚)不健全的; 脆弱的: *a* ~ *heart;* 脆弱的心; 易碎的; 易跌落的。

Dic·ta·phone /'dɪktəfəʊn; 'dɪktə,fon/ n (P) office machine that records words spoken into it and then reproduces them (for transcription, etc). (商标) (办公室中用以录话供以后抄写等的)录音机; 口授留声机.

dic·tate /dɪk'teɪt US: 'dɪkteɪt; 'dɪktet/ vt, vi 1 [VP 6A, 2A, 14] ~ (to), say or read aloud (words to be written down by another or others): 大声讲或读; 口授 (字句以供他人听写): to ~ a letter to a secretary. 向秘书口授信稿. The teacher ~d a passage to the class. 教师读一段文章要全班听写. 2 [VP6A, 14] ~ (to), state with the force of authority: 指示; 指定; 指令: to ~ terms to a defeated enemy. 向战败的敌人指定条款. 3 [VP3A] ~ to, order: I won't be ~d to, I refuse to accept orders from you. 我不接受你的命令. □ n /'dɪkteɪt; 'dɪktet/ (usu pl) direction or order (esp given by reason, conscience, etc): (通常用复数)指示; 指令(尤指发自理智, 良心等者): the ~s of common sense. 根据常识的判断. Follow the ~s of your conscience, Do what your conscience tells you to do. 遵照良心的指示 (凭良心行事).

dic·ta·tion /dɪk'teɪʃn; dɪk'teʃən/ n 1 [U] dictating; being dictated to: 口授; 听写; 命令: The pupils wrote at their teacher's ~. 教师口授, 学生听写. 2 [C] passage, etc that is dictated. 口授听写的一段文字等.

dic·ta·tor /dɪk'teɪtə(r) US: 'dɪkteɪtə; 'dɪkteɪtə/ n ruler who has absolute authority, esp one who has obtained such power by force or in an irregular way. 独裁者(有绝对权力的统治者, 尤指以武力或非常的手段获此权力者). ~·ship /-ʃɪp; -,ʃɪp/ n [C, U] (country with) government by a ~. 独裁政治; 独裁国家. dic·ta·torial /,dɪktə'tɔːrɪəl; dɪktə'tɔrɪəl/ adj of or like a ~: 独裁者的; 似独裁者的: ~ial government; 独裁政治; overbearing; fond of giving orders: 盛气凌人的; 喜发号施令的: his ~ial manner. 他那种盛气凌人的态度. dic·ta·tori·ally /-əlɪ; -əlɪ/ adv

dic·tion /'dɪkʃn; 'dɪkʃən/ n [U] choice and use of words; style or manner of speaking and writing. 用词; 措辞; 句法.

dic·tion·ary /'dɪkʃənrɪ US: -nerɪ; 'dɪkʃən,ɛrɪ/ n (pl -ries) book listing and explaining the words of a language, or the words or topics of a special subject, eg the Bible, architecture, and arranged in ABC order. 字典(将字按字母顺序编列出并解释字义者); 辞典(解释专门学科如圣经, 建筑学等之名辞或论题者).

dic·tum /'dɪktəm; 'dɪktəm/ n (pl ~s, -ta /-tə; -tə/) formal expression of opinion; saying. 正式发表的意见; 格言.

did /dɪd; dɪd/ ⇨ do.

di·dac·tic /dɪ'dæktɪk US: daɪ-; daɪ'dæktɪk/ adj 1 intended to teach: 说教的; 教训的; 教海的: ~ poetry. 说教的诗. 2 having the manner of a teacher: 表现教训态度的: A teacher should not be ~ outside the classroom. 教师走出教室就不应再持教训的态度. di·dac·ti·cally /-klɪ; -klɪ/ adv

diddle /'dɪdl; 'dɪdl/ vt [VP6A, 14] ~ sb (out of sth), (colloq) cheat. (口)欺骗; 诈欺.

die[1] /daɪ; daɪ/ n 1 (pl dice ⇨ dice. 2 (pl dies /daɪz; daɪz/) block of hard metal with a design, etc cut in it, used for shaping coins, type[1](3), medals, etc or stamping paper, leather, etc so that designs stand out from the surface. 铸钱币, 奖章等刻有阴纹图案的钢印模(在纸, 皮革等上压印凸纹图案的钢印模). '**die-cast** adj made by casting metal in a mould: 印模铸造的: die-cast toys, eg. small models of cars. 印模铸造的玩具(如小汽车模型).

die[2] /daɪ; daɪ/ vi (pt, pp died, pres part dying) 1 [VP2A, C, D] come to the end of life; cease to live: 生命结束; 死亡; 死去: Flowers soon die if they are left without water. 花如不浇水, 不久即枯死. (Note the preps): (注意介词): to die of an illness/a disease/hunger/grief; 死于疾病(疾病, 饥饿, 悲伤); to die by violence; 惨死; 横死; to die by one's own hand, ie

commit suicide; 自杀; to die from a wound; 受伤不治而死; to die for one's country; 为国捐躯; to die through neglect; 因疏忽而送命; to die in battle; 战死; to die happy/poor; 在幸福(穷困)中死亡; to die a beggar/a martyr. 乞丐(殉道)而死. 2 (various phrases) (各种成语) die in one's bed, of old age or illness. 老死床榻; 寿终正寝. die with one's boots on, while still vigorous, while fighting. 横死; 暴毙; 战死. die in the last ditch, fighting desperately to defend sth. 战斗到底. die game, facing death bravely. 勇敢地面对死亡; 至死不屈. die hard, only after a struggle. 经一番挣扎方才死去; 不易死去. ⇨ 5 below. 参看下列第 5 义. die in harness, while still at one's usual occupation, still working. 死在岗位上; 殉职. 3 [VP3A, 4C] be dying for sth/to do sth, have a strong wish: 有强烈的愿望; 渴望: We're all dying for a drink. 我们都渴得要死. She's dying to know where you've been. 她渴望知道你到哪里去了. 4 [VP2A, C] pass from human knowledge; be lost: 无人知晓; 被遗忘: His fame will never die. 他的名声将永垂不朽. His secret died with him, He died without telling it to anyone. 他的秘密至死未告他人.

5 '**die-hard**, (often attrib) person who obstinately resists being compelled to do anything; politician who obstinately opposes new policies and fights hard in defence of old policies. (常用作定语)死硬派; 倔强的人(坚不屈服的人或坚决反对新政策而拼命卫护旧政策的从政者). 6 [VP2C] (with various adverbial particles): (与各副词性小品词连用): die away, lose strength, become faint or weak: 减低力量; 渐消; 渐弱: The breeze died away. 风渐息. The noise died away. 闹声渐消.

die back, (of plants) die down to the roots, which remain alive and send up shoots the next growing season: (指植物) 茎死根不死 (至下一季再发幼苗): The dahlias died back when the frosts came. 大利花打霜以后暂时枯萎.

die down, (of a fire in a fireplace, etc) burn with less heat; (of excitement, etc) become less violent; (of noise, etc) become less loud. (指炉火等)渐熄; (指骚动等)渐平息; (指闹声等)渐消失.

die off, die one by one: 先后死去; 一一死去: The leaves of this plant are dying off. 这植物的叶子在凋落中.

die out, become extinct; come to a complete end: 死光; 绝种: With the death of the fifth earl, this old family had died out. 随着第五位爵之死, 这个老世家就绝后了. Many old customs are gradually dying out. 许多旧习俗都在日渐消失中.

di·er·esis /daɪ'erɪsɪs; daɪ'srɛsɪs/ ⇨ **diaeresis.**

die·sel /'diːzl; 'dizl/ n (attrib) ~-**electric locomotive**, one that generates its own electric current from a ~ engine. 狄塞尔电动机车; 内燃电力传动机车(由柴油机发电以行驶者). '~ **engine**, oil-burning engine (as used for buses, locomotives) in which ignition is produced by the heat of suddenly compressed gas. 狄塞尔内燃机; 柴油机(其发火系由突然受压缩气体的热力产生, 如用于公共汽车或火车机车中者). '~ **oil**, heavy fuel oil. 柴油.

diet[1] /'daɪət; 'daɪət/ n [C] 1 sort of food usually eaten (by a person, community, etc): (个人, 社区等)通常所吃的食物: the Japanese ~ of rice, vegetables and fish. 日本人所常吃的食物: 米, 蔬菜和鱼. Too rich a ~ (= Too much rich food) is not good for you. 太油腻的食物对你不好. 2 sort of food to which a person is limited, eg for medical reasons: 被限制食用的食物(因医疗的理由等): The doctor put her on a ~. 医生限制她的饮食. No potatoes for me—I'm on a ~. 不要给我马铃薯——我在吃规定的饮食. □ vt, vi [VP6A, 2A] restrict (oneself, sb), be restricted, to a ~(2): 规定或限制(自己或他人)的饮食; 实行节食: She became so fat that she had to ~ herself, 她身材太胖, 所以不得不实行节食. My doctor is ~ing me very strictly. 我的医生正极严格地限制我的饮食. Is he still ~ing? 他仍在节食吗? **die·tary** /'daɪətərɪ US: -terɪ; 'daɪə,tɛrɪ/ adj of

~: 限制饮食的: *~ary rules; 饮食规则*; *~ary taboos, eg pork for Muslims.* 饮食方面的禁忌(例如伊斯兰教徒之不食猪肉). **die·tet·ics** /ˌdaɪə'tetɪks; ˌdaɪə'tɛtɪks/ *n* (*sing v*) science of *~*. (用单数动词)饮食学; 营养学. **die·tician, die·titian** /ˌdaɪə'tɪʃn; ˌdaɪə'tɪʃən/ *n* expert in dietetics. 饮食学家; 营养学家.

diet² /'daɪət; 'daɪət/ *n* series of meetings for discussion of national, international or church affairs. 会议(包括一连串的集会, 讨论国内、国际或教会事务等).

dif·fer /'dɪfə(r); 'dɪfɚ/ *vi* [VP2A, C, 3A] 1 ~ (from), be unlike; be distinguishable: 不同; 有异: *The two brothers are like each other in appearance, but ~ widely in their tastes.* 这两兄弟相貌相象, 但趣味却大不相同. *French ~s from English in having gender for all nouns.* 法语与英语不同: 法语所有的名词都有性别. *Tastes ~, Different people have different interests.* 趣味人各不同. 2 ~ from sb (about/on sth), disagree; have another opinion: 不同意; 持异议: *I'm sorry to ~ from you about/on that question.* 对不起, 关于那个问题我与你的看法不同. **agree to ~**, give up the attempt to convince each other. 同意各持己见(不欲互相说服).

dif·fer·ence /'dɪfrəns; 'dɪfərəns/ *n* [C, U] ~ (between), 1 the state of being unlike: 不同; 相异; 差别: *the ~ between summer and winter.* 冬夏之别. 2 amount, degree, manner, in which things are unlike: 相差之数额, 程度或方式; 差数; 差别之处: *The ~ between 7 and 18 is 11.* 7 与 18 的差数是 11. *What a great ~ there is in the temperature today!* 今天气温差别好大啊! *There are many ~s between the two languages.* 这两种语言有许多不同之处. **split the ~**, ⇨ **split**. 3 **make a/some/no/any/not much/a great deal of ~**, be of some/no, etc importance: 有(颇有, 没有, 有何, 没有多大, 有很大)重要性: *It won't make much ~ whether you go today or tomorrow.* 你今天去或明天去没有多大关系. *Does that make any ~,* Is it important, need we consider it? 那是否有重要性?我们是否需要考虑它? **make a ~ between**, treat differently. 区别对待. 4 disagreement: 不同意; 歧见: *Why can't you settle your ~s and be friends again?* 你们为何不消除歧见而言归于好?

dif·fer·ent /'dɪfrənt; 'dɪfərənt/ *adj* 1 not the same: 不同的; 相异的: *They are ~ people with the same name.* 他们名叫同样, 却大有异. *The two boys are ~ in their tastes.* 这两个孩子的兴趣不同. *She is wearing a ~ dress every time I see her.* 我每次看见她, 她都穿一件不同的衣服. ~ **from/to/** (US) **than**, 与...不同: *Your method is ~ from/to mine.* 你的方法与我的不同. (Note: ~ **than** may be used when ~ is not immediately followed by its *prep*: 注意: different 后面未紧接介词时可用 than: *How ~ life today is than what it was fifty years ago*, where ~ is followed immediately by *from*. 此句中 different 后紧接介词 from.) 2 separate; distinct: 分别的; 各不相同的: *I called three ~ times, but he was out.* 我打了三次电话, 他都不在家. *They are sold in ~ colours,* a variety of colours. 它们以各种不同的颜色出售. ~ **·ly** *adv*

dif·fer·en·tial /ˌdɪfə'renʃl; ˌdɪfə'renʃəl/ *adj* 1 of, showing, depending on, a difference: 有分别的; 基于差别的: *~ tariffs*, that differ according to circumstances. 差别的税率(根据情况不同而异). ~ **calculus**. 2 ~ **(gear)**, arrangement of gears (in a motor-car, etc) that allows the rear wheels to turn at different speeds on curves. 差动(速)齿轮(装于汽车断件, 使后轮在转弯时以不同速度转动). □ *n* **(wage)** ~, difference (expressed in a percentage) in wages between skilled and unskilled workers in the same industry: (在同一种行业内, 技术工与非技术工之)工资差别(按百分比计算): *They opposed a flat increase for all workers because that would upset the wage ~.* 他们反对给所有的工人平等的加薪, 因为那样就破坏了工资差别制度.

dif·fer·en·ti·ate /ˌdɪfə'renʃɪeɪt; ˌdɪfə'renʃɪˌet/ *vt* 1

[VP6A, 14] ~ **(from)**, see as different; show to be different: 区别; 分别; 辨别: *to ~ varieties of plants;* 辨别各种植物; *to ~ one variety from another.* 区别一种与另一种. *The report does not ~ the two aspects of the problem.* 此报告未能将问题的两方面加以区别. *One aspect is not ~ed from the other.* 一方面未与另一方面区别. 2 [VP3A] ~ **between**, treat as different: 差别对待: *It is wrong to ~ between pupils according to their family background.* 按照家庭背景而区别对待学生是不对的. **dif·fer·en·ti·ation** /ˌdɪfərenʃɪ'eɪʃn; ˌdɪfəˌrenʃɪ'eʃən/ *n*

dif·fi·cult /'dɪfɪkəlt; 'dɪfəklt/ *adj* 1 not easy; requiring effort, strength, skill or ability: 不容易的; 困难的; 需要用力的; 需要技巧或能力的: *a ~ problem/language.* 困难的问题(语言). *He finds it ~ to stop smoking.* 他觉得戒烟是件难事. *The sound is ~ to pronounce.* 这个音不容易发. *It is a ~ sound to pronounce.* 它是一个难发的音. *The place is ~ to reach/~ of access.* 那个地方不易到达. *He was placed in ~ circumstances.* 他被置于困境. 2 (of persons) not easily pleased or satisfied; easily offended: (指人)不易取悦或满足的; 易恼怒的: *He's a ~ man to get on with.* 他是个不易相处的人. *The famous actress was being rather ~,* was causing trouble, eg to the other members of the cast. the producer. 那个著名的女演员相当难对付(例如对别的演员, 制片人都感到麻烦). *Please don't be so ~.* 请不要那样别扭.

dif·fi·culty /'dɪfɪkəltɪ; 'dɪfəˌkʌltɪ/ *n* 1 [U] the state or quality of being difficult: 困难; 艰难; 费力: *Do you have any ~ in understanding spoken English?* 你听英语口语有无困难? *There was some ~ in getting everybody here in time.* 使每一个人都按时到达这里曾经过相当的周折. *He did the work without ~/without any/much ~.* 他毫不费力地做好了那工作. *He did it, but with ~.* 他做成了, 但颇为费力. 2 [C] (*pl* **-ties**) sth difficult, hard to do or understand: 难事; 难做的事; 难懂的事: *the difficulties of Greek syntax;* 希腊文句法的困难之处; *to be working under difficulties,* in difficult circumstances; 在不利的环境中工作; *to be in financial difficulties,* short of money, in debt, etc. 处于经济困难中(如缺钱, 负债等). *If you knew the difficulties I am in!* 你完全不知道我遭遇了何种困难! *Mary's father raised/made difficulties when she said she wanted to marry a poor school-teacher,* He objected to, opposed, the proposal. 玛丽说她想娶一个穷教员时, 她父亲提出了异议.

dif·fi·dent /'dɪfɪdənt; 'dɪfədənt/ *adj* not having, not showing, much belief in one's own abilities; lacking in self-confidence: 对自己的能力没有信心的; 缺乏自信心的: *to be ~ about doing sth;* 对做某事缺乏信心的; *to speak in a ~ manner.* 说话没有自信心的样子. ~ **·ly** *adv* **dif·fi·dence** /-dəns; -dəns/ *n* [U] being ~; shyness. 无自信心; 羞怯.

dif·fract /dɪ'frækt; dɪ'frækt/ *vt* [VP6A] break up (a beam of light) into a series of dark and light bands or the coloured bands of the spectrum. 分解(光线)使成为明暗或七彩的光谱; 使衍射. ⇨ the illus at **spectrum**. 参看 spectrum 之插图. **dif·frac·tion** /dɪ'frækʃn; dɪ'frækʃən/ *n*

dif·fuse¹ /dɪ'fjuːz; dɪ'fjuz/ *vt, vi* 1 [VP6A] send out, spread, in every direction: 散布; 传播; 传布; 漫射: *to ~ learning/knowledge/good humour/light/heat/a scent/an odour;* 传播学问(知识, 高兴, 光, 热, 气味); ~*d lighting,* contrasted with direct lighting. 漫射灯光(与直射灯光相对). 2 [VP6A, 2A] (of gases and liquids) (cause to) mix slowly. (指气体及液体)(使)慢慢混合; (使)扩散. **dif·fu·sion** /dɪ'fjuːʒn; dɪ'fjuʒən/ *n* [U] diffusing or being ~d: 散布; 传播; 扩散: *the diffusion of knowledge through books and lectures;* 知识经由书籍及演讲的传播; *the diffusion of gases and liquids,* their moving without external force. 气体和液体不经外力的自然混合.

dif·fuse² /dɪ'fjuːs; dɪ'fjus/ *adj* 1 using too many

words: 用词太多的; 冗赘的: *a ~ writer/style*. 冗赘的作家(文体). **2** spread out; scattered: 散布的; 散播的; 扩散的; 漫射的: *~ light*. 漫射光. **~·ly** *adv* **~ness** *n*

dig[1] /dɪg; dɪg/ *vt, vi* (*pt, pp* **dug** /dʌg; dʌg/) **(-gg-)** **1** [VP6A, 15B, 2C] use a tool (eg a spade), a machine, claws, etc to break up and move earth, etc; make a way (*through, into,* etc) by doing this; make (a hole, etc) by doing this; get (sth) by doing this: 用工具(如铁铲), 机器, 爪子等挖掘泥土地等; 挖穿(与...通用); 挖(洞等); 挖掘; 掘出: *It is difficult to dig the ground when it is frozen hard*. 地面冻硬时不易挖掘. *They are digging through the hill to make a tunnel/digging a tunnel through the hill*. 他们正在穿山凿一隧道. *He dug a deep hole*. 他挖了一个深洞. *The soldiers were digging trenches*. 士兵们(那时)正在挖战壕. **2** [VP6A] (sl) enjoy; appreciate; understand; follow: (俚)喜欢; 欣赏; 了解; 懂: *I don't dig modern jazz*. 我不欣赏现代爵士乐. **3** [VP15B, 3A, 2C] (uses with *adverbial particles* and *preps*): (与副词性小品词及介词连用的用法):

dig in; dig into sth, serve oneself with food, begin eating, with appetite: 津津有味地进食; 开始津津有味地吃: *dig into a pie*. 津津有味地吃一馅饼. *The food's here, so dig in!* 食物在这里, 吃罢!

dig sth in, mix with the soil by digging: 混入土壤中: *The manure should be well dug in*. 肥料应该均匀地混入土壤. *dig sth into sth, dig sth into sth*, push, thrust, poke: 推; 插入; 刺: *to dig a fork into a pie/a potato*. 将叉子插入馅饼(洋芋)中. *The rider dug his spurs into the horse's flank/dug his spurs in*. 骑者以马刺刺马的侧腹. *dig oneself in*, **(a)** protect oneself by digging a trench, etc. 挖壕沟等以藏身. **(b)** (fig, colloq) establish oneself securely (in a position, etc). (喻, 口)巩固自己的职位等. *dig sb in the ribs*, poke one's elbow in his ribs, eg to call attention to sth funny. 用肘拐触某人的肋骨(如为促其注意可笑的事物).

dig sb/sth out (of sth), **(a)** get out by digging: 挖出; 掘出; 挖地而逼出: *They dug out the fox/dug the fox out of its hole*. 他们挖地逼出那狐狸(将狐狸自洞中逼出). *He was buried by the avalanche and had to be dug out*. 他为雪崩所埋, 必须让人挖出来. **(b)** get by searching: 探索: *to dig information out of books and reports*; 自书中与报告中探索知识; *to dig out the truth*. 寻求实情.

dig sth up, **(a)** break up (land) by digging: 翻(土): *to dig up land for a new garden*. 翻土建一新花园. **(b)** remove from the ground by digging: 自地上挖掉: *We dug the tree up by the roots*. 我们把那树连根挖起. **(c)** bring to light (what has been buried or hidden) by digging: 挖出(被湮埋之物): *An old Greek statue was dug up here last month*. 一尊古希腊雕像上个月在此地被挖出. **(d)** (fig) (喻): *The newspapers love to dig up scandals*.报纸喜欢揭露丑闻.

dig[2] /dɪg; dɪg/ *n* **1** push or thrust: 推; 戳; 刺: *give sb a dig in the ribs*. 推推某人的肋骨. *That was a dig at me*, a remark directed against me. 那句话是对我而发的. **2** site being excavated by archaeologists. 考古学家所挖掘的地点. **3** (*pl*) (GB, colloq) lodgings: (复)(英, 口)寄宿舍: *Are you living at home or in digs?* 你住在家里还是住在宿舍?

di·gest[1] /'daɪdʒest; 'daɪdʒest/ *n* [C] short, condensed account; summary: 摘要; 纲要: *a ~ of the week's news*. 一周新闻摘要.

di·gest[2] /dɪ'dʒest; də'dʒest/ *vt, vi* [VP6A, 2A] **1** (of food) change, be changed, in the stomach and bowels, so that it can be used in the body: (指食物)消化(在胃肠中起变化以便身体吸收); 被消化: *Some foods ~/are ~ed more easily than others*. 某些食物较其他的食物易于消化. **2** take into the mind; make part of one's knowledge; reduce (a mass of facts, etc) to order: 吸收于脑中; 使成为自己的知识的一部分; 将(一堆事实等)归类: (系统地)整理; 透彻了解: *Have you ~ed everything*

that is important in the book? 你是否已将书中每一要点透彻了解? **~·ible** /dɪ'dʒestəbl; də'dʒestəbl/ *adj* that can be ~ed. 可消化的. **~i·bil·ity** /dɪ,dʒestə'bɪlɪtɪ; də,dʒestə'bɪlətɪ/ *n*

di·ges·tion /dɪ'dʒestʃən; də'dʒestʃən/ *n* [U] digesting: 消化; 吸收: *food that is easy/difficult of ~*; 易(难)于消化的食物; [C] power of digesting food: 消化力: *to have a poor/good ~*. 消化力弱(强).

di·ges·tive /dɪ'dʒestɪv; də'dʒestɪv/ *adj* of digestion (of food): 消化(食物)的: *suffer from ~ trouble*. 患消化系统的疾病. **the '~ system**, the alimentary canal. 消化系统.

dig·ger /'dɪgə(r); 'dɪgə/ *n* **1** (usu in compounds) person who digs: (通常用于复合词中)挖掘者: *'gold-~*, one who tries to find gold in a gold-field. 采金者; 淘金者. **2** mechanical excavator. 挖掘机. **3** (sl) Australian. (俚)澳大利亚人.

dig·ging /'dɪgɪŋ; 'dɪgɪŋ/ *n* [U] action of digging; [C] (often *pl*) place where men dig or search for metal, esp gold. 挖掘; (常用复数)采矿场(尤指采金矿).

digit /'dɪdʒɪt; 'dɪdʒɪt/ *n* **1** any one of the ten Arabic numerals 0 to 9: 阿拉伯数字: *The number 57306 contains five ~s*. 57306 一数中含五个数字. **2** finger or toe. 手指; 趾. **digi·tal** /'dɪdʒɪtl; 'dɪdʒɪtl/ *adj* of ~s. 数字的; 指或趾的. **~al clock/watch**, one without hands, showing the time by ~s (eg 07.45) only. (没有时针分针而用数字表示时间的)电子钟(表); 数字钟. **~al computer**, one showing its calculations by ~s (binary or decimal). 数字计算机(以二进或十进数字表示计算结果者).

dig·nify /'dɪgnɪfaɪ; 'dɪgnə,faɪ/ *vt* [VP6A, 14] ~ **(with)**, cause to appear worthy or honourable; give dignity to: 使显得有价值或可尊敬; 使显赫; 使高贵: *to ~ a small collection of books by calling it a library/~ it with the name library*. 称少数的藏书为图书馆, 以提高其身价. **dig·ni·fied** *part adj* having or showing dignity: 可敬的; 高贵的: *a dignified old lady*. 高贵的老妇人.

dig·ni·tary /'dɪgnɪtərɪ US: -terɪ; 'dɪgnə,terɪ/ *n* (*pl* **-ries**) person holding a high office. 高僧; 权贵.

dig·nity /'dɪgnɪtɪ; 'dɪgnətɪ/ *n* **1** [U] true worth; the quality that earns or deserves respect: 真实价值; 可尊敬的品格: *the ~ of labour*. 劳动的真正价值; 劳工神圣. *A man's ~ depends not upon his wealth or rank but upon his character*. 人的真正价值不在财富或地位, 而在品格. **2** [U] calm and serious manner or style: 尊严; 威严: *If you're afraid of losing your ~ (eg of being made to look foolish), you can't expect to learn to speak a foreign language*. 如果你怕失去尊严, 你就不能期望学会说一种外国语. *beneath one's ~*, below one's moral, social, etc standards: 有失身份: *It is beneath your ~ to answer such a rude remark*. 回答这种租野的话有伤你的尊严. *stand on/upon one's ~*, insist upon being treated with proper respect; refuse to do what one considers to be below one's moral, social, etc standards: 坚持礼遇; 保持尊严(拒绝做有失身份的事). **3** [C] (*pl* **-ties**) high or honourable rank, port or title: 高位显爵: *The Queen conferred the ~ of a peerage on him*. 女王授他以贵族身分.

di·graph /'daɪgrɑːf US: -græf; 'daɪgræf/ *n* two letters that represent a single sound (eg sh /ʃ/, ea /i:/ in *sheaf*). 代表单一语音的两个字母(如 sheaf 中 sh 代表 /ʃ/ 音, ea 代表 /i:/ 音).

di·gress /daɪ'gres; də'gres/ *vi* [VP2A, 3A] ~ **(from)**, (esp in speaking or writing) turn or wander away (from the main subject). (尤指演说或写作时)离开(本题); 转入枝节. **di·gression** /daɪ'greʃn; də'greʃn/ *n* [U] ~ing; [C] instance of this. 离题; 转入枝节.

digs /dɪgz; dɪgz/ *n pl* (GB, colloq) lodgings. (英, 口)宿舍; 住地.

dike, dyke /daɪk; daɪk/ *n* **1** ditch (for carrying away water from land). (排水的)沟. **2** long wall of earth, etc (to keep back water and prevent flooding).

堤(阻水或防洪的长壁，以土等筑成)。**3** ⚠ (derog sl) (masculine) lesbian. (讳)(贬俚)(男性化之)同性恋女子。□ vi, vt [VP2A, 6A] make or provide with a ~ or ~s. 筑堤。

a dike

dil·api·dated /dɪˈlæpɪdeɪtɪd; dəˈlæpə‚detɪd/ adj (of buildings, furniture, etc) falling to pieces; in a state of disrepair: (指建筑物,家具等)残破的; 失修的; 倒塌的: a ~-looking car; 破烂不堪的汽车; a ~ old house. 残破的古屋。 **dil·api·da·tion** /dɪ‚læpɪˈdeɪʃn; də‚læpəˈdeʃən/ n [U] being or becoming ~. 残破不堪; 失修倒塌。

di·late /daɪˈleɪt; daɪˈlet/ vi, vt 1 [VP6A, 2A] (cause to) become wider, larger, further open: (使)扩大; 膨胀; 张大: The pupils of your eyes ~ when you enter a dark room. 当你进入暗室, 你的眼睛的瞳孔就会扩大。The horse ~d its nostrils. 那马张大它的鼻孔。2 [VP3A] ~ upon, (formal) speak or write comprehensively about: (正式用语)详述(说或写): If there were time, I could ~ upon this subject. 假如有时间, 我对此题目即可以详述。 **di·la·tion** /daɪˈleɪʃn; daɪˈleʃən/ n [U] dilating or being ~d. 扩大; 膨胀; 详述。

dila·tory /ˈdɪlətərɪ US: ‚ˈdɪlə‚tɔrɪ/ adj slow in acting; causing delay. 做事缓慢的; 拖延的。

di·lemma /dɪˈlemə; dəˈlemə/ n situation in which one has to choose between two things, two courses of action, etc both unfavourable or undesirable. 进退两难之境; 两条路均不如意的困境。 be in/place sb in a ~: 处(使处)于进退两难之境: You place me in something of a ~. 你使我进退两难。

dil·et·tante /‚dɪlɪˈtæntɪ; ‚dɪləˈtæntɪ/ n (pl ~s -ti:z; -tiz/ or -ti /-tɪ; -tɪ/) one who studies sth, but not seriously and not with real understanding. 研究某事物不认真且不甚了解的人。

dili·gence /ˈdɪlɪdʒəns; ‚ˈdɪlədʒəns/ n [U] ~ (in), steady effort; showing care and effort (in what one does). 勤勉; 细心而用功。

dili·gent /ˈdɪlɪdʒənt; ‚ˈdɪlədʒənt/ adj ~ (in), hard-working; showing care and effort (in what one does). 勤勉的; 努力的; 细心而用功的。 ~·ly adv

dill /dɪl; dɪl/ n herb with spicy seeds, eg as used for flavouring pickles. 草茴香; 莳萝(草本植物,子有香味,用作泡菜等之香料)。

dilly-dally /ˈdɪlɪ ˈdælɪ; ‚ˈdɪlɪ‚dælɪ/ vi [VP2A] dawdle; waste time (by not making up one's mind). (因犹豫不决而)浪费时间。

di·lute /daɪˈljuːt US: -ˈluːt; daɪˈlut/ vt [VP6A, 14] ~ (with), make (a liquid or colour) weaker or thinner (by adding water or other liquid): (加水等使液体或颜色)变薄; 变淡; 稀释: to ~ wine with water; 加水于酒以冲淡之; (fig) weaken the force of (by mixing): (喻)(由混合而)减弱···之力量: to ~ skilled labour, eg by employing a proportion of unskilled workers. 如熟练的工人中掺入不熟练的工人。□ adj (of acids, etc) weakened by diluting. (指酸液等)稀释的; 冲淡的; 掺水的。 **di·lu·tion** /daɪˈljuːʃn US: -ˈluː-; daɪˈluʃən/ n [U] diluting or being ~d; [C] sth that is ~d. 稀释; 冲淡; 掺水; 稀释或冲淡之物。

dim /dɪm; dɪm/ adj (-mmer, -mmest) 1 not bright; not clearly to be seen: 不亮的; 看不清楚的; 朦胧的; 模糊的: the dim light of a candle; 微弱的烛光; the dim outline of buildings on a dark night; 在黑夜里建筑物之

朦胧的轮廓; dim memories/recollections of my childhood. 对于儿时之模糊的记忆。 **2** (of the eyes, eyesight) not able to see clearly: (指眼睛,目力)看不清楚的: eyes dim with tears. 为泪水所模糊的眼睛。 His eyesight is getting dim. 他的目力逐渐模糊。 take a dim view of, (colloq) regard with disapproval or pessimism. (口)对···不赞成或不抱乐观。 **3** (colloq, of persons) lacking intelligence. (口,指人)愚钝的。 □ vt, vi (-mm-) [VP 6A, 2A] make or become dim: (使)变微弱,朦胧,模糊: The light of a candle is dimmed by sunlight. 烛光在太阳光下变得微弱。 **dim·ly** adv in a dim manner: 模糊地; 朦胧地; a dimly lit room. 灯光微弱的房间。 **dim·ness** n

dime /daɪm; daɪm/ n coin of US and Canada worth ten cents. (美国及加拿大银币)一角。

di·men·sion /dɪˈmenʃn; dɪˈmenʃən/ n 1 [U, C] measurement of any sort (breadth, length, thickness, height, etc): 任何一种度量(宽、长、厚、高等): What are the ~s of the room? 这房间的长、宽、高是多少? **2** (pl) size; extent: (复)大小; 面积; 体积; 范围; 程度: a building of great ~s; 庞大的建筑物; the ~s of the problem. 问题的范围。 **3** (algebra) number of unknown quantities contained as factors in a product: (代数)维; 次元(乘积之因子数): x^3, x^2y and xyz are of three ~s. x^3, x^2y, xyz 都是三次式。 ~al /-ˈʃənl; -ʃənl/ adj having a (certain number of) ~s: ···次元的: two-/three-~al figures. 二(三)次元的数字。 **3D** /‚θriː ˈdiː; ‚θriˈdi/ (abbr of three-~al) (three-dimensional 之略) stereoscopic, giving the illusion of depth in perspective (as well as height and breadth). 立体的(给人不但有高、阔, 且有深度的幻觉)。

dim·in·ish /dɪˈmɪnɪʃ; dəˈmɪnɪʃ/ vt, vi [VP6A, 2A] make or become less: (使)减少; 缩小: ~ing food supplies; 日渐减少的食品供应; a war that seriously ~ed the country's wealth; 严重消耗国家财富的战争; a currency that has ~ed in value. 已贬值的货币。

dim·inu·endo /dɪ‚mɪnjuˈendəʊ; də‚mɪnjuˈendo/ n (pl ~s /-dəʊz; -doz/) [C] (music) gradual decrease in loudness: (音乐)声音渐弱: a sudden ~. 声音突然减弱。

dim·in·ution /‚dɪmɪˈnjuːʃn US: -ˈnuːʃn; ‚dɪməˈnjuʃən/ n [U] diminishing or being diminished; [C] amount of this: 减少; 缩小; 减少量; 缩小量: to hope for a small ~ in taxes. 希望税捐略微减低。

dim·inu·tive /dɪˈmɪnjutɪv; dəˈmɪnjətɪv/ adj 1 unusually or remarkably small. 较通常为小的; 小得多的。 **2** (gram, of a suff) indicating smallness. (语法, 指词尾)表示'小'的。 □ n word formed by the use of a suff of this kind, eg streamlet, a small stream, lambkin, a small lamb. 由此种词尾所构成的词(如 streamlet 小溪, lambkin 小羊)。

dim·ity /ˈdɪmɪtɪ; ‚ˈdɪmətɪ/ n [U] (kinds of) cotton cloth woven with raised strips or designs, used for bedroom hangings, etc. (各种)有棱条或凸出之花样的棉布(用作卧室帷幔等)。

dimple /ˈdɪmpl; ‚ˈdɪmpl/ n small natural hollow in the chin or cheek (either permanent, or which appears eg when a person smiles); slight hollow on water (made eg by a breeze). 面颊上的酒窝; 笑靥; 风吹水面所起的涟漪。 □ vt, vi [VP6A, 2A] make ~ on; form ~s. (使)现酒窝; (使)起涟漪。

din /dɪn; dɪn/ n [U] (or a din) loud, confused noise that continues: 不断的喧闹声; 嘈杂声: The children were making so much din/such a din that I couldn't study. 孩子们吵闹得非常厉害, 我简直不能读书。 They made/kicked up such a din at the party. 那次聚会中他们吵闹得真凶。 □ vt, vi (-nn-) 1 [VP2C] make a din: 喧嚣; 发嘈杂声: The cries of his tormentors were still dinning in his ears. 那些折磨他的人的叫吼声仍然在他的耳朵里响个不停。 **2** din sth into sb, tell him again and again, in a forcible manner. 再三叮嘱; 三番五次地告诫。

dine /daɪn; daɪn/ vi, vt 1 [VP2A] (formal) have

dinner. (正式用语)吃饭; 进餐. **~ out**, dine outside one's home (eg at the house of friends, or at a restaurant). 在外面吃饭(在朋友家或餐馆吃饭). **2** [VP 6A] give a dinner for: 设宴款待; 请(客): *The great man was wined and ~d wherever he went*, People gave dinner-parties for him. 那大人物无论走到哪里都受到酒宴招待. **'dining-car**, railway coach in which meals are served. (火车的)餐车. **'dining-room**, room in which meals are eaten. 餐厅; 饭厅. **'dining-table**, table used for eating on. 餐桌.

diner /'daɪnə(r); 'daɪnɚ/ *n* **1** person who dines. 吃饭者; 进餐者. **2** dining-car on a train. (火车的)餐车. **3** (US) restaurant shaped like a ~(2). (美)外形似餐车般的餐馆.

ding-dong /'dɪŋ 'dɒŋ; 'dɪŋ,dɒŋ/ *n, adv* (with the) sound of bells striking repeatedly. (钟反复敲击的)叮咚声; 叮叮咚咚地. **a ~ struggle/battle**, one in which each of two contestants has the advantage alternately. 双方互有胜败的比赛; 旗鼓相当的竞争.

din·ghy /'dɪŋɪ; 'dɪŋɪ/ *n* (*pl* **-ghies**) (kinds of) small open boat; inflatable rubber boat (eg carried by an aircraft for use if forced down on water). 无篷小船; (飞机等携带以备迫降水上用的可以充气的)橡皮艇.

dingle /'dɪŋgl; 'dɪŋgl/ *n* deep dell, usu with trees. 深谷(通常有树木).

dingy /'dɪndʒɪ; 'dɪndʒɪ/ *adj* (**-ier, -iest**) dirty-looking; not fresh or cheerful: 样子肮脏的; 不清爽的; 昏暗的: *a ~ manufacturing town*; 肮脏的制造工业城镇; *a ~ room in a ~ boarding-house*. 昏暗的寄宿舍中一个昏暗的房间. **ding·ily** *adv* **dingi·ness** *n*

dining /'daɪnɪŋ; 'daɪnɪŋ/ ⟹ **dine**.

dinky /'dɪŋkɪ; 'dɪŋkɪ/ *adj* (**-ier, -iest**) (GB, colloq) pretty; neat: (英, 口)漂亮的; 精致的; 精致的: *What a ~ little hat!* 多么精致的一顶小帽!

din·ner /'dɪnə(r); 'dɪnɚ/ *n* main meal of the day, whether eaten at midday or in the evening (note the *preps* and the use and omission of the articles): 一日间的主餐(无论中午吃或晚间吃.注意连用的介词以及冠词的使用和省略): *It's time for ~/~-time*. 吃饭的时间到了. *Have you had* (US 美 = *eaten*) *~ yet?* 你吃了饭没有? *They were at ~/having ~ when I called*. 当我访晤时, 他们正在吃饭. *He ate too much ~*. 他饭吃得太多. *The ~ was badly served*. 饭菜上得不好. *Shall we give a ~* (= '**~-party**) *for her?* 我们需要宴请她一次吗? *Four ~s at £5 a head*. 四客饭, 每客五英镑. *Shall we ask him to ~?* 我们要请他吃饭吗? '**~-jacket**, black jacket worn by men in the evening for formal occasions. 男人在晚间正式场合所穿的黑色礼服. (Cf *dress coat*, with tails, and US *tuxedo*.) (参较有燕尾之 dress coat, 及美国间之 tuxedo.) '**~-service**, '**~-set**, set of plates, dishes, etc for ~. (杯盘碗碟等)餐具.

dino·saur /'daɪnəsɔ(r); 'daɪnə,sɔr/ *n* large extinct reptile. 恐龙(已绝迹的巨大爬虫).

a dinosaur

dint /dɪnt; dɪnt/ *n* **1** [C] = **dent**. **2** *by ~ of*, by means of: 由于; 凭借: *He succeeded by ~ of hard work*. 他凭苦干而成功.

dio·cese /'daɪəsɪs; 'daɪə,sɪs/ *n* bishop's district. (主教的)教区. **di·ocesan** /daɪ'ɒsɪsn; daɪ'ɑsəsn/ *adj, n* (of a) ~. 教区(的).

di·ox·ide /daɪ'ɒksaɪd; daɪ'ɑksaɪd/ *n* (chem) oxide

formed by combination of two atoms of oxygen and one atom of a metal or other element: (化学)二氧化物(二氧原子和一金属或其他元素之原子之化合物): *carbon ~*, (CO₂). 二氧化碳.

dip¹ /dɪp; dɪp/ *vt, vi* (**-pp-**) **1** [VP6A, 14] *dip in/into*, put, lower, (sth) into a liquid: 使某物浸入液体中; 沾: *to dip one's pen into the ink*; 将笔伸入墨水中(沾墨水); *to dip sheep*, immerse them in a liquid that disinfects them, kills vermin; 用消毒水洗羊(以消灭害虫等); *to dip candles*, make them by dipping wick into melted fat; 用烛心沾蜡油以制蜡烛; *dip a garment*, put it in a liquid dye to change its colour. 将衣物浸入染料中染衣服. '**dip-stick**, stick or rod (to be) dipped into a tank or other container to measure the depth of liquid in it (eg oil in the sump of an engine). 探条(伸入液体容器中以探测其中液体深度, 如探测发动机贮油槽中的油用作者). **2** [VP3A] *dip into*, (fig): (喻): *to dip into one's purse*, spend money; 花钱; 支付; *to dip into the future*, try to imagine what it will be like; 预想未来的事情; *to dip into a book/an author, etc*, make a cursory study of its colour. 浏览一本书(一个作家的作品). **3** [VP 2A, C] go below a surface or level: 沉入; 降至(某平面)以下: *The sun dipped below the horizon*. 太阳沉入地平线以下. *The birds rose and dipped in their flight*. 鸟上下飞翔. **4** [VP6A, 2A] (cause to) go down and then up again: (使)一低一扬; 降下复升起: *to dip a flag*, as a salute, eg to another ship; 行点旗礼(将旗下降复升起, 以示向另一船敬礼); *to dip the headlights of a car*, lower their beams (in order not to dazzle the driver of another car). 使汽车前灯之光度减弱(以免使另一汽车的驾驶员目眩); 打近灯. *The land dips gently to the south*. 地面向南方微弱倾斜.

dip² /dɪp; dɪp/ *n* **1** [C] act of dipping, esp (colloq) quick bathe or swim: 浸; 沾; (尤指, 口)短促的沐浴或游泳: *to have/take/go for a dip*. 作短促的沐浴(或游泳). **2** [U] cleansing liquid in which sheep are dipped. 洗羊的消毒水. **3** [C] downward slope: 斜坡: *a dip in the road*; 路上的斜坡; *a dip among the hills*. 山中的斜坡. **4** [U] position of a flag when it is dipped(4): 旗帜下降示意的位置; 点旗: *at the dip*. 在下降示意的位置.

diph·theria /dɪf'θɪərɪə; dɪf'θɪrɪə/ *n* [U] serious contagious disease of the throat causing difficulty in breathing. 白喉(喉部严重的传染病, 使呼吸困难).

diph·thong /'dɪfθɒŋ US: -θɔːŋ; 'dɪfθɔŋ/ *n* union of two vowel sounds or (more usu *digraph*) vowel letters, eg the sounds /aɪ; aɪ/ in *pipe* /paɪp; paɪp/, the letters *ou* in *doubt*. 二重元音; 双元音(合读一音的两个元音); 合读一音的两个元音字母(digraph 较常用).

di·ploma /dɪ'pləʊmə; dɪ'plomə/ *n* [C] educational certificate of proficiency: 毕业证书; 文凭: *a ~ in architecture*. 建筑学系毕业证书.

di·plo·macy /dɪ'pləʊməsɪ; dɪ'ploməsɪ/ *n* [U] **1** management of a country's affairs by its agents abroad (ambassadors and ministers), and their direction by the Ministry of Foreign Affairs at home; skill in this. 外交; 外交手段. **2** art of, skill in, dealing with people so that business is done smoothly. (为业务进行顺利, 对人的)交际手腕.

diplo·mat /'dɪpləmæt; 'dɪplə,mæt/ *n* **1** person engaged in diplomacy for his country (eg an ambassador). 外交官(例如大使). **2** person clever at dealing with people. 善于应付人者; 善于办交涉者.

diplo·matic /ˌdɪplə'mætɪk; ˌdɪplə'mætɪk/ *adj* **1** of diplomacy: 外交的: *the '~ service* (2); 外交界; 外交官的总称; *the '~ corps/body*, all the ambassadors, ministers and their officers in the capital of a country. 外交使节团; 一国首都的所有外交使节. **2** tactful; having diplomacy(2): 圆通的; 圆滑的; 有交际手腕的: *a ~ answer*; 圆通的答复; *to be ~ in dealing with people*. 对人有交际手腕. **diplo·matically**/ -klɪ; -klɪ/ *adv*

di·ploma·tist /dɪ'pləʊmətɪst; dɪ'plomətɪst/ *n* = **diplomat**.

dip·per /'dɪpə(r); 'dɪpɚ/ n 1 cup-shaped vessel with a long handle, for ladling out liquids. 有长柄的舀水勺。2 (US) **the Big D∼, the Little D∼**, groups of stars in the northern sky. (美)大熊星及小熊星之北斗七星。⇨ bear¹(3), plough(4).

dip·so·ma·nia /ˌdɪpsə'meɪnɪə; ˌdɪpsə'menɪə/ n [U] insatiable craving for alcoholic drink. 嗜酒狂。**dip·so·maniac** /ˌdɪpsə'meɪnɪæk; ˌdɪpsə'menɪˌæk/ n person suffering from ∼. 嗜酒狂患者。

dip·tych /'dɪptɪk; 'dɪptɪk/ n painting or carving, esp an altarpiece, on two hinged panels that can be closed like a book. (尤指祭坛上方或背后)似书般可折合的双连画或雕刻。

dire /'daɪə(r); daɪr/ adj dreadful; terrible: 可怕的; 可怕的: ∼ news; 可怕的消息; extreme: 极度的: to be in ∼ need of help. 非常需要帮助。

di·rect¹ /dɪ'rekt; də'rɛkt/ adj 1 (going) straight; not curved or crooked; not turned aside: 直(进)的; 不弯曲的; 不曲折的: in a ∼ line; 成一直线; a ∼ hit/shot, not turned aside by hitting sth else first; 直接命中; the ∼ rays of the sun, not reflected from sth. 太阳的直射光线。2 with nothing or no one in between; in an unbroken line: 直接的; 直系的: to be in ∼ contact with sb; 与某人直接连络; as a ∼ result of this decision. 此一决定之直接结果。He's a ∼ descendant of the Duke of Bumford. 他是巴穆富公爵的直系子孙。3 straightforward; going straight to the point; frank; unhesitating: 直率的; 直截了当的; 坦白的; 爽快的: He has a ∼ way of speaking/acting. 他说话直率(做事直截了当)。He made a ∼ answer to the charges brought against him. 他对于被控的罪名做直率的答复。2 exact, diametrical: 恰好的; 全然的: a ∼ contradiction; 完全矛盾; the ∼ opposite/contrary. 正好相反。5 (various uses): (各种不同的用法): ∼ action, use of strikes by workmen to get their demands. 直接行动(工人为达到要求而从事罢工)。∼ current, electric current flowing in one direction. 直流电。⇨ alternate. ∼ speech, speaker's actual words. 直接引语。⇨ indirect. '∼ tax, one levied on the person who pays it (eg income tax), not (eg purchase tax) on goods, etc. 直接税(例如所得税, 而非购买税等)。☐ adv without interrupting a journey; without going by a round-about way: 直接地; 一直: The train goes there ∼. 火车直达那里。He came to London. 他直接来到伦敦。⇨ directly. ∼ness n

di·rect² /dɪ'rekt; də'rɛkt/ vt, vi [VP6A, 14] ∼ sb (to), tell or show (sb) how to do sth, how to get somewhere: 指点; 指示方向; 指引: Can you ∼ me to the post office? 你能指示我去邮局的路吗? They ∼ed me wrongly. 他们把我指引错了。2 [VP6A, 14] ∼ sth (to), address (a letter, parcel, etc): 书写(信件, 包裹等之)地址: Shall I ∼ the letter to his business address or to his home address? 这封信我写他的办公地址还是他的住宅地址? 3 [VP14] ∼ sth to sb, speak or write to: 对某人说…; 写…给某人: My remarks were not ∼ed to all of you. 我的话并非指你们全体说的。4 [VP6A] manage; control: 管理; 支配; 指挥; 指导: Who is ∼ing the women? 谁在指挥工人? Who ∼ed the film? 谁导演这部影片的? 5 [VP14] ∼ to/towards, turn: 指向: We ∼ed our steps towards home. 我们走向回家的路。Our energies must be ∼ed towards higher productivity. 我们必须努力谋求增产。6 [VP17, 9] order: 命令: The officer ∼ed his men to advance/that his men should advance. 那军官命令部下前进。

di·rec·tion /dɪ'rekʃn; də'rɛkʃən/ n 1 [C] course taken by a moving person or thing; point towards which a person or thing looks or faces: 方向; 方位: Tom went off in one ∼ and Harry in another ∼. 汤姆朝着一个方向去, 哈里朝另一个方向去。The aircraft was flying in a northerly ∼. 那飞机在向北飞行中。When the police arrived, the crowd scattered in all ∼s. 警察来时, 群众向四方散去。(fig) (喻) Reforms are needed in numerous ∼s. 许多方面需要改革。'∼-finder, radio

device that shows the ∼ from which wireless signals are coming. 无线电定向仪; 探向器(指示无线电信号发来之方向者)。2 [U] have a good/poor sense of ∼, be able/unable to determine well one's position with regard to one's surroundings when there are no known or visible landmarks. 有(无)方向感(指无可见的陆标时, 能或不能决定自己的位置和周遭方位的能力)。3 (often pl) information or instructions about what to do, where to go, how to do sth, etc: (常用复数)说明; 指引: D∼s about putting the parts together are printed on the card. 组合各种零件的说明印在卡片上。He gave me full ∼s to enable me to find his house. 对我详细说明如何去他的家。4 (pl) address on or for a letter, parcel, etc: (复)(信件, 包裹等上面之)地址: The parcel was returned to the sender because the ∼s were insufficient. 这包裹因地址不详细而退还寄件人。5 [U] management; control; guidance: 管理; 指挥; 指导: ∼ of labour, movement of workers from one area, one kind of work, to another. 劳工管理(将工人自一地区转至另一地区, 或由一工作转另至一工作)。He did the work under my ∼. 他在我的指导下做这事。She feels the need of ∼, wants sb to guide and advise her. 她感到需要有人指导她。∼al /-ʃənl; -ʃənl/ adj of ∼ in space (esp of radio signals transmitted over a narrow angle): 定向的(尤指关于无线电信号呈狭小的角度发送者): a ∼al aerial. 定向天线。

di·rec·tive /dɪ'rektɪv; də'rɛktɪv/ n [C] general or detailed instruction. 一般或详细的指令; 训令。

di·rect·ly /dɪ'rektlɪ; də'rɛktlɪ/ adv 1 in a direct manner; 直接地; 一直: He was looking ∼ at us. 他直视着我们。2 at once; without delay: 即刻; 立刻: Come in ∼. 即刻进来。3 in a short time: 不久: I'll be there ∼. 我马上就到那里。☐ conj (colloq) as soon as: (口)刚一…就; 立即: D∼ I had done it, I knew I had made a mistake. 我刚一做完这事, 就知道我做错了。

di·rec·tor /dɪ'rektə(r); də'rɛktɚ/ n person who directs, esp one of a group (called the Board of D∼s) who manage the affairs of a business company; (theatre, cinema, TV) person who supervises and instructs the actors and actresses, the camera crew, etc. 指导者; (尤指)董事(董事会称作the Board of Directors); (戏剧, 电影或电视之)导演。∼·ship /-ʃɪp; -ˌʃɪp/ n position of a company ∼; time during which he holds his position. 董事之职; 董事之任期。

di·rec·tor·ate /dɪ'rektərət; də'rɛktərɪt/ n 1 office or position of a director. 指导者, 董事或导演的职位。2 board of directors. 董事会。

di·rec·tory /dɪ'rektərɪ; də'rɛktərɪ/ n (pl -ries) (book with a) list of persons, business firms, etc in a district; list of telephone subscribers (and usu addresses) in A B C order. 姓名住址录; 电话簿(按字母顺序排列者)。

dire·ful /'daɪəfl; 'daɪrfəl/ adj (liter) dire; terrible. (文)可怕的; 可怖的; 悲惨的。∼ly /'daɪəfəlɪ; 'daɪrfəlɪ/ adv

dirge /dɜːdʒ; dɝdʒ/ n song sung at a burial or for a dead person. 挽歌。

diri·gible /'dɪrɪdʒəbl; 'dɪrədʒəbl/ n [C] balloon (used as an airship) that can be steered; zeppelin. 可驾驶的气球; 飞船; 飞艇。

dirk /dɜːk; dɝk/ n kind of dagger. 一种短剑; 匕首。

dirndl /'dɜːndl; 'dɝndl/ n full-skirted dress with a close-fitting bodice. 一种连裙的上半身为紧身的女装。

dirt /dɜːt; dɝt/ n [U] 1 unclean matter (eg dust, soil, mud) esp when it is where is not wanted (eg on the skin, clothes, in buildings): 污秽物(例如皮肤, 衣服, 建筑物上的灰尘, 泥土等): His clothes were covered with ∼. 他的衣服上满是脏东西。How can I get the ∼ off the walls? 我怎样除掉墙上的脏东西? 2 loose earth or soil: 松土: a ∼ road, (US) unpaved, not macadamized. (美)未经修葺的道路; 泥土路。as cheap/common as ∼, vulgar; low-class. 贱如粪土的; 低级的。

fling/throw ~ at sb, say slanderous things about him. 诽谤某人。 **treat sb like ~**, treat him as if he were worthless. 轻待某人。 **'~ farmer**, (US) one who does all his own work. (美)自耕农。 **,~·cheap**, very cheap, almost valueless. 很贱的； 几乎毫无价值的。 **'~·track**, one made of cinders, etc (for eg motor-cycle races). (由泥土、煤渣等铺成的)赛车跑道。 **3** unclean thought or talk. 肮脏的思想或言语。

dirty¹ /'dɜːtɪ; 'dɜtɪ/ adj (-ier, -iest) **1** not clean; covered with dirt: 污秽的； 脏的； 覆满污秽物的： ~ hands/clothes; 脏的手(衣服)； causing one to be ~: 会把人弄脏的： ~ work. 会把人弄脏的工作。 **2** (of the weather) rough; stormy: (指天气)有暴风雨的： I'm glad I haven't to go out on such a ~ night. 我很高兴，因为在这样一个暴风雨夜里我不必外出。 **3** unclean in thought or talk; obscene: 思想或言语猥亵的； 淫猥的： scribble ~ words on lavatory walls. 在厕所墙上乱写猥亵的文字。 **4** (colloq) mean, dishonourable, underhand: (口)卑鄙的； 可耻的； 欺瞒的： play a ~ trick on sb, play a mean trick on him; 以卑鄙的手段对付某人； get/give sb a ~ look, one of severe disapproval or disgust. 被(对某人)瞪一眼。 **dirt·ily** adv

dirty² /'dɜːtɪ; 'dɜtɪ/ vt, vi [VP6A, 2A] make or become dirty: 弄脏； 变脏： Don't ~ your new dress. 不要弄脏你的新衣服。 White gloves ~ easily. 白手套易脏。

dis·abil·ity /,dɪsə'bɪlətɪ; ,dɪsə'bɪlətɪ/ n (pl -ties) **1** [U] state of being disabled; incapacity. 无能力； 失去能力。 **2** [C] sth that disables or disqualifies one: 使人无能力的事物； 使人无资格的事物： Mr Hill has a ~ and a pension from the government, eg because he lost a leg while he was in the army. 希尔先生领有一笔政府发给的伤残抚恤金(例如因其在军中时断过腿)。

dis·able /dɪs'eɪbl; dɪs'ebl/ vt [VP6A] make unable to do sth, esp take away the power of using the limbs: 使无能力； (尤指)使残废： ~d ex-service men, former soldiers, crippled in war. 残废的退役军人。 **~·ment** n

dis·abuse /,dɪsə'bjuːz; ,dɪsə'bjuz/ vt [VP6A, 14] ~ (of), (formal) free (sb, his mind) from false ideas; put (a person) right (in his ideas): (正式用语)使(某人、某人的心灵)免除虚妄的观念；(在观念上)矫正(某人)； 解惑； 开导： to ~ a man of silly prejudices. 开导某人的愚妄的偏见。

dis·ad·van·tage /,dɪsəd'vɑːntɪdʒ US: -'væn-; ,dɪsəd'væntɪdʒ/ n **1** [C] unfavourable condition, sth that stands in the way of progress, success, etc: 不利的条件； 妨碍进步、成功等的事物： It is a ~ to be small when you're standing in a crowd to look at a football game. 站在人群中看足球比赛时，身材矮小是一个不利的条件。 His inability to speak English puts him at a ~ when he attends international conferences. 他不会说英语，使他在参加国际会议时处于不利的情况。 **2** [U] loss; injury: 损失； 伤害： rumours to his ~, that hurt his reputation, etc. 损害其名誉等的谣言。 **~·ous** /,dɪs,ædven'teɪdʒəs; dɪs,ædvən'tedʒəs/ adj ~ous (to), causing a ~: 不利的： a ~ous place. 处于不利的地位。 **~·ous·ly** adv

dis·af·fected /,dɪsə'fektɪd; ,dɪsə'fektɪd/ adj discontented; rebellious; disloyal. 不满的； 反叛的； 不忠的。 **dis·af·fec·tion** /,dɪsə'fekʃn; ,dɪsə'fekʃən/ n [U] political discontent; disloyalty. 政治不满； 不忠； 背叛。

dis·af·for·est /,dɪsə'fɒrɪst US: -'fɔːr-; ,dɪsə'fɔrɪst/ vt = disforest.

dis·agree /,dɪsə'griː; ,dɪsə'gri/ vi [VP2A, 3A] ~ (with), take a different view; have different opinions; not agree: 持不同的意见； 意见不合； 不同意； 不一致： Even friends sometimes ~. 即使是朋友，有时也会意见不合。 I'm sorry to ~ with you/with what you say/with what you say. 很抱歉，我不同意你的意见/(你的声明，你所说的话)。 reports from Rome ~ with those from Milan. 来自罗马的报导与来自米兰的报导不一。 **2** [VP3A] ~ with sb, (of food, climate) have bad effects on; prove unsuitable for: (指食物、气候)对…有

不良影响；不适宜： The climate ~s with me. 这气候对我不适宜。 **~·able** /-əbl; -əbl/ adj unpleasant: 令人不愉快的： ~able weather; 讨厌的天气； bad-tempered: 脾气坏的： a ~able fellow. 一个坏脾气的人。 **~·able·ness** n **~·ably** /-əblɪ; -əblɪ/ adv

dis·agree·ment /,dɪsə'griːmənt; ,dɪsə'grimənt/ n **1** [U] disagreeing; absence of agreement: 意见不合； 不一致； 不适合； 不调合： to be in ~ with sb or sth. 与某人的意见不合或与某事物不调合。 **2** [C] instance of this; difference of opinion; slight quarrel: 意见不合的实例； 争论； 小争执： ~s between husbands and wives. 夫妻间的小争执。

dis·al·low /,dɪsə'laʊ; ,dɪsə'laʊ/ vt [VP6A] refuse to allow or accept as correct: 不准； 不承认； 不接受： The judge ~ed the claim. 法官驳回该要求。

dis·ap·pear /,dɪsə'pɪə(r); ,dɪsə'pɪr/ vi [VP2A] go out of sight; be seen no more: 不见； 消失： Let's hope our difficulties will soon ~, vanish. 希望我们的困难不久便可以消除。 The snow soon ~ed, melted. 雪很快地融化了。 **~·ance** /-rəns; -rəns/ n ~ing. 不见； 消失。

dis·ap·point /,dɪsə'pɔɪnt; ,dɪsə'pɔɪnt/ vt [VP6A] fail to do or be equal to what is hoped for or expected: 使失望： The book/match/meeting ~ed me. 这本书(比赛、会议)令我失望。 Please don't ~ me, don't fail to do what you have promised. 请不要使我失望。 **2** prevent a hope, plan, etc from being realized: 阻碍(希望、计划等)实现： I'm sorry to ~ your expectations. 我很抱歉使你的期望落空。 **~ed part adj ~ed (in/at sth) (with sb)**, sad at not getting what was hoped for, etc: 失望的； 受挫折的： We were ~ed to hear/~ed when we heard that you could not come. 听说你不能来，我们感到失望。 I was ~ed at not finding/~ed not to find her at home. 我发现她不在家，感到失望。 We were ~ed in our hopes. 我们的希望落空了。 What are you looking so ~ed about? 什么事情使你显得如此失望？ I'm ~ed with you. 我对你感到失望。 **~·ed·ly** adv ~ing adj causing sb to be ~ed: 令人失望的： The weather this summer has been ~ing. 今年夏天的天气一直令人失望。

dis·ap·point·ment /,dɪsə'pɔɪntmənt; ,dɪsə'pɔɪntmənt/ n **1** [U] being disappointed: 失望： To her great ~, it rained on the day of the picnic. 野餐的那一天下雨，使她大为失望。 **2** [C] sb or sth that disappoints: 令人失望的人或物： He had suffered many ~s in love, Many women had not returned his love. 他在恋爱方面，曾经遭受多次失意。

dis·ap·pro·ba·tion /,dɪs,æprə'beɪʃn; ,dɪsæprə'beʃən/ n (formal) disapproval. (正式用语)不赞成。

dis·ap·prove /,dɪsə'pruːv; ,dɪsə'pruv/ vi, vt [VP2A, 3A, 6A] ~ (of), have, express, an unfavourable opinion: 不赞成： She wants to train for the theatre but her parents ~. 她想训练自己做戏剧演员，但她的父母不赞成她的意图。 **dis·ap·proval** /-'pruːvl; -'pruvl/ n [U] disapproving: 不赞成： He shook his head in disapproval, 不以为然地： He shook his head in disapproval. 他摇头表示不赞成。 **dis·ap·prov·ing·ly** /-ɪŋlɪ; -ɪŋlɪ/ adv in a way that shows disapproval: 不以为然地： When Mary lit a cigarette, her father looked at her disapprovingly. 玛丽点起一支香烟，她父亲不以为然地望着她。

dis·arm /dɪs'ɑːm; dɪs'ɑrm/ vi, vt **1** [VP6A] take away weapons and other means of attack from: 缴械； ~ed. 除…的武装： Five hundred rebels were captured and ~ed. 五百名叛军被俘并被缴械。 **2** [VP2A] (of nations) reduce the size of, give up the use of, armed forces: (指国家)裁减军备： It is difficult to persuade the Great Powers to ~. 要说服列强裁军是很困难的。 **3** [VP6A] make it difficult for sb to feel anger, suspicion, doubt: 消除某人之愤怒、猜忌或怀疑： By frankly admitting that he was not a scholar, he ~ed criticism. 他坦白承认他不是一位学者，因而消除了旁人对他的非议。 I felt angry, but he smiles ~ed me. 我很生气，但他的微笑使我的怒气消失了。 **dis·arma·ment** /dɪs'ɑːməmənt; dɪs'ɑrməmənt/ n [U] ~ing or being ~ed(2): 裁减军备： ~ament

conferences; 裁军会议; *new proposals for ~ament.* 新的裁军建议。

dis·ar·range /ˌdɪsəˈreɪndʒ, ˌdɪsəˈrendʒ/ *vt* [VP6A] disturb; upset; put into disorder: 扰乱; 使乱; 使紊乱: *to ~ sb's plans/hair.* 扰乱某人之计划(弄乱某人的头发)。 ~ment *n*

dis·ar·ray /ˌdɪsəˈreɪ, ˌdɪsəˈre/ *n, vt* [VP6A] (put into) disorder: (使)紊乱: *The troops were in ~.* 军队混乱。

dis·as·so·ci·ate /ˌdɪsəˈsoʊʃɪeɪt, ˌdɪsəˈsoʃɪˌet/ *vt* [VP14] ~ *from* = **dissociate**.

dis·as·ter /dɪˈzɑːstə(r) US: -ˈzæs-; dɪzˈæstɚ/ *n* 1 [C] great or sudden misfortune; terrible accident (eg a great flood or fire, an earthquake, a serious defeat in war, the loss of a large sum of money): 大灾难; 突然的灾祸; 灾祸(例如洪水或大火, 地震, 战争大败, 大量金钱的损失)。 2 [U] great misfortune or suffering: 重大的不幸或灾难: *a record of ~.* 灾难的记录。 **dis·as·trous** /dɪˈzɑːstrəs US: -ˈzæs-; dɪzˈæstrəs/ *adj* causing ~: 招致灾祸的: *disastrous floods;* 损失惨重的水灾; *a defeat that was disastrous to the country.* 使国家蒙受灾祸的失败。 **dis·as·trous·ly** *adv*

dis·avow /ˌdɪsəˈvaʊ, ˌdɪsəˈvaʊ/ *vt* [VP6A] (formal) deny belief in, approval or knowledge of: (正式用语)否认, 不承认: *He ~ed my share in the plot.* 他否认我曾参与这项密谋。 ~al /-ˈvaʊəl; -ˈvaʊəl/ *n*

dis·band /dɪsˈbænd; dɪsˈbænd/ *vt, vi* [VP6A, 2A] (of organized groups) break up: (指团体)解散; 裁撤: *The army (was) ~ed when the war ended.* 战事结束后, 军队(被)裁撤了。 ~ment *n*

dis·be·lieve /ˌdɪsbɪˈliːv, ˌdɪsbəˈliv/ *vi* [VP6A, 2A, 3A] ~ *in*, refuse to believe (sb or sth); be unable or unwilling to believe in. 不肯相信(某人或某事); 不能或不愿相信。 **dis·be·lief** /ˌdɪsbɪˈliːf, ˌdɪsbəˈlif/ *n* [U] lack of belief; refusal to believe. 不相信; 不肯相信。

dis·bud /dɪsˈbʌd; dɪsˈbʌd/ *vt* (-dd-) [VP6A] remove buds from (a plant, etc) (eg to get stronger or better shoots from those that are left). 摘去(草木等)之嫩芽(例如以使余下部分长成较佳之新芽)。

dis·bur·den /dɪsˈbɜːdn; dɪsˈbɚdn/ *vt* [VP6A, 14] ~ *(of)*, (formal) relieve of a burden; unburden (the more usu word). (正式用语)卸除~的重负 (unburden 为较常用之词)。

dis·burse /dɪsˈbɜːs; dɪsˈbɚs/ *vt, vi* [VP6A, 2A] pay out (money). 支付(钱)。 ~ment *n* [U] paying out (of money); [C] sum of money paid out. (金钱的)支付; 付出之款; 支出。

disc, disk /dɪsk; dɪsk/ *n* [C] thin, flat, round plate, eg a coin, a gramophone record; round surface that appears to be flat: 薄平的圆盘状物(如铜币、唱片); 扁平的圆状表面: *the sun's ~.* 日轮。 '~ **brake,** brake which operates when a flat plate is brought into contact with another (rotating) plate at the centre of a (car) wheel. 圆盘煞车。 '~ **harrow,** one with ~s instead of teeth. 圆盘耙(非带齿者)。 '~ **jockey,** radio or TV broadcaster who introduces performers and comments on records and tapes of (esp) light, and popular music. 电台或电视室唱片音乐节目主持人。 2 (anat) layer of cartilage between vertebrae. (解剖)椎间盘(脊椎骨间的一片软骨)。 *a slipped ~,* one that is slightly dislocated. 略微突出的椎间盘。

dis·card /dɪˈskɑːd; dɪsˈkɑrd/ *vt* [VP6A] throw out or away; put aside, give up (sth useless or unwanted): 抛弃; 放弃; 摒弃; 抛开(无用或不需要之物): *to ~ one's winter underclothing when the weather gets warm;* 天气转暖时抛开冬天穿着的内衣; *to ~ old beliefs.* 摒弃旧信仰。 □ /ˈdɪskɑːd; ˈdɪskɑrd/ *n* card or cards ~ed in a card game. 被抛掷的无用之牌。

dis·cern /dɪˈsɜːn; dɪˈsɝn/ *vt* [VP6A] see clearly (with the eyes or with the mind); (esp) see with an effort: (用目或用心)辨明(光指努力以认清): *We ~ed the figure of a man clinging to the mast of the wrecked ship.* 我们看出有一人紧抱着破船的桅。 *It is often difficult to ~ the truth of an event from a newspaper report.* 要从报纸的报导去辨明一个事件的真实性常是困难的。 ~**ing** *adj* able to see and understand well. 眼光好的; 有辨识力的。 ~**ible** /-əbl; -əbl/ *adj* that can be ~ed. 可辨明的。 ~**ment** *n* [U] ~ing; ability to ~; keenness in judging, forming opinions. 辨明; 眼力; 辨认力; 敏于判断。

dis·charge¹ /ˈdɪstʃɑːdʒ; dɪsˈtʃɑrdʒ/ *n* 1 [U] discharging or being discharged (all senses, the numbers refer to *discharge²*): 卸货; 放出; 流出; 发射; 遣走; 放行; 偿还: *How long will the ~(1) of the cargo take?* 卸完货需要多久? *The ~(2) of water from the reservoir is carefully controlled.* 水库的放水被慎重的控制着。 *After his ~(4) from the army, he emigrated to Canada.* 退役后, 他移居加拿大。 *The prisoners were glad to get their ~(4).* 犯人们获释都很高兴。 *He is faithful in the ~(5) of his duties.* 他忠于执行他的职守。 *Will £50 be enough for the ~(5) of your liabilities?* 五十英镑够不够还清你的债务? 2 [U, C] that which is discharged: 放出物; 流出物: *The wound hasn't healed—there's still some/a ~.* 这伤口尚未治好好——仍然有东西流出来。

dis·charge² /dɪsˈtʃɑːdʒ; dɪsˈtʃɑrdʒ/ *vt, vi* [VP6A, 14] 1 unload (cargo from) a ship. 卸(船上之货); 自(船)上卸货。 2 give or send out (liquid, gas, electric current, etc): 放出; 流出(液体、气体、电流等): *Where do the sewers ~ their contents?* 阴沟里的水流往哪里? *The Nile ~s itself* (= flows) *into the Mediterranean.* 尼罗河注入地中海。 *Lightning is caused by clouds discharging electricity.* 闪电系由云层放电所造成的。 *The wound is still discharging pus.* 这伤口仍在流脓。 3 fire (a gun, etc); let fly (an arrow or other missile). 开(枪等); 发射(箭或其他投射物)。 4 send (sb) away; allow (sb) to leave: 遣走(某人); 让(某人)离去: *to ~ a patient from hospital.* 让病人出院。 *The accused man was found not guilty and was ~d.* 这被告因无罪而获释放。 *The members of the jury were ~d,* set free from their duties. 陪审员们被解除了职务。 5 pay (a debt); perform (a duty): 偿还(债务); 执行(职责): *a ~d bankrupt,* man who, after being made bankrupt, has done what the court requires and is now free to act as he wishes. 债务消除的破产者(已履行法院规定之处置后可自由行动的破产者)。

dis·ciple /dɪˈsaɪpl; dɪˈsaɪpl/ *n* follower of any leader of religious thought, art, learning, etc. 信徒; 弟子。 **the Twelve D~s,** the twelve personal followers of Jesus Christ. 耶稣十二门徒。

dis·ci·pli·nar·ian /ˌdɪsəplɪˈneərɪən; ˌdɪsəplɪnˈɛrɪən/ *n* person able to maintain discipline(2): 维持纪律的人: *a good/strict/poor ~.* 能(严格, 不能)维持纪律的人。 *He's no ~,* does not or cannot maintain discipline. 他不能维持纪律。

dis·ci·pline¹ /ˈdɪsɪplɪn; ˈdɪsəplɪn/ *n* 1 [U] training, esp of the mind and character, to produce self-control, habits of obedience, etc: 训练(尤指头脑和品行的训练, 以培养自制, 服从的习惯等): *school ~;* 学校训练; *military ~.* 军事训练。 2 [U] the result of such training; order kept (eg among school-children, soldiers): 上述训练的结果: (学生, 士兵等之)纪律; 风纪: *The soldiers showed perfect ~ under the fire of the enemy.* 在敌人的炮火下, 那些士兵表现了良好纪律。 *The children were clever, but there was not much ~ in the school.* 那些孩子们很聪明, 但学校里缺少纪律。 3 [C] set rules for conduct; method by which training may be given: 戒律; 训练方法: *Pronunciation drill and question and answer work are good ~s for learning a foreign language.* 发音练习和问答是学习外国语言的良好方法。 4 [U] punishment. 惩罚。 5 [C] branch of knowledge; subject of instruction. 学科; 科目。 **dis·ci·pli·nary** /ˈdɪsɪplɪnərɪ US: -nerɪ; ˈdɪsəplɪnˌɛrɪ/ *adj* of or for ~: 训练的; 纪律的; 训练方法的; 惩罚的; 学科的: *to take disciplinary measures;* 采取惩戒的措施; *disciplinary punishment.* 惩

戒的处分。

dis·ci·pline² /'dɪsɪplɪn; 'dɪsə,plɪn/ vt [VP6A] apply discipline(1) to; train and control the mind and character of; punish: 训练; 训导; 熏陶; 惩罚: to ~ badly behaved children. 惩罚行为不良的儿童。

dis·claim /dɪs'kleɪm; dɪs'klem/ vt [VP6A, C] say that one does not own, that one has no connection with: 否认有; 否认与…有关: to ~ responsibility for sth; 否认对某事有责任; to ~ all knowledge of an incident. 否认对一事件知情。~er n statement that ~s: 否认的声明: to issue/send sb a ~er. 发表(致某人)否认的声明。

dis·close /dɪs'kləʊz; dɪs'kloz/ vt [VP6A, 14] ~ (to), uncover; allow to be seen; make known: 揭发; 使显露; 透露: to refuse to ~ one's name and address; 拒绝透露自己的姓名和住址; to ~ a secret. 揭发秘密。**dis·clos·ure** /dɪs'kləʊʒə(r); dɪs'kloʒɚ/ n [U] disclosing or being ~d; [C] that which is ~d (esp what has been kept secret). 揭发; 显露; 被显露的事物(尤指秘密)。

disco /'dɪskəʊ; 'dɪsko/ n (colloq) [C] = **discotheque**.

dis·col·our (US = -lor) /dɪs'kʌlə(r); dɪs'kʌlɚ/ vt, vi [VP2A] change, spoil, the colour of: 使变色; 使褪色; 使变污: walls ~ed by damp. 被湿气污污的墙壁。 2 [VP2A] become changed in colour: 变色; 褪色: materials that ~ in strong sunlight. 遇强烈阳光而褪色的料子。**dis·col·our·ation** (US = -lor-) /,dɪs,kʌlə-'reɪʃn; ,dɪskʌlə'reʃən/ n [U] ~ing or being ~ed; [C] ~ed place; stain. 变色; 褪色; 变色之处; 污点。

dis·com·fit /dɪs'kʌmfɪt; dɪs'kʌmfɪt/ vt [VP6A] baffle; confuse; embarrass. 使困惑; 使混乱; 使窘迫。**dis·com·fi·ture** /dɪs'kʌmfɪtʃə(r); dɪs'kʌmfɪtʃɚ/ n [U] ~ing or being ~ed. 困惑; 混乱; 窘迫。

dis·com·fort /dɪs'kʌmfət; dɪs'kʌmfɚt/ n 1 [U] absence of comfort; uneasiness of mind or body. 不舒服; 不安。 2 [U] sth that causes uneasiness; hardship: 令人不舒适之物; 困苦: the ~s endured by explorers in the Antarctic. 南极探险家忍受的艰难。

dis·com·mode /,dɪskə'məʊd; ,dɪskə'mod/ vt [VP 6A] (formal) put (sb) to inconvenience. (正式用语)使(某人)不方便。

dis·com·pose /,dɪskəm'pəʊz; ,dɪskəm'poz/ vt [VP 6A] disturb the composure of: 使不安; 使烦乱: Don't let their objections ~ you. 不要让他们的反对使你不安。**dis·com·posure** /-əʊʒə(r); -oʒɚ/ n [U] state of being ~d. 不安; 心情烦乱。

dis·con·cert /,dɪskən'sɜːt; ,dɪskən'sɝt/ vt [VP6A] upset the calmness or self-possession of: 使不安; 使慌乱: The Manager was ~ed to discover that he had gone to the office without putting in his false teeth. 经理发现他未戴假牙而来办公室时感到很窘。

dis·con·nect /,dɪskə'nekt; ,dɪskə'nɛkt/ vt [VP6A, 14] ~ (from), detach from; take (two things) apart: 使分开; 拆开(两物): You should ~ the TV set (eg by pulling out the plug) before you make adjustments inside it. 你应将电视机的插头拔掉, 始可做内部的调整。~ed adj (of speech or writing) having the ideas, etc badly connected. (指演说或写作)无系统的; 不连贯的。

dis·con·so·late /dɪs'kɒnsələt; dɪs'kɑnsəlɪt/ adj unhappy at the loss of sth; without hope or comfort; inconsolable. (因失去某物而)不愉快的; 无希望或安慰的; 无法安慰的。~·ly adv

dis·con·tent /,dɪskən'tent; ,dɪskən'tɛnt/ n [U] dissatisfaction; absence of contentment; [C] cause of this; grievance. 不满意; 不满的原因; 不满。□ (of) [VP6A] (usu in the pp) make dissatisfied: (通常用过去分词)使不满意: to be ~ed with one's job. 对自己的工作不满。~·ed·ly /-ɪdlɪ; -ɪdlɪ/ adv

dis·con·tinue /,dɪskən'tɪnjuː; ,dɪskən'tɪnju/ vt, vi [VP6A, C, 2A] cease; give up; put an end to; come to an end: 停止; 放弃; 结束; 中止: I'm so busy that I shall have to ~ (paying) these weekly visits. 我太忙, 故必须停止这些每周的往访。**dis·con·tinu·ance** /-'tɪnjʊəns; -'tɪnjʊəns/ n

dis·con·tinu·ous /,dɪskən'tɪnjʊəs; ,dɪskən'tɪnjʊəs/ adj not continuous. 不继续的; 中断的。

dis·cord /'dɪskɔːd; 'dɪskɔrd/ n 1 [U] disagreement; quarrelling: 不一致; 争吵: What has brought ~ into the family, caused its members to be quarrelsome? 什么事情使得这一家人争吵? 2 [C] difference of opinion; dispute. 意见不和; 争论。 3 [U] (music) lack of harmony between sounds, notes, etc sounded together; [C] instance of this, offending the ear; clashing sound that lacks harmony. (音乐)(声音、音调等)不和谐; 刺耳的声音; 嘈杂声。**dis·cor·dance** /dɪ'skɔːdəns; dɪs'kɔrdns/ n [U] want of harmony; disagreement. 不和谐; 不一致。**dis·cor·dant** /dɪ'skɔːdənt; dɪs'kɔrdnt/ adj 1 not in agreement: 不一致的: ~ant opinions. 不一致的意见。 2 (of sounds) not harmonious; harsh: 刺耳的; 不和谐的; 刺耳的: the ~ant noises of motor-car horns. 汽车喇叭的噪音。**dis·cor·dant·ly** adv

dis·co·theque /'dɪskətek; 'dɪskətɛk/ n (colloq abbr 口语略作 **disco** /'dɪskəʊ; 'dɪsko/) club or party where people dance to amplified recorded music played by a disc jockey. 由唱片伴奏的舞厅或舞会; 迪斯科舞会。

dis·count¹ /'dɪskaʊnt; 'dɪskaʊnt/ n [C, U] amount of money which may be taken off the full price, eg of goods bought by shopkeepers for resale, of an account if paid promptly, of a bill of exchange not yet due for payment: 折扣(例如自下列情况中获得者: 批发的货物, 立即付现款, 未到期的期票); 贴现: We give a) 10 per cent ~ for cash, for prompt payment instead of payment at a later date. 现金付款, 我们予以九折优待。 '~ broker n (comm) broker who gets a fee for acting as an intermediary between buyers and sellers. (商)贴现掮客。 '~ house n (comm) establishment which specializes in the ~ing of bills of exchange. (商)票据贴现所。 ⇒ **discount**²(1). at a ~, (of goods) not in demand; easily obtained; (fig) not in high esteem. (指货物)无销路的; 易获得的; (喻)不受重视的: Is honesty at a ~ today? 诚实在今天不受重视吗?

dis·count² /dɪs'kaʊnt US: 'dɪskaʊnt; 'dɪskaʊnt/ vt [VP6A] 1 (comm) give or receive the present value of a bill of exchange not yet due. (商)贴现。 2 refuse complete belief to a piece of news, a story, etc; allow for exaggeration: 不全部信(一消息、故事等); 认为有夸张之处: You should ~ a great deal of what appears in the newspapers. 你对报上的消息, 要打一个大折扣。

dis·coun·ten·ance /dɪs'kaʊntɪnəns; dɪs'kaʊntɪnəns/ vt [VP6A] (formal) refuse to approve of; discourage. (正式用语)不赞成; 劝阻。

dis·cour·age /dɪs'kʌrɪdʒ; dɪs'kɝɪdʒ/ vt 1 [VP6A] lessen, take away, the courage or confidence of: 使气馁; 使沮丧: Don't let one failure ~ you: try again. 勿因一次失败而气馁, 再试试看。 2 [VP14] ~ sb from doing sth, put difficulties in his way; make it seem not worth while; try to persuade him not to do it: 阻碍; 使认为某事不值得做; 劝阻: We tried to ~ him from climbing the mountain without a guide. 我们设法劝他无向导不要去爬山。~·ment n [U] discouraging or being ~d; [C] sth that ~s. 挫折; 气馁; 令人气馁的事物; 障碍。

dis·course /'dɪskɔːs; 'dɪskɔrs/ n [C] speech; lecture; sermon; treatise. 演讲; 讲道; 讲论; 论文。□ vi /dɪ'skɔːs; dɪ'skɔrs/ ~ upon, (formal) talk, preach or lecture upon (usu at length). (正式用语)谈论; 讲道; 讲述(通常为详细地)。

dis·cour·teous /dɪs'kɜːtɪəs; dɪs'kɝtɪəs/ adj not courteous; impolite: 不礼貌的; 失礼的: It was ~ of you to arrive late. 你迟到是失礼的。~·ly adv **dis·cour·tesy** /dɪs'kɜːtɪsɪ; dɪs'kɝtɪsɪ/ n [U] impoliteness; (pl -sies) impolite act. 失礼; 失礼的行为。

dis·cover /dɪs'kʌvə(r); dɪ'skʌvɚ/ vt [VP6A, 9, 8, 10, 25] find out; get knowledge of, bring to view (sth existing but not yet known); realize (sth new or unexpected): 发现(存在而未为人知之物); 发觉(新奇或

意外之物）: *Columbus ~ed America, but did not explore the new continent.* 哥伦布发现了美洲, 但未探勘此新大陆。*Harvey ~ed the circulation of the blood.* 哈维发现了血液的循环。*It was never ~ed how he died.* 他是如何死去的, 始终未被发现。*I never ~ed how to start the engine.* 我从来不知道怎样将发动这引擎。*We suddenly ~ed that it was too late to catch the train.* 我们突然发觉已来不及赶上火车了。*We have ~ed him to be* (more usu 比较常用 *that he is*) *quite untrustworthy.* 我们已发觉他很不可靠。~**er** *n* person who has made a ~y. 发现者; 发觉者。

dis·cov·ery /dɪ'skʌvərɪ; dɪ'skʌvərɪ/ *n* **1** [U] discovering or being discovered: 发现; 发觉: *a voyage of ~;* (企图)有所发现的航海; 探测航行; *the ~ of new chemical elements;* 新化学元素的发现; *the ~ by Franklin that lightning is electricity.* 富兰克林之发现闪电即是电。**2** [C] (*pl* -**ries**) sth that is discovered: 被发现之物: *He made wonderful scientific discoveries.* 他完成了惊人的科学发现。

dis·credit[1] /dɪs'kredɪt; dɪs'krɛdɪt/ *vt* [VP6A] refuse to believe or have confidence in; cause the truth, value or credit of sth or sb to seem doubtful: 不相信; 不信任; 怀疑; 使(某事物或某人的真情、价值或信誉)显得可疑: *His theories were ~ed by scientists.* 他的理论受到科学家们的怀疑。*The judge advised the jury to ~ the evidence of one of the witnesses.* 法官劝陪审员不要相信一位证人的证词。

dis·credit[2] /dɪs'kredɪt; dɪs'krɛdɪt/ *n* **1** [U] loss of credit or reputation: 不名誉; 丢面子: *If you continue to behave in this way, you will bring ~ upon yourself.* 如果你继续做出这样的行为, 你会玷辱了你的名誉。**2** *a ~ to,* person, thing, causing such loss to: 玷辱名誉的人或物: *a ~ to the school /to your family.* 破坏学校(家庭)名誉的人或物。**3** [U] doubt; disbelief. 怀疑; 不相信。~·**able** /-əbl; -əbl/ *adj* bringing ~: 不名誉的; ~**able** *conduct.* 不名誉的行为。~·**ably** /-əblɪ; -əblɪ/ *adv*

dis·creet /dɪ'skri:t; dɪ'skrit/ *adj* careful, tactful, in what one says and does; prudent: 谨慎的; 有智虑的: *to maintain a ~ silence.* 保持谨慎的沉默。~·**ly** *adv*

dis·crep·ancy /dɪ'skrepənsɪ; dɪ'skrɛpənsɪ/ *n* (*pl* -**cies**) [C, U] (of statements and accounts) difference; absence of agreement: (指言论和记述)不同; 不符合: *There was* (*a*) *considerable ~/There were numerous discrepancies between the two accounts of the fighting.* 这两段关于战事的叙述颇有出入(有差多不符之处)。

dis·crete /dɪ'skri:t; dɪ'skrit/ *adj* discontinuous; individually distinct. 不连续的; 分立的。~·**ness** *n*

dis·cre·tion /dɪ'skreʃn; dɪ'skrɛʃən/ *n* [U] **1** being discreet; prudence: 谨慎; 考虑周到: *You must show more ~ in choosing your friends.* 你择友时须更加谨慎。*years /age of ~,* the age at which one is fit to judge and decide for oneself. 责任年龄(自己可判断事物的年龄)。*D~ is the better part of valour,* (prov) used jokingly to excuse oneself for not taking unnecessary risks. (谚)慎重即勇过半矣(为不做无谓冒险的借口, 用以解嘲)。**2** freedom to act according to one's own judgement, to do what seems right or best: 自由处理; 自由决定: *Use your ~.* 由你自行决定。*It is within your own ~,* You are free to decide. 此事可由你自作决定。*You have full ~ to act.* 你可完全随意行事。~·**ary** /dɪ'skreʃənərɪ *US:* -nerɪ; dɪ'skrɛʃən,ɛrɪ/ *adj* having ~(2): 可自由处理的; 可自由决定的: *an official with ~ary powers.* 有擅自处理权的官员。

dis·crimi·nate /dɪ'skrɪmɪneɪt; dɪ'skrɪmə,net/ *vt, vi* **1** [VP14, 3A] ~ *one thing from another; ~ between two things,* be, make, see, a difference between: 区别; 辨别: *Can you ~ good books from bad / ~ between good and bad books?* 你能区别好书和坏书吗? **2** [VP2A, 3A] ~ (*against*), treat differently; make distinctions: 以不同方式对待; 歧视: *laws which do not ~ against anyone,* that treat all people in the same way. 不歧视任何人的法律(对所有人民一视同仁)。**dis·crimi·nat·**

ing *adj* **1** able to see or make small differences: 有辨别力的: *a discriminating taste in literature.* 对文学的辨识鉴赏力。**2** giving special or different treatment to certain people, countries, etc; differential(1): 对某些人民、国家等待遇不同的; 歧视的; 差别的: *discriminating tariffs /rates /duties.* 差别关税(地方税, 国家税)。

dis·crimi·na·tion /dɪˌskrɪmɪ'neɪʃn; dɪ,skrɪmɪ'neʃən/ *n* [U] discriminating: ability to discriminate: 区别; 辨别; 差别待遇; 歧视: *D~ against goods from foreign countries is usually done by means of tariffs.* 对外国货的差别待遇通常借关税行之。*Is there racial ~ in your country?* 在你们的国家内有种族歧视吗? **dis·crim·i·na·tory** /dɪ'skrɪmɪnətərɪ *US:* -tɔːrɪ; dɪ'skrɪmənə,torɪ/ *adj* discriminating(2): 差别待遇的; 歧视的: *discriminatory legislation.* 不公平的法律。

dis·cur·sive /dɪ'skɜːsɪv; dɪ'skɜsɪv/ *adj* (of a person, what he says or does, his style) wandering from one point or subject to another. (指人, 人的言行、文体)散漫的。~·**ly** *adv* ~·**ness** *n*

dis·cus /'dɪskəs; 'dɪskəs/ *n* heavy, round plate of stone, metal or wood, thrown in ancient Roman and Greek athletic contests and in modern contests (eg the Olympic Games): 铁饼(石头、金属或木制的重的圆形盘状物, 在古罗马希腊运动会及现代运动会如奥林匹克运动会中投掷者); *the ~ throw,* name used for this contest. 掷铁饼(此种比赛之名称)。

throwing the discus

dis·cuss /dɪ'skʌs; dɪ'skʌs/ *vt* [VP6A, 8, 10, 14] ~ (*with*), examine and argue about (a subject): 讨论(题目); 商讨: *to ~ a question with sb;* 与某人讨论一问题; *to ~* (*with one's friends*) *what to do /how to do it /how something should be done.* (与友人)商讨做何事(如何做一事)。

dis·cus·sion /dɪ'skʌʃn; dɪ'skʌʃən/ *n* [U, C] discussing or being discussed; talk for the purpose of discussing: 讨论; 商讨; 议论: *after much ~;* 经详细讨论后; *after several long ~s.* 经数度长时间的讨论后。*We had a long ~ about the question.* 关于该问题我们会做长时间的讨论。*When will the matter come up for ~?* 此事将于何时提出讨论? *under ~,* being discussed: 在讨论中: *The question is still under ~.* 这问题仍在讨论中。

dis·dain /dɪs'deɪn; dɪs'den/ *vt* [VP6A, C, 7A] look on with contempt; think (it) dishonourable (to do sth); be too proud (to do sth): 轻视; 藐视; 不屑为: *A good man should ~ flattery.* 人应藐视谄媚。*He ~ed to notice the insult.* 他不屑计较这侮辱。*He ~ed my offer of help.* 他轻视我的援助之意。□ *n* [U] contempt; scorn: 轻视; 藐视: *No one likes to be treated with ~.* 没有人喜欢受到轻视。~·**ful** /-fʊl; -fəl/ *adj* showing ~: 表示轻视的; 藐视的: *~ful looks.* 轻视的样子。~·**fully** /-fəlɪ; -fəlɪ/ *adv*

dis·ease /dɪ'zi:z; dɪ'ziz/ *n* [U] illness; disorder of body or mind or of plants; [C] particular kind of illness or disorder: 病; 疾病; 植物的病害; 某种疾病: *The business of doctors is to prevent and cure ~.* 医生的职务为防止和治疗疾病。*Measles, mumps and influenza are common ~s.* 麻疹、流行性腮腺炎和流行性感冒是普

dis·eased /dɪ'ziːzd; dɪ'zizd/ part adj suffering from, injured by, ~: 有病的; 为疾病伤害的: ~d vines; 有病害的葡萄树; ~d in body and mind. 身心有病的.

dis·em·bark /ˌdɪsɪm'bɑːk; ˌdɪsɪm'bɑrk/ vt, vi [VP6A, 14, 2A, C] ~ (from), put, go, on shore (from a ship). (自船上)登于岸上; 登岸; 上岸. **dis·em·bar·ka·tion** /ˌdɪsɪmbɑː'keɪʃn; ˌdɪsɛmbɑr'keʃən/ n

dis·em·barrass /ˌdɪsɪm'bærəs; ˌdɪsɪm'bærəs/ vt [VP14] ~ of, (formal) rid (sb, oneself) from embarrassment; rid (sb, oneself) of a burden: (正式用语)使 (某人、自己)脱离困窘; 使(某人、自己)摆脱负担: to ~ oneself of a burden/charge/responsibility. 使自己摆脱一负担(责任). ~·ment n

dis·em·body /ˌdɪsɪm'bɒdɪ; ˌdɪsɪm'bɑdɪ/ vt [VP6A] (chiefly in pp) separate, set free (the soul or spirit) from the body: (主要用过去分词)使(灵魂或精神)脱离躯体: a building haunted by a disembodied spirit. 一所有幽灵出没的建筑物.

dis·em·bowel /ˌdɪsɪm'baʊəl; ˌdɪsɪm'baʊəl/ vt (-ll-) (US also -l-) [VP6A] cut out the bowels of. 切腹取出…的肠子.

dis·en·chant /ˌdɪsɪn'tʃɑːnt US: -'tʃænt; ˌdɪsɪn'tʃænt/ vt [VP6A] free from enchantment or illusion: 使解除魔力或幻想: He is quite ~ed with the Tory Government. 他对保守党政府不再存有幻想. ~·ment n

dis·en·cum·ber /ˌdɪsɪn'kʌmbə(r); ˌdɪsɪn'kʌmbə/ vt [VP6A, 14] ~ (from), (formal) free from encumbrance: (正式用语)使解除障碍或负累: ~ed of his heavy responsibilities. 卸下他的重负.

dis·en·franchise /ˌdɪsɪn'fræntʃaɪz; ˌdɪsɪn'fræntʃaɪz/ vt = disfranchise.

dis·en·gage /ˌdɪsɪn'geɪdʒ; ˌdɪsɪn'gedʒ/ vt, vi [VP6A, 14, 2A, C] ~ (from), separate, detach (oneself or sth): 分开; 使(自己或某物)脱离: Two enemy battalions (were) ~d from the battle after suffering heavy casualties. 在遭受严重伤亡后, 敌人的两营士兵脱离了战斗. **dis·en·gaged** pp (of a person) free from engagements: (指人)无约会的; 空闲的: If the Manager is ~d ..., if he is free .... 如果经理有空的话…. ~·ment n (condition of) being ~d: 脱离; 解脱: the military and economic ~ment of the USA from SE Asia. 美国在军事和经济上之脱离东南亚.

dis·en·tangle /ˌdɪsɪn'tæŋgl; ˌdɪsɪn'tæŋgl/ vt, vi 1 [VP6A, 14] ~ (from), free from complications, tangles or confusion: 使解除纠缠或混乱状态: to ~ truth from falsehood. 分真伪. 2 [VP2A] unravel; become clear of tangles: 解开; 解开缠结: This skein of wool won't ~, cannot be ~d. 这一束毛线解不开了. ~·ment n

dis·equi·lib·rium /ˌdɪsiːkwɪ'lɪbrɪəm; dɪsˌikwə'lɪbrɪəm/ n [U] absence, loss, of equilibrium; instability. 不平衡; 失去平衡; 不稳定.

dis·es·tab·lish /ˌdɪsɪ'stæblɪʃ; ˌdɪsəˈstæblɪʃ/ vt [VP6A] end, break up, an established state of affairs, esp the constitutional connection between a national Church (eg the Church of England) and the State. 废除既成状态; (尤指)废除国教(例如英国国教)制; 使(教会)与政府分离. ~·ment n

dis·favour (US = -favor) /ˌdɪs'feɪvə(r); dɪs'fevə/ n [U] state of being out of favour; disapproval: 不喜欢; 不赞成: to regard sth with ~; 不赞成某事; to be in ~; 受冷遇; to fall into ~; 失宠; to incur sb's ~. 引起某人的反对. □ vt [VP6A] regard with ~; disapprove of. 不喜欢; 不赞成.

dis·figure /dɪs'fɪgə US: -gjər; dɪs'fɪgjə/ vt [VP6A] spoil the appearance or shape of: 损毁…之外表或形状: beautiful scenery ~d by ugly advertising signs; 被丑陋的广告招牌损毁的美丽的风景; a face ~d by a broken nose/an ugly scar. 被残缺的鼻子(难看的伤疤)所毁的面貌. ~·ment n [U] disfiguring or being ~d; [C] sth that ~s. 损毁外表或形状; 损毁外表或形状之物.

dis·for·est /dɪs'fɒrɪst US: -'fɔːr-; dɪs'fɑrɪst/ vt [VP6A] clear (land) of forests. 砍伐(某地)之森林.

dis·fran·chise /dɪs'fræntʃaɪz; dɪs'fræntʃaɪz/ vt [VP6A] deprive of rights of citizenship; (esp) deprive (a place) of the right to send a representative to parliament or (a citizen) of the right to vote for a parliamentary representative. 褫夺公权; (尤指)剥夺(某地或某人)之议员选举权. ~·ment /-'fræntʃɪzmənt; -'fræntʃɪzmənt/ n

dis·gorge /dɪs'gɔːdʒ; dɪs'gɔrdʒ/ vt [VP6A] throw up or out from, or as from, the throat; (fig) give up (esp sth taken wrongfully). 吐; 吐出; (喻)放弃(尤指非法获得之物).

dis·grace¹ /dɪs'greɪs; dɪs'gres/ n 1 [U] loss of respect, favour, reputation: 耻辱; 不名誉; 丧失体面: A man who commits a crime and is sent to prison brings ~ on himself and his family. 因犯罪而被关入监狱的人玷辱了自己和他的家族. There need be no ~ in being poor. 贫穷并不足为耻. **be in ~**, be in a state of having lost respect, etc: 处于不受他人尊重的状态: He told a lie and is in ~. 他说谎而不受他人的尊重. **2 a** ~, thing, state of affairs, person, that is a cause of shame or discredit: 招致耻辱的人或物: These slums are a ~ to the city authorities. 这些贫民窟为市当局的耻辱. The continued use of armed forces to settle disputes is a ~ to the rulers of all countries. 不断用武力解决纠纷实乃各国元首之耻. ~·ful /-fl; -fəl/ adj bringing or causing ~: 可耻的; 不名誉的: ~ful behaviour. 可耻的行为. ~·fully /-fəlɪ; -fəlɪ/ adv: to behave ~fully. 行为可耻.

dis·grace² /dɪs'greɪs; dɪs'gres/ vt [VP6A] 1 bring disgrace on; be a disgrace to: 玷辱; 使蒙羞: Don't ~ the family name. 勿玷辱家声. 2 put (sb) out of favour. 使(某人)不再受宠; 使失宠.

dis·gruntled /dɪs'grʌntld; dɪs'grʌntld/ adj ~ (at sth/with sb), discontented; in a bad mood. 不满意的; 不高兴的.

dis·guise¹ /dɪs'gaɪz; dɪs'gaɪz/ vt [VP6A, 16B] 1 change the appearance, etc of, in order to deceive or to hide the identity of: 伪装; 假扮: He ~d his looks but he could not ~ his voice. 他伪装了外貌, 但无法伪装他的声音. He ~d himself as a woman/~d himself by wearing a wig. 他假扮成一个女人(戴上假发伪装自己). 2 conceal; cover up: 隐藏; 掩饰: He ~d his sorrow beneath a cheerful appearance/by appearing cheerful. 他以欢乐的外貌掩饰他的悲苦. There is no disguising the fact that ..., The fact that ... cannot be concealed. …的事实是无法掩饰的.

dis·guise² /dɪs'gaɪz; dɪs'gaɪz/ n 1 [U] disguising; disguised condition: 伪装; 假扮; 掩饰; 伪装或掩饰的状态: He went among the enemy in ~. 他化装混入敌人中. He went to the ball in the ~ of a clown. 他假扮成一个小丑去参加舞会. 2 [C, U] dress, actions, manner, etc used for disguising: 用以伪装的衣服、行动、态度等: a clever ~. 巧妙的伪装. He had tried all sorts of ~s. 他尝试过各种伪装. She made no ~ of her feelings, did not hide them. 她不掩饰她的情感.

dis·gust¹ /dɪs'gʌst; dɪs'gʌst/ n [U] ~ (at sth/with sb), strong feeling of dislike or distaste (eg caused by a bad smell or taste, a horrible sight, evil conduct): 厌恶; 嫌恶(例如由恶臭或恶味, 可怕的景象, 邪恶的行为所引起者): He turned away in ~. 他厌恶地把脸转开. His ~ at the government's policy caused him to resign. 他对政府的政策的厌恶促使他辞职.

dis·gust² /dɪs'gʌst; dɪs'gʌst/ vt [VP6A] cause disgust in: 使人厌恶: His behaviour ~ed everybody. 他的行为使每一个人都厌恶. We were ~ed at/by/with what we saw. 我们讨厌我们所看到的东西. ~·ing adj: ~ing political opinions. 令人厌恶的政见. ~·ing·ly adv: He is ~ingly (colloq □ = extremely) mean with his money. 他对金钱极为吝啬(他对金钱的吝啬令人憎恶). ~·ed·ly /-ɪdlɪ; -ɪdlɪ/ adv with ~: 厌恶地:

He looked ~edly at the dirty room. 他厌恶地望着那肮脏的房间。

dish¹ /dɪʃ; dɪʃ/ n **1** shallow, flat-bottomed (often oval or oblong) vessel, of earthenware, glass, metal, etc from which food is served at table: 盘; 碟: *a 'meat-~.* 盛肉盘。 **~·ful** /-ful; -ˌful/ n as much as a ~ will contain. 一碟或一盘之量。 **2 the ~es,** all the crockery (plates, bowls, cups and saucers, etc) used for a meal: 进餐时所用的全部盘碟杯碗等: *to wash up the ~es.* 将盘碟洗净。 **~·cloth,** cloth for washing ~es, etc. 洗碗布; 抹布。 **'~·washer,** power-operated machine for washing dishes, cutlery, ect. 洗碗机。 **'~·water,** water in which ~es have been washed. 洗碗水。 **3** food brought to table on or in a ~: 盘中的食物; 菜: *His favourite ~ is steak and kidney pie.* 他最喜爱的菜是牛排和腰子饼。 **4** ~-shaped object, esp a large concave reflector for the reception of radio-waves from outer space, or in radio telescopes, etc. 盘碟状之物; (尤指用以接收太空的电波或用于无线电望远镜等中的)凹形的)反射器。 ⇨ the illus at **radio telescope.** 参看 radio telescope 之插图。 **5** (sl) attractive person: (俚)漂亮的人: *She's quite a ~.* 她真漂亮。 **~·y** adj **(-ier, -iest)** (sl) (of a person) attractive. (俚)(指人)漂亮的; 动人的。

dish² /dɪʃ; dɪʃ/ vt **1** [VP15B] ~ **sth up,** put on or into a ~ or ~es: 盛于盘碟中: *to ~ (up) the dinner,* get it ready for serving; 将饭菜盛于盘碟中准备开饭。 (fig) prepare, serve up facts, arguments, etc: (喻)准备并提出(事实、论据等): *to ~ up the usual arguments in a new form.* 以新方式提出平常的论据。 ~ *sth out,* distribute it. 分配。 **2** [VP6A] (colloq) upset; thwart: (口)破坏; 挫败: *to ~ one's opponents.* 挫败对手。 *The scandal ~ed his hopes of being elected.* 毁谤破坏了他当选的希望。

dis·habille /ˌdɪsæ'biːl; ˌdɪsæ'bil/ n [U] (usu 通常用 *in* ~) (usu of a woman) the state of being negligently or partly dressed. (通常指妇女)衣着随便; 服装不整。

dis·har·mony /dɪs'hɑːmənɪ; dɪs'hɑːrmənɪ/ n [U] lack of harmony; discord. 不和谐; 不调和。 **dis·har·moni·ous** /ˌdɪshɑː'məʊnɪəs; ˌdɪshɑːr'monɪəs/ adj

dis·hearten /dɪs'hɑːtn; dɪs'hɑːrtṇ/ vt [VP6A] cause to lose courage or confidence: 使沮丧; 使气馁: *Don't be ~ed by a single failure.* 勿因一次失败而气馁。

di·shev·elled (US = **-eled**) /dɪ'ʃevld; dɪ'ʃɛvld/ adj with the hair uncombed; (of the hair and clothes) in disorder; untidy. 头发蓬乱的; (指头发和衣服)散乱的; 不整齐的。

dis·hon·est /dɪs'ɒnɪst; dɪs'ɑnɪst/ adj not honest; intended to cheat, deceive or mislead. 不诚实的; 欺骗的; 欺诈的。 **~·ly** adv **dis·hon·esty** /dɪs'ɒnɪstɪ; dɪs'ɑnɪstɪ/ n [U] being ~; [C] ~ act, etc. 不诚实; 欺骗; 欺骗的行为等。

dis·hon·our (US = **-honor**) /dɪs'ɒnə(r); dɪs'ɑnə/ n [U] **1** disgrace or shame; loss, absence, of honour and self-respect: 不名誉; 耻辱: *to bring ~ on one's family.* 玷辱家声。 **2** *a ~ to,* person or thing that brings ~ to: 不名誉的人或物: *He was a ~ to his regiment.* 他是他那一团的耻辱。 □ vt [VP6A] **1** bring shame, discredit, loss of honour on (sb or sth). 玷辱(某人或某物)。 **2** (of a bank) ~ *a cheque/bill of exchange,* refuse to pay money on it (because the bank's customer has not enough credit). (指银行)退票(因顾客无足够存款而拒绝兑现)。 **~·able** /-əbl; -əbl/ adj without honour; shameful. 不名誉的; 可耻的。 **~·ably** /-əblɪ; -əblɪ/ adv

dis·il·lusion /ˌdɪsɪ'luːʒn; ˌdɪsɪ'luʒən/ vt [VP6A] set free from mistaken feelings: 使从错误信念中醒悟; 使觉醒; 使幻想破灭: *They had thought that the new colony would be a paradise, but they were soon ~ed.* 他们原以为新殖民地是一个天堂, 但不久便幻想破灭了。 □ n [U] the state of being ~ed. 醒悟; 觉醒。 **~·ment** n [U] freedom from illusions: 醒悟; 幻想破灭: *in a state*

of complete ~(ment). 彻底自幻想中醒悟。

dis·in·cen·tive /ˌdɪsɪn'sentɪv; ˌdɪsɪn'sɛntɪv/ n [C] act, measure, etc that tends to discourage efforts, production, etc: 使努力受挫, 阻碍生产等的行动、措施等; 阻力; 障碍: *Is high taxation a ~ to members of the managerial class?* 高税对经理人员的工作情绪有妨碍吗?

dis·in·cli·na·tion /ˌdɪsɪnklɪ'neɪʃn; ˌdɪsɪnklɪ'neʃən/ n [U, C] ~ *(for sth/to do sth),* (usu with indef art) unwillingness: (通常与不定冠词连用)不愿意: *Some schoolboys have a strong ~ for work.* 有些男学生极不愿意工作。 *His ~ to meet people worries his wife, who is very sociable.* 他的不喜与人接触使他那位很爱交际的妻子烦恼。

dis·in·cline /ˌdɪsɪn'klaɪn; ˌdɪsɪn'klaɪn/ vt [VP17, 14] (usu passive) (通常用被动语态) *be ~d for sth; be ~d to do sth,* be reluctant or unwilling: 不愿意: *He was ~d to help me.* 他不愿帮助我。 *The hot weather made him feel ~d for work.* 炎热的天气使他感到不愿工作。

dis·in·fect /ˌdɪsɪn'fekt; ˌdɪsɪn'fɛkt/ vt [VP6A] make free from bacterial infection: 使免受细菌的传染; 消毒: *The house was ~ed after Tom had had scarlet fever.* 汤姆患过猩红热后, 这房子曾经过消毒。 **dis·in·fec·tant** /ˌdɪsɪn'fektənt; ˌdɪsɪn'fɛktənt/ adj, n ~ing (chemical), 消毒的; 消毒剂。 **dis·in·fec·tion** /ˌdɪsɪn'fekʃn; ˌdɪsɪn'fɛkʃən/ n [U] (act of) ~ing. 消毒; 消毒作用。

dis·in·fest /ˌdɪsɪn'fest; ˌdɪsɪn'fɛst/ vt [VP6A] get rid of vermin. 消灭害虫或害兽。 **dis·in·fes·ta·tion** /ˌdɪsɪnfe'steɪʃn; dɪs.ɪnfɛs'teʃən/ n [U]: ~ation officer, person employed to get rid of vermin (eg a rat-catcher). 消灭害虫或害兽(例如捕鼠)的官员。

dis·in·fla·tion /ˌdɪsɪn'fleɪʃn; ˌdɪsɪn'fleʃən/ n (process of) returning from a state of inflation to a stable or more normal level (in which prices, wages, etc do not vary much). 通货紧缩(由通货膨胀返回原来物价, 工资等稳定或较正常的状态); 通货紧缩的过程。

dis·in·genu·ous /ˌdɪsɪn'dʒenjʊəs; ˌdɪsɪn'dʒɛnjʊəs/ adj (formal) insincere; not straightforward. (正式用语)不真诚的; 不坦白的。 **~·ly** adv **~·ness** n

dis·in·herit /ˌdɪsɪn'herɪt; ˌdɪsɪn'hɛrɪt/ vt [VP6A] take away the right (of sb) to inherit. 剥夺(某人的)继承权。 **dis·in·heri·tance** /ˌdɪsɪn'herɪtəns; ˌdɪsɪn'hɛrɪtəns/ n [U] being ~ed. 剥夺继承权。

dis·in·te·grate /dɪs'ɪntɪgreɪt; dɪs'ɪntəˌgret/ vt, vi [VP6A, 2A] (cause to) break up into small parts or pieces: (使)分裂成小块: *rocks ~d by frost and rain.* 被霜和雨蚀裂成碎块的岩石。 **dis·in·te·gra·tion** /dɪs.ɪntɪ'greɪʃn; dɪs.ɪntə'greʃən/ n

dis·inter /ˌdɪsɪn'tɜː(r); ˌdɪsɪn'tɝ/ vt **(-rr-)** [VP6A] (formal) dig up from the earth (eg from a grave). (正式用语)自地中(如坟墓中)掘出。 **~·ment** n

dis·in·ter·ested /dɪs'ɪntrəstɪd; dɪs'ɪntərɪstɪd/ adj not influenced by personal feelings or interests: 不为个人情感或利害所影响的; 公正无私的; *His action was not altogether ~.* 他的行动并不完全公正。 ⇨ **uninterested.** **~·ly** adv **~·ness** n

dis·joint /dɪs'dʒɔɪnt; dɪs'dʒɔɪnt/ vt [VP6A] separate at the joints; take to pieces: 自关节处拆开; 拆散: *to ~ a chicken.* 自关节处切开一只鸡。

dis·jointed /dɪs'dʒɔɪntɪd; dɪs'dʒɔɪntɪd/ adj (eg of speech and writing) not connected; incoherent. (指说话和写作等)不连贯的; 无系统的。 **~·ly** adv **~·ness** n

dis·junc·tive /dɪs'dʒʌŋktɪv; dɪs'dʒʌŋktɪv/ adj ~ conjunction, (gram) one expressing opposition of or contrast between ideas (eg *either ... or*). (语法)转折连词(例如 either ... or)。

disk n ⇨ **disc.**

dis·like /dɪs'laɪk; dɪs'laɪk/ vt [VP6A, C] not like: 不喜欢; 厌恶: *to ~ getting up early/being disturbed.* 不喜欢早起(受打扰)。 *If you behave like that, you'll get yourself ~d,* become unpopular. 如果你的行为那个样子, 你会使人厌恶。 □ n [U, C] feeling of not liking;

feeling against: 不喜欢;厌恶: to have a ~ of/for cats; 不喜欢猫; to feel ~ for sb. 不喜欢某人。 **take a ~ to sb**, begin to ~ him. 厌恶某人。 **tikes and ~s** /'dɪslaɪks; 'dɪslaɪks; preference and aversions: 喜爱和厌恶之物; He has so many likes and ~s that he is difficult to please. 他喜爱很多东西,也讨厌很多东西,故而他是个难以取悦的人。

dis·lo·cate /'dɪsləkeɪt US: -ləʊk-; 'dɪslo,ket/ vt [VP 6A] **1** put (esp a bone in the body) out of position: (尤指身体某部)脱离原位;使脱臼: He fell from his horse and ~d his collarbone. 他从马上跌下,而使锁骨脱臼了。 **2** put traffic, machinery, business, etc out of order: 使(交通、机器、事务等)混乱: Traffic was badly ~d by the heavy fall of snow. 大雪使交通十分紊乱。 **dis·lo·ca·tion** /,dɪslə'keɪʃn US: -ləʊk-; ,dɪslo'keʃən/ n [U, C] dislocating or being ~d: 脱臼;混乱: the dislocation of trade caused by the blocking of the canal. 运河受阻引起的贸易混乱。

dis·lodge /dɪs'lɒdʒ; dɪs'lɑdʒ/ vt [VP6A, 14] ~ **(from)**, move, force (sb or sth) from the place occupied: (自其占有的位置)移去或驱逐(人或物): to ~ a stone from a building/the enemy from their positions. 自一建筑物移去一石(将敌人自阵地逐出)。 **~·ment** n

dis·loyal /dɪs'lɔɪəl; dɪs'lɔɪəl/ adj ~ **to**, not loyal to. 对…不忠的。 ~**·ly** /-'lɔɪəlɪ; -'lɔɪəlɪ/ adv ~**·ty** /-'lɔɪəltɪ/ n [U] ~**·ty (to)**, being ~ (to); [C] (pl **-ties**) ~ act, etc. (对…)不忠;不忠的行为等。

dis·mal /'dɪzməl; 'dɪzml/ adj sad, gloomy; miserable; comfortless: 悲哀的; 阴郁的; 忧愁的; 不愉快的: a ~ weather; 阴沉的天气; in a ~ voice. 以忧郁的声音。 ~**·ly** /'dɪzməlɪ; 'dɪzmlɪ/ adv

dis·mantle /dɪs'mæntl; dɪs'mæntl/ vt [VP6A] **1** take away fittings, furnishings, etc from: 拆除…之装备等: The old warship was ~d, Its guns, armour, engines, etc were taken out. 旧战舰上的装备(即枪炮、装甲、发动机等)被拆除了。 **2** take to pieces: 拆散: to ~ an engine. 拆散一发动机。 ~**·ment** n [U] dismantling (now the usu word). 拆除装备。拆 散 (现在较常用dismantling)。

dis·may /dɪs'meɪ; dɪs'me/ n [U] feeling of fear and discouragement: 惊慌; 丧胆: The news that the enemy were near filled/struck them with ~. 敌人逼近的消息使他们惊慌。 He looked at me in (blank) ~. 他惊慌(茫然不知所措)地望着我。 □ vt [VP6A] fill with ~: 使惊慌: We were ~ed at the news. 听到这消息,我们感到惊慌。

dis·mem·ber /dɪs'membə(r); dɪs'mɛmbə/ vt [VP 6A] **1** tear or cut the limbs from: 割断…的四肢; 肢解: Poor fellow! He was ~ed by a pack of wolves. 可怜的家伙!他被一群狼给肢解了。 **2** (fig) divide up (a country, etc). (喻)瓜分(国家等)。 ~**·ment** n

dis·miss /dɪs'mɪs; dɪs'mɪs/ vt [VP6A, 14] ~ **(from)**, **1** send away (from one's employment, from service): 解雇; 撤职; 开革: The servant was ~ed for being lazy and dishonest. 这仆人因懒惰和不诚实而被解雇。 The officer was ~ed from the service for neglect of duty. 这军官因疏于职守而被撤职。 **2** allow to go: 使退去; 解散: The teacher ~ed his class when the bell rang. 铃声响,老师就让学生下课。 **3** put away from the mind; stop thinking or talking about: 自心中摒除; 不再考虑或谈论: to ~ all thoughts of revenge. 摒除一切报复的念头。 **4** (cricket, of the team that is fielding) put a batsman/a team out: (板球,指防守的球队)使(击球员或球队)出局: The fast bowler ~ed Smith for ten runs. 那位快速投球手在第十分时就使史密斯出局。 ~**·al** /-'mɪsl; -'mɪsl/ n [U, C] ~ing or being ~ed: 解雇; 撤职; 开除; 退去: a ~al from the Navy. 自海军解职。

dis·mount /dɪs'maunt; dɪs'maunt/ vi, vt **1** [VP2A, 3A] ~ **(from)**, get down (from sth on which one is riding): 下马(或自所骑之物)下来: to ~ from one's horse/bicycle. 从马车(脚踏车上)下来。 (Cf alight from a bus, taxi, tram or train.) (参较alight表示下公共汽车、计

程车、电车或火车。) **2** [VP6A] remove (sth) from its mount: 自托架上移下(某物): to ~ a gun (from the gun-carriage). (自炮架)将炮卸下。 **3** [VP6A] cause to fall (from a horse, etc). 使(从马上等)跌下。 ⇨ **joust**. ~**ed** part adj (of cavalry) fighting as infantry. (指骑兵部队)似步兵作战的。

dis·obedi·ence /,dɪsə'biːdɪəns; ,dɪsə'bidɪəns/ n [U] ~ **(to)**, failure or refusal to obey: 不服从; 违命: acts of ~; 违命的行动; ~ to orders. 违抗命令。 **dis·obedi·ent** adj ~ (to), not obedient. 不服从的; 违命的。 **dis·obedi·ent·ly** adv

dis·obey /,dɪsə'beɪ; ,dɪsə'be/ vt, vi [VP6A, 2A] pay no attention to orders; not obey a person, a law, etc. 不服从命令;违命;不服从(某人、法律等)。

dis·oblige /,dɪsə'blaɪdʒ; ,dɪsə'blaɪdʒ/ vt [VP6A] (formal) refuse to be helpful or to think about another person's wishes or needs: (正式用语)拒绝帮助; 不考虑别人的愿望或需要: I'm sorry to ~ you, but last time I lent you money you did not repay me. 我很抱歉不能帮助你,但上次我借钱给你,你没有还我。

dis·order /dɪs'ɔːdə(r); dɪs'ɔrdə/ n **1** [U] absence of order; confusion: 无秩序; 混乱: The burglars left the room in great ~. 窃贼将这房间弄得乱七八糟。 The enemy retreated in ~. 敌人狼狈地退却。 **2** [U] absence of order caused by political troubles: 骚动; 骚乱: (政治纠纷引起的)骚动; 骚乱: Troops were called out to deal with the ~s in the capital. 军队被召去镇压首都的骚乱。 **3** [C, U] disturbance of the normal working of the body or mind: 身心不适; 疾病: a ~ of the digestive system; 消化系统的毛病; suffering from mental ~; 患精神病; ~s of the mind. 精神方面的毛病。 □ vt [VP 6A] put into ~: 使紊乱: a ~ed imagination/mind. 紊乱的想像(心绪)。

dis·order·ly /dɪs'ɔːdəlɪ; dɪs'ɔrdəlɪ/ adj **1** in disorder: 无秩序的; 混乱的: a ~ room/desk. 乱七八糟的房间(书桌)。 **2** causing disturbance; unruly; lawless: 造成混乱的; 骚乱的; 不守法的: ~ crowds; 骚乱的群众; a ~ mob; 骚乱的暴民; ~ behaviour. 不守法的行为。 **a ~ house**, a brothel or a place where illegal gambling is carried on. 败坏风纪的场所; 妓院; 赌场。

dis·or·gan·ize /,dɪs'ɔːgənaɪz; dɪs'ɔrgə,naɪz/ vt [VP 6A] throw into confusion; upset the working or system of: 使紊乱; 破坏…的工作或组织: The train service was ~d by fog. 火车班次被雾搅乱了。 **dis·or·gan·iz·ation** /dɪs,ɔːgənaɪ'zeɪʃn US: -nɪ'z-; dɪs,ɔrgənə'zeʃən/ n [U].

dis·orien·tate /dɪs'ɔːrɪentent; dɪs'ɔrɪən,tet/ vt (also, esp US) **dis·orient** /dɪs'ɔːrɪent; dɪs'ɔrɪ,ɛnt/ vt [VP 6A] (lit, fig) confuse (sb) as to his bearings(4). (字面,喻)使(某人)迷失方向。

dis·own /dɪs'əun; dɪs'on/ vt [VP6A] say that one does not know (sb or sth), that one has not, or no longer wishes to have, any connection with (sb or sth): 否认(某人或某物);不承认与(某人或某物)有关系;声明与(某人)脱离关系: The boy was so wicked that his father ~ed him. 这男孩太顽劣, 所以他父亲声称与他脱离父子关系。

dis·par·age /dɪ'spærɪdʒ; dɪ'spærɪdʒ/ vt [VP6A] say things to suggest that (sb or sth) is of small value or importance. 贬抑; 藐视。 ~**·ment** n **dis·par·ag·ing·ly** adv in a disparaging manner. 贬抑地; 藐视地。

dis·par·ate /'dɪspərɪt; 'dɪspərɪt/ adj that cannot be compared in quality, amount, kind, etc; essentially different. (性质、数量、种类等)不可比较的; 根本不同的。 □ n pl things so unlike that comparison is impossible. 差异太大而无法比较之物。

dis·par·ity /dɪ'spærɪtɪ; dɪ'pærətɪ/ n **1** [U] inequality; difference; [C] (pl **-ties**) instance or degree of this: 不等; 不同; 不等或不同的实例或程度: ~ in age/rank/position; 年龄(阶层、职位)之不同; the disparities in the newspaper accounts of the accident. 报纸对这事件之报道的不同。

dis·pas·sion·ate /dɪˈspæʃənət; dɪsˈpæʃənɪt/ *adj* free from passion; not taking sides, not showing favour (in a quarrel, etc between others). 冷静的; 不偏私的; (对他人的争执等)态度公平的. ~**·ly** *adv* ~**ness** *n*

dis·patch[1], **des·patch** /dɪˈspætʃ; dɪˈspætʃ/ *n* **1** [U] dispatching or being dispatched (all senses): 派遣; 发送; 迅速结束; 杀死; 处死: *Please hurry up the ~ of these telegrams.* 请赶紧将这些电报发出去. **2** [C] sth dispatched(1), esp a government, military or newspaper report: 发送之物; (尤指)政府、军事文电或新闻(电讯)报道: *London newspapers receive ~es from all parts of the world.* 伦敦的报纸收到世界各地发来的新闻电讯. *The soldier was mentioned in ~es*, had his name recorded in accounts of fighting, etc because of his bravery, etc. 发出的文件中提到了这个士兵(因其英勇的战绩等,在战事报道中记载了他的姓名). ⇨ *citation* at *cite.* '~**·box**, one for official ~es. 公文递送箱. '~**·rider**, man who carries military ~es (usu on a motor-bike). 递送军公文者(通常乘摩托车). **3** [U] promptness; speed: 迅速; 急速: *to act with ~.* 迅速行动.

dis·patch[2], **des·patch** /dɪˈspætʃ; dɪˈspætʃ/ *vt* **1** [VP6A, 14] ~ (*to*), send off; to a destination, on a journey, for a special purpose: 派遣; 发送: *to ~ letters/telegrams;* 发出信件(电报); *to ~ a cruiser to the island to restore order.* 派一远洋舰至该岛以恢复秩序. **2** [VP6A] finish, get through, business, a meal quickly. 迅速结束(事务,餐膳). **3** [VP6A] kill; give the death blow to: 杀死; 处死: *The executioner quickly ~ed the condemend man.* 行刑者迅速将该犯处决了.

dis·pel /dɪˈspel; dɪˈspɛl/ *vt* (-ll-) [VP6A] drive away; scatter: 驱逐; 驱散: *The wind soon ~led the fog.* 风不久就把雾驱散了. *How can we ~ their doubts and fears?* 我们如何才能消除他们的怀疑和恐惧?

dis·pens·able /dɪˈspensəbl; dɪˈspɛnsəbl/ *adj* that can be done without; not necessary. 不必要的; 不需要的.

dis·pens·ary /dɪˈspensərɪ; dɪˈspɛnsərɪ/ *n* (*pl* -ries) place where medicines are dispensed (eg in a hospital). 发药处(例如医院中);药局.

dis·pen·sa·tion /ˌdɪspenˈseɪʃn; ˌdɪspɛnˈseʃən/ *n* **1** [U] the act of dispensing(1) or distributing: 分配; 分给; 施给: *the ~ of justice/charity/food.* 法律之执行(放赈; 食物的分配). **2** [U] ordering or management, esp of the world by Providence; [C] sth arranged by Nature or Providence; 天道(上帝对人世的治理; 造物主或上帝所安排的事物); 神意: *A bereavement* (eg the death of a very old person) *is sometimes called a ~ of Providence.* 亲属的丧亡(例如高龄者之去世)有时被称作上天的安排. **3** [C, U] permission to do sth that is usually forbidden, or not to do sth that is usually required, esp by ecclesiastical law: 特准; 特免(尤指教规所禁止或规定者): *to be granted a ~ from fasting during a journey.* 旅途中特免斋戒. **4** [C] religious system prevalent at a period: 某一时代的宗教制度: *the Mosaic ~*, that of the time of Moses. 摩西时代的律法.

dis·pense /dɪˈspens; dɪˈspɛns/ *vt, vi* **1** [VP6A, 14] ~ (*to*), deal out; distribute; administer: 分配; 分给; 施给: *to ~ charity/alms/one's favours to people;* 对人们放赈(施舍, 施恩); (legal) (法律) *to ~ justice* (in law courts). (在法庭)执法. **2** [VP6A] mix; prepare, give out (medicines): 配制并分发(药物): *to ~ a prescription;* 照药方配药; *a dispensing chemist,* one qualified to do this. 药剂师. **3** [VP3A] ~ **with,** (a) do without: 无需; 不用; 没有也可以: *He is not yet well enough to ~ with the doctor's services.* 他尚未痊愈, 仍需医生的照看. (b) render unnecessary: 使不必要; 使多余: *The new machinery ~s with hand-labour.* 新机器使手工成为多余. **dis·penser** *n* **1** person who ~s, esp medicines. (尤指)配药者; 药剂师. **2** container from which sth can be withdrawn, ejected or otherwise obtained without removing a cover, lid, etc: 一种不需要拿开盖子便可取物的容器: *a ~r for liquid soap/*

toilet powder/paper cups. 免开盖式肥皂水容器(扑粉盒, 纸杯盒).

dis·perse /dɪˈspɜːs; dɪˈspɝs/ *vt, vi* [VP6A, 2A] (cause to) go in different directions; scatter: 驱散; 散开: *The police ~d the crowd.* 警察驱散群众. *The crowd ~d when the police arrived.* 警察来时, 群众散了. *The soldiers were ~d* (= stationed at different points) *along a wide front.* 兵士们散驻在广阔的前线上. *A prism ~s light,* breaks it up into its coloured rays. 三棱镜可使光色散(使其散为彩色光线). **dis·per·sal** /dɪˈspɜːsl; dɪˈspɝsl/ *n* [U, C] dispersing or being ~d. 驱散; 散开. **dis·per·sion** /dɪˈspɜːʃn *US:* -ʒn; dɪˈspɝʒən/ *n* = **dispersal,** esp of light. (尤指光的)色散. **the Dispersion,** the Jews ~d among the Gentiles. 散居在异邦人中间的犹太人. ⇨ **Diaspora.**

dis·pirit /dɪˈspɪrɪt; dɪˈspɪrɪt/ *vt* [VP6A] discourage; dishearten (chiefly in *pp*): 使沮丧; 使气馁(主要用过去分词): *to look ~ed.* 显得神情沮丧. ~**ed·ly** *adv*

dis·place /dɪsˈpleɪs; dɪsˈples/ *vt* [VP6A] **1** put out of the right or usual position. 自正常位置移走; 移置. ,~**d 'person,** refugee left homeless, unable or unwilling to return to his own country. 不能或不愿返国的难民. **2** take the place of; put sth or sb else in the place of: 代替; 替换: *The volunteers were ~d by a professional army.* 志愿军被正规军替换. *Tom has ~d Harry in Mary's affections.* 在玛丽的感情上, 汤姆已代替了哈里的位置.

dis·place·ment /dɪsˈpleɪsmənt; dɪsˈplesmənt/ *n* **1** [U] displacing or being displaced: 移置; 代替: *the ~ of human labour by machines.* 人力之被机器代替. **2** [C] amount of water displaced by a solid body in it, or floating in it: 排水量: *a ship with a ~ of 10000 tons.* 一艘有一万英吨排水量的船.

dis·play[1] /dɪsˈpleɪ; dɪsˈple/ *vt* [VP6A] **1** show; place or spread out so that there is no difficulty in seeing: 展示; 陈列: *Department stores ~ their goods in the windows.* 百货公司将货物陈列在橱窗内. *The peacock ~ed its fine tail feathers.* 那孔雀展示它尾巴上美丽的羽毛. **2** allow to be seen; show signs of having: 显露; 表露: *to ~ one's ignorance.* 显示自己的无知. *She ~ed no sign of emotion when she was told of her son's death.* 她听到儿子去世的消息时并未显得悲哀.

dis·play[2] /dɪsˈpleɪ; dɪsˈple/ *n* [C, U] displaying; show or exhibition: 展示; 陈列; 显露; 表现: *a fashion ~*, a showing of new styles in clothes, etc; 时装等展览; *a fine ~ of courage;* 勇气的充分表现; *a ~ of bad temper;* 坏脾气的表现; *to make a ~ of one's knowledge,* show what a lot one knows; 炫耀自己的知识; *to make a ~ of one's affection,* show great affection (whether genuine or not). 显得非常亲切(不论真或假).

dis·please /dɪsˈpliːz; dɪsˈpliz/ *vt* [VP6A] not please; offend; annoy; make indignant or angry: 使不高兴; 触怒; 使厌烦; 使生气: *to ~ one's wife;* 使妻子不悦; *to be ~d with sb* (*for doing sth*); 对某人(因做某事)不高兴; *to be ~d at sb's conduct.* 不满某人的行为. **dis·pleas·ing** *adj* ~ (*to*), not pleasing. 使人不高兴的; 令人厌恶的. **dis·pleas·ing·ly** *adv*

dis·pleasure /dɪsˈpleʒə(r); dɪsˈplɛʒɚ/ *n* [U] displeased feeling; dissatisfaction: 不悦; 不满: *He incurred his father's ~.* 他引起他父亲的不悦. *He looked with ~ at the meal that was set before him.* 他不满地望着摆在他面前的食物.

dis·port /dɪsˈpɔːt; dɪsˈport/ *vt* [VP6A] ~ **oneself,** (formal) play; amuse oneself, eg in the sea or in the sunshine. (正式用语)玩乐; 在(海上或阳光下等)嬉戏.

dis·pos·able /dɪsˈpəʊzəbl; dɪsˈpozəbl/ *adj* made so that it may be (easily) disposed of after use: 使用后易处理的: 用后易处置的: ~ *nappies/panties,* made of soft paper which disintegrates quickly in water. 用后易处置的尿布(短内裤)(用软纸制成,容于水中易碎易弃的).

dis·posal /dɪsˈpəʊzl; dɪsˈpozl/ *n* [U] ~ (*of*), **1** the act of disposing(1,2): 处理; 处置; 除去; 布置: *the ~ of*

property, eg by selling it, leaving it to sb in one's will; 财产的处理(如将其售卖, 或照遗嘱赠与某人); *the ～ of rubbish*, getting rid of it; 垃圾的清理; *a waste～ unit*, kind of machine that shreds waste products so that they can be washed away down the drains; 废物处理机(可将废物弄碎, 使其由沟中流走); *a bomb ～ squad*, group of men who, when unexploded bombs are found, try to make them harmless and remove them; 未爆弹清除队 (清除未爆炸的炸弹者); *the ～ of troops*, the method of using them, placing them in position, etc; 军队的部署; *the ～ of business affairs*, settling them. 业务的处理。**2** control; management: 控制; 支配: *In time of war the government must have entire ～ of all material resources.* 在战时政府必须完全控制全国的物资。*at one's ～*, to be used as one wishes: 任意使用: *He placed £50 at my ～.* 他留下五十英镑任我使用。*My car is at your ～.* 我的车随便你使用。

dis·pose /dɪˈspəʊz; dɪˈspoz/ *vi, vt* **1** [VP3A] ～ *of*, finish with; get rid of; deal with: 处理; 除去; 处置: 置: *～ of rubbish.* 除去垃圾。*He doesn't want to ～ of* (eg sell) *the land.* 他不想处理(例如卖掉)那块地。*I think we have ～d of all his arguments*, answered them, proved them unsound. 我认为我们已答复了他所有的论点(证明其不确)。*The dictator soon ～d of his opponents*, eg by putting them in prison. 那独裁者不久就把那些反对他的人清除了(例如将他们下狱)。**2** [VP6A, 2A] place (persons, objects) in good order or in suitable positions: 置(人或物)于适当位置; 布置: *The cruisers were ～d in line abreast.* 巡洋舰被布置为横队。*Man proposes, God ～s*, (prov) Men may propose things, but God determines what shall happen. (谚)谋事在人, 成事在天。**3** [VP17] ～ *sb to do sth*, (formal) make willing or ready: (正式用语)使愿意或准备做某事: *Your news ～s me to believe that ....* 你的消息使我相信…。*The low salary did not ～ him to accept the position.* 菲薄的待遇使他不愿接受这工作。*I'm not ～d/don't feel ～d to help that lazy fellow.* 我不愿帮助那个懒惰的人。*be well/ill ～d (towards)*, be/not be friendly and helpful: (对…)有好(恶)感; (对…)友善(不友善): *Most of the newspapers seem to be well ～d towards the new government.* 大多数的报纸似乎对新政府的态度友善。

dis·po·si·tion /ˌdɪspəˈzɪʃn; ˌdɪspəˈzɪʃən/ *n* [C] **1** arrangement; placing in order: 排列; 布置: *a clever ～ of furniture in a room*; 房间内家具的布置: *a clever ～ of troops.* 军队之巧妙的部署。**2** person's natural qualities of mind and character: 性情; 气质: *a man with a cheerful ～*; 性情开朗的人; *a ～ to jealousy/to take offence easily.* 喜妒忌/易发怒的性情。**3** inclination: 倾向: *There was a general ～ to leave early*, Most people seemed to wish to leave early. 大多数人似乎想早些动身。**4** power of ordering and disposing: 支配权; 处理权: *Who has the ～ of this property*, the power or authority to dispose of it? 谁有处置这项财产之权?

dis·pos·sess /ˌdɪspəˈzes; ˌdɪspəˈzes/ *vt* [VP14] ～ *sb of sth*, take away (property, esp land) from; compel (sb) to give up (the house he occupies): 剥夺(某人的财产, 尤指土地); 霸占(某人之房屋): *The nobles were ～ed of their property after the Revolution.* 贵族们的财产于革命后被剥夺。**dis·pos·session** /ˌdɪspəˈzeʃn; ˌdɪspəˈzeʃən/

dis·proof /dɪsˈpruːf; dɪsˈpruf/ *n* [U] disproving; [C] that which disproves; proof to the contrary. 证明为误;反证物;反证。

dis·pro·por·tion /ˌdɪsprəˈpɔːʃn; ˌdɪsprəˈpɔrʃən/ *n* [U] the state of being out of proportion: 不均衡; 不相称: *～ in age.* 年龄的不相称。**～·ate** /-ˈpɔːʃənət; -ˈpɔrʃənɪt/ *adj* ～ *(to)*, out of proportion; relatively too large or small, etc: 不相称的; 比较而言过大或过小等的: *to give a ～ate amount of one's time to games*; 以过量的时间游戏; *pay that is ～ate to the work done.* 与工作不相称的待遇。**～·ate·ly** *adv*

dis·prove /ˌdɪsˈpruːv; dɪsˈpruv/ *vt* [VP6A] prove

---

to be wrong or false. 证明为误;证明为伪。

dis·put·able /dɪˈspjuːtəbl; dɪˈspjutəbl/ *adj* that may be disputed; questionable. 可能引起辩论的; 有问题的。

dis·pu·tant /dɪˈspjuːtənt; ˈdɪspjutənt/ *n* person who disputes. 辩论者;争论者。

dis·pu·ta·tion /ˌdɪspjuːˈteɪʃn; ˌdɪspjuˈteʃən/ *n* [U] disputing; [C] debate, controversy. 辩论;争论。

dis·pu·ta·tious /ˌdɪspjuːˈteɪʃəs; ˌdɪspjuˈteʃəs/ *adj* fond of disputing; inclined to dispute. 爱辩论的; 喜争论的。**～·ly** *adv*

dis·pute¹ /dɪˈspjuːt; dɪˈspjut/ *n* **1** [U] debate, argument. 辩论; 争论。*in ～: The matter in ～* (= being disputed) *is the ownership of a house.* 目下争论的事是一所房子的所有权。*beyond/past (all) ～*, unquestionably; undoubtedly: 无疑是有关此问题最好的一本书。*This is beyond ～ the best book on the subject.* 这无疑是有关此问题最好的一本书。*in ～ with*, engaged in a ～ with: 与…辩论; 与…争论: *The workers' union is in ～ with the management.* 工会与经理人员争论。*without ～*, without fear of contradiction. 不会引起反驳地。**2** [C] quarrel; argument; controversy: 争吵; 争辩; 争论: *There were many religious ～s in England during the 17th century.* 十七世纪在英国有过多宗教上的争论。

dis·pute² /dɪˈspjuːt; dɪˈspjut/ *vi, vt* **1** [VP2A, 3A] ～ *(with/against sb)*, argue, debate, quarrel in words: (与某人)辩论; 争论: *Some people are always disputing.* 有些人总喜欢争论。**2** [VP6A, 8, 10] discuss, question the truth or validity of: 讨论; 怀疑…的真实性或妥当性: *to ～ a statement/a claim/a decision.* 讨论一声明(要求, 决策)的真实性或妥当性。*The election result was ～d*, eg it was said that the votes had been counted wrongly. 选举的结果引起异议(如据说选票被数错)。*The will was ～d*, eg it was said that it had not been made in correct legal form. 这遗嘱的真实性受到怀疑(如据说系未经合法手续而立者)。*They were disputing whether to start at once or wait.* 他们讨论是立刻开始还是等待。*They ～d (about) how to get the best results.* 他们讨论如何获得最佳结果。**3** [VP6A] fight for, try to win: 争夺; 竞争: *Our team ～d the victory until the last minute of the game.* 我们的队取胜利直到比赛的最后一分钟。

dis·qual·ify /ˌdɪsˈkwɒlɪfaɪ; dɪsˈkwɑləˌfaɪ/ *vt* [VP6A, 14] ～ *sb (for sth/from doing sth)*, make unfit or unable; 使不适合; 使不能; 使不合格: *His weak eyesight disqualified him for military service.* 他的目力欠佳使他不能服兵役。*As he was a professional, he was disqualified from taking part in the Olympic Games.* 由于他是个职业运动员, 他没有资格参加奥林匹克运动会。**dis·quali·fi·ca·tion** /ˌdɪsˌkwɒlɪfɪˈkeɪʃn; ˌdɪskwɑləfəˈkeʃən/ *n* [U] ～ing or being disqualified; [C] that which disqualifies. 不适合;无能力;不合格;不合格的原因。

dis·quiet /ˌdɪsˈkwaɪət; dɪsˈkwaɪət/ *vt* [VP6A] make troubled, anxious, uneasy: 使不安; 使烦乱: *～ed by rumours of war.* 由于战争的谣言而不安。□ *n* [U] anxiety; troubled condition: 忧虑;不安: *The President's speech caused considerable ～ in some European capitals.* 总统的演说在欧洲的某些首都中引起很大的不安。**～·ing** *adj* causing ～: 引起不安的: ～*ing news.* 令人不安的消息。**～·ing·ly** *adv* in a way that causes ～: 引起不安地: *a ～ingly high percentage of errors in the examination papers.* 考卷中令人忧虑的百分比很高的错误。**～·ude** /dɪsˈkwaɪətjuːd US: -tuːd; dɪsˈkwaɪəˌtjud/ *n* state of ～; uneasiness. 忧虑;不安。

dis·qui·si·tion /ˌdɪskwɪˈzɪʃn; ˌdɪskwəˈzɪʃən/ *n* [C] ～ *on sth*, long, elaborate speech or piece of writing. 精心做出的长篇演说或写作;专题演讲;专论。

dis·re·gard /ˌdɪsrɪˈɡɑːd; ˌdɪsrɪˈɡɑrd/ *vt* [VP6A] pay no attention to; show no respect for: 不注意; 忽视: *to ～ a warning/sb's objections to a proposal.* 不理一项警告(某人对一建议的反对)。□ *n* [U] inattention; indifference; neglect: 不注意; 忽视; 不理: ～ *of a rule*; 忽视一规则; ～ *for one's teachers.* 漠视老师。

dis·re·pair /ˌdɪsrɪ'peə(r)/ ; /ˌdɪsrɪ'per/ *n* [U] the state of needing repair: 需要修理; 失修: *The building was in bad ~,* in great need of being repaired. 这建筑物急需修理.

dis·repu·table /dɪs'repjutəbl/ ; dɪs'repjətəbl/ *adj* having a bad reputation: 名誉不好的; 声名狼藉的: *~ bars and clubs;* 声名狼藉的酒吧和俱乐部; not respectable in appearance: 外表不雅的: *a ~-looking fellow.* 外表不雅的人. *~ to,* reflecting badly on: 玷辱名声的: *incidents ~ to his character as a priest.* 有损他做为牧师的品格的事件. **dis·repu·tably** /-təblɪ/ ; -təblɪ/ *adv*

dis·re·pute /ˌdɪsrɪ'pjuːt/ ; ˌdɪsrɪ'pjut/ *n* [U] condition of being disreputable; discredit: 不名誉; 不名誉: *The hotel has fallen into ~,* no longer has a good reputation. 这旅馆已名誉扫地了.

dis·re·spect /ˌdɪsrɪ'spekt/ ; ˌdɪsrɪ'spekt/ *n* [U] rudeness; want of respect: 无礼; 不敬: *He meant no ~ by that remark,* did not intend to be impolite. 他说那句话并无不敬之意. **~·ful** /-fʊl; -fəl/ *adj* showing ~: 无礼的; 不敬的: *to be ~ful to sb.* 对某人无礼. **~·fully** /-fʊlɪ; -fəlɪ/ *adv: to speak ~fully of/about sb.* 无敬意地谈论某人.

dis·robe /dɪs'rəʊb/ ; dɪs'rob/ *vi, vt* [VP6A, 2A] undress; take off (esp official or ceremonial robes): 脱衣(尤指官服或礼服): *The Queen ~d after the coronation ceremony.* 女王于加冕礼后脱去王袍.

dis·rupt /dɪs'rʌpt/; dɪs'rʌpt/ *vt* [VP6A] break up, split, separate by force a State, an empire, communications, other non-physical things: 分裂 (国家, 帝国, 交通或其他无形之物): *Their quarrels seem likely to ~ the Coalition.* 他们的争执似乎可能使联盟分裂. **dis·rup·tion** /dɪs'rʌpʃn/ ; dɪs'rʌpʃən/ *n* [U] ~ing or being ~ed: 分裂; 被分裂: *the ~ion of the Roman Empire.* 罗马帝国的分裂. **dis·rup·tive** /dɪs'rʌptɪv/ ; dɪs'rʌptɪv/ *adj* causing ~ion: 造成分裂的: *~ive forces.* 造成分裂的力量; 迅裂力.

dis·sat·is·fac·tion /ˌdɪsˌsætɪs'fækʃn/ ; ˌdɪssætɪs'fækʃən/ *n* [U] ~ *(with sb/sth) (at doing sth),* the state of being dissatisfied. 不满.

dis·sat·is·fy /dɪs'sætɪsfaɪ/ ; dɪs'sætɪsˌfaɪ/ *vt* [VP6A] (usu passive) fail to satisfy; make discontented. (通常用被动语态)使不满; 使不满足. *be dissatisfied (with sb/sth) / (at doing sth): to be dissatisfied with one's salary/at not getting a better salary.* 对薪金(不能获较高薪金)不满.

dis·sect /dɪ'sekt/ ; dɪ'sekt/ *vt* [VP6A] **1** cut up (parts of an animal body, plant, etc) in order to study its structure. 解剖(动植物各部). **2** (fig) examine (a theory, argument, etc) part by part, to judge its value. (喻)详细研究或分析(学说, 论据等). **dis·sec·tion** /dɪ'sekʃn/ ; dɪ'sekʃən/ *n* [U] ~ing or being ~ed; [C] (part of) sth that has been ~ed. 解剖; 解剖体; 详细研究或分析; 经过详细研究或分析的事物.

dis·semble /dɪ'sembl/ ; dɪ'sembl/ *vt, vi* [VP6A, 2A] (formal) speak, behave, so as to hide one's real feelings, thoughts, plans, etc, or give a wrong idea of them: (正式用语)以言语或行动掩饰(真正情感, 思想, 计划等, 或令人对它们有一种错误的想法): *to ~ one's emotions.* 掩饰感情. **dis·sem·bler** /-blə(r)/ ; -blə/ *n* person who ~s; deceiver. 以言语或行动做掩饰者; 欺骗者.

dis·semi·nate /dɪ'semɪneɪt/; dɪ'semə,net/ *vt* [VP6A] distribute or spread widely ideas, doctrines, etc. 传播; 散布(思想, 教义等). **dis·semi·na·tion** /dɪˌsemɪ'neɪʃn/; dɪˌsemə'neʃən/ *n*

dis·sen·sion /dɪ'senʃn/ ; dɪ'senʃən/ *n* [U] angry quarrelling; [C] angry quarrel: 纷争; ~*(s) between rival groups in politics.* 敌对政党间的纷争.

dis·sent[1] /dɪ'sent/ *n* [U] dissenting; (expression of) disagreement: 意见不同; 不信奉英国国教; 不同意(的表示): *to express strong ~.* 表示极不赞同.

dis·sent[2] /dɪ'sent/ ; dɪ'sent/ *vi* **1** [VP3A] ~ *from,*

have a different opinion from; refuse to assent to: 与…意见不同; 不同意: *I strongly ~ from what the last speaker has said.* 我十分不同意刚才这位发言者的话. **2** [VP2, 3A] ~ *(from),* (esp) refuse to accept the religious doctrine of the Church of England. (尤指)不信奉英国国教. **~·er** *n* (often *D~*) one who ~s (esp as in 2 above). 意见不同者; (常作大写)不信奉英国国教者.

dis·ser·ta·tion /ˌdɪsə'teɪʃn/; ˌdɪsɚ'teʃən/ *n* [C] long written or spoken account (eg as submitted for a higher university degree): 长篇论文或演说(例如为获得大学较高学位而提出者): *a ~ on/upon/concerning sth.* 关于某事物的长篇论文或演说.

dis·ser·vice /dɪs'sɜːvɪs/; dɪs'sɝvɪs/ *n* [U, C] *(a) ~ (to),* harmful or unhelpful action: 有害的行动; 损害: *to do sb a ~.* 损害某人. *The spreading of such ideas is of great ~* (= is very harmful) *to the State.* 散播这种思想对国家极为有害.

dis·sever /dɪ'sevə(r)/; dɪ'sevɚ/ *vt* [VP6A] sever. 切断; 割开.

dis·si·dent /'dɪsɪdənt/; 'dɪsədənt/ *adj* disagreeing. 意见不同的. □ *n* person who disagrees; dissenter. 不同意者; 意见不同者. **dis·si·dence** /-dəns/ ; -dəns/ *n* [U] disagreement. 意见不同; 持异议.

dis·simi·lar /dɪ'sɪmɪlə(r)/; dɪ'sɪmɪlɚ/ *adj* ~ *(from/to),* not the same; not similar: (与…)不相同的; 不相似的: *people with ~ tastes.* 嗜好不同的人们. **~·ity** /ˌdɪsɪmɪ'lærətɪ; dɪˌsɪmə'lærətɪ/ *n* [U] lack of similarity; [C] (*pl* **-ties**) point of difference. 不相似; 不同之点. **dis·simi·li·tude** /ˌdɪsɪ'mɪlɪtjuːd; *US:* -tuːd/; /ˌdɪssɪ'mɪlə,tjud/ *n* unlikeness. 不相似; 不相似; 不相似; 不相似; 不相似.

dis·simu·late /dɪ'sɪmjuleɪt/; dɪ'sɪmjə,let/ *vt, vi* [VP 6A, 2A] (formal) dissemble. (正式用语)以言语或行动掩饰. **dis·simu·la·tion** /dɪˌsɪmju'leɪʃn/; dɪ'sɪmjə'leʃən/ *n*

dis·si·pate /'dɪsɪpeɪt/; 'dɪsə,pet/ *vt, vi* **1** [VP6A, 2A] (cause to) disperse, go away: 驱散; 消失: *to ~ fear/doubt/ignorance.* 消除恐惧(怀疑, 愚昧). **2** [VP 6A] waste (time, money) foolishly: 浪费(时间, 金钱): *He soon ~d his fortune.* 他不久便将他的财产荡尽了. *Don't ~ your efforts.* 不要浪费你的精力. **dis·si·pated** *part adj* given up to foolish and often harmful pleasures: 放荡的; 闲游浪荡的: *to lead a ~d life;* 过放荡的生活; *to fall into ~d ways.* 染于闲游浪荡.

dis·si·pa·tion /ˌdɪsɪ'peɪʃn/; ˌdɪsə'peʃən/ *n* [U] dissipating or being dissipated: 驱散; 消散; 浪费; 放荡: *a life of ~;* 放荡的生活; *unwise ~ of one's energy.* 不智的浪费精力.

dis·so·ci·ate /dɪ'səʊʃɪeɪt/; dɪ'soʃɪ,et/ *vt* [VP6A, 14] ~ *(from),* separate (in thought, feeling); not associate with: (在思想, 情感上)与…分离; 与…无关系: *It is difficult to ~ the man from his position,* to think of the man without also thinking of his work and duties. 将一个人和他的职位分开来是困难的(想到某人便想到他的工作和职务). *A politician's public and private life should be ~d.* 从政者的公私生活应分开. *I wish to ~ myself from what has just been said.* 我真希望自己与刚才所说的话毫无关系. **dis·so·cia·tion** /dɪˌsəʊsɪ'eɪʃn/; dɪˌsosɪ'eʃən/ *n* [U] dissociating or being ~d: (思想, 情感上的)分离; 无关系. *dissociation of ideas,* keeping them distinct. 将各种观念分开.

dis·sol·uble /dɪ'sɒljubl/; dɪ'saljəbl/ *adj* that can be dissolved or disintegrated; (of non-material things) that can be annulled: 可溶解的; 可解散的; (指无形物)可作废的; 可解除的: *Is marriage ~?* 婚姻是可以解除的吗? **dis·solu·bil·ity** /dɪˌsɒlju'bɪlətɪ; dɪˌsaljə'bɪlətɪ/ *n*

dis·so·lute /'dɪsəljuːt *US:* -luːt/; 'dɪsə,lut/ *adj* (of persons) given up to immoral conduct; (of behaviour, etc) evil; vicious: (指人)荒淫的; (指行为等)邪恶的; 放荡的; 不道德的: *to lead a ~ life;* 过荒淫的生活; *~ conduct.* 邪恶的行为. **~·ly** *adv*

dis·sol·ution /ˌdɪsə'luːʃn/; ˌdɪsə'luʃən/ *n* [C, U] ~ *(of),* breaking up; undoing or ending (of a marriage,

partnership, etc); (esp) ending of Parliament before a general election. 分解;解除(婚约,合伙关系等);(尤指)普通前国会之解散。

dis·solve /dɪˈzɒlv; dɪˈzɑlv/ *vt, vi* **1** [VP6A] (of a liquid) soak into a solid so that the solid itself becomes liquid: (指液体)溶解: *Water ~s salt.* 水溶解盐。 **2** [VP2A, 3A] *~ (in)*, (of a solid) become liquid as the result of being taken into a liquid: (指固体在液体中)溶解: *Salt ~s in water.* 盐在水中溶解。 **3** [VP6A, 14] *~ (in)*, cause (a solid) to: 使(固体)溶解: *He ~d the salt in water.* 他使盐在水中溶解。 **4** [VP2A, C] disappear; fade away: 消失;消散: *The view ~d in mist.* 那景象在雾中消失了。 **5** [VP6A, 2A] bring to, come to, an end: 结束: *to ~ a business partnership/a marriage / Parliament.* 结束商业上的合伙关系(解除婚约;解散国会)。 *Parliament ~d.* 国会解散了。

dis·son·ance /ˈdɪsənəns; ˈdɪsənəns/ *n* [U] discord; [C] combination of notes that is discordant. 不和谐; 不和谐的音调; 不协和音。

dis·son·ant /ˈdɪsənənt; ˈdɪsənənt/ *adj* not harmonious; harsh in tone. 不和谐的; 刺耳的。

dis·suade /dɪˈsweɪd; dɪˈswed/ *vt* [VP6A, 14] *~ sb (from sth/from doing sth)*, advise against; (try to) turn (sb) away: 劝阻; 戒戒(某人): *to ~ a friend from marrying.* 劝阻友人结婚。 **dis·sua·sion** /dɪˈsweɪʒn; dɪˈsweʒən/ *n*

dis·taff /ˈdɪstɑːf *US*: -tæf; ˈdɪstæf/ *n* stick round which wool, flax, etc, is wound for spinning by hand. (手纺用的)缠线杆。 *on the '~ side*, on the mother's side of the family. 属于母系的。

dis·tance /ˈdɪstəns; ˈdɪstəns/ *n* [C, U] **1** measure of space, between two points, places, etc; being far off: 距离; 远: *In the USA ~ is measured in miles, not in kilometres.* 在美国测量距离用英里,不用公里。 *The house stands on a hill and can be seen from a ~ of two miles, from two miles away.* 那房子在山顶上,从二英里外可以看到。 *The town is a great ~ off,* a long way off. 那城市很遥远。 *My house is within easy walking ~ of the shops,* near enough for me to walk to them easily. 我家离商店很近,走几步就到了。 *at a ~,* not too near. 不太近; 在远处。 *in the ~,* far away. 在远处。 *keep sb at a ~,* refuse to let him become familiar; treat him with reserve. 不与某人亲近; 对某人保持相当距离。 *keep one's ~,* (fig) not be too friendly or familiar. (喻)不与亲近。 *no ~,* near. 在近处。 *some ~,* fairly far away. 相当远。 **long-~** *adj* **(a)** (of races, journeys, etc) covering an extensive length, area, etc: (指竞赛、旅行等)长距离的: *long-~ runners.* 长距离的赛跑者。 **(b)** (of telephone calls) to/from a distant place. (指电话)长途的。 **middle-~** *adj* (of races, etc) covering a medium-size length or area. (指竞赛等)中距离的。 **the middle-~** *n* that part of a view between the foreground and the background. 中景(前景与背景间)。 **2** space of time: 时间的距离: *to look back over a ~ of fifty years;* 回顾过去五十年的时间; *at this ~ of time.* 在如此长久的时间。 □ *vt* [VP6A, 14] *~ (from),* place or keep at a ~. 使远离;不与…接近。

dis·tant /ˈdɪstənt; ˈdɪstənt/ *adj* **1** *~ (from),* far away in space or time: 远离的; 远隔的; 遥远的: *The school is three miles ~ from the station.* 这学校距车站三英里。 *We had a ~ view of Mt Qomolangma:* 我们远眺珠穆朗玛峰。 **2** far off in family relationship: 亲属关系远的; 远房的: *She is a ~ cousin of mine.* 她是我的一位远房表妹。 **3** (of degree of similarity) not easily seen: (指相似程度)不易见的: *There is a ~ resemblance between the cousins.* 这两位堂兄弟隐约相像。 **4** reserved; not showing familiarity: 冷淡的; 不表示亲近的: *Instead of stopping to speak, she passed by with only a ~ nod.* 她没有停下来谈话,只冷淡的点一下头走了过去。 **~·ly** *adv* in a ~ manner: 遥远地; 远房地; 不易见地; 冷淡地: *He is ~ly related to me.* 他是我的远亲。

dis·taste /dɪsˈteɪst; dɪsˈtest/ *n* [U, C] **(a)** *~ (for)*;

dislike; aversion: 厌恶; 憎厌: *a ~ for hard work.* 讨厌苦干的工作。 *He turned away in ~.* 他厌恶地走开了。 **~·ful** /-fl; -fəl/ *adj* **~ful (to)**, disagreeable; unpleasant: 讨厌的; 令人不愉快的: *It is ~ful to me to have to say this, but ....* 我不得不这样说,是使我很不愉快的,但是…。 **~·fully** /-fəlɪ; -fəlɪ/ *adv* **~·ful·ness** /-fəlnɪs; -fəlnɪs/ *n*

dis·temper[1] /dɪsˈtempə(r); dɪsˈtempɚ/ *n* [U] (method of painting with) colouring matter (to be) mixed with water and distributed on walls and ceilings. 胶画颜料(与水混合,用以涂刷墙壁和天花板的一种颜料); 用胶画颜料作画的方法。 □ *vt* [VP6A, 22] colour with ~: 用胶画颜料将墙壁粉刷成绿色。 *We ~ed the walls green.* 我们用胶画颜料将墙壁粉刷成绿色。

dis·temper[2] /dɪsˈtempə(r); dɪsˈtempɚ/ *n* [U] disease of dogs and some other animals, with coughing and weakness. 犬瘟热(狗和某些其他动物所患的一种温热病,有咳嗽及虚弱的现象)。

dis·tend /dɪsˈtend; dɪsˈtend/ *vt, vi* [VP6A, 2A] (cause to) swell out (by pressure from within): (使)扩张; (使)膨胀(由内部压力所致): *a ~ed stomach/vein.* 扩张的胃(静脉)。 **dis·ten·sion** (US = **-tion**) /dɪsˈtenʃn; dɪsˈtenʃən/ *n* ~ing or being ~ed. 扩张;膨胀。

dis·til (US = **-till**) /dɪsˈtɪl; dɪsˈtɪl/ *vt, vi* (-ll-) **1** [VP6A, 15B, 14] *~ sth (from sth)*; *~ sth off / out*, change (a liquid) to vapour by heating, cool the vapour and collect the drops of liquid that condense from the vapour; purify (a liquid) thus; drive out or off impurities thus; make (whisky, essences) thus: 蒸馏(液体);用蒸馏法净化(液体);用蒸馏法除去不纯之物(与out或off连用); 用蒸馏法制造(威士忌酒,香精等): *Salt water can be ~led and made into drinking water.* 咸水可被蒸馏成为饮用的水。 **2** [VP6A, 2A] fall, let fall, in drops: 滴下; 使滴下: *flowers that ~ nectar.* 滴出花蜜的花。 **dis·til·la·tion** /ˌdɪstɪˈleɪʃn; ˌdɪstlˈeʃən/ *n* **1** [U] ~ling or being ~led: 蒸馏; 由蒸馏法净化或制造: *the ~lation of malted barley (to make whisky).* 蒸馏发芽的大麦(以制威士忌酒)。 **2** [C, U] substance obtained by ~ling. 蒸馏物。

dis·til·ler /dɪsˈtɪlə(r); dɪsˈtɪlɚ/ *n* person who distils (esp whisky). 蒸馏者; (尤指以蒸馏法制造威士忌酒者); 制酒者。 **dis·til·lery** /-lərɪ; -lərɪ/ *n* (*pl* **-ries**) place where liquids (eg gin, whisky) are distilled. 蒸馏所; 造酒厂。

dis·tinct /dɪsˈtɪŋkt; dɪsˈtɪŋkt/ *adj* **1** easily heard, seen, understood; plain; clearly marked: 清楚的; 明白的; 明晰的; 明显的: *a ~ pronunciation.* 清晰的发音。 *The earth's shadow on the moon was quite ~.* 月球上的地球阴影是十分清晰的。 *There is a ~ improvement in her typing.* 她的打字有显著的进步。 **2** *~ (from),* different in kind; separate: 种类不同的; 分开的: *Keep the two ideas ~,* the one from the other. 将这两个观念彼此分别清楚。 *Hares and rabbits are ~ animals.* 野兔和家兔是不同的动物。 **~·ly** *adv* in a ~ manner: 清楚地; 清晰地: *to speak / remember ~ly.* 说话(记得)清楚。 **~·ness** *n*

dis·tinc·tion /dɪsˈtɪŋkʃn; dɪsˈtɪŋkʃən/ *n* **1** [U] being, keeping things, different or distinct(2); distinguishing, being distinguished, as different; [C] instance of this: 种类不同; 分别; 区别: *The President shook hands with everyone, without a ~.* 总统与每个人握手,不分地位等级。 *The ~s of birth* (= The different classes of society into which people are born) *are less important than they used to be.* 出身贵贱之分在今日不像往时那样重要了。 *It is difficult to make exact ~s between all the meanings of a word.* 对一个词的各种意义详加区别是困难的。 *a ~ without a difference,* no real difference at all. 无差异的区别(假的区别)。 **2** [C] point of difference; that which makes one thing different from another: 不同之点; 差别之处: *the ~ between poetry and prose.* 诗与散文之不同处。 **3** [U] quality of being superior, excellent, distinguished: 优越; 卓越; 非凡: *a*

writer / novel of ~. 卓越的作家(小说). **4** [C] mark of honour; title; decoration; reward: 荣誉; 荣衔; 殊勋; 奖赏: *academic ~s*, eg a doctor's degree; 学术上的荣誉 (例如博士学位); *to win ~s for bravery.* 因英勇而获殊勋.

dis·tinc·tive /dɪˈstɪŋktɪv; dɪˈstɪŋktɪv/ adj serving to mark a difference or make distinct: 表示有别的; 区别的; 有特色的: *Soldiers wear a ~ uniform.* 军人穿特殊的制服. **~·ly** adv

dis·tin·guish /dɪˈstɪŋgwɪʃ; dɪˈstɪŋgwɪʃ/ vt, vi **1** [VP14, 3A] ~ *one thing from another;* ~ *between two things,* see, hear, recognize, understand well, the difference: 辨别; 区别: *People who cannot ~ between colours are said to be colour-blind.* 不能辨别颜色的人谓之色盲. *The twins were so much alike that it was impossible to ~ (the) one from the other.* 这对孪生子像得使人无法分辨. *It is not easy to ~ cultured pearls from genuine pearls.* 辨别真珍珠与养珠不易. **2** [VP6A] make out by looking, listening, etc: 辨识; 认明: *A person with good eyesight can ~ distant objects.* 眼力好的人能看清远处的物体. **3** [VP14] ~ *from,* be a mark of character, difference: 作为…的特性; 使别于: *speech ~es man from the animals.* 言语使人与动物有别. *What ~es the hare from the rabbit?* 野兔与家兔有何不同? **4** [VP6A] ~ *oneself,* behave so as to bring credit to oneself: 显扬自己; 使自己扬名: *to ~ oneself in an examination.* 考试成绩出众. *He ~ed himself by his courage.* 他因英勇而扬名. **~·able** /-əbl; -əbl/ adj **~·able (from),** able to be ~ed from sb/sth else: 可辨别的; 可区别的: *Tom is hardly ~able from his twin brother.* 汤姆与他的孪生哥哥(弟弟)几乎令人分辨不出. *The coast was hardly ~able* (= could hardly be seen) *through the haze.* 从薄雾中几乎无法看清海岸. **~ed** adj famous; well known; remarkable; showing distinction(3): 著名的; 卓越的; 非凡的: *He is ~ed for his knowledge of economics / ~ed as an economist.* 他在经济学方面的知识是卓越的(他是一位著名的经济学家). *He has had a ~ed career in the diplomatic service.* 他在外交界具有不寻常的经历.

dis·tort /dɪˈstɔːt; dɪˈtɔrt/ vt [VP6A] **1** pull, twist, out of the usual shape: 使变形; 扭曲: *a face ~ed by pain.* 因痛苦而扭曲的面孔. *A curved mirror ~s the features.* 弯曲的镜面使容貌变形. **2** give a false account of; twist out of the truth: 歪曲; 曲解: *Newspaper accounts of international affairs are sometimes ~ed.* 报纸对国际事件的报道有时是歪曲事实的. *You have ~ed my motives.* 你曲解了我的动机. **dis·tor·tion** /dɪˈstɔːʃən; dɪˈstɔrʃən/ n [U] ~ing or being ~ed; [C] instance of this; sth that is ~ed. 变形; 扭曲; 歪曲; 曲解; 被扭曲或曲解的事物.

dis·tract /dɪˈstrækt; dɪˈstrækt/ vt [VP6A, 14] ~ *from,* draw away sb's attention from sth: 转移注意力; 使分心: *The noise in the street ~ed me from my reading.* 街上的嘈杂声使我不能专心读书. *What can we do to ~ her mind from the sorrow caused by her child's death?* 我们怎样减轻她丧子的痛苦呢? **~ed** adj **~ed (with/by),** with the mind confused or bewildered: 心情纷乱的; 困扰的; 迷惑的: *to be ~ed with/by anxiety/grief.* 为忧虑(悲伤)所烦扰. **~·ed·ly** adv in a ~ed manner. 心情纷乱地; 困扰地; 迷惑地.

dis·trac·tion /dɪˈstrækʃn; dɪˈstrækʃən/ n **1** [U] distracting or being distracted. 转移注意力; 分心. **2** [C] sth that distracts, sth annoying and unwelcome: 分心的事物; 使人烦扰的事物: *Noise is a ~ when you are trying to study.* 在你要读书时, 嘈杂声是分散注意力的. **3** [C] sth that holds the attention and gives pleasure: 吸引心神而令人快乐的事物; 娱乐; 消遣: *He complained that there were not enough ~s in the small village.* 他抱怨说在那小村子里没有足够的娱乐. *There are plenty of ~s* (= interesting and amusing things to see and do) *in a large city.* 大城市里有许多有趣的事物. **4** [U] wildness or confusion of mind: 发狂; 精神错乱. **to ~:**

He loves her to ~, loves her wildly, passionately. 他爱她爱得发狂. *You will drive me to ~ with your silly questions.* 你的傻问题将使我发狂.

dis·train /dɪˈstreɪn; dɪˈstren/ vi [VP2A, 3A] ~ **(upon),** (legal) seize goods to compel a person to pay money due (esp rent): (法律)扣押物品强使一人付清到期的款项(尤指租金): *to ~ upon a person's furniture for rent.* 扣押一人的家具以抵偿租金. **dis traint** n ~ing. (法律)扣押物品.

dis·trait /dɪˈstreɪ; dɪˈstre/ adj (F) absent-minded; not paying attention. (法)心不在焉的; 不注意的.

dis·traught /dɪˈstrɔːt; dɪˈstrot/ adj distracted; violently upset in mind: 心情纷乱的; 狂乱的: ~ *with grief.* 悲痛得发狂.

dis·tress¹ /dɪˈstres; dɪˈstres/ n [U] **1** (cause of) great pain, discomfort or sorrow; (suffering caused by) want of money or other necessary things: 痛苦; 痛苦的原因; 穷困; 贫苦: *At the end of the Marathon race several runners showed signs of ~.* 当马拉松赛跑结束时, 几位参加赛跑的人显示出痛苦的迹象. *His wild behaviour was a great ~ to his mother.* 他的放荡的行为使他的母亲极为苦恼. *He spent his fortune in relieving ~ among the poor.* 他以财产解除穷人的困苦. **2** serious danger or difficulty: 严重的危机或困难: *The lifeboat went out to a ship in ~.* 救生船去救一艘遇险的船只. *The ship was flying a ~ signal.* 这船悬起遇险的信号.

dis·tress² /dɪˈstres; dɪˈstres/ vt [VP6A] cause distress(1) to: 使痛苦; 使忧愁; 使贫苦: *I am much ~ed to hear the news of your wife's death.* 听到你妻子去世的消息我很难过. *What are you looking so ~ed about?* 什么事情使你着有此苦恼? *Don't ~ yourself,* Don't get worried. 不要担忧. **~ed 'area,** part of a country where there is serious and continued unemployment. 一国之贫苦地区. **~·ful** /-fəl; -fəl/, **~·ing** adj causing or experiencing ~. 使人痛苦的; 苦恼的. **~·fully** /-fəlɪ; -fəlɪ/, **~·ing·ly** advv in a manner that causes distress. 使人痛苦地; 苦恼地.

dis·trib·ute /dɪˈstrɪbjuːt; dɪˈstrɪbjʊt/ vt [VP6A, 14] ~ **(to/among),** **1** put (parts of a set of things) in different places; give or send out: 分配; 分给. **2** spread out (over a larger area): 散布(于广大地区); 分布: *to ~ manure over a field.* 施肥于田地. **3** put into groups or classes. 分类; 区分. **dis·tribu·tor** /-tə(r); -tər/ n person or thing that ~s. 分配者; 分配机; 散布者; 散布机; 分布器.

dis·tribu·tion /ˌdɪstrɪˈbjuːʃn; ˌdɪstrəˈbjuʃən/ n [U] distributing or being distributed; manner of being distributed; [C] instance or occasion of distributing: 分配; 分布; 被分配或分布的状态; 分配或分布的实例: *They could not agree about the ~ of the profits.* 他们对于利润的分配意见不一致. *Is the ~ of wealth uneven in your country?* 在你们的国家内财富分配得不均吗? *The pine-tree has a very wide ~,* is found in many parts of the world. 松树的分布很广(见于世界许多地方).

dis·tribu·tive /dɪˈstrɪbjʊtɪv; dɪˈstrɪbjʊtɪv/ adj **1** of distribution: 分配的; 分布的: *the ~ trades,* eg railways, shop-keeping. 运销业(例如铁路, 开店). **2** (gram) referring to each individual, each member of a class: (语法)个体的: '*Each*', '*every*', '*either*' *and* '*neither*' *are ~ pronouns.* Each, every, either 和 neither 是个体代词. **~·ly** adv

dis·trict /ˈdɪstrɪkt; ˈdɪstrɪkt/ n **1** part of a country: 地区; 区域: *a mountainous ~;* 山区; *purely agricultural ~s.* 纯粹农业区域. *the Lake D~,* in north-west England. 英格兰西北部的湖区. **2** part of a town or country marked out for a special purpose: 为特殊目的而划出的区: *the London postal ~,* eg NW5, EC4. 伦敦的邮政区(例如 NW5, EC4). ⇨ *postcode* at *post³(4); rural and urban ~s,* for purposes of local

government. 乡区和市区(为地方行政目的所做之划分). ~ **nurse**, one who visits people in their homes. 区域护士(至家里访视或看护病人者). **the D~ of Columbia**, the city of Washington, the Federal government area of the US. 哥伦比亚特区[美国首都华盛顿的行政区, 属联邦政府].

dis·trust /dɪsˈtrʌst; dɪsˈtrʌst/ *n* [U, C] *(a)* ~ *(of)*, doubt or suspicion; want of trust or confidence: 怀疑; 疑惑;不信任;不相信: *The child looked at the big stranger with* ~. 那小孩怀疑地望着那个高大的陌生人。*He has a* ~ *of foreigners*. 他不信任外国人。 □ *vt* [VP6A] have no trust in; be doubtful about: 不信任; 猜疑: *He would* ~ *his own friends.* 他信任他自己的朋友。*He ~ed his own eyes.* 他不信任他自己的眼睛。 ~·**ful** /-ful/, -fəl/ *adj* unwilling to trust; suspicious: 不信任的; 猜疑的: *I was* ~*ful of his motives*. 我怀疑他的动机。 ~·**fully** /-fəlɪ; -fəlɪ/ *adv* ~·**ful·ness** *n*

dis·turb /dɪˈstɜːb; dɪˈstɜːb/ *vt* [VP6A] break the quiet, calm, peace or order of; put out of the right or usual position; upset: 扰乱; 惊动; 搅乱; 使骚动; 使紊乱; 使不安: *He put his oars in the water and* ~*ed the smooth surface of the lake*. 他把桨放入水中, 搅乱了平静的湖面。 *She opened the door quietly so as not to* ~ *the sleeping child.* 她静静地开门以免惊扰了睡着的孩子。*Don't* ~ *the papers on my desk*. 不要乱动我桌上的文件。*He was* ~*ed to hear of your illness/was* ~*ed by the news of your illness.* 他听到你生病的消息感到不安。 ~ **the peace**. (legal) cause disorder, rioting, etc. (法律)扰乱治安。

dis·turb·ance /dɪˈstɜːbəns; dɪˈstɜːbəns/ *n* [U] disturbing or being disturbed; [C] instance of this; sth that disturbs; disorder (esp social or political): 扰乱; 动乱; 不安; 引起动乱或不安的事物; (尤指社会或政治上的)骚动: *Were there many political* ~*s in the country last year?* 这个国家去年有很多政治上的骚动吗?

dis·union /dɪsˈjuːnɪən; dɪsˈjunjən/ *n* [U] breaking of what unites; lack of union; dissension. 分裂; 不统一;纷争。

dis·unite /ˌdɪsjuːˈnaɪt; ˌdɪsjuˈnaɪt/ *vt, vi* [VP6A, 2A] (cause to) become separate. (使)分开; (使)分裂。

dis·unity /dɪsˈjuːnətɪ; dɪsˈjunətɪ/ *n* [U] lack of unity; dissension. 不统一; 分裂; 纷争。

dis·use /dɪsˈjuːs; dɪsˈjus/ *n* [U] state of no longer being used: 不用: *rusty from* ~; 因不用而生锈; *words that have fallen into* ~. 废而不用的词。~**d** /dɪsˈjuːzd; dɪsˈjuzd/ *part adj* no longer used: 废弃: *a* ~*d well*. 废井。

di·syl·labic (US = **dis·syl·labic**) /ˌdaɪsɪˈlæbɪk; ˌdɪsɪˈlæbɪk/ *adj* of two syllables. 双音节的。 **di·syl·lable** (US = **dis·syl·lable**) /daɪˈsɪləbl; dɪˈsɪləbl/ *n* ~ word or metrical foot. 双音节的词或音步。

ditch /dɪtʃ; dɪtʃ/ *n* narrow channel dug in or between fields, or at the sides of a road, etc to hold or carry off water. (田里或路边等用以储水或排水的)沟。*dull as* '~ *water*, very dull(3) indeed. 极其乏味的。 ⇨ **die²(2)**. □ *vt, vi* **1** [VP6A, 2A] make, clean, repair or provide with ~es. 挖沟; 清理沟; 修沟; ⋯开沟。**2** [VP6A] send or throw into a ~ (or, sl, the sea): (fig, sl) abandon: 把⋯驶入沟中; 丢入沟中; (喻, 俚)抛弃: *The drunken man* ~*ed his car*, drove it into one. 那醉汉将车驶入沟中。*The pilot had to* ~ *his plane*, make a forced landing on the sea. 那飞行员被迫将飞机降落海上。*He* ~*ed his girlfriend*, (sl) suddenly stopped seeing her. (俚)他突然抛弃了他的女友。

dither /ˈdɪðə(r); ˈdɪðɚ/ *vi* [VP2A, C] (old use) tremble; (colloq) hesitate about what to do; be unable to decide. (旧用法)颤抖; (口)踌躇; 犹豫。□ *n* trembling: 颤抖: *be all of/in a* ~; 浑身发抖; *have the* ~*s*; 发抖; (colloq) nervous, uncertain, indecisive state: (口)紧张不安; 犹豫不决: *be all of a* ~; 神经紧张; *have the* ~*s*. 紧张不安。

ditto /ˈdɪtəʊ; ˈdɪto/ *n* (abbr 略作 **d°, do**) the same thing (used in lists to avoid writing a word or words again): 同上(用于表格中以避免重复前面的字): *One hat at £2.25;* ~ *at £4.50.* 一顶帽子 2.25 英镑; 一顶帽子 4.50 英镑。*say* ~ *to*, (colloq) say the same thing as; agree with. (口)说与⋯相同的话; 同意⋯。

ditty /ˈdɪtɪ; ˈdɪtɪ/ *n* (*pl* **-ties**) short, simple song. 小曲; 小调。

di·ur·nal /daɪˈɜːnl; daɪˈɝnl/ *adj* (formal) of the daytime; (astron) occupying one day. (正式用语)昼间的; (天文)日的; 周日的。

di·va·gate /ˈdaɪvəɡeɪt; ˈdaɪvəˌɡet/ *vi* [VP2A, 3A] ~ *(from)*, (formal) stray; wander from the point. (正式用语)入歧途; 离题。 **di·va·ga·tion** /ˌdaɪvəˈɡeɪʃn; ˌdaɪvəˈɡeʃən/ *n*

di·van /dɪˈvæn; ˈdaɪvæn/ US: /dɪˈvæn; ˈdaɪvæn/ *n* **1** long, low, soft, backless seat. 无靠背的长沙发椅。 '~-**bed** such a seat that can be converted into a bed. 可变为床铺的无靠背的长沙发椅。**2** (in Muslim countries) public audience room; State council or council room. (伊斯兰国家的)会议室; 国务会议或会议室。

dive¹ /daɪv; daɪv/ *n* **1** the act of diving: 跳水; 潜水: *a graceful* ~. 优美的跳水。**2** (colloq) disreputable place for the sale of drink, or for gambling. (口)下流的饮酒或赌博场所。

dive² /daɪv; daɪv/ *vi* (US alternative *pt* 美国用法之过去式亦作 **dove** /dəʊv; dov/) [VP2A, C] ~ *(off/ from/into)*, **1** go head first into water: 跳水: *He* ~*d from the bridge and rescued the drowning child.* 他从桥上跳入水中, 救起那快要溺死的小孩。**2** (of a submarine) go under water; (of divers) go under water in a special dress: (指潜艇)潜水; (指潜水者)着特种服装潜水: *to* ~ *for pearls.* 潜水取珍珠。 '**diving-bell**, open-bottomed apparatus which can be lowered into water, supplied with air pumped through pipes, and used by underwater workers. 潜水钟(底部敞开的一种潜水装置, 借气管供给空气, 可供水下工作人员使用)。 '**diving-board**, flexible board from which to ~ (eg into a swimming pool). 跳水踏板(如游泳池中所设者)。 '**diving-dress** /-**suit**, suit with weighted boots and an air-tight helmet into which air is pumped through tubes, used by divers. 潜水衣(一种附有重靴与不透气头盔的衣服, 借管将空气通入盔内, 供潜水者用)。 **3** go quickly to a lower level; move sth (eg the hand) quickly and suddenly downwards (into sth): 迅速向下去;(手等)突然向下插入: *The aircraft* ~*d steeply.* 那架飞机垂直俯冲。*The rabbit* ~*d into its hole.* 那兔子突然钻入它的洞内。*He* ~*d into his pocket and pulled out a handful of coins.* 他突然把手伸入口袋, 掏出来一把钱币。 '~-**bomb**, *vi* (of an aircraft, **a** '~-**bomber**) drop bombs at the end of a steep dive. (指飞机, 俯冲轰炸机)俯冲轰炸。 **diver** *n* person who ~s, esp a person who works under water in a diving-suit. 跳水者; (尤指)潜水员(着潜水衣在水下工作者)。

di·verge /daɪˈvɜːdʒ; dəˈvɝdʒ/ *vi* [VP2A, 3A] ~ *(from)*, (of lines, paths, opinions, etc) get farther apart from a point or from each other as they progress; turn or branch away from. (指线条, 道路, 意见等)分歧; 离题; 逸出。 **di·ver·gence** /-dʒəns; -dʒəns/, **-gency** /-dʒənsɪ; -dʒənsɪ/ *n* [U] diverging; [C] (*pl* **-ces**, **-cies**) instance of this: 分歧; 离题; 逸出: *divergencies from the normal.* 脱离正轨。 **di·ver·gent** /-dʒənt; -dʒənt/ *adj*

di·vers /ˈdaɪvɜːz; ˈdaɪvəz/ *adj* (old use) several; more than one. (旧用法)若干的; 数个的。

di·verse /daɪˈvɜːs; dəˈvɝs/ *adj* of different kinds: 种类不同的: *The wild life in Africa is extremely* ~. 非洲野生动物的种类十分不同。 ~·**ly** *adv*

di·ver·sify /daɪˈvɜːsɪfaɪ; dəˈvɝsəˌfaɪ/ *vt* [VP6A] make diverse; give variety to: 使不同; 使变化: *a landscape diversified by hills and woods.* 由于山林穿插而变化有致的景色。 **di·ver·si·fi·ca·tion** /daɪˌvɜːsɪfɪˈkeɪʃn; dəˌvɝsəfəˈkeʃən/ *n*

di·ver·sion /daɪˈvɜːʃn US: -ʒn; dəˈvɜʒən/ n 1 [U] diverting; the act of turning sth aside or giving it a different direction: 转向; 改道: the ~ of a stream; 河流的改道; [C] instance of this: 转向或改道的实例: traffic ~s, eg when traffic is directed by different routes because of road repairs. 交通改道(例如因修补马路所致). 2 [C] sth which turns the attention from serious things; sth giving rest or amusement: 消遣; 娱乐: Chess and billiards are his favourite ~s. 国际象棋和台球是他最喜爱的消遣. 3 [C] method used to turn the attention from sth that one does not wish to be noticed, as when, in war, the enemy's attention is drawn from one place to another by an unexpected attack at another place: 一种分散注意力的方法(例如在作战时突袭乙地而转移敌人对甲地之注意力); 牵制(转移); 声东击西: to create/make a ~. 声东击西. 分散其注意力; 声东击西. ~**ary** /daɪˈvɜːʃənərɪ US: -ˈʒenerɪ; dəˈvɜʒən,ɛrɪ/ adj: a ~ary raid. 牵制性的突袭. ~**·ist** n person who engages in disruptive or subversive activities. 从事破坏活动者.

di·ver·sity /daɪˈvɜːsətɪ; dəˈvɜsətɪ/ n [U] the state of being diverse; variety. 异样; 不同; 各式各样.

di·vert /daɪˈvɜːt; dəˈvɜt/ vt [VP6A, 14] ~ (from), 1 turn in another direction: 使转向; 使改道: to ~ the course of a river; 使河改道; to ~ a river from its course; 使河改道; to ~ water from a river into the fields. 将河水导入田间. 2 amuse; entertain; turn the attention away: 娱乐; 消遣; 使转变注意力: Some people are easily ~ed. 有些人的注意力容易转变. How can we ~ her thoughts from her sad loss? 我们如何使她不再想她的可悲的损失? ~**ing** adj amusing. 有趣的. ~**·ing·ly** adv

Dives /ˈdaɪviːz; ˈdaɪviz/ n (typical name for a) rich man. 富翁; 财主(代表有钱人的名称). ⇨ **Luke 16: 19.** 参看路加福音16章19节.

di·vest /daɪˈvest; dəˈvɛst/ vt [VP14] ~ sb of, 1 (formal) take off (clothes): (正式用语)脱去(衣服): to ~ a king of his robes. 脱去国王的王袍. 2 take away from: 剥夺: to ~ an official of power and authority. 剥夺一官员的权柄. 3 (reflex) get rid of: give up: (反身)去除; 放弃: I cannot ~ myself of the idea, It comes back to my mind. 我无法摒除这个念头.

di·vide[1] /dɪˈvaɪd; dəˈvaɪd/ vt, vi 1 [VP6A, 15B, 14, 2A, C] ~ sth (up/out); ~ sth between/among sb; ~ sth from sth, separate; split or break up: 分开; 划分; 分割: We ~d (up/out) the money equally. 我们将钱均分. They ~d the money between / among themselves. 他们分那笔钱. The river ~s my land from his. 这条河将我的地和他的地隔开. The Nile ~s near its mouth and forms a delta. 尼罗河于近河口处分岔, 形成一个三角洲. He ~s his time between London and Cairo. 他把时间花在伦敦、开罗. How shall we ~ the work up/up the work? 我们怎样划分这工作? 2 [VP14] ~ into; ~ by, find out how often one number is contained in another: 除: If you ~ 6 into 30 / ~ 30 by 6, the answer is 5. 以6除30, 答案为5. (With passive force): (含被动意味): 12 ~s by 3, can be ~d by 3. 12可被3除尽. 3 [VP 14] ~ into, form into smaller parts: 分成若干较小部分: The house was divided into flats. 那房屋被隔成数套房间(公寓). 4 [VP6A] cause disagreement; cause to disagree: 使不和; 使意见不合: Please don't let such a small matter ~ us. 请不要让这小事使我们失和. Opinions are ~d on the question, There are opposed opinions. 对于这问题, 意见不一致. 5 [VP2A, 6A] (in Parliament, at debates, etc) part in order to vote; cause to part for this purpose: (在议会, 辩论时等)分组以做正反之表决; 使分组以做正反之表决: After a long debate, the House ~d, voted on the question. 经长时间辩论后, 议院就该问题付诸表决. The Opposition does not propose to ~ the House on this question, does not insist upon the taking of a vote. 反对党不主张议院表决这一问题.

di·vide[2] /dɪˈvaɪd; dəˈvaɪd/ n sth that divides, esp a watershed (a line of high land that separates two

different river systems). 使分开之物; (尤指)分水界(将两条河分开的高地); 分水岭; 分水线.

divi·dend /ˈdɪvɪdend; ˈdɪvə,dend/ n 1 [U] number to be divided by another. (数学)被除数. ⇨ **divisor** 2 (comm) (usu periodical) payment of a share of profit, to shareholders in a business company, or of assets to creditors (eg of an insolvent company), or to a policy holder in a mutual insurance company: (商)(通常为定期的)股息; 红利; 破产债权人之偿金: to pay a ~ of 10 per cent. 付一成股息. '~-**warrant**, order on a bank to pay a ~. 股息支付券; 股息单.

di·vid·ers /dɪˈvaɪdəz; dəˈvaɪdɚz/ n pl (pair of) ~, pair of measuring compasses, used for dividing lines or angles, measuring or marking distances, etc. 两脚规; 分线规.

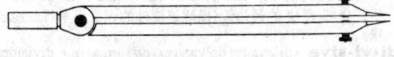

dividers

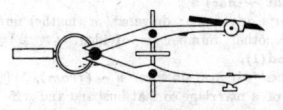

a compass

div·i·na·tion /ˌdɪvɪˈneɪʃn; ˌdɪvəˈneʃən/ n [U] divining, ⇨ **divine**[3], discovery of the unknown or the future by supernatural means; [C] clever guess or forecast. 占卜; (借超自然的方法)发现或预知; 巧妙的猜测或预测.

di·vine[1] /dɪˈvaɪn; dəˈvaɪn/ adj 1 of, from, or like God or a god: 神的; 神发出的; 如神的: King Charles I claimed to rule by ~ right, right given to him by God. 查理王一世认为他的王权是神授的. **D~ Service**, the public worship of God. 对于上帝之礼拜. 2 (colloq) excellent; very beautiful: (口)极好的; 很美的: ~ weather; 极好的天气; a ~ hat. 一顶漂亮的帽子. She looks ~ in that new dress. 她穿起那件新衣服美极了. ~**·ly** adv

di·vine[2] /dɪˈvaɪn; dəˈvaɪn/ n person (usu a priest) learned in theology. 神学家; 神学者(通常为牧师).

di·vine[3] /dɪˈvaɪn; dəˈvaɪn/ vt, vi [VP6A, 10, 2A] discover or learn (sth) about future events, hidden things, etc by means not based on reason: (借非根据理智的方法)预测; 占卜: to ~ sb's intentions; 预测某人的意向; to ~ what the future has in store. 预卜未来.

di·viner /dɪˈvaɪnə(r); dəˈvaɪnɚ/ n person who divines, esp one who claims to have the power of learning the presence of subterranean water, metal, etc by using a Y-shaped stick or rod (called 称作 a di'vining-rod). 预测者; (尤指)用一丫形杖探测水源, 金属等者. ⇨ **dowsing**.

di·vin·ity /dɪˈvɪnətɪ; dəˈvɪnətɪ/ n 1 [U] the quality of being divine, ⇨ **divine**[1]: 神性: the ~ of Christ; 基督之神性; [C] (pl -**ties**) divine being. 神. 2 [U] the study of theology: 神学: the ~ school at Oxford; 牛津大学神学院; a doctor of ~ (abbr 略作 **DD**). 神学博士.

di·vis·ible /dɪˈvɪzəbl; dəˈvɪzəbl/ adj (maths) that can be divided without remainder: (数学)可除尽的: 8 is ~ by 2. 8可被2除尽.

di·vi·sion /dɪˈvɪʒn; dəˈvɪʒən/ n 1 [U] dividing or being divided: 分开; 划分; 除; 除法: the ~ of time into months, weeks and days; 时间之划分为月, 周, 日; a simple problem in ~ (eg 50÷5); 简单的除法(例如50÷5); the ~ of labour, sharing work, giving different kinds of work to different people, according to their capabilities. 分工(技能力将各种工作分给不同的人). 2 [C] the effect of dividing; one of the parts into which sth is divided:

分开的结果; 成分的一部分: *the export ~ of a business company.* 一商业公司的出口部门。*Is that a fair ~ of the money?* 那样分款公平吗? **3** [C] line that divides: 分界线: *A hedge forms the ~ between his land and mine.* 一道树篱形成他的土地和我的土地之间的分界线。*The ~s between the various classes of society are not so sharply marked as they used to be.* 现在社会各阶级的区分不如过去那样显明了。**4** [C, U] disagreement; separation in thought, feeling, etc: 不和; 思想, 情感等分裂: *a nation in ~.* 分裂中的国家。**5** [C] (army) unit of two or more brigades. (陆军)师。**6** [C] (Parliament, etc) separation into two groups for the counting of votes: (议会等)(为便于计算正反票数而)分为两组表决: *The Bill was read for the second time without a ~.* 这议案无须分组即进入二读。*'~ bell,* bell rung to warn members (who are outside the House) that there is to be a ~. 分组表决的通知铃(提醒议院外的议员将举行分组表决)。

di·vi·sive /dɪ'vaɪsɪv; də'vaɪsɪv/ *adj* creating divisions or differences between people: 造成分裂的; 造成不和的: *~ actions/ideas/policies.* 造成分裂的行为(意见, 政策)。
~·ly *adv* **~·ness** *n*

div·isor /dɪ'vaɪzə(r); də'vaɪzə/ *n* (maths) number by which another number is divided. (数学)除数。⇨ **dividend(1).**

di·vorce¹ /dɪ'vɔːs; də'vɔrs/ *n* ~ *(from),* **1** [U] legal ending of a marriage so that husband and wife are free to marry again; [C] instance of this: 离婚; 离婚的实例例: *to sue for a ~;* 请求离婚; *to take/start ~ proceedings;* 提出离婚诉讼; *to obtain a ~ (from...).* 获准(与…)离婚。**2** [C] ending of a connection or relationship: 断绝关系; 分裂: *the ~ between religion and science,* as when science claims or seems to show that religious beliefs have no foundation. 宗教与科学间的分裂(如科学主张或似乎表示宗教信仰缺乏根据的时候)。

di·vorce² /dɪ'vɔːs; də'vɔrs/ *vt* [VP6A, 14] ~ *(from),* **1** put an end to a marriage by law: 使离婚: *Did Mr Hill ~ his wife or did she ~ him?* 是希尔先生要和他太太离婚, 还是他太太要和他离婚呢? **2** (fig) separate (things usually together): (喻)使(通常在一起的东西)分开: *the ~ between state and religion* 政教分离。**di·vor·cee** /dɪ,vɔː'siː; də,vɔr'si/ *n* ~ed person. 离了婚的人。

divot /'dɪvət; 'dɪvət/ *n* piece of turf sliced off by a golf club in making a bad stroke. (击高尔夫球时, 击出不佳, 球棒削起的)一块草土。

di·vulge /daɪ'vʌldʒ; də'vʌldʒ/ *vt* [VP6A, 14] ~ *(to),* make known (sth secret). 泄露(秘密)。**di·vul·gence** /-dʒəns; -dʒəns/ *n*

divvy /'dɪvɪ; 'dɪvɪ/ *n* (*pl* **-vies**) (colloq *abbr* of) dividend(2), eg as formerly paid by a cooperative society. (口, dividend 之简写)股息; 红利。

dixie /'dɪksɪ; 'dɪksɪ/ *n* large iron pot in which tea, stew, etc is made or carried (by soldiers, campers, etc). 士兵, 露营者等用以煮茶, 炖菜等的)大铁锅。

dizzy /'dɪzɪ; 'dɪzɪ/ *adj* (**-ier, -iest**) **1** (of a person) feeling as if everything were turning round, as if unable to balance; mentally confused: (指人)晕眩的; 昏乱的。**2** (of places, conditions) causing such a feeling: (指地点, 情况)使人晕眩的: *a ~ height.* 使人晕眩的高度。□ *vt* make dizzy. 使晕眩。**diz·zily** *adv* **diz·zi·ness** *n*

djinn /dʒɪn; dʒɪn/ *n* = **genie.**

do¹ /də; də; *strong form* duː; du/ *anom fin* (*1st and 2nd person sing pres t neg* **don't** /dəunt; dont/, *3rd person sing pres t* **does** /dʌz; dʌz/, *strong form* dʌz/, *neg* **doesn't** /'dʌznt; 'dʌznt/, *pt* **did** /dɪd; dɪd/, *neg* **didn't** /'dɪdnt; 'dɪdnt/, *pp* **done** /dʌn; dʌn/) 第一第二人称, 单数, 现在时, 否定为 don't, 第三人称, 单数, 现在时为 does, 否定为 doesn't, 过去时为 did, 否定为 didn't, 过去分词为 done。**1** used with the *main verb* to form *neg sentences* with *not:* 与 not 一起用于否定句: (**a**) for *neg sentences* with *not:* 起用于否定句: *He didn't go.* 他没有走。*Don't go yet.* 现

在不要走。(**b**) for *interr sentences:* 用于疑问句: *Does/Did he want it?* 他需要它吗? (**c**) after a front-shifted *adverbial,* etc: 用于倒装句中移置句前的副词等之后: *So hard did they work that...;* 他们如此辛苦地工作, 以致…; *Not only did they promise to help, but....* 他们不仅答应援助, 而且…。(**d**) to emphasize the positive or negative nature of a sentence (declarative, interr or imper), always stressed: 用以加重句子(陈述句,疑问句或祈使句)的语气(重重读): *That's exactly what he said.* 那正是他所说的话。*I tell you I don't like him.* 我告诉你我根本不喜欢他。*'Do stop that noise!* 不要吵! **2** used alone, to refer to a *main verb* or *verb phrase:* 单独使用, 以代替 '动词' 或 '动词短语': (**a**) in comparisons: 用于比较句中: *She plays the piano better now than she did* (ie played) *last year.* 她现在弹钢琴比去年(弹得)好。(**b**) in question phrases: 用于疑问短语中: *He lives in London, doesn't he?* 他住在伦敦, 不是吗? *So you want to be a doctor, do you?* 所以你想要做一个医生, 是吗? (**c**) in answers, comments, etc: 用于回答, 评论等中: *'They work hard'.*—'Oh, do they?' '他们工作努力。'——'哦, 真的吗?' *'Who broke the window?'—'I did!'* '谁打破了窗子?'——'是我!'

do² /duː; du/ *vt, vi* (For uses with *adverbial particles* and *preps* ⇨ **15** below.) (与副词性小品词及介词连用的用法参看下列第 15 义。) **1** (**a**) [VP2A, 6A] perform, carry out (an action); busy oneself with: 做; 做出(动作); 忙于: *What are you doing now?* 你现在做些什么? *What shall I do next?* 我下一步做什么? *I will do what I can.* 我愿尽我所能去做。*What does he do for a living,* What is his occupation? 他做何事谋生(他的职业是什么)? *I have nothing to do.* 我没有事情做。*Are you doing anything tomorrow?* 明天你有什么事情要做吗? *There's nothing to do here,* ie no means of passing the time. 此地无事可做(无法消磨时间)。*What's done cannot be undone.* 做过的事无法挽回; 覆水难收。*See what kindness will do,* Try the effect of kindness. 和气一些试试看。*do it yourself* (abbr 略作 **DIY**), (esp) do house decorating, furnishing, upkeep, etc oneself (instead of employing professional workers): 自己做(尤指家庭装饰、维护保养等工作, 自己动手, 不请专业人员): (attrib) (用作定语) *do-it-yourself kits,* materials, etc for doing work of this kind. 自己做所需用的一套工具。*easier said than done,* easier to talk about than to do. 说来容易做着难。*No sooner said than done,* done at once. 说做就做。*Well begun is half done,* A good start makes it easy to finish sth. 好的开始是成功的一半。(**b**) [VP2C] act; behave: 行动; 行为: *When in Rome do as the Romans do.* 入境从俗; 入乡问俗。*You would do well* (ie be wise) *to take your doctor's advice.* 你最好听医生的劝告。**2** [VP6A, 12B, 13B] (combined with *nouns* in many senses) (与名词相连于许多意义) (**a**) produce; make: 产生; 制作: *Patience and perseverance will do wonders,* produce remarkable results. 耐心和毅力可产生奇迹(产生非凡的结果)。*I have done* (ie made) *six copies.* 我已复制了六份。*I will do* (ie make) *a translation for you/do you a translation.* 我愿替你翻译。(**b**) work at; be busy with: 工作; 忙于: *She's doing her lessons/homework,* etc. 她正在做功课(作业等)。(**c**) perform: 实行; 履行: *Do your duty.* 尽你的责任。*He still has to do his military service.* 他仍须服兵役。*do the* + *gerund: Who'll do the cooking,* Who'll cook, who'll undertake the task of cooking? 谁来烧饭? *also* ⇨ *get sth done at* **get(2).** (**d**) study; learn: 攻读; 学习: *Are you doing science at school?* 你在学校里学科学吗? *He has been doing engineering at Sheffield University.* 他一直在过菲尔德大学攻读工程。(**e**) solve; find the answer to: 解决; 求出…的答案: *I can't do this sum/this problem in algebra.* 我不会做这个算术(代数)题。(**f**) put in order; arrange: 整理; 布置: *Please do the flowers,* arrange them in vases, etc. 请你插一下花。(**g**) make tidy: 使整洁: *Go and do your hair.* 去梳一梳你的头发。*Has* (ie brushed) *your teeth?* 你刷过牙齿没有有? (**i**) deal with; attend to: 处理; 照料: *I will do you next,*

sir, (eg at the barber's) I will attend to you next. 我下一个照看你，先生 (例如在理发店: 我下一个给您理)。*I have a lot of correspondence to do.* 我有很多信件要处理。 **(j)** use, exert: 用; 运用: *do one's best /utmost*: 尽力做; *do all one can*; 尽己所能; *do everything in one's power*. 尽力做每一件事。*He did his best to help us.* 他尽最大能力帮助我。 ⇨ also **credit**[1](7), **favour**[1](4), **good**[2], **harm, homage, honour**[1](1), **injury, justice,** *kindness* at **kind**[2], **mischief, service,** *a good /bad turn* at **turn,** **wrong. do-gooder** /ˌduːˈɡʊdə(r)/ *n* (colloq; often pej) person who is (over-)zealous to improve people, conditions, etc. (口, 常作蔑) (过份) 热心改良社会的人。 **3** (the *pp* and perfect tenses) bring to an end; finish: (用过去分词和完成时态) 结束; 完成: [VP6A] *It's done.* 做完了。*I've done it.* 我已做完。*Will he ever have /be done?* 他有没有完的时候呀? [VP3A] *Have you done* (ie finished) *with my pen yet?* 你用我的钢笔用好了没有了? [VP6 C] *I've done talking—I'm going to act.* 我话已说完——我要采取行动了。 **4** [VP3A, 6A] **do (for),** be good, satisfactory or convenient, enough (for a purpose, for sb): 可用; 可以; 方便; 适用 (与 for 连用, 后接目的或人): *These shoes won't do* (ie are not strong enough) *for mountain-climbing.* 这些鞋子爬山不适用 (不够牢)。*This log will do for a seat /do for us to sit on.* 这圆木材可以用作座位(可以供我们坐)。*This room will do me quite well,* will serve my needs. 这房间很适合我的需要。**make sth do /make do (with sth),** make sth suffice, provide for a need: 使足以敷用; 使凑合应需: *Can you make £5 do,* make this sum cover your expenses? 你能设法使五英镑足敷你的费用吗? *Can't you make that shirt do* (ie wear it) *for another day?* 那件衬衫你不能再穿一天吗? *It isn't much but I will make it do /make do with it,* manage with it. 这不够多, 但我会设法应付过去。⇨ **make**[1](14). **5** [VP2A] be fitting, suitable, tolerable: 适合; 行; 可以: *This will never do,* cannot be accepted or allowed! 这事绝不可以! *That will do!* You've said or done enough! 够了; 行了! *be done,* be considered polite; be the usual custom: 有礼貌; 合乎风俗: *It's not done to talk with your mouth full.* 嘴里满含着食物时讲话是不礼貌的。**6** [VP2A] (with passive force; colloq) happen: (有被动意味; 口)发生: *He came to ask what was doing, being done,* happening. 他来问发生了什么事。'*Can you lend me 50 p?*'—'*Nothing doing!*' (sl) 'No!' '你能借给我五十便士吗?'——(俚) '不行!' **7** [VP2C] **(a)** fare; get on well, badly, etc: 进行; 发展(好, 坏等): *Everything in the garden is doing* (= growing) *well.* 花园里的一切欣欣向荣(= growing)。*Roses do well in a clay soil.* 蔷薇在粘土里生长得很好。*He's doing well at school.* 他在学校里成绩很好。**(b)** (esp of health) make progress: (尤指健康)进步: *The patient is doing quite well.* 这病人大有起色。*How do you do?* (formula used when people are formally introduced) 你好(人们初次介绍后用的客套话)。**8** [VP2B, 15A] complete (a journey); travel (a distance); go (at a certain speed): 完成(旅行); 走过(距离); (以某种速度)行走: *How many miles a day did you do during your tour?* 你们旅行时每天走多少英里? *We've done eighty miles since lunch.* 吃过午饭后我们已走了八十英里了。*We did the journey in six hours.* 我们用了六小时内走完了这段旅程。*The car was doing sixty miles an hour.* 那汽车正以时速六十英里行驶。**9** [VP6A] play the part of: 扮演; 充当一角色: *He does Hamlet well.* 他善于演汉姆雷特这个角色。*He does the host admirably,* is an admirable host. 他是个令人赞赏的主人。*I suppose we must do the polite thing,* (colloq) be sociable, chat, etc. (口)我认为我们必须和气相处。**10** [VP6A, 15B] **do sb (out of sth),** (colloq) cheat, swindle, get the better of: (口)骗取; 欺诈: *Please don't do* '*I'm trying to do you.* 请不要以为我想欺骗你。*I'm afraid you've been done.* 我恐怕你已受骗了。*She was done out of her money.* 她被人骗走了钱。*He once tried to do me out of my job,* supplant me. 他一度想抢夺我的职位。**11** *do sb /oneself well,* (colloq) provide food, comforts etc for: (口)款

待; 招待: *They do you very well at the Bristol Hotel.* 布里斯托旅社招待得很好。*He does himself well,* provides well for his own comfort. 他的生活舒适(养尊处优)。**12** [VP6A] (colloq) visit as a sightseer; see the sights of: (口)观光; 参观: *Have you done the British Museum yet?* 你参观过大英博物馆吗? **13** [VP15A] cook in the right degree: 烹调至适当的程度: *Mind you do the beef well.* 记住将牛肉烧透。*How would you like your mutton chop done?* 你的羊排要煎到什么程度? ⇨ **underdone, overdone** at **overdo.** *do sth to a 'turn,* extremely well cooked: 烧得恰到好处: *The steak was done to a turn,* cooked perfectly. 这牛排煎得恰到好处。**14** [VP7B] (with *have*) **have to do with,** be connected with; result from: 与…有关; 由…而产生: *I know he behaves badly—It all has to do with the way he was brought up.* 我知道他的行为不端——这和他所受的教养有关。**have sth /nothing /not much /a great deal, etc to do with,** be /not be connected or concerned with; contribute to: 与…有(无, 无多少, 有很大等)关系; 促成: *He had something to do with* (= was in some way connected with, perhaps was responsible for) *my decision to teach English.* 我决定教英语,同他是有关系的(我的决定多少或直接受他的影响)。*Hard work had a great deal to do with* (= contributed greatly to) *his success.* 他的成功与工作努力大有关系。**15** [VP2C, 3A, 15B] (uses with *adverbial particles* and *preps*): (与副词性小品词及介词连用的用法): *do a'way with,* abolish, get rid of: 废除; 除去: *That department was done away with two years ago.* 那一部门于两年前被废除了。*That's a practice that should be done away with.* 那是个应该废除的习惯。*Our dog is getting so old and blind that we shall have to do away with him,* have him put to death. 我们的狗变得又老又瞎, 我们不得不将他弄死。

do well /badly by sb, treat, deal with, well /badly: 善待(对待不善): *A good employer always does well by good workmen.* 一个好的雇主总是善待他的工人。**(be) hard 'done by,** (be) treated unfairly: 受不公平对待: *He complains that he has been hard done by.* 他抱怨说他受到不公平的对待。,*Do as you would be 'done by,* (prov) Treat others as you would like to be treated. (谚)你愿意旁人怎样对待你, 你就怎样对待旁人(以己所欲施之于人)。

do sb down, (colloq) (口) **(a)** get the better of sb (by outwitting or cheating him). (以计谋或欺骗)胜过某人。**(b)** speak ill of. 说某人坏话。⇨ *run sb down* at **run**[1](26).

do for sb /sth, (colloq) (口) **(a)** act as housekeeper for, perform, esp domestic services, for: 为…料理家务; 做家事: *Old Mrs Green has been doing for me since my wife died.* 自从我的妻子死后, 格林老太太一直为我料理家务。*He won't employ a housekeeper; he prefers to do for himself.* 他不愿意雇女管家, 宁愿自己料理家务。**(b)** manage: 设法: *What /How will you do for water* (= manage to have supplies of water) *while you're crossing the desert?* 穿过沙漠时, 你将如何获得水的供应? **(c)** (usu passive) ruin; destroy; kill: (通常用被动语态)毁掉; 破坏; 杀死: *These shoes are done for,* worn out, useless. 这些鞋都破烂了。*Poor fellow, I'm afraid he's done for,* according to context, ruined in his career, likely to die, etc. 可怜的人, 我恐怕他是完了(事业毁掉、可能死去等, 视上下文而定)。*The country's done for,* ruined. 这国家毁灭了。

do sb in, (sl) kill him. (俚)杀死某人。**be done in,** exhausted: 筋疲力竭: *The horse was done in after the race.* 那匹马在竞赛后已筋疲力竭了。

do sth out, sweep or clean out; put in order: 扫除; 整理: *Tell Tom to do out the stables.* 吩咐汤姆打扫马厩。*This room needs doing out.* 这房间需要清扫。*do sb out of sth,* ⇨ **10** above. 参看上列第10义。

do sth over, redecorate: 再装饰; 重装修: *The dining-room needs doing over.* 餐厅需要重装修。*do sb over,* (sl) assault sb. (俚)袭击某人。

do sth up, (a) restore, repair, renovate: 修复；整修；刷新: *The house needs to be done up/needs doing up*, repainted, restored, etc. 这房屋需要重新修葺刷刷一番。(b) change the shape of, put new trimmings, etc on: 改变形式；重新装饰: *She has been doing up her last summer's hat*. 她一直在重新装饰她去年夏季的帽子。(c) tie or wrap up; make into a bundle or parcel: 捆好；包好；束起: *Please do up these books and post them to Mr Smith*. 请将这些书包扎好寄给史密斯先生。(d) fasten (a dress or other garment) with buttons, hooks and eyes, etc: 用扣、领钩等系牢(衣服): *She asked me to do up her dress for her at the back*. 她要我把她衣服的背后扣好。(e) (of a dress, etc) fasten with buttons, etc: (指衣服等)用钮扣等扣起: *This dress does up at the back*. 这衣服是从背后扣的。(f) (usu passive) tire out: (通常用被动语态)使极为疲倦: *He/His horse was done up (done in is more usu) after the long ride*. 经长途乘骑后, 他(他的马)疲乏不堪了 (done in 较常用)。

do with sb/sth, (a) (meanings as in the examples): (含义见下列例句): *What did you do with my umbrella*, Where did you put it, leave it, etc? 你把我的伞放到哪里去了? *What are we to do with* (= How shall we deal with) *this naughty boy?* 我们怎样处置这个顽皮的男孩? *She didn't know what to do with herself*, how to occupy her time. 她不知道做些什么才好。*Tell me what you did with yourselves* (= how you passed the time) *on Sunday*. 告诉我你们星期天是怎样度过的。*The children didn't know what to do with themselves for joy/excitement/impatience*, were so happy, excited, etc that they could not control their feelings. 孩子们高兴(兴奋, 急躁)得无法控制自己。(b) tolerate: 忍受: *I can't do with him and his insolence*. 我无法忍受他和他的傲慢。(c) (with *can, could*) expressing a need or wish: (与 can, could 连用) 表示需要或愿望: *You look as if you could do with* (= as if you need) *a good night's sleep*. 你看来似乎需要好好睡上一夜。*That man could do with* (= would look better if he had) *a shave*. 那个人能够刮刮脸就好了。*I think we can do with* (= will need) *two extra loaves today*. 我认为今天我们需要多加两条面包。*I could do with a cup of tea*. 我需要一杯茶。

do without sb/sth, dispense with; manage without: 不需要；不用: *He can't do without the services of a secretary*. 他离要一位秘书的襄助。*We shall have to do without a holiday this summer*. 今年夏天我们不能有假日了。*The hens haven't laid any eggs; we shall have to do without*. 母鸡未生蛋, 我们只好没有鸡蛋了。

do³ /duː/ du / *n* (*pl* **dos** or **do's** /duːz/ duz/) **1** (sl) swindle: (俚)欺诈: *The scheme was a do from the start*. 这方案从开始便是骗局。**2** (colloq) entertainment; party: (口)款待；庆祝或娱乐性的集会: *We're going to a big do at the Fotherington's this evening*. 我们今晚要去参加佛林顿家的盛大宴会。**3** customs, rules: 风俗；规则: *Some teachers have too many do's and don'ts*. 有些教师的规矩太多。**4** *fair dos/do's*, (GB sl) (as an exclamation) fair shares; let's be fair (eg in sharing something). (英俚)(作为感叹词)公平分配；要公平(例如在分配东西时)。

do⁴ /ˈdɪtəʊ/ ˈdɪto/ (abbr of) **ditto**. = ditto 之略。

do⁵, **doh** /dəʊ/ do/ *n* (music) first and eighth of the notes in the musical octave. (音乐)音阶的第一音和第八音。

dob·bin /ˈdɒbɪn/ ˈdɑbn/ *n* (pet name for a) farm horse. (呢称)农场用的马。

doc·ile /ˈdəʊsaɪl/ US: /ˈdɒsl/ ˈdɑsl/ *adj* easily trained or controlled: 易训练或管制的; 温顺的: *a ~ child/horse*. 温顺的小孩(马)。 **do·cil·ity** /dəʊˈsɪlɪtɪ/ do'sɪlətɪ/ *n* [U] the quality of being ~. 驯良；温顺。

dock¹ /dɒk/ dɑk/ *n* **1** place in a harbour, river, etc with gates through which water may be let in and out, where ships are (un)loaded or repaired: 船坞(港口、河流等处供船只装卸货物或修理船只的地方, 有门可将水放入和排出): *to go into/enter/leave ~*; 入(进, 离)船坞;

to be in ~. 在船坞中。**'dry/'graving ~**, one from which water may be pumped out. 干船坞(坞中水可排除者)。**'floating ~**, floating structure that may be used as a dry. ~ 浮坞(一种漂浮的构造物, 可做干船坞使用)。**'wet ~**, one in which the water may be kept at high-tide level. 船渠; 湿坞(坞中水可保持高潮之高度者)。**'~-dues**, money paid for the use of a ~. 使用船坞的费用。**2** (*pl*) number or row of ~s with the wharves, sheds, offices, etc round them. (复)(连带码头, 棚库, 办公室等的)一排船坞。**'~-yard**, enclosure with ~s and facilities for building and repairing ships: 造船厂；修船所: *the naval ~yard at Chatham*. 查塔姆的海军造船厂。**3** (US) wharf; ship's berth. (美)码头；碇泊处。**~·er** *n* ~yard labourer. 船坞工人。

dock² /dɒk/ dɑk/ *vi*, *vt* **1** [VP2A] (of a ship) come or go into a dock. (船)入坞。**2** [VP6A] bring, take, (a ship) into a dock. 使(船)入坞。**3** [VP6A] couple (two or more spacecraft) in space; [VP2A] perform this manoeuvre. 在太空中对接(两个或多个太空船)；做此种演习。

dock³ /dɒk/ dɑk/ *n* enclosure in a criminal court for the prisoner: 法庭上的犯人席; 被告席: *to be in the ~*. 在被告席; 为被告。

dock⁴ /dɒk/ dɑk/ *vt* [VP6A, 14] (~ *off*), **1** cut short (an animal's tail). 剪短(动物的尾巴)。**2** make wages, allowances, supplies, less: 减少(工资, 津贴, 供应物): *to ~ a workman's wages*; 减少一工人的工资; *to have one's salary ~ed*; 薪金被减少; *to ~ the soldiers off part of their rations*. 减少士兵一部分口粮。

dock⁵ /dɒk/ dɑk/ *n* common weed with large leaves and small green flowers. 酸模; 羊蹄(生有大叶和小绿花的一种普通野草)。

docket /ˈdɒkɪt/ ˈdɑkɪt/ *n* **1** summary of the contents of a letter, document, etc. 信件, 文件等的摘要。**2** (comm) list of goods delivered, jobs done, etc; label on a package listing the contents, or giving information about use, method of assembly, etc. (商)送货单; 工作程序表; 载明内容, 用途, 装配方法等的标签。□ *vt* [VP6A] enter in or write on a ~; label. 摘记; 加标签。

doc·tor /ˈdɒktə(r)/ ˈdɑktə/ *n* **1** person who has been trained in medical science. 医生。 ⇨ **physician, surgeon**. **2** person who has received the highest university degree: 博士: *D~ of Philosophy*. 哲学博士。□ *vt* [VP6A] **1** (colloq) give medical treatment to: (口)医治: *a ~ cold/a child*; 医治伤风(一小孩); *a ~ed tomcat*, one that has been neutered, ⇨ **neuter**(*v*). 阉割过的雄猫。**2** make (esp food, drink) inferior by adding sth; add drugs to. 掺杂(尤指食物和饮料); 搀混; 加香。**3** (fig) falsify accounts, evidence. (喻)假造(帐目, 证据)。**~·ate** /ˈdɒktərət/ ˈdɑktərɪt/ *n* ~'s degree. 博士学位。

doc·tri·naire /ˌdɒktrɪˈneə(r)/ ˌdɑktrɪˈnɛr/ *n* person who wants his doctrines to be put into practice without allowing for circumstances, considering their suitability for particular cases, etc. 空论家(欲使其理论实现而不考虑环境及对于某些特殊状况的适合性等的理论家)。□ *adj* theoretical; unpractical; dogmatic: 理论的; 不合实际的; 武断的: *~ socialism*. 空论的社会主义。

doc·trinal /dɒkˈtraɪnl/ US: /ˈdɒktrɪnl/ ˈdɑktrɪnl/ *adj* of doctrines. 教义的; 主义的; 学说的。

doc·trine /ˈdɒktrɪn/ ˈdɑktrɪn/ *n* [C, U] body of teaching; beliefs and teachings of a church, political party, school of scientists, etc: 教旨; 教义; 学说: *a matter of ~*; 教旨问题; *the ~ that the Pope is infallible*. 教皇永不会错的说法。

docu·ment /ˈdɒkjʊmənt/ ˈdɑkjəmənt/ *n* sth written or printed, to be used as a record or in evidence (eg birth, marriage and death certificates): 文件; 公文; 证件(例如出生, 结婚, 死亡证明书): *~ of title*, providing evidence of rights, ownership, etc; 契据; 房地契; *a human ~*, number of facts or incidents that illustrate

human nature. 人性记录(说明人性的事实或事件)。□ / 'dɒkjument; ˌdɑkjəˌmɛnt/ vt [VP6A] prove by, supply with, ~s: 用文件证明; 供以公文或证件: to be well ~ed. 有许多文件证明。**docu·men·ta·tion** /ˌdɒkjumen-'teɪʃn; ˌdɑkjəmen-'teʃən/ n [U].

docu·men·tary / ˌdɒkju'mentrɪ; ˌdɑkjə'mɛntərɪ/ adj consisting of documents: 有文件的; 有证件的: ~ proof/evidence. 文书证据(证明文件)。~ ('film), cinema or TV film showing some aspect of human or social activity (eg the work of the post-office, the lives of fishermen). 记录影片(说明人类或社会活动的电影或电视影片,例如说明邮政工作,渔民生活等)。

dod·der /'dɒdə(r); 'dɑdɚ/ vi [VP2A, C] (colloq) walk, move, in a shaky way, as from weakness or old age: (口)(因体弱或年迈)蹒跚; 步履不稳; 震颤: to ~ along. 蹒跚而行。~er n person who ~s. 蹒跚而行者;因体弱或年迈而震颤者。~·ing, ~·y adj trembling; weak and uncertain in movement. 震颤的; 行动不稳的。

dodge¹ /dɒdʒ; dɑdʒ/ n 1 quick movement to evade sth. 闪避; 躲闪。2 (colloq) trick; piece of deception: (口)诡计; 蒙骗: He's up to all the ~s, knows them all. 他诡计多端。3 (colloq) plan; method; ingenious way of doing sth. (口)计划;方法;巧妙的方法。

dodge² /dɒdʒ; dɑdʒ/ vt, vi [VP2A, 3A, 6A] 1 move quickly to one side, change position or direction, in order to escape or avoid sth: 闪避; 躲闪: He ~d cleverly when I threw my shoe at him. 我将我的鞋子掷向他时, 他机敏地躲开了。I ~d behind a tree so that he should not see me. 我躲在树后使他看不见我。You need to be quick in order to ~ the traffic in London nowadays. 要躲避今日伦敦的车辆, 你需要机敏。2 get round (difficulties), avoid (duties, etc) by cunning or trickery: 以巧计或诡计规避(困难), 逃避(责任等): to ~ military service. 逃避兵役。**dodger** n person who ~s, esp an artful or cunning person. 狡猾的逃避者。

dod·gem / 'dɒdʒəm; 'dɑdʒəm/ n (colloq) (at fun fairs, etc) small car, electrically propelled, (to be) driven on a special platform where there are many others which have to be avoided or dodged. (口)(游乐园等中)电动小汽车(在一特设的平台上行驶, 而且必须闪避台上许多其他车辆)。

dodgy /'dɒdʒɪ; 'dɑdʒɪ/ adj (colloq) (口) 1 artful. 狡猾的; 诡计多端的。2 involving risk or loss. 冒险性或有

损失的。

dodo /'dəudəu; 'dodo/ n (pl ~, es~s /-dəuz/ -doz/) extinct, large, flightless bird of Mauritius. 渡渡鸟(产于毛里求斯岛的一种巨鸟, 已绝种)。

doe /dəu; do/ n female fallow-deer, rabbit or hare. 母鹿;雌兔。'~ skin n skin of a ~; [U] soft leather made from this skin. 母鹿皮;母鹿皮革。

doer / 'du:ə(r); 'duɚ / n person who does things (contrasted with persons who merely talk, etc): 实行者; 做事者(以别于空谈者等): He's a ~, not a talker. 他是个实行者, 不是个空谈者。(Also in compounds, as evil-doer). (亦用于复合词中, 如 evil-doer)。

does /dʌz; dʌz/, **doesn't** /'dʌznt; 'dʌznt/ ⇨ do¹.

doff /dɒf US: dɔːf; daf/ vt [VP6A] (old use) take off one's hat, coat, etc. (旧用法)脱(衣帽等)。

dog¹ / dɒg US: dɔːg; dɔg / n 1 common domestic animal, a friend of man, of which there are many breeds; male of this animal and of the wolf and the fox: 犬; 狗; 雄狗; 雄狼; 雄狐。⇨ **bitch**. 2 (phrases): (短语): *a case of dog eat dog,* situation, eg in business, where ruthless methods are used. 互相残害(例如商业上之使用无情手段)。*die like a dog; die a 'dog's death,* die in shame or misery. 潦倒而死。*a dog in the manger,* person who prevents others from enjoying sth that is useless to himself. 狗占马槽; 占着茅坑不拉屎的人。*dressed like a dog's dinner,* (colloq) in the height of fashion. (口)穿着极讲究。*give/throw sth to the dogs,* throw it away as worthless, or as a sacrifice to save oneself. 丢弃某物; 牺牲某物以自保。*give a dog a bad name (and hang him),* (prov) give a person a bad reputation, slander him, and the bad reputation will remain. (谚)一旦加给某人一个坏名, 他就永远洗不干净。*go to the dogs,* be ruined. 堕落; 败坏。*help a lame dog over a stile,* help a person in trouble. 助人于危难, *lead a 'dog's life,* be troubled all the time. 过困苦的生活。*lead sb a 'dog's life,* give him no peace; worry him all the time. 使不安宁; 使某人经常苦恼。*let sleeping dogs lie,* (prov) let well alone; not look for trouble. (谚)勿惹睡狗; 勿惹事生非。*look like a dog's breakfast/dinner,* (colloq) very untidy; messy. (口)凌乱的; 乱七八糟的。*love me, love my dog,* (prov) if you want me as a friend, you must accept my friends as yours. (谚)爱屋及乌。*not stand (even) a 'dog's*

dogs

dogs

chance, have no chance at all of beating a stronger enemy, surviving a disaster, etc. 毫无希望(击败强敌, 度过灾难等). **be top dog,** be in a position where one rules. 居于高位. **be (the) 'underdog,** be in a position where one must always submit. 处于永远听命他人的地位. **3** (colloq) (口) **the dogs,** greyhound race-meetings. 赛狗; 猎犬比赛. **4** (old use; of a man) worthless, wicked or surly person. (旧用法, 指人)卑鄙的小人; 乖戾的人. **5** (with *adj,* colloq) person: (与形容词连用, 口)人; 家伙:*He's a dirty/sly/lucky/gay dog.* 他是个肮脏(狡诈, 幸运, 快乐)的人. **6** (kinds of) mechanical device for gripping, etc. (各种)抓、扣等机械装置; 铁钩. **7** (*pl,* also 亦作 **'fire-dogs**) metal supports for logs in a fireplace. (复)炉中铁架; 薪架. **8** (compounds) (复合词) **'dog-biscuit,** hard, thick biscuit for feeding dogs. 喂狗饼干(硬而厚者). **'dog-cart,** high, two-wheeled cart, pulled by a horse, with two seats back to back. (车身很高, 有两个背对背座位的)二轮单马车. **'dog-collar,** (colloq) clerical collar. (口) (神父所戴的)硬白领. **'dog-days,** period of very hot weather (July and August). 酷热的暑天(七、八月); 三伏天. **'dog-eared,** (of a book) having the corners of the leaves turned down with use. (指书)书页折角的. **'dog-fish,** small kind of shark. 角鲛(一种小鲨). ⇨ the illus at **sea.** 参看 sea 之插图. **'dog-house,** (US) kennel. (美)狗舍. *in the doghouse,* (colloq) in disgrace or disfavour. (口)失体面; 失宠. **'dog paddle,** simple swimming stroke in which the arms and legs are moved in short, quick splashing movements. 狗扒式游泳(手臂和双腿作短暂急促溅水动作的一种游泳). **'dogs-body,** drudge. 服贱役者; 做苦工的人. **,dog-'tired,** tired out, exhausted. 极度疲乏. **'dog-tooth,** small pyramid-shaped ornament (in stonework, Norman and Early English architecture). (诺曼第和早期英国建筑之石工上的)角锥形装饰. **'dog's-tooth,** checked pattern (in cloth for men's suits, overcoats, etc). (男子西服, 大衣等衣料上的)方格花样. **'dog-trot,** gentle, easy trot. (徐缓从容的)小跑. **'dog-watch,** (on ships) one of the two-hour watches (4 to 6pm, 6 to 8pm). (船上)夜更(下午四至六时为上春更, 六至八时为下春更). **'dog-wood,** tree with large white or pinkish flowers in spring. 山茱萸; 水木(一种树, 春天开大而白或略带粉红色的花). **'dog-like** *adj* like or as of a dog, 如狗的, esp 尤用于 *doglike devotion,* the kind of devotion given by a dog to its master. 如狗一般的忠实. **doggy, doggie** /'dɒgɪ *US:* 'dɔːgɪ/ *n* (child's word for a) dog. (儿语)狗; 狗狗.

dog² /dɒg *US:* dɔːg/ *vt* (-gg-) [VP6A] keep close behind, in the footsteps of: 追随; 尾随:*dog a suspected thief;* 尾随一有嫌疑的小偷; (fig) (喻) *dogged by misfortune.* 被灾祸紧紧随着的.

doge /dəʊdʒ; dodʒ/ *n* elected chief magistrate in the former republics of Venice and Genoa. (昔时威尼斯和热那亚共和国之)总督.

dog·ged /'dɒgɪd *US:* 'dɔːg-; 'dɔgɪd/ *adj* obstinate; stubborn. 顽强的; 固执的. **~·ly** *adv* ~·**ness** *n*

dog·gerel /'dɒgərəl; 'dɔgərəl/ *n* [U] irregular, inexpert verse. 歪诗; 打油诗.

doggo /'dɒgəʊ *US:* 'dɔːg-; 'dɔgo/ *adv* **lie ~,** (sl) lie without making a movement or sound. (俚)一动也不动或一声不响地静卧着.

dogma /'dɒgmə *US:* 'dɔːg-; 'dɔgmə/ *n* **1** [C] belief, system of beliefs, put forward by some authority (esp the Church) to be accepted as true without question. 教条; 信条. **2** [U] such beliefs collectively. 教条或信条的总称.

dog·matic /dɒg'mætɪk *US:* dɔːg-; dɔg'mætɪk/ *adj* **1** put forward as dogmas: 做为教条而提出的: ~ *theology.* 教条神学. **2** (of a person) making purely personal statements as if they were dogmas: (指人或言论)武断的. **dog·mati·cally** /-klɪ; -klɪ/ *adv*

dog·ma·tism /'dɒgmətɪzəm *US:* 'dɔːg-; 'dɔgmə,tɪzəm/ *n* [U] the quality of being dogmatic; being dogmatic: 教条主义; 武断; 独断:*His ~ aroused their opposition.* 他的武断引起了他们的反对.

dog·ma·tize /'dɒgmətaɪz *US:* 'dɔːg-; 'dɔgmə,taɪz/ *vi, vt* [VP2A] make dogmatic statements; [VP6A] express (a principle, etc) as a dogma. 作武断的主张; 武断地提出(主义等); 当做教条提出.

doh ⇨ do⁵.

doily /'dɔɪlɪ; 'dɔɪlɪ/ *n* (*pl* **-lies**) small, round piece of linen, lace, etc placed under a dish on a table or under an ornament on a shelf. (垫于盘碟或架上饰物下的)小圆布巾; 小圆垫.

do·ings /'duːɪŋz; 'duɪŋz/ *n pl* (colloq) things done or being done: (口)所做之事:*Tell me about all your ~ in London.* 告诉我你在伦敦所做的一切.

dol·drums /'dɒldrəmz; 'dɑldrəmz/ *n pl* **in the ~,** (colloq) in low spirits. (口)精神沮丧.

dole /dəʊl; dol/ *vt* [VP15B] **~ out,** distribute food, money, etc in small amounts. 布施; 少量分配(食物, 金钱等). □ *n* **1** [C] sth ~d out. 布施之物; 分与物. **2** [U] **the ~,** (colloq term for) weekly payment made under various Insurance Acts in GB (from contributions made by workers, employers and the State) to an unemployed worker. (口)(依据英国各种保险法案, 由工人、雇主及政府每周所给与失业人员的)失业救济金. *be/go on the ~,* receive/begin to receive such payments. 因失业而(开始)接受救济金.

dole·ful /'dəʊlfl; 'dolfəl/ *adj* mournful; dismal. 悲哀的; 忧愁的. **~·ly** /-fəlɪ; -fəlɪ/ *adv*

doll¹ /dɒl; dɑl/ *n* **1** model of a baby or person, usu for a child to play with. 玩偶; 洋娃娃. **2** (sl) (pretty but silly) girl or woman. (俚)(美丽而无头脑的)女人.

doll² /dɒl; dɑl/ *vt, vi* [VP15B, 2C] **~ up,** (colloq) dress (oneself) up smartly: (口)漂亮地打扮(自己):*She was all ~ed up for the party.* 她打扮得漂漂亮亮的去参加那宴会.

dol·lar /'dɒlə(r); 'dɑlɚ/ *n* unit of money (symbol $) in the US, Canada, Australia and other countries. 圆; 元(美国, 加拿大, 澳大利亚等国家的货币单位, 符号为$).

dol·lop /'dɒləp; 'dɑləp/ *n* (colloq) shapeless quantity of food, etc: (口)一团(食物等); 一块食物:*a ~ of cold rice pudding.* 一团冷的米布丁.

dolly /'dɒlɪ; 'dɑlɪ/ *n* (*pl* **-lies**) **1** (child's word for a) doll. (儿语)洋娃娃; 玩偶. **2** small wheeled frame or platform for moving heavy objects; mobile platform for a heavy camera. 运送重物的小辘车; 安放重摄影机的轮台. **3** (sl) attractive, fashionably dressed but silly girl or young woman. (俚)漂亮而打扮入时的傻女郎.

dol·men /'dɒlmen; 'dɑlmən/ *n* = **cromlech.**

dol·our (US = **-lor**) /'dɒlə(r); 'dolɚ/ *n* (poet) grief; sorrow. (诗)悲伤; 忧愁. **~·ous** /-rəs; -rəs/ *adj* sorrowful; distressed; distressing. 悲哀的; 忧愁的; 令人烦恼的.

dol·phin /'dɒlfɪn; 'dɑlfɪn/ *n* sea animal like a porpoise. 海豚. ⇨ the illus at **sea.** 参看 sea 之插图.

dolt /dəʊlt; dolt/ *n* stupid fellow; blockhead. 愚蠢的人; 傻瓜. **~·ish** *adj* stupid. 愚蠢的.

do·main /dəʊ'meɪn; do'men/ *n* lands under the rule of a government, ruler, etc; (fig) field or province of thought, knowledge, activity: 领土; 版图; 领域; 领地; (喻)(思想, 知识, 活动的)范围:*in the ~ of science.* 在科学范围中.

dome /dəʊm; dom/ *n* rounded roof with a circular base; sth shaped like a ~: 圆屋顶; 近圆屋顶之物:*the rounded ~* (= summit) *of a hill.* 圆形山顶. **domed** *adj* rounded; 圆的; 圆顶的:*a man with a ~d forehead.* 额头隆起的人.

Domes·day Book /'duːmzdeɪ bʊk; 'dumz,de bʊk/ *n* record of the inquiry, made by King William I in 1086, into the ownership of all the lands in England

domes

英格兰土地记录书(威廉一世于一〇八六年勘查英格兰土地所有权后编成者)。

do·mes·tic /də'mɛstɪk; də'mɛstɪk/ *adj* **1** of the home, family, household: 家庭的; 家务的: *He has had a good many ~ troubles.* 他有许多家庭纠纷。*What a charming ~ scene!* eg of members of a family happy together at home. 这是多么可爱的一个家庭情景啊!(例如一家人欢聚在家里)。*She's a very ~ sort of woman*, prefers home life to social activities outside the home. 她是个十分喜欢家庭生活的女子。**2** not foreign; native; of one's own country: 非外国的; 国内的; 本国的: *The government could get neither foreign nor ~ loans*, could not borrow money either abroad or at home. 该政府既无法借得外债,亦无法借到内债。*This newspaper provides more foreign news than ~ news.* 这家报纸刊登的国外消息多于国内消息。**3** (of animals, etc) kept by, living with, man: (指动物等)由人饲养的; 与人生活在一起的: *Horses, cows and sheep are ~ animals.* 马、牛和羊是家畜。⇨ **wild. domes·ti·cally** /-klɪ; -klɪ/ *adv*

do·mes·ti·cate /də'mɛstɪkeɪt; də'mɛstə,ket/ *vt* [VP6A] **1** (chiefly in *pp*) make fond of, interested in, household work and duties: (主要用过去分词)使喜欢家庭生活; 使喜欢家务: *She's not at all ~d*, is not fond of, skilled in, cooking, house-keeping, etc. 她丝毫不喜(不谙)家务。**2** tame (animals). 驯服(动物)。**do·mes·ti·ca·tion** /də,mɛstɪ'keɪʃn; də,mɛstə'keʃən/ *n*

do·mes·tic·ity /,dɒmɛs'tɪsətɪ; ,domɛs'tɪsətɪ/ *n* [U] home or family life. 家庭生活。

domi·cile /'dɒmɪsaɪl; 'dɑməsl/ *n* (formal) dwelling-place; (legal) place where a person lives permanently. (正式用语)住处; (法律)永久居住地。

dom·i·cili·ary /,dɒmɪ'sɪlɪərɪ US: -lɪɛrɪ; ,dɑmə'sɪl,ɛrɪ/ *adj* (formal) of or to a dwelling-place: (正式用语)住处的; 至住处的: *a ~ visit*, one made to a house, etc (eg by officials to search or inspect it, or by a doctor to a patient). 住宅访查(例如官方的搜查或视察,或是医生之探访病人)。

domi·nant /'dɒmɪnənt; 'dɑmənənt/ *adj* **1** having control or authority; dominating; most important or influential: 有统治权的; 有支配力的; 最有势力的; 占优势的: *the ~ partner in a business*. 商店中最有势力的股东。**2** (of heights) overlooking others: (指高处)高于其他的: *a ~ cliff.* 耸立的绝壁。□ *n* (music) fifth note of a scale. (音乐)全阶的第五音。**~·ly** *adv* **domi·nance** /-nəns; -nəns/ *n* being ~. 统治; 支配; 优势。

domi·nate /'dɒmɪneɪt; 'dɑmə,net/ *vt, vi* [VP6A, 2A, 3A] ~ **(over)**, **1** have control, authority or influence: 统治; 支配; 控制: *A great man can ~ (over) others by force of character.* 伟人能以人格的力量支配他人。*The strong usually ~ (over) the weak.* 强者通常统治弱者。**2** (of a place, esp a height) overlook: (地点,尤指高处)俯临: *The whole valley is ~d by this mountain.* 这座山俯临着整个的山谷。**domi·na·tion** /,dɒmɪ'neɪʃn; ,dɑmə'neʃən/ *n* [U] dominating or being ~d. 统治; 支配; 控制; 俯临。

domi·neer /,dɒmɪ'nɪə(r); ,dɑmə'nɪr/ *vi* [VP2A, 3A] ~ **(over)**, act, speak, in a dominating manner; behave like a tyrant; be overbearing: 压制; 跋扈; 擅权; 专横: *Big boys sometimes ~ over their small sisters.* 大的男孩们有时压制他们的小妹妹。**~·ing** *adj*: *He's a very ~ing sort of fellow*, likes to ~ over others. 他是个非常跋扈的人。**~·ing·ly** *adv*

Dom·ini·can /də'mɪnɪkən; də'mɪnɪkən/ *n, adj* (friar or nun) of the religious order founded in 1212 by St Dominic. (一二一二年圣多明尼克所创之)圣多明尼克

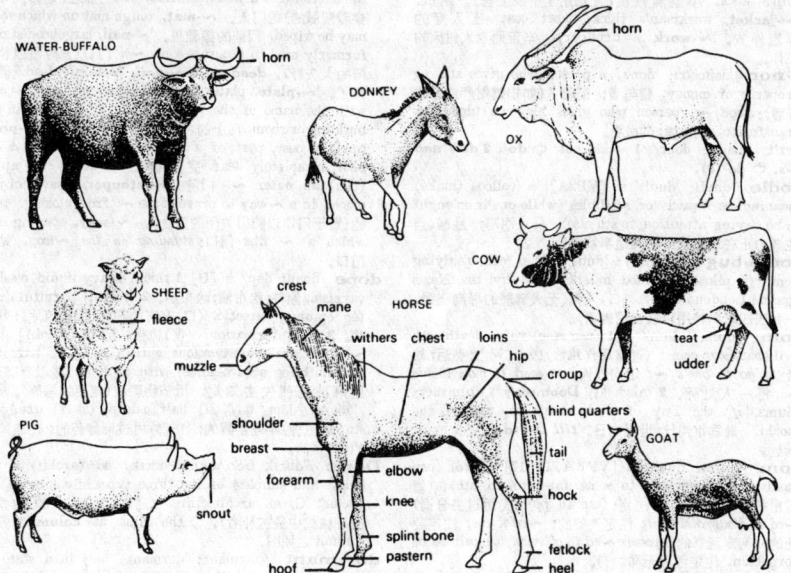

domestic animals

教派的;圣多明尼克教派僧侣或修女。

domi·nie /'dɒmɪnɪ; 'dɑmənɪ/ n (Scot) schoolteacher. (苏)教师。

do·min·ion /də'mɪnjən; də'mɪnjən/ n 1 [U] ~ (over), authority to rule; control (over). 统治权;主权;支配。2 [C] territory of a sovereign government. 领土;版图。3 [C] (old use) one of the self-governing territories of the British Commonwealth of Nations. (旧用法)英联邦的自治领。

dom·ino /'dɒmɪnəʊ; 'dɑmə,no/ n (pl ~es or ~s /-nəʊz; -noz/) 1 small, flat, oblong piece of wood or bone, marked with spots. 骨牌(小而扁的长方形木块或骨块,刻有黑点)。2 (pl with sing v) table game played with 28 of these. (复,与单数动词连用)四二十八枚骨牌玩的)骨牌戏。3 loose cloak with a mask for the upper part of the face, worn at parties, fancy-dress balls, etc. (宴会、化装舞会等所穿的)带有面罩可将面孔上部遮住的一种宽松外衣。

don[1] /dɒn; dɑn/ n 1 (GB) teaching member of a university staff. (英)大学教师。2 Spanish gentleman; Spanish title (used before a man's name): 西班牙绅士;先生(西班牙人的尊称,冠于男子的名之前): Don Juan. 胡安先生;唐璜。**don·nish** /'dɒnɪʃ; 'dɑnɪʃ/ adj of or like a don(1). 大学教师的;似大学教师的。

don[2] /dɒn; dɑn/ vt (-nn-) [VP6A] (old use) put on clothing, etc. (旧用法)穿上(衣服等)。⇨ **doff**.

do·nate /dəʊ'neɪt US: 'dəʊneɪt; 'donet/ vt [VP6A, 14] ~ (to), give (eg money, to a charity, etc); contribute. 捐赠(例如捐钱给慈善机关等);赠送。**do·na·tion** /dəʊ'neɪʃn; do'neʃən/ n [U] giving; [C] sth given: 捐赠;捐赠之物: donations to the Red Cross/the refugee fund. 对红十字会(救济难民基金)的捐款。

done /dʌn; dʌn/ ⇨ **do**[1].

don·jon /'dɒndʒən; 'dʌndʒən/ n large, strongly fortified main tower of a castle. (城堡之)主楼;主塔。

don·key /'dɒŋkɪ; 'dɑŋkɪ/ n (pl ~s /-kɪz; -kɪz/) (the common and usu word for an) ass. 驴(较ass常用)。⇨ the illus at **domestic**. 参看 domestic 之插图。'~ engine, small auxiliary steam-engine, esp one on a ship's deck. 小型蒸汽机(尤指用于甲板上者);副机。'~jacket, workman's thick, short coat. 工人穿的厚短外衣。'~work n drudgery. 辛苦而令人讨厌的工作。

do·nor /'dəʊnə(r)'; 'donə/ n person who gives sth, eg property or money: 赠与者;捐赠者(如捐赠财产或金钱等者): blood ~, person who gives his own blood for transfusion. 捐血者;供血者。

don't /dəʊnt; dont/ 1 = do not; ⇨ **do**[1]. 2 do's and ~s, ⇨ **do**[2](3).

doodle /'duːdl; 'dudl/ vi [VP2A], n (colloq) (make) meaningless scrawls or scribbles (while one is or ought to be paying attention to sth else). (口)胡写; 乱画(当注意力正在或应该集中于其他事物时)。

doodle·bug /'duːdlbʌg; 'dudl,bʌg/ n (colloq) flying bomb (a pilotless guided missile) used by the Nazis against London in 1944. (口)飞弹(无人驾驶的导向飞弹,一九四四年纳粹用以袭击伦敦者)。

doom[1] /duːm; dum/ n 1 (usu sing) ruin; death; sth evil that is to come: 通常用作单数)毁灭;死亡;恶运;劫数: to go to one's ~, 走向毁灭; to send a man to his ~. 将一人处死。2 (also 亦作 **Doomsday** /'duːmzdeɪ; 'dumz,de/) the Day of Judgement; the end of the world. 最后审判日;世界末日。till D~sday, for ever. 永远。

doom[2] /duːm; dum/ vt [VP6A, 14, 17] ~ to, (usu passive) condemn (sb to some fate/to do sth); (通常用被动态会) 判定;注定: (esp in pp) (尤用过去分词) ~ed to disappointment, 注定失望的; ~ed to die, 注定要死的; 判定死罪的; poems ~ed to oblivion, certain to be forgotten. 注定湮没无闻的诗。

door /dɔː(r); dor/ n 1 that which closes the entrance to a building, room, cupboard, safe, etc: 门;户: to open/

close/lock, etc the ~; 开(关, 锁)门; hinged/sliding/revolving ~s. 有铰链的门(拉门;旋转门)。The ~ opened/was opened and a man came out. 门开了, 一个人走了出来。back ~, at the back of the house (to the yard, garden, etc). 后门(通庭院、花园等者)。front ~, chief ~ from a house to the street or road. 前门;大门(通街道者)。next ~, (in/to) the next house: (在/到)隔壁: Who lives next ~ (to you)? 谁住在(你的)隔壁? I'm just going next ~ to see Mrs Jones. 我正要去隔壁探望琼斯太太。next ~ to, (fig) nearly, almost. (喻)几乎。two/three, etc ~s away/down/off, in the next house but one/two, etc: 过去第二(三等)家: My brother lives three ~s away. 我哥哥(弟弟)住在从这里过去第三家。from ~ to ~, (a) from the ~ of one building to the ~ of another: 沿门;从一家门口到另一家门口: It was raining heavily, but the taxi took us from ~ to ~. 雨下得很大, 但计程车把我们送到每一家的门口。(b) from house to house: 逐家; 挨户: He went from ~ to ~ delivering the milk/selling encyclopaedias. 他挨户送牛奶(推销百科全书)。Hence, 由此产生, ~-to-~ adj = ~-to-~ salesman. 挨户推销的售货员。out of ~s, in the open air: It's cold out of ~s; put an overcoat on. 户外冷, 穿上一件大衣罢。within ~s, inside; in the house. 在户内; 在屋内。at death's ~, near death. 垂死。lay sth at sb's ~, say that he is responsible for it. 归咎于某人。show sb the ~, lead him out to it (esp when he is unwelcome). 将某人逐出门外。2 (fig) means of obtaining or approaching sth: (喻)门路;途径: a ~ to success; 成功之道; to close the ~ against an agreement upon disarmament, make it impossible. 拒作裁军的协定; 使裁军协议无实现之可能。3 (compounds) (复合词) '~-bell, bell inside a building, operated by a button, etc outside. 门铃。'~-case/-frame, framework into which a ~ fits. 门框。'~-handle, one which releases the latch to open a ~. 门的把手。'~-keeper, person on duty or on guard at a ~ or other entrance. 门房;守门人。'~-knob, round knob turned to release the lock on a ~. 门的球形把手。'~-knocker, knocker. 门环。'~-man /-mən/ -men/ (pl -men) uniformed attendant at the entrance to a hotel, cinema, etc. (旅社,电影院等之)穿着制服的司门人。'~-mat, rough mat on which shoes may be wiped. 门前的擦鞋垫。'~-nail, largeheaded nail formerly used to decorate some ~. 门钉(昔时用以装饰门的大头钉)。dead as a ~-nail, certainly dead. 确实死了。'~-plate, plate (usu brass) fastened to a ~ and with the name of the person living or working in the building or room. 门上的名牌(通常是铜做的)。'~-post, upright post, part of a frame. 门柱。deaf as a ~-post, completely deaf. 完全聋的。'~-step, step up to (usu) an outer ~. 门阶。'~-stopper, heavy object placed in a ~way to prevent the ~ from closing. 制门物(置于门口以防门关闭的重物)。'~-way, opening into which a ~ fits: standing in the ~way. 站在门口。

dope /dəʊp; dop/ n [U] 1 thick, heavy liquid used as varnish. 涂料; 涂布液; 涂布油。2 (colloq) harmful drug (eg opium); narcotic. (口)有害的药物(例如鸦片); 麻醉药。3 (sl) information. (俚)情报。□ vt [VP6A] give ~(2) to; make unconscious with a drug or narcotic; stimulate (eg a race-horse) with a drug. 施以麻醉药; 用麻醉药使失去知觉; 用药物刺激(竞赛的马等)。~y /'dəʊpɪ; 'dopɪ/ adj (sl) half asleep (as if) drugged; stupid. (俚)半睡半醒的;(仿佛)用过麻醉药的;迷迷糊糊的;鲁钝的。

Doric /'dɒrɪk US: 'dɔːr-; 'dorɪk/ adj (archit) (of the oldest and simplest of the three types of column(1) in ancient Greek architecture. (建筑)陶立克式的(古希腊三种柱式中最古朴者)。⇨ the illus at **column**. 参看 column 之插图。

dor·mant /'dɔːmənt; 'dɔrmənt/ adj in a state of inactivity but awaiting development or activity: 潜伏的; 蛰伏的: a ~ volcano; 休火山; ~ facilities, mental

powers capable of being developed; 潜在的能力; *plants which are ~/lie ~ during the winter*, alive but not growing. 冬季停止生长的植物。

dor·mer /'dɔːmə(r); 'dɔrmɚ/ n (usu 通常作 '~-window) upright window built from a sloping roof. (屋顶斜坡上凸出的)天窗。 ⇨ the illus at **window**. 参看 window 之插图。

dor·mi·tory /'dɔːmɪtrɪ US: -tɔːrɪ; 'dɔrmə,tɔrɪ/ n (pl **-ries**) sleeping-room with several or many beds, esp in a school or institution. (有几张床或很多的)大寝室; (尤指学校或机关团体的)宿舍。

dor·mouse /'dɔːmaʊs; 'dɔr,maʊs/ n (pl **dormice** /'dɔːmaɪs; 'dɔr,maɪs/) small animal (like a mouse or squirrel) that sleeps during cold weather in winter. 睡鼠; 冬眠鼠。

dor·sal /'dɔːsl; 'dɔrsl/ adj (anat) of, on, near, the back: (解剖)背部的; 背上的; 近背部的:*the ~ fin*, eg of a shark. (鲨等的)脊鳍。 ⇨ the illus at **sea**. 参看 sea 之插图。

dory[1] /'dɔːrɪ; 'dɔrɪ/ n (pl **-ries**) ship's light, flat-bottomed rowing-boat (eg as used by cod-fishers in N America). 平底小船(如北美洲捕鳕渔人所用者)。

dory[2] /'dɔːrɪ; 'dɔrɪ/ n (also 亦作 **John 'D~**) edible seafish. 海鲂(一种可食的海鱼)。

dos·age /'dəʊsɪdʒ; 'dosɪdʒ/ n [U] giving of medicines in doses; quantity of a single dose. 下药; 剂量; 服用的药量。

dose /dəʊs; dos/ n [C] **1** amount (of a medicine/drug) to be taken at one time: 剂量; 一服; 一剂:*The bottle contains six ~s*. 这瓶内装有六次的药量。 ⇨ **salt**(4). **2** (fig, colloq) sth given or taken; (喻)给与或接受的东西:*give sb a ~ of flattery*. 向某人灌迷汤。 **3** (sl) venereal disease: (俚)性病:*give sb a ~*: 使某人感染性病。 ▷ vt [VP6A, 15B, 14] give ~(s) to: 使服药:*to ~ oneself with quinine*. 服奎宁。

doss /dɒs; das/ vi (GB sl) [VP2C] ~ **down**, go to bed. (英俚)就寝; 睡觉。 **'~-house** n cheap lodging-house. 下等旅馆; 小客栈。 **dos·ser** /-sə(r); -sɚ/ n tramp (n, 3). 飘泊者。

dos·sier /'dɒsɪeɪ US: 'dɔːs-; 'dɑsɪ,e/ n set of papers giving information about a person or event, esp a person's record. 记录文件(尤指有关个人的记录)。

dost /dʌst; dʌst/ v old form, used in *Thou* ~, You do. 古语中 do 的第二人称单数, 与 thou 连用。

dot /dɒt; dɑt/ n **1** small round mark (as over the letters i and j); decimal points: 小点(如 i 和 j 上面者); 小数点:*dots and dashes*, the marks (· — · · ·) used for morse signals. 电报符号; 摩尔斯电码。 **on the dot**, (colloq) at the precise moment. (口)准时。 **2** sth like a dot in appearance: 似小点之物:*We watched the ship until it was a mere dot on the horizon*. 我们注着那条船, 一直到它在水平线上变成了一个小点。 ▷ vt (**-tt-**) **1** mark with a dot. 加以小点。 **dot one's/the i's and cross one's/the t's**, (fig) make (sth) clear and definite. (喻)使(某事)明确。 **2** make with, cover with, dots: 用点制成; 覆以点:*dotted about*, scattered here and there; 散落在各处的; 星散的;*a field dotted with sheep*, with sheep here and there; 到处是羊的田野;*a dotted line*, eg on a document, for a signature. 虚线(例如文件上的签名处)。 **sign on the dotted line**, (fig) agree without hesitation or protest. (喻)毫不迟疑地同意。

do·tage /'dəʊtɪdʒ; 'dotɪdʒ/ n [U] weakness of mind caused by old age: 因年老而心力衰迈; 老耄; 老朽:*He is in his ~*, is growing foolish, is unable to remember things, fails to notice things, etc. 他年迈昏愦了。 **do·tard** /'dəʊtəd; 'dotɚd/ n person in his ~. 年迈昏愦之人。

dote /dəʊt; dot/ vi [VP3A] ~ **on/upon**, show much, or too much, fondness; centre one's affections (on): 溺爱; 宠爱:*She ~s on her grandson*. 她溺爱她的孙子。 *He's a doting (= very loving) husband*. 他是个很疼太太的

丈夫。

doth /dʌθ; dʌθ/ old form used for *does*. does 的古时拼法。

dottle /'dɒtl; 'dɑtl/ n small quantity of tobacco left unsmoked in a pipe. 烟斗中吸剩的少量残烟。

dotty /'dɒtɪ; 'dɑtɪ/ adj (**-ier, -iest**) (colloq) feeble-minded; idiotic; eccentric. (口)智力不足的; 愚鲁的; 古怪的。

double[1] /'dʌbl; 'dʌbl/ adj **1** twice as (much, large, etc): 加倍的(多, 大等); 两倍的:*His partner is ill and he has to do ~ work*. 他的伙伴病了, 他必须做双倍的工作。 *His income is ~ what it was five years ago*. 他的收入是五年前的两倍。 *There was a ~ knock at the door*, two knocks in quick succession. 门口有连续两次的敲门声。 *Two ~ whiskies, please*, two glasses of whisky, each with twice the usual portion. 请倒两杯原来的量加倍的威士忌酒。 **2** having two of the same things or parts: 成双的; 成对的:*a gun with a ~ barrel*: 双管枪;*a railway with a ~ track*; 双轨铁路;*~ doors*; 双扇门;*~-glazing / ~ windows* (used in cold countries); 双重窗(为气候寒冷冷国家所用);*a man with a ~ chin*, with a fold of loose flesh below the chin; 双下巴的人;*a ship/box / trunk with a ~ bottom*; 双层底的船(盒, 箱);*a sword with a ~ edge*; 双刃剑;*a ~ exposure*, (photo) two exposures on the same plate or section of film. (摄影)双重曝光。 ⇨ **single**. **3** made for two persons or things: 供二人或二物用的:*a ~ bed*; 双人床;*a ~ harness*, for two horses. 双马具。 **4** combining two things, qualities, etc: 将两种东西、性质等联合在一起的; 两种的:*a ~ advantage*; 两种利益; 一举两得;*a piece of furniture that serves a ~ purpose*, eg one that is a settee and can be opened out to make a bed; 两用家具(例如可打开做床铺用的长靠椅);*a man with a ~ character*, eg Jekyll and Hyde; 有双重性格的人(例如 Jekyll 和 Hyde); *to engage in ~ dealing*, be dishonest and deceitful. 从事欺诈。 **5** (of flowers) having more than one set or circle of petals: (指花)重瓣的:*~ daffodils*. 重瓣水仙花。

double[2] /'dʌbl; 'dʌbl/ adv **1** twice (as much): 加倍地:*Many things now cost ~ what they did a few years ago*. 许多东西现在比数年前贵了一倍。 **2** in twos; in a pair; in pairs or couples: 成双地; 成对地:*to see ~*, to see two things when there is only one; 将一物看成两物; 眼花;*to sleep ~*, two to a bed. 双宿; 二人共一床。

double[3] /'dʌbl; 'dʌbl/ n **1** twice the quantity: 加倍; 两倍:*Ten is the ~ of five*. 十为五的两倍。 **~ or quits**, the decision by chance (eg by throwing dice) whether a person shall pay twice what he owes, or nothing at all. 靠运气(如掷骰子)决定一人是否加倍清还欠债或一笔勾销。 **2** person or thing that looks exactly, or almost exactly, like another: 相貌相似的人或物;*She is the ~ of her sister*. 她和她的妹妹象极了。 **3** (pl) (tennis) game with two pairs. (复)(网球)双打。 **mixed ~s**, a man and woman against another man and woman. 男女混合双打。 **4 at the ~**, (colloq) quickly. (口)很快地; 迅速地。 **5** [C] (bridge) act of doubling. (桥牌)加倍; 赌倍。 ⇨ **double**[4](6).

double[4] /'dʌbl; 'dʌbl/ vt, vi **1** [VP6A, 2A] make or become twice as great: 使加倍; 增加一倍:*to ~ one's income*. 使收入加倍。 *Money earning good interest will ~ itself in time*. 以优利放存的款到时候会增加一倍。 **2** [VP6A, 15B] ~ (**up/over/across**), bend or fold in two: 折叠; 对折:*Let me ~ (over) the shawl and put it round you*. 让我把这披巾折起来围在你身上。 *He ~d his fists*, clenched them as if ready to fight. 他握紧了拳头(似欲打架)。 **3** [VP2A, C] ~ (**back**), turn sharply back in flight (when running to escape pursuit): (逃避追逐时)急忙转身而逃:*The fox ~d (back) on its tracks*. 这狐狸突然转身循着原路急急逃走。 **4** [VP15B, 2C] ~ **back**, turn or fold (sth) back. 折叠(某物)。 ~ **up**, (**a**) fold (sth) up: 折叠(某物):*He ~d up his legs and kicked out*,

eg when swimming. 他将腿弯起又伸开(如游泳时所作者). **(b)** be capable of folding up or rolling up: 可折叠:可卷起: *This carpet is too thick to ~ up.* 这地毯太厚, 无法折起来. **(c)** (of persons) (cause to) bend the body with pain or in helpless laughter: (指人)(使)痛或笑得弯下了身: *The stone struck him in the stomach and ~d him up.* 那石头打在他的腹部, 使他痛得弯下了身. *He ~d up with the pain of the blow.* 他因受击而痛得弯下了身. **5** [VP2C, 6A] do two jobs at the same time; (of an actor) act two parts in the same play: 一身兼两个工作; (指演员)在同一剧中扮演两角: *doubling as / doubling the parts of king and slave.* 兼演国王和奴隶. **6** (bridge) bid to cause the points, lost or won by the opponents on the hand (**13c**), to be twice as much as they would normally have been. (桥牌)加倍; 赌倍.

double⁵ /'dʌbl; 'dʌbl/ *adj, adv* (in compounds) (用于复合词中), **~-'barrelled** *adj* (of a gun) having two barrels; (fig, of a compliment, etc) ambiguous; (of a surname) compound, hyphened (as *Smith-Jones*). (指枪)双管的; (喻, 指恭维语等)暧昧的; 含糊的; (指姓氏)复合的(如 Smith-Jones). **~-'bass** *n* largest and lowest-pitched instrument in the violin family. 低音部的最大提琴; 低音提琴. ⇨ the illus at **string**. 参看 string 之插图. **~-'bedded** *adj* (of a room) with two beds or a ~ bed. (指房间)有两张床的; 有双人床的. (Cf *single-/twin-bedded*.) **~ 'bind** *n* dilemma. 进退两难之境. **~'breasted** *adj* (of a coat or waistcoat) made so as to overlap across the front of the body. (指上衣或大衣)对襟的; 双排扣的. **~-'check** *vt* check¹(1), twice in order to be certain. 检查两次. **~-'cross** *vt* [VP6A] (colloq) cheat or betray. (口)欺骗或出卖. **~** *n* act of this kind. 欺骗; 出卖. **~-'dealer** *n* person who says one thing and means another; deceiver. 口是心非之人; 骗子. **~-'dealing** *n, adj* deceit(ful) (esp in business). (尤指在商业上)诈欺(的). **~-'decker** *n* ship, tram, bus with two decks. 两层甲板的船; 双层的电车或公共汽车. ⇨ **deck¹(2)**. **~-'dutch** *n* (colloq) gibberish. (口)无意义的声音; 叽哩咕噜的谈话. **~-'dyed** *adj* (chiefly fig) having certain qualities to a very high degree: (主作喻)深重的; 彻头彻尾的: *a ~-dyed scoundrel,* deeply stained with guilt. 一个彻头彻尾的恶汉. **~-'edged** *adj* with two cutting edges; (fig, of an argument, compliment) that can be understood as being either for or against. 双刃的; (喻, 指论据或恭维)正反两可的; 双关的. **~-'entry** *n* system of book-keeping in which each transaction is entered (written) on the debit side of one account and the credit side of another. 复式簿记(每笔帐在借方与贷方均登记一次的簿记方法). **~-'faced** *adj* (= *two-faced*) insincere. 口是心非的. **~-'first** *n* a first-class honours degree in two principal subjects gained at the same time. 双重优等奖(同时获得两门主要科目的最高荣誉). **~-'jointed** *adj* having joints that allow the fingers (or arms, legs) to move or bend in unusual ways. 有可作不寻常活动或弯曲之关节的. **~-'park** *vt, vi* park a car at the side of a car already parked at the side of a street. 将车停在街边另一部车的旁边. **~-'quick** *adj, adv* very quickly: 极迅速的(地): *in ~quick time.* 非常快. **~ 'take** *n* delayed reaction to a situation. 反应迟钝. **'~-talk** *n* kind of talk that really means the opposite of, or sth quite different from, what it seems to mean. 反语; 所表示的意义与字面意义相反或相距甚远的谈话. **~-'think** *n* ability to believe two contradictory things. 相信二种矛盾事物的能力; 矛盾思想.

doub·let /'dʌblɪt; 'dʌblɪt/ *n* **1** close-fitting garment for the upper part of the body, worn by men (about 1400—1600). (十五、十七世纪男子穿的)一种紧身上衣. **2** one of a pair, esp one of two words with the same origin but which have become different in form or meaning, eg *hospital / hostel.* 两个异形或异义的同源词中的一个(例如 hospital 和 hostel).

doub·loon /dʌb'lu:n; dʌ'blun/ *n* (hist) Spanish gold coin. (史)西班牙的金币名.

a doublet and hose   **a jerkin**

doubly /'dʌblɪ; 'dʌblɪ/ *adv* (used before *adjj*) to twice the extent or amount: (用于形容词前)加倍地: *to be careful / sure.* 加倍小心(有信心).

doubt¹ /daut; daut/ *n* uncertainty of mind; [C] feeling of uncertainty: 怀疑; 疑问; 疑惑: *I have no ~ that you will succeed / no ~ of your ability.* 我相信你会成功的(你的能力). *There is not much ~ about his guilt,* He is almost certainly guilty. 他有罪是没有多少问题的(是几乎可以确定的). *She had her ~s whether he would come.* 她拿不准他是否会来. *I have my ~s as to / about this being true.* 我怀疑这件事是否属实. *There is no room for ~,* We can be quite certain about it. 没有怀疑的余地(我们可以确信). *There is no ~ about it,* It is certain. 这是确实的. *It became a matter of ~* (= became uncertain) *whether....* 是否…尚未确定. *in ~,* uncertain: 拿不准; 不能确定: *When in ~ about the meaning of a word, consult a dictionary.* 你不能确定一个词的意义时, 就去查一下词典. *He is in ~* (*about*) *what to do.* 他尚未确定做些什么. *beyond / past (all) ~; without (a) ~,* certainly: 无疑地: *Don't worry; he'll come back without ~.* 不要担心, 他一定会回来. *no ~,* very probably: 多半; 十有八九: *He meant to help, no ~, but in fact he has been a hindrance.* 他原意是很想帮忙, 但事实上他变成一个障碍了. *throw ~ upon sth,* suggest that it is not to be regarded as certain or reliable. 怀疑. ⇨ **benefit.**

doubt² /daut; daut/ *vt* [VP6A, 9, 10] **~** (*if / whether*), feel/doubt about; hesitate to believe; question the truth of: 怀疑; 不相信; 拿不准; 不能确定: *You cannot ~ your own existence.* 你不能怀疑你的存在. *I ~ the truth of this report.* 我怀疑这项报告的真实性. *Do you ~ my word,* think I am not telling the truth? 你不相信我的话吗? *I don't ~ that he will come.* 我相信他会来. *Can you ~ that he will win?* 你能不相信他将得胜吗? *I ~ whether he will come.* 我拿不准他是否会来. *I ~ if that was what he wanted.* 我不能确定那是否是他所要的.

doubt·ful /'dautfl; 'dautfəl/ *adj* **~** (*about / of*), feeling doubt; causing doubt; unreliable: 怀疑的; 不能确定的; 可疑的; 不可靠的: *I am / feel ~* (*about*) *what I ought to do.* 我不能确定应该做些什么. *The future looks very ~.* 前途堪忧. *The weather looks very ~.* 天气看来不可靠. *This is a ~ blessing,* may or may not be one. 这件事也许是福, 也许不是. *Are you ~ of success?* 你怀疑是否能成功吗? *He's a ~ character,* perhaps dishonest. 他是一个不可靠的人. *It is a ~ neighbourhood,* one with a bad reputation, one where ~ characters live. 这是一个名誉不佳的地区. **~ly** /-fəlɪ; -fəlɪ/ *adv*

doubt·less /'dautlɪs; 'dautlɪs/ *adv* very probably. 很可能; 十有八九.

douche /du:ʃ; duʃ/ *n* stream of water applied to a part of the body (outside or inside) for cleaning it or for medicinal purposes; instrument for forcing out such a stream of water. 灌洗身体(外部或内部)的水; 灌洗器.

dough /dəu; do/ *n* [U] mixture of flour, water, etc in a paste (for making bread, pastry, etc); (sl) money. (做面包、点心等的)生面团; (俚)金钱. **'~-nut,** sweetened ~ cooked in deep fat, usu in the shape of a ring or a

ball. 油炸圈饼. **~·y** /'dəʊɪ; 'doɪ/ adj of or like ~; soft; flabby. 生面团的; 似生面团的; 软的; 软松的.

doughty /'daʊtɪ; 'daʊtɪ/ adj (old use, or joc) brave and strong; bold: (旧用法或谑) 勇敢的; 坚强的: a ~ warrior; 勇敢的战士; ~ deeds. 英勇的事迹.

dour /dʊə(r); dʊr/ adj severe; stern; obstinate: 严厉的; 冷峻的; 执拗的: ~ looks; 严厉的面容; ~ silence. 冷寂. **~·ly** adv

douse, dowse /daʊs; daʊs/ vt [VP6A] put into water; throw water over; (colloq) extinguish (a light). 浸入水; 泼以水; (口) 熄灭(灯).

dove¹ /dʌv; dʌv/ n 1 kind of pigeon; symbol of peace. 鸽; 和平的象征. **'~-cote** /'dʌvkət; 'dʌv‚kɒt/ n small shelter or house with nesting-boxes for ~s. 鸽舍; 鸽房. **flutter the ~-cotes,** alarm quiet people. 惊扰安静的人们. 2 (colloq) member of a group promoting peace. (口)提倡和平的人; 鸽派人物. ⇨ **hawk¹(2)**.

dove² /dəʊv; dəv/ (US) alternative pt form of **dive²**. (美) dive² 之另一过去式.

dove·tail /'dʌvteɪl; 'dʌv‚tel/ n joint for two pieces of wood. 楔形接榫; 鸠尾榫. □ vt, vi [VP6A, 2A, 3A] **~ (with/into),** join together by means of ~s; (fig) fit (together): 用鸠尾榫接合; (喻)吻合; 密合: My plans ~ed with his. 我的计划和他的计划吻合.

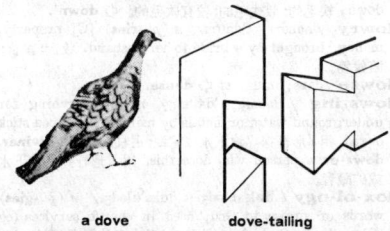

a dove   dove-tailing

dowa·ger /'daʊədʒə(r); 'daʊədʒə/ n 1 woman with property or a title from her dead husband: 承受亡夫的遗产或爵位的寡妇: the ~ duchess. 公爵的未亡人. 2 (colloq) dignified elderly lady. (口)年长的贵妇.

dowdy /'daʊdɪ; 'daʊdɪ/ adj (-ier, -iest) (of clothes, etc) shabby or unfashionable; (of a person) dressed in ~ clothes. (指衣服等)褴褛的; 不雅观的; (指人)衣衫褴褛的; 衣冠不整的. **dow·di·ly** adv **dow·di·ness** n

dowel /'daʊəl; 'daʊəl/ n headless nail or peg for keeping two pieces of wood, metal, stone, etc together. 缘缝钉; 合钉; 暗销.

dower /'daʊə(r); 'daʊə/ n 1 widow's share of her husband's property. 寡妇得自亡夫的财产. 2 dowry. 嫁妆; 妆资; 陪嫁物. 3 gift of nature (eg beauty, intelligence). 天赋; 禀赋 (例如美貌, 智慧). □ vt provide with a ~. 给与(寡妇)财产; 给与嫁妆; 赋与才赋.

down¹ /daʊn; daʊn/ n [U] first, soft feathers of young birds; soft under-feathers of birds (as used for pillows and cushions); fine soft hair, eg the first hair that comes on a boy's face; the soft hair on some plants and seeds (eg the thistle). (雏鸟的)软毛; 羽绒(如用以填枕头、靠垫者); (初生于男孩面孔上的)细软胡须; (某些植物和种子上的)茸毛(例如蓟毛).

down² /daʊn; daʊn/ adv part 1 (with vv of motion) from a high(er) level to a low(er) level: (与表示动作之动词连用)向下; 自高至低: The sun went ~. 太阳下山了. The flag was hauled ~ at sunset. 旗于日落时被降下. If you can't jump ~, climb ~. 如果你不能跳下来, 就爬下来. Some kinds of food go ~ (= can be swallowed) more easily than others. 有些食物比别的食物更易吞下去. 2 (with vv of motion) from an upright position to a horizontal position: (与表示动作的动词连用)倒下; 自直

立的位置到横躺的位置: He was knocked ~ by a bus. 他被公共汽车撞倒了. If you're tired, go and lie ~. 如果你累了, 就去躺下. He's ~ (= ill in bed) with flu. 他因患流行性感冒而卧床. Don't hit a man when he's ~, (fig) attack him when he has suffered misfortune, etc. (喻)不要落井下石; 不要打落水狗. 3 (with vv indicating change of stance but not of position in space) to or in a lower position or direction: (与动词连用表示姿态的变动, 而非位置的移动)至较低位置; 朝下: Sit ~, please. 请坐. The man bent ~ to speak to me. 那高个子弯下腰对我讲话. 4 (with vv indicating position or state): (与动词连用表示位置或状态): Mary isn't ~ yet, is not yet dressed and downstairs. 玛丽还没有穿好衣服下楼来. We can't use the telephone—the lines are all ~, on the ground, eg after a storm. 我们不能打电话——电话线都掉在地上了(例如暴风雨后). The river is ~, (fig) back to its normal height, eg after a flood. 河水退了(例如泛滥后)退至正常水位). 5 from a more important place (eg the capital) to a less important place; from an inland place to the coast; from the university: 自重要地点(例如首都)至次要地点; 自内陆至海岸; 自大学: We went ~ to Brighton (eg from London) for the weekend. 我们去布赖顿(例如从伦敦)度周末. The Bill was sent ~ (from the House of Lords) to the House of Commons. 该项议案(自上议院)送往下议院. 6 (used with vv to indicate reduction to a smaller volume, a lower degree, a state of less activity, etc): (与动词连用, 表示数量、程度、活动性等的减少): The heels of my shoes have worn ~. 我的鞋后跟磨坏了. Boil the fat ~. 将脂肪熬一熬. The wind died ~. 风势渐渐弱了. The sea is ~/has calmed ~, is, has become, calm. 海浪已平静了. The fire is burning ~, getting low. 火势减弱了. One of the back tyres is ~, is flat or getting flat. 有一个后胎泄气了. The clock has run ~, needs to be wound up. 钟停了. The temperature has gone ~. 温度已降低. The price of fruit is ~. 水果的价格跌了. 7 (used with reference to writing) on paper: (用以指书写)于纸上; 于某事记下; to write sth ~; to get sth ~, write it. 写下某事. Please take ~ this letter, write it (eg in shorthand) as I dictate it. 请将这封信笔录下来(例如经我授而用速记录下). Put me ~/Put my name ~ for 50p, eg as willing to give this sum. 请把我的名字登记下来, 我准备出五十便士(例如愿意缴此款项时). I see your ~ (= your name appears in the programme) for a speech at the next meeting. 我知道下次开会你要演说(节目表上有你的名字). 8 from an earlier time (to a later time): 自较早时间(至较晚时间): the history of Europe ~ to 1914; 自古以迄一九一四年的欧洲史; looking ~ through the ages; 纵观古今; coming ~ to modern times. 以迄近代. 9 including the lower limit in a series: (指一系列中)由上至下; 由大至小: from ocean liners ~ to rowing-boats. 从班轮到划艇. 10 (in various phrases) (用于各种短语中) **D~ with,** let us be rid of: 打倒: D~ with the grammarians! 打倒语法学家! **~ under,** (colloq) on the other side of the world from Europe (eg Australia). (口)与欧洲对跖之地(例如大洋洲). **up and ~,** to and fro: 往返地; walking up and ~. 走来走去. **money/cash '~,** payment at the time of purchase (contrasted with credit): 付现金(与 credit 相对): You must pay £10 ~. 你必须付十英镑现金. Hence, 由此产生, **'~ payment.** (分期付款的)首次款. **be ~ and out,** (colloq) (口) **(a)** (boxing) be knocked out, unable to resume the fight. (拳赛)被击倒而不能继续比赛. **(b)** (fig) be beaten in the struggle of life; be unemployed and without money. (喻)失败潦倒; 落魄. Hence, 由此产生, **‚~-and-'out** n [C] **get ~ to work/business,** start work in real earnest. 认真开始工作. **be ~ on sb,** feel ill-will towards him. 对某人不怀善意; 仇视某人. **~ in the dumps,** (colloq) dejected; in low spirits. (口)沮丧; 心情不好. **~ in the mouth,** (colloq) sad-looking. (口)面容忧戚的. **~ on one's luck,** (colloq) having suffered misfortune. (口)倒霉的. **come '~ in the world,** fall to a lower social position. 社会地位降

低；潦倒。 **come ～ on sb**, scold or rebuke him sharply. 严斥某人。 **～-to-'earth** adj concerned with realities; practical (contrasted with *impractical, vague, idealistic*)：现实的；实际的(与 *impractical, vague, idealistic* 相对)：He's a ～-to-earth sort of fellow. 他是个现实的人。

down³ /daun; daʊn/ prep **1** from a high(er) to a low(er) level: 自高处向下：to run ～ a hill. 自山上跑下。The tears ran ～ her face. 眼泪顺着她的脸流下。Her hair was hanging ～ her back. 她的头发披在她的背上。**2** at a lower part of: 在…之较低处：Oxford is farther ～ the river. 牛津在这条河的下游。**3** along (not necessarily with reference to a lower level): 沿；循(不一定相较低处)：I was walking ～ the street. 我沿着街道走。He has gone ～ town, from one of the outlying parts, eg a suburb, to the business or shopping quarters of the town. 他已进城去了(例如自郊区至闹区)。 ⇨ downtown. ～ (the) wind, (of a boat) with the wind behind. (指船)顺风的。**4** (of time) from a farther to a nearer period: (指时间)自较远至较近的时期：～ the ages. 由古至今。

down⁴ /daun/ vt [VP6A] (colloq) bring, put, knock, down: (口)打倒；击倒：to ～ a player with a tackle; 以擒抱动作绊倒一球员；to ～ a glass of beer, empty the glass. 喝干一杯啤酒。～ **tools**, (of workers) refuse to work, go on strike. (指工人)罢工。

down⁵ /daun; daʊn/ n **ups and ～s**, changes in fortune, prosperity, etc: 时运等的变化：have one's ups and ～s; 有好运也有厄运；the ups and ～s of life. 人生的荣枯(浮沉)。 **have a ～ on sb**, feel ill-will towards him. 对某人不怀善意，仇视某人。

down·beat /'daunbi:t; 'daʊn,bit/ n (music) first beat of a bar (when the conductor's hand moves down). (音乐)强拍。

down·cast /'daunka:st US: -kæst; 'daʊn,kæst/ adj (of a person) depressed; discouraged; sad; (of eyes) looking downwards. (指人)沮丧的；气馁的；悲哀的；(指眼睛)向下视的。

down·fall /'daunfo:l; 'daʊn,fol/ n (usu sing) (通常作单数) **1** heavy fall (of rain, etc). (雨等的)大降。**2** (fig) ruin; fall from fortune or power: (喻)毁灭；败落：His ～ was caused by gambling and drink. 他的身败名裂是由赌博和酗酒造成的。

down·grade /ˌdaun'greid; 'daʊn,gred/ vt [VP6A] reduce to a lower grade or rank. 使降级。

down·hearted /ˌdaun'ha:tid; 'daʊn'hartɪd/ adj in low spirits; depressed. 郁闷的；沮丧的。

down·hill /ˌdaun'hil; 'daʊn,hɪl/ adv in a downward sloping direction. 向下地。go ～, (fig) get worse (in health, fortune, etc). (喻)(健康、运气等)每况愈下。

Down·ing Street /'daunɪŋ stri:t; 'daʊnɪŋ strɪt/ n street in London with official residence of the Prime Minister; (hence) the British Government: 唐宁街(伦敦一街道名，有英国首相的官邸)；(由此产生)英国政府：What does ～ think of the matter? 英国政府对此事情何想法?

down·pour /'daunpo:(r); 'daʊn,por/ n (usu sing) heavy fall (esp of rain): (常用单数)大降(尤指雨)；倾盆大雨：to be caught in a ～. 赶上倾盆大雨。

down·right /'daunrait; 'daʊn,rait/ adj **1** forthright; honest; frank: 直爽的；诚实的；坦白的：He has a ～ manner. 他有坦白的态度。He is a ～ sort of person. 他是个直爽的人。**2** thorough; complete: 彻底的；完全的；纯粹的：It's a ～ lie. 这完全是谎言。It's ～ nonsense. 这完全是一派胡言。□ adv thoroughly: 彻底地：He was ～ rude. 他真是太粗鲁了。**～·ness** n

downs /daunz; daʊnz/ n **1** expanse of open high land. 广阔的高地。**the North／South D～**, the chalk uplands of S England. 北部(南部)高地(英格兰南部含有石灰石的高地)。**2 the D～**, the sea off the coast of Kent (SE England) (英格兰东南)肯特郡之外海：anchor in the D～. 在肯特郡外海抛锚。

down·stairs /ˌdaun'steəz; 'daʊn'stɛrz/ adv to, at, on, of, a lower floor; down the stairs: 至楼下；在楼下；属于楼下；下楼地：He went ～ to breakfast. 他下楼吃早餐。Our neighbours ～ (= on the lower floor) are very noisy. 我们楼下的邻居很吵闹。Your brother is waiting ～. 你哥哥(弟弟)在楼下等着。□ **down·stair(s)** adj: the ～(s) rooms. 楼下的房间。

down·town /'dauntaun; 'daʊn'taʊn/ adv (esp US) to or in the lower part of a town; to or in the main or business part of a town: (尤美)至或在城市的较低地区；至或在闹区；至或在商业区：(attrib)(用作定语) ～ New York; 纽约的商业区：a ～ movie theatre. 在闹区的电影院。

down·trod·den /'dauntrɔdn; 'daʊn'tradn̩/ adj oppressed; kept down and treated badly. 受压迫的；被蹂躏的。

down·ward /'daunwəd; 'daʊnwəd/ adj moving, leading, going, pointing, to what is lower: 向下的；下降的；下行的：a ～ slope; 一个下坡；a ～ path; 往一向下倾斜的小路上；prices with a ～ tendency. 有下跌趋势的物价。**down·ward(s)** adv towards what is lower: 向下地：He laid the picture face ～s on the table. 他把那幅画反放在桌上。The monkey was hanging head ～s from the branch. 那猴子头向下倒挂在树枝上。

downy /'dauni; 'daʊni/ adj of, like, covered with, down. 软毛的；似软毛的；覆有软毛的。 ⇨ **down¹**.

dowry /'dauəri; 'daʊri/ n (pl **-ries**) [C] property, money, brought by a bride to her husband. 妆奁；嫁妆；陪嫁物。

dowse /daus; daʊs/ vt ⇨ **douse**.

dows·ing /'dauzɪŋ; 'daʊzɪŋ/ n [U] searching for underground water or metals by using a Y-shaped stick or rod. 用Y形杆探寻地下水或矿藏；占杖测水。 ⇨ **diviner**. **dows·er** n person who does this. 用 Y 形杆探寻地下水或矿藏者。

dox·ol·ogy /dɔk'sɔlədʒi; daks'alədʒɪ/ n (pl **-gies**) words of praise to God, used in church services (eg 'Glory be to God...'). (礼拜时)对上帝的赞颂(例如：'荣耀归于上帝…')。

doyen /'dɔiən; 'dɔiən/ n senior member of the diplomatic corps in a capital city, or a society, profession, etc. 外交使节团团长；(社团或某一行业等之)高级代表。

doy·ley, doyly n = **dolly**.

doze /douz; doz/ vi [VP2A, C] sleep lightly; be half asleep. 假寐；假寐。**～ off**, fall lightly asleep: 打瞌睡：He ～d off during the sermon. 他在做礼拜时打瞌睡。 □ n [C] short, light sleep. 瞌睡；假寐。

dozen /'dʌzn; 'dʌzn/ n (also used attrib, pl unchanged) (亦作定语，复数不变)。**1** twelve: 十二个；一打：Eggs are 35p a ～. 鸡蛋三十五便士一打。I want three ～ of these. 这些我要三打。Pack them in ～s, in sets or groups of twelve. 把它们一打一打地包装起来。**talk nineteen to the ～**, talk incessantly. 不停地谈话；刺刺不休。**2** (pl) ～**s of**, a large number of: (复)很多的：I've been there ～s of times. 我曾去过那里很多次。

drab /dræb; dræb/ adj **1** (also as n) dull muddy brown. (亦做名词用)土褐色(的)。**2** (fig) dull; uninteresting; monotonous: (喻)乏味的；单调的：a ～ existence. 单调的生活。**～·ly** adv **～·ness** n

drachm /dræm; dræm/ n **1** = **dram(1)**. **2** (archaic) small quantity. (古)小量；微量。

drachma /'drækmə; 'drækmə/ n ancient Greek silver coin; modern Greek unit of currency. 古希腊的银币名；近代希腊货币单位。

dra·co·nian /drə'kəuniən; dre'kɔniən/ adj of a rigorous law or code of laws; harsh: 严峻法典的；严厉的：～ measures. 严厉的手段。

draft¹ /dra:ft US: dræft; dræft/ n [C] **1** outline (usu in the form of rough notes) of sth to be done: 草稿：a ～ for a speech／letter; 一篇演说(一封信)的草稿；preliminary version: 草案：a ～ for a Parliamentary

Bill; 一項國會議案的草案; rough sketch: 草圖: *a ~ for a machine.* 一部機器的草圖. **2** written order for payment of money by a bank; drawing of money by means of such an order: 匯票; 匯票的支付; 提款: *a ~ for £500 upon London,* eg one written by a Paris bank upon its London branch. 在倫敦提取的五百英鎊的(此一張匯票(例如由巴黎的銀行開出至倫敦分行者). Hence, 由此產生, '**bank-~. 3** group of men chosen from a larger group for a special purpose; (US) group of men conscripted for the armed forces. 特遣部隊; 分遣隊; (美)徵召的兵員隊. **the ~,** conscription. 征兵. '**~ card,** card summoning a man to serve in the armed forces. 征召令. **4** (US) (美) = draught.

draft² /drɑːft US: dræft; dræft/ vt [VP6A] **1** make a draft(1) of: 作⋯的草圖、草案、草圖; 草擬: *a ~ a speech.* 草擬一演說稿. **2** choose men for a draft(3); (US) conscript (a man) for the armed forces: 選拔做為特遣隊; (美)征召服役: *to be ~ed into the Army.* 被征召當兵. **~ ·ee** /ˌdrɑːfˈtiː US: ˌdræfˈtiː; ˌdræfˈtiː/ n (US) man ~ed for military service. (美)被征召的士兵. **~ ·ing** n the act of ~ing; way in which sth is ~ed(1): 起草; 草擬; 起草的方式: *a ~ing committee,* eg of a Parliamentary Bill. (國會議案等的)起草委員會. *The ~ing of this section of the Bill is obscure.* 草案上的這一項含糊不清.

drafts·man /ˈdrɑːftsmən US: ˈdræfts-; ˈdræftsmən/ n (pl **-men**) man who prepares drafts(1), esp in engineering and architecture; person responsible for the careful and exact wording of a legal document, or a (clause in a) parliamentary bill. 作草圖者; 作圖樣者; 繪圖員; 法案或議案的起草人.

drafty /ˈdrɑːftɪ US: ˈdræftɪ; ˈdræftɪ/ adj (-ier, -iest) (US) (美) = **draughty.**

drag¹ /dræg; dræg/ n **1** sth that is dragged, eg a net ('~net) pulled over the bottom of a river (eg to catch fish); a heavy harrow pulled over the ground to break up the soil. 被拖曳的東西(例如拖網, 亦稱 drag-net); 重耙(耕土用者). **2** (colloq) sth or sb that slows down progress because heavy, dull, etc: (口)拖累之物; 阻礙物: *His wife has been a ~ on him all his life,* has hindered him in his career. 他的妻子是他一生事業上的累贅. *Do we have to take your sister with us? She's such a ~.* 我們必須帶着你的妹妹嗎? 她真是個累贅. ⇨ drag² (3). **3** [U] (sl) woman's clothes worn by a man: (俚)男扮女裝用的衣服: '*As You Like It' performed in ~,* with the women's parts acted by men dressed as women. 由男扮女裝演出的「如願」. **4** (sl) puff at a cigarette or cigar. (俚)吸一口(香煙或雪茄).

drag² /dræg; dræg/ vt, vi (-gg-) **1** [VP6A, 15B, 14] pull along (esp with effort and difficulty): 拖; 曳; 用力拉: *to ~ a heavy box out of a cupboard.* 把一個箱子從櫥里拖出來. *The escaped prisoner was ~ged from his hiding-place.* 那逃犯被人從他隱藏之處拖了出來. **~ sb into doing sth,** involve him unwillingly in an undertaking: 使某人勉強做一事: *He hates parties; we had to ~ him into going.* 他不喜歡聚會; 我們不得不勉強他參加. **2** [VP6A, 15B, 2A, C] (allow to) move slowly and with effort; (allow to) trail: (使)緩慢而費力地行動; (使)拖曳而進: *to walk with ~ging feet.* 踢躅而行. *He could scarcely ~ himself along.* 他几乎走不動了. *The ship ~ged its anchor / The ship's anchor ~ged during the night,* it failed to hold, was drawn along the sea bottom. 這船的錯在夜里拖動了(錯沒有鈎牢, 沿着海底拖動). **~ one's feet,** go forward slowly, unwillingly (often fig): 拖曳前進; 緩慢而勉強地前進(常作喻): *We suspect the Government of ~ging their feet.* 我們懷疑政府在拖延. **~ up (a child),** (colloq) (contrasted with **bring up**) educate, train, etc it badly. (口)未能適當地管教(小孩) (與 bring up 相對). **3** [VP2A, C] (~ on), (of time, work, an entertainment) go on slowly in a dull manner: (指時間、工作、娛樂)緩慢而單調地進行: *Classwork often ~s towards the end of term,* pupils lose interest. 學期近

結束時, 功課常是松懈而乏味地進行. *The performance ~ged on.* 表演緩慢而單調地進行着. *Time seemed to ~.* 時間好像走過得很慢. **~ out,** make longer (in time): 拖延(時間): *~ out a meeting / an argument / a performance.* 拖延會議(辯論、表演)的時間. **4** [VP6 A, 2A] use nets, tools, etc to search the bottom of a river, lake, etc (usu for sth lost or missing): (用網、工具等)在河底、湖底等撈取; 打撈: *They ~ged the river for the missing child.* 他們打撈河底尋找這失蹤的孩子.

drag·gled /ˈdrægld; ˈdrægld/ adj (often 常作 **be·~**) wet, dirty or muddy (as if dragged through mud, etc). 潮濕而泥污的(如在泥漿等中曳過).

drago·man /ˈdrægəʊmən; ˈdrægəmən/ n (pl **~s**) guide and interpreter (esp in Arabic-speaking countries). 通譯(尤指在說阿拉伯語的國家中者).

dragon /ˈdrægən; ˈdrægən/ n fabulous creature like a crocodile or snake, often with wings and claws, able to breathe out fire, often guarding a treasure; (colloq) fierce person. 龍(神話中似鱷魚或蛇的一種動物, 常生有翅及爪, 能吐火, 常守護一寶藏); (口)凶狠的人.

a dragon

drag·on·fly /ˈdrægənflaɪ; ˈdrægənˌflaɪ/ n (pl **-flies**) insect with a stick-like body and two pairs of large wings. 蜻蜓. ⇨ the illus at **insect.** 參看 insect 之插圖.

dra·goon /drəˈguːn; drəˈgun/ n horse-soldier; cavalryman. 騎兵. □ vt [VP6 A, 14] **~ sb (into doing sth),** force him (to do sth), harass him. 逼迫某人(做某事).

drain¹ /dreɪn; dren/ n **1** pipe, channel, trench, etc for carrying away water, sewage and other unwanted liquids; (pl) system of pipes and sewers for carrying away waste liquid, etc from buildings; (US) plug-hole: 水管; 下水道; 陰溝; (復)排水系統; 排水裝置; (美)消防右水裝置: *There's a bad smell; something wrong with the ~s, I suppose.* 有難聞的氣味, 我覺得排水道有毛病. **go down the ~,** (fig) be wasted. (喻)被浪費; 白費. '**~-pipe,** pipe used in a system of ~s. 排水管. **2** (fig) sth that continually uses up force, time, wealth, etc; cause of weakening or loss: (喻)不斷消耗力量、時間、財富等之事物; 衰弱或損失的原因: *Military expenditure has been a great ~ on the country's resources.* 軍費消耗國家的財源甚大. *All this extra work was a ~ on his strength.* 所有這些額外的工作是耗損他體力的原因. '**brain ~,** movement of trained technical and scientific personnel from one country to another (because of better opportunities, etc). 人才外流(由于機會較好等, 一國之技術和科學人才流向另一國). **3** (colloq) small drink; mouthful: (口)小飲; 一口之量: *Don't drink it all; leave me a ~!* 不要把它喝光, 給我留一口!

drain² /dreɪn; dren/ vt, vi **1** [VP15B, 2C] **~ away/off,** (of liquid) (cause to) run or flow away: (指液體) (使)排出; (使)流出: *Dig trenches to ~ the water away / off.* 挖溝以排水. *The water will soon ~ away / off.* 水不久便會流去了. **2** [VP2A, C, 6A] (of land, etc) make, become, dry as water flows away: (指土地等)使干涸; 因水流出而變干: *to ~ swamps / marshes.* 排出沼澤的水. *Land must be well ~ed for some crops.* 土地必須相當地的排水以適合某些作物. *These fields ~ into the river.* 這些田地的水流入河中. *Leave the dishes on the board to ~.*

将盘碟放在水槽旁边的板上晾干。'~-**ing-board**, board at the side of a sink, on which washed dishes, etc are placed to ~. 滴干板(在洗涤槽旁边,可置放洗过的盘碟等使之晾干)。 **3** [VP6A, 15B, 14, 2C] ~ (*away* /*off*); ~ (*of*), (fig) (cause to) lose (strength, wealth, etc) by degrees: (喻)(使)逐渐消耗(力量、财富等): *The country was ~ed of its man-power and wealth by war.* 这个国家因战争而逐渐耗尽了人力和财富。 *His life was slowly ~ing away,* eg of a man bleeding to death. 他的生命逐渐枯竭了(例如因流血而死的人)。 **4** [VP6A, 22] drink; empty: 饮; 饮干: *to ~ a glass dry.* 饮干一杯(酒等)。

drain·age /'dreɪnɪdʒ; 'drenɪdʒ/ n [U] **1** draining or being drained. 排水; 疏水。 '~-**basin**, area drained by a river. 某一河流排水的区域; 流域。 **2** system of drains(1). 排水系统; 排水装置。 **3** that which is drained away or off; sewage. 排出之物; 下水道中之污物。

drake /dreɪk; drek/ n male duck. 公鸭。

dram /dræm; dræm/ n **1** unit of weight: (apothecaries' weight) 60 grains (8 drams = 1 oz or 31.1 grams); (avoirdupois weight) 27¹/₃ grains (16 drams = 1 oz or 28.35 grams). 打兰(衡量单位, 在药量中等于60喱, 8 打兰等于1 啊或31.1克; 在常衡中等于27¹/₃喱, 16 打兰等于1啊或28.35克)。 ⇨ **App 5.** 参看附录五。 **2** small drink of alcoholic spirits: 少量的酒: *He's fond of a ~,* eg of whisky. 他喜欢喝一点酒(例如饮威士忌)。

drama /'drɑːmə; 'dromə/ n **1** [C] play for the theatre, radio or TV; [U] (**the**) ~, composition, presentation and performance of such plays: 剧本; 戏剧; 戏剧的制作及演出: *a student of* (*the*) ~; 研究戏剧的人; *to be interested in* (*the*) ~. 对戏剧有兴趣。 **2** [C, U] series of exciting events. 一连串紧张刺激的事件。

dra·matic /drə'mætɪk; drə'mætɪk/ adj **1** of drama(1): 剧本的; 戏剧的: ~ *performances;* 戏剧的演出; ~ *criticism.* 戏剧批评。 **2** sudden or exciting, like an event in a stage play: 如舞台剧般紧张刺激的; 戏剧性的: ~ *changes in the international situation.* 国际局势之戏剧性的变化。 **3** (of a person, his speech, behaviour) showing the feelings or character in a lively or exaggerated way. (指人或人的言行)生动或夸张地表现情感或性格的。 **dra·mati·cally** /-klɪ; -klɪ/ adv in a ~ manner. 戏剧性地。 **dra·mat·ics** n (usu with sing v) (通常与单数动词连用) **1** ~(1) works or performances by amateurs: 业余者的戏剧作品或演出: *Are you interested in amateur ~s?* 你对于业余演戏有兴趣吗? **2** ~(3) speech, behaviour, etc. 夸张情感的言词、行为等。

drama·tis per·sonae /ˌdræmətɪs pɜː'səʊnaɪ; 'dræmətɪspɑ'soni/ n (Lat) (list of the) characters in a play. (拉)剧中人; 登场人物。

drama·tist /'dræmətɪst; 'dræmətɪst/ n writer of plays. 剧作家; 戏剧作者。

drama·tize /'dræmətaɪz; 'dræmə,taɪz/ vt [VP6A] **1** put a story, novel, etc into the form of a drama. 改编(小说等)为戏剧。 **2** treat (a situation, etc) as if it were a drama. 戏剧性地处理(事态等)。 **drama·tiz·ation** /ˌdræmətaɪ'zeɪʃn US: -tɪ'z; ˌdræmətə'zeʃən/ n [C, U].

drank /dræŋk; dræŋk/ pt of **drink.**

drape /dreɪp; drep/ vt [VP6A, 14] **1** ~ (*round* /*over*), hang curtains, cloth, a cloak or other garment in folds round or over sth: 用(窗帘、布、斗篷或其他织物)覆盖某物: *to ~ curtains over a window;* 用窗帘遮起窗子; *to ~ a cloak over one's shoulders* /*a flag over the coffin.* 将斗篷披在肩上(将旗覆于棺上)。 **2** ~ (*with*), cover or decorate: 覆盖或装饰: *walls ~d with flags;* 挂着旗子的墙壁; *a doorway ~d with a heavy curtain.* 悬有厚帘的门口。 **3** ~ (*round* /*over*), allow to rest loosely: 使松弛地停靠于: *He ~d his legs over the arms of his chair.* 他将两腿松弛地放在椅臂上。 □ n [C] (chiefly US) cloth hung in folds; curtain. (主美)成褶而下垂的布; 帘。

dra·per /'dreɪpə(r); 'drepɚ/ n (GB) shopkeeper who sells cloth, linen, clothing, etc. (英)布商。 ~**y** n **1** [U] ~'s trade, goods or business: 布业; 呢绒业; 布商所售之货: (attrib) (用作定语) *a ~y business* /*store.* 布业(店)。 **2** [C, U] (pl -**ies**) materials used for garments, hangings, curtains, etc; such materials arranged in folds. 用以制衣服、帐、帏、帘等的布料; 成褶的衣料、帐、帏、帘等。

dras·tic /'dræstɪk; 'dræstɪk/ adj (of actions, methods, medicines) having a strong or violent effect: (指行动、方法、药品)激烈的; 猛烈的: ~ *measures to cure inflation,* eg a steep increase in the bank rate; 抑制通货膨胀之激烈的措施(例如银行贴现率之突增); ~ *remedies to cure an illness.* 治疗某一疾病的烈性药物。 **dras·ti·cally** /-klɪ; -klɪ/ adv.

drat /dræt; dræt/ vt (-**tt-**) (used chiefly in exclamations, dated, colloq) curse: (主要用于感叹句; 过时用语, 口头语; 该咒; 讨厌: *D~ that child!* 那个该死的小鬼! *That ~ted* (= cursed) *boy!* 那个该死的男孩!

draught (US = **draft**) /drɑːft US: dræft; dræft/ n **1** [C, U] current of air in a room, chimney or other enclosed place: 通风; 气流: *You'll catch cold if you sit in a ~.* 如果坐在风口上, 你会伤风。 *Turn the electric fan on and make a ~.* 把电扇打开通一下风。 *There's not enough ~ up the chimney; that's why the fire doesn't burn well.* 烟囱里的通风不足; 那便是火烧不旺的原因。 **2** [C] depth of water needed to float a ship: 船底没入水中的深度; 船的吃水: *vessels of shallow ~;* 吃水浅的船只; *a ship with a ~ of ten feet.* 吃水十英尺的船。 ⇨ *draw²*(13). **4** [U] drawing of liquid from a container (eg a barrel): 自容器(例如桶)中汲取: *beer on ~;* ~ *beer.* 桶装啤酒。 Cf 参较 *bottled beer.* **5** [C] (amount drunk during) one continuous process of swallowing: 一饮(之量): *a ~ of water;* 一口饮下之水; *to drink half a pint of beer at a ~.* 一口气饮下半品脱啤酒。 **6** (pl, with sing v) (US = *checkers*) table game for two players using 24 round pieces (called 称作 '~s(men)') on a board with 32 black and 32 white squares. (复用单数动词)国际象棋。 (供二人娱乐的一种桌上游戏, 用二十四个圆形棋子, 在一有三十二黑方格与三十二白方格的棋盘上进行)。 □ vt *draft².* '~-**horse**, one that pulls heavy loads. 拖马。 ⇨ *packhorse* at **pack¹**(1). **draughts·man** /'drɑːftsmən US: 'dræ-; 'dræftsmən/ n (pl -**men**) **1** = **draftsman.** **2** piece used in ~s, ⇨ **6** above. 国际象棋子(参看上列第6义)。

draughty (US = **drafty**) /'drɑːftɪ US: 'dræftɪ; 'dræftɪ/ adj (-**ier, -iest**) with draughts(1) blowing through: 通风的: *a ~ room.* 一通风的房间。

draw¹ /drɔː; drɔ/ n **1** the act of drawing (in various senses): 拉; 牵; 抽; 拉; 拔; 拔; 拔取; 吸引; 吸入; 逗人吐露情感等; 变长; 移动; 绘; 写; 吃水; 不分胜负; 结束; 吸取精华: *the ~ for the fourth round of the tennis tournament.* 网球赛第四局之平手。 *When does the ~ take place,* When will the winning numbers for the lottery, etc, be drawn? 何时开始抽奖? *The game ended in a ~,* neither side won. 比赛不分胜负。 *Our team has had five wins and two ~s this season.* 我们的队本季赢了五次, 打平二次。 **2** sb or sth that attracts attention, ⇨ **draw²**(5): 吸引注意力的人或物: *Mr A is always a great ~ at political meetings,* is a popular speaker. A 君在政治性的集会中是十分引人注意的人物。 *The new play is a great ~,* many people are going to the theatre to see it. 这出新戏很卖座。 **3** *be quick*/*slow on the ~,* quick/slow at pulling out a sword, revolver, etc; (fig) quick/slow to understand. 拔剑、枪等迅速(缓慢); (喻)思想敏捷(迟钝)。

draw² /drɔː; drɔ/ vt, vi (pt **drew** /druː; dru/, pp **drawn** /drɔːn; drɔn/) **1** [VP6A, 15B, 14] move by pulling: 拉; 牵: *to ~ a boat* (*up*) *out of the water*/*on to the beach;* 将一小船拉出水(至滩上); *to ~ one's chair up to the table;* 把椅子拉至桌旁; *to ~ sb aside,* eg to speak

to him quietly; 将某人拉到一边(例如与其悄悄说话); to ~ *on/off one's socks/gloves/tights;* 穿上(脱下)袜子(手套,紧身衣); *to ~ a curtain across a window;* 将窗帘拉上; *to ~ down the blinds* (of windows); 将百叶窗拉下; *to ~ one's belt tighter;* 拉紧裤带; *to ~ one's pen through a word,* cross it out. *The fisherman drew in his net.* 那渔民将网拉起。**2** [VP6A, 15B] (esp) move by pulling after or behind: (尤指)拖; 曳: *a train ~n by two locomotives;* 由两个机车牵引的火车; *tractor-~n ploughs.* 曳引机拖动的犁。*The wagon was being ~n by two horses.* 这货车由两匹马拖着。**3** [VP6A, 15B, 14] ~ **(out);** ~ **(from/out of),** take or get out by pulling; extract: 抽出; 拔出: *to ~ a cork, out of a bottle;* (自瓶上)拔出软木塞; *to ~ nails from a plank;* 自厚板上拔出钉; *to have a tooth ~n;* 拔牙; *to ~ stumps,* (cricket) pull them out at the end of play; (板球戏)比赛终了时拔去标柱; *to ~ trumps,* (in card games such as bridge) cause them to be played; (牌戏,例如桥牌)吊王牌; *to ~ cards from a pack;* 自一副纸牌中抽取纸牌; *to ~ for partners,* eg when about to play a card game, allow this to decide the question; (玩牌等)抽牌以决定伙人; *to ~ lots,* ⇨ **lot²(1);** 抽签; *to ~ the winner,* get a ticket, etc at a lottery, on which there is a payment, prize, etc; 抽彩; 抽彩: *to ~ a gun* (on *sb*), take it from its holster, ready for use. 拔枪(对着某人)。~ *a blank,* find nothing. 落空; 未发现任何东西。~ *sb's teeth,* make him harmless. 使无害。**4** [VP6A, 14] ~ **(from/out of),** obtain from a source: 自一来源获取; 提取: *to ~ water from a well;* 由井中汲水; *to ~ cider/beer from a cask/barrel;* 由桶中汲取苹果酒(啤酒); *to ~ one's salary;* 领薪; *to ~ money from the bank/from one's account;* 自银行(本人帐户)中提款; *to ~ rations,* get, receive, supplies (of food, etc) from a store; 自店中取得粮食; *to ~ inspiration from nature.* 由大自然获得灵感。*What moral are we to ~ from this story?* 我们从这个故事里体会到什么教训?~ *it mild,* (orig of beer; fig) be moderate; not exaggerate. (最初指啤酒,现为比喻用法)适度; 不夸张。~ *tears/applause, etc,* be the cause of: 引起眼泪,(鼓掌等): *Her singing drew long applause.* 她的歌声引起历时甚久的掌声。**5** [VP6A, 14, 15B, 2A] ~ **(to),** attract: 吸引: *Street accidents always* ~ *crowds.* 街上发生的祸事总是吸引群众。*The film drew large audiences.* 这影片吸引了许多观众。*He drew* (= called) *my attention to a point I had overlooked.* 他提醒我注意我忽略的一点。*She didn't feel ~n towards him,* There was nothing in his character, behaviour, etc that attracted her.她对他没有好感(他的性格,举止等不能吸引她)。**6** [VP6A, 15B] take in: 吸入: *to ~ a deep breath,* 深深吸一口气; *stop to ~ breath,* to rest after exertion. 歇息。~ *one's first/last breath,* be born/die. 降生(死亡)。**7** [VP2A] (of a chimney, etc) allow a current of air to flow through; be built so that air and smoke pass up or through: (指烟囱等)通风; 通气: *This chimney ~s badly.* 这烟囱的通风情况不佳。*This cigar does not ~ well.* 这支雪茄不太通气。**8** [VP6A, 15B] ~ *sb* **(out),** cause, persuade, (a person) to talk, show his feelings, etc: 使(一人)吐露其情感等: *He was not to be ~n,* He refused to say anything about the matter. 他不愿吐露真情。*He has many interesting stories of his travels if you can ~ him out.* 如果你能诱使他讲述,关于他的旅行的有趣的故事讲给你听。**9** [VP2C, D] move; come (in the direction indicated by the *adv,* etc): 移动; 来(移动方向按照其后之副词等而定): *Christmas is ~ing near.* 圣诞节快到了。*The day drew to its close.* 这一天要过完了。*The two ships drew level.* 这两条船并排行驶。*The favourite began to ~* (= gain) *on the other runners.* 那匹众所认为会获胜的马开始逼近其他的马。*The Queen's horse quickly drew away from the others,* went ahead of them. 女王的马迅速地越过了其他的马。*Everyone drew back in alarm.* 每个人都惊慌而后退。*When the enemy saw how strong our forces were, they drew off,* went back. 敌人发现我们的兵力是多么强大时,

他们就撤退了。**10** [VP6A, 15B] cause to move or come (in the direction indicated by the *adv,* etc): 使移动(其方向按照后面的副词等而定): *He drew himself up to his full height,* stood in an erect, stiff attitude. 他笔直地站着。**11** [VP6A, 2A] make with a pen, pencil, chalk, etc: 绘; 画: *to ~ a straight line/a circle;* 绘(画)一直线(圆周); *to ~ a picture/plan/diagram;* 绘制图画(平面图,图表); *to ~ a horse.* 画一匹马。*She ~s well.* 她画得好。(fig) describe in words: (喻)描写; 描绘: *The characters in Jane Austen's novels are well ~n.* 简·奥斯汀的小说里的人物描写得很好。~ *a distinction (between),* point out differences; show the dividing line. 指出(…之)异; 指出界线。~ *a parallel/comparison/analogy (between),* show how two things are alike. 指出(…之)相似处。~ *the line (at),* set limits; declare what cannot be allowed; refuse to go as far as or beyond: 限制; 划定界限; 宣布不许做之事; 不肯做到或超越某种程度: *I don't mind lending him my razor, but I ~ the line at lending him my toothbrush.* 把剃刀借给他我不介意,但我不能把我的牙刷借给他。**12** [VP6A, 15B] write out: 写出: ~ *a bill/a cheque/an order* (on a banker, etc, for a sum of money). 开票据(支票, 汇票)(与 on 连用,后接银行业者等; 与 for 连用,后接开出的款处)。**13** [VP6A] (of a ship) require (a certain depth of water) in order to float; (指船)吃(水): *The ship ~s 20 feet of water.* 这船吃水二十英尺。**14** [VP6A, 2A] end (a game, etc) without either winning or losing: 不分胜负地结束(比赛等): *a football or cricket match;* 不分胜负地结束一足球或板球赛; *a ~n game;* 不分胜负的比赛; *to ~ 2—2.* 二比二平手。*The teams drew.* 这些队赛成平手。**15** [VP6A, 2A, B] extract the essence of: 吸取…之精华: *to let the tea ~ for three minutes.* 让茶泡三分钟。**16** (usu in *pp*) (of the features) pull out of shape: (通常用过去分词)(指面貌)拉之使变形: *a face ~n with pain/anxiety;* 因痛苦(忧虑)而扭曲的面孔; *with ~n features.* 眉蹙嘴苦。**17** [VP2C, 3A, 14, 15B] (special uses with *preps* and adverbial *particles*): (与介词及副词性小品词连用的特殊用法):

draw back, (fig) show unwillingness: (喻)表示不愿意: ~ *back from a proposal.* 不愿接受建议。⇨ **drawback(1).**

draw in, (of a day) (指白昼) **(a)** reach its end. 结束。**(b)** become shorter: 变短: *The days begin to ~ in after midsummer.* 仲夏之后白昼开始变短了。

draw on, (of a period of time) approach: (指一段时间)接近: *Night drew on.* 夜即来临。~ *on sth/sb,* take or use as a source: 用做来源: *If newspapermen cannot get facts for their stories, they sometimes ~ on their imaginations.* 如果记者们采访不到事实真相来写报道,他们有时就凭想象力去编造。*We mustn't ~ on our savings.* 我们不可动用我们的积蓄。*You may ~ on me for any sum up to £500,* get sums up to this maximum from me or my agents. 五百英镑以内的款项我可以借给你。~ *sb on,* attract, entice him. 吸引某人,诱惑某人。

draw out, (of a day) become longer: (指白昼)变长: *Christmas passed and the days began to ~ out.* 圣诞节过了,白昼开始变长。~ *sth out,* stretch; cause to become longer: 伸展; 使变长: *He heated the metal and drew it out into a long wire.* 他将那金属烧热,并将它拉成一条长的金属线。*There was a long-~n-out discussion.* 有过长时间的讨论。*He has ~n out the subject into three volumes.* 他将这题目加以引伸,写了三卷。~ *sb out,* ⇨ **8** above. 参看上列第 8 义。

draw (sth/sb) up, **(a)** (of a vehicle) (cause to) come to a stop: (指车辆)(使)停止: *The taxi drew up in front of the station.* 计程车驶至车站前面停下。**(b)** prepare; compose: 预备; 草拟: *to ~ up a contract.* 草拟一合约。**(c)** (usu passive) (of troops, etc) bring into regular order: (通常用被动语态)(指军队等)使排列整齐; 列队: *The troops were ~n up ready for the inspection.* 军队排列整齐准备接受检阅。

draw·back /'drɔːbæk; 'drɔ,bæk/ *n* **1** [C] sth which

lessens one's satisfaction, or makes progress less easy; disadvantage *(to)*. 缺陷; 障碍; 不利(与 to 连用). **2** [U] amount of import duty paid back when goods are exported again. 退还之关税.

draw·bridge /'drɔːbrɪdʒ; 'drɔ,brɪdʒ/ *n* bridge that can be pulled up at the end(s) by chains (eg across the moat of a castle in ancient times to prevent passage, or across a river or canal to allow ships to pass). (可拉起或放下的)活动桥; 吊桥(例如古时设于防御城堡之壕沟上以控制通行者, 或设于河上可拉起让船通行者).

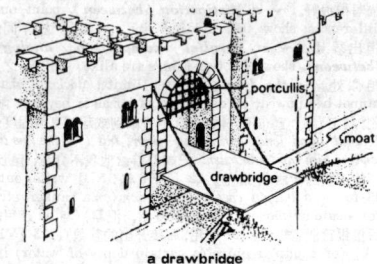

a drawbridge

drawer /drɔː(r); drɔr/ *n* **1** box-like container (with a handle or handles) which slides in and out of a piece of furniture, etc. 抽屉. **chest of '~s**, piece of furniture consisting of a set of ~s. 带抽屉的橱柜. **2** *(pl)* old-fashioned two-legged undergarment for the lower part of the body; knickers. (复)旧式的内裤; 灯笼短裤. **3** /'drɔːər; 'drɔə/ person who draws pictures; person who draws a cheque, etc. 绘图画者; 开支票等者.

draw·ing /'drɔːɪŋ; 'drɔːɪŋ/ *n* [U] the art of representing objects, scenes, etc by lines, with a pencil, chalk, etc; [C] sth made in this way; a sketch, plan, etc. 绘画; 制图; 图画; 图样; 图案. **out of ~**, incorrectly drawn. 不合画法; 画错. **'~-board**, flat board on which to fasten paper for ~, used eg by a draftsman; (fig) planning stage. 制图板; (喻)计划阶段. **'~-pin**, (US 美 = *thumb-tack*) flat-headed pin for fastening paper to a ~-board, notice-board, etc. 图钉.

draw·ing-room /'drɔːɪŋ rum US: ruːm; 'drɔ·ŋ,rum/ *n* room in which guests are received. 客厅.

drawl /drɔːl; drɔl/ *vi, vt* [VP2A, C, 6A, 15B] speak so that the sounds of the vowels are longer than usual. 拖长语调地说; 慢吞吞地说话: *The speaker ~ed on.* 那位发言者慢吞吞地继续说. *Don't ~ (out) your words.* 不要慢吞吞地说话. □ *n* slow way of speaking. 慢吞吞的说话方式.

drawn /drɔːn; drɔn/ *pp* of **draw²**; ⇨ esp **2, 14, 16.**

dray /dreɪ; dre/ *n* low, flat, four-wheeled cart, without sides, for heavy loads, eg barrels from a brewery. 低平而无侧板的四轮载货马车(例如自酒厂运桶装酒者).

dread /dred; drɛd/ *n* [U] (also 亦作 *a ~ of*) great fear and anxiety: 恐惧; 忧惧: *to be in ~ of sb or sth;* 怕某人或某物; *to live in constant ~ of poverty.* 经常担忧贫穷. *Cats have a ~ of water.* 猫怕水. □ *vt, vi* [VP 6A, C, 7A] fear greatly: 畏惧: *to ~ a visit to/~ having to visit the dentist.* 害怕看牙医. *I ~ to think of what may happen.* 我怕想可能发生的事. **~ed** *part adj* greatly feared: 非常可怕的: *a ~ful disaster.* 可怕的灾难. *What a ~ful story!* 多么可怕的故事啊! **2** (colloq) unpleasant: (口)令人不愉快的: *What a ~ful weather!* 多么讨厌的天气! **~·fully** /-fulɪ; -fəlɪ/ *adv* **~·ful·ness** *n*

dread·nought /'drednɔːt; 'drɛd,nɔt/ *n* type of battleship in the early years of the 20th century. 二十世纪初期一种战舰; 无畏战舰.

dream¹ /driːm; drim/ *n* [C] **1** sth which one seems to see or experience during sleep: 梦: *to have a ~ (about sth);* 做梦(梦见某事物); *to awake from a ~.* 自梦中醒来. **'~·land; '~·world**, region outside the laws of nature, as experienced in sleep or in the imagination. 梦乡; 梦境. **2** state of mind in which things going on around one seem unreal: 梦一般的感觉; 幻然若梦: *live/go about in a ~.* 梦--般地过日子(四处走动). **3** mental picture(s) of the future: 幻想; 梦想: *~s of wealth and happiness.* 梦想财富和幸福. **4** (colloq) beautiful or pleasing person, thing, experience, etc: (口)美丽或悦人的人, 事物, 经验等: *His holiday by the sea was a ~.* 他在海滨的度假是一种快乐的经验. **~·less** *adj* without ~s. 无梦的. **~·like** /'driːmlaɪk; 'drim,laɪk/ *adj* like a ~. 梦一般的.

dream² /driːm; drim/ *vi, vt* (*pt, pp* ~ed /driːmd; drimd/ or **dreamt** /dremt; drɛmt/) **1** ~ *(about/of)*, have ~s; see, experience, in a dream; imagine; suppose: 做梦; 梦见; 想象; 假想: *He often ~s.* 他常做梦. *The soldier often ~t of/about home.* 这士兵常梦到家. *He ~t that he was at sea.* 他梦见他在航海. *I certainly didn't promise you £100; you must have ~t it.* 我的确未答应你一百英镑; 一定是你在做梦. *I wouldn't ~ of doing such a thing,* The idea would never occur to me. 我绝不会想到做这件事. *He little ~ed that....* did not imagine or suppose that.... 他做梦也不会想到.... **2** [VP15 B] ~ *away,* spend idly: 虚度: *~ away one's time/the hours.* 虚度光阴. **3** [VP 15 B] ~ *up,* (colloq) imagine (a plan, etc). (口)构思(计划等). **~·er** *n* person who ~s; person with impractical ideas, plans, etc. 做梦者; 梦者; 梦想家.

dreamy /'driːmɪ; 'drimɪ/ *adj* (-ier, -iest) **1** (of a person) with thoughts far away from his surroundings or work. (指人)心不在焉的. **2** (of things, experiences) vague; unreal: 朦胧的, 模糊的; 不真实的: *a ~ recollection of what happened;* 对往事的模糊回忆: (colloq) pleasing; soothing: (口)悦人的; 予人慰藉的: *~ music.* 轻柔而予人慰藉的音乐. **dream·ily** /-ɪlɪ; -ɪlɪ/ *adv*

dreary /'drɪərɪ; 'drɪrɪ/ *adj* (-ier, -iest) (poet 诗 **drear** /drɪə(r); drɪr /) dull; gloomy; causing low spirits: 沉闷的; 阴沉的; 使人忧郁的: *~ work/weather/people.* 沉闷的工作(阴沉的天气; 忧郁的人们). **drear·ily** /-ɪlɪ; -əlɪ/ *adv*

dredge¹ /dredʒ; drɛdʒ/ *n* apparatus for bringing up mud, oysters, specimens, etc from the bed of the sea, rivers, etc. 捞泥机; 捞泥船. □ *vt, vi* [VP6A, 15B, 2A, 3A] ~ *(up),* bring up with a ~; clean with a ~: 用捞泥机捞取; 用捞泥机捞取; 用捞泥机清除: ~ *(up) mud;* 挖泥; *to ~ (for) oysters;* 捞取牡蛎; *to ~ a channel/harbour.* 疏浚河床(港口). **dredger** *n* boat carrying a ~. 捞泥船; 疏浚船; 挖捞船.

dredge² /dredʒ; drɛdʒ/ *vt* [VP6A, 14] sprinkle or scatter: 撒; 撒布: *to ~ meat with flour;* 将面粉撒在肉上; *to ~ sugar over a cake.* 把糖撒在糕上. **dredger** *n* box with holes in the lid for sprinkling flour, sugar, etc on food. (盖上有孔, 可用以撒面粉, 糖等于食物上的)撒布盒.

dregs /dregz; drɛgz/ *n pl* **1** bits of worthless matter which sink to the bottom of a glass, bottle, barrel, etc of liquid. 渣滓. **drink/drain to the ~,** drink and leave only the ~. 喝干. **2** (fig) worst and useless part: (喻)最劣和无用的部分: *the ~ of society/humanity.* 社会(人类)的渣滓.

drench /drentʃ; drɛntʃ/ *vt* [VP6A] make wet all over, right through: 使湿透: *to be ~ed with rain/~ed to the skin.* 被雨淋透(湿透). *They were caught in a downpour and came back ~ed.* 他们遭逢大雨, 回来时湿透了. **~·ing** *n* thorough wetting: 湿透: *We got a ~ing.* 我们湿透了.

dress[1] /dres; drɛs/ n 1 [C] one-piece outer garment with a bodice and skirt worn by a woman or girl; gown or frock. 妇女的外衣; 妇女的长服。 2 [U] clothing in general (for both men and women), esp outer garments: 衣服(男女服装的总称, 尤指外衣): *She doesn't care much about* ～, is not much interested in clothes. 她不太注意衣着。 '～ **circle**, lowest gallery in a theatre, in which evening ～ was formerly required. 戏院楼座中之最低座; 楼座前排(昔时须着晚礼服始能入座)。 '～ **coat**, black, swallow-tailed coat worn by men for evening ～. 燕尾服。 '～**maker**, woman who makes women's ～es. 制女服的女裁缝。 '～ **rehearsal**, final rehearsal of a play, at which actors wear the costumes to be worn at actual performances. (演员着剧中人服装之)最后排演; 彩排。 'evening ～, clothing worn at, formal social occasions (eg dinners, evening parties). 晚礼服。 full '～, kind of clothes worn on special occasions: 盛装; 礼服: *ambassadors, naval and military officers, all in full* ～. 大使们, 海陆军军官, 均着礼服。

dress[2] /dres; drɛs/ vt, vi 1 [VP6A, 2A] put on clothes: 给～穿衣服; 穿衣服: *Mary was* ～*ing her doll.* 玛丽正为她的洋娃娃穿衣服。 *Jim isn't old enough to* ～ *himself.* 吉姆未到自己会穿衣服的年纪。 *Have you finished* ～*ing?* 你衣服穿好了没有? *How long does it take you to* ～ *(yourself)?* 你穿衣服需要多少时间? [VP15B, 2C] ～ **up**, put on special clothes, as for a play, a fancy dress ball, etc: (为演戏, 参加化装舞会等)着特殊服装: *The children* ～*ed (themselves) up as pirates.* 孩子们打扮成海盗。 2 [VP2A, C] put on evening dress: 着晚礼服: *We don't* ～ *for dinner nowadays.* 现今我们不再着晚礼服了。 *You've just time to* ～ (= change into evening dress) *before we leave for the theatre.* 在我们赴剧院前, 你刚好有时间换好晚礼服。 3 [VP2C] (of what is habitual) wear clothes: (指惯常的)穿衣: *He has to* ～ *well in his position.* 以他的地位他必须穿得很整齐。 4 *be* ～*ed in*, be wearing: 穿着: *She was* ～*ed in white.* 她穿着白色的衣服。 *They were* ～*ed in the height of fashion,* wearing the most fashionable clothes. 他们穿着最时髦的衣服。 5 [VP6A] provide clothes for: 供以衣服: *How much does it cost them a year to* ～ *their children?* 他们一年花多少钱供给子女的衣服? 6 [VP6A] make ready to use; prepare: 处置妥当; 准备; 调制: to ～ *leather*, make it soft and smooth: 鞣革; 制革(使软而光滑); to ～ *a salad*, ⇨ **dressing**(3); 加调味油于生菜; to ～ *a chicken*, clean it ready for cooking. 剖洗一鸡。 7 [VP6A, 15B] brush and comb, arrange (one's hair): 梳理(头发); 整刷(毛): to ～ *down a horse*, brush its coat well. 梳理马毛。 ～ **sb down**, (fig) scold him severely; thrash him. (喻)严斥某人; 笞打某人。 Hence, 由此产生, '～*ing*-'**down** severe scolding. 严斥。 8 [VP6A] clean and bandage (a wound, etc). 包扎(伤处等)。 9 [VP6A] make cheerful and attractive: 使悦目动人; 装饰: to ～ *a shop-window*, eg with attractive goods: (以美观的货品等)装饰商店橱窗; to ～ *the streets*, eg with flags; (以旗帜等)装饰街道; to ～ *a Christmas-tree*. 装饰圣诞树。 10 [VP6A, 2A] (mil) get or bring (soldiers) into a straight line: (军)整列(士兵): ～ *the ranks*. 整列队伍。

dress·age /'dresa:ʒ; 'drɛsɑʒ/ n [U] (F) training of horses (for show-jumping, etc). (法)训练马(使表演跳跃等)。

dresser[1] /'dresə(r); 'drɛsə/ n person who dresses, 穿衣者, 装饰者, 处理者, esp 尤指 **(a)** one who helps a surgeon to dress wounds in a hospital: (医院中帮助外科医生的)裹伤者; **(b)** person who helps actors and actresses to dress ready for the stage. (剧场中帮助演员着装的)服装师。

dresser[2] /'dresə(r); 'drɛsə/ n 1 piece of kitchen furniture with shelves for dishes, and cupboards below often with drawers for cutlery, etc. 碗柜。 2 (US) dressing-table. (美) 梳妆台。

dress·ing /'dresɪŋ; 'drɛsɪŋ/ n 1 [U] process of

dressing (putting on clothes, cleaning and bandaging a wound, etc). 穿衣; 裹伤。 '～-**case**, one for brushes, bottles and other articles of toilet, when travelling. 化妆箱(旅行时装钮, 瓶, 及其他化妆用品者)。 '～-**gown**, (US 美 = *bath-robe*) loose gown worn over pyjamas, etc before dressing, etc. 晨衣; 睡袍。 '～-**table**, one with a mirror, used in a bedroom. 化妆台; 梳妆台。 2 [C, U] sth used for dressing wounds, eg an ointment, bandage, etc. 包伤用品(例如药膏, 绷带等)。 3 [C, U] mixture of oil, vinegar, condiments, etc used as a sauce for salads and other dishes. 调味酱(油, 醋, 作料等调和后置于生菜等食物上者)。 4 [U] substance used to stiffen silk, cotton, etc during manufacture. 浆丝、棉等的材料。

dressy /'dresɪ; 'drɛsɪ/ adj (-ier, -iest) (colloq) (of persons) fond of, looking smart in, fine clothes; (of clothes) stylish. (口)(指人)讲究穿的; 衣着考究的; (指衣服)时髦的。

drew /dru:; dru/ pt of **draw**[2].

dribble /'drɪbl; 'drɪbl/ vt, vi [VP6A, 2A] 1 (of liquids) flow, allow to flow, drop by drop or in a slow trickle (esp from the side of the mouth): (指液体)使滴下; 滴下(尤指自口边): *Babies often* ～ *on their bibs.* 婴儿常流口水在围嘴上。 2 (football) take (the ball) forward by means of quick, short kicks, either between the feet of one player, or by short passes from one player to another. (足球)盘(球); 短传(球)。 **drib·bler** n person who ～s. 流口水者; 盘球者。

drib·let /'drɪblɪt; 'drɪblɪt/ n falling drop; small amount: 小滴; 小量; 微量: *in/by* ～*s*, a little at a time. 一点点地。

dribs and drabs /ˌdrɪbz n 'dræbz; 'drɪbz ən 'dræbz/ n pl (colloq) small amounts. (口)小量; 微量。

dried /draɪd; draɪd/ pt, pp of **dry**[2].

drier /'draɪə(r); 'draɪə/ comp adj ⇨ **dry**[1]; n ⇨ **dry**[2].

drift[1] /drɪft; drɪft/ n 1 [U] drifting movement; being carried along by currents: 漂流; 飘动: *the* ～ *of the tide.* 潮汐的流动。 *The general* ～ *of the current was northerly.* 这水流常向北流。 '～-**age** /-ɪdʒ; -ɪdʒ/ n (of a ship) general movement off course due to currents, winds, tides, etc. (指船)(由于水流, 风向, 潮流等造成的)漂动; 航差。 '～-**net**, large net into which fish ～ with the tide. 漂网(捕鱼的一种大网, 鱼可随潮流入内)。 2 [C] sth caused by drifting: 由飘动或漂流造成之物; 刮刮而成之物; 漂刮而成之物: *Big* ～*s of snow / Big snow* ～*s made progress slow and difficult.* 大的雪堆使前进缓慢而困难。 *It was buried in a* ～ *of dead leaves.* 它被埋在一堆枯叶中。 '～-**ice**, broken ice carried along on the surface of the sea, a river, etc in masses by currents of water or air. 流冰。 '～-**wood**, wood carried along by currents and washed up on beaches. 由水冲至岸边的木头; 漂流木。 3 [U] general tendency or meaning: 大意; 要旨: *I caught the* ～ *of what he said.* 我懂得他所说的大意。 *Did you get the* ～ *of the argument?* 你懂得这论据的要旨吗? 4 [U] the way in which events, etc tend to move: 趋势; 倾向: *The general* ～ *of affairs was towards war.* 当时的情势是趋向战争。 5 [U] the state of being inactive and waiting for things to happen: 不采取行动; 等待事情发展: *Is the government's policy one of* ～? 政府是采取观望政策吗?

drift[2] /drɪft; drɪft/ vi, vt 1 [VP2A, C] be carried along by, or as by, a current of air or water; (fig, of persons) go through life without aim, purpose or self-control: 飘动; 漂流; (喻, 指人)无目的地生活: *The boat* ～*ed out to sea.* 那只小船漂往海里去了。 *We* ～*ed down the stream.* 我们顺流而下。 *The snow had* ～*ed everywhere.* 雪飘至各处。 *Is the factory / the corporation* ～*ing towards bankruptcy?* 这家工厂(企业)在盲目地走向破产之路吗? *She* ～*s from one job to another.* 她无目的地更换着工作。 2 [VP6A, 15B, 14] cause to ～: 使飘动; 使漂流: *The logs were* ～*ed down the stream to the saw-mills.* 圆木

料顺流漂至锯木厂。*The wind had ~ed the snow into high banks.* 风把雪飘积成高堆。**~er** *n* **1** boat used in ~-net fishing and, during war, for minesweeping. 带有漂网的渔船; 扫雷船。⇨ **drift¹(1).** **2** person who ~s(1). 生活无目的之人; 流浪者。

drill¹ /drɪl; drɪl/ *n* instrument with a pointed end or cutting edges for making holes in hard substances: 钻; 手钻; 锥: *a dentist's ~.* 牙医用的钻子。 □ *vt, vi* [VP6A] make a hole with a ~: 用钻钻孔(孔): *~ a hole in a stone wall;* 在一石墙上钻孔。 [VP2A] use a ~. 钻孔。'~·ing-rig, ⇨ **rig¹(2).**

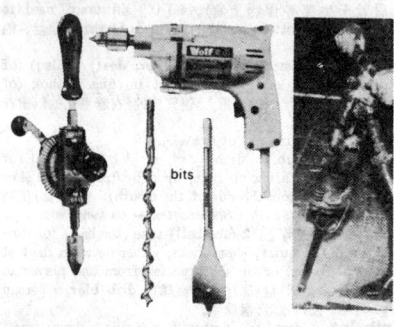

bits

drills

drill² /drɪl; drɪl/ *n* [C, U] **1** army training in the handling of weapons; formal movements, eg marching, turning, to develop alertness: 军事训练; 操练: *'bayonet ~;* 劈刺操练; '*gun-~.* 炮操练。*The soldiers were at ~ in the barrack square.* 兵士们在营房的操场上操练。 **2** thorough training by practical experiences, usu with much repetition: 练习: *~s in the English vowel sounds.* 英语元音发音练习。 **3** routine procedure to be followed, eg in an emergency: (应付紧急情况之)例行步骤: *'fire-~;* 救火演习; 消防演习; *'lifeboat ~.* 救生艇演习。 □ *vt, vi* [VP6A, 14, 2A] train, be trained, by means of ~s: 训练; 操练; 练习: *~ troops on a parade ground;* 在阅兵场训练军队; *a well-~ed crew.* 训练有素的船员。

drill³ /drɪl; drɪl/ *n* furrow; machine for making furrows, sowing seeds in them, and covering the seeds; row of seeds sown in this way. 犁沟; 播种机; 用播种机播下的一排种子。 □ *vt* [VP6A] sow (seeds) in ~s. 一排排地播(种子)。

drill⁴ /drɪl; drɪl/ *n* [U] heavy, strong linen or cotton cloth. 坚实的斜纹布(一种厚而压牢的麻布或棉布)。

drill⁵ /drɪl; drɪl/ *n* kind of West African baboon. (西非产的一种)黑面狒狒; 鬼狒。

drily /'draɪlɪ; 'draɪlɪ/ *adv* ⇨ **dry¹.**

drink¹ /drɪŋk; drɪŋk/ *n* [C, U] **1** liquid for drinking: 饮料: *We should die without food and ~.* 我们如果没有饮食必死。*We have plenty of bottled ~s,* beer, lemonade, etc in bottles. 我们有很多瓶装饮料(瓶装啤酒, 柠檬水等)。 **2** alcoholic liquor: 酒: *What about a ~?* 来杯酒如何? *I'll bring in the ~s,* eg the gin, whisky, sherry. 我去把酒拿来。*He's too fond of ~.* 他太爱喝酒。**be in ~/the worse for ~/under the influence of ~,** intoxicated: 酒醉: *He's a good husband except when he's in ~.* 他在不醉酒的时候是一个好丈夫。*drive sb to ~,* cause him to take to ~: 使某人嗜酒: *Mrs Bell's bad temper drove her husband to ~.* 贝尔太太的坏脾气使得她丈夫到汗酒。**take to ~,** acquire the habit of drinking regularly and too much. 嗜酒。**the ~,** (sl) the sea. (俚)海。

drink² /drɪŋk; drɪŋk/ *vt, vi* (*pt* **drank** /dræŋk; dræŋk/, *pp* **drunk** /drʌŋk; drəŋk/) **1** [VP6A, 15B, 2A] take (liquid) into the mouth and swallow: 饮; 喝: *to ~a*

pint of milk. 饮一品脱牛奶。 **~ sth down/off/up,** the whole of it (esp at once). 喝光(尤指一口气喝乾)。 **2** [VP6A, 15B] **~ (in/up),** (of plants, the soil, etc) take in, absorb (liquid): (指植物, 土壤等)吸收(水分): *The thirsty plants drank (up) the water I gave them.* 乾旱的植物把我浇的水都吸收了。*The parched soil drank (in) the rain.* 乾透了的土地吸收了雨水。 **3** [VP15B] **~ sth in,** (fig) take into the mind eagerly or with pleasure: (喻)欣赏: *The boy drank in every word of the sailor's story of his adventures.* 这男孩全神倾听着那水手叙述他冒险故事的每一句话。 **4** [VP6A, 15B, 2A] take alcoholic liquors, beer, wine, etc, esp in excess: 纵饮(酒); (尤指)纵饮: *He ~s far too much.* 他过度纵饮。*He ~s half his earnings,* spends it on alcoholic liquors. 他赚来的钱半花在饮酒上。*He will ~ himself to death.* 他将因纵饮而致死。 **5** [VP6A, 3A] **~ (to),** wish good (to sb) while raising one's glass: 举杯祝贺(某人): *to ~ a person's health;* 举杯祝某人一人健康; 举杯祝贺(某人); *to ~ a toast to sb;* 举杯祝贺(某人); *to ~ to sb's success;* 举杯祝某人成功; *to ~ to sb's health.* 举杯祝某人健康。 **~·able** /-əbl; -əbl/ *adj* suitable or fit for ~ing. 可饮用的。 **~·er** *n* (esp) person who ~s alcoholic liquor too often or too much: (尤指)纵饮者; 酒徒: *He's a heavy ~er.* 他是个豪饮者。 **~·ing** *n* process or habit of taking liquid(s), esp alcoholic liquor: 饮酒: *He's fond of ~ing.* 他喜欢饮酒。 '**~·ing-bout,** long spell of ~ing. 酒宴。 '**~·ing-fountain,** device for providing a supply of ~ing-water in a public place. (设于公共地方的)饮水器。 '**~·ing-song,** one to be sung at a ~ing party; one celebrating the joys of ~ing. 饮酒歌。 '**~·ing-water,** water fit for ~ing. 饮用水。

drip /drɪp; drɪp/ *vi, vt* (**-pp-**) [VP2A, C, 6A] (of a liquid) fall, allow to fall, in drops: (指液体)滴落; 滴下: *The rain was ~ping from the trees.* 雨从树上滴下。*The tap was ~ping.* 龙头在滴水。*Sweat was ~ping from his face.* 汗从他脸上滴下。*He was ~ping sweat.* 他大汗淋漓。*Blood was ~ping from his hand.* 血从他的手滴下。*His hand was ~ping blood.* 他的手在滴血。 **~ping wet,** very wet. 很湿的; 湿透的。 '**~·dry** *adj* (of a fabric) able to dry quickly, without previous squeezing or wringing out, when hung up to ~: (指织物)可用滴干法(洗后不用拧绞, 任其滴干)的; 快干的; *~-dry shirts.* 可快速晾干的衬衣。 □ *vt* dry in this way. 滴干。 *n* **1** the drop-by-drop falling of a liquid: 滴; 滴落: *the ~s from the trees/of the rain.* 自树上滴下的水(雨滴)。 **2** (sl) a dull, insipid person. (俚)乏味的人; 无风趣的人。

drip·ping /'drɪpɪŋ; 'drɪpɪŋ/ *n* **1** [U] fat melted out of roasted meat, used for frying, or spread on bread: 烤肉时滴落之油渣(用以煎炸或敷于面包上): *a slice of bread and ~.* 一片涂有烤肉油的面包。 '**~-pan,** pan in which ~ collects when meat is roasted. 烤肉时用以接油滴之锅或盘。 **2** (*pl*) liquid that drips or has dripped from sth: (复)滴落之物: *the ~s from the roof.* 檐上滴落的雨水。

drive¹ /draɪv; draɪv/ *n* **1** driving or being driven (in a car, etc, not in a public vehicle): 驾驶; 乘坐(非公共车辆):*to go for a ~;* 驾车一游; *to take sb for a ~.* 驾车载某人一游。*The station is an hour's ~ away.* 从此地驾车到车站有一个小时的路程。 **2** (in US also 美亦作) **~way** private road through a garden or park to a house. 穿过花园或邸园至一住宅的私人车路。 **3** (in games played with a ball, eg golf) [U] force given to a ball when it is struck; [C] stroke or hit: (球赛, 如高尔夫)击球之力; 一击: *a ~ to the boundary.* 击往边界。 **4** [U] energy; capacity to get things done: 精力; 魄力: *young men with brains, ~ and initiative.* 有头脑, 精力和进取精神的青年。*The new headmaster lacks ~/is lacking in ~.* 新校长缺乏魄力。 **5** organized effort or campaign: 有组织的努力或运动: *a 'sales ~,* one made to increase sales, eg by reducing prices; 推销运动(例如借减价); *the 'export ~,* to increase exports. 外销运动。*The school made a*

great ~ to raise £5000 for a new sports ground. 这学校发动筹募五千英镑以建筑一新的运动场。**6** tournament: 比赛；竞赛: *a 'bridge-~.* 桥牌比赛。**7** (mech) apparatus for driving: (机械) 传动装置: *front/rear ~,* with power that operates the front/rear wheel(s); 前(后)轮传动装置; *a four-wheel ~,* with four wheels connected to the source of power; 四轮传动; *right-/left-hand ~,* (of a motor vehicle) having the steering and other controls on the right/left side. (指汽车) 驾驶控制在右(左)方的。

drive² /draɪv; draɪv/ *vt, vi* (*pt* drove /drəʊv; drov/, *pp* driven /'drɪvn; 'drɪvən/) **1** [VP6A, 15B, 14] cause animals, people to move in some direction by using cries, blows, threats or other means: 驱；逐；赶；撵: to ~ cattle to market; 把牛赶向市场; *to ~ the enemy out of their positions.* 将敌人逐出阵地。~ *sb into a corner,* (fig) force him (eg during an argument) into a position from which escape will be difficult. (喻) 逼入死角; 逼入绝境(例如在辩论时驳倒某人)。**2** [VP6A, 2A] operate, direct the course of a railway engine, bus, motor-car or other vehicle; control, direct the course of an animal or animals drawing a cart, plough, etc: 驾驶; 驾驭: to ~ *a taxi/cart;* 驾驶计程车(驾一辆二轮马车); *to take driving lessons.* 上驾驶课。*D~ with caution.* 小心驾驶。**'driving licence,** licence to ~ a motor vehicle. 驾驶执照。**'driving school,** one for teaching persons to ~ a motor vehicle. 驾驶学校。**'driving test,** test which must be passed to obtain a driving licence. 驾驶执照考试。**3** [VP2A, C] travel in a car, etc which is at one's disposal (Cf *ride* in a bus, train or other public vehicle): 驾汽车旅行(乘汽车，火车等公共交通工具用ride): *We drove right up to the front door.* 我们将车一直开到大门。*Shall we ~ home or walk?* 我们驾车回家还是步行? *We are merely driving through,* travelling through (the place) without intending to stay. 我们只是开车从此地经过。**'~-in** *n* (and attrib) (也用作定语) restaurant, cinema, etc at which persons get service while in their cars: 驾车人内的餐馆，电影院等(可在车内进餐或看电影等): *a ~-in cinema/bank.* 驶车人内的电影院(银行)。**4** [VP15B, 14] carry, convey, (sb) in a car, etc from a public vehicle): (非公共车辆) 载送(某人): *He drove me to the station.* 他开车送我到车站。**5** [VP6A] (usu passive) (of steam, electricity or other kind of power) set or keep going; be the power to operate: (通常用被动语态) (指蒸汽, 电或其他动力)发动; 推动: *The machinery is ~n by steam/water-power, etc.* 这些机器是由蒸汽(水力等)推动。**'driving-belt,** belt that carries motion from an engine, motor, etc to machinery. 传动带; 掣带。**'driving-wheel,** one that communicates power to other parts of a machine. 传动轮; 主动轮。**6** [VP15B, 14] (of wind, water) send, throw, (lifeless things) in some direction: (指风, 水)推动(无生命之物): *The gale drove the ship on to the rocks.* 大风将这船吹至岩滩上。*The ship was ~n out of its course.* 这船被吹(冲)离了航线。*The wind was driving the rain against the window-panes.* 风吹雨点打在玻璃窗上。**7** [VP2C] go or move along fast or violently: 迅速行动; 猛烈行动: *The ship drove on the rocks/was driving along before the wind.* 船触礁(乘风而驶)。*The clouds drove across the sky.* 云在天空疾驰。*The rain was driving in our faces.* 雨疾落在我们的脸上。**8** [VP15B, 14] ~ *sth in;* ~ *sth into sth,* force a nail, screw, stake, etc into sth: 钉入(钉子, 螺丝, 木桩等): *With one blow he drove the nail into the plank.* 他一锤便将钉子钉入木板。**9** [VP6A, 15B, 14, 2A] hit or strike with force: 击: (cricket) (板球) to ~ *a ball to the boundary;* 把球击至边界; (tennis) (网球) *to ~ a ball out of the court.* 击球出界。(golf) (高尔夫球) *hit ~ well.* 他打得好。~ *sth home,* (fig) impress deeply on the mind. (喻)使印象深刻。*let ~ at,* aim a blow at; send a missile at: 打击; 射击: *He let ~ at me with his left,* aimed a blow at me with his left fist. 他用左拳打我。**10** [VP15B, 17, 22] cause or compel (sb) to be (in

a certain state); cause or compel (sb to do sth): (迫)使(某人)处于(某种状态); (迫)使(某人做某事): *Failure drove him to despair/desperation.* 失败使他绝望。*You'll ~ me mad/to my wits' end.* 你会把我气疯的(使我穷于应付的)。*He was ~n by hunger to steal.* 他为饥饿所迫而偷窃。**11** [VP15A, 2C] (cause to) work very hard: (使) 努力工作; 使~n. 他工作辛苦。*He ~ himself very hard.* 他努力地工作。*Don't ~ the workers too hard.* 不要使工人工作过度。~ *away at* (one's work), work very hard at it. 努力做(工作)。**12** [VP6A, 15B, 14] bore (a tunnel); make (a horizontal excavation): 挖(隧道); 开凿(横的坑道): *to ~ a tunnel/gallery through a hill;* 掘一隧道(通道)通过小山; *to ~ a railway across a hilly district.* 筑一铁路通过山区。**13** [VP6A] manage; bring about: 经营; 引起: to ~ *a roaring trade,* sell a lot of things very fast. 生意兴隆。~ *a hard bargain,* not give way easily to another person in a business deal. 谈生意不轻易让步。**14** [VP3A] ~ *at,* (in the progressive tenses only) mean, intend: (只用于进行时)用意; 意欲: *What's he driving at,* What's he trying to do, explain, etc? 他的用意何在? **15** [VP14] postpone; defer: 延缓; 展期: *Don't ~ it to the last minute.* 不要延至最后一分钟。

drivel /'drɪvl; 'drɪvl/ *vi* (**-ll-,** US **-l-**) [VP2A, C] talk nonsense; talk childishly: 胡说八道; 谈话幼稚: *What's he ~ling about?* 他胡说些什么么? *He's still ~ling on.* 他仍在胡说八道。□ *n* [U] silly nonsense; foolish talk. 胡说; 乱说。~ **-ler,** *n* ~er /'drɪvələ(r); 'drɪvlə/ *n* person who ~s. 胡言乱语者。

driven /'drɪvn; 'drɪvən/ *pp* of **drive².**

driver /'draɪvə(r); 'draɪvə/ *n* **1** person who drives (vehicles): 驾驶人; 司机: *a 'taxi-~;* 计程车司机; *a 'bus-~.* 公共汽车司机。⇨ **chauffeur.** *in the ~'s seat,* in control. 居于控制地位。**2** person who drives animals. 驱赶动物者。⇨ *drover* at **drove²,** *slave-* at **slave-. 3** (mech) part of a machine, etc that receives power directly, eg the drivingwheel of a locomotive. (机械)机器等直接接受动力部分(例如机车的主动轮)。**4** (golf) wooden club for driving the ball long distances from the tee. (高尔夫球)长打棒。

drizzle /'drɪzl; 'drɪzl/ *vi* [VP2A] rain (in many small fine drops): 下毛毛雨: *It ~d all day.* 下了一天的毛毛雨。□ *n* [U] fine rain. 毛毛雨。**drizz·ly** /'drɪzlɪ; 'drɪzlɪ/ *adj* drizzling: 下毛毛雨的: *drizzly weather.* 下毛毛雨的天气。

drogue /drəʊg; drog/ *n* **1** sea anchor (sth like a bag, dragged in the sea to steady a boat's movement). 浮锚; 海锚(一种袋状物, 拖在船后, 以平衡船身者)。**2** wind-sock, ⇨ **wind**¹(8). 风向指示袋。**3** cone towed by one aircraft as a target for use by others in firing practice. 斗形拖靶(由一飞机拖曳供其他飞机练习射击之用)。**4** '~ **parachute,** small parachute used to pull a large parachute from its pack. 小降落伞(用以将大降落伞拖出者)。

droll /drəʊl; drol/ *adj* causing amusement (because strange or peculiar). (因其怪异而)有趣的。~·**ery /-erɪ /-ərɪ/** *n* [U] jesting; [C] (*pl* **-ries**) sth peculiar and amusing; amusing trick. 滑稽; 奇特而有趣之物; 诙谐。

drom·edary /'drɒmedərɪ US: -ederɪ; 'drɑmə‚derɪ/ *n* (*pl* **-ries**) fast, one-humped riding-camel. 单峰骆驼。

drone /drəʊn; dron/ *n* **1** male bee; person who does no work and lives on others. 雄蜂; 不工作而依赖他人为生者。**2** [U] low humming sound (as) made by bees: 嗡嗡之声(如蜜蜂所发出者): *the ~ of an aeroplane high in the sky/of distant motorway traffic.* 高空飞机(远处高速公路车辆)的嗡嗡声。**3** [C] monotonous speech, sermon, speaker: 单调的演说, 说教或演说者: *He's a boring old ~.* 他是个令人厌烦的讲话单调的老人。□ *vi, vt* [VP15B, 2C] **1** make a ~ (2). 发嗡嗡声。**2** talk or sing, say (sth) in a low, monotonous way. 单调而低沉地说或唱: *children droning through their lessons.* 以单调而低沉的声音读书的孩子们。*The parson ~d out the*

psalm. 牧师以单调而低沉的声音诵赞美诗。

drool /druːl; drul/ *vi* ~ (*over*), drivel; slobber. 胡说; 乱说.

droop /druːp; drup/ *vi, vt* 1 [VP2A, C] bend or hang downwards (through tiredness or weakness): (由于疲倦或衰弱而)低垂; 下垂: *The flowers were ~ing for want of water*. 这些花因缺水而垂萎. *Her head ~ed sadly*. 她悲哀地垂着头. *His spirits ~ed, He became sad, low-spirited*. 他的精神委顿. 2 [VP6A] let (the head, face, eyes) move forward or down. 使(头, 面孔, 眼睛)下垂或朝下. □ *n* ~ing attitude or position. 低垂; 垂下. ~**ing·ly** *adv*

drop[1] /drɒp; drɑp/ *n* 1 (a) very small quantity of liquid, usu round- or pear-shaped: 滴, 点滴: '*rain~s*. 雨点. *He emptied the glass to the last ~*. 他一滴不留地饮干了那一杯. (b) (*pl*) liquid medicine taken in ~s: (复)滴使用的药水; 滴剂: *ear/eye/nose ~s*. 滴耳(点眼, 滴鼻)药水. *in ~s; by ~, slowly, one ~ at a time*. 一滴一滴地. 2 very small quantity. 极少量. *only a ~ in the bucket/ocean*, a negligible quantity. 沧海一粟; 九牛一毛. 3 (glass of) intoxicating liquor. (一杯)酒: *He has had a ~ too much*, is drunk. 他已喝醉了. 4 sth like a ~ in shape or appearance: 滴状物: '*acid ~s*, of boiled sugar; (熬糖做成的)一种圆形小糖果; '*ear~*, ⇨ **ear**[1](1). 5 movement from a higher to a lower level, esp distance of a fall: 下跌; (尤指)落下之距离: *a sudden ~ in the temperature*, eg from 30°C to 20°C; 温度之突降(例如自三十摄氏度降至二十度); *a ~ in the price of wheat*. 小麦价格之下跌. *There was a ~ of 10 metres from the window to the ground*. 从窗子到地上的距离为十公尺. *at the ~ of a hat*, at once; readily or willingly. 立刻; 自愿地. 6 thing that drops or is dropped(1): 滴落之物; 落下之物: *a ~ in a gallows*, platform or trap-door which falls from under the feet of a person executed by hanging. 绞台上犯人脚下陷落的踏板. '*~-curtain*, curtain lowered between the acts of a play in a theatre. 剧院中之垂幕. '*~-kick*, (Rugby football) one in which the ball is dropped and kicked as it rises. (橄榄球)落地踢(将球放落地面, 趁弹起时踢出之动作). '*~-hammer*; '*~-press*, machine for shaping or stamping, eg metal sheets for motor-car bodies, using the power of a dropped weight. 落锤(一种用重力压金属的机器, 例如压造汽车车身的金属板者).

drop[2] /drɒp; drɑp/ *vt, vi* (-pp-) (For uses with *adverbial particles* and *preps*, ⇨ 13 below.) (与副词性小品词和介词连用之用法, 参看下列第13义。) 1 [VP2A, C, 6A] (of liquids) fall, cause to fall, in drops. (指液体)滴落; 使滴下. ⇨ **drip**. 2 [VP6A, 2A, C, 14, 15B] fall (by the force of gravity, by not being held, etc); allow to fall: (因地心引力, 未能握住等)降落; 使落下: *It was so quiet you could hear a pin ~*. 那时是如此的安静, 你可以听到一根针落地的声音. *The apple blossom is beginning to ~*. 苹果树上的花开始落了. *The teapot ~ped out of her hand*. 茶壶从她手上落下. *She ~ped the teapot*. 她把茶壶掉落了. *~ anchor*, lower the anchor; come to anchor. 下锚. *~ a brick*, ⇨ **brick**. *~ a stitch*, (knitting) let it slip off the needle. (编织)使漏一针. 3 [VP2A, C, 6A, 15A] (allow to) become weaker or lower; (allow to) fall in amount, degree, pitch, condition, etc: (使)变弱或降低; (使)减低; (使)减少: *The wind/temperature has ~ped*. 风势已减(温度已下降). *His voice ~ped/He ~ped his voice to a whisper*. 他的声音降低(他的声音降低成耳语). *Don't ~ your voice at the end of a sentence*. 不要在句尾时降低你的声音. *Our boat gently ~ped* (= moved with the current) *downstream*. 我们的小船慢慢顺流而下. ⇨ **drift**[2](1). 4 [VP2A, C, 6A, 15A] (cause to) fall or sink to the ground, etc: (使)跌落; (使)跌倒: *They were ready to ~ with fatigue*, were so tired that they could scarcely stand. 他们疲乏得随时要倒下了. *She ~ped into a chair, utterly worn out*. 她一下子坐在椅子上, 显得精疲力竭. *He ~ped (on) to his knees*, knelt down. 他跪下. *Supplies were ~ped*

by parachute. 补给品由降落伞空投. Hence, 由此产生, '*~pingzone*, area where men, supplies, etc are ~ped by parachute. (人员, 补给等的)降落地区. *The enemy were still ~ping* (= firing) *shells into the town*. 敌人仍在炮轰这城市. *He ~ped a bird* (= hit one and caused it to fall) *with every shot*. 他每射一发便击落一鸟. *He ~ped* (= hit) *the ball to the back of the court*. 他把球打到球场后面去了. 5 [VP6A, 12A, 13A] utter or send casually: 偶然说出; 偶然寄出: *to ~ sb a hint*, give him one; 偶对于某人一暗示; *to ~ a word in sb's ear*; 有意地将一话说给某人听; *to ~ sb a postcard/a few lines*, a note. 寄给某人一张明信片(一封短信). ⇨ **let**[1](4) for *let ~*. 6 [VP6A] omit; fail to pronounce, write or insert: 略去; 遗漏; 未读出, 写出或置入: *He ~ s his h's*, eg by saying 'at for hat. 他略去 h 音(例如将 hat 读作 'at). *The relative pronoun is often ~ped if it is the object*, eg in '*the man* (*whom*) *we met yesterday*'. 关系代词做宾语时常被省略(如 the man whom we met yesterday 中之 whom). 7 [VP15A] set down; stop a car, etc to allow (sb) to get out: 使下车; 停下汽车等让(某人)下车: *Where shall I ~ you?* 你要我在什么地方停下来让你下车? *Please ~ me at the Post Office*. 请让我在邮局下车. 8 [VP6A] cease to associate with (sb): 停止与(某人)交往: *He seems to have ~ped his friends, no longer meets them*. 他好像与大多数的朋友不再来往了. 9 [VP6A] give up: 放弃: *to ~ a bad habit*. 革除一恶习. 10 [VP6A, 2A] (cause to) come to an end; no longer deal with or discuss: (使)结束; 不再讨论: *The correspondence ~ped*. 通讯停止了. *We ~ped the subject*. 我们不再讨论这问题. *The subject* (*was*) *~ped*. 这问题不再讨论了. *We couldn't agree about the matter, so we decided to let it ~*. 我们对此事意见不一致, 所以我们决定不再讨论了. *Let's ~ it*, stop talking about it. 我们不要再谈论此事了. 11 [VP6A] (colloq) lose (money, esp in gambling or a risky enterprise): (口)损失(金钱, 尤指在赌博或投机事业方面): *He ~ped 1000 francs at the Casino last night*. 他昨夜在赌场输了一千法郎. 12 (Rugby football) (橄榄球) *~ a goal*, score one by a *~*-kick, ⇨ **drop**[1](6). 13 [VP 2C, 3A, 15B] (special uses with *adverbial particles* and *preps*): (与副词性小品词和介词连用的特殊用法):

drop across sb/sth, (= run across, which is more usu) meet or find by chance. 偶然遇到或发现(某人或某事物, run across 较常用).

drop away, = ~ **off**(a).

drop back; drop behind, come to a position behind: 落后: *The two lovers ~ped back*. 这对情侣落在后面. *They ~ped behind the rest of the party*. 他们落在他人的后面.

drop in on sb; drop by/in/over/round, pay a casual visit: (to): 偶然拜访: *I wish he wouldn't ~ in on me so often*. 我希望他不要时常来访我. *Some friends ~ped in to tea/~ped by to see me*. 有几位朋友偶然来喝茶(偶然来访).

drop off, (a) become fewer or less: 减少: *His friends ~ped off one by one*. 他的朋友一个个地弃他而去. *The doctor's practice has ~ped off*, He now has fewer patients. 这医生的病人愈来愈少了. (b) fall asleep; doze: 睡着; 打瞌睡: *He ~ped off during the sermon*. 讲道时他在睡着了. *drop sth/sb off (at sth*), deliver (sb) to: 将某人(某物)送到(某处): *The bus will ~ you off at the station*. 这公共汽车送你到车站下车. ⇨ **drop**(7) above. 参看上列第 7 义.

drop out, (a) (of persons taking part in a contest, etc) cease to compete: (指人参加比赛等)弃权: *Three of the runners ~ped out*. 三位赛跑者弃权. (b) (of persons engaged, or about to engage, in an activity, etc) not take part; give up the idea: (指从事或即将从事某项活动等之人)不参加; 放弃: *Smith has ~ped out of the team*. 史密斯不参加那个队了. (c) (colloq) withdraw from conventional social activities, attitudes. (口)脱离传统的社会活动和观念等. Hence, 由此产生, '*~-out n*

(a) person who ~s out, eg one who withdraws from a course of instruction: 放弃者(例如退学者): *University* ~*-outs*, who do not finish their courses. 大学退学者。 **(b)** person who withdraws from conventional society. 退出传统社会者。

drop through, (colloq) come to nothing; be no longer discussed: (口) 毫无结果; 不再被讨论: *The big scheme he was busy with seems to have ~ped through.* 他所忙着的那个大计划似乎已成泡影。

drop·sy /'drɒpsɪ; 'drɑpsɪ/ n [U] disease in which watery fluid collects in some part of the body, eg the legs. 水肿; 浮肿。 **drop·si·cal** /'drɒpsɪkl; 'drɑpsɪkl/ adj suffering from ~; of or like ~. 患水肿的; 水肿的; 似水肿的。

drosh·ky /'drɒʃkɪ; 'drɑʃkɪ/ n (pl **-kies**) light, four-wheeled, open horse-carriage, as formerly common in Russia. 一种轻便,四轮,敞篷马车(如昔时俄国所用者)。

dross /drɒs US: drɔːs; drɔs/ n [U] waste material rising to the surface of melted metals; (fig) anything considered to be worthless, mixed with sth else. 浮渣 (熔化金属浮至表面的废物); (喻)任何与他物混在一起的无用之物。

drought /draʊt; draʊt/ n [C, U] continuous (period of) dry weather causing distress; want of rain. 久旱; 干旱时期; 旱灾。

drove¹ /drəʊv; drov/ pt of **drive²**.

drove² /drəʊv; drov/ n large number of animals (a flock of sheep, a herd of cattle) being driven together; crowd of people moving together: 被驱赶的一群动物(牛羊等); 行动中的一群人: ~*s of sightseers*, 一群群的游览者; *visitors in* ~*s*. 一群一群的访客。 **drover** n man who drives cattle, sheep, etc to market; cattle-dealer. 驱赶牛羊等至市场的人; 牛羊商人。

drown /draʊn; draʊn/ vt, vi 1 [VP6A, 2A] (cause sb to) die in water because unable to breathe: (使某人) 溺死; 淹死: *a* ~*ing man*. 快要淹死的人。 *He* ~*ed the kittens.* 他溺死了那些小猫。 *Do cats* ~ *easily?* 猫容易淹死吗? *He fell overboard and was* ~*ed*. 他从船上掉下水里淹死了。 2 [VP6A, 15B] ~ *(out)*, (of sound) be strong enough to prevent another sound from being heard: (指声音)淹没(另一声音): *The noises in the street* ~*ed out the teacher's voice.* 街上的喧声淹没了老师的声音。 3(fig): (喻): *a face* ~*ed in tears*, wet with tears; 泪流满面; ~*ed in sleep*, in a deep sleep (eg caused by exhaustion); 酣睡(例如疲惫不堪以后); *to* ~ *one's sorrows in drink*, to deaden them by getting drunk. 借酒浇愁。

drowse /draʊz; draʊz/ vi, vt [VP15B, 2A, C] ~ *(away)*, be half asleep; pass (time) half asleep: 假寐; 打盹睡; 以假寐度过(时间): *to* ~ *away a hot afternoon.* 整个炎热的下午都在打瞌睡。 □ n half-asleep condition: 假寐; 瞌睡: *in a* ~. 在瞌睡。

drowsy /'draʊzɪ; 'draʊzɪ/ adj (-ier, -iest) feeling sleepy; half asleep; making one feel sleepy. 欲睡的; 半睡的; 使人昏昏欲睡的。 **drows·ily** /-əlɪ; -ɪlɪ/ adv **drow·si·ness** n

drub /drʌb; drʌb/ vt (-bb-) [VP6A, 14] give repeated blows to; hit with a stick; (fig) beat an idea, a notion *into* or *out of* sb. 连续打击; 棒打; (喻)强使某人接受或放弃(观念,) or into and out of 运用)。 ~·**bing** n beating: 殴打: *give sb a good/sound* ~*bing*, beat him well. 痛殴某人。

drudge /drʌdʒ; drʌdʒ/ n person who must work hard and long at unpleasant tasks. 做苦工的人。 □ vi [VP 2A, C, 3A] ~ *at*), work as a ~ does: 做苦工; 辛苦地工作: *to* ~ *at dictionary-making*. 辛苦地编词典。 **drudg·ery** /-ərɪ; -ɪrɪ/ n [U] hard, unpleasant, uninteresting work. 辛苦而令人讨厌的工作。

drug /drʌg; drʌg/ n [C] 1 substance used for medical purposes, either alone or in a mixture; substance that changes the state or function of cells, organs or organisms. 药物; 药剂; 药材。 '~·**store** n (US) place

where a wide variety of articles is sold, where prescriptions can be made up, and where food and drink may be bought and eaten. (美) 药房 (兼卖杂货,并出售食物,饮料); 杂货店。 2 substance (often habit-forming) inducing sleep or producing stupor or insensibility, eg opium, cocaine: 麻醉药(例如鸦片,古柯碱):*the* ~ *habit*, the habit of taking harmful ~s; 服用麻醉品的习惯; *a* '~ *addict*; 有吸毒瘾的人; '~ *addiction*. 耽溺于麻醉品; 毒瘾; 药瘾; *a* '~ *pedlar*. 麻醉药贩子。 **3** *a* ~ *on the market*, an article that cannot be sold because there is no demand. 滞销货。 □ vt [VP6A] **(-gg-) 1** add harmful ~s to (food and drink): 下麻醉药于(食物和饮料): *His wine had been* ~*ged, and they stole his money while he was sleeping heavily.* 他的酒中被人下了麻醉药,乘他酣睡时他们偷走了他的钱。 **2** give ~s to, esp in order to make unconscious: 用药麻醉; 用麻醉药使昏迷: *They* ~*ged the caretaker and then robbed the bank.* 他们用药将看守人麻醉,然后抢劫了这银行。

drug·get /'drʌgɪt; 'drʌgɪt/ n [C, U] (floor covering of) heavy coarse woollen material. 粗毛毡; 粗毛呢; 粗毛地毯。

drug·gist /'drʌgɪst; 'drʌgɪst/ n **1** (GB) tradesman who sells drugs; pharmacist. (英)药商; 药剂师。 **2** (US) person who sells medicines, toilet articles and other goods, and usually food and drinks. (美)杂货商。 ⇨ *drug-store* at **drug**(1).

Druid, druid /'druːɪd; 'druɪd/ n member of the priesthood among the Celts of ancient Gaul, Britain and Ireland. (古高卢,不列颠及爱尔兰之凯尔特族中)督伊德教之僧侣。

drum¹ /drʌm; drʌm/ n **1** (music) percussion instrument made of a hollow cylinder or hemisphere with parchment stretched over the open side(s), ⇨ the illus at **percussion**; sound of a ~ or ~s, or sound as of ~s. (音乐) 鼓 (参看 percussion 之插图); 鼓声; 似鼓之声。 '~·*fire*, heavy continuous rapid fire from big guns. 猛烈的连珠炮火。 ~·**head court-martial**, one held while military operations are in progress, in order to try an offender without delay. 战地临时军法审判。 ~·**head service**, open-air military church service in which ~s form an altar. (军中之)野外礼拜式 (用鼓形成祭坛)。 ~·'**major**, sergeant in charge of drummers, and leader of a regimental band on the march; (US) (also 亦作 ~·**majo'rette** /ˌmeɪdʒə'ret; ˌmedʒə'ret/ leader of any marching band. 领导鼓手和团乐队的士官; (美)乐队队长。 '~·**stick**, **(a)** stick for beating a ~. 鼓槌。 **(b)** lower part of the leg of a cooked chicken, turkey, etc. 鸡腿(指煮熟的鸡,火鸡等的腿的下部)。 **2** sth like a ~ in shape, eg a cylindrical container for oil, a cylinder or barrel on which thick wire or cable is wound. 鼓状物(例如装油的圆筒状容器,缠绕粗铁丝或缆的卷轴)。 ⇨ **ear¹**(1).

drum² /drʌm; drʌm/ vt, vi (-mm-) **1** [VP2A, C] play the drum. 击鼓。 **2** [VP6A, 14, 2C, 3A] ~ *(on)*, make drum-like sounds; beat or tap continuously: 作似鼓之声; 连续敲击: *to* ~ *on the table with one's fingers;* 用手指连续敲敲桌子; *to* ~ *the floor with one's feet;* 用脚连续敲踏地板; ~*ming on the piano / at the door.* 连续弹奏钢琴(咚咚敲门)。 **3** [VP15B] ~ *up*, summon by ~*ming*: 击鼓召集: (fig) (喻) ~ *up* (= get, find) *support for a cause.* 争取对一运动的支持。 **4** [VP14] ~ *sth into sb/into sb's head*, cause him to remember it by repeating it often. 反覆述说一事使某人记住。 ~·**mer** n person who plays a drum; (colloq, esp US) commercial traveller. 鼓手; (口,尤美)旅行推销员。

drunk /drʌŋk; drʌŋk/ adj (usu pred) (pp of **drink²**) intoxicated; overcome by drinking alcoholic liquor: (通常用作表语) 醉的: *He was dead/blind/half* ~. 他烂醉如泥(酩酊大醉); 半醉。 *I've never seen anyone so* ~. 我从没有看到过喝得这么醉的人。 **get** ~, become intoxicated: 醉: *It's easy to get* ~ *on brandy.* 喝白兰地容易醉。 ~ **with sth**, (fig) elated: (喻)陶醉: *He was* ~

with joy / success. 他陶醉于快乐(成功)中。□ n person who is ～; man charged (at a police-station) with drunkenness. 酒醉者; 醉汉; 酗酒者。～·**ard** /-əd; -əd/ n man who is ～, or who often gets ～. 醉汉; 酒徒。

drunken /'drʌŋkən; 'drʌŋkən/ adj (usu attrib)(通常用作定语) **1** intoxicated; in the habit of drinking; often drunk: 酒醉的; 嗜酒的; 常酒醉的: a ～ and dissolute man. 一个嗜酒而又放荡的人。**2** caused by drinking; showing the effects of drinking: 因饮酒而引起的; 显示酒力的: a ～ frolic. 酒后狂欢。～·**ly** adv ～·**ness** n

drupe /druːp; drup / n (bot) fruit with juicy flesh, usu with a hard stone enclosing a seed, eg an olive, a plum, a peach. (植)核果(例如橄榄, 李子, 桃子)。

dry[1] /draɪ; draɪ/ adj (**drier, driest**) **1** not wet; free from moisture: 干的; 干燥的: Is this wood dry enough to burn? 这木柴是否很干可以燃烧了? *dry as a 'bone*; ,bone-'dry, quite dry. 十分乾的。**2** not rainy: 无雨的; dry weather; 无雨的天气; having a low annual rainfall: 年雨量少的: a dry climate. 干燥的气候。**3** not supplying water: 缺水的: a dry well; 干涸的井; 枯井; not supplying milk: 无奶的: The cows are dry. 这些母牛无奶。**4** solid, not liquid: 固体的; 非液体的: dry goods, ⇨ **12** below. 参看下列第12义。**5** without butter: 无奶油的: dry bread / toast. 无奶油的面包(烤面包片)。**6** (of wine, etc) not sweet, not fruity in flavour: (指酒等)不甜味的; 无水果味的: dry wines; 无甜味的酒; a dry martini, a kind of cocktail. 无甜味的马丁尼酒(一种鸡尾酒)。**7** (colloq) thirsty; causing thirst: 口乾口渴的; 令人口渴的: to feel dry; 觉得口渴; dry work. 令人口渴的工作。**8** uninteresting; dull: 无趣味的; 枯燥的: a dry lecture / book / subject. 枯燥的演讲(书, 问题)。*dry as 'dust*, very dull. 十分枯燥无味的。**9** unemotional; undemonstrative: 感情不露于外的; 不形于色的: dry humour / sarcasm; 冷峻的幽默(讽刺); a dry fellow. 感情不形于色的人。**10** plain; undisguised: 明白的; 赤裸的: dry facts. 赤裸裸的事实。**11** not connected with liquid: 与液体无关的: a dry cough, without phlegm; 干咳; a dry death, not by drowning: 死于陆上; a dry shampoo, one in which water is not used. 不用水的洗发剂; 干洗(发)。**12** (compounds) (复合词) ,dry **'battery**, electric battery with two or more dry cells. 干电池组。,dry-**bulb ther'mometer**, one of two thermometers, one dry and the other kept wet, used for measuring the humidity of the atmosphere. 干球温度计(一对干湿温度计中之干温度计, 用以测量大气的湿度)。dry **'cell**, cell in which the chemicals are in a firm paste which does not spill. 干电池。,dry-**'clean** v clean (clothes, etc) by using spirits (eg petrol) instead of water. (用干洗法)干洗(衣服等)。Hence, 由此产生, ,dry-**'cleaner**; ,dry-**'cleaning** nn. **'dry dock**, ⇨ **dock**[1](1). dry **'goods**, (also called 亦称作 soft goods), (contrasted with meat, groceries, etc) (与 meat, groceries 等相对) corn; (esp US) textiles, drapery. 谷类;(尤用于美国)绸缎呢绒。,dry **'ice**, solid carbon dioxide (used for refrigerating). 干冰(固体的二氧化碳, 用以冷却)。,dry **'measure**, measure of capacity for dry goods such as corn. 干量(量干物如谷类等的容量单位)。**'dry nurse**, not suckling the baby she is caring for. (不喂奶的)保姆。,dry **'rot** n decay of wood (causing it to crumble to powder), occurring when there is no movement of air over its surface; (fig) hidden or unsuspected moral or social decay. 木之干腐;(喻)隐伏或未料到的道德或社会之腐败。**'dry-shod** adj, adv without wetting the feet; with dry feet or shoes. 未湿脚的(地); 脚或鞋未湿的(地)。,dry-**'walling**, building of stone walls (eg for a field) without mortar. 不涂灰泥而造石墙(例如围于田地者)。drily / 'draɪlɪ; 'draɪlɪ/ adv dry·**ness** n

dry[2] /draɪ; draɪ/ vt, vi (pt, pp **dried**) **1** [VP6A, 15B, 2A, C] dry (out), make or become dry: 使干; 变干: Dry your hands on this towel. 用这毛巾擦干你的手。We

were drying our clothes in front of the fire. 我们正在火前烘干我们的衣服。Our clothes soon dried out. 我们的衣服不久便干了: 使完全干; 完全变干: The long drought dried up all the wells. 长期的干旱使所有的井干涸了。The stream dries up during the hot summer. 河流在炎热的夏季干涸了。His imagination seems to have dried up. 他的想像力似乎已枯竭了。Dry up! (sl) Stop talking! Be quiet! (俚)停止谈话! 安静! **2** [VP6A] (usu the pp) preserve by extracting moisture: (通常用过去分词)脱水以保藏: dried eggs / milk. 蛋(奶)粉。**dryer, drier** /'draɪə(r); 'draɪə/ n **1** substance mixed with oilpaints and varnish to quicken drying. 干燥剂。**2** (in compounds) thing that dries: (用于复合词中)干燥器: an electric 'hair-dryer; 电动吹发器; thing on or in which clothes, etc are placed to dry: 使衣服等变干之机器: a 'clothes-drier; 烘干机; a 'spindrier. 旋转式脱水机。

dryad /'draɪæd; 'draɪəd/ n (GK myth) tree nymph (希神)森林女神。

dual /'djuːəl US: 'duːəl; 'djuəl/ adj of two; doubled divided in two: 二的; 双重的; 分为二的: ～ control, for or by two persons; 二人管辖; 双重管辖; 双操纵; ～ ownership; 二人共有; ,～ 'carriageway (US 美 = divided highway); 双车道公路; ,～ 'purpose, adapted so as to, intended to, serve two purposes. 两用的。

dub /dʌb; dʌb/ vt (-**bb**-) **1** [VP22, 23] make (sb) a knight by touching him on the shoulder with a sword; give (sb) a nickname: 以剑轻击(某人)肩膀以授与爵士位; 给(某人)起绰号: They dubbed him 'Shorty' because he was so tall. 因为他长得这么高, 他们给他起一个绰号叫 '矮子'。**2** [VP6A] replace or add to the sound-track of a film or magnetic tape, esp in a different language. (尤指用不同的语言)为(影片或录音带)配音。

dub·bin /'dʌbɪn; 'dʌbɪn/ n [U] kind of thick grease used to make leather soft and waterproof. 保护皮革油; 皮革用防水软油。

du·biety /djuː'baɪətɪ US: duː-; dju'baɪətɪ/ n [U] (formal) feeling of doubt; [C] (pl -**ties**) doubtful affair. (正式用语)怀疑; 可疑之事。

du·bious /'djuːbɪəs US: 'duː-; 'djubɪəs/ adj **1** ～ (of / about), (of persons) feeling doubt: (指人)怀疑的: I feel ～ of his honesty. 我怀疑他的诚实。I feel ～ about / as to what to do next. 我不知下一步该怎么办。**2** (of persons) causing doubt (because probably not very good or reliable): (指人)(由于可能不十分好或不大可靠而)可疑的: He's a ～ character. 他是个可疑的人物。**3** (of things, actions, etc) causing doubt; of which the value, truth, etc is doubtful: (指事物, 动作等)可疑的; 其价值, 真实性等有问题的; 未定的: a ～ compliment; 含意不明的恭维; a ～ blessing. 不可确定的幸福。The result is still ～. 结果仍未定。～·**ly** adv ～·**ness** n

du·cal /'djuːkl US: 'duːkl; 'djukl/ adj of or like a duke. 公爵的; 似公爵的。

ducat /'dʌkət; 'dʌkət/ n gold coin formerly used in many European countries. (昔时欧洲许多国家所用的)金币名。

Duce /'duːtʃeɪ; 'duːtʃe/ n (I) leader (esp as used of Mussolini, Italian Fascist leader). (意)总裁; 领袖(尤指意大利法西斯领袖墨索里尼)。

duch·ess /'dʌtʃɪs; 'dʌtʃɪs/ n wife or widow of a duke; woman whose rank is equal to that of a duke. 公爵夫人; 公爵未亡人; 女公爵; 公国之女君主。

duchy /'dʌtʃɪ; 'dʌtʃɪ/ n (pl -**chies**) (also 亦作 dukedom) land ruled by a duke or duchess. 公爵之领地; 公国。

duck[1] /dʌk; dʌk/ n (pl -**s**, but often unchanged when collective)(用作集合名词时常无复数变化) **1** [C] common water-bird, both wild and domestic; female of this, ⇨ **drake**; cf the illus at **fowl**; [U] its flesh as food. 鸭; 母鸭(参看 fowl 之插图); 食用之鸭肉。,lame '～, disabled person or ship; business or commercial organization in financial difficulties. 行动失灵的人或

船; 有财务困难的商业机构。 *(take to sth) like a ~ to water,* (begin doing, being etc it) naturally, without fear, hesitation or difficulty. (做某事)自然地; 毫无疑惧或困难。 *like water off a ~'s back,* without producing any effect. 毫无效果或影响。 *~s and drakes,* game in which flat stones are made to skip along water. 用石使其在水上漂跃的游戏; 打水漂游戏。 *play ~s and drakes with* (eg one's money), squander, waste. 挥霍 (金钱等); 浪费无度。 **2** (colloq, also 亦 口, 亦作 *~y*) (GB) darling; delightful person. (英)可爱的人。 **3** vehicle (also 亦作 **DUKW** /dʌk; dʌk/) able to travel on land and water, used as a landing-craft by troops. 水陆两用车辆; 两栖载重车。 **4** (cricket, 板球, also sometimes 有时亦作 *~'s egg*) batsman's score of nought, 0: 零分:to make a ~; 获零分; be out for a ~. 因零分而出局。 **5** (compounds) (复合词) **'~·bill, ,~·billed 'platypus ⇨ platypus. '~·boards,** boards with narrow slats fixed across, for use on soft or muddy ground. 铺于泥泞地面上之木板道。 **'~·weed,** small flowering plant growing on the surface of shallow water (eg on ponds). (池塘等中所生的)水萍。 **'~·ling** /-lɪŋ; -lɪŋ/ *n* young ~. 小鸭。 *ugly '~·ling,* plain or stupid child who grows up to be attractive or brilliant. 丑小鸭 (指小时不好看或愚笨,长大后变得漂亮或聪明的人)。

duck² /dʌk; dʌk/ *vt, vi* [VP6A, 2A] **1** move quickly down (to avoid being seen or hit): 迅速俯下(以免被望见或闪避打击):to ~ one's head. 迅速低下头。 **2** go, push (sb), quickly under water for a short time: 短时没入水中; 将(某人)短时浸入水中:The big boy ~ed all the small boys in the swimmingpool. 那大男孩将游泳池中所有的小男孩都短时浸入水中。 □ *n* quick downward or sideways movement of the head or body; quick dip below water (when bathing in the sea, etc). 头部或身体迅速俯下或侧闪的动作; (海上游泳等)突将头浸入水中。 **~·ing** *n* thorough wetting: 湿透:to give sb a ~ing, eg by pushing him into or under the water. 使某人全身湿透(例如将其推入水中)。 *It rained heavily and we all got a ~ing.* 雨下得很大, 我们都湿透了。 **'~ingstool,** (hist) one (attached to a pole) on which a person was tied and ~ed into a pond, river, etc, as a punishment. (史)没刑椅(将一人缚于其上, 浸入水中, 以作惩罚)。

duck³ /dʌk; dʌk/ *n* [U] strong linen or cotton cloth used for outer clothing of sailors; *(pl)* trousers made of this. (供制船员外衣布)一种坚实的麻布或棉布; (复)此种布制成的裤子。

duct /dʌkt; dʌkt/ *n* **1** tube or canal through which liquid is conveyed, esp in the body: 管(尤指身体内者):'tear-~s. 泪管。 **2** metal tube and outlet for air (to ventilate, eg an aircraft): 通气的金属管(例如飞机上者); 通风管:The air ~s above your seat may be adjusted to your convenience. 你可任意调整你座位上方的通气管。

duc·tile /'dʌktaɪl US: -tl; 'dʌktl/ *adj* **1** (of metals) that can be pressed, beaten or drawn into shape while cold, eg copper. (指金属, 不必加热)可延展的; 可拉长的(例如铜)。 **2** (fig of a person, his character) easily influenced, managed or directed; docile. (喻, 指人或其性格)易指使的; 驯良的。 **duc·til·ity** /dʌk'tɪlətɪ; dʌk'tɪlətɪ/ *n* [U] the quality of being ~(1). 延展性; 韧性。

dud /dʌd; dʌd/ *n, adj* (sl) (thing or person) of no use, eg a shell or bomb that fails to explode or a banknote or cheque of no value. (俚)无用的(人或物)(例如未能爆炸的炮弹或炸弹, 失效的钞票或支票)。

dude /djuːd US: duːd; djuːd/ *n* (US) dandy. (美)纨袴子弟; 花花公子。 *'~ ranch,* ranch organized for tourists. 供观览的农场。

dudg·eon /'dʌdʒən; 'dʌdʒən/ *n in high ~,* offended and feeling indignation, or sullen anger: 极为愤怒:He went off in high ~. 他极为愤怒地离去了。

duds /dʌdz; dʌdz/ *n pl* (sl) clothes, esp old or ragged

clothes. (俚)衣服(尤指破旧者)。

due¹ /djuː US: duː; djuː/ *adj* **1** due (to), to be paid: 当付的; 应付给的:When is the rent due? 何时应付房租? The wages due to him will be paid tomorrow. 他应得的工资明天付给他。 **2** (attrib only) suitable; right; proper: (仅用作定语)适当的; 正当的; 适宜的:after due consideration; 经过适当考虑后; in due course, at the right and proper time. 在适当时期; 时机一至。 **3** (to be) expected; appointed or agreed (for a certain time or date): 预期的; 应到的; 预定的:When is the steamer due? 轮船预定何时到达?The train is due (in) at 1.30. 火车应一点半到达。 *Mr Hill is due to speak/lecture twice tomorrow.* 希尔先生预定明天演讲两次。 **4** *due to,* that may be ascribed or attributed to: 由于; 起因于: The accident was due to careless driving. 车祸起因于驾驶疏忽。(Cf 参较 owing to: Owing to (= Because of) his careless driving, we had a bad accident. 由于他驾驶疏忽, 我们发生了一次大车祸)。 □ *adv* (of points of the compass) exactly, directly: (指罗盘方位)正向:due east/ north. 向正东(北)。

due² /djuː US: duː; djuː/ *n* **1** (sing only) that which must be given to sb because it is right or owing: (仅用单数)应得之物:give the man his due. 给予那人应得之物。 *give the devil his due,* (prov) be fair to a person even though he is not a friend, or does not deserve much. (谚)对恶人亦公平相待; 勿掩恶人之善(纵非其友, 或无甚价值, 亦予以应得之对待)。 **2** *(pl)* sums of money to be paid, eg for membership of a club, legal charges paid. (复)应付之款(例如会费, 诉讼费等); 应缴之费。

duel /'djuːəl US: 'duːəl; 'djuəl/ *n* (hist) fight (usu with swords or pistols) agreed between two persons, esp to decide a point of honour, at a meeting arranged and conducted according to rules, in the presence of two other persons called seconds; any two-sided contest: (史)决斗(通常用剑或手枪);双方的斗争:a ~ of wits. 二人斗智。 □ *vi* (-ll-, *US* also -l-) fight a ~ or ~s. 决斗。 **~·list, ~·ist** /'djuːəlɪst US: 'duː-; 'djuelɪst/ *n* person who fights ~s. 决斗者。

du·enna /djuːˈenə US: duː-; djuˈɛnə/ *n* (esp in a Spanish or Portuguese family) elderly woman acting as governess and companion in charge of girls; chaperon. (尤指西班牙或葡萄牙家庭中)少女的保姆; 陪媪。

duet /djuːˈet US: duː-; djuˈet/ *n* piece of music for two voices or for two players. 二部曲; 二重唱; 二重奏。

duf·fer /'dʌfə(r); 'dʌfə/ *n* (colloq) slow-witted, unintelligent or incompetent person. (口)笨拙无能之人。

duffle (also **duf·fel**) /'dʌfl; 'dʌfl/ *n* [U] coarse woollen cloth with a thick nap. 一种厚毛的粗呢。 *'~ bag,* a cylindrical kitbag (of cloth or canvas). (圆筒状, 布或帆布做的)行裹; 行李袋。 *'~ coat,* one of this material, usu with toggles instead of buttons, and a hood. 此种粗呢制成的上衣(通常以套索代替钮扣并有一兜帽)。

dug¹ /dʌg; dʌg/ *pt, pp* of **dig.**

dug² /dʌg; dʌg/ *n* udder or teat of a female mammal. (雌性哺乳动物之)乳房; 乳头。

du·gong /'duːgɒŋ; 'dugɑŋ/ *n* large sea mammal with flippers and a forked tail. 儒艮(一种大的海洋哺乳动物, 生有鳍状肢和叉形之尾)。 ⇨ **manatee.**

dug-out /'dʌg aʊt; 'dʌg,aʊt/ *n* **1** rough covered shelter made by digging, esp by soldiers for protection in war. 掩蔽壕; (尤指)避弹壕。 **2** canoe made by hollowing out a tree trunk. 独木舟。

duke /djuːk US: duːk; djuk/ *n* nobleman of high rank (next below a prince); (in some parts of Europe) independent sovereign ruler of a small State. 公爵; 欧洲某些公国之君主。 **~·dom** /-dəm; -dəm/ *n* **1** position and duties, rank of a ~. 公爵的爵位; 公国君主的地位。 **2** (=**duchy**) land ruled by a ~ who is a sovereign ruler.

公爵管辖地；公国。

dul·cet /'dʌlsɪt; 'dʌlsɪt/ adj (usu of sounds) sweet; pleasing. (通常指声音)美妙的；悦耳的。

dul·ci·mer /'dʌlsɪmə(r); 'dʌlsɪmə/ n (often portable) musical instrument like a zither with strings struck with two hammers. (常是可以携带的)洋琴；德西马琴(类似齐特琴,用双锤击打)。

dull /dʌl; dʌl/ adj (-er, -est) 1 not clear or bright: 不清楚的；不鲜明的:a ~ colour/sound/mirror/day/sky; 暗晦的颜色(模糊的声音；不明亮的镜子；阴天；阴暗的天空)；~ weather; 阴沉的天气；~ of hearing, unable to hear well. 听觉不良。2 slow in understanding. 头脑迟钝的；愚笨的: ~ pupils; 愚笨的学生；a ~ mind. 迟钝的头脑。3 monotonous; uninteresting; not exciting or appealing to the imagination: 单调的；无趣味的；枯燥的:a ~ book/speech/sermon/play. 枯燥无味的书(演说,说教,戏)。4 not sharp: 钝的:a ~ knife; 钝的刀子；a knife with a ~ edge; 口钝的刀子；(of pain) not felt distinctly: (指痛)隐约感觉到的:a ~ ache. 隐约感到的痛。5 (of trade) not active; (of goods) not in demand. (指贸易)萧条的；(指货物)滞销的。□ vt, vi [VP6A, 2A] make or become ~: (使)变钝；使不清楚；(使)变迟钝:to ~ the edge of a razor; 使剃刀口变钝；drugs that ~ pain. 减轻痛苦的药物。~y /'dʌli; 'dʌli/ adj ~·ness n

dull·ard /'dʌləd; 'dʌləd/ n mentally dull person. 愚笨的人。

duly /'djuːli US: 'duː-; 'djuli/ adv in a right or suitable manner; at the right time. 适当地；及时地。

dumb /dʌm; dʌm/ adj (-er, -est) 1 unable to speak: 哑的: ~ from birth. 生来即哑。We must be kind to ~ animals, ie also to animals other than human beings. 我们必须慈善对待不能言语的动物。2 temporarily silent: 暂时沉默的: The class remained ~ when the teacher asked a difficult question. 老师问一难题时,全班皆沉默无言。strike ~, make speechless, unable to talk because of surprise, fear, etc: (因惊奇, 恐惧等)说不出话；使吓呆: He was struck ~ with horror. 他吓得不能出声。'show n the communication of ideas by means of acting, etc but without words. 哑剧；哑剧。3 (US colloq) stupid; dull. (美口)笨的；愚蠢的。~·ly adv ~·ness n

dumb·bell /'dʌmbel; 'dʌm,bel /n short bar of wood or iron with a metal ball at each end, used in pairs (one in each hand) for exercising the muscles of the arms and shoulders. 哑铃(两端有金属球的短木棒或铁棒,同时用一对,每手持一个,以锻炼臂肩之肌肉)。

dumb·found (US also **dum·found**) /dʌm'faʊnd; dʌm'faʊnd/ vt [VP6A] astonish; strike dumb with surprise. 使惊愕；使呆。

dumb·waiter /dʌm'weɪtə(r); 'dʌm'wetə/ n 1 stand with (usu revolving) shelves for food, dishes, etc used at a dining-table. (回转式)食品台。2 (US; in GB food-lift) box with shelves, pulled up and down a shaft, to carry food, etc from one floor to another, eg in a restaurant. (美)递送食物的升降器。吊斗(英国指 food-lift)。

dum·dum /'dʌmdʌm; 'dʌmdʌm/ n '~ bullet, softnosed bullet which expands on contact, causing a gaping wound. 达姆弹(一种软头子弹, 击中会扩散, 造成严重伤害)。

dummy /'dʌmi; 'dʌmi/ n 1 object made to look like and serve the purpose of the real person or thing: 模型: a tailor's ~, for fitting clothes; 服装店之人像模型； a baby's ~, sucked like the nipple of a mother's breast. 橡皮奶头。2 (attrib) sham, imitation: (用作定语)假的;伪造的:a ~gun. 假枪。3 (in card games, esp bridge) player whose cards are placed upwards on the table and played by his partner; the cards so placed. (牌戏,尤指桥牌)明家(将牌摊起于桌面者);这些纸牌。4 person who is present at an event, etc, but who takes no real part, eg because he is a substitute for sb else. 名义代表(参与一事并不实际有所作为, 而系代表他人之人);傀儡。

5 (attrib) (用作定语),~ 'run, a trial or practice attack, shoot, performance, etc. 攻击,射击,演习等之试验或练习。

dump /dʌmp; dʌmp/ n 1 place where rubbish, etc may be unloaded and left; heap of rubbish, etc. 垃圾场；垃圾堆。2 (place where there is a) temporary store of military supplies: 军需品之临时贮存(站): an ,ammu'nition ~. 军火临时堆积所。3 (sl; pej) poorly cared for, dirty or ugly place (eg a village or town): (俚; 蔑)肮脏或丑陋的地方(例如一村镇): I should hate to live in a ~ like this. 我不愿住在这样肮脏的地方。□ vt [VP6A, 15A] 1 put on or into a ~(1); put or throw down carelessly; let fall with a bump or thud: 倒在垃圾场; 随便倾倒; 砰然倒下: Where can I ~ this rubbish? 我把这垃圾倒在什么地方？They ~ed the coal outside the shed instead of putting it inside. 他们把煤倒在棚外, 而不倒在棚内。2 (comm) sell abroad at low prices goods which are unwanted in the home market. (商)向国外廉价倾销国内市场不需要的货物。~er n (also 亦作 '~ truck) vehicle with a bin that can be tilted, for carrying and emptying soil, rubble, etc (eg for road building). (铺路时)运土, 碎石等的卡车。

dump·ling /'dʌmplɪŋ; 'dʌmplɪŋ/ n 1 small round mass of dough steamed or boiled with meat and vegetables. 与肉和蔬菜蒸或煮的面团。2 baked pudding made of dough with an apple or other fruit inside it. (将苹果等放在面团里烘制而成之)苹果布丁；水果布丁。

dumps /dʌmps; dʌmps/ n pl (down) in the ~ (colloq) in low spirits; feeling gloomy. (口)沮丧的；忧郁的。

dumpy /'dʌmpi; 'dʌmpi/ adj (-ier, -iest) short and fat. 矮胖的。

dun[1] /dʌn; dʌn/ adj, n dull greyish-brown. 暗褐色的；暗褐色。

dun[2] /dʌn; dʌn/ vt (-nn-) (continue to) demand payment of a debt or debts: (连续)催讨债款: a dunning letter. 讨债的信。□ n person who duns; debt-collector; importunate demand for payment. 讨债人；催债者；催付。

dunce /dʌns; dʌns/ n slow learner (esp a child at school); stupid person. 迟钝的学习者(尤指学童)；笨人。'~'s cap, pointed paper cap which a ~ was formerly given to wear in class as a punishment. 昔时劣等生受罚所戴的圆锥形纸帽。

dun·der·head /'dʌndəhed; 'dʌndə,hed/ n blockhead; stupid person. 蠢材；笨人。

dune /djuːn US: duːn; djun/ n mound of loose, dry sand formed by the wind, esp near the seashore. 沙丘(尤指海边被风吹积成者)。

dung /dʌŋ; dʌŋ/ n [U] excrement dropped by animals (esp cattle), used on fields as manure: 家畜的粪便(尤指牛粪,可用作肥料): to cart and spread ~. 用车装送并施粪。'~·hill, heap of ~ in a farmyard. 粪堆。

dunga·rees /ˌdʌŋɡə'riːz; ˌdʌŋɡə'riz/ n pl overalls of (usu) coarse calico. 粗布制成的工作服。

dun·geon /'dʌndʒən; 'dʌndʒən / n (hist) dark underground cell used as a prison. (史)地牢。

dunk /dʌŋk; dʌŋk/ vt [VP6A, 14] dip (a piece of food) into a liquid: 浸泡(食物): ~ a doughnut in one's coffee. 把油炸圈饼在咖啡中浸一下。

duo·deci·mal /ˌdjuːəʊ'desɪml US: ˌduːə'd-; ˌdjuə'desəml/ adj of twelve or twelfths; proceeding by twelves: 十二的；十二分算的；十二进法的:a ~ notation. 十二进法。

duo·denum /ˌdjuːəʊ'diːnəm US: ˌduːə-; ˌdjuə'dinəm/ n (anat) first part of the small intestine immediately below the stomach. (解剖)十二指肠。⇨ the illus at alimentary. 参看 alimentary 之插图。**duodenal** /ˌdjuːə'diːnl US: ˌduːə-; ˌdjuə'dinl/ adj of the ~: 十二指肠的:a duodenal ulcer. 十二指肠溃疡。

duo·logue /'djuːəlɒɡ US: 'duːəlɔːɡ; 'djuə,lɔɡ/ n conversation between two persons. 对话。

dupe /djuːp US: duːp; djup/ vt [VP6A] cheat; make a fool of; deceive. 欺骗; 欺瞒。 □ n person who is ~d. 受骗者。

du·plex /'djuːpleks US: 'duː-; 'djupleks/ adj double; twofold: 二倍的; 二重的: a ~ (oil-)lamp, one with two wicks; 双灯心的(油)灯; a ~ apartment, (US) one with rooms on two floors with an inner staircase. (美)跨两层楼的公寓套房; 楼中楼的公寓。

du·pli·cate[1] /'djuːplɪkət US: 'duː-; 'djuplɪkɪt/ adj **1** identical: 完全相同的: ~ keys for the front door of a house. 开启前门用的几把相同的钥匙。 **2** with two corresponding parts; doubled; twofold. 双联的; 加倍的; 双重的。 □ n [C] thing that is exactly like another. 完全相同之物。 in ~, (of documents, etc) with a ~ copy. (指文件等)一式两份。

du·pli·cate[2] /'djuːplɪkeɪt US: 'duː-; 'djuplə,ket/ vt [VP6A] **1** make an exact copy of (a letter, etc); produce copies of. 复写(信件等); 复制。 **2** double. 加倍。 **du·pli·ca·tor** /-tə(r); -tɚ/ n machine, etc that ~s sth written or typed. 复印机。 **du·pli·ca·tion** /ˌdjuːplɪ'keɪʃn US: ˌduː-; ˌdjuplə'keʃən/ n [U] duplicating or being ~d; [C] copy. 复写; 复制; 加倍; 复制物; 副本。

du·plic·ity /djuː'plɪsətɪ US: duː-; dju'plɪsətɪ/ n [U] deliberate deception. 欺骗。

dur·able /'djʊərəbl US: 'dʊə-; 'djʊrəbl/ adj likely to last for a long time: 耐久的: a ~ pair of shoes, not soon worn out or needing repair. 一双耐穿的鞋子。 □ n (usu pl) (often 常作 **consumer** ~s) goods bought and expected to last a long time (eg vacuum cleaners). (通常作耐久)耐用消费品; 可久用的货物(例如吸尘器)。 **dura·bil·ity** /ˌdjʊərə'bɪlətɪ US: ˌdʊə-; ˌdjʊrə'bɪlətɪ/ n [U]

du·rance /'djʊərəns US: 'dʊə-; 'djʊrəns/ n (old use) imprisonment. (旧用法)禁锢; 监禁。

dur·ation /djʊ'reɪʃn US: dʊ-; dju'reʃən/ n [U] time during which sth lasts or exists: 持续时间; 期间: for the ~ of the war; 战争进行的期间; of short ~. 短期的。

dur·bar /'dɜːbɑː(r); 'dɝbɑr/ n (hist) Indian ruler's court; reception given by a ruler in India. (史)印度王的宫廷; 印度王的接见。

dur·ess /'djʊəres US: djʊ-; 'djʊrɪs/ n threats, imprisonment, or violence, used to compel sb to do sth: 强迫某人做某事所用的威胁、监禁或暴行: under ~, compelled by such means. 受胁迫。

dur·ing /'djʊərɪŋ US: 'dʊər-; 'djʊrɪŋ/ prep **1** throughout the duration of: 在⋯期间: The sun gives us light ~ the day. 太阳在白天给我们阳光。 **2** at some point of time in the duration of: 在⋯期间之某一时间: He called to see me ~ my absence. 我不在的时候他来看过我。

durst /dɜːst; dɝst/ old pt form of **dare**. 旧时 dare 的过去式。

dusk /dʌsk; dʌsk/ n [U] time just before it gets quite dark: 黄昏; 薄暮: scarcely visible in the ~. 在黄昏时几乎看不见的。

dusky /'dʌskɪ; 'dʌskɪ/ adj (-ier, -iest) rather dark; dark-coloured; dim. 颜暗的; 黑暗的; 暗淡的。

dust[1] /dʌst; dʌst/ n **1** [U] dry earth or other matter in the form of fine powder, lying on the ground or the surface of objects, or blown about by the wind: 灰尘; 尘土: The ~ was blowing in the streets. 街上尘土飞扬。 When it rains ~ turns into mud. 下雨时尘土变成了泥。 **bite the** ~, (sl) fall wounded or killed. (俚)受伤倒地或倒毙。 (**humbled**) **in**(**to**) **the** ~, humiliated (as if lying at the feet of an enemy). 受屈辱(如倒在敌人脚下)。 **shake the** ~ **off one's feet**, leave in anger or scorn. 愤然离去。 **throw** '~ **in a person's eyes**, mislead him; prevent him from seeing the truth. 蒙骗一人; 欺瞒一人。 '~**bowl**, area that is denuded of vegetation by drought, unwise farming methods, etc. 因旱灾、种植方法不良等而缺乏植物的地区。 ,~**coat**, coat worn to keep ~ off or out. 御灰尘的外衣; 风衣。 '~**jacket**,

-wrapper, removable paper cover to protect the binding of a book. 书皮; 包书纸。 '~**pan**, pan into which ~ is swept from the floor. 畚箕; 簸箕。 '~**sheet**, n one for covering furniture not in use. 遮盖不用的家具之防尘布。 **2 a** ~, cloud of ~: 云状尘埃; 烟尘: What a ~! 灰尘漫天! (fig) commotion. (喻)骚动。 **kick up**/**make**/**raise a** ~, (sl, fig) cause a commotion. 闹事。(俚、喻)引起骚动。 **3** (in compounds) (用于复合词中) (GB; Cf 参较 US 美 refuse, trash, garbage) household refuse. (英)垃圾。 '~**bin**, box for such refuse. (Cf 参较 US 美 ash-can, garbage-box.) '~**cart**, vehicle into which ~bins are emptied. 垃圾车。 '~·**man** /-mən; -mən/ (pl **-men**) man employed (by municipal authorities, etc) to empty ~bins and cart away refuse. 清除垃圾的工人。 **4** (old use, poet or liter) remains of a dead human body: 遗骸: buried with the ~ of (= in the same grave as) one's ancestors. 与祖先遗骸葬在一起。

dust[2] /dʌst; dʌst/ vt **1** [VP6A, 15B] **dust sth** (**down**/**off**), remove dust from, by wiping, brushing, flicking: 拭去灰尘; 拂去灰尘: ~ the furniture; 拭去家具上的灰尘; ~ down the seat of a car. 拭去汽车座位上的灰尘。 ~ sb's jacket, (colloq) beat him. (口)殴打某人。 '~-up n (colloq) fight; quarrel. (口)打斗; 吵闹。 **2** [VP15A] sprinkle with powder: 撒以粉: to ~ a cake with sugar; 撒糖于糕上; sprinkle (powder, etc): 撒(粉等): to ~ sugar on to a cake. 将糖撒在糕上。 ~**er** n cloth for removing dust from furniture, etc. 擦布; 抹布; 掸子。

dusty /'dʌstɪ; 'dʌstɪ/ adj (-ier, -iest) covered with dust; full of dust; like dust; dry as dust. 覆有灰尘的; 满是灰尘的; 似灰尘的; 灰尘般干燥的。 ~ **answer**, answer that is not pleasing or satisfactory (to the receiver). 不满意的回答。

Dutch /dʌtʃ; dʌtʃ/ adj **1** of or from the Netherlands (Holland), its people, their language: 荷兰的; 荷兰人的; 荷兰语的: ~ cheese. 荷兰乳酪。 **2** (colloq uses) (口语用法) ~ auction, sale at which the price is reduced by the auctioneer until a buyer is found. 拍卖者自动落价直至有买主时的拍卖。 ~ courage, that obtained by drinking (spirits, etc). 酒后之勇。 ~ treat, meal, entertainment, etc at which each person pays for himself. 各自付费的聚餐、娱乐等; 打平伙。 **go** ~ (**with sb**), share expenses. (与某人)各自付帐。 **talk to sb like a** ~ **uncle**, lecture him candidly but severely. 谆谆告诫; 严厉斥责。 □ n **1 the** ~, the people of Holland. 荷兰人。 **2** their language. 荷兰语。 **double** ~, unintelligible language. 无法了解的语言。 ~**man** /-mən; -mən/ n (pl **-men**) native of Holland. 荷兰人。

du·teous /'djuːtɪəs US: 'duː-; 'djutɪəs/ adj (formal) dutiful (the more usu word); obedient. (正式用语)尽职的 (dutiful 较常用); 服从的。

duti·able /'djuːtɪəbl US: 'duː-; 'djutɪəbl/ adj on which customs duties must be paid: 应纳关税的; 应纳税的: ~ goods. 应纳关税的货物。 Tobacco is ~ in most countries. 在多数国家烟草须纳税。 ⇨ duty(3).

duti·ful /'djuːtɪfl US: 'duː-; 'djutɪfl/ adj ~ (**to**), doing one's duty well; showing respect and obedience: 尽职的; 恭敬服从的; 孝顺的: a ~ son. 孝顺的儿子。 ~**ly** /-fəlɪ; -fəlɪ/ adv

duty /'djuːtɪ US: 'duːtɪ; 'djutɪ/ n (pl **-ties**) **1** [C, U] what one is obliged to do by morality, law, a trade, a calling, conscience, etc; inner voice urging one to behave in a certain way: 任务; 义务; 责任; 本分; 孝道; 敬意: When ~ calls, no man should disobey. 当有义务需要履行时, 任何人都义不容辞。 Do not forget your ~ to your parents. 不要忘记对父母应尽的责任。 His sense of ~ is strong. 他的责任感很强。 What are the duties of this post? 这个工作岗位的职责是什么? The ~ of a postman is to deliver letters and parcels. 邮差的职责是递送信件和包裹。 **on**/**off** ~, actually engaged/not engaged in one's regular work: 值(不值)班; 上(下)班:

He goes on ~ at 9am and comes off ~ at 5pm. 他上午九时上班，下午五时下班。 **(as) in ~ bound,** as required by ~. 基于义务；有义务。 **do ~ for,** be used instead of; serve for: 充作；当作…之用: *An old wooden box did ~ for a table.* 一个旧木箱充作桌子。 **2** (attrib) moral obligation. (用作定语)道德上的义务。 **'~call,** visit one makes from a sense of ~, not because one expects to enjoy it. 出于义务感所作的拜访。 **3** [C, U] ~ (on), payment demanded by the government on certain goods exported or imported ('customs duties), or manufactured in the country ('excise duties), or when property, etc is transferred to a new owner by sale ('stamp duties) or death (e'state ~). 税: 关税 (customs duties); 消费税 (excise duties); 印花税 (stamp duties); 遗产税 (estate duty)。 **,~·'free,** (of goods) allowed to enter a country without the payment of customs duties: (指货物)免关税的: ~-free shops, (eg at airports) selling ~-free goods. 免税商店(例如飞机场中者)。

duvet /'dju:veɪ US: du:'veɪ; dju'veɪ/ n bed quilt (filled with feathers, eg swan's-down, or an artificial substitute) used in place of blankets. 绒毛(如天鹅毛或人造毛)制成的褥垫。

dwarf /dwɔ:f; dwɔrf/ n (pl ~s) person, animal or plant much below the usual size; (in fairy tales) small being with magic powers; (attrib) undersized. 矮子；侏儒；较一般矮小的动物或植物；(神仙故事)小妖；(用作定语)矮小的。 **~ish** adj like a ~; undersized: 似侏儒的; 矮小的: ~ish trees/fingers. 矮小的树(短小的手指)。 □ vt [VP6A] **1** prevent from growing to full size. 阻碍发育。 **2** cause to appear small by contrast or distance: 使相形之下显得矮小或渺小: The big yacht ~ed our little launch. 这艘大游艇使我们的小汽船相形之下显得小了。

dwell /dwel; dwel/ vi (pt dwelt /dwelt; dwelt/) [VP3A] (liter)(文) **1 ~ in/at,** reside. 居住。 **2 ~ on/upon,** think, speak or write at length about: 细思；详论；详述: *She ~ too much upon her past.* 她过于详细地叙述她的过去。 **~er** (in compounds) inhabitant:(用于复合词中)居民: 'town-~ers; 城市里的人; 'cliff-~ers; 崖洞的居民; 'cave-~ers. 穴居者。 **~ing** n place of residence (a house, flat, etc). 住处；住宅。 **'~ing-house,** one used for living in, not as an office, workshop, etc. 住宅。

dwindle /'dwɪndl; 'dwɪndl/ vi [VP2A] become less or smaller by degrees. 减少；缩小。

dy·archy n = diarchy.

dye[1] /daɪ; daɪ/ vt, vi (3rd pers sing pres t, **dyes,** pt, pp **dyed,** pres part **dyeing**) **1** [VP6A, 22] colour, usu by dipping in a liquid: 染:to dye a white dress blue; 将白色衣服染成蓝色; *to have a dress dyed.* 把衣服送去染。 *dye in the wool/in grain,* dye while the material is in the

raw state, so that the process is thorough. 生染(未织前即染，故可染透)。 **,dyed-in-the-'wool** adj (fig) thorough; complete. (喻)彻底的；完全的。 **2** [VP6A] give colour to: 着色于: *Deep blushes dyed her cheeks.* 她的面颊发红。 **3** [VP2A] take colour from dyeing: 染色: *This material does not dye well.* 这料子染不好。

dye[2] /daɪ; daɪ/ n [C, U] substance used for dyeing cloth; colour given by dyeing. 染料；染色。 *a villain/scoundrel of the blackest/deepest dye,* of the worst kind. 穷凶极恶的人；恶汉。 **'dye-stuff,** substance yielding a dye or used as a dye. 染料。 **'dye-works,** one where dyeing is done. 染厂。 **dyer** n one who dyes cloth. 染布工人；染匠。

dy·ing ⟹ **die**[2].

dyke n = **dike**.

dy·namic /daɪ'næmɪk; daɪ'næmɪk/ adj **1** of physical power and forces producing motion. 动力的。 ⟹ **static.** **2** (of a person) having energy, force of character: (指人)精悍的；精力充沛的:a ~ personality. 精力充沛的人。 □ n **1** (pl with sing v) branch of physics dealing with matter in motion. (复数，与单数动词连用)力学；动力学。 **2** moral force that produces activity or change: 引起活动或变化的道德力量: driven by an inner ~. 受内心道德力量的驱使。 **dy·nami·cally** /-klɪ; -klɪ/ adv **dy·na·mism** /'damemɪzəm; 'dame,mɪzəm/ n [U] (of a person or a thing) power, energy. (指人或物)活力；精力；动力。

dyna·mite /'daɪnəmaɪt; 'daɪnə,maɪt/ n [U] powerful explosive (used in mining and quarrying). 炸药。 □ vt [VP6A] blow up with ~. 用炸药炸开或炸毁。

dy·namo /'daɪnəməʊ; 'daɪnə,mo/ n (pl ~s /-məʊz; -moz/) machine for changing steam-power, waterpower, etc into electrical energy. 发电机。

dyn·ast /'dɪnæst; 'daɪnæst; 'dæmæst/ n lord; hereditary ruler. 君主；世袭的统治者。 **~y** /'dɪnəsɪ US: 'daɪ-; 'daɪnəstɪ/ n (pl **-ties**) succession of rulers belonging to one family: 朝代；王朝: the Tudor ~y (in England). (英国)都铎王朝。 **~tic** /dɪ'næstɪk US: daɪ-; daɪ'næstɪk/ adj of a ~y. 朝代的；王朝的。

dyne /daɪn; daɪn/ n unit of force in the metric system. 达因(公制中力的单位)。

dys·en·tery /'dɪsntrɪ US: -terɪ; 'dɪsn,terɪ/ n [U] painful disease of the bowels, with discharge of mucus and blood. 痢疾；赤痢。

dys·lexia /dɪs'leksɪə; dɪs'leksɪə/ n [U] disturbance in the ability to read. 阅读能力失常；读字困难。 **dys·lexic** /-'leksɪk; -'leksɪk/ adj

dys·pep·sia /dɪs'pepsɪə; dɪ'spepʃə/ n [U] indigestion. 消化不良症。 **dys·pep·tic** /dɪs'peptɪk; dɪ'speptɪk/ adj of ~. 消化不良的。 □ n person suffering from ~. 消化不良患者。

Ee

E, e /i:; i/ (pl **E's, e's** /i:z; iz/), fifth letter of the English alphabet. 英文字母之第五个字母。

each /i:tʃ; itʃ/ adj (of two or more) every one, (thing, group, person, etc) taken separately or individually: (指二或二以上之物，群人等)每一；各个: *He was sitting with a child on ~ side of him.* 他坐在那里，两边各有一个小孩。 *On ~ occasion I just missed the target.* 我每次总是不能中的。 *He had words of encouragement for ~ one of us.* 他对我们每人都勉励一番。 □ pron **1 ~** thing, person, group, etc: 各个每物，每人，每组等): *E~ of them wants to try.* 他们每人都要试一试。 *E~ of the boys had a try.* 每个男孩子都试了一次。 *He had good advice for ~ of us.* 他对我们每人都赠以良言。 **2** used in apposition, like all and both: (用作同位语，类似 all 和 both) 各自；各: *We ~ took a big*

risk. 我们各自冒了一次大险。 *Tom, Dick and Harry ~ put forward a different scheme.* 汤姆，迪克和哈里各提出了一个不同的计划。 **3** used adverbially meaning 'apiece': (用作状语)每个；每件；每人: *He gave the boys 50p ~.* 他给男孩子们每人五十便士。 *The oranges are 6p ~.* 橙子卖六便士一个。 **4 ~ other,** used as the object of a v or prep; both words usu unstressed; often replaced by one another when the reference is to a number more than two: 互相(用做动词或介词的宾语；两字通常都不重读；如多于两个时，常用 one another 代替): *We see ~ other (= ~ of us sees the other) at the office every day.* 我们每天在办公室见面。 *They are afraid of ~ other.* 他们互相惧怕。

eager /'i:gə(r); 'igɚ/ adj ~ (for sth/to do sth)- full of, showing, strong desire: 热切的；渴望的: ~ for

success; 渴望成功; ~ *to succeed.* 急欲成功。~ **'beaver,** (colloq) hardworking and (over) enthusiastic person. (口)工作努力并(过分)热心之人。~**·ly** *adv* ~**·ness** *n*

eagle /'i:gl; 'igl/ *n* large, strong bird of prey of the falcon family with keen sight. 鹰。⇨ the illus at **prey.** 参看 prey 之插图。~**·'eyed** *adj* keen-sighted. 目光锐利的。**eag·let** /'i:glɪt; 'iglɪt/ *n* young ~. 小鹰。

ear[1] /ɪə(r); ɪr/ *n* **1** organ of hearing. 耳; 耳朵。⇨ illus here and the illus at **head.** 参看本条及 head 之插图。**be all ears,** be listening eagerly. 专心倾听。**fall on deaf ears,** pass unnoticed. 未受注意。**feel one's ears burning,** imagine that one is being talked about. 觉得耳朵在发烧(想象正被人谈论)。**give one's ears (for sth/to do sth),** make any sacrifice, pay any price. 不惜任何牺牲;不惜任何代价。**go in (at) one ear and out (at) the 'other,** said of sth that, although heard, makes no impression. 左耳进右耳出; 当作耳边风。**have an ear to the ground,** be alert for what may be happening in secret. 注意秘密中可能发生的事。**(have) a word in sb's ear,** (say) sth in confidence: 私下说出一事: *May I have a word in your ear?* 我可以和你私下谈句话吗? **have / win sb's ear(s),** his favourable attention. 获得某人的好感; 对某人讲话有力。**over head and ears,** deeply (in debt, etc). 深陷(债务等中)。**prick up one's ears,** become suddenly attentive. 显出突然注意或关切的神情。**set (persons) by the ears,** set them quarrelling. 挑拨离间。**turn a deaf ear (to),** refuse to help. 拒绝帮助。**up to the/one's 'ears in (work, etc),** overwhelmed by it. 工作等极繁忙。**wet behind the ears,** naïve. 天真的。**'ear·ache,** pain in the inner ear. 耳痛。**'ear·drop,** earring with a hanging ornament. 耳环; 耳坠。**'ear·drum,** thin membrane (in the inner ear) which vibrates when sound-waves strike it. 耳鼓; 鼓膜。⇨ the illus **here.** 参看本条之插图。**'ear·ful** /-ful; -ful/, as much (usu abusive or unsolicited) that one can endure. 一个人听对方(通常含有辱骂性或令人觉得多余的)说话所能容忍的限度。**'ear·mark** *n* mark on the ear of a sheep, etc, to mark ownership; (fig) special characteristic. 耳号(置于羊等之耳上, 以示所有权); (喻)特征。□ *vt* [VP 6A, 14] *earmark sb/sth (for sth),* put an earmark on (an animal); (fig) keep sb in mind for a special purpose, work, etc; set sth aside for a special purpose: 加耳号于(某动物); (喻)指定某人担任特殊任务, 工作等; 指定某物做特殊用途: *earmark sb for an important post;* 指定某人担任一件重要的工作; *earmark a sum of money for research.* 拨款做研究费用。**'ear·piece,** earphone of a telephone receiver. (电话机之)听筒。**'ear·phone,** head-phone. 耳机。**'ear·ring,** ring worn in or on the

lobe of the ear as an ornament. 耳环。**'ear·shot,** hearing distance: 听力所及之距离: *out of/within earshot.* 在听力所及之距离外(内)。**'ear·trumpet,** trumpetshaped tube formerly used by partly deaf people. (昔时半聋之人用的喇叭状)助听器; 耳筒。⇨ *hearing·aid* at **hearing. 'ear·wax,** waxy substance secreted in the ear. 耳垢。**2** sense of hearing. 听觉。**have a good ear for music,** be able to discriminate sound. 音感好的; 能辨音的。**(play sth) by ear,** (play) without printed music, or without having memorized it; (fig) (do it) unprepared. 凭听过一次后不用乐谱演奏; (喻)无准备(而做某事)。**3** earshaped thing, esp the handle of a pitcher. 耳状物; (尤指)水壶耳。**(-)eared,** used in compounds: 用于复合词中: *,long-'eared,* having long ears. 长耳的。

ear[2] /ɪə(r); ɪr/ *n* seed-bearing part of a cereal (corn, barley, etc): (玉蜀黍, 大麦等之)穗: *corn in the ear,* with ears developed. 正在长穗的玉蜀黍。⇨ the illus at **cereal.** 参看 cereal 之插图。

earl /ɜ:l; ɜl/ *n* (fem *countess*) title of a British nobleman. (英)伯爵(女伯爵为 countess)。~**·dom** /-dəm; -dəm/ *n* rank of an ~. 伯爵爵位。

early /'ɜ:lɪ; 'ɜlɪ/ (**-ier, -iest**) *adj, adv* near to the beginning of a period of time, sooner than usual or than others: 早; 初; 初期的: *in the ~ part of this century;* 本世纪的初叶; *in ~ spring;* 在初春; *an ~ breakfast,* eg 5 am: 很早的早餐(例如早于上午五点钟进食者); *~ peaches,* ripening ~ in the season; 早熟的桃子; *~·'closing day,* (GB) on which shops, etc are closed during the afternoon. (英)商店等早停止营业(下午停止营业)的日子。*He's an ~ riser,* gets up at an ~ hour. 他惯于早起。*Please come at your earliest convenience,* as soon as it is convenient for you to do so. 得便请尽可能早来。*He keeps ~ hours,* gets up, goes to bed, ~. 他早睡早起。*It's better to be too ~ than too late.* 太早比太迟好(不怕早只怕晚)。*Come as ~ as possible.* 尽量早来。*The ~ bird gets/catches the worm,* (prov) The person who arrives, etc ~ will (probably) succeed. (谚)早起的鸟能捕到虫(意谓早到等的人可能会成功)。*~ days (yet),* too soon to tell how sth will develop. 言之过早。*earlier on,* at an earlier stage. 初时;在较早的阶段。Cf 参较 *later on* at **late**[2](1). *,~-'warning* *adj* (of radar) giving early indication of the approach of enemy aircraft, missiles, etc: (指雷达)预先警报的(可早期指示敌机, 导弹等之逼近的): *an ~ warning system.* 预先警报系统。

earn /ɜ:n; ɜn/ *vt* [VP6A, 12B, 13B] get in return for work, as a reward for one's qualities or in payment for a loan: 赚; 挣得; 博得: *to ~ £10000 a year;* 一年赚

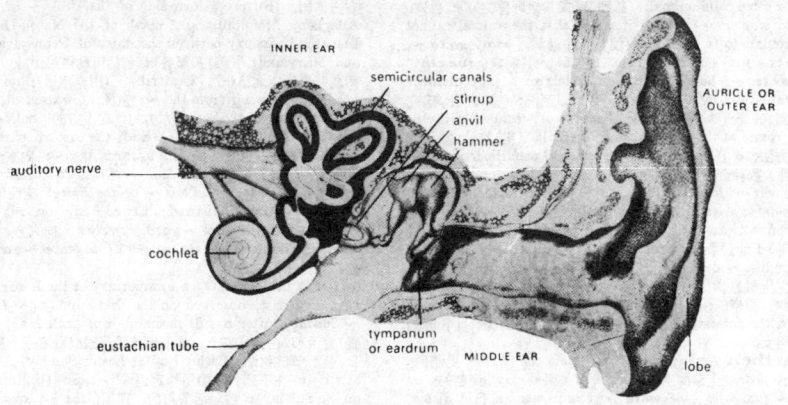

the ear

一万英镑; *to ~ one's living/one's livelihood/one's daily bread.* 谋生. *The money ~s 7% interest.* 这笔钱得利息七厘. *His achievements ~ed him respect and admiration.* 他的成就使他受到尊敬和钦佩. *His eccentricities had ~ed for him the nickname 'The Madman'.* 他的怪癖已为他博得'疯子'的绰号. *I had a well-~ed rest.* 我得到应得的休息了. **~ings** *n pl* money ~ed: 赚得的钱: *He has spent all his ~ings.* 他把赚来的钱都花光了. **~ings yield,** (comm) ratio between annual profit and capital. (商)年利润与资本间的比率.

ear·nest¹ /'ɜːnɪst; 'ɜnɪst/ *adj* serious; determined: 认真的; 坚决的: *an ~ worker/pupil;* 认真的工作者(学生); *a terribly ~ young man,* perhaps over-serious, over-conscientious. 过于认真的青年. □ *n in ~,* in a determined manner; seriously: 郑重; 认真: *If you work in ~, you will succeed.* 如果你认真工作, 你会成功的. *I'm perfectly in ~,* am not joking. 我完全是正经的(不是开玩笑). *It is raining in real ~,* heavily, and likely to continue. 雨真的下大了. **~·ly** *adv* in an ~ manner: 认真地; 坚决地: *We ~ly hope that ....* 我们真正希望…. **~·ness** *n*

ear·nest² /'ɜːnɪst; 'ɜnɪst/ *n* **1** (also 亦作 '**~-money**) part payment made as a pledge that full payment will follow. 定金. **2** sth coming in advance as a sign of what is to come after: 预兆: *As an ~ of my good intentions I will work overtime this week.* 本周我愿加班以示我的善意.

earth /ɜːθ; ɜθ/ *n* **1 (the) ~,** this world; the planet on which we live: 地球; 世界: *The moon goes round the ~ and the ~ goes round the sun.* 月亮绕地球运转, 而地球绕太阳运转. *Who do you think was the greatest man on ~?* 你认为谁是世界上最伟大的人? ⇨ the illus at **planet.** 参看 planet 之插图. **2** [U] land surface of the world; land contrasted with the sky: 陆地; 大地: *The balloon burst and fell to ~.* 气球爆了, 落在地上. **come down/back to ~,** stop daydreaming; return to practical realities. 返回现实. **move heaven and ~ (to do sth),** make every possible effort. 用尽办法; 竭力. *how/why/where/who, etc on ~,* how/why, etc ever ... (used for emphasis; ⇨ **ever**). 究竟如何(为何, 在何处, 是谁等)(用以加强语气). **3** [U] soil: 泥土: *to fill a pit with ~;* 用泥土填坑; *to cover the roots of a plant with ~.* 将植物的根用泥土埋上. **'~-closet,** latrine; substitute for a lavatory in places where there is no supply of water from mains, etc. (无抽水设备场所的)厕所. **'~-nut,** groundnut. 落花生. **'~-work,** embankment of ~ used in fortifications as a defence. 泥土筑成的防御工事. **'~-worm,** common kind of worm that lives in the soil. 蚯蚓. **4** [C] hole of a fox, badger or other wild animal: (狐狸、獾或其他野兽之)洞; 兽穴: *to stop an ~,* block it before the hunt so that the animal cannot return to it. 填塞兽洞(使其无法返回). **run/go to ~,** (of a fox) go into its hole. (指狐)入其洞穴. **run sth/sb to ~,** hunt (a fox) to its burrow; (fig) discover (sth/sb) by searching. 追寻(狐)至洞; (喻)查明; 追究到底. **5** [C, U] (electr) (means of) contact with the ground at the completion of a circuit. (电)接地; 接地的方法. **6** [C] (chem) one of several metallic oxides. (化学) 数种金属氧化物之一. □ *vt* **1** [VP15B] **~ up,** cover with ~: 覆以土: *to ~ up the roots of a newly-planted shrub.* 用土埋起新植灌木之根. **2** [VP6A] (electr) connect (apparatus, etc) with the ~. (电) 接(装置等)于地. ⇨ **5** above. 参看上列第 5 义. **~·y** *adj* **1** of or like ~ or soil: 泥土的; 土状的: *an ~y smell.* 土味; 泥土气息. **2** (fig) grossly material; unaffected, unrefined: (喻) 粗俗的; 纯朴的: *the ~y and robust men and women in the paintings of Rubens.* 鲁宾斯画中的纯朴而壮健的男女.

earthen /'ɜːθn; 'ɜθən/ *adj* made of earth: 土制的: *~ floors;* 土铺的地板; made of baked clay: 陶制的: *an ~ jar.* 陶瓶. **'~-ware** /-weə(r); -ˌwɛr/ *n* [U] dishes, etc made of baked clay: 陶器; (attrib) (用作定语) *an*

~ware casserole. 陶制炻锅.

earthly /'ɜːθlɪ; 'ɜθlɪ/ *adj* **1** of this world, not of heaven: 现世的; 尘世的: ~ *joys/possessions.* 尘世的享乐(财产). **2** (colloq) possible; conceivable: (口)可能的; 可想象的: *You haven't an ~ (chance),* no chance at all. 你根本没有机会. *no ~ use,* quite useless. 完全无用.

earth·quake /'ɜːθkweɪk; 'ɜθˌkwek/ *n* [C] sudden, violent movement of the earth's surface. 地震.

ear·wig /'ɪəwɪɡ; 'ɪrˌwɪɡ/ *n* small harmless insect with pincers at the rear end of its abdomen. 蠼螋(无害的小虫, 腹部后端生有鳌); 小蜈蚣. ⇨ the illus at **insect.** 参看 insect 之插图.

ease¹ /iːz; iz/ *n* [U] freedom from work, discomfort, trouble, difficulty, anxiety: 安逸; 舒适; 不费力; 安宁: *a life of ~;* 舒适的生活; ~ *of body and mind.* 身心的舒适. **at ~,** comfortable; comfortably: 舒适的(地); 安逸的(地): *a mind at ~;* 心情安适; *sitting at ~.* 悠闲地坐着; 安适地坐着. **ill at ~,** anxious or embarrassed. 局促不安. **stand at ~,** (as a mil command) with the legs apart and the hands behind the back. (军队口令)稍息. (Cf 参较 at **attention, stand easy**). **take one's ~,** stop working or worrying. 悠闲. **with ~,** without difficulty. 无困难地.

ease² /iːz; iz/ *vt, vi* **1** [VP6A, 14] ~ **(of),** give relief to (the body or mind) from pain, discomfort, anxiety: 使(身心)舒适; 使安心; 减轻(身心之痛苦, 不安, 忧虑): ~ *sb's anxiety;* 减轻某人的忧虑; ~ *sb of his pain/trouble.* 减轻某人的痛苦(烦恼). *Can I ~ you of your burden?* 我能减轻你的负担吗? **2** [VP6A, 15A, B, 2C] make looser, less tight; lessen speed, efforts: 放松; 减低(速度或努力): ~ *a coat under the armpits;* 将上衣的腋下部分放宽松; ~ *a drawer,* make it so that sticks fast or opens with difficulty: 使一抽屉易于开关; ~ *(down) the speed of a boat.* 减低船速. *E~ off a bit, we're going too fast.* 慢一点, 我们走得太快了. **3** [VP 2A,C] ~ **(off/up),** become less tense or troublesome: 缓和; 减少紧张或麻烦: *the easing of tension between the two countries.* 两国间紧张局势的缓和. *The situation has ~d off/up.* 局势缓和了.

easel /'iːzl; 'izl/ *n* wooden frame to support a blackboard or a picture (while the artist is working at it). 黑板架; 画架.

east /iːst; ist/ *n* **1 the ~,** point of the horizon where the sun rises. 东; 东方. ⇨ the illus at **compass.** 参看 compass 之插图. **the ˌFar 'E~,** China, Japan, etc. 远东(中国, 日本等). **the ˌMiddle 'E~,** countries from Egypt to Iran. 中东(埃及及伊朗间诸国). **the ˌNear 'E~,** Turkey, etc. 近东(土耳其等). **the E~, (a)** the Orient. 东方诸国. **(b)** the eastern side of the USA ~ of the Allegheny Mountains and north of the Mason-Dixon line (the boundary between the states of Pennsylvania and Maryland). (美)东部各州(包括阿勒格尼山脉以东, 南北分界线以北诸州). **2** (attrib) (用作定语): *an ~ wind,* one blowing from the ~; 东风; towards, at, in the direction of the ~: 向东方的; 在东方的: *on the ~ coast.* 在东部海岸. **the ˌE~ 'End,** the eastern part of London. 伦敦东区. □ *adv* towards the ~: 向东: *to travel ~;* 向东方旅行; *to face ~;* 朝东; *to sail due ~;* 向正东航行; *a town that lies ~ of the Rhine.* 莱茵河东岸一城. **~·ward** /'iːstwəd; 'istwəd/ *adj* towards the ~: 向东方的: *in an ~ward direction.* 向东方的. **~ward(s)** *adv* towards the ~: 向东: *to travel ~wards.* 向东旅行.

Easter /'iːstə(r); 'istɚ/ *n* anniversary of the Resurrection of Christ, observed on the first Sunday (~ **Day,** ~ **Sunday**) after a full moon on or after 21 Mar. (基督)复活节(在三月二十一日或该日后月圆以后第一个星期日, 复活节日称作, Easter Day 或 Easter Sunday). Used attrib in the following compounds: 在下列各例中用作定语: '**~-week** (beginning on ~ Sunday); 自复活节起的一周间; *the ~ holidays.* 复活节假期. '**~ egg,** egg with a painted or dyed shell,

or an egg made of chocolate. 复活节彩蛋(蛋壳涂有彩色，或由巧克力制成者)。

east·er·ly /'i:stəlɪ; 'istəlɪ/ *adj, adv* in an eastern direction or position; (of the wind) coming from the east. 在东方; (指风)来自东方的(地)。

east·ern /'i:stən; 'istən/ *adj* (attrib) of, from, living in, the east part of the world: (用作定语形)东方的; 自东方的; 居于东方的: ~ *religions*. 东方的宗教。the E~ **Church,** the Greek Orthodox Church. 东方教会(希腊正教)。the E~ **Hemisphere,** Africa, Asia and Europe. 东半球(非洲，亚洲及欧洲)。**~·most** / -məust; -,most/ *adj* farthest east. 最东的; 极东的。

easy /'i:zɪ; 'izɪ/ *adj* (**-ier, -iest**) **1** not difficult: 容易的: *an* ~ *book.* 易读的书。*The place is* ~ *to reach.* 那地方容易到达。*It is an* ~ *place to reach.* 那是个容易到达的地方。**2** free from pain, discomfort, anxiety, trouble, etc: 舒适的; 安心的; 轻松的: *to lead an* ~ *life;* 过舒适的生活; *in* ~ *circumstances,* having enough money to live comfortably; 生活优裕; *an* '~ *chair,* one that is soft and restful; 安乐椅; 柔软舒适的椅子; ~ *manners,* not showing stiffness or embarrassment; 从容的态度; (*to buy furniture*) *on* ~ *terms,* trade term for hire-purchase; (购家具)分期付款; *persons who are* ~ *to get on with,* people who are informal, not stiff. 容易相处的人。,~·'going, (of persons) placid and tolerant; casual; lazy and careless; lax. (指人) 温和宽容的; 随便的; 懒惰并马虎的; 不严格的。**3** (comm) (of goods and money on loan) not much in demand. (商)(指货物与贷款)需求不殷的; 松动的。**tight.** □ *adv* in an ~ manner: 安适地; 轻松地: *E~! (as a command)* Move (it) gently. (命令)轻轻地移动(它)! *take it/things* ~, don't work too hard or too energetically. 轻松一点; 勿太紧张。*go* ~ *on/with,* (colloq) be careful or moderate with: (口)小心对待; 温和对待: *Go* ~ *on the brandy—it's the last bottle!* 白兰地要省着点喝——这是最后一瓶了! *Easier said than done,* It is easier to say one will do it than to do it. 说来容易做来难。*Stand* ~! (as a mil command) Stand with more freedom of movement than when *at ease,* ⇨ **ease¹.** (军队口令)休息(比站立时享有更多活动的自由)。**eas·ily** /'i:zəlɪ; 'izɪlɪ/ *adv* **1** with ease. 容易地; 安适地。**2** without doubt: 无疑地: *easily the best TV programme.* 无疑为最佳的电视节目。**3** possibly: 可能地: *That may easily be the case.* 情况可能就是那样。

eat /i:t; it/ *vt, vi* (*pt* **ate** /et US: eɪt; et/, *pp* **eaten** /'i:tn; 'itn/) **1** [VP6A, 15B, 2A, C, 4A] *eat (up),* take (solid food, also soup) into the mouth and swallow it: 吃; 食: *to eat one's dinner;* 吃正餐; *to eat up (=* finish eating) *one's food.* 吃光食物。我们到哪儿吃饭? *He was too ill to eat.* 他病重得不能吃东西了。*We should eat to live, not live to eat,* not make eating the most important thing in life. 我们应为生活而吃饭，不应为吃饭而生活。*eat its head off,* (of a horse) cost more to feed than it is worth. (指马)饲养的费用较其本身价值高; 吃得太多。*eat one's heart out,* suffer in silence; be very sad. 默默忍受痛苦; 极为悲伤。*eat one's words,* take a statement back, say in a humble way that one was wrong. 收回前言; 低声下气地认错。**2** [VP6A, 3A, 15B] destroy as if by eating: 侵蚀; 啃; 蛀蚀: *Acids eat into metals.* 酸能腐蚀金属。*He is eaten up with pride.* 他被骄傲冲昏了头(他一味的骄傲)。*The river had eaten away the banks.* 河水侵蚀了两岸。*The moths have eaten holes in my coat.* 蛀虫将我的上衣蛀了一些小洞。**'eating-apple** *n* suitable for eating uncooked. 适于生吃的苹果。**'eating-house,** restaurant. 餐馆。**eats** *n pl* (sl) food: (俚)食物: *There were plenty of eats, but not enough drinks.* 有许多食物，但无足够的饮料。**eat·able** /-əbl; -əbl/ *adj* fit to be eaten; good to eat: 可食的; 好吃的: *The prison food was scarcely eatable.* 狱中的伙食几乎不能吃。~**s** *n pl* (usu pl) food. (通常用复数)食物。~**er** *n* **1** one that eats: 食者: *He's a big eater,* eats large quantities. 他的食量很大。

2 apple, pear, etc for dessert, good when eaten uncooked. 生吃的苹果，梨等(做为餐后水果)。

eau /əʊ; o/ *n* **eau de Cologne** /,əʊ də kə'ləʊn; ,odeko'lon/ *n* (F) perfume made at Cologne. (法)德国科伦所产的香水。**eau-de-vie** /,əʊ də 'vi:; ,ode'vi/ *n* (F) brandy. (法)白兰地酒。

eaves /i:vz; ivz/ *n pl* overhanging edges of a roof: 屋檐: *icicles hanging from the* ~. 屋檐上垂下的冰柱。

eaves·drop /'i:vzdrɒp; 'ivz,drɑp/ *vi* (**-pp-**) [VP 2A,3A] listen secretly to private conversation: 窃听: ~ *on a discussion.* 窃听一讨论。~**·per** /-drɒpə(r); -,drɑpə/ *n* person who does this. 窃听者。

ebb /eb; ɛb/ *vi* [VP2A, C] **1** (of the tide) flow back from the land to the sea. (指潮水)退落。**2** (fig) grow less; become weak or faint: (喻)减少; 衰落: *His fortune's beginning to ebb.* 他的财产开始减少了。*Daylight was ebbing away.* 白昼渐逝。□ *n* **1** the flowing out of the tide: 退潮; 落潮: *the ebb and flow of the sea/the tide.* 海潮之涨落。*The tide is on the ebb,* is going out. 正在退潮。**2** (fig) low state; decline or decay: (喻)衰退; 衰落: *His health is at a low ebb.* 他的健康在衰退中。**,ebb·'tide** *n* = ebb.

eb·on·ite /'ebənaɪt; 'ɛbən,aɪt/ *n* [U] (comm) hard black insulating material made by vulcanising rubber. (商)硬橡胶。

eb·ony /'ebənɪ; 'ɛbənɪ/ *n* [U] hard, black wood. 黑檀; 乌木。□ *adj* made of, black as, ~: 乌木制的; 乌木色的: *the* ~ *keys on a piano.* 钢琴上乌木色的键。

ebul·lient /ɪ'bʌlɪənt; ɪ'bʌljənt/ *adj* exuberant. 充溢的。**ebul·lience** /-əns; -əns/ *n* exuberance; outburst (of feeling). 充溢; (感情的)奔放。

ec·cen·tric /ɪk'sentrɪk; ɛk'sɛntrɪk/ *adj* **1** (of a person, his behaviour) peculiar; not normal or conventional. (指人或其举动)怪癖的; 古怪的。**2** (of circles) not having the same centre, ⇨ the illus at **concentric;** (of orbits) not circular; (of planets, etc) moving in an ~ orbit. (指圆)不同中心的(参看 concentric 之插图); (指轨道)偏心的; 离心的; (指行星等)在离心轨道运行的; 呈偏心运动的。□ *n* **1** ~ person. 古怪的人。**2** (mech) device for changing circular motion into backward-and-forward motion. (机械)偏心器; 偏心轮。

ec·cen·tric·ity /,eksen'trɪsətɪ; ,ɛksɛn'trɪsɪtɪ/ *n* **1** [U] quality of being eccentric; strangeness of behaviour, etc: 怪癖; 古怪: ~ *in dress.* 衣着古怪。**2** [C] (*pl* **-ties**) instance of this; strange or unusual act or habit: 古怪的行动或习惯: *One of his eccentricities is sleeping under the bed instead of in it.* 他的怪癖之一是睡在床底下，而不睡在床上。

ec·clesi·as·tic /ɪ,kli:zɪ'æstɪk; ɪ,klɪzɪ'æstɪk/ *n* clergyman. 传教士; 牧师。**ec·clesi·as·ti·cal** /-kl; -kl/ *adj* of the Christian Church; of clergymen. 基督教会的; 教士的; 牧师的。**ec·clesi·as·ti·cally** /-klɪ; -klɪ/ *adv*

eche·lon /'eʃəlɒn; 'ɛʃə,lɑn/ *n* step-like formation of troops, aircraft, ships, etc as shown in illus: (军队，飞机，船只等的)梯队(如图)。*flying in* ~. 成梯队飞行。

echo¹ /'ekəʊ; 'ɛko/ *n* (*pl* ~**es** /-əʊz; -oz/) **1** [C, U] sound reflected or sent back (eg from a wall of

flying in echelon

rock): 回声; 回音(例如由石壁返回者): *The speaker was cheered / applauded to the ~*, long and loudly: 这演说者受到了热烈的喝彩(掌声). '*~* **chamber**, natural or artificial space for producing *~*es. 回声室. '*~*-**sounding**, method of ascertaining distances (eg of the ocean bed or underwater objects) by measuring the time taken for waves of sound, etc to be echoed back. 回音测深(利用回音的时间以测距离的方法,例如测海底或水底物体之距离). Hence, 由此产生, '*~*-**sounder** *n* instrument used for this. 回音测深器. **2** [C] person who, statement etc which, is a copy or repetition of another. 附和者;应声虫;重复的陈述.

echo² /'ekəʊ/ *vi*, *vt* [VP6A, 15B, 2A, C] *(back)*, **1** (of places) send back an echo: (指地方)发回声: *The valley ~ed as he sang.* 他唱歌时山谷发出回声. *The hills ~ed back the noise of the shot.* 山中发出枪声的回音. **2** (of sounds) be sent back as an echo: (指声音)被传回: *The shot ~ed through the woods.* 林中传出枪声的回音. **3** be an echo of; repeat the words, etc of another: 随声附和; 重复旁人的话等: *They ~ed every word of their leader.* 他们随声附和他们首领的每一句话.

éclair /eɪ'kleə(r); eɪ'kler/ *n* (F) small cylindrical pastry iced on top and filled with cream. (法) 一种奶油馅, 顶上有糖霜的长形小饼.

éclat /eɪ'klɑː; eɪ'klɑ/ *n* [U] (F) brilliant, conspicuous success; applause from everyone: (法) 显赫的成功; 大众的喝彩: *with great ~.* 极为成功地; 在大众喝彩声中.

ec·lec·tic /ɪ'klektɪk; ɪk'lɛktɪk/ *adj* (of persons, methods, etc) choosing, accepting, freely from various sources.(指人,方法等)选择或随意取材的.**ec·lec·ti·cism** /-tɪsɪzəm; -tɪ,sɪzəm/ *n*

eclipse /ɪ'klɪps; ɪ'klɪps/ *n* [C] **1** total or partial cutting off of the light of the sun (when the moon is between it and the earth), or of the reflected light of the moon (when the earth's shadow falls on it). 日蚀; 月蚀. **2** (fig) loss of brilliance, power, reputation, etc: (喻)光亮,权力,声望等的丧失; 失色; 晦暗: *After suffering an ~ he is now again famous.* 声望一度跌落后, 现在他已重振声威. *An author's reputation is often in ~ for some years after his death.* 作家的名声在其死后常有几年的晦暗时期. □ *vt* [VP6A] **1** (of the moon, a planet, etc) cause an ~; cut off the light from. (指月球,行星等)蚀; 掩蔽…之光. **2** (fig) make (sb or sth) appear dull by comparison; outshine: (喻)使(某人或某物)黯然失色;超越: *She was so beautiful that she ~d every other woman at the ball.* 她的美丽使舞会中其他妇女黯然失色.

corona

a total eclipse of the sun

eclip·tic /ɪ'klɪptɪk; ɪ'klɪptɪk/ *n* the path of the sun in the sky. (天文)黄道.

ecol·ogy /iː'kɒlədʒɪ; ɪ'kɑlədʒɪ/ *n* [U] branch of biology that deals with the habits of living things, esp their relation to their environment. 生态学(研究生物之习惯,尤其是生物与环境的关系). **eco·logi·cal** /,iːkə'lɒdʒɪkl; ,ɪkə'lɑdʒɪkl/ *adj* of ~; 生态学的: *the ecological effects of industry*, eg the pollution of the atmosphere, of rivers, etc. 工业对生物环境之影响(例如

空气,河流等之污染). **eco·logi·cally** /-klɪ; -klɪ/ *adv* **ecol·ogist** /iː'kɒlədʒɪst; ɪ'kɑlədʒɪst/ *n* student of; expert in, ~. 生态学家. **eco·system** /'iːkəʊ,sɪstəm, 'ɪkə,sɪstəm/ *n* = ecological system. 生态系.

econ·omic /,iːkə'nɒmɪk *US*: ,ek-; ,ɪkə'nɑmɪk/ *adj* **1** of economics (⇨ below): 经济学的; 国家经济状态的; 经济的 (参看 economics): *the government's ~ policy.* 政府的经济政策. **2** designed to give a profit: 企图给予利润的;为生利而设计的: *an ~ rent*, one that compensates the owner for the cost of the land, building, etc. 足以补偿地主或房主土地, 建筑等费用的租金. **3** connected with commerce and industry: 与工商业有关的: ~ *geography*, studied chiefly in connection with industry. 经济地理(以研究与产业有关者为主).

econ·omi·cal /,iːkə'nɒmɪkl *US*: ,ek-; ,ɪkə'nɑmɪkl/ *adj* careful in the spending of money, time, etc and in the use of goods; not wasteful: 经济的; 节俭的: *to be ~ of time and energy;* 节省时间和精力; *an ~ fire*, one that does not waste fuel. 省燃料的炉火.~*ly* /-klɪ; -klɪ/ *adv*

econ·omics /,iːkə'nɒmɪks *US*: ,ek-; ,ɪkə'nɑmɪks/ *n* (with *sing v*) [U] science of the production, distribution and consumption of goods; condition of a country as to material prosperity. (与单数动词连用)经济学;国家的经济状况. **econ·om·ist** /ɪ'kɒnəmɪst; ɪ'kɑnəmɪst/ *n* **1** expert in ~; person who writes or lectures on ~ or political economy. 经济学家; 经济学专家. **2** person who is economical or thrifty. 节俭的人.

econ·om·ize /ɪ'kɒnəmaɪz; ɪ'kɑnə,maɪz/ *vt*, *vi* [VP 6A, 2A, 3A] ~ *(on sth)*, be economical; use or spend less than before, cut down expenses: 节俭; 俭省; 节约: *He ~d by using buses instead of taking taxis.* 他改乘公共汽车而不乘计程车以节省钱. *We must ~ on light and fuel.* 我们必须节省灯光和燃料.

econ·omy /ɪ'kɒnəmɪ; ɪ'kɑnəmɪ/ *n* (*pl* -**mies**) **1** [C, U] (instance of) avoidance of waste of money, strength or anything else of value: 经济;节俭;节约: *to practise ~.* 实行节约. *In the long run, it is an ~ to buy good quality goods, even though they cost more.* 购买质料好的货物, 虽然价格较贵, 到头来是经济的. *By various little economies, she managed to save enough money for a holiday.* 在许多小地方节省,她设法储够了度假的钱. '*~* **class**, cheapest class of travel (esp by air). 经济舱(尤指客机者). **2** [U] control and management of the money, goods and other resources of a community, society or household: 理财: *political ~;* 政治经济学; *domestic ~.* 家庭经济; 家政. **3** [C] system for the management and use of resources: 经济制度: *the totalitarian economies of Germany and Italy before the Second World War.* 第二次世界大战前德意两国的极权经济制度.

ec·stasy /'ekstəsɪ; 'ɛkstəsɪ/ *n* (*pl* -**sies**) [U, C] (feeling of) great joy and spiritual uplift: 狂喜; 心醉神迷: *in an ~ of delight;* 喜极; *to be in / go into / be thrown into ~ / ecstasies (over sth).* (对某物)心醉神迷. **ec·static** /ɪk'stætɪk; ɪk'stætɪk/ *adj* of, in, causing, ~. 狂喜的; 心醉神迷的; 使人狂喜的. **ec·stati·cally** /-klɪ; -klɪ/ *adv*

ec·to·plasm /'ektəplæzəm; 'ɛktə,plæzəm/ *n* [U] substance supposed to flow from a spiritualistic medium during a trance. 外质; 一种假想的;从恍惚状态的灵媒体放射出的物质.

ecu·meni·cal /,iːkjuː'menɪkl; ,ɪkju'mɛnɪkl/ *adj* **1** of or representing the whole Christian world or universal Church: 全基督教会的: *an E~ Council*, eg of all the RC church as summoned by the Pope. 全基督教会会议(例如由教皇召集之全天主教会会议). **2** seeking to restore the unity of the Christian churches: 促进基督教会团结的: *the ~ movement.* 促进基督教会团结的运动.

ec·zema /'eksɪmə; 'ɛksəmə/ *n* [U] itching skin disease. 湿疹.

eddy /'edɪ; 'ɛdɪ/ n (pl **-dies**) (of wind, smoke, fog, mist, dust, water) circular or spiral movement: (风、烟、雾、尘土、水之)漩流; 涡流: *Eddies of mist rose from the valleys.* 缕缕雾气自谷中升起。*The car went past in an ~ of dust.* 这汽车在一阵滚滚的尘土中驶过。□ *vi* [VP2A, C] move in small circles; move in or like eddies; whirl. 旋涡; 旋转.

edel·weiss /'eɪdlvaɪs; 'edl,vaɪs/ n small Alpine plant with white leaves and small flowers, growing among rocks. 火绒草(一种高山植物,有白色的叶及小花,生于岩石中).

Eden /'iːdn; 'idn/ n (Bible) garden where Adam and Eve lived; place of delight. (圣经)(亚当与夏娃所居之)伊甸园; 乐园.

edge¹ /edʒ; ɛdʒ/ n 1 sharp, cutting part of a knife, sword or other tool or weapon: 刀; 刀口: *a knife with a sharp ~;* 有利刃之刀: *to put an ~ on a knife,* sharpen it. 使刀口锋利. **be on ~,** be excited or irritable. 激动; 急躁. **give sb the ~ on,** rebuke him sharply. 严斥某人. **have the ~ on sb,** (colloq) have an advantage over him. (口)较某人占优势; 胜过某人. **set sb's 'teeth on ~,** upset his nerves (as when a scraping sound or a sharp, acid taste causes physical revulsion). 使某人牙齿发酸; 刺激其神经(如刮刺耳声或尝酸酸物后引起身体上之急剧反应). **take the ~ off sth,** dull or soften; reduce, eg one's appetite. 使某物变钝; 挫其锋芒; 减弱(胃口等). **2** (line marking the) outer limit or boundary of a (flat) surface; 边沿; 边缘: *a cottage on the ~ of a forest;* 位于林边的茅舍; *the ~ of a lake;* 湖边; *trim the ~s of a lawn,* cut the grass there. 修剪草地之边缘。*Don't put the glass on the ~ of the table; it may get knocked off.* 不要把杯子放在桌边上, 它可能被碰碎。*He fell off the ~ of the cliff.* 他自崖边跌下。~, 激动的; 急躁的.

edgy /'edʒɪ; 'ɛdʒɪ/ adj having one's nerves on ~. 激动的; 急躁的.

edge² /edʒ; ɛdʒ/ vt, vi 1 [VP6A, 14] ~ **(with),** supply with a border: 加以边: *to ~ a handkerchief with lace/a garden path with plants;* 在手帕上加花边(在花园小径两边植花木); form a border to: 形成…之边: *a road ~d with grass.* 两边沿种有草的道路。**2** [VP6A] sharpen (a tool, etc). 使(工具等)锐利. **3** [VP15A, B, 2C] (cause to) move slowly forward or along: (使)慢慢向前移动; 渐移: *~ oneself/~ one's way through a crowd;* 在人群中慢慢挤向前移动; *~ along a narrow ledge of rock;* 沿着突出的狭窄岩石慢慢移动; *~ a piano through a door;* 将钢琴慢慢挪进门; *~ one's chair nearer to the fireplace.* 将椅子移近壁炉.

edge·ways, edge·wise /'edʒweɪz, -waɪz; 'edʒ,wez, -,waɪz/ adv with the edge outwards or forwards. 以刃向外或向前; 以边缘向外或向前. **not get a word in ~,** be unable to say anything when a very talkative person is speaking. 一极健谈者谈话时插不进嘴.

edg·ing /'edʒɪŋ; 'edʒɪŋ/ n narrow border: 窄边: *an ~ of lace on a dress.* 一件衣服上的花边. **'~·shears,** tool for trimming grass on the edges of a lawn. 修剪草地边缘的剪刀; 修边剪刀.

ed·ible /'edɪbl; 'edəbl/ adj fit to be eaten; not poisonous. 可食的; 无毒的. □ n (usu pl) things fit to be eaten. (通常用复数)可食之物. **edi·bil·ity** /,edɪ'bɪlətɪ, ,edə'bɪlətɪ/ n

edict /'iːdɪkt; 'idɪkt/ n order or proclamation issued by authority; decree. 敕令; 诏书; 法令; 告示.

edi·fi·ca·tion /,edɪfɪ'keɪʃn; ,ɛdəfə'keʃən/ n [U] mental or moral improvement. 开导; 启发; 熏陶.

edi·fice /'edɪfɪs; 'ɛdəfɪs/ n [C] building (esp a large or imposing one); (fig) sth built up in the mind: 大厦; (喻)心中构思之物: *The whole ~ of his hopes was destroyed.* 他心中整个的希望都毁了.

edify /'edɪfaɪ; 'edə,faɪ/ vt (pt, pp **-fied**) [VP6A] improve in morals or mind: 开导; 启发; 熏陶: *~ing books.* 陶冶人性的书籍.

edit /'edɪt; 'ɛdɪt/ vt [VP6A] 1 prepare (another person's writing) for publication (as a book, or in a newspaper or other periodical); 编辑(他人之作品成书或发表于报纸或其他刊物); 刊行: *~ a newspaper;* 编辑一报纸; *~ a Shakespeare play for use in schools.* 编印莎士比亚的一个剧本供学校之用. **2** do the work of planning and directing the publication of a newspaper, magazine, book, encyclopaedia, etc. 主编(报纸, 杂志, 书, 百科全书等). **3** prepare a cinema film, tape recording by putting together parts in a suitable sequence. 剪辑(影片, 录音). **4** arrange data for computer processing. 编排资料供电脑处理.

edi·tion /ɪ'dɪʃn; ɪ'dɪʃən/ n 1 form in which a book is published: 版本: *a cheap ~;* 廉价版; *a 'pocket ~.* 袖珍版. **2** total number of copies (of a book, newspaper, etc) issued from the same types: (书籍, 报纸等)一版所刊印的总数: *the first ~;* 初版; *a revised ~.* 修订版. ⇨ impression (3).

edi·tor /'edɪtər; 'ɛdɪtə/ n person who edits (esp a book, newspaper, periodical, radio news programme) or who is in charge of part of a newspaper: 编辑; 主笔: *the 'sports/fi'nancial ~.* 体育(金融)新闻编辑.

edi·tor·ial /,edɪ'tɔːrɪəl; ,ɛdə'tɔrɪəl/ adj of an editor: 编辑的; 主笔的: *the ~ office;* 编辑部; *~ work.* 编辑工作. □ n [C] special article or discussion of news in a newspaper, etc usu written by the editor. 社论.

edu·cate /'edʒukeɪt; 'ɛdʒə,ket/ vt [VP6A, 15A, 16A] give intellectual and moral training to; train: 教育; 训练: *The boy had to ~ himself in the evening after finishing his work.* 这个男孩只能在工作做完后晚上自修。*I was ~d for the law.* 我是学法律的。*You should ~ your children to behave well.* 你应教导你的孩子们守规矩. **edu·ca·tor** /-tə(r); -tə/ n person who ~s. 从事教育者; 教育家.

edu·ca·tion /,edʒu'keɪʃn; ,ɛdʒə'keʃən/ n [U] 1 systematic training and instruction (esp of the young, in school, college, etc): 教育(尤指学校中对青年的教育): *No country can afford to neglect ~.* 任何国家都不容忽视教育。*Is ~ free and compulsory in your country?* 贵国是实行免费的义务教育吗? **2** knowledge and abilities, development of character and mental powers, resulting from such training. (学识、能力、品格、智力的)培养; 教养. **~·al** /-ʃənl; -ʃnəl/ adj of, connected with, ~: 教育的; 与教育有关的: *~ work,* 教育工作; *an ~·al magazine.* 教育杂志. **~·ist** /-ʃənɪst; -ʃnɪst/, **~·al·ist** /-ʃənəlɪst; -ʃnlɪst/ nn expert in ~. 教育家.

educe /ɪ'djuːs US: ɪ'duːs; ɪ'djus/ vt [VP6A] (formal) bring out, develop (from what is latent or potential). (正式用语)引出; 自潜在物中引发.

eel /iːl; il/ n long, snake-like fish. 鳗; 鳝. ⇨ the illus at sea. 参看 sea 之插图. **as slippery as an eel,** very difficult to hold; (fig) (of a person) untrustworthy; difficult to manage. 似鳝鱼般滑溜; 难以握住; (喻)(指人)不可靠的; 难以控制的.

e'en /iːn; in/ adv (poet) (诗) = even.

e'er /eə(r); ɛr/ adv (poet) (诗) = ever.

eerie, eery /'ɪərɪ; 'ɪrɪ/ adj (-ier, -iest) causing a feeling of mystery and fear: 引起神秘而恐怖感觉的: *an ~ shriek.* 凄惨的怪叫. **eer·ily** /'ɪərəlɪ; 'ɪrɪlɪ/ adv **eeri·ness** n

eff /ef; ɛf/ vi (sl, euphem for △ fuck): (俚, fuck 的委婉语): *I told him to eff off.* 我叫他走开。*What an effing nuisance!* 真令人讨厌!

ef·face /ɪ'feɪs; ɪ'fes/ vt [VP6A] 1 rub or wipe out; make indistinct, (fig) obliterate: 抹掉; 涂抹; 使不清楚; (喻) 忘却: *~ an inscription;* 使铭刻不清楚; *unpleasant memories of the past.* 忘却过去不愉快的记忆. **2** **~ oneself,** keep in the background in order to escape being noticed; make oneself appear to be unimportant. 隐于幕后以期不为人所注意; 埋没自己. **~·ment** n

ef·fect /ɪ'fekt; ɛ'fɛkt/ n 1 [C, U] ([U] in phrases of degree or extent) result; outcome: (用作不可数名词时指程度或限度)结果; 效果: *the ~ of heat upon metals;*

热对于金属所发生的效应; *the ~s of the hot weather.* 炎热天气之苦。 *Did the medicine have any ~/a good ~?* 这药有效吗? *Punishment had very little ~ on him, did not reform him, frighten him, etc.* 惩罚对他没有什么效果(不能使他改过,生畏等)。 *Our arguments had no ~ on them, did not influence them.* 我们的议论对他们没有影响。 *of no ~,* useless, not doing what was intended or hoped for. 无用; 无效。 *in ~,* **(a)** in fact, really; for practical purposes. 事实上; 实际上。 **(b)** (of a rule, law, etc) in operation: 现行施行的(依法等实施中); 有效: *The rule is still in ~.* 本规则仍在实施中。 *bring/carry/put sth into ~,* cause it to operate; 实行(某事物);实施: *The plans will soon be carried into ~.* 这些计划不久便可实施。 *come into ~,* reach the stage of being operative: 实行;实施: *The new tax regulations came into ~ last week.* 新税法上周已开始实施。 *give ~ to,* cause to become active or have a result. 使生效。 *take ~,* **(a)** produce the result intended or required. 生效;奏效。 **(b)** come into force; operate; become active. 实施; 实行; 起作用。 **2** [C, U] impression produced on the mind of a spectator, hearer, reader, etc: 印象; 感触: *wonderful 'cloud ~s,* impressions produced by light on clouds, eg at sunset; 阳光射在云上形成的奇异景象(例如日落时); *'sound ~s,* (in broadcasting, etc) sounds characteristic of a scene, or incidental to an event, eg the noise of a train. (广播等)音响效果(表示某一情景或事件的声音,例如火车的噪音); *Everything he says and does is calculated for ~,* designed to impress spectators or hearers. 他的一言一行都是想给别人造成一个印象。 **3** *to this/that ~,* with this/that meaning: 大意是: *That is what he said, or words to that ~,* words with the same general meaning. 那便是他说的话, 或者大意是如此。 *to the ~ that ...,* stating: 大意是说···: *I have received a cable to the ~ that ...,* with the information that .... 我收到一封电报,大意是说···, *to the same ~,* giving the same information: 具有同样意思; 意思一样: *I sent a telegram and wrote a letter to the same ~.* 我发出一份电报, 并以同样意思写了一封信。 **4** (*pl*) goods; property: (复)所有物; 财产: *The hotel-keeper seized her personal ~s because she could not pay her bill.* 因为她付不起帐,旅馆主人扣留了她私人的所有物。 *no ~s,* written (often 常略作 N/E) by bankers on a cheque which is dishonoured. 无存款(银行职员书于空头支票上者)。 □ *vt* [VP6A] bring about; accomplish: 产生; 引起; 实现; 完成: *~ one's purpose.* 达到目的。 *a cure;* 完成治疗; 治愈; *~ (= take out) an insurance policy.* 取得保险单;加入保险。

ef·fec·tive /ɪˈfektɪv; əˈfɛktɪv/ *adj* **1** having an effect; able to bring about the result intended: 有效的; 奏效的: *~ measures to cure unemployment.* 消除失业的有效措施。 **2** making a striking impression: 予人深刻印象的: *an ~ scheme of decoration.* 引起深刻印象的装饰法。 **3** actual or existing: 实际的; 真存的; 现行的: *the ~ membership of the society;* 现在有效的会员资格; (of a military force, soldiers, sailors, etc) fit for service: (指军队,士兵,船员等)适于任务的: *the ~ strength of the army.* 军队的现有员额。 *~·ly* *adv* *~·ness* *n*

ef·fec·tual /ɪˈfektʃʊəl; əˈfɛktʃʊəl/ *adj* (not used of persons) bringing about the result required; answering its purpose: (不用以指人)有效的; 奏效的: *an ~ remedy/punishment;* 有效的治疗(惩罚); *to take ~ steps.* 采取有效步骤。 *~·ly* /-lɪ; -lɪ/ *adv* *~·ness* *n*

ef·femi·nate /ɪˈfemɪnət; əˈfɛmɪnɪt/ *adj* (of a man, derog) feminine. (指男人, 贬)女人气的; 无丈夫气概的。 *ef·femi·nacy* /ɪˈfemɪnəsɪ; əˈfɛmɪnəsɪ/ *n*

ef·fendi /eˈfendɪ; ɛˈfɛndɪ/ *n* (old use, in Turkey) sir; (in Arab countries) educated or powerful person. 先生(土耳其昔时对男人之尊称); (阿拉伯国家)受过教育的人, 有势力的人。

ef·fer·vesce /ˌefəˈves; ˌɛfəˈvɛs/ *vi* [VP2A] give off bubbles of gas; (of gas) issue in bubbles; (fig, of persons) be gay and excited. 起气泡; (指气)冒泡; (喻,指人)愉快而兴奋。 *ef·fer·ves·cence* /ˌefəˈvesns; ˌɛfəˈvɛsns/ *n* [U] *ef·fer·ves·cent* /-snt; -snt/ *adj*

ef·fete /ɪˈfiːt; ɛˈfiːt/ *adj* exhausted; weak and worn out: 筋疲力竭的; 衰弱不堪的: *~ civilizations/empires.* 衰落的文明(帝国)。 *~·ness* *n*

ef·fi·ca·cious /ˌefɪˈkeɪʃəs; ˌɛfɪˈkeɪʃəs/ *adj* (not used of persons) producing the desired result: (不用以指人)有效的: *an ~ cure for a disease.* 对一病之有效治疗。 *~·ly* *adv* **ef·fi·cacy** /ˈefɪkəsɪ; ˈɛfəkəsɪ/ *n* [U] state or quality of being ~. 有效; 效能。

ef·fi·cient /ɪˈfɪʃnt; əˈfɪʃənt/ *adj* **1** (of persons) capable; able to perform duties well: 能胜任的: *an ~ secretary/staff of teachers.* 能干的秘书(教师)。 **2** producing a desired or satisfactory result: 有效力的: *~ methods of teaching.* 有效的教学方法。 *~·ly* *adv* **ef·fi·ciency** /ɪˈfɪʃnsɪ; əˈfɪʃənsɪ/ *n* [U] state or quality of being ~. 有能力; 能胜任; 效力; 效能; 效率。

ef·figy /ˈefɪdʒɪ; ˈɛfədʒɪ/ *n* (*pl* **-gies**) [C] representation of a person (in wood, stone, etc). (木, 石等制的)肖像; 雕像。 *in ~,* as an ~: 作为肖像: *hang/burn a person in ~,* make an ~ of him and hang/burn it (as a sign of hatred, etc). 悬吊(焚毁)某人之肖像(以泄恨等)。

ef·flor·es·cence /ˌefloˈresns; ˌɛfloˈrɛsns/ *n* [U] (formal) flowering; bursting out into flower. (正式用语)开花。 *ef·flor·es·cent* /-snt; -snt/ *adj*

ef·flu·ent /ˈefluənt; ˈɛfluənt/ *n* **1** [C] stream flowing from a larger stream or from a lake. 自河, 湖等流出之水道;支流。 **2** [U] discharge of waste liquid matter, sewage, etc, eg from a factory. 废水或污水(例如自工厂流出者)。

ef·flux /ˈeflʌks; ˈɛflʌks/ *n* [U] flowing out of liquid, gas, etc; [C] that which flows out. (液体,气体等的)流出; 流出之物。

ef·fort /ˈefət; ˈɛfət/ *n* [U] trying hard; use of strength and energy (*to do* sth); [C] vigorous attempt: 努力; 尽力(与不定式连用); 努力的尝试: *He lifted the big rock without ~.* 他不费力地举起了那块大石。 *It doesn't need much ~.* 这事不需要费什么力气。 *Please make an ~ to arrive early.* 请劳驾早到。 *Does it require a great ~ of will to give up smoking?* 戒烟需要坚强的毅力吗? *I will make every ~ (= do all I can) to help you.* 我愿尽我的力量帮助你。 *His ~s at clearing up the mystery failed.* 他企图揭开此一奥秘之努力失败了。 **2** (*n*) (colloq) result of ~; sth done with ~: (口)努力的结果; 精心之作: *That's a pretty good ~,* ie you have done well. 那是努力的良好成果(你做得不错)。 *~·less* *adj* making no ~; without ~; easy: 不尽力的; 不费力的; 容易的: *done with ~less skill.* 容易做成的。

ef·front·ery /ɪˈfrʌntərɪ; ɛˈfrʌntərɪ/ *n* [U] shameless boldness; impudence: (*pl* **-ries**) instance of this: 厚颜; 无耻; 厚颜无耻的行为: *How can you have the ~ to ask for another loan?* 你怎能厚着脸皮再来借钱?

ef·ful·gent /ɪˈfʌldʒənt; ɛˈfʌldʒənt/ *adj* (liter) radiant; resplendent. (文)光辉的; 灿烂的。 **ef·ful·gence** /-dʒəns; -dʒəns/ *n* radiance. 光辉; 灿烂。

ef·fu·sion /ɪˈfjuːʒən; əˈfjuːʒən/ *n* **1** [U] sending or pouring out (of liquid, eg blood); [C] quantity poured out. 流出(指液体, 例如血液)倾注; 流出之量。 **2** [C] (esp unrestrained) outpouring of thought or feeling: (尤指未加抑制的)思想或感情的流露: *poetical ~s;* 诗情奔放; *~s in love letters.* 情书中感情的盈溢。

ef·fu·sive /ɪˈfjuːsɪv; əˈfjuːsɪv/ *adj* (of the feelings, signs of pleasure, gratitude, etc) pouring out too freely: (指感情, 表露的快乐, 感激等)洋溢的; 充溢的; 过分流露的: *~ thanks;* 感激之言; *~ in one's gratitude.* 感激之情溢于言表。 *~·ly* *adv* *~·ness* *n*

eft /eft; eft/ *n* newt. 水蜥。

egali·tar·ian /ɪˌɡælɪˈteərɪən; ɪˌɡæləˈtɛrɪən/ *n*, *adj* (person) favouring the doctrine of equal rights,

benefits and opportunities for all citizens. 主张人人平等的(人). Cf 参较 **elitist**. ~·**ism** /-ɪzəm; -ɪzəm/ n

egg[1] /eg; ɛg/ n female reproducing cell; ovum, (esp an embryo enclosed in a shell, eg of a hen, used as food): 卵; 蛋: *Birds, reptiles and insects come from eggs*. 鸟, 爬虫及昆虫均系卵生。 *Chickens are hatched from eggs*. 小鸡是由鸡蛋孵出的。 *The hen laid an egg*. 这只鸡下了一个蛋。 *Will you have your eggs boiled or fried?* 你的蛋是煮着吃还是煎着吃? [U] *You've got some egg* (ie a bit of a cooked egg) *on your chin*. 你的下巴上沾有一点蛋。 ⇨ the illus at **amphibian**, prey 参看 amphibian, prey 之插图。 *a bad egg*, (colloq) a worthless or dishonest person. 坏蛋; 坏人。 *as sure as eggs is eggs*, (colloq) undoubtedly. (口)无疑地。 *in the egg*, at an early stage; undeveloped. 在初期; 未发展的。 *put all one's eggs in one basket*, risk everything one has in a single venture, eg by investing all one's money in one business. 孤注一掷(例如将全部金钱投资于一项事业)。 *teach one's grandmother to suck eggs*, give advice to sb who has much more experience than oneself. 班门弄斧。 **'egg-cup**, small cup for holding a boiled egg. 吃煮蛋用的小杯。 **'egg-head** n (colloq) intellectual person; theorist. (口)知识分子; 理论家。 **'egg-plant**, plant with large, purple (rather egg-shaped) fruit (= aubergine), used as a vegetable. 茄子。 ⇨ the illus at **vegetable**. 参看 vegetable 之插图。 **'egg-shell**, shell of an egg: 蛋壳: *egg-shell china*, very thin kind; 薄瓷器; *egg-shell paint*, kind that gives a finish that is neither glossy nor matt. 蛋壳漆(一种光泽既不亮亦不暗的漆)。 **'egg-whisk**, utensil for beating eggs. 搅蛋器。

egg[2] /eg; ɛg/ vt [VP15B] **egg sb on**, urge him (*to do sth*). 怂恿某人(做某事, 与不定式连用)。

eg·lan·tine /'egləntaɪn; 'ɛglən,taɪn/ n [U] kind of rose; sweet-briar. 多花蔷薇。

ego /'egəʊ US: 'iːgəʊ; 'igo/ n **(the) ego**, (psych) individual's perception or experience of himself; individual's capacity to think, feel and act; self-esteem. (心理)自我; 个人的思想, 感觉和行动的能力; 自尊; 自负。 **'ego·trip** n (colloq) self-centred or self-seeking act. (口)以自我为中心或自私自利的行为。 □ vt act in this way. 行为自私自利。

ego·cen·tric /ˌegəʊ'sentrɪk; ˌiːg-; ˌigo'sɛntrɪk/ adj self-centred; egoistic. 以自我为中心的; 利己主义的。

ego·ism /'egəʊɪzəm US: 'iːg-; 'igo,ɪzəm/ n [U] **1** (phil) theory that our actions are always caused by the desire to benefit ourselves. (哲)利己主义; 自我主义。 **2** systematic selfishness; state of mind in which one is always thinking of oneself. 自私; 利己心。 ⇨ **altruism**. **ego·ist** /-ɪst; -ɪst/ n believer in ~. 利己主义者; 自我主义者。 **ego·istic** /ˌegəʊ'ɪstɪk US: ˌiːg-; ˌigo'ɪstɪk/, **ego·isti·cal** /-kl; -kəl/ adj of ~; of an egoist. 利己主义的; 利己主义者的; 自私的; 利己主义者的。 **ego·isti·cal·ly** /-klɪ; -klɪ/ adv

ego·tism /'egəʊtɪzəm US: 'iːg-; 'igo,tɪzəm/ n [U] practice of talking too often or too much about oneself; self-conceit; selfishness. 自我吹嘘; 自负; 自私。 **ego·tist** /-tɪst; -tɪst/ n person who practises ~; selfish person. 自夸者; 自负者; 自私者。 **ego·tis·tic** /ˌegəʊ'tɪstɪk US: ˌiːg-; ˌigo'tɪstɪk/ adj of ~; of or like an egotist. 自夸的; 自负的; 自私的; 自夸者的; 自负者的; 自私者的。 **ego·tis·ti·cal·ly** /-klɪ; -klɪ/ adv

egre·gi·ous /ɪ'griːdʒɪəs; ɪ'gridʒəs/ adj (formal) outstanding, exceptional (used of sb or sth bad): (正式用语)显著的; 异常的(用以指不良的人或事物): ~ *folly*, 惊人的愚蠢; *an ~ blunder*. 大错。

egress /'iːgres; 'igrɛs/ n (formal) [U] (right of) going out; [C] way out; exit. (正式用语)外出权; 出路; 出口。

egret /'iːgret; 'igrɪt/ n kind of heron with beautiful long feathers in the tail and on the back; bunch of these feathers as an ornament. 白鹭(尾部及背部有美丽的长羽毛); 装饰用的白鹭羽毛。

Egyp·tian /ɪ'dʒɪpʃn; ɪ'dʒɪpʃən/ adj, n (native) of Egypt. 埃及的; 埃及人。

eh /eɪ; e/ int used to express surprise or doubt, or to invite agreement. 呃! 嗯! (表示惊奇, 疑问, 或征求同意)。

eider·down /'aɪdədaʊn; 'aɪdɚdaʊn/ n (bed-covering filled with) soft breast feathers of large, wild duck (called 称作 '*eider*). 棉凫之绒毛; 鸭绒(被)。

eight /eɪt; et/ adj, n **1** the number 8. 八; 八个。 ⇨ **App 4**. 参看附录四。 *have one over the ~*, drink too much. 饮酒过量。 **2** crew of ~ in a rowingboat. 划艇之八名选手。 ⇨ **bow**[3](2), **stroke**[1](3). **eighth** /eɪtθ; etθ/ adj, n **eighth·ly** adv ~·**pence** /'eɪtpəns US: -pens; 'etpəns/ n ~·**penny** /'eɪtpənɪ US: -penɪ; 'et,penɪ/ adj ~·**een** /ˌeɪ'tiːn; e'tin/ adj, n the number 18. 十八; 十八个。 ~·**eenth** /ˌeɪ'tiːnθ; e'tinθ/ adj, n ~·**y** /'eɪtɪ; 'etɪ/ adj, n the number 80. 八十; 八十个。 **the eighties**, 80—89. 80 至 89。 ~·**ieth** /'eɪtɪəθ; 'etɪəθ/ adj, n

a rowing eight

eight·some /'eɪtsəm; 'etsəm/ n lively Scottish dance (a *reel*) for eight dancers. 一种活泼的苏格兰八人舞。

eis·tedd·fod /aɪ'steðvɒd; e'stɛðvɑd/ n (in Wales) annual gathering of poets and musicians for competitions. (威尔士的)诗人与音乐家之竞赛年会。

either /'aɪðə(r); 'iːðɚ; 'iðɚ, 'aɪðɚ/ adj, pron **1** ~ **(of)**, (Cf the use of *any*, or *any one of*, when the number is greater than two) one or the other (of two): 二者之一(如为三者以上, 参较 any 或 any one of 的用法): *Take ~ half; they're exactly the same*. 你任选一半; 它们完全相同。 *E~ of them / E~ one will be satisfactory*. 二者中任何一个都会令人满意。 *You must not favour ~ side in the dispute*. 你不可偏袒争论中的任何一方。 *In ~ event / ~ of these events you will benefit*. 两种情况都会对你有利。 **2** ~ **(of)**, (Cf the use of *both* and *each*, which are more usu) one and the other (of two): 二者(参较 both 和 each 的用法, 此二字较为常用): *There was an armchair at ~ end of the long table*. 长桌的两端各有一张扶手椅。 □ adv, conj **1** used in statements after *not*; 用于陈述句中 not 之后; (Cf the use of *neither*): (参较 neither 的用法): *I don't like the red one, and I don't like the pink one*, ~, ie I dislike both of them. 我不喜欢那个红的, 也不喜欢那个粉红的。 *A: 'I haven't been to Paris yet.' B: 'I haven't been there yet*, ~.' (= Neither have I). A: '我没有到过巴黎'。 B: '我也没有去过'。 **2** (used after a negative phrase) moreover; furthermore: 用于否定短语后)而且; 再者: *There was a time, and not so long ago* ~, *when she could walk twenty miles a day*. 有一段时期, 而且不是很久以前, 她一天能够步行二十英里。 **3** ~ ... *or*, (used to introduce the first of two or more alternatives): (用以介绍两个或多个可选择的事物中之第一项): *He must be* ~ *mad or drunk*. 他不是疯了, 就是醉了。 *Please* ~ *come in or go out: don't stand there in the doorway*. 请你或是进来, 或是出去: 不要站在门口。 *E~ the dog or the cat has eaten it*. 不是狗就是猫把它吃了。

ejacu·late /ɪ'dʒækjuleɪt; ɪ'dʒækjə,let/ vt [VP6A] **1** say suddenly and briefly. 突然而简短地说出。 **2** eject

(fluid, eg semen) from the body. 自体内射出(液体,例如精液). **ejacu·la·tion** /ɪˌdʒækjʊ'leɪʃn; ɪˌdʒækjə'leʃən/ *n* **1** [C] exclamation; sth said suddenly. 呼喊; 突然说出的话. **2** discharge or ejection of fluid (eg semen) (from the body). (自体内)射出液体(例如精液).

eject /ɪ'dʒekt; ɪ'dʒɛkt/ *vt*, *vi* [VP6A, 14] ~ *(from)*, **1** compel (sb) to leave (a place); expel: 强迫(某人)离开(某地); 逐出: *They were ~ed because they had not paid their rent for a year.* 他们因为已经一年未付房租而被赶出去了. **2** send out (liquid, etc): 喷出(液体等); 射出: *lava ~ed from a volcano.* 自火山喷出的熔岩. **3** [VP2A] make an emergency exit, with a parachute, from an aircraft. (自飞机)紧急跳伞. **ejec·tion** /ɪ'dʒekʃn; ɪ'dʒɛkʃən/ *n* **ejec·tor** /-tə(r); -tɚ/ *n* sth that ~s. 喷出物; 射出物. **e'jector-seat**, one in an aircraft for ~ing the pilot so that he may descend by parachute. (飞机上之)弹射座椅(可将驾驶员弹出,以便跳伞降落).

eke /iːk; ik/ *vt* [VP15B] *eke sth out*, make (small supplies of sth) enough for one's needs by adding sth; make (a living) by doing this: 补足; 力求维持(生活): *eke out one's coal by saving the cinders for further use;* 留着煤渣再用,以弥补煤的不足; *eke out one's livelihood.* 力谋生计.

elab·or·ate /ɪ'læbərɪt; ɪ'læbərɪt/ *adj* worked out with much care and in great detail; carefully prepared and finished; complicated: 精心做成的; 细心完成的; 复杂的: ~ *plans;* 细心完成的计划; *an* ~ *design;* 精心设计的; *an* ~ *dinner,* eg with many courses. 精致的餐食(例如有许多道菜). □ *vt* /ɪ'læbəreɪt; ɪ'læbəˌret/ [VP6A] work out, describe, in detail: 精心做成; 详尽描述: *Please* ~ *your proposals a little.* 请将你的建议详细数述一下. ~**ly** *adv* ~**ness** *n* **elab·or·ation** /ɪˌlæbə'reɪʃn; ɪˌlæbə'reʃən/ *n* [U] elaborating or being ~d; [C] that which is added; detail that ~s. 精心做成; 详细描述; 增加物; 细节.

élan /eɪ'lɑːn; e'lɑ̃/ *n* [U] (F) vivacity; impetuosity; enthusiasm. (法)活力; 冲劲; 热心.

eland /'iːlənd; 'ilənd/ *n* kind of S African antelope. 非洲旋角大羚羊.

elapse /ɪ'læps; ɪ'læps/ *vi* [VP2A] (of time) pass. (指时间)经过; 逝去.

elas·tic /ɪ'læstɪk; ɪ'læstɪk/ *adj* **1** having the tendency to go back to the normal or previous size or shape after being pulled or pressed: 有弹性的: ~ *bands.* 橡皮带; *Rubber is* ~. 橡皮是有弹性的. *Sponges are* ~. 海绵有弹性. **2** (fig) not firm, fixed or unalterable; able to be adapted: (喻)非固定或不可改变的; 可以伸缩的: ~ *rules;* 有伸缩性的规则; *an* ~ *temperament,* eg of a person who soon becomes cheerful again after being sad. 开朗的性情(例如能迅速自悲伤的心情转为愉快). □ [U] cord or material made ~ by weaving rubber into it: 橡皮筋; 松紧带: *a piece of* ~; 一条松紧带(橡皮筋); (attrib) (用作定语) ~ *braces,* made of this material. 松紧吊裤带. ~**·ity** /ˌelæ'stɪsətɪ US: ɪ'læ-; ɪˌlæs'tɪsəti/ *n* [U] the quality of being ~; 弹性; 伸缩性: *elasticity of demand,* (comm) change in demand because of price changes. (商)需求的弹性(因物价波动造成者).

elate /ɪ'leɪt; ɪ'let/ *vt* [VP6A] (usu passive) stimulate; make high-spirited: (通常用被动语态)鼓舞; 使得意: *He was* ~*d at the news/by his success.* 这消息(他的成功)使他得意. **ela·tion** /ɪ'leɪʃn; ɪ'leʃən/ *n* [U] high spirits: 得意扬扬; 兴高采烈: *filled with elation.* 得意扬扬.

el·bow /'elbəʊ; 'ɛl,bo/ *n* **1** (outer part of the) joint between the two parts of the arm, ⇨ the illus at **arm**; corresponding part of a sleeve (in a jacket, etc). 肘(参看**arm**之插图); (衣服的)肘部. *at one's* ~, close to; near by. 靠近; 在近旁. *out at* ~*s,* (a) (of a garment) worn-out. (指衣衫)褴褛的. (b) (of a person) in worn-out clothes. (指人)衣衫褴褛的. '~ **grease** *n* [U] vigorous polishing; hard work. 费力的擦; 费力的工作. '~ **room** *n* [U] room to move freely. 可自由活动的余

地. **2**~-shaped bend, corner or joint (eg in a pipe or chimney). 弯管; 肘管; 弯头(例如管子或烟囱之转接处). □ *vt* [VP6A, 15B, 14] push or force (one's way through, forward, etc): 挤进(与 through, forward 等连用): *to* ~ (*also shoulder*) *one's way through a crowd.* 自人群中挤过(shoulder 亦可用作此义).

el·der [1] /'eldə(r); 'ɛldɚ/ *adj* (attrib only; 仅用作定语; cf 参较 *older*) (of members of a family, esp closely related members, or of two indicated members) older; senior: (指家庭中的分子,尤指近亲,或指两个指明的分子)年纪较长的: *My* ~ *brother is in India.* 我的哥哥在印度. *The* ~ *sister is called Mary.* 姐姐名叫玛丽. *the* ~, (before or after a person's name to distinguish that person from another of the same name): (用于人名后,以别于同姓名之人)老的; 年长的: *Pliny the* ~; 老普利尼; *the* ~ *Pitt.* 老皮特. ~ **'statesman** /-stɛtsmən; -stɛtsmən/, (*pl* -**men**), person (usu retired from office) whose unofficial advice is sought and valued because of his long experience. 元老. □ *n* **1** (*pl*) persons of greater age: (复)年长者; 长辈: *Should we always follow the advice of our* ~*s and betters?* 我们应当永远听从长辈和前辈的劝告吗? **2** official in some Christian churches, member of a governing body (session) in Presbyterian churches. 某些教会中之职员;(长老会中之)长老. **3** *the* ~ *sb's* ~, older of two persons: 二人中之较长者: *He is my* ~ *by several years.* 他比我大几岁.

el·der [2] /'eldə(r); 'ɛldɚ/ *n* (kinds of) bush or small tree with clusters of white flowers and red or black berries. 接骨木(有白花和红或黑果的一种矮树). '~-**berry 'wine,** wine made from these berries. 接骨木果实制成的酒.

el·der·ly /'eldəlɪ; 'ɛldɚlɪ/ *adj* getting old; rather old. 渐老的; 年龄相当大的.

el·dest /'eldɪst; 'ɛldɪst/ *adj* (attrib only; 仅用作定语; cf 参较 *oldest*) first-born or oldest surviving (member of a family): (家族中)最年长的: *my* ~ *son/brother.* 我的长子(大哥).

El Dorado /ˌel də'rɑːdəʊ; ˌɛldə'rɑdo/ *n* (*pl* ~**s** /-dəʊz; -doz/) fictitious country or city rich in precious metals. 传说中的黄金国.

elect [1] /ɪ'lekt; ɪ'lɛkt/ *adj* **1** (after the *n*) chosen, selected: (用于名词后)被选出的: *the bishop* ~, not yet in office. 被选出而尚未就职的主教. **2** *the* ~, those persons specially chosen, or considered to be the best. 特别精选出来的人.

elect [2] /ɪ'lekt; ɪ'lɛkt/ *vt* **1** [VP6A, 25, 23, 14] ~ *(to)*, choose (sb) by vote: 选举: *to* ~ *a president;* 选举总统; *to* ~ *Smith (to be) chairman;* 选举史密斯做主席; *to* ~ *Green to the Academy.* 推选格林为该学院院士. **2** [VP7A] choose; decide: 选择; 决定: *He had* ~*d to become a lawyer.* 他已决定做律师.

elec·tion /ɪ'lekʃn; ɪ'lɛkʃən/ *n* [U] choosing or selection (of candidates for an office, etc) by vote; [C] instance of this: 选举: (attrib) (用作定语) ~ *results.* 选举结果. **,general '~,** of representatives, (GB members of the House of Commons), for the whole country. (议员等)普选; 大选; (英)下议院议员选举. **,local '~,** of representatives, (GB the councillors), for a town/borough/district council. 市, 郡等议员选举; 地方议员选举. **'by-~,** of one member, to fill a vacancy. 补选. ~**·eer·ing** /ɪˌlekʃə'nɪərɪŋ; ɪˌlekʃən'ırıŋ/ *n* [U] working on ~s, eg by canvassing, making speeches. 竞选(如借游说,发表演讲等).

elec·tive /ɪ'lektɪv; ɪ'lɛktɪv/ *adj* **1** having the power to elect: 有选举权的: *an* ~ *assembly.* 有选举权的大会. **2** chosen or filled by election: 被选出的; 选任的: *an* ~ *office.* 选任的职位. **3** (US) not compulsory; that may be chosen: (美)非强迫的; 可以选择的: ~ *subjects in college.* 大学中的选修科目. ⇨ *optional* at **option**.

elec·tor /ɪ'lektə(r); ɪ'lɛktɚ/ *n* person having the right to elect (esp by voting at a parliamentary election). 有选举权者; 选举人(尤指选议员时有投票权

者). **~al** /ɪˈlektərəl; ɪˈlɛktərəl/ *adj* of an election; of ~s: 选举的; 选举人的: *the ~al roll / register*, the list of ~s. 选举人名录. *The E~al College in the USA elects the President.* 在美国, 由选举团选举总统. **~·ate** /ɪˈlektərət; ɪˈlɛktərɪt/ *n* whole body of qualified ~s. 选举团; 选民.

elec·tric /ɪˈlektrɪk; ɪˈlɛktrɪk/ *adj* of, worked by, charged with, capable of developing, electricity: 电的; 用电的; 带电的; 发电的: *an ~ current / torch / iron / shock*; 电流(电筒; 电熨斗; 电震); *~ light*; 电灯; *~ flex / cord*; 花线; 皮线; *the ~ chair*, used for electrocuting criminals; 电椅(用做刑具); *~ blue*, steely blue; 钢青色; *an ~ guitar*, one that has amplifiers for the sound; 电吉他; *an ~ eye*, a photo-electric cell. 光电池; 电眼.

elec·tri·cal /ɪˈlektrɪkl; ɪˈlɛktrɪkl/ *adj* 1 relating to electricity: 关于电的: *~ engineering*. 电机工程学. 2 (fig) (eg of news) causing strong and sudden emotion. (喻)(指新闻等)震撼性的; 刺激性的. **~ly** /-klɪ; -klɪ/ *adv*

elec·tri·cian /ɪˌlekˈtrɪʃn; ɪˌlɛkˈtrɪʃən/ *n* expert in setting up, repairing and operating electrical apparatus. 电机师; 电器技师; 电机匠.

elec·tric·ity /ɪˌlekˈtrɪsətɪ; ɪˌlɛkˈtrɪsətɪ/ *n* [U] 1 all the phenomena associated with electrons (negative charge) and protons (positive charge); the study of these phenomena. 电; 电学. 2 supply of electric current: *When did ~ come to the village?* 这村庄何时开始有电力供应?

elec·trify /ɪˈlektrɪfaɪ; ɪˈlɛktrəˌfaɪ/ *vt* (*pt*, *pp* **-fied**) [VP6A] 1 charge (sth) with electricity. 使带电; 充电. 2 equip (a railway, etc) for the use of electric power. 电气化 (铁路等). 3 (fig) excite, shock, as if by electricity: (喻)震撼; 使惊骇: *to ~ an audience by an unexpected announcement.* 以意外的宣布使听众震惊. **elec·tri·fi·ca·tion** /ɪˌlektrɪfɪˈkeɪʃn; ɪˌlɛktrəfəˈkeʃən/ *n* ~ing, eg the conversion of a steam railway to an electric railway. 充电; 电气化(例如将一使用蒸汽的铁路电气化).

elec·tro- /ɪˈlektrəʊ; ɪˈlɛktro/ *pref* (in compounds) involving electricity: (用于复合词)电: **,~·cardio-gram** /-ˈkɑːdɪəʊɡræm; -ˈkɑrdɪəˌɡræm/ curve traced by an ~cardiograph, used in the diagnosis of heart disease. 心电图(诊断心脏疾病所作者). **,~·ˈcardio·graph** /-ˈkɑːdɪəʊɡrɑːf US: -ɡræf; -ˈkɑrdɪəˌɡræf/ apparatus which detects and records electric activity in the muscles of the heart. 心电图仪. **,~·ˈchem·is·try**, electricity as applied to chemistry. 电化学. **,~·ˈmag·net**, piece of soft iron that becomes magnetic when an electric current is passed through wire coiled round it. 电磁铁; 电磁体. **,~·ˈmag·ˈnetic** *adj* having both electric and magnetic character. 有电磁性的; 电磁铁的. From 由此产生, **,~·ˈmag·net·ism** *n* '~**plate** *vt* coat with a thin layer of metal (eg silver) by electrolysis. 电镀(例如镀以银面). □ *n* [U] articles plated with silver in this way. 镀银电镀器.

elec·tro·cute /ɪˈlektrəkjuːt; ɪˈlɛktrəˌkjut/ *vt* [VP 6A] kill accidentally, put to death, by means of an electrical current. 误触电而致死; 处以电刑. **elec·tro·cu·tion** /ɪˌlektrəˈkjuːʃn; ɪˌlɛktrəˈkjuʃən/ *n*

elec·trode /ɪˈlektrəʊd; ɪˈlɛktrod/ *n* solid conductor by which an electric current enters or leaves a vacuum tube, etc. 电极; 电极棒. ⇨ **anode, cathode.**

elec·tro·ly·sis /ɪˌlekˈtrɒləsɪs; ɪˌlɛkˈtrɑləsɪs/ *n* [U] separation of a substance into its chemical parts by electric current. 电解.

elec·tron /ɪˈlektrɒn; ɪˈlɛktrɑn/ *n* [C] (phys) subatomic particle of matter having a negative electric charge. (物理)电子. **~ microscope**, using ~s instead of visible light. 电子显微镜. **~·ic** /ɪˌlekˈtrɒnɪk; ɪˌlɛkˈtrɑnɪk/ *adj* of ~s; operated by, based on, ~s. 电子的; 电子操作的; 以电子为基础的. **~ic music**, produced

by manipulating natural or artificial sounds by means of electric or ~ic equipment. 电子音乐(用电化或电子设备制作的). **,~ic ˈdata ˈprocessing**, (abbr 略作 EDP) use of ~ic computers to derive information or to achieve a required order of data. 电子数据处理. **~·ics** *n* (with *sing v*) the science and technology of ~ic phenomena, devices and systems, as in radio, TV, tape recorders, computers, etc.(与单数动词连用)电子学.

elee·mosy·nary /ˌeliːˈmɒsɪnərɪ US: -nerɪ; ˌɛləˈmɑsnˌɛrɪ/ *adj* (formal) of, dependent upon, alms; charitable. (正式用语)依赖施舍的; 施舍的; 慈善的.

el·egant /ˈelɪɡənt; ˈɛləɡənt/ *adj* showing, having, good taste; graceful; done with care, skill and taste: 雅的; 优美的; 优雅的; 精美的: *an ~ young man*; 文雅的青年; *~ manners*; 文雅的举止; *leading a life of ~ ease.* 过着风雅的生活. **~·ly** *adv* **el·egance** /-əns; -əns/ *n* [U].

el·egiac /ˌeliˈdʒaɪək; ˌliˈdʒaɪˌæk/ *adj* 1 (of metre) suited to elegies: (指诗的韵律)适于挽歌的: *~ couplets.* 挽歌对句. 2 mournful. 哀悼的. □ *n pl* ~ verses. 挽歌; 哀歌.

el·egy /ˈelədʒɪ; ˈɛlədʒɪ/ *n* (*pl* **-gies**) poem or song of sorrow, esp for the dead. 挽歌; 挽诗.

el·ement /ˈelɪmənt; ˈɛləmənt/ *n* 1 (science) substance which cannot be split up into a simpler form by ordinary chemical methods: (科学)元素: *Water is a compound containing the ~s hydrogen and oxygen.* 水是含有氢和氧元素的化合物. 2 (according to the ancient philosophers): (根据古代哲学家的说法): *the four ~s*, earth, air, fire and water (out of which the material universe was thought to be composed). 四行(即土、风、火、水, 认为宇宙即由此四行构成). *in / out of one's ~*, in / not in suitable or satisfying surroundings: 在(不在)适当或满意的环境中: *He's in his ~ when taking part in a political debate*, is doing sth that pleases and satisfies him. 他参加政治辩论时, 真是得其所哉(可以大展所长). *I'm out of my ~ when people start talking about economics.* 当人们开始谈论经济学时, 我就成了外行了. 3 (*pl*) (复) **the ~s**, the forces of nature, the weather, etc: 自然力; 风雨等的力量: *exposed to the fury of the ~s*, to the winds, storms, etc. 暴露于风, 暴风雨等中. 4 (*pl*) beginnings or outlines of a subject of study; parts that must be learnt first: 初步; 大纲; 基本原理: *the ~s of geometry.* 几何学的初步. 5 necessary or characteristic feature: 要素; 特色: *Justice is an important ~ in good government.* 公正为善治的要素. 6 suggestion, indication, trace: 提示; 表示; 小量: *There's an ~ of truth in his account of what happened.* 对所发生的事之叙述略有一些是真实的. ⇨ **atom**(2). 7 resistance wire in an electrical appliance (eg a heater). 电阻线(例如电热器中者). **el·emen·tal** /ˌelɪˈmentl; ˌɛləˈmɛntl/ *adj* of the four ~s(2); of the ~s(3): 四行的; 自然力的: *the ~al fury of the storm.* 风雨的狂暴.

ele·men·tary /ˌelɪˈmentrɪ; ˌɛləˈmɛntərɪ/ *adj* of or in the beginning stage(s); not developed; simple: 初步的; 基本的; 未发展的; 简单的: *the ~ rules of social conduct*; 社会行为的基本守则; *~ arithmetic.* 初等算术. **ele·men·tar·ily** /ˌelɪˈmentərəlɪ US: ˌɛlɪmənˈtɛrəlɪ; ˌɛləmənˈtɛrəlɪ/ *adv*

el·eph·ant /ˈelɪfənt; ˈɛləfənt/ *n* largest four-footed animal now living, with curved ivory tusks and a long trunk (proboscis). 象. ⇨ the illus at **large**. 参看 large 之插图. **~ white**, costly or troublesome possession useless to its owner. 昂贵而无用的东西; 累赘. **el·ephan·ti·asis** /ˌelɪfənˈtaɪəsɪs; ˌɛləfənˈtaɪəsɪs/ *n* [U] skin disease causing great enlargement of limbs. 象皮病; 结节瘤. **ele·phan·tine** /ˌelɪˈfæntaɪn; ˌɛləˈfæntɪn/ *adj* of or like ~s; heavy; clumsy: 象的; 似象的; 重的; 笨拙的: *an ~ine task*; 累赘的工作; *~ine humour.* 笨拙的幽默; *an ~ine memory*, extremely reliable one. 绝对可靠的记忆.

el·ev·ate /'eliveit; 'ɛlə,vet/ vt [VP6A, 14] ~ **(to)**, (formal) lift up; raise; (fig) make (the mind,, morals) higher and better: (正式用语)举起;提高;(喻)使(思想,道德)高尚: ~ the voice, speak louder; 提高讲话声音; ~ a man to the peerage, make him a peer; 晋升一人为贵族; an elevating book/sermon; 激励人心的书(讲道); an ~d railway/railroad, one built on piers (usn in a town) to run overhead. 高架铁路.

el·ev·ation /,eli'veiʃn; ,ɛlə'veʃən/ n 1 [U] elevating or being elevated; 举起; 提高; 激励人心: ~ to the peerage; 晋身为贵族; [C] instance of this. 举起或提高的实例. 2 [U] grandeur or dignity: 高尚;庄严: ~ of thought/style/language. 思想(风格,语言)的高尚. 3 [C] height (esp above sea-level); hill or high place: 高度(尤指海拔);山;高地: an ~ of 2000 metres. 海拔二千米. 4 [C] angle (eg of a gun) with the horizon. 仰角(例如炮之仰角). 5 [C] plan (drawn to scale) of one side of a building. (建筑物之一面的)立视图. ⇨ **plan**. ⇨ the illus at perspective. 参看 perspective 之插图.

el·ev·ator /'eliveitə(r); 'ɛlə,vetɚ/ n 1 machine like a continuous belt with buckets at intervals, used for raising grain, etc. (运送谷类等之)升降机. 2 storehouse for grain. 谷仓. 3 thing that elevates, eg part of an aircraft that is used to gain or lose altitude. 使升起之物(例如飞机之升降舵). 4 (US) lift n (2). (美)电梯.

eleven /i'levn; i'lɛvən/ adj, n the number 11, ⇨ **App 4**; a team of eleven players for football, hockey or cricket. 十一; 十一个(参看附录四); 由十一名球员组成的足球, 曲棍球或板球队. **elev·enth** /i'levnθ; i'lɛvənθ/ adj, n at the ~th hour, at the latest possible time. 在最后一刻;刚好来得及. **elev·enses** /i'levnziz; i'lɛvnziz/ n pl (GB) snack and drink taken during the morning. (英)早前茶点(上午十一时左右进食的点心和饮料).

elf /elf; ɛlf/ n (pl elves /elvz; ɛlvz/) small fairy; mischievous little creature. 小精灵; 小妖精. **elfin** /'elfin; 'ɛlfɪn/ adj of elves: 小精灵的; 小妖精的: elfin dances/laughter. 小妖精的舞蹈(欢笑). **elf·ish** /'elfiʃ; 'ɛlfɪʃ/ adj mischievous. 恶作剧的.

eli·cit /i'lisit; ɪ'lɪsɪt/ vt [VP6A, 14] ~ **sth (from sb)**, draw out; cause to come out: 引出; 使发出: to ~ the truth/a reply 使吐露真情(作出回答). **eli·ci·ta·tion** /i,lisi'teiʃn; ɪ,lɪsɪ'teʃən/ n

elide /i'laid; ɪ'laɪd/ vt [VP6A] leave out a vowel or syllable in pronunciation. 发音时省略(一元音或音节). ⇨ **elision**.

eli·gible /'elidʒəbl; 'ɛlɪdʒəbl/ adj ~ **(for)**, fit, suitable, to be chosen; having the right qualifications: 适于被选的;合格的: ~ for promotion/a position/a pension/membership in a society; 有资格升级(充任一职,领养老金,为会员); an ~ young man, eg one who would be a satisfactory choice as a husband. 合格的青年(例如可以选择为丈夫者). **eli·gi·bil·ity** /,elidʒə'biləti; ,ɛlɪdʒə'bɪlɪtɪ/ n [U] the state of being ~. 合格;有资格.

elim·in·ate /i'limineit; ɪ'lɪmə,net/ vt [VP6A, 14] ~ **(from)**, remove; take or put away, get rid of (because unnecessary or unwanted): 除去;剔除;淘汰: ~ slang words from an essay; 将俚语自一篇文章中剔除; ~ a possibility, set it aside and pay no consideration to it; 对一种可能性不予考虑; ~ waste products from the body, excrete them. 自体内排泄废物. **elim·in·ation** /i,limi'neiʃn; ɪ,limə'neʃən/ n

eli·sion /i'liʒn; ɪ'lɪʒən/ n (from 出自 elide) [U] leaving out of a vowel or syllable in pronunciation (as in let's); [C] instance of this. 省略; 发音时一元音或一音节之省略(例如 let's).

élite /ei'li:t; ɪ'lit/ n group in society considered to be superior because of the power, talent, privileges, etc of its members: (因其权力,才能,特权等而被视为)优秀的团体; 杰出的人物; 精华: an educated ~. 有教养的优秀人才. ⇨ **egalitarian**, **élitism** /-tizəm; -tɪzəm/ n

[U] belief that the education system, etc should aim at developing ~s. 认为教育目标应培植优秀人才的主张. **élitist** /-tist; -tɪst/ n

elixir /i'liksə(r); i'lɪksɚ/ n [C] 1 preparation by which medieval scientists hoped to change metals into gold or (~ of life) to prolong life indefinitely. (中古时期科学家希望能变铁成金的)炼金药; 长生不老药(亦作 elixir of life). 2 remedy that cures all ills. 万灵药.

Eliza·bethan /i,lizə'bi:θn; ɪ,lɪzə'biθən/ adj of the time of Queen Elizabeth I of England: 英国伊丽莎白女王一世时代的: the '~ age; 伊丽莎白一世时代; ~ drama. 伊丽莎白女王一世时代的戏剧. □ n person who lived during her reign, eg Shakespeare. 伊丽莎白一世时代的人(例如莎士比亚).

elk /elk; ɛlk/ n one of the largest kinds of living deer, found in N Europe, N Asia, and (called a moose) N America. 麋(产于北欧、北亚及北美, 在北美此种鹿称作 moose).

el·ipse /i'lips; i'lɪps/ n regular oval. 椭圆. **el·lip·tic** /i'lɪptɪk; ɪ'lɪptɪk/, **el·lip·ti·cal** /-kl; -kl/ adj shaped like an ~. 椭圆形的.

el·lip·sis /i'lipsis; i'lɪpsɪs/ n (pl -pses /-psi:z; -psiz/) [U] omission from a sentence of words needed to complete the construction or meaning; [C] instance of this. 一句中字的省略;省略法. **el·lip·ti·cal** /i'lɪptɪkl; ɪ'lɪptɪkl/ adj containing ~: 省略之处的: an elliptical sentence. 含有省略之句子.

elm /elm; ɛlm/ n [C] common deciduous tree that grows to a great size and height, ⇨ the illus at tree; [U] its hard, heavy wood. 榆树(参看 tree 之插图); 榆木.

elo·cu·tion /,elə'kju:ʃn; ,ɛlə'kjuʃən/ n [U] art or style of speaking well, esp in public. 演说术; 雄辩术. **~·ary** /-ʃənri US: -ʃəneri; -ʃnerɪ/ adj of ~. 演说术的; 雄辩术的. **~·ist** /-ʃənist; -ʃənɪst/ n expert in ~. 演说家; 雄辩家.

elon·gate /'i:lɒŋgeit US: i'lɔ:ŋ-; i'lɔŋget/ vt, vi [VP6A, 2A] make or become long(er) in space. 伸长; 延长. **elon·ga·tion** /,i:lɒŋ'geiʃn US: lɔ:ŋ-; i,lɔŋ'geʃən/ n [U] making longer; [C] the part (of a line, etc) produced this way. 伸长;延长; (线等)延长部分.

elope /i'ləup; i'lop/ vi [VP2A, C, 3A] ~ **(with)**, (of a woman) run away from home or a husband (with a lover). (指女子)私奔. **~·ment** n

elo·quence /'eləkwəns; 'ɛləkwəns/ n [U] skilful use of language to persuade or to appeal to the feelings; fluent speaking. 口才; 雄辩; 滔滔而言. **elo·quent** /-ənt; -ənt/ adj having or showing ~. 有口才的; 善辩的. **elo·quent·ly** adv

else /els; ɛls/ adv 1 (with indef or interr pron) besides; in addition: (与不定或疑问代词连用)此外; 别的: Did you see anybody~, any other person(s)? 你还看到别的人没有? Have you anything ~ to do? 你有别的事情做没有? Ask somebody ~ to help you. 去请别人帮助你. That must be somebody ~'s (= some other person's) hat; it isn't mine. 那一定是别人的帽子, 不是我的. Nothing ~ (= Nothing more), thank you. 没有别的事了, 谢谢你. We went nowhere ~, to no other place. 我们没有去别的地方. What ~ should I do? 我还应该做些什么? Who ~ was there? 还有谁在那里? How ~ (= In what other way) would you do it? 你还有别的做法吗? little ~, not much more. 没有多少了;没有什么了. 2 otherwise; if not: 否则; 不然的话: Run (or) ~ you'll be late. 快跑,否则你要迟到了. He must be joking, or ~ he's mad. 他一定是开玩笑,不然他就是疯了.

else·where /,els'weə(r) US: -'hweər; 'ɛls,hwɛr/ adv somewhere else; in, at or to some other place. 在别处; 至别处.

elu·ci·date /i'lu:sideit; ɪ'lusə,det/ vt [VP6A] (formal) make clear; explain; throw light on (a problem, difficulty). (正式用语)阐明; 说明(问题,困难). **elu·ci·da·tion** /i,lu:si'deiʃn; ɪ,lusə'deʃən/ n

elude /ɪˈluːd/ ɪˈlud/ vt [VP6A] escape capture by (esp by means of a trick); avoid: 逃避(尤指借诡计); 躲避: ~ one's enemies; 逃避敌人; ~ observation. 避人耳目.

elu·sive /ɪˈluːsɪv/ ɪˈlusɪv/ adj tending to elude or escape: 逃避的; 躲避的: an ~ criminal; 逃犯; tending to escape from the memory; not easy to recall: 难记忆的; 不易记起的: an ~ word. 难记忆的字.

el·ver /ˈelvə(r)/ ˈelvə/ n young eel. 小鳗鲕.

elves /elvz/ ɛlvz/ pl of **elf**.

elv·ish /ˈelvɪʃ/ ˈelvɪʃ/ adj = **elfish**.

Ely·sium /ɪˈlɪzɪəm/ ɪˈlɪʒɪəm/ n (Gk myth) home of the blessed after death; place or state of perfect happiness. (希神)极乐世界; 福地. **Ely·sian** /ɪˈlɪzɪən/ ɪˈlɪʒən/ adj of ~; heavenly; blissful. 极乐世界的; 福地的; 天堂的; 幸福的.

em /em; em/ pron (colloq) (口) = them.

ema·ci·ate /ɪˈmeɪʃɪeɪt/ ɪˈmeʃɪˌet/ vt [VP6A] make thin and weak (usu passive): 使瘦弱(通常用被动语态): ~d by long illness. 由于长期生病而瘦弱了. **emaci·ation** /ɪˌmeɪsɪˈeɪʃn/ ɪˌmeʃɪˈeʃən/ n [U].

ema·nate /ˈeməneɪt/ ˈeməˌnet/ vi [VP3A] ~ from, (formal) come, flow, proceed from. (正式用语)发出; 流出; 生出. **ema·na·tion** /ˌeməˈneɪʃn/ ˌeməˈneʃən/ n [U] emanating; [C] sth that ~s. 发出; 流出; 生出; 发出物; 流出物; 生出物.

eman·ci·pate /ɪˈmænsɪpeɪt/ ɪˈmænsəˌpet/ vt [VP 6A, 14] ~ (from), set free (esp from legal, political or moral restraint): 解放(尤指自法律, 政治或道德的约束中解脱): ~ slaves; 解放奴隶; an ~d young woman, one who has freed herself from the conventions or restrictions of the community to which she belongs. 解放了的女青年.

eman·ci·pa·tion /ɪˌmænsɪˈpeɪʃn; ɪˌmænsəˈpeʃən/ n [U] emancipating or being emancipated: 解放; 被解放: the ~ of women, giving or obtaining all or some of the rights, opportunities, etc that men have; 妇女的解放; ~ from the authority of one's parents. 摆脱父母的管束 (获得法定自立权).

emas·cu·late /ɪˈmæskjʊleɪt/ ɪˈmæskjəˌlet/ vt [VP 6A] deprive of (masculine) vigour; weaken; impoverish. 使阉; 使无丈夫气. **emas·cu·la·tion** /ɪˌmæskjəˈleɪʃn; ɪˌmæskjəˈleʃən/ n

em·balm /ɪmˈbɑːm; ɪmˈbɑm/ vt [VP6A] preserve (a dead body) from decay by using spices or chemicals; preserve from oblivion; fill with fragrance. 以香料或药物防止(尸体)腐烂; 使之不被遗忘; 使弥漫香气. ~·ment n

em·bank·ment /ɪmˈbæŋkmənt; ɪmˈbæŋkmənt/ n [C] wall or mound of earth, stone, etc to hold back water or support a raised road or railway; roadway supported by such a wall: 堤; (铁路等的)路基; 填基; 路堤: of earth or stone; the Thames E~. 泰晤士河河堤.

em·bargo /ɪmˈbɑːgəʊ; ɪmˈbɑrgo/ n (pl ~es /-gəʊz; -goz/) order that forbids trade, movement of ships, etc; stoppage of commerce, or of a branch of commerce: 禁止贸易令; 封港令; 禁运; 禁止通商: a gold ~, one that forbids or restricts the buying and selling of gold; 禁止买卖黄金; (fig) blocking; prohibition. (喻)阻止; 障碍. **lift/raise/remove an ~ (from sb)**, start trading (with him) again. 解禁; 重新开放贸易. **place/lay sb under (an) ~; put an ~ on sb**, do no trade with him. 禁止贸易. □ vt (pt, pp ~ed /-gəʊd; -god/)[VP6A] lay under an ~; seize (ships or goods) by government authority, for the service of the State. 禁止贸易; 禁止(船只或货物)出入; 扣押(船只或货物)以供国家之用.

em·bark /ɪmˈbɑːk; ɪmˈbɑrk/ vi, vt 1 [VP2A, C, 6A] go, put or take on board a ship: 乘船; 装于船上; 装载: The soldiers ~ed for Malta. 士兵乘船赴马他. The ship ~ed passengers and cargo. 这船装载旅客和货物. 2 [VP3A] ~ on/upon, start, take part in: 开

始; 从事: ~ upon a new business undertaking. 从事一新的商业.

em·bar·ka·tion /ˌembɑːˈkeɪʃn; ˌembɑrˈkeʃən/ n [U] ~ing; [C] instance of this; that which is ~ed. 乘船; 装载; 开始; 从事; 装载物.

em·bar·rass /ɪmˈbærəs; ɪmˈbærəs/ vt [VP6A] 1 make to feel awkward or ashamed; cause mental discomfort or anxiety to: 使困窘; 使局促不安; 使焦急: ~ing questions; 令人困窘的问题; ~ed by lack of money. 因缺钱而窘迫. 2 (old use) hinder the movement of: (旧用法)阻碍; 妨碍: He fell into the river and, because he was ~ed by his heavy overcoat, only just managed to swim to the bank. 他跌入河中, 因受其厚大衣的妨碍, 很勉强地游至岸边. ~·ing adj ~·ing·ly adv ~·ment n [U] ~ing or being ~ed; [C] that which ~es: 困窘; 局促不安; 焦急; 阻碍; 令人困窘的事物: financial ~ments; 财务的困难; an ~ment (= an over-abundance) of riches. 财富过多的烦恼.

em·bassy /ˈembəsɪ; ˈembəsɪ/ n (pl -ssies) duty and mission of an ambassador; his official residence; ambassador and his staff: 大使之职务; 大使馆; 大使馆全体人员: to go/come/send sb on an ~ (to sb); 去(来, 派某人)任大使; the French ~ in London; 伦敦的法国大使馆; (attrib) (用作定语) ~ officials. 大使馆官员.

em·battled /ɪmˈbætld; ɛmˈbætld/ adj (of an army, etc) drawn up ready for battle; (fig) in a condition of defence; (of a tower or building) having battlements. (指军队等)布阵以待的; (喻)在防御状态中的; (指城楼或建筑物)有雉堞的.

em·bed /ɪmˈbed; ɪmˈbɛd/ vt (-dd-) [VP6A,14] (usu passive) ~ (in), fix firmly (in a surrounding mass): (通常用被动语态) 嵌入(周围物体中): stones ~ded in rock; 嵌入岩石内的石头; (fig) (喻) facts ~ded in one's memory. 深留记忆中的事实.

em·bel·lish /ɪmˈbelɪʃ; ɪmˈbɛlɪʃ/ vt [VP6A, 14] ~ (with), make beautiful; add ornaments or details to: 美化; 装饰; 修饰: ~ a dress with lace and ribbons; 用花边及缎带来修饰衣服; ~ a story, eg by adding amusing but perhaps untrue details. 修饰一故事(例如加以有趣味而或许不真实的细节). ~·ment n [U] ~ing or being ~ed; [C] that which ~es; artistic addition. 美化; 装饰; 装饰物; 美化物.

em·ber /ˈembə(r); ˈembə/ n (usu pl) small piece of burning wood or coal in a dying fire; (pl) ashes of a dying fire. (通常用复数)燃屑; (复)余烬.

em·bezzle /ɪmˈbezl; ɪmˈbezl/ vt [VP6A] use (money placed in one's care) in a wrong way for one's own benefit. 挪用(公款); 盗用. ~·ment n [U] embezzling; [C] instance of this. 挪用公款; 盗用公款.

em·bit·ter /ɪmˈbɪtə(r); ɪmˈbɪtə/ vt [VP6A] arouse bitter feelings in: 使痛苦; 使难过: ~ed by repeated failures. 因连续失败而难过. ~·ment n

em·blazon /ɪmˈbleɪzn; ɛmˈblezn/ vt [VP6A,14] ~ (with), 1 adorn (eg a shield or banner) with heraldic devices: 以纹章装饰(盾或旗): ~ed with the coat of arms of the family. 饰有家族盾徽的. 2 extol; exalt. 颂扬; 赞扬.

em·blem /ˈembləm; ˈembləm/ n symbol; device that represents sth: 象征; 标记: an ~ of peace, eg a dove; 和平的象征(例如鸽子); an ~ of love, eg a heart. 爱的象征(例如一颗心). ~·atic /ˌembləˈmætɪk; ˌembləˈmætɪk/ adj ~ (of), serving as an ~. 作为象征的; 作为标记的.

em·body /ɪmˈbɒdɪ; ɪmˈbɑdɪ/ vt (pt, pp -died) [VP6A, 14] ~ (in), 1 give form to ideas/feelings, etc: 具体表现(思想, 感情等): ~ one's ideas in a speech. 在一篇演说中体现自己的思想. 2 include; comprise: 包括; 包含: The latest locomotives ~ many new features. 最新的火车头含有许多新的特色. 3 clothe (a spirit) with a body: 赋(灵魂)以躯体: an embodied spirit. 有躯体的灵魂. **em·bodi·ment** /ɪmˈbɒdɪmənt; ɪmˈbɑdɪmənt/ n

[C] that which embodies sth or is embodied: 能具体表现他物者; 化身; 被具体表现者: *She is the embodiment of kindness.* 她是仁慈的化身。

em·bolden /ɪm'bəʊldən; ɪm'boldn/ vt [VP6A, 17] give courage or confidence to: 给与勇气或信心: *Their sympathy ～ed me to ask them for help.* 他们的同情使我有勇气向他们求助。

em·bon·point /ˌɒmbɒn'pwɑ:ŋ; ɑ̃bõ'pwæ̃/ n (F) plumpness (used as a polite way of saying that sb, usu a woman, is very fat). (法) 福泰 (通常用以说女子肥胖的客气话)。

em·boss /ɪm'bɒs US: -'bɔ:s; ɪm'bɒs/ vt [VP6A, 14] ～ (with), cause a pattern, figure, etc to stand out on (the surface of sth); raise the surface of sth into a pattern: 使(花样,图案等)浮凸于(某物之平面)上; 使有浮雕花纹: ～ed notepaper, with the address ～ed on it; 有浮凸的地址之信纸; *a silver vase ～ed with a design of flowers.* 饰有浮起花卉图案的银瓶。

em·brace /ɪm'breɪs; ɪm'bres/ vt, vi 1 [VP6A, 2A] take (a person, etc) into one's arms, as a sign of affection: 拥抱: ～ *a child.* 拥抱一小孩。*They ～d.* 他们互相拥抱。2 [VP6A] accept; make use of: 接受; 利用: ～ *an offer/opportunity.* 接受提议 (利用机会)。3 [VP 6A] (of things) include: (指事物) 包括: ～ *many examples in a single formula.* 将许多例子包括在一个公式内。□ n [C] act of embracing: 拥抱: *He held her to him in a warm ～.* 他热情地拥抱她。

em·brasure /ɪm'breɪʒə(r); ɛm'breʒə/ n 1 [C] bevelled opening in a parapet for a gun. (胸墙上之)射口;炮(枪)眼。2 bevelled opening (esp interior side of a doorway or window), eg in an old stone castle. 四周内宽外窄的开口(尤指门窗之内侧,如古老石堡中者)。

em·bro·ca·tion /ˌembrə'keɪʃn; ˌembro'keʃən/ n [U] liquid (a liniment) for rubbing a bruised or aching part of the body. 擦剂(揉擦于伤处或痛处之液剂)。

em·broider /ɪm'brɔɪdə(r); ɪm'brɔɪdə/ vt, vi 1 [VP 6A, 2A] ornament (cloth) with needlework: 绣花于(布); 刺绣: ～ *one's initials on a handkerchief;* 将姓名的起首字母绣在手帕上; *a design ～ed in gold thread.* 用金线绣成的图样。2 [VP6A] (fig) add fanciful details to a story. (喻)添加想象的细节于故事中; 修饰一故事。～y /-dərɪ; -dərɪ/ n [U] ～ed needlework. 刺绣; 刺绣品。

em·broil /ɪm'brɔɪl; ɛm'brɔɪl/ vt [VP6A, 14] ～ *sb/oneself (in),* cause (sb, oneself) to be mixed up in a quarrel: 使(某人或自己)卷入纠纷: *I don't want to become ～ed in their quarrels.* 我不愿被卷入他们的争端中。

em·bryo /'embrɪəʊ; 'ɛmbrɪ,o/ n (pl -s /-əʊz; -oz/) [C] offspring of an animal in the early stage of its development before birth (or before coming out of an egg); (fig) sth in its rudimentary stage. 胚胎; (喻)在萌芽期的事物。*in ～,* (lit, fig) still undeveloped. (字面, 喻)尚未发展的; 在萌芽时期的。**em·bry·onic** /ˌembrɪ'ɒnɪk; ˌɛmbrɪ'ɑnɪk/ adj in ～: 胚胎期的; 萌芽期的: *an ～nic plan.* 萌芽阶段的计划。

emeer /e'mɪə(r); ɛ'mɪr/ n = **emir**.

emend /ɪ'mend; ɪ'mɛnd/ vt [VP6A] take out errors from: 修正; 订正; 修改: ～ *a passage in a book.* 修正书中的一节。**emen·da·tion** /ˌiːmen'deɪʃn; ˌimɛn'deʃən/ n [U] ～ing; the result of this. 修正; 修改; 被修正之处。

em·er·ald /'emərəld; 'ɛmərəld/ n bright green precious stone; colour of this. 祖母绿; 纯绿宝石; 翠玉; 翠绿色。

emerge /ɪ'mɜːdʒ; ɪ'mɝdʒ/ vi [VP2A, 3A] ～ *(from),* 1 come into view; (esp) come out (from water, etc): 出现; (尤指从水中等)现出: *The moon ～d from behind the clouds.* 月亮自云后现出。2 (of facts, ideas) appear; become known: (指事实, 意见)出现; 暴露: *No new ideas ～d during the talks.* 谈论中没有新的意见出现。

emerg·ence /-dʒəns; -dʒəns/ n [U] emerging. 出现; 现出; 显露。**emerg·ent** /-dʒənt; -dʒənt/ adj emerging: 出现的; 现出的: *(the recently ～d and) emergent countries of Africa,* those changing from dependence to independence, becoming modernized, etc. 非洲的新兴国家。

emerg·ency /ɪ'mɜːdʒənsɪ; ɪ'mɝdʒənsɪ/ n (pl -cies) 1 [U, C] serious happening or situation needing prompt action: 紧急事件; 紧急情况: *This fire extinguisher is to be used only in (an) ～.* 这灭火器只在紧急情况时使用。2 (attrib use): (用作定语): *an '～ exit;* 太平门; *an '～ fund,* one to be used in an ～. 应急基金。

emeri·tus /ɪ'merɪtəs; ɪ'mɛrətəs/ adj (Lat) retired from service but retaining an honorary title: (拉)退休但仍保留荣誉头衔的; 名誉退休的: ～ *professor.* 名誉退休教授。

em·ery /'emərɪ; 'ɛmərɪ/ n [U] hard metal used (esp in powdered form) for grinding and polishing: 钢玉粉; 刚石粉; 金刚砂(磨擦用): '～-cloth /-paper /-wheel, with ～ on the surface. 砂布(砂纸, 砂轮)。

em·etic /ɪ'metɪk; ɪ'mɛtɪk/ n medicine causing a person to vomit, eg when suffering from food-poisoning. 催吐剂(例如食物中毒时所用者)。

emi·grate /'emɪgreɪt; 'ɛmə,gret/ vi [VP2A, 3A] ～ *(to) (from),* go away (from one's own country to another to settle there). 自本国移居他国。⇨ **immigrate**. **emi·grant** /'emɪgrənt; 'ɛməgrənt/ n person who ～s: 自本国移居他国者: *emigrants to Canada;* 移居加拿大的人; (attrib) (用作定语) *emigrant labourers.* 移居他国的劳工。**emi·gra·tion** /ˌemɪ'greɪʃn; ˌeməˈgreʃən/ n [U] emigrating; instance of this. 自本国移居他国; 移民。

émi·gré /'emɪgreɪ US: ˌemɪ'greɪ; 'ɛmə,gre/ n (F) person who has left his own country, usu for political reasons. (法)因政治原因而离国者。

emi·nence /'emɪnəns; 'ɛmənəns/ n 1 [U] state of being famous or distinguished; superiority of position: 著名; 卓越; 显赫; 显要: *reach ～ as a doctor;* 成为名医; *win ～ as a scientist.* 成为卓越的科学家。2 [C] area of high or rising ground. 高地。3 *His / Your E～,* title used of / to a cardinal. 对红衣主教之尊称。

emi·nent /'emɪnənt; 'ɛmənənt/ adj 1 (of a person) distinguished: (指人)著名的; 卓越的: ～ *for her virtues;* 以她的美德著名; *an ～ sculptor.* 卓越的雕刻家。2 (of qualities) remarkable in degree: (指性质)优良的: *a man of ～ goodness.* 品德优良的人。～·ly adv

emir /e'mɪə(r); ə'mɪr/ n (title of a) Muslim ruler. 酋长; 穆斯林国家统治者(的尊称)。～·ate /e'mɪərɪt; ə'mɪrɪt/ n rank, lands, etc of an ～: 酋长区; 穆斯林国家统治者的地位, 土地等: *the great ～ates of Northern Nigeria.* 尼日利亚北部的酋长国。

em·iss·ary /'emɪsərɪ; 'ɛmə,sɛrɪ/ n (pl -ries) person sent to deliver a message (often of an unpleasant and secret kind). 使者; 密使。

emission /ɪ'mɪʃn; ɪ'mɪʃən/ n ～ *(of),* [U] sending out or giving off (of light, heat, smell, etc); [C] that which is sent out or given off. (光, 热, 气味等之)发出; 发射; 散发; 发出之物; 散发之事。

emit /ɪ'mɪt; ɪ'mɪt/ vt (-tt-) [VP6A] give or send out: 发出; 放射: *A volcano ～s smoke and ashes.* 火山喷出烟和灰。

emolu·ment /ɪ'mɒljʊmənt; ɪ'mɑljəmənt/ n [C] (usu pl) (formal) profit from official employment; fee; salary. (通常用复数)(正式用语)报酬; 酬金; 薪金。

emo·tion /ɪ'məʊʃn; ɪ'moʃən/ n 1 [U] stirring up, excitement, of the mind or (more usu) the feelings; excited state of the mind or feelings: (心情或感情的)激动: *He thought of his dead child with deep ～.* 他想起他死去的孩子就变得非常激动。*He spoke in a voice touched with ～.* 他以激动的声音说话。2 [C] strong feeling of any kind: 激情; 情感; 情绪: *Love, joy, hate, fear and*

grief are ~s. 爱, 喜, 恨, 惧和悲哀是情感。 *He appealed to our* ~s *rather than to our reason.* 他诉诸我们的情感而非我们的理智。 ~·**less** *adj* without ~. 无情感的。 ~**al** /-ʃənl; -ʃənl/ *adj* **1** of, directed to, the ~s: 情感的; 情绪的; 诉诸情感的: *an* ~*al appeal;* 诉诸情感的请求; ~*al music.* 抒情音乐。 **2** having ~s that are easily excited; capable of expressing ~s: 感情易激动的; 能表达情感的: *an* ~*al woman/actor/nature.* 多情的女子(能表达情感的演员; 易激动的性情)。 ~·**ally** /-ʃənlɪ; -ʃənlɪ/ *adv* emot·**ive** /ɪ'məʊtɪv; ɪ'motɪv/ *adj* of, tending to excite, the ~s. 情感的; 易激动情感的。

em·pale /ɪm'peɪl; ɪm'pel/ *vt* = **impale**.

em·panel /ɪm'pænl; ɪm'pænl/ *vt* (**-ll-**, US also **-l-**) [VP6A] enter (a person's name) on a panel; enrol (a jury). 将(人名)列入陪审员名簿; 选任(陪审员)。

em·pa·thy /'empəθɪ; 'empəθɪ/ *n* [U] (*psych*) (power of) projecting oneself into (and so fully understanding, and losing one's identity in) a work of art or other object of contemplation; (power of) sharing another person's feelings. (心理)神入(全神贯入一艺术品或其他引人沉思的事物以达忘我的境界); 神入的能力; 移情(能体会到别人的情感); 移情的能力。

em·peror /'empərə(r); 'empərɚ/ *n* ruler of an empire. 皇帝。 ⇨ **empress**.

em·pha·sis /'emfəsɪs; 'emfəsɪs/ *n* (*pl* **-ases** /-əsiːz/ -əsiz/) [C, U] force or stress laid on a word or words to make the significance clear, or to show importance; (the placing of) special value or importance: 加强语气; (赋予)特殊价值或重要性: *Some schools lay/put special* ~ *on language study.* 有些学校特别注重语言的学习。 *I insist, with all the* ~ *at my command, that ....* 我全力坚持…。 **em·pha·size** /'emfəsaɪz; 'emfə,saɪz/ *vt* [VP6A] put ~ on; give ~ to: 强调; 加强…的语气: *He emphasized the importance of careful driving.* 他强调小心驾驶的重要。 **em·phatic** /ɪm'fætɪk; ɪm'fætɪk/ *adj* having, showing, using, ~: 语气强的; 强调的; 表示强调的: *an emphatic gesture/opinion;* 强调的手势(意见); *an emphatic person.* 表示强调的人。 **em·phati·cally** /-klɪ; -klɪ/ *adv*

em·pire /'empaɪə(r); 'empaɪr/ *n* **1** [C] group of countries under a single supreme authority: 帝国(在一个皇帝统治下的若干国家): *the Roman E*~. 罗马帝国。 **2** [U] supreme political power: 至高的政治权力: *the responsibilities of* ~. 至高政治权力的责任。 **the First E**~, (in France) period of the reign of Napoleon I (1804—1815); (**E**~, attrib) of the style of furniture or dress fashionable in this period. (法国)第一帝国(一八〇四至一八一五年间拿破仑一世统治时期); (**E**~, 用作定语)第一帝国当代流行的(家具和服装式样)。 **the Second E**~, the period of the reign of Napoleon III (1852—1870). 第二帝国(一八五二至一八七〇年间拿破仑三世统治期)。

em·piric, em·piri·cal /ɪm'pɪrɪk, -kl; ɪm'pɪrɪk, -kl/ *adj* relying on observation and experiment, not on theory. 全凭观察和实验的。 **em·piri·cally** /-klɪ; -klɪ/ *adv* **em·piri·cism** /ɪm'pɪrɪsɪzəm; ɪm'pɪrə,sɪzəm/ *n* ~ practice. 全凭观察和实验; 经验主义。 **em·pir·i·cist** /-sɪst; -sɪst/ *n* ~ person. 全凭观察和实验的人; 经验主义者。

em·place·ment /ɪm'pleɪsmənt; ɪm'plesmənt/ *n* prepared position for a heavy gun or guns. 炮兵阵地。

em·plane /em'pleɪn; ɛm'plen/ *vi, vt* [VP2A, 6A] go, put, on board an aircraft. 乘飞机; 装入飞机。

em·ploy /ɪm'plɔɪ; ɪm'plɔɪ/ *vt* [VP6A,16B,14] **1** give work to, usu for payment: 雇用: *They* ~ *five waiters.* 他们雇用五个侍者。 *He is* ~*ed in a bank.* 他在一家银行任职。 **2** make use of: 使用: *How do you* ~ *your spare time?* 你怎样利用你的暇时? □ *n* **in the** ~ **of,** ~ed by, working for. 为…所雇用; 替…工作。 ~·**able** /-əbl; -əbl/ *adj* that can be ~ed. 可雇用的; 可使用的。 ~·**er** /-ə(r); -ɚ/ -ə / *n* person who ~s others. 雇主。 ~·**ee**

/ˌemplɔɪ'iː; ˌɪm'plɔɪ·i/ *n* person ~ed for wages. 受雇者; 雇工; 雇员; 职员。

em·ploy·ment /ɪm'plɔɪmənt; ɪm'plɔɪmənt/ *n* [U] employing or being employed; one's regular work or occupation: 雇用; 受雇; 使用; 工作; 职业: *to find* ~; 找工作; 求职; *to give* ~ *to sb;* 雇用某人; *the men in my* ~; 我所雇用的人员; *to be thrown out of* ~. 被解雇; 失业。 **be in/out of** ~, have/not have a job. 有工作(失业)。 '~ **agency,** business establishment which helps persons (for a fee) to find ~. 职业介绍所(收介绍费用者)。 '~ **exchange,** Government office which puts employers and unemployed persons in touch and where unemployment benefits are paid. 劳工介绍所(政府机构, 并发放失业救济金)。

em·por·ium /ɪm'pɔːrɪəm; ɛm'pɔrɪəm/ *n* centre of commerce; market; large retail store. 商业中心; 市场; 大零售商店。

em·power /ɪm'paʊə(r); ɪm'paʊɚ/ *vt* [VP17] ~ *sb to do sth,* give power or authority to act. 授权给某人(做某事)。

em·press /'emprɪs; 'emprɪs/ *n* woman governing an empire; wife of or widow of an emperor. 女皇; 皇后。

empty¹ /'emptɪ; 'emptɪ/ *adj* having nothing inside; containing nothing: 空的; 内中无物的: *an* ~ *box;* 空匣; ~ *promises,* not meaning anything, not giving satisfaction; 空洞的诺言; *feeling* ~, (colloq) hungry; (口)感觉饿的; *words* ~ *of meaning,* meaningless words. 无意义的话。 *The house was* ~, unoccupied. 那房子是空着的。 ~-'**handed** *adj* bringing back nothing; carrying nothing away. 空手的; 徒手的。 ~-'**headed** *adj* witless; lacking in common sense. 愚蠢的; 无脑筋的。 □ *n* (usu *pl*) box, bottle, crate, etc that has been emptied: (通常用复数)空匣, 空盒, 空瓶, 空箱等: *Empties* (eg ~ beer bottles) *are not taken back,* the brewery will not accept them and allow credit for them. 空瓶(例如啤酒瓶)不收回。 **emp·ti·ness** /'emptɪnɪs; 'emptɪnɪs/ *n*

empty² /'emptɪ; 'emptɪ/ *vt, vi* (*pt, pp* **-tied**) [VP6A, 15B, 2A, C, 3A] ~ **(out),** make or become empty, remove what is inside (sth): 使空; 变空: ~ *one's glass,* drink everything in it; 干杯; 喝干; ~ *(out) a drawer;* 腾空一抽屉; ~ *a box of rubbish into a rubbish-cart;* 将一箱垃圾倒入垃圾车; ~ *one's pockets of their contents.* 将衣袋中之物全部取出。 *The streets soon emptied/were soon emptied when the rain started.* 一旦始下雨, 街上立即空无行人。 *The Rhone empties* (= flows) *into the Mediterranean.* 罗讷河注入地中海。 *The water empties* (= flows out) *slowly.* 这水慢慢地流出。 *The cistern empties* (= becomes empty) *in five minutes.* 这贮水池五分钟流干。

em·purpled /ɪm'pɜːpld; ɛm'pɝpld/ *adj* made purple. 使成紫色的。

em·py·rean /ˌempaɪ'riːən; ˌɛmpə'rɪən/ *n* the highest heaven; the visible heavens. 最高空; 天空。 □ *adj* heavenly; celestial. 天空的; 天上的。

emu /'iːmjuː; 'imju/ *n* large flightless Australian bird that runs well. 食火鸡(澳大利亚产, 不会飞, 但跑得快); 鸸鹋。 ⇨ the illus at **rare**. 参看 rare 之插图。

emu·late /'emjʊleɪt; 'emjə,let/ *vt* [VP6A] try to do as well as or better than. 欲赶上或超过; 与…竞争。

emu·la·tion /ˌemjʊ'leɪʃn; ˌemjə'leʃən/ *n* [U] emulating; 竞争; 争胜: *in a spirit of* ~; 以竞争的精神; *in* ~ *of each other.* 互相争胜。

emu·lous /'emjʊləs; 'emjələs/ *adj* ~ **(of),** (formal) wishing or anxious to do as well as or better than: (正式语)竞争心切的; 求胜心切的: ~ *of all rivals;* 欲胜过所有的竞争者; imitating (others) in a jealous spirit, desiring to obtain: 出于忌妒而仿效(他人)的; 急欲获得的: ~ *of fame/honours.* 好名。 ~·**ly** *adv*

emul·sion /ɪ'mʌlʃn; ɪ'mʌlʃən/ *n* [C, U] (kinds of) creamy liquid in which particles of oil or fat are suspended: 乳状液; 乳剂; 乳胶: ~ *paint,* in which the

colour is in an ~-like liquid. 乳状漆。 **emul·sify** /ɪˈmʌlsɪfaɪ; ɪˈmʌlsəˌfaɪ/ vt (pt, pp -fied) [VP6A] make an ~ of. 使成乳状液; 使成乳剂; 乳浆化。

en·able /ɪˈneɪbl; mˈebl/ vt [VP17] make able, give authority or means (to do sth): 使能够; 使可以; 授以权柄或方法 (与不定式连用): The collapse of the strike ~d the company to resume normal bus services. 罢工的失败使公司恢复了正常的公共汽车营业。 **en·abling**/ɪˈneɪblɪŋ; mˈeblɪŋ/ part adj making possible: 可能的: enabling legislation. 可行的法律。

en·act /ɪˈnækt; mˈækt/ vt 1 [VP6A, 9] make (a law); decree; ordain: 制定 (法律); 颁令; 规定: as by law ~ed. 如法律所规定。 Be it further ~ed that .... (legal style). 再进一步规定…(法律文体)。 2 [VP6A] perform on, or as though on, the stage of a theatre. 演出 (戏); 扮演 (剧中或现实生活中的角色)。 ~ment n [U] ~ing or being ~ed; [C] law. 制定; 规定; 颁令; 法律。

en·amel /ɪˈnæml; ɪˈnæml/ n [U] 1 glass-like substance used for coating metal, porcelain, etc, for decoration or as a protection: 瓷釉; 搪瓷; 珐琅: '~ware, manufactured goods with ~ surfaces; 搪瓷器; '~ paint, paint which dries to make a hard, glossy surface. 亮漆。 2 hard outer covering of teeth. (牙齿的)珐琅质。 □ vt (-ll-, US also -l-) cover, decorate, with ~ (esp with designs or decorations). 以瓷釉涂 (尤指花样)于; 涂以搪瓷。

en·amour (US = -amor) /ɪˈnæməʊ(r); mˈæmə/ vt [VP6A] (usu in passive) (通常用被动语态) be ~ed of, fond of, delighted with and inclined to use: 喜欢; 恋慕; 迷恋: ~ed of one's own voice. 喜爱自己的声音。

en·camp /ɪˈnkæmp; mˈkæmp/ vt, vi [VP6A, 2A] settle in a camp; lodge in tents. 扎营; 露营。 ~·ment n place where troops, etc are camped. 扎营地; 露营地。

en·case /ɪˈnkeɪs; mˈkes/ vt [VP6A, 14] ~ (in), put into a case; surround or cover as with a case: 装在箱内; 纳入套内; 包围; 包裹: a knight ~d in armour. 披着甲胄的武士。

en·caus·tic /enˈkɔːstɪk; ɪnˈkɔstɪk/ adj prepared by using heat: 以热力制成的; 上釉烧的: ~ bricks/tiles, inlaid with coloured clays that are burnt in. 琉璃砖 (瓦)。

en·cepha·li·tis /ˌenkefəˈlaɪtɪs; ˌɛnsɛfəˈlaɪtɪs/ n [U] inflammation of the brain. 脑炎。

en·chain /ɪˈntʃeɪn; ɛnˈtʃen/ vt [VP6A] fasten with chain(s); (fig) hold fast (the attention, etc). 用锁链锁住; (喻)抓牢(注意力等)。

en·chant /ɪˈntʃɑːnt US: -ˈtʃænt; mˈtʃænt/ vt [VP6A] 1 charm; delight: 使心醉; 使喜悦: She was ~ed/by the flowers you sent her. 她极喜爱你送她的花。 2 use magic on; put under a magic spell: 施魔法于; 蛊惑: the ~ed palace, as in a fairy tale. 魔宫 (例如神话中者)。 ~·er /-ə(r); -ɚ/ n man who ~s. 施魔法的男人; 妖人。 ~·ress /-trɪs; -trɪs/ n woman who ~s. 施魔法的女人; 妖女。 ~·ing·ly adv ~·ment n 1 [U] being ~ed. 心醉; 销魂; 着迷。 2 [C] sth which ~s; magic spell. 蛊惑之物; 法术。 3 [U] charm; delight: 诱惑力; 乐趣: the ~ment of moonlight. 月光的魅力。

en·circle /ɪˈnsɜːkl; mˈsɝkl/ vt [VP6A] surround; form a circle round: 环绕; 包围: a lake ~d by trees; 被树林环绕着的湖; ~d by enemy forces. 被敌军包围。 ~·ment n

en clair /ˌɒn ˈkleə(r); ɑ̃ˈklɛr/ adv phrase (F) (used in telegrams, official dispatches, etc) (= in clear) in ordinary language, not in code or cipher. (法)(指电报、官方发出的文件等)用普通文字(非电码或密码)。

en·clave /ˈenkleɪv; ˈɛnklev/ n [C] territory wholly within the boundaries of another. 被外国领地包围的土地。

en·close /ɪˈnkləʊz; mˈkloz/ vt [VP6A, 14] ~ (with), 1 put a wall, fence, etc round; shut in on all sides: 围以墙、篱等; 包围: ~ a garden with a wall. 用墙

将花园围起; ~ common land, put fences, etc round land which has been used by everyone. 用篱等将公地围起。 2 put in an envelope, parcel, etc: 将(某物)装入 (信封, 包裹等)中; 封入: I'll ~ your letter with mine. 我将你的信装在我的信内寄出。 A cheque for £5 is ~d. 附上五英镑支票一张。 E~d, please find ..., (comm style) You will find, ~d with this .... (商业文体)兹附上…。

en·clos·ure /ɪˈnkləʊʒə(r); mˈkloʒɚ/ n 1 [U] enclosing; 围以墙篱等; 包围: ~ of common land; 公地之用篱围起; [C] instance of this. 围以墙篱或包围的实例。 2 [C] sth that is enclosed (esp with a letter). 装入物; (尤指)函中附件。

en·code /ɪˈnkəʊd; ɛnˈkod/ vt [VP6A] put in a code. 译成密码。 ▷ code v.

en·co·mium /ɪˈnkəʊmɪəm; ɛnˈkomɪəm/ n (usu pl) (formal) very high praise. (通常用复数)(正式用语)极高的颂赞或赞美。

en·compass /ɪˈnkʌmpəs; mˈkʌmpəs/ vt [VP6A] encircle; surround; envelop; comprise. 围绕; 包围; 含; 包括。

en·core /ˈɒŋkɔː(r); ˈɑŋkɔr/ int Repeat! Again! 再来一个! 再一次! □ vt, n [VP6A] (call for a) repetition (of a song, etc) or further performance by the same person(s): 要求再唱或再演: The violinist got an ~. 这小提琴家被听众要求再演奏。 The singer gave three ~s. 这歌唱家应听众之请而加唱三支歌。 The audience ~d the pianist. 听众要求那钢琴家再奏一曲。

en·coun·ter /ɪˈnkaʊntə(r); mˈkaʊntɚ/ vt [VP6A] find oneself faced by (danger, difficulties, etc); meet(an enemy or enemies): meet (a friend, etc) unexpectedly. 遭遇 (危险, 困难等); 遭逢 (敌人); 邂逅 (友人等)。 □ n [C] ~ (with), sudden or unexpected (esp hostile) meeting. 遭遇(尤指与敌人)。

en·cour·age /ɪˈnkʌrɪdʒ; mˈkɝɪdʒ/ vt [VP6A, 14, 17] ~ sb in sth/to do sth, give hope, courage or confidence to; support: 鼓励; 激励; 支持; 援助: ~ a man to work harder; 鼓励一人更加努力工作; ~ a boy in his studies; 鼓励孩子用功; feel ~d by the progress one has made. 由于自己的进步而感到鼓舞。 Don't ~ him in his idle ways. 不要助长他的懒惰。 ~·ment n [U] encouraging: 鼓励; 支持: cries of ~ment; 鼓励的呼声; [C] sth that ~s: 鼓励之物; 支持之物: Praise acts as an ~ment to the young. 称赞对于青年是一种鼓励。

en·croach /ɪˈnkrəʊtʃ; mˈkrotʃ/ vi [VP3A] ~ on/upon, go beyond what is right or natural or desirable: 超出正当范围; 侵入; 侵害: ~ (up) on sb's rights (time, land). 侵害某人的权利(占用某人的时间, 土地)。 The sea is ~ing (up) on the land, washing it away. 海水浸蚀了土地。 ~·ment n [U] ~ing; [C] sth gained by ~ing; advance beyond the original limits: 侵入; 侵害; 侵占之物; 超出范围: ~ments made by the sea upon the land. 海水对陆地的侵蚀。

en·crust /ɪˈnkrʌst; mˈkrʌst/ vt, vi 1 [VP6A, 14] ~ (with), cover with a crust; overlay (a surface) with a crust of ornamental or costly material: 包以外壳; 覆以装饰性或贵重的外层: a gold vase ~ed with precious stones. 镶有宝石的金瓶。 2 [VP2A] form into a crust. 形成壳。

en·cum·ber /ɪˈnkʌmbə(r); mˈkʌmbɚ/ vt [VP6A, 14] ~ (with), 1 get in the way of, hamper, be a burden to: 阻碍; 妨害; 牵累: be ~ed with a large family; 为一大家庭所累; an estate ~ed with mortgages; 被抵押的土地; ~ed with unnecessary luggage. 使为无必要的行李所累。 2 crowd; fill up: 堆满; a room ~ed with old and useless furniture. 堆满了旧而无用的家具的房间。 **en·cum·brance** /ɪˈnkʌmbrəns; mˈkʌmbrəns/ n [U] thing that ~s; burden. 阻碍物; 累赘; 负担。

en·cyc·li·cal /ɪˈnsɪklɪkl; ɛnˈsɪklɪkl/ adj, n (letter written by the Pope) for wide circulation. 广泛传送的; 传阅的; 传阅的教皇通谕。

en·cy·clo·pedia (also **-paedia**) /ɪnˌsaɪklə'piːdɪə; ɪnˌsaɪklə'pɪdɪə / n book, or set of books, giving information about every branch of knowledge, or on one subject, with articles in ABC order. 百科全书. **en·cy·clo·pedic, -paedic** /ˌɪnsaɪklə'piːdɪk; ɪnˌsaɪklə'pɪdɪk / adj dealing with, having knowledge of, a wide variety of subjects. 有关各种学科的; 学识渊博的.

end¹ /end; ɛnd/ n 1 farthest or last part: 端; 终点; 末梢: the end of a road /stick /line, etc; 路之终点 (杖, 线等之末端); the house at the end of the street: 在街道末端的房屋; (attrib) (用作定语) the end house; 最末尾的房屋; the last end carriage, the last carriage in a train; 末节车 (火车之末节车厢); the west /east end of a town, the parts in the west /east; 城之西(东)区; the ends of the earth, most remote parts, parts difficult of access. 最遥远的地方; 天涯海角. **begin /start at the wrong end**, in the wrong way, at a wrong point. 开始即错误. **get hold of the wrong end of the stick**, have a completely mistaken idea of what is intended or meant. 完全误解. **keep one's 'end up**, (GB)continue cheerful, full of fighting spirit, in the face of difficulties, etc. (英)面对困难等时能保持愉快和战斗精神. **at a loose end**, unoccupied, having nothing important or interesting to do. 无事可做. **on end**, (a) upright: 竖起; 直立着: Place the barrel /box on (its) end. 将这桶(箱子)竖起来放. The ghost story set their hair on end. 那个鬼故事使他们毛发竖立. (b) continuously: 继续地: two hours on end. 一连两小时. **end on**, with the ends meeting: 两端相遇: The two ships collided end on, The stern (or bows) of one struck the stern (or bows) of the other. 这两条船的船尾(或船首)相碰. **end to end**, in a line with the ends touching: 头尾相接地成一行: Arrange the tables end to end. 把这些桌子衔接着摆起来. **go (in) off the 'deep end**, express strong feeling without trying to control it. 情绪失去控制; 变得非常激动. **make (both) ends meet**, live within one's income, balance one's income with one's expenditure. 量入为出; 使收支相抵. **(reach) the end of the line /road**, (fg) (reach) the point at which no more of what has happened before is possible or desirable. (喻)到此为止. 2 small piece that remains; remnant: 残片; 残余: candle ends; 蜡烛头; a cigarette end. 香烟头. **'end-papers**, (usu) blank pages pasted to the inside covers of a book. 衬页(书籍卷首卷尾的空白页). ⇨ **odds(5)**. 3 finish; conclusion: 结束; 结局: at the end of the day /the century; 一日 (世纪)之末; the end of a story /adventure. 故事(冒险)的结局. We shall never hear the end of the matter, It will be talked about for a long time to come. 我们将永远听不到这件事情的结尾(在未来的长时期内, 此事将谈论下去). **(be) at an end; at the end (of)**: 结束; 穷尽; 到⋯之尽头: The war was at an end, finished. 战争结束了. She was at the end of her patience /tether, had no patience left. 她已忍无可忍了. He was at the end of his resources. 他已智穷力竭(山穷水尽)了. **come to an end**, finish: 结束; 完毕: The meeting came to an end at last. 会议终于结束了. **come to a bad end**, be led by one's actions to ruin, disgrace, punishment, etc: 遭到恶报; 得到报应: If you don't give up crime, you'll come to a bad end, eg be sent to prison for life as a murderer. 如果你不停止犯罪, 你会得到报应的(例如因行凶而被判处无期徒刑). **draw to an end**: As the year drew to its end ... : 当岁暮之时⋯. **make an end of sth; put an end to sth**, finish it, get rid of it (according to context): 结束一事; 消除一事物(根据上下文确定其意义): We must put an end to these abuses. 我们必须除去这些弊端. Death put an end to his wicked career. 死亡结束了他邪恶的一生. **in the end**, finally, at last: 最后; 终于: He tried many ways of earning a living; in the end he became a farm labourer. 他尝试过许多谋生的方法, 最后他做了农场工人. **no end of**, (colloq) very many or much, very great, etc: (口)很多; 非常: We met no end of

interesting people. 我们遇到很多有趣的人. He thinks no end of himself, has a high opinion of his abilities, etc. 他自命不凡. **without end**, never reaching an end: 无尽的; 无休止的: We had trouble without end. 我们有无尽的困难. 4 death: 死亡: He's nearing his end, is dying. 他离死期不远了. She came to an untimely end, died young. 她夭折了. 5 purpose, aim: 目的; 目标: gain /win /achieve one's end(s); 达到目的; With this end in view; 以此为目的; for /to this end; 为达到此一目的; to the end that, intention: 为了; 其目的在于; to no end, in vain. 无结果; 徒劳. **The end justifies the means**, (prov) for a good purpose even wrong or unfair methods may be allowed. (谚)只要目的正当, 可以不择手段.

end² /end; ɛnd/ vi, vt [VP2A, C, 3A, 6A, 15B] (cause to) come to an end; reach an end: 结束; 终止: The road ends here, goes no farther. 这条路到此为止了. How does the story end? 这故事的结局如何? Let's end our quarrel. 我们不要再吵了. **end in sth**, have as a result: 以⋯为结果: The scheme ended in failure. 这计划终于失败了. He ended his days in peace, the last period of his life was peaceful. 他在平静中度过了晚年. **end (sth) off**, finish: 结束: He ended off his speech with some amusing stories. 他以一些有趣的故事结束了他的演说. **end (sth) up**, finish: 结束: If you continue to steal, you'll end up in prison, will one day be sent to prison. 如果你继续行窃, 总有一天你要坐牢. We started with soup, and had fruit to end up with. 我们开始时喝汤, 最后吃水果. **end-all** ⇨ **be²(4)**. **end·ing** n [C] end, esp of a word or a story. 终止; 末尾; (尤指)词尾; 故事的结局.

en·dan·ger /ɪn'deɪndʒə(r); ɪn'dendʒɚ/ vt [VP6A] put in danger; cause danger to: 使受危险; 危及: ~ one's chances of success. 危及成功的机会.

en·dear /ɪn'dɪə(r); ɪn'dɪr/ vt [VP14] ~ sb /oneself to, make dear or liked: 使受喜爱; 使为人爱: ~ oneself to everyone; 使自己为大家所喜爱; an ~ ing smile. 可爱的微笑. ~**·ing·ly** adv ~**·ment** n [C, U] act, word, expression, of affection: 表示亲爱的行为, 言语或表情: a term of ~ment, eg darling; 表示亲密的称呼(例如: 亲爱的); the ~ments that a wife expects from her husband. 妻子期望于丈夫的亲爱的表示.

en·deav·our (US = **-vor**) /ɪn'devə(r); ɪn'dɛvɚ/ n [C] (formal) effort, attempt: (正式用语)努力; 尽力; 企图: Please make every ~ to be early. 请尽量早点. His ~ to persuade her to go with him failed. 他尽力劝她同他一道去, 但是失败了. □ vi [VP4A] (formal) try: (正式用语)试图; 努力: ~ to please one's wife. 尽量使妻子快乐.

en·demic /en'demɪk; ɛn'dɛmɪk/ n, adj (disease) prevalent or often recurring in a country or area, or among a particular class of people, eg miners. 某一国家, 地区或人群(例如矿工)经常有的(疾病); 地方性的(病). ⇨ **epidemic**.

en·dive /'endɪv US: -daɪv; 'ɛndaɪv/ n [C] kind of curly-leaved chicory, used as salad. 苣荬菜; 菊苣苣(生菜食品).

end·less /'endlɪs; 'ɛndlɪs/ adj having no end; never; stopping: 无穷尽的; 永不停的: a woman with ~ patience 有无限耐心的女子; an ~ belt /chain /cable, one with the ends joined, to pass continuously over wheels, etc to transmit power in a machine. 环带(链, 缆)(两端相连接, 绕于轮等之上, 循环不息地转动, 以传递动力). ~**·ly** adv

en·dorse /ɪn'dɔːs; ɪn'dɔrs/ vt [VP6A] 1 write one's name on the back of (a cheque), write comments, etc in, on the back of (a document): 签名于(支票)的背面; 背书; 批注(文件): His driving licence has been ~d, a record of a motoring offence has been entered in it. 他的驾驶执照上曾有违规的记录. 2 approve, support a claim, statement, etc. 认可; 赞同(要求, 言论等). ~**·ment** n [U]endorsing; [C]instance of this; statement,

etc that ~s. 签名于支票背面; 背书; 签注; 认可; 签注或认可的记载.

en·dow /ɪn'dau; ɪn'dau/ vt [VP6A, 14] ~ **(with)**, 1 give money, property, etc to provide a regular income for (eg a college): 捐赠 (金钱, 财产等), 例如捐助基金与办大学): ~ a bed in a hospital; 在医院中捐助一个病床 (即给经常资助一名住院病人的全部医疗费用); ~ a school. 捐赠基金办一学校. 2 (usu passive) (通常用被动语态) be ~ed with, possess naturally, be born with (qualities, etc): 赋有 (资质等): be ~ed by nature with great talents. 赋有很大的才能. ~·ment n 1 [U] ~ing. 捐赠; 捐助. 2 [C] money, property, etc given to provide an income: 捐赠的金钱, 财产等: The Oxford and Cambridge colleges have numerous ~ments. 牛津和剑桥大学获有许多的捐款. 3 [C] talent: 禀赋; 才能: natural ~ments, eg a good ear for music. 天资; 天赋(例如辨音的能力).

en·due /ɪn'dju; US: -'du:; ɪn'dju/ vt [VP14] (usu passive) (通常用被动语态) be ~d with, be furnished, supplied, with. 赋予; 供以.

en·dur·ance /ɪn'djuərəns US: -'duə-; ɪn'djurəns/ n [U] ability to endure: 忍耐力: He showed remarkable powers of ~. 他显示了非凡的忍耐力. He came to the end of his ~. 他已忍无可忍了. past/beyond ~, to an extent that can no longer be endured. 忍无可忍的. ~·test, test of how long sb or sth can endure sth. 耐力试验; 持久测验.

en·dure /ɪn'djuə(r) US: -'duər; ɪn'djur/ vt, vi 1 [VP6A, 2A, C] suffer, undergo pain, hardship, etc: 忍受; 忍耐(痛苦, 艰难等): ~ toothache. 忍受牙痛. If help does not come, we must ~ to the end, suffer until death comes. 如无援助到来, 我们必须忍耐到底(即到死为止). 2 [VP6A, D, 17, esp in neg] bear; put up with: (尤用于否定句)容忍: I can't ~ that woman. 我无法容忍那个女人. She can't ~ seeing ~ to see animals cruelly treated. 她不能容忍看到动物受虐待. 3 [VP2A] last; continue in existence: 持久; 持续: as long as life ~s; 一直到死; 有生之年; fame that will ~ for ever. 永垂不朽的声名. **en·dur·able** /-rəbl; rəbl/ adj that can be ~d; bearable. 可忍受的; 可容忍的. **en·dur·ing** adj lasting: 持久的; an enduring peace. 持久的和平. **en·dur·ingly** adv

end·ways /'endweɪz; 'end,wez/, **end·wise** /-waɪz; -,waɪz/ adv with the end towards the spectator; end forward; end to end. 末端朝旁观者; 末端向前; 两端相接.

en·ema /'enɪmə; 'enəmə/ n (syringe used for an) injection of liquid into the rectum. 灌肠; 灌肠器.

en·emy /'enəmɪ; 'enəmɪ/ n (pl -mies) ~ (of/to), 1 one who tries or wishes to harm or attack; one who has ill feeling or hatred towards sb or sth: 敌人; 仇人; 仇敌: A successful man often has many enemies. 一个成功的人往往有许多敌人. Don't make an ~ of him, Do nothing that will cause him to be your ~. 不要使他变成你的敌人. He's an ~ of reform. 他反对改革. 2 the ~, armed forces of a nation with which one's country is at war: 敌军: ~-occupied territory. 敌军占领的土地. The ~ were forced to retreat; 敌军被迫撤退了; (attrib) of the ~: (用作定语)敌人的; 敌军的: aircraft/ships. 敌军的飞机(舰舰). 3 member of such a hostile force. 敌军中的一员. 4 anything that harms or injures: 为害之事物: Laziness is his chief ~. 懒惰是他的主要敌人. Idleness is an ~ to discipline, weakens discipline. 闲散危害纪律.

en·ergy /'enədʒɪ; 'enədʒɪ/ n 1 [U] force, vigour; capacity to do things and get things done: 精力; 活力; 能力: He had so much ~ that he did the work of three men. 他的精力旺盛, 能做三个人的工作. He's full of ~. 他的精力充沛. 2 (in pl, -gies) (person's) powers available for working, or as used in working: (复) (个人的)工作能力: apply/devote all one's energies to a task. 倾全力去做一工作. 3 [U] (science) capacity for,

power of, doing work: (科学)能量; 能: electrical ~; 电能; kinetic ~; 动能; potential ~. 位能; 势能. **en·er·getic** /,enə'dʒetɪk; ,enɚ'dʒɛtɪk/ adj full of, done with, ~ (1). 精力充沛的; 需要精力去做的; 奋力完成的. **en·er·geti·cally** /-klɪ; -klɪ/ adv

en·er·vate /'enəveɪt; 'enɚ,vet/ vt [VP6A] cause to lose physical (sometimes moral) strength: 使失去身体的, 精神的力量; 使衰弱: a country with an enervating climate. 其气候使人衰弱无力的国家.

en famille /,ɒn fæ'mi:; ,ɑnfæ'mi/ adv (F) at home; among one's family. (法)在家; 在家中.

en·fant ter·rible /,ɒnfɒn te'ri:bl; ,ɑnfɑnts'ribl/ n (F) young or new person whose behaviour, ideas, etc cause annoyance or embarrassment to those who hold conventional opinions. (法) 其行为, 思想等使持有传统思想的人厌恶或困窘的青年或新潮派的人; 肆无忌惮的人.

en·feeble /ɪn'fi:bl; ɪn'fibl/ vt [VP6A] make feeble. 使衰弱.

en·fold /ɪn'fəuld; ɪn'fold/ vt [VP6A,14] ~ sb (in), enclose (esp in one's arms). 拥抱.

en·force /ɪn'fɔːs; ɪn'fɔrs/ vt [VP6A,14] 1 ~ (on/upon), compel obedience to; make effective; impose: 迫使服从; 实施; 厉行: ~ a law; 实施法律; ~ discipline/silence; 强制执行纪律(迫令安静); ~ a course of action upon sb. 以一项行动强行加诸某人. 2 give force or strength to: 加强: Have you any statistics that would ~ your argument? 你有无任何统计资料可加强你的论点? ~·able /-əbl; -əbl/ adj that can be ~d. 可强行的; 可实施的. ~·ment n [U] enforcing or being ~d: 强制; 实施; 加强: strict ~ment of a new law. 一项新法律的严格执行.

en·fran·chise /ɪn'fræntʃaɪz; ɛn'fræntʃaɪz/ vt [VP6A] 1 give political rights to (esp, the right to vote at parliamentary elections): 给予政治上的权利 (尤指选举国会议员的投票权): In Great Britain women were ~d in 1918. 在英国妇女于一九一八年获得选举议员的投票权. 2 set free (slaves). 解放(奴隶). ~·ment /ɪn'fræntʃɪzmənt; ɛn'fræntʃɪzmənt/ n

en·gage /ɪn'geɪdʒ; ɪn'gedʒ/ vt, vi 1 [VP6A, 16B] obtain the right to employ: 雇用: ~ a servant; 雇用一仆人; ~ sb as a guide/as an interpreter; 雇用一人做向导(译员); get the right to use or occupy: 使用; 占用; 预定: ~ a taxi (hire is the preferred word). 租一计程车 (hire 较常用). 2 [VP7A, 17, 9, 3A] promise; undertake; bind (oneself); guarantee: 允诺; 答应; 约束(自己); 担保: I will ~ (myself) to manage the business if you will ~ (yourself) to provide the capital. 如果你答应出资本, 我答应经管这个事业. Can you ~ that all his statements are trustworthy? 你能担保他的话都可靠吗? That is more than I can ~ for, guarantee, take responsibility for. 那事我尚不能担保. 3 [VP3A] ~ in, take part in; busy oneself with: 从事; 忙于: ~ in politics. 从事于政治. 4 be ~d to/to marry, be bound by a promise to marry: 订婚: Tom and Anne are ~d. 汤姆与安妮订婚了. Tom is ~d to Anne. 汤姆已与安妮订婚. 5 be ~d (in), be busy, be occupied (with); take part in: 忙于; 做着; 参加: be ~d in business/in writing a novel. 忙着工作(写小说). My time is fully ~d. 我的时间完全被占去了. The line/number is ~d, (telephoning) Someone else is using the line. (电话用语)电话线(号码)被占着(有人在讲话). 6 [VP6A] (usu passive) attract: (通常用被动语态)吸引: Nothing ~s his attention for long. 没有散物可长久吸引他的注意. Her attention was ~d by the display of new sweaters in the shop window. 她的注意力被商店橱窗内展览的新毛线衫吸引住了. 7 [VP6A, 2A] attack; begin fighting with: 攻击; 与…交战: The general did not ~ the enemy. 那将军未与敌军交战. Our orders are to ~ at once. 我们的命令是即刻进攻. 8 [VP2A, 3A, 6A, 14] ~ (with), (of parts of a machine) lock together; (cause to) fit into: (指机器各部)衔接; (使)啮合: The two cog-wheels ~

这两个齿轮相啮合。*The teeth of one wheel ～ with those of the other.* 一轮之齿与另一轮之齿相啮合。(motoring) (驾车) *E～ the clutch/the first gear.* 使离合器啮合(挂第一挡)。**en·gag·ing** *adj* likely to ～ the attention; charming. 引人注意的; 美丽动人的: *an engaging smile/manner.* 迷人的一笑(姿态)。**en·gag·ingly** *adv*

en·gage·ment /ɪnˈgeɪdʒmənt; ɪnˈgedʒmənt/ *n* [C] **1** (formal) promise or undertaking, esp one that is formal or made in writing: (正式用语)约定; 契约: *He has only enough money to meet his ～s,* to make the payments he has undertaken to make. 他仅有约定要付的款。**2** agreement to marry: 婚约: *Their ～ was announced in the papers.* 他们订婚的消息登报了。**～-ring**, one given by a man to a woman when they agree to marry. 订婚戒指。**3** arrangement to go somewhere, meet someone or do sth, at a fixed time: 约会: *I have numerous ～s for next week.* 我在下周有很多约会。**4** battle: 战争; 交战: *The admiral tried to bring about an ～,* to make the enemy fight. 海军上将设法迫使敌人交战。**5** [C, U] engaging (of part of a machine, etc): (指机器之一部分等)啮合: *～ of first gear.* 第一排挡的啮合。

en·gen·der /ɪnˈdʒendə(r); ɪnˈdʒɛndɚ/ *vt* [VP6A] be the cause of (a situation or condition): 产生(某种局势或情况); 造成: *Crime is sometimes ～ed by poverty.* 犯罪有时因贫穷而产生。

en·gine /ˈendʒɪn; ˈɛndʒən/ *n* **1** machine that converts energy into power or motion: 引擎; 发动机; 机车: a 'steam-/'oil-～; 蒸汽机(石油发动机); *a new ～* (petrol or diesel) *for a motor-vehicle.* 机动车辆的新引擎(汽油或柴油机)。⇨ the illus at **motor.** 参看 motor 之插图。**'～-driver** *n* (esp) man who drives a railway ～. (尤指) 火车司机。**2** (old use) machine or instrument: (旧用法)机器; 器械: *～s of war,* eg cannons. 战争工具(例如大炮)。

en·gin·eer /ˌendʒɪˈnɪə(r); ˌɛndʒəˈnɪr/ *n* **1** person who works in a branch of engineering; person who designs engines, machines, bridges, railways, docks, etc: 工程师; 设计引擎, 机器, 桥梁, 铁路, 船坞等的人: *a civil/mining/electrical ～.* 土木(采矿, 电机)工程师。**2** skilled and trained person in control of an engine or engines: 机师; 机工: *the chief ～ of a ship;* 船上的轮机长; (US) man who drives a locomotive. (美)火车司机。**3** member of the branch of an army (called the **E～s**) that builds roads and bridges, controls communications, etc. 工兵。⇨ *vt, vi* [VP6A, 2A] **1** act as an ～; construct or control as an ～. 做工程师或机械师; 建造; 监督。**2** (colloq) arrange or bring about skilfully: (口) 巧妙地安排或完成: *～ a scheme/plot;* 巧妙地拟定一项计划(阴谋); *～ that ….* 巧妙地安排…。

en·gin·eer·ing /ˌendʒɪˈnɪərɪŋ; ˌɛndʒəˈnɪrɪŋ/ *n* [U] the application of science for the control and use of power, esp by the use of machines; the technology, work or profession of an engineer: 工程学; 工程; 工程业: *chemical/mechanical/electrical ～;* 化学工程(机械工程; 电机工程); *a triumph of ～,* eg a magnificent bridge; 十分成功的工程(例如一座宏伟的桥梁); *an ～ works.* (电机等)工程厂。

Eng·lish /ˈɪŋglɪʃ; ˈɪŋglɪʃ/ *n* [U] the ～ language. 英语; 英文. *in plain ～,* in language so simple that the meaning is quite clear. 用浅易明白的英语。the **Queen's/King's '～,** standard, educated English. 标准英语; 纯正英语。□ *adj* **1** of England. 英国的; 英格兰的。**the ～,** (pl) ～ people. (复)英国人。**2** of, written in, spoken in, the ～ language. 英语的; 用英语写的; 用英语说的。**～·man** /-mən; -mən/ (pl **-men**) *n* **～·woman** /-wʊmən; -wʊmən/ (pl **-women**) *n*

en·graft /ɪnˈgrɑːft US: -ˈgræft; ɛnˈgræft/ *vt* [VP6A, 14] ～ (into/upon), insert (a shoot of one tree into another). 接(枝)。～ (in), (fig) implant (principles in the mind or character). (喻)灌输(思想至

心灵或性格中)。

en·grave /ɪnˈgreɪv; ɪnˈgrev/ *vt* **1** [VP6A, 14] ～ on/upon, cut or carve (lines, words, designs, on) a hard surface: 雕刻(线条, 文字, 图案)于…一硬面上: ～ *a design on a metal plate* (for printing); 刻图案于金属板上(印刷用); *a name ～d on a tombstone.* 刻于墓碑上的姓名。**2** [VP14] ～ *with,* mark such surfaces with (an inscription, etc). 将(文字等)刻于硬面上。**3** [VP14] ～ on/upon, (fig) impress deeply (on the memory or mind). (喻)深印于(心上); 使铭记。**en·graver** *n* person who ～s designs, etc on stone, metal, etc. 雕刻师。

en·grav·ing /ɪnˈgreɪvɪŋ; ɪnˈgrevɪŋ/ *n* [U] art of cutting or carving designs on metal, stone, etc; 雕刻术: copy of a picture, design, etc printed from an ～d plate. 雕刻术; 雕版印成的图画, 图案等。

en·gross /ɪnˈgrəʊs; ɪnˈgros/ *vt* **1** [VP6A] (usu passive) take up all the time or attention of: (通常用被动语态)占去…所有的时间或注意力; 使全神贯注: ～ed in his work; 全神贯注于他的工作; an ～ing story. 引人入胜的故事。**2** (legal) write (eg a legal document) in large letters or in formal legal style. (法律)用大字或正式的法律文体写(法律文件等)。

en·gulf /ɪnˈgʌlf; ɪnˈgʌlf/ *vt* [VP6A] swallow up (as in a gulf): 吞没(如被漩涡吞噬): *a boat ～ed in/by the sea/waves.* 被海浪吞没了的小舟。

en·hance /ɪnˈhɑːns US: -ˈhæns; ɪnˈhæns/ *vt* [VP6A] add to (the value, attraction, powers, price, etc). 增加(价值, 吸引力, 力量, 价格等)。

enigma /ɪˈnɪgmə; ɪˈnɪgmə/ *n* [C] question, person, thing, circumstance, that is puzzling. 谜; 令人迷惑的问题, 人或情况。**enig·matic** /ˌenɪgˈmætɪk; ˌɛnɪgˈmætɪk/ *adj* puzzling; mysterious. 令人迷惑的; 神秘的。**enig·mati·cally** /-klɪ; -klɪ/ *adv*

en·join /ɪnˈdʒɔɪn; ɪnˈdʒɔɪn/ *vt* [VP6A, 17, 9, 14] ～ (on sb), give an order for; urge; prescribe; command: 命令; 催促; 指示; 吩咐: ～ *silence/obedience;* 命令肃静(服从); ～ *on sb the necessity for economy;* 嘱咐某人须节俭; ～ *a duty on sb;* 交给某人一项责任; ～ *sb to obey the rules;* 命令某人遵守规则; ～ *that sth should be done.* 下令做某件事。

en·joy /ɪnˈdʒɔɪ; ɪnˈdʒɔɪ/ *vt* [VP6A, C] **1** get pleasure from; take delight in: 享受…之乐趣; 乐于: ～ *one's dinner.* 津津有味地吃饭。*I've ～ed talking to you about old times.* 我很高兴曾经和你话旧。**2** have as an advantage or benefit: 享有: ～ *good health/a good income.* 享有健康之福(好的收入)。**3** ～ *oneself,* experience pleasure; be happy. 感到快乐; 玩得愉快。**～·able** /-əbl; -əbl/ *adj* giving joy; pleasant. 令人快乐的; 令人愉快的。**～·ably** /-əblɪ; -əblɪ/ *adv*

en·joy·ment /ɪnˈdʒɔɪmənt; ɪnˈdʒɔɪmənt/ *n* **1** [U] pleasure; joy; satisfaction: 享乐; 快乐; 满意: *to think only of/live for ～.* 只想到(生活只为了)享乐。**2** [U] possession and use: 享受; 享有: *be in the ～ of the full possession of one's faculties,* be physically and mentally well. 享有身心健康。**3** [C] sth that gives joy and pleasure. 令人快乐的事物; 乐事。

en·kindle /ɪnˈkɪndl; ɛnˈkɪndl/ *vt* [VP6A] cause (flame, passion, etc) to flare up; inflame (with passion, etc). 使燃起(火焰, 激情等); 煽动; 动之以激情。

en·large /ɪnˈlɑːdʒ; ɪnˈlɑrdʒ/ *vt, vi* **1** [VP6A, 2A] make or become larger: 扩大; 增大: ～ *a photograph/one's house.* 放大相片(扩建房屋)。*Will this print ～ well,* Will it be good if it is reproduced on a larger scale? 这张照片可放大得好吗? **2** [VP3A] ～ *on/upon,* say or write more about: 详述: *I need not ～ upon this matter; you all know my views.* 我不需要详述此事; 你们都知道我的意见。**～·ment** *n* [U] enlarging or being ～d; [C] result of this, esp a photograph. 扩大; 增大; 扩大的结果(尤指放大的照片)。

en·lighten /ɪnˈlaɪtn; ɪnˈlaɪtn/ *vt* [VP6A, 14] ～ (on), give more knowledge to; free from ignorance,

misunderstanding or false beliefs: 教导；启迪；开导: *Can you ~ me on this subject,* help me to understand it better? 你能帮助我明白这一问题吗? **~ed** *part adj* free from ignorance, prejudice, superstition, etc: 文明的；不迷信的；开通的: *in these ~ed days.* 值此文明的时代。**~·ment** *n* [U] **~ing** or being ~ed: 教导；启迪；开导；开明；开通: *living in an age of ~ment;* 生活于文明的时代; *work for the ~ment of mankind.* 为启迪人类而努力。**the E~ment,** the period (esp 18th c) when men believed that reason and science (and not religion) would advance human progress. 启蒙运动(尤指十八世纪，人类相信理智和科学(而非宗教)为推动人类进步的力量)。

en·list /ɪnˈlɪst; ɪnˈlɪst/ *vt, vi* 1 [VP6A, 14, 16B, 2A, C] ~ *(in),* take into, enter, the armed forces: 使入伍; 从军: *a recruit;* 征募一新兵; ~ *as a volunteer;* 志愿从军; *~ed men,* soldiers, etc: 士兵; ~ *in the army.* 从军。**2** [VP6A, 14] ~ *(in/for),* obtain; get the support of: 获得; 得到…的支持: *sb's sympathy and help in a charitable cause/for the Red Cross.* 获某人对一慈善运动(红十字会)的同情与赞助。**~·ment** *n* [U] ~ing or being ~ed; [C] instance of this. 使入伍; 从军; 被征入伍; 获得。

en·liven /ɪnˈlaɪvn; ɪnˈlaɪvn/ *vt* [VP6A] make lively: 使活泼；使有生气: *How can we ~ the party?* 我们怎样使这聚会热闹起来?

en masse /ˌɒn ˈmæs; ɛnˈmæs/ *adv* (F) in a mass; all together. 全体；一起。

en·mesh /ɪnˈmeʃ; ɛnˈmɛʃ/ *vt* [VP6A, 14] ~ *(in),* take (as) in a net; entangle. 使陷入网;使陷入。

en·mity /ˈenmətɪ; ˈɛnmɪtɪ/ *n* [U] condition of being an enemy; hatred: 仇恨; 憎恨: *be at ~ with one's neighbours;* 与邻人不睦; [C] *(pl* **-ties**) particular feeling of hostility or hatred. 某种仇恨心。

en·noble /ɪˈnəʊbl; ɪˈnobl/ *vt* [VP6A] **1** make (sb) a member of the nobility. 使(某人)成为贵族;授以爵位。**2** (fig) make morally noble; make dignified. (喻)使崇高;使高贵。**~·ment** *n*

en·nui /ɒnˈwiː; ˈɑnwɪ/ *n* [U] (F) weariness of mind caused by lack of any interesting occupation; [C] instance of this. (法)(因缺乏有兴趣的工作而)倦怠;无聊。

enor·mity /ɪˈnɔːmətɪ; ɪˈnɔrmətɪ/ *n* **1** [U] great wickedness: 极恶; 凶恶: *Does he realize the ~ of his offence?* 他知道他的罪恶深重吗? **2** [C] *(pl* **-ties**) serious crime. 严重的罪行; 大罪。**3** [U] immense size: 极大: *the ~ of the problem of feeding the world's population in AD 2000.* 公元二〇〇〇年供应全球人口粮食的问题。

enor·mous /ɪˈnɔːməs; ɪˈnɔrməs/ *adj* very great; immense: 极大的;巨大的;广大的: *an ~ sum of money.* 巨额金钱。**~·ly** *adv* to an ~ extent: 极大地; 巨大地: *The town has changed ~ly during recent years.* 近年来这城市大为改变了。**~·ness** *n*

enough /ɪˈnʌf; əˈnʌf/ *adj, n* (of a quantity) as great as is needed; as much or as many as necessary (数量)足够;充分 (as an *adj* ~ occurs in the pattern 做形容词用时 enough 的句型为 ~ + *noun* or *noun* + ~): *There's ~ food/food ~ for everybody.* 有足够大家吃的食物。*Have you had ~ peanuts?* 你花生吃够了吗? (as a *noun* ~ occurs in the pattern 做名词用时 enough 的句型为 ~ *(of the/this/that/his* etc+*noun) (for sb/to do sth)*): *Will £5 be ~ for you/~ to cover the journey?* 五英镑够你用吗? Have you had ~ of this TV programme yet? 这电视节目你看够了吗? *I've had ~ of your grumbling and groaning.* 我已听够了你的抱怨和牢骚。*~ is as good as a feast,* I'm glad that you have had as much as you needed. 吃得刚饱就等于吃一顿盛宴; 足食犹如盛宴。*more than ~,* too much. 过多; 太多。□ *adv of degree* 表示程度的副词 (placed after *adj,* *adv* and *pp*; also after a *noun* used as an *adj,* as when *fool* means *foolish;* used in the pattern 置于形容

词，副词和过去分词之后；亦置于做形容词用的名词之后，如 fool 作 foolish 解时; 用于下列句型 *adj + ~ (for sb/to do sth)*) **1** to the right or necessary degree; sufficiently: 充分地; 足够地: *The meat is not cooked ~.* 这肉火候不够。*Are you warm ~?* 你觉得够暖和吗? *You know well ~ (= quite well) what I mean.* 你很懂得我的意思。*I was fool (= foolish) ~ to believe her.* 我相信了她，真是够傻的。*He wasn't man (= manly) ~ to admit his mistake.* 他没有勇于认错的丈夫气概。*You're old ~ to know better.* 你已届懂事的年龄了。*This book is easy ~ for a six-year-old child to read.* 这本书容易到六岁的孩子都可以读得懂。**2** sometimes used in a disparaging way, suggesting that sth could be better, etc: 有时含有贬抑之意,暗示某事可以做得更好等: *It's interesting ~ in its way,* moderately interesting. 还有一点趣味。*She sings well ~,* indicating faint praise. 她唱得还可以(表示勉强的称赞)。**3** *oddly/curiously/strangely* etc *~,* in a way that is odd, etc. 很奇怪地。*sure ~,* in a degree that satisfies doubt; as one expected. 确实地; 正如所料。

en·plane /enˈpleɪn; ɛnˈplen/ *vi, vt* ⇨ **emplane.**

en·quire, en·quiry /ɪnˈkwaɪə(r), ɪnˈkwaɪərɪ; ɪnˈkwaɪr; ɪnˈkwaɪrɪ/ *v, n* = **inquire, inquiry.**

en·rage /ɪnˈreɪdʒ; ɪnˈredʒ/ *vt* [VP6A] fill with rage: 激怒; 触怒: *~d at/by sb's stupidity.* 因某人的愚蠢而愤怒。

en·rap·ture /ɪnˈræptʃə(r); ɪnˈræptʃɚ/ *vt* [VP6A] fill with great delight or joy. 使狂喜。

en·rich /ɪnˈrɪtʃ; ɪnˈrɪtʃ/ *vt* [VP6A, 14] ~ *(with),* make rich; improve in quality, flavour, etc: 使丰富: (在品质、味道等方面)改进: ~ *the mind (with knowledge);* (以知识)充实心智; *soil ~ed with manure.* 由于施肥料而肥沃的土壤。**~·ment** *n*

en·roll, en·rol /ɪnˈrəʊl; ɪnˈrol/ *vt, vi* [VP6A, 14, 16B, 2A, C] ~ *(in),* (cause to) become a member (of): (使)成为会员或社员; 登记; 注册: *to ~ in evening classes;* 在夜间部注册上课; *to ~ (sb)* as a member of a *society/club;* 登记(某人)为会员; *to be ~ed in a register of electors;* 被登入选举人名册; *to ~ new students.* 收新生。**~·ment** *n* [U] ~ing or being ~ed; [C] number ~ed: 登记为会员; 注册; 登记或注册的人数: *a school with an ~ment of 800 pupils.* 有八百学生注册的学校。

en route /ˌɒn ˈruːt; ɑnˈrut/ *adv* ~ *(from/to),* on the way (from/to): 在途中: *We stopped at Paris ~ from Rome to London.* 我们从罗马至伦敦的途中曾在巴黎停留。

en·sconce /ɪnˈskɒns; ɛnˈskɑns/ *vt* [VP14] ~ *oneself in,* establish oneself in (a safe, comfortable, etc place). 安置(自己于一安全, 隐秘, 舒适等之地)。

en·semble /ɒnˈsɒmbl; ɑnˈsɑmbl/ *n* [C] (F) **1** sth viewed as a whole; general effect. (法)整体; 总效果。**2** (music) passage of music in which all the performers unite; group of musicians who play together regularly (smaller than an orchestra). (音乐)重奏; 合奏; 合奏的一段; 经常在一起演奏的乐队 (小于管弦乐队)。**3** (trade use) woman's matched clothing outfit (dress, coat, etc designed to be worn together). (商业用语)妇女之全套服装(衣服, 上衣等设计在一起者)。

en·shrine /ɪnˈʃraɪn; ɛnˈʃraɪn/ *vt* [VP6A, 14] ~ *(in),* (formal) place or keep in, or as in, a shrine; serve as a shrine for: (正式用语)置于神龛内; 奉祀于神殿内; 奉为神龛: 珍藏; 作为…的神龛或圣物: *the casket that ~s the relics;* 珍藏遗物的小箱; *memories ~d in her heart;* 深藏在她内心的记忆; *basic human rights ~d in the constitution.* 宪法所保证的人类的基本权利。

en·shroud /ɪnˈʃraʊd; ɛnˈʃraʊd/ *vt* [VP6A] cover completely: 遮蔽; 掩蔽: *hills ~ed in mist.* 为雾所遮蔽的群山。

en·sign /ˈensən; ˈɛnsɪn/ *n* **1** (esp naval) flag or banner: (尤指海军的)旗帜: *white ~,* used by the

Royal Navy; 英国皇家海军旗 (白色); *red* ~, used by British merchant ships; 英国商船旗(红色); *blue* ~, used by the Royal Naval Reserve. 英国皇家海军预备舰队旗(蓝色). **2** (US) lowest commissioned officer in the navy. (美)海军少尉. **3** /'ensən; 'ɛnsəɪn/ (old uses) badge or symbol (showing office, authority, etc); infantry officer who carried the regimental colours. (旧用法)徽章(表示职位, 权威等);陆军团中的掌旗官.

en·si·lage /'ensɪlɪdʒ; 'ɛnsɪlɪdʒ/ *n* = **silage.**

en·slave /ɪn'sleɪv; ɪn'slev/ *vt* [VP6A] make a slave of. 使成为奴隶;奴役.

en·snare /ɪn'sneə(r); ɛn'snɛr/ *vt* [VP6A, 14] ~ **(in),** catch in, or as in, a snare or trap. 使入罗网;使人陷阱.

en·sue /ɪn'sju: US: -'su:; ɛn'su/ *vi* [VP2A, 3A] ~ **(from),** happen later; follow, happen as a result: 随着发生;续起;因而发生: *the trouble that* ~*d from this misunderstanding;* 由此误会而产生的麻烦; *in the ensuing* (= next) *year.* 翌年.

en·sure (US = **in·sure**) /ɪn'ʃuə(r); ɪn'ʃʊr/ *vt, vi* **1** [VP9] make sure; guarantee: 确定;使确实;保证: *I can't* ~ *that he will be there in time.* 我不能确定他会及时到那里. **2** [VP14, 3A] ~ **(sb)** *against sth,* make safe: 使安全: *We* ~ *(ourselves) against possible disappointment.* 我们避免可能产生的失望. *You should* ~ *(yourself) against loss of heat by having double glazing.* 你应该装置双重玻璃以免散热. **3** [VP12A, 13A] secure; assure: 获得;保证得到: *These documents* ~ *to you the authority you need.* 这些文件使你获得你需要的职权. *I cannot* ~ *you a good post.* 我不能担保你获得一个好的职位. **4** (formerly). (昔时) = **insure.**

en·tail /ɪn'teɪl; ɪn'tel/ *vt* [VP6A, 14] ~ **(on),** **1** make necessary; impose (expense, etc on sb): 使必要; 使负担(花费等, 与 on 连用, 后接某人.): *That will* ~ *an early start.* 那将使你着手要有准备. *These plans* ~ *great expense on us.* 这些计划需要花费我们引很大的经费. **2** (legal) leave, settle, (land) to a line of heirs so that none of them can give it away or sell it: (法律)限定(地产)继承人: ~ *an estate on sb.* 限定某人继承地产. □ *n* [U] settlement of landed property in this way; [C] the property so settled. 限定继承;限定继承的地产.

en·tangle /ɪn'tæŋgl; ɪn'tæŋgl/ *vt* [VP6A, 15A, 14] ~ **(in),** **1** catch in a snare or among obstacles: 使纠缠; 缠住: *My fishing line got* ~*d in weeds.* 我的钓鱼线与杂草搅缠在一起了. *The duck flew into the nets and the more it struggled the more it* ~*d itself.* 那鸭子飞入网中, 它越挣扎, 缠得越紧. **2** (fig) put or get into difficulties, in unfavourable circumstances: (喻)使陷入困境;使陷入不利情况: ~ *oneself with money-lenders.* 为放债者所苦. ~·**ment** *n* **1** [U] entangling or being ~d; [C] situation that ~s: 陷入困境;引起纠缠之情况;纠纷: ~*ments with rogues;* 与歹徒间的纠纷; *emotional* ~*ments.* 感情的纠缠. **2** *(pl)* barrier of stakes and barbed wire to impede the enemy's advance. (复)铁丝网(以阻敌人前进者).

en·tente /ɒn'tɒnt; ɑn'tɑnt/ *n* [C] (F) (group of States with a) friendly understanding. (法)国与国间之谅解;互相谅解的国家. ~ **cordi·ale** /ˌkɔːdi'ɑːl; kɔr'djɑl/ *n* ~, esp between two governments. 两国间的谅解.

en·ter /'entə(r); 'ɛntə/ *vt, vi* **1** [VP6A, 2A] come or go into: 进入: ~ *a room.* 进入室内. *The train* ~*ed a tunnel.* 火车驶进隧道. *Where did the bullet* ~ *the body?* 子弹是从哪里进入身体的? (Stage direction in a printed play) (剧本中的舞台说明) *E*~ *Hamlet,* Hamlet comes on to the stage. 哈姆雷特上场. **2** [VP6A] become a member of; join: 加入;参加: ~ *a school/college;* 进学校(大学); ~ *the Army/Navy;* 投效陆军(海军); ~ *the Church,* become a priest; 做教士;做牧师; ~ *a profession.* 从事一职业. **3** [VP3A] ~ *into sth (with sb),* begin, open: 开始: ~ *into conversation with sb;* 与某人开始交谈; ~ *into negotiations with a business*

firm. 与一公司商谈. ~ *into sth,* **(a)** begin to deal with: 开始处理: ~ *into details/particulars.* 着手处理细节. **(b)** sympathize with; be able to understand and appreciate: 同情;领略;体会: ~ *into sb's feelings.* 同情某人的感受; ~ *into the spirit of the occasion.* 领略某一场合的精神. **(c)** form a part of: 成为…之一部: *a possibility that had not* ~*ed into our calculations.* 我们未考虑到的一个可能性. **4** [VP3A] ~ *on/upon,* **(a)** make a start on: 开始; 着手: ~ *upon a new career/one's duties/another term of office.* 开始一新事业(着手工作,开始另一任期). **(b)** take possession of; begin to enjoy: 承受: ~ *upon one's inheritance.* 承受遗产. **5** [VP6A,14,15B] ~ *(in/up)* ~ *(in),* unite, record names, details, etc in a book, etc: 登记姓名, 细节等: ~ *(in/up) an item in an account-book.* 将一笔帐记入帐簿. **6** [VP3A, 14] ~ *for;* ~ *sb for,* give the name of sb for a competition, race, etc: (替…)报名参加(竞赛等): ~ *oneself for an examination.* 报名参加考试; ~ *for the high jump.* 报名参加跳高赛; ~ *a horse for the Derby.* 给一马报名参加英国大赛马.

en·teric /en'terɪk; ɛn'tɛrɪk/ *adj* of the intestines: 肠的: ~ *fever,* typhoid. 肠热病; 伤寒. **en·ter·itis** /ˌentə'raɪtɪs; ˌɛntə'raɪtɪs/ *n* [U] inflammation of the intestines. 肠炎.

en·ter·prise /'entəpraɪz; 'ɛntə.praɪz/ *n* **1** [C] undertaking, esp one that needs courage or that offers difficulty. 事业 (尤指需要勇气或难以进行者); 企业. **2** [U] courage and willingness to engage in ~s(上): 企业心; 事业心: *We need a spirit of* ~ *if we are to overcome our difficulties.* 如欲克服我们的困难, 我们需要进取的精神. *He is a man of great* ~. 他是个事业心很强的人. **3** [U] carrying on of ~s(1): 从事企业或事业: *private* ~ *versus government control of commerce and industry.* 民营企业与工商业由政府控制的问题. ⇨ **free**[1](3); **private**(1). **en·ter·pris·ing** *adj* having, showing, ~(2). 有 或表现企业心的; 具有创业精神的. **en·ter·pris·ing·ly** *adv*

en·ter·tain /ˌentə'teɪn; ˌɛntə'ten/ *vt* [VP6A, 14, 2A] **1** ~ *(to),* receive (people) as guests; give food and drink to: 款待,以食物饮料招待: ~ *friends to dinner.* 请用友们吃饭. *The Smiths* ~ *a great deal/do a great deal of* ~*ing,* often give dinner parties, etc. 史密斯家常款待客人. **2** ~ *(with),* amuse, interest: 使快乐; 使感到兴趣: ~ *the children with tricks.* 变戏法使孩子们快乐. *We were all* ~*ed by his tricks.* 我们都对他的戏法感到兴趣. **3** be ready to consider: 准备考虑: ~ *a proposal;* 准备考虑一建议; have in the mind: 持有; 怀有: ~ *ideas/doubts, etc.* 持有意见(感到怀疑等). ~·**ing** *adj* pleasing; amusing. 令人愉快的; 有趣的. ~·**ing·ly** *adv* ~·**ment** *n* **1** [U] ~ing or being ~ed(2): (使)感到快乐或兴趣: *He fell into the water, much to the* ~*ment of the onlookers.* 他掉进水中, 使旁观者大乐. **2** [C] public performance (at a theatre, circus, etc). (戏院,马戏团等之)娱乐; 游艺; 技艺表演. ~·**er** *n* person who ~s(2), esp professionally. 娱乐节目表演者; (尤指)职业娱乐节目表演者.

en·thral (also, esp US **en·thrall**) /ɪn'θrɔːl; ɪn'θrɔl/ *vt* (-ll-) [VP6A] **1** take the whole attention of; please greatly: 迷住; 使极为喜悦: ~*ed by an exciting story.* 为一动人的故事所迷. **2** enslave (usu fig): 奴役 (通常作喻): ~*ed by a woman's beauty.* 为一女子的美色迷住.

en·throne /ɪn'θrəʊn; ɪn'θron/ *vt* [VP6A] place a king, bishop on a throne; (fig) give a high place to, in one's judgement or affection: 使(国王, 主教)就位; (喻)崇拜; 尊崇; 爱戴: ~ *a ruler* ~*d in the hearts of his subjects.* 为臣民爱戴的君主. ~·**ment** *n*

en·thuse /ɪn'θju:z US: -'θu:z; ɪn'θjuz/ *vi* [VP3A] ~ *over,* (colloq) show enthusiasm for. (口)热心于.

en·thusi·asm /ɪn'θju:zɪæzəm US: -'θu:-; ɪn'θjuzɪ.ˌæzəm/ *n* [U] ~ *(for/about),* strong feeling of admiration or interest: 渴慕;热心;热爱: *arouse* ~ *in*

sb; 引起某人的热爱; *a play that moved the audience to* ~; 使观众狂热的戏剧; *feel no* ~ *for/about sth*; 对某事不热心; *an outburst of* ~. 狂热。

en·thusi·ast /ɪn'θjuːzɪæst US: -'θuː-; ɪn'θjuzɪˌæst/ *n* ~ *(for/about)*, person filled with enthusiasm: 热心者; 渴慕者; ~ *a sports* ~; 酷爱运动者; *an* ~ *for/about politics*. 热中于政治者。

en·thusi·astic /ɪn,θjuːzɪ'æstɪk US: -'θuː-; ɪn,θjuzɪ'æstɪk/ *adj* ~ *(about/over)*, full of enthusiasm: 热心的; 热情洋溢的: ~ *admirers of a film star*; 热烈仰慕某一电影明星者; *become* ~ *over sth*. 热心于某事。 **en·thusi·asti·cally** /-klɪ; -klɪ/ *adv*

en·tice /ɪn'taɪs; ɪn'taɪs/ *vt* [VP6A, 15A, 17] tempt or persuade: 诱惑; 怂恿: ~ *a young girl away from home*; 诱骗一少女出走; ~ *sb into doing sth/to do sth wrong*; 怂恿某人做坏事; ~ *a man from his duty*. 引诱一人失职。 ~·**ment** *n* [U] enticing or being ~d; [C] sth that ~s. 诱惑; 怂恿; 诱惑物。

en·tire /ɪn'taɪə(r); ɪn'taɪr/ *adj* whole, complete; in one piece, unbroken: 整个的; 完全的; 完整的: *The* ~ *village was destroyed*. 整个村庄被毁掉了。*Is your stamp collection still* ~? 你集的邮票还是那样完整吗? ~·**ly** *adv* completely: 完全地; 全然: ~*ly unnecessary/different*. 完全不必要(不同)。*My life is* ~*ly given up to work*. 我的一生全部献给了工作。 ~·**ty** /ɪn'taɪərɪtɪ; ɪn'taɪrtɪ/ *n* [U] the state of being ~; completeness: 全部;完全: *We must examine the question in its* ~*ty*, as a whole, not in parts only. 我们必须就问题整个予以研究一下。

en·title /ɪn'taɪtl; ɪn'taɪtl/ *vt* 1 [VP23] *be* ~*d*, have as a title: 称作; 以…为名: *a book* ~*d 'Adam Bede'*. 书名为《亚当·比得》的一本书。2 [VP14, 17] ~ *sb to sth/to do sth*, (usu in passive) (of conditions, circumstances, qualities, etc) give a right (to): (通常用被动语态)(指条件,情况,特性等)给予权利: *If you fail three times, you are not* ~*d to try any more*. 如果你失败三次,你便无权再尝试了。 ~·**ment** *n* that which ~s(2). 给予权利之条件,情况等。

en·tity /'entɪtɪ; 'ɛntɪtɪ/ *n* (*pl* -ties) 1 [C] sth that has real existence; a thing's existence (contrasted with its qualities, relations, etc). 实在物;实体(与性质,关系等相对)。2 [U] being; existence. 存在;实在。

en·tomb /ɪn'tuːm; ɪn'tum/ *vt* [VP6A] place in a tomb; serve as a tomb for. 埋葬; 作为…之墓。

ento·mol·ogy /,entə'mɒlədʒɪ; ,ɛntə'mɑlədʒɪ/ *n* [U] the study of insects. 昆虫学。 **en·to·mol·ogist** /-dʒɪst; -dʒɪst/ *n* student of, expert in, ~. 昆虫学家。 **en·to·mo·logi·cal** /,entəmə'lɒdʒɪkl; ,ɛntəmə'ladʒɪkl/ *adj*

en·tour·age /,ɒntu'rɑːʒ; ,ɑntu'raʒ/ *n* all those accompanying and attending for an important or high-ranking person: 要人的所有随从: *the President and his* ~. 总统及其随员。

en·tr'acte /'ɒntrækt; ɑn'trækt/ *n* [C] (F) (performance in an) interval between acts in a play. (法)幕与幕间之休息; 幕间休息之插演节目。

en·trails /'entreɪlz; 'ɛntrelz/ *n pl* bowels; intestines. 肠。

en·train /en'treɪn; ɛn'tren/ *vt*, *vi* [VP6A, 2A] get, put troops, etc into a train. 使(军队等)乘火车; 乘火车。

en·trance¹ /'entrəns; 'ɛntrəns/ *n* 1 [C] opening, gate, door, passage, etc by which one enters: 入口; 大门;门;进入之道: *The* ~ *to the cave had been blocked up*. 那个洞的入口已被阻塞。2 [C, U] coming or going in; coming or act upon the stage; entering: 进入; (舞台演员之)出场: *the university* ~ *examination*. 大学入学考试。*E*~ *into/upon ministerial office requires a visit to the Queen*. 就职阁员须觐见女王。*Actors must learn their* ~*s and exits*, when to come upon and leave the stage. 演员必须知道何时出场和退场。3 [C, U] right of entering: 进入权: *to be refused* ~. 被拒绝

进入. '~-fee, '~-money, charge for admission. 入场费。

en·trance² /ɪn'trɑːns US: -'træns; ɪn'træns/ *vt* [VP6A] ~ *(at/with)*, (usu in passive) fill with emotion and delight: (通常用被动语态)使狂喜; 使出神: ~*d with the music*. 听音乐出神。*She stood* ~*d at the sight*. 她站在那里望着那景色出神。

en·trant /'entrənt; 'ɛntrənt/ *n* person who enters to a profession, for a competition, race, etc. 进入者; 开始一种职业者(与 to 连用); 参加比赛者(与 for 连用)。

en·trap /ɪn'træp; ɪn'træp/ *vt* (*-pp-*) [VP6A]=**trap** (the usu word). (trap 一字较常用)。

en·treat /ɪn'triːt; ɪn'trit/ *vt* [VP6A, 17, 14] ~ *(of)*, (formal) ask (sb) earnestly: (正式用语)恳求: ~ *sb to show mercy*; 恳求某人怜悯; *a favour of sb*. 求某人帮忙。 ~·**ing·ly** *adv*

en·treaty /ɪn'triːtɪ; ɪn'tritɪ/ *n* (*pl* -ies) [C, U] earnest request(ing): 恳求; 哀求: *deaf to all entreaties*; 不理睬一切恳求; *with a look of* ~. 以哀求的眼光。

en·trée /'ɒntreɪ; 'ɑntre/ *n* (F) (法) 1 [U] right or privilege of admission. 进入权; 入场权。2 [C] dish served between the fish and the meat course. 鱼与大块肉间的一道菜;旁碟。

en·trench /ɪn'trentʃ; ɪn'trɛntʃ/ *vt* [VP6A] 1 surround or protect with a trench or trenches: 围以壕沟; 以壕沟防护: *The enemy were strongly* ~*ed on the other side of the river*. 敌军在河的彼岸以坚固的壕沟防护自己。2 establish firmly: 确立: *customs* ~*ed by tradition*; 由传统确立的风俗; *legal clauses/provisions*, those (in a constitution(1)) which can be changed only by a special procedure. 确立的宪法条款(须经特殊程序始可更动者)。 ~·**ment** *n*

entre·pot /'ɒntrəpəʊ; 'ɑntrə,po/ *n* (F) storehouse; commercial centre for the import, export, collection and distribution of goods. (法)仓库; 货物集散地。

entre·pre·neur /,ɒntrəprə'nɜː(r); ,ɑntrəprə'nɝ/ *n* person who organizes and manages a commercial undertaking. 企业家。 ~·**ial** /-'nɜːrɪəl; -'nɝɪəl/ *adj*

en·trust /ɪn'trʌst; ɪn'trʌst/ *vt* [VP14] ~ *sth to sb*; ~ *sb with sth*, trust sb to complete or safeguard sth: 委托某事给某人; 信托某人做某事: *Can I* ~ *the task to you/~ you with the task*? 我可以将此事交给你办吗? *Ought I to* ~ *to them/~ them with such confidential and important plans*? 我应该将如此机密和重要的计划交托他们吗?

en·try /'entrɪ; 'ɛntrɪ/ *n* [C] (*pl* -tries) 1 coming or going in: 进入; 进入: *the* ~ *of the USA into world politics*. 美国之参与世界政治。*The army made a triumphal* ~ *into the town*. 这批军队凯旋进入该城。*Thieves had forced an* ~ *into the building*. 窃贼强行进入那建筑物。'~-visa, ⇨ **visa**. 2 [C, U] (place of) entrance; right of entering: 入口; 进入权: *The sign* ~ *means 'No* ~'. 表示'不准入内'。3 item in a list; item noted in an account book: (表中之)条目; 项目; 帐目: *dictionary entries*; 词典中列出之词目; *make an* ~ *of a transaction*; 记一笔交易; *book-keeping by double/single* ~, in which each item is entered twice/once in a ledger. 复(单)式簿记. *bill of* ~, ⇨ **bill³**(6). 4 list, number, of persons, etc entering for a competition: 参加比赛的名单, 人数等: *a large* ~ *for the 5000 metres race*; 参加五千米赛跑的许多人; person or thing that is entered for a competition: 参加比赛的人或物: *nearly fifty entries for the Marathon race*. 几乎有五十位参加马拉松赛跑。

en·twine /ɪn'twaɪn; ɪn'twaɪn/ *vt* [VP6A, 14] ~ *(with/round)*, make by twining; curl (one thing) (with or round another). 编织; 盘绕(一物于另一物, 与 with 或 round 连用)。

enu·mer·ate /ɪ'njuːməreɪt US: ɪ'nuː-; ɪ'njumə,ret/ *vt* [VP6A] count, go through (a list of articles) naming them one by one. 点查; 列举。 **enu·mer·ation**

/ɪˌnjuːməˈreɪʃn *US*: ˌnuː-; ɪˌnjuːməˈreʃən/   *n* [U] enumerating; [C] list. 数;列举;目录。

enun·ci·ate /ɪˈnʌnsɪeɪt; ɪˈnʌnsɪˌet/ *vt, vi* **1** [VP6A, 2A] say, pronounce (words): 念(字);发音: *He ~s (his words) clearly.* 他发音(念字)清晰。 **2** express a theory, etc clearly or definitely. 清楚或确切表明(理论 等). **enun·ci·ation** /ɪˌnʌnsɪˈeɪʃn; ɪˌnʌnsɪˈeʃən/ *n*

en·velop /ɪnˈveləp; ɪnˈveləp/ *vt* [VP6A,14] **~ (in),** wrap up, cover, on all sides: 包围; 掩蔽; 包住: *~ed in mist:* 被雾遮蔽的群山; *a baby ~ed in a shawl;* 包在披肩内的婴儿; *~ a subject in mystery.* 使一问题变得神秘。 **~·ment** *n*

en·vel·ope /ˈenvələup; ˈɛnvəˌlop/ *n* wrapper or covering; esp one made of paper for a letter; covering of a balloon or airship. 封皮; (尤指)信封; 包袋; 气球或飞艇之气囊。

en·venom /ɪnˈvenəm; ɛnˈvɛnəm/ *vt* [VP6A] put poison on or in, eg a weapon; (fig) fill with bitter hate: 置毒药于(例如武器); (喻)使痛恨: *~ed quarrels/tempers.* 充满怨恨的争吵(脾气)。

en·vi·able /ˈenvɪəbl; ˈɛnvɪəbl/ *adj* causing envy; likely to excite envy (used both of the object and the person, etc, possessing it): 令人羡慕的; 可羡慕的(用以 指某物和拥有该物的人);等): *an ~ school record,* one of great success, etc; 令人羡慕的在校成绩; *an ~ woman,* eg one who has a kind, handsome and rich husband. 令人羡慕的女人(例如她丈夫和善,英俊而且富有)。

en·vi·ous /ˈenvɪəs; ˈɛnvɪəs/ *adj* **~ (of),** full of envy; feeling envy; showing or expressing envy: 嫉妒的; 羡慕的; 表示嫉妒或羡慕的: *of sb's success;* 羡慕某人的成功; *~ looks;* 嫉妒的神情; *looking at sth with ~ eyes.* 以羡慕的眼光望着某物。 **~·ly** *adv*

en·viron /ɪnˈvaɪərən; ɪnˈvaɪrən/ *vt* [VP6A] be in a position round; surround: 包围; 环绕: *a town ~ed by/with forests.* 为森林所环绕的城镇。

en·vi·ron·ment /ɪnˈvaɪərənmənt; ɪnˈvaɪrənmənt/ *n* [U, C] surroundings, circumstances, influences: 环境: *a healthy ~.* 有益于健康的环境。 *Students of social problems investigate the home, social and moral ~(s) of different classes of people.* 研究社会问题的学者调查各阶层人民的家庭, 社会和精神上的生活环境。 **Department of the E~,** (GB) Government Department responsible for land planning, construction industries, transport, preservation of public amenities, control of air and water pollution, the protection of the coast and the countryside. (英)环境部(负责土地计划,建筑工业,运输,公共休闲去处,管制空气和水的污染,保护海岸与乡间等)。 **~al** /ɪnˌvaɪərənˈmentl; ɪnˌvaɪrənˈmentl/ *adj* **~·ally** /-təlɪ; -tlɪ/ *adv*

en·virons /ˈenvɪrənz; ɪnˈvaɪrənz/ *n pl* districts surrounding a town, etc. 郊外; 近郊: *Berlin and its ~.* 柏林及其近郊。

en·vis·age /ɪnˈvɪzɪdʒ; ɛnˈvɪzɪdʒ/ *vt* [VP6A] picture in the mind (esp in a particular way): 想象; 设想;(尤指从某一方面): *He had not ~d the matter in that light.* 他没有从那方面设想过此事。

en·voy[1] /ˈenvɔɪ; ˈɛnvɔɪ/ *n* messenger, esp one sent on a special mission; diplomatic agent next in rank below an ambassador. 使者; 特使; 公使。

en·voy[2] (also **en·voi**) /ˈenvɔɪ; ˈɛnvɔɪ/ *n* [C] concluding part of a poem, esp a short stanza at the end of some archaic forms of poetry. 一首诗的结尾; (尤指某些诗体的)结语诗节。

envy[1] /ˈenvɪ; ˈɛnvɪ/ *n* [U] **1 ~ at sth/of sb,** feeling of disappointment and resentment (at another's better fortune): 嫉妒; 羡慕: *He was filled with ~ of me/at my success.* 他十分羡慕我(我的成功). *My success excited his ~.* 我的成功引起了他的羡慕。 *They say such scandalous things about you out of ~.* 他们出于嫉妒才这样毁谤你。 **2** object of such feeling: 羡慕的对象; 嫉妒的对象: *His splendid new car was the ~ of all his friends/an object of ~ to all his friends.* 他那部豪华的

新车是他所有的朋友羡慕的东西。

envy[2] /ˈenvɪ; ˈɛnvɪ/ *vt* (*pt, pp* **-vied**) [VP6A, 12C] feel envy of: 羡慕; 嫉妒: *I ~ you.* 我羡慕你。 *I ~ your good fortune.* 我羡慕你的好运。 *I don't ~ him his bad-tempered wife,* am glad I am not married to her. 我不羡慕他有个坏脾气的妻子。

en·wrap /ɪnˈræp; ɛnˈræp/ *vt* **(-pp-) =** **wrap** (the more usu word). (wrap 较常用)。

en·zyme /ˈenzaɪm; ˈɛnzaɪm/ *n* [C] organic chemical substance (a catalyst) formed in living cells, able to cause changes in other substances without being changed itself. 酶。

eon /ˈiːən; ˈiən/ *n* = **aeon.**

ep·aulet (also **ep·aul·ette**) /ˈepəlet; ˈɛpəˌlɛt/ *n* shoulder ornament on a naval or military officer's uniform. (海军或陆军军官之)肩章。

épée /ˈeɪpeɪ; ˈe,pe/ *n* (F) sharp-pointed slender sword used in fencing. (法)(击剑用的)尖剑。

ephem·er·al /ɪˈfemərəl; əˈfemərəl/ *adj* living, lasting for a very short time. 生命短促的; 短暂的; 瞬息的。

epic /ˈepɪk; ˈɛpɪk/ *n, adj* (poetic account) of the deeds of one or more great heroes, or of a nation's past history, eg Homer's *Iliad;* (colloq) (subject) fit to be celebrated as heroic: 描写英雄事迹的诗(例如荷马的《伊利亚特》);史诗;叙事诗;写英雄事迹的;史诗的;叙事诗的; (口)英勇值得颂扬的(事迹): *an ~ achievement.* 值得颂扬的英勇成就。

epi·centre (US = **-center**) /ˈepɪsentə(r); ˈɛpɪˌsɛntɚ/ *n* point at which an earthquake reaches the earth's surface. 地震中心; 震央; 震中。

epi·cure /ˈepɪkjuə(r); ˈɛpɪˌkjʊr/ *n* person who understands the pleasures to be had from delicate eating and drinking. 喜美食醇酒之人;会享受口福之人。

epi·cur·ean /ˌepɪkjuˈriːən; ˌɛpɪkjuˈriən/ *n, adj* (person) devoted to pleasure (esp refined sensuous enjoyment): 享乐主义者;喜享乐(尤指感官上的享受)的: *an ~ feast.* 盛宴。

epi·demic /ˌepɪˈdemɪk; ˌɛpəˈdɛmɪk/ *n, adj* (disease) spreading rapidly among many people in the same place for a time: 流行病; 传染病; 流行性的: *an influenza ~.* 流行性感冒。 ⇨ **endemic.**

epi·der·mis /ˌepɪˈdɜːmɪs; ˌɛpəˈdɝmɪs/ *n* [U] outer layer of the skin. 外皮; 表皮。

epi·dia·scope /ˌepɪˈdaɪəskəup; ˌɛpɪˈdaɪəˌskop/ *n* optical lantern which projects on a screen transparent objects (eg film-strip) and opaque objects (eg coins, pictures). 实物幻灯机(可映出透明物体如幻灯片,及不透明物体如硬币和画片)。

epi·glot·tis /ˌepɪˈɡlɒtɪs; ˌɛpəˈɡlɑtɪs/ *n* structure of tissue at the root of the tongue, lowered during swallowing to prevent food, etc from entering the windpipe. 会厌软骨(位于舌根,吞食时能降下以阻止食物等进入气管)。 ⇨ the illus at **head.** 参看 head 之插图。

epi·gram /ˈepɪɡræm; ˈɛpəˌɡræm/ *n* short poem or saying expressing an idea in a clever and amusing way. 警句; 隽语。 **~·matic** /ˌepɪɡrəˈmætɪk; ˌɛpəɡrəˈmætɪk/ *adj* short and witty in expression; (of a person) fond of making ~s. 短而机智的; (指人)喜作隽语的。

epi·lepsy /ˈepɪlepsɪ; ˈɛpəˌlɛpsɪ/ *n* [U] nervous disease causing a person to fall unconscious (often with violent involuntary movements). 癫痫病。 **epi·lep·tic** /ˌepɪˈleptɪk; ˌɛpəˈlɛptɪk/ *adj* of ~: 癫痫症的: *an epileptic fit.* 癫痫症突发。 □ *n* person suffering from ~. 癫痫症患者。

epi·logue (US = **-log**) /ˈepɪlɒɡ *US*: -lɔːɡ; ˈɛpəˌlɔɡ/ *n* last part of a literary work, esp a poem spoken by an actor at the end of a play; (radio, TV) religious programme at the end of the day's transmission. 文学作品之结尾; (尤指戏剧结尾由演员念出之)收场白;(广播,电

视)一日播送结束时之宗教节目。

Epiph·any /ɪ'pɪfənɪ; ɪ'pɪfənɪ/ n commemoration (6 Jan) of the coming of the Magi /'meɪdʒaɪ; 'medʒaɪ/ (the *Three Wise Men*) to Jesus at Bethlehem. 主显节 (庆祝一月六日东方三博士至伯利恒礼拜耶稣). Cf 参较 *Twelfth Night*.

epis·co·pal /ɪ'pɪskəpl; ɪ'pɪskəpl/ adj of, governed by, bishops: 主教的;主教管辖的: the E~ *Church*, (esp) the Anglican Church in the US and Scotland. (尤指在美国和苏格兰的)英国国教; 主教派教会; 圣公会。**epis·co·pa·lian** / ɪ,pɪskə'peɪlɪən; ɪ,pɪskə'peɪlɪən / n, adj (member) of an ~ church. 主教派教友; 圣公会教徒; 主教派的; 圣公会的。

epi·sode /'epɪsəʊd; 'epə,sod/ n [C] (description of) one event in a chain of events. 一连串事件中的一个事件; 插曲。**epi·sodic** /epɪ'sɒdɪk; ,epə'sadɪk/ adj sporadic. 时有时无的; 零星的。

epistle /ɪ'pɪsl; ɪ'pɪsl/ n (old use, or joc) letter. (旧用法, 或谑) 书信。the E~s, letters included in the New Testament, written by the Apostles. (新约)使徒书信。**epis·tol·ary** US: -lerɪ; ɪ'pɪstə,lerɪ/ adj of, carried on by, letters. 书信的; 由书信传递的。

epi·taph /'epɪtɑːf US: -tæf; 'epə,tæf/ n [C] words commemorating a dead person (eg as cut on his tombstone). 墓志铭。

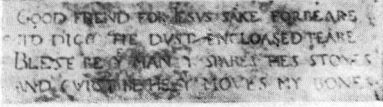

the epitaph on Shakespeare's tombstone

epi·thet /'epɪθet; 'epə,θet/ n adjective or descriptive phrase used to indicate the character of sb or sth, as in 'Alfred the *Great*'. 表性质的形容词; 附于人名后之描述词(例如 Alfred the Great 中之 Great)。

epit·ome /ɪ'pɪtəmɪ; ɪ'pɪtəmɪ/ n short summary of a book, speech, etc; sth which shows, on a small scale, the characteristics of sth much larger; sth or sb that perfectly displays a quality, type, etc: 摘要; 缩影; 完全显示一性质, 型态等的人或物; 典型: the ~ *of a loving mother*. 慈母的典型。**epit·om·ize** /ɪ'pɪtəmaɪz; ɪ'pɪtə,maɪz/ vt [VP6A] make ~ of: 摘要; 为…之缩影; 为…之典型: *She epitomizes a loving mother*. 她是慈母的典型。

ep·och /'iːpɒk US: 'epək; 'epək/ n (beginning of a) period of time in history, life, etc marked by special events or characteristics: (新) 纪元; (历史, 生活等中的特殊事件或特点的)时代: *Einstein's theory marked a new* ~ *in mathematics*. 爱因斯坦的学说在数学上开一新纪元。**'~-making**, beginning a new ~: 划时代的; 开创新纪元的: *an ~-making discovery*, eg of America by Columbus. 划时代的发现(例如哥伦布之发现美洲)。

Ep·som salts /,epsəm 'sɔːlts; ,epsəm 'sɔlts/ n pl hydrated magnesium sulphate ($MgSo_4$), used medically to empty the bowels. 泻盐。

equable /'ekwəbl; 'ekwəbl/ adj steady; regular; not changing much: 稳定的; 固定的; 变化甚小的: an ~ *climate / temper*. 稳定的气候(平和的性情)。**equably** /'ekwəblɪ; 'ekwəblɪ/ adv

equal /'iːkwəl; 'ikwəl/ adj 1 the same in size, amount, number, degree, value, etc: (大小, 数量, 数目, 程度, 价值等)相等的; 同样的; 平等的: ~ *pay for* ~ *work*; 同工同酬; ~ *opportunity*; 机会均等; ~ *in ability*; 能力相等; *divide sth into two* ~ *parts*; 将某物二等分; *two boys of* ~ *height*. 一样高的两个男孩子。He speaks English and Arabic with ~ *ease*. 他说英语和阿拉伯语同样的流利。*Things which are* ~ *to the same thing are* ~ *to one another*. 与一物相同之各物彼此亦相同。2 ~ *to sth / to doing sth*, having strength, courage, ability, etc for: 有…之力量, 勇气, 能力等: *He was* ~ *to the occasion*, was able to deal with it. 他能应付这个局势。*She did*

not feel ~ to receiving visitors. 她的身体不适, 不能接见客人。□ n person or thing ~ to another: 相等的人或物: *Is he your* ~ *in strength?* 他在力气方面和我相等吗? *Let* x *be the* ~ *of* y. 设 x 与 y 相等。□ vt (-ll-, US also -l-) [VP6A, 15A] be ~ to: 等于: *He* ~s *me in strength but not in intelligence*. 他在力气方面和我相等, 但在智力方面却不如我。*He is* ~led *by no one in strength*. 在力气方面无人能比得过他。**~ly** /'iːkwəlɪ; 'ikwəlɪ/ adv in an ~ manner; in ~ shares: 同样地; 同样地: ~ly *clever*. 同样地聪明。*Divide it* ~ly. 将它等分。**~·ity** /ɪ'kwɒlətɪ; ɪ'kwɑlətɪ/ n [U] the state of being ~: 相等; 平等; 同等: *on terms of* ~ *(with)*, on ~ *terms (with)*. 与…平等相处。**~·i·tarian** /ɪ,kwɒlɪ'teərɪən; ɪ,kwɑlə'tɛrɪən / n = egalitarian. **~·ize** /'iːkwəlaɪz; 'ikwə,laɪz/ vt [VP6A] make ~: 使相等; 使平等: ~ize *incomes*. 使收入均等。**~·iz·ation** /iːkwəlaɪ'zeɪʃn US: -lɪ'z-; ,ikwələ'zeʃən/ n

equa·nim·ity /,ekwə'nɪmətɪ; ,ikwə'nɪmətɪ/ n [U] calmness of mind or temper: 平静; 镇定: *bear misfortune with* ~; 对于不幸泰然处之; *disturb sb's* ~. 扰乱某人心中之平静。

equate /ɪ'kweɪt; ɪ'kwet/ vt [VP6A, 14] ~ *(with)*, consider, treat (one thing as being equal): 认为相等; 视为相等: (maths) (数学) ~ *two quantities*. 使二量相等。

equa·tion /ɪ'kweɪʒn; ɪ'kweʒən/ n 1 [C] (maths) statement of equality between two expressions by the sign = as in: $2x+5=11$. (数学)等式; 方程式 (例如: $2x+5=11$). 2[U] ~ *(with)*, making equal, balancing, eg of demand and supply. 使相等; 平衡(例如需要和供给间之平衡)。

equa·tor /ɪ'kweɪtə(r); ɪ'kwetə/ n imaginary line round the earth; line drawn on maps to represent points at an equal distance from the north and south poles. 赤道。⇨ the illus at **projection**. 参看 projection 之插图。**~·ial** /,ekwə'tɔːrɪəl; ,ikwə'tɔrɪəl/ adj of or near the ~: 赤道的; 近赤道的: ~ial *Africa*. 非洲近赤道的地区。

equerry /ɪ'kwerɪ; 'ekwərɪ/ n (pl **-rrie**) officer in the court of a ruler; officer in attendance on a member of the royal family. 王室武官; 王室侍卫官。

eques·trian /ɪ'kwestrɪən; ɪ'kwestrɪən / adj of horse-riding: 骑马的; ~ *skill*; 骑术; an ~ *statue*, of a person on horseback. 骑马者的雕像。□ n person clever at horse-riding. 精通骑术者; 善骑者。

equi·dis·tant /,iːkwɪ'dɪstənt; ,ikwə'dɪstənt/ adj ~ *(from)*, separated by equal distances. 等距的。

equi·lat·eral /,iːkwɪ'lætərəl; ,ikwə'lætərəl / adj having all sides equal: 等边的: an ~ *triangle*. 等边三角形。

equi·lib·rium /,iːkwɪ'lɪbrɪəm; ,ikwə'lɪbrɪəm / n [U] state of being balanced: 平衡; 均势: *maintain / lose one's* ~; 保持(失去)平衡; *scales* (on a balance) *in* ~. 平衡的天秤。

equine /'ekwaɪn; 'ikwaɪn/ adj (formal) of, like, a horse; of horses. (正式用语)马的; 似马的。

equi·noc·tial /,iːkwɪ'nɒkʃl; ,ikwə'nɑkʃəl/ adj of, at or near, the equinox: 昼夜平分时的; 近昼夜平分时的; 春分的; 秋分的: ~ *gales / tides*. 春(秋)分时的风(潮)。

equi·nox /'iːkwɪnɒks; 'ikwə,nɑks/ n time of the year at which the sun crosses the equator and when day and night are of equal length: 昼夜平分时; 春分; 秋分: the *spring* (= vernal) ~, around 20 Mar; 春分(约在三月二十日); the *autumnal* ~, around 22 Sept. 秋分(约在九月二十二日)。

equip /ɪ'kwɪp; ɪ'kwɪp/ vt (-pp-) [VP6A, 14] ~ *(with)*, supply (a person, oneself, a ship, etc) with what is needed, for a purpose: 供给(某人, 自己, 船只等)以所需的东西; 装备: ~ *oneself for a task*; 使自己准备好去做一工作; ~ *a ship for a voyage*; 装备一船以便出航; ~ *soldiers with uniforms and weapons*. 以服装和

武器装备军队. **~·ment** n [U] **1** ~ping or being ~ped: 装备: *The ~ment of his laboratory took time and money.* 装备他的实验室花了很多时间和金钱. **2** (collective noun) things needed for a purpose: (集合名词)装备品; 设备品: *a factory with modern ~ment;* 有现代化设备的一家工厂; '*radar ~ment.* 雷达装置.

equi·page /'ekwɪpɪdʒ; 'ɛkwəpɪdʒ/ n [C] equipment, outfit; carriage, horses and attendants (of a rich person in former times). 装备; 用具; (昔时富人之)马车, 马匹和随从.

equi·poise /'ekwɪpɔɪz; 'ɛkwə,pɔɪz/ n [U] equilibrium; [C] thing that counterbalances. 平衡; 平衡物.

equi·table /'ekwɪtəbl; 'ɛkwɪtəbl/ adj fair; just; reasonable. 公平的; 公正的; 合理的. **equi·tably** /-blɪ; -blɪ/ adv

equity /'ekwɪtɪ; 'ɛkwətɪ/ n **1** [U] fairness; right judgement; (esp, English law) principles of justice outside common law or Statute law, used to correct laws when these would apply unfairly in special circumstances. 公平; 公正; (尤用于英国法律)平衡法(用以纠正在特殊情况下被误用的法律). **2** (often pl) (-ties) ordinary stocks and shares not bearing fixed interest. (常用复数)无固定利息的股票.

equiv·al·ent / ɪ'kwɪvələnt; ɪ'kwɪvələnt/ adj ~ (to), equal in value, amount, meaning: (价值, 数量, 意义)相等的: *What is $5 ~ to in French france?* 五块美金等于法国几法郎? □ n sth that is ~: 相等物; 等同词; the same: *Is there a French word that is the exact ~ of the English word 'home'?* 法语中有没有一个英语'home'的等词同? **equiv·al·ence** /-əns; -əns/ n [U] being ~; [C] sth that is ~. 相等; 相等物.

equivo·cal /ɪ'kwɪvəkl; ɪ'kwɪvəkl/ adj **1** having a double or doubtful meaning; open to doubt: 模棱两可的; 意义不明的; 暧昧的: *an ~ reply.* 模棱两可的答复. **2** questionable; suspicious: 不可靠的; 可疑的: *an ~ success.* 可疑的成功. **equivo·ca·tion** / ɪ,kwɪvə'keɪʃn; ɪ,kwɪvə'keʃən/ n [U] the use of ~ statements to mislead people. 说模棱两可的话. **2** [C] ~ expression. 模棱两可的话; 暧昧语.

era /'ɪərə; 'ɪrə/ n [C] period in history, starting from a particular time or event: 纪元; 时代; 代: *the Christian era.* 耶稣纪元.

eradi·cate /ɪ'rædɪkeɪt; ɪ'rædɪ,ket/ vt [VP6A] pull up by the roots; put an end to, get rid of: 根除; 消灭: *~ crime/typhoid fever.* 根除罪恶(伤寒). **eradi·ca·tion** /ɪ,rædɪ'keɪʃn; ɪ,rædɪ'keʃən/ n

erase /ɪ'reɪz US: ɪ'reɪs; ɪ'res/ vt [VP6A] rub or scrape out; remove all traces of: 擦掉; 抹掉; 抹去: ~ *pencil marks.* 擦去铅笔的笔迹. ~**r** /ɪ'reɪzə(r) US: -sər; ɪ'resɚ/ n thing used to ~: 橡皮擦; 黑板擦: *a pencil ~r* (usu 通常 = *rubber[1](2)).* 铅笔擦. **eras·ure** /ɪ'reɪʒə(r); ɪ'reʒɚ/ n [U] erasing; [C] sth ~d; place where sth has been ~d. 擦去; 被擦之物; 被擦之处.

ere /eə(r); ɛr/ adv, prep (old use, or poet) before, (旧用法或诗)在前; 在…以前.

erect[1] /ɪ'rekt; ɪ'rɛkt/ adj upright; standing on end: 直立的; 竖起的: *stand ~;* 直立; *hold a banner ~.* 握着旗子使其直立. ~**·ly** adv ~**·ness** n

erect[2] /ɪ'rekt; ɪ'rɛkt/ vt [VP6A] **1** build, set up, establish: 建筑; 建立; 设立: ~ *a monument;* 立一纪念碑; ~ *a statue (to sb);* (给某人)立一雕像; ~ *a tent.* 搭帐篷. **2** set upright: 使直立; 竖起: ~ *a flagstaff.* 竖立一旗竿. **erec·tile** US: -tl; ɪ'rɛktl/ adj (physiol) (capable of) becoming rigid from dilation of the blood-vessels: (生理)能勃起的; 勃起性的: ~ *tissue.* 勃起性的组织. **erec·tion** /ɪ'rekʃn; ɪ'rɛkʃən/ n **1** [U] act of ~ing; state of being ~ed; (physiol) hardening and swelling of the penis or clitoris. 建筑; 建立; 竖立; (生理)阴茎或阴蒂之勃起. **2** [C] sth ~ed; building or structure. 建筑物.

ere·mite /'erɪmaɪt; 'ɛrə,maɪt/ n = **hermit**.

erg /ɜːg; ɝg/ n unit of energy in the metric system. 尔格(功的单位).

ergo /'ɜːgəʊ; 'ɝgo/ adv (Lat) (usu hum) therefore. (拉)(通常用作诙谐语)所以.

ergo·nom·ics /ˌɜːgə'nɒmɪks; ˌɝgə'nɑmɪks/ n pl (with sing vb) study of the environment, conditions and efficiency of workers. (与单数动词连用)研究工作者的环境与效率的科学; 人类工程学.

Erin /'erɪn; 'ɛrɪn/ n (old name for) Ireland. (旧称)爱尔兰.

er·mine /'ɜːmɪn; 'ɝmɪn/ n **1** small animal whose fur is brown in summer and white (except for its black-pointed tail) in winter. 貂. **2** [U] its fur; garment made of this fur: 貂皮; 貂皮制的衣服: *dressed in ~;* 穿貂皮衣服; *a gown trimmed with ~.* 饰有貂皮的长服.

erode /ɪ'rəʊd; ɪ'rod/ vt [VP6A] (of acids, rain, etc) wear away; eat into: (指酸, 雨等)侵蚀; 腐蚀: *Metals are ~d by acids.* 金属为酸所侵蚀. **ero·sion** /ɪ'rəʊʒn; ɪ'roʒən/ n [U] eroding or being ~d: 侵蚀; 腐蚀: *soil erosion,* by wind and rain; (风雨所造成的)土壤浸蚀; *coast erosion,* by the sea. (海洋所造成的)海岸侵蚀. **ero·sive** /ɪ'rəʊsɪv; ɪ'rosɪv/ adj

erog·en·ous /ɪ'rɒdʒənəs; ɪ'rɑdʒənəs/ adj (esp in): (尤用于): ~ '**zone**, area of the body particularly sensitive to sexual stimulation. (身体上对性刺激敏感之)动情区.

erotic /ɪ'rɒtɪk; ɪ'rɑtɪk/ adj of sexual desire. 性欲的; 色情的. **erot·ica** /ɪ'rɒtɪkə; ɪ'rɑtɪkə/ n pl books, pictures, etc intended to arouse sexual desire. 黄色书刊; 春宫画片. **eroti·cism** /ɪ'rɒtɪsɪzəm; ɪ'rɑtə,sɪzəm/ n [U] sexual desire. 性欲.

err /ɜː(r) US: eər; ɝ/ vi [VP2A, C] (formal) make mistakes; do or be wrong: [正式用语]犯错; 做错: *It is better to err on the side of mercy,* be too merciful than too severe. 过于仁慈比过于严厉好.

er·rand /'erənd; 'ɛrənd/ n **1** short journey to take or get sth, eg a message, goods from a shop: (短程)差使 (例如送信,取货等): *to go on ~s for sb;* 为某人去办事; *to run ~s.* 出差; 跑腿. **2** object or purpose of such a journey. 差使的目的; 差事. **fool's ~**, one with no real or useful purpose. 无目的之差使; 无谓的奔走.

er·rant /'erənt; 'ɛrənt/ adj erring; mistaken: 犯错的; 错误的: *an ~ husband,* one who is unfaithful to his wife. 对妻子不忠实的丈夫.

er·ratic /ɪ'rætɪk; ə'rætɪk/ adj **1** (of a person or his behaviour) irregular in behaviour or opinion; likely to do unusual or unexpected things. (指人或其行为)乖僻的; 古怪的; 言行反复无常的. **2** (of things, eg a clock) uncertain in movement; irregular. (指物, 例如钟)不稳定的; 不规律的. **er·rati·cally** /-klɪ; -klɪ/ adv

er·ratum /e'rɑːtəm; ɪ'retəm/ n (pl **-ta** /-tə; -tə/) (Lat) error in printing or writing: (拉)印刷或书写错误: *an errata slip,* list of errors, misprints, etc in a printed book. 书中勘误表.

er·ron·eous /ɪ'rəʊnɪəs; ə'ronɪəs/ adj incorrect; mistaken. 错误的. ~**·ly** adv

er·ror /'erə(r); 'ɛrɚ/ n **1** [C] sth done wrong; mistake: 差错; 错误: *spelling ~s;* 拼字错误; *printer's ~s,* misprints; 印刷错误; *an ~ of judgement;* 判断错误; *a clerical ~,* made in writing. 书写错误. 笔误. **2** [U] condition of being wrong in belief or conduct: 谬见; 行为不正: *fall/lead sb into ~;* 误(引某人)入歧途; *do sth in ~,* by mistake. 错做一事.

er·satz /'eəzæts US: 'eərzɑːts; ɛr'zats/ adj (G) imitation, substitute (esp inferior): (德)仿造的; 人造的(尤指品质低劣的): ~ *coffee/whisky/silk.* 仿造的咖啡(威士忌, 丝).

Erse /ɜːs; ɝs/ n Scottish Gaelic or Irish Gaelic. 苏格兰之盖尔语; 爱尔兰之盖尔语.

eruc·ta·tion /ˌiːrʌk'teɪʃn/ /ˌrʌk'teʃən/ n [U, C] (formal) belching, esp of a volcano. (正式用语) (尤指火山之) 喷出。

eru·dite /'eruˌdaɪt/ /ˈeruˌdaɪt/ adj (formal) having, showing, great learning; scholarly. (正式用语) 饱学的; 博学的。 ~·ly adv eru·di·tion /ˌeruː'dɪʃn/ /ˌeru'dɪʃən/ n [U] learning. 学问; 学识。

erupt /ɪ'rʌpt/ /ɪ'rʌpt/ vi [VP2A] (esp of a volcano) break out. (尤指火山) 爆发。 erup·tion /ɪ'rʌpʃn/ /ɪ'rʌpʃən/ n [C] outbreak of a volcano; (fig) outbreak of war, disease, etc: 火山爆发; (喻) (战争, 疾病等之) 爆发; 发作; 暴发: ~ions of ashes and lava; 灰烬和熔岩的喷发; in a state of ~ion. 爆发。

ery·sip·elas /ˌerɪ'sɪpɪləs/ /ˌerə'sɪpləs/ n [U] skin disease that causes fever and produces deep red inflammation. 丹毒 (一种皮肤病, 会引起发烧, 使皮肤发炎而且变成深红色)。

es·ca·late /'eskəleɪt/ /ˈeskəˌlet/ vt, vi [VP2A, 6A] increase, develop, intensify by successive stages. 逐渐增加; 增强; 扩大; 逐步升级。 es·ca·la·tion /ˌeskə'leɪʃn/ /ˌeskə'leʃən/ n

es·ca·la·tor /'eskəleɪtə(r)/ /ˈeskəˌletə/ n moving stairway carrying people up or down between floors or different levels. 自动梯。

es·ca·lope /'eskələup/ /ˈeskələp/ n slice of boneless meat, esp veal. 一片无骨的肉 (尤指小牛肉)。

es·ca·pade /'eskəpeɪd/ /ˈeskəˌped/ n [C] daring, mischievous or adventurous act, often causing gossip or trouble. 大胆的, 恶作剧的或冒险的行为 (常招致闲言或麻烦者)。

es·cape¹ /ɪ'skeɪp/ /ə'skep/ n 1 [C, U] (act of) escaping; fact of having escaped: 逃走; 逃脱; 漏出: E~ from Dartmoor prison is difficult. 从达特木监狱逃走是困难的。 There have been very few successful ~s from this prison. 很少有人成功地自此狱中逃走。 I congratulate you on your ~ from the shipwreck. 恭喜你脱自船难中逃还。 Don't look for an ~ of gas with a lighted match. 不要用燃着的火柴去寻找漏煤气的地方。 '~ velocity, the speed at which a projectile or spacecraft must travel in order to leave a (eg the earth's) gravitational field. 发射体或太空船脱离地心吸力之速度; 逃逸速度。 2 [C] means of escape: 逃脱之方法: a 'fire~; 太平梯; 太平门; an '~-pipe/-valve, for carrying off steam or water. 排气管 (活门); 排水管 (活门)。 3 (sth that provides) temporary distraction from reality or dull routine (eg through music, reading). 消遣 (例如听音乐, 读书等) ; 消遣物。 es·capee /ˌɪskeɪ'piː/ /ˈeske'pi/ n (esp) prisoner who has ~d. (尤指) 越狱的逃犯。 es·cap·ism /ɪ'skeɪpɪzm/ /-ɪzəm/ n [U] habit of escaping from unpleasant realities into a world of fancy. 逃避现实。 es·cap·ist /-ɪst/ /-ɪst/ n person whose conduct is characterized by escapism: 逃避现实者; 逃避主义者: (attrib) (用作定语) escapist literature. 逃避现实的文学。

es·cape² /ɪ'skeɪp/ /ə'skep/ vi, vt 1 [VP2A, 3A] ~ (from), get free; get away; (of steam, fluids, etc) find a way out: 逃脱; 逃走: (指蒸汽, 液体等) 漏出: Two of the prisoners have ~d. 有两个囚犯逃走了。 The canary has ~d from its cage. 金丝雀从笼中逃走了。 Is the gas escaping somewhere? 是不是有个地方漏煤气? Make a hole and let the water ~. 弄一个洞让水流出去。 2 [VP6A, C, 2A] avoid; keep free or safe from: 避免; 免除: You were lucky to ~ punishment/being punished. 你逃过了受罚, 真幸运。 Where can we go to ~ the crowds? 我们去何处才能躲开这群人? How can we ~ observation/being seen? 我们怎样才不会让人发现? 3 [VP6A] be forgotten or unnoticed by: 被…忘记; 未被…注意: His name ~s me for the moment, I cannot recall it. 我一时想不起他的名字来。

es·cape·ment /ɪ'skeɪpmənt/ /ə'skepmənt/ n [C] device in a clock or watch to regulate the movement. 钟表齿轮的擒纵器 (控制速度的装置); 司行轮。

es·carp·ment /ɪ'skɑːpmənt/ /ɪ'skɑrpmənt/ n long

steep slope or cliff separating two areas of different levels. 陡坡; 峭壁。

es·cha·tol·ogy /ˌeskə'tɒlədʒɪ/ /ˌeskə'talədʒi/ n [U] branch of theology concerned with death, judgement, heaven and hell. (神学之一支) 末世学 (研究死亡, 审判, 天堂和地狱) ; 终世论。

es·chew /ɪs'tʃuː/ /es'tʃu/ vt [VP6A] (formal) avoid (the more usu word); keep oneself away from, abstain from: (正式用语) 避免 (一字较常用); 戒除: ~ political debate. 避免政治辩论。

es·cort¹ /'eskɔːt/ /ˈeskɔrt/ n [C] 1 one or more persons going with another or others, or with valuable goods, to protect them, or as an honour: 护送者; 护送队; 仪 (仗) 队: an ~ of soldiers; 一队护送的士兵; under police ~. 在警察护送下。 2 one or more ships, aircraft, etc giving protection or honour: 护航的舰队或飞机等: When the Queen sailed, her yacht had an ~ of ten destroyers and fifty aircraft. 女王航海时, 她的游艇由十艘驱逐舰和五十架飞机担任护航。 3 person or persons accompanying sb for courtesy's sake: 礼貌上的伴随者: Mary's ~ to the ball. 伴随玛丽去舞会的人。

es·cort² /ɪ'skɔːt/ /ɪ'skɔrt/ vt [VP6A, 15B] go with as an escort: 护送; 护航: a convoy of merchant ships ~ed by destroyers. 由驱逐舰护航的商船队。 Who will ~ this young lady home? 谁愿意护送这位小姐回家?

es·cri·toire /ˌeskrɪ'twɑː(r)/ /ˌeskrɪ'twɑr/ n writing-desk with drawers for stationery. 写字台。

es·cutcheon /ɪ'skʌtʃən/ /ɪ'skʌtʃən/ n shield with a coat of arms on it. 饰有纹章的盾。 ⇨ the illus at armour. 参看 armour 之插图。 a blot on one's ~, a stain on one's reputation. 名誉上的污点。

Es·kimo /'eskɪməu/ /ˈeskɪˌmo/ n (pl ~s or ~es /-məuz/ /-moz/), member of a people living in the Arctic regions of N America and E Siberia. 爱斯基摩人。

esopha·gus (also **oesopha·gus**) /iː'sɒfəgəs/ /i'sɑfəgəs/ n passage from the pharynx to the stomach; gullet. 咽管; 食道。 ⇨ the illus at alimentary, head. 参看 alimentary, head 之插图。

eso·teric /ˌesəu'terɪk/ /ˌesə'tɛrɪk/ adj intended only for those who are initiated, for a small circle of disciples or followers, abstruse. 秘密的; 奥传的。

es·palier /ɪ'spælɪə(r)/ /ɛ'spæljɚ/ n (tree or shrub trained on a) trellis or a wire framework. 树棚; 树架; 树架上之树。

es·pecial /ɪ'speʃl/ /ə'spɛʃəl/ adj particular; exceptional: 特别的; 特殊的: a question of ~ importance; 特别重要的问题; for your ~ benefit. 为了你的特殊利益。 in ~, above all. 尤其是。 ~·ly /-ʃəlɪ/ /-ʃli/ adv to an exceptional degree; in particular: 特别地; 尤其: She likes the country, ~ly in spring. 她喜爱乡间, 尤其在春天。

Es·per·anto /ˌespə'ræntəu/ /ˌespə'ranto/ n [U] an artificial language designed for world use. (一种人造的) 世界语。

espion·age /'espɪənɑːʒ/ /ˈespɪənɪdʒ/ n [U] practice of spying or using spies. 侦探; 间谍活动。

es·pla·nade /ˌesplə'neɪd/ /ˌesplə'ned/ n [C] level area of ground where people may walk or ride for pleasure, often by the sea. 游逛的广场 (常指位于海滨者)。

es·pouse /ɪ'spauz/ /ɪ'spauz/ vt [VP6A] 1 give one's support to (a cause, theory, etc). 拥护 (主义, 学说等)。 2 (old use; of a man) marry. (旧用法; 指男子) 娶。 es·pousal /ɪ'spauzl/ /ɪ'spauzl/ n 1 espousing (of a cause, etc). (主义等的) 拥护; 赞助。 2 (old use; usu pl) marriage or betrothal. (旧用法; 通常用复数) 结婚; 婚约。

es·presso /e'spresəu/ /ɛ'prɛso/ n, ~ 'coffee, coffee made by forcing boiling water under pressure through ground coffee. 一种使开水在压力下冲过咖啡粉而煮成的咖啡。

esprit /e'spriː/ /ɛ'spri/ n [U] (F) lively wit. (法) 机智。 ~ de corps /ˌespriː də 'kɔː(r)/ /ɛ'spridə'kɔr/ n

spirit of loyalty and devotion which unites the members of a group or society. 团队精神.

espy /ɪ'spaɪ; ə'spaɪ/ *vt* (*pt, pp* **-pied**) [VP6A] (usu joc) catch sight of. (通常为谑)看见; 发现.

Es·quire /ɪ'skwaɪə(r) *US:* 'es-; es'kwaɪə/ *n* title of courtesy (used in GB and written **Esq**, esp in the address of a letter after a man's family name instead of *Mr* before it): 先生(用于英国, 略作 Esq, 尤用作信件中男子姓氏后的尊称, 以代替用于姓氏前的 Mr): *Edgar Broughton, Esq.* 爱德嘉·布劳顿先生.

es·say[1] /'eseɪ; 'ese/ *n* piece of writing, usu short and in prose, on any one subject. 文章; 短论; 随笔; 小品文. ~·**ist** /-ɪst; -ɪst/ *n* writer of ~s. 散文家; 随笔作家; 小品文作者.

es·say[2] /e'seɪ; e'se/ *vt, vi* [VP6A, 4A] try; attempt: 试验; 企图: ~ *a task*; 试做一工作; ~ *to do sth.* 企图做某事. □ *n* /'eseɪ; e'se/ **1** testing or trial of the value or nature of sth. 对某物价值或性质的试验. **2** attempt. 企图.

es·sence /'esns; 'esns/ *n* **1** [U] that which makes a thing what it is; the inner nature or most important quality of a thing: 要素; 精髓; 精essence: *Is the ~ of morality right intention?* 道德的真髓在于心正吗? *Caution is the ~ of that man's character.* 谨慎是那人性格的本质. *The two things are the same in outward form but different in ~.* 那两样东西在外表上相同, 但在本质上不同. **2** [C, U] extract obtained from a substance by taking out as much of the mass as possible, leaving all its important qualities in concentrated form: 精; 粹: *meat ~s*; 肉汁; ~ *of peppermint.* 薄荷精.

es·sen·tial /ɪ'senʃl; ə'senʃl/ *adj* **1** necessary; indispensable; most important: 必要的; 不可缺少的; 最重要的: *Is wealth ~ to happiness?* 财富对于幸福是必要的吗? *Exercise, fresh air and sleep are ~ for the preservation of health.* 运动, 新鲜空气和睡眠对于保持健康是必要的. *'Wanted, a good secretary: experience ~'.* '征求优良秘书一名: 须有经验者'. **2** of an essence(2): 精的: ~ *oils.* 香精油. **3** fundamental 基本的: *Love of fair play is said to be an ~ part of the English character.* 喜爱公平据说是英国人的性格中的基本性质. □ *n* [C] (usu *pl*) fundamental element: (通常用复数)要素; 要点: the *~s of English grammar.* 英语语法要义. *We've time to pack only the basic ~s*, the minimum amount (of clothes, etc) that is necessary. 我们只有将必要的东西(衣物等)包起来的时间. ~·**ly** /ɪ'senʃlɪ; ə'senʃəlɪ/ *adv* in an ~ (3) manner: 本质上: *We are an ~ly peace-loving people.* 我们基本上是爱好和平的民族.

es·tab·lish /ɪ'stæblɪʃ; ə'stæblɪʃ/ *vt* [VP6A, 14, 16B] **1** set up, put on a firm foundation: 建立; 设立; 确立: *a new state/government/business.* 建立一新国家(政府, 事业). **2** settle, place a person, oneself in a position, office, place, etc: 安置; 使任职; 使定居: *We are now comfortably ~ed in our new house.* 我们现在很舒适地住在我们的新居内了. *Mr X was ~ed as governor of the province.* X 先生被任命为省主席. **3** cause people to accept a belief, claim, custom, etc: 使人民接受(信仰, 要求, 风俗等); 确定: *He succeeded in ~ing a claim to the title.* 他成功地确立了对此权益或名份的要求权. *Newton conclusively ~ed the law of gravity.* 牛顿确立了万有引力的定律. *E~ed customs are difficult to change.* 既有的风俗难以改变. *His honesty is well ~ed.* 他的诚实是大家公认的. **4** make (a church) national by law. 使(教会)成为国教.

es·tab·lish·ment /ɪ'stæblɪʃmənt; ə'stæblɪʃmənt/ *n* **1** [U] establishing or being established: 建立; 设立; 确定: *the ~ of a new state.* 一新国家的建立. **2** [C] that which is established, eg a large organized body of persons (eg the army or navy; a civil service; a business firm, with many employees; a hotel and the staff in it). 经建立的机构(例如陆军, 海军, 政府机关, 有许多人员的公司行号, 旅社及其服务人员等). **3 the E~**, (GB) those persons in positions of power and authority, exercising

influence in the background of public life or other field of activity. (英)当权派.

es·tami·net /e'stæmɪneɪ *US:* eˌstæmɪ'neɪ; estami'ne/ *n* (F) small French café selling beer, wine, coffee, etc. (法)卖啤酒, 葡萄酒, 咖啡等的小店.

es·tate /ɪ'steɪt; ə'stet/ *n* **1** [C] piece of property in the form of land, esp in the country: 地产(尤指在乡间者): *He owns large ~s in Scotland.* 他在苏格兰有大批地产. '~ **agent**, (US 美=*Realtor*) person who buys and sells buildings and land for others. 房地产经纪人. '**housing ~**, area of land on which many houses are built, either by private enterprise or ('**council ~**) by a public authority. 住宅区(或由私人或由公家所建立的). **in'dustrial ~**, area of land development for industrial use (factories, etc). 工业区. **2** [C] (legal) a person's whole property. (法律)一人的全部财产. '**real ~**, land and buildings. 房地产; 不动产. '**personal ~**, money and other kinds of property. 动产. **3** [C] political or social group or class: 政治团体; 社会阶级: *the three ~s of the realm*, the Lords Spiritual (Bishops in the House of Lords), the Lords Temporal (other lords) and the House of Commons; 上议院僧主教议员, 上议院贵族议员与下议院议员; 贵族, 僧侣和平民; *the fourth ~*, the press(3). 新闻界(3). **4** (old use) condition; stage in life: (旧用法)状况; 生活阶段: *reach man's ~*; 成年; *the holy ~ of matrimony.* 神圣的婚姻生活. **5** '~ **car**, (US 美=*station-wagon*) saloon-type motor vehicle with removable or collapsible rear seats and door(s) at the back, for easy loading of luggage, etc. 旅行车 (设有可以移动的座位和后门, 以便易于装行李等).

es·teem /ɪ'stiːm; ə'stim/ *vt* **1** [VP6A] (formal) have a high opinion of; respect greatly: (正式用语)尊重; 尊敬: *No one can ~ your father more than I do.* 没有人比我更尊敬你的父亲了. **2** [VP25] (formal) consider; regard: (正式用语)认为; 以为: *I shall ~ it a favour if…* . 如果…我将深切厚意. *I it a privilege to address this audience.* 我认为能向诸位演讲是一种荣幸. □ *n* [U] high regard: 尊敬; 尊重: *He lowered himself in our ~ by this foolish behaviour.* 由于此一愚行, 他减低了我们对他的尊重. *We all hold him in great ~.* 我们都十分尊敬他.

es·thetic /ˌiːs'θetɪk; es'θetɪk/ = aesthetic.

es·ti·mable /'estɪməbl; 'estəməbl/ *adj* worthy of esteem. 值得尊敬的.

es·ti·mate[1] /'estɪmət; 'estəmɪt/ *n* [C] judgement; approximate calculation (of size, cost, etc): 判断; (大小, 价钱等之) 估计: *I hope the builders don't exceed their ~.* 我希望营造商们不要超过他们的估算. *I do not know enough about him to form an ~ of his abilities.* 我对他的了解不够, 不能对他的能力作估计. *Can you give me a rough ~ of the cost?* 你能将费用大约地估计一下吗? ⇨ **rough**[1](2). **outside** *adj* (2). the **E~s**, figures supplied each year by the Chancellor of the Exchequer showing the probable national expenditure, etc. 政府的岁费预算.

es·ti·mate[2] /'estɪmeɪt; 'estəˌmet/ *vt, vi* [VP9, 14, 3A] ~ (**at**), form a judgement about; calculate the cost, value, size, etc of sth: 评定; 估计(某物的价值, 价值, 大小等): *The firm ~d the cost of the work at £8000.* 这公司估计这工作的费用为八千英镑. *We ~ that it would take three months to finish the work.* 我们估计完成这工作需要三个月. *I ~ his income at / to be about £5000.* 我估计他的收入约为五千英镑. *Ask a contractor to ~ for the repair of the building.* 请个包工估计一下修理这房屋需要多少钱.

es·ti·ma·tion /ˌestɪ'meɪʃn; ˌestə'meʃən/ *n* [U] judgement; regard: 判断; 评价: *in my ~*; 据我的判断; *in the ~ of most people.* 在大多数人的心目中.

es·trange /ɪ'streɪndʒ; ə'strendʒ/ *vt* [VP6A, 14] ~ (**from**), bring about a separation in feeling and sympathy: 使疏远: *foolish behaviour that ~d all his friends*; 使所有朋友们与之疏远的愚行; ~ *sb from his*

friends. 使某人与其朋友们疏远。 *He is ~d from his wife,* living apart from her. 他和妻子分居。 **~·ment** *n* [U] being ~d; [C] instance of this: 被疏远；疏远: *cause an ~ment between two old friends.* 导致两位老朋友间之疏远。

es·tu·ary /'estjʊərɪ US: -ʊerɪ/ 'estʃʊ,ɛrɪ/ *n* (*pl* **-ries**) [C] river mouth into which the tide flows: (与海相连的)河口: *the Thames ~.* 泰晤士河河口。

et cet·era /ɪt 'setərə US: et; ɪt 'setərə/ (Lat, 拉, usu shortened to 通常略作 **etc**) and other things; and so on. 及其他；等等。

etch /etʃ; etʃ/ *vt, vi* [VP6A, 2A] use a needle and acid to make a picture, etc on a metal plate from which copies may be printed; make (pictures, etc) in this way. (用针和酸类在金属板上)蚀刻图画等; 以蚀刻术作(图画等)。 **~·er** *n* person who ~es. 蚀刻师; 用针和酸类在金属板上蚀刻图画等者。 **~·ing** *n* [U] the art of the ~er; [C] copy printed from an ~ed plate. 蚀刻术; 用蚀刻版印出之图画。

eter·nal /ɪ'tɜːnl; ɪ'tɜnl/ *adj* 1 without beginning or end; lasting for ever: 永恒的; 永远的: *the E~,* God; 上帝; *the E~ City,* Rome. 罗马。 *Does the Christian religion promise ~ life?* 基督教许诺永生吗？ 2 (colloq) unceasing; too frequent: (口)不断的; 不停的: *Stop this ~ chatter.* 不要吵嚷个不停。 *the ~ triangle,* situation of conflict in which two men want the same woman or two women the same man. 三角恋爱。 **~·ly** /ɪ'tɜːnəlɪ; ɪ'tɜnlɪ/ *adv* throughout all time; for ever; (colloq) (too) frequently. 永恒地; 久远地; (口)不停地。

eter·nity /ɪ'tɜːnɪtɪ; ɪ'tɜnətɪ/ *n* (*pl* **-ties**) 1 [U] time without end; the future life: 永恒; 来世: *send a man to ~,* to his death. 使某人死去。 2 an ~, period of time that seems endless: 似乎无终止的一段时间: *It seemed an ~ before news of his safety reached her.* 她的平安的消息到达她那里以前，那段时间似乎是漫长无限的。 3 (*pl*) eternal truths. (复)永久不变的真理。

ether /'iːθə(r); 'iθə/ *n* [U] 1 liquid made from alcohol, used in industry, and medically as an anaesthetic. 醚 (由酒精制成的一种无色液体，用于工业，医学上用作麻醉剂)。 2 medium(3) through which, it was once believed, light waves were transmitted through all space. 以太 (一度被认为充满整个空间，可借以传送光波的一种物质)。 3 (poet) the pure, upper air above the clouds. (诗)天空; 苍天。

eth·ereal /ɪ'θɪərɪəl; ɪ'θɪrɪəl/ *adj* 1 of unearthly delicacy; seeming too light or spiritual for this world: 轻妙的; 灵妙的; 超俗的: *~ beauty/music;* 轻妙的美(音乐); *the ~ figure of an angel.* 天使的飘然姿态。 2 (poet) of the pure, upper air above the clouds. (诗)天上的; 苍天的。

ethic /'eθɪk; 'ɛθɪk/ *n* a, system of moral principles, rules of conduct: 道德原则及行为准绳的体系: *Was Islam in Turkey a traditional social code or an ~ for living?* 在土耳其伊斯兰教是一传统的社会法典还是生活上的道德体系？ **eth·ics** *n pl* 1 (with *sing v*) science of morals: (与单数动词连用)伦理学: *E~s is a branch of philosophy.* 伦理学为哲学之一支。 2 (with *pl v*) moral soundness: (与复数动词连用)行为的准绳; 道德规范: *The ~s of his decision are doubtful.* 他的决定的道德准绳令人怀疑。 **ethi·cal** /-kl; -kl/ *adj* of morals or moral questions: 道德的; 伦理的; 道德问题的: *an ~al basis for education.* 教育的道德基础。 **ethi·cally** /-klɪ; -klɪ/ *adv*

eth·nic /'eθnɪk; 'ɛθnɪk/ *adj* of race or the races of mankind; (colloq) of a particular cultural group: 人种的; 种族的; (口)某一特殊文化团体的; 具有种族特色的: ~ *clothes/food/music;* 具有种族特色的服装(食物，音乐); *an ~ restaurant.* 具有种族特色的餐馆。 **eth·ni·cally** /-ɪklɪ; -ɪklɪ/ *adv*

eth·no·gra·phy /eθ'nɒɡrəfɪ; ɛθ'nɑɡrəfɪ/ *n* [U] scientific description of the races of mankind. 人种史; 人种学。 **eth·no·gra·pher** /eθ'nɒɡrəfə(r); ɛθ'nɑɡrəfə/

n **eth·no·graphic** /ˌeθnə'ɡræfɪk; ˌɛθnə'ɡræfɪk/ *adj*

eth·nol·ogy /eθ'nɒlədʒɪ; ɛθ'nɑlədʒɪ/ *n* [U] science of the races of mankind, their relations to one another, etc. 人种学。 **eth·nol·o·gist** /-dʒɪst; -dʒɪst/ *n* student of, expert in, ~. 人种学家; 人种学者。 **eth·no·logi·cal** /ˌeθnə'lɒdʒɪkl; ˌɛθnə'lɑdʒɪkl/ *adj* of ~. 人种学的。

ethos /'iːθɒs; 'iθɑs/ *n* characteristics of a community or of a culture; code of values by which a group or society lives. 社会的特质; 文化精神; 团体或社会的生活准则。

ethyl /'eθɪl; 'ɛθl/ *n* **~ alcohol,** the base of alcoholic drinks, also used as a fuel or solvent. 乙醇; 普通酒精。

eti·ology /ˌiːtɪ'ɒlədʒɪ; ˌitɪ'ɑlədʒɪ/ *n* assignment of a cause; (med) study of the causes of disease. 推究原因; (医)病原学。

eti·quette /'etɪket; 'ɛtɪkɛt/ *n* [U] rules for formal relations or polite social behaviour among people, in a class of society or a profession: 礼节; 礼仪; 规矩; 成规: *medical/legal ~.* 医学(法律)界的成规。

ety·mol·ogy /ˌetɪ'mɒlədʒɪ; ˌɛtə'mɑlədʒɪ/ *n* 1 [U] science of the origin and history of words. 词源学; 语源学。 2 [C] account of the origin and history of a word. 语源之记述。 **ety·mol·ogist** /-dʒɪst; -dʒɪst/ *n* student of ~. 语源学者。 **ety·mo·logi·cal** /ˌetɪmə'lɒdʒɪkl; ˌɛtəmə'lɑdʒɪkl/ *adj* of ~. 语源学的。

euca·lyptus /ˌjuːkə'lɪptəs; ˌjukə'lɪptəs/ *n* sorts of tall evergreen tree (including the Australian gum tree) from which an oil is obtained. 桉树类; 有加利树(包括澳洲橡皮树的数种长青树，自其中可提取一种油)。

Eu·char·ist /'juːkərɪst; 'jukərɪst/ *n* **the E~,** the Lord's Supper; the bread and wine taken at this. 圣餐; 圣餐中食用的面包和酒。 ⇨ **lord(2).**

Eu·clid·ean /juː'klɪdɪən; ju'klɪdɪən/ *adj* of the geometric principles of Euclid, tne Greek mathematician. (希腊数学家)欧几里德几何学的。

eu·gen·ics /juː'dʒenɪks; ju'dʒɛnɪks/ *n pl* (with *sing v*) science of the production of healthy offspring with the aim of improving the human genetic stock. (与单数动词连用)优生学; 人种改良学。

eu·logize /'juːlədʒaɪz; 'julə,dʒaɪz/ *vt* [VP6A] (formal) praise highly in speech or writing. (正式用语)颂扬。 **eu·logist** /-dʒɪst; -dʒɪst/ *n* person who does this. 颂扬者。 **eu·logis·tic** /ˌjuːlə'dʒɪstɪk; ˌjulə'dʒɪstɪk/ *adj* giving or containing high praise. 颂扬的; 歌颂的。 **eu·logy** /'juːlədʒɪ; 'julədʒɪ/ *n* (*pl* **-gies**) [C, U] (speech or writing full of) high praise. 颂扬; 颂词; 颂扬文。

eu·nuch /'juːnək; 'junək/ *n* castrated man, esp one formerly employed in some Oriental courts. 阉人; (尤指昔时东方宫廷的)太监; 宦官。

eu·phem·ism /'juːfəmɪzəm; 'jufə,mɪzəm/ *n* [C, U] (example of the) use of other (mild, vague and indirect) words or phrases in place of what is required by truth or accuracy: 委婉的说法; 委婉的话: *'Pass away' is a ~ for 'die'.* pass away 为die的委婉说法。 *'Pass water' is a ~ for 'urinate'.* pass water 为urinate的委婉说法。 **eu·phem·is·tic** /ˌjuːfə'mɪstɪk; ˌjufə'mɪstɪk/ *adj* of the nature of ~: 委婉的: *euphemistic language/ expressions.* 委婉的言语(措辞)。 **eu·phe·mis·ti·cally** /-klɪ; -klɪ/ *adv*

eu·phony /'juːfənɪ; 'jufənɪ/ *n* [U] pleasantness of sound; [C, U] (*pl* **-nies**) pleasant sound. 声音的谐和; 谐和的声音。

eu·phoria /juː'fɔːrɪə; ju'fɔrɪə/ *n* [U] state of well-being and pleasant excitement; elation. 舒适; 安乐; 兴高采烈。 **eu·phoric** /juː'fɒrɪk US: -'fɔrr-; ju'fɔrɪk/ *adj*

eu·phu·ism /'juːfjuːɪzəm; 'jufju,ɪzəm/ *n* [U] (instance of) elaborately artificial style of writing and speaking (as fashionable in England in the late 16th and early 17th cc). 夸饰的文体(如十六世纪末及十七世纪初英国所盛行的)。

Eur·asia /jʊə'reɪʒə; ju'reʒə/ *n* Europe and Asia. 欧

亚大陆。**Eur·asian** /juə'reɪʒn; ju'reʒən/ *n, adj* (person) of mixed European and Asian parentage; of Europe and Asia. 欧亚混血的(人); 欧亚大陆的。

eu·reka /juə'riːkə; ju'rikə/ *int* (Gk = 'I have found it!') cry of triumph at a discovery. (希) (发现时得意的欢呼) 我找到了!

eu·rhyth·mics (also **eu·ryth-**) /juː'rɪðmɪks; ju'rɪðmɪks/ *n pl* (with *sing v*) harmony of bodily movement, esp as a system of physical training with music. (与单数动词连用) 身体动作的协调; (尤指) 配合音乐的体操; 韵律体操。

Euro·dollar /'juərəʊdɒlə(r); 'jurə,dɑlə/ *n* US dollar put in European bank to act as an international currency and help the financing of trade and commerce. 欧洲美元; 存于欧洲银行的美元(用作国际货币, 以助贸易)。

Euro·pean /ˌjuərə'piən; ˌjurə'piən/ *n, adj* (native) of Europe; happening in, extending over, Europe: 欧洲人; 欧洲的; 发生在欧洲的; 延伸至欧洲的: *~ countries;* 欧洲各国; *a ~ reputation.* 遍及全欧的名声。

Euro·vision /'juərəvɪʒn; 'jurəvɪʒən/ *n* European TV network. 欧洲电视网。

Eu·sta·chian tube /juː'steɪʃn 'tjuːb US: 'tuːb; ju'stekɪən 'tjub/ *n* (anat) duct extending from the middle ear to the pharynx. (解剖) 欧氏管; 耳咽管。⇨ the illus at ear. 参看 ear 之插图。

eu·tha·nasia /ˌjuːθə'neɪzɪə US: -'neɪʒə; ˌjuθə'neʒə/ *n* [U] (bringing about of a) mercifully easy and painless death (for persons suffering from an incurable and painful disease). (患痛苦的不治之症者之) 无痛苦的死亡; 无痛苦致死术。

evacu·ate /ɪ'vækjueɪt; ɪ'vækjuˌet/ *vt* **1** [VP6A] (esp of soldiers) withdraw from; leave empty: (尤指军队) 撤离, 自…撤退: *~ a fort/town.* 撤离一堡垒(城镇)。 **2** [VP6A, 14] *~ sb (from) (to),* remove him from a place or district, eg one considered to be dangerous in time of war: 一到一地区(如战时危险地区)遣走(某人); 疏散: *The children were ~d to the country.* 孩子们被疏散至乡下。 **3** [VP6A] empty (of its contents); (esp) defecate. 排泄; (尤指) 大便。**evacu·ation** /ɪ,vækju'eɪʃn/ *n* [U] evacuating or being ~d; [C] instance of this. 撤离; 疏散; 除清。**evacuee** /ɪ,vækju'iː; ɪ'vækjuˌi/ *n* person who is ~d(2). 被疏散者。

evade /ɪ'veɪd; ɪ'ved/ *vt* [VP6A, C] **1** get, keep, out of the way of: 躲避; 逃避: *a blow/one's enemies/an attack.* 躲避一击(敌人, 攻击)。 **2** find a way of not doing sth: 避免(做某事): *~ paying income tax;* 避付所得税; *~ military service;* 逃避兵役; avoid answering (fully or honestly): 避免(充分或诚实地) 回答: *~ a question.* 避免回答一问题。

evalu·ate /ɪ'væljueɪt; ɪ'væljuˌet/ *vt* [VP6A] find out, decide, the amount or value of. 求出…的数量值; 决定…的数量或价值; 评价; 估计。**evalu·ation** /ɪ,vælju'eɪʃn; ɪ,væljuˈeʃən/ *n*

evan·escent /ˌiːvə'nesnt US: ˌev-; ˌevə'nɛsnt/ *adj* quickly fading; soon going from the memory: 迅速凋落的; 不久便被遗忘的: *~ political triumphs.* 政治上昙花一现的胜利。**evan·escence** /-sns; -sns/ *n*

evan·geli·cal /ˌiːvæn'dʒelɪkl; ˌivæn'dʒɛlɪkl/ *adj* **1** of, according to, the teachings of the Gospel: 福音的; 根据福音的: *~ preaching.* 福音传道。 **2** of the beliefs and teachings of those Protestants who maintain that the soul can be saved only by faith in Jesus Christ. 福音派新教会 (主张只有相信耶稣, 灵魂始能得救的)。**~ism** /-ɪzəm; -ɪzəm/ *n* [U] **~**(2) beliefs or teachings. 福音派新教会之信仰或教义。

evan·gel·ist /ɪ'vændʒəlɪst; ɪ'vændʒəlɪst/ *n* **1** one of the writers (Matthew, Mark, Luke or John) of the Gospels. 四福音书作者 (马太, 马可, 路加, 约翰) 之一。 **2** preacher of the Gospel, esp one who travels and holds religious meetings wherever he goes, preaching to any who are willing to listen. 福音传道者 (尤指旅行传道者)。**evan·gel·is·tic** /ɪ,vændʒə'lɪstɪk; ɪ,vændʒə'lɪstɪk/ *adj*

evap·or·ate /ɪ'væpəreɪt; ɪ'væpə,ret/ *vt, vi* **1** [VP6A, 2A] (cause to) change into vapour: (使) 蒸发: *Heat ~s water.* 热蒸发水。 *The water soon ~d.* 水不久便蒸发了。 **2** [VP6A] remove liquid from a substance, eg by heating: 除去(某物)之水分 (用加热): *~d milk.* 炼乳。 **3** [VP2A] disappear; die: 消失; 死亡: *His hopes ~d,* He no longer felt any hope. 他的希望消失了。**evap·or·ation** /ɪ,væpə'reɪʃn; ɪ,væpə'reʃən/ *n*

evas·ion /ɪ'veɪʒn; ɪ'veʒən/ *n* **1** [U] evading: 躲避; 逃避; 避免: *~ of responsibility.* 逃避责任。 **2** [C] statement, excuse, etc made to evade sth; act of evading: 遁词; 借口; 推托: *His answers to my questions were all ~s.* 他对我的问题的回答均为遁词。

evas·ive /ɪ'veɪsɪv; ɪ'vesɪv/ *adj* tending, trying, to evade: 躲避的; 逃避的; 避免的: *an ~ answer;* 遁词; 推托; *take ~ action,* do sth in order to evade danger, etc. 采取某种行动以求躲避 (危险等)。**~·ly** *adv*~**·ness** *n*

Eve /iːv; iv/ *n* (in the Bible story of the Creation) the first woman. (圣经创世纪中的) 夏娃 (世界第一个女人)。

eve /iːv; iv/ *n* day or evening before a Church festival or any day or event; time just before anything: (宗教节日, 任何日期或事件之) 前日或前夜; 前夕: *Christmas Eve,* 24 Dec; 圣诞节前夕 (十二月二十四日); *New Year's Eve,* 31 Dec; 除夕 (十二月三十一日); *on the eve of great events.* 重大事件之前夕。

even[1] /'iːvn; 'ivən/ *adj* **1** level; smooth: 平坦的; 平滑的: *A billiard-table must be perfectly ~.* 撞球台必须十分平坦。 **2** regular; steady; of unchanging quality: 有规律的; 不变的; 均匀的: *His ~ breathing showed that he had got over his excitement.* 他的均匀的呼吸显示出他已由兴奋转为平静了。 *His work is not very ~,* it is a mixture of good and bad. 他的作品好好坏坏。 **3** (of amounts, distances, values) equal: (指数量, 距离, 价值) 相等的: *Our scores are now ~.* 我们的得分现在相等。 *The two horses were ~ in the race.* 那两匹马竞赛的成绩相等。 *be/get ~ with sb,* have/get one's revenge on him. 向某人报复。 *~ odds,* chances which are the same for or against. 成败或正反的机会相等。 *break ~,* (colloq) make neither a profit nor a loss. (口) 不赚不赔; 得失相等。 **4** (of numbers) that can be divided by two with no remainder: (指数目) 可被二除尽的; 偶数的: *The pages on the left side of a book have ~ numbers.* 一本书左面的页码是偶数。⇨ odd. **5** equally balanced: 公平的; 均衡的: *an ~ chance;* 公平的机会; 均等 (in betting). (赌赛中) 相等的钱。 *~-handed adj* fair: 公正的; *~-handed justice.* 大公无私。 **6** (of temper, etc) calm; not easily disturbed: (指性情等) 平静的; 冷静的: *an ~-tempered baby.* 性情平静的婴孩。□ *vt* [VP6A, 15B] *~ (up),* make ~ or equal: 使平坦; 使平; 使相等: *That will ~ things up,* make them equal. 这可以使事情得其平。**~·ly** *adv* **~·ness** *n*

even[2] /'iːvn; 'ivən/ *adv* **1** (used to invite a comparison between what happened and what might have happened). 甚至; 即使 (用以就所发生者与可能发生者之间做一比较): *He never ~ 'opened the letter* (so he certainly did not read it). 他甚至连那封信都未打开过 (所以他一定没有看过). *He didn't answer ~ 'my letter* (not to mention letters from others). 他甚至连我的信都没有回复 (不用说别人的信了). *It was cold there ~ in Ju'ly* (so you may imagine how cold it was in winter). 那地方即使在七月里也是冷的 (所以你可以想象在冬天是多么寒冷). *E~ a 'child can understand the book* (so adults can certainly do so). 即使小孩子也能看懂那本书 (所以大人一定也能看懂). **2** *~ if/though,* (used to call attention to the extreme nature of what follows): 纵然; 即令 (用以使人注意下文之极端性质): *I'll get there ~ if I have to pawn my watch to get the railway fare.* 纵我必须将表押当做为火车旅费, 我也要到那里去。 *She won't leave the TV set, ~ though her supper's on the table.* 纵使晚餐已摆在桌上, 她也不愿意离开电视机。 **3** (with comparatives) still, yet: (与比较级连用) 更加; 愈加: *You know ~ less about it than I do.* 关于此事你知道的比我更少。 *You seem ~*

more stupid than usual today. 你今天好象比平时更加愚笨. **4 ~ as**, just at the time when: 正当; 恰在…的时候: *E~ as I gave the warning the car skidded.* 正当我提出警告时, 那车子滑到一边去了. **~ now/then**, in spite of these or those circumstances, etc: 甚至此时(那时); 虽然情况如此: *E~ now he won't believe me.* 甚至到现在他还不相信我. *E~ then he would not admit his mistake.* 甚至那时他还不承认错误. **~ so**, though that is the case: 虽然如此: *It has many omissions;* **~ so**, *it is quite a useful reference book.* 那书有许多遗漏之处, 虽然如此, 尚不失为一本有用的参考书.

even[3] /'iːvn; 'ivən/ n (poet) evening. (诗)日暮; 晚间. **'~·song** n Evening Prayer in the Church of England. 英国国教之晚祷. **'~·tide** n (poet) evening. (诗)日暮; 晚间.

even·ing /'iːvnɪŋ; 'ivnɪŋ/ n **1** [C, U] that part of the day between sunset and bedtime: 晚间; 傍晚; 黄昏: *a cool ~*; 凉爽的晚间; *musical ~s*, evenings given to playing or listening to music; 演奏或欣赏音乐之夜; *two ~s ago*; 前天晚上; (no prep) *this/tomorrow/yesterday ~*; 今(明, 昨)晚(前面不用介词); *in the ~*; in the evening; *on Sunday ~*; 在星期日晚间; *on the ~ of the 8th*; 在八日晚间; *one warm summer ~*. 一个暖和的夏夜. **2** (attrib) (用作定语): **~ dress**, dress as worn for formal occasions in the ~. 晚礼服. **,~ 'paper**, newspaper published after midday. 晚报. **,~ 'prayer**, church service; vespers. 晚祷. **the ~ 'star**, planet (Venus or Mercury), seen in the western sky after sunset 晚星; 金星; 水星(日落后西天出现之星).

even·song /'iːvnsɒŋ US: -sɔːŋ; 'ivən,sɔŋ/ ⇨ **even**[3].

event /ɪ'vent; ɪ'vɛnt/ n **1** happening, usu sth important: 事件; 重要事件: *the chief ~s of 1789.* 一七八九年的大事. *It was quite an ~* (often used to suggest that what happened was on an unusual scale, memorable, etc). 那确是一件大事. **in the natural/normal/usual course of ~s**, in the order in which things naturally happen. 按照事情自然发生的程序; 按照自然的趋势. **2** fact of a thing happening: 事情发生的事实: *in the ~ of his death*, if he dies. 如果他死去. **3** outcome; result. 结果. **at 'all ~s**, whatever is so. 无论如何. **in 'any ~**, whatever is so. 无论如何. **in 'either ~**, whichever is so. 无论是这样还是那样; 或此或彼. **in 'that ~**, if that is so. 如果是那样的话. **in the ~**, as it in fact happens. 如事实所发生; 结果. **4** one of the races, competitions, etc in a sports programme: 运动节目表中之一项竞赛: *Which ~s have you entered for?* 你参加了哪几项竞赛? **~·ful** /-fl; -fəl/ adj full of notable ~s: 充满大事的; 多事的: *He had had an ~ful life.* 他的是多彩多姿. *The past year has been ~ful.* 过去的一年是多事之秋.

even·tide /'iːvntaɪd; 'ivən,taɪd/ n ⇨ **even**[3].

event·ual /ɪ'ventʃʊəl; ɪ'vɛntʃʊəl/ adj coming at last as a result; ultimate: 结果的; 最终的: *his foolish behaviour and ~ failure.* 他的愚行及最终的失败. **~·ly** /-tʃʊəlɪ; -tʃʊlɪ/ adv in the end: 最后; 终于: *He fell ill and ~ly died.* 他得了病, 最后去世了. **~·ity** /ɪ,ventʃʊ'ælətɪ; ɪ,vɛntʃʊ'ælətɪ/ n (pl **-ties**) [C] possible event. 可能发生的事件.

ever /'evə(r); 'ɛvɚ/ adv **1** (usu in neg and interr sentences, and in sentences expressing doubt or conditions; usu placed with the v) at any time: (通常用于否定句和疑问句, 以及表示怀疑或条件的句子中; 通常置于动词v)无论何时: *Nothing ~ happens in this village.* 这村子里从未发生过什么事情. *Do you ~ wish you were rich?* 你曾经希望过自己富有吗? *She seldom, if ~, goes to the cinema.* 她很少看电影. *If you ~ visit London....* 你若是去伦敦…. **2** (with the present perfect tense, in questions) at any time up to the present: (用于现在完成时疑问句中)曾经: *Have you ~ been up in a balloon?* 你曾经乘过气球吗? (Note that *ever* is not used in the answer: either 'Yes, I have' or 'No, never', etc.) (注意: *ever* 不用于回答, 回答时用 Yes, I have 或 No, never 等). **3** (after a comparative or superlative): (用

于比较级或最高级之后): *It is raining harder than ~*, than it has been raining so far. 雨比以前大了. *It is more necessary than ~* (= than it has been so far) *for all of us to win.* 我们大家比以往更须要获胜. *This is the best work you have ~ done.* 这是你所做的最好的工作. **4** (chiefly in phrases) at all times; continuously: (主要用于短语中)始终; 老是: *~ afterwards*; 自此以后; *for ~* (*and ~*); 永远; *~ since I was a boy.* 从我孩提时代起. **5** (colloq) (as an intensifier): (口)(用以加强程度): *Work as hard as ~ you can.* 尽量努力工作. *I'll tell her as soon as ~ she arrives.* 她一来到我就告诉她. **'~ so**; **'~ such (a)**, (colloq) very: (口)非常: *~ so rich*; 非常有钱; *~ such a rich man.* 非常有钱的人. **6** (used after interrogatives as an intensifier): 究竟; 到底(用于疑问句之后以增强语势): *When/Where/How ~ did you lose it?* 你到底何时(何处, 怎样)将它遗失的? *What ~ do you mean?* 你究竟是什么意思? **7 did you ~...!** used to express surprise, incredulity, etc: 用以表示惊讶, 怀疑等: *Well, did you ~ hear such nonsense!* 啊, 你们听这一派胡言! **As if...** ~, used in a similar way: 用以表示惊讶, 怀疑等: *As if he would ~ do such a thing!* He would certainly not do it! 就好象他一直做这种事情似的! (其实他决不会做出此事.) **8** (old use) always: (旧用法)永远: *You will find me ~ at your service.* 你会发现我永远听命于你. **9 Yours ~**, used at the end of a letter, informal or familiar style. 你的永久的(朋友)(用于书信末尾签名前的客套语, 不拘礼仪或亲切的用法).

ever·green /'evəgriːn; 'ɛvə,grin/ n, adj (tree, shrub) having green leaves throughout the year: 常绿树; 常绿的: *The pine, cedar and spruce are ~s.* 松, 柏和针枞是常绿树. ⇨ **deciduous**.

ever·last·ing /,evə'lɑːstɪŋ US: -'læst-; ,ɛvə'læstɪŋ/ adj **1** going on for ever: 永久的; 永恒的: *~ fame/glory.* 永久的声誉(光荣). **the E~**, God. 上帝. **2** repeated too often: 重复太多次的: *I'm tired of his ~ complaints.* 我厌倦了他那不断的抱怨.

ever·more /,evə'mɔː(r); ,ɛvə'mɔr/ adv for ever. 永远.

every /'evrɪ; 'ɛvrɪ/ adj (used attrib with *sing* [C] nouns; cf the use of *all* with *pl* nouns and [U] nouns) (用作定语, 与单数可数名词连用; 参较 all 与复数名词以及与不可数名词的用法) **1** (Cf *every* and *each*. When *every* is used, attention is directed to units comprising a whole; when *each* is used, attention is directed simply to the unit) all or each one of a whole: (参较 every 和 each. 用 every 时, 观念着重于全体; 用 each 时则着重于个别)所有的; 每一: *E~ boy in the class* (= All the boys, The whole class) *passed the examination.* 班上所有的男生都考试及格了. (Cf 参较 *Each boy may have three tries.* 每个男孩可以试三次.) *I have read ~ book* (= all the books) *on that shelf.* 我读遍了那书架上所有的书. *Not ~ horse* (= Not all horses) *can run fast.* 并非所有的马都跑得快. **2** (not replaceable by *all* and the plural noun) each one of an indefinite number (the emphasis being on the unit, not on the total or whole): (不可被 all 和复数名词代替) 每 (着重于单位而非整体): *He enjoyed ~ minute of his holiday.* 他享受他的假日的每一分钟. *Such things do not happen ~ day.* 这种事情并非每天发生. *He spends ~ penny he earns.* 他赚来的每一分钱都花掉了. **3** (used with abstract nouns) all possible; complete: (与抽象名词连用)所有可能的; 完全的: *You have ~ reason to be satisfied.* 你没有理由不满意. *I have ~ reason/There is ~ reason to believe that....* 我有充分的理由相信…. *There is ~ prospect of success.* 有百分之百成功的希望. **4** (used with cardinal and ordinal numbers, and with *other* and *few*, to indicate recurrence, or intervals in time or space): (与基数, 序数, other 和 few 连用, 表示重现或时间空间的间隔). 隔行: *Write on ~ other line*, on alternate lines. 隔行写. *There are buses to the station ~ ten minutes.* 每隔十分钟有公共汽车至车站. *I go there ~ other day/~ three days/~ third day/~ few days,* etc. 我每隔一日(每三日, 每逢第三日, 每隔数日等)到那里

去一次。*He was stopped ~ dozen yards by friends who wanted to congratulate him.* 他每走十几码便被向他祝贺的朋友们拦住。~ **now and then/again,** from time to time. 有时；间或；时常。**5** (used with, and placed after, possessives; replaceable by *all+pl*): (用于所有格形容词后,此种用法可由 all+复数名词代替): *His ~ movement was watched,* All his movements.... 他的每一动作都受到注视。*He tries to meet her ~ wish,* all her wishes. 他试图满足她所有的愿望。我们的足球队总是得胜。**6** (in phrases) (用于短语中) ~ **bit,** quite: 完全: *This is ~ bit as good as that.* 这个和那个完全一样好。~ **time, (a)** always: 总是: *Our football team wins ~ time.* 我们的足球队总是得胜。**(b)** whenever: 无论何时；每当: *E~ time I meet him, he tries to borrow money from me.* 每当我遇到他,他便向我借钱。~ **'one of them/us/you,** (placed at the end) without exception: (置于句后)统统；无例外: *You deserve to be hanged, ~ one of you.* 你们该受绞刑,统统都该。**in ~ way,** in all respects: 在各方面: *This is in ~ way better than that.* 这个在各方面比都个好。~ **body** /'evribɒdi; 'ɛvrɪˌbɑdi/, ~ **one** /'evriwʌn; 'ɛvrɪˌwʌn/ *pron* = person: 每个人；人人: *In a small village ~one knows ~one else.* 在一个小村子里人人皆相识。~ **day** /'evrider; 'ɛvrɪˈde/ *adj* (attrib only) happening or used daily; common and familiar: (仅用作定语)每天发生的；每日所用的; *an ~day occurrence;* 日常之事; *in his ~day clothes.* 他穿着便服。**'~place** (US colloq) ~**where.** (美口)各处；到处。~**thing** /'evriθɪŋ; 'ɛvrɪˌθɪŋ/ *pron* **(a)** all things: 一切事物；每样事物: *This shop sells ~thing needed for camping.* 这商店出售一切露营用具。*Tell me ~thing about it.* 告诉我这件事情的始末。**(b)** (pred) thing of the greatest importance: (用作表语)最重要的事物: *Money is ~thing to him.* 金钱对于他什么都重要。*She's beautiful, I agree, but beauty is not ~thing.* 我同意她是美丽的,但美并非最重要者。~**where** /'evriweər; US: -hweer; 'ɛvrɪˌhwɛr/ *adv* in, at, to, ~ place: 各处; 到处。*I've looked ~where for it.* 我曾到处寻找它。*E~where seemed to be quiet.* 各处似乎都很安静。

evict /ɪ'vɪkt; ɪ'vɪkt/ *vt* [VP14] ~ **(from),** expel (a tenant) (from a house or land) by authority of the law: 根据法律将 (房客或佃户) 自房屋或土地逐出: *They were ~ed for not paying the rent.* 他们因欠房租而被逐出。 **evic·tion** /ɪ'vɪkʃn; ɪ'vɪkʃən/ *n* [U] ~ing or being ~ed; [C] instance of this. (根据法律将房客或佃户自房屋或土地)逐出的行动。

evi·dence /'evidəns; 'ɛvədəns/ *n* **1** [U] anything that gives reason for believing sth, that makes clear or proves sth: 证据; 根据: *There wasn't enough ~ to prove him guilty.* 没有充分的证据证明他有罪。*Have you any ~ for this statement?* 你说这话有无根据? *We cannot condemn him on such slight ~.* 我们不能根据这样少的证据而判他的罪。*The scientist must produce ~ in support of his theories.* 这科学家必须提出证据以支持其学说。**(be) in ~,** (be) clearly or easily seen: 明白的; 显著的; 易为人所见的: *She's the sort of woman who likes to be very much in ~,* who likes to be seen and noticed. 她是那种喜欢出风头的女子。*Smith was nowhere in ~,* could not be seen anywhere. 到处找不到见史密斯。**bear/give/show ~ of,** show signs of: 有…的迹象: *When the ship reached port, it bore abundant ~ of the severity of the storm,* ie signs of damage. 船抵港时,船上满是受到暴风雨肆虐的痕迹。**turn Queen's/King's/** (US) **State's ~,** (of a criminal) give ~ in court against accomplices. (指犯人) 在庭上提出不利共犯的证据。**2** (used in *pl*) indication, mark, trace: (用复数)形迹; 迹象; 痕迹: *There were ~s of glacial action on the rocks.* 这些岩石上有冰河留下的痕迹。□ *vt* [VP6A] (rare) prove by ~; be ~ of: (罕)证明; 作为…的证据: *His answer ~d a guilty conscience.* 他的回答证明他良心有愧。

evi·dent /'evɪdənt; 'ɛvədənt/ *adj* plain and clear (to the eyes or mind): 明显的; 显然的: *It must be ~ to all of you that....* 你们显然知道…。*He looked at his twelve*

children with ~ pride. 他以明显的得意态度望着他的十二个儿女。~**ly** *adv*

evil /'iːvl; 'ivl/ *adj* **1** wicked, sinful, bad, harmful: 邪恶的; 罪恶的; 不良的; 有害的: ~ *men/thoughts;* 恶人(恶念); *live an ~ life;* 过着罪恶的生活; *the 'E~ One,* thf Devil. 魔鬼; 恶魔。~**minded** *adj* having ~ thoughts and desires. 有邪恶之念头及愿望的; 恶毒的; 心毒的。**2** likely to cause trouble; bringing trouble or misfortune: 易引起麻烦的; 不吉的; 不幸的: *in an ~ hour;* 在不幸的时刻; 不吉利; *fall on ~ days;* 遭逢厄运, *an ~* (= slanderous) *tongue.* 诽谤的嘴; 恶毒的舌头。~ *eye,* malicious look; supposed power to cause harm by a look or glance. 恶毒的眼光; 凶狠的眼光; 据说一瞥即可造成伤害的力量。□ *n* **1** [U] sin; wrong-doing: 罪恶; 邪恶; 犯罪: *return good for ~;* 以德报怨; *the spirit of ~.* 戾气; 恶魔。**'~doer** *n* person who does ~. 作恶的人; 犯罪者。**2** [C] ~ thing; disaster: 恶事; 不幸; 灾祸: *War, famine and flood are terrible ~s.* 战争, 饥荒和水灾是可怕的灾祸。*be/choose the lesser of two ~s,* the less harmful of two bad choices. 两害相权, 择其小者。~**ly** /'iːvlɪ; 'ivlɪ/ *adv* in an ~ manner: 邪恶地; 罪恶地; 有害地: *He eyed her ~ly.* 他凶狠地瞪着她。

evince /ɪ'vɪns; ɪ'vɪns/ *vt* [VP6A, 9] (formal) show that one has (a feeling, quality, etc): (正式用语)表现(感情, 性质等): *a child who ~s great intelligence.* 表现出极高智慧的儿童。

evis·cer·ate /ɪ'vɪsəreɪt; ɪ'vɪsəˌret/ *vt* [VP6A] disembowel. 取出…之肠。

evoca·tive /ɪ'vɒkətɪv; ɪ'vɑkətɪv/ *adj* that evokes, or is able to evoke: 易引起的; 唤起的: ~ *words,* that call up memories, emotions, in addition to their ordinary meanings. 勾起回忆或感情的言语。

evoke /ɪ'vəʊk; ɪ'vok/ *vt* [VP6A] call up, bring out: 召唤; 引起: ~ *a spirit from the other world;* 召来鬼魂; ~ *admiration/surprise/a smile/memories of the past.* 引起羡慕(惊奇, 微笑, 过去的回忆)。**evo·ca·tion** /ˌiːvəʊ'keɪʃn; ˌɛvo'keʃən/ *n*

evol·ution /ˌiːvə'luːʃn; US: ˌev-; ˌɛvə'luʃən/ *n* **1** [U] evolving; process of opening out or developing: 开展; 发育; 发展: *the ~ of a plant from a seed.* 由种子发育成植物的过程。*In politics England has preferred ~* (= gradual development) *to revolution* (= sudden or violent change). 在政治上英国喜欢渐进, 不喜欢革命。**2** [U] (theory of the)development of more complicated forms of life (plants, animals) from earlier and simpler forms. 进化; 进化论。**3** [C] movement according to plan (of troops, warships, dancers, etc). (军队, 军舰, 舞蹈者之)按照计划的行动。~**ary** /ˌiːvə'luːʃənrɪ US: ˌevə'luːʃənerɪ; ˌɛvə'luʃənˌɛrɪ/ *adj* of, being produced by, ~; developing. 开展的; 进化的; 发展的。

evolve /ɪ'vɒlv; ɪ'vɑlv/ *vi, vt* [VP2A, 6A] (cause to) unfold; develop; be developed, naturally and (usu) gradually: (使)开展; 发展; 自然而逐渐地进展: *The American constitution was planned; the British constitution ~d.* 美国的宪法是依计划制定的, 英国的宪法是自然演进的。*He has ~d a new plan/theory.* 他发展出一项新计划(学说)。

ewe /juː; ju/ *n* female sheep. 牝羊; 母羊。⇨ **ram.**

ewer /'juːə(r); 'juɚ/ *n* large wide-mouthed pitcher for holding water, eg as used with a basin on a wash-stand in a bedroom without a piped supply of water. 大口水罐 (如寝室内无水管装置时与面盆共置于脸盆架上者)。

ex- /eks; ɛks/ *pref* ⇨ **App 3.** 参看附录三。

ex·acer·bate /ɪg'zæsəbeɪt; ɪg'zæsɚˌbet/ *vt* [VP6A] (formal) irritate (a person); aggravate (= make worse) (pain, disease, a situation): (正式用语)激怒(一人); 加重(痛苦, 疾病, 局势); 使恶化。**exacer·ba·tion** /ɪgˌzæsə'beɪʃn; ɪgˌzæsɚ'beʃən/ *n*

exact¹ /ɪg'zækt; ɪg'zækt/ *adj* **1** correct in every detail; free from error: 精确的; 正确的: *Give me his ~ words.* 把他的话一字不差的告诉我。*What is the ~ size of the room?* 这房间的正确面积是多少? *I want ~ directions*

for finding your house. 我需要如何能找到你住处的正确说明。**2** capable of being precise: 严谨的; 精密的: ~ *sciences;* 精密的(严谨的)科学: *an ~ memory;* 精确的记忆: *an ~ scholar.* 严谨的学者。**~·ly** *adv* **1** correctly; quite: 正确地; 完全地: *Your answer is ~ly right.* 你的答案完全对。*That's ~ly* (= just) *what I expected.* 正是我所期待的。**2** (as an answer or confirmation) quite so; just as you say. (作为回答或认可)正是; 不错。**~·ness, ~·i·tude** /ɪgˈzæktɪtjuːd *US:* -tuːd/ ɪgˈzæktə,tjud/ *nn.*

exact² /ɪgˈzækt; ɪgˈzækt/ *vt* [VP6A, 14] **~ (from)**, **1** demand and enforce payment of: 要求偿付; 强制要求付出: ~ *taxes (from people);* (向人民)征税; ~ *payment (from a debtor).* 强制(债务人)还债。**2** insist on: 坚持: ~ *obedience.* 坚持要求服从。**3** (of circumstances) require urgently; make necessary: (指情况)迫切需要; 使之必要: *work that ~s care and attention.* 需要小心和注意的工作。**~·ing** *adj* making great demands; severe; strict: 苛求的; 严厉的; 严格的: *an ~ing piece of work;* 费力的工作; *an ~ing master.* 严厉的主人。**ex·action** /ɪgˈzækʃn; ɪgˈzækʃən/ *n* **1** [U] act of money, etc. (对金钱等的)强求; 强取。**2** [C] that which is ~ed, esp a tax which is considered to be too high; a great demand (on one's time, strength, etc). 索取之物; (尤指)苛税; (对时间, 力量等之)大量需求。

exag·ger·ate /ɪgˈzædʒəreɪt; ɪgˈzædʒə,ret/ *vt, vi* [VP6A, 2A] stretch (a description) beyond the truth; make sth seem larger, better, worse, etc than it really is: 夸张; 夸大: *You ~ the difficulties.* 你夸大了那些困难。*If you always ~, people will no longer believe you.* 如果你老是夸张, 人们便不会相信你了。*He has an ~d sense of his own importance,* thinks he is far more important than he really is. 他过于自大(自视过高)。**exag·ger·ation** /ɪgˌzædʒəˈreɪʃn; ɪgˌzædʒəˈreʃən/ *n* [U] exaggerating or being ~d; [C] ~d statement: 夸张; 夸大; 夸张的陈述: *a story full of exaggerations.* 充满夸张的故事。

exalt /ɪgˈzɔːlt; ɪgˈzɔlt/ *vt* [VP6A] **1** make high(er) in rank, great(er) in power or dignity. 擢升; 提高…之职位。**2** praise highly. 赞扬。**~ed** *adj* dignified; ennobled: 崇高的; 高贵的: *a person of ~ed rank.* 地位崇高之人。**exal·ta·tion** /ˌegzɔːlˈteɪʃn; ˌegzɔlˈteʃən/ *n* [U] (fig) elation; state of spiritual delight. (喻)得意; 意气扬扬。

exam /ɪgˈzæm; ɪgˈzæm/ *n* (colloq abbr of) examination. (口)为 examination 之略。

exam·in·ation /ɪgˌzæmɪˈneɪʃn; ɪgˌzæməˈneʃən/ *n* **1** [U] examining or being examined: 讯问: *On ~, it was found that the signature was not genuine.* 检查时发现此签名不是真的。*The prisoner is still under ~,* being examined. 这犯人仍在受审中。**2** [C] instance of this, esp 检查或讯问之实例, 尤指 **(a)** a testing of knowledge or ability: 考试; 测验: *an ~ in mathematics;* 数学考试; ~ *questions/papers;* 试题(试卷); *an oral ~.* 口试。**(b)** an inquiry into or inspection of sth: 审查; 审查: *an ~ of a botanical specimen;* 审查一植物标本; *an ~ of business accounts;* 审查商业帐目; *an ~ of one's eyes.* 检查眼睛。**(c)** questioning by a lawyer in a law court: 律师在法庭上的质询: *an ~ of a witness.* 律师对证人的质询。

exam·ine /ɪgˈzæmɪn; ɪgˈzæmɪn/ *vt* [VP6A, 14] **1 ~ (for)**, look at carefully in order to learn about or from: 检查; 审查: ~ *old records;* 检查旧记录; *have one's teeth/eyes ~d for decay/weakening;* 检查牙齿是否有蛀牙(检查视力是否衰退); ~ *a new theory.* 审查一新学说。*She needs to have her head ~d,* (colloq) is foolish or impudent. (口)她真该去检查一下她的脑袋了。**2 ~ (in),** put questions to in order to test knowledge or get information: 考试; 询问: ~ *pupils in Latin/on their knowledge of Latin;* 考学生的拉丁文; ~ *a witness in a court of law.* 在法庭上质问一证人。**exam·iner** *n* person who ~s. 检查者; 审查者; 考试者; 审问者。

example /ɪgˈzɑːmpl *US:* -ˈzæmpl; ɪgˈzæmpl/ *n* **1** fact, thing, etc which illustrates or represents a general rule: 实例; 例证: *This dictionary has many ~s of how verbs are used.* 这部词典有许多说明动词用法的实例。**for ~,** (abbr 略作 **eg**) by way of illustration: 例如; 譬如: *Many great men have risen from poverty—Lincoln and Edison, for ~.* 许多伟人由贫苦中崛起, 例如林肯和爱迪生。**2** specimen showing the quality of others in the same group or of the same kind: 样本; 标本: *This is a good ~ of Shelley's lyric poetry.* 这是雪莱的抒情诗的一个良好的例子。**3** [C, U] thing or person, person's conduct, to be copied or imitated: 模范; 榜样: *follow sb's ~:* 模仿某人; *set an ~ to sb;* 给某人树一榜样; *set sb a good ~;* 为某人树立好榜样; *learn by ~.* 模仿; 仿效。**4** warning: 警告: *Let this be an ~ to you.* 这便是给你的警告。**make an ~ of sb,** punish him as a warning to others. 惩一儆百。

exas·per·ate /ɪgˈzæspəreɪt; ɪgˈzæspə,ret/ *vt* [VP6A] irritate; produce ill feeling in; make ill feeling, anger, etc worse: 激怒: 引起…之恶感; 加深(恶感, 愤怒等): ~d by/at sb's stupidity. 因某人之愚笨而愤怒。*It is exasperating to lose a train by half a minute.* 因半分钟之差而误了火车是令人恼火的。**exas·per·ation** /ɪgˌzæspəˈreɪʃn; ɪgˌzæspəˈreʃən/ *n* state of being ~d: 恼怒; 愤怒: *'Stop that noise,' he cried out in exasperation.* '不要吵,' 他愤怒地大声说。

ex·ca·vate /ˈekskəveɪt, vet/ *vt* [VP6A] make, uncover, dig or by digging: 挖掘; 发掘: ~ *a trench/a buried city.* 挖壕 (发掘一个埋在地下的城市)。**ex·cavator** /-tə(r); -tə/ *n* person engaged in, machine used for, excavating. 挖掘者; 挖掘机。**ex·ca·vation** /ˌekskəˈveɪʃn; ˌekskəˈveʃən/ *n* [U] excavating or being ~d; [C] place that is being or has been ~d. 挖掘; 发掘; 被挖掘之地。

ex·ceed /ɪkˈsiːd; ɪkˈsid/ *vt* [VP6A] **1** be greater 比…大; 超乎…之上: *Their success ~s all their expectations.* 他们的成功出乎一切预料。*London ~s Glasgow in size and population.* 伦敦在面积和人口方面大于格拉斯哥。**2** go beyond what is allowed, necessary or advisable: 超出; 超越: ~ *the speed limit,* drive faster than is allowed; 驾车超速; ~ *one's instructions,* do more than one has authority to do. 逾越权限。**~·ing·ly** *adv* extremely; to an unusual degree: 非常; 极度地: *an ~ingly difficult problem.* 一个非常困难的问题。

ex·cel /ɪkˈsel; ɪkˈsɛl/ *vi, vt* (**-ll-**) **~ (in/at), 1** [VP2C, 3A] do better than others, be very good: 优于他人; 胜过他人; 优秀: *He ~s in courage/as an orator.* 他在勇气(演说)方面胜过他人。*The firm ~s in at producing cheap transistor radios.* 这家公司在生产价廉的晶体管收音机方面胜过其他公司。**2** [VP6A, 15A] do better than; surpass (the more usu word): 优于; 胜过 (surpass 一字较常用): *He ~s all of us in/at tennis.* 他的网球胜过我们所有的人。

ex·cel·lence /ˈeksələns; ˈeksləns/ *n* **1** [U] **~ (in/at),** the quality of being excellent; great merit: 优越; 卓越; 优秀: *a prize for ~ in furniture design;* 家具设计特优奖; *his ~ in at all forms of sport.* 他在各项运动方面的优越。**2** [C] thing or quality in which a person excels: 优秀之处; 长处; 优点: *They do not recognize her many ~s.* 他们没有发觉她的许多优点。

Ex·cel·lency /ˈeksələnsɪ; ˈekslənsɪ/ *n* (*pl* **-cies**) title of ambassadors, governors and their wives, and some other officers and officials: 阁下(对大使, 省长, 大使及省长夫人, 以及若干其他官员的尊称): *Your/His/Her ~.* 阁下。

ex·cel·lent /ˈeksələnt; ˈekslənt/ *adj* very good; of high quality. 极好的; 优秀的。**~·ly** *adv*

ex·cel·sior /ek'selsiɔː(r); ɪk'sɛlsɪɔ/ *n* [U] (US) soft, fine wood shavings used for packing easily damaged goods, eg glassware. (美)细刨花(包装时用以填垫玻璃器皿等易损毁之货物)。

ex·cept¹ /ɪkˈsept; ɪkˈsɛpt/ *prep* not including; but

not: 除…之外。但…不包括在内: *He gets up early every day* ~ *Sunday*. 除星期日他每天早起。*Nobody was late* ~ *me*. 除我以外无人迟到。Cf 参较 *Five others were late besides me*. 在我之外尚有五人迟到。*My papers seem to be everywhere* ~ *where they ought to be*. 我的文件似乎完全不在它们应该放置的地方。 ~ *for*, (used when what is excluded is different from what is included): 除…外(用以说明除外者异于包括在内者); 只是: *Your essay is good* ~ *for the spelling*. 你的文章甚好, 只是字母拼写有误。(The comparison is between the spelling, which is not good, and other things, eg ideas, grammar, which are satisfactory). (系就字母拼写与其他方面例如思想, 语法等做一比较, 字母拼写虽不佳, 但他方面令人满意). Cf 参较 *All the essays are good* ~ *John's*. 除了约翰的以外, 所有的文章都好。 ~ *that*, apart from the fact that: 除去…一点之外: *She knew nothing about his journey* ~ *that he was likely to be away for three months*. 关于他的旅行她不清楚, 只知道他大概要离开三个月。□ *conj* (old or liter use) unless: (旧用法或文学用语)除非: (biblical style) (圣经文体) E~ *ye be born again*. 非你们重生。

ex·cept² /ɪkˈsept; ɪkˈsɛpt/ *vt* [VP6A, 14] ~ *(from)*, exclude (from); set apart (from a list, statement, etc): 将…除外; 不包括…在名单, 陈述等内: *I discovered that I had been* ~*ed from the list of those who were being sent to India*. 我发现我并没有包括在派往印度去的人的名单上。*All those who took part in the plot, nobody* ~*ed, were punished*. 凡参与此一阴谋者, 无人例外, 均受到了处分。**present company** ~*ed*, not including those here present. 在场者除外。~*ing* *prep* (used after *not*, *always* and *without*) leaving out; excluding: (用于 *not*, *always*, *without* 之后)除…外: *the whole staff, not* ~*ing the heads of departments*. 全体人员, 包括各部门首长。

ex·cep·tion /ɪkˈsepʃn; ɪkˈsɛpʃən/ *n* 1 [U, C] excepting; sb or sth that is excepted (not included). 除外; (人或事物之)例外。**make an** ~ *(of sb/sth)*, treat (sb/sth) as an ~, a special case: 把…作为例外: *You must all be here at 8am; I can make no* ~*s*, cannot excuse any of you. 你们都必须上午八点钟到此, 我不能特许任何人例外。**with the** ~ **of**, except: 除…外: *I enjoyed all his novels with the* ~ *of his last*. 我喜欢他所有的小说, 最后一部例外。**without** ~, excepting nobody/nothing: 无例外; 争吵: *All men between 18 and 45 without* ~ *are expected to serve in the army during a war*. 凡十八至四十五岁的男子一概应于战时从军。2 [C] sth that does not follow the rule: 规则的例外; 与 a rule of grammar. 语法规则的例外。▷ **prove** (1). 3 [U] objection. 反对。**take** ~ *(to sth)*, object to; protest against; be offended by: 反对抗议; 因…而不悦: *He took great* ~ *to what I said*. 他十分反对我的话。~·**able** /-əbl; -əbl/ *adj* objectionable. 可反对的; 可抗议的。~·**al** /-ʃənl; -ʃənl/ *adj* unusual; out of the ordinary; 异常的; 例外的; 特别的: *weather that is* ~*al for June*; 六月里异常的天气; ~*al advantages*. 特别好的利益。~·**ally** /-ʃənlɪ; -ʃənlɪ/ *adv* unusually: 异常地; 罕有地: *an* ~*ally beautiful boy*. 一个非常美丽的男孩。

ex·cerpt /ˈeksɜːpt; ˈɛksɝpt/ *n* [C] passage, extract, from a book etc, eg one printed separately. 摘录; 引述。

ex·cess¹ /ɪkˈses; ɪkˈsɛs/ *n* 1 **an** ~ **of**, fact of being, amount by which sth is, more than sth else, or more than is expected or proper: 超过; 超越; 过度; 过剩; 过分; 过多之量: *an* ~ *of enthusiasm*; 过分热心; *an* ~ *of imports over exports*. 输入超过输出; 入超。**in** ~ **of**, more than: 多于; 超过: *Luggage in* ~ *of 100kg will be charged extra*. 超过一百公斤的行李要额外收费。**to** ~, to an extreme degree: 过度: *Don't carry your grief to* ~. 不要过度悲伤。*She is generous to* ~. 她过度慷慨。2 [U] immoderation; intemperance. 无节制。3 (*pl*) personal acts which go beyond the limits of good behaviour, morality or humanity: (复)过分的行为; 超

越道德或人性的行为: *The* ~*es* (= acts of cruelty, etc) *committed by the troops when they occupied the capital will never be forgotten*. 那些军队占领首都时所施的暴行将永远不会使人忘记。~·**ive** /ɪkˈsesɪv; ɪkˈsɛsɪv/ *adj* too much; too great; extreme: 过多的; 过度的; 极端的: ~*ive charges*. 过高的索价。~·**ive·ly** *adv*

ex·cess² /ˈekses; ˈɛksɛs/ *adj* extra; additional: 额外的; 附加的: ~ *fare*, eg for travelling farther than is allowed by one's ticket; 额外票价; 补票费; ~ *luggage*, weight above what may be carried free; 超重的行李; ~ *postage*, charged when a letter, etc is understamped: 欠资邮费; ~ *profits duty*, extra tax on profits increased by, eg, war conditions. (战时等)逾限利得税; 过分利得税。

ex·change¹ /ɪksˈtʃeɪndʒ; ɪksˈtʃendʒ/ *n* 1 [C, U] (act of) exchanging: 交换; 互换: *Is five apples for five eggs a fair* ~? 用五个苹果换五个蛋是公平的交换吗? *There have been numerous* ~*s of views between the two governments*. 两国政府间曾多次交换意见。E~ *of prisoners during a war is unusual*. 战时交换俘虏是少有的。*He is giving her French lessons in* ~ *for English lessons*. 他教她法语, 她教他英语。2 [U] the giving and receiving of the money of one country for that of another; relation in value between kinds of money used in different countries: 外币兑换; 兑换率: *the rate of* ~ (between the dollar and the pound, etc). (美元与英镑等之)兑换率。'E~ **Control**, system of protecting gold and reserves of foreign currency. (外币之)汇兑管制。3 [C] place where merchants or financiers meet for business: 交易所: *the* 'Cotton *E*~; 棉花交易所; *the* 'Stock *E*~, for the buying and selling of stocks, shares, bonds. 证券交易所。4 '**labour** ~, (GB) Government offices where unemployed workmen may be put in touch with prospective employers. (英)(政府所设)劳工介绍处。'**telephone** ~, control office where lines are connected. 电话局; 电话交换所。

ex·change² /ɪksˈtʃeɪndʒ; ɪksˈtʃendʒ/ *vt* [VP6A, 14] ~ *sth (for sth) (with sb)*, give, receive (one thing) in place of another: 交换; 互换: ~ *greetings/glances*; 互相问候/凝视; ~ *five apples for five eggs*. 用五个苹果换五个蛋。*Mary* ~*d seats with Anne*. 玛丽和安妮交换座位。~ *blows/words (with)*, fight/quarrel. 打架; 争吵。~·**able** /-əbl; -əbl/ *adj* that may be ~d. 可交换的; 可互换的。

ex·chequer /ɪksˈtʃekə(r); ɪksˈtʃɛkɚ/ *n* 1 **the** E~, (GB) government department in charge of public money. (英)财政部: *Chancellor of the* 'E~, minister at the head of this department (= Minister of Finance in other countries). 财政大臣(相当于其他国家之财政部长)。2 supply of money (public or private); treasury. (公共或私人的)财源; 资金; 国库。

ex·cise¹ /ˈeksaɪz; ˈɛksaɪz/ *n* [U] government tax on certain goods manufactured, sold or used within a country: 国产税; 本国消费税: *the* ~ *on beer/tobacco*; 啤酒(烟草)消费税; ~ *duties* 消费税; *the Commissioners of Customs and E*~. 海关与国产税务司官员。'~·**man** /-mən; -mən/ (*pl* -**men**), 'E~ **Officer**, officer collecting ~ and preventing breaking of ~ laws. 国产税务官。

ex·cise² /ˈekˈsaɪz; ˈekˈsaɪz/ *vt* [VP6A] (formal) remove by, or as if by, cutting (a part of the body, a passage from a book, etc). (正式用语)切除(身体之一部); 删去(书中之一段等)。**ex·cision** /ɪkˈsɪʒn; ɪkˈsɪʒən/ *n* [U] excising or being ~d; [C] sth ~d. 切除; 删去; 被切除或删去的部分。

ex·cite /ɪkˈsaɪt; ɪkˈsaɪt/ *vt* [VP6A, 14, 17] 1 ~ *(to)*, stir up the feelings of; cause (sb) to feel strongly: 激动; 鼓舞; 使兴奋: *Don't* ~ *yourself!* Keep calm! 不要激动! *Everybody was* ~*d by the news of the victory*. 人为为此胜利的消息而兴奋。*It's nothing to get* ~*d about*. 这没有什么值得兴奋的。*Agitators were exciting the people to rebellion/to rebel against their rulers*. 煽动者

鼓动人民叛乱(反叛其统治者)。**2 ~ (in sb)**, get (a feeling) in motion; rouse; bring about: 引起(某种感情); 激起; 招惹: ~ admiration/envy/affection in an audience; 引起观众的钦佩(羡慕, 爱慕); ~ a riot. 引起暴动。**3** cause (a bodily organ) to be active: 使(身体器官)活动; 刺激: drugs that ~ the nerves. 刺激神经的药物。**ex·cit·able** /ɪk'saɪtəbl; ɪk'saɪtəbl/ adj easily ~d. 易兴奋的; 易激动的。**ex·cit·abil·ity** /ɪk,saɪtə'bɪlətɪ; ɪk,saɪtə'bɪlətɪ/ n quality of being excitable. 易兴奋; 易激动。**ex·cit·ed·ly** adv in an ~d manner. 兴奋地; 激动地。

ex·cite·ment /ɪk'saɪtmənt; ɪk'saɪtmənt/ n **1** [U] state of being excited: 兴奋; 激动; 刺激; 骚动: news that caused great ~; 令人极为兴奋的消息; jumping about in ~. 兴奋地跳来跳去。**2** [C] sth that excites; exciting incident, etc: 令人兴奋的事物; 使人激动的事件等: He kept calm amid all these ~s. 他在这些使人激动的事件中保持镇静。

ex·claim /ɪk'skleɪm; ɪk'sklem/ vt, vi [VP9, 2A] cry out suddenly and loudly from pain, anger, surprise, etc: (因痛苦, 愤怒, 惊奇等)呼喊; 惊叫: 'What!' he ~ed. 'Are you leaving without me?' '什么!' 他喊道。'你要丢下我离去吗?'

ex·cla·ma·tion /,eksklə'meɪʃn; ,eksklə'meʃən/ n **1** [U] exclaiming: 呼喊; 惊叫: ~ mark, the mark(!). 感叹号; 惊叹号 (!)。⇨ App 9. 参看附录九。**2** [C] sudden short cry, expressing surprise, pain, etc: 感叹词; 惊叹语: 'Oh!' 'Look out!', and 'Hurrah!' are ~s. '啊!' '小心!' 和 '好哇!' 是感叹词。

ex·clama·tory /ɪk'sklæmətrɪ US: -tɔːrɪ; ɪk'sklæmə,torɪ/ adj using, containing, in the nature of, an exclamation: 惊叹的; 感叹的: an ~ sentence. 惊叹句。

ex·clude /ɪk'skluːd; ɪk'sklud/ vt [VP6A, 14] ~ (from), **1** prevent (sb from getting in somewhere): 拒绝(某人进入): ~ a person from membership of a society/immigrants from a country. 拒绝一人入会(拒绝移民进入一国)。**2** prevent (the chance of sth arising): 排除(某事发生的机会): ~ all possibility of doubt; 排除一切疑虑; leave out of account, ignore as irrelevant: 不予考虑: We can ~ (from the reckoning) the possibility that the money won't arrive. 我们不必考虑(由于计算)该款项不会到达的可能性。**ex·clu·sion** /ɪk'skluːʒn; ɪk'skluʒən/ n [U] ~ (from), excluding or being ~d. 拒绝; 排除。**to the exclusion of**, so as to ~. 以便排除。

ex·clus·ive /ɪk'skluːsɪv; ɪk'sklusɪv/ adj **1** (of a person) not willing to mix with others (esp those considered to be inferior in social position, education, etc). (指人)孤僻的; (尤指)孤傲的。**2** (of a group or society) not readily admitting new members: (指社团)不愿吸收新份子的: He moves in ~ social circles and belongs to the most ~ clubs. 他活动于限制甚严的社交圈内, 而且属于某些最不愿吸收新份子的社团。**3** (of a shop, goods sold in it, etc) of the sort not to be found elsewhere; uncommon. (指商店, 售货等)罕有的; 不平常的; 独家的。**4** reserved to the person(s) concerned: 独有的: ~ privileges; 独有的特权; have ~ rights/an ~ agency for the sale of Ford cars in a town; 享有福特汽车在一城市的专卖权(独家代理权); an ~ story/interview, eg given to only one newspaper. (仅给一家报纸报导)独家报导(访问)。**5 ~ of**, not including: 不包括…在内: The ship had a crew of 57 ~ of officers. 这船上有五十七位水手, 高级船员除外。**6** excluding all but what is mentioned: 唯一的: Dictionary-making has not been his ~ employment. 编词典一直都不是他唯一的工作。**~·ly** adv

ex·cogi·tate /eks'kɒdʒɪteɪt; eks'kɑdʒə,tet/ vt [VP6A] (formal or hum) think out (a plan). (正式用语或诙谐语)想出(计划)。**ex·cogi·ta·tion** /eks,kɒdʒɪ'teɪʃn; eks,kɑdʒɪ'teʃən/ n

ex·com·mu·ni·cate /,ekskə'mjuːnɪkeɪt; ,ekskə'mjunə,ket/ vt [VP6A] exclude (as a punishment) from the privileges of a member of the Christian Church, eg marriage or burial in church, Holy Communion. 把…逐出教会(以作惩罚使不能享受教友特权, 例如在教堂结婚, 埋葬或参加圣餐等)。**ex·com·muni·sa·tion** /,ekskə,mjuːnɪ'keɪʃn; ,ekskə,mjunə'keʃən/ n [U] excommunicating or being ~d; [C] instance of this; official statement announcing this. 逐出教会; 逐出教会的公告。

ex·cori·ate /ɪk'skɔːrɪeɪt; ɪk'skɔrɪ,et/ vt [VP6A] (formal) strip, peel off (skin); (fig) criticize severely. (正式用语)剥(皮); (喻)严厉批评; 批评得体无完肤。**ex·cori·a·tion** /ɪk,skɔːrɪ'eɪʃn; ɪk,skɔrɪ'eʃən/ n

excre·ment /'ekskrɪmənt; 'ekskrɪmənt/ n [U] solid waste matter discharged from the bowels. 粪便。

ex·cres·cence /ɪk'skresns; ɪk'skresns/ n [C] abnormal (usu ugly and useless) outgrowth on an animal or vegetable body. 瘤; 赘疣。

ex·creta /ɪk'skriːtə; ɛk'skritə/ n pl waste(excrement, urine, sweat) expelled from the body. 排泄物; 粪便; 尿; 汗。

ex·crete /ɪk'skriːt; ɛk'skrit/ vt [VP6A] (of an animal or plant) discharge from the system, eg waste matter, sweat. (指动植物)排泄; 分泌。**ex·cre·tion** /ɪk'skriːʃn; ɪk'skriʃən/ n [U] excreting; [C, U] that which is ~d. 排泄; 分泌; 排泄物; 分泌物。

ex·cru·ci·at·ing /ɪk'skruːʃɪeɪtɪŋ; ɪk'skruʃɪ,etɪŋ/ adj (of pain, bodily or mental) acute. (指身心痛苦)剧烈的。**~·ly** adv

ex·cul·pate /'ekskʌlpeɪt; 'ɛkskʌl,pet/ vt [VP6A, 14] ~ (from), (formal) free from blame; say that (sb) is not guilty of wrongdoing: (正式用语)使无罪过; 辩白(某人)无罪: ~ a person from a charge. 申明某人无罪。

ex·cur·sion /ɪk'skɜːʃn US: -ʒn; ɪk'skɝʒən/ n [C] short journey, esp one made by a number of people together for pleasure: 短程旅行; 远足: go on/make an ~ to the mountains; 登山旅行; an '~ train; 游览火车; an '~ ticket, one issued at a reduced fare. (减价的)游览票。**~·ist** n person who makes an ~. 作短程旅行者; 远足者。

ex·cuse[1] /ɪk'skjuːs; ɪk'skjus/ n **1** [C] reason given (true or invented) to explain or defend one's conduct; apology: 借口; 口实; 托词; 辩解; 解释: He's always making ~s for being late. 他总是为他的迟到找借口。He had numerous ~s to offer for being late. 他对迟到有无数的借口。Please give them my ~s. 请将我的解释告诉他们。**2 in ~ of**: 为…辩解: Where the law is concerned, you cannot plead ignorance in ~ of your conduct. 就法律而言, 你无法以不知情来为你的行为辩白。**without ~**: 无故: Those who are absent without (good) ~ will be dismissed. 无故缺席者将被开除。

ex·cuse[2] /ɪk'skjuːz; ɪk'skjuz/ vt **1** [VP6A, C, 14, 19C] ~ (for), give reasons showing, or intended to show, that a person or his action is not to be blamed; overlook a fault, etc: 为…辩解; 原谅; 宽宥(过失)等: ~ sb's conduct. 原谅某人的行为。Nothing can ~ such rudeness. 如此无礼绝不可宽恕。Please ~ my coming late/~ me for being late/~ my late arrival. 请原谅我的迟到。E~ my interrupting you. 原谅我打扰了你。**2** [VP14, 6A] ~ (from), set (sb) free from a duty, requirement, punishment, etc: 使(某人)免除(责任, 规定, 处罚等): He was ~d (from) attendance at the lecture. 他获准可不去听讲。They may be ~d from complying with this regulation. 他们可以不按照这规则行事。**3** E~ me, used as an apology when one interrupts, disagrees, has to behave impolitely or disapprove: 对不起(打搅他人, 不同意, 迫不得已而失礼或不赞成时的道歉语): E~ me, but I don't think that statement is quite true. 对不起, 不过我认为那话不十分真实。⇨ pardon(2); sorry(2). **ex·cus·able** /ɪk'skjuːzəbl; ɪk'skjuzəbl/ adj that may be ~d: 可原谅的; 可宽宥的; 可饶恕的: an excusable mistake. 可原谅的错误。**ex·cus·ably** /-əblɪ; -əblɪ/ adv

ex·di·rec·tory /ˌeksdɪˈrektərɪ; ˌɛksdəˈrɛktərɪ/ adj (of a telephone number) not listed in the telephone directory (for reasons of security, privacy, etc). (指电话号码)(因安全、隐秘等理由而)未列入电话簿中的。

ex·ecrable /ˈeksɪkrəbl; ˈɛksɪkrəbl/ adj very bad; deserving hate: 恶劣的; 可恶的; 可恨的: ~ manners/weather. 恶劣的态度(天气)。

ex·ecrate /ˈeksɪkreɪt; ˈɛksɪˌkret/ vt [VP6A] express or feel hatred of. 憎恨; 嫌恶。 **ex·ecra·tion** /ˌeksɪˈkreɪʃn; ˌɛksɪˈkreʃən/.

ex·ecute /ˈeksɪkjuːt; ˈɛksɪˌkjut/ vt [VP6A] 1 carry out (what one is asked or told to do): 执行; 实现; 实施: ~ sb's commands; 执行某人的命令; ~ a plan/a piece of work/a purpose. 实现一计划(完成一件工作); 达到一目的。 2 (legal) give validity to: (法律)使生效; 实施: ~ a will. 使遗嘱生效。 3 (legal) make legally binding: (法律)使受法律约束: ~ a legal document, by having it signed, witnessed, sealed and delivered. 签发一法律文件。 4 carry out punishment by death on (sb): 处死(某人); 处决: ~ a murderer. 处死一凶手。 5 perform on the stage, at a concert, etc: (在舞台上或音乐会中等)演奏; 表演: The piano sonata was badly ~d. 这钢琴奏鸣曲演奏得不好。 **ex·ecu·tant** /ɪgˈzekjutənt; ɛgˈzɛkjʊtənt/ n person who is a design, etc; person who performs music, etc. 实行者; 演奏者; 表演者。

ex·ecu·tion /ˌeksɪˈkjuːʃn; ˌɛksɪˈkjuʃən/ n 1 [U] the carrying out or performance of a piece of work, design, etc: (工作、计划等的)实行; 实现; 完成: His intention was good, but his ~ of the plan was unsatisfactory. 他的用意甚佳, 但他做起来不令人满意。 put/carry sth into ~, complete it, do what was planned. 完成一计划。 2 [U] skill in performing, eg music: 演奏音乐等的技巧: a pianist with marvellous ~. 技高的钢琴家。 3 [U] (of weapons) destructive effect: (指武器)摧毁效果; 威力: The artillery did great ~, killed and wounded many. 那些大炮的威力惊人。 4 [U] infliction of punishment by death: 处死刑; 处死: ~ by hanging; 以绞刑处死; five ~s last year. 去年的五次死刑执行。 [C] instance of this: 死刑刑; 处死: ~er n public official who ~s criminals. 行刑者; 死刑执行人。

execu·tive /ɪgˈzekjutɪv; ɪgˈzɛkjʊtɪv/ adj 1 having to do with managing or executing(1): 执行的; 实行的; 实现的: ~ duties; 执行的职责; ~ ability. 执行的能力。 2 having authority to carry out decisions, laws, decrees, etc: 有权执行决策、法律、命令等的; 行政的: the ~ branch of the government; 政府的行政部门; the ~ head of the State, eg the President of the US. 一国之行政首长(例如美国的总统)。 ⇨ n 1 the ~, the branch of a government. 政府的行政部门。 ⇨ administration, judiciary, legislature. 2 (in the Civil Service) person who carries out what has been planned or decided. (文职部门)执行计划者; 行政官; 行政人员。 3 person or group in a business or commercial organization with administrative or managerial powers. (大企业或商业机构中的)决策人; 负责制定政策者; 董事会。

execu·tor /ɪgˈzekjutə(r); ɪgˈzɛkjətɚ/ n person who is appointed by the maker of a will to carry out the terms of the will. (立遗嘱者所委托之)遗嘱执行人。 **executrix** /ɪgˈzekjutrɪks; ɪgˈzɛkjətrɪks/ n woman ~. 女遗嘱执行人。

exe·gesis /ˌeksɪˈdʒiːsɪs; ˌeksoˈdʒɪsɪs/ n [U] explanation and interpretation (of a written work). (文字作品之)注释。

exemp·lary /ɪgˈzemplərɪ; ɪgˈzɛmplərɪ/ adj serving as an example or a warning: 作为模范的; 作为警戒的: ~ conduct/punishment. 可作模范的行为(作为警戒的惩罚)。

exemp·lify /ɪgˈzemplɪfaɪ; ɪgˈzɛmpləˌfaɪ/ vt (pt, pp -fied) [VP6A] illustrate by example; be an example of. 例证; 例示。 **exemp·lifi·ca·tion** /ɪgˌzemplɪfɪˈkeɪʃn; ɪgˌzɛmpləˈkeʃən/ n [U] ~ing; [C] example. 例证; 例子。

exempt /ɪgˈzempt; ɪgˈzɛmpt/ vt [VP6A, 14] ~ (from), free (from an obligation): 使免除(义务): Poor eyesight will ~ you from military service. 视力不佳将使你免服兵役。 □ adj ~ (from), not liable; free: 没有义务的; 免除的: ~ from tax. 免税。 **exemp·tion** /ɪgˈzempʃn; ɪgˈzɛmpʃən/ n [U] ~ion (from), ~ing or being ~ed; [C] instance of this. 免除; 解除。

ex·er·cise¹ /ˈeksəsaɪz; ˈɛksɚˌsaɪz/ n 1 [U] employment or practice of (mental or physical powers, of rights): 智力运用; 运动; 权利运用: Walking, running, rowing and horse-riding are all healthy forms of ~. 散步, 跑步, 划船和骑马都是有益健康的运动方式。 The doctor advised her to take more ~. 医生嘱她多运动。E~ of the mental faculties is as important as bodily ~. 智能的锻炼与身体的运动同样重要。 The ~ of patience is essential in diplomatic negotiations. 耐性在外交谈判中是必要的。 His tales showed considerable ~ of the imagination. 他的故事显示他用过人的想象力。 2 [C] activity, drill, etc designed for bodily, mental or spiritual training: 身体, 智力或精神训练之活动; 练习; 操练: vocal/gymnastic/deep-breathing, etc ~s; 声音练习(体操; 深呼吸运动等); ~s for the harp/flute, etc; 竖琴(横笛等)练习; five-finger ~s for the piano; 弹钢琴五指练习; ~s in logic/English composition; 推理(英语作文)练习; spiritual ~s, eg prayer. 精神训练之活动(例如祈祷)。 An ~ in clear thinking would benefit many public speakers. 思考清晰的训练对许多在公共场合演说者有益。 3 (pl) series of movements for training troops, crews of warships, etc: (复) (训练军队, 战舰船员等之)演习: military ~s; 军事演习; The third cruiser squadron has left for ~s in the North Sea. 第三巡洋舰战队已去北海演习。 4 (pl, US) ceremonies: (复, 美)典礼; 仪式: graduation ~s; 毕业典礼; opening ~s, eg speeches at the start of a conference. 开幕仪式。

ex·er·cise² /ˈeksəsaɪz; ˈɛksɚˌsaɪz/ vt, vi 1 [VP6A, 15A, 21] use; practise; give exercise to, ⇨ **exercise¹(1)**: 运动; 锻炼: Horses get fat and lazy if they are not ~d. 马如果不运动会肥胖和懒惰。 He ~s himself in fencing. 他练习剑术。 You don't ~ enough. 你的运动不够。 2 [VP6A] employ; make use of: 运用; 利用: ~ patience; 运用耐力; ~ authority over sb; 对某人使用权威; ~ one's rights. 行使权利。 3 [VP6A] (usu passive) perplex; trouble; worry the mind of: (通常用动语态)使迷惑; 使困扰; 使忧愁: The problem that is exercising our minds ... . 使我们困恼的问题是……。 I am very much ~d about the future/about the education of my son. 我对于未来(对于我儿子的教育)深为担忧。

exert /ɪgˈzɜːt; ɪgˈzɝt/ vt [VP6A,14,16A] 1 ~ (on/upon), put forth; bring into use: 发挥; 运用: ~ all one's strength/influence, etc (to do sth); 发挥个人所有的力量(影响力等)(去做某事); ~ pressure on sb. 对某人施以压力。 2 ~ oneself, make an effort: 努力: ~ oneself to arrive early; 尽力早到; ~ yourself on my behalf. 你尽量帮助我。

exer·tion /ɪgˈzɜːʃn; ɪgˈzɝʃən/ n [U] exerting; [C] instance of this: 发挥; 运用; 努力: E~ of authority is not always wise; persuasion may be better. 运用权威并不永远是明智的, 用说服的方法可能较好。 He failed to lift the rock in spite of all his ~s. 他虽然费尽力气, 仍未能将那岩石抬起。 Now that I am 90, I am unequal to the ~s of travelling. 我因年届九十, 已无力旅行了。

ex·eunt /ˈeksɪənt; ˈɛksɪənt/ (Lat) (as a stage direction) (拉)(舞台说明) ~ Antony and Cleopatra, they leave the stage. 安东尼及克利奥佩特拉退场。 ⇨ **exit**.

ex gratia /ˌeks ˈɡreɪʃə; ɛks ˈɡreʃə/ n (Lat) (拉) ~ pay·ment, payment not legally binding but for which some moral obligation is felt. 基于道德上的义务而付的款。

ex·hale /eksˈheɪl; ɛksˈhel/ vt, vi [VP6A, 2A] breathe out; give off gas, vapour; be given off (as gas or vapour): 呼出; 发出(气体, 蒸气); 被发出(如气体或蒸

气): ~ *air from the lungs.* 自肺中呼出气。 **ex·ha·la·tion** /ˌekshə'leɪʃn; ˌɛksə'leʃən/ n 1 [C] act of exhaling. 呼出; 发出。 2 [U, C] sth ~d. 呼出之气; 发出之气。

ex·haust[1] /ɪg'zɔːst; ɪg'zɔst/ n [C, U] (outlet, in an engine or machine, for) steam, vapour, etc that has done its work. (机器等之)排气口; 排出之废气。 '~-pipe n pipe for this. 排气管。 ⇨ the illus at **motor**. 参看 motor 之插图。

ex·haust[2] /ɪg'zɔːst; ɪg'zɔst/ vt [VP6A] 1 use up completely; 用尽; 耗尽: ~ *one's patience/strength;* 失去耐心/用尽力气; ~ *oneself by hard work;* 因努力工作而疲惫不堪; *feeling* ~*ed;* tired out. 感觉筋疲力竭。 2 make empty: 使空: ~ *a well;* 汲干一井; ~ *a tube of air.* 抽尽管中空气。 他们爬山爬得筋疲力竭。 **3** say, find out, all there is to say about (sth): 详论; 详尽阐述: ~ *a subject.* 详论一问题。

ex·haus·tion /ɪg'zɔːstʃən; ɪg'zɔstʃən/ n [U] exhausting or being exhausted; total loss of strength: 用尽; 竭尽; 疲惫: *They were in a state of* ~ *after climbing the mountain.* 他们爬山爬得筋疲力竭。

ex·haus·tive /ɪg'zɔːstɪv; ɪg'zɔstɪv/ adj thorough, complete: 彻底的; 完全的: *an* ~ *inquiry.* 彻查。 ~·**ly** adv

ex·hibit[1] /ɪg'zɪbɪt; ɪg'zɪbɪt/ n [C] 1 object or collection of objects, shown publicly, eg in a museum: 展览品; 陈列品(例如博物馆内者): *Do not touch the* ~*s.* 不要触摸展览品。 **2** document, object, etc produced in a law court and referred to in evidence, eg a weapon said to have been used by the accused person. (法庭上提出之)证件; 证物; 物证(例如指明被告所用的武器)。 **3** (US) exhibition(1). (美)商展; 工展; 动植物花卉等展览。

ex·hibit[2] /ɪg'zɪbɪt; ɪg'zɪbɪt/ vt [VP6A] 1 show publicly (for pleasure, for sale, in a competition, etc): (为乐趣, 售卖, 竞赛等而)陈列; 展览: ~ *paintings in an art gallery/flowers at a flower show;* 在一美术馆展览画(在花展陈列花); [VP2A, C]: *Mr X* ~*s in several galleries.* 某先生在数处画廊展出作品。 **2** give clear evidence of (a quality): 显示(一种性质): *The girls* ~*ed great powers of endurance during the climb.* 在攀登时, 那些女孩子显示出很大的耐力。 **ex·hibi·tor** /-tə(r); -tə/ n person who ~s at a show of pictures, a flower show, etc. (画展、花展等之)展出者; 参展者。

ex·hi·bi·tion /ˌeksɪ'bɪʃn; ˌɛksə'bɪʃən/ n 1 [C] collection of things shown publicly (eg of works of art); display of commercial or industrial goods for advertisement; public display of animals, plants, flowers, etc (often shown in competition, for prizes, and colloq called a *show*). 展览品(例如艺术品); 商展; 工展; 动植物花卉等展览(常是竞赛性的, 口语用 show)。 **2** (*sing* only) act of showing: (仅作单数)表现; 显示: *an* ~ *of bad manners;* 无礼貌之表现; *an opportunity for the* ~ *of one's knowledge.* 显示个人知识的机会。 *make an* ~ *of oneself,* behave in public so that one receives contempt. 当众出丑。 **3** (GB) money allowance to a student from school or college funds for a number of years. (英) 奖学金。 ~*er* n student to whom an ~(3) is granted. 获得奖学金的学生。 ~·**ism** /-ˌɪzəm; -ˌɪzəm/ n [U] tendency towards extravagant behaviour designed to attract attention to oneself. 表现主义; 风头主义。 ~·**ist** /-ɪst; -ɪst/ n person given to ~ism. 表现主义者; 风头主义者。

ex·hil·ar·ate /ɪg'zɪləreɪt; ɪg'zɪlə,ret/ vt [VP6A] (usu passive) fill with high spirits; make lively or glad: (通常用被动语态) 使高兴; 使兴奋: *exhilarating news.* 令人兴奋的消息。 **ex·hil·ar·ation** /ɪg,zɪlə'reɪʃn; ɪg,zɪlə'reʃən/ n

exhort /ɪg'zɔːt; ɪg'zɔrt/ vt [VP6A, 14, 17] ~ *sb to sth/to do sth,* (formal) urge, advise earnestly: (正式用语)力劝; 劝告: ~ *sb to do good/to work harder.* 劝告某人行善(更加努力); ~ *one's listeners to action.* 劝听众采取行动。 **ex·hor·ta·tion** /ˌeksɔː'teɪʃn; ˌegzɔ-

'teʃən/ n [U] ~ing; [C] earnest request, speech etc that ~s sb. 力劝; 劝告; 劝诫。

exhume US: ɪg'zhjuːm; ɪg'zuːm; ɪg'zjuːm/ vt [VP6A] take out (a dead body) from the earth (for examination). 掘出(尸体)以检验。 **exhum·ation** /ˌekshjuː'meɪʃn; ˌɛkshjuˈmeʃən/ n [U] exhuming or being ~d; [C] instance of this. 掘尸检验。

exi·gency /'eksɪdʒənsɪ; 'ɛksədʒənsɪ/ n (*pl* -**cies**) [C] condition of great need; emergency: 急迫需要; 紧急: *measures to meet the exigencies of this difficult period.* 为应付此困难时期的急迫需要所采取的措施。 **exi·gent** /-dʒənt; -dʒənt/ adj 1 urgent; pressing. 紧急的; 急迫的。 **2** exacting. 严苛的。

exigu·ous /eg'zɪgjʊəs; ɪg'zɪgjʊəs/ adj (formal) scanty: (正式用语)稀少的; 不足的: *an* ~ *diet.* 少量的食物。

exile /'eksaɪl; 'ɛgzaɪl/ n 1 [U] being sent away from one's country or home, esp as a punishment: 放逐; 充军; 流放: *be/live in* ~; 过流亡生活; 亡命他乡; *go/be sent into* ~; 遭放逐; *a place of* ~; 流放之地; [C] instance of this: *after an* ~ *of seven years.* 经七年之放逐。 **2** [C] person who is sent away in this way. 被放逐者。 □ vt [VP6A, 15A] send (sb) into ~: 放逐; 充军: ~ *sb from his country;* 将某人放逐国外; ~*d for life.* 被终身放逐。

exist /ɪg'zɪst; ɪg'zɪst/ vi 1 [VP2A,C] be; have being; be real: 存在; 实在: *The idea* ~*s only in the minds of poets.* 这观念只存在于诗人的心中。 *Do you believe that fairies* ~, *that there really are fairies?* 你相信真有神仙吗? *Does life* ~ *on Mars?* 火星上有生物吗? **2** [VP2A, C, 3A] continue living: 生存: *We cannot* ~ *without food and water.* 没有食物和水我们不能生存。 *She* ~*s on very little.* 她的生活很艰苦。 *How do they* ~ *in such wretched conditions?* 在这样恶劣的环境中他们怎样生存? ~·**ence** /-əns; -əns/ n 1 [U] the state of ~ing: 存在; 实在: *When did this world come into* ~*ence?* 这个世界是何时产生的? *Do you believe in the* ~*ence of ghosts?* 你相信有鬼吗? *This is the oldest Hebrew manuscript in* ~*ence.* 这是现存最早的希伯来文手抄本。 **2** an ~*ence,* manner of living: 生存方式; 生活: *lead a happy* ~*ence.* 过快乐的生活。 ~·**ent** /-ənt; -ənt/ adj ~ing; actual. 存在的; 现有的; 实在的。

exis·ten·tial·ism /ˌegzɪ'stenʃəlɪzəm; ˌɛgzɪs'tɛnʃəl,ɪzəm/ n doctrine (deriving from Kierkegaard and individual popularized by Sartre) that man is unique and isolated in an indifferent or hostile universe, responsible for his own actions and free to choose his destiny. 存在主义 (为充实基所创的, 萨塔特牙引提倡, 认为人在冷漠或有敌意的宇宙中, 是个独特和孤立的分子, 对自己的行为负责, 并可自由选择其命运)。

exit /'eksɪt; 'ɛgzɪt/ n 1 departure of an actor from the stage: (演员之)退场: *make one's* ~, go out or away. 离去。 **2** way out, eg from a theatre or cinema. (戏院或电影院等之)出口。 □ (as a stage direction) (作为舞台说明) *E*~ *Macbeth,* Macbeth goes off the stage. 麦克贝斯退场。 ⇨ **exeunt**.

ex·odus /'eksədəs; 'ɛksədəs/ n [C] (*sing* only) (仅用单数) going out or away of many people: (许多人之)离开; (很多人之)离去: *the* ~ *of people to the sea and the mountains for the summer holidays.* 很多人到海滨和山间度暑假。 **the E**~, the ~ of the Israelites from Egypt, in about 1300 BC. (约在纪元前一三〇〇年以色列人)出埃及。

ex officio /ˌeks ə'fɪʃɪəʊ; ˌɛksə'fɪʃɪ,o/ adv, adj (Lat) because of one's office or position: (拉) 由于职位; 依照官职: *an* ~ *member of the committee;* (委员会中)由于职位而产生的当然委员; *present at the meeting* ~. 依照职权出席一会议。

exon·er·ate /ɪg'zɒnəreɪt; ɪg'zɑnə,ret/ vt [VP6A, 14] ~ *sb (from),* free, clear: 免除: ~ *sb from blame/responsibility.* 免除某人之罪咎(责任)。 **exon·er·ation** /ɪg,zɒnə'reɪʃn; ɪg,zɑnə'reʃən/ n

exor·bi·tant /ɪgˈzɔːbɪtənt; ɪgˈzɔrbətənt/ adj (of a price, charge or demand) much too high or great. (指价格、索价或要求)过高的；过份的。 **~·ly** adv **exor·bi·tance** /-təns; -təns/ n

ex·or·cize /ˈeksɔːsaɪz; ˈeksɔrˌsaɪz/ vt [VP6A, 14] **~** (sth from)/(sb of), drive out (an evil spirit) by prayers or magic. 用祈祷或魔法驱除(妖魔)。

exotic /ɪgˈzɒtɪk; ɪgˈzɑtɪk/ adj 1 (of plants, fashions, words, ideas) introduced from another country. (指植物、时新式样、文字、观念)来自外国的；外来的。 2 foreign or unusual in style; striking or pleasing because colourful, unusual: 样式奇特的；因富有色彩和奇特而引人注意或悦人的： ~ birds. 奇特动人的鸟。

ex·pand /ɪkˈspænd; ɪkˈspænd/ vt, vi [VP6A, 14, 2A, C] **~** (in/into), 1 make or become larger: 使大；扩大；变大： Metals ~ when they are heated. 金属遇热则膨胀。 ⇨ **contract**[3](1). A tyre ~s when you pump air into it. 打了气，轮胎会胀大。 ⇨ **shrink**. The river ~s (= broadens) and forms a lake. 该河扩大而成湖。 The small pocket dictionary was ~ed into a larger volume. 该袖珍词典增订为较大的词典。 Our foreign trade has ~ed during recent years. 我们的对外贸易近年来已获扩展。 2 unfold or spread out: 展开： His face ~ed in a smile of welcome. 他的脸上绽开欢迎的笑容。 The petals of many flowers ~ in the sunshine. 许多花的花瓣在阳光中绽放。 3 (of a person) become good-humoured or genial. (指人)变为愉快和蔼。

ex·panse /ɪkˈspæns; ɪkˈspæns/ n [C] wide and open area: 宽阔的区域： the broad ~ of the Pacific; 浩瀚的太平洋； the blue ~ of the sky; 广袤的蓝天； a broad ~ of brow, eg of a man with a high forehead and bald head. 宽阔的额头。

ex·pan·sion /ɪkˈspænʃn; ɪkˈspænʃən/ n [U] expanding or being expanded(1): 扩大；变大；膨胀： ~ of the currency, by putting more banknotes into circulation: 通货膨胀； ~ of territory, eg by winning new territory; 领土的扩张； the ~ of gases when heated. 气体受热时之膨胀。

ex·pan·sive /ɪkˈspænsɪv; ɪkˈspænsɪv/ adj 1 able, tending, to expand. 可扩大的；可扩展的。 2 (of persons, speech) unreserved, effusive. (指人、言语)率直的；滔滔不绝的。 **~·ly** adv **~·ness** n

ex·pati·ate /ɪkˈspeɪʃɪeɪt; ɪkˈspeʃɪˌet/ vi [VP3A] **~** upon, (formal) write or speak at great length, in detail, about. (正式用语)详述；细说。

ex·patri·ate /eksˈpætrɪət; eksˈpetrɪɪt/ n person living outside his own country: 居于国外之人；侨民： American ~s in Paris; 居于巴黎的美国人； (attrib) (用作定语) ~ Americans 居于国外的美国人。 □ vt /-rɪeɪt; -rɪˌet/ [VP6A] ~ oneself, leave one's own country to live abroad; renounce one's citizenship. 移居国外；脱离国籍。

ex·pect /ɪkˈspekt; ɪkˈspekt/ vt [VP6A, 17, 7A, 9, 14] think or believe that sth will happen or come, that sb will come; wish for and feel confident that one will receive: 预期；盼望；期待；料想： We ~ed you yesterday. 我们昨天期待你来。 We were ~ing a letter from her. 我们当时正期待着她的信。 I ~ to be/~ that I shall be back on Sunday. 我想在星期日回来。 You would ~ there to be/that there would be strong disagreement about this. 你大概以为关于此事将有激烈的争论。 You can't learn a foreign language in a week; it's not to be ~ed. 你无法在一周内学会一种外国语言，那是不可指望的事。 You are ~ing too much of her. 你对她的期望过高。 'Will he be late?'—'I ~ so.' '他会迟到吗？'——'我想会的。' 'Will he need help?'—'No, I don't ~ so' (or)'No, I ~ not.' '他需要帮助吗？'——'不，我想他不需要。' They ~ (= require) me to work on Saturdays. 他们要我在星期六工作。 I ~ (= require) you to be punctual. 我希望你守时。 'Who has eaten all the cake?'—'Oh, I ~ (colloq 口 = suppose) it was Tom.' '谁把整个糕都吃掉了？'——'哦，我猜想是汤姆。' **~·ancy** /-ənsɪ; -ənsɪ/ n the state

of ~ing: 预期；期望；期待： with a look/an air of ~ancy; 以欣羡的神情； life ~ancy. 平均寿命。 **~·ant** /-ənt; -ənt/ adj ~ing: 预期的；期望的；期待的： an ~ant mother, woman who is pregnant. 孕妇。 **~·ant·ly** adv **~ed** adj that is ~ed: 预期的；所预料的；所期望的： an ~ed reply; 预期的回复； ~ed objections. 预料中的反对。

ex·pec·ta·tion /ˌekspekˈteɪʃn; ˌekspɛkˈteʃən/ n 1 [U] expecting; awaiting: 期望；期待： He ate a light lunch in ~ of a good dinner. 他草草用过午餐，期望吃一顿丰富的晚餐。 2 (often pl) thing that is expected. (常用复数)期望的事物。 beyond ~, greater or better than was expected. 出乎意料(较预期者为大或好)。 contrary to ~, in a way different from what was expected. 与期望相违。 fall short of/not come up to one's ~s, be less good than what was expected. 未臻理想。 3 (pl) future prospects, esp sth to be inherited: (复)期望之事物；前途；远景；(尤指)有希望继承之遗产： a young man with great ~s, eg one who has a millionaire uncle who has promised to leave him his wealth. 一位有希望继承大笔遗产的青年。 4 ~ of life, years a person is expected to live: 估计寿命；一个人可望活着的年数： A life assurance company can tell you the ~ of life of a man who is 40 years old. 人寿保险公司能告诉你一个四十岁的人的估计寿命。

ex·pec·tor·ate /ɪkˈspektəreɪt; ɪkˈspɛktəˌret/ vt, vi [VP6A, 2A] (formal) spit; send out (phlegm from the throat, blood from the lungs) by coughing. (正式用语)吐；咳嗽而吐(痰、血)。 **ex·pec·tor·ant** /-rənt; -rənt/ n medicine promoting expectorating. 祛痰剂；助咳药。

ex·pedi·ent /ɪkˈspiːdɪənt; ɪkˈspidɪənt/ adj (usu pred) likely to be useful or helpful for a purpose; advantageous though contrary to principle: (通常用作表语)有用的；有助益的；有利的(纵或不正当)；权宜的： In times of war governments do things because they are ~. 战时政府做一些事情，是因其有利。 Do what you think ~. 做你认为有利的事。 □ n [C] ~ plan, action, device, etc. 有利的计划或行动；权宜之计。 **~·ly** adv **ex·pedi·ence** /-əns; -əns/, **ex·pedi·ency** /-ənsɪ; -ənsɪ/ n [U] suitability for a purpose; being ~; self-interest: 适宜；有利；利己： act from expediency, not from principle. 因有利而行事，而非根据原则。

ex·pedite /ˈekspɪdaɪt; ˈekspɪˌdaɪt/ vt [VP6A] (formal) help the progress of; speed up (business, etc). (正式用语)帮助…之进展；加速发展(事业等)。

ex·pedi·tion /ˌekspɪˈdɪʃn; ˌekspɪˈdɪʃən/ n 1 [C] (men, ships, etc making a) journey or voyage for a definite purpose: (为一确定目的所做的)远征；远征队： a hunting ~; 狩猎(队)； go/send a party of men on an ~ to the Antarctic; 至(派一队人至)南极探险； members of the Mount Qomolangma ~. 珠穆朗玛峰探险队众队员。 2 [U] (formal) promptness; speed. (正式用语)敏捷；迅速。 **~·ary** /-ʃənərɪ US: -nerɪ; -ʃənˌerɪ/ adj of, making up, an ~: 远征(队)的；组成远征队的： an ~ary force, eg an army sent to take part in a war abroad. 远征军。

ex·pedi·tious /ˌekspɪˈdɪʃəs; ˌekspɪˈdɪʃəs/ adj (formal) acting quickly; prompt and efficient. (正式用语)迅速的；敏捷而有效的。 **~·ly** adv

ex·pel /ɪkˈspel; ɪkˈspɛl/ vt (-ll-) [VP6A, 14] **~** (from), send out or away by force: 驱逐；逐出： ~ the enemy from a town; 将敌人逐出一城； ~ a boy from school, as a punishment. 开除一男生。

ex·pend /ɪkˈspend; ɪkˈspɛnd/ vt [VP6A, 14] **~** sth (on/upon sth/in doing sth), 1 spend: 花费；使用： ~ all one's capital on equipment; 将所有资金用于设备； ~ time and care in doing sth. 费时间和精神去做某事。 2 use up: 耗尽；用光： They had ~ed all their ammunition. 他们的弹药已用尽。 **~·able** /-əbl; -əbl/ adj that may be ~ed, esp that may be sacrificed to achieve a purpose: 可消费的；(尤指)为达成某一目的而

可牺牲的: *The general considered that these troops were ~able.* 那将军认为这些部队可以牺牲。

ex·pen·di·ture /ɪk'spendɪtʃə(r); ɪk'spɛndɪtʃɚ/ *n* 1 [U] spending or using: 花费; 使用: *the ~ of money on armaments.* 军费的开支。2 [C,U] amount expended: 花费之量; 开销; 经费: *an ~ of £500 on new furniture.* 花五百英镑购新家具。*Limit your ~(s) to what is essential.* 将你的开销限制在必要范围内。

ex·pense /ɪk'spens; ɪk'spɛns/ *n* 1 [U] spending of money; cost: 花费; 代价: *Most children in Great Britain are educated at the public ~.* 英国大多数的儿童靠公家出钱受教育。*I want the best you can supply; you need spare no ~,* you need not try to economize. 我要你最好的货, 你不必去省钱。 **at the ~ of,** with the sacrifice of: 牺牲; 以…作代价: *He became a brilliant scholar, but only at the ~ of his health.* 他成为一个卓越的学者, 但却牺牲了健康。 **at his/her/my, etc ~, (a)** with him, her, me, etc paying: 由他(她、我等)付钱: *We were all entertained at the director's ~.* 我们全由导演请客。 **(b)** (fig) bringing discredit, ridicule or contempt on him, her, me, etc: (喻)嘲弄或轻视他(她、我等): *We had a good laugh at his ~,* We laughed at him because he had done sth ridiculous, been deceived, etc. 我们对他大加嘲笑一番。 **go to/put sb to the ~ of,** spend /cause him to spend money on: (使某人)花钱于: *It's foolish to go to the ~ of taking music lessons if you never practise.* 花钱上音乐课而从不练习是愚蠢的。*I don't want to put you to the ~ of providing my meals.* 我不想使你破费来为我准备伙食。'~ **account,** record of expenses incurred and either paid out of money supplied by, or to be refunded by, the employer, eg of a business man for travel, entertainment, etc. 费用帐; 支出帐(向雇主提出之报销帐目)。2 (usu *pl*) money used or needed for sth: (通常用复数)费用: *travelling ~s.* 旅费。*Illness, holidays and other ~s reduced his bank balance to almost nothing.* 患病, 度假, 以及其他费用使他在银行内的存款所剩无几了。

ex·pens·ive /ɪk'spensɪv; ɪk'spɛnsɪv/ *adj* causing expense; high priced: 费用大的; 昂贵的: *an ~ education,* 费用庞大的教育; *too ~ for me to buy.* 太贵而使我买不起。~·**ly** *adv*

ex·peri·ence /ɪk'spɪərɪəns; ɪk'spɪrɪəns/ *n* 1 [U] process of gaining knowledge or skill by doing and seeing things; knowledge or skill so gained: 经验; 由经验获得的知识或技术: *We all learn by ~.* 我们都从经验中学习。*Has he had much ~ in/of work of this sort?* 他对这种工作有很多经验吗? *He hasn't had enough ~ for the job.* 他没有足够的经验担当这工作。2 [C] event, activity, which has given one in some way: 经历; 阅历: *an unpleasant /trying /unusual ~.* 一个令人不愉快的(难堪的, 不平凡的)经历。 □ *vt* [VP6A] have ~ of; feel; meet with: 有…之经验; 经历; 感受; 体验: *~ pleasure /pain /difficulty / great hardships.* 经历快乐(痛苦, 困难, 艰苦)。~·**peri·enced** *adj* having ~; having knowledge or skill as the result of ~: 有经验的; 经验丰富的; 熟练的: *an ~d nurse /lover.* 有经验的护士(爱人)。

ex·peri·ment /ɪk'sperɪmənt; ɪk'spɛrəmənt/ *n* test or trial carried out carefully in order to study what happens and gain new knowledge: 实验; 实验: *perform /carry out an ~ in chemistry;* 做化学实验; [U] *learn sth by ~.* 由实验而学得某事。□ *vi* [VP2A, C, 3A] make ~s: 实验; 试验: *~ with new methods;* 以新方法试验; *~ upon dogs.* 以狗做试验。 **ex·peri·men·ta·tion** /ɪk,sperɪmen'teɪʃn; ɪk,spɛrəmen'teʃən/ *n* ~ing. 实验; 试验。

ex·peri·men·tal /ɪk,sperɪ'mentl; ɪk,spɛrə'mentl/ *adj* of, used for, based on, experiments: 实验的; 用做实验的; 根据实验的: *~ methods;* 实验方法; '*an ~ farm.* 实验农场。~·**ly** /-təlɪ; -tlɪ/ *adv*

ex·pert /'ekspɜːt; 'ekspɚt/ *n* person with special knowledge, skill or training: 专家: *an agricultural ~;*

农业专家; *an ~ in economics;* 经济学专家; *get the advice of the ~s.* 获取专家们的意见。 □ *adj* trained by practice; skilful: 熟练的; 老练的: *according to ~ advice /opinions;* 根据专家的意见; *men who are ~ at driving racing cars.* 熟练驾驶赛车的人。~·**ly** *adv* ~·**ness** *n*

ex·pert·ise /,ekspɜː'tiːz; ,ɛkspɚ'tiz/ *n* [U] 1 (comm) expert appraisal; valuation. (商) 专门鉴定; 评价。2 expert's report. 专家的报告。3 expert knowledge and skill. 专门知识和技术。 ⇨ *know-how* at **know.**

ex·pi·ate /'ekspɪeɪt; 'ɛkspɪ,et/ *vt* [VP6A] make amends for, submit to punishment for (wrongdoing): 补偿; 赎(罪); 为(罪)而受惩罚: *~ sin /a crime.* 赎罪。 **ex·pi·ation** /,ekspɪ'eɪʃn; ,ɛkspɪ'eʃən/ *n* [U].

ex·pir·ation /,ekspɪ'reɪʃn; ,ɛkspə'reʃən/ *n* [U] 1 ~ (of), expiring, ending, esp of a period of time: (尤指一段时期之)终止; 满期: *at the ~ of the lease.* 在租期届满时; 于租约终止时。2 (formal) breathing out (of air). (正式用语)(气之)呼出。

ex·pire /ɪk'spaɪə(r); ɪk'spaɪr/ *vi* [VP2A] 1 (of a period of time) come to an end: (指一段时期) 终止; 满期: *His term of office as President ~s next year.* 他当总统的任期明年届满。*When does your driving licence ~?* 你的驾驶执照何时满期? 2 (liter) die. (文)死亡。

ex·piry /ɪk'spaɪərɪ; ɪk'spaɪrɪ/ *n* (*pl* -**ries**) ~ **(of),** expiring, ending, esp of a period of time of a contract or agreement: (尤指一段时期, 合约等之)终止; 满期: *the ~ of a driving licence.* 驾驶执照之满期。

ex·plain /ɪk'spleɪn; ɪk'splen/ *vt* 1 [VP6A, 9, 8, 10, 14] ~ **sth (to sb),** make plain or clear; show the meaning of: 解释; 讲解; 说明: *A dictionary tries to ~ the meanings of words.* 词典解释词的意义。*Please ~ this problem to me.* 请将此问题解释给我听。*Please ~ to me what this means.* 请对我说明这是什么意思。*He ~ed that he had been delayed by the weather.* 他解释说他曾为天气而耽搁。*Please ~ yourself,* make you meaning clear. 请说明你的意思。 ⇨ 2 below. 参看下列第 2 义。 2 [VP6A, 15B] account for: 辩明; 说明…的原因或理由: *Can you ~ his behaviour?* 你能解释他的行为吗? *That ~s his absence.* 那就说明了他缺席的原因。*Please ~ yourself,* give reasons for your conduct. 请说明你这种行为的理由。~ **sth away,** show why one should not be blamed for a fault, mistake, etc: 说明自己可以不应为某项错误等而受责; 辩护: *You will find it difficult to ~ away your use of such offensive language.* 你将发现你很难为说这这种无礼的话辩护。

ex·pla·na·tion /,eksplə'neɪʃn; ,ɛksplə'neʃən/ *n* 1 [U] (process of) explaining: 解释; 说明; 辩明: *Not much ~ will be needed.* 不需多做说明。*I had better say a few words by way of ~.* 我最好以解释的方式说几句话。*Had he anything to say in ~ of his conduct?* 他还有什么话可以为他的行为辩白吗? 2 [C] statement, fact, circumstances, etc that explains: 解释的言语, 事实, 情形等: *an ~ of his conduct /of a mystery;* 为他的行为(一神秘事件) 所作的解释; *after repeated ~s.* 经反复解释后。

ex·plana·tory /ɪk'splænətrɪ US: -tɔːrɪ; ɪk'splænə,torɪ/ *adj* serving or intended to explain. 解释的; 说明的。

ex·ple·tive /ɪk'spliːtɪv US: 'eksplɪtɪv; 'eksplɪtɪv/ *n* [C] violent (often meaningless) exclamation, eg 'My goodness', or an oath such as 'Damn' 强烈的感叹词(常是无意义的, 例如 'My goodness' 或咒语 'Damn' 之类)。

ex·plic·able /ek'splɪkəbl; 'eksplɪkəbl/ *adj* (formal) that can be explained. (正式用语)可解释的; 能说明的。

ex·pli·cate /'eksplɪkeɪt; 'ɛksplɪ,ket/ *vt* [VP6A] (formal) explain and analyse in detail. (正式用语)详细解说和分析。

ex·plicit /ɪk'splɪsɪt; ɪk'splɪsɪt/ *adj* (of a statement, etc) clearly and fully expressed; definite: (指陈述等)

明白表示的; 明确的: *He was quite ~ about the matter,
left no doubt about what he meant.* 他对此事的态度表
示得十分明白。 ~·ly *adv* ~·ness *n*

ex·plode /ɪkˈspləʊd; ɪkˈsplod/ *vt, vi* 1 [VP6A, 2A,
C] (cause to) burst with a loud noise: (使)爆炸: *~ a
charge of gunpowder/a bomb.* 使一个火药包(一枚炸弹)
爆炸。 *When the boiler ~d many people were hurt by the
steam.* 汽锅爆炸时许多人为蒸汽所伤。 *The shell ~d in
the barrel of the gun.* 炮弹在炮管内爆炸了。 2 [VP2A,
C] (of feelings) burst out; (of persons) show violent
emotion: (指感情)激发; (指人)表示强烈感情: *At last
his anger ~d.* 他的怒气终于发作了。 *He ~d with rage/
jealousy.* 他勃然大怒(嫉妒大发)。 3 [VP6A] destroy,
expose (an idea, a theory, etc); show the falsity of: 推
翻(观念, 学说等); 破除; 揭发其为伪: *~ a superstition.*
破除一迷信; *an ~d idea.* 被推翻的一个观念。

ex·ploit[1] /ˈeksplɔɪt; ˈɛksplɔɪt/ *n* [C] bold or adventurous act; brilliant achievement. 英勇的行为; 辉煌的
事迹; 功业。

ex·ploit[2] /ɪkˈsplɔɪt; ɪkˈsplɔɪt/ *vt* [VP6A] 1 use, work
or develop (eg mines, waterpower, other natural
resources of a country). 利用或开发(一国之矿藏、水利
等天然资源)。 2 use selfishly, or for one's own profit:
自私地利用; 用以自肥; 剥削: *~ child labour.* 剥削童工。
ex·ploi·ta·tion /ˌeksplɔɪˈteɪʃn; ˌɛksplɔɪˈteʃən/ *n* [U]
~ing or being ~ed (both senses): 利用; 开发; 自私的
利用; 剥削: *the ~ation of a new country.* 一个新国家的
开发。

ex·plore /ɪkˈsplɔː(r); ɪkˈsplor/ *vt* [VP6A] 1 travel
into or through (a country, etc) for the purpose of
learning about it: 探测; 踏勘(一国家等): *~ the Arctic
regions.* 探测北极地带。 *Columbus discovered America
but did not ~ the new continent.* 哥伦布发现了美洲, 但未
对此新大陆加以探测。 2 examine thoroughly in order to
test, learn about: 探究; 仔细探查: *~ possibilities/
problems.* 仔细探查可能性(问题)。 **ex·plorer** /-rə(r);
-rɚ/ *n* person who ~s. 探测者; 探究者。 **ex·plo·ra·**
tion /ˌeksplɔːˈreɪʃn; ˌɛksplɔˈreʃən/ *n* [U] exploring:
探测; 探究; 探查: *the exploration of the ocean depths.*
海深之探测; [C] instance of this. 探测的实例。 **ex·**
plora·tory /ɪkˈsplɔːrətrɪ *US:* -tɔːrɪ; ɪkˈsplorə,torɪ/
adj for the purpose of exploring. 探测的; 探查的。

ex·plosion /ɪkˈspləʊʒn; ɪkˈsploʒən/ *n* 1 exploding;
(loud noise caused by) sudden and violent bursting: 爆
炸; 爆炸声: *a bomb.* 炸弹的爆炸。 *The ~ was heard
a mile away.* 在一英里以外可听到爆炸声。 2 ~ (of),
outburst or outbreak (of anger, laughter, etc): (愤怒,
大笑等之)爆发; 发作。 3 great and sudden increase: 大
幅度突增; 剧增: *the population ~ after the war.* 战后人
口之剧增。

ex·plo·sive /ɪkˈspləʊsɪv; ɪkˈsplosɪv/ *n, adj* (substance)
tending to or likely to explode: 爆炸物; 炸药; 易爆的:
易发作的: *a shell filled with high ~.* 装有强烈炸药的炮
弹。 *Dynamite and gun-cotton are ~s.* 炸药和火药棉是
易爆炸物。 *The old man has an ~ temper*, often explodes
with anger, etc. 这老人的脾气暴躁。 *That's an ~
issue*, one likely to inflame feeling. 那是个激动感情的
问题。 ~·ly *adv*

expo /ˈekspəʊ; ˈɛkspo/ *n* international exposition (2).
世界商展; 国际商展; 世界博览会。

ex·po·nent /ɪkˈspəʊnənt; ɪkˈsponənt/ *n* ~ (of),
1 person or thing that explains or interprets, or is a
representative or example: 解释者; 阐明者; 代表; 典型:
Huxley was an ~ of Darwin's theory of evolution. 赫胥
黎是达尔文进化论的解说者。 2 (alg) symbol that indicates what power of a factor is to be taken: (代数)指
数: *In a^3, the figure 3 is the ~; in x^n, the symbol^n is
the ~.* 在 a^3 中 3 是指数, 在 x^n 中 n 是指数。

ex·port[1] /ˈekspɔːt; ˈɛksport/ *n* 1 [U] (business of)
exporting: 输出; 输出业: *a ban on the ~ of gold;* 黄金
出口之禁止; (attrib) (用作定语) *the '~ trade;* 出口贸
易; *'~ duties.* 出口税。 2 [C] sth exported: 输出品; 出口

口货: *Last year ~s exceeded imports in value.* 去年输出
品在价值上超过了输入品。 *What are the chief ~s of your
country?* 你的国家有哪些主要的输出品?

ex·port[2] /ɪkˈspɔːt; ɪksˈport/ *vt* [VP6A] send (goods)
to another country for purposes of trade: 输出(货物):
~ cotton goods. 输出棉织品。 ⇨ **import.** ~·er *n* trader
who ~s goods. 出口商。 ~·able *adj* that
can be ~ed. 可输出的。 **ex·por·ta·tion** /ˌekspɔːˈteɪʃn;
ˌɛksporˈteʃən/ *n* [U] the ~ing of goods; goods ~ed.
输出; 输出货。

ex·pose /ɪkˈspəʊz; ɪkˈspoz/ *vt* [VP6A, 14, 15A] ~
(to), 1 uncover; leave uncovered or unprotected: 揭露;
使暴露; 弃置: *~ soldiers to unnecessary risks/to the
enemy's gunfire:* 让士兵们冒不必要的危险(受敌人炮火
的射击); *~d to the wind and rain;* 受风吹雨打; ~d
to ridicule. 遭受讥笑。 2 display: 展览; 陈列: *~ goods
in a shop window.* 陈列货物于商店橱窗内。 3 disclose,
make known: 揭发; 揭穿: *~ a plot/project/plan;* 揭
发一阴谋(计划); reveal the guilt or wrongdoing of;
unmask: 揭穿…之罪恶; 使暴露真相: *~ a crime/
criminal.* 揭穿一罪行(罪犯)。 4 (photo) allow light to
reach (camera film, etc): (摄影)使(软片等)感光; 曝光:
~ 30 metres of cinema film. 曝晒三十米电影
胶片。

ex·posé /ekˈspəʊzeɪ *US:* ˌekspəˈzeɪ; ˌɛkspoˈze / *n*
1 orderly setting out or précis of a body of facts or
beliefs. (对事实或信仰的)有系统的陈述。 2 making
public of discreditable fact(s). 揭发不名誉之事。

ex·po·si·tion /ˌekspəˈzɪʃn; ˌɛkspəˈzɪʃən/ *n* 1 [U]
expounding or explaining; [C] instance of this;
explanation or interpretation of a theory, plan, etc.
解释; (原理, 计划等之)说明。 2 [C] (abbr 略作 **expo**
/ˈekspəʊ; ˈɛkspo/) exhibition of goods, etc: 商品等之
展览: *an industrial ~.* 工业展览。

ex·postu·late /ɪkˈspɒstjʊleɪt; ɪkˈspɑstʃəˌlet/ *vi*
[VP2A, 3A] ~ (with sb) (on/about sth), make a
friendly protest; reason or argue. 忠告; 劝戒。 **ex·**
postu·la·tion /ɪkˌspɒstjʊˈleɪʃn; ɪkˌspɑstʃəˈleʃən/ *n*
[C, U] friendly protest(ing): 告戒; 劝戒: *My expostu-
lation(s) had no results.* 我的劝戒无效。

ex·po·sure /ɪkˈspəʊʒə(r); ɪkˈspoʒɚ/ *n* 1 [U] exposing
or being exposed (all senses): 暴露; 揭露; 展览; 揭发;
揭穿; 曝晒: *The climbers lost their way on the mountain
and died of ~.* 登山者在山间迷失了路而死于冻馁。 *E~
of the body to strong sunlight may be harmful.* 使身体受
强烈的阳光所晒, 可能有害。 *The ~ of the plot against the
President probably saved his life.* 揭发危害总统的阴谋或
许救了他的命。 2 [C] instance of exposing or being
exposed (all senses): 暴露; 揭露; 揭发; 曝晒等的实
例: *As a result of these ~s the government took strong
measures against bribery and corruption.* 由于这些揭发,
政府采取了强硬措施以惩治贿赂与舞弊。 *How many ~s
have you got left?* How many pictures remain on the
(camera) film? 你还剩下多少张底片呀? *An ~ of one-
hundredth of a second will be enough.* 百分之一秒的曝光
就够了。 '~ meter *n* (photo) device to measure
illumination and to indicate correct duration of ~. (摄
影)曝光表。 ⇨ the illus at **camera.** 参看 camera 之
插图。

ex·pound /ɪkˈspaʊnd; ɪkˈspaʊnd/ *vt* [VP6A, 14] ~
(to), explain, make clear, by giving details: 详加解
释; 详细说明: *~ a theory/one's views (to sb).* (对某人)
详细说明一原理(自己的见解)。

ex·press[1] /ɪkˈspres; ɪkˈsprɛs/ *adj* 1 clearly and
definitely stated, not suggested or implied: 明白表示
的; 明确的: *You cannot ignore such an ~ command.* 你
不能忽视如此明确的一项命令。 *It was his ~ wish that
you should not wait for him.* 他明白表示不要你等他。 2
going, sent, quickly; designed for high speed: 迅速地
进行或发出的; 高速的: *an '~ train;* 快车; *'~ delivery*,
by special postal messenger; 快递; 限时专送; *an '~
letter/messenger.* 限时专送的信件(信差)。 '~ **way** *n*

(US) major road for fast travel· (美)高速公路。⇨ (GB) (英) **motorway**. □ adv by ~ delivery; by ~ train: 用快递; 乘快车: *send a parcel* ~; 以快递寄包裹; *travel* ~. **·ly** adv **1** plainly; definitely: 明白地; 确定地: *You were* ~*ly forbidden to touch my papers.* 你绝不可碰我的文件。**2** specially; on purpose: 特意地; 故意地: *a dictionary* ~*ly compiled for foreign students of English.* 一部专为学习英语的外国学生所编的词典。

ex·press² /ik'spres; ik'sprɛs/ n **1** very fast train: 快车: *the 8.00am* ~ *to Edinburgh.* 上午八时去爱丁堡的快车。**2** (US) company t'at undertakes to deliver goods fast and safely. (美)运送公司(送货迅速安全)。**3** [U] service rendered by the post office, railways, road services, etc for carrying goods quickly: 邮局, 铁路, 公路局等之货物迅速递送: *send goods by* ~. (由铁路等)运送货物。

ex·press³ /ik'spres; ik'sprɛs/ vt **1** [VP6A, 10, 15A] make known, show by words, actions: 表示; 以语言, 表情, 动作)表达: *I find it difficult to* ~ *my meaning.* 我发觉我难以表达我的意思。*A smile* ~*ed her joy at the good news.* 微笑表示出对好消息的欣慰。*I cannot easily* ~ (*to you*) *how grateful I am for your help.* 我难以向你表达我是多么感激你的帮助。~ *oneself,* communicate one's thoughts or feelings through words, gestures, etc: 表达自己的意思: *He is still unable to* ~ *himself in English.* 他仍不能用英语表达他的意思。*He* ~*ed himself strongly* (= spoke in a forceful way) *on the subject.* 他强烈地表示了他对此问题的意见。**2** [VP6A] send a letter, goods, etc fast by special delivery. 快递(邮件, 货物等)。**3** [VP6A,14] ~ *(from/out of),* (formal) press or squeeze out juices/oil: (正式用语)榨出(汁, 油): *juice* ~*ed* (*pressed* is more usu) *from grapes.* 自葡萄榨出的汁(*pressed* 较常用)。

ex·press·ion /ik'spreʃn; ik'sprɛʃən/ n **1** [U] process of expressing(1): 表达; 表示: *give* ~ *to one's gratitude,* say or show how grateful one is; 表示感激; *read* (aloud) *with* ~, in a way that shows feeling for the meaning: 带有感情地朗诵; [C] instance of this (esp a look on sb's face): 表情: *There was an* ~ *of discontent on her face,* a discontented look. 她脸上有不满的表情。*beyond* ~ */past* ~, in a manner that cannot be expressed: 无法形容; 无法表达: *The scenery was beautiful beyond* ~, indescribably beautiful. 那风景美丽的无法形容。*find* ~ *in,* be expressed by means of: 由…表现出来: *Her feelings at last found* ~ *in tears.* 她的感情终于由眼泪发泄出来。**2** [C] word or phrase: 辞句; 措辞: *'Shut up'* (= Stop talking) *is not a polite* ~. '住嘴'不是有礼貌的辞句。 *Slang* ~*s should be avoided in an essay.* 文章里应避免用俚语。**3** [C] (maths) group of symbols expressing a quantity, eg 3xy². (数学)式(例如 3xy²)。~ **·less** adj without ~: 无表情的: *in an* ~*less voice;* 以冷冰冰的声音; *an* ~*less face.* 无表情的面孔。

ex·press·ion·ism /ik'spreʃənizəm; ik'sprɛʃn,ɪzm/ n [U] (in painting, music, etc) the symbolic or stylized expression of emotional experience. (绘画, 音乐等)表现主义(以象征的手法或特殊的风格表现内心的经验)。**ex·press·ion·ist** /-ist; -ist/ n

ex·press·ive /ik'spresiv; ik'sprɛsiv/ adj ~ *(of),* serving to express: 表示的; 表现的: *looks* ~ *of despair;* 表示绝望的神情; *a cry* ~ *of pain;* 表示痛苦的哭叫; *a* ~ *smile.* 意味深长的微笑。~ **·ly** adv

ex·pro·pri·ate /eks'prəuprieit; eks'propri,et/ vt [VP 6 A, 14] ~ *(from),* take away (property); dispossess (sb of an estate, etc). 征用(私产); 剥夺(某人之地产等)。**ex·pro·pri·ation** /eks,prəupri'eiʃn; eks,propri'eʃən/ n [U]

ex·pul·sion /ik'spʌlʃn; ik'spʌlʃən/ n [U] ~ *(from),* expelling or being expelled; [C] instance of this: 逐出; 被逐; 驱逐: ~ *of a student from college,* 将一学生自大学开除; *an* '~ *order,* official order

expelling a person from a country. 驱逐出境的命令。

ex·punge /ik'spʌndʒ; ik'spʌndʒ/ vt [VP6A, 14] ~ *(from),* (formal) wipe or rub out words, names, etc from a book, etc. (正式用语)擦去; 删掉; 划掉(字, 姓名等)。

ex·pur·gate /'ekspəgeit; 'ɛkspɚ,get/ vt [VP6A] take out from (a book, etc what are considered to be) improper or objectionable parts: 删除(书籍等)不妥之处: *an* ~*d edition of a novel.* 一小说的删节本; 洁本。**ex·pur·ga·tion** /,ekspə'geiʃn; ,ɛkspɚ'geʃən/ n

ex·quis·ite /'ekskwizit US: ek'skwizit; 'ɛkskwizit/ adj **1** of great excellence; brought to a high state of perfection: 优美的; 精致的: ~ *workmanship;* 优美的技艺; ~ *designs;* 精致的图案; *a piece of* ~ *lace.* 一条精致的花边。**2** (of pain, pleasure, etc) keenly felt. (指痛苦, 快乐等)强烈地感受到的; 极度的。**3** (of power to feel) keen, delicate: (指感觉力)灵敏的; 敏锐的: ~ *sensibility.* 灵敏的感觉能力。~ **·ly** adv ~ **·ness** n

ex·ser·vice /,eks'sɜːvis; 'ɛks'sɝvis/ adj having formerly served in the armed forces. 退役的; 退伍的。~ **·man** /-mən; -mən/ n (pl **-men**) (GB): (英): *an* ~ *men's organization.* 退伍军人协会。

ex·tant /ek'stænt US: 'ɛkstənt; ik'stænt/ adj still in existence (esp of documents, etc): 仍存在的; 现存的(尤指文件等): *the earliest* ~ *manuscript of this poem.* 此诗现存的最早的原稿。

ex·tem·por·ary /ik'stempərəri US: -pərəri; ik-'stempə,rɛri/ adj = **extempore**. **ex·tem·por·ar·ily** /-rəli US: -'rərəli; -,rɛrəli/ adv

ex·tem·pore /ek'stempəri; ik'stempəri/ adv, adj (spoken or done) without previous thought or preparation: 临时地; 无准备地的: *speak* ~, without notes; 临时演说(未备草稿); *an* ~ *address.* 即席演说。**ex·tem·por·aneous** /ek,stempə'reiniəs(li) / ek,stempo'renios(li); ik,stempo'reniəs(li)/ adj, adv = ~. 临时的(地); 即席的(地)。

ex·tend /ik'stend; ik'stɛnd/ vt, vi **1** [VP6A] make longer (in space or time); enlarge: 使(在空间或时间上)伸展; 扩大; 加长: ~ *a railway/a fence/a wall/the city boundaries.* 延长铁路(围墙, 墙壁, 市界)。*Can't you* ~ *your visit for a few days,* stay a few days longer? 你不能多停留几天吗? ~ *credit,* (fin) prolong the time for which credit is given. (财政)延长信用期限。**2** [VP 6A, 15A] lay or stretch out the body, a limb or limbs, at full length: 伸开; 展开(身体或四肢): ~ *one's arm horizontally;* 将胳膊平伸; ~ *one's hand to sb,* shake hands with him. 伸手与某人握手。**3** [VP6A, 14] ~ *sth (to sb),* offer, grant, accord: 给与; 施与: ~ *hospitality/ an invitation/a greeting/a warm welcome to sb;* 款待(邀请, 问候, 热烈欢迎)某人; ~ *help.* 给予帮助。**4** [VP 2B, C] (of space, land, etc) reach, stretch: (指空间, 土地等)达到; 伸展: *a road that* ~*s for miles and miles.* 伸展很多很多英里的道路。*My garden* ~*s as far as the river.* 我的花园伸展到河边。**5** [VP6A, 15A] cause to reach or stretch: 使达到; 延伸: ~ *a cable between two posts.* 在两柱间拉一条钢索。**6** [VP6A] (usu passive) tax or use the powers of a person, horse, etc to the utmost: (通常用及动语态)使竭尽全力: *The horse was fully* ~*ed.* 那匹马已竭尽全力。⇨ *flat out* at **flat²** adv(4).

ex·ten·sion /ik'stenʃn; ik'stɛnʃən/ n **1** [U] extending or being extended: 伸展; 延伸; 扩大: *the* ~ *of useful knowledge;* 有用的知识之推广; *University E*~, teaching for, examination of, part-time or extramural students; 大学附设的补习班; 大学的附设部分; *the* ~ *of socialist influence in Africa.* 社会主义的影响在非洲的扩大。**2** [C] additional part; addition or continuance; enlargement: 附加部分; 增加之物; 延伸部分: *an* ~ *of one's summer holidays;* 暑假之延长期间; *build an* ~ *to a hospital;* 扩建一医院之附设部分; *an* ~ *of time,* eg for paying a debt; 获一延期(例如偿债); *an* ~ *to a sentence,* (gram) word or words amplifying the subject or

predicate; (语法) 扩大主语或谓语的词; *telephone No 01-629-8494*, ~ *15*, ie a line extending from the switchboard to another room or office. 电话号码 01-629-8494 转 15 号分机.

ex·ten·sive /ɪkˈstensɪv; ɪkˈstɛnsɪv/ *adj* extending far; far-reaching: 广阔的; 广泛的; 远及的: an ~ view; 广阔的视野; ~ *repairs/inquiries*; 广泛的修理(调查); *a scholar with an* ~ *knowledge of his subject.* 对其研究科目知识广博的学者. ~·**ly** *adv*

ex·tent /ɪkˈstent; ɪkˈstɛnt/ *n* [U] **1** ~ *(of)*, length; area; range: 长度; 区域; 范围: *From the roof we were able to see the full* ~ *of the park.* 从屋顶上我们能看到公园的全景. *I was amazed at the* ~ *of his knowledge.* 我对他知识的渊博感到惊奇. *They are building a new racing track, six miles in* ~. 他们正在建筑一条六英里长的新跑道. **2** degree: 程度: *to a certain* ~ *to some* ~, partly, somewhat; 部分地; 有些; *to such an* ~ *that …*; 达到此种程度 *to what* ~; 达到什么程度; *in debt to the* ~ *of £100.* 负债达一百英镑.

ex·tenu·ate /ɪkˈstenjueɪt; ɪkˈstɛnjʊ,et/ *vt* [VP6A] make (wrongdoing) less serious (by finding an excuse): 掩饰(罪过); (以借口)使(罪过)减轻: *Nothing can* ~ *his base conduct.* 他的卑鄙的行为无法掩饰. *There are extenuating circumstances in this case.* 此案中有掩饰罪过的情形. **ex·tenu·ation** /ɪkˌstenjuˈeɪʃn; ɪkˌstɛnjʊˈeʃən/ *n* **1** [U] extenuating or being ~d: 掩饰罪过; 以借口减轻罪过: *He pleaded poverty in extenuation of the theft.* 他以贫穷为借口请求减轻他的偷窃罪. **2** [C] sth that ~s; partial excuse. 减轻罪过的借口.

ex·terior /ɪkˈstɪərɪə(r); ɪkˈstɪrɪɚ/ *adj* outer; situated on or coming from outside: 外部的; 在外部的; 来自外部的: *the* ~ *surface of a hollow ball;* 空心球的表面; *the* ~ *features of a building.* 一建筑物之外貌. ⇨ **interior.** □ *n* outside; outward aspect or appearance: 外部; 外面; 外表: *a gentle man with a rough* ~. 一个外貌粗野而性情温和的男人. ~·**ize** *vt* /-raɪz /,raɪz / **externalize.**

ex·ter·mi·nate /ɪkˈstɜːmɪneɪt; ɪkˈstɝmə,net/ *vt* [VP6A] make an end of (disease, ideas, people's beliefs); destroy completely. 消除(疾病, 观念, 信仰); 消灭. **ex·ter·mi·na·tion** /ɪkˌstɜːmɪˈneɪʃn; ɪkˌstɝməˈneʃən/ *n*.

ex·ter·nal /ɪkˈstɜːnl; ɪkˈstɝnl/ *adj* outside; situated on the outside; of or for the outside: 外部的; 在外部的; 外面的: ~ *evidence*, obtained from independent sources, not from what is being examined; 外证; *alcohol for* ~ *use*, for use on the skin, not to be drunk; 外用酒精 (非饮用者); ~ *examination*, one conducted by authorities outside the school, college, etc of the person(s) examined; 校外主持的考试; ~ *examiner*, person (not on the staff of those setting the examination) conducting such an examination. 校外主考人. ⇨ **internal.** □ *n* (usu *pl*) ~ circumstances; outward features: (通常用复数)外部情况; 外貌; 外观: *the* ~*s of religion*, acts and ceremonies (contrasted with inner and spiritual aspects): 宗教的外表形式(指其行为和仪式, 以别于内在的和精神方面的); *judge people by* ~*s.* 以貌取人。~·**ly** /-aɪz/ *vt* [VP6A] make ~. 使在外部; 使在外面. ~·**ly** /ekˈstɜːnəlɪ; ɪkˈstɝnlɪ/ *adv*

ex·ter·ri·tor·ial /ˌeks,terɪˈtɔːrɪəl; ,ɛkstɛrəˈtorɪəl/ *adj* (eg of ambassadors, etc) free from the jurisdiction of the State in which one resides: (指大使等)享有治外法权的: ~ *privileges and rights.* 治外法权.

ex·tinct /ɪkˈstɪŋkt; ɪkˈstɪŋkt / *adj* **1** no longer burning; no longer active: 熄灭的; 不再活动的: *an* ~ *volcano.* 死火山. **2** (of feelings, passions) dead. (指感情)绝灭的. **3** no longer in existence; having died out: 绝种的; 死绝的: *an* ~ *species*: 已灭绝的; *become* ~. 已绝种.

ex·tinc·tion /ɪkˈstɪŋkʃn; ɪkˈstɪŋkʃən/ *n* [U] **1** making, being, becoming, extinct: 扑灭; 消灭; 毁灭; 绝种: *a tribe threatened by* ~; 有绝种之虞的部落; *research that*

may lead to the ~ *of a disease.* 可能导致灭绝某一疾病的研究工作. **2** act of extinguishing: 灭火: *the* ~ *of a fire/of sb's hopes.* 火之熄灭/某人希望之幻灭.

ex·tin·guish /ɪkˈstɪŋgwɪʃ; ɪkˈstɪŋgwɪʃ/ *vt* [VP6A] **1** put out (eg a light, fire). 熄灭(例如灯, 火). **2** end the existence of (eg hope, love, passion, etc). 消灭(例如希望, 爱情, 情感等). **3** wipe out (a debt). 清偿(债务). ~·**er** *n* (kinds of) apparatus for discharging a jet of liquid chemicals for ~ing a fire. 灭火器.

ex·tir·pate /ˈekstəpeɪt; ˈɛkstɚ,pet / *vt* [VP6A] (formal) pull up by the roots; destroy utterly: (正式用语)连根拔起; 根除; 灭绝: ~ *social evils.* 根除社会弊端. **ex·tir·pa·tion** /ˌekstəˈpeɪʃn; ,ɛkstɚˈpeʃən/ *n* [U].

ex·tol /ɪkˈstəʊl; ɪkˈstol/ *vt* (-ll-) [VP6A,15A] praise highly: 颂扬; 极力称赞: ~ *sb to the skies*, greatly; 把某人捧上天; ~ *sb's merits*; 颂扬某人的功德; ~ *sb as a hero.* 将某人当作英雄来颂扬.

ex·tort /ɪkˈstɔːt; ɪkˈstɔrt/ *vt* [VP6A, 14] ~ *(from)*, obtain by violence, threats, etc: 以暴力、威胁等获得; 强取; 勒索: ~ *money from sb.* 向某人勒索钱财. *The police used torture to* ~ *a confession from him.* 警方用刑逼他招供. **ex·tor·tion** /ɪkˈstɔːʃn; ɪkˈstɔrʃən/ *n* [U] ~ing; [C] instance of this. 强取; 勒索; 以暴力或威胁获得.

ex·tor·tion·ate /ɪkˈstɔːʃənət; ɪkˈstɔrʃənɪt/ *adj* (of demands, prices) much too great or high. (指要求, 价格)过高的; 太大的. ~·**ly** *adv*

extra /ˈekstrə; ˈɛkstrə/ *adj* additional; beyond what is usual, expected or arranged for: 额外的; 特别的; 特加的: ~ *pay for* ~ *work*; 额外工作的额外报酬; *without* ~ *charge.* 不额外收费. *There are so many people that the company put on* ~ *buses.* 人数太多, 公司加开了公共汽车. □ *adv* **1** more than usually: 特别地; 非常地: *an* ~ *strong box*; 特别坚牢的箱子; ~ *fine quality.* 特别好的质地. **2** in addition: 除外: *price £1.30, packing and postage* ~. 价格为 1.30 英镑, 包装与邮费除外. □ *n* **1** ~ thing; sth for which an ~ charge is made: 额外的事物; 额外收费的之物: *Her regular school fees are £50 a term; music and dancing are* ~*s.* 她的固定的学费是每学期五十英镑, 音乐和舞蹈另行收费. **2** (cricket) run not scored off the bat. (板球)未击中球而跑得的分数. **3** (cinema, TV, etc) person employed and paid (usu by the day) for a minor part, eg in a crowd scene. (电影, 电视等)临时演员.

ex·tract /ɪkˈstrækt; ɪkˈstrækt/ *vt* [VP6A, 14] ~ *(from)*, **1** take or get out (usu with effort or by force): 拔取; 拔出: ~ *a cork from a bottle*; 拔出一瓶塞; *have a tooth* ~*ed*; 拔掉一颗牙; ~ *a bullet from a wound*; 自伤口取出一子弹; (fig) (喻) ~ *money/information from sb*, who is unwilling to give it. 榨取某人的金钱 (情报). **2** obtain (juices, etc) by pressing, crushing, boiling, etc: 榨出(汁等); 煎出: ~ *oil from cotton-seed/olives.* 自棉子(橄榄)中榨油. **3** select and present words, examples, passages, etc (from a book, speech, etc). (自书籍, 演说等中)摘录; 选取(语句, 例子, 段落等). □ *n* /ˈekstrækt/ **1** [U, C] that which has been ~ed(2) and concentrated: 榨出物; 精; 汁: *vanilla* ~; 香草精; *beef* ~; 牛肉汁; ~ *of malt.* 麦芽精. **2** [C] passage ~ed(3): (自书等中)摘录的段落; 选辑: ~*s from a long poem.* 一首长诗中摘录下的精粹. **ex·trac·tion** /ɪkˈstrækʃn; ɪkˈstrækʃən/ *n* [U] **1** ~ing or being ~ed(1): 拔取; 拔出: *the* ~*tion of a tooth.* 一颗牙齿之拔出. **2** descent; lineage: 世系; 家世: *Is Mr Mansion of French* ~*ion?* 曼逊先生有法国血统吗?

extra·cur·ricu·lar /ˌekstrəkəˈrɪkjʊlə(r); ,ɛkstrəkə-ˈrɪkjəlɚ/ *adj* outside the regular course of academic work or studies: 课外的; 课程以外的: ~ *activities*, eg belonging to a dramatic society. 课外活动(例如参加戏剧社).

ex·tra·dite /ˈekstrədaɪt; ˈɛkstrə,daɪt/ *vt* [VP6A] **1** give up, hand over (a person) from the State where

he is a fugitive to the State where he is alleged to have committed, or has been convicted of, a crime. 引渡(逃犯)。**2** obtain (such a person) for trial. 获得(逃犯)的引渡。**ex·tra·di·tion** /ˌekstrə'dɪʃn; ˌekstrə'dɪʃən/ *n*

extra·ju·dicial /ˌekstrədʒu:'dɪʃl; ˌekstrədʒu'dɪʃəl/ *adj* beyond the authority of a court; outside the (normal) authority of the law. 法院管辖以外的；法律(正常)权限以外的。

extra·mari·tal /ˌekstrə'mærɪtl; ˌekstrə'mærətl/ *adj* outside marriage; ~ *relations*, adultery. 婚姻外的；通奸。

extra·mural /ˌekstrə'mjuərəl; ˌekstrə'mjurəl/ *adj* **1** outside the boundaries (eg of a town). 在界线外的(例如城市边界以外的)。**2** additional to the full-time activities of a university, etc: 大学等之活动范围以外的；校外的: ~ *lectures / studies / students*. 校外演讲(校外研究；大学推广部的学生)。

ex·traneous /ɪk'streɪnɪəs; ɪk'strenɪəs/ *adj* not related (to the object to which it is attached); not belonging (to what is being dealt with); coming from outside: 体外的；与本题无关的: ~ *interference*. 外来的干涉。

extra·ordi·nary /ɪk'strɔ:dnrɪ US: -dəneri; ɪk'strɔrdn,ɛrɪ/ *adj* **1** beyond what is usual or ordinary; remarkable: 非常的；特别的；非凡的; *a man of ~ talents*; 有惊人才干之人; ~ *weather*. 特别的天气。**2**(of officials) additional, specially employed: (指官员)特命的; *envoy ~*. 特使。**ex·tra·ordi·nar·ily** /ɪk'strɔ:dnrəlɪ US: -dənerəlɪ; ɪk'strɔrdn,ɛrəlɪ/ *adv*

extra·sen·sory /ˌekstrə'sensərɪ; ˌekstrə'sensərɪ/ *adj* (esp) (尤用于) ~ **perception** (abbr 略作 **ESP**), perception of external events without the use of any of the known senses. 超感觉力。

extra·terri·tor·ial /ˌekstrəˌterɪ'tɔ:rɪəl; ˌekstrəˌterə'torɪəl/ *adj* = **exterritorial**.

ex·trava·gant /ɪk'strævəgənt; ɪk'strævəgənt/ *adj* **1** wasteful; (in the habit of) wasting (money, etc): 浪费的；奢侈的；挥霍无度的: *an ~ man*; 奢侈的人; ~ *tastes and habits*. 奢侈的嗜好和习惯。**2**(of ideas, speech, behaviour) going beyond what is reasonable, usual or conventional; not properly controlled: (指思想，言论，行为)过度的；过度的: ~ *praise / behaviour*. 过分的赞扬(行为)。~**·ly** *adv* **ex·trava·gance** /-gəns; -gəns/ *n* **1** [U] state of: 奢侈；挥霍无度: *His extravagance explains why he is always in debt*. 他的挥霍无度说明他为何总是负债。**2** [C] statement, act, etc. 过分的言论，行为等。

ex·trava·gan·za /ɪkˌstrævə'gænzə;ɪkˌstrævə'gænzə/ *n* [C] (music, theatre, literature) irregular and fanciful composition; burlesque; spectacular entertainment. (音乐，戏剧，文学之)非正规的奇特的作品；讽刺性滑稽表演；壮观的表演。

ex·treme /ɪk'stri:m; ɪk'strim/ *n* **1** either end of anything; (fig) highest degree: 末端；尽头；(喻)极端；极度: *annoying in the ~*, most annoying. 极为讨厌。**2**(*pl*) qualities, etc as wide apart, as widely different, as possible: (复)极端不同的性质等: *the ~s of heat and cold*. 热与冷之极端不同。*Love and hate are ~s*. 爱和恨是两个极端。**go to / be driven to ~s**, to ~ measures, to do more than is usu considered right or desirable. 走极端。□ *adj* **1** at the end(s); farthest possible: 在尽头的；最远的: *the ~ edge of a field*; 田地之边界; *in ~ old age*; 在极老的时期; *The ~ penalty of the law (in some countries) is the death penalty*. 极刑(在某些国家)就是死刑。**2** reaching the highest degree: 至最高限度的；极度的: ~ *patience / kindness*; 极度的耐心(仁慈); *in ~ pain*. 在极度痛苦中。**3**(of persons, their ideas) far from moderate; going to great lengths in views or actions: (指人或其思想)极端的；偏激的: *hold ~ opinions*; 持偏激的意见; ~**·ly** *adv* (used intensively with *adj* and *adv*) to a very high degree. (与形容词和副词连用，表示强度)极端地；极度地。**ex·trem·ist** /-ɪst; -ɪst/

n person who holds ~ views (esp in politics). 极端主义者；意见偏激者(尤指在政治方面)。**ex·trem·ity** /ɪk'stremɪtɪ; ɪk'streməti/ *n* (*pl* -ties) [C] **1** = point, end or limit; (*pl*) hands and feet. 极点；末端；极限；(复)手足。**2**(*sing* only) ~ degree (of joy, misery, esp of misfortune): (仅用单数) (快乐，痛苦，尤指不幸之)极度: *an extremity of pain*. 极度痛苦。*How can we help them in their extremity*? 我们怎样帮助陷于极端不幸中的他们? **3**(*usu pl*) ~ measures, eg for punishing wrongdoers, taking revenge: (通常用复数)极端的措施；极端手段(例如惩罚犯人或报复者): *Both armies were guilty of extremities*. 两军皆犯有手段激烈之罪。

ex·tri·cate /'ekstrɪkeɪt; 'ɛkstrɪˌket/ *vt* [VP6A, 14] ~ **(from)**, free; disentangle: 使免除；解脱: ~ *oneself from a difficulty*. 使自己免除一困难。**ex·tri·cable** /ek'strɪkəbl; 'ɛkstrɪkəbl/ *adj* that can be ~d. 可免除的；可解脱的。**ex·tri·ca·tion** /ˌekstrɪ'keɪʃn; ˌɛkstrɪ'keʃən/ *n* [U].

ex·trin·sic /ek'strɪnsɪk; ɛk'strɪnsɪk/ *adj* ~ **(to)**, (of qualities, values, etc) not a part of the real character; operating or originating from the outside; not essential. (指性质，价值等)非固有的；外来的；外在的。

ex·tro·vert /'ekstrəvɜ:t; 'ɛkstroˌvɜt/ *n* person more interested in what goes on around him than in his own thoughts and feelings; (colloq) lively, cheerful person; 性格外向的人: (口)活泼愉快的人: (attrib) (用作定语): ~ *behaviour*. 个性外向的行为。⇨ **introvert**. **ex·tro·ver·sion** /ˌekstrə'vɜ:ʃn US: -ʒn; ˌekstrə'vɜʃən/ *n* [U] state of being ~ed. 外向性；外倾。

ex·trude /ɪk'stru:d; ɪk'strud/ *vt* [VP6A, 14] ~ **(from)**, force sb or sth out; shape (eg plastic or metal) by forcing through a die. 逐出；用印模压制(例如塑料或金属)。**ex·tru·sion** /ɪk'stru:ʒn; ɪk'struʒən/ *n*.

ex·uber·ant /ɪg'zju:bərənt US: -'zu:-; ɪg'zjubərənt/ *adj* **1** growing vigorously; luxuriant: 茂盛的；繁茂的; *plants with ~ foliage*. 枝叶茂盛的植物。**2** full of life and vigour; high-spirited; overflowing: 活力充沛的；精神旺盛的；充溢的；丰富的: *children in ~ spirits*; 兴高采烈的孩子们; *an ~ imagination*. 丰富的想象力。~**·ly** *adv* **ex·uber·ance** /-rəns; -rəns/ *n* [U] state or quality of being ~: 茂盛；充溢；繁茂；丰富；活力充沛: *The speaker's exuberance won over an apathetic audience*. 那演说者以充沛的精神和感情说服了那些冷漠的听众。

ex·ude /ɪg'zju:d US: -'zu:d; ɪg'zud/ *vt*, *vi* [VP2A, C, 6A] (of drops of liquid) come or pass out slowly; ooze out: (指水滴)慢慢流出；渗出: *Sweat ~s through the pores*. 汗从毛孔中渗出。

ex·ult /ɪg'zʌlt; ɪg'zʌlt/ *vi* [VP2A, 3A, 4C] rejoice greatly: 狂喜；非常高兴: ~ *at / in a success*; 因成功而狂喜; ~ *to find that one has succeeded*; 发现自己成功后非常高兴; ~ (= triumph) *over a defeated rival*. 将对手击败而得意。~**·ant** /-ənt; -ənt/ *adj* ~ing; triumphant. 狂喜的；欢欣的；得意的。~**·ant·ly** *adv* **ex·ul·ta·tion** /ˌegzʌl'teɪʃn; ˌegzʌl'teʃən/ *n* [U] great joy (*at*); triumph (*over*). 狂喜(与at连用)；欢欣；得意。

eye¹ /aɪ; aɪ/ *n* **1** organ of sight: 眼睛: *We see with our eyes*. 我们用眼睛看。*He opened / closed his eyes*. 他睁开(闭上)了眼睛。*He is blind in one eye*. 他有一只眼失明。*He lost an eye in the war*. 他在战争中丧失一只眼睛。⇨ the illus here and at **head**. 参看本条及 head 之插图。*an eye for an eye*, punishment as severe as the injury suffered; retaliation: 以眼还眼；报复。*eyes right / left / front*, (mil command) Turn the head and look to the right, etc. (军队口令)向右(左，前)看。*if you had half an eye*, if you were not so dull, unobservant. 如果你稍加注意。*in the eyes of the law, etc*, from the point of view of the law, etc; as the law, etc sees it. 就法律等的观点而言。*in the eyes of sb; in my / his, etc eyes*, in the judgement of: 在…的眼里: *You're only a child in his eyes*. 你在他的眼里只是一个孩子。*under /*

before one's very eyes, **(a)** in one's presence, in front of one. 在某人面前。**(b)** with no attempt at concealment. 不欲隐瞒地; 公开地。*up to the eyes in* (work, etc), deeply engaged in. 埋头于(工作等)。*with an eye to,* with a view to, hoping for. 为了要; 指望着。*be all eyes,* be watching intently. 极为注意。*be in the public eye,* be often seen in public; be well known. 常公开出现; 为众所周知。*close one's eyes to,* refuse to see or take notice of. 拒绝看; 拒绝注意。*get one's eye in,* (cricket and other ball games) become able, through practice, to follow with one's eyes the movement of the ball. (板球及其他球戏)由于练习而能用眼睛上球的动向。*give sb a black eye; black sb's eye,* give him a blow so that there is a discoloured bruise round the eye. 将某人的眼圈打成瘀伤; 把某人的眼眶打青。*have an eye for,* be a good judge of, have a proper sense of: 能判断; 能欣赏: *He has a good eye for beauty of the pictures,ue.* 他极会欣赏美(美的东西)。*have an eye to,* have as one's object: 着眼于: *He always has an eye to business,* looks for possibilities of doing business. 他总是着眼于商业。*keep an eye on,* (lit, fig) keep a watch on. (字面, 喻)注意。*make eyes at,* look amorously at. 对…眉目传情; 向…送秋波。*make sb open his eyes,* make him take notice. 使某人注意。*Mind your eye,* (colloq) Take care, Look out. (口) 注意; 当心。*open sb's eyes to,* cause him to realize. 使某人认清。*see eye to eye (with),* agree entirely, have identical views. 完全同意; (与…)有相同的见解。*see sth with half an eye,* see it at a glance. 一目了然。*set/clap eyes on,* see: 看; 看见: *I hope I shall never set eyes on her again.* 我希望我永远不再看到她。*never take one's eyes off,* never stop watching. 永不停止注意。⇨ **catch¹(7), dust¹(1). 2** thing like an eye: 似眼之物; 眼状物: *the eye of a needle,* the hole for the thread; 针眼; *a hook and eye,* fastening with a hook and loop for a dress, etc; (其作用相当于扣扣的)领钩; 钩扣; *the eye of a potato,* point from which a leaf-bud will grow. 马铃薯的芽眼。**3** (compounds, etc) (复合词等) **'eye·ball** *n* the eye within the lids and socket. 眼球。*eyeball to eyeball,* (colloq) face to face. (口)面对面。**'eye-bath; 'eye-cup** *nn* small glass for holding lotion, etc, in which to bathe the eye. 洗眼器; 洗眼杯。**'eye·brow** *n* arch of hair above the eye. 眉; 眉毛。*raise one's eyebrows,* express surprise, doubt, etc. 扬扬眉毛(表示惊奇, 怀疑等)。**'eye·catching** *adj* easy to see and pleasant to look at; attractive. 显明而悦目的; 动人的。**'eye·ful** */-ful/ -,ful/ n* as much as one is capable of viewing; as much as one can see at a glance. 一眼所能看到之物; 一瞥之所见。*have/get an eyeful (of),* have a good long look (at sth that has strongly attracted the attention because one is curious about it). 仔细看看(极使自己好奇之物)。**'eye-glass** *n* lens (for one eye) to help defective sight. (一块)眼镜片; 单眼镜。**'eye-glasses** *n pl* pair of lenses in a frame; spectacles or glasses (the usu words). 一副眼镜(通常用 spectacles 或 glasses)。**'eye·lash** *n* hair, row of hairs, on the edge of the eyelid. 睫毛。**eye·less** *adj* without eyes. 无眼的。**'eye·lid** *n* upper or lower covering of the eye. 眼皮; 眼睑。*hang on by the eyelids,* have a very slight, insecure hold. 一发千钧。**'eye-opener** *n* circumstance,

etc that brings enlightenment and surprise. 令人开眼界并感到惊奇的情形等。**'eye·piece** *n* lens at the end of a telescope or microscope, to which the eye is applied. (望远镜或显微镜之)目镜。**'eye-shadow** *n* [U] cosmetic applied to the eyelids. 眼睑膏; 眼影 (涂眼皮的化妆品)。**'eye·shot** *n* [U] seeing distance: 视界; 视野: *beyond/ out of/in/within eyeshot.* 在视界外(外, 内, 内)。**'eye·sight** *n* [U] power, faculty, of seeing: 视力; 目力: *to have good/poor eyesight.* 目力佳(不佳)。**'eye·sore** *n* ugly object; sth unpleasing to look at. 丑陋的东西; 难看的东西。**'eye-strain** *n* [U] tired condition of the eyes (as caused, for example, by reading very small

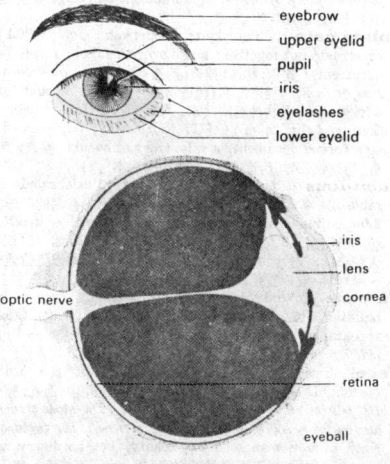

eyebrow
upper eyelid
pupil
iris
eyelashes
lower eyelid

iris
lens
optic nerve
cornea

retina
eyeball

the eye

print). 眼睛疲劳 (例如由阅读印刷字体太小的读物所致)。**'eye-tooth** *n* canine tooth. 犬齿。⇨ the illus at **mouth**. 参看mouth 之插图。**'eye·wash** *n* [U] **(a)** liquid for bathing the eyes. 洗眼药水。**(b)** (colloq) sth said or done to deceive; nonsense. (口)骗人的言语或行动; 胡言乱语。**'eye-witness** *n* person who can bear witness from what he has himself seen: 目击者; 见证人: *an eye-witness account of a crime.* 见证人对于一项罪行的叙述。**-eyed** *suff* (in compounds): (用于复合词中): *a blue-eyed girl,* girl having blue eyes; 蓝眼睛的女郎; *a one-eyed man,* man having only one eye; 一个只有一只眼睛的人; *starry-eyed,* (colloq) idealistic. (口)理想主义者的; 幻想的; 不实际的。

eye² /aɪ; aɪ/ *vt* [VP6A, 15A] observe, watch: 观看: *He eyed me with suspicion.* 他怀疑地望着我。*They were eye/eying us jealously.* 他们嫉妒地看着我们。

eye·let /'aɪlɪt; 'aɪlɪt/ *n* [C] small hole in cloth, in a sail, etc for a rope, etc to go through; metal ring round such a hole, to strengthen it. (布、帆等穿绳等之)小孔; 嵌于上述小孔之金属圈。

eyrie, eyry /'eərɪ; 'ɛrɪ/ *n* ⇨ **aerie.**

Ff

F, f /ef; ɛf/ *(pl* **F's, f's** /efs; ɛfs/) the sixth letter of the English alphabet. 英文字母之第六个字母。

fa /fɑː; fɑ/ *n* fourth note in the musical octave. 大音阶之第四音。

fab /fæb; fæb/ *adj* (dated sl) fabulous(3). (过时俚语)令人惊奇的; 奇妙的。

Fabian /'feɪbɪən; 'febɪən/ *n, adj* **1** (person) using cautious and slow strategy to wear out opposition: 使用谨慎和拖延策略以困败敌手的(人): *a ~ policy.* 拖延的困敌政策。**2** (GB) (person) aiming at gradual socialist change. (英)以缓进手段进行社会改变的(人)。

fable /'feɪbl; 'febl/ *n* **1** [C] short tale, not based on

fact, esp one with animals in it (eg **Aesop's** /'i:sɒps; 'ɪsɑps/ ~**s**) and intended to give moral teaching. 寓言 (例如伊索寓言). **2** [U] (collective *sing*) (集合名词单数) myths; legends: 神话; 传说: *sort out fact from* ~. 自传说中选取真实内容. **3** [C] false statement or account. 无稽之谈. **fabled** /'feɪbld; 'febld/ *adj* celebrated in ~; legendary. 寓言中有名的; 传说的.

fab·ric /'fæbrɪk; 'fæbrɪk/ *n* [C, U] **1** (kind of) textile material: 织物: *woollen/silk* ~*s*; 毛(丝)织物; ~ *gloves*, made of woven material, not of leather. 织造的手套(非皮制的). **2** structure; sth put together: 结构; 构造; 构造物: *the* ~ *of society*; 社会的结构; *funds for the upkeep of the* ~, eg an ancient building. 保养建筑物(如古老建筑物)之专款.

fab·ri·cate /'fæbrɪkeɪt; 'fæbrɪ,ket/ *vt* [VP6A] construct; put together; make up (sth false); forge (a document): 建造; 构造; 捏造; 伪造(文书): ~ *an accusation/a will*; 捏造罪名(伪造遗嘱): *a* ~*d account of adventures*. 虚构的冒险故事. **fab·ri·ca·tion** /ˌfæbrɪ'keɪʃn; ˌfæbrɪ'keʃən/ *n* [U] fabricating; [C] sth ~d, eg a forged document, a false story of events. 捏造; 伪造物; 捏造物(例如伪造的文书、虚构的故事).

fabu·lous /'fæbjʊləs; 'fæbjələs/ *adj* **1** celebrated in fable(2): 神话中有名的: ~ *heroes*. 神话中有名的英雄. **2** incredible or absurd: 难以置信的; 荒谬的: ~ *wealth*. 惊人的财富. **3** (colloq) wonderful; marvellous. (口)令人惊奇的; 奇妙的. ~**ly** *adv* incredibly: 难以置信地: ~*ly rich*. 难以置信的富有.

fa·cade /fə'sɑːd; fə'sɑd/ *n* [C] front or face of a building (towards a street or open place); (fig) false appearance: 建筑物的正面; (喻)虚伪的外表: *a* ~ *of indifference*. 假装冷漠.

face¹ /feɪs; fes/ *n* **1** the front part of the head (forehead, eyes, nose, mouth, cheeks, chin): 面孔; 脸: *He fell on his* ~. 他脸朝下倒下去了. *The stone struck him on the* ~. 石头击在他的脸上. *Her* ~ *is her fortune*, (said of a woman who has beauty, but no dowry or talents). 她的面貌即是她的财产(指一女子有姿色，但无嫁妆或才能). **bring two persons/parties** ~ *to* ~; **bring sb** ~ *to* ~ *with sb*, bring them together so that they confront one another: 使两人面对面: *The two politicians were brought* ~ *to* ~ *in a TV interview*. 这两位从政者曾在一次电视访问中面对面. **come** ~ *to* ~ *with sb*; **meet sb** ~ *to* ~, come into his presence, meet or confront him. 与某人碰面. **look sb in the** ~, look at him steadily. 直视某人. **be unable to look sb in the** ~, be unable to look at sb because of feeling ashamed, bashful, etc. (由于惭愧、害羞等)不敢正视某人. **set one's** ~ *against sb*, oppose him. 反对某人. **show one's** ~, appear, let oneself be seen: 露面; 现身: *How can you show your* ~ *here after the way you behaved last night?* 在你昨夜那种表现之后，你怎能在此露面? **in (the)** ~ *of*, (a) confronted with: 在…面前; 在…之前: *What could he do in the* ~ *of all these difficulties?* 面对着这一切困难，他能做些什么? **(b)** in spite of: 不顾: *He succeeded in* ~ *of great danger*. 他不顾巨大的危险而成功了. **fly in the** ~ *of sth*, openly defy, disregard (eg Providence/public disapproval/the facts): 甘冒大不韪(如悍然不顾天意、公众非议、一切事实): *Your claim flies in the* ~ *of all the evidence*. 你的要求公然违背你所有的证据. **in one's** ~, (a) straight against/at: 正对着: *The sun was shining in our* ~*s*. 太阳正对着我们照射. **(b)** with no attempt at concealment: 公开地: *Death stared him in the* ~. 死神凝视着他(他命在旦夕). *She'll only laugh in your* ~. 她会当面笑你. Cf 参较 *laugh up one's sleeve* at **laugh**(1). *to one's* ~, openly, in one's hearing. 当着某人的面. *I'll tell him so to his* ~, ie I'm not afraid to tell him. 我要当面同他这样说. Cf 参较 *behind one's back* at **back¹**(1). **2** (compounds) (复合词) ~**-ache** *n* neuralgia. 面部神经痛. '~**-card** *n* (playing-card) king, queen, or knave. (纸牌)老 K，女王或杰克. '~

cloth, (esp) small square towel for washing the ~. (尤指) 洗脸毛巾; 小方毛巾. '~**-cream**, cosmetic cream for the skin on the ~. 面脂. '~**-lift(ing)** *n* operation of tightening the skin to smooth out wrinkles and make the ~ look younger. 拉皮(使面部皮肤拉紧以消除皱纹的手术). '~**-pack** *n* paste applied to clean and freshen the skin of the ~. 擦面膏; 面部洁霜. '~**-powder** *n* cosmetic powder for the ~. 扑面粉. **3** look; expression: 面容; 表情: *a sad* ~; 悲伤的面容; *smiling* ~*s*. 微笑的面容. *She is a good judge of* ~*s*, judges the character well from the expression of the ~. 她善于根据面部表情来判断人的性格. **keep a straight** ~, hide one's amusement (by not smiling or laughing). 不露笑容. **make/pull a** ~/~*s (at sb)*, pull the ~ out of shape; make grimaces (at sb). (向某人)扮鬼脸. **put on/wear a (long)** ~, look serious or dismal. 绷着脸; 愁眉苦脸; 拉长了脸. **4** (in various senses) (用于各种意义)**have the** ~ *(to do sth)*, (more usu the *cheek*) (cheek 较常用) be bold or impudent enough. 竟大胆或厚颜得; 竟有脸. **lose** ~, be humiliated, suffer loss of credit or reputation. 丢脸; 失面子. **put a good/bold/brave** ~ *on sth*, make it look well; show courage in dealing with it. 使某物美观; 处置某事时显出勇气. **put a new** ~ *on sth*, alter its aspect, make it look different. 使面目一新; 使改观. **save (one's)** ~, refrain from, evade, shaming oneself openly; avoid losing one's dignity or suffering loss of credit or reputation. 保全面子; 保持尊严. Hence, 由此产生, '~**-saver** *n* act or event that allows this. 保全面子的行动或事件. '~**-saving** *n*, *part adj*: ~*-saving moves*. 保全面子的行动. **on the** ~ *of it*, judging by appearances, when first seen or heard: 就表面判断: *On the* ~ *of it, his story seems unconvincing*. 就表面判断，他的故事似乎不足以令人相信. **5** surface; façade (of a building); front: 表面; (建筑物之)正面; 前面: *the* ~ *of a clock*. 钟面. *He laid the cards* ~ *down on the table*. 他把那些纸牌反放在桌上. *A dice has six* ~*s*. 骰子有六个面. *A diamond crystal has many* ~*s*. 钻石有很多面. *The team climbed the north* ~ *of the mountain*. 该队由山的北面攀登. *They disappeared from/off the* ~ *of the earth*. 他们从地面上消失了. *The miner worked at the coal* ~ *for six hours*. 那矿工在煤矿的采掘面工作了六小时. *The value of a coin or banknote is shown on its* ~. 钱币或钞票的价值见于其表面. Hence, 由此产生, ~ *value*, the nominal value of a coin or banknote; (fig) what sth or sb seems to be from appearances: 票面价值; 票面额; (喻)某事物或某人的表面. **take sth at its** ~ *value*, accept that it is what it seems to be. 相信某事物的表面价值. ⇨ the illus at **crystal; mountain**. 参看 crystal, mountain 之插图. **6** size or style of the surface of a piece of type cast for printing: 印刷活字的大小或字体: *bold*~ *type*. 粗体铅字; 黑体字. ~**-less** *adj* (fig) anonymous; unknown to the general public: (喻)匿名的: *the* ~*less men who have power in commerce and industry*. 工商界有势力的匿名人氏.

face² /feɪs; fes/ *vt, vi* **1** [VP6A, C] have or turn the ~ to, or in a certain direction; 面向; 向: 面对: *Turn round and* ~ *me*. 转过身来对着我. *Who's the man facing us?* 对着我们的那个人是谁? *The window* ~*s the street*. 那窗子面临街道. *The picture* ~*s page 10*. 该图在第十页的对面. *'Which way does your house* ~?' — *'It* ~*s south.'* '你的房子朝哪个方向?' —— '它朝南.' *About/Left/Right* ~! (US mil commands) Turn right round/to the left/right. (美、军队口令)向后转! 向左(右)转! Cf 参较 (GB) (英) *About/Left/Right turn!* **2** [VP6A,15B, 2C] meet confidently or defiantly: 毅然相对; 勇敢相对: ~ *the enemy*; 毅然面对敌人; ~ *dangers*. 勇敢地对付危险. ~ *sth/it out*, refuse to give way, carry it through with courage. 不让步; 坚持到底. ~ *the music*, show no fear at a time of trial, danger, difficulty. 毅然面对考验、危险或困局; 勇敢地承担一切后果. ~ *up to (sth)*, recognize and deal with,

honestly and bravely: 诚实而又勇敢地承认和对付: ~ up to the fact that one is no longer young. 勇敢地面对不再年轻这一事实. **let's ~ it,** (colloq) it must be acknowledged. (口)我们必须承认此事; 我们必须面对事实. **3** [VP6A] recognize the existence of: 承认…的存在: ~ facts/altered circumstances. 承认事实(改变了的情势). **4** [VP6A] present itself to: 呈现于…之前: the problem that ~s us. 摆在我们面前的问题. **5** [VP6A, 14] ~ (with), cover with a layer of different material: 覆以一层不同的东西: ~ a wall with concrete; 用混凝土涂墙壁; a coat of d with silk, eg with silk on the lapels. 镶有绸边的上衣(如在翻领上镶以绸边). **facer** n (GB dated colloq) serious difficulty by which one is suddenly or unexpectedly ~d. (英,过时口语)突然遭遇的重大困难.

facet /'fæsɪt; 'fæsɪt/ n one of the many sides of a cut stone or jewel; (fig) aspect, eg of a problem. 宝石等的小平面; 刻面; (喻)(问题等的)一面.

fa·cetious /fə'siːʃəs; fə'siʃəs/ adj humorously teasing or mocking; fond of, marked by, inappropriate or bitter joking: 诙谐的; 戏谑的; (爱)乱开玩笑的; (爱)挖苦人的: a ~ remark/young man. 诙谐的话(爱乱开玩笑的青年). ~·ly adv ~·ness n

facia /'feɪʃə; 'feʃə/ n = fascia.

fa·cial /'feɪʃl; 'feʃəl/ adj of or for the face: 面孔的; 面部用的: a ~ massage. 面部按摩. □ n ~ massage. 面部按摩.

facile /'fæsaɪl US: -sl; 'fæsl/ adj **1** easily done or obtained: 易做的; 易得的: a ~ victory. 轻易获得的胜利. **2** (of a person) able to do things easily; (of speech or writing) done easily but without attention to quality: (指人)能干的; (指演说或写作)流畅但不重内容的: a ~ liar/remark; 善于说谎的人(流畅而无内容的谈话); a man with a ~ pen/tongue. 文笔流畅(能说会道)的人.

fa·cili·tate /fə'sɪlɪteɪt; fə'sɪlə,tet/ vt [VP6A] (of an object, process) make easy; lessen the difficulty of: (指物件,方式)使容易; 使便利; 减轻…的困难: Modern inventions have ~d housework. 现代的发明物使家务的操作便利了. (Note: ~ is never used when the subject is a person). (注意: ~ 用以人做主语).

fa·cil·ity /fə'sɪlətɪ; fə'sɪlətɪ/ n (pl -ties) **1** [U] quality which makes learning or doing things easy or simple: 灵巧; 熟练: have great ~ in learning languages; 有学习语言的天才; show ~ in performing a task; 在一工作中表现熟练; play the piano with ~. 熟练地弹钢琴. **2** (pl) aids, circumstances, which make it easy to do things: (复)使工作便利的工具或环境; 设备: facilities for travel, eg buses, trains, air services; 便利旅行的工具(例如公共汽车、火车、航空设备); facilities for study, eg libraries, laboratories; 研究设备(例如图书馆、实验室); 'sports facilities, eg running tracks, swimming pools. 运动设备(例如跑道、游泳池).

facing /'feɪsɪŋ; 'fesɪŋ/ n **1** coating of different material, eg on a wall. 不同材料的覆饰; 饰面(例如墙壁上者). **2** (pl) material of a different colour on a garment, eg on the cuffs, collar: (复)衣服上不同颜色的饰物(例如袖口、衣领之饰边): a purple jacket with green ~s. 一件有绿色饰边的紫夹克. ⇨ **face²**(5).

fac·sim·ile /fæk'sɪməlɪ; fæk'sɪməlɪ/ n [C] exact copy or reproduction of writing, printing, a picture, etc: (写作、印刷、图片等)精确的复制; 摹写; 传真: reproduced in ~, exactly. 精确复制的.

fact /fækt; fækt/ n **1** [C] sth that has happened or been done. 已发生或所做之事; 事件; 行为. **accessary before the ~,** (legal) accessary who is not present when a crime is committed. (法律)犯罪前的从犯(犯罪时未在场). **accessary after the ~,** (legal) who knowingly helps another who has committed a crime. (法律)犯罪后的从犯. **2** [C] sth known to be true or accepted as true: 事实: No one can deny the ~ that fire burns. 无人能否认火可燃烧的事实. Poverty and crime

are ~s. 贫穷和犯罪是事实. I know it for a ~, I know that it is really true. 我知道这是真正的事实. a ~ of life, sth that cannot be ignored, however unpleasant. 尽管不愉快而无法更改的事实. **the ~s of life,** (colloq, euphem) details of human sexual reproduction (eg as told to children) (口,委婉语)性知识(例如讲给孩子们听的). **'~-finding** adj: A ~-finding commission has been appointed, one to inquire into ~s, to find out what is true and what is not true. 一个事实调查团已被派定. **3** [U] reality; what is true; what exists: 现实; 真实的事物; 存在的事物: The story is founded on ~. 故事根据现实. It is important to distinguish ~ from fiction. 辨别现实与虚构是重要的. The ~ of the matter is ... , The truth is ... . 此事的真相是 ... . **in ~; as a matter of ~; in point of ~,** really: 事实上; 实际上: I think so; in ~, I'm quite sure. 我想是如此,事实上我十分相信是如此.

fac·tion /'fækʃn; 'fækʃən/ n **1** [C] discontented, often unscrupulous and self-interested group of persons within a party (esp political): 派系; 小派别(尤指政治上的): The party split into petty ~s. 该党分裂成若干小派系. **2** [U] quarrelling among such groups; party strife. 派系间不和; 倾轧; 党争. **fac·tious** /'fækʃəs; 'fækʃəs/ adj of, caused by, ~; fond of ~: 党派的; 由派系间不和而造成的; 喜倾轧的: a factious spirit. 喜倾轧的风气.

fac·ti·tious /fæk'tɪʃəs; fæk'tɪʃəs/ adj (formal) unnatural; artificial; created or developed by design: (正式用语)不自然的; 人为的; 设计而成的: ~ enthusiasm, 虚假的热心; a ~ demand for goods, eg as the result of extensive advertising. 对货物之反需的需要(例如由大规模广告宣传造成的)

fac·tor /'fæktər; 'fæktɚ/ n **1** (arith) whole number (except 1) by which a larger number can be divided exactly: 因子; 因数: factor 2, 3, 4 and 6 are ~s of 12. 2, 3, 4 and 6 是 12 的因数. **2** fact, circumstance, etc helping to bring about a result: 因素: evolutionary ~s, environmental influences, etc that have caused sth to evolve or develop; 进化的因素; ~s in the making of a nation; 构成一个国家的因素; an unknown ~, sth unknown, likely to influence a result; 未知的因素; the ~ of safety, eg in engineering. (工程等中的)安全因素. Hence, 由此产生, **'safety-~** n. 安全因素. **3** agent; person who buys and sells on commission; (in Scotland) land-agent, steward. 代理人; 代理商; (苏格兰)土地经管人. **~·ize** /'fæktəraɪz; 'fæktəˌraɪz/ vt [VP6A] find the ~s of (a number). 分解(某数)的因子.

fac·tory /'fæktərɪ; 'fæktərɪ/ n (pl -ries) **1** building(s) where goods are made (esp by machinery); workshop: 工厂; 制造厂: (attrib) (用作定语) ~ workers. 工厂工人. **F~ Acts,** (in GB) laws dealing with safety regulations, working conditions of employees, etc. (英)工厂法案(规定工人的安全规章、工作条件等). **2** (hist) merchant company's trading station abroad. (史)驻外商店; 代理店.

fac·to·tum /fæk'təʊtəm; fæk'totəm/ n (general) ~, (often hum) servant doing all kinds of work. (常作诙谐语)杂役.

fac·tual /'fæktʃʊəl; 'fæktʃʊəl/ adj concerned with, full of, facts). 与事实有关的; 充满事实的. ~·ly adv

fac·ulty /'fækltɪ; 'fækltɪ/ n (pl -ties) [C] **1** power (of mind); ability (to do sth): 才能; 能力: the mental faculties, the reason; 思想与理解等之能力; 心智能力; the ~ of making friends easily; 善于交友的能力; have a great ~ for learning languages; 极富有学习语言的才能; the ~ of speech; 演说的才能; 口才; be in possession of all one's faculties, be able to see, hear, speak, understand, etc. 有视,听,说,理解等能力. **2** (in a university) department or grouping of related departments: (大学的)系; 学院: the F~ of Law/Science; 法(理)学院; all the teachers, lecturers, professors, etc in one of these: 学院或系科的全体教员: a member of (the) ~; 教授中的

一员; *a* ~ *meeting;* 教员会; (US) the whole teaching staff of a university. 大学的全体教员。

fad /fæd; fæd/ *n* [C] fanciful fashion, interest, preference, enthusiasm, unlikely to last: 新奇的时尚; 一时流行的嗜好或狂热: *Will Tom continue to collect foreign stamps or is it only a passing fad?* 汤姆将继续搜集外国邮票呢, 还是仅将它当作一时的嗜好呢? *She is full of fads and fancies,* has rather silly likes and dislikes. 她有许多怪诞的嗜好 (在爱恶方面颇为奇特). **faddy** /'fædɪ; 'fædɪ/ *adj* having fads; having silly likes and dislikes, eg about food. 有新奇的时尚、嗜好或狂热的; (对食物等) 特别喜爱或特别厌恶的。 **fad·dily** /'fædɪlɪ; 'fædɪlɪ/ *adv*

fade /feɪd; fed/ *vt, vi* ~ *(away),* **1** [VP6A, 2A, C] (cause to) lose colour, freshness or vigour: (使) 褪色; (使) 凋落; (使) 衰弱; 凋谢: *The strong sunlight had* ~*d the curtains.* 强烈的阳光使窗帘褪了色。 *Flowers soon* ~ *when cut.* 花折下不久就会凋谢。 *Will the colour in this material* ~? 这块料子会褪色吗? *She is fading away,* losing strength. 她渐渐衰弱了。 **2** [VP2A,C] go slowly out of view, hearing or the memory: 自视界、听界或记忆中渐渐消失: *Daylight* ~*d away.* 白昼渐渐消失了。 *As evening came the coastline* ~*d into darkness.* 夜晚降临时, 海岸线消失在黑暗中。 *The sound of the cheering* ~*d away in the distance.* 欢呼的声音在远处逐渐消失了。 *His hopes* ~*d.* 他的希望逐渐消逝了。 *All memory of her childhood* ~*d from her mind.* 所有她童年的记忆渐渐自她脑海中消逝了。 **3** [VP15B, 2C, 3A] (cinema, broadcasting) (cause to) decrease or increase in strength: (电影、广播) (使) 渐弱; (使) 渐强; (使) 淡出; (使) 淡入 (使) 渐隐; (使) 渐显: ~ *one scene into another* (on a cinema screen); (银幕上) 使一画面渐渐隐暗而融入另一画面中; ~ *a conversation out/in,* (in broadcasting) gradually reduce/increase the volume of sound to inaudibility/audibility. (广播) 使一音量渐弱 (强)。

faeces (US = **feces**) /'fiːsiːz; 'fisɪz/ *n pl* (med) waste matter excreted from the bowels. (医) 粪便。

faerie, faery /'feərɪ; 'feərɪ/ *n* (old use) fairyland; (attrib) visionary; fancied. (旧用法) 仙境; 仙国; (用作定语) 幻想的; 想象的。

fag[1] /fæg; fæg/ *n* **1** [C,U] (*sing* only) (colloq) tiring job: (仅用单数) (口) 吃力的工作: *What a fag!* 多么费力的工作! *It's too much (of a) fag.* 这工作真使人吃不消。 **2** (formerly at public schools in England) junior pupil who performs certain duties for a senior pupil. (昔日英国公学) 为高年级生服务的低年级生。 **3** (GB sl) cigarette. (英国) 香烟。 **4** = **faggot(3).**

fag[2] /fæg; fæg/ *vi, vt* (**-gg-**) **1** [VP2C, 3A] ~ *(at),* (colloq) do very tiring work: (口) 做极其令人疲倦的工作: *fag (away) at sth/at doing sth.* 辛苦地做某事。 **2** [VP6A, 15B] ~ *(out),* (colloq) (of work) make very tired: (口) (指工作) 使极为疲劳: *Doesn't that sort of work fag you out?* 那种工作不使你疲倦吗? *He was almost fagged out,* exhausted. 他几乎筋疲力尽了。 *Your horse looks fagged.* 你的马看来疲倦了。 **3** [VP2A, 3A] ~ *(for),* act as a fag(2). (英国公学) 为高年级生服务。

fag-end /'fæg end; 'fæg‚ɛnd/ *n* (colloq) inferior or useless remnant; worthless part of anything; cigarette butt. (口) 低劣或无用的剩余物; 无用的部分; 香烟头。

fag·got (US also **fagot**) /'fægət; 'fægət/ *n* **1** bundle of sticks or twigs tied together for burning as fuel. 束薪; 柴捆。 **2** meat ball for frying. 供油煎的肉丸。 **3** △ (US sl, derog) male homosexual. (讳) (美俚, 蔑) 男子同性恋者。

Fahr·en·heit /'færənhaɪt; 'færən‚haɪt/ *n* name of a thermometer scale with freezing-point at 32° and boiling-point at 212°. 华氏温度计 (冰点为 32 度, 沸点为 212 度)。 ⇨ **App 5.** 参看附录五。

fa·ience /feɪˈɑːns; faɪˈɑns/ *n* [U] (F) decorated and glazed earthenware or porcelain. (法) 彩陶; 彩色瓷器。

fail[1] /feɪl; fel/ *n* (only in) (仅用于) *without* ~, for certain, no matter what difficulties, etc there may be; 必定; 不误: *I'll be there at two o'clock without* ~. 我两点钟一定到那里。

fail[2] /feɪl; fel/ *vi, vt* **1** [VP2A, 3A, 4A, 6A] ~ *(in),* be unsuccessful: 失败: ~ *(in) an examination;* 考试不及格; ~ *to pass an examination.* 考试失败。 *All our plans/attempts* ~*ed.* 我们所有的计划 (企图) 都失败了。 **2** [VP6A] (of examiners) reject (a candidate); decide that (a candidate) has ~*ed:* (主试者) 给应考者) 不及格; 不录取 (应考者): *The examiners* ~*ed half the candidates.* 主试者使半数应考者落榜。 **3** [VP2A, C] (often with an *indirect object*) (常接一间接宾语) be not enough; come to an end while still needed or expected: 不足; 短少; 缺乏: *The crops* ~*ed because of drought.* 由于旱灾, 农作物歉收。 *Our water supply has* ~*ed.* 我们的水供应不足了。 *The wind* ~*ed (us),* There was not enough wind for our sails. 风势不足, 吹不动我们的帆船。 *Words* ~ *me,* I cannot find words (to describe my feelings, etc). 我找不出适当的言辞 (来形容我的感情等)。 *His heart* (= courage) ~*ed him.* 他失去了勇气。 '~-**safe** (attrib *adj*), (定语形容词), (of a mechanical device, etc) designed to compensate automatically for a failure (thus eliminating danger, etc). (指机械装置等) 可自动补偿失误 (以免危险等) 的。 **4** [VP2A, C] (of health, eyesight, etc) become weak: (指健康、视力等) 衰退: *His eyesight is* ~*ing.* 他的视力渐衰退了。 *He has suffered from* ~*ing health/has been* ~*ing in health for the last two years.* 这两年来他的健康一直在衰退。 **5** [VP4A] omit; neglect (or, in many cases, simply making, with the *inf,* a neg of an affirm): 忽略; 疏忽 (或在许多情形下与不定式连用形成否定意义): *He never* ~*s to write* (= always writes) *to his mother every week.* 他从未忘记每周写信给他的母亲。 *His promises* ~*ed to* (=did not) *materialize.* 他的诺言未能实现。 *He did not* ~ *to keep* (= he did keep) *his word.* 他未食言。 **6** [VP 2A] become bankrupt: 破产; 倒闭: *Several of the biggest banks* ~*ed during the depression.* 几家最大的银行在不景气的时期倒闭了。 **7** [VP3A] ~ *in,* be insufficiently equipped with; be lacking in: 未充分具有; 缺少: *He's a clever man, but* ~*s in perseverance.* 他是个聪明的人, 但缺少毅力。

fail·ing[1] /'feɪlɪŋ; 'felɪŋ/ *n* [C] weakness or fault (of character); shortcoming: (品行的) 缺点; 短处: *We all have our little* ~*s.* 我们都有小的缺点。

fail·ing[2] /'feɪlɪŋ; 'felɪŋ/ *prep* in default of; in the absence of: 若缺少…时; 如果没有: ~ *this,* if this does not happen; 如果此事不发生; ~ *an answer,* if no answer is received; 若无答复; ~ *Smith,* if Smith is not available. 如果没有史密斯。

fail·ure /'feɪljər; 'feljə/ *n* **1** [U] failing; lack of success: 失败; 不成功: *F*~ *in an examination did not deter you from trying again.* 一次考试不及格不应妨碍你再次的尝试。 *All his efforts ended in* ~, were unsuccessful. 他所有的努力结果都失败了。 **2** [C] instance of failing; person, attempt, or thing that fails: 失败的实例; 失败的人、企图或事物; 失败者: *Success came after many* ~*s.* 经多次失败后, 成功终于到来。 *He was a* ~ *as a teacher.* 他是个不好教师。 **3** [U] state of not being adequate; non-performance of what is normal, expected or required; [C] instance of this: 不足; 缺乏; 未能达到正常, 所要求或所要求的状态; 其实例: '*heart* ~; 心脏衰竭; '*engine* ~*s.* 发动机故障。 *F*~ *of crops often results in famine.* 歉收常引起饥荒。 *Crop* ~*s caused great hardship for the people.* 歉收造成了人民极大的痛苦。 **4** [C] bankruptcy: 破产; 倒闭: *numerous bank* ~*s.* 许多的银行倒闭。 **5** [C, U] neglect, omission, inability (*to do sth*): 忽略; 未做; 无能为力 (与不定式连用): *His* ~ *to help us was disappointing.* 他未能帮助我们令人失望。 *His* ~ *to answer questions made the police suspicious.* 他不回答问题引起警方的不疑。

fain /feɪn; fen/ *adv* (poet, or old use after *would*)

willingly; with pleasure: (诗中或旧时用语, 用于 would 之后) 乐意; 欣然: *I would ~ have stayed at home.* 我当时真想留在家里.

faint[1] /feɪnt; fent/ *adj* (**-er, -est**) **1** (of things perceived through the senses) weak; indistinct; not clear: (指觉察到的东西) 微弱的; 模糊的; 不清楚的: *The sounds of the music grew ~er in the distance.* 音乐的声音在远处渐渐模糊了. *She called for help in a ~ voice.* 她以微弱的声音求救. *Only ~ traces of the tiger's tracks could be seen.* 这老虎的踪迹只有模糊的痕迹可见. **2** (of things in the mind) weak; vague: (指心中的事) 微弱的; 模糊的: *There is a ~ hope that she may be cured.* 她痊愈的希望不大. *I haven't the ~est idea (of) what you mean.* 我一点也不懂你的意思. **3** (of the body's movements and functions) weak; failing: (指身体的动作和机能) 微弱的; 衰退的: *His breathing became ~.* 他的呼吸微弱了. *His strength grew ~.* 他的体力衰退了. **4** (*pred* only) (of persons) likely to lose consciousness; giddy: (仅作表语) (指人) 昏晕的: *She looks/feels ~.* 她看来(感到)快要昏倒似的. **5** (*pred* only) (of persons) weak, exhausted: (仅作表语)(指人)委顿不堪的: *~ with hunger and cold.* 因饥寒而委顿不堪. **6** (of actions, etc) weak; unlikely to have much effect: (指动作等) 无力的; 似无效果的: *a ~ show of resistance;* 无力的抵抗; *make a ~ attempt to do sth.* 勉强尝试做某事. **7** ~ **heart,** timid spirit: 懦弱者; 怯懦者: (pro) (谚) *F~ heart never won fair lady.* 懦弱的人永不会博得美人的欢心. **,~-'hearted** *adj* lacking in courage. 懦弱的; 怯懦的. **~·ly** *adv* ~ **·ness** *n*

faint[2] /feɪnt; fent/ *vi* [VP2A, C] **1** lose consciousness (because of loss of blood, the heat, shock, etc): (因失血、受热、受惊等)昏厥; 昏倒: *He ~ed from hunger.* 他饿昏了. **2** become weak; 衰弱; 委顿: *He was ~ing with hunger.* 他因饥饿而逐渐衰弱. **3** (= fade) become: 消失: *The sounds ~ed away.* 声音渐渐消失了. □ *n* act, state, of ~ing(1). 昏厥; 不省人事. **in a (dead)** ~, (completely) unconscious. (完全)不省人事.

fair[1] /feə(r); fer/ *adj* **1** not showing favour to either person, side, etc; acting in an honest and honourable manner; in accordance with what is deserved or with the rules (of a game, etc): 公平的; 正直的; (游戏等)公正的: *Everyone must have a ~ share.* 每人须得其应得之份(或负担其应负担之部分). *It was a ~ fight,* eg the rules of boxing were observed. 那是一场公正的拳击赛(例如遵守拳击规则). *We charge ~ prices and are content with ~ (= reasonable) profits.* 我们索取公道的价钱, 并满足于公道的利润. *give sb/get a ~ hearing,* an opportunity to defend his conduct, etc, eg in a law court. (在法院等中)给予某人(获得)为其行为等辩护的机会. ~ **play**; **play**[1](2). **,~·'minded,** not prejudiced. 公正的. **2** average; quite good: 平常的; 尚可的; 相当好的; 不算坏的: *a ~ chance of success.* 相当好的成功机会. *His knowledge of French is ~, but ought to be better.* 他的法语还不错, 但应该还要好些. *The goods arrived in ~ condition.* 货物运到, 情况尚佳. *She has a ~ amount of sense.* 她有相当多的见识. **3** (of the weather) good; dry and fine; (of winds) favourable: (指天气)美好的; 晴朗的; (指风)顺的: *hoping for ~ weather.* 希望有好天气. *They set sail with the first ~ wind.* 他们一有顺风就起航. *The glass is at set ~,* The needle of the barometer is stationary (= set) at ~ (indicating a likelihood of good weather). 晴雨表预示有好天气. **,~-weather 'friend,** person who ceases to be a friend when one is in trouble. 不能共患难的朋友. **4** satisfactory; abundant: 令人满意的; 丰富的: *a ~ heritage;* 大量的遗产; promising: 有希望的: *be in a ~ way to succeed,* at the stage where success seems assured; 颇有成功的希望; *in a ~ way of business,* quite prosperous. 生意兴隆. **5** (of the skin, hair) pale; light in colour; blond: (指皮肤、头发) 淡色的; 白皙的: 金黄色的: *a '~-haired girl;* 金发女郎; *a ~ complexion.* 白皙的肤色. **6** (of speeches, promises, etc) carefully

chosen to seem polite and gentle in order to please and persuade: (指演说、诺言等)似乎可信的; 口惠的; 似乎动听的: *put sb off with ~ words/promises:* 以虚与委蛇的言语(诺言)敷衍某人; *the ~ speeches of the politicians,* eg before an election. 政客们花言巧语的演说(例如在选举前). **7** clean; clear; without blemish: 整洁的; 清楚的; 无瑕疵的: *Please make a ~ copy of this letter,* a new one without the errors, corrections, etc. 请将这封信整洁地誊录一遍. *Such behaviour will spoil your ~ name,* good reputation. 此种行为将损毁你的名誉. **8** (old use) beautiful: (旧用法) 美丽的; ~ **a maiden,** 美丽的少女. **the '~ sex,** women. 女性; 妇女. **~·ish** /'feərɪʃ; 'fɛrɪʃ/ *adj* of ~ (2) size or quality. 大小或质量平常的; 尚可的.

fair[2] /feə(r); fer/ *adv* **1** in a fair[1](1) manner: 公平地; 正直地; 公正地: *play ~.* 公正地比赛. ~ **enough,** (colloq) used to indicate agreement or reasonable disagreement. (口)还可以; 还合理(用以表示同意或合理的不同意). **2** in a fair[1](7) manner: 整洁地; 清楚地: *write/copy sth out* 整洁地写(誊录)一文件. **3** (old use) politely, courteously: (旧用法)有礼貌地: *speak sb ~.* 对人彬彬有礼地谈话.

fair[3] /feə(r); fer/ *n* **1** market (esp for cattle, sheep, farm products, etc) held periodically in a particular place, often with entertainments: 集市 (尤指买卖牛羊、农产品等者, 定期举行, 常伴有表演和娱乐). *a day before/after the ~,* too early/late. 太早; 太晚. '~-ground, open space for ~s. 市集场地. **2** large-scale exhibition of commercial and industrial goods: 博览会; 商展; 工展: *a world ~.* 世界博览会. **3** bazaar(3). 义卖会.

fair·ly[1] /'feəlɪ; 'fɛrlɪ/ *adv* **1** in a fair[1](1) manner; honestly: 公平地; 公正地; 诚实地: *treat sb ~;* 公平地对待某人; *come by (= obtain) sth ~,* by honest means. 光明正大地获得某物. **2** (colloq) utterly; completely: (口)完全地: *We were ~ caught in the trap,* had no chance of escape. 我们完全落入陷阱中(无逃脱机会). *He was ~ beside himself with rage,* as angry as he could possibly be. 他简直气得发疯. *His suggestion ~ took my breath away,* left me quite breathless (with surprise, etc). 他的建议真使我大吃一惊.

fair·ly[2] /'feəlɪ; 'fɛrlɪ/ *adv of degree* (Cf *rather,* which may be used with *too* and comparatives; *fairly* cannot be used in this way 参较 *rather,* rather 可与 too 和比较级连用, fairly 则不可) moderately: 相当地; 适度地: *This is a ~ easy book* (not a, therefore, perhaps suitable). 这是一本相当浅易的书(故或许适当). (Cf 参较 *This is a rather easy book,* suggesting 'rather too easy', and, therefore, perhaps unsuitable. 这本书过于浅易(故或许不适当).) *He wants a ~ large car,* not small, but not very large. 他要一部稍稍大一点的汽车. (Cf 参较 *That car is rather larger than he wants.* 那部汽车比他所需要的大了一点.)

fair·way /'feəweɪ; 'fer,we/ *n* **1** navigable channel for ships. 航路; 水路. **2** (golf) part of a golflinks, between a tee and a green, free from hazards. (高尔夫球) 无障碍的一部分球场.

fairy /'feərɪ; 'fɛrɪ/ *n* (*pl* **-ries**) **1** small imaginary being with supernatural powers, able to help or harm human beings; (attrib) of or like fairies: 小仙; (用作定语) 小仙的: *a ~ shape,* beautiful; small, delicate; 小巧可爱的形状; ~ *voices/footsteps.* 娇美的声音(轻巧的脚步). '~ **lamps/lights,** small lamps of coloured glass used for decoration. 彩色小灯. '~·**land** *n* **(a)** home of fairies. 仙境. **(b)** enchanted region; beautiful place. 乐园; 迷人之地. '~·**tale** *n* **(a)** tale about fairies. 神话; 童话. **(b)** untrue account, esp by a child. 谎言(尤指小儿所说的). **2** △ (sl, derog) male homosexual. (讳)(俚, 蔑)男子同性恋者.

fait accompli /,feɪt e'kɒmpliː; US: ekʌm'pli:; fstakɔ'pli/ *n* (F, 法 *= accomplished fact*)sth done and, for this reason, not reversible. 既成事实.

faith /feιθ; feθ/ n 1 [U] ~ *(in sb/sth)*, trust; strong belief; unquestioning confidence: 信任; 信仰; 信心: *have/put one's ~ in God.* 信仰上帝. *Have you any ~ in what he says?* 你相信他的话吗? 你对于此药没有多大信心. *I've lost ~ in that fellow,* can no longer trust him. 我再也不信任那个家伙了. *'~ cure,* one (alleged to be) made through religious ~. 信仰疗法. *'~ -healing,* (belief in) healing (of disease, etc) by prayer, appealing to and strengthening a person's religious ~, apart from the use of medicines, etc. 信仰疗法(相信除了用药物之外由祈祷或加强宗教信仰可以治病). 2 [C] belief in divine truth without proof; religion: 宗教信仰; 宗教: *the Christian, Jewish and Muslim ~s.* 基督教、犹太教和伊斯兰教. 3 [U] promise; engagement. 诺言; 约定. *give/pledge one's ~ to sb,* promise solemnly to support him. 保证拥护某人. *keep/break ~ with sb,* be loyal/disloyal to sb. 对某人守(不守)信用. 4 [U] loyalty; sincerity. 忠实; 诚实. *in bad ~,* with the intention of deceiving. 存心欺诈地. *in good ~,* honestly; sincerely. 诚实地; 诚恳地.

faith·ful /feιθfl; 'feθfəl/ adj 1 keeping faith; loyal and true (*to* sb, *to* a cause, *to* a promise, etc): 守信的; 忠实的(与 to 连用, 后接人、主义、诺言等): *a ~ friend;* 忠实的朋友; *~ to one's promise;* 守信; *~ in* (= in respect of) *word and deed.* 言行忠实. 2 true to the facts; accurate: 真实的; 翔实的; 正确的: *a ~ copy/description/account.* 真实的副本(描写, 报导). 3 **the ~** *n pl* the true believers, esp of Islam and Christianity. 忠实信徒 (尤指伊斯兰教徒和基督教徒). ~ly /-fəli; -fəli/ adv in a ~ manner. 忠实地. *Yours ~ly,* formula for closing a letter in formal or business style. 谨上 (信尾之客套语, 用于正式或商业信件中). ~ness n

faith·less /feιθlιs; 'feθlιs/ adj not trustworthy. 不可信任的; 不可靠的. ~·ly adv ~·ness n

fake /feιk; fek/ n [C] story, work of art, etc that seems genuine but is not; person who tries to deceive by claiming falsely to be or have sth: 杜撰的故事; 伪造的艺术品等; 赝品; 冒充的人; 骗子: (attrib) (用作定语) *a ~ picture.* 假画. □ vt [VP6A, 15B] ~ *(up),* make (eg a work of art, a story) in order to deceive: 伪造(艺术品、故事等): ~ *an oil-painting.* 伪制一幅油画. *There wasn't a word of truth in what he said; the whole story had been ~d (up),* invented. 他说的话没有一句是真的, 整个故事是捏造的.

fakir /feιkιər/ US: fə'k-; fə'kιr/ n Muslim or Hindu religious mendicant who is regarded as a holy man, a prophet, or a wonder-worker. (伊斯兰教或印度教的)行乞僧 (被视为圣者, 先知或异人).

fal·con /fɔ:lkən US: 'fælkən; 'fɔlkən/ n small bird of prey trained to hunt and kill other birds and small animals. 猎鹰. ⇨ the illus at **prey.** 参看 prey 之插图. ~·ry /-rι; -rι/ n [U] sport of hunting with ~s; art of training ~s. 放鹰狩猎; 鹰猎; 训练猎鹰术.

fall¹ /fɔ:l; fol/ n [C] 1 act of falling: 跌落; 降落; 堕落: *a ~ from a horse;* 从马上跌下; *the ~ of an apple from a tree;* 苹果自树上落下; *a ~ in price/temperature;* 物价的下跌 (温度的下降); *the ~ (= collapse) of the Roman Empire.* 罗马帝国之灭亡. *the F~ (of man),* Adam's sin and its results. 亚当之犯罪及其后果; 人类之堕落. *~ guy n* (colloq) (口) (a) dupe; easy victim. 受骗者; 易受害者. (b) scapegoat. 代罪羔羊. 2 amount of rain that falls; distance by which sth falls or comes down: 降雨量; 落差; 落差: *the ~ of the river here is six feet.* 此地的河水降落六英尺. 3 (often *pl*) place where a river falls over cliffs, etc: (常用复数) *Niagara F~s.* 尼亚加拉大瀑布. 4 (US) autumn: (美) 秋季: *in the ~ of 1970:* 一九七〇年的秋天; (attrib) (用作定语) *~ fashions.* 秋季式样.

fall² /fɔ:l; fol/ vi (pt fell /fel; fεl/, pp ~en /'fɔ:lən;

'fɔlən/) (For special uses with *adverbial particles* and *preps,* ⇨14 below.) (与副词性小品词及介词连用之特殊用法, 参看下列第 14 义.) 1 [VP2A, B, C, 3A] ~ *(down/over),* come or go down freely (by force of weight, loss of balance, etc): 落下; 降落; 跌下: *The book fell from the table to the floor.* 那书从桌上掉落在地板上. *He fell over into the water.* 他掉落水里了. *The rain was ~ing steadily.* 雨不停地下. *The leaves ~ in autumn.* 树叶在秋天掉落. *He slipped and fell ten feet.* 他失足跌下十英尺. *This basket is full of eggs — don't let it ~.* 这篮内盛满了蛋, 不要把它打翻了. *The lambs are beginning to ~,* be born. 小羊快要生下来了. ⇨ **drop²(2).** *~ on one's feet,* (fig) be fortunate; get out of a difficulty successfully: (喻) 走好运; 化险为夷; 避过危难: *Some people always seem to ~ on their feet,* be lucky and successful. 有些人似乎总是走好运. *~ short,* (指投射物) 未达目标: *The arrow fell short.* 那箭没有射中目标. *~ short of,* fail to equal; be inferior to: 未达到; 不及: *Your work ~s short of my expectations.* 你的工作未达到我的期望. *~ing 'star,* object (eg a meteor) seen as a bright streak in the sky as it burns up. 陨星; 流星. 2 [VP2A, C, 3A] ~ *(down/over),* no longer stand; come to the ground; collapse; be overthrown: 跌倒; 跌下; 倒塌; 被推倒: *Many trees fell in the storm.* 许多树在那场暴风雨中倒了. *Babies often ~ down when they are learning to walk.* 小儿学步时常会跌跤. *He fell over and broke his left leg.* 他跌倒并将左腿摔断了. *He fell full length.* 他挺直地跌倒在地上. *He fell on/to his knees (= knelt down) and begged for mercy.* 他跪下来乞求怜悯. *He fell in battle,* was killed. 他阵亡了. *Six tigers fell to his rifle.* He shot six tigers. 他用步枪射倒了六只虎. *Six wickets fell before lunch,* (cricket) Six batsmen were out. (板球) 六位击球员在午饭以前退场. ~ *flat,* (fig) fail to have the intended effect: (喻) 未产生预期的效果: *His best jokes all fell flat,* did not amuse his listeners. 他最拿手的笑话都失效了. *The scheme fell flat,* was unsuccessful. 这计划失败了. ~ *flat on one's face,* ~ *face down to the ground.* 面朝下直挺挺地跌倒在地. ~ *to the ground,* ~ **ground¹(1).** ~ *'over oneself,* (a) ~ because one is awkward, clumsy, or in too much of a hurry. 由于笨拙或过于匆忙而跌倒. (b) (fig) be very eager: (喻) 渴望; 极想: *The big firms were ~ing over themselves/each other for the services of this brilliant young scientist.* 那些大公司竟相争取这位卓越的青年科学家的服务. **the ~en,** those killed in war. 阵亡将士. ⇨ 战死者. 3 [VP2C] ~ *(down),* hang down: 垂下; 低垂: *His beard fell to his chest.* 他的胡须垂在胸前. *Her hair/cloak fell over her shoulders.* 她的头发 (斗篷) 披在肩上. 4 [VP2A, B, C, 3A] come or go to a lower level or point; become lower or less: 降低; 减退: *The temperature fell rapidly.* 温度迅速下降. *His voice fell to a whisper.* 他的声音降低成为耳语. *Her spirits fell at the bad news,* She became low-spirited, sad. 她听到这坏消息而精神沮丧. *His face/jaw fell,* He showed dismay. 他显出沮丧的样子. (Cf 参较 *put on a long face at* **face¹(3)**.) *The wind fell during the night,* became less strong. 夜间风势减弱了. 5 [VP2C, D, 3A] ~ *(into),* become; pass into (the state indicated by the *adj* or phrase): 成为; 变为(其后形容词或短语所表示的状态): *His horse fell lame.* 他的马跛了. *He fell silent.* 他变为沉默. *The old man fell asleep.* 那老人睡着了. *He has ~en ill.* 他生病了. *When does the rent ~ due,* When must it be paid? 租金何时该付? *He fell into a doze,* began to doze. 他打瞌睡了. *Don't fall into bad habits!* Don't acquire or adopt them. 不要养成坏习惯! *They have ~en into poverty,* become poor. 他们贫穷了. *She fell an easy prey to him.* 她轻易地被他控制了. ~ *in love (with),* become filled with love (for): 喜爱; 爱上: *He fell in love with an actress.* 他爱上一位女演员. *I've ~en in love with your beautiful house.* 我很喜欢你的漂亮的房子. ~ *out of love (with),* cease to feel love (for).

不再喜爱。⇨ **foul**[1](6). **6** [VP2A, C, 3A] **~ (upon)**, descend (upon): 降临: *Darkness fell upon the scene*, It became dark. 黑暗降临这个地方。*A great stillness had ~en upon everything*, Everything had become quiet and motionless. 万籁俱寂。*Fear fell upon them*, They became frightened. 他们均感恐惧。**7** [PV2A,C] (old use) sin; give way to wrongdoing: (旧用法)犯罪; 堕落: *Eve tempted Adam and he fell*. 夏娃诱惑亚当, 于是他堕落了。**~en 'woman**, (old use) one who has lost her virginity before marriage. (旧用法)堕落的女人; 婚前失贞的女人。**8** [VP2A] (of a city, fort, etc) be captured: (指城市, 要塞等) 沦陷; 失守: *Rome has ~en!* 罗马已经沦陷了! be overcome or defeated: 被征服; 被击败: *The Government has ~en again*. 政府又垮台了。**9** [VP3A] **~ on**, take the direction or position (indicated by the *adv* or phrase): 朝某一方向或占据某一位置(由其后的副词或短语表示): *A shadow fell on the wall*. 一个阴影投落在墙上。*His eye fell on* (= He suddenly saw) *a curious object*. 他突然看见一个奇怪的物体。*Strange sounds fell on our ears*, We heard strange sounds. 我们听到了奇怪的声音。*The lamplight fell on her face*. 灯光照射在她的脸上。*In 'formidable' the stress may ~ on either the first or the second syllable*. 在 formidable 一词中, 重音在第一或第二音节上均可。**10** [VP3A] **~ on / upon / to**, come by chance, design, or right: 由于偶然、计划或权利而来到: *All the expenses fell on me*, I had to pay them. 所有的开销均由我付。*The responsibility/blame, etc fell upon me*. 这责任(过失等)落在我的身上。*It fell to my lot/to me to open the discussion*, I had to speak first. 我必须首先发言。*He has fallen on evil days*, is suffering misfortune. 他遭逢厄运。**11** [VP2C] (of land) slope: (指土地)下斜: *The ground ~s towards the river*. 那土地向河边倾斜。**12** [VP2C] occur, have as date: (做为日期) 发生: *Easter ~s early next year*. 明年的复活节将到得早。*Christmas Day ~s on a Monday this year*. 今年的圣诞节是星期一。**13** [VP2A, C] be spoken: 被说出: *Not a word from his lips*. 他什么话也没有说。*I guessed what she was going to do from the few words that she let fall*, from what she said. 从她所说的几句话中我猜得出她要做些什么。**14** [VP2C, 3A] (special uses with *adverbial particles* and *preps*): (与副词性小品词和介词连用的特殊用法):

fall about (laughing/with laughter), (colloq) laugh uncontrollably: (口)不禁大笑: *They fell about when Sir Harold slipped on the banana skin*. 当哈罗德爵士踏到香蕉皮而滑跤时, 他们不禁大笑。

fall among sb, get mixed up with, come by chance among: 与某人结交; 落入某人之手: *~ among thieves, evil companions*. 落入盗贼之手(交上坏人)。

fall away, (a) desert: 遗弃: *His supporters began to ~ away*. 支持他的人开始疏远他了。**(b)** disappear, vanish: 消失: *In this crisis, prejudices fell away and all classes co-operated well*. 值此危急时期, 各种偏见均已消除, 各阶层合作无间。

fall back, retreat; move or turn back: 撤退; 后退: *Our attack was so vigorous that the enemy had to ~ back*. 我们的攻势凶猛, 敌人不得不撤退了。**~ 'back on sth,** have recourse to; turn to for support: 依靠: 依靠: *If you don't need the money now, bank it — it's always useful to have something to ~ back on*. 如果你目前不需要这笔钱, 便将它存在银行里——有点依靠的东西总是有用的。

fall behind (with sth), fail to keep level (with); lag: 落于…之后; 落后: *We always ~s behind when we're going uphill*. 我们登山时他总是落在后面。*I've ~en behind with my correspondence*, have many unanswered letters. 我积压了许多信函未作复。*Don't ~ behind with your rent, or you'll be evicted*. 不要逾期不缴房租, 否则你将被逐出。

fall down (on sth), (colloq) fail (in a task, in expectation): (口)(在…方面)失败; 未做到: *~ down on one's promises/obligations (to sb)*. (对某人)未实践诺言, 有负所望。

(未尽到责任。)

fall for sth / sb, (colloq) yield to the charms, attractions or merits of (esp when deceived): (口)被…迷住(尤指为骗局情况下); 对…倾倒; 受…的诱惑: *He ~s for every pretty face he sees*. 他见到美丽的面孔便为之倾倒。*Did he ~ for your suggestion*, Did he decide that it was good, and agree to it? 他喜欢你的建议吗?

fall in, (a) collapse; give way: 塌陷; 垮下: *The roof fell in*. 屋顶塌陷了。*The (sides of the) trench fell in*. 壕沟(壕沟的两边)塌陷了。**(b)** (mil) (cause to) go on parade: (军)(使)站队; 集合: *The sergeant ordered the men to ~ in*. 士官命令兵士们集合。**(c)** (of a lease) expire. (指租约)期满。**~ due** (of a debt) become due. (指债务)到期。**~ in with sb / sth, (a)** happen to meet. 偶遇。**(b)** agree to: 同意: *He fell in with my views at once*. 他立刻赞同我的见解。

fall into sth, be naturally divisible into: 自然地分作: *The subject ~s into four divisions*. 这问题可自然地分作四部分。**~ into line (with sth/sb),** agree (to what others are doing or wish to do); accept (a course of conduct, procedure, etc). 同意(别人所做或欲做之事); 接受某种行动, 方法等。

fall off, become smaller, fewer or less: 消减; 减少: *The takings at the football stadium have ~en off*, Less money has been paid for admission. 足球运动的收入减少了。*The daily number of passengers by this line shows a slight ~ing off*. 每日搭乘本航线的乘客数目略见减少。

fall on sth/sb, attack; assault (the enemy). 攻击(敌人)。

fall out, (a) (mil) (cause to) go off parade. (军) 解散; 离队。**(b)** happen: 发生: *It (so) fell out that I could not get there in time*. 结果是我未能及时到那里。*Everything fell out as we had hoped*. 一切均达到我们的愿望。**(c)** discontinue; stop: 停止; 放弃: the *'~out rate*, eg of pupils who give up a course of study. 退出率(例如学生之退选一课程); 放弃率。⇨ **drop-out** at **drop**[2](13). **~ out (with sb),** quarrel (with 与某人) 争吵: 吵架: *The two men fell out*. 那两个人吵架了。*He has fallen out with the girl he was going to marry*. 他和要同他结婚的那位女郎吵架了。**'~-out** [U] radio-active dust in the atmosphere, after a nuclear explosion. (核爆炸后大气中之)放射性尘埃。

fall through, fail; miscarry; come to nothing: 失败; 成为泡影: *His scheme fell through*. 他的计划失败了。

fall 'to, begin to do sth: 开始做某事: *They fell to with a good appetite*. 他们津津有味地开始大吃。**~ to 'doing sth:** *I fell to wondering where to go for my holidays*. 我开始考虑去何处度假。

fall under sth, be classifiable under: 归入…项下: *The results ~ under three heads*. 这些结果分在三个项目下。

fal·la·cy /'fæləsɪ; 'fæləsɪ/ n (pl **-cies**) **1** [C] false or mistaken belief. 谬见; 错误的信念。**2** [U] false reasoning or argument: 谬误的推理; 谬论: *a statement based on ~*. 基于谬误推理之声明。**fal·la·cious** /fə'leɪʃəs; fə'leʃəs/ adj misleading; based on error. 使人误解的; 谬误的。

fallen pp of **fall**[2].

fal·li·ble /'fæləbl; 'fæləbl/ adj liable to error. 易犯错误的。**fal·li·bil·ity** /ˌfælə'bɪlɪtɪ; ˌfælə'bɪlətɪ/ n (state of) being ~. 易犯错误。

Fallopian tube /fəˌloʊpɪən 'tjuːb US: 'tuːb; fə-'lopɪən'tjub/ n (anat) (解剖)=**oviduct**. ⇨ the illus at **reproduce**. 参看 reproduce 之插图。

fal·low /'fæloʊ; 'fælo/ adj, n [U] (land) ploughed but not sown or planted: 犁过而未耕种的(土地); (耕地) 休闲的; 休耕的(土地): *allow land to lie ~*; 让土地休耕; *plough (up) ~ land*. 犁起休耕的田地。

fal·low-deer /'fæloʊ dɪə(r); 'fælo dɪə(r)/ n (pl unchanged) small Eurasian deer with a reddish-yellow coat with, in the summer, white spots. (复数不变) 黇鹿; 梅花鹿(一种欧洲和亚洲产的小鹿, 毛皮呈赤褐色, 夏季有白斑)。

false /fɔːls; fɔls/ adj **1** not right, true or real: 错误的; 不对的; 不真实的: a ~ alarm; 虚假的警报; ~ ideas; 错误的观念; ~ weights, eg one of 90 grammes marked as 100 grammes; 不足的砝码(如将 90 克当作 100 克); take a ~'step, stumble; (fig) act wrongly; 绊跌; 失足; (喻)行为失检; 犯错; sing a ~ note; 唱错音符; ~ shame/pride, based on wrong ideas, etc; 错误的羞耻(自负); make a ~ start, (athletics) start before the signal has been given; (fig) start wrongly. (体育)起步太早(未发信号前即开始); (喻)错误地开始; 不当地开始. **2** deceiving; lying: 欺骗的; 不诚实的: give a ~ impression; 予人以不诚实的印象; bear/give ~ witness, tell lies or deceive (eg in a law court); 作伪证; be ~ to one's word, fail to keep a promise. 不守信. act under ~ pretences, ⇨ pretence. put sb/be in a ~ position, in circumstances that cause misunderstanding or make it necessary for sb to act contrary to principles. (使某人)处于使人误会的立场; (使某人)处于违背原则行事的地位. sail under ~ colours, (a) (of a ship) with a flag which it has no right to use. (指船)挂其他国家的国旗航行. (b) (fig) pretend or appear to be different from what one really is. (喻)冒充. a ~ bottom, a secret compartment in a container such as a suitcase. 假底; (箱底之)秘密夹层. **3** not genuine; sham; artificial: 不真实的; 假的; 人造的: ~ hair/teeth; 假发(牙); ~ coins. 假钱币. **4** improperly so called: 命名不当的: the ~ acacia (not really an acacia tree). 刺槐(非真正的胶树). □ adv (only in) (仅用于) play sb ~, cheat or betray him. 欺骗或出卖某人。~·ly adv in a ~ manner: 错误地; 欺骗地; 不真地: ~ly accused. 被诬告的。~·ness n

false·hood /ˈfɔːlshʊd; ˈfɔlsˌhʊd/ n **1** [C] lie; untrue statement: 谎言; 不实之言: How can you utter such ~s? 你怎能说出这种谎言? **2** [U] telling lies; lying: 说谎; 撒谎: guilty of ~. 犯说谎罪. Truth, if exaggerated, may become ~. 真理如加以夸张, 可能成为谬误.

fal·setto /fɔːlˈsetəʊ; fɔlˈsetɔ/ n (pl ~s) high voice in men; counter-tenor: (男子发出的尖锐的)假声; 上次中音: to sing ~; 唱上次中音; (attrib) of or in such a voice: (用作定语)(以)尖锐假声的: in a ~ tone. 以尖锐的假音调.

fal·sies /ˈfɔːlsɪz; ˈfɔlsɪz/ n pl (colloq) brassieres filled with soft material to exaggerate the size of the breasts. (口)假乳房; 义乳.

fals·ify /ˈfɔːlsɪfaɪ; ˈfɔlsəˌfaɪ/ vt (pt, pp -fied) [VP6A] **1** make false: 使伪的; 伪造; 窜改: ~ records/accounts; 伪造记录(帐目); tell falsely: 伪称: ~ a story. 虚构一故事. **2** misrepresent: 错误表示; 误称: ~ an issue. 误言一问题. falsi·fi·ca·tion /ˌfɔːlsɪfɪˈkeɪʃn, ˌfɔlsɪfɪˈkeɪʃən/ n [U] ~ing or being falsified; [C] change made in order to deceive. 使伪; 伪造; 窜改; 伪称; 误称.

fals·ity /ˈfɔːlsətɪ; ˈfɔlsətɪ/ n **1** [U] falsehood; incorrectness; error. 错误; 不正确; 谬误. **2** [C] (pl -ties) false or treacherous act, statement, etc. 虚伪或奸诈的行为, 言语等.

fal·ter /ˈfɔːltə(r); ˈfɔltɚ/ vi, vt **1** [VP2A, C] move, walk or act in an uncertain or hesitating manner, from either weakness or fear. (由于衰弱或恐惧)摇晃; 蹒跚而行. **2** [VP2A] (of the voice) waver: 吞吐: His voice ~ed as he tried to speak. 他要说话时声音发颤了. [VP15B] ~ (out), (of a person) speak in a hesitating way or with a broken voice: (指人)支吾地说出; 结巴地说出: He ~ed out a few words. 他结结巴巴地说出几个字。~·ing·ly /ˈfɔːltərɪŋlɪ; ˈfɔltɚɪŋlɪ/ adv

fame /feɪm; fem/ n [U] (condition of) being known or talked about by all; what people say (esp good) about sb: 风闻; 传说; 名声; 声誉: He was not anxious for ~. 他不急于想成名. 他死后始获得许久之名. famed adj famous: 著名的: ~d for their courage. 他们以勇敢闻名.

fam·il·iar /fəˈmɪlɪə(r); fəˈmɪljɚ/ adj **1** ~ with, having a good knowledge of: 熟悉; 熟谙: facts with which every schoolboy is ~. 每位学童所熟悉的事实. I am not very ~ with botanical names. 我不太熟悉植物学方面的名称. **2** ~ to, well known to: 为…所熟知: facts that are ~ to every schoolboy; 每位学童所熟知的事实; subjects that are ~ to you. 你所熟知的科目. **3** common; usual; often seen or heard: 日常的; 通常的; 常见的; 常听到的: the ~ scenes of one's childhood; 儿时常见的情景; the ~ voices of one's friends. 常听到的朋友们的声音. **4** close; intimate; personal: 密切的; 亲密的; 个人的: Are you on ~ terms with him as to address him as 'Tom'? 你和格林先生的交情好吗? (譬如你称他 '汤姆' 吗?) Don't be too ~ with him; he's a dishonest man. 不要同他过分亲密, 他不是个诚实的人. **5** claiming a greater degree of amorous friendship than in proper: 过分亲密的: He made himself much too ~ with my wife. 他对我的妻子过分亲密. □ n intimate friend. 亲密的朋友。~·ly adv in a ~ manner; without ceremony. 亲密地; 不拘礼地.

fam·ili·ar·ity /fəˌmɪlɪˈærətɪ; fəˌmɪlɪˈærətɪ/ n (pl -ties) **1** [U] ~ (with/to), (the state of) being familiar: 熟悉; 熟谙; 亲密: His ~ with the languages used in Nigeria surprised me. 他之精通尼日利亚的各种语言使我惊奇. You should not treat her with such ~. 你不应该对她如此亲密. F~ breeds contempt, (prov) When we know sth or sb very well, we may lose respect, fear, etc. (谚)熟悉而生轻视之心; 亲昵生狎侮. **2** (pl) acts that lack ceremony; instances of familiar behaviour: (复)不拘形式的行动; 亲密的动作: She dislikes such familiarities as the use of her first name by men she has only just met. 她讨厌这种不拘礼的行动, 譬如刚见面的男子便呼唤她的名字.

fam·il·iar·ize /fəˈmɪlɪəraɪz; fəˈmɪljəˌraɪz/ vt **1** [VP14] ~ sb/oneself with, make well acquainted with: 使熟习: ~ oneself with a foreign language/the use of a new tool/the rules of a game. 熟习一外国语(新工具的用法, 比赛的规则). **2** [VP6A] make well known: 使闻知: The newspapers and radio have ~d the word 'automation'. 报纸和无线电广播使 "工业自动化" 一词成为家喻户晓了.

fam·ily /ˈfæməlɪ; ˈfæməlɪ/ n (pl -lies) **1** [collective] n) group of parents and children: (集合名词)家庭: Almost every ~ in the village has a man in the army (Note here sing v after collective n). 这村子里几乎每一家都有一男子从军(注意: 此集合名词后用单数动词). My ~ are early risers (Note here pl v after family = members of my family). 我全家都是早起的人(注意: family 在此指家里的人, 故其后动词是复数). **2** (collective n) (集合名词) person's children: 子女: He has a large ~. 他的子女很多. Has he any ~? 他有儿女吗? Tom is the eldest of the ~, the eldest child. 汤姆是最大的孩子. **3** [C] all those persons descended from a common ancestor: 家族: families that have been in Surrey for hundreds of years. 已在萨里居住数百年的各家族. **4** [U] ancestry: 家世: a man of distinguished ~. 家世显赫的人. **5** [C] group of living things (plants, animals, etc) or of languages, with common characteristics and a common source: (动植物等的)族; 科; 系; 语系: animals of the cat ~, eg lions and tigers; 猫科动物(如狮和虎); the Germanic ~ of languages (including German, Dutch, English). 日耳曼语系(包括德语、荷兰语、英语). **6** (attrib) of or for a ~: (用作定语)家的; 家庭的; 家族的: the ~ estate/jewels, etc. 家产(家中的珠宝等). in the ~ way, (sl; of a woman) pregnant. (俚, 指女子)怀孕的. ~ doctor, a general practitioner. 家庭(特约)医师. ~ hotel, one with lower rates for families. 家庭旅馆(为家庭设的经济旅社). ~ likeness, resemblance between members of a ~. 家族各份子间的相似. '~ man, one who is fond of home life with his ~. 喜好家庭生活的人. ~ name, surname. 姓; 氏. ~ planning, (use of birth control,

contraceptives, for) planning the number of children, intervals between births, etc in a ~. 家庭计划；节育；生育控制。 **~ tree**, a genealogical tree or chart. 家谱。

fam·ine /'fæmɪn; 'fæmɪn/ n 1 [U] extreme scarcity of food in a region: (一地区之) 饥荒: *Parts of India have often suffered from ~.* 印度有些地区常闹饥荒。 2 [C] particular occasion when there is such scarcity: 某一饥荒: *a ~ in Ethiopia.* 埃塞俄比亚的一次饥荒。 3 (attrib) caused by ~: (用作定语) 因饥荒而造成的: *~ prices,* high prices. 因饥荒而造成的高价。

fam·ish /'fæmɪʃ; 'fæmɪʃ/ vi, vt 1 [VP2A, 3A] suffer from extreme hunger: 挨饿; 饥饿: *They were ~ing for food.* 他们因缺乏食物而挨饿。*I'm ~ing!* (colloq) very hungry. (口) 我很饿! 2 [VP6A] (usu passive) cause (sb) to suffer from hunger: (通常用被动语态) 使挨饿; 使受饥: *The child looked half ~ed.* 那孩子看来很饿了。*I'm ~ed!* (colloq) very hungry. (口) 我饿死了!

fa·mous /'feɪməs; 'feməs/ adj 1 known widely; having fame; celebrated: 著名的; 出名的; 驰名的: *a ~ scientist.* 著名的科学家。*The town is ~ for its gambling casino / ~ as a gambling resort.* 该城以其赌场驰名 (是个著名的赌博场所)。 2 (dated colloq) excellent. (过时口语) 极好的; 令人满意的。 **~·ly** adv in a ~ (2) manner: 极好; 令人满意地: *get on ~ly with sb;* 与某人相处极为融洽; *do ~ly in / at sth.* 顺利地进行某事。

fan¹ /fæn; fæn/ n (flat, semi-circular, usu folding) object waved in the hand, or (with rotating blades) operated mechanically, for making a current of air (eg to cool a room, oneself or to blow dust, etc away); sth that is like a hand fan in shape, eg the tail of a peacock. 扇子; 风扇; 扇状物 (例如孔雀尾)。 **'fan belt** n rubber belt transferring circular motion to the cooling fan of an engine. 扇带 (传送循环动作至发动机冷却扇的橡皮带)。 **'fan·light** n fan-shaped window over a door. (门上的) 扇形窗。 **,fan 'vaulting** n (archit) style of vaulting in which ribs, like those of a folding fan, rise and spread from a single point. (建筑) 扇形圆屋顶。

fans

fan² /fæn; fæn/ vt, vi (-nn-) 1 [VP6A] send a current of air on to: 扇; 吹向: *fan oneself;* 扇自己; 扇扇子; *fan a fire,* to make it burn up; 扇火; *fan the flame,* (fig) increase excitement or emotion. (喻) 煽动情绪。 2 [VP6A] (of a breeze) blow gently on: (指微风) 徐徐吹在⋯上: *The breeze fanned our faces.* 微风轻轻吹在我们的脸上。 3 [VP2C] **~ out,** open in fan-shaped formation: 作扇形散开: *The troops stormed the enemy's trenches and fanned out across the fields.* 军队猛袭敌人的战壕并在战场上呈扇形散开。 4 [VP6A] spread out (eg playing cards) like a fan. 将 (纸牌等) 展成扇形。

fan³ /fæn; fæn/ n (colloq) keen supporter of sth: (口)

对某事物之狂热者; 迷: *'baseball fans;* 棒球迷; *'fan mail,* letters from fans, eg to a popular singer. 狂热者寄来的信 (例如歌迷寄给歌星者)。

fa·natic /fə'nætɪk; fə'nætɪk/ n person filled with excessive (and often mistaken) enthusiasm, eg in religion: 狂热者 (常是盲目的，例如在宗教方面); 盲信者: *food ~s,* willing to eat only certain kinds of food. 偏食者。 □ adj (also 亦作 **fa·nati·cal** /-kl; -kl/) excessively enthusiastic; of or like a ~: 狂热的; 狂热者的: *~(al) beliefs.* 狂热的信仰。 **fa·nati·cally** /-klɪ; -klɪ/ adv **fa·nati·cism** /-sɪzəm; -sɪzəm/ n [U] violent, unreasoning enthusiasm; [C] instance of this. 狂热; 盲信。

fan·cier /'fænsɪə(r); 'fænsɪr/ n person with special knowledge of and love for some article, animal, etc (the name being prefixed): 对某物品、动物等有特殊知识或爱好之人; 玩赏家 (玩赏的对象名称冠于前): *a 'dog ~;* 玩赏狗的人; *a 'rose ~.* 玩赏玫瑰的人。

fan·ci·ful /'fænsɪfl; 'fænsɪfəl/ adj 1 (of persons) full of fancies(2); led by imagination instead of reason and experience: (指人) 富于幻想的; 为想象力引导的: *a ~ writer.* 富于幻想的作家。 2 unreal; curiously designed: 不真实的; 设计奇特的: *~ drawings.* 构想奇特的图画。 **~·ly** /-fəlɪ; -fəlɪ/ adv

fancy¹ /'fænsɪ; 'fænsɪ/ n (pl -cies) 1 [U] power of creating mental pictures (often a passive process). (⇨ **imagination**, in which the mind is more active): 想象力 (与为消极的过程)。 (参看 **imagination**, 其思想过程较为积极): *a world of mere ~.* 纯想象的世界。 2 [C] sth imagined; unfounded opinion or belief: 想象之物; 空论; 无根据的念头; 幻想: *the fancies of a poet.* 诗人的幻想。 *Did I really hear someone come in or was it only a ~?* 我是真听到有人来，或只是一种幻觉? *I have a ~ (=* vague idea) *that she will be late.* 我仿佛觉得她会迟到。 3 [C] **a ~ (for),** fondness, liking, desire: 爱好; 喜爱: *I have a ~ for some wine with my dinner.* 我喜欢吃饭的时候喝点酒。 **take a ~ to,** become fond of: 喜爱: *The children have taken quite a ~ to their cousin.* 孩子们十分喜欢他们的表兄。 **take / catch the ~ of,** please or attract: 投合⋯的心意; 吸引: *She saw the dress in a shop window and it caught her ~.* 她看到一家商店橱窗内的衣服，而为它所吸引。 *a passing ~,* sth that attracts one's attention and liking for a short period of time only. 一时为人所爱好之物。 **,~-'free** adj not in love; not committed to anything; not taking things seriously. 未在恋爱中的; 无拘束的; 态度不严肃的。 ⇨ **foot¹**(8).

fancy² /'fænsɪ; 'fænsɪ/ adj (usu attrib; not in the comp or superl) (通常用作定语，不用于比较级或最高级) 1 (esp of small things) brightly coloured; made to please the eye: (尤指小东西) 颜色鲜艳的; 悦目的: *~ cakes;* 漂亮的蛋糕; *~ goods.* 精美小物品。 2 not plain or ordinary: 特别装饰的: *~ bread.* 特制面包。 *~ dress,* unusual costume, often historical or exotic, as worn at balls, called *~-'dress balls.* 奇装异服 (如化装舞会 fancy-dress balls 所穿者，常是有历史或外国特色的)。*~ work,* ornamental sewing. 用做装饰的针织物; 刺绣。 3 bred for particular points of beauty: 因其珍奇而特别培育的: *~ dogs / pigeons;* 品种珍奇的狗 (鸽子); *~ pansies,* having two or more colours. 珍品紫罗兰 (有两种或多种颜色)。 4 extravagant: 过度的; 过分的: *~ ideas / prices.* 过分的思想 (高昂的价格)。 5 (US, of goods) superior in quality: (美，指货物) 品质优良的: *'F~ Crab'* (on a label, etc). '精选蟹' (见于标签等)。 6 imagined: 想象的; 空想的: *~ a portrait.* 想象的画像。

fancy³ /'fænsɪ; 'fænsɪ/ vt (pt, pp -cied) 1 [VP6A, 16 B, 19 C] picture in the mind; imagine: 想象; 假想: *Can you ~ me as a pirate?* 你能想象我是一个海盗吗? *I can't ~ his doing such a thing.* 我不能想象他做这种事。 2 [VP25, 9] be under the impression that (without being certain, or without enough reason): (不把握或充分的理由而) 以为: *I rather ~ (that) he won't come.* 我认为他不会来。 *He fancied he heard footsteps behind him.* 他

以为他听到身后有脚步声。*Don't ~ that you can succeed without hard work.* 不要认为你不努力工作而能成功。*When she saw Tom, whom she had fancied (to be) dead, ...* 当她看到她以为已经死去的汤姆时，…。**3** [VP6A] (colloq) have a fancy(3) for: (口) 喜爱: *What do you ~ for your dinner?* 你午(或晚)饭喜欢吃什么? *I don't ~ this place at all.* 我一点也不喜欢这地方。*Do you ~ that girl, find her attractive, likeable?* 你喜欢那个女孩子吗? **4 ~ oneself,** have an excessively high opinion of oneself; be rather conceited: 自负; 自命不凡: *He fancies himself as an orator.* 他认为自己是位了不起的演说家。**5** [VP6A, C] exclamatory style, expressing surprise: 感叹语气，表示惊讶: *F~ her saying such unkind things about you!* 想到有，她竟然说出这些对你无情的话! *F~ that, now!* 嗳呀! *Just ~!* How strange! How surprising! 多奇怪呀! 真想不到!

fan·dango /fænˈdæŋgəʊ; fænˈdæŋgo/ *n* (*pl* ~es /-gəʊz; -goz/) (music for a) lively Spanish or S American dance. 方当果舞 (一种轻快的西班牙或南美洲舞); 方当果舞曲。

fan·fare /ˈfænfeə(r); ˈfæn,fer/ *n* [C] (music) flourish of trumpets or bugles. (音乐) 喇叭或号角之高而急的吹奏; 鼓号曲。

fang /fæŋ; fæŋ/ *n* long, sharp tooth (esp of dogs and wolves); snake's poison-tooth. (犬、狼之)尖牙; (蛇的) 毒牙。

fan·light ⇔ **fan¹.**

fan·ny /ˈfænɪ; ˈfænɪ/ *n* (*pl* -nies) (US sl) buttocks. (美俚)屁股。

fan·tan /ˈfæntæn US: ˈfæntæn; ˈfæn,tæn/ *n* Chinese gambling game. 番摊(中国的一种赌博)。

fan·tasia /fænˈteɪzɪə US: -ˈteɪʒə; fænˈteɪʒə/ *n* artistic composition in which a fanciful style is more important than structure. 幻想曲。

fan·ta·size /ˈfæntəsaɪz; ˈfæntəsaɪz/ *vi, vt* [VP2A, 3A, 6A] ~ (*about*), have a fantasy(2) (of); imagine. 幻想; 想象。**fan·ta·sist** *n* person who ~s. 幻想者; 想象者。

fan·tas·tic /fænˈtæstɪk; fænˈtæstɪk/ *adj* **1** wild and strange; grotesque: 奇异的; 怪诞的: ~ *dreams/shapes/fashions.* 怪异的梦(形状、式样)。**2** (of ideas, plans) impossible to carry out; absurd. (指观念、计划)无法实现的; 荒谬的。**3** (sl) marvellous; wonderful: (俚) 令人惊奇的; 极妙的: *Christina's a really ~ girl!* 克里斯蒂娜真是个奇妙的女孩! **fan·tas·ti·cally** /-klɪ; -klɪ/ *adv*

fan·tasy /ˈfæntəsɪ; ˈfæntəsɪ/ *n* (*pl* -sies) **1** [U] fancy(1); imagination, esp when extravagant: 想象力; 想象; (尤指过度的)幻想; 狂想: *live in a world of ~;* 生活在幻想世界中; (attrib) (用作定语) *one's ~ life,* that part devoted to ~. 个人的幻想生活。**2** [C] product of the imagination: 幻想出的东西: *sexual fantasies.* 性幻想。**3** [C] = **fantasia.**

far¹ /fɑː(r); far/ *adj* (⇔ **farther, farthest, further, furthest**) **1** (usu in liter style) distant: (通常用于文学的文体)远的: *a far country.* 一个远方的国家。*a far cry from,* a long way from; (fig) a very different thing from. 距离…很远; (喻)与…不相同之物。**2 the Far West** 远东。**the Far West,** the Pacific coast area of the US. 美国西部太平洋沿岸地区。**3** (= *farther*) more remote: 较远的: *at the far end of the street;* 在街的那一头; *on the far bank of the river.* 在河的彼岸。

far² /fɑː(r); far/ *adv* (⇔ **farther, farthest, further, furthest**) **1** (indicating a great distance, commonly used in the interr and neg, but not usually, except as shown in **2** below, in the affirm): 远; 遥远(通常用于疑问和否定句，除下列第 **2** 义所列之情形外，不常用于肯定句): *How far did you go?* 你走了多远? *We didn't go far.* 我们没有走远。Cf 参较 (in the affirm): (在肯定句中): *We went a long way.* 我们走了很长一段路。*We went only a short way.* 我们仅走了短短的一段路。**2** (with other *advv* and *preps*) (indicating a great distance): (与副词和介词连用)(表示很远): *far away/off/*

out/back/in; 遥远(深远): *far beyond the bridge;* 远在桥那边; *far above the clouds;* 远在云上; *not far from here;* 距此不远; *far into the night;* 至深夜; *far back in history;* 很久以前; *as far back as 1902.* 远在 1902 年。**far from,** not at all: 毫不; 一点也不; 远非: *Your work is far from (being)* (= is not at all) *satisfactory.* 你的工作一点也不令人满意。*The newspaper accounts are far from (being) true,* are in many points false. 报纸的报导远非事实(有许多地方不确)。*Far from* (= Instead of) *admiring his paintings, I dislike them intensely.* 我不但不钦佩反而十分讨厌他的画。**by far,** (with comp or superl) by a large amount or degree: (与比较级或最高级连用)大量; 甚多: *by far the smallest/heaviest;* 显然最小的(最重的); *better by far.* 好得多。**from far,** from a great distance. 自远处。**go far, (a)** (of persons) be successful; do much: (指人) 成功; 有成就: *He's clever and intelligent, and will go far.* 他又伶俐又聪明，将来会成功的。**(b)** (of money) buy goods, services, etc: (指钱)买货物、劳役等: *A pound does not go so far today as it did five years ago.* 今天的一英镑不如五年前那么顶用了。**go/carry sth too far,** go beyond the limits of what is considered reasonable: 过分: *Don't carry the joke too far.* 不要把玩笑开得太过分。(Cf 参较 It's beyond a joke. 那不是开玩笑的事。) *Don't carry your modesty too far,* Don't be unnecessarily modest. 不要过分谦虚。**go far towards/to doing sth,** help or contribute greatly to: 大有助于; 对…大有贡献: *The loan will go far towards clearing my debt.* 这笔贷款对于清偿我的债务将大有帮助。**far and near/wide,** everywhere: 到处: *They searched far and wide for the missing child.* 他们到处寻找那走失的孩子。*People come from far and near to hear the famous violinist.* 各地的人都来聆听这位著名的小提琴家(演奏)。**far be it from me to do sth,** I would/should/could never do it. 我决不会做某事。**'so far,** until now: 到目前为止: *So far the work has been easy.* 到目前为止，这工作是容易的。**,So far, so 'good,** Up to now everything has gone well. 到目前为止，一切良好。**as/so far as, (a)** to the place mentioned: 至某一指明的地点: *He walked as far as the post office.* 他步行到邮局。**(b)** the same distance: 同样的距离: *We didn't go so far as the others (did).* 我们不如其他的人走得那样远。**(c)** to the extent that (to indicate a limit of advance or progress): 就…之限度; 在…范围内: *So far as I know he will be away for three months.* 就我所知，他将离开三个月。*He will help you as far as he can/as far as (is) possible/as far as lies in his power.* 他会尽力帮助你。*We have gone so far as to collect some useful statistics.* 我们甚至收集了一些有用的统计资料。**3** (with qualifying *adjj* and *advv*) (by) much; considerably; to a great extent: (与性质形容词和副词连用)很; 甚; 极: *This is far better.* 这个要好得多。*It fell far short of our expectations.* 此事远未达到我们的期望。**far and away,** (with comp or superl) by a large amount or degree: (与比较级或最高级连用)很; 甚: *He's far and away the best actor I've seen.* 他是我所看到的最好的演员了。**'far-away** *adj* **(a)** distant, remote: 遥远的; 久远的: *far-away places/times.* 遥远的地方(很久以前的时代)。**(b)** (of a look in a person's eyes) dreamy; as if fixed on sth far away in space or time. (指人的眼睛)迷蒙的; 恍惚的。**,far-'famed** *adj* (rhet) widely known. (修辞)驰名的; 闻名的。**,far-'fetched** *adj* (of a comparison) forced; unnatural. (指一比拟)牵强的; 勉强的。**,far-'flung** *adj* (rhet) widely extended. (修辞)蔓延的; 辽阔的。**,far 'gone,** deeply advanced (into eg illness, madness, drunkenness, debt). 病重; 十分疯狂; 大醉; 负债累累。**far-'off** *adj* = far-away. **,far-'reaching** *adj* likely to have many consequences; having a wide application: 影响广大的; 深远的: *far-reaching proposals.* 深远的建议。**,far-'seeing** *adj* seeing far into the future. 眼光远大的。**,far-'sighted** *adj* **(a)** able to see distant objects more clearly than near objects. 远视的。**(b)** (fig) prudent; having a

good judgement of future needs, etc. (喻)有智慧的; 有先见之明的; 有远见的。

farce /fɑːs; fɑrs/ *n* **1** [C] play for the theatre, full of ridiculous situations intended to make people laugh; [U] this style of drama. 笑剧; 闹剧。 **2** [C] series of actual events like a ~; absurd and useless proceedings: 似笑剧般的一连串事件; 可笑和无谓的行动: *The prisoner's trial was a ~.* 那个囚犯的审讯简直是胡闹。 **far·ci·cal** /ˈfɑːsɪkl; ˈfɑrsɪkl/ *adj* of or like a ~; absurd. 笑剧的; 似笑剧的; 可笑的。 **far·ci·cally** /-klɪ; -klɪ/ *adv*

fare¹ /feə(r); fɛr/ *n* [C] **1** money charged for a journey by bus, ship, taxi, etc. 车费; 船费; 乘客购票所付之费: *All ~s, please!* (cried by the conductor of a bus, etc). 请买票 (公共汽车等售票员用语)! **2** passenger in a hired vehicle: (出租车辆的) 乘客: *The taxi-driver had only six ~s all day.* 那计程车司机一天只载了六位乘客。

fare² /feə(r); fɛr/ *n* [U] food provided at table: 伙食; 饮食: *fine/simple/homely ~.* 美好的(简单的, 家常的)伙食。 **bill of '~,** list of dishes; menu. 菜单。

fare³ /feə(r); fɛr/ *vi* [VP2C] **1** progress; get on: 进展; 进步; 过日子: *How did you ~ during your journey,* What were your experiences? 你旅途好吗? *It has ~d well with him,* He has done well, been fortunate. 他的情况如意。 *You may go farther and ~ worse,* (prov, used to suggest that one should be content with one's present conditions): (谚)走得更远可能情形更坏(劝人安于现状)。 **2** (old use) go, journey. (旧用法) 行; 旅行。 **~ forth,** start out. 动身。

fare·well /ˌfeəˈwel; ˈfɛrˈwel/ *int* goodbye. 再会; 再见。 **(bid/say) ~ to,** (have) no more of. 不再(有)。 □ *n* leave-taking: 告别; 辞别: *make one's ~s,* say goodbye; 辞行; (attrib) (用作定语) *a ~ speech.* 告别演说。

fari·na·ceous /ˌfærɪˈneɪʃəs; ˌfærəˈneʃəs/ *adj* starchy: of flour or meal: 淀粉的; 面粉或谷粉的; ~ *foods,* eg bread, potatoes. 含淀粉的食物(如面包, 马铃薯)。

farm¹ /fɑːm; fɑrm/ *n* **1** area of land (usu divided into fields) and buildings (eg barns), under one management (either owned or rented) for growing crops, raising animals, etc: 农场; 农田; 饲养场: *working on the ~.* 在农场工作。 *Cf* 参较 in the fields. 在田间。 '~·**hand** *n* (US) ~ worker; agricultural labourer. (美) 农场工人; 农场劳动者。 '~·**yard** *n* space enclosed by ~ buildings (sheds, barns, etc). 农家的围院。 **2** (also *attrib*) '~·**house** /-ˌstead/ *sted/; -ˌsted/ farmer's house on a ~. 农舍。

farm² /fɑːm; fɑrm/ *vt, vi* **1** [VP6A, 2A] use (land) for growing crops, raising animals, etc: 耕(田); 耕作; 经营农场; 饲养家畜: *He ~s 200 acres.* 他耕种二百英亩田。 *He is ~ing in Africa.* 他在非洲务农。 *He is engaged in 'sheep-~ing.* 他从事养羊。 **2** [VP15B] ~ **out (to),** (a) send (work) out to be done by others. 招承包工作。 (b) arrange for (a child) to be cared for by others. 寄养 (小孩)。 **~er** *n* man who owns or manages a ~. 农民; 农场主人。 (Cf 参较 *peasant,* a word not used of a ~ in GB or US. 在英国或美国农民不称作 peasant。)

far·rago /fəˈrɑːɡəʊ; fəˈreɡo/ *n* (*pl* ~s, ~es /-ɡəʊz; -ɡoz/) medley; mixture: 混杂; 混杂物: *a ~ of nonsense/useless knowledge.* 一派胡言(一套无用的知识)。

far·rier /ˈfærɪə(r); ˈfærɪə/ *n* smith who shoes horses. 蹄铁匠。

far·row /ˈfærəʊ; ˈfæro/ *vi* give birth to pigs: 产小猪: *When will the sow ~?* 母猪何时产小猪? □ *n* litter of pigs; giving birth to pigs: 一窝小猪; 产小猪: *15 at one ~.* 一胎十五只小猪。

fart /fɑːt; fɑrt/ *vi, n △* (not in polite use) (send out, sending out of) wind through the anus. (诨) (不礼貌的用语)放屁; 屁。

far·ther /ˈfɑːðə(r); ˈfɑrðə/ *adv* (comp of *far*) (far

the比较级) to/at a greater distance/depth: 较远; 更远: *We can't go any ~ without a rest.* 我们如不休息便走不动了。 *They went ~ into the forest.* 他们深入森林。 □ *adj* more distant: 较远的; 更远的: *on the ~ bank of the river;* 在河的彼岸; *at the ~ end of the street.* 在街道的另一端。

far·thest /ˈfɑːðɪst; ˈfɑrðɪst/ *adv, adj* (superl of *far*) (far 的最高级) to/at the greatest distance/depth: 最远(的); 最久(的): *Which village in England is ~ from London?* 在英格兰哪个村庄距离伦敦最远? **(a)** at the greatest distance: 最远: *It's five miles away at the ~,* is not more than five miles away. 最远不超过五英里。 **(b)** (of time) at the latest. (时间)至迟。 in the least. 这事毫无关系(他毫不在乎)。

far·thing /ˈfɑːðɪŋ; ˈfɑrðɪŋ/ *n* (formerly) coin worth one-quarter of a penny. (昔时一钱币名)一便士的四分之一。 *It doesn't matter/He doesn't care a ~,* not in the least. 这事毫无关系(他毫不在乎)。

fas·cia (also **facia**) /ˈfeɪʃə; ˈfeʃə/ *n* dashboard or panel on a motor vehicle, etc (with gauges, dials, etc). (汽车等前部装有计量表, 针盘等之) 仪器板。 ⇨ the illus at **motor.** 参看 motor 之插图。

fas·ci·nate /ˈfæsɪneɪt; ˈfæsn̩ˌet/ *vt* [VP6A] **1** charm, attract or interest greatly: 使着迷; 使神魂颠倒; 使极感兴趣: *The children were ~d by all the toys in the shop windows.* 孩子们被商店橱窗内所有的玩具迷住了。 **2** take away power of movement by a fixed look, as a snake does. 凝视而使之不能动(如蛇所为者); 蛊惑。 **fas·ci·nat·ing** *adj* having strong charm or attraction: 迷人的; 醉人的: *a fascinating voice/story/glimpse.* 迷人的声音(故事, 一瞥)。 **fas·ci·nat·ing·ly** *adv* **fas·ci·na·tion** /ˌfæsɪˈneɪʃn; ˌfæsn̩ˈeʃən/ *n* [U] fascinating or being ~d; power to ~; [C] thing that ~s: 迷惑; 蛊惑; 着迷; 受蛊惑; 魅力; 魔力; 迷人之物: *Girls have a fascination for Brian,* ie they ~ him. 女孩子使布赖恩着迷。 *Brian has a fascination for girls,* ie he ~s them. 布赖恩使女孩子着迷。

fas·cism /ˈfæʃɪzəm; ˈfæʃˌɪzəm/ *n* **F~** 法西斯主义。 **fas·cist** /ˈfæʃɪst; ˈfæʃɪst/ *n* supporter of ~. 法西斯主义者; 法西斯党员。 □ *adj* of ~; extreme right-wing; reactionary. 法西斯主义的; 极端右派的; 反动的。

fashion /ˈfæʃn; ˈfæʃən/ *n* **1 a/the ~,** manner of doing or making sth: 样子; 方式: *He walks in a peculiar ~.* 他走路的样子很奇特。 **after/in a ~,** somehow or other, but not satisfactorily: 略微地(但不令人满意): *He can speak and write English, after a ~.* 他多少会说和写英语(但不太好。 **after the ~ of,** like, in imitation of: 象…一样; 模仿: *a novel after the ~ of Graham Greene.* 模仿格雷厄姆·格林的一部小说。 **2** [C, U] (as shown in the examples) (用于下列例句中) (of clothes, behaviour, thought, custom, etc) prevailing custom; that which is considered most to be admired and imitated during a period or at a place: (指服装, 行为, 思想, 风俗等)风尚; 时髦; 时样; 风气: *dressed in the latest ~.* 装扮入时的。 *F~s for men's clothes change less frequently than ~s for women's clothes.* 男装的时样不及女装的时样多变化。 **be all the ~,** (of dress, behaviour, etc) be very popular. (指服装, 行动等)十分流行。 **come into/go out of ~,** become/no longer be popular: 流行(不流行): *When did that style of dress come into/go out of ~?* 那种衣服式样什么时候变为流行(不流行)? **follow/be in the ~,** do what others do in matters of dress, behaviour, etc. (衣束, 行动等)迎合时尚。 **set the ~,** give the example by adopting new ~s. 开风气; 创新时样。 **a man/woman of ~,** one belonging to fashionable society and conforming to its usages. 上流社会人物; 时髦人物。 '**~·plate** *n* picture showing a style of dress. 时装图样。 □ *vt* [VP 6A, 15A] give form or shape to; mould: 形成; 做成: ~ *the form of: a canoe out of a tree-trunk/a whistle from a piece of wood/a lump of clay into a bowl.* 用树干做成独木舟(用木块制成一口笛; 将粘土塑成一只碗)。

fashion·able /ˈfæʃnəbl; ˈfæʃənəbl/ *adj* following the

fashion(2); used by, visited by, many people, esp the rich: 时新的; 时髦的; 流行的; 有钱人所用的; 有钱人常到的: ~ *clothes*. 流行的服装; *a ~ dressmaker/hotel/ summer-resort*. 有钱人所光顾的裁缝(常去的旅馆, 避暑胜地). **fashion·ably** /-ʃənlɪ; -ʃənlɪ/ *adv* in a ~ manner: 时髦地; 流行地: *fashionably dressed*. 装扮入时的.

fast[1] /fɑːst US: fæst; fæst/ *adj* **1** firmly fixed; not easily moved: 牢固的; 坚固的; 坚牢的: *The post is ~ in the ground*. 那柱子牢牢地埋在地里. *Make the boat ~*, Make it secure. 将船系牢. *Take* (a) ~ *hold of the rope*, hold it tightly. 握紧绳子. **hard and ~ rules**, rigid rules. 不容违犯的规则; 严格的规则. **2** steady; stedfast; loyal; close: 可靠的; 忠实的; 亲密的: *a ~ friend/ friendship*. 忠实的朋友(友谊). **3** (of colours) unfading. (指颜色) 不褪色的. □ *adv* firmly, securely, tightly: 牢固地; 稳固地; 紧紧地; *hold ~ to sth*. 紧握某物. *The ship was ~ aground*, could not be refloated. 那船搁浅了. *She was ~ asleep*, in a deep sleep. 她在酣睡. **stand ~**, not move or retreat; refuse to give way. 立稳; 坚定不移; 不后退; 不屈服. **stick ~**, (a) = stand ~, (b) be unable to make progress. 不能前进. ***F~ bind, ~ find***, (prov) If you make things secure, eg by locking them up, you will not lose them. (谚)锁得牢, 丢不了. ***play ~ and loose with***, repeatedly change one's attitude towards; trifle with: 不断地改变对…的态度; 对…反复无常; 玩弄: *play ~ and loose with a girl's affections*. 玩弄一个女孩子的感情.

fast[2] /fɑːst US: fæst; fæst/ *adj* **(-er, -est) 1** quick; rapid: 迅速的; 快的: *a ~ train/horse*. 快车(马); *a ~ trip*; 迅速之旅行; *a ~ draw*, of a gun from a holster. 拔枪迅速. **2** (dated) (of a person, his way of living) spending too much time and energy on pleasure and excitement; dissipated: (过时用语)(指人, 人的生活方式)耽于游乐的; 放荡的; 放荡的: *lead a ~ life*; 过放荡的生活; *a ~ woman*; 浪漫的女子; *~ society*. 耽于逸乐的人们. **3** (of a watch or clock) showing time later than the true time: (指钟表)走得快的: *My watch is five minutes ~*, eg showing 2.05 at 2.00. 我的表快五分钟. **4** (of a surface) promoting quick motion: (指表面)促成迅速动作的: *a ~ cricket pitch/billiard-table*. 平滑的板球场(撞球台). **5** (of photographic film) suitable for very brief exposures. (指照像软片)适于拍快照的.

fast[3] /fɑːst US: fæst; fæst/ *adv* **1** quickly: 迅速地; 快地: *Don't speak so ~*. 不要说得这样快. *It was raining ~*, heavily. 雨下得很大. *Her tears fell ~*. 她的眼泪簌簌流下. **2 live ~**, live in a dissipated way; use much energy in a short time. 生活放荡; 在短时间耗费很多精力. **3** (old use) close: (旧用法)接近: *~ by/behind the church*. 在教堂旁边(后面)

fast[4] /fɑːst US: fæst; fæst/ *vi* [VP2A, B] go without food, or without certain kinds of food, esp as a religious duty: 禁食; 斋戒: *days devoted to ~ing and penitence*, eg in Lent. 斋戒与忏悔期(例如四旬斋). □ *n* **1** (period of) going without food: 禁食(期); 斋戒(期): *a ~ of three days*; 禁食三日; 斋戒三日; *break one's ~*. 开斋. **2 day ('~-day)** or season of ~ing. 禁食日; 斋日; 斋期.

fas·ten /'fɑːsn US: 'fæsn; 'fæsn/ *vt, vi* **1** [VP6A, 15A, B] ~ **(up/down)**, make fast[1]; fix firmly; tie or join together: 使牢固; 使固定; 系住; 捆在一起: *Have you ~ed all the doors and windows*? 你将所有的门窗关牢没有? *He ~ed the two sheets of paper together*. 他将那两张纸钉在一起. *He ~ed up/down the box*, closed it and made it secure. 他将箱子关牢. **2** [VP14] ~ **on/ upon**, fix (a nickname, accusation, etc) upon sb; direct (one's looks, thoughts, attention, etc) upon sb: 把(绰号, 罪名等)加于某人上; 使(目光, 思想, 注意力等)朝向某人: *He ~ed his eyes on me*. 他用眼睛盯着我. **3** [VP2A, C] become fast[1] or secured: 变为牢固; 变紧: *The door won't ~*. 这门关不牢. *This dress ~s down the back*, has buttons, etc down the back. 这件衣服从背后扣钮扣. **4** [VP3A] ~ **on/upon**, lay hold of, seize

---

upon; single (a person) out for attack: 握住; 抓紧; 选出(某人)作攻击的对象: *He ~ed on the idea*. 他坚持这种想法. **~er** *n* thing that ~s things together: 将东西系牢之物; 系结物: *a paper ~er*; 书钉; 夹子; 回纹针; *a zip-~er*. 拉链. **~ing** *n* thing that ~s, esp a slide or a bolt. 系牢物(尤指发夹或门闩).

fas·tid·ious /fə'stɪdɪəs US: fæ-; fæs'tɪdɪəs/ *adj* hard to please; quick to find fault: 难以取悦的; 吹毛求疵的: *He is ~ about his food/clothes, etc*. 他对于食物(衣服等)很苛求. **~·ly** *adv* ~·**ness** *n*

fast·ness /'fɑːstnɪs US: 'fæs-; 'fæstnɪs/ *n* **1** [C] stronghold; fortress: 要塞; 堡垒: *a mountain ~*, eg of bandits. 山寨(例如盗贼盘据者). **2** [U] the quality of being fast[1](3): 不褪色: *We guarantee the ~ of these dyes*. 我们担保这些颜料不褪色.

fat[1] /fæt; fæt/ *adj* **(fatter, fattest) 1** covered with, having much, fat: 肥的; 胖的: *fat meat*; 肥肉; *a fat man*; 胖子; *fat cheeks*; 肥胖的面颊; *fat cattle*, made fat ready for slaughter. (备宰的)肥牛. **'fat-head** *n* dull, stupid person. 愚蠢的人. **2** thick; well filled: 厚的; 丰满的: *a fat wallet*, one stuffed with banknotes. 装满钞票的钱包. *a 'fat lot*, (sl) a great deal (ironic, = very little): (俚) 很多(作反语用, 表示很少): *A fat lot you care*, ie you don't care at all. 你什么都不管(根本不在乎). **3** rich, fertile: 肥沃的: *fat lands*. 肥沃的土地. **fat·tish** *adj* rather fat. 稍肥的; 略肥的. **fat·ness** *n*

fat[2] /fæt; fæt/ *n* [C, U] (kinds of) white or yellow substance, oily or greasy, found in animal bodies; this substance purified from cooking purposes; oily substance obtained from certain seeds: 脂肪; 肥肉; 食用的动物油; 植物油: *Give me red meat, please; I don't like fat*. 请给我瘦肉, 我不喜欢肥肉. *Fried potatoes are cooked in deep fat*. 炸马铃薯是在很多油里炸成的. *Vegetable cooking fats are sold in tins*. 烹饪用植物油是成罐卖的. **chew the fat**, continue to grumble about sth. 不断抱怨; 不停地发牢骚. **live on/off the fat of the land**, have the best of everything. 享受最好的东西; 生活奢侈. **The fat's in the fire**, What has been done (usu irrevocably) will cause a lot of trouble. 一旦做出无法挽回之事, 将会引起许多麻烦; 闯了大祸. **fat·less** *adj* ⇨ **fatty**.

fat[3] /fæt; fæt/ *vt* **(-tt-)** = fatten: *fatted cattle*. 养肥了的牛. **kill the fatted calf**, (fig) welcome sb back with joy. (喻)热烈欢迎(某人回来).

fatal /'feɪtl; 'feɪtl/ *adj* **1** ~ **(to)**, causing, ending in, death or disaster: 致命的; 悲惨的: *a ~ accident*. 惨祸. *The cyclist was knocked down by a lorry and received ~ injuries*. 那个骑脚踏车的人被卡车撞倒, 受到了致命的伤. *His illness was ~ to our plans*, caused them to fail. 他的病使他的计划成为泡影. **2** like fate; of, appointed by, destiny: 注定的; 命运的; 命运决定的: *the ~ day*. 决定性的一天. **~·ly** *adv* in a ~ manner: 致命地; 悲惨地; 注定地: *~ly injured/wounded*. 受到致命伤.

fatal·ism /'feɪtəlɪzəm; 'feɪtl,ɪzəm/ *n* [U] belief that events are decided by fate(1); submission to all that happens as inevitable. 宿命论; 听天由命. **fatal·ist** /'feɪtəlɪst; 'feɪtl,ɪst/ *n* believer in ~. 宿命论者. **fatal·is·tic** /,feɪtə'lɪstɪk; ,feɪtl'ɪstɪk/ *adj* of ~: 宿命论的: *a fatalistic attitude*. 宿命论的态度.

fatal·ity /fə'tælətɪ; fə-/ *n* (*pl* **-ties**) **1** [C] misfortune, calamity, esp one that causes death and destruction: 灾祸(尤指致命的和导致毁灭的): *floods, earthquakes and other fatalities*. 洪水, 地震和其他的灾祸. **2** [C] death by accident, in war, etc: (意外, 战争等造成的)死亡: *There have been numerous bathing fatalities this summer*, Many people have lost their lives while bathing. 今年夏季有许多人游泳惨遭灭顶. **3** [U] state of being subject to fate(1) or destiny. 听天由命; 天数. **4** [U] fatal influence; deadliness: 致命; 致死: *the ~ of certain diseases*, eg cancer. 某些疾病(例如癌症)之致命.

fate /feɪt; fet/ *n* **1** [U] power looked upon as controlling all events in a way that cannot be resisted; destiny: 命运; 定数: *He had hoped to become President, but ~ decided otherwise.* 他本来希望做总统，但命运使他不能如愿。 *as sure as ~,* quite certain(ly). 必定。 *the* F**~s,** the three Greek goddesses of destiny. 希腊的命运三女神。 **2** [C] the future as decided by ~ for sth or sb; what is destined to happen: 未来的吉凶; 命中注定之事: *They met their various ~s.* 他们遇到种种的祸福。 *They left/abandoned the men to their ~.* 他们丢下那些人让他们自生自灭。 **3** (*sing*) death; destruction; person's ultimate condition, of fate(1); important and 终的结局): *go to one's ~;* 死; *decide a person's ~,* eg whether he shall be killed or allowed to live; 决定某人的生死; *meet one's ~,* be killed, die. 被杀; 死。 □ *vt* [VP17] (usu passive) destine: (通常用被动语态) 命运注定; 命该: *He was ~d to be hanged.* 他命受绞刑。 *It was ~d that...,* F~ decided that...: 命运注定…: *It was ~d that we should fail.* 我们注定要失败。

fate·ful /ˈfeɪtfl; ˈfetfəl/ *adj* **1** controlled by, showing the power of, fate(1); important and decisive: 命运注定的; 显示命运之力量的; 关系重大的; 决定性的: *a ~ decision;* 关系重大的决定; *on this ~ day;* 在此决定性的一天; *these ~ events.* 这些重大事件。 *When the judge pronounced the ~ words...,* eg sentence of death. 当法官宣布决定命运的话时…(例如死刑宣判)。 **2** prophetic. 预言的。 *~·ly* /-fli; -fəli/ *adv*

fa·ther¹ /ˈfɑːðə(r); ˈfɑðɚ/ *n* **1** male parent: 父亲: *You have been like a ~ to me.* 你一直象父亲一般地对待我。 *The property had been handed down from ~ to son for many generations.* 这财产父子相传已经有很多代了。 *The child is ~ to the man,* (prov) One's childhood decides the way in which one will develop in later years. (谚) 童年时代可决定一人之未来; 从小看大。 *The wish is ~ to the thought,* (prov) We are likely to believe what we wish to be true. (谚) 愿望是为思想之父(我们多半会把渴望之事信以为真)。 *'~-in-law* /ˈfɑːðər ɪn lɔː; ˈfɑðɚɪn,lɔ/ *n* (*pl* **~s-in-law**) ~ of one's wife or husband. 岳父; 公公。 *'~ figure,* older man respected because of eg his concern for one's welfare. (因其关心一个人的幸福而)受人尊敬的长者。 **2** (usu *pl*) ancestor(s): (通常用复数)祖先: *sleep with one's ~s,* be buried in the ancestral tomb or grave. 葬在祖坟。 **3** founder or first leader: 创始者; 倡导者: *the F~s of the Church,* Christian writers of the first five centuries; 最初五世纪的基督教作家; *the Pilgrim F~s,* English Puritans who founded the colony of Plymouth, Massachusetts, USA in 1620; 美国的开国先驱(1620年在美国马萨诸塞州建立普利茅斯殖民地之英国清教徒); *the F~ of English poetry,* Chaucer. 英诗鼻祖(乔叟)。 **4** *Our (Heavenly) F~,* God. 我们的天父(上帝)。 **5** priest, esp one belonging to a religious order; head of a monastic house (⊳ **brother** for a monk): 神父; 修道院长(修道士为brother): *the Holy F~,* the Pope. 教宗; 罗马教皇。 **6** title used in personifications: 用做拟人化名词中之称号: *F~ Christmas;* 圣诞老人; *F~ Time.* 时间老人。 *'~·hood* /-hʊd; -,hʊd/ *n* [U] state of being a ~. 做父亲; 父亲的身份。 *'~·land* /-lænd; -,lænd/ *n* one's native country (*mother country* is the normal English usage). 祖国 (mother country是英语的标准用法)。 *~·less adj* without a living ~ or a known ~. 丧父的; 无父的。 *~·ly adj* of or like a ~: 父亲的; 似父亲的: *~ly love/smiles.* 父爱/象如父的笑容。

fa·ther² /ˈfɑːðə(r); ˈfɑðɚ/ *vt* **1** [VP6A] be the originator of an idea, plan, etc. 创始 (思想, 计划等); 创立。 **2** [VP6A] admit oneself to be the father or author of a child, book, etc. 承认是 (某一孩子)的父亲; 承认是 (某书等)的作者。 **3** [VP14] *~ on/upon,* fix the paternity of (a child), the authorship of or responsibility for (sth): 确定 (一孩子)之父亲; 确定…的作者或责任: *Please don't ~ this magazine article on me,* don't lead people to think that I wrote it. 请不要让人

认为杂志上这篇文章是我写的。

fathom /ˈfæðəm; ˈfæðəm/ *n* measure (six feet or 1.8 metres) of depth of water: 英寻(测水深之量度名, 等于6英尺或1.8米): *The ship sank in six ~s.* 该船沉下六英寻。 *The harbour is four ~(s) deep.* 港深四英寻。 □ *vt* [VP6A] find the depth of; get to the bottom of; comprehend: 测出…之深度; 彻底了解; 领悟: *I cannot ~ his meaning.* 我不能彻底了解他的意思。 *~·less adj* too deep to ~. 深不可测的。

fa·tigue /fəˈtiːg; fəˈtig/ *n* **1** [U] condition of being very tired: 疲劳; 疲乏: *Several men dropped with ~ during the long march.* 有几位士兵在长途行军中因疲劳而倒下了。 **2** [U] weakness in metals caused by prolonged stress. (金属经长久应力后的)软化; 疲劳。 **3** [C] tiring task; non-military duty of soldiers, such as cleaning, cooking, etc. 令人劳累的工作; 士兵所做的非军事性劳动服务(如清扫, 烹饪等)。 *'~-party* *n* group of soldiers given such duties. 做劳动服务的一群士兵。 □ *vt* [VP6A] cause ~ to: 使疲劳; 使劳累: *feeling ~d;* 感到疲劳; *fatiguing work.* 令人劳累的工作。

fat·ten /ˈfætn; ˈfætn/ *vt, vi* [VP6A, 15B, 2A, C] *~ (up),* make or become fat: 使肥; 变肥: *~ cattle.* 将牛养肥。

fatty /ˈfætɪ; ˈfætɪ/ *adj* (*-ier, -iest*) like fat; consisting of fat: 象脂肪的; 含脂肪的: *~ bacon.* 很肥的腌肉。

fatu·ous /ˈfætjʊəs; ˈfætʃʊəs/ *adj* without purpose or sense; showing foolish self-satisfaction: 无谓的; 无意义的; 愚昧而自满的: *a ~ smile;* 傻笑; *a ~ young man.* 愚昧而自满的年轻人。 *~·ly adv* **fa·tu·ity** /fəˈtjuːətɪ US: -ˈtuː-; fəˈtjuətɪ/ *n* [U] state of being ~; [C] (*pl -ties*) ~ remark, act, etc. 无意义;愚昧; 自满; 昏聩; 愚昧的言语, 行动等。 *~·ness n*

fau·cet /ˈfɔːsɪt; ˈfɔsɪt/ *n* (esp US) device (*tap* in GB) for controlling the outflow of liquid from a pipe or container. (尤美)(自来水管或容器之)龙头(英国称作tap)。

faugh /fɔː; fɔ (spontaneously, as an explosive puffing sound)/ *int* expression of disgust. 呸; 唯; 啐(厌恶的表示)。

fault /fɔːlt; fɔlt/ *n* **1** [C] sth that makes a person, thing, etc imperfect; defect; blemish; flaw: 缺点; 缺陷; 毛病; 瑕疵: *She loves me in spite of all my ~s.* 虽然我有种种缺点，她仍然爱我。 *Her only ~ is excessive shyness.* 她唯一的缺点是过分怕羞。 *There is a ~ in the electrical system.* 电路系统有了毛病。 *at ~,* in the wrong, at a loss; in a puzzled or ignorant state: 出错; 茫然: *My memory was at ~.* 我记错了; 我忘记了。 *to a ~,* excessively: 过分地: *She is generous to a ~.* 她过分慷慨。 *find ~ (with),* complain (about): 抱怨; (对…)吹毛求疵; 挑剔: *I have no ~ to find with your work.* 我对你的工作无可挑剔。 *He's always finding ~.* 他总是吹毛求疵。 Hence, 由此产生, *'~-finder; '~-finding.* **2** [U] responsibility for being wrong: 过失; 过错; 咎: *Whose ~ is it that we are late?* 我们迟到是谁的过错? *It's your own ~.* 这是你自己的错。 *The ~ lies with you, not with me,* You are to blame. 错在你, 不在我。 **3** [C] thing wrongly done; (tennis, etc) ball wrongly served. 错误; 谬误; (网球等)发球失误。 **4** [C] place where there is a break in the continuity of layers of rock, etc. 断层。 □ *vt* [VP6A] find ~ with: 挑剔; 吹毛求疵: *No one could ~ his performance.* 没有人能挑剔他的表演。 *~·less adj ~·less·ly adv ~·lessness n* no ~ or ~s. 无缺点的; 有过失的; 有错误的。 *~·ily /-ɪlɪ; -ɪlɪ/ adv* in a ~y manner. 有缺点地; 有过失地; 有错误地。

faun /fɔːn; fɔn/ *n* (Roman myth) one of a class of gods of the woods and fields, with a goat's horns and legs. (罗神)农牧神(生有山羊角和山羊腿)。

fauna /ˈfɔːnə; ˈfɔnə/ *n pl* all the animals of an area or an epoch: 某区域或时代的动物之总称: *the ~ of E Africa.* 东非的动物。

faux pas /ˌfəʊ ˈpɑː; ˌfo ˈpɑ/ *n* (F) (*pl unchanged*) indiscreet action, remark, etc esp a social blunder. (法)

a fault in rock   **a faun**

(复数不变)不谨慎的行为,言语等(尤指触犯社会习俗者); 失礼;失言。

fa·vour¹ (US = **fa·vor**) /ˈfeɪvə(r); ˈfevɚ/ n 1 [U] friendly regard; willingness to help, protect, be kind to: 关切;爱护;恩宠: win a person's ~; 获某人的好感或恩宠; look on a plan with ~, approve of it. 赞成一计划. be/stand high in sb's ~, be well regarded by him. 甚受某人的关切与尊重. be in/out of ~ (with sb), have/not have his friendly regard, etc. 受(失去)某人的关切与尊重. find/lose ~ with sb/in sb's eyes, win/lose sb's ~. 邀宠(失宠)于某人; 得到(失去)某人的欢心。2 [U] aid; support. 帮助;支持. in ~ of, (a) in sympathy with; on the side of: 赞成;支持: Was he in ~ of votes for women? 他赞成妇女有选举权吗? (b) on behalf of; to the advantage or account of: 为…的利益, 有利于; 支付给: Cheques should be drawn in ~ of the Society, not in ~ of the Treasurer. 支票应开给会社, 不应开给会计员. in sb's ~, to the advantage of: 对…有利: The exchange rate is in our ~, will benefit us when we change money. 兑换率对我们有利. 3 [U] treatment that is too generous, lenient; partiality: 偏袒; 偏爱: He obtained his position more by ~ than by merit or ability. 他靠别人的偏爱而非靠自己的长处或能力谋得职位. without fear or ~, with impartial justice. 大公无私. 4 [C] act of kindness: 善行; 恩惠: May I ask a ~ of you, ask you to do sth for me? 我可以请你帮忙吗? I would consider it a ~ if you would answer promptly. 若蒙早日赐复则不胜感激. do sb a ~; do a ~ for sb, do sth to help sb: 帮助某人: Do me a ~—turn the radio down while I'm on the phone, will you? 帮个忙——在我打电话时把收音机转小声一点好吗? 5 [C] ornament or decoration, eg a badge, knot of ribbon, given or worn as a sign of favour. (赠与或佩戴以示爱护或支持的)装饰物(例如徽章,花结等); 纪念品. 纪念章.

fa·vour² (US = **fa·vor**) /ˈfeɪvə(r); ˈfevɚ/ vt 1 [VP6A] show favour to; support: 关照; 爱护; 支持: Fortune ~s the brave. 命运爱护勇者. 2 [VP6A] treat with partiality; show more favour to one person, group, etc than to another: 偏爱; 偏袒: A teacher should not ~ any of his pupils. 教师不应偏爱任何学生. **most ~ed nation clause**, clause (in a commercial treaty) agreeing that a nation shall be accorded the lowest scale of import duties. 最惠国条款(通商条约中, 给予某一国家最低进口税的商业条款). 3 [VP14] ~ **sb with sth**, (old use, or formal) oblige; do something for: (旧用法或正式用语)赐助; 为某人做某事: Will you ~ me with an interview? 请准我谒见你好吗? Miss Sharp will now ~ us with a song, will sing for us. 夏普小姐现在最喜为我们唱一支歌. 4 [VP6A] (of circumstances) make possible or easy: (指情况) 便于; 使顺利: The weather ~ed our voyage. 天气使我们的航行顺利. 5 [VP6A] (old use) resemble in features: (旧用法)容貌像; 肖: The child ~s its father, looks more like its father than its mother. 这孩子的面貌象他父亲. **ill/well-~ed** adj having an unpleasing/pleasing appearance. 容貌丑陋(漂亮)的.

fa·vour·able (US = **-vor-**) /ˈfeɪvərəbl; ˈfevərəbl/

adj giving or showing approval; helpful: 赞成的; 有帮助的: a ~ report on one's work; 赞许某人工作的报告; ~ winds. 顺风. Is he ~ to the proposal? 他赞成这建议吗? **fa·vour·ably** /-əblɪ; -əblɪ/ adv in a ~ manner: 赞成地; 有助地: speak favourably of a plan; 赞成一计划; look favourably on sb. 赞许地望着某人.

fa·vour·ite (US = **-vor-**) /ˈfeɪvərɪt; ˈfevərɪt/ n 1 person or thing preferred above all others: 最受喜爱的人或物: He is a ~ with his uncle/a ~ of his uncle's/his uncle's ~. 他是他伯父最喜欢的人. This book is a great ~ of mine. 这本书是我最喜欢读的. 2 the ~, (racing) the horse, etc generally expected to win: (竞赛)公认会获胜的马等; 热门马; 红选手: back the ~, bet money on it. 下赌注于热门马. The ~ came in third. 公认会获胜的马得到第三名. 3 person who receives too much favour, is given unfair advantages. 宠儿; 得宠者. □ attrib adj best liked: 最受喜爱的: He is his uncle's ~ nephew. 他是他伯父最喜欢的侄儿. What is your ~ colour? 你最喜欢什么颜色? **fa·vour·it·ism** (US = **-vor-**) /-ɪzəm; -ˌɪzəm/ n [U] (practice of) having ~s. 偏爱; 偏袒; 徇私.

fawn¹ /fɔːn; fɔn/ n 1 young fallow deer less than one year old. 未满一岁的梅花鹿. 2 light yellowish brown. 浅黄褐色的.

fawn² /fɔːn; fɔn/ vi [VP2A, 3A] ~ **(on)**, 1 (of dogs) show pleasure and affection by jumping about, tail-wagging, etc. (指狗)(以跳来跳去, 摇动尾巴的方式)表示快乐及感情. 2 (of persons) try to win sb's favour by servile behaviour, flattery, etc: (指人) 谄媚; 奉承; 巴结: ~ on a rich relative. 巴结一富有的亲戚.

fe·alty /ˈfiːəltɪ; ˈfɪəltɪ/ n (pl **-ties**) (in feudal times) tenant's or vassal's (acknowledgement of) fidelity to his lord: (封建时期家臣对领主之)效忠: do/make/swear ~ (to one's lord, for one's land); (对领主, 为领地)表示(宣誓)效忠; take an oath of ~. 宣誓效忠.

fear¹ /fɪə(r); fɪr/ n 1 [C, U] feeling caused by the nearness or possibility of danger or evil: 恐惧; 惧怕: They stood there in ~ and trembling, frightened and shaking. 他们站在那里吓得发抖. He was overcome with/by ~. 他吓坏了. The thief passed the day in ~ of discovery. 那贼在惧怕被人发觉的情况下度过了一天. Grave ~s are felt for the safety of the missing climbers. 对失踪的登山者的安全极为担心. A sudden ~ came over him. 他突然感到恐惧. He obeyed from ~. 他由于畏惧而服从. He was unable to speak for ~. 他吓得说不出话来了. for ~ of, because of anxiety about: 惟恐; 生怕: She asked us not to be noisy, for ~ of waking the baby. 她请我们不要吵闹, 因为怕吵醒了婴儿. for ~ (that/lest)..., in order that... should not occur: 惟恐; 以免: I daren't tell you what he did, for ~ (that/lest) he should be angry with me. 我不能将他所做的事告诉你, 因为怕他对我发脾气. 2 [U] ~ **of**, anxiety for the safety of: 担心; 忧虑: He is in ~ of his life. 他为他的生命担忧. 3 [U] likelihood: 可能性: There's not much ~ of my losing the money. 我失去这笔钱的可能性不大. No ~! (colloq) Certainly not! (口)一定不会! 4 [U] dread and reverence: 敬畏: the ~ of God. 对上帝的敬畏. ~·**ful** /-fl; -fəl/ adj 1 causing ~; terrible: 可怕的; 可怖的: a ~ful railway accident; 火车惨祸; (colloq) annoying; very great: (口)讨厌的; 非常的: What a ~ful mess! 简直是一塌糊涂! 2 frightened; apprehensive: 受惊的; 惧怕的: ~ful of wakening sb; 怕吵醒某人; ~ful that/lest the baby should wake up. 恐怕将婴儿吵醒. ~·**fully** /-fəlɪ; -fəlɪ/ adv ~·**ful·ness** n ~·**less** adj without ~: 无畏的; 不怕的: ~less of the consequences. 不计后果. ~·**less·ly** adv ~·**less·ness** n ~·**some** /ˈfɪəsəm; ˈfɪrsəm/ adj (usu jokingly) frightening in appearance: (通常作戏谑语)外貌可怖的: a ~some appearance. 狰狞的幽灵.

fear² /fɪə(r); fɪr/ vt, vi 1 [VP6A, C] feel fear of, be afraid of: 惧怕; 害怕: ~ death. 怕死. These men are not to be ~ed. 这些人并不可怕. 2 [VP2A, 4A] feel

fear; be afraid; hesitate: 感到恐惧；犹豫: *Never ~! Don't be afraid/Don't worry!* 不要怕！放心罢！ *She ~ed to speak in his presence.* 她怕在他的面前说话。 *He did not ~ to die.* 他不怕死。 **3** [VP3A] ~ *for,* feel anxiety about: 担心；忧虑: *We ~ed for his life/safety.* 我们担心他的生命(安全)。 **4** [VP6A, 9] have an uneasy feeling or anticipation of: 担心: ~ *the worst,* be afraid that the worst has happened or will happen. 担心最坏的情况已经或会发生。 *I ~ (that) he has failed.* 我担心他已失败了。 *'Will he get well?'*—*'I ~ not.'* '他会痊愈吗？'——'恐怕不会了。' *'Is he going to die?'*—*'I ~ so.'* '他会死去吗？'——'恐怕会的。' **5** [VP6A] regard with awe and reverence: 敬畏: *F~ God and honour the Queen.* 敬畏上帝尊敬女王。

feas·ible /ˈfiːzəbl; ˈfizəbl/ *adj* **1** that can be done: 可做的；可行的；可能的: *The reconstruction of the destroyed town is ~,* We can, if we choose, do it. 重建这个毁坏的市镇是可以做得到的。 **2** (colloq) that is convenient or plausible; that can be believed: (口)方便的；似乎有理的；可信的: *His story sounds ~,* may be true. 他的故事可能是真的。 **feasi·bil·ity** /ˌfiːzəˈbɪlətɪ; ˌfizəˈbɪlətɪ/ *n*

feast /fiːst; fist/ *n* **1** '~(-day), religious anniversary or festival, eg Christmas or Easter. 宗教节日或节期(例如圣诞节或复活节)。 ⇨ also **movable.** ⇨ **2** splendid meal with many good things to eat and drink; (fig) sth that pleases the mind or senses: 宴会；盛宴；(喻)赏心悦目之事物: *a ~ of colours and sounds.* 赏心悦目的颜色和声音。 □ *vt, vi* **1** [VP6A, 2A, B] take part in a ~; give a ~ to; pass (time) in ~ing: 宴乐；款宴；以宴乐消磨(时间): ~ *one's friends;* 款宴朋友; ~ *all evening.* 整晚宴乐。 *He sat there ~ing (himself).* 他坐在那里大吃大喝。 **2** [VP14] ~ *on,* give sensuous pleasure to: 给予感官上的愉快；使享受: ~ *one's eyes on beauty.* 饱览美色。

feat /fiːt; fit/ *n* sth difficult well done, esp sth showing skill, strength or daring: 技艺；武艺；英勇事绩；伟绩: *brilliant ~s of engineering;* 工程上的伟绩; *perform ~s of valour.* 表演勇敢的技艺。

feather¹ /ˈfeðə(r); ˈfeðɚ/ *n* one of the light coverings that grow from a bird's skin. 羽毛。 ⇨ the illus at **bird, prey, rare, water.** 参看 bird, prey, rare, water 之插图。 *a '~ in one's cap,* sth one may justly be proud of. 的确值得骄傲的事物。 *as light as a ~,* very light indeed. 轻如鸿毛。 *In full/high ~,* in high spirits. 意气洋洋；精神抖擞；高兴。 *birds of a ~ (flock together),* people of the same sort (will be found together). 同类的人(物以类聚)；一丘之貉。 *show the white ~,* show fear. 示弱；胆怯。 ~*bed* n mattress stuffed with ~s. 羽毛床垫。 □ *vt* (-dd-) pamper by giving generous help; make things easy for: 给予大量补助；使方便；使顺利: ~*bed the farmers,* eg by subsidizing them. 给予农民补助。 ~*-'brained* adj empty-headed; flighty. 愚笨的；无头脑的；轻浮的。 '~*weight* n (esp) boxer weighing between 118 and 126 lb (or 53.5 to 57 kg). (尤指)次轻量级拳击手(体重在118至126磅或53.5至57公斤间者)。 ~*y* adj light and soft like ~s: 如羽毛的；轻而软的: ~*y snow.* 羽毛似的雪片。

feather² /ˈfeðə(r); ˈfeðɚ/ *vt* [VP6A] **1** supply with feathers: 装以羽毛；饰以羽毛: ~ *an arrow.* 将羽毛装在箭上。 ~ *one's nest,* make things comfortable for oneself; enrich oneself. 使自己生活舒适；饱私囊。 **2** ~ *one's oar,* (rowing) turn it so as to pass flat along the surface of the water. (划船)放平桨面。

fea·ture /ˈfiːtʃə(r); ˈfitʃɚ/ *n* **1** [C] one of the named parts of the face: 面貌的一部分(口、鼻等): *Her eyes are her best ~.* 她的面貌最好的一部分是眼睛。 **2** (*pl*) the face as a whole: (复)容貌；面貌；相貌: *a man of handsome ~s.* 相貌英俊的男子。 **3** characteristic or striking part: 特色；特征: *the geographical ~s of a district,* eg mountains, lakes; 一地区地理上的特征(例

如山，湖); *unusual ~s in a political programme.* 政纲中不平常的特点。 **4** (often attrib) prominent article or subject in a newspaper; full-length film in a cinema programme, etc: (常作定语)(报纸上的)特写；特别报导；(电影节目中之)正片；长片(等): *a newspaper that makes a ~ of* (= gives special prominence to) *sport.* 特别注重体育新闻的报纸; *a two-~ programme,* ie with two long films. 有两部长片的节目。 □ *vt* [VP6A] be a ~(3) of; make (sb or sth) a ~(3, 4) of; have a prominent part for: 为…之特色；使(人或物)为…之特色；特载；特登: *a film that ~s a new French actress.* 由法国新女星主演的一部影片。 ~*·less* adj uninteresting; with no obvious ~s(3). 无趣味的；平淡无奇的。

feb·rile /ˈfiːbraɪl; ˈfibrəl/ *adj* of fever; feverish. 发烧的；热病的。

Feb·ru·ary /ˈfebruərɪ US: -uerɪ; ˈfɛbru,ɛrɪ/ *n* the second month of the year. 二月。

feces ⇨ **faeces.**

feck·less /ˈfeklɪs; ˈfɛklɪs/ *adj* futile; inefficient; irresponsible. 无用的；无能力的；不负责任的。 ~*·ly* adv ~*·ness* n

fec·und /ˈfiːkənd US ˈfek-; ˈfikənd/ *adj* prolific, fertile. 多产的；丰饶的。 ~*·ity* /fɪˈkʌndətɪ; fɪˈkʌndətɪ/ *n* [U] fertility; productiveness. 丰饶；多产。

fed *pt, pp* of **feed.**

fed·er·al /ˈfedərəl; ˈfɛdərəl/ *adj* **1** of, based upon, federation: 联邦制的；基于联邦制的: *In the USA foreign policy is decided by the ~* (ie central) *government, and ~ laws are made by Congress.* 美国外交政策取决于联邦政府,联邦法律由国会制定。 *F~ Bureau of Investigation* (abbr 缩作 FBI), (US) department which is responsible for investigating violations of ~ law and safeguarding national security. (美)联邦调查局。 ⇨ **state¹(2). 2** relating to, supporting, central (as distinct from individual State) government. 关于联邦政府的；拥护联邦政府的。 ~*·ist* /ˈfedərəlɪst; ˈfɛdərəlɪst/ *n* supporter of ~ union or power. 拥护联邦主义者。 ~*·ism* /-ɪzəm/ *n* -,ɪzəm/ *n*

fed·er·ate /ˈfedəreɪt; ˈfɛdə,ret/ *vt, vi* [VP6A, 2A] (of States, societies, organizations) combine, unite, into a federation. (指州, 社会, 团体)联合；组成联邦；联盟。

fed·er·ation /ˌfedəˈreɪʃn; ˌfɛdəˈreʃən/ *n* **1** [C] political system in which States control most of their internal affairs but leave foreign affairs, defence, etc to the central (Federal) government. 联邦制(大部分内政由各州或邦自理,外交、国防等由联邦政府处理的政治制度)。 **2** [C] such a union of States, eg the US; similar union of societies, trade unions, etc. 联邦政府(类如美国者);(社会、工会等之)联合会。 **3** [U] act of federating. 组成联邦政府；联盟。

fee /fiː; fi/ *n* **1** [C] charge or payment for professional advice or services, eg private teachers, doctors, lawyers, surveyors; entrance money for an examination, club, etc. 费(例如私人教师, 医生, 律师, 测量员等所收的费用);报名费；会费(等)。 **2** [U] (legal) inherited estate: (法律)继承的不动产: *land held in fee simple/fee tail,* with the right to pass it to any class of heirs/one particular class of heirs. 不限定继承人身份的土地(限定继承人身份的土地)。 ⇨ **entail.** □ *vt* [VP6A] pay a fee to, engage for a fee: 缴费给；付费与: *fee a barrister.* 缴费给律师。

feeble /ˈfiːbl; ˈfibl/ *adj* weak; faint; without energy: 衰弱的；虚弱的；无力的: *a ~ old man;* 衰弱的老人; *a ~ cry/argument.* 低弱的呼喊(无力的议论)。 *His pulse was very ~.* 他的脉搏十分微弱。 ~*-minded* /-ˈmaɪndɪd; -ˈmaɪndɪd/ *adj* subnormal in intelligence. 低能的。 **feebly** /ˈfiːblɪ; ˈfibl/ *adv* ~*·ness* n

feed¹ /fiːd; fid/ *n* **1** [C] (chiefly of animals and babies; jokingly of persons) meal: (主要指动物和婴儿;指人, 为诙谐语)一顿;一餐: *We stopped to let the horses have a ~.* 我们停下来让马吃一顿。 **2** [U] food for

animals: 饲料: *There isn't enough ~ left for the hens.* 母鸡的饲料不够了。 **3** [C] pipe, channel, etc through which material is carried to a machine; [U] material supplied. 输送原料至机器的管子，沟槽等；进给管；进给槽；供给的原料。 **'~·back** n [U] **1** return of part of the output of a system to its source (so as to modify it). 反馈(部分产品送回原制作处，以作修正)；回授。 **2** (colloq) information, etc (about a product) given by the user to the supplier, maker, etc; response: (口)使用者供给供应者或制造者(有关某产品)的讯息；反应: *interesting ~back via the market research department.* 经市场研究部门转来的有趣的资料。

feed² /fiːd/ fiˈd/ *vt, vi* (*pt, pp* **fed** /fed; fed/) **1** [VP 6A, 14] **~ (on)**, give food to: 给予食物；喂: *Have the pigs been fed yet?* 猪喂过没有? *Have you fed the chickens?* 你喂过鸡没有? *What do you ~ your dog on, What kind of food do you give it?* 你用什么喂你的狗? **~ oneself,** put food into the mouth: 自己吃东西(不给他人喂): *The baby can't ~ itself yet.* 这婴孩还不会自己吃东西。 [VP 15B] **~ up,** give extra food to, give nourishing food to: 给与额外食物；给与有营养的食物: *There are hundreds of poor children there who need ~ing up.* 那里有几百个贫苦的孩子需要给与营养食物。 **be fed up (with),** (fig, sl) have had too much (of); be discontented (with): (喻, 俚) 因多而厌烦; 不满: *I'm fed up with your grumbling.* 我听够了你的怨言。 **'~ing-bottle** n bottle from which hand-fed infants are given milk, etc. 奶瓶。 **2** [VP14] **~ to,** give to as food: 以…作为食物供养: *~ oats to horses.* 以燕麦喂马。*I wouldn't ~ that stinking meat to my dog.* 我不愿用那臭肉喂我的狗。 **3** [VP2A, C] (chiefly of animals, colloq or hum of persons) eat: (主要指动物; 指人，为口语或诙谐语)吃; 食: *The cows were ~ing in the meadows.* 牛在草地上吃草。*Have you fed yet?* 你吃过饭没有? **4** [VP3A] **~ on,** take as food: 以…为食: *Cattle ~ chiefly on grass.* 牛主要以草为食。 **5** [VP6A, 15A] supply with material; supply (material) to: 供(原料)给: *This moving belt ~s the machine with raw material/~s raw material into the machine.* 这转动的皮带输送原料到机器里。*The lake is fed by two rivers.* 这湖的水是由两条河注入的。

feeder /ˈfiːdə(r); ˈfidɚ/ *n* [C] **1** (of plants and animals, with *adj*) one that feeds: (指动植物，与形容词连用)食者: *This plant is a gross ~,* needs much manure. 达植物需要大量肥料。 **2** child's feeding-bottle or bib. 奶瓶; 围嘴。 **3** (often attrib) branch railway line, airline, canal, etc linking outlying areas with the main line, etc. (常用作定语)(铁路, 航空线, 运河等之)支线。

feel¹ /fiːl; fil/ *n* (*sing* only) (仅用单数) **1** **the ~,** the sense of touch: 触觉: *rough/smooth, etc to the ~,* when touched or felt. 摸起来粗糙(平滑等)。 **2** **the ~,** the sensation characteristic of sth when touching or being touched: 触摸或被触摸时的感觉; 触觉: *You can tell it's silk by the ~.* 你摸一摸就知道是绸子。*The monk didn't like the ~ of the hair shirt they gave him.* 那修道士不喜欢他们送给他的那件毛布衬衫摸起来的感觉。 **3** act of feeling: 触摸: *Let me have a ~.* 让我摸摸看。

feel² /fiːl; fil/ *vt, vi* (*pt, pp* **felt** /felt; felt/) **1** [VP6A, 10] (try to) learn about, explore, by touching, holding in the hands, etc: 触试; 摸摸看; 由触而得知: *Blind persons can often recognize objects by ~ing them.* 盲人常能凭触摸辨识物体。*The doctor felt my pulse.* 医生诊我的脉。*Just ~ the weight of this box!* 试试看这箱子有多么重! *~ whether there are any bones broken.* 摸摸看有没有骨头断了。 **~ one's way, (a)** go forward carefully, as in the dark, or as a blind man does. 摸索着走。 **(b)** be cautious in dealing with sth: 谨慎处理: *They were ~ing their way towards an agreement.* 他们正谨慎地试着达成一项协议。 **2** [VP2C, 3A] **~ (about) (for),** search with the hand(s) (or the feet, a stick, etc): (用手, 足, 杖等)摸索: *He was ~ing about in the dark for the electric-light switch.* 他在黑暗中摸索着找电

灯开关。 *He felt in his pocket for a penny.* 他在口袋里摸索，找一个便士。 *He felt along the wall for the door.* 他沿着墙摸索着找门。 **3** [VP 6A, 18A, 19A] be aware of (through contact): (由接触)感知: *I can ~ a nail in my shoe.* 我感到鞋里有一根钉子。 *I felt something crawl-(ing) up my arm.* 我感到有东西在我臂上往上爬。 **4** [VP6A, 18A, 19A] be aware of, perceive (not through contact): (非由接触)感到; 觉得: *Did you ~ the earthquake?* 你感到地震了吗? *He felt his heart beating wildly.* 他觉得他的心在猛跳。 *She felt apprehension stealing over her.* 她感到恐惧袭上心头。 [VP15B] **~ sb out,** try cautiously to learn the opinion of him: 小心打听某人的意见: *I'll ~ out the members of the committee.* 我会小心地把那些委员的意见打听出来。 **5** [VP2D, C] be consciously; be in a certain physical, moral or emotional state: 感知; 觉得; 处于身体, 精神或情绪的某种状态: *~ cold/hungry/comfortable/sad/happy, etc.* 感觉冷(饥饿, 舒服, 悲哀, 快乐等)。 *How are you ~ing today?* 你今天觉得怎么样? *You will ~ better after a night's sleep.* 经过一夜的睡眠你会觉得好些。 *She doesn't ~ (quite) herself today,* is not as well, calm, self-possessed, etc as usual. 她今天感到不舒服(心慌, 不安等)。 *He ~s confident of success.* 他对成功感到有信心。 *He felt cheated.* 他感到受骗了。 *We don't ~ bound (= obliged) to accept this offer.* 我们并不觉得一定要接受这项提议。 *Please ~ free (= consider yourself welcome) to call on us whenever you like.* 请随时来访。 **6** [VP2A] be capable of sensation: 能感觉; 有知觉: *The dead cannot ~.* 死人不会有知觉。 **7** [VP3A] **~ for/with,** have sympathy (with), compassion (for): 同情(与…相连他); 怜悯(为…连用): *I ~ with you in your sorrow.* 我同情你的烦恼。*I ~ for you.* 我怜悯你。 **8** **~ as if/though,** have, give, the impression that: 仿佛觉得: *She felt as if her head were splitting.* 她仿佛觉得她的头要裂开了。*Her head felt as if it were splitting.* 她的头好象要裂开似的。 **9** [VP2D] give or produce the impression of being: 给与或产生…的印象: *Your hands ~ cold.* 你的手摸起来是冷的。*How does it ~ to be home again after twenty years abroad?* 出国二十年再回家园是一种什么感觉? *This new shirt doesn't ~ right.* 这件新衬衫不太合身。 **10** '**~ like,** (of persons) be in the mood for: (指人)欲; 想要: *I don't ~ like (eating) a big meal now.* 我现在不想吃大餐。*We'll go for a walk if you ~ like it.* 如果你愿意, 我们去散散步。 **~ equal to;** (colloq) (口) **~ up to,** be well enough to, be capable of: 能担任; 有能力做: *I don't ~ equal to the task.* 我不能胜任这工作。*He doesn't ~ up to a long walk.* 他没有走远路的力气了。 **11** [VP6A, C] be sensitive to; suffer because of: 对…敏感; 由于…而受苦: *He doesn't ~ the heat at all,* is not troubled by it. 他一点也不怕热。*He felt the insult keenly.* 那侮辱深深地伤害了他。*She will ~* (be saddened by) *having to sell up her old home.* 必须卖掉她的老家会使她难过。 **12** [VP9, 25] have the idea; be of the opinion: 想到; 以为: *He felt the plan to be unwise/felt that the plan was unwise.* 他认为这计划是不明智的。*We all felt that our luck was about to turn.* 我们都以为我们的运气就要转变了。*He felt in his bones that he would succeed.* 他确信他会成功。 **13** [VP6A] appreciate; understand properly: 察知; 认识清楚: *We all felt the force of his arguments.* 我们都觉得他的议论很有力。*Don't you ~ the beauty of this landscape?* 你不觉得这风景很美吗?

feeler /ˈfiːlə(r); ˈfilɚ/ *n* [C] **1** organ, eg an antenna, in certain animals for testing things by touch. (某些动物的)触须; 触毛; 触角。 ⇨ the illus at **insect.** 参看 insect 之插图。 **2** proposal, suggestion, made to test the opinions or feelings of others, before one states one's own views. 试探性的建议。 **put out ~s/a ~,** test the views of others, by discreet inquiries. 提出试探性的建议。

feel·ing /ˈfiːlɪŋ; ˈfilɪŋ/ *n* **1** [U] power and capacity to feel: 知觉: *He had lost all ~ in his legs.* 他的双腿完

全失去了知觉。**2** [C] physical or mental awareness; emotion: 感觉; 感触; 情绪: *a ~ of hunger /well-being/ discomfort/ gratitude /joy;* 饥饿(幸福, 不适, 感激, 快乐)的感觉; idea or belief not based wholly on reason: 预感: *a ~ of danger /that something dreadful was about to happen;* 感到危险 (可怕的事即将发生); (usu *sing*) general opinion: (通常用单数)一般人的意见: *The ~ of the meeting* (= The opinion of the majority) *was against the proposal.* 与会的人大都反对此项提议。**3** (*pl*) emotional side of a person's nature (contrasted with the intellect): (复) 感情 (与 intellect 相对): *Have I hurt your ~s,* offended you? 我伤了你的感情吗? *The speaker appealed to the ~s of his audience rather than to their reason.* 那演说者诉诸听众的感情而非他们的理智。*No hard ~s, I hope!* ie no bitterness, no ill will. 希望没有恶意(或怨恨)! **4** [U] sympathy; understanding: 同情; 了解: *He doesn't show much ~ for the sufferings of others.* 他对别人的痛苦不十分同情。*She's a woman of ~.* 她是个富有同情心的女子。*good ~,* friendliness. 好感。*ill /bad ~,* bitterness. 恶感。**5** [C, U] excitement of mind, esp of enmity and resentment: 激动; (尤指)愤激; 愤慨: *His speech aroused strong ~(s) on all sides.* 他的演说激起各方面强烈的愤慨。*F~ over the dismissal ran high,* There was much bitterness. 关于这一撤职事件, 人们甚表愤慨。**6** [U] taste and understanding; sensibility: 鉴赏力; 感受力: *He hasn't much ~ for natural beauty.* 他对自然界的美缺少鉴赏力。*She plays the piano with ~.* 她弹钢琴能表现出感受力。□ *adj* sympathetic; showing emotion: 有同情心的; 表现感情的: *a ~ remark.* 同情的话。*~·ly adv* so as to express ~: 表现感情地: *speak ~ly on a subject.* 恳切地谈论一个问题。

feet /fiːt; fit/ *n pl* of **foot**.

feign /feɪn; fen/ *vt* **1** [VP 6A, 9] pretend: 假装: ~ *illness /indifference /death;* 装病(佯作不关心; 诈死); ~ *that one is mad;* 装疯。假装的谦恭。**2** [VP 6A] invent: 虚构; 杜撰: ~ *an excuse.* 捏造一借口。

feint /feɪnt; fent/ *n* **1** pretence (the more usu word): 假装 (pretence 较常用): *make a ~ of doing sth.* 假装做某事。**2** sham attack (in war and boxing) in one place to draw attention away from the place where the real attack is made. (作战或拳击)声东击西。□ *vi* [VP 2A, 3A] make a ~ *at /upon /against.* 假装。声东击西(与 at, upon, against 连用)。

feld·spar, fel·spar /ˈfeldspɑː(r), ˈfelspɑː(r); ˈfeld-ˌspɑr, ˈfel-/ *n* [U] (kinds of) crystalline mineral rock. 长石。

fel·ici·tate /fəˈlɪsɪteɪt; fəˈlɪsəˌtet/ *vt* [VP 6A, 14] ~ *sb (on /upon sth),* (formal) congratulate. (正式用语)祝贺; 道贺。**fel·ici·ta·tion** /fəˌlɪsɪˈteɪʃn; fəˌlɪsəˈteʃən/ *n*.

fel·ici·tous /fəˈlɪsɪtəs; fəˈlɪsətəs/ *adj* (formal) (of words, remarks) well chosen. (正式用语)(指措辞) 精选的; 适当的。*~·ly adv*

fel·ic·ity /fəˈlɪsɪtɪ; fəˈlɪsətɪ/ *n* (formal) (正式用语) **1** [U] great happiness or contentment. 幸福; 满足。**2** [U] pleasing manner of speaking or writing: 言辞的巧妙: *express oneself with ~;* 巧妙地表达自己的意思; [C] (*pl* **-ties**) well-chosen expression or phrase. 精选的措辞; 贴切的措辞。

fe·line /ˈfiːlaɪn; ˈfaɪlaɪn/ *adj* of or like a cat: 猫的; 似猫的: *walk with ~ grace.* 轻巧地行走。

fell[1] *pt* of **fall**[2].

fell[2] /fel; fel/ *adj* (poet) fierce, ruthless, terrible: (诗)凶猛的; 残忍的; 我恶的: *a ~ disease;* 可怕的疾病; *with one ~ blow.* 以狠狠的一击。

fell[3] /fel; fel/ *n* animal's hide or skin with the hair. 兽皮; 毛皮。

fell[4] /fel; fel/ *n* stretch of rocky, bare moorland or bare hilly land (esp in N England): 一片荒地(尤指英格兰北部者): *the Derbyshire F~s.* 德比郡的荒野。

fell[5] /fel; fel/ *vt* [VP 6A] cause to fall; strike down; cut down (a tree): 使倒下; 打倒; 砍伐(树木): *He ~ed his enemy with a single blow.* 他一拳将他的敌人打倒了。

fel·lah /ˈfelə; ˈfelə/ *n* (*pl* ~**in, ~een** /ˌfeləˈhiːn; ˌfeləˈhin/) peasant (in Arab countries). (阿拉伯国家的)农民。

fel·low /ˈfeləʊ; ˈfelo/ *n* **1** (colloq) man or boy: (口)人; 男人或男孩; 家伙: *He's a pleasant ~.* 他是个和气的人。*Poor ~!* 可怜的人! *A ~ must have a holiday occasionally* (used here for 'one' or 'I'). 人总得偶尔度度假。**2** (usu *pl*) comrade, companion: (通常用复数)伙伴; *'school ~s;* 同学; *'bed ~s;* 同床者; ~*s in good fortune /misery.* 共安乐(共患难)的伙伴。*be ˌhail·~·'well·'met with sb,* be (superficially or falsely) on friendly terms with him. (表面地或假地)与某人友善。~·'feeling *n* [U] sympathy. 同情心。**3** (attrib) of the same class, kind, etc: (用作定语)同等级的; 同类的; ˌ~ *'creatures;* 同类动物; 人类; ˌ~·'citizen; 同胞; 同方人; ˌ~·'countryman, person from the same country or nation. 同胞。ˌ~·'traveller *n* **(a)** person travelling with one. 旅伴; 同路人; 同行人。**(b)** one who sympathizes with the aims of a political party (eg the Communist Party) but is not a member. 同情某一政党而非党员之人 (例如共产党的同情者)。**4** member of a learned society: 学术团体之会员: *F~ of the British Academy;* 英国学会会员; member of the governing body of some university colleges; incorporated graduate member of a college. 某些大学之校务委员会委员; 大学的特别研究员。**5** one of a pair: 一对中的一只: *Here's one of my shoes, but where's its ~?* 这里有我一只鞋子, 另一只在哪里?

fel·low·ship /ˈfeləʊʃɪp; ˈfeloˌʃɪp/ *n* **1** [U] friendly association; companionship: 友谊; 交情. *offer sb the hand of ~;* 向某人伸出友谊之手; *enjoy ~ with people;* 享受人们的友情; ~ *in misfortune.* 患难时之交情。**2** [C] number of persons associated together; group or society; [U] membership in such a group: 团体; 会; 会员资格或地位: *admitted to ~.* 被准许入会。**3** [C] position of a college fellow(4). 大学校务委员会委员的地位; 大学特别研究员的地位。

fel·ony /ˈfelənɪ; ˈfelənɪ/ *n* (*pl* **-nies**) [C, U] major serious crime, eg murder, armed robbery, arson. 重罪 (例如谋杀, 持械抢劫, 纵火)。⇨ **misdemeanour. felon** /ˈfelən; ˈfelən/ *n* person guilty of ~. 重罪犯。**fel·oni·ous** /fɪˈləʊnɪəs; fəˈlonɪəs/ *adj* criminal. 犯重罪的。

fel·spar ⇨ **feldspar.**

felt[1] *pt, pp* of **feel**[2].

felt[2] /felt; felt/ *n* [U] wool, hair or fur, compressed and rolled flat into a kind of cloth: 毛毡: (attrib) (用作定语) ~ *hats /slippers.* 毡帽(毡鞋)。

fe·lucca /feˈlʌkə; fəˈlʌkə/ *n* narrow Mediterranean coasting vessel with oars or sails or both. (地中海沿岸之)小船(用桨或帆, 或两者皆用)。

fe·male /ˈfiːmeɪl; ˈfimel/ *adj* **1** of the sex that produces offspring: 女性的; 雌性的: *a ~ child /dog;* 女孩(母狗); (of plants or their parts) fruit-bearing: 结果实的; 雌的; 有雌蕊的。**2** of women: 妇女的: ~ *suffrage;* 妇女选举权; ~ *workers.* 女工。**3** (mech) having a hollow part designed to receive an inserted part, eg a plug. (机械)凹的; 阴的。□ *n* ~ animal; (derog) ~ person. 雌兽; (贬)女人。⇨ **male.**

femi·nine /ˈfemənɪn; ˈfemənɪn/ *adj* **1** of, like, suitable for, women: 妇女的; 似妇女的; 适于妇女的: *a ~ voice.* 女人似的声音。**2** (gram) of the gender proper to the names of females: (语法)阴性的: ~ *nouns and pronouns,* eg actress, lioness, she, her. 阴性的名词和代词(例如 actress, lioness, she, her)。**fem·i·nin·ity** /ˌfeməˈnɪnətɪ; ˌfeməˈnɪnətɪ/ *n* [U] quality of being ~. 妇女的气质。⇨ **masculine.**

fem·in·ism /ˈfemɪnɪzəm; ˈfeməˌnɪzəm/ *n* [U] movement for recognition of the claims of women for rights

(legal, political, etc) equal to those possessed by men. 女权运动; 男女平等主义。 ⇨ lib. **fem·in·ist** /-ɪst, -ɪst/ *n* supporter of ∼. 女权运动者; 男女平等主义者。

fe·mur /'fiːmə(r); 'fimɚ/ *n* (anat) thigh-bone. (解剖) 股骨。 ⇨ the illus at skeleton. 参看 skeleton 之插图。

fen /fen; fɛn/ *n* area of low marshy land. 沼泽; 沼地. **the Fens,** lowlying districts in Cambridgeshire and Lincolnshire. 英国剑桥郡和林肯郡之低洼地区。

fence¹ /fens; fɛns/ *n* [C] barrier made of wooden or metal stakes or rails, or wire, esp one put round a field, garden, etc to keep animals from straying or to keep out intruders. 栅栏; 围墙; 篱笆. **come down on one side or the other of the ∼,** give one's support to one side or the other. 支持一方. **come down on the right side of the ∼,** join the winner. 附和胜利的一方. **mend one's ∼s,** make peace. 谋和; 谈和. **sit on the ∼,** not commit oneself; wait to see where one can win most advantage. 骑墙; 观望. Hence, 由此产生, **(a)** '**∼-sit·ter** *n* person who does this. 骑墙份子; 持观望态度者. **(b)** '**∼-sit·ting** *n* □ *vt* [VP6A, 15B] surround, divide, provide with a ∼ or ∼s: 围以栅栏; 围以篱笆: *Farmers ∼ their fields.* 农民用篱笆将田地围起. *His land is ∼d with barbed wire.* 他的土地由铁丝围着. *The land is ∼d in/round.* 这土地是用栅栏围着的. **fenc·ing** /'fensɪŋ; 'fɛnsɪŋ/ *n* [U] material for making ∼s. 围墙材料。

fence² /fens; fɛns/ *vi* [VP 2A, C, 3 A] practise the art of fighting with long slender swords or foils; (fig) avoid giving a direct answer to a question(er): 斗剑; 击剑; (喻)不做正面答复; 搪塞: ∼ *with a question.* 搪塞一问题. **fencer** *n* person who ∼s. 斗剑者; 击剑者. **fenc·ing** /'fensɪŋ; 'fɛnsɪŋ/ *n* [U] art of fighting with swords. 剑术; 击剑。

fencing

fence³ /fens; fɛns/ *n* (sl) receiver of stolen goods; his place of business. (俚)收藏赃物者; 买卖赃物者; 买卖赃物之处。

fend /fend; fɛnd/ *vt, vi* 1 [VP15B] ∼ **off,** defend oneself from: 抵御; 抵挡: ∼ *off a blow.* 挡开一击. 2 ∼ **for oneself,** look after oneself: 照顾自己: *When his father died, Tom had to ∼ for himself.* 汤姆的父亲死后, 他必须自行谋生. *Most animals let their young ∼ for themselves from an early age.* 大多数的动物让他们的幼仔从小就独立生活。

fender /'fendə(r); 'fɛndɚ/ *n* 1 metal frame bordering an open fireplace (to prevent burning coal, etc from rolling on to the floor). (防止炉炭滚落在地板上的)火炉围栏. 2 (on the front of a vehicle, etc) strong bar, etc, used to lessen shock or damage in a collision. (车辆等前部之)挡板. 3 log of wood, heavy mass of rope, old rubber tyre etc hung on the side of a boat to prevent damage, eg when the boat comes alongside a wharf or another ship. 护舷板; 碰垫(例如当船沿码头或另一船停靠时, 为避免磨损, 系于船侧之木材或粗绳圈). 4 (US) (美) = mudguard, ⇨ mud.

fen·nel /'fenl; 'fɛnl/ *n* [U] yellow-flowered herb, used as a flavouring. 茴香(用来调味)。

feoff /fiːf; fif/ *n* = fief.

fe·ral /'fɪərəl; 'fɪrəl/ *adj* wild; untamed; brutal. 野的; 未驯的; 野蛮的。

fer·ment¹ /'fɜːment; 'fɝmənt/ *n* 1 [C] substance, eg yeast, that causes other substances to ferment. 酵母; 发酵剂. 2 *in a ∼,* (fig) in a state of, eg social, political, excitement. (喻)在骚动中(例如在社会或政治方面)。

fer·ment² /fə'ment; fɚ'mɛnt/ *vt, vi* [VP6A, 2A] 1 (cause to) undergo chemical changes through the action of organic bodies (esp yeast): (使)发酵: *Fruit juices ∼ if they are kept a long time.* 果汁放置日久会发酵. *When wine is ∼ed, it gives off bubbles of gas.* 酒发酵时发出气泡. 2 (fig) (cause to) become excited. (喻)(使)激动; 酝酿. **fer·men·ta·tion** /ˌfɜːmen'teɪʃn; ˌfɝmən'teʃən/ *n* [U] ∼ing or being ∼ed: 发酵: *the ∼ation of milk* (when cheese is being made); (做乳酪时)牛乳之发酵; (fig) excitement and unrest. (喻)激动; 纷扰。

fern /fɜːn; fɝn/ *n* [C] sorts of feathery, green-leaved flowerless plant: 蕨类植物: *hillsides covered with ∼* (collective *sing*) (集合名词单数); 长满蕨类植物的山坡; ∼*s growing in pots.* 长在盆内的蕨类植物。 ∼**y** *adj*

fer·ocious /fə'rəʊʃəs; fə'roʃəs/ *adj* fierce, cruel, savage. 凶猛的; 残忍的; 野蛮的。 ∼**·ly** *adv*

fer·oc·ity /fə'rɒsətɪ; fə'rɑsətɪ/ *n* [U] fierceness; savage cruelty; [C] (*pl* **-ties**) fierce, savage or cruel act. 凶猛; 残暴; 残暴的行为。

fer·ret /'ferɪt; 'fɛrɪt/ *n* small animal of the weasel family, used for driving rabbits from their burrows, killing rats, etc. 雪貂(用以逐兔, 捕鼠等). □ *vt, vi* 1 [VP2A] hunt with ∼s: 用雪貂行猎: *go ∼ing.* 带着雪貂出猎. 2 [VP15B, 2C] ∼ **sth out;** ∼ **about (for sth),** discover by searching; search: 侦察 搜索: ∼ *out a secret;* 侦察一秘密; ∼ *about among old papers and books for sth lost.* 在旧报和书籍中搜寻(某物)。

fer·ro·con·crete /ˌferəʊ'kɒŋkriːt; ˌfɛro'kɑnkrit/ *n* [U] reinforced concrete. 钢筋混凝土; 钢骨水泥。

fer·rous /'ferəs; 'fɛrəs/ *adj* containing or relating to iron: 含有铁的; 关于铁的: ∼ *chloride* (FeCl₂). 氯化亚铁。

fer·rule /'feruːl *US:* 'ferəl; 'fɛrəl/ *n* metal ring or cap placed on the end of a stick (eg of an umbrella) or tube, to prevent splitting; band strengthening or forming a joint. (装于伞把等长杖或管子上的)金属箍或包头; 套圈; 箍。

ferry /'ferɪ; 'fɛrɪ/ *n* (*pl* **-ries**) [C] (place where there is a) boat, hovercraft or aircraft that carries people and goods across a river, channel, etc. 渡口; 渡船; 输送人员货物渡过河或海峡等的飞机. □ *vt, vi* [VP6A, 15A, B, 2A, C] take, go, across in a ∼: 以船渡; 用飞机输送; 乘船渡过; 飞渡: ∼ *people/a boat across a river,* 渡人 (小船) 过河; *aircraft ∼ing motor-cars between England and France.* 英法间输送汽车的飞机。 '∼-**boat** *n* '∼-**man** /-mən, -mən/ (*pl* -**men**) *n*

fer·tile /'fɜːtaɪl *US:* -tl; 'fɝtl/ *adj* 1 (of land, plants, etc) producing much; (of a person, his mind, etc) full of ideas, plans, etc: (指土地, 植物等)肥沃的; 多产的; (指人, 头脑等)有才智的: ∼ *fields/soil;* 肥沃的土地(土壤); *a ∼ imagination.* 丰富的想象力. 2 able to produce fruit, young; capable of developing: 能结果实的; 能生育的; 能生长的: ∼ *seeds/eggs.* 能生长的种子(受精卵)。 ⇨ **sterile. fer·til·ity** /fə'tɪlətɪ; fə'tɪlətɪ/ *n* [U] state of being ∼. 肥沃; 多产; 丰富; 能结果实。

fer·til·ize /'fɜːtəlaɪz; 'fɝtl͵aɪz/ *vt* [VP6A] make fertile or productive: 使肥沃; 使多产: ∼ *the soil* (by using manure); 施肥于土壤; ∼ *flowers* (as bees do when they collect nectar). 使花受粉. **fer·ti·lizer** /-zə(r); -zɚ/ *n* [U] chemical plant food; artificial manure; [C] substance of this kind: 化学肥料; 人造肥料; 肥料: *Bonemeal and nitrates are common fertilizers.* 骨粉和硝酸盐是通常之肥料。 **fer·ti·liz·ation** /ˌfɜːtəlaɪ'zeɪʃn *US:* -lɪ'z-; ͵fɝtl͵ə'zeʃən/ *n* [U] fertilizing or being ∼d. 使肥沃; 使多产; 变为肥沃; 变为多产。

fer·ule /'feruːl *US:* 'ferəl; 'fɛrəl/ *n* flat ruler for punishing children by striking them on the hand. (惩罚小孩的)戒尺。

fer·vent /'fɜːvənt; 'fɝvənt/ *adj* 1 hot, glowing. 热

的；白热的。**2** showing warmth of feeling; passionate: 热烈的；热情的: ~ love/hatred; 热烈的爱(强烈的恨); a ~ lover/admirer. 热情的爱人(景慕者)。~·ly adv

fer·vency /ˈfɜːvənsɪ; ˈfɝvənsɪ/ n

fer·vid /ˈfɜːvɪd; ˈfɝvɪd/ adj fervent(2); spirited; showing earnest feeling: 热烈的; 热心的; 热情的: a ~ orator. 激昂的演说者。~·ly adv

fer·vour (US = -vor) /ˈfɜːvə(r); ˈfɝvɚ/ n [U] strength or warmth of feeling; earnestness. 热诚; 热心。

fes·tal /ˈfestl; ˈfestl/ adj of a feast or festival; festive (the more usu word): 节日的; 欢乐的 (festive 较常用): a ~ occasion, eg a wedding, a birthday party; 欢乐的场合(例如结婚, 过生日); ~ music. 欢乐的音乐。

fes·ter /ˈfestə(r); ˈfestɚ/ vi [VP2A] **1** (of a cut or wound) fill with poisonous matter (pus): (指伤口) 化脓; 溃烂: If the cut gets dirty, it will probably ~. 如果伤口弄脏了, 可能会化脓。**2** (fig) act like poison in the mind; become resentful, embittered: (喻)使人痛苦; 使人气愤; 使人难过: The insult ~ed in his mind. 这侮辱使他心中痛楚。

fes·ti·val /ˈfestɪvl; ˈfestəvl/ n **1** (day or season for) rejoicing; public celebrations: 节日; 节期; 祭; 庆祝: Christmas and Easter are Church ~s. 圣诞节和复活节是教会的节日。**2** series of performances (of music, ballet, drama, etc) given periodically (usu once a year): (音乐, 芭蕾舞, 戏剧等之)节(通常每年一次): the Edinburgh F~; 爱丁堡之戏剧节; a jazz ~. 爵士音乐节。**3** (attrib) festive; of a feast or feast-day. (用作定语)节日的; 欢宴的。

fes·tive /ˈfestɪv; ˈfestɪv/ adj of a feast or festival; joyous: 宴乐的; 节日的; 欢乐的: a '~ season, eg Christmas; 欢乐的季节(例如圣诞节); the ~ board, a table on which a feast is spread. 宴席。

fes·tiv·ity /feˈstɪvətɪ; fesˈtɪvətɪ/ n (pl -ties) **1**[U] rejoicing; merry-making. 欢乐; 宴乐。**2** (pl) festive, joyful events: (复)庆典; 喜庆: wedding festivities. 结婚庆典。

fes·toon /feˈstuːn; fesˈtun/ n [C] chain of flowers, leaves, ribbons, etc hanging in a curve or loop between two points, as a decoration. 花彩; 垂花饰。□ vt [VP6A] make into, decorate with, ~s: 结成花彩; 饰以花彩: a room ~ed with Christmas decorations. 饰有圣诞花彩的房间。

fetch /fetʃ; fetʃ/ vt, vi **1** [VP6A, 15A, B, 13B, 12B] go for and bring back (sb or sth): 接来(人); 取来(物): F~ a doctor at once. 立刻请位医生来。Please ~ the children from school. 请到学校里把孩子们接来。The chair is in the garden; please ~ it in. 椅子在花园里, 请搬进来。Shall I ~ your coat for you/~ you your coat from the next room? 要我去隔壁房间把你的外衣拿来吗? ~ and carry (for), be busy with small duties for; be a servant for: (替…)做杂事; (供…)差遣: He expects his daughter to ~ and carry for him all day. 他希望他的女儿终日供他差遣。**2** [VP6A, 15A] cause to come out; draw forth: 使出来; 使发出: ~ a deep sigh/a dreadful groan; 发出深深的叹息声(可怕的呻吟); ~ tears to the eyes. 使眼泪从眼中流出。**3** [VP 6A, 12B] (of goods) bring in; sell for (a price): (指货物)售得(若干价钱): These old books won't ~ (you) much. 这些旧书卖不了多少钱。**4** [VP12C] (colloq) deal, give (a blow) to:(口)给予(打击): She ~ed me a slap across the face/a box on the ears. 她打了我一耳光, 打了我一记耳光。~·ing adj (colloq) attractive, delightful: 动人的; 迷人的: What a ~ing little hat! 多么漂亮的一顶小帽子! What a ~ing smile! 多么迷人的一笑!

fête /feɪt; fet/ n (usu outdoor) festival or entertainment: (通常在户外)庆祝会; 游乐会: the village ~, often one at which funds are raised. 村民游乐会(常是募捐性质的)。'~-day n saint's-day. 圣徒纪念日;(天主教)祝名日; 生日。⇨ saint(5). □ vt [VP6A] honour by entertaining; make a fuss of: 款待; 热烈欢迎: The hero

was ~d wherever he went. 那英雄不论走到何处, 均受到热烈的欵待。

fetid /ˈfetɪd; ˈfetɪd/ adj stinking. 有恶臭的; 臭的。

fet·ish /ˈfetɪʃ; ˈfitɪʃ/ n **1** object worshipped by pagan people because they believe a spirit lives in it. 物神(认为有神灵而受异教徒崇奉之物)。**2** anything to which abnormal, excessive respect or attention is given; (colloq) obsession: 盲目崇拜物; 过分受到注意之物; 偶像; (口)紫绕心头之事物: Some women make a ~ of clothes. 有些妇女过于注意衣服。

fet·lock /ˈfetlɒk; ˈfetˌlɑk/ n (tuft of hair on a) horse's leg above and behind the hoof. 距毛(马蹄上之丛毛); 簇毛。⇨ the illus at domestic. 参看 domestic 之插图。

fet·ter /ˈfetə(r); ˈfetɚ/ n chain for the ankles of a prisoner or the leg of a horse; (fig, usu pl) sth that hinders progress. (犯人或马之)足械; 脚镣; (喻, 通常用复数)障碍; 束缚。□ vt [VP 6A] put in ~s or chains; (fig) restrain. 上以脚镣; (喻)束缚; 拘束。

fettle /ˈfetl; ˈfetl/ n in fine/good ~, in good (physical) condition; in high spirits. 身体健壮; 神采奕奕。

fe·tus ⇨ foetus.

feud /fjuːd; fjud/ n [C] bitter quarrel between two persons, families or groups, over a long period of time. (二人, 家族或团体间之)长期不和; 夙怨。

feu·dal /ˈfjuːdl; ˈfjudl/ adj of the method (the '~ system) of holding land (by giving services to the owner) during the Middle Ages in Europe: 封建制度的: ~ law; 封建法; the ~ barons. 封建贵族。⇨ vassal. ~·ism /-ɪzəm; -ɪzəm/, -ɪzəm/ n [U] the ~ system. 封建制度。

feuda·tory /ˈfjuːdətərɪ US: -tɔːrɪ; ˈfjudəˌtɔrɪ/ adj owing service to a lord: 臣事的: ~ obligations. 为臣的职责。□ n vassal. 家臣。

fe·ver /ˈfiːvə(r); ˈfivɚ/ n **1** [U, C] condition of the human body with temperature higher than usual, esp as a sign of illness: 发烧; 发热。She hasn't much ~. 她发烧不太厉害。He has a high ~. 他发高烧。~ heat, high temperature of the human body in ~. 高烧。**2** [U] one of a number of diseases in which there is high ~: 热病: yellow/typhoid/rheumatic ~. 热病(肠热病; 风湿病)。**3** (usu常作 a ~) excited state; nervous agitation: 兴奋; 激昂: in a ~ of impatience. 极度暴躁。at/to a ~ pitch, at/to a high level of excitement: 极为激动: The crowd was at ~ pitch. 群众极为激昂。~ed adj affected by a ~: 发烧的; 激动的: a ~ed imagination, highly excited. 狂热的想象。~·ish /-rɪʃ; -rɪʃ/ adj having symptoms of ~; caused by ~; causing ~: 发烧的; 害热病的; 发烧引起的; 引起发烧的: in a ~ish condition; 发烧状态中; ~ish dreams; 发烧引起的梦; ~ish swamps. 产生热病的湿地。~·ish·ly adv

few /fjuː; fju/ adj (-er, -est), pron (contrasted with many; 与many相对; ⇨ little, less, much) **1** (attrib, with a pl n) not many: (用作定语与复数名词连用)不多; 很少: Few people live to be 100 and fewer still live to be 110. 很少人活到一百岁, 活到一百一十岁的人则更少了。Which of you made the fewest mistakes, the smallest number of mistakes? 你们当中谁犯的错误最少? He is a man of few words. He says very little. 他是个沉默寡言的人。no fewer than, as many as: 不下于; 有…之多: No fewer than twenty workers were absent through illness. 因病而缺席的工人不下于二十人。**2** (pred, rare in colloq style): (用于表语中, 罕用于口语): Such occasions are few. 此种场合不多见。We are very few, fewer than at the last meeting of the society. 我们到会的人数不多, 较上次开会的人数还少。**3** a few, a small number (Note that few is neg and a few is positive): 少数; 数个(注意: few 有否定意味, a few 则是肯定的): We are going away for a few days. 我们要离开几天。I'd like a few more red roses. 我想再要几朵红玫瑰。some few; a

good few; quite a few; not a few, a considerable number, a fair number. 相当多; 颇有几个。 **4** *every few minutes/days, etc.* 每隔几分钟 (天等)。 ⇨ **every**(5). **5 the few,** the minority. 少数。 □ *pron* **few of,** (neg) not many of: (否定之义) 不多的人或物; 很少的人或物: *Few of those roses are worth buying.* 那些玫瑰花没有几朵值得购买的。 *a few of,* (positive) a small number of: (肯定之义) 少数的; 数个: *I know a a few of these people.* 这些人当中我认识几个。 **few-ness** *n*

fey /feɪ; fe/ *adj* **1** (Scot) having a feeling of approaching death. (苏) 感到死期近的。 **2** clairvoyant. 有超人洞察力的。 **3** otherworldly. 来世的。

fez /fez; fez/ *n* red felt hat with a flat top and no brim, worn by some Muslim men. (某些伊斯兰教徒戴的平顶无边) 红毡帽。

fi·ancé (fem **fi·ancée**) /fɪˈɒnseɪ US: ˌfiːɑːnˈseɪ; ˌfiən-ˈse/ *n* (F) man (woman) to whom one is engaged to be married. (法) 未婚夫 (fiancé); 未婚妻 (fiancée)。

fi·asco /fɪˈæskəʊ; fɪˈæsko/ *n* (*pl* ~s, US also ~es /-kəʊz; -koz/) complete failure, breakdown, in sth attempted: 彻底失败; 惨败: *The new play at the Ritz Theatre was a* ~. 在里茨戏院演出的新剧完全失败了。

fi·at /ˈfaɪæt US: ˈfiːət; ˈfaɪət/ *n* [C] order or decree made by a ruler. 谕; 命令。

fib /fɪb; fɪb/ *n* (colloq) untrue statement (esp about sth unimportant). (口) 无关紧要的谎言; 小谎。 □ *vi* (-bb-) [VP2A] tell a fib. 撒小谎。 **fib·ber** *n* person who tells fibs. 撒小谎的人。 **fib·bing** *n* [U] telling fibs. 撒小谎。

fibre (US = **fiber**) /ˈfaɪbə(r); ˈfaɪbɚ/ *n* **1** [C] one of the slender threads of which many animal and vegetable growths are formed, eg cotton, wood, nerves, muscles. (棉, 木, 神经, 肌肉等之)纤维; 纤维质。 **2** [U] substance formed of a mass of ~s, for manufacture into various materials: (用以制成纺, 织等材料之)纤维物质: *hemp* ~, for making rope; 大麻纤维 (制绳用者); *cotton* ~, for spinning. 棉花纤维 (纺织用者)。 '~**board** *n* [U] board made of compressed ~. 纤维板。 '~**glass** *n* [U] material of glass ~s in resin, used as an insulating material, and made into structural materials, eg for boat-building. 玻璃纤维; 玻璃棉 (用作绝缘材料, 并制成造船等建筑材料)。 **3** [U] structure; texture: 构造; 结构; 质地: *material of coarse* ~; 粗劣的料子; (fig) character: (喻)品格: *a person of strong moral* ~. 品德很好的人。 **fi·brous** /ˈfaɪbrəs; ˈfaɪbrəs/ *adj* made of, like, ~s. 纤维制的; 似纤维的; 纤维状的。

fib·ula /ˈfɪbjʊlə(r); ˈfɪbjələ/ *n* (anat) outer of the two bones between the knee and the foot. (解剖) 腓骨。 ⇨ the illus at **skeleton**. 参看 skeleton 之插图。

fickle /ˈfɪkl; ˈfɪkl/ *adj* (of moods, the weather, etc) often changing; not constant: (指心情, 天气等) 常变的; 多变的: ~ *fortune;* 变化无常的命运; *a* ~ *lover.* 情意不专的爱人。 ~**ness** *n*

fic·tion /ˈfɪkʃn; ˈfɪkʃən/ *n* **1** [C] sth invented or imagined (contrasted with truth). 虚构之事; 捏造的故事(与 truth 相对)。 *a legal/polite* ~, sth assumed to be true, although it may be false, for legal/social convenience. 法律上的假定(为法律或社会上的方便, 假定某事为真, 虽然此事可能是假的)。 **2** [U] (branch of literature concerned with) stories, novels and romances: (作为文学之一分支的)小说: *works of* ~; 小说作品; *prefer history to* ~. 喜欢历史甚于小说。 *Truth is often stranger than* ~. 事实往往比小说还奇怪。

fic·ti·tious /fɪkˈtɪʃəs; fɪkˈtɪʃəs/ *adj* not real; imagined or invented: 假的; 想象的; 虚构的: *The account he gives of his movements is quite* ~. 他对他的行动之说明完全是虚构的。

fiddle /ˈfɪdl; ˈfɪdl/ *n* **1** (colloq) violin; any instrument of the violin family, eg a cello or viola. (口)小提琴; 提琴类的乐器(例如大提琴或中音提琴)。 *have a face as long as a* ~, look dismal. 板着脸; 显得愁眉苦脸。

fit as a ~, very well; in good health. 精神健旺; 身体健壮。 *play second* ~ *(to),* take a less important part (than). 居于(…的)次位。 '~**-stick** *n* bow[1](2). 拉提琴的弓。 '~**-sticks** *int* Nonsense! 胡说! **2** instance of fiddling; ⇨ 3 below. 虚报帐目等(参看下列第 3 义)。 □ *vt, vi* **1** [VP6A, 2A] (colloq) play the ~; play a tune, etc on the ~. (口)奏小提琴; 以小提琴奏出(一曲调等)。 **2** [VP2A, C] ~ *(about) (with),* make aimless movements; play aimlessly (*with* sth in one's fingers): 做无目的之动作; 用手指无聊地拨弄(与 with 连用, 后接某物): *Stop fiddling!* 不要虚耗光阴! *He was fiddling (about) with a piece of string.* 他无聊地玩弄一条绳子。 **3** [VP6A] (sl) make or keep dishonestly inaccurate records of figures (in business accounts, etc): (俚)虚报帐目等: ~ *an incometax return,* conceal part of it so as to try to escape correct tax payments. 虚报所得税申报书。 **fiddler** *n* person who plays the ~; person who ~s(3). 奏提琴者; 虚报帐目者。 **fid·dling** *adj* (colloq) trivial; futile: (口)琐细的; 无益的: *fiddling little jobs.* 琐细的工作。

fi·del·ity /fɪˈdeləti; faɪˈdɛlətɪ/ *n* [U] **1** ~ *(to),* loyalty, faithfulness: 忠贞; 忠实: ~ *to one's principles/religion/leader/wife.* 忠于主义(宗教, 领袖, 妻子)。 **2** accuracy; exactness: 正确; 精确: *translate sth with the greatest* ~; 极为确实地翻译一篇东西; *high* ~ *equipment,* with high quality sound reproduction. 高度传真性音响设备。 ⇨ **hi-fi.**

fidget /ˈfɪdʒɪt; ˈfɪdʒɪt/ *vi, vt* [VP2A, C, 6A] ~ *(about) (with),* (cause sb to) move the body (or part of it) about restlessly; make (sb) nervous: 坐立不安; (使某人)烦躁不安: *Stop* ~*ing!* 不要坐立不安! *The boy was* ~*ing (about) with his knife and fork.* 那孩子不停地摆动他的刀叉。 *What's* ~*ing you,* making you nervous or uneasy? 何事使你烦躁不安? *Hurry up, your father's beginning to* ~, show signs of impatience. 赶快, 你父亲开始不耐烦了。 □ *n* **1** (usu 通常作 **the** ~s) ~*ing movements:* 坐立不安; 烦躁不安: *Having to sit still for a long time often gives small children the* ~*s.* 必须静坐很久, 往往使小孩们烦躁不安: 坐立不安者; 烦躁不安者: *What a* ~ *you are!* 你真是个坐立不安的人! ~**y** *adj* having ~s; restless: 坐立不安的; 烦躁不安的: *a* ~*y child.* 烦躁的小孩。

fie /faɪ; faɪ/ *int* (usu hum) for shame: (通常为诙谐语)呸! *Fie upon you,* You ought to be ashamed! 呸! 真不要脸!

fief /fiːf; fif/ *n* [C] land held from a feudal lord. 封土; 领地; 采邑。

field[1] /fiːld; fild/ *n* [C] **1** area of land, either grassland for cattle, etc or arable land for crops, usu enclosed by means of hedges, fences, etc (not normally used of unenclosed land or uncultivated land): 田野; 田地 (通常由篱笆等围起, 不用以指未被围起或未开垦的土地): *working in the* ~*s* 在田里工作 (Cf 参较 *on the farm*). *What a fine* ~ *of wheat!* 多么好的一片麦田! **2** (usu in compounds) wide area or expanse; open space: (通常用于复合词中)广阔的区域; 茫茫的一片; 空地; 场地: *an 'ice*~, eg round the North Pole; 冰原 (例如北极周围者); *a 'flying*~, 飞机场; *a 'landing*~ (for aircraft); (飞机的)起落场; *a 'baseball/'cricket/'football* ~. 棒球(板球, 足球)场。 '~ *events n pl* athletic contests such as jumping and discus-throwing, but not races or other contests that take place on a track. 田赛(跳高, 跳远, 掷铁饼等)。 '~ *glasses n pl* long-distance binoculars for outdoor use. (户外用)双筒望远镜。 '~ *sports n pl* hunting, shooting and fishing. 野外运动(狩猎, 射击, 钓鱼)。 **3** (usu in compounds) area of land from which minerals, etc are obtained: (通常用于复合词中)矿田: 产地: '*gold*~*s;* 金矿产地; *a new 'oil*~; 新油田; '*coal*~*s.* 煤田。 **4** province or department of study or activity: (学术或活动)范围; 领域; 界: *the* ~ *of politics/art/science/medicine.* 政治(艺术, 科学, 医学)界。 *That is outside my* ~, is not in the departments of knowledge

that I have studied. 那不在我所学的范围内. '**~ work** n [U] scientific, technical or social investigation made outside laboratories, etc eg by surveyors, geologists or by students of social science who visit and talk to people. 野外调查工作; 实地调查工作(例如测量者, 地质学家或社会科学学者所做的勘察工作). **5** range of operation, activity, use); area or space in which forces can be felt: (动作, 活动或作用之)范围; 力量可被感到的区域: a magnetic ~, have a magnet; 磁场; a wide ~ of vision; 广阔的视野; an object that fills the ~ of a telescope; 由望远镜看到的一个物体; the earth's gravitational ~, the space in which the earth's gravity is exerted. 地心吸引力的范围. **6** place, area, where a battle or war is or was fought: 战场: the ~ of battle ('battle-~); 战场; take the ~, go to war. 开战; 作战. '**~ artillery;** '**~ gun** nn light and mobile, for use in battle. 野战炮. '**~ day** n day on which military operations are practised; (fig) great or special occasion. 野外演习日; (喻)重大事件. **have a ~ day,** (fig) have a celebration or triumph. (喻)庆祝一番; 喜气洋洋; 得意扬扬. '**~-hospital** n temporary hospital near the scene of fighting. 野战医院. '**F~ 'Marshal** n army officer of highest rank. 陆军元帅. '**~-officer** n major or colonel. (陆军)校级军官. '**~-work** n temporary fortification made by troops in the ~. 战地临时筑成的防卸工事. **7** (sports and athletics) (in foxhunting) all those taking part in the hunt; (in a contest, esp a horse-race) all the competitors; (in cricket and baseball) team that is not batting; (cricket) the fielding side. (户外活动及运动)(猎狐)全体猎者的参加比赛者的总称; (赛马)全体参加比赛的马; (板球和棒球)守队; (板球)守队队员; 外场员.

field² /fiːld/ n; fild/ vt, vi **1** [VP6A, 2A] (cricket and baseball) (stand ready to) catch or stop (the ball): (板球和棒球)(准备)接或截(球); 守(球); 做外场员或守队队员: He ~ed the ball smartly. 他很巧妙地地将球接住了. He ~s well. 他截球技术极佳! Well ~ed, sir! 截得好! 守得好! **2** [VP6A] (of football teams, etc) put into the ~: (指足球队等)使入场: Brasil are ~ing a strong team for the World Cup. 巴西派了一支强大的球队参加世界杯赛. **~er; fieldsman** /-mən; -mən/ n (pl -**men**) (cricket, etc) person who ~s: (板球等) 外场员; 守队队员: He doesn't bat well, but he's an excellent ~er. 他击球的技术不好, 但是他是个卓越的外场员. ⇔ the illus at **baseball.** 参看 baseball 之插图.

fiend /fiːnd; find/ n devil; very wicked or cruel person; (colloq) person devoted to or addicted to sth (indicated by the word prefixed): 恶魔; 穷凶极恶的人; (口)耽于某一事物(由其前面一字指明)之人: ~迷; 酷爱之人: a drug ~; 有毒瘾的人; a fresh-'air ~. 喜爱户外生活之人. **~-ish** /-ɪʃ; -ɪʃ/ adj savage and cruel. 凶猛的; 残忍的. **~-ish-ly** adv

fierce /fɪəs; fɪrs/ adj (-r, -st) **1** violent and angry: 凶猛的; 愤怒的: ~ dogs/winds; 猛犬 (强风); look ~; 样子凶恶; have a ~ look on one's face. 面部有凶猛的表情. **2** (of heat, desire, etc) intense: (指热, 欲望等)强烈的: ~ hatred. 痛恨. **~-ly** adv **~-ness** n

fiery /'faɪərɪ; 'faɪrɪ/ adj **1** flaming; looking like, hot as, fire: 燃烧的; 似火的; 炽热的: a ~ sky; 火红的天空; ~ eyes, angry and glaring. 冒着怒火的目光. **2** (of a person, his actions, etc) easily or easily made angry; passionate: (指人, 其行动等)易怒的; 暴躁的; 激烈的: a ~ temper/speech. 暴躁的脾气(激昂的演说). **fier-ily** /-əlɪ; -ɪlɪ/ adv **fieri-ness** n

fi-esta /fɪ'estə; fɪ'estə/ n (Sp) religious festival; saint's day; holiday, festival. (西)宗教节日; 圣徒节; 假日; 节日.

fife /faɪf; faɪf/ n small musical wind instrument like a flute, used with drums in military music: 横笛; 短笛 (与鼓伴奏, 用于军乐): a drum and ~ band. 鼓笛乐队.

fif-teen /ˌfɪf'tiːn; ˌfɪf'tin/ n, adj the number 15. ⇔ App 4; team of Rugby players. 十五; 十五个(参看附录四); 橄榄球队. **~th** /ˌfɪf'tiːnθ; ˌfɪf'tinθ/ n, adj 第十

五(个); 十五分之一(的).

fifth /fɪfθ; fɪfθ/ n, adj next after the 4th; one of five equal parts. 第五; 第五个; 五分之一(的). ⇔ **App 4.** 看附录四. **,~ 'column,** organized body of persons sympathizing with and working for the enemy within a country at war. 第五纵队 (战时同情敌人并在国内替敌人工作的组织). **~-ly** adv in the ~ place. 第五.

fifty /'fɪftɪ; 'fɪftɪ/ n (pl -**ties**), adj the number 50. 五十; 五十个. ⇔ **App 4.** 参看附录四. **the fifties,** 50—59. 50 至 59. **go ~-'~ (with); be on a ~-~ basis (with),** have equal shares (with). 与…平分; 均摊. a **~-~ chance,** equal chance. 机会均等; 各占一半. **fif-ti-eth** /'fɪftɪəθ; 'fɪftɪθ/ n, adj 第五十(个); 五十分之一(的) ⇔ **App 4.** 参看附录四.

fig /fɪg; fɪg/ n (broad-leaved tree having a) soft, sweet, pear-shaped fruit full of small seeds. 无花果; 无花果树. ⇔ the illus at **fruit.** 参看 fruit 之插图. **not care/give a fig (for),** not care in the least; consider as valueless or unimportant. (对…) 毫不介意; 毫不重视. '**~-leaf,** (with reference to the story of Adam and Eve) conventional device for concealing genital organs in old drawings, statues, etc. (源于亚当和夏娃的故事) 无花果之叶(古代的裸体画象, 雕象等常见之阴部覆盖物).

fight¹ /faɪt; faɪt/ n **1** [C] act of fighting: 打斗; 交战; 打架: a ~ between two dogs; 狗打架; the ~ against poverty; 对抗贫穷; a prize-~ (boxing). 拳击赛. **put up a good/poor ~,** fight with/without courage and determination. 奋勇 (畏惧) 地战斗. a free ~, ⇔ **free¹**(3). **a stand-up ~,** ⇔ **stand²**(10). **2** [U] fighting spirit; desire or ability for fighting: 战斗精神及斗志. In spite of numerous defeats, they still had plenty of ~ left in them. 虽然屡遭败绩, 他们仍甚有斗志. The news that their leader had surrendered took all the ~ out of them. 他们首领投降的消息使他们失去了一切斗志. **show ~,** show readiness to fight. 表示战意.

fight² /faɪt; faɪt/ vi, vt (pt, pp **fought** /fɔːt; fot/) **1** [VP2A, B, C, 3A, 4A, 6A] use the force of the body or of weapons (against); use physical force (as in war); use all resources available (against) to defeat: 与…格斗; 打架;战斗; 作战: to ~ poverty/oppression. 消灭贫穷(反抗压迫). When dogs ~, they use their teeth. 狗打架时用牙. The dogs were ~ing over a bone/~ing for the possession of a bone. 那些狗为了争一块骨头而打斗. Great Britain has often fought with (= against) her enemies. 英国常和敌人作战. Great Britain fought with (= on the side of) France. 英国与法国联合作战. They were ~ing for (= in order to secure or maintain) their independence. 他们在为争取 (或维护) 独立而战. They were ~ing to preserve their freedom. 他们为维护自由而战. **~ to a finish,** until there is a decision. 战至分出胜负; 决雌雄. **~ shy of,** keep away from, not get mixed up with. 避开; 不与…接触. **2** [VP6A] ~(1) in: 在…中作战: ~ a battle/a duel/an election. 打仗 (决斗; 竞选). **3** [VP15A, B] ~ sth down, repress; overcome: 镇压; 抑制: ~ down a feeling of repugnance. 抑制厌恶感. **~ sb/sth off,** drive away; struggle against: 驱逐; 抵抗: ~ off a cold, eg by taking aspirin. 治好伤风(例如借服阿斯匹林). **~ one's way forward/out (of),** advance, go forward, by ~ing. 向前(外)打开一条路. **~ it out,** until a dispute is settled. 争论解决为止. **4** [VP6A] manoeuvre (ships, etc) in battle: 调动 (舰队等)作战: The captain fought his ship well. 该舰长善于指挥他的军舰作战. **~er** n person or thing that ~s, esp a fast aircraft designed for attacking bombers. 战斗者; (尤指)战斗机: a jet-'~er. 喷射战斗机; (attrib) (用作定语) a ~er pilot/squadron. 战斗机驾驶员(中队). **~ing** n [U]: 'street ~ing. 街头战; 巷战. a ~ing chance, a possibility of success if great efforts are made. 成功的希望.

fig-ment /'fɪgmənt; 'fɪgmənt/ n [C] sth invented or imagined: 虚构或想象之物: ~s of the imagination. 想象中的事物.

figu·rat·ive/ 'fɪɡjərətɪv; 'fɪɡjərətɪv/ *adj* (of words and language) used not in the literal sense but in an imaginative way (as when *fiery* is used of a man who is easily made angry). (指文字和语言) 比喻的 (如 fiery 一词指暴躁的人). **~·ly** *adv*

fig·ure /'fɪɡə(r) US: 'fɪɡjər; 'fɪɡjəs/ *n* **1** symbol for a number, esp 0 to 9: 数字 (尤指由 0 至 9): *He has an income of six figures, £ 100 000 or more.* 他有六位数字的收入 (至少为 100,000 英镑). *We bought the house at a high/low ~,* for a high/low price. 我们以高(低)价买下那所房屋. **double ~s,** any number from 10 to 99 inclusive. 二位数字(自 10 至 99). **2** (*pl*) arithmetic: (复)算术: *Are you good at ~s?* 你精于算术吗? **3** diagram; drawing to illustrate sth: 图形; 图解; 图表: *The blackboard was covered with geometrical ~s,* ie squares, triangles, etc. 黑板上画满了几何图形(正方形, 三角形等). **4** person's ~ drawn or painted, or cut in stone, etc; drawing, painting, image, of the body of a bird, animal, etc. (绘画, 雕刻等的)人像; 肖像; 鸟兽等的像. **'~·head** *n* **(a)** carved image (either bust of full-length) placed for ornament at the prow of a ship. 船首像(船首所饰之雕像, 半身或全身者). **(b)** person in high position but with no real authority. 有名无实的首领; 傀儡. **5** human form, esp the appearance and what it suggests: 人形; (尤指)体态; 相貌; 身材: *I saw a ~ approaching in the darkness.* 我看见黑暗中有个人影走近. *He has a good/poor/handsome, etc ~.* 他的体型很好(很差, 很漂亮等). *She's a fine ~ of a woman,* is well shaped. 她的身材很美. *I'm dieting to keep my ~,* in order not to grow stout. 我在节食以保持我的身材 (不使身体发胖). *She was a ~ of distress,* Her attitude and appearance suggested distress. 她的样子很穷苦. **cut a fine/poor/sorry ~,** make a fine, etc, appearance. 崭露头角(出洋相; 出丑等). **6** person, esp his character or influence: 人物(尤指其性格或其影响力): *dominating ~s like Napoleon.* 象拿破仑般的有领导力的人物. **7 ~ of speech,** expression, eg a simile or metaphor, that gives variety or force, using words out of their literal meaning. 比喻. □ *vt, vi* **1** [VP 15A] imagine; picture mentally: 想象: ~ *sth to oneself.* 想象某事物. **2** [VP2C] ~ (*in*), appear; have a part; be prominent: 出现; 担任一角色; 露头角: ~ *in history/in a play.* ~ *in history* 在历史上留名(在一剧中扮演一角). *He ~s in all the books on the subject.* 所有关于此一问题的书籍中都提到了他. **3** [VP 15 B] ~ *sth/sb out,* calculate; think about until one understands: 演算出; 理解: *I can't ~ that man out,* He puzzles me. 我不了解那个人. **4** [VP 3A, 9, 25] ~ (*on*), (US) reckon; estimate; conclude: (美)料想; 指望; 推断: *They ~d on your arriving early.* 他们预料你会早到. *I ~d (that) he was honest.* 我想他是诚实的. ~ *him (to be) honest.* 我认为他是诚实的. **fig·ured** *adj* ornamented; decorated: 有装饰的; 装饰过的: *a ~d glass window,* with designs, eg in stained glass; 有图案的玻璃窗 (例如用彩色玻璃); 花玻璃窗; ~*d silk,* with patterns or designs on it. 纹织绸.

fila·ment /'fɪləmənt; 'fɪləmənt/ *n* [C] slender thread, eg of wire in an electric light bulb. 细线(例如电灯泡内之灯丝).

fila·ture /'fɪlətʃə(r); 'fɪlətʃə/ *n* workshop in which raw silk is reeled from cocoons. 缫丝厂.

fil·bert /'fɪlbət; 'fɪlbət/ *n* (nut of a) cultivated hazel. 欧洲榛树; 欧洲榛子.

filch /fɪltʃ; fɪltʃ/ *vt* [VP6A] pilfer; steal (sth of small value). 窃取; 偷(不贵重的东西).

file[1] /faɪl; faɪl/ *n* **1** metal tool with rough surface(s) for cutting or smoothing hard substances. 锉刀; 锉子. ⇨ the illus at **tool.** 参看 tool 之插图. □ *vt* [VP 6A, 22, 15A] use a ~ on; make smooth with a ~; remove, cut through, with a ~: 用锉子锉; 锉平; 锉去; 锉开: ~ *one's fingernails;* 用锉修指甲; ~ *sth smooth;* 锉光某物; ~ *an iron rod in two.* 将一铁棒锉为二. **fil·ings**

/'faɪlɪŋz; 'faɪlɪŋz/ *n pl* bits ~d off or removed by a ~. 锉屑.

file[2] /faɪl; faɪl/ *n* [C] holder, cover, case, box, drawer etc for keeping papers, etc together and in order for reference purposes, usu with wires, metal rods or other devices on which the papers, etc may be threaded: 公文箱(夹, 匣); 卷宗; 文卷档: *Where's the ~ of 'The Times'?* 泰晤士报的合订本在哪里? *We have placed the correspondence on our ~s.* 我们已将信件归入档了. **on ~,** on or in a ~. 存卷; 归档; 汇存. □ *vt* [VP 6A, 15B] place on or in a ~; place on record: 归档; 存卷; 汇存: ~ *an application;* 将一申请书归档; ~ (*away*) *letters;* 将信件归档; *a 'filing clerk,* one who ~s correspondence, etc. 管理档案的职员.

file[3] /faɪl; faɪl/ *n* line of persons or things one behind the other; (mil) man in the front rank and the man or men straight behind him. 行; (军)纵队. **(in) single ~; (in) Indian ~,** one line, one behind the other. (成)单行. **the rank and ~,** soldiers who are not officers; (fig) ordinary, undistinguished persons. 士兵; 行伍; (喻)普通人; 常人. □ *vi* [VP2C] march in ~: 成单行或纵队行进: *The men ~d in/out,* came or went in/out. 士兵们成单行进入(出去).

fil·ial /'fɪlɪəl; 'fɪlɪəl/ *adj* of a son or daughter: 子女的: ~ *duty/piety.* 孝道; 孝心.

fili·bus·ter /'fɪlɪbʌstə(r); 'fɪlɪˌbʌstə/ *n* **1** person who obstructs the making of decisions in meetings, parliament, etc by eg making long speeches. 以冗长的演说等阻碍会议、议会等做成决定之人. **2** such a speech. 此种冗长的演说. □ *vi* act as a ~(1). 以冗长的演说等阻碍会议、议会等做成决定; 阻挠议事.

fili·gree /'fɪlɪɡriː; 'fɪlɪˌɡri/ *n* [U] ornamental lace-like work of gold, silver or copper ware: 金、银或铜丝制成的似花边的细工: (*attrib*) (用作定语) *a ~ brooch;* 金(银)丝胸针; ~ *earrings.* 金(银)丝耳环.

fil·ings /'faɪlɪŋz; 'faɪlɪŋz/ *n* ⇨ **file[1].**

fill[1] /fɪl; fɪl/ *n* **1** [U] full supply; as much as is wanted: 充分的供应; 所需之量: *eat/drink one's ~.* 尽量吃(喝)个够. **have one's ~ of sth,** (colloq) have as much as one can bear. (口)尽量用; 尽吃; 受够了. **2** [C] enough to fill sth: 填满某物之量: *a ~ of tobacco,* enough to fill a pipe. 一斗烟; 一烟斗的烟丝. **~ing** *n* [C] sth put in to ~ sth: 供填塞之物; 充填物: *a ~ing in a tooth.* 补牙之物.

fill[2] /fɪl; fɪl/ *vt, vi* **1** [VP 6A, 14, 15B, 12B, 13B, 2A, C] ~ (*with*), make or become full; occupy all the space in: 使满; 装满; 充塞: ~ *a hole with sand/a tank with petrol.* 用沙填满一洞(将油箱装满汽油). *Tears ~ed her eyes.* 她眼中充满了眼泪. *I was ~ed with admiration.* 我内心充满了景慕. *The smoke ~ed the room.* 烟弥漫了房间. *Go and ~ this bucket with water for me.* 去替我装满一桶水来. (fill me…句法较不常用). *The hall soon ~ed.* 那大厅不久便装满了人. *The wind ~ed the sails.* 风张满了帆. *The sails ~ed* (= swelled out) *with wind.* 帆被风吹张满. ~ *in,* add what is necessary to make complete: 填好: ~ *in an application form,* write one's name, and other particulars required; 填写申请表; ~ *in an outline,* add details, etc. 加细节于大纲. ~ *out,* (*a*) make or become larger, rounded or fatter: 使膨胀; 鼓起; 膨胀; 变圆: *Her cheeks began to ~ out.* 她的脸开始胖了. **(b)** (esp US) (尤美) = ~ in. ~ *up,* make or become quite full: 填满; 装满: ~ *up with petrol;* 装满汽油; ~ *up a tank.* 装满油箱. *The channel of the river ~ed up with mud.* 河道为泥所淤塞. '~·ing station,* place where petrol, oil, etc is sold to motorists. 加油站. Cf 参较 *service station,* where motor repairs may be done. 附带修理车辆等之加油站. **2** [VP 6A] hold a position and do the necessary work; put (sb) in a position: 任职; 使(某人)任某职: *The vacancy has already been ~ed.* 这空缺已递补了. *He ~s the post satisfactorily,* performs the duties well. 他很尽职. ~ *the bill,* (colloq) meet

one's needs: (口) 适合需要; 满足需要: *These new machines really ~ the bill.* 这些新机器的确适合需要。 **3** [VP6A] execute, carry out an order, etc: 执行 (命令等)。 ~ *a doctor's prescription.* 配方。

fil·let /ˈfɪlɪt; ˈfɪlɪt/ *n* **1** band (often ornamental) worn to keep the hair in place. 束发带 (常为装饰用的)。 **2** slice of fish or meat without bones. (无骨的)鱼片或肉片。 □ *vt* [VP6A] cut (fish) into ~s: 切(鱼)成片: ~ed plaice. 鲽片。

fil·lip /ˈfɪlɪp; ˈfɪləp/ *n* [C] quick, smart blow or stroke given with a finger; (fig) incentive or stimulus: 用指弹落的一弹;(喻)刺激: *an advertising campaign that gave a ~ to sales.* 刺激销路的广告活动。

filly /ˈfɪlɪ; ˈfɪlɪ/ *n* (*pl* **-lies**) female foal. 牝驹。 **colt**[1].

film[1] /fɪlm; fɪlm/ *n* **1** [C] thin coating or covering: 薄的一层; 薄膜: *a ~ of dust;* 一层灰尘; *a ~ of oil on water;* 浮于水面的一层油; *a ~ of mist.* 一层薄雾。 **2** [C, U] roll or sheet of thin flexible material for use in photography: 软片; 胶卷: *a roll* (US 美 = *spool*) *of ~;* 一卷软片; *expose 50 feet of ~;* 使五十英尺软片曝光; *~ stock,* cinema ~ not yet exposed: 未曝光的电影胶片; '~-strip, length of ~ with a number of photographs (of scenes, diagrams, etc) to be shown on a screen separately (not as a motion picture). 幻灯式影片 (摄有风景,图表等,可分别放映, 但非活动电影)。 **3** [C] motion picture. 电影。 **the ~,** the cinema. 电影。 '~ **test,** photographic test of sb who wishes to act for the ~s. (希望演电影者之)试镜头。 '~-**star,** well-known cinema actor or actress. 电影明星。 **filmy** *adj* (**-ier, -iest**) like a ~(1): 似薄膜的: ~*y clouds.* 薄云。

film[2] /fɪlm; fɪlm/ *vt, vi* **1** [VP2A, 6A] make a motion picture (of): (将…)拍电影: ~ *a play.* 将一剧拍成电影。 *They've been filming for six months.* 他们已经拍了六个月的电影。 **2** [VP6A, 2A, C] ~ (*over*), cover, become covered, with a film(1): 覆以薄膜;起一层薄膜: *The mirror ~ed over.* 这镜子变得朦胧了。 **3** [VP2A, C] be well, badly suited for reproduction in a motion picture: 适 (不适) 于拍电影: *She ~ s well.* 她适于拍电影。 ~·**able** /-əbl; -əbl/ *adj* (of a novel, etc) suitable for ~ing. (指小说等)适于拍成电影。

fil·ter /ˈfɪltə(r); ˈfɪltə/ *n* apparatus (containing, eg sand, charcoal, paper, cloth) for holding back solid substances in an impure liquid passed through it; coloured glass (as used on a camera lens) which allows light only of certain wave-lengths to pass through; (radio) device which suppresses signals from unwanted frequencies. 过滤器(含有沙,木炭,纸,布等);滤光镜;(无线电)滤波器。 '~ **tip,** cigarette end containing material that acts as a ~ for smoke. 过滤嘴。 Hence, 由此产生, '~-**tipped** *adj* □ *vt, vi* [VP6A, 14, 15B, 2A, C] **1** (cause to) flow through a ~; purify (a liquid) by using a ~. (使)过滤;滤清。 **2** (fig, of a crowd, road traffic, news, ideas, etc) make a way; pass or flow: (喻, 指群众,车辆,新闻,思想等)通过;透出;渗入: *new ideas ~ing into people's minds.* 渗入人心的新思想。 *The news of the defeat ~ed through.* 战败的消息传出来了。 **3** (of traffic in GB) be allowed to pass or turn to the left when traffic going straight ahead or to the right is held up by a red light. (指英国的车辆)亮红灯禁止前行或右转时, 准许通过或左转。

filth /fɪlθ; fɪlθ/ *n* (口) disgusting dirt; obscenity. 脏脏; 猥亵。 ~**y** *adj* (**-ier, -iest**) disgustingly dirty; vile; obscene; (colloq) very dirty. 脏脏的; 邪恶的; 猥亵的; (口)污秽的。 ~**y rich,** (colloq) very rich. (口)很有钱。 ~·**ily** /-ɪlɪ; -əlɪ/ *adv* ~·**i·ness** *n*

fil·trate /ˈfɪltreɪt; ˈfɪltret/ *vt, vi* = **filter** *v*(1). 过滤。 **fil·tra·tion** /fɪlˈtreɪʃn; -ˈtreʃən/ *n* [U] process of filtrating. 过滤; 滤清。 □ *n* /ˈfɪltret; ˈfɪltret/ ~d liquid. 经过滤的液体。

fin /fɪn; fɪn/ *n* projecting part of a fish used in swimming; thing shaped like or used in the same way as a fin, eg the '*tail-fin* of an aircraft. 鳍; 鱼翅; 鳍状物

(例如飞机的直尾翅)。 ⇨ the illus at **fish, sea.** 参看 fish, sea 之插图。

fi·nal /ˈfaɪnl; ˈfaɪnl/ *adj* **1** coming at the end: 最后的;最后的: *the ~ chapter of a book.* 一本书的最后一章。 **2** putting an end to doubt or argument: 确定的; 决定的: *a ~ decision / judgement.* 确定性的决定(判决)。 □ *n* **1** (often *pl*) last of a series of examinations or contests: (常用复数)最后考试;决赛: *the law ~*(*s*); 律师业的最后考试; *take one's ~s*; 参加最后考试(决赛); *the tennis ~s,* at the end of a tournament; 网球决赛; *the Cup F~,* last football match in a series. 足球杯决赛。 **2** (colloq) edition of a newspaper published latest in the day: (口)报纸每日最后发行的一版: '*Late night ~.* 夜晚最后版。 ~·**ist** /-nəlɪst; -nlɪst/ *n* **1** player who takes part in the last of a series of contests. 决赛选手; 获决赛权者。 **2** undergraduate in his ~ year. 大学四年级学生。 ~·**ly** /-nəlɪ; -nlɪ/ *adv* **1** lastly; in conclusion. 最后地; 最后一点。 **2** once and for all: 只此一次: *settle a matter ~ly.* 彻底解决一事。

fi·nale /fɪˈnɑːlɪ US: -ˈnælɪ; fɪˈnɑlɪ/ *n* (music) last movement of an instrumental composition, eg a symphony; closing scene of an opera; end. (音乐)(交响曲等的)最后乐章; 终曲; (歌剧之)终场; 结尾。

fi·nal·ity /faɪˈnælətɪ; faɪˈnælətɪ/ *n* [U] state or quality of being final: 最后; 确定性; 决定性: *speak with an air of ~,* giving the impression that there is nothing more to be said or done. 斩钉截铁地说。

fi·nal·ize /ˈfaɪnəlaɪz; ˈfaɪnl̩aɪz/ *vt* [VP6A] give a final form to. 予以最终形式;使定案。

fi·nance /ˈfaɪnæns US: fɪˈnæns; fəˈnæns/ *n* **1** [U] (science) of the management of (esp public) money: 财政; 财政学: *an expert in ~;* 财政专家; *the Minister of F~* (in GB called 英称作 *the Chancellor of the Exchequer*). 财政部长。 '~ **house / company,** one that provides ~ for hire-purchase facilities. 金融机构; 金融公司 (贷款给分期付款购物者)。 **2** (*pl*) money (esp of a government or a business company): (复)(尤指政府或公司的)财源; 资金: *Are the country's ~s sound?* 这国家的财源殷实吗? □ *vt* [VP6A] provide money for (a scheme, etc). 供(计划等)以经费。

fi·nan·cial /faɪˈnænʃl US: fɪˈnæ-; fəˈnænʃəl/ *adj* of finance: 财政的; 金融的: *in ~ difficulties,* short of money; 财政拮据; *a ~ centre,* eg London or New York. 金融中心 (例如伦敦或纽约)。 *the ~ year,* the annual period for which accounts are made up. 会计年度。 **fi·nan·cially** /-ʃəlɪ; -ʃəlɪ/ *adv*

fin·an·cier /faɪˈnænsɪə(r) US: ˈfɪnənˈsɪər; ˌfɪnənˈsɪr/ *n* person skilled in finance; capitalist. 财政家; 资本家。

finch /fɪntʃ; fɪntʃ/ *n* kinds of small bird (usu with a distinctive epithet or prefix, as '*chaf~,* '*green~,* '*bull~*). 雀类 (通常与表示区别的形容词或前缀连用, 如 '*chaf~,* '*green~,* '*bull~*)。

find[1] /faɪnd; faɪnd/ *n* [C] finding; sth found, esp sth valuable or pleasing: 发现物 (尤指贵重或悦人的); *I made a great ~ in a second-hand bookshop yesterday,* found a rare or valuable old book. 昨天我在一旧书店里发现一本珍贵的旧书。

find[2] /faɪnd; faɪnd/ *vt* (*pt, pp* **found** /faʊnd; faʊnd/) **1** [VP6A, 12B, 13B] get back, after a search, (sth/sb lost, left behind, forgotten, etc): 寻得; 找到; 寻获: *Did you ever ~ that pen you lost?* 你找到你遗失的那支钢笔没有? *Please help Mary to ~ her bag.* 请帮助玛丽找她的提包。 *Please ~ Mary her bag / ~ Mary's bag for her.* 请替玛丽找她的提包。 *The missing child has not been found yet.* 那走失的孩子尚未找回。 ~ **one's place** (in a book, etc), turn to the page where one wishes to continue reading etc. 翻至(书等)要继续读下去的地方。 ~ **one's voice / tongue,** be able to speak (after being silent because of shyness, etc). (因害羞等而沉默之后)说得出话来了。 **2** [VP6A, 12B, 8, 13A, B, 15A, B] get or discover (sth / sb not lost, forgotten, etc) after search, experience or effort: 发现; 找到: ~ *a cure /*

remedy (for sth); 发现治疗(补救)方法; ⇨ *a solution/ an answer (to a problem)*; 发现(一问题的)解答(答案); ~ *(the) time to do sth.* 找到时间做事. *They dug five metres and then found water.* 他们掘了五米便发现了水. *I can ~ nothing new to say on this subject.* 关于此一问题我没有什么新的资料来讨论. *Did you ~ him what he wanted?* 你找到他要的东西了吗? *They couldn't ~ the way in/out/back.* 他们找不到路进去(出去, 回来). *Where will they ~ money for the journey?* 他们到哪里去找这笔旅费? **~ favour with sb,** ⇨ **favour¹(1). ~ fault (with),** ⇨ **fault. ~ one's feet, (a)** be able to stand and walk, eg as a baby does: 能站立和行走(例如婴儿): *How old was the baby when it began to ~ its feet?* 这婴儿开始能站立和行走的时候有多大? **(b)** become able to act independently, without the help and guidance of others. 能独立行动. **~ oneself,** discover one's vocation; learn one's powers and abilities and how to use them. 发现自己适于某种职业; 发现自己的能力并知如何去利用. ⇨ also **5** below. 亦参看下列第5义。 **~ it in one's heart/oneself to do sth,** (chiefly neg and interr with *can/could*) be so unkind or callous as to: (主要用于否定和疑问句, 与 can 和 could 连用) 忍心: *How can you ~ it in your heart to drown these little kittens?* 你怎会忍心把这些小猫淹死? **3** [VP6A, 15 A, B] arrive at naturally: 自然到达; 偶然变成: *Rivers ~ their way to the sea.* 诸河皆流入海. *Water always ~s its own level.* 水总会自然成为平面. **4** [VP6A, 19B, 22, 15A] discover by chance; come across: 偶然发现; 撞见; 碰见: *He was found dying/dead/injured at the foot of a cliff.* 他被人发现在一悬崖的脚下快要死(死去, 受伤)了. *I found him in the cellar drinking my best brandy.* 我撞见他在地窖里喝我最好的白兰地. **5** [VP 9, 15A, 22, 25] become informed or aware of, by experience or trial: (由经验或试验) 发觉; 知道, 觉得: *We found the beds quite comfortable.* 我们觉得那些床很舒服. *We found him (to be) dishonest/found he was dishonest.* 我们发现他不诚实. *They found him to be the right man for the job.* 他们觉得他是最适合这工作的人. *Do you ~ that honesty pays/that it pays to be honest?* 你知道诚实不吃亏吗? *I never ~ the best too good for me.* 我从不认为太好的东西是我最高境界. *You must take us as you ~ us,* accept us as we are, not expect special treatment or ceremony. 我们就是这个样子, 你必须容忍迁就(不要指望受到特殊的待遇或礼遇). *I ~ it difficult to understand him/ ~ him difficult to understand.* 我觉得难以了解他. *I called at Smith's this morning and found him still in bed.* 我今晨去史密斯家, 发现他仍未起床. *I was disappointed to ~ her out* (ie not at home) *when I called.* 我去拜访她时没觉她不在家, 颇感失望. **~ oneself +adj/adv,** discover, realize, that one is: 发觉自己在…; 发觉自己是…: *When he regained consciousness, he found himself in hospital,* eg after a motor accident. 他恢复知觉后, 发觉自己躺在医院里(例如在一车祸发生后). *How do you ~ yourself this morning, How are you feeling?* 你今晨好吗? *He found himself alone with a strange woman.* 他发觉自己跟一个陌生的女人单独在一起. **6** [VP 6A, 15B, 8, 10] **~ (out),** learn by study, calculation, inquiry: (由研究, 计算, 探询) 发现; 探知; 探知: *What do you ~ the total?* 你得到的总数是多少? *Please ~ out when the train starts/whether there is an express train/how to get there.* 请查看一下火车何时开车(有无快车, 如何到达该处). **~ sb out,** detect sb in wrongdoing or error: 查出某人做坏事或犯错: *Do you think the police will ~ us out?* 你看警察会逮到我们吗? **7** [VP 15A] (equivalent to a construction with *there is/are,* etc with no suggestion of discovery or inquiry, the subject being *one* or *you):* 有 (等于 *there is/are* 等, 无发现或任询的含义; 主词为 one 或 you): *One doesn't/You don't ~* (= There isn't) *much vegetation in this area.* 这一地区没有什么植物。 *Pine-trees are found* (= There are pinetrees) *in most European countries.* 大多数欧洲国家内有松树. [VP 6A, 15A] supply, furnish; provide: 供给; 供应:

Who will ~ the money for the expedition? 谁负担这探险的费用? **~ sb/oneself in,** provide with: 供应: *He pays his housekeeper £25 a week and she ~s herself in clothes,* buys them herself, from her wages. 他付给他管家的工资为每周二十五英镑, 服装费由她自己出. **all found,** everything provided: 一切都供给: *Wanted, a good cook, £100 a month and all found,* board, lodging, etc provided free in addition to wages. 兹征求良厨一名: 月薪一百英镑, 供膳食等. **9** [VP 22, 25, 9] (legal) determine and declare; give as a verdict: (法律) 判定; 判决: *How do you ~ the accused?* 你如何判决被告? *The jury found the accused man guilty.* 陪审团认定被告有罪. *They found ~ (= the offence) manslaughter.* 他们判定该项犯罪为过失杀人. **~ for,** (elliptical use) decide in favour of: (省略用法) 判决有利于…之判决: ~ *for the defendant/plaintiff.* 做有利于被告(原告)之判决. **~er** n **1** person who ~s sth: 寻得者; 发现者: *Lost, a diamond ring: ~er will be rewarded.* 兹遗失钻戒一枚: 寻得者将获重酬. **2** device in a camera *('view-~er)* or telescope used to ~ the object to be photographed, examined, etc. (照相机上的)取景器(亦作 viewfinder); (望远镜上的)指导镜; 寻星镜. **~·ing** n (usu pl) (通常用复数) **1** what has been learnt as the result of inquiry: 调查的结果; 发现物: *the ~ings of the Commission.* 调查团的调查结果. **2** what is determined by a jury, etc. (陪审团等的)判决.

fine¹ /faɪn; faɪn/ n [C] sum of money (to be) paid as a penalty for breaking a law or rule. 罚金; 罚款. □ vt [VP6A, 14] **~ (for),** punish by a ~: 处以罚金: ~ *sb for an offence;* 为一犯法行为而处某人以罚金; ~ *sb £5.* 罚某人五英镑. **~·able** (also **finable**) /'faɪnəbl; 'faɪnəbl/ *adj* liable to a ~. 应罚款的; 可罚款的.

fine² /faɪn; faɪn/ n (only in) (仅用于) **in ~,** (old use) in short, finally, to sum up. (旧用法)总之, 最后.

fine³ /faɪn; faɪn/ *adj* (-r, -st) **1** (of weather) bright; clear; not raining: (指天气)晴朗的; 无云的; 不下雨的: *It rained all morning, but turned ~ later.* 一早上都在下雨, 但后来转晴了. **one ~ day,** (in story-telling) one day past or future. (讲故事时)有一天; 某日. **one of these ~ days,** at some (vague) time in the future. 改天; 将来. **2** enjoyable; pleasing; splendid: 可爱的; 悦人的; 美好的: *a ~ view;* 美丽的景色; *have a ~ time;* 有一段快乐的时间; 玩得痛快; ~ *clothes.* 漂亮的衣服. *She has grown up to be a ~ young lady.* 她已长成为美丽的少女. *That's a ~ excuse,* (ironic) a very poor excuse. (反语)那倒是个好借口. *She thinks herself a ~ lady,* considers herself a lady of fashion, too superior to do housework, etc. 她自命为上流社会妇女, 不过该做家务事等. **3** delicate; carefully made and easily injured: 纤细的; 精巧的: ~ *workmanship;* 精巧的手工; ~ *silk.* 细绸. **4** of very small particles: 微小的; ~ *dust.* 微尘. *Sand is ~r than gravel.* 沙比碎石微小. **5** slender; thin; sharp: 细的; 锐利的: ~ *thread;* 细线; *a pencil with a ~ point.* 笔尖尖的铅笔. **not to put too ~ a point on it,** to express it plainly. 明白表达; 直截了当地说. **~ tooth comb** ⇨ **tooth(2). 6** (of metals) refined; pure: (指金属)精制的; 纯的: ~ *gold;* 纯金; *gold 18 carats ~,* with 18 parts of pure gold and 6 of alloy. 十八开金. **7** (to be) seen only with difficulty or effort: 难以辨识的; 精微的: *a ~ distinction;* 精微的区别; capable of delicate perception, able to make delicate distinctions: 能作精微辨识的: *a ~ sense of humour;* 善于领会幽默; *a ~ taste in art.* 对美术的精微鉴赏力. **the ~ arts;** ~ **art,** the visual arts that appeal to the sense of beauty, esp painting and sculpture. 美术(尤指绘画和雕刻). **8** (of speech or writing) too ornate; insincerely complimentary: (指演说或写作)过份激刺的: 华而不实的. **call sth/sb by ~ names,** (a) (of sth) use euphemisms about sth. 委婉地叙述某事物. **(b)** (of sb) flatter him. 奉承某人; 恭维某人. **9** in good health: 健康的: *I'm feeling ~.* 我很好. **~·ly** *adv* **1** splendidly:

美好地; 华丽地; ~*ly dressed.* 衣着华丽。 **2** into small particles or pieces: 微小地; 细微地: *carrots ~ly chopped up.* 切碎的红萝卜。 ~**·ness** *n*

fine⁴ /faɪn; faɪn/ *adj* **1** (colloq) very well: (口) 很好; *That will suit me ~.* 那很适合我。 **2** (in compounds) (用于复合词中) ~*'-drawn,* subtle; 精细的; ~*'-spoken,* insincerely complimentary: 假意奉承的; ~*'-spun,* delicate. 纤细的。 **3** cut it ~, ⇨ cut¹(7).

fin·er·y /'faɪnərɪ; 'faɪnərɪ/ *n* [U] gay and elegant dress or appearance: 华丽的服装; 优雅的外表: *young men in their Saturday night ~,* smart clothes; 穿着漂亮衣服的年轻男士们; *the garden in its summer ~,* with its brightly coloured flowers, green lawns, etc. 妍丽的夏季花园。

fi·nesse /fɪ'nes; fə'nɛs/ *n* [U] artful or delicate way of dealing with a situation: (应付某一情况的) 技巧; 手段: *show ~ in dealing with people,* 表现应付人的手腕; [C] (cards) attempt to win using ~. (纸牌戏) 以技巧得分。

fin·ger /'fɪŋɡə(r); 'fɪŋɡɚ/ *n* one of the five members ('little ~, 'ring ~, 'middle ~, 'index or 'fore~, thumb) at the end of the hand. 手指(小指称称 little finger, 无名指称 ring finger, 中指称 middle finger, 食指称 index 或 forefinger, 大拇指称 thumb)。 ⇨ the illus at **arm**. 参看 arm 之插图。 *There are five ~s (of four ~s and one thumb) on each hand.* 每只手有五个手指(四个手指和一个大拇指)。 *sb's ~s are all thumbs,* he is very clumsy. 某人很笨拙。 ⇨ **thumb.** *burn one's ~s,* suffer because of incautious or meddlesome behaviour, etc. 因不谨慎或管闲事等而吃亏。 *have a ~ in every/the pie,* ⇨ **pie.** *keep one's ~s crossed,* ⇨ **cross²(3).** *lay a ~ on,* touch (however slightly): 触 (不论多么轻微): *I forbid you to lay a ~ on the boy,* to punish him by hitting him, etc. 我不许你碰那孩子。 *lay/put one's ~ on,* point out precisely (where sth is wrong, the cause of a problem). 正确指出(错处,症结之所在)。 *not lift a ~ (to help sb),* do nothing to help when help is needed. 一点也不帮忙。 *put the ~ on sb,* (sl) inform against (a criminal). (俚) 告发 (犯人)。 *slip through one's ~s,* ⇨ **slip²(3).** *twist sb round one's (little) ~,* cajole him; dominate him. 笼络某人; 玩弄某人于股掌之上。 '~**-alphabet** *n* method (using the ~s in various ways) for talking with the deaf. 指语法; 手势语 (与聋人交谈用者)。 '~**-board,** wood (on a guitar, violin, etc) where the strings are held against the neck with the ~s. (吉他、小提琴等颈部之) 指板。 '~**-bowl** *n* one for rinsing the ~s at meals. (吃饭时用的) 洗指钵。 '~**-mark** *n* mark, eg on a wall, made by a dirty ~. 指痕。 '~**-nail** *n* nail at the top of the ~. 指甲。 '~**-plate** *n* one fastened on a door near the handle or key-hole to prevent ~-marks. 门上把手或锁眼附近防指污的板。 '~**-post** *n* signpost giving directions with boards shaped like ~s. 指标; 路路牌。 '~**-print** *n* mark made by ~s when pressed on a surface, used for identifying criminals. ⇨ the illus at **whorl.** 指纹。 参看 whorl 之插图。 '~**-stall** *n* protective cover (worn over an injured ~). (用以保护受伤手指的) 指套。 '~**-tip,** top of a ~. 指尖。 *have sth at one's ~tips,* be thoroughly familiar with it. 熟悉某事物。 □ *vt* [VP6A] touch with the ~s: 以指触摸: *~ a piece of cloth,* touch, feel, it (to test its quality). 用指摸一块布(以试其质量)。

fini·cal /'fɪnɪkl; 'fɪnɪkl/ *adj* too fussy or fastidious about food, clothing. etc. 过份讲究饮食衣着等的; 对衣食苛求的。

fin·icky /'fɪnɪkɪ; 'fɪnɪkɪ/ *adj* = finical.

fi·nis /'fɪnɪs; 'faɪnɪs/ *n* (*sing* only) (Lat) (at the end of a book) the end. (仅用单数)(拉)(用于书尾)完; 结束; 终结。

fin·ish /'fɪnɪʃ; 'fɪnɪʃ/ *vt, vi* **1** [VP6A, C, 2A, C, 15B, 3A] bring or come to an end; complete: 完成…; 结束…; *reading a book.* 读完一书。 *Have you ~ed that book yet,* read it to the end? 你读完

那本书没有? *Term ~es next week.* 学期下星期结束。 *We have ~ed the pie,* eaten all of it. 我们已吃完水果饼。 *That long climb almost ~ed me,* (colloq) almost caused my death. (口) 爬那么久几乎把我累死了。 **~ sb off,** (sl) kill, destroy, him. (俚)杀死某人; 毁掉某人。 *That fever nearly ~ed him off.* 那次发烧几乎使他送命。 **~ sth off/up,** eat up completely: 吃光; *We ~ed up everything on the table.* 我们把桌上的东西全吃光了。 **(~ up) with sth,** have at the end: 最后以…结束: *We had an excellent dinner, and ~ed up with a glass of brandy.* 我们吃了一顿盛餐,最后喝了一杯白兰地。 **~ with sb/sth,** no longer be engaged with sb or busy with sth: 与某人断绝关系; 不再忙于某事物: *I haven't ~ed with you yet,* still have sth to say. 我还有话要跟你说。 *Have you ~ed with that dictionary?* 那部词典你用完了没有? **2** [VP6A] make complete or perfect; polish: 使完美; 润饰: *The woodwork is beautifully ~ed,* smoothed and polished. 那件木器漆得很精美。 *They gave a ~ed performance of the quartet.* 他们做了一次完美的四重奏表演。 *He gave the picture a few ~ing touches.* 他将那幅画润饰了一番。 '~**ing school,** private school preparing girls for social life. 女子精修学校(为准备女子进入社会的私立学校)。 □ *n* (*sing* only) (仅用单数) **1** last part: 最终部分; 终结; 收场: *the ~ of a race.* 竞赛的结尾。 *It was a close ~,* The competitors were close together at the ~. 那是一场结束时很紧张的竞赛。 **be in at the ~,** be present when the fox is killed at the end of the hunt; (fig) be present during the last stage (of a struggle, etc). (狩猎时) 狐狸最后被射死时在场; (喻) 目睹 (战斗等的) 最后一幕。 *a fight to the ~,* until one side is defeated or exhausted. 打到底; 拚出胜负。 **2** [C, U] the state of being ~ed or perfect; the manner in which sth is ~ed: 完美; 润饰过的状态: *woodwork with a smooth ~.* 漆得精美的木器。 *His manners lack ~.* 他的仪态欠优雅。

fi·nite /'faɪnaɪt; 'faɪnaɪt/ *adj* **1** limited; having bounds: 有限度的; 有限度的: *Human understanding is ~,* There are things that man cannot understand. 人类的理解力是有限的。 **2** (gram) agreeing with a subject in number and person: (语法) 限定的 (受数和人称限制的): *'Am', 'is', 'are', 'was', and 'were' are the ~ forms of 'be'; and 'be', 'being' and 'been' are the non-~ forms,* Am, is, are, was and were 是 be 的限定形式; be, being and been 是非限定形式。

Finn /fɪn; fɪn/ *n* native of Finland. 芬兰人。 ~**·ish** *adj, n* (language) of the ~s. 芬兰人的; 芬兰的; 芬兰语。

finnan /'fɪnən; 'fɪnən/ *n* (also 亦作, ~ '**haddock/haddie** /'hædɪ; 'hædɪ/) (kind of) smoked haddock. 熏鳕鱼。

fiord, fjord /fɪ'ɔːd; fjɔrd/ *n* long, narrow arm of the sea, between high cliffs (as in Norway). 峭壁间的狭长海湾; 峡湾(例如在挪威者)。

fir /fɜː(r); fɜ/ *n* conifer with needle-like leaves, ⇨ the illus at **tree;** [U] wood of this tree. 冷杉 (参看 tree 之插图) 枞木。 '**fir-cone** *n*

fire¹ /'faɪə(r); faɪr/ *n* **1** [U] condition of burning: 火: *F~ burns.* 火燃烧。 *There is no smoke without ~,* (prov) There is always some reason for a rumour. (谚) 无火不起烟; 无风不起浪。 *on ~,* burning: 着火; 失火: *The house was on ~.* 这房屋失火了。 *play with ~,* take foolish risks. 玩火。 *set sth on ~; set ~ to sth,* cause it to begin burning: 放火; 焚烧; 纵火: *He set the haystack on ~.* 他将那干草堆燃着。 *not (ever)/never set the 'Thames on ~,* not do anything remarkable: 勿做惊人之举; *Tom's not the sort of boy who will ever set the Thames on ~,* distinguish himself. 汤姆不是那种会做出惊人之举的孩子。 *take/catch ~,* begin to burn: 着火; 开始燃烧: *Paper catches ~ easily.* 纸易着火。 *strike ~ from,* get sparks from (by striking or rubbing): 由…打火; 擦火: *strike ~ from flint.* 由燧石打火。 **2** [U] destructive burning: 火灾: *Have you insured your house against ~?* 你的房子保过火险没有? **~ and sword,**

burning and killing (in war). (战时) 杀人放火。'~ **risk(s)**, possible or likely cause(s) of ~. 可能造成火灾的原因。**3** [C] instance of destructive burning: 火灾的实例: *forest* ~s; 森林火灾; *a* ~ *in a coal-mine.* 煤矿火灾。**4** [C] burning fuel in a grate, furnace, etc to heat a room, building, for cooking, etc: 炉火: *The weather is too warm for* ~s. 天气很暖和, 不需要生炉火。*There's a* ~ *in the next room.* 隔壁房间有炉火。*lay a* ~, put paper, wood, coal, etc together ready for use. 堆起燃料以备生火。*make a* ~, lay a ~ and light it. 生火。*make up a* ~, add fuel as it burns low. 加燃料于火。*electric* ~, heater using an incandescent element(7). 电暖气炉。**'gas** ~, heater using lighted gas(2). 瓦斯炉。**5** [U] shooting (from guns). 炮火。*between two* ~s, shot at from two directions. 在两面炮火夹攻下。*hang* ~, ⇨ hang²(4). *open/cease* ~, start/stop shooting. 开(停)火。*under* ~, being shot at. 在炮火下。*running* ~, **(a)** a succession of shots from a line of troops. (一列士兵之)炮火连发。**(b)** (fig) succession of criticisms, hostile questions, etc. (喻) 一连串的批评, 责难等。**6** [U] strong emotion; angry or excited feeling; enthusiasm: 热情; 愤怒; 兴奋; 热心: *a speech that lacks* ~, is uninspiring; 缺少热情的演说; *eyes full of* ~. 充满热情(愤恨)的眼睛。**7** (compounds) (复合词) **'~-alarm** *n* apparatus (bell, etc) for making known the outbreak of a ~. 火警警报器。**'~-arm** *n* (usu *pl*) rifle, gun, pistol or revolver. (通常用复数)轻武器; 枪炮。**'~-ball** *n* (esp) centre of an exploding atomic bomb. 火球; (尤指)原子弹的爆炸中心。**'~-bird** *n* N American bird with orange and black plumage. 金鹩鸟(北美所产, 有橙黄色和黑色羽毛)。**'~-bomb** *n* one that burns fiercely and causes destruction by ~. 烧夷弹;燃烧弹。⇨ napalm. **'~-box** *n* fuel-chamber of a steam-engine. 蒸汽机之燃烧室;火箱。**'~-brand** *n* piece of burning wood; (fig) person who stirs up social or political strife. 燃烧的木柴; (喻) 煽动社会或政治叛乱者。**'~-break** *n* **(a)** (in a forest) wide strip of land without trees (to lessen the risk of a forest ~ spreading). 防火线(森林中一片无树木的宽长地, 以防火灾蔓延)。**(b)** wall or barrier of incombustible material in a warehouse, factory, etc. (仓库, 工厂等中之)防火墙。**'~-brick** *n* kind of brick, proof against ~, used in grates, furnaces, chimneys, etc. 耐火砖。**'~-brigade** *n* organized team of men who put out ~s. 消防队; 救火队。**'~-bug** *n* (sl) person who commits arson. (俚)纵火犯。**'~-clay** *n* [U] kind used for ~-bricks. 耐火粘土(制耐火砖用)。**'~-control** *n* [U] system of regulating the firing of guns. 射击控制 (调整射击之系统)。**'~-cracker** *n* small ~-work that explodes with a cracking noise. 爆竹; 鞭炮。**'~-damp** *n* [U] gas in coal-mines, explosive when mixed in certain proportions with air. (煤矿坑内之)沼气; 甲烷。**'~-dog** *n* andiron. (炉之)薪架。**'~-drill** *n* practice of routine to be followed when ~ breaks out, eg on a ship. 消防演习; 救火演习(例如船上举行者)。**'~-eater** *n* person who quickly gets angry and ready to fight. 性情暴躁而好斗之人。**'~-engine** *n* machine, manned by ~men, for throwing water on to a ~. 救火车。**'~-escape** *n* outside staircase by means of which people may leave a burning building; apparatus, kind of extending ladder, used by ~men to save people from a burning building. 太平梯; 救火队员所用的救火梯。**'~-extinguisher** *n* portable metal cylinder with chemical substance, etc, inside, for putting out a small ~. 灭火器。**'~-fighter** *n* = ~man(b); (esp) man who fights forest ~s. 消防队员 (尤指救森林火灾者)。**'~-fly** *n* (*pl* **-flies**) winged beetle that sends out phosphorescent light. 萤火虫。**'~-guard** *n* protective metal framework or grating round a ~ in a room. 炉栏。**'~-hose** *n* hose-pipe used for extinguishing ~s. 水龙带。**'~-irons** *n pl* poker, tongs, shovel, etc (kept near a ~place). 火炉用具(拨火棒, 火钳, 火铲等)。**'~-light** *n* light from the ~ in a ~place: 炉火之火光:

sitting in the ~light. 围炉而坐。**'~-lighter** *n* piece or bundle of fuel for kindling a ~(4). 火种;引火物。**'~-man** /-mən; -mən/ *n* (*pl* -men) **(a)** man who looks after the ~ in a furnace or steam-engine. (管理炉火或蒸汽机的)火夫;司炉。**(b)** member of a ~-brigade, 消防队员;救火员。**'~-place** *n* grate or hearth for a ~ in a room, usu of brick or stone in the wall. 壁炉。**'~-plug** *n* connection in a water-main for a ~-hose. 消防栓。**'~-power** *n* [U] capacity to fire(6), expressed as the total number and weight of shells fired per minute: 火力; 火量(以每分钟射出的炮弹总数和重量计算): *the ~-power of a cruiser.* 巡洋舰的火力。**'~-proof** *adj* that does not burn; that does not crack or break when heated. 耐火的; 防火的。**'~-raising** *n* [U] arson. 纵火。**'F~ Service**, (now the official term for) ~-brigade(s). 救火队;消防队(现为正式名称)。**'~-side** *the ~side*, part of a room round the ~place: 炉边: *sitting at the ~side;* 坐在炉边; (fig) home life; (喻)家庭生活; (attrib) (用作定语) *a ~side chair;* 炉边之椅; *a homely ~side scene.* 家常的炉边情景。**'~-station** *n* building for a ~-brigade and its equipment. 消防队驻所。**'~-stone** *n* ~-proof stone (in a ~place, etc). 炉石(壁炉之防火石)。**'~-walking** *n* [U] ceremony of walking barefoot over stones heated by ~, or over white-hot wood-ash, etc. 渡火(赤足在灼热的石上或炭灰等上行走的一种仪式)。Hence, 由此产生, **'~-walker** *n*. **'~-watcher** *n* (in World War II) person whose duty was to watch for ~s started by bombs dropped from the air. (二次世界大战时)空袭失火警戒员。Hence, 由此产生, **'~-watching** *n* [U]. **'~-water** *n* (colloq) spirits such as whisky, gin and rum. (口) 烈酒(如威士忌; 杜松子酒和朗姆酒)。**'~-wood** *n* wood prepared for lighting ~s or as fuel. 柴; 薪。**'~-work** *n* [C] device containing gunpowder and chemicals, used for making a display at night, or as a signal; (*pl*) (fig) display of wit, anger, etc. 烟火; (复)(喻)机智, 愤怒等的表现。

a firework display

fire² /'faɪə(r); faɪr/ *vt, vi* **1** [VP6A] set fire to with the intention of destroying; cause to being burning: 纵火烧; 使燃烧; 点燃: ~ *a haystack.* 点燃一干草堆。**2** [VP6A] use artificial heat on sth in order to change it in some way: 加热使改变: (= bake) *bricks/ pottery in a kiln;* 于窑内烧砖(陶); ~ *tea,* cure it, make green leaves dry and dark. 焙茶。**3** [VP6A] supply (a furnace) with fuel: 加燃料于(炉): *an oil~d furnace.* 油炉。**4** ~ *up,* (of a person) (more usu *flare up*) become excited or angry; (指人, flare up 较常用)激动;光火;恼怒: *She ~s up at the least thing.* 她会为了小事发怒。**5** [VP6A] excite or stimulate. 刺激; 激起。~ *sb with sth,* fill with enthusiasm, zeal. 激发某人的热忱。**6** [VP6A] discharge (a gun, etc); send (a shell, etc) from a gun; explode (a charge of explosive): 放(枪炮等);射出(炮弹,子弹等);使(炸药)爆发: ~ *a gun.* 开炮。*They ~d a salute,* discharged guns as a salute. 他们鸣放礼炮。[VP2A] shoot: 射击;放枪或开炮: *The officer ordered his men to* ~. 那军官下令他的士兵开枪。*at/into/on/upon,* [VP3A] direct fire towards: 对…射击: ~ *at a target;* 对目标射击; ~ *upon a fort/ ship.* 对一堡垒(船只)开炮。*The police ~d into the crowd.*

警察向群众鸣枪。 **~ away**, [VP2C] **(a)** continue firing: 继续开枪;继续发炮: *They were firing away at the enemy.* 他们对敌人继续开枪。 **(b)** (fig) go ahead; begin: (喻) 继续;下去;开始: *I'm ready to answer questions;* ~ *away.* 我准备回答复问题,请问吧。 [VP15B] *They ~d away all their ammunition*, expended it all. 他们将所有的弹药都打完了。 **'firing-line** *n* front line (of trenches) where soldiers ~ at the enemy. 火线;射击线。 **'firing-party/ -squad** *n* number of soldiers ordered to ~ volleys at a military funeral or to carry out a military execution. 鸣枪礼葬(丧礼时鸣放礼枪的一队士兵);行刑班(执行死刑的射击队)。 **7** [VP6A] (colloq) dismiss (an employee): (口) 辞退: *the manager for being incompetent.* 因经理无能而将之辞退。

fir·kin /'fɜːkɪn; 'fɝkɪn/ *n* small cask. 小桶。

firm[1] /fɜːm; fɝm/ *adj* (**-er, -est**) **1** solid; hard; not yielding when pressed: 坚固的;坚硬的;坚实的: *flesh/muscles;* 坚实的肉; ~ *ground*, 陆地; *as ~ as a rock.* 固若磐石。 **be on ~ ground**, be sure of one's facts. 立于稳固的基础上。 **2** not easily changed or influenced; showing strength of character and purpose: 不易改变或受影响的;坚强的;坚决的: *a ~ faith*, 坚定的信心; *take ~ measures*, 采取坚决步骤; *be ~ with children*, insist upon obedience and discipline; 对孩子们严厉; ~ *in/of purpose*, 意志坚定; *be ~ in one's beliefs.* 信仰坚定。 **3** (of a person, his body, its movements, characteristics, etc) steady, stable: (指人、人的身体、动作、特点等的) 稳固的;沉着的;稳定的: *walk with ~ steps.* 以稳定的步伐行走。 *The baby is not very ~ on its feet yet*, does not stand or walk confidently. 这婴儿还站(走)不很稳。 *He spoke in a ~ voice.* 他以沉着的声音说话。 *He gave me a ~ glance.* 他坚定地望了我一眼。 □ *vt, vi* make or become ~. 使坚固;使坚定;使(变坚固)变坚定;变坚定。 □ *adv in a ~ way*: 稳固地;坚定地: *stand ~* (lit or fig); (字面或喻)站稳; *hold ~ to one's beliefs.* 坚守信仰。 **~·ly** *adv* in a ~ way. 稳固地;坚定地。 **~·ness** *n*

firm[2] /fɜːm; fɝm/ *n* [C] (two or more) persons carrying on a business. 商号;公司;商行;厂商。

fir·ma·ment /'fɜːməmənt; 'fɝməmənt/ *n* **the ~**, the sky, thought of as containing the stars, planets, moon and sun. 苍天;天空(包括日月星辰)。

first[1] /fɜːst; fɝst/ *adj* **1** (abbr 略作 **1st**) coming before all others in time or order: 第一的;最早的;最先的: *January, the ~ month of the year;* 一月,一年的第一个月; *the ~ chapter (or Chapter One);* 第一章; *King Edward the F~* (often 常作 King Edward I); 英王爱德华一世; *a ~ edition copy of a book;* 一本书的初版; *the ~ man who arrived/the ~ man to arrive;* 最先到达的那人; *at the ~ (= earliest) opportunity;* 一有机会; ~ *(= basic) principles.* 基本的原理。 **at ~ sight**, when seen or examined for the first time: 一见之下;乍看来: *fall in love at ~ sight.* 一见钟情。 *At ~ sight the problem seemed easy.* 这问题乍看起来很容易。 **in the '~ place**, (in making a list) as a beginning; 首先;第一; ~·ly. 首先; *do sth ~ thing*, as a ~ action; before doing anything else: 第一件事;首先做的事: ~ *thing tomorrow morning.* 明天早上首先要做的事。 **the ~ things ~**, the most important things before the others. 最重要的事优先;要事第一。 **not to know the ~ thing about sth**, to know nothing whatsoever about it. 对某事丝毫不知情。 **2** (special uses, compounds): (特殊用法,复合词): ~ **'aid** *n* [U] treatment given at once to a sick or injured person before a doctor comes. (医生未来之前对伤患所做的)急救。 ~ **'base** *n* (baseball) ~ base[1](6) on the field. (棒球)一垒。 **get to ~ base**, (fig) make a successful start. (喻)有一个成功的开始。 ~ **'class** *n* best accommodation in a train, ship, aircraft, etc. (火车的)头等车;(轮船,飞机等的)头等舱。 ⇒ class(1). ~·**'class** *adj* of the best; excellent; 头等的;头等车的;头等舱的;最好的: ~-*class hotels/cabins/passengers;* 头等旅馆(舱,乘客); *a ~-class* (university) *degree;* 优等学位;

~-*class food/entertainment.* 最好的食物(款待)。 □ *adv* by the ~ class: 乘头等车,船,飞机等: *travel*, ~-'*class.* 乘头等车或舱位旅行。 ~ **'cost** *n* (comm) cost not including profit. (商)最初成本。 ~ **de·gree**, ⇒ **de·gree.** ~ **'floor** *n* (GB) floor immediately above the ground floor; (US) ground floor. (英)二楼; (美)一楼;底层。 ~ **form** *n* (GB) lowest class in secondary schools. (英)中学一年级。 ~-**fruits** *n pl* earliest produce (crops, etc) of the season; (fig) ~ results of one's work. 一季中最早的收成;最初收的收益;最早的产品。 ~ **'gear**, lowest gear(1). 头档。 ~·**'hand** *adj, adv* (obtained) directly from the source: 从发源处直接获得; 第一手的(地); ~-*hand information*, 直接得来的消息;第一手资料; *learn something* ~-*hand*. 直接获知某事。 **at ~ hand**, directly. 直接地。 ~ **'lady** *n* (US) wife of a President or a Governor of a State. (美)总统夫人;州长夫人。 '~ **name** *n* given name (contrasted with family name): 教名; 名(以别于姓): *be on ~ name terms with the boss* (suggesting informality). 可与老板互相直呼其名(表示不拘束)。 ~ **'night** *n* evening on which a play or opera is presented for the ~ time. (戏剧或歌剧之)首演之夜。 Hence, 由此产生, ~-'**nighter**, person who regularly attends ~ nights. 经常观戏剧首演的人。 ~ **'mate** *n* ⇒ **mate**[1](2). ~ **of'fender**, one against whom no previous conviction has been recorded. 初犯。 ~ **'person** (gram) the pronouns *I, me, we, us* (and the verb forms used with them). (语法)第一人称 (I, me, we, us 诸代词及其动词形式)。 ~·**'rate** *adj* of the best class; excellent: 第一流的;最佳的: ~-*rate acting.* 最佳的演出。 □ *adv* (colloq) very well: (口)很好: *getting on* ~-'*rate.* 情形很好。 ~·**ly** *adv* (in making a list) as a beginning; in the ~ place. 首先;第一。

first[2] /fɜːst; fɝst/ *adv* **1** before anyone or anything else (often, for emphasis, ~ **of all**; ~ **and foremost**): 第一; 最初; 最先(加强语气时,常作 first of all, first and foremost): *Which horse came in ~*, won the race? 哪一匹马跑得了冠军? *Women and children ~*, ie before men. 妇孺优先。 **F~ come, ~ served**, Those who come ~ will be served ~. 先到的先招待。 **last in, ~ out**, (esp) the last to be employed are the ~ to be dismissed when dismissals are necessary. (尤指)裁员时最后受雇者最先被裁掉。 **~ and last**, taking one thing with another; on the whole. 整个看来;就全体而论。 ~-**born** *n, adj* eldest (child). 最先出生的;长子;长女。 **2** for the ~ time: 初次: *When did you ~ see him/see him ~?* 你第一次是在什么时候看到他的? **3** before some other (specified or implied) time: 首先 (在另一特指或暗示的时间以前): *I must finish this work ~*, ie before starting sth else. 我必须先完成这件工作。 **4** in preference: 宁愿: *He said he would resign ~*, eg resign rather than do sth dishonest for his employers. 他说他宁愿辞职(例如宁愿辞职而不为雇主做欺诈之事)。

first[3] /fɜːst; fɝst/ *n* **1 at ~**, at the beginning. 最初;当初。 **from the ~**, from the start. 从开始起。 **from ~ to last**, from beginning to end; throughout. 自始至终;始终;一直。 **2** (in examinations, competitions) place in the first class; person who takes this: (考试或比赛的)第一名;冠军: *He got a ~ in Modern Languages.* 他在近代语言一科得第一名。

firth /fɜːθ; fɝθ/ *n* narrow arm of the sea; (esp in Scotland) river estuary. 狭窄的海湾;(尤指苏格兰之)河入海口。

fis·cal /'fɪskl; 'fɪskl/ *adj* of public revenue. 国库岁收的;财政的。 ⇒ **year(4).**

fish[1] /fɪʃ; fɪʃ/ *n* (*pl* ~ or ~**es**) **1** [C] cold-blooded animal living wholly in water and breathing through gills, with fins for swimming: 鱼: *catch a ~/two ~es/a lot of ~.* 捉到一(两,许多)条鱼。 ⇒ the illus here and at **sea.** 参看附图及 sea 之插图。 *a 'pretty kettle of ~*, a state of confusion. 混乱。 **have 'other ~ to fry**, more important business to attend to. 另有要事。 *There's as good ~ in the sea as ever came*

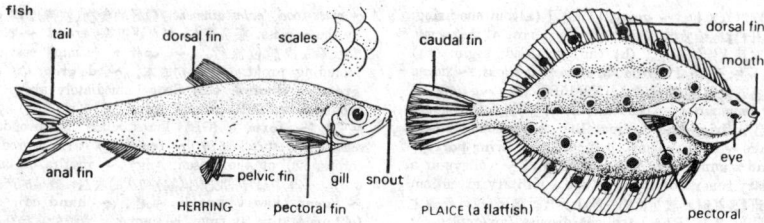

fish
tail — dorsal fin — scales
anal fin — pelvic fin — gill — snout
pectoral fin
HERRING

caudal fin — dorsal fin
mouth
eye
pectoral
PLAICE (a flatfish)

out of it, (prov) Even if one chance, etc has not been seized, there will be plenty of others. (谚) 海里的好鱼多的是(纵然失去一个机会等,尚有许多). **2** [U] ~ as food: 鱼肉: *boiled/fried/grilled* ~; 煮的(炸的,烤的)鱼; *a* ~ *course* (as part of a meal). 一道鱼. **3** (compounds) (复合词) '~·**bone**, bone of a ~. 鱼骨. '~·**cake**, ~ rissole. 鱼饼. ,~ **and** '**chips**, fried fish with fried chips of potato. 炸鱼及炸马铃薯条. ,~·'**finger** (US 美,~ '**stick**), small, long piece of ~, covered with breadcrumbs, eaten fried or grilled. 炸鱼条;烤鱼条. '~·**hook**, metal hook used for catching ~. 鱼钩. '~·**knife**, knife with which ~ is eaten. (吃鱼用之)鱼刀. '~·**monger**, tradesman who sells ~. 鱼贩. '~·**paste**, paste of ~ or shellfish (spread on sandwiches, etc). 鱼酱(鱼或虾蟹等之酱,涂于三明治等上). '~·**slice**, knife for carving and serving ~ at table. 切鱼刀;分鱼刀. '~·**wife**, (colloq) crude, abusive woman. (口)粗野的女人. ~**y** *adj* **1** smelling or tasting like ~: 鱼腥味的: *a* ~**y** *smell*. 鱼腥味. **2** (colloq) causing a feeling of doubt: (口)可疑的; 难以置信的: *a* ~**y** *story*. 难以置信的故事.

fish² /fɪʃ; fɪʃ/ *vi, vt* **1** [VP2A, C] try to catch fish: 钓鱼;捕鱼: *go* ~*ing*; 去钓鱼; ~ *in the sea*; 在海上捕鱼; (fig) try to get, by indirect methods: (喻) 间接探听; 设法获得赞赏: ~ *for information/compliments*. 间接探听消息(沽名钓誉). ~ *in troubled waters*, try to win advantages for oneself from a disturbed state of affairs. 混水模鱼. **2** [VP6A] try to catch ~ in: 在…中钓鱼; 在…中捕鱼: ~ *a river/a pool*; 在河(塘)中钓鱼; try to catch by ~ing: 钓(鱼);捕(鱼): ~ *trout*. 钓鳟鱼. **3** [VP15A, B] ~ *up* (*out of*)/(*from*); ~ *out* (*of/from*), draw or pull (from): 拖出; 拉出; 掏出; 捞出: ~ *out a coin from*/~ *a coin out of one's pocket*; 从口袋里掏出一枚硬币; ~ *up a dead cat out of a canal*. 自沟里拖出一死猫. ~·**ing** *n* [U] catching fish for a living or for pleasure. 捕鱼; 钓鱼. '~·**ing-line** *n* line[1](1) with a ~·hook attached for ~ing. 钓丝;钓线. '~·**ing-rod** *n* long tapered rod (often jointed) to which a ~ing-line is fastened. 钓竿. '~·**ing-tackle** *n* [U] equipment needed for ~ing. 钓具.

fisher /'fɪʃə(r); 'fɪʃɚ/ *n* (old use) fisherman. (旧用法)渔翁;渔人. ~·**man** /-mən; mən/ *n* (*pl* -**men**) man who earns a living by fishing. 渔夫;渔人. ⇨ *angler* at **angle²**.

fish·ery /'fɪʃərɪ; 'fɪʃərɪ/ *n* (*pl* -**ries**) part of the sea where fishing is carried on: 渔场: *in-shore fisheries*, near the coast. 近海渔场: *deep-sea fisheries*. 远洋渔场.

fish·plate /'fɪʃpleɪt; 'fɪʃ,plet/ *n* one of two iron plates used to fasten rails to a sleeper (on a railway track). 接轨夹板(夹接铁轨于枕木的铁板); 鱼尾夹板.

fis·sile /'fɪsaɪl US: 'fɪsl; 'fɪsl/ *adj* that tends to split: 易分裂的: ~ *material*, eg that can be split up in a nuclear reactor. 可裂物质(例如可于核反应器中分裂之物质).

fis·sion /'fɪʃn; 'fɪʃən/ *n* [U] splitting or division, eg of one cell into new cells, or of the nucleus of certain atoms, eg uranium, when an atomic bomb is exploded. 分裂(例如单细胞分裂成新细胞); 裂变(原子弹爆炸时铀的原子核裂变). ~·**able** /-əbl; -əbl/ *adj* that can be split by ~; capable of atomic ~. 可分裂的; 可裂变的.

fis·sip·ar·ous /fɪ'sɪpərəs; fɪ'sɪpərəs/ *adj* (of cells) reproducing by fission. (指细胞)分裂繁殖的.

fis·sure /'fɪʃə(r); 'fɪʃə/ *n* [C] cleft made by splitting or separation of parts. 裂隙; 裂缝.

fist /fɪst; fɪst/ *n* hand when tightly closed (as in boxing): 拳; 拳头: *He struck me with his* ~. 他用拳头打我. *He shook his* ~ *at me*. 他向我挥拳. ⇨ the illus at **arm**. 参看 arm 之插图. ~·**i·cuffs** /'fɪstɪkʌfs; 'fɪstɪ,kʌfs/ *n pl* (usu hum) fighting with the ~s. (通常为谐)斗拳; 互殴.

fis·tula /'fɪstjʊlə; 'fɪstʃʊlə/ *n* long pipe-like ulcer with a narrow mouth. 瘘管.

fit¹ /fɪt; fɪt/ *adj* (fitter, fittest) **1** *fit* (*for*), suitable or suited; well adapted; good enough: 合适的; 切合的; 适宜的; 恰当的: *The food was not fit to eat*, was too bad to be eaten. 那食物不适宜吃. *It was a dinner fit for a king*. 那是一适于王者的盛餐. *That man is not fit for the position*. 那人不适合这职位. *We must decide on a fit time and place for the meeting*. 我们必须决定适当的开会时间和地点. **2** right and proper: 适宜的; 正当的: *It is not fit that you should mock your mother so*. 你如此嘲笑你母亲是不应该的. **think/see fit** (**to do sth**), decide to: 决定; 决心: *He didn't see fit to adopt my suggestion*. 他不采纳我的建议. *Do as you think fit*. 你认为怎么做合适就怎么做. **3** ready; in a suitable condition; (also colloq, as an *adv*): 齐备的; 备妥的; (口语中亦用做副词): *They went on working till they were fit to drop*, ready to drop from exhaustion. 他们继续工作, 直到快要累倒才停. *He was laughing fit to burst himself*, so violently that he seemed ready to burst. 他笑得支持不住了. **4** in good athletic condition; in good health: 强健的; 健壮的: *I hope you're keeping fit*. 我希望你能保持健康. ⇨ **keep¹**(14). *He has been ill and is not fit for work/fit to travel yet*. 他一直在生病, 尚不能工作(旅行). ~·**ly** *adv* **fit·ness** *n* [U] **1** suitability (*for*): 适当; 合宜(与 for 连用): *the fitness of things*, what is right or suitable. 适当的事物; 合宜之事. **2** the state of being physically fit: 健康: *a national fitness campaign*, one for improving the nation's health. 国民健康运动.

fit² /fɪt; fɪt/ *vt, vi* (-**tt**-) **1** [VP6A, 2A] be the right measure, shape and size for: 适合于; 合适: *shoes that fit well*; 很合脚的鞋子; *a badly fitting door*. 不好关的门. *This coat doesn't fit me*. 这件上衣不合我身. *The key doesn't fit the lock*. 这钥匙不合这把锁. **2** [VP15A, B] *fit* (*on*), put on (esp clothing) to see that it is the right size, shape, etc: 试穿(尤指衣服)看是否合身: *have a new coat fitted*. 试穿一新上衣. **3** [VP15A, B] *fit* (*on*), put into place: 安装; 装置: *fit a new lock on a door*. 在门上装一新锁. **4** [VP6A, 14, 16A] *fit* (*for*), make (sb, oneself) suitable or competent: 使(某人或自己)适应或胜任: *fit oneself for one's new duties*. 使自己能胜任新职责. *Military training fits men for long marches*/*to make long marches*. 军事训练能使人适应长途行军. *Can we make the punishment fit the crime?* 我们能使惩罚与犯罪相称吗? **5** [VP15B, 2C] *fit in* (*with*), (cause to) be in a suitable or harmonious relation (with); find, be in, the right or a suitable time or place for: (使)适合(旅行): *I must fit my holidays in with yours*. 我必须使我的假日与你的配合. *My holiday arrangements must fit in with yours*. 我的假期计划必须

配合你的。 **fit** *sb* / *sth* **out** / **up**, supply with what is needed; equip: 供以需品; 装备: *fit out a ship for a long voyage* / *a party for a polar expedition*; 装备一船以作长期航行(一队人以作极地探险); *a hotel primed with modern comforts and conveniences*. 有现代化设备的旅馆。 □ *n* (usu *a* + *adj* + ~) (通常用于 a + adj + ~ 的句型) style, manner, in which sth, eg a garment, fits: (衣服等)适合的样子: *The coat is a tight* / *good* / *excellent fit*. 这上衣很贴身(很合身,十分合身)。

fit³ /fit/ *n* **1** sudden (usu short) attack of illness: 疾病的突然发作(通常是短暂的): *a fit of coughing*; 一阵咳嗽; *a 'fainting fit*. 一阵昏厥。 **2** sudden attack of hysteria, apoplexy, paralysis, with loss of consciousness and violent movements: 歇斯底里症,中风,麻痹的突发(因而失去知觉或发出剧烈动作): *fall down in a fit*. (因中风等)突然昏倒。 **give** *sb* **a fit**, (colloq) do sth that greatly shocks or outrages him. (口) 做某事而使某人大吃一惊或震怒。 **have a fit**, (colloq) be greatly surprised or outraged: (口)大惊;大怒: *She almost had a fit when she saw the bill*. 她看到帐单时几乎大吃一惊。 **3** sudden onset lasting for a short time; outburst: 短时间的发作; 突发: *a fit of energy* / *enthusiasm* / *anger*. 一股干劲(一股热忱,一阵愤怒)。 **by** / **in fits and starts**, in short periods, from time to time, not regularly. 一阵阵地; 间或; 不规则地。 **4** mood: 心情: *when the fit was on him*, when he felt in the right mood (for sth). 与之所至(与 for 连用, 后接某事物)。 **fit·ful** /-fl; -fəl/ *adj* occurring, coming and going, in short periods; irregular: 一阵阵的; 不定的: *a fitful breeze*; 一阵阵的微风; *fitful bursts of energy*. 一阵阵的干劲。 **fit·fully** /-fəlɪ; -fəlɪ/ *adv*

fit·ment /'fɪtmənt; 'fɪtmənt/ *n* piece of furniture or equipment; fittings: 设备: *kitchen* ~s, eg sinks, cupboards, working tables, esp when made as units in a series. 厨房设备(例如洗涤槽,碗橱,料理台,尤指成套者)。

fit·ter /'fɪtə(r); 'fɪtə/ *n* **1** (tailoring and dressmaking) person who cuts out, fits and alters garments. (裁缝)剪裁和试样的裁缝师。 **2** (eng) workman who fits together and adjusts the finished parts of an engine, machine, etc. (工程)装配发动机,机器等之人;装配工。

fit·ting /'fɪtɪŋ; 'fɪtɪŋ/ *adj* proper; right; suitable. 适当的; 适合的。 □ *n* **1** act of fitting: 试衣; 试穿: *go to the tailor's for a* ~. 去裁缝店试衣服。 **2** fixture in a building, esp (*pl*) things permanently fixed: 建筑物中之装置物;(复数尤指)固定装置: *gas and electric light* ~s. 煤气和电灯装置。 **3** (*pl*) furnishings: (复)家具; 设备: *office* ~s, eg desks, chairs, filing cabinets. 办公室的设备(例如桌,椅,档案柜)。

five /faɪv; faɪv/ *n*, *adj* the number 5, ⟹ App 4, 5 五; 五个 (参看附录四, 五): *a* ~*-day week*, one of ~ working days. 有五个工作日的一周。 *'*~*-fold adj* with ~ parts; ~ times as much. 有五部分的; 五重的; 五倍的。 ~*·pence* /'faɪfpəns; 'faɪvpens/ *n* ~ pence. 五便士。 ~*·penny* /'faɪfpənɪ; 'faɪvˌpenɪ/ *adj* costing ~pence. 值五便士的。 **fiver** /'faɪvə(r); 'faɪvə/ *n* (colloq) (GB) £5 note; (US) $5 bill. (口)(英)五英镑钞票;(美)五美元钞票。

fives /faɪvz; faɪvz/ *n* (GB) ball game played with the hands or a bat in a walled court. (英) 一种球戏(用手或球棒在有墙壁围绕的庭院中进行)。

fix¹ /fɪks; fɪks/ *vt*, *vi* **1** [VP6A, 15A, B] make firm or fast; fasten (sth) so that it cannot be moved: 使固定;绑紧;钉牢: *fix a post in the ground* / *a shelf to a wall*; 将一柱装置地上(将一架钉在墙上); *fix facts* / *dates, etc in one's mind*, implant them deeply so that they will not be forgotten. 牢记事实(日期等)。 **2** [VP14] *fix on*, direct (the eyes, one's attention, etc) steadily on or to: 使(眼睛,注意力等)指向;注视;专心于: *fix one's attention on what one is doing*. 专心于自己从事的工作。 *He fixed his eyes on me*. 他注视着我。 **3** [VP6A] (of objects) attract and hold (the attention): (指物体)吸引(注意力): *This unusual sight fixed his attention* / *kept his attention fixed*. 这个不凡的景色吸引了他的注意

力。 **4** [VP6A] determine or decide: 决定; 确定: *fix the rent*; 决定租金; *fix a date for a meeting*; 决定开会日期; *sell goods only at fixed prices*, prices with no discount, with no possibility of bargaining; 定价格出卖货物; 售货不二价: *a man with fixed* (= definite and decided) *principles*. 有定见之人。**fixed odds**, ⟹ **odds(3)**. **5** [VP6A] treat (photographic films, colours used in dyeing, etc) so that light does not affect them. 定(像); 定(影); 使(颜色等)固定不变。 **6** [VP15A] single out (sb) by looking steadily (at him): 凝视(某人): *fix a man with an angry stare*. 以愤怒的眼光瞪着一人。 **7** [VP15B] *fix sb up* (*with sth*); *fix sth up* (*with sb*), arrange; organize, provide for; put in order: 解决; 预备; 整理: *fix sb up with a job*, 为某人安排一工作; *fix up a friend for the night*, give him a bed; 替友人准备一过夜的住处; *fix up a meeting with sb*, 与某人会面; *fix one's room* / *drawers* / *shelves up*. 整理房间(抽屉,架子)。 **8** [VP3A] *fix on* / *upon*, settle one's choice, decide to have: 选定: *They've fixed upon a little bungalow near Rye*. 他们已选定了拉伊附近一所小平房。 **9** [VP6A] (sl) (俚) (a) use bribery or deception, improper influence: 贿赂; 作弊: *You can't fix a judge in Britain*. 在英国你不能贿赂法官。 (b) get even with sb: 报复: *I'll fix him*. 我要向他报复。 **10** [VP6A] (colloq) put in order; prepare: (口)整顿; 修理; 准备: *fix one's hair*, brush and comb it; 梳理头发; *fix a watch*, repair it; 修理表; *fix a salad*, mix and dress it. 调制生菜食品。 **fixed** /fɪkst; fɪkst/ *adj* unchanging: 不变的; 固定的: *fixed costs*, overhead expenses. 固定费用;营业费用。 ⟹ **overhead**; *a fixed idea*, one in which a person persists and which tends to occupy his thoughts too much; 固定观念; *a fixed star*, one that seems to keep the same position relative to others, not changing it as planets do. 恒星。 **fix·ed·ly** /'fɪksɪdlɪ; 'fɪksɪdlɪ/ *adv* in a fixed manner (esp of looking): 固定地 (尤指目光): *look* / *gaze fixedly at sb*. 注视某人。

fix² /fɪks; fɪks/ *n* **1** *be in* / *get oneself into a fix*, a dilemma, an awkward situation. 处于进退两难之境; 陷入困境。 **2** finding of a position, position found, by taking bearings, observing the stars, etc. 确定方位; 确定的方位。 **3** (sl) hypodermic injection of a drug, eg heroin. (俚)注射麻醉药(如海洛英)。

fix·ate /fɪk'seɪt; 'fɪkset/ *vt* **1** stare at. 射视。 **2** (usu passive) cause a fixation(2). (通常用被动语态)引起病态的执着。~*ed (on)*, (colloq) obsessed (with). (口)心神困扰。

fix·ation /fɪk'seɪʃn; fɪks'eʃən/ *n* **1** [U] fixing or being fixed: 固定;决定;装置;安排;定影;定色: *the* ~ *of a photographic film*. 照像软片之定影。 **2** [C] ~ (*on*), (psych) immature and abnormal emotional attachment to another person, with difficulty in forming other, normal, attachments; (colloq) obsession. (心理)执着(病态的眷恋某人);(口)心神困扰;强迫观念。

fixa·tive /'fɪksətɪv; 'fɪksətɪv/ *n* substance that fixes(5) eg photographs, paintings; substance that preserves animal tissue for study under a microscope; substance for keeping hair or dentures in position. 定影剂; 防止褪色剂;(显微镜下固定动物组织之)固定剂; 固定头发或假牙之物。

fix·ture /'fɪkstʃə(r); 'fɪkstʃə/ *n* [C] **1** sth fixed in place, eg (*pl*) built-in cupboards, electric-light fittings, etc which are bought with a building: 固定之物; (复数尤指)建筑物之附属装置(如壁橱,电灯装置等): *The owner of the house charged us for* ~*s and fittings*. 房主要我们付使用附属装置物的费用。 **2** (day fixed or decided for a) sporting event: 运动项目; 预定的运动项目举行日: *football and racing* ~*s*. 足球与赛跑项目。 **3** (colloq) person or thing that appears unlikely to move from or leave a place: (口)不会移动或离开的人或物: *Professor Gravity seems to be a* ~ *in the college*. 格雷维特教授似乎要在这个学院教一辈子。

fizz /fɪz; fɪz/ *vi* [VP2A, C] make a hissing sound (as

when gas escapes from a liquid). 发嘶嘶声 (如气体自液体中冒出之声). □ *n* [U] this sound; aeration by carbon dioxide: 嘶嘶声; 充以二氧化碳: *This soda-water has lost its* ~, has gone flat² (9). 这汽水跑气了. ~**y** *adj* (**-ier, -iest**).

fizzle /'fɪzl; 'fɪzl/ *vi* [VP2A, C] hiss or splutter feebly. 发微弱的嘶嘶声. ~ *out*, end feebly; come to a weak, unsatisfactory end. 虎头蛇尾地结束; 结果失败.

fjord /fɪ'ɔːd; fjɔrd/ = **fiord**.

flab·ber·gast /'flæbəgɑːst *US:* -gæst; 'flæbəˌgæst/ *vt* [VP6A] (colloq) overwhelm with amazement. (口) 使惊愕.

flabby /'flæbɪ; 'flæbɪ/ *adj* (**-ier, -iest**) **1** (of the muscles, flesh) soft; not firm: (指肌肉) 松软的; 松弛的: *A man who never takes exercise is likely to have* ~ *muscles.* 从来不运动的人肌肉会松软. **2** (fig) weak; without moral force: (喻) 软弱的; 无道德力的: *a* ~ *will/character.* 软弱的意志 (性格). **flab·bily** /-ɪlɪ; -əlɪ/ *adv* **flab·bi·ness** *n*

flac·cid /'flæksɪd; 'flæksɪd/ *adj* hanging loose and limp; flabby. 松软的; 软弱的. ~**ity** /flæk'sɪdətɪ; flæk'sɪdətɪ/ *n*

flag¹ /flæg; flæg/ *n* (usu square or oblong) piece of cloth, attached by one edge to a rope, used as the distinctive symbol of a country, or as a signal: 国旗; 旗帜 (通常指方形或长方形者): *the national* ~ *of Great Britain*, the Uninon Jack, ⇨ illus here: 英国国旗 (参看本条之插图); *the Red Cross* ~; 红十字会旗; *streets decorated with* ~s. 饰有旗帜的街道. ~ *of convenience*, ~, eg of Panama, Liberia, used to obscure actual ownership of ships and so evade taxation. 为逃税而隐载船只主权的旗 (例如巴拿马或利比里亚旗). *lower/strike one's* ~, take it down as a sign of surrender. 降旗表示投降. '~**captain** *n* captain of a ~ship. 旗舰舰长. '~**day** (**a**) day on which money is raised for a charitable cause by persons in public places, a small paper ~ being given to those who contribute. 售旗 (小纸旗) 募捐日. (**b**) (US) 14 June, anniversary of the day in 1777 when the Stars and Stripes became the national ~. (美) 国旗纪念日 (为六月十四日, 纪念 1777 年于是日采用星条旗为美国国旗). '~ *officer*, admiral. 海军将官. '~**pole**, pole on which a ~ is flown. 旗竿. '~**ship**, warship having an admiral on board. 旗舰 (驻有海军将官之战舰). ⇨ *also* **black, white**² *and* **yellow.** □ *vt* (**-gg-**) **1** [VP6A] place a ~ or ~s on; decorate with ~s: 插旗于; 饰以旗: *streets* ~ged *to celebrate a victory.* 悬旗庆祝胜利的街道. **2** [VP6A, 15B] ~ (*down*), signal to (sb), stop a train, car, etc by moving one's outstretched arm up and down or waving a ~. 对 (某人) 打旗语; 挥臂或挥旗使 (火车, 汽车等) 停止. ⇨ **semaphore.**

1 St Andrew's 　3 St Patrick's
2 St George's 　4 the Union Jack

flags

flag² /flæg; flæg/ *vi* (**-gg-**) [VP2A] (of plants, etc) droop, hang down, become limp; (fig) become tired or weak: (指植物等) 枯萎; (喻) 疲倦; 衰弱: *My strength/interest/enthusiasm is* ~ging. 我的体力 (兴趣, 热忱) 减退了.

flag³ /flæg; flæg/ *n* (also 亦作 '~·**stone**) flat, square or oblong piece of stone for a floor, path or pavement. (铺地或道路之) 石板.

flag⁴ /flæg; flæg/ *n* kinds of plant with blade-like leaves, growing in moist land, esp kinds of iris. 菖蒲; 香蒲.

flagel·lant /'flædʒələnt; 'flædʒələnt/ *n* person who whips himself or another, eg as a religious penance. (作为宗教赎罪等而) 鞭笞自己或他人者. **flagel·late** /'flædʒəleɪt; 'flædʒəˌlet/ *vt* [VP6A] whip. 鞭笞; 鞭打. **flagel·la·tion** /ˌflædʒə'leɪʃn; ˌflædʒə'leʃən/ *n*

flageo·let /ˌflædʒəʊ'let; ˌflædʒə'let/ *n* small flute, like a whistle, with six stops. 六孔短笛; 哨笛.

flagon /'flægən; 'flægən/ *n* **1** large, rounded bottle in which wine, cider, etc is sold, usu holding about twice as much as an ordinary bottle. 大肚酒瓶 (通常可装一般酒瓶两倍之量). **2** vessel with a handle, lip and lid for serving wine at table. (有把手, 壶嘴和壶盖的) 酒壶.

a flagon 　　　**a flange**

fla·grant /'fleɪgrənt; 'flegrənt/ *adj* (of crime or a criminal, etc) openly and obviously wicked; glaring; scandalous: (指罪恶, 罪犯等) 罪恶昭彰的; 昭然若揭的; 声名狼藉的: ~ *offences/sinners.* 重罪 (恶名昭著的罪人). ~**ly** *adv*

flail /fleɪl; flel/ *n* old-fashioned tool for threshing grain, consisting of a strong stick hinged on a long handle. 连枷 (旧式打谷具). □ *vt* [VP6A] beat with (or as with) a ~. 以连枷打; 似以连枷打.

flair /fleə(r); flɛr/ *n* [U, C] natural or instinctive ability (to do sth well, to select or recognize what is best, most useful, etc): 天才; 本领; 鉴别眼光; 敏锐的觉察力: *have a* ~ *for languages*, be quick at learning them; 有语言天才; *have a* ~ *for bargains*, be good at recognizing them. 有做买卖的眼光.

flak /flæk; flæk/ *n* [U] anti-aircraft guns or gunfire; (fig) criticism: 高射炮; 高射炮火; (喻) 批评: *get/take a lot of* ~. 受到许多批评. '~ *jacket*, protective jacket of heavy material, reinforced with metal. (用厚布料及金属做成的) 防弹背心; 防弹衣.

flake /fleɪk; flek/ *n* [C] small, light, leaf-like piece: 小薄片; '*snow*~s; 雪花; 雪片; ~s *of rust falling from old iron*; 自旧铁上落下的一片片的锈; '*soap*~s. 皂片. □ *vi* [VP2A, C] ~ (*off*), fall off in ~s. 剥落. **flaky** *adj* (**-ier, -iest**) made up of ~s: 小薄片制成的: *flaky pastry.* 酥饼. **flaki·ness** *n*

flam·beau /'flæmbəʊ; 'flæmbo/ *n* (*pl* ~**x** or ~**s** /-bəʊz; -boz/) flaming torch. 火炬; 火把.

flam·boy·ant /flæm'bɔɪənt; flæm'bɔɪənt/ *adj* brightly coloured and decorated; (of a person, his character) florid, showy. 灿烂的; (指人, 性格) 华而不实的; 炫耀的. ~**ly** *adv* **flam·boy·ance** /-əns; -əns/ *n*

flame¹ /fleɪm; flem/ *n* **1** [C, U] (portion of burning) gas; visible part of a fire: 火焰: *The house was in* ~s, was on fire, burning. 这房子失火了. *He put a match to the papers and they burst into* ~s. 他燃一根火柴在那些文件上, 它们便烧着了. '~·**thrower** *n* weapon which projects a steady stream of burning fuel. 火焰喷射器; 喷火器 (一种武器). **2** [C] blaze of light; brilliant colour: 耀目的光辉; 灿烂的颜色: *the* ~s *of sunset.* 夕阳的灿烂光辉. **3** [C] passion: 热情; 激情: *a* ~ *of*

anger/indignation/enthusiasm. 怒火(愤激之火；热情如火). **4** [C] (colloq) sweetheart: (口)爱人: *She's an old ~ of his,* a woman with whom he was once in love. 她是他的老情人。

flame² /fleɪm; flem/ *vi* [VP2A, C] burn with, send out, flames; be or become like flames in colour: 焚烧; 发火焰; 变得红如火焰: *make the fire ~ up;* 使炉火发火焰; *hillsides flaming with the colours of autumn,* eg of maple-trees. 红如火焰的秋天的山坡(例如由枫树的叶之颜色者). *His face ~d with anger.* 他气得面红耳赤。*His anger ~d out.* 他勃然大怒。*The boy's face ~d still redder,* became redder, with anger, embarrassment, etc. 这孩子的面孔红得更厉害了(因愤怒, 困窘等)。**flam·ing** *adj* burning; very hot: 燃烧的; 灼热的: *a flaming sun;* 灼热的太阳; (colloq, vulg) bloody (3): (口, 鄙)非常的; 很大的: *You flaming idiot!* 你这个大笨蛋!

fla·min·go /fləˈmɪŋgəʊ; fləˈmɪŋgo/ *n* (*pl ~s, ~es* /-gəʊz; -goz/) large, long-legged, long-necked wading bird with pink feathers. 红鹤。⇨ the illus at **water.** 参看 water 之插图。

flam·mable /ˈflæməbl; ˈflæməbl/ *adj* (= *inflammable,* but preferred in US and in technical contexts) having a tendency to burst into flames and to burn rapidly. 易燃烧的 (在美国和专门术语中较 inflammable 常用).

flan /flæn; flæn/ *n* [C] tart containing fruit, etc, not covered with pastry. 含有水果等无硬皮的糕点。

flange /flændʒ; flændʒ/ *n* projecting or outside rim or collar, eg of a wheel, to keep sth in position. 凸缘; 轮缘。⇨ the illus at **flagon.** 参看 flagon 之插图。

flank /flæŋk; flæŋk/ *n* **1** fleshy part of the side of a human being or animal between the last rib and the hip 胁腹; 腰窝(人或动物之侧边在肋骨与臀部间的部分)。⇨ the illus at **trunk.** 参看 trunk 之插图。**2** side of a building or mountain. 建筑物或山之侧面。**3** right or left side of an army or body of troops: (军队的)左翼或右翼; 侧翼: *attack the left ~;* 攻击左翼; *make a ~ attack.* 侧击。□ *vt* [VP6A] **1** be situated at or on the ~ of. 在⋯之侧。**2** go round the ~ of (the enemy). 侧翼包围(敌人)。

flan·nel /ˈflænl; ˈflænl/ *n* **1** [U] loosely woven woollen cloth: 法兰绒: *a yard of ~;* 一码法兰绒; *~ trousers/shirts.* 法兰绒裤(衬衫)。**2** (*pl*) ~ trousers used for summer sports and games, eg cricket. (复)夏季运动时所穿的法兰绒裤(例如打板球时所穿的)。**3** [C] piece of ~ for cleaning, rubbing, etc: 抹擦用的法兰绒布块: *a 'face-~.* 擦脸用的法兰绒布块。**4** [U] (sl) nonsense. (俚)胡说八道。**~·ette** /ˌflænɪˈlet; ˌflænˈlet/ *n* [U] cotton material made to look like ~. 棉织法兰绒; 绒布。

flap¹ /flæp; flæp/ *n* [C] **1** (sound of a) flapping blow or movement: 拍打 (声); 轻动 (声): *A ~ from the tail of the whale up set the boat.* 鲸尾轻轻一拍便将那小船打翻了。**2** piece of material that hangs down or covers an opening: 垂下作为覆盖之物: *the ~ of a pocket;* 衣袋的口盖; 口袋盖; *the gummed ~ of an envelope;* 涂有胶的信封口盖; *the ~ of a table,* a hinged section that can hang down when not being used, an on a gate-legged table, ⇨ **gate(1).** 桌子的活边(以铰链与桌相连, 不用时可垂下)。**3** part of the wing of an aircraft that can be lifted in flight to alter its upward direction and speed. (飞机的)襟翼(飞行中可抬起以改变向上的方向和速度)。⇨ the illus at **aircraft.** 参看 aircraft 之插图。**4** *be in/get into a ~,* (sl) a state of nervous excitement or confusion (caused by fear of making errors, being incompetent, etc, eg while awaiting a visit from one's superiors). (俚)惴惴不安; 神经紧张(例如在等待上司来临时, 由于担心犯错、不能胜任等而造成者)。

flap² /flæp; flæp/ *vt, vi* (**-pp-**) [VP2A, VP2C, 6A] (cause to) move up and down or from side to side: (使)上下或左右移动: *The sails were ~ping against the mast.*

帆拍打着桅竿。*The wind ~ped the sails.* 风吹动着帆。*The curtains were ~ping at the open window.* 窗帘在敞开的窗前摆动。*The bird was ~ping its wings.* 那鸟拍动着翅膀。*The heron came ~ping over the water.* 那苍鹭鼓动着翅膀从水面上飞来。**2** [VP6A, 15B] give a light blow to sth with soft and flat: (以软而平之物)轻拍: *~ the flies off/away.* 将苍蝇拍走。**3** [VP2A] (sl) get into a ~¹(4). (俚)惴惴不安; 神经紧张。

flap·jack /ˈflæpdʒæk; ˈflæpˌdʒæk/ *n* [C] sweet oatcake; (US) pancake. 甜煿麦饼; (美)薄煎饼。

flap·per /ˈflæpə(r); ˈflæpɚ/ *n* **1** sth broad and flat (used to swat flies, etc). 拍子; 蝇拍。**2** (fish's) broad fin. (鱼的)宽阔的鳍。**3** (sl use in the 1920's) fashionable young woman. (二十世纪二十年代之俚语)时髦的年轻女子。

flare¹ /fleə(r); fler/ *vi* **1** [VP2A] burn with a bright, unsteady flame: 火焰摇曳地燃烧: *flaring gas-jets.* 闪耀的煤气口火焰。*The candle began to ~.* 烛光开始摇曳。**2** [VP2O] *~ up,* burst into bright flame, (fig) (into a rage; of violence) suddenly break out: 闪耀; (喻)骤然震怒; (指暴乱)突然爆发: *When he was accused of lying, he ~d up.* 当他被控说谎时, 他勃然大怒。*She ~s up at the least thing.* 她为了小事便会突然发怒。*Rioting ~d up again later.* 暴动后来又突然爆发了。Hence, 由此产生, '*~-up n* sudden breaking into flame; short sudden outburst (of anger, etc). 突然发出火焰; (愤怒等)突然爆发。□ *n* **1** [U] flaring flame: 摇曳的火焰; 闪烁的火光: *the ~ of torches;* 火把的摇曳火焰; *the sudden ~ of a match in the darkness.* 黑暗中一根火柴之突然闪耀。**2** [C] device for producing a flaring light, used as a signal, etc: 闪光装置(用以发出信号者): *The wrecked ship was using ~s to attract the attention of the coastguards.* 遇难的船正用闪光信号引起海岸巡逻队的注意。'*~-path n* lit-up landing strip for aircraft. 飞机场之照明跑道。

flare² /fleə(r); fler/ *vi, vt* [VP2A, 6A] (of a skirt, a trouser-leg, the sides of a ship, etc) (cause to) spread gradually outwards; become, make, wider at the bottom. (指裙, 裤腿, 舷侧等)(使)逐渐向外张开; (使)底部变阔。□ *n* gradual widening (eg of a skirt); upward bulge (eg in a ship's sides). (裙等之)逐渐张开; (舷侧等之)向上扩展。

flash¹ /flæʃ; flæʃ/ *n* **1** sudden burst of flame or light: 闪烁; 闪光: *a ~ of lightning;* 闪电: *~es of light from a moving mirror;* 移动的镜中的闪光; *~es from the guns during a battle;* 战争中炮火的闪光; (fig)(喻)*a ~ of wit/merriment/inspiration.* 机智(快乐, 灵感)的闪现。*in a ~,* instantly, at once 瞬间; 即刻。*a ~ in the pan,* an effort that at once ends in failure, or is quickly over and cannot be repeated or developed. 虎头蛇尾; 昙花一现。'*~-back n* (also 亦作 *cutback*) (cinema) part of a film that shows a scene earlier in time than the rest of the film (eg the childhood days of the hero). (电影) 倒叙(例如对男主角童年往事的倒叙)。'*~-bulb n* (photo) bulb giving a momentary bright light. (摄影)闪光灯泡。'*~-gun n* (photo) device to synchronize the release of a ~bulb or electronic light source and a shutter in a camera. (摄影)闪光枪(一种能使闪光灯和快门同时操作的装置)。'*~-light n* (a) light used for signals, in lighthouses, etc. (灯塔等处所用的)闪光信号灯。(b) (also 亦作 *~ photo* or '*photo-*') any device for producing a brilliant ~ of light for taking a photograph indoors or when natural light is too weak. (摄影用的)闪光灯。(c) (US) electric hand-light (GB 英 = *torch*). (美)手电筒。⇨ the illus at **camera.** 参看 camera 之插图。'*~-point n* temperature at which vapour from oil may be ignited. 燃点; 闪点; 发光点。**2** coloured stripe worn as a distinguishing emblem on a military uniform, eg on the shoulder. (佩于军服肩部等之)徽章。Cf 参较 *a badge of rank.* **3** (also 亦作 '**news-**') brief item of news received by telephone, cable, teleprinter, etc. 简短的新闻电报。**4** (attrib use

colloq) showy; smart: (用作定语; 口)过分装饰的; 漂亮的: *a ~ sports car.* 华丽的跑车。

flash² /flæʃ; flæʃ/ *vi, vt* **1** [VP2A, C] send, give out, a sudden bright light: 闪光; 闪烁: *The lightning ~ed across the sky.* 闪电自天空闪过。*A light-house was ~ing in the distance.* 一座灯塔在远方闪出信号。**2** [VP2C] come suddenly (into view; into the mind): 闪现; 掠过(心头): *The idea ~ed into/through his mind.* 这念头掠过他的心头。*The express train ~ed past.* 快车一闪而过。**3** [VP6A, 15A, 12C] send suddenly or instantly: 突然发出; 倏忽发出: *~ a light in sb's eyes;* 用光对着某人的眼睛突然一照; *~ a signal,* eg using a heliograph or torch; (用日光反射信号机或手电筒等)发出信号; *~ news across the world* (by radio or TV). (用无线电或电视)将一消息迅速传遍世界。*She ~ed him a despairing glance.* 她向他投以绝望的眼光。**4** [VP6A] send or reflect like a ~ or ~es: 似闪光般发出或射出: *Her eyes ~ed fire/defiance.* 她的眼睛闪现着热情(反抗)。

flashy /'flæʃɪ; 'flæʃɪ/ *adj* (**-ier, -iest**) brilliant and attractive but not in good taste; given to (rather vulgar) display: 浮华的; 炫耀而庸俗的; 俗丽的: *~ clothes/jewellery;* 浮华的衣服(珠宝); *~ men.* 浮华的人。**flash·i·ly** /-ɪlɪ; -əlɪ/ *adv* in a ~ manner: 浮华地: *a flashily-dressed girl.* 衣着浮华的女郎。

flask /flɑːsk *US*: flæsk; flæsk/ *n* **1** narrow-necked bottle used in laboratories, etc. (实验室等用的)细颈瓶; 烧瓶。**2** narrow-necked bottle for oil or wine. 细颈油瓶或酒瓶。**3** (also 亦作 **'hip-~**) flat-sided bottle of metal or (often leather-covered) glass for carrying spirits in the pocket. (可装在口袋内盛酒用的)扁金属瓶或(有皮套的)玻璃瓶。

flasks

flat¹ /flæt; flæt/ *n* (US 美 = *apartment*) suite of rooms (living-room, bedroom, kitchen, etc) on one floor of a building as a residence: 同一层建筑上组成一个居住单位的数个房间; 一套房间; 公寓: *an old house divided into ~s;* 隔成数套房间的一座古宅; *a new block of ~s;* 新建的一排公寓; *'~-dwellers,* people who live in ~s. 居于公寓中者。**~·let** /-lɪt; -lɪt/ *n* tiny ~. 小公寓。

flat² /flæt; flæt/ *adj* (**-ter, -test**) **1** smooth and level; even; having an unbroken surface: 平坦的; 平的: *A floor must be ~.* 地板必须平坦。*The top of a table is ~.* 桌面是平的。*People used to think that the world was ~; now we know that it is round.* 人们过去以为地球是平的, 现在我们知道地球是圆的。*One of the tyres is ~,* has no or not enough air in it. 有一个轮胎漏气了。**'~-'bottomed** *adj* (of a boat) having a ~ bottom (for use in shallow water). (指船)平底的(行驶于浅水中)。**'~-car** *n* [US] railway carriage without a roof or sides, for carrying freight. (美)平车(无顶篷或边板的铁路货车)。**'~-fish** *n* kinds of fish (including sole, plaice, turbot) having a ~ body and swimming on one side. 比目鱼; 鲽。⇨ the illus at **fish**. 参看 fish 之插图。**,~-'footed** *adj* (a) having feet with flat soles. 脚掌扁平的。(b) (colloq) downright; resolute. (口)直截了当的; 断然的。**'~-iron** *n* ⇨ **iron¹**(2). **'~ racing; the F~,** (horse-racing) over level ground with no obstacles. (赛马)平地比赛。⇨ **steeplechase** at **steeple**. **'~-top** *n* (US colloq) aircraft-carrier. (美口)航空母舰。**2** with

a broad level surface and little depth: 浅的: *~ plates/dishes/pans.* 浅盘(碟, 锅)。*The cake was ~,* had failed to rise while cooking. 糕没有发起来。**3** dull; uninteresting; monotonous: 枯燥的; 平淡无味的; 单调的: *Life seemed ~ to him.* 他似乎觉得生活无味。*The party/conversation was rather ~.* 那聚会(谈话)颇为乏味。*The soup is ~,* lacks flavour. 这汤没有味道。*fall ~,* fail to win applause or appreciation: 未受到喝彩或欣赏: *His best jokes fell ~.* 他最拿手的笑话未能引人发笑。**4** (music) below the true pitch: (音乐)降半音的; 变音的: *sing ~;* 降半音唱; *a ~ note;* 降半音的符号; 变音号; *A ~ (= Ab),* note half a tone lower than A. 降 A 调。⇨ **sharp**(10). **5** absolute; downright; unqualified: 断然的; 直截了当的; 直率的: *give sb a ~ denial/refusal,* deny or refuse sth absolutely. 断然拒绝某人。*And that's ~!* Let there be no doubt about that! 绝对是那样! **6** (comm) '*~ rate,* common price paid for each of different things or services bought in quantity. (商)一律的价格(对于大量购买的不同货物或劳务所定的共同价格)。**7** (of colours, coloured surfaces) uniform, without relief: (指颜色, 有色的表面)无明暗之分的; 无立体感的: *a ~ tint;* 无明暗之分的颜色; *~ paint,* without a gloss. 无光泽的漆。*His paintings all seem rather ~,* lack relief, shading, etc. 他的画都似乎缺少立体感。**8** (of a battery) run down; needing to be recharged. (指电池)变弱的; 需再充电的。**9** (of gaseous or aerated liquids) no longer containing gas: (指充有气的液体)跑气的: *This beer tastes/has gone ~.* 这啤酒喝起来无味(气跑光了)。⇨ **fizz**. **10** '~ 'spin, (a) (often uncontrollable) fast descent of a horizontal, spinning aircraft. 飞机螺旋急降(常指失去控制者)。(b) (colloq) (mental) state of great confusion: (口)精神错乱: *in a ~ spin.* 精神错乱。□ *adv* **1** in a ~ manner: 平坦地; 平直地; 降半音地: *sing ~.* 降半音唱。**2** (lying) spread out; (lying) at full length: 展开地; 挺直地; 平伸地: *He fell ~ on his back.* 他直挺挺地仰面跌倒了。*He knocked his opponent ~.* 他将对手击倒了。*The earthquake laid the city ~,* caused all the buildings to fall. 地震震坍了全城的建筑物。**3** positively: 断然地: *He told me ~ that ....* 他断然地告诉我说……。*He went ~ against orders.* 他断然抗命。*~ broke,* (colloq) with no money at all. (口)一文不名。**4** *~ out,* (a) (colloq) with all one's strength and resources: (口)倾全力; 拼命地: *He was working/running ~ out.* 他拼命工作(跑)。(b) exhausted. 疲惫的。**~·ly** *adv* in a ~ (6) manner: 断然地; 直截了当地: *The suggestions were ~ly opposed.* 那些建议受到断然的反对。*He ~ly refused to join us.* 他断然拒绝跟我们在一起。**~·ness** *n*

flat³ /flæt; flæt/ *n* **1** the ~ (of), flat part of anything: 平的部分: *the ~ of the hand;* 手掌; *with the ~ of his sword.* 以剑面。**2** (usu *pl*) stretch of low flat land, esp near water: (通常用复数)洼地(尤指近水者): *'mud ~s;* 泥沼; *'salt ~s,* near the sea. 盐田(近海者)。**3** (music) flat note; the sign ♭: (音乐)降半音; 降半音的符号(♭): *sharps and ~s,* the black notes on a piano keyboard. 钢琴上的黑键。⇨ the illus at **notation**. 参看 notation 之插图。**4** (esp US) deflated tyre, eg after a puncture. (尤美)瘪气的轮胎。**5** piece of stage scenery on a movable frame. (舞台上的)布景屏。

flat·ten /'flætn; 'flætn/ *vt, vi* [VP6A, 15A, B, 2A, C] *~ (out)*, make or become flat: 使变平; 变平: *a field of wheat ~ed by storms;* 被暴风吹倒的一片麦田; *~ (out) a piece of metal by hammering it;* 将一块金属锤平; *~ oneself against a wall,* eg to avoid being struck by a lorry in a narrow street; (fig) humiliate. 使自己平贴在墙上(例如在狭窄的街道上避免被卡车撞上); (喻)屈辱。*~ out,* (of an aircraft) fly horizontally again. (指飞机)恢复水平姿势。

flat·ter /'flætə(r); 'flætə/ *vt* **1** [VP6A] praise too much; praise insincerely (in order to please). 谄媚; 阿谀。**2** [VP6A] give a feeling of pleasure to: 予以愉快的感觉: *I feel greatly ~ed by your invitation to*

address the meeting. 蒙你邀请在这会上演说，我感到非常愉快。 **3** [VP6A] (of a picture, artist, etc) show (sb) as better looking than he is: (指像片，艺术家等)显示(某人)较其本来面目更漂亮: *This photograph ~s you.* 这照片比你本人面貌漂亮。 **4** ~ *oneself that ...,* be pleased with one's belief that ...: 自认为；自以为: *He ~ed himself that he spoke French with a perfect accent.* 他自以为他说法语的腔调很完美。 **~er** *n* person who ~s. 谄媚者；奉承者。 **~y** *n* [U] ~ing; insincere praise; [C] (*pl* -**ries**) instance of this; ~ing remark: 谄媚；奉承； 阿谀之词所製。 *Don't be deceived by her flatteries.* 勿为她的阿谀之词所製。

flatu·lence /'flætjuləns; 'flætʃələns/ *n* [U] gas in the alimentary canal; feeling of discomfort caused by an accumulation of this. 肠胃气胀；因肠胃气胀而引起的不舒服的感觉。

flaunt /flɔːnt; flɔnt/ *vt, vi* **1** [VP6A] show off complacently; ostentatiously attract attention to: 夸示；炫耀: ~ *oneself*; 炫耀自己； ~ *one's new clothes/riches, etc.* 炫耀新衣服(财富等)。 **2** [VP2A, C] wave proudly: 飘扬: *flags and banners ~ing in the breeze.* 在微风中飘扬的旗帜。

flau·tist /'flɔːtɪst; 'flɔtɪst/ *n* flute-player. 吹笛人。

fla·vour (US = -**vor**) /'fleɪvə(r); 'flevə/ *n* **1** [U] sensation, when eating, of taste and smell: 味；滋味: *When you have a cold, your food sometimes has very little ~.* 患了伤风，食物有时毫无滋味。 **2** [C] distinctive taste; special quality or characteristic: 特殊的味道；特点；特别风味: *a ~ of garlic;* 大蒜味； *various ~s in ice-cream;* 冰淇淋的种种味道； *a newspaper story with a ~ of romance.* 报纸上具有浪漫色彩的故事。 □ *vt* [VP6A] give a ~ to: 调味；加味于；使有特殊风味: ~ *a sauce with onions.* 加洋葱于调味汁以增其味。 **~ing** *n* [C, U] sth used to give ~ to (food, etc): (加于食物等之)调味料；调味品: *too much vanilla ~ing in the cake.* 蛋糕中香草料太多。 *Many ~ings have little or no food value.* 许多调味品没有什么营养价值。 **~less** *adj* having no ~. 无味的；无滋味的；无特殊风味的。

flaw /flɔː; flɔ/ *n* [C] crack (in an object); sth that lessens the value, beauty or perfection of sth: 裂纹；瑕疵；缺陷: ~*s in a jewel/an argument/a person's character.* 珠宝(议论，人格)上的瑕疵。 **~less** *adj* perfect. 完美的；无瑕的。 **~lessly** *adv*

flax /flæks; flæks/ *n* [U] plant cultivated for the fibre obtained from its stem; this fibre (for making linen). 亚麻；亚麻纤维(织亚麻布用)。 **~en** /'flæksn; 'flæksn/ *adj* (of hair) pale yellow. (指毛发)淡黄色的。

flay /fleɪ; fle/ *vt* [VP6A] take the skin or hide off (an animal); (fig) criticize severely or pitilessly: 剥(动物)之皮；(喻)苛评，严责: *The tutor ~ed the idle students.* 导师严责那些懒惰的学生。

flea /fliː; fli/ *n* small wingless jumping insect that feeds on the blood of human beings and some animals. 跳蚤。 ⇨ the illus at **insect**. 参看 insect 之插图。 (*go off/send sb off with a*) *'~ in his ear,* (with a) stinging rebuke. (被)讥诮话(气走)；(用)讥诮话(气走某人)。 *'~-bite* *n* (fig) small inconvenience, sth not very troublesome. (喻)微小之不便；不太伤脑筋的事。 *'~-bitten* *adj* (fig) (of an animal's colouring) speckled. (喻)(指动物的颜色)有斑点的。 *'~ market,* open-air market selling cheap and second-hand goods. (售卖价廉货物和旧货的)露天市场。 *'~·pit* *n* (colloq) old and dirty place of entertainment, eg a cinema, theatre. (口)又旧又脏的娱乐场所(例如电影院或戏院)。

fleck /flek; flek/ *n* [C] **1** small spot or patch: 小点；斑点。 ~*s of colour on a bird's breast;* 一只鸟胸部之彩色斑点； ~*s of sunlight on the ground under a tree.* 树荫下的点点阳光。 **2** small particles (of dust, etc). (灰尘等的)微粒；小粒。 □ *vt* [VP6A] mark with ~: 使有斑点；饰以斑点: *a sky ~ed with clouds.* 布满点点云朵的天空。

fled *pt, pp* of **flee.**

fledged /fledʒd; fledʒd/ *adj* (of birds) with fully grown wing feathers; able to fly. (指鸟)羽毛长成的；会飞的。 **,fully-'~** (fig) *adj* trained and experienced: (喻)有训练和经验的: *a fully-~ engineer.* 有训练和经验的工程师。

fledg(e)·ling /'fledʒlɪŋ; 'fledʒlɪŋ/ *n* young bird just able to fly; (fig) young inexperienced person. 刚会飞的幼鸟；(喻)年轻而无经验之人；初出茅庐之年轻人。

flee /fliː; fli/ *vi, vt* (*pt, pp* **fled** /fled; fled/) [VP2A, C, 6A] run or hurry away (from): 逃跑；逃避；避开；逃离: *The enemy fled in disorder.* 敌人溃逃。 *The clouds fled before the wind.* 云在风前飞驰。 *He killed his enemy and fled the country.* 他杀死了他的敌人，然后逃离那个国家。

fleece /fliːs; flis/ *n* [C, U] **1** woolly covering of a sheep or similar animal; quantity of wool cut from a sheep in one operation: 羊毛；自一只羊身上一次所剪的毛量: *a coat lined with ~.* 羊毛衬里的上衣。 ⇨ the illus at **domestic.** 参看 domestic 之插图。 **2** ~-like head of hair. 似羊毛的头发；蓬松的卷发。 □ *vt* [VP6A,14] ~ *sb (of sth),* (fig) rob (sb) by trickery: (喻)诈取(某人): *He was ~d of his money.* 他的钱被人骗走了。 **fleecy** *adj* (-**ier**, -**iest**) like ~: 似羊毛的: *fleecy clouds/hair/falls of snow.* 白云(蓬松的卷发；纷纷的落雪)。

fleet¹ /fliːt; flit/ *n* [C] **1** number of warships under one commander; all the warships of a country. 舰队；一国所拥有的全部战舰。 **2** number of ships, aircraft, buses, etc moving or working under one command or ownership. 船队；飞机队；公共汽车队等。

fleet² /fliːt; flit/ *adj* (poet. liter) quick-moving: (诗，文学)迅速的；敏捷的: ~ *of foot,* ~-*footed.* 跑得快的。 **~·ly** *adv* **~·ness** *n*

fleet·ing /'fliːtɪŋ; 'flitɪŋ/ *adj* passing quickly: 飞逝的；疾驰的: *pay sb a ~ visit,* a short visit before one goes on to another place; 对某人做短暂的拜访； ~ *happiness,* lasting for a short time. 转瞬即逝的幸福。

Fleet Street /'fliːt striːt; 'flit,strit/ *n* (street in central London where there are many newspaper offices, hence) the press; London journalism. 舰队街(伦敦一街道，为许多报馆所在地)；(由此产生)新闻界；伦敦的报业。

flesh /fleʃ; fleʃ/ *n* [U] **1** soft substance, esp muscle, between the skin and bones of animal bodies: 肌肉；肉: *Tigers are ~-eating animals.* 虎是肉食动物。 ~ *and blood,* human nature with its emotions, weaknesses, etc: 人性(包括其情感、弱点等): *more than ~ and blood can stand,* more than human nature can bear. 非人所能忍受者。 *one's own ~ and blood,* one's near relatives. 骨肉；亲人。 *in the ~,* in life, in bodily form. 活生生的；本人。 *go the way of all ~,* die. 死。 *have (demand one's pound of ~,* insist cruelly on the exact repayment of what was borrowed. 无情地索偿。 ⇨ Shakespeare's Mer of Ven IV, Sc 1. 参看莎士比亚所著《威尼斯商人》第四幕，第一场。 *make a person's '~ creep,* frighten or horrify him (esp with dread of sth supernatural). (尤指以神奇恐怖之事)使某人毛骨悚然。 *put on/lose ~* (more usu *weight*) (weight 较常用)，become fat/thin. 长胖；发胖(变瘦；消瘦)。 *'~·pots* *n pl* (places supplying) good food and material comforts. 美食及物质享受；供美食及物质享受的场所。 *'~-wound* one that does not reach the bone or vital organs. 皮肉之伤；轻伤。 **2** the ~, physical or bodily desires; sensual appetites: 肉欲；色欲；情欲: *the sins of the ~.* 肉欲之罪恶。 **3** the body (contrasted with the *mind* and *soul*). 肉体(与 mind 及 soul 相对)。 *The spirit is willing but ~ is weak,* (of a person who is willing to do sth, but is physically or morally weak or lazy). 心有余而力不足。 **4** pulpy part of fruits and vegetables. 果肉；蔬菜的柔嫩部分。 **~·ly** *adj* (of the body; sensual. 肉体的；肉欲的。 **~y** *adj* fat; of ~. 肥胖的；肉的。

flesh·ings /'fleʃɪŋz; 'fleʃɪŋz/ *n pl* flesh-coloured tights, eg as worn by ballet dancers. 肉色紧身衣(例如

芭蕾舞者所穿者)。

fleur-de-lis, **-lys** /ˌfləː də 'liː; ˌflɝdə'liː/ n (pl **fleurs-de-lis, -lys** pronunciation unchanged) heraldic lily; royal arms of France. (纹章上的)鸢尾; 法国之皇家纹章。 ⇨ the illus at **armour.** 参看 armour 之插图。

flew /fluː; flu/ pt of **fly**[1].

flex[1] /fleks; flɛks/ n [C, U] (length of) flexible insulated cord for electric current. 花线; 皮线; 一段花线或皮线。

flex[2] /fleks; flɛks/ vt [VP6A] bend, eg a limb, one's muscles. 弯曲(例如肢体或肌肉)。

flex·ible /'fleksəbl; 'flɛksəbl/ adj easily bent without breaking; (fig) easily changed to suit new conditions; (of persons) adaptable. 易弯曲的; 柔韧的; (喻)可变通的; 有弹性的; (指人)能适应环境的。 **flexi·bil·ity** /ˌfleksə'bɪlətɪ; ˌflɛksə'bɪlətɪ/ n [U].

flib·ber·ti·gib·bet /ˌflɪbətɪ'dʒɪbɪt; 'flɪbɚtɪˌdʒɪbɪt/ n frivolous person too fond of gossip. 轻浮饶舌之人。

flick /flɪk; flɪk/ n [C] 1 quick light blow, eg with a whip or the tip of a finger. 轻击; 轻弹(例如用鞭或指尖)。 2 short sudden movement; jerk. 短暂而突然的动作; 猛然一动。 '**~-knife** n knife with a blade (inside the handle) which can be brought into position with a **~** for use. 弹簧刀(刀刃藏于柄内, 一揿即可伸出)。 3 (sl) cinema film. (俚)影片。 the **~s**, the cinema. 电影。 □ vt 1 [VP6A, 15A, 22] strike with a **~**, give a **~** with (a whip, etc) touch lightly: 轻击; 以(鞭等)轻击; 轻弹: He **~**ed the horse with his whip/**~**ed his whip at the horse. 他用鞭轻弹他的马。 He **~**ed the switch, eg for electric light. 他轻揿电灯开关。 He **~**ed the knife open. 他轻轻将刀刃弹出。 2 [VP15B] **~** sth away/off, remove with a **~**: 弹去(某物): She **~**ed the crumbs off the table-cloth. 她将桌布上的面包屑弹掉。

flicker /'flɪkə(r); 'flɪkɚ/ vi [VP2A, C] 1 (of a light: fig of hopes, etc) burn or shine unsteadily; flash and die away by turns: (指光; 喻, 指希望等)闪烁不定; 摇曳; 忽隐忽现: The candle **~**ed and then went out. 那蜡烛闪烁不定, 然后即行熄灭。 A faint hope still **~**ed in her breast. 她心中仍闪现着一线希望。 2 move back and forth, wave to and fro: 来回移动; 摆动: leaves **~**ing in the wind; 在风中摆动的树叶; 摇晃的影子; the **~**ing tongue of a snake. 蛇的一吐一伸的舌头。 □ n (usu sing) **~**ing movement: (通常用单数)闪烁不定; 摇曳; 闪动; 摆动: a weak **~** of hope. 闪烁不定的一线希望。

flier /'flaɪə(r); 'flaɪɚ/ = **flyer.**

flight[1] /flaɪt; flaɪt/ n 1 [U] flying through the air: 飞; 飞翔: the art of **~;** 飞行术; study the **~** of birds, how they fly. 研究鸟的飞翔。 in **~,** while flying. 在飞行中。 2 [C] journey by air; distance covered: 航空旅行; 航程: a non-stop **~** from Paris to New York; 从巴黎至纽约的不着陆飞行; **~**s in a balloon; 乘气球旅行; the spring and autumn **~**s of (= seasonal migrations) of birds. 鸟之春秋两季的成群迁徙。 '**~ deck** n (on an aircraft-carrier) deck for taking off from and landing on; (in an airliner) compartment used by the pilot, navigator, engineer, etc. (航空母舰之)飞行甲板; (客机之)驾驶舱。 3 [U] movement (and path) through the air: 空中的行动(及路线): the **~** of an arrow; 箭的飞驰; (attrib) (用作定语) the **~** path of an airliner. 客机的航线。 4 [C] number of birds or objects moving together through the air: 飞行的鸟群或物体; 飞行队: a **~** of arrows/swallows. 连发的飞箭/一队飞燕。 in the first **~,** taking or occupying a leading place. 领头; 占首要地位。 5 [U] swift passing: 飞逝而过: the **~** of time. 光阴的疾驰。 6 [C] soaring; going up above the ordinary: 高耸; 升腾; 飞跃: a **~** of wit/fancy/ambition/the imagination. 才智(幻想, 志向, 想象)之奔放。 7 [C] series (of stairs, etc) without change of direction; stairs between two landings: (阶梯等)之一段; 一段楼梯: My bedroom is two **~**s up. 向上走两段楼梯便是我的卧室。 There was no lift and we had to climb

six **~**s of stairs. 没有电梯, 我们不得不爬六段楼梯。 8 [C] group of aircraft in a country's Air Force. 一国空军之飞行队。 F**~** **Lieutenant,** rank in the Royal Air Force below Squadron Leader. 皇家空军上尉。 F**~** **Sergeant,** rank in the Royal Air Force below Warrant Officer. 皇家空军上士。 □ vt [VP6A] (cricket) move (the ball) sideways when bowling it, so as to deceive the batsman. (板球)侧投(球)以诱骗击球员: a well-**~**ed delivery. 好的侧投。 **~-less** adj (of birds) unable to fly. (指鸟)不会飞的。

flight[2] /flaɪt; flaɪt/ n 1 [U] (act of) fleeing or running away (from danger, etc): 逃走; 逃亡: seek safety in **~;** 逃之大吉; put the enemy to **~,** defeat them and cause them to flee. 击溃敌人。 take **~;** take to **~,** run away. 逃走。 2 [C] instance of this: 逃走的实例: the **~** into Egypt (of Mary with the infant Jesus); 逃亡至埃及(指玛利亚带着婴儿耶稣之逃亡); a **~** of capital, eg when capital is sent abroad during a financial crisis. 资金之外流(如财政危机时资金之被移往国外)。

flighty /'flaɪtɪ; 'flaɪtɪ/ adj (of behaviour, character) influenced by whims; unsteady; fickle. (指行径, 性格) 好作奇想的; 不稳定的; 轻浮的。

flimsy /'flɪmzɪ; 'flɪmzɪ/ adj (-ier, -iest) (of material) light and thin; (of objects) easily injured and destroyed: (指原料)轻而薄的; (指物体)脆弱的; 容易损坏的: a **~** cardboard box; 脆弱的纸板盒; (fig) (喻) a **~** excuse/argument, one that is not convincing. 不住脚的借口(论据)。 □ n [C] thin paper, eg as used when several carbon copies are made on a typewriter. 一种薄纸(例如打字复制时所用者)。 **flim·sily** /-ɪlɪ; -ɪlɪ/ adv **flim·si·ness** n.

flinch /flɪntʃ; flɪntʃ/ vi [VP2A, 3A] **~** (from), draw or move back; wince: 退缩; 畏缩: flinch a tooth pulled out without **~.** 毫不畏缩地去拔牙。 You mustn't **~** from an unpleasant duty. 你不应规避你不愿的职责。

fling /flɪŋ; flɪŋ/ vt, vi (pt, pp flung /flʌŋ; flʌŋ/) 1 [VP6A, 15A, B, 22, 12A, 13A] throw violently: 猛投; 掷; 抛: **~** one's hat up (in the air); 将帽子抛向空中; **~** a stone at sb or sth; 向某人或某物掷石头; **~** one's clothes on, dress hurriedly; 匆匆穿上衣服; **~** the doors and windows open, open them quickly and forcibly; 将门窗猛然推开; be flung into prison; 被投入狱; **~** caution to the winds, act recklessly; 行事鲁莽; **~** off one's pursuers, escape from them. 摆脱追逐的人。 She flung him a scornful look. 她向他投以鄙夷的一瞥。 2 [VP6A, 15A, B] move oneself, one's arms, etc violently, hurriedly, impulsively or angrily: 猛烈移动(身体, 手臂等); 急动: 暴躁地移动: **~** one's arms up/about; 急伸(挥)手臂; **~** oneself into a chair. 猛然坐于椅中; 一屁股坐于椅中。 3 [VP2C] go angrily or violently; rush: 愤然而行; 急行; 冲: He flung out of the room. 他冲出房间。 He flung off without saying goodbye. 他未经告辞即愤然离去。 □ n [C] 1 act of **~**ing; **~**ing movement. 掷; 投; 猛动; 急动; 急冲。 have a **~** at, (shot or go are the more usu words) make an attempt at. 试图 (shot 或 go 为较常用之字)。 2 kind of energetic dance: 一种充满活力的舞蹈: the Highland **~,** as danced in Scotland. 一种充满活力的苏格兰高地舞。 have one's **~,** have a time of unrestricted pleasure. 尽兴; 恣意。

flint /flɪnt; flɪnt/ n [U] hard kind of stone found in lumps like pebbles, steel-grey inside and white outside; 燧石; 火石; 打火石。 [C] piece of this used with steel to produce sparks; [C] piece of hard alloy used in a cigarette-lighter to produce sparks. 燧石; 火石; 打火石。 '**~-lock** n [U] **~**-lock pebbles used for building walls, etc. (筑墙壁等所用之)燧石碟。 **~y** adj (-ier, -iest) very hard, like **~.** 极坚硬的; 似燧石的。

flip /flɪp; flɪp/ vt, vi (-pp-) [VP6A, 15A, B] put (sth) into motion by a snap of the finger and thumb;

throw with a jerk: 以指捻掷; 猝然一挥: ~ *a coin (down) on the counter.* 将一硬币掷在柜台上. **2** quick, light blow. 迅速的轻击. **2** (colloq) short flight in an aeroplane for pleasure. (口)游乐性的短程飞行. □ *adj* (colloq) flippant; glib. (口)不客气的; 油腔滑调的. *the* '~ *side,* (colloq) the reverse side (of a gramophone record). (口)(唱片的)反面.

flip·pant /'flɪpənt; 'flɪpənt/ *adj* not showing deserved respect or seriousness: 不客气的; 无礼的: *a ~ answer/ remark.* 不客气的回答(言语). ~·**ly** *adv* **flip·pancy** /-ənsɪ; -ɛnsɪ/ *n* [U] being ~; [C] ~ remark, etc. 不客气; 不客气的言语等.

flip·per /'flɪpə(r); 'flɪpɚ/ *n* **1** limb of certain sea animals (not fish) used in swimming: (某些海中动物的)鳍状肢: *Seals, turtles and penguins have ~s.* 海豹、海龟和企鹅均有鳍形肢. ⇨ the illus at **sea.** 参看 sea 之插图. **2** device worn on the feet to increase the thrust of leg movements in swimming. 橡皮脚掌; 蛙鞋(穿在脚上的鳍状物, 游泳时可增加腿部动作之冲力). ⇨ the illus at **frogman.** 参看 frogman 之插图.

flirt /flɜːt; flɝt/ *vi* [VP2A, 3A] ~ *(with),* **1** show affection for amusement, without serious intentions: 调情取乐: *She ~s with every handsome man she meets.* 她和她遇到的每个美男子调情. **2** pretend to be interested in; think about, but not seriously: 假装对…有兴趣; 非认真地考虑想了: *He's been ~ing with the idea of going to Moscow.* 他一直有去莫斯科的遐想. □ *n* sb who ~s with many people. 调情者; 卖弄风情者. **flir·ta·tion** /flɜː'teɪʃn; flɝ'teʃən/ *n* [U] ~ing; [C] instance of this: 调情: *carry on a ~ation.* 调情. **flir·ta·tious** /flɜː'teɪʃəs; flɝ'teʃəs/ *adj* fond of ~ing; of ~ing. 喜调情的; 调情的.

flit /flɪt; flɪt/ *vi* (-tt-) **1** [VP2C] fly or move lightly and quickly: 轻快地飞; 轻快地移动: *bees ~ting from flower to flower;* 在花间飞来飞去的蜜蜂; *bats ~ting about in the dusk;* 黄昏时四处飞翔的蝙蝠; (fig) (喻) *fancies that ~ through one's mind.* 掠过心头的幻想. **2** (colloq) remove from one house to another; change one's abode, eg secretly, to avoid paying debts. (口)迁居; 搬家(例如为逃债而悄悄搬走). □ *n* (colloq) act of ~ting(2): (口)悄悄搬家: *do a (moonlight) ~.* (月夜)悄悄搬家.

float¹ /fləʊt; flot/ *n* [C] **1** piece of cork or other light material used on a fishing-line (to indicate when the bait has been taken) or to support the edge of a fishing-net. (钓鱼线或鱼网边上的)浮标; 浮子. **2** hollow ball or other air-filled container, eg to regulate the level of water in a cistern, or to support an aircraft on water. 浮球; 浮筒(例如调节贮水池水位或支持水上飞机者). **3** low platform on wheels, used for showing things in a procession; kind of wagon or cart with a low floor. 游行车; 一种底板低的车.

float² /fləʊt; flot/ *vi, vt* **1** [VP2A, C] be held up in air, gas or (esp) on the surface of liquid; move with moving liquid or air: 飘浮; (尤指)漂; 浮; 漂行; 漂动: *dust ~ing in the air.* 飘浮在空中的灰尘. *Wood ~s on water.* 木头漂浮于水上. *A balloon ~ed across the sky.* 气球飘过天空. *The boat ~ed down the river.* 那船顺河漂行. **2** [VP6A, 15A, B] cause to ~; keep ~ing: 使漂; 使浮动; 使漂动: ~ *a raft of logs down a river.* 使一圆木筏顺河漂下. *The ship was ~ed by the tide,* eg after sticking fast on a sand-bank. 那船被潮水冲动(例如在搁浅于沙洲上之后). *There wasn't enough water to ~ the ship.* 没有足够深的水使船漂浮起来. **3** [VP6A] get (sth financial) support for in order to start; launch: (商)获经济援助以创办; 开办: ~ *a new business company.* 创办一公司. **4** [VP6A] (finance) allow the foreign exchange value of (a currency) to vary (usu within narrow limits): (财政)让货币的国外兑换值浮动(通常是在有限制范围内): ~ *the pound/dollar.* 让镑(金圆)的国外兑换值浮动. **5** circulate: 传播: ~ *a rumour/ an idea.* 传播一谣言(观念). ~·**ing** *adj* **1** fluctuating;

variable: 流动的; 变动的: *the ~ing population,* that part which varies very much, eg sailors in a seaport; 流动性的人口(例如港口的海员): *the ~ing vote,* the votes of those persons who are not committed to a political party. 流动票(不一定投某一政党的选票). **2** ~ing debt, one of which part must be paid on demand, or at a stated time. 流动债务; 短期债务. '~ing rib, (anat) one of the two lower pairs of ribs not attached to the breastbone. (解剖)浮肋.

floa·ta·tion, flo·ta·tion /fləʊ'teɪʃn; flo'teʃən/ *n* [C, U] floating(3) of a business company or enterprise. (公司企业之)创办; 设立.

flock¹ /flɒk; flɑk/ *n* **1** number of birds or animals (usu sheep, goats) of one kind, either kept together or feeding and travelling together: 鸟群; 兽群; (通常指)羊群: *a ~ of wild geese;* 一群雁; ~*s and herds,* sheep and cattle. 羊群和牛群. **2** crowd of people: 人群: *Visitors came in ~s to see the new bridge.* 成群的人来参观这新桥. **3** Christian congregation; number of people together in sb's charge: 基督教会的会众; 受某人管理的一群人: *a priest and his ~.* 牧师和他的教徒. □ *vi* [VP2C, 4A] gather, come or go together in great numbers: 群集; 聚集: *The children ~ed round their teacher.* 孩子们聚集在他们老师的周围. *People ~ed to hear the new prophet.* 人们成群地去听这新的先知演讲.

flock² /flɒk; flɑk/ *n* [C] tuft of wool or hair; (pl) wool or cotton waste for stuffing mattresses, etc. 羊毛丛; 毛丛; (复)填床垫等的羊毛或棉絮.

floe /fləʊ; flo/ *n* [C] sheet of floating ice. 一片浮冰; 浮冰块.

flog /flɒg; flɑg/ *vt* (-gg-) [VP6A] **1** beat severely with a rod or whip. 鞭挞; 鞭笞. ~ *a dead horse,* waste one's efforts. 浪费精力; 徒劳. ~ *sth to death,* be so persistent or repetitive about it (eg a joke, an idea) that people lose interest in it. 努力劝人接受某事物(例如一笑话或观念)以致使人失去兴趣. **2** (sl) sell or exchange (esp sth illicitly obtained, or sth secondhand): (俚)销售或交换(尤指赃物或旧货): ~ *stolen goods/ one's old car.* 销售赃物(旧车). ~·**ging** *n* [U] beating or whipping; [C] instance of this. 鞭打; 鞭笞.

flood¹ /flʌd; flʌd/ *n* [C] **1** (coming of a) great quantity of water in a place that is usually dry: 洪水; 水灾; 泛滥: *The rainstorms caused ~s in the low-lying parts of the town.* 暴风雨在该城的低洼地区造成了水灾. *in ~,* (of a river) overflowing its banks. (指河)泛滥. *the F~;* Noah's F~, (biblical) that described in Genesis. (旧约创世纪中所叙述的)挪亚时代的大洪水. **2** great outpouring or outburst: 大量的流出或发出: ~*s of rain/tears;* 倾盆大雨(泪如泉涌); *a ~ of light/ anger/words/letters.* 一片光明(大发雷霆; 滔滔的言语; 大量的信件). **3** (also 亦作 '~-tide) the flowing in of the tide (form the sea to the land): 涨潮: *The tide is at the ~.* 潮水正在涨. ~ **ebb.** '~-gate *n* gate opened and closed to admit or keep out water, esp the lower gate of a lock. 水门; 水闸. '~-lights *n pl* artificial lighting thrown in a bright and broad beam. 泛光灯; 强力照明灯. '~-light *vt* (pt, pp -lighted, -lit /-lɪt; -lɪt/) light up by this method. 以泛光灯照亮: *The cathedral was ~lit.* 那大教堂被泛光灯照耀着.

flood² /flʌd; flʌd/ *vt, vi* **1** [VP6A, 14, 16A] ~ *(with),* cover or fill with a flood (lit, fig): 淹没; 泛滥(字面, 喻): *The meadows were ~ed.* 草地被淹水淹没了. *The soldiers broke the dikes and ~ed the countryside to keep back the enemy.* 兵士们破堤将那一带地方淹没, 以阻敌人. *We have been ~ed with requests for help.* 我们收到了大批求助的信函. *The stage of the theatre was ~ed with light.* 剧院的舞台被大量的光线照耀着. **2** (of rain) fill (a river) to overflowing; (of streams) 泛滥: *rivers ~ed by heavy rainstorms.* 因暴风雨而泛滥的河流. **3** [VP15B] ~ *out,* compel to leave because of a ~; (fig) inundate: 被洪水迫使离开(喻)泛滥: *Thousands of*

people were ~ed out, forced to leave their homes. 成千上万的人因洪水而被迫离家。 **4** [VP3A] ~ **in**, come in in great quantities or numbers: 涌进: *Applications ~ed in.* 申请书潮涌而来。

floor[1] /flɔː(r); flɔr/ *n* [C] **1** lower surface of a room; part on which one walks: 地板; 室内之地: *sitting on the ~;* 坐在地板上; *a bare ~,* one with no carpet, rugs or other covering. 未铺地毯的地板。 *wipe the ~ with sb,* utterly defeat him, eg in a fight or argument. 彻底击败某人(例如在打斗或辩论中)。 '~**·board** *n* plank of a wooden floor. 一块地板。 '~ **show,** cabaret, entertainment. (餐馆等内的)歌舞表演。 **2** number of rooms, etc on the same level in a building. 楼层。 '**ground ~,** (GB) = level with the street. (英)底层楼; 一楼。 '**first ~,** (GB) = above the ground ~; (US) ground ~. (英)二楼。 (美)一楼。 '**second**/'**third etc ~,** (GB) ~s above the first ~; (US) ~s above the ground ~. (英)三楼, 四楼等; (美)二楼, 三楼等。 *get in on the ground ~,* ⇨ ground[1](10). '~**·walker** *n* (US) = **shop-walker.** **3** bottom of the sea, of a cave, etc. 海底; 洞底; 底部。 **4** part of an assembly hall, eg the Houses of Parliament, Congress, where members sit. 议员席(例如国会中者)。 *take the ~,* speak in a debate. 在辩论中发言。 **5** (opp of *ceiling*) lower limit (of prices). (价格的)最低标准(为 ceiling 之反义词)。 ~**·ing** *n* [U] material, eg boards, used for making ~s. 地板材料。

floor[2] /flɔː(r); flɔr/ *vt* [VP6A] **1** put (a floor) in a building. 铺(地板)。 **2** knock down: 击倒: ~ *a man in a boxing match.* 赛拳时将一人击倒。 **3** (of a problem, argument, etc) puzzle, defeat: (指问题, 议论等)使困惑; 难倒: *Tom was ~ed by two of the questions in the examination paper.* 汤姆被试题中的两个题目难倒了。

floozy, floo·zie /'fluːzɪ; 'fluzɪ/ *n* (sl) slovenly woman, esp a prostitute. 邋遢女人; (尤指)娼妓。

flop /flɒp; flɑp/ *vi, vt* (-pp-) **1** [VP2A, C] move, fall, clumsily or helplessly: 笨拙地移动或落下; 无可奈何地移动或落下: *The fish we had caught were ~ping about in the bottom of the boat.* 我们捕到的那些鱼在船底无可奈何地跳动着。 *He ~ped down on his knees and begged for mercy.* 他咕咚一声跪下来求饶。 **2** [VP15A, B] ~ **down,** put down or drop clumsily or roughly: 笨拙或粗野地抛下: ~ *down a heavy bag.* 笨拙地抛下一重袋。 **3** [VP2A] (sl) (of a book, a play for the theatre, etc) fail. (俚)(指书, 戏剧等)失败。 □ *n* act or sound of ~ping; (sl) failure of a book, play, etc. 笨拙的落下或响声; 笨重的落下声; 扑通声; (俚)(书, 戏剧等之)失败。 □ *adv* with a ~: 扑通落下: *fall ~ into the water.* 扑通一声掉进水里。 ~**py** *adj* (-ier, -iest) inclined to ~; hanging down loosely: 势将扑通落下的; 松松下垂的: *a ~py hat.* 下垂的帽子。

flora /'flɔːrə; 'flɔrə/ *n pl* all the plants of a particular area or period. (某地区或时代的)植物的总称; 植物区系。

floral /'flɔːrəl; 'flɔrəl/ *adj* of flowers: 花的: ~ *designs.* 花的图案。

flori·cul·ture /'flɔːrɪkʌltʃə(r); 'flɔrɪˌkʌltʃə/ *n* [U] the cultivation of flowering plants. 养花; 花卉栽培。

florid /'flɒrɪd; 'flɔrɪd/ *adj* **1** very much ornamented; (too) rich in ornament and colour: 大加装饰的; 过于粉饰的; 华丽的; 绚烂的: ~ *carving;* 过于粉饰的雕刻; *a ~ style,* eg of writing. 华丽的文体。 **2** (of a person's face) naturally 'red': (指人的面孔)红润的: *a ~ complexion.* 面色红润。 ~**·ly** *adv*

florin /'flɒrɪn; 'flɔrɪn/ *n* former name of a British coin worth one tenth of £1 (until 1971, two shillings; now ten pence). 英国昔时硬币名(一九七一年以前值二先令, 现值十便士)。

flor·ist /'flɒrɪst US: 'flɔːr-; 'flɔrɪst/ *n* person who grows or sells flowers. 花商; 经营花卉业者。

floss /flɒs US: flɔːs; flɔs/ *n* [U] rough silk threads on the outside of a silkworm's cocoon; (also 亦作 '~

silk) silk spun from these for needlework. 蚕茧外层的粗丝; (此种粗丝纺成的)刺绣用的丝线。 '**candy-~,** soft, coloured mass of spun sugar, eaten off a stick. 棉花糖。

flo·ta·tion /fləʊ'teɪʃn; flo'teʃən/ = **floatation.**

flo·tilla /flə'tɪlə; flo'tɪlə/ *n* fleet of small warships, eg destroyers. 分遣舰队(小型战舰, 如驱逐舰, 组成的舰队)。

flot·sam /'flɒtsəm; 'flɑtsəm/ *n* [U] (legal) parts of a wrecked ship or its cargo floating in the sea. (法律)遇难船只漂浮在海上的残骸或货物。 ⇨ **jetsam.**

flounce[1] /flaʊns; flaʊns/ *vi* [VP2C] move with exaggerated or impatient movements: 夸张或不耐烦地走动: ~ *out of/about the room.* 不耐烦地离开了屋子(在室内走来走去)。 □ *n* [C] fling; jerk; sudden impatient movement of the body. 急冲; 急转; 因不耐烦身体所作的突然扭动。

flounce[2] /flaʊns; flaʊns/ *n* [C] (often ornamental) strip of cloth or lace sewn by the upper edge to a woman's skirt. 衣裙上之荷叶边装饰。 □ *vt* [VP6A] trim with a ~ or ~s. 饰以荷叶边。

floun·der[1] /'flaʊndə(r); 'flaʊndə/ *vi* [VP2A, C] make violent and vain efforts (as when trying to get out of deep snow, or when one is in deep water and unable to swim); (fig) hesitate, make mistakes, when trying to do sth: 挣扎(如陷入深雪中时或不会游泳而跌入深水中时所作的); (喻)踌躇或错乱地做事: ~ *through a speech,* eg in a foreign language. 错乱地做完一次演说(例如用外国语)。

floun·der[2] /'flaʊndə(r); 'flaʊndə/ *n* small flatfish, used as food. 比目鱼类(可食用)。

flour /'flaʊə(r); flaʊr/ *n* [U] fine meal, powder, made from grain, used for making bread, cakes, pastry, etc. 面粉; 谷类之粉。 □ *vt* [VP6A] cover or sprinkle with ~. 覆以面粉; 撒以粉末。 ~**y** *adj* of, like, covered with, ~. 面粉的; 似面粉的; 粉状的; 覆有粉末的。

flour·ish /'flʌrɪʃ; 'flɝɪʃ/ *vi, vt* **1** [VP2A] grow in a healthy manner; be well and active; prosper: 旺盛; 兴隆; 茂盛: *His business is ~ing.* 他的生意兴隆。 *I hope you are all ~ing,* keeping well. 我希望你们都安好。 **2** [VP6A] wave about and show: 挥舞并显示: ~ *a sword.* 舞剑。 **3** [VP2A] (of a famous person) be alive and active (at the time indicated): (指某一时代的名人)享盛名; 生存并活跃: *When did the troubadours ~?* 吟游诗人何时盛行? □ *n* [C] ~ing movement; curve or decoration, ornament in handwriting, eg to a signature; loud, exciting passage of music; fanfare: 挥舞; 花体字(如签名用者); 响亮而令人兴奋的一段音乐; 鼓号曲: *a ~ of trumpets,* eg to welcome a distinguished visitor. 一段响亮的喇叭乐曲(例如欢迎贵宾时所吹奏者)。

flout /flaʊt; flaʊt/ *vt* [VP6A] oppose; treat with contempt: 反对; 蔑视: ~ *sb's wishes/advice.* 轻视某人的愿望(劝告)。

flow /fləʊ; flo/ *vi* (*pt, pp* ~**ed**) [VP2A, C] **1** move along or over as a river does; move smoothly: 流; 流动: *Rivers ~ into the sea.* 千条大河归大海。 *The tears ~ed from her eyes.* 泪水从她的眼中流出。 *The river ~ed over* (= overflowed) *its banks.* 河水泛滥了。 *Gold ~ed* (= was sent) *out of the country.* 黄金外流。 **2** (of hair, articles of dress, etc) hang down loosely: (指头发, 衣服等)飘垂: *~ing robes;* 飘垂的长袍; *~ing hair* (= 长悬的)领带; *hair ~ing down her back.* 飘垂在她背部的头发。 **3** come from; be the result of: 来自; 为…之结果: *Wealth ~s from industry and economy.* 财富由勤俭而来。 **4** (of the tide) come in; rise: (潮)涨: *The tide began to ~.* 开始涨潮了。 ⇨ **ebb.** □ *n* (*sing only*) ~ing movement; quantity that ~s: 流动; 流动量: 流量: *a good ~ of water;* 大量流水; *a ~ of angry words;* 滔滔的怒言; *the ebb and ~ of the sea.* 海潮的涨落。 *The tide is on the ~,* coming in. 正在涨潮。

flower /'flauə(r); 'flauɚ/ n 1 that part of a plant that produces seeds. 花。 in ~, with the ~s out. 开着花。 '~·bed n plot of land in which ~s are grown. 花坛; 花床。 '~ garden, one with ~ing plants, not vegetables, etc. 花园。 '~-girl n girl who sells ~s, eg in a market. 卖花女。 '~ children/people, (colloq, in the 1960's) hippies favouring universal love and peace. (口, 二十世纪六十年代之) 嬉皮 (主张博爱与和平)。 '~ power, the ideals of these people. 上述嬉皮的理想。 '~·pot n pot, eg of red earthenware or plastic, in which a plant may be grown. 花盆; 花钵。 '~ show n exhibition at which ~s are shown (often in competition for prizes). 花展(常为比赛性的)。 2 the ~ of, the finest part of: 最佳部分; 精华: in the ~ of one's strength; 年轻力壮之时; the ~ of the nation's manhood. the finest men. 一国中最优秀的男子。 3 ~s of speech, ornamental phrases. 华丽的词藻。 □ vi [VP2A, C] produce ~s: 开花: ~ing bushes; 开花的灌木; late-~ing chrysanthemums. 迟开的菊花。 **flow·ered** adj decorated with floral patterns: 饰有花的图样的: ~ed chintz. 印花棉布。 ~·y adj (-ier, -iest) having many ~s: 多花的: ~y fields; 多花的田野; (fig) full of ~s of speech: (喻) 多华丽的词藻的; 绚丽的: ~y language. 绚丽的文辞。 ~·less adj not having, not producing, ~s: 无花的; 不开花的: ~less plants. 不开花的植物。

flown /fləun; flon/ pp of **fly**.

flu /fluː; flu/ n (colloq abbr of) influenza. (口)流行性感冒(为 influenza 之略)。

fluc·tu·ate /'flʌktʃueit; 'flʌktʃu,et/ vi [VP2A, C] (of levels, prices, etc) move up and down; be irregular: (指标准, 价格等)波动; 不规则: fluctuating prices; 波动的物价; ~ between hope and despair. 徘徊于希望与失望之间。 **fluc·tu·ation** /ˌflʌktʃu'eiʃn; ˌflʌktʃu'eʃən/ n [U] fluctuating; [C] fluctuating movement: 变动; 波动: fluctuations of temperature; 温度的变动; fluctuations in the exchange rates. 兑换率的波动。

flue /fluː; flu/ n [C] channel, pipe or tube for carrying heat, hot air or smoke to, from or through a boiler, oven, etc: 烟道; 锅炉通气管; 焰管: clean the ~s of soot. 清除烟道中的煤烟。

flu·ent /'fluːənt; 'fluənt/ adj (of a person) able to speak smoothly and readily: (指人)说话流利的: a ~ speaker; 口若悬河的演说者; (of speech) coming smoothly and readily: (指说话)流畅的; 流利的: speak ~ French. 说流利的法语。 ~·ly adv fluency /'fluːənsi; 'fluənsi/ n [U] the quality of being ~. 流利; 流畅。

fluff /flʌf; flʌf/ n 1 [U] soft, feathery stuff given off by blankets or other soft woolly material; soft fur or down[1]. (毛毯或其他呢绒物之)绒毛; 软毛; 柔毛。 2 bungled attempt. 拙劣的尝试; 失误。 ⇨ 2 below. 参看动词第 2 义。 □ vt 1 [VP6A, 15B] ~ (out), shake, puff or spread out: 抖开; 抖松: ~ out a pillow. 抖松一枕头。 The bird ~ed (out) its feathers. 这鸟抖开它的羽毛。 2 [VP6A] bungle (sth in games, in speaking one's lines in a play, etc): 拙劣地做(比赛失误, 背错台词): ~ a catch, eg fail to catch the ball in cricket. 未接住球(例如在板球戏中)。 ~·y adj (-ier, -iest) of or like ~; covered with ~: 绒毛的; 似绒毛的; 覆有绒毛的: Newly hatched chickens are like ~y balls. 刚孵出的小鸡象绒毛球。

fluid /'fluːid; 'fluid/ adj able to flow (as gases and liquids do); (of ideas, etc) not fixed; capable of being changed: 流动的(如气体和液体); (指思想等)不固定的; 可改变的: ~ opinions/plans. 不固定的意见(计划)。 □ n [C, U] (chem) ~ substance, eg water, air, mercury; (colloq) liquid substance. (化学)流质(例如水, 空气, 水银); (口)流体; 液体。 ~ ounce, ⇨ App 5. 参看附录五。

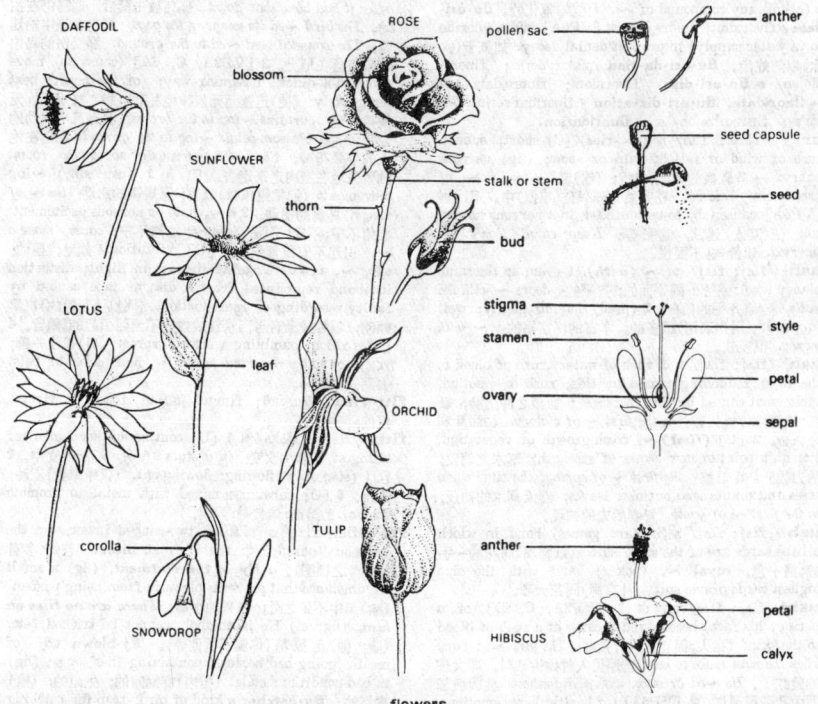

DAFFODIL
ROSE — blossom
SUNFLOWER
thorn
bud — stalk or stem
LOTUS
leaf
ORCHID
corolla
TULIP
SNOWDROP
HIBISCUS
anther
petal
calyx
pollen sac
anther
seed capsule
seed
stigma
stamen — style
ovary — petal
sepal

flowers

~·ity /fluːˈɪdətɪ; fluˈɪdətɪ/ n quality of being ~. 流动性; 流动状态。

fluke[1] /fluːk; fluk/ n [C] sth resulting from a fortunate accident; lucky stroke: 侥幸的结果; 侥幸: win (eg a game of billiards) by a ~. 侥幸得胜(例如撞球比赛)。

fluke[2] /fluːk; fluk/ n 1 broad, triangular flat end of each arm of an anchor. 锚爪; 锚钩。2 either lobe of a whale's tail. 鲸尾二裂片之一。⇨ the illus at sea. 参看 sea 之插图。

fluke[3] /fluːk; fluk/ n parasite flat worm, found in a sheep's liver. (羊肝中之)肝蛭。

flume /fluːm; flum/ n [C] artificial channel for carrying water for industrial use, eg to a waterwheel in a mill, or for carrying logs. 工业用途的人工水道(例如通往磨坊之水车或运送干材用者)。

flum·mox /ˈflʌməks; ˈflʌməks/ vt [VP6A] (colloq) disconcert; confound. (口)使窘狼;使失措。

flung /flʌŋ; flʌŋ/ pt, pp of **fling**.

flunk /flʌŋk; flʌŋk/ vi, vt n (out), [VP2A, 2C,6A, 15B] (US colloq) fail (an examination); fail (a candidate): (美口)考试(某科)不及格; 予以不及格: to ~ Biology／to be ~ed (out) in Biology. 生物学不及格。

flun·key, flunky /ˈflʌŋkɪ; ˈflʌŋkɪ/ n (pl -keys, -kies /-kɪz; -kɪz/) (derog) servant in uniform. (贬)着制服的男仆。

flu·or·escent /fluəˈresnt; ˌfluəˈresn̩t/ adj (of substances) taking in radiations and sending them out in the form of light: (指物质)萤光性的; 发萤光的: ~ lamps／lighting. 萤光灯，日光灯(萤光)。**flu·or·escence** /-sns; -sn̩s/ n

flu·or·ine /ˈfluərin; ˈfluərɪn/ n (chem) (symbol F) pale-yellow gas resembling chlorine. (化学)氟(似氯之淡黄气, 符号为 F)。**flu·or·ide** /ˈfluəraɪd; ˈfluəraɪd/ n (chem) any compound of ~. (化学)氟化物。**flu·ori·date** /ˈfluərɪdet; ˈfluərə̩det/ vt [VP6A] add a fluoride to (a water supply) to prevent dental decay. 加氟于(饮水)以防蛀齿。**flu·ori·da·tion** /ˌfluərɪˈdeʃn; ˌfluərə̩-ˈdeʃn/ n **flu·ori·dize** /ˈfluərɪdaɪz; ˈfluərə̩daɪz/ vt = **fluoridate**. **flu·ori·diz·ation** /ˌfluərɪdaɪˈzeɪʃn US: -dɪˈz-; ˌfluərɪdaɪˈzeʃn/ n = **fluoridation**.

flurry /ˈflʌrɪ; ˈflʌrɪ/ n (pl -ries) [C] short, sudden rush of wind or fall of rain or snow; (fig) nervous hurry: 一阵骤疾的风, 雨或雪; (喻)慌张: in a ~ of excitement／alarm. 在突然一阵兴奋(惊惶)中。□ vt [VP6A] cause (sb) to be confused, in a nervous hurry, etc: 使(某人)迷乱, 慌张等: Keep calm! Don't get flurried. 镇静些! 不要慌。

flush[1] /flʌʃ; flʌʃ/ adj ~ (with), 1 even; in the same plane; level: 同平面的; 同平的; 齐平的: doors ~ with the walls. 与墙齐平的门户。2 (pred) having plenty; well supplied: (用作表语)很多的; 丰富的; 富裕的: ~ with money. 很多钱。

flush[2] /flʌʃ; flʌʃ/ n 1 rush of water; rush of blood to the face; reddening caused by this; rush or emotion, excitement caused by this: 涌; 激流; 血液之冲上脸; 晕红; 脸红; 激动兴奋: in the first ~ of victory. 初尝胜利之兴奋。2 [U] (first) ~, fresh growth of vegetation, etc; high point or new access of strength: 草木之萌发; 活力的充沛; 旺盛: the first ~ of spring, the time when trees and plants send out new leaves; 春天草木的初茂; in the first ~ of youth. 青春活力的初现。

flush[3] /flʌʃ; flʌʃ/ n (in card games) hand in which all the cards are of the same suit. (纸牌戏)同花的一手牌; 清一色。**'royal** ~, (poker) hand with the five highest cards of one suit. (扑克牌)同花大顺。

flush[4] /flʌʃ; flʌʃ/ vi, vt 1 [VP2A, C, D] (of a person, his face) become red because of a rush of blood to the skin: (指人, 面孔)变红; 发红: The girl ~ed (up) when the man spoke to her. 当那男人对她讲话时, 那女孩的脸红了。He ~ed crimson with indignation. 他因愤怒而面孔涨得通红。2 [VP6A] (of health, heat, emotions,

etc) cause (the face) to become red in this way; (fig) fill with pride; encourage: (指健康, 热, 感情等)使(面孔)发红; (喻)使得意; 激励: Shame ~ed his cheeks, 羞愧使他的脸红了。She was ~ed with exercise. 她因运动而脸发红。The men were ~ed with success／joy／insolence. 那些人因胜利而得意(因喜悦而兴奋, 因侮辱而激动)。3 [VP6A] clean or wash with a ~ of water. 冲洗: ~ the drains; 冲洗阴沟; ~ the pan, eg in a lavatory, by emptying the cistern. 冲洗盆状器皿(如抽水马桶)。4 [VP2A, C] (of water) rush out in a flood. (指水)涌出。

flush[5] /flʌʃ; flʌʃ/ vt, vi 1 [VP6A, 2A] (of birds) (cause to) rise suddenly and fly away: 惊起(鸟); (鸟)突然飞走: ~ a pheasant. 惊起一野鸡。2 [VP14] ~ from／out of, chase, drive from a hiding-place: 自隐藏处赶出; 逐出: snipers ~ed from foxholes. 自狙兵坑逐出的狙击兵。

flus·ter /ˈflʌstə(r); ˈflʌstə/ vt [VP6A] make nervous or confused. 使紧张; 使慌乱。□ n nervous state: 紧张; 慌乱: all in a ~. 慌狼不堪。

flute[1] /fluːt; flut/ n musical woodwind instrument in the form of a pipe, blown at the side, with holes stopped by keys. 长笛。⇨ the illus at **brass**. 参看 brass 之插图。□ vi play the ~. 吹笛。**flut·ist** /ˈfluːtɪst; ˈflutɪst/ n (chiefly US) flautist. (主美)吹笛者; 长笛演奏家。

flute[2] /fluːt; flut/ vt [VP6A] make vertical grooves in (a pillar, etc): 在(柱上等)刻凹槽: ~d columns. 饰有凹槽的柱子。**flut·ing** n [U] grooves cut on a surface as a decoration. 装饰性的凹槽。

flut·ter /ˈflʌtə(r); ˈflʌtə/ vt, vi 1 [VP2A, C, 6A, 15A, B] (of birds) move the wings hurriedly or irregularly without flying, or in short flights only; cause (the wings) to move in this way: (指鸟)鼓翼; 拍翅; 鼓(翼); 拍(翅膀): The wings of the bird still ~ed after it had been shot down. 那鸟被击落后, 翅膀仍在拍动。The bird ~ed its wings in the cage. 那鸟在笼中拍翅膀。The wounded bird ~ed to the ground. 那受伤的鸟拍着翅膀落在地上。2 [VP2A, C, 6A] (cause to) move about in a quick, irregular way; (of the heart) beat irregularly: (使)迅速而无规律地乱动; (指心脏)扑动; 无规律地跳: curtains ~ing in the breeze; 在微风中飘动的窗帘; apple-blossom petals ~ing to the ground. 飘落在地上的苹果花瓣。She ~ed nervously about the room. 她紧张地在室内走来走去。□ n 1 (usu sing) ~ing movement: (通常用单数)鼓翼; 无规律的急动: the ~ of wings. 鸟翼的拍动。2 a ~, state of nervous excitement: 心绪不宁; 不安; 心绪不宁; cause／make a ~. 引起不安或紧张。3 [U] vibration: 颤动; 摆动: wing ~, as a defect of an aircraft in flight; distortion in sound reproduced from a disc or tape caused by faulty recording or reproduction. (飞机飞行时的)机翼颤动; (唱片或录音带因杂音或播放不当而引起的)颤音。4 [C] (colloq) gambling venture; spree: (口)孤注一掷的冒险; 欢闹: go to the races and have a ~, make a bet or bets. 去赌场一赌赛马。

flu·vial /ˈfluːvɪəl; ˈfluvɪəl/ adj of, found in, rivers. 河的; 河中的。

flux /flʌks; flʌks/ n 1 [U] continuous succession of changes: 继续的改变: in a state of ~, 不断改变中。2 [C] (sing only) flowing; flowing out. (仅用单数)流动; 流出。3 [C] substance mixed with metal to promote fusion. 助溶剂; 熔接剂; 焊剂。

fly[1] /flaɪ; flaɪ/ n (pl **flies**) two-winged insect, esp the common 'housefly; ⇨ the illus at **insect**. 苍蝇(参看 insect 之插图)。**a fly in the ointment**, (fig) a small circumstance that prevents pleasure from being perfect. (喻)美中不足之处; 扫兴的小事。**There are no flies on him**, (fig) he is no fool, cannot be tricked, etc. (喻; 俚)他很精(你骗不了他等)。**'fly-blown** adj (of meat) (going bad because) containing flies' eggs; (fig) in bad condition; stale. (指肉)有蝇卵的; 生蛆的; (喻)腐坏的。**'fly·catcher** n kind of bird; trap for catching

flies. 鶺; 京燕; 蝇虎类鸟; 捕蝇器。 **'fly-fish** vi [VP2A] fish with artificial flies as bait. 以假蝇做饵钓鱼。 Hence, 由此产生, **'fly-fishing** n [U]. **'fly-paper** n strip of sticky paper used for catching flies. 捕蝇纸。 **'fly-trap** n trap for catching flies. 捕蝇器。 **'fly·weight** n boxer weighing 112 lb (50.8kg) or less. 蝇量级拳击手(体重不超过112磅或50.8公斤的)。

fly² /flaɪ; flaɪ/ vi, vt (pt **flew** /fluː; flu/, pp **flown** /fləʊn; flon/) **1** [VP2A, B, C, D, 4A] move through the air as a bird does, or in an aircraft: 飞; 飞行; 空中航行: birds flying in the air; 天上飞的鸟; fly from London to Paris; 自伦敦飞行至巴黎; fly (across) the Atlantic. 飞越大西洋。 **fly high**, be ambitious. 怀大志; 野心很大。 The bird is/has flown, The person wanted has escaped. 要捕的人跑掉了。 **2** [VP6A, 15A, B] direct or control the flight of (aircraft); transport goods/passengers in aircraft: 驾驶(飞机,飞船等); 以飞机运输(货物,乘客): Five thousand passengers were flown to Paris during Easter weekend. 复活节的周末有五千位乘客飞往巴黎。 **3** [VP2A, C, D, 4A] go or move quickly; rush along; pass quickly: 疾行; 迅速地动: He flew down the road. 他沿着路飞奔。 The children flew to meet their mother. 孩子们跑着迎接他们的母亲。 It's getting late; we must fly. 天色渐渐晚了, 我们必须快跑。 The door flew open. 门突然敞开了。 He paid us a flying visit, a very short, fleeting visit. 他匆忙地拜访我们。 fly at sb, rush angrily at sb. 愤怒地冲向某人。 let fly (at), ⇨ let¹(4). fly off the handle, ⇨ handle. fly in the face of, **(a)** defy openly: 公然反抗: You're flying in the face of the law. 你在公然违法。 **(b)** be quite contrary to: 与…完全相反: This version of what happened flies in the face of all the evidence. 这个对事情发生的经过所作的叙述与证据完全相反。 fly into a rage/passion/temper, become suddenly angry. 勃然大怒。 fly to arms, take up arms eagerly. 急速武装起来。 fly to bits/into pieces, break to bits and scatter. 成碎片而飞散。 make the feathers/fur fly, cause quarrelling or fighting. 引起争吵或争斗。 make the money fly, spend it quickly, recklessly. 挥霍。 send sb flying, strike him so that he falls over or backwards. 将某人击倒或击退。 send things flying, send or throw them violently in all directions. 将东西向四面八方投掷。 **4** [VP6A] cause (a kite) to rise and stay high in the air; raise (a flag) so that it waves in the air. 放(风筝); 悬(旗)。 **5** flee from: 逃离; 逃出: fly the country. 逃出国境。

fly³ /flaɪ; flaɪ/ n (pl **flies**) **1** (also, colloq, pl used with sing meaning) flap of cloth on a garment to contain or cover a zip fastener or buttonholes, eg down the front of a pair of trousers: (口, 复数形式单数意义)衣服上盖拉链或钮扣间的遮盖(例如裤子前面者): John, your fly is/flies are undone! 约翰, 你裤子的拉链未拉上(钮扣未扣好)。 **2** flap of canvas at the entrance to a tent or covered wagon. 帐篷或篷车的门帘。 **3** (old use) one-horse hackney carriage. (旧用法)单马的出租马车。 **4** outer edge of a flag farthest from the flagpole. 旗的外端。

fly⁴ /flaɪ; flaɪ/ adj (sl) cunning; alert; not to be deceived or hoodwinked. (俚)狡猾的; 机警的; 不易受骗的。

flyer, flier /'flaɪə(r); 'flaɪɚ/ n **1** animal, vehicle, etc going with exceptional speed. 行走特快的动物, 车辆等。 **2** airman. 飞行者。

fly·ing /'flaɪɪŋ; 'flaɪɪŋ/ part adj, gerund (in compounds): (用于复合词中): **'~ boat** n form of seaplane without floats and with a fuselage that floats on water. 水上飞机; 飞艇。 **'~·bomb** n rocket filled with explosives that can be fired to a great distance. 飞弹; 自导飞弹。 **~ 'buttress** n (archit) one arching from a column up to a wall, ⇨ the illus at church. (建筑)飞扶拱; 飞扶墙; 拱柱(参看church之插图)。 **'~ club**, club for those interested in ~ as a sport. 航空俱乐部。

~ 'colours, flags on display (as during a ceremony). 展示的旗帜(如飘扬于庆典中者)。 come through/off with ~ colours, ⇨ colour¹(8). **~ 'column**, (mil) body of troops able to move rapidly and act independently. (军)快速突击部队; 别动队。 **~ field**, airfield. 飞机场。 **'~·fish**, (kind of) tropical fish able to rise out of the water and move forward. 飞鱼。 **,~·fox**, (kind of) large fruit-eating bat. 以水果为食的大蝙蝠。 **'F~ Officer**, rank in the Royal Air Force below Flight Lieutenant. (英国皇家空军之)空军中尉。 **~ 'jump**, one made with a running start. 急行跳高。 **,~ 'saucer**, unidentified flying object seen, or thought to have been seen, moving across the sky, eg one said to have arrived from another planet. 飞碟。 **'~·squad**, part of a police force organized (with fast cars) for pursuit of (suspected) criminals. 机动警察队(备有快速汽车, 可迅速追捕犯人或嫌疑犯)。 **~ 'visit**, hasty visit made while passing. 匆匆拜访; 过访。

fly·leaf /'flaɪliːf; 'flaɪ,lif/ n blank leaf at the beginning or end of a book. 扉页; 蝴蝶页(书籍前后的空白页)。

fly·over /'flaɪəʊvə(r); 'flaɪ,ovɚ/ n **1** (US 美 = overpass) roadway, bridge, etc which crosses above another roadway, etc (as on a motorway). 立交桥; 横跨另一道路之上的道路或天桥(如高速公路上者)。 **2** (GB) (英) = flypast.

flyovers

fly·past /'flaɪpaːst US: -pæst; 'flaɪ,pæst/ n flight of aircraft in formation, usu at a low altitude, as part of a military display. 空中分列式(阅兵之项目)。

fly·post /'flaɪpəʊst; 'flaɪpost/ vt [VP6A] post⁶(1) up rapidly (and often illegally). 迅速地(往往是非法地)张贴。 **~er** n sth ~ed; sb who ~s. 迅速(非法)张贴之物; 迅速(非法)张贴之人。

fly·wheel /'flaɪwiːl US: -hwiːl; 'flaɪ,hwil/ n heavy wheel revolving on a shaft to regulate machinery. 飞轮; 整速轮。

foal /fəʊl; fol/ n young horse (colt or filly). 小马; 幼马; 驹。 ⇨ the illus at **domestic**. 参看 domestic 之插图。 in/with ~, (of a mare) pregnant. (指母马)怀孕。 □ vi [VP2A] give birth to a ~. 生小马。

foam /fəʊm; fom/ n [U] **1** white mass of small air bubbles formed in or on a liquid by motion, or on an animal's lips, eg after exertion. 泡沫; 涎沫; 口角飞沫。 **2** (also 亦作 **,~·'rubber**) spongy rubber used in upholstery (eg in seats, mattresses). 泡沫胶(例如座垫中者)。 □ vi [VP2A, C] form ~; break into ~; send out ~ (at the mouth): 起泡沫; 变泡沫; (口)流泡沫: waves ~ing along the beach; 沿着海滩起泡沫的海浪; a glass of ~ing beer, beer with froth on it; 一杯起泡沫的啤酒; (fig) (喻) ~ing with rage, looking angry. 生气的。 **~y** adj

fob /fɒb; fab/ vt (-bb-) [VP15B] fob sth off on sb; fob sb off with sth, get a person to accept sth of little or no value by deceit or trickery. 以劣物哄骗某人。

fo·cal /'fəʊkl; 'fokl/ adj of or at a focus: 焦点的; 在焦点上的: the ~ length/distance of a lens, from the surface of a lens to its focus. 透镜的焦距。

fo'c'sle /'fəʊksl; 'foksl/ n = **forecastle**.

fo·cus /'fəʊkəs; 'fokəs/ n (pl ~es or **foci** /'fəʊsaɪ; 'fosaɪ/) **1** meeting-point of rays of light, heat, etc;

point, distance, at which the sharpest outline is given (to the eye, through a telescope, through a lens on a camera plate, etc): 焦点;焦距: *The image is in/out of* ~. 这影像在焦点上(外)。*Bring the object into* ~ *if you want a good photograph.* 你如果要照一张好像，就要把焦点对准物体。 **2** point at which interests, tendencies, etc meet: 兴趣，趋势等之中心: *the* ~ *of attention;* 注意力的中心; *the* ~ *of an earthquake/storm/disease, etc.* 震源(暴风圈的中心；疾病的主要患部等)。 □ *vt, vi* (**-s-** or **-ss-**) **1** [VP2A, C, 6A, 14] ~ (**on**), (cause to) come together at a ~; adjust (an instrument, etc) so that it is in ~: (使)聚集于焦点;调整(仪器等)使其在焦点上: ~ *the sun's rays on sth with a burning-glass;* 以取火镜使太阳光线聚集于某物上; ~ *the lens of a microscope.* 调整显微镜的透镜以定焦点。 **2** [VP14] ~ *on,* concentrate: 集中: ~ *one's attention/thoughts/ efforts on a problem.* 集中注意力(思想，努力)于一问题。

fod·der /'fɒdə(r); 'fɑdɚ/ *n* [U] dried food, hay, etc for farm animals, horses, etc. 牛马等之饲料[秣;草料.

foe /fəʊ; fo/ *n* (poet) enemy. (诗)敌人。

foe·tus (US = **fe·tus**) /'fiːtəs; 'fitəs/ *n* fully developed embryo in the womb or in an egg. (发育完整的)胎儿;胚胎。 ⇨ the illus at **reproduce**. 参看 reproduce 之插图。 **foe·tal** (US = **fe·tal**) /'fiːtl; 'fitl/ *adj* of, like, a ~. 胎儿的;似胎胎的: *the foetal position* (in the womb). 胎儿(在子宫内)的位置。

fog /fɒg *US:* fɔːg; fag/ *n* **1** [U] vapour suspended in the atmosphere at or near the earth's surface, thicker than mist and difficult to see through: 雾(比 mist 浓): *Fog is the sailor's worst enemy.* 雾是船员最大的敌人。 *in a fog,* (fig) puzzled; in a haze. (喻)迷惑; 困惑; 坠入五里雾中。 'fog·bank *n* dense mass of fog on the sea. 海上的浓雾; 雾堤。 'fog·bound *adj* unable to proceed safely because of fog. 因雾而无法安全行进的。 'fog-horn *n* instrument used for warning ships in fog. 雾角 (用以警告雾中船只的号角)。 'fog·lamp, headlamp (on a motor vehicle) providing a strong beam of light for use in foggy weather. 雾灯(汽车在雾中行驶用的强光灯)。 'fog·signal, device placed on railway lines in fog to explode when a train passes over it and so warn drivers. 浓雾信号; 雾中信号(置于有雾的铁道上，火车经过时则爆炸以警告驾驶人员)。 **2** [C] period of fog; abnormal darkened state of the atmosphere: 有雾时期; 大气反常的昏暗状态: *London used to have bad fogs in winter.* 过去伦敦在冬季有大雾。 **3** [C, U] (area of) cloudiness on a developed photographic plate or film. 照相底片或感光板上之模糊: 底片或感光板上的模糊迹。 □ *vt* (-**gg**-) cover with, as with, fog; bewilder: 雾笼罩于; 使朦胧; 使迷惑: *I'm a bit foggy about it.* 我对那件事有点糊涂了。 **foggy** *adj* (**-ier, -iest**) **1** dense, not clear, because of fog: 有浓雾的; 雾色朦胧的: *a foggy evening;* 有雾的晚上; *foggy weather.* 有雾的天气。 **2** obscure, confused: 模糊的; 迷惑的: *have only a foggy idea of what something means.* 对某事的意义仅有一模糊的观念。 *I haven't the foggiest idea,* I don't know. 我不知道。

fogey (US = **fogy**) /'fəʊgɪ; 'fogɪ/ *n* (*pl* ~**s**, US **fogies**) (*old*) ~, person with old-fashioned ideas which he is unwilling to change. 老顽固。

foible /'fɔɪbl; 'fɔɪbl/ *n* [C] slight peculiarity or defect of character, often one of which a person is wrongly proud. 性格上小的特色或缺点(误误以自负者); 瑕疵; 沾沾自喜的性格特点。

foil[1] /fɔɪl; fɔɪl/ *n* **1** [U] metal rolled or hammered into a thin, flexible sheet: 箔: *lead/tin/aluminium* ~, eg as wrapped round chocolate or cigarettes. 铅 (锡,铝)箔(例如包装巧克力或香烟者)。 **2** [C] person or thing that contrasts with, and sets off strongly, the qualities of another: 衬托的人或物: *A plain old woman serves as a* ~ *to a beautiful young woman.* 一面貌平庸的老妇可作为一美丽的少女的衬托。

foil[2] /fɔɪl; fɔɪl/ *n* light sword without a sharp edge and with a button on the point, for fencing. 钝头剑; 花

梢剑。

foil[3] /fɔɪl; fɔɪl/ *vt* [VP6A] baffle; prevent (sb) from carrying out his plans; make plans/designs ineffective: 挫败; 阻止(某人)实行其计划; 阻挠(计划): *We* ~*ed him/his plans.* 我们阻挠了他(他的计划)。 *He was* ~*ed in his attempt to deceive the girl.* 他企图欺骗那女孩子的计划失败了。

foist /fɔɪst; fɔɪst/ *vt* [VP14, 15A] ~ *sth (off) on sb,* trick him into accepting (a useless article, etc). 混骗; 骗某人接受(无用之物等)。

fold[1] /fəʊld; fold/ *vt, vi* **1** [VP6A, 15B] bend one part of a thing back over on itself: 折叠: ~ *a letter,* before putting it in an envelope; 折叠一信; ~ *a newspaper;* 将报纸折叠; ~ *back the bedclothes.* 把被褥折起来。 **2** [VP2A, C] become ~ed; be able to be ~ed: 折叠起来; 可以折起: ~*ing doors,* having hinged parts; 折门; *a* ~*ing boat/bed/chair,* made so as to occupy a smaller space when not in use. 可折叠的舟(床,椅)。 *The window shutters* ~ *back.* 百叶窗可以折起来。 ~ (*up*), (fig; colloq) collapse; come to an end: (喻;口)垮台; 失败; 结束: *The business finally* ~*ed up last week.* 生意终于在上周垮掉了。 **3** ~ *one's arms,* cross them over the chest. 交臂; 抱臂。 ~ *sb/sth in one's arms,* hold him/it to the breast. 拥抱某人(抱着某物)。 **4** [VP15A, B] cover, wrap up: 包起: ~ *sth (up) in paper;* 将某物用纸包起; ~ *sth round;* 将某物包起来; *hills* ~*ed in mist.* 为雾所笼罩的群山。 **5** (cooking) mix an ingredient (eg beaten eggs) into another (eg flour) by turning them with a wooden spoon. (烹调)以木匙搅合(例如将面粉和打散的蛋搅合)。 □ *n* **1** part that is ~ed: 折叠部分: *a dress hanging in loose* ~*s:* 有宽松褶层的衣服; line made by ~*ing.* 折缝。 **2** hollow in mountains. 山坳;山谷;山窝。 ~*er n* **1** holder (made of ~ed cardboard or other stiff material) for loose papers. 硬纸夹。 **2** ~*ing card or paper with advertisements, railway timetables, etc printed on it, or (US) as a container, eg for matches. (印有广告，火车时间表等的)折叠式卡片;折叠式小册子;(美)折叠式火柴。

fold[2] /fəʊld; fold/ *n* [C] enclosure for sheep; (fig) body of religious believers; members of a Church. 羊栏; (喻)教会团体;某一教会的教徒, *return to the* ~, come or go back home (esp rejoin a body of believers). 回老家(尤指回到教会)。 □ *vt* [VP6A] enclose (sheep) in a ~. 关(羊)入栏。

fo·li·age /'fəʊlɪɪdʒ; 'folɪɪdʒ/ *n* [U] all the leaves of a tree or plant. 树或植物的叶子的总称。

fo·lio /'fəʊlɪəʊ; 'folɪ,o/ *n* (*pl* ~**s**) **1** sheet of paper numbered on one side only; page number of a printed book; (bookkeeping) two opposite pages of a ledger, used for both sides of an account. 单面记页码的一页; (书籍之)页码; (簿记)总帐中左右对记的两页。 **2** large sheet of paper folded once to make two leaves or four pages (of a book); volume made of such sheets: (书本之)对折纸; 对折纸; 对开本; 对折本: ~ *volumes;* 对开本的书卷; *in six volumes* ~. 分成六卷对开本。

folk /fəʊk; fok/ *n* **1** (collective *n*, used with *pl v*) people in general: (集合名词，与复数动词连用)人们; 人民: *Some* ~ *were not satisfied.* 有些人永远不满足。 *Is there more honesty among country* ~ *than among towns* ~? 乡下人较城里人诚实吗? **2** (in compounds) of the common people of a country. (用于复合词中)民间的。 '~-**dance** *n* (music for a) traditional popular dance. 民间舞(曲);土风舞(曲)。 '~-**lore** *n* [U] (study of the) traditional beliefs, tales, etc of a community. 民俗; 民间传说; 民俗学。 '~ **music/song** *n* popular music/song handed down from the past. 民间音乐;民谣;民歌。 '~-**tale** *n* popular story handed down orally from past generations. 民间故事。 **3** (*pl*) (colloq) relatives: (复) (口)亲属;家人: *the old* ~*s at home.* 家里的老人家。

folksy /'fəʊksɪ; 'fɔksɪ/ *adj* (colloq) unpretentious in manners; simple; friendly and sociable. (口)平易的; 朴实的;友善的。

fol·low /'fɒləu; 'falo/ vt, vi 1 [VP2A, B, C, 6A] come, go, have a place, after (in space, time or order): You go first and I will ~ (you). 你先走，我就跟来。Monday ~s Sunday. 星期一在星期日之后。They ~ed us for miles. 他们跟着我们走了好几英里路。One misfortune ~ed (upon) another. 灾祸接踵而来。His arguments were as ~s, as now to be given. 他的意见见如下。~ on, (a) ~ after a period of time. 经过一段时间后再继续。(b) (cricket, of a side) bat again after failing to get the necessary number of runs. (板球，指一方)得分不足后继续攻击。Hence, 由此产生, second innings following the first at once. 一局结束后紧接着举行的第二局。~ through, (a) (tennis, golf, etc) complete a stroke by moving the racker, club, etc after hitting the ball. (网球，高尔夫球等)完成动作(球击出后继续挥动球拍或球棒以完成一击)。Hence, 由此产生, '~-through n [C] such a stroke. (网球、高尔夫球等之)完成动作。(b) complete a task, carry out a promise. 完成工作；实践诺言。2 [VP2A] go along, keep to (a road, etc): 沿…而行；循(路等): F~ this road until you get to the church; then turn left. 顺着这条路一直走到教堂，然后左转弯。3 [VP6A] understand (an argument, sth said, etc): 听得懂(议论，说的话等): Do you ~ my argument? 你听得懂我的意见吗？He spoke so fast that I couldn't ~ him / ~ what he said. 他说得太块，我听不懂他的话。4 [VP6A] engage in as a business, trade, etc: 从事；经营(商业等): ~ the law; 做律师；~ the trade of a builder. 从事建筑业；做营造商。5 [VP6A] take or accept as a guide, an example, etc: 接受(做为指导，例子等): ~ sb's advice; 听从某人的劝告；~ the fashion. 追随时尚；讲究时髦。~ suit, do what has just been done by sb else. 照别例；照样做。6 [VP2A] be necessarily true: 必然是真实的；为必然的结果: Because he is good, it does not ~ that he is wise. 他人好，并不见得就聪明。~s from what you say that.... 根据你的话来推断，则…为必然的结果。7 [VP 15B] ~ sth out, keep to, carry out, to the end: 贯彻；彻底实行: ~ out an enterprise. 贯彻一项事业。~ sth up, pursue, work at further: 追逐；追求: ~ up an advantage / a victory. 乘机(乘胜追出)。Hence, 由此产生, '~-up n (esp) second letter, circular, visit, referring to an earlier one. (尤指)接连的信件，传单，访问。~er n 1 supporter; disciple: 拥护者；信徒；门徒: Mahatma Gandhi and his ~ers. 圣雄甘地及其信徒。2 pursuer. 追捕者；追求者。~ing adj the ~ing, the one or ones about to be mentioned. 下列的。□ n body of supporters: 一批追随者或拥护者: a political leader with a large ~ing. 拥有大批追随者的政治领袖。

fol·ly /'fɒlɪ; 'falɪ/ n (pl -lies) [U] foolishness; [C] foolish act, idea or practice; ridiculous thing. 愚蠢；愚蠢的行为，思想或习惯；荒唐之事。

fo·ment /fəu'ment; fo'mɛnt/ vt [VP6A] 1 put warm water, clothes, lotions, etc on (a part of the body, to lessen pain, etc). (以温水，布布，洗涤剂等)热敷；热罨(身体之患部，以减轻疼痛苦等)。2 (fig) cause or increase (disorder, discontent, ill feeling, etc). (喻)引起或增加(紊乱，不满，恶意等)。fo·men·ta·tion /ˌfəumen'teɪʃn; ˌfomɛn'teʃən/ n [U] ~ing; [C] that which is used for ~ing. 热敷；热罨物；热罨剂。

fond /fɒnd; fand/ adj (-er, -est) 1 (pred only) (仅作表语) be ~ of, like, be full of love for, take pleasure in: 喜欢；喜好: be ~ of music. 爱好音乐。2 loving and kind: 慈爱的: a ~ mother; 慈母; ~ looks.慈爱的样子。3 foolishly loving; doting: 痴爱的；溺爱的: a young wife with a ~ husband. 一少妇与溺爱她的丈夫。4 (of hopes, ambitions) held, but unlikely to be realized. (指希望，抱负)不能实现的。~·ly adv 1 lovingly: 亲爱地；爱怜地: smile ~ly at sb. 爱怜地望着某人。2 in a foolishly optimistic manner: 以一种愚蠢的乐观态度: He ~ly imagined that he could learn French in six weeks. 他天真地想象他能在六个星期内会合法语。~·ness n

fon·dant /'fɒndənt; 'fandənt/ n [C] kind of soft sweet that melts in the mouth. 一种软糖。

fon·dle /'fɒndl; 'fandl/ vt [VP6A] touch or stroke lovingly: 抚弄；抚爱: ~ a baby / a doll / a kitten. 抚弄一婴孔(洋娃娃，小猫)。

fon·due /'fɒndju; 'fandu/ n dish of melted cheese, into which pieces of bread are dipped; dish of hot fat, into which pieces of raw meat are dipped; dish of hot chocolate, into which pieces of fruit are dipped. (蘸面包片的)一碟融化的干酪；(蘸生肉的)一碟热油；(蘸水果片的)一碟热巧克力。

font /fɒnt; fant/ n 1 basin or vessel (often in carved stone) to hold water for baptism; basin for holy water. 洗礼盆(常为一雕刻的石盆)；圣水盆。2 = fount(2).

food /fu:d; fud/ n 1 [U] that which can be eaten by people or animals, or used by plants, to keep them living and for growth: 食物；食料；滋养品: ~ and water; 食物和水; (attrib) (用作定语) ~ rationing; 食物配给; (fig) (喻) ~ for thought / reflection, sth to think / reflect about. 需要思考(考虑)之事。2 [C] kind of ~: 某种食物: breakfast / frozen / packaged ~s. 早餐(冷冻，包装)食品。'~-stuff n material used as ~. 食料；粮食。~·less adj without ~. 无食物的；无食料的。

fool¹ /fu:l; ful/ n 1 person without much sense; stupid or rash person; person whose conduct one considers silly: 蠢人；呆子；傻瓜: What ~s we were not to see the trap! 我们没有看出那个陷阱，多么傻啊！She was ~ enough (= enough of a fool) to believe him. 她会相信他，真是够傻了。be a ~ for one's pains, do sth for which one gets neither reward nor thanks. 做得不到报酬或感激之事。be / live in a ~'s paradise, be / live in a state of carefree happiness that cannot last. 生活在虚幻的乐境中。be sent / go on a ~'s errand, on an errand that is seen in the end to be useless. 做徒劳无功之奔走。make a ~ of sb, trick him; cause him to seem like a ~. 愚弄某人。play the ~, behave stupidly. 做傻样；做傻事。no ~ like an old ~, (prov) said of an aged lover. (谚)痴瓜象老瓜一样傻(指老年恋爱之人)。2 (in the Middle Ages) man employed by a ruler or noble as a clown or jester. (中世纪)帝王或贵族豢养的小丑；弄臣。3 April '~, person deceived, or sent on a ~'s errand, on, All 'F~s' Day, 1st April. 在愚人节(All Fools' Day 四月一日)受愚弄之人。4 (used attrib, colloq) foolish; silly: (用作定语，口)愚蠢的；傻的: a scheme devised by some ~ politician. 某一愚蠢的政客想出的计划。□ vi, vt 1 [VP2A, C] ~ (about / around), behave like a ~; trifle; be idle and silly: 做出似愚人般的行为；玩弄；虚度光阴: If you go on ~ing with that gun, there'll be an accident. 如果你继续玩弄那把枪，就会发生意外。Stop ~ing (about)! 不要做愚蠢无益之事! 2 [VP6A, 14, 15B] ~ sb (out of sth), cheat; deceive: 欺骗: He ~ed her out of her money. 他骗走了她的钱。You can't / don't ~ me! 你骗不了(不要骗)我!

fool² /fu:l; ful/ n creamy liquid of stewed fruit (esp gooseberries), crushed and mixed with cream or custard. 果酱(尤指醋栗酱)与奶油或乳蛋糕制成的食物。

fool·ery /'fu:lərɪ; 'fulərɪ/ n [U] foolish behaviour; (pl -ries) foolish acts, ideas or utterances. 愚行；(复)愚蠢的行动，思想或言语。

fool·hardy /'fu:lha:dɪ; 'ful,hardɪ/ adj foolishly bold; taking unnecessary risks. 有勇无谋的；蛮勇的。fool·hardi·ness n

fool·ish /'fu:lɪʃ; 'fulɪʃ/ adj without reason, sense or good judgement; silly: 蠢的；无头脑的；愚蠢的: How ~ of you to consent! 你竟会同意，多么愚蠢啊! It would be ~ for us to quarrel. 我们争吵是愚蠢的。~·ly adv ~·ness n

fool·proof /'fu:lpru:f; 'ful'pruf/ adj incapable of failure, error or misinterpretation: 不会失败的；不会出错的；不会有误解的: a ~ scheme / design / gadget. 不会有差错的计划(设计，小器具)。

fools·cap /'fuːlskæp; 'ful‚skæp/ n [U] size (17 × 13½ inches) of writing or printing paper. 大页纸(大小为 17×13½ 英寸).

foot[1] /fut; fut/ n (pl **feet** /fiːt; fit/) **1** part forming the lower end of the leg, beginning at the ankle; part of a sock, etc covering the ~: 足; 脚; (袜子等的)脚部: *A dog has four feet.* 狗有四只足. *A dog's feet are called paws.* 狗足称作爪. *He rose to his feet,* stood up. 他站了起来. ⇨ the illus at **leg.** 参看 leg 之插图. **on ~,** (a) walking, not riding. 徒步; 步行. Cf 参较 by bus/car/tram, etc. 乘公共汽车(汽车,电车等). **(b)** (fig) started: (喻)已经开始: *A project is on ~ to build a new tunnel here.* 在此建一新隧道的计划已经开始. **be on one's feet,** (a) be standing: 站着: *I've been on my feet all day.* 我站了一整天. **(b)** rise (to speak): 起立 (以发言): *The Minister was on his feet at once to answer the charge.* 部长即刻起立答复那项指控. **(c)** (fig) be in good health after an illness: (喻)痊愈; 复元: *It's nice to see you on your feet again.* 很高兴看到你已复元了. **fall on one's feet,** (colloq) be fortunate, have good luck. (口)幸运; 有好运. **find one's feet,** ⇨ **find**[2]**(2). have feet of clay,** be weak or cowardly. 衰弱; 怯懦. **have one ~ in the grave,** be near death, eg because of old age. 死期不远; 行将就木(例如因年迈). **keep one's feet,** not fall, eg when walking on ice. 不跌倒(如行走于冰上时). **put one's ~ down,** (colloq) object; protest; be firm. (口)反对; 抗议; 坚持立场. **put one's ~ in it,** (colloq) say or do sth wrong or stupid; blunder. (口)说错话或做错事; 犯错误. **put one's feet up,** (colloq) rest with the legs in a horizontal position. (口)将腿平放着休息. **put one's best ~ forward,** walk (fig, get on with one's work) as fast as one can. 尽快往前走; (喻)全力以赴. **set sth/sb on its/his feet,** make it/him self-supporting, no longer in need of help. 使某事物(或某人)自立. **set sth on ~,** start it; get it going. 发动; 开始. **sweep sb off his feet,** fill him with strong enthusiasm. 使某人狂热. **under ~,** on the ground: 在地上: *wet under ~.* 地上湿. **wait on/bind sb hand and ~,** ⇨ **hand**[1]**(1). 2** step, pace, tread: 脚步; 步法; 步态: *light/swift/fleet of ~,* stepping or walking lightly, swiftly, etc. 脚步轻快(疾速)的. **3** lowest part; bottom: 底部: *at the ~ of the page/ladder/wall/mountain.* 在页底(梯脚, 墙根, 山脚). **4** lower end of a bed or grave. (床铺或坟墓之)尾端. ⇨ **head**[1]**(10). 5** measure of length, = 12 inches: 呎(十二英寸); 英尺: (with pl **unchanged**) (复数不变) *George is very tall—he's six ~ two* (six feet two inches). 乔治很高, 他有六英尺二英寸. **6** division or unit of verse, each with one strong stress and one or more weak stresses, as in: for 'men/may 'come/and 'men/may 'go. 音步(诗行的区分或单位, 每一音步有一重音节和一个或多个非重音节, 如: for 'men/may 'come/and 'men/may 'go). **7** [U] (mil, old use) infantry: (军, 旧用法)步兵: *the Fourth Regiment of F~;* 第四步兵团; *~ and horse,* infantry and cavalry. 步兵和骑兵. **8** (compounds) (复合词): **~-and-'mouth disease,** disease of cattle and other cloven-hoofed animals. 口蹄病; 鹅口疮(牛羊等的一种病). **'~-ball** n [C] inflated leather ball used in games; [U] the game played with it. 足球; 足球戏; 足球运动. ⇨ the illus below and at **Rugby.** 参看附图及 Rugby 之插图. **'~-bath** n (small bath used for a) washing of the feet. 灌足; 灌足具; 洗脚盆. **'~-board** n sloping board for the feet of the driver (in a carriage, etc). (马车等驾驶者之)踏板. **'~-bridge** n one for the use of persons on ~, not vehicles. 人行桥; 天桥. **'~-fall** n sound of a ~step. 脚步声. **'~-fault** n (tennis) service not allowed because the server's feet are wrongly placed. 发球犯规(发球时足部踩线等). **'~-hills** n pl hills lying at the ~ of a mountain or a range of mountains. (山麓或山脉之)山麓小丘. **'~-hold** n support for the ~, eg when climbing on rocks or ice; (fig) secure position. 立足处(如攀登山岩或

American football

GA goal area   PA penalty area   PS penalty spot
CC centre circle   CS centre spot

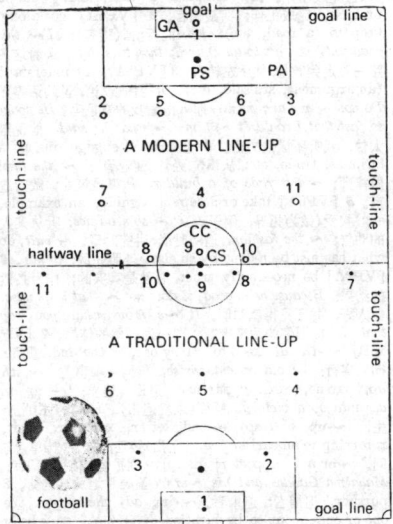

A MODERN LINE-UP

A TRADITIONAL LINE-UP

football

goal line

A TRADITIONAL LINE-UP 1 goalkeeper 2 right back 3 left back 4 right half (back) 5 centre half (back) 6 left half (back) 7 outside right or right winger 8 inside right 9 centre forward 10 inside left 11 outside left or left winger

A MODERN LINE-UP 1 goalkeeper 2 5 6 3 defenders or backs 7 4 11 midfield link men 8 9 10 strikers or forwards

Association football (soccer)

冰时); (喻)据点; 立足点. **'~-lights** n pl row of screened lights at the front of the stage of a theatre. (舞台上的)脚灯. **the ~ lights,** (fig) the profession of an actor. (喻)演员的职业. **'~-loose** adj (also 亦作 **~loose and fancy-free**) independent and without cares or responsibilities. 自由自在的; 无拘束的. **'~-man** /-mən; -mən/ n (pl, **-men**) manservant who admits visitors, waits at table, etc. 男仆; 阍者; 侍者. **'~-mark** n = ~print. **'~-note** n note at the ~ of a page. 脚注; 注脚(印于页底者); 附注. **'~-path** n path for the use of persons on ~, esp one across fields or open country, or at the side of a country road. (田野中的)小径; 小路. Cf 参较 US 美 *trail.* ⇨ **pavement, sidewalk** at **side**[1]**(14). '~-plate** n platform in a locomotive for the driver and fireman: 火车机车上司机和司炉所立之平台: *~plate workers,* drivers and firemen. 火车司机与司炉. **'~-pound** n unit of work (done in lifting 1 lb through 1 ft).

英尺磅(使一磅之物体升高一英尺所做的功)。'~·**print** n impression left on a soft surface by a ~. 足迹; 脚印。'~·**race** n running race between persons. 赛跑; 竞走。'~ **rule** n ruler (strip of wood or metal) 12 inches long. 一英尺长的尺。'~·**slog** vi (colloq) walk, tramp, march far and with effort. (口)长途费力地步行或行军。Hence, 由此产生, '~·**slogger** n (colloq) person who walks or marches long distances. (口)长途步行或行军者。'~·**sore** adj having sore feet, esp from walking. 足痛的(尤指因走路过多而引起者)。'~·**step** n (sound of a) step of sb walking; ~print. 脚步; 脚步声; 足迹; 脚印。follow in the ~steps of sb, do as he did. 效法自己的父亲。'~·**stool** n low stool for resting the feet on. 脚凳。'~·**sure** adj not stumbling; not making false steps. 脚步稳的; 不会走错步的。'~·**wear** n [U] (tradesmen's term for)boots, shoes, etc. (商人用语)脚上穿用之物(如靴, 鞋等)。'~·**work** n [U] manner of using the feet, eg in boxing, dancing. (拳击, 跳舞等之)步法。

foot² /fut; fʊt/ vt, vi **1** [VP6A] knit the ~ of, eg a stocking. 织(袜子等)的足部。**2** ~ **it,** (colloq) go on ~; walk: We've missed the last bus, so we'll have to ~ it. 我们未赶上最后一班公共汽车, 只好步行了。~ **the bill,** (colloq) (agree to) pay it. (口)(同意)付帐。~**ed,** (in compounds) having the kind of feet indicated: (用于复合词中)有…足的: ,wet-'~ed. 脚湿的; ,sure-'~ed; 脚步稳的; ,flat-'~ed. 脚掌扁平的。

foot·age /'futidʒ; 'fʊtɪdʒ/ n [U] length measured in feet, esp length of exposed cinema film. 以英尺计算的长度(尤用于电影胶片)。

footer /'futə; 'fʊtə/ n **1** (colloq) the game of football. (口)足球戏; 足球运动。**2** (compounds)(复合词) a ,six-'footer, a person six feet tall. 六英尺高的人。

foot·ing /'futiŋ; 'fʊtɪŋ/ n [C] (sing only) (仅用单数) **1** placing of the feet; surface for standing on: 立足; 立足处: He lost his ~ (= stumbled, slipped) and fell. 他失足跌倒了。**2** position (in society, a group): 社会地位; 团体中的地位: get a footing in musical circles: 在音乐界取得地位; relationship (with sb); condition⒮. (与人之)关系; 状态。be/get on a ... ~ (with), be/get in a ... relationship/state (with): 与…有某种关系: be on a friendly ~ with Julie's family. 与朱莉一家有友谊关系, **3** conditions; state of the army, etc: 情况; (军队等之)编制: on a peace/war ~, in the state usual for peace/war. 按平时(战时)编制。

footle /'futl; 'fʊtl/ vi, vt (colloq) trifle; play the fool: (口)儿戏; 做傻事。~ about; 做无聊的事。~ away one's time. 虚掷光阴。**foot·ling** /'futliŋ; 'fʊtlɪŋ/ adj insignificant; trifling: 不关紧要的; 微小的: footling little jobs. 无关紧要的工作。

fop /fɔp; fɑp/ n man who pays too much attention to his clothes and personal appearance. 过份注意衣着和外表的人; 纨袴子弟。**fop·pish** /-ɪʃ; -ɪʃ/ adj or like a ~. 纨袴子弟的; 似纨袴子弟的; 浮华的。

for¹ /fɔ(r); fɚ; strong form: fɔː(r); fɔr/ prep **1** (indicating destination, or progress or endeavours towards) (表示目的地, 向…进行或努力) **(a)** (after vv): (用于动词后): set out for home; 动身回家。make for home, turn one's steps towards home; 朝家走; a ship bound for the Baltic. 驶往波罗的海的一艘船。The ship was making for (= sailing towards) the open sea. 那船正向大海行驶。The swimmers struck out for the shore. 那些游泳者用力向岸边游去。**(b)** (after nn): (用于名词后): the train for Glasgow; 开往格拉斯哥的火车; letters for the provinces; 寄往各地的信件; passengers for Cairo. 往开罗的乘客。**2** (indicating what is aimed at, or the attaining of sth, shown by the noun after for) (表示目标或志向, 欲达成之事, 由于后面的名词指出): He was educated for the law/trained for the priesthood. 他受教育准备做律师/(接受训练准备做牧师)。He felt that he was destined for something great. 他觉得他注定要做伟大的事。**3** (indicating eventual possession): (表示最终的所有权): Here's a letter for you. 这里有你一封信。Are

all these for me? 这些都是给我的吗? Save it for me. 为我留着。She made some coffee for us. 她为我们煮了些咖啡。**be 'for it,** (colloq)be likely to be punished, get into trouble; etc. (口)大概要受罚; 惹上麻烦等。**4**(indicating preparation to deal with a situation): (表示准备应付一情况): prepare/preparations for an examination; 准备考试; lay in supplies of coal for the winter; 储煤以备冬日之需; dress for dinner; 穿礼服赴宴; get ready for school. 准备上学。**5** (indicating purpose) (表示目的) **(a)** (used in place of an inf) in order to be, have, obtain, etc; with a view to: (用以代替~不定式)为某种目的; 为了: go for a walk/ride/swim, etc; 去散步(骑一会儿马, 游泳等); run for one's life; 逃命; work for one's living; 为生计而工作; read for pleasure. 读书以求乐趣。**what ... for,** for what purpose: 为何目的; 为什么: What's this tool for? 这工具是做什么用的? What's this hole in the door for? It's for the cat to come in and out by. 门上开出洞的目的何在?它是为了猫的出入而设的。⇨ **24 (g)** below. 参看下列 24 义 (g)。What did you do that for? why did you do that? 你为何做那事? **(b)** (followed by a gerund): (后接~动名词): a mill for (= for the purpose of) grinding coffee; 研磨咖啡的机器; a room for sleeping in. 卧室。**6** (introducing a complement): (引导~补语): They were sold for slaves. 他们被卖为奴。They left him on the battlefield for dead. 他们把他遗留在战场, 以为他已经死了。They chose him for (= as, to be) their leader. 他们选他做首领。**take sb/sth for sth,** mistakenly conclude that he/it is sb/sth else: 将某人或某物误作他(他或他物): He took me for my brother. 他把我误作我哥哥(弟弟)。What do you take me for? You seem to have a mistaken or poor idea of my character, judging from what you say, etc. 你把我当作什么呀? **for certain,** as being certain: 的确; 确实: I cannot say for certain that .... 我不确知…。**7** (followed by an object of hope, wish, search, inquiry, etc): (后接所希望, 愿望, 搜寻, 调查等之人或事物): hope for the best; 盼望最好的情况; pray for peace; 祈求和平; fish for trout; 钓鳟; ask for (= to see) the manager; 求见经理; go to sb for help; 去某人处求援; a cry for help; 呼救; fifty applicants for a post. 一职位而有五十名申请者。**8** (indicating liking, affection, etc): (表示喜欢, 情爱等): have a liking for sb or sth; 喜欢某人或某物; a taste for art; 爱好艺术; no regret for the truth; 不为实情惋惜; a weakness for fine clothes. 特别喜爱漂亮衣服。**9** (indicating aptitude): (表示才能): an aptitude for foreign languages; 学习外国语的才能; a good ear for music; 对音乐的高超鉴赏力; an eye for the picturesque. 审美眼光。**10** (indicating suitability, fitness): (表示适合): bad/good for your health; 有损(益)于你的健康; fit/unfit for food; (不)适于做食物; clothes proper for the occasion. 适于某场合的衣服。This is no place for a young, innocent girl. 这地方不适合天真无邪的年轻女孩子。You are the very man for the job. 你是最适合这个工作的人。**11** (with adjj not otherwise followed by for, in the patterns too+adj+for, or adj+enough+for): (与形容词连用, 用于 too+形容词+for, 或形容词+enough+for 的句型中): too beautiful for words; 美得无法形容; quite risky enough for me. 对我来说是够冒险了。**12** considering (the circumstances, etc); in view of: 就(情况等)而论; 鉴于: It's quite warm for January. 就一月而言, 天气相当暖了。Not bad for a beginner! 就一位初学者而言, 已经不错了! She is tall for her age. 就她的年龄而论, 她算是高的。For all the good you're doing, you may as well stop trying to help. 你做了这么多善事, 你也不必再帮忙了。**for 'all that,** in spite of all that has been said, done, etc. 虽然如此; 尽管如此。**13** representing; instead of; in place of: 代表; 代替: B for Benjamin; B代表Benjamin; the member for Coventry, the person representing Coventry in the House of Commons; 在下议院中代表考文垂城的议员; substitute one thing for another. 以一物代替另一物。Will you please act for me in

the matter? 请你替我处理这件事情好吗? **stand for,** represent: 代表: *The letters MP stand for Member of Parliament and the letters PM stand for Prime Minister.* MP 两字母代表国会议员, PM 两字母代表首相。 **14** in defence or support of; in favour of: 支持; 拥护; 赞成: *Are you for or against the proposal?* 你是赞成这建议还是反对呢? *The rate of exchange is for us, in our favour.* 兑换率对我们有利。 *Three cheers for the President!* 向总统欢呼三声! *I'm all for an early start/for starting early.* 我十分赞成早些动身。 **15** with regard to; so far as concerns: 关于; 至于: *hard up for money;* 需款孔亟; 缺钱; 穷困; *anxious for sb's safety;* 担心某人的安全; *for my part, so far as it concerns me;* 就我而言; 至于我; *speaking for myself, and in the name of all my colleagues.* 为我自己同时也代表我的全体同事发言。 *You may take my word for it, believe me so far as this is concerned.* 关于此事你要相信我。 **16** because of; on account of: 因为; 由于: *for this reason;* 为此原因; *for my sake;* 为了我的缘故; *for the sake of peace;* 为了和平; *for fear of discovery;* 免得被发现; *noted/famous for its scenery;* 以风景著名; *dance/cry for joy;* 快乐得手舞足蹈(大声喊叫); *suffer for one's sins;* 因罪恶而受苦; *sent to prison for stealing;* 因偷窃而被关入狱; *win a medal for bravery.* 因英勇而获勋章。 *She couldn't speak for laughing,* because she was laughing so much. 她笑得说不出话来。 *We trembled for their safety.* 我们担忧他们的安全。 **17** (after a comparative) as the result of; because of: (用于比较级后)…之结果; 由于: *My shoes are the worse for wear.* 我的鞋子穿破了。 *Are you any the better for your long sleep?* 睡了一大觉以后你好些了吗? **18** in spite of; notwithstanding: 虽然; 尽管: *For* (= In spite of) *all you say, I still like her.* 尽管你这样说,我仍然喜欢她。 *For all his wealth, he is unhappy.* 他虽然有钱, 但不快乐。 **19** to the amount or extent of: 达到…的数量或程度: *Put my name down for £5.* 请写上我捐五英镑。 *He drew on his bank for £40.* 他在银行提款四十英镑。 (cricket) (板球) *The score is 157 for 8 wickets.* 八位击球员获得一百五十七分。 *They were all out for 80.* 他们在八十分时都被杀出场。 **20** in exchange for: 交换: *I paid 60 p for the book.* 我出六便士买这本书。 *He did the job for nothing.* 他做那工作没有报酬。 *Don't translate word for word.* 不要逐字翻译。 *Plant a new tree for every tree you cut down.* 你每砍倒一棵树,便植一株新树。 **21** in contrast with: 与…对比: *For one enemy he has fifty friends.* 他的敌人和朋友为一与五十之比。 **22** (indicating extent in time): (表示经过多少时间): *I'm going away for a few days.* 我要离开几天。 *He will be a cripple for life.* 他将终生是一个跛子。 *That's enough for the present.* 目前那是够了。 **for good,** ⇨ **good²(2).** **23** (indicating extent in space; *for* may be omitted if it occurs directly after the *v*): (表示经过若干距离; *for* 如直接在动词后,可以省略): *We walked (for) three miles.* 我们走了三英里路。 *For miles and miles there's not a house to be seen.* 好多英里路望不见一座房屋。 *The road is lined with trees for ten miles.* 沿途长十英里之长两旁种着树。 **24** (in the pattern *for*+*noun/pronoun*+*to-inf*) (用于 for + 名词或代词十不定式的句型中) **(a)** (as the subject of a sentence, usu with preparatory *it*): (做一句之主语, 通常与一预设的 it 连用): *For a woman to divorce her husband is impossible in some countries.* 妇女要与丈夫离婚在某些国家内是不可能的事。 *It's impossible for there to be a quarrel between us.* 我们之间不会发生争执。 *It seemed useless for them to go on.* 他们继续下去似乎是无用了。 **(b)** (as a complement): (做补语): *Their hope was for David to marry a wealthy girl.* 他们希望大卫能娶一富家女。 **(c)** (after *adj*, esp with *too* and *enough*, usu replaceable by a clause): (用于形容词, 尤其是与 too 和 enough 连用的形容词之后, 通常可被一从句代替): *I am anxious for you and my sister to* (= anxious that you and my sister should) *become acquainted.* 我很希望你能和我的妹妹认识。 *This box is too heavy for her to lift.* 这

箱子太重, 她提不动。 **(d)** (after *nn*): (用于名词后): *There's no need for anyone to know* (= that anyone should know). 并不需要让每个人都知道。 *It's time for little girls to be in bed.* 小女孩们就寝的时间到了。 *I'm in no hurry for them to do anything about it yet.* 我不急于让他们对于此事有任何作为。 **(e)** (after *vv*, including some that normally take *for* and others that do not normally take *for*): (用于动词后, 包括某些通常与 for 连用的动词以及通常不与 for 连用者): *We didn't wait for the others to join us.* 我们没有等其余的人参加我们的团体。 *She couldn't bear for Tom and Mary not to be friends.* 汤姆与玛丽不和睦使她难以忍受。 **(f)** (after *than* and *as (if)*): (用于 than 和 as (if) 后): *Is there anything more ridiculous than for a man of 80 to marry a girl of 18?* 还有比一位八十岁的老翁娶一位十八岁的少女更荒唐的事吗? *She had her arms wide apart, as if for the child to run into them.* 她张开两臂, 象是去拥抱那个跑来的孩子。 **(g)** (indicating purpose, design, determination, etc): (表示目的、计划、决心等): *I have brought the books for you to examine.* 我已将这些书带来供你审阅。 *The crowd made way for the procession to pass.* 群众让开路, 使游行的行列通过。 *I'd have given anything for this not to have happened.* 我真愿付出一切使这件事不致发生。 *It's for you to decide.* 此事由你决定。 *For production to be increased we must have efficient organization.* 我们必须有有效的组织, 才能使生产率增加。

for² /fɔ(r)/ fə; strong form: fɔ:(r)/ conj (rare in spoken English; not used at the beginning of a sentence) seeing that; since; the reason, proof, explanation, being that: (罕用于口语中, 不用于句首)鉴于; 因为: *I asked her to stay to tea, for I had something to tell her.* 我请她留下来喝茶, 因为我有事要告诉她。

for·age /'fɒrɪdʒ US: -; 'fɔːrɪdʒ/ n [U] food for horses and cattle. 牛马饲料。 □ vi [VP2A, 3A] ~ **(for),** search (*for* food, etc). 搜寻(与 for 连用, 后接食物)。

for·as·much as /,fɔːrəz'mʌtʃ əz; ,fɔːrəz'mʌtʃ əz/ conj (legal) seeing that; since. (法律)鉴于; 因为。

foray /'fɒreɪ US: 'fɔːreɪ; 'fɔːre/ n [C] raid; sudden attack (*for* food, animals, etc): 侵袭; 突袭(尤指为了获得食物, 动物等); *go on/make a ~.* 侵掠。 □ vi [VP2A] make a ~. 侵掠。

for·bad, for·bade /fə'bæd US: -'beɪd; fə'bæd/ pt of forbid.

for·bear¹ /fɔː'beə(r); fɔr'bɛr/ vt, vi (pt **forbore** /fɔː'bɔː(r); fɔr'bor/, pp **forborne** /fɔː'bɔːn; fɔr'born/) [VP6C, 7A, 2A, 3A] ~ **(from),** (formal) refrain (*from*); not use or mention; be patient: (正式用语)抑制; 自制; 不提及; 忍耐: *I* ~ *to go into details.* 我不欲详述。 *I cannot* ~ *from going into details.* 我不得不详述。 *We begged him to* ~. 我们恳求他忍耐。 **~·ance** /fɔː'beərəns; fɔr'bɛrəns/ n [U] patience; self-control; 耐性; 自制: *show* ~*ance towards sb;* 对某人有耐性; *show* ~*ance in dealing with people.* 待人宽容。

for·bear² (US = **fore·bear**) /'fɔːbeə(r); 'fɔr,bɛr/ n (usu *pl*) ancestor. (通常用复数)祖先。

for·bid /fə'bɪd; fə'bɪd/ vt (pt **forbade** or **forbad** /fə'bæd US: -'beɪd; fə'bæd/, pp **forbidden** /fə'bɪdn; fə'bɪdn/) [VP6A, 17, 12C] order (sb) not to do sth; order that sth shall not be done; not allow: 禁止; 不许: ~ *a girl to marry;* 不许女孩结婚; ~ *a marriage;* 禁止一婚事; ~ *sb to leave;* 不许某人离开; ~ *his departure.* 不许他离去。 *Students are* ~*den the use of the office duplicator.* 不许学生用办公室的复印机。 *I* ~ *you to use that word.* 我不许你用那个词。 *God* ~ *that* ..., used to express a wish that something may not happen. 愿上帝阻止…; 但愿…不会发生。, **den 'fruit,** sth desired because it is not allowed (with reference to Eve and the apple). 因禁止而更欲获得之物; 禁果(由夏娃之食禁果而言)。 **~·ding** *adj* stern; repellent; threatening: 冷峻的, 讨厌的, 险恶的: *a* ~*ding appearance/look;* 冷峻的面貌; *a* ~*ding coast,* one that looks dangerous.

形势险恶的海岸。 ~·**ding·ly** adv

for·bore, for·borne ⇨ forbear¹.

force¹ /fɔːs; fɔrs/ n **1** [U] strength; power of body or mind; physical power: 力量; 气力; 心智的力量; 体力: the ~ of a blow/an explosion/argument, 一击 (爆炸, 论据) 之力; ~ of character; 人格的力量: overcome by the ~ of her emotion; 被她的感情力量所征服; by ~ of contrast. 借对照之力。 The enemy attacked in (great) ~. 敌人猛烈攻击。 He overcame his bad habits by sheer ~ of will. 他全凭意志力克服了他的恶习。 Owing to ~ of circumstances the plans had to be postponed. 由于情势所迫,这些计划不得不延期执行了。 in ~s, (usu of people) in large numbers. (通常指人) 众多的。 **2** [C] person or thing that makes great changes: 引起重大改变的人或事物: the ~s of nature, eg storms, earthquakes. 大自然的力量 (如暴风雨, 地震等)。 Is religion a ~ for good in the lives of people? 宗教在人们的生活当中是一种使人向善的力量吗? The Left and the Right have always been the principle political ~s. 左派和右派一直是主要的政治力量。 **3** [C] organized body of armed or disciplined men: 有组织的武装部队: the armed ~s of a country, the Army, Navy, Air F~; 一国之武装部队 (陆, 海, 空三军); join the F~s; 从军; (attrib) (用作定语) a F~s newspaper, one for members of the armed ~s; 军中报纸: the po'lice ~. 警察队。 **join** ~s (with), unite (with) in order to use combined strength. (与…) 联合以求运用共同的力量。 **4** [C, U] (intensity of, measurement of) pressure or influence exerted at a point, tending to cause movement. 压力; 压力的强度。 **5** [U] (legal) authority; power of binding(6). (法律) 权威; 拘束力。 **in/into** ~, in/into power: 实施: put a law into ~, make it binding. 实施一法律。 When does the new law come into ~? 新法律何时生效? The rule/regulation is no longer in ~. 这规则已不再实行了。

force² /fɔːs; fɔrs/ vt **1** [VP6A, 15A, B, 17, 22] compel, oblige; use force to get or do sth, to make sb do sth; break open by using force: 强迫; 迫使; 强制; 突破; ~ one's way through a crowd; 在人群中挤过去; ~ a way in/out/through; 冲入 (出, 过); ~ an entry into a building, eg by breaking a door; 强行进入一建筑物 (如破门而入); ~ (open a door; 破门而入; ~ a confession from sb; 强迫某人供认; 逼供; ~ sb/oneself to work hard; 强迫某人 (自己) 努力工作; ~ sb into doing sth. 强迫某人做某事。 They said that the war had been ~d upon them, that they had not wanted to make war, but had been compelled to do so. 他们说他们是被迫作战。 ~d 'landing, one that an aircraft is compelled to make, eg because of engine trouble. (飞机因引擎故障等) 强迫降落。 Hence, 由此产生, ~land vt, vi, ~d 'march, eg by soldiers, one requiring special effort, made in an emergency. (军队等之) 强行军; 紧程行军。 ~ sb's hand, make him do sth unwillingly, or earlier than he wished or intended to do it. 逼某人做事; 逼某人提早行动。 **2** [VP6A] cause plants, etc to mature earlier than is normal, eg by giving them extra warmth: 使 (植物等) 提早成熟 (如予以特别的温暖以促成者): (fig) (喻) ~ a pupil, hurry on his education by making him do extra study. 使一学童从事额外的学习以加速其教育之进行。 **3** [VP6A] produce under stress: 强作: ~ a smile, eg when one is unhappy; 强作笑颜; a ~d laugh, one that is not the result of real amusement. 勉强的笑。 The singer had to ~ her top notes. 那歌唱者必须勉强唱出最高音。

force-feed /'fɔːsfiːd; 'fɔrs'fid/ vt (pt, pp **forcefed** /'fɔːsfed; 'fɔrs'fɛd/) [VP6A] compel (an animal, a prisoner or a patient) to take food and drink. 强迫 (动物, 囚犯或病人) 饮食。

force·ful /'fɔːsfl; 'fɔrsfəl/ adj (of a person, his character, of a argument, etc) full of force: (指人, 性格, 辩论等) 有力的: a ~ speaker/style of writing. 有力的演说者 (文体)。 ~·**ly** /-fəlɪ; -fəlɪ/ adv ~·**ness** n

force majeure /ˌfɔːs mæˈʒɜː(r); ˌfɔrs məˈʒɜr/ n [U] (F) (legal) compulsion; superior force. (法) (法律) 不可抗力。

force·meat /'fɔːsmiːt; 'fɔrs'mit/ n [U] meat chopped up finely, mixed with herbs, etc used as stuffing, eg in a roast chicken. 调香料的碎肉 (例如填塞烤鸡等所用者)。

for·ceps /'fɔːseps; 'fɔrsəps/ n (sing or pl) small pincers or tongs used by dentists (when pulling out teeth) and by doctors for gripping things: (牙医用的) 齿镊; 牙钳; (医生用的) 镊子; 钳子: a ~ delivery (of a baby). (胎儿之) 产钳产。

forc·ible /'fɔːsəbl; 'fɔrsəbl/ adj done by, involving the use of, physical force: 强行的; 用力的: a ~ entry into a building; 强行进入一建筑物; ~ expulsion. 强行驱逐。 **2** (of a person, his acts, words, etc) convincing; persuasive. (指人, 行动, 言语等) 动听的; 有说服力的。 **forc·ibly** /-əblɪ; -əblɪ/ adj

ford /fɔːd; fɔrd/ n [C] shallow place in a river where it is possible to walk or drive across. 河流之可涉的浅处。 □ vt [VP6A] cross (a river) by walking or driving through the water. 涉 (河)。 ~·**able** /-əbl; -əbl/ adj that can be ~ed. 可涉的。

fore /fɔː(r); fɔr/ adj (attrib only) situated in the front (opp of back, aft) (仅用作定语) (在前部的 (为 back, aft 之反义词): in the ~ part of the train; 在火车的前部; the ~ hatch, (in a ship). (船) 前舱口。 □ n [U] ~ part (of a ship). (船之) 前部。 **to the** ~, ready to hand; on the spot; prominent: 在手头; 随时可资利用; 当场; 突出; 显著: He has come to the ~ recently, has become prominent. 他近来已出人头地了。 □ adv (naut) in front. (航海) 在前。 ~ **and aft**, at the bow and stern of a ship; lengthwise in a ship: 在船首和船尾; 从船首至船尾: ~ and aft sails/rigged, with sails set lengthwise. 纵帆 (纵帆装置的)。 □ **squa·re-rigged**. □ int (golf) warning (to people in front) that the player is about to drive the ball. (高尔夫) 前面注意 (击球时警告前面的人以免被球所击之呼声)。

fore·arm¹ /'fɔːraːm; 'fɔrˌɑrm/ n arm from the elbow to the wrist or finger-tips. 前臂 (肘至腕或指尖部分)。 □ the illus at **arm**. 参看 arm 之插图。

fore·arm² /ˌfɔːrˈaːm; fɔrˈɑrm/ vt [VP6A] (usu in passive) arm beforehand; prepare for trouble in advance: (通常用被动语态) 预先武装; 警备; 预先准备: To be forewarned is to be ~ed. 预先获得警告即是预先有了准备。

fore·bear n = forbear².

fore·bode /fɔːˈbəʊd; fɔrˈbod/ vt (formal) (正式用语) **1** [VP6A] be a sign of warning of: 预示; 预兆: These black clouds ~ a storm. 这些乌云预示有暴风雨。 **2** [VP6A, 9] have a feeling of (usu sth evil); have a feeling (that): 预感 (通常为不祥之事; 有时与 that 所引导的从句连用): ~ disaster. 预感灾祸。 **fore·bod·ing** n [C, U] feeling that trouble is coming. 凶兆; 预兆。

fore·cast /'fɔːkaːst US: -kæst; fɔrˈkæst/ vt (pt, pp ~ or ~ed) [VP6A] say in advance what is likely to happen. 预言; 预测。 □ n statement that ~s sth: 预言; 预告: inaccurate weather ~s. 不正确的天气预报。

fore·castle, fo'c's'le /'fəʊksl; 'foksl/ n (in some merchant ships) part under the bows where the seamen have their living and sleeping accommodation. 船艏 (某些商船中船首甲板下之水手舱)。

fore·close /fɔːˈkləʊz; fɔrˈkloz/ vt, vi [VP2A, 3A, 6A] ~ (on), (legal) use the right (given by a mortgage) to take possession of property (when interest or capital has not been paid at the required time): (法律) (利息或资金未能按期缴付时) 取消赎取抵押品之权利: The Bank ~d (on) (the mortgage). 银行取消了此一赎取抵押品之权利。 **fore·closure** /fɔːˈkləʊʒə(r); fɔrˈkloʒə/ n [C, U] (act of) foreclosing a mortgage. 赎取抵押品权利之取消。

fore·court /'fɔːkɔːt; 'fɔrˌkort/ n enclosed space in front of a building. 前院。

fore·doom /fɔː'duːm; fɔr'dum/ vt [VP6A, 14] (usu passive) ~ (to), destine (to): (通常用被动语态) 预先注定: an attempt that was ~ed to failure. 注定失败的一个尝试。

fore·father /'fɔːfɑːðə(r); 'fɔr,faðɚ/ n (usu pl) ancestor. (通常用复数)祖先。

fore·fin·ger /'fɔːfɪŋgə(r); 'fɔr,fɪŋgɚ/ n first finger, next to the thumb; index finger. 食指。⇨ the illus at **arm**. 参看 arm 之插图。

fore·foot /'fɔːfʊt; 'fɔr,fʊt/ n (pl forefeet /'fɔːfiːt; 'fɔr,fit/) one of the front feet of a four-legged animal. (四足动物之)前足。

fore·front /'fɔːfrʌnt; 'fɔr,frʌnt/ n the ~, most forward part: 最前部: in the ~ of the battle; 在最前线; in the ~ of my mind. 在我心头。

fore·gather ⇨ forgather.

forego[1] /fɔː'gəʊ; fɔr'go/ vt, vi (pt forewent /fɔː'went; fɔr'wɛnt/, pp foregone /fɔː'gɒn US: -'gɔːn; fɔr'gɔn/) precede (but rarely used except in) 在前 (除下列形式外极为少用) **fore·going** adj preceding, already mentioned. 前面的; 前述的。**fore·gone** /'fɔːgɒn US: -gɔːn; 'fɔr,gɔn/ adj a foregone conclusion, ending that can be seen or could have been seen from the start. 自开始即可察知的结果; 必然的结果。

forego[2] ⇨ forgo.

fore·ground /'fɔːgraʊnd; 'fɔr,graʊnd/ n 1 part of a view (esp in a picture) nearest to the observer. 前景(尤指图书上最靠近观赏者的部分)。2 (fig) most conspicuous position: (喻)最引人注意的地位: keep oneself in the ~, where one is most easily seen or noticed. 使自己处于最引人注意的地位。

fore·hand /'fɔːhænd; 'fɔr,hænd/ adj (of a stroke at tennis, etc) made with the palm turned forward. (打网球等)正击的; 正手的。(Cf 参较 backhand = stroke made with the back of the hand turned forward and from the left side of the body, by a right-handed player 反手的击球)。

fore·head /'fɒrɪd US: 'fɔːrɪd; 'fɔrɪd/ n part of the face above the eyes. 额。⇨ the illus at **head**. 参看 head 之插图。

foreign /'fɒrən US: 'fɔːr-; 'fɔrɪn/ adj 1 of, in, from, another country, not one's own: 外国的; 在外国的; 来自外国的: ~ languages/countries; 外国语言(外国); ~ trade. 对外贸易。the 'F~ Office, the department of state dealing with ~ affairs; its building in London. (伦敦之)英国外交部。,F~ 'Secretary, head of the F~ Office. 外交部长。2 ~ to, not natural to, unconnected with: 非…所原有的; 不适于; 与…无关连: Lying is ~ to his nature. 说谎不是他的本性。3 coming or introduced from outside: 来自外部的; 外来的: a ~ body in the eye, eg a bit of dirt blown into it by the wind. 眼中一异物(如被风吹入的一粒灰尘)。~er n person from, living in, or born in a ~ country. 外国人。

fore·knowl·edge /ˌfɔː'nɒlɪdʒ; ˌfɔr'nɑlɪdʒ/ n [U] knowledge of sth before its occurrence or existence. 预知; 先知。

fore·land /'fɔːlənd; 'fɔrlənd/ n cape; promontory. 岬; 海角。

fore·leg /'fɔːleg; 'fɔr,lɛg/ n one of the front legs of a four-footed animal. (四足动物之)前腿。

fore·lock /'fɔːlɒk; 'fɔr,lɑk/ n lock of hair growing just above the forehead. 长在额头上方的毛发; 额发; 额毛。take time by the ~, not let an opportunity slip by; use an opportunity promptly. 把握时机; 立即利用一个机会。

fore·man /'fɔːmən; 'fɔrmən/ n (pl -men /-mən; -mən/) 1 workman in authority over others. 工头; 领班。2 chief member and spokesman of a jury. 陪审团之主席。

fore·mast /'fɔːmɑːst US: -mæst; 'fɔr,mæst/ n mast nearest the bow of a ship. 船之前桅。⇨ the illus at **barque**. 参看 barque 之插图。

fore·most /'fɔːməʊst; 'fɔr,most/ adj first; most notable; chief: 第一的; 首要的; 最著名的: the ~ painter of his period. 在他那个时期最重要的画家。□ adv first in position. 在最前面。first and ~, before all else; in the first place. 首先; 首要。

fore·name /'fɔːneɪm; 'fɔr,nem/ n (as used in official style, eg on forms) name preceding the family name. 名(用于表格等正式文件中)。

fore·noon /'fɔːnuːn; fɔr'nun/ n (old use) part of the day between sunrise and noon. (旧用法)上午; 午前。

for·en·sic /fə'rensɪk; fə'rɛnsɪk/ adj of, used in, courts of law: 法庭的; 用于法庭的: ~ skill, skill as needed by barristers, etc; 律师等在法庭上的辩论才能; ~ medicine, medical knowledge as needed in legal matters, eg a poisoning trial. 法医学(法律事件, 如用毒案件, 所需要的医学知识)。

fore·or·dain /ˌfɔːrɔː'deɪn; ˌfɔrɔr'den/ vt [VP6A, 14, 17] determine or appoint beforehand: 预定; 预先注定: what God has ~ed. 上帝所注定者。

fore·run·ner /'fɔːrʌnə(r); 'fɔr,rʌnɚ/ n 1 sign of what is to follow: 预兆; 前兆: swallows, the ~s of spring. 燕子, 春天的前兆。2 person who prepares for the coming of another. 先驱; 先锋。

fore·sail /'fɔːseɪl; 'fɔr,sel/ n principal sail on the foremast. 前桅帆。⇨ the illus at **barque**. 参看 barque 之插图。

fore·see /fɔː'siː; fɔr'si/ vt (pt foresaw /fɔː'sɔː; fɔr'sɔ/, pp foreseen /fɔː'siːn; fɔr'sin/) [VP6A, 9, 10] know beforehand or in advance: 预知; 预见: ~ trouble; 预知困难; ~ what will happen/how things will turn out/that things will go well. 预知将发生之事(事情的结局, 事情顺利)。~·able /-əbl; -əbl/ adj that can be known beforehand. 可预知的。the ~able future, period from the present for which events can reasonably be predicted. 在可预见的将来。

fore·shadow /fɔː'ʃædəʊ; fɔr'ʃædo/ vt [VP6A] be a sign or warning of (sth to come). 预示(将来临之某事物)。

fore·shore /'fɔːʃɔː(r); 'fɔr,ʃɔr/ n part of the shore between the sea and land that is cultivated, built on, etc. 前岸; 河滩。

fore·shorten /fɔː'ʃɔːtn; fɔr'ʃɔrtn/ vt [VP6A] (in drawing pictures) show (an object) by the use of perspective(1). (绘画)用透视法显示(物体)。

fore·sight /'fɔːsaɪt; 'fɔr,saɪt/ n [U] ability to see future needs; care in preparing for these: 先见; 远见; 深谋远虑: If you had had more ~, you would have saved yourself a lot of trouble. 如果那时你有更多的远虑, 你就会免除许多麻烦了。

fore·skin /'fɔːskɪn; 'fɔr,skɪn/ n fold of skin covering the end of the penis. (男性生殖器之)包皮。

for·est /'fɒrɪst US: 'fɔːr-; 'fɔrɪst/ n 1 [C, U] (large area of) land covered with trees and (often) undergrowth; the trees growing there: 森林地带; 森林。~s stretching for miles and miles; 延伸无数英里的森林地带; (attrib) (用作定语): ~ animals/fires. 森林动物(森林火灾)。2 (GB) area where game (eg deer) is or was hunted (and preserved), not necessarily wooded; (with proper name prefixed, as Sherwood F~) district that was formerly ~ but is now partly under cultivation: (英)狩猎场(并不一定树木繁茂); (冠以专名词, 如舍伍德林区)昔时的林区(现在已部分开垦): the deer ~s in Scotland. 苏格兰的猎鹿场。3 (fig) sth that suggests ~ trees: (喻)林立之物: a ~ of masts, eg in a harbour. (港内)林立之帆樯。~er n officer in charge of a ~ (protecting wild animals, watching for fires, etc); man who works in a ~. 林务官; 林务员; 林中工作者。~ry n [U] (science of) planting and caring for ~s. 森林学; 造林与森林管理。

fore·stall /fɔː'stɔːl; fɔr'stɔl/ vt [VP6A] do sth first and so prevent another from doing it; upset (sb, his

plans) by doing sth unexpectedly early: 先采取行动以阻止; 先发制人: ~ *a competitor*. 比一竞争者占先.

fore·swear /fɔːˈsweə(r); forˈswer/ *vt* = forswear.

fore·taste /ˈfɔːteɪst; ˈforˌtest/ *n* ~ (of), partial experience (of sth) in advance: 预先得到的经验: *a ~ of suffering/pleasure*. 预尝到的苦(乐).

fore·tell /fɔːˈtel; forˈtel/ *vt* (*pt, pp* foretold /fɔːˈtəuld; forˈtold/) [VP6A, 9, 10, 12A, 13A] tell beforehand; predict: 预言; 预测: 预卜某人的未来. *Is this the prophet whose coming was foretold (to) us?* 这便是预言要来的那位先知吗?

fore·thought /ˈfɔːθɔːt; ˈforˌθot/ *n* [U] careful thought or planning for the future. 先虑; 预谋.

fore·told *pt, pp* of foretell.

fore·top /ˈfɔːtɒp; ˈforˌtɑp/ *n* (naut) platform at the head of a foremast. (航海)前檣的平台; 前桅楼. ⇨ the illus at **barque**. 参看 barque 之插图.

for·ever /fəˈrevə(r); fəˈɛvə/ *adv* always; at all times; endlessly. 永远地; 无穷尽地.

fore·warn /fɔːˈwɔːn; forˈworn/ *vt* [VP6A] warn beforehand. 预先警告.

fore·woman /ˈfɔːwumən; ˈforˌwumən/ *n* (*pl* -women /-wɪmɪn; -ˌwɪmɪn/) woman in authority over other women workers. 女工头; 女工监督.

fore·word /ˈfɔːwɜːd; ˈforˌwɜd/ *n* [C] introductory remarks to a book, printed in it, esp by someone not the author of the book. 前言; 序; 引言.

for·feit /ˈfɔːfɪt; ˈforfɪt/ *vt* [VP6A] (have to) suffer the loss of sth as a punishment or consequence, or because of rules: (作为惩罚或结果, 或由于规则等而)丧失; 被没收: ~ *the good opinion of one's friends*; 失去朋友的好感; ~ *one's health*. 丧失健康. □ *n* [C] 1 sth (to be) ~ed: 丧失之物; 没收物: *His health was the ~ he paid for overworking*. 他因工作过度而丧失健康. 2 (*pl*) game in which a player gives up various articles if he makes an error and can redeem them by doing sth ludicrous: (复)罚物游戏(参加者如犯错误, 必须放弃种种物品, 如要赎回那些物品, 须受罚做可笑的事): *Let's play ~s.* 让我们来玩罚物游戏. ~·**ure** /ˈfɔːfɪtʃə(r); ˈforfɪtʃə/ *n* [U] losing; 丧失; 没收: *(the) ~ure of one's property*. 财产之被没收.

for·gather, fore·gather /fɔːˈgæðə(r); forˈgæðə/ *vi* [VP2A, C] come together. 聚会.

for·gave /fəˈgeɪv; fəˈgev/ *pt* of forgive.

forge[1] /fɔːdʒ; fordʒ/ *n* [C] 1 workshop with fire and anvil where metals are heated and shaped, esp one used by a smith for making shoes for horses, repairing agricultural machinery, etc. 铁工厂; 铁匠店. 2 (workshop with) furnace or hearth for melting or refining metal. 锻炉; 锻铁场.

forge[2] /fɔːdʒ; fordʒ/ *vt* [VP6A] 1 shape by heating and hammering: 锤炼成; 打制; 锻造: ~ *an anchor*; 打制一锚; (fig) (喻) *Their friendship was ~d by shared adversity*. 他们的友谊是由于共患难而结成的. 2 make a copy of sth, eg a signature, a banknote, a will, in order to deceive. 伪造(签名, 钞票, 遗嘱等). **forger** *n* person who ~s (2). 伪造者. **forg·ery** /ˈfɔːdʒərɪ; ˈfɔrdʒərɪ/ *n* 1 [U] forging (2) of a document, signature, etc. (文件, 签名等的)伪造. 2 [C] (*pl* -ries) ~d document, signature, etc. 伪造的文件, 签名等. **forg·ing** *n* [C] piece of metal that has been ~d(1) or shaped under a press. 锻造过的一块金属; 锻件.

forge[3] /fɔːdʒ; fordʒ/ *vi* [VP2C] ~ *ahead*, make steady progress; take the lead (in a race, etc). 稳定而徐缓地前进; (竞赛等)领先.

for·get /fəˈget; fəˈget/ *vt, vi* (*pt* forgot/ fəˈgɒt; fəˈgat/; *pp* forgotten/ fəˈgɒtn; fəˈgatn/) 1 [VP6A, C, D, 8, 9, 10, 2A, 3A] ~ (*about*), lose remembrance of; fail to keep in the memory; fail to recall: 忘记; 忘却: *I ~/I've forgotten her name*. 我忘了她的名字. *I shall never ~ your kindness to me*. 我永远不会忘记你对我的厚意. *Did you ~ (that) I was coming?* 你忘了我要

来吗? *I have forgotten how to do it/where he lives/whether he wants it*. 我忘记怎样做(他住的地方, 他是否需要它)了. *I forgot all about it*. 我一点也记不得了. *I shall never ~ hearing Chaliapin singing the part of Boris Godunov*. 我永不会忘记听沙利亚宾唱波里·高德诺夫一角. **forget-me-not** /fəˈget mɪ nɒt; fəˈgetmɪˌnɑt/ *n* small plant with blue flowers. 琉璃草; 勿忘草. 2 [VP7A] neglect or fail (to do sth): 疏忽; 忘记(做某事): *Don't ~ to post the letters*. 不要忘了寄出这些信. *He has forgotten to pay me*. 他忘了付钱给我. 3 [VP6A, 2A] put out of the mind; stop thinking about: 不以…为意; 不再思念: *Let's ~ our quarrels*. 我们忘却我们的争执吧. *Forgive and ~*. 不念旧恶. 4 [VP6A] omit to pay attention to: 忽略: *Don't ~ the waiter*, Give him a tip. 别忘了给侍者小账. 5 ~ *oneself*, (a) behave thoughtlessly in a way not suited to one's dignity, to the circumstances. 忘形; 忘掉自己的身分. (b) act unselfishly, thinking only of the interests of others. 为他人而忘我. ~·**ful** /-fl; -fəl/ *adj* in the habit of ~ting: 健忘的: *He's very ~ful of things*. 他十分健忘. *Old people are sometimes ~ful*. 老年人有时很健忘. ~·**fully** /-fəlɪ; -fəlɪ/ *adv* ~·**ful·ness** *n*

for·give /fəˈgɪv; fəˈgɪv/ *vt, vi* (*pt* forgave /fəˈgeɪv; fəˈgev/; *pp* forgiven /fəˈgɪvn; fəˈgɪvn/) [VP6A, 14, 12C, 2A] 1 ~ *sb (sth/for doing sth)*, say that one no longer has the wish to punish sb; no longer have the wish to punish sb for an offence, a sin; pardon or show mercy to (sb); no longer have hard feelings towards (sb): 宽恕(某人); 赦免; 饶恕; 原谅: ~ *sb for being rude/~ his rudeness*. 宽恕某人的卤莽. *Am I ~n?* 我被饶恕了吗? *F~ us our trespasses*. 赦免我们的罪. *Your sins will be ~n you*. 你的罪将被赦免. 2 not demand repayment of (a debt); not demand repayment of a debt from (sb): 不索取(债务); 宽免(某人)之债: *He forgave the debt*. 他放弃了索债. *Will you ~ me the debt?* 请宽免我的债好吗? **for·giv·able** /-əbl; -əbl/ *adj* that can be ~n. 可宽恕的; 可原谅的. **for·giv·ing** *adj* ready or willing to ~: 宽仁的; 宽大的: *a forgiving nature*. 宽仁的天性. **for·giv·ing·ly** *adv* ~·**ness** *n* [U] forgiving or being ~n; willingness to ~: 宽恕; 饶恕; 宽仁: *ask for/receive ~ness*; 请求(受到)宽恕; *full of ~ness*. 富有宽仁之心.

forgo /fɔːˈgəu; forˈgo/ *vt* (*pt* forwent /fɔːˈwent; forˈwent/; *pp* forgone/ fɔːˈgɒn *US*: -ˈgɔːn; forˈgɔn/) do without; give up: 弃绝; 放弃: ~ *pleasures in order to study hard*. 为了努力用功而放弃享乐.

for·got, for·got·ten ⇨ forget.

fork /fɔːk; fork/ *n* [C] 1 implement with two or more points (*prongs*), used for lifting food to the mouth, carving, etc. 叉(用以进食, 切开食物等). '~ *lunch/supper*, one (for more persons than can be seated at table) at which food is served as a buffet where guests serve themselves. 自助午餐(晚餐)(人数多于席位时而设). 2 farm or gardening tool for breaking up the ground, lifting hay, straw, etc. 草叉. ⇨ the illus at **tool**. 参看 tool 之插图. 3 place where a road, tree-trunk, etc divides or branches; part of a bicycle to which a wheel is fixed. 路; 树等之分岔处; 岔口; (脚踏车上固定轮之)叉状支架; 前叉. ⇨ also *tuning-* at **tune**. 4 ~-*lift* 'truck, powered truck or trolley with mechanical means of lifting and lowering goods (to or from storage space, or for loading and unloading). 叉车; 叉式起重车; 又动车. □ *vt, vi* 1 [VP6A, 15A, B] lift, move, carry, with a ~: 以叉叉; ~ *hay/straw*; 用叉叉干草(稻草); ~ *in manure*, dig it into the ground with a ~; 用叉将肥料埋入土中; ~ *the ground over*, turn the soil over with a ~. 用叉翻土. 2 [VP2A, C] (of a road, river, etc) divide into branches; (of persons) turn (left or right): 分岔; (指道路之)分岔; (指人)转向(左或右): *We ~ed right at the church*. 我们自教堂向右走. 3 [VP15B, 2C] ~ *sth out*, ~ *up/out*, (colloq) hand over; pay: (口)交出; 支付: *I've got*

to ~ out a lot of money to the Collector of Taxes this year. 今年我必须付许多钱给税务征收员。 **~ed** *adj* branching; dividing into two or more parts: 有叉的; 分叉的: *a ~ed road;* 岔路; *the ~ed tongue of a snake;* 蛇的分叉的舌; *a bird with a ~ed tail;* 尾部分叉的鸟; **~ed** *lightning.* 叉状闪电。

a fork-lift truck

for·lorn /fə'lɔːn; fɚ'lɔrn/ *adj* (poet or liter) unhappy; uncared for; forsaken. (诗或文)不幸的; 孤寂的; 被遗弃的。 **~ hope,** desperate enterprise; plan or enterprise which has very little likelihood of success. 希望甚微而不惜冒险的事业; 绝少成功希望的计划或事业。 **~·ly** *adv* **~·ness** *n*

form[1] /fɔːm; form/ *n* **1** [U] shape; outward or visible appearance: 形状; 外形; 外貌: *without shape or ~;* 不成形状的; *take ~,* begin to have a (recognizable) shape; 成形; [C] person or animal as it can be seen or touched: 人形; 形体: *A dark ~ could be seen in the distance.* 在远处可看到一个黑影。 *Proteus was a Greek sea-god who could appear in the ~ of any creature he wished.* 普洛提由斯是一希腊海神, 他能随心所欲的以任何动物的形体出现。 *He has a well-proportioned ~,* a well-shaped body. 他有匀称的体型。 **2** [U] general arrangement or structure; way in which parts are put together to make a whole or a group; style or manner of presentation: 形式; 结构; 表现的方式: *a piece of music in sonata ~;* 奏鸣曲式的乐章; *have a sense of ~ in painting* (~ being contrasted with colouring); 在绘画中对形式之美具有灵敏的感觉('形式'为'色彩'之对)。 *literary ~* (~ being contrasted with subject-matter). 文学形式 (为题材之对)。 **3** [C] particular kind of arrangement or structure; manner in which a thing exists; species, kind or variety: 特殊的形式; 存在方式; 种类: *~s of government;* 政治制度; 政体; *~s of animal and vegetable life.* 动植物的生活方式。 *Ice, snow and steam are ~s of water.* 冰、雪和蒸汽是水的各种形态。 **4** [U] (gram) shape taken by a word (in sound or spelling): (语法)一词的读音或拼写形式; 词形: *change ~;* 改变形式; *different in ~ but identical in meaning;* 形式不同但意义相同; [C] one of the shapes taken by a word (in sound or spelling): 一词(在发音或拼法上)的某种形式: *The word 'brother' has two plural ~s, 'brothers' and 'brethren'.* brother 一词有两种复数形式, 一为 brothers, 一为 brethren. *The past tense ~ of 'run' is 'ran'.* run 的过去式是 ran. **5** [U] manner of behaving or speaking fixed, required or expected by custom or etiquette: 礼貌; 礼节: *do sth for ~'s sake,* ie because it is usual, not because one wishes to do it or likes doing it; 为了礼节而做某事(并非因为喜爱而做); *say 'Good morning' as a mere matter of ~,* ie not because one is really pleased to see the person to whom the words are spoken. 只是为了礼貌问题而说'早安'(并非因真喜欢见到对方而说)。 **good/bad '~,** behaviour according to/not according to custom or etiquette. 有礼貌(失礼)。 **6** [C] particular way of behaving, etc; greeting, utterance, act, as required by custom or etiquette; established practice or ritual: 行为等之特殊的方式; 习惯或礼貌所要求的招呼, 言语或动作; 礼仪; 仪式: *the ancient ~s observed at the coronation of a sovereign;* 国王加冕时所遵守的古代仪式; *pay too much*

attention to ~s; 过于拘礼; *a ~ of prayer used at sea;* 航海时的祈祷式; *~s of worship.* 礼拜式。 **7** [C] printed paper with space to be filled in: 表格: *'telegraph ~s;* 电报纸; *appli'cation ~s;* 申请表格; *printed or typewritten letter sent out in great numbers* (also called 亦称作 **a ~ letter**). 大量发出的印刷或打字的信件。 **8** [U] condition of health and training (esp of horses and athletes): 健康和训练情况(尤指马和运动员者): *If a horse is not in good ~ it is unlikely to win a race.* 如果一匹马的健康和训练情况不佳, 它多半不会在赛马中得胜。 *On ~* (= Judging from recent performances as evidence of condition and training), *the Aga Khan's horse is likely to win the race.* 根据近况判断, 那位伊斯兰苏教首领的马可能获胜。 **in/out of ~; on/off ~,** in good/bad condition: 情况良好(不好): *Smith is out of ~/is not on ~/is off ~ and is unlikely to run in the 100 metres race tomorrow.* 史密斯的情况失常, 大概不会参加明天的百米赛跑。 **9** [U] spirits: 精神; 心境: *Jack was in great ~ at the dinner party,* in high spirits, lively. 杰克在那宴会上十分愉快。 **10** [C] long wooden bench, usu without a back, for several persons to sit on. 长凳(通常无靠背, 可以坐数人)。 **11** [C] class in GB schools, the youngest boys and girls being in the first ~ and the oldest in the sixth ~. (英国学校的)年级; 级 (自一年级至六年级)。 **~·less** *adj* without shape. 无形状的; 无形式的。 **~·less·ly** *adv*

form[2] /fɔːm; form/ *vt, vi* **1** [VP6A, 15A] give shape or form to; make; produce: 形成; 作成; 制作: *~ words and sentences;* 形成词和句子; *~ the plural of a noun by adding -s or -es;* 加 s 或 es 以形成一名词的复数式; *~ one's style* (in writing) *on good models.* 模仿良好的模范以形成自己的文体。 **2** [VP6A] develop, build up, conceive: 养成; 培养; 想出: *~ good habits;* 养成良好习惯; *~ a child's character/mind,* by training, discipline, etc; 陶冶一个孩子的品性(心性); *~ ideas/plans/judgements/opinions/conclusions.* 形成(计划, 意见, 结论)。 **3** [VP6A, 15A] organize: 组织; 编组: *~ a class for beginners in French.* 编组一法语初级班。 *They ~ed themselves into a committee.* 他们组织成一个委员会。 **4** [VP6A] be (the material of), be (one or part of): 作为(…的材料); 为(…的一员或一部份): *What ~s the basis of this compound?* 这化合物的主要成分是什么? *This series of lectures ~s part of a complete course on French history.* 这一系列的演讲为一门法国史课程的一部份。 **5** [VP14, 2C] ~ *into,* (mil) (cause to) move into a particular order: (军)(使)排列; (使)成队形: *~ a regiment into columns;* 将一团排成纵队; *~ into line.* 排成行。 *The company was ~ed into three ranks.* 该连排成三列。 **6** [VP2A, C] come into existence; become solid; take shape: 生出; 形成; 凝固; 成形: *The idea ~ed in his mind.* 这观念在他心中形成了。 *The words would not ~ on her lips,* She could not bring herself to speak them. 她说不出那些话来。 *Ice ~s at the temperature of 0°C.* 冰之形成是在摄氏零度时。

for·mal /ˈfɔːml; ˈforml/ *adj* **1** in accordance with rules, customs and convention: 正式的; 合于习俗的; 合于礼仪的: *pay a ~ call on the Ambassador;* 正式拜会大使; *~ dress,* as required by custom for certain occasions; 礼服; *make a ~* (= ceremonial) *bow to sb;* 对某人深深地鞠躬; *a ~ receipt,* according to commercial custom, regular and in good order. 正式收据。 **2** regular or geometric in design; symmetrical: 整齐的; 井然有序的; 匀称的: *~ gardens,* eg with flower beds, hedges, etc in geometrical patterns. 形式整齐的花园 (例如有整齐而有系统之格式的花床, 树篱等)。 **3** of the outward shape or appearance (not the reality or substance): 形式上的; 外表上的: *a ~ resemblance between two things.* 两物在外表上的相似。 **4** ~ '**grammar,** of the forms of words, of rules (of syntax, etc). 规范语法(讨论词的形式, 句法规则等)。 **~·ly** /-məlɪ; -mlɪ/ *adv* **~·ism** /-ɪzəm; -ˌɪzəm/ *n* [U] exact observance of forms and ceremonies, eg in religious duties,

in behaviour. 形式主义;拘泥礼仪。

for·mal·de·hyde /fɔː'mældɪhaɪd; fɔr'mældə,haɪd/ *n* [U] (chem) colourless gas (**HCHO**) used, dissolved in water, as a preservative and disinfectant. (化学)甲醛(一种无色气体, 溶于水用作防腐剂和消毒剂)。 **for·malin** /'fɔːməlɪn; 'fɔrmə,lɪn/ *n* [U] (chem) solution of ～ used as a disinfectant. (化学)甲醛液(用作消毒剂);福马林。

for·mal·ity /fɔː'mælətɪ; fɔr'mælətɪ/ *n* (*pl* **-ties**) **1** [U] strict attention to rules, forms and convention: 严守礼仪; 拘泥形式: *There was too much ～ in the Duke's household.* 公爵的家里过份拘泥形式。 **2** [C] formal act; sth required by custom or rules: 正式行动; 礼节; 仪式; 手续: *legal formalities;* 法律上的正式手续; *comply with all the necessary formalities.* 遵守一切必要的礼仪。 *a mere ～,* sth one is required or expected to do, but which has little meaning or importance. 仅为形式而已; 只是手续而已。

for·mat /'fɔːmæt; 'fɔrmæt/ *n* **1** shape and size of a book, including the type, paper and binding: (书籍的)版式: *reissue a book in a new ～.* 以新的版式重新出版一书。 **2** arrangement; procedure; style: 安排; 程序;格式: *the ～ of a meeting/conference/interview.* 会议(讨论会, 访问)的程序。

for·ma·tion /fɔː'meɪʃn; fɔr'meʃən/ *n* **1** [U] forming or shaping: 形成: *the ～ of character/of ideas in the mind;* 性格(观念)之形成; [C] that which is formed: 形成之物: *Clouds are ～s of condensed water vapour.* 云乃凝聚的水蒸气所形成者。 **2** [U] structure or arrangement: 构造; 排列: *troops/warships in 'battle ～;* 成战斗队形的军队(战舰); *military aircraft flying in ～;* 编队飞行的军机; (attrib) (用作定语) *flying / dancing;* 编队飞行(舞蹈); [C] particular arrangement or order: 特殊的排列: *rock ～s;* 岩层; [C] the arrangement of the players at the start of a (football, Rugby) match. (足球, 橄榄球比赛开始时)在场球员之排列。

for·ma·tive /'fɔːmətɪv; 'fɔrmətɪv/ *adj* **1** giving, or tending to give, shape to: 使成形的; 形成的: ～ *influences,* eg on a child's character. 影响力(如造成儿童性格的影响力)。 **2** pliable: 易受影响的: *the ～ years of a child's life,* the years during which its character is formed. 儿童性格的形成时期。

for·mer /'fɔːmə(r); 'fɔrmə/ *adj* **1** of an earlier period: 早先的; 以前的; 从前的: *in ～ times;* 往昔, 从前; *my ～ students;* 我从前的学生; *customs of ～ days.* 昔时的风俗。 *She looks more like her ～ self,* eg looks well again after her illness. 她恢复她从前的样子了(例如病后复元)。 **2** (also as *pron*) (亦作代词) *the ～* (contrasted with *the latter*), the firstmentioned of two: 前者(与 the latter 相对): *I prefer the ～ alternative to the latter.* 就此两者之间我愿选择前者; *Of these alternatives I prefer the ～.* 就此两者之间我愿选择前者。 ～·**ly** *adv* in ～ times. 从前; 以前; 往昔。

for·mic /'fɔːmɪk; 'fɔrmɪk/ *adj,* ～ **'acid,** the acid (used to make insecticides, fumigants, etc) contained in the fluid emitted by ants but now usu produced synthetically. 甲酸(用以制杀虫药, 熏蒸消毒剂等, 现在通常可由人工制造。

For·mica /fɔː'maɪkə; fɔr'maɪkə/ *n* [U] (P) heat-resistant plastic made in sheets (for covering surfaces). (商标)一种耐热塑胶薄板(用以做餐桌等家具的表面)。

for·mi·dable /'fɔːmɪdəbl; 'fɔrmɪdəbl/ *adj* **1** causing fear or dread: 可怕的; 令人畏惧的: *a man with a ～ appearance.* 面目可怕的人。 **2** requiring great effort to deal with or overcome: 难以克服的; 难缠的; 艰难的: *obstacles/opposition/enemies/debts.* 难以克服的障碍(难以平服的反抗; 难以对付的敌人, 难清偿的债务)。 **for·mi·dably** /-əblɪ; -əblɪ/ *adv*

for·mula /'fɔːmjələ; 'fɔrmjələ/ *n* (*pl* ～**s,** or, in scientific usage, 在科学用语中作 ～**e** /-liː; -lɪ/) **1** form of words used regularly (as 'How d'you do?', 'Excuse

me', 'Thank you'); phrase or sentence regularly used in legal documents, church services, etc: 客套语(如'你好', '对不起', '谢谢你'); (法律文件,宗教仪式等之)惯用语: ～ *used in baptism.* 受洗时的惯用语。 **2** statement of a rule, fact, etc esp one in signs or numbers, as in mathematics; (chem) expression in symbols of the constituent parts of a substance, eg **H₂O** (water). (数学)公式; (化学)分子式(例如水的分子式为 H₂O)。 **3** set of directions, usu in symbols, for a medical preparation: 药方; 处方: *a ～ for a cough mixture.* 配咳嗽药的药方。

for·mu·late /'fɔːmjʊleɪt; 'fɔrmjə,let/ *vt* [VP6A] express clearly and exactly: 明确地表达: ～ *one's thoughts / a doctrine.* 明确地表达个人的思想(学说)。 **for·mu·la·tion** /ˌfɔːmjʊ'leɪʃn; ˌfɔrmjə'leʃən/ *n* [U] formulating; [C] exact and clear statement. 明确的表达; 明确的陈述。

for·ni·ca·tion /ˌfɔːnɪ'keɪʃn; ˌfɔrnɪ'keʃən/ *n* [U] voluntary sexual intercourse between persons not married to one another, esp when both are unmarried. 通奸; 私通(未婚男女彼此间自愿发生的性行为)。 ⇨ **adultery. for·ni·cate** /'fɔːnɪkeɪt; 'fɔrnɪ,ket/ *vi* [VP2A] commit ～. (未婚男女与异性)通奸; 私通。

for·ra·der /'fɒrədə(r); 'fɔrədə/ *adv* (colloq) more forward: (口)更向前: *can't get any ～,* can't make any progress. 毫无进展。

for·sake /fə'seɪk; fə'sek/ *vt* (*pt* **forsook** /fə'sʊk; fə'sʊk/, *pp* **forsaken** /fə'seɪkən; fə'sekən/) [VP6A] give up; break away from; desert: 放弃; 弃绝; 遗弃: ～ *one's wife and children;* 遗弃妻儿; ～ *bad habits.* 革除恶习。 *His friends forsook him when he became poor.* 当他穷困时, 他的朋友们背弃了他。

for·sooth /fə'suːθ; fə'suθ/ *adv* (used in irony) no doubt; in truth. (用作反语)的确; 确实。

for·swear /fɔː'sweə(r); fɔr'swɛr/ *vt* (*pt* **forswore** /fɔː'swɔː(r); fɔr'swɔr/, *pp* **forsworn** /fɔː'swɔːn; fɔr'sworn/) [VP6A] **1** give up doing or using (sth): 放弃; 戒绝: ～ *bad habits/smoking.* 革除恶习(戒烟)。 **2** ～ *oneself,* perjure oneself. 作伪誓; 背誓。

for·sythia /fɔː'saɪθɪə US: fər'sɪθɪə; fə'sɪθɪə/ *n* [U] shrub with bright yellow flowers in spring. 连翘(春季开鲜黄色花朵的灌木)。

fort /fɔːt; fɔrt/ *n* building or group of buildings specially erected or strengthened for military defence. 要塞; 堡全; 碉堡; 城垒。

forte¹ /'fɔːteɪ US: fɔrt; fɔrt/ *n* person's special talent; sth a person does particularly well: (人的)长处; 特长: *Singing is not my ～,* I do not sing well. 我不擅长唱歌。

forte² /'fɔːteɪ; 'fɔrtɪ/ *adj, adv* (I; music) (abbr 略作 **f**) loud (ly). (意;音乐)强音的; 用强音。

forth /fɔːθ; forθ/ *adv* **1** (archaic) out. (古)向外。 **2** (formal) onwards; forwards: (正式用语)向前: *from this day ～.* 自今日起。 *and so ～,* and so on. 等等。 *back and ～,* to and fro (which is more usu). 前后; 来回 (to and fro 较常用)。 **3** *hold ～,* ⇨ hold¹(14).

forth·com·ing /ˌfɔːθ'kʌmɪŋ; 'forθ'kʌmɪŋ/ *adj* **1** about to come out; 即将出现的: *a list of ～ books,* books about to be published. 即将出版的书籍的目录。 **2** (pred) ready for use when needed: (用作表语)需要时即可供给的; 随要随有的; 现成的: *The money/help we hoped for was not ～,* We did not receive it. 我们所期待的那笔款(那项帮助)没有来到。 **3** ready to be helpful, give information, etc: 热心的; 肯帮忙的; 乐意提供消息的: *The girl at the reception desk was not very ～.* 接待处那位小姐服务不太热心。

forth·right /'fɔːθraɪt; forθ'raɪt/ *adj* outspoken; straightforward. 坦白的; 直率的。

forth·with /ˌfɔːθ'wɪθ US: -'wɪð; forθ'wɪθ/ *adv* at once; without losing time. 立刻; 即刻。

for·ti·eth /'fɔːtɪəθ; 'fɔrtɪəθ/ ⇨ **forty.**

for·tify /'fɔːtɪfaɪ; 'fɔrtə,faɪ/ *vt* (*pt, pp* **-fied**) [VP 6A, 14] ～ (*against*), strengthen (a place) against

attack (with walls, trenches, guns, etc); support or strengthen oneself, one's courage, etc: 加强防卫(地方);加强(自己,勇气等): ~ *a town against the enemy*; 加强防卫—城以对付敌人; *a fortified city/zone*; 设防的城市(地带); ~ *oneself against the cold*, eg by wearing a fur coat; 加强自己(例如穿—皮外衣)以御寒冷; *fortified with the rites of the Church*, prepared, by having received the Sacraments, for death. 临终前领有圣体(对死已有准备). **fortified wine**, wine, eg sherry, strengthened by the addition of grape brandy. 加有葡萄白兰地的酒(例如雪利酒). **for·ti·fi·ca·tion** /ˌfɔːtɪfɪ'keɪʃn/ ˌfɔːtəfə'keʃən/ n [U] ~**ing**; [C] (often *pl*) defensive work(s), tower(s), earthwork(s), etc. 加强防卫;(常用复数)防御工事.

for·tis·simo /fɔː'tɪsɪməʊ/ fɔː'tɪsə,mo/ *adj*, *adv* (I; music) (abbr 略作 **ff**) very loud(ly). (意;音乐)非常响亮的;用最强音.

for·ti·tude /'fɔːtɪtjuːd US: -tuːd/ 'fɔrtə,tjud/ n [U] calm courage, self-control, in the face of pain, danger or difficulty. 不屈不挠的精神;坚忍不拔;刚毅.

fort·night /'fɔːtnaɪt/ 'fɔrtnaɪt/ n period of two weeks: 两星期; 两礼拜: *a* ~*'s holiday*; 两礼拜的假期; *go away for a* ~; 离开两星期; *a* ~ (= *a* ~ *from*) *today/tomorrow/next Monday*; 从今天(明天,下星期一)算起两星期以后(或以后); *a* ~ *ago yesterday*. 从昨天算起两星期前. ~·**ly** *adj*, *adv* happening or occurring every ~: 每两星期的; 隔周: ~*ly sailings to Bombay*; 每两周驶往孟买一次; *go* ~*ly*. 隔周行驶;隔周去一次.

for·tress /'fɔːtrɪs/ 'fɔrtrɪs/ n fortified building or town. 堡垒;要塞;城堡.

for·tu·itous /fɔː'tjuːɪtəs US: -'tuː-/ fɔr'tjuetəs/ *adj* (formal) happening by chance: (正式用语)偶然发生的: *a* ~ *meeting*. 偶遇. ~·**ly** *adv*

for·tu·nate /'fɔːtʃənɪt/ 'fɔrtʃənɪt/ *adj* favoured by fortune; lucky; prosperous; having, bringing, brought by, good fortune: 幸运的; 运气好的; 吉利的; 带来好运的;好运带来的: *be* ~ *in life*. 一生幸运. *You were* ~ *to escape being injured*. 你没有受伤真是幸运. *He was* ~ *enough to have a good income*. 他很幸运,有一笔好收入. *That was* ~ *for you*. 你的运气真好. *You were* ~ *in your choice/in winning his sympathy*. 你作这样的选择(能获得他的同情)很幸运. ~·**ly** *adv* in a ~ manner: 幸运地: ~*ly for everybody*. 为每人带来幸运.

for·tune /'fɔːtʃuːn/ 'fɔrtʃən/ n **1** [C, U] chance, chance looked upon as a power deciding or influencing sb or sth; fate; good or bad luck coming to a person or undertaking: 机会; 运气; 命运; 好运或坏运: *have* ~ *on one's side*, be lucky. 走好运. *the* ~(*s*) *of war*, what may happen in war. 战争中可能发生之事; 战争中的运气. *try one's* ~, take a risky step. 碰运气. *tell sb his* ~, say, eg as gypsies do, from a reading of playing cards, or the lines on his palm, what will happen to him. (用纸牌或据掌纹等)为某人算命; 为某人看相. '~ **teller** n person who claims to be able to do this. 算命者; 看相者. **2** [C, U] prosperity; success; great sum of money: 兴隆; 成功; 巨富; 巨资: *a man of* ~; 富人; *seek one's* ~ *in a new country*. 至一新国家淘金(寻出路). **come into a** ~, inherit a lot of money. 继承大笔遗产. **make a** ~, make a lot of money. 发财; 致富. *marry a* ~, marry sb who is or will be rich, eg an heiress. 娶—有钱或将来会有钱(例如女继承人)的女人. *a small* ~, a lot of money: 许多钱: *spend a small* ~ *on clothes*. 花许多钱买衣服. '~ **hunter** n man seeking a rich woman to marry. 欲娶富有女子为妻者; 欲发妻财者.

forty /'fɔːtɪ/ 'fɔrtɪ/ *adj*, *n* the number 40: 四十; 四十个: *a man of* ~, aged 40: 四十岁的人; *under/over* ~. 四十以下(上). ⇨ **App 4**. 参看附录四. **the forties, 40-49**. 四十至四十九. *have* ~ *winks*, ⇨ **wink**. **for·ti·eth** /'fɔːtɪəθ/ 'fɔrtɪθ/ *adj*, *n* ⇨ **App 4**. 参看附录四.

fo·rum /'fɔːrəm/ 'forəm/ n (in ancient Rome) public place for meetings; any place for public discussion: (古

罗马)集会的广场; 论坛: *TV is an accepted* ~ *for the discussion of public affairs*. 电视是公认的讨论公共事务的论坛.

for·ward¹ /'fɔːwəd/ 'fɔrwəd/ *adj* (⇨ **backward**) **1** directed towards the front; situated in front; moving on, advancing: 向前的; 在前的; 向前进行的: *a* ~ *march/movement*; 前进(向前移动); *the* ~ *ranks of a column of troops*; —纵队军队的前几排; ~ *planning*, for future needs, etc; 预先的谋划; *be well* ~ *with one's work*. 工作进度很快. **2** (of plants, crops, seasons, children) well advanced; making progress towards maturity: (指植物,农作物,季节,儿童)早的; 早熟的: *a* ~ *spring*. 早临的春天. **3** eager or impatient; ready and willing: 急切的; 热心的: ~ *to help others*; 热心助人; *too eager*; rather presumptuous: 过于急切的; 孟浪的: *a* ~ *young girl*. 孟浪的少女. **4** advanced or extreme: 前进的; 急进的: ~ *opinions*. 急进的意见. **5** (comm) relating to future produce: (商)有关将来出品的: ~ *prices*; for goods to be delivered later; 期货价目; *a* ~ *contract*. 期货契约. □ n one of the first-line players in football (now often called 现在常称作 a *striker*), hockey, etc. (足球,曲棍球等之)前锋. ⇨ the illus at **football**. 参看 football 之插图. ~·**ness** n [U] the state of being ~(2): 早; 早熟: *the* ~*ness of the season*. 季节之早临.

for·ward² /'fɔːwəd/ 'fɔrwəd/ *vt* [VP6A, 12A, 13A, 15A] **1** help or send forward; help to advance; 协助; 促进: ~ *sb's plans*. 协助某人的计划. **2** send, dispatch: 发送; 递送: ~ *goods to sb*. 送给某人. *We have today* ~*ed you our new catalogue*. 我们今天已将我们的新目录寄给你了. '~**ing agent** n person or business company that ~s goods. 运输业者; 运输行业. '~**ing instructions**, instructions concerning the destination, etc of goods. (有关货物之目的地等之)运送指示. **3** send a letter, parcel, etc after a person to a new address: 转递(信件,包裹等): *Please* ~ *my letters to this address*. 请将我的信件转到这个地址.

for·ward(s) /'fɔːwəd(z)/ 'fɔrwəd(z)/ *adv* (Note: ~s is not much used except as in 4 below.) (注意: 除下列第 4 义外, ~s 的形式极少用). **1** onward so as to make progress: 向前; 前进: *rush/step* ~, 冲(跨步)向前; *go* ~. 走向前; 进步. ⇨ **carriage(3)**; **forrader**. **2** towards the future; onwards in time: 至未来; 至将来: *from this time* ~; 从此以后; *look* ~, think ahead, think about the future. 前瞻; 考虑将来. *look* ~ *to sth*, ⇨ **look**¹(7). **3** to the front; into prominence: 至前面; 至显要处: *bring* ~ (= call attention to) *new evidence*; 提出新证据; *come* ~, offer oneself for a task, a post, etc. 自愿做—工作或担任—职务. **4** *backward(s) and* ~(*s*), to and fro. 来回;前后.

fosse /fɒs/ fɔs/ n [C] long, narrow ditch or trench, eg a moat, or as a fortification. 壕(例如防御城堡或御御工事者).

fos·sil /'fɒsl/ 'fɑsl/ n [C] **1** recognizable (part, trace or imprint of a) prehistoric animal or plant once buried in earth, now hardened like rock: 化石: *hunt for* ~s; 寻觅化石; (attrib) (用作定语) ~ *bones/shells*; 成化石的骨头(贝壳); ~ *ferns in coal*. 煤层中成化石的羊齿植物. **2** (colloq) person who is out of date and unable to accept new ideas: (口)守旧的人; 落伍的人: *Isn't Professor Baboon an old* ~! 巴布恩教授真是个落伍的人!

a fossil

~·**ize** /'fɒsəlaɪz; 'fɑsl̩ˌaɪz/ vt, vi [VP6A, 2A] change or turn into stone; (fig) make or become out of date or antiquated. 使成化石; 变为化石; (喻)使古旧; 变为古旧。 ~·**iz·ation** /ˌfɒsəlaɪ'zeɪʃn US: -əl1'z-; ˌfɑsl̩'zeɪʃn/ n

fos·ter /'fɒstə(r) US: 'fɔst-; 'fɒstə/ vt [VP6A] care for; help the growth and development of; nurture: 照顾; 抚育; 养育; 培养。 ~ a child, bring it up as one's own without legally adopting it; 养育一小孩(作为家庭之一员, 但未合法收养为养子或养女); ~ the sick; 照顾病人; ~ musical ability; 培养音乐才能; ~ evil thoughts / a desire for revenge. 心怀恶念(复仇的欲望)。 '~-**brother** /-**sister** n one by one's parent(s). 义兄弟(姐妹)。 '~-**child** n one brought up by ~ parents. 养子; 义子; 螟蛉子。 '~-**parent** /-**mother** /-**father** nn one who acts as a parent in place of a natural parent, but without legal guardianship. 养母; 义母; 养父, 义父。 ⇨ **adopt.**

fought /fɔːt; fɔt/ pt, pp of **fight.**

foul[1] /faʊl; faʊl/ adj 1 causing disgust; having a bad smell or taste; filthy: 令人厌恶的; 有恶臭的; 味恶的; 污秽的: a ~ prison cell; 污浊的小牢房; medicine with a ~ taste; 味恶的药; ~-smelling drains; 有恶臭的阴沟; a ~ meal, (sl) a poor meal. (俚)令人发腻的饭。 2 wicked; evil; (of language) full of oaths; obscene; (of the weather) stormy, rough. 邪恶的; (指言语)粗鄙的; 猥亵的; (指天气)暴风雨的; 恶劣的。 '~·'**spoken** /'~-'**mouthed** adj using ~ language. 言语粗鄙的。 by ˌfair means or /~, somehow or other, whether by good or evil methods. 用正当或不正当的手段; 用种种手段; 不择手段。 ~ **play**, (a) (in sport) sth contrary to the rules. (运动)犯规。 (b) violent crime, esp murder: 凶暴罪; (尤指)谋杀: Is ~ play suspected, Do the police think this is a case of murder? 警方猜疑到这是一件谋杀案吗? 4 entangled: 纠缠的: a ~ rope. 纠缠着的绳子。 5 (of a flue, pipe, gun-barrel, etc) clogged up, not clear: (指通烟道, 水管, 枪管等)堵塞的; 阻塞的: The fire won't burn; perhaps the chimney is ~, needs sweeping. 火生不着, 或许是烟囱塞住了。 6 fall ~ of, (a) (of a ship) run against, collide with, become entangled with. (指船)与…相撞; 与…纠缠在一起。 (b) (fig) get into trouble with: (喻)招致…的困难; 陷入困境: fall ~ of the law. 招致法律上的困难。 □ n 1 [C] (sport) sth contrary to the rules; irregular stroke or piece of play. (运动)犯规。 2 [U] through fair and ~, through good and bad fortune; through everything. 不论遭遇好运或恶运; 在任何情形下。 ~·ly /'faʊllɪ; 'faʊllɪ/ adv in a ~ manner: 污秽地; 发恶臭地; 味恶地; 邪恶地; 粗鄙地: He was ~ly murdered. 他被人以残暴的手段杀害了。 ~·ness n

foul[2] /faʊl; faʊl/ vt, vi [VP6A, 2A, 2C] ~ (up), 1 make or become foul: 弄脏; 弄污秽; 使臭; 变污秽; 变臭; 玷污: factory chimneys that ~ up the air with smoke; 冒烟使空气污浊的工厂烟囱; ~ one's name /reputation; 玷污名声; ~ a drain / gun-barrel. 阻塞阴沟(枪管)。 2 collide; collide with; make or become entangled: 碰撞; 与…相撞; (使)纠缠; 纠结: The rope ~ed the anchor chain. 绳与锚链缠在一起了。 His fishing-line got ~ed up in the weeds. 他的钓丝和杂草缠在一起了。 3 (sport) commit a ~(1) against: (运动)对…犯规: ~ an opponent. 向对手犯规。

found[1] /faʊnd; faʊnd/ pt, pp of **find.**

found[2] /faʊnd; faʊnd/ vt 1 [VP6A] start the building of; lay the base of; establish: 建立; 立…的基础; 设立: ~ a new city / a factory in a new country. 建一新城市(在一新的国家建立工厂)。 2 [VP6A] get sth started by providing money (esp endowments): 捐资兴办; 捐资办(尤指捐款)兴办: ~ a new school. 捐款兴办一新学校。 3 [VP14] ~ sth on /upon, base on: 根据: a novel ~ed on fact; 根据事实写成的一部小说; arguments ~ed on fact. 基于事实的论据。

foun·da·tion /faʊn'deɪʃn; faʊn'deʃən/ n 1 [U] founding or establishing (of a town, school, church or

other institution). (城市, 学校, 教堂或其他机关之)建立; 创立; 建设。 2 [C] sth that is founded, eg a college, monastery, hospital; fund of money for charity, research, etc: 建立物(例如学院, 寺院, 医院); (慈善, 研究等)基金: the Ford F~. 福特基金。 3 [C] (often pl) strong base of a building, usu below ground-level, on which it is built up: (常用复数)地基; 屋基: the ~(s) of a block of flats. 一排公寓的地基。 The huge lorries shook the house to its ~s. 大卡车驶过连屋基都震动了。 '~-**stone** n stone laid at a ceremony to celebrate the founding of a building. 基石。 4 [C, U] that on which an idea, belief, etc rests; underlying principle; basis; starting-point: (思想, 信仰等之)基础; 根据; 根本; 出发点: the ~s of religious beliefs; 宗教信仰的基础; lay the ~(s) of one's career; 为事业奠立基础; a story that has no ~ in fact /is without ~. 无事实根据的故事。 '~ **garment**, (trade use) woman's corset or other garment to shape and support the body (often with a bra attached); (商业用语)女用紧身胸衣(常连奶罩一起); '~ **cream**, (cosmetics) cream used on the skin before other cosmetics are applied. (化妆品)粉底霜。

foun·der[1] /'faʊndə(r); 'faʊndə/ n person who founds or establishes a school, etc. (学校等之)创立人; 建立者。 **found·ress** /'faʊndrɪs; 'faʊndrɪs/ n woman ~. 女创立人; 女建立者。

foun·der[2] /'faʊndə(r); 'faʊndə/ vi, vt [VP2A, 6A] 1 (of a ship) (cause to) fill with water and sink. (指船)(使)进水而沉没。 2 (of a horse) fall or stumble (esp in mud or from overwork); cause (a horse) to break down from overwork. (指马)跌倒在泥中; 因过度疲劳而跌倒; 使(马)工作过度而衰弱。 3 (of a plan, etc) fail. (计划等)失败。

found·ling /'faʊndlɪŋ; 'faʊndlɪŋ/ n deserted or abandoned child of unknown parents. 弃儿; ~ **hospital**, (formerly) institution where ~s are taken in and cared for. (昔时)弃儿养育院。

foun·dry /'faʊndrɪ; 'faʊndrɪ/ n (pl **-dries**) place where metal or glass is melted and moulded: 铸造厂; 玻璃厂: a 'type ~, where type for printing is made. 铸字工厂。

fount /faʊnt; faʊnt/ n 1 (poet) spring of water. (诗)泉; 喷泉。 2 (also 亦作 font) set of printer's type of the same size and face. 一套活字。 3 (poet or rhet) source. (诗或修辞)来源; 根源。

foun·tain /'faʊntɪn US: -tn; 'faʊntn/ n 1 spring of water, esp one made artificially with water forced through holes in a pipe or pipes for ornamental purposes. 喷泉(尤指人造的装饰用者); 喷水池。 '**drink·ing-~** n fountain that supplies drinking-water in a public place. (设于公共场所之)饮用喷水。 '~-**pen** n pen with a supply of ink inside the holder. 自来水笔。 '**soda-~**, ⇨ **soda.** 2 (fig) source or origin: (喻)源泉; 源流: the ~ of justice. 正义的源泉。 '~-**head** n original source. 根源; 源头。

four /fɔː(r); for/ n, adj the number 4: 四; 四个: a child of ~, ~ years old; 四岁的小孩; a coach and ~, with ~ horses; 四匹马拉的马车; the ~ corners of the earth, the farthest parts; 天涯海角; scatter sth to the ~ winds, in all directions. 使某物向四面八方飞散。 ⇨ **App 4.** 参看附录四。 '~-**letter** '**word**, word of ~ letters, eg shit, which is regarded as obscene. 四个字母的字(指某些四个字母的下流语, 例如 shit)。 **on all ~s**, (crawling) on the hands and knees. 匍匐; 爬着; 全部 on **all ~s (with)**, be quite the same (as). (与…)完全相同。 a ~, a rowing-boat with a crew of ~; 四人划行之船; (cricket) hit for ~ runs. (板球)得四分的一击。 '~-**in-hand** n vehicle (coach or carriage) pulled by ~ horses and with no outrider. 无骑马侍从的四马车。 '~-**part** adj (music) arranged for ~ voices to sing. (音乐)四部合唱的。 '~·**pence** /'fɔːpəns; 'fɔrpəns/ n the sum of 4p. 四便士: apples, ~pence each. 苹果, 四便士一个。 ~·**penny** /'fɔːpnɪ US: -penɪ; 'fɔrˌpenɪ/ adj

costing 4p: 值四便士的: *a ~penny loaf.* 四便士一条的
面包。'~·**ply** *adj* (of wool, wood, etc) having ~ strands
or thicknesses. (指毛线、木材等)四股的; 四层的:
'**poster** *n* bed with ~ posts to support a canopy or
curtains. 有四柱和帐帷的床。,~·'**pounder** *n* gun
throwing a 4 lb shot. 发射四磅重炮弹的炮。'~·**score**
adj, *n* 80. 八十。'~·'**square** *adj* square-shaped; (fig)
steady; solidly based. 方形的;四方的;(喻)稳固的;巩固
的。,~·'**wheeler** *n* hackney carriage with ~ wheels
(not a hansom cab): 四轮出租马车。~·**fold** /'fɔːfəʊld;
'fɔr'fold/ *adj, adv* repeated ~ times; having ~ parts;
~ times as much or as many. 重复四次的;四重的:有四
部分的;四倍的(地)。~·**some** /'fɔːsəm; 'fɔrsəm/ *n*
game (esp of golf) between two pairs: 四人分为两组的
比赛(尤指高尔夫球): 双打: *a mixed ~some,* with one
man and one woman in each pair. 每边一男一女的对赛;
男女混合双打。~·**teen** /,fɔː'tiːn; fɔr'tin/ *n, adj* the
number 14; ⇨ **App 4.** 十四; 十四个(参看附录四)。
~·**teenth** /,fɔː'tiːnθ; fɔr'tinθ/ *n, adj* ⇨ **App 4.** 参看
附录四。**fourth** /fɔːθ; fɔrθ/ *n, adj* ⇨ **App 4.** 参看附
录四。**Fourth of July,** (US) anniversary of the
Declaration of Independence (1776). 美国独立纪念日。
fourth·ly *adv*

fowl /faʊl; faʊl/ *n* **1** (old use) any bird: (旧用法)鸟;
禽: *the ~s of the air.* 飞禽。**2** (with a *pref*) one of the
larger birds: (冠以前级)较大的鸟: '**wild~**, 猎鸟,
'**water~**. 水鸟。**3** domestic cock or hen: 家禽; 鸡: *keep
~s.* 养家禽。'~·**pest** *n* infectious disease of ~s. 家禽
疫病;鸡瘟。'~·**run** *n* piece of (usu enclosed) land
where ~s are kept. 养鸡场。**4** [U] flesh of ~s as food:
禽肉;鸡肉: *roast ~ for dinner.* 烤禽供餐食。□ *vi* (usu
as gerund) catch, hunt, snare, wild~: (通常用作动名
词)捕鸟; 猎鸟: *go ~ing.* 去猎鸟。'~·**ing-piece** *n* light
shot-gun used in ~ing. 鸟枪。'~·**er** *n* person who shoots
or traps wild birds for food. 猎野禽者;捕鸟者。

fox¹ /fɒks; faks/ *n* (fem **vixen** /'vɪksn; 'vɪksṇ/) wild
animal of the dog family, with (usu) red fur and a
bushy tail, preserved in Britain for hunting, and
proverbial for its cunning. 狐。⇨ the illus at **small.**
参看 small 之插图。'**fox·glove** *n* plant with tall-
growing spikes of purple or white flowers. 指顶花(一种
开紫色或白色花的长穗花)。'**fox·hole** *n* (mil) hole in
the ground used as a shelter against enemy fire and as a
firing-point. (军)散兵坑。'**fox·hound** *n* kind of hound

bred and trained to hunt foxes. 猎狐犬。'**fox·hunt** *n*,
vi chasing of, chase, foxes with hounds. 以猎犬猎狐。
,**fox-'terrier** *n* small and lively short-haired dog used
for driving foxes from earths, or kept as a pet. 一种猎
狐小犬(活泼的短毛小犬, 用以自狐穴中逐狐, 或养作宠
物)。'**fox·trot** *n* (music for a) ballroom dance with
slow and quick steps. 狐步舞; 狐步舞曲。**foxy** *adj*
crafty; crafty-looking. 狡猾的;样子狡猾的。

fox² /fɒks; faks/ *vt* [VP6A] (colloq) deceive by
cunning, confuse; puzzle: (口)用狡计欺骗; 使迷惑; 使
困惑: *He was completely foxed.* 他完全受骗了。

foyer /'fɔɪeɪ *US:* 'fɔɪər; 'fɔɪə/ *n* large space in a
theatre for the use of the audience during intervals;
entrance hall of a cinema or hotel. 戏院中观众休息处;
电影院或旅社入口厅堂。

fra·cas /'fræka: *US:* 'freɪkəs; 'frekəs/ *n* (*pl* GB ~
/-ka:z; -kaz/; *US* **~es** /-kəsəz; -kəsɪz/) noisy quarrel.
吵闹。

frac·tion /'frækʃn; 'frækʃən/ *n* **1** small part or bit.
小块;碎片。**2** number that is not a whole number 分数;
小数 (eg 如 1/3, 5/8, 0.76). ~**al** /-ʃənl; -ʃənl/ *adj* of
or in ~s: 小块的; 断片的; 分数的: ~**al distillation,**
partial separation of liquids, eg petroleum, having
different boiling-points by gradual heating. 分馏法。

frac·tious /'frækʃəs; 'frækʃəs/ *adj* irritable; peevish;
bad-tempered. 易怒的; 乖张的; 脾气坏的。~·**ly** *adv*
~·**ness** *n*

frac·ture /'fræktʃə(r); 'fræktʃə/ *n* [U] breaking or
being broken, eg of a bone, a pipe-line; [C] instance
of this: 折断; 断裂(例如骨或管线);破裂: *compound/
simple ~s,* with /without skin wounds. 复合骨折(单纯
骨折)。□ *vt, vi* [VP6A, 2A] break; crack: 折断; 破
碎: ~ *one's leg;* 折断腿; *bones that ~ easily.* 易断
的骨。

frag·ile /'frædʒaɪl *US:* -dʒəl; 'frædʒəl/ *adj* easily
in jured, broken or destroyed: 易受伤害的; 易碎的; 易
毁坏的: ~ *china/health/happiness.* 易碎的瓷器(虚弱
的体质; 易失去的幸福)。**fra·gil·ity** /frə'dʒɪləti; fræ-
'dʒɪləti/ *n* [U].

frag·ment /'frægmənt; 'frægmənt/ *n* [C] part broken off; separate or incomplete part: 断片; 碎片; 破片:
try to put the ~s of a broken vase together; 试将一破花
瓶的碎片拼起来; *overhear ~s of conversation.* 无意中听
到谈话的片断。□ /fræg'ment; 'fræg,mɛnt/ *vi* [VP

crest
PHEASANT
PARTRIDGE
DUCK
wattle
GROUSE
QUAIL
COCK
HEN
TURKEY
GOOSE
webbed foot

fowl

2A] break into ~s: 破碎; 成为碎片: *The shell ~s on impact.* 贝壳受撞击会破碎. **frag·men·tary** /ˈfrægməntri US: -teri; ˈfrægmənˌtɛri/ *adj* incomplete: 不完整的; 片断的: *a ~ary report of an event.* 关于一事件之不完整的报导. **frag·men·ta·tion** /ˌfrægmenˈteɪʃn; ˌfrægmənˈteʃən/ *n* '~**ation bomb,** one that breaks up into small ~s. 杀伤炸弹; 爆炸时裂成碎片的炸弹.

fra·grant /ˈfreɪɡrənt; ˈfreɡrənt/ *adj* sweet-smelling: 芳香的; 馥郁的: ~ *flowers;* 芳香的花; (fig) pleasant: (喻)愉快的: *sweet ~ memories.* 甜蜜的回忆. **fra·grance** /-əns; -əns/ *n* [C, U] sweet or pleasing smell. 香味; 香气.

frail /freɪl; frel/ *adj* weak; fragile: 虚弱的; 薄弱的; 脆弱的: *a ~ child,* one with a weak constitution; 体质虚弱的孩子; *a ~ support;* 不坚实的支柱; ~ *happiness.* 不稳固的幸福. ~**ty** /ˈfreɪlti; ˈfrelti/ *n* [U] the quality of being ~: 虚弱; 薄弱; 脆弱: *the ~ty of human life;* 人的生命之脆弱; [C] (*pl* -**ties**) fault; moral weakness: 过失; 品德上的弱点: *He loved her in spite of her little frailties.* 虽然她在品德上有些小缺点, 他依然爱她.

frame¹ /freɪm; frem/ *n* [C] **1** skeleton or main structure, eg steel girders, brick walls, wooden struts, of a ship, building, aircraft, etc which makes its shape, esp in the process of building: (船、建筑物、飞机等之)骨架. '~ **aerial** n one in which the wire is round a ~ (instead of being stretched out between two poles, etc). 框形天线. '~ **house** n one with a wooden skeleton covered with wooden boards or shingles. 木架屋; 木屋. **2** border of wood or other material in which a picture, photograph, window or door is enclosed or set; structure that holds the lenses of a pair of spectacles. 框架; 画框; 相框; 窗框; 门框; 眼镜框. ⇨ the illus at **window.** 参看 window 之插图. **3** human or animal body: 身体: *a girl of slender* ~. 身体细长的女孩子. *Sobs shook her* ~. 她哭得身体发抖. **4** box-like structure of wood and glass for protecting plants from the cold: 保护植物的玻璃温室: *a cold /heated* ~. 冷(热)室. **5** ~ **of mind,** temporary condition of mind; temper: 心境; 心情: *in a cheerful ~ of mind;* 心情愉快; *in the ~ of mind to welcome any diversion.* 有娱乐的心情. **6** (more usu 较常用 '~**work**) established order or system: 组织; 体制: *the ~ of society.* 社会组织. **7** single exposure on a roll of photographic film. 一卷照片软片中的一个画面. ~**work** n that part of a structure that gives shape and support: 构架; 结构; 组织: *a bridge with a steel ~work;* 钢架桥; *the ~work of a policy.* 政策的大纲.

frame² /freɪm; frem/ *vt, vi* **1** [VP6A] put together; shape; build up: 构造; 组织; 建筑: ~ *a plan /theory / sentence;* 拟订计划(建立学说; 造句); *a man not ~d for severe hardships,* unable to endure them well. 不能吃苦的人. **2** [VP6A] put a frame(2) round; enclose in a frame: 加以框; 装框于: ~ *a photograph;* 给照片装框; *have an oil-painting ~d;* 为油画装框; serve as a frame: 作为框架: *a landscape ~d in an archway.* 经由拱门所看到的风景. **3** [VP2A, C] develop; give promise of developing: 发展; 有发展的希望: *plans that ~ well /badly.* 发展顺利不顺利的计划. **4** [VP6A] (sl) form a plan to make (sb) appear guilty of sth; put together a false charge against (sb): (俚)陷害(某人); 诬告(某人): *The accused man said he had been ~d.* 被告说他是被人陷害了. '~**-up** n (sl) scheme or conspiracy to make an innocent person appear guilty. (俚)诬陷之计; 阴谋.

franc /fræŋk; fræŋk/ *n* standard unit of a decimal currency in eg Belgium, France, Switzerland. 法郎(如比利时,法国,瑞士通用的货币名).

fran·chise /ˈfræntʃaɪz; ˈfræntʃaɪz/ *n* **1** [U] the ~, full rights of citizenship given by a country or town, esp the right to vote at elections. 公民权; (尤指)选举权; 投票权. **2** [C] (chiefly US) special right given by public authorities to a person or company: (主美)政府给予个人或团体的特权: *a ~ for a bus service.* 设公共

汽车之特权. □ *vt* [VP6A] (US) grant a ~(2) to. (美)给予特权.

Fran·cis·can /frænˈsɪskən; frænˈsɪskən/ *n, adj* (friar or nun) of the religious order founded in 1209 by St Francis /ˈfrɑːnsɪs; ˈfrænsɪs/ of Assisi /əˈsiːsɪ; əˈsɪzɪ/. 圣芳济会(1209年圣芳济所建立之教会)的; 圣芳济会修道士或修女.

Franco- /ˈfræŋkəʊ; ˈfræŋko/ *pref* (used in compounds) French: (用于复合词中)法国的; the ~-*German 'War of 1870-71;* 1870至1871年间的法德战争; '~**phile,** (one who is) friendly towards France; 亲法的(人); '~**phobe,** (one who is) hostile towards France. 反法的(人).

Frank /fræŋk; fræŋk/ *n* member of the Germanic tribes that conquered Gaul (= France) in the 6th c AD. (日耳曼民族中之)法兰克人(于六世纪征服了高卢).

frank¹ /fræŋk; fræŋk/ *adj* showing clearly the thoughts and feelings; open: 坦白的; 率直的: *a ~ look /smile / face;* 率直的神色(微笑, 面孔); *make a ~ confession of one's guilt;* 坦白认罪; *be quite ~ with sb (about sth).* 对某人(某事)十分坦白. ~**ly** *adv* ~**ness** n

frank² /fræŋk; fræŋk/ *vt* [VP6A] put a stamp or a mark on (a letter, etc) to show that postage has been paid. 加印记于(信件等)表示邮资已付. '~**ing-machine** n machine that automatically stamps letters etc passed through it, with a counting mechanism to show the total charge. 自动邮资盖印机(附有计算装置, 可表明邮资总额).

frank·furter /ˈfræŋkfəːtə(r); ˈfræŋkfɔːtə/ *n* seasoned and smoked sausage made of beef and pork. 牛肉和猪肉制的腊肠.

frank·in·cense /ˈfræŋkɪnsens; ˈfræŋkɪnˌsɛns/ *n* [U] kind of resin from trees, giving a sweet smell when burnt. 乳香(一种树脂, 燃时发出香气).

frank·lin /ˈfræŋklɪn; ˈfræŋklɪn/ *n* (in GB, 14th and 15th cc) landowner not of noble birth, higher in rank than a yeoman. (英国十四和十五世纪之)非贵族出身的地主(地位高于自耕农).

fran·tic /ˈfræntɪk; ˈfræntɪk/ *adj* wildly excited with joy, pain, anxiety, etc; (因喜悦、痛苦、焦虑等而)狂乱的: ~ *cries for help;* 狂呼求救; *drive sb ~.* 使某人狂乱. **fran·ti·cally** /-klɪ; -klɪ/ *adv*

fra·ter·nal /frəˈtɜːnl; frəˈtɜːnl/ *adj* brotherly: 兄弟般的: ~ *love.* 手足之情. ~**ly** /-nəlɪ; -nlɪ/ *adv*

fra·ter·nity /frəˈtɜːnətɪ; frəˈtɜːnətɪ/ *n* (*pl* -**ties**) **1** [U] brotherly feeling. 手足之情; 友爱; 博爱. **2** [C] society of men, eg monks, who treat each other as equals; men who are joined together by common interests: 彼此平等相待的团体(如修道团体);为共同利益而结合的团体: *the ~ of the Press,* newspaper writers. 报界同人. **3** [C] (US) society of students, with branches in various colleges, usu with names made up of Greek letters. (美)大学中的兄弟会(通常以希腊字母为名). ⇨ **sorority.**

frat·er·nize /ˈfrætənaɪz; ˈfrætəˌnaɪz/ *vi* [VP2A, C, 3A] ~ (*with*), become friendly (with): 变为友善; 与…友善: *Men from the two armies stopped fighting and ~d on Christmas Day.* 两军的士兵于圣诞节停止交战并友善地交往. **frat·er·niz·ation** /ˌfrætənaɪˈzeɪʃn US: -nɪˈz-; ˌfrætənɪˈzeʃən/ n

frat·ri·cide /ˈfrætrɪsaɪd; ˈfrætrəˌsaɪd/ *n* [C, U] (person guilty of) wilful killing of one's brother or sister. 杀害兄弟或姐妹; 杀害兄弟或姐妹者.

Frau /frau; frau/ *n* (*pl* **Frauen** /ˈfrauən; ˈfrauən/) (G) (of a German wife or widow) Mrs; German woman. (德)(指德国妇人或寡妇)太太(冠于姓名前); 德国妇人.

fraud /frɔːd; frɔd/ *n* **1** [U] criminal deception; [C] act of this kind: 欺诈; 欺诈的行为: *get money by ~.* 骗得钱. **2** [C] person or thing that deceives: 欺诈者; 行骗的人; 骗人的事物: *This hair-restorer is a ~; I'm as bald as ever.* 这生发剂是骗人的玩意, 我还是和从前一样

的秃顶。~**u·lent** /'frɔːdjʊlənt US: -dʒʊ-; 'frɔdʒələnt/ adj acting with ~; deceitful; obtained by ~: 欺诈的; 诈骗的; 骗得的: ~ulent gains. 骗得的财物。~**u·lent·ly** adv

fraught /frɔːt; frɔt/ pred adj **1** involving; attended by; threatening (unpleasant consequences): 牵涉…的; 伴随…的; 预示…之恶兆的: an expedition ~ with danger. 充满危险的探险。**2** filled with: 充满…的: ~ with meaning. 充满意义的。

Fräu·lein /'frɔɪlaɪn; 'frɔɪlaɪn/ n (G) (of an unmarried German woman) Miss; German spinster. (德) (指未婚德国女子)小姐(冠于姓名前); 德国未婚女子。

fray[1] /freɪ; fre/ n (lit, fig) fight; contest: (字面,喻) 打斗; 争吵; 争辩: eager for the ~. 急欲争斗。

fray[2] /freɪ; fre/ vt, vi [VP6A, 2A, C] (of cloth, rope, etc) become worn, make worn, by rubbing so that there are loose threads: (指布、绳等)磨破; 磨损: ~ed cuffs, eg on a coat sleeve; 磨破了的袖口; (fig) become strained; become exasperated: (喻)变得紧张; 变得恼怒: ~ed nerves/tempers. 神经紧张(脾气急躁)。

frazzle /'fræzl; 'fræzl/ n exhausted state: 疲惫不堪: worn to a ~. 身心疲惫的。

freak /friːk; frik/ n **1** abnormal or unusual idea, act or occurrence: 怪诞的思想、行动或事件: (作定语) a ~ storm. 极其反常的暴风。**2** (also 亦作 ~ **of 'nature**) person, animal or plant that is abnormal in form, eg a five-legged sheep. 畸形的人、动物或植物 (例如五只腿的羊)。□ vi, vt [VP2C, 15B] ~ **out**, (sl) (cause to) have an intense emotional experience as from hallucinatory drugs. (俚)(使)感到非常兴奋(如服用迷幻药后)。Hence, 由此产生, ~**-out** n ~**·ish** /-ɪʃ; -ɪʃ/ adj abnormal: 不正常的: ~ish behaviour. 怪异的行为。~**·ish·ly** adv ~**·ish·ness** n ~y adj = ~ish.

freckle /'frekl; 'frɛkl/ n one of the small light-brown spots on the human skin; (pl) such spots on the face and hands caused by sunburn. 雀斑; (复)面部和手因日晒而生的斑点。□ vt, vi [VP6A, 2A] (cause to) become covered with ~s: (使)生雀斑或斑点: a ~d forehead. 生有雀斑的额头。Some people ~ more easily than others. 有些人较他人易生斑点。

free[1] /friː; fri/ adj (freer /'friːə(r); 'friə/, freest /'friːɪst; 'friɪst/) **1** (of a person) not a slave; not in the power of another person or other persons; not in prison; having personal rights and social and political liberty: (指人)自由的; 不受别人控制的; 不受监禁的; 有个人权利及社会和政治自由的: The prisoners were pardoned and set ~. 那些囚犯获赦并被释放。Were the Pyramids built by slave labour or by ~ labour? 金字塔是由奴隶的劳工还是自由劳工筑成的? ⇨ also **~labour** below. 亦参看下列之 ~ labour。'~**·born** adj inheriting liberty and rights of citizenship. 生而自由的。'~**·man** /-mən; -mən/ n (pl -**men**) person who is not a slave or a serf. 自由人; 自由民。⇨ also ~**man** at (9) below. 亦参看下列第 9 义之 freeman。**2** (of a State, its citizens, and institutions) not controlled by a foreign government; having representative government in which private rights are respected: (指国家、国民,机关)非由外国政府管辖的; 自主的; (政府)民主的: democracies; 自由民主国家; Ruritania, the land of the ~. 理想国, 自由人民的国家。**3** not fixed or held back; able to move about without hindrance; unrestricted; not controlled by rules, regulations or conventions: 松的; 可不受阻碍而移动的; 不受约束的; 无拘束的; 随便的: leave one end of the rope ~, loose; 放松绳子的一端; ~ hydrogen, not combined with another element. 游离氢。You are ~ to go or stay as you please. 请随便你的便。Please feel ~ to ask questions. 请随便发问。She is not ~ to marry, cannot do so, eg because she has to look after her parents. 她不能结婚(例如因为必须照料双亲)。One of the parts has worked ~, become loose, out of position. 有一部分松脱了。allow sb / give sb / have a ~ hand, permission or discretion to do what seems best without consulting

others. 给予某人(有)处理的自由。~ **'agent** n person who is ~ to act without restrictions. 行动不受限制的人。~**-and-easy** adj unceremonious. 不拘礼的。**F~ 'Church**, n **(a)** nonconformist Church. 非国教派教会。**(b)** Church not under State control. 独立教会。~ **'enterprise** n the conduct of trade and industry with the minimum of State control. 自由企业(工商业之经营不受国家控制)。~ **'fall** n fall from an aircraft at a great height without use of a parachute (until this is needed): 自由降落(高空跳伞时跳伞者最初不将伞打开,至必要时始打开): a ~-fall parachutist. 自由降落的跳伞者。~ **'fight**, one in which anyone present may join; one without rules. 在场的任何人皆可参加的打斗; 混战。'~**-for-all** n dispute, quarrel, etc in which all are allowed to express their views, fight for their own points of view, etc. 可自由参加的争辩等。'~**·hand** adj (of drawings) done by hand with easy movements, no rules, compasses or other instrument being used: (指绘画)凭手画的(不借仪器的): a ~hand sketch. 手画的略图。~**·'handed** adj generous; giving and spending money generously. 慷慨的; 出手大方的。'~**·hold** n (legal) (holding of) land in absolute ownership. (法律)完全保有的土地; 土地之完全保有。⇨ leasehold at **lease**. ~**·holder** n person who possesses ~hold estate. 地产之完全保有人。⇨ **1** above. 参看上列第 1 义。~ **house** n (GB) public-house not controlled by a brewery, and able, for this reason, to stock and sell all brands of beer, etc. (英)售卖各种酒的酒店(未受某家酒厂特约,可售卖各种牌子的酒)。⇨ tied house at **tie**[2]. ~ **'kick** n (football) kick allowed for a penalty without opposition from any other player. (足球)罚自由球。~ **'labour** n workers not belonging to trade unions. 不属于工会的工人。⇨ **1** above. 参看上列第 1 义。~**·lance** /-lɑːns US: -læns; -'læns/ n **(a)** (in the Middle Ages) soldier ready to serve anyone for pay. (中世纪之)佣兵。**(b)** independent journalist, writer, etc earning his living by selling his services, wherever he can. 借别处出卖文稿等为生的自由记者、作者等。□ vi work in this way: 做自由写作者: He gave up his regular job in order to ~lance. 他放弃了有固定的工作以便做自由投稿的写作者。~**·'liver** n person who indulges ~ly in (esp) food and drink; 纵情享受(尤指吃喝)的人; hence, 由此产生, ~**·'living** adj, n [U]. ~**·'load** vi [VP2A] (sl) (俚) = **sponge(3)**; hence, 由此产生, ~**·'loader** n ~ **'love** n [U] (old use) agreed sexual relations without marriage. (旧用法)自由性爱(同意无须结婚而发生性关系)。~ **port** n port open to all traders alike, with no trade restrictions, taxes, import duties, etc. 自由港。~**·'range** adj (of poultry) allowed to range freely (contrasted with **battery** birds). (指家禽)自由散放的(以别于饲养于固定房舍内者)。~ **'speech** n [U] right to speak in public without interference from the authorities. 言论自由。~**·'spoken** adj not concealing one's opinions; speaking or spoken frankly. 坦白的; 直言的。~**·'standing** adj not supported; standing independently so that it may be viewed from all sides. 不需要支持物的; 独立的(故自四方皆可观赏)。~**·'stone** n (U) easily sawn sandstone and limestone. 易锯断的砂石或石灰石; 软石。'~**·style** n [U] (swimming) race where the competitors choose their own stroke, usually the crawl. (游泳)自由选择方式的比赛(通常为自由式)。~**·'thinker** n person not accepting traditional religious teaching, but basing his ideas on reason. 不接受传统宗教信仰而根据理智思考的人; 自由思想者。Hence, 由此产生, ~**·'thinking** adj, ~**·'thought** n [U]. ~**·'trade** n [U] trade not hindered by customs duties to restrict imports or protect home industries; 自由贸易(不以其税收限制进口货或保护国内工业之贸易); hence, 由此产生, ~**·'trader** n supporter of this principle. 赞成自由贸易者。~ **trans'lation** n not word for word, but giving the general meaning. 意译。~ **'verse** n [U] without regular metre and rhyme. 自由体诗。'~**·way** n (US) highway with several lanes;

expressway. (美)高速公路。 **~-'wheel** *vi* [VP2A, C] move along on a bicycle with the pedals at rest (as when going downhill); (fig) act or live without effort or constraint. 不踩踏板任脚踏车滑行(如下坡时); (喻)不费力或无约束地行动或生活。 **,~ 'will** *n* [U] individual's power of guiding and choosing his actions (subject to limitations of the physical world, social environment, and inherited characteristics): 自由意志: *do sth of one's own ~ will*, without being required or compelled. 自愿做某事。 **'~-will** *adj* voluntary: 自愿的: *a ~will offering*. 自愿的奉献。 **4 ~ from**, without: 无…的: *~ from blame/error/anxiety*; 不会受责难(无错误, 无忧虑)的; released or exempt from: 免去…的: *~ from the ordinary regulations*. 免去通常规则的。 **~ of, (a)** outside: 在…之外: *as soon as the ship was ~ of the harbour*. 当船刚刚刚出港时。 **(b)** without: 无…的: *a harbour ~ of ice*. 不冻港。 *At last I am ~ of her*, have got away from her. 我终于离开了她。 **5** without payment; costing nothing: 免费的: *~ tickets for the theatre*; 免费戏票; *give sth away ~*; 免费赠送某物; *50 p post ~*, 50 p including cost of postage; 五十便士, 邮费在内; *admission ~*; 免费入场; *~ of income tax*, on which income tax need not be paid, or has been paid in advance (eg dividends on shares). 免所得税(不需付所得税, 或已预付过所得税, 例如股息)。 **(get sth) for ~**, (colloq) without charge or payment. (口)不要钱; 免费(获得某物)。 **'~-list** *n* **(a)** list of persons (to be) admitted ~, eg to a theatre or concert-hall. 准许免费入场者(例如戏院或音乐厅的优待者)之名单。 **(b)** list of goods (to be) admitted ~ of customs duties. 免税货物表。 **,~ 'pass** *n* authority to travel etc without paying. (旅行等的)免费乘车证; 免费证。 **~ on 'board**, (abbr 略作 **fob**) (comm) where the exporter pays all the charges for putting the goods onto the ship. (商)船上交货; 出口港离岸交货(出口商负担到货物上船费用)。 **6** (of place or time) not occupied or engaged; not being used; (of persons) not having time occupied; not doing anything: (指地点或时间)未被占用的; 空着的; (指人)有空的; 闲着的: *There will be no rooms ~ in the hotel until after the holidays*. 旅馆的房间要在假期过后才有空。 *Her afternoons are usually ~*. 她下午通常有空。 *She is usually ~ in the afternoon(s)*. 她通常下午闲着。 *have one's hands ~*, **(a)** have them empty, not being used. 手空着。 **(b)** be in a position to do as one likes; have no work or duties that demand attention. 可以自由行动; 没有需要料理的工作或职务。 ⇨ *be tied up at* **tie²**. **7** coming or given readily; lavish; profuse: 随时有的; 慷慨的; 丰富的: *a ~ flow of water*; 水的畅流; *~ with his money*; 他用钱爽爽; *~ bloomers*, plants that have a large number of blooms. 多花的植物。 *He is very ~ with his advice*, willingly gives plenty of advice. 他很喜欢劝告别人。 **8** without restraint: 无拘束的: *He is somewhat ~ in his conversation*, not quite as proper or decent as he ought to be. 他讲话有点随便(讲话有些放肆)。 *make ~ with sth/sb*, use property, persons as if they were one's own: 随意使用他人之物; 对某人随便: *He seems to have made ~ with my whisky while I was away*. 在我离开时, 他好象随便饮用了我的威士忌。 *He is/makes rather too ~ with the waitresses/the wives of his friends*, is too familiar or impudent in his behaviour. 他对女侍(朋友之妻)有些放肆。 **9** *make sb ~ of*, give him the right to share in the privileges of a company, citizenship of a city; give him the unrestricted use of one's library, etc. 给予某人分享公司特权或市民资格之权利; 让某人任意利用书房等。 *~·man /-mən, -mən/ n* (*pl* **-men**) one who has been given the privileges of a city, usu a distinguished person. 享有市民特权的人; 市民; 荣誉市民。 ⇨ **1** above. 参看上列第1义。 **~·ly** *adv* in a ~ manner; readily. 自由地; 直率地; 随意地; 爽快地。
free² /fri:; fri/ *vt* (*pt*, *pp* **freed** /fri:d; frid/) [VP 6A, 14] *~ (from/of)*, make free (*from*); rid (*of*);

set at liberty: 使自由; 免除; 释放: *~ an animal from a trap*; 自一陷阱释放一动物; *~ a country of cholera*; 使一国家免受霍乱之灾; *~ oneself from debt*. 还清债务。
freed·man /'fri:dmən; 'fridmən/ *n* (*pl* **-men**) slave set free. 被解脱奴隶身份的人。
free·booter /'fri:bu:tə(r); 'fri,butɚ/ *n* pirate; buccaneer. 海盗。
free·dom /'fri:dəm; 'fridəm/ *n* [U] condition of being free (all senses); [C] particular kind of ~: 自由; 自主; 无拘束; 率直; 随便; 特权; 出人权; 使用权: *the four ~s*, of speech, of religion, ~ from fear, ~ from want; 四大自由(言论自由、信仰自由、免于恐惧的自由、免于匮乏的自由); *give slaves their ~*; 给奴隶以自由; *give sb ~ to do what he thinks best*; 给某人随意处理事务的自由; *speak with ~*, without constraint, fearing nothing; 侃侃而言; 直言; *the ~ of the seas*, (in international law) the right of ships of neutral countries to sail the seas without interference from warships of countries at war; (国际公法)战时中立国船只之自由航海权; *give a friend the ~ of one's house/library*, allow him to use it freely. 让朋友随便使用自己的房屋(书房)。 *give sb/receive the ~ of a town/city*, full rights of citizenship (as an honour for distinguished services). 给某人(接受)市民权(作为卓越贡献的荣誉)。
Free·mason /'fri:meisn; 'fri,mesn/ *n* member of a secret society (with branches in many parts of Europe and America) for mutual help and fellowship. 互助会(在欧美有许多分布各分会的一种互济的秘密结社)。 **~ry** *n* [U] system and institutions of the ~s; (**f~ry**) instinctive sympathy between people of similar interests, the same sex: 互助会之制度; (且趣相同或同性别的人之间的)本然的同情共鸣; 默契: *the f~ry of the Press*. 报界的默契。
free·sia US: /'fri:ziə; 'fri:ʒə/ *n* kinds of flowering bulbous plant. 小苍兰属植物; 鸢尾科植物。
freeze /fri:z; friz/ *vt*, *vi* (*pt* **froze** /frouz; froz/, *pp* **frozen** /'frouzn; 'frozn/) **1** [VP2A, C] (impers) be so cold that water turns into ice: (无人称用法)冷至结冰; 酷寒: *It was freezing last night*. 昨夜天气酷寒。 *What freezing weather!* 多么冷的天气啊! *It froze hard yesterday*. 昨天的天气真冷。 **'~ing-point** *n* temperature at which a liquid (esp water) turns solid. (液体的)凝固点; (尤指水的)冰点。 **2** [VP2A, C] *~ (over/up)*, (of water) become ice; (of other liquids) become solid; (of other substances) become hard or stiff from cold: (指水) 结冰; (指其他液物)冻凝或变硬: *Water ~s when the temperature falls below 0°C (32° F)*. 当温度降至零摄氏度(32华氏度)以下时, 水会结冰。 *The lake froze over*, became covered with ice. 湖面全结了冰。 *make one's blood ~*, fill one with terror. 令人战栗。 **3** [VP2A, C] be or feel very cold: 冰冷; 感觉很冷: *I'm freezing*. 我觉得很冷。 *Two of the men froze to death*, died of cold. 有两个人冻死了。 **4.** [VP6A, 15B] *~ (over/up)*, make cold; make hard; cover with ice: 使冷; 使冻结; 使结冰; 覆以冰: *frozen food*, preserved by being kept very cold, 冰冻的食物; 冷藏的食物, ⇨ *refrigeration* at **refrigerate**; *frozen roads*, with the surface of mud, snow, etc hardened by frost. 结冻的道路。 *The lake was frozen over*. 湖面全结了冰。 *If this frost lasts the ships in the harbour will be frozen in*, be fast in the ice. 如果这种严寒的天气继续下去, 港内的船只将被冻结住了。 *one's blood*, fill one with terror. 使人战栗。 **'freezing-mixture** *n* one of salt, snow, etc used to ~ liquids. 冷冻剂(盐、雪等之混合物, 以冷冻液体者)。 **5** [VP6A] (fin) make assets, credits, etc temporarily or permanently unable to be exchanged for money; stabilize prices, wages: (财政)冻结; 冻结(财产、信用等); 稳定(价格、工资): '*price-freezing* and '*wage-freezing* (as methods to cure inflation)'. 平定物价与稳定工资(作为防止通货膨胀的方法)。 **6** [VP15B] *~ out*, (colloq) exclude him from business, society, etc by competition, cold behaviour, etc. (口)(以竞争、冷淡态度等)逼走某

人. **7** [VP2C] ~ **on to sth,** (colloq) take or keep a very tight hold of it. (口)紧握; 紧执某物。**8** [VP2A, C] become motionless, eg of an animal that stands quite still to avoid attracting attention. 不动(例如动物为避免引起注意而静立)。 [VP2C] ~ **up,** (of an actor) be unable to speak, move, etc on the stage. (指演员)在舞台上说不出话或做不出动作(时); 穿帮。 □ **n 1** period of freezing weather. 冰冻期; 严寒期。 **2** (fin) severe control, stabilization, of incomes, wages, dividends, etc: (财政)稳定(收入、工资、股息等): *a* ~*wage*—. 稳定工资。 **3** **deep-**~, (part of a) refrigerator where a very low temperature is used. 冰柜; 冰箱之冷冻库。 ⇨ also *deep-freeze* at **deep**[2].

freezer /ˈfriːzə(r); ˈfrizɚ/ *n* (part of a) refrigerator or room for storing food etc at a very low temperature for a long time. 冰柜; 冰库; 冷冻库。

freight /freit; fret/ *n* [U] (money charged for) the carriage of goods from place to place by water (in US also by land); the goods carried. 货物之水上运输(美国亦指陆上运输); 运费; 运输的货物。 '~**liner** *n* linertrain, ⇨ **liner**(2). 长途快速货运火车。 '~**train** *n* (US) goods train, ⇨ **goods**(2). (美)货运火车。 □ *vt* [VP6A, 14] ~ (*with*), load (a ship) with cargo; send or carry (goods): 装货于(船); 运输(货物): *a ship* ~*ed with wheat;* 载小麦的船; *a boat with fruit.* 将水果装在船上。 ~**er** *n* ship or aircraft that carries mainly ~ (cargo). 货船; 运货机。

French /frentʃ; frentʃ/ *adj* of France or the people of France. 法国的; 法国人的。 **take** ~ **leave,** do sth, go away, without asking permission or giving notice. 未经许可而而贸然做某事; 不辞而别。 ,~ '**bread**/**loaf** *n* long, thin, crisp, light, white bread/loaf. 法国面包。 ,~ '**dressing** *n* [U, C] salad dressing of oil and vinegar. 法国式生菜调味品(有油和醋)。 ,~ '**fries** *n pl* (US) potato chips. (美)炸马铃薯条。 ,~ '**horn** *n* brass wind instrument. 法国号; 圆喇叭(一种铜管乐器)。 ⇨ the illus at **brass**. 参看 brass 之插图。 ,~ '**letter** *n* (GB colloq) protective sheath. (英口)保险套。 ⇨ **sheath**(2). ,~ '**window** *n* one that is both a window and a door, opening on to a garden or balcony. 落地窗。 ⇨ the illus at **window**. 参看 window 之插图。 □ *n* the ~ language. 法语; 法文。 '~**man** /-mən; -mən/ '~**woman** *man*/*woman* of ~ birth or nationality. 法国男人; 法国女人。

fren·etic /frəˈnetɪk; frəˈnɛtɪk/ *adj* frenzied; frantic. 狂乱的; 发狂的。

frenzy /ˈfrenzɪ; ˈfrɛnzɪ/ *n* [U] violent excitement: 狂乱; 极为激动: *in a* ~ *of despair*/*enthusiasm;* 在一阵绝望(热情)的狂乱中; *rouse an audience to absolute* ~. 使听众们极为激动。 **fren·zied** /ˈfrenzɪd; ˈfrɛnzɪd/ *adj* driven to ~; wildly excited. 狂乱的; 狂暴的。 **fren·zied·ly** *adv*

fre·quency /ˈfriːkwənsɪ; ˈfrikwɛnsɪ/ *n* **1** [U] frequent occurrence: 时常发生; 频繁: *the* ~ *of earthquakes in Japan.* 日本地震之频繁。 **2** [C] (*pl* -**cies**) rate of occurrence; number of repetitions (in a given time): 频率; 周率; 发生次数(在某一时间内): *a* ~ *of 25 per second,* eg of an alternating electric current. (如交流电之)每秒 25 频率。

fre·quent[1] /ˈfriːkwənt; ˈfrikwənt/ *vt* [VP6A] go often to (a place); be often found in or at: 常去(一地点); 常在…见到: *Frogs* ~ *wet places.* 青蛙常在湿地见到。 *He no longer* ~*s bars.* 他不再常去泡吧了。

fre·quent[2] /ˈfriːkwənt; ˈfrikwənt/ *adj* often happening; habitual: 时常发生的; 惯常的: *Hurricanes are* ~ *here in autumn.* 在秋天此地时常有飓风。 *He's a* ~ *visitor.* 他是常来的客人。 ~**ly** *adv* often: 时常地: *~ly occurring hurricanes.* 时常发生的飓风。

fresco /ˈfreskəʊ; ˈfreskɔ/ *n* (*pl* ~**s**, ~**es** /-kəʊz, -koz/) **1** [U] pigment applied to moist plaster surfaces and allowed to dry; method of painting with this pigment: 壁画颜料; 壁画法: *painting in* ~. 作壁画。 **2**

[C] picture painted in this way: 壁画; 用壁画法作成之画: *the* ~*(es) in the Sistine Chapel, Rome.* 罗马西斯汀教堂中的壁画。 □ *vt* paint (a wall, etc) in ~. 用壁画法作画于(墙壁等)。

fresh /freʃ; freʃ/ *adj* (-**er**, -**est**) **1** newly made, produced, gathered, grown, arrived, etc: 新做的; 新制的: ~ *flowers*/*fruit*/*eggs*/*milk;* 新鲜的花(水果、蛋、牛奶); ~ *paint* (= still wet); 刚刷上的漆; *a man* ~ *from the country;* 刚从乡间来的人; *a boy* ~ *from school,* who has only recently finished his school course. 刚从学校毕业的男孩子。 ⇨ *faded* at **fade.** '~·**man** /-mən; -mən/ *n* (*pl* -**men**) student in his first year at a college or university. 大学一年级学生。 **2** (of food) not salted, tinned or frozen: 没腌过的; 未加盐的; 未保存在罐头中的; 未冰冻的: ~ *butter*/*meat;* 淡牛油(鲜肉); (of water) not salt; not sea-water. (指水)淡的。 ~·**water** *adj* ~ water, not of the sea: 淡水的: ~*water fish;* 淡水鱼; ~*water fishermen.* 在淡水捕鱼的人。 **3** new or different: 新奇的; 不同的: *Is there any* ~ *news?* 有什么新的消息吗? *Take a* ~ *sheet of paper and start again.* 另外拿一张纸重新开始。 *He didn't throw much* ~ *light* (= give much new information) *on the subject.* 关于这问题他没有提供很多新的见解或资料。 **break** ~ **ground,** (fig) start sth new, find new facts. (喻)开辟新园地; 着手新事业; 寻求新事实。 **4** (of the air, wind, weather) cool; refreshing: (指空气、风、天气)凉爽的, 清新的: *go out for some* ~ *air;* 出外呼吸新鲜空气; *in the* ~ *air,* out of doors. 在户外。 ~ **breeze**/**wind,** blowing rather strongly. 凉爽的风; 清风。 **5** bright and pure: 鲜艳的: ~ *colours;* 鲜艳的颜色; bright and pure in colour: 气色好的: *a* ~ *complexion.* 气色好的面容。 **6** (US colloq) presumptuous, impudent (esp towards sb of the opposite sex): (美口)卤莽的; 无礼的(尤指对于异性): *Tell that young man not to get*/*be so* ~ *with your sister.* 告诉那个年轻人不要对你的姐姐(妹妹)如此无礼。 □ *adv* (in hyphened compounds) ~**ly,** newly: 刚于(加有连字符的复合词中)新近地: ~*-caught fish;* 方才捕到的鱼; ~*-killed meat;* 新宰的肉; ~*-painted doors.* 新漆的门。 ~·**ly** *adv* (only with *pp,* without hyphen) recently: (仅与过去分词连用, 无连字符)新近地: ~*ly picked peaches.* 新采下来的桃子。 ~**er** *n* = ~**man.** ~·**ness** *n*

freshen /ˈfreʃn; ˈfreʃən/ *vi, vt* [VP2A, C, 6A, 15B] ~ (*up*), become or make fresh; revive: 使新鲜; 变为新鲜; (使)复活: *feel* ~*ed up after a shower;* 淋浴后感到舒畅; *give a drink,* add more to it; 加添饮料; *the breeze* ~*ed,* grew stronger. 风力增强。

fret[1] /fret; fret/ *vi, vt* (-**tt-**) **1** [VP2A, C, 3A, 15A] worry; (cause) to be discontented or bad-tempered: 烦恼; (使)不满或烦躁: *What are you* ~*ting about?* 你为何烦躁不安? *Don't* ~ *over trifles.* 勿为琐事烦恼。 *She* ~*s at even the slightest delays.* 稍微晚一点她都要发脾气(着急)。 *Small babies often* ~ *in hot weather.* 天热时婴儿常烦躁。 *She'll* ~ *herself to death one of these days.* 不久她会急死。 **2** [VP6A] wear away by rubbing or biting at: 磨损; 侵蚀: *a horse* ~*ting its bit;* 咬着口衔的马; ~*ted rope,* 磨损了的绳子; *a channel* ~*ted through the rock by a stream.* 溪流侵蚀岩石而成的水道。 □ *n* state of irritation or querulousness: 急躁; 烦躁; 牢骚满腹: *in a* ~. 焦急地; 烦躁地。 ~·**ful** /-fl; -fəl/ *adj* discontented; irritable: 不满的; 烦躁的: *a* ~*ful baby.* 烦躁的婴儿。 ~·**fully** /-fl; -fəl/ *adv*

fret[2] /fret; fret/ *vt* (-**tt-**) [VP6A] decorate (wood) with patterns made by cutting or sawing. 以格子细工装饰(木)。 '~·**saw** *n* very narrow saw, fixed in a frame, for cutting designs in thin sheets of wood. 细工锯; 钢丝锯。 '~·**work** *n* [U] work in decorative patterns; wood cut with such patterns by using a ~saw. 格子细工; 凸花细工; 饰有格子细工之木。

fret[3] /fret; fret/ *n* one of the metal ridges set at intervals across the fingerboard of a guitar, banjo, etc to act as a guide for the fingers to press the strings

at the correct place. (吉他、班究琴等指板上的)柱;马;品。

Freud·ian /'frɔɪdɪən; 'frɔɪdɪən/ adj of the psychoanalytic theories of Sigmund Freud. 弗洛伊德之精神分析学说的。 **~ 'slip,** (colloq) instance when a speaker accidentally says something contrary to what was intended and which seems to reveal his true thoughts. (口)偶然说出心中不觉讲的话。

fri·able /'fraɪəbl; 'fraɪəbl/ adj easily crumbled. 易碎的。 **fria·bil·ity** /,fraɪə'bɪlətɪ; ,fraɪə'bɪlətɪ/ n

friar /'fraɪə(r); 'fraɪə/ n man who is a member of one of certain religious orders. 修道士。

fric·assee /'frɪkəsiː; ,frɪkə'siː/ n [C, U] (dish of) meat or poultry cut up, fried or stewed, and served with sauce. 一种由细切之肉或鸡煎成或炖成后加以酱汁的食品。 □ vt /,frɪkə'siː; ,frɪkə'siː/ make a ~ of. 将…制成上述之食品。

frica·tive /'frɪkətɪv; 'frɪkətɪv/ adj, n (phon) (consonant) produced with audible friction when the air is expelled through a narrowing of the air passage: (语音)由摩擦而产生的; 摩擦辅音: The sounds /f, v, θ/ are ~s. /f, v, θ/ 是摩擦辅音。

fric·tion /'frɪkʃn; 'frɪkʃən/ n 1 [U] the rubbing of one thing against another, esp when this wastes energy. 摩擦。 2 [C, U] (instance of a) difference of opinion leading to argument and quarrelling: 不和; 冲突: political ~ between two countries; 两国间政治上的不和; ~(s) between parents and children. 父母与子女间之冲突。

Fri·day /'fraɪdɪ; 'fraɪdɪ/ n sixth day of the week. 星期五; 礼拜五。 **Good '~,** the ~ before Easter; the anniversary of the crucifixion of Jesus. 耶稣受难日(复活节前的星期五)。 **,man '~,** (from the story of Robinson Crusoe) faithful servant. 忠仆(源自鲁宾逊漂流记)。

fridge /frɪdʒ; frɪdʒ/ n (abbr of) refrigerator. 冰箱 (refrigerator 之略)。

fried /fraɪd; fraɪd/ pt, pp of **fry.**

friend /frend; frɛnd/ n 1 person, not a relation, whom one knows and likes well: 朋友; 友人: We are great/good ~s. 我们是好朋友。 He has been a good ~ to me. 他一向是我的好朋友。 be ~s with be a ~ of. 是…的朋友。 **make ~s,** become mutual ~s. 交上朋友; 成为朋友。 **make '~s again,** become ~s again after a disagreement, etc. 言归于好。 **make '~s with; make a '~ of,** become the ~ of. 与…交朋友。 2 helpful thing or quality: 有帮助的东西或性质: Among these wild young people, her shyness was her best ~. 置身在这些放荡的青年当中, 她的羞怯给予她最大的帮助。 3 helper or sympathizer: 赞助者; 同情者: a good ~ of the poor. 乐于帮助贫穷的人。 4 **F~,** member of the Society of F~s; Quaker. 基督教教友派教徒。 **~·less** adj having no ~s. 没有朋友的。 **~·less·ness** n

friend·ly /'frendlɪ; 'frɛndlɪ/ adj (-ier, -iest) acting, or ready to act, as a friend; showing or expressing kindness: 作为朋友而做出的; 友善的; 亲切的: be ~ with sb; 对某人友善; be ~ to a cause; 赞助一事业; a ~ smile; 亲切的微笑; be on ~ terms with sb; 与某人友好; a ~ match/game, one not played in competition for a prize, etc. 友谊赛。 **'F~ Society,** one for the mutual benefit of its members, eg during illness, unemployment, old age. 互助会。 **friend·li·ness** n [U] ~ feeling and behaviour. 友善; 友好; 亲切。

friend·ship /'frendʃɪp; 'frɛndʃɪp/ n 1 [U] being friends, the feeling or relationship that exists between friends: 友爱; 友情; 友谊: live together in ~; 友善地生活在一起; my ~ for her. 我对她的友谊。 2 [C] instance or period of this feeling: 友情的实例; 友谊期间: a ~ of twenty years; 二十年的友谊; never to forget old ~s. 永不忘记旧时的友谊。

frieze /friːz; friːz/ n [C] ornamental band or strip along a wall (usu at the top), eg a horizontal band of

sculpture on the outside of a building, or a strip of wallpaper with a special design just below the ceiling of a room. 檐壁(沿墙的饰带,通常在墙的上端, 例如建筑物外部之雕刻的横饰带,或紧接天花板下, 墙头上印有图案的一条壁纸)。 ⇨ the illus at **column.** 参看 column 之插图。

frig·ate /'frɪgət; 'frɪgɪt/ n fast sailing-ship formerly used in war; (modern use) (GB) fast escort vessel; (US) medium sized warship. 旧时挂帆的快速战舰; (近代用法)(英)快速护航舰; 巡防舰; (美)中型战舰。

fright /fraɪt; fraɪt/ n 1 [U] great and sudden fear: 惊骇: die of ~, 惊骇至死; take ~ (at sth); (因某事物)吃惊; [C] instance of this. 惊骇的实例。 **give sb/get/have a ~.** 使某人吃惊(感到吃惊)。 2 [C] (colloq) ridiculous-looking person or thing: (口)怪样子的人或物: What a ~ you look in that old hat! 你戴着那顶旧帽子样子多么可笑啊! □ vt (poet) frighten. (诗)使吃惊; 使惊骇。

frighten /'fraɪtn; 'fraɪtn/ vt [VP6A, 15B, 14] fill with fright or terror; alarm suddenly: 使吃惊; 使惊骇; 使害怕: Did the noise ~ you? 那声音使你吃惊吗? The barking of the dog ~ed the burglar away. 狗吠声将那窃贼吓跑了。 She was nearly ~ed out of her life. 她几乎吓死。 **~ sb into/out of doing sth,** cause him to do/not to do sth by ~ing him. 恐吓某人做(不做)某事。 **fright·ened** adj (colloq) afraid: (口)害怕的: be ~ed of sb or sth; 害怕某人或某物; alarmed: 受惊的: ~ed at the idea of sth happening. 想到某事之发生而惊恐。 **~·ing** adj causing fright or terror: 可怕的; 令人恐怖的: a ~ing experience. 可怕的经验。

fright·ful /'fraɪtfl; 'fraɪtfəl/ adj 1 causing fear; dreadful: 可怕的; 令人恐怖的: a ~ accident. 可怕的事故。 2 (colloq) very great; unpleasant: (口)极大的; 讨厌的: a ~ mess; 乱七八糟; a ~ journey, a very uncomfortable one. 一次极不舒服的旅行。 **~·ly** /-fəlɪ; -fəlɪ/ adv 1 in a ~ way. 可怕地; 令人恐怖地。 2 (colloq) very. (口)非常地。 **~·ness** n

frigid /'frɪdʒɪd; 'frɪdʒɪd/ adj 1 cold: 寒冷的: a ~ climate; 寒冷的气候; the ~ zones, those within the polar circles. 寒带。 2 unfriendly; without ardour or sympathy; apathetic: 无情的; 冷淡的; 缺乏情感的: a ~ welcome; 冷淡的欢迎; a ~ manner; 冷淡的态度; ~ conversation; 冷淡的谈话; a ~ woman, lacking in sexual desire. 性冷感的女人。 **~·ly** adv **frigid·ity** /frɪ'dʒɪdətɪ; frɪ'dʒɪdətɪ/ n [U].

frill /frɪl; frɪl/ n 1 ornamental border on a dress, etc. (衣服等的)饰边。 2 (pl) unnecessary adornments, eg to speech or writing; airs[1](6b), affectations: 装腔作势; 虚饰: (喻)矫饰(如言语或写作中者); 装腔作势; 虚饰。 **frilled** adj having ~s(1). 有饰边的: a ~ed skirt. 有饰边的裙子。 **frilly** adj having ~s; (colloq) too much ornamented. 有饰边的; (口)过份装饰的。

fringe /frɪndʒ; frɪndʒ/ n 1 ornamental border of loose threads, eg on a rug or shawl. (地毯或围巾等之)须边; 缨; 流苏。 2 edge (of a crowd, forest, etc): (人群, 森林等之)边缘: on the ~(s) of the forest. 在森林之边缘。 **'~ area,** area on the border of a district (eg) (fig) less important area. 边界地区; (喻)不太重要的地区。 **'~ benfiets,** eg a rent-free house, the use of a car, additional to wages or salary. 薪资外, 尚有不收租金的房屋, 可使用汽车等)。 **'~ group,** group of persons loosely attached to a larger group or party (but who may be rebellious or nonconformist in some respects); 边缘团体; 外围团体(不太密切地隶属于一较大团体或政党, 但在某些方面可能不一致行动); hence, 由此产生, (in) 'medicine/theatre, etc. 辅药(外围或院等)。 3 part of hair cut short and allowed to hang over the forehead. 额头之垂发; 刘海。 □ vt [VP 6A] put a ~ on; be a ~ to: 加饰边于; 作为…之边缘: a roadside ~d with trees. 植有树的路边。

frip·pery /'frɪpərɪ; 'frɪpərɪ/ n [U] needless ornament, esp on dress; [C] (pl -ries) cheap ornament or

useless trifle. 不需要的装饰(尤指衣服上者); 贱价的装饰品; 琐屑无用之物。

Fris·bee /'frɪzbiː; 'frɪzbi/ *n* (P) piece of light plastic, shaped like a plate, thrown between players in a game. (商标)飞盘(一种抛着玩的塑料盘)。

frisk /frɪsk; frɪsk/ *vi, vt* **1** [VP2A, C] jump and run about playfully. 欢跃; 雀跃。 **2** [VP6A] pass the hands over (sb) to search for concealed weapons. 搜查 (某人有无私藏武器)。 **~y** *adj* lively; ready to ~: 活泼的; 好欢跃的: *as ~y as a kitten*. 象小猫一样活泼。 **'~ily** /-ɪlɪ; -ɪlɪ/ *adv*

fris·son /'friːsɒn US: friːˈsɒn; friˈsɒn/ *n* (F) emotional thrill: (法)震颤; 战栗: *a ~ of delight/horror*. 高兴(害怕)得发抖。

frit·ter[1] /'frɪtə(r); 'frɪtə/ *vt* [VP15B] ~ *sth away*, waste it on divided aims: 零碎地消耗: ~ *away one's time/energy/money*. 零碎地消耗时间(精力, 金钱)。

frit·ter[2] /'frɪtə(r); 'frɪtə/ *n* [C] piece of fried batter, usu with sliced fruit in it. 油炸饼(通常以水果为馅)。

frivol /'frɪvl; 'frɪvl/ *vi, vt* **(-ll-) 1** [VP2A] behave in a silly, time-wasting way. 作无聊和浪费时间的行动。 **2** [VP15B] ~ *away*, waste time, money, etc foolishly. 浪费(时间, 金钱等)。

friv·ol·ous /'frɪvələs; 'frɪvələs/ *adj* **1** not serious or important: 不庄重的; 不重要的: ~ *remarks/behaviour*. 不庄重的言谈(举动)。 **2** (of persons) not serious, pleasure-loving. (指人)轻浮的; 喜享乐的。 **~·ly** *adv* **friv·ol·ity** /frɪˈvɒlətɪ; frɪˈvɑlətɪ/ *n* **1** [U] ~ behaviour; lightness of character. 行为不庄重; 轻浮。 **2** [C] (*pl* **-ties**) ~ act or utterance. 不庄重的行动或言语。

frizz /frɪz; frɪz/ *vt* [VP6A] form into masses of small curls. (指毛发)使卷曲。 **~y** *adj* (of hair) ~ed. (指毛发)卷曲的。

frizzle[1] /'frɪzl; 'frɪzl/ *vt, vi* [VP6A, 2A] cook, be cooked, with a spluttering noise: 烹煎时发咝咝声: *bacon frizzling in the pan*. 在锅内煎至发咝咝声的脆肉。

frizzle[2] /'frɪzl; 'frɪzl/ *vt, vi* [VP2C, 15B] ~ *up*, (of hair) twist in small, crisp curls. (指毛发)卷曲; 使卷曲。

fro /frəʊ; fro/ *adv* *to and fro*, backwards and forwards: 往返地; 来回地: *walking to and fro*; 来回走; *journeys to and fro between London and Paris*. 伦敦与巴黎间往返的旅行。

frock /frɒk; frɑk/ *n* **1** woman's or girl's dress. (女子的)洋装。 **2** monk's long gown with loose sleeves. 僧袍。 **3** **~'coat** *n* long coat, usu with square corners, formerly worn by men in the 19th c (now replaced by the *morning-coat*). 十九世纪男子所穿的一种方领角的长外衣(现已被晨礼服所代替)。

frog /frɒg; frɑg/ *n* **1** small, cold-blooded, tailless jumping animal living in water and on land. 蛙。 ⇨ the illus at **amphibian**. 参看 amphibian 之插图。 **'~·man** /-mən; -mən/ *n* (*pl* **-men**) person skilled in swimming under water with the aid of flippers on the feet and breathing apparatus. 蛙人。 **'~·march** *vt* [VP6A] carry (a prisoner) away, face downwards, by four men holding his arms and legs. 蛙式抬运(令囚犯面向下, 由四人执其四肢而抬运之)。 **2** long button and loop for fastening to it, used to fasten cloaks, etc. (外衣等的)长扣; 花扣。

a frogman

frolic /'frɒlɪk; 'frɑlɪk/ *vi* (*pt, pp* **-ked**) [VP2A, C] play about in a gay, lively way. 嬉戏。 □ *n* [C] outburst of gaiety or merrymaking; wild or merry prank. 嬉戏; 作乐。 **~·some** /-səm; -səm/ *adj* inclined to ~; playful and merry. 爱嬉戏的; 欢乐的。

from /frəm; frəm; *strong form:* frɒm; fram/ *prep* **1** (used to introduce the place, point, person, etc that is the starting-point): 自; 从(表示起点): *jump (down) ~ a wall*; 从墙上跳下; *travel ~ London to Rome*; 自伦敦旅行至罗马; *bees going ~ flower to flower*. 逐花飞行的蜜蜂。 **2** (used to indicate the starting of a period of time): 自; 从(表示时期的起始): *~ the first of May*; 从五月一日起; *~ childhood*; 自童年起; *~ day to day*; 日复一日; *~ beginning to end*. 自始至终。 **3** (used to indicate the place, object, etc whose distance, absence, etc is stated): 距; 离: *ten miles ~ the coast*; 距海岸十英里; *stay away ~ school*; 缺课; *be/go away ~ home*; 离家; *far ~ blaming you*, not in any way doing so. 绝不责备你。 **4** (showing the giver, sender, etc): 由…发出: *a letter ~ my brother*; 我哥哥(弟弟)的来信; *a present ~ his father*. 他父亲给他的一件礼物。 *Tell him ~ me that* …. 替我转告他…。 **5** (art, showing the model, etc): (艺术, 表示模仿的题材等): *painted ~ nature/life*, with the actual scene, object, etc in front of the artist. 写生。 **6** (showing the lower limit): (表示较低的限度): *We have good Italian wine ~ £1.50 a bottle*, at this price and at higher prices. 我们有好的意大利酒, 售价自1.50英镑起。 *There were ~ ten to fifteen boys absent*. 有十至十五个男孩子缺席。 **7** (used to indicate the source from which sth is taken): 由(表示来源): *quotations ~ Shakespeare*; 由莎士比亚作品中引来的文句; *draw water ~ a well*; 由井中汲水; *draw conclusions ~ the evidence*; 由证据获得结论; *judge ~ appearances*; 以貌取人; *~ this point of view*. 由此观点。 **8** (showing the material, etc used in a process, the material being changed as a result); (表示原料等在制造过程中有所改变): *Wine is made ~ grapes*. 葡萄酒是用葡萄酿制的。 *Steel is made ~ iron*. 钢是铁炼成的。 Cf 参较 *That bridge is made of steel*. 那座桥是用钢建造的。 **9** (used to indicate separation, removal, prevention, escape, avoidance, deprivation, etc. ⇨ *v/ n +~*, in *v* and *n* entries): (表示分离, 除去, 阻止, 逃避, 避免, 剥夺等): 参看动词及名词各条中之 *v/n+~*): *Take that knife (away) ~ the baby*. 将那刀子从那婴儿身旁拿走。 *When were you released ~ prison?* 你是什么时候出狱的? *What prevented/stopped/hindered you ~ coming?* 何事阻止你前来? **10** (used to indicate change): (表示变化): *Things are going ~ bad to worse*. 事情愈来愈糟了。 *The price has been increased ~ 20 p to 25 p*. 价格已由二十便士增至二十五便士。 **11** showing reason, cause or motive: 由于; 因为: *collapse ~ fatigue*; 累倒; *suffer ~ starvation and disease*; 因饥饿和疾病而患病; *do sth ~ necessity, not ~ a sense of duty*. 因需要而做某事, 并非由于责任感。 *F~ his looks you might think him stupid*. 由外表看来你可能认为他是愚蠢的。 *F~ what I heard, the driver was to blame*. 就我所听到的, 驾驶人应受指责。 **12** (showing distinction or difference): (表示区别): *distinct/different ~ others*; 与其他的不同的; *to differ ~ others*. 与其他的不同。 *How would you know an Englishman ~ an American?* 你怎样分辨英国人和美国人? **13** (governing *advs* and *prep* phrases): (限制副词和介词短语): *seen ~ above/below*; 由上(下)而看; *looking at me ~ above/under her spectacles*. 她从眼镜上面(下面)看我。

frond /frɒnd; frand/ *n* leaf-like part of a fern or palm-tree. 羊齿植物或棕榈等的复叶。

front /frʌnt; frʌnt/ *n* **1** *the ~*, foremost or most important side: 正面; 前面: *the ~ of a building*, that with the main entrance; 建筑物的正面; *the east/west ~ of the Palace*; 宫殿之东(西)面: *sitting in the ~ of the class*, in one of the foremost rows facing the teacher 坐在班上前排 (cf 参较 *standing in ~ of the class*, facing

the pupils 站在全班学生面前); (attrib): (用作定语): *a ~ seat*; 前排座; *the ~ garden*; 前花园; *a ~ room*, one in the ~ of a house; 前面的房间; *the ~ page of a newspaper*, page 1; 报纸的第一版; *~-page news*, important enough for the ~ page; 登在第一版的重要新闻; *a seat in the ~ part of the train.* 火车前部的座位。 **(be) in the ~ rank,** (fig) (be) well known or important. (喻)著名; 显要. **come to the ~,** (fig) become conspicuous, well known, etc. (喻)出名。 *in ~ (adv),* 在前面, *in ~ of (prep)*: 在…的前面: *Please go in ~.* 请走前面走。*There are some trees in ~ of the house.* 那房屋前有几棵树。*~ 'runner n* (In an election, etc) person likely to win. (选举等中)可能获胜者; 领先者。⇨ also **bench, door. 2** [C] (war) part where the fighting is taking place: 前线; 前方: *go/be sent to the ~;* 上前线; *a ~ of 500 miles:* 长达五百英里的前线; (fig) organized body or department of activity: (喻)有组织的团体或活动部门: *How are things on the domestic ~,* (colloq) at home? (口)国内的情形如何? **3** road, promenade bordering the sea; 海滨之步道; 环湖的道路: *have a walk along the ('sea) ~;* 在海滨散步; *drive along the lake ~;* 驶车于湖滨; *a house on the ~,* facing the sea. 位于海滨的一所房屋。**4** [U] *have the ~ (to do sth),* be impudent enough. 厚颜(做某事)。 *put on/show/present a bold ~,* face a situation with (apparent) boldness. (表面上)勇敢地面对某情况。 **5 ('shirt) ~,** breast of a shirt (esp the starched ~ part of a man's (dress) shirt). 衬衫的胸部(尤指男子衬衫浆硬的胸部)。**6** (theatre) auditorium; part where the audience sits. (戏院)大厅。**7** (met) boundary between masses of cold and warm air: (气象)锋(冷热气团间的交界面): *a cold/warm ~.* 冷(热)锋。**8** (poet, rhet) forehead; face. (诗, 修辞)额; 面孔。**9** apparent leader ('~ **man**) or group of persons (~ **organization**) serving as a cover for the secret or illegal activities of an anonymous person or group. 秘密或不法活动份子的掩护人; 幌子(亦称 '~ man 或 '~ organization)。□ *vt, vi* **1** [VP6A, 2A, C] face: 面向; 朝: *hotels that ~ the sea;* 朝海的旅社; *windows ~ing the street;* 朝街的窗子; *a house ~ing north;* 朝北的房子。**2** [VP6A] (old use) confront; oppose: (旧用法)面对; 对抗: ~ *danger.* 面对危险。

front·age /'frʌntɪdʒ; 'frʌntɪdʒ/ *n* [C] extent of a piece of land or a building along its front, esp bordering a road or river: 土地或建筑物之正面长度; 土地或建筑物之前沿(尤指临道路或河川者); 临街面: *For sale, office buildings with ~s on two streets:* 面临两街之办公大楼出售; *factory premises with a good river ~;* 厂房连同一片良好的面河的空地; *a building site with a road ~ of 500 metres.* 一块建筑用地, 五百米临路。

frontal /'frʌntl; 'frʌntl/ *adj* of, on or to, the front: 正面的; 在正面的; 至正面的: *a ~ attack*, 正面攻击; *full ~ nudity*, of the whole of the front of the body. 正面全部裸体。⇨ **flank; rear.**

fron·tier /'frʌntɪə(r) US: frʌn'tɪər; frʌn'tɪr/ *n* [C] **1** part of a country bordering on another country; (land on each side of a) boundary: 国境; 边疆; 边界: *a town on the ~;* 位于边区的城市; (attrib) (用作定语) *disputes/incidents;* 边疆的争端(事件); (esp US, in the past) farthest part of a country to which settlement has spread, beyond which there is wild or unsettled land. (尤指昔时美国之)新开辟地。*~s·man* /-zmən; -zmən/ *n* (*pl* -**men**) man who lives on a ~; pioneer in a newly settled district near the ~. 边疆居民; 拓荒者。**2** (fig) extreme limit: (喻)极限: *the ~s of knowledge;* 知识的极限; *underdeveloped area* (eg of scientific research). 未开发的领域(如科学研究方面者)。

front·is·piece /'frʌntɪspiːs; 'frʌntɪs͵piːs/ *n* illustration placed opposite the title-page of a book. (书籍之)与书名页相对的插画; 卷头插画。

frost /frɒst US: frɔːst; frɔst/ *n* **1** [U] weather condition with temperature below the freezing-point of water; [C] occasion or period of such weather: 严寒的天气; 温度在冰点以下的天气; 严寒期: *plants killed by ~*; 为寒天所摧毁的植物; *ten degrees of ~*; 冰点下九度(二十二华氏度); *early ~s*, ie in autumn; 早寒(在秋季者); *late ~s*, ie in spring. 春寒。**Jack 'F~,** (fig) personified. (拟人语)严寒。**'~-bite** *n* [U] injury to tissue in the body from freezing. 冻疮; 冻伤。**'~-bitten** *adj* having, suffering from, ~-bite. 被冻伤的; 受冻伤的。**'~-bound** *adj* (of the ground) made hard by ~. (地面)冻硬的。**2** [U] white powder-like coating of frozen vapour on the ground, roofs, plants, etc: 霜: 'white/'hoar ~, with this coating; 白霜; 'black ~, without it. 无霜的酷寒; 严寒。**3** [C] (colloq) event which fails to come up to expectations or to arouse interest: (口) 未达期望或引不起兴趣的事: *The party was a ~*, no one enjoyed it. 那聚会使人不感兴趣。□ *vt, vi* **1** [VP6A] cover with ~(2): 覆以霜: *~ed window-panes,* 覆有霜的窗玻璃; *cake, etc) with finely powdered sugar.* 以糖粉覆于(蛋糕等)之上。**2** [VP6A] injure or kill (plants, etc) with ~(1). 冻坏或冻死(植物等)。**3** [VP6A] give a roughened surface to (glass) to make it opaque: 给与(玻璃)不透明之面: *~ed glass.* 不透明的玻璃; 磨砂玻璃; 毛玻璃。**4** [VP2A, C] ~ (*over/up*), become covered with ~(2): 覆有霜; 结霜: *The windscreen of my car ~ed over during the night.* 我车子上的挡风玻璃夜里结了霜。**~·ing** *n* [U] icing(1). 糖霜(覆于蛋糕上之糖与蛋白等的混合物)。

frosty /'frɒstɪ US: 'frɔːstɪ; 'frɔstɪ/ *adj* **1** cold with frost: 下霜的; 严寒的: ~ *weather;* 下霜的天气; *a ~ morning.* 寒冷的早晨。**2** (fig) unfriendly; without warmth of feeling: (喻)冷淡的; 无情的: ~ *smiles/looks;* 冷淡的笑(表情); *a ~ welcome.* 冷淡的欢迎。 **frost·ily** *adv* **frosti·ness** *n*

froth /frɒθ; frɔθ/ *n* [U] **1** creamy mass of small bubbles; foam: 泡沫: *a glass of beer with a lot of ~ on it.* 有许多泡沫的一杯啤酒。**2** light, worthless talk or ideas. 肤浅的谈话或观念。□ *vi* [VP2A, C] have, give off, ~: 起泡沫: *A mad dog may ~ at the mouth.* 疯狗可能嘴流泡泡沫。**~·y** *adj* (-**ier, -iest**) of, like, covered with, ~: 泡沫的; 似泡沫的; 起泡沫的: ~*y beer/conversation.* 起泡沫的啤酒(肤浅的谈话)。**~·ily** /-ɪlɪ; -elɪ/ *adv* **~·i·ness** *n*

fro·ward /'frəʊəd; 'froəd/ *adj* (old use) perverse; not easily controlled. (旧用法)刚愎的; 顽逆的。

frown /fraʊn; fraʊn/ *vi* [VP2A, 3A] draw the eyebrows together, causing lines on the forehead (to express displeasure, puzzlement, deep thought, etc): 蹙眉; 皱眉头; 蹙额(表示不悦, 迷惑, 沉思等): ~ *at sb.* 对某人蹙眉。~ *on/upon,* disapprove of: 不赞成: *Gambling is very much ~ed upon here.* 此地十分反对赌博。□ *n* [C] ~ing look; drawing together of the eyebrows: 蹙眉; 皱眉头; 蹙额: *a ~ of disapproval.* 皱眉头表示不赞成。*There was a deep ~ on his forehead.* 他深深皱着额头。**~·ing·ly** *adv*

frowsty /'fraʊstɪ; 'fraʊstɪ/ *adj* (of the atmosphere of a room) warm and musty; fuggy. (指房间内的空气)闷热而有霉味的; 污浊的。

frowzy /'fraʊzɪ; 'fraʊzɪ/ *adj* **1** ill-smelling; stuffy (like an overheated room). 臭的; 闷气的(如一过于闷热的房间)。**2** untidy; uncared for. 不整洁的; 无人照管的。

froze, frozen ⇨ **freeze.**

fruc·tify /'frʌktɪfaɪ; 'frʌktə͵faɪ/ *vt, vi* (*pt, pp* -**fied**) [VP6A, 2A] (formal) make or become fruitful or fertile. (正式用语)(使)结果实; (使)多产。**fruc·ti·fi·ca·tion** /͵frʌktɪfɪ'keɪʃn; ͵frʌktəfə'keʃən/ *n*

fru·gal /'fruːgl; 'frugl/ *adj* ~ (of), careful, economical (esp of food, expenditure); costing little: 节俭的(尤指食物和开销方面, 可与 of 连用); 俭省的; 节约的:

a ~ meal; 俭省的餐食; *a ~ housekeeper;* 节俭的女管家; *be ~ of one's time and money.* 俭省时间与金钱. ~·**ly** /-gǝlɪ; -glɪ/ *adv* ~·**ity** /fruːˈgælǝtɪ; fruˈgæləti/ *n* [U] being ~; [C] (*pl* **-ties**) instance of this. 节俭; 俭省; 节约.

fruit /fruːt; frut/ *n* **1** [U] (collective *n*) that part of a plant or tree that contains the seeds and is used as food, eg apples, bananas; [C] kind of ~: (集合名词) 水果; 一种水果: *People are eating more ~ than they used to.* 人们现在吃水果较以往多了. *F~ is expensive these days.* 水果近来很贵. *Is a tomato a ~?* 蕃茄是水果吗? '~**-cake** *n* rich cake containing dried currants, peel, etc. 含有葡萄干,果皮等的饼糕; 水果蛋糕. '~**-fly** *n* (*pl* **-flies**) small fly that feeds on decaying ~. 果蝇 (以腐烂果实为食). '~ **knife** *n* one with an acid-proof blade, for cutting ~ at meals. 水果刀. ‚~ '**salad** *n* [U, C] (GB) various kinds of ~, cut up and mixed in a bowl, often served with cream; (US) jelly (2) prepared with pieces of fruit in it. (英)水果沙拉(各种水果混合一起食用); (美)水果冻. **2** [C] (bot)

that part of any plant in which the seed is formed. (植物)果实. **3** *the ~s of the earth*, those plant or vegetable products that may be used for food, including grain, etc. 可用作食物的植物或蔬菜产物(包括谷类等). **4** (fig, often *pl*) profit, result or reward (of labour, industry, study, etc): (喻, 常用复数)收获; 成果: *the ~s of industry.* 勤劳的收获. *I hope your hard work will bear ~.* 我希望你的辛苦工作会有收获. *His knowledge is the ~ of long study.* 他的知识是长期求学的成果. **5** '~**-machine** *n* (GB colloq) coin-operated gambling machine. (英口)吃角子老虎; 由硬币操纵的赌具. □ *vi* (of trees, bushes, etc) bear ~: (指树木等)结果实: *These trees ~ well.* 这些树结的果实很多. ~**er** /ˈfruːtǝ(r); ˈfrutǝr/ *n* person who sells ~. 水果商. ~**ful** /-fl; -fǝl/ *adj* producing ~ or (fig) 多产的: *a ~ful career.* 成功的事业. *The last session of Parliament was particularly ~ful,* much useful work was accomplished. 上次国会开会特别成功(完成甚多有用的工作). ~**fully** /-fǝlɪ;-fǝlɪ/ *adv* ~**ful·ness** *n* ~**·less**

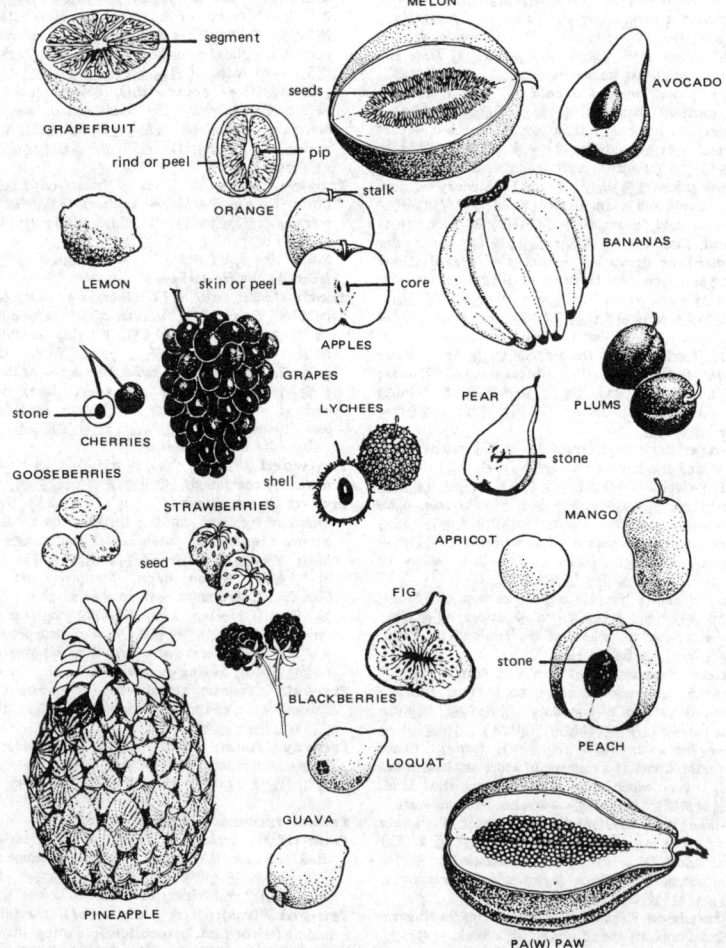

MELON
segment
seeds
GRAPEFRUIT
AVOCADO
rind or peel
pip
ORANGE
stalk
LEMON
BANANAS
skin or peel
core
APPLES
GRAPES
PEAR
PLUMS
LYCHEES
stone
CHERRIES
stone
GOOSEBERRIES
shell
STRAWBERRIES
MANGO
APRICOT
seed
FIG
stone
BLACKBERRIES
PEACH
LOQUAT
PINEAPPLE
GUAVA
PA(W) PAW

adj without ~ or (fig) results or success; profitless: 不结果实的; 无果实的; (喻)无结果的; 失败的; 无收获的: ~*less efforts.* 徒劳. ~·**less·ly** *adv* ~·**less·ness** *n* ~**y** *adj* **1** of or like.~ in smell or taste. 水果的; 有水果香味的; 有水果滋味的. **2** (colloq) full of rough (often suggestive) humour: (口)充满不雅(常为猥亵的)之戏谑的: *a* ~*y novel.* 充满不雅之戏谑的小说. **3** (colloq) rich; mellow; florid: (口)丰映的; 圆润的; 华丽的: *a* ~*y voice.* 圆润的声音.

fru·ition /fruːˈɪʃn; fruˈɪʃən/ *n* [U] realization of hopes; getting what was wanted: 希望之实现; 达到愿望: *aims brought to* ~; 实现的目的; *plans that come to* ~. 完成的计划.

frump /frʌmp; frʌmp/ *n* person dressed in old-fashioned and dowdy clothes. 衣着旧式而遢遢的人. ~·**ish** /-ɪʃ; -ɪʃ/, ~**y** *adj*

frus·trate /frʌˈstreɪt *US:* ˈfrʌstreɪt; ˈfrʌstret/ *vt* [VP6A, 15A] prevent (sb) from doing sth; prevent (sb's plans) from being carried out: 阻止(某人)做某事; 破坏(某人的计划): ~ *an enemy in his plans/the plans of an enemy;* 破坏敌人的计划; *be* ~*d in an attempt to do sth.* 欲做某事而遭受挫折. **frus·tra·tion** /frʌˈstreɪʃn; frʌsˈtreʃən/ *n* [U] frustrating or being ~d; [C] instance of this; defeat or disappointment: 阻止; 破坏; 挫折; 顿挫: *embittered by numerous frustrations.* 受到多多挫折之苦.

fry¹ /fraɪ; fraɪ/ *vt, vi* (*pt, pp* **fried**/ fraɪd; fraɪd/) [VP6A, 2A] cook, be cooked, in boiling fat: 油煎; 油炸: *fried chicken.* 炸鸡. *The sausages are frying/being fried.* 香肠正在煎着. **'fry·ing-pan,** (*US also* 美亦作 **'fry-pan**) *n* shallow pan with a long handle used for frying. 煎锅(有长柄的浅锅). *out of the frying-pan into the fire,* from a bad situation to one that is worse. 每况愈下. **fryer; frier** /ˈfraɪər; ˈfraɪɚ/ *n* small young chicken for frying. 炸食用的小鸡.

fry² /fraɪ; fraɪ/ *n pl* newly hatched fishes. 鱼苗; 鱼秧. **'small fry,** young or insignificant creatures; persons of no importance. 幼小或弱小的生物; 不重要的人物.

fuchsia /ˈfjuːʃə; ˈfjuʃə/ *n* shrub with bell-like drooping flowers, pink, red or purple. 晚樱科植物.

fuck /fʌk; fʌk/ *vt, vi* △ (sl) [VP6A, 2A] have sexual intercourse (with). (讳;俚)(与…)性交. ~ *(it)!* (int, used to express irritation, anger, etc.) 混帐! 滚开! (用以表示恼怒, 愤怒等). ~ *off,* (esp imper) go away. (尤用于祈使语气)走开. ~ *sth up,* spoil, ruin-it. 把某事物弄糟. Hence, 由此产生, ~*ed (up),* spoilt, ruined. 弄糟了. **'~-all** *n* nothing. 没什么. ~*er n* fool. 傻瓜; 笨蛋. ~*ing adj* (used to express irritation, etc, but often meaningless) 该死的; 讨厌的(用以表示恼怒等, 但常常没有意义) ~*ing well,* surely(1). 当然; 一定.

fuddle /ˈfʌdl; ˈfʌdl/ *vt* [VP6A, 15A] confuse, stupefy, (esp with alcoholic drink): 使迷糊; 使烂醉: ~ *oneself/one's brain with gin;* 喝杜松子酒喝得烂醉; *in a* ~*d state.* 烂醉如泥.

fuddy-duddy /ˈfʌdɪ ˌdʌdɪ; ˈfʌdɪˌdʌdɪ/ *n* (*pl* -**dud-dies**) (colloq) fussy and old-fashioned person. (口)唠叨而守旧的人.

fudge /fʌdʒ; fʌdʒ/ *n* [U] sort of soft sweet made with milk, sugar, chocolate, etc. 一种由牛奶、糖、巧克力等制成的软糖. □ *int* (dated) Nonsense! (过时用语)胡说!

fuel /ˈfjuːəl; ˈfjuəl/ *n* [U] material for producing heat or other forms of energy, eg wood, coal, oil, uranium; [C] kind of ~; (fig) sth that inflames the passions. 燃料(例如木、煤、油、铀); (喻)刺激感情之物. *add* ~ *to the flames,* make passions stronger. 火上加油; 使情绪更为激烈. □ *vt, vi* (**-ll-,** *US also* **-l-**) [VP 6A, 2A] supply with or obtain ~: 加燃料; 给…燃料: *a power station* ~*led by uranium;* 以铀做燃料的发电所; *a ship;* 给船加燃料; *a '*~*ling station,* one where oil, coal, etc may be obtained. 加油站; 燃料供应站.

fug /fʌg; fʌg/ *n* (colloq) stuffy atmosphere (as in an overcrowded or badly ventilated room, etc): (口)污浊难闻的空气(如一人数过多或通风不良的房间内的情形): *What a fug!* 空气多么污浊! **fuggy** *adj*

fugi·tive /ˈfjuːdʒɪtɪv; ˈfjudʒətɪv/ *n* ~ *(from),* person running away from justice, danger, etc: 逃亡者;逃犯; 亡命徒: ~*s from an invaded country;* 自受侵国家逃出的难民; ~*s from justice;* 逃犯; (attrib) (用作定语) *a* ~ *prisoner.* 逃跑的犯人. □ *adj* (attrib) of temporary interest or value; lasting a short time only: (用作定语)只有暂时的兴趣或价值的; 短暂的: ~ *verses.* 即兴的诗.

fugue /fjuːg; fjug/ *n* [C] musical composition in which one or more themes are introduced by the different parts or voices in turn and then repeated in a complex design. 赋格曲; 遁走曲(有一个或多个主题, 经不同部分或声音轮流引出, 然后予以重复而复杂的音乐曲目).

ful·crum /ˈfʊlkrəm; ˈfʌlkrəm/ *n* (*pl* -**s** or **fulcra** /ˈfʊlkrə; ˈfʌlkrə/) point on which a lever turns. 杠杆. ⇨ the illus at **lever.** 参看 lever 之插图.

ful·fil (*US also* **ful·fill**) /fʊlˈfɪl; fʊlˈfɪl/ *vt* (**-ll-**) [VP6A] perform or complete a task, duty, etc; do what is required (by conditions, etc): 履行(工作、任务等); 做(根据条件等需要做的事): ~ *one's duties/a command/an obligation/sb's expectations or hopes.* 尽职(执行命令); 尽义务; 满足某人的期望). ~·**ment** *n* ~ling or being ~led. 履行; 完成; 实践.

full /fʊl; fʊl/ *adj* (-**er,** -**est**) **1** ~ *(of),* holding or having plenty *(of),* holding or having as much or as many *(of)* as possible; completely filled: 满的; 装满的; 充满的: *pockets* ~ *of money;* 装满钱的口袋; *a lake* ~ *of fish;* 有很多鱼的湖; *a girl* ~ *of vitality.* 活力充沛的女孩. *The box is* ~. 这箱子满了. *The room was* ~ *of people.* 房间里挤满了人. ~ *up,* (colloq) completely ~: (口)全满的: *The greedy girl ate and ate until she was* ~ *up.* 那个贪心的女孩不停地吃, 直到吃得很饱为止. *The drawers were* ~ *to overflowing.* 抽屉满得装不下了. **2** ~ *of,* completely occupied with thinking of: 充满某种思想的: *She was* ~ *of the news,* could not refrain from talking about it. 她脑海里尽想着这个消息(禁不住谈论这消息). *He was* ~ *of himself/his own importance,* could talk of nothing else. 他只为自己打算(自以为很了不起). **3** plump; rounded: 丰满的; 圆的: *a* ~ *figure;* 丰满的身材; *rather* ~ *in the face.* 面孔颇圆. **4** (of clothes) (指衣服) **(a)** having material arranged in wide folds: 有宽折的: *a* ~ *skirt.* 有宽折的裙子. **(b)** easy fitting: 宽松的: *Please make this coat a little* ~ *across the back.* 请将这上衣的背部做宽松些. **5** reaching the usual or the specified extent, limit, length, etc: 达到通常或指定的限度,长度等的: *apple-trees in* ~ *blossom;* 盛开着花的苹果树; *wait a* ~ *hour,* not less than an hour. 等了足足一个钟头. *He fell* ~ *length,* so that he was lying stretched out on the floor/ground. 他直挺挺地跌在地上. *Her dress was a* ~ *three inches below the knee.* 她的衣服达膝盖下足有三英寸. **6** (esp in comp and superl) complete: (尤与比较级和最高级连用)完全的: *A* ~/~*er account will be given later.* 以后将有完整的报告. *This is the* ~*est account yet received.* 这是迄今最完整的报告. **7** (phrases and compounds) (短语和复合词) *at* ~ *speed,* at the highest possible speed. 倾全速. *in* ~, without omitting or shortening anything: 未省略地; 完全地: *write one's name in* ~, eg John Henry Smith, *not* J H Smith; 写全名(例如 John Henry Smith 即是, 不写作 J H Smith); *pay a debt in* ~, pay the whole of what is owed. 还清全部债务. *in* ~ *career,* while at the maximum rate of progress. 在以最大的速率行进中; 以全速力. *to the* ~, to the utmost extent: 至极限: *enjoy oneself to the* ~. 尽情享乐. ~·**back** *n* player (defender) placed farthest from the centre line, behind the half-backs (in football, etc). (足球等的)后卫. ⇨ the illus at **football.** 参看 football 之插图. ~·**blooded** *adj* **(a)** vigorous; hearty. 精力旺盛的; 精神饱满的. **(b)** of unmixed ancestry or race. 纯种的. ~·**blown** *adj*

(of flowers) completely open. (指花)盛开的。 ~ '**dress** n [U] dress as worn on ceremonial occasions. 盛装。

,~-'**dress** adj formally complete: 正式的; 全副的: a ~-dress rehearsal, (theatre) with the costumes, etc that are to be worn at public performances; (戏剧)(穿着剧中服装的)彩排; a ~-dress debate (in Parliament) on an important question. (国会)对一重要问题的正式辩论。

,~-'**face** n with the face turned to the viewer(s): 正面的脸: a ~-face portrait. 正面肖像。 ⇨ **profile.** ,~-'**fashioned** adj (trade use, of garments) made to fit the shape of the body: (商业用语, 指衣服)完全合身的: ~-fashioned stockings / sweaters. 完全合腿形的长袜(合身的毛线衫)。 ,~-'**fledged** adj (of a bird) having all its flight feathers; able to fly; (fig) having completed training, etc: (指鸟)毛长全的; 能飞的; (喻)完成训练等的: a ~-fledged barrister. 有充分资格的律师。 ,~-'**grown** adj having reached maturity. 成熟的, 长成的。 ,~ '**house** n (theatre) with no unoccupied seats. (戏院)客满。 ,~-'**length** adj (of a portrait) showing the whole figure. (指肖像)全身的。 **(b)** of standard or usual length: 标准长度的; 通常长度的: a ~-length novel. 通常字数的小说。 ,~ '**marks** n pl highest marks[1](5) possible 满分。 ,~ '**moon** n seen as a complete disc. 满月; 圆月; 望月。 ⇨ the illus at **phase.** 参看 phase 之插图。 ,~-'**page** adj filling a whole page: 全页的: a ~-page advertisement in a newspaper. 报纸上全页的广告。 ,~-'**scale** adj (of drawings, plans, etc) of the same size, area, etc as the object itself; (colloq) complete. (指绘图, 设计图等)与原物大小相等的; 原尺寸的; (口)完全的; 全部的。 ,~ '**stop**, the punctuation mark (.) ⇨ **App 9.** 句点(参看附录九)。 **come to a ~ stop**, stop completely. 完全停止。 ,~-'**time** n the end of a game of football, etc. 足球等比赛之结束。 ,~-'**time** adj, adv occupying all normal working hours: 全时间的(地); 专职的(地): a ~-time worker; 专职的工作者; working ~-time; 全时间工作; It's a ~-time job, one that leaves no time for leisure or other work. 这是个专职的工作。 ⇨ part-time at **part**[1](1). ,~**y** /'fʊlɪ; 'fʊlɪ/ adv 1 completely: 完全地; 全部地: ~y satisfied; 完全满意的; a ~y paid up debt. 我觉得我已得到充分的报酬。 I feel ~y rewarded. 我觉得我已得到充分的报酬。 2 at least: 至少: The journey will take ~y two hours. 这行程至少要花费两小时。 ,~-**y-fashioned**/**fledged**/ **grown** ⇨ above. 参看上列第 7 义。 ,~-**ness** n [U] state of being ~: 满; 充满; 完全; 丰满: have a feeling of ~ness after a meal. 饭后有饱胀之感。 **in the ~ness of time**, at the appointed time; eventually. 在预定的时候; 终于。

fuller /'fʊlə(r); 'fʊlə/ n person who cleans and thickens freshly woven cloth. 漂布者; 浆洗布匹者。 ,~'**s 'earth**, kind of clay used for cleaning and thickening textile materials. 漂布泥; 漂土。

ful·mar /'fʊlmə(r); 'fʊlmə/ n seabird like a petrel, about the size of a seagull. 鹱; 管鼻鹱(一种似海燕的海鸟, 大小与海鸥相若)。

ful·mi·nate /'fʌlmɪneɪt US: 'fʊl-; 'fʌlmə,net/ vi [VP2A, 3A] ~ (**against**), protest loudly and bitterly: 猛烈抗议; 严词谴责: ~ against the apparent idleness of the younger generation. 严词谴责青年一代人的懒散。 **ful·mi·na·tion** /,fʌlmɪ'neɪʃn US: ,fʊl-; ,fʌlmə'neʃən/ n [U] fulminating; [C] instance of this; bitter denunciation or protest. 严词谴责; 猛烈攻击; 抨击。

ful·some /'fʊlsəm; 'fʊl-/ adj (of praise, flattery, etc) excessive and insincere. (指称赞, 谄媚等)过分而虚伪的。 ~**ly** adv ~**ness** n

fumble /'fʌmbl; 'fʌmbl/ vi, vt 1 [VP2A, C] feel about uncertainly with the hands; use the hands awkwardly: 摸索; 笨拙地用手: ~ in one's pockets for a key; 在口袋里摸索钥匙; ~ at a lock, eg, as a drunken man might; 乱摸弄一锁(如一醉汉所为者); ~ in the dark. 在黑暗中摸索。 2 [VP6A, 2A] handle or deal with (sth) nervously or incompetently: 紧张或无能地处理(事物): ~ a ball, eg in cricket. 失球(例如在板球戏

中)。 **fumbler** /'fʌmblə(r); 'fʌmblə/ n person who ~s. 摸索者; 笨手笨脚的人; 紧张或无能地处理事物者。

fume /fjuːm; fjum/ n 1 (usu pl) strong-smelling smoke, gas or vapour: (通常用复数)气味强烈的烟, 气或汽: air thick with the ~s of cigars; 充满雪茄烟味的空气; petrol ~s; 强烈的汽油味; ~s of incense. 浓郁的香的烟味。 2 (liter) excited state of mind: (文)激动的心绪: in a ~ of anxiety. 一阵焦虑。 □ vi, vt 1 [VP2A, C; 3A] ~ (**at**), give off ~s; pass away in ~s; (fig) betray repressed anger or irritation: 发散出强烈的烟气; 以浓烈的气味蒸发; (喻)发怒: ~ because one is kept waiting; 因久等而生气; ~ at sb's incompetence. 为某人的无能而生气。 2 [VP6A] treat (wood, etc) with ~s (to darken the surface, etc): 熏黑(木材等): ~d oak. 黑橡木。

fu·mi·gate /'fjuːmɪgeɪt; 'fjumə,get/ vt [VP6A] disinfect by means of fumes: 以烟熏消毒: a room used by someone with an infectious disease; 以烟熏消毒一传染病患者住过的房间; ~ rose-bushes, to kill insect pests. 熏玫瑰树(以除害虫)。 **fu·mi·ga·tion** /,fjuːmɪ'geɪʃn; ,fjumə'geʃən/ n

fun /fʌn; fʌn/ n [U] 1 amusement; enjoyment; playfulness: 娱乐; 快乐; 嬉戏: What fun the children had at the seaside, How they enjoyed themselves! 孩子们在海边玩得真开心! He's full of fun. 他很风趣。 I don't see the fun of doing that, do not think it is amusing. 我不觉得做那事有什么趣味。 '**fun·fair** n amusement park. 儿童乐园; 游乐场。 ⇨ **amuse. fun and games**, (colloq) lively merry-making; pranks. (口)欢乐; 开玩笑。 **make fun of; poke fun at**, ridicule; cause people to laugh at: 嘲弄; 取笑: It is cruel to make fun of a cripple. 取笑一跛者是残忍的。 **for/in fun**, as a joke, for amusement; not seriously: 开玩笑地; 闹着玩地; 非认真地: He said it only in fun. 他只是说着玩的。 2 that which causes merriment or amusement: 有趣的人或物: Your new friend is great fun, is very amusing. 你的新朋友很有趣。 3 (attrib, colloq): (用作定语, 口): a 'fun car / hat / fur, used, worn, for amusement. 娱乐用的汽车(帽子, 毛皮衣)。

func·tion /'fʌŋkʃn; 'fʌŋkʃən/ n [C] 1 special activity or purpose of a person or thing: 职责; 作用; 功能: the ~s of a judge / an officer of state; 法官(部长)的职责; the ~ of the heart, ie to pump blood through the body; 心脏的功能(即司血液循环); the ~s of the nerves; 神经的机能; the ~ of education. 教育的功能。 2 public ceremony or event; social gathering of an important and formal kind: 祝典; 正式集会; 典礼: the numerous ~s that the Queen must attend. 女王必须参加的无数集会。 3 (maths) variable quantity, dependent in value on another. (数学)函数。 □ vi [VP2A, C] fulfill a ~(1); operate; act: 尽职责; 有效用: The telephone was not ~ing, was out of order. 电话坏了。 Some English adverbs ~ as adjectives. 英语的某些副词有形容词的作用。 ~**al** /-ʃənl; -ʃənl/ adj of a ~; having, designed to have, a ~s(1): 职责的; 功能的; 机能的; 有作用的; 有功能的: a ~al disorder, an illness caused by the failure of an organ of the body to perform its ~; 官能病; ~al architecture, designed to serve practical purposes, beauty of appearance being secondary; 实用的建筑(以功用为主, 美观其次); schools designed according to ~al principles. 根据实用的原则而设计的学校。 ~**al·ism** /-ʃənlɪzəm; -ʃənl,ɪzəm/ n principle that the ~ of objects, etc should determine their design, the materials used, etc. (生产, 建筑等)实用主义; 效用主义。 ~**al·ist** /-ʃənlɪst; -ʃənlɪst/ n adherent of ~alism. 实用主义者。

func·tion·ary /'fʌŋkʃənərɪ US: -nerɪ; 'fʌŋkʃən,ɛrɪ/ n (pl -**ries**) (often derog) person with official functions. (常含贬抑意味)公务员; 官员。

fund /fʌnd; fʌnd/ n [C] 1 store or supply (of non-material things): 贮藏物(指非物质的东西): a ~ of common sense / humour / amusing stories. 大量的常识(幽默, 有趣的故事)。 2 (often pl) sum of money available

for a purpose: (常用复数)专款;基金: *a re'lief* ~, eg to help sufferers from a flood or other disaster: 救济基金; '*school* ~*s*, to finance schools. 学校基金(经费). **the (public)** ~**s**, the stock of the national debt as a form of investment: 公债: *have £5000 in the* ~*s*. 有五千英镑的公债. **no** ~**s**, notice (given by a bank) that the person who has drawn a cheque on it has no money in his account. 无存款(银行通知开空头支票者之用语). □ *vt* [VP6A] **1** provide with money: 供以款项: *a project* ~*ed by the government*. 经费由政府补助的一项计划. **2** (fin) convert (a short-term debt) into a long-term debt at fixed interest. (财政)将(短期债)改为长期债.

fun·da·men·tal /ˌfʌndəˈmentl/ *adj* ~ **(to)**, of or forming a foundation; of great importance; serving as a starting-point: 基本的; 基础的; 十分重要的: 作为起点的: *the* ~ *rules of arithmetic*, those which must be learnt first and on which everything that follows depends. 算术的基本规则. □ *n* essential part. 基本. **the**, ~ **s** rules or principles: 基本规则; 基本原理: *the* ~*s of mathematics*. 数学的基本原理. ~**·ly** /-təlɪ; -tlɪ/ *adv* ~**·ism** /-ɪzəm; -ɪzəm/ *n* [U] maintenance of the literal interpretation of the traditional beliefs of the Christian religion (such as the accuracy of everything in the Bible), in opposition to more modern teachings. 原教旨主义(相信圣经所记载的传统的基督教信仰,反对较为近代的教义). ~**·ist** /-ɪst/ *n* supporter of ~ism. 原教旨主义信徒.

fu·neral /ˈfjuːnərəl; ˈfjunərəl/ *n* [C] **1** burial or cremation of a dead person with the usual ceremonies. 葬礼. **2** (attrib use) of or for a ~: (用作定语)葬礼的; 送葬的; 出殡用的: *a* '~ *procession*; 送葬的行列; *a* '~ *march*, sad and solemn piece of music; 送葬曲; *a* '~ *pile/pyre*, pile of wood, etc on which a corpse is burnt; 火葬柴堆; *a* '~ *parlor*, (US) undertaker's offices. (美)殡仪馆. *it's/that's* '*my*/'*your etc* ~, (colloq) it's/that's my/your etc concern, worry etc. (口)这是我(你等)所开心的事(烦恼等). **fu·ner·eal** /fjuːˈnɪərɪəl; fjuˈnɪrɪəl/ *adj* of or like a ~; gloomy; dismal; dark: 葬礼的; 似葬礼的; 忧郁的; 阴森的; 阴沉的: *a funereal expression*. 忧郁的表情.

fun·gus /ˈfʌŋɡəs; ˈfʌŋɡəs/ *n* (*pl* **-gi** /-ɡaɪ; -dʒaɪ/ or ~**es** /-ɡəsɪz; -ɡəsɪz/) plant without leaves, flowers or green colouring matter, growing on other plants or on decaying matter, eg old wood: 真菌类: *Mushrooms, toadstools and mildew are all fungi*. 蘑菇、蕈与霉都是真菌类. **fun·gi·cide** /ˈfʌndʒɪsaɪd; ˈfʌndʒəˌsaɪd/ *n* [U, C] substance that destroys fungi. 杀真菌类剂. **fun·goid** /ˈfʌŋɡɔɪd; ˈfʌŋɡɔɪd/ *adj* of or like fungi. (似)真菌类的. **fun·gous** /ˈfʌŋɡəs; ˈfʌŋɡəs/ *adj* of or like, caused by, fungi. (似)真菌类的;真菌类引起的.

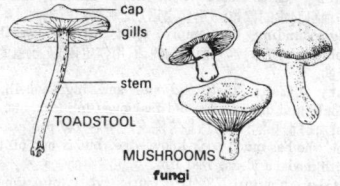
cap / gills / stem / TOADSTOOL / MUSHROOMS
fungi

fu·nicu·lar /fjuːˈnɪkjʊlə(r); fjuˈnɪkjələ/n ~ **(railway)**, railway on a slope, worked by a cable and a stationary engine. 缆索铁路.

funk /fʌŋk; fʌŋk/ *n* (colloq) (口) **1** great fear: 惊惶; 恐惧: *be in a* ~. 大为恐惧. **2** coward. 怯懦者. □ *vi, vt* [VP6A, 2A] show fear; (try to) escape (doing sth) because of fear. 畏惧; 畏缩; 因畏惧而(试图)避免(做某事). ~**y** *adj* (US sl) (of music) emotional and rhythmic. (美俚)(指音乐)有感情和节奏的.

funnel /ˈfʌnl; ˈfʌnl/ *n* **1** tube or pipe wide at the top 'ınd narrowing at the bottom, for pouring liquids or

powders into a small opening. 漏斗. **2** outlet for smoke (ie smoke-stack, metal chimney) of a steamship, locomotive etc. (轮船,火车等的)烟囱. ⇨ the illus at **ship**. 参看 ship 之插图. ~, **two-**/**three-**/**~s**, having two/three ~s. 有两(三)个烟囱的. □ *vt, vi* (**-ll-**, US **-l-**) [VP6A, 2A] (cause to) move through, or as if through, a ~. (使)通过漏斗或烟囱; (使)仿佛通过漏斗或烟囱.

funny /ˈfʌnɪ; ˈfʌnɪ/ *adj* (**-ier, -iest**) **1** causing fun or amusement: 有趣的; 好玩的: ~ *stories*. 有趣的故事. **2** strange; queer; causing surprise: 奇特的; 古怪的; 令人惊奇的: *There's something* ~ *about the affair*, sth strange, perhaps not quite honest or straightforward. 这件事有点奇怪(或许其中有不诚实或不坦白之处). '~**-bone** *n* part of the elbow over which a very sensitive nerve passes. (肘的)尺骨端. **the funnies**, *n pl* (colloq) comic strips. (口)连环图画. **fun·nily** /-ɪlɪ; -ɪlɪ/ *adv* in a ~ way: 有趣地; 奇特地: *funnily* (= strangely) *enough*. 十分古怪. **fun·ni·ness** *n*

fur /fɜː(r); fɜ/ *n* **1** [U] soft thick hair covering certain animals, eg cats, rabbits. (猫,兔等动物之)软毛. *make the 'fur fly*, cause a disturbance. 引起骚动. *fur and feather*, furred animals and birds. 兽类. **2** [C] animal skin with the fur on it, esp when made into garments: 兽类的毛皮; (尤指)毛皮衣: *a fine fox fur*; 上等狐皮; *wearing expensive furs*; 穿着昂贵的皮衣; (attrib) (用作定语) *a fur coat*, one made of furs. 皮上衣. **3** [U] rough coating on a person's tongue when ill; crust forming on the inside of a kettle, boiler, etc when the water heated in it contains lime. 舌苔; 壶、锅等的水锈. □ *vt, vi* (**-rr-**) [VP6A, 2A, C] ~ **(up)**, cover, be or become covered, with fur: 覆以毛皮; 覆有舌苔; 生有水锈: *a furred animal/tongue/kettle*. 有毛皮的动物(有舌苔的舌; 生水锈的壶). **furry** /ˈfɜːrɪ; ˈfɜɪ/ *adj* (**-ier, -iest**) of or like fur; covered with fur. 毛皮的; 似毛皮的; 覆有毛皮的.

fur·be·low /ˈfɜːbɪləʊ; ˈfɜbˌlo/ *n* (often used in 常用于 *frills and* ~**s**) (old-fashioned) piece of elaborate or unnecessary trimming (on a dress, etc). (衣服等上)(旧式的)精巧或不必要的装饰.

fur·bish /ˈfɜːbɪʃ; ˈfɜbɪʃ/ *vt* [VP6A] polish, eg by removing rust from; make like new (esp sth that has not been used for a long time): 擦亮; 刷新: ~ *a sword*; 擦亮一剑; *newly* ~*ed skills*. 最近温习过的技能.

furi·ous /ˈfjʊərɪəs; ˈfjurɪəs/ *adj* violent; uncontrolled; full of fury: 猛烈的; 狂暴的; 狂怒的: *a* ~ *struggle/ storm/quarrel*; 猛烈的斗争(暴风雨,争吵); *running at a* ~ *pace*; 急奔; *be* ~ *with sb/at what sb has done*. 对某人(某人所做之事)发狂怒. *fast and* ~, uproarious, wild: 狂放般的; 狂热般的: *The fun was fast and* ~. 狂欢般地玩乐. ~**·ly** *adv*

furl /fɜːl; fɜl/ *vt, vi* [VP6A, 2A] (of sails, flags, umbrellas, etc) roll up: (指帆,旗,伞等)卷起; 折起: ~ *the sails of a yacht*. 卷起一轻舟的帆. *This fan/ umbrella doesn't* ~ *neatly*. 这扇(伞)不能整齐地收叠起来.

fur·long /ˈfɜːlɒŋ US: -lɔːŋ; ˈfɜlɔŋ/ *n* 220 yards (= 201 metres); eighth of a mile. 浪(长度名,合 220 码或 201 米;一英里的八分之一).

fur·lough /ˈfɜːləʊ; ˈfɜlo/ *n* [C, U] (permission for) absence from duty (esp civil officials, members of the armed forces, working abroad): 休假(尤指在国外的公务员, 军人): *going home on* ~; 返乡度假; *six months'* ~; 六个月的休假; *have a* ~ *every three years*. 每三年休假一次. ⇨ **leave**[2].

fur·nace /ˈfɜːnɪs; ˈfɜnɪs/ *n* **1** enclosed fireplace for heating buildings with hot water or steam in pipes. 火炉. **2** enclosed space for heating metals, making glass, etc. 熔炉.

fur·nish /ˈfɜːnɪʃ; ˈfɜnɪʃ/ *vt* [VP6A, 14] ~ *sth* (**to sb**); ~ *sb*/*sth with sth*, supply or provide; put furniture in: 供给; 布置家具于: ~ *a library with books*;

供给一图书馆书籍; ~ *an army with supplies* / ~ *supplies to an army*; 供给军队补给品; ~ *a room* / *an office*; 以家具布置一房间(办公室); *a ~ed house* / *flat*, one rented with the furniture. 备有家具的出租房屋(公寓). ~·**ings** n pl furniture and equipment. 家具与陈设品.

fur·ni·ture /'fɜːnɪtʃə(r); 'fɝnɪtʃɚ/ n [U] all those (usu) movable things such as chairs, beds, desks, etc needed in a house, room, office, etc. 家具.

fu·rore (US = **fu·ror** /fjuə'rɔːr; 'fjuːrɔːr; 'fjuror/ n general uproar: 轰动; 骚动: *The new play at the National Theatre created a ~*, was received with general excitement. 在国家剧院演出的新剧轰动一时.

fur·rier /'fʌrɪə(r); 'fɝɪɚ/ n person who prepares, or who deals in, furs. 修整毛皮之人; 毛皮衣商.

fur·row /'fʌrəu; 'fɝo/ n [C] **1** long cut in the ground made by a plough: 犁沟; 畦: *newly turned ~s*. 新犁的犁沟. **2** wrinkle; line in the skin of the face, esp the forehead. (额上的)皱纹. ▷ vt [VP6A] make ~s in: 犁; 使起皱纹: *a forehead ~ed by old age* / *anxiety, etc*. 因年迈(焦虑等)而起皱纹的额头.

furry /'fɜːrɪ; 'fɝɪ/ adj ⟹ **fur.**

fur·ther /'fɜːðə(r); 'fɝðɚ/ adv, adj **1** (often used for *farther*) more far: (常用作 farther 之义)较远的(地); 更远的(地): *It's not safe to go any ~*. 再走这些就不安全了. **2** (not interchangeable in this sense with *farther*) more; in addition; additional: (用作此义不可与 farther 互用)更多的; 添加的; 另外的; 更进一步的(地): *We must get ~ information*. 我们必须获得更多的消息. *The Museum will be closed until ~ notice*. 该博物馆将关闭, 开放时另行通知. *We need go no ~ into the matter*, need make no more inquiries. 我们不需要进一步调查此事. *I'll offer you £50 but I can't go any ~*, offer more. 我愿出价五十英镑, 但不能再多了. **3** (also 亦作 *~more*, ⟹ below 参看下面) moreover; also; besides: 而且; 此外; 并且: *He said that the key was lost and, ~, that there was no hope of its being found*. 他说那钥匙遗失了, 而且也没有希望找回来. ▷ vt [VP6A] help forward; promote: 增进; 促进: *~ sb's interests*; 提高某人的兴趣; *~ the cause of peace*. 促进和平. ~·**ance** /-rəns; -rəns/ n [U] ~ing; advancement: 增进; 促进: *for the ~ance of public welfare*; 为促进大众的福利; *in ~ance of your aims*. 为促进你的目标. ~·**more** /,fɜːðə'mɔː(r); 'fɝðɚ,mor/ adv moreover; in addition. 而且; 此外. '~·**most** /-məust; -,most/ adj most distant; furthest. 最远的.

fur·thest /'fɜːðɪst; 'fɝðɪst/ adj, adv ⟹ **farthest.**

fur·tive /'fɜːtɪv; 'fɝtɪv/ adj done secretly so as not to attract attention; having or suggesting a wish to escape notice: 偷偷摸摸的; 鬼鬼祟祟的: *a ~ glance* / *manner*; 偷瞧(鬼鬼祟祟的样子); *~ behaviour*; 偷偷摸摸的行为; *be ~ in one's movements*. 行动鬼祟. ~·**ly** adv ~·**ness** n

fury /'fjuərɪ; 'fjʊrɪ/ n (pl **-ries**) **1** [U] violent excitement, esp anger: 狂暴; (尤指)愤怒: *filled with ~*; 气愤填胸; *the ~ of the elements*, wild storms, winds; 狂风暴雨; *in the ~ of battle*. 在激战中. **2** [C] outburst of wild feelings: 愤怒之爆发: *She was in one of her furies*. 她在愤怒中. *He flew into a ~ when I refused to lend him the money*. 当我拒绝借钱给他时, 他勃然大怒. **3** [C] violently furious woman or girl: 愤怒的女子; 泼妇: *What a little ~ she is!* 她真是个小泼妇! **4 the Furies**, snake-haired goddesses in Greek mythology sent from the underworld to punish crime. (希腊神话中生有蛇发的)复仇女神.

furze /fɜːz; fɝz/ n [U] = **gorse.**

fuse¹ /fjuːz; fjuz/ n [C] tube, cord, etc for carrying a spark to explode powder, etc, eg in a firecracker, bomb or blasting charge; (US 美 = *fuze*) part of a shell or mine that detonates the explosive charge. 导火线; 引信; 信管. '**time-~** n one that does this after a pre-arranged interval of time. 定时信管.

fuse² /fjuːz; fjuz/ vt, vi **1** [VP6A, 15A, B, 2A] make or become liquid as the result of great heat; join, become joined, as the result of melting: 熔化; 熔合: ~ *two pieces of wire together*. 将两条金属丝熔合起来. **2** [VP2A] (of an electric circuit, or part of it) be broken through melting of the fuse²: (指电路, 或其部分)因保险丝熔断而中断: *The light has ~d*. 保险丝烧断, 灯不亮了. **3** [VP6A, 15A, B] (fig) make into one whole. (喻)使成为一体; 合并. ▷ n [C] (in an electric circuit) short piece of wire which melts and breaks the circuit if the circuit is overloaded. (电路中的)保险丝. '~ **wire** n [U] kinds of wire used for this purpose. 保险丝.

fu·sel·age /'fjuːzəlɑːʒ; 'fjuzlɪdʒ/ n body of an aircraft (to which the engine(s), wings and tail are fitted). (飞机之)机身. ⟹ the illus at **air.** 参见 air 之插图.

fu·sil·ier /,fjuːzə'lɪə(r); ,fjuzl'ɪr/ n soldier (of certain British regiments) formerly armed with a light musket. (英军某些团中)昔时持有轻滑膛枪的枪手.

fus·il·lade /,fjuːzɪ'leɪd US: -sə'lɑːd; ,fjuzl'ed/ n [C] continuous discharge of firearms. 枪炮的连发.

fusion /'fjuːʒn; 'fjuʒən/ n [C, U] mixing or uniting of different things into one: 融合; 熔合; 联合: *the ~ of copper and tin*; 铜与锡之熔合; *a ~ of races* / *political parties*. 种族之融合(政党之合并). '~ **bomb** n hydrogen bomb; ⟹ **atomic.** 氢弹.

fuss /fʌs; fʌs/ n [U] unnecessary nervous agitation, esp about unimportant things; [C] nervous state: 小题大做; 大惊小怪; 无谓扰乱; 紧张; 急躁: *Don't make so much ~* / *get into such a ~ about trifles*. 不要因细故而大事纷扰(如此急躁). **make a ~, (a)** be nervously agitated. 激动; 纷扰. **(b)** be ostentatiously active. 夸张地活动. **(c)** complain vigorously. 猛烈地抱怨. **make a ~ of,** pay ostentatious attention to: 过于注意: *Don't make so much ~ of the children*. 不过分注意孩子们. '~·**pot** n (colloq) very ~y person. (口)很爱小题大做的人. ▷ vt, vi [VP6A, 2A, C] make a ~; cause (sb) to be in a ~: 小题大做; 急躁; 使(某人)为琐事烦扰: *Stop ~ing*. 不要大惊小怪. *She ~ed about, unable to hide her impatience*. 她无谓烦扰, 无法掩饰她的急躁. *Don't ~ over the children so much*. 不要为孩子们过于操心. *Don't ~ me*, make me nervous. 不要以琐事烦扰我. ~·**y** adj **(-ier, -iest) 1** nervously active or agitated. 紧张的; 大惊小怪的. **2** full of, showing, close attention to detail: 多纷扰的; 为琐事担忧的: *be too ~y about one's clothes* / *food*. 过于挑剔衣服(食物). **3** (of dress, style, etc) over-ornamented; having too many unimportant details, etc. (指衣服, 文体等)装饰过分的; 有太多不重要的细节的. ~·**ily** /-ɪlɪ; -əlɪ/ adv ~·**i·ness** n

fus·tian /'fʌstɪən US: -tʃən; 'fʌstʃən/ n [U] **1** thick, strong, coarse cotton cloth; (used as attrib) made of this cloth. 一种粗而厚的棉布; (用作定语)此种棉布所制的. **2** (fig) high-sounding but empty talk; (attrib) worthless; bombastic. (喻)浮夸而空洞的话(用作定语)无价值的; 夸大的.

fusty /'fʌstɪ; 'fʌstɪ/ adj stale-smelling; smelling of mould and damp; (fig) old-fashioned in ideas, etc: 腐臭的; 有霉湿味的; (喻)思想守陈腐的: *a ~ old professor*, eg one who has much book knowledge, but is out of touch with modern ideas, real life. 思想陈腐的老教授.

fu·tile /'fjuːtaɪl US: -tl; 'fjutl/ adj **1** (of actions) of no use; without result: (指行动)无用的; 无效果的: *a ~ attempt*. 无效的尝试. **2** (of persons) unlikely to accomplish much; vain or frivolous: (指人)无成就的; 轻浮的; 不足取的. **fu·til·ity** /fjuː'tɪlətɪ; fju'tɪlətɪ/ n (pl **-ties**) [U] the state of being ~; [C] ~ action or utterance. 无用; 无效; 无用的行动或言语.

fu·ture /'fjuːtʃə(r); 'fjutʃɚ/ n, adj [U, C] (time, events) coming after the present: 将来的时间或事件; 将来; 未来; 将来的; 未来的: *The ~ must always be uncertain*. 未来的一切难以预卜. *I hope you have a happy ~ before you*. 我希望你有一个幸福的将来. *I've given*

up my job; there was no ~ *in it /it didn't have a* ~, no prospects of higher salary, advancement, etc. 我已放弃了我的工作；那工作没有前途。*for the* ~, with ~ time in mind: 在将来: *Have you provided for the* ~, saved money, taken out an insurance policy, etc? 你为将来作准备没有(储蓄,保险等)? *in* ~, from this time onwards: 从今以后: *Try to live a better life in* ~. 今后要努力过更好的生活。**2** (*adj*, or attrib use of the *n*) of or in the ~: (形容词或以名词用作定语) 属于未来的; 在将来的~: *the* ~ *life, after death of the body*; 来世; *his* ~ *wife*, the woman he will marry. 他将与之结婚的女子。**3** (*pl*) (comm) (orders for) goods and stocks bought at prices agreed upon at the time of purchase, but to be paid for and delivered later. (复) (商)期货; 期货定单。~·**less** *adj* having no (successful) ~. 无前途的; 前途无望的。

fu·tur·ism /ˈfjuːtʃərɪzəm; ˈfjutʃɔˌɪzəm/ *n* [U] (early 20th c) movement in art and literature marked by a complete abandonment of tradition in favour of expressing the energy of contemporary life as influenced by modern machinery. 未来派(二十世纪初期，因受现代机械的影响,文艺界欲彻底打破传统,主张表达当代生活精力的一种运动). **fu·tur·ist** /-ɪst; -ɪst/ *n* supporter of ~. 未来派文艺家。

fu·tur·ity /fjuːˈtjuərətɪ US: -ˈtuər-; fjuˈturɪ/ *n* (*pl* -**ties**) [U] future; [U, C] future events. 未来; 将来; 未来的事件。

fuze /fjuːz; fjuz/ *n* (US) = **fuse**¹.

fuzz /fʌz; fʌz/ *n* [U] fluff; fluffy or frizzed hair. 绒毛;细毛。*the* ~, (US sl) the police. (美俚)警察。

fuzzy /ˈfʌzɪ; ˈfʌzɪ/ *adj* (-**ier, -iest**) like fuzz; blurred, indistinct (in shape or outline); frayed or fluffy. 似绒毛的; 模糊的;(形状或轮廓)不清楚的; 有绒毛的。

Gg

G, g /dʒiː; dʒi/ (*pl* **G's, g's** /dʒiːz; dʒiz/) the seventh letter of the English alphabet; (US sl) one thousand dollars. 英文字母之第七个字母; (美俚)一千元。

gab /gæb; gæb/ *n* [U] (colloq) talk(ing): (口)谈话: *Stop your gab*, (sl) be quiet. (俚)住嘴。**have the gift of the gab**, be good at speaking eloquently. 有口才。

gab·ar·dine, gab·er·dine /ˈgæbəˈdiːn; ˈgæbɔˌdin/ *n* [U] strong, smooth twill-woven cloth. 轧别丁(坚牢平滑的斜纹布料)。华达呢。

gabble /ˈgæbl; ˈgæbl/ *vt, vi* [VP6A, 15B, 2A, C] speak, say things, quickly and indistinctly: 急促而不清楚地说话: *The little girl* ~*d her prayers and jumped into bed*. 那小女孩急急说过祈祷词, 就跳上了床。*Listen to those children gabbling away*. 听那些孩子叽哩咕噜地说个没完。□ *n* [U] fast, confused, unintelligible talk. 急促而不清楚的谈话。

gable /ˈgeɪbl; ˈgebl/ *n* [C] three-cornered part of an outside wall, under sloping roofs. (双斜面屋顶形成的)山(形)墙。**gabled** /ˈgeɪbld; ˈgebld/ *adj* having a ~ or ~s: 有山形墙的: *a* ~*d house*. 有山形墙的房屋。⇨ the illus at **window**. 参看 window 之插图。

gad¹ /gæd; gæd/ *vi* (-**dd-**) [VP2C] *gad about*, (colloq) go from place to place for excitement or pleasure. (口)闲游; 游荡。**ˈgad·about** *n* person who does this. 闲游者;游荡者。

gad² /gæd; gæd/ *int* (also 亦作 *By* '**gad!**) (old-fashioned) used to express surprise, etc. (旧式用语)(表示惊讶等)嗳呀! 天哪!

gad·fly /ˈgædflaɪ; ˈgædˌflaɪ/ *n* (*pl* -**flies**) fly that stings horses and cattle. 牛蝇; 牛虻。

gadget /ˈgædʒɪt; ˈgædʒɪt/ *n* (colloq) small (usu mechanical) contrivance or device: (口)小器具; 小机械: *a new* ~ *for opening tin cans*. 开罐头用的新器具。~**ry** *n* [U] ~s collectively. (集合名词)小器具; 小机械。

Gael /geɪl; gel/ *n* Scottish or Irish Celt. 盖尔人(苏格兰或爱尔兰的塞尔特人)。~**ic** /ˈgeɪlɪk; ˈgelɪk/ *adj, n* (language) of the Scottish or Irish Celts. 盖尔人的; 盖尔人(苏格兰或爱尔兰的塞尔特人)的(语言)。

gaff¹ /gæf; gæf/ *n* stick with an iron hook for landing fish caught with rod and line. 鱼叉;鱼钩(将钓得之鱼钩至岸上所用的工具)。

gaff² /gæf; gæf/ *n blow the* ~, (sl) let out a secret; disclose the plot. (俚)泄露秘密;泄露计划。

gaffe /gæf; gæf/ *n* blunder; indiscreet act or remark. 过失;出丑;言行的失态。

gaffer /ˈgæfə(r); ˈgæfɔ/ *n* (colloq) elderly man, esp a countryman; foreman (for a gang of workmen). (口)年长者(尤指乡下老汉);工头。⇨ **boss**¹, **guvnor**.

gag /gæg; gæg/ *n* [C] **1** sth put in a person's mouth to keep it open (eg by a dentist), or into or over it to prevent him from speaking or crying out. 置于口中使口撑开之物(例如牙医所用之张口器); 塞入口中或覆于口上使不能谈话或哭喊之物。**2** words or action added to his part by an actor in a play. 演员临时插入的台词或动作。**3** joke, funny story, esp as part of a comedian's act (in the theatre, on radio or TV). (剧院, 广播或电视)插科打诨。□ *vt, vi* (-**gg-**) **1** [VP6A] put a gag(1) into or over the mouth of; silence; (fig) deprive (sb) of free speech. 塞物于…之口中; 覆物于…之口上; 使闭口无言; (喻)禁止发言; 剥夺(某人)言论自由。**2** [VP2A] (of an actor, etc) use gags(2, 3). (指演员等)插科打诨。**3** [VP2A] (colloq) retch. (口)作呕。

gaga /ˈɡɑːɡɑː; ˈgaga/ *adj* (sl) in senile dotage; crazy. (俚)老朽的; 疯狂的。

gage¹ /geɪdʒ; gedʒ/ *n* **1** (old use) sth given as security or a guarantee; pledge. (旧用法)抵押物;担保物。**2** = *gauntlet*) glove thrown down (by knights in the Middle Ages) as a challenge to a fight. 中古武士抛于地上表示挑战的手套。□ *vt* [VP6A] (old use) give or offer as a ~; pledge as a guarantee. (旧用法)以…做抵押; 以…为担保。

gage² /geɪdʒ; gedʒ/ ⇨ **gauge**.

gaggle /ˈgæɡl; ˈgæɡl/ *n* flock (of geese); (hum) group (of talkative girls or women). 鹅群; (谐)一群(饶舌妇女)。

gai·ety /ˈgeɪətɪ; ˈgeətɪ/ *n* **1** [U] being gay; cheerfulness; bright appearance: 欢乐; 愉快; 欢乐的气象: *flags and bunting that added to the* ~ *of the scene*. 在那场面增加欢乐气氛的旗帜。**2** (*pl* -**ties**) merrymaking; joyful, festive occasions: (复)作乐; 欢乐的场合: *the gaieties of the Christmas season*. 圣诞节期间的欢乐场合。

gaily /ˈgeɪlɪ; ˈgelɪ/ *adv* ⇨ **gay**.

gain¹ /geɪn; gen/ *n* **1** [U] increase of possessions; acquiring of wealth: 财物的增加; 财富的获取: *the love of* ~; 爱财; *interested only in* ~. 只想发财。**2** (*pl*) (复) **capital** ~**s**, ⇨ **capital**. **ill-gotten** ~**s**, dishonestly obtained profits, etc. 以不正当手段获得的钱财等。**3** [C] increase in amount or power: 数量或力量的增加: 增进: *a* ~ *in weight/health*; 体重增加(健康之增进); *a* ~ *to knowledge*. 知识的增进。~**ful** /-fl; -fel/ *adj* yielding money: 有报酬的; 赚钱的: ~*ful occupations*. 有报酬的职业。~**fully** /-fəlɪ; -felɪ/ *adv* in a ~ful manner: 有报酬地: ~*fully employed*. 受雇有酬。

gain² /geɪn; gen/ *vt, vi* **1** [VP6A, 14, 12B, 13B] obtain (sth wanted or needed); acquire: 获得(需要之物); 增加: ~ *experience/momentum/weight*; 得到经验 (增加动量)(增加重量); ~ *an advantage over a*

competitor; 胜过对手；占上风。~ *strength,* eg become strong again after an illness. 恢复体力(例如病后)。~ *ground,* make progress. 进步。~ *time,* improve one's chances by delaying sth, making pretexts, etc. 拖延时间。~ *the upper hand,* be victorious. 得胜；占上风。**2** [VP2A, B, C] ~*(from),* make progress; be improved; benefit: 进步；改进；获益。从获益中获益。*She is* ~*ing in* (more usu 较常用 putting on) *weight.* 她的体重在增加。**3** [VP2A, B] (of a watch or clock) become fast, ahead of the correct time: (指钟表)快于正确的时间: *This watch neither* ~ *nor loses.* 这表不快也不慢。*The clock* ~*s three minutes a day.* 这钟每天快三分钟。**4** [VP3A] ~ *on / upon,* **(a)** get closer to (the person or thing pursued): 逼近(被追的人或物)；赶上: ~ *on the other runners in a race.* 在赛跑中赶上其他的选手。**(b)** go faster than, get farther in advance of: 跑得较…快；超过: ~ *on one's pursuers.* 跑得比追赶者快。**(c)** (of the sea) advance gradually and eat away (the land). (指海)逐渐侵蚀(陆地)。**5** [VP6A] reach, arrive at (a desired place, esp with effort): 抵达(心中想去的地方,尤指经过一番努力): ~ *the top of a mountain.* 到达山顶。*The swimmer* ~*ed the shore.* 那游泳者抵达岸上。~*ings* n pl earnings; profits; winnings. 收入；收益；赢得之物。

gain·say /ˌgeinˈsei; ˌgenˈse/ vt (pt, pp **-said** /ˈsed; -ˈsed/) [VP6A] (liter) (chiefly in neg and interr) deny; contradict: (文)(主要用于否定和疑问句)否认；反驳: *There is no* ~*ing his honesty,* We cannot deny that he is honest. 我们不能否认他的诚实。

gait /geit; get/ n manner of walking or running: 步态；步法: *an awkward / slouching* ~. 难看(垂头丧气)的步态。

gai·ter /ˈgeitə(r); ˈgetə/ n cloth or leather covering for the leg from knee to ankle, or for the ankle: 绑腿；皮腿套: *a pair of* ~*s.* 一副绑腿。

gal /gæl; gæl/ n (dated colloq) girl. (过时口语) 女郎。

gala /ˈgɑːlə US: ˈgeilə; ˈgelə/ n festive occasion; 节日; (attrib): (用作定语): *a* ~ *night,* eg at a theatre, with special features. 欢乐之夜(例如剧院中有特别节目之夜)。

ga·lac·tic /gəˈlæktik; gəˈlæktik/ adj of a galaxy or the Galaxy: 太空星群的；银河系的；天河的: *extra-*~ *systems,* systems outside the Galaxy. 银河外面的星系。

gal·an·tine /ˈgæləntiːn; ˈgælən,tin/ n white meat, boned, spiced, cooked in the form of a roll, and served cold. 去骨,加香料煮成的冷食的肉卷。

gal·axy /ˈgæləksi; ˈgæləksi/ n (pl **-xies**) **1** any of the large-scale clusters of stars in outer space. 太空中任何大规模的星群；星系。**the G**~, that which includes our solar system, visible as a luminous band known as 'the Milky Way'. 银河系；天河。**2** brilliant company of persons: 一群显赫的人: *a* ~ *of talent /beautiful women.* 一群才子(美女)。

gale /geil; gel/ n **1** strong and violent wind: 强风；大风: *The ship lost her masts in the* ~. 这艘的桅樯被强风吹断了。*It was blowing a* ~. 刮着大风。**2** noisy outburst: 一阵喧闹: ~*s of laughter.* 阵阵笑声。

gall¹ /gɔːl; gɔl/ n [U] **1** bitter liquid (bile) secreted by the liver. 胆汁。'~ **bladder** n (anat) vessel attached to the liver containing and discharging ~. (解剖)胆囊。⇨ the illus at **alimentary**. 参看 alimentary 之插图。'~**stone** n hard mass that forms in the ~ bladder. 胆石。**2** bitter feeling: 恶毒；怨恨；痛苦: *with a pen dipped in* ~, used of a writer who makes bitter attacks. 以恶毒的笔调。**3** (colloq) impudence: (口)厚颜; 卤莽: *Of all the* ~! 脸皮真厚！

gall² /gɔːl; gɔl/ n [C] painful swelling on an animal, esp a horse, caused by rubbing (of harness, etc); place rubbed bare. 擦伤(尤指马的)；擦伤之处。□ vt **1** [VP6A] rub sore. 磨伤；擦伤。**2** (fig) hurt the feelings of; humiliate: (喻)伤害…之感情；侮辱: ~ *sb with one's remarks.* 用言语伤害某人的感情。*It was* ~*ing to him to*

have to ask for a loan. 必须向人求贷使他感到屈辱。

gall³ /gɔːl; gɔl/ n unnatural growth produced on a tree by insects, eg on the oak. 虫瘿(例如橡树上者)；没食子；五倍子。

gal·lant /ˈgælənt; ˈgælənt/ adj **1** (archaic) brave: (古)勇敢的；英勇的: *a* ~ *knight,* 勇敢的骑士; ~ *deeds.* 英勇的事迹。**2** fine; grand; stately: 华丽的；堂皇的；壮丽的；雄伟的: *a* ~*-looking ship,* 华丽的船只; *a* ~ *display.* 华丽的展览。**3** (also 亦作 /gəˈlænt; gəˈlænt/) showing special respect and courtesy to women: 对妇女特别殷勤的: *He was very* ~ *at the ball.* 他在舞会中对妇女大大献殷勤。□ (also 亦作 /gəˈlænt; gəˈlænt/) n young man of fashion, esp one who is fond of and attentive to women. 时髦的青年(尤指喜欢女人并对女人献殷勤者)。~·**ly** adv ~**ry** n **1** [U] bravery. 勇敢；英勇。**2** [U] devotion, chivalrous attention, to women. 尊崇妇女；扶助妇女。**3** [C] (pl **-ries**) elaborately polite or amorous act or speech to a woman. 对妇女殷勤的言行。

gal·leon /ˈgælən; ˈgælən/ n Spanish sailing-ship (15th to 17th cc) with a high stern. (十五至十七世纪的)西班牙大帆船(船尾很高)。

galleons

gal·lery /ˈgæləri; ˈgæləri/ n (pl **-ries**) **1** room or building for the display of works of art. 美术品陈列室；美术陈列馆；画廊。**2** (people in the) highest and cheapest seats in a theatre. (戏院中)票价最便宜的最高楼座；楼座观众。*play to the* ~, try to win approval or popularity by appealing to the taste of the masses. 设法迎合大众趣味。**3** raised floor or platform extending from an inner wall of a hall, church, etc: (大厅,教堂等中自内壁伸展出去的)廊台: *the 'press* ~ *of the House of Commons,* used by newspaper reporters. 下议院的记者席。**4** covered walk or corridor, partly open at one side; colonnade. 走廊；柱廊。**5** long, narrow room: 狭长的房间: *a 'shooting-*~, for indoor target practice. 室内靶场。**6** horizontal underground passage in a mine. (横)坑道。⇨ **shaft**.

gal·ley /ˈgæli; ˈgæli/ n (pl ~**s**) **1** (hist) low, flat single-decked ship, using sails and oars, rowed by slaves or criminals; ancient Greek or Roman warship. (史)(昔时奴隶或犯人划行的用帆与桨的)单甲板平底船；古希腊或罗马的战舰。'~-**slave** n person condemned to row in a ~. 被罚划船的奴隶；船役囚犯。**2** ship's kitchen. 船上厨房。**3** oblong metal tray in which type is assembled by compositors. 长方形活字盘；检字盘。'~-**proof** n proof(4) on a long slip of paper, before division into pages. 尚未分成页的校样；长条校样。

Gal·lic /ˈgælik; ˈgælik/ adj of Gaul or the Gauls; (often hum) French. 高卢的；高卢人的；(常为谐语)法国的。**gal·li·cism** /ˈgælisizəm; ˈgælə,sizəm/ n [C] French way of saying sth, used in another language. 外语中的法国语风。

gal·li·vant /ˌgæliˈvænt; ˈgælə,vænt/ vi [VP2C] ~ *about/off,* (not used in the simple tenses) (不用于简单时态) = gad about, ⇨ **gad¹:** *Where are you* ~*ing off to now?* 你现在要到哪里去游逛？

gal·lon /ˈgælən; ˈgælən/ n measure for liquids, four quarts (4.5 litres). 加仑(液量名,合四夸脱或 4.5 公升)。⇨ **App 5.** 参看附录五。

gal·lop /'gæləp; 'gæləp/ n (of a horse, etc) fastest pace with all four feet off the ground at each stride; period of riding at such a pace: (马等四蹄同时离地之) 飞奔; 疾驰; 骑马飞奔之期间: He rode away at a ~/at full ~. 他骑着马疾驰而去. Shall we go for a ~? 我们 去骑一阵快马如何? □ vi, vt 1 [VP2A, B, C, 6A](cause to) go at a ~: 疾驰; 使飞奔: He ~ed across the field. 他 骑马驰过田野. 2 [VP2A, B, C] hurry: 匆匆地做: ~ through one's work / lecture: 匆匆赶完工作 (演说); progress rapidly: 迅速进行: in a ~ing consumption, ill with tuberculosis which is rapidly getting worse. 患有 马痨(即急剧恶化的肺结核病).

gal·lows /'gæləʊz; 'gæloz/ n pl (usu with sing v) wooden framework on which to put criminals to death by hanging: (通常用单数动词)绞架: send a man to the ~, condemn him to be hanged. 处某人以绞刑。He'll end up on the ~, will end by being hanged. 他总有一天 要受绞刑的。'~-bird n person who is thought by some to deserve hanging. 应受绞刑的人.

Gal·lup poll /'gæləp pəʊl; 'gæləp'pol/ n questioning of a representative sample of people to assess general public opinion about sth, eg how they will vote at a general election, esp as a means of making a forecast. (盖洛普)民意测验.

ga·lore /gə'lɔ:(r); gə'lor/ adv in plenty: 丰富地: a meal with beef and beer ~. 有牛肉和啤酒的丰盛的一餐.

ga·loshes /gə'lɒʃɪz; gə'laʃɪz/ n pl (pair of) ~, rubber overshoes worn in wet weather. (雨天用) 胶 套鞋.

ga·lumph /gə'lʌmf; gə'lʌmf/ vi (made from gallop and triumph) prance clumsily or noisily in triumph. (由 gallop 和 triumph 二字转成)得意扬扬而行; 昂首阔步.

gal·van·ism /'gælvənɪzəm; 'gælvə,nɪzəm/ n [U] (science of, medical use of) electricity produced by chemical action from a battery. 由化学作用自电池产生 的电;流电;流电学; 电疗. **gal·vanic** /gæl'vænɪk; gæl-'vænɪk/ adj 1 of ~. 化学电池之电流的;流电的;用流电 的; 流电学的. 2 (fig) (of smiles, movements, etc) sudden and forced (as if produced by an electric shock). (喻) (指微笑, 动作等) 突然而勉强的 (如被电击 般).

gal·van·ize /'gælvənaɪz; 'gælvə,naɪz/ vt 1 [VP6A] coat (sheet iron, etc) with metal, eg zinc: 电镀 (铁片 等); 镀锌铁; 白铁. 2 [VP6A, 14] ~ sb (into doing sth), shock or rouse. 惊起或激励 (某人 做某事).

gam·bit /'gæmbɪt; 'gæmbɪt/ n kinds of opening move in chess (in which a player sacrifices a pawn or other piece to secure certain ends); (fig) any initial move: 国 际象棋开局时牺牲一子以达到某目的之着棋; (喻)任何开 始的行动: His opening ~ at the debate was a direct attack on Government policy. 他在辩论开始的演说是对政 府政策的直接攻击.

gamble /'gæmbl; 'gæmbl/ vi, vt 1 [VP2A, B, C] play games of chance for money; take great risks for the chance of winning sth or making a profit: 赌博; 投机: He lost his money gambling at cards / gambling on the Stock Exchange / gambling in oil shares, etc. 他赌纸牌 (买卖股票,投资石油 股等)输(损失)了钱. 2 [VP15B] ~ sth away, lose by gambling: 赌输: He has ~d away half his fortune. 他赌 博输去了一半的财产. □ vi 1 [C] undertaking or attempt with risk of loss and chance of profit or advantage. 冒 险的事业; 赌博; 投机. take a ~ (on sth), risk (it). 冒 险. **gam·bler** n person who ~s. 赌徒;赌博者;为利益 而冒险者; 投机者. **gam·bling** n [U] playing games for money; taking risks for possible advantage: 赌博; 为可能利益 而冒险: fond of gambling. 嗜赌. '**gambling-den**/-**house** n (old use) place where gambling is carried on. (旧用 法)赌窟. ⇨ game[3].

gam·boge /gæm'bu:ʒ; US: -'bəʊʒ; gæm'buʒ/ n [U] deep yellow colouring matter used by artists. 藤黄; 雌

黄(画家所用深黄色颜料).

gam·bol /'gæmbl; 'gæmbl/ n (usu pl) quick, playful, jumping or skipping movements, eg of lambs, children. (通常用复数) (小羊, 小孩等) 雀跃; 嬉戏. □ vi (-ll-, US also -l-) [VP2A, C] make such movements. 雀跃; 嬉戏.

game¹ /geɪm; gem/ n 1 [C] form of play, esp with rules, eg tennis, football, cards: (有规则的)游戏(例如 网球,足球,纸牌): play ~s; 做游戏; have a ~ of whist. 玩惠斯特牌. He plays a good ~ of snooker, is a good player. 他撞球打得很好. **be off one's** ~, be out of form, not playing well. 健康与训练情形不佳, 玩得不 好. **have the** ~ **in one's hands**, be sure to win it, be able to direct it. 有把握获胜. **play the** ~, keep the rules;(fig) be straight forward and honest. 遵守规则; (喻) 正直诚实. '~s-**master**/-**mistress**, teacher in charge of ~s at a school. 教游戏的男 (女) 老师. ~s-**manship** /'geɪmzmənʃɪp; 'gemzmən,ʃɪp/ n (colloq) the art of winning ~s by upsetting the confidence of one's opponents. (口)扰乱对手信心而获胜之道。2 [C] apparatus, etc needed for a ~, eg one played by children with a board and dice and counters, such as ludo and draughts. 游戏器具(例如骰子和国际象棋游戏 的器具). 3(pl) (international)athletic contests: (复)(国 际)运动会: the Olympic / Commonwealth / Highland G~s; 奥林匹克(英联邦,苏格兰高地)运动会; (In Greece and Rome, ancient times) athletic and dramatic contests. (古 希腊和罗马) 运动和戏剧竞赛会. 4 [C] single round in some contests, eg tennis: (网球等比赛之)一次; 一盘;一 场; 一局: win four ~s in the first set; 在第一盘中赢四 局; score needed to win; state of the ~: 比赛的积分; 比 赛状况: The ~ is four all; 双方各得四分; ~ all, equal score; 各赢一次;平手;打平; ~, set and match. 一局,一 盘,一场比赛. 5 [C] scheme, plan or undertaking; dodge or trick: 计划; 策略; 诡计: He was playing a deep ~, engaged in a secret scheme of some sort. 他在从事 一秘密计划. I wish I knew what his ~ is, what he is trying to do. 但愿我能知道他想做些什么. That's a ~ two people can play, said when two people use the same scheme against each other. 那是一场两个人都会玩的把 戏 (意谓两个人彼此向对方玩同一把戏). So that's your little ~, said when one discovers what sb is scheming to do. 原来那就是你的鬼把戏. The ~ is up, The scheme is discovered and thwarted. 计谋被拆穿而成功无望了. You're playing Smith's ~, You are, unintentionally, helping to advance Smith's scheme. 你无意中帮助了史 密斯的计谋. None of your little ~s! Don't try to play tricks on me! 我不会上你的当! 不要耍你那套把戏! You're having a ~ with me, trying to trick me, deceive me, etc. 你在欺骗我. ,give the ~ away, reveal a secret trick, scheme, etc. 泄露秘密诡计诡谋. make ~ of sb, ridicule him. 嘲弄某人. 6 [U] (collective) (flesh of) wild animals and birds hunted for sport or food. (集合 名词)猎物; 野兽或野禽之肉. big ~ n [U] the larger animals (elephants, lions, tigers). 大猎物(象,狮,虎). fair ~, n [U] what may be lawfully hunted or shot; (fig) person or institution that may with reason be attacked or criticized. 不禁猎的鸟兽; (喻)可据理加以攻 击或批评的人或制度. '~-**bag**, bag for holding ~ killed by sportsmen. (盛装猎物之)猎袋. '~-**bird**, wild bird (eg grouse, pheasant) hunted for sport or food. 猎鸟; 猎禽(例如松鸡,雉等). ⇨ illus at **fowl**. 参看 fowl 之插 图. '~-**cock**, of the kind bred for cock-fighting. 斗 鸡. '~-**keeper**, man employed to breed and protect ~, eg pheasants, grouse, on a country estate. 猎物看 守人. '~ **laws**, laws regulating the killing and preservation of ~. 狩猎规则; 狩猎法. '~-**licence**, one to kill and deal in ~. 狩猎许可证; 狩猎执照. **gamy** /'geɪmɪ; 'gemɪ/ adj having the flavour and odour of ~(6), esp when high[1](8). 有猎物气味的(尤指略有臭味 时).

game² /geɪm; gem/ adj 1 brave; ready to go on fighting; spirited. 勇敢的; 奋发的; 精神抖擞的. 2 ~

for / to do sth, spirited enough, willing: 高兴做…的; 愿意…的: *Are you ~ for a 10-mile walk?* 你有兴趣走十英里路吗? *He's ~ to do anything you may suggest.* 不论你做何建议, 他都愿接受。 **~·ly** *adv*

game³ /geɪm; gem/ *vi, vt* [VP2A, C, 15B] gamble. 赌博。 **'gaming-house/-rooms/-table,** house etc (usu licensed) for gambling. 赌场(通常有许可执照)。

game⁴ /geɪm; gem/ *adj* (of a leg, arm, etc) lame; crippled. (指腿, 臂等)跛的; 残废的。

gamma /'gæmə; 'gæmə/ *n* third letter of the Greek alphabet. 希腊字母之第三个字母。⇨ **App 4.** 参看附录四。 **'~-rays** *n pl* rays of very short wave-length emitted by radio-active substances. γ 射线;加马射线(放射性元素所放出的极短波射线)。

gam·mon /'gæmən; 'gæmən/ *n* [C] piece of bacon from the side of a pig, including the hind leg; [U] smoked or cured ham. 腌猪后腿; 腊肉; 熏腿。

gammy /'gæmɪ; 'gæmɪ/ *adj* (colloq) (口)=**game⁴**: *a ~ leg.* 跛的腿。

gamp /gæmp; gæmp/ *n* (hum; dated) umbrella (esp a large, untidy one). (谐; 过时用语)伞(尤指大而不整洁者)。

gamut /'gæmət; 'gæmət/ *n* the **~,** complete extent or scope of sth: 全部; 整个范围: *the whole ~ of feeling,* eg from the greatest joy to the depths of despair or misery. 全部感情历程(例如从极端喜悦至绝望或痛苦)。 *run the ~ (of sth),* experience the whole range (of it). 经验全部历程。

gan·der /'gændə(r); 'gændə/ *n* male goose. 雄鹅。

gang /gæŋ; gæŋ/ *n* **1** group of persons going about or working together, esp for criminal purposes. 帮;一伙 (尤指有犯罪企图者)。⇨ **gangster. 2** (colloq) group of persons going about together, disapproved of by the speaker: (口)一帮(为说话者所不满者): *Don't get mixed up with that ~; they spend too much time drinking and gambling.* 不要同那一帮人混在一起, 他们终日饮酒赌博。 □ *vi* [VP2C] *~ up,* act together as a *~:* 联合起来; 结成一伙: *They ~ up on/against me.* 他们联合起来对付我。 **~·er** /'gæŋə(r); 'gæŋə/ *n* foreman of a *~*(1). 工头。

gan·gling /'gæŋglɪŋ; 'gæŋglɪŋ/ *adj* (of a person) lanky; tall, thin and awkward-looking. (指人)瘦长的; 瘦长而难看的。

gan·glion /'gæŋglɪən; 'gæŋglɪən/ *n* (*pl ~s* or *-lia* /-lɪə; -lɪə/) group of nerve-cells from which nerve-fibres radiate; (fig) centre of force, activity or interest. 神经中枢; 神经结; (喻)(力量, 活动或兴趣的)中心。

gang·plank /'gæŋplæŋk; 'gæŋ.plæŋk/ *n* movable plank placed between a ship or boat and the land, or between two boats or ships. (上下船的)跳板。

gan·grene /'gæŋgriːn; 'gæŋgrin/ *n* [U] death and decay of a part of the body, eg because the supply of blood to it has been stopped: 坏疽: *G~ set in and his leg had to be amputated.* 他的腿生了坏疽, 必须切掉。 □ *vt, vi* [VP6A, 2A] affect, become affected, with *~.* 使生疽; 生疽。 **gan·gren·ous** /'gæŋgrɪnəs; 'gæŋgrənəs/ *adj*

gang·ster /'gæŋstə(r); 'gæŋstə/ *n* member of a gang of armed criminals: 歹徒; 匪徒: (attrib)(用作定语)*~ films.* 警匪片。

gang·way /'gæŋweɪ; 'gæŋ,we/ *n* **1** opening in a ship's side; movable bridge from this to the land. (船边之)梯口; (由梯口至岸上的)舷梯。 **2** (US 美 = *aisle*) passage between rows of seats, eg in the House of Commons, in a theatre or concert-hall, or between rows of people. 两排座位之间人们之间的通道(例如下议院, 剧院或音乐厅中者)。 □ *int* Make way, please! 请让路! 请闪开!

gan·net /'gænɪt; 'gænɪt/ *n* kind of large sea-bird. 塘鹅。

gan·try /'gæntrɪ; 'gæntrɪ/ *n* (*pl* **-ries**) structure of steel bars to support a travelling crane, railway signals over several tracks, etc. (支撑移动起重机, 铁路信号装置等的)桥形台架。

gaol, jail /dʒeɪl; dʒel/ *n* (usu *jail* in US) [C] public prison; [U] confinement in prison: (美国通常用 jail)监牢; 牢狱; 监禁: *three years in ~;* 坐监三年; *be sent to ~.* 被下狱。 **'~-bird** *n* prisoner, esp one who has often been in prison; rogue. 囚犯; (尤指)惯犯; 恶棍。 **'~-break** *n* [C] escape from *~.* 越狱。 □ *vt* [VP6A] put in *~.* 下牢; 监禁。 **gaoler, jailer, jailor** /'dʒeɪlə(r); 'dʒelə/ *nn* man in charge of a *~* or the prisoners in it. 看守监狱者; 狱卒; 狱吏。

gap /gæp; gæp/ *n* **1** break or opening in a wall, hedge, etc: (墙壁, 树篱等之)裂缝; 缺口: *The sheep got out of the field through a gap in the hedge.* 羊从树篱的间隙跑出牧场。 *We must see that there is no gap in our defences.* 我们必须注意不要使我们的防线有漏洞。 **2** unfilled space; interval; wide separation (of ideas, etc): 空白; 间隔; (思想, 意见等之)悬隔; 歧异: *a gap in a conversation,* interval of silence; 谈话的间断; *fill in the gaps in one's education,* study what one failed to learn while at school, etc; 补充一个人的教育; *a wide gap between the views of the two statesmen.* 两位政治家意见之歧异。 *bridge/fill/stop a gap,* supply sth lacking. 补充所缺之物。⇨ stopgap at **stop¹**(8). **credi'bility gap,** failure of one person, group, etc to convince another that he or it is telling the truth. 信用的差距(无法使对方相信所说的话)。 **gene'ration gap,** failure or inability of the younger and older generations to communicate, understand one another. 代沟(年轻一代与年长一代间之不能勾通思想或彼此了解)。 **,gap'-toothed** /'tuːθt; 'tʊθt/ *adj* having teeth which are wide apart. 牙齿间缝隙很大的。 **3** gorge or pass between mountains. 山峡; 山间狭路; 隘口。

gape /geɪp; gep/ *vi* [VP2A, C] **1** *~ (at sb/sth)* open the mouth wide; yawn; stare open-mouthed in surprise: 张口; 打哈欠; 目瞪口呆地注视: *country visitors gaping at the neon lights.* 张口惊视霓虹灯的乡下人。 **2** be or become open wide: 裂开: *a gaping chasm.* 裂缝。 □ *n* open-mouthed stare. 打哈欠; 目瞪口呆; 张口凝视。 the **~s, (a)** disease of poultry causing them to gape until they die (with the beak wide open). 家禽之一种张嘴病。 **(b)** (joc) fit of yawning. (谑)一阵哈欠。

gar·age /'gærɑːʒ US: gə'rɑːʒ; gə'rɑʒ/ *n* **1** building in which to keep a car or cars. 汽车间; 汽车房。 **2** (US 美 = *service station*) roadside petrol and service station. 路边加油站; 修车厂。 □ *vt* [VP6A] put (a motor-vehicle) in a *~.* 将(汽车)送入车房。

garb /gɑːb; gɑrb/ *n* [U] (style of) dress (esp as worn by a particular kind of person): 服装(尤指某一种人所穿者); 装束: *a man in clerical ~.* 穿着牧师服装的人。 □ *vt* [VP6A] (usu passive) dress: (通常用被动语态)装扮: *~ed in motley.* 穿着杂色衣服。

gar·bage /'gɑːbɪdʒ; 'gɑrbɪdʒ/ *n* [U] **1** waste food put out as worthless, or for pigs, etc; (US) rubbish; refuse (of any kind). (丢弃或喂猪等之)剩饭残羹; (美)垃圾。 **'~-can** *n* (US) dustbin. (美)垃圾箱。 **2** (colloq) worthless material; meaningless or irrelevant data in a storage device of a computer. (口)无价值的资料;无意义或不相关的电脑资料。

garble /'gɑːbl; 'gɑrbl/ *vt* [VP6A] make an incomplete or unfair selection from statements, facts, etc, esp in order to give false ideas: 断章取义: *a ~d report of a speech.* 曲解一演说的报导。

gar·den /'gɑːdn; 'gɑrdn/ *n* **1** [C, U] (piece of) ground used for growing flowers, fruit, vegetables, etc: 花园; 果园; 菜园: *a kitchen ~,* for vegetables; 菜园; *a market ~,* for vegetables, fruit and flowers for sale in public markets; 供应市场蔬菜, 水果和花的农圃; (attrib)(用作定语)*a ~ wall;* 花园之墙; *~ flowers/plants.* 园中的花(植物)。 *We have not much ~/only a small ~.* 我们的花园不大。 *lead sb up the ~ path,* (colloq) mislead him. (口)使人歧途; 使迷惑。 **~ 'city/'suburb** *n* one laid out with many open spaces, and

planted with numerous trees. (多空地, 种有大量树木之) 花园城市(市郊)。'~ **party** *n* social gathering held out of doors on a lawn, in a ~ or park, etc. 游园会。**2** (usu *pl*) public park: (通常用复数)公园: *Kensington G~s*, in London; (伦敦之)肯辛顿公园; *botanical~zoological~s.* 植物(动物)园。□ *vi* [VP2A] cultivate a ~: 从事园艺; 种植花木: *He's been ~ing all day.* 他忙做了一整天的园艺工作。~**er** *n* person who works in a ~, either for pay or as a hobby. 园丁; 花匠; 园艺家。~**ing** *n* [U] cultivating of ~s: 园艺; *fond of ~ing;* 爱好园艺; (attrib)(用作定语)~*ing gloves/tools.* 园艺用手套(工具)。

gar·denia /gɑːˈdiːnɪə; gɑrˈdinɪə/ *n* (kind of) tree or shrub with large white or yellow flowers, usu sweetsmelling. 栀子; 栀子属(开白花或黄花的树或灌木, 其花通常有香味)。

gar·gan·tuan /gɑːˈɡæntjʊən; ɡɑrˈɡæntʃʊən/ *adj* enormous; gigantic. 庞大的; 巨大的。

gargle /ˈɡɑːɡl; ˈɡɑrɡl/ *vt, vi* [VP6A, 2A] wash the throat with liquid kept in motion by a stream of breath. 漱喉。□ *n* liquid used for this purpose; act of gargling. 含漱剂; 漱口剂; 漱喉。

gar·goyle /ˈɡɑːɡɔɪl; ˈɡɑrɡɔɪl/ *n* stone or metal spout, usu in the form of a grotesque human or animal creature, to carry off rain-water from the roof of a building ⟨esp Gothic-style churches⟩. 承霤口; 滴水; 笕嘴(通常作古怪之人形或动物形状, 尤指哥德式建筑之教堂上者)。⇨ the illus at **church.** 参看 church 之插图。

gar·ish /ˈɡeərɪʃ; ˈɡerɪʃ/ *adj* unpleasantly bright; over-coloured or over-decorated: 炫耀的; 过于艳丽的; 过份装饰的: ~ *clothes.* 过于艳丽的衣服。~**ly** *adv*

gar·land /ˈɡɑːlənd; ˈɡɑrlənd/ *n* circle of flowers or leaves as an ornament or decoration; this as a prize for victory, etc. (作为装饰或胜利奖品等之)花圈; 花环; 花冠。□ *vt* [VP6A] decorate, crown, with a ~ or ~s. 饰以花圈; 戴以花冠。

gar·lic /ˈɡɑːlɪk; ˈɡɑrlɪk/ *n* [U] onion-like plant with strong taste and smell, used in cooking: 蒜; 蒜头; 大蒜: *a clove of ~,* one of the small bulbs making up the compound bulb of a ~ plant; 一瓣蒜; *too much ~ in the food;* 食物中放太多的蒜; *smelling of ~.* 有大蒜气味。

gar·ment /ˈɡɑːmənt; ˈɡɑrmənt/ *n* [C] article of clothing: 衣服: (US, attrib) (美, 用作定语) *the '~ industry;* 制衣工业; '~ *workers.* 制衣工人。

gar·ner /ˈɡɑːnər; ˈɡɑrnɚ/ *n* (poet, rhet) storehouse for grain, etc (also fig). (诗, 修辞)谷仓; 仓库(亦作喻)。□ *vt* [VP6A, 15B] ~*(in/up),* store, gather. 储藏; 收藏。

gar·net /ˈɡɑːnɪt; ˈɡɑrnɪt/ *n* semi-precious gem of deep transparent red. 石榴石; 柘榴石。

gar·nish /ˈɡɑːnɪʃ; ˈɡɑrnɪʃ/ *vt* [VP6A, 14] ~*(with),* decorate, esp food for the table: 装饰(尤指食物): *fish ~ed with slices of lemon.* 用柠檬片装饰的鱼。□ *n* sth used to decorate a dish of food for the table. 食物上的装饰物。

gar·ret /ˈɡærət; ˈɡærɪt/ *n* room (often small, dark, etc) on the top floor of a house, esp in the roof. 阁楼; 屋顶室(常是小而暗的)。

gar·ri·son /ˈɡærɪsn; ˈɡærəsn/ *n* [C] military force stationed in a town or fort: 卫戍部队; 要塞驻军; 驻军: (attrib)(用作定语) *a ~ town,* one in which a ~ is permanently stationed. 有部队驻防之城市。□ *vt* [VP 6A] supply a town, etc with a ~; place troops, etc on ~ duty. 以卫戍部队驻守(城市等); 派(军队等)驻守。

gar·rotte, ga·rotte /ɡəˈrɒt; ɡəˈrɑt/ *vt* [VP6A] execute (a person condemned to death) by strangling or throttling (a stick being twisted to tighten a cord over the windpipe); murder (sb) in this way. 执行绞刑(扭动一棒, 拉紧绳索, 勒喉咙以绞杀); 绞杀(某人)。□ *n* this method of capital punishment; apparatus used for it. 以上述方法所作的绞刑; 上述绞刑所用的刑具。

gar·ru·lous /ˈɡærələs; ˈɡærələs/ *adj* talkative; talk-ing too much about unimportant things. 爱说话的; 絮聒的。**gar·ru·lity** /ɡəˈruːlətɪ; ɡəˈruləti/ *n* [U].

gar·ter /ˈɡɑːtər; ˈɡɑrtɚ/ *n* (elastic) band worn round the leg to keep a stocking in place. (弹性)袜带。**the G~,** (badge of) the highest order of English knighthood. 嘉德勋位(英国爵士之最高勋位); 嘉德勋章。

gas /ɡæs; ɡæs/ *n* (*pl* **gases** /ˈɡæsɪz; ˈɡæsɪz/ **1** [C] kind of air-like substance (used chiefly of those that do not become liquid or solid at ordinary temperatures): 气体(主要用在通常温度下不会变为液体或固体的气体): *Air is a mixture of gases.* 空气是各种气体的混合物。*Hydrogen and oxygen are gases.* 氢和氧是气体。**2** [U] pure gas or mixture of gases used for lighting and heating, eg natural gas or the kind manufactured from coal; gas manufactured for use in war *(poison gas),* or occurring naturally, eg in a coal mine: 天然气; 煤气; 瓦斯; 毒气: *put the kettle on the gas,* ie on the gas-ring or cooker. 将壶放在煤气炉上。'**gas-bag** *n* **(a)** bag for holding gas, eg in an airship. 蓄气囊(例如飞艇中者)。**(b)** (colloq) person who talks too much without saying anything useful or interesting. (口)废话连篇的人。'**gas-bracket** *n* pipe with one or more burners projecting from a wall. 墙上伸出的有喷嘴的煤气管。'**gas chamber** *n* room filled with gas for lethal purposes. 毒气室。'**gas-cooker** *n* stove (with gas-rings and an oven) for cooking by gas. 煤气炉。'**gas fire** *n* one for heating a room by gas. 煤气暖炉。'**gas-fitter** *n* workman who provides a building with gas-fittings. 安装煤气装置的工人。'**gas-fittings** *n pl* apparatus, eg pipes, burners, etc for heating or lighting with gas. 煤气装置(如用煤气加热或点灯之管道, 灯头、炉心等)。'**gas-helmet** *n* = **gas-mask.** '**gas-holder** *n* = **gasometer.** '**gas-light** *n* [U] light produced by burning coal-gas. 煤气灯; 煤气灯光。'**gas-mask** *n* breathing apparatus to protect the wearer against harmful gases. 防毒面罩; 防毒面具。'**gas-meter** *n* meter for registering the amount of gas that passes through it. 煤气表(记录煤气用量的量具)。'**gas-oven** *n* (a) one heated by gas. 煤气炉。**(b)** = **gas chamber.** '**gas-poker** *n* metal rod with holes in one end, connected to a supply of gas, used to light fires in a fireplace. 煤气火棒(一端有孔之金属棒, 与煤气源相接, 用以在火炉中燃火者)。'**gas-ring** *n* metal ring with numerous small holes and supplied with gas for cooking, etc. (有环梁喷火孔的轻便)煤气炉。'**gas-stove** *n* = **gas-cooker.** '**gas-tar** *n* [U] coal-tar produced during the manufacture of coal-gas. (制煤气时产生的)煤焦油。'**gas-works** *n pl* (*sing v*) place where coal-gas is manufactured. (后接单数动词)煤气厂。**3** (also 亦作 *'laughing-gas*) nitrous oxide (N₂O) used by dentists as an anaesthetic. 笑气(牙医用作麻醉剂的氧化亚氮)。**4** (US colloq) (abbr of *gasoline*) petrol. (美口)汽油(为 gasoline 之略)。*step on the gas,* press down the accelerator pedal; increase speed. 踩加速器; 加速。'**gas-engine** *n* one from which power is obtained by the regular explosion of gas in a closed cylinder. 燃气(发动)机。'**gas-station,** (US) = petrol station. (美)加油站。**5** (fig, colloq) empty talk; boasting. (喻, 口)空谈; 吹牛。□ *vt, vi* (**-ss-**) **1** [VP6A] poison or overcome by gas. 以毒气毒害; 以毒气克服。**2** [VP2A, C] (colloq) talk for a long time without saying much that is useful. (口)空谈; 瞎扯。

gas·eous /ˈɡæsɪəs; ˈɡæsɪəs/ *adj* of or like gas: 气体的; 似气体的: *a ~ mixture.* 气体混合物。

gash /ɡæʃ; ɡæʃ/ *n* [C] long deep cut or wound. 长而深的切痕或伤口。□ *vt* [VP6A] make a ~ in. 长而深地切伤。

gas·ify /ˈɡæsɪfaɪ; ˈɡæsəˌfaɪ/ *vt, vi* [VP6A, 2A] (cause to) change into gas. (使)变成气体; 气化。**gasi·fi·ca·tion** /ˌɡæsɪfɪˈkeɪʃn; ˌɡæsɪfəˈkeʃən/ *n*

gas·ket /ˈɡæskɪt; ˈɡæskɪt/ *n* **1** strip or soft, flat piece of material used for packing a joint, piston, etc to prevent steam, gas, etc from escaping. 垫圈; 垫板; 密合垫; 接合垫料(装于接头处, 活塞周围, 以免漏气等的带形

或软扁的填塞物)。**2** (usu *pl*) (naut) small cords used for tying a furled sail to a yard. (通常用复数)(航海) 束帆索。

gaso·line (also **-lene**) /'gæsəliːn; 'gæsl,in/ *n* [U] (US) petrol; motor spirit. (美)汽油。

gas·ometer /gæ'sɒmɪtə(r); gæs'amətə/ *n* large round tank in which gas is stored and measured (usu at a gas-works) and from which it is distributed through pipes. 气柜; 煤气贮存计量器(通常设于煤气厂中, 装有管子输送煤气)。

gasp /gɑːsp US: gæsp; gæsp/ *vi*, *vt* **1** [VP2A, C] struggle for breath; take short, quick breaths as a fish does out of water: 喘气; 喘息: ~*ing for breath*; 喘息; ~*ing* (= breathless) *with rage/surprise*. 气(惊奇)得喘不过气来。**2** [VP6A, 15B] ~ (**out**), utter in a breathless way: 喘着气说出: *He ~ed out a few words.* 他喘着气说出了几个字。□ *n* [C] catching of the breath through pain, surprise, etc: (因痛苦, 惊奇等)喘气; 屏息: *at one's last* ~, exhausted; at the point of death. 奄奄一息; 即将断气。

gassy /'gæsɪ; 'gæsɪ/ *adj* of or like gas; full of gas; (of talk, etc) empty; vain and boastful. 气体的; 气状的; 充满气体的; (指谈话等)空洞的; 夸张的。

gas·tric /'gæstrɪk; 'gæstrɪk/ *adj* of the stomach: 胃的: *a* ~ *ulcer;* 胃溃疡; ~ *fever;* 胃热; ~ *juices.* 胃液。**gas·tri·tis** /gæ'straɪtɪs; gæs'traɪtɪs/ *n* [U] inflammation of the stomach. 胃炎。

gas·tron·omy /gæ'strɒnəmɪ; gæs'trɑnəmɪ/ *n* [U] art and science of choosing, preparing and eating good food. 美食术; 美食学。**gas·tron·omic** /,gæstrə'nɒmɪk; ,gæstrə'nɑmɪk/ *adj* of ~. 美食术的; 美食学的。

gate /geɪt; get/ *n* **1** opening in the wall of a city, hedge, fence or other enclosure, capable of being closed by means of a barrier; barrier that closes such an opening, either of solid wood or of iron gratings or bars, usu on hinges; barrier used to control the passage of water, eg into or out of a lock on a canal: 城门; 篱笆门; 围墙门; 大门; 门扇; 扉; 闸门: *He opened the garden* ~ *and went into the street.* 他打开花园的门走到街上去。*He jumped over the* ~ *into the field.* 他跳过栅门进入田野。'**~crash** *vt* [VP6A] enter (a building at which there is a private social occasion of some sort) without invitation or payment. 未被邀请或付费而参加(私人社交场合); 擅自入场。Hence, 由此产生, '**~crasher** *n.* '**~house** *n* house built at the side of, or over, a ~, eg at the entrance to a park, the house being used by a '~*keeper.* 门房 (例如公园入口处供守门人所用者)。,**~legged** '**table**, table with legs that can be moved out to support a folding top. (桌脚可拉开以支撑折迭式桌面的)折迭式桌子。'**~ money** *n* total sum paid for admission to a public spectacle in a stadium, etc. 入场费。'**~post** *n* post on which a ~ is hung or against which it is closed. 门柱。*between you (and) me and the* ~-**post**, in strict confidence. 极秘密的; 严守秘密的。'**~way** *n* way in or out that can be closed by a ~ or ~-post, etc; (fig) means of approach: 门口; 通路; (喻)接近的手段: *a* ~*way to fame/ knowledge.* 求取名誉(知识)之门径。**2** = ~ **money**, ⇨ 1 above. 参看上列第 1 义。**3** '**starting** ~, barrier

a gate-legged table

(either of horizontal ropes that are lifted or of rows of stalls with barriers) at the start of a horse or greyhound race. (赛马或赛狗时的)起跑门; 起赛栅门。□ *vt* [VP 6A] confine (a student) to college or school (as a penalty). (大学或中学)禁止(学生)外出(作为惩罚)。

gâ·teau /'gætəʊ US: gæ'toʊ; ga'to/ *n* (*pl* ~**x** /-təʊz; -toz/ or ~**s**) (F) rich fancy cake, often served in slices. (法)一种味浓特制的糕饼(常切成片食用)。

gather /'gæðə(r); 'gæðə/ *vt*, *vi* **1** [VP6A, 15A, B, 2 A, C] get, come or bring together: 集合; 聚集: *He soon* ~*ed a crowd round him.* 他不久便聚合了一群人在他周围。*A crowd soon* ~*ed round him.* 一群人不久便聚集在他的周围。*The clouds are* ~*ing; it's going to rain.* 云在集结, 天要下雨了。*be* ~*ed to one's fathers,* (liter or rhet) die. (文或修辞)死。**2** [VP6A, 12B, 13B] pick (flowers, etc); collect: 采集(花等); 收集: ~ *one's papers and books together.* 将文件和书籍收集起来。*Please* ~ *me some flowers/* ~ *some flowers for me.* 请为我采一些花。**3** [VP6A] obtain gradually; gain little by little: 逐渐获得; 渐增: ~ *information/impressions/experience.* 逐渐获得消息(印象, 经验)。*The train* ~*ed speed as it left the station.* 火车离站时速度渐增。**4** [VP6A, 19] understand; conclude: 了解; 推断: *What did you* ~ *from his statement?* 你推想他的声明是什么意思? *I* ~, *from what you say, that….* 从你的话中, 我得到的结论是…。**5** [VP6A, 15A, B] (in sewing) pull together into small folds by putting a thread through; draw parts of material, a garment closer together: (缝纫)缝长褶; 打褶: *a skirt* ~*ed at the waist.* 腰部打褶的裙子。**6** [VP2 A] (of an abscess or boil) form pus and swell up; come to a head. (指脓肿或疖)化脓; 出头。~·**ing** *n* [C] **1** coming together of people; meeting. 聚集; 集合。**2** swelling with pus in it. 脓肿。

gauche /gəʊʃ; goʃ/ *adj* socially awkward; tactless. 不善交际的; 不圆滑的; 无手腕的。**gauch·erie** /'gəʊʃərɪ US: ,gəʊʃə'riː; ,goʃə'ri/ *n* [U] ~ behaviour; [C] ~ act, movement, etc. 不善交际; 无手腕; 笨拙的行动。

gaucho /'gautʃəʊ; 'gautʃo/ *n* (*pl* ~**s**) cowboy of mixed European and American Indian descent. 有欧洲与美洲印第安人混合血统的牧人。

gaud /gɔːd; gɔd/ *n* [C] showy ornament. 华丽的装饰物。

gaudy[1] /'gɔːdɪ; 'gɔdɪ/ *adj* (**-ier**, **-iest**) too bright and showy; gay or bright in a tasteless way: 炫丽的; 华丽而俗气的: ~ *decorations;* 华而俗气的装饰品; *cheap and* ~ *jewels.* 价廉而炫丽的珠宝。**gaud·ily** /-ɪlɪ; -əlɪ/ *adv*

gaudy[2] /'gɔːdɪ; 'gɔdɪ/ *n* annual college dinner, given to former members. 大学每年为校友举行的宴会。

gauge (US also **gage**) /geɪdʒ; gedʒ/ *n* **1** [U] standard measure; extent: 标准度量; 程度: 范围: *take the* ~ *of (eg sb's character),* estimate, judge. 估计; 判断(某人的品行等)。**2** [U, C] distance between rails (or between opposite wheels on a vehicle that runs on rails): 铁道两轨间的距离; 轨距; 轨幅: *standard* ~; 标准轨距; *broad* ~, more than 4 ft 8¹/₂ in.; 宽轨(宽于 4 英尺 8.5 英寸); *narrow* ~, less than 3 ft 8¹/₂in. 窄轨(窄于 3 英尺 8.5 英寸)。**3** [U] thickness of wire, sheet-metal, etc; diameter of a bullet, etc. 金属线的直径; 金属板的厚度; 子弹等的直径。**4** [C] instrument for measuring, eg rainfall, strength of wind, size, diameter, etc of tools, wire, etc. 计量器(例如雨量计, 风力计, 量度工具, 金属线等的大小、直径等的仪器): ~ *the diameter of wire/the contents of a barrel/the strength of the wind;* 计量金属线的直径(桶之容积, 雨量, 风力); (fig) make an estimate, form a judgement, of: (喻)估计; 判断: ~ *a person's character.* 估量一人的品格。

Gaul /gɔːl; gɔl/ *n* Celt of ancient ~ (the area now known as France and Belgium). 高卢人 (古代高卢地区之克尔特人, 所居地区即现今之法国和比利时)。

gaunt /gɔːnt; gɔnt/ *adj* (of a person) lean, haggard, as from hunger, ill-health or suffering; (of a place)

grim or desolate: (指人)憔悴的; 形容枯槁的; 枯萎的(如因饥饿, 不健康或受苦而形成的); (指地方)荒凉的: *a ~ hillside*. 荒凉的山坡。 ⇨·**ness** *n*

gaunt·let¹ /ˈɡɔːntlɪt; ˈɡɔntlɪt/ *n* **1** glove with metal plates worn by soldiers in the Middle Ages. (中古士卒所戴的)铁手套。 ⇨ the illus at armour. 参看 armour 之插图。 **throw down / pick up / take up the ~**, give/ accept a challenge to a fight. 挑(应)战。 **2** strong glove with a wide cuff covering the wrist, used for driving, fencing, etc. (驾驶, 击剑等所戴的)宽口大手套。

gaunt·let² /ˈɡɔːntlɪt; ˈɡɔntlɪt/ *n* (only in) (仅用于) **run the ~**, run between two rows of men who strike the victim as he passes; (fig) be exposed to continuous severe criticism, risk, danger: 在两排人中跑过并受众人夹笞; (喻)受严厉批评; 冒大险: *He ran the ~ of their criticism / scorn*. 他受到他们严厉的批评(尖刻的嘲笑)。

gauze /ɡɔːz; ɡɔz/ *n* [U] thin, transparent net-like material of silk, cotton, etc (for medical use) or of wire (for screening windows against insects, etc). 薄纱; 纱布 (医用); 铁纱; 纱网(做纱窗等用者)。 **gauzy** *adj*

gave /ɡeɪv; ɡev/ *pt* of **give**.

gavel /ˈɡævl; ˈɡævl/ *n* hammer used by an auctioneer or a chairman as a signal for order or attention. 拍卖者或主席所用的槌。

ga·votte /ɡəˈvɒt; ɡəˈvɑt/ *n* [C] (music for an) old French dance like the minuet but more lively. 嘉禾舞 (昔时法国一种似小步舞而更为活泼的一种舞蹈); 嘉禾舞曲。

gawk /ɡɔːk; ɡɔk/ *n* awkward or bashful person. 笨拙或害羞的人。 **~y** *adj* (**-ier, -iest**) (of persons) awkward, bashful, ungainly. (指人)笨拙的; 害羞的; 愚蠢的。 **~i·ness** *n*

gawp /ɡɔːp; ɡɔp/ *vi* [VP2A, 3A] **~ (at)**, look at in an intense, foolish way: 呆呆地看: *What are they all ~ing at?* 他们都在呆呆地看什么?

gay /ɡeɪ; ɡe/ *adj* (**-er, -est**) **1** light-hearted; cheerful; happy and full of fun: 快乐的; 愉快的; 欢欣的: *the gay voices of young children*; 小孩们欢乐的声音; *gay looks / laughter*. 快乐的表情 (笑声)。 **2** suggesting happiness and joy: 表示快乐的: *gay colours*; 轻快的音乐; *gay colours*; 缤纷的色彩; *streets that were gay with flags*. 旗帜飘扬的街道。 **3** (colloq) homosexual. (口)同性恋爱的。 □ *n* [C] (colloq) homosexual. (口)同性恋的人。 **gaily** /ˈɡeɪlɪ; ˈɡelɪ/ *adv* in a gay manner. 快乐地; 欢欣地。 **gay·ness** *n*

gaze /ɡeɪz; ɡez/ *n* (*sing* only) long, steady look: (仅用单数)凝视; 注视: *with a bewildered ~*. 以茫然的凝视。 □ *vi* [VP2A, C, 3A] **~ (at)**, look long and steadily: 凝视; 注视: *What are you gazing at?* 你在凝视什么? *Stop gazing round*. 不要左顾右盼。 **~ on / upon**, (formal) set eyes on: (正式用语)看: *She was the most beautiful woman he had ever ~d upon*. 她是他所见过的最美丽的女子。

ga·zelle /ɡəˈzel; ɡəˈzel/ *n* small, graceful kind of antelope. 小羚羊; 瞪羚。

ga·zette /ɡəˈzet; ɡəˈzet/ *n* **1** official periodical with legal notices, news of appointments, promotions, etc of officers and officials. 政府的公报。 **2** (as part of a title) newspaper: 报纸(作为报纸名称之一部分): *the Marlowe G~*. 马洛报。 □ *vt* (usu passive) (通常用被动语态) **be ~d**, be published in the official ~: 刊载于公报上: (of an army officer) *be ~d to a regiment*. (指军官)刊载于公报上被调派至某团任职。

ga·zet·teer /ˌɡæzəˈtɪə(r); ˌɡæzəˈtɪr/ *n* index of geographical names, eg at the end of an atlas. 地名索引(例如附于地图集之后者)。

ga·zump /ɡəˈzʌmp; ɡəˈzʌmp/ *vi, vt* [VP2A, 6A] (colloq) cheat by increasing the price demanded for property between the date of acceptance of an offer and the date for signing the contract. (口)出售房地产价格议成后于签约前提高价钱。

gear /ɡɪə(r); ɡɪr/ *n* **1** [C] set of toothed wheels

working together in a machine, esp such a set to connect the engine of a motor-vehicle with the road wheels: 齿轮组(尤指联系汽车引擎与车轮者); 汽车之排档: *change ~*; 换排档; particular state of adjustment of such a set: 排档之排列: *a car with five ~s, first, second, third, fourth and reverse*. 一辆有五档的汽车, 即头档, 二档, 三档, 四档和倒档。 ⇨ the illus at **bicycle, motor**. 参看 bicycle, motor 之插图。 **high / low ~**, mechanism causing the driven part to move relatively fast / slowly, low ~ being used when starting, or when driving on a steep hill. 高(低)速齿轮; 高(低)速排档。 **in / out of ~**, engaged / disengaged from the mechanism. 搭上(脱下)齿轮。 **top / bottom ~**, highest / lowest ~. 最高(低)速齿轮。 **'~-box / -case**, case that encloses the ~ mechanism. (汽车等之)齿轮箱。 **~-shift / lever / stick**, device for engaging or disengaging ~s. 操纵杆(变速杆)。 **2** [C] apparatus, appliance, mechanism, arrangement, of wheels, levers, etc for a special purpose: 轮与杠杆等装置: *the 'steering-~ of a ship*; 船只的操舵机; *the 'landing-~ of an aircraft*. 飞机的起落架。 **3** [U] equipment in general: 装备; 用具: *'hunting-~*; 狩猎用具; (modern colloq) clothes: (现代口语)衣服: *party ~*. 宴(舞)会穿的衣服。 □ *vt, vi* [VP15A, 14, 2 A, C, 3A] **~ up / down**, (= change up / down) put into a higher / lower ~. 换快(慢)速齿轮相连; 开快(慢)车。 **~ to**, adjust one thing to the working of another, make dependent on: 使一物的作用与另一物搭配: *The country's economics must be ~ed to wartime requirements*. 这国家的经济必须配合战时的需要。

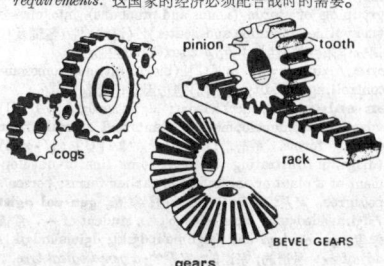

gears

gecko /ˈɡekəʊ; ˈɡeko/ *n* (*pl* ~s, ~es /-kəʊz; -koz/) kind of small house lizard, found in warm countries. (热带国家房中所见到的)壁虎类。

gee¹ (also **gee-up**) /ˌdʒiːˈʌp; ˌdʒi(ˈʌp)/ *int* (command to a horse) go on; go faster. (驭马用语)前进! 加快! **gee-gee** /ˈdʒiː dʒiː; ˈdʒidʒi/ *n* (child's word for a) horse. (小儿语)马。

gee² (also **gee whiz**) /ˌdʒiː ˈwɪz; ˌdʒi ˈwɪz/ *int* (US) mild exclamation indicating surprise, admiration, etc: (美)啊(表示惊奇, 赞赏等的感叹语): *Gee, I like your new hat!* 啊! 我喜欢你的新帽子!

geese /ɡiːs; ɡis/ *n pl* of **goose**.

geezer /ˈɡiːzə(r); ˈɡizɚ/ *n* (sl) (old) person, esp if eccentric. (俚)(老)人(尤指古怪的)。

Geiger /ˈɡaɪɡə(r); ˈɡaɪɡɚ/ *n* (esp 尤用于'**~ counter**) metal tube containing an electrode, used for detecting and measuring radio-activity. 盖氏计算器(为含有电极的金属管, 用以测量放射作用)。

geisha /ˈɡeɪʃə; ˈɡeʃə/ *n* Japanese girl or woman trained to entertain men by singing and dancing at parties, etc. (日本的)艺妓。

gel /dʒel; dʒel/ *n* semisolid like a jelly. 凝胶; 胶滞体。 □ *vi* (**-ll-**) **1** set into a jelly. 成为凝胶状; 胶化。 **2** = **jell**.

gela·tine /ˌdʒeləˈtiːn US: ˈdʒelətɪn; ˈdʒelətɪn/ (also 亦作 **gela·tin** /ˈdʒelətɪn; ˈdʒelətṇ/) *n* [U] clear, tasteless substance, made by boiling bones and waste parts of animals, dissolved in water to make jelly. 明

胶; 骨胶。动物胶。**gel·ati·nous** /dʒi'lætɪnəs; dʒə-'lætənəs/ adj of or like ～; jelly-like in consistency, etc. 骨胶的; 似骨胶的; 胶质的: 胶状的。

geld /geld; geld/ vt [VP6A] castrate. 阉割; 去势。～**·ing** n ～ed animal, esp a horse. 被阉割的动物(尤指马)。

gel·ig·nite /'dʒelɪgnaɪt; dʒelɪg,naɪt/ n [U] explosive made from nitric acid and glycerine. 爆炸胶(一种含有硝酸和甘油的炸药)。

gem /dʒem; dʒem/ n 1 precious stone or jewel, esp cut or polished. 宝石; 珠宝。2 sth valued because of great beauty; sth much prized: 珍爱的美丽之物; 珍贵之物: the gem of the collection, the most valued item in it. 所搜集物品中之逸品。**gemmed** part adj adorned with, or as with, gems: 似饰有宝石的: the night sky, gemmed with stars. 点缀着晶莹的星星的夜空。

Gem·ini /'dʒemɪnɪ; 'dʒemə,naɪ/ n third sign of the zodiac. 双子星座; 双子宫。⇨ the illus at **zodiac**. 参看zodiac之插图。

gen /dʒen; dʒen/ n (sl) (the) gen, information. (俚)情报。□ vt [VP15B] gen up, provide with information. 供以情报。

gen·darme /'ʒɒndɑːm; 'ʒɑndɑrm/ n (in France and some other countries, but not GB or US) member of a military force employed in police duties. (在法国或其他国家, 但非英美的)宪兵。～**·rie** /ʒɒn'dɑːmərɪ; ʒɑn-'dɑrmərɪ/ n (collective sing) force of ～s. (集合名词单数)宪兵队。

gen·der /'dʒendə(r); 'dʒendə/ n 1 grammatical grouping of words (nouns and pronouns) into classes (masculine, feminine and neuter). (语法)性(名词及代词分作阳性, 阴性与中性)。2 sex(1). 性别。

gene /dʒiːn; dʒin/ n [C] (biol) unit in chromosome controlling heredity. (生物)遗传因子; 基因。

gen·eal·ogy /,dʒiːnɪ'ælədʒɪ; ,dʒinɪ'ælədʒɪ/ n 1 [U] science of the development of plants and animals from earlier forms. 系谱学; 系谱学。2 [C] (pl -gies) (diagram illustrating the) descent or line of development of a plant or animal from earlier forms; person's pedigree. 家系; 血统; 宗谱; 系谱; 家谱。**gen·eal·ogist** /,dʒiːnɪ'ælədʒɪst; ,dʒinɪ'ælədʒɪst/ n student of ～. 系谱学者。**genea·logi·cal** /,dʒiːnɪə'lɒdʒɪkl; ,dʒinɪə'lɒdʒɪkl/ adj of ～: 系谱的; 宗谱的; 家系的: a genealogical tree, a diagram (a table like a tree with branches showing the descent of a family or species. 家谱; 系谱图。**genea·logi·cally** /-klɪ; -klɪ/ adv

gen·era /'dʒenərə; 'dʒenərə/ n pl of **genus**.

gen·eral /'dʒenrəl; 'dʒenərəl/ adj 1 of, affecting, all or nearly all; not special, local or particular: 普遍的; 全面的; 非特殊或地方性的; 一般人的: a matter of ～ interest, one in which all or most people are likely to be interested; 引起大众兴趣的事; a ～ meeting, one to which all members (of a society, etc) are invited; 全体大会; a ～ strike, one by workmen of all, or nearly all, the trade unions; 集体罢工; 总罢工; a good ～ education, in all the chief subjects; 良好的普通教育; a word that is in ～ use, used by all people; 一般人普遍使用的一个词; the ～ opinion on this subject, what most people think about it. 大多数人对此问题的意见。The cold weather has been ～, has been experienced in all or most parts of the country. 这些时全国大部分地区天气寒冷。as a ～ rule: in ～, in most cases; usually. 概言之; 一般说来; 通常。'～ degree, nonspecialist university degree involving a course in two or more subjects. 普通学位(在大学专修两个或多个专业所得的大学学位)。'～ 'election, one for representatives in Parliament from the whole country. 大选。Cf 参较 by-election, local election. ～ 'knowledge, of a wide variety of subjects. 一般知识; 各方面的知识。Cf 参较 common knowledge, knowledge (of a particular fact, etc) possessed by every member of a class or community of people. 常识。～ 'practice, work of a ～ prac'titioner (abbr 略作 GP),

(GB) doctor who is not a specialist or consultant. (英)全科医师(非专科医生)的业务。2 not in detail; not definite: 概括的; 大概的: a ～ outline of a scheme, 一个计划的大纲; have a ～ idea of what a book is about; 对一本书的内容有一概括的观念; explain something in ～ terms. 概括地说明某事物。3 (after an official title) chief: (用于官衔后)首要的: ,postmaster-'～, 邮务部长; in,spector-'～. 首席监察官; 督察署署长。□ n army officer with the highest rank below Field Marshal (and also, by courtesy, of Lieu,tenant-'～ and ,Major-'～) 陆军上将; 将官(礼貌上亦指中将及少将)。

gen·er·al·is·simo /,dʒenərə'lɪsɪməu; ,dʒenərəl'ɪsə,mo/ n (pl ～s) commander of combined military and naval and air forces, or of combined armies. 大元帅; 司令官。最高统帅。

gen·er·al·ity /,dʒenə'rælətɪ; ,dʒenə'rælətɪ/ n (pl -ties) 1 [C] general rule or statement; vague or indefinite remark, etc: 通则; 概论; 概说: I wish you would come down from generalities to particularities. 希望你不要谈一般性的, 谈谈特殊的。2 [U] the ～ (of), majority or greater part: 大多数; 大部分: The ～ Swedes are blonde. 大多数瑞典人都是头发金黄皮肤白皙的。3 [U] quality of being general: 普遍性; 一般性: a rule of great ～, one with few exceptions. 普遍性的法则。

gen·er·al·iz·ation /,dʒenrəlaɪ'zeɪʃn US: -lɪ'z-; ,dʒenərəle'zeʃən/ n 1 [U] generalizing: 一般化; 归纳; 概论: It is unwise to be hasty in ～. 急于归纳是不明智的。2 [C] statement or proposition obtained by generalizing, esp one based on too few examples. 概括的叙述或命题(尤指根据很少的例子而作的)。

gen·er·al·ize /'dʒenrəlaɪz; 'dʒenərəl,aɪz/ vi, vt 1 [VP2A, 3A] ～ (from), draw a general conclusion; make a general statement. 归纳; 泛论。2 [VP6A, 14]. ～ (from), state (sth) in general terms or principles: 概括地说(某事物): draw a conclusion from a collection of instances or facts. 从一些事例中做出结论。3 [VP6A] bring into general use: 推广; 普及: ～ the use of a new invention. 推广一新发明物的使用。

gen·er·ally /'dʒenrəlɪ; 'dʒenərəlɪ/ adv (usu with the finite v) (通常与限定动词连用) 1 usually; as a general rule: 通常: I ～ get up at six o'clock. 我通常六时起床。2 widely; for the most part: 广泛地; 普通地: The new plan was ～ welcomed, was welcomed by most people. 新计划受到普通的欢迎。3 in a general sense; without paying attention to details: 一般地; 概括地: ～ speaking. 一般言之。

gen·er·ate /'dʒenəreɪt; 'dʒenə,ret/ vt [VP6A] cause to exist or occur; produce: 使发生; 产生: ～ heat; electricity; 生热(发电); hatred ～d by racial prejudices. 因种族偏见而产生的仇恨。

gen·er·ation /,dʒenə'reɪʃn; ,dʒenə'reʃən/ n 1 [U] generating; bringing into existence: 产生; 发生: the ～ of electricity by steam or water-power; 用蒸汽或水力发电; the ～ of heat by friction. 摩擦生热。2 [C] single stage or step in family descent: 家族中的一代; 一世: three ～s, children, parents, grandparents. 三代(儿女, 父母, 祖父母)。3 [C] average period (regarded as 30 years) in which children grow up, marry, and have children: 一代(自子女长成, 结婚再生子女, 通常为三十年): a ～ ago. 一代以前。'～ gap, ⇨ gap(2). 4 [C] all persons born about the same time, and, therefore, of about the same age: 同时代的人: the present/past/ coming ～; 现在(过去, 未来)的一代人; the rising ～, the young ～. 青年。

gen·er·at·ive /'dʒenərətɪv; 'dʒenə,retɪv/ adj able to produce; productive. 能生产的; 有生产力的。

gen·er·ator /'dʒenəreɪtə(r); 'dʒenə,retə/ n [C] machine or apparatus that generates (electricity, steam, gas, vapour, etc) (US 美 = dynamo). 发电机; 蒸汽发生器; 发生器。

gen·eric /dʒɪ'nerɪk; dʒə'nɛrɪk/ adj of a genus;

common to a whole group or class, not special. 属的；类的；一般的。 **gen·eri·cally** /-klɪ; -klɪ/ adv

gen·er·os·ity /ˌdʒenəˈrɒsɪtɪ; ˌdʒenəˈrɑsətɪ/ n **1** [U] the quality of being generous; nobility of mind; greatness of heart: 慷慨；大度；宽大：show ~ in dealing with a defeated enemy. 对一战败敌人表示宽大。 **2** [C] (pl **-ties**) generous act, etc. 慷慨的行为，宽大的行为。

gen·er·ous /ˈdʒenərəs; ˈdʒenərəs/ adj **1** giving, ready to give, freely; given freely; noble-minded: 慷慨的；大方的；宽大的；思想高尚的：He is ~ with his money/~ in giving help. 他用钱大方(慷于助人)。 It was ~ of them to share their house with the refugees. 他们真慷慨，让难民住在他们家里。 What a ~ gift! 多么大方的礼物啊！ He has a ~ nature. 他禀性宽厚。 **2** plentiful: 丰富的：a ~ helping of meat and vegetables; 一份丰富的肉和蔬菜；a ~ harvest. 丰收。 ~·ly adv

gen·esis /ˈdʒenɪsɪs; ˈdʒenəsɪs/ n **1** beginning; starting-point: 开始；起源：the ~ of civilization. 文明的起源。 **2** G~, the first book of the Old Testament. (旧约)创世纪。

gen·etic /dʒɪˈnetɪk; dʒəˈnɛtɪk/ adj of genes; of ~s. 遗传因子的；遗传的。 **gen·etics** n pl (with sing v) science (branch of biology) dealing with heredity, the ways in which characteristics are passed on from parents to offspring. (与单数动词连用)遗传学；发生学(生物学之一支)。 **gen·eti·cist** /dʒɪˈnetɪsɪst; dʒəˈnɛtəsɪst/ n specialist in ~s. 遗传学家。

ge·nial /ˈdʒiːnɪəl; ˈdʒinjəl/ adj **1** kindly, sympathetic; sociable: 亲切的；和蔼的；友善的：a ~ old man; 一位和蔼的老人；~ smiles; 亲切的微笑；under the ~ influence of good wine. 在好酒暖意之下。 **2** favourable to growth; mild; warm: 利于生长的；温和的；温暖的：a ~ climate; 温和的气候；~ sunshine. 和煦的阳光。 ~·ly adv ~·ity /ˌdʒiːnɪˈælətɪ; ˌdʒinɪˈælətɪ/ n [U] quality of being ~; [C] (pl **-ties**) ~ look, act, utterance, etc. 亲切；和蔼；温和；亲切的表情，行动，言谈等。

ge·nie /ˈdʒiːnɪ; ˈdʒinɪ/ n (pl ~s or genii /ˈdʒiːnɪaɪ; ˈdʒiːnɪˌaɪ/) (in Arabic stories) spirit or goblin with strange powers. (阿拉伯故事中的)神怪；妖怪。

geni·tal /ˈdʒenɪtl; ˈdʒenətl/ adj of generation(1) or of animal reproductive organs. 生产的；生殖的；生殖器的。 ~s n pl external sex organs. 外阴部；生殖器。

geni·tive /ˈdʒenətɪv; ˈdʒenɪtɪv/ adj ~ (case), (gram) showing source or possession. (语法)所有格；属格。

gen·ius /ˈdʒiːnɪəs; ˈdʒinjəs/ n (pl ~es, but ⇨ **5** below 参看下列第 5 义) **1** [U] great and exceptional capacity of the mind or imagination; creative or inventive capacity: 天才；创造能力：men of ~. 有天才的人。 **2** [C] person having this capacity: 天才；才子：Einstein was a mathematical ~. 爱因斯坦是一位数学天才。 **3** a ~ for, natural ability for: 天资；天赋：have a ~ for languages/acting/making friends. 有语言(表演，交友)的才能。 **4** the ~ (of), guardian spirit of a person, place or institution, (hence, by extension) special and inborn character, spirit or principles of a language, a period of time, an institution, etc; prevalent feeling, opinions, taste, etc of a race of people: 守护神；保佑的神灵；(由此引申)语言，时代，制度等的民族的特征：the French ~; 法国人的特征；the ~ of the British Constitution/the Renaissance period in Italy. 英国宪法(意大利的文艺复兴时期)的精神。 ~ loci /ˈləʊsaɪ; ˈləʊsaɪ/ n (sing only) (Lat) associations, atmosphere, etc of a place. (仅用单数)(拉)一地方的风气。 **5** (pl genii /ˈdʒiːnɪaɪ; ˈdʒinɪˌaɪ/) supernatural being. 神灵；精灵。 one's good/evil ~, spirit or angel working for one's salvation/damnation; person who has a strong influence upon one for good/ill. 使人得救的神(使人堕灭的魔鬼)；予人以好(坏)影响的人。

geno·cide /ˈdʒenəsaɪd; ˈdʒenəˌsaɪd/ n [U] extermination of a race or community by mass murder, or by imposing conditions that make survival impossible. 种族灭绝；灭绝种族的屠杀。

genre /ˈʒɑːnrə; ˈʒɑnrə/ n **1** (F) kind; style; category (esp of literary form, eg poetry, drama, the novel). (法)种类；式样；类型(尤指诗歌，戏剧，小说等文学上的形式)。 **2** (also attrib '~-painting) portrayal of scenes, etc, from ordinary life. 浮世绘；以日常生活为题材的绘画；世态画。

gent /dʒent; dʒent/ n (colloq abbr of) gentleman. (口)绅士(为 gentleman 之略)。 **the /a G~s** n (GB colloq) public toilet for men. (英口)公共男厕。

gen·teel /dʒenˈtiːl; dʒenˈtil/ adj (usu ironic in modern use, but serious in former use) polite and well-bred; elegant; characteristic of, suitable for, the upper classes of society: (近代用法通常为反语，但昔时为认真的用语)有教养的；文雅的；有上流社会之特点的；适于上流社会的：living in ~ poverty, trying to maintain the style of the upper classes, although too poor to do so. 过着穷苦而摆阔的生活；打肿脸充胖子。 ~·ly adv

gen·tian /ˈdʒenʃn; ˈdʒenʃən/ n (kind of usu) blue-flowered plant growing in mountainous districts. 龙胆属植物(生于山区，通常开蓝花)；龙胆；陵游。

gen·tile /ˈdʒentaɪl; ˈdʒentaɪl/ n, adj (person) not Jewish. 非犹太人；非犹太人的。

gen·til·ity /dʒenˈtɪlətɪ; dʒenˈtɪlətɪ/ n [U] state of being genteel: 有教养；文雅：living in shabby ~, trying, without real success, to keep up an appearance of being genteel. 硬充上流。

gentle /ˈdʒentl; ˈdʒentl/ adj (**-r, -st**) **1** mild, quiet, careful; not rough, violent, severe: 和善的；友善的；温柔的；温和的；文雅的；轻柔的：a ~ nature/heart/look/voice/call/touch; 温和的性情(仁慈的心肠)和善的面貌；柔和的声音；低声的呼唤；轻轻的触摸；~ manners; 温和的态度；a ~ breeze; 和风；a ~ heat, ie not too hot; 暖和；a ~ slope, ie not steep. 不太陡的斜坡。 **2** (of a family) with good social position: (指家庭)有社会地位的：a person of ~ birth. 出身名门的人。 ~·folk n pl persons of ~ birth. 出身名门的人；有身分的人；上流人士。 ~·ness n

gentle·man /ˈdʒentlmən; ˈdʒentlˌmən/ n (pl **-men** /-mən; -mən/) **1** man who shows consideration for the feelings of others, who is honourable and courteous. 绅士；君子；~'s agreement, one that is binding in honour, but cannot be enforced at law. 君子协定。 **2** (hist) man of good family attached to a court or the household of a great noble: (史)国王或贵族的侍从：one of the king's gentlemen. 国王的一位侍从。 ~-at-'arms, one of the sovereign's bodyguard. 国王的侍卫。 **3** (hist) man entitled to bear arms but not a member of the nobility. (史)有资格从军的平民。 **4** (dated use) man of wealth and social position, esp one who does not work for a living: (过时用语) 有钱和社会地位的人 (尤指无需工作以谋生者)：'What does he do for a living?'——'Nothing; he's a ~.' '他做什么谋生？'——'什么也不做，他是个有钱不需工作的人。' ~ 'farmer, ~ who has a farm, but does no manual work himself. (拥有农场，但不从事体力工作的)乡绅。 **5** polite form of address to men (eg in an audience): 诸位先生(对男性听众的礼称)：Gentlemen! 诸位先生！ Ladies and Gentlemen! 诸位女士和先生！ Also used instead of Sirs or Dear Sirs when writing to a business firm, etc. (在商业信件中亦代替Sirs 或 Dear Sirs)。 ~·ly adj feeling, behaving, or looking like a ~: 绅士风度的；似绅士的；合乎绅士的：a ~(1): suitable or right for a ~(1): a ~ly apology. 绅士似的道歉。

gentle·woman /ˈdʒentlwʊmən; ˈdʒentlˌwʊmən/ n (pl **-women** /-wɪmɪn; -ˌwɪmɪn/) lady. 女士；淑女；贵妇。

gent·ly /ˈdʒentlɪ; ˈdʒentlɪ/ adv in a gentle manner: 和善地；温和地；温柔地；轻轻地：Hold it ~, carefully. 小心地拿着它。 Speak ~ (= softly, kindly) to the child. 对孩子温和地谈话。 The road slopes ~ (= gradually) to the sea. 那条路逐渐向海边倾斜下去。

gen·try /ˈdʒentrɪ; ˈdʒentrɪ/ n pl (**the**) people of

good social position next below the nobility. 绅士; 上等人。 **gen·tri·fy** /'dʒentrɪfaɪ; 'dʒɛntrɪ,faɪ/ vt [VP6A] (colloq) modernize, smarten, restore (a house, area, etc) to make suitable for middle-class occupiers: (口)将(一房屋、地区等)现代化, 翻新, 改建(俾适于中产阶级之人居住): *the gentrifying of inner city working-class districts*. 市中心劳工住宅区的现代化。

genu·flect /'dʒenjuːflekt; 'dʒɛnju,flɛkt/ vi [VP2A] bend the knee, esp in worship. 屈膝(尤指礼拜); 跪拜。 **genu·flec·tion, genu·flex·ion** /,dʒenjuː'flekʃn; ,dʒɛnju-'flɛkʃən/ nn

genu·ine /'dʒenjʊɪn; 'dʒɛnjʊɪn/ adj true; really what it is said to be: 真正的; 真实的: *a ~ picture by Rubens*; 鲁宾斯的真迹(画); *~ pearls*; 真珍珠; *~ sorrow*; 真正的悲戚; *a ~ signature*. 亲笔签名。 **~·ly** adv **~·ness** n

ge·nus /'dʒiːnəs; 'dʒinəs/ n (pl **genera** /'dʒenərə; 'dʒɛnərə/) **1** (biol) division of animals or plants within a family: (生物) (动植物的)类; 属: *~ 'Homo* /'həʊməʊ; 'homo/, mankind. 人类。 **2** sort; kind; class. 种类。

geo- /,dʒiːəʊ; ,dʒio/ pref (form of Greek word for 'earth', used in combinations): (希腊词)形, 表示'地'或'地球'之义,用于复合词中): **geo·cen·tric** /,dʒiːəʊ'sentrɪk; ,dʒio'sɛntrɪk/ adj having or representing the earth as centre. 以地球为中心的。 **geo·phys·ics** /,dʒiːəʊ'fɪzɪks; ,dʒio'fɪzɪks/ n pl (sing v) study of the earth's magnetism, meteorology, etc. (接单数动词)地球物理学。 **geo·physi·cal** /-'fɪzɪkl; -'fɪzɪkl/ adj **geo·poli·tics** /,dʒiːəʊ'pɒlətɪks; ,dʒio'pɑlətɪks/ n pl (sing v) country's politics as determined by its geographical position. (接单数动词)地缘政治学。

ge·ogra·phy /dʒɪ'ɒɡrəfɪ; dʒi'ɑɡrəfɪ/ n [U] science of the earth's surface, physical features, divisions, climate, products, population, etc. 地理学。 **geo·gra·pher** /dʒɪ'ɒɡrəfə(r); dʒi'ɑɡrəfɚ/ n authority on ~. 地理学家。 **geo·graphi·cal** /,dʒiːə'ɡræfɪkl; ,dʒiə'ɡræfɪkl/ adj of ~. 地理学的。 **geo·graphi·cally** /-klɪ; -klɪ/ adv

ge·ol·ogy /dʒɪ'ɒlədʒɪ; dʒi'ɑlədʒɪ/ n [U] science of the earth's history as shown by its crust, rocks, etc. 地质学。 **ge·ol·ogist** /dʒɪ'ɒlədʒɪst; dʒi'ɑlədʒɪst/ n authority on ~. 地质学家。 **geo·logi·cal** /,dʒiːə'lɒdʒɪkl; ,dʒiə'lɑdʒɪkl/ adj of ~. 地质学的。 **geo·logi·cally** /-klɪ; -klɪ/ adv

ge·ometry /dʒɪ'ɒmɪtrɪ; dʒi'ɑmətrɪ/ n [U] science of the properties and relations of lines, angles, surfaces and solids. 几何学。 **geo·met·ric, -metri·cal** /,dʒiːə-'metrɪk(l); ,dʒiə'mɛtrɪk(l)/ adj of ~; of or like the lines, figures, etc used in ~: 几何学的; 几何学中所用的线条, 图形等的; 似几何线条图形等的: *geometrical patterns*. 几何图案。 **geo,metrical pro'gression**, series of numbers with a constant ratio between successive quantities, the numbers either increasing by a common multiplier, or decreasing by a common divisor, as 1:3: 9:27:81. 几何级数: 等比级数(如 1:3:9:27:81)。 **geo·met·ri·cally** /-klɪ; -klɪ/ adv

George /dʒɔː; dʒɔrdʒ/ n **1** St ~, patron saint of England; 圣乔治(英国的守护神); *St '~'s day*, 23 Apr; 守护神日(四月二十三日); *St ,~'s 'Cross*, vertical and horizontal red bars crossing in the centre. 圣乔治十字(在中心交叉之红色十字形)。 ⇨ the illus at **flag**. 参看 flag 之插图。 **2** (sl) automatic pilot of aircraft. (俚)飞机的自动驾驶仪。 □ int *by ~l* (dated) exclamation of surprise, determination, etc. (过时用语) (表示惊讶、决心的感叹词)的确!

geor·gette /dʒɔː'dʒet; dʒɔr'dʒɛt/ n [U] thin silk dress material. 乔其纱(一种做衣料的薄绸纱)。

Geor·gian /'dʒɔːdʒən; 'dʒɔrdʒən/ adj **1** of the time (1714—1811) of any of the Kings George I, II and III of Britain: (一七一四至一八一一)英王乔治一世至三世时期的: (esp) (尤指) *~ architecture*. 英王乔治一世至三

世时期的建筑。 **2** of Geor·gia /'dʒɔːdʒə; 'dʒɔrdʒə/ (republic in USSR, of state in US). (苏联之)格鲁吉亚共和国的; (美国之)佐治亚州的。

ger·anium /dʒə'reɪnɪəm; dʒə'renɪəm/ n kind of garden plant with red, pink or white flowers. 天竺葵(长红色, 粉红色或白色的花)。

geri·atrics /,dʒerɪ'ætrɪks; ,dʒɛrɪ'ætrɪks/ n pl (sing v) medical care of old people. (接单数动词)老人医学; 老年卫生学。 **geri·atric** adj of ~: 老人医学的; 老年卫生学的: *the geriatric ward*, of a hospital. 老人病房。 **geria·tri·cian** /,dʒerɪə'trɪʃən; ,dʒɛrɪə'trɪʃən/ n expert in ~. 老人医学专家; 老人病科医师。

germ /dʒɜːm; dʒɝm/ n [C] **1** portion of a living organism capable of becoming a new organism; (fig) beginning or starting-point (of an idea, etc). 芽胞; 胚芽; 幼芽; (喻) (观念等的)起源; 根源。 **2** microbe or bacillus, esp one causing disease: 细菌; 病菌: *~ warfare*, use of bacteria as a weapon in war. 细菌战。

Ger·man /'dʒɜːmən; 'dʒɝmən/ adj of Germany and its people. 德国的; 德国人的。 **,~ 'shepherd** n (US) (美) = **Alsatian (dog)**. □ n native of Germany; language of the ~ people. 德国人; 德语。 **~ic** /dʒɜː'mænɪk; dʒɝ'mænɪk/ adj of the group of languages now including German, English and Dutch. 日耳曼语(现包括德, 英, 荷语的)。

ger·mane /dʒə'meɪn; dʒɝ'men/ adj ~ (to), relevant, pertinent (to). 适切的。

ger·mi·cide /'dʒɜːmɪsaɪd; 'dʒɝmə,saɪd/ n substance used to destroy germs (esp bacteria). 杀菌剂。

ger·mi·nate /'dʒɜːmɪneɪt; 'dʒɝmə,net/ vi, vt [VP 2A, 6A] (of seeds) (cause to) start growth. (指种子) (使)发芽; 萌芽。 **ger·mi·na·tion** /,dʒɜːmɪ'neɪʃn; ,dʒɝmə'neʃən/ n [U] germinating; sprouting. 发芽; 萌发。

ger·on·tol·ogy /,dʒerɒn'tɒlədʒɪ; ,dʒɛrən'talədʒɪ/ n [U] branch of science concerned with the processes of growing old, esp in human beings. (尤指人类)老年医学。

gerry·man·der /'dʒerɪ'mændə(r); 'dʒɛrɪ,mændɚ/ vt [VP6A] manipulate (a constituency, etc by division into voting areas) so as to give unfair advantages to one party or class in elections; practise trickery. 操纵(选举区, 如借划分)而为己党图利; 欺诈。 □ n such a falsification. 借划分操纵选举区而为己党图利; 欺诈。

ger·und /'dʒerənd; 'dʒɛrənd/ n **1** form of a verb when used as a noun. 动名词(动词用做名词的形式)。 **2** the -ing form of an English verb when used as a noun (as in 'fond of *swimming*'). (英语)动名词(由动词加–ing 形成, 如 fond of swimming 中之 swimming)。

Ges·tapo /ge'stɑːpəʊ; gə'stɑpo/ n German secret State police of the Nazi regime. 盖世太保(德国纳粹掌权时期的秘密警察)。

ges·ta·tion /dʒe'steɪʃn; dʒɛs'teʃən/ n carrying or being carried in the womb between conception and birth; this period. 怀孕; 怀孕期。

ges·ticu·late /dʒe'stɪkjuleɪt; dʒɛs'tɪkjə,let/ vi [VP 2A] use movements of the hands, arms or head instead of, or to accompany, speaking. 做表达情意的动作或姿态; 做手势等。 **ges·ticu·la·tion** /dʒe,stɪkju'leɪʃn; ,dʒɛstɪkjə'leʃən/ n [U] gesticulating; [C] movement used in this. 做表达情意的动作; 做手势; 表达情意的动作。

ges·ture /'dʒestʃə(r); 'dʒɛstʃə/ n **1** [C] movement of the hand or head to indicate or illustrate an idea, feeling, etc or sth done to convey a friendly intention: 手势; 姿态; 友善的表示: *a ~ of refusal*; 拒绝的手势; *make a friendly ~ to sb*. 向某人做友善的表示。 **2** [U] use of expressive movements: 表情的运用: *an actor who is a master of the art of ~*. 一个精于表情的演员。 □ vi [VP2A] gesticulate. 做表达情意的动作或姿态; 做手势等。

get /get; get/ *vt, vi* (*pt* **got** /gɒt; gɑt/, *pp* **got**, (US) **gotten** /'gɒtn; 'gɑtn/) (For uses with *adverbial particles* and *preps* ⇨ 15, 16, 17, below.) (与副词性小品词和介词连用的用法，参看下列第 15, 16, 17 义。) **1** [VP2D] (cause oneself to) become; pass from one state to another: (使自己)变成；变得: *get dressed/excited/lost/married/tired/wet.* 好穿衣服(变得兴奋；迷路；结婚；感到疲倦；变得潮湿)。 *He went out and got drunk.* 他到外面去喝醉了。*She'll soon get well/better again.* 她不久就会康复的。*You'll soon get used to the climate here.* 你不久即可适应此地的气候了。*It's time you got married.* 你该结婚了。*Get lost!* (sl) Go away! (俚)走开! **get even with sb,** ⇨ **even¹(3).** ⇨ also **wise¹. 2** [VP22, 24C] bring to a certain condition; cause to be or become: 使成为某种状态；使变成某种情况或结果: *She soon got the children ready for shool.* 她很快就给孩子们准备好让他们去上学。*I must get the breakfast ready/cooked.* 我必须准备好早餐。*Did you get the sum right,* produce the correct answer? 你算对了吗? *He got his wrist broken,* broke it by accident. 他折断了手腕。**get sth done,** complete it: 完成某事; 做好某事: *The farmer got his planting done before the rains came.* 那农民在雨季前完成了他的种植。**3** [VP2E] reach the stage where one is doing something: 达到(做某事)的阶段: *Get going!* Start! 开始! *It's time we got going,* made a start. 我们现在该开始了。*Things haven't really got going yet,* are not yet at the stage of full activity. 事情尚未展开(一切尚未充分活动)。*When these women get talking, they go on for hours.* 这些女人一谈便是几小时。**4** [VP19B] bring sb/sth to the point where he/it is doing sth: 使(人或物)达到时候之某一点: *Can you really get that old car going again,* restart or repair it? 你真的能发动(修好)那部旧车吗? *It's not hard to get the children talking; the problem is to stop them.* 让孩子们谈话不难，停止他们的谈话却有问题。*We'll soon get things going.* 我们不久便要展开活动。**5** [VP4A] reach the stage where one knows, feels, etc sth: 达到认识，感觉等之阶段: *When you get to know him you'll like him.* 等你了解他的时候，你就会喜欢他。*They soon got to be (= became) friends.* 他们不久便成了朋友。*After a time you get to realize that...* 一段时期你便会了解...。*One soon gets to like it here.* 一个人不久便会喜欢此地。*How did you get to know (= learn) that I was here?* 你怎么知道我在此地吗? **6** [VP17, 24C] bring, persuade, cause (sb/sth) to do sth or act in a certain way: 使(人或物)以某种方式做某事或行动: *You'll never get him to understand.* 你无法使他了解。*I can't get this old radio to work.* 我无法使这架旧收音机工作。*I can't get her to talk.* 我无法使她说话。*I can't get anyone to do the work/can't get the work done by anybody.* 我找不到人做这工作。(Cf 参较 *I must get my hair cut/get somebody to cut my hair.* 我必须去理发。) **7** [VP6A, 14] **get sth (of),** receive; have; obtain; procure; acquire: 收到; 获得; 得到; 取得: *get news/knowledge/possession of sth.* 获得消息(知识，某物)。*I've got (= now have) your telegram.* 我已经收到你的电报。*This room gets (= receives, admits) very little sunshine.* 这房间几乎晒不到太阳。*I'll come as soon as I get time.* 我一有时间便会来。*The soldier got leave (= permission) to go home.* 士兵请假探亲。*He got (= received) a nasty blow on the head.* 他的头部受到凶险的一击。*The bullet got him/The soldier got it in the leg,* He was injured there. 子弹打中了他(这士兵腿部中弹)。*Where did you get that hat?* 你那顶帽子在哪里买的? *How does he get (= earn) his living?* 他怎样谋生? *If we divide 12 by 4, we get 3.* 我们如以 4 除 12, 便得 3。*Can you get (= receive) distant stations on your transistor?* 你的半导体收音机能收到远处的电台吗? *Go and get (= take, eat) your breakfast.* 去吃你的早餐。**8** [VP12B, 13B] *Get me a ticket, please.* 请给我准备一张票。*Get yourself a haircut/get your hair cut.* 去理个发吧! *Get some more food for the guests.* 再给客人拿些食物来。**'get one,** ⇨ **get one's goat,** ⇨ **goat. get the better/best of,** ⇨ **better³** and **best³.**

get the boot, ⇨ **boot¹(1). get a glimpse of,** ⇨ **glimpse. get hold of sth,** ⇨ **hold²(1). get the sack,** ⇨ **sack². get (a) sight of,** ⇨ **sight¹(2). get the upper hand (of),** ⇨ **upper. get one's own way,** ⇨ **way. get wind of,** ⇨ **wind¹(4). get the wind up,** ⇨ **wind¹(1). get the worst of,** ⇨ **worst. 8** [VP6A] catch (an illness): 生(病); 得(病); 患(病): *get the measles;* 得麻疹; *get religion,* (colloq) be converted (from disbelief or indifference): (口)信仰宗教。**9** [VP6A] receive as a penalty: 受到: *get six months,* be sentenced to six months' imprisonment. 被判处六个月的徒刑。**get told off,** (colloq) be admonished: (口)受训诫: *I daren't be late home again or I'll get told off.* 我再也不敢晚回家了，否则会挨骂的。**10** [VP6A] (colloq) understand: (口)了解: *I don't get you/your meaning.* 我不明白你的意思。*She didn't get the joke.* 她没有听懂那个笑话。*Get it?* Do you understand? 懂吗? (明白了吗?) *You've got it wrong,* have misunderstood it. 你误会了。*I didn't get (= hear) your name.* 我没有听清楚你的姓名。**11** [VP6A] (esp in the perfect tenses) puzzle; catch in an argument; bring an accusation against sb to which he cannot supply a good answer: (尤用于完成时)使迷惑; 难住; 问倒: *Ah! I've got you there!* 我可将你难住了! *That's got him!* 那问题难住了他! **12** [VP7A] **have got,** have, eg as a possession or characteristic: 有(拥有或具有): *We've got a new car.* 我们有一辆新车。*That ugly teeth he's got!* 他的牙齿真难看! **13** [VP7B] **have got to,** must, be compelled or obliged: 必须: *It has got to (= must) be done today.* 此事今天必须做好。*She's got to work hard for her living.* 为了生活她必须辛苦地工作。*You haven't got to (= needn't) go to the office today, have you?* 你今天不须要上班, 对不对? ⇨ **have³(1). 14** [VP7A] (US) succeed: (美)能够: *Do you ever get to see him,* have opportunities of seeing him? 你有机会见到他吗? **15** [VP2C, 3A] (non-idiomatic intransitive uses with *adverbial particles* and *preps;* for idiomatic uses, ⇨ 17 below) move to or from a specified point or in a particular direction: (下列例句中与副词性小品词及介词连用系非成语用法, 至于成语用法,参看下列第 17 义) to; 去到; 移动; 移向: *He gets about a good deal.* 他常旅行。*A car makes it easier to get about.* 汽车使行动容易多了。*The bridge was destroyed so we couldn't get across,* couldn't cross the river. 桥被毁坏, 所以我们无法过河。*Did you manage to get away (= have a holiday) this Easter?* 这次复活节你有没有去度假呀? *Get back!* (imper) Move backwards, get away from danger: (祈使)退后! (例如离开危险): *When did you get back (= return) from the country?* 你何时从乡下回来的? *She got back into bed.* 她回到床上。*Please let me get by,* pass. 请让我过去。*He got down from the bus.* 他下公共汽车。*I can't get in/out,* I can't enter/leave. 我进不去(出不来)。*I'm getting off (= leaving the train) at the next station.* 我下一站下火车。*When did you get here/there,* arrive here/there? 你何时到此地(那里)的? *Dust got into his eyes.* 灰尘进入他的眼睛。*Get off the grass/my toes!* 不要践踏草地(我的脚趾)! *Get a move on!* Hurry up! 快点! *Can you get over that wall?* 你能爬过那墙吗? *We didn't get to bed until 2 am.* 我们直到凌晨二时才睡觉。*Where have they got to?* 他们到哪里去了? *Where can it have got to?* Where can it be? 它到哪里去了? **get (sb) under one's skin,** ⇨ **skin(1). get somewhere/anywhere/nowhere,** obtain some/any/no result; make some/any/no progress: 有(有任何, 无)结果; 有(有任何, 无)进展。**'get there,** (colloq) succeed; accomplish sth. (口)成功; 有成就 **16** [VP15A, B] (non-idiomatic transitive uses with *adverbial particles* and *preps;* for idiomatic uses, ⇨ 17 below) cause to move to or from a point, or in a particular direction: (下列例句中与副词性小品词及介词连用系非成语及物用法, 至于成语用法,参看下列第 17 义) 使移动; 使移向: *The general had to get his troops across the river.* 这个将军必须使他的部队过河。*He never lends books; he says it's too difficult to get*

them back. 他从来不借书给别人；他说书借出去以后很难收回来。 If you'll come and help me, I promise to get you back (= see that you reach home again) before dark. 如果你愿意来帮助我，我担保在天黑以前送你回去。 He's drunk again—we'd better call a taxi and get him home. 他又喝醉了——我们最好叫辆计程车送他回家。 It was nailed to the wall and I couldn't get it off. 它被钉在墙上，我无法将它取下。 Get (= Put) your hat and coat on. 戴上你的帽子，穿上你的上衣。 I can't get the lid on/off. 我盖不上(打不开)这盖子。 We couldn't get the piano through the door. 我们无法将钢琴从此门搬进去。 **17** [VP2C,15B, 3A, 14] (idiomatic uses with adverbial particles and preps): (与副词性小品词及介词连用之成语用法): **get about, (a)** (of sb who has been ill) be no longer confined to bed, to the house: (指病人)可以走动: He's getting about again after his accident. 经此意外事件后，他又可以走动了。 **(b)** (of news, rumours, stories) spread from person to person, usu by gossip: (指新闻,谣言,故事)传开(通常系由口传): The news of his resignation soon got about. 他辞职的消息很快就传开了。

get a'bove oneself, have a feeling of self-satisfaction not in strict proportion to one's merits; have too high an opinion of oneself. 自傲；自视过高。 ⇨ swollen-headed at **swell**.

get sth across (to sb), (cause sth to) be understood: 使(某事物)被人了解: I spoke slowly, but my meaning didn't get across. 我慢慢地讲，但我的意思仍不被人了解。 I failed to get my joke across to the crowd. 我未能使群众了解我的笑话。

get ahead (of sb), go forward and pass sb; make progress: 前进并越过(某人)；有进展: Tom has got ahead of all the other boys in the class. 汤姆胜过了班上其他的男孩子。

get along, (a) manage: 过活；生活: We can't get along without money. 没有钱我们无法生活。 **(b)** make progress: 进展: How are you getting along? 你好吗？ How is he getting along with his French? 他的法语学习的情况如何？ **get along (with sb)**, be friendly and in harmony: (与某人)和好相处；相处和谐: He gets along well with his boss. 他和他的上司相处甚好。 He and his boss get along well. 他同他的上司相处甚好。 **Get a'long with you!** (colloq imper) Go away! (or) Don't expect me to believe that! (口,祈使)走开! 去你的! 胡说!

get at sb/sth, reach; gain access to: 到达；得到；接近: The books are locked up and I can't get at them. 书被锁起来了，我无法拿到它们。 Hence, 由此产生, **get-'at-able** /'get'ætəbl/, ,get'ætəbl/ adj accessible. 可以到的；可进入的。 **get at sb, (a)** bribe, corrupt: 贿赂；行贿: One of the witnesses had been got at. 一位证人曾受贿赂。 **(b)** taunt: 责骂；辱骂: He's always getting at his wife. 他总是责骂他的妻子。 **get at sth**, discover; lay bare: 发现: get at the truth / the facts. 发现真情(事实)。 **be getting at**, (colloq) be implying; be trying to say or suggest: (口)暗指: What are you getting at? 你的意思是什么？

get away, manage to leave; escape: 设法离开；逃脱: Two of the prisoners got away. 两位犯人逃走了。 Hence, 由此产生, **'get-away** n: make one's get-away; escape; 逃走; (attrib) (用作定语) The get-away car had been stolen. 那部用来逃走的汽车是偷来的。 **get away with sth**, pursue successfully a course of action which might usually be expected to result in blame, punishment or misfortune: 避开责备、惩罚或灾难而能顺利行事: The thieves got away with the contents of the safe. 这些贼顺利地将保险柜内之物窃走。 If I cheat in the examination, do you think I might get away with it? 如果我考试作弊，你想我能避开惩罚吗？ **Get a'way with you!** Get along with you! 走开! ⇨ **get along** above. 参看上列之 get along.

get back, return to power or prominence after losing it for a time: (失去后)恢复力量: 东山再起: The Democrats hope to get back at the next election. 民主党人希望在下次选举中重振威势。 **get 'back at sb / get one's**

'own back (on sb), have one's revenge: 报复: He tricked me this time but I'll get my own back one day. 这次他骗了我，可是我有一天要向他报复。

get by, (a) pass; be accepted, without comment or criticism: 通过； 未受批评而被接受: I have no formal clothes for this occasion; perhaps I can get by in a dark suit. 我没有参加这个场合的礼服，或许我穿深色服装可以应付过去。 **(b)** manage; survive: 设法；继续存在: How can he get by on such low wages? 以如此低微的工资他如何能度日？ She can't get by without him. 没有他她无法生活。

get down, leave the table, after a meal. 饭后离开餐桌。 **get sb down**, (colloq) depress: (口)使沮丧: Don't let this cold weather get you down. 不要让这寒冷的天气使你沮丧。 **get sth down, (a)** swallow: 吞下: The medicine was bitter, and she couldn't get it down. 药很苦，她咽不下去。 **(b)** write down: 记下: Did you get that telephone message down? 你将电话里所留的话记下来没有？ **get down to sth**, deal seriously with; tackle: 认真应付；处理: get down to one's work after the holidays; 假期过后静心工作; get down to the facts, deal with them, ignoring speculations, etc. 认真研究事实。 **get down to brass tacks**, ⇨ **brass**.

get home (to) sb, be fully understood (by): 被充分了解: That remark of yours about Sally got home, She understood (and reacted). 萨利听懂了你针对她所说的话(而且有所反应)。

get in, (a) arrive: 到达: The train got in five minutes early. 那班火车早到了五分钟。 **(b)** be elected: 当选: He got in (= was elected MP) for Islington. 他当选为伊斯灵顿的国会议员。 **get sb in**, call sb to one's house, etc to perform a service: 使某人到家中等做事: We must get someone in to repair the TV. 我们必须请个人来修理电视机。 **get sth in, (a)** collect; gather: 收集； 收割: get in the crops / the harvest; 收割庄稼; get in debts / taxes. 收回借款(收税)。 **(b)** obtain a supply of sth: 获某物之供应: get coal in for the winter; 贮藏以备冬日用煤; get in more wine for Christmas. 多备酒以供圣诞节之用。 **get one's hand / eye in, not get a word in edgeways, get a blow in**, ⇨ **hand**[1](5), **eye**[1](1), **edgeways**, and **blow**[3](1).

get into sth, (a) put on: 穿上: I can't get into these shoes—they're two sizes too small! 这双鞋我穿不进—它们小了二号。 **(b)** pass into a particular condition: 进入特殊状态: get into trouble / a rage / a temper; 惹上麻烦(发怒; 发脾气); 负债。 **get a girl into trouble**, (colloq) make her pregnant. (口)使一女子怀孕。 ⇨ also **get with** below. 亦参看下列之 get with. **(c)** acquire: 得到: get into bad habits. 养成恶习。 **(d)** associate with: 结交: get into undesirable company. 结交不良的朋友。 **(e)** learn by experience or experiment: 由经验或实验而学得: get into the way / habit / routine of doing something. 学会做事的方法(养成做某事的习惯；学得做某事之常规)。 **get it into one's head that...; get 'this into your head that...**, become convinced, understand, that.... 相信...; 了解...。

get off, start: 出发: We got off immediately after breakfast. 早餐后即刻出发。 **get off lightly / cheaply**, escape severe punishment or suffering. 未受重罚或痛苦。 **tell sb where to get off / where he gets off**, (colloq) tell him how far his misbehaviour, impudence, etc will be tolerated, or that it will no longer be tolerated (= put sb in his place). (口)告诉某人其行为、无礼等将被容忍到什么地步。 **get off sth / sb**, send: 送; 传递: get letters / parcels off in good time; 按时寄出信件(包裹); get the children off to school. 送孩子们去上学。 **get off one's chest / hands**, ⇨ **chest**(2), **hand**[1](1). **get sb off**, save from punishment or a penalty: 使某人免于受罚: His youth and inexperience got him off. 他的年轻和无经验使他免于受罚。 A clever barrister may be able to get you off. 一位聪明的律师可能为你开脱罪行。 **get sb off to sleep**, help him to fall

asleep: 助某人入睡: *She got the baby off to sleep*, eg by rocking it. 她要助婴儿入睡(例如摇动婴儿)。 **get sth off**, remove: 脱下; 除下: *get a ring off one's finger*; 脱下指环; *get off one's gloves*. 脱下手套。 **get sth off (by heart)**, learn it until the words can be repeated mechanically. 能机械般地背诵出来。 **get off with sb**, (colloq) have a romantic or sexual encounter with him: (口)同某人勾搭(与某人发生恋情或性关系): *The nurse got off with a young doctor at the dance.* 那护士在舞会中与一位年轻的医生勾勾搭搭。 **get off with sth**, escape more severe punishment or misfortune: 逃脱较严重的惩罚或灾祸: *He got off with only a fine*, eg instead of possible imprisonment. 他仅受到罚款(例如代替监禁)。

get on, (a) become older. 年事渐高。 (b) make progress; advance: 进步; 进展: *How's Jim getting on at school?* 吉姆的学业有进步吗? *He is getting on well.* 他颇有进步。 *Time is getting on*, is passing. 时光流逝。 **get on sth**, mount: 登上; 骑上: *He got on his bike／horse／ the train.* 他骑上脚踏车(骑上马, 登上火车)。 **get on one's feet**, stand; (fig) recover after a set-back: 站立; (喻)经挫折后而复元: *The industry will need time to get on its feet again.* 工业需要一段时期才能恢复旧观。 **get on one's nerves**, ⇨ **nerve**(2). **be getting 'on for**, (of age or time) be approaching: (指年龄或时间)接近: *He's getting on for seventy*, will soon be 70 years old. 他快七十岁了。 *It's getting on for midnight.* 快到半夜了。 **get 'on to sb**, (a) get in touch with, eg by telephone; make contact with: 与某人联络(例如以电话): *If you're not satisfied with the firm's service, get on to the manager.* 如果你对公司的服务不满意, 请和经理联系。 (b) (colloq) succeed in recognizing, eg dishonesty, deceit: (口)认清某人之虚伪, 欺骗等: *He has tricked many of us but people are beginning to get on to him at last.* 他骗过我们当中许多人, 但是人们才开始认清了他的面目。 **get on (with sb)**, work or live in a sociable way: (与某人)相处: *The new manager is easy to get on with.* 新经理易于相处。 *They don't get on at all well (together).* 他们相处得一点也不好。 **get on (with sth)**, continue: 继续: *Please get on with your work.* 请继续你的工作。

get out, become known: 为人知道; 泄露: *The secret got out.* 秘密泄露了。 *If the news gets out there'll be trouble.* 如果这消息泄露出去, 将会引起麻烦。 **get sth out**, (a) utter: 说出: *He managed to get out a few words of thanks.* 他勉强说出几句感谢的话。 (b) produce; publish; distribute: 生产; 出版; 分配: *Will we get the new dictionary out by the end of the year?* 我们在年底可将新词典出版吗? **get out of (doing) sth**, (a) (fig) avoid; escape (from): (喻)避免; 逃避: *I wish I could get out of (going to) that wedding.* 我希望我能不参加那场婚礼。 (b) (fig) abandon gradually: (喻)逐渐放弃: *get out of bad habits.* 逐渐弃绝恶习。 **get sth out of sb**, extract: 设法取得: *The police have got a confession out of him*, have made him confess. 警方已使他招供。 *Just try getting money out of him!* 设法从他那里弄点钱看看!

get over sb, (colloq) forget: (口)忘记: *He never got over Jane, you know*, She stayed in his memory. 你知道, 他永远忘不掉简。 **get over sth**, (a) recover from, eg illness, surprise, a loss: (自疾病, 惊讶, 损失等情况中)恢复; 痊愈; 复元: *I can't get over his rudeness.* 我无法忘怀他的无礼。 *Fred didn't remarry; he never got over the shock of losing Jane.* 弗雷德没有再婚, 他永远忘不掉失去简时所受的震惊。 (b) overcome: 克服: *She can't get over her shyness.* 她不能克服她的羞怯。 **get sth over (with)**, reach the end of sth unpleasant or troublesome: 结束不愉快的事: *I have to see my dentist today; I'll be glad to get it over with.* 今天我得去看牙齿, 希望能就此结束这件恼人的事。 **get sth over (to sb)**, cause (him) to understand it. 使(某人)了解某事。

get round sb, persuade sb into some action to which he was at first opposed or indifferent; influence sb in one's favour; coax: 说服某人去做其最初反对或不热心的事; 笼络某人; 哄诱: *Alice knows how to get round her father.* 艾

丽斯知道如何说服她的父亲。 **get round sth**, evade, eg a law or regulation, but without committing a legal offence; circumvent: 逃避某事物(例如法律或规则)但不违法; 钻(法律)漏洞: *A clever lawyer might find ways of getting round that clause.* 聪明的律师可能有办法逃避那条法律。 **get round to (doing) sth**, deal with it (when more important matters have been dealt with): (较重要之事处理完毕后)处理某事: *I'm very busy this week but I hope to get round to (answering) your request next week.* 我本周内很忙, 但是我希望下周能处理(答复)你的请求。

get through (to sb), arrive; reach (sb); make contact (with sb): 到达某人处; (与人)接触: *I left as soon as your message got through (to me).* 一接到你的信我就离开了。 *I rang you several times yesterday but couldn't get through.* 我昨天打了几次电话给你, 但是都找不到你。 **get through (sth)**, pass, eg an examination: 通过(例如考试): *Tom failed but his sister got through.* 汤姆不及格, 但他的妹妹及格了。 **get through (with) sth**, reach the end of: 结束; 完成: *I've got through a lot of correspondence today.* 今天我写了许多信。 *He has got through (= spent) all his money.* 他已将他所有的钱花光了。 *As soon as I get through (with) my work, I'll join you.* 我一做完我的工作, 就去找你们。 **get through to sb that...**, communicate to him that...: 通知某人说…: *Try to get through to him that he's ruining his own life.* 设法告诉他他正在摧毁他的一生。 **get sb through (sth)**, help to pass an examination: 帮助某人考试及格: *get pupils through (an examination).* 让学生们考试及格。 **get sth through**, ensure that it is done; make it law: 使完成; 使通过为法律: *get the proposal through the committee*, have it discussed and accepted; 使提议为委员会所接受; *get a Bill through Parliament.* 使一法案在国会通过。

get to sth, reach (a place, state, person, etc): 到达(某地, 某种状态, 某人等): *When she got to the station, the train had already left.* 她到达车站时, 火车已经开走了。 *He got to thinking (= began to think) that she wouldn't come after all.* 他开始觉得她毕竟不会来了。 **get to work**, ⇨ **work¹**(1).

get together (with sb), come or meet together, eg for discussion or for social purposes: (与某人)聚会(例如为讨论或为社交活动): *get together for a friendly chat*; 聚在一起闲话家常; *get together with sb to discuss a problem.* 与某人聚在一起讨论问题。 Hence, 由此产生, **'get-together** n [C]. 聚会; 叙旧。

get it／sth together, (colloq) organize or manage it; put it in order. (口)组织; 管理; 整顿。 **get oneself together**, (colloq) get control of oneself, one's feelings, etc. (口)控制自己, 自己的感情等。

get people／things together, collect them: 聚集: *The rebel leader couldn't get an army together.* 叛军首领无法召集一支军队。

get sth under control, ⇨ **control**. **get sth under way**, ⇨ **way**(8).

get up, (a) rise: 起床; 起立: *When do you get up, ie from bed?* 你早上几点钟起床呢? *He got up (= stood up) to sing.* 他站起来唱歌。 Hence, 由此产生, **get-up-and-'go** n [U] (colloq) energy. (口)精力; 活力。 (b) mount (a horse). 登上; 乘; 骑。 (c) begin to be violent: 开始强烈; 变剧烈: *The wind／sea is getting up.* 风势开始增强(海浪开始汹涌)。 **get sb／sth up**, (a) cause to rise, be out of bed: 使起立; 使起床: *Get the children up and dressed for school.* 让孩子们起床, 穿好衣服去上学。 (b) arrange sb's／sth's appearance: 装扮某人之外表; 整理某物之外表: *got up to look like an Arab princess.* 装扮成阿拉伯公主的样子。 *The book is well got up*, well printed and bound. 这本书印刷和装订得很好。 Hence, 由此产生, **'get-up** n (colloq) (口) (a) style or arrangement, eg of a book, periodical. (书籍刊物的)装订形式。 (b) style of dress, esp if unusual: 衣服式样(尤指特别的): *I wouldn't be seen dead with you in that get-up!* 你穿着那种怪衣服, 我说什么也不愿意同你在一

起! **get sth up,** organize: 组织；筹划：*We're getting up a party for his birthday.* 我们正在筹划为他的生日举行一个庆祝会。 **get up steam,** ⇨ **steam. get up to sth,** (a) reach: 到达：*We got up to page seventy-two last lesson.* 我们上一课上到第七十二页。 *We soon got up to the others, caught up with them.* 我们不久便赶上其他的人了。 (b) become involved in (sth unusual): 专心于(不平常之事)：*What will they get up to next?* 他们下一步计划做些什么？
get sb with child, (archaic) make her pregnant. (古)使一女子怀孕。 **get with it,** (colloq) (口) ⇨ with(12).

geum /'dʒiːəm; 'dʒiəm/ *n* [C] kind of small garden plant. 水杨梅属。

gey·ser /'giːzə(r) *US:* 'gaɪzər; 'gaɪzɚ/ *n* 1 natural spring sending up at intervals a column of hot water or steam. 天然喷泉(间歇地喷出一股温水或蒸气)。 2 (GB) apparatus for heating water, eg by gas, in a kitchen, bathroom, etc. (英) (厨房、浴室间等的)热水器；热水锅炉。

a geyser

gharry /'gæri; 'gæri/ *n* (*pl* -ries) (in India, etc) (horse-drawn) carriage. (印度等地之)马车。

ghast·ly *US:* 'gɑːstli; 'gæstli/ *adj* (-ier, -iest) 1 death-like; pale and ill: 死一般的；惨白的：*looking ~.* 面色惨白的。 (also as *adv*): (亦作副词)：*~ pale.* 惨白。 2 causing horror or fear: 可怖的；可怕的：*a ~ accident.* 可怕的意外。 3 (colloq) very unsatisfactory or unpleasant: (口)十分令人不满或不快的：*a ~ dinner.* 糟糕的一顿饭。

ghat /gɑːt; gɔt/ *n* [C] (in India) flight of steps leading to a landing-place on a river bank. (印度)河岸上下之阶梯。 *'burning ~,* level area at the top of a ~ on which Hindus cremate their dead. 河旁的火葬场。

ghee /giː; gi/ *n* [U] clarified Indian buffalo-milk butter, (印度)酥油(将水牛乳煮沸澄清而成)。

gher·kin /'gɜːkɪn; 'gɝkɪn/ *n* small, green cucumber for pickling. (供腌泡用的)小黄瓜。

ghetto /'getəʊ; 'geto/ *n* (*pl* -s /-təʊz; -toz/) 1 (formerly, in some countries) Jewish quarter of a town. (昔时某些国家中)城市中犹太人的居留区。 2 section of a town, lived in by underprivileged classes, or people who are discriminated against, eg because of race or religion. 城市中未享受正当权利的阶级或遭受歧视的人民居住的地区。

ghost /gəʊst; gost/ *n* 1 spirit of a dead person appearing to sb still living: 鬼；幽灵：*He looked as if he had seen a ~,* looked frightened. 他的样子好象碰见了鬼。 *I don't believe in ~s.* 我不相信有鬼。 2 (old use) spirit of life. (旧用法)灵魂。 **give up the ~,** die. 死。 3 Spirit of God: 上帝之灵：(only in) (仅用于) **the Holy G~,** the Third Person of the Trinity. 圣灵(三位一体之第三位)。 4 sth shadowy or without substance. 幻影；一丝；一点；些微：*'~ town,* one now deserted, eg an area where gold was once mined, but is now abandoned. 鬼城(例如昔时曾有金矿而现被遗弃的城镇)。 **not have the '~ of a chance,** no chance at all. 一点机会也没有。 5 (also 亦作 **'~-writer**), person who does literary or artistic work for which his employer takes the credit.

为人代笔的作家；捉刀人。 6 duplicated image on a television screen. 电视屏幕上重复的影像。 □ *vt, vi* act as a ~-writer (for): 为人代笔；为人捉刀(~ed memoirs, compiled by a ~-writer. 由他人代笔撰写的回忆录。

ghost·ly /'gəʊstli; 'gostli/ *adj* 1 of, like, suggesting, a ghost: 鬼的；似鬼的；鬼状的：*vague shapes, looking ~ in the darkness.* 黑暗中看来似鬼魂的模糊的影子。 2 (archaic) spiritual; from a priest: (古)精神上的；来自教士的：*~ comfort / counsel.* 精神上的安慰(教士的劝诫)。 **ghost·li·ness** *n*

ghoul /guːl; gul/ *n* 1 (in stories) spirit that robs graves and feeds on the corpses in them. (故事中)食尸鬼。 2 person with gruesome and unnatural tastes and habits. 嗜好和习惯古怪可怕的人。 *~·ish* /-ɪʃ; -ɪʃ/ *adj* gruesome; revolting. 可怕的；使人嫌恶的。

GI /,dʒiː'aɪ; ,dʒi'aɪ/ *n* enlisted soldier of the US army: 美国兵：*a GI bride,* bride, (in or from a country other than the US) of such a soldier. 美国兵的(外国)新娘。

gi·ant /'dʒaɪənt; 'dʒaɪənt/ *n* 1 (in fairy tales) man of very great height and size. (童话中)巨人。 2 man, animal or plant much larger than normal; (fig) person of extraordinary ability or genius. 特别大的人、动物或植物；(喻)伟人；天才。 3 (attrib) of great size or force: (用作定语)巨大的：*~ strength,* 巨大的力量；*a ~ cabbage.* 一颗特大的卷心菜。 *~ess* /'dʒaɪəntɪs; 'dʒaɪəntɪs/ *n* female ~. 女巨人。

gib·ber /'dʒɪbə(r); 'dʒɪbɚ/ *vi* [VP2A, C] talk fast or make meaningless sounds (like an ape, or as when the teeth knock together through cold or fear): 叽哩咕噜地谈话；作无意义的声音(如猿，或因寒冷恐惧等牙齿震颤时然)。 *~·ish* /'dʒɪbərɪʃ; 'dʒɪbərɪʃ/ *n* [U] meaningless sounds; unintelligible talk. 无意义的声音；叽哩咕噜的谈话。

gib·bet /'dʒɪbɪt; 'dʒɪbɪt/ *n* 1 (hist) gallows. (史)绞架。 2 wooden post with an arm, on which corpses of executed criminals were formerly exposed as a warning. 示众架(昔时将已处死的犯人的尸体陈列其上，以儆他人)。 3 death by hanging. 绞刑。 □ *vt* put to death by hanging; expose on a ~; (fig) hold up to contempt or ridicule. 绞死；陈列于示众架；(喻)当众侮辱或嘲弄；使人出丑或丢人。

gib·bon /'gɪbən; 'gɪbən/ *n* kinds of long-armed ape. 长臂猿。 ⇨ the illus at **ape.** 参看 ape 之插图。

gib·bous /'dʒɪbəs; 'dʒɪbəs/ *adj* 1 (of the moon) having the bright part greater than a semicircle and less than a circle. (指月亮)凸圆的(大于半月小于满月的)。 ⇨ the illus at **phase.** 参看 phase 之插图。 2 humped; hunchbacked. 隆起的；驼背的。

gibe, jibe /dʒaɪb; dʒaɪb/ *vi* [VP2A, 3A] *~ (at),* jeer or mock; make fun of: 讥笑或嘲弄；提弄：*~ at a boy's mistakes.* 讥笑一孩子的错误。 □ *n* taunt; cruel joke: 笑骂；嘲弄：*cheap ~s,* easy but unnecessary mockery. 轻易的但是不必要的嘲笑。 **gib·ing·ly** /'dʒaɪbɪŋlɪ; 'dʒaɪbɪŋlɪ/ *adv*

gib·lets /'dʒɪblɪts; 'dʒɪblɪts/ *n pl* heart, liver, gizzard, etc of a goose, hen, etc taken out before the bird is cooked: 鹅、鸡等的杂碎：*giblet soup,* soup made from these parts. 鸡(鹅等)杂汤。

giddy /'gɪdɪ; 'gɪdɪ/ *adj* (-ier, -iest) 1 causing, having, the feeling that everything is turning round; feeling that one cannot stand firm: 令人眩晕的；头晕的：*look down from a ~ height.* 从一令人眩晕的高处向下望。 *If you turn round quickly fifty times, you will feel ~.* 如果你很快地转五十次，你会感到头晕。 2 too fond of pleasure; not serious; without steady principles: 过于喜欢享乐的；轻佻的；轻浮的：*a ~ young girl,* 一位轻佻的少女；*a ~ life of pleasure.* 放荡的生活。 **play the ~ goat,** ⇨ **goat. gid·dily** /*adv* **gid·di·ness** *n*

gift /gɪft; gɪft/ *n* 1 [C] sth given: 礼物；赠品：*~s to charities;* 捐赠给慈善事业的东西；*'~ vouchers / coupons.* 礼券。 Cf 参较 **birthday** and **Christmas presents.** 2 [C]

natural ability or talent: 天赋; 天才; *have a ~ for art/
languages*; 有艺术(语言)天才; *a woman of many ~s*,
talented by nature. 多才多艺的女子。 *look a ~horse
in the mouth*, ⇨ *mouth¹(1)*. **3** [U] right or power to
give: 授予权: *The post is in the ~ of the Prime Minister*,
He has the right to bestow it. 这职位的委派权在首相手
中。 □ *vt* [VP6A] bestow, eg land, as a ~ to sb. 赠
与(例如土地)。 **~ed** *adj* having great natural ability:
有天才的; *~ed with rare talents*; 有罕见的天才; *a ~ed
pianist.* 天才钢琴家。

gig /gɪg; gɪg/ *n* **1** (hist) small, light two-wheeled
carriage pulled by one horse. (史)小型轻便的二轮单马
车。 **2** (naut) ship's small boat for oars or sails, eg for
the captain's use. (航海)(大船上的)小艇。 (舰长)座艇。
3 (colloq) (pop or jazz music) engagement to play. (口)
(流行或爵士音乐)预订表演期间。

gi·gan·tic /dʒaɪˈgæntɪk; dʒaɪˈgæntɪk/ *adj* of immense
size: 巨大的; 庞大的: *He has a ~ appetite, and eats ~
meals.* 他的食量很大, 能吃很多食物。

giggle /ˈgɪgl; ˈgɪgl/ *vi, vt* [VP2A] laugh lightly in
a nervous or silly way; [VP6A] express by
giggling: 咯咯地笑; 傻笑; 咯咯地笑着表示: *She ~d
her appreciation of my silly joke.* 她咯咯地笑着表示欣赏
我愚蠢的笑话。 □ *n* laugh of this kind. 咯咯的笑; 傻笑。

gig·olo /ˈʒɪgələʊ; ˈʒɪgəˌlo/ *n* (*pl* **~s** /-ləʊz; -loz/)
professional male dancing-partner who may be hired by
wealthy women; paid male companion of a wealthy older
woman. 职业性的男舞伴(可受有钱妇女所雇用者); 有钱
而较年长的妇女雇用的男伴。

Gilbertian /gɪlˈbɜːtɪən; gɪlˈbɜːtɪən/ *adj* a ~ *situation*, humorously ridiculous or paradoxical situation as
in Gilbert and Sullivan operas. 可笑或荒谬的诙谐场面
(如吉尔伯特和沙利文喜歌剧中者)。

gild¹ /gɪld; gɪld/ *vt* (*pp* usu **~ed**, sometimes **gilt** /gɪlt;
gɪlt/), ⇨ **gilt** below) (过去分词通常用 ~ed, 有时用 gilt,
参看下列之 gilt) [VP6A] cover with gold leaf or gold-
coloured paint; make bright as if with gold: 镀金于;
以金箔; 涂以漆以金色; 使有金子般的光彩: *a picture-
frame.* 给画框镀金。 *~ the lily*, spoil the beauty of sth
by unnecessary embellishment. 过份装饰而破坏某物之
美; 画蛇添足。 *~ the pill*, make an unpleasant necessity
seem attractive. 使讨厌之必需品显得可爱; 虚饰外观。
~ed youth, young people of fashion and wealth. 纨袴
子弟。 **~er** *n* person who ~s (picture-frames, etc). 镀
金工; 镀金者。 **~ing** *n* [U] material with which things
are ~ed. 镀金用的材料。

gild² ⇨ **guild**.

gill¹ /gɪl; gɪl/ *n* (usu *pl*) **1** organ (one on
each side) with which a fish breathes. 鳃。 ⇨ the illus
at **fish**. 参看 fish 之插图。 **2** one of the many thin
vertical sheets on the under side of a mushroom. 菌褶。
⇨ the illus at **fungus**. 参看 fungus 之插图。 **3** (*pl*)
person's flesh under the ears and jaw. (复)(人之)腮。
be green/white about the ~s, be sick/afraid. 有病
(害怕)。

gill² /dʒɪl; dʒɪl/ *n* one-quarter of a pint liquid measure.
吉尔(液量单位, 合四分之一品脱)。 ⇨ **App 5**. 参看附
录五。

gil·lie /ˈgɪlɪ; ˈgɪlɪ/ *n* man or boy attending a sportsman
in Scotland while fishing or shooting. 苏格兰钓鱼或游猎
者的仆从(或向导)。

gilt /gɪlt; gɪlt/ *n* [U] gilding. 镀金材料。 ⇨ **gild**.
take the ~ off the gingerbread, (prov) take away
the most attractive feature. (谚)除去最诱人的外貌。
,~-edged 'stocks/se'curities, investments that are
considered safe. 优良股票(证券); 金边股票(证券)(即可
靠的股票或证券)。

gim·bals /ˈgɪmblz; ˈdʒɪmblz/ *n* (usu *pl*) contrivance
(of rings and pivots) for keeping instruments, eg a
compass, horizontal on a ship at sea. (通常用复数)(罗
盘等的)平衡环; 水平环。

gim·crack /ˈgɪmkræk; ˈdʒɪmˌkræk/ *adj* worthless,

flimsy and badly made: 制造粗劣而无价值的: *~ ornaments.* 做得粗劣而无价值的装饰品。

gim·let /ˈgɪmlɪt; ˈgɪmlɪt/ *n* small tool, with a handle
usu fixed crosswise, used for boring holes in wood, etc.
螺丝锥; 木钻; 手锥。 ⇨ the illus at **tool**. 参看 tool 之插
图。 *~ eye*, piercing glance. 锐利的眼光。

gim·mick /ˈgɪmɪk; ˈgɪmɪk/ *n* [C] (colloq) trick,
device, catchword, mannerism, article of wear, etc
used for publicity purposes, to identify sth or sb. (口)
为宣传某物或某人所用的花样, 策略, 妙句, 怪样, 衣着等;
噱头。

gin¹ /dʒɪn; dʒɪn/ *n* **1** trap or snare for catching animals,
etc. 陷阱。 **2** (**cotton**) **~**, machine for separating raw
cotton from its seeds. 轧棉机。 □ *vt* (**-nn-**) [VP6A]
1 catch (animals, etc) in a trap or snare. 以陷阱诱捕
(动物等)。 **2** treat (cotton) in a gin. 以轧棉机除去(棉
花)之子。

gin² /dʒɪn; dʒɪn/ *n* [U] colourless alcoholic drink
distilled from grain or malt and flavoured with juniper
berries, often drunk with tonic water, and used in many
kinds of cocktail. 杜松子酒。

gin·ger /ˈdʒɪndʒə(r); ˈdʒɪndʒə/ *n* [U] **1** (plant with)
hot-tasting root used in cooking, as a flavouring and
for making a kind of wine. 生姜; 姜。 **2** liveliness:
spirit; energy: 活泼; 元气; 精力: *a ~ group*, (in
Parliament) group of MP's that urges the Government
to be more active. (国会中)督促政府更加积极行事的一
群议员。 **3** (also as *adj*) light reddish-yellow colour: (亦
用作形容词) 淡赤黄色(的): *~ hair.* 淡赤黄色的头发。
4 *'~ 'beer/'ale*, kinds of non-alcoholic aerated drink
flavoured with ~. 姜啤酒。 *'~-bread* *n* dark-coloured
cake or biscuit flavoured with ~. 姜饼; 姜汁饼干。
~ 'gilt, '~nut*, biscuit flavoured with ~. 姜汁饼干。
□ *vt* [VP6A, 15B] *~ (up)*, make more vigorous or
lively. 使更有生气; 使更为活泼。

gin·ger·ly /ˈdʒɪndʒəlɪ; ˈdʒɪndʒəlɪ/ *adv* with great
care and caution to avoid harming, making a noise, etc;
极为小心地(以避免伤害或弄出声音): *set about sth ~.* 极
为小心地开始做。 □ *adj* cautious: 小心的; 谨慎的: *in a
~ fashion.* 小心翼翼。

ging·ham /ˈgɪŋəm; ˈgɪŋəm/ *n* [U] printed cotton
or linen cloth, usu with designs in stripes or checks. 印
花棉布(印花麻布(通常有条纹或方格图案)。

gingko /ˈgɪŋkəʊ; ˈgɪŋko/ *n* (*pl* **~s**, **~es** /-kəʊz; -koz/)
tree native to China and Japan with fan-shaped leaves.
白果树; 银杏。

gin·seng /ˈdʒɪnseŋ; ˈdʒɪnseŋ/ *n* [U] plant of which
the aromatic root is used in medicine. 人参。

gipsy, Gypsy /ˈdʒɪpsɪ; ˈdʒɪpsɪ/ *n* (*pl* **-sies**) **1** gipsy,
(playfully) attractive or mischievous person, esp one
with black, sparkling eyes. (戏谑语)漂亮或顽皮的人
(尤指有黑色明亮的眼睛者)。 **2** **Gypsy**, member of a
wandering, originally Asiatic people, who move about
in caravans and make camps from time to time, and
earn a living by collecting scrap material, horse-dealing,
fortune-telling, basket-making, etc: 吉普赛人(亚洲一
流浪民族, 原居于欧洲各地, 乘马拉的篷车流浪, 随时露
营, 以收废料、贩马、算命、制篮等谋生): (attrib) (用作
定语) *a ~ girl/camp/orchestra.* 吉普赛女郎(营地, 管
弦乐队)。

gi·raffe /dʒɪˈrɑːf US: -ˈræf; dʒəˈræf/ *n* African
animal with a very long neck and legs and dark patches
on its coat. 长颈鹿。 ⇨ the illus at **large**. 参看 large 之
插图。

gird /gɜːd; gɜd/ *vt* (*pt, pp* **girded** or **girt** /gɜːt; gɜt/)
(poet or rhet) (诗或修辞) **1** [VP15B] *~ on*, fasten,
attach: 系结; 佩带: *~ on a sword.* 佩带剑。 **2** [VP15B]
~ up, raise and fasten, eg with a belt or sash: 以带等
系紧; 束以带: *~ up one's clothes.* 束紧衣服。 *~ up one's
loins*, prepare for action. 准备行动。 **3** encircle: 围起;
围绕: *a sea-girt isle*, surrounded by the sea. 四面环海的
小岛。

girder /'gə:dər/; 'gɜdə/ n wood, iron or steel beam to support the joists of a floor; compound structure of steel forming the span of a bridge, roof, etc. 大梁; 桁; 梁。

girdle¹ /'gə:dl/; 'gɜdl/ n 1 cord or belt fastened round the waist to keep clothes in position. 腰带。2 corset. 妇人的紧身褡。3 sth that encircles like a ~: 似腰带状的围绕物: a ~ of green fields round a town. 围绕在城市四周的一片绿野。□ vt encircle: a lake ~d with trees. 四周植有树的湖。

girdle² /'gə:dl/; 'gɜdl/ n (Scot) (苏) = **griddle**.

girl /gə:l/; gɜl/ n female child; daughter; young woman; woman working in a shop, office, etc. 女孩; 女儿; 少女; 女店员; 女职员。'~·(friend) regular companion with whom one may or may not be in love. 爱人; 女友。(GB) (英)G~ 'Guide, (US)(美)G~ 'Scout, member of an organization for ~s, with principles and aims similar to those of the Scout Association. 女童子军。'~·hood /-hud/; -hʊd/ n [U] state or time of being a ~. 少女时代。~·ish /-ɪʃ; -ɪʃ/ adj of, for, like a ~: 女孩的; 少女的; 似女孩的: ~ish games/behaviour/laughter. 女孩子们的游戏(行为, 大笑)。~·ish·ly adv ~·ish·ness n

giro /'dʒaɪərəʊ/; 'dʒaɪro/ n [U] (comm) system of credit transfer between banks. (商)若干合资银行集体清算帐目的一种制度。**National G~**, (GB) similar system operated by the Post Office. (英)邮局采用的类似上述的制度。

girt /gə:t; gɜt/ ⇨ **gird**.

girth /gə:θ; gɜθ/ n 1 leather or cloth band tightened round the body of a horse to keep the saddle in place. (马的)肚带。⇨ the illus at **harness**. 参看 harness 之插图。2 measurement round anything that is roughly like a cylinder in shape: 周围的长度: a tree 10 metres in ~, in circumference; 周长十米的树; my ~, my waist measurement. 我的腰围。

gist /dʒɪst; dʒɪst/ n **the ~**, main points or substance; general sense: 要点; 要旨; 要义: Tell me the ~ of what he said. 告诉我他所说的要点。

give¹ /gɪv; gɪv/ vt, vi(pt gave /geɪv; gev/, pp given /'gɪvn; 'gɪvən/) (For uses with adverbial particles and preps, ⇨ **13** below.) (与副词性小品词和介词连用的用法, 参看下列第13义。) **1** [VP12A, 13A, 2A] ~ (to), hand over (to sb) without payment or exchange, eg as a present or gift: 给予: I gave David a book. 我给了大卫一本书。I gave a book to each of the boys. 我给每个孩子一本书。Each of the boys was ~n a book. 每个孩子得到一本书。A book was ~n to each of them. 他们每人得到一本书。I gave it him (= to him). 我把它给了他。G~ me one. 给我一个。G~ one to me. 拿一个给我。He ~s generously, is generous in giving money, etc. 他很慷慨。**2** [VP12B, 16A] ~ for sth; ~ to do sth, cause (sb) to have (sth) in exchange for sth else, for payment, as compensation, for: 付给; 报答: How much will you ~ me for my old car? 你愿意给多少钱买我的旧车?I would ~ anything to know what happened. 我愿付出一切以探究竟竟发生了什么事。**3** [VP 12A, 13A] ~ (to), allow (sb or sth) to pass into the care or safekeeping or custody of; entrust (to): 交付; 委托: G~ the porter your bags. 把你的提包交给搬运行李的人。G~ your money to the hotel manager to be looked after. 把你的钱交给旅馆经理保管。**4** [VP12A] allow (sb) to have, eg time; cause (sb) to have, eg trouble; concede; grant: 使(某人)有时间等; 使(某人)遭受麻烦等; 让与; 容许: You'd better ~ yourself half an hour for the journey. 你最好打算以半小时走完这段路程。G~ me five minutes and I'll change the wheel. 给我五分钟的时间, 我来换轮子。They gave me a week to make up my mind. 他们给我一周的时间作决定。'The car has a good engine' 'OK, I'll ~ you that (= concede that you're right on that point) but the body's very rusty'. '这部汽车的引擎很好' '不错, 你说得很对, 但是车身很锈了'。~ sb (some/no/any, etc) trouble,

cause or make trouble to: 使有(有些, 没有, 任何等)麻烦: Did you ~ your parents much trouble when you were young? 你小的时候给你父母许多麻烦吗?**5** [VP6A, 12A, 13A] furnish; supply; provide: 供; 供应: The sun ~s us warmth and light. 太阳供给我们温暖和光。You should ~ (more usu set) (set before) them a good example. 你应当给他们做个好榜样。You should ~ a good example to your young brothers and sisters. 你应当给你的弟弟妹妹们做个好榜样。**6** [VP12A, 13A] be the source or origin of: 为…的来源; 为…的起因: You've ~ me your cold, I've caught a cold from you. 你把感冒传染给我了。**7** [VP6A, 13A Note that 12A is not used 注意不用于 12A 型] devote; dedicate: 致力; 献身: He gave his life to the cause of peace. 他终生献身于和平。**8** [VP 12A] (used in the imper to show preference): (用于祈使句表示偏爱或选择): G~ me liberty or ~ me death, If I cannot have liberty, I prefer to die. 不自由毋宁死。G~ me Bach and Beethoven, not these modern crash-bang-tinkle composers. 我喜欢巴赫与贝多芬, 不喜欢这些近代的喧嚣的作曲家。**9** [VP6A, 12A, 13A] (used with a n in a pattern that may be replaced by one in which the n is used as a v): (与一名词连用, 此种句型可由将该名词换作动词之句型代替): ~ a groan/laugh/sigh/yell, groan, laugh, sigh, yell: 呻吟(大笑; 叹气; 号叫); ~ a shrug of the shoulders, shrug the shoulders; 耸肩; ~ three cheers, cheer three times; 欢呼三次; ~ sb a kick/push/shove, kick/push/shove him; 踢(推, 撞)某人; ~ sb a ring, phone him. 给某人打电话。**10** (in fixed phrases) (用于固定短语中) ~ birth (to), ⇨ **birth**. ~ chase (to), ⇨ **chase**¹. ~ currency (to), ⇨ **currency**. ~ one's ears, ⇨ **ear**¹(1). ~ evidence of, ⇨ **evidence**. ~ ground, ⇨ **ground**¹(2). ~ place to, ⇨ **place**¹(10). ~ rise to, ⇨ **rise**¹(5). ~ or take..., plus or minus: 加或减: She'll be here at 4 o'clock, ~ or take a few minutes. 她大概四点钟到此地, 或早或迟几分钟。He's six feet tall, ~ or take an inch or two. 他身高大约六英尺, 不会超过一两英寸的差别。Cf 参较 give and take at **give**². ~ sb best, (old use) admit his superiority. (旧用法)承认某人的优越。~ sb to understand that..., inform, assure him, that...: 使某人了解; 告知某人; 使某人相信: I was ~n to understand that you might help me to find employment. 我听说你可能帮我找工作。~ it to sb, (colloq) punish or reprimand him. (口)惩罚或严斥某人。~ sb sth to cry for, ⇨ **cry**¹(2). ~ sb what 'for/ a piece of one's mind, (colloq) punish or scold him. (口)惩罚或责骂某人。~ way, (a) retire, retreat: 退后; 撤退: Our troops had to ~ way. 我们的部队不得不撤退了。(b) fail to support: 不能支持: The ice gave way and we all went through into the water. 冰裂了, 我们都掉进水中。I felt the foundations giving way. 我觉得地基在下陷。The rope gave way, broke, snapped. 绳子断了。~ way (to sth/sb), (a) yield; allow priority to: 顺从; 让...优先: G~ way to traffic coming in from the right. 让从右面来的车辆先走。(b) be replaced by: 被代替: Tears gave way to smiles. 破涕为笑。(c) abandon oneself to: 耽于; 放纵自己: Don't ~ way to despair/grief/tears. 不要绝望(悲痛, 哭泣)。(d) make concessions (to): 让步: We mustn't ~ way to these unreasonable demands. 我们不可对这些不合理的要求让步。**11** [VP 2A] lose firmness; bend; yield to pressure: 垮下; 弯曲; 凹下: The branch gave (eg swung downwards) but did not break. 这树枝弯下来了, 但并未折断。His knees seemed to ~, to feel weak (so that he fell down). 他的膝盖弱得象是直不起来。This chair ~s comfortably, is soft and springy. 这椅子很有弹性。The frost is beginning to ~, is less severe. 严寒减退了。**12** ~n pp (a) (in formal documents) delivered: (在正式文件中)发出的; 签订的: ~n under my hand and seal in this fifth day of May, 1705. 签订于一七〇五年五月五日。(b) granting or assuming that one has, eg as a basis for reasoning: 假定; 倘若: G~n good health, I hope to finish the work this year. 假若健康情况良好, 我希望今年完成这工作。(c) agreed

upon; assigned: 约定的; 指定的: *under the ~n conditions.* 在约定的条件下。 *They were to meet at a ~n time and place.* 他们将在一约定的时间和地点相会。 **(d)** '~n **name,** name ~ to a child in addition to its family name, eg *David* in *David Hume.* 名(例如 David Hume 中之 David)。 **(e) be ~n to sth/doing sth,** have as a habit: 习惯于; 沉溺于; 深爱: *He's ~n to boasting.* 他喜欢自夸。 *I'm not much ~n to wild forecasts.* 我不大喜欢作轻率的预言。 **13** [VP2C, 15B, 3A] (uses with *adverbial particles* and *preps*): (与副词性小品词和介词连用的用法):

give sb away, **(a)** (esp) hand over (the bride) to the bridegroom at a wedding: (尤指)在婚礼中将(新娘)交给新郎: *The bride was ~n away by her father.* 新娘由她父亲将她交给了新郎。 **(b)** ~ *sth away,* **(a)** allow sb else to have; sacrifice: 让别人得去; 牺牲: *You've ~n away a good chance of winning the match.* 你已失掉一个比赛得胜的良好机会。 **(b)** distribute: 分配: 分送: *The Mayor gave away the prizes at the sports meeting.* 市长颁发运动会的奖品。 **(c)** ~ freely, not expecting anything in return: 赠送: *He gave away all his money.* 他把所有的钱都送给别人了。 **(d)** reveal, intentionally or unintentionally: (有意或无意地)泄露; *Don't ~ away my secret.* 不要泄露我的秘密。 *His accent gave him away, made known who or what he was.* 他的口音暴露了他的身分。 Hence, 由此产生, '~-**away** *n* (colloq) (口) **(a)** sth given without charge: 赠品: *airlines which present ~aways (= gifts) to their passengers.* 给乘客赠品的航空公司。 *The last question on the exam paper was a ~away, so easy that it needed no effort, etc.* 考试的最后一项题等于赠送分数。 **(b)** sth revealed, intentionally or unintentionally: (有意或无意)泄露的事: *The expression on the thief's face was a ~away,* showed his guilt. 那窃贼面部的表情显示他有罪。 ~ the '**game away,** ⇨ **game**[1](5).

give sth back (to sb); ~ sb back sth, restore; return: 恢复; 归还: ~ *a thing back to its rightful owner; ~ a man back his liberty;* 恢复一人的自由; *a wall of rock that ~s back loud echoes.* 产生响亮回音的一块岩壁。

give sth forth, (old use or liter) give sth off. (旧用法或文)放出。

give in (to sb), surrender; yield; submit: 投降; 屈服; 归顺: *The rebels were forced to ~ in.* 叛军被迫投降。 *He has ~n in to my views,* has accepted them. 他已接受了我的观点。 *Mary usually has to ~ in to her big brother,* accept his plans, etc and abandon her own. 玛丽通常必须听从她大哥的话。 ~ *sth in,* hand over (papers, etc) to the proper authorities: *Please ~ in your examination papers now.* 现在请将试卷交来。 ~ *one's name in (to sb),* make known one's willingness or readiness for sth, eg a duty, as a candidate, etc. (向某人)公开宣布愿做某事 (如担任某一职务, 做候选人等)。

give sth off, emit, send out, eg smoke, smell, etc. 放出(烟, 气味等)。

give on to, look out on; overlook: 面对; 俯视; 俯瞰: *The bedroom windows ~ on to a courtyard.* 卧室的窗子面对着庭院。

give out, come to an end; be exhausted: 用尽; 耗尽: *Our food supplies began to ~ out.* 我们食物要吃完了。 *Her patience/strength gave out.* 她失去了耐心(她力竭了)。 ~ *sb out/not out,* (cricket of the umpire) say that the batsman has been/has not been defeated. (板球, 指裁判员)判一击球员出局(未出局)。 ~ *sth out,* distribute; send out: 分配; 分发: ~ *out books/handbills.* 分发书籍(传单)。 ~ *sth out to be:* ~ *it out that sb is,* announce: 宣布; 公布: *It was ~n out that Mr Hall would be the chief speaker.* 据宣布, 霍尔先生将为主要的演说者。

give over, (sl) stop: (俚)停止: *Please ~ over crying.* 请不要再哭了。 *Do ~ over!* 停止! ~ *sb/sth over (to sb),* hand (the usu word) over; deliver: 交与 (通常用

hand over): ~ *sb over to the police.* 将某人交与警察。 *be ~n over to sth,* **(a)** be abandoned to (an unesirable state): 沉溺于 (不良的状态): *be ~ over to despair.* 陷于绝望。 **(b)** be devoted to: 专供 ... 之用: *The period after supper was ~n over to games.* 晚饭后的时间用来做游戏。

give up, abandon the attempt (to do sth, to find the answer to sth): 放弃(做某事, 寻求答案等): *I can do nothing more; I ~ up.* 我无能为力, 我放弃。 *I can't answer that puzzle; I ~ up.* 我猜不出那个谜, 我放弃。 ~ *sb up,* **(a)** say that one regard sb, or his estate, as hopeless: 宣称某人或其财产已无希望: *Even his teachers have ~n him up,* have decided that he cannot be reformed. 甚至他的老师们已认为他无可救药。 *The doctors have ~n him up,* say that they cannot cure him. 医生们说他的病已不能治了。 **(b)** (colloq) stop keeping company with him: (口)与(某人)断绝往来: *She was tired of Tom's nagging so she gave him up.* 她厌倦了汤姆唠唠叨叨的责骂, 所以她不同她往来了。 **(c)** no longer expect sb: 不再期待某人: *She was so late that we had ~n her up.* 她到得太迟, 我们以为她不会来了。 ~ *sb up for lost,* no longer expect him to be found or saved. 认为某人不会被发现或得救。 ~ *sb/oneself/sth up (to sb),* surrender; part with: 投降; 自首; 把 ... 交给; 放弃; 让与: ~ *up a fortress,* 放弃一要塞; ~ *up one's seat to sb,* eg in a crowded bus. 将座位让给别人(例如在一拥挤的公共汽车上)。 *Shall we let the thief get ~ (= deliver him) to the police?* 我们是将这窃贼放走呢, 还是将他交给警察? *The escaped prisoner gave himself up.* 那逃犯投案了。 ~ *sth up,* stop (doing) it: 停止 (做某事): *I wish I could ~ up smoking.* 我希望我能把烟戒掉。 ~ *up the ghost,* die. 死。

give upon, ⇨ on to.

give[2] /gɪv; gɪv/ *n* [U] quality of being elastic, of yielding to pressure: 弹性; 弹力: *A good dance floor should have a certain amount of ~ in it.* 好的跳舞用的地板应有相当的弹力。 *A stone floor has no ~ in it;* 石头地面没有弹性; (fig) (of a person) quality of yielding: (喻)(指人)屈服性: 让步: *There's no ~ in him,* He does not concede anything, eg in negotiations, argument: 他丝毫不让步(例如在谈判或争论中)。 ⇨ **give**[1](11). ~ *and take,* compromise; mutual concession; willingness on both sides to give way: 妥协; 互相让步; 双方迁就: *There must be ~ and take if the negotiations to settle an industrial dispute are to succeed.* 解决工业纠纷的磋商如欲成功, 必须双方让步。 (attrib) (用作定语) *Is marriage a ~-and-take affair?* 婚姻是一件互相让步的事吗?

given /gɪvn; gɪvn/ *pp* of **give**[1].

giver /'gɪvər; 'gɪvɚ/ *n* one who gives: 给与者; 施赠者: *a generous/cheerful ~.* 慷慨(乐意)的给与者。

giz·zard /'gɪzəd; 'gɪzɚd/ *n* bird's second stomach for grinding food; (fig, colloq) throat: 砂囊 (鸟的第二胃, 用以将食物磨碎); (喻, 口)喉咙: *It sticks in my ~,* is a proposal, etc that I dislike intensely. 这事我十分厌恶 (不合我的胃口)。

glacé /'glæseɪ US: glæ'seɪ; glæ'se/ *adj* (of fruits) iced, sugared; (of leather, cloth) smooth, polished. (指水果)覆有糖霜的; 加糖的; (指皮革, 布匹)光滑的。

gla·cial /'gleɪsɪəl US: 'gleɪʃl; 'gleɪʃəl/ *adj* of ice or the ice age: 冰的; 冰河时代的: *the ~ era/epoch,* the time when large areas of the northern hemisphere were covered with ice; 冰河时代; (fig) (喻) *a ~ (= icy) manner/smile.* 冷冰冰的态度(笑)。

gla·cier /'glæsɪər US: 'gleɪʃər; 'gleɪʃɚ/ *n* [C] mass of ice, formed by snow on mountains, moving slowly along a valley. 冰河。 ⇨ the illus at **mountain.** 参看 mountain 之插图。

glad /glæd; glæd/ *adj* (-der, -dest) **1** (*pred* only) pleased: (仅用作表语)高兴的: *be/look/feel ~ about something;* 对某事感到高兴; ~ *to see someone.* 看见某人而高兴。 *I am ~ of your success/that you have succeeded.* 你的成功使我高兴。 **2** causing or bringing joy;

joyful: 使人快乐的: 令人愉快的: *Have you heard the ~ news/tidings?* 你听到那喜讯没有了? *All nature seemed ~*, was bright and beautiful, as if rejoicing. 万物欣欣向荣 (灿烂而美丽，象是高兴的样子)。 *give sb the '~ eye*, (sl) give an amorous, inviting look. (俚)向某人投媚眼。 *give sb the ~ hand*, (sl) offer the hand of welcome. (俚)向某人伸出欢迎的手。 *'~ rags*, (sl) clothes for a festive occasion. (俚)庆祝场合所穿的衣服。 **~·den** /'glædn/ *vt* [VP6A] make ~. 使高兴; 使快乐。 **~·ly** *adv* **~·ness** *n* **~·some** /-səm/ *adj* (liter) cheerful; joyful. (文)愉快的;可喜的。

glade /gleɪd; gled/ *n* clear, open space in a forest. 森林中的空地。

gladi·ator /'glædieɪtə(r); 'glædɪˌetɚ/ *n* (in ancient Rome) man trained to fight with weapons at public shows in an arena. (古罗马) 在斗技场公开作打斗表演的)斗士。 **gladia·tor·ial** /ˌglædɪə'tɔːrɪəl; ˌglædɪə'torɪəl/ *adj* of ~: ~ *ial combats*. 斗技。

gladi·olus /ˌglædɪ'əʊləs; ˌglædɪ'oləs/ *n* (*pl* **-li** /-laɪ; -laɪ/ or **~es**) plant with sword-shaped leaves and spikes of brightly coloured flowers. 剑兰; 唐菖蒲。

glam·our (US also **glamor**) /'glæmə(r); 'glæmɚ/ *n* [U] **1** charm or enchantment; power of beauty or romance to move the feelings: 魅力; 魔力; 迷人的力量: *the ~ of moonlight on the sea*. 海上迷人的月色。 **2** alluring beauty or charm, often with sex-appeal. 诱惑力(常是性感的)。 **glamor·ous** /-əs; -əs/ *adj* full of ~: 富有魅力的: *glamorous film stars.* 富有魅力的电影明星。 **glamor·ize** /-aɪz; -aɪz/ *vt* [VP6A] make glamorous: 使有魅力: *newspapers that glamorize the lives of film stars.* 把影星的生活描写得十分动人的报纸。 **glamor·iz·ation** /ˌglæmərɑɪ'zeɪʃn US: -rɪ'z-; ˌglæmərɪ'zeʃən/ *n*

glance /glɑːns US: glæns; glæns/ *vi, vt* **1** [VP2C, 3A] *~ at/over/through/round*, take a quick look: 瞥视; 匆匆一看: *~ at the clock*; 匆匆看一下钟; *~ over/through a letter*; 略读一封信; *~ round a room.* 略略环视一房间。 *She ~d shyly at him from behind her fan.* 她羞怯地从她的扇子后面看了他一眼。 [VP15A] *He ~d his eye down the classified advertisements.* 他浏览分类广告栏。 **2** [VP3A] *~ off*, (of a weapon or a blow) quickly slip or slide: (武器或一击)擦过: *The arrow ~d off his armour.* 箭擦过他的甲胄。 **3** [VP2C] (of bright objects, light) flash: (指明亮的物体，光)闪耀; 闪光: *Their helmets ~d in the sunlight.* 他们的钢盔在阳光下闪耀着。 □ *n* **1** quick look: 匆匆一看; 匆匆一瞥: *take a ~ at the newspaper headlines*; 浏览报上的标题; *loving ~s.* 脉脉含情的眼神。 *at a ~*, immediately on looking. 一瞥之下。 *at first ~*, = at first sight, ⇨ **sight¹(2)**. **2** (sudden movement producing a) flash of light: 闪烁; 发闪光的突然动作: *a ~ of spears in the sunlight.* 矛在阳光下的闪烁。

gland /glænd; glænd/ *n* simple or complex organ that separates from the blood substances that are to be used by or expelled from the body: 腺: *a snake's poison ~s*; 蛇的毒腺; *milk-producing ~s in a female*; 雌性动物的乳腺; *sweat ~s.* 汗腺。 **~ular** /'glændjulə(r) US: -dʒu-; 'glændʒələ/ *adj* of, like, or involving a gland. 腺的; 似腺的。

glan·ders /'glændəz; 'glændɚz/ *n* [U] contagious disease of horses with swellings below the jaw, and sores in the nose and throat. 马的鼻疽病。

glare¹ /gleə(r); glɛr/ *n* **1** [U] strong, fierce, unpleasant light: 强烈刺目的光: *the ~ of the sun on the water*; 水面上刺目的阳光; (fig) (喻) *in the full ~ of publicity*, public attention directed towards one. 众目睽睽之下。 **2** [C] angry or fierce look; fixed look: 怒目而视; 瞪视: *look at someone with a ~.* 怒视某人。

glare² /gleə(r); glɛr/ *vi, vt* **1** [VP2A, C] shine in a dazzling or disagreeable way: 发强烈的光; 发刺眼的光: *The tropical sun ~d down on us all the day.* 热带的太阳整日灼照着我们。 **2** [VP2A, C, 3A] *~ (at)*, stare angrily or fiercely: 怒目而视: *They stood glaring at each other.*

他们站着互相怒目而视。 [VP6A, 14] *~ (at)*, They *~d defiance/hate at me.* 他们以轻蔑(仇恨)的眼神瞪着我。 **glar·ing** *adj* **1** dazzling: 耀目的; 刺目的光: *a car with glaring headlights*; 有刺目的前灯的汽车; *glaring neon signs.* 耀目的霓虹灯广告。 **2** angry; fierce: 愤怒的; 凶恶的: *glaring eyes.* 愤怒的眼光。 **3** gross; conspicuous: 显著的; 易见的: *a glaring error/blunder*; 显著的谬误; *glaring injustice.* 昭彰的不公。 **4** (of colours) crude; gaudy. (指颜色)粗俗的; 华丽而俗气的。

glass /glɑːs US: glæs; glæs/ *n* **1** [U] hard, brittle substance (as used in windows), usu transparent: 玻璃: *bottles made of ~*; 玻璃瓶; *a man with a ~ eye.* 装有假眼的人。 **2** [C] article made of this substance. 玻璃制品。 **(a)** ~ drinking vessel or its contents: 玻璃杯; 酒杯; 一杯之量; 杯内之饮料: *have a ~ too much*, drink too much alcoholic liquor, be rather drunk. 酒喝得过多。 **(b)** (also 亦作 '**looking-~**) mirror made of ~. 镜子。 **(c)** telescope: 望远镜: *The sailor looked through his ~.* 那船员由望远镜瞭望。 **(d)** barometer: 晴雨表: *The ~ is falling.* 晴雨表在下降。 **(e)** (*pl*) (rarely 罕 '**eye-~es**) spectacles: 眼镜: *She can't read without ~es.* 不戴眼镜她无法看书。 **(f)** (*pl*) binoculars. (复)双筒望远镜。 **(g)** '*magnifying ~*, lens on a handle for making writing, etc appear larger. 放大镜。 ⇨ the illus at **magnet**. 参看 magnet 之插图。 **3** [U] vessels and articles made of ~: 玻璃器皿: *There's plenty of ~ in the house*, plenty of drinking ~s, wine ~es, ~ bowls and dishes, etc. 这房屋内有许多玻璃器皿。 *There are many acres of ~ in Jersey*, acres covered with ~houses (for growing plants). 在泽西有许多英亩的温室。 **4** (compounds) (复合词) '**~-blower** *n* workman who blows molten ~ to shape it into bottles, etc. 吹制玻璃器皿。 '**~-cutter** *n* workman who cuts designs on ~; tool for cutting ~. 玻璃雕切匠; 割切玻璃之器具; 割玻璃刀。 '**~·house** *n* building with ~ sides and roof (for growing plants); (sl) military prison. 温室; 暖房; (俚)军人监狱。 *People who live in ~houses shouldn't throw stones*, (prov) People with faults shouldn't criticize those of others. (谚)人居温室不可投石(自己有毛病不可批评他人)。 '**~·ware** /-weə(r); -wɛr/ *n* [U] articles made of ~. 玻璃器皿。 '**~·wool** *n* [U] fine ~ fibres used for filtering and in man-made fibres. 玻璃绒; 玻璃纤维。 '**~·works** *n pl* (with *sing v*) factory where ~ is manufactured. (接单数动词)玻璃工厂。 □ *vt* [VP6A, 15B] *~ (in)*, fit with ~; glaze: 装以玻璃; 镶以玻璃: *a ~ed-in veranda.* 装有玻璃的走廊。 **~·ful** /-ful; -ˌfʊl/ *n* as much as a drinking ~ will hold. 一杯之量。 **~·y** *adj* (**-ier, -iest**) like ~ in appearance: 形象如玻璃的: *a ~y calm*; 平静如镜; (of the sea, etc) smooth and shiny; (指海洋等)平稳如镜的; *a ~y stare/look/eye*, lifeless, expressionless, fixed. 呆滞的凝视(目光;眼神)。

glau·coma /glɔ:'kəumə; glɔ'komə/ *n* [U] eye disease involving gradual loss of sight. 绿内障; 青光眼(使眼睛逐渐失明的疾病)。

glau·cous /'glɔːkəs; 'glɔkəs/ *adj* **1** dull greyish green or blue. 淡灰绿色的; 淡灰蓝色的。 **2** (of leaves, grapes, etc) covered with bloom(3). (指叶、葡萄等)有粉衣的; 有霜粉的。

glaze /gleɪz; glez/ *vt, vi* **1** [VP6A, 15B] *~ (in)*, fit glass into: 装以玻璃: *~ a window/house*; 给窗子(房屋)装玻璃; *~ in a porch/veranda*, enclose it with glass. 给走廊装上玻璃。 **2** [VP6A, 15B] *~ (over)*, cover with a glass-like surface: 覆以玻璃状的表面; 上釉: *~ pottery/porcelain/bricks.* 给陶器(瓷器,砖)上釉。 **3** [VP2A, C] *~ (over)*, (of the eyes) become glassy: (指眼神)变为呆滞: *His eyes ~d over.* 他的目光呆滞。 *His eyes were ~d in death.* 他死时目光呆滞。 □ *n* [C, U] (substance used for, surface obtained by giving, a) thin glassy coating: 釉; 上釉的表面; 光滑的薄面: *a Satsuma vase with a fine crackle ~.* 饰有上等纹釉的萨摩瓷花瓶。

glaz·ier /'gleɪzɪə(r) US: -ʒə(r); 'gleʒɚ/ *n* workman who

fits glass into the frames of windows, etc. 装玻璃的工人。

gleam /gli:m; glim/ n [C] **1** beam or ray of soft light, esp one that comes and goes: 一丝光线; 微弱的闪光: *the ~ of a distant lighthouse*; 远处灯塔的闪光; *the first ~s of the morning sun.* 曙光。 **2** (fig) brief show of some quality or emotion: (喻)某种性质或感情的闪现: *a novel with an occasional ~ of humour/intelligence*; 偶尔闪现着幽默(智慧)的一部小说; *a ~ of hope*; 一线希望。 *a man with a dangerous ~ in his eye*, with a threatening look. 眼中闪现凶光的一个人。 □ vi [VP2A, C] send out ~s: 发闪光; 闪烁: *a cat's eyes ~ing in the darkness*; 在黑暗中闪烁的猫眼; *glass reflector studs ~ing in the roadway.* 在车道上闪烁的玻璃反光钉。

glean /gli:n; glin/ vi, vt [VP2A, 6A] pick up grain left in a harvest field by the workers; (fig) gather news, facts in small quantities: 拾(穗); (喻)一点点地搜集(消息,事实): *~ a field*; 在田中拾落穗; *~ corn.* 拾谷谷。 ~**er** n person who ~s. 拾落穗者; 搜集消息或事实者。 ~**ings** n pl (usu fig) small items of knowledge ~ed from various sources. (通常作哟)自各处汇集的零碎知识。

glebe /gli:b; glib/ n **1** (poet) earth; field. (诗)大地; 土地。 **2** portion of land that forms part of a clergyman's benefice. 作为牧师俸给之一部分的土地。

glee /gli:; gli/ n **1** [U] feeling of joy caused by success or triumph: (由于成功或胜利而产生的)欢欣; 高兴: *shout with ~.* 欢呼。 *She was in high ~ when she learnt the news.* 她得悉此消息高兴之至。 **2** [C] song for three or four voices singing different parts in harmony. 格里(三部或四部重唱曲)。 ~·**ful** /-fl; -fəl/ adj full of ~; joyous. 高兴的; 愉快的。 ~·**fully** /-fəli; -fəli/ adv

glen /glen; glen/ n narrow valley. 狭谷; 幽谷。

Glen·garry /,glen'gæri; glen'gæri/ n(pl -**ries**) kind of cap worn in the Highlands of Scotland. 苏格兰高地人所戴的一种帽子。

glib /glib; glib/ adj (-**bber, -bbest**) (of a person, what he says or how he says it) ready and smooth, but not sincere: (指人,言语, 说话方式)口齿伶俐但不真诚的; 油腔滑调的: *a ~ talker*; 口齿伶俐的谈话者; *~ excuses*; 流利但不真实的托词; *~ in finding excuses*; 找借口时口齿伶俐; *have a ~ tongue.* 有伶俐的口舌。 ~·**ly** adv ~·**ness** n

glide /glaid; glaid/ vi [VP2A, C] move along smoothly and continuously: 滑行; 滑动; 滑翔: *The skier ~d skilfully down the snow-covered slope.* 那滑雪者熟练地自陡坡上滑下。 *The skaters ~d across the ice.* 那些溜冰者滑过冰面。 *A boat ~d past.* 一只小船滑过。 □ n gliding movement or sound. 滑动; 滑行; 滑音。 ~r /'glaidə(r); 'glaidə/ n aircraft without an engine. 滑翔机。 **glid·ing** n sport of flying in ~rs. 滑翔运动。

glim·mer /'glimə(r); 'glimə/ vi [VP2A, C] send out a weak, uncertain light: 发出闪烁的微光: *lights ~ing in the distance.* 远处忽隐忽现的灯光。 □ n weak, faint, unsteady light: 微弱的闪光: *a ~ of light through the curtains*; 透过窗帘的一线微弱的闪光; (fig) (喻) *a ~ of hope*; 一线希望; *not the least ~ of intelligence.* 毫无智力(情报)。

glimpse /glimps; glimps/ n short look (at sth or sb). 一瞥(与此连用, 后接人或物)。 *get/catch a ~ of sb/ sth*, have a quick, imperfect view: 一瞥; 瞥见: *catch/ catch a ~ of something from the window of a train.* 自火车的窗中瞥见某物。 □ vt [VP6A, 19A] catch a ~ of. 瞥见。

glint /glint; glint/ vi gleam. 闪烁。 □ n gleam or flash: 闪烁; 闪光: *~s of gold in her hair.* 她头发中的金黄色闪光。

glis·sade /gli'seid US: -'sa:d; gli'sad/ vi (mountaineering) slide on the feet down a steep slope of ice or snow (usu with the support of an ice-axe); (ballet) make a sliding step. 滑(登山)(通常以破冰斧支撑自覆有冰雪之陡坡)滑下; (芭蕾舞)滑步。 □ n such a slide or step. 下滑; 滑步。

glissando /gli'sændəu; gli'sando/ adv, adj (music) passing quickly up or down the scale. (音乐)滑奏。

glis·ten /'glisn; 'glisn/ vi [VP2A, C] (esp of wet or polished surfaces, tear-filled eyes) shine brightly; sparkle: (尤指潮湿或光泽的表面,充满眼泪的眼睛)闪耀; 闪烁: *dew-drops*; 晶莹的露珠; *eyes ~ing with tears.* 泪光闪闪的眼睛。

glis·ter /'glistə(r); 'glistə/ vi, n (poet) glitter. (诗)闪烁。

glit·ter /'glitə(r); 'glitə/ vi [VP2A, C] shine brightly with flashes of light; sparkle: 闪烁: *stars ~ing in the frosty sky*; 闪烁在寒空的星斗; *~ing with jewels.* 珠光灿烂。 □ n [U] brilliant, sparkling light: 灿烂的光辉: *the ~ of the Christmas tree decorations.* 圣诞树上装饰品的光辉。 ~·**ing** adj brilliant; attractive: 灿烂的; 动人的: *~ing prizes.* 灿烂的奖品。

gloam·ing /'gləumiŋ; 'glomiŋ/ n the ~, (poet) evening twilight. (诗)薄暮; 黄昏。

gloat /gləut; glot/ vi [VP2A, 3A] ~ (**over sth**), look at with selfish delight: 怀着自私心理的喜悦去看; 幸灾乐祸地看: *~ over one's wealth*; 心满意足地看自己的财富(幸灾乐祸地看着敌对者的败落); *a miser ~ing over his gold.* 心满意足地望着他的金子的守财奴。 ~·**ing·ly** adv

glo·bal /'gləubl; 'globl/ adj world-wide; embracing the whole of a group of items, etc. 全球性的; 包括一切的。

globe /gləub; glob/ n **1** object shaped like a ball; model of the earth; spherical chart of the earth or the constellations. 球形体; 球体; 地球仪; 天体仪。 **the ~**, the earth. 地球。 **2** spherical glass vessel, esp a lampshade or a fishbowl. 球状玻璃器(尤指灯罩或金鱼缸)。 **3** '~**fish** n fish able to inflate itself into the shape of a ~. 河豚。 '**~-trot** vi [VP2A] travel hurriedly through many foreign countries. 匆匆游历世界。 '**~-trotter** n person who does this. 匆匆游历世界者。

glob·ule /'globju:l; 'globjul/ n tiny drop, esp of liquid. 小球状物; (尤指)水珠; 点滴。 **globu·lar** /'globjulə(r); 'globjələ/ adj globe-shaped; made of ~s. 球状的; 由点滴集成的。

glock·en·spiel /'globkənspi:l; 'glakən,spil/ n musical instrument consisting of metal bars which are struck with two light hammers. 钟琴(由金属棒构成之一种乐器,以二小锤击之); 铁琴。 ⇨ the illus at **percussion**. 参看 percussion 之插图。

gloom /glu:m; glum/ n [C, U] **1** semi-darkness; obscurity. 阴暗; 幽暗; 朦胧。 **2** feeling of sadness and hopelessness: 忧郁; 愁闷: *The future seems to be filled with ~.* 前途似乎充满了暗淡。 *The news cast a ~ over the village.* 这消息给整个村子罩上了一层忧郁。

gloomy /'glu:mi; 'glumi/ adj (-**ier, -iest**) **1** dark, unlighted. 黑暗的; 幽暗的。 **2** depressed; depressing: 阴郁的; 令人沮丧的: *a ~ outlook over roofs and chimneys*; 笼罩在屋顶和烟囱上的一片阴沉的景色; *feeling ~ about the future.* 感到前途暗淡。 **gloomily** /-ili; -ili /adv

glor·ify /'glo:rifai; 'glore,fai / vt (pt, pp -**fied**) [VP6A] **1** give adoration and thanksgiving to (God); worship; give honour and glory to (a hero). 赞美(上帝); 礼拜; 褒扬(英雄)。 **2** invest (sth common or simple) with splendour; make (sth or sb) seem more imposing: (使普通或朴素之物)增色; 美化: *His weekend cottage is only a glorified barn.* 他的周末别墅只是一个美化了的谷仓。 **glori·fi·ca·tion** /,glo:rifi'keiʃn; ,glorefə'keʃən/ n [U] ~ing or being glorified. 赞美; 礼拜; 褒扬。

glori·ous /'glo:riəs; 'glories/ adj **1** splendid; magnificent: 辉煌的; 壮丽的: *a ~ sunset/view.* 光辉灿烂的落日(景色)。 **2** illustrious; honourable; possessing or conferring glory: 显赫的; 光荣的; 辉煌的: *a ~ victory*; 光荣的胜利; *the ~ reign of Queen Elizabeth I.* 英国女王伊利莎白一世的辉煌朝代。 **3** (colloq) enjoyable: (口)愉快的: *have a ~ time.* 过一段愉快的时间; *~ fun.* 愉快的情趣。 **4** (ironic) dreadful: (反语)

可怕的: *What a ~ mess!* 真是乱七八糟! **·ly** adv

glory /'glɔːrɪ; 'glɔrɪ/ n [U] **1** high fame and honour won by great achievements. 光荣; 荣誉。**2** adoration and thanksgiving offered to God: (对上帝的)赞美; 赞颂: '*G~ to God in the highest.*' '荣耀归于至高的上帝.' **3** quality of being beautiful or magnificent: 壮丽; 灿烂; 辉煌: *the ~ of a sunset.* 落日的灿丽。**4** (sometimes [C] *pl* **-ries**) reason for pride; subject for boasting; sth deserving respect and honour: 值得骄傲可爱的名词分的原因; 夸耀的事物; 荣耀的事: *the glories of ancient Rome.* 古罗马的光荣事迹。**5** heavenly splendour: 天国的荣耀: *the saints in ~.* 天国的圣徒。**6** (colloq uses) **go to ~,** die; 死; **send sb to ~,** kill him. 杀死某人。'**~-hole** n room, drawer, filled untidily with miscellaneous articles. 装满杂乱物件的房间或抽屉。□ vi [VP3A] **~ in,** rejoice in, take great pride in: 为 … 而得意; 以 … 而自豪: *~ in one's strength / in working for a good cause.* 因强壮(从事有益人群的工作)而自豪。

gloss[1] /glɒs; glɔs/ n **1** [U] smooth, bright surface: 光滑的表面: *the ~ of silk and satin,* 绸缎之光滑的表面; *material with a good ~.* 表面光滑的料子。~, '**paint** n paint which, when dry, leaves a ~ (usu washable) surface. 亮光漆。**2** (usu *fig* a ~) deceptive appearance: 欺人的表面; 虚饰: *a ~ of respectability,* eg over a life of secret wrongdoing. 金玉其外的声望(例如掩饰暗中犯罪生活的)。□ vt [VP6A] **~ over,** give a ~ (2) to; cover up or explain away (an error, etc): 予以光滑的表面; 掩饰(错误等): *~ over sb's faults.* 掩饰某人的过失。~**y** adj (**-ier, -iest**) smooth and shiny: 光滑的; 有光泽的: *a ~y photographic print;* 光面的相片; ~*y hair;* 光滑的头发; ~*y periodicals,* those printed on high quality ~y paper, with photographs, coloured illustrations, etc, esp those periodicals dealing with clothes, fashions, etc. 由光滑的上等纸印成的有照片, 彩色插图等的刊物(尤指介绍服装, 时尚等者)。~**·ily** /-ɪlɪ; -ɪlɪ/ adv ~**·iness** n

gloss[2] /glɒs; glɔs/ n [C] explanation (in a footnote, or in a list at the end of an article, a book, etc) of a word in the text; comment; interpretation. 注释; 评注; 解释。□ vt [VP6A] add a ~ or ~es to (a text); write ~es on; make comments on. 注释(本文); 注解; 评注。

gloss·ary /'glɒsərɪ; 'glɑsərɪ/ n (*pl* **-ries**) [C] collection of glosses; list and explanations of special, eg technical, obsolete, words. 词汇; 语汇; 术语汇编。

glot·tis /'glɒtɪs; 'glɑtɪs/ n opening between the vocal cords at the upper part of the windpipe. 声门。⇨ the illus at **head.** 参看 head 之插图。**glottal** /'glɒtl; 'glɑtl/ adj of the ~. 声门的。**glottal stop,** speech sound produced by a complete closure of the ~, followed by an explosive release of breath. 喉塞音; 声门塞音。

glove /glʌv; glʌv/ n covering of leather, knitted wool, etc for the hand, usu with separated fingers. 手套。⇨ the illus at **base.** 参看 base 之插图。**fit like a ~,** fit perfectly. 十分相合。**be hand in ~ (with),** be in close relations (with). (与…)关系密切。**take off the ~s to sb; handle sb without ~s,** argue or contend in earnest, without mercy. 认真地或不留情地与某人争辩或争斗。'**~-compartment** n compartment in the dashboard of a car, for small articles. 汽车仪器板上放零星物件的隔间。

glow /gləʊ; glo/ vi [VP2A, C] **1** send out brightness or warmth without flame: 发炽热; 发光辉; 无焰地燃烧: ~*ing embers/charcoal;* 炽燃的余烬(木炭); ~*ing metal from the furnace.* 自熔炉中取出的炽热的金属。**2** (*fig*) be, look, feel, warm or flushed (as after exercise or when excited): (喻)身体发热或面孔发红(如运动后或兴奋时): ~*ing with enthusiasm/health/pride.* 热情洋溢(容光焕发; 得意扬扬)。**3** show strong or warm colours: 显示鲜艳的颜色: *woods and forests ~ing with autumn tints.* 带有鲜艳秋色的树林。□ n (*sing* only, with *def* or *indef art*) ~*ing* state; warm or flushed look; warm

feeling: (仅用单数, 与定冠词或不定冠词连用)炽热; 容光焕发; 热情: *in a ~ of enthusiasm;* 热情洋溢地; *cheeks with the ~ of health on them;* 红润的面颊; *(all) in a ~ after a hot bath;* 洗过热水澡后浑身通红; *the ~ of the sky at sunset.* 落日余晖。'**~-worm** n insect of which the wingless female gives out a green light at its tail. 萤火虫。~**·ing** adj showing warm colour or (*fig*) enthusiasm: 颜色鲜明的; (喻)热心的; 热烈的: *give a ~ing account of what happened;* 热烈地叙述所发生之事; *describe an event in ~ing colours.* 生动地描述一事件。~**·ing·ly** adv

glower /'glaʊə(r); 'glaʊə/ vi [VP2A, 3A] ~ (**at**), look in an angry or threatening way. 怒目而视; 凶狠地瞪着。~**·ing·ly** adv

glu·cose /'gluːkəʊs; 'glukos/ n [U] grape sugar. 葡萄糖。

glue /gluː; glu/ n [U] thick, sticky liquid used for joining things, eg broken wood, crockery. 胶(粘接断木、陶器等者)。□ vt (*pt, pp* **glued;** *pres p* **gluing**) [VP 6A, 15A, B] ~ (**to**), **1** stick, make fast, with ~: 用胶粘合; ~ *two pieces of wood together;* 将两块木头粘在一起; ~ *a piece of wood on to something.* 将一块木头粘在某物上。**2** put tightly or closely: 使密结; 使固着: *His eyes were/His ear was ~d to the keyhole.* 他的眼睛(他的耳朵)紧贴在钥匙孔上。*Why must you always remain ~d to your mother,* 你为何总是离不开你的母亲? ~**y** /'gluːɪ; 'gluɪ/ adj sticky, like ~. 粘的; 似胶的。

glum /glʌm; glʌm/ adj (**-mmer, -mmest**) gloomy; sad. 阴郁的; 忧愁的。~**·ly** adv ~**·ness** n

glut /glʌt; glʌt/ vt (**-tt-**) [VP6A, 14] ~ (**with**), **1** supply too much to: 过多地供应; 过度供给; 充斥: ~ *the market (with fruit, etc).* (水果等)充斥市场。**2** overeat; satisfy to the full; fill to excess: 过量地食饱; 使过量; 使过量: ~ *one's appetite.* 吃得过饱; ~ *oneself with rich food,* 吃太多油腻的食物; ~*ted with pleasure.* 纵情享乐。□ n [C] supply in excess of demand: 过量供应: *a ~ of pears in the market.* 市场上梨子的供应过剩。

glu·ten /'gluːtən; 'glutn/ n [U] sticky substance (protein) that is left when starch is washed out of flour. 面筋; 麸质。**glu·ti·nous** /'gluːtɪnəs US: -tənəs; 'glutənəs/ adj of or like ~; sticky. 面筋的; 似面筋的; 粘的。

glut·ton /'glʌtn; 'glʌtn/ n person who eats too much: 贪食者; 食用过量者: *You've eaten the whole pie, you ~!* 你把整个馅饼都吃掉了, 你这个好吃鬼! *He's a ~ for work,* (*fig*) is always willing and ready to work. (喻)他是个爱工作的人。~**·ous** /'glʌtənəs; 'glʌtnəs/ adj very greedy (for food). 贪吃的。~**·ous·ly** adv ~**y** /-tənɪ; -tnɪ/ n [U] habit or practice of eating too much. 吃过量的习惯; 贪食; 暴食。

gly·cer·ine (US = **gly·cer·in**) /'glɪsəriːn US: -rɪn; 'glɪsrɪn/ n [U] thick, sweet, colourless liquid made from fats and oils, used in medical and toilet preparations and explosives. 甘油; 丙三醇。

G-man /'dʒiːmæn; 'dʒimæn/ n (US colloq) federal criminal investigation officer. (美口)联邦调查局的探员。

gnarled /nɑːld; nɑrld/ adj (of tree trunks) twisted and rough; covered with knobs: (指树干)歪扭而粗糙的; 多瘤节的: *a ~ old oak;* 多瘤节的老橡树; ~ (= knotty, deformed) *hands/fingers.* 粗节的手(手指)。

gnash /næʃ; næʃ/ vi, vt **1** [VP2A] (of the teeth) strike together, eg in rage. (指牙齿)切齿; 咬牙(例如愤怒时)。**2** [VP6A] (of a person) cause (the teeth) to do this: (指人)咬(牙); 切(齿): *wailing and ~ing of teeth.* 大声吼叫并咬牙切齿。

gnat /næt; næt/ n small two-winged fly that stings; (*fig*) insignificant annoyance. 蚋; 蠓虫; (喻)小烦扰。**strain at a ~,** hesitate over a trifle. 为琐碎事而迟疑。

gnaw /nɔː; nɔ/ vt, vi **1** [VP6A, 15B, 3A] ~ (**at**), bite steadily or with effort (at sth hard): 咬; 啃; 嚼(硬物): *The dog was ~ing (at) a bone.* 那狗在啃一根骨头。*The*

rats had ~ed away some of the woodwork. 老鼠将一些木器咬坏了。 *He was ~ing his finger-nails with impatience.* 他焦灼地咬着他的指甲。 **2** [VP6A, 3A] **~ (at)**, torment; waste away: 使苦恼; 折磨; 消耗; 侵蚀: *fear and anxiety ~ing (at) the heart;* 磨噬内心的恐惧和焦虑; *the ~ing pains of hunger.* 饥饿的痛苦。

gnome /nəʊm; nom/ *n* (in tales) small goblin living under the ground (often guarding treasures of gold and silver). (故事中)地下的小妖魔; 地精(常常保护金银珍藏)。

gnu /nu::; nu/ *n* wildebeest. 牛羚,非洲产的一种大羚羊。 ⇨ the illus at **large**. 参看 large 之插图。

go[1] /gəʊ; go/ *vi* (*3rd pers sing t* **goes** /gəʊz; goz/, *pt* **went** /went; wɛnt/, *pp* **gone** /gɒn US: gɔːn; gɔn/) (For idiomatic uses with *adverbial particles* and *preps*, ⇨ **29** below.) (与副词性小品词和介词连用的习惯用法, ⇨ 下列第 29 义。) **1** [VP2A, C, 3A, 4A] (with a *prep* or *adv* of place or direction, present or implied; ⇨ **come**) (与表示地点或方向的介词或副词连用) **go (from/to)**, move, pass, *from* one point to another and away from the speaker, etc (cf 参较 **come from/to**): 走动; 走过; 行走; 离去: *Shall we go (there) by train or by plane?* 我们乘火车还是飞机去(那里)? *He has gone to China,* is now in, or on his way to, China. 他到中国去了。 *He has gone to see his sister.* 他探望他的姐姐(妹妹)去了。 *Go and get your hat.* 去拿你的帽子。 *Let's go to the cinema.* 我们去看电影吧。 *Let's go,* Let's leave. 我们走吧。 *They came at six and went* (= left) *at nine.* 他们六时来到, 九时离去。 *I must be going now,* must leave now. 我现在必须走了。 *I wish this pain would go (away).* 我希望这疼痛会消失。 *All hope is gone* (more usu today, has gone). 一切希望都没有了(现较常用 has gone)。 *Be gone! Go away!* (the more usu expression today). 走开! (现较常用 go away)。 *Who goes there?* (challenge from a sentry = Say who you are). 谁? (哨兵盘问时用语)。 **2** [VP2C] **(a)** be placed; have as a usual or proper position: 被安置; 以…为通常或适当的位置: *Where do you want your piano to go?* 你要我们把你的钢琴放到哪里? *'Where does this teapot go?' 'In that cupboard.'* '这茶壶放在何处?' '放在那个食橱里。' *This dictionary goes on the top shelf.* 这部词典是放在顶层书架上的。 **(b)** be fitted or contained in: 纳入; 被包容: *My clothes won't go into this small suitcase.* 我的衣服装不进这小提箱。 *7 into 15 won't go,* 15 does not contain exact multiples of 7. 七除十五除不尽。 **3** [VP2A, B, C, 3A] **go (from/to)**, reach, extend; last; (of a person's behaviour, remarks, achievements, etc) reach certain limits: 到达; 延及; 持续; (指人的行为, 言论, 成就等)达到某种限度: *This road goes to London.* 这条路通伦敦。 *I want a rope that will go from the top window to the ground.* 我要一条能从顶上的窗户伸到地上的绳子。 *Differences between employers and workers go deep,* Their views are far apart. 雇主与工人间意见上的冲突甚大。 **go a long way, (a)** last: 持续: *She makes a little money go a long way,* buys many things, etc by careful spending. 她能用很少的钱买很多的东西。 *A little of this paint goes a long way,* covers a large area. 这种漆一点点便可漆一大块面积。 **(b)** (colloq) be as much as one can bear: 所能忍受的限度: *A little of his company goes a long way,* One can endure his company for a short time only. 同他在一起只要短时间就够了。 **go a long way/go far towards doing sth,** make a considerable contribution towards: 对…有相当的贡献: *The Prime Minister's statement went a long way towards reassuring the nation.* 首相的话, 在使国民恢复信心方面, 甚为收效。 **go (very) far, (a)** last: 维持: *A pound doesn't go far nowadays,* doesn't last, doesn't buy much. 现在一英镑不当用了。 **(b)** (of a person, future tense) succeed: (指人, 用于将来时)成功: *He will go far in the diplomatic service,* will win promotion, etc. 他将来在外交界会有所成就。 **go too far,** go beyond acceptable limits: 过份: *That's going too far,* saying or doing more than is right. 那太过份了。 *You must apologize at once—you've gone too far,* exceeded the limits of accepted behaviour, etc. 你必须立刻道歉——你太过份了。 **go (any) further,** go beyond a certain point: 进一步: *I'll give you £50, but I can't go any further.* 我愿意给你五十英镑, 但我不再多给了。 *Need I go any further,* do or say anything more? 还有需要我做(说)的吗? **go as/so far as to do sth,** do or say sth to a certain limit: 做事或说话至某种限度: *I won't go as far as to say he's dishonest,* won't accuse him of this, even though I may suspect him of it. 我不愿意说他是不诚实(纵然我怀疑他, 我不愿意这样指控他)。 *I would go so far as to suggest that the House of Lords should be abolished.* 我甚至想建议废除上议院。 **as far as it goes,** to a limited extent: 至一限度: *That's all very well as far as it goes,* The limitations of statement, explanation, etc must be realised. 就目前情形而言, 一切良好。 *What he says is true as far as it goes,* suggesting that further information, knowledge, etc is needed or desirable. 就某种程度而言, 他的话是对的。 **go to great lengths/trouble/pains (to do sth),** take care to do sth well: 费心将某事做好: *He went to great trouble to make his guests comfortable.* 他尽力让他的客人感到舒服。 **go to one's head,** ⇨ **head**[1](19). **go as low/high as,** (of a price) reach a certain level: (指价格)达到某一标准: *I'll go as high as £250,* will offer this sum, eg at an auction. 我愿意出二百五十英镑(例如在拍卖中)。 **go one better (than sb),** improve on what he has done: 较某人所做更佳: *I hit the target 17 times out of 20, but Tom went one better and scored 18.* 我在二十次中击中了目标十七次, 但汤姆胜我一筹, 击中了十八次。 *It all/just goes to show/prove that,* tends or helps to show/prove that. 一切显示出(证明了)…。 **4 go on a journey/trip/outing,** make a journey, take a trip, have an outing, etc. 去旅行(旅行, 远足)。 **go for a walk/swim, etc,** go out in order to walk, swim, etc. 去散步(游泳等)。 **go walking/swimming, etc,** take part in the activity of walking, swimming, etc: 散步(游泳等)(指参与散步, 游泳等活动): *Do they often go sailing?* Is sailing sth they often do? 他们时常去驾船吗? (Cf 参较 *Let's go for a walk,* referring to a specified occasion. 指特殊场合。 *Bill has gone (out) shopping,* has gone to buy things in the shops. 比尔买东西去了。 **5** (in the pattern, **go into + prep + n**) (用于 go + 介词 + 名词句型中) **(a)** pass into/from the state indicated by the *n*. 变成某种状态。 **go into abeyance,** ⇨ **abeyance. go from bad to worse,** ⇨ **bad**[1](4). **go into a coma/trance,** ⇨ **coma, trance. go out of fashion,** ⇨ **fashion. go into liquidation,** ⇨ **liquidation** at **liquidate. go to pieces,** ⇨ **piece**[1](1). **go to pot,** ⇨ **pot**[1](2). **go to rack and ruin,** ⇨ **rack**[4]. **go into retirement,** ⇨ **retirement** at **retire. go to seed,** ⇨ **seed. go to sleep,** ⇨ **sleep**[1](3). **go out of use,** ⇨ **use**[1](1). **go to war,** ⇨ **war. (b)** go to the place, etc indicated for the purpose associated with it. 到一指明的地点等做与其有关之事。 **go to the block/stake,** ⇨ **block**[1](3), **stake. go to church,** attend a church service. 做礼拜。 **go to hospital,** ⇨ **hospital. go to market,** ⇨ **market. go to school/college/university,** attend school, etc in order to learn or study. 上学(大学)。 **go to sea,** become a sailor. 做海员。 **go on the stage,** ⇨ **stage. go on the streets,** ⇨ **street. (c)** have recourse to. 求助于; 诉诸。 **go to the country,** ⇨ **country. go to law,** ⇨ **law**(6). **6** [VP3A] **go to sb,** pass into sb's possession; be allotted to: 归某人所有; 归某人所得: *Who did the property go to when the old man died,* Who inherited it? 那老人死后, 财产归谁所有? *Honours do not always go to those who merit them.* 荣誉并不总是归于应得之人。 *The first prize went to Mr Hill.* 头奖为希尔先生所得。 **7** [VP2D] become; pass into a specific condition: 变成; 进入某种特殊的情况: *go blind/mad, etc.* 变瞎(疯等)。 *He went purple with anger/grey with worry.* 他气得脸色发紫(忧愁得头发灰白了)。 *Fish soon goes bad* (=

rotten) *in hot weather*. 鱼在热天不久便变坏了。*The children went wild with excitement*. 孩子们兴奋得发狂。*This material has gone a nasty colour*. 这料子变成脏兮兮的颜色。*Kensington went Labour at the by-election*, changed politically by returning the Labour candidate to Parliament. 肯辛顿于补选会议员时改投工党竞候选人的票。*Will the country go Democrat next year?* 该国明年会变成民主党的天下吗？ **go berserk, ⇨ berserk. go broke,** become penniless. 破产。 **go dry,** ⇨**dry¹(12). go flat,** (of liquid) lose its gas content: (指液体)跑气: *This beer has gone flat*. 这啤酒跑气了。 **go haywire, ⇨ hay. go native,** adopt the mode of life of the natives of the country in which one is living. 过当地人的生活。 **go phut,** (colloq) (of machines) collapse: (口)(指机器)垮了；不灵光了：*The old car went phut half way up the hill*: 那部老爷车在爬山的半途抛锚了；(fig): (喻)：*His plan/scheme/project has gone phut*. 他的计划泡汤了。 **go scotfree/unchallenged/unpunished,** be free from penalty or punishment; escape being challenged. 未受罚；未受诘难。 **8** [VP2A, C] be moving, working, etc: 正在活动，工作等：*This clock doesn't go*. 这钟不走了。*Is your watch going?* 你的表在走吗？*Her tongue was going nineteen to the dozen*, ⇨ **dozen.** 她噼噼不休(话讲个没完)。 (口)那出戏非常叫座。⇨ **go down** in **28** below. 参看下列第 28 义之 go down。 **a going concern**, a business in working order, operating well. 营业情况良好的商行。 **9** [VP2C, D] be or live habitually in a specific state or manner: 习惯于某种状态；过惯某种生活：*Refugees often go hungry*. 难民时常挨饿。*The men of this tribe used to go naked*. 这个部落里的男子过去常是裸体的。*He went in fear of his life*. 他经常恐惧会丧失生命。*You'd better go armed (= carry a weapon) while in the jungle*. 在丛林中最好持携带武器。*She is six months gone*, six months pregnant. 她已怀孕六个月了。 **10** [VP2C, D, E] (after *How*) progress: (用于'How'之后)进展：*How's everything going*. 事情发展情形如何？ *How's work going? How goes work?* 工作进展情况如何？ *How goes it?* (colloq) How are you? (口)你好吗？ (with an *adv* or *adj* equivalent, eg *adj*j such as *slow, easy*, indicating manner of progress): (与副词或相当于副词如 *slow, easy* 等形容词连用，表示进行的状态)：*go badly/well*, (of work, events) proceed (un)satisfactorily: (指工作，事件)进行(不)满意：*All has gone well with our plans*, they've succeeded. 我们的计划顺利进行。*Things went better than had been expected*. 事情的进行较预期者令人满意。*go easy (on/with/sb/sth),* be less strenuous, less severe; handle gently or carefully: 轻松一些；不要紧张；不要太严厉：*Go easy with/on the butter, that's all we have*, don't be wasteful. 不要浪费牛油，我们只有那么多了。*Go easy with her, she's too young to realize her mistake*. 对她不要太严厉，她太年轻而不知道犯了错误。 **go slow, (a)** (of traffic) move forward slowly. (指交通)慢行。 **(b)** (of workers in factories, etc) work slowly, esp to reduce output, as a protest against sth or to draw attention to demands. (指工厂等的工人)怠工以示抗议。 Hence, 由此产生，**'go-slow** *n* [C] such slow work. 怠工。 **c. be going strong**, be proceeding vigorously; be still flourishing: 有力地进行；仍然旺盛：*He's ninety and/but still going strong*. 他九十岁了，但仍然健壮。 **11** [VP2A, C] work; operate: 运转：*This machine goes by electricity*. 这机器由电推动。*I've been going hard (at it) all day and I'm exhausted*. 我一整天辛苦地工作，我感到疲惫了。 **12** [VP2A, C] (in progressive tenses only) be available, be offered: (仅用于进行时)可获得；被提供：*Are there any jobs going?* 有什么工作机会吗？ **13** [VP2C, 3A] *go (to sb) for*, be sold (to sb) for: (以…的价钱)被卖出(被售与某人)：*The house went cheap*. 这房子卖得便宜。*I shan't let mine go (= sell it) for less than £8000*. 少于八千英镑我的就不卖。 **go for a song**, ⇨ **song. Going! Going! Gone!** (used at an auction to announce the

closing of the bidding). (拍卖时用语)要卖掉了！要卖掉了！卖掉了！ **14** [VP3A] *go on/in*, (of money) be spent on: (指金钱)用于；花在…上：*How much of your money goes on food and clothes/in rent?* 你的钱有多少花费在食物和衣服(房租)上？*Half the money he inherited went in gambling debts*. 他所继承的金钱一半付了赌债。 **15** [VP2A, C] be given up, abandoned, lost: 被放弃，废除或失去：*I'm afraid the car must go*, We can no longer afford to run it, so must sell it. 我恐怕这车子必须卖掉了。*My sight is going*, I'm losing my ability to see. 我的视力正在减退。 **16** [VP2A, C] be current or accepted; be commonly thought of or believed: 流通；流传：*The story goes that…*. It is said that…. 据说…。 **17** [VP2A] *as people/things go*, considering the average person/thing: 照一般人，东西等而论：*They're good cars as cars go nowadays*, judging them from the average or usual type today. 就目前一般汽车而论，它们是好汽车。*Five pounds for a pair of shoes is not bad as things go today*, in view of how much things cost today. 照如今一般物价而言，一双鞋卖五英镑不算贵。 **18** [VP2A] fail; collapse; give way; break off: 失败；坍塌；折裂；中断：*First the sails and then the mast went in the storm*. 在那暴风雨中先是帆坏了，其次桅也断了。*The bank may go (= fail) any day*. 这家银行随时可能倒闭。*He's far gone*, is critically ill or (colloq) is mad. 他的病况甚为严重；(口)他疯狂了。 **let oneself go**, relax, enjoy oneself, etc. 放松自己；享乐。 **19** die: 死：*He is going/has gone, poor fellow!* 他要死了(已死了)，可怜的人！ *dead and gone*, dead and buried. 死去并已埋葬了。 **20** [VP2A, C] be decided: 被决定：*The case (te in a law court) went against him*, he lost. 他官司打输了。*The case went in his favour*, he won. 他官司打赢了。*How did the election go at Hull*, Who was elected? 赫尔城的选举结果如何？ *Does promotion go by favour in your firm?* 你们公司中的升迁是凭主管的偏爱吗？ **21** (various phrases) (各种短语) **go bail (for sb)**, ⇨ **bail¹. go Dutch (with sb)**, ⇨ **Dutch. go shares/halves (in sth with sb)**, ⇨ **share¹(1), half. go sick**, ⇨ **sick¹(2).** **'go it**, (colloq) act vigorously, indulge in wild spending, etc. (口)使劲干；浪费金钱等。 **go it alone**, act by oneself, without support. 自己干。 **22** [VP2A, C] **(a)** have a certain wording or tune: 有某种语法或调子：*I'm not quite sure how the words go/tune goes*. 我不大清楚那些话是怎么说的(那个曲调是怎么唱的)。 **(b)** (of a verse or song) be adaptable (to a certain tune): (指诗歌)可适合(某曲调)：*It goes to the tune of 'Three Blind Mice'*. 它可适合 'Three Blind Mice' 的调子。 **23** (colloq) (followed by *and* and another *v*) proceed to do sth: (口)(后接 *and* 及另一动词)去做某事：*Go and shut the door, would you?* (as an informal request). 去把门关上好吗？ (作为非正式的请求)。*Go and ask that policeman the way*. 去向那个警察问路。*Now you've gone and done it*, (sl) have made a mistake, blundered. (俚)如今你犯了一个大错。 **24** [VP2A, C] make a specific sound: 发某种声音：*The clock goes 'tick-tock, tick-tock'*. 时钟发出'滴答滴答'的声音。*'Bang!' went the gun*. '砰'! 枪声响了。 **25** (in bridge²) [VP6A] bid; declare: (桥牌)叫牌：*go two spades/three no trumps*. 叫二黑桃(三无王)。 **26** [VP2A] begin an activity: 开始动作：*One, two, three, go!* or *Ready, steady, go!* (eg as a signal for competitors in a race to start). 一，二，三，开始! (竞赛开始的口令)。*Well, here goes!* (used to call attention to the fact that one is about to start to do sth). 喂，开始了! (用以使人注意将要开始做某事。 **27** (used to express the future) (用以表示未来) **be going to do sth, (a)** indicating what is intended, determined or planned: 表示打算，决定或计划做某事：*We're going to spend our holidays in Wales this year*. 今年我们要在威尔士度假。*I'm going to have my own way*. 我要照自己的意思去做。*We're going to buy a house when we've saved enough money*. 我们存够了钱的时候，打算买一栋房子。 **(b)** indicating what is considered likely or probable: 表示可能会发生…事: *Look at those

black clouds—we're going to have/there's going to be a storm. 看那些乌云——暴风雨要来了。 (c) expressing the immediate or near future (= about to): 表示即将发生: *I'm going to tell you a story.* 我要给你们讲一个故事。 *I'm going to be twenty next month.* 我下个月就二十岁了。 **28** (compounds) (复合词) **'go-ahead** n ⇨ **go ahead** in **29** below. 参看下列 29 义之 go ahead。**,go-as-you-'please**, attrib adj untroubled by regulations. 无拘束的；自由行动的。**'go-by**, ⇨ **go by** in **29** below. 参看下列 29 义中之 go by。**,go-'slow**, ⇨ **10** above. 参看上列第 10 义。**,go-to-'meeting**, attrib adj (dated colloq of hats, clothes, etc) worn on special occasions, eg for church: (过时口语，指衣帽等)为某种场合(例如赴教堂)而穿戴的: *wearing their Sunday go-to-meeting clothes.* 穿着他们星期日做礼拜的衣服(体面衣服，最好的衣服)。 **29** [VP2C, 15B, 3A] (idiomatic uses with *adverbial particles* and *preps*): (与副词性小品词及介词连用的习惯用法):

go about, **(a)** move from place to place; pay visits: 走来走去；四处走动: *I don't go about much anymore.* 我不再经常四处走动了。 **(b)** (of rumours, stories, etc) pass from person to person, usu verbally; be current: (指谣言，故事等)流传(通常为口头上地): *A story/rumour is going about that...* 据传说(谣传)...。 **(c)** (of a ship) change course or tack(3). (指船)改变航行方向。 **go about sth**, set to work at: 着手于: *You're not going about that job in the right way.* 你做那事的方法不对。 *We'll have to go about it more carefully.* 我们必须细心去做此事。 **go about one's business**, deal with one's own affairs (rather than with sb else's). 处理自己的事(勿管他人之事)。 **go about with sb**, spend time (in public) regularly with him: 经常(公开地)与某人在一起: *go about with a bunch of thugs.* 跟一群恶棍鬼混。 **go after sb/sth**, try to win or obtain: 设法追求某人(获得某物): *He's going after that pretty Swedish girl, is trying to win her interest or affection.* 他正在追求那位美丽的瑞典女郎。 *He's gone after a job in the City.* 他去伦敦老城求职。 **go against sb**, **(a)** oppose: 反对: *Don't go against your father.* 不要反对你的父亲。 **(b)** have an unsatisfactory outcome: 结果不令人满意: *The war is going against them, They seem likely to be defeated.* 战争似乎对他们不利。 ⇨ also **20** above. 亦参看上列第 20 义。 **go against sth**, be contrary to: 与…相反: *It goes against my principles/interests.* 这与我的主张(利益)相反。 **go against the grain**, ⇨ **grain**.

go ahead, **(a)** make progress: 进步: *He's going ahead fast.* 他进步很快。 *The Joneses are very go-ahead (= progressive) people; it's difficult to keep up with them.* 琼斯一家人很进步，令人难以赶上。 **(b)** proceed without hesitation: 不犹豫地进行: '*May I start now?' 'Yes, go ahead.*' '我可以动身吗?' '是的，动身罢。' Hence, 由此产生, **'go-ahead** n permission to proceed: 准许进行: *give them the go-ahead.* 准许他们进行。

go along, proceed: 进行: *You may have some difficulty first but you'll find it easier as you go along.* 最初你或许有些困难，但过些时你会觉得较为容易。 **go along with sb**, **(a)** accompany: 陪伴: *I'll go along with you as far as the main road.* 我将陪你走到大路。 **(b)** agree with: 同意: *I can't go along with you on that point.* 我不同意你的那一点。 **go at sb/sth**, **(a)** rush at; attack: 冲向；攻击: *They went at each other furiously.* 他们猛烈地互相扑打。 *They went at it tooth and nail/hammer and tongs, fought furiously.* 他们猛烈地攻击。 **(b)** take sth in hand, deal with it energetically: 努力去做；努力对付: *They were going at the job for all they were worth, making the utmost possible effort to do the work.* 他们在尽最大努力做此事。

go away, leave. 离去。 **go away with sb/sth**, take with, abscond with: 带走；卷逃: *He has gone away with my razor, has taken it with him.* 他把我的剃刀带走了。 **go back**, **(a)** return. 回来。 **(b)** extend backwards in

space or time: 回溯: *His family goes back to the time of the Norman Conquest, can be traced back to then.* 他的家族可追溯至诺曼第人征服英国的时代。 **go back on/upon**, fail to keep; break or withdraw from, eg a promise: 违背；背弃(例如诺言): *He's not the sort of man who would go/to go back on his word.* 他不是那种背信的人。

go before (sth), precede: 居前: *Pride goes before a fall.* 骄者必败。

go behind sth, search for sth: 寻求某物: *go behind a person's words*, look for a hidden meaning in what he says. 探求一人言语中的含义。 **go behind sb's back**, do or say sth without his knowledge. 瞒着某人做或说某事。

go beyond sth, exceed: 超过: *You've gone beyond your instructions.* 你已逾越你所受到的指示。 *That's going beyond a joke, is too serious to be amusing.* 那样开玩笑是太过火了。

go by, pass: 经过: *Time went by slowly.* 时间慢慢逝去。 *We waited for the procession to go by.* 我们等着那行列走过。 **'go by sth**, be guided or directed by: 受…之指导: *I shall go entirely by what my solicitor says, shall follow his advice.* 我将完全遵照律师的指示。 *That's a good rule to go by, to be guided by.* 那是个可遵守的好规则。 **(b)** form an opinion or judgement from: 凭…而判断: *Have we enough evidence to go by?* 我们有足够的证据以资判断吗? *It's not always wise to go by appearances.* 由外表判断未必一定是明智的。 *I go by what I hear.* 我根据我听到的而判断。 **,go by the 'book**, follow the rules closely. 按照规则行事。 **go by/under the name of**, use the name of; be called. 称为; 叫做。 **'go-by** n. **give sb/sth the go-by**, (colloq) ignore; disregard; slight or snub: (口)忽视; 不理; 轻视; 冷落: *He gave me the go-by in the street yesterday, ignored me completely.* 他昨天在街上视我为路人。

go down, **(a)** (of a ship, etc) sink. (指船只等)沉没。 **(b)** (of the sun, moon, etc) set. (指日，月等)下落。 **(c)** (of food and drink) be swallowed: (指食物与饮料)被吞下: *This pill won't go down, I can't swallow it.* 这药丸吞不下去。 **(d)** leave a university for the vacation, having graduated, etc. 离开大学去度假: 已毕业。 **(e)** (of the sea, wind, etc) become calm: (指海，风等)平静; 平息: *The wind has gone down a little, is less strong.* 风势减弱了。 **(f)** (of prices) go lower: (指物价)跌落: *The price of eggs/The cost of living has gone down.* 鸡蛋的价格(生活费用)下跌了。 **(g)** **go down to the sea/country etc,** pay a visit to the seaside, countryside, etc. 去海滨(乡村)等。 **go down before sb,** be defeated or overthrown: 被击败; 被推翻: *Rome went down before the barbarians.* 罗马被野蛮人征服。 **go down (in sth)**, be written in; be recorded or remembered in: 被记录下来; 被记得: *It all goes down in his notebook.* 他将它都记在笔记簿里了。 *He'll go down in history as a great statesman.* 他将成为历史上伟大的政治家。 **go down to,** be continued or extended as far as: 继续至; 延续至: *This 'History of Europe' goes down to 1970.* 这部 '欧洲史' 记述至一九七〇年止。 **go down (with sth),** **(a)** (of an explanation or excuse) be accepted or approved (by the listener, reader, audience, etc): (指解释或借口，故事，戏剧等)为听者，读者，听众等接受或赞许: *The new play went down well/like a bomb (= extremely well) with provincial audiences.* 这新戏甚为(深为)地方观众赞赏。 *That explanation won't go down well with me.* 我不相信那种解释。 *The new teacher doesn't go down well with his pupils.* 新教师不受学生们的欢迎。 **go down (with sth),** fall ill (with an illness): 染病: *Poor Peter—he's gone down with flu.* 可怜的彼得—他染上了流行性感冒。

go for sb, **(a)** go to fetch: 去取来或接来: *Shall I go for a doctor?* 要我去请一位医生吗? **(b)** attack: 攻击: *The dog went for the postman as soon as he opened the garden gate.* 邮差一打开花园的门，那狗便向他扑了过去。 *Go for*

him! (said to a dog to urge him to attack). 去咬他! (对狗说的话). *They went for me in the correspondence columns of the papers.* 他们在报纸通信栏内攻击我. **(c)** be applicable to: 可以应用于: *What I have said about Smith goes for you, too.* 我听说的有关史密斯的话也可以用在你的身上. **go for nothing / little,** be considered of no / little value: 被认为无价值: *All his work went for nothing.* 他的一切工作都归于零(被认为无何价值).

go forth, (formal) be published or issued: (正式用语)公布; 发表: *The order went forth that....* 命令宣布说....

go forward, (a) advance: 前进: *A patrol went forward to investigate.* 一支巡逻队前去调查. **(b)** make progress: 进步: *The work is going forward well.* 工作进展良好.

go in, (a) enter: 进入: *The key won't go in (the lock).* 这钥匙塞不进(锁里)去. *This cork's too big; it won't go in.* 这软木塞太大了, 塞不进去. *She went in to cook the dinner.* 她进去烧饭. **(b)** (of the sun, moon, etc) be obscured by clouds: (指日, 月等)被云遮蔽: *The sun went in and it grew rather cold.* 太阳被云遮蔽, 天气变得有些冷了. **(c)** (cricket, etc) begin an innings: (板球等)开始一局比赛: *Who goes in next?* 下一局谁进了? **(d)** enter as a competitor: 参加比赛: *Go in and win!* (used as a form of encouragement). 去好好比赛一场! (用以鼓励参加比赛者). **go in for sth,** (a) take, enter (an examination or competition). 参加(考试或比赛). **(b)** have an interest in, have a hobby, etc: 以…为兴趣, 嗜好等; 爱好: *go in for golf / stamp-collecting / growing orchids.* 爱好高尔夫球(集邮, 种兰).

go into sth, (a) enter: 进入; 加入: *go into business*; 从商; *go into the Army / the Church / Parliament.* 从军(做传教士; 当国会议员). *When did Britain go into Europe, join the EEC?* 英国在何时加入了欧洲共同市场? **go into details,** ⇨ **detail¹(2).** **(b)** investigate; examine carefully: 调查; 审查: *go into the evidence;* 调查证据; *go deeply into a question.* 深究一问题. *This problem will need a lot of going into,* will need thorough investigation. 这问题需要彻底调查. **(c)** (allow oneself to) pass into (a certain state): (使自己)进入(某种状态): *go into fits of laughter / hysterical fits.* 发出阵阵笑声(歇斯底里症发作). **go into mourning,** wear black clothes as a symbol of mourning. 着丧服.

go off, (a) explode; be fired: 爆炸; 发射: *The gun went off by accident.* 这枪走火了了. **(b)** lose good quality; deteriorate: 变质; 变坏: *The cooking in the hotel has started to go off.* 旅馆内的烹调已开始变坏了. *This milk has gone off,* turned sour. 这牛奶变酸了. *Meat and fish go off quickly in hot weather.* 肉和鱼在热天很快会变坏. **(c)** become unconscious, either in sleep or in a faint: (睡眠或晕倒时)失去知觉: *Hasn't the baby gone off yet?* 这婴儿还没有睡着吗? *She went off into a faint.* 她晕倒昏迷过去了. **(d)** (of goods) be got rid of by sale: (指货物)卖掉; 售出: *The goods went off quickly.* 那些货物很快地卖掉了. **(e)** (of events) proceed well, etc: (指事件)进行良好等: *The performance / concert went off well.* 表演(音乐会)进行甚佳. *How did the sports meeting go off?* 运动会进行的情况如何? **(f)** (as a stage direction in a printed play) leave the stage; exit / exeunt: (剧本中的演出说明)下场: *Hamlet goes off.* 哈姆雷特下. **go off sb / sth,** lose interest in or one's taste for: 对某人(某物)失去兴趣或不再喜欢彼得了: *Jane seems to have gone off Peter.* 简好像不再喜欢彼得了. *I've gone off beer.* 我不喜欢啤酒了. **go off the beaten track,** ⇨ **beaten. go off the deep end,** ⇨ **end¹(1). go off one's head,** ⇨ **head¹(19). go off with sb / sth,** go away with, esp abscond with or steal: 带走; (尤指)拐带(某人或某物): *He's gone off to Edinburgh with his neighbour's wife.* 他已与邻居的妻子私奔至爱丁堡. *The butler went off with some of the duke's treasured possessions.* 那管事席卷公爵的一些珍藏而逃.

go on, (a) (of time) pass: (指时间)过去: *As the months went on, he became impatient.* 一月月地过去, 他变得不耐烦了. **(b)** conduct oneself; behave, esp in a wrong,

shameful or excited way: 举动(尤指错误, 可耻或激动地行动): *If you go on like this you'll be thrown out.* 如果你继续此种行为, 你将被开除. **(c)** happen; take place; be in progress: 发生; 进行: *What's going on there?* 那里出了什么事? *There's nothing interesting going on here at present.* 这里目前没有有趣的事情发生. *Harvesting was going on in the south.* 南部在收割. *Things are going on much as usual.* 一切如常. **(d)** (theatre) appear on the stage: (戏剧)出场: *She doesn't go on until Act Two.* 她要到第二幕才出场. **(e)** take one's turn at doing sth; (eg cricket) begin bowling: 轮到做某事; (例如板球)投球: *The captain told Snow to go on next.* 队长叫斯诺下一个投球. **'go on sth,** take or accept, as evidence: 接受(作为证据等): *What evidence have we got to go on,* to be guided by in reaching a decision, etc? 我们必须接受什么证据? **go on the dole / social security / (US) (美) welfare,** obtain, eg when unemployed, payments under various government schemes. 接受失业津贴. **go on the pill,** start using contraceptive pills. 服用避孕药丸. **go on about sth,** talk persistently and often irritatingly about: 不断地谈(常是令人气愤地)谈论: *I wish you'd stop going on about my smoking.* 请不要再谈论我抽烟的事. **go on (at sb),** rail; nag; scold: 责骂; 埋怨; 挑剔: *She goes on at her husband continually.* 她不停地埋怨她的丈夫. *Oh, you do go on!* 哎呀, 你真在骂人! **be going on (for),** (of age or time) be approaching: (指年龄或时间)接近: *He's going on (for) seventy.* 他快七十岁了. **be gone on,** (sl) be infatuated with: (俚)迷恋: *It's a pity Peter's so gone on Jane.* 彼得如此迷恋着简真是遗憾. **go on to sth / to do sth,** do or say it next; proceed to it; 接着做; 接着说: *Let's now go on to the next item on the agenda.* 现在让我们接着讨论议程的下一项. *He went on to say that...,* He next said that.... 他接着说.... *I shall now go on to deal with our finances.* 现在我要接着处理我们的财务. **go on (with sth / doing sth),** continue, persevere, with: 继续; 保持: *Go on with your work.* 继续你的工作. *How much longer will this hot weather go on?* 这种热天气还要继续多久? *That's enough to go on with / to be going on with,* enough for our immediate needs. 那足够目前的需要了. **Go on trying.** 继续尝试. *I hope it won't go on raining all day.* 我希望不会整天下雨. **Go on (with you)!** (colloq) Don't expect me to believe that! Don't be so silly! etc, according to context. (口)不要胡说! 我才不信呢! 别傻! **,goings-'on** *n pl* (colloq) (often with *such strange / queer*) happenings; behaviour: (口)(常与 such strange, such queer 连用)发生的事情; 举动: *I've never seen such queer goings-on!* 我从未见过这种怪事! **'on-going** *adj* continuing; progressing; evolving. 继续的; 进行的; 发展的. **go out, (a)** leave the room, building, etc: 离开房间、建筑物等: *She was (all) dressed to go out,* wearing outdoor clothes. 她打扮好准备外出. *Out you go!* 出去去! *Do you often go out riding* (ie on a horse)? 你常出外骑马吗? **(b)** attend social functions, go to parties, dances, etc: 参加社交活动; 参加聚会、舞会等: *She still goes out a great deal, even at seventy-five.* 她虽然已七十五岁, 仍时常参加社交活动. **go out on a spree / on the town,** ⇨ **spree, town. (c)** be extinguished: 熄灭: *The fire* (eg the fire burning in the grate) *has gone out.* 火已熄灭. *There was a power cut and all the lights went out.* 停电了, 所有的灯都熄灭. **(d)** become unfashionable: 不再流行: 过时: *Has the fashion for boots / Have boots gone out?* 长靴已过时了吗? **(e)** (of a government) retire from power. (指政府)下台. **(f)** (as used by workers of themselves) strike: (工人们用语)罢工: *Are we likely to gain anything by going out?* 我们罢工能得到什么好处吗? **come out (of) in come(16). (g)** (of a year, etc) end: (指岁月)结束: *The year went out gloomily.* 那一年悲惨地结束了. **go out on a limb,** ⇨ **limb(2). go out to,** leave, eg one's own country, and go to: 离开(例如本国)而去: *He couldn't get work at home* (eg in England) *so went out to Australia.* 他在国内(例如英国)找不到工作,

所以去了澳大利亚。**go out to sb,** (of the heart, feelings) be extended to: (指心、感情)给与; 施与: *Our hearts/sympathies go out to those poor children orphaned by war.* 我们同情他们是因战争而变成孤儿的可怜的孩子。**go out with sb,** (colloq) be regularly in sb's company: (口)经常陪伴某人: *How long has Jane been going out with David? How long have Jane and David been going out together?* 简和大卫交往有多久了?

go over, (colloq) make an impression: (口)予人以印象: *I wonder whether this new play will go over,* whether it will impress the public, be favourably received. 我不知道这新剧是否给予观众良好印象。*David didn't go over well with Jane's parents at the weekend.* 大卫在周末给简的父母的印象不太好。**go over sth,** (a) examine the details of: 仔细检查: *We must go over the accounts carefully before we settle them.* 在结帐以前, 我们必须将这帐目仔细核对一番。**(b)** look at; inspect: 看; 视察: *We should like to go over the house before deciding whether we want to buy it.* 我们要将这房屋查看一遍, 然后再决定是否要买。**(c)** rehearse; study or review carefully: 演习; 温习: *Let's go over this chapter/lesson/the main facts/Scene 2 again.* 我们将这一章一课、主要事实(第二场)再温习一遍。Hence, 由此产生, **,going-'over** n (*pl* **goings-over**) (colloq) process of examining or putting in good working order: (口)检查; 核对: *The document will need a careful going-over before we can make a decision.* 在我们作决定以前, 需要将这文件仔细看一下。*The patient was given a thorough going-over by/from the doctor.* 那病人由医师彻底检查了一下。**(b)** (sl) beating: (俚)毒打: *The thugs gave him a thorough going-over, beat him repeatedly.* 流氓们将他毒打一顿。**go over to sb/sth,** change one's political party, side, a preference, etc: 变党; 倒戈; 投向; 改用: *I'm going over to a milder brand of cigarettes.* 我现在改抽一种较淡的香烟。

go round, (a) be enough, in number or amount, for everyone to have a share: (在数量上)足够分配: *There aren't enough apples/isn't enough whisky to go round.* 苹果(威士忌)不够分配了。**(b)** reach one's destination by using a route other than the usual or nearest way: 绕道: *The main road to Worcester was flooded and we had to go (a/the long way) round.* 在伍斯特特的要道被洪水淹没, 我们必须绕道(绕得远)。**go round (to a place/to do sth),** visit: 拜访: *We're going round to my mother's/to see my mother at the weekend.* 我们打算在周末去拜望我的母亲。**go round the bend,** (colloq) become hysterical, enraged, mad, etc. (口)变为歇斯底里、激怒、疯狂等。

go through, (a) (= get through) be passed or approved: 被通过: *The Bill (ie in Parliament) did not go through.* 这议案未被通过。**(b)** be concluded: 被订立: 被缔结: *The deal did not go through.* 这项交易未谈成。**go through sth, (a)** discuss in detail: 详细讨论: *Let's go through the arguments again.* 我们将要把这些论据再详细讨论一遍。**(b)** search: 搜查: *The police went through the pockets of the suspected thief.* 警察搜查那个窃盗嫌疑犯的口袋。**(c)** perform; take part in: 履行: *She made him go through both a civil and religious wedding.* 她使他举行了照约的和宗教仪式的婚礼。*How long will it take to go through (= complete) the programme?* 整个节目要多久结束? **(d)** undergo; suffer: 经历; 遭受: *go through hardships.* 经历艰难。*If you only knew what she had to go through with that husband of hers!* 你要是知道她得跟着她那位丈夫受什么样的苦, 就好啦! **(e)** (of a book) be sold: (指书)被售出: *The book went through ten editions,* Ten editions were sold out. 这本书卖完了十版。**(f)** reach the end of; spend: 至…之尽头; 花费: *go through a fortune/all one's money.* 耗尽财产(所有的金钱)。**go through with sth,** complete; not leave unfinished: 完成; 做完: *He's determined to go through with the marriage in spite of his parents' opposition.* 他不顾父母的反对, 决

心要完成这婚事。

go to/towards sth, contribute to, be contributed to: 有助于; 促成: *What qualities go to the making of a statesman?* 要有什么条件才能做一个政治家? *This money can go towards the motor-bike you're saving up for.* 你可以用这笔钱加上你你的存款买部你所需要的摩托车。

go together, (a) (of two or more things) be a normal accompaniment (of one another): (指两件以上的事物)经常(互相)伴随: *Disease and poverty often go together.* 疾病与贫穷常常互相伴随。**(b)** match; be suitable together: 相配; 调和: *Do my green shirt and my blue jeans go together?* 我的绿衬衫与蓝牛仔裤相配吗? ⇨ **go with (c)** below. 参看下列之 go with (c)。

go under, (a) sink: 沉没。**(b)** (fig) fail; succumb; become bankrupt: (喻)失败; 屈从; 破产: *The firm will go under unless business improves.* 这家公司如不改进业务将会倒闭。

go up, (a) rise: 上升: *The barometer/temperature/thermometer is going up.* 气压计(温度, 寒暑表)上升。*Everything went up (ie in price) in the budget except pensions.* 预算中样样都增加了, 只有养老金例外。**(b)** be erected: 被建立: *New office blocks are going up everywhere.* 新办公大楼到处建立起来。**(c)** be blown up; be destroyed by explosion or fire: 被炸毁; 被焚毁: *The bridge went up with a roar when the mine exploded.* 地雷爆炸时, 那桥梁轰然一声被炸毁了。*The whole building went up in flames.* 整个建筑物为火所焚毁。**(d)** enter a university or travel to a town, esp the capital: 进大学; 进城(尤指首都)*go up to London/to town.* 去伦敦(进城)。*When will you go up (eg to Cambridge)?* 你何时进大学(例如进剑桥大学)? **go up sth,** climb: 攀登: *go up a tree/ladder/wall/hill.* 爬树(登梯; 攀墙; 爬山)。**go up the wall** ⇨ **wall.**

go with sb/sth, (a) accompany: 陪伴: *I'll go with you.* 我陪你一道去。*We must go with the times/tide,* do as others do nowadays. 我们必须跟上时代(潮流)。*He always goes with his party,* votes, etc as the party does. 他总是追随他的政党行事。**(b)** take the same view as: 与…有相同的观点: *I can't go with you on that,* can't agree with you. 关于那一点我不同意你的看法。**(c)** be a normal accompaniment of: 通常伴随; 附带; 连同: *Five acres of land go with the house,* become the property of the buyers or are for the use of the tenant. 这所房子附带有五英亩空地。*Disease often goes with squalor, but it is wrong to say that crime always goes with poverty.* 疾病通常因不洁而起, 但如果说罪恶永远因贫穷而生则是不正确的。**(d)** match; be fitting and suitable with: 配合; 适合: *These new curtains don't go well with your carpet,* don't suit them. 这些新窗帘与你的地毯不太调合。*I want some shoes to go with these trousers.* 我要一些配这些长裤的鞋子。**(e)** (colloq) (of a young man or girl) be often in the company of a person of the opposite sex possibly with a view to marriage: (口)(指青年男女)常与…在一起(希望能结婚): *go with a girl,* ⇨ **go out with sb** above. 常和一女孩子在一起, (参看上列之 go out with)。

go without (sth), endure the lack of: 忍受没有…之苦: *The poor boy often has to go without supper.* 这可怜的男孩时常没有晚饭吃。*There's no money for a holiday this year; we'll just have to go without.* 今年无钱度假, 我们只好不度假了。**go without saying,** be understood or naturally being stated: 不用说; 不待言: *It goes without saying that she's a good cook.* 她是个好厨师, 自不待言。

go² /gəʊ/ go/ n (*pl* **goes** /gəʊz/ goz/) (all uses colloq) (口) **all systems go,** (of launching or operating eg a spacecraft) all is ready to proceed. (指太空船等之发射或操作)一切就绪, 等着开始。**all the go,** very popular, fashionable: 流行的; 时髦的: *Leather pyjamas were all the go last year.* 宽松的皮裤去年极为流行。**at one go,** at one attempt: 一举; 一气; 一次: *He blew out all the candles on his birthday cake at one go,* at one breath. 他一口气把生日蛋糕上的蜡烛都吹灭了。**be full of go; have plenty of go,** be full of energy, enthusiasm. 精力充沛; 热心。**be on the**

go, be busy, active: 忙碌; 活躍: *She's been on the go all day*, has had no rest. 她終日忙碌。

have a go (at sth), make an attempt: 企圖; 嘗試(做某事): *He had several goes at the high jump before he succeeded in clearing it.* 他嘗試跳高數次，最後才跳了過去。*The police warned the public not to have a go because the bank raiders were armed*, not to try to intercept, catch them. 警方警告群眾不要嘗試攔截，因為那些搶劫銀行的暴徒帶著武器。

near go, narrow escape. 驚險的逃脫。**no go, (a)** false start. 錯誤的開始; 不適當的開始。**(b)** impossible or hopeless situation: 不可能; 不行: *It'll be no go to ask / asking for a rise when you arrive so late.* 你到得這麼晚而要求加薪是不可能的。**,no-'go area**, one to which access is prohibited to those who do not live there. 禁止外地人進入之地區。

goad /gəʊd/ *god*/*n* pointed stick for urging cattle on; (fig) sth urging a person to action. 驅畜之刺棒; 刺激物。□ *vt* [VP6A, 15B, 14, 17] ~ *sb (on)*; ~ *sb into doing sth*, urge, drive forward: 驅策; 激勵: ~ *sb into a fury*; 激怒某人; *be* ~*ed by hunger into stealing.* 為飢餓所迫而行竊。

goal /gəʊl/ *gol*/ *n* **1** point marking the end of a race; (football) posts between which the ball is to be driven in order to score; point(s) made by doing this: (賽跑之)終點; (足球)球門; 踢球門所得之分: *score / kick a* ~; 得(踢得)一分; *win by three* ~*s to one*; 以三比一之分數獲勝; *keep* ~, protect the ~. 守球門。**'~·keeper**, (colloq) (口) **~·ie** /'gəʊlɪ; 'golɪ/ *n* player whose duty is to keep the ball out of the ~. (足球)守門員。**'~·kick** *n* (Association football) kick by the defending side after the attacking side sends the ball over the ~-line; (Rugby football) attempt to kick a ~. (英式足球)球門球; (橄欖球)射門。**'~-line** *n* (football) line behind the ~ posts, reaching to the touch-lines. (足球)球門線。⇨ **touch-line** at **touch¹(7);** ⇨ the illus at **football, Rugby.** 參看 football, Rugby 之插圖。**2** (fig) object of efforts or ambition: (喻)目標: *one's* ~ *in life*; 生活的目標; *the* ~ *of his desires.* 他的欲望的目標。

goat /gəʊt/ *got*/ *n* small, active horned animal, ⇨ the illus at **domestic.** 山羊(參看 domestic 之插圖)。**'she-~** (or *'nanny-*~), female goat, kept for its milk. 牝山羊。**'he-~** (or *'billy-*~), male goat. 雄山羊。⇨ **kid¹(1).** **get one's** ~, (sl) irritate or annoy one. (俚)激怒某人; 令某人煩躁。**play/act the giddy** ~, play the fool; behave in a foolish and carefree way. 行為如小丑。**separate the sheep from the** ~**s**, the good from the bad. 將好的與壞的分開。**'~-herd** *n* person who looks after a flock of ~s. 照看山羊者。**'~-skin** *n* [C, U] (garment made of) skin of a goat. 山羊皮; 山羊皮衣。**~·ee** /gəʊ'tiː/ *n*; go'ti/ *n* small tuft of hair on the chin like a ~'s beard. 山羊胡子(似山羊之須者)。

gob¹ /gɒb; gab/ *n* (vulg) clot or lump of slimy substance. (鄙)粘稠塊。

gob² /gɒb; gab/ *n* (derog sl) mouth. (貶俚)嘴。

gob³ /gɒb; gab/ *n* (US sl) sailor. (美俚)水兵。

gob·bet /'gɒbɪt; 'gabɪt/ *n* [C] lump or chunk, esp of meat. 一塊(尤指肉); 一厚塊。

gob·ble¹ /'gɒbl; 'gabl/ *vt, vi* [VP6A, 15B, 2A] ~ *(up)*, eat fast, noisily and greedily. 狼吞虎咽。

gob·ble² /'gɒbl; 'gabl/ *vi* [VP2A, C] (of a turkeycock) make the characteristic sound in the throat; (of a person) make such a sound when speaking, because of rage, etc. (指火雞)作咯咯聲; (指人)因憤怒等而發出咯咯聲。□ *n* characteristic sound made by a turkeycock. (火雞的)咯咯聲。

gobble·dy·gook /'gɒbldɪguːk; 'gabldɪ,guk/ *n* [U] incomprehensible or pompous specialist's jargon. 不能理解的或浮夸的專門術語。

gob·bler /'gɒblə(r); 'gablə/ *n* (US) male turkey. (美)雄火雞。

go-between /'gəʊbɪtwiːn; 'gobə,twin/ *n* messenger or

negotiator for two persons or groups who do not or cannot meet: 中間人; 掮客; 媒人: *In some countries marriages are arranged by* ~s. 在有些國家，婚姻系由媒人撮合的。

gob·let /'gɒblɪt; 'gablɪt/ *n* glass or pottery drinking-vessel with a stem and base and no handle. (無把手之)高腳玻璃杯或瓷杯。

gob·lin /'gɒblɪn; 'gablɪn/ *n* mischievous demon; ugly-looking evil spirit. 惡鬼; 丑妖怪。

go-cart /'gəʊ kɑːt; 'go,kɑrt/ *n* light handcart. 輕便手推車。

god /gɒd; gad/ *n* **1** being regarded or worshipped as having power over nature and control over human affairs; image in wood, stone, etc to represent such a being: 神; 神像: *the blind god* (or *god of love*), Cupid; 愛神; *the god of the sea*, Neptune; 海神; *a feast / sight for the gods*, something extraordinary, exquisite, etc. 不尋常的事物; 精美的事物。**2 God**, the Supreme Being, creator and ruler of the universe. (大寫)上帝。*God (almighty)! Good God! int* (colloq) exclamations of surprise, shock etc. (口)(表示驚異、震驚等)上帝啊! 老天啊! *God willing*, if circumstances permit. 如情況許可。*God knows*, = *goodness knows*, ⇨ **goodness(3).** **3** person greatly adored or admired; very influential person; sth to which excessive attention is paid: 受尊崇之人; 極有影響力的人; 極受注意之事物: *make a god of one's belly*, think excessively about food and drink. 尊崇自己的肚子; 非常重視飲食。*He thinks he's a (little) tin god*, used eg of an official who expects undeserved and excessive respect. 他認為他自己是个很了不起而且極受尊崇的人物(用以指希望受別不應得的過分尊崇的官員等)。**4** (theatre) **the gods**, (persons in the) gallery seats. (戲院)最高樓座(之觀众)。**5** (compounds) (复合詞) **'god·child, 'god·daughter, 'god·son** *nn* person for whom a godparent acts as sponsor at baptism. 教子; 教女(受洗時由教父或教母担保其宗教教育的孩子)。**'god·dam(ed)** (US) **'god·dam** /'gɒdæm; 'gad'dæm/ *adj, adv* △ (sl; intensive) very; very great. (諱; 俚; 增強語氣之词)很; 很大。**'god·father, 'god·mother** *nn* person who, when a child is baptized, takes on the responsibility for its welfare. 教父; 教母(孩子受洗時, 担保其宗教教育之人)。**'god·fearing** *adj* reverent; living a good life and sincerely religious. 虔誠的; 虔敬的。**'god·for·saken** *adj* (of places) dismal; wretched. (指地方)陰森的; 荒涼的。**God's 'acre** *n* (old use) churchyard. (舊用法)教堂墓地。**'god·send** /-send; -,send/ *n* piece of good fortune coming unexpectedly; sth welcome because it is a great help in time of need. 意外的好運; 緊急時大有幫助因而受歡迎之物; 天賜之物。**god·'speed** *n bid / wish sb godspeed*, wish him success on a journey, etc. 祝某人一帆風順; 祝某人一路平安。

god·dess /'gɒdɪs; 'gadɪs/ *n* female god, esp in Greek and Latin mythology: 女神 (尤指希臘羅馬神話中者): *Diana, the* ~ *of hunting.* 戴安娜, 狩獵之女神。

god·head /'gɒdhed; 'gadhed/ *n* [U] being God or a god; divine nature. 為神; 神性。**the G~**, God. 上帝。

god·less /'gɒdlɪs; 'gadlɪs/ *adj* wicked; not having belief in God; not recognizing God. 邪惡的; 不信上帝的; 不承認上帝存在的。**~·ness** *n*

god·like /'gɒdlaɪk; 'gad,laɪk/ *adj* like God or a god in some quality. 似神的; 如神的。

god·ly /'gɒdlɪ; 'gadlɪ/ *adj* (**-ier, -iest**) loving and obeying God; deeply religious. 敬愛神的; 虔誠的。**god·li·ness** *n*

go·down /'gəʊdaʊn; 'go'daʊn/ *n* (in the East) warehouse. (東方之)倉庫。

go-get·ter /'gəʊ getə(r); 'go'getə/ *n* (colloq) pushing, enterprising person. (口)積極而進取之人。

goggle /'gɒgl; 'gagl/ *vi* [VP2A, 3A] ~ *(at)*, roll the eyes about (or *at* sth); stare at with bulging eyes: 轉動眼睛望著; 睜視: *He* ~*d at her in surprise.* 他驚奇地

瞪视她. *The frog's eyes seemed to be goggling out of its head.* 青蛙的眼睛从头上凸出，像是要掉下来似的. '~-**box** *n* (sl) TV set. (俚)电视机. '~-**eyed** *adj* having staring, prominent, or rolling eyes. 睁视的；眼睛凸出的；眼睛转动的.

goggles /'gɒglz; 'gɑglz/ *n pl* large round spectacles with hoods to protect the eyes from the wind, dust, water etc (worn by racing motorists, frogmen etc). (赛车驾驶人、蛙人等所戴的)护目镜；遮灰镜；风镜. ⇨ the illus at **frog**. 参看 frog 之插图.

go·ing /'gəʊɪŋ; 'goɪŋ/ *n* (⇨ also **go**[1]) **1** [U] condition of the ground, a road, a race-course, etc, for walking, riding, etc: 地面、道路、跑道等供行走或驾驶等的状况: *The ~ is hard over this mountain road.* 在这山路上行走甚为吃力. **2** [U] method or speed of working or travelling: 工作或行驶的方法或速度: *For a steam train, 70 miles an hour is good ~.* 以蒸汽火车而论，每小时行驶七十英里是快的速度. **3** (usu *pl*) (通常作复数) *comings and ~s,* (lit or fig) arrivals and departures: (字面或喻)到达和离去；来往: *the comings and ~s in the corridors of power.* 来往于权力的走廊上. □*adj a ~ concern,* ⇨ **go**[1](8).

goitre (US = **goi·ter**) /'gɔɪtər; 'gɔɪtɚ/ *n* morbid swelling of the thyroid gland (in the neck). (颈部之)甲状腺肿.

go-kart /'gəʊ kɑːt; 'go ͵kɑrt/ *n* small low racing car with open framework. 一种车身低的小赛车.

gold /gəʊld; gold/ *n* [U] precious yellow metal used for making coins, ornaments, jewellery, etc: 黄金；金子: *currencies backed by ~;* 以黄金为准备金的通货; *£500 in ~,* in ~ coins; 五百英镑金币; (attrib) (用作定语) *a ~ watch/bracelet.* 金表(手镯). *worth one's weight in ~,* invaluable; indispensable. 无价的；不可缺少的. **2** money in large sums; wealth. 大量金钱；财富. **3** (fig) brilliant or precious things or qualities: (喻)华丽或美丽之物; 华贵的性质: *a heart of ~;* 高贵的心; *a voice of ~.* 甜美的声音. **4** colour of the metal: 金黄色: *the red and ~ of the woods in autumn;* 秋季树林中的红色和金黄色; *old ~,* a dull, brownish-golden yellow. 古金色；暗黄褐色. **5** (compounds) (复合词) '~-**leaf** *n* person whose trade is to beat ~ into ~-leaf. 金箔工人. '~-**digger** *n* person who digs for ~; (sl) girl or woman who uses her attractions to extract money from men. 掘金者；(俚)以美色骗取男人金钱的女人. '~-**dust** *n* in the form of dust, as often found in ~ fields. 砂金. '~-**field** *n* district in which ~ is found. 金田；采金区. '~-**finch** *n* bright-coloured song-bird with yellow feathers in the wings. 金翅雀. '~-**fish** *n* small red carp kept in bowls or ponds. 金鱼. '~-**foil**, '~-**leaf** *n* [U] ~ beaten into thin sheets. 金箔；金叶. '~-**mine** *n* place where ~ is mined; (fig) source of wealth, eg a shop that is very successful in making money. 金矿；(喻)富源(例如非常赚钱的商店). '~-**plate** *n* [U] articles (spoons, dishes and other vessels) made of ~. 金器；金制品、盘等容器. '~-**rush** *n* rush to a newly discovered ~field. 涌向新金矿之热潮；淘金潮. '~-**smith** *n* smith who makes articles of ~. 金匠. '~-**standard,** ⇨ **standard**(4).

golden /'gəʊldən; 'goldn/ *adj* **1** of gold or like gold in value or colour: 黄金的；价值似金的；金黄色的: *~ hair.* 金黄色的头发. **2** precious; excellent; important: 可贵的；极好的；重要的: *a ~ opportunity.* 绝好的机会. **the** ͵~ '**age,** (in Gk stories) the earliest and happiest period in history; period in a nation's history when art or literature was most flourishing. (希腊故事)黄金时代；一国历史上的黄金时代(文学或艺术最兴盛的时代). ͵~ '**handshake,** (usu large) sum of money given to a high-ranking member of a company when he retires (in recognition of good work and loss of continuation of salary). (高级职员退休时公司给付之)大笔退休金(以酬谢其过去的服务并弥补其因停薪后之损失). **the** ͵~ '**mean,** the principle of moderation. 中庸之道. **the** ͵~ '**rule,**

any important rule of conduct (esp **Matt 7: 12,** *Treat others as you would like them to treat you*). 金科玉律；金箴(尤指马太福音第 7 章第 12 节者, 例如: 以期待别人对你之心对待他人). ͵~ '**wedding,** fiftieth wedding anniversary. 金婚纪念(结婚五十周年纪念).

golf /gɒlf; gɑlf/ *n* [U] game played by two or four persons, each with a small, hard '~-**ball,** driven with a '~-**club,** into a series of 9 or 18 holes on smooth greens(4) over a stretch of land (a '~-**course**/**links**). 高尔夫球(由二或四人比赛, 用球棒将小球打人场中九或十八个洞中, 其球场称作 golf-course 或 links). □ *vi* play ~. 打高尔夫球. '~-**er** *n* person who plays ~. 打高尔夫球者.

Gol·i·ath /gə'laɪəθ; gə'laɪəθ/ *n* giant. 巨人. ⇨ **1 Sam 17.** 参看旧约圣经撒母耳记上第 17 章.

gol·li·wog /'gɒlɪwɒg; 'gɑlɪ͵wɑg/ *n* black-faced doll with thick stiff hair. 黑面竖发之木偶.

golly /'gɒlɪ; 'gɑlɪ/ *int* (sl) used to express surprise. (俚)表惊异之声; 天哪.

go·losh *n* ⇨ **galosh.**

gon·dola /'gɒndələ; 'gɑndələ/ *n* long, flat-bottomed boat with high peaks at each end, used on canals in Venice. (威尼斯运河中航行之)长形平底轻舟. **gon·do·lier** /͵gɒndə'lɪər; ͵gɑndə'lɪr/ *n* man who propels a ~. 威尼斯运河中驾长形平底轻舟者.

a gondola

gone /gɒn US: gɔːn; gɔn/ *pp* of **go.**

goner /'gɒnər US: 'gɔːn-; 'gɔnɚ/ *n* (sl) person or thing in desperate straits, ruined or doomed. (俚)即将灭亡之人或物; 无可救药者.

gong /gɒŋ; gɔŋ/ *n* metal disc with a turned rim giving a resonant note when struck with a stick, esp as a signal, eg for meals. 锣(尤指击之以作为信号, 如通知用膳等者). □ *vt* (of traffic police) direct (a motorist) to stop by striking a ~. (指交通警察)敲锣使(驾驶汽车者)停车.

gonna /'gɒnə; 'gɑnə/ (US sl) (美俚) = going to ⇨ **go**[1](27).

gon·or·rhea (also **-rhoea**) /͵gɒnə'rɪə; ͵gɑnə'rɪə/ *n* [U] contagious venereal disease which causes an inflammatory discharge from the genital organs. 淋病.

goo /guː; gu/ *n* [U] (sl) sticky wet material; sentimentality. (俚)粘而湿的东西; 伤感. **gooey** /'guːɪ; 'guɪ/ *adj* sticky. 粘的.

good[1] /gʊd; gʊd/ *adj* (**better, best**) **1** having the right or desired qualities; giving satisfaction: 美好的; 良好的; 令人满意的: *a ~* (eg sharp) *knife,* 一把好刀; *a ~ fire,* one that is bright and cheerful, giving warmth; 明亮旺盛的炉火; *~* (= fertile) *soil.* 肥沃的土壤. *Is raw herring ~ eating,* Is it enjoyable to eat it? 生鲱好吃吗? **2** beneficial; wholesome: 有益的; 对健康有益的: *Is this water ~ to drink,* Is it clean and pure? 这水适于喝吗? *Milk is ~ for children.* 牛奶对小孩有益. *Exercise is ~ for the health.* 运动有益于健康. **3** efficient; competent; able to do satisfactorily what is required: 能胜任的; 有能力的; 能干的: *a ~ teacher/driver/ worker;* 好教师(驾驶, 工作者); *a ~ man for the position;* 对某一职位之适当人选; *~ at mathematics/languages/ describing scenery.* 擅长数学(语言, 描写风景). *She has been a ~ wife to him.* 她一直是他的好妻子. **4** pleasing; agreeable; advantageous: 令人快乐的; 悦人的; 有利的: *~ news.* 好消息. *It's ~ to be home again.* 重回家园是令人快乐的. *have a ~ time,* enjoy oneself. 过得很快乐. Hence, 由此产生, '~-**time girl,** (colloq) one whose chief aim is enjoyment. (口)以享乐为目的之女子. *(all)*

in ~ time, at a suitable or advantageous time. 在适当或有利的时刻. *be a ~ thing*, be sth that one approves of: 为人所赞成之事: *Do you think lower taxes are a ~ thing?* 你赞成降低纳税吗? *be a ~ thing that...*, be fortunate that.... 幸好⋯; 好在⋯. *have a good/bad night*, sleep well/badly. 睡得好(不好). *put in/say a ~ word for sb*, say sth in his favour. 为某人说几句好话. *start/arrive/leave in ~ time*, early. 及早动身(到达, 离去). **5** kind; benevolent; willing to help others: 和善的; 仁慈的; 乐于助人的: *It was ~ of you to help them.* 你真好, 帮了他们的忙. *Will you be ~ enough to/be so ~ as to come early?* 请早些来好吗? *How ~ of you!* 你真好! Cf *do sb a ~ turn*, a turn, (in exclamations of surprise, shock, etc.) (在惊叹句中) *G~ 'God!* 天啊! *G~ 'Gracious!* 天啊! *G~ 'Heavens!* 天啊! *G~ 'God!* 天啊! *G~ 'Heavens!* 天啊! **6** thorough; sound; complete: 彻底的; 痛快的; 完全的: *give sb a ~ beating/scolding;* 痛殴(责)某人; *have a drink;* 喝个痛快; *find a ~ excuse;* 找一充分的借口; *go for a ~ long walk.* 作一次痛快而距离远的散步. *have a ~ mind (to do sth)*, feel a strong desire to: 很想做; 极有意: *I've a ~ mind to report you to the police.* 我很想将你报警. **7** strong; vigorous: 强健的; 有力的: *His eyesight is still ~.* 他的目力仍然很强. *The children were in ~ spirits.* 孩子们都兴高采烈. ⇨ *low spirits* at **low[1](6)**. **8** amusing: 有趣的: *a ~ story/joke;* 有趣的故事(笑话); *as ~ as a play.* 像戏剧般有趣; 十分有趣. **9** fresh; eatable; untainted: 新鲜的; 可食的; 未腐败的: *Fish does not keep ~ in hot weather.* 鱼在热天不能保持新鲜. *This meat doesn't smell quite ~.* 这肉的气味不太新鲜. **10** reliable; safe; sure: 可靠的; 安全的; 确实的: *a car with ~ brakes;* 煞车可靠的汽车; *~ debts, debts that will certainly be paid.* 确可偿还的债. *~ bad debts at bad[1](4).* *He's a ~ life*, is healthy and is, therefore, likely to be acceptable for life assurance. 他是保险公司乐意承保的健康的人. *~ for, (a)* safely to be trusted for (the amount stated): 可信赖或托付 (列明的款数): *His credit is ~ for £5000.* 他的信用可以转帐五千英镑. *(b)* (of a draft, etc) drawn for (the amount stated): (指汇票等)可支付(列明的款数): *~ for £5.* 可支付五英镑. *(c)* having the necessary energy, inclination, etc for: 有必要的精力、意愿等: *He's ~ for several years' more service.* 他还有精力再服务几年. *My car is ~ for another five years.* 我的汽车还可以再用五年. *Are you ~ for a five-mile walk?* 你有气力走五英里路吗? *(d)* valid: 有效: *The return half of the ticket is ~ for three months.* 回程票有效期为三个月. *~-for-nothing, ~-for-naught adjj, nn* worthless (person). 无用的; 无用之人. **11** (esp of a child) well behaved; not giving trouble: (尤指儿童) 守规矩的; 听话的: *Try to be a ~ boy.* 尽量做个乖孩子. *as ~ as gold*, giving no trouble. 不惹麻烦. **12** morally excellent; virtuous: 品行优良的; 有品德的: *a ~ and holy man;* 有品德的人; *live a ~ life.* 过高尚的生活. *~ 'works*, charitable deeds, helping the poor, the sick, etc. 慈善事业. **13** right; proper; expedient: 正当的; 适合的; 权宜的: *Ee thought it ~ to offer his help.* 他认为他应该提供帮助. (As an *int*, expressing approval): (用做感叹词, 表示赞同): *'You will come with us?' 'G~!'* 你和我们一道去吗? '好的!' **14** in forms of greeting and farewell: 用于问候和告别词句中: *G~ morning/afternoon/evening/night.* 早(午, 晚, 晚)安. **15** as a polite (but often ironical, patronizing or indignant) form of address: 作为客气(但常是讥讽、傲慢或愤慨)的称呼: *my ~ sir/man/friend;* 我的好先生(人, 朋友); or as a polite (but often condescending) description: 或作为客气(但常含上对下关系)的描述: *How's your ~ man (ie your husband)?* 你的先生好吗? *How's the ~ lady (ie your wife)?* 你的太太好吗? *the ~ people*, the fairies. 小神仙. **16** as a form of commendation: 作为赞扬之词: *~ men and true.* 善良诚实的君子; 温厚笃实之士. *G~ old Smith!* 厚道的老史密斯! *That's a ~ 'un!* 这个, 'gudn; (colloq) an amusing lie or story. (口) 那是个有趣的谎言或故事! **17** considerable in number, quantity,

etc: 相当多的: *a ~ deal of money;* 很多金钱; *a ~ many people;* 很多人; *a ~ few*, a considerable number. 相当多的数目. *We've come a ~ way*, quite a long way. 我们已走了相当远了. **18** not less than; rather more than: 不少于⋯的; 颇多于⋯的: *We waited for a ~ hour.* 我们等了整整一小时. *It's a ~ three miles to the station.* 到车站足足有三英里路. *He ate a ~ half of the duck.* 他至少吃掉了半只鸭子. **19** *as ~ as*, practically, almost: 实际上; 几乎: *He as ~ as said I was a liar*, suggested that I was a liar without actually using the word 'liar'. 他实际上等于说我是个说谎者. *My car is as ~ as new, even though I've had it a year.* 我的汽车虽用了一年, 几乎还是新的. *The matter is as ~ as settled*, We may look upon it as being settled. 这事等于解决了. **20** *make ~*, accomplish what one attempts; prosper: 有成就; 成功: *He went to Canada, where he soon made ~.* 他去到加拿大, 在那里不久便很有成就了. [VP22] *make sth ~*, (a) compensate for; pay for (sth lost or damaged): 补偿; 赔偿(损失): *make a loss or theft.* 赔偿损失或失窃. (b) effect (a purpose): 实现(目的): *make ~ one's escape.* 顺利逃脱. (c) prove the truth of an accusation, a statement, etc. 证实(控告之罪、言论等). (d) restore to sound condition: 修复: *The plaster will have to be made ~ before you paint it.* 在你粉刷前, 灰泥必须修补好. **21** (phrases and compounds) (短语与复合词) *,~ 'fellowship n* sociability. 友善; 亲睦. *,~ 'humour n* cheerful mood; happy state of mind. 愉快; 高兴. *,~ 'humoured adj* cheerful, amiable. 愉快的; 亲切的. *,~ 'looks n pl* personal beauty. 美貌. *,~ 'looking adj* (usu of persons) handsome. (通常指人)貌美的; 漂亮的. *,~ 'money, (a)* genuine money. 真正的钱. (b) (colloq) high wages. (口)高的工资. *throw ~ money after bad*, lose money in trying to regain money lost. 为了夫人又再拆夫; 一亏再亏. *,~ 'natured adj* kind; ready and willing to help others, even by sacrificing one's own interests. 和蔼的; 不计自身利益乐于帮助他人的. *,~ 'neighbourliness n* friendly conduct and relations. 亲睦; 交情. *,~ 'sense n* [U] soundness of judgement; practical wisdom. 判断正确; 见识. *,~ 'tempered adj* not easily irritated or made angry. 好脾气的.

good[2] /gud; gʊd/ *n* [U] **1** that which is ~; what is morally right, beneficial, advantageous, profitable, etc; what has use, worth, value. 良好的事物; 善良; 善行; 利益; 好处(等). *do ~*, help: 行善; *Social workers do a lot of ~.* 社会工作者做了许多善事. ⇨ *do-gooder* at **do[2](2)**. *(do sth) for the ~ of*, in order to benefit: (做某事)为⋯之利益: *He works for the ~ of the country.* 他为国家谋福利. *I'm giving you this advice for your ~.* 我这样劝你是为了你好. *Is it right to deceive people, even if it's for their own ~?* 即使为了人们好而去欺骗他们是正当的吗? *do sb ~*, benefit him: 对某人有益: *Eat more fruit: it will do you ~.* 多吃些水果, 那会对你有益. *Smoking does you more harm than ~.* 吸烟对你有害无益. *Much ~ may it do you*, (usu ironic, meaning) You won't get much benefit from it. 但愿这对你有很大的好处 (通常作反语, 意谓: 这对你不会有多大好处). *be up to no ~*, be engaged in sth wrong, mischievous, etc. 做坏事; 恶作剧. *be no/not much/any/some ~ (doing sth)*, be no, not much, etc use, of no, little, etc value: (做某事)没有(有些)用; 没有(有些)价值: *It's no ~ (my) talking to him.* (我)同他谈没有用. *Was his advice ever any ~?* 他的劝告有用吗? *What ~ was it?* 有什么用处? *This gadget isn't much ~.* 这小器具没有什么大价值. **2** *for ~ (and all)*, permanently; finally: 永久地; 决定性地: *He says that he's leaving the country for ~*, intending never to return to it. 他说他出国后便不再回来了. **3** *to the ~*, as balance on the right side, as net profit: 作为盈余; 作为纯益: *We were £5 to the ~.* 我们净赚了五英镑. **4** (*adj* as *pl n*) good or virtuous persons: (形容词用作复数名词) 好人: *G~ and bad alike respected him.* 不分好人与坏人都尊敬他.

good·bye /ˌgud'baɪ; gʊd'baɪ; *fast or informal:* gu'baɪ;

gu'baɪ/ *int, n* (saying of) farewell: 再见；再会: '*I must say* ~ *now*', It is time for me to leave. 我必须告辞了。 *Have you said all your* ~s? 你向大家告别了没有？

good·ish /'gudɪʃ; 'gudɪʃ/ *attrib adj* rather large, extensive, etc: 颇大的；相当的: *It's a* ~ *step from here*, quite a long way. 距此颇远。

good·ly /'gudlɪ; 'gudlɪ/ *adj* (**-ier, -iest**) (liter) (文) 1 handsome; pleasant-looking. 漂亮的；美丽的。 2 of considerable size: 相当大的: *a* ~ *sum of money*, 相当大的一笔钱; *a* ~ *heritage*. 相当可观的遗产。

good·ness /'gudnɪs; 'gudnɪs/ *n* [U] 1 quality of being good; virtue: 善良；美德: ~ *of heart*. 心地之善良。 *have the* ~ *to*, be kind enough to: 有…之善意; 恳请: *Have the* ~ *to come this way, please*. 请从这边走。 2 strength or essence: 真髓; 精华: *meat with the* ~ *boiled out*. 精华被煮掉了的肉。 3 (in exclamations) used instead of *God!*: (在感叹句中)用以代替 God: *G*~ *Gracious!* 啊呀! 啊呀! *G*~ *me!* 啊呀! *For* ~ *sake!* 看在老天爷的面上! 务请! *Thank* ~! 谢天谢地! *I wish to* ~ *that…*, wish very strongly that…. 万祈…。 *G*~ *knows*, (**a**) I do not know. 天晓得; 我不知道。 (**b**) I appeal to Heaven to witness: 上天作证: *G*~ *knows I've tried hard*. 上天作证, 我确实努力尝试过。

goods /gudz; gudz/ *n pl* 1 movable property; merchandise: 动产；货物: *He buys and sells leather* ~. 他买卖皮货。 *Half his* ~ *were stolen*. 他半数的财产(货物)被人偷走了。 '~ *and* '*chattels*, (legal) personal belongings. (法律) 有体动产。 2 things carried by rail, etc (contrasted with passengers): 火车等所运之货物(与passengers 相对): *a* '~ *agent/station*. 货运代理行(站)。 '~ *train*, ie not a passenger train (US 美 = *freight train*). (火车)货车。 *piece of* ~, (colloq) person: (口) 人: *She's a sexy little piece of* ~, a sexy young girl. 她是个性感的女郎。

good·will /ˌgud'wɪl; 'gud'wɪl/ *n* [U] 1 friendly feeling: 亲善: *a policy of* ~ *in international relations*. 国际关系上的亲善政策。 2 privilege of trading as the successor to a well-established business: 一个老店铺所享有的信誉; 商誉: *The* ~ *is to be sold with the business*. 商誉将连同其商誉一并售出。

goody /'gudɪ; 'gudɪ/ *n* (colloq) sweetmeat; desirable thing. (口)糖果; 想要的东西。

goody-goody /'gudɪ gudɪ; 'gudɪ'gudɪ/ *adj, n* (person who is) primly or pretentiously virtuous. 道学的; 道学先生。

gooey /'guːɪ; 'guɪ/ *adj* ⇨ **goo**.

goof /guːf; guf/ (sl) (俚) *n* silly or stupid person. 愚蠢的人。 □ *vi, vt* [VP2A, 6A] make a mess (of). 弄乱; 弄糟。 ~**y** *adj* silly, stupid, crazy. 愚蠢的; 蠢笨的。

goog·ly /'guːglɪ; 'guglɪ/ *n* (*pl* **-lies**) (cricket) ball bowled as if to break in one way that actually breaks in the opposite way. (板球)曲球(先向一方, 继而转向相反方向的球)。

goon /guːn; gun/ *n* (sl) stupid or awkward person (俚) 愚笨之人; 笨拙之人。

goose /guːs; gus/ *n* (*pl* **geese** /giːs; gis/) 1 water bird larger than a duck; female of this, ⇨ **gander**; ⇨ the illus at **fowl**; [U] its flesh as food. 鹅; 雌鹅(参看 fowl 之插图)。 鹅肉。 *cook sb's* ~, put an end to his hopes; prevent him from being a nuisance, etc. 使某人绝望, 阻止某人做一讨厌的人等。 *kill the* ~ *that lays the golden eggs*, (prov) sacrifice future gains to satisfy present needs. (谚) 杀鸡取卵 (为满足目前需要而牺牲将来的财源)。 *be unable to say 'boo' to a* ~, be very timid. 非常胆小。 *All one's geese are swans*, One overestimates or exaggerates the good qualities of persons and things. (某人)喜欢夸大。 '~**-flesh** *n* [U] rough bristling skin caused by cold or fear. (因寒冷或恐惧皮肤上所生的)鸡皮疙瘩。 '~**-step** *n* way of marching without bending the knees. 正步。 2 simpleton:

傻瓜; 笨蛋: *You silly* ~! 你这个笨蛋!

goose·berry /'guzbərɪ US: 'guːsberɪ; 'gus,berɪ/ *n* (*pl* **-ries**) [C] (bush with) green, smooth berry (used for jam, tarts, etc). 醋栗(绿色光滑的浆果, 用做果酱, 果馅糕点等)。 ⇨ the illus at **fruit**. 参看 fruit 之插图。 *play* ~, be present with two persons, eg lovers, who prefer to be alone. 陪伴两个想单独在一起的人(例如情侣); 当电灯泡。

go·pher /'gəufə(r); 'gofə/ *n* burrowing rat-like animal in N America. 北美产的一种地鼠; 衣囊鼠。

Gor·dian /'gɔːdɪən; 'gɔrdɪən/ *adj* (only in) (仅用于) ~ *knot*, knot difficult or impossible to untie; difficult problem or task. 难解的结; 难题。 *cut the* ~ *knot*, solve a problem by force or by disregarding the conditions. 用强硬手段解决难题; 以快刀斩乱麻的手段解决问题。

gore[1] /gɔː(r); gɔr/ *n* [U] (liter, chiefly in descriptions of fighting) thickened blood from a cut or wound. (文, 主要用于描写战斗)伤口的凝血。

gore[2] /gɔː(r); gɔr/ *vt* [VP6A] pierce, wound, with the horns or tusks: 用角或长牙抵: ~*d to death by an infuriated bull*. 被一发狂的公牛用角抵死。

gorge[1] /gɔːdʒ; gɔrdʒ/ *n* 1 narrow opening, usu with a stream, between hills or mountains. 峡。 2 gullet; contents of the stomach: 食道; 咽下之物; 胃内之物: *His* ~ *rose at the sight/It made his* ~ *rise*, He was sickened or disgusted. 他看到那景象就作呕。

gorge[2] /gɔːdʒ; gɔrdʒ/ *vi, vt* [VP6A, 14, 2A, C] ~ (*oneself*) (*on/with sth*), eat greedily; fill oneself: 狼吞虎咽; 塞饱: ~ *on rich food*; 贪婪地吃着油腻的食物; ~ *oneself with meat*. 肚子里塞满了肉。 □ *n* act of gorging; surfeit. 狼吞虎咽; 塞饱。

gorg·eous /'gɔːdʒəs; 'gɔrdʒəs/ *adj* 1 richly coloured; magnificent: 华丽的; 灿烂的: *a* ~ *sunset*. 光辉灿烂的落日。 2 (colloq) giving pleasure and satisfaction: (口) 宜人的; 令人满意的: ~ *weather*; 宜人的天气; *a* ~ *dinner*. 盛餐。 ~**ly** *adv*

Gor·gon /'gɔːgən; 'gɔrgən/ *n* (Gk myth) one of three snake-haired sisters whose looks turned to stone anyone who saw them. (希神)三蛇发女怪之一 (人或其貌则化为石)。

Gor·gon·zola /ˌgɔːgən'zəulə; ˌgɔrgən'zolə/ *n* [U] rich creamy blue-veined cheese (from ~ in Italy). 一种味浓, 含多量乳脂, 有蓝色纹理的干酪(因产于意大利哥根索拉市而得名)。

gor·illa /gə'rɪlə; gə'rɪlə/ *n* man-sized, tree-climbing African ape. (非洲)大猩猩。 ⇨ the illus at **ape**. 参看 ape 之插图。

gor·man·dize /'gɔːməndaɪz; 'gɔrmən,daɪz/ *vi* eat, devour, greedily for pleasure. 狼吞虎咽。

gorse /gɔːs; gɔrs/ *n* [U] yellow-flowered evergreen shrub with sharp thorns, growing on waste land (also called *furze* or *whin*). 金雀花(生黄花之长青灌木, 有尖刺, 生长于荒地, 亦称 furze 或 whin)。

gory /'gɔːrɪ; 'gorɪ/ *adj* (**-ier, -iest**) covered with blood; of bloody physical violence: 血污的; 染满血的; 流血暴乱的: ~ *details/incidents*. 血污的详情 (流血暴乱的事件)。

gosh /gɒʃ; gɑʃ/ *int* (sl) (also 亦作 *by* ~) by God. (俚) 哎呀!

gos·ling /'gɒzlɪŋ; 'gɑzlɪŋ/ *n* young goose. 小鹅。

gos·pel /'gɒspl; 'gɑspl/ *n* the **G**~ [U] (the life and teachings of Jesus as recorded in the) first four books of the New Testament; [C] any one of these; set of principles that one acts upon or believes in: (大写) 新约圣经四福音书; 四福音书中所记载之耶稣生平及教训; 四福音之一; (小写) 信条; 主义: *the* ~ *of health*; 健康之道; *the* ~ *of soap and water*, (hum for) firm belief in the value of cleanliness. (谐)清洁主义。

gos·sa·mer /'gɒsəmə(r); 'gɑsəmə/ *n* 1 [C, U] (thread of) fine silky substance of webs made by small spiders, floating in calm air or spread on grass, etc.

蛛丝；游丝。**2** [U] soft, light, delicate material: 薄纱: *as light as ~*; 轻如薄纱的; (attrib) (用作定语)*a ~ veil*. 薄面纱。

gos·sip /ˈgɒsɪp; ˈgɑsəp/ *n* **1** [U] idle, often ill-natured, talk about the affairs of other people: 闲话: *Don't believe all the ~ you hear*. 不要相信你所听到的一切闲话。*She's too fond of ~*. 她太喜欢说闲话。**2** [C] instance of this; friendly chat: 闲谈；聊天: *have a good ~ with a neighbour over the garden fence*. 隔着花园篱笆同一邻居愉快地聊天。**3** [U] informal writing about persons and social happenings, eg in letters or in newspapers: 随笔；漫谈: (attrib) (用作定语)*the '~ column, of a newspaper*; (报上的)随笔栏；*a '~ writer/columnist*. 随笔作家(专栏作家)。**4** [C] person who is fond of ~: 喜闲谈之人; *She's an old ~*. 她是个老长舌妇。□ *vi* (**-p-** or **-pp-**; US **-p-**) [VP2A, C] talk or write ~. 闲谈；漫谈。

got *vt*, *pp* of **get**.

Goth /gɒθ; gɑθ/ *n* member of a Germanic tribe that invaded the Roman Empire in the 3rd and 4th cc; rough, uncivilized person. 哥特人(于三、四世纪侵略罗马帝国的日耳曼人之一支)；野蛮人。⇨ **Vandal**.

Gothic /ˈgɒθɪk; ˈgɑθɪk/ *adj* **1** of the Goths or their language. 哥特人的；哥特语的。**2** of the style of architecture common in Western Europe in the 12th to 16th cc, characterized by pointed arches, clusters of columns, etc. 哥特式建筑的(哥特式为十二至十六世纪常见于西欧之建筑风格，以尖拱、簇柱等为特色)。⇨ the illus at **church**. 参看 church 之插图。**3** of an 18th c style of fantastic, romantic literature: 哥特式文学的(十八世纪一种怪异幻想文学风格的): *~ novels*. 哥特式小说。**4** (of printing type) thick or heavy, as formerly used for German. (指活字)哥特体的；粗黑体的。□ *n* ~ language: ~ architecture; ~ type. 哥特语；哥特式建筑；粗黑体活字。

gotta /ˈgɒtə; ˈgɑtə/ (US sl) (美俚) = have got to. ⇨ **get(13)**.

got·ten *pp* (in US) of **get**. (美) get 的过去分词。

gouache /guˈɑːʃ; guˈɑʃ/ *n* [U] opaque watercolour paint; method of painting using this material. 树胶水彩；树胶水彩画法。

gouge /gaʊdʒ; gaʊdʒ/ *n* tool with a sharp semicircular edge for cutting grooves in wood. 半圆凿。□ *vt* [VP6A, 15B] ~ (*out*), cut with a ~; shape with a ~; force out with, or as with, a ~: (用半圆凿)凿；挖；凿成；挖成；挖出: ~ *out the stone from a horseshoe*. 自马蹄铁中将石头挖出。

gou·lash /ˈguːlæʃ; ˈguːlæʃ/ *n* [C, U] (dish of) stew of steak and vegetables, seasoned with paprika. 菜炖牛肉(肉片与蔬菜煮成并加辣椒调味)；一道菜炖牛肉。

gourd /gʊəd; gɔrd/ *n* (large, hard-skinned fleshy fruit of) kind of climbing or trailing plant; bottle or bowl consisting of the dried skin of this fruit. 葫芦；结葫芦的攀缘植物；葫芦制的瓶；葫芦瓢。

decorated gourds

gour·mand /ˈgʊəmənd; ˈgʊrmənd/ *n* lover of food. 贪吃的人；喜美食者。

gour·met /ˈgʊəmeɪ; ˈgʊrme/ *n* person who enjoys, and is expert in the choice of, delicate food, wines, etc. 讲究美食，美酒等者。

gout /gaʊt; gaʊt/ *n* [U] disease causing painful swellings in joints, esp toes, knees and fingers. 痛风(使足趾，膝盖，手指关节肿痛的一种病)。~y *adj* suffering from ~. 患痛风病的。

gov·ern /ˈgʌvn; ˈgʌvən/ *vt*, *vi* **1** [VP6A, 2A] rule (a country, etc); control or direct the public affairs of (a city, country, etc): 统治(国家等); 治理(城市，国家等): *In Great Britain the sovereign reigns but does not ~*. 在英国，君主临国但不治理。**2** [VP6A] control: 控制: ~ *one's temper*. 控制自己的脾气。**3** [VP6A] (usu passive) determine; influence: (通常为被动语态) 支配; 影响: *be ~ed by the opinions of others*. 受他人意见的影响。*Don't be ~ed by what other people say*. 不要被别人的话所左右。**4** (gram, esp of a *v* or *prep*) require, make necessary (a certain case or form of another word). (语法，尤指动词或介词)需用 (某一词之某种格或形式)。~ing *adj* having the power or right to ~: 有统治权的: *the ~ing body of a school/college etc*. 学校(学院等)的行政部门。

gov·ern·ance /ˈgʌvnəns; ˈgʌvənəns/ *n* [U] (formal) act, fact, manner, of governing; sway, control. (正式用语)统治；统治之法；权势；支配。

gov·ern·ess /ˈgʌvənɪs; ˈgʌvənɪs/ *n* woman who is employed to teach young children in a private family. 女家庭教师。

gov·ern·ment /ˈgʌvənmənt; ˈgʌvərnmənt/ *n* **1** [U] governing; power to govern: 统治；统治权: *What the country needs is strong ~*. 这国家所需要的是有力的统治。**2** [U] method or system of governing: 统治方法; 政体: *We prefer democratic ~*. 我们比较喜欢民主政体。**3** [C] body of persons governing a State: 内阁; 政府: *The Prime Minister has formed a G~*, *has chosen his colleagues, selected Ministers for the Cabinet*. 首相已组阁。*The G~* (collectively 集合用法) *has welcomed the proposal*. 政府接受了这项建议。*The G~* (its members 政府成员) *are discussing the proposal*. 政府当局正在讨论这项建议。**G~ House**, official residence of the Governor (of a province, etc). 州长 (总督，省长等) 的官邸。**G~ securities**, bonds, exchequer bills, etc, issued by the state. 政府证券，公债券等。~al /ˌgʌvn-ˈmentl; ˌgʌvənˈmentl/ *adj* connected with ~. 统治的；政府的。

gov·ernor /ˈgʌvənə(r); ˈgʌvənə/ *n* **1 G~**, person who governs a province or colony or (US) a State: 省主席；省长；总督; (美)州长: *the G~ of New York State*. 纽约州州长。Cf 参较 *the Mayor of New York City*. 纽约市市长。**G~-'General** *n* (in the British Commonwealth) representative of the Crown, having no special powers: (英联邦中代表王室的)总督: *the G~-General of Canada*. 加拿大总督。**2** member of the governing body of an institution (eg a school in England, a college, a hospital) (英国学校，学院，医院等内之)主管人员；管理者；理事。**3** (colloq) chief; employer; father. (口)首长；雇主；父亲。**4** regulator in a machine, automatically controlling speed or the intake of gas, steam, etc. (机械)调速器；调节器。

gown /gaʊn; gaʊn/ *n* **1** woman's dress, esp one for special occasions: 女人穿的长服 (尤指为特殊场合所穿者): *a 'ball-/'night-~*. 舞会长服(睡袍)。**2** loose, flowing robe worn by members of a university, judges, etc. 大学学人，法官等所穿的长服。⇨ the illus at **judge**. 参看 judge 之插图。□ *vt* (chiefly *pp*) dress in a ~: (主要用过去分词)使穿着长服: *beautifully ~ed women*. 穿着美丽长袍的妇女。

grab /græb; græb/ *vt*, *vi* (**-bb-**) [VP6A, 3A] ~ (*at*), take roughly; selfishly or eagerly snatch: 抢夺；攫取: *The dog ~bed the bone and ran off with it*. 那狗抢了骨头就跑。*Don't ~!* 不要抢! *He ~bed at the opportunity of going abroad*. 他抢着抓住出国的机会。□ *n* [C] **1** sudden snatch: 攫取; 突攫: *make a ~ at something*. 攫取某物。**2** mechanical device for taking up and holding

sth to be lifted or moved. 搅取机；抓斗；抓子。 **~·ber** *n* person who ~s; greedy person whose chief aim in life appears to be making money. 抢夺者；以赚钱为人生目的之贪财者。

grace /greɪs; gres/ *n* **1** [U, C] quality of being pleasing, attractive or beautiful, esp in structure or movement: 优美;优雅(尤指在结构或动作上): *She danced with ~/with a ~ that surprised us.* 她的舞姿优美(优雅得使我们惊奇)。 **2** [C] (*usu pl*) pleasing accomplishment; elegance of manner. (通常用复数)文雅；温雅。 *airs and ~s,* ways of speaking and behaving that are intended to impress and attract people. (说话与举止之)做作态度；装模作样。 **3** [U] favour; goodwill. 恩赐；善意。 *an act of ~,* sth freely given, not taken as a right. 恩典;仁慈的行为。 *days of ~,* time allowed by the law or custom after the day on which a payment, eg of a bill of exchange, an insurance premium, is due. 付款(如付汇票、保险费)之法定或习惯的宽限日期。 *give sb a day's/week's, etc ~,* allow him an extra day, etc before requiring him to fulfil an obligation. 给与某人一日(一周等)的宽限。 *be in sb's good ~s,* enjoy his favour and approval. 受某人之宠爱。 **4** [U] *have the ~ to do sth,* realize that it is right and proper, and do it: 明理地做某事: *He had the ~ to say that he was sorry.* 他明理地道歉。 *do sth with a good/bad ~,* do it willingly/reluctantly. 乐意地(勉强地)做某事。 **5** [U, C] short prayer of thanks before or after a meal: 饭前或饭后简短的谢恩祷告: *say (a) ~.* 作谢恩祷告。 **6** [U] God's mercy and favour towards mankind; influence and result of this. 上帝对人类的慈悲；天恩的影响与结果。 *in the year of ~ 19...,* in the 19...th year after the birth of Jesus. 在纪元一九…年。 *in a state of ~,* being influenced by the strength and inspiring power of God, having been pardoned; having received the Sacraments. 受天惠；受上帝的恩宠；受圣礼。 *fall from ~,* fall to a lower moral state after being in a state of ~. 失上帝恩宠；堕落。 **7** as a title, used when speaking of or to an archbishop, duke or duchess: 对大主教、公爵或公爵夫人之尊称;阁下;夫人: *His/Her/Your G~.* 阁下；夫人。 **8** the G~s, (Gk myth) three beautiful sister goddesses who gave beauty, charm and happiness. (希神)赐人美丽、魅力与快乐的三位美丽的姐妹女神。 □ *vt* [VP6A] add ~ to; confer honour or dignity on; be an ornament to: 使优美；作增光；为…之装饰: *The occasion was ~d by the presence of the Queen.* 女王之驾临使场面为之增色。 *Her character is ~d with every virtue.* 她的品格因具有一切美德而显得高尚。

grace·ful /ˈgreɪsfl; ˈgresfʊl/ *adj* having or showing grace (1,4): 优雅的；优美的；得体的: *a ~ dancer;* 优美的舞者; *a ~ letter of thanks.* 得体的谢函。 **~·ly** /-fəlɪ; -fəlɪ/ *adv*

grace·less /ˈgreɪslɪs; ˈgreslɪs/ *adj* without grace(4); without a sense of what is right and proper: 不知礼的;不明理的: *~ behaviour.* 粗野的行为。 **~·ly** *adv*

gra·cious /ˈgreɪʃəs; ˈgreʃəs/ *adj* **1** (of persons and their behaviour) kind; generous; courteous: (指人及其行为)亲切的；和善的；大方的；有礼的: *her Majesty the Queen.* 女王陛下。 *It was ~ of her to come.* 蒙她劳临,不胜感激。 **2** (of God) merciful. (指上帝) 仁慈的。 **3** (in exclamations) expressing surprise: (在感叹句中) 表示惊奇: *Good(ness) G~! G~ me!* 天啊! 哎呀! **~·ly** *adv* **~·ness** *n*

gra·da·tion /grəˈdeɪʃn US: greɪ-; greˈdeʃən/ *n* [C, U] step, stage, degree in development; gradual change from one thing to another or from one state to another: 进展的过程，阶段，程度；渐变: *the ~s of colour in the rainbow.* 彩虹中颜色的渐变。

grade¹ /greɪd; gred/ *n* [C] **1** step, stage or degree in rank, quality, value, etc; number or class of things of the same kind: 阶级；品等；等级;同类或同等级的事物: *The rank of major is one ~ higher than that of captain.* 少校的等级较上尉者高一级。 *Potatoes are sold in ~s,*

and G~ A potatoes are of the best quality. 马铃薯分等售出，甲等马铃薯品质最好。 *This pupil has a high ~ of intelligence.* 这个学生的智力很高。 **2** (US) division of the school course; one year's work; pupils in such a division: (美)班级；年级；同一班或年级的全体学生: *An elementary school in the US has eight ~s and is called a "~ school".* Its teachers are called "~ teachers". 美国的小学分为八个年级，因而称作 ‘grade school’。小学教师称作 ‘grade teachers’。 **3** the mark, eg 80%, or rating, eg 'Excellent' or 'Fair', given to a pupil for his work in school. (学校中给学生的)分数(例如用 80 分); 等级(例如优或尚佳)；成绩。 *make the ~,* (colloq) reach a good standard; do as well as is required. (口)达到良好标准；合乎要求。 **4** (US) slope of a road, railways, etc (GB ＝ *gradient*). (美)道路、铁路等的坡度。 *on the 'up/'down ~,* rising/falling: 上升(下降)；兴盛(衰败): *Business is on the up ~,* is improving. 商业兴隆。 *~ crossing,* (US) level crossing. (美)平交道;铁路、公路的平面交叉。

grade² /greɪd; gred/ *vt* [VP6A] **1** arrange in order in grades or classes: 分等；分类；分级: ~ *potatoes;* 将马铃薯分成等级; ~*d by size.* 按大小分类。 **2** make land (esp for roads) more nearly level by reducing the slope. 减少土地(尤指道路用地)之斜度使坡近于水平。 **3** [VP6A, 15B] ~ (*up*), cross (cattle) with a better breed. 使(牛)与优良种交配。

gradi·ent /ˈgreɪdɪənt; ˈgredɪənt/ *n* degree of slope: 坡度;倾斜度；斜率；梯度: *a ~ of one in nine;* 九比一的倾斜度(约合仰角6.34度); *a steep ~.* 陡峭的坡度。

grad·ual /ˈgrædʒʊəl; ˈgrædʒʊəl/ *adj* taking place by degrees; (of a slope) not steep: 逐渐的；(指斜坡)不陡峭的: *a ~ increase in the cost of living.* 生活费的逐渐增高。 **~·ly** /-dʒʊlɪ; -dʒəlɪ/ *adv* by degrees. 逐渐。 **~·ness** *n*

grad·uate¹ /ˈgrædʒʊət; ˈgrædʒʊɪt/ *n* **1** (GB) person who holds a university degree, esp the first, or Bachelor's, degree: (英)获大学学位(尤指学士学位)者；大学毕业生: *Oxbridge ~s;* 牛津或剑桥大学毕业生; *a ~ student;* 研究生; *post-~ studies.* 研究所的课程。 **2** (US) one who has completed a course at an educational institution: (美)毕业生: *high school ~s;* 高中毕业生; *a ~ nurse,* one from a College or School of Nursing. 护理学校毕业的护士。 (Cf 参较 *trained nurse* in GB 英国称 trained nurse.)

grad·uate² /ˈgrædʒʊeɪt; ˈgrædʒʊˌet/ *vt, vi* **1** [VP6A] mark with degrees for measuring: 刻度数于: *a ruler ~d in both inches and centimetres;* 刻有英寸及厘米的尺; *a ~d glass,* for measuring quantities of liquid. 量杯(上有刻度;量液体用)。 **2** [VP6A] arrange according to grade. 分等级；定以等第。 **3** [VP2A, C] take an academic degree: (自大学)毕业；获学位: *He ~d from Oxford/~d in law.* 他毕业于牛津大学(获得法学学位)。 (US, of other institutions): (在美国亦指自其他学校毕业): ~ *from the Boston School of Cookery.* 毕业于波士顿烹饪学校。 **4** [VP6A] (chiefly US) give a degree or diploma to: (主美)授以学位；准予毕业: *The university ~d 350 students last year.* 该大学去年有350位学生毕业。 *He had been ~d from Maryland College in the Class of 1868.* 他毕业于马里兰学院一八六八年级。 **gradu·ation** /ˌgrædʒʊˈeɪʃn; ˌgrædʒʊˈeʃən/ *n* graduating or being ~d; (US) ceremony at which degrees are conferred. 刻度;分等级；毕业;授学位;获学位;(美)毕业典礼;授学位典礼。

graf·fito /grəˈfiːtəʊ; greˈfito/ *n* (*pl* -ti /-tiː; -ti/) (usu *pl*) (I) drawing, words, scratched on a hard surface, esp a wall. (通常用复数)乱刻于墙上等的画或文字。

graft¹ /grɑːft US: græft; græft/ *n* **1** shoot from a branch or twig of a living tree, fixed in a cut made in another tree, to form a new growth. 接枝;接木。 **2** (surgery) piece of skin, bone, etc from a living

person or animal, transplanted on another body or another part of the same body. (外科) 移植物; 移植的皮肤、骨骼等。 □ *vt, vi* [VP6A, 15A, B, 2A] put a ~ in or on: 接木于; 接枝; 移植: ~ *one variety on/upon/in/into another;* 将一品种接到另一品种上; ~ *on briar roots;* 接枝于石南枝上; ~ *new skin.* 移植新皮肤。

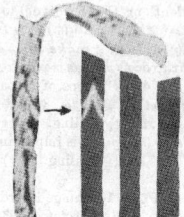 

grafting   wood grain

graft² /grɑːft *US:* græft; græft/ *n* [C, U] (instance of) getting business advantages, profit-making, etc through illegal or unethical means, eg by taking wrong advantage of connections in politics, by bribery etc. 贪污; 受贿; 渎职。 □ *vi* practise ~. 贪污; 受贿; 渎职。

grail /greɪl; grel/ *n* (usu 通常作 **the Holy G~**) platter or cup used by Jesus at the Last Supper and in which one of his followers is said to have received drops of his blood at the Crucifixion. 圣盘; 圣杯(耶稣在最后晚餐时所用, 据说耶稣被钉于十字架上时, 其门徒之一曾用以盛装耶稣的血)。

grain /greɪn; gren/ *n* **1** [U] (collective *sing*) small, hard seed of food plants such as wheat and rice: (集合名词单数)谷类: ~ *imports;* 谷类输入; *a cargo of* ~. 一船谷类; '~ *elevator,* storehouse for ~, with devices for lifting ~. 谷仓。 ⇨ the illus at **cereal**. 参看 cereal 之插图。 **2** [C] single seed of such a plant: 谷粒: *give a beggar a few* ~*s of rice;* 给一乞丐少许的米饭; *eat up every* ~ *of rice in one's bowl.* 将碗中的米饭吃得一粒也不剩。 **3** [C] tiny, hard bit: 小硬粒: ~*s of sand/salt/gold;* 沙(盐, 金)粒; (fig) small amount: (喻)少许: *a boy without a* ~ *of sense;* 没有一点头脑的男孩; *receive a few* ~*s of comfort.* 得到些许安慰。 **4** smallest unit of weight, 1/7000 lb or 0.065 gm. 喱, 谷(最小的重量单位, 等于 1/7000 磅或 0.065 克)。 ⇨ **App 5**. 参看附录五。 **5** [U] natural arrangement or pattern of the lines of fibre in wood, etc as seen on a surface that has been sawn or cut: 木等之纹; 纹理: *woods of fine/coarse* ~. 细(粗)纹木。 *be/go against the* ~, (fig) contrary to one's nature or inclination. (喻)不合自己的性情或意图。

gram /græm; græm/ *n* metric unit of weight. 克。 ⇨ **App 5**. 参看附录五。

gram·mar /ˈɡræmə(r); ˈɡræmɚ/ *n* **1** [U] study or science of, rules for, the combination of words into sentences (*syntax*), and the forms of words (*morphology*). 语法; 语法规则。 **2** [C] book containing the rules of ~ of a language. 语法书。 '~ **school**, (in GB) type of secondary school which provides academic (contrasted with technical) courses. (英国之)语法学校(一种中等学校, 设有文学或古典作品的课程, 以别于工艺或技术学校)。 ~**·ian** /ɡrəˈmeərɪən; ɡrəˈmerɪən/ *n* expert in ~. 语法学者; 语法家。

gram·mat·i·cal /ɡrəˈmætɪkl; ɡrəˈmætɪkl/ *adj* of, conforming to, the rules of grammar: 语法的; 合乎语法规则的: *a* ~ *error/explanation/sentence.* 语法上的错误(语法的解释, 合语法的句子)。 ~**ly** /-klɪ; -klɪ/ *adv*

gramme /græm; græm/ *n* = **gram**.

gramo·phone /ˈɡræməfəʊn; ˈɡræməˌfon/ *n* (US 美 = *phonograph*) machine for reproducing music and speech recorded on flat discs (*record-player* is now the usu word). 留声机; 唱机(现较常用 record-player)。

gram·pus /ˈɡræmpəs; ˈɡræmpəs/ *n* large dolphin-like sea animal; person who breathes loudly. 逆戟鲸; 鲦(一种大海豚); 呼吸粗浊之人。

gran·ary /ˈɡrænərɪ; ˈɡrænərɪ/ *n* (*pl* **-ries**) storehouse for grain. 谷仓。

grand /grænd; grænd/ *adj* **1** (in official titles) chief; most important: (用于官衔中)主要的; 最高级的: *G~ Master,* eg of some orders of knighthood; 骑士团的首领; *a* ~ *master,* chess champion; 国际象棋王(国际象棋冠军); *G~ Vizier,* (former title of) chief minister of Turkey. 昔时土耳其的首相。 **2** of most or greatest importance: 最重要的: *the* ~ *finale;* 大结局; 大终曲; *the* ~ *question;* 最重要的问题; *the* ~ *staircase/entrance,* of a large building. 主要的楼梯(入口)。 **3** magnificent; splendid: 壮丽的; 堂皇的: *a* ~ *view;* 壮丽的景色; *living in* ~ *style;* 过豪华生活; ~ *clothes.* 华丽的服装。 **4** self-important; proud: 自大的; 骄傲的: *He puts on a* ~ *manner/air.* 他的态度骄傲。 **5** (colloq) very fine or enjoyable: (口)极好的; 快乐的: *We had a* ~ *time.* 我们玩得很愉快。 *What* ~ *weather!* 天气真好！ **6** full; complete: 完全的; 全部的: *a* ~ *orchestra,* one with all kinds of instruments (not strings only); 大管弦乐队(配有各种乐器, 不限于弦乐器); *the* ~ *total,* including everything; 总计; *the* ~ *result of our efforts.* 我们努力的总结果。 **7** impressive because of high moral or mental qualities: 崇高的; 高贵的: *Lincoln had a* ~ *character.* 林肯有崇高的人格。 *Gladstone was called the G~ Old Man.* 格拉斯通被称作伟大的长者。 **8** (phrases) (短语) **the ,G~ 'National,** annual steeplechase at Liverpool. 利物浦每年举行的越野障碍大赛马。 **,~ 'opera,** in which there are no spoken parts, everything being sung. 大歌剧(无对白, 全部为歌唱者)。 **~ pi'ano,** large piano with horizontal strings. 平台钢琴。 ⇨ the illus at **keyboard**. 参看 keyboard 之插图。 **,baby '~,** small-size ~ piano. 小型平台钢琴。 **G~ Prix** /ˌɡrɑːn ˈpriː; ˌɡrɑnˈpri/, (F) (motor-racing) one of several international races. (法)国际大赛车。 **'~·stand,** rows of roofed seats for spectators at races, sports-meetings, etc. (赛马场, 运动场等之)大看台。 **the ,G~ 'Tour,** (formerly) tour of the chief towns, etc of Europe, completing the education of a wealthy young person. (昔时)教育旅行(富家子弟至欧洲各大都市之旅行, 做为教育之最后一个阶段)。 ~**ly** *adv*

grand- /grænd; grænd/ *pref* **'~·child, '~·daughter, '~·son** *nn* daughter or son of one's son or daughter. 孙(外孙); 孙女(外孙女); 孙子(外孙)。 **'~·parent, '~·father, '~·mother** *nn* father or mother of one's father or mother. (外)祖父或(外)祖母; (外)祖父; (外)祖母。 **'~·nephew, '~·niece** *nn* son or daughter or one's nephew or niece. 侄孙(侄外孙); 侄外孙女(侄外孙女)。 **'~·uncle, '~·aunt** *nn* uncle or aunt of either of one's parents. 伯祖(叔祖, 姑公, 舅公); 伯祖母(叔婆, 姑婆, 姨婆, 舅婆)。 **'~·father clock** *n* clock worked by weights in a tall wooden case. 装于高木匣中有摆的大钟。

grand-dad, gran·dad /ˈɡrændæd; ˈɡrænˌdæd/ *n* (colloq for) grandfather. (口)爷爷; 外公。

gran·dee /ɡrænˈdiː; ɡrænˈdi/ *n* (hist) Spanish or Portuguese nobleman of high rank. (史)大公(西班牙或葡萄牙之贵族)。

gran·deur /ˈɡrændʒə(r); ˈɡrændʒɚ/ *n* [U] greatness; magnificence: 伟大; 壮丽: *the* ~ *of the Swiss Alps.* 瑞士境内阿尔卑斯山之壮丽。

gran·dilo·quent /ɡrænˈdɪləkwənt; ɡrænˈdɪləkwənt/ *adj* using, full of, pompous words: 夸张的; 夸大的: *a* ~ *speaker;* 说话夸大的人; *written in a* ~ *style.* 文体浮华的。 **gran·dilo·quence** /-əns; -əns/ *n* [U].

gran·di·ose /'grændɪəʊs; 'grændɪ,os/ *adj* planned on a large scale; imposing. 宏伟的; 堂皇的。

grand·ma /'grænmɑː; 'grænmɑ/ *n* (colloq for) grandmother. (口)奶奶; 外婆。

grand·pa /'grænpɑː; 'grænpɑ/ *n* (colloq for) grandfather. (口)爷爷; 外公。

grange /greɪndʒ; grendʒ/ *n* country house with farm buildings attached. 农庄。

gran·ite /'grænɪt; 'grænɪt/ *n* [U] hard, usu grey, stone used for building. 花岗岩; 花岗石。

granny, gran·nie /'grænɪ; 'grænɪ/ *n* (colloq for) grandmother. (口)奶奶; 外婆。 **~ knot**, reef-knot crossed the wrong way and therefore insecure. 祖母结 (交叉错误的方结, 故而不牢)。 ⇨ the illus at **knot.** 参看 knot 之插图。

grant /grɑːnt; grænt/ *vt* 1 [VP6A, 12A, 13A] consent to give or allow (what is asked for): 允许; 准许; 答应给与: ~ *a favour / request;* 答应一项帮助(请求); ~ *sb permission / a request to do sth.* 准许某人做某事。 *He was ~ed a pension.* 他获得年金。 2 [VP6A, 9, 25] agree (that sth is true): 承认(某事为真): ~ *the truth of what someone says;* 承认某人的话是真的; ~ *ing this to be true / that this is true.* 姑认此系真情。 *I ~ his honesty / ~ that he is honest.* 我承认他是诚实的。 *He's an honest man, I ~ you.* 我保证他是个诚实的人。 **take sth for ~ed**, regard it as true or as certain to happen. 认为真实; 视为当然。 **take sb for ~ed**, treat his presence and actions as a due rather than a favour. 认为某人之到场和行动是应该的(而非恩惠)。 *n* sth ~ed, eg money or land from a government: 赐与之物(例如由政府授与的金钱或土地): ~ *towards the cost of a university education;* 给与大学生的助学金; ~*-aided schools / students.* 获有补助金的学校(学生)。

granu·lar /'grænjʊlə(r); 'grænjələ/ *adj* of or like grains. 小粒的; 粒状的。

granu·late /'grænjʊleɪt; 'grænjə,let/ *vt, vi* [VP6A, 2A] form into grains; roughen the surface of: (使)成粒; 粒化; 使⋯之表面粗糙: ~*d sugar*, sugar in the form of small crystals. 砂糖。

gran·ule /'grænjuːl; 'grænjul/ *n* [C] small grain. 小粒。

grape /greɪp; grep/ *n* green or purple berry growing in clusters on vines, used for making wine: 葡萄: *a bunch of ~s.* 一串葡萄。 ⇨ the illus at **fruit.** 参看 fruit 之插图。 *sour ~s; the ~s are sour,* said when sb says that sth he wants but cannot get has little or no value. 酸葡萄(得不到某种东西便说那种东西不好)。 '**~-shot** *n* [U] (hist) cluster of small iron balls fired together from a cannon to make a hail of shot. (史)同时发生的一群小弹丸; 葡萄弹。 '**~-sugar** *n* dextrose or glucose, a kind of sugar found in ripe ~s and other kinds of fruit. 葡萄糖。 '**~-vine** *n* **(a)** kind of vine on which ~s grow. 葡萄藤。 **(b)** (fig) means by which news gets about, eg in an office, school or a group of friends: (喻)(办公处、学校或朋友间等)传达消息的方法: *I heard on the ~-vine that Jill is to be promoted.* 我听别人说吉尔要升级了。

grape·fruit /'greɪpfruːt; 'grep,frut/ *n* (*pl* ~ or ~s) [C] fruit like a large orange but with an acid taste. 葡萄柚。 ⇨ the illus at **fruit.** 参看 fruit 之插图。

graph /grɑːf; græf/ *n* [C] diagram consisting of a line or lines (often curved) showing the variation of two quantities, eg the temperature at each hour. 图; 图表; 曲线图(例如表明每小时之温度变化者)。 '**~-paper**, paper with small squares of equal size. 方格纸; 坐标纸。

graphic /'græfɪk; 'græfɪk/ *adj* **1** of visual symbols (eg lettering, diagrams, drawings): 文字的; 书写的; 图表的; 绘画的: *a ~ artist;* 书画雕刻艺术家; ~ *displays;* 图表展示; *the ~ arts.* 书画雕刻艺术; 平面艺术。 **2** (of descriptions) causing one to have a clear picture in the mind: (指描写)生动的: *a ~ account of the battle.* 对该

战役生动的叙述。 □ *n pl* ~**s**, lettering, drawings, etc. 文字, 图样等。 **graphically** /-klɪ; -klɪ/ *adv* by writing or diagrams; (fig) vividly. 用书写或图表; (喻)生动地。

graph·ite /'græfaɪt; 'græfaɪt/ *n* [U] soft, black substance (a form of carbon) used in lubrication, as a moderator in atomic piles, and in making lead pencils. 石墨。

grap·nel /'græpnl; 'græpnəl/ *n* **1** anchor with many flukes[2]; instrument as used for dragging along the bed of a river, lake, etc when searching for sth. 多爪锚; 抓机(例如为寻物而用以拖抓河床, 湖床等者)。 **2** instrument like this formerly used in sea battles for holding enemy ships. 昔时海战中用以钩住敌船的战具。

grapple /'græpl; 'græpl/ *vi* [VP2A, C, 3A] ~ (*with*), seize firmly; struggle with sb / sth at close quarters; (fig) try to deal with (a problem, etc): 提牢; 抓住; 互扭; 格斗; (喻)设法对付(问题等): ~ *with an enemy.* 与敌人格斗。 *The wrestlers ~d together.* 摔角选手揪在一起。 '**grappling-iron** *n* grapnel. 抓机; 多爪锚。

grasp /grɑːsp US: græsp; græsp/ *vt, vi* **1** [VP6A] seize firmly with the hand(s) or arm(s); understand with the mind: 抓住; 紧握; 抱住; 领悟: ~ *sb's hand / a rope;* 抓住某人的手(一根绳); ~ *an argument / sb's meaning.* 领会一论点(某人的意思)。 **2** [VP3A] ~ *at,* try to seize; accept eagerly: 欲抓住; 急欲接受: ~ *at an opportunity.* 欲抓住一机会。 *A man who ~s at too much may lose everything.* 贪得无厌的人可能毫无所得。 □ *n* (usu *sing*) firm hold or grip; (power of) grasping: (通常用单数)紧握; 把握; 抓紧; 把握力; 领悟力: *in the ~ of a wicked enemy;* 在一邪恶的敌人的掌握中; *have a thorough ~ of the problem;* 彻底理解一问题; *a problem within / beyond my ~,* that I can / cannot understand. 我所能(不能)了解的一个问题。 ~**ing** *adj* eager to ~; greedy (for money, etc): 急欲抓住的; 贪婪的: *a ~ing rascal.* 贪婪的恶汉。

grass[1] /grɑːs US: græs; græs/ *n* **1** [U] kinds of common, wild, low-growing plant of which the green blades and stalks are eaten by cattle, horses, sheep, etc. 青草; 草。 *not let the ~ grow under one's feet,* (fig) waste no time in doing sth. (喻)及时行动。 **2** [C] (*pl* ~**es**) any species of this plant (including, in botanical use, cereals, reeds and bamboos). 禾本科植物(在植物学上的用法, 包括谷类、芦苇和竹)。 **3** [U] grazing land; pasture: 牧地; 草原; 草地: (of animals) (指动物) *at ~,* grazing. 在吃青草。 *put / send / turn animals out to ~,* put them to graze. 放动物出去吃草。 ~**land** /-lænd; -lænd/ *n* area of land covered with ~ where there are few trees. 草原。 **~·roots** *n pl* (often attrib) ordinary people remote from political decisions, but who are affected by these decisions: (常作定语用)(不参与政治决策但受其影响的)一般人民: *a ~roots movement / rebellion.* 一般民众的运动(叛乱)。 *We must not neglect the ~roots.* 我们不可忽视一般民众。 ~ *widow* ~*n* wife whose husband is temporarily not living with her. 独守空闺的妻子。 ~**y** *adj* (-ier, -iest) covered with ~. 长满草的; 多草的。

grass[2] /grɑːs US: græs; græs/ *vt, vi* **1** [VP6A, 15B] ~ (*over*), cover with turf; [VP6A] (US) feed with grass. 以草覆盖; 铺以草皮; 以青草; 放牧。 **2** [VP2A, 3A] ~ (*on sb*), (GB sl) inform (on); betray. (英俚)向警方告发; 告密; 出卖。

grass·hopper /'grɑːshɒpə(r) US: 'græs-; 'græs,hɑpə/ *n* jumping insect which makes a shrill, chirping noise. 蚱蜢。 ⇨ the illus at **insect.** 参看 insect 之插图。

grate[1] /greɪt; gret/ *n* (metal frame for holding coal, etc, in a) fireplace. 壁炉; 炉条; 炉格子; 炉栅。

grate[2] /greɪt; gret/ *vt, vi* **1** [VP6A, 15A] rub into small pieces, usu against a rough surface; rub small bits off: 磨碎; 擦碎; 磨损: ~ *cheese into beaten eggs,* eg

when making a cheese omelette. 磨碎干酪置入搅过的蛋中(中用以做干酪煎蛋卷时). **2** [VP6A, 2A, 3A] ~ **(on)**, make a harsh noise by rubbing; (fig) have an irritating effect (on a person, his nerves): 因磨擦而发刺耳声;(喻)刺激; 激怒 (人或其神经): *His bad manners ~d on everyone.* 他的无礼使大家都不愉快。 *Out-of-date slang ~s.* 过时的俚语听来刺耳。 *The gate ~s on its hinges.* 那大门开关时铰链吱吱作响。 **grat·ing·ly** *adv* ~ **r** n device with a rough surface for grating food, etc: (将食物等磨成碎块的)擦子: *a 'nutmeg ~r.* 磨豆蔻的擦子。

grate·ful /ˈgreitfl; ˈgretfəl/ *adj* **1** ~ **(to sb) (for sth)**, feeling or showing thanks: 感激的; 感谢的: *We are ~ to you for your help.* 我们感激你对我们们的帮助。 **2** (liter) pleasant; agreeable; comforting: (文)令人愉快的; 悦人的; 使人舒适的: *trees that afford a ~ shade.* 有树荫可供人乘凉的树木。 **~ly** /-fəli; -fəli/ *adv*

grat·ify /ˈgrætifai; ˈgrætə.fai/ *vt (pt, pp -fied)* [VP 6A] **1** give pleasure or satisfaction to: 使高兴; 使满意: *We were all gratified with/at the result.* 我们都对此结果感到欣慰。 *It gratified me to learn that you had been successful.* 获悉你成功了, 我很高兴。 **2** indulge; give what is desired to: 使满足; 给与所希望获得的东西: ~ *a person's whims/his fancies for something;* 满足一人的奇想(满足他想要某物的愿望); ~ *a child's thirst for knowledge.* 满足一儿童的求知欲。 **~·ing** *adj: It is always ~ing to have one's efforts rewarded.* 努力而有收获, 总是令人高兴的。 **grati·fi·ca·tion** /ˌgrætifiˈkeiʃn; ˌgrætəfəˈkeʃən/ n [U] **1** ~ing or being gratified; state of being pleased or satisfied: 喜悦; 满意; 满足: *I have the gratification of knowing that I have done my duty.* 得悉我已尽到职责, 我很高兴。 **2** [C] that which causes one to feel gratified. 令人满意的事物。

grat·ing /ˈgreitiŋ; ˈgretiŋ/ n [C] framework of wooden or metal bars, either parallel or crossing one another, placed across an opening, eg a window, to keep out burglars or to allow air to flow through. 格子;格栅(例如装于窗上以防盗贼所用者)。

gra·tis /ˈgreitis; ˈgretis/ *adv, adj* free of charge: 免费的(地): *be admitted ~.* 受免费招待。

grati·tude /ˈgrætitjuːd US: -tuːd; ˈgrætə.tjud/ n [U] ~ **(to sb) (for sth)**, thankfulness; being grateful. 感谢; 感激。

gra·tu·itous /grəˈtjuːitəs US: -ˈtuː-; grəˈtjuətəs/ *adj* **1** given, obtained or done, without payment: 不收费的; 免费的: ~ *service/information/help/advice.* 免费的服务(消息, 帮助, 忠告)。 **2** done or given, acting, without good reason: 无故的; 无理由的: *a ~ insult;* 无故的侮辱; *a ~ lie/liar.* 无故的谎言(无故扯谎者)。 **~·ly** *adv*

gra·tu·ity /grəˈtjuːəti US: -ˈtuː-; grəˈtjuəti/ n (pl **-ties**) **1** gift (of money in addition to pay) to a retiring employee for services. 退休雇员的奖金。 **2** tip (for service). 小帐。

grave[1] /greiv; grev/ *adj* (**-r, -st**) serious; requiring careful consideration: 严重的; 严肃的: ~ *news;* 重大的新闻; *make a ~ mistake;* 犯一严重的错误; *as ~ as a judge.* 象法官一样严肃。 *The situation is more ~ (ie serious) now than at any time since the end of the war.* 战争结束以来, 目前局势为最严重的时期。 **~·ly** *adv*

grave[2] /greiv; grev/ n hole dug in the ground for a corpse; the mound of earth or the monument over it. 墓穴; 坟墓; 墓上建筑物。 **have one foot in the ~,** be nearing death, be very old. 行将就木; 十分年迈。 '~**-clothes** n pl wrappings in which a corpse is buried. 死人所穿的衣服; 寿衣。 '~**-stone** n stone over a ~, with the name, etc of the person buried there. 墓碑。 (参阅church之插图。 '~**-yard** n burial ground. 墓地。

grave[3] /grɑːv; grɑv/ n (also 亦作 ~ **accent**) mark placed over a vowel to indicate how it is to be

sounded (as in French mère). 抑音符(例如法语 mère 中之 `).

grave[4] /greiv; grev/ *vt (pp **graven** /ˈgreivn; ˈgrevn/) (archaic or liter)* carve: (古或文)雕刻: ~ *on my memory,* indelibly fixed. 铭记心头。 **~n 'image,** an idol. 雕像; 偶像。

gravel /ˈgrævl; ˈgrævl/ n [U] small stones with coarse sand, as used for roads and paths: (铺路用的)砂砾; 砾石; 碎石和粗砂: *a load of ~;* 一车(担等)碎石; (attrib) (用作定语) *a ~ path/pit.* 碎石路(坑)。 **grav·elly** /ˈgrævəli; ˈgrævli/ *adj* (of a voice) deep and rough. (指声音) 低沉而沙哑的。 □ *vt* (**-ll-,** US also **-l-**) [VP6A] **1** cover with ~: 铺碎石于: ~ *a road;* 铺碎石于道路; ~*led paths.* 碎石路。 **2** (colloq) perplex; puzzle. (口)使困窘; 使困惑。

grav·ing dock /ˈgreiviŋ dɒk; ˈgreviŋ dɑk/ n dry dock in which the outside of a ship's hull may be cleaned. 干船坞。

gravi·tate /ˈgræviteit; ˈgrævə.tet/ *vi* [VP3A] ~ **to/towards**, move or be attracted: 移动; 被吸引: *Young people in the country districts seem to ~ towards the cities.* 乡村的青年有向都市移动的趋势。 **gravi·tation** /ˌgræviˈteiʃn; ˌgrævəˈteʃən/ n [U] process of gravitating; gravity(1). 吸引作用;万有引力;地心吸力。

grav·ity /ˈgrævəti; ˈgrævəti/ n [U] **1** (phys) force of attraction between any two objects, esp that force which attracts objects towards the centre of the earth. (物理)万有引力;(尤指)地心吸力;重力。 **2** (phys) weight: (物理)重量: *centre of ~.* (物体的)重心。 **spe,cific '~,** relation between the weight of a substance and that of the same volume of a standard substance (usu water for liquids and solids, and air for gases). 比重。 **3** quality of being serious or solemn: 严重; 严肃: *the ~ of the international situation;* 国际局势的严重; *the ~ of his appearance.* 他外表的严肃。 *He could hardly keep his ~, could with difficulty refrain from smiling or laughing.* 他几乎保持不住庄重的态度(禁不住要笑)。

gra·vure /grəˈvjuə(r); ˈgrevjər/ n = **photogravure**.

gravy /ˈgreivi; ˈgrevi/ n [U] **1** juice which comes from meat while it is cooking; sauce made from this. 肉汁; 调味肉汁。 '~**-boat** n vessel in which ~ is served at table. 盛调味肉汁的器皿。 **2** (sl) money or profit easily or unexpectedly acquired. (俚)轻易或意外获得之钱财。 '~ **train** n source of much and easy money, etc: 可轻易赚大钱的机会: *get on the ~ train,* get a job where such money, etc is easily acquired. 获一可轻易赚大钱的工作。

gray /grei; gre/ *adj, n* = **grey**.

graze[1] /greiz; grez/ *vi, vt* **1** [VP2A, C] (of cattle, sheep, etc) eat growing grass: (指牛羊等)吃草: *cattle grazing in the fields.* 在田野中吃青草的牛群。 **2** [VP6A] put (cattle, etc) in fields to ~: 放牧(牛羊等): ~ *sheep;* 放羊; use grassland for cattle: 做牧地: ~ *a field.* 用一田野做牧地。 '**grazing-land** n land used for grazing cattle. 放牧(牛羊之)草地。 **graz·ier** /ˈgreiziə(r) US: ˈgreiʒə(r); ˈgreʒə/ n person who feeds cattle for market. 畜牧业者。

graze[2] /greiz; grez/ *vt, vi* **1** [VP6A] touch or scrape lightly in passing; rub the skin from: 轻擦; 擦去⋯之皮: *The bullet ~d his cheek.* 子弹擦伤了他面颊上的皮肤。 **2** [VP2C] pass and touch while going *against/along/by/past.* 经过时触及;擦过。 □ *n* place where the skin is ~d. 皮肤擦伤之处。

grease /griːs; gris/ n [U] **1** animal fat melted soft 熔化之软脂肪。 **2** any thick, semi-solid oily substance: 油脂; 滑脂: *axle* ~, used to lubricate axles. 滑润轮轴之油; 车轴脂。 '~**-gun** n device for forcing ~ into the parts of an engine, machine, etc. 滑脂枪(向机器挤入引擎, 机器等之一种装置)。 '~**-paint** n [U] mixture of ~ and paint used by actors to make up their faces. 演员化装用之油彩。 □ *vt* put ~ or rub ~ on or in (esp parts of a machine). 涂以油脂; 搽以油(尤指机器之各部分)。 ~ *sb's palm,* bribe him. 贿赂某人。 **~r** n man who ~s

machinery, eg a ship's engines. 搽油工人(例如为船只引擎搽油者)。

greasy /'gri:sɪ; 'grisɪ/ adj (-ier, -iest) covered with grease; slippery: 涂有油脂的; 油污的; 油腻的; 滑的: ~ fingers; 涂有油脂的手指; a ~ road. 滑溜的道路。 **greas·ily** /-ɪlɪ; -əlɪ/ adv **greasi·ness** n

great /greɪt; gret/ adj (-er, -est) **1** well above the average in size, quantity or degree: (体积, 数量, 程度) 超出一般标准的; 巨大的; 很多的; 非常的: take ~ care of sth; 对某事物特别用心照顾(对某事项): an essay that shows ~ ignorance of grammar; 显示出语法十分不通的一篇文章; a ~ friend of mine, one for whom I feel more than ordinary friendship. 我的一位亲密的朋友。 ~ **with child**, (old use) pregnant. (旧用法)怀孕的。 '~-**coat** n heavy overcoat. 厚大衣。 **2** of remarkable ability or quality: 伟大的: ~ men; 伟人; a ~ painter/painting/musician. 伟大的画家(画, 音乐家)。 **3** important; noted; of high rank or position: 重要的; 著名的; 地位高的: a ~ occasion; 重大的场合; the G~ Powers of Europe; 欧洲列强; a ~ lady; 贵妇人; Alexander the G~. 亚历山大大帝。 **4** (colloq, preceding another adj which is often weakly stressed; implying surprise, indignation, contempt, etc according to context): (口)(用在另一个常轻读的形容词前; 表示惊异, 愤怒, 轻蔑等, 视上下文而定): See what a ~ big fish I've caught! 看我捉到多么大的一条鱼啊! Take your ~ big head out of my light! 把你的大头移开, 不要遮住我的光线! What a ~ thick stick! 多么粗的一根棍子啊! **5** (also 亦作 **G~er**) used as a distinctive epithet of the larger of two. 用做区别性质的形容词, 指两者中之较大者。 **the G~ Bear**, ⇒ bear¹(3). **G~ Britain**, (abbr 略作 **GB**) England, Wales and Scotland, excluding Northern Ireland. 英国; 大不列颠(包括英格兰, 威尔士与苏格兰; 北爱尔兰除外)。 **the G~ Lakes**, series of five large lakes in N America along the boundary between Canada and the US. 大湖(加拿大与美国之间的五个大湖)。 **G~er London**, an administrative area of local government that includes inner London and the outer suburbs. 大伦敦(包括伦敦市及其郊区)。 **the G~ War**, that of 1914–18. 第一次世界大战。 **6** (attrib only) (仅用作定语) fully deserving the name of: 应得...之名的: He's a ~ liar. 他是个名副其实的说谎者。 They are ~ friends. 他们是真正的朋友。 **7** (with agent nouns; attrib only) doing or being sth to a high degree: (与表示动作者的名词连用; 仅用作定语)非常的: He's a ~ reader/eater, reads/eats very much. 他书读得很多(食量很大)。 He's a ~ landowner, owns a large area of land. 他是个大地主。 **8** combined with words indicating quantity, etc: 与表示数量等的词连用: a ~ deal, very much; 很多; a ~ number; 很多; a ~ while ago; 许久以前; the ~ majority, much the larger part. 大多数。 **9** (colloq) splendid; satisfactory: (口)绝妙的; 快乐的; 令人满意的: We had a ~ time in Paris. 我们在巴黎的那段时期很快乐。 Wouldn't it be ~ if we could go there again! 如果我们能够再去那里该多么好啊! **10** (colloq, pred only) (口; 仅用作表语) ~ at, clever or skilful at. 擅长; 精于。 ~ **on**, having a good knowledge of. 精通。 **11** prefixed to a kinship words in grand- to show a further stage in relationship: 冠于以grand起首表示亲属之词前, 以示更高或低一辈的亲属关系: ~'grand-father, one's father's or mother's grandfather; 曾祖; 外曾祖。 ~-'grandson, grandson of one's son or daughter. 曾孙; 外曾孙。 **~ly** adv much; by much: 很; 非常: ~ly amused. 很高兴。 **~·ness** n

greaves /gri:vz; grivz/ n pl pieces of armour to protect the shins. 护胫; 胫甲。 ⇒ the illus at **armour**. 参看 armour 之插图。

grebe /gri:b; grib/ n kind of short-bodied diving bird. 鸊鷉。 ⇒ the illus at **water**. 参看 water 之插图。

Gre·cian /'gri:ʃn; 'griʃən/ adj (eg of architecture, pottery, culture and features of the face) Greek. (指建筑, 陶器,文化, 面貌等)希腊的。

greed /gri:d; grid/ n [U] strong desire for more food, wealth, etc, esp for more than is right or reasonable. (对食物, 财富等之)贪心; 贪婪。

greedy /'gri:dɪ; 'gridɪ/ adj (-ier, -iest) **1** ~ (for sth/to have sth), filled with greed: 贪心的; 贪婪的: not hungry, just ~; 不饿, 只是贪食而已; looking at the cakes with ~ eyes; 以贪婪的目光望着蛋糕; ~ for gain/honours. 贪财(名)。 **2** ~ (to do sth), intensely desirous. 渴望(做某事)的; 急欲(做某事)的。 **greed·ily** /-ɪlɪ; -əlɪ/ adv **greedi·ness** n

Greek /gri:k; grik/ n [C] member of the Greek people, either of ancient Greece or modern Greece; [U] the Greek language. 希腊人; 希腊语。 ~ **to one**, be beyond one's knowledge or understanding: 不了解; 完全不懂。 □ adj of Greece, its people, or the Greek language. 希腊的; 希腊人的; 希腊语的。

green¹ /gri:n; grin/ adj (-er, -est) **1** of the colour between blue and yellow in the spectrum, the colour of growing grass, and the leaves of most plants and trees: 绿色的: a ~ Christmas, Christmas season when the weather is mild and there is no snow. 绿色的圣诞节(天气温暖, 没有下雪的圣诞节)。 ~ '**belt**, wide area of land round a town, where building is controlled (by town-planning) so that there are ~ fields, woods, etc. 都市四周之绿化地带(按都市计划控制建筑, 故有绿野, 树林等)。 **give sb/get the ~ light**, (colloq, from the ~ of traffic lights) permission to go ahead with a project, etc. (口, 源于交通灯之绿灯)准许某人(得到许可)照计划等行事, 予(获得)许可。 **2** (of fruit) not yet ripe: (指水果)未成熟的: ~ apples; 未熟的苹果; ~ figs, young and tender figs; 嫩无花果; (of wood) not yet dry enough for use: (指木材)未干燥的: G~ wood does not burn well. 未干燥的木柴不易燃烧。 **3** inexperienced; undeveloped; gullible; untrained: 无经验的; 未发展的; 易受骗的; 无训练的: a boy who is still ~ at his job. 对其工作尚无经验的青年。 I'm not so ~ as to believe that. 我不会无知至相信那事。 **4** (fig) flourishing; full of vigour: (喻)旺盛的; 精力充沛的: live to a ~ old age; 老当益壮; keep a person's memory ~, not allow it to fade. 使记忆不忘。 **5** (of the complexion) pale; sickly looking. (指脸色)苍白的; 有病容的。 **~-eyed** adj jealous. 嫉妒的。 **the ~-eyed 'monster**, jealousy. 嫉妒。 ~ **with envy**, very envious. 非常嫉妒的。 **6** (special uses and compounds): (特殊用法与复合词): ~-**back** n US banknote, the back printed in ~. 美钞(背面印成绿色)。 ~ '**fingers** n (colloq) skill in gardening. (口)园艺才能。 ~-**fly** n (collective pl; [U]) kinds of aphis. (集合名词复数)绿蚜虫; 蚜蚁之一种。 ~-**gage** /-geɪdʒ; -ˈgedʒ/ n kind of plum with greenish-yellow skin and flesh and fine flavour. 青梅。 ~-**grocer** n shopkeeper selling vegetables and fruit. 卖蔬菜及水果的商人; 果菜商。 ~-**grocery** n (pl -ries) business of, things sold by, a ~ grocer. 果菜业; 蔬菜水果店; 蔬菜水果类。 ~-**horn** n inexperienced and easily deceived person. 无经验易受骗的人。 ~-**house** n building with sides and roof of glass, used for growing plants that need protection from the weather. 温室; 花房。 ~ **room** n room in a theatre for actors and actresses when they are not on the stage. 演员休息室。 '~-**stuffs**, ~ n pl ~ vegetables. 绿色蔬菜。 '~**sward** n [U] turf. 草皮。 '~ '**tea** n tea made from steam-dried leaves. 绿茶。 '~-**wood** n woodlands, esp in summer; forest in full leaf, esp as the home of outlaws in olden times. 林地(尤指夏季者); 青郁的森林; 绿林(尤指古时不法之徒落草之地)。

green² /gri:n; grin/ n **1** [U, C] green colour; what is green: 绿色; 绿色的东西: a girl dressed in ~; 着绿衣的女郎; a picture in ~s and blues, with various shades of ~ and blue. 以各种绿色和蓝色绘成之图画。 **2** (pl) green leaf vegetables, eg cabbage, spinach, before or after cooking; vegetation: (复)青菜(如未煮或煮过的甘蓝, 菠菜); 植物: (US) Christmas ~s, eg branches of fir and holly for decoration. 圣诞节结采用的树枝 (例如枞树树枝和冬青的树枝)。 **3** [C] area of land with

growing grass. 草原; 草地. **(a)** public or common land: 公有草地: *the village* ~. 村中公有草地. **(b)** for the game of bowls: 滚球戏所用的草地: *a 'bowling* ~. 滚球场. **(c)** surrounding a hole on a golf course: 高尔夫球场上球洞四周之草地: *a 'putting* ~. 穴周之轻打区域.

green·ery /'griːnəri; 'grinərɪ/ n [U] green foliage; verdure: 绿叶; 绿色草木; 葱翠: *the* ~ *of the woods in spring.* 春天树林的青葱.

green·ish /'griːnɪʃ; 'grinɪʃ/ adj somewhat green: 浅绿色的; 带绿色的: (in compounds) (用于复合词中) ~·'yellow; 黄绿色; ~·'brown. 褐绿色. ~·ness n

Green·wich /'grenɪtʃ; 'grɪnɪdʒ/ n suburb of London, east and west of whose meridian longitude is measured. 格林威治(伦敦一郊区, 经度由该地作起点, 向东西计算). ~ 'mean time (abbr 略作 GMT), mean² time for the meridian of ~, used as a basis for calculating time in most parts of the world (now called 现称作 *Universal time*). 格林威治时间; 世界标准时间.

greet /griːt; grit/ vt [VP6A, 14] **1** say words of welcome to; express one's feelings on receiving (news, etc); write (in a letter) words expressing respect, friendship, etc: 致意(消息等)时而表现某种感情; (以书信)致敬: ~ *a friend by saying 'Good morning!;'* 向一友人道'早安'致候; ~ *someone with a smile.* 含笑欢迎某人. *The news was* ~ *ed with dismay.* 那消息令人惊慌. *They* ~ *ed me with a shower of stones.* 他们纷纷向我投掷石头. **2** (of sights and sounds) meet the eyes and ears: (指景象和声音)映入眼帘; 入耳: *the view that* ~ *ed us at the hill-top.* 在山顶上收入我们眼底的景色. ~·ing n first words used on seeing sb or in writing to sb; expression or act with which sb or sth is ~ed: 与人见面(写信)时最初所说的话(所写出的字); 问候之词; 致敬; 致敬之动作: *'Good morning' and 'Dear Sir' are* ~*ings;* '早安' 与 '敬启者' 为问候和致敬之词; *a '*~*ings telegram*, one sent with, eg birthday, ~ings. 贺电(例如祝贺生日者).

greg·ari·ous /grɪ'geərɪəs; grɪ'gɛrɪəs/ adj living in groups or societies; liking the company of others. 群居的; 合群的. ~·ly adv ~·ness n

Greg·or·ian /grɪ'gɔːrɪən; grɛ'gɔrɪən/ adj **1** ~ chant, the kind of church music (*plainsong*) named after Pope Gregory I (540–604). 格列高里圣歌(以教皇格列高里一世为名之圣歌). **2** ~ **calendar**, the calendar introduced by Pope Gregory XIII (1502–85), with the days and months arranged as now. 格列高里历(教皇格列高里十三世所倡用, 即今之阳历). ⇨ **Julian**.

grem·lin /'gremlɪn; 'grɛmlɪn/ n goblin said to cause mechanical trouble. (传说可使机械发生故障的)小妖怪.

gre·nade /grɪ'neɪd; grɪ'ned/ n small bomb thrown by hand ('*hand*-~) or fired from a rifle ('*rifle*-~). 手榴弹; 枪榴弹.

grena·dier /ˌgrenə'dɪə(r); ˌgrɛnə'dɪr/ n (formerly) soldier who threw grenades; (昔时)手榴弹兵; (now) soldier in the *G*~*s, the G~ Guards*, British infantry regiment. (现今)英国近卫步兵团之士兵.

grew /gruː; gru/ pt of **grow**.

grey, gray /greɪ; gre/ adj between black and white coloured like ashes, or the sky on a dull, cloudy day: 灰色的: *His hair has turned* ~. 他的头发已灰白. '~·**beard** n old man. 老人. '~·'**headed** adj old; of long service. 老的; 服务久的. '~ **matter**, material of the brain: (脑的)灰白质: *a boy without much* ~ *matter,* a not very intelligent boy. 智力低的男孩. □ n [U, C] ~ colour; ~ clothes: 灰色; 灰色衣服: *dressed in* ~. 着灰色衣服. □ vt, vi [VP6A, 2A] make or become ~. 使成灰色; 变灰白.

grey·hound /'greɪhaʊnd; 'gre,haʊnd/ n slender, long-legged, keen-sighted dog, able to run fast, used in chasing live hares and, as a modern sport (~ *racing*), mechanical hares moved along a rail. 灵猩(一种躯瘦, 腿长, 眼光锐利的猎犬, 奔跑迅速, 用以追野兔或在现代游戏中用以追赶沿一轨道移动之机械假兔).

grey·ish /'greɪɪʃ; 'greɪʃ/ adj somewhat grey. 带灰色的; 略灰的.

grid /grɪd; grɪd/ n [C] **1** system of overhead cables carried on pylons, for distributing electric current over a large area. (架设于铁塔上, 将电流输送至广大地区之)高压输电线路网. **2** network of squares on maps, numbered for reference. 地图上的方格(标有号码备参考). **3** grating: 格子; 栅栏: *a little* ~, one placed at a gate, etc designed to prevent cattle from straying on to a road, etc. 牛防栏 (装于大门口等, 以防牛走失者). **4** frame of spaced parallel spirals or networks of wires in a radio valve. 真空管中之栅极. **5** gridiron. 铁架架子; 烤架.

griddle /'grɪdl; 'grɪdl/ n circular iron plate used for baking cakes. (烤饼用的)浅铁锅.

grid·iron /'grɪdaɪən; 'grɪd,aɪən/ n **1** framework of metal bars used for cooking meat or fish over a clear fire. (架在明火上烤肉或鱼用的)铁格架子; 烤架. **2** field for American football (marked with numerous parallel lines). 橄榄球场(标有许多平行线).

grief /griːf; grif/ n **1** [U] deep or violent sorrow: 悲伤; 忧伤: *driven almost insane by* ~; 因忧伤而几乎疯狂; *die of* ~. 忧伤而死. **2** [C] sth causing ~: 伤心事; 令人悲伤之事物: *His taking to drugs was a great* ~ *to his parents.* 他的吸毒成瘾是他父母的一大伤心事. **3 bring sb/come to** ~, (cause sb to) meet with misfortune, injury or ruin. (使某人)遭受不幸, 伤害或灾难.

griev·ance /'griːvns; 'grivəns/ n [C] ~ (*against*), real or imagined cause for complaint or protest: 冤情; 委屈; 不满: *The trade union leader spoke about the* ~*s of the workers.* 工会的领袖述说工人们的苦情.

grieve /griːv; griv/ vt, vi [VP6A] **1** cause grief to: 使悲伤: ~ *one's parents.* 使父母伤心. **2** [VP2A, C] feel grief: 悲伤; 伤心: ~ *for the dead/over sb's death;* 为死者悲伤/因某人之死而悲伤; ~ *about one's misfortunes/at bad news.* 因不幸(噩耗)而悲伤.

griev·ous /'griːvəs; 'grivəs/ adj **1** causing grief or suffering: 令人悲伤或痛苦的: *a* ~ *railway accident.* 悲惨的火车车祸; ~ *wrongs.* 令人痛心的过失. **2** severe: 严重的: ~ *pain;* 剧痛; ~ *bodily harm.* (法律)严重的人身伤害. ~·ly adv

grif·fin /'grɪfɪn; 'grɪfɪn/ (also 亦作 **grif·fon, gry·phon** /'grɪfən; 'grɪfən/) n (Gk myth) fabulous creature with the head and wings of an eagle and a lion's body. (希神)传说中头翼似鹰, 躯体似狮之怪兽. ⇨ the illus at **armour**. 参看 armour 之插图.

grill /grɪl; grɪl/ n [C] **1** grating; grille; gridiron. 铁格子; 铁格窗; 烤架. **2** dish of meat, etc cooked directly over or under great heat: 烧烤食品: *a mixed* ~, steak, liver, bacon, etc. 什锦烤肉(牛排, 肝, 咸肉等). **3** (also 亦作 '~·**room**) room (in a hotel or restaurant) where ~s are cooked and served. (饭店或餐馆中之)烤肉间. □ vt, vi [VP6A, 2A, C] cook, be cooked, on a gridiron, or over great heat; expose oneself to great heat: 烤; 受烤; 炙; 使自己受酷热之苦: *lie* ~*ing in the hot sun.* 卧于酷热的阳光下. **2** [VP6A] (eg of the police) question closely and severely. (指警察等)严加盘问.

grille /grɪl; grɪl/ n screen of parallel bars used to close an open space, eg in a convent; similar screen over a counter, eg in a post office or bank as a protection. 铁栅(例如装于修女院门上者); (邮局或银行窗口)柜台前之格栅.

grim /grɪm; grɪm/ adj (-mmer, -mmest) stern; severe; forbidding; without mercy: 严厉的; 严酷的; 恶毒的; 冷酷的: *a* ~ *struggle;* 生死之斗; *a* ~ *smile/ expression;* 狞笑(冷酷的表情); *looking* ~; 表情冷酷的; *a* ~ *joke,* one with an element of cruelty in it. 内容有残忍成分的笑话(故事). **hold on like** ~ *death,* very firmly. 坚持. ~·ly adv ·ness n

gri·mace /grɪˈmeɪs US: ˈgrɪmɪs; grɪˈmes/ n [C] ugly, twisted expression (on the face), expressing pain, disgust, etc or intended to cause laughter. (表示痛苦, 厌恶等, 或欲使人发笑之)面部的歪扭; 苦相; 鬼脸。□ vi [VP2A] make ~s. 扮鬼脸。

grime /graɪm; graɪm/ n [U] dirt, esp a coating on the surface of sth or on the body: 污秽物 (尤指东西或身体表面之一层污秽物): the soot and ~ of a big manufacturing town; 大工业城市的煤烟与尘垢; a face covered with ~ and sweat. 满是污垢与汗水的面孔。□ vt [VP6A] make dirty with ~: 使覆有污秽物; 使脏: ~d with dust. 被灰尘弄脏。**grimy** /ˈgraɪmɪ; ˈgraɪmɪ/ adj (-ier, -iest) covered with ~: 覆有污秽物的; 肮脏的: grimy faces/roofs/windows. 肮脏的面孔(屋顶, 窗户)。

grin /grɪn; grɪn/ vi, vt (-nn-) **1** [VP2A, C] smile broadly so as to show the teeth, expressing amusement, foolish satisfaction, contempt, etc: 露齿而笑(表示高兴, 愚蠢的满足, 轻蔑等): ~ning with delight; 高兴得露齿而笑; ~ from ear to ear. 咧着嘴笑。**~ and bear it**, endure pain, disappointment, etc, uncomplainingly. 不抱怨地忍受痛苦, 失望等; 逆来顺受。**2** [VP6A] express by ~ning: 露齿笑着表示: He ~ned his approval. 他露齿一笑表示赞许。□ n [C] act of ~ning: 露齿笑: the tigerish ~ on the murderer's face; 那凶手之露齿狞笑; ~s of derision. 露齿哂笑。

grind /graɪnd; graɪnd/ vt, vi (pt, pp **ground** /graʊnd; graʊnd/) **1** [VP6A, 15A, B] ~ (down) (to/into), crush to grains or powder between millstones, the teeth, etc: (用磨, 牙齿等)磨碎; 磨成粉状; 嚼碎: ~ sth to pieces; 将某物磨碎; ~ sth down; 碾碎某物; ~ coffee beans; 磨碎咖啡豆; ~ wheat in a mill; 用磨粉机磨小麦; ~ corn into flour. 将谷磨成粉。**2** [VP2A, C] be capable of ~ing: 可被磨碎; 可磨成粉状: This wheat ~s well. 这种小麦易磨成粉。This wheat will not ~ fine, cannot be ground fine. 这种小麦没法子磨细。**3** [VP6A] produce in this way: 磨成; 碾成: ~ flour. 磨成面粉。**4** [VP6A, 15A, B] ~ (down), (usu passive) (fig) oppress or crush: (通常用被动语态)(喻)压迫; 折磨: people who were ground (down) by poverty/tyranny/tyranny; 受穷困(苛税, 暴政)折磨的人民; tyrants who grind down the poor. 压榨贫民的暴君。**5** [VP6A] polish or sharpen by rubbing on or with a rough, hard surface: 磨光; 磨尖锐: ~ a knife/lens. 磨刀(镜片)。**have an axe to ~,** ⇨ **axe.** **6** [VP6A, 15A, B] rub harshly together, esp with a circular motion: 摩擦 (尤指旋转摩擦): ~ one's teeth (together); 切齿; 磨牙齿; a ship ~ing on the rocks; 触礁的船; ~ one's heel into the ground. 用脚跟碾地。**~ to a halt**, (of a vehicle) stop noisily (with brakes that ~); (车辆)嘎的一声煞住; (fig) (of a process) stop slowly: (指车辆)嘎的一声煞住; (喻)(指过程)慢慢停止: The strikes brought industry ~ing to a halt. 罢工使工业渐停顿。**7** [VP6A, 15A] work by turning; produce by turning: 转动; 旋转而生~; a hand-mill/coffee-mill/barrel-organ; 转动手摇机 (咖啡磨, 筒风琴); ~ out a tune on an organ; 用筒风琴奏出一曲; (fig) (喻) ~ out some verses, produce them slowly and with effort. 搜索枯肠作成几句诗。**8** [VP2C, 15B] **~ (away) (at),** (cause to) work or study hard and long: (使)刻苦用功: ~ away at one's studies; 用功读书; ~ for an exam. 刻苦用功准备考试。□ n (colloq) long, monotonous task: 长期而枯燥的工作: the examination ~, the task of preparing for an examination. 长期辛苦的准备考试。Do you find learning English a ~? 你觉得学习英语是件苦事吗?

grind·er /ˈgraɪndə(r); ˈgraɪndə/ n **1** thing that grinds, eg a molar tooth, apparatus for grinding coffee: 研磨之物; 研磨机(如臼齿, 磨咖啡机): a 'coffee-~. 磨咖啡机。**2** (in compounds) person who grinds: (用于复合词中)研磨者; 磨光者; 转动者: a 'knife-~; 磨刀人; an 'organ-~, person who produces tunes by turning the handle of a barrel-organ. 摇动筒风琴奏曲者。

grind·stone /ˈgraɪndstəʊn; ˈgraɪndˌstɔn/ n stone shaped like a wheel, turned on an axle, used for sharpening tools. 磨石。**keep sb's nose to the ~,** force him to work hard without rest. 使某人不停地劳动。

grip /grɪp; grɪp/ vt, vi (-pp-) take and keep a firm hold of; seize firmly: 紧握; 抓紧: The frightened child ~ped its mother's hand. 那受惊的孩子紧抓住他母亲的手。The brakes failed to ~ and the car ran into a wall. 煞车失灵, 汽车撞在一堵墙上。The speaker ~ped the attention of his audience. 演说者吸引住听众的注意力。The film is a ~ping story of love and hate. 这电影是一个扣人心弦的爱与恨的故事。□ n **1** (sing only except as shown) act, manner, or power of ~ping: (除见于下列句中外, 仅作单数)紧握; 抓紧; 紧握的方式; 紧握力: let go one's ~ of sth; 松开所握之物; take a ~ on a rope; 抓紧一绳索; have a good ~ (fig, = understanding) of a problem; (喻)深入了解一问题; have a good ~ on an audience, hold their attention and interest. 能吸引听众的注意力及兴趣。**be at ~s with; come/get to ~s with,** be attacking, begin to stand, in earnest; be in close combat: 猛攻; (与…)肉搏; get to ~s with a problem. 认真处理一难题。**take a '~ on oneself,** (colloq) stop being idle and inattentive. (口)不再懒散; 集中注意力。**2** [C] (in a machine, etc) part that ~s or clips; clutch; part that is to be ~ped. (机器等之)把手; 柄; 夹。**3** [C] (also 亦作 '~·sack) (US) traveller's handbag: (美)旅行袋; 手提包: a leather ~. 皮制旅行袋。

gripes /graɪps; graɪps/ n pl (the) ~, (colloq) violent pains in the abdomen. (口)肚子痛; 腹绞痛。

grippe /griːp; grɪp/ n the ~, influenza. 流行性感冒。

gris·ly /ˈgrɪzlɪ; ˈgrɪzlɪ/ adj causing horror or terror; ghastly. 恐怖的; 可怕的。

grist /grɪst; grɪst/ n [U] grain to be ground (chiefly in fig phrases). 准备磨成粉的谷物(主要用于比喻的词句中)。**It's all ~ to the mill; All is ~ that comes to his mill,** (prov) He makes use of everything. (谚)他善于利用每件事物。

gristle /ˈgrɪsl; ˈgrɪsl/ n [U] tough, elastic tissue in animal bodies, esp in meat: 软骨; 脆骨(尤指食用肉中者): I can't eat this meat—it's all ~. 我不能吃这肉——它全是软骨。

grit /grɪt; grɪt/ n [U] **1** (collective sing) tiny, hard bits of stone, sand, etc: (集合名词单数)砂砾: spread ~ on icy roads. 撒砂砾于覆有冰的道路上。I've got some ~ in my shoe. 我鞋子里进去了一些砂子。**2** quality of courage and endurance: 勇气和毅力: The soldiers showed that they had plenty of ~. 那些士兵表现得很有勇气和毅力。□ vt (-tt-) ~ one's teeth, keep one's jaws tight together; (fig) show courage and endurance. 咬紧牙关; (喻)勇敢坚忍。~**ty** adj (-ier, -iest) of or like ~ (1): 砂砾的; 似砂砾的: The sandstorm made the food ~ty. 大风砂使这食物尽是砂子。

grits /grɪts; grɪts/ n pl husked but unground oats; coarse oatmeal. 去壳而未碾细的燕麦; 粗燕麦片。

grizzle /ˈgrɪzl; ˈgrɪzl/ vi (colloq) (esp of children) cry fretfully. (口)(尤指儿童)号哭。

griz·zled /ˈgrɪzld; ˈgrɪzld/ adj grey; grey-haired. 灰色的; 灰色头发的。

griz·zly /ˈgrɪzlɪ; ˈgrɪzlɪ/ n (also 亦作 ~ bear) large, fierce grey bear of N America. 北美的凶猛的灰熊。⇨ the illus at bear. 参看 bear 之插图。

groan /grəʊn; gron/ vi, vt **1** [VP2A, C] make a deep sound forced out by pain, expressing despair or distress: 呻吟: The wounded men lay there ~ing, with no one to help them. 受伤的人们躺在那里呻吟, 而无人去救助他们。The teacher ~ed with dismay. 那老师因惊慌而呻吟。The people ~ed under injustice. 人民受尽了不公正的压迫。**2** [VP2A, C] (of things) make a noise like that of ~ing: (指东西)作似呻吟之声: The ship's timbers ~ed during the storm. 船骨在暴风雨中发出响声。The table ~ed with food, (fig) was weighed down with large quantities of food. (喻)桌上摆满大量食物, 快把桌子压

垮了。 **3** [VP6A, 15B] ~ *(out)*, express with ~ing: 呻吟着表示~: *He* ~*ed out a sad story.* 他呻吟着说出一个悲惨的故事。 **4** [VP15B] ~ *down*, silence by ~ing: 以似呻吟之声使停止作声: *The speaker was* ~*ed down by his audience,* They prevented him from being heard. 那演说者的声音被听众起哄的声音压倒了。 □ *n* [C] deep sound made in ~ing: 呻吟; 似呻吟之深沉声: *the* ~*s of the injured men;* 伤者的呻吟; *give a* ~ *of dismay;* 发出惊慌的呻吟; *a speech interrupted by* ~*s of disapproval.* 被起哄声打断的演说。

groat /grəʊt; grot/ *n* (hist) (14th to 17th cc) English silver coin worth fourpence. (史)(十四至十七世纪间)英国的银币(值四便士)。

groats /grəʊts; grots/ *n pl* (crushed) grain, esp oats, that has been hulled. 去壳的谷(尤指燕麦)/(去壳而压碎的)燕麦片。

grocer /'grəʊsə(r); 'grosɚ/ *n* shopkeeper who sells food in packets, tins, or bottles, and general small household requirements. 杂货商(贩卖包装, 罐装及瓶装食品, 以及一般零星家庭必需品的). ~**y** *n* 1 [U] ~'s trade: 杂货业: *a* ~*'y business.* 杂货店。 **2** *(pl)* ~**ies**, things sold by a ~. (复)杂货。

grog /grɒg; grɑg/ *n* [U] (a word used by sailors) drink of spirits mixed with water. (船员用语)酒(烈酒与水的混合饮料)。

groggy /'grɒgɪ; 'grɑgɪ/ *adj* (**-ier, -iest**) **1** unsteady; likely to collapse or fall: 不稳的; 摇摇欲坠的: *The legs of that chair look rather* ~. 那椅子的腿看来很不稳。 **2** weak and unsteady as the result of illness, shock, lack of sleep, etc: (因生病, 震惊, 缺少睡眠等而显得)软弱的: *That last attack of flu left me rather* ~. 上次患流行性感冒使我颇为软弱无力。

groin /grɔɪn; grɔɪn/ *n* **1** depression between the stomach and the thigh. 鼠蹊(腹与股间之凹处)。 ⇨ the illus at **trunk**. 参看 trunk 之插图。 **2** (archi) curved edge where two vaults meet (in a roof). (建筑)弧棱; 穹棱; 穹窿交叉线。 ⇨ the illus at **church**. 参看 church 之插图。 **3** (US) = **groyne**. □ *vt* build with ~s. 使成弧棱。

groom /gruːm; grum/ *n* **1** person in charge of horses. 马夫。 **2** bridegroom. 新郎。 □ *vt* [VP6A] **1** feed, brush and in other ways look after (horses); (of apes, monkeys) clean the fur and skin of: 喂(马); 刷(马); 照看(马); (指猿, 猴)清理~之毛皮: *a female ape* ~*ing her mate.* 清理其伴侣毛皮之母猿。 **2** (usu in the *pp*, of persons): (通常用过去分词, 指人): *well / badly* ~*ed,* well / badly dressed (esp of the hair, beard and clothes). 修饰得好(不好)(尤指发, 胡须与衣服)。 **3** (colloq) prepare (sb for a career, etc). (口)准备(让某人从事某一事业等); 推荐; 培植。

groove /gruːv; gruv/ *n* **1** long, hollow channel in the surface of hard material, esp one made to guide the motion of sth that slides along it, eg a sliding door or window; spiral cut on a gramophone disc (in which the needle or stylus moves). 沟; 凹槽(尤指可使物体在上面滑动者, 如使门窗滑动的); 唱片上的纹路。 **2** way of living that has become a habit. 生活习惯。 *get into / be stuck in a* ~, become set in one's ways, one's style of living. 落成一种习惯。 *in the* ~, (dated sl) in the right mood (for sth); exhilarated. (过时俚语)有心情 (做某事); 兴高采烈。 □ *vt* make ~s in: 作槽于: *a* ~*d shelf.* 有槽的架子。 ~**r** *n* (sl) up-to-date person. (俚)时髦的人。 **groovy** *adj* (sl) up-to-date; in the latest fashion (esp of young people): (俚)新式的; 时髦的(尤指年轻人):

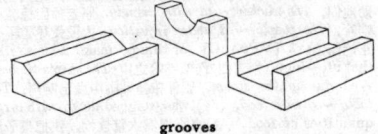

grooves

a groovy restaurant; 新式的餐馆; *groovy clothes / people.* 时髦的衣服(人)。

grope /grəʊp; grop/ *vi, vt* [VP2A, C, 3A, 15A] ~ *(about) (for / after),* (lit or fig) feel or search about as one does in the dark: (字面或喻)摸索; 搜寻: ~ *for the door-handle / the light switch / an answer.* 摸索着找门柄(电灯开关, 搜寻答案)。 *We* ~*d our way along the dark corridor.* 我们在黑暗的走廊上摸索着走。 **grop·ing·ly** *adv* in the manner of one who ~s 摸索着。

gross¹ /grəʊs; gros/ *n* (*pl* unchanged) twelve dozen; 144. (复数不变)十二打; 笔。 ⇨ **App 4.** 参看附录四。

gross² /grəʊs; gros/ *adj* **1** vulgar; not refined; coarse in mind or morals: 粗鄙的; 不雅的; 粗野的: ~ *language / jokes / morals.* 粗鄙的言语(笑话, 品行)。 **2** (of food) coarse, greasy; liking such food: (指食物)粗糙而油腻的; 喜欢粗糙而油腻之食物的: *a* ~ *eater.* 喜欢粗糙而油腻之食物者。 **3** (of the senses) heavy and dull. (指感觉)迟钝的。 **4** flagrant; glaring; clearly seen: 罪恶昭彰的; 显著的; 易见的: ~ *injustice / negligence;* 显著的不公(疏忽); *a* ~ *error / overcharge.* 显然的错误(索价过高)。 **5** (of vegetation) luxuriant: (指草木)茂密的: *the* ~ *vegetation of the tropical rain forest.* 热带雨林中茂密的植物。 **6** (of persons) repulsively fat. (指人)过于肥胖的。 **7** (opposite of *net*) total, whole: (为 net 之反义词)全部的; 整个的; 总的; 毛的: *the* ~ *amount;* 总额; *his* ~ *income.* 他的全部收入。 ~ **national product** (abbr 略作 GNP), annual total value of goods produced, and services provided, in a country. 国民生产总值。 **8** *in (the)* ~, wholesale; in bulk; in a general way. 批发; 大体上; 一般地。 □ *vt* [VP6A] make as a total amount: 总共赚得: *His last film* ~*ed five million pounds.* 他最后制的影片总共获利五百万英镑。 ~**·ly** *adv* extremely: 极度地; 十分地: ~*ly unfair / fat.* 极不公平(十分肥胖)。 ~**·ness** *n*

grot /grɒt; grɑt/ *n* (poet) grotto. (诗)洞穴; 洞室。

gro·tesque /grəʊ'tesk; gro'tɛsk/ *adj* **1** absurd; fantastic; laughable because strange and incongruous: 可笑的; 怪诞的; 因古怪与不协调而可笑的: *a* ~ *appearance;* 可笑的外表; ~ *manners.* 古怪的样子。 **2** (in art) combining human, animal and plant forms in a fantastic way; made up of comically distorted figures and designs. (艺术)奇形怪状的; 滑稽奇异的。 **1** ~ person, animal, figure or design. 奇形怪状的人, 动物, 图形或图案。 **2** *the* ~, painting, carving, etc in which the ~ style appears. 怪异的图画, 雕刻等。 ~**·ly** *adv* ~**·ness** *n*

grotto /'grɒtəʊ; 'grɑto/ *n* (*pl* ~**es**, ~**s** /-təʊz; -toz/) cave, esp one made artificially as a garden shelter. 洞穴; (尤指)花园中的人造洞室。

grotty /'grɒtɪ; 'grɑtɪ/ *adj* (sl) unpleasant; ugly. (俚)令人不悦的; 难看的。

grouch /graʊtʃ; graʊtʃ/ *vi* (colloq) complain. (口)抱怨。 □ *n* fit of ill temper; sulky, discontented person. 愠怒; 愠怒的人; 爱发牢骚的人。 ~**y** *adj* sullenly discontented. 愠怒的; 不满的。

ground¹ /graʊnd; graʊnd/ *n* **1** *the* ~, solid surface of the earth: 地面: *lie on / sit on / fall to the* ~. 躺在(坐在, 落在)地上; (in compounds): (用于复合词中): ~*-to-air missiles,* fired from the ~ (at aircraft). (自地面向天空射击飞机的)地对空导弹。 *The airliner made a* ~*-controlled approach,* approached the runway directed by the control tower. 该客机作由地面控制的降落(由人在塔台引导飞机降于跑道)。 *above* ~, alive. 活着。 *below* ~, dead and buried. 死掉被埋葬。 *fall / be dashed to the* ~, (cause to) fail, be disappointed: (使)失败; 失望: *The scheme / Our plans fell to the* ~. 这计划(我们的计划)失败了。 *Our hopes were dashed to the* ~. 我们的希望破灭了。 *get off the* ~, (of an aircraft) rise into the air; (fig, of an undertaking or scheme) pass from the planning stage and make a start. (指飞机)升空; (喻, 指事业或计划)开始进行或行动。 **2** [U] position, area or distance

on the earth's surface. 在地面上的位置，区域或距离。 **cut the ~ from under sb's feet**, anticipate his plans, arguments, defences, etc and in this way embarrass him. 先发制人；使某人之计划、论据、答辩等失去凭借；使站不住脚。 **cover(much, etc)~, (a)** travel: 旅行: *We've covered a great deal of ~ today*, have come a long way. 我们今天走了很长一段路。 **(b)** (fig, of a lecture, report, inquiry, etc) deal with a variety of subjects; be far-reaching: (喻)演讲说，报告，询问等)牵涉许多方面；范围很广: *The committee's report covers much new ~*, deals with many new matters. 委员会的报告涉及许多新问题。 **gain ~**, make progress; win a success or an advantage. 进步；前进；获胜；获利。 **give/lose ~**, retreat; fail to keep one's position or advantage. 撤退；让步。 **hold/stand/keep one's ~**, stand firm; not yield; maintain one's claim, intention, argument, etc. 坚守；不让步；坚持立场。 **shift one's ~**, change one's argument, etc. 改变立场。 **suit sb down to the ~**, suit him thoroughly: 十分适合某人: *Her new hairstyle/job suits her down to the ~*. 她的新发型(工作)很适合她。 **common ~**, subject on which two or more persons or parties are in agreement or on which they have similar views. (两个以上的人或团体之间的) 一致之处；共同的立场。 **forbidden ~**, subject that must be avoided. 必须避免的问题；犯忌讳的论题。 **3** [U] soil; earth: 泥土；土地: *till the ~*. 耕地。 *The frost has made the ~ hard.* 严寒使土地冻硬了。 **break fresh/new ~, (a)** cultivate land that has not been cultivated before. 开垦处女地。 **(b)** (fig) do sth new; deal with a subject for the first time. (喻)着手一件新事业；初次处理一问题。 **4** [C] area or piece of land for a special purpose or a particular use: 场地(供特殊用途的一块地): *a 'football/'cricket/'sports ~*; 足球(板球，运动)场; *a pa'rade/,recre'ation ~*; 校阅场(娱乐场); *a 'play ~*; 运动场；游戏场; *'hunting/'fishing-~s*, areas used for hunting/fishing. 狩猎场(渔场)。 **5** (always *pl*) land, gardens, round a building, often enclosed with walls, hedges or fences: (经常用复数) 房屋四周的土地和花园 (常用墙或篱围起); 庭园: *the ~s of Buckingham Palace*. 白金汉宫的庭园。 *The mansion has extensive ~s.* 这大厦四周的庭园广阔。 **6** [U] bottom of the sea or of any other body of water: 海底；水底; (chiefly in) (主要用于) **touch ~**, (of a ship) strike the bottom. (指船)达水底；搁浅。 ⇨ **aground**. **7** (*pl*) particles of solid matter that sink to the bottom of a liquid: (复数)沉淀物；渣滓: (esp) (尤用于) *'coffee-~s*. 咖啡渣滓。 **8** (*pl sing pl*) reason(s) for saying, doing or believing sth. 理由；根据。 **be/give/have ~s for,** be/give/have a cause or reason for: 有…之理由: *There are no ~s for anxiety*. 没有理由有忧虑。 *I have good ~s for believing his version of events*. 我有相当理由相信他对事件的说明。 *They don't give me much ~/many ~s for complaint*. 我没有理由抱怨他们。 *What are the ~s for divorce in this country*, What is recognized as a basis for an action of divorce? 在这个国家哪些理由可离婚? **on the ~s of,** because of: 因为: excused *on the ~s of youth*; 因年轻而被原谅; *reject a man on 'medical ~s*. 拒绝一个身体不合格的人。 *On what ~s do you suspect him?* 你根据什么怀疑他? **9** [U] surface on which a design is painted, printed, cut, etc; undecorated part: (图案之绘制，印刷，雕刻等的)底子; 板面: *a design of pink roses on a white ~*. 白底粉红玫瑰的花样。 **10** (compounds) (复合词) **'~-bait** *n* [U] food thrown to the bottom of a fishing-~ to attract fish. 投入水底诱鱼之饵。 **'~-fish** *n* fish living at or near the bottom. 生活于水底之鱼。 **'floor** *n* the floor of a building level with the ~. 建筑物平地面的一层；地面层；一楼。 **be/get in on the ~ floor**, (colloq) join an enterprise at its beginning. (口) 从某企业开始创立时即已加入。 **'~-nut** *n* kind of pea with pods ripening under the ~ (also called *earthnut* and *peanut*). 落花生 (亦称作 earthnut 和 peanut)。 **'~-plan** *n* plan of a building at ~ level. 房屋的底层平面图。 **'~-rent** *n* rent paid for the use of land leased for

building. (租用土地盖房屋的)地租。 **~s·man** /-mən; -mən/ *n* (*pl* **-men**) man employed to look after a cricket ~. 板球场管理员。 **'~·sheet** *n* waterproof sheet spread on the ~, eg under bedding in a tent. 铺于地面之防水布 (例如帐篷内铺在被褥下面者)。 **'~ speed** *n* aircraft's speed on the ~ (contrasted with *air speed*). (航空器之)地面速度(与 air speed 相对)。 **'~ staff/crew** *n* mechanics who service aircraft on the ~; non-flying members of the staff of an airfield, etc. (飞机等的)地勤人员。 **'~·swell** *n* [U] heavy, slow-moving waves caused by a distant or recent storm. 由远处或刚过去的暴风引起的移动缓慢的巨浪; 长浪。 **'~·work** *n* [U] (usu fig) foundation; basis. (通常作喻)基础; 根基。

ground² /graund; graʊnd/ *vt, vi* **1** [VP6A, 2A] (of a ship) (cause to) touch the sea bottom; (of aircraft, airmen) compel to stay on the ground: (指船) (使)触海底; 搁浅; (指飞机，飞行员)强迫停留在地面; 停飞: *Our ship ~ed in shallow water*. 我们的船在浅水中搁浅了。 *All aircraft at London Airport were ~ed by fog yesterday.* 伦敦机场的所有飞机在昨天因雾而被迫停飞。 **2** [VP6A] **~ arms**, (mil) lay (esp rifles) on the ground. (军)将 (尤指步枪)放在地上。 **3** [VP14] **~ sth on sth**, base (the more usu word) (a belief, etc) on: 建立(信仰等)于(…之)基础上 (较常用 base): *one's arguments on facts*; 根据事实以立论: *a well-~ed theory*. 基础稳固的学说。 **4** [VP14] **~ sb in sth**, give (sb) good teaching or basic training in: 给(某人)良好的教导或基本训练: *The teacher ~ed his pupils in arithmetic*. 该教师给他的学生打下了良好的算术基础。 **5** [VP6A] connect (a piece of electrical apparatus) with the ~ as conductor, as a safety precaution (*earth* is the usu word). 使(电器)接地(以地面作为导体，以策安全，通常用 earth); 接地; 通地。 **~·ing** *n* thorough teaching of the elements of a subject: 对一科目在基础上彻底的教授; 基础; 底子: *a good ~ing in grammar*. 对于基本语法的良好的教授; 良好的语法基础。

ground³ /graund; graʊnd/ *pt, pp* of **grind**: **~ rice**, reduced to fine powder. 用米磨成的粉。 **~ glass**, made non-transparent by grinding. 毛玻璃。

ground·less /'graundlɪs; 'graʊnd‚lɪs/ *adj* without foundation or good reason: 无根据的; 无理由的: *~ fears/anxieties/rumours*. 无理由的恐惧(无理由的焦虑;无根据的谣言)。 ⇨ **ground¹(8)**.

ground·sel /'graunsl; 'graʊnsl/ *n* [U] kinds of weed, the commonest kind of which is used as food for some cage-birds. 蔡吾属之杂草 (最普通者常用以饲鸟)。

group /gruːp; grup/ *n* [C] number of persons or things gathered or placed together, or naturally associated; number of jointly-controlled business companies, eg as the result of a merger: 群; 团体; 组; 类; 公司的联合组织(例如由于合并之结果):*a ~ of girls/trees/houses*; 一群女孩子(一片树)，一片房屋); *people standing about in small ~s*; 三五成群散立着的人们; *the Germanic ~ of languages*. 日耳曼语系。 **'G~ captain**, Air Force officer. (英国)空军上校。 □ *vt, vi* [VP6A, 15A, B, 2C] form into, gather in, a ~ or ~s: 使成群; 集合; 类集: *The police ~ed (themselves) round the demonstrators*. 警察围聚在示威者的四周。 *G~ the roses together*. 将蔷薇集在一处。

grouse¹ /graus; graʊs/ *n* (*pl* unchanged) (复数不变) bird with feathered feet, shot for sport and food: 松鸡; 松鸡类: **~ shooting**, the shooting of red ~ on the moors of Scotland and northern England. (在苏格兰与英格兰北部之松鸡猎场上)猎红松鸡。 ⇨ the illus at **fowl**. 参看 fowl 之插图。

grouse² /graus; graʊs/ *vi* [VP2A, C] (colloq) grumble; complain. (口)抱怨; 发牢骚。 □ *n* complaint. 抱怨。

grove /grəʊv; grov/ *n* group of trees; small wood. 树丛; 小树林。

grovel /'grɒvl; 'grɑvl/ *vi* (**-ll-**; US also **-l-**) [VP2A,

C] lie down on one's face, crawl, in front of sb whom one fears, (as if) begging for mercy; (fig) humble oneself; behave in a way that shows one has no self-respect: 匍匐(作乞怜状); (喻)奴颜婢膝; 卑躬屈节: ~ *at the feet of a conqueror.* 向征服者屈膝。~·ler *n* person who ~s. 奴颜婢膝者。

grow /grəʊ; gro/ *vi, vt* (*pt* grew /gruː; gru/, *pp* grown /grəʊn; gron/) **1** [VP2A, C, D] develop; increase in size, height, length, etc: 发育; 生长; 长大; 增长: *Rice ~s in warm climates.* 稻生长在温暖的地区。*How quickly you are ~ing!* 你长得真快啊! *How tall you've ~n!* 你长得好高啊! *She has decided to let her hair ~,* not have it cut short. 她已决定留头发。*A full~ elephant is very large.* 长成了的象很大。*He has ~n into a fine young man.* 他已长成为英俊的年轻小伙子。*Plants ~ from seeds.* 植物由种子长大。**(b)** become too old for; cease to practise; abandon: 年龄增长而革除; 停止做; 戒绝: *He has ~n out of the bad habits of his boyhood days.* 他已长大, 戒掉儿时的坏习惯了。**(c)** have as a source: 由…而生: *His troubles grew out of his bad temper.* 他的烦恼是由于他的坏脾气所引起的。**~ up, (a)** (of persons, animals) reach the stage of full development; become adult or mature: (指人, 动物)长大; 成年; 成熟: *When the boys ~ up....* 当孩子们长大时…。*He has a ~n-up son.* 他有一个成年的儿子。**(b)** develop: 发展: *A warm friendship grew up between the two men.* 温暖的友谊在他们两人之间滋长。'**~·ing-pains** *n pl* **(a)** pains in the limbs of young children, popularly believed to be caused by rapid growth. 儿童或少年时期的一种关节痛(一般认为系因发育迅速所导致)。**(b)** (fig) problems arising while a new enterprise is developing: (喻)新事业发展过程中所产生的问题: *The business is still suffering from ~ing pains.* 这事业仍面临许多难题。'**~n-up** /'grəʊnʌp; 'gronˌʌp/ *n* [C] adult person (contrasted with a child). 成年人(与 child 相对)。□ *adj* adult; mature. 成年人的; 成熟的。**2** [VP2D] become: 变成; 渐变: *grow older; ~ smaller.* 渐大。*It began to ~ dark.* 天渐渐暗了。**3** [VP4A] ~ *to be/like, etc,* reach the point or stage where one is/likes, etc: 达到某一点或阶段; 达到喜欢的程度: *One ~s to like what one is accustomed to.* 人渐渐会喜欢习惯的事物。*My friendship with them grew to be* (= by degrees became) *considerable.* 我与他们间的友谊渐增。**4** [VP 6A, 12B, 13B] cause or allow to: 使生长; 种植; 蓄; 留: ~ *roses.* 种玫瑰。*He's ~ing a beard.* 他留胡须。*Will you ~ some herbs for me/~ me some herbs this year?* 你今年为我种些香草好吗? **5** [VP3A] ~ *on/upon,* **(a)** become more deeply rooted: 变为更根深蒂固: *a habit that ~s on you.* 在你身上日益根深蒂固的习惯。**(b)** come to have a greater attraction for; win the liking of: 更加吸引; 受…的喜爱: *a book/a piece of music that ~s on you.* 你所喜爱的一本书(一支曲)。~**er** *n* **1** person who ~s things: 种植者: *a 'fruit~er.* 果果木者; '*rose~ers.* 种蔷薇者。**2** plant, etc that ~s in a certain way: 按某种方式生长的植物者: *a free/rapid ~er.* 自由生长(生长快)的植物。

growl /graʊl; graʊl/ *vi, vt* **1** [VP2A, C] (of animals, men, thunder) make a low, threatening sound: (指动物, 人, 雷)作低沉的怒吼声: 作隆隆声: *The dog ~ed at me.* 那狗向我咆哮。*We heard thunder ~ing in the distance.* 我们听见远处隆隆的雷声。**2** [VP6A, 15B] ~ **(out),** say in a ~ing manner: 咆哮着说: *He ~ed (out) his answer.* 他咆哮着回答。□ *n* [C] low threatening sound; angry complaint. 低沉的怒吼; 咆哮; 忿怒不平。~**·ing·ly** *adv*

growler /'graʊlə(r); 'graʊlɚ/ *n* (old colloq use) four-wheeled horse-drawn cab. (昔时口语用法)四轮马车。

grown /grəʊn; gron/ *pp* of grow: *a ~ man,* a mature

man. 成人。

growth /grəʊθ; groθ/ *n* **1** [U] growing; development; process of growing: 生长; 发展; 生长过程: *the rapid ~ of our economy.* 我们的经济之迅速成长。*At what age does an elephant reach full ~,* its greatest size? 象到了几岁才达到发育完成的阶段? **2** [U] increase: 增加: '*~ shares,* thought likely to increase in value. 有希望增值之股票。**3** [U] cultivation: 种植; 栽培: *apples of foreign ~,* grown abroad. 外国产的苹果。**4** [C] sth that grows or has grown: 生长物; 长成物: *a thick ~ of weeds:* 浓密的野草; *a three-days' ~ of beard.* 长了三天的胡须。**5** [C] diseased formation in the body, eg a cancer. 身体内部的肿瘤(例如癌)。

groyne (US = **groin**) /grɔɪn; grɔɪn/ *n* [C] structure of wood, etc, or a low, broad wall of stone, concrete, etc built to prevent sand and pebbles from being washed away by the sea, the current of a river, etc. (木或石与三合土等作成的)丁坝; 丁坝。

grub[1] /grʌb; grʌb/ *n* **1** [C] larva of insect. 蛴螬; 蛆。**2** [C] (sl) food. (俚)食物。

grub[2] /grʌb; grʌb/ *vt, vi* (**-bb-**) [VP6A, 15B, 2C] turn over the soil, esp in order to get sth up or out: 挖土; 掘(尤指为掘出某物): ~*bing up weeds.* 掘除杂草。*The pigs were ~bing about among the bushes.* 那些猪在树丛中到处乱挖。

grubby /'grʌbɪ; 'grʌbɪ/ *adj* (**-ier, -iest**) **1** dirty; unwashed. 肮脏的; 不洁的。**2** having grubs in it. 有蛴螬的。

grudge /grʌdʒ; grʌdʒ/ *vt* [VP12A, 13A, 6C] be unwilling to give or allow: 不愿给; 吝惜: *I don't ~ him his success,* I admit that he deserves it. 我认为他的成功是应该的。*His cruel master ~d him even the food he ate,* gave him his food unwillingly. 他那残忍的主人甚至连他吃的食物也不大愿意给他。*I ~ paying £2 for a bottle of wine that is not worth 50p.* 我不愿为一瓶不值五十便士的酒付出二英镑。□ *n* [C] feeling of ill-will, resentment, envy or spite: 恶意; 怨恨; 嫉妒; 遗恨: *I bear him no ~.* 我对他没有怨恨。*He has a ~ against me.* 他对我怀恨。*I owe that man a ~,* think I have good reason to feel ill-will towards him. 我有充分理由对那人怀恨。**grudg·ing·ly** *adv* in a grudging manner: 不情愿地; 吝惜地; 勉强地: *His employer grudgingly raised his salary.* 他的雇主很勉强地替他加了薪。

gruel /'gruːəl; 'gruəl/ *n* [U] liquid food of oatmeal, etc boiled in milk or water. 用燕麦等煮于牛奶或水中的粥。

gruel·ling (US = **gruel·ing**) /'gruːəlɪŋ; 'gruəlɪŋ/ *adj* severe; exhausting: 严厉的; 使人筋疲力竭的: *a ~ling race.* 令人筋疲力竭的竞赛。

grue·some /'gruːsəm; 'grusəm/ *adj* filling one with horror or disgust; frightful. 使人毛骨悚然的; 讨厌的; 可怕的。~·**ly** *adv* ~·**ness** *n*

gruff /grʌf; grʌf/ *adj* (of a person, his voice, behaviour) rough; surly. (指人, 声音, 行为)粗野的; 粗暴的。~·**ly** *adv* ~·**ness** *n*

grumble /'grʌmbl; 'grʌmbl/ *vi, vt* **1** [VP2A, C, 3A] ~ **(at/about/over sth),** complain or protest in a bad-tempered way: 发怨言; 鸣不平: *He's always grumbling* 他老是发牢骚。*He ~d at the low pay offered to him.* 他抱怨给他的待遇低微。**2** [VP6A, 15B] ~ **(out),** say in a sullen, dissatisfied way: 抱怨地说出: ~ **(out)** *a reply.* 抱怨地回答。**3** [VP2A, C] make a low, growling sound: 作隆隆声: *thunder grumbling in the distance.* 远处隆隆的雷声。□ *n* [C] (usu bad-tempered) complaint or protest: (通常为坏脾气的)怨言; 不平: *That fellow is full of ~s.* 那家伙满腹牢骚。**grum·bler** /'grʌmblə(r); 'grʌmblɚ/ *n* person who ~s. 埋怨者; 发牢骚的人。

grumpy /'grʌmpɪ; 'grʌmpɪ/ *adj* (**-ier, -iest**) bad-tempered; surly. 脾气坏的; 脾气暴躁的。**grump·ily** /-ɪlɪ; -ɪlɪ/ *adv* **grumpi·ness** *n*

Grundy·ism /'grʌndɪɪzm; 'grʌndɪɪzm̩/ n [U] conventional propriety; prudery. 拘泥习俗;过分守礼.

grunt /grʌnt; grʌnt/ vi, vt 1 [VP2A] (of animals, esp pigs) make a low, rough sound; (of persons) make a similar sound expressing disagreement, boredom, irritation, etc. (指动物, 尤指猪)作咕噜声; (指人)发类似的哼声(表示不满, 厌烦, 激怒等). 2 [VP6A, 15B] ~ (out), utter in a ~ing way: 咕噜地说出: ~ (out) an answer. 咕噜着回答. □ n [C] low, rough sound. 咕噜声.

gry·phon /'grɪfən; 'grɪfən/ n = **griffin**.

guano /'gwɑːnəʊ; 'gwɑno/ n (pl -nos /-nəʊz; -noz/) [C] dung dropped by sea-birds, used as fertilizer. 海鸟粪(用作肥料).

guar·an·tee[1] /ˌgærən'tiː; ˌgærən'ti/ n [C] 1 (in law, **guaranty**) promise or undertaking (usu in writing or print) that certain conditions agreed to in a transaction will be fulfilled: (法律上用 guaranty) (交易中某些同意的条件将会实现的)保证; 保证书: a year's ~ with a watch, a promise to keep it in good repair, etc. 手表使用一年的保证. 2 (in law, **guaranty**) undertaking given by one person to another that he will be responsible for sth to be done, eg payment of a debt, by a third person. (法律上用 guaranty) 担保; 保证(某人将做某事, 例如偿还债务). 3 (in law, **guarantor**) person who gives such an undertaking: (法律上用 guaranty) 担保人; 担保人: be ~ for a friend's good behaviour. 保证一位朋友品行良好. If I try to borrow £1000 from the bank, will you be my ~? 如果我从银行设法借一千英镑, 你能做我的保证人吗? 4 (in law, **guaranty**) sth offered, eg the deeds of a house or other document of ownership of property, as security for the fulfilling of conditions in a (1, 2): (法律上用 guaranty) 抵押品; 作为保证之物(例如房契或其他所有权证书): 'What ~ can you offer?' 'I can offer my house and land as a ~.' '你能以什么做抵押?' '我能以我的房屋和地产做抵押品.' 5 (colloq) sth that seems to make an occurrence likely: (口)似乎使一事件可能发生的事物: Blue skies are not always a ~ of fine weather. 蔚蓝的天空并不永远保证晴朗的天气.

guar·an·tee[2] /ˌgærən'tiː; ˌgærən'ti/ vt [VP6A, 7A, 25, 9, 12A, 13A] 1 give a guarantee(1, 2, 3) for (sth or sb): 担保; 担保: ~ a man's debts, 保证一人的债务; ~ to pay a man's debts; 保证为一人还债; ~ that the debts will be paid; 保证债会付清; ~ the payment of the debts. 保证偿还债务. We cannot ~ the punctual arrival of trains in foggy weather. 雾天我们不能担保火车准时到达. This clock is ~ for one year. 此钟保用一年. We can't ~ our workers regular employment. 我们不能保证我们的工人经常受雇. 2 (colloq) promise (without legal obligation): (口) 约定; 许诺(无法律上的义务): Many shopkeepers ~ satisfaction to customers. 许多商店老板保证使顾客满意.

guar·an·tor /ˌgærən'tɔː(r); ˈgærəntɔ/ n (legal word for) guarantee(3). (法律名词)保证人; 担保人.

guar·an·ty /'gærəntɪ; 'gærəntɪ/ n (legal word for) guarantee(1, 2, 4). (法律名词)保证书; 担保; 保证; 抵押品; 作为保证之物.

guard[1] /gɑːd; gɑrd/ n 1 [U] state of watchfulness against attack, danger or surprise: 警戒; 戒守; 守望: The sentry/soldier is on ~, at his post, on duty. 那哨兵(士兵)在担任警戒. The soldier was ordered to keep ~. 那士兵奉命守望. 2 [U] attitude of readiness to defend oneself, eg in fencing, boxing, bayonet-drill. (剑术, 拳击, 劈刺等)防御的姿势; 防备. be on/off one's ~, be prepared/unprepared against an attack or surprise: (未)戒备着: Be on your ~ against pickpockets. 谨防扒手. He struck me while I was off my ~. 他在我不提防时袭击我. 3 [C] soldier or party of soldiers keeping ~; sentry. 卫兵; 警卫队; 哨兵. change ~, (mil) replace one ~ by another. (军)换哨; 换岗. Hence, 由此产生, the changing of the ~, eg at Buckingham Palace. 换岗(例如白金汉宫之更换警卫). mount ~,

take up one's post as a sentry. 放哨; 去站岗. relieve ~, take the place of a sentry who has finished his period of duty. 接班(担任警戒); 换哨. stand ~, act as a sentry. 当哨. 4 man (also called warder) or group of men in charge of a prison. 监狱之看守; 典狱官(亦称 warder). 5 (GB) official in charge of a railway train (US 美 = brakeman). (英) (火车之)列车长. 6 (pl) G~s, (in GB and some other countries) troops employed originally to protect the sovereign: (复)(英国及某些国家之)禁卫军; 警卫部队: the G~s; 禁卫队; the Royal Horse G~s; 禁卫骑兵队; a G~s officer. 禁卫队军官. '~s·man /-mən; -mən/ n (pl -men /-men; -mən/) soldier of the G~s. 禁卫队之士兵. 7 [C] body of soldiers with the duty of protecting, honouring or escorting a person: 卫士队; 仪仗队: The Duke, on his arrival, inspected the ~ of honour at the station. 公爵莅临时, 在车站检阅仪仗队. ⇨ also rear~ at **rear**[1](4), Home G~ at **home**[1](7). 8 (esp in compounds) (part of) an article or apparatus designed to prevent injury or loss: (尤用于复合词中)保护器; 防护物; 防护物: a 'fire~, in front of a fireplace; 围护火炉的铁丝网; a 'mud~ (over the wheel of a bicycle, etc); (脚踏车等的)挡泥板; the ~ of a sword, the part of the hilt that protects the hand. 剑的护手. 9 (compounds) (复合词) '~·boat n one sent round a fleet of warships in harbour. 警戒舰; 巡逻艇. '~·house n (mil) building for a military ~ or one in which prisoners are kept. (军)卫兵室; 哨房; 禁闭室. '~·rail n rail, eg on a staircase, to prevent falling or (elsewhere) to prevent persons from danger, eg from traffic. (楼梯等处之)护栏. '~·room n room for soldiers on ~ or for soldiers under ~. 卫兵室; 禁闭室. '~·ship n ship protecting a harbour. (保护港口之)警戒舰.

guard[2] /gɑːd; gɑrd/ vt, vi 1 [VP6A, 15A] protect; keep from danger: 保护; 护卫: a camp; 守营; ~ one's life/one's reputation; 保护一人的生命(名誉); ~ prisoners, prevent them from escaping. 看守囚犯. 2 [VP3A] ~ against, use care and caution to prevent: 预防: ~ against disease/bad habits/suspicion. 预防疾病(杜绝恶习; 避免嫌疑). ~ed adj (of statements, etc) cautious: (指言论等) 谨慎的: a ~ed answer; 慎重的回答; be ~ed in what one says. 言语谨慎. ~ed·ly adv cautiously. 谨慎地.

guard·ian /'gɑːdɪən; 'gɑrdɪən/ n (official or private) person who guards, esp (legal use) one who is responsible for the care of a young or incapable person and his property. (官方或私人的)保护人; (尤指) (法律)监护人. ~ 'angel, spirit watching over a person or place. 守护神. '~·ship /-ʃɪp; -ʃɪp/ n position or office of a ~. 监护人的职责.

guava /'gwɑːvə; 'gwɑvə/ n (tropical tree with) pink edible fruit surrounded by a light yellow outer skin. (产于热带之)番石榴树; 番石榴(的红色果实, 包有一层浅黄色外皮); 芭乐. ⇨ the illus at **fruit**. 参看 fruit 之插图.

gu·ber·na·torial /ˌguːbənə'tɔːrɪəl; ˌgjubənə'tɔrɪəl/ adj (US, Nigeria, etc) of a (state) Governor. (美, 尼日利亚等)州长的.

gudg·eon /'gʌdʒən; 'gʌdʒən/ n small freshwater fish used as bait. 白鮈鱼(用以作饵的一种小淡水鱼)

guel·der rose /'geldə rəʊz; 'geldə,roz/ n plant with round bunches of white flowers; snowball tree. 雪球(生有一束束白花的一种植物).

guer·rilla, guer·illa /gə'rɪlə; gə'rɪlə/ n person, not a member of a regular army; engaged in fighting in small, secret groups. 游击队员. ~ warfare n [U] such fighting. 游击战. ~ war n [C] war fought by ~s on one side or both sides. 游击战. urban ~ n ~ who operates in towns only. 都市游击队员.

guess /ges; ges/ vt, vi [VP6A, 25, 9, 8, 10, 2A, C, 3A] ~ (at), form an opinion, give an answer, make a statement, based on supposition, not on careful thought, calculation or definite knowledge: 猜想; 臆测;

推测: *Can you ~ my weight/what my weight is/how much I weigh?* 你能猜出我的体重吗？ *I should ~ his age at 50/~ him to be 50/~ that he is 50.* 我猜想他有五十岁了。 *Can't you even ~ at her age?* 你甚至连她的年龄也猜不出吗？ *G~ what I'm thinking.* 你猜我在想什么。 *You've ~ed right/wrong.* 你猜对(错)了。 *I ~* (US colloq 美口 = *suppose*) *you're right.* 我想你是对的。 □ *n* [C] opinion formed by ~ing: 猜测: *make/have a ~ (at sth).* 猜想。 *One man's ~ is as good as another's.* 无论谁的猜测都是一样(猜测终归是猜测)。 *it's anybody's ~,* no one can be sure about it. 此事无人能确定。 *at a ~,* making a ~: 依猜测: *At a ~ I should say there were 50 people present.* 凭猜测我认为有五十人在场。 *by ~,* by the use of ~ing: 凭推测: *Don't answer by ~; work the problem out.* 不要凭推测作答，把这个问题解出来。 '~·timate /'gestɪmət; 'gɛstɪmɪt/ *n* (modern colloq 现代口语) estimate made by combining ~ing with reasoning. (现代口语)(凭猜测的)估计。 '~-work *n* [U] ~ing; result of ~ing. 猜测; 臆断。

guest /gest; gɛst/ *n* person staying at or paying a visit to another's house or being entertained at a meal: 宾客; 客人: *We're expecting ~s to dinner.* 我们在等候着客人进餐。 '~-room *n* bedroom kept for the use of ~s. 供宾客留宿的寝室。 '~-house *n* boarding-house. 上等寄宿舍; 宾馆。 '~-night *n* evening on which members of a club, college, mess等, etc may bring in and entertain their friends as ~s. (俱乐部, 学院等)招待来宾之夜晚。 ,paying '~ *n* boarder in sb's house. 寄宿客。 ⇨ **board**[1] (8), **board**[2](2).

guf·faw /gə'fɔː; gʌ'fɔ/ *vi, n* (give a) noisy laugh. 哄笑。

guid·ance /'gaɪdns; 'gaɪdns/ *n* [U] guiding or being guided; leadership. 引导; 指导; 领导。

guide /gaɪd; gaɪd/ *n* **1** person who shows others the way, esp a person employed to point out interesting sights on a journey or visit. 向导。 **,Girl 'G~.** ⇨ **girl.** **2** sth that directs or influences (conduct, etc): 指导或影响(品行等)之物: *Instinct is not always a good ~.* 本能并不永远是一良好的指导者。 '~-line *n* (usu *pl*) advice (usu from sb in authority) on policy, etc: (通常用复数(政策等的)指导方针; 指标: ~-*lines on prices and incomes.* 物价和收入方面之指标。 **3** (also 亦作 '~·book) book for travellers, tourists, etc with information about a place: 指南: *a ~ to the British Museum;* 大英博物馆指南; *a ~ to Italy.* 意大利旅行指南。 **4** book of information; manual: 入门书; 手册: *a G~ to Poultry Keeping.* 家禽饲养手册。 **5** bar, rod or part of a machine or apparatus that keeps other parts, etc, moving as desired. 导杆; 导体; 导机。 □ *vt* [VP6A, 15A, B] act as ~ to: 引导; 领导: ~ *sb to a place;* 引导某人至一地; ~ *sb in/out/up, etc.* 引导某人进入(出去, 上去等)。 *You must be ~d by your sense of what is right and just.* 你必须受正义感的引导。 ,~d 'missile, rocket (for use in war) which can be ~d to its destination while in flight by electronic devices. 导弹; 电导飞弹; 导向飞弹。

guild /gɪld; gɪld/ *n* (older spelling 昔时拼作 **gild**) society of persons for helping one another, forwarding common interests, eg trade, social welfare. 互助会; 行会; 同业公会。 **G~-'hall** *n* hall in which members of a ~ met in the Middle Ages. (中古时公会的)会馆。 **the 'G~-hall,** hall of the Corporation of the City of London, used for banquets, receptions, etc. 伦敦市政厅之会堂(供举行宴会, 招待会等者)。 ~ **socialism,** system by which an industry is to be controlled by a council of its members. 基尔特社会主义。

guilder /'gɪldə(r); 'gɪldə/ *n* unit of currency of the Netherlands. 盾; 基尔德(荷兰之货币单位)。

guile /gaɪl; gaɪl/ *n* [U] deceit; cunning: 诈欺; 狡猾: *a man full of ~;* 奸诈之人; *get sth by ~.* 诈取某物。 ~·**less** *adj* ~·**ful** /-fl; -fəl/ *adj*

guille·mot /'gɪlɪmɒt; 'gɪlɪˌmɑt/ *n* kinds of arctic

sea-bird. 海鸠。 ⇨ the illus at **water.** 参看 water 之插图。

guillo·tine /'gɪlətiːn; 'gɪlə,tin/ *n* **1** machine for beheading (criminals in France) with a heavy blade sliding in grooves dropped from a height (法国处决犯人之)断头台。 **2** kind of machine for cutting the edges of books during manufacture, trimming sheets of paper, etc. 切纸机。 **3** (in Parliament) method of stopping obstruction of a bill (by excessive debate) by fixing times for taking votes. (国会中)决定投票时间以防止(借过多辩论)阻碍议案的措施。 □ *vt* [VP6A] use the ~ on. 处以斩刑; 切(纸); 规定(议案之)投票时间。

guilt /gɪlt; gɪlt/ *n* [U] condition of having done wrong; responsibility for wrong-doing: 犯罪; 罪状; 有罪: *The ~ of the accused man was in doubt.* 被告之罪有疑问。 ~·**less** *adj* ~·**less (of),** innocent; without ~: 无罪的; 无罪的: ~·*less of the offence;* 无罪; not having knowledge or possession. 不知; 没有。 ~·**y** *adj* (-ier, -iest) ~·**y (of), 1** having done wrong: 有罪的; 犯罪的: *plead* ~·*y to a crime;* 服罪; 认罪: *be ~y of a crime.* 有罪。 **2** showing or feeling guilt: 表示有罪的; 感觉有罪的: *look* ~*y;* 象有罪的样子; 心虚; ~*y looks;* 感到有罪的表情; *a* ~*y conscience.* 内疚。 ~·**ily** /-ɪlɪ; -əlɪ/ *adv* ~·**iness** *n*

guinea /'gɪnɪ; 'gɪnɪ/ *n* (*pl* ~s abbr 复数略作 **gns**) (called 称作 *money of account,* ⇨ **account**[1](2)) formerly the sum of twenty-one shillings (now £1.05, or 105p), for which there was neither coin nor banknote, used in stating prices of goods, professional fees, charges, subscriptions, etc: 畿尼; 基尼(昔时值 21 先令, 现值 1.05 英镑或 105 便士, 非硬币亦非纸币, 用以计算货物价格、专业人员之收费、费用、订费等): *the 2000 Gns race,* horse-race with a prize of 2000 ~s. 二千畿尼奖金的赛马。

guinea-fowl /'gɪnɪ faʊl; 'gɪnɪ faʊl/ *n* (*pl* unchanged) domestic fowl of the pheasant family, with dark grey feathers spotted with white. 珍珠鸡(一种属于雉类的家禽, 生有带白点的深灰色羽毛)。

guinea-pig /'gɪnɪ pɪg; 'gɪnɪ pɪg/ *n* **1** short-eared animal like a big rat, often used in scientific experiments; sb allowing himself to be used in medical or other experiments. 豚鼠(常供科学实验用); 供医学或其他实验的人。 ⇨ the illus at **small.** 参看 small 之插图。

Guin·ness /'gɪnɪs; 'gɪnɪs/ *n* (P) kind of bitter stout; bottle or glass of this: (商标)一种黑啤酒; 一瓶或一杯此种黑啤酒: *A pint of draught ~, please.* 请来一品脱桶装黑啤酒。

guise /gaɪz; gaɪz/ *n* [C] **1** (old use) style of dress: (旧用法)装束: *in the ~ of a monk.* 作和尚的装束。 **2** *in/under the ~ of,* assuming a particular manner or appearance: 伪装; 假装: *under the ~ of friendship.* 假装友善。

guitar /gɪ'tɑː(r); gɪ'tɑr/ *n* (usu) six-stringed musical instrument, plucked with the fingers or a plectrum. 吉他; 六弦琴(一种通常为六弦的乐器, 用手指或琴拨弹奏)。 ⇨ the illus at **string.** 参看 string 之插图。

gulch /gʌltʃ; gʌltʃ/ *n* (US) deep, narrow, rocky valley. (美)峡谷。

gul·den /'gʊldən; 'gʊldən/ *n* = **guilder.**

gulf /gʌlf; gʌlf/ *n* **1** part of the sea almost surrounded by land: 海湾: *the G~ of Mexico.* 墨西哥海湾。 **the 'G~ Stream,** warm ocean current flowing north from the G~ of Mexico to Europe. 墨西哥湾流(自墨西哥海湾向北流向欧洲的暖流)。 **2** deep hollow; chasm; abyss; (fig) dividing line, division (*between* opinions, etc). 深坑; 深渊; (喻)隔膜; 鸿沟(在 between 连用, 后接意见等)。

gull[1] /gʌl; gʌl/ *n* large, long-winged sea-bird. 鸥。 ⇨ the illus at **water.** 参看 water 之插图。

gull[2] /gʌl; gʌl/ *vt* [VP6A, 15A] cheat; deceive: 欺

骗; 诈欺: ~ *a fool out of his money.* 骗取傻子的钱. □ *n* person who is easily ~ed. 易受欺骗的人. ~·**ible** /-əbl; -əbl/ *adj* easily ~ed. 易受欺骗的. ~·**i·bil·ity** /ˌɡʌləˈbɪlɪtɪ; ˌɡʌləˈbɪlətɪ/ *n*

gul·let /'ɡʌlɪt; 'ɡʌlɪt/ *n* food passage from the mouth to the stomach; throat. 食道; 咽喉. ⇨ the illus at **head**. 参看 head 之插图.

gully /'ɡʌlɪ; 'ɡʌlɪ/ *n* (*pl* **-lies**) narrow channel cut or formed by rainwater, eg on a hillside, or made for carrying water away from a building. (山腰等地之)水冲沟; 壑; 溪谷; 沟渠.

gulp /ɡʌlp; ɡʌlp/ *vt, vi* [VP2A, 6A, 15B] ~ (*down*), swallow (food or drink) quickly or greedily: 吞食; 吞饮; 狼吞虎咽: ~ *down a cup of tea;* 一口气喝下一杯茶; hold back or suppress (as if swallowing sth); make a ~ing motion. 抑制(若吞下去一般); 吞. □ *n* [C] act of ~ing: 吞食; 吞饮: *empty a glass at one* ~; 一口气喝完一杯; amount that is ~ed; mouthful, esp of sth liquid: 吞食或吞饮之量; 一大口(尤指液体): *a* ~ *of cold tea.* 一大口冷茶.

gum[1] /ɡʌm; ɡʌm/ *n* (usu *pl*) firm, pink flesh round the teeth: (通常用复数)齿龈: *The dog bared its gums at me.* 那狗对着我露出而吠. ⇨ the illus at **mouth**. 参看 mouth 之插图. **gum·boil** /'ɡʌmbɔɪl; 'ɡʌm,bɔɪl/ *n* boil or abscess on the gums. 龈溃疡; 龈脓肿.

gum[2] /ɡʌm; ɡʌm/ *n* **1** [U] sticky substance exuded from some trees, used for sticking things together. 树胶; 树脂. **2** [U] gum that has been specially prepared in some way: 经过特殊方法处理的树胶: *chewing-gum;* 口香糖; [C] (also 亦作 '*gumdrop*) hard, transparent sweet made of gelatine, etc. 橡皮糖. **3** (also 亦作 '*gum-tree*) eucalyptus tree. 橡皮树; 橡胶树. *up a gum-tree,* (sl) in difficulties. (俚)有困难; 在困境. '**gum·boot,** high rubber boot. 长统橡皮靴. '**gum·shoe,** (US) (美) (a) rubber shoe or overshoe. 橡胶鞋或套鞋. (b) (sl) detective. (俚)侦探. □ *vt* (**-mm-**) [VP6A, 15A, B] stick together with gum; spread gum on the surface of: 以树胶粘合; 涂以树胶: *gum sth down;* 用胶粘住某物; *gum two things together.* 将两物用胶粘起. **gummy** *adj* (**-ier, -iest**) sticky. 粘的.

gum[3] /ɡʌm; ɡʌm/ *n* (esp N England) (in oaths, etc) God: (尤用于北英格兰)(誓语等中)上帝: *By gum!* 凭上帝发誓!

gum·bo /'ɡʌmbəʊ; 'ɡʌmbo/ *n* (US) thick okra soup. (美)加秋葵荚之浓汤.

gump·tion /'ɡʌmpʃn; 'ɡʌmpʃən/ *n* [U] (colloq) common sense and initiative; qualities likely to bring success: (口)常识与进取精神; 可以使人成功的性质: *The lad lacks* ~. 这孩子缺乏进取精神.

gun /ɡʌn; ɡʌn/ *n* **1** general name for any kind of firearm that sends shells or bullets from a metal tube: 炮; 枪: *a warship with 16-inch guns;* 装有十六英寸口径大炮的战舰; *machine-guns.* 机关枪. ⇨ **cannon, carbine, musket, pistol, revolver, rifle**[1]. *be going great guns,* be proceeding vigorously and successfully. 正在努力而且顺利地进行. *blow great guns,* (of the wind) blow violently. (指风)狂吹. *stick to one's guns,* maintain one's position against attack or argument. 坚守阵地; 坚守立场. '**gun·boat** *n* small warship carrying heavy guns, or long-range missiles. 炮艇. *gunboat diplomacy,* (fig) diplomacy backed by the threat of force. (喻) 炮艇外交 (以武力威胁作后盾之外交政策). '**gun·carriage** *n* wheeled support of a big gun, or part on which a gun slides when it recoils. 炮架. '**gun-cotton** *n* [U] explosive of acid-soaked cotton. 强棉药; 硝化棉. '**gun·fire** *n* [U] firing of gun(s). 炮火. '**gun·man** /-mən; -mæn/ *n* (*pl* **-men**) man who uses a gun to rob or kill people. 持枪抢劫或杀人的歹徒. '**gun-metal** *n* alloy of copper and tin or zinc; dull blue-grey colour. 炮铜; 青铜(铜与锡或锌的合金); 铁灰色. '**gun·powder** *n* explosive powder used in guns, fireworks, blasting, etc. 火药. **the 'Gunpowder Plot,** plot to blow up the Houses of Parliament, 5 Nov 1605. 火药阴谋 (一六〇五年十一月五日阴谋炸毁英国国会的事件). '**gun·room** *n* (in a warship) room for junior officers. (战舰中)下级军官室. '**gun-running** *n* [U] introduction of firearms, secretly and illegally, into a country, eg to help a revolt. 私运军火(以帮助叛乱等). '**gun-runner** *n* person engaged in this. 私运军火者. '**gun·shot** *n* (a) [C] shot fired by a gun. (射出之)炮弹. (b) [U] range of a gun: 炮的射程: *be out of/ within gunshot.* 在大炮射程以外(内). '**gun-smith** *n* person who makes and repairs small firearms. 造枪工人; 修枪匠. **2** person using a sporting gun, as a member of a shooting party. 狩猎队员. **3** big gun, (colloq) important or powerful person. (俚)重要或有权势的人物. □ *vt* [VP6A, 15B] **gun sb (down),** shoot with a gun. 用枪将某人射倒.

gun·ner /'ɡʌnə(r); 'ɡʌnɚ/ *n* (in the army) soldier in the artillery; (in the navy) warrant officer in charge of a battery of guns. (陆军)炮兵; (海军)枪炮士官长. ~·**y** *n* [U] construction and management of large guns. 射击学; 枪炮学; 炮术.

gunny /'ɡʌnɪ; 'ɡʌnɪ/ *n* [U] strong, coarse material used for making sacks, bales, bags, etc. (制袋, 包, 囊等的)粗麻布.

gun·wale /'ɡʌnl; 'ɡʌnl/ *n* (naut) upper edge of the side of a boat or a small ship. (航海)舷缘(小船船舷的上缘). ⇨ the illus at **row**. 参看 row 之插图.

gurgle /'ɡɜːɡl; 'ɡɝɡl/ *n* [C, U] bubbling sound as of water flowing from a narrow-necked bottle: 汩汩声(如水自一窄颈瓶内倒出的声音): ~*s of delight.* 咯咯的笑声. □ *vi* make this sound: 作汩汩声: *The baby was gurgling happily.* 那婴儿高兴得咯咯咕作声.

Gur·kha /'ɡʊəkə; 'ɡʊrkə/ *n* member of a ruling group in Nepal who became famous as soldiers in the British Indian army. 廓尔喀人(尼泊尔的主要种族, 在英印军中为着名的军人).

guru /'ɡuruː; 'ɡuru/ *n* Hindu spiritual teacher; (colloq) respected and influential teacher or authority. 印度之宗教师; (口)受人尊敬和具有影响力的教师或权威.

gush /ɡʌʃ; ɡʌʃ/ *vi* [VP2A, C, 3A] **1** burst, flow, out suddenly: 涌出; 迸出: *oil* ~*ing from a new well;* 从新油井中涌出的油; *blood* ~*ing from a wound.* 伤口涌出的血. **2** talk with excessive enthusiasm: 滔滔不绝地说: *young mothers* ~*ing over their babies;* 滔滔不绝地谈论她们婴儿的年轻母亲; *girls who* ~ *over handsome film stars.* 过分热心谈论漂亮电影明星的女孩子. □ *n* sudden outburst or outflow: 涌出; 迸发: *a* ~ *of oil / anger / enthusiasm.* 油的涌出(一阵愤怒; 热情的奔放). ~**er** *n* oil-well with a strong natural flow (so that pumping is not needed). 喷油井(自动流出的油井). ~·**ing** *adj:* ~*ing compliments.* 滔滔不绝的问候. ⇨ **2** above. 参看上列第 2 义. ~·**ing·ly** *adv*

gus·set /'ɡʌsɪt; 'ɡʌsɪt/ *n* [C] (usu triangular or diamond-shaped) piece of cloth inserted in a garment to strengthen or enlarge it. 为加强或加大衣服而插接于衣服中的一块布(通常为三角形或菱形); 衬; 裆.

gust /ɡʌst; ɡʌst/ *n* [C] sudden, violent rush of wind; burst of rain, hail, fire or smoke; (fig) outburst of feeling: 突然一阵狂风; 雨, 雹, 火或烟之突然的一阵; (喻)感情的爆发: *The wind was blowing in* ~*s.* 狂风阵阵吹来. ~**y** *adj* (**-ier, -iest**) stormy; with wind blowing in ~s. 有风暴的; 有阵阵狂风的.

gus·ta·tion /ɡʌˈsteɪʃn; ɡʌsˈteʃən/ *n* [U] (formal) tasting. (正式用语)尝味.

gusto /'ɡʌstəʊ; 'ɡʌsto/ *n* [U] enjoyment in doing sth. 趣味; 喜好.

gut /ɡʌt; ɡʌt/ *n* **1** (*pl*) (colloq) intestines; bowels: (复)(口)内脏; 肠: *stick a bayonet into a man's guts.* 将

刺刀戳入一人的内脏. **hate sb's guts,** (sl) hate him intensely. (俚)恨死某人; 恨之入骨. **2** (*pl*) (colloq) contents of anything: (复)(口)内容: *His speech had no guts in it,* no real arguments, force, etc. 他的演说没有内容。*The real guts* (= The essence) *of his speech is....* 他的演说之要义为…. **3** (*pl*) (colloq) courage and determination. (复)(口)勇气与决心; 胆量: 魄力: *a man with plenty of guts.* 很有魄力的人. **4** [U] strong cord made from the intestines of animals, used for the strings of violins, etc. (用做提琴弦等的)肠线. ⇨ catgut. □ *vt* (**-tt-**) [VP6A] **1** take the guts(1) out of (a fish, etc). 取出(鱼等的)内脏. **2** destroy the inside of or the contents of: 毁坏…的内部或内容: *a building gutted by fire.* 内部为火焚毁的房屋。 **gut·less** *adj* lacking in guts(3). 缺少勇气和决心的; 没有胆量的.

gutta-per·cha /ˌgʌtə ˈpɜːtʃə; ˈgʌtəˈpɝtʃə/ *n* [U] rubber-like substance made from the juice of various Malayan trees. 马来树胶; 古塔波胶.

gut·ter¹ /ˈgʌtə(r); ˈgʌtə/ *n* [C] **1** channel or trough (usu metal) fixed under the edge of a roof to carry away rainwater; channel at the side of a road for the same purpose. (檐下之)承霤; 天沟; 屋顶边沟; (道旁之)阴沟; 排水沟. **2 the ~,** (fig) poor or debased state of life: (喻)贫苦低级的生活: *the language of the ~,* low and vulgar language: 下流粗鄙的言语。 **take a child out of the ~,** remove it from poor and wretched conditions, 使孩子离开贫困环境。 **the 'gutter press,** newspapers giving much space to salacious stories, scandals, etc. 低级趣味的报纸(以大量篇幅刊登淫秽故事, 丑行等者). **'~- snipe** /-snaɪp; -ˌsnaɪp/ *n* poor, badly-dressed child who plays in town streets. 街头流浪儿.

gut·ter² /ˈgʌtə(r); ˈgʌtə/ *vi* [VP2A] (of a candle) burn unsteadily so that the melted wax flows down the sides. (指蜡烛)燃烧不稳而融化流下; 淌蜡.

gut·tural /ˈgʌtərəl; ˈgʌtərəl/ *n, adj* (sound that seems to be) produced in the throat: (似)喉间发出的; (似)喉间发出的声音: *~ consonants.* 喉间发出的辅音。 **~·ly** *adv*

guv·nor /ˈgʌvnə(r); ˈgʌvnə/ *n* (GB sl) boss. (英俚)老板; 工头.

guy¹ /gaɪ; gaɪ/ *n* [C] rope or chain used to keep sth steady or secured, eg to hold a tent in place. (支帐篷等的)支索; 牵索; 拉索.

guy² /gaɪ; gaɪ/ *n* **1** figure in the form of a man, dressed in old clothes (eg as burned on 5 Nov in memory of Guy Fawkes's Gunpowder Plot). 着旧时衣服的偶像(例如为纪念发觉 Guy Fawkes 之火药阴谋于每年十一月五日所焚者). **2** person dressed in a strange or queer-looking way. 衣着古怪的人. **3** (sl) man. (俚)人。 ⇨ *fall-guy* at **fall¹(1).** □ *vt* (*pt, pp* **guyed**) [VP6A] ridicule; exhibit (sb) in effigy. 嘲弄; 以肖像展示(某人).

Guy's /gaɪz; gaɪz/ *n* (used for) Guy's Hospital (in London). (用于指伦敦之)盖氏医院.

guzzle /ˈgʌzl; ˈgʌzl/ *vi, vt* [VP2A, 6A, 15B] (colloq) eat or drink greedily: (口)狼吞虎咽: *be always guzzling;* 老是狼吞虎咽; *~ beer.* 狂饮啤酒. **guz·zler** /-zlə(r); -zlə/ *n* person who ~s. 狼吞虎咽者; 狂饮者.

gybe (US **jibe**) /dʒaɪb; dʒaɪb/ *vi, vt* [VP2A, 6A] (naut) (of a sail or boom) swing from one side of the ship to the other; (of a ship or a ship's crew) cause this to happen. (航海)(指帆或其下桁)自船之一侧转向另一侧; (指船或船员)使帆自一侧转向另一侧; (使)改变航道. ⇨ the illus at **barque.** 参看 barque 之插图.

gym /dʒɪm; dʒɪm/ *n* (sl) (short for) gymnasium, gymnastics: (俚)体育馆; 健身房; 体操(为 gymnasium 及 gymnastics 之略): 'gym-shoes; 运动鞋; *the 'gym mistress.* 女体育教师. **'gym-slip** *n* sleeveless tunic worn in GB by some girls as part of school uniform. 无袖的束腰外衣 (英国某些女学生做为制服).

gym·khana /dʒɪmˈkɑːnə; dʒɪmˈkɑnə/ *n* public display of athletics, horse-riding or vehicle-driving competitions. 运动会; 赛马会; 赛车会.

gym·nasium /dʒɪmˈneɪzɪəm; dʒɪmˈneɪzɪəm/ *n* (*pl* ~s) room or hall with apparatus for physical training. 体育馆; 健身房.

gym·nas·tic /dʒɪmˈnæstɪk; dʒɪmˈnæstɪk/ *adj* of physical training. 体操的; 体育的. ~**s** *n pl* (forms of) exercises for physical training. 体操. **gymnast** /ˈdʒɪmnæst; ˈdʒɪmnæst/ *n* expert in ~s. 体操家.

gynae·col·ogy (US = **gyne-**) /ˌgaɪnɪˈkɒlədʒɪ; ˌdʒaɪnɪˈkɑlədʒɪ/ *n* [U] science of the diseases of women and pregnancies. 妇科(医)学. **gynae·cologist** (US = **gyne-**) *n* expert in ~. 妇科医生. **gynae·co·logi·cal** (US = **gyne-**) /ˌgaɪnɪkəˈlɒdʒɪkl; ˌdʒaɪnɪkəˈlɑdʒɪkl/*adj*

gyp¹ /dʒɪp; dʒɪp/ *vt* [VP6A] (sl) cheat. (俚)欺骗.

gyp² /dʒɪp; dʒɪp/ *n* **give sb gyp,** (sl) scold or punish him without mercy. (俚)严斥或严惩某人.

gyp·sum /ˈdʒɪpsəm; ˈdʒɪpsəm/ *n* [U] mineral (calcium sulphate, $CaSO_4$) from which plaster of Paris is made; also used as a fertilizer. 石膏(亦可用做肥料).

Gypsy /ˈdʒɪpsɪ; ˈdʒɪpsɪ/ *n* ⇨ **gipsy.**

gy·rate /dʒaɪˈreɪt US: ˈdʒaɪreɪt; ˈdʒaɪret/ *vi* move round in circles or spirals; revolve. 旋转; 回旋. **gy·ra·tion** /dʒaɪˈreɪʃən; dʒaɪˈreʃən/ *n* [C, U] revolving; revolution. 旋转; 回转.

gyro /ˈdʒaɪərəʊ; ˈdʒaɪro/ *n* (colloq abbr of) **gyroscope** (口)为 gyroscope 之略.

gyro·scope /ˈdʒaɪrəskəʊp; ˈdʒaɪrəˌskop/ *n* wheel which, when spinning fast, keeps steady the object in which it is fixed. 回转仪; 环动仪(快速旋转时可使装有此器之物体保持稳定). **gyro·scopic** /ˌdʒaɪrəˈskɒpɪk; ˌdʒaɪrəˈskɑpɪk/ *adj*

a gyroscope

H h

H, h /eɪtʃ; etʃ/ (*pl* **H's, h's** /ˈeɪtʃɪz; ˈetʃɪz/), the eighth letter of the English alphabet. 英语字母的第八个字母. **drop one's h's,** omit the sound /h/; h/, eg by saying, '*ot* for *hot.* 略去 h 之音(如读时为 'ot 为 hot).

ha /hɑː; hɑ/ *int* used to express surprise, joy, triumph, suspicion, etc. When repeated in print ('*Ha! Ha! Ha!*') it indicates laughter. 哈!(表示惊异、快乐、得意、怀疑等) 如连续写出或印出则表示大笑声.

ha·beas cor·pus /ˌheɪbɪəs ˈkɔːpəs; ˈhebɪəs ˈkɔrpəs/ (Lat; legal) (拉; 法律) (*writ of*) ~, order requiring a person to be brought before a judge or into court, esp to investigate the right of the law to keep him in prison. 人身保护令(要求将人移送法院处理之令状, 特别为调查应否受拘留者).

hab·er·dasher /ˈhæbədæʃə(r); ˈhæbəˌdæʃə/ *n* shopkeeper who sells clothing, small articles of dress,

pins, cotton, etc. 卖零星服饰、针线等的商人。 **~y** n [U] **~'s** goods or business. 服饰杂货;服饰杂货业。

ha·bil·i·ments /həˈbɪlɪmənts; həˈbɪləmənts/ n pl (liter or hum) clothing. (文或谐)衣服.

habit /ˈhæbɪt; ˈhæbɪt/ n **1** [C] sb's settled practice, esp sth that cannot easily be given up: 习惯: the ~ of smoking; 吸烟的习惯; ~-forming drugs. 易于上瘾的麻醉药物. **be in/fall into/get into the ~** of, have, acquire, the ~ of. 有…的习惯; 养成…习惯. **fall/get into bad ~s**, acquire them: 养成坏习惯: Don't let yourself get into bad ~s. 不要让你自己养成坏习惯. **get sb into the ~ of/into bad ~s**, cause him to have the ~ of/bad ~s: 使养成(坏)习惯: Don't let him get you into the ~ of taking drugs. 不要让他使你养成吸毒的习惯. **fall/get out of the ~ of**, abandon the ~ of. 革除…的习惯. **make a ~ of sth**, do it regularly. 经常做某事. **2** [U] usual behaviour: 脾性; 习性; 惯常的行为: H~ is second nature. 习惯成自然. **creature of ~**, sb whose life is marked by many ~s(1). 受习性驱使的人。 **do sth/act from force of ~**, because it is one's ~. 习惯使然而做某事. **do sth out of ~**, because it is one's ~. 因习惯而做某事。 **3** [C] (old use) condition, general quality (of mind or body): (旧用法)心境; 体质: a cheerful ~ of mind. 心情愉快. **4** [C] dress worn by members of a religious order: 表示宗教级别的服装: a monk's ~. 僧袍. **'riding ~**, woman's coat and skirt for horse-riding. 女子骑马装.

hab·it·able /ˈhæbɪtəbl; ˈhæbɪtəbl/ adj fit to be lived in: 适于居住的: The old house is no longer ~. 这古老的房屋已不适于居住了.

habi·tat /ˈhæbɪtæt; ˈhæbɪˌtæt/ n (of plants, animals) usual natural place and conditions of growth; home. (指动植物)产地;栖息地.

habi·ta·tion /ˌhæbɪˈteɪʃn; ˌhæbəˈteʃən/ n **1** [U] living in: 居住: houses that were not fit for ~. 不适于居住的房屋. **2** [C] (liter) place to live in. (文)住所: On these plains there was not a single human ~. 在这些平原上没有一处人的住所.

ha·bit·ual /həˈbɪtʃʊəl; həˈbɪtʃʊəl/ adj **1** regular, usual: 惯常的; 通常的: He took his ~ seat at the dining-table. 他坐于餐桌旁他惯常所坐的座位上. **2** acting by habit; having a regular habit: 惯常做的; 有习惯的: a ~ liar/drunkard/cinema-goer. 惯于说谎(经常喝醉的人; 爱看电影者). **~ly** /-tʃʊlɪ; -tʃʊlɪ/ adv as a habit: 习惯性地: Tom is ~ly late for school. 汤姆上学惯于迟到.

ha·bitu·ate /həˈbɪtʃʊeɪt; həˈbɪtʃʊˌet/ vt [VP14] ~ sb/oneself to sth, (formal) accustom; get (sb/oneself) used to (sth): (正式用法)使熟习; 使(某人、自己)习惯于(某事物): ~ oneself to hard work/getting up early/a cold climate; 使自己惯于艰苦的工作(早起, 寒冷的气候); ~ a horse to the sound of gunfire. 使一马习惯于炮火声.

habi·tude /ˈhæbɪtjuːd; US: -tuːd; ˈhæbəˌtjud/ n [U] (formal) custom; tendency; habitual way of acting or doing things. (正式用语)习惯; 嗜性; 习性.

ha·bitué /həˈbɪtjueɪ; həˈbɪtʃuˌe/ n person who regularly goes to a place: 常至某一地方的人; 常客: a ~ of the orchestral concerts/of the Café Royal. 常听管弦乐队演奏会者(皇家饭店的常客).

haci·enda /ˌhæsɪˈendə; ˌhɑsɪˈendə/ n (pl ~s) (in Latin American countries) large landed estate with a house. (拉丁美洲国家的)庄园;大田庄.

hack¹ /hæk; hæk/ vt, vi [VP6A, 15A, B, 2A, C, 3A] ~ (at), cut roughly or clumsily; chop: 乱砍; 劈; 砍: After the murderer had killed his victim, he ~ed the body to pieces. 凶手杀死受害者后, 将其尸体砍碎. He ~ed at the branch (at it) until it fell to the ground. 他砍那树枝, 直到它落在地上. **~ing cough**, short, dry cough. 短促的干咳. **'~-saw** n one with a replaceable blade in a frame, for cutting through metal. 弓形钢锯(锯金属用者). ⇨ the illus at **tool**. 参看tool之插图.

hack² /hæk; hæk/ n **1** horse that may be hired. 出租之马. **2** person paid to do hard and uninteresting work as a writer: (受雇从事辛苦而又乏味之写作的)文丐: publisher's ~s. 出版商雇用的文人. □ vi ride on horseback on roads, at an ordinary pace: 以普通速度在路上骑马: go ~ing. 以普通速度骑马.

hackles /ˈhæklz; ˈhæklz/ n pl long feathers on the neck of the domestic cock: 雄鸡颈上的长羽毛: with his ~ up, (of a cock, dog or man) angry; ready to fight. (指雄鸡, 狗或人)发怒; 准备打斗. **have one's ~ up**, be, make sb angry, ready to fight. (使某人)愤怒欲战.

hack·ney /ˈhæknɪ; ˈhæknɪ/ n ordinary kind of horse for riding or driving. 普通骑乘或驾车之马. **'~-carriage**, one that may be hired. 出租马车. **~-ed** /ˈhæknɪd; ˈhæknɪd/ adj (esp of sayings) too common; repeated too often. (尤指格言)陈旧的; 陈腐的.

had /hæd; hæd/ ⇨ **have¹**.

had·dock /ˈhædək; ˈhædək/ n (pl unchanged) seafish much used for food, esp smoked ~. (复数不变)黑斑鳕; 黑线鳕(食用甚广, 尤用于制成熏鱼).

Hades /ˈheɪdiːz; ˈhediz/ n (Gk myth) the underworld; place where the spirits of the dead go. (希神)冥府; 黄泉.

Hadji /ˈhædʒɪ; ˈhædʒɪ/ n (title of a) Muslim pilgrim who has been to Mecca. 至圣地麦加朝拜过的伊斯兰教徒(之头衔).

haem- ⇨ **hem-**.

haft /hɑːft; US: hæft; hæft/ n handle of an axe, knife, dagger, etc. (斧、刀、匕首等之)柄.

hag /hæg; hæg/ n witch; ugly old woman, esp one who does, or is thought to do, evil. 女巫; 老丑妇(尤指做或被认为是会做坏事者). **'hag-ridden**, afflicted by nightmares; harassed. 受梦魇搅扰的; 被困扰的.

hag·gard /ˈhægəd; ˈhægəd/ adj (of a person, his face) looking tired and lined, esp from worry, lack of sleep. (指人, 人的面孔)憔悴的; 枯槁的(尤指由于忧愁或缺少睡眠所致).

hag·gis /ˈhægɪs; ˈhægɪs/ n Scottish dish of various parts of a sheep, cut up, mixed with oatmeal, and cooked in a sheep's stomach. (苏格兰)将羊杂切碎加麦片纳入羊胃中煮成的食物.

haggle /ˈhægl; ˈhægl/ vi [VP2A, 3A] ~ (with sb) (about/over sth), argue, dispute, esp the price of sth or the terms of a bargain. 争论; (尤指)讨价还价.

hagi·ol·ogy /ˌhægɪˈɒlədʒɪ; ˌhægɪˈɑlədʒɪ/ n literature of the lives and legends of saints. 圣徒传; 圣徒言行录.

haha /ˈhɑːhɑː; ˈhɑˌhɑ/ n wall or fence bounding a park or garden, sunk in a hollow so as not to interfere with the view. (筑于公园或花园四周之沟中以免妨碍视线之)矮墙; 矮篱.

hail¹ /heɪl; hel/ n **1** [U] frozen raindrops falling from the sky. 雹. **'~-stone** n [C] small ball of ~: 冰雹: ~-stones as big as peas. 象豌豆般大小的雹粒. **'~-storm** n storm with fall of ~. 雹暴. **2** (usu coming a ~ of) sth coming in great numbers and force: 大量和猛烈到来的事物: a ~ of blows/curses. 一阵打击(咒骂). □ vi, vt **1** (impers) (of ~) come down: (无人称)(指雹)下降: It ~ed in the late afternoon. 傍晚时下了雹. **2** [VP2C, 15B] ~ (sth) down (on sb), (of blows, etc) come, send down, hard and fast (on): (指打击等)猛烈迅速地落下: Blows ~ed down on his back. 他的后背挨了一阵狠狠的抽打. They ~ed curses down on us. 他们猛烈地咒骂我们.

hail² /heɪl; hel/ vt, vi **1** [VP6A, 16B, 23] greet; give a welcoming cry to; call out to (so as to attract attention): 欢迎; 向…欢呼; 向…招呼(以引其注意): Cheerful voices ~ed us as we entered the hall. 我们进入会堂时, 向我们欢呼之声四起. They ~ed him (as) king. 他们高呼拥他为王. He was ~ed as a hero. 他受到了英雄式的欢迎. Let's ~ a taxi, shall we? 我们叫一辆计程车好吗? **2** [VP3A]

~ from, come from: 来自: *Where does the ship ~ from*, Which is her home port?* 这只船来自何处(原属何港)? (colloq, of persons) (口, 指人) *They ~ from all parts of the country.* 他们来自全国各地。 *~ n* greeting; *~*ing cry. 欢迎; 欢呼; 招呼. *within ~*, (esp of ships) near enough to be *~*ed. (尤指船舶)在可以招呼的距离内. *be ,~fellow-well-'met (with sb)*, be very familiar and friendly. 极亲密; 很要好.

hair /heə(r); her/ *n* **1** [U] (collective *sing*) all the thread-like growths on the skin of animals, esp on the human head, ⇨ the illus at **head**; threadlike growth on the stems and leaves of some plants; lifelike thing: (集合名词单数)毛发; (尤指)头发(参看 head 之插图); 植物的茸毛; 毛状物: *brush one's ~*; 梳头发; *have one's '~ cut*; 理发: *a cat with a fine coat of ~.* 长有一身好毛的猫. [C] single thread of a ~: 一根毛: 一根发: *find a ~ in the soup;* 在汤内发现了一根毛(发); *two blonde ~s on his coat collar;* 他上衣领上的两根金黄色头发; (archaic) (*pl*, in collective sense): (古)(复数, 作集合之义)一人的全部头发: *It will bring down my grey ~s in sorrow to the grave,* cause me, who am old, to die of sorrow. 这将使我在老年忧心至死. *get sb by the 'short ~s,* (sl) have him at one's mercy; get complete control of him. (俚)支配某人; 完全操纵某人. *keep your '~ on,* (sl) keep cool; don't lose your temper. (俚)保持镇静; 勿发脾气. *let one's '~ down,* (of a woman) remove the pins and allow the *~* to fall over the shoulders; (fig) relax after a period of being formal. (指女子)拿下发针使发垂落散肩头, (喻)经过一段拘谨后使身心放松一下. *lose one's ~,* (a) become bald. 秃头. (b) lose one's temper. 发脾气. *make one's ~ stand on end,* fill one with fright or horror. 使之毛发悚然. *put one's '~ up,* arrange it so that it is rolled up on one's head. 束发; 结鬓. *split ~s,* make or pretend to see differences of meaning, distinctions, etc. so small as to be unimportant. 作无谓的细微的分析. Hence, 由此产生, *'~-splitting n* [U] acting in this way. 作无谓的细微的分析. *tear one's ~,* show great sorrow or vexation. 表示极度悲伤或烦恼. *not turn a ~,* give no sign of being troubled. 毫不受干扰; 若无其事不为所动. *to a ~,* (of describing sth) exactly. (描写事物)精确地. **2** (compounds) (复合词) *'~'s* breadth *n* very small distance: 极短的距离; 一发之距: *escape by a ~'s-breadth; have a ~-breadth escape,* a very narrow one. 间不容发; 幸免于难. *'~-brush n* a toilet brush for the *~.* 发刷. ⇨ the illus at **brush**. 参看 brush 之插图. *'~-cloth n* cloth made of a mixture of fabric and animal's *~* for various purposes. 毛与其它织物组成之布(做各种用途). *'~-cut n* act or style of cutting the *~* (by a barber or dresser). 理发; 做头发; 发型; 发式. *'~-do n* (colloq) haircut. (口)理发; 做头发; 发型. *'~-dresser n* person who dresses and cuts *~.* 理发师; 美容师. ⇨ **barber.** *'~-dye n* dye for the *~.* 染发剂. *'~-line n* area where the roots of *~* join the forehead; width of a *~*; (attrib) very narrow: 额部生发部分之轮廓; 一发之幅(形容语)极窄的: *a ~ line space/fracture.* 极窄的空间(细微的裂缝). *'~-net n* net for keeping the *~* in place. 发网. *'~-oil n* oil for dressing the *~.* 发油. *'~-piece n* tress of false *~.* 假发. *'~-pin n* (woman's) pin for keeping the *~* in place. (女子的)发夹. *'~pin 'bend n* sharp bend on a road, esp on a steep road, as that the road doubles back. 道路(尤指陡路)之 U 字形急弯. *'~-raising adj* terrifying. 恐怖的; 令人毛发悚然的. *'~-shirt n* shirt made of *~*cloth, uncomfortable to wear, for ascetics. 毛布做的衬衣(穿在身上不舒适, 为苦行者所用). *'~-slide n* metal clip for keeping *~* tidily in place. 发夹. *'~-spring n* very delicate spring in a watch, controlling the balance-wheel. 表内的游丝(控制平衡轮之极细的弹簧). *'~-style n* style of haircut. 发型. *'~-stylist n '~-dresser.* 理发师; 美容师. *'~-trigger,* one that fires a gun, etc at the slightest pressure. (枪之)微力扳机. *~-less adj* without *~*; bald.

无毛的; 无发的; 秃头的. *'~-like adj ~y adj* (-ier, -iest) of or like *~*; covered with *~*: 毛的; 毛状的; 长有毛的: *a ~y chest.* 长有毛的胸部. *~i·ness n*

hairpin bends

hake /heik; hek/ *n* (*pl* unchanged) fish of the cod family, used as food. (复数不变)鳕鱼类(用作食物).

hal·berd /'hælbəd; 'hælbəd/ *n* weapon used in the Middle Ages, a combined spear and battle-axe on a long handle. 戟(中古一种枪钺两用的长柄武器). **hal·ber·dier** /,hælbə'dɪə(r); ,hælbə'dɪr/ *n* soldier armed with a *~.* 戟兵.

hal·cyon /'hælsɪən; 'hælsɪən/ *adj* calm and peaceful: 平静的; 太平的: *~ days/weather.* 太平的日子(平静的天气).

hale /heil; hel/ *adj* (rare except in) (通常指老年人)(rare except in) 康健的(除下列用法外极为少用) *~ and hearty,* strong and healthy. 矍铄的; 健壮的.

half /hɑːf US: hæf; hæf/ *n* (*pl* halves /hɑːvz US: hævz; hævz/) *adj, adv* **1** one of two equal or corresponding parts into which a thing is divided: 一半; 半个: *The ~ of 6 is 3/H~ of 6 is 3.* 六的一半是三. *Two halves make a whole.* 两个一半成为整个. *Two pounds and a ~/Two and a ~ pounds.* 两磅半. *H~ of the fruit is bad.* 水果的一半坏了. *H~ (of) the plums are bad.* 半数的李子坏了. *I want ~ as much again,* one and a ~ the amount. 我要一倍半. *Cut it in ~/into halves.* 把它切成两半. *(do sth) by halves,* incompletely, imperfectly. (做某事)不完全地; 不完善地. *go halves (with sb) (in sth),* share equally. (与人)平分(某事物). *too clever, etc by ~,* far too clever, etc. 过于聪明等. *one's ~,* (colloq) one's wife, husband, etc. (口)妻子,丈夫等. **2** (as *adv*) (作副词) to the extent of a *~*; to a considerable degree; nearly: 一半地; 相当程度地. 几乎: *meat that is only ~ cooked;* 半熟的肉; *~-cooked cabbage;* 半熟的包心菜; *not ~* (= not nearly) *long enough;* 根本就不够长; *~ dead,* (colloq) tired out, exhausted; (口)筋疲力竭的; *not ~ bad,* (sl) not at all bad; quite good. (俚)相当好. *not ~,* (sl) to the greatest possible extent: (俚)极端地: *He didn't ~ swear,* He swore very violently. 他破口大骂. '*Was she annoyed?' 'Not ~!'* (ie she was intensely annoyed). '她受到烦扰吗?' '被烦扰得很厉害!' **3** (in compounds) (用于复合词中) *a* '*crown,* **a** ,~'crown *n* (before 1971) coin or amount of 2½ shillings (12½p). (1971 以前) 2½先令 (12½便士). *~ a 'dozen n* six. 半打; 六个. *~ and ~ n* what is ~ one thing and ~ the other, eg a mixture of beer and lemonade. 两者各半混成之物(例如啤酒与柠檬水混成之饮料). *'~-back n* (in football/hockey, etc) (position of) player (defender) between the forwards and the backs. (足球, 曲棍球等) 中卫(的位置). *,~-'baked adj* (colloq) half-witted; crude and inexperienced: (口)愚笨的; 粗鲁而又无经验的: *a ~-baked young man;* 粗鲁而又缺乏经验的青年; foolish; of poor quality: 愚蠢的; 质劣的: *~-baked ideas.* 愚蠢的思想. *'~-blood n* (relationship of a) person having one parent in common with another. 同父异母或同母异父的兄弟或姊妹; 此种血统关系. *'~-breed n* **(a)** person with parents of different races. 混血儿. **(b)** offspring of two animals or plants of different species. 动植物的杂种; 混合种. *'~-brother n* brother by one parent only. 同父异母或同母异父的兄弟. *'~-caste n ~-breed person. 混血儿. *'~-'cock n* position of the hammer of a gun when pulled *~*-way back. 枪机半击发

之位置。 go off at ~ cock, (fig) act too soon and fail. (喻)行动过早而失败。 ,~·'hardy adj (of plants) requiring protection from frost but otherwise suitable for growing in the open. (指植物)适于户外生长但不耐霜雪的。 ,~·'hearted adj done with, showing, little interest or enthusiasm: 无兴趣的;不热心的; a ~-hearted attempt. 不热心的尝试。 Hence, 由此产生, ,~·'heartedly adv, ~·'holiday n day of which ~ (usu the afternoon) is free from work or duty. 半日(通常是半天)休假。 ,~ an 'hour, a ,~·'hour nn period of 30 minutes. 半小时; 三十分钟。 ,~·'hourly adj, adv done, occurring every 30 minutes: 每半小时(做成或发生)的; 每半小时地: a ~-hourly bus service. 每半小时一班的公共汽车。 ,~·'length adj (of a portrait) of the upper ~ of a person. (指画像)半身的。 at ,~·'mast, (of a flag) at the position, near the middle of a mast, to indicate mourning: (指旗)下半旗(在旗杆中部的位置以表示哀悼): Flags were at ~-mast everywhere on the day of the President's funeral. 总统安葬之日一律下半旗。 ,~·'pay n [U] reduced pay given to sb when not fully employed but not yet retired: 半薪(半退休者所领的核减过的薪水): placed on ~-pay. 领半薪。 ~penny /'heɪpnɪ US: 'hæfpenɪ; 'hepnɪ/ n British coin worth ~ a penny (1/2 d before 1971, 1/2 p now). 英国半便士铜币。 ~·'penny-worth /'heɪpnɪwз:θ US: hæf'penɪwзθ; 'hepenɪ,wзθ/, ha'p'orth /'heɪpəθ; 'hepəθ/ n as much as 1/2 d would buy before 1971; now chiefly fig. 值半便士之价。 ⇨ App 5. 参见附录五。 ,~·'price adv at ~ the usual price: 以半价: Children admitted ~-price. 儿童入场半价收费。 ,~-'seas-'over prd adj (colloq) ~ drunk. (口)半醉的。 '~-sister n sister by one parent only. 同父异母或同母异父的姊妹。 ,~·'size adj ~ the usual or regular size. 为通常大小之一半的。 ,~·'timbered adj (of a building) having walls of a wooden framework filled in with brick, stone or plaster. (指建筑物)半露木的(墙壁为木架加填石或灰泥筑成的)。 ,~·'time n [U] (a) work and pay for ~ the usual time: 半工半薪: Owing to the business depression the workers are on ~-time this month. 由于商业萧条,工人们本月半工半薪。 (b) the interval between the two halves of a game of football, etc: (足球等比赛中)上半场与下半场间的休息时间: The score at ~-time was 2—2. 上半场结束时的比分为二比二。 ~-tone n black and white photograph reproduced on paper, eg as an illustration in a book. (印在纸上做出中间调的)黑白图片。 ~·'track n troop-carrying vehicle with tracks(5) on both sides at the rear and wheels at the front. 半履带军车。 Hence, 由此产生, ,~·'tracked adj '~-truth n statement that conveys only a part of the truth. 部分真实的陈述。 ,~·'way adj (a) situated at an equal distance from two places. 位于两地中途的。 (b) going ~ the way; not thorough: 至中途的;不彻底的: In an emergency ~-way measures are usually unsatisfactory. 在紧急时,不彻底的措施通常是不能令人满意的。 □ adv to or at ~ the distance: 至半途; 中途地: meet a person ~-way, be ready to make a compromise. 愿意跟某人妥协;迁就某人。 ,~·'witted adj weak-minded. 鲁钝的。 Hence, 由此产生, '~-wit n ~-witted person. 鲁钝的人。 ,~·'yearly adj, adv (done, occurring) every ~ year. 每半年(完成或发生的); 每半年地。

hali·but /'hælɪbət; 'hæləbət/ n (pl unchanged) large, flat sea-fish used as food. (复数不变)星蝶; 大比目鱼。

hali·tosis /,hælɪ'təʊsɪs; ,hæle'tosɪs/ n [U] badsmelling breath. 口臭。

hall /hɔ:l; hol/ n 1 (building with) large room for meetings, concerts, public business, etc: 厅; 堂; 会堂; 礼堂: the Town/City H~; 市政厅; the County H~; 州会堂; the H~ of Justice; 审判厅; the Festival H~, for concerts, in London; (伦敦之)音乐厅; 'dance-~s. 舞厅。 2 [U] (in colleges at English universities) large room for meals: (英国大学各学院的)餐厅: dine in ~. 在餐厅

进餐。 3 building for university students: 供大学生使用之建筑物: a ~ of residence. 大学的宿舍。 4 (in England) large country house, usu one that belongs to the chief landowner in the district. (英国)大地主的府第。 5 passage, space, into which the main entrance or front door of a building opens: 正门厅廊; 门厅; 穿堂: Leave your hat and coat in the ~. 把你的帽子和大衣放在门厅里。 '~-stand n piece of furniture for hats, coats, umbrellas, etc. 衣帽架(挂衣帽,伞等的家具)。 6 building of a guild: 公会会馆: Saddlers' H~. 马具公会会馆。

hal·le·lu·jah /,hælɪ'lu:jə; ,hæle'lujə/ n, int praise to God. 哈利路亚(赞美上帝之语)。

hal·liard /'hæljəd; 'hæljəd/ n = halyard.

hall·mark /'hɔ:lmɑ:k; 'hɔl,mɑrk/ n mark used for marking the standard of gold and silver in articles (as a guarantee of quality); (fig) distinguishing characteristic (usu of excellence). 证明金银器纯度的印记; 盖印(证明纯度);(喻)特殊优之性质。 □ vt stamp a ~ on. 在…上压印纯度证明印记。

hallo /hə'ləʊ; hə'lo/ int = hullo.

hal·loo /hə'lu:; hə'lu/ int, n cry to urge on hounds; shout to attract attention. 唤使猎犬的呼声; 引人注意的喊叫。 □ vi shout 'H~'!, esp to hounds. 呼叫(尤指对猎犬)。

hal·low[1] /'hæləʊ; 'hælo/ vt [VP6A] (usu passive) make holy; regard as holy: (通常用被动语态)使神圣; 视为神圣: ground ~ed by sacred memories. 因宗教上之纪念而视为神圣的土地。

hal·low[2] /'hæləʊ; 'hælo/ n (only in) (仅用于) **All H~'s Day,** ⇨ hall(6).

Hal·low·e·en /,hæləʊ'i:n; ,hælo'in/ n 31 Oct, eve of All Saints' Day or All Hallows' Day. 万圣节之前夕(十月三十一日)。

hal·luci·na·tion /hə,lu:sɪ'neɪʃn; hə,lusn'eʃən/ n [C, U] (instance of) seeming to see sth not present, sth imagined: 幻觉; 幻觉中的事物: Drunken men are sometimes subject to ~s. 酒醉者有时易生幻觉。 **hall·uci·na·tory** /hə'lu:sɪnətrɪ US: -tɔ:rɪ; hə'lusnə,torɪ/, **hal·luci·no·genic** /hə,lu:sɪnə'dʒenɪk; hə,lusnə'dʒenɪk/ adjj (of drugs) inducing ~. (指药物)产生幻觉的。

halma /'hælmə; 'hælmə/ n [U] game played on a board of 256 squares where pieces are moved from one corner to the other. 一种跳棋(棋盘有256格)。

halo /'heɪləʊ; 'helo/ n (pl ~es, ~s -ləʊz; -loz/) circle of light round the sun or moon or (in paintings) round or above the heads of Christ or sacred figures. 晕(环绕着日月的光轮); 光圈; (绘于耶稣或神像头上之)光环。

halt[1] /hɔ:lt; hɔlt/ n 1 (chiefly mil, of soldiers) (主要为军语, 指士兵) **call a ~ (to),** make a short stop on a march or journey: (行进中)下令停止前进: The officer called a ~. 军官下令停止前进。 It's time to call a ~ to vandalism, (fig) end it. (喻)故意破坏天然环境的行为应该予以制止了。 2 (more general use) **come to a ~,** make a stop or pause: (较普通用法)停止: The train came to a ~. 火车停了。 ⇨ grind(6). 3 stopping-place (smaller than a station) on a railway-line, where trains stop for a short time only. 火车短暂停留的小站。 □ vi, vt 1 [VP2A] (as a mil command) stop marching; come to a ~. 停(队伍行进); 停止行进。 2 [VP6A] bring to a ~: 使停止行进: The officer ~ed his troops for a rest. 军官令军队停止行进,休息一下。

halt[2] /hɔ:lt; hɔlt/ vi [VP2A, C] hesitate; walk in a hesitating way: 犹豫; 踌躇: ~ between two opinions; 踌躇于两个意见之间; in a ~ing voice. 嗫嚅地说。 3 (archaic) lame. (古)跛的: the ~ and the blind. 跛者与盲者。 ~·ing·ly adv in a ~ing way. 犹豫地; 踌躇地。

hal·ter /'hɔ:ltə(r); 'hɔltə/ n 1 rope or leather strap put round a horse's head (for leading or fastening the horse). 缰绳; 马缰。 2 rope used for hanging a person.

绞刑用之绳索。

halve /hɑːv US: hæv; hævz/ vt [VP6A] **1** divide into two equal parts: 二等分；分成两半: ~ an apple. 将一苹果分成两半。 **2** lessen by one half: 减半: The newest planes have ~d the time needed for crossing the Atlantic. 最新式的飞机使横越大西洋所需的时间减少了一半。

halves /hɑːvz US: hævz; hævz/ pl of half.

hal·yard /ˈhæljəd; ˈhæljəd/ n rope for raising or lowering a sail or flag. 帆或旗的升降索。

ham /hæm; hæm/ n **1** [C] upper part of a pig's leg, salted and dried or smoked: 火腿: hams hanging on hooks; 挂在钩上的火腿; [U] this as meat: 火腿肉: a slice of ham; 一片火腿; a ham sandwich. 火腿三明治。 **2** [C] (chiefly used of animals) back of the thigh, thigh and buttock. (主要指动物)大腿的后部；大腿及臀部。 **3** (sl) poor actor or performer; amateur who sends and receives radio messages: (俚)拙劣的演员；无线电收发报业余爱好者: a radio ham; 无线电收发报业余爱好者; (attrib) (用作定语) ham actors/acting/radio. 拙劣的演员(拙劣的演出；业余爱好者的用的无线电收发报机)。 ,ham-'handed/-'fisted adj clumsy in using the hands. 手笨的。 □ vt, vi (-mm-) [VP2A, 6A, 15B] ham (up), (colloq) act in a deliberately artificial, exaggerated way. (口)作过火之表演。

hama·dryad /ˌhæməˈdraɪəd; ˌhæməˈdraɪəd/ n nymph living and dying with the tree she inhabited; poisonous Indian snake. 树神(与其所栖守的树共存亡的女神)；印度的一种毒蛇。

ham·burger /ˈhæmbɜːgə(r); ˈhæmbɜːgə/ n **1** ground or chopped beef made into round flat cakes and fried. 汉堡包；汉堡牛排；牛肉饼(牛肉绞碎煎成的圆饼)。 **2** sandwich or bread roll filled with this. 汉堡牛排三明治；汉堡包；牛肉饼三明治。

ham·let /ˈhæmlɪt; ˈhæmlɪt/ n group of houses in the country; small village, esp one without a church. 乡间的一片房屋；小村(尤指无教堂者)。

ham·mer /ˈhæmə(r); ˈhæmə/ n **1** tool with a heavy metal head used for breaking things, driving in nails, etc. 锤；榔头。⇨ the illus at **tool**. 参看 tool 之插图。 be/go at it ~ and tongs, fight, argue, with great energy and noise. 猛烈喧腾地打斗或争论。 throwing the ~, athletic competition in which a heavy long-handled ~ is thrown as far as possible. 掷锤球(一种运动比赛，掷一长柄重锤，掷得越远越好)。 **2** (in a piano, etc) one of the ~-like parts that strike the strings. (钢琴等之)琴槌。 **3** part of the firing device of a gun that strikes and explodes the charge. (枪之)击铁。 **4** wooden mallet used by an auctioneer. (拍卖者所用的)木槌。 be/come under the ~, be sold by auction. 被拍卖。 **5** (anat) bone in the ear. 锤副(耳之槌骨)。⇨ the illus at **ear**. 参看 ear 之插图。 □ vt, vi **1** [VP6A, 22, 15B, 2A, C, 3A] ~ (in/out/down); ~ (at), strike or beat with a ~, or as if with a ~; 锤打；似用锤般敲击打: ~ nails into wood; 将钉子锤进木头; ~ down the lid of a box, fasten it down by ~ing; 用锤将盒盖钉上; ~ in a nail/~ a nail in; 用锤敲进一钉; ~ a piece of metal flat; 将一片金属锤平; ~ sth out, make it flat or smooth by ~ing; 锤平某物; ~ at the door, eg with a stick, one's fists; 敲打门(例如用杖或拳); ~ at the keys, play the piano loudly, without feeling. (无感情地)猛弹钢琴。 **2** (fig) (喻) [VP15B] ~ out, produce by hard work: 辛勤做成: ~ out a scheme; 苦心想出一计划; [VP3A] ~ at, work hard at: 辛勤工作: ~ away at a problem/a solution/a compromise; 苦研一问题(解答，折衷之道)；[VP6A] force: 强迫: ~ an idea into sb's head. 将一观念灌入某人的头脑中。 **3** (colloq) inflict heavy defeats on (sb) in war or in games. (口)使(某人)在战争或比赛中惨败。

ham·mock /ˈhæmək; ˈhæmək/ n hanging bed of canvas or rope network, eg as used by sailors, or in gardens. 吊床(例如船员或花园中所用者)。

ham·per¹ /ˈhæmpə(r); ˈhæmpə/ n packing-case or basket with a lid, esp one used for sending food: 有盖的盒或篮(尤指送食物所用者): a Christmas ~, one sent as a present, with food, wine, etc. 装有食物、酒等做为圣诞礼物的盒或篮。

ham·per² /ˈhæmpə(r); ˈhæmpə/ vt [VP6A] hinder; prevent free movement or activity: 阻碍；使不能任意行动: ~ed by a heavy overcoat. 受一件厚大衣的妨碍。

ham·ster /ˈhæmstə(r); ˈhæmstə/ n rodent like a large rat, kept by children as a pet. 仓鼠(一种似大鼠的啮齿动物，儿童养做玩物)。

ham·string /ˈhæmstrɪŋ; ˈhæmstrɪŋ/ vt (pt, pp ~ed or **hamstrung** /ˈhæmstrʌŋ; ˈhæmstrʌŋ/) [VP6A] cripple (a person or animal) by cutting the tendon(s) at the back of the knee(s); (fig) destroy the power or efficiency of. 割断腘筋使(人或动物)残废；(喻)摧毁…之力量或效能。

hand¹ /hænd; hænd/ n **1** part of the human arm beyond the wrist: 手: with his ~s in his pockets. 他的手放在口袋中。⇨ the illus at **arm**. 参看 arm 之插图。 at ~, near; within reach: 在近处；在手边；即将到来: He lives close at ~, quite near. 他住在近处。 The examinations are at ~. 考试即将举行了。 at sb's ~s, from sb: 出自某人之手: I did not expect such unkind treatment at your ~s. 我未料到你会如此无情。 bind sb ~ and foot, (lit, fig) make him completely helpless. (字面，喻)把某人的手脚全绑起来；使某人完全无助。 serve/wait on sb ~ and foot, attend to his every wish; perform every sort of service for him. 竭力侍候；忠心侍奉。 by ~, (a) without the use of machinery: 手工做的: Are your socks knitted by ~/~-knitted or machine-made? 你的袜子是手工织的还是机器织的? **(b)** without the use of the post office: 专人送的: The note was delivered by ~, by a messenger. 这短简是专人送来的。 bring up a baby/a calf, etc by ~, rear it by feeding from a bottle: 以奶瓶喂养婴儿、小牛等: The lamb had to be brought up by ~. 这小羊必须以奶瓶喂养。 eat/feed out of one's ~, (eg of a bird) be quite tame. (指鸟等)十分驯服。 **(b)** (fig) be ready to obey without question. (喻)十分顺从。 from ~ to ~, directly, from one person to another: 用手传递；自甲手到乙手: Buckets of water were passed from ~ to ~ to put the fire out. 一桶桶的水用手传递着去救火。 fight ~ to ~, at close quarters. 肉搏；短兵相接。Hence, 由此产生，~-to-~ fighting. 肉搏战。 give/lend (sb) a ~ (with sth), help with, take a part in, doing sth: 帮助；参与: Give (me) a ~ with the washing-up, please. 请帮我洗餐具。 give one's ~ on a bargain, take sb's ~ and clasp it to seal the bargain. 与某人握手表示成交。 be in glove (with sth). ⇨ **glove**. have one's ~s full, have all the work one can do; be fully occupied. 忙碌。 have/get the upper ~ (of sb), ⇨ **upper**. have a free ~; give/allow sb a free ~, ⇨ **free¹**(3). ~ in ~, holding ~s; together: 手牵手；一起: They walked away ~ in ~. 他们携手离去。 (fig) (喻) War and misery go ~ in ~. 苦难与战争形影不离。 H~s off! Don't touch or interfere! 不许摸(干涉)! H~s up! Put your ~s up! Surrender! 举起手来! 投降! ~ over ~, with each ~ used alternately (as when climbing, etc); (fig) rapidly and steadily. 双手交互地(如攀登时)；(喻)迅速而稳定地。 in ~, (a) in reserve, available for use: 保有；可用: I still have some money in ~. 我手头还有些钱。 Cash in ~, £27.25. 手头现金，二十七英镑二十五便士。 **(b)** receiving attention; in course of completion: 在处理或从事中: The work is in ~ and will be finished by the end of the month. 这工作在进行中，本月底将完成。 We have the situation well in ~, are dealing with it satisfactorily. 我们充分掌握了局势。 in ~, being looked after or managed by. 由…的照顾中；由…管理。 in good ~s, being well cared for. 在妥为照顾中。 lay (one's) ~s on sth/sb, ⇨ **lay¹**(2). lend a ~,

⇨ give a ~, above. 参看上列之 give a ~. **not lift a ~; not do a ~'s turn,** make not the least attempt to help. 毫不帮助. **lift / raise a ~ / one's ~ against sb,** threaten, attack him. 威胁某人; 打击某人. **live from ~ to mouth,** precariously, spending money as soon as it is received. 赚一个用一个; 生活不稳定. Hence, 由此产生, **~-to-mouth existence.** 做一日吃一日的生活. **(get sth) off one's ~s,** taken from one's responsibility: 卸除责任: *I'd be glad to get it off my ~s,* to rid myself of responsibility for it. 我愿意摆脱对此事的责任. **on ~,** available: 可用; 握有: *We have some new woollen goods on ~,* in our shop, warehouse, etc. 我们现有一些新的毛货(在商店, 仓库等中). **on one's ~,** resting on one as a responsibility: 做为一项责任而仰赖着某人; 由某人负责: *I have an empty house on my ~s,* one for which I want to find a buyer or tenant. 我有一所空房屋待来找出租. *Time hangs heavy on his ~s,* seems burdensome, passes slowly. 时间慢得使他难以度过. **out of ~, (a)** out of control; undisciplined: 难控制的; 无纪律; 无法约束: *The football fans have got quite out of ~.* 足球迷们变得难以控制了. **(b)** at once, without hesitation: 即刻; 无犹豫地: *The situation needs to be dealt with out of ~.* 这情势须要即刻处理. **shake ~s with sb; shake sb's ~,** grasp his ~ as a greeting, or to express agreement, etc. 与某人握手. **take a ~ (in),** help, play a part (in sth). 帮助; 参与. **take sth / sb in ~,** take charge of; undertake to control or manage. 负责照料; 管理. **be to ~,** (comm style for) be received: (商业文体用语)收到: *Your letter is to ~,* has reached me and is receiving attention. 大函敬悉. **wash one's ~s of,** say that one will no longer be responsible for. 声称不再对某事负责; 洗手不干. **win ~s down,** win easily. 轻易地赢得. **(rule) with a heavy ~,** oppressively; severely. 压制地; 严格地(统治). **win a lady's ~,** win her consent to marriage. 获某女子同意结婚. **2 (pl)** power; possession; responsibility. (复)掌握; 拥有; 责任. *in sb's hands: The property is no longer in my ~s,* is no longer mine, or my responsibility. 这财产已非我所有(我所管). *The matter is in your ~s,* You must decide how to deal with it. 这事你必须处理. *He's still in the ~s of the money-lenders.* 他仍受高利贷者的剥削. **change ~s,** pass to another owner: 易手; 易主: *The property has changed ~s recently,* has been sold. 这财产最近已易主. **3 (sing only)** influence or agency: (仅用单数)势力; 作用: *The ~ of an enemy has been at work here.* 敌人已在此处活动. **4 (sing only)** person from whom news, etc comes. (仅用单数)提供消息等的人. **(only in)** (仅用于) **at first ~,** directly, without any intermediary: 直接地: *I heard / learnt the news at first ~.* 我直接听到(得悉)这消息. **at second ~,** indirectly. 间接地. **5 (sing only)** skill in using one's ~s: (仅用单数)技巧: *She has a light ~ at pastry,* makes it with skill. 她做点心做得心灵手巧. *Why don't you try your ~ at editing the staff magazine,* see whether you have the skill needed? 你为何不去尝试一下编辑职员刊物呢? **get one's ~ in,** acquire or return to one's usual degree of skill by practice. 经练习而获得或恢复平时的技术. **keep one's '~ in,** practise a skill, in order to retain it: 借练习保持技术: *practise the piano every day to keep one's ~ in.* 每天练钢琴以保持熟练. **6 [C]** person who does what is indicated by the context; performer: 做某事的人(所做之事由上下文表示): *a good ~ at fencing,* a good fencer. 剑术家, *He's an old ~ at this sort of work,* has long experience of it. 他做这种工作很有经验. *He's an old ~ at parliamentary ~,* a person with long experience of parliamentary duties. 他是精通议会事物的人. **7** workman, eg in a factory or dockyard; member of a ship's crew: (工厂或船坞等)工人; 船员: *The factory has taken on 200 extra ~s.* 工厂额外雇用了二百名工人. *All ~s on deck!* All seamen are needed on deck! 所有船员都要报告上来! **8** turn; share in an activity. 轮值; 活动中的一份. **have a ~ (in sth),** have a share: 参与(某事): *Let me have a ~ now.* 让我参

加一份. *Do you think he had a ~ in it,* was involved? 你认为他参与了此事吗? **9 [C]** pointer or indicator on the dial of a watch, clock or other instrument: 钟面或表面等上之针: *the 'hour / 'minute / 'second ~ of a watch.* 表的时(分, 秒)针. **10** position or direction (to right or left). 方面; 方向. **on every / either ~; on all ~s,** to or from all quarters. 向四面八方; 从四面八方. **on the one ~ ... on the other ~,** used to indicate contrasted points of view, arguments, etc. 一方面…, 另一方面…. **11 (sing only)** handwriting: (仅用单数)笔迹; 书法: *He writes a good / legible ~.* 他的书法很好(写得很清楚). **12 (formal)** signature: (正式用语)签名: *set one's ~ to a document.* 在一文件上签名. *Given under my ~ and seal,* authenticated by my signature and seal. 由我的签名及印鉴证明. **13** (card games, eg bridge)(桥牌等牌戏) **(a)** (number of) cards dealt to, held by, a player at one time. 一手牌; 手中牌. **have a good / bad / poor ~,** good / bad, etc cards. 拿到一手好(坏)牌. **play a good / bad ~,** play well / badly. 玩得好(差). **take a ~ at sth,** join in and play it. 参加打牌. **play into sb's ~s,** do sth that is to his advantage. 上某人的当; 让某人占便宜. **(b)** player at cards: 牌手; 玩牌者: *We only have three players—we need a fourth ~.* 我们只有三个牌手, 我们需要第四位. **(c)** one round in a game of cards: 牌戏中之一局: *Let's play one more ~, shall we?* 我们再来一局如何? **14 [C]** unit of measurement, about four inches (10.16 cm), the breadth of the ~, used for the height of a horse (from the ground to the top of the shoulder). 一手之宽(约为四英寸或10.16厘米, 用以量马从地面到肩头的高度). **15 (colloq)** applause by clapping. (口)拍手喝彩. **give sb / get a good ~,** a lot of applause. 对某人(获得)热烈拍手喝彩. **16** (compounds) (复合词) **'~-bag** n woman's bag for money, keys, handkerchief, etc. (US ≃ purse.) 女用手提包. **'~-barrow** n light two-wheeled barrow. 轻便双轮手推车. **'~-bill** n printed advertisement or announcement distributed by ~. 传单. **'~-book** n small book giving useful facts; guide-book. 手册; 指南. **'~-brake** n auxiliary brake in a motor-vehicle, used when the vehicle is stationary. 手煞车. **'~-cart** n small cart pushed or pulled by ~. 手车; 手推车. **'~-clap** n clapping: 拍手: *a slow ~clap,* slow rhythmical clapping to show impatience. 缓慢而有节奏的拍手(喝倒彩). **'~-cuff** n (usu pl) one of a pair of metal rings joined by a chain, fastened round a prisoner's wrists. (通常用复数)手铐. □ *vt* put ~cuffs on. 加手铐于. **-ful /-ful/, -ful/** n (pl ~**fuls**) **1** as much or as many as can be hold in one ~. 一握之量; 一把. **2** small number: 少数: *Only a ~ful of people came to the meeting.* 只有少数人到会. **3 (colloq)** person or animal difficult to control: (口)难控制的人或动物: *That young boy of hers is quite a ~ful,* is lively and unruly. 她那个小儿子极难管束. **'~-grenade** n grenade thrown by hand. 手榴弹. **hold** n (esp) anything a climber may grip, eg on a rock face. (尤指)攀登者可抓紧之物(如岩石表面上者). **'~-luggage** n luggage light enough to be carried by hand. 手提的轻便行李. **~-made** adj made by ~. 手工制的(与machine-made相对). with machine-made. **'~-maid** n (archaic) woman servant or attendant. (古)女仆; 侍女. **'~-me-down** n sth passed on (esp sth used and discarded, eg clothes) to another. 给予别人的旧东西(例如旧衣服). **'~-organ** n portable barrel-organ with a crank turned by ~. 手摇风琴. **'~-picked** adj carefully selected. 精选的; 仔细挑选的. **'~-rail** n railing along the edge of a staircase, etc. 栏杆; 扶手. **'~-saw** n saw used with one hand only. 手锯. **'~-shake** n greeting given by grasping a person's ~ with one's own. 握手. **'~-stand** n acrobatic feat of supporting oneself in an upright position on the ~s: 以手着地倒立: *do a ~stand.* 竖蜻蜓. **'~-work** n [U] work done by ~, not by machinery. 手工. **'~-writing** n [U] (person's style of) writing by ~: 笔

迹; 书法: *Whose ~ writing is this?* 这是谁的笔迹? ,**off-'~** *adj* ⇨ **off-hand.**

hand² /hænd/ *vt* [VP12A, 13A, 15A, B] give or pass (to sb); help with the ~(s): 交给; 传递; 用手帮助: *Please ~ me that book.* 请把那本书递给我. *He ~ed the book to the man at his side.* 他把书递给他旁边的那个人. *He ~ed (= helped) his wife out of the railway carriage.* 他扶他的太太下火车. **~ sth down (to sb),** pass by tradition, inheritance, etc: 传递: *We cannot always observe the traditions ~ed down to us from the past.* 我们不能永远遵守过去传下来的传统. **~ sth on (to sb),** send, give, to another: 传给: *Please ~ on the magazine to your friends.* 请将这杂志传给你的朋友们看. **~ sth out (to sb),** distribute; (colloq) give as alms. 分配; (口) 施舍. Hence, 由此产生, **'~-out (a)** prepared statement given, eg by a politician, to newspaper men; leaflet, etc, distributed free of charge. (政治人物等)交给记者的备妥的声明; (免费的)印刷品, 传单等. **(b)** sth given as alms, eg food or money to a beggar at the door. 施舍的东西(例如给予门口乞丐的食物或金钱). **~ sth over (to sb),** deliver a person to authority: 将某人交给当局: *~ sb over to the police.* 将某人交给警局. **~ sth over (to sb),** transfer: 交给他人: *You can't play with my gun—hand it over at once.* 你不能玩弄我的枪, 把它立刻交给我. *I've ~ed over my place on the committee.* 我已将我在委员会中的职位移交他人. **~ it to sb,** (colloq) give him the credit that is his due: (口)给予某人应得之荣誉; 归功于某人: *He's done well! You've got to ~ it to him.* 他做得好! 你必须归功于他.

handi·cap /'hændɪkæp; 'hændɪ,kæp/ *n* [C] **1** (competition, race, in which there is a) disadvantage imposed on a competitor to make the chances of success more nearly equal for all, eg a weight to be carried by a horse. (竞赛时为使得胜机会近乎相等)给与优者的不利条件(例如赛马时使一马负由或与他马比赛); 使用此种障碍的比赛; 让分比赛. **2** anything likely to lessen one's chance of success: 障碍; 阻碍: *Poor eyesight is a ~ to a student.* 视力不良是学生的障碍. □ *vt* **(-pp-)** [VP6A] give or be a ~ to: 加障碍于; 为...之障碍: *~ped by ill health;* 受健康不良的障碍; *~ped children,* suffering from some disability. 残疾儿童.

handi·craft /'hændɪkrɑːft US: -kræft; 'hændɪ,kræft/ *n* [C] art or craft needing skill with the hands, eg needlework, pottery, woodwork, weaving. 手工; 手工艺(例如缝纫, 制陶, 木工, 纺织).

handi·work /'hændɪwɜːk; 'hændɪ,wɝk/ *n* [U] work done, [C] thing made, by the hands; sth done by a named person: 手工; 手工制品; 某人所做之事物: *That's some of Smith's ~.* 那是史密斯所做的一些手工品.

hand·ker·chief /'hæŋkətʃɪf; 'hæŋkətʃɪf/ *n* square piece of cotton, silk, linen, etc carried in the pocket or handbag, for blowing the nose into or wiping the face; similar square worn for ornament, eg round the neck. 手帕; 手绢; 装饰用的方巾(例如围巾).

handle /'hændl; 'hændl/ *n* **1** part of a tool, cup, bucket, door, drawer, etc by which it may be held in the hand. (工具, 杯, 桶, 门, 抽屉等之)柄; 把手; 提手. **'~·bar** *n* (usu *pl*) bar with a ~ at each end, for steering a bicycle, etc. (通常作复数)脚踏车等的把手. ⇨ the illus at **bicycle.** 参看 bicycle 之插图. **fly off the ~,** (colloq) get into a rage and lose self-control. (口)十分激怒; 大怒. **give a ~ (to sb) (against sb),** provide an excuse or pretext that may be taken advantage of and used: 予以可乘之隙; 予以把柄: *Your indiscreet behaviour may give your enemies a ~ against you.* 你的不慎重的行为会给你的敌人可乘的机会. **2** (sl) title: (俚)头衔: *have a ~ to one's name,* have, eg 'Sir' or 'Lord' as part of it. 姓名前有一头衔(例如 Sir, Lord 等). □ *vt* [VP6A] **1** touch with, take up in, the hands: 用手触摸; 用手拿起: *Gelignite is dangerous stuff*

to ~. 爆炸胶是不可随便触摸的危险之物. *Wash your hands before you ~ my books, please.* 在你拿我的书之前, 请你先洗手. **2** manage; deal with; control (men): 管理; 处理; 控制(人): *An officer must know how to ~ men.* 一个军官必须知道如何对待士兵. *Can you ~ the situation, deal with it?* 你能处理这情况吗? **3** treat; behave towards: 对待; 对付: *The speaker was roughly ~d by the crowd.* 那演说者受到了群众的侮辱. **4** (comm) buy and sell: (商) 买卖; 经销: *This shop does not ~ imported goods.* 这家商店不经销进口货. **han·dler** /'hændlə(r); 'hændlɚ/ *n* person who trains and controls an animal, eg a police dog. 训练动物(例如警犬)者.

hand·some /'hænsəm; 'hænsəm/ *adj* **1** of fine appearance; (of men) good-looking, having virile beauty; (of women) having a fine figure, vigour and dignity: 美观的; (指男子)漂亮的; 英俊的; (指女子)身材秀丽, 充满活力而仪态高贵的: *What a ~ horse you have!* 你的这匹马真漂亮! *What a ~ old building it is!* 多么美观的一座古老的建筑啊! *Would you describe that woman as ~ or beautiful?* 你觉得那女子是俊俏还是美丽? **2** (of gifts, behaviour) generous: (指礼物, 行为)慷慨的; 大方的: *He said some very ~ things about you.* 他说了一些称赞你的话. *£500 is quite a ~ birthday present.* 五百英镑是相当大方的生日礼物. **H~ is as that ~ does,** (prov) A fine person is one who acts generously. (谚)行为善者始为美; 唯善为美. **~·ly** *adv* in a ~ (2) manner: 慷慨地; 大方地: *He came down ~ly, made a generous gift.* 他出手大方.

handy /'hændɪ; 'hændɪ/ *adj* **(-ier, -iest) 1** (of persons) clever with the hands: (指人)手巧的. **'~·man** /-mæn; -mæn/ *n* (*pl* **-men**) person clever at doing odd jobs of various kinds. 做杂事灵巧的人. **2** (of things, places) convenient; useful: (指东西, 地方)方便的; 便利的: *A good toolbox is a ~ thing to have in the house.* 家庭里如果预备一个好的工具箱就方便多了. **come in ~,** be useful some time or other: 迟早有用: *Don't throw that plastic bag away; it may come in ~.* 不要把那塑料袋丢掉, 它迟早会有用的. **3** not far away; available for use: 近便的; 可利用的: *Always keep a first-aid kit ~.* 手边要经常保有一个急救箱. **hand·ily** /-ɪlɪ; -ɪlɪ/ *adv* **handi·ness** *n*

hang¹ /hæŋ; hæŋ/ *n* (*sing* only) (仅用单数) **1** way in which a thing hangs: 悬, 挂, 吊, 垂的状态: *the ~ of a coat/skirt.* 上衣(裙子)下垂的样子. **2 get the ~ of sth,** (colloq) **(a)** see how sth, eg a machine, works or is managed: 查看某物(如机器)工作或管理情形: *I've been trying to get the ~ of this new electric typewriter.* 我一直想知道这部新的电动打字机的用法. **(b)** see the meaning or significance of sth said or written: 了解言语或文字的意义: *I don't quite get the ~ of your argument.* 我不十分了解你的论据的意义. **3 not give/care a ~,** (colloq) (euphem for damn) not care at all. (口) (damn之委婉语) 毫不在乎.

hang² /hæŋ; hæŋ/ *vt, vi* (*pt, pp* **hung** /hʌŋ; hʌŋ/, or, for 2 and 3 below, 下列第 2 义和第 3 义用, **~ed**) (⇨ Used with *adverbial particles and preps,* ⇨ **7** below.) (与副词性小品词和介词连用之用法, 参看下列第 7 义.) **1** [VP6A, 15A, B, 2A, C] support, be supported, from above so that the lower end is free: 悬; 挂; 垂; 吊: *~ a lamp from the ceiling;* 将一灯吊在天花板上; *curtains ~ing over the window;* 挂在窗上的窗帘; *windows hung with curtains;* 挂着窗帘的窗子; *pictures ~ing on the wall.* 挂在墙上的图画. *She hung the washing out in the garden.* 她把洗好的衣服晾在花园里. *H~ your coat on that hook.* 把你的外套挂在那个钩上. *A dog's tongue ~s out when it runs fast.* 狗快跑时舌头伸在外面. **2** (*pt, pp* **~ed**) put, be put, to death by hanging with a rope around the neck: 施以绞刑; 绞死; 被绞死: *He was ~ed for murder.* 杀人而被绞死. *He said he would ~ himself,* commit suicide by ~ing. 他说他要自缢. **3** (dated sl; mild

equivalent of *damn*.) (过时俚语；相当于 damn 但较温和之用语)。 **4** (various uses) (各种用法) ~ *wallpaper*, attach it to a wall with paste; 贴壁纸; ~ *bells*, fit them (eg in a belfry); 悬钟(例如悬于钟楼中)。 ~ *a door*, fasten it on hinges so that it swings freely to and fro, 将门安装在绞链上。 ~ *by a hair / a single thread*, (of a person's fate etc) be in a delicate state, depend upon sth small. (指人的命运等)千钧一发。 ~ *one's head*, let it fall forward (eg when ashamed). 低下头(如因羞愧时)。 ~ *fire*, **(a)** (of a gun) be slow in going off. (指枪炮)发火慢。 **(b)** (of events) be slow in developing. (指事件)发展缓慢。 *let things go* ~, (colloq) be indifferent to them; take no interest in or care of them. (口)对事情不关心。 ~ *in the balance*, (of a result, decision, etc) not be certain. (指结果、决定等)尚未确定；仍旧是个未知数。 **5** [VP6A, 2B] leave, eg meat, ~ing until in the right condition for eating: 悬挂(肉等)至可食用的状态: *Hares and pheasants need to be well hung*. 野兔和野鸡需要挂起来吹晾许久方可食用。 *How long has this meat hung for?* 这肉已晾了多久了？ **6** (compounds) (复合词) '~*dog attrib adj* (of sb's look) sly and ashamed. (指人的外表)狡猾而羞缩的。 ~*man* /-mən; -mən/ *n* (*pl* -men) executioner who ~s criminals. 执行绞刑者；绞刑吏。 '~*over* ~ *n* unpleasant after-effects of excessive drinking. 过度饮酒后不舒服的感觉；宿醉。 **(b)** (fig) survival of out-of-date news, rules, etc. (喻)残存的过时新闻，规则等。 **7** [VP 2C, 15B, 3A] (with *adverbial particles and preps*): (与副词性小品词和介词连用):

hang about / (a)round, be standing or loitering about, doing nothing definite: 无所事事地徘徊; 闲荡: *men ~ing about at street corners, waiting for the pubs to open.* 闲待在街道拐角上等着酒店开门的人们。 *There's thunder ~ing about*, Thunder seems likely at any time. 随时可闻雷声。

hang back, hesitate; show unwillingness to act or advance: 犹豫; 踌躇不前: *When volunteers were asked for, not one man hung back.* 当征求志愿者时，没有一人退缩。

hang on, **(a)** hold tight: 紧握: *He hung on until the rope broke.* 他紧握着绳子，直到绳断为止。 **(b)** persevere: 坚忍: *It's hard work, but if you ~ on long enough you'll succeed.* 这是艰苦的工作，但如果你坚持下去，你会成功的。 *H~ on (a minute)!* (colloq) Wait (a minute)! (口)等一下！ ~ *on / upon sb's words*, listen attentively to them. 仔细听某人的话。 ~ *on to sth*, hold it tightly. 紧握某物。

hang out, (sl) live; lodge: (俚)居住: *Where are you ~ing out now?* 你现在住在哪里? ~ *sth out*, **(a)** hang (wet clothes, etc) out to dry: 晾(湿衣等): *She's in the yard, ~ing out the washing.* 她在院子里晾洗好的衣服。 **(b)** display: 展示: ~ *out flags for the Queen's visit.* 悬旗以迎接女王的莅临。

hang together, **(a)** (of persons) support one another; act in unison: (指人)团结一致; 行动一致: *If we all together, our plan will succeed.* 如果我们大家团结一致，我们的计划会成功。 **(b)** fit well together: 和谐一致: *Their accounts of what happened don't ~ together*, are inconsistent, contradictory. 他们对于发生之事报导不一致(有矛盾之处)。

hang up, replace the receiver at the end of a telephone conversation: 挂断电话: *She hung up on me*, (colloq) hung up the receiver before I had said all I wanted to say. (口)她未等我把话说完就把电话挂断了。 *be hung up*, (colloq) (口) **(a)** be delayed or frustrated. 被拖延; 受挫折。 **(b)** be emotionally inhibited or disturbed. 情绪受抑制或骚扰。 Hence, 由此产生, '~*up* ~ *n* **(a)** difficulty. 困难。 **(b)** inhibition; obsession; neurosis. 抑制; 强迫观念; 神经官能症。

hang·ar /ˈhæŋə(r); ˈhæŋɚ/ *n* building in which aircraft are housed. (停放飞机的)棚厂; 飞机库。

hang·er /ˈhæŋə(r); ˈhæŋɚ/ *n* device, loop, etc to, on

or by which sth is hung; 挂物之环，钩，架等; (in compounds): (用于复合词中): '*dress-/'clothes-/'coat-* ~, device on which dresses, etc are hung. 挂衣架。 ~-*on* /ˌhæŋər 'ɒn; ˌhæŋɚ'ɑn/ (*pl* -s-on) *n* person who forces his company upon another or others in the hope of profit or advantage. 食客; 希望获得利益而缠依他人的人。 '*paper-*~, person who hangs (= pastes) wallpaper on to walls. 裱贴壁纸者; 裱糊匠。

hang·ing /ˈhæŋɪŋ; ˈhæŋɪŋ/ *n* **1** [U, C] death by hanging: 绞刑; 绞死: *There were three ~s here last month.* 上月此地有三起绞刑。 **2** (usu *pl*) curtains, drapery, etc with which walls are hung. (通常用复数)窗帘，帷幕等。

hang·nail /ˈhæŋneɪl; ˈhæŋˌnel/ *n* loose skin near the root of a finger-nail. 逆剥(指甲根上的肉刺)。

hank /hæŋk; hæŋk/ *n* (twisted) coil of wool, silk, etc thread: (扭绞的)一束毛线，丝等; 一仔丝: *wind a* ~ *of wool into balls.* 将一束毛线缠成线球。

han·ker /ˈhæŋkə(r); ˈhæŋkɚ/ *vi* [VP3A] ~ *after / for sth*, have a strong desire: 渴望: ~ *for sympathy*; 渴望得到同情; ~ *after wealth.* 渴望得到财富。 '~*ing* *n* strong desire: 渴望: *have a ~ing for / after fame.* 渴望成名。

hanky /ˈhæŋkɪ; ˈhæŋkɪ/ *n* (*pl* -kies) (child's word for) handkerchief. (小儿语)手帕。

hanky-panky /ˌhæŋkɪ 'pæŋkɪ; ˈhæŋkɪˈpæŋkɪ/ *n* [U] (colloq) underhand dealing; trickery. (口)欺诈; 骗术。

Han·sard /ˈhænsɑːd; ˈhænsɚd/ *n* official report of proceedings in Parliament. 英国国会议事录。

han·som /ˈhænsəm; ˈhænsəm/ *n* (also 亦作, ~ '*cab*) (hist) two-wheeled horse-drawn cab for two passengers, with the driver's seat high at the back and reins going over the roof. (史)汉孙式马车 (为一种双轮供二人乘坐的马车，御者座位高踞车后，缰绳自车顶越过)。

a hansom cab

hap /hæp; hæp/ *n* (archaic) chance; luck. (古)机会; 幸运。 □ *vi* (-pp-) come about by chance; happen. 偶然发生; 发生。

hap·haz·ard /hæp'hæzəd; ˌhæp'hæzɚd/ *adj, adv* without order or plan; (at) random. 随便的(地); 偶然的(地)。 ~*·ly adv*

hap·less /ˈhæplɪs; ˈhæplɪs/ *adj* (archaic) unlucky. (古)不幸的。

hap·ly /ˈhæplɪ; ˈhæplɪ/ *adv* (archaic) by chance; perhaps. (古)偶然; 或许。

ha'p'orth /ˈheɪpəθ; ˈhepəθ/ *n* (colloq) half penny-worth. (口)值半便士之物。 □ **half(3).**

hap·pen /ˈhæpən; ˈhæpən/ *vi* **1** [VP2A, 3A] ~ (*to*), take place; come about: 发生: *How did the accident* ~? 这事故是怎样发生的？ *What* ~*ed next?* 以后怎么样了？ *Accidents will* ~, They are to be expected. 意外事件总会发生。 *If anything ~s to him* (= If he meets with an accident), *let me know.* 如果他发生什么意外，请通知我。 **2** [VP2A, 4E] chance; have the fortune: 偶然发生; 碰巧: *I* ~*ed to be out when he called.* 他来访时碰巧我出去了。 *It so* ~*ed that I had no money with me.* 恰巧我身上没有钱。 *as it* ~*s*, by chance: 偶然: *As it* ~*s, I have my cheque-book with me.* 碰巧我带着支票簿。 **3** [VP3A] ~ *on / upon*, find by chance: 偶然发现: *I*

~ed on just the thing I'd been looking for. 我偶然发现我一直在寻找的东西。 ~·ing /'hæpəŋɪŋ; 'hæpənɪŋ/ n (often pl) event: (常用复数)事件: There have been strange ~ings here lately. 此地近来发生了一些奇怪的事件。

happy /'hæpɪ; 'hæpɪ/ adj (-ier, -iest) 1 fortunate; lucky; feeling or expressing pleasure, contentment, satisfaction, etc: 幸运的; 幸福的; 快乐的; 满足的: Their marriage has been a ~ one. 他们的婚姻一直很幸福。 He is ~ in having congenial work. 他很幸运, 有一份适合他的工作。 as ~ as the day is long, very ~. 非常快乐。 2 (in polite formulas) pleased: (客套语)高兴的; 愉快的: We shall be ~ to accept your kind invitation. 我们乐于接受你的邀请。 3 (of language, conduct, suggestions) well suited to the situation: (指言语, 行为, 建议)很适当的: a ~ thought / idea, etc. 一个很适当的想法(观念等)。 ~-go-lucky /,hæpɪ gəʊ 'lʌkɪ; ,hæpɪ,gɔ'lʌkɪ/ adj taking what fortune brings; carefree: 乐天知命的; 无忧无虑的: She goes through life in a ~-go-lucky fashion. 她过着无忧无虑的日子。 hap·pily /-ɪlɪ; -ɪlɪ/ adv hap·pi·ness n

hara-kiri /,hærə 'kɪrɪ; 'hærə'kɪrɪ/ n [U] suicide by disembowelment as practised in the past by Japanese samurai when they believed they had failed in their duty. (过去日本武士或军官之)切腹自杀; 剖腹。

har·angue /hə'ræŋ; hə'ræŋ/ n long, loud (often scolding) talk or speech. 长篇而高声的(常是斥责性的)讲话或演说。 □ vt, vi [VP6A, 2A] make a ~ (to). (对...)作长篇而高声的讲话或演说。

har·ass /'hærəs US: hə'ræs; 'hærəs/ vt [VP6A] 1 trouble; worry: 使烦恼; 使忧愁: ~ed by the cares of a large family, 为照顾一大家庭所苦; ~ed-looking housewives. 愁容满面的家庭主妇。 2 make repeated attacks on: 一再袭击: In olden days the coasts of England were ~ed by the Vikings. 古时英国沿海一带一再受到北欧海盗的侵扰。 ~·ment n [U] ~ing or being ~ed. 烦恼; 困苦; 侵扰。

har·bin·ger /'ha:bɪndʒə(r); 'ha:bɪndʒə/ n sb or sth that foretells the coming of sb or sth: 先驱; 前兆: The crowing of the cock is a ~ of dawn. 鸡啼为黎明之前兆。 The cuckoo is a ~ of spring. 杜鹃鸟是春的前兆。

har·bour (US = -bor) /'ha:bə(r); 'ha:bə/ n 1 place of shelter for ships: 港: a natural ~, eg an inlet of the sea; 天然港(例如海湾); an artificial ~, one made with sea-walls, breakwaters. (以海堤, 防波堤造成之)人工港。 '~ dues n pl money (to be) paid for anchoring or mooring a ship in a ~. 船停在港中之碇泊费; 入港税。 2 (fig) any place of safety or shelter. (喻)安全地方; 避难所。 □ vt, vi 1 [VP6A] give lodging or shelter to; protect; conceal: 庇护; 保护; 藏匿: ~ an escaped criminal. 藏匿一逃犯。 My dog has long, thick hair that ~s fleas. 我的狗生有长而厚的毛, 易藏跳蚤。 2 [VP6A] hold in the mind: 心怀: ~ thoughts of revenge. 心怀报复之念头。 3 [VP2A] come to anchor (in a ~). 停泊(于港内)。 ~·age /'ha:bərɪdʒ; 'ha:bərɪdʒ/ n (place of) shelter. 庇护; 庇护所; 避难所。

hard¹ /ha:d; ha:d/ adj (-er, -est) 1 (contrasted with soft) (与 soft 相对)firm; not yielding to the touch; not easily cut; solid: 坚硬的; 坚固的; 坚实的: as ~ as rock; 坚硬如岩石; ground made ~ by frost. 冻硬的土地。 Teak is a ~ kind of wood. 柚木是一种坚硬的木材。 a ~ nut to crack, (fig) a difficult problem; person difficult to deal with or influence. (喻)难题; 难以对付或接受影响的人。 2 (contrasted with easy) (与 easy 相对)difficult (to understand or explain); needing mental or moral effort: 难以了解或解释的; 困难的: ~ words, difficult for learners, (also ⇨ 4 below); 难解释的字; 难懂的字(参看下列第 4 义); a ~ problem / book / language; 困难的问题(书, 语言); a subject that is ~ to understand. 难了解的课题。 She found it ~ to make up her mind. 她发觉她

难以下决心。 That man is ~ to please / He is a ~ man to please. 那人(他)是个难以取悦的人。 It's ~ to say which is better. 很难说哪一个较好。 It's ~ for an old man to change his way of living. 老年人难以变更自己的生活方式。 3 causing unhappiness, discomfort, or pain; difficult to endure: 引起不快, 不适或痛苦的; 难以忍受的: have / be given a ~ time, experience difficulties, misfortunes, etc; 经历一段困苦的日子; in these ~ times, in these times of money shortage, unemployment, etc when life is difficult. 值此困苦时期(缺钱, 失业等生活困苦时期)。 (find sth) ~ going, (find progress) difficult. (觉得某事)很难进行。 (find sb) ~ going, (find him) difficult (to understand), or boring (to listen to) (觉得某人)很难了解, 言谈乏味。 learn (sth) the ~ way, with perseverance and hardship. 艰苦地学习。 4 severe; harsh: 严厉的; 苛刻的: a ~ father, one who treats his children severely; 严父; ~ words, harsh, showing lack of sympathy. 严厉的言语。 be ~ on sb, treat him severely. 对某人严厉。 drive a ~ bargain, ⇨ bargain. take a ~ line, be uncompromising. 不妥协。 Hence, 由此产生, ~-liner n person who is uncompromising. 不妥协的人。 ⇨ line¹(21). 5 (of the body) having ~ muscles and not much fat: (指身体)结实的: Regular physical exercises soon made the boys ~. 经常的运动不久便使那些男孩的身体结实了。 as ~ as nails, (a) strong and muscular. 强健的。 (b) (fig) without sentiment, or sympathy; ~-hearted. 硬心肠的; 没有感情的; 硬心肠的。 6 done, doing (sth), with much effort or force; strenuous: 辛苦的; 费力的; 猛烈的: a ~ blow; 重击; go for a ~ gallop; 去骑一阵快马; a ~ worker. 辛苦的工作者。 7 (of the weather) severe: (指天气)酷烈的: a ~ winter / frost. 严冬(寒)。 8 (of sounds) (指声音)The letter 'c' is hard in 'cat' and soft in 'city'. 字母 'c' 在 'cat' 一字中是硬音, 在 'city' 一字中是软音。 The letter 'g' is ~ in 'gun' and soft in 'gin'. 字母 'g' 在 'gun' 一字中是硬音, 在 'gin' 一字中是软音。 9 (various uses) ~ and fast (rules, etc), that cannot be altered to fit special cases. 不许变更的; 严格的(规则等)。 ~ of hearing, rather deaf. 重听; 耳背。 '~-back / ~-cover n book bound in a ~ (=stiff) cover (contrasted with paper-backed books): 精装书(硬书皮装订)与平装书相对): The book has just appeared in ~back. 这书刚有精装本出版。 Hence, 由此产生, '~-backed / ~-covered / ~-bound adj. '~-board /-bɔ:d; -bɔrd/ n [U] kind of material like plywood in appearance and use, made by compressing waste wood that has been ground up finely. 高压板(由木屑压成, 外观与用途都很象夹板)。 ~ 'cash n [U] coins and notes, not a cheque or a promise to pay. 现金; 现款。 '~ core n (a) broken brick, rubble, etc (as used for foundations, roadmaking). (作为地基, 路基用的)碎砖, 碎石等。 (b) solid central, basic or underlying part; nucleus: 坚实的中心, 基底或底层; 核心: the ~ core of the opposition / rebellion. 反对党(叛党)的中坚分子。 '~ court n (tennis) court with a ~ surface, not of grass. (网球)硬地球场(非草地)。 '~ currency n one that is reliable and stable. 可靠稳定之货币。 ~ 'drug n one likely to lead to addiction, eg heroin. 麻醉药 (例如海洛英)。 '~-headed /'hedɪd; 'hedɪd/ adj practical; not sentimental; business-like. 讲求实际的; 不感情用事的; 事实求是的。 '~-hearted /'ha:tɪd; 'ha:rtɪd/ adj unfeeling; lacking in sympathy or the gentler emotions. 无情的; 硬心肠的。 ~ 'labour n [U] imprisonment with ~ physical labour as a punishment. 劳役; 苦役。 ~ 'liquor / 'drink n [U] with high alcoholic content eg whisky. 烈酒(酒精成分多的, 例如威士忌)。 ~ 'luck / 'lines n [U] worse fortune than is deserved. 倒霉。 Hence, 由此产生, '~'luck story, one seeking pity, sympathy (for oneself). (用以取得怜悯, 同情等的)倒霉事。 ~ 'shoulder n ~ surface at the side of a motorway, to be used in an emergency: 高速公路之路侧(紧急情况时使用): The lorry driver pulled over to the ~ shoulder when one of the tyres burst.

有一个轮胎爆裂,卡车司机连忙把车开到高速公路的路侧。 **'~ 'standing** n [U] area of ~ surface, eg, concrete, for the parking of vehicles. 硬地面(例如由混凝土铺成可停放车辆者). **'~·top** n car with a steel top and no sliding roof. 有固定金属篷(非活动顶篷)之汽车。 **'~· ware** n [U] **(a)** ironmongery; metal goods for domestic use, eg pans, nails, locks. 铁器类; 五金类(如锅,钉,锁等). **(b)** military ~ware, weapons and equipment, eg armoured vehicles. 武器和装备(例如装甲车辆)。 **(c)** computer ~ware, mechanical equipment (contrasted with information and programmes, called software). 硬件; 计算机硬件(与称作 software 之资讯及程式相对)。 **'~·water** n [U] containing mineral salts that interfere with the lathering of soap. 硬水 (含有干扰肥皂起泡之矿盐)。 **'~·wood** n [U] = heavy wood, eg oak, ebony, teak, contrasted with soft wood, eg pine, fir; 硬材 (例如橡木, 乌木, 柚木, 与松木, 枞木等软木相对): (attrib) (用作定语) ~wood floors. 硬木地板。 **~·ness** n

hard[2] /hɑːd/ hard/ adv 1 with great energy; strenuously; with all one's force: 努力地; 费力地; 费尽全力地: work / study / think / pull / push ~. 努力工作(读书, 思考, 拉, 推); try ~ to succeed; 努力以期成功; drink / swear ~. 拚命喝(诅咒). **,~·'hitting** adj vigorous, direct: 强烈的; 直接的: a ~-hitting speech. 猛烈的演说。 **,~·'working** adj working with care and energy. 努力工作的。 **2** severely; heavily: 剧烈地; 猛烈地: freezing / raining ~. 酷寒(下大雨). **3** with difficulty; with a struggle; painfully: 困难地; 劳苦地; 辛苦地: my ~-earned money 我辛辛苦苦赚来的钱 ⊳ **hardly(5).** be ~ hit, be suffering severely, eg by financial losses, the death of sb much loved. 受严重打击(例如财务受损失, 深爱之人去世等)。 be ~ pressed (for sth), be under pressure, strained. 受压迫; 处困境。 be ~ 'put to it (to do sth), find it difficult: 难以(做某事): He was ~ put to it to explain what had happened. 他难以说明发生了些什么事。 be ~ 'up, be short of money. 缺钱。 be ~ 'up for (sth), in want of; at a loss for: 缺乏; 不知所措: He's ~ up for ideas / something to do. 没有事情做). **4** so as to be ~ (1), solid: 坚硬地; 坚固地: boil eggs ~. 把蛋煮硬。 **,~·'baked** adj baked until ~. 烤硬的。 **,~·'boiled,** (eg of eggs) boiled ~; (fig) callous. (指蛋等)煮老了的; (喻)无情的。 **,~·'bitten** adj (of a person) stubborn in fighting; tough because of a difficult life, etc. (指人)不屈服的; 顽强的; 坚忍的。 **5** closely; immediately: 接近地; 紧随地: follow ~ after / upon / behind someone. 紧随某人。 ~ by, close by; not far away. 在近旁; 在近处; 附近。 run sb ~, pursue him closely. 紧追某人。

harden /hɑːdn/ 'hɑːdn/ vt, vi [VP6A, 2A] make or become hard, strong, hardy, etc: 使硬; 使坚强; 使坚强; 使变硬; 变坚强: ~ steel; 硬化钢; ~ the heart; 硬起心肠; a ~ed criminal, one who is callous, who shows no signs of shame or repentance; 怙恶不悛的罪犯; ~ the body, eg by taking exercise. 锻炼身体 (例如借运动). be ~ed to, made insensitive to. 对...麻木; 对...无动于衷. [VP15B, 2C] ~ off, (of young plants, esp seedlings) make or become hardy, ready for planting outside. (指植物幼苗)(使)变耐寒(以备露天种植)。

hardi·hood /hɑːdɪhud/ 'hɑːdɪ,hud/ n [U] boldness; audacity. 大胆; 胆识。

hard·ly /hɑːdlɪ/ 'hɑːdlɪ/ adv 1 only just; not quite; scarcely: 刚刚; 不十分; 简直没有: I ~ know her, have only a very slight acquaintance with her. 我跟她不熟。 We had ~ got / H~ had we got into the country when it began to rain. 我们刚到乡间就下雨了。 (Cf 参较 No sooner... than.) I'm so tired I can ~ walk. 我太累, 简直走不动了。 **2** (used to suggest that sth is improbable, unlikely or unreasonable): (用以表示某事大概不会发生或不合理): He can ~ have arrived yet. 他大概还没有到。 You can ~ expect me to lend you money again. 你别

希望我再借钱给你。 **3** (neg in meaning) almost no; almost not: (否定意义)几乎没有; 几乎不: He ~ ever (= very seldom) goes to bed before midnight. 他很少在午夜以前就寝。 Cf 参较 His wife almost always goes to bed before midnight. 他的妻子几乎总是在午夜以前就寝。 I need ~ say (= It is almost unnecessary for me to say) that I am innocent. 我几乎用不着说我是无罪的。 There's ~ any coal left. 几乎没有煤剩下了。 H~ anybody (= Very few people) came to the meeting. 几乎没有人到会。 **4** (from hard[1](4)) severely: (由 hard[1] 第4义而来)严厉地: ~ treated. 受严苛对待。 **5** (from hard[1](6)) with effort or difficulty. 费劲地; 辛苦地。 For this sense the adv 'hard' is usu preferred. 指此义时, 通常多用副词 'hard'. (Cf 参较 hard-earned money 辛苦赚来的钱 and salary that was ~ (ie only just, barely) earned. 仅仅能够赚到的薪水; 勉强赚到的薪水。

hard·ship /hɑːdʃɪp/ 'hɑːdʃɪp/ n 1 [C] circumstance that causes discomfort or suffering: 困苦的情况; 艰辛的情形: the ~s borne by soldiers during a war. 战争时士兵所忍受的艰辛。 **2** [U] severe suffering; 艰苦; 苦难: bear ~ without complaining. 毫无怨言地忍受困苦。

hardy /hɑːdɪ/ 'hɑːdɪ/ adj (-ier, -iest) 1 strong; able to endure suffering or hardship: 强壮的; 能吃苦的: A few ~ men broke the ice on the lake and had a swim. 几个健壮的人打破湖上的冰游泳。 **2** (of plants) able to endure frost without being injured: (指植物) 耐寒的: ~ annuals. 耐寒的一年生植物。 **3** bold; ready to face danger. 勇敢的; 勇于面对危险的。 **hardi·ness** n

hare /heə(r)/ hɛr/ n fast-running field animal with long ears and a divided upper lip, like but larger than a rabbit. 野兔。 ~ and hounds, paperchase, a game in which two persons called 'hares' run across country dropping torn-up bits of paper and are followed by others, called 'hounds', who try to catch them. 追纸戏 (由二人扮'兔', 在田野中一面跑一面撒下碎纸, 由其他称作'猎犬'的人在后追逐)。 run with the ~ and hunt with the hounds, try to keep the favour of both sides in a dispute; play a double game. 在争论中欲两面讨好; 骑墙。 mad as a March ~, very mad or wild 十分疯狂的; 野性大发的。 start a ~, raise a topic, argument, etc unrelated to the main issue. 提出一个与主题无关的话题, 议论等。 **'~·bell** n round-leaved plant with blue bell-like flowers 蓝铃花 (in Scotland called 苏格兰称作 bluebell)。 **'~·brained** adj rash; foolish; 轻率的; 愚蠢的: ~-brained schemes. 愚蠢的计划。 **'~·lip** n person's upper lip divided (from birth) like that of a ~. 兔唇; 唇裂; 豁嘴; 缺唇。 □ vi [VP2C] run fast or away: 快跑; 逃走: They ~d off. 他们跑掉了。

harem /hɑːriːm/ 'hɛrəm/ n women's part of a traditional Muslim household; women living in it. 伊斯兰教徒之闺房; 伊斯兰教徒之女眷。

hari·cot /hærɪkəu/ 'hærɪ,ko/ n (also 亦作 ~ bean) kidney bean; French bean. 扁豆。

hark /hɑːk/ hɑːk/ vi 1 (chiefly imper) (主作祈使) ~ at, (colloq, teasing) listen to: (口, 揶揄语)听: Just ~ at him! 听听他! **2** ~ back (to), refer back to sth done or said earlier. 言归(正传)。

har·le·quin /hɑːlɪkwɪn/ 'hɑːrləkwɪn/ n character in Italian comedy; mute character in English pantomime, full of tricks and very lively, wearing a mask and multi-coloured costume; (hence) person fond of practical jokes; buffoon. 意大利喜剧中一角色; 英国哑剧中一诙谐角色 (戴面具, 着彩衣); (由此产生)喜爱玩笑的人; 丑角。 **~·ade** /hɑːlɪkwɪneɪd/ ,hɑːrləkwɪn'ed/ n part of a pantomime in which a ~ plays the chief part. 哑剧中丑角主演的部分。

Har·ley Street /hɑːli striːt/ 'hɑːrlɪ strɪt/ n London street where many fashionable doctors and surgeons live.

哈莱街(伦敦一街道，有许多名医居于此)。

har·lot /ˈhɑːlət; ˈhɑːrlət/ n (archaic, or as a term of abuse) prostitute. (古，或辱骂语)娼妓。

harm /hɑːm; hɑːrm/ n [U] damage; injury: 损害; 伤害: He probably meant no ~, did not intend to hurt anyone or anyone's feelings. 他大概没有恶意。There's no ~ in your staying up late occasionally, no reason why you should not do so. 你偶尔迟睡并无害处。do sb ~, cause injury to him: 伤害某人: A few drinks will do you no ~. 稍微喝几杯对你不会有害。out of ~'s way, in a place of safety. 在安全的地方。□ vt [VP6A] cause ~ to: 伤害; 损害: It hasn't ~ed you, has it? 那没有伤害你吧, 对吗? ~·ful /-fl; -fəl/ adj causing ~ (to). (对···)有害的(与 to 连用)。~·fully /-fəlɪ; -fəlɪ/ adv ~·less adj 1 not doing ~ (to): (对···)无害的(与 to 连用): ~less snakes. 无毒的蛇。2 innocent; inoffensive: 无辜的; 无恶意的: Several ~less spectators were wounded during the rioting. 在骚乱中有几个无辜的旁观者受伤了。~·less·ly adv

har·mat·tan /ˌhɑːməˈtæn; ˌhɑːrməˈtæn/ n cold, dry wind from the north that blows in W Africa from December to March. 非洲西部十二月至三月所吹的寒冷干燥北风。

har·monic /hɑːˈmɒnɪk; hɑːrˈmɑːnɪk/ n (music) higher note produced (by vibration of strings) with a note that is played, and having a fixed relation to it. (音乐)泛音; 和声(由弦之颤动而产生的音高于基音,并与基音有固定的关系)。

har·mon·ica /hɑːˈmɒnɪkə; hɑːrˈmɑːnɪkə/ n mouth-organ. 口琴。

har·moni·ous /hɑːˈməʊnɪəs; hɑːrˈmoʊnɪəs/ adj 1 pleasingly or satisfactorily arranged: 调和的; 协调的; 排列悦目的: a ~ group of buildings. 一片调和的建筑物。2 in agreement; free from ill feeling: 和谐的; 和睦的: ~ families / neighbours. 和睦的家庭(邻居)。3 sweet-sounding; tuneful. 音调和谐的; 悦耳的。~·ly adv

har·mo·nium /hɑːˈməʊnɪəm; hɑːrˈmoʊnɪəm/ n small musical keyboard instrument (like an organ), with the notes produced by air blown through metal reeds. 簧风琴(类似风琴的小键盘乐器,借空气振动金属簧片而发音)。

har·mon·ize /ˈhɑːmənaɪz; ˈhɑːrməˌnaɪz/ vt, vi 1 [VP6A, 14] ~ (with), bring (one thing) into harmony (with another); (music) add notes (to a melody) to make chords. 使调和; (音乐)加音(于乐曲)使成和弦。2 [VP2A, C] ~ (with), be in harmony or agreement: 调和; 和谐: colours that ~ well (with the decorations/with each other). (与装饰物, 彼此之间)很调和的色彩。har·mon·iz·ation /ˌhɑːmənaɪˈzeɪʃn US: -nɪˈz-; ˌhɑːrmənərˈzeʃən/ n

har·mony /ˈhɑːmənɪ; ˈhɑːrmənɪ/ n (pl -nies) 1 [U] agreement (of feeling, interests, opinions, etc): (感情, 兴趣, 意见等的)和睦; 一致: There was not much ~ in international affairs during those years. 那些年国际事

态不很协调。be in ~ (with), match; agree (with): 相配; (与···)一致: His tastes are in ~ with mine. 他的爱好与我的相同。2 [C, U] (instance or example of) pleasing combination of related things: 调和; 协调: the ~ of colour in nature, eg the greens, browns, etc of trees in autumn. 自然界色彩的协调(例如秋季树木绿色, 褐色等)。3 [C, U] (music) pleasing combination of notes sounded together to make chords. (音乐)和声学; 和声。

har·ness /ˈhɑːnɪs; ˈhɑːrnɪs/ n (collective sing) all the leather-work and metal-work by which a horse is controlled and fastened to the cart, waggon, plough, etc, that it pulls. (集合名词单数)马具(将马系于车或犁上, 及御马用的所有皮制与金属用具); 挽具。⇨yoke. in ~, doing one's regular work. 在做经常所做的工作。die in ~, die while engaged in one's regular work, not after retiring. 殉职; 在工作中死去。work/run in double ~, work with a partner, or with a husband or wife. 与伙伴共同工作; 夫妻双双工作。□ vt [VP6A] 1 put a ~ on (a horse). 套马具于(马)。2 use (eg a river, waterfall, etc) to produce (esp electric) power. 利用(河, 瀑布等)产生动力(尤指电力)。

harp /hɑːp; hɑːrp/ n freestanding musical instrument with vertical strings played with the fingers. 竖琴。⇨ the illus at **string**. 参看 string 之插图。□ vi 1 play the ~. 弹竖琴。2 ~ on sth, (fig) talk repeatedly or tiresomely about: (喻)反复地唠或令人厌倦地谈论: She is always ~ing on my faults. 她老是反复述说我的缺点。~er, ~ist /-ɪst; -ɪst/ nn player on the ~. 弹竖琴者。

har·poon /hɑːˈpuːn; hɑːrˈpun/ n spear on a rope, thrown by hand or fired from a gun, for catching whales and other large sea animals. 鱼叉(系于绳上, 由手于抛出, 或用炮射出, 用以捕鲸及其他大的海生动物)。□ vt strike with a ~. 用鱼叉叉。

harp·si·chord /ˈhɑːpsɪkɔːd; ˈhɑːrpsɪˌkɔrd/ n piano-like instrument used from the 16th to the 18th cc (and today for music of these centuries). 大键琴(一种似钢琴的乐器, 风行于十六至十八世纪, 今日用以奏这世纪的音乐)。⇨ the illus at **keyboard**. 参看 keyboard 之插图。

harpy /ˈhɑːpɪ; ˈhɑːrpɪ/ n (pl -pies) 1 (Gk myth) cruel creature with a woman's face and a bird's wings and claws. (希神)生有女人面孔及鸟翅与爪的残酷怪物。2 cruel, greedy, hard-hearted woman. 残酷, 贪婪, 无情的女人。

har·ri·dan /ˈhærɪdən; ˈhærədən/ n worn-out, bad-tempered old woman. 面容枯瘦, 脾气暴躁的老妇。

har·rier /ˈhærɪə(r); ˈhærɪə/ n 1 hound used for hunting hares; (pl) pack of these with huntsmen. 猎兔犬; (复)一群猎兔犬及猎人。2 cross-country runner. 越野赛跑者。

har·row /ˈhærəʊ; ˈhæro/ n heavy frame with metal teeth or discs for breaking up ground after ploughing. 耙。□ vt [VP6A] pull a ~ over (a field, etc); (fig)

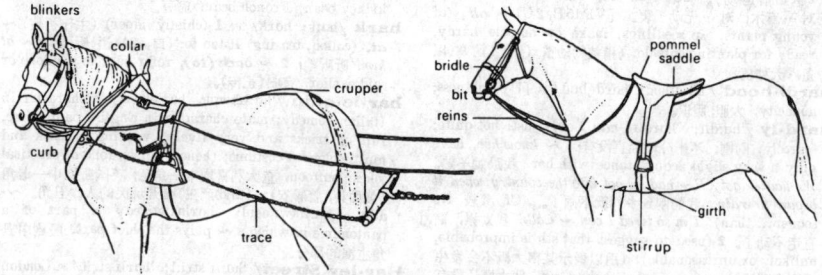

a horse's harness

distress (the feelings): 把(地等); (喻)使(感情)痛苦; 使伤心: a ~ing tale of misfortunes. 一个令人伤心的不幸的故事.

harry /'hærɪ; 'hærɪ/ vt (pt, pp **-rried**) [VP6A] **1** lay waste and plunder; attack frequently: 蹂躏; 时常侵袭: The Vikings used to ~ the English coast. 北欧海盗过去常常侵袭英国沿海地方. **2** annoy or worry: 使苦恼: money-lenders ~ing their debtors. 苦逼债务人的放债者.

harsh /haːʃ; harʃ/ adj (**-er, -est**) **1** rough and disagreeable, esp to the senses: 粗糙而令人不快的(尤指在感官上): a ~ texture/voice/contrast; 粗糙的织物(刺耳的声音; 刺目的对比); ~ to the ear. 刺耳. **2** stern, cruel, severe: 苛刻的; 残酷的; 严厉的: a ~ judge/judgement/punishment. 严厉的法官(判决, 惩罚). ~·ly adv ~·ness n

hart /haːt; hart/ n adult male of (esp red) deer; stag. 牡鹿(尤指红鹿).

harum-scarum /ˌheərəm 'skeərəm; 'herəm'skerəm/ adj, n (colloq) reckless, impulsive (person). (口)轻率的(人); 冒失鬼.

har·vest /'haːvɪst; 'harvɪst/ n **1** (season for) cutting and gathering in of grain and other food crops; quantity obtained: 收获; 收获季; 收获量: this year's wheat ~; 今年小麦的收获; a succession of good ~s. 连续的丰收. ~ 'festival n service of thanksgiving in Christian churches after the ~ has been gathered. (基督教会所举行的)收获感恩礼拜. ~ 'home n festival given by farmers to their workers when the ~ is gathered. 收获宴(收割后农民为雇工所举行者). ~ 'moon n full moon nearest to the autumn equinox. 秋分前后之满月. **2** (fig) consequences of action or behaviour: (喻)行动或行为的结果: reap the ~ of one's hard work, be rewarded for it. 获得辛勤工作的成果. □ vt [VP6A] cut, gather, dig up, a crop: 收割; 收获: ~ rice/potatoes. 收割稻谷(马铃薯). ~er n **1** person who ~s; reaper. 收割者. **2** machine for cutting and gathering grain, esp the kind that also binds the grain into sheaves or (**,combine-**~'er) threshes the grain. 收割机(尤指连带捆谷与打谷者).

has ⇨ **have**[1].

has-been /'hæz biːn; 'hæz,bɪn/ n (colloq) person who, or thing which, has lost a quality, skill, etc formerly possessed; sb or sth now out of date. (口)曾具有某种性质, 技术等的人或物; 过时的人或物.

hash /hæʃ; hæʃ/ vt [VP6A, 15B] ~ (up), chop or cut up (meat) into small pieces. 把(肉)切丁或切碎. □ n **1** [U] (dish of) cooked meat, ~ed and recooked. 回锅肉丁(将熟肉切丁再行烹制的菜肴). **2** make a ~ of sth, (fig) do it very badly, make a mess of it. (喻)弄糟某事物. settle sb's ~, deal with him in such a way that he gives no more trouble. 使某人不再找麻烦. **3** (colloq) hashish. (口)印度大麻.

hash·ish /'hæʃiːʃ; 'hæʃɪʃ/ n [U] dried hemp leaves made into a drug for smoking or chewing; cannabis. 由干大麻叶制成的吸食或嚼用的麻醉品; 印度大麻.

hasn't /'hæznt; 'hæznt/ = has not. ⇨ **have**[1].

hasp /haːsp US: hæsp; hæsp/ n metal fastening for a door, window, etc used with a staple. 门窗等之搭扣(与U 形钉连用). ⇨ the illus at **padlock**. 参看 padlock 之插图.

has·sle /'hæsl; 'hæsl/ n (colloq) (口) **1** difficulty; struggle: 困难; 挣扎: a real ~ to get on the train. 上火车时的争先恐后. **2** argument; quarrel. 争辩; 争吵. □ vi, vt **1** [VP2A, 3A] ~ (with sb), argue; quarrel. 争辩; 争吵. **2** [VP6A] bother; annoy: 打扰; 烦扰: Don't keep hassling me! 不要老找我!

has·sock /'hæsɒk; 'hæsɑk/ n cushion for kneeling on, eg in church. 膝垫(例如教堂内所用者).

hast /hæst; hæst/ (archaic): (古): thou ~, you have.

haste /heɪst; hest/ n [U] quickness of movement; hurry: 急速; 匆忙: Why all this ~? Why are you in

---

such a hurry? 为何如此匆忙? He went off in great ~. 他匆匆离去. Make ~! Hurry! 赶快! More ~, less speed, (prov) The more you hurry, the less real progress you will make. (谚)欲速则不达.

hasten /'heɪsn; 'hesn/ vi, vt **1** [VP2A, C, 4A] move or act with speed: 急忙; 赶快: ~ away/home/to the office; 急忙离去(回家, 到办公室); ~ to tell sb the good news. 急忙把好消息告诉某人. **2** [VP6A] cause (sb) to hurry; cause (sth) to be done or to happen quickly or earlier: 催促(某人); 促进(某事物): Artificial heating ~s the growth of plants. 人工加热法加速植物的生长.

hasty /'heɪstɪ; 'hestɪ/ adj (**-ier, -iest**) said, made or done (too) quickly: 急忙的; 匆促的; 过于匆忙的; 轻率的: ~ preparations for flight; 急忙准备逃走; a ~ departure; 匆匆离去; ~ words that are regretted afterwards. 事后懊悔的轻率言词. **hast·ily** /-ɪlɪ; -ɪlɪ/ adv **hasti·ness** n

hat /hæt; hæt/ n covering for the head, usu with a brim, worn out of doors. 帽(一种盖头之物, 通常有边, 在户外戴). (Cf 参较 cap and bonnet without a brim, cap and bonnet 没有边.) go/come hat/cap in hand, obsequiously, apologetically. 卑躬屈节地; 歉然地. send/pass round the hat, ask for, collect, contributions of money (usu for sb who has suffered a loss). 募捐(通常指为遭受损失者募款). take one's hat off to, (fig) express admiration for. (喻)对…表示敬佩. Hence, 由此产生, Hats off to…! Let us congratulate…! 让我们祝贺…! talk through one's hat, (sl) talk foolishly. (俚)说愚蠢的话. a bad hat, (sl) bad person. (俚)坏人. 'hat-band n band round the crown of a hat, above the brim. 帽带(围绕帽顶的宽带, 在帽缘上面). 'hat-pin n long pin used (formerly) by women to fasten a hat to the hair. 帽针(昔时妇女将帽固定在头发上的长针). 'hat trick n (cricket) taking of three wickets with successive balls; similar success in other sports or activities. (板球)连续使三个击球员退场; 其他运动或活动中类似的成就. hat·ful /-fʊl; -fʊl/ n as much as a hat holds. 一帽所容之量. hat·less adj not wearing a hat. 未戴帽的. hat·ter n man who makes or sells hats. 制帽人; 帽商. as mad as a hatter, very mad. 极为疯狂.

hatch[1] /hætʃ; hætʃ/ n **1** (movable covering over an) opening in a door or floor, esp ('~·way) one in a ship's deck through which cargo is lowered and raised; opening in a wall between two rooms, esp a kitchen and a dining room, through which dishes, etc are passed. 门上或地板上之开口; (尤指甲板上装卸货物之)舱口 (亦称 hatchway); 门或地板上之开口可移动的盖; 舱口盖; 两室间门墙壁上的开口 (尤指厨房与餐厅间用以传递菜肴者). under ~es, below deck. 在甲板下. **2** lower half of a divided door. 上下开合门之下半扇门.

hatch[2] /hætʃ; hætʃ/ vt, vi **1** [VP6A, 2A] (cause to) break out (of an egg): 孵(卵); 孵(鸡); 使(自卵中)孵出: ~ an egg; 孵卵; ~ chickens. 孵小鸡. When will the eggs ~? 这些蛋何时孵出小鸡? Three chickens ~ed today. 今天有三只小鸡孵出来了. Don't count one's chickens before they're ~ed, (prov) Don't rely too much upon sth which is uncertain. (谚)不要在蛋尚未孵出时先数鸡(勿过分指望没有把握之事). **2** [VP6A] think out and produce (a plot, etc). 策划 (计谋等). ~·ery /'hætʃərɪ; 'hætʃərɪ/ n (pl -ries) place for ~ing (esp fish): 孵卵处之(尤指鱼卵孵化处): a 'trout-~ery. 鳟鱼孵化处. Cf 参较 incubator, for chicks. 孵鸡器.

hatch[3] /hætʃ; hætʃ/ vt [VP6A] draw or engrave (a surface) with parallel lines. 在(一平面)绘制或雕刻影线. ~·ing n [U] such lines. 影线.

hatchet /'hætʃɪt; 'hætʃɪt/ n light, short-handled axe. 手斧; 斧头. ⇨ the illus at **tool**. 参看 tool 之插图. bury the ~, stop quarrelling or fighting and be friendly.

媾和; 言归于好。

hatch·way /'hætʃweɪ; 'hætʃ,we/ n ⇨ **hatch**¹.

hate /heɪt; het/ vt [VP6A, D, 7A, 17, 19] have a strong dislike or for; (colloq) regret: 憎恨; 憎恶; (口) 抱歉; 遗憾: My cat ~s dogs. 我的猫恨狗。I ~ to trouble you. 我不愿麻烦你。She ~s getting to the theatre late. 她不喜欢到戏院时迟到。She ~s anyone listening while she's telephoning. 她打电话时讨厌别人听。□ n [U] strong dislike or ill-will: 憎恶: He was filled with ~ for his opponent. 他对他的对手满怀憎恨。

hate·ful /'heɪtfl; 'hetfəl/ adj exciting hatred or strong dislike: 可恨的; 可恶的; 讨厌的: The sight of food was ~ to the seasick girl. 那晕船的女孩看到食物就感到厌恶。**~ly** /-fəlɪ; -fəlɪ/ adv

hath /hæθ; hæθ/ (archaic) 3rd pers sing pres t of have. (古) have 的第三人称, 单数, 现在式。

hatred /'heɪtrɪd; 'hetrɪd/ n ~ of/for, hate; strong dislike: 憎恨; 憎恶: He looked at me with ~. 他以憎恨的眼光望着我。

hat·ter /'hætə(r); 'hætə/ n ⇨ **hat**.

hau·berk /'hɔːbɜːk; 'hɔbɚk/ n coat of chain mail (as worn by soldiers in the Middle Ages); ⇨ the illus at armour. (中古时武士所着之) 锁子铠 (参看 armour 之插图)。

haughty /'hɔːtɪ; 'hɔtɪ/ adj (-ier, -iest) arrogant; having or showing a high opinion of oneself: 傲慢的; 骄傲的: The nobles used to treat the common people with ~ contempt. 贵族在过去惯于傲慢和轻蔑地对待平民。**haught·ily** /-ɪlɪ; -l̩ɪ/ adv **haughtiness** n

haul /hɔːl; hɔl/ vt, vi [VP6A, 15A, B, 2C, 3A] pull (with effort or force): 拖; 拉; 牵; 曳: elephants ~ing logs: 拖木材的象; ~ timber to a saw-mill; 将木材拖到锯木厂; ~ at/upon a rope. 拖绳子。They ~ed the boat up the beach. 他们把船拖到岸上。~ down one's flag/colours, surrender. 投降。~ sb over the coals, scold him severely (for wrongdoing). (因其过失) 严责某人。□ n [C] 1 act of ~ing; distance along which sth is ~ed: 拖; 拉; 拖曳的距离: long ~s on the railways. 铁路上长距离的拖运。2 amount gained as the result of effort, esp of fish ~ed up in a net: 努力所获致的结果; (尤指)一网打起之鱼量: a good ~ of fish. 满满一网鱼。The thief made a good ~, What he stole was valuable. 那贼偷了不少值钱的东西。

haul·age /'hɔːlɪdʒ; 'hɔlɪdʒ/ n [U] transport (of goods): (货物之) 运输: the road ~ industry, concerned with carriage of goods by road in lorries, etc; 公路货运业; a ~ contractor. 货运承办者。

haul·ier /'hɔːlɪə(r); 'hɔljɚ/ n person or firm that owns lorries, and contracts to carry goods by road; haulage contractor. 承办陆路货运者。

haulm /hɔːm; hɔm/ n (collective sing) stems and stalks of peas, beans, potatoes, etc, esp after the crop is gathered. (集合名词单数) 豆、马铃薯等之茎 (尤指收获后者); 豆秸。

haunch /hɔːntʃ; hɔntʃ/ n (in man and animals) part of the body round the hips, or between the ribs and the thighs: (人与动物之) 腰臀部分: a ~ of venison. 腰臀部鹿肉。The dog was sitting on its ~es. 那狗蹲着。

haunt /hɔːnt; hɔnt/ vt [VP6A] 1 visit, be with, habitually or repeatedly: (esp of ghosts and spirits) appear repeatedly in: 常至; 常去; (尤指鬼和幽灵) 常出没于: The old castle is said to be ~ed. 那座古堡据说闹鬼。2 return to the mind repeatedly: 萦绕心头: a ~ing melody/face. 萦绕心头的曲子(面孔)。A wrongdoer is constantly ~ed by fear of discovery. 做恶者经常提心吊胆, 怕被别人发觉。□ n place frequently visited by the person(s) named: (某人) 常去的地方: a ~ of criminals; 罪犯常去的地方; revisit the ~s of one's schooldays, the places where one spent one's time there. 重游学生时代常去的地方。

haut·boy /'həʊbɔɪ; 'hobɔɪ/ n = oboe.

hau·teur /əʊ'tɜː(r); ho'tɚ/ n [U] haughtiness of manner. 傲慢。

Ha·vana /hə'vænə; hə'vænə/ n cigar made at ~ or elsewhere in Cuba. 哈瓦那或古巴其他地方所制的雪茄烟。

have¹ /usu form after 'I, we, you, they': v; v; usu form after a pause: həv; həv; usu form elsewhere: əv; əv; strong form: hæv; hæv/ aux v (3rd pers sing has /usu form: z; z; after p, t, k, f, θ only: s; s; after s, z, ʃ, ʒ, tʃ, dʒ only: əz; əz; after a pause: həz; həz; strong form: hæz; hæz/, pt had /usu form after 'I, we, you, they': d; d; usu form after a pause: həd; həd; usu form elsewhere: əd; əd; strong form: hæd; hæd/; neg forms: haven't /'hævnt; 'hævn̩t/, hasn't /'hæznt; 'hæzn̩t/, hadn't /'hædnt; 'hædn̩t/) 1 used in forming the perfect tenses and the perfect inf: 用以形成完成时态以及不定式的完成式: I ~/I've finished. 我已做完了。He has/He's gone. 他走了。H~ you done it? 你做了吗? Yes, I ~. 是的, 我做了。No, I ~n't. 不, 我没有。I shall ~ done it by next week. 我将于下周前做完(它)。You ought to ~ done it. 你应该做了这事。2 (By inverting the finite had with the subject, the equivalent of an if-clause is obtained): (以其限定形式 had 与主词倒装, 成为一表示条件的从句): Had I (= If I had) known, ... 如果我那时知道的话, ...。⇨ if(1).

have² /hæv; hæv/ anom v (3rd pers sing has /hæz; hæz/; pt, pp had /hæd; hæd/; neg forms haven't /'hævnt; 'hævn̩t/, hasn't /'hæznt; 'hæzn̩t/, hadn't /'hædnt; 'hædn̩t/) (conjugated (for the neg and interr forms) without the aux v 'do' in GB usage, but not always in US usage; iu GB colloq style often replaced by have¹ got, eg I've got for I ~) (其否定和疑问形式变化, 在英国不需要助动词 do, 但在美国的用法则不尽然。在英国口语中常与 got 连用, 例如 I've got 以代替 I have) 1 (in sentences that can be recomposed with the v 'be'): (在可以用 be 重组成的句中): [VP6B] I ~ no doubt (= There is no doubt in my mind) that.... 我确信...。Has the house (= Is there with the house) a good garden? 那房子有一个好花园吗? 2 [VP6B] possess; own (sth concrete): 拥有; 有 (具体之物): He's (got) a house in the country. 他在乡间有一栋房子。How many books ~ you/do you ~? 你有多少本书? 3 [VP6B] possess or show as a mental or physical characteristic (often equivalent to a construction with be): 据有; 有 (指精神或身体的特点, 常相当于某种 be 的结构): Has she blue eyes or brown eyes? Are her eyes blue or brown? 她的眼睛是蓝色的还是棕色的? He hasn't a good memory, His memory isn't good. 他的记忆力不好。(Notes: In US usage aux do is common: 注意: 在美国通常用助动词 do: Does she ~ blue eyes? 她的眼睛是蓝色的吗? Do you ~ a good memory? 你的记忆力好吗? In GB colloq styles, the pp got is common: 在英国口语中常用过去分词 got: Has she got blue eyes? 她的眼睛是蓝色的吗?) 4 [VP6B] used to indicate various connections: 用以表示各种关系: How many children ~ they? 他们有多少孩子? He hasn't many friends here. 他在此地没有多少朋友。(The notes above on GB and US usage apply here, too.) (上述英美用法上的不同亦适用于此)。5 (followed by an abstract n + to-inf, in a construction equivalent to be + adj + to-inf): (后接抽象名词及不定式, 相当于 be 加形容词及不定式): Will you ~ the kindness/goodness, etc (= Please be kind or good enough) to hand me that book? 请将那本书递给我好吗? How dare you ~ the impudence (= be so impudent as) to say that! 你竟敢如此无礼, 说出那种话来! Had she/Did she ~ the cheek (= Was she cheeky enough) to ask for more money? 她还有脸要更多的钱吗? 6 (in colloq style usu with got) hold or keep in the mind; exercise some quality of the mind; experience (some emotion): (在口语中或与 got 连用) 心中有; 心存; 经历 (某种情感): H~ you (got)/Do you ~ any idea where he lives? 你知道他住在哪里吗? What

reason ~ you (got) for thinking that he's dishonest? 你凭什么认为他不诚实? *What kind of holiday ~ you in mind?* 你打算怎样度假? **7** [VP 6 A, 18 C, 19 B] (in the inf only and always stressed) allow; endure: (仅用其不定式, 并须重读) 允许; 忍受: *I won't '~ such conduct.* 我不容许这种行为. *I won't '~ you saying such things.* 我不容许你讲这种话.

have³ (for pronunciations ⇨ **have²**) vt (Used in the neg and interr with or without the *aux v* 'do'. The distinction is not always clear and there can be recommendations only, not rules. When the reference is to sth regular or habitual, the use of do for neg and interr is to be preferred. When the reference is to a particular occasion, constructions without do, and, in colloq style, with got, are to be preferred.) (用于否定和疑问句时, 用助动词 do 或不用皆可, 其间的区别不太分明, 并无规则可循, 仅有下列的提示可供参考:指通常或习惯上的事情时, 在否定和疑问句中多用 do;指一特殊事例时, 多不用, 并且在口语中多与 got 连用.) **1** [VP7B] *~ to do sth,* (have to = /'hæf tə; 'hæftə/; has to = /'hæs tə; 'hæstə/; had to = /'hæt tə; 'hædtə/) expressing obligation or necessity: (表示义务或必要) 必须 (做某事): *Do you often ~ to go to the dentist's?* 你必须常常去看牙吗? *H~ you (got) to go to the dentist's today?* 你今天必须去看牙吗? *The children don't ~ to go to school on Sundays, do they?* 孩子们星期日不须上学, 是吗? *You ~n't (got) to go to school today, ~ you?* 你今天不须上学, 是吗? *I ~ to be getting along (= must leave) now.* 现在我必须走了. *He's so rich that he doesn't ~ to work.* 他很富有, 不须工作. *We had to leave early.* 我们必须早些离去. *Had you / Did you ~ to leave early?* 你们必须早些离去吗? *These shoes will ~ to be repaired.* 这些鞋子必须修补了. ⇨ **must²**, **need²**. **2** [VP 6 A] (in various senses as shown in these examples): (用于下列例句中的各种用法): *Do you often ~ (= suffer from) colds?* 你时常感冒吗? *H~ you (got) (= Are you suffering from) a cold now?* 你感冒了吗? *Do you ~* (ie as a rule, generally) *much time for reading?* 你平常有很多时间读书吗? *H~ you (got)* (ie now, or on the occasion specified) *time to come with me?* 你现在有时间 (现指在或特定的时间) 同我去吗? *Has your dog (got) any puppies now?* 你的狗生小狗了吗? *How often does your dog ~* (ie give birth to) *puppies?* 你的狗多久生一次小狗? *Can you ~* (= take and look after) *the children for a few days?* 你能把孩子们带去照顾几天吗?

have⁴ (for pronunciations ⇨ **have²**) non-anom v (neg and interr always with the *aux v* 'do') **1** [VP 6 A] take; receive; accept; obtain: 吃; 饮; 接受; 得到: *There was nothing to be had,* obtained. 一点东西也得不到. *Do you ~ tea or coffee for breakfast?* 你早餐时饮茶还是喝咖啡? *What shall we ~ for dinner?* 我们晚餐吃什么? **2** [VP6A] (with a n, so that have and the n are equivalent to a v identical with the n): (与一名词连用, 等于与该名词相当的动词的意义): *~ a swim/walk/wash/rest.* 去游泳 (散步, 盥洗, 休息). *Let me ~ a try/look.* 让我试一试 (看一看). *Go and ~ a lie down.* 去躺下休息一会儿. *Do you ever ~ dreams?* 你做过梦吗? **3** [VP6A] experience; undergo: 经历; 遭受: *We didn't ~ much difficulty.* 我们没有遭受什么困难. *Did you ~ a good holiday?* 你过了一个快乐的假日吗? *You've never had it so good,* never had so much, or such good quality, of it before. 你从未得到这样多 (过得这样好). *let him / them ~ it,* (sl) shoot, punish sb, etc according to the situation. (俚) 射杀或惩罚某人. *~ had it,* (sl) not be going to receive or enjoy sth: (俚) 得不到或享不到: *Here come the police—I'm afraid we've had it!* 警察来了——我恐怕我们得不到了! **4** [VP24C] *~ sth done,* cause (sb to do sth): 使 (某人做某事): *I must ~ these bad tooth pulled out.* 我必须把那颗蛀牙拔掉. *I must ~ these shoes repaired.* 我必须把这些鞋子拿去修. *When did you last*

~ your hair cut? 你上一次理发是什么时候? ⇨ **get(2)**. ⇨ also **6** below. 亦参看下列第 6 义. **5** [VP18C] *~ sb do sth,* want him to do it: 要 (某人做某事): *I would ~ you know that...,* I want you to know that.... 我要让你知道...。 *What would you ~ me do?* 你要我做什么? *I wouldn't ~ you do that,* should prefer you not to do it. 我不愿你做那事. *~ to do with,* ⇨ **do²(14)**. **6** [VP 24B] *~ sth done,* experience or suffer it: 蒙受: *He had his pocket picked,* sth stolen from his pocket. 他被人扒窃. *Charles I had his head cut off.* 查理一世遭到断头之祸. **7** [VP6A] (colloq) (口) **(a)** trick; deceive: 欺骗: *I'm afraid you've been had.* 我恐怕你受骗了. *Mind he doesn't ~ you.* 当心别让他骗你. **(b)** beat; win an advantage over: 击败; 胜过: *He had me in that argument.* 他在那次辩论中战胜了我. *You had me there!* 你击败我了! **8** (with it and a clause) express; maintain: (与 it 及一从句连用) 表示; 坚持: *Rumour has it (= There is a rumour) that the Prime Minister is going to resign.* 传闻首相将要辞职. *He will ~ it (= He insists) that our plan is impracticable.* 他会坚持说我们的计划行不通. *...as Plato has it* (used when giving a quotation, etc). 如柏拉图所说...(用于引用文句等时). **9** [VP15B] (uses with *adverbial particles* and *preps*): (与副词性小品词及介词连用的用法):

have sth back: *You shall ~ it back* (= It will be returned to you) *next month.* 下月把它还给你. *Let me ~ it back soon.* 快些把它还给我.

have sb down, entertain sb as a visitor or guest: 请某人作客; 款待某人: *We're having the Greens down* (eg from London) *for a few days.* 我们将请格林一家人来住几天 (例如从伦敦来).

have sb in, receive him in the room, house, etc: 请某人到房屋等内: *We shall be having the decorators in next month,* The men will be decorating the house. 我们下月将请人来装饰房屋. *~ sth in,* possess in the house, etc: 置备某物于房屋等内: *Do we ~ enough coal in for winter?* 我们贮备的煤够冬季用吗?

have it off / away (with sb), ⚠ (sl) *~ sexual intercourse* (with). (讳) (俚) (与某人) 发生性关系.

have sb on, (colloq) play a trick on him, deceive him. (口) 欺骗某人. ⇨ **7** above. 参看上列第 7 义. *~ sth on,* **(a)** be wearing: 穿着; 戴着: *He had nothing on,* was naked. 他赤裸着. **(b)** ~ an engagement: 有约会: *I ~ nothing on tomorrow evening,* I am free. 我明天晚上没有约会.

have sth out, cause sth to be taken out: 使某物在外; 将某物去除: *~ a tooth out.* 拔掉一牙. *~ one's sleep out,* continue sleeping until one wakes naturally: 继续睡到自己醒来: *Let her ~ her sleep out.* 让她继续睡够. *~ it out with sb,* reach an understanding about sth by frank discussion. 坦白地与某人讨论某事以达成谅解.

have sb over / round, be visited at home by him: 请某人到家来: *We had Sue and Steve round for dinner last night.* 昨晚我们请休和史蒂夫来家中晚餐.

have sb up, **(a)** receive sb as a visitor (up to one's room, up from the country, etc). 请某人来作客 (至室内或由乡下来等). **(b)** (usu passive) (colloq) cause sb to appear before a magistrate, in a court of law, etc: (通常用被动语态) (口) 使某人受控告, 出庭等: *He was had up* (= was prosecuted) *for exceeding the speed limit.* 他因超速而受控告.

have⁵ /hæv; hæv/ n pl *the ~s and the '~-nots,* the rich and the poor (of people and countries). 富人与穷人; 富国与穷国.

ha·ven /'heɪvn; 'hevən/ n harbour; (fig) place of safety or rest. 港; (喻) 安全地方; 避难所; 休息处.

hav·er·sack /'hævəsæk; 'hævɚ,sæk/ n canvas bag, esp as used by soldiers, hikers and others, for carrying food, etc. 帆布袋 (尤指士兵, 远足者等用以携带食物等); 干粮袋.

havoc /'hævək; 'hævɚk/ n [U] widespread damage; destruction: 大破坏; 毁坏: *The floods caused terrible ~.*

那洪水造成了可怕的灾害。*play ~ with / among*; *make ~ of*, destroy or injure. 破坏; 伤害。

haw[1] /hɔː; hɔ/ *n* fruit (a red berry) of the hawthorn bush. 山楂; 山楂的果实(一种红浆果)。

haw[2] /hɔː; hɔ/ *vi*, *n* ⇨ **hum(4)**.

haw-haw /'hɔːhɔː; 'hɔ'hɔ/ *n*, *int* boisterous laugh. 哈哈大笑。

hawk[1] /hɔːk; hɔk/ *n* **1** strong, swift, keen-sighted bird of prey. 鹰。⇨ the illus at **prey**. 参看 prey 之插图。 **,~-'eyed** *adj* having keen sight. 眼光锐敏的。 **2** person who favours the use of military force in foreign policy. 鹰派成员(外交政策上主战者)。 ⇨ **dove**.

hawk[2] /hɔːk; hɔk/ *vt* [VP 6 A, 15 B] **~** *(about/around)*, offer (goods) for sale, by going from house to house, street to street, etc; (fig) spread: 沿街叫卖; (喻)散播: *~ news / gossip about.* 散播消息(谣言)。 **~er** *n* person who ~s goods (usu from a barrow or cart). 沿街叫卖之小贩(通常推一小车)。 ⇨ **pedlar**.

haw·ser /'hɔːzə(r); 'hɔzə/ *n* thick, heavy rope; thin steel cable (used on ships). 大索; 小钢缆(用于船上)。

haw·thorn /'hɔːθɔːn; 'hɔ,θɔrn/ *n* thorny shrub or tree with white, red or pink blossom and small red berries (called *haws*), often used for hedges in GB. 山楂(一种有刺的灌木或树, 开白色、红色或粉红色花, 结小红浆果, 称作山楂子, 在英国常被用来做围篱)。

hay /heɪ; he/ *n* [U] grass cut and dried for use as animal food. 秣; 干草(用作牲口饲料)。 *make hay*, turn it over for exposure to the sun; 翻草让日晒以制干草; (hence)(由此产生)**'hay-maker, 'hay-making** *nn* make *hay of*, throw into confusion. 使混乱; 弄乱。 *make 'hay while the 'sun shines*, (prov) make the earliest use of one's opportunities. (谚)把握时机。 **'hay·cock** *n* cone-shaped pile of hay in a field, to be carted away when dry. 圆锥形之干草堆(干后以备用车运走)。 **'hay fever** *n* [U] disease affecting the nose and throat, caused by pollen or dust. 枯草; 花粉热(由植物花粉或尘埃引起感染鼻与喉的病)。 **'hay-fork** *n* long-handled two-pronged fork for turning and lifting hay. 干草叉。 **'hay-rick, 'hay·stack** *nn* large pile of hay firmly packed for storing, with a pointed or ridged top. 大干草堆(顶端呈尖形或拱起, 贮以备用)。 **'hay·wire** *n* [U] wire for tying up bales of hay. 捆干草束用的铁丝。 □ *pred adj* (colloq) out of order; excited or distracted. (口)紊乱的; 狂乱的。 *go haywire*, (of persons) become distraught; (of sth, eg a plan) become badly disorganised. (指人)狂乱的; (指事物, 例如一计划)紊乱。

haz·ard /'hæzəd; 'hæzəd/ *n* **1** [C] risk; danger: 冒险; 危险: *health ~s*, eg smoking cigarettes; 健康上的冒险(例如抽烟); *a life full of ~s.* 充满冒险的一生。 *at all ~s*, whatever the risks may be. 不顾任何危险。 **2** [U] game at dice, with complicated chances. 一种机会复杂的掷骰子之戏。 □ *vt* [VP 6 A] **1** take the risk of; expose to danger: 冒…之险; 使遭受危险: *Rock-climbers sometimes ~ their lives.* 攀岩石者有时冒着生命的危险。 **2** venture to make: 冒险而作: *~ a guess / remark.* 冒险试作猜测(评论)。 **~ous** /-əs; -əs/ *adj* risky: 冒险的; 危险的: *a ~ous climb.* 危险的攀登。 **~ously** *adv*

haze[1] /heɪz; hez/ *n* [C, U] thin mist; (fig) mental confusion or uncertainty. 薄雾; 霭; (喻)疑惑; 心中不定。

haze[2] /heɪz; hez/ *vt* (US) harass (sb) by making him perform humiliating jobs; bully or persecute. (美)使做丢脸之事而折磨(某人); 欺侮。

hazel /'heɪzl; 'hezl/ *n* [C] bush with edible nuts; [U] (esp of eyes) colour of the shell of the nut, reddish brown. 榛(一种小树, 结可食之坚果); 榛果壳的颜色; 红褐色(尤指眼睛的颜色)。

hazy /'heɪzɪ; 'hezɪ/ *adj* (-ier, -iest) misty: 有薄雾的;

~ weather; 有薄雾的天气; (fig) vague; slightly confused; uncertain: (喻)模糊的; 有些困惑的; 不定的: *~ about what to do next.* 不知下一步该做什么。 **hazi·ly** /-ɪlɪ; -lɪ/ *adv* **hazi·ness** *n*

H-bomb /'eɪtʃbɒm; 'etʃbɑm/ *n* hydrogen bomb: 氢弹。

he /*strong or initial form*: hiː; hi; *medial weak form*. iː; i/ *pron* **1** male person or animal previously referred to: 他(代表前面所提及的男子或雄性动物): *Where's your brother? He's in Paris.* 你哥哥(弟弟)在哪里? 他在巴黎。 **2** (as *pref*) male: (作为前级)雄性; 男性: *'he-goat.* 雄山羊。 **'he-man** /-mæn; -mæn/ *n* (*pl* -**men**) (facet) strong man. (玩笑语)健壮的男人。 **3** (liter style) *he who*, the one who, anyone who. (文学用语)凡…者。

head[1] /hed; hed/ *n* **1** that part of the body which contains the eyes, nose, mouth and brain: 头; 头部; 首: *They cut his ~ off.* 他们割下他的头。 *Hit him on the ~* (note: *the ~*, not *his ~*). 打他的头(注意: on 后用 the 而不用 his)。 *It cost him his ~*, his life. 那使他丧失了生命。 *Many nobles lost their ~s during the French Revolution.* 法国大革命期间许多贵族断送了性命。 ⇨ the illus here and at **insect**. 参看本条及 insect 之插图。 **2** (as a measure) ~'s length: (量度单位)一头之长: *The Queen's horse won by a ~.* 王后的马以一头之先获胜。 *Tom is taller than Harry by a ~.* 汤姆比哈里高一头。 *be ~ and 'shoulders above sb*, (fig) be considerably superior in intelligence or ability. (喻)在智慧或能力上超越他人很多。 **3 ~ (s)**, that side of a coin on which the ~ of a person appears, the other side being *tails* or the *tail*. (硬币之)正面(即有人像的一面, 另一面称做背面)。 *H~s or tails?* (said when spinning a coin to decide sth by chance): 要正面还是背面?(掷钱以凭机会决定某事物): *H~s—I win!* 正面——我赢了! *be unable to make ~ or tail of sth*, be unable to understand it in the least. 一点也不明白。 **4** person: 人: *50 dinners at £1. 50 a ~.* 每人一英镑半一餐的饭五十份。 **5** (*pl* unchanged) unit of a flock or herd: (复数不变)牲畜之头数: *50 ~ of cattle*; 五十头牛; *a large ~* (= number) *of game.* 很多猎物。 **6** intellect; imagination; power to reason: 智力; 想象力; 理解力: *He made the story up out of his own ~*, It was an original story, not one that he had heard or read. 这故事是他自己想出来的。 **7** natural aptitude or talent: 天资; 天才: *He has a good ~ for business.* 他很有经商的天才。 **8** sth like a ~ in form or position, eg the part that is pressed (*the ~ of a pin*), struck (*the ~ of a nail*), used for striking (*the ~ of a hammer*) or for cutting (*the ~ of an axe*); *a tape-recorder ~*, attachment that holds or contains an electronic device to record, read or erase material on magnetic tape, disc, etc. 形状或位置似头的东西(例如针头, 钉头, 锤头或斧的头); (录音机的)录音头。 **9** top: 顶端: *at the ~ of the page*; 在该页之顶端; *standing at the ~ of the staircase*; 站在楼梯的顶端; *at the ~ of the poll*, having received most votes at an election. 获最多的选票。 **10** upper end: 上端: *the ~ of a lake*, the end at which a river enters it; 湖的源头; *the ~-waters of the Nile*, its sources and upper streams; 尼罗河的上游; *the ~ of a bed*, where a person's ~ rests. 床头(放头的部分)。 **11** (of plants) mass of leaves or flowers at the top of a stem or stalk: (指植物)茎顶端的一团叶或花: *a fine ~ of cabbage*; 一颗好的卷心菜; *a ~ of lettuce*; 一头莴苣; *a flower ~*; 菖蓿花; *a 'flower ~.* 花头; 头状花。 **12** (often attrib) ruler; chief; position of command: (常用作定语)(统治者; 领袖; 首长地位: *~s of government*, eg the President of the US, the Prime Minister of GB; 政府首长(例如美国总统, 英国首相); *the crowned ~s of Europe*, the kings and queens; 欧洲的国王和女王们; *the ~ of the family*; 家长; *the ~ office*, the chief or most important office (contrasted with *branch* offices); 总店; 总公司(与 branch 的分店相对); *the ~ waiter.* 侍者领班; 茶房头。 **H~ of 'State** *n* (*pl* **H~s of State**) the chief public representative of a country,

who may also be the head of government. 国家之元首。
13 front; front part: 前面; 前部: *at the ~ of the procession*; 在游行行列的前排; *marching at the ~ of the regiment*. 行军时在团的前排。*The ship was down by the ~*, with the bows deeper in the water than the stern. 船首吃水较深。**14** (chiefly in proper names) cape or promontory: (主要用于专有名词)岬; 海角: *Beachy H~*. 俾赤岬。⇨ *headland* in 20 below. 参看下列第 20 义中之 **headland**. **15** body of water kept at a certain height (eg for a water-mill or a hydro-electric power station); pressure or force (per unit of area) of a confined body of steam, etc: 水头(保持某种高度的水源, 例如水车或水力发电站所用); 水位差; 蒸汽等的压力; 水压: *They kept up a good ~ of steam*. 他们保持良好的蒸汽压。**16** main division in a discourse, essay, etc: 演讲, 文章等之要项: *a speech arranged under five ~s*; 分为五项的一篇演说; *treat a question under several ~s*. 分几点讨论一问题。⇨ **heading**. **17** foam of liquid (esp liquor) that has been poured out: 倾出后的液体(尤指酒)所生的泡沫: *the ~ on a glass of beer*. 一杯啤酒上的泡沫。**18** point rising from a boil or other swelling on the flesh, esp when the boil is ripening and about to burst: 疖等之脓包(尤指成熟而要出头者): *The boil came to a ~*. 这疖快要出脓头了。*come to a ~*, (fig) reach a crisis, culminate: (喻)至严重关头; 达于顶点: *Discontent has come to a ~*. 不满之情绪达于顶点。**19** (various phrases) (各种短语) *above/over one's ~*, (in a way that is) too difficult for one to understand: 难以理解的; 难以理解: *be/talk above one's ~*; 难以理解; *go above one's ~*, be too difficult for one. 太难。*an old ~ on young shoulders*, wisdom in a young person. 年轻而有见识; 少年老成。*bite sb's '~ off*, scold them angrily. 怒责某人。*eat one's ~ off*, (of a horse) eat a great deal and do little work. (指马)食量大而工作少。*give sb his ~*, allow him to act freely, unchecked. 任其随意行为。*go to one's ~*, (a) (of liquor) intoxicate: (指酒)上头; 使人醉: *The whisky went to his ~*. 他喝那威士忌酒喝醉了。**(b)** excite. 使激动: *His successes have gone to his ~*, made him over-confident, conceited, etc. 成功使他变得自负了(成功冲昏了他的头脑)。*have a ,good '~ on one's shoulders*, have practical ability, common sense, etc. 有实际才能, 常识等。*~ over heels*, topsy-turvey; (fig) deeply or completely: 头朝下; 颠倒地; (喻)深深地或完全地: *~ over heels in debt / in love*. 负债累累(深深坠入情网)。

keep one's ~, keep calm. 保持镇静。*keep one's above water*, (fig) stay out of debt, difficulty, etc. (喻)未欠债; 未遭受困难。*keep one's ~ down*, avoid danger or distraction. 避免危险或分心。*laugh/scream one's '~ off*, laugh/scream loudly, with great energy. 大笑(大叫)。*lose one's ~*, become confused or over-excited. 冲动; 失去理智。*(go) off one's ~*, (become) crazy. (变得)精神错乱。*(stand, etc) on one's ~*, with feet in the air: 倒立: *I could do it (standing) on my ~*, (colloq) It is very easy. (口)我做这事轻而易举。*on one's own ~ be it*, the consequences will rest on one. 某人应负责。*over one's ~*, = *above one's ~*. *(be promoted) over another's ~/over the ~s of others*, before another or others with prior or stronger claims. (得晋升)至他人之上; 升迁比别人快。*'put our /your/ their '~s together*, consult together. 聚议; 在一起商量。*put sth into a person's ~*, suggest it to him. 将某事提示给某人。*put sth out of one's ~*, stop thinking about it; give up the idea: 不再想某事; 放弃一念头: *You'd better put the idea of marriage out of your ~*. 你最好放弃结婚的念头。*put sth out of sb's ~*, make him forget it: 使某人忘记某事: *An interruption put it out of my ~*. 一打岔我就把这事忘了。*take sth into one's ~*, come to believe it: 相信某事: *He took it into his ~ that I was secretly opposing him*. 他相信我在秘密地反对他。*talk one's '~ off*, talk too much. 说得太多。*talk sb's '~ off*, weary him with talk. 谈得使某人厌倦。*turn sb's ~*, make him conceited. 使自负。*Two ~s are bettr than one*, (prov) The opinions, advice, etc of a second person are valuable. (谚)集思胜过独断。*(be) weak in the ~*, (be) not very intelligent. 智慧低。**20** (compounds) (复合词) *'~·ache n* [C, U] **(a)** continuous pain in the ~. 头痛: *suffer from ~ache(s)*, 患头痛; *have a bad ~ache*. 头痛得很厉害。**(b)** (sl) troublesome problem: (俚)头痛的问题: *more ~aches for the Department of the Environment*. 更多使环境卫生部头痛的问题。*'~·band n* band worn round the ~. 束发带。*'~·dress n* covering for the ~, esp woman's ornamental kind. 头巾(尤指妇女做装饰用者)。*'~·gear n* hat, cap, ~dress. 帽子; 头巾。*'~·hunter n* savage who cuts off and keeps as trophies the ~s of his enemies; (fig) ruthless recruiter. 割取敌人之头以作战利品的野蛮人; (喻)无情的征募人员者。*'~·lamp n* = **headlight**. *'~·land* /-lənd; -,lænd/ *n* promontory, cape. 岬; 海角。

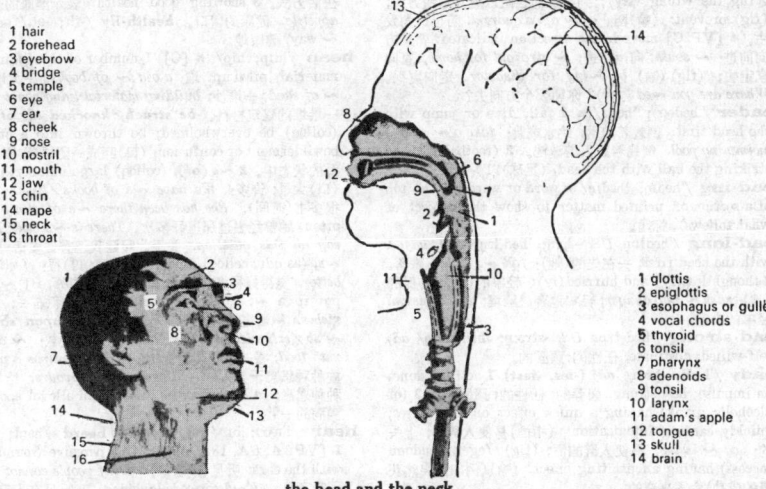

1 hair
2 forehead
3 eyebrow
4 bridge
5 temple
6 eye
7 ear
8 cheek
9 nose
10 nostril
11 mouth
12 jaw
13 chin
14 nape
15 neck
16 throat

1 glottis
2 epiglottis
3 esophagus or gullet
4 vocal chords
5 thyroid
6 tonsil
7 pharynx
8 adenoids
9 tonsil
10 larynx
11 adam's apple
12 tongue
13 skull
14 brain

the head and the neck

'~-light n large lamp on the front of a locomotive, motor-car, etc. (火车，汽车等的)前灯。⇨ the illus at **bicycle, motor.** 参看 bicycle, motor 之插图。**'~-line** n newspaper heading; line at the top of a page containing title, etc; (pl) summary of broadcast news: 报纸的标题；页头标题：(复)新闻广播提要：'Here are the news ~lines.' '现在报告新闻提要。' **'~-man** /-mæn; -mən/ n (pl-men) chief men of a village, tribe, etc. 村长；首长(等)。**'~-master /·'mistress** nn principal master/ mistress of a school. 校长(女校长)。**'~·on** adj, adv (of collisions) with the front parts (of vehicles) meeting: (指相撞)(车辆)正面的(地)：a ~on collision; 正面相撞；meet/strike ~on. 正面互撞。**'~·phones** n pl receivers fitting over the ~ (for radio, etc) : earphones. (收听无线电等之)耳机。**(b)** (colloq) helmet. 盔。**(b)** (colloq) intelligence; brains. (口)智力；头脑。**,~·quarters** n (sing or pl) place from which (eg police, army) operations are controlled. (单或复)(警察，军队等之)总局；司令部。**'~·rest** n sth that supports the ~. (牙医诊所、理发店坐椅的)垫头之物；靠头之物。**'~·room** n = clearance(2). **'~·set** n ~phones. 耳机。**'~·ship** /-ʃɪp; -ʃɪp/ n position of a ~master or ~mistress: 校长的职位：apply for a ~ship. 申请做校长。**'~·stall** n part of a bridle or halter that fits round the ~. 马笼头。**'~·stone** n stone set up at the ~ of a grave. 墓碑。**'~·waters** n pl ⇨ **10** above. 参看上列第10义。**'~·way** n [U] progress. 前进；进步。**make some/no ~way,** (not) make progress. (无)有进展。**'~·wind** n one that blows directly into one's face, or against the course of a ship, etc. 顶头风；逆风。**'~·word** n word used as a heading, eg the first word, in heavy type, of a dictionary entry. 作为标题的词(例如词典中用粗体字所列的词目)；首词。**~ed** adj (in compounds) (用于复合词)，three-'~ed, having three ~s, 有三个头的；long-'~ed, having a long skull. 长脑壳的。**~·less** adj having no ~. 无头的。

head² /hed; hed/ vt, vi **1** be at the head or top of: 在…前头；为…之首；在…的顶部：~ a procession; 在游行行列的前排；~ a revolt/rebellion, act as the leader. 领导叛乱。Smith's name ~ed the list. 史密斯的名字在表上的最上端。**2** [VP6A] strike, touch, with the head (eg the ball in football). 用头撞，顶，触(例如足球中用头顶球)。**3** [VP15B] ~ sth/sb off, get in front of, so as to turn back or aside: 到…的前面使其回转或转向；拦截：~ off a flock of sheep (to prevent them from going the wrong way); 到羊群前拦阻以免其走错方向；(fig) prevent: (喻)防止：~ off a quarrel. 防止口角发生。**4** [VP2C] move in the direction indicated: 朝某方向前进：~ south; 向南行进；~ straight for home, 直向家里去；(fig) (喻) be ~ing for disaster. 走向灾祸。Where are you ~ed (for)? 你朝哪个方向去？

header /'hedə(r); 'hedɚ/ n **1** fall, dive or jump with the head first: 倒栽着跌落，跳水或跳：take a ~ into a swimming pool. 倒栽着跳入游泳池。**2** (football) act of striking the ball with the head. (足球)以头顶球。

head·ing /'hedɪŋ; 'hedɪŋ/ n word or words at the top of a section of printed matter to show the subject of what follows). 标题。

head·long /'hedlɒŋ US: -lɔ:ŋ; 'hed,lɔŋ/ adv, adj **1** with the head first: 头在先的(地)：fall ~: 头向下跌落。**2** thoughtless(ly) and hurried(ly): 轻率的(地)；匆促的(地)：rush ~ into danger; 轻率地奔赴险境；a ~ decision. 轻率的决定。

head·strong /'hedstrɒŋ US: -strɔ:ŋ; 'hed,strɔŋ/ adj self-willed; obstinate. 任性的；顽固的。

heady /'hedɪ; 'hedɪ/ adj (-ier, -iest) **1** acting, done, on impulse; headstrong. 卤莽的；任性的；顽固的。**2** (of alcoholic drink) having a quick effect on the senses; quickly causing intoxication: (酒)易使人醉的；上头的：a ~ wine; 易使人醉的酒；(fig) (eg of sudden success) having an exciting effect. (喻)(例如突然获得的成功)令人兴奋的。

heal /hi:l; hil/ vt, vi **1** [VP6A, 2A, C] (esp of wounds) (cause to) become healthy and sound: (尤指伤口)治愈；痊愈：The wound is not yet ~ed, the new skin has not yet covered it. 这伤口尚未痊愈(尚未长出新皮)。The wound ~ed slowly. 这伤口痊愈得很慢。It soon ~ed up/over. 不久即告痊愈。**2** [VP6A] (archaic or biblical) restore (a person) to health; cure (a disease): (古或圣经文体) 恢复(某人)的健康；医治(疾病)：~ sb of a disease (cure is now the usu word). 医治某人的病(现在则用 cure)。⇨ also faith-~ing at **faith. 3** [VP6A] end: 结束：~ a quarrel. 平息口角。Time is all sorrows. 时间可医治一切忧伤。**~·er** n person or thing that ~s: 治疗的人或物：Time is a great ~er. 时间是很有效的治疗的。**~·ing** adj having the power to ~: 有治疗功能的；能治愈的：~ing ointments. 药膏。

health /helθ; helθ/ n **1** [U] condition of the body or the mind: 人体或精神的状况：be in/enjoy/have good/poor ~. 身体好(不好)。Fresh air and exercise are good for the ~ (more colloq good for you). 新鲜空气和运动有益于健康(用 good for you 较通俗)。**~ food** n [U] food that is nutritious and free of artificial substances: (未加工食物)营养食品：(attrib) (用作定语) a ~ food restaurant/shop. 营养食品餐馆(商店)。**2** (in names of organizations, etc): (用于机构等名称中)：the World'H~ Organization (abbr 缩作 **WHO**); 世界卫生组织；the Department of H~ and Social Security (in GB, 英, abbr 略作 **DHSS**); 卫生和社会保险部；the National'H~ Service (in GB, 英, abbr 略作 **NHS**). 国家卫生局。**3** [U] state of being well and free from illness: 健康：restored to ~. 恢复健康。**4** drink sb's ~; drink a ~ (to sb), (as a social custom) raise one's glass and wish good ~ to him. (按照社交习惯) 举杯祝贺(某人)健康。**~·ful** /-fl; -fəl/ adj -giving; good for the ~. 卫生的；有益于健康的。

healthy /'helθɪ; 'helθɪ/ adj (-ier, -iest) **1** having good health; well, strong and able to resist disease: 健康的；健壮的：The children look very ~. 孩子们看来很健康。The children are quite ~, although they have slight colds at present. 孩子们虽然目前患轻微的伤风，但他们十分健康。(Note that well is the usu word when the reference is to a specific occasion: eg I hope you're quite well.) (注意：指特殊的健康状况时通常用 well，例如：I hope you're quite well. 我希望你身体很好。)**2** likely to produce good health: 有益于健康的；卫生的：a ~ climate; 有益于健康的气候；a ~ way of living. 卫生的生活方式。**3** showing good health: 表示健康的：a ~ appetite. 健康的胃口。**health·ily** /-ɪlɪ; -əlɪ/ adv in a ~ way. 健康地。

heap /hi:p; hip/ n [C] **1** number of things, mass of material, piled up: 堆：a big ~ of books; 一大堆书；a ~ of sand; 一堆沙；building material lying about in ~s. 一堆堆的建筑材料。**be struck/knocked all of a ~**, (colloq) be overwhelmed; be thrown into a state of bewilderment or confusion. (口)吓成一团；陷入困惑或慌乱的状态中。**2 ~s (of),** (colloq) large number; plenty: (口)大量；许多：We have ~s of books/time. 我们有很多书(时间)。She has been there ~s of times, very often. 她曾经去过那里好多次。There is ~s more I could say on this question. 关于此问题我还有许多话可说。**3 ~s,** (as adv; colloq) much: (作副词；口)很：feeling ~s better. 觉得好得多。□ vt **1** [VP6A, 15A, B] ~ (up), put in a ~: 堆积：~ (up) stones; 堆积石头；~ up riches. 积财富。**2** [VP14] ~ sth on/upon sb/sth; ~ sb/sth with sth, fill; load: 装满；装载：~ a plate with food; 将一盘子装满食物；~ favours upon a person, 施种种恩惠于某人；~ a person with favours: 给与某人种种恩惠；a ~ed spoonful, more than a level spoonful. 满满的一匙。

hear /hɪə(r); hɪr/ vt, vi (pt, pp heard /hɜ:d; hɝd/) **1** [VP2A, 6A, 18A, 19A, 24A] perceive (sound, etc) with the ears: 听见(声音等)：Deaf people cannot ~. 聋子听不见。I ~d someone laughing. 我听见有人笑。He

was ~*d to groan.* 有人听见他呻吟。 *Did you* ~ *him go out?* 你听见他走出去吗? *Have you ever* ~*d that song sung in Italian?* 你听过那支歌用意大利语演唱吗? *We listened but could* ~ *nothing.* 我们注意听，但什么也听不见。 *She doesn't/can't* ~ *very well.* 她的听力不大好。 (Note the frequent use of *can-could* when an effort of perception is implied.) (注意: 如含有努力听之义, 用 can 或 could。) **2** [VP6A, 9, 3A] be told or informed: 听说; 闻知: *Have you* ~*d the news?* 你听到那消息没有? *I* ~*d that he was ill.* 我听说他病了。 *I've heard (say) that your country is beautiful.* 我听说你的国家很美丽。 ~ *about sth,* be given information about; learn about: 听说; 得悉: *I've heard* ~ *about his dismissal / illness.* 我刚听说他被解雇(生病)了。 *You will* ~ *about this later,* sometimes implying that there will be a rebuke, etc. 你过些时便会听说这事(有时暗示将有指责等之义)。 ~ *from sb,* receive a letter, news, etc: 收到某人的信件, 消息等: *How often do you* ~ *from your sister?* 你多久接到你姐姐(妹妹)一次信? ~ *of sb/sth,* have knowledge of: 知道某人(某事物): *I've never* ~*d of her / the place,* know nothing of her / the place. 我从来没有听说过她(那地方)。 ~ *tell of,* ~ people talking about: 听人谈起: *I've often* ~*d tell of such happenings.* 我常听人谈起这类事情(的发生)。 **3** [VP6A, 10, 15A, 3A] listen to; pay attention to; (of a judge in a law court) try (a case): 听; 注意; (指法官)审理(案件): *You'd better* ~ *what they have to say.* 你最好听他们要说些什么。 *The court* ~*d the evidence.* 法官们听取证词。 *Which judge will* ~ *the case?* 哪位法官将审理这案件? ~ *sb out,* listen to the end: 听某人说完: *Don't judge me before I've finished my explanation:* ~ *me out, please.* 在我未解释完以前不要批评我, 请听我说完。 *not* ~ *of,* (usu with *will, would*) refuse to consider or allow: (通常与 will, would 连用)不予考虑; 不允许: *I won't* ~ *of such a thing!* 我不同意此事! *She wouldn't* ~ *of it.* 她拒绝考虑。 **4** *,H*~*! 'H*~*!* used as a form of cheering to express approval or agreement, but also ironically. 好哇! 好哇! (用以喝彩, 表示赞同, 但有时亦有讥讽之意)。 ~*er n* person who hears, eg in an audience. 听者; 听众。

hear·ing /'hɔːrɪŋ; 'hɪrɪŋ/ *n* **1** [U] perception by sound: 听觉: *Her* ~ *is poor,* she is rather deaf. 她的听觉不好。 *hard of* ~, rather deaf. 有点聋; 重听。 '~*-aid n* electronic device for helping deaf people to hear. 助听器。 **2** [U] distance within which one can hear: 听力所及的距离: *In some countries it is unwise to talk about politics in the* ~ *of strangers,* where strangers may hear. 在某些国家内, 在陌生人听得见的范围内谈论政治是不智的。 *within/out of* ~, near enough/not near enough to hear or be heard: 在听得见(听不见)的距离内: *Please keep within* ~. 请保持在听得见的距离内。 **3** [U] opportunity of being heard (esp in self-defence). 发言的机会; (尤指)申诉。 *gain a* ~, an opportunity to be heard. 获得申诉的机会。 *give sb/get a fair* ~, an opportunity of being listened to impartially. 公平地听某人申诉(获得申诉机会)。 **4** (legal) trial of a case at law, esp before a judge without a jury. (法律)听讼; 审讯(尤指无陪审团在场者)。

hearken /'hɑːkən; 'hɑrkən/ *vi* (archaic) listen *(to).* (古)倾听(与 to 连用)。

hear·say /'hɔːseɪ; 'hɪr,se/ *n* [U] common talk; rumour; what one has heard another person or other persons say: 道听途说; 谣言: *I don't believe it; it's merely* ~. 我不相信, 这仅是谣传罢了。 *H*~ *evidence is not accepted in law courts.* 传闻的证据在法庭上是不予接受的。

hearse /hɜːs; hɜrs/ *n* carriage, car, for carrying a coffin at a funeral. 枢车; 灵车。

heart /hɑːt; hɑrt/ *n* **1** that part of the body which pumps blood through the system: 心; 心脏: *When a man's* ~ *stops beating, he dies.* 一个人的心脏停止跳动时, 他便死了。 *He had a '*~ *attack,* a sudden illness with irregular and violent beating of the ~. 他的心脏病发

作了。 ⇨ the illus at **respiratory**. 参看 respiratory 之插图。 **2** centre of the emotions, esp love; deepest part of one's nature: 内心; 爱心; 衷心; 心地; 心肠; 心境: *a man with a* ~; 心肠仁慈的人; *a kind*~*ed man.* 好心肠的人。 *sb after one's own* ~, of the sort one very much likes or approves of. 正合自己意之人。 *at* ~, deep down; basically. 在内心; 基本上。 *have sth at* ~, be deeply interested in it, anxious to support or encourage it. 对某事甚为关心; 急于赞助某事。 *from (the bottom of) one's* ~, sincerely. 真诚地。 *in one's* ~ *of* ~*s,* in one's inmost feelings. 在内心深处。 *to one's* ~*'s content,* as much as, for as long as, etc one wishes. 心满意足; 尽情。 *with all one's* ~, completely and willingly: 全心地; 欣然: *I love you with all my* ~. 我全心全意地爱你。 ~ *and soul,* completely: 完全地: *I'm yours* ~ *and soul.* 我是完全属于你的。 *break a person's* ~, make him very sad. 使人伤心; 令人断肠。 Hence, 由此产生, **,broken**~*'*~*ed,* **,broken** *adj.* *cry one's* ~ *out,* pine or brood over sth, esp in secret. 痛哭欲绝; (尤指)为某事暗自忧伤。 *do one's '*~ *good,* cause one to feel encouraged, cheerful, etc. 使人欢欣鼓舞。 *(get/learn/know sth) by* ~, from memory. 熟记; 能背出。 *have a* ~, show sympathy, understanding. 同情; 谅解。 *(have) a change of* ~, (experience) a change of opinion. 改变主意。 *have the* ~ *to,* (usu *neg,* or *interr* with *can-could*) be hard-~ed or unsympathetic enough to: (通常用于否定或疑问句, 与 can 或 could 连用)硬心肠; 忍心: *How can you have the* ~ *to drown the kittens?* 你怎能忍心把这些小猫淹死呢? *have one's* ~ *in sth,* be interested in it and fond of it. 对某事物有兴趣; 喜欢某事物。 *have one's* ~ *in one's boots,* be greatly discouraged, feel hopeless. 深为沮丧; 绝望。 *have one's* ~ *in one's mouth,* be badly frightened. 深为惊恐。 *have one's* ~ *in the right place,* have true or kind feelings. 有热诚; 怀善意。 *have one's* ~ *set on sth,* desire greatly. 渴望; 极想。 *lose* ~, be discouraged. 灰心。 *lose one's* ~ *to sb/sth,* become very fond of; fall in love with. 十分喜爱某人或某物; 倾心于。 *set one's* ~ *on sth/having sth/doing sth, etc,* be very anxious (to have, to do, etc). 渴望(某事物或做某事)。 *take (fresh)* ~ *(at sth),* be confident. (对…)有信心; 振起精神。 *take sth to* ~, be much affected by it, grieve over it. 深为某事所感动; 为某事物感到悲伤。 *wear one's* ~ *on/upon one's sleeve,* show one's feelings quite openly. 表露自己的感情。 **3** central part: 中心部分: *in the* ~ *of the forest;* 在森林的中心; *the* ~ *of the matter,* the essence: 事情的要点; *get to the* ~ *of a subject/mystery;* 抓住一问题(谜团)的中心; *a cabbage with a good solid* ~. 一棵卷得很好的包心菜。 **4** [U] (of land) fertility: (土地之)生产力; 肥沃程度: *in good* ~, in good condition; 肥沃的; *out of* ~, in poor condition. 不肥沃。 **5** ~*-shaped* thing, esp the design used on playing-cards: 心形物 (尤指纸牌上的红心): *The ten/queen/etc of* ~*s.* 红心十点 (女王等)。 *H*~*s are trumps.* 红心是王牌。 ⇨ the illus at **card.** 参看 card 之插图。 **6** (as a term of endearment to a person) (作为对某人表示亲爱之词) dear ~; 亲爱的; '*sweet* ~. 情人; 爱人。 **7** (compounds) (复合词). '~*-ache n* [U] deep sorrow. 悲痛; 伤心。 '~*-beat n* [C] movement of the ~ (about 70 beats a minute). 心搏; 心跳(每分钟约七十次)。 '~*-break n* [U] overwhelming sorrow. 心碎; 伤心。 '~*-breaking* adj causing ~*break.* 令人伤心的; 令人心碎的。 '~*-broken* adj crushed by ~*break.* 伤心的; 心碎的。 '~*-burn n* [U] burning sensation in the lower part of the chest, caused by indigestion. (由于消化不良引起的)胃灼热。 '~*-burn-ing n* [U] (and also in *pl*) envious, discontented feeling(s), usu caused by disappointment. (亦用复数) (通常由失望引起的) 嫉妒; 不满。 '~*-disease n* [U] disease of the ~. 心脏病。 '~*-failure n* [U] failure of the ~ to function. 心脏衰竭; 心脏麻痹。 '~*-felt* adj sincere: 诚意的; 至诚的: ~*felt emotion/thanks.* 衷诚 (衷心感激)。 '~*-rending* adj causing deep grief. 使人

深为悲痛的; 使人伤心的. '~'s-ease n [U] (old name for) pansy. (旧称)三色堇. '~-sick adj low-spirited. 郁闷的; 垂头丧气的. '~-strings n pl deepest feelings of love: 最深挚的爱情; 心弦: play upon sb's ~strings, touch his feelings. 打动某人的心弦. ~ed adj in compounds: 用于复合词中: hard-~ed; 硬心肠的; sad-~ed; 悲伤的; faint-~ed, lacking in courage. 懦弱的. ~·less adj unkind; without pity. 无情的; 残酷的. ~·less·ly adv ~·less·ness n

hearten /'hɑːtn; 'hɑrtn/ vt [VP6A] give courage to; cheer: 鼓励; 使振奋: ~ing news. 使人振奋的消息.

hearth /hɑːθ; hɑrθ/ n floor of a fireplace; (fig) fireside as representing the home: 炉床; (喻)炉边(代表家庭): fight for ~ and altar, (rhet) in defence of one's home and religion. (修辞)为保卫家庭与宗教而战. '~-rug n rug spread out in front of the ~. 炉前地毯.

heart·ily /'hɑːtɪlɪ; 'hɑrtlɪ/ adv 1 with goodwill, courage or appetite: 热忱地; 奋勇地; 有好胃口地: set to work ~; 热忱地着手工作; eat ~. 痛快地吃. 2 very: 十分; 很: ~ glad that..., 十分高兴...; ~ sick of this wet weather. 十分厌恶这雨天.

hearty /'hɑːtɪ; 'hɑrtɪ/ adj (-ier, -iest) 1 (of feelings) sincere: (指感情)诚恳的: give sb a ~ welcome; 竭诚欢迎某人; give one's ~ approval/support to a plan. 衷心赞同(支持)一项计划. 2 strong; in good health: 强健的; 健康的: still hale and ~ at eighty-five. 八十五岁仍很健壮. 3 big: 大的: a ~ meal/appetite. 丰盛的一餐(很好的食欲).

heat[1] /hiːt; hit/ n 1 [U] (the) ~, high temperature: 热; 高温: the ~ of the sun's rays. 阳光的热力. Cold is the absence of ~. 冷即热的不存在. She's suffering from the ~, from the hot weather. 她深受炎热天气之苦. ,prickly '~, ⇨ prickle. 2 [U] (the) ~, (fig) intense feeling: (喻)热烈; 激烈: speak with considerable ~; 讲话颇为激昂; in the ~ of the debate/argument. 在激烈辩论期间. 3 [C] competition the winners of which take part in (the further competitions leading to) the finals: 预赛 (得胜者可参加复赛或决赛): trial/preliminary ~s. 预赛; 初赛. ⇨ also dead ~, at dead(6). 4 [U] (of female mammals) period or condition of sexual excitement: 指雌性哺乳动物)性欲冲动期; 交尾期性欲之冲动. be in/on/at ~. 性欲冲动. 5 (compounds)(复合词)'~ barrier n = thermal barrier, ⇨ thermal. '~-flash n intense ~, eg as released from the explosion of an atomic bomb. 强热 (例如原子弹爆炸所发出者). '~ pump n machine that transfers ~ from a substance at a relatively low temperature to one at a higher temperature, eg for ~ing a building. 热泵, 变热机(将低温变为高温之机器,如供一建筑物暖气所用者). '~-shield n device (esp on the nose-cone of a spacecraft) that gives protection against excessive ~. 挡热罩,热屏(尤指用于太空船之鼻锥体上者,以抵抗高温). '~-spot n mark or point on the skin caused by or sensitive to ~. 热灸点; 痱子(皮肤上感觉发热处). '~-stroke n sudden illness, prostration, caused by excessive ~. 中暑. '~-wave n unbroken period of unusually hot weather. 一段非常炎热的期间; 热浪.

heat[2] /hiːt; hit/ vt, vi [VP6A, 15B, 2C] ~ (up), make or become hot: 使热; 变热: ~ (up) some water; 烧热一些水; ~ up the cold meat for supper; 将冷肉热一热以备晚餐食用. ~ed adj excited; passionate: 热烈的; 激烈的: a ~ed discussion, one during which feelings are roused; 激昂的讨论; get ~ed with wine. 因喝酒而兴奋. ~·ed·ly adv in a ~ed manner. 热烈地; 激烈地. ~er n device for supplying warmth to a room, or for heating water, etc: 暖气设备; 火炉;热水器: a 'gas-~er; 煤气炉; an 'oil-~er. 煤油炉. ~·ing n means of creating ~: 暖气装置: electric/gas/oil ~ing. 电(煤气,煤油)暖气装置. ⇨ central.

heath /hiːθ; hiθ/ n 1 [C] area of flat unused land, esp if covered with ~. 荒地; (尤指)石南荒地. 2 [C,U] (kind of) low evergreen shrub with small purple, pink

or white bell-shaped flowers, eg ling and heather. 石南属常绿灌木(生有紫色、粉红色或白色钟形小花, 如 ling 及 heather 等石南).

hea·then /'hiːðn; 'hiðən/ n 1 [C] (pl ~s or, collectively, the ~) believer in a religion other than the chief world religions: 所相信之宗教非世界上主要的宗教者; 异教徒: The Saxons who invaded England were ~. 侵略英格兰的撒克逊人是异教徒. He went abroad to preach Christianity to the ~. 他去国外向异教徒宣传基督教. 2 [C] (colloq) person whose morals, etc are disapproved of: (口) 道德败坏的人: They've allowed their daughter to grow up as a young ~, wild, ill-mannered, without moral training. 他们听任他们的女儿长大成为道德败坏的年轻人. 3 (attrib): (用作定语): ~ land; 信异教的地方; ~ customs. 异教社会的风俗. ~·ish(-ɪʃ; -ɪʃ] adj of or like ~s; barbarous. 异教徒的; 似异教徒的; 野蛮的.

heather /'heðɚr; 'heðɚ/ n [U] variety of heath(2), with small light-purple or white flowers, common in Scotland. 石南属植物. take to the ~, (in olden times) become an outlaw. (古时) 做歹徒; 做亡命之徒. '~-mixture n cloth of mixed colours supposed to be like ~. 杂色呢.

heave /hiːv; hiv/ vt, vi (pl, pp ~d or (6 and 7 below), nautical use, hove /həʊv; hov/) 1 [VP6A] raise, lift up (sth heavy): 举起(重物). ~ the anchor. 起锚. 2 [VP6A] utter; produce: 发出一声叹息(呻吟). ~ a sigh/groan. 发出一声叹息(呻吟). 3 [VP6A, 15A, B] (colloq) lift and throw: (口) 投掷; 扔; 抛: ~ sth overboard; 将某物掷出船外; ~ a brick through a window. 把一块砖自窗中抛出. 4 [VP2A, C, 3A] ~ (at/on sth), pull (at a rope, etc): 拖; 拉 (绳等): ~ (away) at the capstan. 起锚. H~ away! 用力拉! H~ ho! (sailors' cries when pulling at ropes or cables). 用力拉呀! (水手拖绳或缆时的呼声). 5 [VP2A] rise and fall vigorously and regularly: 猛烈而又规律地升降: a heaving chest; 起伏的胸部; the heaving billows, ie waves. 汹涌的波涛. 6 [VP2C, 15B] ~ to, (of a sailing-ship) (cause to) come to a standstill (without anchoring or mooring): (帆船未抛锚或碇泊而)停止; 使停止. 7 ~ in sight, become visible. 可以看得见; 进入视线范围. □ n act of heaving: 举; 抛; 拖; 起伏: with a mighty ~, a strong pull or throw. 用力拉或抛.

heaven /'hevn; 'hɛvən/ n 1 home of God and the saints: 天堂;天国: die and go to ~. 死后进天堂. 2 H~, God, Providence: 上帝: It was the will of H~. 这是天意. H~ forbid! 上帝不容许! Thank H~ you were not killed. 谢谢天, 你未被杀死. Also in exclamations: 亦用于感叹句中: For H~'s sake! 看在老天爷的份上! Good H~s! 天啊! ,~·'sent adj providential: 由神而来的; 天赐的: a ~sent opportunity. 天赐良机. 3 place, state, of supreme happiness: 极乐之地; 至福. 4 (often 常作 the ~s) the firmament: 天空; 苍天: the broad expanse of ~/the ~s. 一望无际的苍天. move ~ and earth, do one's utmost. 竭尽全力. ~·ward(s) /-wəd(z); -wəd(z)/ adj, adv towards ~. 向天空的(地); 向天国的(地).

heav·en·ly /'hevnlɪ; 'hɛvnlɪ/ adj 1 of, from, like, heaven: 天国的; 自天国的; 似天堂的; 天空的; 自天空的: a ~ angel/vision. 天使(天国的幻景). the ~ bodies, ie the sun, moon, planets, etc. 天体(日,月,星辰). the ~ city, Paradise. 天堂. 2 of more than earthly excellence. 超绝的. 3 (colloq) very pleasing: (口)极为可爱的: What ~ peaches! 多么可爱的桃子啊!

Heavi·side layer /'hevɪsaɪd leɪɚr; 'hɛvɪ,saɪd 'leɚ/ ⇨ ionosphere.

heavy /'hevɪ; 'hɛvɪ/ adj (-ier, -iest) 1 having weight (esp great weight); difficult to lift, carry or move: 重的; 难以举起,携带或移动的: It's too ~ for me to lift. 它太重了, 我举不起来. Lead is a ~ metal. 铅是重金属. '~-weight n boxer weighing 175 lb (79.3 kg) or more. 重量级拳手(体重在 175 磅或 79.3 公斤以上). 2 of more

than usual size, amount, force, etc: 超出一般大小, 数量, 力量等的: ~ *guns/artillery*, of the largest class; 重炮(炮兵); ~ (= abundant) *crops*; 丰收; ~ *rain*; 大雨; ~ *work*; 繁重的工作; *a* ~ *blow*, one with great force behind it; 重击; *a* ~ *fall* one likely to cause shock; 重重的跌倒; *a* ~ *heart*, made sad; 沉重的心情; ~ *tidings*, bad news; 坏消息; ~ *soil*, difficult to cultivate; 难耕种的土地; ~ *roads*, muddy and sticky, difficult to travel over; 泥泞的道路; *a* ~ *sky*, dark with clouds; 阴沉的天空; *a* ~ *sea*, rough, with big waves; 汹涌的大海; ~ *food*, rich, difficult to digest; 油腻而难消化的食物; ~ *bread*, dense, sticky, like dough; 没有发起来的面包; *a* ~ *day*, full of difficult work; 工作艰苦的一天; *a* ~ *sleep/sleeper*, a deep sleep/a person who is difficult to wake up; 熟睡(睡得很熟的人); *a* ~ *drinker/smoker*, sb who drinks (alcoholic drink)/smokes much; 酒鬼(老烟枪); ~ *reading*, difficult to read. 难读的读物。, ~' **hydrogen**, isotope of hydrogen with atoms twice the normal weight. 重氢(氢的同位素, 其原子量大一倍)。, ~' **water**, water whose molecules consist of two ~ hydrogen atoms and one ordinary oxygen atom. 重水(其分子含有两个重氢原子和一个普通的氧原子)。 **3** (of persons) slow in speech or thought; (of writing or painting) dull, tedious; (of parts in a play for the theatre) serious or solemn: (指人)谈话或思想迟缓的; (指写作或绘画)沉闷的; 乏味的; (指剧中角色)严肃的; 庄重的: *play the part of the* ~ *father*; 扮演严肃的父亲; (of bodily states) inactive: (指身体状况)不活动的; 迟钝的: ~ *with sleep/wine*. 因睡眠(饮酒)而呆滞。 (*find sth*) ~ *going*, (find progress) difficult. (觉得某事)很难。 (*find sb*) ~ *going*, (find him) difficult (to understand), or boring (to listen to). (觉得某人) 很难了解; (觉得某人) 所说的话很乏味。 *make* ~ *weather of sth*, ⇨ **weather**(1). **4** (US sl) dangerous; troublesome. (美俚) 危险的; 麻烦的。 **5** (compounds) (复合词) , ~·**handed** *adj* awkward, clumsy. 笨拙的。, ~·**hearted** *adj* melancholy. 忧郁的。 □ *adv* heavily: 沉重地: *The crime lies* ~ *on his conscience*. 那罪行沉重地压在他心上。 *Do you ever find time hangs* ~ *on your hands*, Does it ever pass too slowly? 你曾经发现时间不易度过吗? , ~·**laden** *adj* carrying a ~ load; (fig) having a ~ (= sad) heart. 负重的; 载重的; (喻) 心情沉重的。 **heav·ily** /ˈhevɪlɪ/ *adv* in a ~ manner: 沉重地: *a heavily loaded lorry*. 装载很重的卡车。 **heavi·ness** *n*

heb·doma·dal / hebˈdɒmədl; hɛbˈdɑmədl / *adj* weekly: 一周的; 每周一次的: *H*~ *Council*, one that meets weekly. 每周召开一次的会。

He·braic /hiːˈbreɪɪk; hiˈbreˑɪk/ *adj* Hebrew. 希伯来人的; 希伯来语的。

He·brew /ˈhiːbruː; ˈhibru/ *n* **1** [C] Jew; Israeli. 希伯来人; 犹太人; 以色列人。 **2** [U] language used by the ancient ~s (as in the Old Testament); language now spoken by the people of Israel. 古希伯来语(如旧约圣经中所用者); 现代希伯来语(即现今以色列人的语言)。 □ *adj* of the ~ language or people. 希伯来语的; 希伯来人的。

heca·tomb / ˈhekətuːm; ˈhekəˌtom / *n* (in ancient Greece) great public sacrifice; blood-offering (esp of 100 oxen). (古希腊)大祭; 百牲祭(尤指一次祭一百头牛者)。

heck /hek; hɛk/ *n* (sl, euphem) hell (used in exclamations): (俚, 婉)地狱(用于感叹句中): *Oh! What the* ~! 唉! 去他的! 我才不在乎呢! 嗳! 干吗那么大惊小怪的!

heckle /ˈhekl; ˈhɛkl/ *vt* [VP6A] interrupt and ask many troublesome questions at a public meeting: (在公开会议中)诘问; 质问: ~ *the Socialist candidate*. 诘问社会党候选人。 **heck·ler** /ˈheklər; ˈhɛklɚ/ *n*

hec·tare / ˈhekteə(r); ˈhɛktɛr / *n* measure of area in the metric system, 10000 sq metres (= 2.471 acres). 公顷(合 10000 平方米或 2.471 英亩)。 ⇨ **App 5.** 参看附录五。

hec·tic /ˈhektɪk; ˈhɛktɪk/ *adj* **1** unnaturally red; feverish; consumptive: 红得不自然的; 患热病的; 患肺结核病的: ~ *cheeks*; 潮红的双颊; *a* ~ *colouring*. 不自然的红色。 **2** (colloq) full of excitement and without rest: (口)极为兴奋的; 紧张忙碌的: *have a* ~ *time*; 兴高采烈; *lead a* ~ *life*; 过着紧张忙碌的生活; *for one* ~ (= exciting) *moment*. 一段兴奋的时刻。

hecto- /ˈhektəʊ; ˈhɛktə/ *pref* (in comb) hundred: (用于复合词)一百: *~gram(me)*, 100 grammes. 百克 ⇨ **App 5.** 参看附录五。

hec·tor /ˈhektə(r); ˈhɛktɚ/ *vt*, *vi* bully; bluster. 威吓; 欺凌。

he'd /*strong or initial form*: hiːd; hid; *medial weak form*: iːd; id/ = he had; he would.

hedge /hedʒ; hɛdʒ/ *n* **1** row of bushes, shrubs or tall plants, etc usu cut level at the top, forming a boundary for a field, garden, etc: (围于田地、花园等周围之)树篱: *a* '*beech*~. 山毛榉树篱。 *Will this* ~ *keep the sheep in the field*? 这树篱可将羊群围在这田地中吗? '~·**hop** *vi* fly (an aircraft) not much above ground level, eg when spraying crops. (驾飞机) 超低空飞行 (例如喷洒杀虫剂时)。 '~·**row** *n* row of bushes forming a ~. 一排树篱。 '~·**sparrow** *n* common GB and US bird. 篱雀(常见于英国和美国的一种鸟)。 **2** (fig) means of defence against possible loss: (喻)防备损失的对策: *buy gold/diamonds as a* ~ *against inflation*. 购买黄金(钻石)以防通货膨胀。 □ *vt*, *vi* **1** [VP6A, 15A, B] put a ~ or (fig) barrier round: 围以树篱; (喻)妨碍: ~ *a field*; 用树篱围起田地; ~ *a person in/round with rules and regulations*, restrict his freedom of action. 以种种规则限制一人使其不能自由行动。 **2** [VP2A] refuse to commit oneself; avoid giving a direct answer to a question: 不答应负责; 避免作正面答复; 闪烁其词: *Answer 'yes' or 'no'—don't* ~! 回答'是'或'否'——别回避问题! **3** [VP2A, 6A] (colloq) secure oneself against loss, esp when betting, by compensating transactions: (口)作两面买卖以防损失; (尤指)(赌博为防损失而)两面下注以防…之损失: ~ *one's bets*. 两面下注。 **4** [VP2A] make or trim a ~s. 围树篱; 修剪树篱。

hedge·hog /ˈhedʒhɒg US: -hɔːg; ˈhɛdʒˌhɑg/ *n* insect-eating animal covered with spines, that rolls itself up into a ball to defend itself. 猬。 ⇨ the illus at **small**. 参看 small 之插图。

he·don·ism /ˈhiːdənɪzəm; ˈhidnˌɪzəm/ *n* [U] belief that pleasure is the chief good. 享乐主义。 **he·donist** /-ɪst; -ɪst/ *n* believer in ~. 享乐主义者。 **hedon·is·tic** /ˌhiːdəˈnɪstɪk; ˌhidəˈnɪstɪk/ *adj*

heed /hiːd; hid/ *vt* [VP6A] (formal) pay attention to: (正式用语)注意: ~ *a warning*; 注意一项警告; ~ *what a person says*. 注意某人说的话。 □ *n* [U] *pay/give* ~ *(to); take* ~ *(of)*, give attention, notice: 注意: *pay no* ~ *to'a warning*. 不注意一项警告。 ~·**ful** /-fl; -,ful/ *adj* ~**ful (of)**, attentive: 注意的: *be more* ~*ful of advice*. 多留心忠告。 ~·**less** *adj* ~**less (of)**, inattentive: 不注意的: ~*less of danger*. 不注意危险。

hee·haw /ˈhiːhɔː; ˈhiˌhɔ/ *n* ass's bray; loud laugh. 驴叫; 大笑。

heel [1] /hiːl; hil/ *n* **1** back part of the human foot; part of a sock, stocking, etc covering this; part of a shoe, boot, etc supporting this. 足跟; 踵; 袜等的踵部; 鞋、靴等的后跟。 ⇨ the illus at **leg**. 参看 leg 之插图。 *at/on the* ~*s of sth*; *at/on sb's* ~*s*, close behind it/him: 紧跟在某物(某人)之后: *Famine often follows on the* ~*s of war*. 饥荒常常随战争而至。 *The thief ran off with an angry crowd at his* ~*s*. 那小偷在前面跑, 一群愤怒的人紧随后面追。 *bring/come to* ~, (of a dog) bring/come close behind its master, under control; (fig) submit to discipline and control. (指狗)(使)紧随主人之后; (喻)(使)服从训练和管制。 *down at* ~, (of shoes) with the ~s badly worn down; (of a person) wearing such shoes, or untidy and slovenly in appearance. (指鞋)后跟穿破的; (指人)穿着后跟破了的鞋的; 邋遢的; 潦倒

的. **head over ~s**, upside down, in a somersault; (fig) completely. 倒转; 颠倒; (喻) 完全地; 彻底地. **kick/ cool one's ~s**, be kept waiting. 等候; 久等. **kick up one's ~s**, behave excitedly (esp to show joy at freedom). 狂欢; 手舞足蹈; (尤指) 尽情享乐. **lay sb by the ~s**, confine or imprison him. 监禁某人. **show a clean pair of ~s**, escape in a great hurry. 匆匆逃脱. **take to one's ~s**, run away 逃走. **turn on one's ~**, turn sharply round. 急转身. **under the ~ of**, (fig) dominated by. (喻) 在…支配之下. **2** [US sl] cad; lowdown person. (美俚)恶汉; 下流人. ▯ *vt* [VP6A] put a ~ on: sole and ~ a pair of shoes. 上一双鞋的鞋底及鞋跟. **well-'~ed** *adj* (sl) very rich. (俚)很富有的.

heel² /hiːl; hil/ *vi, vt* [VP2A, C, 15B] ~ **(over)**, (of a ship) (cause to) lean over to one side. (船倾) (使) 倾向一边.

hef·ty /'heftɪ; 'hɛftɪ/ *adj* (**-ier, -iest**) (colloq) big and strong: (口)大而壮的: *a ~ farm worker*. 粗大体壮的农工.

he·gem·ony /hɪ'gemənɪ US: 'hedʒəməunɪ; hɪ'dʒɛmənɪ/ *n* (*pl* **-nies**) [U, C] (formal) leadership, authority, influence, esp of one state in a group of states. (正式用语)领导权; 霸权(尤指数国中之盟主权); 权威; 势力.

He·gira, He·jira /'hedʒɪrə US: hɪ'dʒaɪrə; hɪ'dʒaɪrə/ *n* **the ~**, Muhammad's flight from Mecca to Medina; Muslim era reckoned from this (AD 622). 穆罕默德从麦加到麦地那之逃亡; 伊斯兰教纪元(公元 622 年).

heifer /'hefə(r); 'hɛfə/ *n* young cow that has not yet had a calf. 小牝牛.

heigh·ho /,heɪ'həʊ; 'heɪ,ho/ *int* used to express disappointment, boredom, etc. 嗨嗬! (用以表示失望, 厌烦等).

height /haɪt; haɪt/ *n* **1** [U, C] measurement from bottom to top; distance to the top of sth from a level, esp sea-level: 高度; 海拔: *the ~ of a mountain*. 一山之高度. *What is your ~*, How tall are you? 你有多高? *He is six feet in ~*. 他有六英尺高. **2** [C] high place: 高地: *on the mountain ~s*. 在山冈上. **3** [U] utmost degree: 顶点; 极度: *the ~ of his ambition*; 他的最高志愿; *dressed in the ~ of fashion*. 打扮得最为时髦. *The storm was at its ~*. 风暴达到最猛烈的程度.

heighten /'haɪtn; 'haɪtn/ *vt, vi* [VP6A, 2A] make or become high(er); make greater in degree: 提高; 加高; 变高; 增强; 增加; 增大: ~ *a person's anger*; 增加一人之怒气; ~ *an effect*; 增加效果; *her ~ed colour*, the increased colour in her face, eg caused by emotion. 她逐渐变红的面孔(例如因感情的激动所致).

hei·nous /'heɪnəs; 'henəs/ *adj* (of crime) odious; atrocious. (指罪行)极恶的; 凶暴的. ~**ly** *adv* ~**ness** *n*

heir /eə(r); ɛr/ *n* person with the legal right to receive a title, property, etc when the owner dies: 继承人: *The eldest son is usually the ~*. 长子通常为继承人. *He is ~ to a large fortune*. 他是一大笔财产的继承者. *Who is ~ to the throne*? 谁是王位继承人? ~ **ap'parent** *n* (*pl* **~s apparent**) ~ whose right cannot be superseded by the birth of a nearer ~. 指定继承人 (其继承权不因较近亲属的诞生而受影响). **,~ pre'sumptive** *n* whose right of inheritance may be lost by the birth of a nearer ~. 假定继承人 (其继承权可能因较近亲属的诞生而失去). ~**·ess** /'eərɪs; 'ɛrɪs/ *n* female ~. 女继承人.

heir·loom /'eəluːm; 'ɛr'lum/ *n* sth handed down in a family for several generations. 祖传物; 传家宝.

He·jira /'hedʒɪrə US: hɪ'dʒaɪrə; hɪ'dʒaɪrə/ *n* = **Hegira**.

held /held; hɛld/ *pt, pp* of **hold**.

heli·cop·ter /'helɪkɒptə(r); 'hɛlɪ,kɑptə/ *n* kind of aircraft with horizontal revolving blades or rotors, able to take off and land in a very small space and remain stationary in the air. 直升飞机.

he·lio·graph /'hiːlɪəɡraːf US: -ɡræf; 'hilɪə,ɡræf/ *n* apparatus formerly used for sending signals by reflecting flashes of sunlight. 日光反射信号器. ▯ *vt*

send (a message) by ~. 以日光反射信号器发出 (消息).

he·lio·trope /'hiːlɪətrəʊp; 'hiljə,trop/ *n* plant with small, sweet-smelling purple flowers; colour of these. 天芥菜属植物(生有芬香的小紫花); 淡紫色.

heli·port /'helɪpɔːt; 'hɛlɪ,port/ *n* airport for helicopters. 直升飞机场.

he·lium /'hiːlɪəm; 'hilɪəm/ *n* [U] light, colourless gas (symbol He) that does not burn, used in balloons and airships. 氦(无色, 不燃的轻气体, 符号为 He).

hell /hel; hɛl/ *n* **1** (in some religions) home of devils and of damned souls after death. (某些宗教)地狱; 冥府. **2** place, condition, of great suffering or misery: 痛苦的地方; 苦境: *suffer ~ on earth*; 受人间之苦; *life a ~*. 使某人的生活象地狱般的苦. *We gave the enemy ~*. 我们让敌人吃尽苦头. **3** (colloq, in exclamations, to express anger, or to intensify a meaning) (口, 在感叹句中表示愤怒或加强意义)*H~! 混蛋! What the ~ do you want?* 你到底要什么? *He ran like ~*, very fast. 他跑得极快. *I like him a ~ of a lot*. 我非常喜欢他. *What a ~ of a noise!* 真是吵死人了! *for the ~ of it*, for no particular reason. 无特别理由地. *ride ~ for leather*, as quickly as possible. 尽快地驰骋. ~**·cat** *n* spiteful or furious person. 恶人; 泼辣的人. ~**·ish** /-ɪʃ; -ɪʃ/ *adj* horrible; devilish. 可怕的; 如恶魔的. *be ,~-'bent on sth*, (sl) be recklessly determined to do it. (俚)不顾一切地做某事.

he'll /strong or initial form: hiːl; hil; medial weak form often: ɪːl; il/ = he will; he shall.

Hel·lene /'heliːn; 'hɛlin/ *n* subject of modern Greece; person of genuine Greek race in ancient times. 近代希腊国民; 古希腊人. **Hel·lenic** /he'liːnɪk US: he'lenɪk; hɛ'lɛnɪk/ *adj* of the Greeks, their arts, culture, etc. 希腊人的; 希腊之艺术, 文化等的.

hello /hə'ləʊ; hɛ'lo/ *int* = **hullo**.

helm¹ /helm; hɛlm/ *n* handle (also called 亦称作 *tiller*) or wheel for moving the rudder of a boat or ship: 舵柄; 舵轮; 驾驶盘: *the man at the ~*, the steersman, (fig) leader; 舵手; (喻)领袖; *the ~ of state*, (fig) the government of the nation. (喻)国家的政府. ~**s·man** /-zmən; -zmən/ *n* (*pl* **-men**) man at the ~. 舵手.

helm² /helm; hɛlm/ *n* (archaic) helmet. (古)盔.

hel·met /'helmɪt; 'hɛlmɪt/ *n* protective head-covering worn by soldiers, firemen, miners, motorbike riders, divers (as part of a diving-suit), and some policemen. (士兵, 救火人员, 矿工, 摩托车骑士, 潜水者, 以及某些警察所戴的)头盔; 钢盔. ⇨ the illus at **armour**. 参看 armour 之插图. ⇨ also *sun~* at **sun**. ~**ed** *adj* wearing, provided with, a ~. 戴盔的.

helot /'helət; 'hɛlət/ *n* one of a class of slaves in ancient Sparta; (fig) member of any social class that is despised and kept in subjection. 古斯巴达的奴隶阶级之一员; (喻)任何受鄙视与奴役的社会阶级之一员.

help¹ /help; hɛlp/ *n* **1** [U] act of ~ing: 帮助; 救助. *Thank you for your kind ~*. 谢谢你的惠助. *be of ~* **(to sb)** *be (of) any /much /no /some ~ (to sb)*, be ~ful: 有助于; 对…有(很有, 没有, 有些)帮助: *Can I be of any ~ to you?* 我能帮助你吗? *It wasn't much ~*, didn't ~ much. 它没有多大帮助. *He is ~, sb or sth that ~s*: 帮助者; 帮助的人或事物: *Your advice was a great ~*. 你的劝告是一很大的帮助. *Far from being a ~ to me, you're a hindrance*. 你不但对我没有帮助, 反而是个障碍. **3** [U] remedy: 补救方法: *There's no ~ for it*,

a helicopter

it can't be ~ed. 没有办法了。 ⇨ **help²(3). 4** [C] (usu non-resident) person who ~s with the housework: (通常是不住宿的)仆人；佣人：*a home ~,* ⇨ **home¹(3).** *The ~ hasn't come this morning.* 佣人今早还没有来。~ **·ful** /-fl; -fəl/ *adj* giving ~: 有帮助的；有益的：*be ~ful to one's friends.* 对朋友有帮助。~ **·fully** /-fəlɪ; -fəlɪ/ *adv* ~ **·ful·ness** *n* ~ **·less** *adj* **1** without ~; not receiving ~. 无助的；未受帮助的。 **2** unable to act; dependent upon others: 不能行动的；不能自立的；依赖他人的：*a ~less invalid; 倚赖他人的病人; as ~less as a baby.* 象婴儿般依赖他人。~ **·less·ly** *adv* ~ **·less·ness** *n* ~ **er** *n* person who ~s. 帮助者。~ **·ing** *n* (esp) portion of food served at a meal; 一客：*three ~ings of pie;* 三份水果馅; *a generous ~ing of pudding.* 丰富的一客布丁。

help² /help/ *vt, vi* **1** [VP6A, 17, 18B, 15A, B, 2A, C] do part of the work of another person; make it easier for (sb) to do sth or for (sth) to happen; do sth for the benefit of (sb in need): 帮助；帮忙；援助；资助：*I can't lift this box alone, please ~ me.* 我一个人提不起这箱子，请帮助我。*I ~ed him (to) find his things.* 我帮他找到他的东西。(The omission of *to* is more usual in US than in GB usage.) (help 之后的不定式省去 to, 在美国用法中较在英国习见。) *Please ~ me up/down/out, etc with this heavy trunk.* ~ me to carry it up, etc. 请帮我把这重箱子抬起来(放下去，抬出去等)。*Will you ~ me on with my overcoat, please,* ~ me to put it on? 请你帮我把大衣穿上好吗? *We ~ed the injured man off with his clothes.* ~ed him to get them off. 我们帮助那负者，将他的衣服脱下。*Tom has to ~ his father, who is too old to work.* 汤姆必须帮助他父亲，他父亲太老了不能工作。*Would it ~ you to know that...,* if I told you that...? 如果我告诉你…对你会有帮助吗? ~ **out,** give ~ (esp in a crisis). 帮助(尤指在危机时)。**2** [VP6A, 14] ~ **sb/ oneself (to sth),** serve with food, drink, etc: 替某人(自己)取(食物，饮料等)：*May I ~ you to some more meat?* 再来一点肉好吗? *H~ yourself to the fruit/cigarettes.* 请随便用水果(香烟)。**3** [VP6A, C] *can ~ sth/doing sth,* avoid; refrain; prevent: 避免；抑制；阻止：*Don't tell him more than you can ~,* more than you must. 不要把不应该告诉他的话告诉他（不要告诉他太多了）。*I can't ~ thinking he's still alive.* 我不能不认为他还活着。*She burst out crying; she couldn't ~ it.* 她放声大哭，无法抑制自己。*I can't ~ my husband having so many dull relations.* 我丈夫有这么多呆笨的亲戚，我也没有法子。*It can't be ~ed,* is inevitable. 这是不可避免的。*So ~ me God,*(in an oath) (as I speak the truth, etc) may God ~ me. (用于誓言)(由于我在说实话等)愿上帝帮助我。

help·mate /'helpmeɪt; 'hɛlp,met/, **help·meet** /'helpmiːt; 'hɛlp,mit/ *nn* helpful partner, esp a wife or husband. 良伴(尤指妻子或丈夫)。

hel·ter-skel·ter /ˌheltə'skeltə(r); ˌhɛltɚ'skɛltɚ/ *adv* in disorderly haste. 手忙脚乱地。 □ *n* tall spiral slide¹(2) in a fairground, etc. (露天市场等供儿童游乐之)高螺旋滑梯。

helve /helv; hɛlv/ *n* handle of a tool, esp an axe. 工具的柄(尤指斧柄)。

hem¹ /hem; hɛm/ *n* border or edge of cloth, esp one on an article of clothing, when turned and sewn down. 布的边缘；(尤指)衣服的边缘。 **'hemming-stitch** *n* style of sewing hems on dresses, skirts, etc by joining the turned edge to the length of material using diagonal stitches. 缝衣边之对角针法。 **'hem·line** *n* (esp) lower edge of a skirt or dress. (尤指) 裙子或衣服的下摆：*lower/raise the hemline,* make a skirt, etc longer/ shorter. 将下摆放低(提高); 使裙子变长(短)。 □ *vt* (-mm-) **1** [VP6A] make a hem on ~: 缝…之边：*hem a handkerchief.* 缝一条手帕的边。 **2** [VP15B] ~ *about/around/in,* enclose; confine; surround: 包围; 关闭; surrounded by the enemy. 被敌人包围。

hem² (also **h'm**) /hem, hm; hɛm, hm/ *int* sound used to indicate doubt or sarcasm, or to call attention. (表示疑

惑或讥讽，或促使人注意的声音)哼! □ *vi* (-mm-) make this sound; hesitate in speech. 发哼声; 结结巴巴地说话。 *hem and haw/ha,* = *hum and haw/ha,* ⇨ **hum.**

he·ma·tite (also **hae-**) /'hemətaɪt; 'hemə,taɪt/ *n* iron oxide (Fe_2O_3) the main ore of iron. 赤铁矿(Fe_2O_3)。

hemi·sphere /'hemɪsfɪə(r); 'hɛməs,fɪr/ *n* half a sphere; half the earth. 半球; 地球的一半。 **the Northern ~, Southern ~,** north/south of the equator. 北(南)半球 (赤道以北或以南)。 **the Eastern ~,** Europe, Asia, Africa and Australia. 东半球(指欧，亚，非，大洋四洲)。 **the Western ~,** N and S America. 西半球(指南北美洲)。

hem·lock /'hemlɒk; 'hɛmlɑk/ *n* plant with finely divided leaves and small, white flowers, from which a poison is made. 毒人参(生有羽状分裂的叶和小白花, 可制毒药)。 **'~ spruce** *n* evergreen tree, common in America and Asia, valuable for its timber. 一种松柏科铁杉属的常绿树(常见于美洲及亚洲,其木料甚有价值);加州铁杉。

he·mo·glo·bin (also **hae-**) /ˌhiːmə'gləʊbɪn; ˌhimə'globɪn/ *n* [U] substance present in the red corpuscles of the blood. 血红蛋白; 血红素。

he·mo·philia (also **hae-**) /ˌhiːmə'fɪlɪə; ˌhimə'fɪlɪə/ *n* [U] (usu hereditary) tendency of blood (from a wound, etc) not to clot, so that bleeding continues. 血友病(通常是遗传的)出血不止症, 血友症。 **he·mo·phil·iac** (also **hae-**) /ˌhiːmə'fɪlɪæk; ˌhimə'fɪlɪæk/ *n* person having ~. 患出血不止症者; 血友病者。

hem·or·rhage (also **hae-**) /'heməridʒ; 'hɛmərɪdʒ/ *n* [U] bleeding; [C] escape of blood. 出血; 溢血。

hem·or·rhoids (also **hae-**) /'hemərɔɪdz; 'hɛmərɔɪdz/ *n pl* swelling of a vein or veins, esp at or near the anus; piles. 痔; 痔疮。

hemp /hemp; hɛmp/ *n* [U] (kinds of) plant from which coarse fibres are obtained for the manufacture of rope and cloth. 大麻。 **(Indian) ~,** narcotic from the flowering tops, seed and resin of such plants, 大麻制的麻醉剂, also called 亦称作 *bhang, cannabis, hashish, marijuana.* ~ **en** /'hempən; 'hɛmpən/ *adj* made of ~; like ~: 大麻制的; 似大麻的: *a ~en rope.* 大麻制的绳。

hem·stitch /'hemstɪtʃ; 'hɛm,stɪtʃ/ *vt, n* (ornament the hem of a handkerchief, dress, skirt, towel, etc with a) decorative stitch made by pulling out some of the threads and tying the cross-threads in groups. 垂缝; 抽丝结缝; 缝接于布、手帕、衣服、裙子、毛巾等边缘以作装饰。

hen /hen; hɛn/ *n* **1** female of the common domestic fowl. 母鸡。 ⇨ **cock¹(1).** ⇨ the illus at **fowl.** 参看 fowl 之插图。 **'hen·bane** *n* (narcotic obtained from a) poisonous plant. 天仙子, 莨菪; 菲天斯(一种毒草); 由莨菪提取的麻醉剂。 **'hen-coop** *n* coop for keeping poultry in. 鸡窝; 鸡棚。 **'hen-house** *n* (usu wooden) building for poultry. (通常是木造的)鸡舍。 **'hen-party** *n* (colloq) party for woman only. (口)女人的聚会。 ⇨ **stag party** at **stag. 'hen-pecked** *adj* (of a man) ruled by his wife. (指男子)妻子管治的; 惧内的。 **'hen-roost** *n* place where fowls roost at night. 鸡窝。 **2** female (of the bird named): (某种鸟的)雌性: *guinea-hen,* 雌珠鸡, *pea-hen.* 雌孔雀。

hence /hens; hɛns/ *adv* (formal) (正式用语) **1** from here; from now on: 从此处; 从此时: *a week ~,* in a week's time. 从现在起一星期的时间; 今后一星期。 **2** for this reason. 因此; 由是。 ~ **·'forth,** ~ **·'forward** *advv* from this time on; in future 从今以后; 今后。

hench·man /'hentʃmən; 'hɛntʃmən/ *n* (*pl* **-men** /-mən; -mən/) faithful supporter, esp a political supporter who obeys without question the orders of his leader: 忠实的支持者(尤指在政治上无条件服从其领袖的支持者): *the Dictator and his henchmen.* 独裁者及其亲信。

henna /'henə; 'hɛnə/ *n* [U] (plant, kind of Egyptian privet, producing) reddish-brown dye stuff for colouring leather, the finger-nails, the hair, etc. 散沫

花; 指甲花(埃及产的一种水蜡树类植物); 指甲花所产的一种红褐色的染料(可染皮革, 指甲, 头发等)。 **hen·naed** /'henəd; 'hɛnəd/ adj dyed with ~. 以指甲花染料染过的。

hep /hep; hɛp/ adj ⇨ **hip.⁴**

hepa·ti·tis /ˌhepə'taɪtɪs; ˌhɛpə'taɪtɪs/ n [U] inflammation of the liver. 肝炎。

hep·ta·gon /'heptəgɒn US: -gɑn; 'hɛptəˌgɑn/ n plane figure with 7 (esp equal) sides. 七边形; (尤指)等边七角形。

her /strong or initial form: hɜː(r); hɝ; medial weak form: ɜː(r); ə/ pers pron (as an object, corresponding to she): 她(为 she 的宾格): She's in the garden; I can see her. 她在花园里, 我看得见她。 Give her the book. 把这本书给她。 □ poss adj belonging to her: 她的: Mary's mother is dead but her father is alive. 玛丽的母亲死了, 但她的父亲还健在。 That's her hat, not yours. 那是她的帽子, 不是你的。 **hers** /hɜːz; hɝz/ poss pron belonging to her: 她的: Is that his or hers? 那是他的还是她的? I've borrowed a book of hers, one of her books. 我借了她的一本书。

her·ald /'herəld; 'hɛrəld/ n **1** (hist) person making public announcements from, and carrying messages from, a ruler. (史)传令官; 使者。 **2** person or thing foretelling the coming of sb or sth: 先驱; 预兆: In England the cuckoo is a ~ of spring. 在英国杜鹃鸟预示春天的来临。 **3** official who keeps records of families that have coats of arms. 司宗谱纹章的官。 **H~s' College**, corporation that records pedigrees and grants coats of arms. 司宗纹章院。 □ vt [VP6A] proclaim the approach of. 宣布…之将临。 **her·al·dic** /he'rældɪk; hɛ'rældɪk/ adj of ~s or ~ry. 使者的; 司宗谱纹章之官的; 纹章学的。 **~ry** n [U] science dealing with the coats of arms, descent, and history of old families. 纹章学。

herb /hɜːb US: ɜːrb; ɝb/ n low-growing, soft-stemmed plant which dies down at the end of the growing season; plant of this kind whose leaves or seeds, because of their scent or flavour, are used in medicine or for flavouring food, eg sage, mint, dill. 草本植物; 药草; 香草(因其叶或种子的气味, 故可制药或香料, 例如鼠尾草、薄荷、蒔萝)。 **~ beer** a drink made from ~s. 药草制的饮料。 **~·age** /-ɪdʒ; -ɪdʒ/ n [U] ~s colletively; grass and other field plants. 草本植物的总称; 草类。 **~al** /'hɜːbl US: 'ɜːrbl; 'ɜrbl/ adj of (esp) medicinal ~s: (尤指)药草的: ~al remedies. 药草治疗法。 **~·al·ist** /'hɜːbəlɪst US: 'ɜːrb-; 'ɜrbəlɪst/ n person who grows or sells ~s for medical use. 种植或售卖药草者。 **~·bivor·ous** /hɜː'bɪvərəs US: ɜːr-; hɝ'bɪvərəs/ adj (of animals) feeding on ~age. (指动物)食草的。 ⇨ carnivorous at **carnivore.**

her·ba·ceous /hɜː'beɪʃəs; hɝ'beʃəs/ adj (of plants) having stems that are not woody: (指植物)草本的: a ~ border, (in a garden) border with plants which come up and flower year after year (not shrubs, annuals, etc). (庭园中)种有多年生花草的边缘(非种有灌木及一年生的植物等者)。

her·cu·lean /ˌhɜːkju'liːən; hɝ'kjulɪən/ adj having, needing, great powers of body or mind: 有大体力或智力的; 需要大的体力或智力的: a ~ task. 艰巨的任务。

herd /hɜːd; hɝd/ n **1** number or company of animals, esp cattle, feeding or going about together: 兽群(尤指牛群): a ~ of cattle/deer/elephants. 一群牛(鹿, 象)。 **2** (chiefly in compounds) keeper of a ~: (主要用于复合词中)牧人: 'cow~; 牧牛人; 'goat~. 牧羊人。 **3** (derog) (贬) the common/vulgar ~, the mass of common people; 群众; the ~ instinct, the instinct to act, feel, think, etc like the mass of people, and to be with the mass. 群众本能(行动、感觉、思想等与群众相似并且想跟群众在一起的本能)。 □ vi, vt [VP2C, 15A, B] (cause to) gather into a ~ or as in a ~; look after a ~: (使)成群; 放牧: people who ~ed/were ~ed together like cattle. 像兽群般集结的人们。 **~s·man** /-mən; -mən/ n (pl -men) keeper of a ~. 牧人。

here /hɪə(r); hɪr/ adv **1** in, at, to this point of place: 在这里; 向这里: come ~. 到这里来。 I live ~. 我住在这里。 Put the box ~. 把盒子放在这里。 Look ~. 看这里。 **2** (with front position, and inversion of the subject and finite v if the subject is a n, but not if the subject is a pers pron): (位于句首, 如主语为一名词, 则主语与限定动词倒置, 如主语为一人称代词, 则不倒置): H~ comes the bus! 公共汽车来了! H~ it comes! 它来了! H~ are the others! 其余的在这里! H~ they/we are! 他们 (我们) 终于到了! H~'s something interesting. 这里有个有趣的东西。 H~ you are/it is! H~ is what you asked for are looking for, etc according to context. 你所要的东西在这里! 你要找的东西在这里! (视上下文之意义而定)。 **3** at this point (in a series of events, in a process, etc): (在一连串事件、某一过程等中)此时; 这时: H~ he stopped reading and looked up. 这时他停止看书, 抬起头来往上看。 H~ the speaker paused to have a drink. 这时那说话的人停下来喝了一口水。 H~ goes! Now I'm going to make a start, have a go. 现在我要开始了! **4** (after preps): (在介词后): Come over ~, near to where I am. 到我这里来。 Do you live near ~, near this place? 你住在这附近吗? **5** ~ and there, in various places. 各处; 在不同的地方。 ~, there and everywhere, in all parts; all round. 到处; 处处。 neither ~ nor there, (colloq) irrelevant. (口)不切题; 不相干。 **6** (used after a n to call attention, or for emphasis): (用于名词后以引人注意或加强语气): My friend ~ was a witness of the accident. 我的朋友就是这意外事件的见证。 **7** (used when drinking to sb's health, wishing success to an enterprise, etc): (用于敬酒时祝某人健康, 事业成功等): H~'s to the bride and bridegroom! 敬新娘新郎一杯! ~·abouts /ˌhɪərə'bauts; ˌhɪrə'bauts/ adv near or about ~. 在附近; 在这一带。 ~·after /hɪər'ɑːftə(r); hɪr'æftə/ adv, n (in the) future; the life to come. (在)将来; 来世。 ~·by /hɪə'baɪ; hɪr'baɪ/ adv (legal) by means or by reason of this. (法律)借此; 由此。 ~·in /hɪər'ɪn; hɪr'ɪn/ adv (legal) in this. (法律)在这当中; 于此处。 ~·of /hɪər'ɒv; hɪr'ʌv/ adv (legal) of or about this. (法律)于此; 关于此点。 ~·to /hɪə'tuː; hɪr'tu/ adv (legal) to this (法律)至此。 ~·to·fore /ˌhɪətu'fɔː(r); ˌhɪrtə'for/ adv (legal) until now; formerly. (法律)直到此时之; 以前。 ~·upon /ˌhɪər'pɒn; ˌhɪr'pɑn/ adv (formal) at this point; in consequence of this (正式用语)于此; 于是。 ~·with /ˌhɪə'wɪð US: -wɪθ; hɪr'wɪθ/ adv (comm) with this. (商)同此; 并此; 附此。

her·edita·ment /ˌheri'dɪtəmənt; ˌhɛrə'dɪtəmənt/ n (legal) property that can be inherited. (法律)可继承的财产; 世袭财产。

her·ed·itary /hɪ'redɪtri US: -teri; hə'rɛdəˌtɛri/ adj passed on from parent to child, from one generation to following generations: 世袭的; 代代相传的; 遗传的: ~ rulers/beliefs/diseases. 世袭的统治者(代代相传的信仰; 遗传病)。

her·ed·ity /hɪ'redɪti; hə'rɛdətɪ/ n [U] tendency of living things to pass their characteristics on to offspring, etc; characteristics, qualities, etc so passed on: 遗传性; 遗传; 遗传的特征、性质等: ~ factors/genes. 遗传因素(因子)。

her·esy /'herəsi; 'hɛrəsɪ/ n (pl -sies) [C, U] (holding of a) belief or opinion contrary to what is generally accepted, esp in religion: 异端邪说(尤指宗教方面的); 信奉异端邪说: fall into ~; 陷入旁门左道中; be guilty of ~; 犯了异端邪说罪; the heresies of the Protestants. 新教徒的异端。 **her·etic** /'herətɪk; 'hɛrətɪk/ n person guilty of ~ or supporting a ~; person who holds an unorthodox opinion. 持异端邪说者; 异教徒。 **her·eti·cal** /hɪ'retɪkl; hə'rɛtɪkl/ adj of ~ or heretics: 异端邪说的; 持异端邪说者的: heretical beliefs. 异端邪说。

heri·table /'herɪtəbl; 'hɛrɪtəbl/ adj (legal) capable of inheriting or being inherited. (法律)可继承的; 可传让的。

heri·tage /'herɪtɪdʒ; 'hɛrɪtɪdʒ/ n that which has been or may be inherited. 遗产; 继承物。

her·maph·ro·dite /hɜːˈmæfrədaɪt; hɝˈmæfrə‚daɪt/ *n* [C] animal or other creature, eg an earth-worm, which has both male and female sexual organs or characteristics. 具有雌雄两性的动物 (例如如蚯蚓); 雌雄同体.

her·metic /hɜːˈmetɪk; hɝˈmetɪk/ *adj* completely airtight: 不透气的; 密封的: *a ~ seal.* 密封. **hermetically** /-klɪ; -klɪ/ *adv* ~*ally sealed,* sealed so as to keep all the air in or out. 密封的.

her·mit /ˈhɜːmɪt; ˈhɝmɪt/ *n* person (esp man in early Christian times) living alone. 隐士 (尤指基督教早期者). ~·**age** /-ɪdʒ; -ɪdʒ/ *n* cell or living-place of a ~ or groups of ~s. 隐士隐居之处.

her·nia /ˈhɜːnɪə; ˈhɝnɪə/ *n* [U, C] rupture, esp one caused by a part of the bowel being pushed through a weak point of the muscle wall of the abdomen. 脱肠; 疝气; 疝.

hero /ˈhɪərəʊ; ˈhɪro/ *n* (*pl* ~**es** /-rəʊz; -roz/) **1** person respected for bravery or noble qualities. 英雄; 豪杰. **2** chief person in a poem, story, play, etc. (诗, 小说, 戏剧等中之) 男主角. **'~·ine** /ˈherəʊɪn; ˈhɛro·ɪn/ *n* female ~. 女英雄; (诗, 小说, 戏剧等中之) 女主角. ~·**ism** /ˈherəʊɪzəm; ˈhɛro‚ɪzəm/ *n* [U] quality of being a ~; courage. 英雄气概; 英勇.

her·oic /hɪˈrəʊɪk; hɪˈro·ɪk/ *adj* **1** of, like, fit for, a hero: 英雄的; 英雄般的; 适于英雄的; 英勇的: ~ *deeds/tasks.* 英勇的事迹(工作). *use ~ remedies,* hazardous remedies but worth trying. 采取冒险但值得一试的补救法. **2** of a size larger than life: 大于真人或实物的: *a statue of ~ size/on a ~ scale.* 大于真人的雕像. **3** of poetry dealing with heroes. 叙述英雄故事之诗篇的; 史诗的. ~'**verse,** lines of ten syllables and five stresses, rhyming in pairs. 英雄诗体(每行有十个音节, 五个重音, 每两行押韵). **4** (of language) grand; attempting great things; (指语言) 堂皇的; 夸大的; (hence) (由此产生) ~**s** *n pl* high-flown or high-sounding talk or sentiments. 夸大的言谈或意见. **he·roi·cally** /-klɪ; -klɪ/ *adv*

her·oin /ˈherəʊɪn; ˈhero·ɪn/ *n* [U] narcotic drug prepared from morphine, used medically to cause sleep or relieve pain, or used by drug addicts. 海洛因, 二乙酰吗啡.

heron /ˈherən; ˈhɛrən/ *n* long-legged water-bird living in marshy places. 苍鹭. ⇨ the illus at **water.** 参看 water 之插图. ~**ry** *n* (*pl* -**ries**) place where ~s breed. 苍鹭繁殖之处.

Herr /heə(r); hɛr/ *n* (*pl* **Herren** /ˈherən; ˈhɛrən/) German equivalent of *Mr;* German gentleman. (德) 先生(相当于 Mr); 德国绅士.

her·ring /ˈherɪŋ; ˈhɛrɪŋ/ *n* (*pl* unchanged) sea-fish, usu swimming in immense shoals, valued as food (fresh, salted, or dried). (复数常不变) 鲱; 青鱼. ⇨ the illus at **fish.** 参看 fish 之插图. '~**-bone** *n* [U] pattern (like the spine and bones of a ~) used for stitching, designs on cloth, etc. 鱼脊型 (鲱鱼骨状形, 用做缝钉的式样, 布的图案等). ‚**red** '~, ⇨ **red** (3).

hers /hɜːz; hɝz/ ⇨ **her.**

her·self /hɜːˈself; həˈself; *weak form:* ɜː'sɪ-; ɝ's-/ *reflex, emph pron* **1** (reflex) (反身) *She hurt ~.* 她伤了自己. *She ought to be ashamed of ~.* 她应当自感惭愧. **(all) by ~, (a)** alone. 孤独; 单独. **(b)** without help: 独力: *Can she do it by ~ or does she need help?* 她能自己做还是需要帮助? **2** (emph) (强调气) *She told me the news.* 她亲自将这消息告诉我的. *I saw Mrs Smith ~,* ie not one of her family, on her staff, etc. 我看见史密斯太太本人了. **3** *She's not quite ~ today,* not in her normal state of health or mind. 她今天不大舒服; 她今天有些不正常. *She has come to ~,* is now in her normal mental state. 她的心理状态恢复正常了. (Cf 参较 *She has come to,* has regained consciousness. 她清醒过来了.)

hertz /hɜːts; hɝts/ *n* (symbol **Hz**) unit of frequency equal to one cycle per second. 赫 (每秒周波数, 符号为

Hz).

Hertz·ian /ˈhɜːtsɪən; ˈhɝtsɪən/ *adj* ~ **waves,** electromagnetic waves as used in radio. 赫兹波; 电磁波(如无线电中者).

he's /*strong or initial form:* hiːz; hiz; *medial weak form:* iːz; ɪz/ = he is; he has.

hesi·tant /ˈhezɪtənt; ˈhezətənt/ *adj* tending or inclined to hesitate. 犹豫的; 踌躇的. ~·**ly** *adv* **hesitance** /-əns; -əns/, **hesi·tancy** /-ənsɪ; -ənsɪ/ *nm* [U] (formal) state or quality of being ~. (正式用语) 犹豫; 踌躇.

hesi·tate /ˈhezɪteɪt; ˈhɛzə‚tet/ *vi* [VP2A, 3A, B, 4C] show signs of uncertainty or unwillingness in speech or action: 犹豫; 踌躇; 不愿: *He's still hesitating about joining/over whether to join the expedition.* 他对于是否参加这探险队仍在犹豫. *He ~s at nothing.* 他对什么都毫不迟疑. *I ~ to spend so much money on clothes.* 我不愿花这么多钱做衣服. *He ~d (about) what to do next.* 他对于下一步做什么犹豫不定. **hesi·tat·ing·ly** *adv*

hesi·ta·tion /‚hezɪˈteɪʃn; ‚hɛzəˈteʃən/ *n* [U] state of hesitating; [C] instance of hesitating: 犹豫; 踌躇: *She agreed without the slightest ~.* 她毫不犹豫地同意了. *I have no ~ in stating that….* 我愿意说出…. *There's no room for ~.* 没有踌躇的余地. *His doubts and ~s were tiresome.* 他的疑虑和犹豫令人厌烦.

hes·sian /ˈhesɪən US: ˈheʃn; ˈheʃən/ *n* [U] strong, coarse cloth of hemp or jute; sack-cloth. 一种结实的粗麻布; 麻袋布.

het·ero·dox /ˈhetərədɒks; ˈhetərə‚dɑks/ *adj* not orthodox. 非正统的. ~·**y** /-sɪ; -sɪ/ *n* [U] opposite of orthodoxy. 反正统; 异端.

het·ero·ge·neous /‚hetərəʊˈdʒiːnɪəs; ‚hetərəˈdʒinɪəs/ *adj* made up of different kinds: 由不同种类组成的: *the ~ population of the USA,* of many different races. 由不同种族形成的美国人口. ⇨ **homogeneous.**

het·ero·sex·ual /‚hetərəʊˈsekʃʊəl; ‚hetərəˈsɛkʃʊəl/ *adj* sexually attracted to persons of the opposite sex. 异性爱的; 异性恋的. □ *n ~* person. 异性恋者. ~·**ity** /‚hetərəʊ‚sekʃʊˈælətɪ; ‚hetərə‚sɛkʃʊˈælətɪ/ *n* [U] the condition of being ~. 异性恋.

het-up /‚het'ʌp; ‚het'ʌp/ *adj* excited; over-wrought. 激动的; 过度兴奋的.

heu·ris·tic /hjʊəˈrɪstɪk; hjuəˈrɪstɪk/ *adj* of the theory in education that a learner should discover things for himself. 启发式教学法的. ~**s** *n* method of solving problems by inductive reasoning, by evaluating past experience and moving by trial and error to a solution. 借归纳检讨寻解决问题的方法.

hew /hjuː; hju/ *vt, vi* (*pt* **hewed,** *pp* **hewed** or **hewn** /hjuːn; hjun/) [VP6A, 15A, B, 2A, C] **1** cut (by striking or chopping); aim cutting blows (*at, among):* 砍; 伐; 劈; 砍向(与, 或 之间 连用): *hew down a branch.* 砍下一树枝. *He hewed his enemy to pieces,* eg with his sword. 他将敌人劈成数段 (例如用剑). **2** shape by chopping: 砍成某种形状: *hewn timber,* roughly shaped by hewing. 租劈的木材. **3** make by hard work: 辛苦做成: *hew one's way through dense jungle,* cut out and beat a path: 在浓密的森林里开辟一条路; *hew out a career for oneself.* 艰苦地创一番事业. **hewer** *n* person who hews, esp a man who cuts out coal in a mine: 砍伐者; (尤指) 采煤夫: *hewers of wood and drawers of water,* persons doing hard menial work. 劈柴挑水的人. (⇨ **Josh 9:21.**)(参看圣经约书亚记第 9 章第 21 节.)

hexa·gon /ˈheksəgən US: -ˌgɒn; ˈhɛksə‚gɑn/ *n* plane figure with 6 (esp equal) sides. 六边形; (尤指) 等边六角形. **hex·ag·onal** /heks'ægənl; hɛks'ægənl/ *adj* six-sided. 六边的.

hex·am·eter /heks'æmɪtə(r); hɛks'æmətɚ/ *n* (kind of) line of verse (esp Gk or Lat) with six feet. 六音步的诗或诗行(尤指希腊或拉丁文者).

hey /heɪ; he/ *int* used to call attention, or to express surprise or interrogation. (用以促使注意, 表示惊异或询

问的声音)嘿! 喂! ,**Hey 'presto!** conjuror's phrase used to announce the completion of a trick. (魔术师宣布戏法已完成的用语)说变就变!

hey·day /ˈheɪdeɪ; ˈheˌde/ n (sing only) time of greatest prosperity or power: (仅用单数)全盛时期: *in the ~ of youth.* 在年轻力壮的时候。 *The 19th century was the ~ of steam railways.* 十九世纪为蒸汽火车最盛时期。

hi /haɪ; haɪ/ int **1 = hey. 2** (esp US) (尤美) = **hullo.**

hi·atus /haɪˈeɪtəs; haɪˈetəs/ n (pl **~es** /-sɪz; -sɪz/) gap in a series, making it incomplete; break in continuity. 脱漏之处; 中断。

hi·ber·nate /ˈhaɪbəneɪt; ˈhaɪbəˌnet/ vi [VP2A] (of some animals) pass the whole of the winter in a torpid state. (指某些动物)冬眠; 蛰伏。 **hi·ber·na·tion** /ˌhaɪbəˈneɪʃn; ˌhaɪbəˈneʃən/ n [U]

hi·bis·cus /hɪˈbɪskəs US: haɪ-; haɪˈbɪskəs/ n [U] cultivated plant or shrub with brightly coloured flowers (chiefly in the tropics). 木槿(属)。 ⇨ the illus at **flower.** 参看 flower 之插图。

hic·cup, hic·cough /ˈhɪkʌp; ˈhɪkʌp/ vi, n (have a) sudden stopping of the breath with a cough-like sound. 打嗝; 打呃。 **(the)~s,** an attack of ~s: 打嗝: *have the ~s.* 打嗝。

hick /hɪk; hɪk/ n, adj (sl; derog) (of a) country-man, yokel. (俚; 贬) 乡巴佬(的)。

hick·ory /ˈhɪkərɪ; ˈhɪkrɪ/ n (pl **-ries**) (hard wood of a) N American tree with edible nuts. (北美所产之)山胡桃树; 山胡桃木。

hid, hidden ⇨ **hide¹.**

hide¹ /haɪd; haɪd/ vt, vi (pt **hid** /hɪd; hɪd/, pp **hidden** /ˈhɪdn; ˈhɪdn/ or (archaic) **hid**) **1** [VP 6 A, 14] ~ **(from),** put or keep (sb, sth, oneself) out of sight; prevent from being seen, found or known: 隐藏; 藏起; 遮掩: *Quick, ~ yourself!* 快点, 躲起来! *The sun was hidden by the clouds.* 太阳为云遮掩。 *The future is hidden from us.* 未来是我们难以预卜的。 *She tried to ~ her feelings.* 她设法掩藏她的感情。 *His words had a hidden meaning.* 他的话里有话。 **2** [VP2A] be or become hidden: 被隐藏; 躲藏起来: *You had better ~.* 你最好躲起来。 *Where is he hiding?* 他躲在哪里? ~**and-seek** /ˌhaɪd n ˈsiːk; ˈhaɪdnˌsik/ n [U] children's game in which one child ~s and others try to find him. 捉迷藏。 □ n (US 美 = *blind*) place where wild animals, birds, etc may be observed, eg by photographers, without alarming them. (摄影者等观察野生动物和鸟类之) 隐藏处。 '~**out/away** nn (colloq) hiding-place: (口) 隐匿之处: *a guerrilla ~out in the mountains.* 游击队在山中的隐藏处。 **hid·ing** n [U] (used of persons) (用以指人)*be in/go into hiding,* be hidden /~ oneself. 躲藏起来。 **come out of hiding,** show oneself. 出现; 现身。 **hiding-place** n place where sb or sth is or could be hidden. 藏匿处; 隐藏处。

hide² /haɪd; haɪd/ n **1** [C] animal's skin, esp as an article of commerce and manufacture. 兽皮; (尤指作为商业和制造业货品的)皮革。 **2** [U] (colloq) human skin. (口)人皮。 *save one's ~,* save one self from a beating, from punishment. 避免挨打; 避免受罚。 *tan sb's ~,* give him a beating. 打某人一顿。

hide·bound /ˈhaɪdbaʊnd; ˈhaɪdˌbaʊnd/ adj narrow-minded; having, showing, too much respect for rules and traditions. 心地狭窄的; 过份重视规则和传统的; 墨守成规的。

hid·eous /ˈhɪdɪəs; ˈhɪdɪəs/ adj very ugly; filling the mind with horror; frightful: 十分丑恶的; 恐怖的; 可怕的: *a ~ face/crime/noise.* 丑恶的面孔(极恶的罪行)可怕的声音)。 ~**·ly** adv

hid·ing /ˈhaɪdɪŋ; ˈhaɪdɪŋ/ n [C] beating; thrashing: 打; 鞭笞: *give sb/get a good ~.* 把某人痛打一顿(挨一顿痛打)。

hie /haɪ; haɪ/ vi (archaic, or joc) go quickly (to). (古或谑)快走; 疾行(与 to 连用)。

hi·er·archy /ˈhaɪərɑːkɪ; ˈhaɪəˌrɑrkɪ/ n (pl **-chies**) [C] organization with grades of authority from lowest to highest: 阶级组织; 等级制度: *the ~ of the Civil Service,* group of persons in authority; 文官阶级组织; group of bishops of a country. (一个国家之)主教团。 **hi·er·archi·c(al)** /ˌhaɪəˈrɑːkɪk (I); ˌhaɪəˈrɑrkɪk(I)/ adj

hi·ero·glyph /ˈhaɪərəglɪf; ˈhaɪərəˌglɪf/ n picture or figure of an object, representing a word, syllable or sound, as used in the writing of the ancient Egyptians and Mexicans; other secret or unintelligible written symbol. 象形文字(如古埃及与墨西哥人所用者); 秘密的或难解的符号。 ~**ic** /ˌhaɪərəˈglɪfɪk; ˌhaɪərəˈglɪfɪk/ adj of, written in, ~s. 象形文字的; 用象形文字写成的。 ~**ics** n pl = ~s.

hieroglyphics

hi-fi /ˌhaɪ ˈfaɪ; ˌhaɪˈfaɪ/ n, adj (colloq abbr of) high fidelity; apparatus producing this: (口)高度传真的 (为 high fidelity 之略); 高度传真音响设备: *a ~ (set).* 一套高度传真音响设备。 ⇨ **high(12).**

hig·gledy-pig·gledy /ˌhɪgldɪ ˈpɪgldɪ; ˈhɪgldɪˈpɪgldɪ/ adj, adv (collog) mixed up; without order. (口)混杂的(地); 杂乱无章的(地)。

high¹ /haɪ; haɪ/ adj (**-er, -est**) (For combinations of ~ and nn, participles, etc with meanings not at once to be identified from the meanings in the definitions, ⇨ **12** below) (与名词、分词等构成之复合词, 其意义不能自各定义中即刻辨出者, 参看下列第 12 义)。 **1** extending far upwards; measuring (the distance given) from the base to the top. 高的; 有若干高度的。(Note that *tall* is used for human beings and for a few things which have great height in relation to breadth, eg *a tall building/tower*): (注意: tall 指人或某些就宽高关系而言高度特别突出的物体, 例如 a tall building/tower 一座高建筑物(塔)): *There was an aeroplane ~ in the sky.* 有一架飞机高高在天空。 *How ~ is Mt Qomolangma?* 珠穆朗玛峰有多高? ~ *and dry,* **(a)** (of a ship) stranded; aground; out of the water. (指船)出水; 搁浅。 **(b)** (fig) abandoned; isolated; out of the current of events. (喻)被弃的; 孤立的; 脱离社会潮流的。 *be/get on one's ~ horse,* ⇨ **horse(1).** *(do sth) with a ~ hand,* arrogantly (~*handed(ly)* is preferred)。 (做事)专横地; 做慢地 (high-handed(ly) 较常用)。 **2** chief; important: 高级的; 重要的: *a ~ official;* 高级官员; *a ~ caste;* 高的社会阶级; *the ~ altar,* in a church; 主祭坛; *the Most H~.* (in the Bible) God; (圣经)上帝; ~ *society,* the upper classes. 上流社会。 ~ *and low,* all classes of society. 社会各阶层。 **3** (of sounds) at or near the top of the scale; shrill; sharp: (指声音)尖锐的: *speak in a ~ tone/key.* 以尖锐的嗓音说话。 **4** extreme; intense; great: 极度的; 强烈的; 大的: ~ *prices/temperatures;* 高价(高温); *bought at a ~ cost;* 以巨资购买; *a ~ wind;* 劲风; 大风; *in ~ favour;* 极为得宠; *have a ~ opinion of sb;* 极器重某人; *in ~ spirits;* 兴致勃勃; 高兴; ~ (= angry) *words;* 愤怒之言; *in ~ latitudes,* near the Poles; 在高纬度地区(近南北极); *have a ~* (= enjoyable) *time;* 过一段愉快的时间; *a ~* (= luxurious) *living;* 奢侈的生活; *~ noon/summer,* at or near its peak. 正午(盛夏)。 **5** ~ *time,* time when sth should be done at once: 应该即刻做某事的时间: *It's ~ time you started,* You should start at once. 你该动身了。 *It's ~ time to go,* We must go at once. 我们应马上就走。 **6** noble; virtuous: 高尚的; 良好的: *a woman of ~ character;* 品格高尚的女子; ~ *aims/ideals;* 高尚的目标(理想); *a ~ calling,* eg ~ of a priest, doctor or nurse. 高尚的职业(例如做牧

师、医生或护士)。 **7 H~ Church,** that section of the C of E that gives an important place to the authority of bishops and priests, to ritual and the sacraments. (英国)高教会派 (英国国教中注重主教和牧师权威，以及仪式及圣事的教派)。 Hence, 由此产生, **H~ Churchman. 8** (of food, esp meat and game) slightly tainted. (食物，尤指肉和猎物)略微腐坏的。 **9** (colloq) drunk. (口) 酒醉的。 **10** (colloq) under the influence of hallucinatory drugs: (口)受迷幻药影响的: ~ *on marijuana.* 沉醉于大麻烟中。 **11** (as *n*) (作为名词) ~ level: 高水准; 高峰; 高处: *from (on)* ~, from Heaven. 自天空; 自上苍。 *Shares* (ie on the Stock Exchange) *reached a new* ~ (= the ~est recorded level) *last month.* 股票上月达到了一个新的最高点。 **12** (compounds) (复合词) ~ **'ball** *n* (US) spirits with soda water, ginger ale, etc, served with ice in a tall glass. (美)加汽水或姜汁啤酒等的烈酒 (加冰并用高杯盛装)。 '~·**born** *adj* of noble birth. 出身高贵的; 出身名门的。 '~·**boy** *n* (US) tallboy. (美)高衣柜。 '~·**brow** *n, adj* (person) with tastes and interests considered to be superior (or who wishes to great extremes to get what he aims at. 野心勃勃不择手段的人。 ~·**'flown** *adj* exalted; bombastic and pretentious for *intellectual*): 嗜好和兴趣高雅的(人)(常用做 intellectual 之轻蔑语): ~*brow drama/music.* 适合嗜好和兴趣高雅的人们的戏剧(音乐)。 ~·**'chair** *n* one on ~ legs for an infant at table, or a baby's chair with a hinged tray attached to it. (婴儿用餐时坐的)高腿椅。 **H~ 'Church** *n* ⇨ **7** above. 参看上列第 **7** 义。 ~·**'class** *adj* first-class. 高级的; 第一流的。 ~·**'colour** *n* reddish complexion. 微红的面色。 **H~ Com'missioner** *n* representative of one Commonwealth country in another, equivalent to an ambassador. 英联邦各国相互派驻的大使级代表。 **'H~ Court** *n* supreme court of justice. 最高法院。 ~·**day** *n* festival 节日 (only in) (仅用于): ~ *days and holidays* 节日和假日。 **'~·er-ups** *n pl* (colloq) persons ~er in rank or status. (口)阶级或地位较高的人。 ~·**ex'plosive** *n* very powerful explosive, eg TNT. 高爆炸药(例如 TNT)。 ~·**fa'lutin** /fəˈluːtɪn/ *adj* (colloq) ridiculously pompous, bombastic or pretentious: (口) 过分夸张的; 虚饰的: ~-*falutin ideas/ language.* 夸张的思想(语言)。 ~·**fi'delity** *n, adj* (abbr 略作 **hi-fi**) (of radios, records, tapes and equipment for reproducing sound) (quality of) giving faithful reproduction by the use of a wide range of sound waves. (指收音机、唱片、录音带及唱机、录音机等)高度传真的。 ~·**'flier** / ~·**'flyer** *n* ambitious person who goes to great extremes to get what he aims at. 野心勃勃不择手段的人。 ~·**'flown** *adj* exalted; bombastic and pretentious: 崇高的; 夸张的; 虚饰的: *a* ~*flown style,* eg of writing. 夸张的风格(例如写作)。 ~·**'flying** *adj* (fig) (of persons) ambitious. (喻)(指人)充满野心的。 ~·**'frequen·cy** *n* (abbr 略作 **hf**) radio frequency between 3 and 30 megacycles per second. 高频率; 高周率(每秒 3 至 30 百万周)。 **H~ German** *n* literary German; standard spoken German. 德文的文言文; 标准德语。 ~·**'grade** *adj* of ~ or superior quality. 品质优良的。 ~·**'handed** *adj* domineering; using power or authority without consideration for the feelings of others. 专横的; 高压的。 ~·**'handed·ly** *adv,* ~ **'hat** *adj* (*n*) snobbish (person). 势利的(人)。 □ *vt* treat (sb) in a snobbish or condescending way. 势利地对待(某人)。 ~·**'jack** *vt* (variant spelling of) **hijack.** 为 hijack 之不同拼法。 ~·**'jinks,** ⇨ **jinks. the '~ jump** *n* athletic contest for jumping over an adjustable horizontal bar: 跳高: *enter for/win the* ~ *jump.* 参加跳高(跳高得胜)。 *be for the* ~ *jump,* (sl) due for severe punishment. (俚)应受严刑。 ~·**'keyed** *adj* (⇨ **3** above) (参看上列第 **3** 义) having a ~ pitch; (fig) easily excited or made nervous. 调子高的; (喻)易兴奋或紧张的。 '~·**land** /-lənd; -lənd/ *n* mountainous region; (*pl*) mountainous parts of a country (esp **The H~lands,** those of N W Scotland). 高地; 丘陵地; (复)一国之丘陵地区(大写时尤指苏格兰西北高地)。 **'H~land 'fling** *n* Scottish reel[3]. 苏格兰利尔舞。 **'H~·lander** *n* one who lives in The

H~lands; soldier in a (Scottish) H~land regiment. 苏格兰高地人; 苏格兰高地兵团之士兵。 ~·**'level** *adj* (attrib only) (of conferences, etc) conducted by persons in ~ position, eg in government, commerce. (仅用作定语)(指会议等)高阶层的。 '~ **life** *n* [U] (a) fashionable and luxurious style of living. 奢侈的生活。 (b) (in W Africa) popular kind of music and dance. (非洲西部)一种流行的音乐和舞蹈。 ~·**light** *n* (usu *pl*) luminous area on a photograph, picture, etc which shows reflected light; reflection of light on a shiny object; (fig) most conspicuous or prominent part: (通常用复数)像片、图画等光亮的部分; (0光体上光的反射, (喻)最显著部分; 最精采部分: *the ~lights of the week's events.* 一周事件中之最重要者。 □ *vt* give prominence or emphasis to. 使显著; 使精采; 加强。 ~·**'Mass** *n* (R C Church) (天主教) ⇨ **Mass.** ~·**'minded** /ˈmaɪndɪd/ /ˈmaɪndɪd/ *adj* of morally ~ character; having ~ ideals or principles. 品格高尚的; 有崇高理想或原则的。 Hence, 由此产生, ~·**'minded·ly** *adv,* ~·**'minded·ness** *n.* ~·**'necked** *adj* (of a dress) with the neckline cut ~. (指女服)领口高的。 ~·**'octane** *adj* having a ~ octane number. 高辛烷的。 ⇨ **octane.** ~·**'pitched** *adj* **(a)** (of sounds) shrill. (指声音)尖锐的。 **(b)** (of roofs) having a steep slope. (指屋顶)坡度陡的。 ~·**'powered** *adj* having, using, great power: 很有能力的; 强有力的: *a* ~*powered salesman,* aggressive in selling his goods. 精力充沛的推销员。 ~·**'pressure** *n* [U] pressure ~er than normal, esp ~er than atmospheric pressure: (fig) aggressive and persistent: 高压; (尤指)高气压; (喻)有冲劲而且坚持的: ~*pressure salesmanship.* 强行推销术。 ~·**'priced** *adj* expensive. 高价的; 昂贵的。 ~·**'priest** *n* chief priest. 主教; 大祭司。 ~·**'principled** *adj* honourable. 光明正大的。 ~·**'ranking** *adj* (of officers, etc) having ~ rank. (指军官等)高级的。 ~·**re'lief** *n* **relief**[2](1). '~·**'rise** *adj* (attrib only) used of tall buildings with many storeys or levels, reached by lifts (elevators): (仅用作定语)(指有电梯的建筑物)有很多层的; 高耸的: ~*rise flats.* 有很多层的公寓。 ⇨ **tower-block** at **tower.** '~·**road** *n* main road; (fig) most direct way: 大道; (喻)捷径: *Is there a* ~*road to happiness?* 有达到幸福的捷径吗? **'H~ School** *n* secondary school giving more advanced education than primary or elementary schools. 中学。 **the** ~·**seas** *n pl* all parts of the seas and oceans beyond territorial waters. 外洋; 外海; 公海。 ~·**'sounding** *adj* (of style) impressively pretentious. (指文体)夸饰的。 ~·**'speed** *adj* (able to be) operated at very fast speeds. 高速度的。 ~·**'spirited** *adj* lively; (of a horse) frisky. 有生气的; (指马)乱蹦乱跳的。 '~ **spot** *n* outstanding feature, memory, event, etc. 特色; 显著的记忆、事件等。 ~·**'street** *n* (esp in proper names) main street of a town: (尤用于专有名词中)大街: *There are three banks in the* ~ *street.* 大街上有三家银行。 ~·**'table** *n* table (on a dais) where senior members of a college dine. 大学餐厅中教师用的餐桌。 ~ **'tea** *n* (GB) early evening meal (or late tea) in homes where dinner is not eaten in the evening, usu with meat or fish. (英)黄昏茶点(不在黄昏进晚餐的家庭所食用，通常有肉或鱼)。 ~·**'tension** *n* (electr) (of wires) having a ~ voltage. (电)(指电线)高压的。 ~·**'tide** *n* (time at which the) tide is at its ~est level. 高潮; 高潮时期。 ~ **'time** *n* ⇨ **5** above. 参看上列第 **5** 义。 ~·**'toned** *adj* socially or intellectually superior: 高尚的; 时髦的; 优秀的: *a* ~*toned finishing school for girls.* 高尚的女子精修学校。 ~·**'treason** *n* [U] treason against the State or a sovereign. 叛国; 叛逆。 ~·**'up** *n* (colloq) person of ~ rank or great importance. (口)社会地位高的人; 要人。 ~ **'water** *n* [U] ~ tide. 高潮。 ~·**'water mark** *n* mark showing the ~est point reached by the tide (or any body of water); (fig) ~est point of achievement. 高潮线; 高水标; 高水位线; (喻)成就的最高峰。 ~·**'way** *n* main public road; main route (by air, sea or land); (fig) easiest or most direct way. 公路; 大道;

主要航路; (喻)捷径. **H~·way 'Code** *n* official guide-book for users of public roads. 公路旅行指南. **'~·way-man** /-mən; -mən/ *n* (*pl* **-men**) (formerly) man (usu on horseback) who robbed travellers on ~ways by using, or threatening to use, violence. (昔时)拦路的强盗(通常骑着马).

high² /haɪ; haɪ/ *adv* in or to a ~ degree: 高; 高度地: *climb* ~; 向高处攀登; *aim* ~; 向高处瞄准; 悬着高目标; 怀大志; (lit, fig) (字面, 喻) *pay* ~, pay a ~ price; 付高价; *play* ~, play a card of ~ value, eg an ace; 出大牌(例如么点); *live* ~, on rich, luxurious food and drink. 过奢侈的生活. *fly* ~, (fig) have great ambitions. (喻)有雄心. *hold one's head* ~, be proud. 骄傲. *run* ~, **(a)** (of the sea) have a strong current with a ~ tide. (指海)起大风浪; 波涛汹涌. **(b)** (of the feelings) be excited: (指感情) 激动: *Popular feelings/passions ran* ~, were strong. 群情激昂. *search/hunt/look* ~ *and low (for sth)*, look everywhere (for it). 到处寻找(某物).

high·ly /'haɪlɪ; 'haɪlɪ/ *adv* in or to a high degree: 高度地; 非常地: *a* ~ *paid official;* 薪俸优厚的官员; *a* ~ *amusing film;* 非常有趣的影片; *think* ~ *of sb*, have a high opinion of him; 器重某人; *speak* ~ *of sb*, praise him. 称赞某人.

high·ness /'haɪnɪs; 'haɪnɪs/ *n* **1** [U] (opposite of *lowness*) state or quality of being high: (为 lowness 之反义词)高; 高贵; 高尚: *the* ~ *of his character, aims.* 他的品格(志向)之高尚. **2** title used of and to British and various foreign princes: 殿下; 阁下 (对英国和其他国家皇族的尊称): *His/Her/Your/Royal/Imperial H~.* 殿下/阁下.

hi·jack (also **high·jack**) /'haɪdʒæk; 'haɪˌdʒæk/ *vt* [VP6A] **1** steal goods from (an aircraft or vehicle) by stopping it in transit. 劫取(飞机或车辆之)货物. **2** use force, or the threat of force, against those in control of an aircraft or vehicle, in order to achieve certain aims or to reach a desired destination. 劫持(飞机或车辆). □ *n* [C] instance of ~ing. 劫持. **-er** *n* person taking part in a ~. 劫持飞机或车辆者.

hike /haɪk; haɪk/ *vi, n* (colloq) (go for a) long walk in the country, taken for pleasure or exercise. (口) 远足; 健行; 徒步旅行. **~r** *n* person who ~s. 远足者; 健行者; 徒步旅行者. ⇨ **hitchhike**.

hil·ari·ous /hɪ'leərɪəs; həˈlɛrɪəs/ *adj* noisily merry. 热闹的. **~·ly** *adv* **hil·ar·ity** /hɪ'lærətɪ; həˈlærətɪ/ *n* [U] noisy merriment; loud laughter. 热闹; 欢笑.

hill /hɪl; hɪl/ *n* **1** natural elevation on the earth's surface, lower than a mountain. 丘陵; 小山. **'~·side** *n* side of a ~. 山坡. **'~·top** *n* top of a ~. 山顶. **2** slope, eg on a road: (道路等之)斜坡: *push a bicycle up a steep* ~. 把脚踏车推上陡坡. **3** heap of earth: 土堆: *'ant~s;* 蚁丘; *'mole~s.* 鼹鼠窝; 鼹鼠丘. **~y** *adj* (**-ier, -iest**) having many ~s: 多丘陵的; 多小山的; 多斜坡的: *~y country;* 丘陵地带; *a ~y road.* 多斜坡的路.

hill-billy /'hɪl bɪlɪ; 'hɪlˌbɪlɪ/ *n* (*pl* **-lies**) (colloq, often used derog) farmer, farm-worker, etc from the mountains in the S E of the US; (attrib) of these people: (口, 常用作贬抑语)美国东南部山区的农民; (用作定语)美国东南部山地农民的: ~ *music.* 美国东南部山地音乐.

hill·ock /'hɪlək; 'hɪlək/ *n* small hill(1). 小丘.

hilt /hɪlt; hɪlt/ *n* handle of a sword or dagger. 刀柄; 剑柄. ⇨ the illus at **sword**. 参看 sword 之插图. *(up) to the* ~, completely: 完全地: *His guilt was proved to the* ~. 他的罪完全证实了.

him /strong form: hɪm; hɪm; medial weak form: ɪm; ɪm/ *pers pron* used as object form of *he*: 他 (he 的宾格): *Mr Smith is in the town; I saw him yesterday.* 史密斯先生在城里, 我昨天见过他. *Give him the money.* 把钱给他. *That's him*, (colloq) That's he. (口)就是他.

him·self /hɪm'self; hɪm'sɛlf; weak form: ɪm's-; ɪm's-/ *reflex, emph pron* **1** (reflex) (反身) *He cut* ~. 他割伤

了自己. *He ought to be ashamed of* ~. 他应该为自己感到羞愧. *(all) by* ~, **(a)** alone. 孤独; 单独. **(b)** without help. 独力. **2** (emph) (强调气) *He* ~ *says so.* 他亲口这样说的. *He says so* ~. 他亲口这样说的. *Did you see the manager* ~? 你看见经理本人了吗? **3** *He's not quite* ~ *today*, not in his normal state of health or mind. 他今天不大舒服; 他今天有些失常.

hind¹ /haɪnd; haɪnd/ *adj* (of things in pairs, front and back; cf *fore*) at the back: (指前后成对的东西; 较 fore) 在后的; 后面的: *the* ~ *legs of a horse.* 马的后腿. *,~ 'quarters n pl* = legs and loin of the carcass of lamb, mutton, beef, etc. (羊, 牛等宰后的) 后腿肉. **'~·most** /-məʊst; -most/ *adj* farthest behind or back. 最后面的; 最后方的. *,~·'sight* /-saɪt; -saɪt/ *n* [U] perception of an event after its occurrence. 事后的领悟; 事后聪明.

hind² /haɪnd; haɪnd/ *n* female of (esp the red) deer. 雌鹿; (尤指)红雌鹿.

hin·der /'hɪndə(r); 'hɪndə/ *vt* [VP6A, C, 15A] obstruct; delay; get in the way of: 阻碍; 妨害; 妨碍: *Don't* ~ *me in my work.* 不要妨碍我的工作. *I was ~ed from getting here earlier.* 我受阻不能早些到此. *I have much business that has ~ed my answering your letter.* 我有很多事, 使我不能早日回复你的信.

Hindi /'hɪndiː; 'hɪndɪ/ *n, adj* (of) one of the official languages of N India. 印地语的(的)(为印度北部官方语言之一).

hin·drance /'hɪndrəns; 'hɪndrəns/ *n* [C] sth or sb that hinders: 妨碍的人或物; 阻碍者: *You are more of a* ~ *than a help.* 你与其说是助手, 不如说是障碍.

Hin·du /ˌhɪn'duː; US: 'hɪnduː; 'hɪndu/ *n* person, esp of N India, whose religion is ~ism. 信奉印度教者; 印度人; (尤指)信奉印度教之北部印度人. □ *adj* of the ~s. 印度人的; 北部印度人的; 印度教徒的. **~ism** /'hɪnduːˌɪzəm; 'hɪndu,ɪzəm/ *n* religion of most of the ~s. 印度教.

Hin·du·stani /ˌhɪnduː'stɑːnɪ; ,hɪndʊ'stænɪ/ *n, adj* (of) a form of Hindi. 兴都斯坦语的(的)(为印地语的一种形式).

hinge /hɪndʒ; hɪndʒ/ *n* joint on which a lid, door or gate turns or swings; (fig) central principle on which sth depends: 铰链; (喻)重点; 主旨; 关键: *Take the door off its* ~s *and rehang it.* 把这门自铰链拿下来重装. □ *vt, vi* **1** [VP6A] support, attach with, a ~ or ~s. 装以铰链. **2** [VP3A] ~ *on/upon*, turn or depend on: ~ 而定: *Everything* ~s *upon what happens next.* 一切以下一步发展而定.

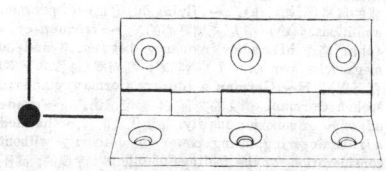

hinges

hint /hɪnt; hɪnt/ *n* [C] slight or indirect indication or suggestion: 提示; 暗示: *She gave him a* ~ *that she would like him to leave.* 她向他暗示希望他离开. *drop (sb) a* ~, indicate or suggest sth indirectly (to sb). 暗示(某人). *take a* ~, realise and do what is suggested. 接受暗示. □ *vt, vi* **1** [VP9, 6A] ~ *(to sb)*, suggest indirectly; give a ~: 暗示; 示意: *I* ~*ed that he ought to work harder.* 我暗示他应该更努力工作. *He* ~*ed to me nothing of his intentions.* 他没有向我暗示他的心意. **2** [VP3A] ~ *at*, refer indirectly to: 间接提及: *He* ~*ed at my extravagance.* 他间接提到我的奢侈.

hin·ter·land /'hɪntəlænd; 'hɪntɚ,lænd/ *n* parts of a country behind the coast or a river's banks. 海岸或河岸的后方地区; 内地; 腹地.

hip[1] /hɪp; hɪp/ n part on either side of the body where the bone of a person's leg is joined to the trunk: 臀部; 髋部: *He stood there with his hands on his hips.* 他两手叉腰站在那里。⇨ the illus at **trunk**. 参看 trunk 之插图。 **'hip-bath** n small tub in which one can sit immersed up to the hips. 小浴盆 (坐入可将下半身浸入水中)。 **'hip-flask** n small flask (for brandy, etc) to be carried in the hippocket. 一种装白兰地等的小酒瓶, 可放在臀部口袋里携带。 **hip-'pocket** n pocket (in a pair of trousers) on the hip. 臀部口袋。

hip[2] /hɪp; hɪp/ n fruit (red when ripe) of the wild rose. 野蔷薇的子(熟时为红色)。

hip[3] /hɪp; hɪp/ int (only in) (仅用于) **,Hip, hip, hur-'rah!** cry, cheer, of satisfaction or approval. 表示满意或赞同的呼声。

hip[4] /hɪp; hɪp/ adj (also 亦作 *hep*) (sl) aware of, in keeping with, advanced trends. (俚)知道最新发展的; 内行的; 跟上发展趋势的。

hip·pie /'hɪpɪ; 'hɪpɪ/ n ⇨ **hippy**.

hippo /'hɪpəʊ; 'hɪpo/ n (pl ~**s** -pəʊz; -poz/) (colloq abbr of) hippopotamus. (口)河马(为 hippopotamus 之略)。

Hip·po·cratic /,hɪpə'krætɪk; ,hɪpə'krætɪk/ adj ,~ **'oath,** oath to observe the medical code of ethical and professional behaviour, sworn by entrants to the profession. 新开业医生所立之誓言。

hip·po·drome /'hɪpədrəʊm; 'hɪpə,drom/ n place for horse- or chariot-races in ancient Greece and Rome. (古希腊, 罗马之)赛马或战车竞赛场。

hip·po·pota·mus /,hɪpə'pɒtəməs; ,hɪpə'pɑtəməs/ n (pl ~**es** -sɪz; -sɪz/ or **-mi** -maɪ; -maɪ/) large, thick-skinned African river animal. 河马。⇨ the illus at **large.** 参看 large 之插图。

hippy, hip·pie /'hɪpɪ; 'hɪpɪ/ n (pl **-pies**) (late 1960's) person who rejects established social conventions and institutions and expresses his personality by unusual styles of dress, living habits, etc. 嬉皮士; 嬉痞。

hire /'haɪə(r); haɪr/ vt [VP6A, 15B] ~(**out**), obtain or allow the use or services of in return for fixed payment: 租; 雇用: ~ *a horse/a concert-hall;* 租一匹马(一音乐厅); ~ *out boats.* 出租小船。(Cf 参较 *rent a house.* 租房屋用 rent。) □ n [U] (money paid for) hiring: 雇用; 雇用; 租金; 工资: *bicycles on ~, 50p an hour;* 脚踏车出租, 每小时五十便士; *pay for the ~ of a hall;* 付会堂租金; *work for ~.* 做雇工。 (**pay for/ buy sth) on ~ purchase,** (abbr 略作 **HP**) (buy by a contract to pay by instalments, and the right to use it after the first payment. 以分期付款方式 (购某物)。 ~**ling** /'haɪəlɪŋ; 'haɪrlɪŋ/ n (derog) person whose services may be ~d. (贬)可被人雇用者。

hir·sute /'hɜːsjuːt; 'hɜsut/ adj (formal) hairy; rough; shaggy (eg of a man with untidy long hair and beard). (正式用语)多毛的; 蓬乱的; 毛发蓬松的 (例如指生有蓬乱的长发和胡须的人)。

his /strong or initial form: hɪz; hɪz; medial weak form: ɪz; ɪz/ adj, pron belonging to him: 他的: *He hurt his hand.* 他弄伤了自己的手。*That book is his, not yours.* 那本书是他的, 不是你的。*I'm a friend of his.* 我是他的朋友。

hiss /hɪs; hɪs/ vi, vt 1 [VP2A] make the sound /s/, or the noise heard when water falls on a very hot surface: 发 /s/ 声; 发嘶嘶声: *The snake raised its head and ~ed.* 那蛇抬起了头并发出嘶嘶声。*The steam escaped with a ~ing sound.* 蒸汽嘶嘶地漏出。 2 [VP6A, 15A, 3A] ~(**off**), ~(**at**), show disapproval by making this sound: 发嘘声表示反对: ~ *an actor off the stage;* 将一演员嘘下台; ~(*at*) *a new play.* 嘘一新剧。 □ n [C] hissing sound: 嘶嘶声; 嘘声: *The speaker was received with a mixture of applause and ~es.* 那演说者同时获得了喝彩声与嘘声。

his·tor·ian /hɪ'stɔːrɪən; hɪs'tɔrɪən/ n writer of history. 历史学家。

his·toric /hɪ'stɒrɪk; US: -'stɔːr-; hɪs'tɔrɪk/ adj 1 notable or memorable in history; associated with past times: 历史上著名的; 与过去时代有关的: *a ~ spot/ event/speech.* 历史上著名的地点(事件, 演说)。 ~ **times,** of which the history is known and recorded (contrasted with *prehistoric times*). 有历史记载的时期(与 prehistoric times 相对)。 2 **the ~ present,** (gram) simple present tense used for events in the past (to make the description more vivid). (语法)历史现在时态(为描述较为生动起见, 用简单现在时态叙述过去事件)。

his·tori·cal /hɪ'stɒrɪkl; US: -'stɔːr-; hɪs'tɔrɪkl/ adj 1 belonging or pertaining to history (as contrasted with legend and fiction): 历史上的(以别于传说或虚构的): ~ *events and people,* real, not imaginary; 历史上的事件和人物(真实的, 非想象的); *a ~ novel/play/ film/painting, etc,* one dealing with real events in history. 历史小说(戏剧, 影片, 绘画等)。 2 having to do with history: 有关历史的: ~ *studies;* 对历史之研究; *the ~ method of investigation.* 依据历史的研究方法。 ~**ly** -klɪ; -klɪ/ adv

his·tory /'hɪstrɪ; 'hɪstrɪ/ n (pl **-ries**) 1 [U] branch of knowledge dealing with past events, political, social, economic, of a country, continent or the world: 历史学; 历史: *a student of ~.* 史学者。 **make ~,** do sth which will be recorded in ~. 创造历史。 **ancient ~,** to AD 476, when the Western Roman Empire was destroyed. 古代史(至纪元后 476 年西罗马帝国灭亡)。 **medieval ~,** to 1453. when Constantinople was taken by the Turks. 中古史(至 1453 年君士坦丁堡被土耳其人占领)。 **modern ~,** since 1453. 近代史(1453 年至今)。 2 [C] orderly description of past events: 对过去事件按顺序的描述: *a new ~ of Europe.* 新著欧洲大事记。 3 [C] train of events connected with a person or thing; interesting or eventful past career: 有关某人或某事物的连续事件; 沿革; 有趣的或重要的经历: *a house with a strange ~;* 有一段奇怪来历的房屋: *the inner ~ of the papal conclave.* 罗马天主教会秘密会议的内幕。 4 **natural '~,** systematic account of natural phenomena. 博物学。

his·tri·onic /,hɪstrɪ'ɒnɪk; ,hɪstrɪ'ɑnɪk/ adj 1 of drama, the theatre, acting: 戏剧的; 剧场的; 演剧的: ~ *ability.* 演剧的才能。 2 theatrical; insincere. 做戏的; 不诚恳的。 **his·tri·on·ics** n pl 1 theatrical performances. 戏剧的演出。 2 dramatic or theatrical manners, behaviour, etc, esp when exaggerated to create an effect. 戏剧化的举止, 行动等(尤指为求效果而夸张时所做)。

hit /hɪt; hɪt/ vt, vi (**-tt-**; pt, pp **hit**) 1 [VP6A, 15A, 12C] give a blow or stroke to; strike (a target, an object aimed at); come against (sth) with force. 击; 打; 击中; 碰; 撞: *hit a man on the head,* 打一人的头; *be hit by a falling stone;* 被落石击中; *hit sb a hard blow;* 痛击某人; *hit the mark/target;* 中的(击中目标); *hit a ball over the fence.* 将一球打过围墙。*He hit his forehead against the kerb when he fell.* 当他跌倒时, 他的额头撞在街道的边石上。 *hit a man when he's down; hit a man below the belt,* act contrary to the rules of boxing; (fig) take an unfair advantage. 违犯拳击规则; (喻)用不正当的手段。 *hit it; hit the nail on the head,* guess right; say or do exactly the right thing. 猜对了; 一语说中; 完全做对了。 *hit it off (with sb/together),* agree, get on well: 相处得很好; 相处融洽: *They hit it off well.* 他们相处得很好。 *hit-and-'run attrib adj* (of a road accident) in which a pedestrian or vehicle is hit by a vehicle which does not stop. 肇事后即逃逸的。 2 *hit sb hard,* cause him to suffer: 使某人痛苦: *The slump hit his business hard.* 物价暴跌使他的生意大受打击。*He was hard hit by his financial losses.* 他深受财务损失的打击。*He has fallen in love and is hard hit.* 他已坠入情网, 甚为痛苦。 3 [VP6A] go to; find; reach: 至; 发现; 到达: *hit the right path,* find it during a journey. 找到正确的道路。 *hit the headlines,* (colloq, of news) be printed prominently in the headlines (because

sensational, etc). (口, 指新闻, 由于耸动等)以显著标题登出。 **hit the road,** (colloq) set out on the road. (口)出发；上路。 **4** [VP2C] strike: 打击: *Hit hard!* 用力打! **hit out (against),** strike vigorously; (fig) attack strongly: 用力打; (喻)猛烈攻击: *The Minister hit out against trade union leaders.* 部长猛烈攻击工会领袖们。 **5** [VP3A] **hit on/upon sth,** find by chance or unexpectedly: 偶然发现; 无意中遇见: *hit upon an idea/ the right answer/a plan for making money.* 偶然想到一个主意(正确的答案, 赚钱的计划)。 **6** [VP15B] **hit sth /sb off,** (colloq) describe briefly and accurately (in words); make a quick sketch of. (口)(用文字)简明正确地描写; 略述。 **7** [VP6A] (cricket) score: (板球)得分: *He quickly hit 60 runs.* 他很快得到六十分。 □ *n* **1** blow; stroke: 打; 击: *three hits and five misses;* 三次击中五次未中; *a clever hit.* 巧妙的一击。 **'hit man** *n* (sl) person who is paid to kill sb. (俚)(受雇的)凶手。 **2** successful attempt or performance: 成功的尝试或表演: *hit songs, song hits,* songs that win wide popularity; 流行歌曲; *a lucky hit.* 侥幸成功。 *The new play is quite a hit,* has been welcomed by the public. 这新戏十分成功。 **make a hit (with sb),** (colloq) make a very favourable impression (with him). (口)予(某人)良好印象。 **'hit parade** *n* list of top selling popular records. 畅销唱片排行榜。 **3** stroke of sarcasm, etc: 讽刺; 抨击: *That was a hit at me,* the words were directed against me. 那是抨击我的。

hitch /hɪtʃ; hɪtʃ/ *vt, vi* **1** [VP6A, 15B] ~ *sth up,* pull up with a quick movement; 迅速拉上; 急拉: ~ *up one's trousers.* 迅速穿起裤子。 **2** [VP15A, 2C] fasten, become fastened, on or to a hook, etc, or with a loop of rope, etc: 系于钩等上; 用绳套住; 被钩住; 被套住: ~ *a horse to a fence;* 将马栓于栅栏上; ~ *a rope round a bough of a tree.* 将绳绕系于树枝上。 *Her dress ~ed on a nail.* 她的衣服被钉子钩住了。 **3** [VP2A, 6A] ~ *(a ride/ lift),* (colloq) ask the driver of a vehicle for a ride (口)搭便车。 ⇨ hitchhike. □ *n* **1** sudden pull or push. 急拉; 急推。 **2** kind of noose or knot used by sailors. 船员用的一种绳套或索结。 ⇨ the illus at knot. 参看 knot 之插图。 **3** temporary stoppage or impediment: 暂时的阻碍: *Everything went off without a ~,* quite smoothly, without difficulty. 一切进行顺利。 *The blast-off was delayed by a technical ~.* 由于技术上临时的障碍, 火箭的发射受到延误。

hitch·hike /'hɪtʃhaɪk; 'hɪtʃ‚haɪk/ *vi* [VP2A] (colloq abbr 口语略作 *hitch*) get a free ride by signalling for one (from a passing car, folty, etc) 搭乘人便车。 **hitch·hiker** *n*

hither /'hɪðə(r); 'hɪðɚ/ *adv* (old use) to this place. (旧用法)向此处; 到此处。 ~·**to** /‚hɪðə'tuː; ‚hɪðɚ'tu/ *adv* until now. 迄今; 至今。

hive /haɪv; haɪv/ *n* **1** (also 亦作 **'bee·~**) box (of wood, straw etc) for bees to live in; the bees living in a ~. (木, 草等制成的)蜂房; 蜂箱; 居于蜂房内之蜂群。 **2** place full of busy people: 喧闹的地区: *What a ~ of industry!* 多么喧嚷的工业区! □ *vt, vi* **1** [VP6A] cause (bees) to go into a ~: 使(蜂)进入蜂房: ~ *a swarm;* 使蜂群进蜂房: (of bees) store (honey) in a ~. (指蜂)贮(蜜)于蜂房。 **2** [VP2C] enter a ~; live close together as bees do. 进入蜂房; 如蜂般聚居。 ~ *off (from),* (fig) become a separate (and perhaps self-governing) body (as when a colony of bees leaves a ~ and forms a new ~); separate and make independent (a part of an organization): 变成单独的(或自治的)团体(如一群割离蜂房另建蜂巢者然); 使脱离组织而独立: ~ *off parts of the nationalized steel industry.* 开放部分国营钢铁工业(为民营)。

hives /haɪvz; haɪvz/ *n pl* skin disease with red patches and itching. 荨麻疹。

h'm /hm; hm/ ⇨ **hem**[2].

ho /həʊ; ho/ *int* expressing surprise, admiration, etc. (表示惊愕, 羡幕等之声)嗬!

hoar /hɔː(r); hɔr/ *adj* (liter) (of hair) grey or white with age; (of a person) having such hair. (文)(指头发)灰白的; 斑白的; (指人)有白发的。 '~·**frost** *n* [U] white frost; frozen dew on grass, the surface of leaves, roofs, etc. 白霜; (草, 叶, 屋顶等上的)霜。

hoard /hɔːd; hɔrd/ *n* carefully saved and guarded store of money, food or other treasured objects; collection of coins, valuable objects, etc dug up, eg one dating from Saxon times in GB: 节省下来并妥为贮藏的金钱, 食物或其他宝物, 密藏物; 窖藏; 挖掘出来的一批金币, 贵重物件等(例如英国萨克逊时代的古物): *a miser's ~;* 守财奴的窖藏; *a squirrel's ~ of nuts.* 松鼠贮藏的坚果。 □ *vt, vi* [VP6A, 15B] ~ *(up),* save and store: 贮藏; ~ *gold;* 贮藏黄金; ~ *up treasure.* 聚藏财宝。 ~·**er** *n* person who ~. 贮藏者。

hoard·ing /'hɔːdɪŋ; 'hɔrdɪŋ/ *n* (US 美 = *billboard*) (often temporary) fence of boards round waste land, building work, etc, frequently used for posting advertisements. 广告于荒地, 建筑工程等,常被用以张贴广告的)栅墙(常为临时性的)。

hoarse /hɔːs; hɔrs/ *adj* (of the voice) rough and harsh; (of a person) having a ~ voice: (指声音)粗哑的; 嘶哑的; (指人)声音嘶哑的: *He shouted himself ~.* 他的嗓子都喊哑了。 ~·**ly** *adv* ~·**ness** *n*

hoary /'hɔːrɪ; 'hɔrɪ/ *adj* (-ier, -iest) grey or white with age; very old: 因年迈而灰白的; 古老的: *the ~ ruins of English abbeys.* 古老英国寺院的遗迹。 **hoari·ness** *n*

hoax /həʊks; hoks/ *n* [C] mischievous trick played on sb for a joke. 恶作剧; 戏弄。 □ *vt* [VP6A, 14] deceive (sb) in this way: 欺骗; 戏弄(某人): ~ *sb into believing or doing sth foolish.* 骗某人相信或做愚蠢之事。 ~·**er** *n*

hob /hɒb; hɑb/ *n* flat metal shelf at the side of a fireplace(with a surface level with the top of the grate) where pots and pans can be kept warm or a kettle boiled. 壁炉旁边的金属平架(其面与炉架顶平), 置锅于上可以保温, 或置以开水壶保持沸腾。

hobble /'hɒbl; 'hɑbl/ *vi, vt* **1** [VP2A, C] walk as when lame, or as when the feet or legs are impeded: 跛行; 蹒跚: *The old man ~d along with the aid of his stick.* 那老人借手杖之助蹒跚而行。 **2** [VP6A] tie two legs of a horse or donkey to prevent it from going far away. 捆绑马或驴之双腿, 以阻其远离。 □ *n* stumbling or limping way of walking. 蹒跚; 跛行。 '~·**skirt** *n* very narrow skirt which caused the wearer to walk with short steps. 一种很窄之裙, 穿者须碎步行走。

hobble·de·hoy /'hɒbldɪhɔɪ; 'hɑbldɪ‚hɔɪ/ *n* awkward overgrown youth. 笨拙而且过于高大的青年。

hobby /'hɒbɪ; 'hɑbɪ/ *n* (pl **-bies**) [C] occupation, not one's regular business, for one's leisure time. eg stamp-collecting, growing roses. 嗜好 (例如集邮, 种植蔷薇)。

hobby·horse /'hɒbɪhɔːs; 'hɑbɪ‚hɔrs/ *n* [C] wooden horse on rockers as a child's toy, or on a merry-go-round; long stick with a horse's head; figure of a horse (in wickerwork) fastened to a dancer (in the morris-dance); (fig) favourite topic (of conversation, etc): 木马(装于摇轴上作儿童玩具, 或装置于旋转游乐台上); 装有马头形物之长棒; (乡村化装舞会中)系于跳舞者身上的柳条编成的马; (喻)(指谈话等的)喜爱的话题: *Now he's started on his ~,* begun to talk on his favourite subject. 现在他开始谈论他最喜爱的话题。

hob·gob·lin /‚hɒb'gɒblɪn; 'hɑb‚gɑblɪn/ *n* [C] mischievous imp; ugly and evil spirit. 小妖魔; 恶鬼。

hob·nail /'hɒbneɪl; 'hɑb‚nel/ *n* short nail with a heavy head used for the soles of heavy shoes and boots, eg for mountain-climbing. (钉于爬山等所用笨重鞋靴底上的)粗大短钉。 ~·**ed** *adj* (of boots, etc) set with ~s. (指鞋靴)装有粗头短钉的。

hob·nob /'hɒbnɒb; 'hɑb‚nɑb/ *vi* (**-bb-**) [VP2A, 3A] ~ *(together)/(with sb),* have friendly social relations: 亲切地与人交往: *I used to ~ with the rich*

and famous. 我过去常与富有而又著名的人交往。

hobo /'həʊbəʊ; 'hobo/ *n* (*pl* ~s, ~es /-bəʊz; -boz/) (US, sl) unemployed worker who wanders from place to place; vagrant. (美俚) 无业游民; 流浪汉。

Hob·son's choice /ˌhɒbsnz'tʃɔɪs; 'hɑbsn̩z'tʃɔɪs/ *n* ⇨ **choice.**

hock¹ /hɒk; hak/ *n* middle joint of an animal's hind leg. 跗关节(动物后腿中间的关节); 踝关节)。 ⇨ the illus at **dod, domestic.** 参看 dog, domestic 之插图。

hock² /hɒk; hak/ *n* [U] (kind of) German white wine. (一种)德国产的白葡萄酒。

hock³ /hɒk; hak/ *vt* (sl) [VP6A] pawn²(1). (俚)典当; 抵押。 □ *n in* ~, pawned. 当掉。

hockey /'hɒkɪ; 'hakɪ/ *n* [U] '**field** ~, game played with sticks on a field by two teams of eleven players each and a ball. 曲棍球; 陆上曲棍球(各有有十一人之两

†ield hockey

队, 在运动场上用一球及曲棍所进行的球戏)。 '**ice** ~. game played on ice by two teams of six players each wearing skates and with sticks and a rubber disc (a *puck*). 冰上曲棍球(由各有六人之两队, 穿冰鞋在冰上用曲棍及一橡皮圆盘 (puck) 所进行的球戏)。 '~ **stick,** long curved or angled stick used to hit the ball or puck. 曲棍球棒。

ice hockey

ho·cus-po·cus /ˌhəʊkəs 'pəʊkəs; 'hokəs'pokəs/ *n* [U] talk, behaviour, designed to draw one's attention away from sth; deception. 故意使人转移注意力的言谈或行动; 欺骗。

hod /hɒd; had/ *n* light open box with a long handle used by workmen for carrying bricks, etc on the shoulder. 砖斗(轻便无盖之箱状工具, 有长柄, 工人用以肩负搬运砖瓦等)。

hodge-podge /'hɒdʒpɒdʒ; 'hadʒ,padʒ/ *n* [U] = hotchpotch.

hoe /həʊ; ho/ *n* tool for loosening the soil, uprooting weeds among growing crops, etc. 锄头。 ⇨ the illus at **tool.** 参看 tool 之插图。 **Dutch hoe,** the kind pushed forward by the user. 锄。 □ *vt, vi* (*pt, pp* **hoed**) [VP 6 A, 15 B, 2 A] work with a hoe: 锄: *hoeing up weeds.* 锄草。

hog /hɒg US: hɔ:g; hag/ *n* castrated male pig reared for meat, ⇨ **boar(2), sow¹;** (fig) greedy, dirty, selfish person. (阉过的供食用的)公猪; (喻)贪婪、肮脏、自私的人。 *go the whole hog,* do sth thoroughly. 彻底做某事。

'**hog·wash** *n* swill(2); (fig) nonsense; rubbish (esp of sth said or written). (喂猪之)泔水; 泔水; (喻)胡说; 废话。 □ *vt* [VP6A] take more than one's fair share of; take greedily and selfishly. 取用超出应得的一份; 贪婪而自私地取用。 **hog·gish** /-ɪʃ; -ɪʃ/ *adj* greedy and selfish. 贪婪而且自私的。

Hog·ma·nay /'hɒgmənel; ,hagmə'ne/ *n* (Scotland) New Year's Eve (and its festivities). (苏格兰)除夕(及其庆祝活动)。

hogs·head /'hɒgzhed US: 'hɔ:g-; 'hagz,hed/ *n* large barrel for beer; liquid measure (52½ gallons in GB or about 238.5 litres. 62 gallons in US or about 234.5 litres). 大啤酒桶; 豪格海(液量名, 在英国合 52½ 加仑或约 238.5 公升, 在美国合 62 加仑或约 234.5 公升)。

hoi pol·loi /ˌhɔɪ pə'lɔɪ; 'hɔɪpə'lɔɪ/ *n* the ~, (pej) the masses; the rabble. (蔑)民众; 贱民。

hoist /hɔɪst; hɔɪst/ *vt* [VP6A, 15B] lift with an apparatus of ropes and pulleys or a kind of elevator (用绳索及滑轮装置或一种升降机)升起; 举起: ~ *a flag /sail;* 升旗(帆); ~ *casks and crates aboard;* 将桶和篓装上船。 将小船从水面吊至甲板上。 □ *n* apparatus for ~ing: 吊机; 起重机; 升起装置: *an ammunition* ~ (on a warship); (军舰上)弹药起卸机; (colloq) pull or push: (口)拉; 推: *give sb a* ~, eg when he is climbing a wall. 将某人向上推一下(例如当其爬墙时)。

hoity-toity /ˌhɔɪtɪ 'tɔɪtɪ; 'hɔɪtɪ'tɔɪtɪ/ *adj* (colloq): supercilious and haughty. (口)傲慢的。 □ *int* used to a ~ person to express disapproval of him or her. 对一傲慢的人所用的感叹词; 表示对其不满。

hold¹ /həʊld; hold/ *vt, vi* (*pt, pp* **held** /held; held/) (For uses with *adverbial particles* and *preps*, ⇨ **14** below.) (与副词性小品词及介词连用的用法, 参看下列第 14 义)。 **1** [VP 6 A, 15 A, B] have or keep in one's possession, keep fast or steady, in or with the hand(s), arm(s) or other part of the body, eg the teeth, or with a tool: 执住; 握住; 拿住: *The girl was* ~*ing her father's hand.* 那女孩握住她父亲的手。 *They held hands/held each other's hands.* 他们互相握住手。 *She held me by the sleeve.* 她扯住我的袖子。 *She was* ~*ing up an umbrella.* 她打着雨伞。 *He held the knife in his teeth as he climbed the tree.* 他爬树时用牙齿叼着刀子。 ~ *the line,* keep a telephone connection (eg while the person at the other end goes away to find sth or sb). 不把电话挂断; 继续维持通话。 ⇨ also **baby, brief²(1).pistol. 2** [VP6A, 15A, B] restrain; keep back; control: 压抑; 阻止; 抑制; 控制: *The police held back the crowd.* 警察阻止了群众。 *It took three of us to* ~ *the madman.* 我们三个人合力制住那个疯子。 *Try to* ~ *the thief until the police arrive.* 设法制住那小偷, 等警察到来。 *He held his attacker at arm's length.* 他把攻击者阻止在一臂之外。 *The dam gave way; it was not strong enough to* ~ *the flood waters.* 水坝坍塌了; 它不够坚固, 挡不住洪水。 ~ *one's breath,* eg from excitement or fear: (例如因兴奋或恐惧而)屏息: *The watchers held their breath as the acrobat crossed the tightrope.* 当表演者走过绷索时, 观众都屏息。 ~ *(one's) fire,* stop shooting for a time. 停火。 ~ *one's tongue /peace,* be quiet. 缄默; 住嘴。 *There is no* ~*ing sb/ sth,* It is impossible to restrain or control him/it: 无法约束或控制某人(某物): *There was no* ~*ing her,* eg because she was so determined or high-spirited. 没有办法阻止她(例如因为她太坚决或太高兴)。 **3** [VP 15 A, B, 2C] keep or maintain sb/sth in a specified position, manner, attitude or relationship: 使某人或某物保持特定位置, 态度, 姿势或关系: *H*~ *your head up.* 把你的头抬起来。 *H*~ *your arms up/out.* 把你的手臂举起来(伸出来)。 *H*~ *yourself still for a moment while I take your photograph.* 我给你拍照的那一刹那, 你不要动。 ~ *oneself in readiness (for),* be prepared (for sth, an emergency). 准备好(做某事, 应付紧急事件)。 ~ *one's sides with laughter,* laugh heartily. 捧腹大笑。 **4** [VP6A] maintain a grip of: 抓紧; 握牢: *This new car* ~s *the*

road well/has good road-~ing qualities, is stable, eg when cornering at speed. 这部新汽车很稳(例如在快速转弯时). **5** [VP6A] support; bear the weight of: 支持; 承受重量: *This nail won't ~ such a heavy mirror.* 这钉子支持不住这样重的镜子. *Come down—that branch won't ~ you!* 下来——那树枝承受不了你的重量! **6** [VP6A] be filled by; have the capacity to contain or accommodate: 装; 盛; 能够容纳: *Will this suitcase ~ all your clothes?* 这衣箱能装下你所有的衣服吗? *This barrel ~s 25 litres.* 这桶能盛 25 公升. *What does the future ~ for us?* 我们将来的命运如何? *He ~s (= has) strange views on religion.* 他对宗教持有奇怪的看法. **~ sth in one's head,** retain, not forget, eg a mass of details, statistics. 牢记; 记住(细节, 统计数字等). **(not) ~ water,** (not) be sound, valid, logical: 站得住(站不住); (不) 正确; (不) 合乎逻辑: *Your argument does not ~ water.* 你的论点站不住. **7** [VP6A, 22] keep the interest or attention of: 维持…兴趣或注意力:*The speaker held his audience spellbound.* 演说者使听众听得入迷. **8** [VP9, 15A, B, 22, 25] consider; regard; believe; affirm: 认为; 视为; 相信; 确定: *~ a man to be a fool/~ that he is foolish,* 认为某人是傻子; *~ the view that a plan is/~ a plan to be impracticable.* 认为某计划不切实际. *The President is not held in great respect.* 那位总统并不十分受人尊敬. *He does not ~ himself responsible for his wife's debts.* 他并不认为他应该对妻子的债务负责. **~ sb in high/low esteem,** have a high/low regard for him. 非常(不很)尊敬某人. **~ sth dear/ cheap,** place a high/low value on it: 重视 (不重视) 某事物: *He ~s his reputation dear.* 他重视他的名誉. **9** [VP6A] defend; keep possession of: 防守; 保持: *They held the fort against all attacks.* 他们坚守那堡垒, 抵抗所有的进攻. **~ the fort,** (fig) be in charge during sb's absence: (喻) 当某人不在时, 代理职掌: *Jane had to ~ the fort* (be in charge of the house) *while her mother was in hospital.* 在她母亲住医院期间, 简只好代理掌家. **~ one's ground,** stand firm, not retreat: 坚守阵地; 不撤退: *Our soldiers held their ground bravely.* 我们士兵英勇地坚守阵地. **~ one's own,** not give way: 坚持立场; 不让步: *The patient is still ~ing his own,* maintaining his strength. 那病人仍然在支撑着. *Mr Green held his own,* eg in a debate, maintained his position (by arguing well). 格林先生坚持自己立场(例如在辩论中, 立论精辟). **10** [VP6A] be the legal owner or possessor of: 保有; 拥有: *~ shares/stock.* 保有股份(股票). ⇨ land¹er at **land**¹(6). *share¹er* at **share**¹(3), *stock¹er* at **stock**¹(5). **11** [VP6A] occupy; have the position of: 占有; 在位: *The Social Democrats held office then,* were the government. 当时是社会民主党执政. Hence, 由此产生, **'office-~er.** **12** [VP6A] have; conduct; cause to take place: 举行: *~ a meeting/debate/ examination.* 举行会议(辩论, 考试). *We ~ a General Election every four or five years.* 我们每四年或五年举行大选. *The Motor Show is usually held in October.* 汽车展览会通常在十月举行. *~ court,* (fig) entertain, welcome, admirers: (喻)接待敬慕者: *a film-star ~ing court at London Airport.* 一位电影明星在伦敦机场接待影迷. ⇨ court¹(2). **13** [VP2A, D] remain unbroken, unchanged, secure, under strain, pressure, etc. (在紧张, 压力等下)不破; 不变; 安全. ⇨ **5** above. 参看上列第 5 义. *How long will the anchor ~,* stay fast in the sea bed? 这锚会固定在海底多久? *How long will this fine weather ~,* continue? 这好天气能继续多久? ⇨ **break**¹(5). *The argument still ~s (good/true),* is still valid. 这论据仍旧有效. **14** [VP15B, 3A, 2C, 14] (uses with *adverbial particles* and *preps;* for non-idiomatic uses ⇨ **1, 2, 3** above): (与副词性小品词及介词连用的用法; 非习惯用法参看上列第 1, 2, 3 义): **hold sth against sb,** allow sth to influence one's opinions adversely: 由于受某事的影响而对某人持不好的看法: *Don't ~ his criminal convictions against him.* 不要因为他判过刑而对他存有偏见.

hold (oneself) aloof, ⇨ **aloof.**

hold back, hesitate; show unwillingness: 踌躇; 退缩: *Buyers are ~ing back,* making few or no offers. 买主们不愿出价. *When danger came, no one held back.* 危险来到时, 无人退缩. **~ sb/sth back, (a)** ⇨ **2** above. 参看上列第 2 义. **(b)** hinder the progress of: 阻碍; 阻止: *His poor education is ~ing him back.* 他的教育程度差阻碍了他的发展. **(c)** keep secret or to oneself: 隐而不宣; 不公开: *~ back information.* 隐藏着消息不宣布.

hold sb/sth down, (a) ⇨ **3** above. 参看上列第 3 义. **(b)** oppress; keep down or under: 控制; 压制: *rulers who ~ the people down,* oppress them. 压迫人民的统治者. *We must ~ (= keep) prices down.* 我们必须抑低物价. **~ a job down,** (colloq) keep it by proving one's capabilities. (口)表现才能而保持住职位.

hold forth, speak pompously, as if in public. 高谈阔论. **~ sth forth,** (~ *sth out,* below is preferred) offer; propose. 提供; 提议 (hold sth out 较常用).

hold sth in, check: restrain; 抑制; 压抑: *~ in one's temper;* 抑制自己的脾气; *~ oneself in,* control one's feelings, eg of indignation. 压抑自己的感情(例如愤慨).

hold off, (a) remain at a distance: 保持距离: *The storm held off.* 风暴滞留在远处. *Will the rain ~ off until after the picnic?* 雨会延缓到野餐之后下吗? **(b)** delay action. 延搁行动: *H~ off for a minute.* 延缓一分钟. **~ sb/sth off,** keep at a distance: 使保持距离: *H~ your dog off!* 别让狗走近! *His cold manner ~s (better keeps) people off,* deters them from trying to be friendly. 他的冷淡态度使人不敢亲近(用 keeps 较佳).

hold on, (a) stand firm when there is danger, difficulty, etc: 坚定: *How much longer do they think we can ~ on?* 他们以为我们还能支持多久? **(b)** (usu imper) stop: (通常作祈使用法) 停止: *H~ on a minute!* Not so fast! Don't go further in what you're doing. 停一停! **~ on to, (a)** keep one's grip on; not let go of: 抓住; 不放手: *~ on to one's hat on a windy day.* 在大风的日子抓住自己的帽子. *The boy held on to the bush until someone climbed down the cliff to rescue him.* 这男孩抓住那矮树, 直到有人爬下悬崖去救他. **(b)** not give up the ownership of: 不放弃拥有; 不出让: *You should ~ on to your oil shares.* 你应该掌握你的石油股份. **~ sth on,** keep in position: 使固定: *These bolts and nuts ~ the wheels on.* 这些螺栓及螺帽使车轮子固定.

hold out, (a) maintain resistance; not give way: 抵抗; 不退让: *How long can we ~ out against these attacks?* 我们对这些攻击能抵抗多久? **(b)** last: 维持; 继续: *How long will our food supplies ~ out?* 我们的贮粮还能维持多久? *I can't ~ out* (= retain my urine) *much longer—I must find a toilet.* 我内急不能再久等了——我必须找个厕所. **~ out for,** continue to demand: 继续要求; 坚持: *The workers are still ~ing out for higher wages,* insisting on being granted their demands. 工人们仍旧坚持更高工资. **~ out on,** refuse to deal with: 拒绝与…来往: *He's still ~ing out on me,* still opposing my wishes, refusing my request. 他仍然拒绝跟我来往. **sb/sth out, (a)** ⇨ **3** above. 参看上列第 3 义. **(b)** offer: 给予: *The doctors ~ out little hope of recovery.* 医生们对痊愈的希望甚微.

hold sth over, defer; postpone; adjourn: 延搁; 延期; 休会: *The matter was held over until the next meeting.* 这件事被延至下次会议解决. **~ sth over sb,** use it as a threat: 以某事要挟某人: *He's ~ing my past record over me.* 他用我过去的记录威胁我.

hold to sth, (a) remain loyal or steadfast to: 忠实; 坚定: *He held to his convictions/choice/course of action.* 他忠于他的信仰(抉择, 行动方针). **(b)** keep to: 遵行: *The ship held to a Southerly course.* 那艘船遵行南方航线. **~ sb to sth,** make sb keep, eg a promise: 使某人遵守(诺言): *We must ~ the contractors to their estimates,* not allow them to exceed them. 我们一定要承包商遵守他们的估价. **~ sb (up) to ransom,** demand

money by threatening penalties, etc; blackmail: 以处罚
等作威胁而索取金钱; 勒索; 敲诈: *Those strikers were
not ~ing the country (up) to ransom.* 那些罢工者并不是
在向全国敲诈。 ⇨ **ransom.**

hold together, (a) be and continue whole: 在一起; 成
一整体: *The bodywork of this old car hardly ~s together,*
is falling apart, eg from rust. 这部旧汽车的车身由于生
锈等几乎要散落开了。 **(b)** remain united: 团结一起:
We always ~ together in times of crisis. 我们在危急时期
永远团结在一起。 ~ **sb/sth together,** cause to remain
together; unite: 使结合在一起; 使团结: *The country
needs a leader who will ~ the nation together.* 那国家需要
一个能使全国团结的领袖。

hold sb/sth up, (a) ⇨ 1, 2 above. 参看上列第 1, 2 义。
(b) delay: 延搁; 阻滞: *They were held up by the
immigration authorities.* 他们为雾(移民当局)所延搁。
(c) stop by the use or threat of force, for the purpose
of robbery: 拦路抢劫: *The travellers were held up by
bandits.* 旅客遭强盗拦劫。 Hence, 由此产生, **'~-up:** a
~up on the Underground, eg by a power failure; 地下
火车运输因为停电等的延搁; a bank ~up, eg one by
armed robbers. 银行被持械强盗等抢劫。 **(d)** put forward as an example: 举出作为例证: *Don't ~ me up as a
model husband.* 不要拿我作为模范丈夫的例子。 ~ *sb up
to derision/scorn/ridicule,* expose him to derision,
etc. 嘲笑某人。

hold with sth, approve of: 赞成某事: *Do you ~ with
nudity on the stage?* 你赞成舞台上裸体么?

hold² /hʊld/ n 1 [C, U] act, manner, power
of holding: 抓; 握; 把握; 把持力: *catch/get/take/lay
/seize* ~ *of sth;* 抓住某物; *let go/lose (one's) ~ of
sth.* 松手; 对某物失去把持力。 *He has a great ~* (=
influence) *over his younger brother.* 他对他弟弟很有影
响力。 *How long can the Government keep its ~ over the
district,* keep the district under control? 政府在该地区
的统治权能维持多久? 2 [C] sth that may be used for
holding on to: 可抓握之物; 可踏脚之处: *The rock face
afforded few ~s to climbers.* 该岩石的正面很少有攀登者
可以踏脚之处。 ⇨ *foothold* at **foot¹(8).** 3 (boxing and
wrestling) (kinds of) grip: (拳击与摔角)抓紧; 擒拿法:
all-in wrestling, with no ~s barred. 自由式的摔角, 不经
擒拿。

hold³ /hʊld; hʊld/ n part of a ship below deck, where
cargo is stored. 货舱。

hold-all /'hʊld ɔːl; 'hʊld,ɔl/ n portable bag or case
large enough to hold clothes, etc when travelling. 装衣
物用的轻便旅行袋。 ⇨ **hold¹(6).**

holder /'hʊldə(r); 'hʊldɚ/ n person or thing that
holds: 支持之人或物; 持有者; 保持者: *a 'share~;* 股东;
a ciga'rette-~; 香烟嘴; *an 'office-~;* 公务员; 职员; *a
'kettle-~,* cloth for handling a hot kettle. 用来拿热水壶
的布。

hold·ing /'hʊldɪŋ; 'hʊldɪŋ/ n sth (esp land) held or
owned; tenure or ownership (esp of land). 所有物(尤
指土地); (尤指土地)所有权或所有权。 **'small-~** n
small area of land farmed by the tenant himself. 佃农
自己耕种的小块土地。 **a '~ company,** one formed to
hold the shares of subsidiary companies. 股权公司(控制
附属公司股份的公司)。

hold-up /'hʊld ʌp; 'hʊld,ʌp/ n ⇨ **hold¹(14).**

hole /hʊl; hol/ n 1 opening or hollow place in a solid
body; 洞; 孔; 坑: *a ~ in a tooth;* 牙齿上的空洞; *roads
full of ~s;* 满是坑洼的道路; ~*s in the walls and roof of
a building,* caused by shell fire; 一建筑物墙壁及屋顶上
炮弹击成的洞孔; *wear one's socks into ~s,* wear them
until there are ~s. 把袜子穿破。 *make a ~ in,* use a
large amount of: 用去一大笔钱: *The hospital bills made
a large ~ in his savings.* 住院费花掉他储蓄的一大半。
pick ~s in, find fault with, eg an argument. 找 (论据
等)的漏洞。 *a square peg in a round ~,* 吹毛求疵。 *a
person not fitted for the position he occupies.* 不适于其
职位的人。 2 (colloq) awkward situation: (口)窘境:

You've put me in a bad ~. 你使我十分困窘。 3 animal's
burrow: 兽穴: *a mouse's ~/'mouse-~;* 鼠穴; *the ~
of a fox;* 狐穴; (fig) small, dark, wretched place; den;
hiding-place: (喻)狭小, 阴暗, 卑陋的地方; 巢穴; 隐匿处:
What a wretched little ~ he lives in! 他住的房子多么狭
小简陋啊! **,~-and-'corner** adj (colloq, attrib) secret;
underhand: (口, 用作定语)秘密的; 偷偷摸摸的: *We don't
like these ~-and-corner methods.* 我们不喜欢这些不光明
正大的方法。 4 (golf) hollow into which the ball must
be hit; point scored by a player who gets his ball from
one ~ to another with the fewest strokes: (高尔夫)球
洞; 自一高尔夫球洞至另一洞间, 球员以最少杆数进球所得
的分数: *win the first ~.* 在第一洞时领先。 □ *vt, vi* 1 [VP6A]
make a ~ or ~s in or through: 凿洞于; 穿孔于: *a
ship,* eg by striking a rock. 使船撞破(例如由于碰撞到
岩石)。 2 [VP6A, 15B, 2C] ~ **(out),** get (a ball) into
a ~ (in golf, etc): (高尔夫球类)打(球)入洞: ~ *out in
one,* get the ball from the tee into the ~ with only one
stroke. 一击而使球入洞。 3 [VP2C] ~ **up,** (sl) hide.
(俚)藏; 躲避。

holi·day /'hɒlədeɪ; 'halə,de/ n 1 day of rest from
work: 假日: *Sunday is a ~ in Christian countries;
Friday is a ~ in Muslim countries.* 星期天在基督教国
家中是假日; 星期五在伊斯兰教国家中是假日。 ⇨ also
bank ~ at bank³(1). 2 (often *pl*) (US 美 = *vacation*)
period of rest from work: (常用复数)假期: *the school
~s;* 学校的假期; *the Christmas ~s;* 圣诞节假期; *take a
month's ~ in summer;* 度一个月的暑假; (attrib) (用作
定语) *'~ camps.* 度假营。 **on ~,** having a ~: 在度假:
休假: *Our typist is away on ~ this week.* 我们的打字员
本周休假。 **'~-maker** n person on ~. 度假者。

holi·ness /'hʊlɪnɪs; 'holɪnɪs/ n 1 [U] being holy
or sacred. 神圣。 2 **His/Your H~,** title used of or to
the Pope. 教皇陛下(对教皇的尊称)。

hol·ler /'hʊlə(r); 'halɚ/ *vi, vt* (sl) yell (to indicate
excitement, etc): (俚)喊叫(表示兴奋等): *Stop ~ing —
nobody's going to hurt you!* 别叫了——没有人要伤害你!

hol·loa /'hʊləu; 'halo/ *n, vi, int* shout, esp to hounds
(during a fox-hunt). 呼喊(尤指猎狐时对猎犬的吆喝)。

hol·low /'hɒləu; 'halo/ adj 1 not solid; with a hole or
empty space inside: 空的; 中空的: *a ~ tree;* 中空的树;
a ~ ball. 中空的球。 2 (of sounds) as if coming from
sth ~: (指声音)空洞的; 重浊的: *a ~ voice/groan.* 沉重
的声音(呻吟)。 3 (fig) unreal; false; insincere: (喻)不
真实的; 虚假的; 虚伪的: *~ sympathy/words/promises;*
虚伪的同情(言语, 允诺); *a ~ laugh;* 虚伪的笑声; *~
joys and pleasures,* not giving true happiness; 空幻的
欢乐; *a ~ victory,* one without real value. 空虚的胜利。
4 sunken: 凹陷的: ~ *cheeks;* 凹陷的双颊; ,~-'eyed. 双
眼凹陷的。 5 (colloq, as adv) (口, 用作副词) *beat sb ~,*
completely. 彻底击败某人。 □ *n* hole; ~ place: 洞; 空;
坑; 凹地: *a ~ in the ground;* 地上的坑; small valley:
小山谷: *a wooded ~,* small valley with trees. 有树林的
小山谷。 □ *vt* [VP6A, 15A, B] ~ **(out),** make a ~
or ~s in; bend into a ~ shape: 挖空; 使成空洞; 弯曲成
凹形: *river banks ~ed out by rushing water.* 为急流冲
刷而凹下进去的河岸。

holly /'hɒlɪ; 'halɪ/ n [U] evergreen shrub with hard,
shiny, dark-green sharp-pointed leaves and, in winter,
red berries. 冬青; 冬青属灌木(生有坚硬、有光泽、深绿色
的尖叶, 冬季结红色浆果)。

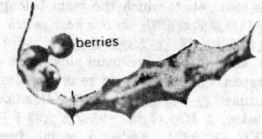

holly

holly·hock /'hɒlɪhɒk; 'halɪ,hak/ n [C] tall garden plant with brightly coloured flowers. 蜀葵（一种高的园艺植物，长有鲜艳的花）.

Holly·wood /'hɒlɪwud; 'halɪ,wud/ n centre of the US film industry: 好莱坞（美国电影工业中心）: ~ films/stars. 好莱坞影片（明星）.

holm-oak /'həum əuk; 'hom ok/ n [C] evergreen oak, ilex. 圣栎; 冬青栎.

holo·caust /'hɒləkɔːst; 'halə,kɔst/ n [C] large-scale destruction, esp of human lives by fire, etc: 大规模的毁灭（尤指人命毁于火灾等）: a nuclear ~. 大规模的核毁灭.

holo·graph /'hɒləgrɑːf US: -græf; 'halə,græf/ n document written wholly by the person in whose name it appears. 亲笔文书.

hol·ster /'həulstə(r); 'holstə/ n leather case for a pistol or revolver. 手枪皮套.

holy /'həulɪ; 'holɪ/ adj (-ier -iest) 1 of God; associated with God or with religion: 上帝的; 神圣的; 与上帝或宗教有关的: the H~ Bible; 圣经; H~ Writ. the Bible; 圣经; the H~ Land, where Jesus lived; 圣地（耶稣居住之地）; the H~ City Jerusalem; 圣城（耶路撒冷）: 'H~ Week, the week before Easter Sunday; 复活节前一周; H~ Communion; 圣餐; the H~ Father, the Pope; 教皇; the H~ Office, the Inquisition; 宗教法庭; the H~ Ghost/Spirit, the Third Person of the Trinity; 圣灵; ~ ground, land held in religious awe; 神圣的土地; ~ water, water blessed by a priest; 圣水; 净水; a ~ war, one (said to be) fought in defence of sth sacred. 圣战（据称为保卫神圣事物的战争）. 2 devoted to religion: 献身于宗教的; 虔诚的: a ~ man; 献身于宗教的人; live a ~ life. 过圣洁的生活. 3 a ~ terror, (sl) formidable person; mischievous, embarrassing child. （俚）可怕的人; 淘气的孩子. □ n the ,H~ of 'Holies, (a) most sacred inner chamber in a Jewish temple, entered by the High Priest once a year. 犹太教堂中之至圣所（祭司长每年进入一次）. (b) (fig) any sacred place. （喻）任何神圣之地.

holy·stone /'həulɪstəun; 'holɪ,ston/ n [U] soft sandstone used for scrubbing the wooden deck of a ship. （磨木甲板用的）磨石. □ vt scrub with ~. 以磨石摩擦.

hom·age /'hɒmɪdʒ; 'hamɪdʒ/ n [U] 1 expression of respect; tribute paid (to sb, his merits). 尊敬; 敬意; 尊崇（与 to 连用, 后接某人或其功绩）. do/pay (to sb): express respect for: （向某人）表示尊崇: Many came to do the dead man ~. 很多人前来向死者致敬. We pay ~ to the genius of Shakespeare. 我们对莎士比亚的天才表示敬意. 2 (in feudal times) formal and public acknowledgement of loyalty to a lord or ruler. （封建时期对君主或统治者正式公开表示的）效忠; 臣服.

home¹ /həum; həm/ n 1 place where one lives, esp with one's family: 家; 家庭: He left ~ at the age of 16, left his parents and began an independent life. 他十六岁离开了家（离开父母过过独立生活）. He looks forward to seeing the old ~ again, eg his birthplace. 他盼望能再看到老家. He was born in England, but he now looks on Paris as his ~. 他生在英国，但现在将巴黎当作他的家乡. When I retire I shall make my ~ in the country. 我退休后将在乡间安家. He left India for ~, for his own country. 他离开印度回国去了. at ~, (a) in the house: 在家里: I've left my books at ~. 我把我的书留在家里了. Is there anybody at ~? 有人在家吗? (b) (football, etc) in the town, etc to which the team belongs: （足球赛等）在球队所属的城市里: Is our next match at ~ or away? 我们下次比赛是在本地还是在他处举行? Hence, 由此产生, the '~ team, the team playing at ~. 地主队. (c) expecting and ready to receive visitors at an appointed time: 在一指定的时间会客: 'Mrs Carr will be at ~, Monday, 1 May, 6pm.' 卡尔太太将于五月一日，星期一，下午五时会客. at-'~ n social function at which guests are expected at a time announced. 约定

时日之接待宾客. **not at ~ (to)**, not receiving visitor. 不会客: Mrs Hill is not at ~ to anyone except relatives. 希尔太太不会客, 但亲属除外. **make oneself/be/feel at ~**, as if in one's own house; at one's ease. 觉得如在自己家中; 无拘束: The boy did not feel at ~ in such a splendid house. 那男孩在这样堂皇的房子内感到拘束. **at ~ in**, familiar with, accustomed to: 熟悉; 习惯: Is it difficult to feel at ~ in a foreign language, to feel easy and confident while using one? 精通一种外国语言困难吗? **be ~ and dry**, (colloq) succeed. （口）成功. **a ~ from ~**, a place where one is as happy, comfortable, etc as in one's own ~: 象家一样安适的处所: Prison is not usually a ~ from ~. 监狱通常不是象家一样安适的处所. **nothing to write ~ about**, (colloq) nothing remarkable. （口）乏善可陈; 平淡无奇. 2 institution or place (for the care of children, old or sick people, etc): （照顾儿童, 老弱, 残疾者之）机构或处所: an 'orphans' ~; 孤儿院; a 'nursing ~; 疗养院; ma'ternity ~. 妇女收容所. 3 (often attrib) family or domestic life: （常用作定语）家庭生活: the pleasures of ~; 天伦之乐; 家庭生活之乐; ~ comforts/joys; 家庭生活的舒适（欢乐); ~ life. 家庭生活. ,~ eco'nomics = housecraft. ,~ 'help n (GB) person employed to help the elderly, infirm or ill (and who are without the help of relatives or friends). （英）帮做家务的人（雇用以协助年长, 体弱或生病, 而无亲友协助之人们）. 4 (= habitat) place where an animal or plant is native or most common: 动植物的栖息地或生长地: the ~ of the tiger and the elephant, eg the jungle; 虎及象之栖息地（例如丛林地带）; the ~ of the fur-seal. 海狗的生长地. 5 (in sport and in various games) goal; place where a player is safe and cannot be caught, put out, etc. （运动及多种游戏中）终点; 安全之处; 不能被捉住、逐出等之处. the '~ plate, (baseball) base at which the batsman stands to bat. （棒球）本垒. ,~ 'run, (baseball) one made after a hit which enables the batsman to go round all the bases without stopping. （棒球）本垒打; 全垒打（打出一球后, 可安全跑完一圈, 经过各垒, 不必停留). the ,~ 'straight/'stretch, last part of a track, near the winning-post. 跑道直道; 接近终点的一段跑道. 6 (attrib) of the ~; of one's own country (=domestic inland, contrasted with foreign)(用作定语)家庭的; 国内的(as opp to foreign 相对): ~ industries/products; 国内工业（产品）; the ~ trade/market. 国内贸易(市场). one's ,~ 'town, town (not necessarily one's birthplace) in which one lives permanently. 永久居住地（并不一定是出生地）. the ,H~ 'Counties, those round London. 伦敦附近各郡. the 'H~ Office, department controlling local government, police, etc in England and Wales, under the minister called the H~ Secretary, or Secretary of State for H~ Affairs (US 美 = Department of the Interior). 内政部(在英国内政部长称作 Home Secretary 或 Secretary of State for Home Affairs). 7 (compounds) (复合词) ,~'baked adj (of bread, etc) baked at ~, not bought from a shop. （指面包等）家里烘制的, 不是从商店买来的. ,~'brewed adj (of beer, etc) brewed at ~ (contrasted with beer from a brewery). （指啤酒等）家里酿制的（以别于酿造厂酿制的）. ,~'coming n arrival at ~, coming to one's ~: 到家; 回家; 回国: ~coming weekend, (US) when alumni or alumnae return to their school, etc. （美）校友返回母校之周末. ,~'cured adj (of food, esp bacon) treated (by smoking, salting, etc) at ~ (contrasted with food cured in factories). （食物, 尤指咸肉）在家里处理的（以别于在工厂中处理的）. '~-farm n farm that supplies the needs of a large estate or establishment (contrasted with farmland that is rented out). 供应一大家庭或产业的农场（以别于租给佃户的农场）; 家庭农场. the ,~ 'front, the civilians (in a country at war). （战时一个国家的）后方民众; 所有平民. ,~'grown adj (of food, etc) produced in the country (contrasted with what is imported). （指食物等）国产的（以别于进口的）. ,H~ 'Guard n (member of the) British citizen army

(1940-1957). 1940-1957 年间的英国国民军(队员)。 '~·**land** /-lænd/ ; -ˌlænd/ *n* native land; country from which one's ancestors came. 故乡; 祖国。 ,~-'**made** *adj* (of bread, cakes, etc) made at ~ (contrasted with what is bought from shops). (指面包、糕饼等)家庭制的; 自制的(以别于商店中买来的)。 ,H~ '**Rule**, government of a country by its own citizens. 地方自治; 独立自主。 '~·**sick** *adj* sad because away from ~; 想家的; 怀乡的; Hence, 由此产生。 '~·**sick·ness** *n* \~·spun *adj*, *n*(cloth made of yarn) spun at ~; 手织的(布); (fig)(anything) plain and homely. (喻)朴素的(任何东西)。 '~·**stead** /-sted/ ; -ˌsted/ *n* house with the land and outbuildings round it; farmhouse; (US) land given to sb by the state on condition that he lives on it and cultivates it. 家园; 农舍; (美) 分给人民开垦的土地。 \~ **thrust** *n* attack (with a weapon or in words) that is effective. (以武器或言语) 命中要害的一击。 ,~ '**truth** *n* unpleasant fact that one is made aware of. 明了后令人不愉快的事实。 '~·**work** *n* [U] **(a)** work which a pupil is required to do at ~ in the evening and take to his teacher(s) at school. (在晚间作好, 再带去学校交给老师的)课外作业。 **(b)** (colloq) preparatory work, eg for a report or discussion. (口)报告或讨论等之)准备工作。 ⇨ **housework** at home¹(7). \~·**less** *adj* having no ~. 无家可归的。 \~·**like** *adj* like ~. 如在家般的。 \~·**ward** /-wəd/ ; -wəd/ *adj* going towards ~. 向家的。 \~·**ward(s)** /-wəd(s); -wəd/ *adv* towards ~. 向家地。

home² /həum; hom/ *adv* **1** at, in or to one's ~ or country: 在家; 到家; 向家; 在国内; 向国内: Is he ~ yet? 他到家了吗? I saw him on his way ~. 我看见他在回家的路上。 He went ~. 他回家去了。 Send the children ~. 把孩子们送回家去。 We ought to turn back and get ~, ie to the starting-point, whether this is or is not one's usual place of residence. 我们应当返回原地(即原出发点, 不论其是否为平常居所)。 **2** to the point aimed at; so as to be in the right place: 中的地; 适切地; 彻底地: drive a nail ~, strike it so that it is completely in. 将钉完全打进。 **bring sth/come ~ to sb**, (cause sb to) realize fully: (使某人) 彻底了解: The stupidity of his behaviour was brought/came ~ to him. 他彻底明白了他行为的愚蠢。 **drive a point/an argument ~**, cause its full force to be understood. 使一论点为人彻底明白。

home·ly /həumlɪ; 'homlɪ/ *adj* (-ier, -iest) **1** simple and plain; of the sort used every day: 朴素的; 家常的: a ~-looking old lady, not trying to seem important or dignified; 容貌朴素的老妇人(不欲作显贵之态者); a ~ meal. 家常便饭。 **2** causing one to think of home or feel at home: 令人思家的; 令人有在家之感的: a ~ atmosphere. 如在家中般的气氛。 **3** (US) (of people, their features) not attractive or good-looking. (美, 指人或其容貌)不吸引人的; 不漂亮的。 **home·li·ness** *n*

Ho·meric /həu'merɪk; ho'merɪk/ *adj* of, in the style of, Homer or his epics. 荷马的; 荷马风格的; 荷马之史诗的。 \~ **laughter**, loud, boisterous laughter like that of the gods in Homer's epics. 纵声大笑(如荷马史诗中诸神所作者)。

homey /həumɪ; 'homɪ/ *adj* (US colloq) like home; cosy. (美口)似家的; 舒适的。

homi·cide /'hɒmɪsaɪd; 'hɑməˌsaɪd/ *n* [U] killing of a human being; [C] person who kills a human being: 杀人; 杀人者: H~ is not criminal when committed in self-defence. 为自卫而杀人无罪。 ~ **squad**, (US)group of police officers who investigate ~s. (美)调查杀人案件之警察小组。 ⇨ **murder**. **homi·cidal** /ˌhɒmɪ'saɪdl/; ˌhɑmə'saɪdl/ *adj* of ~: 杀人的; 杀人者的: a homicidal lunatic; 杀人狂者; homicidal tendencies. 杀人的癖性。

hom·ily /'hɒmɪlɪ; 'hɑmɪ/ *n* (pl -lies) [C] sermon; long and tedious moralizing talk. 讲道; 冗长而令人厌倦的说教。 **homi·letic** /ˌhɒmɪ'letɪk; ˌhɑmə'letɪk/ *adj* of homilies. 讲道的; 说教的。 **homi·let·ics** *n* pl art of preachning 讲道术。

hom·ing /'həumɪŋ; 'homɪŋ/ *adj* (of pigeons) having the instinct to fly home (when released a long way from home); (of torpedoes, missiles) fitted with electronic devices that enable them to reach a predetermined target: (指鸽子) (在离巢很远处被释放) 有归家本能的; (指鱼雷, 飞弹)装有电子装置能使其击中预定目标的; 追踪的: ~ devices; 追踪装置(能使鱼雷等击中预定目标); a ~ 'guidance system. 追踪导向系统。

hom·iny /'hɒmɪnɪ; 'hɑmənɪ/ *n* [U] ground maize boiled in water or milk: 碎玉米粥(用水或牛奶煮成者): ~ grits, biscuits made from ground maize 用碾碎之玉米做成的饼干。

homo /'həuməu; 'homo/ *n* (Lat) man. (拉)人。 ,~ 'sapiens /'sæpɪenz; 'sepɪˌɛnz/, modern man regarded as a species. 现代人类。

ho·moe·opathy (US = **ho·me·o-**) /ˌhəumɪ'ɒpəθɪ; ˌhomɪ'ɑpəθɪ/ *n* [U] treatment of disease by drugs (usu in small doses) that, if given to a healthy person, would produce symptoms like those of the disease. (以毒攻毒疗法; 类似疗法; 顺势医疗(予患者以微量药物, 此种药物如施予健康之人, 将产生与患者类似的症状)。 **ho·moeo·path** (US = **ho·meo-**) /'həuməupæθ; 'homɪˌpæθ/ *n* person who practises ~. 使用类似疗法之医师。

ho·mo·gene·ous /ˌhɒmə'dʒiːnɪəs; ˌhomə'dʒinɪəs/ *adj* (formed of parts) of the same kind. 同类的; 同性质的; 由同类之部分组成的。 ⇨ **heterogeneous**. **ho·mo·gene·ity** /ˌhɒmədʒɪ'niːɪtɪ; ˌhomədʒə'niɪtɪ/ *n* quality of being ~. 同类; 同质。 **hom·ogen·ize** /hə'mɒdʒɪnaɪz; hə'mɑdʒəˌnaɪz/ *vt* [VP6A] make ~; (esp) make milk more uniform in consistency by breaking down and blending the particles of fat. 使性质相同; (尤指) (将脂肪粒搅碎并加以混合)使(牛奶)成分均匀。

homo·graph /'hɒməgrɑːf; US: -ɡræf/ 'haməˌɡræf/ *n* word spelt like another but with a different meaning or pronunciation, eg bow¹/bəu/; bo/; bow² /bau/; bau/. 同形异义词(例如 bow¹, bow²)。

homo·nym /'hɒmənɪm; 'haməˌnɪm/ *n* homograph or homophone; word that is the same in form and sound as another but different in meaning, eg see¹; see². 同形异义词; 同音异义词(例如 see¹, see²)。

homo·phone /'hɒməfəun; 'haməˌfon/ *n* word pronounced like another but different in meaning, spelling or origin, eg some/sum /sʌm; sʌm/; knew/new /njuː; nju/. 同音词(同音但意义, 拼法或字源不同的词, 例如 some 和 sum, knew 和 new)。

homo·sex·ual /ˌhɒmə'seksjuəl; ˌhomə'sɛkʃuəl/ *adj* sexually attracted to persons of one's own sex. 同性恋的。 ~ *n* person. 同性恋者。 ~·**ity** /ˌhɒməsekʃu'ælətɪ; ˌhoməsɛkʃu'ælətɪ; *n* [U] the condition of being ~. 同性恋。

hone /həun; hon/ *n* [C] stone used for sharpening tools (eg old-style razors). 磨刀石(例如用以磨旧式剃刀者)。 □ *vt* [VP6A] sharpen on a ~. 在磨刀石上磨。

hon·est /'ɒnɪst; 'ɑnɪst/ *adj* **1** not telling lies; not cheating or stealing; straightforward: 诚实的; 忠实的; 坦白的: an ~ man; 诚实的人; ~ in business, 在商业方面诚实; give an ~ opinion. 提出坦诚的意见。 **to be quite ~ about it**, phrase used before a statement that one wishes to be believed. 说老实话; 老实说(用于希望别人相信之陈述的前面)。 **earn an ~ penny**, earn money fairly. 以正当手段赚钱。 **2** showing, resulting from, an ~ mind: 显示出心地诚实的; 由诚意产生的: an ~ face; 一副诚实的面孔; look ~; 看来诚实; an ~ piece of work, done conscientiously; 一件尽责做成的工作; ~ weight, not short weight. 够秤头; 斤两不少。 **make an ~ woman of sb**, (dated use) marry her after seducing her. (过时用语)诱奸某女子后再娶她。 ~·**ly** *adv* in a manner; really: 诚实地; 实在地: Honestly, that's all the money I have. 说实在地, 我所有的钱就是这些。 **hon·esty** *n* [U] the quality of being ~; freedom from deceit, cheating, etc. 诚实; 老实。

honey /'hʌnɪ; 'hʌnɪ/ *n* **1** [U] sweet, sticky yellowish

substance made by bees from nectar; (fig) sweetness. 蜂蜜。(喻)甜蜜。'~·bee n ordinary kind of bee that lives in hives. 蜜蜂。'~·dew n [U] (a) sweet, sticky substance found on the leaves and stems of plants in hot weather. 树蜜(植物的叶和茎在热天所分泌的甜而粘的东西)。(b) tobacco sweetened with molasses. 加有糖蜜的烟草。'~·suckle /'hʌnɪsʌkl; 'hʌnɪˌsʌkl/ n [U] climbing shrub with sweet-smelling tube-shaped yellow or reddish flowers. 忍冬; 金银花(攀缘灌木, 生有黄色或淡红色的管状有香味的花)。2 [C] (pl ~s) (colloq) sweetheart; darling: (口)爱人; 亲爱的人: Come here, my ~s, eg a mother to her children. 到这儿来, 亲爱的(例如母亲召唤孩子们)。~ed /'hʌnɪd; 'hʌnɪd/ adj sweet as ~: 甜如蜜的: ~ed words. 甜言蜜语。

honey·comb /'hʌnɪkəum; 'hʌnɪˌkom/ n [C, U] wax structure of six-sided cells made by bees for honey and eggs; (piece of) ornamental work in a ~ pattern. 蜂房; 蜂巢; 蜂巢图案装饰物。☐ vt [VP6A] fill with holes, tunnels, etc: 使有许多孔洞: *The rock at Gibraltar is ~ed with galleries.* 直布罗陀的岩石有很多孔道。

honeycomb

honey·moon /'hʌnɪmuːn; 'hʌnɪˌmun/ n holiday taken by a newly married couple; (fig) period of harmony at the start of an undertaking, etc. 蜜月; (喻)事业等开始时的和谐期间。☐ vi spend a ~: 度蜜月: *They will ~ in Paris.* 他们将在巴黎度蜜月。

honk /hɒŋk; hɔŋk/ n cry of the wild goose; sound made by (the old style of) motor horn. 野鹅叫声; (旧式之)汽车喇叭声。☐ vi make a ~. (野鹅)叫; (旧式汽车喇叭)声。

hon·or·ar·ium /ˌɒnəˈreərɪəm; ˌɑnəˈrɛrɪəm/ n fee offered (but not claimed) for professional services. 酬劳金; 谢礼。

hon·or·ary /'ɒnərərɪ US: 'ɒnəreri; 'ɑnəˌrɛri/ adj 1 (shortened in writing to 缩写为 **Hon**) (of a position) unpaid: (指职位)无薪给的; 无报酬的; 义务的: *the ~ secretary.* 做事而不支薪的秘书; 义务秘书。2 (of a degree, rank) conferred as an honour, without the usual requirements: (指学位, 等级)作为一种荣誉而授与的; 名誉的: *an ~ degree/doctorate;* 名誉学位(博士学位); holding an ~ title or position: 拥有名誉头衔或职位的: *an ~ vice-president.* 名誉副会长。

hon·or·ific /ˌɒnəˈrɪfɪk; ˌɑnəˈrɪfɪk/ n, adj (expression) implying respect: 尊敬的言语; 含有敬意的: *the ~s so frequently used in oriental languages.* 东方语言中十分常用的敬语。

hon·our¹ (US = **honor**) /'ɒnə(r); 'ɑnə/ n 1 [U] great respect; high public regard: 尊敬; 敬重: *win ~ in war;* 立战功; *a ceremony in ~ of those killed in battle;* 纪念阵亡将士的仪式; *show ~ to one's parents.* 尊敬父母。*do sb ~; do ~ to sb,* show courtesy to, esteem of: 向某人致敬: *Twenty heads of state attended the Queen's coronation to do her ~.* 二十位国家元首参加女王加冕典礼以向她致敬。*maid of '~,* lady in attendance upon a queen, princess, etc. 宫女。*guard of '~,* number of soldiers chosen to escort or welcome a distinguished person as a mark of respect. 仪(仗)队。2 [U] good personal character; reputation for good behaviour, loyalty, truthfulness, etc. 人格; 名誉; 荣誉; 信誉。*on one's ~,* on one's reputation for telling the truth. 以人格担保。*an affair of ~,* (hist)duel fought

to settle a question of ~. (史)决斗。*be/feel in ~ bound to do sth,* required to do it as a moral duty, but not by law, 道义上(觉得)应做某事。*one's word of ~,* guarantee to fulfil an obligation, keep a promise, etc. 名誉担保。*pay/incur a debt of ~,* one that need not be paid legally, but which one's good name requires one to pay. 偿还(欠负)(法律上不能追索的)信用借款。*put sb on his ~,* trust him, his ~ being lost if he fails to do what is required, breaks a promise, etc. 信其人以人格担保。3 (in polite formulas) (用于客套语中)giving of ~. 荣幸。*do sb the ~ of; have the ~ of/to:* 给某人…之荣幸; 有…之荣幸: *May I have the ~ of your company at dinner?* 敬备菲酌, 恭请光临。*Will you do me the ~ of dining with me this evening?* 今晚备有便餐, 敬请赏光。(formal style) (正式文体) *I have the ~ to inform you that….* 敬启者。4 *Your/His H~,* title of respect used to/of some judges. 阁下(对某些法官之尊称)。5 *an ~,* person or thing bringing credit: 带来光荣的人或物: *He is an ~ to his school/family.* 他是他的学校(家庭)引以为荣的人。6 (pl) marks of respect, distinction, etc; titles; civilities. (复)荣誉的标识; 官衔; 爵位; 礼仪。*birthday ~s,* (in GB) list of titles, decorations, etc conferred by the Sovereign on her or his birthday. (在英国)国君诞辰授予的勋爵, 勋章等。*New Year H~s,* similar list awarded on 1 Jan. 元旦所授予的勋爵, 勋章等。*full military ~s,* ceremonies, mark of respect, paid by soldiers at the burial of a soldier to distinguished visitors, eg Presidents. 军葬礼; (向总统等贵宾致敬之)军礼。*do the ~s,* (colloq) (of the table, house, etc) act as host(ess), guide, etc and do what politeness requires; perform some small ceremony, eg propose a toast. (口)(席间、房屋等内)尽主人、向导等之谊; 执行某种小礼仪(例如提议举杯祝愿健康)。7 (pl) (in universities) (place in) top division of marks in degree examinations; special distinction for extra proficiency. (复)(大学)学位考试的优等; 特优之荣誉。*~s degree,* one requiring some specialization. 优等学位(需要专修某科目而获得者)。⇨ **general, pass¹**(1). 8 (in card games, whist and bridge) card of highest value, eg 10, knave, queen, king, ace of trumps. (惠斯特及桥牌等牌戏中)价值最高的牌(王牌之 10, J, Q, K, A)。

hon·our² (US = **honor**) /'ɒnə(r); 'ɑnə/ vt [VP6A] 1 respect highly, feel honour for; confer honour on: 尊敬; 以…为荣; 给与荣誉: *Fear God and ~ the Queen.* 敬畏上帝, 尊敬女王。*I feel highly ~ed by the kind things you say about me.* 你恭维我的话使我感到十分荣幸。*Will you ~ me with a visit?* 如蒙造访, 十分荣幸。2 (comm) accept and pay when due: (商)承认并如期支付; 承兑: *~ a bill/cheque/draft, etc;* 承兑票据(支票, 汇票等); *~ one's signature,* agree that one has signed a bill, note, etc and pay the money. 承认自己的签名并付款。

hon·our·able (US = **hon·or-**) /'ɒnərəbl; 'ɑnərəbl/ adj 1 possessing or showing the principles of honour; consistent with honour (1, 2): 可敬的; 高尚的; 光明正大的; 光荣的: *~ conduct;* 高尚的行为; 光明的: *~ peace;* 缔结光荣的和约; *~ burial.* 光荣的葬礼。2 H~ (abbr 略作 **Hon**) title given eg to judges, to the children of peers below the rank of Marquis, and (during debates) to members of the House of Commons: 对法官、低于侯爵的贵族子弟, 以及(辩论时)对下议院议员之尊称: *my H~ friend the member for Chester.* 吾友却斯特城议员。*Right H~,* (abbr 略作 **Rt Hon**) title given eg to cabinet ministers, privy councillors and peers below the rank of Marquis. 对阁员、枢密顾问官、以及低于侯爵的贵族之尊称。**hon·our·ably** /-əblɪ; -əbli/ adv

hooch /huːtʃ; hutʃ/ n [U] (US sl) alcoholic liquor. (美俚)烈酒。

hood¹ /hud; hʊd/ n 1 bag-like covering for the head and neck, often fastened to a cloak so that it can hang down at the back when not in use; (in universities)

fold of cloth worn over an academic gown showing by its colour the degree gained by the wearer and the university by which it was conferred. 兜帽；头巾(呈口袋状，常连在外衣上，不用时则垂在背后；(大学)垂布(加在学位服外，以其颜色表示学位及授予学校)。 **2** anything like a ~ in shape or use: folding roof over a carriage (for protection against rain or sun), or over an open motor-car; (US) hinged cover over the engine of a motor-car (GB 英 = *bonnet*). 任何形状或作用似兜帽或头巾之物；马车或敞篷汽车上可折合的车篷；(美)汽车引擎盖(覆盖引擎，装有铰链之盖)。 ⇨ the illus at **motor**. 参看 motor 之插图。 □ *vt* (chiefly in *pp*) cover with, or as with, a ~: (主要用过去分词)覆以头巾；加以车篷；覆盖: *a ~ed falcon*. 戴着头罩的鹰。

hood² /hʊd; hʊd/ *n* (US *sl*) (abbr of) hoodlam. (美俚)

hood·lum /'hu:dləm; 'hudləm/ *n* (*sl*) gangster; dangerous criminal. (俚)盗匪；歹徒；暴徒。

hoo·doo /'hu:du:; 'hudu/ *n* (chiefly US) person or thing regarded as bringing(s) bad luck. (主美)恶运；带来恶运的人或物；不祥之人或物。 □ *vt* render unlucky. 使不幸；使倒霉。

hood·wink /'hʊdwɪŋk; 'hʊd,wɪŋk/ *vt* [VP6A, 14] ~ *sb* (*into*), deceive; trick; mislead. 欺骗；欺瞒；蒙骗。

hooey /'hu:ɪ; 'huɪ/ *n* [U] (*sl*) humbug; nonsense. (俚)骗人的鬼话；废话；胡说八道。

hoof /hu:f; hʊf/ *n* (*pl* ~s or hooves /hu:vz; huvz/) horny part of the foot of a horse, ox or deer. (马、牛或鹿之)蹄: *buy cattle on the ~*, alive. 买活牛。 ⇨ the illus at **domestic**. 参看 domestic 之插图。

hook¹ /hʊk; hʊk/ *n* **1** curved or bent piece of metal or other material, for catching hold of sth, or for hanging sth on: 钩: *a 'fish-~*; 钓鱼钩; *a 'crochet-~*; 钩针; *a 'clothes-~*; 挂衣钩; *a ~ and eyes*, for fastening a dress. 领钩和钩扣。 ~, *line and sinker*, (from fishing) (fig) entirely; completely. (出自钓鱼)(喻)整个地；完全地。 *be on the ~*, (colloq) in a position where one has problems, difficult or distressing decisions to make. (口)处于困难或难以作决定的境地。 *be/get off the ~*, no longer in such a position. 脱离困境。 *sling one's ~*, ⇨ **sling**(1). '~-nosed *adj* having a nose shaped like a ~ (or like the nose of an eagle). 钩鼻的；鹰钩鼻的。 '~-worm *n* worm that infests the intestines of men and animals, the male of which has ~-like spines. 钩虫；十二指肠虫。 **2** curved tool for cutting (grain, etc) or for chopping (branches, etc): 镰刀；弯刀: *a 'reaping-~*; (收割用的)镰刀; *a 'bill-~*. 砍树枝用的弯刀。 *by ~ or by crook*, by one means or another. 用种种方法。 **3** (cricket, golf) kind of stroke; (boxing) short blow with the elbow bent: (板球，高尔夫球)一种击法; 左曲球；(拳击)钩击: *a left ~*. 左钩拳。

hook² /hʊk; hʊk/ *vt, vi* **1** [VP6A, 15A, B, 2C] fasten, be fastened, catch, with a ~ or ~s: 用钩钩住；被钩住住: *a dress that ~s/is ~ed at the back*; 背后用钩扣住的女服; ~ *something up*; 将某物扣住于钩上(钩住某物); ~ *a fish*; 用钩钓鱼; ~ *a husband*, (fig) catch a man and marry him. (喻)钓个丈夫；钓个金龟婿。 **2** make into the form of a ~: 弯曲成钩形: ~ *one's finger*. 弯曲手指。 **3** ~ *it*, (*sl*) run away. (俚)逃跑。 **4** '~-*up* *n* network of broadcasting stations connected to transmit the same programme: 广播电台联播网: *speak over an international ~-up*. 经联播网向国外广播。 ~*ed adj* **1** ~-shaped: 钩形的: *a ~ed nose*; 鹰钩鼻; furnished with hooks. 有钩的。 **2** ~*ed* (*on*), (*sl*) addicted to; completely committed to: (俚)上瘾；耽溺于；着迷于；完全受摆布: *be /get ~ed on heroin*. 吸海洛因成瘾。 *My aunt is ~ed on package holidays in Spain*. 我的姑母着迷于旅行社包办的西班牙度假。

hookah /'hʊkə; 'hʊkə/ *n* tobacco pipe (also called 亦称作 a *hubble-bubble*) with a long flexible tube through which smoke is drawn through water in a vase and so cooled. 水烟袋。

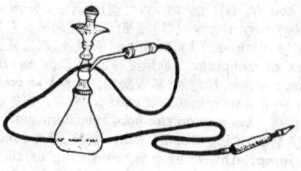

a hookah

hooky /'hʊkɪ; 'hʊkɪ/ *n* *play* ~, (US *sl*) play truant. (美俚)逃学。

hoo·li·gan /'hu:lɪɡən; 'hulɪɡən/ *n* one of a gang of disorderly persons making disturbances in the streets or other public places. 流氓；阿飞，不良少年。 ~·**ism** /-ɪzəm/ *n*.

hoop¹ /hu:p; hʊp/ *n* **1** circular band of wood, metal etc. 箍；铁环。 **2** small iron arch fixed in the ground. through which balls are hit in the game of croquet. 槌球戏中的弓形铁门。 **3** large ring with paper stretched over it through which circus riders and animals jump. 马戏团用的大铁环(用纸蒙起，由骑师或动物自中间跳过)。 *put sb/go through the* ~(*s*), (fig) undergo an ordeal. (喻)(使某人)受磨炼。 □ *vt* bind (a cask, etc) with ~s. 加箍于桶。

hoop² /hu:p; hʊp/ *vt* = **whoop**.

hoop-la /'hu:p lɑ:; 'hʊp,lɑ/ *n* [U] game in which rings are thrown at small objects which are won if the rings encircle them. 投环套物游戏(如套中，则得该物)。

hoo·ray /hu:'reɪ; hʊ're/ *int* = **hurrah**.

hoot /hu:t; hut/ *n* **1** cry of an owl. 枭叫声。 **2** sound made by a motor-car horn, steam-whistle, foghorn, etc. 汽车喇叭，汽笛，雾笛等发出的声音。 **3** shout or cry expressing disapproval or scorn. 表示不满或轻蔑的叫器。 *not care a ~/two ~s*, (*sl*) not care at all. (俚)毫不在乎。 □ *vi, vt* **1** [VP2A, C] make a ~ or ~s: 枭叫; (汽车等)鸣叫；鸣笛; (表示不满或轻蔑而)叫嚣: *an owl ~ing in the garden*. 在花园里叫的猫头鹰。 *The crowd ~ed and jeered at the speaker*. 群众向那演说者叫嚣嘲弄。 **2** [VP6A, 15A, B] make ~s at, drive away by doing this: 向~叫嚣; 以叫嚣驱逐: ~ *an actor*; 向一演员叫嚣; ~ *a speaker down/off/away*. 借叫嚣把演说者轰下台(走走)。 ~·**er** *n* siren or steam-whistle, esp as a signal for work to start or stop; similar device in a motor-vehicle to attract attention from other motorists, pedestrians, etc. 汽笛(尤指表示上下班者)；警笛；汽车喇叭。

Hoover /'hu:və(r); 'huvə/ *n* (P) kind of vacuum cleaner. (商标名)一种真空吸尘器；胡佛真空吸尘器。 □ *vt* [VP6A] (colloq) clean (carpets, etc) with a vacuum cleaner. (口)用真空吸尘器清洁(地毯等)。

hooves /hu:vz; huvz/ *pl* of **hoof**.

hop¹ /hɒp; hɑp/ *n* [C] tall climbing plant with flowers growing in clusters; (*pl*) ripe cones (seedvessels) of this plant, dried and used for giving a bitter flavour to beer, etc. 蛇麻草(一种高的攀绕植物，开花成丛)；(复)蛇麻子(此种植物所结之球果，干后用以使啤酒等带苦味)。 '*hop-garden/-field* *nn* field for the cultivation of hops. 蛇麻草园。 '*hop·pole* *n* tall pole to support wires on which hop plant is trained. 支撑蛇麻草蔓的杆子。 '*hop·picker, hopper* *nn* worker, machine, employed to pick hops. 摘蛇麻子的人或机器。 □ *vi* (-*pp*-) gather hops: 摘蛇麻子: *go hopping in Kent*. 去肯特采收蛇麻子。

hop² /hɒp; hɑp/ *vi, vt* (-*pp*-) **1** [VP2A, C] (of persons) jump on one foot; (of other living creatures, eg birds, frogs, grasshoppers) jump with both or all feet together: (指人)单足跳跃；(指鸟，青蛙，蚱蜢等)双足或齐足跳跃: *Sparrows were hopping about on the lawn*. 麻雀在草地上跳来跳去。 *He had hurt his left foot and*

had to hop along. 他的左脚受伤,不得不单足跳行。**hop off; hop it,** (sl) go away. (俚)走开。**hopping mad,** (colloq) very angry. (口)极怒;气得跳起来。2 [VP6A] cross (a ditch, etc) by hopping. 跃过(沟等)。□ **n 1** the action of hopping. (单足或双足)跳跃。**on the hop,** active, restless. 活动的;不安静的。**catch sb on the hop,** when he is unprepared, off guard. 乘某人疏忽或不注意时抓住他。**keep sb on the hop,** keep him active, alert. 使某人活跃,机敏。2 short jump. 短跳。**hop, skip/step and jump,** athletic exercise consisting of these three movements one after the other. (运动)三级跳远。3 (colloq) informal party and dance, with popular music. (口)放流行音乐之非正式舞会。4 (flying) one stage in a long-distance flight: (飞行)长途飞行中的一段: *from Berlin to Tokyo in three hops.* 分三段从柏林飞行至东京。

hop·scotch /'hɒpskɒtʃ; 'hɑp,skɑtʃ/ n [U] children's game of throwing a stone into numbered squares, etc marked on the ground, and hopping from square to square to collect it. 跳房子(儿童游戏)。

hope[1] /həʊp; hop/ n [C, U] feeling of expectation and desire; feeling of trust and confidence: 希望; 信心: *There is not much ~ that they are/of their being still alive.* 他们仍然活着的希望不大。**hold out some/ no/little/not much ~ (of sth),** give some, etc encouragement or expectation: (对某事)抱一些希望(不抱希望,抱很少希望,不大抱希望): *The doctors could hold out no ~ of recovery.* 医生们不抱痊愈的希望。**be past /beyond ~; not have a ~,** be without possibility of success, recovery, etc. (成功,痊愈等)无望。**in the ~ of doing sth,** hoping to do it: 希望做某事: *I called in the ~ of finding her at home.* 我希望能在家去看她。**live in ~(s) (of sth),** have ~(s) (of): 对某事物抱着希望: *I haven't much money now but live in ~.* 我现在钱不多,但是抱着希望。*We live in ~s of better times.* 我们希望情况会好转。**raise sb's ~s,** give him encouragement of better fortune, etc: 给予某人希望: *Don't raise his ~s too much.* 不要给他太多希望。2 [C] person, thing, circumstance, etc on which ~ is based: 属望的人,事情,情况等: *He was the ~ of the school.* 他是全校所属望的人。*You are my last ~; if you can't help, I'm ruined.* 你是我最后的指望,如果你不能帮助我,我就完了。'~chest n (US) chest or drawer used by a young woman for storing linen, articles for household use, etc in anticipation of marriage (GB 英 = *bottom drawer*). (美)嫁妆箱(未出嫁少女收藏家庭用品,床单等,以备结婚使用之箱或抽斗)。

hope[2] /həʊp; hop/ vt, vi [VP7A, 9, 2A, 3A] expect and desire: 希望;期望: *We ~ to see you soon.* 我们希望不久能见到你。*I ~ you haven't hurt yourself.* 我希望你没有受伤。*'Will it be fine tomorrow?'—'I ~ so.'* '明天是晴天吗?'—'我希望是。'*'Will it rain tomorrow?'—'I ~ not.'* '明天会下雨吗?'—'我希望不会下。'*Let us ~ for the best.* 我们抱乐观态度(往最好处想)吧。*We've had no news from him but we're still hoping.* 我们没有他的消息,但仍旧希望能有他的消息。**~ against ~,** even though there is only a mere possibility. 抱一线希望。

hope·ful /'həʊpfl; 'hopfəl/ adj 1 having hope: 抱有希望的: *be/feel ~ about the future;* 对前途感到乐观; *feel ~ of success/that he will succeed.* 对成功(他的成功)抱着希望。2 giving hope; promising: 有希望的;有前途的: *The future does not seem very ~.* 前途似不太乐观。*He seems quite a ~ pupil,* likely to do well. 他似乎是个相当有前途的学生。3 (as n) (作名词) **(young)** ~, boy or girl who seems likely to succeed. 有希望的青年。**~·ly** /-fəlɪ; -fəlɪ/ adv 1 in a ~ way. 抱有希望地。2 = 'I hope' or 'it is to be hoped'. 希望;可望。**~·ness** n

hope·less /'həʊplɪs; 'hoplɪs/ adj 1 feeling no hope; giving or promising no hope: 不抱希望的; 绝望的: *give way to ~ grief;* 陷入绝望的悲哀中; *a ~ case,* 无希望的情况; *a ~ illness.* 绝症。2 incurable: 不可救

药的: *a ~ idiot.* 不可救药的呆子。**~·ly** adv **~·ness** n

hopped-up /hɒpt 'ʌp; 'hɑpt ˌʌp/ adj (US sl) souped up, supercharged: (美俚)增加过马力的: *a ~ engine.* 增加过马力的引擎。

hop·per[1] /'hɒpə(r); 'hɑpɚ/ n hop-picker. 采蛇麻子的人或机器。⇨ **hop**[1].

hop·per[2] /'hɒpə(r); 'hɑpɚ/ n 1 structure like an inverted cone or pyramid through which grain passes to a mill, coal or coke to a furnace, etc; any similar contrivance for feeding materials into a machine. etc. (碾磨机,煤炉等的)漏斗;将原料注入机器等的任何漏斗状装置;给料漏斗。2 any hopping insect, eg a flea, a young locust; (in Australia) kangaroo. 任何跳的昆虫(例如跳蚤,小蝗虫);(澳大利亚)袋鼠。

horde /hɔːd; hɔrd/ n 1 wandering tribe (of nomads): 游牧部落: *a Gypsy ~;* 吉卜赛人部落; *~s of Tartars.* 鞑靼人各部落。2 (usu contemptuous) crowd; great number: (通常为轻蔑语)群众;大群: *~s of people.* 大群的人。3 multitude: 大批;众多: *a ~ of locusts.* 大批蝗虫。

hor·izon /hə'raɪzn; hə'raɪzn/ n 1 the ~, line at which the earth or sea and sky seem to meet: 地平线;海平线: *The sun sank below the ~.* 太阳沉落在地平线以下了。2 (fig) limit of one's knowledge, experience, thinking, etc: (喻)一个人的知识, 经验, 思想等的限度或范围;眼界; 见识。**hori·zon·tal** /ˌhɒrɪ'zɒntl US: ˌhɔːr-; ˌhɔrə'zɑntl/ adj parallel to the ~; flat or level: 与地平线平行的; 平的; 水平的: *a ~tal line;* 水平线; *~tal bars,* above the floor for gymnastic exercises. 单杠。⇨ **vertical.** ⇨ *n ~tal line, bar, etc.* 水平线等。**~·tally** /-təlɪ; -tlɪ/ adv

hor·mone /'hɔːməʊn; 'hɔrmon/ n (kinds of) internal secretion that passes into the blood and stimulates the bodily organs; medical preparation made from a secretion of this kind. 荷尔蒙(人体之内分泌, 进入血液可刺激器官功能); 荷尔蒙制剂。

horn /hɔːn; hɔrn/ n 1 [C] one of the hard, pointed, usu curved, outgrowths on the heads of cattle, deer, and some other animals. (牛,鹿等动物的)角。⇨ the illus at **domestic, large.** 参看 domestic, large 之插图。⇨ **bull**[1](1). 2 [U] substance of these outgrowths: 角质: *a knife with a handle of ~/a ~ handle;* 角柄小刀; *a ~ spoon.* 角质匙。'**~-rimmed** adj (of spectacles) with the frame made of material that resembles ~. (指眼镜)镜框由似角质材料制成的。3 article made from this substance (or a modern substitute): 角制品; 似角质制品: *a 'shoe-~.* (用角质制成的)鞋拔。**a ~ of plenty,** = **cornucopia.** 4 (music) wind instrument: (音乐)管乐器; 吹奏乐器; 号角; 喇叭: *a 'hunting ~,* 猎号。**(French) ~,** brass orchestral instrument. 法国号;圆喇叭。⇨ the illus at **brass.** 参看 brass 之插图。**English ~,** (also, 亦作, esp GB 尤英 **cor anglais** /ˌkɔːr 'ɒŋgleɪ US: ˌɒŋgleɪ; ˌkɔr ɑn'gle/) woodwind instrument like, but larger than, an oboe, and lower in pitch. 英国管 (一种双簧木管乐器)。5 device for making warning sounds: 示警装置: *a 'fog-~;* 雾笛; *a 'motor-~.* 汽车喇叭。6 ~-like part, eg on the head of a snail. 角状部份(例如蜗牛的触角)。'**~-bill** n bird with a ~like growth on its beak. 犀鸟。**draw in one's ~s,** (fig) draw back, show less zeal for an undertaking. (喻)退缩; 对一事不再热心。7 either of the ends of the crescent moon. 新月的钩尖。⇨ the illus at **phase.** 参看 phase 之插图。**on the ~s of a dilemma,** faced with a choice between things that are equally undesirable, etc. 进退维谷。□ vi (sl, only in) (俚, 仅用于) **~ in (on),** intrude; join in without being invited. 闯入; 侵入; 打岔; 干涉。**~ed** adj having ~s(1): 有角的; *~ed cattle;* 有角的牛; *the ~ed owl,* with tufts like ~s. 鸱鸮\猫头鹰, 其头上毛簇似角。**~·less** adj without ~s: 无角的: *~less cattle.* 无角的牛。'**~·like** adj ~y adj (-ier, -iest) made of ~; hard like ~: 角制的; 坚硬似角的: *hands ~y from hard work.*

由于辛苦工作而粗硬的手.

horn·beam /'hɔ:nbi:m; 'hɔrn,bim/ n small tree with hard wood. 榛类; 角树(木质坚硬的小树).

hor·net /'hɔ:nɪt; 'hɔrnɪt/ n large insect of the wasp family, able to inflict a severe sting. 大黄蜂. **stir up a '~s' nest; bring a '~s' nest about one's ears,** stir up enemies; cause an outburst of angry feeling. 树敌招怨; 自找麻烦.

horn·pipe /'hɔ:npaɪp; 'hɔrn,paɪp/ n [C] (music for a) lively dance (usu for one person, esp a sailor). 号管舞(一种活泼的舞蹈, 通常由一人, 尤其是一水手来跳); 号管舞曲.

hor·ol·ogy /hɒ'rɒlədʒɪ; hə'rɑlədʒɪ/ n [U] art of designing and constructing clocks. 钟表制造术.

horo·scope /'hɒrəskəʊp; 'hɔrə,skop/ n diagram of, observation of, positions of planets at a certain time, eg a person's birth, for the purpose of forecasting future events; such a forecast. (算命用的) 天宫图; 占星; 占星术; 依天宫图算命.

hor·rible /'hɒrəbl US: 'hɔ:r-; 'hɔrəbl/ adj 1 exciting horror: 可怕的; 令人恐怖的: ~ cruelty/crimes. 可怕的残忍(罪行). 2 (colloq) unpleasant: (口)令人不愉快的: ~ weather. 讨厌的天气. **hor·ribly** /-əblɪ; -əblɪ/ adv

hor·rid /'hɒrɪd US: 'hɔ:rɪd; 'hɔrɪd/ adj 1 frightful; terrible. 可怕的;可怖的. 2 (colloq) disagreeable: (口) 讨厌的: ~ weather. 讨厌的天气. **~·ly** adv **~·ness** n

hor·rific /hə'rɪfɪk; hɔ'rɪfɪk/ adj (colloq) horrifying. (口)可怕的.

hor·rify /'hɒrɪfaɪ US: 'hɔ:r-; 'hɔrə,faɪ/ vt (pt, pp -fied) [VP6A] fill with horror; shock; 使恐怖; 使惊骇: We were horrified by what we saw. 我们看到那惨景感到恐怖. Don't let the children see such ~ing scenes. 不要让孩子们看到如此骇人的景象.

hor·ror /'hɒrə(r) US: 'hɔ:r-; 'hɔrə/ n [C, U] (sth that causes a) feeling of extreme fear or dislike: 恐怖; 极端厌恶; 令人恐怖或极端厌恶的事物: She recoiled in ~ from the snake. 她看见那条蛇而吓得退避. She expressed her ~ of cruelty. 她表示她对残忍的憎恶. To her ~ she saw her husband knocked down by a bus. 见她丈夫被公共汽车撞倒时吓坏了. We have all read about the ~s of modern warfare. 我们都曾读到有关现代战争的惨状. **,chamber of '~s,** collection of objects, representations, etc, connected with crime, cruelty, etc. 恐怖之室(与犯罪, 残忍有关之一批物件、模型等). '~ **fiction/comics/films,** in which the subject matter and treatment are intended to arouse feelings of ~. 恐怖小说(连环图画, 影片). '~**struck/-stricken** adj overcome with ~. 惊恐的.

hors de com·bat /,ɔ: də 'kɒmbɑ:; 'ɔrdə'kɑmbɑ/ pred adj (F) unable to take further part in fighting because wounded or disabled. (法)因受伤或残废而失去战斗力的.

hors d'oeuvres /,ɔ: 'dɜːvrə US: 'dɜːv; ɔr'dœvrə/ n pl dishes of food served at the beginning of a meal as a relish. 主菜前所上的开胃小菜.

horse /hɔːs; hɔrs/ n 1 four-legged solid-hoofed animal with flowing mane and tail, used from early times to carry loads, for riding, etc. 马. ➪ the illus at domestic. 参看 domestic 之插图. ➪ **colt**[1], filly, foal mare, stallion. a dark ~, person whose chances of success are not yet known, or have been overlooked. 黑马; 获胜之成算尚未得知之人; 爆出冷门的获胜者. a ~ of another colour, quite a different matter. 完全是另一回事. back the wrong ~, support the loser in a contest. 支持竞争中的失败者. be/get on one's high ~, insist on being treated with proper respect. 摆架子; 趾高气扬; 倨傲作态; 盛气凌人. eat/work like a ~, eat a lot/work hard. 大吃(努力工作). flog a dead ~, ➪ flog. hold one's ~s, hesitate; show restraint. 迟豫; 自制. look a gift ~ in the mouth, accept sth ungratefully esp by examining it critically for faults (because a ~'s teeth indicate its age): 接受礼物不知感

激反而挑剔、批评(因马齿可表示其年龄). **put the cart before the ~,** ➪ cart. (straight) from the ~'s mouth, (of tips, advice, information) from a first-hand source (指秘密消息, 劝告, 情报)直接得来的. 2 (collective sing) cavalry; (集合名词单数)骑兵: ~ and foot, cavalry and infantry; 骑兵和步兵; light ~, lightly armed mounted soldiers; 轻骑兵; ~ artillery, light artillery with mounted gunners; 骑炮兵; the 'H~ Guards,' ➪ **guard**[1](6). 3 framework with legs, on which sth is supported: 支架(常带有腿的): a 'clothes-~, on which clothes may be dried in front of a fire; 烘衣架; a 'vaulting-~, block used in a gymnasium for vaulting over. (体操用的)木马. 4 (compounds) (复合词) '~·back n (only in) (仅用于) on ~back, on a ~. 在马上; 骑着马. '~·box n closed vehicle for taking a ~ by rail, or towing behind a car, etc. (铁路上或拖于汽车后面之)运马用的有篷货车. ,~·'chestnut n large tree with spreading branches and clusters of white or pink blossom; shiny reddish-brown nut of this tree. 七叶树(一种树枝展开,开白色或粉红色花簇的大树);七叶树之明亮的红褐色坚果. '~·flesh n (a) flesh of ~s as food. 马肉(用作食物). (b) ~s collectively: 马(总称): He's a good judge of ~ flesh. 他是个鉴别马匹的行家. '~·fly n (pl -flies) large insect troublesome to ~s and cattle. 虻; 马蝇. '~·hair n [U] hair from the mane or tail of ~s, formerly used for stuffing sofas, etc. 马鬃; 马尾(昔时用做沙发填塞料等). '~·laugh n loud, coarse laugh. 呵呵大笑. '~·man /-mən; -mən/ n (pl -men) rider on ~back, esp one who is skilled. 骑马者. '~·man·ship /-ʃɪp; -,ʃɪp/ n [U] art of riding, skill in riding, on ~back. 马术. '~-meat n ~ flesh. '~·play n [U] rough, noisy fun or play. 喧闹的娱乐. '~·pond n pond for watering and washing ~s. 饮马池; 洗马池. '~·power n [U] (shortened to 略作 **hp**) unit for measuring the power of an engine, etc (550 foot-pounds per second). 马力(测量引擎等动力的单位, 一匹马力为每秒 550 英尺磅). To '~·race n race between ~s with riders. 赛马. '~·racing n [U]. '~·radish n [U] (plant with a) hot-tasting root which is ground or scraped to make a sauce (eaten with beef). 辣根(有辣味, 磨碎或刮碎可制成一种调味品, 与牛肉共食). '~·sense n ordinary wisdom. 常识. '~·shoe /'hɔːʃuː; 'hɔrʃ,ʃu/ n U-shaped metal shoe for a ~; sth of this shape, eg a ~-shoe table. 马蹄铁; 马掌; 马蹄铁形物(例如马蹄形桌). '~·whip n, vt (-pp-) (thrash with a) whip for ~s. 马鞭;用马鞭鞭打. '~·woman n woman who rides on ~back. 女乘马者; 女骑师.

horsy /'hɔːsɪ; 'hɔrsɪ/ adj concerned with, fond of, horses or horse-racing; showing by dress, conversation, manners, etc familiarity with horses, horse-racing, grooms, jockeys, etc. 关于马的; 关于赛马的; 爱马的; 爱赛马的; 衣着、谈吐、态度等表现出熟悉马、赛马、马夫、赛马骑师等的.

hor·ta·tive /'hɔːtətɪv; 'hɔrtətɪv/ adj (formal) exhorting; serving to encourage. (正式用语)劝告的; 鼓励的.

hor·ti·cul·ture /'hɔːtɪkʌltʃə(r); 'hɔrtɪ,kʌltʃə/ n [U] (art of) growing flowers, fruit and vegetables. 园艺; 园艺学. **hor·ti·cul·tural** /,hɔːtɪ'kʌltʃərəl; ,hɔrtɪ'kʌltʃərəl/ adj of ~; 园艺的; 园艺学的: a horticultural show/society. 园艺展览(协会). **hor·ti·cul·tur·ist** /,hɔːtɪ'kʌltʃərɪst; ,hɔrtɪ'kʌltʃərɪst/ n person who practises ~. 园艺家; 园艺家.

ho·sanna /həʊ'zænə; ho'zænə/ n, int cry of praise and adoration (to God). 和散那(赞美上帝之语).

hose[1] /həʊz; hoz/ n [C, U] (length of) flexible tubing (of rubber, canvas or plastic) for directing water on to fires, watering gardens, cleaning streets, etc: 软管(橡皮、帆布或塑胶制成, 用以输水救火、浇花、清除街道等): 一段软管: 60 feet of plastic ~: 六十英尺塑胶管; plenty of fire ~s in the building. 建筑物中的许多消防水管. '~·pipe. □ n length of ~. (一段)软管. □ vt

[VP 6 A, 15 B] ~ *(down)*, water (a garden, etc) with a ~: wash (a motorcar, etc) by using a ~: 用软管输水浇(花园等); 用软管输水洗(汽车等): ~ *(down) the car.* 用软管输水洗汽车。

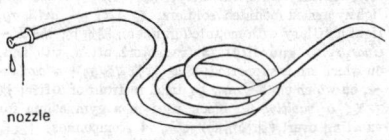

nozzle

a hosepipe

hose² /həʊz; hoz/ *n* **1** (collective, as *pl*) (trade name for) stockings and socks: (集合名词, 作复数用)(商品名称)长统袜及短袜: *six pair of* ~. 六双长统袜(短袜)。 **2** (hist) garment from the waist to the knees or feet worn by men in former times; tights: (史) 昔时男子穿的紧身裤(由腰部至膝部或脚部);紧身衣: *dressed in doublet and* ~. 穿着紧身上衣和紧身裤。 ⇨ the illus at doublet. 参看 doublet 之插图。

ho·sier /'həʊzɪə(r) US: -ʒə(r); 'hoʒə/ *n* tradesman who sells hose²(1) and knitted underwear. 售卖长袜、短袜、针织内衣之商人。 **ho·siery** /'həʊzɪərɪ US: 'həʊʒərɪ; 'hoʒərɪ/ *n* [U] goods sold by a ~. 长袜、短袜、内衣等货品。

hos·pice /'hɒspɪs; 'hɑspɪs/ *n* **1** house of rest for travellers. 供旅客休息的旅舍。 **2** hospital for dying people. 为垂死者而设立之医院。

hos·pit·able /hɒ'spɪtəbl; 'hɑspɪtəbl/ *adj* giving, liking to give, hospitality: 好客的: 好客的: *a* ~ *man/household.* 好客的人(家庭). **hos·pit·ably** /-əblɪ; -əblɪ/ *adv*

hos·pi·tal /'hɒspɪtl; 'hɑspɪtl/ *n* place where people are treated for, nursed through, their illness or injuries: 医院: *He's still in* ~. 他仍在住院。 *I'm going to the* ~ *to see my brother.* 我要去医院看望我的哥哥(弟弟). *His sister is a* ~ *nurse.* 他姐姐(妹妹)是个医院护士. *go to* ~, enter a ~ as a patient. 入医院。 ~·**ize** *vt* send to, admit into, ~. 送入医院。允许住院。 ~·**iz·ation** /ˌhɒspɪtlaɪ'zeɪʃn US: -lɪ'z-; ˌhɑspɪtlɪ'zeʃən/ *n* state of being ~ized. 入院/住院治疗。

hos·pi·tal·ity /ˌhɒspɪ'tælətɪ; ˌhɑspɪ'tælətɪ/ *n* [U] friendly and generous reception and entertainment of guests, esp in one's own home. 对客人的殷勤款待(尤指在自己家中); 好客。

host¹ /həʊst; host/ *n* **1** great number *(of)*: 多数; 许多 (与 of 连用): *He has* ~*s of friends.* 他有很多朋友。 *We are faced with a* ~ *of difficulties.* 我们面临许多困难。 **2** (archaic) army: (古) 军队: *Lord of H*~*s*, Jehovah, God of the Hebrews. 万军之主(耶和华, 希伯来人的上帝)。

host² /həʊst; host/ *n* **1** person who entertains guests: (款待客人的)主人: *As Mr Hill was away, Tom, the eldest son, acted as* ~ *at the dinner party,* welcomed the guests, etc. 希尔先生不在家, 汤姆做家总的主人。 (In the *pl* this word may be common gender.) (复数时此词可指通性)。 *The Parnwells are such good* ~*s.* 巴威尔一家真是善于款待客人的主人。 **2** inn-keeper; hotel-keeper. 旅馆老板。 *reckon without one's* ~, make calculations, plans, etc without consulting the chief person(s) concerned; overlook possible opposition. 作计划、考虑等时未与有关的主要人士磋商; 忽略可能的反对。 **3** (biol) organism which harbours a parasite. (生物)寄生动植物之宿主;寄主。 □ *vt* [VP6A] (US colloq) act as ~ to or at. (美口)作东; 款待。

Host /həʊst; host/ *n the* ~, bread eaten at Holy Communion. (圣餐礼仪式上之)圣饼。

hos·tage /'hɒstɪdʒ; 'hɑstɪdʒ/ *n* person (less often, a thing) given or left as a pledge that demands will be satisfied: 人质; 作抵押的人或物(多指人): *take sb* ~. 把

某人做为人质。 *The bandits demanded that one of the travellers should stay with them as a* ~. 匪徒要一位旅客留下来做人质。 *give* ~*s to fortune,* by an unwise step, take the risk of being harmed in future. 由于不智的步骤, 冒将来受到伤害之险。

hos·tel /'hɒstl; 'hɑstl/ *n* **1** building in which board and lodging are provided (with the support of the authorities concerned) for students, workmen in training, etc: (由有关当局赞助而为学生、训练中的工人等所设的)寄宿舍; 招待所: *a YMCA* ~. 青年会寄宿舍。 '**youth** ~, one for young people walking, riding or cycling on holiday tours, used by members of the International Youth H~ Association. 青年招待所(招待国际青年招待所协会徒步、骑马或骑脚踏车作假期旅行之会员), 招待旅行之游客。 **2** (archaic) inn. (古) 旅馆。 ~·**ry** *n* (archaic) inn. (古) 旅馆。 ~·**ler** /'hɒstələ(r); 'hɑstlə/ *n* person travelling from ~ to ~, esp youth ~lers. 沿途投宿招待所(尤指青年招待所)之旅客。

host·ess /'həʊstɪs; 'hostɪs/ *n* **1** woman who entertains guests; wife of one's host. (款待客人的)女主人。 **2** woman inn-keeper. 旅馆女老板。 **3** '**air** ~, ⇨ **air¹**(7).

hos·tile /'hɒstaɪl US: -tl; 'hɑstl/ *adj* **1** of an enemy: 敌人的: *a* ~ *army.* 敌军。 **2** feeling or showing enmity *(to);* unfriendly: 怀敌意的; 表示敌意的; 对任何人无敌意; show ~ to sb. 对某人表示敌意。 **2** *(pl,* ~**ties)** (acts of) war: (复)战争; 战斗: *at the outbreak of hostilities,* 战争爆发时; *open/ suspend hostilities,* begin/stop fighting. 开(停)战。

hos·til·ity /hɒ'stɪlətɪ; hɑs'tɪlətɪ/ *n* **1** [U] enmity; ill will: 敌意; 敌意: *feelings of* ~; 敌视的情绪; 敌意; *feel no* ~ *towards anyone,* 对任何人无敌意; *show* ~ *to sb.* 对某人表示敌意。 **2** *(pl,* ~**ties)** (acts of) war: (复)战争; 战斗: *at the outbreak of hostilities,* 战争爆发时; *open/ suspend hostilities,* begin/stop fighting. 开(停)战。

hot /hɒt; hat/ *adj* (-**ter,** -**test**) **1** having a high temperature: 热的: *hot weather;* 热天气; *a hot day;* 热天; *feel hot.* 感觉热。 *I like my food hot.* 我喜欢吃热食。 *This coffee is too hot to drink.* 这咖啡太热了, 不能喝。 *be in/get into hot water,* in trouble or disgrace (because of foolish behaviour, etc). (因愚蠢的行为等)惹来麻烦或羞辱。 *be/get hot under the collar,* angry, excited, indignant. 发怒; 兴奋; 愤慨。 *make a place/ make it too hot for sb,* (fig) compel him to leave by rousing hostility against him. (喻)以敌视态度强迫某人离开一地方; 排挤某人。 **2** producing a burning sensation to the taste: 辛辣的: *This curry is too hot.* 这咖喱太辣了。 *Pepper and mustard are hot.* 胡椒和芥末是辣的。 **3** fiery; eager; intense; violent; impetuous: 激情的; 热烈的; 急烈的; 激烈的; 猛烈的: *get hot over an argument;* 辩论时十分激动; *a man with a hot temper,* 一个脾气暴躁的人; *in the hottest part of the election campaign.* 在竞选活动最激烈的部分。 *be hot on the trail of sb/on sb's tracks,* near to what is being pursued; close behind. 逼近追求物; 紧追不舍。 **4** (in hunting, of the scent) fresh and strong. (指对猎物野兽的气味)新鲜而强烈的。 **5** (of music, esp jazz) strongly rhythmical and emotional. (指音乐, 尤指爵士乐)富有节奏和情感的。 **6** (sl) (of stolen goods) difficult to dispose of (because of determined efforts made by the police to trace them): (俚)(指赃物)不易脱手的 (由于警察决心努力追踪该项物品): *These articles are too hot to handle/hold.* 这些赃物太不容易脱手, 所以太不便买卖(持有)。 **7** (as adv) (作为副词) (a)recently: 最近地: *hot off the press.* 最新出版的。 ⇨ **hot news** below. 参看下列 hot news, (b) **blow hot and cold,** (fig) be by turns favourable and unfavourable. (喻)无定见; 反复不定。 (c) *give it sb hot,* punish or scold severely. 严惩或严斥某人。 (这些赃物太不容易脱手, 所以太不便买卖(持有)。 *(with* nn *and participles)* (与名词及分词连用之特殊用法),**hot 'air** *n* [U] meaningless talk, promises, etc. 无意义的话、许诺等; 空话。 hot-air balloon ⇨ **balloon.** '**hot-bed** *n* bed of earth heated by rotting manure to promote growth of plants; (fig) place favourable to growth, esp of sth evil: (培养植物之)温床; (喻)(尤指邪恶事物)便于

滋长的地方: *a hotbed of vice/crime.* 罪恶(犯罪)之温
床。 ˌhot-'blooded *adj* passionate. 热情的。 ˌhot cross
'bun *n* one with a cross marked on it, eaten on Good
Friday. 上有十字架形花饰的圆形小面包, 于耶稣受难节
食用。 ˌhot 'dog *n* hot sausage served with onions and
mustard in a sandwich or bread roll. 热狗(三明治或圆
形面包中, 夹热香肠配以碎洋葱及芥末之食品)。 ˌhot.'foot
adv eagerly; in great haste: 急忙; 火急: *run hotfoot
after the pickpocket.* 急追扒手。 □ *vi* go hastily: 急走;赶
去: *hotfoot it down to the swimming-pool.* 急忙赶到游泳池。
ˌhot 'gospeller *n* (colloq) fervent evangelist preacher.
(口)热情的福音传道者。 'hot·head *n* impetuous person.
性急的人。 ˌhot-'headed *adj* impetuous. 性急的。 hot-
house *n* heated building, usu made of glass, for growing
delicate plants. 温室; 暖房。 'hot line *n* direct line of
communication (telephone or teleprinter) between heads
of governments, eg between Moscow and Washington.
热线(两国政府首脑之间, 例如莫斯科与华盛顿之间, 直接
联络的电话或电传打字电报机专线)。 ˌhot 'money *n* [U]
short-term funds moved from one financial centre to
another by speculators seeking high interest rates and
security. 流动的国际短期资金(投机者为谋高利及不受起
值损失, 由一金融中心转移至另一金融中心者)。 ⇨ also **6**
above. 亦参看上列第 6 义。 ˌhot 'news *n* [U] recent
(esp sensational) news. 最近(尤指轰动的)消息。 'hot-
plate *n* flat surface of a cooking-stove; similar surface
(not part of a stove) that can be heated, eg electrically,
for cooking, boiling water, etc. 火炉上之平顶炊具;可加
热的平面炊具(非火炉之一部分, 例如用电者, 供烹饪、烧
水等用。 ˌhot po'tato *n* (fig, colloq) sth difficult or
unpleasant to deal with: (喻, 口)棘手之事; 使人厌恶之
事: *The issue is a political hot potato.* 这问题是政治上棘
手之事。 'hot rod *n* (US *sl*) supercharged car. (美俚)马
力强大之汽车。 the 'hot seat *n* electric chair (for the
electrocution of murderers); (fig) position of sb who
has to make difficult, often agonizing, decisions, eg of
a head of state. 电椅(对谋杀者施电刑之用); (喻)(国
家元首等必须作困难而且往往痛苦的决定时所处之)困境。
ˌhot 'spring *n* naturally heated spring[1](2). 温泉。 ˌhot
'stuff *n* [U] (sl) sth/sb of first-rate quality. (俚)第一
流的人或事物。 ˌhot-tempered *adj* easily angered. 性急
的; 脾气暴躁的。 ˌhot-'water-bottle *n* container (often
of rubber) to be filled with hot water for warmth in
bed. (往往是橡皮制的, 使床铺温暖的)热水袋。 □ *vt, vi*
(-tt-) [VP 2C, 15 B] *hot* (*sth*) *up*, (colloq) make or
become hotter or (fig) more exciting: (口)使或成为更
热;(喻)使或成为更令人兴奋: *Things are hotting up.* 事
情热闹起来了。 ˌhot·ly *adv* passionately; excitedly: 激烈
地; 热烈地: *He replied hotly that...;* 他怒气冲冲地回
答...; *It was a hotly contested match.* 那是一场竞争激烈
的比赛。

hotch·potch /'hɔtʃpɒtʃ/ *n* jumble; number of things mixed together without order: 杂乱的一
堆东西; 杂混在一起的东西: *His essay was a ～ of other
people's ideas.* 他的文章系将别人的思想凑合而成。

ho·tel /həʊ'tel; hoˈtɛl/ *n* (either *a* or *an* ～)(可用冠
词 a 或 an)building where meals and rooms are
provided for travellers. 旅社; 旅馆。 ～·ier /həʊ'telɪeɪ
US: ˌhəʊtɛl'jeɪ, ˌhoˈtɛl'je/ *n a* ～-keeper. 旅馆老板。

hound /haʊnd; haʊnd/ *n* **1** (kinds of) dog used for
hunting and racing: 猎犬;猎狗: 'fox～; 猎狐犬; 'blood～;
血猎; 'grey～. 灵猴。 (When not in a compound, ～ usu
means fox～.) (不用于复合词时, hound 通常指猎狐
犬)。 *follow the* ～*s; ride to* ～*s,* hunt with a pack of
～s. 带一群猎犬狩猎。 *Master of H*～*s,* the master of a
hunt(2). 猎狐会会长。 **2** (dated colloq) mean, wretched,
contemptible fellow. (过时口语)卑鄙之徒; 卑鄙之流。 □
vt [VP 6A] chase or hunt with, or as with, ～s; harass:
用猎犬追逐或狩猎; 追逼: *be ～ed by one's creditors,*
worried by requests for payment of money owing. 为债
主所追逼。

hour /aʊə(r); aʊr/ *n* **1** twenty-fourth part of a day;

---

60 minutes: 小时; 钟头: *hire a horse by the* ～; 按钟头租
用一匹马; *walk for* ～*s (and* ～*s);* 走好几个钟头; *a
three* ～' *journey,* 三小时的旅程; *the happiest* ～ (=
period) *of my life;* 我一生中最快乐的时期; *work a
forty-* ～ *week;* 每周工作四十小时; *18.00* ～*s,* time calculated on a 24-～ basis, = 6.00 pm, 十八点(按每天廿四
小时推算), 即下午六点。 ⇨ **App 4.** 参看附录四。 *at the
eleventh* ～, when almost too late. 在最后时刻; 在危
急之时。 *the 'small* ～*s,* the three or four ～*s* after
midnight. 午夜后的三或四个小时。 '～·glass *n* sand-
glass which runs out in one ～. 沙漏; 更漏(所盛之沙于
一小时后漏尽)。 '～ hand *n* small hand on a clock or
watch, pointing to the ～. 时针。 **2** time of day; point
or period of time: 时刻; 钟点: *The church clock was
striking the* ～ *as we got home.* 我们回家时, 教堂的钟正
在报时。 *This clock strikes the* ～*s and the half-*～*s, but
not the quarters.* 这钟每到一小时及半小时均报时, 但每刻
钟不报时。 *Please come at an early* ～. 请早些来。 *They
disturb me at all* ～*s of the day and night,* constantly. 他
们日夜不断地打扰我。 **3** (*pl*) fixed periods of time, esp
for work: (复)固定的时间(尤指工作时间): *'school* ～*s,*
上课时间。 *'Office* ～*s, 9 am to 5 pm.* 办公时间, 上午九点
至下午五点。 *after* ～*s,* after the period of regular
business, etc. 下班后。 *out of* ～*s,* outside (before or
after) regular ～*s of duty etc.* 非上班时间; 非办公时
间。 *keep good/bad/early/late/regular, etc* ～*s,*
get up, go to bed, start/stop work, leave/arrive
home, etc, early/late, etc. 按(不按)时作息; 早(晚)
起; 早(晚)睡; 早(晚)开始工作; 早(晚)停止工作; 早(晚)
离家; 早(晚)到家等。 **4** a particular, or the present,
point in time: 某一时刻; 现时: *questions of the* ～, now
being discussed; 目前所谈的问题; *in the* ～ *of danger/
temptation;* 在危险(诱惑)之时; *in a good/evil* ～, at a
lucky/unlucky time. 在幸运(不幸)之时。

houri /'hʊəri; 'hʊri/ *n* young and beautiful woman
of the Muslim Paradise. 伊斯兰天堂之美女。

hour·ly /'aʊəli; 'aʊrli/ *adv* **1** every hour; once every
hour: 每小时; 每小时一次: *This medicine is to be taken
*～. 这药每小时服一次。 **2** at any hour: 随时:
We're expecting news ～. 我们时时期待着消息。 □ *adj*
1 done or occurring every hour: 每小时一次的: *an* ～
service of trains; 每小时一班的火车; *an* ～ *bus service.*
每小时一班的公共汽车。 **2** continual: 不断的: *live in* ～
dread of discovery. 时时刻刻怕被人发觉。

house[1] /haʊs; haʊs/ *n* (*pl* ～s /'haʊzɪz; 'haʊzɪz/) **1**
building made for people to live in, usu for one family
(or a family and lodgers, etc): 房屋; 住宅: *New* ～*s
are going up everywhere.* 到处在建筑新房屋。 *I've bought
a* ～. 我买了一幢房子。 ⇨ **home[1](1).** *get on like a* '～
on fire, (of people) quickly become friendly and jolly
together. (指人)很快地成为好友。 *under* ～ *arrest,*
forbidden by law to leave one's ～ or receive visitors.
(依法)软禁在家中。 **2** (usu with a *pref*) building made
or used for some particular purpose or occupation: (通
常加一前缀)作特殊用途的建筑物: *'hen*～; 鸡舍; *'cow*～;
牛栏; *'store*～; 仓库; *'ware*～; 仓库; *'alms*～; 贫民院;
养老院; *'bake*～; 面包厂; *'custom*～, 海关, etc, ⇨ these
entries. 参看各项。 *the H*～ *of God,* church or chapel.
教堂。 ～ *of cards,* one built by a child out of playing
cards; (fig) scheme likely to collapse. 儿童用纸牌做的
房屋; (喻)不可靠的计划。 ～ *of ill fame,* (old use)
brothel. (旧用法)妓院。 *on the* ～, at the expense of
the inn, firm, etc. 由乡村旅馆、商号等负担费用的。 **3**
(building used by any assembly: 议会; 议会所用的建筑
物: *the H*～ *of Commons/Lords.* (英国)下(上)议院。
the H～*s of Parliament.* (英国)国会两院。 *the H*～,
(colloq, GB) (口, 英) **(a)** the Stock Exchange. 证券交
易所。 **(b)** the H～ of Commons or Lords: 下(上)议院:
enter the H～, become an MP. 成为国会议员。 **(c)** (US)
the H～ of Representatives. (美)众议院。 **(d)** business
firm. 商号; 公司。 **4** [U] *keep* ～, manage the affairs
of a ～hold. 料理家务; 管家。 *keep a good* ～, provide

good food and plenty of comfort. 使家庭丰衣足食。 *keep open* ~, be ready to welcome guests at any time. 随时欢迎客人；开门揖客。 *set/put one's* ~ *in order*, put one's affairs straight. 整顿本身事务；清理自己事务。 **5** household; family line; dynasty: 家族；家系；朝代: *the H* ~ *of Windsor*, the British Royal family; 英国王室；英国皇族: *an ancient* ~; 古老的家族: *an old trading* ~, business firm. 历史悠久的贸易商行。 **6** spectators, audience, in a theatre: 观众；听众: *anybody could be heard in every part of the* ~; 使自己的声音能让戏院中所有的听众听到; *a full* ~, every seat occupied. (戏院)客满。 *The second* ~ (= performance) *starts at 9 o'clock*. 第二场戏九点开始。 *Is there a doctor in the* ~? 观众中有医生吗? *bring down the* ~; *bring the* '~ *down*, win very great applause and approval. 博得满堂喝彩。 **7** (compounds) (复合词) '~ **agent** *n* (GB) person who sells or lets ~s for others. (英) 房屋经纪人。 ⇨ (US) (美) **realtor**. '~**·boat** *n* boat fitted up as a place to live in, eg on a river or estuary. 船宅；屋艇(河上或河口等处可居住的船只)。 '~**·bound** *adj* confined to the ~, eg through ill-health: 被迫困居于室内的(例如因健康不佳): *Should wives with children be* ~*bound?* 有小孩的太太们应该留在家里吗? '~**·breaker** *n* **1** person who enters another's ~ by day to steal. 白日侵入家宅行窃者。 ⇨ **burglar. 2** (US 美 = ~**·wrecker**) workman employed to pull down old buildings. 拆屋工人。 '~**·coat** *n* usu cotton or silk coat worn by women in the house during the day. 妇女日常家居所着之外衣 (通常为棉或丝质)。 '~**·craft** *n* [U] theory and practice of running a home[1]. 治家(学)。 '~**·dog** *n* dog trained to guard a ~. 守门犬；看门狗。 '~**·father** *n* man in charge of children in an institution. 男舍监。 '~ **flag** *n* flag flown by a firm's ships. 商船公司旗号；挂顶公司旗。 ⇨ **5** above. 参看上列第 5 义。 '~**·fly** *n* (*pl* **-flies**) ⇨ **fly**[1]. ~**·ful** /-ful/ -/ful/ *n* as much as a ~ can contain or accommodate. 一屋量。 '~**·hold** *n* all persons (family, lodgers, etc) living in a ~: 同居在一家的人(家人及房客)；全家的人: ~*hold cavalry/troops*, employed to guard the Sovereign; (护卫国王的)禁卫骑兵队; 御林军; ~*hold duties/expenses*. 家务(家庭开销)。 '~**·hold** '**word**, commonly used word or name. 家喻户晓的词或名字。 '~**·holder** *n* person leasing or owning and occupying a ~, not sb living in a hotel, lodgings, etc. 住家的人(非指住在旅舍，寄宿舍等的人)。 '~**·keeper** *n* person employed to manage the affairs of a ~hold. 管家。 '~**·lights** *n pl* lights in the auditorium of a theatre, cinema, etc. 戏院、屯影院等观众席之灯光。 '~**·maid** *n* female servant in a ~, esp one who cleans rooms, etc. 女仆(尤指清洁房间等者)。 ~**·maid's** '**knee**, inflammation of the kneecap due to kneeling. (因跪下工作而引起的)膝盖粘液囊肿。 '~**·man** /-mən; -mən/ *n* (*pl* **-men**) (GB) doctor who is an assistant to a physician or surgeon in a hospital (US 美 = **intern**). (英) 住在医院中之见习医生。 '~**·martin** *n* common bird which nests in the walls of ~s and cliffs. 筑巢于墙壁或绝壁上的燕子。 '~**·master** *n* teacher in charge of a school boarding-~. 男舍监。 '~**·mother** *n* woman in charge of children in an institution. 女舍监。 '~**·party** *n* party of guests being entertained for several days at a country ~, etc. 连续数日在乡间府第等地接受招待之全体宾客。 ⇨ **physician** *n* one who resides in a hospital. 住院内科医师。 '~**·proud** *adj* very much concerned with the care of the ~, with the appearance of the furnishings, etc. 十分关心家事，家俱陈列等的。 '~**·room** *n* space: 空间: *I wouldn't give that table* ~*room*, would not have it in my ~, would not accept it even as a gift. 我不要那桌子(即使送给我也不要)。 '~ **sparrow** *n* common grey and brown bird. 家雀。 '~ **surgeon** *n* one who resides in a hospital. 住院外科医师。 '~**·top** *n* (chiefly in) used in) *cry/publish/proclaim sth from the* ~*tops*, make known to all; declare publicly. 宣布；公开宣扬某事物。 '~**·trained** *adj* (of domestic pets) trained not to

defecate and urinate inside buildings. (指家庭宠物)受过训练而知道不在室内便溺的。 '~**·warming** *n* party given to friends by a person who moves into a new ~. 迁入新居之庆宴。 '~·**wife** *n* **1** woman head of a family, who runs the home, brings up the family, etc. 主妇。 **2** /'hʌzif; 'hʌzɪf/ (dated) case for needles and thread. (过时用语)针线盒。 '~·**wife·ly** *adj* of a ~wife(1). 主妇的。 '~**wifery** /-wɪfəri; -,waɪfri/ *n* [U] work of a ~wife. 家务；家政。 '~·**work** *n* [U] work done in a ~, cleaning, cooking, etc. 家务。 ⇨ **homework** at **home**[1](7).

house[2] /haʊz; haʊz/ *vt* [VP6A] **1** provide a house or shelter for; find room for: 供以房屋: *We can* ~ *you and your friends if the hotels are full*. 如果旅馆已住满，我们可供给你和你的朋友们住处。 **2** store (goods, etc): 贮藏(货物等): ~ *one's old books in the attic*. 将旧书藏置顶楼。

hous·ing /'haʊzɪŋ; 'haʊzɪŋ/ *n* [U] accommodation in houses, etc: 供给房屋；住宅；房屋: *More* ~ *is needed for old people*. 需要更多的老年人住宅。 *The* ~ *in this part of the town is sub-standard*. 城里这一部分的住宅低于标准。 ~ **association** *n* non-profitmaking society for the construction and provision of ~. 住宅协会 (建筑及供应住宅之非营利组织)。 ~ **estate** *n* area of houses planned and built either by a local authority or other organization, to be let or sold. 住宅区；社区(由当地政府或其他机构计划及兴建，供出租或出售者)。

hove /həʊv; hoʊv/ *pt*, *pp* of **heave**.

hovel /'hɒvl US: 'hʌvl; 'hʌvl/ *n* small house or cottage that is unfit to live in; open-sided shed or outhouse. 不适于居住的小屋；棚；外屋。

hover /'hɒvə(r) US: 'hʌvər; 'hʌvə/ *vi* [VP2A, C] **1** (of birds) remain in the air at one place: (指鸟) 翱翔；盘旋: *a hawk* ~*ing overhead*/~*ing over its prey*; 在头上盘旋 (在猎物头顶盘旋) 的一只鹰; *a helicopter* ~*ing over the house*. 盘旋于房屋上空的一架直升飞机。 '~**·craft** *n* craft capable of moving over land or water while supported on a cushion of air made by jet engines. 气垫船(车)(由喷射引擎造成的气垫所支持，可在地面及水面上方移动)。 **2** (of persons) wait about; remain at or near: (指人) 守在附近; 留在一地或附近: (fig) (喻) ~ *between life and death*. 处于生死关头。

a hovercraft

how /haʊ; haʊ/ *adv* **1** in what way or manner; by what means: 怎样；用何方法: *How is the word spelt?* 这词怎样拼法? *Tell me how to spell the word*. 告诉我如何拼这词。 *How did you escape?* 你怎样逃的? *Tell me how you escaped*. 告诉我你如何脱逃的。 **2** (in questions and exclamations) to what extent; in what degree; (用于疑问句及惊叹句中)多么; 何等: *How old is he?* 他多大年纪了? *How often do you go there?* 你多久去那里一次? *How many are there?* 有多少? *How much do you want?* 你要多少? *How dirty the house is!* 这房屋多么脏啊! *How kind you are!* 你多么客气啊! *How he snores!* ie he snores very loudly. 他的鼾声多么大啊! *How well you look!* 你看来多么强健啊! *And how!* (emphatic) Yes! (强语气)是的! 当然! **3** in what state of health: 健康情况如何: *How are you?* 你好吗? *How's your father?* 你父亲好吗? *How do you do?* (formula used as a conventional greeting, esp when persons are formally introduced; used only with the *pron* you.) 你好(用于一般的问候，尤其是初次见面经人正式介绍后的客套语；只可用于代词

you.) **how-d'ye-do** / ˈhaʊ djə du:; ˈhaʊdjeˈdu/ n (colloq) awkward state of affairs: (口)令人困窘的情况: Well, here's a pretty how-d'ye-do! 啊, 这真令人为难! **4** (introducing an indirect statement) 等于 that: He told me how (= that) he had read about it in the newspapers. 他告诉我他在报上获悉此事. **5** used in asking for an opinion, decision, explanation, etc: 如何(用以询人之意见、决定、解释等): How about going (= What do you think about going) for a walk? 去散散步怎么样? How do you find your new job? Do you like. etc? 你对你的新工作觉得怎样? **How come...,** (colloq) Why is it that...: (口)为何…: How come we don't see you more often? 为什么我们不常看到你? **How's that? (a)** What's the explanation of that? 那是怎么回事? **(b)** What's your opinion of that? 你对那个的意见如何(例如指着一物何)? **(c)** (in cricket, to the umpire) Is the batsman out or not out? (板球赛中询问裁判)那击球员怎么样? **How so?** Can you prove that it is so? 为什么是这样? 你能证明其是如此吗? **how-beit** /haʊˈbi:ɪt; haʊˈbi:t/ conj (archaic) nevertheless. (古)然而; 虽然如此. **how-ever** /haʊˈevə(r)/ adv **1** in whatever way or degree: 无论如何: He will never succeed, however hard he tries. 无论他如何努力尝试, 他都不会成功. We must do something, on however humble a scale. 我们必须做些事, 不论多么微不足道. **2** (also conj) although that is/may be/was, etc so: 然而; 依然: Later, however, he decided to go. 后来, 他仍然决定去了. He was mistaken, however. 可是他错了.

how-dah /ˈhaʊdə; ˈhaʊdə/ n seat (usu with a canopy) on an elephant's back. 象舆(象背上的座位, 通常有篷盖).

how-it-zer /ˈhaʊɪtsə(r); ˈhaʊɪtsə/ n short gun for firing shells at a high angle at short range. 榴弹炮.

howl /haʊl; haʊl/ n [C] long, loud cry, eg of a wolf; long cry of a person in pain, or of sb expressing scorn, amusement, etc: 号叫; 哀号; 高声叫嚷: wolves ~ing in the forest. 在森林中嗥叫的狼. The wind ~ed through the trees. 风在林间怒号. The boys ~ed with laughter. 男孩子们高声大笑. **2** [VP6A, 15A, B] ~ (down), utter ~s at; utter with ~s: 对…吼叫; 吼叫着说出: ~ defiance at the enemy. 吼叫对敌人挑战; ~ down a speaker, prevent him from being heard. 用吼叫声掩盖演说者的声音. **~er** n (colloq) foolish and laughable mistake. (口) 愚蠢可笑的错误. **~ing** adj (sl) extreme; glaring: (俚)极端的; 显而易见的: a ~ing shame. 奇耻大辱.

hoy-den /ˈhɔɪdn; ˈhɔɪdn/ n boisterous girl. 顽皮喜闹的女孩. **~ish** /-ɪʃ; -ɪʃ/ adj of or like a ~. (似)顽皮女孩的;

hub /hʌb; hʌb/ n central part of a wheel from which the spokes radiate, ⇨ the illus at **bicycle**; (fig) central point of activity or importance: 毂轮; 轮轴(参看 bicycle 之插图); (喻)中心; 中枢: a hub of industry/commerce. 工业(商业)中心. He thinks that Boston is the hub of the universe. 他认为波士顿是世界的中心.

hubble-bubble /ˈhʌbl bʌbl; ˈhʌbl ˌbʌbl/ n = **hookah**.

hub-bub /ˈhʌbʌb; ˈhʌbʌb/ n [U] confused noise, eg of many voices; uproar. 嘈杂; 喧嚣.

hubby /ˈhʌbɪ; ˈhʌbɪ/ n (GB) (colloq) husband. (英) (口)丈夫.

hu-bris /ˈhjuːbrɪs; ˈhjubrɪs/ n [U] (GK) arrogant pride. (希)傲慢.

hucka-back /ˈhʌkəbæk; ˈhʌkəˌbæk/ n strong, rough, cotton or linen material used for towels, etc.做毛巾等用的一种坚固的粗棉布或麻布.

huckle-berry /ˈhʌklˌberɪ US: -berɪ; ˈhʌklˌbɛrɪ/ n (pl **-ries**) (small, dark-blue berry of a) low shrub common in N America. 越橘属(北美之一种矮灌木); 越橘(越橘树产的深蓝色的小浆果).

huck-ster /ˈhʌkstə(r); ˈhʌkstə/ n hawker. 沿街叫卖

之小贩.

huddle /ˈhʌdl; ˈhʌdl/ vt, vi **1** [VP2C] crowd together: 挤在一起: sheep huddling together for warmth. 挤成一团以取暖的羊. **2** [VP2C] ~ up (against), curl or coil up against: 缩成一团(紧靠); 蜷起身体(紧靠): Tom was cold, so he ~d up against his brother in bed. 汤姆感觉冷, 所以他在床上缩成一团, 紧靠着他哥哥(弟弟). **3** [VP15A, B] heap up in a confused mass: 杂乱地堆起: ~ things together/up/into sth. 把东西混在一起(堆起来, 塞入某物). □ n number of things or persons close together without order or arrangement: 杂乱无章的一堆东西或一群人: be in/go into a ~, (colloq, of persons) be/get together to confer. (口, 指人)在一起商议.

hue[1] /hjuː; hju/ n [C] (shade of) colour: 颜色; 色度: the hues of the rainbow; 虹之色彩; the dark hue of the ocean. 海洋之暗色. **hued** /hjuːd; hjud/ (in compounds) having the hue(s) indicated: (用于复合词中)有…颜色的: 'dark-hued; 暗色的; 'many-hued, 有许多颜色的.

hue[2] /hjuː; hju/ n (only in) (仅用于) **hue and cry**, /ˌhjuː ən ˈkraɪ; ˈhju ən ˈkraɪ/ general outcry of alarm (as when a criminal is being pursued, or when there is opposition to sth): (追捕犯人或表示反对之)喊叫: raise a hue and cry against new tax proposals. 叫嚣反对新税的提议.

huff[1] /hʌf; hʌf/ n fit of ill temper. 发怒: be in/get into a ~, 发怒. **~ish** /-ɪʃ; -ɪʃ/, **~y** adj/ in a ~; taking offence easily. 发怒的; 易生气的. **~ily** /ɪlɪ; -əlɪ/ adv

huff[2] /hʌf; hʌf/ vi puff; blow. 吹气; 喷气.

hug /hʌɡ; hʌɡ/ vt (-gg-) [VP6A] **1** put the arms round tightly, esp to show love: 紧抱(尤指表示亲爱); 搂抱: The child was hugging her doll. 那小孩紧抱着她的洋娃娃. **2** cling to: 固执; 坚持: hug cherished beliefs. 坚持所抱的信念. **3** hug the shore, (of a ship) keep close to it. (指船)紧靠海岸. **4** hug oneself (with pleasure/delight) over sth, be very pleased with oneself, congratulate oneself. 窃喜; 深自庆幸. □ n [C] tight embrace: 紧抱: She gave her mother a big hug. 她紧紧地抱着她母亲.

huge /hjuːdʒ; hjudʒ/ adj very great. 巨大的. **~ly** adv enormously; very much. 极大地; 十分地.

hug-ger-mug-ger /ˈhʌɡə mʌɡə(r); ˈhʌɡəˌmʌɡə/ n, adj, adv secrecy; secret(ly); confusion; confused(ly). 秘密; 混乱; 秘密的(地); 混乱的(地).

Hu-gue-not /ˈhjuːɡənɒt; ˈhjuɡəˌnɑt/ n (16th and 17th cc) French Protestant. (十六、十七世纪)法国新教徒.

hula /ˈhuːlə; ˈhulə/ n native Hawaiian dance. 夏威夷土风舞; 草裙舞.

hulk /hʌlk; hʌlk/ n **1** old ship no longer in use or used only as a storehouse; (formerly) old ship used as a prison. 废船; 用作仓库之旧船; (昔时)囚船. **2** big, clumsy ship, thing or person. 笨大之船、物或人. **~ing** adj clumsy; awkward: 笨大的; 笨拙的: Get out of my way, you ~ing great idiot! 给我滚开, 你这个大笨蛋!

hull[1] /hʌl; hʌl/ n outer covering of some fruits and seeds. esp the pods of peas and beans (某些果实和种子的)壳 (尤指)豆荚. □ vt remove the ~s of. 去…之壳; 去荚.

hull[2] /hʌl; hʌl/ n body or frame of a ship. 船壳. ⇨ the illus at **barque**. 参看 barque 之插图. ~ down **(a)** (of a ship almost below the horizon) with only the mast(s), funnel(s) etc, visible. (指几乎隐于水平线下之船)不见船身, 只露出桅、烟囱等. **(b)** (of a tank) with only the turret showing. (指坦克)只露出炮塔.

hul-la-ba-loo /ˌhʌləbəˈluː; ˈhʌləbəˌlu/ n uproar; disturbance: 喧嚣; 骚扰: What a ~! 多吵闹啊! What's all this ~ about? 吵些什么?

hullo (also **hallo, hello**) /həˈləʊ; həˈlo/ int used as a greeting, to call attention, to express surprise, and to answer a call, eg on the telephone. (打招呼, 引人注意, 表示惊讶及回答之呼声, 例如打电话招呼声)喂!

hum /hʌm; hʌm/ vi, vt (-mm-) [VP6A, A, C] 1 make a continuous sound ·like that made by bees; sing with closed lips: 作嗡嗡声; 哼唱: *She was humming a song to herself.* 她自己在哼唱着。 *The bees were humming in the garden.* 蜜蜂在花园里嗡嗡叫着。 **hum·ming·bird** n name used of several species, usu small and brightly coloured,that make a humming sound by vibration of the wings. 蜂鸟(通常体小而毛色鲜艳, 鼓动翅膀发嗡嗡声)。 **'humming-top** n top that hums when it spins. 响簧陀螺。 2 be in a state of activity: 活跃: *make things hum;* 使事情活跃起来; *a factory humming with activity.* 忙碌的工厂。 3 (sl) smell unpleasantly: (俚)发臭味: *This ham is beginning to hum.* 这火腿开始发臭了。 4 usu 通常作 **hum and haw / ha,** (colloq) make sounds expressing hesitation or doubt. (口) 发咕哝声 (表示迟疑)。 □ n humming noise: 嗡嗡声: *the hum of bees / of distant traffic;* 蜜蜂(远处往来之车辆)之嗡嗡声; *a hum of voices / conversation from the next room.* 邻室之嗡嗡的谈话声。

hu·man /'hjuːmən; 'hjumən/ adj 1 of man or mankind (contrasted with animals, God): 人的; 人类的(以别于动物的或上帝的): *a ~ being;* 人; *~ nature.* 人性; *affairs.* 人事。 *'To err is ~, to forgive divine.'* '犯错是人之常情, 宽恕是超凡入圣的'。 2 having, showing, the qualities that distinguish man: 有人情味的; 有人性的: *His cruelty suggests that he is less than ~.* 他的残忍表示他没有人性。 ~·ly adv (esp) by ~ means; without divine help: (尤指)用人力: *The doctors have done all that is ~ly possible.* 医生们已尽了所有的人事。 ,~·'kind n [U] mankind. 人类。

hu·mane /hjuːˈmeɪn; hjuˈmen/ adj 1 tender; kindhearted: 仁慈的; 好心肠的: *a man of ~ character;* 厚道的; 仁者; *a ~ officer.* 有恻隐之心的军官。 ~ **killer,** instrument for the painless killing of animals. 无痛屠宰机(无痛苦的屠宰动物的工具)。 2 (of branches of study) tending to refinement; polished. (指学科) 高尚的; 文雅的。 ⇨ **humanity(4).** ~·ly adv.

hu·man·ism /'hjuːmənɪzəm; 'hjumənˌɪzəm/ n [U] 1 devotion to human interests; system that is concerned with ethical standards (but not with theology), and with the study of mankind. 人性; 人道; 人文主义。 2 literary culture (of about the 14th to 16th cc) based on Greek and Roman learning. 人文学; 古典文化之研究(约自十四至十六世纪基于希腊及罗马学术思想的)古典文学。

hu·man·ist /'hjuːmənɪst; 'hjumənɪst/ n 1 student of human nature or human affairs (as opposed to theological subjects). 人性学者; 人本学者; 人文学者。 2 supporter of humanism. 人本主义者; 人文主义者。 3 (esp in the 14th to 16th cc) student of Greek and Roman literature and antiquities. (尤指十四至十六世纪)研究希腊罗马之古典文化学者。

hu·mani·tar·ian /hjuːˌmænɪˈteərɪən; hjuˌmænəˈterɪən/ adj, n (of, holding the views of, a) person who works for the welfare of all human beings by reducing suffering, reforming laws about punishment, etc. 人道主义的; 人道主义者的; 持人道主义者之观点的。 ~·ism /-ɪzəm; -ˌɪzəm/ n

hu·man·ity /hjuːˈmænətɪ; hjuˈmænətɪ/ n [U] 1 the human race; mankind: 人类: *crimes against ~.* 对人类有害的罪恶。 2 human nature. 人性。 3 quality of being humane(1): 仁爱; 仁慈: *treat people and animals with ~.* 以仁慈对待人和动物。 4 (pl) **the humanities,** the branches of learning concerned with ancient Greek and Latin culture: the Arts subjects. esp literature, history and philosophy. (复)古典文学(与古希腊及拉丁文化有关的学科); 人文学(尤指文学、历史和哲学)。

hu·man·ize /'hjuːmənaɪz; 'hjumənˌaɪz/ vt, vi [VP 6A,2A] make or become human or humane. 使成为人; 赋与人性; 变为有人性。

humble /'hʌmbl; 'hʌmbl/ adj (-r, -st) 1 having or showing a modest opinion of oneself, one's position, etc: 谦恭的; 谦逊的: *He is very ~ in the company of his* superiors. 他跟上级在一起时非常谦恭。 **eat ~ pie,** make an abject apology, humiliate oneself. 低声下气地道歉; 丢脸。 2 (of persons) low in rank or position; obscure and unimportant; (of things) poor; mean: (指人)微贱的; (指物)卑下的: *men of ~ birth;* 出身微贱的人; *a ~ home;* 简陋的家; *a ~ occupation.* 卑下的职业。 □ vt [VP 6A] make ~; make lower in rank or self-opinion: 使卑下; 贬抑: *~ one's enemies;* 挫敌人的锐气; *~ sb's pride;* 挫某人的气焰; *~ oneself before God.* 在上帝面前表示谦下。 **hum·bly** adv in a ~ way: 谦恭地; 微贱地: *beg most humbly for forgiveness;* 极谦恭地恳求饶恕; *humbly born,* of ~ parents. 出身微贱的。

hum·bug /'hʌmbʌg; 'hʌmˌbʌg/ n [C, U] (instance of) dishonest and deceiving behaviour or talk; [C] dishonest deceitful person. 欺诈的言行; 骗子。 2 (GB) hard boiled sweet flavoured with peppermint. (英)一种熬成的薄荷糖。 □ vt (-gg-) [VP6A, 14] deceive or trick (sb *into* or *out of* sth): 欺骗(骗某人做某事与 *into* 连用, 骗去某人之物与 *out of* 连用): *Don't try to ~ me!* 不要想骗我! □ int Nonsense! 胡说!

hum·dinger /,hʌmˈdɪŋə(r); ,hʌmˈdɪŋə/ n (US sl) sth marvellous or extraordinary. (美俚)奇妙的或特殊的事物。

hum·drum /'hʌmdrʌm; 'hʌmˌdrʌm/ adj dull; commonplace; monotonous: 单调的; 平凡的; 单调的: *live a ~ life;* 过单调的生活; *engaged in ~ tasks.* 从事乏味的工作。

hu·merus /'hjuːmərəs; 'hjumərəs/ n (anat) bone of the upper arm in man. (解剖)上膊骨; 肱骨。 ⇨ the illus at **skeleton.** 参看 skeleton 之插图。

hu·mid /'hjuːmɪd; 'hjumɪd/ adj (esp of air, climate) damp. (尤指空气或气候)潮湿的。 ~·ify /hjuːˈmɪdɪfaɪ; hjuˈmɪdəˌfaɪ/ vt (pt, pp -fied) make ~. 使潮湿。 ~·ity /hjuːˈmɪdɪtɪ; hjuˈmɪdətɪ/ n /U] (degree of)moisture (in the air). 潮湿; 湿气; (空气的)湿度。

hu·mili·ate /hjuːˈmɪlɪeɪt; hjuˈmɪlɪ,et/ vt [VP6A] cause to feel ashamed; put to shame; lower the dignity or self-respect of: 使蒙羞; 使丢脸; 屈辱; 使失面子: *a country that was ~d by defeat;* 因战败而受屈辱的国家; *humiliating peace terms.* 屈辱的和平条款。 **hu·mili·ation** /hjuːˌmɪlɪˈeɪʃn; hjuˌmɪlɪˈeʃən/ n [U] humiliating or being ~d; [C] instance of this: 蒙羞; 丢脸; 屈辱: *the humiliation of having to surrender.* 被迫投降之耻辱。

hu·mil·ity /hjuːˈmɪlɪtɪ; hjuˈmɪlətɪ/ n [U] humble condition or state of mind. 谦恭; 谦让; 谦卑。

hum·ming·bird /'hʌmɪŋbɜːd; 'hʌmɪŋˌbɜd/ n ⇨ **hum(1).**

hum·mock /'hʌmək; 'hʌmək/ n hillock; rising ground in a marsh; hump in an ice-field. 小丘; 沼泽中之小高地; 冰丘。

hu·mor·ist /'hjuːmərɪst; 'hjumərɪst/ humorous talker or writer; facetious person. 谈话幽默者; 幽默作家; 诙谐的人。

hu·mor·ous /'hjuːmərəs; 'hjumərəs/ adj having or showing a sense of humour; funny: 有幽默感的; 诙谐的: *a ~ writer,* eg Mark Twain. 幽默作家(例如马克吐温)。 *~ remarks.* 幽默语。 ~·ly adv

hu·mour (US = **hu·mor**) /'hjuːmə(r); 'hjumə/ n 1 [U] (capacity to cause or feel) amusement: 幽默; 诙谐; 幽默感: *a story full of ~;* 富于幽默的故事: *have no / not much / a good sense of ~.* 无(不大有, 很有)幽默感。 2 [U] person's state of mind (esp at a particular time); temper: 心情(尤指某一时间的); 心境: *in a good / bad ~;* 高兴(心情不佳); *not in the ~ for work,* not feeling inclined to work. 无心工作; *in no ~ to trifle;* 无心嬉玩; *when the ~ takes him,* when he feels so inclined. 在他高兴的时候。 **out of ~,** displeased; in a bad mood. 不高兴; 心情不好。 3 [C] (old use) one of four liquids (blood, phlegm, choler, melancholy) in the body, said to determine a person's mental and physical qualities. (旧用法)(血液, 粘液, 胆汁, 忧郁液四种)体液之一(据说能决定人之精神与身体情况)。 □ vt

[VP6A] give way to, gratify: 迁就; 使满足: *When a person is ill he may have to be ~ed*, his wishes may have to be granted even it they are senseless. 一个人生病时，别人都得迁就他。*Is it wise to always ~ a child*, give it everything it wants? 老是纵容小孩是明智的吗？

hump /hʌmp; hʌmp/ *n* **1** round lump, eg on a camel's back or (as a deformity) on a person's back. 圆形隆起物; 驼峰; 人背上之畸形隆肉。 ⇨ the illus at **large**. 参看 large 之插图。 '**~·back** *n* (person having a) back with a ~. 驼背; 驼背之人。 '**~-backed** *adj* having such a back. 驼背的; 伛偻的。 **2** *have / give sb the ~*, (sl) fit of depression or irritation. (俚) 感觉 (令某人) 心情抑郁或烦燥。 □ *vt* [VP6A, 15B] ~ (*up*), make ~-shaped; gather the shoulders into a ~: 使隆起成圆形; 弓起(背): *The cat ~ed (up) her back when she saw the dog.* 这猫看见那狗时便弓起她的背。

humph /hʌmf; hʌmf *or spontaneously as a grunt with lips closed and then puffed open/ int* used to show doubt or dissatisfaction. (表示怀疑或不满)哼!

hu·mus /'hju:məs; 'hjuməs/ *n* [U] earth formed by the decay of vegetable matter (dead leaves, plants). 腐植土; 腐植质。

Hun /hʌn; hʌn/ *n* member of an Asiatic race which ravaged Europe in the 4th and 5th cc. 匈奴人(亚洲一种族之一员, 曾于第四、五世纪蹂躏欧洲)。

hunch /hʌntʃ; hʌntʃ/ *n* **1** thick piece; hunk; hump. 厚块; 厚片; 圆形隆起物。 '**~-back(ed)**, = **humpback(ed)**. **2** *have a ~ that...*, (colloq) think it likely that.... (口)预感到…。 □ *vt* [VP6A, 15B] ~ (*up*), arch to form a hump. 弯曲而使之隆起; 拱起: *sitting at the table with his shoulders ~ed up.* 耸着肩坐在桌旁。

hun·dred /'hʌndrəd; 'hʌndrəd/ *n, adj* the number 100: 百; 百个: *two and five, 205;* 二百零五; *a few ~ people;* 数百人; *~s of people.* 数以百计的人。 ⇨ App **4.** 参看附录四。 '**~·weight** *n* (often written 常写为 **cwt**) 1/20 of one ton, 112 lb (in US 100 lb). 英担; 一吨之 1/20; 112 磅(在美国为 100 磅)。 ⇨ App **5.** 参看附录五。 '**~·fold**, (US) ~·'**fold** *adv one ~* times as much or as many. 百倍地。 ~**·th** /'hʌndrədθ; 'hʌndrədθ/ *n, adj* next after the 99th; one of a ~ equal parts. 第一百(的); 百分之一。

hung /hʌŋ; hʌŋ/ *pt, pp* of **hang**.

hun·ger /'hʌŋɡə(r); 'hʌŋɡɚ/ *n* **1** [U] need, desire for food: 饥饿: *die of ~;* 饿死; *satisfy one's ~.* 充饥。 *be / go on (a)* '**~-strike**, (eg of a prisoner) refuse to take food as a protest, in order to win release, etc. (指囚犯等)绝食抗议(以求释释等)。 '**~-march** *n* one undertaken, eg by unemployed workers, to call attention to sufferings, etc. 饥饿游行(例如失业者所作的)。 Hence. 由此产生, '**~-marcher** *n.* **2** (fig) any strong desire: (喻)欲望; 渴望: *a ~ for excitement / adventure.* 寻求刺激(冒险)的欲望。 □ *vi* [VP2A, 3A, 4C] ~ (*for / to do sth*), feel, suffer from, ~; have a strong desire: 饥饿; 渴望: *~ for news.* 渴望消息。

hun·gry /'hʌŋɡrɪ; 'hʌŋɡrɪ/ *adj* (**-ier, -iest**) feeling, showing signs of, causing, hunger: 感到饿的; 显出饥饿的; 引起饥饿的: *be / go ~* look. 那男孩显出饥饿的样子。 *Hay-making is ~ work.* 晒干草是易使人感到肚子饿的工作。 *The orphan child was ~ for affection.* 这孤儿渴望着爱。 **hun·grily** /'hʌŋɡrəlɪ; 'hʌŋɡrɪlɪ/ *adv*

hunk /hʌŋk; hʌŋk/ *n* thick piece cut off: (切下的) 厚片; 厚块: *a ~ of bread / cheese / meat.* 厚厚的一块面包(干酪, 肉)。

hun·kers /'hʌŋkəz; 'hʌŋkəz/ *n pl* (colloq) haunches, (口)臀部, esp 尤用于 *on one's ~*, in a squatting position. 蹲着。

hunt¹ /hʌnt; hʌnt/ *n a* the ~, **1** act of ~ing: 狩猎; 搜寻: *have a good ~;* 做一次满意的狩猎; *find sth after a long ~*, search. 经长期搜寻后发现某物。 **2** (esp in GB) group of persons who regularly ~ foxes and stags with

horses and hounds; the area in which they do this: (尤用于英国)经常骑马带着猎狗狩猎狐及鹿之狩猎队; 其狩猎地区: *The Quorn H~;* 库恩猎狐队; *a member of the ~.* 猎狐队中一员; 猎狐队队员。 '**~·ball,** ball organized by members of a ~. 猎人舞会。

hunt² /hʌnt; hʌnt/ *vi, vt* **1** [VP6A, 2A, C] go after (wild animals) for food or sport: 狩猎: ~ *big game;* 猎大动物; *go out ~ing.* 去打猎。 *Wolves ~ in packs.* 狼成群猎食。 ⇨ *shooting at* **shoot. 2** [VP2A, 3A, 15B] search for. 搜索; 寻找。 ~ *down*, pursue and find; bring to bay: 追寻而且捕获; 穷追: ~ *down a criminal / an escaped prisoner.* 捕获一罪犯(逃犯)。 ~ *for*, search for; try to find: 寻找; 寻求: ~ *for a lost book.* 寻找一本遗失的书。 ~ *out*, (try to) find by searching (sth that has been put away and forgotten): 寻出(藏置起来而被遗忘之物): ~ *out an old diary / a black tie that hasn't been needed for years.* 寻出一旧日记(数年未用的黑领带)。 ~ *up*, search for (sth hidden or difficult to find): 寻找(隐藏或难发现之物): ~ *up old records / references / quotations.* 搜寻旧记录(参考资料, 引用之文句)。 **3** [VP6A, 15A] drive or chase away: 驱逐: ~ *the neighbour's cats out of the garden.* 将邻家的猫逐出花园。 **4** [VP6A] (special uses in GB; foxhunting) follow the hounds through or in (a district): (英国之特殊用法; 指猎狐)在(一地区)狩猎: ~ *the county;* 在此郡中狩猎; employ (a horse) in ~ing: 骑(马)狩猎: ~ *one's horse all winter;* 整个冬季骑马狩猎; act as master or huntsman of (a pack of hounds): 带领(一队猎犬)狩猎: ~ *the hounds.* 带着猎犬狩猎。 ~**er** *n* **1** person who ~s: 狩猎的人; 猎人; 搜寻者: ~*ers of big game in Africa.* 狩猎非洲大猎物之猎人。 (Note that in GB a person who ~s foxes, etc on horseback or shoots grouse, pheasants, etc is not called a ~er. 'Do you hunt / shoot?' is preferred to 'Are you a ~er?') (注意: 在英国骑马猎狐等或以枪打猎松鸡、雉等之人, 不称为 hunter。 Do you hunt / shoot? 较 Are you a hunter? 为佳)。 **2** horse used in fox-hunting. 猎马(猎狐用者)。 **3** pocket watch with a metal cover protecting the glass face. 猎人表(有金属盖保护表面之怀表)。 ~**·ing** *n* [U] **1** the act of ~ing; (esp in GB) fox-~ing: 狩猎; (尤用于英国)猎狐: *He's fond of ~ing.* 他喜欢打猎。 **2** (attrib) (用作定语) *a '~ing-man;* 猎人; *a '~ing-horn.* 猎人用的号角。 '**~ing ground**, (fig) place where one may search for sth with hope of success. 猎场; (喻)可寻获某物之处。 ~**·ing 'pink**, shade of red worn by huntsmen. 猎人装常采用的红色。 ~**·ress** /'hʌntrɪs; 'hʌntrɪs/ *n* (liter) woman who ~s, eg the goddess Diana. (文)女猎人; 狩猎女神(月神)。

hunts·man /'hʌntsmən; 'hʌntsmən/ *n* (*pl* **-men**) **1** hunter(1). 狩猎之人; 猎人。 **2** man in charge of the hounds during a hunt(2). 猎狐时管理猎犬者。

hurdle /'hɜːdl; 'hɝdl/ *n* **1** (GB) movable upright oblong frame of wood, etc used for making temporary fences, eg for sheep pens. (英)作临时栅栏(如羊圈)用的长方形木架等; 临时围栏。 **2** light upright frame to be jumped over in a '~-race. 跳栏赛跑用的栏架。 **3** (fig) difficulty to be overcome. (喻)障碍。 □ *vt, vi* **1** [VP 15B] ~ *off*, fence with ~s. 围以临时围栏。 **2** [VP2A] jump over a ~; run in a ~-race. 跳栏; 跳栏赛跑。

hurdling

hur·dlor n person who makes ~s(1); person who runs in ~-races. 制临时围栏者; 跳栏赛跑者。

hurdy-gurdy /'hɜːdɪ gɜːdɪ; 'hɝdɪ,gɝdɪ/ n street piano or barrel organ, usu mounted on wheels, played by turning a handle. 摇弦琴(街头钢琴或筒风琴, 通常装于轮上, 演奏时旋转一柄)。

hurl /hɜːl; hɝl/ vt [VP6A, 15A, B] throw violently: 用力投掷; 猛投: ~ a spear at a tiger. 向一虎投掷矛。 They ~ed themselves at/upon the enemy and attacked them violently. 他们扑向敌人并猛烈攻击他们。 □ n violent throw. 用力的投掷。

hurl·ing /'hɜːlɪŋ; 'hɝlɪŋ/ n [U] Irish ball game resembling hockey. 类似曲棍球的爱尔兰球戏。

hurly-burly /'hɜːlɪ bɜːlɪ; 'hɝlɪ,bɝlɪ/ n [U] noisy commotion; uproar. 喧嚣; 骚动。

hur·rah /hʊ'rɑː; həˈrɔ/ (also **hur·ray** /hʊ'reɪ; hə're/) int expressing joy, welcome, approval, etc: 欢呼声(表示欣喜, 欢迎, 赞成等): H~ for the Queen! 女王万岁! Hip, hip, ~! 欢呼之声! vi shout ~; 欢呼。

hur·ri·cane /'hʌrɪkən US: '-keɪn; 'hɝɪ,ken/ n [C] violent windstorm, esp a W Indian cyclone. 飓风(尤指西印度群岛之旋风)。 '~ lamp/lantern nn kind with the light protected from the wind. 防风灯。

hurry /'hʌrɪ; 'hɝɪ/ n [U, C] eager haste; wish to get sth done quickly; (with neg, or in the interr) need for haste: 急忙; 匆忙; (用于否定或疑问句中) 匆忙的必要: Everything was ~ and excitement. 一切都是匆忙与兴奋。 Why all this ~? 为什么这样匆忙? Is there any/a ~, need for ~? 有急忙的必要吗? Don't start yet—there's no ~, there's plenty of time. 还不要动身一时同还早。 **in a** ~, (a) impatient; acting, anxious to act, quickly: 急忙的; 匆忙的; 慌忙的: He was in a ~ to leave. 他急着要离去。 In his ~ to catch the train, he left his luggage in the taxi. 他慌忙地去赶火车的时候, 把行李忘在计程车上了。 (b) (colloq) soon, willingly: (口)不久, 愿意地: I shan't ask that rude man to dinner again in a ~. 我不愿再请那个粗鲁的人吃饭了。 (c) (colloq) easily: (口)容易地: You won't find a better specimen than that in a ~. 你不容易找到比那更好的样品。 □ vt, vi (pt, pp **-ried**) [VP 6 A, 15A, B, 2 A, C] (cause to) move or do sth quickly or too quickly: (使)匆忙; 赶快; 慌张; 催促; 急赶: Don't ~; there's plenty of time. 不要忙, 时间还多哩。 It's no use ~ing her/trying to make her ~. 催她是无用的。 If we ~ the work, it may be spoiled. 要是我们赶工, 可能将工作弄糟。 He picked up his bag and hurried off. 他拿起提包匆匆离去。 More soldiers were hurried to the front line. 更多的军队被急急调往前线。 H~ up! Make haste. 赶快! H~ him up! Make him ~. 催他赶快! **hur·ried** adj done, etc in a ~: showing haste: 匆忙的; 急促的; 慌忙的: a hurried meal: 匆忙的一顿饭; write a few hurried lines. 草草写几行。 **hur·ried·ly** adv

hurt /hɜːt; hɝt/ vt, vi (pt, pp hurt) **1** [VP6A, B,2A] cause bodily injury or pain (to); damage: (使)受伤; (使)疼痛; 伤害: He ~ his back when he fell. 他跌倒时伤了背部。 He was more frightened than ~. 他受惊较受伤更重。 Did you ~ yourself? 你弄伤自己了吗? These shoes are too tight; they ~ (me). 这双鞋太紧, 使我的脚痛。 **2** [VP6A] pain a person, his feelings: 伤害(某人, 其感情); 使伤心: Their criticisms have ~ him deeply. 他们的批评使他非常伤心。 She was ~ to find that no one admired her performance. 她发现无人赞赏她的表演而感到伤心。 **3** [VP2A] suffer injury; come to harm; have a bad effect: 受损伤; 有不良影响: It won't ~ to postpone the matter for a few days. 将此事搁置几天并无妨碍。 □ n (U) (or with indef art) harm; injury: (或与不定冠词连用)伤害; 损害: I intended no ~ to his feelings. 我无意伤害他的感情。 It was a severe ~ to his pride. 那对他的自尊心是个严重的创伤。 ~·ful /-fl; -fəl/ adj causing ~: 造成伤害的; 有害的: ~ful to the health. 有害于健康。

hurtle /'hɜːtl; 'hɝtl/ vi [VP2C] rush or fly violently: 猛冲; 急飞: During the gale chimney-pots and rooftiles came hurtling down. 狂风期间, 烟囱顶管和屋顶瓦急急速地落下。

hus·band /'hʌzbənd; 'hʌzbənd/ n man to whom a woman is married. 丈夫。 □ vt [VP6A] use sparingly: 节省; 节用: ~ one's resources/strength. 节用资金(体力)。

hus·band·man /'hʌzbəndmən; 'hʌzbəndmən/ n (pl -men /-mən; -mən/) (old use) farmer. (旧用法)农民。 **hus·bandry** /'hʌzbəndrɪ; 'hʌzbəndrɪ/ n [U] farming; management: 耕作; 饲养; 管理: animal husbandry; 畜牧; 畜牧学; good/bad husbandry. 管理(不)得法。

hush /hʌʃ; hʌʃ/ vt, vi [VP2A, 15A, B] make or become silent or quiet: 使肃静; 使安静; 变为安静: H~! Be silent! 肃静! She ~ed the baby to sleep. 她使婴儿安睡入睡。 ~ sth up, prevent it from becoming public knowledge: 秘而不宣: She tried unsuccessfully to ~ up the fact that her husband was an ex-convict. 她企图隐瞒她丈夫以前犯过案的事实, 但未成功。 □ n a/the ~, silence; stillness: 肃静; 安静: in the ~ of night. 在夜的寂静中。 There was a sudden ~. 突然肃静下来。 '~-money n money paid to ~ sth up (usu sth scandalous or discreditable). (为防止某人泄露丑闻或不名之事等而予以贿赂之)缄口钱; 遮羞费。 ,~-'~ adj (colloq) (to be) kept very secret: (口)极秘密的; 需要高度保密的: ~ affair. 极秘密的事。

husk /hʌsk; hʌsk/ n (usu pl) dry outer covering of seeds, esp of grain: (通常用复数)外壳; 外皮(尤指谷类者): rice in the ~, with the ~s not removed; 稻谷; (fig) worthless outside part of anything. (喻)无价值的外部。 ⇨ the illus at **cereal**. 参看 cereal 之插图。 □ vt remove ~s from. 去~。

husky /'hʌskɪ; 'hʌskɪ/ adj (**-ier**, **-iest**) **1** (dry) like husks. 似谷壳的; 似谷壳般干燥的。 **2** (of a person, his voice) hoarse; with a dry and almost whispering voice: (指人及人声)嘶哑的; 嘎声的: a ~ voice/cough. 嘶哑之声(干咳)。 You sound ~ this morning. 今早你的声音有些哑。 **3** (colloq) big and strong: (口)高大强壮的: a fine ~ woman, excellent as a farmer's wife 高大强壮的好女子, 农民理想的妻子。 □ n **1** thick-coated dog of N American Eskimos. 北美洲爱斯基摩人的厚毛狗。 **2** = (3) person, 高大强壮的人。 **husk·ily** /-ɪlɪ; -əlɪ/ adv **huski·ness** n

hus·sar /hʊ'zɑː; hʊ'zɑr/ n soldier of a light cavalry regiment. 轻骑兵。

hussy /'hʌsɪ; 'hʌsɪ/ n (pl -sies) worthless woman; ill-mannered girl. 贱妇; 粗野的女子。

hus·tings /'hʌstɪŋz; 'hʌstɪŋz/ n pl the ~, proceedings (canvassing, speech-making, etc) leading up to a parliamentary election. 国会议员之竞选程序(游说; 讲演等)。

hustle /'hʌsl; 'hʌsl/ vt, vi [VP6A, 15A, 2A, C] **1** push or jostle roughly; (force sb to) hurry: 粗野地推; 匆忙; 催促: The police ~d the thief into their van. 警察将那窃贼粗野地推进囚车中。 I don't want to ~ you into a decision. 我不想催促你作决定。 **2** (esp US) (colloq) sell or obtain sth by energetic (esp deceitful) activity. (尤美)(口)以积极的(尤指狡诈的)行动卖出或得到某物。 **3** (US sl) engage in prostitution. (美)做娼妓。 □ n (sing only) quick and energetic activity: (仅用单数)迅速而有力的活动: The railway station was a scene of ~ and bustle. 火车站是喧嚣扰攘的场所。 **hus·tler** n person who ~s; (US sl) prostitute. 猛推者; 催促者; (美盼)娼妓。

hut /hʌt; hʌt/ n **1** small, roughly made house or shelter: 简陋的小屋: Alpine huts, for the use of mountain climbers. 阿尔卑斯山上的小屋.(为爬山者所设)。 **2** temporary wooden building for soldiers. 临时的木造营房。 **'hut·ment** n encampment of huts. 临时营区; 临时营房。 **hut·ted** adj: hutted camp, with huts, not tents (for troops) etc) 临时营房(有木造营房, 而非帐篷, 供军

队等使用）。

hutch /hʌtʃ; hʌtʃ/ n box or cage with a front of wire netting, esp one used for rabbits. 正面用铁丝网网起的箱或笼；(尤指)兔笼.

hya·cinth /'haɪəsɪnθ; 'haɪə,sɪnθ/ n plant growing from a bulb; its sweet-smelling flowers. 风信子；风信子之花.

'water ~, wild plant that grows in floating masses on rivers, lakes, etc and may hinder navigation. 一种大批漂浮于河流、湖泊等上并可能妨碍航行之野生植物.

hy·aena /haɪ'iːnə; haɪ'inə/ ⇨ **hyena.**

hy·brid /'haɪbrɪd; 'haɪbrɪd/ n, adj (animal, plant, etc) from parents of different species or varieties: 杂种的(动植物等)；杂种；混合之物；混合的: A mule is a ~ animal. 骡是杂种动物. 'Cablegram' is a ~; half the word is Latin and half is Greek. cablegram 一词是混合语,半为拉丁语,半为希腊语。 **~·ize** /-aɪz; -,aɪz/ vt, vi [VP6A, 2A] (cause to) produce ~s; interbreed. (使)产生杂种；杂交繁殖.

hy·dra /'haɪdrə; 'haɪdrə/ n (GK myth) great sea serpent with many heads that grew again if cut off. (希神)海蛇怪(生有许多头,斩去后仍会生出).

hy·drangea /haɪ'dreɪndʒə; haɪ'drendʒə/ n shrub with large round heads of white. blue or pink flowers. 八仙花属；紫阳花(有白、蓝或粉红色大花球).

hy·drant /'haɪdrənt; 'haɪdrənt/ n pipe from a water-main (esp in a street) with a nozzle to which a hose can be attached for street-cleaning, putting out fires, etc. (尤指街上的)给水栓；消防栓.

hy·drate /'haɪdreɪt; 'haɪdret/ n chemical compound of water with another substance. 水合物；水化物. □ vt, vi combine with water to make a ~; become a ~. 使与水结合而成水化物；成为水化物.

hy·drau·lic /haɪ'drɔːlɪk; haɪ'drɔlɪk/ adj of water moving through pipes; worked by the pressure of a fluid, esp water: 通过水管流动之水的；用液体(特指水)的压力控制的；水力的；水压的；用水发动的: a ~ lift; 水力升降机; ~ brakes. in which the braking force is transmitted by compressed fluid; 水力制动器(制动之力量由压缩之液体传送)；hardening under water: 在水中变硬的；水硬的: ~ cement. 水硬水泥. **hy·drau·lics** n pl science of using water to produce power. 水力学.

hy·dro·car·bon /,haɪdrə'kɑːbən; ,haɪdro'karbən/ n [C] substance formed of hydrogen and carbon, eg benzene, paraffin, coal-gas. 烃, 碳化氢 (例如苯, 石蜡, 煤气).

hy·dro·chloric / ,haɪdrə'klɒrɪk US: -'klɔːr-; ,haɪdrə'klɔrɪk/ adj: ~ acid. acid (HCl) containing hydrogen and chlorine. 氢氯酸；盐酸 (HCl).

hy·dro·elec·tric /'haɪdrəʊɪ'lektrɪk, ,haɪdro·ɪ'lektrɪk/ adj of electricity produced by water-power. 水力发电的.

hy·dro·foil /'haɪdrəfɔɪl; 'haɪdro,fɔɪl/ n boat equipped with plates or fins which, when the boat is in motion, raise the hull out of the water. 水翼船.

hy·dro·gen /'haɪdrədʒən; 'haɪdrədʒən/ n gas (symbol H) without colour, taste or smell, that combines with oxygen to form water. 氢(无色, 无味, 无臭的气体, 符号为H, 与氧化合变成水). '~ bomb (also 亦作 fusion bomb) variety of atomic bomb, ⇨ **atomic.** 氢弹, ~ pe'roxide n solution of peroxide of ~. (H_2O_2), used as an antiseptic and bleaching agent. 过氧化氢；双氧水 (H_2O_2, 用作防腐剂或杀菌剂以及漂白剂).

hy·drop·athy /haɪ'drɒpəθɪ; haɪ'drɑpəθɪ/ n [U] use of water (internally and externally) in the treatment of disease. 水疗法. **hy·dro·pathic** /,haɪdrə'pæθɪk; ,haɪdrə'pæθɪk/ adj of ~. 水疗法的.

hy·dro·pho·bia /,haɪdrə'fəʊbɪə; ,haɪdrə'fobɪə/ n [U] rabies; disease marked by strong contractions of the muscles of the throat and consequent inability to drink water. 狂犬病；恐水症.

hy·dro·plane /'haɪdrəpleɪn; 'haɪdrə,plen/ n hydrofoil; motor-boat with a flat bottom, able to skim very fast over the surface; (old name for) seaplane. 水翼船；水上滑行艇；(旧称)水上飞机.

hy·dro·pon·ics /,haɪdrə'pɒnɪks; ,haɪdrə'pɑnɪks/ n pl art of growing plants without soil, in water to which necessary chemical food is supplied. 水栽法(不用土壤, 而用水加以化学养料培植植物的方法).

hy·ena, hy·aena /haɪ'iːnə; haɪ'inə/ n flesh-eating wild animal, like a wolf, with a laughing cry. 鬣狗；土狼. ⇨ the illus at large. 参看 large 之插图.

hy·giene /'haɪdʒiːn; 'haɪdʒin/ n [U] science of, rules for, healthy living; cleanliness. 卫生学；卫生. **hygienic** /haɪ'dʒiːnɪk US: ,haɪdʒɪ'enɪk; ,haɪdʒɪ'enɪk/ adj of ~; likely to promote health; free from disease germs: 卫生学的；保健的；卫生的: hygienic conditions. 卫生环境. **hy·gieni·cally** /-klɪ; -klɪ/ adv

hy·men /'haɪmen; 'haɪmən/ n 1 **H~,** Greek god of marriage. 海门(希腊神话中司婚姻之神). **2** (anat) fold of tissue partly closing the vagina of a virgin girl or woman. (解剖)处女膜.

hymn /hɪm; hɪm/ n song of praise to God, esp one for use in a religious service. 赞美诗；圣歌. □ vt praise (God) in ~s; express (praise) in ~s. 唱圣歌赞美(上帝)；以圣歌表示(赞美). **hym·nal** /'hɪmnəl; 'hɪmnəl/ n book of ~s. 赞美诗集.

hy·per·bola /haɪ'pɜːbələ; haɪ'pɜbələ/n curve produced when a cone is cut by a plane passing anywhere except through its point. 双曲线.

hy·per·bole /haɪ'pɜːbəlɪ; haɪ'pɜbə,li/ n [U] (use of) exaggerated statement(s) made for effect and not intended to be taken literally; [C] instance of this, eg waves as high as Qomolangma. 夸张法；夸张的叙述(例如, 象珠穆朗玛峰一般高的海浪).

hy·per·criti·cal /,haɪpə'krɪtɪkl; ,haɪpə'krɪtɪkl/ adj too critical, esp of small faults. 吹毛求疵的；苛评的.

hy·per·market /'haɪpəmɑːkɪt; 'haɪpə,markɪt/ n immense supermarket occupying an extensive area, outside a town, with a large car park, selling all varieties of goods. 大型超级市场(在市镇之外, 占地甚广, 有大停车场, 销售各种货品).

hy·phen /'haɪfn; 'haɪfən/ n the mark (-) used to join two words together (as in Anglo-French), or to show that a word has been divided between the end of one line and the beginning of another 连字号；短横；短划(用以连接一复合词. 如 Anglo-French, 或在转行时用以划分一词的音节). ⇨ **App 9.** 参看附录九. □ vt join (words) with a ~; write (a compound word) with ~. 以连字号连接 (字)；用连字号连接 (复合词). **~·ate** /-eɪt; -,et /vt = ~.

hyp·no·sis /hɪp'nəʊsɪs; hɪp'nosɪs/ n (pl -ses /-siːz; -siz/) [U, C] state like deep sleep in which a person's acts may be controlled by another person. 催眠状态. **hyp·notic** /hɪp'nɒtɪk; hɪp'nɑtɪk/ adj of ~ in a hypnotic state 在催眠状态中. **hyp·not·ism** /'hɪpnətɪzəm; 'hɪpnə,tɪzəm/ n [U] artificial production of ~. 催眠；催眠术. **hyp·not·ize** /'hɪpnətaɪz; 'hɪpnə,taɪz/ vt [VP 6A] produce ~ in (sb) 施催眠术于(某人). **hyp·not·ist** /'hɪpnətɪst; 'hɪpnətɪst/ n person able to produce ~. 能施催眠术者.

hypo /'haɪpəʊ; 'haɪpo/ n (colloq abbr of) sodium thiosulphate ($Na_2S_2O_3$), used in photography as a fixing agent. (口, sodium thiosulphate 之略)低亚硫酸钠 ($Na_2S_2O_3$. 在摄影中用作定影剂).

hy·po·chon·dria /,haɪpə'kɒndrɪə; ,haɪpə'kandrɪə/ n [U] state of mental depression either without apparent cause or due to unnecessary anxiety about one's health. 疑病(症)；忧郁症. **hy·po·chon·driac** /,haɪpə'kɒndrɪæk; ,haɪpə'kandrɪ,æk/ adj of, affected by, ~. 疑病症的；患疑病症的. □ n person who suffers from ~. 疑病症患者.

hy·poc·risy /hɪ'pɒkrəsɪ; hɪ'pɑkrəsɪ/ n (pl -sies) [C, U] (instance of) falsely making oneself appear to be virtuous or good. 伪善；虚伪. **hyp·ocrite**/ 'hɪpəkrɪt;

'hɪpəˌkrɪt / n person guilty of ~. 伪君子; 伪善者。 **hy·po·criti·cal** /ˌhɪpə'krɪtɪkl/; ˌhɪpə'krɪtɪkl/ / adj of ~ or a hypocrite. 伪善的; 伪君子的; 虚伪的。 **hy·po·criti·cally** /-klɪ; -klɪ/ adv

hy·po·der·mic /ˌhaɪpə'dɜːmɪk; ˌhaɪpə'dɝmɪk/ adj (of drugs, etc) injected beneath the skin: (指药物等)皮下注射的: ~ injections; 皮下注射; a ~ needle/syringe, used for giving such injections. 皮下注射针(器)。 ⇨ the illus at **syringe**. 参看 syringe 之插图。 □ n ~ injection or syringe. 皮下注射; 皮下注射器。

hy·pot·en·use /haɪ'pɒtənjuːz US: -tnuːs; haɪ'pɑtnˌus/ n side of a right-angled triangle opposite the right angle. (直角三角形之)斜边; 弦。

hy·poth·ecate /haɪ'pɒθɪkeɪt; haɪ'pɒθəˌket / vt (legal) pledge; mortgage. (法律)抵押; 质押。

hy·poth·esis /haɪ'pɒθəsɪs; haɪ'pɑθəsɪs/ n (pl **-ses** /-siːz; -ˌsiz /) idea, suggestion, put forward as a starting-point for reasoning or explanation. 假设; 假说。

hy·po·theti·cal /ˌhaɪpə'θetɪkl; ˌhaɪpə'θetɪkl/ adj of, based on, a ~; not based on certain knowledge. 假说的; 假定的; 臆度的。

hys·sop /'hɪsəp; 'hɪsəp/ n strong-smelling plant formerly used in medicine. 海索草; 牛膝草(一种气味浓烈的植物, 昔时用作药品)。

hys·teria /hɪ'stɪərɪə; hɪs'tɪrɪə/ n [U] 1 disturbance of the nervous system, with outbursts of emotion, often uncontrollable. 癔病; 歇斯底里症(一种精神系经病, 患者情绪无常, 常不能自制)。 2 senseless, uncontrolled excitement, eg in a crowd at a football match. 无意义的不可抑制的兴奋(例如群众观看足球赛时)。 **hys·teri·cal** /hɪ'sterɪkl; hɪs'terɪkl/ adj caused by, suffering from, ~: 歇斯底里症引起的; 患歇斯底里症的: hysterical laughter; 狂笑; an hysterical outburst of fury. 勃然大怒。 **hys·teri·cally** /-klɪ; -klɪ/ adv **hys·ter·ics** /hɪ'sterɪks; hɪs'terɪks/ n pl attack of ~: 歇斯底里症的发作: go into hysterics, become hysterical. 发歇斯底里症。

I i

I[1] **i** /aɪ; aɪ/ (pl **I's i's** /aɪz; aɪz/), the ninth letter of the English alphabet; symbol for Roman numeral 1, ⇨ **App 4**. 英文字母之第九个字母; 罗马数字的1(参看附录四)。

I[2] /aɪ; aɪ/ pers pron used by a speaker or writer to refer to himself. 我(说话者或作者指自己)。 Cf 参较 me, object form, and we, us, plural forms. 宾格为 me, 复数为 we 及 us。

iamb /'aɪæm; 'aɪæmb/ n = iambus.

iam·bus /aɪ'æmbəs; aɪ'æmbəs/ n (pl ~es or **-bi** /-baɪ; -baɪ/) (prosody) metrical foot of one unaccented and one accented syllable eg a'lone. (韵律)抑扬格(即一轻音节及一重音节构成的音步, 例如 a'lone)。 **iam·bic** /aɪ'æmbɪk; aɪ'æmbɪk/ adj of, containing, ~es: 抑扬格的; 含有抑扬格的: iambic feet, 抑扬格音步, eg 例如 I 'come/from 'haunts/of 'coot/and 'fern. □ n pl **iam·bics** iambic verse. 抑扬格的诗。

ibex /'aɪbeks; 'aɪbeks/ n wild goat (of the Alps and Pyrenees) with large curved horns. (阿尔卑斯山和比利牛斯山之)生有大弯角的野山羊。

ibi·dem /'ɪbɪdem; ɪ'baɪdem/ adv (abbr 略作 ibid)(Lat) in the same book, chapter, etc (previously quoted). (拉)在(前所引用之)同一书、章等中; 出处同上。

ibis /'aɪbɪs; 'aɪbɪs/ n large wading bird (like a stork or heron) found in lakes and swamps in warm climates. 鹮; 朱鹭(大的涉禽, 似鹳或苍鹭, 见于温带之湖泊与沼泽中)。

ice[1] /aɪs; aɪs/ n 1 [U] frozen water; water made solid by cold: 冰: Is the ice thick enough for skating? 这冰的厚度可以溜冰吗? **break the ice**, (fig) get people on friendly terms; overcome formality or reserve; take the first steps in a delicate matter. (喻)使人们融洽; 打破拘束或矜持; 着手做一须慎重处理之事。 **cut no ice (with sb)**, have little or no effect or influence (on him), 对(某人)无作用, 无影响力。 **keep sth on ice**, in a refrigerator, (fig) reserve for later use. 贮藏于电冰箱中; (喻)保留供日后使用。 **be skating on thin ice**, (fig) in a dangerous or delicate situation. (喻)如履薄冰; 在危险或须慎重将事的境况中。 **dry ice**, ⇨ **dry**[1](12). 2 [C] frozen sweet of various kinds: 冰冻的各种甜食: water-ice; 冰糕; 果汁棒; cream ices; 冰淇淋; two strawberry ices. 两份草莓冰。 ⇨ **ice-cream** below. 参看下列之 ice-cream. 3 (compounds) (复合词) **'Ice Age** n time when much of the N hemisphere was covered with glaciers; glacial period. 冰河时代。 **'ice-axe** n axe used by mountain climbers for cutting steps in ice. (爬山者所用之)破冰斧。 **'ice·berg** n mass of ice (broken off a

glacier) moving in the sea; (fig) unemotional person: 冰山(漂浮于海上之大块冰层, 为水中的断离部份); (喻)冷淡的人: his iceberg of a wife. 他那冷冰冰的妻子。 **'ice·boat** n boat fitted with runners and sails for travelling

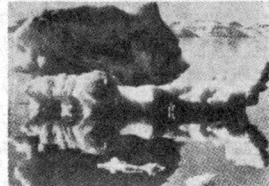
an iceberg

icicles

on a frozen lake or sea. 冰上滑行的船。 **'ice·bound** adj (of harbours, etc) obstructed by ice. (指海口等)冰封的。 **'ice·box** n box in which ice is used to keep food cool; (US)refrigerator. 冰箱; (美)电冰箱。 **'ice·breaker** n ship with strong curved bows used for breaking a passage through ice. 破冰船。 **'ice·cap** n permanent covering of ice sloping down on all sides from a high centre. 冰帽; 冰台 (永积的冰层, 自中心向各方倾斜)。 **ice-'cream** n [C, U] (portion of) cream or custard (or various modern substitutes), sweetened, and flavoured and frozen. (一份)冰淇淋。 **'ice-cube** n cube of ice made in an icetray in a refrigerator. (冰箱内结冰盘中制成的)冰块。 **'ice-fall** n steep part of a glacier, like a frozen waterfall. 冰布(冰河之陡峭部分, 似结冰之瀑布)。 **'ice-field** n large expanse of (esp marine) ice in the Polar regions. 两极地区之(尤指海上)冰原。 **'ice-floe** /-fləʊ; -ˌflo/ n large sheet of floating ice. 大浮冰。 **'ice-free** adj (of a port or harbour) free from ice. (指港口)不冻的。 ⇨ **icebound** above. 参看上列之 icebound。 **'ice hockey**, ⇨ **hockey**. **'ice-house** n building often partly or wholly underground for storing ice in winter for use in summer. 储冰库(常是部分或整个建于地下, 在冬季把冰以备夏季之用)。 **ice-'lolly** n flavoured ice on a stick. 冰棒。 **'ice-man** /-mæn; -ˌmæn/ n (pl **-men**) (US) man who retails and delivers ice (for use in iceboxes, etc). (美)冰商; 送冰人。 **'ice-pack** n (a) stretch of sea covered with broken ice that has drifted into masses. (海中的)冰积块。 (b) bag of broken ice used as an application eg to the head, for fever. 冰袋 (作为敷用物, 例如发烧时置于头上者)。 **'ice-pick** n tool

for breaking ice. (将冰击碎之)冰锄。 **'ice·rink** *n* indoor skating-rink with a floor of artificial ice. 用人造冰作冰池之室内溜冰场。 **'ice-show** *n* variety entertainment in which the performers are on ice-skates (on a floor of artificial ice). (在人造冰上之)溜冰表演。 **'ice-skate** *n* thin metal runner or blade on a boot for skating on ice. 溜冰鞋底之滑刀或冰刀。 □ *vi* skate on ice. 溜冰。 ⇨ the illus at **skate**. 参看 skate 之插图。 **'ice-tray** *n* one kept in the deep-freeze compartment of a refrigerator, for making cubes of ice. 冰箱内制冰块的盘。

ice² /aɪs; aɪs/ *vt, vi* 1 [VP6A] make very cold: 使冰冷: *ice a bottle of beer;* 冰一瓶啤酒; *iced water.* 冰水。 2 [VP2C, 15B] ~ *over/up,* cover, become covered, with a coating of ice: 用冰层覆盖; 覆有冰层: *The pond (was) iced over.* 池水表面结了冰。 *The wings of the aircraft had iced up.* 飞机的两翼覆有冰。 3 [VP6A] cover (a cake) with sugar icing. 加糖霜于(糕)上。 ⇨ **icing.**

ich·neu·mon /ɪkˈnjuːmən US: ·ˈnuː-; ɪkˈnjumən/ *n* 1 small brown weasel-like animal noted for destroying crocodiles' eggs. 猫鼬(棕色小鼬小动物,善于破坏鳄卵)。 2 (also *~-fly*) insect which lays its eggs in or on the larva of another insect. 姬蜂(产卵于其他昆虫之幼虫体上或体内的一种昆虫)。

icicle /ˈaɪsɪkl; ˈaɪsɪkl/ *n* pointed piece of ice formed by the freezing of dripping water. 冰柱。

icing /ˈaɪsɪŋ; ˈaɪsɪŋ/ *n* [U] 1 mixture of sugar, white of egg, flavouring, etc for covering cake(s). (糖, 蛋白, 香料等混合覆于糕点上的) 糖衣; 糖霜。 2 formation of ice on the wings of aircraft. 积冰(机翼上的结冰现象)。

icon /ˈaɪkɒn; ˈaɪkɑn/ *n* (in the Eastern Church) painting, carving or mosaic of a sacred person, itself regarded as sacred. (东方正教中被视为神圣物的)圣象。

icons

icono·clast /aɪˈkɒnəklæst; aɪˈkɑnəˌklæst/ *n* person who took part in the movement against the use of images in religious worship in the churches of Eastern Europe in the 8th and 9th cc (also applied to Puritans in England, 17th c); (fig) person who attacks popular beliefs or established customs which he thinks mistaken or unwise. (第八、九世纪东欧教会中)反对崇拜偶像者(亦指十七世纪英国的清教徒); (喻)抨击一般信仰与既定习俗者。

icy /ˈaɪsɪ; ˈaɪsɪ/ *adj* (-ier, -iest) very cold, like ice: 极冷的;冰冷的: *icy winds;* 寒风; covered with ice: 覆着冰的: *icy roads;* 覆盖着冰的道路; (fig) (喻) *an icy welcome/manner.* 冷淡的欢迎(态度)。 **icily** /ˈaɪsɪlɪ; ˈaɪsɪlɪ/ *adv* (lit, fig) in an icy manner. (字面,喻)冰冷地;冷冰冰地。

id /ɪd; ɪd/ *n* (psych) **(the)** ~, person's unconscious instincts and impulses. (心理)本我(人类不知觉的本能与冲动)。

I'd /aɪd; aɪd/ = I had; I would.

idea /aɪˈdɪə; aɪˈdie/ *n* 1 thought; picture in the mind: 思想;概念: *This book gives you a good* ~ *of life in ancient Greece.* 这本书使你对于古希腊的生活得到清楚的概念。 2 plan; scheme; design; purpose: 计划;主意;计策; 目的: *That man is full of new* ~*s.* 那人有很多新主意。 3 opinion: 意见: *You shouldn't force your* ~*s on*

other people. 你不应该强迫别人听从你的意见。 4 vague belief; fancy; feeling that sth is probable: 模糊的想法;想象;认为某事可能发生的感觉: *I have an* ~ *that she will be late.* 我认为她会迟到。 5 conception: 观念: *What* ~ *can a man who is blind from birth have of colour?* 生来即盲的人对颜色会有何观念? *Picnicking is not my* ~ *of pleasure.* 我觉得野餐没有什么乐趣。 *You can have no* ~ *(of) how anxious we have been.* 你不知道我们有多么着急。 **put** ~*s into sb's head,** give him expectations that are not likely to be realized. 使存幻想; 使抱空想。 6 (in exclamations): (用于感叹句): *The* ~ *of such a thing! What an* ~! (used to suggest that what has been suggested is unrealistic, outrageous, etc). (用以表示所建议者不切实际,骇人听闻等)竟然有这样的念头! 多么奇怪的念头啊! 7 way of thinking: 想法: *the young* ~, the child's mind. 孩子的想法。

ideal /aɪˈdɪəl; aɪˈdiəl/ *adj* 1 satisfying one's idea of what is perfect: 理想的; 完美的: ~ *weather for a holiday.* 理想的假日天气。 2 (contrasted with *real*) existing only in the imagination or as an idea; not likely to be achieved: (与 real 相对)想象中的;理想中的: ~ *happiness;* 想象中的快乐; ~ *plans for reforming the world.* 改造世界的理想中的计划。 □ *n* [C] idea, example, looked upon as perfect: 理想;理想的东西: *the high* ~*s of the Christian religion.* 基督教的崇高的理想。 *She's looking for a husband but hasn't found her* ~ *yet.* 她正在找丈夫, 但尚未找到一位理想的。 **~ly** /aɪˈdɪəlɪ; aɪˈdiəlɪ/ *adv*

ideal·ism /aɪˈdɪəlɪzəm; aɪˈdiəlˌɪzəm/ *n* [U] 1 living according to, being guided by, one's ideals. 根据个人理想的生活。 2 (in art) (opposite of *realism*) imaginative treatment, showing beauty and perfection even if this means being untrue to facts. (艺术) (为 realism 之反义词)理想主义; 想象的创作手法(表现完美的境界而不同是否与事实相符)。 3 (in philosophy) system of thought in which ideas are believed to be the only real things or the only things of which we can know anything. (哲学)观念论;唯心论。 **ideal·ist** /-ɪst; -ɪst/ *n* person who believes in ~. 理想主义者; 唯心论者。 **ideal·istic** /aɪˌdɪəlˈɪstɪk; aɪˌdiəlˈɪstɪk/ *adj* of idealists and idealism. 理想主义(者)的;唯心论(者)的。

ideal·ize /aɪˈdɪəlaɪz; aɪˈdiəlˌaɪz/ *vt* [VP6A] see, think of, as perfect: 使合于理想;视为理想;理想化: *Some biographers* ~ *their subjects.* 有些传记作家将他们的写作对象理想化了。 **ideal·iz·ation** /aɪˌdɪəlaɪˈzeɪʃn US: -lɪˈz-; aɪˌdiəloˈzeʃən/ *n*

idem /ˈaɪdem; ˈaɪdɛm/ *n, adj* (Lat) (by) the same author, etc; the same word, book, authority. etc (already mentioned): (拉) 同作者; 同一词、书、根据等; 同上;同前。

ident·ical /aɪˈdentɪkl; aɪˈdɛntɪkl/ *adj* ~ **(to/with),** 1 the same: 同一的: *This knife is* ~ *to the one with which the murder was committed.* 这便是谋杀所用的那把刀子。 2 exactly alike; agreeing in every way: 完全相同的;完全一样的: *The fingerprints of no two persons are* ~. 没有两个人的指纹是完全相同的。 *Our views of what should be done are* ~. 我们对于应该采取的行动持完全相同的看法。 *40 inches is* ~ *with 3 feet 4 inches.* 四十英寸和三英尺四英寸是相等的。 3 ~ **'twins,** twins from one single fertilized ovum. 同卵孪生; 同卵双胎。 **~ly** /-klɪ; -klɪ/ *adv*

ident·ify /aɪˈdentɪfaɪ; aɪˈdɛntəˌfaɪ/ *vt, vi* (pt, pp **-fied**) [VP6A, 14, 3A] 1 say, show, prove, who or what sb or sth is; establish the identity of: 认出; 认明; 鉴定: *Could you* ~ *your umbrella among a hundred others?* 你能在一百把你的伞叩(中)认出来吗? *His accent was difficult to* ~. 他的口音甚难辨出是什么地方的。 2 ~ *sth with sth,* treat (sth) as identical (with); equate (one thing with another). 认为同一; 视(甲与乙)为相等。 3 ~ *(oneself) with sb/sth,* give support to, be associated with; feel close to: 支持; 与…认同; 觉得与…接近。 *He refused to* ~ *himself/become identified with the new*

political party. 他拒绝支持该一新政党。 **identi·fi·ca·tion** /aɪˌdentɪfɪˈkeɪʃn; aɪˌdɛntəfəˈkeʃən/ n [U] ~ing or being identified: 认出; 认明; 鉴定; 视为同一: *the identification of persons killed in a road accident, finding out who they are.* 查明路上车祸死者的姓名和身份。

iden·ti·kit /aɪˈdentɪkɪt; aɪˈdɛntɪkɪt/ n composite drawing of the face of an unidentified person (esp a suspected criminal), from features recalled by those who saw him. 根据目击者所忆及的面部特征对身份不明之人(尤指嫌疑犯)所作之面部画像。

ident·ity /aɪˈdentətɪ; aɪˈdɛntətɪ/ n (pl -ties) 1 [U] state of being identical; absolute sameness; exact likeness. 同一; 绝对相同; 完全相同。 2 [C,U] who sb is; what sth is: 身份; 本身; 本体: *There is no clue to the ~ of the thief,* nothing to show who he is. 没有线索查明这窃贼是谁。 *The cheque will be cashed upon proof of ~.* 这支票于验明取款人身份后即可兑现。 *He was arrested because of mistaken ~.* 他因身份被误认而被捕。'~ **card/disc/ certificate,** card, etc that gives proof of one's ~. 身份证。

ideo·gram /ˈɪdɪəɡræm; ˈɪdɪəˌɡræm/, **ideo·graph** /ˈɪdɪəɡrɑːf US: -ɡræf; ˈɪdɪəˌɡræf/ nn written or printed character, used in making up words, that symbolizes the idea of a thing without indicating the sounds that make up the word, eg as used in Chinese writing. 表意文字(如中文)。 **ideo·graphic** /ˌɪdɪəˈɡræfɪk; ˌɪdɪəˈɡræfɪk/ adj

ideograms

ideol·ogy /ˌaɪdɪˈɒlədʒɪ; ˌaɪdɪˈɑlədʒɪ/ n (pl -gies) 1 [C] manner of thinking, ideas, characteristic of a person, group, etc, esp as forming the basis of an economic or political system: (代表个人,团体等,尤指形成一经济或政治制度基础的)思想方式; 意识形态。 2 [U] unproductive thought. 空想。 **ideo·logi·cal** /ˌaɪdɪəˈlɒdʒɪkl; ˌaɪdɪˈlɑdʒɪkəl/ adj **ideo·logi·cally** /-klɪ; -klɪ/ adv

ides /aɪdz; aɪdz/ n pl (in the calendar of ancient Rome) the 15th of March, May, July, Oct or the 13th of other months. (古罗马历)三月,五月,七月,十月的十五日; 其他月份的十三日。

id est /ˌɪd ˈest; ˌɪd ˈɛst/ (abbr 略作 **ie**) (Lat) that is to say. (拉)即。

di·ocy /ˈɪdɪəsɪ; ˈɪdɪəsɪ/ n 1 [U] state of being an idiot; extreme stupidity. 白痴; 极愚蠢。 2 [C] (pl -cies) extremely stupid act, remark, etc. 极愚蠢的行为; 言语等。

idio·lect /ˈɪdɪəlekt; ˈɪdɪəˌlɛkt/ n the total of a person's language that he knows and uses at any stage of his language development:—个人在其语言发展过程的任何阶段所知晓及使用的语言的总和; 个人习语; 个人语汇: *Is the word 'psychosis' part of your~?* 你知道 psychosis 这个词吗?

id·iom /ˈɪdɪəm; ˈɪdɪəm/ n 1 language of a people or country; specific character of this, eg one peculiar to a country, district, group of people, or to one individual:—民族或国家的语言; (国家,地区,团体或个人的)特殊语法: *the French~;* 法国人的语法; *the~ of the New England countryside,* ie the kind of English used by country people there; 新英格兰乡间的方言; *Shakespeare's ~,* the method of expression peculiar to him. 莎士比亚的语法。 2 [C] phrase or sentence whose meaning is not obvious through knowledge of the individual meanings of the constituent words but must be learnt as a whole, eg 成语; 惯用语。 eg *give way, in order to, be put to it.* **idio·matic** /ˌɪdɪəˈmætɪk; ˌɪdɪəˈmætɪk/ adj 1 in accordance with the ~s(2) of a language, dialect, etc:

合于某一语言, 方言等之语法的: *speak ~atic English.* 说合乎习惯用法的英语。 2 full of ~s(2): 多成语的: *an ~atic language.* 多成语的语言。 **idi·om·ati·cally** /ˌɪdɪˈmætɪklɪ; ˌɪdɪˈmætɪklɪ/ adv

idio·syn·crasy /ˌɪdɪəˈsɪŋkrəsɪ; ˌɪdɪəˈsɪŋkrəsɪ/ n (pl -sies) [C] way of thinking or behaving that is peculiar to a person; personal mannerism. 个人的癖性; 个人特有的气质; personal mannerism. 个人的癖性; 个人特有的气质。 **idio·syn·cratic** /ˌɪdɪəsɪnˈkrætɪk; ˌɪdɪəsɪnˈkrætɪk/ adj

id·iot /ˈɪdɪət; ˈɪdɪət/ n 1 person so weak-minded that he is incapable of rational conduct. 白痴; 下愚者。 2 (colloq) fool: (口)愚蠢之人: *I've left my suitcase in the train. What an~ I am!* '我把提箱忘在火车上了,我真是个糊涂虫!' **idi·otic** /ˌɪdɪˈɒtɪk; ˌɪdɪˈɑtɪk/ adj stupid. 愚蠢的。 **~i·cally** /-klɪ; -klɪ/ adv

idle /ˈaɪdl; ˈaɪdḷ/ adj (-r, -st) 1 doing no work; not employed; not active or in use; (of time) not spent in doing something: 不做事的; 无工作的; 停顿的; 未用的; (指时间)空闲的: *When men cannot find employment they are~* (though not necessarily lazy). 当人们找不到工作时,他们是闲着的(并不一定是懒惰的)。*During the business depression half the machines in the factory were~.* 在商业萧条的期间,这工厂里的机器半数是停顿的。*We spent many~ hours during the holidays.* 假期内我们过了许多悠闲的时刻。 2 (of persons) not willing to work; lazy (which is the commoner word for this sense): (指人)不愿工作的; 懒惰的 (lazy 一词较常用): *an~, worthless girl.* 懒惰无用的女孩。 3 useless; worthless: 无用的; 无价值的: *Don't listen to~ gossip/tales.* 不要听无益的闲言。 *It's~ to expect help from that man.* 指望那人帮忙是无用的。 □ vi, vt 1 [VP2A, C] be~: 不做事; 懒散; 闲手好闲: *Don't~ (about).* 不要闲混。 2 [VP15B] ~ **away,** spend in an~ manner: 虚度: *Don't~ away your time.* 不要虚度光阴。 3 (of a car engine) run slowly in neutral gear. (指汽车发动机)放空档; 空转。 **idler** /ˈaɪdlə(r); ˈaɪdlə/ n person who ~s. 闲散者; 懒人。 **idly** /ˈaɪdlɪ; ˈaɪdlɪ/ adv ~**ness** n state of being ~: 闲散; 懒惰: *live in~ness.* 游手好闲。

idol /ˈaɪdl; ˈaɪdḷ/ n 1 image in wood, stone, etc of a god; such an image used as an object of worship; false god. (木, 石等制的)神象; 偶像; 假神。 2 sb or sth greatly loved or admired: 极被宠爱或崇拜的人或物: *He was an only child, and the~ of his parents.* 他是个独子, 是他父母的宠儿。 *Don't make an~ of wealth.* 不要崇拜财富。 ~·**ater** /aɪˈdɒlətə(r); aɪˈdɑlətə/ n 1 worshipper of ~s. 偶像崇拜者。 2 devoted admirer (of...). 崇拜...者(与 of 连用)。 ~·**atress** /aɪˈdɒlətrɪs; aɪˈdɑlətrɪs/ n woman ~ater. 崇拜偶像的女人; 女崇拜者。 ~·**atrous** /aɪˈdɒlətrəs; aɪˈdɑlətrəs/ adj (of a person) worshipping ~s; of the worship of ~s. (指人)崇拜偶像的; 偶像崇拜的。 ~·**atrous·ly** adv ~·**atry** /aɪˈdɒlətrɪ; aɪˈdɑlətrɪ/ n 1 [U] the worship of ~s; excessive devotion to or admiration of (sb or sth). 偶像崇拜; (对某人或某事物的)过分崇拜。 2 [C] (pl -ries) instance of this. 偶像崇拜的实例; 过分崇拜的实例。 ~·**ize** /ˈaɪdəlaɪz; ˈaɪdḷˌaɪz/ vt [VP6A] make an~ of; love or admire to excess. 偶像化; 过分崇拜。 ~·**iz·ation** /ˌaɪdəlaɪˈzeɪʃən US: -lɪˈz-; ˌaɪdḷəˈzeʃən/ n ~izing or being ~ized. 偶像化; 过分崇拜。

idyll /ˈɪdɪl US: ˈaɪdɪl; ˈaɪdḷ/ n short description, usu in verse, of a simple scene or event, esp of country life; period of great peace and happiness. 田园诗(尤指对乡村生活纯朴的情景作简短描述的诗歌); 安详快乐的一段时间。 **idyl·lic** /ɪˈdɪlɪk US: aɪd-; aɪˈdɪlɪk/ adj suitable for, like, an~; simple, peaceful and pleasant. 适于田园诗的; 似田园诗的; 纯朴安详而宜人的。

if /ɪf; ɪf/ conj 1 on the condition that; supposing that: 假使; 如果: **(a)** (Present or Present Perfect Tense in the *if-*clause, indicating that sth is possible, probable, or likely): (if 从句中用现在时或现在完成时, 表示某事可能发生): If you are ready, we'll help you. 如果你准备好, 我们就帮助你。 *If (it is) necessary, I can come at six.* 必要时我可以六点钟来。 *If you have finished with*

that book, take it back to the library. 假使你已看完那本书,便将它还回图书馆。**(b)** (with *should* in the *if*-clause, to indicate that an event is unlikely or improbable): (if 从句中用 should 表示不大可能发生之事): *If anyone should call, please let me know.* 万一有人来访,请通知我。*If it should be necessary, I could come at six.* 若有必要我可以六点钟来。**(c)** (with *will* in an *if*-clause, not to show future time, but as part of the polite formula 'Will you, please'): (if 从句中用 will, 并非表示将来事,而是客套语 Will you, please 的一部分): *If you will wait a moment* (= Please wait a moment and) *I'll go and tell the manager that you are here.* 请等一下,我去告诉经理你已经来了。**(d)** (Past Tense in the *if*-clause, indicating a condition that cannot be, or is unlikely to be realized, or is one put forward for consideration): (if 从句中用过去时,表示不可能实现,大概不会实现,或提出作为考虑的假定条件): *If you were a bird, you could fly.* 假使你是只鸟,你便会飞了。*If I asked him/If I were to ask him for a loan, would he agree?* 如果我向他借钱,他会答应吗?*If you would lend me £5 until Monday, I should be grateful.* 如果你愿意借给我五英镑,到下星期一偿还,我将感谢你。**(e)** (Past Perfect Tense in the *if*-clause, indicating that the condition was not fulfilled, eg because it was an impossible one, or through sb's failure to act): (if 从句中用过去完成时,表示过去未实现的条件,例如由于不可能实现或某人之未能实行): *If they'd started earlier, they would have arrived in time.* 要是他们早些动身,他们便可及时到达了。*If they had not started when they did, they wouldn't be here now.* 如果他们那时不动身,现在他们就不会在此地了。(After some *vv*, eg *think, remember, ask*, the main clause depending upon the condition is usu omitted); (在某些动词,例如 think, remember, ask 之后,依条件而定的主要从句通常省略): *If you think about it,* (you realize that) *there were many bright boys in that class.* 如果你想一想,(你就知道)那一班级中有许多聪明男孩。*If you ask me,* (I will tell you) *he's a fool.* 如果你问我,(我会告诉你)他是个笨蛋。**2** (In literary style *if* may be omitted, and an inversion of subject and *aux v*, esp *were/had/should*, used instead): (在文学体中, if 有时可省略, 然后将主语与所用的助动词,尤其是 were, had, should 倒置): *Should it* (= If it should) *be necessary...; 倘若必定要...; Were I* (=If I were) *in your place...;* 如果我处于你的地位...; *Had I* (= If I had) *known earlier...;* 如果我早一些知道..。**3**(When *if* is used meaning 'when' or 'whenever', so that there is no condition, tenses in the main clause and the *if*-clause may be the same): (if 做当…时'或'无论何时'解而不含条件之义时, if 从句中的时态可与主句中者相同): *If you mix yellow and blue you get green.* 你来黄色与蓝色混合, 便会得到绿色。*If she wants the steward she rings the bell.* 每当她需要仆人时, 她便按铃。**4** (*even*) *if,* granting or admitting that: 就算: *If I'm mistaken, you're mistaken, too.* 就算我错了, 你也错了。*Even if he did say that, I'm sure he didn't intend to hurt your feelings.* 就算他真的那样说, 我相信他并无意伤你的感情。**5** (*even*) *if,* although: 即使; 纵然: *I'll do it, even if it takes me all the afternoon.* 即使花费我一下午的时间, 我还是要做这事。**6** (colloq) (*if* replacing *whether,* to introduce an interrogative clause): (口) (if 可代替 whether, 引导一疑问从句): *Do you know if Mr Smith is at home?* 你知道史密斯先生是否在家吗? *She asked if that was enough.* 她问那是否够了。(Note: *if* should not replace *whether* in cases where there may be ambiguity: 注意:如果意义含糊时, if 不可代替 whether: cf 参较 *Let me know whether you are coming,* (information wanted in either case). 告诉我你是否要来(不管来与不来均须回复)。*Let me know if* (= only if) *you are coming,* (information wanted only in the one case). 如果你要来,'就请通知我(决定要来时始回复)。)**7** *as if, as it would be if* (*it isn't as if* .. suggests that the contrary of what follows is true): 仿佛; 好象 (It isn't as if .. 表示与下列所述相反者为事实): *It isn't as if*

we were rich, ie We are *not* rich. 我们不象富有的样子(即我们不富有)。*It isn't as if he doesn't know the rules,* ie He *does* know the rules. 他不象不懂得规则的样子(即他懂得规则)。(*As if* often introduces an exclamation): (As if 常引导一感叹句): *As if I would allow it!* ie I would certainly *not* allow it! 好象我会答应似的!(即我才不答应哩!) ⇨ **as²**(11). **8** *if only,* (often introduces a wish, or indicates an unfulfilled condition, esp in exclamations): (常表示愿望或未实现的条件, 尤用于感叹句): *If only he arrives in time!* 他若能及时到达就好了! *If only she would marry me!* 但愿她肯嫁给我! *If only she had known about it* (but she did *not* know)! 她那时要是知道(但她不知道)这事就好了! *If only you could/If you could only have seen it.* 我真希望你当时能看到它! **9**(*if,* followed by a *v* in the neg, is used in exclamations to indicate dismay, surprise, etc): (if 后接否定动词, 用于感叹句中, 表示沮丧、惊奇等): *Well, if I haven't left my umbrella in the train!* 真倒霉, 我把雨伞丢在火车上了! *And if he didn't try to knock me down!* What do you think he did? He tried to knock me down! 你猜他想做什么?他竟然想把我击倒!

ig·loo /'ɪɡluː; 'ɪɡlu/ *n* (*pl* ~s) dome-shaped hut made of blocks of hard snow, used by the Eskimos. 爱斯基摩人所居住的用硬雪砖砌成的圆顶小屋。

ig·neous /'ɪɡnɪəs; 'ɪɡnɪəs/ *adj* (of rocks) formed by volcanic action. (指岩石)火成的。

ig·nis fatuus /ˌɪɡnɪs 'fætjuəs; ˌɪɡnɪs'fætʃuəs/ *n* (*pl* **ignes fatui** /ˌɪɡniːz 'fætjuaɪ; 'ɪɡnɪs'fætʃu,aɪ/) **1** = **will-o'-the-wisp.** **2** (colloq) sth misleading. (口)使人发生错误或引入歧途的事物。

ig·nite /ɪɡ'naɪt; ɪɡ'naɪt/ *vt, vi* [VP6A,2A] set on fire; take fire. 点燃; 发火。 **ig·ni·tion** /ɪɡ'nɪʃn; ɪɡ'nɪʃən/ *n* igniting or being ~d; (in a petrol engine) electrical mechanism for igniting the mixture of explosive gases: 点燃; 发火; 着火; (汽油发动机的)点火电门(俗称: 电门开关): *switch on the ignition.* 开开(汽车的)点火电门。⇨ the illus at **motor.** 参看 motor 之插图。

ig·noble /ɪɡ'nəʊbl; ɪɡ'nobl/ *adj* **1** dishonourable. shameful: 不名誉的; 可耻的: *an ~ man/action;* 可耻的人(行为); *an ~ peace.* 不光荣的和平。 **2** (old use) of low birth. (旧用法)出身微贱的。 **ig·nobly** /-'nəʊblɪ; -'nobli/ *adv*

ig·nom·ini·ous /ˌɪɡnə'mɪnɪəs; ˌɪɡnə'mɪnɪəs/ *adj* bringing contempt, disgrace, shame; dishonourable: 可鄙的; 可耻的; 可耻的; 可耻的行为: *an ~ behaviour;* 可耻的行为: *an ~ defeat.* 不光荣的失败。 **~·ly** *adv*

ig·nom·iny /'ɪɡnəmɪnɪ; 'ɪɡnə,mɪnɪ/ *n* **1** [U] public dishonour or shame. 不名誉; 耻辱。 **2** [C] (*pl* -nies) dishonourable or disgraceful act; [U] dishonourable behaviour. 可耻的行动; 不名誉的行为。

ig·nor·amus /ˌɪɡnə'reɪməs; ˌɪɡnə'reməs/ *n* (*pl* ~es /-sɪz; -sɪz/) ignorant person. 无知的人。

ig·nor·ance /'ɪɡnərəns; 'ɪɡnərəns/ *n* [U] ~ (*of*), the state of being ignorant; want of knowledge: 无知: *We are in complete ~ of his plans.* 我们完全不知道他的计划。*If he did wrong, it was from/through ~.* 要是他做错了, 那是由于无知。

ig·nor·ant /'ɪɡnərənt; 'ɪɡnərənt/ *adj* **1** ~ (*of*), (of persons) knowing little or nothing; not aware: (指人)无知识的; 无知的: *He's not stupid, merely ~.* 他不是愚蠢, 只是无知。*You are not ~ of the reasons for her behaviour.* 你不是不知道她的行为的原因。*What his plans are I am quite ~ of.* 我一点也不知道他的计划是什么。 **2** showing ignorance; resulting from ignorance: 显示无知的; 因无知而产生的: *an ~ reply;* 无知的回答; *~ conduct.* 无知的行为。 **~·ly** *adv*

ig·nore /ɪɡ'nɔː(r); ɪɡ'nor/ *vt* [VP6A] take no notice of; refuse to take notice of: 不理; 不顾; 忽视: *~ rude remarks;* 不理无礼的谈话; *be ~d by one's superiors.* 被上级忽视。

iguana /ɪ'ɡwɑːnə; ɪ'ɡwɑnə/ *n* large tree-climbing lizard of tropical America. 鬣蜥, 鬣蜥蜴(美洲热带所产

之善爬树大蜥蜴)。

ikon /'aɪkɒn; 'aɪkɑn/ n = icon.

ilex /'aɪleks; 'aɪleks/ n holm-oak; (bot) genus of trees including the common holly. 冬青树;(植物)冬青属。

ilk /ɪlk; ɪlk/ n of that/his etc ilk, (colloq, hum) of that/his etc family, set, type. (口,谐)属于那个(他那个等)家族,种类等的。

I'll /aɪl; aɪl/ = I will; I shall.

ill /ɪl; ɪl/ adj 1 (usu pred) in bad health; sick: (通常作叙述用法)健康不佳的;生病的: She was ill with anxiety. 她因忧虑而病了。 fall/be taken ill, become ill. 生病。 ⇨ worse, worst. 2 (attrib) bad: (用作定语)恶劣的;坏的: ill health; 不健康; in an ill temper/humour; 心情不好; ill repute; 声名狼藉; do sb an ill turn; 危害某人; have ill luck; 遭恶运; a bird of ill omen. 凶兆之鸟;带来恶运的人。 It's an ill wind that blows 'nobody any good, (prov) An affair must be very bad indeed if it does not benefit somebody. (谚)任何人都有得不到好处的事,可真是一件坏事(意谓:世上没有对人人皆不利的事)。 Ill weeds grow apace, (prov) Harmful things grow or spread rapidly. (谚)莠草易滋;有害之事蔓延迅速。 ,ill-'breeding n bad manners. 无教养; 粗鲁无礼。 ,ill-'favoured adj (of a person) unpleasant to look at; ugly. (指人)难看的; 丑的。 ,ill-'mannered adj having bad manners; rude. 无礼貌的; 粗野的。 ,ill-'natured adj bad-tempered. 脾气坏的。 ,ill-'omened adj destined to misfortune. 不吉祥的;恶兆的。 ,ill-'starred adj born under an evil star; unlucky. 星宿不利的;命运坏的。 ,ill-'treatment /-'usage n [U] cruelty; harsh treatment. 虐待。 ,ill 'will n enmity; unkind feeling. 敌意;恶意。 □ n 1 [U] evil; injury: 罪恶; 伤害: do ill. 作恶;为害。 2 [C] misfortune; trouble: 不幸; 灾难: the various ills of life. 人生的种种不幸。 □ adv badly; imperfectly; unfavourably: 恶劣地; 不完美地; 不利地: They were ill (= insufficiently) provided with ammunition. 他们的军火供应不足。 We could ill (= hardly, not easily) afford the time and money. 我们无力负担所需的时间与金钱。 It ill becomes you to criticize him. It is not right or proper for you to do this. 你不宜批评他。 be/feel ill at ease, uncomfortab e, embarrassed. 觉得不自在;觉得困窘。 speak ill of sb, in an unkind or unfavourable way. 说某人的坏话。 ,ill-ad'vised adj unwise; imprudent. 不智的; 卤莽的。 ,ill-af'fected (towards) adj not well-disposed; not feeling favour. 不怀好意的; 没有好感的。 ,ill-'bred adj badly brought up; rude. 无教养的; 粗野的。 ,ill-dis'posed (towards) adj (a) wishing to do harm (to). 怀恶意的。 (b) unfavourable (towards a plan, etc). 不赞成(计划等)的。 ,ill-'fated adj destined to misfortune; bringing misfortune. 命运的;不吉的;招致不幸的。 ,ill-gotten 'gains n pl money gained by evil or unlawful methods. 以卑鄙或不法手段得到的钱财; 不义之财。 ,ill-'judged adj done at an unsuitable time; showing poor judgement: 不合时宜的; 缺乏判断力的; 判断失当的: an ill-judged attempt. 不合时宜之举。 ,ill-'timed adj badly timed; done at a wrong or unsuitable time. 不合时宜的; 失时机的。 ,ill-'treat /-'use vt treat badly or cruelly. 虐待。

il·legal /ɪ'liːgl; ɪ'ligl/ adj not legal; contrary to law. 不合法的; 违法的。 ~ly /-gəlɪ; -glɪ/ adv ~ity /ɪlɪ-'gælətɪ; ɪlɪ'gælətɪ/ n [U] being ~; [C] (pl -ties) ~ act. 不合法;违法;违法的行为。

il·leg·ible / ɪ'ledʒəbl; ɪ'lɛdʒəbl / adj difficult or impossible to read. 难认的; 无法辨认的; 不清楚的。 **il·leg·ibly** /-əblɪ; -əblɪ/ adv **il·leg·ibil·ity** /ɪ,ledʒə-'brlɪtɪ; ɪ,lɛdʒə'brlɪtɪ/ n [U].

il·legit·imate /ɪlɪ'dʒɪtəmɪt; ,ɪlɪ'dʒɪtəmɪt/ adj 1 not authorized by law; contrary to law. 未经法律允许的;不合法的;违法的。 2 born of parents who were not married to each other: 私生的: an ~ child; 私生子; of ~ descent. 私生的。 3 (of a conclusion in an argument, etc) not logical; wrongly inferred. (指辩论的结论等)不合逻辑的; 推理错误的。 □ n an ~ person. 没有合法身分的

人; 私生子。 ~·ly adv il·legit·imacy /,ɪlɪ'dʒɪtɪməsɪ; ,ɪlɪ'dʒɪtəməsɪ/ n [U].

il·lib·eral /ɪ'lɪbərəl; ɪ'lɪbərəl/ adj not befitting a free man; narrow-minded; intolerant; ungenerous; mean. 无教养的; 气量狭小的; 不容异己的; 吝啬的; 卑鄙的。 ~·ly /-rəlɪ; -rəlɪ/ adv ~·ity /ɪ,lɪbə'rælɪtɪ; ɪ,lɪbə'rælətɪ/ n

il·licit /ɪ'lɪsɪt; ɪ'lɪsɪt/ adj unlawful; forbidden: 非法的; 被禁止的: the ~ sale of opium. 非法贩卖鸦片。 ~·ly adv

il·limit·able /ɪ'lɪmɪtəbl; ɪ'lɪmɪtəbl/ adj boundless; without limits: 无边际的;无限的: ~ space/ambition. 无限的空间(雄心)。

il·lit·er·ate /ɪ'lɪtərət; ɪ'lɪtərɪt/ adj with little or no education; unable to read or write; showing such ignorance: 未受教育的;目不识丁的;文字不通的: an ~ letter, one full of spelling and grammatical errors. 一封错字连篇、文句不通的信。 □ n ~ person. 目不识丁者;文盲。 il·lit·er·acy /ɪ'lɪtərəsɪ; ɪ'lɪtərəsɪ/ n [U, C] (instance of) being ~. 未受教育;目不识丁。

ill·ness /'ɪlnɪs; 'ɪlnɪs/ n 1 [U] state of being ill (contrasted with health): 不健康;疾病(与 health 相对): There has been no/not much/a great deal of ~ in the village this winter. 今年冬季这村里没有(没有什么, 有许多)疾病。 2 [C] specific kind of, occasion of, ~: 某种疾病;生病: ~es of children; 儿童所患的各种疾病; a serious ~; 重病; one ~ after another. 一次又一次的生病。

il·logi·cal /ɪ'lɒdʒɪkl; ɪ'lɑdʒɪkl/ adj without logic; contrary to logic. 不合逻辑的; 不合理的。 ~·ly /-klɪ; -klɪ/ adv ~·ity /ɪ,lɒdʒɪ'kælɪtɪ; ɪ,lɑdʒɪ'kælətɪ/, ~·ness nn [U, C] (instance of) being ~. 不合逻辑;不合理。

il·lume /ɪ'luːm; ɪ'lum/ vt (poet) illuminate. (诗)照亮;照光。

il·lumi·nate /ɪ'luːmɪneɪt; ɪ'lumə,net/ vt [VP6A] 1 give light to; throw light on: 使明亮; 照亮: a street ~d by oil lamps; 油灯照明的街道; poorly ~d rooms. 灯光不够亮的房间。 2 decorate (streets, etc) with bright lights as a sign of rejoicing. 以明灯装饰(街道等)以示欢欣。 3 decorate (initial letters in a manuscript) with gold, silver and bright colours (as was the custom in the Middle Ages). 在古代的习俗中)以金、银、鲜艳颜色装饰(稿件上的起首字母)。 4 make clear; help to explain: 说明; 阐明: ~ a difficult passage in a book. 阐明书中一难解的段落。 il·lumi·na·tion / ɪ,luːmɪ'neɪʃn; ɪ,lumə'neʃən/ n 1 [U] illuminating or being ~d. 照明; 明亮; 说明。 2 (usu pl) lights, etc. used to ~ (2) a town for a special occasion. (通常用复数)为特殊节庆装饰一城市所用的明灯等; 灯彩 装饰。 3 (pl) decorations on a manuscript. (复)文稿上的装饰物; 加有装饰的起首字母。 il·lu·mine /ɪ'luːmɪn; ɪ'lumɪn/ vt (poet) (liter) enlighten spiritually; make bright. (文)启发; 使明亮。

il·lu·sion /ɪ'luːʒn; ɪ'luʒən/ n 1 [C] (the seeing of) sth that does not really exist, or of sth as different from the reality; false idea or belief: 幻象; 幻影; 错觉; 错误的观点或信念: an optical ~. 视错觉。 be under an ~, be deceived by one. 产生错觉;搞错。 cherish an ~/the ~ that ..., like to believe .... 没以为…。 have no ~s about sb/sth, have no false beliefs about him/it. 对某人(某事)不存幻想。 2 [U] state of mind in which one is deceived in this way. 错觉。 ~·ist /-ɪst; -ɪst/ n person who produces optical ~s on the stage; conjurer. 幻术师;魔术师。

il·lu·sive /ɪ'luːsɪv; ɪ'lusɪv/, **il·lu·sory** /ɪ'luːsərɪ; ɪ'lusərɪ/ adj/adj deceptive; based on illusion. 欺骗的;虚幻的。

il·lus·trate / 'ɪlʌstreɪt; 'ɪlostret / vt [VP6A] 1 explain by examples, pictures, etc. 举例或以图画等说明。 2 supply a book, article, lecture, etc with pictures, diagrams, etc: 以图画、图表等插入(书籍,文章,演讲等): a well-~d textbook. 一本插图丰富的教科书。 il·lus·tra·tor /-tə(r); -tɚ/ n person who ~s books, etc. 为书籍等作插图的人; 插图画家。 il·lus·tra·tion /ˌɪlə'streɪʃn; ,ɪlos'treʃən/ n 1 [U] illustrating or being ~d: 举例或以图表等说明; 例证: cite instances in illustration of a theory. 举例说明一理论。 Illustration is often more useful than

definition for giving the meanings of words. 就赋予单词之意义而言，举例说明常较下定义有用。**2** [C] sth that ~s; picture, diagram, etc. 证证; 插图; 图解等。**il·lus·tra·tive** /ˈɪləstrətɪv US: ɪˈlʌstrətɪv; ɪˈlʌstrətɪv/ adj serving to ~, as an explanation or example (of sth). 说明的; 作为(某事物之)例证的(与 of 连用)。

il·lus·tri·ous /ɪˈlʌstrɪəs; ɪˈlʌstrɪəs/ adj greatly distinguished; celebrated. 极为杰出的; 著名的。~·ly adv

I'm /aɪm; aɪm/ = I am. ⇨ be[1].

im·age /ˈɪmɪdʒ; ˈɪmɪdʒ/ n [C] **1** likeness or copy of the shape of sb or sth, esp one made in wood, stone, etc: 像; 肖像(尤指以木, 石等制成者): an ~ of the Virgin Mary; 圣母玛利亚像; graven ~s, ~s carved in wood, etc and regarded as gods. 雕刻的神像。**2** close likeness; counterpart: 极为相象; 与同一个极为相象的人或物: Did man create God in his own ~? 人是照他自己的形象创造上帝的吗? be the (very/spitting) ~ (of sth/sb), be exactly like it/him. 酷似某物或某人。**3** mental picture or idea; concept of sth or sb, eg a politician, political party, commercial firm, product, held by the public: 心象; 意象; 形象; 观念; 公众对某事物或某人(例如政界人士, 政党, 商行, 制品之)观念: How can we improve our ~? 我们如何才能增进公众对我们的好感? **4** simile; metaphor: 直喻; 隐喻: speak in ~s, use figures of speech that bring pictures to the mind. 用比喻说。**5** reflection seen in a mirror or through the lens of a camera. 映象; 影象。⇨ the illus at **camera**. 参看 camera 之插图。□ vt [VP6A] **1** make an ~ of, portray. 作…之象; 作…之肖像; 描绘。**2** reflect; mirror. 反映; 映照。~ry /ˈɪmɪdʒərɪ; ˈɪmɪdʒrɪ/ n [U] the use of ~s(4), or figures of speech, in writing; ~s(1) collectively. 写作中直喻或比喻的使用; 像或肖象的总称。

im·agin·able /ɪˈmædʒɪnəbl; ɪˈmædʒɪnəbl/ adj that can be imagined: 可想象的: We had the greatest difficulty ~ getting here in time. 我们为了及时赶到这里, 而经历了所能想得到的最大困难。

im·agin·ary /ɪˈmædʒɪnərɪ US: -əneri; ɪˈmædʒəˌneri/ adj existing only in the mind; unreal. 想象中的; 不真实的。

im·agin·ation /ɪˌmædʒɪˈneɪʃn; ɪˌmædʒəˈneʃən/ n **1** [C, U] power of the mind to imagine: 想象力: He hasn't much ~. 他缺乏想象力。Novelists use their ~. 小说家善用他们的想象力。Children are encouraged to use their ~s. 儿童受到鼓励去运用他们的想象力。**2** what is imagined: 想象的事物: You didn't really see a ghost—it was only ~. 你并没有真正看到鬼——那只是你想象中的东西。**im·agin·ative** /ɪˈmædʒɪnətɪv US: -əneɪtɪv; ɪˈmædʒəˌneɪtɪv/ adj of, having, using, ~: 想象的; 有想象力的; 运用想象力的: imaginative writers. 富有想象力的作者。

im·ag·ine /ɪˈmædʒɪn; ɪˈmædʒɪn/ vt [VP6A, C, 9, 10, 16B, 19A, C, 25] form a picture of in the mind; think of (sth) as probable: 想象; 认为(某事物)可能发生或存在: wild imaginings. 妄想的事物。Can you ~ life without electricity and other modern conveniences? 你能想象出没有电和其他现代化设备时的生活情形吗? I~ yourself (to be) on a desert island. 想象你自己在一个荒岛上的情景。I~ you've been shipwrecked. 想象你遭受了船难。I ~ him as a big, tall man. 我以为他是个高大的人。Can you ~ him/yourself becoming famous as an actor? 你能想象他(你自己)成为一个名演员时候的情形吗? I can't ~ (my) marrying a girl of that sort. 我难于想象(我)与那种女子结婚后的情形。Don't ~ (= get the idea) that I can lend you money every time you need it! 不要认为每当你需要钱的时候, 我便会借给你。

imam /ɪˈmɑːm; ɪˈmɑm/ n prayer leader in a mosque. 伊斯兰教寺院中祈祷时之领导人。**I~**, title of various Muslim leaders. 伊斯兰教首领之尊称。

im·bal·ance /ˌɪmˈbæləns; ɪmˈbæləns/ n absence of balance between two totals, eg payments; lack of proportion: 两总数的不相等(例如支付); 不均衡: the country's ~ in world payments, the state that exists when the total sum paid for imports, etc, is unequal to

the total received for exports, services, etc; 该国在国际贸易收支上的不均衡(进口等付出之款与出口、劳务等收入不相等); the increasing ~ between rich and poor countries, the increasing wealth of some and the increasing poverty of others. 富有国家与贫穷国家间日益增加的不均衡。

im·be·cile /ˈɪmbəsiːl US: -sl; ˈɪmbəsl/ adj weak-minded; stupid: 低能的; 鲁钝的: ~ remarks/conduct. 愚蠢的言谈(行为)。□ n ~ person: fool. 低能者; 愚蠢之人。**im·be·cil·ity** /ˌɪmbəˈsɪlətɪ; ˌɪmbəˈsɪlətɪ/ n [U] stupidity; [C] (pl -ties) stupid act, remark, etc. 愚蠢; 愚蠢的行动, 言语等。

im·bed /ɪmˈbed; ɪmˈbed/ vt (-dd-) = embed.

im·bibe /ɪmˈbaɪb; ɪmˈbaɪb/ vt (formal) drink; take in: (正式用语)饮; 吸收: ~ ideas/knowledge. 吸收思想(知识)。

im·bro·glio /ɪmˈbrəʊlɪəʊ; ɪmˈbroljo/ n (pl ~s /-z; -z/) complicated, confused or embarrassing (esp political or emotional) situation. 复杂错综的情势(尤指政治或情绪上者)。

im·bue /ɪmˈbjuː; ɪmˈbju/ vt (pt, pp -bued) [VP14] ~ with, (formal) fill, inspire: (正式用语)使充满; 激起: ~d with patriotism/hatred, etc; 充满爱国心(仇恨等); politicians ~d with a sense of their own importance. 自大的政客。

imi·tate /ˈɪmɪteɪt; ˈɪmə,tet/ vt [VP6A] **1** copy the behaviour of; take as an example: 仿效…的行为; 模仿: You should ~ great and good men. 你应仿效伟大善良的人。**2** mimic (consciously or not): (自觉或不自觉地)模拟: Parrots ~ human speech. 鹦鹉学人语。**3** be like; make a likeness of: 看似; 仿造: wood painted to ~ marble. 漆成大理石样子的木材。**imi·ta·tor** /-teɪtə(r); -ts/ n

imi·ta·tion /ˌɪmɪˈteɪʃn; ˌɪməˈteʃən/ n **1** [U] imitating: 仿效; 模仿; 模拟: I~ is the sincerest form of flattery. 仿效是最真诚的恭维。He sets us a good example for ~. 他为我们树立一个可效法的楷模。She was pirouetting in ~ of her teacher. 她在学着老师跳脚尖旋转舞。**2** (attrib) not real: (用作定语)假的: ~ leather/jewellery. 人造的皮革(珠宝)。**3** [C] sth made or done in ~: 仿造物; 模拟之物: ~s of the cries of birds and animals. 模拟鸟兽的鸣叫声。Beware of ~s. 谨防假冒。

imi·tat·ive /ˈɪmɪtətɪv US: -teɪtɪv; ˈɪmə,teɪtɪv/ adj following the model or example of: 模仿的; 仿效的; 模拟的: the ~ arts, painting and sculpture; 模仿艺术(指绘画与雕刻); ~ words, eg bozz, plop, the sound of the word being considered similar to the sound it represents: 形声词; 拟声词(例如 buzz, plop 等); as ~ as a monkey. 象猴子般喜模仿。

im·macu·late /ɪˈmækjʊleɪt; ɪˈmækjəlɪt/ adj **1** pure; faultless: 纯洁的; 无瑕疵的: ~ conduct. 纯洁的行为。the I~ Conception, (RC church) teaching that the Virgin Mary was free of Original Sin. (天主教)圣母玛利亚生来纯洁而无原罪之教义。**2** perfectly clean; without a flaw; right in every detail: 洁净的; 完美的; 处处都对的: an ~ suit/record. 一套洁净的衣服(完美的记录)。~·ly adv: ~ly dressed. 衣着整洁。

im·ma·nent /ˈɪmənənt; ˈɪmənənt/ adj ~ (in), (of qualities) present; inherent; (of God) ~ permanently pervading the universe. (指性质)存在的; 固有的; (指上帝)无所不在的。**im·ma·nence** /-əns; -əns/ n

im·ma·terial /ˌɪməˈtɪərɪəl; ˌɪməˈtɪrɪəl/ adj ~ (to), **1** unimportant: (对…)不重要的: ~ objections. 不重要的反对意见。That's quite ~ to me. 那对我无关紧要。**2** not having physical substance: 无实质的: as ~ as a ghost. 象鬼魂般的虚幻。

im·ma·ture /ˌɪməˈtjʊə(r) US: -ˈtʊər; ˌɪməˈtjʊr/ adj not yet fully developed: 未发育完全的; 未成熟的: an ~ girl; 一个未成熟的女孩; the ~ minds of young children. 孩子们未成熟的心理。**im·ma·tur·ity** /ˌɪməˈtjʊərɪtɪ; ˌɪməˈtjʊrɪtɪ/ n [U].

im·measur·able /ɪˈmeʒərəbl; ɪˈmeʒərəbl/ adj that

cannot be measured. 不能衡量的。

im·medi·ate /ɪˈmiːdɪət; ɪˈmidɪɪt/ *adj* (of time or space) (指时间或空间) **1** without anything coming between; nearest: 最接近的; 最接近的: *two objects in* ~ *contact;* 直接接触的两个物体; *the* ~ *heir to the throne,* the next in succession, not a remote heir; 王位的直接继承人; *my* ~ *neighbours;* 我的紧邻; ~ *in formation,* first-hand or direct, not secondhand. 直接的消息。 **2** occurring, done, at once: 即刻的; 立即的: *an* ~ *answer;* 即刻的答复; *take* ~ *action.* 立刻采取行动。 **im·medi·acy** /-əsɪ; -əsɪ/ *n* [U] being ~. 直接; 即刻。 ~·ly *adv* **1** at once; without delay. 立刻; 立即。 **2** directly or closely. 直接地; 紧接地。 ~ *conj* as soon as: 一等…立即: *You may leave* ~*ly he comes.* 他一来到, 你可立即离开。

im·mem·or·ial /ˌɪməˈmɔːrɪəl; ˌɪməˈmɔrɪəl/ *adj* going back beyond the reach of memory: 人所不能记忆之往昔的; 久到难以追忆的: *the* ~ *privileges of the House of Commons.* 由来已久的(英国)下议院特权。 *from time* ~, for a very long time back. 自古以来。

im·mense /ɪˈmens; ɪˈmɛns/ *adj* very large. 极大的。 ~·ly *adv* in an ~ degree; (colloq) very much: 极度; (口)非常: *They enjoyed themselves* ~*ly.* 他们极为高兴。 **im·men·sity** /ɪˈmensətɪ; ɪˈmɛnsətɪ/ *n* [U] great size; (*pl* -**ties**) things that are ~. 巨大; 巨大之物。

im·merse /ɪˈmɜːs; ɪˈmɝs/ *vt* [VP6A, 14] ~ (*in*), **1** put under the surface of (water or other liquid): 浸入(水或其他液体): ~ *one's head in the water.* 将头浸入水中。 **2** absorb, involve deeply: 使专心; 使陷入: *be* ~*d in a book/thought/work/one's business.* 专心阅读一本书(陷入沉思; 专心工作; 专心于自己的事业)。 **im·mer·sion** /ɪˈmɜːʃn US: -ʒn; ɪˈmɝʃən/ *n* immersing or being ~d; (esp) baptism by putting the whole body into water. 浸入; 沉溺; (尤指)浸礼(将全身浸入水中的洗礼)。 **im'mersion heater,** electric water-heater (usu one that is fixed in a hot-water tank): 浸入式电热器(通常指装置于热水箱中者)。

im·mi·grate /ˈɪmɪɡreɪt; ˈɪməˌgret/ *vi* [VP2A, 3A] ~ (*to/into*), come as a settler (to/into another country), not as a tourist or visitor. 移民(另一国家)。 移民。 **im·mi·grant** /ˈɪmɪɡrənt; ˈɪməɡrənt/ *n* person who ~s: 移民; 移居另一国者: *European immigrants in Australia.* 在澳大利亚的欧洲移民。 **im·mi·gra·tion** /ˌɪmɪˈɡreɪʃn; ˌɪməˈɡreʃən/ *n* [U] immigrating; (*C*) instance of this: 移民别国; 移民之实例: *the numerous immigrations into the US:* 移入美国的大批移民。

im·mi·nent /ˈɪmɪnənt; ˈɪmənənt/ *adj* (of events, esp dangers) likely to come or happen soon: (指事件, 尤指危险)逼近的; 即将发生的: *A storm is* ~. 暴风雨即将来临。 *He was faced with* ~ *death.* 他面临迫近的死亡。 ~·ly *adv* **im·mi·nence** /-əns; -əns/ *n* [U] being ~. 逼近; 即至。

im·mo·bile /ɪˈməʊbaɪl US: -bl; ɪˈmobl/ *adj* not able to move or be moved; motionless. 不能移动的; 不动的。 **im·mo·bil·ize** /ɪˈməʊbəlaɪz; ɪˈmobl̩ˌaɪz/ *vt* [VP 6A] make ~; render armed forces, vehicles, etc incapable of being moved; take capital, specie out of circulation. 使不动; 使(军队、车辆等)不能行动; 停止(资金、硬币)之流通。 **im·mo·bil·iz·ation** /ɪˌməʊbəlaɪˈzeɪʃn US: -lɪˈz-; ɪˌmobl̩əˈzeʃən/ *n* [U] being ~. 不动; 不能移动。

im·mod·er·ate /ɪˈmɒdərət; ɪˈmɑdərɪt/ *adj* excessive; extreme: 无节制的; 极端的: ~ *eating and drinking.* 暴食暴饮。 ~·ly *adv*

im·mod·est /ɪˈmɒdɪst; ɪˈmɑdɪst/ *adj* **1** lacking in modesty; indecent or indelicate: 不谦虚的; 不庄重的; 不礼貌的; 粗野的: *an* ~ *dress;* 不庄重的衣着; ~ *behaviour.* 粗鲁的行为。 **2** impudent: 厚颜的; 无耻的: ~ *boasts.* 厚颜的自夸。~·ly *adv* ~·y *n* [U] ~ behaviour; boldness; [C] (*pl* -**ties**) ~ act or remark. 不适当的行为; 厚颜; 粗野的行动或言语。

im·mo·late /ˈɪməleɪt; ˈɪməˌlet/ *vt* [VP6A, 14] ~

(to), (formal) kill as an offering; sacrifice (one thing *to* another). (正式用语)为祭神而杀; 杀…作为祭品; 牺牲。 **im·mo·la·tion** /ˌɪməˈleɪʃn; ˌɪməˈleʃən/ *n* [U] immolating or being ~d; [C] instance of this. 为祭神而杀; 杀之以作祭品; 牺牲; 殉死。

im·moral /ɪˈmɒrəl US: ɪˈmɔːrəl; ɪˈmɔrəl/ *adj* contrary to morality; wicked and evil: 不道德的; 邪恶的: ~ *conduct.* 不道德的行为。 *You* ~ *swindler!* 你这个邪恶的骗子! ~·ly /-rəlɪ; -rəlɪ/ *adv* ~·ity /ˌɪmə-ˈrælətɪ; ˌɪməˈrælətɪ/ *n* [U] ~ conduct: 不道德的行为: *a life of* ~*ity;* 不道德(淫邪)的生活; [C] (*pl* -**ties**) ~ act. 不道德的行为。

im·mor·tal /ɪˈmɔːtl; ɪˈmɔrtl/ *adj* living for ever: 不朽的; 永远生存的: *the* ~ *gods/soul;* 永生不死的神祇(灵魂); never forgotten: 永不为人遗忘的; 永垂不朽的: ~ *poetry/music;* 不朽的诗歌(音乐); ~ *fame.* 不朽的名誉。 □ *n* ~ being. 不朽的人物; 永生不死者, **the** ~**s,** the gods of ancient Greece and Rome. 古希腊罗马的神祇。 ~·**ity** /ˌɪmɔːˈtælətɪ; ˌɪmɔrˈtælətɪ/ *n* [U] endless life or fame. 不朽; 不朽的生命或声名。 ~·**ize** /ɪˈmɔːtəlaɪz; ɪˈmɔrtl̩ˌaɪz/ *vt* [VP6A] give endless life or fame to. 使不朽; 赋与不朽的生命或声名。

im·mov·able /ɪˈmuːvəbl; ɪˈmuvəbl/ *adj* **1** that cannot be moved: 不能移动的: ~ *property,* eg buildings, land. 不动产(例如建筑物, 土地)。 **2** steadfast: 坚定不移的: ~ *in purpose.* 目的坚定不移。 **im·mov·ably** /-əblɪ; -əblɪ/ *adv*

im·mune /ɪˈmjuːn; ɪˈmjun/ *adj* ~ (*from/against/to*), free, secure: 免除的; 安全的: ~ *from smallpox as the result of vaccination;* 由于种痘的结果而不会感染天花; ~ *to/against poison/disease/infection/criticism/attack.* 免受中毒(疾病, 传染, 批评, 攻击)。 **im·mun·ity** /ɪˈmjuːnətɪ; ɪˈmjunətɪ/ *n* [U] safety, security (*from* disease, etc); exemption (*from* taxation, etc): 免疫(与 *from* 连用); (捐税等的)免除(与 *from* 连用): *diplomatic immunity.* 外交豁免权。 **im·mu·nize** /ˈɪmjunaɪz; ˈɪmjəˌnaɪz/ *vt* [VP6A, 14] ~ (*against*), make ~ (*against*). 使免除。 **im·mu·niz·ation** /ˌɪmjunaɪˈzeɪʃn US: -nɪˈz-; ˌɪmjunəˈzeʃən/ *n* [U] **im·mu·nology** /ˌɪmjuˈnɒlədʒɪ; ˌɪmjəˈnɑlədʒɪ/ *n* study of resistance to infection. 免疫学。

im·mure /ɪˈmjʊə(r); ɪˈmjʊr/ *vt* [VP6A] (formal) imprison; shut (oneself) up: (正式用语) 监禁; 幽禁(自己): ~*d in a windowless prison cell;* 被监禁在没有窗户的小牢房里; ~ *oneself in one's study to work undisturbed.* 将自己关在书房内读书以免受干扰。

im·mut·able /ɪˈmjuːtəbl; ɪˈmjutəbl/ *adj* (formal) that cannot be changed. (正式用语)不可改变的。 **im·mut·ably** /-əblɪ; -əblɪ/ *adv* **im·muta·bil·ity** /ɪˌmjuː-təˈbɪlətɪ; ɪˌmjutəˈbɪlətɪ/ *n*

imp /ɪmp; ɪmp/ *n* child of the devil; little devil; (playfully) mischievous child. 魔鬼之子; 小魔鬼; 顽童; 小淘气。

im·pact /ˈɪmpækt; ˈɪmpækt/ *n* ~ (*on*), **1** [C] collision. 碰撞; 撞击。 **2** [U] force exerted by one object when striking against another: 撞击力: *The car body collapses on* ~, when it collides with sth. 汽车的车身在碰撞时塌陷。 **3** strong impression or effect: 强烈印象或影响: *the* ~ *of new ideas on discontented students.* 新观念对情绪不满之学生的巨大影响。 □ *vt* /ɪmˈpækt; ɪmˈpækt/ pack, drive or wedge firmly together: 装紧; 紧压; 插紧: *an* ~*ed tooth,* not able to grow out of the jawbone. (紧压在颚骨中长不出来的)箝闭齿; 阻生牙。

im·pair /ɪmˈpeə(r); ɪmˈpɛr/ *vt* [VP6A] weaken; damage: 使弱; 损害: ~ *one's health by overwork.* 因工作过度而损及健康。 ~·**ment** *n*

im·pala /ɪmˈpɑːlə; ɪmˈpɑlə/ *n* (kind of) African antelope. (一种)非洲羚羊; 黑斑羚。

im·pale /ɪmˈpeɪl; ɪmˈpel/ *vt* [VP6A, 15A] pierce through, pin down, with a sharp-pointed stake, spear, etc. (以尖桩, 矛等)刺穿, 刺住。 ~·**ment** *n*

im·pal·pable /ɪmˈpælpəbl; ɪmˈpælpəbl/ *adj* that

cannot be touched or felt; not easily grasped by the mind. 摸不到的; 感觉不到的; 难以理解的。

im·panel /ɪmˈpænl; ɪmˈpænl/ = empanel.

im·part /ɪmˈpɑːt; ɪmˈpɑrt/ vt [VP6A, 14] ~ (to), (formal) give, pass on, a share of sth, a quality, a secret, news, etc: (正式用语)(把一份物品,性质等)给予; 传予;(把秘密,新闻等)通知; 告知: *I have nothing of interest to ~ to you.* 我没有有趣的事情告诉你。

im·par·tial /ɪmˈpɑːʃl; ɪmˈpɑrʃəl/ adj fair (in giving judgements, etc); not favouring one more than another. (作判断等时)公平的; 不偏袒的; 无私的。 ~·ly adv **im·par·tial·ity** /ˌɪmˌpɑːʃɪˈælətɪ, ˌɪmpɑrˈʃælətɪ/ n [U] the quality of being ~. 公平; 无私。

im·pass·able /ɪmˈpɑːsəbl US: -ˈpæs-; ɪmˈpæsəbl/ adj impossible to travel through or on: 不可通行的: *country roads / Alpine passes ~ in winter.* 在冬季无法通行的乡村道路(阿尔卑斯山道)。

im·passe /ˈæmpɑːs US: ˈɪmpæs; ɪmˈpæs/ n blind; alley; place, position, from which there is no way out; deadlock. 死巷;死路; 绝境; 僵局。

im·pas·sioned /ɪmˈpæʃnd; ɪmˈpæʃənd/ adj full of, showing, deep feeling: 充满热情的; 显示热情的: *an ~ speech.* 一篇热情的演说。

im·pass·ive /ɪmˈpæsɪv; ɪmˈpæsɪv/ adj showing no sign of feeling; unmoved. 冷淡的; 无感觉的; 不动感情的。 ~·ly adv ~·ness, **im·pass·iv·ity** /ˌɪmpæˈsɪvətɪ; ˌɪmpæˈsɪvətɪ/ nn

im·pa·tient /ɪmˈpeɪʃnt; ɪmˈpeʃənt/ adj 1 ~ (at sth/with sb), not patient: 不耐烦的; 急躁的: ~ at the delay; 对延误感到不耐烦; ~ with a tired child. 对疲倦的孩子感到不耐烦。 ~ of sth, (formal) intolerant of it. (正式用语)无法容忍某事物。 2 ~ (for sth/to do sth), eager: 急切的; 渴望的: ~ for a journey to start; ~ to start a journey. 急着要去旅行。 *The audience are growing ~.* 观众渐渐急躁不安。 ~·ly adv **im·pa·tience** /ɪmˈpeɪʃns; ɪmˈpeʃəns/ n [U].

im·peach /ɪmˈpiːtʃ; ɪmˈpitʃ/ vt 1 (formal) question, raise doubts about (sb's character, etc): (正式用语)指摘;责问; 表示怀疑(某人的品行等): *Do you ~ my motives,* suggest that they are dishonourable? 你对我的动机表示怀疑吗? 2 [VP14] ~ sb for / of / with sth; ~ sb for doing sth, (legal) accuse sb of wrongdoing; (esp) accuse (sb) of a crime against the State: (法律)控告(某人); (尤指)检举; 弹劾(某人)叛国或渎职: ~ a judge for taking bribes; 检举一法官受贿; ~ sb of a crime. 控告某人犯罪。 ~·ment n [U] ~ing or being ~ed; [C] instance of this. 指摘;责问;控告;弹劾。

im·pec·cable /ɪmˈpekəbl; ɪmˈpekəbl/ adj (formal) faultless; incapable of doing wrong: (正式用语)无瑕疵的; 不会作错的; 完美的: *an ~ character / record.* 完善的品行(纪录)。

im·pe·cuni·ous /ˌɪmpɪˈkjuːnɪəs; ˌɪmpɪˈkjunɪəs/ adj (formal) having little or no money. (正式用语)无钱的; 贫困的。

im·pede /ɪmˈpiːd; ɪmˈpid/ vt [VP6A] get in the way of; hinder: 阻碍; 妨碍: *What ~s your making an early start?* 何事妨碍你早些动身?

im·pedi·ment /ɪmˈpedɪmənt; ɪmˈpedəmənt/ n [C] sth that hinders, esp a defect in speech, eg a stammer. 妨碍物; 障碍(尤指说话方面的缺点,例如口吃)。 **im·pedi·menta** /ɪmˌpedɪˈmentə; ɪmˌpedəˈmentə/ n pl baggage (esp of an army). 行李;(尤指)军队之辎重。

im·pel /ɪmˈpel; ɪmˈpel/ vt (-ll-) [VP17, 14] ~ (to), drive, force, urge: 推进; 驱使: 驱策: *He said he had been ~led to crime by poverty.* 他说他是为穷困所逼而犯罪。 *The President's speech ~led the nation to greater efforts.* 总统的演说激励全国更加努力。 ~·ler n rotor or rotor blade (of a jet engine). 转轮;(喷射引擎之)旋转翼。

im·pend /ɪmˈpend; ɪmˈpend/ vi (chiefly in pres part) (formal) be imminent; be about to come or happen: (主要用现在分词)(正式用语)逼近; 即将来到或发生: *her*

~ing arrival; 她的即将来临; the ~ing storm; 迫近的暴风雨; the danger ~ing over us. 逼近我们的危险。

im·pen·etrable /ɪmˈpenɪtrəbl; ɪmˈpenətrəbl/ adj ~ (to), that cannot be penetrated: 不能穿过的; 不能透过的;不能制入的: ~ forests and swamps; 无法通过的森林与沼泽; dig down to ~ rock; 挖掘至坚不可破的岩石; ~ darkness; 漆黑。 *men who are ~ to reason.* 不可理喻的人。

im·peni·tent /ɪmˈpenɪtənt; ɪmˈpenətənt/ adj (formal) not penitent. (正式用语)不悔悟的。 ~·ly adv **im·peni·tence** /-əns; -əns/ n

im·pera·tive /ɪmˈperətɪv; ɪmˈperətɪv/ adj 1 urgent; essential; needing immediate attention: 紧急的; 必要的; 急切的: *Is it really ~ for them to have such a large army?* 他们真的迫切需要如此庞大的一支军队吗? *Is it ~ that they should have / for them to have six cars?* 他们必须要六部汽车吗? 2 not to be disobeyed; done, given with, authority: 必须服从的; 强制的: *The duke's orders were ~.* 公爵的命令必须服从。'*Go at once!*', he said, *with an ~ gesture.* '立刻去!' 他说, 并作了个强制的手势。 3 (gram) (also n) (of the) form of a verb or a sentence expressing a command: (语法)(亦作名词用)祈使的;祈使动词;祈使句: *the ~ mood.* 祈使语气。 ~·ly adv

im·per·cep·tible /ˌɪmpəˈseptəbl; ˌɪmpəˈseptəbl/ adj that cannot be perceived; very slight or gradual. 觉察不到的; 不可觉的; 极轻微或逐渐的。 **im·per·cep·tibly** /-əblɪ; -əblɪ/ adv

im·per·fect /ɪmˈpɜːfɪkt; ɪmˈpɜfɪkt/ adj 1 not perfect or complete. 不完善的; 不完全的。 2 ~ tense, (gram) that denotes action in progress but not completed (also called 亦称作 progressive or continuous tenses). (语法)未完成过去时(指尚在进行中的动作) as in eg 例如: 'I am / was / have been / will be speaking.' □ n ~ tense. 未完成过去时。 ~·ly adv **im·per·fec·tion** /ˌɪmpəˈfekʃn; ˌɪmpəˈfekʃən/ n [U] state of being ~; [C] fault. 不完善;不完全; 缺点。

im·perial /ɪmˈpɪərɪəl; ɪmˈpɪrɪəl/ adj 1 of an empire or its ruler(s): 帝国的; 皇帝的: ~ trade; 帝国的贸易; *His I~ Majesty.* 皇帝陛下; 皇上。 2 majestic; august; magnificent: 威严的; 崇高的; 堂皇的: *with ~ generosity* 以宽宏的精神。 3 (of weights and measures) used by law in the United Kingdom: (指度量衡)英国法定的: *an ~ pint / gallon.* 英国法定一品脱(加仑)。 □ n small, pointed beard grown beneath the lower lip. 留在下唇下面的尖形小须;皇帝须。 ~·ly /-rɪəlɪ; -rɪəlɪ/ adv

im·peri·al·ism /ɪmˈpɪərɪəlɪzəm; ɪmˈpɪrɪəlˌɪzəm/ n belief in the value of colonies; policy of extending a country's empire and influence. 帝国主义;扩大一国版图及势力的政策。 **im·per·ial·ist** /-ɪst, -ɪst/ n supporter of, believer in, ~. 帝国主义者。 **im·per·ial·is·tic** /ɪmˌpɪərɪəˈlɪstɪk; ɪmˌpɪrɪəˈlɪstɪk/ adj of ~: 帝国主义的: *imperialistic views.* 帝国主义的观点。

im·peril /ɪmˈperəl; ɪmˈperəl/ vt (-ll-, US also -l-) [VP6A] (liter) put or bring into danger. (文)使陷于危险;危及。

im·peri·ous /ɪmˈpɪərɪəs; ɪmˈpɪrɪəs/ adj (formal) (正式用语) 1 commanding; haughty; arrogant: 专横的; 傲慢的;自大的: ~ gestures / looks. 专横的姿态(样子)。 2 urgent; imperative. 急切的; 紧急的。 ~·ly adv ~·ness n

im·per·ish·able /ɪmˈperɪʃəbl; ɪmˈperɪʃəbl/ adj (formal) that cannot perish; that will never pass away: (正式用语)不灭的;不朽的: ~ fame / glory. 不朽的声名(光荣)。

im·per·ma·nent /ɪmˈpɜːmənənt; ɪmˈpɜmənənt/ adj (formal) not permanent. (正式用语)非永久的。 **imper·ma·nence** /-əns; -əns/ n

im·per·me·able /ɪmˈpɜːmɪəbl; ɪmˈpɜmɪəbl/ adj ~ (to), (formal) that cannot be permeated (esp by fluids); impervious. (正式用语)不被(尤指液体)渗透的; 不透水的。

im·per·sonal /ˌɪmˈpɜːsənl; ɪmˈpɜsnl/ adj 1 not

influenced by personal feeling; not referring to any particular person: 不受个人感情影响的; 非特指某人的; 和个人无关的: ~ *remarks;* 非特指某人的评论; *an ~ discussion.* 和个人无关的讨论. ~ *pronoun,* the pronouns **one**⁴ and **you**(2). 非特指某人的代词(即 one⁴ 及 you(2)). 泛指性的代词. **2** having no existence as a person: 不具人格的: ~ *forces,* eg those of nature. 非人的力量(例如自然力). **3** (of verbs) used after 'it' to make general statements such as '*It is raining/freezing*'. (指动词)非人称的; 无主的(用于 it 之后作一般陈述, 例如: It is raining/freezing 中的动词). ~**ly** /-nǝlɪ/ *adv*

im·per·son·ate /ɪm'pɜːsǝneɪt; ɪm'pɝsn̩ˌet/ *vt* [VP 6A] **1** act the part of (in a play, etc); pretend to be (another person). (在剧中等)扮演…的角色; 假扮(另一人). **2** personify. 拟人化; 赋与人格. **im·per·son·ation** /ɪmˌpɜːsǝ'neɪʃn; ɪmˌpɝsn̩'eʃǝn/ *n* **1** [U] impersonating or being ~d. 扮演; 被扮演或假扮; 人格化; 被人格化. **2** [C] instance of this: 上述的实例: *He gave some clever impersonations of well-known men.* 他巧妙地扮演了几位名人. **im·per·son·ator** /-neɪtǝ(r); -neta/ *n* person who ~s. 扮演某角色的人; 假扮他人之人.

im·per·ti·nent /ɪm'pɜːtɪnǝnt; ɪm'pɝtn̩ǝnt/ *adj* **1** not showing proper respect; impudent; saucy: 无礼的; 失礼的; 厚颜的; 莽撞的: ~ *remarks;* 鲁莽的言词; *an ~ boy.* 失礼的男孩. **2** not pertinent; not pertaining to the matter in hand. 不切题的; 离题的. ~**ly** *adv* **im·per·ti·nence** /-ǝns, -ǝns/ *n* [U] being ~; [C] ~ act or remark. 无礼; 粗鲁; 不切题; 无礼的行为或言语; 不适当的行动或言词.

im·per·turb·able /ˌɪmpǝ'tɜːbǝbl; ˌɪmpɝ'tɝbǝbl/ *adj* (formal) not capable of being excited; calm. (正式用语) 不会激动的; 镇静的. **im·per·turb·abil·ity** /ˌɪmpǝˌtɜːbǝ-'brlǝtɪ; ˌɪmpǝˌtɝbǝ'bɪlǝtɪ/ *n* [U].

im·per·vi·ous /ɪm'pɜːvɪǝs; ɪm'pɝvɪǝs/ *adj* ~ (to), **1** (of materials) not allowing (water, etc) to pass through: (指材料)不为水等渗透的: *Rubber boots are ~ to water.* 橡胶靴是不透水的. **2** (fig) not moved or influenced by: (喻)不为所动的; 不受影响的: ~ *to criticism/argument.* 不为批评(争论)所动的.

im·pe·tigo /ˌɪmpɪ'taɪgǝʊ; ˌɪmpɪ'taɪgo/ *n* [U] contagious skin disease. 脓疱病(一种接触传染性皮肤病).

im·petu·ous /ɪm'petʃʊǝs; ɪm'pɛtʃʊǝs/ *adj* moving quickly or violently; acting, inclined to act, on impulse, energetically but with insufficient thought or care; done or said hastily: 急促或猛烈的; 冲动的; 卤莽的; 轻率妄动的: *Children are usually more ~ than old people.* 孩童们通常较老年人冲动. *Your ~ remarks will get you into trouble.* 你轻率的言谈会给你带来麻烦. ~**ly** *adv* **im·petu·os·ity** /ˌɪmˌpetʃʊ'ɒsǝtɪ; ˌɪmpetʃʊ'ɑsǝtɪ/ *n* [U] quality of being ~; [C] (*pl* **-ties**) ~ act, remark, etc. 急促; 猛烈; 冲动; 卤莽; 冲动的言语、行动等.

im·pe·tus /'ɪmpɪtǝs; 'ɪmpǝtǝs/ *n* (*pl* ~**es** /-sɪz, -sɪz/) **1** [U] force with which a body moves. 动力; 冲力. **2** [C] impulse; driving force: 刺激; 推动力. *The treaty will give an ~ to trade between the two countries.* 这条约将促进两国间的贸易.

im·pi·ety /ɪm'paɪǝtɪ; ɪm'paɪǝtɪ/ *n* (formal) (正式用语) **1** [U] lack of reverence or dutifulness. 不尊敬; 不恭. **2** [C] (*pl* **-ties**) act, remark, etc that shows lack of reverence or dutifulness. 不恭敬的行为; 言语等.

im·pinge /ɪm'pɪndʒ; ɪm'pɪndʒ/ *vi* [VP3A] ~ *on/upon,* (formal) make an impact on. (正式用语)撞击; 冲击. ~**·ment** *n*

im·pi·ous /'ɪmpɪǝs; 'ɪmpɪǝs/ *adj* (formal) not pious. (正式用语)不虔敬的. ~**·ly** *adv*

imp·ish /'ɪmpɪʃ; 'ɪmpɪʃ/ *adj* of or like an imp; mischievous. 小魔鬼的; 似小魔鬼的; 顽皮的. ~**·ly** *adv* ~**·ness** *n*

im·plac·able /ɪm'plækǝbl; ɪm'plekǝbl/ *adj* (formal) that cannot be appeased; relentless: (正式用语)不能平息的; 无情的: *an ~ enemy;* 残酷的敌人; ~ *hatred/love.* 深仇(深爱).

im·plant /ɪm'plɑːnt *US:* -'plænt; ɪm'plænt/ *vt* [VP 6A, 14] ~ *in,* fix or put ideas, feelings, etc in: 灌输, 注入(思想、感情等): *deeply ~ed hatred;* 深植内心的仇恨; ~ *sound principles in the minds of children.* 将健全的原则灌输在儿童心中.

im·ple·ment¹ /'ɪmplɪmǝnt; 'ɪmplǝmǝnt/ *n* tool or instrument for working with: 工具; *farm ~s;* 农具; *stone and bronze ~s made by primitive man.* 原始人所制的石器和青铜器. ⇨ the illus at **tool.** 参看 tool 之插图.

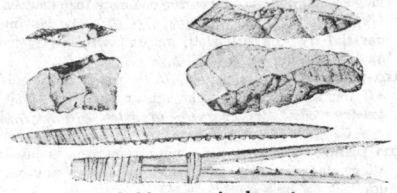

primitive stone implements

im·ple·ment² /'ɪmplɪmǝnt; 'ɪmplǝˌmɛnt/ *vt* [VP6A] carry an undertaking, agreement, promise into effect: 实现; 完成(任务等); 履行(协定; 诺言): ~ *a scheme.* 实现一计划. **im·ple·men·ta·tion** /ˌɪmplɪmen'teɪʃn; ˌɪmplǝmen'teʃǝn/ *n*

im·pli·cate /'ɪmplɪkeɪt; 'ɪmplɪˌket/ *vt* [VP6A, 14] ~ *(in),* (formal) show that (sb) has a share (in a crime, etc): (正式用语)使(某人)牵连于(罪行等中); 显示(某人)和(罪行等)有连带关系: ~ *officials in a bribery scandal.* 显示一些官员与受贿丑闻有所牵连. ⇨ **involve.**

im·pli·ca·tion /ˌɪmplɪ'keɪʃn; ˌɪmplɪ'keʃǝn/ *n* (formal) (正式用语) **1** [U] implicating or being implicated (in a crime, etc). 牵连于罪行等中). **2** [C] what is implied; sth hinted at or suggested, but not expressed: 含意; 暗示: *What are the ~s of this statement?* What is implied by it? 这一声明的含意是什么?

im·pli·cit /ɪm'plɪsɪt; ɪm'plɪsɪt/ *adj* (formal) (正式用语) **1** ~ *(in),* implied though not plainly expressed: 暗示的; 含蓄的: *an ~ threat;* 暗示的恐吓; ~ *in the contract.* 在契约中暗示的. ⇨ **explicit.** **2** unquestioning: 不置疑的: ~ *belief.* 绝对相信; 盲信. ~**·ly** *adv*

im·plore /ɪm'plɔː(r); ɪm'plor/ *vt* [VP6A, 17, 14] ~ *(for),* request earnestly: 恳求; 哀求: ~ *a judge for mercy;* 恳求法官给予怜悯; ~ *a friend to help one;* 恳求一位友人帮助; *an imploring glance.* 哀求的眼光. **im·plor·ing·ly** *adv*

im·plo·sion /ɪm'plǝʊʒn; ɪm'ploʒǝn/ *n* [U, C] bursting inward, collapse, of a vessel, eg an electric light bulb, from external pressure. (由外界压力引起的)向内破裂或陷入(例如电灯泡). ⇨ **explosion.**

im·ply /ɪm'plaɪ; ɪm'plaɪ/ *vt* (*pt, pp* **-plied**) [VP6A, 9] give or make a suggestion (*that*); involve the truth (of sth not definitely stated): 暗示; 含有 … 的意思: *an implied rebuke.* 暗示的指责. *Silence sometimes implies consent,* Failure to say 'No' may be taken to mean 'Yes'. 沉默有时含有同意的意思. *Are you ~ing that I am not telling the truth?* 你的意思是说我没讲实话吗?

im·po·lite /ˌɪmpǝ'laɪt; ˌɪmpǝ'laɪt/ *adj* not polite. 不礼貌的. ~**·ly** *adv* ~**·ness** *n*

im·poli·tic /ɪm'pɒlǝtɪk; ɪm'pɑlǝtɪk/ *adj* (formal) not politic; not expedient. (正式用语)失策的; 不利的.

im·pon·der·able /ɪm'pɒndǝrǝbl; ɪm'pɑndǝrǝbl/ *adj* **1** (phys) that cannot be weighed or measured (物理)不可称量的. **2** of which the effect cannot be estimated. 其结果无法估计的. □ *n* ~ thing; (esp *pl*) qualities, emotions, etc of which the effect cannot be estimated. 不可称量之物; (尤用复数)其结果无法估计的性质, 感情等.

im·port /ɪm'pɔːt; ɪm'port/ *vt* **1** [VP6A, 14] ~ *(from) (into),* bring in, introduce, esp goods from a foreign country: 输入; 进口: ~ *wool from Australia.*

自澳大利亚输入羊毛。 **2** [VP6A, 9] (formal) mean; signify; make known(that): (正式用语) 含有 …之意; 表示; 说明: *What does this ~? What is its significance?* 这事的意义是什么？ □ *n* /ˈɪmpɔːt/ 'import/ **1** (usu *pl*) goods ~ed: (通常用复数) 输入品; 进口货: *~s of raw cotton*, 输入的原棉; *food ~s*. 进口的食品。 **2** [U] act of ~ing goods. 输入; 进口。 **3** [U] what is implied; meaning: 含义; 意义: *What is the ~ of his statement?* 他的声明的意义是什么？ **4** [U] (formal) importance: (正式用语)重要: *questions of great ~*. 极为重要的问题。 **~er** *n* person (usu a merchant) who ~s goods. 进口商人。 **im·port·ation** /ˌɪmpɔːˈteɪʃn; ˌɪmpɔrˈteʃən/ *n* [U] act of ~ing (goods); [C] sth ~ed. 输入; 进口; 输入品; 进口货。

im·port·ant /ɪmˈpɔːtnt; ɪmˈpɔrtn̩t/ *adj* **1** of great influence; to be treated seriously; having a great effect: 重要的; 严重的; 重大的: *~ decisions/statements, etc.* 重大的决定(重要的声明等)。 **2** (of a person) having a position of authority. (指人)显要的; 位尊的。 **~·ly** *adv* **im·port·ance** /-tns; -tn̩s/ *n* [U] being ~: 重要; 重大; 显要: *The matter is of great/no/not much/little importance to us.* 这事对我们极为(不, 不太)重要。 *He spoke with an air of importance.* 他神气十足地说话。

im·por·tu·nate /ɪmˈpɔːtʃunət; ɪmˈpɔrtʃənt/ *adj* (formal) (正式用语) **1** (of persons) making repeated and inconvenient requests: (指人)不断作予人不便之要求的; 缠扰不休的: *an ~ beggar.* 缠扰不休的乞丐。 **2** (of affairs, etc) urgent: (指事务等) 急切的: *~ demands/claims.* 急切的要求。 **~·ly** *adv* **im·por·tun·ity** /ˌɪmpɔ-ˈtjuːnɪtɪ US: -ˈtuː-; ˌɪmpɔrˈtjunɪtɪ/ *n* [U] being ~(1); (*pl* -ties) instance of this. 不断作予人不便的要求; 缠扰不休; (复)上述的实例。

im·por·tune /ˌɪmpɔˈtjuːn; ˌɪmpɔˈtjun/ *vt* [VP6A,9, 14, 17] **~** (*for*), (formal) (正式用语) **1** beg urgently and repeatedly: 再三要求; 不断请求: *She ~d her husband for more money/with requests for money/to give her more money.* 她不断请求丈夫多给她些钱。 **2** (of a prostitute) solicit(2). (指娼妓)拉客。

im·pose /ɪmˈpəuz; ɪmˈpoz/ *vt, vi* **1** [VP14] **~** *on*, lay or place a tax, duty, etc on: 加(税, 义务等于: *New taxes ~d on wines and spirits.* 酒类加征新税。 *I must perform the task that has been ~d upon me.* 我必须要做已加在我身上的工作。 **2** [VP14] **~** *on sb*, force (sth oneself, one's company) on sb: 强使(某人接受某事物, 自己); 硬缠着某人: *Don't ~ yourself/your company on people who don't want you.* 不要缠着不愿和你在一起的人。 **3** [VP3A] **~** *upon sth*, take advantage of: 利用: *~ upon sb's good nature.* 利用某人的好心肠。 **im·pos·ing** *adj* making a strong impression because of size, character, appearance: 因体积, 性格, 外貌而予人强烈印象的; 壮丽的; 堂皇的: *an imposing old lady;* 仪态雍容的老妇人; *an imposing display of knowledge.* 在学识方面令人赞叹的表现。 **im·pos·ing·ly** *adv*

im·po·si·tion /ˌɪmpəˈzɪʃn; ˌɪmpəˈzɪʃən/ *n* **1** [U] the act of imposing(1): 征税; 课税: *Everyone grumbled at the ~ of new taxes.* 每个人都对新课的税不满。 **2** [C] sth imposed, eg a tax, burden, punishment, unwanted guest. 征收的物(例如税, 负担, 惩罚, 不速之客)。

im·poss·ible /ɪmˈpɔsəbl; ɪmˈpasəbl̩/ *adj* **1** not possible: 不可能的: *an ~ scheme/story.* 不可能的计划 (故事)。 *the ~,* that which is ~: 不可能之事: *Don't ask me to do the ~.* 别要求我作不可能的事。 **2** that cannot be endured: 无法忍受的: *It's an ~ situation!* 这种局势令人无法忍受! *He's an ~ person.* 他是个令人无法忍受的人。 **im·poss·ibly** /-əblɪ; -əblɪ/ *adv* **im·possi·bil·ity** /ɪmˌpɔsəˈbɪlɪtɪ; ɪmˌpasəˈbɪlɪtɪ/ *n* [U] state of being ~; [C] (*pl* -ties) sth that is ~. 不可能; 不可能的事。

im·pos·tor /ɪmˈpɔstə(r); ɪmˈpastɚ/ *n* person pretending to be sb he is not. 冒充者; 骗子。

im·pos·ture /ɪmˈpɔstʃə(r); ɪmˈpastʃɚ/ *n* [C] act of deception by an impostor; [U] fraudulent deception:

冒充; 蒙骗: *make a living by lying and ~.* 以说谎及蒙骗为生。

im·po·tent /ˈɪmpətənt; ˈɪmpətənt/ *adj* 'lacking sufficient strength (to do sth); unable to act; (of males) wholly lacking in sexual power. 无力(做某事)的; 无行动能力的; (指男子)阳萎的, 无性交能力的。 **~·ly** *adv* **im·po·tence** /-əns; -əns/ *n* [U] state of being ~: 无力; 无行动能力; 阳萎: *We have reduced the enemy to impotence,* made them quite powerless. 我们已彻底消灭敌人的战斗力。

im·pound /ɪmˈpaund; ɪmˈpaund/ *vt* [VP6A] **1** take possession of by law or by authority. 收押; 扣押; 没收; 充公。 **2** (in former times) shut up (cattle that had strayed) in a pound. (昔时) 将 (迷途的牛) 关入栏中。 ⇨ **pound²**.

im·pov·er·ish /ɪmˈpɔvərɪʃ; ɪmˈpavərɪʃ/ *vt* [VP6A] (formal) cause to become poor; take away good qualities: (正式用语)使穷困; 除去优点。 *~ed by doctors' bills;* 因付医药费而穷困; *~ed soil,* eg when crops are grown year after year without the use of fertilizers, 贫瘠的土壤(例如年复一年种植作物而不使用肥料); *~ed rubber,* rubber that has lost its elasticity. 失去弹性的橡皮。 **~·ment** *n*

im·prac·ti·cable /ɪmˈpræktɪkəbl; ɪmˈpræktɪkəbl̩/ *adj* **1** that cannot be put into practice: 不能实行的: *an ~ scheme.* 不能实行的计划。 **2** (of routes) impassable; that cannot be used. (指道路或航线)不能通行的; 不能使用的。 **im·prac·ti·cably** /-əblɪ; -əblɪ/ *adv* **im·prac·ti·ca·bil·ity** /ɪmˌpræktɪkəˈbɪlətɪ; ɪmˌpræktɪkəˈbɪlətɪ/, **~·ness** *n*

im·prac·ti·cal /ɪmˈpræktɪkl̩; ɪmˈpræktɪkl̩/ *adj* not practical. 不切实际的; 不能实行的。

im·pre·cate /ˈɪmprɪkeɪt; ˈɪmprɪˌket/ *vt* [VP14] **~** *on/upon sb,* (formal) invoke, call down (evil on sb): (正式用语)求天降(祸于某人); 诅咒。 **im·pre·ca·tion** /ˌɪmprɪˈkeɪʃn; ˌɪmprɪˈkeʃən/ *n* [C] curse. 咒语。

im·preg·nable /ɪmˈpreɡnəbl; ɪmˈpreɡnəbl̩/ *adj* that cannot be overcome or taken by force; able to resist all attacks: 不能克服的; 不能以暴力取得的; 攻不破的; *an ~ fortress;* 巩固的堡垒; *~ defences/arguments.* 攻不破的防御工事(驳不倒的论点)。 **im·preg·nably** /-əblɪ; -əblɪ/ *adv* **im·preg·na·bil·ity** /ɪmˌpreɡnəˈbɪlətɪ; ɪmˌpreɡnəˈbɪlətɪ/ *n*

im·preg·nate /ˈɪmpreɡneɪt US: ɪmˈpreɡ-; ɪmˈpreɡnet/ *vt* [VP6A, 14] **~** *(with),* **1** make pregnant; fertilize, eg an ovum. 使怀孕; 授胎; 使(卵子等)受精。 **2** fill, saturate: 灌满; 浸透; 使饱和: *water ~d with salt.* 饱含食盐的水。 **3** imbue, fill with feelings, moral qualities, etc. 使充满(感情, 美德等); 灌输。

im·pre·sario /ˌɪmprɪˈsɑːrɪəu; ˌɪmprɪˈsɑrɪ,o/ *n* (*pl* -s / -z; -z /) manager of an operatic or concert company; sponsor of commercial public entertainment. 歌剧团或音乐团的经理人; 商业性娱乐节目的赞助人。

im·press /ɪmˈpres; ɪmˈpres/ *vt* [VP6A,14] **~** *(on/upon)/(with),* **1** press (one thing on or with another); make (a mark, etc) by doing this: 以一物压(另一物); 盖(印); 压印(记号等): *~ wax with a seal;* 用印盖在火漆上; *~ a seal on wax;* 盖印于火漆上; *~ a figure/design on sth.* 将一图形(图案)印于某物上。 **2** have a strong influence on; fix deeply (on the mind, memory): 给予强烈影响; 使留深刻印象; 使铭记: *His words are strongly ~ed on my memory.* 他的话深深铭记在我心头。 *The book did not ~ me at all,* I did not think it good, useful, etc. 这书没有我任何印象。 *~ed on him the importance of his work,* 我使他知晓他工作的重要性。 *He ~ed me unfavourably,* I formed an unfavourable opinion of him. 我对他的印象不好。 □ *n* /ˈɪmpres; ˈɪmpres/ mark made by stamping a seal, etc on sth. 印记。

im·pression /ɪmˈpreʃn; ɪmˈpreʃən/ *n* [C] **1** mark made by pressing: 印记: *the ~ of a seal on wax.* 盖于火漆上的印记。 **2** print (of an engraving, etc). (雕版等)版图; 版画; 印出的图画。 **3** (product of) any one

printing operation: 一版; 一次印刷; 一次印行之书刊: *a first ~ of 5000 copies.* 第一次印刷的五千册. *Forty ~s* (= reprints without resetting; ⇨ **edition**) *of this book have been sold so far.* 此书迄今已销了四十版(指原版第四十次印刷). **4** effect produced on the mind or feelings: 印象: *It's my ~ that ...;* 我的印象是 …; *The speech made a strong ~ on the House.* 这演说给下议院议员们留下深刻的印象. *I'm surprised you got an unfavourable ~ of him.* 我很惊讶你对他印象不佳. *What were your first ~s of London?* 你对伦敦的最初印象如何? *First ~s are often misleading.* 第一印象时常使人发生错觉. **5** (vague or uncertain) idea, belief: (模糊或不确定的) 观念; 意念: *It's my ~ that he doesn't want to come.* 我觉得他好象不想来. **be under the ~ that ...** , have a vague idea, think, that.... 以为; 认为. **~·ism** /-ɪzəm; -ɪzəm/ *n* [U] method of painting or writing so as to give the general effect without elaborate detail. (绘画或写作之) 印象派; 印象主义. **~·ist** /-ɪst; -ɪst/ *n* person who uses this method. 印象主义者; 印象主义画家. **im·pres·sion·is·tic** /ɪm,preʃə'nɪstɪk; ɪm,preʃə'nɪstɪk/ *adj* **1** of, characteristic of, ~ism or ~ists. 印象主义(者)的. **2** giving only a general ~. 仅给予一般印象的.

im·pres·sion·able /ɪm'preʃənəbl; ɪm'preʃənəbl/ *adj* easily influenced: 易受影响的; 易受感动的: *children who are at the ~ age,* adolescent; 青春期的孩子; *an ~ young lady,* eg one who easily falls in love. 容易动感情的少女(例如易坠入情网者).

im·pres·sive /ɪm'presɪv; ɪm'presɪv/ *adj* making a deep impression on the mind and feelings: 给人深刻印象的: *an ~ ceremony.* 予人以深刻印象的典礼. **~·ly** *adv* **~·ness** *n*

im·pri·ma·tur /,ɪmprɪ'meɪtə(r); ,ɪmprɪ'meɪtə/ *n* (RC Church) official permission to print; (fig) sanction, approval. (天主教)印书许可证; (喻)许可; 准许.

im·print /ɪm'prɪnt; ɪm'prɪnt/ *vt* [VP14] **~ with/ on,** print; stamp: 印; 盖印于: *a postmark/a postmark on a letter;* 盖邮戳于信件上; *ideas ~ed on the mind.* 铭记于心中的观念. □ *n* /'ɪmprɪnt; 'ɪmprɪnt/ [C] that which is ~ed: 印象; 印迹: *the ~ of a foot* (= footprint); 脚印; 足迹; *the ~ of suffering on a person's face;* 苦难在人脸上留下的痕迹; *a publisher's/printer's ~,* his name, address, etc on the title-page or at the end of the book. 书籍内书名页或封底所印的出版者或印刷者的姓名、地址等资料.

im·prison /ɪm'prɪzn; ɪm'prɪzn/ *vt* [VP6A] put or keep in prison. 监禁; 下狱. **~·ment** *n* [U] ~ing or being ~ed: 监禁; 坐牢: *sentenced to one year's ~ment.* 被判有期徒刑一年.

im·prob·able /ɪm'prɒbəbl; ɪm'prɑbəbl/ *adj* not likely to be true or to happen: 似不可信的; 不大可能发生的: *an ~ story/result.* 似不可信的故事/不大可能的结果). *Rain is ~.* 不象要下雨的样子. **im·prob·ably** /-əblɪ; -əblɪ/ *adv* **im·prob·abil·ity** /ɪm,prɒbə'bɪlətɪ; ɪm,prɑbə'bɪlətɪ/ *n* [U]; [C] (*pl* **-ties**) sth which is or seems ~: 似不确实; 不大可能; 不大可能发生的事: *Don't worry about such improbabilities as floods and earthquakes.* 不要为象洪水和地震等不大可能发生的事而忧虑.

im·promptu /ɪm'prɒmptju: US: -tu:; ɪm'prɑmptu/ *adj, adv* without preparation: 未事先准备的: *an ~ speech;* 即席的演说; *speak ~.* 作即席演讲. □ *n* musical composition that seems to have been improvised. 似是演奏中临时作成的乐曲; 即兴曲.

im·proper /ɪm'prɒpə(r); ɪm'prɑpə/ *adj* **1** not suited for the purpose, situation, circumstances, etc: 不适当的; 不合式的: *Laughing and joking are ~ at a funeral.* 在葬礼时大笑和开玩笑是不适合的. **2** incorrect: 不正确的; 错误的: *~ diagnosis of disease.* 对疾病的错误诊断. **3** indecent: 不道德的; 下流的: *~ stories.* 低级故事. **~·ly** *adv*

im·pro·pri·ety /,ɪmprə'praɪətɪ; ,ɪmprə'praɪətɪ/ *n*

(formal) [U] incorrectness; unsuitability; [C] (*pl* **-ties**) improper act, remark, etc. (正式用语)不正确; 不适当; 不适当的行动、言语等.

im·prove /ɪm'pruːv; ɪm'pruv/ *vt, vi* **1** [VP6A, 2A] make or become better: 改良; 改善: *This is not good enough; I want to ~ it.* 这还不够好, 我要加以改进. *He came back from his holiday with greatly ~d health.* 他度假回来, 健康大为增进. *He is improving in health.* 他的健康状况正在好起来. *His health is improving.* 他的健康正在增进. [VP3A] **~ on/upon,** produce sth better than: 改良; 改进: *Your complexion is wonderful; don't try to ~ upon nature.* 你的肤色好得很; 不要企图改良天生的肤色. **2** [VP6A] make good use of; turn to account: 用; 利用: *~ the occasion.* 善用时机. **~·ment** *n* **1** [U] improving or being ~d: 改良; 进步: *This is need for improving in your handwriting.* 你的书法需要改进. *Little / no / not much ~ment seemed possible.* 似乎很少有 (没有, 不太有) 改善的可能了. **2** [C] sth which ~s, which adds to beauty, usefulness, value, etc: 改良的事物; 增加美, 用途, 价值等的事物: *I have noticed a number of ~ments in the town since I was here six years ago.* 我发现这城镇, 自从我六年前来过后, 有许多进步之处. *We all hope for an ~ment in the weather.* 我们都希望天气好转. *This is an ~ment upon your first attempt.* 这比你第一次所做的进步.

im·provi·dent /ɪm'prɒvɪdənt; ɪm'prɑvədənt/ *adj* (formal) wasteful; not looking to future needs. (正式用语)浪费的; 不顾将来需要的. **~·ly** *adv* **im·provi·dence** /-əns; -əns/ *n*

im·pro·vise /'ɪmprəvaɪz; 'ɪmprə,vaɪz/ *vt, vi* [VP 6A, 2A] **1** compose music while playing, compose verse while reciting, etc: 演奏时临时作曲; 朗诵时临时作诗; 即席作曲或诗: *If an actor forgets his words, he has to ~* 如果一个演员忘记了台词, 他必须随时作编作. *The pianist ~d an accompaniment to the song.* 那钢琴家为那首歌作了即兴伴奏. **2** provide, make or do sth quickly, in time of need, using whatever happens to be available: (为配合需要利用任何可用材料)临时凑成; 临时准备: *an ~d meal for unexpected guests;* 为不速之客临时准备的一餐饭; *an ~d bed,* eg one made up on a couch. 临时作成的床铺(例如在长沙发椅上所作的). **im·pro·vis·ation** /,ɪmprəvaɪ'zeɪʃn US: -vɪ'z-; ,ɪmprəvaɪ'zeʃən/ *n* [U, C].

im·prud·ent /ɪm'pruːdnt; ɪm'prudnt/ *adj* rash; indiscreet: 轻率的; 不谨慎的: *Isn't it ~ of you to marry while your salary is so low?* 在你薪水这样低之际结婚, 不是欠考虑吗? **~·ly** *adv* **im·prud·ence** /-ns; -ns/ *n* [U] being ~; [C] ~ act, remark, etc. 轻率; 不谨慎; 轻率的行动, 言语等.

im·pu·dent /'ɪmpjʊdənt; 'ɪmpjədənt/ *adj* shamelessly rude; rudely disrespectful: 厚颜的; 卤莽的; 冒昧的: *He was ~ enough to call me a fool.* 他无礼之极, 竟敢把我称作傻瓜. **~·ly** *adv* **im·pu·dence** /-əns; -əns/ *n* [U] being ~; ~ words and actions: 厚颜; 卤莽; 厚颜的言语和行动: *None of your impudence!* 不要如此卤莽! *He had the impudence to thumb his nose at me.* 他竟然厚脸皮瞒弄我.

im·pugn /ɪm'pjuːn; ɪm'pjun/ *vt* [VP6A] (formal) challenge, express doubt about (a statement, act, quality, etc). (正式用语)指疑(一声明, 行为, 性质等); 责难; 抨击.

im·pulse /'ɪmpʌls; 'ɪmpʌls/ *n* **1** [C] push or thrust; impetus: 推动; 推进力: *give an ~ to trade/education.* 促进贸易(教育). **2** [C] sudden inclination to act without thought about the consequences: 冲动; seized with an ~ to do sth; 情不自禁地欲做某事; *feel an irresistible ~ to jump out of a window,* eg during a fit of insanity. 感觉到了无法抵抗的冲动, 欲跳出窗外(例如当疯狂发作时). **3** [U] state of mind in which such inclinations occur; tendency to act without reflection: 冲动的心理状态; 不加思索而行事的倾向: *a man of ~.* 易冲动的人. **on (an) ~,** without reflection or planning: 凭冲动地; 未经思考或计划地: *phone sb on ~.* 一时冲动打电话给某人.

'**~-buy** vt, vi buy on ~. 未经考虑或计划而购买。**4** (science) sudden, brief force. (科学)脉冲;冲量。

im·pul·sion /ɪmˈpʌlʃn; ɪmˈpʌlʃən/ n [U] impelling; driving or being driven forward; [C] impetus; mental impulse. 驱使;推进;推动力;冲动。

im·pul·sive /ɪmˈpʌlsɪv; ɪmˈpʌlsɪv/ adj **1** (of persons, their conduct) acting on impulse; resulting from impulse: (指人,人的行为)凭冲动行事的; 由冲动造成的: a girl with an ~ nature. 天性易冲动的女郎。**2** (of a force) tending to impel. (指力量)推进的。~·ly adv ~·ness n

im·pun·ity /ɪmˈpjuːnɪtɪ; ɪmˈpjunɪtɪ/ n [U] freedom from punishment. 免受惩罚。**with ~,** without risk of injury or punishment. 不受损害或惩罚地。

im·pure /ɪmˈpjʊə(r); ɪmˈpjʊr/ adj not pure: 不纯的; 不纯洁的: the ~ air of towns; 城市中不洁的空气; ~ milk; 不纯的牛奶; ~ motives. 不纯洁的动机。**im·pur·ity** /-ətɪ; -ətɪ/ n [U] state of being ~; [C] (pl -ties) ~ thing: 不纯;不纯洁;不纯洁之物;杂质: impurities in food. 食物中的杂质。

im·pute /ɪmˈpjuːt; ɪmˈpjut/ vt [VP14] ~ to, (formal) consider as the act, quality, or outcome of: (正式用语)认系…之行为,性质或结果;归于;归咎于;诿于: They ~d the accident to the driver's carelessness. 他们将这次车祸归咎于驾驶的疏忽。He was innocent of the crime ~d to him. 对于所加之于他的罪,他是无罪的。**im·pu·ta·tion** /ˌɪmpjuːˈteɪʃn; ˌɪmpjuˈteʃən/ n [U] act of imputing; [C] accusation or suggestion of wrong-doing, etc: 归咎;归罪;非难: imputations on a person's character. 对一人品格的种种责难。

in¹ /ɪn; ɪn/ adv part (contrasted with out) (与 out 相对) **1** (used with many vv, in obvious meanings, as come in (=enter) and meanings that are not obvious, as give in (= surrender); ⇨ the v entries for these). (与多动词连用, 有时意义明显, 如 come in 中之 in, 有时意义不明显, 如 give in 中之 in; 参看动词各项). **2** be in, **(a)** at home: 在家; 未外出: Is there anyone in? 有人在家吗? My husband won't be in until six o'clock. 我先生要到六点才在家。**(b)** arrive: 到达: Is the train in yet, Has it arrived? 火车到了吗? **(c)** (of crops) harvested; brought in from the fields: (指农作物)收割了的; 已收获的: The wheat crop/the harvest is safely in. 小麦(收获物)安全地收割完了。**(d)** in season; obtainable: 当时的时令; 可获得的: Strawberries are in now. 草莓正当时令。When will oysters be in? 蚝什么时候上市? **(e)** in fashion: 流行: Long skirts are in again. 长裙子又流行了。**(f)** elected; in power; in office: 当选;掌握政权;执政: The Democrats are in. 民主党在执政。The Liberal candidate is in, has been elected. 自由党候选人已当选。**(g)** burning: 燃烧着: Is the fire still in? 火仍在燃烧吗? **(h)** (cricket, baseball) batting: (板球;棒球)击球: Which side is in? 哪一边在击球? He was bowled before he had been in (= at the wicket) five minutes. 他击球尚未到五分钟便被迫退场了。**3** be in for sth, **(a)** likely to have or experience (esp sth unpleasant): 可能尝受或经验(尤指不愉快的事): I'm afraid we're in for a storm. 我恐怕我们要遭受暴风雨了。You're in for an unpleasant surprise. 你可能遇到不愉快的意外之事。**(b)** committed to; having agreed to take part in: 答应; 同意参加: I'm in for the competition, shall be a competitor. 我将参加比赛。Are you in for the 1000 metres race? 你参加一千米赛跑吗? **have it in for sb,** be wanting to take revenge on him. 欲惩罚某人。**be in on sth,** (colloq) participate in; have a share in: (口)参加;加入: I'd like to be in on this scheme. 我想参与这件事情。**day in, day out; week in, week out; year in, year out,** day after day, week after week, etc in a monotonous way. 一天又一天;一周又一周;年复一年。**in and out,** now in and now out: 时进时出: He's always in and out of hospital, is frequently ill and in hospital. 他时常生病住院。**be (well) in with sb,** be on good terms with him (and likely to benefit from his friendship). 与某人相

处甚好(并可能因其友谊而获益)。**4** (preceding a n): (用于名词前): an 'in-patient, one who lives in a hospital while receiving treatment (contrasted with 'out-patient). 住院病人(与 out-patient 相对)。

in² /ɪn; ɪn/ prep (For the use of in with many nn and vv, ⇨ the n and v entries. 与许多名词和动词连用的用法, 请参看名词和动词各项, eg 例如 in print, in memory of, fail in an examination). **1** (of place: ⇨ **at**): (指地点): the highest mountain in the world; 世界上最高的山; in Africa; 在非洲; in the east of Asia; 在亚洲东部; in Denmark; 在丹麦; in the provinces; 在各省; in Kent; 在肯特郡; in London; 在伦敦; the village in which he was born; 他出生的那个村子; the only shop in the village; 这村中唯一的商店; islands in the Pacific Ocean; 太平洋的岛屿; sailing in British waters, ie on the seas round Britain; 在英国近海航行; in every quarter of the town; 在城中每一地区; children playing in the street; 在街上游玩的孩子们; not a cloud in the sky; 天空中没有一片云; swimming in the lake; 在湖中游泳; standing in the corner of the room. 站在该房间的角落里。Cf 参较 the house at the corner; working in the fields/in coal-mines; 在田野(煤矿)工作; a picnic in the woods; 林中的野餐; a holiday in the country/in the mountains. 在乡间(山间)所度的一个假日。Cf 参较 at the seaside; a light in the distance; 在远处的灯; in the background/foreground; 在暗中(在显著地方); lying in bed. 躺在床上。Cf 参较 sitting on the bed; sitting in an armchair. 坐在有扶手的椅上。Cf 参较 on a chair without arms; in school/church/prison; 在学校(在教堂;在狱中); a ride in a motor-car. 乘汽车兜风。He was wounded in the leg. 他的腿部受伤。The key is in the lock. 钥匙在锁中。There were plants in the window, ie on the window-sill, framed by the window. 窗槛上有花木。What would you do in my place, if you were situated as I am situated? 你如果处在我的地位将怎样做呢? I read about it in the newspapers. 我在报上看到有关此事的报导。He had a stick in his hand and a cigar in his mouth. 他手上拿着一根手杖, 嘴里衔着一支雪茄。You will find the verse in the second chapter of Genesis.: 你在创世记第二章会找到这一节。**2** (of direction): (指方向): in this/that direction; 朝此(那)方向; in all directions. 四面八方; 各处。**3** (indicating direction of motion or activity) into: (指运动或动作的方向)进入: He dipped his pen in the ink. 他将他的笔尖浸入墨水中。He put his hands in his pockets. 他把手放进口袋里。Cut the apple in two, into halves. 把这苹果切成两半。Cut/break it in two. 把它切(破)成两半。Throw it in the fire. 把它丢到火中。They fell in love. 他们在恋爱。**4** (of time when): (指时间): in the 20th c; 在二十世纪里; in 1970; 在一九七〇年; in the reign of Queen Anne; 在安女王统治时期; in spring/summer, etc; 在春季(夏季等); in my absence; 在我不在的时间; in his youth; 在他年轻时; in old age; 在晚年; still in her teens; 在她还是十几岁时; in these/those days; 近来(在那些日子里); in the morning/afternoon/evening. 在早晨(下午、晚间)。Cf 参较 on Monday morning; in the daytime; 在白昼; at ten o'clock in the night. 在晚上十点钟。Cf 参较 at night; in (the) future; 今后(在将来); in the past; 在过去; in the end, finally; 最后; in time of war; 在战时; in the hour of victory/death, etc. 在胜利(死亡等)的时刻。He has met many famous men in his time, 他一生中遇到过许多名人。She was a famous beauty in her day, during her best years. 她年轻时是一位著名的美人。The school was quite small in my time, when I was there. 我在那里的时候这学校还很小。**5** (of time) in the course of; within the space of: (指时间)过(若干时间); 在(若干时间)内: I shall be back in a short time/in a few days/in a week's time, etc. 我过一会儿(几天、一星期等)回来。Can you finish the work in an hour? 你能在一小时内完成这工作吗? I'll be ready in a moment. 我过一会儿我便准备好了。Cf also 亦参较 in time. **6** (indicating inclusion): (表示包含之义): seven days in a week; 一星期有七天; four

quarts in a gallon; 一加仑有四夸脱; *a man in his 'thirties,* 1e between 30 and 39 years of age; 一个三十多岁(自 30 至 39 岁)的男子; *in the early thirties of this century,* 1e between 1930 and 1934 or 1935. 在本世纪三十年代的初期(在一九三〇年或一九三四或一九三五年之间). *There is 10 per cent for service in the (hotel) bill.* 这(旅馆)帐单中有百分之十的服务费. *He has nothing of the hero in him,* Heroism is not among his characteristics. 他没有英雄气概. *He has in him the makings of a good soldier,* has qualtties, abilities, etc that will help him to become a good soldier. 他具有成为一个优秀军人的资质. **7** (indicating ratio): (表示比率): *a slope/gradient of one in five.* 五分之一的斜坡(坡度)(约合仰角 11¹/₂度). *He paid his creditors 25 p in the pound.* 他向他的债权人按每英镑二十五便士(即原值的四分之一)偿还. *Not one in ten of the boys could spell well.* 这些男孩中拼字正确的不到十分之一. **8** (of dress, etc): (指衣服等)穿着; 戴着: *dressed/clothed in rags;* 衣衫褴褛; *the man in the top hat;* 那个戴着高顶礼帽的男子; *a prince in disguise;* 乔装的王子; *the woman in white,* wearing white clothes; 那个穿白衣服的女子; *in uniform;* 穿着制服; *in mourning;* 穿着丧服; *in brown shoes;* 穿着棕色皮鞋; *in his shirt sleeves,* not wearing a jacket or coat; 仅穿着衬衫(未穿外套); *a prisoner in irons.* 戴着镣铐的囚犯. **9** (indicating physical surroundings, circumstances, etc): (表示环境或境遇等)在…环境下: *go out in the rain;* 冒雨出去; *sitting in the sun (shine);* 坐在阳光下; *standing outside in the cold;* 站在外面受寒冷; *sleep in the open;* 在露天睡眠; *a temperature of 95°F in the shade;* 在荫凉处 95 华氏度的气温; *lose one's way in the dark;* 在黑暗中迷了路; *unable to work in this heat;* 在这种炎热的天气无法工作; *go for a walk in the moonlight.* 在月光下散步. **10** (indicating state or condition): (表示情况或状态): *in a troubled state;* 在烦恼中; *in good order;* 整齐; 情况良好; *in poor health;* 健康不佳; *in good repair;* 情况良好; *in a good humour;* 心情好; *in a fever of excitement;* 极为兴奋; *in despair;* 在绝望中; *in a rage;* 在愤怒中; *in tears;* 在哭泣; *in a hurry;* 匆忙中; *living in luxury;* 生活奢侈; *in poverty;* 在贫困中; *in ruins;* 在颓废状态中; *not in the mood for work;* 没有心情工作; *in debt;* 负债; *in love;* 恋爱中; *in doubt;* 怀疑; *in wonder;* 惊奇; *in public;* 公开地; *in secret;* 秘密地; *in fun/jest/joke;* 玩笑地; *in earnest.* 认真地; 热心地. **11** (indicating form, shape, arrangement): (表示形式, 形状, 排列): *a novel in three parts;* 分作三部分的一本小说; *books packed in bundles of ten;* 每十本一包的书籍; *men standing about in groups;* 成群地站在各处的人们; *children sitting in rows;* 排排坐的孩子们; *wolves hunting in packs;* 成群猎食的狼; *words in alphabetical order;* 按字母顺序排列的词; *with her hair in curls/in ringlets;* 她的头发卷曲着; *dancing a ring;* 围成一圆圈跳舞; *cloth hanging in folds.* 折着悬挂的布. **12** (indicating the method of in expression, the medium, means, material, etc): (表示表达的方法, 媒介, 工具, 材料等): *speaking/writing in English;* 用英语说(写); *a message in code;* 以密码发出的消息; *written in ink/pencil;* 用墨水(铅笔)写的; *(printed) in italic type;* 以斜体(印刷)的; *in two colours;* 以二种颜色; *in writing;* 书写地; *in a few words;* 简言之; *in round numbers,* eg 200 000 for 197 563; 以约略数字言之(例如以 200 000 代替 197 563); *talking in a loud voice;* 大声谈话; *bound in leather;* 皮面装订的; *painted in oils;* 油彩画的; *carved in oak;* 橡木雕刻的; *cast in bronze;* 青铜铸的; *a statue in marble;* 大理石雕像; *payment in cash/in kind.* 现金(实物)给付. **13** (indicating degree or extent): (表示程度或限度): *in large/small quantities;* 大(少)量; *in great numbers;* 许多; *in some measure;* 有几分; *in part.* 一部分; 有几分. *They appeared in great strength.* 敌人的兵力似乎很强. *in all,* as the total: 合计: *We were fifteen in all.* 我们共有十五位. **14** (indicating identity): (表示同一人或物): *You will always have a good friend in me,* I shall always befriend you. 我永远是你的朋友.

We have lost a first-rate teacher in Jim, Jim, who has left us, was a first-rate teacher. 我们失去了第一流的教师吉姆. *The enemy lost 200 in killed and wounded,* 200 of them were killed or wounded. 敌人伤亡二百名. **15** (indicating relation, reference, respect): (表示关系, 方面): *in some/all respects;* 在某些(各)方面; *in every way;* 各方面; *inferior in physique but superior in intellect;* 体格较差但智力较高; *young in years but old in wisdom;* 年纪虽轻但智慧甚高; *weak in the head,* not intelligent; 智力低; *deficient in courage,* 缺少勇气; *a country rich/poor in minerals;* 矿物丰富(缺乏)的国家; *blind in the left eye;* 左眼失明; *my equal in strength;* 力量与我相等之人; *ten feet in length/depth/diameter, etc;* 长度(深度, 直径等)为十英尺; *wanting/lacking in judgement.* 缺乏判断力. **16** (indicating occupation, activity, etc): (表示职业, 活动等): *He's in the army/in insurance/in the motor business/in the Cabinet/in the Air Ministry.* 他在陆军(保险业, 汽车业, 内阁, 空军部)服务. *He's in politics,* is a politician. 敌人从政. *He was killed in action,* while fighting in war. 他于作战时阵亡. *How much time do you spend in reading?* 你花费多少时间阅读? **17** (used in numerous prepositional phrases of the pattern *in*+*n*+*prep*, ⇨ the *n* entries, eg): (用于许多介词短语中, 其后跟一名词, 名词后再接一介词, 参看各该名词, 例如): *in defence of;* 保卫; *in exchange for;* 交换; *in justice to;* 对…公平; *in memory of;* 纪念; *in touch with.* 接触. **18** *in camera,* (legal) in private, in the judge's private room, not in open court; (colloq) secretly. (法律)不公开审讯; 闭庭审讯; (口)秘密地. *in that,* since, because; 由于; 因为: *The higher income tax is harmful in that it may discourage people from trying to earn more.* 所得税增高是有害的, 因为它可能使人不愿多赚钱. *in as/so far as,* in such measure as; to the extent that: 就…之限度; 至于…的程度; 就…而论: *He is a Russian in so far as he was born in Russia,* but he became a French citizen in 1920. 就他出生在俄国而言, 他是个俄国人, 但他在一九二〇年入了法国籍. *in itself,* in its own nature; absolutely; considered apart from other things: 在本质上; 完全地; 就其本身言: *Card playing is not harmful in itself;* it is only when combined with wild gambling that it may be harmful. 玩牌本身并无害处, 但若加上狂赌, 则有害处.

in³ /ɪn; ɪn/ *n* (only in) (仅用于) *the ins and (the) outs,* (a) political party in office and political party out of office. 执政党与在野党. (b) the different parts; the details and complexities: 详情; 细节: *know all the ins and outs of a problem.* 熟悉一问题之详情.

-in /ɪn; ɪn/ *suff* added to another word (usu a *v*) to indicate participation in a group activity, etc. 附加于另一词(通常为一动词)后, 表示参与集体活动等, ⇨ the *v* entries, 参看动词各项, eg 例如 *sit-in, teach-in.*

in·abil·ity /ˌɪnəˈbɪlətɪ; ˌɪnəˈbɪlətɪ/ *n* [U] ~ *(to do sth),* being unable; lack of power or means. 无能力; 无力量; 无方法.

in·ac·cess·ible /ˌɪnækˈsesəbl; ˌɪnækˈsesəbl/ *adj* ~ *(to),* (formal) not accessible. (正式用语)不能接近的; 不能进入的; 不能达到的. **in·ac·cessi·bil·ity** /ˌɪnækˌsesə-ˈbɪlətɪ; ˌɪnəkˌsesəˈbɪlətɪ/ *n* [U].

in·ac·cur·ate /ɪnˈækjurət; ɪnˈækjərɪt/ *adj* not accurate. 不准确的. ~ **·ly** *adv* **in·ac·cur·acy** /-əsɪ; -əsɪ/ *n* [U] being ~; [C] (*pl* -cies) ~ statement, etc. 不准确; 不正确的陈述等.

in·ac·tion /ɪnˈækʃn; ɪnˈækʃən/ *n* [U] doing nothing; lack of activity. 不做事; 不活动.

in·ac·tive /ɪnˈæktɪv; ɪnˈæktɪv/ *adj* not active. 不活动的; 不活跃的. **in·ac·ti·vate** /ˌɪnˈæktɪveɪt; ɪnˈæktə͵vet/ *vt* make ~: 使不活动: *inactivate a virus.* 使遏过性病原体停止活动. **in·ac·tiv·ity** /ˌɪnækˈtɪvətɪ; ˌɪnækˈtɪvətɪ/ *n* [U].

in·ad·equate /ɪnˈædɪkwət; ɪnˈædəkwɪt/ *adj* ~ *(for sth/to do sth),* not adequate; insufficient. 不适当的; 不充分的. ~ **·ly** *adv* **in·ad·equacy** /ɪnˈædɪkwəsɪ; ɪnˈædəkwəsɪ/;

ɪn'ædəkwəsɪ/ n [U].

in·ad·miss·ible /ˌɪnəd'mɪsəbl; ˌɪnəd'mɪsəbl/ adj that cannot be admitted or allowed: 不能承认的; 不可允许的: ~ evidence; 不能承认的证据; ~ in evidence. 不能作为证据的。

in·ad·ver·tent /ˌɪnəd'vɜːtənt; ˌɪnəd'vɜrtənt/ adj (formal) not paying or showing proper attention; (of actions) done thoughtlessly or not on purpose. (正式用语)不注意的; 不当心的; (指行动)疏忽或无意中所做的。 ~·ly adv in·ad·ver·tence /-təns; -təns/ n [U] the quality of being ~; [C] oversight or error which is the result of being ~. 不注意; 粗心; 疏忽。

in·alien·able /ɪn'eɪlɪənəbl; ɪn'eljənəbl/ adj (formal) (of rights, etc) that cannot be given away or taken away. (正式用语)(指权利等)不能让与的; 不可剥夺的。

in·ane /ɪ'neɪn; ɪn'en/ adj silly; senseless: 愚蠢的; 无意义的: an ~ remark. 无意义的话。 ~·ly adv in·an·ity /ɪ'nænətɪ; ɪn'ænətɪ/ n [U] being ~; [C] (pl -ties) ~ remark, act, etc. 愚蠢; 无意义; 愚蠢或无意义的言语, 行动等。

in·ani·mate /ɪn'ænɪmət; ɪn'ænəmɪt/ adj 1 lifeless: 无生命的: ~ rocks and stones. 无生命的岩石。 2 without animal life: 非动物的: ~ nature, outside the animal world. 非动物界。 3 spiritless; dull: 无生气的; 单调的: ~ conversation. 枯燥的谈话。

in·ani·tion /ˌɪnə'nɪʃn; ˌɪnə'nɪʃən/ n [U] (formal) (正式用语) 1 emptiness. 空虚。 2 extreme weakness from lack of food. 因饥饿而极端虚弱; 营养不足。

in·ap·pli·cable /ɪn'æplɪkəbl; ɪn'æplɪkəbl/ adj ~ (to), not applicable. 不适用的。

in·ap·preci·able /ˌɪnə'priːʃəbl; ˌɪnə'priʃəbl/ adj not worth reckoning; too small or slight to be perceived: 不值得计算或估价的; 微不足道的: an ~ difference. 细微不可辨的差异。

in·ap·pro·pri·ate /ˌɪnə'prəʊprɪət; ˌɪnə'proprɪɪt/ adj ~ to, not appropriate or suitable. 不合宜的。

in·apt /ɪn'æpt; ɪn'æpt/ adj unskilful; not bearing on the subject: 拙劣的; 不适切的: ~ remarks. 不适切的言语。 in·ap·ti·tude /ɪn'æptɪtjuːd US: -tuːd; ɪn'æptə,tjud/ n [U] being ~. 拙劣; 不适切。

in·ar·ticu·late /ˌɪnɑː'tɪkjʊlət; ˌɪnɑr'tɪkjələt/ adj 1 (of speech) not clear or distinct; not well joined together; (of a person) not speaking distinctly; not able to express himself clearly and fluently; not of the nature of speech: (指说话)不清楚的; 不连贯的; (指人)说话不清楚的; 不能清楚和流利地表达的; 不似说话的: ~ rage/sounds/letters. 气得说不出话(不清楚的声音; 不知所云的letters). 2 not jointed: 无关节的: an ~ body, eg a jelly-fish. 无关节的身体(例如水母)。

in·as·much as /ˌɪnəz'mʌtʃ əz; ˌɪnəz'mʌtʃ əz/ conj since; because. 由于; 因为。

in·at·ten·tion /ˌɪnə'tenʃn; ˌɪnə'tenʃən/ n [U] lack of, failure to pay, attention. 缺少注意力; 不注意。 in·at·ten·tive /ˌɪnə'tentɪv; ˌɪnə'tentɪv/ adj not attentive. 不注意的。

in·aud·ible /ɪn'ɔːdəbl; ɪn'ɔdəbl/ adj that cannot be heard. 听不见的。 in·audi·bil·ity /ɪnˌɔːdə'bɪlətɪ; ɪnˌɔdə'bɪlətɪ/ n [U].

in·aug·ural /ɪ'nɔːgjʊrəl; ɪn'ɔgjərəl/ adj of or for an inauguration: 就职的; 就职典礼的: an ~ lecture. 就职演说。 □ n ~ address. 就职演说。

in·aug·ur·ate /ɪ'nɔːgjʊreɪt; ɪn'ɔgjəˌret/ vt [VP6A] 1 introduce (a new official, professor, etc) at a special ceremony: 为(一新的官员, 教授等)举行就职典礼: ~ a president. 举行总统就职典礼。 2 enter, with public formalities, upon (an undertaking); open an exhibition / a new public building with formalities: 以公开仪式开始(某一事业); 为展览会(新公共建筑物)举行开幕式或落成典礼。 3 be the beginning of: 为...之始: The invention of the internal combustion engine ~d a new era in travel. 内燃机之发明为旅行开一新纪元。 **in·aug·ur·ation**

/ɪˌnɔːgjʊ'reɪʃn; ɪnˌɔgjə'reʃən/ n [U, C] inaugurating or being ~d: 就职典礼; 开创; 举行开幕式; 落成: the inauguration of the President of the US (20 Jan). 美国总统的就职典礼(一月二十日)。

in·aus·pi·cious /ˌɪnɔː'spɪʃəs; ˌɪnɔ'spɪʃəs/ adj not auspicious; not of good omen. 不吉祥的。 ~·ly adv

in·board /'ɪnbɔːd; 'ɪn,bord/ adj within the hull of a ship: 在船内的: an ~ motor. 船内马达。 ⇨ **outboard**.

in·born /ˌɪn'bɔːn; ɪn'bɔrn/ adj (of a quality) possessed (by a person or animal) at birth; implanted by nature: (指人或动物的性质)天生的; 天赋的: a boy with an ~ love of mischief; 生来喜欢恶作剧的男孩子; an ~ talent for art. 天赋的艺术才能。

in·bound /'ɪnbaʊnd; 'ɪn'baʊnd/ adj (of a ship) inward or homeward bound. (指船)归航的; 开向本国的。

in·bred /ˌɪn'bred; ɪn'bred/ adj 1 inborn; innate: 天生的; 与生俱来的: ~ courtesy. 天生的谦恭有礼。 2 bred for several or many generations from ancestors closely related. 近亲繁殖的。 **in·breed·ing** /ɪn'briːdɪŋ; 'ɪn,bridɪŋ/ n [U] breeding from closely related ancestors, stocks, etc. 近亲繁殖; 血族交配。

in·built /'ɪnbɪlt; 'ɪn'bɪlt/ adj = built-in, ⇨ **build**[1](3).

in·cal·cu·lable /ɪn'kælkjʊləbl; ɪn'kælkjələbl/ adj 1 too great to be calculated: 不可胜数的; 极大的: This has done ~ harm to our reputation. 这已经对我们的名誉造成极大的伤害。 2 that cannot be reckoned beforehand. 不能预计的。 3 (of a person, his character, etc) uncertain: (指人, 性情等)捉摸不定的; 善变的: a lady of ~ moods. 情绪捉摸不定的妇人。

in·can·descent /ˌɪnkæn'desnt; ˌɪnkən'desn̩t/ adj giving out, able to give out, light when heated: 遇热发光的; 白热的; 白炽的: an ~ filament, eg in an electric-light bulb. 白炽灯丝(例如电灯丝)。 **in·can·descence** /-sns; -sn̩s/ n [U] being or becoming ~. 遇热发光; 白热; 白炽。

in·can·ta·tion /ˌɪnkæn'teɪʃn; ˌɪnkæn'teʃən/ n [C, U] (the use of) (a form of) words used in magic; charm or spell. 咒语; 魔法; 咒符; 念咒。

in·capable /ɪn'keɪpəbl; ɪn'kepəbl/ adj ~ (of), not capable: 无能力的; 不能...的: ~ of telling a lie, too honest to do so. (因太诚实)不会说谎。 drunk and ~, helplessly drunk. 烂醉如泥。 **in·capa·bil·ity** /ɪnˌkeɪpə'bɪlətɪ; ˌɪnkepə'bɪlətɪ/ n [U].

in·ca·paci·tate /ˌɪnkə'pæsɪteɪt; ˌɪnkə'pæsə,tet/ vt [VP6A, 14] ~ sb (for/from), 1 make incapable or unfit: 使不能或不适合: His poor health ~d him for work / from working. 他的健康不佳使他不能工作。 2 disqualify. 使失去资格。

in·ca·pac·ity /ˌɪnkə'pæsətɪ; ˌɪnkə'pæsətɪ/ n [U] ~ (for sth/for doing sth/to do sth), inability; powerlessness: 无能力; 无力。

in·car·cer·ate /ɪn'kɑːsəreɪt; ɪn'kɑrsə,ret/ vt [VP6A] (formal) imprison. (正式用语)监禁。 **in·car·cer·ation** /ɪnˌkɑːsə'reɪʃn; ɪnˌkɑrsə'reʃən/ n

in·car·nate /ɪn'kɑːnət; ɪn'kɑrnɪt/ adj 1 having a body; (esp) in human form: 具有肉体的; (尤指)成为人形的: That prison officer is a devil ~/an ~ fiend. 那狱吏是恶魔的化身。 2 (of an idea, ideal, etc) appearing in human form: (指思想, 理想等)以人形显现的; 具体化的: Liberty ~. 自由的化身。 □ vt /'ɪnkɑːneɪt; ɪn'kɑrnet/ [VP6A] 1 make ~. 使成为...的化身; 使成为人形。 2 put (an idea, etc) into a real or material form. 使(思想等)具体化; 实现。 3 (of a person) be a living form of (a quality): (指人)为(某性质)之化身: a wife who ~s all the virtues. 具有所有美德之妻子。

in·car·na·tion /ˌɪnkɑː'neɪʃn; ˌɪnkɑr'neʃən/ n 1 the I~, the taking of bodily form by God in Jesus. 上帝之化身为耶稣基督。 2 [C] person looked upon as a type of a quality: 被视为某性质之典型的人; 化身: She looked the ~ of every desirable quality. 她看来象是各种美德的化身。

in·cau·tious /ɪn'kɔːʃəs; ɪn'kɔʃəs/ adj not cautious;

rash. 不谨慎的; 卤莽的。 ~·ly adv

in·cen·di·ary /ɪnˈsendɪərɪ US: -dɪerɪ/ ɪnˈsɛndɪˌɛrɪ/ n (pl -ries), adj 1 (person) setting fire to property unlawfully and with an evil purpose; (person) tending to stir up violence: 纵火的; 纵火者; 煽动的; 煽动者: an ~ speech/newspaper article. 煽动的演说 (报纸文章)。 2 (bomb)causing fire. 引起燃烧的; 燃烧弹。 in·cen·di·ar·ism /ˈɪnˌsendɪərɪzəm/ ɪnˈsɛndɪəˌrɪzm/ n [U].

in·cense¹ /ˈɪnsens/ ˈɪnsɛns/ n [U] (smoke of a) substance producing a sweet smell when burning. (焚烧时)可产生香气的)香; 香发出的烟。

in·cense² /ɪnˈsens/ ɪnˈsɛns/ vt [VP6A] make angry: 激怒: ~d by sb's conduct; 被某人的行为激怒; ~d at sb's remarks. 被某人的言语激怒。

in·cen·tive /ɪnˈsentɪv/ ɪnˈsɛntɪv/ n ~ (to sth/to do sth/to doing sth), [C, U] that which incites, rouses or encourages a person: 刺激; 动机; 鼓励; 诱因: He hasn't much ~/many ~s to work hard/to hard work. 他并没有努力工作的强烈动机。

in·cep·tion /ɪnˈsepʃn/ ɪnˈsɛpʃən/ n (formal) start. (正式用语)开始。

in·cer·ti·tude /ɪnˈsɜːtɪtjuːd US: -tuːd/ ɪnˈsɝtəˌtjud/ n [U] (formal) uncertainty. (正式用语)不确定。

in·cess·ant /ɪnˈsesnt/ ɪnˈsɛsnt/ adj continual; often repeated: 不断的; 不停的: a week of ~ rain. 连续下了一星期的雨。 ~·ly adv

in·cest /ˈɪnsest/ ˈɪnsɛst/ n [U] sexual intercourse between near relations, eg brother and sister. 乱伦(例如兄妹相奸)。 in·ces·tuous /ɪnˈsestjuəs/ ɪnˈsɛstʃʊəs/ adj of ~; guilty of, involving, ~. 乱伦的; 犯乱伦罪的; 涉及乱伦的。

inch /ɪntʃ/ ɪntʃ/ n 1 measure of length, one-twelfth of a foot: 英寸(一英尺的十二分之一): six ~es of rain in one day. 一天的雨量达六英寸。 ⇨ App 5. 参看附录五。 2 small amount. 少量。 ~ by ~, by degrees. 逐渐地。 by ~es, (a)only just: 刚刚: The car missed me by ~es. 那辆汽车差一点撞上我。 (b) bit by bit: gradually. 一点一点地; 逐渐地: He's every ~ a soldier. 他是个十足的军人。 within an ~ of, very near, almost: 距离很近; 几乎: He came within an ~ of being struck by a falling tile. 他差一点被落下的瓦打着。 not yield an ~, not give way at all. 丝毫不让步。 ⇨ vt, vi [VP15A, B, 2C] move by ~s; edge one's way: 慢慢移动; 渐进: ~ one's way forward; 慢慢前进; ~ along a ledge on a cliff. 沿悬崖之突出部分蠕动而进。

in·cho·ate /ɪnˈkəʊɪt/ ɪnˈkoɪt/ adj (formal) just begun; in an underdeveloped, half-formed state. (正式用语)刚开始的; 未开展的; 未形成的。 in·choa·tive /ɪnˈkəʊətɪv/ ɪnˈkoətɪv/ adj expressing the beginning of an action or state: 表示一动作或状态之开始的: (gram) (语法) inchoative verbs, eg get in get dark, fall in fall ill. 表始动词(例如 get dark 中之 get, fall ill 中之 fall)。

in·ci·dence /ˈɪnsɪdəns/ ˈɪnsədəns/ n way in which sth affects things: 发生的方式; 影响事物的方式: the ~ of a disease, the range or extent of its effect, the number and kind of people who catch it; 发病率(某疾病蔓延的范围, 病患的数目及种类); the ~ of a tax, the way it falls to certain people to pay it. 征税的方式; 赋税归宿。

in·ci·dent¹ /ˈɪnsɪdənt/ ˈɪnsədənt/ adj ~ to, (formal) forming a natural or expected part of; naturally connected with: (正式用语)形成…的自然的或预料中的一部分; 自然与…相关连的; 随带的: the risks ~ to the life of a test pilot; 飞机试飞员生活中易遭遇的危险; the social obligations ~ to life in the diplomatic service. 与外交界生活相关的社交义务。

in·ci·dent² /ˈɪnsɪdənt/ ˈɪnsədənt/ n 1 event, esp one of less importance than others: 事件(尤指比较不重要的小事件): frontier ~s, eg disputes between forces on a frontier. 边境纠纷(例如边境上两方部队间的争执)。

2 happening which attracts general attention. 引起公众注意的事件。 3 (modern use) happening, eg rebellion, bomb explosion, war, which for various reasons persons in authority do not wish to describe precisely. (现代用法)事变(例如叛乱, 爆炸, 战争等, 当局人士因各种原因不愿说明的事件)。 4 separate piece of action in a play or poem. (戏剧或诗中的)插曲; 枝节。

in·ci·den·tal /ˌɪnsɪˈdentl/ ˌɪnsəˈdɛntl/ adj ~ (to), 1 accompanying but not forming a necessary part: 附属的; 随带的: ~ music to a play. 戏剧的配乐; 剧乐。 2 small and comparatively unimportant: 微小而较不重要的: ~ expenses, additional to the main expenses. 杂费。 3 liable to happen or occur: 易发生的: discomforts ~ to exploration in a wild country. 荒野探险易遭遇到的艰苦。 ~·ly /-tlɪ; -tlɪ/ adv in an ~ manner; by chance. (戏剧或诗中的)插曲; 偶然地。

in·cin·er·ate /ɪnˈsɪnəreɪt/ ɪnˈsɪnəˌret/ vt [VP6A] burn to ashes. 烧成灰。 in·cin·er·ator /-tə(r)/ -tɚ/ n furnace, enclosed fireplace, for burning rubbish, etc. (垃圾等之)焚化炉。 in·cin·er·ation /ɪnˌsɪnəˈreɪʃn/ ˌɪnsɪnəˈreʃən/ n [U] burning up: 烧尽; 焚化: Household and industrial waste disposal—the choice is between tipping and incineration. 家庭及工业废物处理——其方式是丢弃或焚化。

in·cip·ient /ɪnˈsɪpɪənt/ ɪnˈsɪpɪənt/ adj beginning; in an early stage: 开始的; 初期的; 初发的: ~ decay of the teeth. 牙齿的初期蛀坏。

in·cise /ɪnˈsaɪz/ ɪnˈsaɪz/ vt [VP6A] make a cut in; engrave. 切割; 雕刻。 in·ci·sion /ɪnˈsɪʒn/ ɪnˈsɪʒən/ n [U] cutting (into sth); [C] cut, eg one made in a surgical operation. 割切; 切开; 切口(例如外科手术中所作者)。

in·cis·ive /ɪnˈsaɪsɪv/ ɪnˈsaɪsɪv/ adj sharp and cutting; (of a person's mind, remarks) acute; clear-cut: 锋利的; (指人的思想)敏锐的; (指言论)清晰中肯的: ~ criticism. 清晰中肯的批评。 ~·ly adv

in·cisor /ɪnˈsaɪzə(r)/ ɪnˈsaɪzɚ/ n (in human beings) any one of the eight sharp-edged front cutting teeth, four in the upper and four in the lower jaw. (人之)前齿; 门牙。 ⇨ the illus at mouth. 参看 mouth 之插图。

in·cite /ɪnˈsaɪt/ ɪnˈsaɪt/ vt [VP6A, 14, 17] ~ sb (to sth/to do sth), stir up, rouse: 激励; 煽动: Insults ~ resentment. 侮辱激起愤恨。 The soldier was shot for inciting his comrades to rise against their officers. 那士兵因煽动同志反叛其长官而被枪决。 ~·ment n [U] inciting or being ~d; [C] instance of this; sth that ~s. (被)激励; (被)煽动; (被)煽动或激励之实例; 煽动物; 激励物。

in·civ·il·ity /ˌɪnsɪˈvɪlətɪ/ ˌɪnsəˈvɪlətɪ/ n (formal) [U] impoliteness; [C] (pl -ties) impolite act, remark, etc. (正式用语)无礼; 无礼的行动, 言语等。

in·clem·ent /ɪnˈklemənt/ ɪnˈklɛmənt/ adj (formal) (of weather or climate) severe; cold and stormy. (正式用语)(指天气或气候)酷寒的; 寒冷而有狂风暴雨的。 in·clem·ency /-ənsɪ/ -ənsɪ/ n [U] being ~. 酷寒; 寒冷而有暴风雨。

in·cli·na·tion /ˌɪnklɪˈneɪʃn/ ˌɪnkləˈneʃən/ n 1 [C] bending; bowing; slope; slant: 倾斜; 弯曲; 斜度; 倾度: an ~ of the head, a nod; 点头; an ~ of the body, a bow; 鞠躬; the ~ of a roof, its degree of slope. 屋顶的斜度。 2 [C, U] ~ (to sth/to do sth), mental leaning; liking or desire; disposition: 意向; 癖性; 爱好; 性向: Are you usually ready to sacrifice ~ to duty, put on one side what you like doing in order to do your duty? 你通常愿意为了尽忠职守而牺牲个人的爱好吗? He showed no ~ to leave. 他没有表示离去的意思。 She is not free to follow her own ~s, even in the matter of marriage. 她无法照自己的意思行事, 甚至在婚姻方面也是如此。 He has an ~ (=tendency) to stoutness/to grow fat. 他有发胖的趋势。

in·cline¹ /ɪnˈklaɪn/ ɪnˈklaɪn/ vt, vi [VP6A, 15A, 2A] (cause to) lean, slope or slant; bend (the head, body, oneself) forward or downward: 倾斜; 使倾斜; 俯 (首)

弯(身): ~ *the head in prayer.* 低下头祈祷. **2** [VP17] (liter) dispose; direct: (文)使偏向; 指令: '*I ~ our hearts to keep this law.*' '让我们倾心遵守此戒律'. **3** [VP17] (usu passive) direct the mind in a certain direction; cause (sb) to have a tendency or wish(*to do* sth): (通常用被动语态) 使心向; 使(某人)有意(作某事, 与不定词连用): *The news ~s me / I am ~d to start at once.* 这消息使我想(我想)立刻动身. *His letter ~s me to believe that he doesn't want to come.* 他的来信使我相信他不要来. *I am ~d to think* (= I have a feeling or idea) *that he is opposed to the plan.* 我觉得他反对这计划. *He's ~d to be lazy.* 他性懒散. *We can go for a walk if you feel so ~d.* 假如你愿意的话, 我们可以去散步. **4** [VP4C] tend; be disposed: 倾向; 愿意: *I ~ to believe in his innocence.* 我愿相信他的无辜. **5** [VP3A] ~ *to / towards* sth, have a physical or mental tendency: 身心的倾向; 有某种体质: *He ~s to leanness.* 他体质瘦型. *She ~s towards melancholia.* 她有忧郁症的倾向.

in·cline² /ˈɪnklaɪn; ˈɪnklaɪn/ *n* slope; sloping surface: 斜坡; 斜面: *run down a steep ~;* 跑下一陡坡; *an ~ of 1 in 5.* 斜度为五分之一的斜坡. ⇨ **gradient.**

in·close, in·clos·ure /ɪnˈkləʊz; ɪnˈkloʊz(r)/; ɪn-ˈkloz, ɪnˈkloʒə/ = **enclose, enclosure.**

in·clude /ɪnˈkluːd; ɪnˈklud/ *vt* [VP6A, C] bring in, reckon, as part of the whole: 包括; 包含: *This atlas contains fifty maps, including six of North America.* 这部地图集含有五十幅地图, 包括北美地图六幅. *Price £2.75, postage ~d.* 价格2.75 英镑, 邮费包括在内. *Your duties ~ putting the children to bed.* 你的职责包括照顾孩子们就寝. **in·clu·sion** /ɪnˈkluːʒn; ɪnˈkluʒən/ *n* [U] including or being ~d; 包括; 包含.

in·clus·ive /ɪnˈkluːsɪv; ɪnˈklusɪv/ *adj* ~ (*of*), **1** including: 包括的; 包含的: £ 10, ~ *of interest:* 十英镑, 包括利息在内; *from 1 May to 3 June* ~, 1 May and 3 June being included. 从五月一日至六月三日, 首尾两日包括在内. ⇨ (US) (美) **through²** (4). **2** including much or all: 包括许多或一切的: ~ *terms,* (at a hotel, etc) without any extra charges. (旅馆等) 包括一切费用的价目. ~**·ly** *adv*

in·cog·ni·to /ɪnˈkɒɡniːtəʊ; ɪnˈkɑɡnɪ,to/ *adj* concealed under a disguised identity; with an assumed name: 隐藏原来身份的; 使用化名的: *a king* ~. 微服而行的国王. □ *adv* with one's name, identity, etc concealed: 隐姓埋名地; 隐藏身份的: *The millionaire called himself Dick Brown and travelled* ~. 那富豪自称迪克·布朗而化名旅行.

in·co·her·ent /ˌɪnkəʊˈhɪərənt; ˌɪnkoˈhɪrənt/ *adj* not coherent: 思想不连贯的; 语无伦次的: *so drunk as to be quite* ~. 醉得语无伦次. ~**·ly** *adv* **in·co·her·ence** /-əns; -əns/ *n*

in·com·bus·tible /ˌɪnkəmˈbʌstəbl; ˌɪnkəmˈbʌstəbl/ *adj* (formal) that cannot be consumed by fire. (正式用语) 不能燃烧的.

in·come /ˈɪnkʌm; ˈɪn,kʌm/ *n* money received during a given period (as salary, receipts from trade, interest from investments, etc): 收入; 所得(指某一段时间内所得而言, 如薪金, 商业收益, 投资所获利润等): *live within one's* ~, spend less than one receives. 量入为出. *Tax was payable on ~ over £ 2000.* 收入在二千英镑以上者应该缴税. ~**·tax** /ˈɪnkəm tæks; ˈɪnkəm tæks/ *n* tax levied on ~ above a certain level. 所得税(所得超过某一标准所抽之税).

in·com·ing /ˈɪnˌkʌmɪŋ; ˈɪnˌkʌmɪŋ/ *adj* coming in: 进来的; 来到的: *the ~ tide / tenant.* 涨潮(住进来的房客).

in·com·men·sur·ate /ˌɪnkəˈmenʃərət; ˌɪnkəˈmenʃərɪt/ *adj* ~ (*to / with*), **1** not comparable (*to*) in respect of size; not worthy to be measured (*with*): 大小不成比例的; 不值得计量的: *His abilities are ~ to the task he has been given.* 他的能力与给予他的工作不相称. **2** that cannot be compared; having no common measure. 不能相比较的; 无共同单位可计量的.

in·com·mode /ˌɪnkəˈməʊd; ˌɪnkəˈmod/ *vt* [VP6A] (formal) cause trouble or inconvenience to: (正式用语) 使为难; 使不方便: *Will it ~ you if I don't pay what I owe you until next year?* 如果我明年才偿还所欠你的钱, 你会感到不方便吗?

in·com·muni·cado /ˌɪnkəˌmjuːnɪˈkɑːdəʊ; ˌɪnkə-ˌmjunɪˈkɑdo/ *adj* (of sb in confinement) not permitted to communicate with persons outside. (指被监禁者)不准与外面的人接触的.

in·com·par·able /ɪnˈkɒmpərəbl; ɪnˈkɑmpərəbl/ *adj* ~ (*to / with*), not to be compared; without equal: 不能比较的; 无匹的: *her ~ beauty.* 她那举世无双的美. **in·com·par·ably** /-əblɪ; -əblɪ/ *adv*

in·com·pat·ible /ˌɪnkəmˈpætəbl; ˌɪnkəmˈpætəbl/ *adj* ~ (*with*), opposed in character; unable to exist in harmony; inconsistent: 性质相反的; 不能和谐并存的; 矛盾的: *Excessive drinking is ~ with good health.* 纵酒与健康是不能并存的. *They are sexually ~.* 他们二人性生活不合谐. **in·com·pati·bil·ity** /ˌɪnkəmˌpætəˈbɪlətɪ; ˌɪnkəmˌpætəˈbɪlətɪ/ *n* [U] being ~: 性质相反; 无法合谐存; 矛盾: *Incompatibility of temper may cause friction between husband and wife.* 性情不合可能造成夫妻间的摩擦.

in·com·pe·tent /ɪnˈkɒmpɪtənt; ɪnˈkɑmpətənt/ *adj* not qualified or able: 不合格的; 不能胜任的: ~ *to teach science / for teaching science as a teacher of science.* 无资格担任科学教职的. ~**·ly** *adv* **in·com·pe·tence** /-əns; -əns/, **in·com·pe·tency** /-ənsɪ; -ənsɪ/ *nn* [U] being ~. 不合格; 不能胜任.

in·com·plete /ˌɪnkəmˈpliːt; ˌɪnkəmˈplit/ *adj* not complete. 不完全的. ~**·ly** *adv*

in·com·pre·hen·sible /ɪnˌkɒmprɪˈHensəbl; ɪn-ˌkɑmprɪˈhensəbl/ *adj* (formal) that cannot be understood. (正式用语)不能理解的. **in·com·pre·hen·si·bil·ity** /ɪnˌkɒmprɪˌhensəˈbɪlətɪ; ɪnˌkɑmprɪˌhensəˈbɪlətɪ/ *n* [U].

in·com·pre·hen·sion /ɪnˌkɒmprɪˈhenʃn; ˌɪnkɑm-prɪˈhenʃən/ *n* [U] failure to understand. 不能理解.

in·com·press·ible /ˌɪnkəmˈpresəbl; ˌɪnkəmˈpresəbl/ *adj* (formal) that cannot be compressed; hard and unyielding. (正式用语)不能压缩的; 坚硬的.

in·con·ceiv·able /ˌɪnkənˈsiːvəbl; ˌɪnkənˈsivəbl/ *adj* that cannot be imagined; (colloq) hard to believe; very remarkable. 无法想象的; (口)难以相信的; 非凡的.

in·con·clus·ive /ˌɪnkənˈkluːsɪv; ˌɪnkənˈklusɪv/ *adj* (of evidence, arguments, discussions, actions) not decisive or convincing; not bringing a definite result. (指证据, 论据, 讨论, 行动)非决定性的; 不能使人信服的; 不能产生明确效果的. ~**·ly** *adv*

in·con·gru·ous /ɪnˈkɒŋɡruːəs; ɪnˈkɑŋɡruəs/ *adj* ~ (*with*), not in harmony or agreement; out of place. 不和谐的; 不一致的; 不适宜的; 不调和的. ~**·ly** *adv* **in·con·gru·ity** /ˌɪnkɒŋˈɡruːətɪ; ˌɪnkɑŋˈɡruətɪ/ *n* [U] the quality of being ~; [C] (*pl* **-ties**) sth ~. 不合谐; 不调合; 不和谐或不调合之事物.

in·con·sequent /ɪnˈkɒnsɪkwənt; ɪnˈkɑnsəˌkwent/ *adj* not following naturally what has been said or done before: 前后不符的; 先后不连贯的: *an ~ remark;* 前后不符的话; (of a person) saying or doing ~ things. (指人)言行前后不符的. ~**·ly** *adv* **in·con·sequen·tial** /ɪnˌkɒnsɪˈkwenʃl; ˌɪnkɑnsəˈkwenʃəl/ *adj* = ~; unimportant. 前后不符的; 先后不连贯的; 不重要的.

in·con·sid·er·able /ˌɪnkənˈsɪdrəbl; ˌɪnkənˈsɪdərəbl/ *adj* not worth considering; of small size, value, etc. 不值得考虑的; 微不足道的.

in·con·sid·er·ate /ˌɪnkənˈsɪdərət; ˌɪnkənˈsɪdərɪt/ *adj* (of a person, his actions) thoughtless; lacking in regard for the feelings of others: (指人或其行动)卤莽的; 轻率的; 不顾及别人感情的: ~ *children;* 卤莽的孩子; ~ *remarks.* 轻率的言语. ~**·ly** *adv*

in·con·sist·ent /ˌɪnkənˈsɪstənt; ˌɪnkənˈsɪstənt/ *adj* ~ (*with*), **1** not in harmony: 不一致的: *actions that are ~ with one's principles.* 与自己的原则不一致的行动.

2 contradictory; having parts that do not agree. 矛盾的; 各部分不协调的: *His account of what happened was* ~. 他对于所发生事情的叙述前后矛盾。 ~**·ly** *adv*
in·con·sist·ency /-ənsɪ; -ənsɪ/ *n* [U] the quality of being ~; [C] (*pl* -**cies**) instance of this. 不一致; 矛盾; 不协调; 此种事例。
in·con·sol·able /ˌɪnkən'səʊləbl; ˌɪnkən'soʊləbl/ *adj* that cannot be consoled: 不能安慰的; 无法慰藉的: ~ *grief*. 无法安慰的忧伤。 *The widow was* ~. 那寡妇悲伤不已。
in·con·spicu·ous /ˌɪnkən'spɪkjʊəs; ˌɪnkən'spɪkjʊəs/ *adj* not conspicuous: 不显著的; 不引人注目的: *The shy girl tried to make herself as* ~ *as possible*, tried to avoid attention. 那个怕羞的女孩尽量使自己不被人注意。 *She always dresses in* ~ *colours*, colours that are not striking or obvious. 她总是穿颜色不显眼的衣服。 ~**·ly** *adv*
in·con·stant /ɪn'kɒnstənt; ɪn'kɑnstənt/ *adj* (formal) (of persons) changeable in feelings, intentions, purpose, etc: (正式用语) (指人, 在感情, 用意, 目的等方面) 多变的; 无常的; 不专的: *an* ~ *lover*. 用情不专的爱人。 **in·con·stancy** /-ənsɪ; -ənsɪ/ *n* [U]; being ~; [C] instance of this. (感情, 用意, 目的等) 善变; 无常; 不专。
in·con·test·able /ˌɪnkən'testəbl; ˌɪnkən'tɛstəbl/ *adj* that cannot be disputed. 无法争辩的; 不容置疑的。
in·con·ti·nent /ɪn'kɒntɪnənt; ɪn'kɑntɪnənt/ *adj* lacking in self-control or self-restraint (med) unable to control excretion or urination. 不能自制的; (医) 排泄或小便失禁的。 **in·con·ti·nence** /-əns; -əns/ *n* [U].
in·con·tro·vert·ible /ˌɪnˌkɒntrə'vɜːtəbl; ˌɪnˌkɑntrə'vɜtəbl/ *adj* (formal) that cannot be disputed. (正式用语) 无争辩余地的; 不容置疑的。
in·con·ven·ience /ˌɪnkən'viːnɪəns; ˌɪnkən'vinjəns/ *n* [C, U] (cause or instance of) discomfort or trouble: 不便; 麻烦; 困难; 不便或困难的原因; 不便或困难之处: *I was put to/I suffered great* ~. 我感到极大不便。 *They have been at great* ~ *in order to help us*. 为了帮助我们, 他们遭遇了极大的困难。 *Think of the* ~*s of living in such a small house with a large family*. 想想一大家人住在这样小的房子内的不便之处。 □ *vt* [VP6A] cause ~ to. 使感不便; 使感困难。
in·con·ven·ient /ˌɪnkən'viːnɪənt; ˌɪnkən'vinjənt/ *adj* causing discomfort, trouble or annoyance. 使人不便的; 引起困扰的。 ~**·ly** *adv*
in·con·vert·ible /ˌɪnkən'vɜːtəbl; ˌɪnkən'vɜtəbl/ *adj* that cannot be converted, eg paper money that cannot be exchanged for gold. 不能变换的(例如不能兑换成黄金的纸币)。 **in·con·ver·ti·bil·ity** /ˌɪnkənˌvɜːtə'bɪlətɪ; ˌɪnkənˌvɜtə'bɪlətɪ/ *n*
in·cor·por·ate¹ /ɪn'kɔːpərət; ɪn'kɔrpərɪt/ *adj* incorporated; formed into, united in, a corporation. 合并的; 组成或联合成为法人组织或公司的。
in·cor·por·ate² /ɪn'kɔːpəreɪt; ɪn'kɔrpəˌret/ *vt, vi* [VP6A, 14, 23, 2A, 3A] ~ (*in/into/with*), make, become, united in one body or group; (legal) form into, become, a corporation (2): 使结合; 使合并; 结合; 合并; (法律) 使组成或成为法人组织或公司: *Hanover was* ~*d into Prussia in 1886*. 汉诺威于一八八六年被并入普鲁士。 *He was* ~*d a member of the college*. 他成为该学院的一员。 *Your suggestions will be* ~*d in the plan*. 你的建议将并入这计划中。 *The firm* ~*d with others*. 这公司与别家合并了。 **in·cor·por·ation** /ɪnˌkɔːpə'reɪʃn; ɪnˌkɔrpə'reʃən/ *n* incorporating or being ~d. 结合; 合并; 形成法人或公司组织。
in·cor·por·eal /ˌɪnkɔː'pɔːrɪəl; ˌɪnkɔr'pɔrɪəl/ *adj* (formal) not composed of matter; having no bodily form. (正式用语) 无实体的; 无形体的。
in·cor·rect /ˌɪnkə'rekt; ˌɪnkə'rɛkt/ *adj* not correct. 不正确的。 ~**·ly** *adv* ~**·ness** *n*
in·cor·ri·gible /ɪn'kɒrɪdʒəbl; ɪn'kɔrɪdʒəbl/ *adj* (of a person, his faults, etc) that cannot be

cured or corrected: (指人, 其缺点等)不可救药的; 难以矫正的: *an* ~ *liar*; 无药可救的说谎者; ~ *bad habits*. 难以矫正的恶习。
in·cor·rupt·ible /ˌɪnkə'rʌptəbl; ˌɪnkə'rʌptəbl/ *adj* that cannot decay or be destroyed; that cannot be corrupted, esp by being bribed: 不腐朽的; 不能毁坏的; 不贪污受贿的: *an* ~ *as an English judge*. 象英国法官一样廉正。 **in·cor·rupti·bil·ity** /ˌɪnkəˌrʌptə'bɪlətɪ; ˌɪnkəˌrʌptə'bɪlətɪ/ *n*
in·crease¹ /'ɪnkriːs; 'ɪnkris/ *n* [U] *(in)*, increasing; growth; [C] amount by which sth ~s: 增加; 增大; 增多; 繁殖; 增加量: *I*~ *in population made emigration necessary*. 人口的增加使他向外移民成为必要。 *There was a steady* ~ *in population*. 人口一直在增加。 **on the** ~, growing: 在增加中: *Is the consumption of beer still on the* ~? 啤酒的消耗量仍在增加中吗?
in·crease² /ɪn'kriːs; ɪn'kris/ *vt, vi* [VP6A, 2A] make or become greater in size, number, degree, etc: 增加; 增大; 增多: *The population has by 300,000 to 50,000,000*. 人口已增加了二十万, 达到五千万的总数。 *The driver* ~*d speed*. 司机加速行驶。 *Our difficulties are increasing*. 我们的困难正在增多。 **in·creas·ing·ly** /ɪn'kriːsɪŋlɪ; ɪn'krisɪŋlɪ/ *adv* more and more. 逐渐地; 渐增地。
in·cred·ible /ɪn'kredəbl; ɪn'krɛdəbl/ *adj* that cannot be believed; (colloq) difficult to believe; surprising. 不能相信的; (口)难以置信的; 可惊的。 **in·cred·ibly** /-əblɪ; -əblɪ/ *adv* **in·credi·bil·ity** /ɪnˌkredə'bɪlətɪ; ɪnˌkrɛdə'bɪlətɪ/ *n*
in·credu·lous /ɪn'kredjʊləs; ɪn'krɛdʒələs/ *adj* unbelieving; showing disbelief: 不相信的; 表示怀疑的: ~ *looks/smiles*. 怀疑的表情(微笑)。 ~**·ly** *adv* **in·cred·ul·ity** /ˌɪnkrɪ'djuːlətɪ; ˌɪnkrə'dulətɪ/ *n*
in·crement /'ɪnkrəmənt; 'ɪnkrəmənt/ *n* **1** [U] profits; increase: 利润; 增加: *unearned* ~, increased value of sth, eg land, due not to the owner's labour but to other causes, eg a big demand for land. (土地增值之)不劳增值(非因所有者的劳力, 而由于其他因素, 例如土地之大量需求, 而产生的增值。) **2** [C] amount of increase: 增加量: *'Salary £ 4000 per annum, with yearly* ~*s of £ 250 to a maximum of £ 5500.'* '年薪四千英镑, 每年增加二百五十英镑, 直到最高额额五千五百英镑。'
in·crimi·nate /ɪn'krɪmɪneɪt; ɪn'krɪmə,net/ *vt* [VP 6A] say, be a sign, that (sb) is guilty or wrongdoing: 控告; 显示(某人)有罪: *Don't say anything that may* ~ *your friends*. 不要说任何可能牵连你朋友入罪的话。
in·crus·ta·tion /ˌɪnkrʌ'steɪʃn; ˌɪnkrʌs'teʃən/ *n* [U] encrusting; [C] crust; hard coating. 覆以硬壳; 外皮; 硬壳。
in·cu·bate /'ɪnkjʊbeɪt; 'ɪnkjə,bet/ *vt, vi* [VP6A, 2A] **1** hatch (eggs) by sitting on them or by artificial warmth; sit on eggs. 孵(卵); 人工孵(卵); 孵卵。 **2** (of bacteria, etc) develop under favourable conditions. (指细菌等)有有利情况下培养。 **in·cu·ba·tion** /ˌɪnkjʊ'beɪʃn; ˌɪnkjə'beʃən/ *n* **1** hatching (of eggs): 孵卵; 孵化: *artificial incubation*, hatching by artificial warmth. 人工孵卵。 **2 incubation (period)**, (path) (of a disease) period between infection and the appearance of the first symptoms. (病理) (指疾病)潜伏期。 **in·cu·ba·tor** /-tə/; -tə/ *n* apparatus for hatching eggs by artificial warmth or for rearing small, weak babies (esp those born prematurely). 人工孵卵器; 育婴箱 (培育身体弱小之婴儿, 特指早产儿。)
in·cu·bus /'ɪnkjʊbəs; 'ɪnkjəbəs/ *n* (*pl* ~**es** /-sɪz; -sɪz/, or -**bi** /-baɪ; -,baɪ/) nightmare; evil spirit supposed to lie on a sleeping person and weigh him down; sb or sth, eg a debt, an approaching examination, that oppresses one like a nightmare. 梦魇; 梦魇; 传说中压在熟睡者身上的魔鬼; 如梦魇般压迫人的人或事物(例如债务, 即将来临的考试等)。

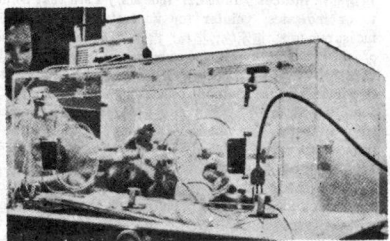

an incubator

in·cul·cate /'ɪnkʌlkeɪt US: ɪn'kʌl-; ɪn'kʌlket/ vt [VP6A, 14] ~ sth (in sb), (formal) fix (ideas, etc) firmly by repetition: (正式用语)反复灌输(思想等)；谆谆教诲: ~ in young people the duty of loyalty. 以忠贞之道谆谆教诲青年年轻人。

in·cul·pate /'ɪnkʌlpeɪt US: ɪn'kʌl-; ɪn'kʌlpet/ vt [VP6A] (formal) involve (sb) in a charge or wrong-doing; blame. (正式用语)连累(某人)受控；责难。

in·cum·bent /ɪn'kʌmbənt; ɪn'kʌmbənt/ adj be ~ on/upon sb (to do sth), (formal) be his duty: (正式用语)负有义务；负某种责任: It is ~ upon you to warn the boy of the danger of smoking. 你有责任去警告那男孩吸烟的危险。 □ n person holding an official position. 在职者；有正式职位者。 **in·cum·bency** /-ənsɪ; -ənsɪ/ n (pl -cies) position of an ~. 职位。

in·cur /ɪn'kɜː(r); ɪn'kɜ/ vt (-rr-) [VP6A] bring upon oneself: 招致；蒙受: ~ debts; 负债; ~ hatred; 招致仇恨; ~ great expense. 引起很大的花费。

in·cur·able /ɪn'kjʊərəbl; ɪn'kjʊrəbl/ adj that cannot be cured: 不能治疗的；不可救药的: ~ diseases/habits. 不治之症(无法矫正的习惯)。 □ n person who is ~: 患不治之症者: a home for ~s. 患不治之症者的收容所。 **in·cur·ably** /-əblɪ; -əblɪ/ adv

in·cur·ious /ɪn'kjʊərɪəs; ɪn'kjʊrɪəs/ adj (formal) having no curiosity; not inquisitive; inattentive. (正式用语)无好奇心的；不追根究底的；不注意的。

in·cur·sion /ɪn'kɜːʃn US: -ʒn; ɪn'kɜʒən/ n ~ on/upon, sudden attack or invasion (not usu made for the purpose of permanent occupation): 侵入；侵犯(通常为不欲作永久占领者): the Danish ~s on our coasts in early times; 古时丹麦人对我国(指英国)沿岸的侵犯; (fig)(喻) ~s upon my leisure time. 我闲暇时间之受打扰。

in·curved /ˌɪn'kɜːvd; ɪn'kɜvd/ adj curved inwards; bent into a curve. 内曲的；变成曲线的。

in·debted /ɪn'detɪd; ɪn'detɪd/ adj ~ to sb, owing money or gratitude: 负债的；欠情的；感恩的: I am greatly ~ to you for your help. 我非常感激你对我的帮助。 **~·ness** n

in·de·cent /ɪn'diːsnt; ɪn'disn̩t/ adj 1 (of behaviour, talk, etc) not decent(2); obscene. (指行为、言语等)不流的；粗鄙的；猥亵的。 2 (colloq) improper: (口)不合适的: leave a party in ~ haste, eg as if to suggest that one is glad to escape from boredom. 匆忙而欠妥地离开一社交集会(仿佛暗示乐于逃避其枯燥等)。 **~·ly** adv **in·de·cency** /-nsɪ; -nsɪ/ n [U] being ~; [C] (pl -cies) act, gesture, expression, etc that is ~. 粗鄙；下流；猥亵；粗鄙的行动、姿态、言语等。

in·de·cipher·able /ˌɪndɪ'saɪfrəbl; ˌɪndɪ'saɪfrəbl/ adj that cannot be deciphered. 无法解释的；无法阐明的。

in·de·ci·sion /ˌɪndɪ'sɪʒn; ˌɪndɪ'saɪʒn/ n the state of being unable to decide; hesitation. 无决断力；犹豫。

in·de·cis·ive /ˌɪndɪ'saɪsɪv; ˌɪndɪ'saɪsɪv/ adj not decisive: 非决定性的: an ~ battle/answer; 非决定性的战役(答复); ~ evidence; 非决定性的证据; hesitating; uncertain: 犹豫不决的；不定的: a man with an ~ manner. 一个样子优柔寡断的人。 **~·ly** adv

in·dec·or·ous /ɪn'dekərəs; ɪn'dɛkərəs/ adj (formal) in bad taste; not in accordance with good manners. (正式用语)不雅的；不合礼节的。 **~·ly** adv

in·de·cor·um /ˌɪndɪ'kɔːrəm; ˌɪndɪ'korəm/ n [U] lack of decorum; improper behaviour. 没有礼貌；不适当的行为；不雅的举止。

in·deed /ɪn'diːd; ɪn'did/ adv 1 really; as you say; as you may imagine: 实在地；的确；真地: I was ~ very glad to hear the news. 我听到了这消息,的确很高兴。 'Are you pleased at your son's success?'—'Yes, ~' (or) 'I~, yes.' '你对于你儿子的成功感到高兴吗?' '是的,实在高兴。' 2 (to intensify) (加强语气) Thank you very much ~. 实在感激你。 It was very kind ~ of you to help. 承蒙协助,至为感激。 3 used as a comment to show interest, surprise, irony, etc: 用作批评语,表示兴趣、惊奇、讥刺等: 'He spoke to me about you.'—'Oh, ~!' 'Oh, did he?' '他对我谈起了你。'—'噢,真的!' 'Who is this woman?'—'Who is she, ~?' 'That's what we all want to know!' '这位女士是谁?'——'她到底是谁?'(我们都想知道她是谁。)

in·de·fati·gable /ˌɪndɪ'fætɪgəbl; ˌɪndɪ'fætɪgəbl/ adj (formal) untiring; that cannot be tired out: (正式用语)不疲倦的；不屈不挠的: ~ workers. 不倦的工作者。

in·de·feas·ible /ˌɪndɪ'fiːzəbl; ˌɪndɪ'fizəbl/ adj (formal) that cannot be forfeited or done away with: (正式用语)不能取消的；不能废除的: ~ rights/claims. 不能取消的权利(要求权)。

in·de·fens·ible /ˌɪndɪ'fensəbl; ˌɪndɪ'fensəbl/ adj that cannot be defended, justified or excused. 不能防守的；无法辩护的；不可原谅的。

in·de·fin·able /ˌɪndɪ'faɪnəbl; ˌɪndɪ'faɪnəbl/ adj that cannot be defined. 不能下定义的；难以描述的。

in·defi·nite /ɪn'defnət; ɪn'defənɪt/ adj vague; not clearly defined or stated: 不确定的；模糊的; has rather ~ views on the question. 他对此问题的观念相当模糊。 He gave me an ~ answer, neither 'Yes' nor 'No'. 他给我一个含糊的答复(不置可否)。 the ~ 'article, a or an. 不定冠词(a 或 an)。 **~·ly** adv

in·del·ible /ɪn'deləbl; ɪn'deləbl/ adj (of marks, stains, ink or (fig) of disgrace) that cannot be rubbed out or removed: (指记号、污迹、墨迹或比喻用法指耻辱)不能擦掉的；不能洗雪的: an ~ pencil; 笔迹难擦掉的铅笔; ~ shame. 洗雪不掉的耻辱。 **in·del·ibly** /-əblɪ; -əblɪ/ adv

in·deli·cate /ɪn'delɪkət; ɪn'delɪkət/ adj (of a person, his speech, behaviour, etc) lacking in refinement; immodest: (指人、其言行等)不雅的；粗鄙的: ~ remarks. 粗鄙的言语。 **in·deli·cacy** /-kəsɪ; -kəsɪ/ n [U] being ~; [C] (pl -cies) ~ act, utterance, etc. 不雅；粗鄙；粗鄙的言行等。

in·dem·nify /ɪn'demnɪfaɪ; ɪn'dɛmnəˌfaɪ/ vt (pt, pp -fied) 1 [VP6A, 14] ~ sb (from/against), (legal, comm) make (sb, oneself) safe: (法律,商)使(某人、自己)安全；保障；保护: ~ a person against harm/loss. 使某人不受伤害(损失)。 2 [VP6A,14] ~ sb (for sth), pay sb back: 偿付(某人): I will ~ you for any expenses you may incur on my behalf. 我会偿付你为了我而负担的任何花费。 **in·dem·ni·fi·ca·tion** /ˌɪndemnɪfɪ'keɪʃn; ɪnˌdɛmnəfəˈkeʃən/ n [U] ~ing or being indemnified; [C] sth given or received as compensation or repayment. 使安全；保障；免受伤害或损失；赔偿；赔偿物。

in·dem·nity /ɪn'demnɪtɪ; ɪn'dɛmnɪtɪ/ n (pl -ties) 1 [U] security against damage or loss; compensation for loss. 保证；保障；赔偿；补偿。 2 [C] sth that gives security against damage or loss; sth given or received as compensation, esp a sum of money, or goods, demanded from a country defeated in war. 保证物；赔偿物；(尤指向战败国索取的)赔款；作为赔偿金的货物。

in·dent /ɪn'dent; ɪn'dɛnt/ vt, vi 1 [VP6A] break into the edge or surface of (as if with teeth): 使成锯齿状；使凹凸不平: an ~ed (= very irregular) coastline. 犬牙交错的海岸线。 2 [VP6A] start (a line of print or writing) farther from the margin than the others: 缩

进(一行印刷或书写文字): *You must ~ the first line of each paragraph.* 你必须将每段的第一行缩进书写(或排印). **3** [VP3A] *~ (on sb) for sth,* (comm) order goods by means of an ~: *The firm ~ed for new machinery.* 这家公司以订货单购新机器. □ *n* /'ɪndent; 'ɪndənt/ (comm) trade order placed in the United Kingdom for goods to be exported; official requisition for stores. (商)在英国订购出口货物的订货单; 征用物资命令. **in·den·ta·tion** /ˌɪnden'teɪʃn; ˌɪndɛn'teʃən/ *n* **1** [U] ~ing or being ~ed. (使)成锯齿状; (使)成犬牙交错. **2** [C] deep recess in a coastline; notch; space left at the beginning of a line of print or writing. 海岸线凹入之处; 缺口; 印刷或书写文字一行开始处所留的空格.

in·den·ture /ɪn'dentʃə(r); ɪn'dɛntʃə/ *n* agreement of which two copies are made, each one binding an apprentice to his master. 契约(一式两份,尤指约束学徒对师傅尽义务者). *take up one's ~s,* receive them back at the end of the period of training. 做学徒期满领回学徒契约. □ *vt* [VP6A] bind (a person) by ~s (as an apprentice). 以契约束缚(某人,使作学徒).

in·de·pen·dence /ˌɪndɪ'pendəns; ˌɪndɪ'pɛndəns/ *n* [U] ~ (from), the state of being independent: 独立; 自立; 自主: *When a boy leaves college and begins to earn money he can live a life of ~.* 男孩子大学毕业开始赚钱时, 便可独立生活了. *Several of these colonies have claimed and have been given ~ from the mother country.* 这些殖民地中有几个曾经向它们的母国要求独立并已获得独立. **'I~ Day,** 4 July, celebrated in the US as the anniversary of the day, in 1776, on which the Declaration of I~(that the American colonies were free and independent of GB) was made. 美国独立纪念日(为七月四日,纪念一七七六年是日发表独立宣言).

in·de·pen·dent /ˌɪndɪ'pendənt; ˌɪndɪ'pɛndənt/ *adj* **1** ~ *(of),* not dependent on or controlled by (other persons or things); not relying on others; not needing to work for a living: 独立的; 不依赖他人或得不受他人控制的; 不劳而能生活的: *If you have a car you are ~ of trains and buses.* 如果你有汽车, 你就不需乘火车和公共汽车了. *They went camping, so as to be ~ of hotels.* 他们去露营, 免得住旅馆. *~ means,* private means. 私人财力. **2** self-governing: 自治的: *when the colony become ~.* 当该殖民地独立时. **3** acting or thinking upon one's own lines; free from control; not influenced by others: 行动或思想自主的; 不受控制的; 不受他人影响的: *an ~ thinker; an ~ witness;* 不受人左右的证人; *~ proof/research,* resulting from ~ work, not related to the work of others. 独立的证据(研究)(由独立的工作达成, 与他人的工作无关联者). □ *n* (esp) MP, candidate, etc who does not belong to a political party: (尤指)无党派的国会议员,候选人等: *Vote for the ~s!* 请投无党派人士一票! *~ly adv*

in·de·scrib·able /ˌɪndɪ'skraɪbəbl; ˌɪndɪ'skraɪbəbl/ *adj* that cannot be described. 难以描述的. **in·de·scrib·ably** /-əblɪ; -əblɪ/ *adv*

in·de·struct·ible /ˌɪndɪ'strʌktəbl; ˌɪndɪ'strʌktəbl/ *adj* that cannot be destroyed: 不能毁灭的: *~ plastics.* 不能毁灭的塑胶. **in·de·struct·ibil·ity** /ˌɪndɪˌstrʌktə'bɪlɪtɪ; ˌɪndɪˌstrʌktə'bɪlɪtɪ/ *n* [U].

in·de·ter·mi·nate /ˌɪndɪ'tɜːmɪnət; ˌɪndɪ'tɝmɪnət/ *adj* not fixed; vague or indefinite: 不固定的; 模糊的或不确定的: (maths)(数学) *an ~ quantity,* with no fixed value. 不定数. **in·de·ter·min·able** /ˌɪndɪ'tɜːmɪnəbl; ˌɪndɪ'tɝmɪnəbl/ *adj* that cannot be determined, decided or (esp of an industrial dispute) be settled. 不能确定的; 不能决定的; (尤指工业界争端)不能解决的. **in·de·ter·min·ably** /-əblɪ; -əblɪ/ *adv* **in·de·ter·man·icy** /-sɪ; -əsɪ/ or **-cy** /-sɪ; -əsɪ/ *n* the state or quality of being ~. 不固定; 模糊; 不确定: *the indeterminacy of small-scale physical events,* the impossibility of determining them in advance. 小规模的自然界变化之难以预测.

in·dex /'ɪndeks; 'ɪndɛks/ *n* (*pl* **~es** or, in science, 科学

用语亦作 **indices** /'ɪndɪsiːz; 'ɪndɪˌsiz/) **1** sth that points to or indicates; pointer (on an instrument) showing measurements: 指示物; 指标; 指针: *The increasing sale of luxuries was an ~ of the country's prosperity.* 奢侈品销售之增加显示出这个国家的繁荣. **the '~ finger,** the finger next to the thumb, used for pointing. 食指. ⇨ the illus at **arm.** 参看 arm 之插图. **2** list of names, subjects, references, etc in ABC order, at the end of a book, or on cards (a '**card** ~) in a library, etc. 索引(名称、科目、参考书等之名单, 按照字母顺序排列, 附于书后或载于图书馆等之索引卡上). **the I~,** (hist) list of books not to be read by members of the RC Church without permission. (史)天主教徒未经准许不得阅读之书目单. **3** '~ **number/figure,** one that indicates the relative level of prices or wages at a particular date compared with the figure 100 (for an earlier period) as a standard: (物价、工资等之)指数: *the cost of living ~;* 生活费指数; (of wages, pensions) (指薪资、退休金) *~ linked/related,* adjusted accordingly. 按照指数调整的. **4** (alg) exponent: (代数)指数: *In b^3-x^n, 3 and n are indices.* 在 b^3+x^n 中, 3 和 n 是指数. □ *vt* [VP6A] make an ~ for a book, collection of books, etc: put a word, reference, etc in an ~: 为(书籍等)编索引; 将(一词、参考指示等)编入索引中: *The book is not well ~ed.* 这本书的索引编得不好. **~er** *n* person who prepares an ~(2). 索引编者.

In·dia /'ɪndɪə; 'ɪndɪə/ *n* '~ **paper** *n* very thin paper, eg for airmail editions of newspapers. 印度纸; 圣经纸(一种很薄的纸, 例如报纸的航空版所采用者). '~**man** /-mən; -mən/ *n* (*pl* -**men**) (formerly) sailing-ship engaged in the trade with India. (昔时)从事对印度贸易的帆船. ,~'**rubber** *n* [C] piece of rubber for rubbing out pencil or ink marks. (擦铅笔字或墨水迹用的)橡皮.

In·dian /'ɪndɪən; 'ɪndɪən/ *adj, n* **1** (native) of the Republic of India. 印度的; 印度人. **2** A,**merican '~,** (one) of the original inhabitants of America. 美洲印第安人的; 印第安人. ,**West '~,** (native) of the West Indies. 西印度群岛的; 西印度群岛人. **3** (various uses) (各种用法) '~ **club,** bottle-shaped club, for use in gymnastic exercises. 瓶状棒; 棍棒(体操用具). '~ **corn,** [U] maize. 玉蜀黍; 玉米. *in ~ file,* in single file, one behind the other. 成一路纵队. ,~ '**hemp,** ⇨ **hemp.** ,~ '**ink,** black ink made in China and Japan (used when writing ideographs with a brush). (中国及日本制造,写毛笔字所用)墨; 墨汁. ,~ '**red,** (soil of a) yellowish-red colour. 浅黄红色; 浅黄红色土壤. ,~ '**summer,** period of calm, dry hazy weather in late autumn, esp in the northern part of the US; (fig) revival of the feelings of youth in old age. 小阳春; 秋老虎(尤指美国北部深秋时之无风、干燥、有薄雾的天气); (喻)回春期.

in·di·cate /'ɪndɪkeɪt; 'ɪndəˌket/ *vt* [VP6A, 9, 14] point to; point out; make known; be a sign of; show the need of; state briefly: 指示; 指出; 表示; 象征; 表示需要; 简单地陈述: *A sign-post ~d the right road for us to follow.* 路标指示我们应走的路. *He ~d that the interview was over.* 他简短地说接见结束了. *The sudden rise in temperature was indicating the use of penicillin.* 体温突然上升表示需要使用盘尼西林. *A fresh approach to industrial relations is ~d,* is necessary or advisable. 劳资关系需要采取新的步骤. **in·di·ca·tion** /ˌɪndɪ'keɪʃn; ˌɪndə'keʃən/ *n* **1** [U] indicating or being ~d. 指示; 指出; 表示. **2** [C, U] sign or suggestion; that which ~s: 象征; 暗示; 征候: *Did he give you any indication of his feelings?* 他向你表示过他的感情吗? *There was not much indication/were not many indications that the next few years would be peaceful.* 没有多少迹象显示以后数年将会太平.

in·dica·tive /ɪn'dɪkətɪv; ɪn'dɪkətɪv/ *adj* **1** (gram) stating a fact or asking questions of fact: (语法)陈述的; 直陈的; 直陈问句的: *the ~ mood.* 陈述语气; 直说法. **2** ~ *of/that,* giving indications (of): 指示的; 表示的:

Is a high forehead ~ of great mental power? 前額高表示智慧高嗎?

in·di·ca·tor /'ɪndɪkeɪtə(r); 'ɪndə,ketɚ/ n person, thing, that points out or gives information, eg a pointer, needle, recording apparatus, on a machine, etc showing speed, pressure, etc: 指示者; 指示物; 指示剂; 指示器(例如机器上表示速度,压力等的指针或记录器); *Litmus paper can be used as an ~ of the presence or not of acid in a solution;* 石蕊试纸可用于指示溶液中是否含有酸; *('traffic-~)* (on a motor vehicle) flashing light or other device to indicate a change of direction; *('train~)* one in a railway station showing times of arrivals and departures of trains, their platform numbers, etc. (汽车等的)方向指示器; 方向灯; (火车站内表示火车来往时刻,其月台号码等的)火车指示牌。

in·di·ces /'ɪndɪsiːz; 'ɪndə,siz/ pl of **index**.

in·dict /ɪn'daɪt; ɪn'daɪt/ vt [VP6A, 14, 16B] (legal) accuse (sb): (法律)控诉; 控告: ~ *sb for riot/as a rioter/on a charge of rioting.* 以暴乱罪控告某人。 **in·dict·able** /-əbl; -əbl/ adj liable to be ~ed; for which one may be ~ed: 可提起诉讼的; 可控告的: ~*able offences,* that may be tried by jury. 刑事罪。 ~·**ment** n [C] written statement that ~s sb: 起诉书; 诉状: *bring in an ~ment against sb.* 控告某人。 *This is a clear ~ment of government mismanagement.* 这显然是对政府管理不善的指控。 [U] ~ing or being ~ed. 控诉; 被控。

in·dif·fer·ence /ɪn'dɪfrəns; ɪn'dɪfrəns/ n [U] ~ *(to),* the state of being indifferent; absence of interest or feeling: 不关心; 不重视; 无兴趣; 冷淡: *He treated my request with ~.* 他不重视我的请求。 *Success or failure cannot be a matter of ~ to you.* 成败对你不可能是件无足轻重的事。 *His ~ to future needs is unfortunate.* 他对未来的需要不关心真令人遗憾。

in·dif·fer·ent /ɪn'dɪfrənt; ɪn'dɪfrənt/ adj 1 ~ *(to),* having no interest in; neither for nor against; not caring for: 对…不感兴趣的; 漠不关心的; 不管的: *How can you be so ~ to the sufferings of these children?* 对于这些孩子的苦难你怎能如此漠不关心? *The explorers were ~ to the discomforts and dangers of the expedition.* 那些探险家对于那次探险的艰苦与危险不以为意。 *We cannot remain ~ (= neutral) in this dispute.* 在这场争辩中,我们不能保持中立。 *It is quite ~ to me whether you go or stay,* I don't care which you do. 你的去留对我都无所谓。 2 commonplace; not of good quality or ability: 平常的; 品质或能力欠佳的: *an ~ book;* 一本平凡的书; *a very ~ footballer.* 技术甚差的足球员。 ~·**ly** adv

in·di·gen·ous /ɪn'dɪdʒɪnəs; ɪn'dɪdʒənəs/ adj ~ *(to),* native, belonging naturally (to): 土生的; 天生的: ~ *language,* that of the people regarded as the original inhabitants of an area. 某一地区土著所用之语言; 土语。 *Kangaroos are ~ to Australia.* 袋鼠原产于澳洲。

in·di·gent /'ɪndɪdʒənt; 'ɪndədʒənt/ adj (formal) poor. (正式用语) 贫穷的。 **in·di·gence** /-əns; -əns/ n [U] poverty. 贫穷。

in·di·gest·ible /,ɪndɪ'dʒestəbl; ,ɪndə'dʒɛstəbl/ adj difficult or impossible to digest. 难消化的; 不能消化的。

in·di·ges·tion /,ɪndɪ'dʒestʃən; ,ɪndə'dʒɛstʃən/ n [U] (pain from) difficulty in digesting food: 消化困难; 不消化; 消化不良症: *suffer from ~;* 患消化不良症; *have an attack of ~.* 患消化不良。

in·dig·nant /ɪn'dɪgnənt; ɪn'dɪgnənt/ adj angry and scornful, esp at injustice or because of undeserved blame, etc: (尤指对不平或受冤屈等而)愤慨的; 愤怒的: ~ *at a false accusation;* 对诬告愤愤不平; ~ *with a cruel man.* 对一残忍的人感到愤慨。 ~·**ly** adv

in·dig·na·tion /,ɪndɪg'neɪʃn; ,ɪndɪg'neʃən/ n [U] anger caused by injustice, misconduct, etc: 愤慨; 义愤: *arouse the ~ of the people;* 引起公愤; *to the ~ of all decent people.* 激起所有正直人士的义愤。 *They felt strong ~ against their teachers.* 他们对他们的教师们感到强烈愤慨。

in·dig·nity /ɪn'dɪgnətɪ; ɪn'dɪgnətɪ/ n [U] rude or unworthy treatment causing shame or loss of respect; [C] 侮辱; 轻蔑; 侮辱的言行: *The hijackers subjected us to all sorts of indignities.* 劫持者对我们施以各种侮辱。

in·digo /'ɪndɪgəʊ; 'ɪndɪ,go/ n [U] deep blue dye (obtained from plants). (自植物中提取的)靛; 靛青; 蓝靛。 ~ **(blue),** blue-violet. 紫蓝色。 ⇨ the illus at **spectrum.** 参看 spectrum 之插图。

in·direct /,ɪndɪ'rekt; ,ɪndə'rɛkt/ adj 1 not straight or direct; not going straight to the point: 非直接的; 间接的; 迂回的: *an ~ road;* 迂回的道路; *make an ~ reference to sb,* not mentioning his name although making clear who is referred to; 间接提到某人(暗指某人); *an ~ answer to a question;* 对一问题的间接答复; ~ *lighting,* by reflected light. 间接照明(以反射光照明)。 2 (of taxes) not paid direct to a tax-collector, but in the form of higher prices for taxed goods. 间接的(非直接交给收税员,而是以对课税货物付出较高价格的方式): *the ~ taxes on tobacco, wines, etc.* 烟草,酒等的间接税。 3 ~ '**object,** person etc secondarily affected by the v, and replaceable by *to/for*+object, eg *him (= to him)* in *Give him the money.* 间接宾语(间接受到动词动作影响者,可以 to 或 for 加宾语代替, 例如 Give him the money 或 Give the money to him 中之 him 即是)。 ,~ '**question,** question in ~ speech. 间接问句(以间接叙述法表达的疑问句)。 ,~ '**speech,** speech as it is reported with the necessary changes of pronouns, tenses, etc, eg *He said he would come* for *He said 'I will come'.* 间接叙述法(例如以 He said he would come 代替 He said 'I will come')。 4 not directly aimed at: 非直接作为目标的: *an ~ result.* 间接的结果。 ~·**ly** adv ~·**ness** n

in·dis·cern·ible /,ɪndɪ'sɜːnəbl; ,ɪndɪ'zɝnəbl/ adj that cannot be discerned. 无法辨认的; 看不清楚的。

in·dis·ci·pline /ɪn'dɪsɪplɪn; ɪn'dɪsəplɪn/ n [U] absence of discipline. 缺少训练; 无纪律。

in·dis·creet /,ɪndɪ'skriːt; ,ɪndɪ'skrit/ adj not wary, cautious or careful. 不稳重的; 不慎重的; 轻率的。 ~·**ly** adv **in·dis·cre·tion** /,ɪndɪ'skreʃn; ,ɪndɪ'skrɛʃən/ n [U] ~ conduct; lack of discretion; [C] ~ remark or act; offence against social conventions. 不稳重; 不谨慎; 轻率的言行; 不检点的行为。

in·dis·crete /,ɪndɪ'skriːt; ,ɪndɪ'skrit/ adj not formed of distinct or separate parts. 密合不分的。

in·dis·crimi·nate /,ɪndɪ'skrɪmɪnət; ,ɪndɪ'skrɪmənɪt/ adj acting, given, without care or taste: 不分皂白的; 不加选择的; 不加鉴别的: ~ *in making friends;* 交友不加选择; *give ~ praise;* 不加鉴别,一味赞扬; *deal out ~ blows,* hit out at anyone, whether an enemy or not. 不分敌我地乱打。 ~·**ly** adv

in·dis·pens·able /,ɪndɪ'spensəbl; ,ɪndɪ'spɛnsəbl/ adj ~ *to,* that cannot be dispensed with; absolutely essential: 不可缺少的; 绝对必要的: *Air, food and water are ~ to life.* 空气,食物与水都是维持生命所不可缺的。 **in·dis·pen·sa·bil·ity** /,ɪndɪ,spensə'bɪlətɪ; ,ɪndɪ,spɛnsə'brlɛtɪ/ n [U]

in·dis·posed /,ɪndɪ'spəʊzd; ,ɪndɪ'spozd/ adj 1 unwell; 身体不适的: *She has a headache and is ~.* 她头痛,感到不适。 2 ~ *for* or *to do sth,* not inclined: 不愿意的: *He seems ~ to help us.* 他似乎不愿意帮助我们。

in·dis·po·si·tion /,ɪndɪspə'zɪʃn; ,ɪndɪspə'zɪʃən/ n [C,U] 1 ill health; slight illness. 身体不适; 微恙。 2 ~ *for/to do sth,* feeling of unwillingness or disinclination; feeling of aversion. 不愿; 嫌恶。

in·dis·put·able /,ɪndɪ'spjuːtəbl; ,ɪndɪ'spjutəbl/ adj that cannot be disputed. 不容置辩的。

in·dis·sol·uble /,ɪndɪ'sɒljʊbl; ,ɪndɪ'saljəbl/ adj (formal) that cannot be dissolved or broken up; firm and lasting: (正式用语)不能溶解的; 不能分解的; 坚固不变的: *the ~ bonds of friendship between my country and yours.* 贵国和我国间不渝的友谊。 *The Roman Catholic Church regards marriage as ~.* 天主教会视婚姻为不可分拆的。

in·dis·tinct /ˌɪndɪˈstɪŋkt ; ˌɪndɪˈstɪŋkt/ *adj* not distinct: 不清楚的；模糊的: ~ *speech*; 含糊不清的言语; ~ *sounds/memories*. 模糊的声音 (记忆)。 **~·ly** *adv* **~·ness** *n*

in·dis·tin·guish·able /ˌɪndɪˈstɪŋgwɪʃəbl; ˌɪndɪˈstɪŋgwɪʃəbl/ *adj* that cannot be distinguished. 不能分辨的。

in·dite /ɪnˈdaɪt; ɪnˈdaɪt/ *vt* [VP6A] (archaic) put into words; compose. (古) 撰写；著作。

in·di·vid·ual /ˌɪndɪˈvɪdʒʊəl, ˌɪndəˈvɪdʒʊəl / *adj* 1 (opp of *general*) specially for one person or thing: (为 general 之反义词) 个别的: *A teacher cannot give* ~ *attention to his pupils if his class is very large.* 如果班上的人数很多，教师便不能对他的学生个别注意了。 2 characteristic of a single person, animal, plant or thing: 独特的: *an* ~ *style of speaking/dressing.* 独特的谈话 (衣着) 风格。 □ *n* 1 any one human being (contrasted with *society*): 个人 (与 society 相对): *Are the rights of the* ~ *more important or less important than the rights of society as a whole?* 个人的权利与整个社会的权利孰轻孰重？ 2 (colloq) person: (口) 人: *What a scruffy* ~ *he is!* 他是多么肮脏的一个人啊！ **~·ly** /-dʒʊəlɪ; -dʒʊəlɪ/ *adv* (opp of *collectively*) separately; one by one: (为 collectively 之反义词) 个别地；逐一地: *speak to each member of a group* ~*ly.* 对一团体中每一个成员个别谈话。

in·di·vid·ual·ism /ˌɪndɪˈvɪdʒʊəlɪzəm, ˌɪndəˈvɪdʒʊəl-ˌɪzəm/ *n* [U] 1 social theory that favours the free action and complete liberty of belief of individuals (contrasted with the theory favouring the supremacy of the state). 个人主义 (一种社会学理论，主张个人行动及信仰完全自由，与国家主义相对)。 2 feeling or behaviour of a person who puts his own private interests first; egoism. 利己的想法或行为；利己主义。 **in·di·vid·ual·ist** /-ɪst; -ɪst/ *n* supporter of ~. 个人主义者。 **in·di·vid·ual·is·tic** /ˌɪndɪˌvɪdʒʊəˈlɪstɪk; ˌɪndəˌvɪdʒʊəlˈɪstɪk/ *adj* of ~ or its principles. 个人主义的；利己主义的。

in·di·vid·ual·ity /ˌɪndɪˌvɪdʒʊˈælɪtɪ, ˌɪndəˌvɪdʒʊˈælɪtɪ/ *n* (*pl* **-ties**) 1 [U] all the characteristics that belong to an individual and that mark him out from others: 个性；个人的特性: *a man of marked* ~. 个性特别的人。 2 state of separate existence. 独立存在状态；个别存在状态。 3 (usu *pl*) individual tastes, etc. (通常用复数) 个人的嗜好等。

in·di·vid·ual·ize /ˌɪndɪˈvɪdʒʊəlaɪz, ˌɪndəˈvɪdʒʊəlˌaɪz/ *vt* [VP6A] 1 give an individual or distinct character to: 使有个性；使有特性: *Does your style of writing* ~ *your work?* 你的写作风格使你的作品具有个性吗？ 2 specify; treat separately and in detail. 指明；个别详述。

in·di·vis·ible /ˌɪndɪˈvɪzəbl, ˌɪndəˈvɪzəbl/ *adj* that cannot be divided. 不能分割的；除不尽的。

Indo- /ˈɪndəʊ, ˈɪndo/ *pref* (in compounds 用于复合词中) =Indian. **~·Euro'pean,** of the family of languages spoken in Europe and parts of western Asia, esp Iran, Pakistan and India. 印欧语系 (欧洲及西亚尤其伊朗、巴基斯坦及印度等地所使用之语言系统)。

in·doc·tri·nate /ɪnˈdɒktrɪneɪt; ɪnˈdɑktrɪnˌet/ *vt* [VP6A, 14] ~ *sb with,* fill the mind of (sb) (with particular ideas or beliefs). (以某种思想或信仰) 灌输 (某人)。 **in·doc·tri·na·tion** /ɪnˌdɒktrɪˈneɪʃn; ɪnˌdɑktrɪˈneʃən/ *n* [U].

in·do·lent /ˈɪndələnt; ˈɪndələnt/ *adj* lazy; inactive. 懒惰的；怠惰的。 **~·ly** *adv* **in·do·lence** /-əns; -əns/ *n* [U].

in·domi·table /ɪnˈdɒmɪtəbl; ɪnˈdɑmɪtəbl/ *adj* that cannot be subdued or conquered; unyielding: 不可征服的；不屈的: ~ *courage;* 不屈不挠的勇气; *an* ~ *will.* 不屈的意志。

in·door /ˈɪndɔː(r); ˈɪnˌdor/ *adj* (attrib only) belonging to, carried on, situated, inside a building: (仅用作定语) 户内的；室内的: ~ *games/photography;* 室内游戏 (室内摄影); *an* ~ *swimming-bath.* 室内游泳池。

in·doors /ˌɪnˈdɔːz; ˈɪnˈdorz/ *adv* in or into a building:

在户内；入户内: *go/stay* ~; 进入室内 (留在室内); *kept* ~ *all week by bad weather.* 因天气不好而整周留在户内。

in·dorse /ɪnˈdɔːs; ɪnˈdɔrs/ *vt* = **endorse.**

in·drawn /ˌɪnˈdrɔːn; ˈɪnˈdrɔn/ *adj* drawn in: 吸入的: *an* ~ *breath.* 吸入的一口气。

in·dubi·table /ɪnˈdjuːbɪtəbl US: -ˈduː-; ɪnˈdjubɪtəbl/ *adj* (formal) that cannot be doubted. (正式用语) 不容置疑的。

in·duce /ɪnˈdjuːs US: -ˈduːs; ɪnˈdjus/ *vt* 1 [VP17] ~ *sb to do sth,* persuade or influence; lead or cause: 劝诱；诱导；促使 (某人做某事): *What* ~*d you to do such a thing?* 什么促使你作这种事的？ *We couldn't* ~ *the old lady to travel by air.* 我们无法劝服那老太太乘飞机旅行。 2 [VP6A,14] bring about: 导致；招致: *illness* ~*d by overwork;* 工作过度而引起的病; ~ *labour,* (in childbirth) by artificial means; 人工分娩; ~ *magnetism in a piece of iron,* by holding it near a magnet. (将铁置于磁铁旁) 使一块铁产生磁性。 ~·**ment** *n* [C,U] that which ~s; incentive: 诱因；引诱物；动机: *He hasn't much* ~*ment/many* ~*ments to study English.* 他没有什么学习英语的动机。

in·duct /ɪnˈdʌkt; ɪnˈdʌkt/ *vt* [VP6A, 14, 16B] ~ *sb (to/into/as),* install formally or with ceremony in position or office; admit as a member of. 使正式就职；使入会。

in·duc·tion /ɪnˈdʌkʃn; ɪnˈdʌkʃən/ *n* 1 inducting or being inducted: 正式就职；入会: *an* ~ *course,* designed to provide general knowledge of future activities, requirements, etc. 就职课程 (使就职者对将来工作上的活动、需求等有通盘了解)。 2 method of reasoning which obtains or discovers general laws from particular facts or examples; production of facts to prove a general statement. 归纳 (法)；归纳推理。 ⇨ **deduction.** 3 the bringing about of an electric or magnetic state in a body by proximity (without actual contact) of an electrified or magnetized body: (电或磁之) 感应: ~ *coils/motors.* 感应线圈 (电动机)。 ⇨ **induce(2).**

in·duc·tive /ɪnˈdʌktɪv; ɪnˈdʌktɪv/ *adj* 1 (of reasoning) based on induction(2). (指推理) 归纳的。 2 of magnetic or electrical induction. (磁或电之) 感应的。

in·due /ɪnˈdjuː US: -ˈduː; ɪnˈdju/ = **endue.**

in·dulge /ɪnˈdʌldʒ; ɪnˈdʌldʒ/ *vt, vi* 1 [VP6A] gratify; give way to and satisfy (desires, etc); overlook the faults of: 使满足；放纵 (欲望等); 纵容; 放任: *It is sometimes necessary to* ~ *a sick child.* 放纵一个生病的小孩 (满足一个生病小孩的喜好) 有时是必要的。 2 [VP3A] ~ *in,* allow oneself the pleasure of: 耽溺于；纵情于；尽情享受: *He occasionally* ~*s in the luxury of a good cigar.* 他偶尔享受一枝好雪茄。 **in·dul·gent** /-ənt; -ənt/ *adj* inclined to ~: 纵容的；放纵的: *indulgent parents,* parents who ~ their children. 溺爱子女的父母。 **in·dul·gent·ly** *adv*

in·dul·gence /ɪnˈdʌldʒəns; ɪnˈdʌldʒəns/ *n* 1 [U] indulging(1); the state of being indulged(1). 纵容; 受到纵容。 2 [U] ~ (*in*), (the habit of) gratifying one's own desires, etc: 耽溺; 纵情: *Constant* ~ *in bad habits brought about his ruin.* 经常耽溺于恶习导致了他的毁灭。 3 [C] sth in which a person indulges(2): 耽溺的事物; 嗜好: *One pint of beer a day and an occasional game of billiards are his only* ~*s.* 每天一品脱啤酒及偶尔打打撞球是他仅有的嗜好。 4 [U] (in the RC Church) granting of freedom from punishment still due for sin after sacramental absolution; [C] instance of this. (天主教) 赦免; 免罪。

in·dus·trial /ɪnˈdʌstrɪəl; ɪnˈdʌstrɪəl/ *adj* of industries: 工业的;产业的: *the* ~ *areas of England* (contrasted with *agricultural,* etc). 英国之工业地区 (与农业地区等相对)。 ~ *action,* striking[2](5). 罢工。 *take* ~ *action,* strike[2](5) 罢工。 ~ *alcohol,* for ~ use (unfit for drinking). 工业用酒精 (不可饮用)。 ~ *dispute,* one between workers and management. 工业纠纷; 劳资纠纷。 ~ *estate,* area of land planned and used for the

building of factories (to be rented to manufacturers). 工业用地; 工业区(分租于厂家作修建厂房之用)。 **the ~ revolution,** the changes brought about by mechanical inventions in the 18th and early 19th cc. 工业革命(由于机器的发明所导致之改革, 发生于十八世纪及十九世纪初期)。 **~·ism** /-ɪzəm; -ɪzəm/ *n* social system in which large-scale industries have an important part. 工业社会制度; 工业主义。 **~·ist** /-ɪst; -ɪst/ *n* owner of a large-scale ~ undertaking; supporter of ~ism. 工业家; 工业主义者。

in·dus·tri·ous /ɪnˈdʌstrɪəs; ɪnˈdʌstrɪəs/ *adj* hard-working; diligent. 勤勉的; 刻苦的。 ⇨ **industry** (1). **~·ly** *adv*

in·dus·try /ˈɪndəstrɪ; ˈɪndəstrɪ/ *n* (*pl* **-tries**) **1** [U] quality of being hard-working; always employed usefully: 勤勉; 工作努力: *His success was due to ~ and thrift.* 他的成功是由于勤勉和节俭。 **2** [C, U] (branch of) trade or manufacture (contrasted with distribution and commerce): 工业; 产业; 生产(或其分支)(与分配及商业相对): *the cotton and woollen industries.* 棉毛工业。

in·dwell·ing /ˌɪnˈdwelɪŋ; ˌɪnˈdwelɪŋ/ *adj* (formal) living, always present, in the mind or soul. (正式用语)在心中的; 经常在心中的。

in·ebri·ate /ɪˈniːbrɪeɪt; ɪnˈibrɪˌet/ *vt* [VP6A] (formal or joc) make drunk; intoxicate. (正式用语或谑)使醉; 使大醉。 □ *n, adj* /ɪˈniːbrɪət; ɪnˈibrɪɪt/ (person who is habitually) drunk: 醉汉; 酒徒; 酒醉的: *an institution for ~s.* 酗酒者收容所。 **in·ebri·ation** /ɪˌniːbrɪˈeɪʃən; ɪnˌibrɪˈeʃən/, **in·ebri·ety** /ˌɪnɪˈbraɪətɪ; ˌɪnɪˈbraɪɪtɪ/ *nn* [U] drunkenness. 酒醉。

in·ed·ible /ɪnˈedɪbl; ɪnˈedəbl/ *adj* (formal) (of a kind) not suitable to be eaten. (正式用语)(指某类东西)不可食的。

in·ef·fable /ɪnˈefəbl; ɪnˈɛfəbl/ *adj* (formal) too great to be described in words: (正式用语)难以言语形容的; 不可名状的: *~ joy/beauty.* 说不出的高兴(美) **in·ef·fably** /-əblɪ; -əblɪ/ *adv*

in·ef·fec·tive /ˌɪnɪˈfektɪv; ˌɪnəˈfɛktɪv/ *adj* not producing the effect(s) desired; (of a person) inefficient. 无效力的; (指人)无效率的。 **~·ly** *adv* **~·ness** *n*

in·ef·fec·tual /ˌɪnɪˈfektʃʊəl; ˌɪnəˈfɛktʃʊəl/ *adj* without effect; unsuccessful; lacking confidence and unable to get things done: 无效的; 不成功的; 缺乏信心而不能成事者; 不称职的: *an ~ teacher/leader.* 不称职的教师(领袖)。 **~·ly** /-tʃʊəlɪ; -tʃʊəlɪ/ *adv*

in·ef·fic·ient /ˌɪnɪˈfɪʃnt; ˌɪnəˈfɪʃənt/ *adj* (of persons) wasting time, energy, etc in their work or duties: (指人)无效率的: *an ~ management/administration;* 无效率的经理人员(行政当局); (of machines, processes, etc) wasteful; not producing adequate results. (指机器、程序等)浪费的; 不能产生适当出成果的; 效率低的。 **~·ly** *adv* **in·ef·fic·iency** /-nsɪ; -ənsɪ/ *n* [U].

in·elas·tic /ˌɪnɪˈlæstɪk; ˌɪnɪˈlæstɪk/ *adj* not flexible or adaptable; unyielding: 无弹性的; 无适应性的; 不变通的: *an ~ programme/timetable.* 毫无弹性的计划(时间表)。

in·el·egant /ɪnˈelɪɡənt; ɪnˈɛləɡənt/ *adj* not graceful or refined. 不雅的。 **~·ly** *adv* **in·el·egance** /-əns; -əns/ *n*

in·eli·gible /ɪnˈelɪdʒəbl; ɪnˈɛlɪdʒəbl/ *adj* ~ (**for**), not eligible; not suitable or qualified: 不合格的; 无资格的: *~ for the position.* 无资格任该职。 **in·eli·gi·bil·ity** /ɪnˌelɪdʒəˈbɪlətɪ; ɪnˌelɪdʒəˈbɪlɪtɪ/ *n* [U].

in·eluc·table /ˌɪnɪˈlʌktəbl; ˌɪnɪˈlʌktəbl/ *adj* (formal) that cannot be escaped from: (正式用语)不能避免的: *the victim of ~ fate.* 无法逃过命运之牺牲者。

in·ept /ɪˈnept; ɪnˈept/ *adj* unskilful; said or done at the wrong time: 笨拙的; 不适当的; 非其时的: *~ remarks.* 不适当的谈话。 **~·ly** *adv* **in·ep·ti·tude** /ɪˈneptɪtjuːd; ɪnˈeptəˌtjud/ *n* [U] quality of being ~; [C] ~ action, remark, etc. 笨拙; 不适当; 笨拙或不当的言行等。

in·equal·ity /ˌɪnɪˈkwɒlətɪ; ˌɪnɪˈkwɑlətɪ/ *n* (*pl* **-ties**)

1 [U] want of, absence of, equality in size, degree, circumstances, etc; difference in size, rank, wealth, etc; [C] instance of this: (大小、程度、情况等)不相等; 不平均; 不平等; (大小、地位、财富等的)差别: *Great inequalities in wealth cause social unrest.* 贫富过于悬殊会引起社会不安。 **2** (*pl*) (of a surface) irregularity: (复)(指表面)不平坦: *the inequalities of the landscape,* the rise and fall of the ground, etc. 地形的起伏不平。

in·equi·table /ɪnˈekwɪtəbl; ɪnˈekwɪtəbl/ *adj* (formal) unjust; unfair: (正式用语)不公正的; 不公平的: *an ~ division of the profits.* 利润的分配不公平。

in·equity /ɪnˈekwətɪ; ɪnˈekwɪtɪ/ *n* (*pl* **-ties**) [C, U] (instance of) injustice or unfairness. 不公正; 不公平。

in·eradi·cable /ˌɪnɪˈrædɪkəbl; ˌɪnɪˈrædɪkəbl/ *adj* that cannot be rooted out; firmly and deeply rooted: 不能根除的; 根深蒂固的: *an ~ fault/failing.* 根深蒂固的缺点。

in·ert /ɪˈnɜːt; ɪnˈɜt/ *adj* **1** without power to move or act: 无运动力的: *~ matter.* 无运动力的物质。 **2** without active chemical properties: 不起化学作用的: *~ gases.* 不生化学作用的气体; 惰性气体。 **3** heavy and slow in (mind or body). (身或心)迟钝的; 呆滞的。 **in·er·tia** /ɪˈnɜːʃə; ɪnˈɜʃə/ *n* [U] **1** state of being ~ (3). 迟钝; 呆滞。 **2** property of matter by which it remains in a state of rest or, if it is in motion, continues in the same direction and in a straight line unless it is acted upon by an external force. 惰性; 惯性。

in·es·cap·able /ˌɪnɪˈskeɪpəbl; ˌɪnəˈskepəbl/ *adj* not to be escaped from: 不可逃避的: *We were forced to the ~ conclusion that he was an embezzler.* 我们无法避免的结论是, 他盗用了公款。

in·es·ti·mable /ɪnˈestɪməbl; ɪnˈestəməbl/ *adj* too great, precious, etc to be estimated. (因过大, 过于贵重等)不能估计的; 难评价的。

in·evi·table /ɪnˈevɪtəbl; ɪnˈevətəbl/ *adj* **1** that cannot be avoided, that is sure to happen. 不可避免的; 必然发生的。 **2** (colloq) so frequently seen, heard, etc that it is familiar and expected: (口) 因时常看到或听到而熟悉及预料中的; 照例的; 惯常的: *a tourist with his ~ camera.* 一个惯常带着照像机的游客。 **in·evi·ta·bil·ity** /ɪnˌevɪtəˈbɪlətɪ; ɪnˌevətəˈbɪlətɪ/ *n*

in·ex·act /ˌɪnɪɡˈzækt; ˌɪnɪɡˈzækt/ *adj* not exact. 不正确的; 不精确的。 **in·ex·acti·tude** /ˌɪnɪɡˈzæktɪtjuːd; ˌɪnɪɡˈzæktəˌtjud/ *n* [U] being ~; [C] instance of this: 不正确; 不精确: *terminological ~itudes.* (joc euphem for) lies. (戏谑性委婉语)谎言。

in·ex·cus·able /ˌɪnɪkˈskjuːzəbl; ˌɪnɪkˈskjuzəbl/ *adj* that cannot be excused: 不可原谅的; 不可辩解的: *~ conduct/delays.* 不可原谅的行为(耽搁)。

in·ex·haust·ible /ˌɪnɪɡˈzɔːstəbl; ˌɪnɪɡˈzɔstəbl/ *adj* that cannot be exhausted: 取之不竭的; 无穷尽的: *My patience is not ~.* 我的忍耐是有限度的。

in·exor·able /ɪnˈeksərəbl; ɪnˈeksərəbl/ *adj* relentless; unyielding: 无情的; 坚决不变的: *~ demands/pressures.* 坚决的要求(无情的压力)。 **in·exor·ably** /-əblɪ; -əblɪ/ *adv*

in·ex·pedi·ent /ˌɪnɪkˈspiːdɪənt; ˌɪnɪkˈspidɪənt/ *adj* not expedient. 不合时宜的; 不适宜的。 **in·ex·pedi·en·cy** /-ənsɪ; -ənsɪ/ *n* [U] quality of being ~. 不得当; 不合权宜。

in·ex·pen·sive /ˌɪnɪkˈspensɪv; ˌɪnɪkˈspɛnsɪv/ *adj* not expensive; low-priced. 不贵的; 廉价的。 **~·ly** *adv*

in·ex·pe·ri·ence /ˌɪnɪkˈspɪərɪəns; ˌɪnɪkˈspɪrɪəns/ *n* [U] lack of experience: 无经验; 缺经验: *He didn't get the job because of his ~.* 他由于无经验而未获得该职。 **in·ex·pe·ri·enced** *adj* lacking experience. 无经验的; 缺乏经验的。

in·ex·pert /ɪnˈekspɜːt; ɪnˈɪksˌpɜt/ *adj* unskilled: 缺乏技巧的; 不熟练的: *~ advice/guidance.* 无技巧的劝告(指导)。 **~·ly** *adv*

in·ex·pi·able /ɪnˈekspɪəbl; ɪnˈeksˌpɪəbl/ *adj* (formal) (of an offence) that cannot be expiated; (of resentment, hatred, etc) that cannot be appeased. (正式用语)(指罪

过)不可赎的;(指憎恨等)不能化解的;不能平息的。

in·ex·plic·able /ˌɪnɪk'splɪkəbl; ɪn'eksplɪkəbəl/ *adj* that cannot be explained. 无法解释的。

in·ex·press·ible /ˌɪnɪk'spresəbl; ˌɪnɪk'spresəbl/ *adj* that cannot be expressed in words: 言语无法表达的: ~ *sorrow/anguish*. 无法以言语表达的忧伤(痛苦)。

in·ex·tin·guish·able /ˌɪnɪk'stɪŋgwɪʃəbl; ˌɪnɪk'stɪŋgwɪʃəbl/ *adj* that cannot be extinguished or quenched: 不能扑灭的;不能消除的: ~ *hatred*. 无法化解的仇恨。

in·ex·tri·cable /ˌɪnɪk'strɪkəbl; ɪn'ekstrɪkəbl/ *adj* that cannot be 无法整理的;不能解决的;不能脱身的: reduced to order, solved, untied, or escaped from: 逃不出的: ~ *confusion/difficulties*. 无法整理的紊乱(无法解决的困难)。

in·fal·lible /ɪn'fæləbl; ɪn'fæləbl/ *adj* 1 incapable of making mistakes or doing wrong: 不会犯错的;不会做错事的: *None of us is ~*. 我们当中没有人不会犯错的。 2 never failing: 绝对可靠的: ~ *remedies/cures/methods/tests*. 万无一失的药(治疗法,方法,测验)。 **in·fal·li·bil·ity** /ˌɪnˌfælə'bɪlətɪ; ɪnˌfælə'bɪlətɪ/ *n* complete freedom from the possibility of being in error. 绝无错误。

in·fa·mous /'ɪnfəməs; 'ɪnfəməs/ *adj* wicked; shameful; disgraceful: 邪恶的;可耻的;不名誉的: ~ *behaviour*; 可耻的行为; *an ~ plot/traitor*. 邪恶的阴谋(无耻的卖国贼)。 **in·famy** /'ɪnfəmɪ; 'ɪnfəmɪ/ *n* 1 [U] being ~; public dishonour: 邪恶;无耻;不名誉: *hold a person up to infamy*. 使某人名誉扫地。 2 [U] ~ behaviour; [C] (*pl -mies*) ~ act. 无耻的行为;不名誉的行动。

in·fancy /'ɪnfənsɪ; 'ɪnfənsɪ/ *n* [U] 1 state of being, period when one is, an infant; early childhood; (legal, in GB) minority(1), period before one reaches 18. 幼稚状态;幼儿期;(英国法律)未成年(未满十八岁)。⇨ **minority**. 2 early stage of development or growth: 发展或成长的初期: *the ~ of a nation;* 一国家立国之初期; *When aviation was still in its ~*. 当航空仍在萌芽阶段。

in·fant /'ɪnfənt; 'ɪnfənt/ *n* 1 child during the first few years of its life; (legal) minor. 幼儿; 婴儿; (法律)未成年者。 2 (attrib) (用作定语) ~ *voices*; 童音; ~ *food*; 婴儿食品; *an '~-school*, part of a primary school for children under 7; 幼儿园, 幼稚园(小学之一部, 为七岁以下之儿童而设); ~ *industries*, new, in an early stage. 新建的工业(新创并在初期之工业)。

in·fan·ti·cide /ɪn'fæntɪsaɪd; ɪn'fæntə,saɪd/ *n* [U] crime of killing an infant; the custom, among some peoples in the past, of killing unwanted new-born children. 杀害婴儿罪;昔日某些民族杀害其不要的新生儿之风俗。

in·fan·tile /'ɪnfəntaɪl; 'ɪnfən,taɪl/ *adj* characteristic of infants; 婴儿的;幼儿的; 幼稚的: ~ *diseases/pastimes;* 小儿病(幼儿的娱乐); ~ *paralysis*, name formerly used for poliomyelitis. 小儿麻痹症(脊髓灰白质炎之旧名)。 **in·fan·til·ism** /ɪn'fæntɪlɪzəm; 'ɪnfæntɪlɪzm/ *n* [U] mentally and physically under-developed or arrested state. 幼稚病(心智及身体发育不足之状态); 幼稚状态。

in·fan·try /'ɪnfəntrɪ; 'ɪnfəntrɪ/ *n* (collective *sing*) [U] soldiers who fight on foot: (集合名词单数)步兵: *two regiments of ~;* 两团步兵; *an ~ regiment.* 一个步兵团。 *'~·man /-mən; -mən/, n (pl -men)* soldier in an ~ regiment. 步兵。⇨ **cavalry.**

in·fatu·ate /ɪn'fætʃueɪt; ɪn'fætʃu,et/ *vt* be ~*d with/by sb*, be filled with a wild and foolish love for: 疯狂迷恋: *He's ~d with that girl.* 他疯狂地爱恋着那个女郎。 **in·fatu·ation** /ɪnˌfætʃu'eɪʃn; ɪnˌfætʃʊ'eʃən/ *n* [U] infatuating or being ~d; [C] ~ *(for)*, instance of this; unreasoning love or passion. 疯狂迷恋;痴迷。

in·fect /ɪn'fekt; ɪn'fɛkt/ *vt* [VP6A, 14] ~ *(with)*, contaminate; give disease, (fig) feelings, ideas, to a person, his body or mind: 污染; 传染疾病; (喻)使某人、其身或心受情感或思想的感染: ~ *a wound;* 使一伤口受到感染; ~ed *with cholera.* 染上了霍乱。 *Mary's high*

spirits ~ed *all the girls in the class.* 玛莉的兴高采烈感染了班上所有的女孩。

in·fec·tion /ɪn'fekʃn; ɪn'fɛkʃən/ *n* 1 [U] infecting or being infected; communication of disease, esp by agency of the atmosphere or water, ⇨ **contagion.** 污染; 被污染; 传染病; 传染疾病(尤指借空气或水)。 2 [C] disease, (fig) influence, that infects. 传染病; (喻)影响力。

in·fec·tious /ɪn'fekʃəs; ɪn'fɛkʃəs/ *adj* 1 infecting with disease; (of disease) that can be spread by means of bacteria carried in the atmosphere or in water. 传染疾病的; (指疾病)可借空气或水中细菌传染的。⇨ **contagious.** 2 (fig) quickly influencing others; likely to spread to others: (喻)迅速影响他人的; 易传播的: ~ *humour.* 易感染他人感受的幽默。

in·fer /ɪn'fɜː(r); ɪn'fɝ/ *vt* (-rr-) [VP6A, 9, 14] ~ *(from sth)(that …)*, conclude; reach an opinion (from facts or reasoning): 推断; (由事实或推理)推知: *Am I to ~ from your remarks that you think I am a liar?* 你的话是否表示你认为我说谎呢? ~ *ence* /'ɪnfərəns; 'ɪnfərəns/ *n* 1 [U] process of ~ring: 推断; 推论; 推知: *by ~ence,* as the result of drawing a conclusion. 根据推断。 2 [C] that which is ~red; conclusion. 推断的结果; 结论: *Is that a fair ~ence from his statement?* 对于他的声明那样推断合乎吗? ~ **en·tial** /ˌɪnfə'renʃl; ˌɪnfə'rɛnʃəl/ *adj* that may be ~red. 可以推断的; 可以推知的。

in·ferior /ɪn'fɪərɪə(r); ɪn'fɪrɪə/ *adj* lower(er) in rank, social position, importance, quality, etc: 级别低的; 社会地位低的; 次要的; 劣势的; 质劣的; 次等的; 较低劣的的: *goods/workmanship;* 低劣的货物(手艺); *an ~ officer/court of law;* 下级军官(低等法院); *make sb feel ~.* 使人感到自卑。 □ *n* person who is ~ (in rank, ability, etc). (级别, 能力等) 较低之人。 ~·ity /ɪnˌfɪərɪ'ɒrətɪ US: -'ɔːr-; ɪn,fɪrɪ'ɔrətɪ/ *n* state of being ~; 较低; 较不重要; 低劣。 '~·ity complex, state of mind in which a person who has a morbid feeling of being ~ to others may try to win recognition for himself by boasting and being aggressive. 自卑感 (一种病态心理, 自觉不如他人, 欲借吹嘘和出风头以获取他人的赞誉)。

in·fer·nal /ɪn'fɜːnl; ɪn'fɝnl/ *adj* of hell; devilish; abominable: 地狱的; 恶魔般的; 可憎的: ~ *regions;* 地狱; ~ *cruelty.* 恶魔般的残忍。 ~·ly /-nəlɪ; -nlɪ/ *adv*

in·ferno /ɪn'fɜːnəʊ; ɪn'fɝno/ *n* (*pl ~s* /-nəʊz; -noz/) hell; scene of horror, eg a blazing building in which people are trapped. 地狱; 恐怖的景象(例如有人困于熊熊大火的建筑物中)。

in·fer·tile /ɪn'fɜːtaɪl US: -tl; ɪn'fɝtl/ *adj* not fertile; barren. 不肥沃的; 不结果实的; 不能生育的。 **in·fer·til·ity** /ˌɪnfə'tɪlətɪ; ɪnfə'tɪlətɪ/ *n*

in·fest /ɪn'fest; ɪn'fɛst/ *vt* [VP6A] (of rats, insects, etc) be present in large numbers: (指老鼠, 虫类等)大批出动; 成群出现: *warehouses ~ed with rats;* 老鼠横行的仓库; *clothes ~ed with vermin/lice.* 生满跳蚤(虱子)的衣服。 **in·fes·ta·tion** /ˌɪnfe'steɪʃn; ˌɪnfɛs'teʃən/ *n* [U, C] (instance of) ~ing or being ~ed. (老鼠, 虫类等)大批出现。

in·fi·del /'ɪnfɪdəl; 'ɪnfədl/ *n* 1 (hist) person with no belief in a religion, esp in what is considered to be the true religion. (史)不信仰宗教(尤指正统宗教)者; 宗教信仰者。 2 (attrib) unbelieving; of unbelievers: (用作定语)不信教的; 异教徒的: *He showed an ~ contempt for sacred places.* 他对圣地表示一种异教徒的轻蔑。

in·fi·del·ity /ˌɪnfɪ'delətɪ; ˌɪnfə'dɛlətɪ/ *n* (*pl -ties*) [C,U] (formal) (act of) disloyalty or unfaithfulness; adultery: (正式用语)不忠实; 不贞; 不贞的行为; 通奸: *conjugal ~,* ~ *to one's husband or wife.* 对配偶的不忠。

in·field /'ɪnfiːld; 'ɪn,fild/ *n* (cricket) (opp of *outfield*) part of the ground near the wicket; fieldsmen stationed there; baseball diamond. (板球) (为 outfield 之反义词)内场; 内野区(为 outfield 之反义词)内场。

in-fight·ing /'ɪn faɪtɪŋ; 'ɪn,faɪtɪŋ/ *n* [U] boxing at rather close quarters; (colloq) often ruthless competition between colleagues or rivals (esp in commerce and

industry). (拳击)接近战; 短打; (口)(特指工商业界)同ุ
或对手间时常无情的竞争。

in·fil·trate /'ɪnfɪltreɪt; ɪn'fɪltreɪt/ vt, vi [VP6A,
14,2A,3A] ~ sth (into sth), ~ (into/through),
(cause to) pass through or into by filtering; (of troops)
pass through defences without attracting notice; (of
ideas) pass into people's minds. (使)渗透; (指军
队)悄悄越过对方防线; 渗透; (指思想)渗入人的心中。
in·fil·tra·tion /ˌɪnfɪl'treɪʃn; ˌɪnfɪl'treʃən/ n [U]
infiltrating or being ~d; (esp) gradual and unnoticed
occupation of land by small groups, eg of soldiers or
settlers. 渗透; 被渗透; (尤指)渗透运动; 渗透侵占(例
如小股军队或殖民者的不为人注意之逐渐占领或侵占土
地)。

in·fi·nite /'ɪnfɪnət; 'ɪnfənɪt/ adj endless; without
limits; that cannot be measured, calculated, or
imagined: 无穷的; 无限的; 无法计量或想象的: ~ space;
无穷的太空; the ~ goodness of God; 上帝的无限恩典;
Such ideas may do ~ harm. 这种思想可能会造成极大的
害处。the l~, God. 上帝。~·ly adv in an ~ degree:
无穷地; 无限地; 无法计量或想象地: Atoms and molecules
are ~ly small. 原子与分子极小。 **in·fini·tesi·mal**
/ˌɪnfɪnɪ'tesɪml; ˌɪnfɪnə'tesəml/ adj ~ly small. 极微
小的。

in·fini·tive /ɪn'fɪnətɪv; ɪn'fɪnətɪv/ adj, n (gram)
(in English) non-finite form of a v used with or without
to, eg let him go; allow him to go. (语法)不定式的; 不
定式(英语中一动词的非限定形式,可与to或不与to连用,
例如let him go 中的go, 及 allow him to go 中的to go)。
in·fini·tude /ɪn'fɪnɪtjuːd US: -tuːd; ɪn'fɪnə,tjud/ n
[U] (formal) the state of being endless or boundless;
boundless number or extent (of): (正式用语)无限; 无限
的数目或范围(与of连用): the ~ of God's mercy; 上帝
慈悲的无限; [C] infinite number, quantity, or extent:
无数; 无限量; 无限范围: an ~ of small particles. 无数
的微小粒子。

in·fin·ity /ɪn'fɪnətɪ; ɪn'fɪnətɪ/ n [U] the state of
being endless or boundless; (maths) infinite quantity
(expressed by the symbol ∞). 无限; (数学)无限大(符号
为∞)。

in·firm /ɪn'fɜːm; ɪn'fɝm/ adj 1 physically weak (esp
through age): 体弱的; (尤指由于年迈): walk with ~
steps. 以虚弱的步子行走。2 mentally or morally weak.
懦弱的; 意志薄弱的。~ of purpose, not purposeful;
undecided. 意志薄弱的; 犹豫不决的。 **in·firm·ity**
/ɪn'fɜːmətɪ; ɪn'fɝmətɪ/ n (pl -ties) (particular
form of) weakness: 体弱; 虚弱: I~ity often comes with
old age. 虚弱常与老年俱来。 Deafness and failing
eyesight are among the ~ities of old age. 耳聋与眼花是
年老体衰的现象。

in·firm·ary /ɪn'fɜːmərɪ; ɪn'fɝmərɪ/ n (pl -ries)
1 hospital. 医院。2 (in a school, institution, etc) room
used for people who are ill or injured. (学校, 机关等的)
医务室。

in·flame /ɪn'fleɪm; ɪn'flem/ vt, vi [VP2A, 6A]
(cause to) become red, angry, overheated: 使红; 使怒;
使红肿; 使发炎; 使炽热; 变红; 发炎; 被激怒; 变热:
~d eyes; 红肿的眼睛; an ~d boil, red and angry
looking; 红肿的疖子; speeches that ~d popular feeling,
roused people to anger, indignation, etc; 煽动群情的演
说; ~d with passion. 情绪激动。

in·flam·mable /ɪn'flæməbl; ɪn'flæməbl/ adj easily set
on fire or (fig)excited: 易燃的; (喻)易激动的: Petroleum—
Highly I~! 汽油—极易燃烧! ⇨ **flammable**.

in·flam·ma·tion /ˌɪnfləˈmeɪʃn; ˌɪnfləˈmeʃən/ n
[U] inflamed condition (esp of some part of the body):
激怒; 炽热; (尤指)发炎: ~ of the lungs/liver; 肺部
(肝部)发炎; [C] instance of this; place on or in the
body where there is redness, swelling and pain. 发炎
之处。

in·flam·ma·tory /ɪn'flæmətrɪ US: -tɔːrɪ; ɪn-
'flæmə,torɪ/ adj 1 tending to inflame: 易使人愤怒

的; 煽动性的: ~ speeches. 煽动性的演说。2 of, tending
to produce, inflammation: 发炎的; 引起发炎的; 炎性
的: an ~ condition of the lungs, eg as a symptom of
pneumonia. 肺部发炎的炎性的症候)。

in·flate /ɪn'fleɪt; ɪn'flet/ vt, vi [VP6A,14,2A,C] ~
sth (with), 1 fill a tyre, balloon, etc with air or gas;
(cause to) swell: 灌气于(轮胎, 气球等); 使膨胀; 膨胀:
(fig) (喻) ~d with pride; 傲气十足; ~d language,
full of high-sounding words but containing little
substance. 浮夸的言词。2 take action to increase the
amount of money in circulation so that prices rise. 使
(通货)膨胀而引起物价上涨。⇨ **deflate**. **in·flat·able**
/-əbl; -əbl/ adj that can be ~d: 可充气的; 可使之膨胀
的: an inflatable rubber dinghy. 一条可充气的橡皮艇。

in·fla·tion /ɪn'fleɪʃn; ɪn'fleʃən/ n [U] act of
inflating; state of being ~d; (esp) (rise in prices
brought about by the) expansion of the supply of bank
money, credit, etc. 灌气; 膨胀; (尤指)通货膨胀; 信用
膨胀; 因通货或信用膨胀而引起的物价上涨。 **in·fla·tion·
ary** /ɪn'fleɪʃnrɪ US: -nerɪ; ɪn'fleʃən,ɛrɪ/ adj of,
caused by, inflation: 膨胀的; 通货膨胀的; 由膨胀或
通货膨胀所引起的: the inflationary spiral, economic
situation in which prices and wages rise in turn as the
supply of money is increased. 螺旋性通货膨胀(因通货
膨胀而引起物价及工资上涨的经济状况)。

in·flect /ɪn'flekt; ɪn'flɛkt/ vt [VP6A] 1 (gram)
change the ending or form of (a word) to show its
relationship to other words in a sentence. (语法)
发生屈折变化; 变化(一词)之词尾或形式(以表示该词与
句中其他词间的关系)。2 modulate (the voice); bend
inwards; curve. 改变(声音)的声调; 使向内弯折; 弯曲。

in·flec·tion /ɪn'flekʃn; ɪn'flɛkʃən/ n 1 [U] inflecting.
词尾变化; 词形变化; 改变声调; 弯曲。2 [C] inflected
form of a word, eg am, are, is; suffix used to inflect,
eg -ed, -ing. 曲折形式; 一词变化的形式(例如 am, are,
is); 表示变化的词尾(例如 -ed, -ing)。3 [C] rise and
fall of the voice in speaking. 讲话声调的抑扬变化。~·al
/-ʃənl; -ʃənl/ adj of ~: 词形变化的; 词尾变化的;
音调变化的: ~al endings/forms, eg -ed. 变化词形的词
尾(形式)(例如 -ed)。

in·flexion /ɪn'flekʃn; ɪn'flɛkʃən/ n = **inflection**.

in·flict /ɪn'flɪkt; ɪn'flɪkt/ vt [VP6A, 14] ~ sth
(on/upon), give (a blow, etc); cause to suffer, impose:
予以(打击等); 使受痛苦; 强加于之: ~ a blow/a severe
wound upon sb. 予某人以打击(严重伤害)。The judge
~ed the death penalty upon the murderer. 法官处该杀人
犯以死刑。I'm sorry to have to ~ myself/my company
upon you, force my company upon you. 我很抱歉不得不
打搅你。 **in·flic·tion** /ɪn'flɪkʃn; ɪn'flɪkʃən/ n [U] ~ing
or being ~ed: 打击; 伤害; 强加; 施加痛苦; 受苦: the
unnecessary ~ion of pain and suffering; 不必要的施予
痛苦; [C] sth ~ed; painful or troublesome experience.
所受的痛苦或处罚; 痛苦的经验。

in·flor·escence /ˌɪnflɔː'resns; ˌɪnflo'rɛsns/ n [U]
arrangement of a plant's flowers on the stem; collective
flower of a plant; (lit or fig) flowering. 花序; 花(一植
物上花的总称); (字面或喻)开花。⇨ the illus at **flower**.
参看 flower 之插图。

in·flow /'ɪnfləʊ; 'ɪn,flo/ n [U] flowing in; [C, U]
that which flows in: 流入; 流入物: an ~ of capital/
investment; 资本(投资)的流入; an ~ of 25 litres an
hour; 每小时流入 25 公升; (attrib) (用作定语) an ~
pipe. 流入管道。

in·flu·ence /'ɪnfluəns; 'ɪnfluəns/ n ~ on/upon,
1 [U] power to affect sb's character, beliefs or actions
through example, fear, admiration, etc; [C] person,

fact, etc that exercises such power; [U] the exercise of such power. 影响力; 感化力; 有影响力的人, 事实等; 影响; 感化: *Many a woman has had a civilizing ~ upon her husband.* 许多妇女对其丈夫有感化力。*He's an ~ for good in the town.* 他在本市具有使人向善的影响力。*Heredity and environment are ~s on character.* 遗传与环境是影响性格的因素。*He was under the ~ of alcohol,* had had too much to drink. 他喝醉了。 **2** [U] action of natural forces: 自然力的作用: *the ~ of the moon (on the tides);* 月亮(对于潮汐)的影响; *the ~ of climate (on vegetation).* 气候(对于植物)的影响。 **3** [U] power due to wealth, position, etc: 势力; 权力: *Will you please use your ~ with the manager on my behalf?* 请你对经理运用你的权力, 帮我忙好吗? *Will you use your ~ to get me a job?* 你愿意运用你的影响力替我找一份工作吗? □ *vt* [VP6A] exert an ~ on; have an effect on: 影响; 对…作用: *Can the planets ~ human character, as astrologers claim?* 行星能象占星家所宣称那样对人的性格有所影响吗? *Don't be ~d by bad examples.* 勿受坏榜样的影响。

in·flu·en·tial /ˌɪnfluˈenʃl; ˌɪnfluˈɛnʃəl/ *adj* having influence: 有影响力的; 有势力的: *~ politicians;* 有影响力的政界人士; *considerations which are ~ in reaching a decision.* 对于作决定有影响的因素。 **~ly** /-ʃəlɪ; -ʃəlɪ/ *adv*

in·flu·enza /ˌɪnfluˈenzə; ˌɪnfluˈɛnzə/ *n* [U] (colloq abbr 口语略作 **flu**) infectious disease with fever, muscular pain and catarrh. 流行性感冒。

in·flux /ˈɪnflʌks; ˈɪnˌflʌks/ *n* [U] flowing in; [C] (*pl* **~es**) constant inflow or large numbers or quantities: 流入; 注入; 巨大数目或量的经常流入: *repeated ~es of visitors;* 访客的川流不息; *an ~ of wealth.* 财富的涌入。

in·form /ɪnˈfɔːm; ɪnˈfɔrm/ *vt, vi* **1** [VP6A, 11, 14, 21] ~ *sb* (*of sth*)/(*that ...*), give knowledge to: 通知; 报告; 告诉: *We were ~ed that two prisoners had escaped.* 我们听说有两个囚犯逃跑了。*Keep me ~ed of fresh developments.* 随时告诉我新的发展。*He's a well-~ed man.* 他是个消息灵通的人。*Have you ~ed them of your intended departure?* 你通知了他们你想离去吗? **2** [VP6A] ~ *against/on sb,* (legal) bring evidence or an accusation against him (to the police). (法律)(向警方)告发某人。**~·ant** /-ənt; -ənt/ *n* person who gives information; (ling) native speaker of a language who helps a foreign scholar who is making an analysis of it. 提供消息的人; 通知者; (语言学)(协助外国学者分析研究本国语言之)讲说本国语者。~·**er** *n* person who ~s(2), esp against a criminal or fugitive. 告发者(特指告发罪犯或逃犯)。

in·for·mal /ɪnˈfɔːml; ɪnˈfɔrml/ *adj* not formal(1,2); irregular; without ceremony or formality: 非正式的; 非正规的; 不规则的; 不拘礼仪的: *an ~ visit;* 非正式的访问; *~ dress;* 便服; *~ conversations between the statesmen of two countries,* no official records being kept. 两国政治家之间非正式的谈话(不列入官方记录者)。**~·ly** /-məlɪ; -mlɪ/ *adv* **~·ity** /ɪnfɔːˈmælətɪ; ˌɪnfɔrˈmælətɪ/ *n* [U] being; [C] (*pl* **-ties**) ~ act, etc. 不正式; 不拘礼仪; 非正式的行动等。

in·for·ma·tion /ˌɪnfəˈmeɪʃn; ˌɪnfəˈmeʃən/ *n* [U] ~ *on/about,* **1** informing or being informed. 通知; 报告; 接到通知。 **2** sth told; news or knowledge given: 消息; 情报; 知识: *That's a useful piece/bit of ~.* 那是一项重要的情报(知识)。*Can you give me any ~ on/ about this matter?* 关于此事你能供给我任何消息吗? *The ~ bureau may be able to help you.* 新闻局可能对你有所帮助。

in·for·ma·tive /ɪnˈfɔːmətɪv; ɪnˈfɔrmətɪv/ *adj* giving information; instructive: 供给消息的; 给予知识的: *~ books;* 增益知识的书; *an ~ talk.* 有助益的谈话。 **~·ly** *adv*

in·fra /ˈɪnfrə; ˈɪnfrə/ *adv* (Lat, formal) below; farther or later on (in a book, etc): (拉, 正式用语) 在下; (书中等)以下: *See ~, p 21,* See p 21 farther on in

this book. 参看以下第 21 页。 *~ **dig** /dɪɡ; dɪɡ/ pred adj* beneath one's dignity. 有失身份的。 □ *pref* *~·* **'red** *adj* of those invisible rays below the red in the spectrum. 红外线的。 **'~·structure** *n* the parts of a system that compose the whole; (esp) permanent military installations forming a basis for defence. 形成整体的各部分; (尤指)永久性军事防卫设施。 ⇨ supra.

in·frac·tion /ɪnˈfrækʃn; ɪnˈfrækʃən/ *n* [U] breaking of a rule, law, etc; [C] instance of this. 犯规; 违法。

in·fre·quent /ɪnˈfriːkwənt; ɪnˈfrikwənt/ *adj* not frequent; rare. 罕见的; 少有的。 **~·ly** *adv* **in·fre·quency** /-kwənsɪ; -kwənsɪ/ *n* [U].

in·fringe /ɪnˈfrɪndʒ; ɪnˈfrɪndʒ/ *vt, vi* **1** [VP6A] break (a rule, etc); transgress; violate: 违背(规章等); 触犯; 侵犯: *~ a rule/an oath/copyright/a patent.* 违犯规章(违背誓言; 侵犯版权; 侵害专利权)。 **2** [VP3A] ~ *upon,* encroach: 侵占; 侵害: *Be careful not to ~ upon the rights of other people.* 当心不要侵害别人的权利。 **~·ment** *n* [U] infringing; [C] ~*ment of,* instance of this, eg the unlawful use of a trade name or of copyright material. 违背; 侵犯; 侵占; (如冒用商标或侵害版权)。

in·furi·ate /ɪnˈfjʊərɪeɪt; ɪnˈfjʊrɪˌet/ *vt* [VP6A] fill with fury or rage: 使狂怒; 激怒: *infuriating delays.* 令人非常愤怒的耽搁。

in·fuse /ɪnˈfjuːz; ɪnˈfjuz/ *vt, vi* (formal) (正式用语) **1** [VP14] ~ *into/with,* put, pour (a quality, etc *into*); fill (*sb with*): 灌输(性质等); 向(某人)灌输: *~ fresh courage/new life into soldiers.* 给士兵们灌输新勇气(新生命); *~ soldiers with fresh courage.* 灌输士兵们以新勇气。 **2** [VP6A] pour (hot) liquid on (leaves, herbs, etc) to flavour it or to extract its constituents: 沏或泡(叶子、草药等), 使液体加味或提出其成分): *~ herbs.* 浸泡草药。 **3** [VP2A] undergo infusion: 经过泡制: *Let the herbs ~ for three minutes.* 将草药泡三分钟。

in·fu·sion /ɪnˈfjuːʒn; ɪnˈfjuʒən/ *n* **1** [U] infusing or being infused. 灌输; 泡制。 **2** [C] liquid made by infusing. 泡浸制成的液体; 浸剂; 泡剂。 **3** [U] pouring in; mixing: 注入; 混合: *the ~ of new blood into old stock,* the use of new breeds to improve old breeds. 用新品种以改良旧种。

in·gath·er·ing /ˈɪnɡæðərɪŋ; ˈɪnˌɡæðərɪŋ/ *n* [C] (formal) gathering in; harvest. (正式用语) 采集; 收获。

in·geni·ous /ɪnˈdʒiːnɪəs; ɪnˈdʒinjəs/ *adj* **1** (of a person) clever and skilful (at making or inventing); showing skill, etc: (指人) 有发明天才的; 机敏的; 灵巧的: *an ~ mind.* 灵巧的心智。 **2** (of things) skilfully made: (指物) 制作精巧的: *an ~ toy/tool.* 精巧的玩具(工具)。 **~·ly** *adv* **in·genu·ity** /ˌɪndʒɪˈnjuːɪtɪ; ˌɪndʒəˈnuətɪ/ *US:* /-nuː-; -ˌnu/ *n* [U] cleverness and skill; originality in design. 灵巧; 机敏; 设计之创新; 创造力。

in·gé·nue /ˈænʒeɪnjuː; ˈændʒənuː/ *US:* /ˈændʒənuː; ˈændʒəˌnu/ *n* (F) (formal) simple, innocent girl, esp as a type in dramas; actress playing such a part. (法)(正式用语) 天真无邪的女郎(尤指戏剧中此种角色); 扮演此种角色之女演员。

in·genu·ous /ɪnˈdʒenjʊəs; ɪnˈdʒɛnjʊəs/ *adj* (formal) frank; open; innocent; natural: (正式用语) 坦白的; 直率的; 天真的; 自然的: *an ~ smile.* 坦率的微笑。 **~·ly** *adv* **~·ness** *n*

in·gest /ɪnˈdʒest; ɪnˈdʒɛst/ *vt* [VP6A] (formal) (lit or fig) take in (food, etc) by, or as if by, swallowing. (正式用语)(字面或喻) 吞咽(食物等); 吸收。

ingle-nook /ˈɪŋɡl nʊk; ˈɪŋɡlˌnʊk/ *n* chimney-corner (in a wide old-fashioned fireplace) where the fire burns on an open hearth. (旧式宽阔的壁炉之) 炉边; 炉隅; 炉角。

in·glori·ous /ɪnˈɡlɔːrɪəs; ɪnˈɡlɔrɪəs/ *adj* **1** shameful; ignominious. 可耻的; 不名誉的。 **2** obscure. 默默无闻的。 **~·ly** *adv*

in·go·ing /ˈɪnɡəʊɪŋ; ˈɪnˌɡoɪŋ/ *adj* going in: 进来的: *the ~* (= new) *tenant of a house/flat.* 一所房屋(公寓)的新来房客。

in·got /ˈɪŋgət; ˈɪŋgət/ n [C] (usu brick-shaped) lump of metal (esp gold and silver), cast in a mould. (尤指金、银之)铸块(通常为砖形); 锭.

in·graft /ɪnˈgrɑːft US: -ˈgræft; ɪnˈgræft/ v = engraft.

in·grained /ˌɪnˈgreɪnd; ɪnˈgrend/ adj 1 (of habits, tendencies, etc) deeply fixed; thorough: (指习惯、倾向等)深染的; 根深蒂固的; 彻底的: ~ prejudices/honesty. 根深蒂固的偏见(绝对的诚实). 2 going deep: 变深的: ~ dirt. 深陷的泥土.

in·grati·ate /ɪnˈgreɪʃɪeɪt; ɪnˈgreʃɪ,et/ vt [VP14] ~ oneself with sb, bring oneself into favour, esp in order to gain an advantage: 讨好; 逢迎(某人)(尤指以利益为目的者): with an ingratiating smile. 带着讨好的微笑. **in·grati·at·ing·ly** adv

in·grati·tude /ɪnˈgrætɪtjuːd US: -tuːd; ɪnˈgrætə,tjud/ n [U] want of gratitude. 忘恩负义.

in·gredi·ent /ɪnˈgriːdɪənt; ɪnˈgridɪənt/ n [C] one of the parts of a mixture: (混合物的)成分: the ~s of a cake; 糕饼的各种成分; the ~s of a man's character, all those qualities, etc that together form it. 形成一个人的性格的种种因素.

in·gress /ˈɪngres; ˈɪɪŋgrɛs/ n [U] (formal) going in; (right of) entrance: (正式用语)进入; 进入权; 入场权: a means of ~. 进入的方法. ⇨ egress.

in·grow·ing /ˈɪngrəʊɪŋ; ˈɪn,groɪŋ/ adj growing inwards: 向内生的: an ~ toe-nail, one growing into the flesh. (向内里生长的)嵌趾甲.

in·habit /ɪnˈhæbɪt; ɪnˈhæbɪt/ vt [VP6A] live in; occupy. 居住于. 住于. 可居住的. **in·hab·it·able** /-əbl; -əbl/ adj that can be lived in. 可居住的. **in·hab·it·ant** /-ənt; -ənt/ n person living in a place. 居住者; 居民.

in·hale /ɪnˈheɪl; ɪnˈhel/ vt, vi [VP6A, 2A] draw into the lungs: 吸入肺部: ~ air/gas/tobacco smoke. 吸入空气(气体, 烟草之烟气). I~! Exhale! Breathe in! Breathe out! 吸入! 呼出! **in·haler** n device for producing a chemical vapour to make breathing easier. 产生化学气体以协助呼吸困难者之装置; 吸入器.

in·har·moni·ous /ˌɪnhɑːˈməʊnɪəs; ˌɪnhɑrˈmonɪəs/ adj not harmonious. 不和谐的; 不协调的.

in·herent /ɪnˈhɪərənt; ɪnˈhɪrənt/ adj ~ (in), existing as a natural and permanent part or quality of: 固有的; 生来的; 天生的: Weight is an ~ quality of matter. 重量是物质固有的特性. He has an ~ love of beauty. 他天生爱美. The power ~ in the office of President must not be abused. 总统一职所具有的权力不得滥用.

in·herit /ɪnˈherɪt; ɪnˈhɛrɪt/ vt, vi [VP6A, 2A] 1 receive property, a title, etc as heir: 继承(财产, 爵位等): The eldest son will ~ the title. 长子将继承爵位. 2 derive (qualities, etc) from ancestors: 由遗传而得(特质等): She ~ed her mother's good looks and her father's bad temper. 她继承了母亲的美貌和父亲的坏脾气. **in·herit·ance** /-əns; -əns/ n [U] ~ing: 继承; 遗传: receive sth by ~ance; 由继承而获得; [C] (lit, fig) what is ~ed: (字面,喻)继承或遗传之物; 遗产; 天禀: an ~ance of ill-feeling. 遗留下来的怨恨.

in·hibit /ɪnˈhɪbɪt; ɪnˈhɪbɪt/ vt [VP6A, 14] ~ sb (from sth/doing sth), hinder, restrain: 阻止; 禁止; 抑制: ~ wrong desires and impulses; 抑制不正当的欲望和冲动; an ~ed person, one who is unable or unwilling to express his feelings. 无能力或不愿表示情感的人; 抑制感情者. **in·hi·bi·tion** /ˌɪnhɪˈbɪʃn; ˌɪnhɪˈbɪʃən/ n [U] (psych) restraint on, habitual shrinking from, an action for which there is an impulse or desire; [C] instance of this: (心理)抑制; 抑制的念头; Wine weakens a person's ~ions. 酒能减弱人的抑制力. **in·hibi·tory** /ɪnˈhɪbɪtrɪ US: -tɔːrɪ; ɪnˈhɪbə,tɔrɪ/ adj tending to ~; of an inhibition. 有抑制倾向的; 抑制的.

in·hos·pi·table /ˌɪnhɒˈspɪtəbl; ɪnˈhɑsprtəbl/ adj not hospitable; (of a place, coast, etc) not affording shelter: 待客不亲切的; 冷淡的; (指地点, 海岸等)无遮蔽

处的; 荒凉的: an ~ coast. 荒凉的海岸.

in·hu·man /ɪnˈhjuːmən; ɪnˈhjumən/ adj cruel; unfeeling; 无情的; 无情的: 虐待. **~·ity** /ˌɪnhjuːˈmænətɪ; ˌɪnhjuˈmænətɪ/ n [U] ~ conduct or behaviour. 残忍; 残忍的行为: man's ~ity to man; 人类的自相残杀; [C] (pl -ties) ~ act. 残忍的举动.

in·hu·mane /ˌɪnhjuːˈmeɪn; ˌɪnhjuˈmen/ adj not humane; cruel; without pity. 不人道的; 残忍的; 无怜悯心的. **~·ly** adv

in·imi·cal /ɪˈnɪmɪkl; ɪnˈɪmɪkl/ adj ~ (to), (formal) unfriendly or harmful: (正式用语)不友善的; 有害的: actions ~ to friendly relations between countries. 对两国友善关系有害的行动.

in·imi·table /ɪˈnɪmɪtəbl; ɪnˈmetəbl/ adj (formal) too good, clever, etc to be imitated: (正式用语)(太好, 太聪明等而)无法模仿的. **in·imi·tably** /-əblɪ; -əblɪ/ adv

in·iqui·tous /ɪˈnɪkwɪtəs; ɪˈnɪkwətəs/ adj (formal) very wicked or unjust: (正式用语)极邪恶的; 极不公正的: an ~ system/regime. 极邪恶的体系(政权). **~·ly** adv wickedly. **in·iquity** /ɪˈnɪkwɪtɪ; ɪˈnɪkwətɪ/ n (formal) [U]; [C] (pl -ties) ~ act. 极邪恶; 极不公正; 极邪恶或极不公正的行为.

in·itial /ɪˈnɪʃl; ɪˈnɪʃəl/ adj of or at the beginning: 开始的; 起初的: the ~ letter of a word; 一词起首的字母; the ~ stages of an undertaking. 一事业最初的阶段. □ n = letter, esp (pl) first letters of a person's names, as GBS (for George Bernard Shaw). 起首的字母; (尤指)(复)姓名起首的各字母(例如 GBS 代表 George Bernard Shaw). □ vt (-ll-, US also -l-) mark, sign, with one's ~s: 标识或签名记姓名的起首各字母于: ~ a note or document. 在一短简或文件上签上自己姓名的起首各字母. **~·ly** /-ʃəlɪ; -ʃəlɪ/ adv at the beginning. 在起初; 在开始.

in·iti·ate /ɪˈnɪʃɪeɪt; ɪˈnɪʃɪ,et/ vt 1 [VP6A] set (a scheme, etc) working: 开始; 着手(一计划等): ~ a plan. 推动一计划. 2 [VP14] ~ sb into sth, admit or introduce sb to membership of (a group, etc). 准许或介绍某人加入成为(某一团体等). 3 [VP14] ~ sb into sth, give sb elementary instruction, or secret knowledge of: 传授(某人)入门知识或秘密知识: ~ students into the mysteries of interstellar communication. 传授星际通讯的奥秘教给学生. □ n, adj /ɪˈnɪʃɪət; ɪˈnɪʃɪɪt/ (person) who has been ~d(2,3): 被准许或介绍加入的(人); 被传授秘识的(人): an ~ member of a secret society. 一秘密会社的新社员. **in·iti·ation** /ɪˌnɪʃɪˈeɪʃn; ɪˌnɪʃɪˈeʃən/ n [U] initiating or being ~d; being made acquainted with the rules of a society, etc: 开始; 着手; 传授秘密知识; 熟悉一会社等的规章: (attrib) (用作定语) initiation ceremonies. 入会仪式.

in·iti·ative /ɪˈnɪʃətɪv; ɪˈnɪʃɪ,etɪv/ n 1 [U,C] first or introductory step or move: 初步的阶段或行动: peace ~s. 和平的初步. act/do sth on one's own ~, without an order or suggestion from others. 主动地作某事. have the ~, be in the position to make the first move, eg in war. 处于主动的地位(例如在战争中). take the ~ (in doing sth), make the first move towards it. 采取(作某事之)初步行动. 2 [U] capacity to see what needs to be done and enterprise enough to do it: 创始力; 进取心: A statesman must have/ show/display ~. 政治家必须有(表示, 表现)开创精神. 3 [C] power or right of citizens outside the legislature to put forward proposals for legislation (as in Switzerland). (公民的)创制权(如瑞士所实行者).

in·ject /ɪnˈdʒekt; ɪnˈdʒɛkt/ vt [VP6A, 14] ~ sth (into sb/sth); ~ sb/sth (with sth), drive or force a liquid, drug, etc into sth with, or as with, a syringe; fill (sth with a liquid, etc) by ~ing: 注射(液剂, 药物等于); (用注射器)注入: ~ penicillin into the blood-stream; 将盘尼西林注射入血液; ~ sb's arm with morphia; 给某人的臂注射吗啡; (fig, colloq) (喻, 口) His appointment may ~ some new life into the committee.

他的任命可能给这委员会注入新生命。**in·jec·tion** /ɪnˈdʒekʃn; ɪnˈdʒekʃən/ n [U] ~ing; [C] instance of this: 注射; 注入: *five* ~*ions of glucose;* 注射了五针葡萄糖; *an* ~*ion in the left buttock;* 在左臀注射的一针; [C] liquid, etc that is ~ed. 注射剂; 针药. '**fuel injection**, method by which liquid fuel is converted to vapour and sprayed into the cylinders of an internal combustion engine. 燃料注射 (将液体燃料变为气体并喷入一内燃引擎的汽缸之方法)。

in·ju·di·cious /ˌɪndʒuˈdɪʃəs; ˌɪndʒuˈdɪʃəs/ adj (formal) not well-judged: (正式用语)欠考虑的; 不智的: ~ *remarks.* 不智的言词。 ~·**ly** adv

in·junc·tion /ɪnˈdʒʌŋkʃn; ɪnˈdʒʌŋkʃən/ n [C] authoritative order, esp a written order from a law court, demanding that sth shall or shall not be done (called an *interdict* in Scotland). 必须服从的命令; (尤指法院发布之书面)强制令; 禁止令(在苏格兰称为 interdict)。

in·jure /ˈɪndʒə(r); ˈɪndʒɚ/ vt [VP6A] hurt; damage. 伤害; 损害。 **in·jured** adj wounded; hurt; wronged; offended: 受伤的; 被伤害的; 受冤屈的; 感情受伤害的: ~*d looks;* 受冤屈的样子; 感情受到伤害的样子; *in an* ~*d voice;* 以不高兴的声音; *the dead and the* ~*d,* those people killed and hurt (in an accident, etc). (意外事件等中)死者及伤者。

in·juri·ous /ɪnˈdʒʊərɪəs; ɪnˈdʒʊrɪəs/ adj ~ (**to**), (formal) causing, likely to cause, injury; hurtful: (正式用语)引起伤害的; 可能引起伤害的; 有害的: *beha-viour that is* ~ *to social order;* 妨害社会治安的行为; *habits that are* ~ *to health.* 有害健康的习惯。

in·jury /ˈɪndʒərɪ; ˈɪndʒərɪ/ n (pl -ries) 1 [U] harm; damage; wrongful treatment: 伤害; 损害; 不公平的待遇: *If you knock a man down with your car, and then call him a fool, you are adding insult to* ~. 如果你开汽车撞倒一人, 然后说他是个傻瓜, 你是在伤害以外又加上了侮辱。 *do sb an* ~, cause sb harm. 伤害某人。 2 [C] place (in the body) that is hurt or wounded; act that hurts; insult: (身体的)受伤之处; 伤害的行动; 侮辱: *The cyclist suffered severe injuries.* 那骑脚踏车的人受了严重的伤。 *This attack was a severe* ~ *to his reputation.* 这项攻击对他的名誉是严重的伤害。

in·jus·tice /ɪnˈdʒʌstɪs; ɪnˈdʒʌstɪs/ n [U] lack of justice, 不公正; 不讲道义; 不公正的行动等。 *do sb an* ~, judge him unfairly. 冤枉某人。

ink /ɪŋk; ɪŋk/ n [U] (kinds of) coloured liquid used for writing and printing; black liquid ejected by cuttlefish, etc: 墨水; 墨汁; 油墨; (乌贼等喷出的)墨汁: *written in ink;* 用墨水写的; 钢笔写的; *a pen and ink drawing.* 钢笔画。 '**ink-bottle**/-**pot** nn for holding ink: 墨水瓶. '**ink-pad** n pad for ink used on rubber stamps. 印墨; 打印台. '**ink·stand** n stand for one or more ink-bottles, with grooves or a tray for pens, etc. 墨水瓶架 (旁有凹槽或盘可置笔). '**ink-well** n ink-pot that fits into a hole in a desk. 墨水池 (镶于嵌入凹洞中之墨水瓶)。 □ vt [VP6A, 15B] ~ (**in**), mark with ink: 涂以墨汁: *ink one's fingers;* 以墨水染污手指; *ink in a drawing,* mark with ink lines previously drawn in pencil. (将铅笔画的线条)用墨水描过. **inky** adj (-**ier**, -**iest**) marked with ink: 涂有墨水的; 涂有油墨的; *inky fingers;* 染有墨水或油墨的手指; black like ink: 墨黑的; 深黑的: *inky darkness.* 漆黑。

ink·ling /ˈɪŋklɪŋ; ˈɪŋklɪŋ/ n [C] *give sb/have/get an*/*some* /*no* ~ (*of sth*), slight understanding of it. (使某人)对(某事)略有(一无)所知。

in·laid /ˌɪnˈleɪd; ɪnˈled/ pt, pp of inlay.

in·land /ˈɪnlənd; ˈɪnlənd/ adj 1 situated in the interior of a country, far from the sea or border: 内陆的; 内地的: ~ *towns;* 内陆城市; *the I~ Sea of Japan,* area of sea almost enclosed by large islands. 日本濑户内海。 2 carried on, obtained, within the limits of a country: 国内的: ~ (= domestic) *trade.* 国内贸易。

the ,I~ '**Revenue**, (GB) money obtained by taxation within the country (excluding taxes on imported goods); (colloq) department responsible for collecting these taxes. (英国)国内税收(输入货物之税除外); (口)负责征收国内税款之部门。 □ adv /ɪnˈlænd; ˈɪnˌlænd/ in or towards the interior. 在内陆地; 向内陆地。

in-laws /ˈɪn lɔːz; ˈɪnˌlɔz/ n pl (colloq) relatives by marriage: (口)姻亲: *All my* ~ *will be visiting us this summer.* 我所有的姻亲今年夏天都要来探望我们。

in·lay /ˌɪnˈleɪ; ɪnˈle/ vt (pt, pp inlaid /-ˈleɪd; -ˈled/) [VP6A,14] ~ (*in/into/with*), set pieces of (designs in) wood, metal, etc in the surface of another kind of wood, metal, etc so that the resulting surface is smooth and even: 镶; 嵌: *gold inlaid into ivory;* 嵌入象牙的黄金; *ivory inlaid with gold.* 嵌金的象牙。 □ n /ˈɪnleɪ; ˈɪnˌle/ 1 [U] inlaid work; materials used for this; [C] design, pattern, made by ~ing. 镶嵌细工; 镶嵌所用材料; 镶嵌图案。 2 [C,U] (dentistry) (method of making a) solid filling of gold, plastic, etc for a cavity in a tooth. (牙科)(用以镶填牙洞之金质、塑胶等)镶体; 此种镶填牙齿之方法。

in·let /ˈɪnlet; ˈɪnˌlet/ n 1 strip of water extending into the land from a larger body of water (the sea, a lake), or between islands. 湾; (海、湖之)汊。 2 sth let in or inserted, eg a piece of material inserted into a garment. 插入物; 镶入物(例如镶入衣服中的一块衣料). 3 (attrib) that lets in: (用作定语)进入的通道: ~ *and outlet channels,* eg in a reservoir. 入水和出水的通道(例如水库中者)。

in loco par·en·tis /ɪn ˌləʊkəʊ pəˈrentɪs; ɪnˈlokoˈrentɪs/ (Lat) in the place or position of a parent: (拉)代替父或母; 以父或母之地位: *I stood towards him* ~. 我以父母的立场对待他。

in·mate /ˈɪnmeɪt; ˈɪnmet/ n one of a number of persons living together, esp in a hospital, prison or other institution. 许多同居人中之一(尤指医院、监狱或其他机构中者)。

in mem·or·iam /ˌɪn məˈmɔːrɪəm; ˌɪnmeˈmorɪˌæm/ (Lat) (used in epitaphs, on gravestones) in memory of; as a memorial to. (拉)(用于墓志铭中或墓碑上)纪念; 悼念。

in·most /ˈɪnməʊst; ˈɪnˌmost/ adj most inward; farthest from the surface; (fig) most private or secret: 最内部的; 最内里的; (喻)最秘密的; 秘藏心中的: *my* ~ *feelings.* 秘藏我心底的感情。

inn /ɪn; ɪn/ n 1 public house where lodgings, drink and meals may be had, usu (today) in the country. 酒馆兼供宿, 酒及餐食者; 兼营旅馆之酒馆(目前通常在乡间)。 ⇨ **hotel.** '**inn-keeper** n person who keeps an inn. 此种旅馆主人。 2 ,**Inn of** '**Court**, (building of) one of four law societies in London having the exclusive right of admitting persons to the bar. (伦敦之)四律师学校之一(独享检定律师之权。名为 law societies, 实为学校); 四律师学校之校址。 ⇨ **bar**[1](12).

in·nards /ˈɪnədz; ˈɪnədz/ n pl (colloq) (口) 1 stomach and bowels; entrails. 胃肠; 内脏。 2 any inner parts. 内部; 内在部分。

in·nate /ɪˈneɪt; ɪˈnet/ adj (of a quality, etc) in one's nature; possessed from birth: (指性质等)天生的; 与生俱来的; 先天的: ~ *aggression.* 天生的好攻击。 ~·**ly** adv

in·ner /ˈɪnə(r); ˈɪnɚ/ adj (of the) inside: 在内的; 内部的: *an* ~ *room.* 内室。 ,~ '**city**, the oldest parts of a city, at or near its centre: 内城; 旧市区: ~ *city decay.* 内城的衰败。 '~ **tube**, circular tube, filled with air, in a pneumatic tyre. (轮胎之)内胎. *the* ~ *man,* (**a**) sb's soul or mind (contrasted with *body*). 灵魂; 心(与body相对). (**b**) (joc) the stomach: (谑)肚子: *satisfy the* ~ *man.* 填饱肚子。 ~·**most** /-məʊst; -ˌmost/ adj = inmost.

in·ning /ˈɪnɪŋ; ˈɪnɪŋ/ n 1 (baseball) division of a game in which each team bats. (棒球)一局。 2 ~**s,**

(with *sing v*) (cricket) time during which a player or team is batting: (用单数动词)(板球)一局: *Our team made 307 runs in its first ~s.* 我们球队在第一局获307分. *The first batsman had a short ~s.* 第一位击球员的一局甚短. (fig)period of power, eg of a political party, or of opportunity to show one's ability, period of active life: (喻)(例如一政党之)当权时期; 表现能力的机会; 活跃时期: *have a good ~s,* (colloq) have a long and happy life. (口)长寿而且幸福.

in·no·cent /'ɪnəsnt; 'ɪnəsnt/ *adj* 1 ~ (*of*), not guilty: 清白的; 无罪的; 无辜的: *~ of the charge/accusation.* 无罪(无所控的罪行). 2 harmless: 无害的: *~ amusements.* 无害的娱乐. 3 knowing nothing of evil or wrong: 天真无邪的: *as ~ as a new-born babe.* 如新生婴儿一般的天真无邪. 4 foolishly simple: 无知的; 头脑简单的: *Don't be so ~ as to believe everything the politicians say.* 不要太天真, 竟至相信政客们说的每一句话. □ *n* ~ person, esp a young child. 无罪的人; 天真无邪的人(尤指小孩). **~·ly** *adv* **in·no·cence** /-sns; -sns/ *n* [C] quality or state of being ~. 清白; 无罪; 无害; 天真无邪; 无知.

in·nocu·ous /ɪ'nɒkjʊəs; ɪ'nɑkjʊəs/ *adj* causing no harm: 无害的: *~ snakes/drugs.* 无害的蛇(良性的药物).

in·no·vate /'ɪnəveɪt; 'ɪnə,vet/ *vi* [VP2A] make changes; introduce new things. 改革; 革新; 创新. **in·no·va·tor** /-tə(r); -tɚ/ *n* person who ~s. 改革者; 革新者; 创新者. **in·no·va·tion** /,ɪnə'veɪʃn; ,ɪnə'veʃən/ *n* [U] innovating; [C] instance of this; sth new that is introduced: 改革; 革新; 创新; 新事之处: *technical innovations in industry.* 工业技术上的创新.

in·nu·endo /,ɪnjuː'endəʊ; ,ɪnju'endo/ *n* (*pl* **~es** /-dəʊz; -doz/) indirect reference (usu sth unfavourable to a person's reputation): 间接诽及; 影射 (通常指间接的诽谤): *If you throw out such ~es against the Minister, you'll be sued for libel.* 如果你这样间接诽谤部长, 你将被控诬谤罪.

in·numer·able /ɪ'njuːmərəbl US: ɪ'nuː-; ɪ'njumərəbl/ *adj* too many to be counted. 数不清的; 无数的.

in·ocu·late /ɪ'nɒkjʊleɪt; ɪn'ɑkjə,let/ *vt* [VP6A, 14] ~ *sb* (*with sth*) (*against sth*), inject a serum or vaccine into him to give him a mild form of the disease to safeguard him against it: 接种; 注射血清或疫苗于(人或动物使其预防该疾病): *~ sb against cholera;* 给某人注射以预防霍乱; (fig) fill the mind with opinions, etc. (喻)向...灌输(思想等): *~d with evil doctrines.* 被灌输以邪恶的主义. **in·ocu·la·tion** /ɪ,nɒkjʊ'leɪʃn; ɪn,ɑkjə'leʃən/ *n* [U] inoculating or being ~d; [C] instance of this: 接种; 注射疫苗而预防; 灌输; 上述之实例: *have inoculations against cholera and yellow fever.* 接受预防霍乱和黄热病的注射. ⇨ **vaccinate.**

in·of·fen·sive /,ɪnə'fensɪv; ,ɪnə'fɛnsɪv/ *adj* not giving offence; not objectionable: 无碍的; 不令人讨厌的: *an ~ remark/person.* 不令人讨厌的言语(人).

in·op·er·able /ɪn'ɒpərəbl; ɪn'ɑpərəbl/ *adj* (of tumours, etc) that cannot be cured by a surgical operation. (肿瘤等)无法以手术治愈的.

in·op·er·ative /ɪn'ɒpərətɪv; ɪn'ɑpə,retɪv/ *adj* (of laws, rules, etc) not working or taking effect; invalid. (指法律, 规章等)无效果的; 不生效果的.

in·op·por·tune /ɪn'ɒpətjuːn US: -tuːn; ,ɪnɑpɚ'tjun/ *adj* (esp of time) not appropriate: (尤指时间)不适当的; 不合时宜的: *at an ~ moment.* 我们在不适当的时机. **~·ly** *adv*

in·or·di·nate /ɪ'nɔːdɪnət; ɪn'ɔrdnɪt/ *adj* (formal) not properly restrained or controlled; excessive: (正式用语)无节制的; 过度的: *~ passions;* 奔放的热情; *the ~ demands of the Tax Collector.* 收税员过度的要求. **~·ly** *adv*

in·or·ganic /,ɪnɔː'gænɪk; ,ɪnɔr'gænɪk/ *adj* 1 not having an organized physical structure, esp as plants and animals have; not forming part of the substance of living bodies: 无机的(无动植物之有机体组织的); 不形成生物体质之一部的: *~ chemistry.* 无机化学. *Rocks and metals are ~ substances.* 岩石及金属是无机物. 2 not the result of natural growth: 非自然生长而形成的: *an ~ form of society.* 一种非由自然发展而形成的社会形式. **in·or·gani·cally** /-klɪ; -klɪ/ *adv*

in·pa·tient /'ɪnpeɪʃnt; 'ɪn,peʃənt/ *n* person who lives in hospital while receiving treatment. 住院病人. ⇨ **out-patient.**

in·pour·ing /'ɪnpɔːrɪŋ; 'ɪn,pɔrɪŋ/ *n, adj* (formal) pouring in: (正式用语)倾入; 倾入的: *an ~ of spiritual comfort.* 大量的精神安慰.

in·put /'ɪnpʊt; 'ɪn,pʊt/ *n* [U] ~ (*to*), what is put in or supplied, eg data for processing in a computer, power supplied to a machine. 置入或供应之物(例如供电子计算机处理的资料, 供机器所用的动力); 输入.

in·quest /'ɪnkwest; 'ɪnkwɛst/ *n* ~ (*on*), official inquiry to learn facts, esp concerning a death which may not be the result of natural causes. 侦讯; 审讯(尤指调查非自然死亡者); 验尸.

in·quie·tude /ɪn'kwaɪɪtjuːd US: -tuːd; ɪn'kwaɪə,tjud/ *n* [U] (formal) uneasiness of mind; anxiety. (正式用语)不安心; 焦虑.

in·quire /ɪn'kwaɪə(r); ɪn'kwaɪr/ *vt, vi* 1 [VP6A, 8, 10, 14, 2A] ~ *sth* (*of sb*), ask to be told: 询问: *~ a person's name;* 询问某人的姓名; *~ what a person wants/where to stay/how to do sth/at the railway station;* 问人需要什么(问那里可以住宿; 问如何作某事; 在火车站询问); *~ of sb the reason for sth.* 问某人某事的原因. 2 [VP3A] ~ *about/concerning/upon,* ask for information about: 查问; 查明: *~ about trains to London.* 查询去伦敦的火车. I~ *within every-thing,* eg as the title of a small encyclopaedia. 本书解答一切疑难值(例如一小型百科全书的标题). ~ *after,* ask about (sb's health, welfare): 问候. ~ *for,* ask for (goods in a shop), ask to see (sb): 查询(商店中之货物); 求见(某人): *~ for a book in a shop;* 在一店中查询一书; *~ for the manager.* 求见经理. ~ *into,* try to learn the facts about; investigate: 查究; 调查: *We must ~ into the matter.* 我们必须调查此事. **in·quirer** *n* person who ~s. 询问者; 调查者. **in·quir·ing** *adj* in the habit of asking for information: 爱询问的; 喜探究的: *an inquiring mind;* 喜爱探究的精神; showing a desire to learn: 显示好奇的: *inquiring looks.* 好奇的神情. **in·quir·ing·ly** *adv*

in·quiry /ɪn'kwaɪərɪ US: 'ɪnkwərɪ; ɪn'kwaɪrɪ/ *n* (*pl* **-ries**) 1 [U] asking; inquiring: 询问; 探问: *learn sth by ~.* 询问得知某事. *on ~,* when one has asked. 有人询问时. **court of ~,** (mil) one to investigate charges brought against sb. (军)调查庭. 2 [C] question; investigation: 质询; 调查: *make inquiries about sb or sth;* 调查某人或某事物; *hold an official ~ into sth.* 正式调查某事物.

in·qui·si·tion /,ɪnkwɪ'zɪʃn; ,ɪnkwə'zɪʃən/ *n* 1 [U] thorough search or investigation; [C] instance of this, esp a judicial or official inquiry. 彻底调查; (尤指法庭或官方的)调查或审讯. 2 **the I~,** (also called 亦称作 *the Holy Office*) court appointed by the Church of Rome to suppress heresy (esp active in 15th and 16th cc) and to compile the Index(2). (尤指十五及十六世纪之)天主教宗教法庭(以镇压邪说并编撰天主教禁书目录).

in·quisi·tive /ɪn'kwɪzətɪv; ɪn'kwɪzətɪv/ *adj* fond of, showing a fondness for, inquiring into other people's affairs. 喜欢打听别人的事情的; 好管闲事的; **~·ly** *adv* **~·ness** *n*

in·quisi·tor /ɪn'kwɪzɪtə(r); ɪn'kwɪzətɚ/ *n* investigator, esp an officer of the Inquisition(2); person appointed by law to make an inquiry. 调查者; 审讯者(尤指天主教宗教法庭调查官); 司法机关任命之调查者或审讯者. **in·quisi·tor·ial** /ɪn,kwɪzɪ'tɔːrɪəl; ɪn,kwɪzə'torɪəl/ *adj* of or like an ~. 天主教宗教法庭调查官的; 审讯者的; 似调查官的.

in·road /'ɪnrəʊd; 'ɪn,rod/ n sudden attack (into a country, etc), esp one made for the purpose of plunder. 袭击；突袭(与 in 连用，后接地区等，尤指目的为劫掠者): *make ~s on/upon*, encroach: 侵占: *make ~s upon one's leisure time/one's savings.* 侵占一人的空闲时间(积蓄)。

in·rush /'ɪnrʌʃ; 'ɪn,rʌʃ/ n rushing in: 涌入；闯入: *an ~ of water/tourists.* 水(游客)之涌入。

in·sane /ɪn'seɪn; ɪn'sen/ adj mad; senseless: 疯狂的；愚蠢的: *an ~ person.* 疯子; *an ~ asylum*, place where ~ people are cared for, usually called a mental hospital or home. 疯人院(现在通常称作精神病院)。 **~·ly** adv **in·san·ity** /ɪn'sænətɪ; ɪn'sænətɪ/ n [U] madness. 疯狂；癫狂。

in·sani·tary US: -teri; ɪn'sænə,terɪ/ adj not sanitary: 不卫生的: *living under ~ conditions.* 生活在不卫生的环境中。

in·sa·tiable /ɪn'seɪʃəbl; ɪn'seʃəbl/ adj ~ (of/for), (formal) that cannot be satisfied; very greedy: (正式用语)不能满足的; 极贪心的: *~ appetites;* 无厌的食欲; *politicians who are ~ of power.* 贪权的政客。 **in·sa·tiably** /-ʃəblɪ; -ʃəblɪ/ adv

in·sa·tiate /ɪn'seɪʃɪɪt/ adj (formal) never satisfied. (正式用语)永不满足的。

in·scribe /ɪn'skraɪb; ɪn'skraɪb/ vt [VP6A, 15A] ~ (on/in/with), write (words, one's name, etc in or on); mark (sth with words, etc): 题写(文字, 姓名等); (以文字等)铭刻(某物): *~ names on a war memorial/one's name in a book;* 铭刻姓名于阵亡将士纪念碑上(题记姓名于书中); *~ a tomb with a name.* 铭刻姓名于墓碑上。 **~d stock**, (comm) stock of which the names of the holders are recorded in lists or registers. (商)记名股票。 **in·scrip·tion** /ɪn'skrɪpʃn; ɪn'skrɪpʃən/ n [C] sth ~d, esp words cut on a stone, eg a monument, or stamped on a coin or medal. 题名; 题字; 刻制文字; 铭文(尤指刻于纪念碑石上, 或压印于硬币或奖章等上者)。 ⇨ the illus at **epitaph**. 参看 epitaph 之插图。

in·scru·table /ɪn'skruːtəbl; ɪn'skrutəbl/ adj that cannot be understood or known; mysterious: 不可了解的; 神秘的: *the ~ ways of Providence;* 难解之天道; *the ~ face of the Sphinx.* 狮身人面像的神秘的面部。

in·sect /'ɪnsekt; 'ɪnsɛkt/ n sort of small animal, eg ant, fly, wasp, having six legs and no backbone and a body divided into three parts (head, thorax, abdomen): (incorrect but pop usage) similar tiny, crawling creature, eg spider. 昆虫(例如蚂蚁,苍蝇,黄蜂等);(不正确但普遍的用法)小虫(例如蜘蛛)。 **'~-powder** n powder for killing or driving away ~s. 杀虫粉; 驱虫粉。

in·sec·ti·cide /ɪn'sektɪsaɪd; ɪn'sɛktə,saɪd/ n preparation used for killing ~s, eg DDT. 杀虫剂(例如 DDT)。

in·sec·tivor·ous /,ɪnsek'tɪvərəs; ,ɪnsɛk'tɪvərəs/ adj eating ~s as food: 以昆虫为食的: *Swallows are ~ivorous.* 燕子以虫为食。

in·se·cure /,ɪnsɪ'kjʊə(r); ,ɪnsɪ'kjʊr/ adj 1 not safe; not providing good support; not to be relied on: 不安全的;不坚固的;不可靠的: *have an ~ hold on sth*, eg when rock-climbing. 未抓牢某物(例如攀登岩壁时)。 2 feeling unsafe; without protection; lacking confidence. 感觉不安全的; 没有保护的; 缺乏自信心的。 **~·ly** adv **in·se·cur·ity** /,ɪnsɪ'kjʊərətɪ; ,ɪnsɪ'kjʊrətɪ/ n [U]: *suffer from feelings of insecurity.* 因为没有安全感而觉得痛苦。

in·semi·nate /ɪn'semɪneɪt; ɪn'sɛmə,net/ vt [VP6A] sow seed into; introduce semen into. 播种于; 栽植; 授精于。 **in·semi·na·tion** /ɪn,semɪ'neɪʃn; ɪn,sɛmə'neʃən/ n [U] inseminating. 播种; 使受胎; 授精。 **,artificial in,semi'nation**, the introduction of semen; taken, eg from a pedigree animal, into the generative organs of a female animal so that offspring may be produced without sexual union. 人工授精。

in·sen·sate /ɪn'senseɪt; ɪn'sɛnset/ adj (formal) (正式用语) 1 without the power to feel or experience: 无感觉力的;无知觉的: *~ rocks.* 顽石。 2 unfeeling; without sensibility; foolish: 无情的; 迟钝的; 愚蠢的: *~ rage/cruelty.* 无理的愤怒(残忍)。

in·sen·si·bil·ity /ɪn,sensə'bɪlətɪ; ,ɪnsɛnsə'bɪlətɪ/ n [U] (formal) lack of mental feeling or emotion; state of being unable to know, recognize, appreciate: (正式用语)无感情; 无知觉; 不了解; 不会欣赏: *~ to pain/beauty/art;* 对痛苦无感觉(不会欣赏美,不会欣赏艺术); *in a state of ~*, unconscious. 无知觉; 失去知觉。

in·sen·sible /ɪn'sensəbl; ɪn'sɛnsəbl/ adj 1 unconscious as the result of injury, illness, etc: (因受伤,生病等)昏迷的,不省人事的: *The rock struck her on the head and she was ~ for nearly an hour.* 石块打在她头上,使她昏迷了将近一小时。 2 ~ (of), unaware (of): 不知道的: *He seemed to be ~ of his danger.* 他似乎不知道他的危险。 *I'm not ~ how much I owe to your help.* 我并非不知道你曾予我甚多帮助。 3 ~ (to), without feeling: 无感觉的: *When your hands are frozen they become ~*, numb. 当你的手冻僵时, 它们就麻木了。 4 unsympathetic; emotionless; callous. 无同情心的; 无感情的; 硬心肠的。 5 (of changes) too small or gradual to be perceived: (指变化)太小或太慢而难以觉察的: *by ~ degrees.* 极缓慢地。 **in·sen·sibly** /-əblɪ; -əblɪ/ adv

in·sen·si·tive /ɪn'sensətɪv; ɪn'sɛnsətɪv/ adj ~ (to), not sensitive (to touch, light, the feelings of other people). (对接触, 光, 他人的感情等)感觉迟钝的。 **~·ly** adv **in·sen·si·tiv·ity** /ɪn,sensə'tɪvətɪ; ,ɪnsɛnsə'tɪvətɪ/ n [U].

in·sen·tient /ɪn'senʃnt; ɪn'sɛnʃɪənt/ adj (formal) inanimate; without feeling or awareness. (正式用语)无生命的;无感觉的;无知觉的。

in·sep·ar·able /ɪn'sepərəbl; ɪn'sɛpərəbl/ adj ~ (from), that cannot be separated: 不能分离的: *~ friends.* 不能分开的朋友。

in·sert /ɪn'sɜːt; ɪd'sɜ't/ vt [VP6A, 15A] put, fit, place (sth in, into, between, etc): 插入; 嵌进 (某物, 后接 in, into, between 等): *~ a key in a lock/an advertisement in a newspaper/a new paragraph in an essay.* 插钥匙于锁中(将广告插刊于报纸; 将一新段落加入一文章中)。 □ n /'ɪnsɜːt; 'ɪnsɚt/ sth ~ed, eg in a book. 插入部分; 插入之物(例如在一书中)。 **in·ser·tion** /ɪn'sɜːʃn; ɪn'sɚʃən/ n [U] ~ing or advertisement in a newspaper, a piece of lace, etc ~ed in a dress. 插入; 被插入; 被插入之物(例如报纸上的启事或广告; 衣裙上的花边等)。

in·ser·vice /'ɪn ˌsɜːvɪs; 'ɪn'sɚvɪs/ attrib adj while in service (contrasted with pre-service training, etc): 在职中的 (与 pre-service training 相对): *the ~ training of teachers.* 教师的在职训练。 Cf 参较 refresher course.

in·set /'ɪnset; 'ɪn,sɛt/ n [C] extra page(s) inserted in a book, etc; small map, diagram, etc within the border of a printed page or of a larger map; piece of material, eg lace, let into a dress. (书等中的)插页; (一页印刷品或大地图中嵌入的,小地图, 图解, 插图等; (衣裙上的)镶料(如花边)。 □ vt /,ɪn'set; ɪn'sɛt/ (pt, pp inset) put in; insert. 嵌入; 插入。

in·shore /,ɪn'ʃɔː(r); 'ɪn,ʃor/ adj, adv close to the shore: 近海岸的(地): *an ~ current;* 近海流; *~ fisheries.* 近海渔场。

in·side /ɪn'saɪd; 'ɪn'saɪd/ n 1 inner side or surface. part(s) within: 内侧; 内面; 内部: *the ~ of a box;* 盒的内部; *a door bolted on the ~.* 自里面闩住的门。 □ adj /'ɪnsaɪd; 'ɪn'saɪd/ with the inner side out: 内部翻到外面的; 翻转的: *He put his socks on ~ out.* 他的袜子穿反了。 *The wind blew her umbrella ~ out.* 风把她的伞吹反过来了。 *The burglars turned everything ~ out*, put drawers, boxes, etc and their contents into great disorder. 窃贼将所有的东西都翻得乱七八糟。 *He knows the subject ~ out*, knows it thoroughly. 他对这个科目了解得很透彻。 2 part of a road, track, etc on the inner side of a curve; part of a pavement or footpath farthest from the road. 道路、跑道等转弯处的内侧; 人行道或步行小径等的内侧。 3 (colloq) stomach and bowels: (口)内脏; 肠胃

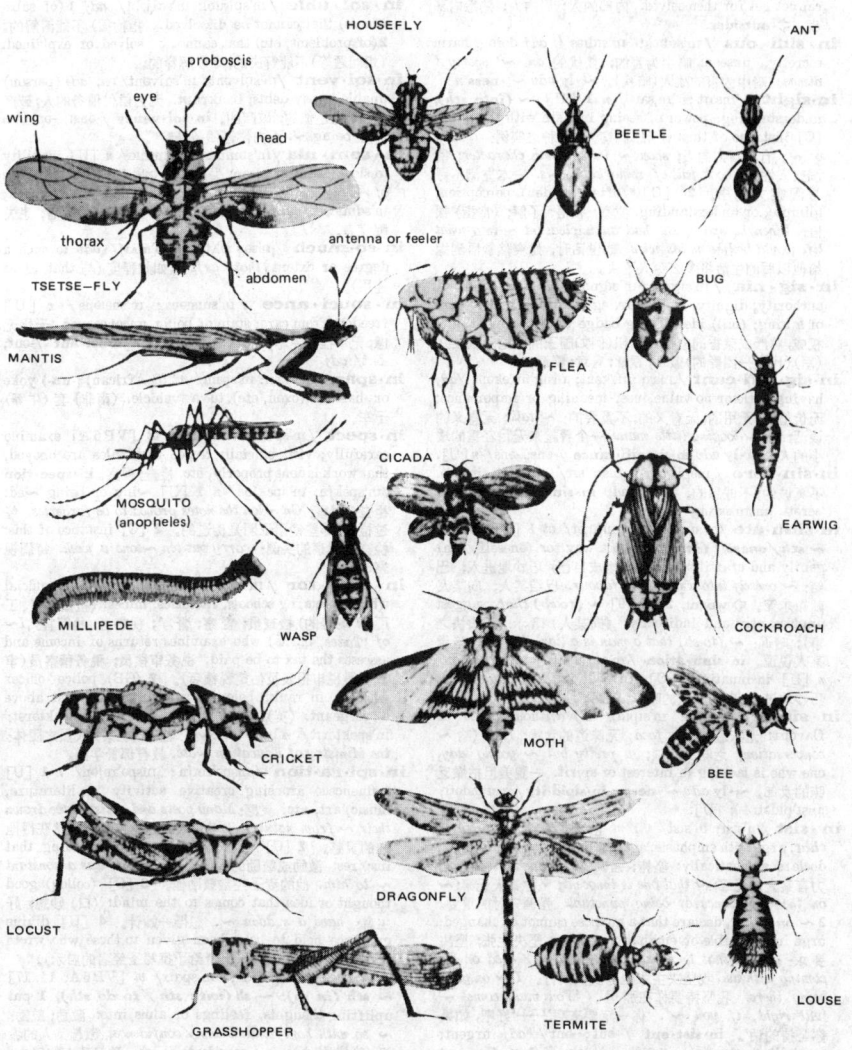

Insects

a pain in his ~. 肚子痛。 □ *adj* (or *n* used attrib) /'insaid; in'said/ situated on or in, coming from the ~: (或名词用作定语)在内部的；自内部的：*the ~ pages of a newspaper* 报纸的里页。 **~ 'left/'right.** (football, etc) player in the forward (attacking) line immediately to the left/right of the centre-forward. (足球等)左内锋(右内锋)。 ⇨ the illus at **football.** 参看 football 之插图。 **the '~ track,** (in racing) track nearest to the inner edge of a curve, giving an advantage to those using it; (fig) a position of advantage. (赛跑)跑道的内圈(使用者可占便宜)；(喻)有利之地位。 **an '~ job,** (sl) theft committed by, or with the help of, sb employed in a building. (俚)内贼所作的窃案；有内应的

窃案。 □ *adv* **1** on or in or in to the ~: 在里面；在内部；向里面：*Is this coat worn with the fur ~ or outside?* 这件上衣的毛皮穿在里面还是外面？ *Look ~.* 向里面看。 *Go ~.* 进去。 *There's nothing ~.* 里面什么也没有。 **~ of,** (colloq) in less than: (口)在(某数额)以内；不到：*We can't finish the work ~ of a week.* 我们无法在一周之内完成这工作。 **2** (GB sl) in prison: (英俚)在狱中；受监禁：*Jones is ~ for three years.* 琼斯入狱服刑三年。 □ *prep* on the inner side of: 在…之内；在…里面：*Don't let the dog come ~ the house.* 不要让狗进入房子里。 *She was standing just ~ the gate.* 她正好站在大门的内侧。 **in·sider** /in'saidə(r); in'saidɚ/ *n* person who, because he is a member of some society, organization, etc is in a position to obtain

facts and information, or win advantages, that others cannot get for themselves. 内部的人；局内人；熟悉内幕者。⇨ **outsider**.

in·sidi·ous /ɪnˈsɪdɪəs; ɪnˈsɪdɪəs/ *adj* doing harm secretly, unseen: 暗中为害的；隐伏的: *an ~ enemy/disease.* 暗中为害的敌人(暗疾). **~·ly** *adv* **~·ness** *n*

in·sight /ˈɪnsaɪt; ˈɪnˌsaɪt/ *n* 1 [U] **~ (into sth)**, understanding; power of seeing into sth with the mind; [C] instance of this: 了解；洞察力；此种之实例: *a man of ~;* 有洞察力的人; *show ~ into human character;* 能洞察人性; *a book full of remarkable ~s.* 一本充满不寻常洞察力的书. 2 [C] (often sudden) perception, glimpse, or understanding: 觉察；领悟；了解;(常指)顿悟: *When he spoke, she had an unpleasant ~ into what life would be like as his wife.* 他说话时，她突然领悟到嫁给他以后的生活将多么令人不快.

in·sig·nia /ɪnˈsɪɡnɪə; ɪnˈsɪɡnɪə/ *n pl* symbols of authority, dignity, or honour, eg the crown and sceptre of a king; (mil) identifying badge of a regiment, etc. 权威，尊严或荣誉的象征或标帜(例如国王的王冠及权杖);(军)(代表一团等的)徽章；领章；肩章；臂章.

in·sig·nifi·cant /ˌɪnsɪɡˈnɪfɪkənt; ˌɪnsɪɡˈnɪfɪkənt/ *adj* having little or no value, use, meaning or importance: 无价值的；无用的；无意义的；不重要的: *~ talk;* 无意义的谈话; *an ~-looking little man.* 一看起来无足轻重的矮小的人. **~·ly** *adv* **in·sig·nifi·cance** /-əns; -əns/ *n* [U].

in·sin·cere /ˌɪnsɪnˈsɪə(r); ˌɪnsɪnˈsɪr/ *adj* not sincere. 不真诚的；不诚恳的。**~·ly** *adv* **in·sin·cer·ity** /ˌɪnsɪnˈserətɪ; ˌɪnsɪnˈserətɪ/ *n* [U].

in·sinu·ate /ɪnˈsɪnjʊeɪt; ɪnˈsɪnjʊˌet/ *vt* 1 [VP6A, 14] **~ sth/oneself (into)**, make a way for (oneself/sth) gently and craftily: 使(某事物或自己)巧妙地进入；巴结: *~ oneself into a person's favour.* 巴结某人；向某人献媚求宠. ⇨ **worm.** 2 [VP9] **~ (to sb) that,** suggest unpleasantly and indirectly: (向某人)暗示(不愉快之事)；暗讽: *~ (to sb) that a man is a liar.* (向某人)暗示某人说谎. **in·sinu·ation** /ɪnˌsɪnjʊˈeɪʃn; ɪnˌsɪnjʊˈeʃən/ *n* [U] insinuating; [C] sth ~d; indirect suggestion. 巧妙地进入；令人不快的暗示；暗讽.

in·sipid /ɪnˈsɪpɪd; ɪnˈsɪpɪd/ *adj* without taste or flavour: 无味道的: *~ food;* 无味道的食物; (fig) *~ conversation;* 乏味的言谈; *a pretty but ~ young lady,* one who is lacking in interest or spirit. 一个漂亮但枯燥乏味的女郎. **~·ly** *adv* **~·ness** *n* **in·sipid·ity** /ˌɪnsɪˈpɪdətɪ; ˌɪnsɪˈpɪdətɪ/ *n* [U].

in·sist /ɪnˈsɪst; ɪnˈsɪst/ *vi, vt* [VP3A, B] 1 **~ on/that,** urge with emphasis, against opposition or disbelief; declare emphatically: 坚持；强调: *~ on one's innocence;* 力言某人无罪; *~ that one is innocent;* 坚持说某人无罪; *~ on the importance of being punctual.* 强调守时的重要. 2 **~ on/that,** declare that a purpose cannot be changed; urge in a forcible or emphatic manner: 坚决主张；坚决要求: *I ~ed that he should come with us / ~ed on his coming with us.* 我坚决主张他与我们同行. *I ~ on your being there.* 我坚持要你在那里。*'You must come' — 'All right, if you ~.'* '你一定要来啊'—'好吧，如果你坚持的话'. **in·sist·ent** /-ənt; -ənt/ *adj* urgent; compelling attention: 迫切的；坚持的；紧急的: *the ~ent demands of the Commander-in-Chief for more troops.* 总司令对增加军队所做的迫切要求. **in·sist·ence** /-əns; -əns/ *n* [U] ~ing or being ~ed: 坚持；坚决主张: *the officer's ~ence on strict obedience.* 军官之强调绝对服从。

in·situ /ˌɪnˈsɪtjuː; ɪnˈsaɪtjʊ/ (Lat) in its (original) place. (拉)在其位置；在原处.

in·so·far /ˌɪnsəˈfɑː(r); ˌɪnsəˈfɑr/ (US) (美) = in so far. ⇨ **in²(18)**

in·sole /ˈɪnsəʊl; ˈɪnˌsol/ *n* inner sole of a shoe. 鞋子的内底；鞋垫.

in·so·lent /ˈɪnsələnt; ˈɪnsələnt/ *adj* **~ (to),** insulting; offensive; contemptuous. 侮辱的；无礼的；傲慢的. **~·ly** *adv* **in·so·lence** /-əns; -əns/ *n* [U] being ~. 侮辱；无

in·sol·uble /ɪnˈsɒljʊbl; ɪnˈsɑljəbl/ *adj* 1 (of substances) that cannot be dissolved. (指物质)不能溶解的. 2 (of problems, etc) that cannot be solved or explained. (指问题等)不能解决的；难以解释的.

in·sol·vent /ɪnˈsɒlvənt; ɪnˈsɑlvənt/ *n, adj* (person) unable to pay debts; bankrupt. 无力偿付债务的人；破产者；无力还债的；破产的. **in·sol·vency** /-ənsɪ; -ənsɪ/ *n* [U] being ~. 无力偿还债务；破产.

in·som·nia /ɪnˈsɒmnɪə; ɪnˈsɑmnɪə/ *n* [U] inability to sleep; want of sleep: 失眠；缺少睡眠: *ill after weeks of ~.* 经数周失眠而生病. **in·som·niac** /ɪnˈsɒmnɪæk; ɪnˈsɑmnɪˌæk/ *n* person suffering from ~. 失眠者；患失眠症者.

in·so·much /ˌɪnsəʊˈmʌtʃ; ˌɪnsəˈmʌtʃ/ *adv* to such a degree or extent *(that/as).* 至如此程度(与 that 或 as 连用).

in·souci·ance /ɪnˈsuːsɪəns; ɪnˈsusɪəns/ *n* [U] freedom from care; state of being unconcerned. 无忧无虑；无牵挂；漠不关心；漫不经心。**in·souci·ant** /-ənt; -ənt/ *adj*

in·span /ɪnˈspæn; ɪnˈspæn/ *vt* (S African) **(-nn-)** yoke or harness (oxen, etc) to a vehicle. (南非)套(牛等)于车.

in·spect /ɪnˈspekt; ɪnˈspekt/ *vt* [VP6A] examine carefully; visit officially to see that rules are obeyed, that work is done properly, etc. 检查；视察。**in·spec·tion** /ɪnˈspekʃn; ɪnˈspekʃən/ *n* 1 [U] ~ing or being ~ed: 检查；视察: *On ~ion the notes proved to be forgeries.* 经过检查，那些钞票证明是伪造的. 2 [C] instance of this: 检查或观察的实例: *carry out ten ~ions a week.* 每周视察十次.

in·spec·tor /ɪnˈspektə(r); ɪnˈspektə/ *n* 1 official who inspects, eg schools, factories, mines: (检查学校、工厂、矿场等的)检查员；督察；督学；视察者；检阅官: *I~ of Taxes,* official who examines returns of income and assesses the tax to be paid. 税务审核员；税务稽查员(审查所得税申报表及估定税额者). 2 (GB) police officer who is, in rank, below a superintendent and above a sergeant. (英)(警察)巡官。**~·ate** /ɪnˈspektərət; ɪnˈspektərɪt/ *n* body of ~s: 检查(视察)人员之团体: *the Ministry of Education ~ate.* 教育部督学团.

in·spi·ra·tion /ˌɪnspəˈreɪʃn; ˌɪnspəˈreʃən/ *n* 1 [U] influence(s) arousing creative activity in literature, music, art, etc: 灵感: *Many poets and artists have drawn their ~ from nature.* 许多诗人和艺术家从大自然获得他们的灵感. 2 [C] **~ (to/for),** person or thing that inspires: 激励或鼓励的人或物: *His wife was a constant ~ to him.* 他的妻子经常鼓励他. 3 [C] (colloq) good thought or idea that comes to the mind: (口)妙想；好主意: *have a sudden ~.* 忽得一妙计. 4 [U] divine guidance held to have been given to those who wrote the Bible. 神灵之启示(上帝给予撰写圣经者的启示).

in·spire /ɪnˈspaɪə(r); ɪnˈspaɪr/ *vt* [VP6A, 14, 17] **~ sth (in sb); ~ sb (with sth / to do sth),** 1 put uplifting thoughts, feelings or aims into: 激励；鼓励: *~ sb with hope/enthusiasm/confidence;* 激起某人的希望（热情;信心); *~ confidence in sb.* 激起某人的信心. *What ~d him to give such a brilliant performance?* 什么鼓励了他因而作出如此精采的表演？2 fill with creative power: 使充满创造力；予以灵感: *~d poets/artists;* 具有灵感的诗人(艺术家); *in an ~d moment.* 在有灵感的时刻. 3 (pp) **~d,** (of sth written or spoken) one secretly suggested by an influential person who has special information: (指文章或谈话)(由拥有特殊消息之有势力人士)授意的.

in·sta·bil·ity /ˌɪnstəˈbɪlətɪ; ˌɪnstəˈbɪlətɪ/ *n* [U] lack of stability (usu of character, moral qualities). (通常指性格或精神方面)不稳定；无常.

in·stall (also **in·stal**) /ɪnˈstɔːl; ɪnˈstɔl/ *vt* [VP6A, 14] **~ sb/sth (in sth),** 1 place (sb) in a new position of authority with the usual ceremony: (以例行仪式)使

(某人) 就新职: ~ *a priest*. 使一教士就职. **2** place, fix (apparatus) in position for use: 装设 (器械): ~ *a heating or lighting system*. 装置暖气或照明设备. **3** settle (sb/oneself) in a place: 安置 (某人或自己) 于某处: *be comfortably ~ed in a new home*. 舒适地安居于新家之内. *She ~ed herself in her father's favourite chair*. 她坐在她父亲最心爱的椅子上. **in·stal·la·tion** /ˌɪnstə'leɪʃn; ˌɪnstə'leʃən/ *n* [U] ~ing or being ~ed; [C] sth that is ~ed, esp apparatus: 装设; 装置; 安置; 装置物 (尤指器械): *a heating ~ation*. 暖气装置.

in·stal·ment (US also **in·stall·ment**) /ɪn'stɔːlmənt; ɪn'stɔlmənt/ *n* [C] **1** any one of the parts in which sth is presented over a period of time: 一段时期中所供应之物的任一部分; 一期; 一批; 一段: *a story that will appear in ~s*, eg in a periodical. 将分段连载的故事 (例如在定期刊物中). **2** any one of the parts of a payment spread over a period of time: 分期付款: *We're paying for the television by monthly ~s*. 我们按月分期付款以偿付电视机价款. **'~ plan**, (chiefly US) this method of paying for goods (also called, chiefly GB, 英亦称作 *hire purchase*). (主美) 分期付款购物法.

in·stance /'ɪnstəns; 'ɪnstəns/ *n* [C] **1** example; fact, etc supporting a general truth: 例; 实例: *This is only one ~ out of many*. 这不过是许多例子中的一个. **for ~**, by way of example. 例如. **in the first ~**, firstly. 首先; 第一. **2** *at the ~ of*, at the request of. 应…之请求. □ *vt* [VP6A] give as an example. 引以为例.

in·stant¹ /'ɪnstənt; 'ɪnstənt/ *adj* **1** coming or happening at once: 即刻的; 立刻的: *feel ~ relief after taking a dose of medicine*. 服用一剂药后立即感到舒适. *The novel was an ~ success*. 这本小说立即获得成功. **2** urgent: 紧急的: *in ~ need of help*. 急需帮助. **3** (abbr 略作 **inst**) (comm; dated style) of the present month: (商: 过时文体) 本月的: *in reply to your letter of the 9th inst*. 为答复本月九日的贵函. **4** (of food preparations) that can be made ready for use quickly and easily: (指食品) 可迅速备好供食用的; 速食的; 即溶的: ~ *coffee*, prepared by adding boiling water or milk to a powder. 即溶咖啡 (加沸水或牛乳于咖啡粉就可以饮用). **~·ly** *adv* at once. 立即; 即刻. □ *conj* as soon as …就. 一…就.

in·stant² /'ɪnstənt; 'ɪnstənt/ *n* **1** precise point of time: 即时; 即刻: *Come here this ~!* at once! 即刻到这里来! *He left that ~/on the ~*, immediately. 他立即离开了. *I sent you the news the ~ (that) I heard it*, as soon as I heard it. 我一听到这消息, 便立刻通知你了. **2** moment: 瞬间; 刹那; 时刻: *I shall be back in an ~*. 我马上就回来. *Help arrived not an ~ too soon*. 帮助及时来到了 (来得恰是时候).

in·stan·taneous /ˌɪnstən'teɪnɪəs; ˌɪnstən'teɪnɪəs/ *adj* happening, done, in an instant: 即时的; 瞬间的: *Death was ~*, eg in an accident. 瞬间就死了 (例如在意外事件中). **~·ly** *adv*

in·stead /ɪn'sted; ɪn'sted/ *adv* as an alternative or substitute: 代替; 更换: *If Harry is not well enough to go with you, take me ~*. 如果哈里不舒服不能跟你去, 那就带我去好了. *The water here is not good, so I'm drinking beer ~*. 此地的水不好, 所以我改喝啤酒. ~ *of*, *prep phrase* in place of; as an alternative to or substitute for (followed by a *n*, *pron*, *gerund*, or *prep phr*): 代替 (后接名词, 代词, 动名词或介词短语): *Shall we have fish ~ of meat today?* 我们今天不吃肉改吃鱼如何? *I will go ~ of you*. 我代替你去. *He has been playing all afternoon ~ of getting on with his work*. 他整个下午一直在游玩, 而不继续工作. *We'll have tea in the garden ~ of in the house*. 我们将在花园里用茶, 而不在室内用.

in·step /'ɪnstep; 'ɪnˌstep/ *n* upper surface of the human foot between the toes and the ankle; part of a shoe, etc covering this. 足背; 跗; 鞋等之足背部分; 鞋面. ⇨ the illus at **leg**. 参看 leg 之插图.

in·sti·gate /'ɪnstɪgeɪt; 'ɪnstəˌget/ *vt* [VP6A, 17] ~ *sth/sb to do sth*, incite; goad (sb to do sth); cause

(sth) by doing this: 鼓动; 教唆 (某人作某事); 煽动 (某事): ~ *workers to down tools*; 鼓动工人罢工; ~ *a strike*. 煽动罢工. **in·sti·ga·tor** /-tə(r); -tə/ *n* **in·sti·ga·tion** /ˌɪnstɪ'geɪʃn; ˌɪnstə'geʃən/ *n* instigating or being ~d. 鼓动; 被煽动.

in·stil (US = **in·still**) /ɪn'stɪl; ɪn'stɪl/ *vt* (**-ll-**) [VP6A, 14] ~ *sth into sb*, introduce (ideas, etc) gradually. 逐渐灌输(思想等). **in·stil·la·tion** /ˌɪnstɪ'leɪʃn; ˌɪnstɪ'leʃən/ *n*

in·stinct /'ɪnstɪŋkt; 'ɪnstɪŋkt/ *n* **1** [U] natural tendency to behave in a certain way without reasoning or training: 本能: *Birds learn to fly by ~*. 鸟学飞系出于本能. **2** [C] innate impulse or intuition; instance of ~(1): 本性的冲动; 直觉; 凭本能行事的实例: *He seems to have an ~ for always doing and saying the right thing*. 他好像有做事说话永永不出错的本能. □ *pred adj* /ˌɪn'stɪŋkt; ɪn'stɪŋkt/ ~ *with*, filled with, animated by: 充满; 受…的鼓舞: *a picture ~ with life*; 充满生气的一幅画; *a poem ~ with passion*. 充满热情的一首诗. **in·stinc·tive** /ɪn'stɪŋktɪv; ɪn'stɪŋktɪv/ *adj* based on ~, not coming from training or teaching: 凭本能的; 天生的: *Animals have an ~ive dread of fire*. 动物天生怕火. **in·stinc·tive·ly** *adv*

in·sti·tute¹ /'ɪnstɪtjuːt US: -tuːt; 'ɪnstəˌtjut/ *n* [C] society or organization for a special (usu a social or educational) purpose; its office(s) or building(s). (社会或教育等方面之) 会, 社, 协会, 学会; 会馆; 社址.

in·sti·tute² /'ɪnstɪtjuːt US: -tuːt; 'ɪnstəˌtjut/ *vt* **1** [VP6A] establish, start, an inquiry, custom, rule, etc: 设立; 制定(风俗, 规则等); 着手(调查等): ~ *legal proceedings against sb*; 对某人提起诉讼; ~ *an action at law*; 提起诉讼; 采取法律行动; ~ *restrictions on the use of pesticides*. 对杀虫药的使用予以限制. **2** [VP6A, 14] ~ *sb (to)*, appoint him (to an official position). 任命(某人充任一职).

in·sti·tu·tion /ˌɪnstɪ'tjuːʃn US: -'tuːʃn; ˌɪnstə'tjuʃən/ *n* **1** [U] instituting or being instituted: 设立; 制定; 任命: *the ~ of customs/rules, etc* 风俗(规则等)的创立: ~ *as a bishop*. 任命为主教. **2** [C] long-established law, custom, or group (eg a club or society); familiar object or person. 由来已久的法律, 风俗习惯或团体(如会, 社, 协会等); 熟悉的人或物. **3** (building of) organization for social welfare, eg an orphanage, a home for old people. 慈善机关; 社会福利机构(例如孤儿院, 养老院). **~al** /-ʃənl; -ʃənl/ *adj* of or connected with an ~: 慈善机关的: *old people in need of ~al care*. 需要慈善机关照顾的老年人. **~·al·ize** /-ʃənəlaɪz; -ʃənlˌaɪz/ *vt* [VP6A] make into an ~(2). 使制度化; 使成为习俗.

in·struct /ɪn'strʌkt; ɪn'strʌkt/ *vt* **1** [VP6A, 15A] teach a school subject, a skill: 教; 教授: ~ *a class in history*: 教授一班级历史; ~ *recruits ~ a class of apprentices*. 教授新兵(一班学徒). **2** [VP17, 20, 21] give orders or directions to: 命令; 指导: ~ *sb to start early*; 命令某人早动身; ~ *sb how to do his work*. 指导某人如何工作. **3** [VP11, 20, 21] inform: 通知: *I have been ~ed by my agent that you still owe me £50*. 我的代理人通知我, 你尚欠我五十英镑. **in·struc·tor** /-tə(r); -tə/ *n* person who ~s; trainer. 教师; 教练. **in·struc·tress** /-trɪs; -trɪs/ *n* woman who ~s. 女教师; 女教练.

in·struc·tion /ɪn'strʌkʃn; ɪn'strʌkʃən/ *n* **1** [U] instructing or being instructed: 教授; 教导; 被教导: ~ *in chemistry*; 教授化学; *give/receive ~*. 教授(受教). **2** (*pl*) directions; orders: (复)指令; 命令; 指导: *give ~s to arrive early*; 命令某人早到起身; ~*s* (=coded commands) *to a computer*. 给予电子计算机之指示(代号指令). **~al** /-ʃənl; -ʃənl/ *adj* educational: 教育的: ~*al films*, eg of industrial processes. 教育影片(例如介绍工业过程者).

in·struc·tive /ɪn'strʌktɪv; ɪn'strʌktɪv/ *adj* giving or containing instruction: 教导的; 教训的: ~ *books*. 教育性的书籍. **~·ly** *adv*

in·stru·ment /'ɪnstrʊmənt; 'ɪnstrəmənt/ *n* [C] **1** implement, apparatus, used in performing an action,

esp for delicate or scientific work: 器具; 工具; 器械; 仪器(尤指精细工作或科学上所用者): *optical ~s*, eg a microscope; 光学仪器(例如显微镜); *surgical ~s*, eg a scalpel. 外科器械(例如解剖刀). Cf 参较 *tools* used by labourers and craftsmen. tools 指工人和工匠用的工具。 **2** apparatus for producing musical sounds, eg a piano, violin, flute or drum. 乐器(例如钢琴, 小提琴, 笛或鼓)。 ➪ the illus at **brass, percussion, string.** 参看 brass, percussion, string 各条之插图。**3** person used by another for his own purposes: 被人利用的人; 傀儡: *be made the ~ of another's crime.* 被利用作他人犯罪的工具。**4** formal (esp legal) document: 正式文件(尤指法律上的): *The King signed the ~ of abdication.* 国王签署了退位的正式文件。 **in·stru·men·ta·tion** /ˌɪnstrumenˈteɪʃn; ˌɪnstrəmɛnˈteʃən/ *n* [U] arrangement of music for ~s; the development and manufacture of ~s for scientific use. 器乐的谱曲; 乐器法; 乐器学; 科学仪器之发展及制造。

in·stru·men·tal /ˌɪnstruˈmentl; ˌɪnstrəˈmɛntl/ *adj* **1** serving as an instrument or means: 作为工具或手段的; 有帮助的: *be ~ in finding well-paid work for a friend.* 有助于一友人获得待遇优厚的工作。**2** of or for musical instruments: 乐器的; 供乐器用的: *~ music.* 器乐。 **~·ist** /-təlɪst; -tlɪst/ *n* player of a musical instrument. 乐器演奏者; 器乐家。 **~·ity** /ˌɪnstrumenˈtælətɪ, ˌɪnstrəmənˈtælətɪ/ *n* [U] agency: 工具; 媒介: *by the ~ity of*, by means of. 凭借; 以⋯为工具的媒介。

in·sub·or·di·nate /ˌɪnsəˈbɔːdɪnət; ˌɪnsəˈbɔrdɪnt/ *adj* disobedient; rebellious. 不服从的; 犯上的。 **in·sub·or·di·na·tion** /ˌɪnsəˌbɔːdɪˈneɪʃn US: -dɪˈneɪʃn; ˌɪnsəˌbɔrdnˈeʃən/ *n* [U] being ~; [C] instance of this. 不服从; 犯上; 此等之实例。

in·sub·stan·tial /ˌɪnsəbˈstænʃl; ˌɪnsəbˈstænʃəl/ *adj* **1** not solid or real; lacking substance: 非实在的; 无实体的: *an ~ vision.* 幻像。**2** without good foundation: 无根据的: *an ~ accusation.* 无稽的指控。

in·suf·fer·able /ɪnˈsʌfrəbl; ɪnˈsʌfrəbl/ *adj* overproud; unbearably conceited; unbearable: 过度骄傲的; 非常自负的; 令人难以忍受的: *~ insolence.* 令人难以忍受的傲慢。

in·suf·fi·cient /ˌɪnsəˈfɪʃnt; ˌɪnsəˈfɪʃənt/ *adj* not sufficient: 不充足的; 不够的: *~ evidence/grounds.* 证据(理由)不充分。 **~·ly** *adv* **in·suf·fi·ciency** /-ʃnsɪ; -ʃənsɪ/ *n*

in·su·lar /ˈɪnsjulə(r) US: -sələr; ˈɪnsələ/ *adj* **1** of an island: 岛屿的: *an ~ climate.* 海岛气候。**2** of or like islanders: (esp) narrow-minded: 岛民的; 似岛民的; (尤指)心胸偏狭的: *~ habits and prejudices.* 褊狭的习惯与偏见。 **~·ism** /-ɪzəm; -ɪzm/, **in·su·larity** /ˌɪnsjuˈlærətɪ US: -sə'l-; ˌɪnsəˈlærətɪ/ *nn* [U] state of being ~ (esp 义 2). 岛民心理; (尤指)心胸褊狭。

in·su·late /ˈɪnsjuleɪt US: -səl-; ˈɪnsəˌlet/ *vt* [VP6A, 14] *~ (from)*, **1** cover or separate (sth) with nonconducting materials to prevent loss of heat, prevent passage of electricity, etc: 使绝热; 使绝缘: *~ a cooking-stove with asbestos;* 以石棉使一烹调用的炉灶绝热; *'insulating tape,* as used for covering joins in flex for electric current. 绝缘胶带(如包于电线接头处者)。**2** separate (sb or sth) (from): 使(某人或某物)隔绝: *children carefully ~d from harmful experiences.* 使人小心隔离, 以免接触有害经验的孩子们; isolate. 使孤立。 **in·su·la·tor** /-tə(r)/ *-ts/ n* [C] substance, device, for insulating, esp a device of porcelain used for supporting bare electric wires and cables. 绝缘体; 绝热器; 绝缘器(尤指架设裸电线用的瓷绝缘器)。 **in·su·la·tion** /ˌɪnsjuˈleɪʃn US: -sə'l-; ˌɪnsəˈleʃən/ *n* [U] insulating or being ~d; materials used for this. 绝热; 绝缘; 隔离; 绝缘材料。

in·su·lin /ˈɪnsjulɪn US: -səl-; ˈɪnsəlɪn/ *n* [U] substance (a hormone) prepared from the pancreas of sheep, used in the medical treatment of sufferers from diabetes. 胰岛素(一种荷尔蒙, 由羊的胰脏提炼而得, 用于治疗糖尿病患者)。

in·sult /ɪnˈsʌlt; ɪnˈsʌlt/ *vt* [VP6A] speak or act in a way that hurts or is intended to hurt a person's feelings or dignity. 侮辱; 侮慢。 □ *n* /ˈɪnsʌlt; ˈɪnsʌlt/ [C, U] remark or action that ~s. 侮辱; 侮辱的言行。 **~·ing** *adj* **~·ing·ly** *adv*

in·super·able /ɪnˈsjuːprəbl US: -ˈsuː-; ɪnˈsupərəbl/ *adj* (of difficulties, etc) that cannot be overcome: (指困难等)不能克服的: *~ barriers.* 不能克服的障碍。

in·sup·port·able /ˌɪnsəˈpɔːtəbl; ˌɪnsəˈpɔrtəbl/ *adj* unbearable; that cannot be endured. 不堪的; 不能忍受的。

in·sur·ance /ɪnˈʃʊərəns; ɪnˈʃʊrəns/ *n* **1** [U] (undertaking, by a company, society, or the State, to provide) safeguard against loss, provision against sickness, death, etc in return for regular payments. 保险; 保险业。**2** [U] payment made to or by such a company, etc: 保险费; 保险金额: *When her husband died, she received £20000 ~.* 她丈夫去世后, 她得到二万英镑的保险金。 *He pays out £110 in ~ / in ~ premiums every year.* 他每年付保险费一百一十英镑。 '**~ policy** *n* contract made about ~. 保险单。**3** [C] = policy: 保险单: *How many ~s have you?* 你保了多少种险? **4** any measure taken as a safeguard against loss, failure, etc: 保险; 预防损失、失败等之措施: *He's sitting an entrance exam at Leeds University as an ~ against failure at York.* 他正参加里兹大学的入学考试以备约克大学考不取。

in·sure /ɪnˈʃʊə(r); ɪnˈʃʊr/ *vt* [VP6A, 14] *~ (against)*, make a contract that promises to pay, secures payment of, a sum of money in case of accident, damage, loss, injury, death, etc: 保险; 投保: *~ one's house against fire;* 将自己房屋保火险; *~ oneself / one's life for £50000.* 自己保寿险五万英镑。 *Insurance companies will ~ ships and their cargoes against loss at sea.* 保险公司会给船只及其货物作海上保险。 **the ~d**, the person to whom payment will be made. 被保险人; 保险户。 **the ~r**, the person or company undertaking to make payment in case of loss, etc. 承保人; 保险公司。 **the insurant** /ɪnˈʃʊərənt; ɪnˈʃʊrənt/, (legal) the person who pays the premiums. (法律)付保险费者; 被保险人; 投保人。

in·sur·gent /ɪnˈsɜːdʒənt; ɪnˈsɝdʒənt/ *adj* (rarely *pred*) rebellious; in revolt: (罕作表语)叛乱的; 暴动的: *~ troops.* 叛军。 □ *n* rebel soldier. 叛乱的士兵。

in·sur·mount·able /ˌɪnsəˈmaʊntəbl; ˌɪnsɚˈmaʊntəbl/ *adj* (of obstacles, etc) that cannot be surmounted or overcome. (指障碍等)无法超越的; 不能克服的。

in·sur·rec·tion /ˌɪnsəˈrekʃn; ˌɪnsəˈrɛkʃən/ *n* [U] rising of people in open resistance to the government; [C] instance of this. 起义; 叛乱; 此种实例。

in·tact /ɪnˈtækt; ɪnˈtækt/ *adj* untouched; undamaged; complete: 未触动的; 未损伤的; 完整的: *He lived on the interest and kept his capital ~.* 他靠利息生活, 本金不动。

in·taglio /ɪnˈtɑːlɪəʊ; ɪnˈtæljo/ *n* (*pl ~s* /-z; -z/) [U] (1) (process of) carving in depth; [C] (gem with) figure or design made by cutting into the surface of metal or stone. (意)凹刻; 凹刻术; 凹刻之花纹或刻有此种花纹之宝石。 ➪ **cameo.**

in·take /ˈɪnteɪk; ˈɪnˌtek/ *n* [C] place where water, gas, etc is taken into a pipe, channel, etc. (水、气体等流入管、沟等之)入口; 进水口; 进气口。**2** [C, U] quantity, number, etc entering or taken in (during a given period): (一定时期内的)引入之量: *an annual ~ of 100000 men*, eg for military service. 每年征召十万人(如征兵)。**3** (area of) land reclaimed from a moor, marsh or the sea. 开发荒野, 填充沼泽或海而成之地。

in·tan·gible /ɪnˈtændʒəbl; ɪnˈtændʒəbl/ *adj* that cannot be touched or grasped; (esp) that cannot be grasped by the mind: 不可触摸的; 无形的; (尤指)捉摸不定的: 难以明了的: *~ ideas;* 难以明了的观念; *~ assets,* assets (of a business) which cannot be measured, eg a good reputation. (一商业机构之)无形资产(例如其良好

商誉）。 **in·tan·gi·bil·ity** /ɪnˌtændʒə'bɪlətɪ; ɪnˌtændʒə-'bɪlətɪ/ n

in·te·ger /'ɪntɪdʒə(r); 'ɪntədʒɚ/ n whole number (contrasted with *fraction*): 整数（与 fraction 相对）: *1, 3 and −3 are* ~*s*, ³/₄ *is not an* ~. 1, 3 及 −3 是整数,³/₄ 不是整数。

in·te·gral /'ɪntɪgrəl; 'ɪntəgrəl/ adj **1** necessary for completeness: 构成整体所需要的: *The arms and legs are* ~ *parts of a human being.* 臂和腿是构成完整的人体所需要的。 **2** whole; having or containing all parts that are necessary for completeness. 完整的; 整个的。 **3** (maths) of, denoted by, an integer; made up of integers. (数学) 整数的; 由整数表示的; 整数组成的; 积分的。 ⇨ **calculus.** ~·ly /-grəlɪ; -grəlɪ/ adv

in·te·grate /'ɪntɪgreɪt; 'ɪntə,gret/ vt, vi [VP6A, 2A] **1** combine (parts) into a whole; complete (sth that is imperfect or incomplete) by adding parts: 连接(各部)使成一整体; 使完全; 使成完整之物; 结合成一体: *an* ~*d personality,* person whose physical, mental and emotional components fit together well. 完整人格(身体、心理及情绪各方面配合良好的人)。 ~*d* '**circuit** n very small circuit (4) made of a single chip of eg silicon. 集成电路。 **2** bring or come into equality by the mixing of groups or races. 使打成一片; 种族融合。 **in·te·gra·tion** /ˌɪntɪ'greɪʃn; ˌɪntə'greʃən/ n [U] integrating or being ~d: 使完整; 合而为一; 整合: *the integration of black children into the school system in the Southern States of America.* 美国南部各州的(白人)学校之准许黑人子弟入学。

in·teg·rity /ɪn'tegrətɪ; ɪn'tɛgrətɪ/ n [U] **1** quality of being honest and upright in character: 廉正; 诚实: *a man of* ~, 正直的人; *commercial* ~. 商业上的诚实。 **2** state or condition of being complete: 完整的: *The old Roman walls may still be seen, but not in their* ~. 古代罗马人筑的城墙仍然可见, 但已残缺不全了。 *Wasn't this Treaty supposed to guarantee our territorial* ~? 这一条约不是认为可以保证我们领土的完整吗?

in·tegu·ment /ɪn'tegjʊmənt; ɪn'tɛgjəmənt/ n (formal) (usu natural) outer covering, eg skin, a husk, rind or shell. (正式用语)覆盖物(通常为天然者, 例如皮肤, 外皮, 硬壳或外壳)。

in·tel·lect /'ɪntəlekt; 'ɪntḷ,ɛkt/ n **1** [U] power of the mind to reason (contrasted with feeling and instinct): 理解力; 推理力; 悟力; 智力(与感情及本能相对): *I*~ *distinguishes man from the animals.* 智力使人异于禽兽。 *He's a man of* ~. 他是有思辨力的人。 **2** (collective *sing*, or in *pl*) person(s) of good understanding, reasoning power, etc: (集合名词单数, 或用复数)知识分子; 有推理力者; 智者: *the* ~*(s) of the age.* 当代的知识分子。

in·tel·lec·tual /ˌɪntə'lektʃʊəl; ˌɪntḷ'ɛktʃʊəl/ adj **1** of the intellect: 智力的: *the* ~ *faculties.* 智能。 **2** having or showing good reasoning power; interested in things of the mind (the arts, ideas for their own sake): 有理解力的; 有智力的; 显示智力的; 对需要用智力之事(如艺术, 思想等)有兴趣的: ~ *people;* 有智力的人; ~ *interests* / *pursuits.* 需用智力的爱好(消遣)。 □ n [C] ~ person: 有智力者; 知识分子: *a play* / *book for the* ~*s.* 为知识分子而编写的剧本(书)。 ~·ly /-tʃʊəlɪ; -tʃʊəlɪ/ adv

in·tel·li·gence /ɪn'telɪdʒəns; ɪn'tɛlədʒəns/ n [U] **1** the power of perceiving, learning, understanding and knowing; mental ability: 智力; 才智: *a boy who shows little* ~. 智力不高的男孩。 *The children were given an* ~ *test.* 那些孩子们接受了智力测验。 *When the water-pipe burst, she had the* ~ *to turn the water off at the main.* 当水管裂开时, 她很有头脑, 连忙把总水管关起来。 **2** news; information, esp with reference to important events: 消息; 情报 (尤指与重要事件有关者): *have secret* ~ *of the enemy's plans;* 获得有关敌方计划之秘密情报: *the* I~ *Department* / *Service,* eg of an army or navy, collecting and studying information useful in war. 情报部门 (例如陆军或海军中搜集及研究战时有用之情报资

料者)。 **intel·li·gent** /-ənt; -ənt/ adj having, showing, ~: 有智力的; 有才智的; 聪明的: *intelligent questions* / *answers;* 聪明的问题(答复); *an intelligent child;* 聪明的孩子; *an intelligent expression on sb's face.* 某人脸上聪明的表情。 **in·tel·li·gent·ly** adv

in·tel·li·gent·sia /ɪnˌtelɪ'dʒentsɪə; ɪnˌtɛlə'dʒɛntsɪə/ n (usu collective *sing* 通常为集合名词单数 **the** ~) that part of a community which can be regarded (or which regards itself) as intellectual and capable of serious independent thinking. 知识分子; 知识界。

in·tel·li·gible /ɪn'telɪdʒəbl; ɪn'tɛlɪdʒəbl/ adj that can be easily understood; clear to the mind: 易了解的; 易领悟的: ~ *speech;* 清晰的言语; 可了解的言语; *an* ~ *explanation.* 明白的解释。 **in·tel·li·gibly** /-əblɪ; -əblɪ/ adv **in·tel·li·gi·bil·ity** /ɪnˌtelɪdʒə'bɪlətɪ; ɪn'tɛlɪdʒəbɪlətɪ/ n the quality of being ~. 易领悟性。

in·tem·per·ate /ɪn'tempərət; ɪn'tɛmpərɪt/ adj (formal) (of a person or his behaviour) not moderate; showing lack of self-control: (正式用语)(指人或其行为)放纵的; 无节制的: ~ *habits.* (esp) habits of excessive drinking. 无节制的习惯(尤指无节制的饮酒)。 ~·ly adv **in·tem·per·ance** /-pərəns; -pərəns/ n [U].

in·tend /ɪn'tend; ɪn'tɛnd/ vt [VP6A, D, 7A, 9, 14, 17] **1** ~ (*for*), have in mind as a purpose or plan: 意欲; 打算: *What do you* ~ *to do?* ~ *doing today?* 你今天打算做些什么? *They* ~ *that this reform shall be carried through this year.* 他们计划今年完成此一改革。 *We* ~ *them to do it* / *that they shall do it.* 我们打算让他们做那事。 *His son is* ~*ed for the medical profession.* 他计划让他的儿子行医。 *This book is* ~*ed for you,* is to be given to you. 这本书是要给你的。 *Is this sketch* ~*ed for me, Is it a sketch of me?* 这张素描画的是我吗? *Does he* ~ *marriage or is he only flirting with her?* 他打算跟她结婚, 还是仅仅跟她调情? *Let me introduce you to my* ~*ed,* (sl 俚 for 'my future wife'). 让我向你介绍我未来的妻子。 **2** ~ (*by*), (old use) mean: (旧用法) 意指; 意谓: *What do you* ~ *by this word?* 你说这话是什么意思?

in·tense /ɪn'tens; ɪn'tɛns/ adj **1** (of qualities) high in degree: (指性质)强烈的; 剧烈的; 高度的: ~ *heat.* 酷热。 **2** (of feelings, etc) ardent; violent; (of persons) highly emotional: (指感情等)热烈的; 激烈的; (指人)热情的: ~ *political convictions.* 热烈的政治信仰。 ~·ly adv

in·ten·sify /ɪn'tensɪfaɪ; ɪn'tɛnsə,faɪ/ vt, vi (*pt, pp* -fied) [VP6A, 2A] make or become more intense. 使更剧烈; 使更强烈; 加强; 变得更剧烈; 变得更强烈。 **in·ten·si·fi·ca·tion** /ɪnˌtensɪfɪ'keɪʃn; ɪnˌtɛnsəfə'keʃən/ n [U, C].

in·ten·sity /ɪn'tensətɪ; ɪn'tɛnsətɪ/ n [U] state or quality of being intense; strength or depth (of feeling, etc); [C] instance of these. 强烈; 剧烈; 紧张; (感情等之)强度; 深度。

in·ten·sive /ɪn'tensɪv; ɪn'tɛnsɪv/ adj **1** characterized by, relating to, intensity (as opposed to extent); deep and thorough: 强烈的; 关于深度(与广度相反)的; 精深的; 密集的: *make an* ~ *study of a subject;* 就一题目作精深的研究; ~ *methods of horticulture,* producing large quantities by concentrating labour and care on small areas of land; 精耕园艺; 密集园艺法(集中劳力照料小块土地, 使之大量生产的方法); *an* ~ *bombardment.* 密集炮击。 ~ *care* n medical treatment with constant observation etc of the patient. 重症治疗; 加意护理(给予病人密切观察等之医疗方法)。 ~ '**care unit**, part of a hospital where this is given. (医院中之)重症病房; 加护病房。 **2** (gram) giving force and emphasis: (语法)加强语气的: *In 'a bloody difficult book' and 'a terribly hot day', 'bloody' and 'terribly' are used colloquially as* ~ *words.* 在 a bloody difficult book 和 a terribly hot day 中, bloody 及 terribly 用作口语中加强语气的词。 ~·ly adv

in·tent[1] /ɪn'tent; ɪn'tɛnt/ adj **1** (of looks) eager: earnest: (指样子)急切的; 热心的: *There was an* ~ *look*

on her face as she watched the game. 她看比赛时脸上显出急切的样子. **2** ~ **on/upon** *sth/doing sth*, (of persons) with the desires or attentions directed towards: (指人) 专心的; 热中的: *He was* ~ *on his work/on getting to the office in time.* 他专心于他的工作(一心一意要及时赶到办公室). ~**·ly** *adv* ~ **·ness** *n*

intent² /ɪnˈtent; ɪnˈtɛnt/ *n* **1** [U] (chiefly legal) purpose; intention: (主要为法律用语)目的; 意向: *shoot with* ~ *to kill;* 存心开枪杀人; *with good/evil/malicious* ~. 好(恶)意地. **2** (*pl*) (复) **to all** ~**s and purposes,** in all essential points. 就各要点看来; 实际上.

in·ten·tion /ɪnˈtenʃn; ɪnˈtɛnʃən/ *n* [C, U] intending; thing intended; aim; purpose: 意图; 意向; 目的; 意旨: *If I've hurt your feelings, it was quite without* ~. 如果我伤害了你的感情, 那完全是无意的. *He went to Paris with the* ~ *of learning French.* 他去巴黎目的在学法语. *His* ~*s are good, but he seldom carries them out.* 他的目的很好, 但极少实现. *Has he made known his* ~*s,* said what he intends to do? 他表示过他的意向没有? **(-) in·ten·tioned** *adj*: *well-'* ~*ed,* having good ~s: 好意的; *ill-'* ~*ed,* having bad, wrong, etc ~s. 恶意的.

in·ten·tional /ɪnˈtenʃənl; ɪnˈtɛnʃənl/ *adj* intended; done with purpose: 有意的; 故意的: *If I hurt your feelings, it was not* ~. 如果我伤害了你的情感, 那并不是有意的. ~**·ly** /-ʃənlɪ; -ʃnlɪ/ *adv* with purpose. 故意地; 有意地.

in·ter /ɪnˈtɜː(r); ɪnˈtɝ/ *vt* (**-rr-**) (formal) place (a corpse) in a grave or tomb; bury. (正式用语) 埋葬(尸体).

in·ter·act /ˌɪntərˈækt; ˌɪntɚˈækt/ *vi* act on each other. 相互作用; 相互影响. **in·ter·ac·tion** /-ˈækʃn; -ˈækʃən/ **in·ter·ac·tive** /-ˈæktɪv; -ˈæktɪv/ *adj*

in·ter alia /ˌɪntər ˈeɪlɪə; ˈɪntɚˈelɪə/ (Lat) among other things. (拉)除了其他事物以外.

in·ter·breed /ˌɪntəˈbriːd; ˌɪntɚˈbrid/ *vt, vi* (*pt, pp* **-bred** /-ˈbred; -ˈbrɛd/) [VP6A, 2A] crossbreed; produce hybrids. (使)杂交繁殖; 生育杂种.

in·ter·ca·lary /ɪnˈtɜːkələrɪ US: -lerɪ; ˌɪntɚkəˌlɛrɪ/ *adj* (of a day or month) added to make the calendar year correspond to the solar year; (of a year) having such an addition. (指月或日)闰的; (指年)闰的(即有闰月或闰日的).

in·ter·cede /ˌɪntəˈsiːd; ˌɪntɚˈsid/ *vi* [VP3A] ~ (*with sb*) (*for sb*), plead (as a peacemaker, or to obtain a favour): (作为调停者或为获得赞助而)(向某人, 为某人)说项; 求情: ~ *with the father for/on behalf of the daughter.* 替女儿向父亲求情. **in·ter·ces·sion** /ˌɪntəˈseʃn; ˌɪntɚˈsɛʃən/ *n* [U] interceding; [C] prayer or entreaty for another. 说项; 求情; 代祷; 代为求情.

in·ter·cept /ˌɪntəˈsept; ˌɪntɚˈsɛpt/ *vt* [VP6A] stop, catch(sb or sth) between starting-point and destination: 中途阻止或拦截(某人或某物); ~ *a letter/a messenger.* 中途截取一信(拦阻一信差). *Can our fighter-planes* ~ *the enemy's boombers?* 我们的战斗机能拦截敌人的轰炸机吗? **in·ter·cep·tion** /ˌɪntəˈsepʃn; ˌɪntɚˈsɛpʃən/ *n* [U, C]. **in·ter·cep·tor** /-tə(r); -tɚ/ *n* sth or sb that is, eg a fast fighter-plane. 中途阻止或拦截的人或物(例如一架快速的战斗机).

in·ter·change /ˌɪntəˈtʃeɪndʒ; ˌɪntɚˈtʃendʒ/ *vt, vi* **1** [VP6A] (of two persons, etc) give and receive; make an exchange of: (指二人等)交换; ~ *views/gifts/letters.* 交换意见(交换礼物; 互通书信). **2** [VP6A, 2A] put (each of two things) in the other's place. 使(二物)互换; 轮换. ~**·able** /-əbl; -əbl/ *adj* that can be ~d: 可交换的; 可轮换的: *True synonyms are* ~*able.* 真正的同义词是可以交替互用的. *This machine has* ~*able parts.* 这部机器有互换零件. □ *n* /ˈɪntətʃeɪndʒ; ˈɪntɚˌtʃendʒ/ [U, C] interchanging: 交换; 互换; 轮换: *an* ~ *of views.* 意见的交换.

in·ter·col·legi·ate /ˌɪntəkəˈliːdʒɪət; ˌɪntɚkəˈlidʒɪɪt/ *adj* carried on, etc between colleges: 大学间的; 学院间的: ~ *games/debates.* 学院间的运动(辩论)比赛.

in·ter·com /ˈɪntəkɒm; ˈɪntɚˌkɑm/ *n* (colloq) system of (inter) communication, eg in aircraft: (口)内部通话装置(例如飞机内的对讲装置): *receive a message on/over the* ~. 接到对讲机传话.

in·ter·com·mu·ni·cate /ˌɪntəkəˈmjuːnɪkeɪt; ˌɪntɚkəˈmjunəˌket/ *vi* communicate with one another: 互通; 互通消息或电码互通消息. **in·ter·com·mu·ni·ca·tion** /ˌɪntəkəˌmjuːnɪˈkeɪʃn; ˌɪntɚkəˌmjunəˈkeʃən/ *n* [U].

in·ter·com·mu·nion /ˌɪntəkəˈmjuːnɪən; ˌɪntəkəˈmjunjən/ *n* mutual communion, esp between different Churches, eg Catholic and Orthodox. 互相交往; 特别不同教会间的互相交往(例如天主教与希腊正教间的互相交往).

in·ter·con·ti·nen·tal /ˌɪntəˌkɒntɪˈnentl; ˌɪntɚˌkɑntəˈnɛntəl/ *adj* between continents: 洲际的; 洲与洲间的: ~ *ballistic missiles,* that can be fired from one continent to another. 洲际弹道导弹.

in·ter·course /ˈɪntəkɔːs; ˈɪntɚˌkors/ *n* [U] **1** social dealings between individuals; exchanges of trade, ideas, etc between persons, societies, nations, etc: 交际; 交往: (贸易, 思想等的)交流: *our commercial* ~ *with S America.* 我们与南美洲的通商. **2** (sexual) ~, =**coitus**.

in·ter·de·nomi·na·tional /ˌɪntədɪˌnɒmɪˈneɪʃənl; ˌɪntɚdɪˌnɑməˈneʃənl/ *adj* common to, shared by, different religious denominations, eg Methodist, Baptists, Catholic. 各不同宗教派别(例如美以美会, 浸信会, 天主教)间所共有的.

in·ter·de·pen·dent /ˌɪntədɪˈpendənt; ˌɪntɚdɪˈpɛndənt/ *adj* depending on each other. 互相依赖的; 相依的. **in·ter·de·pen·dence** /-əns; -əns/ *n*

in·ter·dict /ˌɪntəˈdɪkt; ˌɪntɚˈdɪkt/ *vt* [VP6A] (formal) prohibit (an action); forbid (the use of sth); (RC Church) exclude from sacraments and church services. (正式用语) 禁止 (行动); 禁止 (某物的使用); (天主教)禁止参加各种圣体及弥撒; 停止···的权力. □ *n* /ˈɪntədɪkt; ˈɪntɚˌdɪkt/ [C] formal or authoritative prohibition, esp (RC Church) an order debarring a person or place from sacraments and church services: 正式禁止; (尤指天主教之)停止职权令; 停止宗教活动之命令: *lay a priest/a town under an* ~. 停止一神父的职权(停止一城市的宗教活动). **in·ter·dic·tion** /ˌɪntəˈdɪkʃn; ˌɪntɚˈdɪkʃən/ *n* [U, C] ~*ing;* ~(*n*). 禁止; 禁止参加各种圣礼及弥撒; 停止教权.

in·ter·dis·ci·plin·ary /ˌɪntəˌdɪsɪˈplɪnərɪ; ˌɪntɚˌdɪsəˈplɪnɛrɪ/ *adj* of more than one branch of learning: 各学科间的; 科际的; 跨越学科的: ~ *studies/degrees.* 各学科间的研究(学位).

in·ter·est /ˈɪntrəst; ˈɪntərɪst/ *n* **1** [U] condition of wanting to know or learn about sth or sb: 兴趣; 关心: *feel/take no/not much/a great* ~ *in politics;* 对政治不感(不太感, 很感)兴趣; *events that arouse great* ~. 引起很多人关心的事件. ⇨ **lose. 2** [U] quality that arouses concern or curiosity, that holds one's attention: 引起关心或好奇心的性质; 趣味: *a matter of considerable/not much* ~. 一件相当(不太)令人感兴趣的事. *Suspense adds* ~ *to a story.* 悬疑增加一个故事的趣味. **3** [C] sth with which one concerns oneself: 爱好的事物; 嗜好: *Her chief* ~ *seems to be horse-racing.* 她主要的嗜好似乎是赛马. *His two great* ~*s in life are music and painting.* 他生活中的两大爱好是音乐及绘画. **4** [C] (often *pl*) advantage; profit; well-being: (常用复数)利益; 裨益; 福利: *look after one's own* ~*s;* 照顾自己的利益; *work in the* ~(*s*) *of humanity;* 为人类谋福利; *travel in Asia in the* ~*s of a business firm.* 为一商行的利益而旅行于亚洲. *It is to your* ~ *to go.* 去对你有利. **5** [C] legal right to a share in sth, esp in its profits: 股份; 权益: *have an* ~ *in a brewery,* eg by owning shares; 在一酿啤酒厂有股份; *have an* ~ *in an estate,* a legal claim to part of it; 在一地产中有部分产权; *American* ~*s in the Caribbean,* eg capital invested in the countries of

that area; 美国在加勒比海地区的权益(例如在该地区国家中的投资金额); *He has sold his ~ in the company.* 他已售出他在那公司中的股份. **6** [U] money charged or paid for the use of money: 利息: *rate of ~/* $^1/_4$ *~ rate,* payment made by a borrower for a loan, expressed as a percentage, eg 5%; 利率(四分之一利率)(以百分比表示, 例如利率 5%); *pay 6 per cent ~ on a loan.* 借款付六厘息. *with~,* (fig) with increased force: (喻)加强地; 加重地: *return a blow/sb's kindness with ~,* give back more than one received. 加重回击(加重报答某人的善意). **7** (often *pl*) group of persons engaged in the same trade, etc or having sth in common: (常用复数)同业; 同行; 同道: *the landed ~s,* landowners collectively; 地主们; *the business ~s,* large business firms collectively; 公司业者; *the brewing ~,* brewers collectively. 酿啤酒业者.

in·ter·est² /'ɪntrɪst; 'ɪntərɪst/ *vt* [VP6A, 14] ~ *sb (in sth),* cause (sb) to give his attention to: 使注意; 使关心; 使感兴趣: *Can I ~ you in this question?* 我可以请你注意这个问题吗? *He is ~ed in shipping,* **(a)** likes to know and learn about ships. 他对船舶感兴趣. **(b)** has money invested in the shipping industry. 他投资于航运业. *~ed adj ~ed (in),* **1** having an interest(5) in; not impartial: 有利害关系的; 有权益的; 偏私的: *When manufacturers demand higher tariffs, we may suspect them of having ~ed motives.* 厂商要求提高关税时, 我们会怀疑他们有自私的动机. **2** showing interest (1): 表现出兴趣的: *an ~ed look,* 一副有兴趣的神情. **3** taking an interest(1) in: 感兴趣的: *~ed spectators;* 感兴趣的观众. *not ~ed in botany/his work.* 对植物学/(他的工作)不感兴趣. *I shall be ~ed to know what happens.* 我很想知道将要发生什么事. *~·ing adj* holding the attention; arousing interest(1): 有趣味的; 令人发生兴趣的: *~ing men/books/conversation.* 有趣的人(书籍, 谈话). *~·ing·ly adv*

in·ter·face /'ɪntəfeɪs; 'ɪntəˌfes/ *n* **1** surface common to two areas. 界面; 分界面. **2** (fig) area common to two or more systems, processes, etc: (喻)(两个或多个系统, 程序等之)共同范围: *at the ~ of creative art and experimental science.* 创作艺术与实验科学的共同范围.

in·ter·fere /ˌɪntə'fɪə(r); ˌɪntə'fɪr/ *vi* **1** [VP2A, 3A] ~ *(in sth),* (of persons) break in upon (other person's affairs) without right or invitation: (指人)干预(他人之事): *Please don't ~ in my business.* 请不要干涉我的事. *Isn't she an interfering old lady!* 她真是个爱管闲事的老太婆! *It's unwise to ~ between husband and wife.* 干预别人夫妻间的事是不智的. **2** [VP2A, 3A] ~ *(with),* (of persons) meddle; tamper (with): (指人)干涉; 乱弄: *Do not ~ with this machine.* 不要乱动这部机器. **3** [VP3A] ~ *with,* (of events, circumstances, etc) come into opposition; hinder or prevent: (指事件, 环境等)妨害; 妨碍; 干扰: *Do you ever allow pleasure to ~ with duty?* 你曾为了玩乐而妨碍了你的职责吗? **in·ter·fer·ence** /ˌɪntə'fɪərəns; ˌɪntə'fɪrəns/ *n* [U] interfering: 干涉; 妨碍; 干扰: *interference from foreign broadcasting stations,* eg when these have a wave-length close to that of the station one wishes to receive; 外来广播电台的干扰(如当外来广播电台的波长与某人欲收听的电台波长接近时); (computers) existence of unwanted signals in a communications circuit. (电子计算机)通讯电路中的干扰.

in·terim /'ɪntərɪm; 'ɪntərɪm/ *n* **1** *in the ~,* meanwhile; during the time that comes between. 在其时; 在其间. **2** (attrib) as an instalment: (用作定语)作为一段时间所供应物之一部; 期间的: *~ dividends,* paid between annual dividends as advance payments; 期中利; provisional or temporary: 临时的; 暂时的: *an ~ report,* one that precedes the final report. 暂时的报告(在最终报告前所作者).

in·terior /ɪn'tɪərɪə(r); ɪn'tɪrɪə/ *adj* **1** situated inside; of the inside. 在内的; 内部的. **2** inland; away from the coast. 内地的; 内陆的. **3** home or domestic (contrasted

with *foreign*). 国内的(与 foreign 相对). □ *n* **the ~,** **1** the inside: 内部: (used attrib) (用作定语) *~ decorators,* those who decorate the inside of a building (with paint, wall-paper, etc). 室内装璜设计师; 室内装饰工匠. **2** inland areas. 内地. **3** (department dealing with the) domestic affairs of a country: 内政; 内政部门: (US) (美) *the Department of the I~.* 内政部. (Cf 参较 *Home Office in GB.* 英国称 Home Office。)

in·ter·ject /ˌɪntə'dʒekt; ˌɪntə'dʒɛkt/ *vt* [VP6A] put in suddenly (a remark, etc) between statements, etc made by another. (他人讲话时) 突然插入 (评语等). **in·ter·jec·tion** /ˌɪntə'dʒekʃn; ˌɪntə'dʒɛkʃən/ *n* word or phrase used as an exclamation, eg *Oh! For goodness sake!* 感叹词(例如: 啊! 看在老天爷的面上!).

in·ter·lace /ˌɪntə'leɪs; ˌɪntə'les/ *vt, vi* [VP6A, 2A, 14] ~ *(with),* join, be joined, by weaving or lacing together, one with another; cross as if woven: (使)交织; (使)交错: *interlacing branches.* 交错的树枝.

in·ter·lard /ˌɪntə'lɑːd; ˌɪntə'lɑrd/ *vt* [VP14] ~ *with,* (formal) mix writing, speech, etc with foreign phrases, etc: (正式用语)使(写作, 演说等)杂有(外国词句等): *essays ~ed with quotations from the poets.* 混有引用诗人文句的文章.

in·ter·leave /ˌɪntə'liːv; ˌɪntə'liv/ *vt* [VP6A, 14] ~ *(with),* insert (usu blank leaves) between the leaves of (a book, etc): 在(书等)之各页中插以(空白纸等): *a diary ~ed with blotting-paper.* 插有吸墨纸的日记簿.

in·ter·link /ˌɪntə'lɪŋk; ˌɪntə'lɪŋk/ *vt, vi* [VP6A, 2A] link together. 使连锁; 连环; 环结.

in·ter·lock /ˌɪntə'lɒk; ˌɪntə'lɑk/ *vt, vi* [VP6A, 2A] lock or join together; clasp firmly together. 连结; 结合; 连锁; 互锁.

in·ter·locu·tor /ˌɪntə'lɒkjʊtə(r); ˌɪntə'lɑkjətə/ *n* person taking part in a discussion or dialogue. 讨论者; 对话者.

in·ter·lo·per /'ɪntələʊpə(r); 'ɪntəˌlopə/ *n* person who, esp for profit or personal advantage, pushes himself in where he has no right. 闯入者(尤指为个人利益而妨害他人者).

in·ter·lude /'ɪntəluːd; 'ɪntəˌlud/ *n* **1** interval of different character between two events or two periods of time: 二事件间不同性质的穿插事件; 两段时期中间的时间; 间隔的时间: *~s of bright weather.* 间隔的睛朗天气. **2** interval between two acts of a play, two scenes of an opera or between parts of a psalm, hymn etc; music played during such an interval. 戏剧两幕间, 歌剧两场间, 圣诗, 赞美诗等两段间之间歇; 上述间歇时的插曲; 间奏.

in·ter·marry /ˌɪntə'mærɪ; ˌɪntə'mærɪ/ *vi* (*pt, pp* -**married**) [VP2A, 3A] ~ *(with),* (of tribes, races, etc) become connected by marriage with other tribes, etc. (指不同部落, 种族等) 通婚. **in·ter·mar·riage** /ˌɪntə'mærɪdʒ; ˌɪntə'mærɪdʒ/ *n* [U] marriage between members of different families, tribes, castes, etc. (不同家族; 部落, 阶级等间的) 通婚.

in·ter·medi·ary /ˌɪntə'miːdɪərɪ US: -dɪərɪ; ˌɪntə'midɪˌɛrɪ/ *n* (*pl* -**ries**), *adj* **1** ~ *(between),* (sb or sth) acting as a link between (persons and groups); go-between; mediator. 居间的 (人或物); 斡旋的; 中人; 调解人. **2** (sth) intermediate. 中间物; 中间; 中间的.

in·ter·medi·ate /ˌɪntə'miːdɪət; ˌɪntə'midɪɪt/ *adj* situated or coming between in time, space, degree, etc: (时间, 空间, 程度等) 中间的: *at an ~ stage,* eg the cocoon stage of development of a butterfly; 在中间的阶段 (如蝴蝶的作茧期). *~ courses,* between elementary and advanced; 中级课程; *~-range ballistic missiles.* 中程弹道导弹. □ *n* sth that is ~. 中间物. *~·ly adv*

in·ter·ment /ɪn'tɜːmənt; ɪn'tɜmənt/ *n* [U] being buried; [C] instance of this; burial. 被埋葬; 埋葬; 葬礼.

in·ter·mezzo /ˌɪntə'metsəʊ; ˌɪntə'metso/ *n* (*pl* **-s** /-tsəʊz; -tsoz/ or -**zzi** /-tsɪ; -tsɪ/) short musical composition to be played between the acts of a drama or an

opera, or one that connects the main divisions of a large musical work such as a symphony. 幕间插曲; 间奏曲.

in·ter·mi·nable /ɪn'tɜːmɪnəbl; ɪn'tɝmɪnəbl/ adj endless; tedious because too long: 无终止的; 冗长的: an ~ debate/sermon. 冗长的辩论(讲道). **in·ter·mi·nably** /-əblɪ; -əblɪ/ adv

in·ter·mingle /ˌɪntə'mɪŋgl; ˌɪntɚ'mɪŋgl/ vt, vi [VP 6A, 14, 2A, 3A] ~ (with), mix together (two things, one with the other); mingle; 互相混合; 混合: The conference delegates ~d over coffee. 会议代表们一面喝咖啡一面互相交谈.

in·ter·mission /ˌɪntə'mɪʃn; ˌɪntɚ'mɪʃən/ n pause; interval: The film lasted for three hours without ~/with a short ~ half-way through. 那电影演出三小时没有休息(中间有片刻的休息).

in·ter·mit·tent /ˌɪntə'mɪtnt; ˌɪntɚ'mɪtnt/ adj pausing or stopping at intervals; stopping and starting again: 间歇的; 继续的: ~ fever. 间歇热. **~·ly** adv

in·ter·mix /ˌɪntə'mɪks; ˌɪntɚ'mɪks/ vt, vi = mix (the usu word). (mix 较常用). **~·ture** /-tʃə(r); -tʃɚ/

in·tern¹ /ɪn'tɜːn; ɪn'tɝn/ vt [VP6A] compel (a person, esp an enemy alien during a war) to live within certain limits or in a special building, camp, etc. 拘留 (尤指战时敌国之人)于某地. **~·ment** n [U] ~ing or being ~ed: 拘留; 被拘留: '~ment camp. 拘留营. **~·ee** /ˌɪntɜː'niː; ˌɪntɝ'ni/ n person who is ~ed.拘留留者.

in·tern² (US also **in·terne**) /'ɪntɜːn; 'ɪntɝn/ n (US) young doctor who is completing his training by residing in a hospital and acting as an assistant physician or surgeon there. (美)住院实习医生; 住院助理医师. (GB 英 = houseman.)

in·ter·nal /ɪn'tɜːnl; ɪn'tɝnl/ adj 1 of or in the inside: 内部的;在内部的: suffer ~ injuries in an accident. 在一些事件中受内伤; ~ bleeding, eg in the bowels. 内出血(例如在肠中). **~ combustion**, the process by which power is produced by the explosion of gases or vapours inside a cylinder (as in the engine of a car). 内燃(由气缸内气体的爆发而产生动力的方法, 如汽车的内燃机). 2 domestic; of the home affairs of a country: 国内的; 内政的: ~ trade/revenue, (also 亦作 Inland Revenue). 国内贸易(税收). 3 derived from within the thing itself: 由本身得来的: ~ evidence, eg of when an old book was written, or of the date of an old manuscript. 内证据(例如在考证一古书或稿件的日期时, 由该书或稿件本身获得证据). **~·ly** /-nəlɪ; -nlɪ/ adv

in·ter·na·tional /ˌɪntə'næʃənl; ˌɪntɚ'næʃənl/ adj existing, carried on, between nations: 国际的: ~ trade/law/agreements/conferences. 国际贸易(法, 协定, 会议). **~money order**, one which may be cashed in a country other than the country of origin. 国际汇票(可在他国兑现者). □ n the **1st/2nd/3rd I~**, three socialist or communist associations for workers of all countries, formed in 1864, 1889 and 1919. 第一(二, 三)国际(先后成立于一八六四, 一八八九, 一九一九年的三个国际社会主义或共产主义组织). **~·ism** /-nəlɪzəm; -nl‚ɪzəm/ n 国际主义. **~·ist** /-ɪst; -ɪst/ n person who supports and advocates ~ism. 国际主义者. **~·ize** /-fənəlaɪz; -fənl‚aɪz/ vt [VP6A] make ~; bring under the combined control or protection of all or many nations: 使国际化; 使以国际共管: Should the Suez and Panama Canals be ~ized? 苏伊士运河和巴拿马运河应归国际共管吗? **~·iz·ation** /ˌɪntəˌnæʃənəlaɪ'zeɪʃn US: -lɪ'z-; ˌɪntɚˌnæʃənlə'zeʃən/ n [U] . **~·ly** adv

in·ter·na·tio·nale /ˌɪntənæʃə'nɑːl; ˌɪntɚˌnæʃə'nɑl/ n The I~, (revolutionary) socialist song. 国际歌.

in·terne /'ɪntɜːn; 'ɪntɝn/ n ⇨ intern².

in·ter·necine /ˌɪntə'niːsaɪn; ˌɪntɚ'nisɪn/ adj (usu of war) causing destruction to both sides. (通常指战争)互相毁灭的; 两败俱伤的.

in·ter·nee /ˌɪntɜː'niː; ˌɪntɝ'ni/ n ⇨ intern¹

in·ter·pel·late /ɪn'tɜːpəlɪt US: ˌɪntə'pelɪt; ˌɪntɚ'pɛlɪt/ vt [VP6A] (in some Parliaments, eg the

French and Japanese) interrupt the proceedings and demand a statement or explanation from (a Minister). (某些国会中, 例如在法国和日本)议员于会中阻挠议程并要求(部长)加以说明; 质询. **in·ter·pel·la·tion** /ɪn‚tɜːpə'leɪʃn US: ˌɪntɚ-; ˌɪntɚpə'leʃən/ n [U] interpellating or being ~d; [C] instance of this. 质询; 被质询.

in·ter·phone /'ɪntəfəʊn; 'ɪntɚ‚fon/ n (US) (美) = intercom.

in·ter·plan·etary /ˌɪntə'plænɪtrɪ US: -terɪ; ˌɪntɚ'plænə‚tɛrɪ/ adj between planets: 行星间的: an ~ journey in a spacecraft. 乘太空船作行星间的旅行.

in·ter·play /'ɪntəpleɪ; 'ɪntɚ‚ple/ n [U] operation of two or more things on each other: 相互作用: the ~ of colours, their combined effect. 颜色的相互作用.

in·ter·pol /'ɪntəpɒl; 'ɪntɚ‚pɑl/ n International Police Commission. 国际刑警委员会.

in·ter·po·late /ɪn'tɜːpəleɪt; ɪn'tɝpə‚let/ vt [VP6A] make (sometimes misleading) additions to a book, etc. 加添(有时会引起误解的)字句于一书等. **in·ter·po·la·tion** /ɪn‚tɜːpə'leɪʃn; ɪn‚tɝpə'leʃən/ n interpolating; [C] sth ~d. 加添字句; 加添的字句.

in·ter·pose /ˌɪntə'pəʊz; ˌɪntɚ'poz/ vt, vi 1 [VP6A] put forward an objection, a veto, etc as an interference: 提出(异议, 否决等): Will they ~ their veto yet again? 他们又将提出否决吗? 2 [VP6A, 2A] say (sth) as an interruption; make an interruption. 插入(言语)打断谈话; 插嘴. 3 [VP2A, 3A,14] ~ (oneself) between; ~ in, place oneself, be, between others: 介入二者之间: ~ between two persons who are quarrelling; 介入两个吵架的人的中间; mediate (in a dispute). 调停(争端). **in·ter·po·si·tion** /ˌɪntəpə'zɪʃn; ˌɪntɚpə'zɪʃən/ n [U] interposing; [C] sth ~d. 提出异议, 否决等; 插嘴; 介入; 调停; 插入物.

in·ter·pret /ɪn'tɜːprɪt; ɪn'tɝprɪt/ vt, vi 1 [VP6A] show, make clear, the meaning of (either in words or by artistic performance); (用言语或表演)解释; 说明: ~ a difficult passage in a book; 解释艰涩难文字; ~ (of an actor) (指演员) a role; 演出一角色; (of a conductor)(指乐队指挥) ~ a symphony. 指挥一交响乐. Poetry helps to ~ life. 诗有助于阐释人生的意义. 2 [VP6A, 16B] consider to be the meaning of; 认为是…的意思; We ~ed his silence as a refusal. 我们认为他的沉默是拒绝的表示. 3 [VP2A] act as ~er: 口译; 通译: Will you please ~ for me, translate what is (to be) said? 请你为我翻译一下好吗? **~·er** n person who gives an immediate oral translation of words spoken in another language. 口译者; 通译者; 译员. **in·ter·pre·ta·tion** /ɪn‚tɜːprɪ'teɪʃn; ɪn‚tɝprɪ'teʃən/ n [U] interpreting; [C] result of this; explanation or meaning: 解释;解释的结果; 说明; 翻译; 含意: The announcement may be given several ~ations. 这段声明可能有几种不同的解释.

in·ter·racial /ˌɪntə'reɪʃl; ˌɪntɚ'reʃəl/ adj between, involving, different races. 各族间的.

in·ter·reg·num /ˌɪntə'regnəm; ˌɪntɚ'regnəm/ n pl ~s, -na /-nə; -nə/ period during which a State has no normal or legitimate ruler, esp between the end of a Sovereign's reign and the beginning of his successor's reign; pause or interval. 国家无正常统治者的时期(尤指一君主的统治权结束而继任者尚未执政的一段时间); 休止时间; 空位期.

in·ter·re·late /ˌɪntə'leɪt; ˌɪntɚ'let/ vt, vi [VP6A, 2A] come or bring together in reciprocal relationship: (使) 相互关连: ~d studies, of separate but related subjects as a single unit group, eg politics, philosophy and economics. 相关的学科(例如政治学, 哲学和经济学). **in·ter·re·la·tion** /ˌɪntəri'leɪʃn; ˌɪntɚrɪ'leʃən/ n ~ of/between, mutual relation. 相互关系. **~·ship** /-ʃɪp; -ʃɪp/ n mutual relationship. 相互关系.

in·ter·ro·gate /ɪn'terəgeɪt; ɪn'tɛrə‚get/ vt [VP6A] put questions to esp closely or formally: 询问(尤指严密地或正式地): ~ a prisoner. 审问一犯人. **in·ter·ro·ga·tor** /-tə(r); -tɚ/ n person who ~s. 询问者; 审问者; 质问

者. **in·ter·ro·ga·tion** /ɪnˌterəˈgeɪʃn; ɪnˌterəˈgeʃən/ *n*
1 [U] asking questions. 讯问；发问. **interrogation
point**, question mark; the mark (?). 问号(?). 2 [C, U]
oral examination; inquiry: 审问；侦讯: *long and tiring
interrogations by police officers.* 受警官长期和令人疲倦
的审问.

in·ter·roga·tive /ˌɪntəˈrɒgətɪv; ˌɪntəˈrɑgətɪv/ *adj*
1 showing or having the form of a question; of inquiry:
表示疑问的；疑惑的；疑问的；询问的: *an ~ look / glance;*
疑惑的样子(目光); *in an ~ tone.* 以疑问的声调。2
(gram) used in questions: (语法)用于疑问句的:
pronouns / adverbs, eg who, why. 疑问代词(副词)(例如
who, why). □ *n* = word, esp a pronoun. 表示疑问的词
(尤指疑问代词). **~·ly** *adv*

in·ter·roga·tory /ˌɪntəˈrɒgətərɪ US: -tɔːrɪ; ˌɪntə-
ˈrɑgəˌtɔrɪ/ *adj* of inquiry: 疑问的；质问的: *in an ~
tone.* 质问的口气。

in·ter·rupt /ˌɪntəˈrʌpt; ˌɪntəˈrʌpt/ *vt, vi* [VP6A,
2A] 1 break the continuity of: 使中断；阻断: *The war
~ed the flow of commerce between the two countries.* 战
争使该两国间的通商中断了. *Traffic was ~ed by floods.*
交通被洪水阻断. *Those trees are growing so high that
they ~* (= obstruct) *the view.* 那些树长得过高而遮住了
视线. 2 break in upon (a person's action, speech, etc):
打断(某人的行动, 言语等); 打岔; 插嘴; 打扰: *Don't ~
(me) while I'm busy.* 在我忙的时候不要打搅我. *Don't
~ the speaker; ask your questions afterwards.* 不要打断
那演说者的演说, 等他讲完后再问问题。**~er** *n* person or
thing that ~s. 使中断者; 打断者; 打岔者。 **in·ter·rup·
tion** /ˌɪntəˈrʌpʃn; ˌɪntəˈrʌpʃən/ *n* [U] ~ing or being
~ed; [C] instance of this; sth that ~s: 阻断; 打断; 打
岔; 打扰; 使中断的事物: *Numerous ~ions have prevented
me from finishing the work.* 无数的打岔的事使我未能完
成此工作.

in·ter·sect /ˌɪntəˈsekt; ˌɪntəˈsekt/ *vt, vi* 1 [VP6A]
divide by cutting, passing or lying across. 横断; 横切;
贯穿. 2 [VP6A, 2A] (of lines) cut or cross each other:
(指线条)相交; 交叉: *The lines AB and CD ~ at E.* 直线
AB 与直线 CD 相交于 E 点. *The line AB ~s the line
CD at E.* 直线 AB 和直线 CD 于 E 点相交. **in·ter·sec·
tion** /ˌɪntəˈsekʃn; ˌɪntəˈsekʃən/ *n* [U] ~ing or being
~ed; [C] point where two lines, etc ~. 横断; 横切;
相交; 交叉; 交叉点。

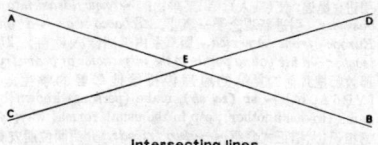

Intersecting lines

in·ter·sperse /ˌɪntəˈspɜːs; ˌɪntəˈspɜrs/ *vt* [VP14] ~
among / between, place here and there. 散置。 ~ *with,*
diversify: 使有变化; 穿插; 点缀: *a speech ~d with witty
remarks.* 穿插着妙语的一篇演说。

in·ter·state /ˌɪntəˈsteɪt; ˌɪntəˈstet/ *adj* (US) between
States: (美)州与州间的; 州际的: ~ *commerce.* 州际
贸易。

in·ter·stel·lar /ˌɪntəˈstelə(r); ˌɪntəˈstelə/ *adj* between the stars: 星与星间的; 星际的: ~ *matter,* eg the
masses of gas between stars; 星际的物质(例如气团); ~
communications. 星际通讯系统。

in·ter·stice /ɪnˈtɜːstɪs; ˈɪntɜstɪs/ *n* crack; chink;
crevice: 罅隙; 空隙; 裂缝: ~*s* (= very small spaces)
between stones in a heap. 一堆石头间狭小的空隙。

in·ter·tribal /ˌɪntəˈtraɪbl; ˌɪntəˈtraɪbl/ *adj* between
tribes: 种族间的; 部族间的: ~ *wars.* 部族间的战争。

in·ter·twine /ˌɪntəˈtwaɪn; ˌɪntəˈtwaɪn/ *vt, vi* [VP
6A, 2A] twine or twist together; become twined or
twisted together: 纠缠; 缠绕在一起: *a lattice ~d with
vines.* 攀附着藤蔓的格子窗。

in·ter·val /ˈɪntəvl; ˈɪntəvl/ *n* 1 time (between two
events or two parts of an action); (esp) time between
two acts of a play, two parts of a concert, etc: (两件
事或两部分动作间)间隔的时间; 间歇; (尤指)戏剧两幕间或
音乐会上下半场间的间歇: *buses leaving at short ~s,* ie
very frequently. 开出班次频繁的公共汽车。2 space
between (two objects or points): 间隔: *arranged at ~s
of ten feet.* 以十英尺的间隔排列。3 (music) difference of
pitch between two notes on a given scale. (音乐)音程.

in·ter·vene /ˌɪntəˈviːn; ˌɪntəˈvin/ *vi* 1 [VP2A]
(of events, circumstances) come between (others) in
time: (指事件或情况)插入 (其他的事件或情况之间)
发生: *I shall leave on Sunday if nothing ~s.* 如果没有
别的事, 我星期天动身。2 [VP2A, 3A] ~ *(in),* (of
persons) interfere so as to prevent sth or change the
result: (指人)干涉; 阻挠; 调停: ~ *in a dispute;* 调停争
端; ~ *between people who are disputing.* 调停他人间的
争端。3 [VP2A] (of time) come or be between: (指时
间)介于其间: *during the years that ~d.* 在其间的几年
中。 **in·ter·ven·tion** /ˌɪntəˈvenʃn; ˌɪntəˈvenʃən/ *n*
[U] intervening (esp 2 above): 插入; 介于其间; (尤指)
干涉; 阻挠; 调停: *armed intervention by one country in
the affairs of other countries:* 一国对他国内政之武力干
涉; [C] instance of this. 干涉或调停的实例。

in·ter·view /ˈɪntəvjuː; ˈɪntəˌvju/ *n* [C] meeting
with sb for formal consultation or examination, eg
between employers and applicants for posts; meeting
(of a reporter, etc) with sb whose views are requested:
接见; 会见 (例如雇主与求职者间者); 新闻记者的访问:
*The Ambassador refused to give any ~s to journalists
or TV men.* 该大使拒绝任何新闻或电视记者的访问。□
vt [VP6A] (of a reporter, etc) have or obtain an ~
with. (指记者等)访问; 会见; 接见。

in·ter·weave /ˌɪntəˈwiːv; ˌɪntəˈwiv/ *vt* (*pt* **-wove**
/-ˈwəʊv; -ˈwov/, *pp* **-woven** /-ˈwəʊvn; -ˈwovən/) [VP
6A, 14] ~ *(with),* weave together (one with another).
交织。

in·tes·tate /ɪnˈtesteɪt; ɪnˈtestet/ *adj* not having
made a will before death occurs: 未留遗嘱而死: *die ~.*
未留遗嘱而死。

in·tes·tine /ɪnˈtestɪn; ɪnˈtestɪn/ *n* (usu *pl*) lower
part of the food canal from below the stomach to the
anus: (通常用复数)肠: *small / large ~,* parts of this.
小(大)肠. **in·tes·ti·nal** /ɪnˈtestɪnl; ɪnˈtestɪnl/ *adj* of
the ~s: 肠的: *intestinal disorders.* 肠疾。 ⇨ **abdominal;**
⇨ the illus at **alimentary.** 参看 alimentary 之插图。

in·ti·mate¹ /ˈɪntɪmət; ˈɪntəmɪt/ *adj* 1 close and
familiar: 亲近的; 亲密的: ~ *friends.* 密友; 知己. *be /
get on ~ terms (with),* eg when one calls a man
'Jack' instead of 'Mr Hill'. 与某人很亲近(例如对希尔
先生直呼其名杰克). 2 innermost; private and personal:
最内部的; 私人的; 秘密的: *tell a friend the ~ details of
one's life;* 将一生中个人的琐碎私事告诉一友人; *an ~
diary,* one in which one records experiences, thoughts,
emotions, etc usu kept secret. 私人日记。3 resulting
from close study or great familiarity: 精湛的; 仔细研究
而得的; 熟悉的: *an ~ knowledge of Greek philosophy.*
对希腊哲学的精湛的知识。□ *n* ~ friend. 密友; 知己。
~·ly *adv* **in·ti·macy** /ˈɪntɪməsɪ; ˈɪntəməsɪ/ *n* (*pl*
-cies) 1 [U] the state of being ~; close friendship or
relationship; (euphem) sexual relations. 亲密; 亲近; (委
婉语)性关系。2 (*pl*) ~ actions, eg caresses or kisses.
(复)亲密的抚摸或动作。

in·ti·mate² /ˈɪntɪmeɪt; ˈɪntəˌmet/ *vt* [VP6A, 9, 14]
~ *sth (to sb);* ~ *(to sb) that...,* make known; show
clearly: 宣布; 明白表示: ~ *one's approval of a plan /that
one approves of a plan.* 表示赞成一计划. *He ~d to me
his intention of leaving early / that he intended to leave
early.* 他告诉我他有意早些离去。**in·ti·ma·tion** /ˌɪntɪ-
ˈmeɪʃn; ˌɪntəˈmeʃən/ *n* [U] intimating; [C] sth ~d;
notification; suggestion. 宣布; 明白表示; 明白表示的事
物; 通知; 暗示。

in·timi·date /ɪn'tɪmɪdeɪt; ɪn'tɪmə,det/ vt [VP6A,
14] ~ (into), frighten, esp in order to force (sb into
doing sth): 胁迫; 恐吓 (某人做某事): ~ a witness,
eg by threatening him. 恐吓一证人. **in·timi·da·tion**
/ɪn,tɪmɪ'deɪʃn; ɪn,tɪmə'deʃən/ n [U] intimidating or
being ~d: 胁迫; 威迫: surrender to intimidation. 屈服于
胁迫.

into /'ɪntə; 'ɪntə; strong form: 'ɪntuː; 'ɪntu/ prep 1
(indicating motion or direction to a point within): (表
示向内的动作或方向)进入…之内; 向内: Come ~ the house
/garden. 到房屋(花园)里来. Throw it ~ the fire. 把
它丢到火中去. He worked late ~ the night. 他工作至深夜.
2 (indicating change of condition, result): (表示状况的
变化或结果)变成…之状况: She burst ~ tears. 她突然
号啕大哭. Don't get ~ trouble. 不要惹麻烦. The rain
changed ~ snow. 雨变成了雪. He poked the fire ~ a
blaze, poked it so that it blazed up. 他拨火拨大了.
Collect them ~ heaps. 把它们聚成堆. He frightened her
~ submission. 他恐吓她使她顺从. be ~ sth, (mod use,
colloq) be involved in, concerned with, it: (现代用法,
口) 牵扯; 与…有关: She's heavily ~ vegetarianism. 她
十分主张素食. 3 (maths): (数学)除: 5 ~ 25 (= 25
divided by 5) goes 5. 5 除 25 得 5.

in·tol·er·able /ɪn'tɒlərəbl; ɪn'talərəbl/ adj that
cannot be tolerated or endured: 无法忍受的; 不能忍
耐的: ~ heat/insolence. 无法忍受的热(侮辱). Is the
world becoming an ~ place to live in? 这世界渐渐变成一
个无法居住的地方了吗? **in·tol·er·ably** /-əblɪ; -əblɪ/
adv

in·tol·er·ant /ɪn'tɒlərənt; ɪn'talərənt/ adj ~ (of),
not tolerant: 不能容纳异己的; 不宽容的: a man who is
~ of opposition. 不能容忍反对的人. ~·ly adv **in·tol·
er·ance** /-əns; -əns/ n

in·ton·ation /,ɪntə'neɪʃn; ,ɪntə'neʃən/ n [U] the
rise and fall of the pitch of the voice in speaking; this
as an element of meaning in language. 说话时声音的升
降; 语调; 音调.

in·tone /ɪn'təʊn; ɪn'ton/ vt, vi [VP6A,2A] recite a
prayer, psalm, etc in a singing tone; speak with a
particular tone. 吟诵 (祈祷文, 赞美诗等); 以特殊音调
说话.

in toto /ɪn 'təʊtəʊ; ɪn'toto/ (Lat) totally; altogether.
(拉)整个地; 全部.

in·toxi·cant /ɪn'tɒksɪkənt; ɪn'taksəkənt/ adj, n
intoxicating (liquor). 醉人的; 酒类饮料.

in·toxi·cate /ɪn'tɒksɪkeɪt; ɪn'taksə,ket/ vt [VP6A]
1 make stupid with, cause to lose self-control as the
result of taking, alcoholic drink: 使醉: If a man drinks
too much whisky, he becomes ~d. 如果一人饮过多的威士
忌, 他会醉. 2 excite greatly, beyond self-control: 使极
度兴奋; 使陶醉: ~d by success; 因成功而极度兴奋;
~d with joy. 高兴极了. **in·toxi·ca·tion** /ɪn,tɒksɪ-
'keɪʃn; ɪn,taksə'keʃən/ n [U] being ~d; alcoholic
poisoning. 醉; 极度兴奋; 酒精中毒.

in·trac·table /ɪn'træktəbl; ɪn'træktəbl/ adj not
easily controlled or dealt with; hard to manage: 难控制
的; 难对付的; 难处理的: ~ children; 难管教的孩子们;
an ~ temper. 顽强的脾气. **in·trac·ta·bil·ity** /ɪn-
,træktə'bɪlətɪ; ɪn,træktə'bɪlətɪ/ n

in·tra·mural /,ɪntrə'mjʊərəl; ,ɪntrə'mjʊrəl/ adj
1 existing, done, within the walls of a town, building,
etc: 在城市内的; 在一建筑物内的: ~ burial, inside a
church instead of in the churchyard. 教堂内的葬礼(而
非葬于毗连教堂的墓地中). 2 intended for full-time,
residential students, 为住校正式生而设的; 校内的. ⇨
extramural.

in·tran·si·gent /ɪn'trænsɪdʒənt; ɪn'trænsədʒənt/ adj
(formal) uncompromising, esp in politics. (正式用语)不
妥协的; 不让步的 (尤指在政治上). **in·tran·si·gence**
/-əns; -əns/ n

in·tran·si·tive /ɪn'trænsɪtɪv; ɪn'trænsətɪv/ adj (of
verbs) used without a direct object. (指动词)不及物的.

~·ly adv ⇨ **transitive**.

in·tra·uter·ine /,ɪntrə 'juːtəraɪn; ,ɪntrə'jutəraɪn /
adj (med) within the uterus. (医)子宫内的. ~ **device**,
(abbr 缩作 **IUD**), loop or spiral inserted in the uterus
as a contraceptive. 子宫环(一种避孕器).

in·tra·venous /,ɪntrə'viːnəs; ,ɪntrə'vinəs/ adj within
a vein or veins: 静脉内的: ~ injections, and so into the
blood stream. 静脉注射.

in·trench /ɪn'trentʃ; ɪn'trentʃ/ = **entrench**.

in·trepid /ɪn'trepɪd; ɪn'trepɪd/ adj fearless. 无畏的.
~·ly adv **in·trep·id·ity** /,ɪntrɪ'pɪdətɪ; ,ɪntrə'pɪdətɪ/
n [U] fearlessness; [C] (pl -ties) fearless act. 无畏; 无
畏的行动.

in·tri·cate /'ɪntrɪkət; 'ɪntrəkɪt/ adj complicated;
puzzling; difficult to follow or understand: 复杂的; 使
人迷惑的; 难了解的: a novel with an ~ plot; 情节复杂的
一部小说; an ~ piece of machinery. 一部复杂的机器.
~·ly adv **in·tri·cacy** /'ɪntrɪkəsɪ; 'ɪntrəkəsɪ/ n (pl
-cies) [U] the quality of being ~; (pl) ~ things,
events, etc. 复杂; 难了解; (复)复杂的事物, 事件等.

in·trigue /ɪn'triːg; ɪn'trig/ vi, vt 1 [VP2A, 3A] ~
(with sb) (against sb), make and carry out secret
plans or plots: 搞阴谋; 密谋: ~ with Smith against
Robinson. 与史密斯密谋对付鲁宾逊. 2 [VP6A] arouse
the interest or curiosity of: 激起…的兴趣或好奇心: The
news ~d all of us. 这消息引起我们大家的兴趣. □ n 1
[U] secret plotting. 密谋; 搞阴谋. 2 [C] plot; secret
plan; secret love affair. 阴谋; 秘密计划; 私通.

in·trin·sic /ɪn'trɪnsɪk US: -zɪk; ɪn'trɪnsɪk/ adj (of
value, quality) belonging naturally; existing within,
not coming from outside: (指价值或性质)固有的; 内在
的: a man's ~ worth, eg such qualities as honour and
courage, contrasted with extrinsic qualities, eg family
connections: 一个人内在的优点(例如荣誉、勇敢等, 与家
世关系等外在的优点相对); the ~ value of a coin, the
value of the metal in it, usu less than its face value.
一钱币的内在价值(指其所含金属的价值, 通常低于面值).
in·trin·si·cally /-klɪ; -klɪ/ adv

in·tro·duce /,ɪntrə'djuːs US: -'duːs; ,ɪntrə'djus/ vt
[VP6A, 15A] 1 bring in; bring forward: 提出: ~ a Bill
before Parliament. 向国会提出一法案. 2 [VP14] ~
into/to, bring (sth) into use or into operation for the
first time; cause (sb) to be acquainted with (sth): 采用;
引进; 提倡; 使(某人)认识某事物: ~ new ideas into a
business. 引进新观念于一事业. Tobacco was ~d into
Europe from America. 烟草系由美洲传入欧洲. The
teacher ~d his young pupils to the intricacies of geometry.
那教师把几何的复杂的原理传授给他年轻的学生. 3
[VP6A, 14] ~ sb (to sb), make (persons) known by
name (to one another), esp in the usual formal way: 介
绍相识(尤指正式介绍): ~ two friends. 介绍两位朋友相
识. He ~d me to his parents. 他把我介绍给他的父母.
The chairman ~d the lecturer to the audience. 主席将演
说者介绍给听众. 4 [VP6A, 14] ~ (into), insert: 插
入: ~ a tube into a wound; 将一管插入伤口; ~ a
subject into a conversation. 将一题目引入谈话中.

in·tro·duc·tion /,ɪntrə'dʌkʃn; ,ɪntrə'dʌkʃən/ n
1 [U] introducing or being introduced: 提倡; 采用; 介
绍: a letter of ~, one that introduces the bearer to
friends of the writer; 介绍信; foreign words of recent
~, recently introduced into the language. 最近采用的
外来语. 2 [C] introducing of persons to one another:
介绍人们相识: It was necessary to make ~s all round,
to introduce many people to one another. 需要将大家一
一互为介绍. 3 [C] sth that leads up to sth else; the
opening paragraph of a letter, essay, speech, etc;
explanatory article at or before the beginning of a
book. 导引之事物; 引言; 序言; 序论. 4 [C] elementary
textbook: 入门(书); 初步: 'An I~ to Greek Grammar'.
希腊语法入门.

in·tro·duc·tory /,ɪntrə'dʌktərɪ US: -tɔːrɪ; ,ɪntrə-
'dʌktərɪ/ adj serving to introduce: 介绍的; 导引的: an

~ *chapter;* 序篇; *a few ~ remarks by the chairman.* 主席的简短的介绍词。

in·tro·spect /ˌɪntrəˈspekt; ˌɪntrəˈspɛkt/ *vi* [VP2A] (formal) examine one's own thoughts and feelings. (正式用语)内省;反省。 **in·tro·spec·tion** /ˌɪntrəˈspekʃn; ˌɪntrəˈspɛkʃən/ *n* [U] ~ing. 内省;反省。 **in·tro·spec·tive** /-tɪv; -tɪv/ *adj* inclined towards, based on, ~ion. 好内省的;根据内省的。

in·tro·vert /ˈɪntrəvɜːt; ˈɪntrəˌvɜrt/ *vt* [VP6A] turn (the mind, thought) inward upon itself. 使(心性, 思想)内向。 □ *n* /ˈɪntrəvɜːt; ˈɪntrəˌvɜrt/ person who habitually does this; one who is more interested in his own thoughts and feelings than in things outside himself. 惯于内省之人;内向性格的人。 **in·tro·ver·sion** *n* [U] state of being ~ed. 内向。 ⇨ **extrovert.**

in·trude /ɪnˈtruːd; ɪnˈtrud/ *vt,vi* [VP14, 2A, 3A] ~ *(oneself) on/upon sb;* ~ *(oneself/sth) into sth,* force (sth, oneself, upon, into a place); enter without invitation: 强使(某人)接受(某事物, 自己);强行进入(某地);闯入;侵入;侵扰: *the thought/suspicion that ~d itself into my mind;* 侵入我心中的念头 (怀疑); ~ *oneself into a meeting;* 闯入一会议; ~ *upon a person's time/privacy.* 侵扰一人的时间(静居)。 *I hope I'm not intruding.* 我希望没有打扰你。 **in·truder** *n* person or thing that ~s: 闯入者;侵入者; (attrib)(用作定语) ~*r aircraft;* 突袭飞机; ~*r patrols,* ie intruding into the enemy's country. 闯入敌国的巡逻队。

in·tru·sion /ɪnˈtruːʒn; ɪnˈtruʒən/ *n* ~ *(on/upon/into),* [U] intruding: 闯入;侵扰: *guilty of unpardonable* ~ *upon sb's privacy;* 犯不可原谅的侵扰某人静居罪; [C] instance of this: 闯入或侵扰的实例: *angry at numerous ~s on one's privacy by rude journalists.* 因无礼的记者屡次侵扰其清静生活而发怒。 **in·tru·sive** /ɪnˈtruːsɪv; ɪnˈtrusɪv/ *adj* intruding: 闯入的;侵扰的; 侵入的: *the intrusive 'r',* eg the r-sound often heard in eg 'awe and wonder'. 插入的 r 音(例如 awe and wonder 读音中的)。

in·trust /ɪnˈtrʌst; ɪnˈtrʌst/ = **entrust.**

in·tuit /ɪnˈtjuːɪt *US:* -ˈtuː-; ˈɪntjuɪt/ *vt, vi* [VP2A, 6A] sense by intuition. 直觉。

in·tu·ition /ˌɪntjuːˈɪʃn *US:* -tuː-; ˌɪntjuˈɪʃən/ *n* **1** [U] (power of) the immediate understanding of something without conscious reasoning or study. 直觉;直觉力。 **2** [C] piece of knowledge gained by this power. 直觉的知识。 **in·tu·itive** /ɪnˈtjuːɪtɪv *US:* -ˈtuː-; ɪnˈtjuɪtɪv/ *adj* of ~: 直觉的: *intuitive knowledge;* 直觉的知识; possessing ~: 有直觉力的: *Are women more intuitive than men?* 女子较男子更具有直觉力吗? **in·tu·itive·ly** *adv*

in·tu·mescence /ˌɪntjuːˈmesns *US:* -tuː-; ˌɪntjuˈmesns/ *n* (med) process or condition of swelling or expanding. (医)肿大;膨胀。

in·un·date /ˈɪnʌndeɪt; ˈɪnənˌdet/ *vt* [VP6A, 14] ~ *(with),* flood; cover (with water) by overflowing; (fig, esp passive) overwhelm: 泛滥;淹没;(喻,尤用于被动语态)压倒: *be ~d with requests for help/applications for a post.* 因请求援助(求职信)过多而不胜其扰。 **in·un·da·tion** /ˌɪnʌnˈdeɪʃn; ˌɪnənˈdeʃən/ *n* [U] flooding; [C] instance of this; flood. 泛滥;淹没;洪水。

in·ure /ɪˈnjʊə(r); ɪnˈjʊr/ *vt* [VP14] ~ *oneself/sb to,* (usu passive) accustom: (通常用被动语态)使惯于: *Living in the far North had ~d him to cold.* 居于极北部使他惯于寒冷。 *He had become ~d to ridicule.* 他已受惯了他人的讥笑。

in·vade /ɪnˈveɪd; ɪnˈved/ *vt* [VP6A] **1** enter (a country) with armed forces in order to attack; (fig) crowd into; enter: 侵略(一国);侵犯;(喻)蜂拥而至;涌入: *a city ~d by tourists;* 游客蜂拥而至的城市; *a mind ~d by worry and anxiety.* 充满忧伤和焦虑的心境。 **2** violate; interfere with: 侵害;干扰: ~ *sb's rights.* 侵害某人的权利。 **in·vader** *n* person or thing that ~s. 侵略者;侵犯者;侵入物。

in·valid¹ /ɪnˈvælɪd; ɪnˈvælɪd/ *adj* not valid: 无效的;作废的: ~ *excuses/claims/arguments;* 无效的辩解(要求, 论据); *an ~ will/cheque,* eg one without a signature; 无效的(例如未签字的)遗嘱(支票); *declare a marriage* ~. 宣告一婚姻无效。 **in·vali·date** /ɪnˈvælɪdeɪt; ɪnˈvælədet/ *vt* [VP6A] make ~. 使无效;使作废。 **in·vali·da·tion** /ɪnˌvælɪˈdeɪʃn; ɪnˌvæləˈdeʃən/ *n* [U] state of being ~; [C, U] (act of) rendering sth ~: 无效;作废;使某事物无效(之行动): *the invalidation of a passport.* 一护照之无效。 **in·val·id·ity** /ˌɪnvəˈlɪdətɪ; ˌɪnvəˈlɪdətɪ/ *n* [U] state of being ~. 无效。

in·va·lid² /ˈɪnvəlɪd; ˈɪnvəlɪd/ *adj* **1** weak or disabled through illness or injury: 因生病或受伤而虚弱或残废的;病弱的;伤残的: *a home of rest for ~ soldiers.* 伤病士兵之休养所。 **2** suitable for an ~: 适于伤病的: *an ~ chair,* one with wheels; 病人坐的轮椅; *an ~ diet.* 病人用的饮食。 □ *n* ~ person. 伤残者;病人。 □ *vt* [VP15A] (esp of members of the armed forces) remove from active service as an ~; send (*home*) as an ~: 因伤病而使(尤指军中人员)退役; 因伤病而遣返家乡: *be ~ed home;* 因伤病而退役回乡; ~*ed out of the army.* 因伤病而退役。 ~*·ism* /-ɪzəm; -ɪzəm/ *n* chronic ill health. 久病衰羽;慢性虚弱病。

in·valu·able /ɪnˈvæljuəbl; ɪnˈvæljəbl/ *adj* ~ *(to),* of value too high to be measured: 价值高到无法估量的;无价的: *Her services are* ~ *to me.* 她的服务对我是非常珍贵的。

in·vari·able /ɪnˈveərɪəbl; ɪnˈvɛrɪəbl/ *adj* never changing; unchangeable; constant: 永不变的;无变化的;恒久的: *an ~ pressure/temperature.* 不变的压力(气温)。 **in·vari·ably** /-əblɪ; -əblɪ/ *adv*

in·va·sion /ɪnˈveɪʒn; ɪnˈveʒən/ *n* [U] invading or being invaded; [C] instance of this: 侵略;侵犯;被侵袭;侵害: *an ~ of privacy.* 侵扰清居。

in·vas·ive /ɪnˈveɪsɪv; ɪnˈvesɪv/ *adj* making invasion; tending to spread. 侵略的;侵入的;蔓延性的。

in·vec·tive /ɪnˈvektɪv; ɪnˈvɛktɪv/ *n* [U] abusive language: 抨击的言语; 谩骂: *speeches filled with* ~; 充满抨击的演说; (*pl*) curses; violent expressions: (复)咒语;骂人的话: *a stream of coarse ~s.* 一连串下流的骂人话。

in·veigh /ɪnˈveɪ; ɪnˈve/ *vi* [VP3A] ~ *against sb/sth,* speak bitterly; attack violently in words. 痛骂;用言语猛烈抨击。

in·veigle /ɪnˈveɪgl; ɪnˈvigl/ *vt* [VP14] ~ *sb into (doing) sth,* trick by using flattery, deception, etc: 诱骗: ~ *sb into investing his money unwisely.* 诱骗某人将钱乱投资。

in·vent /ɪnˈvent; ɪnˈvɛnt/ *vt* [VP6A] **1** create or design (sth not existing before): 发明;创造: *When was the steam engine ~ed?* 蒸汽机是何时发明的? Cf 参较 *discover,* find sth existing before, but unknown. 指发现早已存在, 但不为人们所知的东西。 **2** make up, think of: 虚构;杜撰: ~ *a story/an excuse.* 虚构一故事(借口)。 **in·ven·tive** /ɪnˈventɪv; ɪnˈvɛntɪv/ *adj* able to ~: 有发明力的;有创造力的;有发明才智的: *an ~ive mind;* 有创造力的头脑; ~*ive powers.* 发明力。 **in·ven·tor** /-tə; -ɪzom/ *n* person who ~s things. 发明者。

in·ven·tion /ɪnˈvenʃn; ɪnˈvɛnʃən/ *n* **1** [U] inventing: 发明;创造;虚构: *the ~ of the telephone;* 电话的发明; capacity for inventing: 发明之才能; 杜撰之才: *Necessity is the mother of* ~. 需要为发明之母。 **2** [C] sth invented: 发明物; 虚构的事物: *the numerous ~s of Edison;* 爱迪生发明的许多东西; *newspapers that are full of ~s,* invented, untrue stories. 充满不实报导的报纸。

in·ven·tory *US:* -tɔːrɪ; ˈɪnvənˌtɔrɪ/ *n* (*pl* -**ries**) detailed list, eg of household goods, furniture, etc. 详细目录(例如动产, 家具等的清单);财产清册;存货;盘存。

in·verse /ɪnˈvɜːs; ɪnˈvɜrs/ *adj* inverted; reversed in position, direction or relations: 倒转的;〈位置, 方向或关系〉颠倒的: ~ *ratio/proportion,* that between two

quantities one of which increases proportionately as the other decreases. 反比 (反比例)。 □ *n* /ɪnvɜːs; ɪnˈvɜːs/ [U] inverted state. 倒转; 颠倒。 ~·ly *adv*

in·vert /ɪnˈvɜːt; ɪnˈvɚt/ *vt* [VP6A] put upside down or in the opposite order, position or arrangement: 倒转; 上下倒置; 前后颠倒。 *a glass*, so that it is bottom upwards. 倒放杯子。 **~ed 'commas**, quotation marks (" " or ' '). 引号 (" " 或 ' ')。 ⇨ **App 9.** 参看附九。 **in·ver·sion** /ɪnˈvɜːʃn US: -ʒn; ɪnˈvɚʃən/ *n* [U] ~ing or being ~ed; [C] instance of this; sth ~ed. 倒转; 倒置; 倒转物; 倒置物。

in·vert·ebrate /ɪnˈvɜːtɪbrɪt; ɪnˈvɚtəbrɪt/ *adj* not having a backbone or spinal column, eg molluscs, insects, worms; (fig) weak-willed. 无脊椎的(例如软体动物, 昆虫, 蠕虫); (喻)意志薄弱的。 □ *n* ~ animal. 无脊椎动物。

in·vest /ɪnˈvest; ɪnˈvest/ *vt, vi* 1 [VP6A, 14] ~ (*in*), put (money in): 投资; 投资于: ~ £1000 *in government stock*; 投资一千英镑于公债; ~ *one's savings in a business enterprise*. 将储金投资于一企业。 2 [VP3A] ~ *in*, (colloq) buy (sth considered useful): (口)购买(认为有用之物): ~ *in a new kettle*. 买一把新的开水壶。 3 [VP14] ~ *with*, clothe; endow; decorate; surround (with qualities): 包覆; 授与; 授以勋章; 使笼罩(某种性质): *The military governor has been ~ed with full authority*. 该军政长官被授以全权。 *The old ruins were ~ed with romance*. 那古废墟富有传奇色彩。 4 [VP6A] surround a fort, town, etc with armed forces; lay siege to. 包围(要塞, 城镇等); 围攻。 ~**or** /-tə(r); -tɚ/ *n* person who ~s money. 投资者。 ~**·ment** *n* 1 [U] ~ing money: 投资: *By careful ~ment of his capital, he obtained a good income*. 由于慎重的投资, 他获得很好的收入。 2 [C] sum of money that is ~ed; that in which money is ~ed: 投入的资本; 投资额; 投资的对象: *an ~ment of £500 in oil shares*; 投资五百英镑于石油股票; *wise and profitable ~ments*. 明智而有利的投资。 3 [U] act of ~ing a town, fort, etc; blockade. 包围(城, 要塞等); 封锁。 4 = **investiture**.

in·ves·ti·gate /ɪnˈvestɪgeɪt; ɪnˈvestəˌget/ *vt* [VP6A] examine, inquire into; make a careful study of: 调查; 审查: ~ *a crime*; *the causes of a railway accident*; 调查一犯罪案(火车失事原因); ~ *the market for sales of a product*. 为一产品的销路调查市场。 **in·ves·ti·ga·tor** /-tə(r); -tɚ/ *n* person who ~s. 调查者; 审查者。 **in·ves·ti·ga·tion** /ɪnˌvestɪˈgeɪʃn; ɪnˌvestəˈgeʃən/ *n* [U] careful and thorough inquiry; [C] instance of this: 调查; 审查: *The matter is under investigation*. 此事在调查中。

in·ves·ti·ture /ɪnˈvestɪtʃə(r) US: -tʃʊər; ɪnˈvestətʃɚ/ *n* (from **invest**(3)) ceremony of investing sb *with* an office, rank, power or dignity. (由 invest 第 3 义而来)授权, 授爵, 授权等之仪式(与 with 连用)。

in·vest·ment ⇨ **invest**.

in·vet·er·ate /ɪnˈvetərət; ɪnˈvetɚrɪt/ *adj* (esp of habits, feelings) deep-rooted; long-established: (尤指习惯, 感情)根深蒂固的; 由来已久的: *an ~ smoker*; 积习已久的抽烟者; ~ *prejudices*. 根深蒂固的偏见。

in·vid·i·ous /ɪnˈvɪdɪəs; ɪnˈvɪdɪəs/ *adj* likely to cause ill-feeling (because of real or apparent injustice): (由于真正的或表面上的不公)易引起反感的; 易招怨恨的: *make ~ distinctions*. 造成易引起反感的差别。 ~**·ly** *adv*

in·vigi·late /ɪnˈvɪdʒɪleɪt; ɪnˈvɪdʒəˌlet/ *vi, vt* [VP2A, 6A] watch over (eg students during examinations.) 监考。 **in·vigi·la·tor** /-tə(r); -tɚ/ *n* person who ~s. 监考员。 **in·vigi·la·tion** /ɪnˌvɪdʒɪˈleɪʃn; ɪnˌvɪdʒɪˈleʃən/ *n* [U, C].

in·vig·or·ate /ɪnˈvɪgəreɪt; ɪnˈvɪgəˌret/ *vt* [VP6A] make vigorous; give strength or courage to: 使有生气; 鼓舞: *an invigorating climate/speech*. 令人奋发的气候(演说)。

in·vin·cible /ɪnˈvɪnsəbl; ɪnˈvɪnsəbl/ *adj* too strong to be overcome or defeated: 不能克服的; 不能征服的;

an ~ will. 坚强的意志。 **in·vin·cibly** /-əblɪ; -əblɪ/ *adv* **in·vin·ci·bil·ity** /ɪnˌvɪnsəˈbɪlətɪ; ɪnˌvɪnsəˈbɪlətɪ/ *n* [U].

in·vio·lable /ɪnˈvaɪələbl; ɪnˈvaɪələbl/ *adj* (formal) not to be violated, dishonoured or profaned: (正式用语)不可侵犯的; 不容亵渎的: *an ~ oath/law*. 不容违背的誓言(法律)。

in·vio·late /ɪnˈvaɪələt; ɪnˈvaɪəlɪt/ *adj* (formal) kept sacred; held in respect; not violated: (正式用语)神圣的; 受敬重的; 不可侵犯的: *keep an oath/a promise/rule ~*; 坚守一誓约(诺言, 规则); *remain ~*. 保持不可侵犯。

in·vis·ible /ɪnˈvɪzəbl; ɪnˈvɪzəbl/ *adj* that cannot be seen: 看不见的: *stars that are ~ to the naked eye*. 肉眼看不见的星星。 ~ **exports/imports**, money that goes out of/comes into a country as interest on capital, payments for shipping services, tourist expenditure, etc. 无形输出(入)(如投资的利息, 运费, 观光费等收支)。 ~ **ink**, ink which, when used for writing, can be seen only after treatment by heat, etc. 隐形墨水(经加热等始显出的一种墨水)。 ~ **mending**, repair of woven materials, silk stockings, etc by interweaving threads so that the repair is hardly noticeable. 看不出的修补(编织物, 丝袜等几乎看不出的修补); 绣补。 **in·vis·ibly** /-əblɪ; -əblɪ/ *adv* **in·visi·bil·ity** /ɪnˌvɪzəˈbɪlətɪ; ɪnˌvɪzəˈbɪlətɪ/ *n* [U].

in·vite /ɪnˈvaɪt; ɪnˈvaɪt/ *vt* 1 [VP15A, B, 17] ask (sb to do sth, come somewhere, etc): 邀请: ~ *a friend to dinner/to one's house*. 请一朋友吃饭(到家里来)。 *He didn't ~ me in*. 他未请我人内。 *We are old now, and seldom get ~d out*. 我们现在老了, 很少受邀外出。 2 [VP6A] ask for: 要求; 请求: ~ *questions/opinions/confidences*. 请人提出问题(发表意见, 说出心里的秘密)。 3 [VP6A, 17] encourage: 鼓励; 引诱: *The cool water of the lake ~d us to swim*. 清凉的湖水使我们想游泳。 *Don't leave the windows open—it's inviting thieves to enter*. 不要让窗子开着—那会引诱盗贼进入。 ~ /ˈɪnvaɪt; ˈɪnvaɪt/ (sl) = **invitation**(2). **in·vit·ing** *adj* tempting; attractive. 诱惑的; 动人的。 **in·vit·ing·ly** *adv* in an inviting way: 诱惑地; 动人地: *The doors were invitingly open*, open in a way that ~d people to enter. 门大开着像是邀人人内。 **in·vi·ta·tion** /ˌɪnvɪˈteɪʃn; ˌɪnvɪˈteʃən/ *n* 1 [U] inviting or being ~d: 邀请; 被邀请: *a letter of invitation*; 邀请函; *admission by invitation only*. 非请勿入。 2 [C] request to come or go somewhere, or do sth: 邀请的表示; 请帖; 招待券: *send out invitations to a party*. 发出宴客请帖。

in·vo·ca·tion /ˌɪnvəˈkeɪʃn; ˌɪnvəˈkeʃən/ *n* ⇨ **invoke**.

in·voice /ˈɪnvɔɪs; ˈɪnvɔɪs/ *vt, n* [VP6A] (make a) list of goods sold with the prices charged: (开)发票; (开)发货单: ~ *sb for goods*. 给某人开货物发货单。

in·voke /ɪnˈvəʊk; ɪnˈvok/ *vt* 1 [VP6A] call upon God, the power of the law, etc for help or protection. 祈求(上帝, 法律的力量等)帮助或保护。 2 [VP6A, 14] ~ *sth on/upon*, request earnestly; call down from heaven: 恳求; 迫切地要求; 祈求天降…: ~ *vengeance on one's enemies*. 祈求天神向敌人报仇。 3 [VP6A] summon up (by magic): (以法术)召唤: ~ *evil spirits*. 召唤邪鬼。 **in·vo·ca·tion** /ˌɪnvəˈkeɪʃn; ˌɪnvəˈkeʃən/ *n* [U] invoking or being ~d; [C] prayer or appeal that ~s. 祈求; 祈祷; 恳求; 以法术召唤; 召魂或诱惑贼进人的咒语。

in·vol·un·tary /ɪnˈvɒləntrɪ US: -terɪ; ɪnˈvɑlənˌterɪ/ *adj* done without intention; done unconsciously: 非本意的; 不随意的; 不知不觉的: *an ~ movement of fear*. 由于恐惧所引起的不随意的动作。 **in·vol·un·tar·ily** /ɪnˈvɒləntrəlɪ US: ɪnˌvɒlənˈterəlɪ; ɪnˈvɑlənˌterəlɪ/ *adv*

in·vo·lute /ˈɪnvəluːt; ˈɪnvəˌljut/ *adj* complex; intricate: (bot) curled spirally. 复杂的; 错杂的; (植物)内旋的; 卷成螺状的。 **in·vo·lu·tion** /ˌɪnvəˈluːʃn; ˌɪnvəˈluʃən/ *n* anything internally complex or intricate. 任何内部复杂错综之物。

in·volve /ɪnˈvɒlv; ɪnˈvɑlv/ *vt* 1 [VP6A, 14] ~

(in), cause (sb or sth) to be caught or mixed up (in trouble, etc); get (sb or sth) into a complicated or difficult condition: 使陷于(麻烦等中); 使卷入复杂或困难的情况: *They are deeply ~d in debt.* 他们债台高筑. *Don't ~ yourself in unnecessary expense.* 勿做不必要的花费. **2** [VP6A, B, 19C] have as a necessary consequence: 产生某种必然结果; 牵涉; 包含: *To accept the position you offer would ~ my living in London.* 若接受你所提出的职位, 我必然得住在伦敦了. *The war ~d a great increase in the national debt.* 那战争使国债大为增加. **~d** *adj* **1** complex: 复杂的: *an ~d sentence/ explanation;* 复杂的句子(说明); *Henry James's ~d style of writing.* 亨利·詹姆斯的复杂文体. **2** *be/become/get ~d in sth/with sb,* be, etc concerned with sth/connected with sb: 与某事(某人)有关连: *become ~d in criminal activities;* 与犯罪活动有关连; *get emotionally ~d with sb.* 与某人相爱. **~·ment** *n*

in·vul·ner·able /ɪn'vʌlnərəbl; ɪn'vʌlnərəbl/ *adj* that cannot be wounded or hurt: 不能伤害的: (fig)(喻) *in an ~ position.* 处于无懈可击的地位.

in·ward /'ɪnwəd; 'ɪnwəd/ *adj* **1** situated within; inner: 在内的; 内部的: *~ happiness,* ie of the spirit: 内在的快乐(即精神的快乐); *one's ~* (ie mental or spiritual) *nature.* 一个人内在的性情(或心性). **2** turned towards the inside: 向内的: *an ~ curve.* 向内的弧线. **~·ly** *adv* in mind or spirit: 内心或精神方面: *grieve ~ly,* ie so as not to show one's grief. 苦在心里(不将痛苦表现出来). **~·ness** *n* (person's) inner nature; spiritual quality: (人之)心性; 本性; 本质: *the true ~ness of Christ's teaching.* 基督教义真正的本质. **~(s)** *adv* towards the inside; into or towards the mind or soul. 向内; 入人心中; 向心灵.

in·wrought /ˌɪn'rɔːt; ɪn'rɔt/ *adj* (of a fabric) decorated *(with a pattern,* etc); (of a pattern or design) worked or woven *(in* or *on).* (指织物) 绣有 (花型等) 的 (与 with 连用); (指花型或图案) 绣入的(与 in 或 on 连用).

iod·ine /'aɪədiːn US: -daɪn; 'aɪə,daɪn/ *n* [U] nonmetallic element (symbol **I**) found in seawater and seaweed, widely used as an antiseptic (in the form *tincture of ~*) and in photography. 碘(存于海水和海藻中的非金属元素, 符号为 I, 制成碘酒普遍用做消毒剂, 亦用于摄影).

ion /'aɪən; 'aɪən/ *n* electrically charged particle formed by losing or gaining electrons. Such particles make a solution of certain chemicals a conductor of electricity. 离子. **ion·ize** /'aɪənaɪz; 'aɪə,aɪz/ *vi, vt* [VP2A, 6A] be converted or convert into ions. (使)变成离子; 电离. **ion·iz·ation** /ˌaɪənaɪ'zeɪʃn US: -nɪ'z-; ,aɪənɪ'zeʃən/ *n* [U]. **iono·sphere** /aɪ'ɒnəsfɪə(r); aɪ'anə,sfɪr/ *n* (also known as 亦称作 the *Heaviside Layer)* set of layers of the earth's atmosphere, which reflect radio waves and cause them to follow the earth's contour. 电离层(大气之一层, 反射电波并传送至地球各处).

Ionic /aɪ'ɒnɪk; aɪ'anɪk/ *adj* (archit) of the type of column (I) in ancient Greek architecture having scrolls on the capital (4). (建筑) 爱奥尼亚式的(古希腊之一种建筑式, 其柱头有涡卷形装饰). ⇨ the illus at **column.** 参看 column 之插图.

iota /aɪ'əʊtə; aɪ'otə/ *n* the Greek letter ι; (fig) smallest amount: 希腊字母(ι); (喻)极小量: *not an ~ of truth in the story,* nothing at all. 故事中毫无真实性.

I O U /ˌaɪ əʊ 'juː; ,aɪ,o'ju/ *n* (= *I owe you*) signed paper acknowledging that one owes the sum of money stated. 借据; 欠条(其本义为'我欠你'或'兹借到').

ipse dixit /ˌɪpsɪ 'dɪksɪt; 'ɪpsɪ'dɪksɪt/ (Lat) (= *he himself said it*) dogmatic statement made on sb's unsupported word. (拉)武断的陈述; 武断的言谈.

ipso facto /ˌɪpsəʊ 'fæktəʊ; 'ɪpso'fækto/ *adv phrase* (Lat) by that very fact. (拉)就该事实而而论.

iras·cible /ɪ'ræsəbl; aɪ'ræsəbl/ *adj* (formal) easily made angry. (正式用语) 易怒的; 性情暴躁的. **iras·ci·bil·ity** /ɪˌræsə'bɪlətɪ; aɪ,ræsə'bɪlətɪ/ *n* tendency to anger; angry behaviour. 易怒; 性情暴躁.

irate /aɪ'reɪt; 'aɪret/ *adj* (formal) angry. (正式用语) 发怒的; 愤怒的. **~·ly** *adv*

ire /'aɪə(r); aɪr/ *n* (poet or formal) anger. (诗中或正式用语) 发怒; 愤怒. **ire·ful** /-fl; -fəl/ *adj* angry. 愤怒的.

iri·des·cent /ˌɪrɪ'desnt; ,ɪrə'desnt/ *adj* (formal) showing colours like those of the rainbow; changing colour as light falls from different directions. (正式用语) 呈虹彩的; 现晕光的. **iri·des·cence** /-'desns; -'desns/ *n* [U].

irid·ium /ɪ'rɪdɪəm; aɪ'rɪdɪəm/ *n* [U] hard white metal (symbol Ir). 铱(一种坚硬的白色金属, 符号为 Ir).

iris /'aɪərɪs; 'aɪrɪs/ *n* **1** coloured part round the pupil of the eye. 眼球之虹彩; 虹膜. ⇨ the illus at eye. 参看 eye 之插图. **2** kinds of flowering plant with sword-shaped leaves. 鸢尾属植物.

Irish /'aɪərɪʃ; 'aɪrɪʃ/ *adj* of Ireland: 爱尔兰的: *the ~ Free State/the ~ Republic* (also 亦作 *Eire* /'eərə; 'erə/), part of Ireland that became independent in 1922. 爱尔兰自由邦; 爱尔兰共和国(爱尔兰之一部, 于 1922 年独立). *, ~ 'stew,* one of mutton, boiled with onions and other vegetables. (加洋葱和其他蔬菜煮成的)燉羊肉. □ *n* the ~ language (= *Gaelic,* ⇨ *Gael*). 爱尔兰语. the ~, ~ people. 爱尔兰人. **~·man** /-mən; -mən/ *n* (*pl* -men) **· woman** /-wumən; -wumən/ *n* (*pl* -women) native of Ireland. 爱尔兰人; 爱尔兰女人.

irk /ɜːk; ɝk/ *vt* trouble; annoy 使厌烦; 使苦恼 (chiefly in 主要用于): *It irks me to (do sth).* 我讨厌(做某事). **irk·some** /-səm; -səm/ *adj* tiresome. 令人厌烦的.

iron[1] /'aɪən US: 'aɪərn; 'aɪən/ *n* **1** [U] commonest of all metallic elements (symbol Fe), used in various forms. (⇨ *cast* ⇨ *cast[1](3), wrought* ⇨ *wrought*): 铁(符号为 Fe): *~ ore;* 铁矿; *as hard as ~;* 铁一般坚硬; (fig) (喻) *an ~ will.* 坚强的意志. *rule with a rod of ~/with an ~ hand,* with extreme severity. 以铁制; 施高压政策统治. *a man of ~,* a hard, unyielding or merciless man. 铁汉; 意志坚强之人; 铁石心肠之人. *an ~ fist in a velvet glove,* an appearance of gentleness concealing severity, determination. 外柔内刚. *Strike while the ~ is hot,* act while the opportunity is good. 打铁趁热; 把握良机. **the 'I~ Age,** prehistoric period, following the Bronze Age, when ~ came into use for tools and weapons. 铁器时代. *~ curtain,* (fig) frontier between countries, considered as a barrier to information and trade. (喻) 铁幕 (使一国与其他国家在消息和贸易上隔绝的界线). *~ lung,* apparatus fitted over the whole body, except the head, to provide a person with artificial respiration by the use of mechanical pumps. 铁肺(装于身体四周, 头部除外, 借机械气筒造成人工呼吸的装置). *~ rations,* store of food for use in an emergency as for troops/explorers. 铁粮; 携带口粮(应急之用, 例如军队或探测者所用者). **2** [C] (esp in compounds) tool, etc made of ~: (尤用于复合词中)铁器: (*'flat~*), flat-bottomed household implement, heated (usu electrically) and used for smoothing clothes, etc; 熨斗; *'fire~s,* poker, tongs, etc used at a fireplace or stove; 火炉用具 (拨火棒, 火钳等); golf-club with an ~ head; branding tool; 铁头高尔夫球棒; 烙铁; (*pl*) fetters: (复)镣铐: *put sb in ~s,* fasten his wrists and ankles in chains. 给某人加以镣铐. *have too many ~s in the fire,* too many undertakings needing attention at the same time. 同时要办的事太多. **3** (compounds) (复合词) *~·clad adj* protected by ~. 装甲的; 装甲的. *'~·foundry n* foundry where cast ~ is produced. 铸铁厂. *,~·'grey adj, n* (of) the colour of freshly broken cast~. 铁灰色(的). *'~·monger* /-mʌŋɡə(r); -,mʌŋɡə/ *n* dealer in metal goods. 五金商. *'~ mongery* /-mʌŋɡərɪ; -,mʌŋɡərɪ/ *n* business of an ~monger. 五金业. *'~·mould n* discolouration caused by ~ rust or ink. 锈痕; 墨水痕. *'~·side n* one of Oliver Cromwell's cavalry troopers (17thc); (fig) tough, obstinate man. 十七世纪克伦威尔所率骑兵队之队员; (喻) 刚毅固执之人. *'~·ware* /-weə(r); -,wɛr/ *n*

[U] goods made of ~; hardware. 铁器;五金。 '~**work** *n* anything made of ~, eg gratings, rails, railings. 铁制之物(例如栅栏、铁轨等)。 '~-**works** *n* (usu with *sing v*) place where ~ is smelted or where heavy ~ goods are made. (通常用单数动词)炼铁厂;铁工厂。

iron² /'aɪən *US*: 'aɪərn; 'aɪɚn/ *vt, vi* [VP6A, 15A, B, 2A, C] smooth cloth/clothes with an ~ (a 'flat-~): (以熨斗)熨平(衣物)。 ~ *a shirt*. 熨一衬衫。 *Do clothes* ~ *more easily when they are damp?* 衣服潮湿时是否易于熨平? *She's been ~ing all afternoon*. 她一下午都在熨衣服。 ~ **out**, remove by ~ing: 借熨烫而除去: ~ *out wrinkles*; 将皱折熨平; (fig) remove: (喻)消除: ~ *out misunderstandings/points of disagreement*. 消除误会(歧见)。 '~**ing-board** *n* padded board on which to ~ clothes, etc. 熨衣板。

ironic /aɪ'rɒnɪk; aɪ'rɑnɪk/ **ironi·cal** /aɪ'rɒnɪkl; aɪ'rɑnɪkl/ *adj* of, using, expressing, irony: 反语的;用反讽的;讥刺的: *an* ~ *smile/remark/person*. 讥讽的笑(讥刺之言; 喜欢讥讽别人的人)。 **ironi·cally** /-klɪ; -klɪ/ *adv*

irony /'aɪərənɪ; 'aɪrənɪ/ *n* **1** [U] the expression of one's meaning by saying sth which is the direct opposite of one's thoughts, in order to make one's remarks forceful. 反讽; 反语法 (说出与自己思想恰恰相反的话以增强讲话力量之表达法)。 **2** [C] (*pl* **-nies**) event, situation, etc which is itself desirable, but which, because of the circumstances, is of little or no value, thus appearing to be directed by evil fate: 命运的嘲弄; 讥刺性的事件、情况等(本来是一件幸运之事, 但由于环境演变, 而失去价值, 故而象是受了命运的愚弄): *the ~ of fate/circumstances*. 命运(环境)的嘲弄。 *If a poor man inherits a large fortune and dies a month later, one might call it one of life's ironies*. 如果一个穷人继承一大笔财产后一个月便死了, 我们可称之为人生的一大嘲弄。

ir·ra·di·ate /ɪ'reɪdɪeɪt; ɪ'redɪ,et/ *vt* [VP6A] (formal) (正式用语) **1** send rays of light upon; subject to sunlight, ultraviolet rays, or radioactivity; (fig) throw light on (a subject). 照耀; 照射; 使接受阳光或放射线照射; (喻)阐释(一问题); 启发。 **2** light up: 使生辉: *faces ~d with joy*. 因高兴而焕发的面孔。

ir·ra·tional /ɪ'ræʃənl; ɪ'ræʃənl/ *adj* **1** not endowed with reason: 无理性的: *behave like an ~ animal*. 举止像一无理性的野兽。 **2** not guided by reason: 荒谬的; 不合理的: ~ *fears/behaviour*. 荒唐无稽的恐惧(行为)。 ~**ly** /-ʃnəlɪ; -ʃənl,ɪ/ *adv*

ir·rec·on·cil·able /ɪ,rekən'saɪləbl; ɪ'rekən,saɪləbl/ *adj* (formal) (of persons) that cannot be reconciled: (of ideas, actions) that cannot be brought into harmony. (正式用语)(指人)不能和解的; (指思想, 行动)不能调和的。

ir·re·cover·able /ɪrɪ'kʌvərəbl; ,ɪrɪ'kʌvərəbl/ *adj* (formal) that cannot be recovered or remedied: (正式用语)不能挽回的; 不能治疗的; 不能补救的: ~ *losses*. 不可挽回的损失。

ir·re·deem·able /,ɪrɪ'diːməbl; ,ɪrɪ'diməbl/ *adj* **1** (of paper currency) that cannot be exchanged for coin; (of government annuities) that cannot be terminated by repayment. (指纸币)不能兑换的; (指政府年金)不能借偿还而终止的。 **2** that cannot be restored, reclaimed, saved: 不能恢复的; 不可救药的; 不能挽救的: *an ~ loss/misfortune*. 不能挽救的损失(不幸)。

ir·re·den·tist /ɪrɪ'dentɪst; ,ɪrɪ'dentɪst/ *n* person who advocates the reunion to his own country of territory which has been lost to a foreign government, or which is culturally related to his own country, as Italy of Italian-speaking districts. 主张国土统一者(主张收复丧失之领土或将与本国文化相关之地区并入国土之人, 例如有些意大利人想使说意大利语地区并入意大利)。 **ir·ri·den·tism** /-ɪzəm; -ɪzṃ/ *n*

ir·re·duc·ible /ɪrɪ'djuːsəbl *US*: -'duːs-; ,ɪrɪ'djusəbl/ *adj* ~ **(to)**, (formal) (正式用语) **1** that cannot be reduced or made smaller; 不能减低的; 不能缩小的: £250

is the ~ *minimum for repairs to the house*. 二百五十英镑是修理这房子所需要的最低额了。 **2** that cannot be brought (*to* a desired condition). 不能归复(所期望之状态)的。

ir·re·fut·able /ɪrɪ'fjuːtəbl; ɪ'refjʊtəbl/ *adj* that cannot be proved false: 无法驳倒的: *an ~ argument/case*. 无法反驳的论点(诉讼)。

ir·regu·lar /ɪ'regjʊlə(r); ɪ'regjələ/ *adj* **1** contrary to rules, to what is normal and established: 不合常规的;不规则的;非正规的: *an ~ proceeding/marriage*; 非按正规的处置(非正式的婚姻); *be ~ in church attendance*, be absent frequently; 做礼拜的次数不规则(常常不到); ~ *troops*, not trained for, or not forming part of, the regular army. 非正规军。 **2** uneven; not regular in shape, arrangement, etc: 不平坦的; 不整齐的: ~ *lines and figures*; 零乱的线条和图形; *a coast with an ~ outline*, with many bays, inlets, etc. 曲折的海岸线。 **3** (gram) not inflected in the usual way: (语法)变化不规则的: *'Child' has an ~ plural*. Child 一词之复数变化不规则。 ~ *n* (usu *pl*) member of an ~ military force. (通常用复数)非正规军。 ~·**ly** *adv* ~·**ity** /ɪ,regjʊ'lærətɪ; ɪ,regjə'lærətɪ/ *n* (*pl* **-ties**) [U] state or quality of being ~; [C] sth ~: 不合常规; 不规则; 不整齐; 不规则的事物; 不平坦的东西: ~*ities in behaviour*; 行为反常之处; *the ~ities of the earth's surface*. 地球表面的凹凸不平。

ir·rel·evant /ɪ'reləvənt; ɪ'reləvənt/ *adj* ~ **(to)**, not relevant (to); not connected (with): 不切题的;不相关的: ~ *remarks/evidence*. 不切题的话(证据)。 *What you say is ~ to the subject*. 你说的话不切题。 **ir·rel·evance** /-əns; -əns/, **ir·rel·evancy** /-ənsɪ; -ɪnsɪ/ *nn* (*pl* ~**s**, **-cies**) [U] state of being ~; [C] ~ remark, question, etc: 不切题; 不相关; 不相关的言论, 问题等: *Let us ignore these irrelevancies*. 我们不要管这些不相干的问题。

ir·re·li·gious /ɪrɪ'lɪdʒəs; ,ɪrɪ'lɪdʒəs/ *adj* opposed to, showing no interest in, religion: 反宗教的; 对宗教无兴趣的: ~ *acts/persons*. 反宗教的行为(人)。

ir·re·medi·able /ɪrɪ'miːdɪəbl; ,ɪrɪ'midɪəbl/ *adj* that cannot be remedied: 无可救药的; 不能补救的: ~ *acts/faults*. 不能补救的行为与过失。

ir·re·mov·able /ɪrɪ'muːvəbl; ,ɪrɪ'muvəbl/ *adj* that cannot be removed (esp from office). 不能移动的; (尤指)不能撤免其职务的。

ir·rep·ar·able /ɪ'repərəbl; ɪ'repərəbl/ *adj* (of a loss, injury, etc) that cannot be put right or restored: (指损失、伤害等)不能弥补的; 无可挽救的: ~ *harm*. 无可挽救的伤害。

ir·re·place·able /ɪrɪ'pleɪsəbl; ,ɪrɪ'plesəbl/ *adj* of which the loss cannot be supplied. 不能替换的。

ir·re·press·ible /ɪrɪ'presəbl; ,ɪrɪ'presəbl/ *adj* that cannot be held back or controlled: 不能抑制的; 不能控制的: *a girl with ~ high spirits*. 抑制不住兴高采烈的女孩。

ir·re·proach·able /ɪrɪ'prəʊtʃəbl; ,ɪrɪ'protʃəbl/ *adj* free from blame or fault: 无可责难的; 无过失的: ~ *conduct*. 无可非难的行为。

ir·re·sist·ible /ɪrɪ'zɪstəbl; ,ɪrɪ'zɪstəbl/ *adj* too strong, convincing, delightful, etc to be resisted: (过于坚强、有说服力、令人快乐等而)不可抵抗的; 不能压制的; 禁不住的: ~ *desires/temptations*. 不能抗拒的欲望(诱惑)。 *On this hot day the sea was ~*, We couldn't resist the desire to go to or into the sea. 在这种热天, 我们不禁想到海边去玩。

ir·res·ol·ute /ɪ'rezəluːt; ɪ'rezə,lut/ *adj* undecided; hesitating. 无决断的; 犹豫不决的。 **ir·res·ol·ution** /ɪ,rezə'luːʃn; ,ɪrezə'luʃən/ *n* [U].

ir·re·spec·tive /ɪrɪ'spektɪv; ,ɪrɪ'spektɪv/ *adj* ~ **of**, not paying consideration to; not taking into account: 不考虑; 不顾: *He rushed forward to help*, ~ *of the consequences*. 他不顾后果, 冲上前去救助。

ir·re·spon·sible /ɪrɪ'spɒnsəbl; ,ɪrɪ'spɑnsəbl/ *adj* **1** not responsible for conduct, etc; not to be blamed or

punished: (对行为等) 不须负责任的; 不受指责或惩罚的: an ~ child. 不须负责的孩子。 2 (doing things, done) without a proper sense of responsibility; not trustworthy: (做事)无责任感的; 不可靠的: ~ teenagers; 无责任感的青少年; ~ behaviour. 无责任的行为。 **ir·re·spon·si·bil·ity** /ˌɪrɪˌspɒnsə'bɪlətɪ ; ˌɪrɪˌspɑnsə'bɪlətɪ/ n [U].

ir·re·triev·able /ˌɪrɪ'triːvəbl; ˌɪrɪ'trivəbl/ adj that cannot be retrieved or remedied: 不可挽回的; 不能补救的: an ~ loss. 不能补救的损失。

ir·rev·er·ent /ɪ'revərənt; ɪ'revərənt/ adj feeling or showing no respect for sacred things. 不虔敬的; 不恭敬的。 **~·ly** adv **ir·rev·er·ence** /-əns; -əns/ n [U].

ir·re·vers·ible /ˌɪrɪ'vɜːsəbl; ˌɪrɪ'vɜsəbl/ adj that cannot be reversed or revoked: 不能反转的; 不能撤销的: an ~ decision. 不能取消的决定。

ir·revo·cable /ɪ'revəkəbl; ɪ'revəkəbl/ adj final and unalterable; that cannot be revoked: 已确定而不能改变的; 不能取消的: an ~ decision/judgement; 最后的决定(判决); an ~ letter of credit. 不能取消的信用状。

ir·ri·gate /'ɪrɪgeɪt; 'ɪrəˌget/ vt [VP6A] 1 supply (land, crops) with water (by means of rivers, water-channels, overhead pipes, etc): 灌溉(田地, 作物): ~ desert areas and make them fertile. 灌溉荒芜地区使之变为肥沃良田。 2 construct reservoirs, canals, etc for the distribution of water (to fields): 筑水库, 沟渠等以分配水(至农田)。 3 wash out (a wound, etc) with a constant flow of liquid. 冲洗(伤口等)。 **ir·ri·ga·tion** /ˌɪrɪ'geɪʃn; ˌɪrə'geʃən/ [U] irrigating: 灌溉; 冲洗: (attrib) (用作定语) an irrigation project; 灌溉计划; irrigation canals. 灌溉用的沟渠。

ir·ri·table /'ɪrɪtəbl; 'ɪrətəbl/ adj easily annoyed or made angry. 急躁的; 易怒的。 **ir·ri·tably** /-əblɪ; -əblɪ/ adv **ir·ri·ta·bil·ity** /ˌɪrɪtə'bɪlətɪ; ˌɪrətə'bɪlətɪ/ n [U].

ir·ri·tant /'ɪrɪtənt; 'ɪrətənt/ adj causing irritation. 有刺激性的。 □ n ~ substance, eg dust or pepper in the nose; sth that irritates the mind. 刺激物 (例如鼻孔中之灰尘或胡椒); 使精神受刺激的事物。

ir·ri·tate /'ɪrɪteɪt; 'ɪrəˌtet/ vt [VP6A] 1 make angry or annoyed; excite the temper of: 激怒; 使急躁: ~d by the delay. 被耽搁所激怒。 2 cause discomfort to (part of the body); make sore or inflamed: 使 (身体某部) 感到不适; 刺痛; 使痛或发炎: The smoke ~d her eyes. 烟熏得她眼睛不舒服。 **ir·ri·ta·tion** /ˌɪrɪ'teɪʃn; ˌɪrə'teʃən/ n [U] irritating or being ~d; [C] instance of this. (被)激怒; 愤怒; 刺激; 感到痛或发炎。

ir·rup·tion /ɪ'rʌpʃn; ɪ'rʌpʃən/ n sudden and violent entry; bursting in. 突然冲入; 闯入。

is ⇨ **be**[1]

isin·glass /'aɪzɪŋglɑːs US: -glæs; 'aɪzn̩ˌglæs/ n [U] clear white jelly made from the air bladders of some freshwater fish, used for making glue. 鱼胶(由某些淡水鱼之鳔制成, 用以制胶)。

is·lam /'ɪzlɑːm US: 'ɪsləm; 'ɪsləm/ n faith, religion, proclaimed by the Prophet Muhammad; all Muslims; all the Muslim world. 伊斯兰教信仰; 伊斯兰教; 伊斯兰教徒(总称); 伊斯兰教世界。 **~·ic** /ɪz'læmɪk US: ɪs'lɑːmɪk; ɪs'læmɪk/ adj

is·land /'aɪlənd; 'aɪlənd/ n piece of land surrounded by water; sth resembling an ~ because it is detached or isolated: 岛; 岛屿; 孤立似岛之物: a 'traffic ~, a raised place in a busy street where people may be safe from traffic. (马路上之)安全岛。 **~·er** n person born on or living on an ~. 岛人; 岛民。

isle /aɪl; aɪl/ n island (not much used in prose, except in proper names): 岛; 岛屿 (不用于专有名词外, 罕用于散文中): the I~ of Wight; 怀特岛(在英国); the British I~s. 不列颠诸岛。 **is·let** /'aɪlɪt; 'aɪlɪt/ n small island. 小岛; 小岛屿。

ism /'ɪzəm; 'ɪzəm/ n distinctive doctrine or practice:

主义; 学说; 制度: behaviourism and all the other isms of the twentieth century. 二十世纪之行为主义及所有其他的学说。

isn't ⇨ **be**[1].

iso·bar /'aɪsəbɑː(r); 'aɪsəˌbɑr/ n line on a map, esp a weather chart, joining places with the same atmospheric pressure at a particular time. 等压线(地图上, 尤指气象图上, 连接在某一时间内气压相等之各地点的线)。

iso·late /'aɪsəleɪt; 'aɪslˌet/ vt [VP6A, 14] ~ (from), 1 separate, put or keep apart from others: 使隔离; 使孤立; 使隔绝: feel ~d from one's fellows. 在同伴中感到孤立。 When a person has an infectious disease, he is usually ~d. 当一人患传染病时, 他通常是被隔离起来。 Several villages in the north have been ~d by heavy snowfalls. 北部有几个村庄因大雪而与外界隔绝了。 2 (chem) separate a substance, germ, etc from its combinations. (化学) 分解(物质等); 使游离; 使(细菌)分离。

iso·la·tion /ˌaɪsə'leɪʃn; ˌaɪslˈeʃən/ n [U] ~ (from), isolating or being isolated. 隔离; 孤立; 隔绝; 分解; 分离。 in ~, alone; separated: 单独的; 隔离的: consider facts in ~ from others. 单独考虑某些事实。 '~ **hospital**/**ward**, one for persons with infectious diseases. 隔离医院(病房)。 **~·ism** /-ɪzm; -ɪzm/ n (in international affairs) policy of non-participation in the affairs of other countries. (国际事务中的)孤立主义。 **~·ist** /-ɪst; -ɪst/ n supporter of ~ism. 孤立主义者。

isos·celes /aɪ'sɒsəliːz; aɪ'sɑslˌiz/ adj (of a triangle) having two sides equal. (指三角形) 二等边的; 等腰的。

iso·therm /'aɪsəθɜːm; 'aɪsəˌθɜm/ n line on a map joining places having the same mean temperature. 等温线(地图上连接平均温度相等之地点的线)。

iso·tope /'aɪsətəʊp; 'aɪsəˌtop/ n atom of an element, eg heavy hydrogen, having a nuclear mass different from that of other atoms of the same element although chemically identical: 同位素(同一元素中之原子, 其核质量与其他原子不同而化学性质完全相同者, 如氢中之重氢): radio-active ~s, unstable forms used in medicine and industry. 放射同位素。

issue /'ɪʃuː; 'ɪʃu/ vi, vt 1 [VP2A, 3A] ~ (out/forth) (from), come, go, flow, out: 出来; 发出; 流出: smoke issuing from chimneys; 烟囱冒出的烟; blood issuing from a wound. 自伤口流出的血。 2 [VP4,6A,14] ~ (sth to sb), ~ (sb with sth), distribute for use or consumption: 分发; 发给: ~ warm clothing to the troops; 发暖和的衣服给军队; ~ them with warm clothing. 发给他们暖和的衣服。 3 [VP6A, 14] ~ (to), publish (books,etc); put stamps, banknotes, shares[1] (3), etc into circulation. 出版(书等); 发行(邮票, 钞票, 股票等)。 □ n 1 [U] outgoing; outflowing: 发出; 流出: the point or place of ~; 发出点; [C] the act of flowing out; that which flows out: 流出; 流出物: an ~ of blood from the nose. 鼻子流血。 2 [U] putting forth; sending out; publication: 发行; 出版; 印行: the ~ of a newspaper/a new coinage; 报纸(新币)之发行; buy new stamps on the day of ~; 于发行日购买新邮票; [C] that which is sent out, etc: 发行等之物: new ~s of banknotes; 一定新发行的钞票; the most recent ~s of a periodical; 一定期刊物最近的发行等; an ~ of winter clothing to the troops. 发给军队冬衣。 3 [C] question that arises for discussion: 引起讨论的问题: debate an ~; 为一讨论的问题; raise a new ~; 提出一新问题; argue political ~s. 讨论政治问题。 **join/take ~ with sb (on/about sth)**, proceed to argue with him (about it). 与某人争辩(某事)。 the point/matter at ~, the point being discussed. 争论点; 正在讨论的问题。 4 [C] result; outcome; consequence: 结果; 后果: bring a campaign to a successful ~; 使一运动获致良好结果; await the ~. 等待结果。 5 [U] (legal) offspring: (法律) 子孙: die without ~, ie childless. 死时无子嗣。

isth·mus /'ɪsməs; 'ɪsməs/ n (pl ~es /-sɪz; -sɪz/)

neck of land joining two larger bodies of land: 地峡: *the I~ of Panama*. 巴拿马地峡。

it /ɪt/ *pron* (*pl* **they** /ðeɪ/; ðe/, **them** /ðem; ðəm; *strong form* ðem; ðəm/) **1** (used of lifeless things, of animals (when sex is unknown or unimportant) and of a baby or small child when the sex is unknown or a matter of indifference): 它(指无生命的东西, 性别不明或不重要的动物, 亦指性别不明或无关紧要的婴儿或小孩): *This is my watch; it's a Swiss one.* 这是我的表, 它是瑞士制的。 *Where's my book?— Have you seen it?* 我的书在哪里? 你看见它没有? *'Where's the cat?'—'It's in the garden.'* '猫在哪里?'——'它在花园里。' *She's expecting another baby and hopes it will be a boy.* 她又有孕了, 她希望生个男孩。 **2** (used to refer to a group of words which follows, this being the grammatical subject. This may be)(用以指其后的一组词, 该组词可能为)**(a)** an infinitive phrase: 不定式短语: *It is difficult to learn written Chinese?* 学习中国文字很难吗? **(b)** a construction with *for,* a *noun* / *pronoun,* and a *to*-infinitive: 接for + 名词或代词+不定式: *It was hard for him to live on his small pension.* 依靠菲薄的养老金生活使他感到甚为艰苦。 **(c)** a gerundial phrase: 动名词短语: *It doesn't seem much use going on.* 继续下去似乎没有什么好处。 *It's no use your trying to do that.* 你试图那样做是无用的。 **(d)** a clause: 一从句: *It seems unlikely that he will catch the train.* 他大概赶不上火车了。 *I think it a pity that you didn't try harder.* 我认为你未曾更加努力尝试是一憾事。 *It doesn't matter whether we start now or later.* 我们现在开始还是过以后开始都没有关系。 *Does it matter what you do next?* 你下一步所做的事关系重大吗? **3** (used to refer backwards or forwards to identify sb or sth. Note that if the identity of a person is already known, it is not used): (用以指明前述或后述的人或东西。注意: 若已知为某人时, 则不用 it): *'Who's that at the door?'—'It's the postman.'* '谁在门口?'——'是邮差。' (Cf 参较 *Mr Smith is at the door. He wants to see you.* 史密斯先生在门口, 他想要见你。) *'What was that noise?'—'It was a mouse.'* '那是什么声音?'——'那是一只老鼠。' **4** (used as a formal or meaningless word to supply a subject) (用做形式上的或无意义的主语) **(a)** dealing with the weather, atmospheric conditions, etc: 指天气, 大气状况等: *It is raining* / *snowing, etc.* 正在下雨(下雪等)。 *It's warm* / *cold* / *windy, etc.* 天气温暖(寒冷, 有风等)。 *Isn't it a nice day!* 天气真好! *How dark it is!* 好黑呀! **(b)** for time: 指时间: *It's six o'clock.* 六点钟了。 *It is past midnight.* 已过半夜了。 *It's Monday, the 1st of May.* 今天是五月一日了。 *It is three years since I last met you.* 自从我上次遇见你到现在有三年了。 *It's a month to Christmas.* 距圣诞节还有一个月。 **(c)** for distance: 指距离: *It's ten miles to Oxford.* 到牛津有十英里。 *It's only a short way now.* 现在没有多远了。 **(d)** vaguely for the general situation, or for sth that is to be understood from the context: 模糊地指一般情形, 或指由上下文可以了解的事物: *So it seems.* 好象是如此。 *It can't be helped.* 没有办法了。 *Whose turn is it next?* 下一个轮到谁了? *That's the best* / *worst of it!* 那最好(糟)了! *Keep at it,* ie at whatever you are doing. 继续下去! 不要放弃! *You've got what it takes,* have the qualities, etc needed for this job, situation, etc. 你有资格担任此一工作(有办法应付此一情况等)。 *You've had it,* there's nothing more to be had from this situation, experience, etc. 你已够了(从这个情况, 经验中再也得不到什么了)。 *Go it!* Go on with your efforts, etc. 继续努力! *Now you've done it!* ie You've done sth wrong or foolish! 现在可糟了!(你做了错事或傻事了)! *Now you'll catch it!* You'll be reprimanded, punished, etc! 现在你可倒霉了!(你将受责罚等)! *As it happened,...:* 碰巧...; *If it hadn't been for your help,...:* 倘若没有你的帮助…。 **5** (used to bring into prominence one part of a sentence) (用以加强句中某一部分) **(a)** the subject: 主语: *It was his work during the weekend that exhausted him.* 使他疲惫不堪的是他周末的工作。 **(b)** the object of a *v*: 动词的宾语:

It's the red book that I want, not the green one. 我要的是那本红书, 不是绿书。 **(c)** the object of a *prep*: 介词的宾语: *It was John I gave the book to, not Harry.* 我把书交给约翰的, 不是交给哈里的。 **(d)** an adverbial adjunct: 副词修饰语: *It was on Sunday that I saw him, not on Saturday.* 我看见他的那天是星期天, 不是星期六。 **its** /ɪts; ɪts/ *poss adj* of it: 它的: 他的: *The dog wagged its tail.* 那狗摇着尾巴。 *The child fell and hurt its knee.* 那小孩跌伤了膝盖。 *I don't like this hat—its shape is wrong.* 我不喜欢这帽子——它的式样不对劲。 **itself** /ɪt'self; ɪt'self/ *reflex pron:* 反身代词: *The dog got up and stretched itself.* 那狗站起来伸展一下身子。 *emph pron:* 加强语气的代词: *The thing itself is not valuable, but I want it as a keepsake.* 这东西的本身并无价值, 但我要把它留做纪念品。 **by itself, (a)** automatically: 自动地: *The machine works by itself.* 这机器是自动的。 **(b)** alone: 单独地: *The farmhouse stands by itself in the fields.* 那农舍孤零零地座落在田田中。

italic /ɪ'tælɪk; ɪ'tælɪk/ *adj* (of printed letters): sloping: (指印刷字母)斜体的: *This is ~ type.* 这是斜体。 *n pl ~ letters:* 斜体字母: *in ~s.* 用斜体。 **italicize** /ɪ'tælɪsaɪz; ɪ'tælə,saɪz/ *vt* print in ~s. 用斜体印刷。 ⇨ **Roman (1)**.

itch /ɪtʃ; ɪtʃ/ *n* **1** (with *def* or *indef art,* but rarely *pl*) feeling of irritation on the skin, causing a desire to scratch: (与定冠词或不定冠词连用, 但罕用复数)痒: *have* / *suffer from the ~* / *an ~.* 觉得痒。 **2** (usu with the *indef art* or a *poss adj*) restless desire or longing: (通常与不定冠词或所有格形容词连用)热望; 渴望: *have an ~ for money;* 渴望发财; *his ~ to go to the South Seas.* 他之渴望去南太平洋。 □ *vi* **1** [VP 2A,4A] have an ~: 发痒: *scratch where it ~es.* 搔痒处。 *Scratch yourself if you ~.* 如果你觉得痒, 就搔好了。 *Are your mosquito bites still ~ing?* 你被蚊子咬的地方还在痒吗? **2** [VP 3A] ~ *for,* (colloq) long for: (口)渴望: *The boys were ~ing for the lesson to end.* 那些男孩子渴望快点下课。 *have an ~ing palm,* be ~ing for money. 贪财。 **~y** *adj* (**-ier, -iest**) 发痒的。 发痒的皮肤。

item /'aɪtəm; 'aɪtəm/ *n* **1** single article or unit in a list, etc: (目录等的)条款; 项目: *the first ~ on the programme,* 节目中的第一项; *number the ~s in a catalogue.* 把目录中的项目加以编号。 **2** detail or paragraph (of news): (新闻之)一条; 一则: *Are there any interesting 'news ~s* / *~s of news in the paper this morning?* 今晨报上有什么有趣的新闻没有? □ *adv* also (used to introduce successive articles in a list): 又; 亦(用以介绍目录中连续的项目): *I~, one chair; ~, two carpets.* 椅子一把, 又地毯两张。 **~ize** /-aɪz; -aɪz/ *vt* [VP 6A] give, write, every ~ of: 分项列举; 分条列记: *an ~ized account;* 细帐; *~ize a bill.* 详列一帐单。

it·er·ate /'ɪtəreɪt; 'ɪtə,reɪt/ *vt* [VP 6A] say again and again; make (an accusation, etc) repeatedly. 重复地说; 反复予以(控诉等)。 **it·er·ation** /,ɪtə'reɪʃn; ,ɪtə'reʃən/ *n* [U] iterating; [C] sth ~d. 重述; 反复说的话。

i·tin·er·ant /aɪ'tɪnərənt; aɪ'tɪnərənt/ *adj* travelling from place to place: 巡回的: *~ musicians.* 巡回的乐师们。

i·tin·er·ary /aɪ'tɪnərərɪ *US*: -rerɪ; aɪ'tɪnə,rɛrɪ/ *n* (*pl* -ries) [C] plan for, details or records of, a journey; route. 旅行计划; 旅行日志; 旅行路线。

it'll /ɪtl; 'ɪtl/ = it will.

it's /ɪts; ɪts/ = it is; it has.

its, it·self /ɪts, ɪt'self; ɪts, ɪt'self/ ⇨ **it**.

I've /aɪv; aɪv/ = I have.

ivory /'aɪvərɪ; 'aɪvərɪ/ *n* [U] white, bone-like substance forming the tusks of elephants, used for ornaments, piano-keys, etc; (attrib) the colour of ~: 象牙(质), (用做装饰品、钢琴键等); (用作定语)象牙色的: *an ~ skin* / *complexion.* 乳白色的皮肤(面色)。 **~ tower,** place of seclusion or retreat from the realities of life. 象牙塔(与世隔绝之境界)。

ivy /'aɪvɪ; 'aɪvɪ/ n [U] climbing, clinging, evergreen plant with dark, shiny (often five-pointed) leaves. 常春藤 (一种攀附性长青植物，叶子深色发亮，通常有五个尖). **ivied** /'aɪvɪd; 'aɪvɪd/ adj covered with ivy: 长满常春藤的: ivied walls. 长满常春藤的墙壁.

ivy

Jj

J, j /dʒeɪ; dʒe/ (pl **J's, j's** /dʒeɪz; dʒez/) the tenth letter of the English alphabet. 英文字母之第十个字母.

jab /dʒæb; dʒæb/ vt, vi (-bb-) 1 [VP3A] jab at, poke or push at sb/sth with force: 猛戳; 猛推: jab at sb/sth with a knife. 用刀猛戳某人(某物). He jabbed at his opponent, (boxing) aimed a quick blow at him. (拳击)他猛击他的对手. 2 [VP14] jab sth into sth/sb, force sth into sth/sb: 以…猛戳: He jabbed his elbow into my side. 他用肘猛戳我的腰部. 3 [VP15B] jab sth out, force or push out by jabbing: 戳出: Be careful! Don't jab my eye out with your umbrella! 当心你的伞不要戳到我的眼睛! □ n sudden, rough blow or thrust: 猛戳; 猛击; 猛刺: a jab in the arm, (colloq) an injection or inoculation. (口)臂上打针或接种. Have you had your cholera jabs yet? 你打过霍乱预防针了吗?

jabber /'dʒæbə(r); 'dʒæbɚ/ vi, vt 1 [VP2A, C] talk excitedly; talk in what seems to be a rapid and confused manner: 兴奋地说; 似是急促而含糊地讲述: Listen to those children ~ing away! 听听那些孩子们叽哩咕噜地说个不停! 2 [VP6A, 15B] utter (words, etc) rapidly and indistinctly: 急促而模糊地说出(话等): ~ (out) one's prayers. 嘀嘀地祈祷. □ n [U] ~ing; chatter: 急促而含糊的说; 叽哩咕噜的说; 喋喋不休: Listen to the ~ of those monkeys. 听那些猴子吱吱喳喳的叫. ~er n person who ~s. 说话急促含糊的人.

jabot /'ʒæbəʊ; ʒæ'bo/ n [C] ornamental frill on the front of a woman's blouse or a man's shirt. 男女衬衫胸部的装饰绉褶.

jack¹ /dʒæk; dʒæk/ n 1 J~, familiar form of the name John. John 的昵称. J~ Frost, frost personified. (拟人语)霜. 'J~ in office, self-important official who fusses over details. 摆架子的官吏. J~ of 'all trades, person who can turn his hand to anything; workman knowing something of many trades. 百事通; 万能博士; 对许多事都懂一点的人; 博艺而不精的工人. before one can say J~ Robinson, very quickly or suddenly. 迅速地; 突然地. J~ is as good as his master, the workman is the equal of his employer. 伙计不比老板差. 2 (colloq) man. (口)人. every man ~, everybody. 每个人; 人人. 3 (usu portable) device for raising heavy weights off the ground, esp one for raising the axle of a car so that a wheel may be changed. (通常可用手提的)顶重器; (尤指)(支起汽车轮轴的)千斤顶. 4 (in the game of bowls) small white ball towards which bowls are rolled. (滚木球戏中) 小白球(木球即向该球滚去). 5 ship's flag to show nationality. 船舰上表示国籍的旗. the Union J~, flag of the United Kingdom. 英国国旗. ⇨ the illus at flag. 参看 flag 之插图. '~ staff n staff on which a ship's flag is flown to show nationality. 船旗杆(船舰上用以悬挂国旗者). 6 (in a pack of playing-cards) knave. (纸牌中之)杰克. 7 (compounds) (复合词) '~-in-the-box n toy in the form of a box with sth inside which springs up when the lid is opened. 玩偶盒(一种盒状玩具, 盖启开时, 有一玩偶跳出). ,~-o'-'lantern n pumpkin cut to look like a face and used as a lantern (by placing a candle inside) in fun. 鬼火; 南瓜制成的人面形灯笼. '~ rabbit n large hare of Western N America. 北美西部所产之一种大野兔. ~ tar n (old name for a) naval rating; ordinary seaman in the Navy, wearing a jumper and wide-bottomed trousers. 海军兵类之旧称; 普通水兵(穿套头上衣及喇叭裤).

jack² /dʒæk; dʒæk/ vt [VP15B] ~ sth in, (sl) abandon (the work, attempt, etc). (俚)放弃(工作, 企图等). ~ sth up, lift with a jack(3): 用重器或千斤顶抬起: J~ up the car and change the wheel with the punctured tyre. 用千斤顶将汽车抬起, 把跑气的轮胎换掉.

jackal /'dʒækɔːl US: -kl; 'dʒækɔl/ n wild dog-like animal. 胡狼.

jack·a·napes /'dʒækəneɪps; 'dʒækə,neps/ n 1 conceited person. 自负的人. 2 (often playfully of a child) impudent or mischievous person. 无礼或喜恶作剧的人; (常戏指)顽童.

jack·ass /'dʒækæs; 'dʒækæs/ n male ass; foolish person. 公驴; 牡驴; 愚人; 笨伯. laughing ~, (in Australia) giant kingfisher. (澳洲产的)笑鸫; 大鱼狗.

jack·boot /'dʒækbuːt; 'dʒæk,but/ n large boot coming above the knee (as formerly worn by cavalrymen). 过膝之长靴(如骑兵所穿者).

jack·daw /'dʒækdɔː; 'dʒæk,dɔ/ n bird of the crow family (noted for flying off with small bright objects). 穴乌(一种小乌鸦, 因其爱衔走明亮之小东西而著名).

jacket /'dʒækɪt; 'dʒækɪt/ n 1 short, sleeved coat. 短上衣; 夹克. dust a person's ~, beat him. 打某人. 2 outer covering round a boiler, tank, pipe, etc to lessen loss of heat, or (a water ~) to cool an engine. (锅炉, 槽, 管等之)护套(有保温或冷却作用). 3 skin (of a potato): (马铃薯的)皮: baked in their ~s. (指马铃薯)连皮烧的. 4 (also 亦作 'dust-~) loose paper cover in which a hardback book is issued. (精装书的)封面套纸.

jack-knife /'dʒæk naɪf; 'dʒæk,naɪf/ n large pocket-knife with a folding blade. 大折刀. □ vi [VP2A] (esp of an articulated truck) fold and double back like the blade and handle of a ~. (尤指挂接拖车的货车)(如刀刃与刀柄般)回转折合.

jack-plane /'dʒæk pleɪn; 'dʒæk,plen/ n plane² for rough smoothing of wood. 粗刨.

jack·pot /'dʒækpɒt; 'dʒæk,pɑt/ n accumulated stakes in various games (esp poker), increasing in value until won. (尤指扑克牌赌博中)累积的赌注(逐渐增加直到被赢去). hit the ~, have great success or good fortune. 大获成功; 发大财.

Jaco·bean /,dʒækə'bɪən; ,dʒækə'biən/ adj of the reign of James I (1603—25) of England: 英王詹姆士一世时代 (一六〇三至一六二五) 的: ~ literature/architecture/furniture. 英王詹姆士一世时代的文学(建筑, 家具).

Jac·obin /'dʒækəbɪn; 'dʒækəbɪn/ n member of a group of revolutionaries organized in 1789 during the French Revolution. 雅各宾派(一七八九年法国大革命时之一革命党派)之党徒. □ adj violent; extremely radical. 激烈的; 极端激进的. ~·ism /-ɪzəm; -ɪzm/ n (politics) extreme radicalism. (政治)激进主义.

Jac·obite /'dʒækəbaɪt; 'dʒækəbaɪt/ n supporter of James II (reigned 1685—1688) of England after his overthrow or of his descendants who claimed the English

throne. 英王詹姆士二世(在位于一六八五至一六八八年)被推翻后或其争取王位之子孙的拥护者。

jade¹ /dʒeɪd; dʒed/ n [U] hard, usu green stone, carved into ornaments, etc. 碧玉; 玉; 翡翠。

jade² /dʒeɪd; dʒed/ n 1 tired out or worn-out horse. 疲惫之马; 老马。 2 (either contemptuous or playful) woman: (轻蔑或戏谑语) 女人: You saucy little ~! 你这个无礼的女孩子! ~d /dʒeɪdɪd; dʒedɪd/ adj worn out; overworked; dulled; 疲倦的; 工作过度的; 变得迟钝的; He looks ~d. 他看来疲惫不堪。 He has a ~d appetite. 他的食欲不振。

jag¹ /dʒæg; dʒæg/ n sharp projection, eg of rock. 尖锐的突出物(例如尖锐的岩石)。 **jaggy** adj having ~s. 有尖锐突出部分的; 锯齿状的; 凹凸不平的。

jag² /dʒæg; dʒæg/ vt (-gg-) 1 [VP6A] cut or tear in an uneven manner; give an edge like that of a saw to. 不整齐地切或撕; 使成锯齿状。 **jag·ged** /ˈdʒægɪd; ˈdʒægɪd/ adj notched; with rough, uneven edges: 有 V 字形凹痕的; 边缘不整齐的: jagged rocks. 嵬岩。

jag·uar /ˈdʒægjʊə(r); ˈdʒægwɑr/ n large, fierce, cat-like meat-eating animal of Central and South America. 美洲虎(中美及南美产的一种猫科食肉的凶猛大野兽)。 ⇨ the illus at cat. 参看 cat 之插图。

jail /dʒeɪl; dʒeɪl/ ⇨ **gaol**.

jakes /dʒeɪks; dʒeks/ n (sl) water-closet. (俚) (有抽水设备的)厕所。

ja·lopy /dʒəˈlɒpɪ; dʒəˈlɑpɪ/ n (pl -pies) (colloq) old, rickety or battered automobile or aircraft. (口) 破旧的汽车或飞机。

jam¹ /dʒæm; dʒæm/ n [U] fruit boiled with sugar until it is thick, and preserved in jars, pots, tins, etc. 果酱。 **money for jam**, (sl) something for nothing; something coming by good luck. (俚) 白捡的财物; 幸运得来的财物。 '**jam-jar** n pot m one for containing jam. 果酱瓶(罐)。 '**jam session** n impromptu performance by jazz musicians. 爵士乐师的即兴演奏。

jam² /dʒæm; dʒæm/ vt, vi (-mm-) 1 [VP6A, 15A, B, 14, 2A, C] ~ (in / under / between, etc), crush, be crushed, between two surfaces or masses; squeeze, be squeezed: 压紧; 挤紧; 夹住; 被夹住: a ship jammed in the ice. 被夹住在冰中的船。 The logs jammed in the river, become tightly packed. 圆木材挤塞在河里。 2 [VP15B, 2A, C] ~ (on), (of parts of a machine, etc) (cause to) become fixed so that movement or action is prevented: (指机器零件等)卡住不动; (使)发生故障: jam the brakes on / jam on the brakes. 猛然刹车。 The brakes jammed and the car skidded badly. 刹车故障, 汽车向一侧滑冲。 3 [VP6A, 15A, B] push (things) together tightly: 把(东西)挤塞在一起: jam one's clothes into a small suitcase. 把衣服塞入一小箱中。 The corridors were jammed by/ with hordes of school-children. 走廊上挤满了一群群的小学生。 4 [VP6A] make the reception of a broadcast programme impossible or difficult by broadcasting a signal that deliberately interferes: (无线电)干扰: jam the enemy's stations during a war. 战争期间干扰敌人的电台。 □ n [C] 1 number of things or people crowded together so that movement is difficult or impossible: 拥塞之物; 拥挤的人群: 'traffic-jams in our big towns; (交通的)拥塞; a 'log-jam, on a river, etc. (河上等)圆木材拥塞。 2 stoppage of a machine due to jamming(2). 机器之因故障而停顿。 3 (sl) awkward position; difficult situation: (俚) 窘境; 困难的处境: be in / get into a jam. 陷入困难的处境。

jamb /dʒæm; dʒæm/ n vertical side post of a doorway, window frame, etc; (pl) stone sides of a fireplace. 门、窗等之侧柱; 橙子; (复)壁炉两旁的石壁。

jam·boree /ˌdʒæmbəˈriː; ˌdʒæmbəˈri/ n 1 merry meeting. 快乐的聚会。 2 large rally or gathering, esp of Scouts or Guides. 大集会; (尤指)童子军大会。

jam-pack /ˌdʒæmˈpæk; ˈdʒæmˈpæk/ vt [VP6A] (colloq) crowd to capacity: (口) 挤满; 塞满: a stadium ~ed with spectators. 挤满观众的运动场。

jangle /ˈdʒæŋgl; ˈdʒæŋgl/ vt, vi [VP6A, 2A] (cause to) give out a harsh metallic noise; argue noisily. (使) 发出刺耳的金属碰击声; 喧闹地争论。 □ n [U] harsh noise. 刺耳的声音。

jani·tor /ˈdʒænɪtə(r); ˈdʒænətə/ n 1 doorkeeper. 看门者; 管门者。 2 (US) person hired to take care of a building, offices, etc, eg by cleaning, stoking the furnaces. (美)照顾一建筑物, 办公室等(例如扫除烟道, 照料火炉)的人; 工友。

Janu·ary /ˈdʒænjʊərɪ US: -jʊerɪ; ˈdʒænjʊˌerɪ/ n the first month of the year. 一月; 正月。

Ja·nus /ˈdʒeɪnəs; ˈdʒeɪnəs/ n ancient Roman god, guardian of gates and doors, beginnings and ends, represented with two faces, one on the front and the other on the back of his head. 古罗马之门神(司管门户, 开始与结束, 有两个面孔, 一在头的前面, 一在头的后面)。

ja·pan /dʒəˈpæn; dʒəˈpæn/ vt (-nn-), n (cover with) hard, shiny black enamel. 漆; 亮漆; 假漆; 涂以假漆。

jape /dʒeɪp; dʒep/ n (old use) joke. (旧用法)玩笑; 笑话。

ja·pon·ica /dʒəˈpɒnɪkə; dʒəˈpɑnɪkə/ n [U] (sorts of) ornamental variety of pear or quince. 装饰用的梨树或榅桲类植物。

jar¹ /dʒɑː(r); dʒɑr/ n [C] 1 (usu harsh) sound or vibration: (通常指刺耳的)声音或震动; 轧音: We felt a jar when the engine was coupled to the train. 当机车连接到火车上时, 我们感到剧震。 2 shock; thrill of the nerves; discord: 震荡; 震惊; 神经的刺激; 不和; 争吵: The fall from his horse gave him a nasty jar. 他自马上跌下受到剧烈的震荡。 It was an unpleasant jar to my nerves. 那使我神经不安。

jar² /dʒɑː(r); dʒɑr/ n tall vessel, usu round, with a wide mouth, with or without handles, of glass, stone or earthenware; its contents: 坛子; 罐; 广口瓶; 一广口瓶内所盛之物或量: a jar of strawberry jam. 一瓶草莓酱。 **jar·ful** /-ful; -fəl/ n

jar³ /dʒɑː(r); dʒɑr/ vi, vt (-rr-) 1 [VP3A] jar against / on, strike with a harsh unpleasant sound. 以刺耳的声音撞击。 2 [VP3A] jar on, have an unpleasant effect (on): 使有不愉快的感觉: The way he laughs jars on me / on my ears / on my nerves. 他大笑的样子使我有不愉快的感觉(刺激我的耳朵, 刺激我的神经)。 3 [VP6A] send a shock through (the nerves): 震动(神经): He was badly jarred by the blow. 那打击使他的神经震动得很厉害。 She was jarred by this sad news. 她为此不幸的消息而受了刺激。 4 [VP2A, 3A] jar (with), be out of harmony: 不和谐; 不一致: His opinions jar with mine. 他的意见与我的不一致。 Try to avoid colours that jar when choosing curtains and rugs. 选择窗帘和地毯时, 设法避免颜色不调和。 **jar·ring** adj causing disharmony; harsh: 引起不调和的; 刺耳的: a jarring note. 刺耳的音调。 **jar·ring·ly** adv

jar·gon /ˈdʒɑːgən; ˈdʒɑrgən/ n [U] 1 language difficult to understand, because it is badly formed or spoken badly: 因形式不好或说得不好而使人难懂的话; 怪异难懂的话语: Only a mother can understand her baby's ~. 只有母亲能了解她的婴孩说的那种难懂的话。 2 language full of technical or special words: 多专门术语(的话); 行话; 切口: the ~ of radio technicians / linguists. 无线电技术人员(语言学家)用的行话。

jas·mine /ˈdʒæsmɪn; ˈdʒæsmɪn/ n [U] shrub with white or yellow sweet-smelling flowers. 茉莉; 素馨。

jas·per /ˈdʒæspə(r); ˈdʒæspə/ n [U] semi-precious stone, red, yellow or brown. 碧石(红, 黄或褐色的次等宝石)。

jaun·dice /ˈdʒɔːndɪs; ˈdʒɔndɪs/ n [U] disease, caused by stoppage of the flow of bile, marked by yellowness of the skin and the whites of the eyes; (fig) state of mind in which one is jealous, spiteful, envious and suspicious. 黄疸病; 黄胆; (喻)嫉妒, 怨恨, 猜忌的心情。 □ vt (usu passive) affect with ~: (通常用被动语态)使患黄疸病; 使怀嫉妒, 怨恨, 猜忌的心情: take a ~d view,

one influenced by jealousy, spite, etc.(因嫉妒、怨恨等而)
持有偏见。

jaunt /dʒɔːnt; dʒɔnt/ n short journey for pleasure. 短
程游览。 □ vi [VP2A, C] make such a journey. 作短
程游览。 '~·**ing-car** n light, two-wheeled horse-drawn
vehicle with seats back to back, used in Ireland. 爱尔兰
的一种有背靠背座位的双轮轻便马车。

jaunty /'dʒɔːntɪ; 'dʒɔntɪ/ adj (-ier, -iest) feeling or
showing self-confidence and self-satisfaction: 感到自信
和自满的; 扬扬得意的: He wore his hat at a ~ angle,
tipped to one side as a sign of high spirits, etc. 他歪戴
着帽子,显得扬扬得意。 **jaunt·ily** /-ɪlɪ; -əlɪ/ adv **jaunti-
ness** n [U]

javelin /'dʒævlɪn; 'dʒævlɪn/ n light spear for throwing
(usu in sport). (运动用之)标枪。

throwing the javelin

jaw /dʒɔː; dʒɔ/ n 1 (lower/upper) jaw, either of
the bone structures containing the teeth: (下, 上)颚:
Which jaw moves up and down when you talk? 你谈话时
哪个颚上下活动? ⇨ the illus at **head**. 参看 head 之插
图。 '**jaw-bone** n one of the bones in which the teeth
are set. 颚骨; 牙床骨。 '**jaw-breaker** n (colloq) word
hard to pronounce. (口)难发音的词。 2 (pl) framework
of the mouth, including the teeth; (sing) lower part of
the face: (复)颌; (单)下巴: a man with a strong jaw. 下
巴大的人。 3 (pl) narrow mouth of a valley, channel,
etc: (复)山谷、水道等之狭窄入口: (fig) (喻) into/out of
the jaws of death, into/out of great danger. 进入(脱
离)险境。 4 (pl) parts of a tool, machine, etc, eg a
vice, between which things are gripped or crushed.
(复)工具, 机器等 (例如虎头钳) 之钳夹部分; 叉钳。
5 (colloq) talkativeness: (口)唠叨; 多嘴: None of your
jaw! 不要啰唆! 6 (colloq) long, dull talk giving moral
advice. (口)冗长枯燥的教训。 □ vi [VP2A, C, 3A]
jaw (at), (colloq) talk, esp at tedious length; give a
moral talk to: (口)闲谈(尤指喋喋不休); 教训: Stop
jawing at me! 不要向我唠叨!

jay /dʒeɪ; dʒe/ n noisy European bird with brightly
coloured feathers; (fig) impertinent person who chatters
too much. 樫鸟(一种爱叫的欧洲鸟, 有颜色鲜艳的羽毛);
(喻)爱唠叨的无礼之人。 '**jay-walker** n person who
walks erratically across or along streets without paying
attention to traffic. 不遵守交通规则而穿越马路者。
'**jay-walk** vi walk in this way. 不遵守交通规则而穿越
马路。

jazz /dʒæz; dʒæz/ n [U] popular music first played by
Negro groups in Southern USA in the early 20th c,
characterized by improvisation and strong rhythms,
called traditional ~; similar music played by large
bands for dancing; a later variation much influenced
by the blues to produce an unhurried unemotive style,
called modern ~. 爵士乐(二十世纪初期美国南部黑人倡
导的流行音乐, 以即席演奏和明快的节奏为特点, 称之为
传统的爵士乐, 后来受布鲁斯爵士乐之影响, 变为缓慢而不
表现感情的风格, 称之为现代爵士乐)。 '~ **age**, 爵士乐时代; (attrib) (用作定语) ~ music; 爵士
音乐; a '~ band. 爵士乐队。 □ vt, vi 1 [VP6A, 2A]
play or arrange in the style of ~: 奏爵士乐; 改写成爵
士乐: ~ a song/tune; 将一歌曲奏成爵士乐; dance to ~

music. 跳爵士舞。 2 [VP15B] ~ sth up, (fig, colloq)
liven up; put more energy into: (喻, 口)使快乐活泼; 使
有活力: ~ up a party; 使一聚会愉快; ~ things up a bit.
使事情有点生气。 **jazzy** adj (-ier, -iest) (colloq) of or
like ~; flashy, showy: (口)爵士乐的; 似爵士乐的; 浮华
的; 炫丽的: ~y cushions; 颜色刺眼的垫子; a ~y sports
car. 炫丽的跑车。

jeal·ous /'dʒeləs; 'dʒeləs/ adj 1 feeling or showing
fear or ill will because of possible or actual loss of
rights or love: 妒忌的; 妒忌的: a ~ husband; 嫉妒的丈
夫; ~ looks. 妒忌的样子。 2 ~ (of sb/sth), feeling or
showing unhappiness because of the better fortune, etc
of others: 妒羡的; ~ of sb else's success. 妒羡别人的成
功。 3 ~ (of sth), taking watchful care of): 注意
的(与 of 连用): ~ of one's rights; 注意自己的权利; keep
a ~ eye on sb. 注意看守某人。 4 (in the Bible, of God)
requiring exclusive loyalty and whole-hearted worship
and service. (圣经中指上帝) 要求绝对忠实和崇敬的。
~·**ly** adv **jeal·ousy** /'dʒeləsɪ; 'dʒeləsɪ/ n (pl -sies)
1 [U] being a ~: 嫉妒; 妒羡的; a lover's ~y. 爱人的嫉妒。
2 [C] instance of this; act or utterance that shows ~y:
嫉妒或妒羡的实例; 嫉妒或妒羡的行为或言语: I'm tired
of all these jealousies and quarrels. 我已厌倦这些嫉妒和
争吵的事情了。

jean /dʒiːn; dʒin/ n 1 [U] heavy, strong cotton cloth:
斜纹布; (attrib) (用作定语) ~ overalls. 斜纹布的工装
裤。 2 ~s, tough (usu denim) trousers worn informally
by men, women and children. (男子, 女子及儿童穿的)
斜纹布裤; 牛仔裤。

jeep /dʒiːp; dʒip/ n small, light utility motor vehicle
with great freedom of movement, useful on rough
ground. 吉普车(一种小型, 轻便, 活动范围大, 可在崎岖地
面行驶的汽车。

jeer /dʒɪə(r); dʒɪr/ vi [VP2A, 3A, 6A] ~ (at sb),
mock, laugh rudely: 嘲弄; 讥笑: ~ at a defeated enemy;
嘲弄一战败的敌人; ~ (at) the speaker; 讥笑演说者; a
~ing crowd. 讥笑的群众。 □ n [C] ~ing remark; taunt.
讥笑的言语; 嘲笑。 ~·**ing·ly** adv

Je·ho·vah /dʒɪ'həʊvə; dʒɪ'hovə/ n name of God used
in the Old Testament. 耶和华(旧约圣经中对上帝的称
呼)。

je·june /dʒɪ'dʒuːn; dʒɪ'dʒun/ adj (formal) (of writings)
dry; uninteresting; unsatisfying to the mind. (正式用
语)(指写作)枯燥的; 无趣味的; 令人不满意的。 ~·**ly** adv
~·**ness** n [U].

Jekyll and Hyde /ˌdʒekl ən 'haɪd; ˌdʒɪkl ən 'haɪd/
n single person with two personalities, one good (Jekyll)
and one bad (Hyde). 有善恶双重人格者。

jell /dʒel; dʒel/ vi, vt [VP2A, 6A] (colloq) (cause
to) become like jelly; take shape: (口)(使)成冻子状;
(使)结冻; (使)凝结; 成形; 具体化; 明确化: My ideas
are beginning to ~. 我的思想逐渐明确。

jel·laba /dʒə'lɑːbə; dʒə'lɑbə/ n loose hooded cloak worn
by Arab men. 阿拉伯男子所穿有头巾的披风。

jelly /'dʒelɪ; 'dʒelɪ/ n (pl -lies) 1 [U] soft, semisolid
food substance made from gelatin; similar substance
made of fruit juice and sugar. 冻子(一种由胶质制成的
软的半固体食品); 果子冻。 2 [C, U] (portion of) this
substance prepared in a mould, flavoured and coloured,
as a sweet dish. 果冻甜食, 一份果冻甜食。 3 [C, U] ~-
like substance. 冻状物质。 '~-**fish** n ~-like sea animal.
水母; 海蜇。 ⇨ the illus at **sea**. 参看 sea 之插图。 □ vt,
vi [VP6A, 2A] (cause to) become like ~. 使成冻状;
变成冻子。 **jel·lied** adj set in ~; prepared in ~; like
~: 成冻的; 制成冻状的; 冻状的: jellied eels. 鳗冻。

jemmy /'dʒemɪ; 'dʒemɪ/ n (pl -mies) (US 美 =
jimmy) crowbar, esp as used by burglars for forcing
open doors, windows and drawers. 铁撬(尤指窃盗用以
撬门, 窗, 抽屉等的)。

jenny /'dʒenɪ; 'dʒenɪ/ n ⇨ spinning = at spin.

jeop·ard·ize /'dʒepədaɪz; 'dʒepəd,aɪz/ vt [VP6A]
put in danger. 使受危险; 使陷险境。 **jeop·ardy** /'dʒe-

pədɪ; ˈdʒepədɪ/ *n* [U] danger of harm or loss, usu in the phrase: 危险(指伤害或损失,通常用于下列短语中): *be/place/put in jeopardy*, (使)陷入危险。

jer·boa /dʒɜːˈbəʊə; dʒɜˈboʊ/ *n* small rat-like animal of Asia and the N African deserts with long hind legs and the ability to jump well. 跳鼠(产于亚洲及非洲北部沙漠,后腿长,善跳跃)。

jere·miad /ˌdʒerɪˈmaɪæd; ˌdʒerəˈmaɪæd/ *n* long, sad and complaining story of troubles, misfortunes, etc. 苦难不幸等之漫长的哀诉;哀史。

jerk¹ /dʒɜːk; dʒɜˈk/ *n* [C] 1 sudden push, pull, start, stop, twist, lift or throw: 急推; 急拉; 急动; 急停; 急扭; 急抬; 急投:*The train stopped with a ~/a series of ~s.* 火车颠了一下(颠了几下)才停住。 2 sudden involuntary twitch of a muscle or muscles. (肌肉的)痉挛; 反射。 3 physical ~s, (colloq) gymnastic exercises. (口)体操; 运动。 4 (sl) foolish person. (俚)愚笨的人。 □ *vt, vi* [VP6A, 15A, B, 2C] give a ~ to; move with a ~ or ~s: 猛然一推(拉, 动, 停, 扭, 抬, 投):颠簸而行:*He ~ed the fish out of the water.* 他猛地一拉把鱼从水中钓起。 *The train ~ed along/~ed to a stop.* 火车颠簸而行(猛然停住)。 *Don't ~ out your words; try to recite more smoothly.* 不要断断续续地背诵字句, 要背得更流利些。 ~**y** *adj* (-ier, -iest) with ~s; not smooth: 急动的; 不平稳的:*a ~y ride in an old bus.* 乘破旧公共汽车颠簸行进。 ~**ily** /-ɪlɪ; -əlɪ/ *adv* ~**i·ness** *n* [U].

jerk² /dʒɜːk; dʒɜˈk/ *vt* [VP6A] cure (esp beef) by cutting it into long slices and drying it in the sun. 将(尤指牛肉)切成长片晒干; 干制(牛肉)。

jer·kin /ˈdʒɜːkɪn; ˈdʒɜˈkɪn/ *n* short, close-fitting jacket, usu of leather (as worn by men in olden times). (昔时男子所穿之)皮制紧身短上衣。 ⇨ the illus at **doublet**. 参看 doublet 之插图。

jerry /ˈdʒerɪ; ˈdʒerɪ/ *n* (*pl* -ries) 1 '~-**builder/-building**, builder/building of houses of poor quality with bad materials. 偷工减料的营造商(建筑工程)。 Hence, 由此产生, '~-**built** *adj* 2 '~-**can**, army-style metal container used for carrying extra supplies of water or petrol on long journeys. (仿军中样式供长途运输贮备水或汽油用的)金属制液体容器。 3 J~, (army sl) German soldier. (军中俚语)德国兵。 4 (sl) chamber-pot. (俚)尿罐; 便壶。

jer·sey /ˈdʒɜːzɪ; ˈdʒɜˈzɪ/ *n* (*pl* -seys) 1 [U] (~-**wool**) soft, fine knitted fabric used for clothes; [C] close-fitting knitted woollen garment with sleeves. 毛织紧身上衣; 毛织运动衫。 ⇨ **jumper, pullover, sweater**. 2 J~, cow of the breed that originally came from J~, one of the Channel Islands (near the French coast). 泽西乳牛(原产于英国海峡群岛之泽西岛)。

jest /dʒest; dʒest/ *n* [C] 1 joke; sth said or done to cause amusement. 玩笑; 笑话; 戏谑。 *in ~*, as a joke, not in earnest. 开玩笑地; 不认真地。 2 object of ridicule: 笑柄; 嘲笑对象:*a standing ~*, sth or sb always laughed at. 经常被人嘲笑的对象。 □ *vi* [VP2A, 3A] ~ (*with*), make ~s; act or speak lightly: 开玩笑; 取笑; 讲笑话:*Don't ~ about serious things.* 对于重要的事不能儿戏。 *He's not a man to ~ with.* 他是个不能开玩笑的人。 ~**ing** *adj* spoken in ~: 说着玩的; 打趣的:*~ing remarks*, 开玩笑的话; 戏谑的话; fond of ~s: 爱开玩笑的:*a ~ing fellow*. 喜欢开玩笑的人。 ~**ing·ly** *adv*

jest·er /ˈdʒestə(r); ˈdʒestə/ *n* person who jests, esp (in olden times) a man whose duty it was to make jokes to amuse the court or noble household in which he was employed. 开玩笑者; (尤指古时宫庭或贵族豢养的)弄臣。

Jesuit /ˈdʒezjuːɪt; ˈdʒeʒuːɪt/ *n* member of the Society of Jesus, a RC order founded in 1534 by Ignatius Loyola, Spanish priest, taking vows of obedience, poverty and chastity; (as used by opponents of the Society) person who thinks that it may be right to dissemble or prevaricate if this helps to obtain good results. 耶稣会会员(耶稣会为天主教之一派, 一五三四年由西班牙教士伊格那修·罗耀拉所创, 宣誓顺从、刻苦及坚

贞);(反对该会者用语)认为只要能达到良好结果就可以虚伪的人。 ~**i·cal** /ˌdʒezjuˈɪtɪkl US: ˌdʒezjʊ-; ˌdʒeʒuˈɪtɪkl/ *adj* of or like the ~s. 耶稣会会员的; 似耶稣会会员的; 虚伪的。

Jesus /ˈdʒiːzəs; ˈdʒizəs/ *n* the founder of the Christian religion. 耶稣(基督教的创始者)。

jet¹ /dʒet; dʒet/ *n* [C] 1 fast, strong stream of gas, liquid, steam or flame, forced out of a small opening: (气体, 液体或火焰之)喷射:*The pipe burst and a jet of water shot across the kitchen.* 管子破了, 一股水由厨房这边喷到那边。 **jet-pro'pulsion (engine)**, propulsion of aircraft and spacecraft by engines that suck in air at the front, mix the air with gases, and send out the hot, burnt gases in jets at the back. (飞机和太空船之)喷气推进(引擎)。 Hence, 由此产生, **jet** ('**aircraft/'airliner/'fighter**) *n*, **jet-pro'pelled** *adj*. ⇨ the illus at **air**. 参看 air 之插图。 **the 'jet set**, wealthy persons who often travel by jet aircraft for holidays. 常乘喷气式客机旅行度假的有钱人。 2 (*pl*) (often a brief but repeated) stream of liquid, gas, etc: (复)液体, 气体等之阵阵的涌出:*He cut his wrist so badly that jets of blood spurted out.* 他的手腕割伤得很厉害, 血阵阵地涌出。 3 narrow opening from which a jet comes out: 喷射口; 喷嘴:*a 'gas-jet.* 煤气喷嘴; 煤气喷灯。 □ *vi, vt* (-tt-) 1 come, send out, in a jet or jets. 喷出; 喷射。 2 (colloq) travel by jet airliner. (口)乘喷气式客机旅行。

jet² /dʒet; dʒet/ *n* [U] hard, black mineral that takes a brilliant polish, used for buttons, ornaments, etc; the colour of this mineral; (attrib) made of jet; (also 亦作, **jet-'black**) deep, glossy black. 贝煤炭; 黑玉; 黑玉色; (用作定语)黑玉制的; 黑玉色的; 黑黝黝的。

jet·sam /ˈdʒetsəm; ˈdʒetsəm/ *n* [U] goods thrown overboard from a ship at sea to lighten it, eg in a storm; such goods washed up on the sea-shore. 投弃货物(船舶为减轻负担而抛弃的货物, 例如遇有暴风雨时);冲至岸上的投弃货物。 **flotsam and ~**, (fig use) persons whose lives have been wrecked: (比喻用法)流离失所的人:*Sick and starving refugees are the flotsam and ~ of war.* 生病挨饿的难民乃战争中流离失所的人。

jet·ti·son /ˈdʒetɪsn; ˈdʒetɪsn/ *vt* [VP6A] throw (goods) overboard in order to lighten a ship, eg during a storm; abandon, discard (what is unwanted): 为减轻船上负担而抛弃(货物)(例如遇暴风雨时); 投弃; 抛弃(不要的东西): ~ *an unpleasant passenger/an unworkable plan.* 丢弃一使人厌恶的乘客(放弃难实行的计划)。

jetty /ˈdʒetɪ; ˈdʒetɪ/ *n* (*pl* -ties) structure built out into a body of water as a breakwater or as a landing-place for ships and boats. 突堤; 防波堤; 码头。

Jew /dʒuː; dʒu/ *n* person of the Hebrew people or religion. 犹太人; 犹太教徒。 **Jew·ess** /ˈdʒuːɪs; ˈdʒuɪs/ *n* female Jew. 犹太女人; 犹太女人。 **Jew·ish** /ˈdʒuːɪʃ; ˈdʒuɪʃ/ *adj* of the Jews. 犹太人的。

jewel /ˈdʒuːəl; ˈdʒuəl/ *n* 1 precious stone, eg a diamond or a ruby; ornament with a ~ or ~s set in it. 宝石(例如钻石或红宝石); 镶有宝石的装饰品; 珠宝。 2 artificial diamond: 人造钻石:*This watch has 15 ~s.* 这只表有十五个人造钻石。 3 (fig) sth or sb highly valued: (喻)极珍视的东西或人:*His wife is a ~.* 他的妻子是他的宝贝。 □ *vt* (-ll-, US -l-) adorn with ~s; set in (usu in *pp*) (通常用过去分词) *a ~led ring*; 镶有珠宝的戒指; *a ~led watch*, with industrial, not gem diamonds, in the movement. 装有宝石轴承的表。 ~**ler**, (US = ~**er**) /ˈdʒuːələ(r); ˈdʒuːələr/ ~s, a trader in ~s; person who sells ~s. 宝石业者; 珠宝商。 ~**ry**, ~**lery** /ˈdʒuːəlrɪ; ˈdʒuəlrɪ/ *n* [U] ~s collectively, ie precious stones, ornaments set with ~s, etc. 珠宝(总称); 珠宝类。

Jeze·bel /ˈdʒezəbl US: -bel; ˈdʒezəbl/ *n* (as a term of abuse) shameless, immoral woman. (辱骂之词)耶洗别; 无耻放荡的女人。 ⇨ **1 Kings 16: 31**. 参看旧约圣经列王记上第16章第31节。

jib¹ /dʒɪb; dʒɪb/ n **1** small triangular sail (in front of the mainsail). 艏帆; 船首三角帆 (在主帆之前). **,jib-'boom** spar to which the lower part of a jib is fastened. 艏帆斜桅(系船首三角帆之下端的圆木). ⇨ the illus at **barque, sail.** 参看 barque 和 sail 之插图. **the cut of his jib,** his personal appearance. 某人的风采. **2** projecting arm of a crane or derrick. 起重机之臂; 突梁. ⇨ the illus at **crane.** 参看 crane 之插图.

jib² /dʒɪb; dʒɪb/ vi (**-bb-**) [VP2A] (of a horse, etc) stop suddenly; refuse to go forwards; (fig) refuse to proceed: (指马等)突然停止; 不肯前进; (喻)踌躇不前: *On seeing the gate the horse jibbed.* 那马看到了门, 便不肯前进了. [VP3A] *jib at,* (fig) show unwillingness or dislike: (喻)表示不愿或厌恶: *He jibbed at working overtime every day.* 他不愿意每天都加班工作. *My small car sometimes jibs at a steep hill.* 我的小汽车有时遇到陡坡便爬不上去了.

jibe /dʒaɪb; dʒaɪb/ vi (US) (美) **1** = **gibe. 2** =**gybe.**

jiffy /'dʒɪfɪ; 'dʒɪfɪ/ n colloq) moment. (口)瞬间. *in a ~,* very soon. 即刻; 片刻.

jig /dʒɪg; dʒɪg/ n [C] **1** (music for a) quick, lively dance. 基格舞(一种急速轻快的舞); 基格舞曲. **2** appliance that holds a piece of work and guides the tools that are used on it. 可将制品条件夹引导工具工作的机械装置; 钻模; 装夹. □ vi, vt (**-gg-**) **1** [VP2A, C] dance a jig. 跳基格舞. **2** [VP 15B, 2C] move up and down in a quick, jerky way: 活泼地急跳; 跳动: *jigging up and down in excitement:* 兴奋得直蹦直跳; *jig a baby (up and down) on one's knees.* 将一婴儿放在膝上(上下)颠动.

jig·ger /'dʒɪgə(r); 'dʒɪgɚ/ n **1** flea or other parasite that burrows under the skin; (in England) harvest mite. 跳蚤或其他皮肤寄生虫; (英国)秋螨. **2** small measure for liquor (esp spirits), as fitted to bottles in bars. 量酒之小杯(尤指量烈酒者).

jig·gered /'dʒɪgəd; 'dʒɪgɚd/ adj (pred only, colloq) (仅用作表语, 口) **1** amazed: 惊奇的: *Well, I'm ~!* 哪有这种事(真叫人惊奇)! **2** exhausted. 筋疲力竭的.

jig·gery-po·kery /,dʒɪgərɪ 'pəʊkərɪ; 'dʒɪgɚɪ'pokɚɪ/ n [U] colloq) hocus-pocus; humbug. 口)欺骗; 诈骗.

jig·gle /'dʒɪgl; 'dʒɪgl/ vt, vi, n joggle. 摇摆; 摇动.

jig·saw /'dʒɪgsɔː; 'dʒɪg,sɔ/ n **1** machine fretsaw. 锯曲线机. **2** '~ (puzzle), picture, map, etc pasted on thin board or wood and cut in irregularly shaped pieces which are to be fitted together again. 拼图玩具.

ji·had /dʒɪˈhɑːd; dʒɪˈhɑd/ n religious war by Muslims against unbelievers; (fig) campaign for or against a teaching, practice, etc. 伊斯兰教徒对异教徒之战争; (喻)维护或反对教义、教规等之运动.

jilt /dʒɪlt; dʒɪlt/ vt [VP6A] give up, send away, (sb) after giving him encouragement or a promise to marry: 遗弃(情人): *When he lost his job, she ~ed him.* 他失业以后, 她便遗弃了他. □ n person who jilts sb. 负心之人.

Jim Crow /,dʒɪm 'krəʊ; 'dʒɪm'kro/ n △ (US) contemptuous name for a Negro. (讳)(美)对黑人之蔑称.

ji·miny /'dʒɪmənɪ; 'dʒɪmənɪ/ int colloq) exclamation of surprise. (口)表示惊奇的感叹词.

jim-jams /'dʒɪmdʒæmz; 'dʒɪm,dʒæmz/ n pl (sl) **the ~,** the jitters. (俚)神经紧张.

jimmy /'dʒɪmɪ; 'dʒɪmɪ/ n (US) (美) = **jemmy.**

jingle /'dʒɪŋgl; 'dʒɪŋgl/ n [C] **1** metallic clinking or ringing sound (as of coins, keys or small bells). 叮当声(如钱币、钥匙, 或小铃发出的声音). **2** series of the same or similar sounds in words, esp when designed to attract the attention, jingling verse. 一连串同音或类似音反复的文字(尤指欲引人注意者); 叠韵的诗句. □ vt, vi **1** [VP 6A, 15B, 2C] (cause to) make a light, ringing sound: (使)作叮当声: *He ~d his keys.* 他把钥匙弄得叮当地响. *The money in his pocket ~d.* 他口袋里的钱叮当作响. **2** [VP 2A] (of verse) be full of

alliterations and rhymes that make it easy to learn and remember. (指诗)充满头韵和韵脚而易学易记; 押韵.

jingo /'dʒɪŋgəʊ; 'dʒɪŋgo/ n (pl **~es** /-gəʊz; -goz/) person who combines excessive patriotism with contempt for other countries, esp one who supports a warlike policy. (蔑视他国之)极端爱国主义者; (尤指)主张好战政策者. *By ~!* (dated sl) exclamation expressing surprise, pleasure, etc or giving emphasis to a statement. (过时俚语)(表示惊异、快乐等, 或加强语势)嗳呀! 一定! **~ism** /-ɪzəm; -ɪzəm/ n attitude of mind, principles, of ~es. 极端的爱国主义; 侵略主义; 好战主义. **~·ist** /-ɪst; -ɪst/ n ~ is·tic /,dʒɪŋgəʊ'ɪstɪk/ adj characteristic of ~es. 极端爱国的; 侵略主义的; 好战的.

jinks /dʒɪŋks; dʒɪŋks/ n [U] (only in) (仅用于) *high ~,* noisy merrymaking; uncontrolled fun. 狂欢作乐.

jinn /dʒɪn; dʒɪn/ n = **genie.**

jinx /dʒɪŋks; dʒɪŋks/ n colloq) person or thing that brings bad luck. (口)不祥的人或物. *put a ~ on sb,* do sth to bring him bad luck. 做某事使某人倒霉.

jit·ney /'dʒɪtnɪ; 'dʒɪtnɪ/ n (US colloq) **1** (old use) nickel. (旧用法)五分钱; 五分镍币. **2** small motor-bus. 小型公共汽车.

jit·ters /'dʒɪtəz; 'dʒɪtɚz/ n pl **the ~,** (sl) extreme nervousness: (俚)极度紧张; 极为神经过敏: *have/get/give sb the ~.* 觉得极为紧张(使某人极为紧张). **jit·ter·bug** /'dʒɪtə bʌg; 'dʒɪtɚ,bʌg/ n **1** (person who participated in a) lively, popular dance of the 1940's to swing music. 吉特巴舞(一九四〇一一九四九年间流行的一种活泼的伴随摇摆音乐的舞蹈); 跳吉特巴舞的人. **2** (old use) flustered person. (旧用法)紧张的人. **jit·tery** /'dʒɪtərɪ; 'dʒɪtɚɪ/ adj nervous; frightened. 神经紧张的; 害怕的.

jive /dʒaɪv; dʒaɪv/ n style of popular music with a strong beat; dancing to this. 摇摆乐(一种节拍强烈的爵士乐); 摇摆舞. □ vi dance to ~ music. 摇摆舞.

job¹ /dʒɒb; dʒɑb/ n **1** piece of work, either to be done, or completed: 一件工作(将要做或已完成者); 成果; 成品: *Your new Bentley car is a lovely job,* is magnificent. 你的新本特利车很漂亮. *on the job,* (colloq) at work; busy. (口)工作中; 忙碌的. *be paid by the job,* separately for each job. 按件计酬. *make a good/fine job of sth,* do it well. 做得好. *odd jobs,* bits of work not connected with one another. 零碎工作; 散工. **,odd-'job man,** one who makes a living by doing any bits of work he is asked to do. 做零工者; 做短工者. **2** *a good job,* (colloq) a fortunate state of affairs: (口)幸运之事: *He lost his seat in Parliament, and a good job, too!* 他失去了国会中的席位, 这倒也是件好事! *give sb/sth up as a bad job,* (colloq) decide that sb/sth is hopeless. (口)因无希望等而放弃某人(某事物). *make the best of a bad job,* do what one can to remedy an unfortunate state of affairs. (为补救不幸事件而)尽力为之. **3** *be/have a (hard) job doing/to do sth,* be/have a difficult task: 为(有)困难的工作: *It's a (hard) job for a poor man to keep his wife and children clothed and fed.* 一个穷人使他的妻子儿女有衣穿有饭吃不是件容易的事. *You'll have a job convincing your wife that you were really detained at the office.* 让你的妻子相信你是真的被阻留在办公室里不是件容易的事. **4** employment; work: 职业; 工作: *to have/lose a job;* 获得工作(失业); (attrib) (用作定语) *job safety/satisfaction.* 职业保障(补偿). *out of a job,* unemployed. 失业的. *jobs for the boys,* (colloq) positions for one's supporters, friends, etc. (口)做为政治酬庸等之职位. **'job centre,** employment exchange, ⇨ **employment.** 职业介绍所. **5** *job lot,* mixed collection of articles, bought together. 整批买进的各种货物. **6** *just the job,* (colloq) exactly what is wanted. (口)恰为所需. **7** (sl) sth done by intrigue or dishonesty for private profit or advantage: (俚)以阴谋或欺骗手段为私人利益所做之事: *a put-up job.* 意图蒙混之事. ⇨ *put-up* at **put¹(11). 8** (sl) criminal

act, esp theft: (俚)罪行(尤指窃盗): *He got three years for a job he did in Leeds.* 他因在利兹犯窃盗罪行而被判三年徒刑。

job² /dʒɒb; dʒɑb/ *vt, vi* [VP2A] **1** above; do odd jobs: 做零工；做散工 (参看 job¹ 第 1 义): *a jobbing gardener,* one who works for several employers and is paid by the hour/day; 做零工的园丁；*a jobbing printer:* one who prints leaflets, posters, etc. 印刷散页印刷品之商人。 **2** [VP6A] (on the Stock Exchange) act as a broker; buy, sell (stocks and shares) for others. 做股票经纪；代客买卖(公债，股票)。 **3** [VP2A, 14] (colloq) use a position of trust for private advantage or for the benefit of one's friends: (口)假公济私；利用公职为己设或为人谋私；以假公济私的手段牟利: *He jobbed his brother into a well-paid post.* 他假公济私为他哥哥(弟弟)找到一个待遇很好的工作。 **job·ber** *n* **1** dealer in Stock Exchange securities. 股票经纪人。 ⇨ **broker.** **2** person who jobs(1). 做散工者。 **3** person who jobs(3). 假公济私的人。 **job·bery** /'dʒɒbərɪ; 'dʒɑbərɪ/ *n* [U] jobbing; (esp) use of unfair means to gain private advantage. 徇私舞弊；假公济私。

Job /dʒəʊb; dʒob/ *n* (from Job in the Book of Job in the Old Testament) person of great patience. (由旧约圣经约伯记中的约伯而来)非常有耐心之人。 *try the patience of Job,* be very difficult to endure, very vexatious. 令人十分难以忍受；十分使人烦恼。 *a Job's comforter,* one who aggravates the distress of the person he is supposed to be comforting. 增加对方痛苦的安慰者。

jockey /'dʒɒkɪ; 'dʒɑkɪ/ (*pl* ~s) professional rider in horse-races. 赛马的职业骑师。 ⇨ also *disc.* **'J~ Club,** club that controls horse-racing in England. (在英国主持赛马的)赛马俱乐部。 □ *vt, vi* [VP15A, 3A] trick; cheat: 欺骗: *He ~ed Green out of his job.* 他欺骗格林，使他失业。 ~ *for position,* **(a)** (in racing) jostle other riders in order to get a more favourable position. (赛马)挤其他的骑师以图占取有利的位置。 **(b)** (fig) try by skilful management, by tricky manoeuvring, to gain an advantage. (喻)以技巧手段图获利益。

jo·cose /dʒəʊ'kəʊs; dʒo'kos/ *adj* (formal) humorous; playful. (正式用语)诙谐的；开玩笑的。 ~·**ly** *adv* ~·**ness.** /ˌdʒəʊ'kəʊsɪtɪ/ *n* [U].

jocu·lar /'dʒɒkjʊlə(r); 'dʒɑkjələ/ *adj* meant as a joke; given to joking. 滑稽的；喜欢玩笑的。 ~·**ly** *adv* ~·**ity** /ˌdʒɒkjʊ'lærɪtɪ; ˌdʒɑkjə'lærɪtɪ/ *n* (*pl* -**ties**) [U] being ~; [C] ~ act or utterance. 滑稽；诙谐；滑稽的言行。

joc·und /'dʒɒkənd; 'dʒɑkənd/ *adj* (liter) merry; cheerful. (文)欢乐的；愉快的。 ~·**ity** /dʒə'kʌndətɪ; dʒo'kʌndətɪ/ *n* (*pl* -**ties**) [U] being ~; [C] ~ act or utterance. 欢乐；愉快；愉快的言行。

jodh·purs /'dʒɒdpəz; 'dʒɑdpɚz/ *n pl* long breeches for horse-riding, close-fitting from knee to ankle. 骑马裤(膝至踝部分为紧身的长裤)。

jog /dʒɒg; dʒɑg/ *vt, vi* (-**gg**-) **1** [VP6A, 15B] give a slight knock or push to; shake with a push or jerk: 轻撞；轻推；摇动: *The horse jogged its rider up and down.* 那马上下颠动着它的主人。 *He jogged my elbow,* touched it, eg to attract my attention, to warn me, etc. 他轻轻撞我的肘(例如引起我的注意，警告我等)。 *jog sb's memory,* try to make him remember or recall sth. 唤起某人的记忆；提醒某人。 **2** [VP15B] cause to move unsteadily, in a shaking manner: 使颠簸行进: *The old bus jogged us up and down on the rough mountain road.* 那辆旧公共汽车载着我们在崎岖的山路上颠簸前行驶。 **3** [VP2C] *jog along/on,* make slow, patient progress: 缓缓地前进或进行: *We jogged along the bad roads.* 我们沿着那些坏路缓缓前进。 *Matters jog along.* 事情在缓缓进行中。 *We must jog on somehow until business conditions improve.* 我们必须慢慢熬到商业情况改进为止。 **4** [VP2A] (mod colloq) run slowly and steadily for a time, for physical exercise. (现代口语)慢跑(作为运动)。 **jog·ger** /'dʒɒgə(r); 'dʒɑgɚ/ *n* person who

jogs(4). 慢跑者。 **jog·ging** /'dʒɒgɪŋ; 'dʒɑgɪŋ/ *n* [U] the physical exercise of jogging(4). 慢跑。 □ *n* [C] **1** slight push, shake or nudge. 轻推；轻摇；轻撞。 **2** (also *attrib* '**jog-trot**) slow walk or trot. 漫步；缓行。

joggle /'dʒɒgl; 'dʒɑgl/ *vt, vi* [VP6A, 2A] shake, move, by or as if by repeated jerks. 摇；摇摆；摇动。 □ *n* slight shake. 轻摇。

john /dʒɒn; dʒɑn/ *n* (sl) water-closet. (俚)(有抽水设备的)厕所。

John Bull /ˌdʒɒn 'bʊl; 'dʒɑn 'bʊl/ *n* the English nation; typical Englishman. 英国；典型的英国人；约翰牛。

John Doe /ˌdʒɒn'dəʊ; ˌdʒɑn'do/ *n* (esp US) (尤美) **1** (legal) invented name for an unknown person. (法律)某甲，用来称呼不知姓名之人。 **2** ordinary, typical man. 普通人。

joie de vivre /ˌʒwɑ: də 'vi:vrə; ʒwɑde'vivr/ *n* (F) carefree enjoyment of life. (法)无忧无虑的享受生活。

join /dʒɔɪn; dʒɔɪn/ *vt, vi* **1** [VP6A, 14, 15A, B] ~ *sth to sth;* ~ *things together/up,* put together; unite; connect (two points, things) with a line, rope, bridge, etc: 连结；结合；联合: ~ *one thing to another;* 将一物与另一物连接起来; ~ *two things together;* 将二物连接在一起; ~ *the pieces together;* 将片段接合起来; ~ *an island to the mainland (with a bridge);* (以桥梁)将一岛与大陆连接; ~ *two persons in marriage,* make them man and wife. 使二人结为夫妻。 *Where does this stream* ~ *the Danube?* 这条河流在何处与多瑙河会合？ ~ *battle,* begin fighting. 交战。 ~ *hands,* clasp each other's hands; (fig) combine in an enterprise, etc. 握手；(喻)携手共事。 ~ *forces (with...),* unite in action; work together. (与…)联合行动；合作。 **2** [VP2A, C] come together; unite: 交会；连合；相连: *Parallel lines are, by definition, lines that never* ~. 按照定义，平行线是永不相交的线。 *Which two rivers* ~ *at Lyons?* 那两条河在里昂相会合？ **3** [VP6A] become a member of: 参加；加入: ~ *the army/a club.* 从军(加入俱乐部)。 [VP2C] *join up,* (colloq) join the army. (口语)从军。 **4** [VP6A, 15A, 3A] ~ *(sb) in sth,* come into the company of; associate with (sb in sth): 与…在一起；伴随(某人做某事): *I'll* ~ *you in a few minutes.* 我过几分钟将和你们会合。 *Will you* ~ *us in a walk,* come with us? 你愿意和我们一块去散步吗？ *Why doesn't Tom* ~ *in the conversation,* Why is he silent? 汤姆为什么不讲话？ *May I* ~ *in (the game)?* 我可以参加(这游戏)吗？ □ *n* place or line where two things are ~ed: 相交点；连接处: *The two pieces were put together so cleverly that the* ~ *could not be seen.* 这两块接合得很巧妙，故而看不出相接之处。

joiner /'dʒɔɪnə(r); 'dʒɔɪnɚ/ *n* skilled workman who makes the inside woodwork of buildings, etc. 细工木匠。 ⇨ **carpenter, cabinet-maker** at **cabinet. join·ery** *n* [U] work of a ~; 细工；细木作。 *learn* ~*y;* 学习细木工；*lessons in* ~*y.* 细木工课程。

joint¹ /dʒɔɪnt; dʒɔɪnt/ *adj* (attrib only) held or done by, belonging to, two or more persons together: (仅用作定语)共同的；共有的；共享的: ~ *efforts/ownership/responsibility;* 共同的努力(所有权，责任); ~ *heirs to a legacy;* 一遗产之共同继承人；*a* ~ *account,* bank account in the name of more than one person, eg a husband and wife; 二人以上(例如夫妇)共有之银行户头；*a* ~-'*stock company,* a number of persons who carry on a business with capital contributed by all; 股份公司*during their* ~ *lives,* (legal) while they are both (or all) living; (法律)当他们都活着的时候; *settle a trade dispute by* ~ *consultation,* eg workers and management. 共同磋商(例如工人与资方)解决一劳资争议。 ~·**ly** *adv*

joint² /dʒɔɪnt; dʒɔɪnt/ *n* **1** place, line or surface at which two or more things are joined: 连接处；接合点；接缝；接合面: *the* ~*s in a jigsaw puzzle.* 拼图玩具的接缝。 **2** device or structure by which things, eg lengths of pipe, bones, are joined together: 接头，关节: '*finger* ~*s.* 指关节。 *out of* ~, (of bones) dislocated; pushed out of position: (指骨)脱臼；脱节: *He fell and put*

his knee out of ~. 他跌倒了，并且把膝盖摔脱了臼。**put
sb's 'nose out of** ~, (fig) take his place in another's
affections or favour; upset or humble sb who is a
nuisance. （喻）夺某人之宠；骚扰或贬抑一讨厌之人。
3 limb (shoulder, leg) or other division of an ox, a
sheep, etc which a butcher supplies to customers: 牛羊
等的腿肉或肩膊肉；大片肉: *a slice off the* ~, eg of roast
beef. 一大片肉(例如烤牛肉)。 **4** (sl) place visited by
people for gambling, drinking or drug-taking. （俚）下
流场所(赌窟,酒馆或烟馆)。 **'clip** ~, bar, night-club, etc
at which extortionate charges are made (often for
services not rendered). （俚）敲竹杠的酒吧, 夜总会等。**5** (sl)
cigarette containing a drug. （俚）含有麻醉剂的香烟。

joint³ /dʒɔɪnt; dʒɔɪnt/ *vt* [VP6A] **1** provide with a
joint or joints(2): 装以接头或关节: a ~*ed fishing-rod* /
doll. 有接头的鱼竿(有活动关节的洋娃娃)。 **2** divide at a
~ or into ~s(3). 在牛羊等之腿部或肩膊关节处切开; 将
(牛羊等之腿或肩膊)切成大片肉。

join·ture /'dʒɔɪntʃə(r); 'dʒɔɪntʃɚ/ *n* [C] (legal)
property settled on a woman during her marriage, to
be used by her after her husband's death. (法律）(夫生
前指定的)由妻继承的遗产；寡妇所得产。

joist /dʒɔɪst; dʒɔɪst/ *n* one of the parallel pieces of
timber (from wall to wall) to which floor-boards are
fastened; steel beam supporting a floor or ceiling. 地板
的托梁；搁栅。

joke /dʒəuk; dʒok/ *n* sth said (eg a story with a funny
ending) or done to cause amusement, laughter, etc: 笑
话；玩笑: *tell / make a joke*; 说笑话; sth that causes
amusement. 笑料。 **have a** ~ **with sb**, share one
with him. 与某人说笑话。 **make a** ~ **about sb or sth**,
speak lightly or amusingly about. 拿某人或某事开玩笑。
play a ~ **on sb**, cause him to be the victim of a
practical ~. 戏弄某人。 **a practical** ~, a trick played
on sb in order to make him appear ridiculous. 恶作剧。
It's no ~, It's a serious matter. 这可不是闹着玩的事。
the ~ *of the village / town, etc,* the laughing-stock;
person, event, etc which causes great amusement. 村
(镇等)内的笑柄；取笑的对象。 □ *vi* [VP2A, C] make
~s: 开玩笑: *He's always joking.* 他老是爱开玩笑。 *I was
only joking.* 我只是在开玩笑。 **jok·ing·ly** *adv* in a
joking manner. 开玩笑地; 戏谑地。

joker /'dʒəukə(r); 'dʒokɚ/ *n* **1** person who is fond of
making jokes. 诙谐者; 喜开玩笑的人。 **2** (sl) fellow.
（俚）人；家伙。 **3** extra playing card (the 53rd) which is
used in some games as the highest trump or as a
wild(10) card. 纸牌中的百搭 (在某些牌戏中可做最大的
王牌或飞牌)。

jolly /'dʒɒlɪ; 'dʒɑlɪ/ *adj* (**-ier, -iest**) joyful; gay;
merry; slightly drunk. 高兴的；愉快的；欢乐的；微醉的。
'J~ Roger, pirate's black flag (with skull and
crossbones). 海盗的黑旗 (骷髅旗)。 □ *adv* (GB colloq)
very: (英口)非常; 很: *I'll take a ~ good care not to lend
him money again.* 我将特别当心不再借钱给他了。 □ *vt*
[VP6A, 15A, B] (colloq) keep (sb) in a good humour
(esp in order to win his cooperation): （口）使 (某人)高
兴 (尤指欲获彼之合作时): *They jollied me along
until I agreed to help them.* 他们一直奉承我, 直到我答应
帮助他们。 **jol·li·fi·ca·tion** /ˌdʒɒlɪfɪ'keɪʃn; ˌdʒɑləfə-
'keʃən/ *n* [U] merry-making; festivity; [C] instance
of this. 作乐; 欢乐; 欢宴。 **jol·lity** /'dʒɒlɪtɪ; 'dʒɑlətɪ/ *n*
[U] state of being ~. 高兴；愉快；欢乐。

jolly-boat /'dʒɒlɪbəut; 'dʒɑlɪbot/ *n* kind of ship's
boat. 大船所携带的一种小艇。

jolt /dʒəult; dʒolt/ *vt, vi* [VP6A, 15A, B, 2A, C]
give a jerk or jerks to; shake up; (of a vehicle) move
along by jerks: 使颠簸; 摇动; (指车辆)颠簸而行: *The old
bus ~ed us as it went over the stony road.* 旧公共汽车
驶过碎石路时颠簸着前进。 *The bus ~ed along.* 那公共
汽车颠簸而行。 □ *n* jerk; sudden bump or shake; (fig)
surprise, shock. 颠簸；震摇；（喻）惊奇；震惊。 ~**y** *adj*
~ing. 颠簸的；摇动的。

Jo·nah /'dʒəunə; 'dʒonə/ *n* person whose presence
seems to bring ill luck; person who is sacrificed lest he
should bring ill luck. 不祥之人; 因恐其不祥而被牺牲
之人。

jon·quil /'dʒɒŋkwɪl; 'dʒɑŋkwɪl/ *n* kind of narcissus.
长寿花；黄水仙。

joss /dʒɒs; dʒɑs/ *n* (in China) carving in stone, etc,
of a god. 中国的神像；菩萨。 **'~-house** *n* temple. 庙。
'~-stick *n* stick of incense. 香。

jostle /'dʒɒsl; 'dʒɑsl/ *vt, vi* [VP6A, 2C] push
roughly (against); push: 撞; 挤 (与诸词连用); 推:
We were ~d by the crowd. 我们被人群挤来挤去。 *The
pickpocket ~d against me in the crowd.* 那扒手在人群中
撞我。

jot¹ /dʒɒt; dʒɑt/ *n* **a jot**, (usu with neg) small amount:
(通常与否定语连用) 少量; 些许: *There's not a jot of
truth in a story,* no truth at all. 故事中一点真实性都
没有。

jot² /dʒɒt; dʒɑt/ *vt* (**-tt-**) [VP15B] *jot sth down,* make
a quick written note of: 匆匆摘记下来: *The policeman
jotted down my name and address.* 那警察把我的姓名
和住址匆匆记下。 **jot·ter** *n* notebook or pad for rough
notes. 笔记簿；拍纸簿。 **jot·tings** *n pl* notes jotted down.
匆匆记下的东西。

joule /dʒuːl; dʒaul/ *n* (electr) (abbr **J**) unit of energy
or work. (电)焦耳(能量或功的单位,略作 **J**)。

jour·nal /'dʒɜːnl; 'dʒɝnl/ *n* **1** daily newspaper;
other periodical: 日报；杂志；定期刊物: *the Ladies' Home
J~*; 妇女家庭杂志; *the Economic J~*. 经济杂志。 **2** daily
record of news, events, business accounts, etc. 日记；
日志；流水帐。 ~**·ese** /ˌdʒɜːnə'liːz; ˌdʒɝnl'iz/ *n* [U]
style of language full of clichés, common in some ~s,
eg the use of 'prior to interment' for 'before burial'
(常见于某些报纸之多陈辞的) 新闻文体 (例如不用 before
burial 而用 prior to interment)。 ~**·ism** /-ɪzəm; -ɪzəm/
n [U] work of writing for, editing, or publishing ~s.
新闻业；新闻工作；新闻写作；新闻编辑；新闻出版。 ~**·ist**
/-ɪst; -ɪst/ *n* person engaged in ~ism. 从事新闻业者；
报人；新闻记者；为报纸杂志撰稿者。 ~**·is·tic** /ˌdʒɜːnə'-
lɪstɪk; ˌdʒɝnl'ɪstɪk/ *adj* of ~ism; characteristic of
~ism. 新闻事业的；新闻事业特有的。

jour·ney /'dʒɜːnɪ; 'dʒɝnɪ/ *n* (*pl* ~**s**) (distance
travelled (esp on land) in) going to a place, esp a
distant place: 旅行(尤指至遥远地方之旅行); 旅程; 路程:
reach one's ~'s end; 到达旅行目的地; *go / come / send
sb on a ~*; 去旅行(旅行前来); 遣人旅行); *make a ~
half-way round the world.* 旅行半个地球。 ⇨ *flight¹(2)*,
voyage. □ *vi* [VP2A, C] travel; make a ~. 旅行。

jour·ney·man /'dʒɜːnɪmən; 'dʒɝnɪmən/ *n* (*pl* -**men**
/-mən; -mən/) skilled workman who works for a master
(contrasted with an *apprentice*). 熟练的工人(与
apprentice 相对)。

joust /dʒaust; dʒʌst/ *vi, n* (hist) (engage in a) fight
on horseback with lances (as between knights in the
Middle Ages). (史)骑着马用长矛打斗(如中古时代之武
士)。

Jove /dʒəuv; dʒov/ *n* Jupiter, 古罗马之主神, esp (尤
用于) *By ~!* (as an exclamation of surprise, etc). (表
示惊异等的感叹词)啊!

jov·ial /'dʒəuvɪəl; 'dʒovɪəl/ *adj* full of fun and good
humour; merry: 快活的；愉快的；快乐的: *a ~ fellow*.
快活的人; *in a ~ mood*. 心情愉快。 ~**·ly** /-ɪəlɪ; -ɪəlɪ/
adv ~ly. **·ity** /ˌdʒəuvɪ'ælɪtɪ; ˌdʒovɪ'ælɪtɪ/ *n* [C] being
~; good humoured behaviour; [C] (*pl* -**ties**) ~ acts
or utterances. 快活；高兴的行为；快乐的行动或言语。

jowl /dʒaul; dʒaul/ *n* (usu) lower part of the face: 颚；
下颚: *a man with a heavy ~ / a heavy-jowled man,* one
with heavy jaws, a fold or folds of flesh hanging from
the chin. 一个有双下巴的人。 *cheek by ~,* ⇨ *cheek(1).*
~**y** *adj* with a heavy ~. 下颚宽厚的；双下巴的。

joy /dʒɔɪ; dʒɔɪ/ *n* **1** [U] deep pleasure; great gladness:
快乐；欣喜；极为高兴: *I wish you joy.* 祝你快乐。 *We*

judges

词)在壶或罐中煨炖(野鸭等): *jugged hare.* 用罐煨烧的野兔。 **2** (colloq) imprison. (口)监禁。

jug·ger·naut /'dʒʌgənɔːt; 'dʒʌgə,nɔt/ n **1** cause or belief to which persons are sacrificed or to which they sacrifice themselves: 使人为之牺牲的主义或信仰: *the ~ of war.* 使人为之牺牲的战争。 **2** 巨型长途运输车辆. (口)巨型长途运输车辆。huge long-distance transport vehicle.

juggle /'dʒʌgl; 'dʒʌgl/ *vi, vt* **1** [VP2A, 3A] ~ *(with),* do tricks, perform (with balls, plates, etc) to amuse people; play tricks (with facts, figures, etc) to deceive people. (用球,盘等)要把戏; 变戏法; 玩弄事实, 数字等以骗人。 **2** [VP6A, 16A] play tricks with; deceive: 以…要把戏; 诓骗; 欺骗: *The manager ~d his figures to make it seem that the company was prosperous.* 那经理玩弄数字, 以使他的公司显得兴隆。 **jug·gler** n person who ~s. 要把戏者; 变戏法者; 骗子。

jugu·lar /'dʒʌgjulə(r); 'dʒʌgjələ/ *adj* of the neck or throat: 颈部的; 喉部的: ~ *veins,* the large veins of the neck, returning blood from the head to the heart. 颈静脉。

juice /dʒuːs; dʒus/ n [C, U] **1** fluid part of fruits, vegetables and meat: 果汁; 菜汁; 肉汁: *a glass of 'orange ~;* 一杯柑汁; *a mixture of 'fruit ~s.* 综合果汁。 **2** fluid in organs of the body: 体内分泌液; 体液: *gastric/digestive ~s,* those that help to digest food. 胃 (消化)液。 **3** [U] (colloq) electricity, petrol or other source of power. (口)电,汽油,或其他动力的来源。

juicy /'dʒuːsɪ; 'dʒusɪ/ *adj* (**-ier, -iest**) **1** containing much juice: 多汁液的: ~ *oranges.* 多汁的柑。 **2** (colloq) interesting (esp because scandalous, etc). (口)有趣味的 (尤指由于诽谤等)。 **juici·ness** n

ju-jitsu /dʒuː'dʒɪtsuː; dʒu'dʒɪtsu/ n Japanese art of self-defence from which judo was developed. 柔术(柔道系由此发展而来)。

juju /'dʒuːdʒuː; 'dʒudʒu/ n West African charm or fetish; its magic power. 非洲西部的符咒或神物; 其魔力。

ju·jube /'dʒuːdʒuːb; 'dʒudʒub/ n [C] lozenge of gelatin, flavoured and sweetened. (含药物之)胶糖。

juke-box /'dʒuːk bɒks; 'dʒuk,bɑks/ n [C] coin-operated record-player. 用钱币操纵的电唱机; 自动电唱机。

ju·lep /'dʒuːlɪp; 'dʒulɪp/ n (US) spirit (eg whisky), mint and ice: (美)加薄荷和冰的酒(例如威士忌): *mint ~.* 薄荷酒。

Jul·ian /'dʒuːlɪən; 'dʒuljən/ *adj* of Julius Caesar. 凯撒的。 ~ **calendar,** the calendar introduced by him in Rome in 46 BC. 凯撒历(纪元前46年凯撒借用者); 儒略历。 ⇨ **Gregorian.**

July /dʒuː'laɪ; dʒu'laɪ/ n seventh month of the year. 七月。

jumble /'dʒʌmbl; 'dʒʌmbl/ *vi, vt* [VP15B, 2C] ~ *(up),* mix, be mixed, in a confused way: 混杂: *The untidy girl's toys, books, shoes and clothes were all ~d up together in the cupboard.* 那不整洁的女孩子的玩具, 书籍, 鞋子和衣服都乱堆在橱里。 □ n confused mixture; muddle. 杂乱的一堆, 一团糟。 '~-sale n sale of a mixed collection of old or second-hand articles. 旧杂货拍卖。

jumbo /'dʒʌmbəʊ; 'dʒʌmbo/ *adj* unusually large: 巨大的: ~ *jets;* 大型喷气式客机; ~-*sized.* 巨大型的。

jump¹ /dʒʌmp; dʒʌmp/ n **1** act of jumping; sudden spring from the ground. 跳; 跃. **the 'long/'high ~,** athletic competitions in which competitors jump a distance/height. 跳远/跳高。 **2** sudden movement caused by fear. 惊跳. **give sb a ~,** frighten him. 使某人吓一跳。**the ~s,** (colloq) form of nervous excitement with uncontrollable bodily movements. (口)神经性抽动; 舞蹈病; 震颤谵妄。 **3** sudden rise in amount, price, value, etc: (数额, 价格, 价值等之)突增; 突升; 暴涨: *a ~ in car exports.* 汽车出口之突增。 **jumpy** *adj* (**-ier, -iest**) excited and nervous. 激动而紧张的。 **~i·ness** n

jump² /dʒʌmp; dʒʌmp/ *vi, vt* **1** [VP2A, C] move

quickly by the sudden use of the muscles of the legs or (of fish) the tail; rise suddenly (from a seat, etc); move quickly (into sth): 跳; 跃; (自座位等)突然起来; 迅速进入(与 into 连用): ~ *over a fence;* 跳过篱笆; ~ *up out of one's chair;* 突然从椅子上站起来; (fig) (喻) ~ *from one subject to another in a speech.* 演说中自一问题突然转入另一问题。 ~ *down sb's throat,* answer, interrupt, him violently. 粗暴地回答或打断某人的谈话。 **,~ing·'off place,** starting point. 起点; 出发点。 '~ed-up *adj* (colloq) upstart. (口)暴富的; 骤贵的。 **2** [VP6A] pass over by moving in this way: 跳过: ~ *a ditch;* 跃过一沟; cause (a horse, etc) to move in this way: 使(马等)跳过: ~ *a horse over a fence.* 骑马跳过篱笆。 ~ **the rails/track,** (of a train, tram, etc) leave the rails suddenly. (指火车, 电车等)出轨。 **3** [VP2A, C] move with a jerk or jerks from excitement, joy, etc; start suddenly: (因兴奋, 喜悦等)跳动; 惊跳。 ~ *for joy;* 高兴得跳起来; ~ *up and down in excitement.* 兴奋得跳来跳去。 *Her heart ~ed when she heard the news.* 她听到那消息时心跳了起来。 **4** [VP2A, C] rise suddenly in price: 价格突升; 暴涨: *Gold shares ~ed on the Stock Exchange yesterday.* 昨天证券交易所中金子的股票暴跳。 **5** ~ *at,* accept eagerly: 迫不及待地接受; 欣然接受: ~ *at an offer.* 迫不及待地接受一提议。 ~ *to conclusions,* reach them hastily. 匆匆做结论。 ~ *'to it,* act quickly or promptly. 行动迅速。 ~ *on/upon,* attack, reprove severely; scold. 攻击; 谴责; 责骂。 **6** ~ *(one's) bail,* fail to appear for trial, ⇨ **bail¹.** 未能按时到庭应讯; 弃保潜逃。 ~ *a claim,* (colloq) take possession of land or mining rights, eg in a new goldfield, to which another person has already established a claim. (口)霸占土地或采矿权。 ~ **the gun,** start too soon (as from the use of a shot to start a race). 起动过早(由鸣枪起跑而来)。 *(go and)* ~ *in the lake,* (colloq, imper) go away (said dismissively or angrily). (口, 祈使)走开; 滚开(说时含不屑或愤怒)。 ~ **the queue,** (lit or fig) obtain sth without waiting for one's proper turn. (字面或喻)在未轮到前抢先获得某物; 插队。 ~ *a train,* travel illegally by goods train, eg by riding in or under a closed wagon. 违章搭乘运货火车。

jumper /'dʒʌmpə(r); 'dʒʌmpə/ n **1** outer knitted garment, with or without sleeves, pulled on over the head and coming down to the hips, ⇨ **jersey, pullover, sweater;** (US) pinafore. 一种带袖或无袖针织外衣(自头部套下, 下面齐臀部); (美)(小孩的)围兜。 **2** person, animal or insect, that jumps. 跳跃的人, 动物或昆虫。

junc·tion /'dʒʌŋkʃn; 'dʒʌŋkʃən/ n [U] joining or being joined; [C] instance of this: 连接; 会合: *The allied armies hope to effect a ~,* meet and unite. 联军希望能会师。 **2** [C] place where roads, railway lines or sections of an electrical circuit meet or diverge. 道路交叉点; 铁路交叉点; 枢纽站; 联轨站; (电路之)中继线。

junc·ture /'dʒʌŋktʃə(r); 'dʒʌŋktʃə/ n [C] (formal) (正式用语) **1** junction (1). 接合处; 接合点。 **2** state of affairs, esp in the phrase: 事情的状况(尤用于下列短语中): *at this ~,* at this time, when affairs are/were in this state. 在此时; 值此际。

June /dʒuːn; dʒun/ n sixth month of the year. 六月。

jungle /'dʒʌŋgl; 'dʒʌŋgl/ n **1** [U] (usu 通常作 the ~, sing or pl 单数或复数) (land covered with) thickly growing underwood and tangled vegetation: 丛林; 丛林地带: *cut a path through the ~;* 自丛林中开一条路; ~ *warfare;* 丛林战; ~ *birds and animals;* 丛林地带的鸟兽; '~ *fever,* malarial fever. 丛林热(疟疾)。 **the law of the ~,** (fig) ruthless competition or exploitation. (喻)无情的竞争或利用; 优胜劣败; 弱肉强食。 **2** (in compounds) (用于复合词) '~-*cat,* 林猫; '~-*fowl,* 原鸡; 林鸡。 **jun·gly** /'dʒʌŋglɪ; 'dʒʌŋglɪ/ *adj* of, like, from the ~ or its inhabitants. 丛林的; 丛林地带所居的; 似丛林的。

jun·ior /'dʒuːnɪə(r); 'dʒunjə/ n, *adj* **1** (person)

younger, lower in rank, than another: 较年幼的; 地位较低的; 较幼者; 地位较低者: *a ~ high school*; 初中; 初级中学; *~ dress sizes.* 年幼者穿的衣服尺码。 *He is my ~ by two years.* 他比我小两岁。 *He is the ~ partner in the firm.* 他是这公司地位较低的股东。 *Tom Brown, Junior* (or abbr 略作 **Jun, Jnr, Jr**), used of a son having the same first name as his father, or the younger of two boys of the same surname in a school, etc. 小汤姆·布朗 (父子同名时, 用于儿子姓名后, 或同一学校之二男生同姓时, 用于年幼者之名后)。 **2** (US schools and colleges) student in his third year (of four). (美) (四年制的中学或大学) 三年级生。

ju·ni·per /ˈdʒuːnɪpə(r); ˈdʒunəpə/ *n* evergreen shrub with dark berries from which an oil (*oil of ~*) is obtained, used in medicine, etc. 杜松(生有黑色浆果, 可以制杜松子油 oil of juniper, 用于药品等中)。

junk[1] /dʒʌŋk; dʒʌŋk/ *n* [U] old, discarded things of little or no value: 废弃的旧物; 破烂物: *an attic full of ~*; 装满废弃物的顶楼; *a ~ dealer.* 买卖废弃旧物的商人; 旧货商。 **'~-shop,** one selling cheap second-hand goods. 旧货店。

junk[2] /dʒʌŋk; dʒʌŋk/ *n* [C] flat-bottomed Chinese sailing-vessel. (平底的)中国帆船。

a junk

junket /ˈdʒʌŋkɪt; ˈdʒʌŋkɪt/ *n* **1** [C, U] (dish of) milk curdled by the addition of acid, often sweetened and flavoured. (一份)凝乳食品(由牛奶加酸制成, 常调有糖和香料)。 **2** social gathering for a feast; picnic. 宴会; 野宴。 □ *vi* take part in a ~(2). 参加宴会; 参加野宴。 Hence, 由此产生, **~·ing** *n* [U] feasting; merrymaking. 宴乐; 作乐。

junkie, junky /ˈdʒʌŋkɪ; ˈdʒʌŋkɪ/ *n* (sl) drug (esp heroin) addict. (俚)有毒瘾者; 烟毒犯。

Juno·esque /ˌdʒuːnəʊˈesk; ˌdʒunoˈesk/ *adj* (of a woman) having a stately beauty (like the goddess Juno). (指女子)有高贵美的; 端庄的(似女神 Juno 的)。

junta /ˈdʒʌntə US: ˈhʊntə; ˈhʊntə/ *n* (in Spain and Italy) deliberative or administrative council; group of army officers who have seized power by a coup d'état. (西班牙和意大利)评议或行政会议; 以武力夺得政权的军官团。

Jupi·ter /ˈdʒuːpɪtə(r); ˈdʒupɪtə/ *n* (ancient Rome) ruler of gods and men; largest planet of the solar system. (古罗马)主神; 木星(太阳系中最大之行星)。 ⇨ the illus at **planet.** 参看 planet 之插图。

ju·ridi·cal /dʒʊəˈrɪdɪkl; dʒʊˈrɪdɪkl/ *adj* of law or legal proceedings. 法律的; 诉讼程序的。

ju·ris·dic·tion /ˌdʒʊərɪsˈdɪkʃn; ˌdʒurɪsˈdɪkʃən/ *n* [U] administration of justice; legal authority; right to exercise this; extent of this: 法律的执行; 司法; 司法权; 裁判权; 审判的权限; 管辖权; 管辖区域: *The courts have ~ not only over our own citizens but over foreigners living here.* 法庭的裁判权不仅及于我们的国民, 且及于侨居此地的外国人。 *This matter does not come/fall within our ~,* We have no authority to deal with it. 我们无权过问此事。

ju·ris·pru·dence /ˌdʒʊərɪsˈpruːdns; dʒʊrɪsˈprudns/ *n* [U] science and philosophy of human law. 法学; 法理学。

jur·ist /ˈdʒʊərɪst; ˈdʒurɪst/ *n* expert in law. 法学家; 法理学家。

juror /ˈdʒʊərə(r); ˈdʒurɚ/ *n* member of a jury. 陪审团之一员; 陪审员; 评判员。

jury /ˈdʒʊərɪ; ˈdʒurɪ/ *n* (*pl* **-ries**) [C] **1** body of persons (in US and GB twelve) who swear to give a decision (*verdict*) on issues of fact in a case in a court of justice: 陪审团(英美皆由十二人组成): *trial by ~.* 陪审。 *The ~ found the prisoner not guilty.* 陪审团认为囚犯无罪。 **'~-box** *n* enclosure for a ~ in court. 陪审团席。 **2 grand ~,** specially chosen body of 12 to 23 persons who (GB until 1933) inquire into a charge in order to decide whether there is enough evidence to justify a trial or whether the case should be abandoned. 大陪审团(由十二至二十三人组成, 在英国于一九三三年前, 可调查一项指控, 俾决定是否有充分证据应使被告受审, 或对该案不予受理)。 **coroner's ~,** one that decides the cause of a death (if unnatural death, eg suicide or murder, is suspected). 验尸陪审团(于有自杀或谋杀等非自然死亡之嫌疑时鉴定死因者)。 **3** body of persons chosen to give a decision or make an award in a competition: (比赛之)评判委员会; (fig) (喻) *the ~ of public opinion,* the public, thought of as a ~, deciding a question. 舆论。 **'~·man** /-mən; -mən/ (*pl* **-men**) *n* member of a jury; juror. 陪审员。

jury-mast /ˈdʒʊərɪ mɑːst US: mæst; ˈdʒurɪˌmæst/ *n* temporary mast put up in place of one that is broken or lost overboard. 应急桅杆。

just[1] /dʒʌst; dʒʌst/ *adj* **1** in accordance with what is right: 公平的; 公正的; 正直的: *a ~ man;* 正直的人; *a ~ sentence;* 公平的判决; *be ~ to a person.* 对某人公正。 **2** well deserved; fairly earned: 应得的; 应该有的: *get/receive one's ~ deserts,* be rewarded or punished as one deserves. 得到应得的赏罚。 **3** reasonable; based on reasonable grounds: 合理的; 有理的: *a ~ opinion;* 合理的意见; *~ suspicions.* 有根据的怀疑。 **~·ly** *adv: to feel ~ly ashamed.* 应感到惭愧。 **~·ness** *n*

just[2] /dʒʌst; dʒʌst/ *adv* **1** used (GB) in the perfect tenses and (US often) with the simple past tense, placed with the *v,* to indicate an immediate past: 刚才; 方才(在英国用于完成时态, 在美国常用于一般过去时, 置于动词之前): (GB) (英) *I've ~ had dinner.* 我刚才吃完晚饭。 (US) (美) *I ~ had dinner.* 我刚才吃完晚饭。 Cf 参较 *I had dinner an hour ago.* 我在一小时前吃完了晚饭。 *My son had ~ left school.* 我儿子刚刚离开学校(毕业)。 **2** (followed by *nn, n phrases* and *clauses*) exactly; precisely: 正好; 恰好(后接名词, 名词短语和从句): *It's ~ two o'clock.* 现在的时间是两点钟正。 *This is ~ what I wanted.* 这正是我所要的。 *That's ~ what I was going to say.* 那恰好是我正要说的。 *J~ my luck!* 我的运气就是这么坏! *J~ the thing!* 就是这个东西(意思)! **3 ~ as** (*+adj+as*), **(a)** exactly as: 恰如: *Leave everything ~ as (tidy as) you find it.* 让每件东西都保持原样(象原来一样整齐)。 *Come ~ as you are,* Do not make any special preparations. 你就这样来(勿做特别准备)。 *This is ~* (= quite) *as good as the other.* 这个同另外一个简直一样的好。 **(b)** (introducing adverbials of time) when: (引导表示时间的副词短语或从句)当…之时; 其时: *He arrived ~ as I was about to go out/~ as I was shaving.* 他来到时我正要出去(正在刮脸)。 **(c)** (introducing clauses of comparison) in the same way as: (引导表示比较的从句)如同…一样: *J~ as you find it difficult to like Mr Green, so I find it easy to like his wife.* 如同你觉得格林先生难以讨人喜欢一样, 我觉得他的太太容易讨人喜欢。 **4** (with *advv*) exactly: (与副词连用)正确地: *~ here/there.* 就在这里(那里)。 **5** (used to indicate approximation) more or less: (用以表示近似)大约: *I've had ~ about enough of your impudence,* almost more than I can endure. 你的无礼几乎使我无法容忍了。 *Put it ~ over there,* near that place. 把它放在那附近。 *It's ~ about tall enough,* will be satisfactory. 差不多够高了。 **6** at this/that very moment: 此时; 现

在; 那时: *We're ~ off / ~ about to start*. 我们现在正要
出去(动身). *His new book is ~ out / ~ published*. 他的
新书刚刚出版. ~ **now, (a)** at this moment: 此刻; 现在:
I'm busy ~ now. 我现在很忙. **(b)** a short time ago: 刚
才; 方才: *Tom came in ~ now—he's probably upstairs*.
汤姆刚刚刚进来——他大概在楼上. **7 (only) ~,** almost
not; with a very little time / space / margin etc to
spare: 几乎不; 仅仅地: *We (only) ~ caught the train*,
almost missed it. 我们刚好赶上火车. *Jane ~ managed
to pass the exam*. 简妮考试刚好及格. Cf 参较 She *almost
failed*. 她几乎不及格. *I've ~ enough money to last me
till pay-day*. 我的钱刚好够我维持到发薪. **8** (used in
familiar, colloquial style, esp with imperatives, to call
attention to sth, sometimes to soften what follows): (用
于日常的口语中, 尤用于祈使句, 以引起对某事物的注意,
有时可使语气婉转): *J~ listen to him!* and note how
clever / silly / amusing, etc he is! 听他说说看! (看他多
么聪明, 愚蠢, 有趣等)! *J~ taste this!* (so that you may
judge its quality, say whether it is right, etc). 尝尝看!
(以便评定它的品质, 看看是否满意等). *J~ feel it!* and
note how hard, soft, smooth, etc it is! 摸摸看! (看它多
么硬, 软, 光滑等). *J~* (= Please) *come here a moment*.
请过来一下. *J~ a moment, please*, Please wait a
moment. 请稍等片刻. **9** only; merely: 仅; 只: *He's ~
an ordinary man*. 他只是个普通人. *I've come here ~*
(= on purpose) *to see you*. 我专程来此看望你. *Would
you walk five miles ~ to see a film?* 你愿意只是为了看一
场电影而走五英里路吗? **10** (colloq) very; very much:
(口) 很; 十分: *The concert was ~ splendid*. 那音乐会很不
错. *'Did you enjoy yourselves?'* —*'I should ~ say we
did!'* or *'Didn't we ~!'* (emph) We had a most enjoyable
time. '你们玩得痛快吗?'——(强语气) '我们玩得实在痛
快极了.'

jus·tice /'dʒʌstɪs; 'dʒʌstɪs/ n **1** [U] just conduct;
the quality of being right and fair: 公平; 公正; 合理;
公道; 公理; 正义: *treat all men with ~*. 公平对待所有
的人. **in ~ to,** in order to be just to. 公平起见. **
do ~ to,** treat fairly; show that one has a just opinion
of, that one realizes the value of: 公平对待; 公平评判;
赏识: *To do him ~, we must admit that his intentions
were good*. 公平而论, 我们必须承认他的用意是好的. *He
did ~ to the dinner*, showed by eating heartily that the
food was good. 他津津有味地吃那顿饭. **do oneself ~,**
behave in a way that is worthy of one's abilities: 发挥
自己的能力: *You're not doing yourself ~,* You could do
much better if you tried. 你尚未发挥你的能力. **2** [U]
the law and its administration: 法律制裁; 司法; 审判:
a court of ~. 法庭. **bring sb to ~,** arrest, try and
sentence (a criminal). 使(犯人)归案受审. **3** [C] judge
of the Supreme Courts: (英) 高等法院法官; (美) 最高法
院法官: *the Lord Chief J~*; 高等法院的庭长或首席法官;
the Lords J~s; 高等法院法官们: *the Chief J~ of
England;* 英国高等法院的庭长或首席法官; *Mr J~ Smith*.
法官史密斯先生. **4** J~ **of the 'Peace,** (abbr 略作 JP)

magistrate. 保安官; 治安法官. **Department of J~,**
(US) executive department, headed by the Attorney
General, supervising internal security, naturalization,
immigration, etc. (美) 司法部.

jus·tici·ary /dʒʌ'stɪʃ(ə)rɪ *US:* -ʃɪerɪ; dʒʌs'tɪʃɪ,ɛrɪ/ n
(*pl* **-ries**) (jurisdiction of a) judge or chief justice: 司
法官; 法院推事; 裁判权: (in Scotland) (苏格兰) *the High
Court of J~*. 高等法院.

jus·tify /'dʒʌstɪfaɪ; 'dʒʌstə,faɪ/ vt (*pt, pp* **-fied**)
[VP6A, 19C] **1** show that (a person, statement, act,
etc) is right, reasonable or proper: 证明(人, 言论, 行动
等)为正当: *The Prime Minister justified the action of the
Government*. 首相证明政府的该一行动是正当的. *You can
hardly ~ such conduct*. 你几乎无法证明此种行为是正当
的. *You'd be hard put to it to ~ your behaviour*. 你难以
证明你的行为是正当的. **2** be a good reason for: 为…之
好的理由; 为…辩护; 辩明: *Your wish to go for a walk
does not ~ your leaving the baby alone in the house*. 你想
出去散步并不构成将婴儿独自丢在屋中的理由. **3** adjust
(a line of type) to fill a space neatly. 调整(一行铅字)
使排满一空间. **jus·ti·fi·able** /,dʒʌstɪ'faɪəbl; 'dʒʌstɪ-
,faɪəbl/ adj that can be justified: 可证明为正当的; 有理
由的: *justifiable homicide*. 正当杀人. **jus·ti·fi·ably**
/-əblɪ; -əblɪ/ adv **jus·ti·fi·ca·tion** /,dʒʌstɪfɪ'keɪʃn;
,dʒʌstəfə'keʃən/ n [U] **1** sth that justifies: 理由: *His
justification for stealing was that his children were
starving*. 他偷窃的理由是他的儿女快要饿死了. **in
justification (for / of sth / sb),** ~ing sth: 作为
某事物之理由; 为某人辩护: *It can be said in justification
for what he had done that…*. 他所以这样做的理由是….
2 the act of ~ing sth. 证明为正当; 辩明. **3** the state of
being free from blame. 无咎.

jut /dʒʌt; dʒʌt/ vi (**-tt-**) [VP2C] *jut out*, stand out
from; be out of line (from what is around): 突出; 伸
出: *The soldier saw a gun jutting out from a bush*. 那兵
士看见一枝枪自矮树丛伸出来. *The balcony juts out over
the garden*. 阳台在花园上方突出来.

jute /dʒuːt; dʒut/ n [U] fibre from the outer skin of
certain plants, used for making canvas, rope, etc: 黄
麻的纤维: *the ~ mills of Bangladesh*. 孟加拉共和国的黄
麻纤维制造厂.

ju·ven·ile /'dʒuːvənaɪl; 'dʒuvənl/ n young person.
少年. □ adj of, characteristic of, suitable for, ~s:
少年的; 少年特有的; 适于少年的: *~ books*: 少年读物; *a
~ appearance;* 少年的外貌; *a ~ court*, where children
are tried; 少年法庭; *~ delinquency*, law-breaking by
young people; 少年犯罪; *~ delinquent*, young offender;
少年犯; *a ~ sense of humour*, eg in an adult. 少年人的
幽默感(例如用以形容某成年人).

jux·ta·pose /,dʒʌkstə'pəuz; ,dʒʌkstə'poz/ vt [VP6A]
place side by side. 并列; 并置. **jux·ta·po·si·tion**
/,dʒʌkstəpə'zɪʃn; ,dʒʌkstəpə'zɪʃən/ n [U] placing side
by side; the state of being placed side by side. 并列;
并置.

K k

K, k /keɪ; ke/ (*pl* **K's, k's** /keɪz; kez/) the 11th letter
of the English alphabet. 英文字母之第十一个字母.

Kaf·fir /'kæfə(r); 'kæfɚ/ n △ (offensive word for)
black African person. (讳) (蔑) 非洲黑人.

Kaiser /'kaɪzə(r); 'kaɪzɚ/ n Emperor (esp of Germany
before 1918). 皇帝(尤指一九一八年前之德国皇帝).

kake·mono /,kækɪ'məunəu; 'kækɪ'mono/ n Japanese
painting in a hanging scroll of silk or paper. 日本人挂
于墙上的画; 条幅.

kale, kail /keɪl; kel/ n kind of curly-leaved cabbage.
一种甘蓝.

ka·leido·scope /kə'laɪdəskəup; kə'laɪdə,skop/ n [C]

1 tube containing mirrors and small, loose pieces of
coloured glass. When the tube is turned, constantly
changing patterns are seen through the eye-piece. 万花
筒. **2** (fig) frequently changing pattern of bright
scenes: (喻) 时时变化之鲜明景色: *Sunlight and shadow
made the landscape a ~ of colour*. 阳光与阴影使那风景
的颜色化了多变万化. **ka·leido·scopic** /kə,laɪdə'skɒpɪk;
kə,laɪdə'skapɪk/ adj quickly changing. 迅速变化的; 千
变万化的.

kal·ends /'kælendz; 'kælɪndz/ n pl ⇨ calends.

kam·pong /'kæmpɒŋ; 'kæmpaŋ/ n (in Malaysia)
enclosed space; village. (马来西亚之) 房屋四周等围起来

的空地；村庄。

kan·ga·roo /ˌkæŋgə'ru:; ˌkæŋgə'ru/ n Australian marsupial that jumps along on its strong hind legs. The female has a pouch in which its young are carried. (产于澳大利亚)袋鼠。⇨ the illus at **large**. 参看 large 之插图。**~ court**, one set up without authority by workers, prisoners, etc to try someone whom they consider to have acted against their interests. 工人，犯人等私设之法庭。

kao·lin /'keɪəlɪn; 'keɪəlɪn/ n [U] fine white clay used in making porcelain, etc. (制瓷器等之)白陶土；高岭土。

ka·pok /'keɪpɒk; 'kepək/ n [U] soft cotton-like material (from seeds of a tropical tree) used for filling cushions, life-belts, mattresses, etc. 木棉。

ka·put /kə'put; kə'pʊt/ adj (pred only) (G) (sl) done for; ruined; smashed. (以作表语)(俗)(俚)不行了；完了；坏了。

karat /'kærət; 'kærət/ n (US) = **carat**(2).

ka·rate /kə'rɑːtɪ; kə'rɑtɪ/ n [U] Japanese method of unarmed combat using blows made with the hand, foot, head or elbow. (日本之)空手道。

karma /'kɑːmə; 'kɑrmə/ n (in Buddhism) person's acts in one of his successive existences, looked upon as deciding his fate in his next existence. (佛教) 羯磨；业；因果报应(个人在其本轮回生命中之行为，被视为可决定其来生之命运)。

kava /'kɑːvə; 'kɑvə/ n [U] (intoxicating drink made from the roots of a) Polynesian shrub. 卡法树(太平洋波里尼西亚群岛所产之一种灌木)；卡法酒(此种灌木根制成的酒)。

kayak /'kaɪæk; 'kaɪæk/ n Eskimo canoe of light wood covered with sealskins; any small, covered canoe. 爱斯基摩人用的覆有海豹皮的独木舟；任何有覆盖的小独木舟。⇨ the illus at **canoe**. 参看 canoe 之插图。

ke·bab /kə'bæb; kə'bæb/ n dish of small pieces of meat, seasoned and roasted on skewers. 以小木棒或叉串起的烤肉。

ked·ger·ee /'kedʒəri; 'kedʒə,ri/ n [U] rice cooked with fish, eggs, etc. 以米、鱼、蛋等烧成的食品。

keel /kiːl; kil/ n timber or steel structure on which the framework of a ship is built up: 龙骨；船脊骨；lay down a ~, start the building of a ship. 安龙骨(起工造船)。**(keep) on an even ~**, (a) (of a ship) without movement to one side or the other. (指船)平稳的。(b) (fig) steady; steadily; calm(ly). (喻)稳定的(地)；安静的(地)。□ vt, vi 1 [VP6A] turn (a ship) over on one side to repair it, clean the ~, etc. 将(船)翻至一侧(以修理，洗刷龙骨等)。2 [VP15B, 2C] ~ **over**, capsize; upset. (船)倾覆；倾覆。

keen[1] /kiːn; kin/ adj (-er, -est) 1 (of points and edges) sharp: (指尖和刃)锋利的；锐利的：a knife with a ~ edge; 刀刃锋利的小刀；(fig) (喻) a ~ (= cutting) wind; 刺骨的风；~ sarcasm. 尖刻的讽刺。2 (of interest, the feelings) strong; deep: (指兴趣，情感)强烈的；深刻的：He has a ~ interest in his work. 他对他的工作极感兴趣。3 (of the mind, the senses) active; sensitive; sharp: (指心智，感官)敏捷的；敏锐的：~ sight; 敏锐的视力；~'sighted; 视力敏锐的；a ~ intelligence. 敏捷的智力。4 (of persons, their character, etc) eager; anxious to do things: (指人，性格等)切望的；热心的：a ~ sportsman. 热心运动者。He's very ~ to see his birthplace again. 他非常渴望能再见他的故乡。~ **on**, (colloq) interested in, fond of, eager to/for: (口)对…有兴趣；喜欢；渴望：~ on going abroad. 渴望出国。Mrs Hill is ~ on Tom('s) marrying Stella / ~ that Tom should marry Stella. 希尔太太很希望汤姆和斯特拉结婚。Tom is not very ~ on Stella, does not like her much. 汤姆不太喜欢斯特拉。I'm not very ~ on jazz. 我对爵士乐不太感兴趣。~·ly adv ~·ness n

keen[2] /kiːn; kin/ n Irish funeral song accompanied by wailing. 爱尔兰的伴有恸哭的挽歌。□ vi, vt utter this song; lament (a person) in this way. 以哀哭唱出

挽歌；以哀哭唱出挽歌追悼(某人)。

keep[1] /kiːp; kip/ vt, vi (pt, pp **kept** /kept; kɛpt/) (For idiomatic uses with adverbial particles and preps, ⇨ **18** below. For **keep** and **nn** not given here, the n entries, eg ~ pace/step, ~ time, ~ watch, ~ good/early hours.) (与副词连用或介词连用之习惯用法参看下列第18义。keep与名词连用如未列于本词条下者，则参看于各该名词。)1 [VP22, 15A] cause sb/sth to remain in a specified state or position: 使(人或物)保持某种状态：~ the children quiet/happy. 使孩子们安静(快乐)。The cold weather kept us indoors. 寒冷的天气使我们呆在家里。If your hands are cold, ~ them in your pockets. 如果你的手觉得冷，就把它们放在口袋里。Will they ~ me in prison/custody? 他们会监禁(拘留)我吗？Extra work kept (= detained) me at the office. 额外的工作使我留在办公室里。Will you ~ these things safe for me? 你愿意为我保管这些东西吗？~ **an eye on**, (colloq) watch over closely: (口)注意看守：Please ~ an eye on the baby while I'm in the garden. 我去花园里的时候，请照看着这婴儿。~ **sth in mind**, remember it: 记住(某事物)：Do ~ it in mind that we expect a report next week. 千万记住下周提出报告。~ **track of/tabs on/a tab on**, ⇨ **track**(1), **tab**(2). 2 [VP19B] cause a process or state to continue: 使一过程或状态继续：Please ~ the fire burning. 请使火保持燃烧。I'm sorry I've kept you waiting. 我很抱歉使你久等了。~ **sb going**, help him to continue in some way: 帮助某人继续某种活动方式：Will £10 ~ you going until payday, cover your expenses? 十英镑可使你维持到发薪日吗？The doctors manage to ~ me going, help me to remain active. 医生们设法助我活下去。~ **the ball rolling**, ⇨ **ball**[1]. ~ **the pot boiling**, ⇨ **pot**[1](2). 3 [VP14] ~ **sb/sth from doing sth**, prevent, hold back, refrain: 阻止；防止；阻碍：What kept you from joining me? Often shortened to 略作 'What kept you?'. 什么事情使你耽搁了？We must ~ them from getting to know our plans. 我们必须防止他们知道我们的计划。We must do something to ~ the roof from falling in. 我们必须设法防止屋顶塌下来。[VP3A] ~ **from doing sth**, refrain: 抑制：I couldn't ~ from laughing. 我不禁大笑起来。4 [VP15B, 14] ~ **sth (back) (from)**, (a) not let others know about it: 不让他人知道：She can ~ nothing (back) from her friends. 她在她的朋友面前没有秘密。(b) hold back; withhold: 留下；保留：They ~ back £20 a month from my salary for National Insurance. 他们从我的薪金中每月扣下二十英镑付国民保险费。~ **sth to oneself**, (as with imper) not express, eg comments, views, etc: (常为祈使用法)不表示意见等：K~/You may ~ your remarks to yourself, I don't want to hear them. 我不要听你的评论。(b) refuse to share: 不让他人分享：He kept the good news to himself. 他没有把这好消息告诉别人。~ **one's own counsel**, ⇨ **counsel**[1]. ~ **a secret**, ⇨ **secret**. 5 [VP6A] celebrate: 庆祝；过节，庆日等：~ (with an implied complement, eg inviolate) pay proper respect to; be faithful to; observe; fulfil: (含有暗示的补足语，例如 inviolate) 遵守；忠于；履行：~ a promise/a treaty/an appointment/the law. 遵守诺言(条约，约定，法律)。~ **faith with sb**, ⇨ **faith**. 6 [VP6A] celebrate: 庆祝；过节，庆日等：~ the Sabbath, ie ~ it sacred: 守安息日：~ Christmas/one's birthday. 过圣诞节(生日)。7 [VP6A] guard; protect: 保卫；保护：~ goal, ⇨ **goal**, 守球门；~ (cricket) stand behind the wicket to stop or catch the ball, ⇨ **wicket-keeper**. (板球)守三柱门。May God/the Lord bless and ~ you, ie keep you safe. 愿上帝保佑你。8 [VP6A] continue to have; have in one's possession and not give away; not lose; preserve, eg for future use or reference: 保有；保管；保持，保留(以供将来之用或参考)：You may ~ this—I don't want it back. 你可以把这个留下来，我不要了。K~ the change, ie from money offered in payment. 零钱不要找了。Please ~ these things for me while I'm away. 我离开期间请你替我保管这些东西。We'll ~ these for another day. 我们还要将这

些再保留一天。 ~ *hold of*; ~ *a firm*／*tight hold on*, not let go: 握住;紧紧握住:*K~ a tight hold on the horse's reins.* 紧紧握住马缰。 **9** [VP6A, 15A, 22] support; take care of; provide what is needed for; maintain: 赡养; 照顾; 供应所需之物; 养护:*Does he earn enough to ~ himself and his family?* 他的收入够维持自己和家人的生活吗?*He has a wife and children to ~, poor fellow!* 他要养活妻子和十个孩子, 真是个可怜的人! *She lives with her parents but earns enough to ~ herself in clothes,* to buy her own clothes. 她和父母住在一起, 但她赚的钱够添置衣服。 *He ~s sheep in the Highlands.* 他在苏格兰高地养羊。 *He ~s a mistress in Chelsea.* 他在契尔西养了一个情妇 (hence, 由此产生, now dated, 现为过时用语, **kept woman,** one whose needs are provided by a man whose mistress she is 受赡养的情妇)。 **10** [VP6A] have habitually on sale or in stock: 经售:'*Do you sell batteries for transistor sets?'*—'*Sorry, but we don't ~ them.*' '你们经售晶体管收音机的电池吗?'—'对不起, 我们不卖那种电池。' **11** ~ *house,* be responsible for the housework, cooking, shopping, etc: 管家; 料理家务:*His sister ~s house for him.* 他姐姐(妹妹)为他管家。 ~ *housekeeper* at **house**[1]. ~ *open house,* be ready to entertain friends, etc at any time. 随时欢迎客人来临。 **12** [VP6A] own or manage, esp for profit: 经营(尤指为了牟利):~ *hens*／*bees*／*pigs;* 养母鸡(蜜蜂,猪); ~ *a shop*／*an inn.* 经营一商店(旅馆)。 Hence, 由此产生, '**shop**-~**er,** '**inn**-~**er.** **13** [VP6A] make entries in, records of: 记入; 记录:~ *a diary.* 记日记。 ~ *accounts,* records of money paid out and received. 记帐。 ~ *books,* ⇨ here. Hence, 由此产生, '**book**-~**er.** **14** [VP2C, D] continue to be, remain, in a specified condition: 保持(某种状态):*If you've got the flu,* you'd better go to bed and ~ *warm.* 你如已患流行性感冒,最好躺在床上盖暖和些。 *Please ~ quiet!* 请保持安静! *I hope you're ~ing well.* 我希望你保持健康。 *K~ cool!* (fig) Don't get excited! (喻)保持冷静(勿激动)! ~ *fit,* (do physical exercise) to remain in good health: (做运动)保持健康:(attrib) (用作定语)~*-fit classes.* 体育课。 **15** [VP6A, 2C, 3A] ~ *on*／*to,* continue in a particular direction; remain in a particular relationship to a place, etc: 继续朝某方向; 继续循…而行; 保持某种方向; 留在(某地); 保持在(某位置上):*We kept (on) our way*／*course all morning.* 我们整个早上继续前行。 *While that big lorry ~s (to) the middle of the road, we can't possibly overtake it.* 只要那辆大卡车一直沿着路中央行驶, 我们就无法超越它。 *K~ straight on until you get to the church.* 一直向前走, 便可到达教堂。 *Traffic in Britain ~s (to the) left.* 英国往来的行人等多靠左边走的。 *K~ left,* as a traffic sign. 靠左边走(指示交通向左的标志)。 *He was ill and had to ~ to his bed*／*the house for weeks.* 他病了,不得不躺在床上(留在房屋内)好几个礼拜。 *He couldn't ~ her seat,* ie on her horse. 她无法安稳地骑在马上。 **16** [VP2E, 3A] ~ *(on) doing sth,* continue doing sth; do sth frequently or repeatedly: 继续做某事; 不断或反复做某事:*K~ smiling!* 保持笑容! *Why does she ~ (on) giggling?* 她为什么不断吃吃地笑? *My shoe lace ~s (on) coming undone.* 我的鞋带老是松开。 ~ *going,* not stop; not give up; continue to function: 不停止; 不放弃; 继续起作用:*This is exhausting work, but I manage to ~ going.* 这是件累人的工作,但我设法做下去。 *I'm not sure that the company can ~ going,* continue in business. 我不能确定这家公司能否继续营业。 **17** [VP2A] (of food) remain in good condition: (指食物)保持良好状态:*Will this meat ~ till tomorrow?* 这肉能放到明天吗? Cf 参较 ~ *fresh,* ⇨ **14** above. 参看上列第 14 义。 *This news will ~,* (fig) need not be told yet. (喻)这消息目后再宣布吧。 **18** [VP2C, 3A, 14, 15B] (uses with *adverbial particles and preps*): (与副词性小品词及介词连用之用法): **keep** '*at sth,* work at it: 埋头做(某事):*K~ at it,* don't give up! 埋头做下去! ~ **sb** '*at sth,* make him work: 使某人做事:*K~ them at it!* Don't let them get lazy! 让他们做事

(不要让他们偷懒)!

keep away (from sth), avoid coming／going near (to): 远离; 不接近:*K~ away from the water's edge.* 远离水边。 ~ *sb*／*sth away (from),* prevent from going／coming near: 阻止某人或某物前去或接近:*K~ the child away from the water's edge.* 让孩子离水边远一点。

keep back (from sth), remain in the rear, at the back. 留在后面。 ~ *sb back,* restrain sb; prevent sb from advancing: 阻止某人向前。 ~ *sth back,* ⇨ **4** above. 参看上列第 4 义。

keep sb down, hold in subjection; oppress: 压服:~ *down subject nations.* 压服臣属的国家。 ~ *sth down,* **(a)** control: 控制:*He couldn't ~ down his anger.* 他无法控制他的愤怒。 *This chemical will ~ the weeds down.* 这化学药品能消除野草。 **(b)** limit: 限制:*We must ~ down expenses.* 我们必须限制开销。 **(c)** retain: 保留:*He couldn't ~ his food down,* had to vomit. 他将食物吐了出来。

keep in, eg of a coal fire in a grate, continue burning: (例如煤火等)继续烧着; 不熄:*Will the fire ~ in until we get back?* 这火能烧到我们回来吗? Cf 参较 *go out.* ~ **in with sb,** remain on good terms with, continue to be friendly with: 与某人保持友谊:*You must ~ in with your customers,* retain their goodwill. 你必须对顾客保持友善。 ~ *sb in,* (esp) detain (a child in school) as a punishment. (尤指)使(学童)留校作为处罚。 ~ *sth in,* **(a)** see that (a fire) continues to burn; 让(火)燃着:*Shall we ~ the fire in or let it out?* 我们让火烧着还是将它熄灭? **(b)** restrain: 抑制:*He couldn't ~ in his indignation.* 他抑制不住他的愤慨。 Cf 参较 *burst out.*

keep off, remain at a distance; not come: 远离; 不来:*if the rain ~s off,* if it doesn't start to rain. 如果不下雨。 ~ *off sth,* refrain from: 制止; 抑制:*Please ~ off that subject,* say nothing about it. 请不要谈那问题。 *Do please ~ off drugs,* Don't use them. 千万请不要服用麻醉药。 ~ *sb*／*sth off,* hold, cause to remain, at a distance: 使避开; 不让接近:*They made a big fire to ~ wild animals off.* 他们生起大火,不让野兽接近。 *K~ your hands off,* Don't touch it, me, etc. 把手拿开(不要碰它,我等)。

keep on (doing sth), continue; persist: 继续(做某事):~ *on (working) although one is tired.* 虽疲倦仍继续(工作)。 *Don't ~ on asking silly questions.* 不要老是问些可笑的问题。 *Why do the dogs ~ on barking?* 这些狗为什么不停地叫呢? ⇨ also **16** above. 亦参看上列第 16 义。 ~ *sth on,* continue to wear: 继续穿戴:~ *one's hat on.* 一直戴着帽子。 ~ *your hair on,* ⇨ *hair.* ~ *one's shirt on,* ⇨ *shirt*(1). ~ *sb on,* continue to employ: 继续雇用:~ *an old employee on,* not dismiss her／him. 继续雇用着一年老的职员。 ~ *on at sb,* worry with repeated complaints, questions, etc. 以不断的抱怨、发问等困扰某人。

keep out (of sth), remain outside: 留在外面; 置身于(某事物)之外: *Danger! K~ out!* 危险! 不要入内! *K~ out of their quarrels,* Don't get involved in them. 不要卷入他们的纠纷。 ~ *sb*／*sth out(of sth),* prevent from entering: 不让入内: *Shut the window and ~ the cold out.* 把窗子关上, 免得冷风吹进来。 *K~ that dog out of my study.* 不要让那狗进入我的书房。 **keep to sth, (a)** do what one has agreed to do: 履行; 遵守: *He always ~s to his promises*／*an agreement*／*his word.* 他是个守信(约)的人。 **(b)** limit oneself to: 限制自己: *Keep to the subject*／*the point at issue.* 把讨论的主题(要点)。 ~ *(oneself) to oneself,* avoid meeting people. 独居; 不交际。 **keep sb**／*sth under,* control; repress: 控制; 压制: *The firemen managed to ~ the fire under,* prevented it from spreading. 救火人员控制了火势。 *That boy needs ~ing under,* needs discipline. 那孩子需要严格管束。 ~ *sb under observation,* ⇨ *observation*(1).

keep up (with sb*／*sth), progress at the same rate (as sb／sth): 赶上; 不落后: *I can't ~ up with you,* eg walk

as fast as you. 我赶不上你(例如走得没有你那样快)。 *Dave couldn't ~ up with the rest of the class*, eg learn as quickly as his fellow pupils. 德夫赶不上班上的同学。 *Is your salary ~ing up with inflation*, growing as fast? 你的薪水赶得上通货膨胀吗? **keep up with sb/sth**, stay in contact with: 保持联系: *try to ~ up with old friends far away*: 设法与远方的老友保持联系; stay informed about: 经常有…的消息: *Alexander is careful to ~ up with the latest fashions in clothes*. 亚历山大大特别留心最新的服装式样。 **~ up with the Joneses**, compete with one's neighbours, etc (in the purchase of articles, eg clothes, a car, indicating social status). 和邻居一家人比(在购买物品如衣物、汽车等方面与邻人等相比以示社会地位)。 **~ sb up**, delay sb from going to bed: 使迟睡: *It's wrong to ~ the children up so late*, They should go to bed. 这么晚还不让孩子们去睡觉是不对的。 *I don't want to ~ you up; you look sleepy and ready for bed*. 我不想让你熬夜,你象是困倦欲睡了。 **~ sth up, (a)** prevent from sinking or getting low: 振起; 使不低落: *K~ up your courage/spirits*. 鼓起你的勇气(振作精神)。 *K~ your chin up!* Cheer up, have courage, etc. 振作精神! **(b)** observe: 遵守: *~ up old customs*. 遵守古老的风俗。 **(c)** continue: 继续: *They kept up the attack all day*. 他们一整天不断地攻击。 **(d)** maintain in proper condition: 使保持适当的状态; 维护: *How much does it cost you to ~ up your large house and garden?* 维护你的大房子和花园需要多少花费? ⇨ **upkeep, ~ up appearances**, ⇨ **appearance. (e)** continue; carry on: 使继续进行: *~ up a correspondence with an old friend*. 与一老朋友保持通信。 **~ one's end up,** ⇨ **end**¹. *Do you still ~ up your Greek*, still read the Greek classics? 你仍在研读古希腊文学吗? **~ it up,** continue without slackening: 继续下去而不松弛: *He works far too hard; he'll never be able to ~ it up*. 他工作过于努力,他绝对无法继续这样工作下去的。

keep² /kiːp; kip/ *n* **1** [U] (food needed for) support: 生计; 生活所需之食量: *The dog doesn't earn his ~*, is not useful enough to be worth the cost of keeping him. 这条狗不值得养。 **2** [C] tower of a fortress, often in (in olden times): (昔时)要塞、城堡等的高楼: *the castle ~*. 城堡的高楼。 **3 for ~s,** (colloq) permanently: (口)永久地: *Is this mine for ~s?* 这个是永久属于我的吗?

keeper /ˈkiːpə(r); ˈkipɚ/ *n* **1** guard, eg a person who looks after animals in a zoo. 看守者(例如动物园中的照看动物的人)。 **2** (in compounds) person with special duties: (用于复合词)有特别职务的人: *'park-~*; 公园(停车场等)看守人; *'lighthouse-~*; 灯塔看守人; *game-~*, ⇨ **game¹**(6); *'goal-~*, ⇨ **goal**; person who manages a shop, inn, etc: 经营商店、旅馆等之人: *'shop-~*; 店主; *'inn-~*. 旅馆老板。 ⇨ **keep**¹(11, 12, 13).

keep·ing /ˈkiːpɪŋ; ˈkipɪŋ/ *n* [U] **1** care. 保管; 照看。 *in safe ~*, being kept carefully: 安全地保管着: *The valuables are in safe ~*. 贵重物品都安全地保管着。 **2** (in verbal senses): (用动词意义来说): *the ~ of bees*; 蜂之饲养; *'bee-~*. 养蜂。 **in/out of ~ (with)**, in/out of harmony (with): (与…)一致(不一致): *His actions are not in ~ with his promises*. 他的言行不一致。

keep·sake /ˈkiːpseɪk; ˈkipˌsek/ *n* sth kept in memory of the giver: 纪念物: *Please have this ring for a ~*. 请收下这个戒指作为纪念品。

keg /keg; keg/ *n* small barrel, usu of less than 10 gallons: 小桶(通常容量在十加仑以下): *a ~ of brandy*. 一小桶白兰地。

kelp /kelp; kɛlp/ *n* [U] large kinds of seaweed. 大海藻。

kelt /kelt; kɛlt/ *n* = Celt.

ken¹ /ken; kɛn/ *n* [U] (only in) (仅用于) *beyond/outside my ~*, (colloq) not within one's range of knowledge. (口)在我的知识范围以外。

ken² /ken; kɛn/ *vt* **(-nn-)** [VP6A, 9] (Scot) know. (苏)知道。

ken·nel /ˈkenl; ˈkɛnl/ *n* **1** hut to shelter a dog. 狗舍;

狗房。 **2** (establishment for a) pack of hounds; place where dogs are cared for (eg during quarantine). 一群猎犬; 饲养猎犬之场所(例如检疫隔离时期者)。 □ *vt, vi* **(-ll-,** US also **-l-)** put, keep, in a ~; live in a ~. 置于狗舍; 养于狗舍; 居于狗舍。

kepi /ˈkeɪpɪ; ˈkɛpɪ/ *n* French military cap with a horizontal peak. 法国军人戴的平顶帽。

kept /kept; kɛpt/ ⇨ **keep**¹.

kerb (also **curb**) /kɜːb; kɝb/ *n* stone edging to a raised path or pavement. 突起于道路或行人道的石边; 边石; 道的边沿。 **'~·stone** *n* stone forming a part of this. 街道的边沿石。

ker·chief /ˈkɜːtʃɪf; ˈkɝtʃɪf/ *n* [C] (old use) square piece of cloth or lace used by women as a head covering. (旧用法)头巾。

ker·nel /ˈkɜːnl; ˈkɝnl/ *n* [C] **1** softer, inner (usu edible) part of a nut or fruit-stone. 坚果或核果的仁(通常是可食的)。 **2** part of a seed, eg a grain of wheat, within the husk; (fig) central or important part of a subject, problem, etc. (麦粒等的)粒; (喻)(问题等的)要点;实质。

kero·sene /ˈkerəsiːn; ˈkɛrəˌsin/ *n* [U] paraffin oil: 煤油; 火油: (attrib) (用作定语) *a ~ lamp*. 煤油灯。

kes·trel /ˈkestrəl; ˈkɛstrəl/ *n* kind of small hawk. 茶隼(一种小鹰)。

ketch /ketʃ; kɛtʃ/ *n* small two-masted sailing vessel used in coastal trading. 双桅小帆船(用于沿岸贸易)。

ketch·up /ˈketʃəp; ˈkɛtʃəp/ *n* [U] highly-flavoured sauce made from tomato juice, vinegar etc. 蕃茄酱(蕃茄、醋等制成的酱)。

kettle /ˈketl; ˈkɛtl/ *n* metal vessel with lid, spout and handle, for boiling water. (烧开水用的)壶。 *a 'pretty ~ of fish,* ⇨ **fish**¹(1).

kettle·drum /ˈketldrʌm; ˈkɛtlˌdrʌm/ *n* drum shaped like a hemisphere, made of brass or copper, with parchment stretched over the edge. 釜状铜鼓;定音鼓。 ⇨ the illus at **percussion**. 参看 percussion 之插图。 ⇨ **timpani.**

key¹ /kiː; ki/ *n* **1** metal instrument for moving the bolt of a lock: 钥匙: *put the key in the lock*; 把钥匙放入锁中; *turn the key*. 转动钥匙。 ⇨ the illus at **bunch**. 参看 bunch 之插图。 **'master/'skeleton key**, one that will open several locks. 万能钥匙。 **'key·hole** *n* hole in a lock, door, etc, into which a key fits. 钥匙孔。 **'key money** *n* [U] extra payment (requested by some house agents, now illegal in GB) before completion of an agreement about renting a house, flat, etc. 房屋代理人于房屋租约完成前所索的额外费用(在英国现认为不合法)。 **'key-ring** *n* (usu split) ring on which to keep keys. 钥匙环(通常可裂开, 将钥匙装上)。 **2** instrument for winding a clock or a watch by tightening the spring (上钟表发条的)钟匙。 **3 ~ (to)**, (fig) sth that provides an answer to a problem (or mystery). (喻)(问题或神秘事物之)解答; 关键。 **4** set of answers to exercises or problems; translation of sth from a foreign language: 题解; 翻译: *a key for the use of teachers only*, eg to a book of problems in algebra. 专供教师用的题解(例如代数题解)。 **5** (also attrib) place which, from its position, gives control of a route or area: (亦用作定语)在地势上可控制一路线或地区的地方; 要地: *a key position*. 险要的位置。 *Gibraltar has been called the key to the Mediterranean*. 直布罗陀一向被称作地中海的门户。 **6** (attrib) essential: 重要的; (用作定语)基本的: *key industry*, one (eg coal-mining) that is essential to the carrying on of others; 基本工业(例如煤矿工业); *a key man/a man in a key position*, one whose work is essential to the work of others. 重要人物; 中心人物。 **'key·stone** *n* (archit) stone at the top of an arch locking the others into position; (fig) central principle on which everything depends. (建筑)拱顶石; 枢石; 冠石; (喻)根本原理; 主旨。 ⇨ the illus at **window**. 参看 window 之插图。 **7** operating part (lever or button) of a typewriter, piano, organ, flute,

etc pressed down by a finger. (打字机、钢琴、风琴、笛等之)键。⇨ the illus here and at **brass.** 参看本词及 brass 之插图。**'key·board** *n* row of such keys (on a piano, organ, typewriter). (钢琴、风琴、打字机之)键盘。**8** (bot) usu one-seeded winged fruit of some trees, eg the ash and elm. (植物)(秦皮树和榆树等之)翅果。**9** (music) scale of notes definitely related to each other and based on a particular note called the *'keynote*: (音乐)调: *the key of C major*; C 大调; (fig) tone or style of thought or expression: (喻)思想或表达的格调: *in a minor key*, sadly; 忧郁地; *all in the same key*, monotonously, without expression; 无表情地; *speak in a high/low key*, urgently/not urgently. 用急切(缓和)的声调说话。**'key·note** *n* **(a)** (music)note on which a key is based. (音乐)主音。**(b)** (fig) prevailing tone or idea: (喻)主旨; 要旨: *The keynote of the Minister's speech was the need for higher productivity.* 该部长演说的要旨是更高生产力的需要。**'key·less** *adj* not having or needing a key. 无钥匙的; 无键的; 不需要钥匙的; 不需要键的; (指钟表)不需用钥匙上发条的。

key² /kiː; kiː/ *vt* [VP6A] tune (the strings of a musical instrument by tightening or loosening). 调整(乐器之弦); 调音。**key sth 'in,** bring it into harmony. 使和谐。**key sth to sth,** bring sth into harmony with sth; make connections between (the two things). 使一物与另一物相和; 连合(两事物)。**key sb up,** stimulate or raise the standard of(a person, his activity, etc): 激动; 鼓舞(人、其行为等): *The thought of the coming adventure keyed him up to a state of great excitement.* 他一想到即将来临的冒险就使他非常兴奋。*The crowd was keyed up for the football match.* 群众为该足球比赛所鼓舞。

key³ /kiː; kiː/ *n* low island or reef, esp off the coasts of Florida, W Indies. 低岛; 暗礁(尤指美国佛罗里达州和西印度群岛岸外者)。

khaki /'kɑːki; 'kækɪ/ *n, adj* (cloth, military uniform, of a) dull yellowish-brown. 黄卡其布; 黄卡其布军服; 黄褐色; 黄褐色的。

khan¹ /kɑːn; kɑn/ *n* title used by some rulers and officials in Central Asia, Afghanistan, etc; (in olden times) title used by supreme rulers of Turkish, Tartar and Mongol tribes. 中亚细亚, 阿富汗等地对某些统治者或官员的专称; (古时)可汗(土耳其、鞑靼及蒙古对最高统治者的称呼)。

khan² /kɑːn; kɑn/ *n* (in the East) inn built round a court-yard where caravans may rest. (东方)供旅行队停宿的旅馆。

kib·butz /ki'buts; kɪ'buts/ *n* (*pl* **~im** /kɪbu'tsiːm; kɪbu'tsim/) communal farm or settlement in Israel. 以色列之集体农场或农庄。**~nik** /-nɪk; -nɪk/ *n* member of a ~. 以色列集体农场之农民。

kick¹ /kik; kɪk/ *n* **1** act of kicking: 踢: *give a ~ at the door;* 踢门; *give sb a ~ in the arse.* 踢某人的屁股。*The bruise was caused by a ~.* 这瘀伤是脚踢的。**more ~s than halfpence,** more harsh treatment than reward (for what one does). 所受虐待多于优遇; 得不偿失。**'~-back** *n* (US sl) percentage payment made to sb who has enabled one to make money. (美俚)佣金; 回扣。⇨ *rake-off* at **rake¹.** **,~-'start(er)** *n* lever on a motorcycle or lawn-mower which is ~ed to start the engine. 摩托车或除草机之发动杆(借踢此杆, 始可发动)。**2** (colloq) thrill; excitement: (口)快感; 兴奋: *He gets a good deal of ~/a big ~ out of motor-racing.* 他自赛车中得到很大的乐趣。*He gets his ~s by playing football.* 他自踢足球中获得乐趣。for excitement: 为刺激或兴奋而做某事(生活): *I don't expect to win when I bet—I do it for ~s.* 我打赌时并不指望赢——我是为了刺激。**be on a ~,** (sl) be deeply absorbed in a new activity: (俚)全神贯注一新活动: *She's on a health-food ~ at the moment.* 她此刻正全神贯注在有益健康的食物上。**3** [U] (colloq) resilience; strength: (口)弹力; 力气: *He has no ~ left in him,* is exhausted. 他筋疲力尽了。*This beer has a lot of ~ in it,* is strong. 这啤酒有点烈。

kick² /kik; kɪk/ *vt, vi* **1** [VP6A, 15A, B, 2A, C] hit

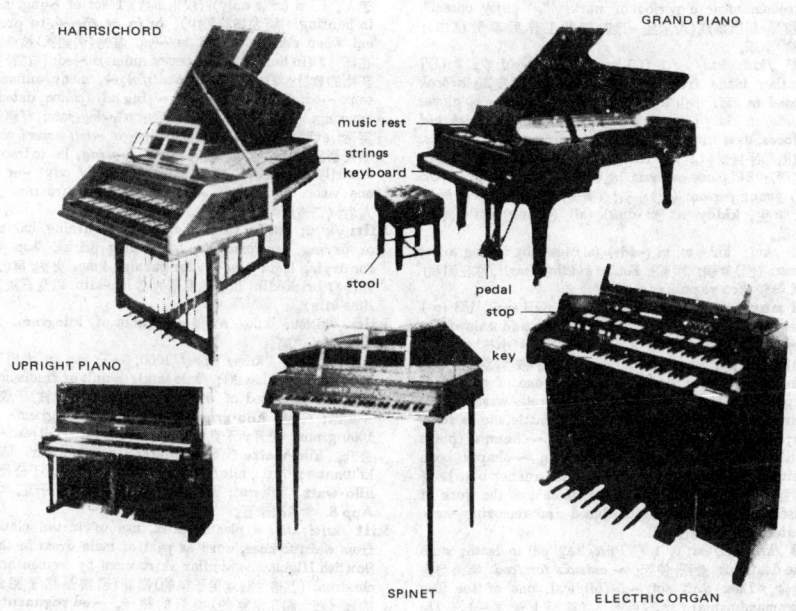

HARPSICHORD · GRAND PIANO · music rest · strings · keyboard · stool · pedal · stop · key · UPRIGHT PIANO · SPINET · ELECTRIC ORGAN

keyboard instruments

with the foot; move the foot; move sth by doing this;
move the foot or feet jerkily: 踢; 跐: ~ *a ball;* 踢一球;
~ *a man on the shin;* 踢某人的胫部; ~ *a hole in sth,*
make one by ~ing. 将某物踢穿一洞。 *The baby was
~ing and screaming.* 那婴儿又踢又叫。 *This horse ~s,*
has the habit of ~ing. 此马有好踢的习惯。 ~ *the
bucket,* (sl) die. (俚)死。 ~ *a goal,* (Rugby football)
score a penalty; convert a try. (橄榄球)罚得一分。 Cf
参较 *score a goal* in Association football. (足球) 踢得
一分。 ~ *one's heels,* be idle (as when forced to waste
time when waiting for sth/sb). 闲着; 苦等; 久候。 ~ *sb
upstairs,* (fig) get sb out of the way, eg from the House
of Commons, by giving him a higher position, eg a
peerage, so that he sits in the House of Lords. (喻)使某
人明升暗降 (例如授以爵位使某人离开下议院去做上议院
议员)。 **2** [VP2A] (of a gun) recoil when fired: (指枪
发射时)反冲; 后坐: *The old rifle ~s badly.* 这枝老式步枪
后坐得厉害。 **3** [VP2A, C, 3A, 15B] (special uses with
adverbial particles and *preps*): (与副词性小品词及介词
连用之特殊用法):
kick against/at, show annoyance; protest: 抱怨; 反对;
抗议: *He ~ed at/against the treatment he was receiving.*
他对他受到的对待表示抗议。
kick off, (football) start the game; resume after half-
time, by making the first ~. (足球)开赛; 开球。 Hence,
由此产生, *'~off n:* ~-off at 2.30. 下午两点半开赛。 ~
sth off, remove by ~ing: 踢掉: *He ~ed off his slippers.*
他踢脱拖鞋。
kick sb out, expel him: 逐出某人: *The drunken man was
~ed out of the bar.* 那醉汉被人从酒吧中逐出。
kick over the traces, ⇨ *trace*[3].
kick sth up, raise by ~ing: 踢起某物: ~ *up the carpet,*
turn up the edge by striking it with the foot. 踢起一
地毯。 ~ *up a fuss/shindy/row/stink,* (colloq)
cause a disturbance, eg by protesting vigorously. (口)
引起骚扰(例如由于激烈地抗议)。 ~ *up one's heels,* (of
a horse) make lively jumps, showing enjoyment of
freedom after a period of work; (fig) enjoy oneself.
(指马)踢腿嬉戏(表示经一段时期的工作后享受自由); (喻)享乐。

kid[1] /kɪd; kɪd/ *n* **1** [C] young goat. 小山羊。 **2** [U]
leather made from skin of this: 小山羊皮革: *a book
bound in kid.* 小山羊皮装的书。 *kid gloves n pl* gloves
made of kid. 小山羊皮制的手套。 *handle sb with kid
gloves,* deal with him gently, avoiding severe methods.
以温和手段对付某人。 Hence, 由此产生, (attrib): (用作
定语): *kid-glove methods.* 温和方法。 **3** (sl) child; (US
sl) young person: (俚)小孩; (美俚)年轻人: *college kids.*
大学生。 **kiddy** *n* (*pl* -dies) (sl) (young) child. (俚)
小孩。

kid[2] /kɪd; kɪd/ *vt, vi* (-dd-) (sl) tease by telling a lie;
hoax: (俚)欺骗; 哄骗: *You're kidding (me)!* 你在骗我!
Cf 参较 *You're pulling my leg!*

kid·nap /'kɪdnæp; 'kɪdnæp/ *vt* (GB **-pp-,** US **-p-**)
steal (a child); carry away (sb) by force and unlawfully
(esp in order to obtain a ransom). 诱拐(小孩); 绑架;
勒赎。 ~ *per n* person who ~s. 诱拐小孩者; 绑匪。

kid·ney /'kɪdnɪ; 'kɪdnɪ/ *n* (*pl* ~s) one of a pair of
organs in the abdomen that separate waste liquid
(urine) from the blood; ~ of sheep, cattle, etc as food.
肾; (牛羊等的)腰子(可用作食物)。 **,~·'bean** *n* (plant
with pod containing) reddish-brown ~-shaped bean
(either the dwarf French bean or the runner bean). 肾
形豆; 菜豆。 **~ machine** *n* one which does the work of
diseased ~s by washing the blood and removing waste
materials. 洗肾机。

kill /kɪl; kɪl/ *vt, vi* **1** [VP6A, 2A] put to death; cause
the death of: 杀死; 使死: ~ *animals for food.* 宰杀动物
为食。 *Thou shalt not ~,* (biblical, one of the Ten
Commandments). 汝不可杀人。 (圣经十诫之一)。 *The
troops were shooting to ~,* eg in a riot, shooting with the
intention of ~ing, not merely to warn or wound the

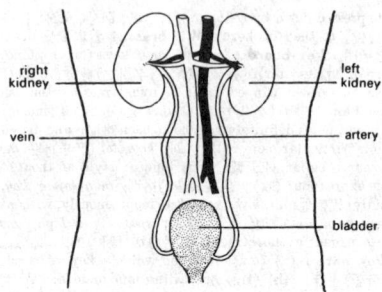

the kidneys and the bladder

rioters. 军队开枪射杀(例如平定暴动时开枪不仅为示警
或伤害, 而欲击毙暴动者)。 *The frost ~ed the flowers.* 严
寒使花枯死了。 ~ *sb/sth off,* [VP15B] get rid of: 除
去; 杀掉: *The frost ~ed off most of the insect pests.* 严寒
杀掉了大半的虫害。 ~ *time,* find ways of passing the
time without being bored, eg when compelled to wait
for sb/sth. 消遣; 消磨时间。 ~ *two birds with one
stone,* ⇨ *bird.* **2** [VP6A] neutralize, make ineffective,
by contrast: 中和; 抵消: *The scarlet carpet ~s (=
deadens) your curtains.* 这猩红色的地毯中和了你的窗帘
的颜色。 **3** [VP6A] cause the failure or defeat of; veto:
使失败; 否决: ~ *a proposal/a Bill in Parliament.* 否决
一建议(国会议案)。 **'~-joy** *n* person who throws gloom
over those who are enjoying themselves. 扫兴之人; 败兴
的人。 **4** [VP6A, 2A] overwhelm; impress deeply. 令人
不胜羡慕; 予人深刻印象。 ~ *sb with kindness,* harm
him by being excessively or mistakenly kind. 盛意对待
某人(使他受害); 宠坏某人。 *(be) dressed/got up to ~,*
dressed elaborately, so as to impress people. 打扮得十分
迷人。 □ *n* (*sing* only) (仅用单数) **1** act of ~ing, esp
in hunting. 杀(尤指狩猎中)。 *be in at the ~,* be present when sth, eg a fox, is ~ed. 某物(例如狐)被杀时
在场。 **2** (in hunting) number of animals ~ed: (狩猎) 猎
获物的数目: *There was a plentiful ~,* many animals
were ~ed. 猎获的动物甚多。 **~·ing** *adj* (colloq, dated)
amusing: (口, 过时用语) 有趣的: *a ~ing joke;* 有趣的
笑话; exhausting: 令人筋疲力竭的: *a ~ing experience.*
令人筋疲力竭的经验。 □ *n make a ~ing,* be extraor-
dinarily successful. 非常成功。 **~·ing·ly** *adv* **~er** *n*
one who, that which, ~s; (journalese) murderer. 杀
人者; (二流新闻文体的)凶手。

kiln /kɪln; kɪl/ *n* furnace or oven for burning, baking
or drying, esp '*brick-~,* for baking bricks; '*hop-~,*
for drying hops; '*lime-~,* for burning lime. 火炉; 窑(如
指砖窑 brick-kiln, 烘干蛇麻草的窑 hop-kiln, 以及石灰窑
lime-kiln)。

kilo /'kiːləʊ; 'kɪlo/ *n* (*pl* ~s) (abbr of) **kilogram.** 为
kilogram 之略。

kilo- /'kɪlə-; 'kɪlə-/ *pref* 1000, 一千 esp in 尤用于
kilo·cycle /'kɪləsaɪkl; 'kɪlosaɪkl/ *n* unit of frequency
of vibration, used of wireless waves. (无线电波)千周;
千周率; 千赫。 **kilo·gram** /'kɪləgræm; 'kɪlə,græm/ *n*
1000 grams. 公斤; 千克。 **kilo·litre** *n* 1000 litres. 千
公升。 **kilo·metre** (US = **-meter**) /'kɪləmiːtə(r) *US:*
kɪ'lɒmɪtər; 'kɪlə,mitə/ *n* 1000 metres. 公里; 千公尺。
kilo·watt /'kɪləwɒt; 'kɪlə,wɑt/ *n* 1000 watts. 千瓦。 ⇨
App 5. 参看附录五。

kilt /kɪlt; kɪlt/ *n* pleated skirt, usu of tartan cloth,
from waist to knee, worn as part of male dress in the
Scottish Highlands; similar skirt worn by women and
children. (苏格兰高地男子穿的)褶裙(通常是格子呢做
的); (妇女和儿童穿的)类似的裙子。 **~ed regiments,**
regiments of Scottish soldiers wearing ~s. 穿褶裙的苏
格兰兵团。

bagpipes
tassel
sporran
tartan kilt

kilts

kim·ono /kɪˈməʊnəʊ US: -nə; kəˈmonə/ n (pl ~s)
1 wide-sleeved long flowing gown, characteristic of
Japanese traditional costume. (日本的)和服。 ⇨ the
illus at **sarong**. 参看 sarong 之插图。 2 style of loose
garment worn as a dressing-gown. 一种宽松的晨衣。

kin /kɪn; kɪn/ n (collective pl) family; relations: (集合
名词复数)家族；亲戚: We are near kin, are closely
related. 我们是近亲。 **next of kin**, nearest relation(s).
最近的亲戚。

kind¹ /kaɪnd; kaɪnd/ adj (-er, -est) having, showing,
thoughtfulness, sympathy or love for others: 亲切的，关
蔼的；仁慈的；慈爱的: be ~ to animals. 爱护动物。Will you
be ~ enough / so ~ as to close the door? 请把门关上。
It was ~ of you to help us. 承蒙惠助，不胜感激。
~·'hearted adj having a ~ nature; sympathetic. 好心
肠的；仁慈的。 **~·ly** adv 1 in a ~ manner: 亲切地；和
善地；仁慈地: speak ~ly to sb; 温和地对某人说话; treat
sb ~ly. 和善地对待某人。 2 (in polite formulas) (用于
客套) Will you ~ly tell me the time? 请告诉我几点钟了?
3 naturally; easily: 自然地；容易地: He took ~ly to his
new duties. 他很喜欢他的新职务。He doesn't take ~ly to
being treated as an inferior. 他不喜欢被当作地位低的人
看待。 **~·ness** n 1 [U] ~ nature; being ~. 亲切；和
蔼；仁慈；慈爱。 **out of ~ness (to sb)**, because of feeling
~ (towards): (对某人)出于仁慈之心: He did it all out
of ~ness, not in the hope of reward. 他做此事完全是出
于仁慈之心 (不希望受报酬)。 2 [C] ~ show sb a ~·
ness, perform a ~ act: 帮助某人: He has done / shown
me many ~nesses. 他帮过我很多忙。

kind² /kaɪnd; kaɪnd/ n 1 race, natural group, of
animals, plants, etc: (动植物等的)类；属;: man'~; 人类;
,human'~. 人类。 2 class, sort or variety: 种类: apples
of several ~s / several ~s of apples. 几种苹果; people
of this ~. 此类人。 What ~ of tree is this? 这是哪一
种树? She's the ~ of woman who likes to help other people.
她是那种喜欢帮助别人的女子。 She's not the ~ (of
person) to talk scandal. 她不是那种诽谤他人的人。
nothing of the ~, not at all like it. 毫不相似;决非
如此。 **something of the** ~, sth like the thing in
question. 类似之事物。 **of a** ~, **(a)** of the same ~: 同
类的: two of a ~. 同类的两个。 **(b)** (implying contempt)
scarcely deserving the name: (含有轻蔑之意)徒有其名
的: They gave us coffee of a ~. 他们给我们品质极劣的
咖啡。 **a** ~ **of...**, used when there is uncertainty: 用以
表示不太确定: a ~ of suspicion (= I vaguely
suspected) that he was cheating. 我有点怀疑他在欺骗。
~ of, (sl, sometimes spelt 俚, 有时拼作 **~a** /'kaɪndə;
'kaɪndə/) adv to some extent: 有点; 有几分: I ~ of
thought this would happen. 我当时就有预感，这事将会发
生。 3 [U] nature; character: 性质；本质: They differ
in degree but not in ~. 他们的程度不同，并非性质不同。
4 in ~, (of payment) in goods or natural produce, not
in money: (指偿付)以货物；以产品；以实物: benefits in
~, benefits other than wages of salary received by employees, eg the right to buy articles at cost price: (薪资
以外之)福利 (例如给予员工以成本价格购物之权利); (of
repayment, fig) with what was received: (指回报，喻)以
所受者: repay insolence in ~, be insolent in return. 以
无礼报无礼。

kin·der·gar·ten /'kɪndəgɑːtn; 'kɪndə,gɑrtn / n
school for children too young to begin formal education.
幼儿园。

kindle /'kɪndl; 'kɪndl/ vt, vi [VP6A, 2A] 1 (cause
to) catch fire or burst into flames or flaming colour:
(使)燃烧; (使)发火焰般的颜色: The sparks ~d the dry
wood. 火星燃着了干木。 This wood is too wet to ~. 此
木柴太湿，不易燃烧。 The setting sun ~d the sky. 落日照
红了天空。 2 rouse, be roused, to a state of strong
feeling, interest, etc: 激起或被激起强烈的情感，兴趣等:
~ the interest of an audience. 引起听众的兴趣。 Her
eyes ~d with excitement. 她的眼睛显出兴奋的神色。
kind·ling /'kɪndlɪŋ; 'kɪndlɪŋ/ n [U] material for
lighting a fire, esp light, dry sticks of wood. 引火柴
(尤指轻的干木柴)。

kind·ly¹ /'kaɪndlɪ; 'kaɪndlɪ/ adj (-ier, -iest) friendly:
友善的；亲切的: speak in a ~ tone; 以亲切的声调说话;
give sb ~ advice. 给予某人友善的劝告。

kind·ly² /'kaɪndlɪ; 'kaɪndlɪ/ adv ⇨ **kind¹**.

kin·dred /'kɪndrɪd; 'kɪndrɪd/ n 1 [U] relationship
by birth between persons: 血亲关系: claim ~ with
sb. 声称与某人有血亲关系。 2 (collective pl) family;
relations: (集合名词复数)家族；亲戚: Most of his ~ are
still living in Ireland. 他的大部分亲戚现仍住在爱尔兰。
□ adj (attrib only) (仅用作定语) 1 related; having a
common source: 有亲戚关系的；同宗的；同源的: ~
languages, eg English and Dutch; 同源的语言(例如英语
和荷兰语); ~ dew, frost and phenomena; 露、霜及其同类
的现象; ~ tribes / races. 同族的部落(同类的种族)。
2 similar: 相似的: ~ natures; 相似的性质; a ~ spirit,
sb whom one feels to be congenial, sympathetic. 性情相
投之人。

kine /kaɪn; kaɪn/ n pl (old form) cows. (古)母牛。

kin·etic /kɪˈnetɪk; kɪˈnɛtɪk/ adj of, relating to, produced
by, motion. 运动的；由运动引起的。 ~ 'art, sculptural
objects parts of which may be in motion, eg from air
currents. 动态雕刻艺术 (例如由于气流而使雕刻品某部
分可运动者)。 ~ 'energy, energy of a moving body
because of its motion. 动能。 **~s** n pl (with sing v)
science of the relations between the motions of bodies
and the forces acting on them. (用单数动词)动力学。

king /kɪŋ; kɪŋ/ n 1 male sovereign ruler (esp one
whose position is hereditary) of an independent state:
国王；君主: the K~ of Denmark. 丹麦国王。 ⇨ **queen**.
K~'s / Queen's Bench, ⇨ **bench**. K~'s / Queen's
Counsel, ⇨ **counsel¹**(3). **turn K~'s / Queen's evidence**, (of one who has shared in a crime) give
evidence against accomplices (often in order to escape
punishment): (指参与犯罪者)提出对共犯不利的证据(常
是自己欲逃脱处罚而为之)。 **~'s evil**, scrofula, formerly
thought to be curable by the touch of a ~. 瘰疬(昔时
认为经君王触摸即可痊愈的一种疾病)。 K~s, either of
two books in the Old Testament, giving the history of
the ~s of Israel and Judah. (旧约圣经之)列王
纪。 2 person of great influence: 极有势力之人: an 'oil
~. 石油大王。 3 principal piece in the game of chess,
⇨ the illus at **chess**; (playing cards) court-card with a
picture of a ~: (国际象棋中的)王；将(参看 chess 之插
图); (纸牌中的)老K: the ~ of spades. 黑桃老K。
4 largest variety of a species; most prominent member
of a group, category, etc: 某一种类中之最大者: 某一
群、类等中之最显著者: the ~ of beasts, the lion; 兽中之
王(即狮子); the ~ of the forest, the oak; 橡树; the ~
of terrors, death; 死亡; ~ cobra / crab / penguin. 一种
大眼镜蛇(鳖;大企鹅)。 5 (compounds) (复合词) '~·cup
n large variety of buttercup; marsh marigold. 毛茛(一
种大金凤花); 立金花。 '~·fisher n small brightly-
coloured bird feeding on fish in rivers, etc. 鱼狗(一种
啄鱼为食，羽色鲜亮的小水鸟)。 ⇨ the illus at **bird**. 参
看 bird 之插图。 '~·pin n vertical bolt used as a pivot;
(fig) indispensable or essential person or thing. 用作轴

的螺钉; (喻) 不可缺少的人或物; 主要的人或物。 **'~-size(d)** adj (in advertising, etc) larger than normal; very large: (用于广告等中) 特大号的; 特大的。 ~-size cigarettes. 特长的香烟。 **'~·like, ~·ly** adjj of, like, suitable for, a ~; majestic; regal. 似王的; 国王的; 适于王的; 俨若君王的; 威严的。 **~·ship** /-ʃɪp; -ʃɪp/ n [U] state or office of a ~. 王位; 王权。

king·dom /'kɪŋdəm; 'kɪŋdəm/ n 1 country ruled by a king or a queen. 王国。 **the United K~ (the UK),** the Union of Great Britain (ie England, Scotland and Wales) and Northern Ireland. 联合王国(包括英格兰、苏格兰、威尔士及北爱尔兰, 即英国)。 **2** the spiritual reign of God: 上帝在世间的统治; 神权: Thy ~ come, May the rule of God be established. 愿你的国降临。 **gone to ~ come,** (colloq) dead, gone to the next world. (口) 死。 **3** any one of the three divisions of the natural world: 自然三界之一: the animal, vegetable and mineral ~s. 动物、植物与矿物界。 **4** realm or province: 领域: the ~ of thought, the mind. 思想领域。

kink /kɪŋk; kɪŋk/ n 1 irregular back-twist in a length of wire, pipe, cord, etc such as may cause a break or obstruction. (金属线、软管、绳索等之)纠结; 缠绕。 **2** (fig) mental twist; sth abnormal in a person's way of thinking. (喻)奇想; 怪念头。 □ vt, vi make a ~ in; form a ~ or ~s: 使纠结; 打结; 纠缠: This hosepipe ~s easily. 这橡皮软管容易纠结。 **~·y** adj (colloq) eccentric; perverted. (口)古怪的; 乖僻的。

kins·folk /'kɪnzfəʊk; 'kɪnz,fok/ n pl relations by blood. 亲戚; 血亲。 **kins·man** /-mən; -mən/ n (pl -men) male relative. 男亲戚。 **kins·woman** n (pl -women) female relative. 女亲戚。

kin·ship /'kɪnʃɪp; 'kɪnʃɪp/ n [U] relationship by blood; similarity in character. 亲戚关系; 血族关系; 性质之相似。

kiosk /'kiːɒsk; kɪ'ɑsk/ n 1 small open-fronted structure, esp a round one, for the sale of newspapers, sweets, cigarettes, etc, eg in a park. 小亭(尤指圆形的, 如公园等内贩卖报纸、糖果、香烟等者)。 **2** small booth for a public telephone. 电话亭; 公共电话间。

kip /kɪp; kɪp/ n (GB sl) (room or bed in a) house where beds may be rented; sleep. (英俚)寄宿舍; 客栈; 客栈的房间或床; 睡眠。 □ vi [VP2A, C] go to bed; sleep: 睡觉: time to kip down. 该睡觉的时间。

kip·per /'kɪpə(r); 'kɪpə/ n kind of salted herring, dried or smoked. 晾干或熏的咸鲱。 ⇨ **bloater.**

kirk /kɜːk; kɜk/ n (Scot) church. (苏格兰)教堂。

kirsch /kɪəʃ; kɪrʃ/ n [U] colourless liqueur made from the juice of wild cherries. 樱桃酒(野樱桃制的无色烈酒)。

kirtle /'kɜːtl; 'kɜtl/ n (archaic) woman's gown or outer petticoat; man's tunic. (古)女子的长袍或外裙; 男子的上衣。

kis·met /'kɪzmet; 'kɪzmɛt/ n [U] destiny; the will of Allah. 命运; (伊斯兰教)阿拉的旨意; 天命。

kiss /kɪs; kɪs/ vt, vi [VP6A, 2A, 15A, B] touch with the lips to show affection or as a greeting: 吻; 接吻(以表示亲密或致意): ~ the children goodnight. 向孩子们道吻道晚安。 He ~ed her (on the) cheek. 他吻她的面颊。 She ~ed the child goodbye. 她吻别那孩子吻别。 She ~ed away the child's tears. 她吻去那孩子的眼泪。 ~ the book, ~ the Bible on taking an oath. 吻圣经宣誓。 ~ the dust / ground, (a) give abject submission to a conqueror. 向征服者屈服。 (b) be killed. 被杀死。 ~ hands / the Queen's hand, the sovereign's hand on being appointed to an office (eg as a member of the Cabinet). 吻君王或女王之手(例如内阁阁员被任命时)。 ~ the rod, accept punishment meekly. 驯顺地接受处罚。 □ n touch, caress, given with the lips. 吻; 接吻。 ~ of life, method of mouth-to-mouth resuscitation, eg for sb rescued from drowning. 口对口的人工呼吸(例如救溺水者)。 **~·er** n (sl) mouth. (俚)嘴。

kit /kɪt; kɪt/ n 1 (collective sing) all the equipment

(esp clothing) of a soldier, sailor or traveller: (集合名词单数)(兵士、海员或旅行者)所有的装备(尤指衣服): 'kit inspection, examination of kit by an officer to see that it is complete, etc. (军官对士兵之)装备检查。 **'kit-bag** n long canvas bag in which kit is carried. 背包; 背袋; 行李袋。 **2** [C] equipment needed by a workman for his trade: 工人的一套工具(例如工人员降落在沙漠地区或森林中所需要者)。 **3** [C, U] outfit or equipment needed for sport or some other special purpose: 运动等的用具: 'shooting / 'golfing / 'skiing kit; 射击(高尔夫、滑雪)用具; a sur'vival kit, articles to be used by a person in distress, eg an airman who has come down in a desert or jungle. (遇难时用之)求生用具(例如飞行人员降落在沙漠地区或森林中所需要者)。 **4** [C] ,do-it-your'self kit, collection of parts, eg for a piece of furniture, or a set, to be assembled by the purchaser. 由买主自己装配的一套零件(例如家具或收音机等)。 □ vt (-tt-) [VP15B] kit sb out / up (with sth), equip. 装备。

kit·chen /'kɪtʃɪn; 'kɪtʃɪn/ n room in which meals are cooked or prepared, and for other forms of housework; (in many homes in GB) general purpose rooms, eg where meals are eaten. 厨房; (英国许多家庭中)厨房; 起居室兼餐厅。 **~ 'garden** n one for fruit and vegetables. 菜圃; 菜园。 **~ sink,** ⇨ **sink1.** **,~-sink 'drama,** drama in GB (late 1950's, early 1960's) portraying working-class family life, showing political, social and educational awareness. (二十世纪五十年代末期与二十世纪六十年代初期在英国)描写工人阶级之家庭生活, 显示政治、社会及教育意识的戏剧。 **'~ unit,** unit combining two or more articles of ~ equipment, eg a sink and a storage cabinet. 一套厨具(包括两件或多件用具, 例如一洗涤槽及一餐具柜)。 **~·ette** /-,kɪtʃɪ'net; ,kɪtʃɪn'et/ n tiny room or alcove used as a ~ (esp in a small flat). 小厨房(尤指小公寓中者)。

kite /kaɪt; kaɪt/ n 1 bird of prey of the hawk family. 鸢。 **2** framework of wood, etc covered with paper or cloth, made to fly in the wind at the end of a long string or wire. 风筝; 纸鸢。 **fly a ~,** (fig) test possible public reactions by means of hints, rumours, etc. (喻)借暗示、谣言等试探大众的反应。 Cf 参较 see which way the wind blows. **'~-balloon,** sausage-shaped captive balloon for military observation. (军事观察用的)系留气球; 风筝气球。

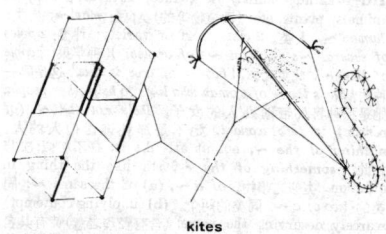

kites

kith /kɪθ; kɪθ/ n (only in) (仅用于) ~ and kin, friends and relations. 亲友。

kitsch /kɪtʃ; kɪtʃ/ adj (in the arts, design, etc) pretentious; superficial; showy. (艺术、设计等)矫饰的; 肤浅的; 炫耀的。

kit·ten /'kɪtn; 'kɪtn/ n young cat. 小猫。 **~·ish** /-ɪʃ; -ɪʃ/ adj like a ~; playful. 似小猫的; 顽皮的。

kitty /'kɪtɪ; 'kɪtɪ/ n 1 (in some card games) pool of stakes to be played for; (colloq) any joint pool or fund, eg of savings. (某些纸牌戏中)赌注; (口)共同的资金(例如储金)。 **2** (bowls) jack1(4). (滚木球戏中)小白球。 **3** child's name for a cat. (儿语)猫咪。

kiwi /'kiːwiː; 'kiwɪ/ n 1 New Zealand bird with undeveloped wings; (sl) New Zealander. 几维; 鹬鸵(产于新西兰的一种无翼鸟); (俚)新西兰人。 ⇨ the illus at

rare, 参看 rare 之插图。

klaxon /'klæksn; 'klæksən/ n (P) powerful electric warning horn(5). (商标)一种声音大的示警用电动喇叭。

kleenex /'kli:neks; 'kli,neks/ n (P) [U, C] tissue paper. (商标)一种卫生纸。 ⇨ **tissue(3).**

klep·to·mania /,kleptə'meinɪə; ,kleptə'menɪə/ n obsessive wish to steal, not necessarily from poverty. 偷窃狂；盗癖。 **klep·to·maniac** /-nɪæk; -nɪæk/ n person with ~. 有偷窃狂的人。

knack /næk; næk/ n (rarely pl) cleverness (intuitive or acquired through practice) enabling one to do sth skilfully: (罕用复数) (直觉的或由练习而得的)技巧; 诀窍: There's a ~ in it, You have to learn by doing it. 这里面有技巧(你必须做方能学会)。 It's quite easy to drive a car when you have／get the ~ of it. 你要是知道窍门驾驶汽车就容易了。

knacker /'nækə(r); 'nækə/ n 1 person who buys and slaughters useless horses (to sell the meat and hides). 购买并屠杀废马之人(为卖马肉和皮)。 2 person who buys and breaks up old houses, ships, etc for the materials in them. 收买废屋、废船等者(买来拆掉取其材料)。 ~'s **yard,** place where old metal goods, etc are broken up for scrap. 拆旧金属物品等之场所。

knap /næp; næp/ vt (-pp-) break (flints for roads) with a hammer. 以锤敲碎(燧石用以铺路)。

knap·sack /'næpsæk; 'næp,sæk/ n [C] canvas or leather bag, strapped to the back and used (by soldiers, travellers) for carrying clothing, food, etc. (士兵、旅行者用的帆布或皮制的)背囊。

knave /neɪv; nev/ n 1 (old use) dishonest man; man without honour. (旧用法)不诚实的人；不名誉的人。 2 (playing cards) court-card between 10 and Queen in value: (纸牌)介于十点与王后间的一张牌; 杰克: the ~ of hearts. 红心 J。 ⇨ **Jack.** **knav·ery** /'neɪvərɪ; 'nevərɪ/ n [U] dishonesty; [C] (pl -ries) dishonest act. 不诚实；不诚实的行为。 **knav·ish** /'neɪvɪʃ; 'nevɪʃ/ adj deceitful: 欺诈的: knavish tricks. 欺诈的手段。 **knav·ish·ly** adv

knead /ni:d; nid/ vt [VP6A] 1 make (flour and water) into a firm paste (dough) by working with the hands; do this with wet clay; make (bread, pots) in this way. 揉(面粉和水)成团；揉(湿的粘土)成团；捏制(面包、陶器)。 2 massage; apply hands to (muscles, etc) as if making dough. 按摩；揉捏(肌肉等)。

knee /ni:; ni/ n 1 joint between the thigh and the lower part of the leg in man, ⇨ the illus at **leg;** corresponding part in animals. (人或动物之)膝；膝盖 (参看 leg 之插图)。be on／go (down) on one's ~s, be kneeling／kneel down (to pray, or in submission). 跪着(祈祷或屈服)。 bring sb to his ~s, force him to submit. 迫使某人屈服。 2 part of a garment covering the ~s: 服装之膝部: the ~s of a pair of trousers. 裤之膝部。 3 (compounds) (复合词) '~-breeches /-brɪtʃɪz; -brɪtʃɪz/ n pl breeches reaching down to or just below the ~s. (长及膝部的)短裤。 '~-cap n (a) flat, movable bone forming the front part of the ~-joint. 膝盖骨。 ⇨ the illus at **skeleton.** 参看 skeleton 之插图。 (b) protective covering for the ~. 护膝之物。 '~-deep adj, adv so deep as to reach the ~s: 深及膝的(地): The water was ~-deep. 水深及膝。 '~-high adj, adv so high as to reach the ~s: 高及膝的(地): The grass was ~-high. 草高及膝。

kneel /ni:l; nil/ vi (pt, pp knelt /nelt; nɛlt/) [VP2A, C] ~ (down), go down on the knees; rest on the knees: 跪下; 跪倒: He knelt down to look for a coin he had dropped. 他跪下找他掉了的一个钱币。 Everyone knelt in prayer. 每个人都跪下来祈祷。

knell /nel; nɛl/ n (sing with a or the) sound of a bell, esp for a death or at a funeral; (fig) sign of the end or death of sth: (单数，与 a 或 the 连用)钟声；(尤指)丧钟声；(喻)结束或死亡之征兆: toll the ~; 敲丧钟; the ~ of

her hopes. 她的希望破灭的征兆。

knelt /nelt; nɛlt/ ⇨ **kneel.**

Knes·set /'kneset; 'knɛsɛt/ n Israeli parliament. 以色列国会。

knew /nju: US: nu:; nju/ ⇨ **know.**

knicker·bock·ers /'nɪkəbɒkəz; 'nɪkə,bakəz/ n pl loose wide breeches gathered in below the knees. 灯笼裤。

knickers /'nɪkəz; 'nɪkəz/ n pl 1 (US) knickerbockers. (美)灯笼裤。 2 (dated) woman's or girl's drawers from the waist to the thighs. (过时用语)女用自腰至股的内裤。 get one's ~ in a twist, (GB sl) become confused. (英俚)混乱；糊涂。

knick-knack /'nɪk næk; 'nɪk,næk/ n small ornament, piece of jewellery, article of dress, piece of furniture, etc. 小装饰品、珠宝、衣服、家具等；小玩意儿。

knife /naɪf; naɪf/ n (pl knives /naɪvz; naɪvz/) sharp blade with a handle, used as a cutting instrument or as a weapon: (有柄的)刀: a 'table ~, used for food at table; 餐刀; a 'pocket ~, one with hinged blade(s). (刀刃可以折合的)小刀。 get one's ~ into sb, have the wish to harm him. 欲伤害某人。 war to the ~, war without mercy; relentless enmity. 惨烈之战；血战。 '~-edge n cutting edge of the blade of a ~. 刀刃。 on a ~-edge, (of a person awaiting) an important outcome, result, etc) extremely uncertain. (指重要结果等)十分不确定的；(指等待重要结果之人)十分不安的。 □ vt [VP 6A] cut or stab with a ~. 用刀切割；用刀刺。

knight /naɪt; naɪt/ n 1 (in the Middle Ages) man, usu of noble birth, raised to honourable military rank (after serving as a page and squire). (中古时代的)武士；骑士。 ,~-'errant /-'erənt; -'ɛrənt/ n (pl ~s-errant) ~ who went about in search of adventure. 游侠骑士。 2 (GB modern use) man on whom a title or honour is conferred (lower than that of baronet) as a reward for services to the State. (The title Sir is always used before the man's first name, with or without his surname, as in Sir Harold; Sir James Hill). (英国现代用法)爵士(低于从男爵之爵位,颁给对国家有贡献者,其名之前冠以 Sir, 带不带姓皆可,例如 Sir Harold; Sir James Hill)。 3 (GB history) (英史) ~ (of the shire), person who represented a shire or county in Parliament. 郡选议员。 4 piece in the game of chess, usu made with a horse's head. (国际象棋)马(有马头的棋子)。 ⇨ the illus at **chess.** 参看 chess 之插图。 □ vt [VP6A] make (sb) a ~. 授以爵士位。 ~·hood /-hʊd; -hʊd/ n 1 [U] rank, character or dignity of a ~; [C] a particular ~hood: 骑士位；骑士或爵士的地位, 身份或尊严; 某一骑士位: The Queen conferred ~hoods on two magicians. 女王授与两位魔术师骑士之位。 2 [U] ~s collectively: 骑士; 爵士(总称): the ~hood of the Commonwealth. 英联邦所有的骑士。 ~·ly adj chivalrous; brave and gentle; like a ~: 侠义的; 勇敢而文雅的; 似骑士的: ~ly qualities. 武士气概。

knit /nɪt; nɪt/ vt, vi (pt, pp ~ted or (old use) (旧用法) **knit,** -tt-) [VP6A, 15A, B, 2A, C] 1 ~ sth (up) (from／into), make (an article of clothing, etc) by looping wool, silk, etc yarn on long needles: 编织 (衣物等): ~ stockings out of wool; 用毛线织长袜; ~ wool into stockings; 织毛线长袜; ~ sth up, repair it by ~ting. 织补某物。 She often ~s while reading. 她常常在看书时织东西。 2 unite firmly or closely: 坚固或密切地结合: ~ broken bones; 接合碎骨; a closely ~ argument. 紧凑的论据。 Mortar is used to ~ bricks together. 灰泥是用来粘合砖的。 The two families are ~ together by common interests. 这两家族因共同的利益而结合在一起。 3 draw together. 皱起。 ~ one's／the brows, frown. 皱眉头。 ~·ter n person who ~s. 编织者。 ~·ting n [U] 1 action of one who ~s. 编织。 2 material that is being ~ted: 编织物: Her ~ting fell from her lap to the floor. 她织的东西从她膝上掉在地板上。 '~·ting-machine n machine that ~s. 针织机。 '~·ting-needle

n long slender rod of steel, wood, etc two or more of which are used together in ~ting. 织针。 **~·wear** /-weə(r); ,war/ *n* [U] (trade use) ~ted garments. (商业用法)编织之衣物。

knives /naɪvz; naɪvz/ ⇨ **knife**.

knob /nɒb; nɑb/ *n* [C] **1** round-shaped handle of a door, drawer, walking-stick, etc; control, eg of a radio or television set: (门、抽屉、手杖等的)圆形把手; 旋钮; 拎头(例如收音或电视机者): *turn the ~ clockwise to switch the set on.* 将旋钮顺时针方向转打开收音机(电视机)。 **2** round-shaped swelling or mass on the surface of sth, eg a tree trunk. 圆形突出物; 节(如树干上者); 球块; 瘤; 疙瘩。 **3** small lump (eg of coal). 小块(例如煤块)。 **'~·ker·rie** /'nɒbkerɪ; 'nɑb,kerɪ/ *n* short stick with a knob at ~ at one end of it, formerly used as a weapon (by S African tribes). 圆头棒(南非土人昔时用作武器)。

knob·ble /'nɒbl; 'nɑbl/ *n* small knob. 小节; 小瘤; 小球块。 **knob·bly** /'nɒblɪ; 'nɑblɪ/ *adj* (-ier, -iest) having ~s: 有圆形突出物的; 有节的; 有疙瘩的; 有球块的: *bly knees.* 有疙瘩的膝盖。

knock¹ /nɒk; nɑk/ *n* [C] **1** (short, sharp sound of a) blow: 击; 打; 敲; 短促的敲击声: *He got a nasty ~ on the head when he fell.* 他跌倒时头部受到严重的碰撞。 *I heard a ~ at the door.* 我听到了敲门声。 *I knew him by his ~,* because of the way he ~ed (at the door). 从他的敲门声我知道是他。 **~ for ~,** situation in a motoring accident when insurance companies agree to pay only for the damage to the vehicle for which they are liable. 车祸发生后保险公司仅赔偿车辆之损坏。 **2** sound of ~ing in a petrol engine. 汽油发动机因故障而发出的爆声。 ⇨ knock²(3), and anti~. **3** (cricket) innings: (板球)一局: *have a good ~.* 好好地打一局球。 **4** (sl) criticism; insult; financial loss: (俚)批评; 侮辱; 财务损失: *He's taken a bad ~,* suffered a financial reverse. 他损失了少量钱。 **~er** *n* person or thing that ~s; (esp) hinged metal device on a door for ~ing on it (now often replaced by an electric bell). 敲击之人或物; (尤指)门环(现多以电铃取代之)。

knock² /nɒk; nɑk/ *vt, vi* **1** [VP6A, 15A, B, 14, 22, 2A, C] hit; strike; cause to be (in a certain state) by hitting; make by hitting: 击; 打; 敲; 击成(某种状态): *Someone is ~ing at the door/on the window.* 有人敲door (窗子)。 *Come in—don't ~.* 进来, 不要敲门。 *He ~ed the bottom out of the box.* 他把箱底打掉了。 *Let's ~ a hole in the wall.* 我们就在墙上打个洞吧。 *He ~ed (= struck by accident) his head on/against the wall.* 他的头撞在墙上了。 *The blow ~ed me flat/senseless.* 那一击把我击倒在地上(使我失去了知觉)。 **~ one's head against a brick wall,** (fig) achieve nothing. (喻)无成就。 **~ sb/sth into a cocked hat,** ⇨ cock³(1). **~ the bottom out of an argument,** ⇨ bottom(7). **~ spots off sth/sb,** ⇨ spot. **2** [VP6A] (sl) surprise; shock: (俚)使惊讶; 使震惊: *What ~s me is his impudence.* 使我大为惊讶的是他的厚颜无耻。 **3** [VP2A] (of a petrol engine) make a tapping or thumping noise (because of a defect that prevents the engine from running smoothly): (指用汽油的发动机)发爆声(因有毛病致机器不能畅动): *The engine of this old car is ~ing badly.* 这部老汽车的引擎发爆声响得厉害。 ⇨ knock¹(2). **4** [VP6A] (sl) criticize unfavourably: (俚)批评; 攻击: *Why must you always ~ my driving?* 你为何总是批评我的驾驶技术? **5** (compounds) (also ⇨ (6) below) (复合词) (亦参看下列第6义) **'~-about** *adj* (of a comic performance) = slapstick; ⇨ slap; (of clothes) suitable for rough wear. (指滑稽演出)喧器的; (指衣服)粗的。 **'~-down** *adj* (of prices, eg at an auction) lowest at which goods are to be sold; reserve price. (指价格, 例如拍卖时)最低的; 起码的; 最低价的。 **(b)** (fig) overwhelming; stunning. (喻)压倒的; 锐不可当的。 **'~-kneed** *adj* having legs curved so that the knees touch when walking. 膝外翻的(两腿向内弯曲, 故行走时两膝互

撞)。 **'~-out** *adj, n* **(a)** (abbr 略作 **KO**) (blow) that ~s a boxer out. (拳击)打倒对手的(一击); 获胜的一击。 **(b)** (of a) tournament or competition for eliminating weaker competitors. 淘汰赛的。 **(c)** (colloq) (person, thing) impressive or attractive: (口)予人印象深刻的; 动人的(人或物): *Isn't she a ~out!* 她多么动人啊! **(d)** (sl) drug, etc which induces sleep or unconsciousness: (俚)迷药: *~out pills.* 迷药丸。 **6** [VP2C, 15B] (uses with *adverbial particles* and *preps*): (与副词性小品词和介词连用的用法):

knock about, (colloq) lead an unsettled life, travelling and living in various places: (口)过漂泊不定的生活: *He has ~ed about all over Asia.* 他曾在亚洲到处漂泊。 **~ about (with sb),** (sl) have a (casual) (sexual) relationship with sb: (俚)与某人发生(随便的)(性)关系: *She's ~ing about with a married man.* 她正同一位已婚的男人有染。 **~ sb/sth about,** hit repeatedly, treat roughly: 接连敲打; 粗鲁地对待: *The ship had been ~ed about by storms.* 那艘曾饱受风暴的摧残。

knock sth back, (sl) drink: (俚)饮: *~ back a pint of beer.* 饮一品脱啤酒。

knock sb down, strike to the ground or floor: 击倒; 打倒: *He was ~ed down by a bus.* 他被公共汽车撞倒了。 *He ~ed his opponent down.* 他将他的对手击倒。 *You could have ~ed me down with a feather,* I was very surprised. 我甚为吃惊。 **~ sth down, (a)** demolish: 拆除: *These old houses are to be ~ed down.* 这些旧房屋将被拆除。 **(b)** take to pieces to save cost and space in transport: 拆散以节省运费和空间: *The machines will be ~ed down before being packed for shipment to Singapore.* 这些机器在包装运往新加坡之前将被拆卸。 Hence, 由此产生, **'~-down** *furniture,* etc, which can be taken to pieces. 可拆卸的家具。 **~ sth down to sb,** (at an auction sale) sell (to a bidder): (拍卖时) 卖 (给出价者): *The painting was ~ed down to Mr Smith for £50.* 那幅画以五十英镑拍卖给史密斯先生了。 **~ sth/sb down (to sth),** (compel sb to lower a price: (强迫某人)减价: *He asked £500 for his car but I managed to ~ him down 10 per cent/~ed his price down to £450.* 他的汽车要卖五百英镑, 但我总算使他减价百分之十(使其价格减低为四百五十英镑)。 Hence, 由此产生, **~-down prices.** 减低的价格。 ⇨ knock-down at (5) above. 亦参看上列第5义中之 knock-down。

knock sth in, strike so that sth goes/stays in: 打入; 敲进: *~ in a nail;* 敲进一钉; *~ in the top of a barrel.* 将桶顶敲进。

knock off (work), stop work: 停止(工作): *It's time to ~ off for tea.* 该停工喝茶了。 **~ sb,** (sl) quickly seduce and then abandon. (俚)迅速诱奸然后遗弃。 **~ sth off, (a)** deduct: 减除: *I'll ~ 50p off the price.* 我愿减价五十便士。 **(b)** compose or finish rapidly: 迅速写成: *~ off an article/some verses for a magazine.* 迅速为一杂志匆匆写一文章(几节诗)。 **(c)** (cricket) score quickly: (板球)迅速得分: *~ off the runs needed to win a match.* 迅速获得赢得比赛所需要的分数。 **(d)** (sl) break into, rob: (俚)抢劫: *~ off a bank.* 抢劫银行。 **K~ it off!** (sl) Stop it! (俚)停止! 住手! 不要吵!

knock on, (Rugby) ~ the ball forward when trying to catch it (a foul). (橄榄球)欲接球时将球击向前(为犯规动作)。 Hence, 由此产生, **~-on** *n.* **'~-on effect** *n* (colloq) (usu unpleasant) consequence. (口)结果; (通常指)不愉快的结果。

knock sb out, (a) (boxing) strike (an opponent) so that he cannot rise to his feet for the count. (拳击)击倒(对手, 使无法于规定时间内站起)。 **(b)** (fig) overwhelm; stun: (喻)使震惊: *She was ~ed out by the news.* 这消息使她非常吃惊。 **(c)** **~ sb out (of),** eliminate him from a competition): (击败某人) 使退出 (比赛)。 (by defeating him). **~ sth out,** empty by ~ing: 敲空: *~ out one's pipe,* ie of ash, etc. 磕烟斗。

knock (things) together, make roughly or hastily: 匆匆凑成: *~ boards together for a camp table.* 用木板匆匆

湊成一露營用的桌子。*The bookshelves had obviously been ~ed together*, not made with care. 那些書架顯然是匆匆拼成的。*~ your/their heads together*, use force to prevent you/them from quarrelling, being foolish or stubborn. 迫使你们/(他们)停止争吵,不再愚蠢或固执。**knock up**, (tennis) practise shots before the start of a match. (网球)赛前练球。 **~ sb up**, **(a)** (GB colloq) waken or rouse sb by ~ing at his door, etc: (英口)敲门等以唤醒: *Please could you ~ me up at seven o'clock.* 请在七点钟敲门叫醒我。 **(b)** (GB colloq) make tired; exhaust: (英口)使疲倦; 使筋疲力竭: *He was ~ed up after the long steep climb.* 经长时间险峻的攀登后, 他已疲惫不堪了。 **(c)** (US sl) attack; beat up. (美俚)攻击; 痛打。 **(d)** △ (US vulg sl) (of a man) have sexual intercourse with; make pregnant. (伟)(美鄙俚)(指男人)与某女子有性关系; 使怀孕。 **~ sth up**, **(a)** drive upwards with a blow: 向上击: *K~ his arm up!* 向上打他的胳臂! **(b)** arrange, put together quickly: 迅速安排; 匆匆凑成: *~ up a meal from whatever there is in the larder*; 用食橱中所有的东西匆匆做好一餐饭。 *~ up a shelter for mountain-climbers.* 为登山者草草搭成一棚。 **(c)** score (runs) at cricket. (板球)得(分)。 **~ up copy**, prepare material for printing (in a newspaper, etc). (为报纸等)预备排印资料。

knoll /nəʊl/ nol/ *n* small hill; mound. 小山; 小丘。

knot /nɒt/ nɑt/ *n* [C] **1** parts of one or more pieces of string, rope, etc, twisted together, usu to make a fastening: (绳索等之)结: *tie a ~ in a rope*; 在绳上打一结; *tie a rope in a firm ~*; 将绳打一牢结; *make a ~*;

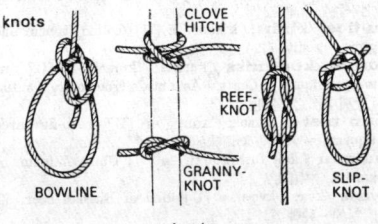

knots CLOVE HITCH REEF-KNOT GRANNY-KNOT BOWLINE SLIP-KNOT

knots

打一结; (fig) sth that ties together: (喻)结合物: *the 'marriage-~.* 婚姻结合。 **2** piece of ribbon, etc twisted and tied as an ornament. (丝带等打成的装饰用的)花结。 **3** difficulty; hard problem. 困难; 难题。 *tie oneself in/up in/into ~s*, get badly confused about sth. 对某事深感困惑。 ⇨ **Gordian**. **4** hard lump in wood where a branch grew out from a bough or trunk; round cross-grained piece caused by this in a board. (树木或木板上的)节; 节瘤; 木节。 **'~-hole** *n* hole (in a board) from which such a piece has come out. 木板上的节疤孔。 **5** group of persons or things: 一群人或物: *People were standing about in ~s, anxiously waiting for news.* 一群人成群伫立, 急切等候消息。 **6** measure of speed for ships: 节(测船速的单位); 海里: *a vessel of 20 ~s, able to sail 20 nautical miles an hour.* 时速二十海里之船。⇨ **App 5.** ⇨ 参看附录五。 □ *vt, vi* (-tt-) [VP6A, 15B, 2A] make a ~ or ~s in; tie sth with ~s; form ~s: 打结于; 包扎; 成结: *~ two ropes together*; 将两绳打一结连起来; *tie a parcel firmly*; 将一包裹扎紧; *string that ~s easily.* 容易打结的绳子。 **~ty** *adj* (-ier, -iest) full of ~s: 多结的; 多节的; 多困难的: *a ~ty board.* 多节的木板。 *a ~ty problem*, one that is difficult to solve. 难题。

know /nəʊ/ no/ *vt, vi* (*pt* **knew** /nju: *US*: nu:/, *pp* **known** /nəʊn/ non/) **1** [VP6A, 8, 9, 10, 17, 25, 2A] have in the mind as the result of experience or of being informed, or because one has learned: 知道; 晓得; 懂得: *Every child ~s that two and two make four.* 每个孩子都知道二加二等于四。 *He ~s a lot of English.* 他懂得许多英语。 *Do you ~ how to play chess?* 你会下国际象

棋吗? *I don't ~ whether he is here or not.* 我不知道他是否在此地。 *I ~ (that) he's an honest man.* 我知道他是个诚实的人。 *I ~ him to be honest.* 我知道他是诚实的人。 *I'm not 'guessing—I really ~.* 我不是在猜想——我真知道。 *Oh, yes, I ~ all about that.* 哦, 是的, 我对那事全知道。 *There's no ~ing* (= It is impossible to ~) *when we shall meet again.* 不知道何时我们能再相见。 [VP17, 18B] (past and perfect tenses only): (仅用于过去时和完成时): *I have never ~n a man (to) die of love, but I have ~n a disappointed lover (to) lose weight.* 我从未看到有人因恋爱而死, 但我曾看到失恋的人消瘦。 **~ one's business/what's 'what/the ropes/a 'thing or two**, have common sense, good judgement, practical experience. 明事理; 有头脑; 精明能干。 **~ better than to do sth**, be wise enough not to...: 明白事理而不至于...: *You ought to ~ better than to go swimming on such a cold day.* 你应该知道在这样冷的天去游泳是不对的。 **2** [VP6A] be acquainted with (a person); be able to distinguish (sb) from others: 认识(一人); 认出: *Do you ~ Mr Hill?* Have you met him, talked with him, etc? 你认识希尔先生吗? (Cf 参较 *Do you ~* (1) *when Napoleon was?* 你知道拿破仑是谁吗?) *I ~ Mr White by sight but have never spoken to him.* 我认识怀特先生, 但从未同他说过话。 *I've ~n Mrs Grey since I was a child.* 我从小便认识格雷太太。 *I was introduced to Miss Wood last week, but I've a bad memory for faces and might not ~* (= recognize) *her again.* 上星期我经介绍认识了伍德小姐, 但我对面孔的记忆力很差, 再见面时可能认不出她来了。 **make oneself ~n to sb**, introduce oneself: 自我介绍: *There's your host; you'd better make yourself ~n to him.* 那边是你(的)主人, 你最好向他做一番自我介绍。 **be ~n to**: 为...所熟知: *He's ~n to the police*, The police have his name in their records, eg because he has been a criminal. 警方认识他(例如因其曾犯过案; 在他们的记录中有他的名字)。 **be ~n as**: 以...著称; 通称为: *He's ~n as* (= has the reputation of being) *a successful architect.* 他以成功的建筑师闻名。 **~ sb from sb**, distinguish from: 辨识: *They're twins and it's almost impossible to ~ one from the other.* 他们是双生, 旁人几乎无法辨别。 **not ~ sb from Adam/from a bar of soap**, (colloq) have no idea who he is. (口)不晓得某人是谁。 **3** [VP6A] have personal experience of: 经历; 遭受: *He knew poverty and sorrow in his early life.* 他早年经历过穷困与忧患。 *He's ~n better days*, has not always been so poor, unfortunate, etc, as he is now. 他曾享受过好日子(并不总是象现在这样穷愁潦倒等)。 **4** [VP6A] be able to recognize: 能辨识: *He ~s a good singing voice when he hears one.* 他有辨识好的歌声的能力。 *He ~s a swallow from a house-martin.* 她分别不出移居的燕和墙上筑巢的燕。 **5** [VP3A] **~ about/of**, have information concerning; be aware of: 知道关于...的事情; 知道: *I knew about that last week.* 我上星期听说了那事。 *I didn't ~ about that, was in ignorance.* 我不知道那事。 *I ~ of an excellent little restaurant near here.* 我听说附近有一家非常好的小餐馆。 *'Has Smith been ill?'—'Not that I ~ of.'* I am not aware of his having been ill. '史密斯病了吗?'—'我没听说。' *I don't actually ~* (2) *the man you mention, but of course I ~ 'of him*, I'm aware of his existence. 我不认识你提到的这个人, 不过我的确听说过他。 **6** (compounds) (复合词) **don't-~** *n* (colloq) person who is unable to give an answer in a poll(2). (口)民意调查中不能回答问题之人。 **'~-all** *n* person who ~s, or claims to ~, everything. 无所不知之人; 自称无所不知之人。 **'~-how** *n* [U] faculty of ~ing how (to do sth); knowledge of methods; ingenuity (contrasted with theoretical knowledge). 技能; 方法上的知识; 技巧(以别于理论上的知识)。 □ *n* (only in) (仅用于) *in the ~*, (colloq) having information not shared by all or not available to all. (口)知道实情的; 熟识内幕的。

know·ing /'nəʊɪŋ/ 'noɪŋ/ *adj* cunning; wide-awake; having, showing that one has, intelligence, sharp wits,

etc: 狡黠的; 机警的; 聪颖的; 伶俐的: *a* ~ *fellow;* 机警的人; ~ *looks.* 狡黠的样子。 ~·**ly** *adv* **1** consciously; intentionally: 有意地; 故意地: *He would never* ~*ly do anything to hurt your interests.* 他绝不会故意做出任何损害你利益的事。 **2** in a ~ manner: 狡黠地; 机警地: *look* ~*ly at someone.* 狡黠地瞧着某人。

knowl·edge /'nɒlɪdʒ; 'nɑlɪdʒ/ *n* [U] **1** understanding: 了解; 理解: *A baby has no* ~ *of good and evil.* 婴儿不了解善恶。 **2** familiarity gained by experience; range of information: 通晓; 知识; 见闻; 消息: *My* ~ *of French is poor.* 我的法语不太好。 *K*~ *of the defeat soon spread.* 战败的消息不久便传播开来。 *It has come to my* ~ (= I have been informed) *that you have been spreading gossip about me.* 我听说你一直在说我的闲话。 *To the best of my* ~ (= As far as I know) *he is honest and reliable.* 据我所知, 他是诚实可靠的。 *She married without the* ~ *of her parents.* 她结婚连她的父母都不知道。 ~·**able** /-əbl; -əbl/ *adj* well-informed; having much ~. 博识的; 有见识的。

knuckle /'nʌkl; 'nʌkl/ *n* **1** bone at a finger-joint: 指节; 指关节: *give a boy a rap over / on the* ~*s.* 责备一男孩。 ⇨ the illus at **arm.** 参看 arm 之插图。 **2** (in animals) knee-joint, or part joining leg to foot (esp as food). 动物的膝关节或足踝(尤指可做食物用者); 肘; 蹄。 □ *vi* ~ **down to,** (of a task, etc) apply oneself earnestly. 专心于(工作等)。 ~ **under,** submit, yield. 屈服; 投降。

ko·ala /kəʊ'ɑ:lə; kə'ɑlə/ *n* Australian tree-climbing tailless mammal, like a small bear. 考拉; 科拉熊(一种澳大利亚产会攀树的无尾哺乳动物, 似小熊)。 ⇨ the illus at **small.** 参看 small 之插图。

kobo /'kɒbəʊ; 'kobo/ *n* (Nigeria) 100th part of a naira; coin of this value. (尼日利亚之)考包(值百分之一奈拉); 价值一考包之硬币。

kohl /kəʊl; kol/ *n* [U] cosmetic preparation used in the East to darken the eyelids. 东方妇女用以把眼皮涂黑的一种化妆品。

kohl·rabi /'kəʊl'rɑ:bɪ; 'kol,rɑbɪ/ *n* [C, U] cabbage with turnip-shaped stem. 一种球茎甘蓝。

kola /'kəʊlə; 'kolə/ *n* W African tree. 可拉树(产于非洲西部)。 '~·**nut** *n* the white or pink bitter edible seed of the ~ tree, used in cooking or to chew. 可拉果(可拉树之白色或粉红色种子, 有苦味, 用于烹饪或嚼食)。

kooka·burra /,kukəbʌrə; 'kʊkə,bʌrə/ *n* large Aus-

tralian kingfisher (also called 亦称 *laughing jackass*). (澳大利亚产的一种)大鱼狗。

ko·peck /'kəʊpek; 'kopek/ *n* = **copeck.**

kopje, kop·pie /'kɒpɪ; 'kɑpɪ/ *n* (in S Africa) small hill. (南非)小山。

Ko·ran /kə'rɑ:n US: 'ræn; ko'rɑn/ *n* sacred book containing the Prophet Muhammad's oral revelations, written in Arabic. 可兰经(载有穆罕默德口述的启示, 用阿拉伯文写成的伊斯兰教经典)。 ~**ic** *adj*

ko·sher /'kəʊʃə(r); 'koʃə/ *n*, *adj* (food, foodshop) fulfilling the requirements of Jewish dietary law. 合于犹太饮食戒律的; 合于犹太戒律的食物或饮食店。

kou·miss /'ku:mɪs; 'kumɪs/ *n* = **kumis.**

kow·tow, ko·tow /,kaʊ'taʊ; kaʊ'taʊ/ *n* (former Chinese custom) touching of the ground with the forehead (as a sign of respect, submission, etc). 叩头; 磕头(昔时中国的风俗, 以示尊敬、屈服等)。 □ *vi* ~ **(to),** make a ~; act obsequiously (to). 叩头; (向…)磕头; (向…)卑躬屈节。

kraal /krɑ:l US: krɔ:l; krɑl/ *n* (in S Africa) fenced-in village of huts; enclosure for domestic animals. (南非)用栅栏围起来的茅舍村庄; 家畜栏。

krem·lin /'kremlɪn; 'kremlɪn/ *n* citadel of a Russian town, esp that of Moscow. (俄国的, 尤指莫斯科的)城堡, 尤指 **the K**~, the Government of the USSR. 克里姆林宫; 苏联政府。

krona /'krəʊnə; 'kronə/ *n* (*pl* **-nor** /-nə; -nɔr/) unit of currency in Sweden. 克朗(瑞典之一种货币单位)。

krone /'krəʊnə; 'kronə/ *n* (*pl* **-ner** /-nə; -nɛr/) unit of currency in Denmark and Norway. 克朗(丹麦及挪威之一种货币单位)。

ku·dos /'kju:dɒs; 'kjudɑs/ *n* [U] (colloq) honour and glory; credit. (口)光荣; 荣誉。

kumis, kou·miss /'ku:mɪs; 'kumɪs/ *n* [U] fermented liquor of Central Asia made from mare's milk. (亚洲中部之)马乳酒。

küm·mel /'kʊml; 'kɪml/ *n* [U] herb-flavoured liqueur. 一种用香草调味的酒。

kung fu /,kʊŋ 'fu:; ,kʊŋ'fu/ *n* [U] Chinese form of karate. 中国功夫。

kvass /kvæs; kvæs/ *n* [U] kind of Russian beer. 俄国制的一种啤酒。

kwela /'kwelə; 'kwelə/ *n* [U] kind of S African jazz music. 一种爵士乐(流行于南非)。

L l

L, l /el; ɛl/ (*pl* **L's l's** /elz; ɛlz/) the 12th letter of the English alphabet; symbol for the Roman numeral 50, ⇨ **App 4.** 英文字母之第十二个字母; 罗马数字的50 (参看附录四)。

la /lɑ:; lɑ/ *n* sixth note of the musical octave. 大音阶的第六音。

laa·ger /'lɑ:gə(r); 'lɑgə/ *n* camp, defensive encampment, esp inside a circle of carts or wagons; (mil) park for armoured vehicles. 扎营(尤指四周以车辆围成一圆阵者); (军)装甲车停车处。

lab /læb; læb/ *n* (colloq abbr of) laboratory. (口)实验室(为 laboratory 之略)。

label /'leɪbl; 'lebl/ *n* piece of paper, cloth, metal; wood or other material used for describing what sth is, where it is to go, etc: 标签; 签条: *plant* ~*s;* 植物标签; *put* ~*s on one's luggage.* 在行李上贴标签。 □ *vt* **(-ll-,** US **-l-)** [VP6A] put a ~ or sth on: 贴标签于: *properly* ~*led luggage,* 标签贴得妥当的行李; (fig) (喻) ~ *sb as a demagogue,* assign him to this class of persons. 指某人为煽动家。

la·bial /'leɪbɪəl; 'lebɪəl/ *adj* of the lips; made with the lips: 唇的: ~ *sounds,* eg /m, p, v/. 唇音(例如m,

p, v/)。

labor /'leɪbə(r); 'lebə/ *n* (US) = **labour.**

lab·ora·tory /lə'bɒrətrɪ US: 'læbrətɔ:rɪ; 'læbrə,torɪ/ *n* (*pl* **-ries**) room or building used for scientific experiments, research, testing, etc esp in chemistry. 实验室(尤指化学方面者)。 ⇨ **language.**

la·bori·ous /lə'bɔ:rɪəs; lə'borɪəs/ *adj* **1** (of work, etc) requiring great effort: (指工作等)艰苦的; 费力的: *a* ~ *task.* 艰苦的工作。 **2** showing signs of great effort; not fluent or easy: 具见苦心的; 艰涩的; 不流畅的: *a* ~ *style of writing.* 艰涩的文体。 ~·**ly** *adv*

la·bour (US = **la·bor**) /'leɪbə(r); 'lebə/ *n* **1** [U] bodily or mental work: (身或心之)劳作; 劳动: *The majority of men earn their living by manual* ~. 大多数的人靠双手劳动以谋生。 **hard** ~ [U] work done by criminals (sentenced to penal servitude) as a punishment. (判处苦役监禁之罪犯所服之)劳役。 ~·**saving** *adj* that reduces the amount of ~ needed: 减轻劳动的; 节省劳力的; 省工的: ~·*saving devices,* eg washing-machines, vacuum cleaners. 省工用具(例如洗衣机, 吸尘器)。 **2** [C] task; piece of work. 工作; 一件工作。 ~ *of love,* task gladly undertaken (eg one for the good

of sb one loves). 出于爱心的工作。**3** [U] workers as a class (contrasted with the owners of capital, etc): 劳动阶级；劳工(与资方等相对): *skilled and unskilled ~*; 技术工与非技术工; *~ relations*, between workers and employers. 劳工与雇主间的关系。'L~ **Exchange**, Government agency used by employers for finding workers and by workers for finding jobs. 劳工介绍所。**the 'L~ Party**, one of the two large political parties in Britain. 工党(英国二大政党之一)。**L~ leaders**, leaders of this party; trade union officials. 工党领袖；工会高级职员。**the L~ vote**, of those who support the L~ Party. 工党票数。'**Labor Day**, (US) first Monday in September, a legal holiday in honour of the working class. (美)劳工节(九月的第一个礼拜一)。'**labor union**, (US) (美) = trade union. **4** [U] process of childbirth: 分娩过程: *a woman in ~.* 分娩中的女人; 产妇。□ *vi, vi* **1** [VP 2A, C, 4A] work; try hard: 工作；劳动；努力: *~ for the happiness of mankind*; 为人类的幸福而努力; *~ at a task*; 努力做一工作; *~ to complete a task*, 努力完成一工作; *~ in the cause of peace.* 为谋和平而努力。**2** [VP 2A, C] move, breathe, slowly and with difficulty: 缓慢吃力地行动或呼吸: *The ship ~ed through the heavy seas.* 船在巨浪汹涌的海上缓慢费力地航行。*The old man ~ed up the hillside.* 那老人缓慢吃力地走上山坡。**3** [VP3A] *~ under sb/sth*, be the victim of, suffer because of: 受害于；苦于: *~ under a delusion / difficulty / disadvantage.* 为幻想(困难，不利条件)所苦。**4** [VP6A] work out in detail; treat at great length: 详细地做; 详细说明或讨论: *There's no need to ~ the point / argument.* 该论点(论据)无需详细说明或讨论。*~ed* adj slow and troublesome: 缓慢而困难的: *~ed breathing.* 缓慢困难的呼吸。**2** not easy or natural; showing too much effort: 不流畅的；艰涩的；具见苦心的: *a ~ed style of writing.* 艰涩的文体。*~er n* man who performs heavy unskilled work: 劳工: *agricultural ~ers*, farm workers. 农场工人。**L~·ite** /-aɪt; -aɪt/ *n* member or supporter of the L~ Party. 英国工党党员; 拥护工党者。

la·bur·num /ləˈbɜːnəm; ləˈbɜrnəm/ *n* small tree with yellow flowers that hang down gracefully and with seeds in long pods. 金链花(一种小树，开美丽下垂的黄花，并生有长荚，内含种子)。

lab·y·rinth /ˈlæbərɪnθ; ˈlæbərɪnθ/ *n* network of winding paths, roads, etc through which it is difficult to find one's way without help; (fig) entangled state of affairs. 迷宫; 迷津; (喻)事情之错综复杂。**laby·rin·thine** /ˌlæbəˈrɪnθaɪn US: -θɪn; ˌlæbəˈrɪnθɪn/ *adj*

lace /leɪs; les/ *n* **1** [U] delicate, ornamental openwork fabric of threads: 花边; 饰带: *a dress trimmed with ~*; 饰有花边的服装; *a ~ collar.* 镶着花边的衣领。**gold / silver ~**, braid used for trimming uniforms, eg of

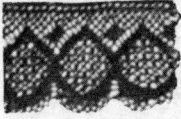

lace

diplomats, army officers. (外交官和军官等服装所饰的)金(银)边。**2** [C] string or cord put through small holes in shoes, etc to draw edges together: 鞋带; 带: *a pair of 'shoe-~s.* 一双鞋带。□ *vt, vi* **1** [VP6A, 15A, B, 2A, C] *~ (up)*, fasten or tighten with *~s* (2): 用鞋带系牢; 用带系紧: *~ (up) one's shoes*; 结好鞋带; *a corset that ~s (up) at the side.* 自侧面用带系紧的女用束腹。**2** [VP3A] *~ into sb*, lash him, beat him. 打某人。**3** [VP14] *~ with*, flavour or strengthen (a liquid) (with some kind of spirit): 搀酒于(饮料): *a glass of milk ~d with rum.* 一杯搀有朗姆酒的牛奶。

lac·er·ate /ˈlæsəreɪt; ˈlæsəˌret/ *vt* [VP6A] tear (the flesh; (fig) the feelings). 划破(肉); (喻)伤害(感情)。**lac·er·ation** /ˌlæsəˈreɪʃn; ˌlæsəˈreʃən/ *n* [U] tearing; [C] tear or injury. 划破; 撕裂; 裂伤; 破口。

lach·ry·mal /ˈlækrɪml; ˈlækrəml/ *adj* of tears: 眼泪的: (esp) (尤用于) *~ glands.* 泪腺。**lach·ry·mose** /ˈlækrɪməʊs; ˈlækrəˌmos/ *adj* tearful; in the habit of weeping. 含泪的; 爱哭的。

lack /læk; læk/ *vt, vi* **1** [VP6B, 3A] *~ (in)*, be without; not have; have less than enough of: 缺乏; 没有; 缺少: *~ wisdom.* 缺乏智慧。*I ~ words with which to express my thanks.* 我无法以言语来表示我的感激。*What I ~ in experience I make up in curiosity.* 我以求知欲弥补我经验的缺乏。**be ~ing in sth**, not have enough of it: 缺乏: *He's ~ing in* (= He ~s) *courage.* 他缺乏勇气。**2** *be ~ing*, be in short supply, not be available: 缺乏; 没有: *Money was ~ing* (= There was no money) *for the plan.* 此一计划尚缺钱。**3** [VP3A] *~ for*, (formal) need: (正式用语)需要: *They ~ed for nothing*, had everything they wanted. 他们什么也不缺少(需要的东西都有了)。□ *n* [U] want, need, shortage: 缺少; 缺乏; 不足: *The plants died for ~ of water.* 那些植物因缺水而枯死了。'**~-lustre** *adj* (of eyes) dull. (指眼睛)无光泽的。

lacka·daisi·cal /ˌlækəˈdeɪzɪkl; ˌlækəˈdezɪk/ *adj* appearing tired, uninterested, unenthusiastic. 无精打采的; 冷漠的。**~ly** /-klɪ; -klɪ/ *adv*

lackey /ˈlækɪ; ˈlækɪ/ *n* (*pl ~s*) manservant (usu in livery); (fig) person who is too obsequious, who obeys orders without question, etc. 男仆(通常着制服); (喻)卑躬屈膝之人。

la·conic /ləˈkɒnɪk; ləˈkɑnɪk/ *adj* using, expressed in, few words: 简洁的; 简明的: *a ~ person / reply.* 说话简洁之人(简明的回答)。**la·coni·cally** /-klɪ; -klɪ/ *adv* **la·coni·cism** /-nɪsɪzəm; -nɪsɪzəm/, **lacon·ism** /ˈlækənɪzəm; ˈlækənɪzəm/ *nn* [U] being ~; [C] instance of this; short, pithy saying. 简洁; 简明; 简洁之语句; 警句。

lac·quer /ˈlækə(r); ˈlækə/ *n* [U] varnish used to give a hard, bright coating to metal (esp brass); varnish used for wooden articles (esp **Japanese ~**); liquid sprayed on the hair to keep it in place. 假漆(用以漆金属，尤其是黄铜); 亮漆(漆木器者，尤指日本漆); (喷在头发上用以固定发型之)发水。□ *vt* [VP6A] coat with *~*. 涂假漆于; 涂以亮漆; 喷以胶水。

la·crosse /ləˈkrɒs US: -ˈkrɔːs; ləˈkrɔs/ *n* [U] outdoor game, popular in N America, played with a ball which is caught in, carried in, and thrown from, a racket with a net (called a *crosse*). 长曲棍球(盛行于北美之一种户外球戏，进行时以一带网的曲棍球棒捕球、持球和掷球)。

lac·tic /ˈlæktɪk; ˈlæktɪk/ *adj* of milk. 乳的。'**~ 'acid**, the acid in sour milk. 乳酸。

la·cuna /ləˈkjuːnə; ləˈkjunə/ *n* (*pl ~s or ~e* /-niː; -nɪ/) blank; empty part; missing portion, esp in writing, or in an argument. 空白; 空隙; 脱漏部分(尤指写作或议论中者); 漏洞。

lacy /ˈleɪsɪ; ˈlesɪ/ *adj* (*-ier, -iest*) of or like lace. 花边的; 似花边的。

lad /læd; læd/ *n* boy; young man. 少年; 青年。

lad·der /ˈlædə(r); ˈlædə/ *n* **1** two lengths of wood, metal or rope, with crosspieces (called *rungs*) used in climbing up and down walls, a ship's side, etc. 梯(梯级称作 rung). ⇨ '**step-~** at **step**²(5). **2** (US 美 = *run*) fault in a stocking caused by stitches becoming undone, so that there is a vertical *~*-like flaw. 袜子因脱线而成的梯形裂缝; 抽丝。'**~-proof** *adj* proof against such flaws. 防抽丝的; 不抽丝的。□ *vi* (of stockings, etc) develop *~s*: (指袜子等)抽丝: *Have you any tights that won't ~?* 你有不会抽丝的紧身衣吗?

lad·die /ˈlædɪ; ˈlædɪ/ *n* = lad.

lade /leɪd; led/ *vt* (*pp laden* /ˈleɪdn; ˈledn/) [VP

6A] load (which is the usu word). 装载 (load 为常用
词).

laden /'leɪdn; 'ledn/ adj ~ **with,** weighted or bur-
dened with: 载满; 装着: *trees* ~ *with apples:* 结满苹果
的树; *a mind* ~ *with grief.* 充满忧伤的心。

la-di-da /ˌlɑː dɪ 'dɑː; ˌlɑdɪ'dɑ/ adj (colloq) pretentious; genteel; affected (esp in pronunciation). (口)装
模作样的; 装作有教养的; 做作的(尤指发音方面)。

lad·ing /'leɪdɪŋ; 'ledɪŋ/ n [U] (naut) cargo; freight.
(航海)船货; 装载的货物。 **bill of '~,** list with details
of a ship's cargo. (船货之)提货单。

ladle /'leɪdl; 'ledl/ n large, deep, cup-shaped spoon
for dipping out liquids: 长柄勺; 勺子: *a 'soup* ~. 汤勺。
□ vt [VP6A, 15B] ~ **(out),** serve with or as from a
~: 以勺舀取; 似以勺给与: ~ *out soup;* 用勺舀汤; (fig)
(喻) ~ *out honours.* 给与荣誉。

lady /'leɪdɪ; 'ledɪ/ n (pl **-dies**) **1** (corresponding to
gentleman) woman belonging to the upper classes; woman
who has good manners and some claim to social position.
(与绅士相对)贵妇; 淑女: 有教养和社会地位的妇女。 '**~-
in-'waiting,** ,~ of the '**bedchamber,** ~ attending
upon a queen. 宫女。 **2** (used courteously for any)
woman of any kind or class, with or without good
manners and refinement. 女士(对所有妇女的客气称呼,
不论其身份或是否有教养)。 **3** (pl only) form of address,
(仅用复数)称呼的套语, esp (尤用于) '*Ladies and Gen-*
tlemen'. '诸位先生和女士'。 **4** (attrib) female: (用作
定语)女性的: ~ *doctor / clerk,* (woman being preferable). 女医生(职员) (woman 较普通)。 **5 Ladies**
(as a sing n), women's public lavatory: (作单数名词)
女厕所; 女盥洗室: *Is there a Ladies near here?* 这附近有
女厕所吗? **6 L~,** (title in GB) used of and to the
wives of some nobles; (prefixed to Christian names)
titles used of and to the daughters of some nobles. (英)
夫人(对某些贵族之妻子之尊称); (冠于教名前)小姐(对某
些贵族之女儿的尊称)。 **7** *My L~,* formal term of
address used to holders of the title *Lady* (as in **6** above).
夫人; 小姐(对贵族的妻女的尊称)。 **8** (compounds) (复
合词) '~**-bird** n reddish-brown or yellow insect (a
small flying beetle) with black spots. 瓢虫(一种红褐
色或黄色会飞的小甲虫, 身上有黑点)。 ,**Our 'L~,** the
Virgin Mary. 圣母玛利亚。 '**L~-chapel,** chapel (in a
large church) dedicated to the Virgin Mary. (大教堂中
之)圣母堂。 '**L~ Day,** the feast of the Annunciation,
25th March. 报喜节(三月二十五日)。 '~**-killer** n man
with the reputation of being very successful with
women. 很会吸引妇女的男人。 '~**'s-maid** n ~'s personal
servant, esp in charge of her toilet. 侍女; (尤指)专管女
主人化妆的女仆。 '~**'s / 'ladies' man,** man fond of the
society of women. 喜欢与妇女交际的男人。 '~**-like** adj
behaving as a ~; befitting a ~; genteel. 行为似
贵妇的; 淑雅的。 '~**-ship,** ,~ / 'ʃɪp; -ʃɪp/ n *Your / Her*
L~ship, used in speaking to or of a titled ~. 夫人; 小
姐(对有 Lady 头衔之妇女的尊称), 当面称 Your Lady-
ship, 谈话中提及称 Her Ladyship)。

lag¹ /læg; læg/ vi **(-gg-)** [VP2A, C] go too slow, not
keep up with: 走得太慢; 落后: *The lame child lagged*
behind. 那跛足的孩子落在后面。 □ n **('time)** lag,
period of time by which sth is slower or later. 迟延的时
间; 时滞。

lag² /læg; læg/ n (sl) person convicted of crime; (俚)
犯人; (esp) (尤用于) *old lag,* one who has served
several sentences of imprisonment. 常坐牢的犯人; 惯犯。

lag³ /læg; læg/ vt **(-gg-)** [VP6A, 14] **lag (with),**
encase (waterpipes, cisterns, etc) with material that
will not conduct heat or cold, esp to prevent freezing of
water in pipes, waste of heat, etc. 以隔热或隔冷的材料
保护(水管, 贮水器等), 以防止管中的水 结冰或散热等)。
lag·ging n [U] material used for this. 隔热或隔冷的
材料。

la·ger /'lɑːgə(r); 'lɑgɚ/ n [U] sort of light beer; [C]
bottle or glass of this. 一种淡啤酒; 一瓶或一杯淡啤酒。

lag·gard /'lægəd; 'lægɚd/ n person who lags behind;
person who is lacking in energy, etc. 落后者; 缺乏精力
者等。

la·goon /lə'guːn; lə'gun/ n (usu shallow) salt-water
lake separated from the sea by sandbank(s) or coral
reef(s); enclosed by an atoll. 由沙湖或珊瑚礁与
海相隔之咸水湖(通常是浅的); 礁湖。 ▷ the illus at
atoll. 参看 atoll 之插图。

laic /'leɪɪk; 'le·ɪk/ adj of the laity; secular. 常人的; 俗
人的; 世俗的。 **lai·cize** /'leɪɪsaɪz; 'leəˌsaɪz/ vt [VP6A]
free from ecclesiastic control; make, eg priest, a
layman. 使不受教会管制; 使还俗。

laid /leɪd; led/ pt, pp of lay¹.

lain /leɪn; len/ pp of lie².

lair /leə(r); lɛr/ n wild animal's resting-place or den.
野兽的窝穴。

laird /leəd; lɛrd/ n (Scot) landowner. (苏)地主。

laissez-faire /ˌleɪseɪ 'feə(r); ˌleˈsɛr/ n [U] (F)
(policy of) allowing individual activities (esp in commerce) to be conducted without government control.
(法)自由竞争(尤指商业上者); 放任政策。

laity /'leɪɪtɪ; 'leətɪ/ n (usu the ~, and a pl v) (通常用
the ~, 与复数动词连用) **1** all laymen (ie all those
persons not in Holy Orders, those who are not clergy).
俗人(以别于僧侣或教士)。 **2** all those persons outside a
particular learned profession (thus, used by a doctor,
the word may mean all those not trained for the medical
profession). 外行人(以别于专家, 例如医生用此词, 则指
未受过医学训练的人)。

lake¹ /leɪk; lek/ n large area of water enclosed by
land. 湖。 the '**L~ District,** the part of N W
England with many ~s. 英格兰西北部之湖泊区。 '**L~**
Poets, poets who lived in this area, esp Coleridge and
Wordsworth. 湖畔诗人(居住在这个湖泊区之诗人, 尤指
科尔里奇与华滋华斯)。 the Great **L~s,** ▷ **great.** '~-
dwelling, ▷ *pile-dwelling* at pile¹.

lake² /leɪk; lek/ n (often crimson ~) dark red
colouring material. 深红色的颜料。

lakh /lɑːk; lɑk/ n (India and Pakistan) 100000. (印
度和巴基斯坦)十万。 ▷ **crore.**

lam /læm; læm/ vt, vi **(-mm-)** (sl) (俚) [VP6A]
thrash. 鞭打。 [VP3A] *lam into sb,* attack him,
physically or verbally. 攻击某人; 攻击某人, 或叱骂某人。

lama /'lɑːmə; 'lɑmə/ n Buddhist monk in Tibet or
Mongolia. 喇嘛(西藏或蒙古的佛教僧人)。 **~·sery** /'lɑː-
məserɪ; 'lɑməˌsɛrɪ/ n (pl **-ries**) monastery of
~s. 喇嘛寺院。

lamb /læm; læm/ n [C] **1** young of the sheep, ▷ the
illus at **domestic;** [U] its flesh as food: 小羊; 羔羊(参
看 domestic 之插图); 羔羊肉(作为食物): *a leg of* ~; 羔
羊腿肉; *roast* ~. 烤羊肉。 **2** innocent, mild-mannered
person; dear person. 天真温和之人; 可爱的人。 *like a*
~, without resistance or protest. 无抵抗或抗议的。 □
vi bring forth ~s: 生小羊: *the '~ing season,* when ~s
are born. 生小羊。 '~**·kin** / -kɪn; -kɪn/ n very
young ~. 很小的羊; 小羔羊。 '~**-skin** [C] skin of a
~ with the wool on it (as used for coats, gloves, etc);
[U] leather made from ~skin. 带毛的羔皮(用做上衣,
手套等); 羔羊皮革。

lam·baste /læm'beɪst; læm'best/ vt (sl) thrash, beat;
scold violently. (俚)打; 打; 严厉责骂。

lam·bent /'læmbənt; 'læmbənt/ adj (liter) (of a
flame or light) moving over the surface with soft
radiance; (of the eyes, sky) shining softly; (of humour,
wit) gently brilliant. (文)(指火或光)轻轻摇曳的; (指眼
睛或天空) 微微发亮的; (指幽默, 机智)巧妙的。 **lam-**
bency /-ənsɪ; -ənsɪ/ n

lame /leɪm; lem/ adj **1** not able to walk normally
because of an injury or defect: 跛的: ~ *in the left leg.*
左腿跛。 ▷ **duck,** ▷ duck¹(1). **2** (of an excuse, argument, etc) unconvincing; unsatisfactory. (指辩解, 论
据等)不能说服人的; 令人不满意的。 **3** (of metre) halting.

(指诗的韵律)不合诗韵的。 □ *vt* make ~. 使跛。 ~·**ly** *adv* ~·**ness** *n*

lamé /'lɑːmeɪ *US*: lɑːˈmeɪ; lɑˈme/ *n* [U] fabric with metal threads interwoven. 金属丝织物。

la·ment /lə'ment; lə'mɛnt/ *vt, vi* [VP6A, 3A, 2A] ~ *(for / over)*, show, feel, express, great sorrow or regret: 悲伤; 哀悼; 惋惜: ~ *the death of a friend*; 哀悼朋友的死; ~ *for a friend*; 为朋友悲伤; ~ *(over) one's misfortunes*. 为自己的不幸而悲伤。 □ *n* [C] expression of grief; (music) song or poem expressing grief: 悲伤; 哀悼; 挽歌; (音乐)悲歌; 哀乐: *a funeral* ~. 送葬的哀乐。 **lam·en·table** /'læməntəbl; 'læmɛntəbl/ *adj* regrettable; to be deplored: 令人惋惜的; 可悲的: *a* ~*able* (= poor, unsatisfying) *performance of an opera*. 一歌剧之令人惋惜的演出(即演出失败)。 **lam·en·tably** /-bli; -əblɪ/ *adv* **lam·en·ta·tion** /ˌlæmen'teɪʃən, ˌlæmən'teʃən/ *n* [U] ~**ing**; [C] ~; expression of grief. 悲伤;哀悼;哀伤。

lami·nate /'læmɪneɪt; 'læmə,net/ *vt, vi* [VP6A, 2A] beat or roll (metal) into thin plates; split into layers; manufacture by placing layer on layer; cover with metal plates: 锤打或碾压(金属)成薄片; 破开使成薄片; 用叠片制造; 覆以金属片: ~*d wood / plastics*, of layers one over the other. 层板(叠合塑胶板);胶合板。

Lam·mas /'læməs; 'læməs/ *n* (hist) 1st August, formerly a harvest festival in England. (史)(昔时英国之)收获节(八月一日)。

lamp /læmp; læmp/ *n* container with oil and wick, used to give light; (in modern times) any apparatus for giving light (from gas, electricity, etc). 油灯; (近代用法)灯(指任何发光之灯, 如煤气灯, 电灯等)。 '~·**black** *n* [U] black colouring matter made from the soot of burning oil, formerly used in making paint and printing-ink. 灯黑;灯烟;油烟(昔时用以制颜料和油墨)。 '~·**light** *n* [U] light from a ~. 灯光: *read by* ~*light*. 借灯光看书。 '~·**lighter** *n* (hist) man who went round the streets to light public ~s (when gas was used). (史)(用煤气灯时代)点燃路灯之灯夫。 '~·**post** *n* (usu metal) post for a street ~. 路灯柱(通常是金属的)。 '~·**shade** *n* globe of glass, screen of silk, parchment, etc placed round or over a lamp. 灯罩。

lam·poon /læm'puːn; læm'pun/ *n* [C] piece of satirical writing attacking and ridiculing sb. 攻击和讥讽的文章。 □ *vt* [VP6A] write a ~ against. 写文章攻击和讥讽。

lam·prey /'læmprɪ; 'læmprɪ/ *n* (*pl* ~**s**) eel-like water animal. 七鳃鳗; 八目鳗(一种似黄鳝的水生动物)。

lance[1] /lɑːns *US*: læns; læns/ *n* (hist) weapon with a long wooden shaft and a pointed steel head used by a horseman; similar instrument used for spearing fish. (史)骑兵用的长矛; 鱼叉。 ~·'**corporal** *n* non-commissioned officer in the army. (英)陆军代理下士(领比上等兵薪水)。 ~·**r** *n* soldier of a cavalry regiment originally armed with ~s. 枪骑兵。 ~**rs** *n pl* (with *sing v*) (music for a) dance for four or more couples. (与单数动词连用)由四对或多于四对所跳的一种舞; 此种舞曲。

lance[2] /lɑːns *US*: læns; læns/ *vt* [VP6A] cut open, prick, with a lancet: 以刺血针切开或割破: ~ *an abscess*. 以刺血针刺破一脓疮。

lan·cet /'lɑːnsɪt *US*: 'læn-; 'lænsɪt/ *n* **1** pointed, two-edged knife used by surgeons. 刺血针;柳叶刀(外科医生用的双刃小尖刀)。 **2** (archit) high, narrow, pointed arch or window. (建筑)尖顶拱门或窗户。

land[1] /lænd; lænd/ *n* **1** [U] solid part of the earth's surface (contrasted with *sea, water*): 陆地(与海, 水相对): *travel over* ~ *and sea*; 在陆上和海上旅行; *come in sight of* ~; 看见陆地; *glad to be on* ~ */ to reach* ~ */ to come to* ~ *again*; 很高兴重登陆地; *a* ~ *breeze*, one blowing from the land towards the sea (after sunset); 陆风(日落后由陆上吹向海上的微风); ~·*based aircraft*, using bases on ~ (contrasted with aircraft

based on carriers). 陆上基地的飞机(以别于航空母舰上者)。 *Are you going by* ~ *or by sea*, by train, car, etc, or by boat? 你将由陆路还是海路去? *make* ~, see, reach the shore. 见到岸;抵岸。 *see / find out how the* '~ *lies*, ⇨ lie[1](4). **2** [U] ground, earth, as used for farming, etc: 土地; 田地: *working on the* ~; 在农田工作; '~·*workers*; 农田工人; *rough and stony* ~. 崎岖多石的土地。 '~ *army*, (GB) body of women farm workers in World War II. (英)二次大战期间的女农工。 **3** [U] property in the form of ~: 地产: *How far does your* ~ *extend*? 你的地产伸展多远? *Do you own much* ~ *here*? 你在此地有很多地产吗? '~·*agent*, (chiefly GB) person employed to manage an estate; person who buys and sells estates (US 美 = *real estate agent*). (主英)地产管理人; 地产经纪人。 **4** (*pl*) estate; area of ~ with the trees, etc on it: (复)地产; (含树木等在内的)所有地: *own houses and* ~*s*. 拥有房地产。 **5** country and its people (liter or emotive in this sense, *country* being the ordinary word): 国土; 国家(为文学上或含有感情的用语, country 一词是普通用语): *my native* ~; 我的祖国; *visit distant* ~*s*. 游历遥远的国家。 *the* ~ *of the living*, this present existence. 现世。 *the Promised L*~, *the L*~ *of Promise*, Canaan / 'keɪnən; 'kenən/, promised by God to the Israelites. 迦南地(上帝应许赐予以色列人的土地)。 **6** (compounds, etc) (复合词等) '~·**fall** *n* approach to ~, esp for the first time during a voyage: 接近陆地(尤指航行中初次发现陆地): *a good* ~*fall*, one that corresponds well to the calculations made by the ship's officers. 如期见到陆地。 '~·**forces** *n pl* military forces (not naval). 陆军。 '~·**holder** *n* owner or (more usu) tenant of ~. 地主; (较常指)租地人。 '~·**lady** *n* (*pl* -**ladies**) woman who owns a house which she leases to a tenant, or who rents a house, rooms of which she sublets to tenants: 女房东: *owe one's* ~*lady a month's rent*. 欠女房东一个月房租。 '~·**locked** *adj* (of a bay, harbour, etc) almost or entirely surrounded by ~. (指海湾,港口等)几乎全为陆地包围的。 '~·**lord** *n* (**a**) person from whom another rents ~ or building(s). 地主; 房东。 (**b**) keeper of an inn, a public house, a boarding-house or lodging-house. 旅社、酒馆或寄宿舍之主人。 '~·**lubber** /'læbə; ˌlʌbɚ/ *n* (used by sailors to describe a) person not accustomed to the sea and ships. (船员用语)不习惯海上生活及船上事物者。 '~·**mark** *n* [C] (**a**) object that marks the boundary of a piece of ~. 界标。 (**b**) object, etc easily seen from a distance and helpful to travellers (eg navigating officers of a ship). 易自远处看得见并对旅行者(例如船上的航行人员)有帮助的目标; 陆标。 (**c**) (fig) event, discovery, change, etc that marks a stage or turning-point: (喻)划时代的大事、发现、变化等; 里程碑: ~*marks in the history of mankind*. 人类历史上划时代的事件。 '~·**mine** *n* [C] explosive charge laid in or on the ground or dropped by parachute and exploded by vehicles passing over it. (埋于地下, 置于地上或由飞机用降落伞投下的)地雷。 '~·**owner** *n* owner of ~. 地主。 'L~·**rover** *n* (P) strongly-built motor vehicle for use over rough ground. (商标)用以行驶崎岖陆地的坚固车辆。 '~·**slide** *n* [C] (**a**) sliding down of a mass of earth, rock, etc from the side of a cliff, hillside, railway cutting, etc. 山崩; 土崩; 坍方。 (**b**) sudden change in political opinion resulting in an overwhelming majority of votes for one side in an election: 选举中获压倒性多数票: *a Democratic* ~*slide*, a great victory for the Democratic party. 民主党的大胜利。 '~·**slip** *n* = ~slide(a). '~**s·man** *n* (*pl* -**men**) person who is not a sailor. 陆居者(以别于海员)。

land[2] /lænd; lænd/ *vt, vi* **1** [VP6A, 2A, C] go, come, put, on ~ (from a ship, aircraft, etc): (自船, 飞机等)(使)登陆; (使)登岸; (使)着陆: *The passengers* ~*ed / were* ~*ed as soon as the ship reached harbour*. 船刚一抵港, 乘客们即迅速地登岸。 *We* ~*ed at Bombay*. 我们在孟买登陆。 *The airliner* ~*ed safely*. 该客机安全降

落了. *The pilot ~ed the airliner safely.* 驾驶员使那客机安全降落. ⇨ also **crash-~** at **crash¹** and **soft-~** at **soft**. **~ on one's feet,** (fig) be lucky; escape injury. (喻) 幸运; 逃脱伤害. **2 ~** *sb/oneself in sth,* get into (trouble, difficulties, etc): 使处于(麻烦、困难等中): *What a mess you've ~ed us all in!* 你看你为我们大家惹来多少麻烦! **~ up,** (colloq) arrive; find oneself: (口) 到达; 处于: *If you go on behaving in this way, you'll ~ up in prison one day.* 你如果继续这种行为, 有一天你会坐牢. *Tom has been away for months, but he'll ~ up one of these days.* 汤姆已离开数月, 但这几天他会回来. *She ~ed up in a strange city without any money or friends.* 她到达一个陌生的城市, 没有钱或朋友. **3** [VP 6A] (colloq) obtain: (口) 得到: *~ a good job/a contract for building a factory.* 获得一良好工作(建一工厂之合同). **4** [VP12C] (sl) strike (a blow): (俚) 击; 打: *She ~ed him one in the eye.* 她在他眼睛上打了一拳. **~ed** *adj* **1** consisting of ~: 含有土地的: *the ~ed property.* 地产. **2** owning ~: 拥有土地的: *the ~ed classes/gentry.* 地主阶级(拥有土地的缙绅). **~·less** *adj* without ~; not owning ~. 无土地的; 无陆地的; 无地产的.

lan·dau /'lændɔː; 'lændo/ *n* (hist) four-wheeled horse-carriage with a folding roof in two sections. (史) 分顶式四轮马车(其折叠式顶篷可分作两半).

land·grave /'lændgreɪv; 'lænd,grev/ *n* (hist) title of some German princes. (史) 德国某些王子的称号.

land·ing /'lændɪŋ; 'lændɪŋ/ *n* **1** act of coming or bringing to land: 登陆; 着陆: *the ~ of the Pilgrim Fathers in America.* 一六二〇年英国清教徒之在美国登陆. *The pilot made an emergency ~.* 该驾驶员作紧急降落. **'~-craft** a ship whose bows can be opened up to allow (usu military) vehicles to get ashore without being lifted out. 登陆艇. **'~-field/-strip** area of land for aircraft to take off from and land on. 飞机起落场(起落地带). **'~-gear** *n* undercarriage and wheels of an aircraft. 飞机起落架(包括起落轮). **'~-net** *n* bag-shaped net on a long handle for landing fish caught with a rod and line. (用以抄取钓上之鱼的长柄)袋网. **'~-party** *n* party of armed men who are landed (eg to keep order). (武装之)登陆队(例如维持治安者). **2** (also 亦作 **'~-place**) place where people and goods may be landed from a boat, etc. (船等)卸货处; 登陆处. **'~-stage** *n* platform (usu floating) on which passengers and goods are landed. 栈桥(通常浮于水上, 供人货登陆者)浮动码头. **3** area at the top of a flight of stairs on to which doors may open. 楼梯平台(一段楼梯顶端之驻脚处, 楼上门户可朝此装设).

land·scape /'lændskeɪp; 'lænskep/ *n* [C] (picture of) inland scenery; [U] branch of art dealing with this. 陆上风景; 风景画; (绘画之一支)山水画. **~·gardening/~·architecture** *n* [U] the laying out of grounds and gardens in imitation of natural scenery. (模仿天然景色的)庭园布置.

lane /leɪn; len/ *n* **1** narrow country road, usu between hedges or banks. 乡村小道(通常在篱或坡间); 小径. **2** (usu as part of a proper name) narrow street or alley between buildings: (通常为专有名称之一部)街: *Drury L~.* 德鲁里巷. **3** passage made or left between lines of persons. 两列人间的通路. **4** route regularly used by ships or aircraft. (船或飞机之定期)航线; 航路. **5** marked division of a wide road for the guidance of motorists; line of vehicles within such a division: (宽大马路上用白线画出的)车道; 行驶的一列车辆: *the inside/nearside ~;* 内车道(外车道); *the outside/offside ~;* 外车道(内车道); *four-~ traffic.* 四线交通. **6** marked course for a competitor in a race (eg on a running track or a swimming pool). 竞赛中为比赛者画出之道(例如赛跑之跑道或游泳之泳道).

lang·syne /ˌlæŋ'saɪn; ˌlæŋ'saɪn/ *adv, n* (Scot) (in) the old days; (in) past time. (苏)昔日; 往时; 往昔.

lan·guage /'læŋgwɪdʒ; 'læŋgwɪdʒ/ *n* **1** [U] human and non-instinctive method of communicating ideas, feelings and desires by means of a system of sounds and sound symbols. 语言. **2** [C] form of ~ used by a group: (一群人所用的)语言: *the ~s of Asia;* 亚洲的各种语言; *foreign ~s.* 外国语. **dead ~,** one no longer in spoken use (eg classical Greek). 死的语言(不再被使用者, 如古希腊语). **'~ laboratory,** classroom(s) where ~s are taught using tape-recorders, etc. 语言教室;语言电化教室. **3** [U] manner of using words: 用语文的方法: *a person with a good command of ~,* person who is fluent or eloquent. 善于词令之人. **4** [U] words, phrases, etc used by a profession or class: 专门语;术语: *technical/legal ~;* 专门(法律)术语; *the ~ of diplomacy.* 外交术语. **5** [U] **bad ~; strong ~,** language full of oaths, violent words, etc. 粗野的话语. **6** [U, C] system of signs used as ~: 用做语言的一套符号: *com'puter ~,* ordered system for giving instructions to a computer; 电脑语言(指示电脑作业的一套方法); *'finger ~,* as used by deaf and dumb persons; 手语(聋哑之人所用者); *the ~ of flowers;* 以花表示情感的方法; *the ~ of algebra.* 代数语.

lan·guid /'læŋgwɪd; 'læŋgwɪd/ *adj* lacking in energy; slow-moving. 无精神的; 不活泼的; 行动迟缓的. **~·ly** *adv*

lan·guish /'læŋgwɪʃ; 'læŋgwɪʃ/ *vi* [VP2A, C] be or become languid; lose health and strength; be unhappy because of a desire (for sth): 无生气; 变得衰弱无力; 因渴望而烦恼(为了、为了连用, 后接某事物): *~ in prison;* 在狱中变得衰弱无力; *~ for love and sympathy.* 因渴望爱情和同情而烦恼. *She gave the young man a ~ing look,* one that suggested a desire for love or sympathy. 她向那青年作渴望爱情或同情的一瞥.

lan·guor /'læŋgə(r); 'læŋgɚ/ *n* [U] weakness of body (as produced by hard work) or of spirit (as produced by sorrow or an unhappy love affair); lack of life or movement; stillness or heaviness: (辛苦工作引起的)身体衰弱; (悲伤或失恋引起的)精神消沉; 无精打采; 沉闷; 低沉: *the ~ of a summer day.* 夏日的沉闷. **2** (often *pl*) soft or tender mood. (常用复数)柔情. **~·ous** *adj;* **~·ous·ly** *adv*

lan·gur /lʌŋ'gʊə(r); lʌŋ'gʊr/ *n* (kind of) long-tailed monkey. 一种长尾猴.

lank /læŋk; læŋk/ *adj* **1** (of hair) straight and lying limp or flat. (指发)平直的. **2** tall and lean. 瘦长的.

lanky /'læŋkɪ; 'læŋkɪ/ *adj* (-ier, -iest) (of a person, his arms or legs) long and lean in an ungraceful way: (指人, 四肢)瘦长的; 细长而难看的: *a ~, overgrown girl.* 一个长得太高的瘦长女孩.

lano·lin /'lænəlɪn; 'lænəlɪn/ *n* [U] fat extracted from sheep's wool used as the basis of ointments for the skin. 羊毛脂(供制润肤膏).

lan·tern /'læntən; 'læntɚn/ *n* case (usu metal and glass) protecting a light from the wind, etc, outdoors. 灯笼;提灯. ⇨ **dark²**(1) **magic**. **'~-jawed** *adj* having long and thin jaws so that the face has a hollow look. 下巴瘦而长的.

lan·yard /'lænjəd; 'lænjəd/ *n* **1** cord (worn by sailors and soldiers) for a whistle or knife. (水手或士兵用以)悬哨子或小刀的绳索. **2** short rope used on a ship for fastening or moving sth. 船上系物或搬动东西之短索;小索.

lap¹ /læp; læp/ *n* front part of a person's legs from the waist to the knees, when sitting, as the place on which a child is nursed or sth held: 人坐着时自腰至膝之部分; 大腿前部(可放置婴儿或东西之处): *The mother had the baby on her lap.* 母亲把婴儿放在腿上. **be/live in the lap of luxury,** in fortunate and luxurious circumstances. 生活在幸福奢侈的环境中. **in the lap of the gods,** (of future events) uncertain. (指未来事件)不确定的. **'lap-dog** *n* small pet dog. 宠爱的小狗.

lap² /læp; læp/ *vt, vi* (**-pp-**) **1** [VP15B] wrap or fold (cloth, etc) *round* or *in.* 包裹; 缠绕(布等)于(后接 *round* 或 *in*). **2** [VP6A, 2A, C] (cause to) overlap;

(使)重叠: *Put the slates on the roof so that they lap over.* 将石板叠盖于屋顶上。 ⇨ **overlap.** □ *n* **1** amount by which one thing laps over. 重叠部分。 **2** one circuit round a track or race-course: (竞赛跑道之)一圈: *Smith overtook the other runners/riders/drivers on the last lap.* 史密斯于最后一圈追上了其他的赛跑者(骑马者, 驾驶者)。

lap³ /læp; læp/ *vi, vt* (-pp-) **1** [VP15B] *lap up,* drink by taking up with the tongue, as a cat does: 舐; 舐食: *The cat quickly lapped up all the milk.* 那猫很快地将所有的牛奶舐光了。 **2** (colloq) (of human beings) take quickly or eagerly: (口)(指人)迅速或急切地接受: *lap up compliments.* 爱听恭维的话。 **3** [VP2A, C] (of water) move with a sound like the lapping up of liquid: (指水)轻拍: *waves lapping on the beach;* 轻拍海滩的波浪; *water lapping against the sides of a canoe.* 轻拍着小舟两侧的水。 **4** [VP6A] (in a race) become ahead of by a lap²(2). (竞赛)以一圈领先。 □ *n* **1** act of lapping: 舐; 舐食: *The dog emptied the plate with three laps of the tongue.* 那狗舐了三次便将盘中的食物舐干净了。 **2** [U] sound of lapping: 水的轻拍声: *the lap of the waves against the side of the boat.* 波浪冲击船侧的轻拍声。

la·pel /lə'pel; lə'pɛl/ *n* part of the breast of a coat or jacket folded back and forming a continuation of the collar. 西服上衣的翻领。

lapi·dary /'læpɪdərɪ US: -derɪ; 'læpəˌderɪ/ *adj* cut on stone; (fig) neat; precise: 刻于石上的; (喻)整齐的; 精确的: *a ~ inscription/speech.* 刻在石上的题铭(精确的演说)。 □ *n* person who cuts, polishes or engraves, gems. 宝石匠。

lap·is la·zuli /ˌlæpɪs 'læzjulɪ US: 'læzəlɪ; 'læpɪs'læzjə,laɪ/ *n* [U, C] bright blue semi-precious stone; its colour. 青金石; 璧琉璃; 金精; 天蓝色。

lapse /læps; læps/ *n* [C] **1** slight error in speech or behaviour; slip of the memory, tongue or pen. 言行上些微的差错; 记错; 失言; 笔误。 **2** ~ *(from) (into),* falling away from what is right: 过失; 错误: *a ~ from virtue;* 道德上的过失(堕落); *a ~ from true belief into heresy.* 背弃真正信仰, 相信异端邪说。 **3** (of time) passing away; interval: (指时间)流逝; 间歇: *the ~ of time;* 时间的流逝; *a long ~ of time.* 一段长时间。 **4** (legal) ending of a right, etc from failure to use it or ask for its renewal. (法律)权利等的终止或丧失(因未加使用或未要求续展而致)。 □ *vi* **1** [VP2A, 3A] ~ *(from) (into),* fail to keep one's position; fall (from good ways into bad ways): 失足; 堕落: *~ from virtue into vice;* 堕落; *~ into bad habits;* 养成恶习; *a ~d Catholic.* 叛教的天主教徒。 **2** [VP2A] (legal) (of rights and privileges) be lost because not used, claimed or renewed. (法律)(指权利及特权因未使用, 未要求或未康续而)终止; 失效。

lap·wing /'læpwɪŋ; 'læp,wɪŋ/ *n* bird of the plover family; pewit. 田凫(千鸟之类); 京燕。

lar·board /'lɑːbəd; 'lɑːrbəd/ *n, adj* left side of a ship when looking forward (now always called 现常称作 the *port side*). 左舷(的)。 ⇨ **starboard.**

lar·ceny /'lɑːsənɪ; 'lɑːrsnɪ/ *n* (*pl* -nies) [U] (legal) stealing; theft; [C] instance of this. (法律)窃盗罪; 偷窃。

larch /lɑːtʃ; lɑːrtʃ/ *n* [C] deciduous tree with small cones and light-green leaves; [U] its wood. 落叶松; 落叶松木。

lard /lɑːd; lɑːrd/ *n* [U] fat of pigs prepared for use in cooking. 猪油。 □ *vt* [VP6A] put ~ on; put pieces of bacon into or on (meat, etc) before cooking, in order to add to the flavour. 涂猪油于; 于烹调前塞填或加添咸肉于(肉等)以增美味。 ~ *with,* (fig, often derog) enrich: (喻,常为贬抑语)以…充实; 润饰: *a speech ~ed with boring quotations.* 充满令人厌恶的引用文句的一篇演说。

lar·der /'lɑːdə(r); 'lɑːrdə/ *n* room or cupboard where

meat and other kinds of food are stored. 肉及其他食品的贮藏室; 伙食房; 食橱。

large /lɑːdʒ; lɑːrdʒ/ *adj* (-r, -st) **1** of considerable size; taking up much space; able to contain much: 大的; 巨大的; 容量大的: *A man with a ~ family needs a ~ house.* 有一大家庭的人需要一所大房子。 *She inherited a ~ fortune.* 她继承了一大笔财产。 *as ~ as life,* ⇨ **life(10).** (Note that *large* is less colloq than *big* and not as emotive as *great.* 'A great city' is large, but the use of 'great' suggests that it is also important or famous. *Large* is seldom used of persons, but note ~ *of limb,* having ~ limbs.) (注意: large 一词不如 big 通俗, 亦不如 great 带有感情。'a great city' 不仅指一城市的面积大, 而且含有'重要'或'著名'的意思。large 很少用以形容人, 但可形容四肢, 如 ~ of limb, 四肢粗大。) *'~-scale adj* (a) extensive: 大规模的; *~-scale operations.* 大规模的军事行动。 (b) made or drawn to a ~ scale: 大比例尺绘制的: *a ~-scale map.* 大比例尺绘制的地图。 **2** liberal; generous; unprejudiced (chiefly in the following): 宽大的; 慷慨的; 大公无私的(主要用于下列词词): *a ~ heart,* 宽大的心胸, hence, 由此产生, *~-'hearted;* 宽大为怀的; *~-'minded,* 宽宏大量的, hence, 由此产生, *~-'mindedness.* 宽宏大量。 **3** of wide range; not confined or restricted: 广阔的; 广泛的; 无限制的: *give an official ~ powers/discretion;* 给予一官员广泛的权力(自由处理权); *a man with ~ ideas;* 思想广阔的人; *~ and small farmers,* men farming on a ~ and a small scale. 大农场主人和小规模自耕农。 □ *n* (only in) (仅用于) *at ~,* (a) at liberty; free: 自由的; 自由行动的: *The escaped prisoner is still at ~.* 该逃犯仍逍遥法外。 (b) at full length; with details: 详细地; 仔细地: *to talk/write at ~.* 详细地说(写)。 (c) in general: 一般的: *Did the people at ~ approve of the government's policy?* 一般老百姓赞成政府的政策吗? (d) at random; without definite aim: 随便地; 无目标地: *scatter accusations at ~.* 随便指控。 □ *adv* **1** (only in) (仅用于) *bulk / loom /writ ~,* ⇨ **bulk, loom²,** **write(6). by** and ~, ⇨ **by¹(4). 2** boastfully: 夸大地: *talk ~.* 夸大其词; 说大话。 *~-'ish* ~-ɪʃ; -ɪ/ *adj* rather ~. 颇大的。 *~ly adv* **1** to a great extent: 大部分; 大半: *His success was ~ly due to luck.* 他的成功大都由于幸运。 **2** generously; freely: 慷慨地; 大方地: *He gives ~ly to charity.* 他慷慨捐助慈善事业。 *~·ness n*

lar·gesse (US also **lar·gess**) /lɑː'dʒes; 'lɑːrdʒɪs /*n* [U] generous or excessive giving; money or other things generously or excessively given. 慷慨的赠与; 慷慨的赠金或赠物。

largo /'lɑːɡəʊ; 'lɑːrɡo/ *n* (*pl* ~**s** /-ɡəʊz; -ɡoz/), *adv* (piece of music, movement) in very slow and solemn time. 缓慢地; 缓慢的音乐或乐章; 最缓板。

lar·iat /'lærɪət; 'lærɪət/ *n* rope for tethering a horse; long rope with a noose; lasso. 系马于桩上之绳; 一端有活结之长绳; 套索。

lark¹ /lɑːk; lɑːrk/ *n* small songbird, esp the skylark. 小鸣禽; (尤指)鹨; 云雀; 百灵鸟。 ⇨ the illus at **bird.** 参看 bird 之插图。

lark² /lɑːk; lɑːrk/ *n* [C] bit of fun; frolic: 欢乐; 嬉戏; 乐趣: *Boys are fond of having a ~.* 男孩子喜欢嬉戏。 *He did it for a ~,* in fun. 他是为了好玩而做的。 *What a ~!* How amusing! 真有趣! □ *vi* [VP2A, C] play pranks: 戏谑; 玩乐: *Stop ~ing about and get on with your work.* 不要玩乐, 去做你的工作。

lark·spur /'lɑːkspɜː(r); 'lɑːrk,spɜ/ *n* tall garden plant with blue, white or pink flowers. 飞燕草(一种高的园艺植物, 开蓝、白或粉红色花)。

larn /lɑːn; lɑːrn/ *vt, vi* (dial) learn. (方)学习。

larva /'lɑːvə; 'lɑːrvə/ *n* (*pl* ~*e* /-viː; -viː/) insect in the first stage of its life-history, after coming out of the egg. 昆虫的幼虫。 ⇨ the illus at **butterfly.** 参看 butterfly 之插图。 **lar·val** /'lɑːvl; 'lɑːrvl/ *adj* of or in the form of a ~. 幼虫的; 幼虫状的。

lar·ynx /'lærɪŋks; 'lærɪŋks/ *n* (anat) upper part of

CAMEL
Hc 167cm

BISON
Hc 189cm

LLAMA
Hc 189cm

KANGAROO
Lc 152cm

hump

ELEPHANT
Hc 350cm

HYENA
Hc 67cm

tusk   trunk

WILDEBEEST
or GNU
Hc 152cm

tine

horn   antlers

RHINOCEROS
Hc 167cm

REINDEER
Hc 167cm

GIRAFFE
Hc 548cm

ZEBRA
Hc 152cm

ANTELOPE
Hc 183cm

large wild animals

the windpipe where the vocal cords are. (解剖) 喉。 ⇨ the illus at **head**. 参看 head 之插图。 **lar·yn·gi·tis** /ˌlærɪnˈdʒaɪtɪs; ˌlærɪnˈdʒaɪtɪs/ n [U] inflammation of the ~. 喉炎。

las·car /ˈlæskə(r); ˈlæskə/ n seaman from the East Indies. 东印度水手。

las·civ·ious /ləˈsɪvɪəs; ləˈsɪvɪəs/ adj feeling, causing, expressing, lust. 淫荡的; 挑动春情的; 猥亵的。 ~·ly adv ~·ness n

laser /ˈleɪzə(r); ˈlezə/ n device for generating, amplifying and concentrating light waves into an intense beam in one specific direction: 激光; 雷射(产生和扩大光波, 并将其聚成强烈光柱之装置): (attrib) (用作定语) ~ beams. 激光束; 雷射光柱。

lash¹ /læʃ; læʃ/ n 1 part of a whip with which strokes are given; (usu leather) thong; blow or stroke given with a ~: 鞭之抽打或皮条部分; 捆绑用的(皮)带; 鞭挞: He was given twenty ~es. 他挨了二十鞭。 the ~, punishment of flogging: 鞭打(刑罚): mutinous sailors sentenced to the ~; 被判鞭打的叛变的水手; (fig) (喻) the ~ of criticism; 严酷的批评; 讥刺; the ~ of an angry woman's tongue. 一愤怒女子的漫骂。 2 = eyelash.

lash² /læʃ; læʃ/ vt, vi 1 [VP6A, 14, 2C] strike violently; make a sudden movement of (a limb, etc): 猛击; 打; 踢; 突然摆动(肢体等): The rain was ~ing (against) the windows. 雨击打着窗子。 The tiger ~ed its tail angrily. 那虎怒摆其尾。 He ~ed his faint-hearted men with his tongue. 他抨击他怯懦的部下。 He ~ed the

horse across the back with his whip. 他用鞭抽打马背。 2 ~ sb into (a state), rouse into: 煽动: The speaker ~ed his listeners into a fury. 那演说者煽动听众, 使之愤怒。 ~ out (against/at sb/sth), attack violently (with blows or words): 攻击; 抨击: The horse ~ed out at me, kicked or tried to kick, me 那马(想)踢我。 The speaker ~ed out against the government. 那演说者抨击政府。 3 [VP15A, B] ~ one thing to another; ~ things together, fasten tightly together (with rope, etc). (用绳等)将一物与另一物牢系在一起。 ~ sth down, make it secure with rope, etc. 捆紧某物。 '~-up n improvised or roughly constructed piece of apparatus. 临时拼凑的器具。

lash·ing /ˈlæʃɪŋ; ˈlæʃɪŋ/ n 1 [C] cord or rope used for binding or fastening. 捆绑用的绳子。 2 [C] whipping or beating. 鞭打。 3 (pl, colloq) plenty: (复,口) 许多: strawberries with ~s of cream; 拌有许多奶油的草莓; ~s of drink/~s to drink. 大量饮料。

lass /læs; læs/ n girl; sweetheart. 少女; 爱人。

las·sie /ˈlæsɪ; ˈlæsɪ/ n = lass.

lassi·tude /ˈlæsɪtjuːd US: -tuːd; ˈlæsəˌtjud/ n [U] tiredness; state of being uninterested in things. 倦怠; 对事物缺乏兴趣; 厌倦。

lasso /læˈsuː; ˈlæso/ n (pl ~s, ~es /-ˈsuːz; -soz/) long rope with a slip-knot, used for catching horses and cattle, esp in America. 套索(一端有活结之长绳, 尤指美洲捕牛马等所用者)。 □ vt catch with a ~. 以套索捕捉。

last¹ /lɑːst US: læst; læst/ adj 1 (contrasted with first.

与 first 相对。⇨ **late**¹.) coming after all others in time or order: 最后的；末尾的：*the ~ month of the year;* 一年的最后一月；*the ~ Sunday in June;* 六月的最后一个星期日；*the ~ time I saw you;* 上次我见到你的时候；*the ~ letters of the alphabet,* ie XYZ; 英文字母中最后的几个字母(即 X Y Z)；*the two ~/the ~ two persons to arrive;* 将最后到达的二位；*a ~-minute appeal,* one made just before sth is to be done, decided, etc. 最后一分钟的恳求。*~ but not least,* coming at the end, but not least in importance. 最后的但非最不重要的。*be on one's ~ legs,* ⇨ **leg**(1). *the L~ Day,* ⇨ Doomsday at **doom**¹. *the ~ post,* ⇨ **post**². *the ~ straw,* ⇨ **straw**. *have the ~ word,* ⇨ **word**. **2** (contrasted with *next*) coming immediately before the present: (与 next 相对) 就在现在以前的；刚过去的：*~ night / week / month / summer / year;* 昨夜(上周；上月；去夏；去年)；*on Tuesday ~;* 刚过去的(上或本)星期二；*~ May;* 刚过去的(去年或今年)五月；*in May ~;* 在去年(或今年)五月；*in/for/during the ~ few days/weeks, etc;* 在过去数日(周数)中；*this day ~ week,* a week ago. 上礼拜的今天；一周前。**3** only remaining: 仅余的；留在最后的：*He had spent his ~ dollar.* 他已用去他所剩的最后一块钱。*He would share his ~ crust with a beggar.* 他愿与乞丐分享他仅剩的面包皮。*This is our ~ hope.* 这是我们唯一的希望了。*I wouldn't marry you if you were the ~ person on earth.* 即使你是这个世界上仅余的一个男人，我也不会嫁给你。**4** least likely, suitable, willing, desirable, etc: 最不可能的；最不适合的；最不愿意的；最不希望的：*She's the ~ woman I want to sit next to at dinner,* I have no wish whatever to do so. 她是我在宴席上最不愿意与之邻座的女人。*That's the ~ thing I should expect him to do,* it seems most improbable that he will do it. 那是他最不可能做的事。**5** final; leaving nothing more to be said or done: 最终的；决定性的；*my ~ word on this question.* 关于此问题我已尽述了我的意见。*This is the ~ thing* (= the newest, the most up-to-date, thing) *in labour-saving devices.* 这是在节省劳力上最新的发明物。□ *adv* **1** (contrasted with *first*) after all others: (与 first 相对) 最后地；最末了：*I am to speak ~ at the meeting.* 我将在会中最后发言。*The horse I bet on came in ~.* 我赌的那匹马最后到达。**2** (contrasted with *next*) on the ~ occasion before the present time: (与 next 相对) 上一次；最近一次：*When did you ~ get a letter from her?* 你是什么时候接到她的信的？*She was quite well when I saw her ~/when I ~ saw her.* 我上次看见她时，她很健康。*When were you ~ in London / in London ~?* 你上次是什么时候在伦敦的？□ *n the ~ of,* that which comes at the end of: 最后的人或事物：*These are the ~ of our apples.* 这些是我们最后的苹果。*James II was the ~ of the Stuart kings.* 詹姆士二世是斯图亚特王朝最后的一个国王。*We shall never hear the ~ of this,* People will always talk about it. 人们将不停地谈论此事。*I hope we've seen the ~ of her,* that we shall never see her again. 我希望我们永远不再见到她。*at (long) ~,* in the end; after (much) delay: 终于；终于：*At (long) ~ we reached London.* 我们终于到达伦敦。*The holidays came at ~.* 假日终于来到了。*to/till the ~,* until the end; (liter or rhet) until death: 至终；到底；(文学或修辞)至死：*faithful to the ~.* 始终忠实。*breathe one's ~,* (liter) die. (文) 死。*~·ly adv* (in making a list) in the ~ place; finally: (列举时)最后；最后一点；*L~ly I must explain that ....* 最后我必须说明…。

last² /lɑːst US: læst/ *vi* [VP2A, B, C] *~ (out),* **1** continue; endure: 继续；延续；持久；维持：*How long will the fine weather ~?* 这好天气会延续多久？*Will Jim ~ out in his new job?* 吉姆的新工作会持久吗？**2** be adequate or enough for: (足够维持：*We have enough food to ~ (us) three days.* 我们有足够维持三天的食粮。*~·ing adj* continuing for a long time: 持久的；恒久的：*a ~ing peace.* 持久的和平。

last³ /lɑːst US: læst/ *n* block of wood shaped like a foot for making shoes on. 鞋楦(制鞋用的模型)。*stick to one's ~,* not try to do things one cannot do well. 守本分；做不好的事情不做。

latch /lætʃ/ *n* **1** simple fastening for a door or gate, the bar falling into a catch and being lifted by a small lever. 门闩。**2** small spring lock for a door opened from outside with a ~key. (自外面用门锁钥匙启开的)小弹簧锁；门锁。*on the ~,* fastened with a ~, but not locked. 栓着门闩(并非锁着)。'~·key, key for releasing or turning back a ~. 弹簧锁钥匙；门锁钥匙。'~·key child, (colloq) one left to look after himself because both parents go out to work. (口)父母外出工作留在家里乏人照顾的孩子。□ *vt, vi* [VP6A, 2A] fasten with a ~: 以门闩栓牢；以门闩关上：*L~ the doors.* 把门栓上。*This door won't ~ properly.* 这门门闩不牢。**2** [VP2C, 3A] *~ on (to),* (colloq) cling to; get possession of; understand. (口)坚守；持有；了解。

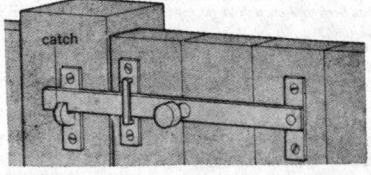

catch

a latch

late¹ /leɪt/ /let/ (-r, -st. ⇨ **last¹**, latter.) *adj* **1** (contrasted with *early*) after the right, fixed or usual time: (与 early 相对) 迟的；晚的：*Am I ~?* 我晚了吗？*Don't be ~ for work.* 上班不要迟到。*The train was ten minutes ~.* 火车误点十分钟。*The crops are ~ this year.* 今年的收获迟了。**2** far on in the day or night, in time, in a period or season: (日夜,时间,季节等)近末尾的；将尽的：*at a ~ hour;* 在深夜；在很晚的时候；*in the ~ afternoon;* 在下午将尽的时候；在接近傍晚的时候；*in ~ summer,* eg in Sept; 在夏末(例如九月)；*in the ~ eighties,* eg of the 19th c, in the years just before 1890; 在八十年代的末期(例如在十九世纪，则指1890年以前数年)；*~ Latin,* between classical Latin and the Latin of the Middle Ages; 古典拉丁语与中世纪拉丁语之间的拉丁语；*keep ~ hours,* ie much after the usual times. 习惯迟起。*The ~ edition of this paper appears at 3 pm; there's a later one at 5 pm;* the final edition comes out at 7 pm. 此报的晚版于下午三时出版,下午五时有较晚版,最晚版于下午七时发行。**3** recent; that recently was: 近时的；近来的：*the ~ political troubles;* 近来政治上的纷争；*the ~ news/fashions;* 最近的消息(风尚)；*the very ~st improvements;* 不久前的改善；*Mr Greene's ~st novel,* the most recently published. 格林先生最近出版的小说。(Cf 参较 *latest* and *last: Mr Greene has said that his ~st novel will be his last,* that he will write no more novels. 格林先生说他新近出版的小说将是他最后一部的了。)**4** former, recent (and still living): 以前的；前任的(现仍在世)：*the ~ prime minister.* 前任首相。**5** former, recent (and not now living): 已故的：*her ~ husband;* 她已故的丈夫；*the ~ King.* 先王。**6** *of ~,* recently. 近来。*at (the) ~st,* before or not later than: 最迟：*Be here on Monday at (the) latest.* 最迟不迟星期一为此止。

late² /leɪt/ /let/ *adv* **1** (contrasted with *early*) after the usual, right, fixed or expected time: (与 early 相对) 迟；晚：*get up/go to bed/arrive home ~;* 起床(睡觉,到家)很晚；*marry ~ in life,* eg at the age of 50; 晚婚(例如五十岁结婚)；*two years ~;* 二年后；*sit/stay up ~,* not go to bed until a ~ hour. 晚睡；熬夜。*Better ~ than never.* 迟做总比不做好。*~ in the day,* ~r than desired or expected. 较期望者为晚。*~r on,* at a ~r time; afterwards: 后来；以后；*as we shall see ~r on.* 正如我们以后将要看到的。*early and ~,* at all hours: 从早到晚：*He's at his desk*

early and ~. 他一天到晚在桌前工作. *sooner or* ~*r,* some time or other. 迟早; 总有一天. **2** recently: 近来; 新近: *I saw him as* ~ *as / no* ~*r than yesterday.* 我昨天还看见过他. **lat·ish** /'leɪtɪʃ; 'letɪʃ/ *adj* rather ~. 稍迟的; 稍晚的.

la·teen /lə'tiːn; læ'tin/ *adj* (naut) (航海) (only in) (仅用于) ~ **sail,** triangular sail on a long yard at an angle of 45° to the mast. 大三角帆(在与桅成 45 度角的长帆桁上).

late·ly /'leɪtlɪ; 'letlɪ/ *adv* (usu in neg and interr sentences, or with *only,* or in *as* ~ *as*) in recent times; recently: (通常用于否定和疑问句, 或与 only 连用, 或用于短语 as lately as 中)近来; 最近: *Have you seen Sam* ~*?* 你近来看见过山姆吗? *I haven't been home* ~. 我最近没有回过家. (Cf 参较 in the affirm: 在肯定句中: *I saw Sam a few days ago.* 我于数日前看见过山姆. *I was home not long ago.* 我不久前在家里). *I saw her as* ~ *as last Sunday.* 我上星期天还看见她. *It is only* ~ *that she has been well enough to go out.* 她身体复元能够外出还是最近的事.

latent /'leɪtnt; 'letnt/ *adj* present but not yet active, developed or visible: 隐藏的; 潜伏的: ~ *bacteria;* 潜伏的病菌; ~ *energy;* 潜能; *the* ~ *image on a photographic film,* not visible until the film is developed; 照相软片上的潜像; ~ *abilities.* 潜在的才能.

lat·eral /'lætərəl; 'lætərəl/ *adj* of, at, from, to, the side(s): 侧面的; 从旁边的; 至侧面的: *Pinch out the* ~ *buds to get large chrysanthemum blooms.* 将侧生的蕾剪除, 使菊花开大.

lat·erite /'lætəraɪt; 'lætə,raɪt/ *n* [U] kind of red soil much used for road-making in the tropics. 红土; 红泥 (热带地方用以铺路).

latex /'leɪteks; 'leteks/ *n* [U] milk-white liquid of (esp rubber) plants; emulsion of rubber globules used in paints, etc. 植物之乳汁; (尤指)橡胶乳汁; (用于油漆等中之)乳胶.

lath /lɑːθ *US:* læθ; læθ/ *n* (pl ~s /lɑːðz *US:* læðz; læðz/) long, thin strip of wood, esp as used in plaster walls and ceilings, and for making trellises, Venetian blinds. 板条(尤指用以做涂灰泥之墙壁和天花板之骨架, 与做格子棚, 百叶窗者).

lathe /leɪð; leð/ *n* machine for holding and turning pieces of wood or metal while they are being shaped, etc. 车床; 旋床.

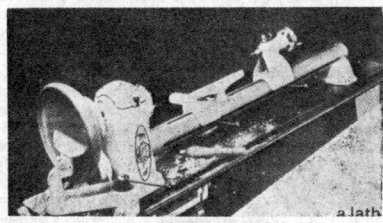

a lathe

lather /'lɑːðə(r); *US:* 'læð-; 'læðə/ *n* [U] **1** soft mass of white froth from soap and water (as made on a man's face before shaving). 肥皂泡沫(如刮脸前涂于脸上者). **2** frothy sweat on a horse. 马的汗沫. □ *vt, vi* **1** [VP6A] make ~ on: 涂以肥皂泡沫; 使生汗沫: ~ *one's chin before shaving.* 刮脸前在下巴上涂肥皂泡沫. *The horse was badly* ~*ed.* 那匹马满身是汗. **2** [VP2A] form ~: (肥皂)起泡沫; (马)冒汗沫: *Soap does not* ~ *in sea-water.* 肥皂在海水中不起泡沫. **3** [VP6A] (colloq) whip or beat. (口)鞭打; 打.

lathi /'lɑːtɪ; 'lætɪ/ *n* long, iron-bound stick used as a weapon (by the police) in India. 包铁长杖(印度警察的武器).

Latin /'lætɪn *US:* 'lætn; 'lætn/ *n* language of ancient

Rome. 拉丁文. □ *adj* of the ~ language; of peoples speaking languages descended from ~ (in Italy, France, Spain, Portugal, etc). 拉丁文的(意大利, 法兰西, 西班牙, 葡萄牙等)拉丁语系民族的). ~ **America,** countries of S and Central America in which Spanish and Portuguese are spoken. 拉丁美洲(南美洲及中美洲说西班牙和葡萄牙语诸国). **the** ~ **Church,** the RC Church. 天主教. ⇨ the illus at **cross.** 参看 cross 之插图. **the '**~ **Quarter,** (in Paris) area on the south bank of the Seine, a centre for students and artists for many centuries. 拉丁区(巴黎塞纳河南岸一地区, 几百年来为学生及艺术家荟集之处). ~·**ist** /-ɪst; -ɪst/ *n* ~ scholar. 拉丁语文学者. ~·**ize** /-aɪz; -aɪz/ *vt* give a ~ form to (a word); put (sth) into ~. 使 (一字)具有拉丁文形式; 译成拉丁文.

lati·tude /'lætɪtjuːd *US:* -tuːd; 'lætə,tjud/ *n* **1** [U] distance north or south of the equator measured in degrees. 纬度. ⇨ the illus at **projection.** 参看 projection 之插图. **2** *(pl)* regions or districts: (复)地区: *high / low* ~*s,* places a long way from / near to the equator; 高(低)纬度地区; 距赤道远(近)的地区; *warm* ~*s.* 热带地区. **3** [U] (measure of) freedom in action or opinion: (行动或言论的)自由; 自由的范围: *Does your government allow much* ~ *in political belief,* allow people to hold widely different political beliefs? 贵国政府在政治信仰上给予人民很多自由吗? **4** (photo) time limits within which a film may safely be under- or over-exposed. (摄影)底片安全曝光的时限. **lati·tudi·nal** /ˌlætɪ'tjuːdɪnl *US:* -'tuːdənl; ˌlætə'tjudənl/ *adj* **lati·tudi·narian** /ˌlætɪtjuːdɪ'neərɪən *US:* -ˌtuːdn'eər-; ˌlætə,tjudn-'erɪən/ *adj, n* (person who is) tolerant, broad-minded (esp in religious beliefs and dogmas). (尤指在宗教信仰和教条方面宽容的); 放任的; (对宗教信仰等)放任的人.

la·trine /lə'triːn; lə'trin/ *n* (in places where there are no sewers, eg camps) pit or trench to receive human urine and excrement. (营地等无下水道地方之)厕所; 便所; 茅坑.

lat·ter /'lætə(r); 'lætɚ/ *adj* **1** recent; belonging to the end of a period): 近来的; (一段时期之)末尾的; 较后的: *the* ~ *half of the year.* 下半年. ~·**day** *adj* modern. 近代的. **2** (also as 亦用作 *pron*) **the** ~, (contrasted with **the former**) the second of two things or persons already mentioned: (与 the former 相对)后者: *Of these two men the former is dead,* but the ~ *is still alive.* 此二人中前者已死, 但后者仍活着. ~·**ly** *adv* of late; nowadays. 近来; 现今.

lat·tice /'lætɪs; 'lætɪs/ *n* framework of crossed laths or metal strips as a screen, fence or door, or for climbing plants to grow over: 板条制成的格子架(作为屏障, 篱, 门或供植物攀缘); 格构: (attrib) (用作定语) *a* ~ *frame / girder / pylon,* made with iron or steel ~·**work.** 格构框架(梁, 塔). ~ **window,** one with small square- or diamond-shaped pieces of glass in a framework of lead. 格子窗. ⇨ the illus at **window.** 参看 window 之插图. ~**d** /'lætɪst; 'lætɪst/ *adj* made in the form of a ~; provided with a ~. 格子状的; 有格子的.

laud /lɔːd; lɔd/ *vt* [VP6A] (formal) praise; glorify. (正式用语)称赞; 赞美. ~·**able** /-əbl; -əbl/ *adj* deserving praise. 值得称赞的. ~·**ably** /-əblɪ; -əblɪ/ *adv*

lauda·num /'lɔːdənəm; 'lɔdənəm/ *n* [U] opium prepared for use as a sedative. 鸦片剂; 鸦片酊(用作镇静剂).

lauda·tory /'lɔːdətərɪ *US:* -tɔːrɪ; 'lɔdə,tɔrɪ/ *adj* (formal) expressing or giving praise. (正式用语)表示称赞的; 赞赏的.

laugh /lɑːf *US:* læf; læf/ *vi, vt* **1** [VP2A, B, C, 3A] make sounds and movements of the face, body, showing amusement, joy, contempt, etc: 笑; 发笑: *The jokes made everyone* ~. 那些笑话使人人都笑了. ~ *at,* **(a)** be amused by: 觉得有趣而发笑: ~ *at a joke / a funny story.* 听到笑话(有趣的故事)而笑. **(b)** make fun of; ridicule: 嘲笑; 讥笑: *It's unkind to* ~ *at a person*

who is in trouble. 嘲笑一个陷入困境的人是不仁慈的。 **(c)** disregard; treat with indifference: 嘲笑讨论；藐视；对···一笑置之: ~ *at difficulties.* 对困难一笑置之。 ⇨ *in sb's face,* defy openly, show contempt for. 公然反抗某人；当面嘲笑某人。 ~ *one's 'head off,* heartily. 痛快地笑。 ~ *on the other side of one's face,* change from joy or triumph to sorrow or regret. 转喜为忧。 ~ *over,* ~ while discussing, examining, etc: 笑着讨论，审查等: ~ *over a letter.* 一面看信一面笑。 ~ *up one's sleeve,* be secretly amused. 窃喜；偷笑。 *He ~s best who ~s last; He who ~s last ~s longest,* (prov) warning against expressing triumph too soon. (谚)勿高兴过早。 **2** [VP15B] ~ *away,* dismiss (a subject) by ~ing: 借笑以驱走某人: ~ *away sb's fears or doubts,* suggest, by ~ing, that they are without real cause. 借笑以驱走某人的恐惧或疑虑。 ~ *down,* silence by ~ing scornfully; reject by ~ing: 以轻蔑的笑使沉默；借笑以拒绝: *They ~ed the speaker/the proposal down.* 他们以笑使那讲演者中止(拒绝那建议)。 ~ *off,* escape from, get rid of, by ~ing: 借笑以逃避或消除: ~ *off an embarrassing situation.* 对尴尬的处境一笑置之。 **3** [VP22, 15A] arrive at a state, obtain a result, by ~ing: 笑至某种状态或结果: ~ *oneself silly/helpless;* 笑傻了(笑得不能停止); ~ *oneself into convulsions;* 笑得前仰后合; ~ *a person out of his depression/out of a foolish belief.* 笑得别人不再沮丧(笑得别人放弃一愚昧的信仰)。 ~ *sb/sth out of court,* dismiss him/it completely by ridicule. 对···一笑置之。 **4** [VP6B] express with or by means of a ~: 以笑来表示否认: *He ~ed his denial.* 他以笑表示否认。 □ *n* [C] sound made in ~ing; act of ~ing: 笑声；笑: *We've had a good many ~s over his foolishness.* 他的愚蠢让我们笑了不够。 *They all joined in the ~.* 他们都一起笑了起来。 *'Oh, yes', she answered with a ~.* '哦，是的，'她笑着回答道。 *have/get the ~ of sb,* score off him. 羞辱某人；驳倒某人。 ⇨ *score²*(4). *have the last ~,* get one's satisfaction. 获得最后胜利。 *'belly-~,* ⇨ *belly¹*(1). ~·*able* /-əbl/ -əbl/ *adj* amusing; causing persons to ~: 有趣的；可笑的: *a ~able mistake.* 可笑的错误。 ~·*ably* /-əblɪ/ -əblɪ/ *adv* showing happiness, amusement, etc: 笑的；带笑的: ~*ing faces.* 带笑的面孔。 *'~ing-gas n* nitrous oxide (N₂O) used in dental surgery. 笑气(氧化亚氮，牙科手术时用之)。 *'~ing-stock n* ⇨ *stock¹*(7). ~·*ing·ly adv*

laugh·ter /'lɑ:ftə(r) US: 'læf-; 'læftɚ/ *n* [U] laughing: 笑: *burst into ~;* 失声大笑; *roar with ~;* 哄然大笑; *an outburst of ~.* 一阵大笑。

launch¹ /lɔ:ntʃ; lɔntʃ/ *vt, vi* **1** [VP6A] set (a ship, esp one newly built) afloat: 使(船，尤指新船)下水: *a new passenger liner.* 使一新的定期客轮下水。 **2** [VP6A, 15A] ~ *sth (against/at),* set in motion; send; aim: 发动；发射; 发射: ~ *an attack;* 发动攻击; ~ *threats at an opponent;* 威胁对手; ~ *a missile/spacecraft into outer space.* 发射飞弹(太空船)至太空。 *'~ing-pad n* base or platform from which spacecraft, etc are ~ed. (太空船等的)发射台。 *'~ing-site n* place for ~ing-pads. (发射)基地。 ⇨ the illus at **rocket.** 参看 **rocket** 之插图。 **3** [VP6A, 15A] (fig) get started; set going: (喻)使开始; 开办: ~ *a new business enterprise;* 创办新企业; ~ *a man into business.* 使一人入商业界。 **4** [VP2C, 3A] ~ *out:* (*out*) *into,* make or start (on): 开始: ~ *out into a new argument/debate;* 开始一新的辩论; ~ *into a new subject;* 开始一新题目; ~ *out into extravagance.* 开始挥霍。 □ *n* act of ~ing (a ship or spacecraft). (船之)下水(太空船之)发射。

launch² /lɔ:ntʃ; lɔntʃ/ *n* mechanically propelled passenger-carrying boat (on rivers and lakes, in harbours). (于河湖及海港上航行之，机器推进的)汽艇。

launder /'lɔ:ndə(r); 'lɔndɚ/ *vt, vi* [VP6A, 2A] wash and press (clothes): 洗熨(衣服): *Send these sheets to be ~ed.* 把这些被单送去洗熨。 *Will these shirts ~ well?* 这些衬衫禁洗吗？

laun·der·ette /lɔ:n'dret; lɔn'dret/ *n* laundry at which members of the public may launder their clothes, etc in coin-operated automatic washing-machines and dryers. (设有投进钱币就能自动操作的自动洗衣机和烘干机的)自助洗衣店。

laun·dress /'lɔ:ndrɪs; 'lɔndrɪs/ *n* woman who earns money by washing and ironing clothes. 洗衣妇。

laun·dry /'lɔ:ndrɪ; 'lɔndrɪ/ *n* (*pl* -**dries**) **1** [C] laundering business; place where clothes, sheets, etc, are sent to be laundered. 洗衣业；洗衣店。 **2** the ~, clothes (to be) laundered: 所洗的衣服；待洗的衣服: *Has the ~ come back yet?* 洗的衣服送回来了吗？ *'~·man /-mæn; -mən/ n* (*pl* -**men**) man who collects and delivers ~. (洗衣店所雇的)取送衣服之男工。

laur·eate /'lɔrɪət US: 'lɔːr-; 'lɔːrɪət/ *adj* crowned with a laurel wreath. 戴桂冠的。 *n* the (,Poet) 'L~, poet officially appointed to the Royal Household in GB. The holder may write poems on great national occasions. 桂冠诗人(英国国王所任命者，视为王室之一员，获此荣誉者于国家大典时可赋写诗庆祝)。

laurel /'lɒrəl US: 'lɔːrəl; 'lɔːrəl/ *n* evergreen shrub with smooth, shiny leaves, used by ancient Romans and Greeks as an emblem of victory, success and distinction. 月桂树(有平滑发亮的树叶的常青灌木，古罗马人及希腊人用以作胜利、成功及荣誉的象征)。 *look to one's ~s,* beware of losing one's reputation; be on the look-out for possible successes among rivals. 爱惜名声；小心保持纪录。 *rest on one's ~s,* be content with one's successes and rest. 对既得之成功心满意足。 *win/gain one's ~s,* win reputation, honour. 博得荣誉。 ~*led adj* crowned with ~. 戴桂冠的。

lav /læv; læv/ *n* (colloq abbr of) lavatory. (口)为lavatory 之略。

lava /'lɑ:və; 'lɑvə/ *n* [U] hot liquid material flowing from a volcano: (火山流出之)熔岩: *a stream of ~;* 熔岩流: this material when it has cooled and hardened: 火山岩(由熔岩凝结而成): *'~ beds.* 火山岩床。 ⇨ **pumice.**

lava·tory /'lævətrɪ US: -tɔːrɪ; 'lævə,tɔrɪ/ *n* (*pl* -**ries**) [C] room for washing the hands and face in; water-closet. 盥洗室；厕所。

lave /leɪv; lev/ *vt* (poet) wash; bathe; (of a stream) flow gently past or against. (诗)洗；沐浴; (指河流)缓慢流过；冲洗。

lav·en·der /'lævəndə(r); 'lævəndɚ/ *n* [U] plant with pale purple sweet-scented flowers; the dried flowers and stalks (sewn up in bags and placed among linen sheets, etc); the colour of ~. 欧薄荷；熏衣草(开淡紫香花的一种植物)；欧薄荷的干花及干茎(装于缝好的袋内，置于床单等内)；淡紫色。 ~ *water n* [U] perfume distilled from ~. 欧薄荷香水。

lav·ish /'lævɪʃ; 'lævɪʃ/ *adj* **1** ~ (*of sth/in doing sth),* giving or producing freely, liberally or generously: 慷慨的；大方的: *He is never ~ of praise/in giving money to charity.* 他吝于称赞他人(捐助慈善事业)。 **2** (of what is given) given abundantly; excessive: (指给予之物)过多的；过度的: ~ *praise/expenditure on luxuries.* 过多的称赞(奢侈品过度的开销)。 □ *vt* [VP14] ~ *on,* give abundantly and generously to: 慷慨给与；不吝惜地给与: ~ *care on an only child.* 对独生子过度溺爱。 ~·*ly adv*

law /lɔː; lɔ/ *n* **1** [C] rule made by authority for the proper regulation of a community or society or for correct conduct in life: 法律；法令: *When a Bill is passed by Parliament and signed by the Sovereign, it becomes a law.* 当一法案由国会通过再经国王签署，即成为法律。 *'law-giver n* man who gives a code of laws (eg Moses in Hebrew history, Solon in Greek history). 立法者(例如希伯来历史上的摩西，希腊历史上的梭伦)。 *'law-officer n* (esp) Attorney or Solicitor-General. (尤指)检察长及副检察长。 ⇨ **regulation, statute.** **2** [U] **the law,** the whole body of laws considered collectively:

法律(集合用法): *If a man fails to observe the law he can be punished.* 一个人如果犯法将受惩罚。*Does the law allow me to do this?* 法律允许我这样做吗？ *break the law,* fail to observe it. 违法；犯法。 *lay down the law,* talk authoritatively, as if one were certain of being right. 独断地说；命令似地说。 **'law-abiding** *adj* obeying the law. 守法的。 **'law-breaker** *n* person who disobeys the law. 犯法者。 **3** [U] controlling influence of the laws: 法治: *maintain law and order,* see that the laws are respected. 维持法治和秩序。 *Necessity knows no law,* When sth cannot be avoided, ordinary laws and rules will be ignored or broken. 需要不知法律(迫不得已时将铤而走险)。 **4** [U] the laws as a system or science; the legal profession: 法律系统；法律学；法律业: *study law;* 研读法学; *law students;* 法科学生; 法律学者; *read law,* study in order to become a lawyer. 学习法律以期做律师。 ⇨ **jurisprudence. 5** [U] (with a defining word) one of the branches of the study of law: (与一说明的词连用)法律学之一支；法律学之一部门: *commercial law;* 商法; *the law of nations;* 国际法; *international law.* 国际法。 **6** [U] operation of the law (as providing a remedy for wrongs). 法律的实施(如对损害等之补偿)。 *go to law (against sb);* have the law on sb,* (colloq) appeal to the law courts. (口)控告某人。 *take the law into one's own hands,* use force to redress a wrong. 私行治罪。 **'law court** *n* court of justice. 法庭。 **'law suit** *n* prosecution of a claim in a law court. 诉讼。 **7** [C] rule of action or procedure, esp in the arts or a game: 规则(尤指艺术或游戏中者)；原则；原理: *the laws of perspective/harmony;* 透视(和声)原则; *the laws of cricket.* 板球规则。 *be a law unto oneself,* disregard rules and conventions; do what one thinks right. 忽视惯例；照自己的意思行事。 **8** [U, C] (also 亦作 *law of nature* or *natural law*) factual statement of what always happens in certain circumstances; regularity in nature, eg the order of the seasons: 自然的法则；自然律(例如四季的循环)；定律: *Newton's law;* 牛顿定律; *the laws of motion;* 运动定律; *the law of supply and demand;* 供求律; *the law of self-preservation,* the instinct of men and animals to behave in a way that will save them from danger. 自卫的本能。 **law·ful** /-fl; -fəl/ *adj* **1** allowed by law; according to law: 合法的；法定的；依法的: *lawful acts;* 合法的行为; *the lawful ruler.* 合法的统治者。 **2** (of offspring) legitimate: (指子孙)合法的: *the lawful heir.* 合法的继承人。 **law·fully** /-fəli; -fəlı/ *adv* **law·less** *adj* not in accordance with the law; not conforming to the law; not restrained by law; unruly: 不法的；不遵守法律的；不受法律控制的；违法的: *lawless acts;* 不法的行为; *lawless tribes.* 法律所不能及的部落。 **law·less·ly** *adv* **law·less·ness** *n* [U].

lawn¹ /lɔːn; lɔn/ *n* [C] area of grass (turf) kept closely cut and smooth, eg in a private garden or a public park; such an area of grass used for a game: (经过修剪而平坦的)草地(例如私人花园或公园里的)；草场(供运动用): *a croquet ~;* 槌球场; *a 'tennis ~.* 草地网球场。 **'~-mower** *n* machine for cutting grass on **~s**. 刈草机；剪草机。 **~ 'tennis** *n* [U] the game of tennis played on an unwalled court, either hard surfaced or turfed. 草地网球。 ⇨ the illus at **tennis.** 参看 tennis 之插图。

lawn² /lɔːn; lɔn/ *n* [U] kind of fine linen used for dresses, blouses and esp for a bishop's sleeves. 细竹布；软洋纱(一种细麻布，用以制女服和罩衫，特别用以制主教法衣之袖)。

law·yer /'lɔːjə(r); 'lɔjə/ *n* person who practises law, esp a barrister or solicitor. 律师。

lax /læks; læks/ *adj* **1** negligent; inattentive; not strict or severe: 疏忽的；不小心的；不严格的: *lax discipline/behaviour;* 不严格的纪律(疏忽的行为); *lax in morals.* 品行不检。 **2** (of the bowels) free in action. (指肠)松弛的；腹泻的。 **lax·ity** /'læksətı; 'læksətı/

[U] being lax; [C] (*pl* **-ties**) instance of being lax. 疏忽；不严松；腹泻。 **lax·ly** *adv*

laxa·tive /'læksətıv; 'læksətıv/ *n, adj* (medicine, drug) causing the bowels to empty. 通便的；通便剂；轻泻剂。

lay¹ /leɪ; le/ *vt, vi* (*pt, pp* **laid** /leɪd; led/) For uses with *adverbial particles* and *preps* ⇨ **12** below. 与副词性小品词和介词连用之用法。参看下列第 12 义。 **1** [VP6A, 15A] put on a surface; put in a certain position, in the proper place for a purpose: 置放；铺设；装于适当位置: *Who will lay the carpet,* spread it out, fasten it down, etc? 谁将铺设地毯? *He laid his hand on my shoulder.* 他把他的手放在我的肩上。 *A new submarine cable was laid between England and Holland.* 英国至荷兰间铺设了新的海底电缆。 *The woodcutter laid his axe to the tree,* began to chop. 那砍柴者举斧砍树。 *A bricklayer is a man who lays bricks.* 砖瓦匠即砌砖之人。 *lay a snare/trap/an ambush (for sb/sth),* prepare one. (为…)设陷阱(埋伏)。 **2** [VP6A, 15B] (of nonmaterial things, and fig uses) place; put. (指非物质事物及比喻用法)安放。 *lay (one's) hands on sth/sb,* **(a)** seize; get possession of: 攫取；占有: *He keeps everything he can lay (his) hands on.* 他占有每一样能得到的东西。 **(b)** do violence to: 对…行凶；伤害: *How dare you lay hands on me?* 你怎敢向我动手? *He laid violent hands on himself* (dated) tried to commit suicide. (过时用语)他企图自杀。 **(c)** find: 寻获: *I have the book somewhere, but can't lay my hands on it just now.* 我是有那本书，不知摆在什么地方，现在就是找不到。 **(d)** (eccles) confirm; ordain; consecrate. (教会)施坚信礼；行按手礼(立为牧师、神父或其他神职人员)。 Hence, 由此产生, *laying-on of hands,* confirmation; ordination; consecration. 坚信礼；按手礼。 *lay the blame (for sth) on sb,* say that he is responsible for what is wrong, etc. 归咎于某人。 *lay a (heavy) burden on sb,* cause sb to be responsible for sth likely to be difficult, to cause suffering, etc. 使负(艰苦)重责。 *lay one's hopes on,* = pin (the more usu word) one's hopes on. *lay a strict injunction on sb (to do sth),* give him strict orders (to do it). 予以严格命令；强制。 *lay great/little store by/on sth,* value very much/little. (不)重视。 *lay stress/emphasis/weight on sth,* treat it as important; emphasize it. 认为重要；强调某事之重要。 *lay a tax on sth,* impose one. 加税于。 **3** [VP15A] cause to be in a certain state, condition, or situation. 使处于某种状态，状况或情势。 *lay sb to rest,* (esp) bury sb: (尤指)埋葬某人: *He was laid to rest in the churchyard.* 他被葬于教堂之墓地。 *lay sb under a/the necessity/obligation,* make it necessary or obligatory for him (to do sth): 使某人(对某事物)有义务: *Your conduct lays me under the necessity of dismissing you.* 你的行为使我必须解除你的职务。 *He was laid under an obligation to support the wife he had deserted.* 他必须赡养被他遗弃的妻子。 *lay sb under contribution,* compel him to contribute money, etc. 强迫某人捐献金钱等。 *lay sth to sb's charge,* hold him responsible. 委过于某人。 *lay claim to sth,* ⇨ **claim.** *lay sth at sb's door,* ⇨ **door.** *lay one's finger on,* ⇨ **finger.** *lay siege to,* ⇨ **siege. 4** [VP22] (*lay* + *n, adj* or *adv phrases*) cause to be in a specified condition. (与名词，形容词或副词短语连用)使处于某指明的状态。 *lay sth bare,* show; reveal: 显示；表露: *lay bare one's heart,* reveal one's inmost feelings, etc. 表明心曲。 *lay sth flat,* cause to be flat: 使倒下: *crops laid flat by heavy rainstorms.* 被暴雨击倒的作物。 *lay sth open,* **(a)** expose, reveal: 显示；揭露: *lay open a plot.* 揭露一阴谋。 **(b)** cut, gash: 刺伤；割伤: *lay open one's cheek,* eg by falling and striking it against a rock. 使面颊受伤(例如跌倒撞在一岩石上)。 *lay oneself open to sth,* render oneself liable to criticism, calumny, etc. 使自己易受(批评，毁谤等)。 *lay sth waste,* ravage, destroy: 蹂躏；破坏: *a countryside laid waste by invading armies.* 被人侵敌军夷为平地的乡间一地区。 **5**

[VP6A] cause to be down, settle: 使倒下; 使降落: *sprinkle water on the roads to lay the dust.* 洒水在路上以使尘土飞扬. **lay sb's doubts,** get rid of them, 消除某人的疑惑 (allay 较常用), **lay a ghost /spirit,** expel or exorcize it; cause it to stop appearing to people. 驱除鬼魂. **6** [VP6A, 2A] (of birds and insects) produce (eggs): (指鸟与昆虫)产 (卵): *Are your hens laying yet?* 你那些母鸡下蛋了吗? *How many eggs does this hen lay each week?* 这只母鸡每星期下多少个蛋? *New laid eggs, 5p each.* 新鲜鸡蛋, 五便士一个. **7** [VP15A] (usu passive) set (a story, etc) in time and place: (通常用被动语态)为(故事等)安排时间和地点: *The scene is laid in Athens, in the third century BC.* 背景是公元前三世纪的雅典. **8** [VP6A] place or arrange by laying (ready for use, etc): 布置 (以备使用): *lay the table (for breakfast),* put out plates, knives, etc; 摆设餐具(准备吃早餐); *lay the cloth,* spread it on the table ready for a meal; 铺餐桌布; *lay a fire,* put wood, coal, etc in a fireplace, ready for lighting. 准备生火. **9** [VP6A, 12C, 14] put down (a sum of money) as a wager or stake (on sth of which the result is uncertain); offer as a bet: 下(若干钱)作为赌注; 打赌: *They laid a wager on the result of the race.* 他们以竞赛的结果打赌. *I'll lay you £5 that he won't come.* 我跟和你赌五英镑, 他不会来. *I'll lay (= make) you a bet that ....* 我和你打赌.... **10** [VP6A, 15A] cover; coat: 覆盖; 覆以一层: *lay carpet on the floor /lay the floor with carpet;* 将地毯铺于地板上; *lay straw over the yard /lay the yard with straw;* 将稻草铺在院中; *lay colours on canvas.* 涂颜料于画布上. ⇨ **lay on** at **12** below. 参看下列第 **12** 义之 **lay on. 11** [VP6A] (sl) have sexual intercourse with. (俚)和…发生肉体关系. **12** [VP2C, 3A, 15B] (uses with adverbial particles and preps): (与副词性小品词及介词连用的用法):

lay about one (with sth), hit out in all directions: 向四周挥打: *When they rushed at him, Harry laid about him with his big stick.* 当他们向他冲去时, 哈里用他的大手杖向四周挥打.

lay sth aside, keep for future use: 储蓄(以备将来之用): *lay aside money for one's old age.* 储蓄金钱以备老年之需. **(b)** put down: 放下: *He laid his book aside to listen to me.* 他放下书听我说话. **(c)** abandon; give up: 抛弃; 放弃: *lay aside bad habits.* 革除恶习.

lay sth back, turn back: 使向后: *The horse laid back its ears.* 那马将耳朵伸向后面.

lay sth by, = lay sth aside(a).

lay sb /oneself down, place in a lying or recumbent position: 使躺下: *Lay the baby down gently.* 将婴儿轻轻放下. *She laid herself down.* 她躺下. **lay sth down, (a)** pay or wager: 付(款); 下(赌注): *How much are you ready to lay down?* 你准备付(付)多少? **(b)** (begin to) build: 开始建筑: *lay down a new ship.* 开始造新船. **(c)** convert (land) to pasture: 使(土地)变为牧场: *lay down land in /to /with /under grass.* 使土地变为草地. **(d)** store (wine) in a cellar: 贮藏(酒)于酒窖: *lay down claret and port.* 贮藏红葡萄酒和紫葡萄酒. **lay sth down; lay it down that ...,** establish: 设立; 制定: *You can't lay down hard and fast rules.* 你不能制定严格的规则. *It was laid down that all applicants should sit a written examination.* 根据规定, 所有申请人均应参加笔试. *These prices have been laid down by the manufacturers.* 这些价格都是厂商规定的. **lay down one's arms,** put one's weapons down as a sign of surrender: 放下武器投降. **lay down the law,** say with (or as if with) authority what must be done. 独断地说; 命令似地说. **lay down one's life,** sacrifice it: 牺牲生命: *He laid down his life for his country.* 他为国捐躯. **lay down office,** resign a position of authority. 罢官; 辞职.

lay sth in, provide oneself with a stock of: 备办: *lay in provisions /stores.* 贮备粮食(货物).

lay off, (colloq) (口**) (a)** discontinue work or activity; rest: 停止工作或活动; 休息: *The doctor told me to lay*

off for a week. 医生要我休息一星期. **(b)** stop doing sth which irritates or annoys: 停止做惹人生气或烦恼之事: *I hear you've been pestering my sister again—Well, you can just lay off.* 我听说你又去纠缠我妹妹了——哼, 你可不可再去缠她了. **lay sb off,** dismiss temporarily: 暂时解雇 *lay off workmen,* eg because of a shortage of materials. 将工人暂时解雇(例如由于原料之缺乏). Hence, 由此产生, **'lay-off** *n* period during which men are temporarily dismissed. 工人被暂时解雇期间.

lay sth on, (a) supply gas, water, electricity to a building: 为建筑物接煤气、自来水、电: *We can't occupy the new house until gas and water are laid on.* 我们要等煤气和水接好始能移居新屋. **(b)** (colloq) provide: (口)准备: *Sightseeing tours were laid on for the distinguished visitors from Poland.* 为波兰来的贵宾安排了观光旅行. **lay it on (thick /with a trowel),** use exaggerated praise, flattery, etc: 过份称赞; 过度奉承: *To call him a genius is laying it on a bit too thick!* 称他是天才是有点过份称赞了! **lay sth out, (a)** spread out ready for use or so as to be seen easily: 展开以便使用或易见: *lay out one's evening clothes;* 取出晚礼服以待客; *the magnificent scene that was laid out before the climbers when they reached the summit.* 当爬山者到达山顶时呈现在他们眼前的壮丽的风景. **(b)** prepare for burial: 准备埋葬: *lay out a corpse.* 准备一尸体以备埋葬. **(c)** spend (money): 用(钱): *lay out one's money carefully.* 谨慎用钱. **(d)** make a plan for; arrange: 计划; 设计: *well laid-out streets and avenues;* 设计良好的街道和马路; *lay out a printed page.* 设计一印刷版面. Hence, 由此产生, **'lay-out** *n* arrangement, plan, design of a printed page, an advertisement, a book, a group of buildings. 布置; 图样; (书, 广告, 房屋等之)设计. **lay oneself out (to do sth),** exert oneself, take pains: 尽力(做某事): *She laid herself out to make her guests comfortable.* 她煞费苦心地款待她的客人.

lay over, (US) (GB 英 = *stop over*) stop at a place during a journey because of a requirement in a schedule. (美)(因行程之需要)中途停留于某地. **'lay-over** *n* such a stop. 中途停留.

lay sth up, (a) save; store: 贮藏: *lay up provisions.* 贮粮. **(b)** ensure by what one does or fails to do that one will have trouble, etc in future: (所做所为)以将招惹麻烦等: *You're only laying up trouble for yourself.* 你简直是在为自己找麻烦嘛. **(c)** put (a ship) out of commission: 使(船)不被使用: *lay a ship up for repairs.* 将船拖入船坞修理. **lay sb up,** (usu passive) force sb to stay in bed: (通常用被动语态)迫使某人卧床: *He's laid up with a broken leg.* 他因一腿折断而卧床. *The flu has laid him up for a few days.* 流行性感冒使他卧床数日.

lay² /leɪ/ le/ *n* (chiefly in) (主要用于) *the lay of the land* (*lie* is more usu), the nature or formation of an area of land. 地形; 地势 (lie 较常用).

lay³ /leɪ/ le/ *n* (sl) partner in sexual intercourse. (俚) 发生肉体关系之对方; 姘夫. ⇨ **lay¹**(11).

lay⁴ /leɪ/ le/ *n* (liter) minstrel's song; ballad. (文)歌谣; 民歌.

lay⁵ /leɪ/ le/ *pt of* **lie².**

lay⁶ /leɪ/ le/ *adj* (attrib only) (仅用作定语) **1** of, for, done by, persons who are not priests: 凡俗的(与神职人员相对而言): 普通人的: *a lay brother /sister,* one who wears the dress and has taken the vows of a religious order, but who does manual work and is excused other duties. 凡入修士(修女)(穿修士或修女服, 并发誓修道, 但从事体力之工作, 不担任其他职务者). ⇨ **laity. 2** non-professional; not expert (esp with reference to the law and medicine): 非属于专门职业的; 外行的(尤指对法律和医学方面而言): *lay opinion,* what non-professional people think. 外行人的意见. *To the lay mind the language of a lawyer seems to be full of jargon.* 对外行人而言, 律师所用的语言中似乎充满了术语. **'lay-man** /-mən/ -mən/ *n* (*pl* -men) lay(2) person: 外行人; 门外

汉: *Where the law is concerned I am only a layman*, I have no expert knowledge. 谈到法律，我不过是个外行人。

lay·about /'leɪəbaʊt; 'leə,baʊt/ n (GB sl) loafer; person who avoids working for a living. (英俚)游荡之人;不务正业者。

lay·by /'leɪbaɪ; 'le,baɪ/ n (GB) area at the side of a road where vehicles may park without hindering the flow of traffic. (英)马路旁边可停车之处。

layer /'leɪə(r); 'leə/ n [C] 1 thickness of material (esp one of several) laid or lying on or spread over a surface, or forming one horizontal division: 层(尤指数层中之一): a ～ of clay. 一层泥土。 '～-cake, one with horizontal divisions separated by cream, jam, etc. 夹心蛋糕。 2 (gardening) shoot of a plant fastened down to take root while still growing from the parent plant. (园艺)压枝; 压条。 3 (of hens) (指母鸡) *good/bad* ～s, hens that lay eggs in large/small numbers. 生蛋多(少)的母鸡。 □ vt [VP6A] fasten down (a shoot of a plant): 压植(植物的枝条): ～ *carnations*. 用压条法培植康乃馨。

lay·ette /leɪ'et; le'et/ n garments, blankets, etc for a new-born baby. 新生婴儿所需的衣物。

lay fig·ure /,leɪ 'fɪɡə(r); ,le'fɪɡɚ/ n jointed wooden figure of the human body (used by artists for arranging drapery, etc); (fig) dummy. (艺术家用以陈列装饰用织物等的)人体模型; (喻)傀儡。

lay·man ⇨ lay⁶.

lazar /'læzə(r); 'læzɚ/ n (archaic) poor and diseased person, esp a leper. (古)贫病交迫者(尤指麻疯病患者)。

laza·retto /,læzə'retəu; ,læzə'reto/ (pl ～s /-təuz; -toz/) (also 亦作 **laza·ret, laza·rette** /,læzə'ret; ,læzə'ret/) nn quarantine station; ship's storeroom. 检疫所;(船上的)贮藏室。

Laz·arus /'læzərəs; 'læzərəs/ n beggar; (in contrasts) very poor man: 乞丐; (用于对比)极穷的人: ～ *and Dives*. 穷人和富人。 ⇨ **Luke 16: 20**. 参看路加福音第16章第20节。

laze /leɪz; lez/ vi, vt [VP2A, C, 15B] ～ *(away)*, be lazy; pass (time) in idleness: 懒散;混(时光): ～ *all day;* 终日懒散; *lazing away the afternoon*. 混这一下午。

lazy /'leɪzɪ; 'lezɪ/ adj (-ier, -iest) unwilling to work; doing little work; suitable for, causing, inducing, inactivity: 懒惰的; 怠惰的; 适于闲散的; 令人闲散的: *a* ～ *fellow;* 懒人; *a* ～ *afternoon*. 令人懒散的下午。 ～ **idle.** '～-**bones** n person. 懒人; 懒骨头。 **lazi·ly** adv **lazi·ness** n

lea /liː; li/ n (poet) stretch of open grass land. (诗)草地;草原。

leach /liːtʃ; litʃ/ vt 1 [VP6A] cause (a liquid) to percolate through some material. 使(液体)过滤。 2 [VP15B] ～ *out/away*, purge (a soluble matter) away or out by the action of a percolating fluid: 滤除(可溶性物质): *the* ～*ing of the soil*, the washing a way, eg by heavy rainfall, of elements in it necessary for plant growth. 土壤中植物成长所需成分之淋溶(例如被大雨冲掉)。

lead¹ /led; led/ n 1 [U] soft, heavy, easily melted metal (symbol **Pb**) of a dull bluish-grey colour used for water- and gas-pipes, as a roofing material, and in numerous alloys. 铅(符号为 Pb)。 '～-**ore** n [U] rock containing ～. 铅矿。 ～ '**poisoning** n diseased condition caused by taking ～ into the system. 铅中毒。 ⇨ **shot, shot**¹(4). ～ **works** n sing place where ～-ore is smelted. (单数)铅矿熔炼厂。 2 [U] (also 亦作 '**black** ～) graphite; stick of graphite as used in a ～-pencil. 石墨;黑铅(如用做铅笔心者)。 3 [C] lump of ～ fastened to a line marked in fathoms for measuring the depth of the sea from ships. (自船上测海水深度的)铅锤;测锤。 *cast/heave the* ～, (naut) take soundings. 投测锤以测深浅。 *swing the* ～, (sl) evade one's proper share of work by pretending to be ill, using tricks, etc. (俚)装病或以其

他欺骗方法逃避份内的工作。 4 (pl) strips of ～ used to cover a roof; area of (esp horizontal) ～-covered roof; ～ frames for glass, eg in a lattice window. (复)屋顶的长条铅板; 铅框铺的屋顶面积(尤指水平之铅板屋顶面积); 装玻璃的铅框(例如格子窗上者)。 ～ed /'ledɪd; 'ledɪd/ adj secured with strips of ～: 用长条铅板固定的: ～*ed windows*. 铅框窗子。 ～ed **light,** ⇨ **light³(9).** ～en /'ledn; 'ledn/ adj 1 made of ～: 铅制的: *a* ～*en coffin*. 铅制的棺材。 2 having the colour or appearance of ～: 铅色的;铅灰色的;似铅的: ～*en clouds*. 铅灰色的云。 3 dull and heavy like ～: 沉闷的; 沉重的: ～*en sleep;* 沉睡; *a* ～*en heart*. 沉重的心。 **take** the ～*en way*. **lead·ing** n [U] space between lines of print. 印刷行间之空间。

lead² /liːd; lid/ n 1 [U, C] (*sing* only) action of guiding or giving an example; direction given by going in front; sth that helps or hints. (仅用单数)领导; 带头;率先;榜样;提示。 *follow sb's* ～, follow his example. 效法某人。 *give sb a* ～, encourage him by doing sth first, or by giving a hint towards the solution of a problem. 带领某人; 提示某人。 *take the* ～, take the leading place, give an example. 领头; 带头; 做榜样。 2 *the* ～, first place or position: 首位;最先之地位; 领先: *have/gain the* ～ *in a race*; 在赛跑中领先; (attrib) (用作定语) *the* ～ *story*, (journalism, news broadcasting) item of news given the greatest prominence. (新闻, 新闻广播)头条新闻。 *a* ～, distance by which one leads: 领先的距离: *have a* ～ *of ten feet*. 领先十英尺。 *take over/lose the* ～, move to the front/fall behind in a race, in business, etc. (竞赛, 商业等)领先(落后)。 3 [C] cord, leather strap, for leading a dog: 牵狗的绳或皮带: *Keep your dog on the* ～ *in these busy streets*. 在这些热闹的街道上要好好牵着你的狗。 4 [C] principal part in a play; actor or actress who plays such a part: 剧中的主角; 扮演主角的演员: *the juvenile* ～, eg the actor who plays the part of the handsome young hero. 扮演英俊年轻男主角的演员。 5 [C] artificial watercourse leading to a mill; channel of open water in an ice-field. 通往磨粉厂的人工水道; 冰间水路。 6 [C] (electr) conductor conveying current from a source to the place where it is used. (电)导线; 引线。 7 [C] (in card games) act or right of playing first: (牌戏)首先出牌;首先出牌权: *Whose* ～ *is it?* 谁先出牌?

lead³ /liːd; lid/ vt, vi (pt, pp **led** /led; led/) 1 [VP6A, 15A, B] guide or take, esp by going in front: 引导: *Our guide led us through a series of caves*. 我们的向导引导我们穿过一连串的洞穴。 *The servant led the visitors in/out/back*. 那仆人引导客人入内(出去, 回去)。 ～ *the way (to)*, go first; show the way. 带路; 引路。 '～-**in** n (a) preliminary remarks, introduction (to). 引语;介绍辞。 (b) wire joining an aerial to a wireless receiver or television set. 引入线(自天线接至收音机或电视机的电线)。 2 [VP6A, 15A, B] conduct (sb) by the hand, by touching him, or by a rope, etc: 牵引: ～ *a blind man;* 牵引一盲人; ～ *a horse*, by holding the halter and walking at its head. 牵马。 ～ *sb astray*, (fig) tempt him to do sth wrong. (喻)将某人引入歧途。 ～ *sb by the nose*, control him completely; make him do everything one wishes him to do. 完全控制某人;牵着某人的鼻子走。 ～ *sb on*, (fig) entice sb to do more than he intended. (喻)怂恿某人做非其心愿之事。 ～ *a woman to the altar*, (joc) marry her. (谑)与一女子结婚。 3 [VP6A, 2A] act as chief; direct by example or persuasion; direct the movements of: 领导; 率领;指挥: ～ *an army/an expedition/a mutiny;* 指挥军队(率领探险队;领头叛变); ～ *the Conservative Party*, 领导保守党; ～ *the fashion*, 开风气;创时尚; ～ *the choir/the singing*. 领导唱诗班(歌唱)。 *Who's going to* ～? 谁将领导? 4 [VP6A, 2A, C] have the first place in; go first: 居于…之首位; 领先: *A brass band led the regiment*. 该团由一铜管队引导。 *Which horse is* ～*ing*, eg in a race? 哪一匹马领先(例如赛马时)? ～ *off*, start:

开始: *Who's going to ~ off?* 谁先开始? *He led off by saying that ....* 他开始时说…. **5** [VP6A, 17, 14] *~ (to)*, guide the actions and opinions of; influence; persuade: 作…的行动和意见; 影响; 劝诱: *What led you to this conclusion?* 什么使你下此结论? *He is easier led than driven.* 他适于诱导而不适于驱使。*I am led to believe* (= Certain facts, etc cause me to believe) *that he is disloyal to us.* 某些事实使我相信他对我们不忠。*What led you to think so?* 什么使你这样想? **6** [VP2C] be a path, way or road to; (fig) have as a result: 通; 达; (喻)导致某种结果: *Where does this road ~?* 这条路通到哪里? *Your work seems to be ~ing nowhere*, getting no result. 你的工作似乎没有什么效果。*This led to great confusion.* 此事导致大的混乱。*~ up to*, be a preparation for or an introduction to; direct the conversation towards: 作为…的准备或前导; 使话题(渐渐)转向: *That's just what I was ~ing up to.* 那正是我要说的。*Chapter One describes the events that led up to the war.* 第一章描写引起战争的一些事件。*All roads ~ to Rome*, (fig) There are many ways of reaching the same result. (喻)条条道路通罗马; 殊途同归。**7** [VP6A, 12C] (cause sb to) pass, go through, spend (life, etc): 过(生活等); 使某人过(生活等): *~ a miserable existence/生活困苦; ~ a double life/a Jekyll and Hyde existence.* 过双重人格的生活。⇨ *sb a (pretty) dance*, dance¹(1). *~ sb a 'dog's life*, make his life wretched. 使某人过困苦的日子。**8** [VP6A, 2A] (in card games) put down, as first player (a certain card or kind of card): (牌戏)首先出(某张或某种牌): *~ the two of clubs*, 首先出梅花2; *~ trumps.* 首先出王牌。**9** [VP 3A] *~ with*, (journalism) have as the main article or news story: (新闻)使成为头条新闻或特别报导: *We'll ~ with the dock strike.* 我们将以船坞罢工作头条新闻。

leader /ˈliːdə(r); ˈlidɚ/ *n* **1** person who leads: 领导者; 率领者; 领袖; 指挥者: *the ~ of an army/an expedition/the Labour Party;* 军队之指挥(探险队之领队); *the ~ of the choir;* 唱诗班的指挥; *the ~ of an orchestra* (usu the first violinist). 管弦乐队的首席(通常为第一小提琴手)。**2** principal counsel in a law court case: 首席法律顾问; 主要辩护人: *the ~ for the defence.* 被告之主要辩护人。**3** (GB) leading article (in a newspaper). (英)(报纸的)社论。⇨ **leading** below. 参看下列之leading。**4** shoot growing at the end of a stem or principal branch. 茎或大枝顶端发出的嫩枝。**5** tendon or sinew. 腱。**~·less** *adj* '**~·ship** /-ʃɪp; -ʃɪp/ *n* [U] being a ~; power of leading; the qualities of a ~. 作为领导者; 领导权; 领导地位; 领导能力。

lead·ing /ˈliːdɪŋ; ˈlidɪŋ/ *adj* chief; most important: 主要的; 最重要的: *the ~ men of the day;* 今日之领导人物; *the ~ topics of the hour*, those now being discussed; 当前主要的论题; *the ~ lady*, the actress with the chief part in a play; (剧中的)女主角; *L~ Aircraftman*, non-commissioned rank in the RAF. 英国皇家空军上等兵。*,~ 'article*, (in a newspaper) one giving editorial opinions on events, policies, etc. (报纸的)社论。*~ 'case*, (legal) one that establishes a precedent. (法律)成为判例之案件。*,~ 'light*, (colloq) prominent person. (口)重要人物。*,~ 'question*, one that suggests the answer that is hoped for. 诱导询问。□ *n* act of leading. 领导; 率领; 领先。'**~-rein** *n* for a horse. 辔。'**~-strings** *n pl* straps, etc with which babies were formerly taught to walk: 昔时教幼儿学步用的引带: *in ~-strings*, (fig) guided and controlled like a young child. 似幼儿般受管束。

leaf /liːf; lif/ *n* (*pl* **leaves** /liːvz; livz/) **1** one of the parts (usu green and flat) growing from the side of a stem or branch or direct from the root of a tree, bush, plant, etc (collectively called *foliage*): 叶(集合用作foliage): *sweep up dead leaves in autumn;* 扫净秋季的枯叶; (colloq) petal (as in *rose-leaves*) (口)花瓣(如蔷薇花瓣)。⇨ the illus at **flower**, **tree**. 参看flower, tree之插图。*in ~*, with the leaves grown: 长叶子的: *The*

trees will soon be in ~. 这些树不久就会长叶子。*come into ~*, grow leaves: 长叶子: *The trees come into ~ in spring.* 树木在春季长叶子。'**~-bud** *n* one from which leaves, not flowers, develop. 叶芽。'**~-mould** *n* [U] soil composed chiefly of decaying leaves. 腐叶土。**2** single sheet of paper forming two pages of a book. (书籍的)一张(即两页)。*take a ~ out of sb's book*, take him as a model. 模仿某人。*turn over a new ~*, make a new and better start. 过新生活; 改过自新; 重新开始。**3** hinged or loose part of an extending table (used to make the table larger). 桌子的活边(支起可使桌子加大)。**4** [U] very thin sheet of metal, esp of gold or silver: (金、银)箔: *gold ~.* 金箔。□ *vi ~ through (a book, etc)*, turn over the pages quickly; glance through. 迅速翻阅(书页等); 浏览。*~·less adj* having no leaves. 无叶的。*~·y adj* (-ier, -iest) covered with leaves; having leaves; made by leaves: 覆有叶的; 生叶的; 叶做成的: *a ~y shade.* 树荫。

leaf·let /ˈliːflɪt; ˈliflɪt/ *n* **1** young leaf. 小叶; 嫩叶。**2** printed sheet (unbound but sometimes folded) with announcements, etc esp one for free distribution. 散页的印刷品(有时是折叠的,尤指免费分送者); 传单。

league¹ /liːɡ; liɡ/ *n* (old) measure of distance (about three miles or 4.8 kms). (旧)里格(长度名, 约等于三英里或4.8公里)。

league² /liːɡ; liɡ/ *n* [C] **1** agreement made between persons, groups or nations for their common welfare, eg to work for peace; the parties that make such an agreement. 盟约(例如为谋和平者)联盟; 同盟; 参加盟约的会员。*the L~ of Nations*, that formed in 1919 after the First World War, with headquarters at Geneva, dissolved in 1946. 国际联盟(成立于1919年第一次世界大战后, 总部设于日内瓦, 1946年解散)。⇨ **United Nations**. *in ~ with*, allied with; having made an agreement with. 与…联盟。**2** group of sports clubs or teams playing matches among themselves: (运动竞赛之)联盟: *~ football matches.* 足球联赛。□ *vt, vi* [VP6A, 15A, B, 2C] form into, become, a ~: 组成联盟; 成为同盟: *countries that are ~d together.* 联盟国家。

leak /liːk; lik/ *n* **1** hole, crack, etc caused by wear, injury, etc through which a liquid, gas, etc may wrongly get in or out: 漏洞; 漏隙: *a ~ in the roof*, allowing rain to enter; 屋顶的漏雨处; *a ~ in the gas-pipe*, allowing gas to escape; 煤气管上的漏气处; (fig) (喻) *a ~ of information;* 情报的泄漏; *an inspired ~*, of news that is deliberately disclosed. 消息之故意泄漏。*spring a leak*, ⇨ **spring³(6)**. **2** the liquid, gas, etc that gets out or in. 漏出或漏进的液体、气体等。□ *vi, vt* **1** [VP2A, C] (allow to) pass out or in through a ~: 漏: *The rain is ~ing in.* 漏雨了。*The ship was ~ing badly.* 那船漏得厉害。**2** [VP2A, 6A, 14] *~ (out) (to)*, (of news, secrets, etc) (cause to) become known by chance or with authority: (指消息、秘密等)(使)泄漏: *The news has ~ed out.* 消息已泄漏出去了。*Who ~ed the news to the press?* 谁将消息泄漏给新闻界的? '**~·age** /-ɪdʒ; -ɪdʒ/ *n* **1** [U] the process of ~ing: 漏; 泄漏: *~age of military secrets.* 军事秘密的泄漏。**2** [C] instance of this; that which ~s in or out; amount that ~s in or out. 漏的实例; 漏入物; 漏出物; 漏泄量。*~·y adj* having a ~: 有漏隙的; 漏的: *a ~y kettle.* 一把会漏水的壶。

leal /liːl; lil/ *adj* (Scot or liter) loyal. (苏或文)忠实的。

lean¹ /liːn; lin/ *adj* (-er, -est) **1** (of persons and animals) having less than the usual proportion of fat; (of meat) containing little or no fat. (指人和动物)瘦的; (指肉)脂肪少的; 无脂肪的。**2** not productive or of poor quality: 无生产力的; 质劣的: *a ~ harvest;* 歉收; *~ years*, years of scarcity. 歉收之年; 荒年。□ *n* [U] meat with little or no fat. 瘦肉。**~·ness** *n*

lean² /liːn; lin/ *vi, vt* (*pt, pp ~t* /lent; lɛnt/ or

leaned /liːnd; liːnd/) 1 [VP2A, C] be or put in a sloping position: 倾斜; ~ *backwards;* 向后倾; ~ *out of a window;* 斜伸出窗外; *trees that* ~ *over in the wind;* 被风吹斜的树; *the L~ing Tower of Pisa.* 比萨斜塔。~ *over backward(s) (to do sth),* (colloq) make a great effort (to please sb, get a result, etc); (口)(为取悦某人, 获一结果等)过份努力; 矫枉过正。 2 [VP2C, 3A] ~ (*on/upon*), rest in a sloping position for support: 倚; 靠: ~ *on a table;* 靠在桌上; ~ *upon one's elbows;* 倚于两肘上; ~ *on sb's arm.* 靠在某人的臂上。 3 [VP15A] cause to rest against and be supported by: 使倚靠: ~ *a ladder against a wall/one's elbows on a table.* 将一梯子靠于墙上(把两肘倚于桌上)。 4 [VP3A] ~ *towards,* have a tendency: 倾向: *Do some oriental philosophies ~ towards fatalism?* 有些东方的哲学倾向于宿命论吗? 5 [VP3A] ~ *on/upon,* depend: 依靠; 依赖: ~ *on a friend's advice;* 依赖某人的忠告; ~ *upon others for guidance.* 依靠别人的指导。~**ing** n [C] tendency (of mind *towards* sth): 倾向(指思想等, 与 *towards* 连用): ~*ings/~ings towards pacificism.* 他有和平主义者的倾向(倾向于和平主义)。'~**-to** n building with the rafters of its roof resting against the side of another building: 披屋 (单斜面屋顶之屋,其屋顶之橡紧靠于另一房屋之墙壁上): (attrib) (用作定语) *a ~to greenhouse.* 单斜面屋顶之温室。

leap /liːp; lip/ *vi, vt* (*pt, pp* **leapt** /lept; lept/ or **leaped** /liːpt; lipt/) 1 [VP2A, C, 3A] jump (*jump* is the usu word; *leap* is used in liter and rhet style): 跳; 跃 (jump 是普通用语, leap 是文学和修辞用语): *He ~t at the opportunity,* seized it eagerly. 他即刻抓住了这机会。*Look before you ~,* ⇨ **look**[1](1). 2 [VP6A, 15A] (cause to) jump over: (使)跳过; 跃过: ~ *a wall;* 跳过墙; ~ *a horse over a fence.* 纵马跃过栏杆。 □ *n* [C] sudden upward or forward movement; 跳; 跃: *a great ~ forward,* (fig) a great advance. (喻)一大进步。*a ~ in the dark,* an attempt to do sth the result of which cannot be foreseen. 后果不可预料的行动; 冒险的行动。*by ~s and bounds,* very rapidly. 极迅速地。'~**-frog** n [U] game in which players jump with parted legs over others who stand with bent backs. 跳蛙游戏; 跳背游戏(部分人弯背而立,供其他参加者两腿分开自上跃过之游戏)。 □ *vt* (**-gg-**) jump over in this way. 跳蛙般地跃过。'~**-year** n in which February has 29 days. 闰年。

learn /lɜːn; lɝn/ *vt, vi* (*pt, pp* ~**t** /lɜːnt; lɝnt/, ~**ed** /lɜːnd; lɜrnd/) [VP2A, 3A, 6A, 7A, 8, 9, 10, 15A, B] 1 gain knowledge of or skill in, by study, practice or being taught: 学习; 学; 学会: ~ *a foreign language;* 学习一外国语文; ~ *to swim/how to ride a horse.* 学游泳(骑马)。*Has he ~t his lessons?* 他的功课都学会了吗? *Some boys ~ slowly.* 有些男孩子学习得慢。~ *sth by heart,* memorize it. 记诵; 能背诵。 2 be told or informed: 闻知; 获悉; 听说: *I'm sorry to ~ of his illness/that he's ill.* 我听说他生病, 甚为难过。*We have not yet ~ed whether he arrived safely.* 我们尚未获悉他是否已安全抵达。 3 (vulg or dialect, sometimes *larn* /lɑːn; larn/) teach: (鄙或方, 有时作 larn) 教: *I'll ~ you* (= punish you and so teach you how unwise it is) *to come into my orchard and steal apples.* 我要叫你知道进入我的果园偷苹果会得到什么教训。~**ed** /'lɜːnɪd; 'lɝnɪd/ *adj* having or showing much knowledge, esp of the humanities: 有学问的 (尤指在人文科学方面): *the ~ed professions,* those needing much knowledge; 需要学问的职业: ~*ed men;* 有学问的人; ~*ed periodicals/societies;* 学术性的书籍(刊物, 社团); *to look ~ed.* 看起来有学问。~**ed·ly** *adv* ~**er** n person who is ~ing; beginner: 学习者; 初学者: *He hasn't passed his driving test yet; he's only a ~er.* 他尚未通过驾驶考试, 他不过刚开始学驾驶。~**ing** n [U] wide knowledge gained by careful study: 学问; 学识: *a man of great ~ing.* 学识丰富的人。

lease /liːs; lis/ *n* [C] contract by which the owner of land or a building (*the lessor*) agrees to let another (*the lessee*) have the use of it for a certain time for a fixed money payment (called *rent*); the rights given under such a contract: (土地或房屋之)租约(出租人称作 lessor, 承租人称作 lessee, 租金称作 rent); 租赁权: *take a farm on a ~ of several years.* 以若干年为期租一农田。*When does the ~ expire?* 租约何时期满? *by/on ~:* 以租借的方式: *We took the land on ~.* 我们租用那块地。*give sb/get a new ~ of life,* a better chance of living longer, or of being happier, more active. (使某人)得以长寿或过更快乐和更有活力的生活。 □ *vt* [VP6A] give, take possession of (land, etc), by ~. 租出, 租得, 租借(土地等)。,~**-'lend** n [U] arrangement (1941) by which the President of the US could supply war materials to countries whose defence he considered important. 租借法案(一九四一年美国所定, 授权美国总统可以战争物质援助在防卫上认为重要的同盟国家)。'~**-hold** n, *adj* (land) (to be) held for a term of years on ~. 租借的; 租借的。 □ *freehold* at **free**[1](3). '~**-holder** n person who holds a ~; lessee. 租借人; 承租人; 租赁人。

leash /liːʃ; liʃ/ *n* [C] leather strap or thong for holding or controlling an animal (esp a hound): 拴动物(尤指猎犬)的皮带条: *hold in ~,* (fig) control. (喻)控制。*strain at the ~,* (fig) show eagerness to be free, to have an opportunity to do sth. (喻)渴望获得自由和有机会做某事。

least /liːst; list/ *adj, n* (contrasted with *most;* ⇨ **less, little**) (与 most 相对; 参看 less, little) 1 (the) ~, smallest in size, amount, extent, etc: 最小的; 最少的; 最小; 最少: *A has little, B has less, and C has (the)* ~. A 所有的不多, B 所有的更少, C 所有的最少。*There isn't the ~ wind today,* no wind at all. 今天一点风也没有。*That's the ~ of my anxieties.* 那是我最不担心的。*The ~ said the better,* The best thing is silence. 说得愈少愈好(最好不说)。*L~ said soonest mended,* (prov) Talking only makes things worse. (谚)话越少越好; 话说多了反而糟糕。 2 (phrases) (短语) *at ~:* 至少: *It will cost at ~ five pounds,* five pounds and perhaps more. 它至少值五英镑。*I can at ~ at all as you.* 他至少和你一样高。*You should at ~ have warned her.* 你至少也应该警告她。*You can at ~ try.* 你至少可以试试看。*(not) in the ~,* 一点(也)不; 毫不: *It doesn't matter in the ~.* 一点也没有关系。*I don't understand in the ~ what this author is trying to say.* 我丝毫不明白这位作者在说些什么。*'Would you mind holding this box?' 'Not in the ~.'* I do not mind at all. '请你拿着这个箱子好吗?' '好的。' *to say the ~ (of it),* without saying more; without exaggeration: 至少可以这样说; 不夸张地说: *It wasn't a very good dinner, to say the ~ of it.* 至少可以这样说, 那宴会不太好。 □ *adv* (**the**) ~, to the smallest extent: 最少的; 最小的: *He works hardest and is being paid* ~. 他工作最辛苦, 待遇却最低。*This is the ~ useful of the four books.* 这是四本书中用处最少的。~ *of all:* 最不: *None of you can complain, Charles ~ of all,* Charles has the ~ reason for complaining. 你们谁都不应抱怨, 查尔斯尤不应该。*L~ of all would I want to hurt your feelings,* That is sth I would never do. 我绝对没有意思要伤害你的感情。'~**-wise** /-waɪz; -,waɪz/ '~**-ways** /-weɪz; -,weɪz/ *advv* or at least; or rather. 至少; 不如; 或者。

leather /'leðə(r); 'leðɚ/ *n* [U] material made by curing animal skins, used for making shoes, gloves, bags, etc: 皮革; 皮革: ~ *upholstery,* eg for the seats of a car. 皮椅套(例如汽车座位上者)。'~**-jacket** n grub of the crane-fly. 长脚蝇的蛆。'~**-neck** n (US, sl) marine. (美.俚)海军陆战队兵。~**-y** *adj* like ~: 似皮革的: ~ *meat,* hard, tough. 坚韧的肉。'~**-ette** /-'ret; -'rɛt/ n imitation ~. 假皮; 人造皮。

leave[1] /liːv; liv/ *vt, vi* (*pt, pp* **left** /left; lɛft/) 1 [VP6A, 2A, 3A] go away from: 离开: *When did*

you ~ *London?* 你什么时候离开伦敦的? *It's time for us to ~/time we left.* 我们现在该走了。 **~ for,** go away to: 到…地方去; 去某地: *We're leaving for Rome next week.* 我们下星期要到罗马去。 **2** [VP6A, 15A, 2A] go away finally or permanently; no longer live (in a place); cease to belong to a school, society, etc; give up working for (an employer, etc): 永久离开; 不再居于(某地); 退出(学校、社团等); 不再为(某雇主等)工作: *When did you ~ school?* 你是什么时候离开学校的? *The secretary has threatened to ~.* 那秘书曾威胁说要辞职。 *The boy left home and went to sea.* 那男孩离开家去做船员。*He left medicine for the law, changed from the medical to the legal profession.* 他离开医界而转入法学界。*My typist has left me, has resigned.* 我的打字员已辞职了。*be/get nicely left,* (colloq) be tricked, deceived or deserted. (口)上当; 受骗; 被遗弃。 **3** [VP15A, B] neglect or fail to take, bring or do sth: 忽略或忘记拿、带或做; 遗忘: *I've left my umbrella in the train.* 我把伞忘在火车上了。*I left my books on the table.* 我把书忘在桌上了。*He left half his work until the next day.* 他留下一半的工作到第二天才做。 **~ sth behind,** neglect or forget to bring or take: 留下; 遗落; 忘记携带: *The luggage has been left behind!* 行李忘记带了! *Don't ~ me behind!* 别把我忘了! **4** [VP15A, B, 22, 19B, 2C, 24A, 25] allow or cause to remain in a certain place or condition: 听任其在某处; 使保持某一状态: *L~ your hat and coat in the hall.* 把你的帽子和上衣放在门厅里好了。 *Always ~ things where you can find them again.* 永远把东西放在你能再找到的地方。 *Did you ~ the doors and windows firmly fastened?* 你把门窗关牢了吗? *Who left that window open?* 谁让窗开着了? *His illness has left him weak.* 他的病使他身体衰弱了。 *Don't ~ her waiting outside in the rain.* 不要让她在外面雨中等待。 **~ sb/sth alone,** not touch, spoil or interfere with: 不要干涉某人或某事: *L~ the cat alone,* Don't tease it. 不要逗那猫。 **~ well alone,** (prov) try to improve what is already satisfactory. (谚)事情已经够好了,不要再去管它; 不要画蛇添足。 **~ off,** stop: 停止: *Has the rain left off yet?* 雨停了吗? *We left off at the end of Chapter Five.* 我们在第五章末尾停止。 **~ sth off, (a)** stop: 停止: *It's time to ~ off work.* 该停工了。*Do ~ off biting your nails, Jane!* 简, 千万别再咬你的指甲了! **(b)** no longer wear: 不再穿: *They left off their woollen underwear when the weather got warm.* 天气转暖的时候,他们就不再穿羊毛内衣。 **~ sth/sb out,** omit; fail to consider: 忽略; 遗漏: *~ out a possibility;* 忽略一个可能性; *~ out a letter,* eg spell *embarrass* with one r instead of two r's. 遗漏一个字母(如拼写 embarrass 时遗漏了一个 r)。*Don't ~ me out, please!* Don't forget me—I want a share, a place, etc. 请不要把我忘了(不要忘记我, 我也要一份)。 **~ sth over,** postpone: 延后: *That matter can be left over until the committee meets next week.* 此事可延至下周委员会开会时再行处理。 **~ it at that,** do or say nothing more: 不再做或说什么; 就那样好了: *There's nothing we can do; we must ~ it at that.* 我们无能为力, 我们必须听其自然。 **~ sb to himself/to his own devices,** not try to control or direct his activities: 不要管某人; 任其自由行动: *The children were left very much to themselves during the holidays,* were allowed to do what they liked, without guidance or help. 孩子们在假期中的行动未受管束。 **~ sth unsaid,** not say it: 不要说出来: *Some things are better left unsaid,* It is better to remain silent about them. 有些事情最好不要说出来。 **much/a lot/sth/nothing to be desired,** be (un)satisfactory: 不令人满意(令人满意): *His behaviour ~s a lot/nothing to be desired,* is very unsatisfactory/ is quite satisfactory. 他的行为不令人满意(令人十分满意)。 **~ go/hold (of sth),** (more usu let go) cease holding: 放掉; 放手 (let go 较常用): *L~ go of my hair, you brute!* 放开我的头发, 你这个可恶的人! **5** [VP6A, 12B, 13B, 14] (cause to) remain; allow to remain;

(使)留下; 剩余; 剩下: *Three from seven ~s four* (7 − 3 = 4). 七减三余四。 *When I've paid all my debts, there'll be nothing left.* 等我把所有的债还清, 便什么也不剩了。 *Have you left anything for me/left me anything?* 你有没有留下什么东西给我呀? *To be left until called for,* used as a direction for a letter, package, etc which is to be collected. 留待来取(如书信、包裹等)。 **6** [VP6A, 14, 12B, 13B] hand over before going away: (离开之前)交给;遗留: *Did the postman ~ anything for me?* 邮差给我留下什么信件吗? **~ word (with sb) (for sb),** give a message etc: 留言: *Please ~ word (for me) with your secretary if you get news of what happened.* 如果你对发生之事有了消息, 请留话给你的秘书。 **7** [VP16A, 14] entrust; commit; hand over: 委托; 托付; 交给: *I'll ~ the matter in your hands/~ it to you/~ you to attend to the matter.* 我将这事交给你办(我委托你办此事)。*He left his assistant in charge of the shop/left the shop in his assistant's charge.* 他让他的助手管理店铺 (将店铺交给他的助手管理)。 **8** [VP6A, 12A, 13A, 15A, 22] **~ sth (to sb) ~ sb sth,** bequeath by will; leave at the time of one's death: 遗赠(给某人); 死后留下: *She left all her money to charity.* 她将所有的钱遗留给慈善团体。 *He left me £500.* 他遗留给我五百英镑。*He died leaving nothing but debts.* 他死后只留下一身债。 *He ~s a widow and two sons.* 他遗下寡妻和两个儿子。 *He left her poor.* 他死后使她受穷。 **9** [VP15A] pass beyond (a place, etc) so that it is in the direction or relation indicated: 经过(某个地方等): *L~ the church on your left and go on up the hill.* 经过左手边的教堂, 然后上那座山。

leave² /li:v/ liv/ n **1** [U] permission; consent; authority, esp to be absent from duty or work: 许可; (尤指职务或工作之)请假许可; 准假: *You have my ~ to stay away from the office tomorrow.* 我准许你明天不上班。 **~ of absence,** permission to be absent: 请假许可: *The soldier asked for ~ of absence.* 那士兵请假。 **on ~,** absent with permission: 告假中: *He went home on ~.* 他请假回家了。 **by/with your ~,** with your permission. 如果你允许的话。 **(take) French ~,** absence without permission. 未获许可而离开;擅离职守; 不辞而别。 **2** [C] period of such absence; occasion of being absent from duty, etc: 假期; 请假; 休假: *have only two ~s in six years;* 六年中仅有两次假; *a six months' ~.* 六个月的假。 **3** [U] departure. 离去。 **take (one's) ~ (of sb),** say goodbye. (向某人)告别; 辞别。 Hence, 由此产生, '**~-taking** n **take ~ of one's senses,** behave as if mad. 举止若狂。

leaven /'levn; 'levən/ n [U] substance, eg yeast, used to make dough rise before it is baked to make bread; (fig) quality or influence spreading in and changing sth. 酵母; 酵素; (喻)散布其间而具有改变力量的性质或影响力。 □ vt [VP6A] add ~ to; act like ~ upon. 使发酵; 使发酵; 影响。

leaves /li:vz; livz/ pl of **leaf.**

leav·ings /'li:vɪŋz; 'livɪŋz/ n pl what is left, esp sth unwanted or of little value: 剩余物(尤指不需要或无价值者): *Give the ~* (eg unwanted food) to the dog. 把残余的食物给狗吃。

lech·er·ous /'letʃərəs; 'letʃərəs/ adj lustful; having, giving way to, strong sexual desires. 淫荡的; 好色的。 **lecher** /'letʃə(r); 'letʃə/ n ~ person. 淫荡的人; 好色之徒。 **lech·ery** /'letʃərɪ; 'letʃərɪ/ n [U] lust; [C] (pl -ries) lustful or lascivious act. 淫荡; 淫乱的行为。

lec·tern /'lektən; 'lektən/ n sloping reading-desk as for a Bible in church. 讲经台; 讲桌。

lec·ture /'lektʃə(r); 'lektʃə/ n [C] **1** talk (to an audience or class) for the purpose of teaching: 教导性的演讲; 讲课; 讲演 /give/read a ~. 演讲(讲学)。 *a course of ~s on Greek philosophy;* 关于希腊哲学的一系列的演讲; *go on a ~ tour.* 作讲学旅行。 **2** reproof: 谴责; 训诫: *give sb a ~,* scold or reprove him. 训诫某人。 □ vi, vt

1 [VP2A, 3A] ~ *(on)*, give a ~ or course of ~s: 演讲; 讲课: ~ *on modern drama*. 讲授现代戏剧。 **2** [VP 6A, 14] ~ *sb (for)*, scold, reprove: 责骂; 谴责: *The teacher* ~*d the boys for being lazy*. 教师责骂那些男孩子懒惰。 ~**r** /'lektʃərə(r); 'lɛktʃərə/ *n* person, lower in rank than a professor, who gives ~s, esp at a college or university. (大学之)讲师。 ~**ship** /-ʃɪp; -ˌʃɪp/ *n* post as a ~r at a university, etc. 大学讲师之职位。

led /led; lɛd/ *pt, pp of* **lead**[3].

ledge /ledʒ; lɛdʒ/ *n* **1** narrow horizontal shelf coming out from a wall, cliff or other upright surface: (墙壁、悬崖或其他直面上)突出的狭长部分: *a 'window* ~; 窗台; *a* ~ *for chalk at the bottom of a blackboard*. 黑板底边的粉笔槽。 **2** ridge of rocks under water, esp near the shore. 礁石(尤指近岸者)。

ledger /'ledʒə(r); 'lɛdʒə/ *n* **1** book in which a business firm's accounts are kept. 分类帐。 **2** (music) '~ (or *'leger) line*, short line added above or below the stave for outside notes. (音乐)加线。 ⇨ the illus at **notation.** 参看 notation 之插图。

lee /liː; li/ *n* [U] (place giving) protection against wind. 下风; 背风处。 **lee (side)**, the side away from the wind (contrasted with the *windward* or *weather* side): 背风面(与 windward side 或 weather side 相对): *the lee side of a ship*; 船的背风面; *a 'lee shore*, on the lee side of one's ship; 下风岸; *a 'lee tide*, one flowing in the same direction as the wind. 下风潮。

leech /liːtʃ; litʃ/ *n* **1** small blood-sucking worm living in wet places of which one kind was formerly used by doctors for bleeding patients: 水蛭(有一种水蛭昔时被医生用以吸取病人之血): *stick like a* ~, (fig) be very persistent, be difficult to get rid of. (喻)纠缠不休。 **2** (fig) person who sucks profit out of others. (喻)榨取他人利益者; 吸血鬼。 **3** (old use) doctor. (旧用法)医生。

leek /liːk; lik/ *n* onion-like vegetable with a long, slender white bulb. 青葱的一种; 韭。 ⇨ the illus at **vegetable.** 参看 vegetable 之插图。

leer /lɪə(r); lɪr/ *n* [C] sly, unpleasant look that suggests evil desire or ill will. 含恶意的一瞥; 不怀好意的一瞥。 □ *vi* [VP2A, 3A] ~ *(at sb)*, look with a ~: 不怀好意地瞥视: ~*ing at his neighbour's pretty young wife*. 色迷迷地瞥视邻居漂亮的年轻太太。

lees /liːz; liz/ *n pl* dregs; sediments (of wine, etc); basest part; refuse (as at the bottom of a cask, etc). 渣滓; (酒等的)沉渣; 沉淀部分; 糟粕; (桶等底部之)废物。 *drink/drain to the* ~, (fig) experience the last extremes of suffering, passion, etc. (喻)尝尽辛酸。

lee·ward /'liːwəd; 'liwəd/ (among sailors: 海员读作: /'luːəd; 'luəd/) *adj, adv* on or to the sheltered side (contrasted with *windward*). 在下风; 向下风(与 windward 相对)。 □ *n* [U] lee side; sheltered side: 下风面; 背风面: *on the* ~; 在下风方向; *steer to* ~. 向下风行驶。

lee·way /'liːweɪ; 'liˌwe/ *n* [U] sideways drift (of a ship) in the direction towards which the wind is blowing; (fig) freedom to vary (while still being tolerated or safe). 风压差; 偏航(船只因风之作用向下风方向之偏航); (喻)变化之余地; 改变之余地。 *make up* ~, make up for lost time; get back into position. 赶上; 回到原来的位置。

left[1] *pt, pp of* **leave.**

left[2] /left; lɛft/ *adj, n, adv* (opposite of *right*) (of, in, on, the) side of a person's body which is towards the west when he faces north: (为 right 之反义词) 左边的; 左方的; 左方; 左侧; 在左边; 左侧: *Not many people write with the* ~ *hand*. 没有多少人用左手写字。 *The* ~ *bank of a river is on your* ~ *as you face the direction in which it flows*. 当你面向河水所流的方向时, 河的左岸在你的左方。 *Come and sit on my* ~, ie at my ~ side. 来坐在我的左边。 *Turn (to the)* ~ *at the pub*. 在酒馆那里向左转。 **the L~ (Wing)**, more radical group(s), party or parties, eg socialists, communists: 左翼(激进的党派, 例如社会党员、共产党员): (attrib) (用作定语) ~-*wing militants*. 左翼的好战份子。 '~-**hand** *adj* of, situated on, the ~ side: 左方的; 左边的: *a house on the* ~-*hand side of the street*; 在街道左侧的一所房屋; *a* ~-*hand blow/stroke*. 用左手的一击。 ~-'**handed** *adj* (of a person) using the ~ hand more easily or with more skill than the right. (指人)惯用左手的。 *a* ~-**handed** *compliment*, one that is ambiguous, of doubtful sincerity. 暧昧的恭维; 无诚意的恭维。 '~-**ist** /-ɪst; -ɪst/ *n* supporter of socialism or radicalism. 左翼份子; 激进分子。

leg /leg; lɛg/ *n* **1** one of the parts of an animal's or a person's body used for walking, esp (of a human body) the part above the foot: 腿; 腿部: *have a leg of mutton for dinner*. 以一只羊腿佐餐。 *He lost his right leg in the war*. 他在战争中失去了右腿。 *be all legs*, (of a person) be overgrown, lanky and thin. (指人)个子过高而细瘦。 *be off one's legs*, resting: 休息: *Poor woman! She's never off her legs*, is always working. 可怜的女人! 她永远得不到休息。 *be on one's legs*, (or joc, 或谑, *on one's hind legs*), **(a)** be standing, esp to make a speech. 站立者(尤指演说)。 **(b)** (after an illness) be well enough to walk about again. (病后)开始能走路。 *be on one's last legs*, **(a)** fatigued, exhausted. 疲倦; 疲惫。 **(b)** near one's death or end. 将死。 *feel/find one's legs*, *(feet* is more usu) (feet 较常用) **(a)** (of a baby) get the power of standing or walking. (指婴儿)会站立; 会走。 **(b)** (fig) begin to realize one's powers, abilities, etc; become self-confident. (喻)开始认识自己的能力; 有了自信。 *find one's 'sea-legs*, ⇨ **sea**(7). *give sb a leg up*, (lit) help him to mount a horse or to climb up sth; (fig) help him in time of need. (字面)扶人上马; 助某人攀登; (喻)助某人一臂之力。 *pull sb's leg*, try, for a joke, to make him believe sth that is untrue. 愚弄某人以作为玩笑。 Hence, 因此, '**leg-pull** [C] and '**leg-pulling** [U] *nn. run sb off his legs*, tire him by keeping him constantly busy. 使某人疲于工作。 *shake a leg*, (colloq) dance; (imper) start. (口)跳舞; (祈使)开始。 *show a leg*, (colloq) get out of bed; (imper) do sth with more effort. (口)起床; 下床; (祈使)加劲做事。 *not have a* ~*leg to 'stand on*, have nothing to support one's opinion, defence, etc. 没有立论根据; 站不住脚。 *stretch one's legs*, go for a walk (esp to take exercise after sitting for a long time). 出外散步(尤指久坐后作为运动者)。 *take to one's legs*, *(heels* is more usu) (heels 较常用) run away. (heels 较常用)逃走。 *walk one's 'legs off; walk sb off his legs*, tire oneself/him out with walking. 使自己(某人)走累。 **2** that part of a garment that closely covers a leg: 衣物的腿部: *the leg of a stocking*; 袜筒; *the legs of a pair of trousers*. 裤腿。 **3** support of a chair, table, etc: (桌椅等之)腿; 脚: *a stool with three legs*; 三脚凳; *the legs of a bed*. 床腿。 *be on its last legs*, weak and likely to collapse. 不稳而欲倒塌。 **4** [U] (cricket) part of the field to the left rear of a right-handed batsman in position (or vice versa): (板球)右手击球员之左后方场地; 左手击球员右后方场地; *leg-stump*, stump nearest to this; 击球员后方三柱门之柱; *hit a ball to leg*. 击球至后方场地。 ⇨ the illus at **cricket.** 参看 cricket 之插图。 **5** one section of a journey, esp by air: 旅行(尤指空中者)的一段路程: *the first leg of a round-the-world flight*; 环球飞行之第一段路程; *one of a series of games in a competition*. (竞赛中一连串比赛之)一场; 一局; 一项; 一段赛程。 -**legged** /legd; lɛgd/ *adj* (in compounds) (用于复合词) ,*long-'legged*, having long legs; 长腿的; ,*three-'legged*, having three legs, eg a stool; 三条腿的(例如凳); 三脚的; ,*bare-'legged*, having bare legs. 赤着腿的。 ,**three-'legged** /legɪd; 'lɛgɪd/ *race n* race for pairs with two legs tied together. 三足赛跑(令二人为一组, 将其相靠之二足扎在一起)。

leg·acy /'legəsɪ; 'lɛgəsɪ/ *n* (*pl* -**cies**) [C] **1** money, etc (to be) received by a person under the will of and

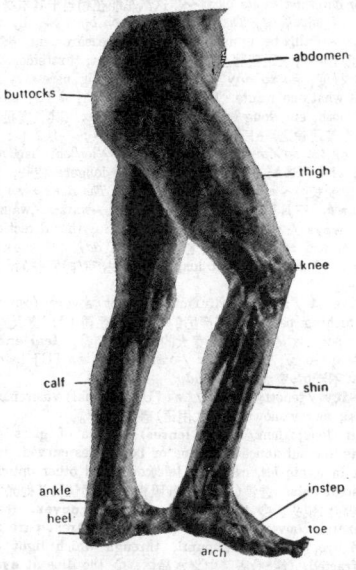

abdomen

buttocks

thigh

knee

calf

shin

ankle

instep

heel

toe

arch

the leg and the foot

at the death of another person. 遗产; 遗赠(物). **2** (fig) sth handed down from ancestors or predecessors: (喻)祖先或先辈留下来的东西: *a ~ of ill will*. 宿恨; 世仇。

legal /'li:gl; 'ligl/ *adj* connected with, in accordance with, authorized or required by, the law: 法律上的; 合法的; 法律承认的; 法律要求的; 法定的: *~ affairs*; 法律事务; *my ~ adviser/representative*, eg a solicitor; 我的法律顾问(代表)(例如律师); *take ~ action (against sb)*; 提起诉讼(控告某人); *the ~ fare*; 诉讼费; *~ tender*, form of money which must be accepted if offered in payment; 法币; 法偿; *a ~ offence*, one against the law, contrasted with an offence against convention; 违法(以别于违反习俗); *free ~ aid*, help (from lawyers paid by the State) given to persons unable to pay the usual charges. (由政府花钱聘请律师给予无钱请辩护律师者的)免费的诉讼上的援助。**~·ly** /'li:gəlɪ; 'ligli/ *adv* '**~·ism** /-ɪzəm; -,ɪzəm/ *n* [U] strict adherence to, undue respect for, the law and ~ forms. 绝对遵守法律;墨守法规;条文主义。

legal·ity /li:'gælətɪ; lɪ'gælətɪ/ *n* [U] the state or quality of being legal: 合法: *the ~ of an act*. 一行动之合法。

legal·ize /'li:gəlaɪz; 'liglˌaɪz/ *vt* [VP6A] make legal: 使合法; 使成为法定: *~ the sale of alcoholic drinks*. 使贩卖酒类合法。**legal·iz·ation** /ˌli:gəlaɪ'zeɪʃn US: -lɪ'z-; ˌiglə'zeʃən/ *n*.

leg·ate /'legɪt; 'legət/ *n* the Pope's ambassador to a country. 罗马教皇的使节。

lega·tee /ˌlegə'ti:; ˌlegə'ti/ *n* [C] (legal) person who receives a legacy. (法律)遗产继承人。

leg·ation /lɪ'geɪʃn; lɪ'geʃən/ *n* [C] (house, offices, etc, of a) diplomatic minister below the rank of ambassador, with those under him, representing his government in a foreign country. 公使馆全体人员; 公使馆; 公使职权。

le·gato /lɪ'gɑːtəʊ; lɪ'gɑto/ *adj*, *adv* (musical direction) (to be played) smoothly, without breaks. (乐谱记号)滑畅而无中断的(地)(演奏); 圆滑的(地)。

leg·end /'ledʒənd; 'ledʒənd/ *n* **1** [C] old story handed

down from the past, esp one of doubtful truth: 传奇; 秘史: *the ~s of King Arthur*. 亚瑟王的秘史。**2** [U] literature of such stories: 传奇文学: *heroes who are famous in ~*. 传奇文学中著名的英雄。**3** [C] inscription on a coin or medal; explanatory words on a map, a picture, etc. (地图、图画等之)说明; 图例; 题词。**~·ary** /'ledʒəndrɪ US: -derɪ; 'ledʒəndˌɛrɪ/ *adj* famous, known only, in ~s: 传奇中著名的; 只有秘史中记载的: *~ary heroes*. 传奇故事中著名的英雄。

leger /'ledʒə(r); 'ledʒɚ/ ⇨ **ledger** (2).

leger·de·main /ˌledʒədə'meɪn; ˌledʒədɪ'men/ *n* [U] juggling; quick and clever performance of tricks with the hands; (fig) deceitful argument. 戏法; 魔术的明快的手法; (喻)诡辩。

leg·ging /'legɪŋ; 'legɪŋ/ *n* (usu *pl*) outer covering, of leather or strong cloth, for the leg up to the knee, or (for small children) for the whole of the leg: (通常用复数)(皮或坚牢之布制成的)护胫; 绑腿; (小孩之)胫衣: *a pair of ~s*. 一双护胫。

leggy /'legɪ; 'legɪ/ *adj* having long legs (esp of young children, puppies and colts). (尤指小孩、小狗和小马)腿长的。

leg·horn /le'gɔːn US: 'legɔrn; 'legɚn/ *n* **1** kind of domestic fowl. 来亨鸡。**2** hat made of the kind of straw imported from Leghorn (also called 亦称作 Livorno), a town in NW Italy. (用意大利西北部来亨城所产的一种草所制成的)来亨草帽。

leg·ible /'ledʒəbl; 'ledʒəbl/ *adj* (of handwriting, print) that can be read easily. (指字迹、印刷物)易读的; 清楚的。**leg·ibly** /-əblɪ; -əblɪ/ *adv* **legi·bil·ity** /ˌledʒə'bɪlətɪ; ˌledʒə'bɪlətɪ/ *n*

legion /'li:dʒən; 'lidʒən/ *n* **1** division of several thousand men in the armies of ancient Rome; (fig) great number: 古罗马的军团(由数千人组成); (喻)众多: *Their numbers are ~*. 他们的数目众多。**2 British L~**, national association of ex-service men formed in 1921. 英国退伍军人协会(创立于一九二一年)。**(French) Foreign L~**, body of non-French volunteers who serve in the French army, usu overseas. 法国军队中之外籍志愿兵团(通常驻在海外)。**L~ of Honour**, high French decoration (civilian and military). 法国高级勋章(授与文武官员)。**3** (in liter or rhet style) vast host or number. (文学或修辞用语)众多。**legion·ary** /'li:dʒənərɪ US: -nerɪ; 'lidʒənˌɛrɪ/ *adj* (*pl* -ries), *n* [C] (member) of a ~, esp the (French) Foreign L~. 古罗马之军团的(士兵); 英国退伍军人协会的(会员); (尤指)(法国)外籍兵团的(士兵)。

legis·late /'ledʒɪsleɪt; 'ledʒɪsˌlet/ *vi* [VP2A, 3A] make laws: 立法; 制定法律: *~ against gambling*. 立法以禁止赌博。**legis·la·tion** /ˌledʒɪs'leɪʃn; ˌledʒɪs'leʃən/ *n* [U] making laws; the laws made. 立法; 法律。

legis·lat·ive /'ledʒɪslətɪv US: -leɪtɪv; 'ledʒɪsˌletɪv/ *adj* (of) law-making: 立法(的); 有关立法的: *~ assemblies*; 立法会议; *~ reforms*. 关于立法上的改革。

legis·la·tor /'ledʒɪsleɪtə(r); 'ledʒɪsˌletɚ/ *n* member of a law-making body. 立法委员; 国会议员。

legis·la·ture /'ledʒɪsleɪtʃə(r); 'ledʒɪsˌletʃɚ/ *n* law-making body, eg Parliament in GB. 立法机关(例如英国的国会)。

le·git·imate /lɪ'dʒɪtɪmət; lɪ'dʒɪtəmɪt/ *adj* **1** lawful, regular: 合法的; 正规的: *the ~ king*; 正统的国王; *use public money only for ~ purposes*. 公款只能用作合法的用途上。**2** reasonable; that can be justified: 合理的; 可说明为正当的: *a ~ reason for being absent from one's work*. 未上班工作之正当的理由。**3** born of persons married to one another; the result of lawful marriage: 婚生的; 嫡出的: *a ~ child*; 嫡子; 婚生子; *of ~ birth*. 嫡出。**4** *the ~ theatre*, drama, not revue or musical comedy etc. 正统的戏剧(非时事讽刺剧或音乐喜剧等)。**~·ly** *adv* **le·git·imacy** /lɪ'dʒɪtɪməsɪ; lɪ'dʒɪtəməsɪ/ *n* [U] being ~. 合法; 合理; 嫡出。**le·git·ima·tize**

leguminous/**less**

/lɪ'dʒɪtɪmətaɪz; lɪ'dʒɪtəmə,taɪz/ *vt* make ~. 使合法;使合理;立为嫡嗣。

leg·umin·ous /lɪ'gju:mɪnəs; lɪ'gjumənəs/ *adj* of, like, the botanical family that includes peas and beans (and other seeds in pods). 豆科的;似豆科的。

lei /leɪ; 'le·ɪ/ *n* garland of flowers worn round the neck (as in Polynesian islands). (波利尼西亚群岛等之人戴于颈上的)花环。

lei·sure /'leʒə(r) US: 'li:ʒər; 'liʒə/ *n* [U] **1** spare time; time free from work: 闲暇; 空闲: *have no ~ for sport*. 没有空闲做户外活动。 *at ~*, (when) not occupied: 空闲的;闲暇中的: *I am seldom at ~*. 我很少有空闲。 *at one's ~*, when one has free time: 在空闲之时: *Please look through these papers at your ~*. 请你在闲暇时翻阅这些报纸。 **2** (attrib) (用作定语) *~ time/ hours/ clothes*. 空闲时间(空闲时刻; 闲暇时穿的衣服)。 ~·**ly** *adv* without haste or hurry: 不匆忙地; 从容地: *work ~ly*. 从容地工作。 □ *adj* unhurried; deliberate: 不匆忙的; 从容的: *~ly movements*. 从容的动作。~**d** /'leʒəd US: 'li:ʒərd; 'liʒəd/ *adj* having plenty of ~: 有许多空暇的: *the ~d classes*. 有闲阶级。

lem·ming /'lemɪŋ; 'lemɪŋ/ *n* small arctic migratory rodent like a field-mouse. 旅鼠(产于北极,似田鼠)。

lemon /'lemən; 'lemən/ *n* **1** (tree with) pale yellow fruit with acid juice used for drinks and flavouring. 柠檬;柠檬树。 ⇨ the illus at **fruit**. 参看 fruit 之插图。'~ **drop** *n* piece of boiled sugar flavoured with ~. 柠檬糖。 '~ **'squash** *n* drink of ~-juice and water or soda-water. 柠檬水; 柠檬汽水。 '~ **'squeezer** *n* device for pressing juice out of a ~. 柠檬榨汁器。 '~ **'sole** *n* kind of edible flatfish, like a plaice. 一种鲽。 **2** (GB sl) silly and plainlooking person. (英俚)带有傻气而不漂亮的人。 ~·**ade** /,lemə'neɪd; ,lemən'ed/ *n* [U] drink made from ~-juice, sugar and water. 柠檬水。

lemur /'li:mə(r); 'limə/ *n* nocturnal animal of Madagascar, similar to a monkey but with a fox-like face. 狐猴(马达加斯加岛所产之夜间活动的动物,状似猴但面孔似狐)。

lend /lend; lɛnd/ *vt* (*pt, pp* **lent** /lent; lɛnt/) **1** [VP6A, 12A, 13A, 14] ~ *sth to sb:* ~ *sb sth*, give (sb) the use of (sth) for a period of time on the understanding that it or its equivalent will be returned: 借出; 借与; 把(某物)借给(某人)使用: *I will ~ you £100, but I can't ~ money to everyone.* 我愿意借给你一百英镑, 但我不能借钱给每一个人。 ~ *a hand (with sth)*, help. 帮助。 '~ **ing-library**, one from which books may be borrowed. 书可借出的图书馆。 **2** [VP14] ~ *sth to sth*, contribute: 贡献: *facts that ~ probability to a theory*. 使一理论可能成立的事实。 **3** [VP14] ~ *oneself to sth*, give; accomodate: 参与; 适于: *Don't ~ yourself to such dishonest schemes*. 你不要参与此种欺诈的计划。 *This peaceful garden ~s itself to* (= is favourable for) *meditation*. 这个恬静的花园适合冥想。 ~·**er** *n* person who ~s. 借出者;贷款人。

length /leŋθ; leŋθ/ *n* **1** [U] measurement from end to end (in space or time): (空间的)长;长度;(时间的)长短;期间: *the ~ of a road/ field/ stick;* 道路(田地, 手杖)的长度; *a river 300 miles in ~;* 长达三百英里的一条河; *a room 8 metres in ~ and 6 in breadth;* 长八米宽六米的一间屋子; *a river navigable for most of its ~;* 大部分河道均可航行的一条河; *make a stay in Rome for some ~,* for a considerable period of time; 在罗马停留一段时期; *the ~ of time needed for the work.* 完成该工作所需之时间。 *at ~,* **(a)** at last; finally: 终于; 最后。 **(b)** for a long time: 长时间地: *speak at (great) ~.* (极)长时间地演说。 **(c)** in detail; thoroughly: 详细地;彻底地: *treat a subject at ~.* 详细处理一问题。 *(at) full ~,* with the body stretched out and flat: 全身平伸地: *lying at full ~ on the grass.* 全身平伸地躺在草地上。 *keep sb at arm's ~,* avoid being friendly with him. 避免与某人亲近。 **2** [C] measurement of a particular thing from end to end: 某一物体之长度: *The*

car can turn in its own ~. 这汽车能在相当于其本身长度的空间内转弯。 *The horse/ boat won by a ~*, by its own ~, this being used as a unit of measurement. 那马(艇)以一身之距获胜。 **3** [U, C] extent; extreme. 程度;极度。 *go to any ~(s)*, do anything necessary to get what one wants. 尽一切力量达到目的。 **4** [C] piece of cloth, etc, long enough for a purpose: (其长度足以供作某用途之)一段(布料等): *a 'dress ~;* 一块衣料; *a ~ of tubing/ pipe*. 一段管子。 '~·**en** /'leŋθən; 'leŋθən/ *vt, vi* [VP6A, 2A] make or become longer: 使长; 加长; 变长: *~en a skirt*. 将一裙放长。 *The days ~en in March*. 三月里的白昼变长。 '~·**wise** /-waɪz; -,waɪz/, '~·**ways** /-weɪz; -,wez/ *adv, adj* in the direction from end to end. 纵长地(的)。 ~·**y** *adj* (of speech, writing) very long; too long. (指演说,写作)冗长的;过长的。

leni·ent /'li:nɪənt; 'linɪənt/ *adj* not severe (esp in punishing people): 不严厉的(尤指在惩罚上); 宽大的: ~ *parents/ judges*. 宽大的父母(法官)。 **leni·ence** /-əns; -əns/, **leni·ency** /-ənsɪ; -ənsɪ/ *nn* [U] being ~. 不严厉; 宽大。~·**ly** *adv*

len·ity /'lenətɪ; 'lenətɪ/ *n* [U] (formal) mercifulness; mercy shown. (正式用语)慈悲;宽厚。

lens /lenz; lɛnz/ *n* (*pl* **lenses**) **1** piece of glass or glasslike substance with one or both sides curved, for use in spectacles, cameras, telescopes and other optical instruments. 透镜(用于眼镜,照相机,望远镜及其他光学仪器);镜头。⇨ the illus at **camera, convex**. 参看 camera, convex 之插图。 **2** (anat) transparent part of the eye, behind the pupil, through which light is refracted. (解剖)眼睛中之水晶体。⇨ the illus at **eye**. 参看 eye 之插图。

lent /lent; lɛnt/ *pt, pp* of **lend**.

Lent /lent; lɛnt/ *n* (in Christian Churches) period of forty days before Easter, the weekdays of this period being observed by devout persons as a period of fasting and penitence. (基督教)四旬斋(复活节前四十日,在此期内非星期日时需斋戒和忏悔); 封斋期。~ **lily**, daffodil. 水仙。 '~·**en** /'lentən; 'lɛntən/ *adj* of: ~ *services* (in church); (教会中)四旬斋期的礼拜; sparse: 稀少的: ~*en fare*. 稀少的饮食。

len·til /'lentl; 'lɛntl/ *n* [C] kind of bean plant; edible seed of this: 扁豆: ~ *soup*. 扁豆汤。

lento /'lentəʊ; 'lɛnto/ *adj, adv* (musical direction) slow(ly). (乐谱说明)缓慢的(地)。

Leo /'li:əʊ; 'lio/ *n* the fifth sign of the zodiac. 狮子宫(黄道带之第五宫)。⇨ the illus at **zodiac**. 参看 zodiac 之插图。

leo·nine /'li:ənaɪn; 'liə,naɪn/ *adj* of or like a lion. 狮子的;似狮子的。

leop·ard /'lepəd; 'lɛpəd/ *n* large African and South Asian flesh-eating animal with a yellowish coat and dark spots. 豹。⇨ the illus at **cat**. 参看 cat 之插图。 ~·**ess** /,lepə'des; 'lɛpədɪs/ *n* female ~. 母豹。

leper /'lepə(r); 'lɛpə/ *n* person suffering from leprosy. 麻风病患者。

lep·re·chaun /'leprəkɔ:n; 'lɛprə,kɔn/ *n* (in Irish folklore) fairy or sprite. (爱尔兰民间传说中之)妖精。

lep·rosy /'leprəsɪ; 'lɛprəsɪ/ *n* [U] skin disease that forms silvery scales on the skin, causes local insensibility to pain, etc and the loss of fingers and toes. 麻风病。 **lep·rous** /'leprəs; 'lɛprəs/ *adj* of, having, ~. 麻风病的;患麻风病的。

les·bian /'lezbɪən; 'lɛzbɪən/ *n* homosexual woman. 同性恋爱之女子。 ~·**ism** /-zəm; -ɪzm/ *n*

lese maj·esty /,leɪz 'mædʒɪstɪ US: ,li:z-; 'liz'mædʒɪstɪ/ *n* [U] treason; (joc) presumptuous conduct on the part of inferiors. 叛逆; (谑)地位低者的僭越行为。

lesion /'li:ʒn; 'liʒən/ *n* [C] harmful change in the tissues of a bodily organ, caused by injury or disease. (因受伤或疾病而引起的)身体上的损害。

less /les; lɛs/ *adj* (~ is contrasted with *more*. It is an

independent comparative, with no real corresponding positive. ⇨ **little, least.**) (与 more 相对, 乃一独立的比较级, 无真正相当的原级。) **1** (used with a *n* that stands for what is measured by amount or quantity or degree; *fewer* is used before a *pl n*) not so much; a smaller quantity of: 少量的; 较少的;(与可用数量或程度量度的名词连用; 在复数名词前用 fewer): ~ *butter.* 较少的奶油。Cf 参较 *fewer eggs; ~ food.* 较少的食物。Cf 参较 *fewer meals; ~ manpower.* 较少的人力。Cf 参较 *fewer workers; ~ shipping.* 较少的船舶。Cf 参较 *fewer ships; pay ~ money for the house.* 付较少的房租。Cf 参较 *pay a lower rent; have ~ difficulty with one's work.* 工作较少困难。Cf 参较 *meet with fewer difficulties; ~ size means ~ weight;* 较小即较轻; *of ~ value/importance.* 价值较少(较不重要)的。**2** (followed by *than*): (其后与 than 连用): *I have ~ money than you.* 我的钱比你的少。□ *adv* **1** (modifying *vv*) to a smaller extent; not so much: (修饰动词)较少; 少: *Eat ~, drink ~, and sleep more.* 少吃, 少饮酒, 多睡眠。**2** (with *adjj, participles* and *advv*) not so: (与形容词, 分词, 副词连用) 不如; 不及; 不如此: *Tom is ~ clever than his brother.* 汤姆不及他的哥哥(弟弟)聪明。*Please behave ~ foolishly.* 请不要这样愚蠢。Note that *less ... than* may be replaced by *not so ..., as,* 注意: *less ... than* 可由 *not so...as* 代替, eg 例如 *He was ~ hurt than frightened.* 他受的伤不重, 但是被吓得厉害。Cf 参较 *He was not so hurt as frightened.* 不要这样急躁。Cf 参较 *Try not to be so impatient.* **3 the ~:** *I was the ~ surprised as I had been warned,* My surprise was ~ because .... 因为我事先受到警告, 故不十分吃惊。*The ~ you worry about it the better it will be.* 你越不为此事担心越好。⇨ **the. any the ~,** in a lower degree: 程度较少: *I don't think any the ~ of him* (= My opinion of him is not lower) *because of this one failure.* 我并不因为此一失败而轻视他。**even / still ~,** and certainly not: 而且当然不会: *I don't suspect him of robbery, still ~ of robbery with violence.* 我不怀疑他会抢劫, 更不用说用暴力打劫了。**no less(...) than ...,** not a smaller amount (of sth) than ...: 不少于; 不减于: *He won no ~ than £50 in the lottery/He won £50, no ~, in the lottery* (expressing surprise at the amount). 他居然中了五十英镑的奖券(表示对此数额的惊奇)。*Our soldiers fought with no ~ daring than skill,* Their daring equalled their skill. 我们的士兵作战的英勇不亚于他们的战技。**none the ~,** but for all that; all the same: 仍旧; 依然: *Though he cannot leave the house, he is none the ~* (= he is, in spite of that) *busy and active.* 虽然他不能离开房屋, 但他依旧是忙碌和活跃的。□ *n* [U] smaller amount, quantity, time, etc: 较少的数额, 数量, 时间等: *in ~ than an hour.* 不到一小时。*I won't sell it for ~ than £50.* 少于五十英镑我不卖。*I want ~ of this and more of that.* 我少要些这个, 多要些那个。Cf 参较 *fewer of these and more of those. I expect to see ~ of her* (= to see her ~ often) *in future.* 我希望今后少同她见面。□ *prep* minus; with the deduction of: 减除: *£30 a week ~ £2 for National Insurance contribution.* 每周三十英镑, 扣除二英镑国民保险费。

les·see /le'siː; lɛs'i/ *n* person who holds land, a building, etc on a lease. 租地人; 租屋人; 承租者。

les·sen /'lesn; 'lɛsn/ *vt, vi* **1** [VP6A, 2A] make or become less: 减少; 变少: *to ~ the impact/effect of sth.* 减少某事物之冲击力(影响)。**2** [VP6A] cause (sth) to appear smaller, less important; belittle: 使变小; 使较不重要; 贬抑: ~ *a person's importance.* 贬抑某人的重要性。

les·ser /'lesə(r); 'lɛsɚ/ *adj* (attrib only) not so great as the other: (仅用作定语)较小的; 次要的: *choose the ~ evil.* (两祸害中) 选择较轻的祸害。**in / to a ~ degree,** not so much as the other. 程度较轻。

les·son /'lesn; 'lɛsn/ *n* **1** sth to be learnt or taught; period of time given to learning or teaching: 课; 一节课; 课程: *'English ~s;* 英语课; *a ~ in music.* 音乐课。

2 (*pl*) children's education in general: (复)儿童的功课; 课业: *Tom is very fond of his ~s.* 汤姆很喜欢他的课业。**3** sth experienced, esp sth serving as an example or a warning: 经验(尤指作为警戒者); 教训: *Let his fate be a ~ to all of you!* 让他的下场给你们大家一个教训! **4** passage from the Bible read aloud during a church service. 礼拜仪式中诵读的一段圣经。

les·sor /'lesɔː(r); 'lɛsɔr/ *n* (legal) person who grants a lease. (法律)出租土地, 房屋等者; 出租人。

lest /lest; lɛst/ *conj* **1** for fear that; in order that ... not: 恐; 以免: *He ran away ~ he should be seen.* 他因为怕被人看见而逃跑了。**2** (after *fear, be afraid / anxious etc*) that: (用于 fear, be afraid/anxious 等之后, 等于) that: *We were afraid ~ he should get here too late.* 我们恐怕他会来得太迟。

let¹ /let; lɛt/ *vt, vi* (*pt, pp* let) (-tt-) (For uses with *adverbial particles* and *preps* ⇨ **8** below.) (与副词性小品词和介词连用的用法, 参看下列第 8 义。) **1** [VP18B] (followed by a *noun/pronoun* and an *infinitive* without to; rarely used in the passive in this sense) allow to: 允许; 让(其后跟一名词或代词, 再接一没有 to 的不定式; 用于此义罕作被动): *Her father will not let her go to the dance.* 她父亲不会让她去参加舞会。*She wants to go to the party but her father won't let her* (ie let her *go.* The omission of the *infinitive* is frequent when it may be inferred from the context). 她要去参加那聚会, 但她父亲不允许她去 (her 之后省略了 go, 当有上下文可以推知时, 此种不定式常省略)。*Please let me know* (ie inform me) *what happens.* 请告诉我发生了什么事情。*Don't let the fire go out.* 勿要让火熄灭。**2** [VP18B] (used with first and third person *pronouns* to supply an indirect imperative): (与第一人称和第三人称的代词连用, 形成间接的祈使句): *Let's start at once, shall we?* 我们即刻动身吧, 好吗? *Don't let's start yet!* 还不要开始! *Let me see—where did I leave my hat?* 让我想一想——我的帽子放到哪儿去了呢? *Let us both have a try!* 让我们两人都试试看! *Let her do it at once.* 让她马上做此事。*Let there be no mistake about it,* Don't make any mistake, don't misunderstand me, etc. 此事不要弄错了, 勿有误解我, 等等。**Live and let live,** ⇨ **live²(2). 3** [VP18B] (*let,* in the imperative, may also indicate an assumption. It may also indicate permission, with a suggestion of defiance): (let 在祈使句中亦可指假设, 有时亦指许可, 但含有挑战的意味): *Let AB be equal to CD.* 假设 AB 等于 CD。*Let ABC be an angle of ninety degrees.* 假设 ABC 为一九十度角。*Let them do their worst!* I defy them to do their worst! 让他们蛮干好啦(我不相信他们敢蛮干)! *Let them all come!* 让他们都来吧! **4** [VP18B] (The pattern *let + noun + infinitive,* as in *let the waitress go,* is sometimes replaced by the pattern *let + infinitive + noun,* as in *let drop a hint.* In some cases, eg in *let fly,* the object of *let* is omitted): (let + 名词+不定式之句型, 例如: let the waitress go, 有时可改作 let + 不定式+名词, 例如: let drop a hint, 有时 let 的宾语可以省略, 例如: let fly). Note the following: 注意下列者: *let sb/sth be,* allow to be quiet or unworried: 不搅扰某人或某物: *Let me be,* Don't worry me. 不要打扰我。*Let the poor dog be,* Don't tease it. 不要捉弄那只可怜的狗。*let drive (at sb/sth),* aim a blow (at); throw sth (at): 瞄击; 向…投掷: *He let drive with his left fist.* 他用左拳击出。*He let drive at me with a stone.* 他拿一石头对我掷来。*let sb/sth drop,* allow to drop; (fig) utter (on purpose or by chance): 使跌下; 丢下;(喻)(故意或偶然)说出。*let sth fall,* allow to fall; (fig) allow to be heard: 使跌倒; 丢下;(喻)说出; 吐露出: *He let fall a hint of his intentions.* 他吐露出一点他的意向。*let fly (at sb/sth),* discharge; send out violently; shoot; strike out (at): 发出; 猛烈地发出;射出; 击出: *He aimed carefully and then let fly* (ie fired) *at the ducks.* 他仔细地瞄准, 然后射向那些鸭子。*The angry man let fly a volley of oaths.* 那愤怒的人发出一连串的咒语。*let sb/ sth go; let go of sb/sth,* release one's hold of him/

it: 放手; 松手; 放开: *Don't let the rope go/let go of the rope.* 不要松开那绳子。 *Let me go! Take your hands off me; don't hold or keep me.* 放开你的手!不要拉我!让我走! **let oneself go,** give way to, no longer hold back, one's feelings, desires, impulses, etc: 尽量发泄情感、欲望、冲动等: *He let himself go on the subject.* 他畅谈此一问题。 **let it go at that,** say no more about it; dismiss the subject: 不再谈论某事; 停止讨论一问题: *I don't agree with all you say but we'll let it go at that.* 我并不全同意你说的话, 但我们不要再谈此事了。 **let sth pass,** overlook; disregard: 忽略; 忽视: *It's not a serious error; we can let it pass, I think.* 这不是个严重的错误, 我想我们可以不必重视它。 **let sth slip, (a)** miss (an opportunity, etc). 错过(机会等)。 **(b)** = let sth drop / fall, (see above). **5** [VP22] (combined with *adj*) (与形容词连用) **let sb / sth alone,** allow (sb) to do sth unaided; not interfere with: 不管; 不要干涉: *Let it alone!* 不要管它! **Let well alone,** (prov) Don't try to improve sth that is already satisfactory: (谚)对已感满意之事不要再求改善; 不要画蛇添足。 **let alone,** (colloq) to say nothing of; not to mention: (口)遑论; 至于…更不必说了: *There were seven people in the car, let alone a pile of luggage and three dogs.* 那部汽车载了七个人, 更不必说还有一堆行李和三只狗了。 **let sb / sth loose (on sb / sth),** allow to be free (somewhere); (fig) release (one's anger, etc on sb): 释放; 放掉; (喻)发泄(愤怒等): *Don't let that dog loose.* 不要放开那条狗。 **6** [VP6A, 14, 22, 24A] ~ **sth (to),** give the use of (buildings, land) in return for regular money payments: 出租(房屋, 土地): *This house is to be let.* 此屋出租。 *The house would let (= could be let) easily.* 这房子容易出租。 *She has let her house furnished.* 她已将她备有家具的房屋租出。 **to let,** offered for renting. 出租。 **let out,** put out to hire: 出租: *He used to let out horses by the day.* 他以前按日出租马。 **7** [VP6A] (surgery) ~ **blood,** cause it to flow. (外科)放血。 Hence, 由此产生, **'blood-letting** *n* [U] **8** [VP15A, B, 2C, 14] (used with *adverbial particles* and *preps*): (与副词性小品词和介词连用之用法):

let sth down, lower; put or take down: 放低; 放下: *Please let the window down.* 请放下窗子。 *This skirt needs letting down,* lengthening by lowering the hemline. 这条裙子需要放长。 *She let down her hair.* 她松下她的头发。 *That chair has a broken leg, it might let you down,* might not support you. 那椅子有一条腿断了, 它可能会使你跌倒。 **let sb down,** (fig) disappoint; fail to help: (喻)使某人失望; 不帮助: *Harry will never let you down,* You can rely on him to help you always. 哈里永不会置你于不顾(你永远可以依赖他的帮助)。 *I've been badly let down,* placed in a difficult or awkward situation through the failure of others to support me. 我非常失望(由于别人不支持我而陷入困境)。 Hence, 由此产生, **'let-down** *n* feeling of having been let down; disappointment. 失望。 *let the side down,* **side¹(10).**

let sb / sth in / into sth, allow to enter: 允许进入; 放入: *Windows let in light and air.* 窗子使光线和空气进入。 *These shoes let in water.* 这些鞋子会进水。 *He let himself in / into the flat with a latchkey,* opened the door using the key. 他用钥匙打开弹簧锁而进入公寓。 *Who let you into the building?* 谁让你进入那房屋的? **let sth in,** make (a garment, etc) narrower: 将(衣物等)改窄: *This skirt needs letting in at the waist.* 这裙子的腰部需要改窄。 **let sb in for sth,** involve in loss, difficulty, hard work, etc: 使陷入(损失, 困难, 辛苦工作等): *He didn't know what a lot of unpaid work he was letting himself in for when he agreed to become secretary of the society.* 当他同意担任该社的秘书时, 他不知道他将做许多无报酬的工作。 **let sb into sth,** allow to share (a secret): 使知道(秘密): *She has been let into (= told) the secret.* 她已知道这秘密了。 **let sth into sth,** put into the surface of:

嵌进: *We must let another window into this wall.* 我们必须在这墙上再装一个窗户。 **let sb off,** excuse; not compel; not punish; not punish severely: 原谅; 不强迫; 不惩罚; 使免受重罚: *He was let off with a fine instead of being sent to prison.* 他没有坐牢, 只是受罚款了事。 *You have let him off lightly,* by excusing him from too much work, by punishing him lightly, etc. 你轻易地放过了他(例如免除他过多的工作, 减轻惩罚等)。 **let sth off,** fire off: 放(枪炮, 烟火等): *The boys were letting off fireworks.* 男孩子们在放烟火。

let on (that …), (colloq) reveal a secret: (口)泄露秘密: *He knew where the boy was hiding but he didn't let on, didn't tell anyone.* 他知道那男孩藏在哪里, 但他不泄露给别人。 **let sb / sth out,** allow to go (flow, etc) out: 使出去; 使流出; 放出: *He let the air out of the tyres.* 他将轮胎的气放掉。 *He let the water out of the bathtub.* 把浴盆中的水放掉。 **let sth out,** make (a garment, etc) looser, larger, etc: 放宽(衣服等): 放大: *He's getting so fat that his trousers need to be let out round the waist.* 他愈来愈胖, 故而他的裤腰需要放宽。 ⇨ also **6** above. 亦参看上列第 6 义。 **let out at sb,** aim a violent blow, kick, etc, at him; (fig) use violent language to him. 猛击某人; (喻)猛烈地攻讦某人: *Be careful! That mule has a habit of letting out at people.* 当心! 那匹骡子有踢人的习惯。

let sb / sth through (sth), allow to pass (an examination, etc): 使通过(考试等): *He got only 40%, so the examiners couldn't possibly let him through.* 他只得到四十分, 所以主试者不可能让他通过。 **let up,** become less strong, etc: 减弱: *Will the rain never let up?* 雨势永不会减弱吗? **'let-up** *n* (colloq) cessation; diminution: (口)停止; 中止; 减小: *There has been no let-up in the rain yet.* 雨一直没有停过。 *I've been working ten hours without a let-up.* 我已工作了十小时未曾中断。 **let up on sb,** (colloq) treat more leniently. (口)对待某人比较宽大。

let² /let/ *n* (from **let¹(6)**) letting; lease: (出自动词第 6 义)出租; 租出: *I can't get a let for my house,* can find no one willing to rent it from me. 我的房子租不出去。 **'let·ting** *n* [C] property that is let: 出租的房屋等: *a furnished letting,* a furnished house or flat that is let. 备有家具的出租的房屋或公寓。

let³ /let/ *vt* (archaic) hinder; obstruct. (古)妨碍; 阻碍。 □ *n* **1** hindrance, esp in the legal phrase: 阻碍 (特别作法律上用语): *without let or hindrance.* 毫无阻碍。 **2** (tennis) ball which when served, strikes the net before dropping into the opponent's court. (网球)(发球时)球触网。

lethal /'li:θl; 'liθəl/ *adj* causing, designed to cause, death: 致命的: *a ~ dose of poison,* 一剂致命的毒药; *~ weapons,* 凶器; *a ~ chamber,* eg in which sick animals may be put to death painlessly. 致命室(例如可使有病动物无痛苦地死去者)。

leth·argy /'leθədʒɪ; 'lɛθəɪdʒɪ/ *n* [U] (state of) being tired, uninterested; want of energy. 倦怠; 无兴趣; 无生气。 **leth·ar·gic** /lɪ'θɑːdʒɪk; lɪ'θɑɪdʒɪk/ *adj* sleepy; lacking in energy; caused by, likely to cause, ~. 困倦的; 无力气的; 倦怠所引起的; 易引起倦怠的。 **leth·ar·gi·cally** -klɪ; -klɪ/ *adv*

Lethe /'li:θɪ; 'liθɪ/ *n* (Gk myth) (river in Hades, the Greek underworld, producing) forgetfulness of the past. (希神)冥界的遗忘河(饮其水令人遗忘过去); 忘却往事。

let's /lets; lɛts/ = let us. ⇨ **let¹(2).**

let·ter /'letə(r); 'lɛtə/ *n* **1** character or sign representing a sound, of which words in writing are formed: 字母: *the 26 ~s of the English alphabet;* 英文的二十六个字母; *capital ~s* (A, B, C, etc) *and small ~s* (a, b, c, etc). 大写字母 (A, B, C 等)和小写字母 (a, b, c 等)。 Cf 参较 *phonetic symbol.* **2** written message,

request, account of events, etc sent by one person to another: 书信; 函件: *I have some ~s to write.* 我有几封信要写。 *Inform me by ~ of your plans.* 写信告诉我你的计划。 *~ of 'credit,* ⇨ **credit¹(1).** **'~-box** *n* (US 美 = *mail box*) **(a)** box (in the street, at a post office) in which ~s are posted; pillar-box. (街道上或邮局之)邮箱; 邮筒。 **(b)** box (in a building) for receiving ~s from the post. (房屋等内之)信箱。 **'~-card** *n* folded card with a gummed edge for use instead of notepaper and an envelope. 邮简; 封缄信片。 **'~-case** *n* pocket-book for holding ~s. 夹信件的小夹。 **'~-head** *n* (sheet of paper with a) printed name and address, eg of a business firm. 印于信纸上的信头(例如公司行号的名称和地址); 有信头的信纸。 **'~-press** *n* [U] contents of an illustrated book other than the pictures; printing from type. 有插图的印刷物中的文字部分; 本文(以别于插图); 活字印刷; 凸板印刷。 **3** (phrases) (短语) *keep (to) the ~ of the law/an agreement,* carry out the stated conditions without regard to its spirit or true purpose. 拘泥于法律(协约)的条文而忽略其精神或宗旨。 *to the ~,* paying strict attention to every detail: 严密周详地: *carry out an order to the ~.* 彻底执行命令。 **4** (*pl*) literature and learning: (复)文学; 文学修养: *the profession of ~s;* 文人的职业; 著作业; *a man of ~s.* 文学家; 文人。 *~ed* /'letəd; 'lɛtəd/ *adj* having a good knowledge of books: 有学问的: *a ~ed young man.* 有学问的青年。 *~ing* /'letərɪŋ; 'lɛtərɪŋ/ *n* [U] ~s, words, esp with reference to their style and size: 文字(尤指就其字体和大小而言): *the ~ing on a book cover;* 一书封面上所印的文字; *poor ~ing on a gravestone.* 墓碑上拙劣的雕刻文字。

let·tuce /'letɪs; 'lɛtɪs/ *n* [C] garden plant with crisp green leaves used in salads; [U] these leaves as food. 莴苣; 莴苣叶; 生菜。 ⇨ the illus at **vegetable.** 参看 vegetable 之插图。

leu·co·cyte (US = **leu·ko·cyte**) /'luːkəsaɪt; 'luːkə-ˌsaɪt/ *n* [C] white blood-cell. 白血球。

leu·kae·mia (US = **leu·ke·mia**) /luːˈkiːmɪə; luːˈkimɪə/ *n* [U] disease in which there is an excess of leucocytes, with changes in the lymph glands. 白血球过多症; 血癌。

Lev·ant /lɪˈvænt; ləˈvænt/ *n* the ~, Eastern part of the Mediterranean, its countries and islands. 地中海东部诸国家和岛屿。 *~·ine* /-aɪn/; -aɪn/ *n, adj* (native) of the ~. 地中海东部诸国家和岛屿的(人)。

lev·ant /lɪˈvænt; ləˈvænt/ *vi* abscond; leave (esp without paying gambling losses). 潜逃; 离去(尤指未付赌债而逃走)。

levee¹ /'levɪ; ləˈvi/ *n* (hist) formal reception; (GB) assembly held by a king or his representative at which men only were received. (史)正式接见; (英)君王或其代表为男士们所举行的接见会。

levee² /'levɪ; 'lɛvɪ/ *n* (US) embankment built to protect land from a river in flood: (美)防洪堤; 河堤: *the ~s along the Mississippi.* 密西西比河沿岸的防洪堤。

level¹ /'levl; 'lɛvl/ *adj* having a horizontal surface: 平的; 水平的: *~ ground;* 平地; *make a surface ~.* 使一表面变平。 *~ crossing,* (US 美 = *grade crossing*) place where a road and a railway cross on the same ~. 平交道。 **2** on an equality: 同等的; 相等的: *a ~ race,* one in which the competitors keep close together; 势均力敌的赛跑; *draw ~ with the other runners.* 与其他赛跑者相齐。 **3** *have a ~ head,* be steady and well-balanced, able to judge well. 有稳健清晰的头脑。 Hence, 由此产生, *~-'headed adj. do one's ~ best,* do all that one can do, do everything possible. 尽最大的努力。

level² /'levl; 'lɛvl/ *n* **1** [C] line or surface parallel with the horizon; such a surface with reference to its height: 水平线; 水平面; 就其高度而论的平面: *1000 metres above sea ~.* 海拔一千米。 *The water rose until*

it was on a ~ with the river banks. 河水涨至与河岸相平的高度。 *Water always finds its own ~.* 水总会找到它的水平面(水往低处流直到形成水平水面)。 **2** natural or right position, stage, social standing, etc: 自然或适当的位置, 阶段, 社会地位等: *He has found his own ~,* (fig) has found the kind of people with whom he is morally, socially or intellectually equal. (喻)他已找到与他相称的人(指在品行、身分或智力方面相当者)。 *They'll rise to higher ~s* (= advance in civilization, etc) *very quickly.* 他们在文明方面将会很迅速地提高。 **3** [U] (group of persons having) equal position or rank: 相等的地位或阶级; 同等地位的人: *consultations at cabinet ~,* among members of the cabinet; 内阁阁员间的磋商; *top-level talks,* talks between persons in the highest positions (in government, etc). 政府等中的高阶层会议。 (Cf 参较 *summit talks.*) '**O-**/'**A-~ (examination)** *n* [C] = of achievement(Ordinary/Advanced)in the school-leaving examination in England and Wales: (英格兰和威尔士)普通(高级)毕业标准考试: *a girl with five O~s and three A~s.* 通过五次普通考试和三次高级考试的女孩。 **4** on the ~,** (colloq) honest(ly); straightforward(ly): (口)诚实的(地); 坦率的(地): *Is he on the ~?* 他诚实吗？ ⇨ **crooked(2).** **5** '**spirit ~,** ⇨ **spirit(11).**

level³ /'levl; 'lɛvl/ *vt, vi* (-**ll-,** US **-l-**) **1** [VP6A, 15A, B] make or become ~ or flat: 使平; 使平坦; 变平: *~ a building with the ground.* 拆除一建筑物。 *Death ~s all men,* makes them equal by ending social distinctions, etc. 死使一切人皆平等(死使社会地位等无差别)。 *~ sth down/up,* make (incomes, marks, standards, surfaces, etc) equal by lowering the higher or raising the lower. (借降低高者或提高低者)使(收入, 分数, 标准, 表面等)相等。 **2** [VP6A, 14, 2C, 3A] bring or come into a horizontal plane: 使成平面; 变成平面: *~ a gun at a tiger,* raise it and aim. 举枪瞄准一虎。 *~ sth against sb,* put forward (a charge, an accusation, etc). 控诉某人。 *~ sth off/out,* cause an aircraft to fly parallel to the earth's surface: 使飞机平飞: *On reaching 1000 metres, the pilot ~led off.* 到达一千米高时, 那驾驶员便作水平飞行。 **(b)** (fig) reach a point in one's career beyond which no further progress is likely: (喻)事业到达不大可能再有发展的阶段: *You're unlikely to get further promotion—we all have to ~ off some time.* 你大概不会得到擢升——我们的事业必定会到达不再有发展的时候。 *~·ler,* US *~er* /'levlə(r); 'lɛvlə/ *n* (esp) person who wishes to abolish social distinctions. (尤指)主张社会地位平等者。

lever /'liːvə(r) US: 'lɛvə(r); 'lɛvə/ *n* bar or other tool turned on a fulcrum to lift sth or to force open, eg a window or drawer; (fig) means by which moral force may be exerted. 杠杆; (喻)激发道德力量的方法。 □ *vt* [VP6A, 15B] move (sth *up, along, into/out of position,* etc) with a ~. 用杠杆移动(与up, along, into position, out of position 等连用)。 *~·age* /-ɪdʒ; -ɪdʒ/ *n* [U] action of, power or advantage gained by, using, a ~. 杠杆作用; 由杠杆获得的力量或利益; 杠杆利率。

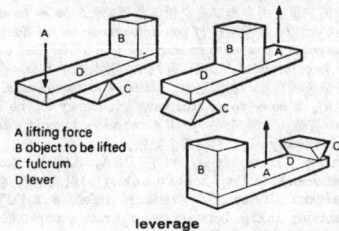

A lifting force
B object to be lifted
C fulcrum
D lever

leverage

lev·eret /'levərɪt; 'lɛvərɪt/ *n* young (esp first-year) hare. 小野兔(尤指未满一年者)。

lev·ia·than /lɪˈvaɪəθən; ləˈvaɪəθən/ *n* **1** (in the

Bible) sea animal of enormous size. (圣经中)巨大海兽；鳄鱼。 **2** anything of very great size and power. 任何巨大有力的东西。

levis /'liːvaɪz; 'liːvaɪz/ *n pl* (P) jeans. (商标)牛仔裤。

levi·tate /'levɪteɪt; 'levə͵tet/ *vt, vi* [VP6A, 2A] (with reference to powers claimed by spiritualists) (cause to) rise and float in the air in defiance of gravity. (关涉招魂论者所声称的力量) (使)飘浮在空中。 **levi·ta·tion** /͵levɪ'teɪʃn; ͵levə'teʃən/ *n*

lev·ity /'levɪtɪ; 'levətɪ/ *n* [U] (formal) tendency to treat serious matters without respect; lack of seriousness; [C] (*pl* **-ties**) instance of this. (正式用语)轻率；轻浮。

levy /'levɪ; 'levɪ/ *vt, vi* (*pt, pp* **levied**) **1** [VP6A, 14] ~ (**on**), impose; collect by authority or force: 征收；强迫收集：~ *a tax/a fine/a ransom on sb*; 向某人征收税(罚金，索取赎金)；~*ing an army/troops*, using compulsion to get men as soldiers. 征集军队。 **2** ~ *war upon/against*, declare, make, war on after ~ing men and supplies. 向…开战。 **3** [VP3A] ~ *on*, seize by law: 扣押：~ *on a person's property/estate*, seize this in order to get money for an unpaid debt. (为未付欠债)扣押某人的财产。 □ *n* (*pl* **levies**) [C] act of ~ing; amount of men, number of men, so obtained. 征收；征集；征集的员额。 **capital** ~ ⇨ **capital²**.

lewd /ljuːd *US:* luːd; lud/ *adj* indecent; lustful. 猥亵的；淫荡的。 ~**·ly** *adv* ~**·ness** *n*

lexi·cal /'leksɪkl; 'leksɪkl/ *adj* (contrasted with *grammatical*) of the vocabulary of a language. (与 *grammatical* 相对)词汇的；语词的。 ~**·ly** /-klɪ; -klɪ/ *adv* **lexis** /'leksɪs; 'leksɪs/ *n* [U] vocabulary. 词汇。

lexi·cogra·phy /͵leksɪ'kɒgrəfɪ; ͵leksə'kɑgrəfɪ/ *n* [U] dictionary compiling. 词典编纂。 **lexi·cogra·pher** /͵leksɪ'kɒgrəfə(r); ͵leksə'kɑgrəfə/ *n* person who compiles a dictionary. 词典编纂人。

lexi·con /'leksɪkən *US:* -kɒn; 'leksɪkɑn/ *n* dictionary (esp of Greek, Latin or Hebrew). 词典；字典(尤指希腊，拉丁或希伯来语者)。

ley /leɪ; le/ *n* [C] area of land temporarily under grass; 暂时长满草之可耕地；休耕地：*new-sown leys.* 刚播过种的休耕地。

lia·bil·ity /͵laɪə'bɪlɪtɪ; ͵laɪə'bɪlətɪ/ *n* (*pl* **-ties**) **1** [U] the state of being liable: 应负责；有义务；易遭受：有责任倾向：~ *to pay taxes*; 纳税的义务；~ *for military service*, in a country where there is conscription; (在行征兵制度的国内)服兵役的义务；~ *to disease.* 易患疾病。*Don't admit* ~ *for the accident*, eg because of car insurance claims. 不要承认此意外事件负责(例如由于汽车保险之要求)。**limited** ~ **company,** ⇨ **limit².** **2** (*pl*) debts; sums of money that must be paid (contrasted with *assets*). (复)债务；负债(与 assets 相对)。 **3** (colloq) handicap: (口)阻碍；不利：*His wife is more of a* ~ *at a party than an asset.* 在宴会中他的妻子是得力助手，反而是个碍事的人。

li·able /'laɪəbl; 'laɪəbl/ *adj* (usu *pred*) (通常用作表语) **1** ~ **for,** responsible according to law: 应负责任：*Is a man* ~ *for his wife's debts in your country?* 在你的国家里丈夫应为其妻之债务负责吗？ **2** *be* ~ *to sth,* be subject to: 易遭受：*If you drive a car to the danger of the public, you make yourself* ~ *to a heavy fine, or even to imprisonment.* 如果你开汽车危及公众的安全，你就可能受到重的罚款，甚或坐牢。*He is* ~ *to seasickness.* 他易晕船。 **3** *be* ~ *to do sth,* have a tendency to, be likely to: 有做…的倾向；易为：*We are all* ~ *to make mistakes occasionally.* 我们有时都会犯错。

li·aise /lɪ'eɪz; lɪ'ez/ *vi* [VP2A, 3A] ~ (**with/ between**), (colloq) act as a link. 联络；联络。

li·aison /lɪ'eɪzn *US:* 'liːəzɒn; ͵lie'zõ/ *n* **1** [U] connection; linkage between two separate groups. 联络；团体间的联系，'~ **officer,** one who keeps two such groups in touch with each other; member of a committee, etc acting as a link between the committee and other people. 联络员；委员会之联络人。 **2** [C] illicit (eg sexual) relationship. (男女间的)私通；通奸。

li·ana /lɪ'ɑːnə *US:* -'ænə; lɪ'ænə/ *n* climbing and twining tropical plant. (热带的)攀缘植物；葛藤类。

liar /'laɪə(r); 'laɪə/ *n* person who tells an untruth or who has told an untruth; person who habitually tells lies. 说谎者；惯于说谎者。

lib /lɪb; lɪb/ *n* (colloq abbr for) liberation. (口)为 liberation 之略。 **gay/women's lib,** movement (early 1970's) for the liberation of homosexuals/women from legal, social, economic and self oppression. 二十世纪七十年代早期同性恋(妇女)解放运动。

li·ba·tion /laɪ'beɪʃn; laɪ'beʃən/ *n* [C] (pouring out of an) offering of wine, etc to a god: 奠酒；灌奠(倾酒于地以祭神)：*make a* ~ *to Jupiter.* 向罗马主神祭酒。

li·bel /'laɪbl; 'laɪbl/ *n* **1** [U, C] (the publishing of a) written or printed statement that damages sb's reputation: 诽谤人的文字；出版或刊登诽谤性文字：*sue a newspaper for* ~; 控告某报刊登诽谤性文字；*utter/ publish a* ~ *against sb.* 诽谤某人(发表文字诽谤某人)。 **2** [C] ~ **on,** (colloq) anything that brings discredit upon or fails to do justice to: (口)有损名誉或对人不公平的东西：*The portrait is a* ~ *on me.* 这画像把我画得太难看。 □ *vt* (**-ll-,** *US* **-l-**) [VP6A] publish a ~ against; fail to do full justice to. 发表诽谤…的文字；对…不公平。 ~**·lous,** *US* ~**·ous** /'laɪbələs; 'laɪbləs/ *adj* containing a ~; in the nature of a ~: 含有诽谤文字的；诽谤性的：~*lous reports,* 诽谤性的报导；in the habit of uttering ~s: 有诽谤习惯的；爱诽谤的：*a* ~*lous person/periodical.* 爱诽谤的人(定期刊物)。

lib·eral /'lɪbərəl; 'lɪbərəl/ *adj* **1** giving or given freely; generous: 慷慨的；大方的；丰富的；充足的；不吝啬的：*a* ~ *giver to charities;* 对慈善事业慷慨的施舍者；*a* ~ *supply of food and drink;* 食物和饮料的充分供给；*a* ~ *table*, one with plenty of food and drink. 丰盛的一餐。*He is* ~ *of promises but not* ~ *of money*, gives plenty of promises but not much money. 他在承诺上慷慨，但给钱时吝啬(口惠而实不至)。 **2** open-minded; having, showing, a broad mind, free from prejudice. 大度的；磊落的；无偏见的。 **3** (of education) directed chiefly towards the broadening of the mind, not specially to professional or technical needs. (指教育)着重于开阔智力而不在于专业和技术的需要。**the** ~ **arts,** eg philosophy, history, languages. 文(理)科(例如哲学，历史，语言)。 **4** (politics in GB) of the party (dominant until the 1920's), favouring moderate democratic reforms. (英国政治)自由党的(自由党于二十世纪二十年代前很有势力，主张缓和性的民主改革)。 □ *n* person in favour of progress and reform and opposed to privilege. 自由主义者。**L~,** member of the L~ party in GB. 英国自由党员。 ~**·ism** /-ɪzəm; -ɪzəm/ *n* [U] ~ views, opinions and principles. 自由主义。 ~**·ize** /'lɪbrəlaɪz; 'lɪbərəl͵aɪz/ *vt* make ~; free from narrow-mindedness. 使磊落；使心胸宽大。 ~**·iz·ation** /͵lɪbrəlaɪ'zeɪʃn *US:* -lɪ'z-; ͵lɪbərəlɪ'zeʃən/ *n*

lib·er·al·ity /͵lɪbə'rælətɪ; ͵lɪbə'rælətɪ/ *n* (*pl* **-ties**) **1** [U] generosity; free giving; quality of being broad-minded; freedom from prejudice. 慷慨；大方；胸襟开阔；无偏见。 **2** (*pl*) instances of generosity: (复)慷慨施的实例：*He has made himself poor by his liberalities.* 他由于慷慨好施而致穷了。

lib·er·ate /'lɪbəreɪt; 'lɪbə͵ret/ *vt* [VP6A, 14] ~ (**from**), set free: 解放；使获自由：~ *slaves;* 解放奴隶；~ *the mind from prejudice.* 解除心中的偏见。 **lib·er·ator** /-tə(r); -tə/ *n* **lib·er·ation** /͵lɪbə'reɪʃn; ͵lɪbə'reʃən/ *n* [U] liberating or being ~d. 解放；获自由。 ⇨ **lib.**

lib·er·tine /'lɪbətiːn; 'lɪbə͵tin/ *n* licentious person. 淫佚放荡之人；浪子。**chartered** ~, person whose irregularities and eccentricities of behaviour are tolerated. 被宽容的浪子。

lib·erty /'lɪbətɪ; 'lɪbətɪ/ *n* (*pl* **-ties**) **1** [U] state of being free (from captivity, slavery, imprisonment,

despotic control, government by others); right or power to decide for oneself what to do, how to live, etc: 自由; 自由权: *They fought to defend their ~.* 他们为保卫自由而战. **at ~,** (of a person) free; not imprisoned: (指人)自由的; 未被监禁的: *You are now at ~ to leave any time,* 你现在随时可以离去. **set sb at ~,** release: 释放: *set prisoners/slaves at ~.* 释放囚犯(奴隶). **~ of conscience,** freedom to have one's own (esp religious) beliefs without interference. 信仰(尤指宗教上的)自由. **~ of speech,** freedom to say openly, in public, what one thinks, eg on social and political questions. 言论自由. **~ of the press,** freedom to write and print in periodicals, books, etc whatever one wishes without interference. 出版自由. **2** [U] ungrained and sometimes improper familiarity: setting aside of convention. 冒昧; 失礼. **take the ~ of doing sth/to do sth:** 冒昧地做某事: *I took the ~ of borrowing your lawn-mower while you were away on holiday.* 当你外出度假时我借用你的刈草机, 甚为冒昧. **take liberties with:** 对…太随便: *You must stop taking liberties with the young woman,* stop treating her with too much familiarity. 你不能对那年轻女子太随便. **3** (pl) privileges or rights granted by authority: (复)当局的特许权或权利: *the liberties of the City of London.* 伦敦市的特权.

li·bid·in·ous /lɪˈbɪdɪnəs; lɪˈbɪdnəs/ adj lustful. 淫荡的; 好色的.

li·bido /lɪˈbiːdəʊ; lɪˈbaɪdo/ n [U, C] (psych) sexual desire; emotional energy or cravings. (心理)性欲; 情欲.

Libra /ˈliːbrə; ˈlaɪbrə/ n the seventh sign of the zodiac (also called 亦称作 'the scales' or 'the balance'). 天秤宫(黄道之第七宫). ⇨ the illus at **zodiac.** 参看 zodiac 之插图.

li·brary /ˈlaɪbrərɪ US: -brerɪ; ˈlaɪˌbrɛrɪ/ n (pl -ries) **1** room or building for a collection of books kept there for reading; the books in such a room or building: 图书室; 图书馆; 图书馆或图书室的藏书: *the public ~,* maintained by a town or city council, etc; 公立图书馆; a 'circulating ~,* one that lends books for profit, members paying a subscription fee; 流通图书馆(借书以牟利者, 借书者须付订阅费); 'reference ~,* one in which books may be consulted but not taken away. 参考图书室(书籍只供参考, 不可借出者). **2** (attrib) (用作定语) a '~ book: 图书馆的书; a '~ edition, book usu of large size and print and with a strong binding. 图书馆版(通常为大字本, 装订牢固者). **3** writing and reading room in a private house. 书房. **4** series of books issued by a publisher in uniform binding and connected in some way: 丛书; 文库: *the Home University L~.* 家庭大学丛书. **li·brar·ian** /laɪˈbreərɪən; laɪˈbrɛrɪən/ n person in charge of a ~. 图书馆长; 图书馆员; 图书管理员. **li·brar·ian·ship** n [U] the work of a librarian. 图书馆长或馆员的工作.

li·bretto /lɪˈbretəʊ; lɪˈbrɛto/ n (pl ~s -təʊz; -toz/ or -tti/ -tiː; -ti/) book of words of an opera or musical play. 歌剧或乐剧之脚本. **li·bret·tist** /lɪˈbretɪst; lɪˈbrɛtɪst/ n writer of a ~. 歌剧或乐剧的脚本作者.

lice /laɪs; laɪs/ n pl of **louse.**

li·cence (US = **li·cense**) /ˈlaɪsns; ˈlaɪsns/ n **1** [C] (written or printed statement giving) permission from someone in authority to do sth; [U] authorization: 执照; 特许; 许可; 特许: a ~ to drive a car/a 'driving ~; 驾驶执照; a ~ to practise as a doctor; 医师开业执照; *marry by (special) ~* (contrasted with banns): 获得特许而结婚(与banns相对); a ~ for the sale of alcoholic drinks. 卖酒特许证. **'~-plate** n (US) number-plate, ⇨ number(2). (美)(汽车等之)号码牌. **'on-~** n [C] (GB) licence for the sale of alcoholic drinks to be consumed on the premises. (英)贩卖的酒只准许在酒店内饮用之许可证. **'off-~** n [C] (GB) licence for the sale of liquor to be taken away; shop where liquor is

sold and taken away. (英)贩卖的酒准许带走的许可证; 贩卖的酒可带走的酒店. **2** [U] wrong use of freedom; disregard of laws, customs, etc; licentious behaviour: 放肆; 不顾法律, 风俗等; 放纵: *The ~ shown by the troops when they entered enemy territory disgusted everyone.* 那些部队进入敌人领土所表现的放肆使人厌恶. **poetic ~,** freedom from the ordinary rules of language, eg of word order, allowed in verse. 诗的破格(写诗所特许的可打破语言之一般规格的自由, 例如文字顺序上的破格).

li·cense (also **li·cence**) /ˈlaɪsns; ˈlaɪsns/ vt [VP6A, 17] give a licence to: 许可; 特许; 给予执照或特许证: *shops ~d to sell tobacco,* 特许卖烟之商店; a ~ doctor to practise medicine, 许可医师行医; a ~d house/~d premises, where the sale of alcoholic drinks is allowed, eg hotels, restaurants; 特许的卖酒处(例如旅馆, 饭店); a ~d victualler, 有贩卖酒类许可证的酒店店主; the ~d quarters, (in some countries) part of a town where there are ~d brothels. (某些国家中)公娼区. **li·cen·see** /ˌlaɪsənˈsiː; ˌlaɪsnˈsi/ n person holding a licence (esp to sell alcohol). 领有执照者; (尤指)持有卖酒特许证者.

li·cen·tiate /laɪˈsenʃɪət; laɪˈsɛnʃɪt/ n person who has a licence or certificate showing that he is competent to practise a profession. 持有证件证明其在某一专门职业内有相当资格之人.

li·cen·tious /laɪˈsenʃəs; laɪˈsɛnʃəs/ adj immoral (esp in sexual matters); not held back by morality. 淫荡的; 淫秽的; 放纵的. **~·ly** adv **~·ness** n

li·chee, li·chi /ˈlaɪtʃiː; ˈlitʃi/ = **lychee.**

li·chen /ˈlaɪkən; ˈlaɪkɪn/ n [U] dry-looking plant that grows on rocks, walls, tree-trunks, etc, usu green, yellow or grey. 石耳; 地衣.

lich·gate, lych·gate /ˈlɪtʃɡeɪt; ˈlɪtʃˌget/ n roofed gateway of a churchyard, where, at a funeral, the coffin used to await the arrival of the clergyman. 教堂墓园之有顶盖的门口(葬礼时停棺等处等候牧师来临).

licit /ˈlɪsɪt; ˈlɪsɪt/ adj lawful; permitted. 合法的; 许可的.

lick /lɪk; lɪk/ vt, vi **1** [VP6A, 15A, B, 22] pass the tongue over or under: 舐: *The cat was ~ing its paws.* 猫在舐爪. *He ~ed the spoon clean.* 他将那调羹舐干干净了. **~ sb's boots,** cringe before sb; be abject, servile. 在某人面前卑躬屈膝; 拍人马屁. **~ one's lips,** show eagerness or satisfaction. 表示垂涎或满足. **~ one's wounds,** try to recover after a defeat. 失败后求复元; 重整旗鼓. **~ sth off,** remove by ~ing: 舐掉某物: *The boy ~ed the jam off his lips.* 那男孩舐掉他唇上的果酱. **~ sth up,** take it up by ~ing: 舐尽: *The cat ~ed up the milk.* 那猫舐光了牛奶. **~ into shape,** (fig) make presentable, efficient, properly trained: (喻)使象样; 整顿: *The recruits were soon ~ed into shape by the drill sergeants.* 新兵不久便被教育班长训练得像样样了. **~ the dust,** (rhet) fall to the ground, defeated or killed. (修辞)被击倒; 被打败; 被杀死. **2** [VP6A] (esp of waves, flames) touch lightly: (尤指波浪和火焰)冲洗; 卷烧: *The flames ~ed the sides of the fireplace.* 火焰卷烧壁炉边. **3** [VP6A] (colloq) overcome; triumph over; give a whipping to: (口)克服; 征服; 打击: *Well, that ~s everything!* That is more surprising than anything I've ever seen or heard! 嗯, 那真是闻所未闻, 见所未见的事! **4** [VP2A] (sl) go; hurry: (俚)走; 匆忙: *He went off as hard as he could ~.* 他飞快地跑走了. □ n **1** act of ~ing with the tongue. 舐. **give sth a ~ and a promise,** a hasty attempt to clean, polish, etc (with a promise of sth more thorough later). 马马虎虎地洗擦某物(准备以后再好好洗擦). **2** (also 亦作 'salt-~) place to which animals go for salt. 动物祗盐之处. **3** (sl) **at a great; at full ~,** at a great pace. (俚)极速地; 急忙. **~·ing** n (colloq) beating; defeat: (口)打败; 击败: *Our football team got a ~ing yesterday.* 我们的足球队昨天败了.

licor·ice /ˈlɪkərɪs; ˈlɪkərɪs/ n ⇨ **liquorice.**

lid /lɪd; lɪd/ n **1** movable cover (hinged or detachable)

for an opening, esp at the top of a container: 盖(尤指容器上者): *the lid of a kettle/box*; 壶(箱)盖; *the 'teapot lid.* 茶壶盖。 **2** eyelid. 眼睑。 **~·less** *adj*

lido /'li:dəu; 'lido/ *n* (*pl* **~s** /-dəuz; -doz/) public open-air swimming pool or bathing beach. 公共露天游泳池; 海滨浴场。

lie[1] /laɪ; laɪ/ *vi* (*pt, pp* **lied**, *pres p* **lying**) [VP2A] make a statement that one knows to be untrue: 说谎: *He lied to me.* 他对我说谎。 *He's lying.* 他在撒谎。 □ *n* such a statement: 谎言: *He's telling lies.* 他在说谎。 *What a pack of lies!* What a lot of untrue statements! 真是一派谎言! *He lived a lie*, deceived without using words. 他以行为欺骗。 **white lie**, ⇨ **white**[1](2). *give sb the lie*, accuse him of lying. 责某人说谎。 **'lie-detector** *n* device which records physiological changes, eg heart beats, rate of breathing, caused by emotional stresses while a person is being questioned. 测谎器(人受质询时, 由于情绪紧张而引起生理上的变化, 如心脏跳动、呼吸的速率等, 根据此种变化记录出以测是否说谎)。

lie[2] /laɪ; laɪ/ *vi* (*pt* **lay** /leɪ; le/, *pp* **lain** /leɪn; len/, *pres p* **lying**) [VP2A, C, D, 3A] **1** be, put oneself, flat on a horizontal surface or in a resting position: be at rest: 卧; 躺: *lie on one's back/side*; 仰卧(侧卧); *lie face downwards.* 俯卧。 *Don't lie in bed all morning!* 不要整个早上都躺在床上! *His body lies* (= He is buried) *in the churchyard.* 他被葬于教堂的墓地里。 *He lay on the grass enjoying the sunshine.* 他躺在草地上享受阳光。 *lie back*, get into, be in a resting position: 向后靠: *lie back in an armchair.* 向后靠着坐在扶手椅上。 *take sth lying down*, submit to a challenge, an insult without protest. 甘受挑战或侮辱。 *lie down under (an insult, etc)*, fail to protest, resist, etc. 未抗议或抵抗(侮辱等)。 *lie in*, (a) stay in bed after one's usual time for getting up. 睡懒觉。 Hence, 由此产生, **,lie-'in** *n*: *have a nice lie-in on Sunday morning.* 星期天早上好好睡个懒觉。 **(b)** remain in bed to give birth to a child: 分娩; 待产: *The time had come for her to lie in.* 她生产的时间到了。 **,lying-'in hospital**, (old use) maternity hospital. (旧用法)产科医院。 *lie in ambush*, ⇨ **ambush**. *lie low*, (colloq) ⇨ **low**[1](12). *lie up*, stay in bed or in one's room (from illness, etc). (因病等)卧床不起; 不能离室。 *lie with*, (old use, biblical, now usu *sleep with*) have sexual intercourse with. 〈旧用法, 圣经文体, 现在通常用 sleep with〉与…性交。 *Let sleeping dogs lie*, (prov) Avoid discussing problems that are likely to cause trouble. (谚)莫惹事生非; 不要讨论麻烦问题。 **'lie-abed** /-əbed; -əbed/ *n* lazy person who lies in bed instead of getting up. 睡懒觉的人。 **2** (of things) be resting flat on sth: (指物)平放在某物之上; 在某处: *The book lay open on the table.* 那本书在桌上打开着。 *How long has your bicycle been lying out on the wet grass?* 你的脚踏车放在外面潮湿的草地上有多久了? **3** be kept, remain, in a certain state or position: 保持在某种状态或位置: *money lying idle in the bank*; 闲存在银行内的钱; *towns lying in ruins*; 成废墟状态的城市; *men who lay* (= were) *in prison for years.* 坐牢数载的人。 *The snow lay thick on the ground.* 雪厚厚的堆积在地上。 *The fields lay thickly covered with snow.* 田野积着厚厚的雪。 *lie heavy on sth*, cause discomfort, trouble, distress to it: 使不舒服, 烦恼, 痛苦: *The lobster lay heavy on his stomach.* 那龙虾使他的肚子难受。 *The theft lay heavy on his conscience.* 那次偷窃使他良心不安。 *lie over*, be left for action at a future time: 延期处理; 搁延: *Let the matter lie over until the next committee meeting.* 将此事搁延至委员会下次会议。 **4** be spread out to view; extend: 展现; 展开: *The valley lay before us.* 那山谷展现在我们的眼前。 *The coast lay undefended and lay open to attack.* 该海岸未设防, 易受攻击。 *If you are young, life still lies before you.* 如果你年轻, 你仍有远大的前途。 *find out/see how the 'land lies*, (fig) learn how matters stand, what the state of affairs is. (喻)探知事情的真相。 **5** be situated: 位于: *ships lying*

at anchor. 停泊着的船只。 *The ship is lying at No 5 berth.* 该船停于五号碇泊处。 *The fleet lay off the headland.* 舰队停在岬处。 *lie 'to*, (of a ship) come almost to a stop, facing the wind. (指船)因逆风而几乎不能前进。 **6** (of abstract things) exist; be in a certain position or manner: (指抽象事物)存在; 在某种情况或状态之中: *The trouble lies* (= is) *in the engine.* 毛病发生在引擎。 *The answer to this difficulty lies in not putting too much pressure on the engine.* 解决这毛病的方法是不要给引擎加太大的压力。 *He knows where his interest lies*, where he may win an advantage, make a profit. 他知道他的利益之所在。 *I will do everything that lies in* (= that is within) *my power.* 我愿就我能力范围尽量去做。 *lie at sb's door*, be attributable to: 归于: *At whose door should the blame/fault/responsibility lie.* Who should we attribute it to? 我们应该归咎于谁? (Cf 参较 *lay sth at sb's door*, ⇨ **door**(1).) *lie with sb*, be sb's duty or responsibility: 为某人的责任: *The solution/The burden of proof lies with you.* 解决问题的办法(举证的责任)落在你身上。 *It lies with you* (= It is your duty) *to accept or reject the proposal.* 接受或拒绝此提议自由你做主。 *as far as in me lies*, to the best of my power. 尽我的力量。 **7** (legal) be admissible: (法律)可承认; 成立: *The appeal will not lie*, is not according to law, cannot be admitted. 该上诉不能成立。 □ *n* (*sing* only) the way sth lies; (golf) the position of a ball when it comes to a stop. (仅用单数)位置; 形势; (高尔夫球)球停下来的位置。 *the lie of the land*, the natural features (esp the contours) of an area; (fig) the state of affairs. 地势; (喻)情势; 情况。

lied /li:t; lit/ *n* (*pl* **~er** /'li:dər; 'lidə/) (G) German song or lyric. (德)德国歌曲或抒情曲。 **'~er-singer**, person who sings **~**er. 唱德国歌曲或抒情曲者。

lief /li:f; lif/ *adv* (archaic or liter) willingly: (古或文)欣然: *I would/had as ~ join the Crusade as anything*, would do this more willingly than anything else. 参加十字军是我最乐意的事。

liege /li:dʒ; lidʒ/ *adj* (only in) (仅用于) *'~ lord/sovereign*, (feudal times) ruler, landowner, entitled to receive service and homage. (封建时代之)君主; 王侯。 **'~·man** /-mən; -mən/ *n* (*pl* **-men**) feudal vassal; faithful follower. 封建时代的家臣; 忠实的部下。 □ *n* *~ lord; ~man.* 君主; 王侯; 家臣。

lien /'lɪən; lin/ *n* (legal) legal claim (*upon* property) until a debt on it is repaid: (法律)留置权(对财产以待偿还借款的权利, 后接 upon): *A shipping company has a ~ upon cargo until the freight is paid.* 航运公司对于运费有留置到运费付清始可提取的货物的权利。

lieu /lu:; lu/ *n* (only in) (仅用于) *in ~ (of)*, instead (of). 代替。

lieu·ten·ant /lef'tenənt US: lu:'t-; lu'tenənt/ *n* **1** army officer below a captain; (/lə'tenənt; lu'tenənt/) junior officer in the Navy. 陆军中尉; 海军上尉。 **2** (in compounds) (用于复合词) officer with the highest rank under: 仅次于复合词中后一词所示官职的官员: *~-'general*; 陆军中将; 空军中将; *,~-'colonel*; 陆军中校; 空军中校; *,~-com'mander*; 海军少校; *,~'governor*, official under a governor-general. 副总督。 **3** deputy or substitute; one who acts for a superior. 副职官员; 代理上级官员。 **Lord L~ (of the County)**, the Queen's representative in a county. 女王驻郡代表。 **L~ of the Tower**, (ie the Tower of London). 伦敦塔的副主官。 **lieu·ten·ancy** /-ənsɪ; -ənsɪ/ *n* rank, position, of a **~**. 陆军中尉, 海军上尉, 代理上级官员的等级或职位。

life /laɪf; laɪf/ *n* (*pl* **lives** /laɪvz; laɪvz/) **1** [U] condition that distinguishes animals and plants from earth, rock, etc: 生命: *How did ~ begin?* 生命是怎样开始的? *Where did ~ come from?* 生命是从哪里来的? **life force**, vital energy thought of as working for the survival of the human race and the individual. 生命力。 **2** [U] living things collectively, in general; plants, animals, people: 生物(集合用法); 动植物和人:

Is there any ~ on the planet Mars? 火星上有生物吗? *A naturalist studies animal and plant ~.* 博物学者研究动植物。 **3** [U] state of existence as a human being: 人生; 人的生存: *L~ is sweet.* 人生是甜美的。 *The battle was won, but only with great loss of ~,* many were killed. 那一战虽然胜了, 但伤亡惨重。 **bring to ~,** cause to live; cause to recover from a faint, an illness thought to be fatal, etc. 使复活; 使苏醒; 使康复。 **come to ~,** recover consciousness, recover from a faint, etc: 苏醒: *We all thought he was drowned, but after an hour's artificial respiration he came (back) to ~.* 我们都认为他淹死了, 但经过一小时的人工呼吸后, 他又苏醒了。 **run for one's ~ / for dear ~,** in order to, or as if to, save oneself from death. 逃命。 **a matter of ~ and / or death,** one on which sb's continued existence depends. 生死关头; 生死攸关之事。 **kiss of ~,** ⇨ **kiss.** **this ~, ~ on earth.** 此生; 现世。 **the 'other ~; future / eternal / everlasting ~,** conscious existence, the state of existence, after bodily death. 来世; 永生。 **with all the pleasure in ~,** with the greatest possible pleasure. 极高兴地。 **4** [C] state of existence, as an individual living being: 性命: *How many lives were lost in the disaster?* 在那灾祸中丧失了多少性命? **take sb's ~,** kill him. 杀死某人。 **take one's own ~,** kill oneself; commit suicide. 自杀。 **a ~ for a ~,** phrase used to express the view that murder must be revenged by the killing or execution of the murderer or (in a vendetta) by the killing of a member of his family. 一命抵一命(此短语用以表示凶手必须被杀或处死,以为死者报仇,若为冤冤相报之血仇,必须杀死对方家族一份子以偿命)。 **cannot for the '~ of one,** cannot, however hard one tries: 怎么也不能; 要了命也不能: *For the ~ of me I couldn't recall her name.* 我怎么样也想不起她的名字来了。 **Not on your ~!** (colloq *int*) Quite definitely not. (口,感叹词)绝对不。 **5** [C] period between birth and death, or between birth and the present, or between the present and death: 一生; 一辈子; 终身: *He lived all his ~ in London.* 他一生都住在伦敦。 *I have lived here all my ~.* 我自出生即住在此地。 *The murderer received a ~ sentence / was sentenced to imprisonment for ~.* 该杀人犯被判无期徒刑。 *The murderer is doing ~ / was given ~,* (sl) imprisonment for ~. (俚)那杀人犯在服无期徒刑(被判无期徒刑)。 **~ annuity,** one that will be paid for the rest of a person's ~. 终身年金; 终身俸。 **'~ cycle,** progression through different stages of development: 生命环; 生命周期(经过不同发育阶段之过程): *the ~ cycle of a frog,* from the egg to the tadpole to the final stage. 青蛙之生命环(自卵至蝌蚪至最后阶段)。 **~ interest,** (legal) benefit valid (from property, etc) during a person's ~. (法律)终身权益。 **~ peer,** member of the House of Lords, whose title is not inherited by his heirs. 英国国会中其头衔不为子孙承袭的上议院议员。 **early / late in ~,** during the early / late part of one's ~: 一生中之早(晚)期; 早年(晚年): *marry early / late in ~.* 早(晚)婚。 **have the time of one's ~,** (colloq) enjoy oneself immensely, as never before. (口)享受从未有过的快乐。 **6** [U] human relations; the business, pleasures, social activities, etc, of the world: 社交关系; 社交生活; 世事; 人世繁华: *Sailors don't earn much money, but they do see* ~, see how people everywhere live. 船员的收入虽不多, 但他们的阅历极广。 *There is not much ~* (eg social activity) *in our small village.* 我们的小村子里没有多少社交活动。 **true to ~,** (of a story, drama, etc) giving a true description of how people live. (指故事,戏剧等)描写真实; 与实际生活相同。 **7** [C, U] (way of) living; career: 生活; 生活方式; 生涯: *Some people have easy lives.* 有些人生活舒适。 *Which do you prefer, town ~ or country ~?* 你比较喜欢都市生活还是乡村生活? *That's the ~ for me!* That's how I should like to live. 那才是我向往的生活。 **'high ~,** ⇨ **high¹(12). 8** [C] written account of sb's ~; biography: 言行录; 传记: *Do you enjoy*

reading the lives of great men? 你喜欢读伟人的传记吗? *He has written a new ~ of Newton.* 他写了一部新的牛顿传。 **'~ story,** biography. 传记。 **9** [U] activity, liveliness, interest: 活力; 生气; 兴趣: *The children are full of ~,* are active and cheerful. 孩子们生气勃勃。 *Put more ~ into your work.* 你工作时要提起精神。 **the ~ (and soul) of the party,** person who is the most lively and amusing member of a social gathering. 社交场合的灵魂人物(最活泼而又风趣之人)。 **10** [U] living form or model: 活人; 实物; 模特儿: *a portrait / picture taken from (the) ~;* 以活人做模特儿的画像; *a '~ drawing;* 实物图画; *a '~ class,* (in an art school) one in which students draw or paint from living models. (美术学校中之)人体写生课。 **to the ~,** with great fidelity or exactness: 逼真: *draw / portray / imitate sb to the ~.* 将某人画得栩栩如生(模仿某人很逼真)。 ⇨ **lifelike** below. 参看下列之 lifelike。 **as large as ~,** **(a)** of natural or ordinary size: 与真人或真物一样大的: *a statue as large as ~.* 与真人一样大的雕像。 **(b)** (colloq and in joke) in person; without possibility of doubt or error. (口,谑)亲自; 无容置疑。 **11** [C] fresh start or opportunity after a narrow escape from death, disaster, etc: (死里逃生后之)新生命; 新机会: *The batsman was given a ~,* eg when the fielders missed an easy catch. 那击球员获一新机会(例如当外场员未能接住一易接的球时)。 *They say a cat has nine lives.* 据说猫有九条命。 **12** [C] period during which sth is active or useful: 一物之活动或有用的时期; 寿命: *the ~ of a steamship / a government.* 轮船(政府)的寿命。 **13** '~ **assurance / insurance,** ⇨ these words. 参看 assurance, insurance, **expectation of ~; '~ expectancy,** (insurance) statistically determined number of years that a person at a particular age may expect to live. (保险业)(某一年龄者所能活的)平均寿命。 **a good / bad ~,** person who is likely to pass / not to reach this average. 可能活过(不到)平均寿命者。 **14** (compounds) (复合词) **'~·belt** *n* belt of cork or other buoyant material to keep a person afloat in water. 救生带; 浮带。 **'~·blood** *n* [U] blood necessary to ~; (fig) vitalizing influence; sth that gives strength and energy. 保持生命的血液; (喻)元气; 活力的来源。 **'~·boat** *n* **(a)** boat specially built for going to the help of persons in danger at sea along the coast. (岸边的)救生艇。 **(b)** boat carried on a ship for use in case the ship is in danger of sinking, is on fire, etc. (大船上的)救生艇。 **'~·buoy** *n* ~belt in the form of a ring, through which a person puts his head, shoulders and arms. 救生圈。 **'~ cycle** *n* ⇨ 5 above. 参看上列第 5 义。 **'~·estate** *n* property that a person enjoys for ~, but cannot dispose of further. (仅限于一代的)终身财产。 **'~-giving** *adj* that strengthens or restores physical or spiritual ~. 赋与生命的; 给与生气的。 **'~·guard** *n* **(a)** expert swimmer on duty at dangerous places where people swim. (游泳场的)救生员。 **(b)** bodyguard of soldiers. 侍卫; 卫队。 **'L~ Guards** *n pl* cavalry regiment in the British army. (英国陆军中的)禁卫骑兵团。 **'~ 'history** *n* (biol) record of the ~ cycle of an organism. (生物)(生物体之)生活史。 **'~-jacket** *n* one of cork or other buoyant material or one that can be inflated. 救生衣。 **'~·less** *adj* **1** never

a life-buoy

a life-jacket

having had ~; 无生命的: *~less stones.* 无生命的石头. **2** having lost ~; dead. 失去生命的; 死的. **3** dull; not lively: 枯燥无味的; 无生气的: *answer in a ~less manner.* 要死不活地回答. **~·less·ly** *adv* '**~·like** *adj* **1** resembling real ~; looking like the person represented: 栩栩如生的; 酷似维肖的: *a ~like portrait.* 栩栩如生的画像. **2** like a living thing: 似生物的: *a ~like cloud.* 一片似生物的云. '**~·line** *n* rope used for saving ~, eg one attached to a ~buoy, or one fastened along the deck of a ship during a storm, for persons to cling to; 救生索(例如系于救生圈或暴风雨中系于船甲板上供人攀附之绳索); diver's line for signalling to the ship from which he is working; 潜水员上系于潜水人员以信号之绳索; (fig) anything on which one's ~ depends; (喻)生命寄托之物; (palmistry) line across the palm of the hand, alleged to show one's length of ~, major events in one's ~, etc. (手相)生命线. '**~·long** *adj* continuing for a long time; lasting throughout ~. 长期的; 终身的. '**~·office** *n* life assurance office or business. 人寿保险公司办事处; 人寿保险业. ~ **peer** *n* ⇨ **5** above. 参看5义第5义. '**~·preserver** *n* **(a)** (GB) short stick with a heavy, weighted end, used as a weapon of defence. (英) 护身棒 (用作防御武器之一端重的短棒). **(b)** (US) (美) = ~-jacket. **lifer** /'laɪfə(r); 'laɪfɚ/ *n* **1** (with *adj* prefixed) person who lives a certain kind of ~: (前面冠以形容词)过某种生活者: *a simple-lifer.* 生活简朴的人. **2** (sl) (one who is serving a) sentence of ~ imprisonment. (俚)无期徒刑; 被判无期徒刑者. '**~·saver** *n* (esp in Australia) ~guard (a). (尤用于澳洲)救生员. '**~·size(d)** *adj* (of pictures, statues, etc) having the same size, proportions, etc, as the person represented. (指图画, 雕像等)与真人一般大小的. '**~·span** *n* (biol) longest period of ~ of an organism known from the study of it. (生物) 寿命(某生物体的最长生命期). ~ **sup·port system**, equipment in a spacecraft which provides an artificial environment in which astronauts may live. 太空生活装备(太空船中供太空人生活之装置). '**~·time** *n* duration of a person's ~. 一生; 终身. *the chance of a ~time*, an opportunity that comes only once. 一生只有一次的机会. '**~·work** *n* task that occupies one's whole ~ or to which one devotes all one's ~. 毕生的工作; 终身的事业.

lift /lɪft; lɪft/ *vt, vi* **1** [VP6A, 15A, B] raise or higher level or position: 举起; 抬起: *~ (up) a table;* 抬起一桌子; *~ sth out of a box / a child out of his cot.* 从箱中将某物抽出(把小孩从小儿床中抱出). *This box is too heavy for me to ~ (it).* 这箱子太重, 我搬不动. *This piece of good luck raised her spirits.* 这次幸运使她非常高兴. *~ up one's eyes (to …),* look up (at). 向上看. *have one's face ~ed,* have a face-lift; ⇨ **face¹(2)**. 做面部拉皮(使面部拉紧以消除皱纹). *not ~ a finger,* ⇨ **finger**. *~ up one's voice,* raise it, cry out. 高呼. **2** [VP2C] *~ off,* (of a rocket, spacecraft) rise from the launching site. (指火箭、太空船)升空; 发射. Hence, 由此产生, '**~·off** *n: We have ~off.* 我们的火箭(太空船)升空了. **3** [VP2A] yield to an attempt to ~: 被举起; 被抬起: *This window won't ~,* won't go up. 这窗子推不上去. **4** [VP2A] (of clouds, fog, etc) rise; pass away: (指云雾等)消散: *The mist began to ~.* 雾开始消散. **5** [VP6A] dig up (root crops); remove (plants, shrubs, etc) from the ground: 掘出 (块根作物); 掘除(植物、灌木等): *~ potatoes.* 掘马铃薯. **6** [VP6A] steal: 偷窃: *~ articles in a supermarket.* 在一超级市场内偷窃. '**shop-,** ⇨ **shop(1)**. take without permission or proper acknowledgement: 偷取; 剽窃: *Long passages in that textbook have been ~ed from other authors.* 那教科书中几段长的文字系窃自其他作者. **7** [VP6A] end a ban, prohibition, blockade, siege. 解除 (禁令、封锁、包围). □ *n* [C] **1** act of ~ing. 举起; 抬起. *give sb / get a ~*, **(a)** offer sb / be offered a ride in a car or other vehicle: 让某人搭自己的车(获得搭别人的车): *Can you give me a ~ to the station?* 你能

让我搭你的车到车站吗? ⇨ also *air ~* at **air¹(7)**. **(b)** (of a person's spirits) become / make more cheerful, contented: (指人的心情)变为(使)更愉快、满足: *The big increase in her salary gave her a tremendous ~.* 她的薪水大幅度增加使她极为振奋. **2** (US 美 = *elevator*) box-like apparatus in a building for taking people up or down to another floor: 电梯: *take the ~ to the tenth floor.* 乘电梯至十楼. '**~·man** /-mæn; -mən/ *n* one who operates a ~. 电梯管理员.

liga·ment /'lɪgəmənt; 'lɪgəmənt/ *n* [C] band of tough, strong tissues that holds two or more bones together in the body. (连接体内骨骼之)韧带.

liga·ture /'lɪgətʃə(r); 'lɪgə,tʃʊr/ *n* [C] **1** bandage, piece of thread, etc used in tying, esp cord used to tie up a bleeding artery. 绑缚用的绷带. **2** (printing) two or more letters joined, eg *f* and *l* joined as fl. (印刷)连字(例如 f 和 l 连成fl).

light¹ /laɪt; laɪt/ *adj* (-er, -est) (opposite of *dark*). (为 dark 之反义词) **1** (of a place) well provided with light³(1): (指地方)光线充足的; 明亮的: *a ~ room.* 光线充足的房间. *It's beginning to get ~.* 天开始亮了. **2** pale-coloured: 淡色的; 浅色的: *~ hair;* 淡色的头发; *~ complexion;* 白皙的肤色; *~ blue / green / brown.* 淡蓝(绿/棕)色. '**~·coloured** *adj* having a ~ colour: 淡色的; 浅色的: *a ~-coloured dress.* 浅色的女装.

light² /laɪt; laɪt/ *adj* (-er, -est) (opposite of *heavy*). (为 heavy 之反义词) **1** not heavy; not having much weight (for its size): 不重的; 轻的; 没有多少重量的(与体积相较): *as ~ as air / as a feather;* 像空气(羽毛)一样轻; *a ~ fall of snow;* 雪花轻飘; *a pair of ~ shoes;* 一双轻便的鞋; *a ~ cart or van,* one made for ~ loads and quick movement; 轻快的马车或货车; *~ clothing,* for summer; 轻便的衣服(夏季穿用); *a ~ building / bridge,* 轻巧的建筑物(桥梁); *a ~ railway,* for ~ traffic; 轻便铁道(供交通不拥挤的地区使用); *a ~ cruiser,* with ~ armour and guns. 轻巡洋舰. *~ horse,* light-armed cavalry: 轻骑兵: *a ~ (horse) brigade,* with ~ equipment and weapons. 轻装备(骑兵)旅. Hence, 由此产生, '**~·armed** *adj* **2** gentle; delicate: 轻柔的; 轻盈的: *give sb a ~ touch on the shoulder;* 轻轻一拍某人的肩头; *walk with ~ footsteps / movements;* 轻轻地走; *have a ~ hand for pastry,* have delicacy of touch that gives good results. 在做面点方面手很巧. Hence, 由此产生, '**~·handed** *adj* having a ~ hand. 手艺巧的. '**~·handedly** *adv* '**~·fingered** *adj* skilful in using the fingers; clever at stealing, eg as a pickpocket. 手指灵巧的; 偷窃技术高明的(例如扒手). **3** below the correct weight, amount, etc: 重量(分量)不够的: *~ coin;* 分量不够的钱币; *give ~ weight.* 未给足够分量. *We're about 50p ~ on the petty cash,* 50p short. 我们短少五十便士的零用金. **4** (of beer, wines) not very strong; (of food) easily digested; (of meals) small in quantity: (指啤酒或葡萄酒)味淡的; (指食物)易消化的; (指餐食)少量的: *a ~ supper,* 少量的晚餐, (hence) (由此产生) *a ~ eater;* 饭量小的人; (of sleep) not deep; easily disturbed; (of sleepers) easily waked; (of books, plays, music) primarily for amusement, not for serious entertainment or study: (指睡眠)不沉的; 易受骚扰的; (指睡眠者)容易惊醒的; (指书籍, 戏剧, 音乐)娱乐性的; 轻松的: *~ reading / music / comedy;* 轻松的读物(音乐, 喜剧); *a ~ comedian;* 轻松的喜剧演员; (of soil) easily broken up; (of work) easily done; (of taxes, punishment) not difficult to bear; (of a syllable) not stressed, unemphatic. (指土壤)松的; (指工作)容易做的; (指税, 惩罚)轻微的; (指音节)非重音的; 弱音的: *~ work of sth,* do it without much effort. 轻易地做某事. **5** not serious or important: 不严重的: *a ~ attack of illness.* 不严重的疾病发作. *make ~ of,* treat as of no or little importance: 轻视; 不把…当一回事: *He makes ~ of his illness.* 他不把他的病当一回事. **6** thoughtless; frivolous; jesting: 轻率的; 轻浮的; 开玩笑的: *~ conduct;* 轻浮的行为; *a man of ~ character,*

not troubling much about moral questions. 性格轻率的人。 **~-'minded** adj frivolous. 轻浮的。 Hence, 由此产生, **~-'mindedness** n **7** cheerful: free from sorrow; 愉快的; 无忧无虑的: a ~ heart. 愉快的心情。 Hence, 由此产生, **~-'hearted** adj, **~-'heartedly** adv **~-'heartedness** n **8** without moral discipline; wanton: 放荡的; 不贞洁的: a ~ woman. 水性杨花的女人。 **9** dizzy, delirious: 晕眩的; 昏迷的 (chiefly in) (主要用于) **,~-'headed** adj, **~-'headedly** adv and **,~-'headedness** n **10** (compounds) (复合词) **~-'heavyweight** n (esp) boxer weighing between 160 and 175 lb (or 72.5 to 79.3 kg). (尤指)重乙级(体重在 160 至 175 磅或 72.5 至 79.3 公斤间之拳击家)。 **~-o'-'love** n fickle woman; harlot. 荡妇; 娼妓。 **'~-weight** n, adj (man or animal) below average weight; (esp, boxing) boxer weighing between 126 and 135 lb (or 57 to 61 kg); (fig) (person) not important or serious. 平均重量以下的; 平均重量以下的人或动物; (尤指,拳击)体重在 126 磅至 135 磅 (57 至 61 公斤)间的拳击家; 轻量级(拳击家); ~(喻:不重要的人); 不认真的(人)。 □ adv in a ~ manner: 轻: tread/ sleep ~; 轻轻走(小睡); travel ~, with little luggage; 带很少的行李旅行; get off ~(ly), (colloq) escape without heavy punishment. (口)逃过严厉的惩罚。 **~-ly** adv **~-ness** n

light[3] /laɪt/ n (opposite of dark[1] or darkness) (为 dark[1] 或 darkness 之反义词) **1** [U] (and with indef art and adjj) that which makes things visible: (亦可与不定冠词及形容词连用的)光; 光线: the ~ of the sun/a lamp/the fire; 阳光(灯光; 火光); read by the ~ of a candle; 借烛光读书; a bright/dim ~ 明亮(朦胧)的光线; go for a walk by 'moon~; 月光下散步; bathed in 'sun~. 接受日光浴; 晒太阳。 We need more ~. 我们需要更多的光线。 The ~ (ie day-~) began to fail, It began to get dark. 天开始黑了。 in a good/bad ~, (a) so as to be seen well/badly: 在亮处(在暗处): The picture has been hung in a bad ~. 那幅画被挂在光线不好的地方。 (b) (fig) so as to make a good/bad impression: (喻)给人以良好(不好)的印象: Press reports always make him appear in a bad ~. 新闻报导总是使他给人不良的印象。 see the ~, (a) (liter or rhet) be born. (文学或修辞)降生。 (b) be made public. 被公开。 (c) realize the truth of sth that one has been obstinate about. 认清自己所固执的事情之真相。 (d) undergo religious conversion. 改信某一宗教。 be/stand in sb's ~, (a) obscure what he is looking at. 遮住某人的光线。 (b) (fig) hamper, hinder (sb's chances of success, progress). (喻)妨碍某人成功,进步等的机会。 **stand in one's own ~**, (a) so as to obscure one's work, etc. 遮住自己的光线; 背光。 (b) (fig) act against one's own interests. (喻)损害自己的利益; 使自己受损。 **'~ year**, (astron) unit of measurement for distances between stars; distance travelled by ~ in one year (about 6 million million miles). (天文)光年; 光一年所行的距离 (约为 6,000,000,000,000 英里)。 **2** [C] source of ~; sth that gives ~, eg a candle or lamp: 光源; 发光物(例如蜡烛或灯): 'traffic ~s; 交通灯; 红绿灯; navi'gation ~s. 航行灯。 L~s were burning in every room. 每个房间里都点着灯。 Turn/Switch the ~s on/off. 把灯打开(关掉)。 Put that ~ out! 把那灯熄掉! All the ~s went out—there was a power failure. 所有的灯都熄了——停电了。 L~s out, (bugle call signalling) the time when ~s are to be turned out. 熄灯时间; 熄灯号。 **northern/southern ~s**, ⇨ **aurora**. **3** [C] flame; spark; sth used for producing a spark or flame: 火焰; 火花; 引火物: Can you give me a ~, please? eg for a cigarette or pipe. 请借个火好吗? (例如用以抽香烟或烟斗)。 Note that fire is not used in this sense. 注意: fire 不可用作此义。 Strike a ~, make a ~ by striking a match. 擦火柴。 **4** [U] expression of brightness or liveliness in a person's face (esp in the eyes), suggesting happiness or other emotion: 表示快乐等的面部光彩(尤指眼睛发出者): The ~ died out of her eyes,

Her looks changed from happiness to sadness, from liveliness to lack of interest. 她眼中的光彩消失了(她的表情由快乐转为悲伤,由活泼转为冷淡)。 **the ~ of sb's countenance**, (biblical) his favour, approval. (圣经)恩惠; 赞许。 **5** [U] knowledge or information that helps understanding; [C] fact or discovery that explains. 见解; 见识; 帮助说明的事实或发现。 **come/bring sth to ~**, become/cause sth to be visible or known: 显露; 揭露: Much new evidence has come to ~/has been brought to ~ in recent years. 近年来许多新证据已纷纷出现。 **shed/throw ~ (a) new ~ on sth**, make sth clearer, provide new information: 帮助说明某事物: These facts shed (a) new ~ on the matter. 这些事实有助说明此事。 **by the ~ of nature**, without the help of revelation or teaching. 本能地; 自然而然地。 **in the ~ of**, with the help given by or gained from. 借助; 征诸; 按照; 根据。 **6** [C] aspect; way in which sth appears: 观点; 外貌: I cannot view your conduct in a favourable ~, cannot approve of it. 我不能赞成你的行为。 I have never looked upon the matter in that ~. 我从未就该观点看此事。 In the ~ of the new evidence, it was decided to take the manufacturers to court. 根据新的证据, 决定向法院控告那些制造商。 **7** (pl) (natural or acquired) abilities; mental powers. (复)(先天或后天的)能力; 智力。 **according to one's ~s**, to the best of one's abilities. 尽个人之所能。 **8** [C] famous person; person (to be) regarded as an example or model: 名人; 被视作模范的人: one of the leading/shining ~s of our age. 我们这个时代的领导(显赫)人物之一。 **9** [C] window or opening in a wall or roof for the admission of ~ (esp in a roof): 进光的窗户; (尤指)天窗: a 'sky~; 天窗; compartment of glass in the side or roof of a greenhouse or frame (used for ventilation). (温室侧墙或屋顶上所开之)通风玻璃窗。 **leaded ~**, small pane or panel of glass, secured in strips of lead, often coloured, forming part of a larger window. 铅框小玻璃窗(常是彩色的, 形成大窗户之一部分)。 ⇨ also **quarter~** at **quarter(16)**. **10** [C] (painting) part of a picture shown as lighted up: (绘画)图画的明亮部分: 'high ~s, the brightest parts; 最明亮的部分; ~ and shade. 明与暗。 **11** (compounds) (复合词) **'~-house** n tower or other tall structure containing beacon ~s for warning or guiding ships at sea. 灯塔。 **'~-ship** n ship moored or anchored and provided with beacon ~s for the same purpose as those in a ~house. 灯船; 信号船。

a lighthouse

light[4] /laɪt/ vt, vi (pt, pp **lit** /lɪt/; lɪt/ or **~ed**) (~ed is more usu as an attrib adj, as in a ~ed candle). (lighted 较常用做置于名词前的形容词, 例如: a lighted candle)。 **1** [VP6A] cause to begin burning or to give out ~: 点燃; 使发光: ~ a lamp/candle/cigarette; 点燃一灯(蜡烛, 香烟); ~ a fire, put a burning match to the material in a fireplace, etc. 点火。 **2** [VP6A] provide lights[3](2) in or for: 供以光源: Is your flat ~ed/lit by gas or by electricity? 你们的公寓用煤气灯还是电灯? Our streets are ~ed/lit by electricity. 我们的街道用电照明。 **3** [VP15B] ~ sth up, cause to become bright: 使明亮: The shops were brilliantly lit up. 那些商店灯光明亮。 The burning building lit up the

whole district. 那燃烧的建筑物照亮了整个的地区。**4** [VP2C] ~ *up,* **(a)** switch on (electric) ~s; turn on gas-lamps, etc: 开(电)灯; 点亮煤气灯等: *It's getting dark—time to ~ up.* 天渐渐黑了——该点灯了。Hence, 由此产生, ~*ing·'up time* n time at which, according to regulations, lamps in the roads and on vehicles must be lit. (法令规定之)街道和行车开灯时间。**(b)** (colloq) begin to smoke a pipe or cigarette: (口)开始抽烟斗或香烟: *He struck a match and lit up.* 他撩燃一根火柴, 点上烟斗(香烟)。**5** [VP2C, 15B] ~ *up (with),* (of a person's face or expression) (cause to) become bright: (指人的面孔或表情)使容光焕发; 春风满面: *Her face lit up with pleasure.* 她的脸上焕发着喜色。*A smile lit up her face.* 微笑使她容光焕发。**6** [VP15A] guide with or by a light: 以灯引导: ~ *a person on his way.* 用灯替某人引路。

light[5] /laɪt; laɪt/ *vi* (*pt, pp* **lit** /lɪt; lɪt/ or ~**ed**) [VP3A] ~ *on/upon,* come upon a find by chance: 偶遇; 偶然发现: ~ *upon a rare book in a secondhand bookshop.* 在一旧书店里偶然发现一珍本书。

lighten[1] /'laɪtn; 'laɪtn/ *vt, vi* [VP6A, 2A] make or become less heavy; reduce the weight of: 使轻; 变轻; 减轻: ~ *a ship's cargo;* 减轻船上的载货; ~ *a ship of her cargo;* 减轻一船的负载; ~ *taxes.* 减税轻收。*Her heart ~ed when she heard the news.* 她听到这消息心情轻松了。

lighten[2] /'laɪtn; 'laɪtn/ *vt, vi* **1** [VP6A] make light or bright: 使亮; 使光明: *A solitary candle ~ed the darkness of the cellar.* 一枝烛烛照耀着黑暗的地窖。**2** [VP2A] become light or bright: 变亮; 变光明: *The eastern sky ~ed.* 东方的天空亮了。**3** [VP2A] send out lightning: 闪电: *It's thundering and ~ing.* 雷电交作。

lighter[1] /'laɪtər; 'laɪtə/ *n* [C] **1** device for lighting cigarettes or cigars. 打火机。**2** (chiefly in compounds) person or thing that lights: (主要用于复合词)点火的人或物: 'lamp-~, man who went round the streets with a ladder to light gas-lamps. 点街灯者。

lighter[2] /'laɪtər; 'laɪtə/ *n* boat, usu flat-bottomed, used for loading and unloading ships not brought to a wharf, and for carrying goods in a harbour or river: 驳船; 平底船: *a tug with a string of ~s behind it.* 拖着一些驳船的拖船。□ *vt* remove (goods) in a ~. 以驳船运(货)。~·**age** /-ɪdʒ; -ɪdʒ/ *n* fees charged for carrying goods in a ~s. 驳船运货费。

light·ning /'laɪtnɪŋ; 'laɪtnɪŋ/ *n* [U] flash of bright light produced by natural electricity between clouds in the sky or clouds and the ground, with thunder: 闪电: *struck/killed by ~;* 为闪电所击(遭闪电击死); *like ~;* *with ~ speed,* very fast. 风驰电掣似。~ **bug,** (US) firefly. (美)萤火虫。'~·**rod**/-**conductor** *nn* metal rod fixed on the top of a high building, etc and connected with the earth, to prevent damage by ~. 避雷针。~ **strike** *n* strike, of workers, started without warning. 工人的突然罢工。

lightning

lights /laɪts; laɪts/ *n pl* lungs of sheep, pigs, bullocks, etc used as food. (羊、猪、阉牛等之)肺脏(用做食物)。

light·some /'laɪtsəm; 'laɪtsəm/ *adj* **1** graceful. 优雅的。**2** merry; light-hearted; frivolous. 快活的; 愉快的; 轻浮的。~·**ly** *adv* ~·**ness** *n*

lig·neous /'lɪgnɪəs; 'lɪgnɪəs/ *adj* (of plants) woody. (指植物)木质的; 木本的。⇨ **herbaceous.**

lig·nite /'lɪgnaɪt; 'lɪgnaɪt/ *n* [U] soft, brownish-

black coal. 褐煤。

lik·able, like·able /'laɪkəbl; 'laɪkəbl/ *adj* of a kind that is, or deserves to be, liked; pleasing: 可爱的; 悦人的; 讨人喜欢的: *a ~ man/tune.* 可爱的人(曲子)。

like[1] /laɪk; laɪk/ *adj* ⇨ **alike.** (used attrib and pred) similar; having the same or similar qualities, etc; having a resemblance: (可用作定语和表语)相似的; 同样的: *The two girls are very ~.* 这两个女孩子很相似。*L~* (ie similar) *causes produce* ~ (ie similar) *results.* 相似的原因产生相似的结果。*He writes well on this and ~ subjects.* 他对于这个和类似的题目写得很好。*They are as ~ as two peas.* 他们一模一样。*L~ father, ~ son; ~ master, ~ man,* (prov) As the one is, so the other will be. (谚)有其父必有其子; 有其主必有其仆。~·'**minded** /'maɪndɪd; 'maɪndɪd/ *adj* having the same tastes, aims, etc. 志趣相投的。□ *adv* **1** ~ *as,* (archaic) in the same manner as. (古)如同。**2** probably: 大概: (only in) (仅用于) ~ *enough; most/very ~; as ~ as not,* very probably (*likely* is more usu, ⇨ **likely(2)**). 大概: 很可能 (*likely* 较常用, 参看 *likely* 第 2 义)。□ *conj* **1** as (common use among those who have not been taught to avoid it; considered incorrect, but found in many good writers): (用作 as) 像; 如(为不知避免此种用法的人所常用, 此用法被认为不正确, 但许多好的作者也这样用): *She can't cook ~ her mother does.* 她烹饪的技术不如她的母亲。*Don't think you can learn grammatical rules ~ you learn the multiplication tables.* 不要以为你学习语法规则就像背乘法表一样。**2** (non-standard use) as if: (不标准的用法, 用作 as if) 仿佛: *It rained ~ the skies were falling.* 雨下得就象天要塌下来的样子。□ *n* **1** ~ person or thing; that which is equal or similar to sth else: 相似的人或事物; 与他物相等或相似之物: *That was acting, the ~ of which we shall not see again,* We shall not see acting equally good. 我们再也看不到那样的的演技了。*Music, painting and the ~,* and similar branches of the arts. 音乐、绘画等等。*I never heard the ~ (of it),* anything so strange, etc according to context. 我从未听说过这种事(这样奇怪的事等, 随上下文而定)。**2** *the ~s of,* (colloq) person(s), thing(s), similar to: (口)类似的人、物等: *the ~s of us/them.* 与我们(他们)类似的人。*Have you ever seen the ~s of this?* 你看到过和这个相同的吗? □ *prep* **1** (Often governing a *pron, n,* or *gerund;* originally ~ *to/unto,* this being now archaic or poet) such as; resembling: (常用于代词、名词或动名词之前; 最初 like 后接 to 或 unto 的用法, 现已作废或仅用于诗中)象; 如; 似: *What is he ~?* What sort of person is he—in looks, behaviour, etc, according to the situation? 他是个什么样的人? *He was wearing a hat rather ~ this one.* 他戴着一顶很象这一顶的帽子。*It looks ~ gold,* has the appearance of gold. 它看来象是金子。*This is nothing ~ as good,* not nearly so good. 这个差多了。*nothing ~,* nothing to equal; nothing to be compared with: 无物能及; 无物能与之相比: *There's nothing ~* (= nothing as good as) *leather.* 没有比皮革更好的了。*There's nothing ~ walking as a means of keeping fit.* 做为保持健康的方法, 再没有比散步更好的了。*something ~,* nearly; about: 几乎; 大约: 有点象: *The cost will be something ~ five pounds.* 费用约为五英镑。*This is something '~ a dinner!* This is a remarkably good or satisfactory dinner! 这才象是一顿盛餐! **2** '*feel ~,* be in a state or mood right or suitable for: 适于; 心情适合; 想要: *Do you feel ~ having a rest?* 你想休息吗? *She felt ~ crying.* 她想哭。*We'll go for a walk if you feel ~ it.* 如果你想散步, 我们就去吧。'*look ~,* look as if sb/it might be (used to show probability or likelihood): 好象; 似乎: *He looks ~ winning,* It seems likely that he will win. 他好象要胜了。*It looks ~ being a fine day,* Appearances suggest that the day will be fine. 天气好象不错。*It looks ~ rain.* 好象要下雨。**3** characteristic of: 表现出…之特点的: *That's just ~*

him! He has behaved, spoken, etc just as one would expect! 那正象他那个人！ *It's (just) ~ her to think of others before thinking of herself.* 先想到别人再想到自己，这正象她的为人。 **4** in the manner of; to the same degree as: 象；象……一样: *Don't talk ~ that,* in that way. 不要那样说话。 *If I were to behave ~ you ...,* in the way you behave .... 如果我的行为象你一样，…。 *If everyone worked ~ me, ...* 如果每一个人都象我一样的工作，…。 *It fits him ~ a glove,* closely, tightly. 它恰好适合于他。 *He drinks ~ a fish.* 他喝酒喝得很凶。 **5** (colloq, sl) (口, 俚) ~ **anything,** as hard, etc as can be expected or imagined: 极其努力等; 非常: *She works ~ anything when she's interested.* 她有兴趣时工作非常努力。 ~ **mad/crazy,** as if crazy: 象疯狂一般地; 猛烈地: *He complains ~ mad when things go wrong.* 事情不对劲的时候, 他猛烈地抱怨。 ~ **hell/blazes, (a)** furiously; energetically: 猛烈地; 奋力地: *He moans ~ hell when he loses a bet.* 他赌输了便猛烈地抱怨。 **(b)** (as an *int*) of course (not)!: (作为感叹词)当然不！: *'But you were there, weren't you?' 'I~ hell, I was!'* I certainly wasn't! '但是你在那里, 是不是？' '我当然没有在那里！'

like² /laɪk; laɪk/ *vt* **1** [VP6A, D, 7A] be fond of; have a taste for; find satisfactory or agreeable: 喜欢; 喜爱; 爱好; 中意: *Do you ~ fish?* 你喜欢鱼吗？ *I ~ to read in bed but I don't ~ having meals in bed.* 我喜欢躺在床上看书, 但我不喜欢在床上吃饭。 *She ~s him but she doesn't love him.* 她喜欢他但并不爱他。 *I ~ his impudence!* (ironic, meaning that his impudence is preposterous or amusing). (反语)他真不怕难为情! *Well, I ~ that!* (ironic, meaning that what has been said or done is surprising, unexpected, etc). (反语)哎呀, 你竟说得出口! 真出乎意料! **2** [VP6D, 7A] (in *neg* sentences) be unwilling or reluctant: (用于否定句)不愿意: *I didn't ~ to disturb you.* 我不愿打搅你。 *I don't ~ troubling her.* 我不愿麻烦她。 **3** [VP6A, 7A] (with *should, would*) used to indicate a wish: (与 should, would 连用)表示愿望: *I should ~ to go there,* if it were possible, if I were invited, etc. 我想去那里(如果可能、如我被邀请的话)。 *I shouldn't ~ to do that,* have no wish to do it. 我不愿意做那事。 *She would ~ a cup of tea, I think.* 我觉得她想喝一杯茶。 *I should ~ to know/to see ...,* often ironic, meaning that it would be difficult to explain, show, etc. (常作反语)我倒想了解一下(看一看)。 *They would want to come ....* 他们本来想来。 **4** [VP6A, 7A, 17, 19B, C,22] prefer; choose; wish: 比较喜欢; 宁择; 希望: *I ~ people to tell the truth.* 我喜欢人讲实话。 *How do you ~ your tea?* 你喜欢喝什么样的茶？ *I ~ (= prefer) it rather weak.* 我比较喜欢淡一点的。 *I ~ this more (or, colloq better) than that.* 我比较喜欢这个, 不太喜欢那个(口语中用 better 代替better)。 *You wouldn't ~ there to be another war, would you?* 你不会希望再有一次战争的, 对吗？ *I don't ~ you to smoke/you smoking/your smoking.* 我不喜欢你抽烟。 **if you ~,** used to express consent to a request or suggestion: 如果你高兴的话(用以表示同意一请求或建议): *I will come if you ~.* 你高兴我就来, 我愿意来。 **5** [VP6A] suit the health of: 适合……的健康: *I ~ lobster but it doesn't ~ me,* ie it gives me indigestion. 我喜欢吃龙虾, 但它不宜于我的健康(使我消化不良)。 □ *n* (*pl,* only in) (复, 仅用于) **~s and 'dis~s,** ⇨ **dislike.**

like·ly /'laɪklɪ; 'laɪklɪ/ *adj* (**-ier, -iest**) **1** that is expected: 可能发生的; 有希望的: *the ~ winner of the contest.* 很可能在比赛中获胜的人。 *Is he ~ to win?* 他有希望获胜吗？ **2** that seems reasonable, suitable, or right for a purpose: 似乎合理的; 好象适当的; 恰当的: *That's a ~ story/excuse* (often used ironically). 那似乎是合理的故事(借口)(常用作反语)。 *This looks a ~ field for mushrooms.* 这块地似乎适合于长蘑菇。 *What do you think is the likeliest/the most ~ time to find him at home?* 你认为什么时候最可能在他家里找到他？ *Which are the most ~ candidates,* those with the best chance

of success? 哪些是最有希望当选的人？ **3** ~ + to-inf: ~ *that ...,* to be expected: 很可能的: *He is not ~ to succeed.* 他大概不会成功。 *It's highly (= very) ~ that he will succeed.* 他成功的可能性很大。 *An incident ~ to lead to war is reported from X.* 某方面报导出一可能导致战争的事件。 *That is not ~ to happen.* 那事不大可能发生。 □ *adv* most/very ~, probably. 或许; 大概; 很可能。 *I shall very ~ be here again next month.* 我下个月很可能再来此地。 **as ~ as not,** with greater probability: 多半: *He will succeed as ~ as not.* 他多半会成功。 *He'll forget all about it as ~ as not.* 他多半会将此事忘记了。 □ **like·li·hood** /-hʊd; -hʊd/ *n* [U] probability: 可能性: *In all likelihood* (= Very probably), *we shall be away for a week.* 我们很可能离开一个星期。

liken /'laɪkən; 'laɪkən/ *vt* [VP14] ~ *sth to sth,* point out the likeness of one thing (to another): 指出一物与另一物的相似; 将…比喻作: ~ *the heart to a pump.* 将心脏比作唧筒。

like·ness /'laɪknɪs; 'laɪknɪs/ *n* **1** [U] resemblance; being like: 相似; 相象: *I can't see much ~ between the two boys.* 我看不出这两个男孩子有多少相似。 **in the ~ of,** in the form, shape or external appearance of. 状似; 貌似。 **2** [C] point of resemblance; instance of being like: 相似点; 相似的实例: *There's a family ~ in all of them.* 他们之间有一种家族的相似之处。 **3** [C] representation (in a portrait, picture, photograph, etc): 肖像; 画像; 像片: *The portrait is a good ~.* 这画像很像本人。

like·wise /'laɪkwaɪz; 'laɪk,waɪz/ *adv* in the same or a similar way: 同样地; 照样地: *Watch him and do ~.* 注意着看他并且照样做。 □ *conj* also; moreover. 亦; 而且。

lik·ing /'laɪkɪŋ; 'laɪkɪŋ/ *n* (**a**) ~, fondness. 爱好; 喜爱。 **have a ~ for,** be fond of. 喜欢。 **to one's ~,** as one likes it; satisfactory: 投某人之所好; 合某人之意: *Is everything to your ~?* 一切都合你的意吗？

li·lac /'laɪlək; 'laɪlək/ *n* **1** shrub with sweet-smelling pale purple or white blossom: 紫丁香: *an avenue of ~s,* ~ shrubs; 两旁种着紫丁香的道路; a *bunch of ~* (sing for the blossom). 一束紫丁香花(单数指花)。 **2** pale purple or pinkish-purple: 淡紫色; 淡紫红色: a ~ *dress.* 淡紫色衣服。

Lil·li·pu·tian /ˌlɪlɪ'pjuːʃn; ˌlɪlə'pjuʃən/ *n* native of Lilliput /'lɪlɪpʌt; 'lɪlə,pʌt/ (the country described in Swift's *Gulliver's Travels*). (斯威夫特所著格利佛游记中的)小人国的人, □ *adj* very small. 很小的。

lilt /lɪlt; lɪlt/ *n* [C] (lively song or tune with a) well-marked rhythm or swing. 明显的韵律或旋律; 节拍显明而又活泼的歌曲。 □ *vt, vi* go, sing with a ~: 活泼轻快地走动或唱出: *a ~ing waltz.* 活泼轻快的华尔兹。

lily /'lɪlɪ; 'lɪlɪ/ *n* (*pl* **-lies**) (kinds of) plant growing from a bulb, of many sizes, shapes and colours: 百合; 百合花: *~ of the 'valley;* 铃兰; *'water lilies;* 睡莲; *'Easter lilies;* 白百合; *'calla lilies.* 茨菇花; 白星海芋。 **~-livered** /'lɪlɪ lɪvəd; 'lɪlɪ'lɪvɚd/ *adj* cowardly. 怯懦的; 胆小的。 **~-'white** *adj* as white as a ~; pure white. 如百合般白的; 纯白的。

limb /lɪm; lɪm/ *n* **1** leg, arm or wing (the more usu words): 肢; 臂; 手足; 翼 (leg, arm 或 wing 较常用): *rest one's tired ~s,* 让疲倦的四肢休息; *be torn ~ from ~ by wolves;* 被狼撕肢解; *escape with life and ~,* without serious injury. 逃出而未受严重伤害。 **2** bough (of a tree). (树之)大枝。 **leave sb/be/go out on a ~,** (colloq) leave sb/be/put oneself in a vulnerable position, eg because separated from supporters. (口)(使)处于易受伤害或攻击的地位(例如因脱离拥护者而孤立)。 **3** (colloq) (口) ~ **of the devil/of Satan,** mischievous child. 恶作剧的小孩; 顽童。 **-limbed** /lɪmd; lɪmd/ *suff* (in compounds) (用于复合词) *long-/strong-'~ed,* having long/strong ~s. 四肢长(强健)的。

lim·ber /'lɪmbə(r); 'lɪmbɚ/ *adj* flexible, pliable. 柔软

的；易曲折的。 □ *vt, vi* [VP15B, 2C] ~ *(oneself) up*, make oneself (one's muscles) pliant, flexible. 使(自己或肌肉)柔软。

limbo /ˈlɪmbəʊ; ˈlɪmboʊ/ *n* (*pl* ~**s** /-bəʊz; -boz/) **1** [U] *in* ~, in a condition of being forgotten and unwanted: 被遗忘；被遗弃: (colloq) *The idea of forming a staff association is in* ~ (= has been put to one side) *until the new Manager is appointed.* 成立职员协会的计划被搁置了，要等到新的经理上任后才能再推出。 **2** [C] place for forgotten and unwanted things. 丢弃废物的地方。 **3** (usu 通常作 L~) region for souls of unbaptized infants and pre-Christian righteous persons. 未受洗礼的婴儿与基督诞生前的善人死后所去的地方。

lime¹ /laɪm; laɪm/ *n* [U] **1** white substance (calcium oxide, **CaO**) obtained by burning limestone, used in making cement and mortar. 石灰。 '**quick-~**, ~ before water is added. 生石灰(未加水的石灰)。 **,slaked** '~, ~ after being acted upon by water. 熟石灰(加水者)。 ⇨ **calcium**. '~**·kiln** *n* kiln in which ~stone is burnt. 石灰窑。 '~**·light** *n* [U] intense white light produced by heating ~ in a very hot flame, formerly used for lighting the stage in theatres. 石灰光(在极热的火焰中烧石灰棒所产生的强烈白光，昔时为舞台照明所用)。 *the* ~**light**, publicity: 受注目；出风头: *fond of the* ~*light.* 喜引人注目；爱出风头。 *in the* ~**light**, receiving publicity. 受注目；出风头。 '~**·stone** *n* [U] (kinds of) rock containing much ~, quarried for industrial use. 石灰石。 **2** [U] ('**bird-**)~, sticky substance made from holly bark for catching small birds. 粘鸟胶(冬青属灌木皮制成，用以捕捉小鸟)。 □ *vt* [VP6A] put ~ on (fields, etc) (to control acidity). 撒石灰于(田地等中)(以控制酸度)。

lime² /laɪm; laɪm/ *n* (also 亦作 '~**·tree**) tree with smooth heart-shaped leaves and sweet-smelling yellow blossoms. 菩提树。

lime³ /laɪm; laɪm/ *n* (tree with) round juicy fruit like, but more acid than, a lemon. 宜母子(一种似柠檬但较柠檬更酸的果物)；宜母子树。 '~**·juice** *n* juice of this fruit used for flavouring, as a drink, and medicinally. 宜母子汁(用作调味、饮料和医药用途)。

lim·er·ick /ˈlɪmərɪk; ˈlɪmərɪk/ *n* humorous or nonsense poem of five lines. 五行打油诗。

limey /ˈlaɪmɪ; ˈlaɪmɪ/ *n* (*pl* ~**s**) (US sl) British person. (美俚)英国人。

limit¹ /ˈlɪmɪt; ˈlɪmɪt/ *n* [C] line or point that may not or cannot be passed; greatest or smallest amount, degree, etc of what is possible: 界线；边界；界限；(最大或最小的)额；限度: *within the city* ~*s*, boundaries: 在该城界线内； *within a* ~ *of five miles* , *a five-mile* ~. 在五英里内。 *We must set a* ~ *to the expense of the trip*, fix a sum not to be exceeded. 我们必须对这次旅行的费用定一个限度。 *As we grow older we learn the* ~*s of our abilities*, learn what we can do and what we cannot do. 当我们的年龄渐长时，我们就会知道自己能力的限度。 *His greed knows no* ~. 他的贪心是无止境的。 *There is a* ~ *to my patience.* 我的耐心是有限度的。 *She reached the* ~ *of her patience.* 她已达到忍耐的极限。 *within* ~*s*, in moderation: 适度地；有限度地: *I'm willing to help you, within* ~*s.* 我愿意有限度地帮助你。 *without* ~, to any extent on degree: 无限地；无限制地: *If only the banks would lend money without* ~! 但愿银行能无限制地贷款！ *off* ~*s*, (US) (美) = out of bounds. ⇨ **bound¹**. *That's the* ~, (colloq) that is as much as (or more than) can be tolerated. (口)无法再忍耐了。 '**~age** = *n* age¹(1) given as a ~ for participation in an activity, etc. 年龄限制。

limit² /ˈlɪmɪt; ˈlɪmɪt/ *vt* [VP6A, 14] ~ *sb/sth (to sth)*, put a limit or limits to; be the limit of: 限制；限定: 作为…的界限: *We must* ~ *the expense to what we can afford.* 我们必须限制开销不超出我们经济能力的范围。 *I shall* ~ *myself to three aspects of the subject.* 我将限制自己就三方面讨论此问题。 '**~ed** *pp* small;

restricted; narrow: 少的；有限制的；有限的；狭小的: *~ed edition*, one ~ed to a specified number of copies. 发行有限的版本。 *Our accommodation is very* ~*ed.* 我们住宿的地方极为有限。 *He seems to have only a* ~*ed intelligence.* 他的智力似乎有限。 '**~ed 'lia·bility com·pany,**(abbr 略作 **Ltd**, placed after the name 置于名称之后) business company whose members are liable for its debts only to the extent of the capital sum they have provided. 股份有限公司。 '**~ed 'monarchy**, one that is restricted by the constitution. 君主立宪政体。 ⇨ **absolute(2)**. '**~·less** *adj* without ~: 界限的；无限制的: *the* ~*less ocean*; 茫茫大海； *a dictator whose ambitions were* ~*less.* 有无限野心的独裁者。

limi·ta·tion /ˌlɪmɪˈteɪʃn; ˌlɪməˈteʃən/ *n* **1** [U] limiting; condition of being limited. 限制；受限制。 **2** [C] condition, fact or circumstance that limits; disability or inability: 限制的条件、事实或环境；无能力；能力上的缺陷: *He knows his* ~*s*, knows well that in some respects his abilities are limited. 他知道他在能力上的缺陷(他的能力有限)。

limn /lɪm; lɪm/ *vt* (old use) paint (a picture); portray (in drawing or in words). (旧用法)绘(画)；(用图画或文字)描写。

limou·sine /ˈlɪməziːn; ˈlɪməˌzin/ *n* large, luxurious motor-car with an enclosed body, the front seats being separated by means of a partition (as in a London taxi). 大型豪华轿车(驾驶人座位被玻璃板隔开者，如伦敦之计程车)。 (Cf 参较 *saloon-car*, with no partition behind the driver. 驾驶人背后未用玻璃板隔开之大轿车。)

limp¹ /lɪmp; lɪmp/ *adj* not stiff or firm; lacking strength: 柔软的；软弱的；无力的: *The book is bound in* ~ *cloth*; 这本书是用软布装订的； *a* ~ *edition of a book.* 一书之软布面装订本。 *The flowers looked* ~ *in the heat.* 花在热天显得软弱无力。 '**~·ly** *adv* ~**·ness** *n*

limp² /lɪmp; lɪmp/ *vi* [VP2A, C] walk lamely or unevenly as when one leg or foot is hurt or stiff: 跛行；一瘸一瘸地走: *The wounded soldier* ~*ed off the battlefield.* 那负伤的兵士一瘸一瘸地离开了战场。 *The damaged ship* ~*ed* (= managed with difficulty to get) *back to port.* 那受损坏的船费力地驶回港口。 □ *n* (usu 通常作 **a** ~) lame walk: 跛行: *walk with/have a bad* ~. 跛得厉害。

lim·pet /ˈlɪmpɪt; ˈlɪmpɪt/ *n* small shellfish that fastens itself tightly to rocks, ⇨ the illus at **mollusc**; (fig) person who sticks tightly to an office, a position or another person. 蛾(一种紧贴在礁上的贝，参看 mollusc 之插图)；(喻)坚守职位者；紧缠他人者。 '**~ mine,** explosive mine (to be) placed in position against the hull of a ship, eg by frogmen. 蛾雷(蛙人等附置于敌舰舰体上的水雷)。

lim·pid /ˈlɪmpɪd; ˈlɪmpɪd/ *adj* (lit, fig, rhet) (of liquids, the atmosphere, the eyes) clear; transparent: (字面，喻，修辞)(指液体、大气、眼睛)清澈的；清澄的；明晰的；清晰的。 '**~·ly** *adv* ~**·ity** /lɪmˈpɪdətɪ; lɪmˈpɪdətɪ/ *n* [U] quality or state of being ~. 清澄；明晰；清晰。

linch·pin /ˈlɪntʃpɪn; ˈlɪntʃˌpɪn/ *n* iron pin passed through the end of an axle to keep the wheel in position; (fig) vital part; person who, because of his work, etc, keeps an organization, etc together. (轴端之)轮辖；制轮楔；(喻)重要部分；关键；枢纽人物。

Lin·coln green /ˌlɪŋkən ˈɡriːn; ˈlɪŋkən ˌɡrin/ *n* bright green cloth as made at Lincoln: 英国林肯城所产的鲜绿色的布: *Robin Hood and his men, dressed in* ~. 着鲜绿色服装的罗宾汉及其一伙人。

lin·den /ˈlɪndən; ˈlɪndən/ *n* (also 亦作 '~**·tree**) = **lime²**.

line¹ /laɪn; laɪn/ *n* **1** piece or length of thread, string rope or wire for various purposes: 线；索；绳: *'fishing* ~*s*; 钓鱼线； *'telephone* ~*s*. 电话线。 *Hang* (out) *the clothes on the* ~, (ie *the 'clothes-*~). 把这些衣服挂在晒

衣绳上。*L~ fishing is quite different from net-fishing.* 用线钓鱼和用网捕鱼完全不同。*He's clever with rod and ~,* is a good angler. 他很会钓鱼。*The ~s* (ie telephone, etc ~s) *are all down as a result of the blizzard.* 暴风雪将电线通通吹落了。*Give me a ~,* please, (to the operator of a telephone switchboard) Connect me to the Exchange, please (so that I can dial direct). (对接线生用语)请接中继线(以便直接拨号)。*L~ engaged!* (US 美 *L~ busy*) used of a telephone ~ already in use. (指电话线路)有人讲话! **crossed ~,** ⇨ **cross²(5).** 'hot ~, ⇨ **hot(8).** 'party/shared ~, telephone ~ serving two or more subscribers. 数家共用的电话线路。**2** long, narrow mark made on a surface: 线条;纹线: *L~s may be straight, crooked or curved.* 线条可能是直的, 扭曲的或弯曲的。*Draw a ~ from A to B.* 从 A 到 B 画一条线。*In mathematics a ~ is defined as having length but not breadth or thickness.* 数学上线的定义是有长度但无宽度或厚度。**3** [U] the use of ~s(2) in art, etc: 艺术等中线条之使用: *a '~drawing,* eg with a pen or pencil; 线条画(例如用钢笔或铅笔画); '~-engraving, done with ~s cut on a surface; 线雕(以线条刻于平面显示形象者); *the beauty of ~ in the work of Botticelli;* 包提柴里作品中线条的美; *translate life into ~ and colour,* represent living things by means of ~s and colour. 以线条和色彩表现生命。**4** (in games) mark made to limit a court or ground, or special parts of them: (竞技)运动场的界线; 场线: *Did the ball cross the ~?* 那球过线了吗? ⇨ **lineman. 5** mark like a ~ on the skin of the face; furrow or wrinkle; one of the marks on the palm of the hand: (面部等的皮肤上的)皱纹; 掌纹: *There were deep ~s on her face.* 她的脸上有很深的皱纹。**6** (pl) contour; outline: (复)轮廓; 外形: *a ship of fine ~s,* with a graceful outline; 外貌美观的船; *the delicate ~s of Gothic architecture;* 哥德式建筑之精致的外貌; (in shipbuilding) plans, esp of horizontal, vertical and oblique sections. (造船)船体线图。**7** row of persons or things: (人或物之)排; 列: *a ~ of trees/chairs/people waiting to go into a cinema;* 一排树(椅子, 等待进入电影院的人); *manufactured goods on the assembly ~;* 在装配线上的成品; *a long ~ of low hills.* 一长列小山。*be in (a) ~,* forming a ~: 成行; 排队: *The boys were standing in (a) ~.* 男孩子们排成队站着。*in ~ for,* next in order for: 下一个即轮到; *He's in ~ for promotion.* 他即将晋升。*on the ~,* (of objects exhibited, esp paintings) with the centre about level with the eyes of the viewer. (指展览的物件, 尤指图画)中心与参观者的眼睛平行的。**8** edge, boundary, that divides: 边界: *cross the ~ into Canada* (ie from US); (自美国)越过边界至加拿大; equator: 赤道: *cross the ~.* 越过赤道。*draw the ~ (at),* ⇨ **draw²(11). 9** railway; single track of railway ~s: 铁路; 铁轨: *the 'up/'down ~* to/from the chief terminus; 上(下)行铁路线; *the main ~;* 铁路干线; *a 'branch ~.* 铁路支线。*Cross the ~ by the bridge.* 自此(天)桥越过铁道。*reach the end of the ~,* (fig, eg of a relationship) reach the point where it breaks down, ends. (喻, 指关系等)破裂。**10** organized system of transport under one management and giving a regular service: 运输系统; 运输公司: *an 'air~;* 航空公司; *a new 'bus ~;* 一条新辟的公共汽车路线; *a 'steamship ~.* 轮船公司。**11** direction; course; track; way of behaviour, dealing with a situation, etc: 方向;路线; 行程; 行为的方式; 处理情况等的方法: *the ~ of march of an army;* 军队行军的路线; *communi'cation ~s.* 交通路线。*Don't stand in the ~ of fire! You'll get shot!* 不要站在发射方向! 你会被射到! *You should keep to your own ~,* be independent of others. 你应该单独行动。*choose/follow/take the ~ of least resistance,* the easiest way of doing things. 采取最简便的方法。*take a strong/firm ~ (over sth),* deal with a problem, etc resolutely: 断然处理一问题等: *Should the government take a stronger ~ over inflation?* 政府应以较坚决的态度处理通货膨胀的问题吗? *What ~*

do you intend to take, How will you approach the problem? 你准备如何处理此问题? *do sth along/on sound/correct, etc ~s,* use good, etc methods: 用良好或正确的方法处理事物: *He is studying the subject on sound ~s/on the wrong ~s.* 他正以正确的(错误的)方法研究此问题。*I shall proceed along/on these ~s until further notice.* 在未获进一步的通知前, 我将以如此方式进行。*(be) in/out of ~ (with),* in agreement/disagreement (with). 与…一致(不一致)。*bring sth into ~,* cause sth to conform. 使某事物一致; 使某事物符合。*come/fall into ~ (with),* accept views, conform, agree. 服从; 遵守; 同意。*toe the ~,* (fig) submit to discipline, accept the ideas, programme, etc of a (political, etc) party. (喻)服从纪律; 接受团体(政党等)的思想、计划等。*the party ~,* the agreed or established policy of a political party: 政党的路线; 党的政策: *follow the party ~,* vote, speak, write, etc in accordance with this policy. 遵守党的政策。**12** connected series of persons following one another in time, esp of the same ancestry: 一连串接续有关的人(尤指同世系者); 家系: *a long ~ of great kings;* 一长系列伟大的君主; *the last of his ~;* 他的家系中的最后一人; *trace back one's family ~,* one's ancestry: 追溯自己的家世; *a descendant of King David in the direct ~/in the male ~.* 大卫王的直系(男系)子孙。**13** row of words on a page of writing or in print: (文字的)一行: *page 5, ~ 10.* 第5页第10行。*'L~s to a friend on her birthday',* eg as the title of a poem. '友人华诞祝词'(例如作为一首诗的题目)。*drop sb a ~,* (colloq) write to sb: (口)给某人写信: *Drop me a ~ to say how you're getting on.* 来封信告诉我你的生活情形。*read between the ~s,* (fig) find more meaning than the words appear to express. (喻)领会言外之意。*'marriage ~s,* (GB colloq) certificate of marriage. (英口)结婚证书。*~s, (a)* words of an actor's part: (演员之)台词: *The leading actor was not sure of his ~s.* 那男主角记不清台词。*(b)* form of punishment by which a schoolchild is required to write out a specified number of ~s. 罚写(处罚小学生的一种方法)。**14** series of connected military defence posts, trenches, etc: (碉堡、战壕等连成的)防线: *go into the front ~(s),* the area nearest to the enemy's ~s; 至前线; *high-ranking officers well behind the ~s.* 离防线很远的高级军官。*all along the ~,* at every point; in every way. 在每一点上, 在每一方面。*go up the ~,* leave base for the front ~(s). 离开基地至前线。**15** (mil) row of tents, huts, etc in a camp: (军)营地中的一排帐篷、临时木造营房等: *inspect the ~s;* 视察营帐: *the 'horse ~s.* 马棚。**16** the ~, (GB army) regular infantry regiments (excluding the Guards and Rifles): (英军)战列步兵(禁卫军及步枪队除外的正规队)。*regiments of the ~;* 战列步兵团; *a ~ regiment;* 一团战列步兵; *infantry of the ~;* 战列步兵; (US army) regular fighting forces of all classes. (美军)战斗兵; 战列部队(包括各兵种)。**17** [U] (mil) double row (front and rear ranks) of men standing side by side (contrasted with *file* and *column*): (军)二列横队(与 file 和 column 相对): *The troops attacked in extended ~.* 那些军队以展开的二列横队攻击。*The men formed into ~.* 兵士们成二列横队。**18** (naval) ~ *abreast,* (number of parallel ships) abreast of each other. (海军)横阵; 舰队并列。~ *astern,* (number of ships) in a ~ one behind the other. 纵阵; 舰队队列。*ship of the ~;* ~-*of-battle ship,* (in former times) ship of 74 or more guns; largest type of warship. (昔时之)主力舰(配有七十四门以上的炮)。**19** department of activity; business; occupation: 活动的范围; 行业; 事业; 职业: *He's in the 'drapery ~.* 他从事绸布业。*His ~ is stockbroking/banking.* 他从事证券经纪(银行业)。*That's not much in my ~,* I don't know much about it, am not much interested in it. 那不是我的本行(我对此行业不大清楚, 没有什么兴趣)。**20** (trade use) class of commercial goods: (贸易用语)商品的一种: *a cheap ~ in felt hats;*

一种便宜的毡帽; *the best-selling ~ in woollen underwear.* 最畅销的一种羊毛内衣。**21** *Hard ~s!* Bad luck! 你真倒霉! 你的运气实在太坏了! **22** (sl) (俚) *shoot a ~,* brag, boast. 吹嘘; 吹牛。Hence, 由此产生, **'~-shooting, '~-shooter** *nn* **23** (colloq) (口) *give sb/ get/have a ~ on sth,* give etc information about it. 给予某人(获得,有关…)的消息。

line² /laɪn; laɪn/ *vt, vi* **1** [VP6A, 15B] mark (sth) with lines: 划线于: *~d paper,* with lines printed on it. 有横线格的纸。*~ in a contour,* on a blank map; 画地图区分线; *~ sth out on paper,* mark it out with ~s. 用线条在纸上标出某物。**2** [VP6A] cover with lines: 使起皱纹: *a ~d face;* 生皱纹的面孔; *a face ~d with anxiety.* 因忧虑而起皱纹的面孔。*Pain had ~d her forehead.* 痛苦使她的额上生了皱纹。**3** [VP2C, 15B] *~ up,* (cause to) be in a line, get into a line: 排成行列; 使成行: *The general ~d up his troops.* 将军整列他的队伍。*The soldiers quickly ~d up.* 士兵们迅速地排好了队。*~ up (for sth),* (US) queue (for it). (美) 排队(做某事)。**4** [VP6A] form, be placed, in a line or lines along: 沿着…形成行列: *a road ~d with trees;* 旁边有着一排排树的道路; *a road ~d with police.* 排列着警察的道路。*Crowds of people ~d the kerb to see the funeral procession.* 成群的人排列在人行道上去看那送葬的队伍。

line³ /laɪn; laɪn/ *vt* [VP6A, 14] *~ sth (with sth),* **1** provide with an inside covering; add a layer of (usu different) material to the inside of (bags, boxes, articles of clothing): 加以衬里; 衬里于(袋、箱、衣物): *fur~d gloves;* 毛皮里的手套; *an overcoat ~d with silk.* 衬有绸里的大衣。⇨ **lining. 2** (fig) fill (one's purse, pocket, stomach, etc): (喻)填装(钱袋、口袋、胃等): *He has ~d his purse well,* made a lot of money. 他赚了很多钱。

lin·eage /'lɪnɪɪdʒ; 'lɪnɪɪdʒ/ *n* [U] family line; ancestry; line of descent. 家系; 世系; 血统。

lin·eal /'lɪnɪəl; 'lɪnɪəl/ *adj* in the direct line of descent (from father to son, etc): 直系的; 嫡系的: *a descendant / heir.* 嫡系后裔(继承人)。**~·ly** /-ɪəlɪ; -ɪəlɪ/ *adv*

lin·ea·ment /'lɪnɪəmənt; 'lɪnɪəmənt/ *n* (formal) (usu *pl* except after *each* and *every*) line, detail, distinctive feature or characteristic (of the face): (正式用语)(除在 each 和 every 后,通常用复数)(面部之)轮廓; 外貌; 特征: *the ~s of a Mongol face.* 蒙古人面孔的特征。

lin·ear /'lɪnɪə(r); 'lɪnɪə/ *adj* **1** of or in lines: 线的; 线状的: *a ~ design.* 线构成的图案。**2** of length: 长的; 长度的: *~ measure,* eg feet and inches or metres. 长度(例如英尺、英寸或米)。⇨ **App 5.** 参看附录五。

line·man /'laɪnmən; 'laɪnmən/ *n* **1** man who puts up and maintains telegraph and telephone lines. 架设和保养电报线和电话线的工人; 线工。**2** (US) = **linesman.**

linen /'lɪnɪn; 'lɪnɪn/ *n* [U] cloth made of flax; articles made from this cloth, esp shirts and collars, bedsheets, tablecloths and table napkins: 亚麻布; 亚麻布制成之物(尤指衬衫、衣领、床单、桌布和餐巾): (attrib) (用作定语) *~ handkerchiefs.* 亚麻布制的手帕。**'~-draper** *n* person who sells ~ and cotton goods. 卖亚麻布及棉布制品的布商。*wash one's dirty ~ in public,* discuss family quarrels, unpleasant personal affairs, etc in the presence of other people. 宣扬家丑。

liner /'laɪnə(r); 'laɪnə/ *n* **1** ship or aircraft of a line(10) of ships or aircraft: (轮船公司的)邮轮; 班轮; (航空公司的)班机: *a fast 'air~;* 迅速的班机; *a trans-Atlantic ~.* 航行大西洋的班轮。⇨ the illus at **ship.** 参看 ship 之插图。**2** '~ (-train) (also 亦作 'freight ~), long distance express goods train between industrial centres and seaports, with facilities for fast (un)loading of goods. 长途货运快车(行驶于工业中心和海港间之快速货运火车,有快速装卸货物之设备)。

lines·man /'laɪnzmən; 'laɪnzmən/ *n* (sport) person who helps the umpire or referee by saying whether or where the ball touches or crosses one of the lines. (运动)(球赛中协助裁判认定球是否或在何处触线或出界之)巡边员; 司线员。

line-up /'laɪn ʌp; 'laɪn‚ʌp/ *n* **1** way in which persons, states, etc are arranged or allied; alignment: (人民、国家等联合的)阵容; 联盟: *a new ~ of Afro-Asian powers;* 亚非国家之新阵容; *a ~ of men in an identification parade.* 一列供指认人指认的人。**2** formation of players ready for action (in a game such as baseball or football). (棒球、足球等)在场运动员之排列; 配置。**3** programme of items (esp for radio or TV): 节目(尤指广播电台或电视台者): *This evening's ~ includes an interview with the Chairman of British Rail.* 今晚的节目包括访问英国铁路工会主席。

ling¹ /lɪŋ; lɪŋ/ *n* [U] (kinds of) heather. 石南。

ling² /lɪŋ; lɪŋ/ *n* long, slender N European seafish (usu salted) for food. 北欧产的一种长身鳕鱼(通常用盐腌后食用)。

lin·gam /'lɪŋgəm; 'lɪŋgəm/ *n* phallic emblem (as a symbol of the Hindu god Siva /'ʃiːvə; 'sivə/). 男性生殖器像(印度神 Siva 之象征)。

lin·ger /'lɪŋgə(r); 'lɪŋgə/ *vi* [VP2A, C] be late or slow in going away; stay at or near a place: 逗留; 徘徊: *~ on after everyone else has left;* 于他人皆离去后逗留; *~ about/around.* 徘徊。*The custom ~s on,* is still observed but is now weak. 该风俗历久犹存(但不若往昔的盛行)。**~·ing** *adj* long; protracted: 拖久的; 延长的: *a ~ing illness;* 缠绵的疾病; *a ~ing look,* one showing regret, unwillingness to leave or give up sth; 恋恋不舍的表情; *a few ~ing (remaining) doubts.* 几个萦绕于心的疑问。**~·ing·ly** *adv* **~er** *n* person who ~s. 逗留者; 徘徊者。

linge·rie /'læ̃ʒəri; US: ‚lɑːndʒə'reɪ; 'lænʒə,ri/ *n* [U] (F) (trade name for) women's underclothing. (法)(商品名)女内衣。

lingo /'lɪŋgəʊ; 'lɪŋgə/ *n* (*pl* **~es** /-gəʊz; -goz/) (hum or derog) language, esp one that one does not know; way of talking, vocabulary, of a special subject or class of people: (谐或贬)语言(尤指某人所不懂者); 专门术语; 某一等级的人所用的语汇: *the strange ~ used by experts in radio and television.* 广播和电视专家用的奇怪术语。

lin·gua franca /‚lɪŋgwə 'fræŋkə; 'lɪŋgwə'fræŋkə/ *n* language adopted for local communication over an area in which several languages are spoken, eg Swahili in E Africa. (使用数种语言的地区内所采用的)共同语言(语言如东非的斯瓦西里语)。

lin·gual /'lɪŋgwəl; 'lɪŋgwəl/ *adj* of the tongue, speech or languages, esp in compounds, 舌头的; 说话的; 语言的(尤用于复合词), as eg of **audio-'~,** (of methods, devices, etc) requiring one to listen and speak: 指方法器材等)听和说的: *audio-~ aids,* eg a tape-recorder. 听和说的教具(例如录音机), **,bi'~,** speaking two languages. 说两种语言的, **,multi-'~,** speaking many languages. 说多语言的。

lin·guist /'lɪŋgwɪst; 'lɪŋgwɪst/ *n* **1** person skilled in foreign languages: 精通数种外国语言者: *She's a good ~.* 她精通数国语文。*I'm no ~,* am poor at foreign languages. 我不精外国语。**2** one who makes a scientific study of language(s). 语言学家。

lin·guis·tic /lɪŋ'gwɪstɪk; lɪŋ'gwɪstɪk/ *adj* of (the scientific study of) languages: 语言的; 语言学的; 语言研究的: *the ~ study of literature,* centred on the language. 对文学作品之语文研究。**~s** *n pl* (with *sing v*) the science of language, eg of its structure, acquisition relationship to other forms of communication. (与单数动词连用)语言学。**ap‚plied '~s,** this study put to practical uses, esp in the teaching of languages. 应用语言学(尤指语言教学研究)。

lini·ment /'lɪnɪmənt; 'lɪnɪmənt/ *n* [C, U] (kind

of) liquid usu made with oil for rubbing on stiff or aching parts of the body. (一种)擦剂(通常为油质液体, 擦于身体的疼痛部位)。

lin·ing /'laɪnɪŋ; 'laɪnɪŋ/ *n* **1** [C] layer of material added to the inside of sth: 衬里; 里子: *an overcoat with a fur ~;* 毛皮里的大衣; *a jewel-box with a velvet ~.* 用天鹅绒做衬里的珠宝盒。*Every cloud has a silver ~.* (prov) There is sth good in every evil. (谚)祸中有福。 **2** [U] material used for this purpose. 衬料。

link¹ /lɪŋk; lɪŋk/ *n* **1** one ring or loop of a chain. 链环; 环。**2** (usu *pl*) one of a pair of fasteners for the sleeves of a shirt: (通常用复数)(衬衫的)臂袖链扣之一; 链扣: *'cuff-~s.* (衬衫袖口的)链扣。**3** person or thing that unites or connects two others: 连接的人或物; 连锁物: *a ~ in a chain of evidence;* 一串证据中之一环; *the ~ between the past and the future.* 过去与未来间的桥梁; 承先启后者。**missing ~,** that which is needed to complete a series; animal supposed to have existed, of a type between the apes and man. 缺少的一环; 被认为是曾存在过的一种介于猿与人之间的动物。'**~·man** /-mæn; -mən/ *n* (*pl* **-men**) person who provides the connecting ~ between two groups. 两团体间的连络人。**4** measure of length, one hundredth of a chain; 7.92 inches or about 20 centimetres. 令(长度名, 为 chain 的百分之一, 合 7.92 英寸或 20 厘米左右)。⇨ **App 5.** 参看附录五。□ *vt, vi* [VP6A, 15A, B, 2A, C] **(up),** join, be joined, with, or as with, a ~ or ~s: 连接; 接合: ~ *things together:* 将诸物连接起来; ~ *one's arm in/through another person's arm;* 挽着他人的臂; *two towns ~ed by a canal;* 由一运河连接的两个城镇; *~ing verbs,* eg *be.* 连系动词(例如 be)。*How do religion and philosophy ~ up?* 宗教与哲学如何连接? Hence, 由此产生, '**~-up** *n* act or result of ~ing. 连接; 接合。

link² /lɪŋk; lɪŋk/ *n* (hist) torch formerly used for lighting people along streets. (史)昔时街上行人用以照明的火把。'**~·boy,** '**~·man** /-mæn; -mən/ *nn* one formerly employed to carry ~s and guide people through badly lighted streets. 火把僮(昔时受雇持火把引导行人走过晦暗街道之男孩或男子)。

links /lɪŋks; lɪŋks/ *n* (with *pl v*) grassy land, esp sand-hills, near the sea. (用复数动词)近海岸的草地(尤指沙丘)。**2** (often **a ~,** with *sing v*) golf-course. (常作 a ~, 与单数动词连用)高尔夫球场。

lin·net /'lɪnɪt; 'lɪnɪt/ *n* small brown songbird, common in Europe. 红雀(常见于欧洲之一种小的褐色鸣禽)。

lino /'laɪnəʊ; 'laɪnoʊ/ *n* [U] (abbr for) linoleum. 为 linoleum 之略。'**~-cut** *n* [C] design cut in relief on a block of linoleum; print made from this. 油毡浮雕; 油毡浮雕版:油毡浮雕的印刷图样。

lin·oleum /lɪ'nəʊlɪəm; lɪ'noʊlɪəm/ *n* [U] strong floorcovering of canvas treated with powdered cork and oil. 油地毡(一种坚牢的地板布, 由帆布涂以软木屑及油制成)。

lino·type /'laɪnəʊtaɪp; 'laɪnoʊ,taɪp/ *n* (P) machine (with a keyboard like that of a typewriter) used for setting type, each line of type being cast in the form of a complete bar of metal. (商标)长条活字铸造机(有一似打字机般的键盘, 可将一行活字成条铸出)。

lin·seed /'lɪnsiːd; 'lɪn,sid/ *n* [U] seed of flax. 亚麻子。~ **oil** *n* [U] oil pressed from ~, used in making printing-ink, linoleum, etc. 亚麻子油(用以制造油墨, 油地毡等)。

lin·sey-wool·sey /ˌlɪnzɪ 'wʊlzɪ; 'lɪnzɪ'wʊlzɪ/ *n* [U] strong, coarse material made from inferior wool woven with cotton. 棉毛织品。

lint /lɪnt; lɪnt/ *n* [U] linen, with one side scraped so as to be fluffy, used for dressing wounds: 内伤用的亚麻布: (attrib) (用作定语) *a ~ bandage.* 亚麻布绷带。

lin·tel /'lɪntl; 'lɪntl/ *n* horizontal piece of wood or stone forming the top of the frame of a door or

window. 楣; (门窗上面的)过梁。⇨ the illus at **window.** 参看 window 之插图。

lion /'laɪən; 'laɪən/ *n* **1** large, strong, flesh-eating animal found in Africa and S Asia, called 'the King of Beasts' because of its fine appearance and courage. 狮。⇨ the illus at **cat.** 参看 cat 之插图。the '~'s **share,** the larger or largest part. 较大或最大部分。'**~-hearted** *adj* brave. 勇敢的。**2** person whose company is very much desired at social gatherings, eg a famous author or musician. 社交场合的宠儿; 名人(如著名的作家或音乐家)。'**~·hunter** *n* person who tries to get ~s as guests at dinner parties, etc. 巴结名人者。**~·ess** /-es; -ɪs/ *n* female ~. 母狮。⇨ the illus at **cat.** 参看 cat 之插图。'**~·ize** /-aɪz; -aɪz/ *vt* [VP6A] treat as a ~(2): 奉为社交场合的宠儿; 奉为名士: *The famous explorer was ~ized when he returned home.* 那著名的探险家返乡后被奉为社交场合的宠儿。

lip /lɪp; lɪp/ *n* **1** one or other of the fleshy edges of the opening of the mouth: 唇: *the lower/upper lip;* 下(上)唇; *a man with a cigar between his lips.* 口里衔着一枝雪茄的人。*She refused to open her lips,* wouldn't say anything. 她拒绝开口。⇨ the illus at **mouth.** 参看 mouth 之插图。*bite one's lip,* show vexation. 咬唇(表示烦恼)。*curl one's lip,* show scorn. 撇嘴(表示轻蔑)。*give/pay 'lip-service to sth,* make promises, express regret, admiration etc about it, not sincerely felt. 口惠而实不至。*hang on/upon sb's lips,* listen eagerly to every word he says. 急切地倾听某人说的每一个字。*keep a stiff upper lip,* show no emotion, sign of fear, anxiety, etc. 不显示激动, 恐惧, 忧虑等。*lick/smack one's lips,* show (anticipation of) enjoyment. 舐(咂)嘴唇(表示享受或垂涎)。'**lip-reading** *n* [U] method (taught to deaf people) of understanding speech from lip movements. 读唇法(教导耳聋者由嘴唇的动作了解说话的方法)。Hence, 由此产生, '**lip-read** *vt.* '**lip·stick** *n* [C, U] (stick of) cosmetic material for reddening the lips: 唇膏; 口红: *buy three lipsticks;* 买三支口红; *use too much lipstick.* 搽太多的口红。**2** edge of a hollow vessel or opening: 凹陷的器皿的边; 洞边: *the lip of a saucer/crater.* 碟(火山口)边。**3** [U] (sl) impudence: (俚)冒昧; 无礼: *None of your lip!* Don't be impudent! 不要冒失地说话! **-lipped,** in compounds: (在复合字中): 'thick-/'dry-'lipped, having thick/dry lips. 嘴唇厚(干)的。

liquefy /'lɪkwɪfaɪ; 'lɪkwə,faɪ/ *vt, vi* (*pt, pp* **-fied**) [VP6A, 2A] make or become liquid. 液化; 使液化。**lique·fac·tion** /ˌlɪkwɪ'fækʃn; ˌlɪkwɪ'fækʃən/ *n* [U] making or becoming liquid; being liquified. 液化。

li·ques·cent /lɪ'kwesnt; lɪ'kwɛsnt/ *adj* becoming, apt to become, liquid. 液化的; 易液化的。

li·queur /lɪ'kjʊə(r) US: -'kɜːr; lɪ'kɜ/ *n* strong usu sweet alcoholic drink for taking in small quantities: 味甜性烈的酒(适于少量饮用): ~ *brandy,* of special quality for drinking as a ~; 适于少量饮用的特种白兰地; ~ *glass,* very small for ~s. 小酒杯。

liquid /'lɪkwɪd; 'lɪkwɪd/ *n* **1** [C, U] substance like water or oil that flows freely and is neither a solid nor a gas: 液体: *Air is a fluid but not a ~; water is both a fluid and a ~.* 空气是流体不是液体, 水是流体也是液体。*You have added too much ~ to the mixture.* 这混合物中你加了过多的液体。**2** (phon) the consonants /r/ or /l/. (语音)流音(即 /r/ 或 /l/)。□ *adj* **1** in the form of a ~; not solid or gaseous: 液态的; 液体的: ~ *food,* soft, easily swallowed, suitable for sick people; 液体食物(适合病人的易吞咽的流质食物); ~ *mud,* so soft that it can be poured. 稀泥。~ *gas,* gas reduced to a ~ state by intense cold. 液态气体。**2** clear, bright and moist-looking: 清澈的; 明亮的; 水汪汪的: ~ *eyes,* bright and shining; 明亮的眼睛; *a ~ sky.* 清澈的天空。**3** (of sounds) clear; pure; not guttural: (指声音)清澈的; 纯正的; 流畅的: *the ~ notes of a blackbird.* 山鸟的清脆的鸣声。**4** not fixed; easily changed: 不定的;

易变的: ~ opinions. 不定的意见。 **5** (in finance) easily sold or changed into cash: (财务)易变卖的: ~ assets. 易变卖的资产; 流动资产。

liqui·date /'lɪkwɪdeɪt; 'lɪkwɪˌdet/ vt, vi **1** [VP6A] pay or settle (a debt). 偿付(债务)。 **2** [VP6A] bring (esp an unsuccessful business company) to an end by dividing up its property to pay debts; [VP2A] (of a company) go through this process. 清理(尤指商业失败的公司)债务以作结束; (指公司)清理; 清算; 结束。 **3** [VP6A] (colloq or newspaper style) get rid of, put an end to; kill: (口语或新闻用语)清除; 肃清; 杀掉: gangsters who ~ their rivals. 将对手杀掉的匪徒。 **liqui·da·tion** /ˌlɪkwɪ'deɪʃn; ˌlɪkwɪ'deʃən/ n [U] liquidating or being ~ed. 清偿; 清理债务以作结束; 清算; 清除。 **go into liquidation**, become bankrupt. 破产。 **liq·ui·da·tor** /-tə(r); -tɚ/ n official who ~s(2). 清理公司债务之官员; 破产管理人; 清盘人。

li·quid·ity /lɪ'kwɪdətɪ; lɪ'kwɪdətɪ/ n [U] state of being liquid(5); state of being able to raise funds easily by selling assets. 资产之易变卖; 资产流动性。

liquid·ize /'lɪkwɪdaɪz; 'lɪkwəˌdaɪz/ vt [VP6A] crush, eg fruit, vegetables, to a liquid pulp. 榨(水果, 蔬菜)成汁。 ~**r** n device (usu with an electric motor) for liquidizing fruit, etc. 果汁机(通常为电动)。

liquor /'lɪkə(r); 'lɪkɚ/ n [C, U] **1** (GB) any alcoholic drink: (英)酒; 酒类: under the influence of ~, partly drunk; 有些醉; the worse for ~, drunk; 喝醉; malt ~, beer; 麦酒; brandy and other spirituous ~s. 白兰地和其他烈酒。 **2** (US) any distilled alcoholic drink: (美)蒸馏法制造的酒类: ~ store. 酒店。 **3** liquid produced by boiling or fermenting a food substance. 煮出的汁; 发酵而成的汁液。

liquor·ice (US = **licor·ice**) /'lɪkərɪs; 'lɪkərɪs/ n [U] (plant from whose root is obtained a) black substance used in medicine and in sweets. 甘草。

lira /'lɪərə; 'lɪrə/ n (pl **lire** /'lɪəreɪ, 'lɪərə; 'lɪrə/ or ~**s**) unit of money in Italy. 里拉(意大利货币单位)。

lisle /laɪl; laɪl/ n [U] fine, hard-twisted cotton fabric, used for stockings, gloves, etc. 一种光滑坚韧的棉线(用以制袜, 手套等)。

lisp /lɪsp; lɪsp/ vi, vt [VP2A, 6A, 15B] fail to use the sounds /s/ and /z/ correctly, eg by saying /θɪk-'θɪn; θɪk'θɪn/ for sixteen; say in a ~ing manner: 发不正确 /s/ 和 /z/ 的音(例如将 sixteen 读作 /θɪk-'θɪn; θɪk'θɪn/); 口齿不清地说话: She ~s. 她发不清楚 /s/ 和 /z/ 的音。The ~ed (out) his words. 他口齿不清地说出他的话。 □ n lisping way of speaking: 口齿不清: The child has a bad ~. 这孩子的口齿十分不清。 ~**ing·ly** adv

lis·som, lis·some /'lɪsəm; 'lɪsəm/ adj lithe; quick and graceful in movement. 柔软的; 轻快而优雅的。 ~**ness** n

list[1] /lɪst; lɪst/ n number of names (of persons, items, things, etc) written or printed: 名单; 目录; 一览表; 名册: a 'shopping ~; 购物单; make a ~ of things one must do; 将必须做的事情列一表; put sb's name on/take his name off the list. 将某人的姓名列入名单(自名单中除掉)。 ~ **price**, (comm) published or advertised price. (商)价目表所列之价格; 标价。 **the active** ~, ~ of officers in the armed forces who may be called upon for service. 现役军官名册。 **the free** ~, **(a)** those goods admitted into a country free of duty. 海关免税品目录。 **(b)** those persons who are admitted to a cinema, theatre, concert hall, etc without payment. 免费入场观众名单。 □ vt [VP6A] make a ~ of; put on a ~: 造表; 造册; 编目录; 列于表上: ~ all one's engagements; 将自己的约会列一表; ~ sb's name. 将某人的姓名列于表上。

list[2] /lɪst; lɪst/ vi [VP2A, C] (esp of a ship) lean over to one side, eg because the cargo has shifted: (尤指船)横倾侧(例如因货物之移动引起者): The ship ~s to starboard. 这船向右舷倾侧。 □ n ~ing of a ship: 船

之倾侧: a bad ~ to port. 向左舷倾侧得厉害。

list[3] /lɪst; lɪst/ vt, vi (old use) listen (to). (旧用法)倾听(与……连用)。

list[4] /lɪst; lɪst/ vi (old use) please; choose: (旧用法)高兴; 愿意: 'The wind bloweth where it ~eth.' '风任意地吹。'

lis·ten /'lɪsn; 'lɪsn/ vi [VP2A, C, 3A] **1** try to hear; pay attention: 倾听; 留心听: We ~ed but heard nothing. 我们留心听, 但没有听见什么。The boys heard their father's voice but were not ~ing to what he was saying. 男孩们听见了他们父亲的声音, 但并没有留心听他说话的话。Please ~ carefully for the telephone while I'm upstairs. 我在楼上时请你注意听电话。 ~ **in (to)**, **(a)** listen to a broadcast programme: 听广播节目: Did you ~ in to the Prime Minister yesterday evening? 你昨晚收听首相的广播没有? **(b)** ~ in to a conversation, eg by tapping telephone lines or using an extension telephone receiver. 用搭线或分机听他人在电话中的谈话。 **2** agree to a suggestion, request, etc: 同意一建议, 请求等: Don't ~ to him; he wants to get you into trouble. 不要听他的话, 他想使你陷入困境。 ~**er** n one who ~s. 倾听者。

list·less /'lɪstlɪs; 'lɪstlɪs/ adj too tired to show interest or do anything. 倦怠的; 无精打采的。 ~**·ly** adv ~**ness** n

lists /lɪsts; lɪsts/ n pl (hist) (palisades enclosing an) area of ground for fights between men on horseback wearing armour and using lances. (史)比武场。 **enter the ~ (against sb)**, (fig) challenge (sb) or accept a challenge (from sb) to a contest. (喻)向人挑战; 接受挑战。

lit /lɪt; lɪt/ pt, pp of **light**[4]. **lit up**, (sl) drunk. (俚)喝醉。

lit·any /'lɪtənɪ; 'lɪtnɪ/ n (pl -**nies**) form of prayer for use in church services, recited by a priest with responses from the congregation. 连祷; 启应式祈祷。 **the L ~**, that in the Book of Common Prayer of the Church of England. (英国国教公祷书中之)连祷文; 启应祷文。

lit·chi /'laɪtʃiː; 'lɪtʃɪ/ n = **lychee**.

liter /'liːtə(r); 'litɚ/ ⟹ **litre**.

lit·er·acy /'lɪtərəsɪ; 'lɪtərəsɪ/ n [U] ability to read and write. 会读书和写字。

lit·eral /'lɪtərəl; 'lɪtərəl/ adj **1** connected with, expressed in, letters of an alphabet: 与字母有关的; 用字母表达的: a ~ error, a misprint. 字母上的错误(印刷错误)。 **2** corresponding exactly to the original: 完全按照原文的: a ~ transcript/copy of an old manuscript; 一旧稿的精确的誊本; a ~ translation. 直译。(Cf 参较 free translation.) **3** (contrasted with figurative) taking words in their usual and obvious sense, without allegory or metaphor: (与 figurative 相对)按照字义的; 不是讽喻或比喻的: I hear nothing in the ~ sense of the word, (ie of the word 'hear') get no news by hearing people speak (though I may get news from letters, etc). 我并未'听'到什么(不过我也许自书信等中知道的)。 **4** (of a person) prosaic; matter of fact; lacking in imagination: (指人)平凡的; 求实际的; 缺乏想象力的: He has a rather ~ mind. 他的头脑没有什么想象力。 □ n ~ error; misprint. 字母上的错误; 印刷错误。 ~**ly** /'lɪtərəlɪ; 'lɪtərəlɪ/ adv **1** word for word; strictly: 逐字地; 严格地: translate ~ly; 直译; 逐字翻译; carry out orders too ~ly. 过份严格执行命令。 **2** (informal use, to intensify meaning) without exaggeration: (非正式用法, 以加强含义)不夸张地; 简直: The children were ~ly starving. 孩子们简直是在挨饿。

lit·er·ary US: /'lɪtərerɪ; 'lɪtəˌrɛrɪ/ adj of literature or authors: 文学的; 作家的: the ~ profession; 著作业; a ~ man, either an author or a man interested in literature; 作家; 文人; 对文学有兴趣的人; ~ style, as used in literature contrasted with colloquial, etc. 文体; 文言(以别于白话等); ~ **property**, the right of

an author to fees, royalties, etc coming from his writings. (作者的)版权。

lit·er·ate /ˈlɪtərət; ˈlɪtərɪt/ *adj* **1** able to read and write. 会读书和写字的。 **2** cultured; well-read: 文雅的; 博学的: *He's a remarkably ~ young man.* 他是个十分博学的青年。 □ *n ~* person. 会读书和写字的人。

lit·er·ati /ˌlɪtəˈrɑːtiː; ˌlɪtəˈreɪtaɪ/ *n pl* the literary intelligentsia. 文学界; 文人。

lit·era·ture /ˈlɪtrətʃə(r) *US:* -tʃʊər; ˈlɪtərətʃər/ *n* **1** [U] **1** (the writing or the study of) books, etc valued as works of art (drama, fiction, essays, poetry, biography, contrasted with technical books and journalism). 文学; 文学作品(之写作或研究)。 **2** (also with *indef art*) all the writings of a country (*French ~*) or a period (*18th century English ~*); books dealing with a special subject: 亦与不定冠词连用)一国之文学(如法国文学); 一时代之文学(如十八世纪英国文学); 关于某一专门科目的文献: *travel ~;* 旅行文献; *the ~ of poultry-farming.* 家禽饲养学的文献。 *There is now an extensive ~ dealing with the First World War.* 现在有大量关于第一次世界大战的文献。 **3** printed material describing or advertising sth, eg pamphlets: 说明或广告性质的印刷品(例如小册子): *We shall be glad to send you some ~ about our refrigerators/package holidays.* 我们愿意寄给你一些关于我们的冰箱(假日旅行)的说明。

lithe /laɪð; laɪð/ *adj* (of a person, a body) bending twisting or turning easily: (指人, 身体)易弯曲的; 柔软的: *~ movements;* 柔软的动作; *make one's muscles ~.* 使肌肉柔软。

lith·ogra·phy /lɪˈθɒɡrəfɪ; lɪˈθɑɡrəfɪ/ *n* [U] process of printing from parts of a flat stone or sheet of zinc or aluminium that are prepared to receive a greasy ink. 平版印刷术; 石版印刷术; 金属版印刷术。 **litho·graph** /ˈlɪθəɡrɑːf *US:* -ɡræf; ˈlɪθəˌɡræf/ *n* sth (esp a picture) printed by this process. 平版印刷物; (尤指)石版画。 □ *vt, vi* print by this process. 平版印刷; 石版印刷。 **litho·graphic** /ˌlɪθəˈɡræfɪk; ˌlɪθəˈɡræfɪk/ *adj* of ~. 平版印刷术的; 石版印刷术的。

liti·gant /ˈlɪtɪɡənt; ˈlɪtəɡənt/ *n* person engaged in a lawsuit. 诉讼当事人。

liti·gate /ˈlɪtɪɡeɪt; ˈlɪtəˌɡet/ *vi, vt* **1** [VP2A] go to law; make a claim at a court of law. 诉讼; 打官司。 **2** [VP6A] contest (sth) at a court of law. 在法庭上争论(某事物); 讼争。 **liti·ga·tion** /ˌlɪtɪˈɡeɪʃn; ˌlɪtəˈɡeʃən/ *n* [U] litigating; going to law. 诉讼; 打官司; 讼争。 **lit·igious** /lɪˈtɪdʒəs; lɪˈtɪdʒəs/ *adj* **1** fond of going to law. 好诉讼的; 爱打官司的。 **2** that can be disputed at law. 可诉讼的。

lit·mus /ˈlɪtməs; ˈlɪtməs/ *n* blue colouring-matter that is turned red by acid and can then be restored to blue by alkali. 石蕊(一种蓝色素, 遇酸变红, 再遇碱恢复蓝色)。 *~-paper,* paper stained with ~ and used as a test for acids and alkalis. 石蕊试纸(试验酸和碱者)。

li·totes /ˈlaɪtəʊtiːz; ˈlaɪtəˌtiz/ *n* understatement used ironically, esp using a negative to express the contrary, as 'I shan't be sorry when it's over' meaning 'I shall be very glad', or 'It was no easy matter' for 'It was very difficult'. 意重语轻的反语法(例如用 '此事结束后我不会难过' 代替 '我将很高兴' 或 '此事不容易' 代替 '此事很困难')。

litre (US = **liter**) /ˈliːtə(r); ˈlɪtə/ *n* unit of capacity in the metric system. 1 ~ = about 1¾ pints. 升; 公升(约合1¾ 品脱)。 **⇨ App 5.** 参看附录五。

lit·ter¹ /ˈlɪtə(r); ˈlɪtə/ *n* **1** (hist) couch or bed (often with a covering and curtains) in which a person may be carried about, eg on men's shoulders, and as used in ancient Rome. (史)轿(如古罗马所用者)。 **2** sort of stretcher for carrying a sick or wounded person. 担架; 舁床。

lit·ter² /ˈlɪtə(r); ˈlɪtə/ *n* **1** [U] odds and ends, bits of paper, discarded wrappings, bottles, etc left lying about in a room or public place: (在室内或公共场所乱

丢的)杂物; 垃圾(如纸屑, 不要的包装纸, 空瓶等): *Pick up your ~ after a picnic.* 野餐后将丢在地上的杂物收拾好。 *'~-bin/~-basket n* bin, basket, into which to place ~. 垃圾箱; 垃圾筒。 *'~-lout n* (colloq) person who leaves ~ about in public places. (口)在公共场所乱丢杂物者。 **2 a ~,** state of untidiness that results when things are left lying about instead of being put away: 杂乱; 零乱: *Her room was in such a ~ that she was ashamed to ask me in.* 她的房间十分零乱, 故而不好意思请我进去。 **3** [U] straw and dung of a farmyard; straw and similar material, eg dry bracken, used as bedding for animals or for protecting plants from frost. 农家院中的稻草和粪; 厩肥; 铺给兽类睡眠或遮盖植物以防霜的草荐。 **4** [C] all the newly born young ones of an animal: 哺乳类动物的小兽; 一窝: *a ~ of puppies;* 一窝小狗; *ten little pigs at a ~.* 一窝十只小猪。 □ *vt, vi* **1** [VP6A, 15A, B, 14] *~ sth (up) with sth,* make untidy with odds and ends; scatter ~(1): 使杂乱; 使零乱; 乱丢杂物: *~ a desk with papers;* 将桌上零乱地堆满了文件(或纸张); *~ up one's room.* 把自己房间弄得乱七八糟。 **2** [VP6A, 15B] *~ sth (down),* supply (a horse, etc) with straw; make a bed for an animal: 给(马等)以草荐; 为兽作窝: *~ down a horse/a stable.* 铺草给马(铺草于马厩)。 **3** [VP2A] (of animals, esp dogs and pigs) bring forth a ~ of young ones. (指动物, 尤指狗和猪)产一窝小狗或小猪。

little /ˈlɪtl; ˈlɪtl/ *adj* (In senses 1, 2 and 4 ~ has no real *comp* and *superl*; ~r and ~st are occasionally used but are better avoided; ⇨ **less** and **least** for senses 3 and 5.) (用于第 1, 2, 4 义, little 无真正的比较级和最高级; littler 和 littlest 虽偶尔可用, 但最好避免用; 第3,5 两义请参看 less 和 least。) **1** small, or small in comparison: 小的: (as a distinctive epithet) (作区别性的形容词) *the ~ finger/toe.* 小指(趾)。 **2** (often preceded by another *adj* with no connotation of smallness, to indicate affection, tenderness, regard, admiration, or the contrary, depending upon the preceding *adj*): (其前常与未有'小'之含义的形容词连用, 表示感情, 亲切, 关心, 羡慕或相反之义, 视其前之形容词而定): *Isn't he a ~ devil!* (indicating affectionate regard). 你看他是不是个小淘气! (表示感情上的关切)。 *What a pretty ~ house!* 多么漂亮的小房子啊! *That poor ~ girl!* (indicating sympathy). 那个可怜的小女孩! (表示同情)。 *What horrid ~ children!* 多么讨厌的小鬼! *She's a nice ~ thing* (indicating tenderness or regard, but possibly patronage, or a feeling of superiority). 她是个可爱的小东西(含有亲切或爱护之意, 但亦可能表示屈尊或一种优越感)。 *Such a dear ~ man* (suggesting benign patronage) *came round and fixed my central heating.* 这样一个可爱的人(表示善意的屈尊)到这里来装修我的暖气系统设备。 *He's quite the ~ gentleman!* (suggesting patronage). 他可以说是个相当温雅的人! (表示屈尊)。 *the '~ people/folk,* (esp in Ireland) fairies; elves. (尤用于爱尔兰)小仙; 小神。 **3** short (in time, distance, stature): (指时间, 距离, 身材)短的; 矮的: *Won't you stay a ~ time with me?* 你不愿意陪我一会儿吗? *Come a ~ way with me.* 陪我走一小段路。 **4** young: 年轻的: *How are the ~ ones,* the children? 孩子们都好吗? *Here come the ~ Smiths,* the Smith children. 史密斯家的孩子们来了。 **5** not much: 很少的: *He gained ~ advantage from the scheme.* 他从这计划中没有获得什么利益。 *I have very ~ time for reading.* 我很少有时间读书。 *He knows ~ Latin and less Greek.* 他对拉丁文懂得很少, 对希腊文懂得更少。 **6 a ~,** some but not much; a small quantity of: 少许的; 少量的: *He knows a ~ French.* 他懂一点法文。 *A ~ care would have prevented the accident.* 稍微注意一点此一意外就不会发生了。 *Will you have a ~ cake,* a piece or slice of cake? 你要吃一点糕吗? (Cf 参较 *Will you have a cake,* one of these cakes? 你要吃一块糕吗?) *not a ~,* (euphem) much: (委婉语)很多: *It has caused me not a ~ anxiety,* considerable anxiety. 此事曾使我相当焦虑。

□ *adv* **1** not much; hardly at all; only slightly: 很少; 几乎一点也不; 些微地: *He is ~ known.* 很少有人知道他。 *She slept very ~ last night.* 她昨夜没有睡什么觉。 *I see him very ~* (ie rarely) *nowadays.* 近来我很少看见他。 *He left ~ more than an hour ago.* 他不过是一小时前离开的。 *That is ~ short of* (= is almost) *madness!* 那几乎近于疯狂！ *He is ~ better than* (= is almost as bad as) *a thief.* 他和一个小偷没有什么差别。 **a ~,** (used *adverbially* meaning) (做副词用，意为) rather; somewhat: 有几分；稍微: *She seemed to be a ~ afraid.* 她好象有点害怕。 *This hat is a ~ too large for me.* 这帽子对我有点嫌大了。 *He was not a ~ annoyed,* was considerably annoyed. 他相当苦恼。 **2** (with such *vv* as *know, think, imagine, guess, suspect, realize,* and always placed before the v) (用于 *know, think, imagine, guess, suspect, realize* 等动词时) not at all: 毫不: *They ~ suspect/L~ do they suspect that their plot has been discovered.* 他们丝毫没有想到他们的阴谋已被人发现了。 *He ~ knows/L~ does he know that the police are about to arrest him.* 他一点也不知道警察就要逮捕他了。 **~·ness** *n* [U] the quality of being ~. 小; 少。 □ *n* (⊙ **less, least**). **1** not much; only a small amount: 少许；少量: *You have done very ~ for us,* have not helped us much. 你没有帮我们多少忙。 *I see very ~ of him,* do not see him often or for long. 我很少看见他。 *The ~ of his work that I have seen seems excellent.* 我所看到的他仅有的那一点工作似乎做得非常好。 *I got ~ out of it,* not much advantage or profit. 我从这当中没有得到什么好处。 *He did what ~ he could.* 他已尽到他仅有的一点力量了。 *Every ~ helps.* 任何小东西都有用。 **~ by ~,** gradually; by degrees. 逐渐; 渐渐地。 **~ or nothing,** hardly anything. 几乎没有东西。 **in ~,** on a small scale. 小规模的(地)。 **2 a ~,** a small quantity; something (*a ~* is positive; *~* is negative): 少许，一点 (*a little* 是肯定的，*little* 含否定之义): *He knows a ~ of everything.* 他什么都懂得一点。 *A ~ makes some people laugh.* 只懂一点皮毛会招致某些人的讥笑。 *Please give me a ~.* 请给我一点。 **after/for a ~,** after/for a short time or distance. 经过一段短时间或距离。

lit·toral /ˈlɪtərəl; ˈlɪtərəl/ *n, adj* (part of a country which is) along the coast. 沿海地的; 沿海地区。

lit·urgy /ˈlɪtədʒɪ; ˈlɪtədʒɪ/ *n* (*pl* **-gies**) [C, U] fixed form of public worship used in a church. 礼拜仪式。 **li·turgi·cal** /lɪˈtɜːdʒɪkl; lɪˈtɜdʒɪkl/ *adj*

liv·able, live·able /ˈlɪvəbl; ˈlɪvəbl/ *adj* (of life) tolerable. (指生活)过得去的。 **~ (in),** (of a house, room, climate, etc) fit to live in. (指房屋，房间，气候等)适于居住的。 **~ (with),** (of persons) easy to live with. (指人)易共同生活的；易处的。

live[1] /laɪv; laɪv/ *adj* (rarely pred; ⊙ **living** and **alive** for pred uses). (罕用作表语；参看 *living* 和 *alive* 在表语中的用法)。 **1** having life: 有生命的；活的: *~ fish;* 活鱼; (joc) actual, not pretended: (谑)真正的；不是假装的: *There's a real ~ burglar under my bed!* 我床底下有一个真正的窃贼！ **2** burning or glowing: 燃烧的；炽热的: *~ coals/embers;* 燃烧着的煤(余烬); unexploded: 未爆炸的: *a ~ shell/cartridge/bomb;* 未爆炸的炮弹(子弹,炸弹); 实弹; not used: 未用过的: *a ~ match;* 未用过的火柴; charged with electricity: 充电的: *a ~ rail,* carrying current for trains. 带电的铁轨。 *a ~ wire,* (fig) a lively energetic person. (喻)精力充沛有生气的人。 **3** (of broadcast) not recorded in advance (on tape or records): (指广播内容)非预先录音的; 现场播出的: *It was a ~ broadcast, not a recording.* 那是现场广播，不是录音广播。 **4 '~-birth** *n* (contrasted with *still-birth*) baby born alive: 生下后活着的婴儿; 活着生下来的婴儿(与 *still-birth* 相对): *the ratio of ~-births to still-births.* 活产与死产之比率。 **5** full of energy, activity, interest, importance, etc: 充满精力，活动力，兴趣，重要性等的: *a ~ question/issue,* one in which there is great interest. 最为人关心的问

题。 □ *adv* (from **3** above): 现场播出地: *The concert will be broadcast ~.* 那音乐会将现场播出。

live[2] /lɪv; lɪv/ *vi, vt* **1** [VP2A] have existence as a plant or animal; be alive (the more usu phrase: 比较常用语: *He's still alive* is preferable to *He still ~s*). 生存; 活着 (be alive 较 live 常用，例如: *He's still alive* 较 *He still lives* 常用)。 **2** [VP2A, B, C, 4A] continue to be alive; remain alive: 继续活着; 继续生存: *~ to be old/ to a great age;* 活到老(高龄); *~ to see all one's grandchildren married.* 活到看到自己的孙儿辈结婚。 *She's very ill—the doctors don't think she will ~.* 她病得很重，医生们认为她难能活了。 *Can he ~ through the night?* 他能活得过今夜吗? **~ on,** continue to ~: 继续活着: *The old people died but the young people ~d on in the village.* 村子里的老年人死了，但年轻人还继续活着。 **~ through,** experience and survive: 经历…而未死: *He has ~d through two wars and three revolutions.* 他亲历两次战争和三次革命。 *You/We ~ and learn,* phrase used when one hears sth new, esp sth surprising. 活到老学到老。 **~ and 'let ~,** be tolerant; ignore the failings of others in order that one's failings may be ignored. 待人要容忍; 待人宽容如待己。 **3** [VP3A] **~ by doing sth,** earn one's livelihood by doing it. 以…为生。 **~ by one's wits,** get money by ingenious and irregular methods, not necessarily honest. 靠小聪明过日子(以机敏和不合常规的方法，但不一定是诚实的方法赚钱度日)。 **~ off the land,** use its agricultural products for one's food needs. 以农产品为食。 **~ on sth,** have it as food or diet: 以…为食: *~ on fruit/a milk diet:* 以水果(规定的乳类饮食)为食; depend upon for support, etc: 靠…过活: *~ on one's salary/on £3000 a year/on one's wife's income.* 靠薪金(一年三千英镑，妻子的收入)过活。 **~ on one's name/reputation,** keep one's position, continue to earn money, because one has been successful in the past. 靠好的名声过活(由于过去有成就，故能继续保持职位或赚钱度日)。 **4** [VP 2C, 3A] **~ (in/at),** make one's home; reside: 居; 住: *~ in England;* 住在英国; *~ at home;* 住在家里; *~ abroad:* 居于国外; *~ in lodgings/an hotel.* 住在寄宿舍(旅馆)。 *Where do you ~?* 你住在那里? **~ in/out,** (esp of domestic servants, shop assistants, workers) lodge in/out of the building where one is employed. (尤指仆人,店员,工人)(不)住在主人家; (不)住在工作处。 **~ together,** live in the same house, etc; (of two persons of opposite sex) live as if married: 住在一起; (指异性)同居: *I hear that Jane and Bill are living together.* 我听说简和比尔目前在一起同居。 **5** [VP 6B, 2D] (with cognate object) spend, pass, experience: (与同源宾语连用)度过…生活: *~ a happy life/a virtuous life;* 过快乐的(有德性的)生活; *~ a double life,* act two different parts in life. 过双重生活。 *He ~d the life of a Christian.* 他过着基督徒的生活。 *He ~d and died a bachelor.* 他终生未娶。 **6** [VP2C, D] conduct oneself; pass one's life in a specified way: 处身; 做人; 以某种方式生活: *~ honestly/happily;* 诚实地(快乐地)生活; *~ like a saint;* 象圣徒一般地生活; *~ well,* live a life satisfying all the appetites. 生活优裕。 **~ a lie,** express a lie by one's manner of living. 过虚伪的生活。 **~ to oneself,** in isolation, without trying to make friends. 过孤独的生活。 **7** [VP15B] **~ sth down,** live in such a way that (past guilt, scandal, foolishness, etc) is forgotten: 过新的生活以忘却(往日的罪恶，丑行，愚蠢等): *He hopes to ~ down the scandal caused by the divorce proceedings.* 他希望借新的生活忘却那因离婚而引起的丑闻。 [VP2C] **~ up to sth,** put (one's faith, principles, etc) into practice; reach the standard that may be expected: 实行(信仰,主义等); 达到预期的标准: *It's difficult to ~ up to the principles of the Christian religion.* 实行基督教的教条是困难的。 *He didn't ~ up to his reputation.* 他的往昔的生活和他的名声不符。 **~ with sth,** accept and endure it: 接受并忍受某事物: *I don't like the noise of these jet aircraft, but I've learnt*

to ~ *with it.* 我厌恶这些喷射机的噪音，但我已学会去忍受它了。 **8** [VP2A] (of things without life) remain in existence; survive: (指无生命的东西)继续存在; 仍在: *His memory will always* ~, He will never be forgotten. 他将永远被人记着。 *No ship could* ~ *in such a rough sea.* 任何船只都不能在这汹涌的海上安然航行。 **9** [VP2A] enjoy life intensely: 享受人生: *I want to* ~,' *she said,* 'I don't want to spend my days cooking and cleaning and looking after babies.' '我要享受人生,'她说,'我不要把我的日子花费在烧饭,清洗和照顾孩子上。' ➪ *it up,* live a life of hectic enjoyment. 享受人生。

live·li·hood / ˈlaɪvlɪhʊd; ˈlaɪv،lɪhʊd / n means of living; way in which one earns money: 生计;营生;谋生之道: *earn/gain one's* ~ *by teaching;* 靠教书生活; *earn an honest* ~; 规规矩矩地谋生; *deprive a man of his* ~. 剥夺一人的生计。

live·long / ˈlɪvlɒŋ US: ˈlaɪvlɔːŋ; ˈlɪv،lɔŋ/ *adj* (only in) (仅用于) *the* ~ *day/night,* the whole length of the day / night (implying, according to context, weariness or delight): 整整的一天(夜)(含厌恶或喜悦之意,视上下文而定)。

live·ly /ˈlaɪvlɪ; ˈlaɪvlɪ/ *adj* (-ier, -iest) **1** full of life and spirit; gay and cheerful: 有生气的; 活泼的; 愉快的;快活的: *She's as* ~ *as a kitten.* 她快活得象只小猫。 *The patient seems a little livelier/a little more* ~ *this morning.* 那病人今晨似乎精神好些了。 *He has a* ~ *imagination.* 他有活泼的想象力。 *They had a* ~ *time exciting,* perhaps with an element of danger. 他们有一段够刺激的(或许是惊险的)经历。 *look* ~, move more quickly, show more energy. 较前活泼且精力充沛。 *make things* ~ *for sb,* make it exciting and perhaps dangerous for him. 使(某人)感到惊险刺激。 **2** (of colour) bright; gay. (指颜色)鲜明的; 鲜艳的。 **3** (of non-living things) moving quickly or causing quick movement: (指无生命的东西)动作迅速的; 引起迅速动作的: *a* ~ *ball;* 快速直球; *a* ~ *(cricket) pitch.* 迅速的(板球)一投。 **4** lifelike; realistic: 生动的; 真实的: *a* ~ *description of a football game;* 对一场足球比赛生动的描写; *give sb a* ~ *idea of what happened.* 使某人对发生的事情有身历其境的感觉。 **live·li·ness** n [U] state of being ~. 有生气; 活泼; 快活; 鲜明; 生动。

liven /ˈlaɪvn; ˈlaɪvən/ *vt, vi* [VP15B, 2O] ~ *up,* make or become lively: 使有生气; 使活泼; 活泼有力: *How can we* ~ *things up?* 我们怎样能使事情有生气呢? *The party is beginning to* ~ *up.* 这宴会现在开始活泼起来了。

liver[1] /ˈlɪvə(r); ˈlɪvə/ n **1** [C] large, reddish-brown organ in the body which secretes bile and purifies the blood. 肝脏。 ➪ the illus at **alimentary**. 参看 alimentary 之插图。 **2** [U] animal's ~ as food. (动物的)肝(指做食物用者)。 **~·ish** /-ɪʃ; -ɪʃ/, ~·y *adjj* (colloq) suffering from ~ trouble; bilious (口)患肝病的; 脾气坏的。

live[2] /ˈlɪvə(r); ˈlɪvə/ n person who lives in a specified way: 过某种生活者: *an evil/clean/loose* ~. 过着罪恶(清白,放荡)生活的人。

liver·wurst /ˈlɪvəwɜːst; ˈlɪvə،wɜst/ n (US) sausage of chopped liver, popular in sandwiches. (美)肝制腊肠(常用于三明治)。

liv·ery /ˈlɪvərɪ; ˈlɪvərɪ/ n (pl -ries) **1** special dress or uniform worn by men servants in a great household (esp of a king or noble) or by members of one of the city companies of London (trade or craft guilds). (帝王贵族等家庭仆从所穿的)仆从制服; (伦敦市某同业工会会员所穿的)会员制服。 *in/out of* ~, wearing/not wearing such dress or uniform. 穿(不穿)着制服。 '~ **company,** one of the London trade guilds that have a distinctive uniform. (有特殊制服的)伦敦市同业工会之一。 **2** (fig, poet) dress; covering: (喻:诗)衣服; 覆盖: *trees in the* ~ *of spring,* with new green leaves; 春季生出新叶的树; *birds in their winter* ~. 长着冬季羽毛孔的鸟。 **3** '~ **(stable),** stable where horses are kept

for their owners, fed and looked after for payment: stable from which horses may be hired. 马房(付费后可寄马和饲马之处); 租马处。 **liv·er·ied** /ˈlɪvərɪd; ˈlɪvərɪd/ *adj* wearing ~(1). 穿特殊制服的。 '~·man /-mən; -mən/ n (pl -men) **1** member of a ~ company. 伦敦市穿特殊制服的同业公会会员。 **2** keeper of, workers in, a ~ stable. 代人饲马者; 出租马者。

lives /laɪvz; laɪvz/ *pl* of **life**.

live·stock /ˈlaɪvstɒk; ˈlaɪv،stak/ n [U] (esp farm) animals kept for use or profit, eg cattle, sheep, pigs. 家畜(尤指农家者;例如牛,羊,猪等)。

livid /ˈlɪvɪd; ˈlɪvɪd/ *adj* of the colour of lead, bluegrey; (of a person or his looks) furiously angry: 铅色的; 蓝灰色的; (指人或面容)狂怒的: ~ *marks/bruises on the body;* 身上青灰色的斑记(瘀伤); ~ *with cold/rage.* 冻(气)得脸发青。 **~·ly** *adv*

liv·ing[1] /ˈlɪvɪŋ; ˈlɪvɪŋ/ *adj* **1** alive, esp now existent: 活着的; (尤指)现存的: ~ *languages.* 现行的语言。 *No man* ~ (= No man who is now alive) *could do better.* 当代的人没有一个能做得比这更好的了。 *within/in* ~ *memory,* within the memory of people now alive. 在当今人的记忆中。 **2** (of a likeness) true to life: (指相似以其或物)逼真的: *He's the* ~ *image of* (= is exactly like) *his father.* 他跟他父亲长得一模一样。 **3** strong; active; lively: 强烈的; 活泼的; 生动的: *a* ~ *hope/faith.* 强烈的希望(信心)。 *the* ~ *theatre,* the ordinary theatre (contrasted with the cinema, TV, etc). 舞台剧(指一般的戏剧,以别于电影或电视剧等)。 □ n *the* ~, (with *pl v*) those now alive: (用复数动词)现世的人: *He's still in the land of the* ~. 他尚活在人间。

liv·ing[2] /ˈlɪvɪŋ; ˈlɪvɪŋ/ n **1** means of keeping alive, of earning what is needed for life: 生存之道; 生计: *earn/gain/get/make a* ~ *as a car salesman.* 做汽车推销员以谋生。 **2** [U] manner of life: 生活方式: *good* ~, having good food, etc; 优裕的生活; *plain* ~ *and high thinking,* having plain, simple food and leading a philosophic life; 朴素的生活与崇高的思想(过简朴达观的生活); *the high cost/standard of* ~ *in the US;* 美国的生活费用(水准)很高; *the art of* ~. 生活的艺术。 '~ '**wage,** minimum wage for a worker and his family to live on. 使工人能够维持一家人生活的工资。 '~·**room** n room for general use during the day (often a general purpose room, used for meals, recreation, etc). 起居室; 客厅。 '~·**space** n area of land considered by a State as necessary for further expansion. 某一国家认为未来扩展所必需的地区; 生存空间。 **3** (Church of England) benefice. (英国教会)牧师的俸禄。

liz·ard /ˈlɪzəd; ˈlɪzəd/ n small, creeping, long-tailed, four-legged reptile. 蜥蜴; 四脚蛇; 石龙子。 ➪ the illus at **reptile**. 参看 reptile 之插图。

llama /ˈlɑːmə; ˈlɑmə/ n S American animal with a thick woolly coat, used as a beast of burden. 美洲驼; 骆马(南美洲产的一种毛厚的驮兽)。 ➪ the illus at **large**. 参看 large 之插图。

Lloyd's /lɔɪdz; lɔɪdz/ n society of underwriters in London. 伦敦劳埃德船舶协会。 *A 1 at* ~, (dated sl) excellent. (过时俚语)第一流的; 最好的。 ~*'s Register,* annual list of ships in various classes. 在劳埃德协会每年登记的各种船舶名单。

lo /ləʊ; lo/ *int* (old use) Look! See! (旧用法)看! 瞧! *Lo and behold!* This will surprise you. 看哪!真会叫你惊讶。

load[1] /ləʊd; lod/ n [C] **1** that which is (to be) carried or supported, esp if heavy; (fig) weight of care, responsibility, etc: 负荷物; 载荷物(尤指沉重者); (喻)负担: *a heavy* ~ *on one's shoulders;* 肩上的重担; *a 'coach-*~ *of passengers.* 一马车乘客。 *take a* ~ *off sb's mind,* relieve him of anxiety, etc. 解除某人的忧虑等。 ~*s of,* (colloq) a large amount of: (口)大量的: ~*s of friends/money/time.* 许多朋友(金钱,时间)。 '~·**line** = **Plimsoll line.** 载重线。 **2** amount which a cart, etc can take: 车等负载之量; 装载量: *a 'cart-*~ *of hay;* 一车干草; *two 'lorry-*~s *of coal.* 两卡车煤。 ➪ also

payload at **pay**¹. **3** amount of work that a dynamo, motor, engine, etc is required to do; amount of current supplied by a generating station or carried by an electric circuit. (发电机, 发动机, 引擎等之) 载荷; (发电厂或电路的) 负载; 负荷。 '~-shedding n cutting off the supply of current on certain lines when the demand for current is greater than the supply. (电源不胜负担时) 切断某些电路的电源。

load² /ləʊd; lod/ vt, vi **1** [VP6A, 14, 15A, B, 2A, C] ~ sth into/on to sth/sb; ~ sth/sb (with sth), put a ~ in or on: 装货物于; 装载 (货物); 使负担: ~ sacks on to a cart/a donkey; 装货于一车 (驴); ~ a cart with coal; 装煤于车; ~ a lot of work on to one's staff; 将许多工作交给下属去做; a poor old woman ~ed (down) with her shopping; 背着大包小包购物的可怜的老妇人; (fig) (喻) ~ a man with favours/honours; 使一人备受恩宠 (荣誉); a heart ~ed with sorrow. 满怀悲伤的心。 ~ (sth) up, fill with goods, materials, etc: 装载货物于: Have you finished ~ing up (the van) yet? 你将货物装上 (货车) 了吗? **2** [VP6A, 2A] put a cartridge or shell into (a gun) or a length of film into (a camera): 装弹于 (枪炮); 装胶卷于 (照相机): Are you ~ed? Is there a cartridge in your gun? 你的枪里装有子弹吗? **3** [VP6A] weight with lead; add extra weight to: 用铅以加重; 加重: a ~ed cane/stick, one having lead added to make the cane useful as a weapon; 铅头杖 (用做武器); ~ed dice, so weighted as to fall with a certain face, eg the six, uppermost. 填有铅的骰子 (掷时某一面, 例如六点, 恒向上); 假骰子。 ~ the dice (against sb), (fig) do sth that gives one an unfair advantage (over him). (喻) 使用欺诈手段 (不利于某人)。 a ~ed question, one that is intended to trap a person into making an admission which may be harmful. 另有用意的问题 (欲引诱某人作对其不利之承认的一个问题)。 ~ed adj (sl) having much money. (俚) 很有钱的。

load-star, load-stone ⇨ **lode**.

loaf¹ /ləʊf; lof/ n (pl loaves /ləʊvz; lovz/) **1** mass of bread cooked as a separate quantity: 一条面包: a two-pound ~. 一条两磅重的面包。 Half a ~ is better than none/'no bread, It is better to take what one can get or is offered than to run the risk of having nothing. 半条面包比没有面包强; 聊胜于无。 **2** 'sugar-~ [C] cone-shaped mass of sugar, as formerly made and sold. (昔时制卖售的) 圆锥形糖块。 '~-sugar n [U] sugar cut into small lumps. 方块糖。 **3** [C, U] (quantity of) food shaped and cooked: 一块食物 (之量): (a) meat ~, made of minced meat, eggs, etc. 剁碎之肉和蛋等制成的菜。 **4** (sl) use one's ~, think intelligently; reflect. (俚) 动动脑筋; 好好想一想。

loaf² /ləʊf; lof/ vi, vt [VP2A, C, 15A, B] (colloq) waste time; spend time idly: (口) 浪费时间; 虚掷光阴: out-of-work men ~ing at street corners. 在街道转角处闲荡的失业男子。 Don't ~ about while there's so much work to be done. 当有这么多工作要做时, 不要闲荡。 Don't ~ away your time. 不要浪费你的时光。 □ n (sing only) ~ing. (仅用单数) 虚掷光阴。 ~er n person who ~s. 虚掷光阴者; 游手好闲者。

loam /ləʊm; lom/ n [U] rich soil with some sand or a little clay, and with much decayed vegetable matter in it. (含有少量沙或一点粘土及大量腐烂植物的) 沃土; 壤土。 ~y adj of or like ~: 上述沃土的; 似上述沃土的: ~y land. 沃地。

loan /ləʊn; lon/ n **1** [C] sth lent, esp a sum of money: 借出物; (尤指) 借款; 贷款: government ~s, sum lent to the government; 公债; domestic and foreign ~s. 内债和外债。 **2** [U] lending or being lent. 借出。 have the ~ of sth; have sth on ~ (from sb), have it as a borrower: 借得某物: May I have the ~ of your sewing-machine? 我可以借用你的缝纫机吗? I have the book on ~ from the library. 我从图书馆里借出那本书。 '~-collection n number of pictures, etc lent by

their owners for exhibition. 借自收藏家的展览品。 '~-office n one for lending money to private borrowers. 贷款处。 '~-word n word taken from another language. 外来语。 □ vt [VP6A, 14] ~ sth (to sb), lend (which is the more usu word except in formal style). 借出; 借 (除正式文体外, lend 一词较常用)。

loath, loth /ləʊθ/ adj (pred only) (仅用作表语) ~ to do sth, unwilling. 不愿意做某事。 nothing ~, quite willing. 十分乐意。

loathe /ləʊð; loð/ vt [VP6A, C] **1** feel disgust for; dislike greatly: 厌恶; 嫌恶: She was seasick, and ~d the smell of greasy food. 她晕船, 厌恶油腻食物的气味。 **2** (colloq) dislike: (口) 不喜欢: He ~s travelling by air. 他不喜欢坐飞机旅行。 loath-ing n [U] disgust. 厌恶。 loath-ly, (rare) (罕), loath-some /-səm; -səm/ adj disgusting; causing one to feel shocked: 可厌的; 令人震惊的: a loathsome disease. 讨厌的疾病。

loaves /ləʊvz; lovz/ pl of loaf¹.

lob /lɒb; lab/ vi, vt (-bb-) ~ sth in a high arc (in tennis). (网球) 高击 (球)。 □ n ball bowled underhand at cricket or hit high up into the air at tennis. (板球) 下手球; (网球) 高球。

lobby /'lɒbɪ; 'labɪ/ n (pl -bies) **1** porch, entrance-hall, anteroom, corridor: 门廊; 入口的厅堂; 大厅; 通道; 走廊: the ~ of a hotel/theatre. 旅馆 (戏院) 的休息室。 **2** (in the House of Commons, etc) large hall used for interviews between members and the public; group of people who try to influence members, eg of the House of Commons, the Senate in Washington, DC, to support or oppose proposed legislation. (下议院或参议院等中的) 民众接待厅; 游说者的一群人。 **3** (di'vision) ~, (House of Commons) one of two corridors to which members vote in this way. (英国下议院分组表决时) 议员前往投票的两走廊之一。 □ vt, vi [VP6A, 15A, 2A, C] (try to) influence the members of a law-making body; get (a bill) passed or rejected in this way: 游说议员; 运动议员使 (议案) 通过或不通过: ~ a bill through the Senate; 运动议员使参议院通过一议案; the National Union of Farmers ~ing in order to maintain subsidies/~ing for higher subsidies/~ing their MP's. 为维持补助金 (增加补助金) 而游说议员的全国总农会。 '~-ist /-ɪst; -ɪst/ n person who lobbies. 游说议员者; 运动议员使议案通过或不通过者。

lobe /ləʊb; lob/ n **1** lower rounded part of the external ear. 耳垂。 ⇨ the illus at **ear**. 参看 ear 之插图。 **2** subdivision of the lungs or the brain. 肺叶; 脑叶。 ⇨ the illus at **respiratory**. 参看 respiratory 之插图。 ~d adj having ~s. 有耳垂的; 有肺叶或脑叶的。

lob-ster /'lɒbstə(r); 'labstɚ/ n [C] shellfish with eight legs and two claws, bluish-black before and scarlet after being boiled. 龙虾。 ⇨ the illus at **crustacean**. 参看 crustacean 之插图。 '~-pot n basket in which ~s are trapped. 捕捉龙虾的篮或篓。 **2** [U] its flesh as food. 龙虾肉 (食用)。

lo·cal /'ləʊkl; 'lokl/ adj **1** of, special to, a place or district: 地方的; 本地的: the ~ doctor, living in the district; 当地的医生; ~ customs; 地方风俗; a column of ~ news; 地方新闻栏; ~ government. 地方政府。 ~ colour, details of the scenes and period described in a story, added to make the story more real. 地方色彩 (对地方背景和时代详细的描述, 以增加故事的真实性)。 ~ option/veto, (in some countries) system by which people may decide, by voting, whether they do or do not want sth, eg the sale of alcoholic drink, in their district. (某些国家) 地方人民的选择 (否决) 权 (例如决定是否应贩卖酒类)。 ~ time, time at any place in the world as calculated from the position of the sun: 地方时: L~ time changes by one hour for every 15° longitude. 经度每差十五度当地时间就差一小时。 **2** affecting a part, not the whole: 局部的: a ~

pain/injury; 局部疼痛(伤害); *a ~ anaesthetic.* 局部麻醉剂。 □ *n* **1** (usu *pl*) inhabitant of a particular district. (通常用复数)当地人; 本地人。 **2** item of ~ news in a newspaper. 地方新闻。 **3** (colloq) ~ public house: (口)当地酒店: *pop into the ~ for a pint.* 匆匆进入本地酒店去买一品脱酒。 **~·ly** /-kəlɪ; -kəlɪ/ *adv*

lo·cale /ləʊˈkɑːl US: -ˈkæl; ləˈkæl/ *n* [C] scene of an event; scene of a novel, etc. 事件的现场; 小说等发生的地点。

lo·cal·ism /ˈləʊkəlɪzəm; ˈlokḷˌɪzəm/ *n* **1** [U] interest in a district, esp one's own; favouring of what is local; narrowness of ideas that may be the result of this. 对于地方(尤指自己的乡土)的关心; 乡土偏爱; (由乡土偏爱产生的)思想的偏狭; 地方主义。 **2** [C] local idiom, pronunciation, etc. 土话; 方言; 土音。

lo·cal·ity /ləʊˈkæləti; loˈkæləti/ *n* (*pl* **-ties**) **1** [C] thing's position; place in which an event occurs; place, district, neighbourhood. 位置; 发生地; 所在地; 地方; 地区。 **2** [U] faculty of remembering and recognizing places, features of the landscape, etc, esp as a help in finding one's way: 记忆地方的能力; 辨认地方的能力: *She has a good sense of ~.* 她能记忆地方的能力很强。

lo·cal·ize /ˈləʊkəlaɪz; ˈlokḷˌaɪz/ *vt* [VP6A] **1** make local, not general; confine within a particular part or area: 使限于局部; 使限于一区域: *There is little hope of localizing the disease.* 没有希望使疾病限于局部。 **2** invest with local characteristics. 使带有地方色彩。 **lo·cal·iz·ation** /ˌləʊkəlaɪˈzeɪʃn US: -lɪˈz-; ˌlokḷəˈzeʃən/ *n*

lo·cate /ləʊˈkeɪt US: ˈləʊkeɪt; ˈloket/ *vt* [VP6A, 15A] **1** discover, show, the locality of: 找出…的位置; 指出…的位置: *~ a town on a map.* 在地图上找出一城市的位置。 **2** establish in a place: 在一地点设置: *a new school to be ~d in the suburbs.* 将设于郊区的一所新学校。 *Where is the new factory to be ~d?* 新工厂将设于何处? **3** *be ~d,* be situated. 位于。 **lo·ca·tion** /ləʊˈkeɪʃn; loˈkeʃən/ *n* **1** [U] locating or being ~d. 指出位置; 定位置。 **2** [C] position or place: 位置; 地方: *suitable locations for new factories.* 适于建工厂的位置。 **3** place, not a film studio, where (part of) a cinema film is photographed. (电影之)外景拍摄地。 **on location,** shooting film in this way. 拍外景。 **4** (in S Africa) suburb where Africans are constrained to live. (南非)非洲土著被迫居住之城郊。

loch /lɒk; lɑk/ *n* (Scot) (苏) **1** long, narrow arm of the sea almost enclosed by land. 长窄的海湾。 **2** lake. 湖。

loci /ˈləʊsaɪ; ˈlosaɪ/ *pl* of **locus**.

lock[1] /lɒk; lɑk/ *n* portion of hair that naturally hangs or clings together; (*pl*) hair of the head: 一绺头发; (复)头发: *my scanty ~s.* 我的稀少的头发。

lock[2] /lɒk; lɑk/ *n* **1** appliance, mechanism, by which a door, gate, lid, etc may be fastened with a bolt that needs a key to work it. 锁。 *keep sth/put sth/be under ~ and key,* in sth fitted with a ~. 将某物锁着 (被锁着)。 **'~·smith** *n* maker and mender of ~s. 锁匠。 **2** mechanism by which a gun is fired. 枪机。~,

stock and barrel, the whole of the thing; completely. 全部; 完全地。 **3** enclosed section of a canal or river at a point where the water level changes, for raising or lowering boats by the use of gates fitted with sluices. (运河或河流之)闸河。 **'~·gate,** gate on a lock. 闸门。 **'~·keeper** *n* keeper of a canal or river ~, who opens and shuts the gates to allow boats to pass through. 水闸管理人。 **4** [U] condition of being fixed or jammed so that movement is impossible. 固定; 塞紧。 **'~·jaw** *n* [U] form of disease (tetanus) that causes the jaws to be firmly locked together. 牙关锁闭症; 破伤风。 **'~·nut** *n* extra nut screwed over another to prevent its turning. 锁紧螺母(使另一螺母固定之螺母)。 **'~·stitch** *n* sewing-machine stitch by which two threads are firmly joined together. (缝纫机之)双线连锁缝法。 ⇨ also *air ~* at **air**[1](7). **5** (motoring) extent of the turning arc of a steering wheel: (驾驶汽车)方向盘旋转弧度: *full ~,* with the steering wheel turned (right or left) as far as it will go. (方向盘)可(左右)任意旋转。

lock[3] /lɒk; lɑk/ *vt, vi* **1** [VP6A, 15A, B] fasten a door, box, etc with a lock. 锁(门, 箱等)。 *~ the stable door after the horse has bolted/has been stolen,* take precautions when it is too late. 亡羊补牢; 贼去关门。 *~ sth away,* put it away in a ~ed box, drawer, etc; (fig) keep securely: 将某物锁藏起来; (喻)安全地保存: *have a secret safely ~ed (away) in one's breast.* 把一秘密隐藏在心底。 *~ sb in,* put sb in a room of which the door is ~ed on the outside. 将某人锁在房内。 *~ oneself in,* ~ the door so that no one can enter from outside, or so that one cannot open it again. 将自己锁在房内。 *~ sb out,* keep him outside, prevent him from entering, by ~ing the gate or door(s) on the inside: 将某人锁在房外: *If you don't get back before midnight, you'll be ~ed out.* 如果你在半夜以前还不回来, 你将被锁在房外。 **'~·out** *n* refusal of employers to allow workmen to enter their place of work until certain conditions are agreed to or demands given up. 闭厂; 停业(雇主与工人间之条件未获协议前抵制工人的行动)。 ⇨ **strike**[1]. *~ sth/sb up,* (a) make safe by placing in sth that ~s: 锁妥当; 锁好: *L~ up your jewellery before you go away.* 在你离开前把你的珠宝好好锁藏起来。 (b) shut up a house, etc by ~ing all the doors. 关锁房门。 (c) put (a person) in a ~ed room, a prison, a mental home, etc. 将(某人)锁在房间、监狱、疯人院等内。 (d) invest (money) in such a way that it cannot easily or quickly be exchanged for cash: 使(资本)固定: *All his capital is ~ed up in land.* 他所有的资金都投资在土地上。 **'~-up** *n* place where prisoners may be kept temporarily; (colloq) any prison. 拘留所; (口)监狱。 □ *adj* (attrib only) that can be ~ed: (仅用作定语)可以锁的: *a ~-up garage,* one, eg at a hotel, that can be ~ed. 可上锁的汽车间(例如旅馆中者)。 **2** [VP2A] have a ~; become ~ed; be capable of being ~ed: 有锁; 锁住; 能被锁上: *This trunk doesn't ~,* has no lock or has a lock that does not work. 这箱子没有锁(或有锁而锁不住)。 *The door ~s easily.* 那门容易锁。 **3** [VP6A,

a canal lock

2A, C] (cause to) become fixed, unable to move: 使固定; 固定: *His jaws were tightly ~ed.* 他的牙关紧闭。 *He ~ed the wheels of the car to prevent its being stolen.* 他固定住汽车的轮胎以防被窃。 *They were ~ed together in a fierce struggle.* 他们扭扭在一起猛烈地格斗。 *They were ~ed in each other's arms.* 他们紧紧拥抱着。 *The parts ~ into each other,* interlock. 各部分互相锁着。 **4** **[VP2C]** **~ on to,** (of a missile, etc) find and automatically follow (a target) by radar. (指飞弹等) 用雷达自动追踪(目标); 锁定(目标)。

locker /'lɒkər; 'lɑkɚ/ *n* **1** small cupboard, esp one of a number used for keeping one's clothes, eg at a swimming-pool or golf-club. 有锁的小橱柜(尤指供储放衣物用的许多小橱之一, 例如游泳池或高尔夫球场附近者)。 **2** box or compartment in a ship used for clothes, stores, ammunition, etc. 内务箱(船上储放衣服, 物品, 军火等的箱柜或小舱)。 *be in*/*go to Davy Jones's ~,* be drowned at sea. 淹死在海中。

locket /'lɒkɪt; 'lɑkɪt/ *n* small (often gold or silver) case for a portrait, a lock of hair, etc, usu worn round the neck on a chain. (以项链悬于颈上的)小盒(装画像, 或一绺头发等, 常是金或银质的)。

loco /'ləʊkəʊ; 'loko/ *adj* (sl) mad. (俚)疯的。

lo·co·mo·tion /ˌləʊkəˈməʊʃn; ˌlokəˈmoʃən/ *n* [U] moving, ability to move, from place to place. 运动; 移动; 运动力; 移动力。 **lo·co·mo·tive** /ˌləʊkəˈməʊtɪv; ˌlokəˈmotɪv/ *adj* of, having, causing, ~. 移动的; 有移动力的; 引起运动的。 *n* self-propelled engine for use on railways: 火车机车; 火车头: *steam*/*Diesel*/*electric locomotives.* 蒸汽(柴油, 电动)机车。

locum /'ləʊkəm; 'lokəm/ (also ~ **'tenens** /'tiːnenz; 'tininz/) *n* doctor or priest performing the duties of another who is away, eg on holiday. 临时代理的医师或牧师。

lo·cus /'ləʊkəs; 'lokəs/ *n* (*pl* loci /'ləʊsaɪ; 'losaɪ/) exact place of sth. 所在地; 场所。 **~ classicus** /klæˈsɪkəs; 'klæsɪkəs/, best known or most authoritative passage on a subject. 关于一问题最著名或最具权威的章节。

lo·cust /'ləʊkəst; 'lokəst/ *n* **1** (kinds of) migratory African and Asian winged insect which flies in great swarms and destroys crops and vegetables. 蝗虫。 ⇨ the illus at **insect**. 参看 insect 之插图。 ⇨ **hopper**²(2). **2** '~(-tree),** (kind of) tree, esp *carob* and a N American tree, *false acacia.* 刺槐属(尤指槐豆及北美产刺槐)。

lo·cu·tion /ləˈkjuːʃn; loˈkjuʃən/ *n* [C] style of speech; way of using words; [C] phrase or idiom. 语风; 语法; 语句; 惯用语。

lode /ləʊd; lod/ *n* vein of metal ore. 矿脉。 '~·star* *n* star by which a ship may be steered; the polestar; (fig) guiding principle. 指示船航行方向之星; 北极星; (喻)指导原则。 '~·stone* *n* magnetized iron ore. 天然磁铁矿。

lodge¹ /lɒdʒ; lɑdʒ/ *n* **1** small house, esp one at the entrance to the grounds of a large house, occupied by a gatekeeper, gardener or other employee of the estate. 小屋(尤指大宅第入口处守门人, 园丁, 或其他仆从所住者)。 **2** country house used in the hunting or shooting season: 狩猎季节供人使用的房舍: *a 'hunting ~ in the Highlands;* 苏格兰高地供狩猎者用的房室; (US) hut or cabin for temporary use: (美)暂时用的小屋: *a 'skiing ~.* 滑雪时用的小屋。 **3** porter's room(s) in the chief gateway or entrance to a college, factory, block of flats, etc. 学院, 工厂, 公寓等的传达室; 门房。 **4** (GB) residence of the head of a college. (英)大学院长之住宅。 **5** (place of meeting for) members of a branch of a society such as the Freemasons. 会社(如共济会)支部的全体会员; 支部会员集会处。 **6** beaver's lair. 海狸的巢穴。

lodge² /lɒdʒ; lɑdʒ/ *vt, vi* **1** **[VP6A, 15A]** supply (sb) with a room or place to sleep in for a time; receive as a guest: 供以临时住宿处; 留宿: *The ship-wrecked sailors were ~d in the school.* 那些遭船难的船

员暂时住在学校里。 **2** **[VP3A]** **~ at**/**with,** live as a paying guest: 寄宿: *Where are you lodging now?* 你现在寄宿在何处? *I'm lodging at Mrs P's*/*with Mr and Mrs X.* 我现在寄宿在 P 太太(X 夫妇)家。 **3** **[VP3A]** **~ in,** enter and become fixed: 进入并固定: *The bullet ~d in his jaw.* 子弹射入他的颚。 **4** **[VP6A, 15A]** **~ (in),** cause (sth) to enter and become fixed (*in*); put or place (in a particular place): 使进入并固定于(与in连用); 置于(某一地方): *~ a bullet in a man's brain.* 将一子弹射入某人的头部。 **5** **[VP6A, 15A]** put (money, etc) for safety: 存放(金钱等): *~ one's valuables in the bank while away from home on holiday.* 离家度假时将贵重物品存放在银行里。 **6** **[VP6A, 14]** **~ sth (with sb) (against sb),** place (a statement, etc) with the proper authorities: 向当局提出(声明等)(以控告某人): *~ a complaint against one's neighbours with the authorities.* 向当局控诉邻居。 **~r** *n* person paying for rooms, etc in sb's house: 房客; 寄宿人: *The widow makes a living by taking in lodgers.* 那寡妇以收房客维持生活。

lodge·ment (also **lodg·ment**) /'lɒdʒmənt; 'lɑdʒmənt/ *n* **1** [U] act or process of lodging: 向当局提出: *the ~ of a complaint.* 控诉之提出。 ⇨ **lodge**²(6). **2** [C] sth that has accumulated or been deposited: 聚积物; 沉淀物: *a ~ of dirt in a pipe.* 管内积存的脏物。 **3** [C] (mil) position gained in enemy territory: (军)(在敌军领土占领的)立足点; 据点: *gain a ~ on an enemy-held coast.* 在敌方海岸取得一据点。

lodg·ing /'lɒdʒɪŋ; 'lɑdʒɪŋ/ *n* (usu *pl*) room or rooms (not in a hotel) rented to live in: (通常用复数)出租的房间; 寄宿舍: *It's cheaper to live in ~s than in a hotel.* 住寄宿舍比住旅馆便宜。 *Where can we find ~s for the night?* 我们今晚在哪里找一寄宿处? '~-house* *n* house in which ~s are let (usu by the week). 出租房间的公寓(通常按周出租); 寄宿舍。

lo·ess /'ləʊɪs; 'lo·ɪs/ *n* [U] deposit of fine yellowish-grey soil, found esp in northern China, central USA and central Europe. (在中国北部, 美国中部, 以及欧洲中部一带所见到的)黄土。

loft¹ /lɒft US: lɔːft; lɔft/ *n* **1** room, place, used for storing things, in the highest part of a house, under the roof; space under the roof of a stable or barn, where hay or straw is stored. (屋顶下存放东西的)阁楼; 顶楼; (贮放干草的)厩楼。 **2** gallery in a church or hall: 教堂或厅堂的廊台; 楼厢: *the 'organ-~.* 教堂内的风琴台。

loft² /lɒft US: lɔːft; lɔft/ *vt* **[VP6A]** (golf, cricket) hit (a ball) high: (高尔夫, 板球)击(球)高飞: *~ a ball over the fielders' heads.* 将球击出自外场员头上飞过。

lofty /'lɒftɪ US: 'lɔːftɪ; 'lɔftɪ/ *adj* (**-ier, -iest**) **1** (not used of persons) of great height: (不用以指人)极高的: *a ~ tower*/*mountain.* 高塔(山)。 **2** (of thoughts, aims, feelings, etc) distinguished; noble: (指思想, 目的, 情感等)高超的; 高尚的: *~ sentiments;* 高尚的情操; *a ~ style.* 高超的风格。 **3** haughty; proud; consciously superior: 高傲的; 骄傲的; 傲慢的: *a ~ appearance;* 高傲的样子; *in a ~ manner.* 态度高慢地。 **loft·ily** /-ɪlɪ; -ɪlɪ/ *adv* **lofti·ness** *n*

log¹ /lɒg US: lɔːg; lɔg/ *n* [C] rough length of tree-trunk that has fallen or been cut down; short piece of this for a fire: (未经砍削的)干材; 圆材; 圆木; 圆形短木柴: *a raft of logs,* floating down a river. (顺流漂下之)圆木排。 *like a log,* unconscious; immovable. 无知觉的; 不能动的。 *sleep like a log,* sleep soundly and with little or no movement. 酣睡; 熟睡得毫无块木头。 'log-'cabin* *n* cabin with walls and roof made of logs. not boards. 木屋(墙和屋顶均用圆木构成, 而不用木板者)。 'log-jam* *n* mass of floating logs tightly mixed together; (US) deadlock. 河流中圆木阻塞; (美)僵局; 停滞状态。 'log-rolling* *n* practice of giving support to others in return for support from them, eg by author-reviewers who praise each other's books. 互相标榜(例如作者兼书评家间的互捧)。 **log·ging** *n* work of cutting down forest

trees for timber: 伐木工作; 伐木业: *a logging camp.* 伐木营.

log² /lɒg US: lɔːg; lɔg/ *n* **1** device attached to a knotted line, trailed from a ship, to measure its speed through the water: (船用)测程仪: *sail by the log,* calculate a ship's position by means of information gained from the log. 用测程仪测量船的位置. **2** (also 亦作 **'log-book**) book with a permanent daily record or events during a ship's voyage (esp the weather, ship's position, speed, and distance as recorded by the log); (by extension) any record of performance, eg of a car or aircraft. 航海日志; (引伸用法)任何进度记录(例如汽车或飞机行驶里程,保养等记录). **3** (colloq) registration book (of a motor-vehicle). 口 汽车主登记表册. 口 *vt* **(-gg-)** [VP6A] enter (facts) in the log-book of a ship or aircraft. 记载(事实)于航海日志或飞行日志.

log³ /lɒg US: lɔːg/ (colloq abbr for) **logarithm.** (口)对数(为 logarithm 之略).

lo·gan·berry /'lɒʊɡənberɪ; 'loɡən,bɛrɪ/ *n* (*pl* **-ries**) large dark-red berry from a plant that is a cross between a blackberry and a raspberry. 洛干杨莓; 大杨莓(系黑莓与蘩莓子的交配种).

log·a·rithm /'lɒɡərɪðəm US: 'lɔːɡ-; 'lɔɡə,rɪðəm/ *n* (arith) one of a series of numbers set out in tables which make it possible to work out problems in multiplication and division by adding and subtracting (算术)对数.

log·ger·heads /'lɒɡəhedz; 'lɔɡə,hɛdz/ *n* (only in) (used用作) *at* **(*with*),** disagreeing or disputing: (与…)不和; 相争: *He's constantly at ~ with his wife.* 他经常与妻子不和.

log·gia /'lɒdʒɪə; 'lɑdʒɪə/ *n* (I) open-sided gallery or arcade; part of a house with one side open to the garden. (意)凉廊; 房屋敞向花园的部分.

logic /'lɒdʒɪk; 'lɑdʒɪk/ *n* [U] science, method, of reasoning; (person's) ability to argue and convince: 逻辑(学); 论理学; 理则学; (人之)辩论和说服的能力: *argue with learning and ~.* 有学问而正直合逻辑地辩论。 **logi·cal** /-kl; -kl/ *adj* in accordance with the rules of ~; able to reason correctly: 合逻辑的; 条理分明的; 能正确地推理的: *a ~al mind/argument/conclusion;* 合理的头脑(条理分明的辩论; 合逻辑的结论); *~al behaviour.* 合理的行为。 **logi·cally** /-klɪ; -klɪ/ *adv* **logi·cal·ity** /ˌlɒdʒɪ'kælətɪ; ˌlɑdʒɪ'kælətɪ/ *n* [U] being ~al. 合乎逻辑; 条理分明. **lo·gician** /lə'dʒɪʃn; lo-'dʒɪʃən/ *n* person skilled in ~. 逻辑学家; 论理学家; 理则学家.

lo·gis·tics /lə'dʒɪstɪks; lo'dʒɪstɪks/ *n* (with *sing v*) supply, distribution and replacement of materials and personnel, eg for the armed forces. (与单数动词连用) 后勤(学).

loin /lɔɪn; lɔɪn/ *n* **1** (*pl*) the lower part of the body on both sides of the spine between the ribs and the hip-bones. (复)腰; 腰部。口 the illus at dog, domestic. 参看 dog, domestic 之插图。 *gird (up) one's ~s,* (biblical) prepare for a journey; make ready for action. (圣经)准备旅行; 准备行动。 **'~-cloth** *n* piece of cloth covering the middle of the body, folded between the legs, and fastened round the ~s. 缠腰布。 **2** joint of meat which includes the ~s: 腰肉: *~ of mutton.* 羊腰肉.

loi·ter /'lɔɪtə(r); 'lɔɪtɚ/ *vi, vt* [VP2A, C, 15B] go slowly and stop frequently on the way somewhere; stand about; pass (time) thus: 边走边停; 闲荡; 徘徊; 闲散以度过(时间): *~ on one's way home;* 在回家路上边走边玩; *~ the hours away;* 虚度时光; *~ over a job.* 工作闲散。 *~er* *n* *~ing* person. 闲荡者; 闲散的人.

loll /lɒl; lɑl/ *vi, vt* [VP2A, C] *~ (about / around),* rest, sit or stand (*about*) in a lazy way. 懒洋洋地躺卧, 坐着或站着。 **2** [VP2C, 15B] *~ out,* (of the tongue) (allow to) hang: (舌头)垂伸; 任其垂伸: *The dog ~ed its tongue out.* 那狗垂伸着舌头。 *The dog's*

tongue was ~ing out. 那狗的舌头垂伸在外.

lol·li·pop /'lɒlɪpɒp; 'lɑlɪ,pɑp/ *n* large sweet of boiled sugar on a stick, held in the hand and sucked. 棒棒糖。 **'~ man/woman,** (colloq) one who carries a pole with a disc marked 'Stop! Children crossing', to conduct children across busy roads, eg outside a school. (口)引导学童穿越闹区马路的男人或女人(手持一杆, 杆头有一圆盘状板, 上书'止步! 孩子们在过马路! ').

lolly /'lɒlɪ; 'lɑlɪ/ *n* **1** (colloq) lollipop. (口)棒棒糖。 **ice(d) ~,** quantity of frozen fruit juice on a stick. 冰棒。 **2** (sl) money, (esp money easily earned and lavishly spent). (俚)金钱(尤指容易赚得并挥霍掉者).

lone /lɒʊn; lon/ *adj* (attrib only; 只用作定语; ⇨ **alone** and **lonely,** which are more usu) solitary; without companions; unfrequented: (仅用作定语; 参看 alone 和 lonely, 此二词较为常用)孤身的; 孤独的; 人迹罕至的: *play a ~ hand,* (fig) do sth without the help or support of others, esp sth not very popular. (喻)独力做某事(尤指不太普遍之事).

lone·ly /'lɒʊnlɪ; 'lonlɪ/ *adj* (**-ier, -iest**) **1** without companions: 孤单的: *a ~ traveller.* 孤单的旅客。 **2** sad or melancholy because one lacks companions, sympathy, friendship: 寂寞的; 寂寞的: *a ~-looking girl;* 样子孤寂的女孩; *feel ~.* 感到寂寞。 **3** (of places) not often visited; far from inhabited places or towns: (指地点)人迹罕至的; 偏僻的: *a ~ house;* 孤僻的房屋; *a ~ mountain village.* 荒凉的山村。 **lone·li·ness** *n* [U] state of being ~: 孤独; 孤寂; 寂寞: *suffer from loneliness.* 备尝孤寂之苦.

lone·some /'lɒʊnsəm; 'lonsəm/ *adj* **1** sad because alone: 寂寞的; 孤寂的: *feel ~;* 感到寂寞; causing a feeling of loneliness: 令人感到孤寂的: *a ~ journey.* 孤单的旅行。 **2** solitary, unfrequented: 偏僻的; 人迹罕至的: *a ~ valley.* 人迹罕至的山谷.

long¹ /lɒŋ; lɔŋ/ *adj* (**-nger** /-ŋɡə(r); -ŋɡə/, **-ngest** /-ŋɡɪst; -ŋɡɪst/) **1** of extent in space; measuring much from end to end: (指空间)长的: *How ~ is the River Nile?* 尼罗河有多长? *The new road is twenty miles ~.* 新路长达二十英里。 *Your car is ~er than mine.* 你的汽车比我的长。 *What a lot of men have ~ hair nowadays!* 现下留长头发的男人真多! *What a lot of ~-haired men we see today!* 今天我们看到留长头发的男人真多啊! *put on a ~ face,* ⇨ **face¹(3).** **2** in phrases indicating (great) extent. 用于表示(广大)范围之短语中。 *have a ~ arm,* be able to make one's power felt far. 能使势力远伸。 *the ~ arm of the law,* its far-reaching power. 法律之远及的力量。 *make a ~ arm for sth,* reach out for sth, eg at table. 伸手取物(例如用餐时)。 *it's as broad as it's ~,* ⇨ **broad¹(9).** **3** expressing duration or extent in time: (指时间)长的: *the ~ vacation,* the summer vacation of law courts and universities. 长的假期(如法院和大学的暑假)。 *He was ill for a ~ time.* 他病了一段长时间。 *How ~ are the holidays?* 假日有多久? *They're six weeks ~.* 有六周之久。 *He won't be ~ (in) making up his mind,* will soon do so. 他很快就会作决定。 *Don't be too ~ about it,* Do it soon or quickly. 快点做。 *~ time no see!* (colloq; as greeting) We haven't met for a long time. (口; 作为寒暄语)好久不见了! **4** (of vowel sounds) usually taking more time to utter than others: (指元音)长音的: 'Sit' has a short vowel and 'seed' has a ~ vowel. 'Sit' 有一短元音, 'seed' 有一长元音. The 'u' in 'rude' is ~. 'rude' 中之 'u' 是长音. **5** (in phrases concerned with extent in time) (用于与期限有关的短语中) *a ~ bond,* (fin) which mature in 20 years or more. (财政)长期债券(二十年以上到期者). *take a ~ cool / hard look at sth,* consider facts, problems shrewdly and at length. 明智细密地考虑事实或问题. *take the ~ view,* consider events, factors, etc a ~ time ahead, rather than the present situation, etc. 眼光远大. *in the ~ run,* ⇨ **run¹(7).** *in the ~ term,* looking ahead for a ~ time. 长期. Hence, 由此产生, **~-'term** *attrib adj* lasting

for a ~ time: 长期的: ~-*term agreements/contracts/ investments*. 长期的协定(合约,投资). **6** (compounds) (复合词) '~·**boat** n sailing-ship's largest boat. 帆船所携带之最大的艇. '~·**bow** n bow drawn by hand, equal in length to the height of the archer, used with feathered arrows. 大弓; 长弓(长度与射手手臂高相当,射出装有羽毛的箭). ⇨ **crossbow**. *draw the ~bow*, tell exaggerated or invented stories. 说大话; 吹牛. '~·**distance** attrib adj covering a ~ distance: 长距离的; 长途的: ~-*distance runners* (in sport); (运动)长途赛跑者; a ~-*distance telephone call*; 一次长途电话; a ~-*distance lorry driver*. 跑长途的卡车司机。 ~ **drink** n large quantity, eg of beer, served in a tall glass (contrasted with a *short drink*, eg neat whisky). 大量饮酒(例如用高杯饮啤酒; 以别于 short drink, 例如纯威士忌). *a ~ dozen*, thirteen. 十三个. '~·**hand** n [U] ordinary handwriting (contrasted with *shorthand and typing*). 普通写法(与 shorthand 和 typing 相对). ,~·'**haired** adj (a) ⇨ **1** above. 参看上列第 1 义。 (b) intellectual; artistic; unconventional. 有智力的; 志趣高尚的; 不守旧的. *a ~ haul*, ⇨ **haul**. ,~·'**headed** adj shrewd; having foresight. 精明的; 有头脑的; 有先见的. **the** '~ **jump**, (athletic contest) measured along the ground for distance. (运动比赛)跳远. ⇨ *high jump* at **high**[1](12). ~ **measure**, ⇨ **App 5**. 参看附录五。~ **metre** n [U] stanza of four eight-syllable lines. 长律(每节四行, 每行有八音节的诗)律。 ~ **odds** n pl (in betting) very uneven, eg 50 to 1. (打赌)悬殊(例如 50 比 1). ,~·**play(ing)** '**disc**/'**record** n (abbr 略作 **LP**) playing (at slow speed) for a ~er time than earlier kinds. 长时间唱片(以慢速放出)。 '~·**range** attrib adj of ~ periods of time or ~ distances: 长期的; 久远的; 长距离的; 远程的: *a ~range weather forecast*, eg for one month ahead; 长期气象预报(例如一月前所作); ~*range planning*, eg in ten years; 长远计划(例如十年计划); ~*range missiles*. 远程飞弹. '~·**shore·man** n man who works on shore (on wharves, in dockyards) loading and unloading ships. 码头上装卸船货的工人. *a ~ shot*, ⇨ **shot**[1](2). ,~·**sighted** adj able to see things a great distance away; (fig) prudent; having foresight. 能远视的; (喻)审慎的; 有远见的。 *a ~ suit*, ⇨ **suit**[1](5). '~ **stop** n [U] (cricket) player who fields straight behind the wicket-keeper. (板球)站在三柱门守门员正后方的外场员. ⇨ the illus at **cricket**. 参看 cricket 之插图。 '~·**time** attrib adj that has lasted for a long time: 长时间的: *a ~time acquaintance*. 长时期的结识。 ~ **wave** n 2240 lb. 长吨 (2240 磅). '~·**wave** n [U] (radio telegraphy) one having a wavelength of 1000 metres or over. (无线电)长波(波长在一千米以上者). ,~·**winded** adj tedious and diffuse in speaking or writing: (喻)冗长而令人生厌的: *a ~winded and boring lecturer*. 冗长而令人生厌的演说者. Hence, 由此产生, ,~·'**windedness**.

long[2] /lɒŋ US: lɔːŋ; lɔŋ/ n **1** [U] ~ time or interval: 长期间: *I shall see you before ~*. 我不久就可以见到你了. *The work won't take ~*. 这工作不会花太长的时间. *Shall you be away for ~?* 你将离开很久吗? *at (the) ~est*, to give the most distant date, etc: 最久; 最长; 最多: *I can wait only three days at ~est*, not after the third day from now. 我最多只能等三天. *the ~ and the short of it*, all that need be said; the general effect or result. 要言之; 总之. **2** [C] ~ syllable, esp in Latin verse: 长音节(尤指拉丁诗中者): *four ~s and six shorts*. 四个长音节和六个短音节.

long[3] /lɒŋ US: lɔːŋ; lɔŋ/ adv (-**er** /-ŋgə(r)/; -ŋgə/, -**est** /-ŋgɪst; -ŋgɪst/) **1** (**for**) ~, for a long time: 长期地; 长久地: *Stay (for) as ~ as you like*. 你愿意停留多久皆可. *I've ~ wanted to meet her*. 我很久以来就想见她. *as/so ~ as*, on condition that, provided that: 只要; 如果: *You may borrow the book so ~ as you don't lend it to anyone else*. 只要你不把它借给别人, 你多会借这本书. **2** (in numerous compounds): (用于许多复合词

中): ,~·**drawn·'out** adj extended; unduly prolonged: 延长的; 过分延长的: *a ~drawn-out visit from my mother-in-law*. 我岳母的过长的访问. ,~·'**lived** adj having a long life; destined for a long time: 长命的; 长存的: *a ~lived family*. 历史悠久的家族. '~·**standing** adj that has lasted for a long time: 存在已久的: *a ~standing invitation to visit the Browns*. 为时甚久的邀请去拜访布朗一家人. ,~·'**suffering** adj patient and uncomplaining in spite of trouble, provocation, etc: 能忍受的; 长期受苦的: *his ~suffering wife*. 他那位能吃苦的妻子. **3** at a long time (from a point of time): (自时间的某一点起)在长时间: ~ *ago/before/ after/since*. 很久以前(远在…之前; 远在…之后; 很久以后). *That happened ~ ago*. 那事发生在很久以前. **4** (with nn indicating duration) throughout the specified time: (与表示持续时期的名词连用)经过该段时间: *all day ~*, throughout the whole day; 整天; *all my life ~*. 我毕生; 我一辈子. **5** *no/any/much ~er*, after a certain point of time: 在某一时刻以后: *I can't wait any/much ~er*. 我不能再等了(等太久). *He's no ~er living here*. 他已不住在此处.

long[4] /lɒŋ US: lɔːŋ; lɔŋ/ vi [VP3A, 4C] ~ *for sth/ for sb to do sth*, desire earnestly; wish for very much: 渴望; 渴慕: *She ~ed for him to say something*. 她渴望他说几句话. *I'm ~ing to see you*. 我渴望见到你. *The children are ~ing for the holidays*. 孩子们渴望着假日. ~·**ing** n [C, U] (an) earnest desire: 渴望; 热望: *a ~ing for home*. 思家. ☐ adj longing or showing an earnest desire: 渴望的; 表示渴望的: *a ~ing look*; 渴望的样子; *with ~ing eyes*. 以渴望的眼神. ~·**ing·ly** adv

lon·gev·ity /lɒn'dʒevətɪ; lɑn'dʒevɪtɪ/ n [U] long life. 长寿; 长命.

longi·tude /'lɒndʒɪtjuːd US: -tuːd; 'lɑndʒə,tjud/ n distance east or west (measured in degrees) from a meridian, esp that of Greenwich, in London. 经度. ⇨ the illus at **projection**. 参看 projection 之插图. **longi·tudi·nal** /,lɒndʒɪ'tjuːdɪnl US: ,lɑndʒə'tjudnl/ adj **1** of ~. 经度的. **2** of or in length. 长度的. **3** running lengthwise: 纵的: *longitudinal stripes*, eg in a flag. 纵条纹(例如旗帜上者).

long·ways /'lɒŋweɪz US: 'lɔːŋ-; 'lɔŋ,wez/, **long·wise** /'lɒŋwaɪz US: 'lɔːŋ-; 'lɔŋ,waɪz/ adv = **lengthways**.

loo /luː/ n (GB colloq) water-closet. (英口)厕所.

loo·fah, loofa /'luːfə; 'lufə/ n [C] dried pod of a plant (kind of gourd or pumpkin) used as a sponge. 丝瓜络.

look[1] /lʊk; lʊk/ vi, vt (pt, pp ~**ed**) (For uses with *adverbial particles* and *preps* ⇨ **7** below.) (与副词性小品词和介词连用的用法, 参看下列第 7 义.) **1** [VP2A, C, 3A, 4A] ~ (**at**), use one's sight; turn the eyes in some direction; try to see: 看; 视; 望: ~ (*up*) *at the ceiling*; (向上)看天花板; ~ (*down*) *at the floor*. (向下)看地板. *We ~ed but saw nothing*. 我们看了, 但没有看见什么. *I happened to be ~ing another way*, in a different direction. 我碰巧朝另一方向看了. *L~ to see whether the road's clear before you cross*. 穿越以前看看路上是否安全. *to ~ at him/it, etc*, judging by the outward appearance: 由外貌判断: *To ~ at her you'd never guess that she was a university teacher*. 由外貌判断你绝对想不到她是位大学教师. *L~ before you leap*, (prov) Avoid acting hastily, without considering the possible consequences. (谚)慎思而后行. '~·**ing·glass** n mirror made of glass. 镜子. **2** [VP2D, 4D] seem to be; have the appearance of being: 看来象是; 现出某种样子: *sad/ill/tired*. 面现愁容(病容, 倦容). *The town always ~s deserted on Sunday mornings*. 在星期日的早晨这座城市总显得冷清清的样子. *It ~s very suspicious to me*, I suspect that it is not strictly honest, straightforward, etc. 我觉得此事有点蹊跷. *The girl ~ed puzzled*. 那女孩显得很困惑. (**not**) ~ **oneself**, (not) have one's normal appearance: 看起来跟平常一样(不一样): *You're not ~ing yourself today*, You're ~ing ill, worried,

etc. 你看来有点异样(象是病了, 担忧等). *He's beginning to ~ himself again,* ~ well again, eg after an illness. 他开始复元了(例如病后). ~ **one's age,** have an appearance that conforms to one's age: 看起来与年龄相符: *She ~s her age,* seems as old as she in fact is. 她看起来和她的年龄相符. *You don't ~ your age,* look younger than you are. 你看起来比你的实际年龄年轻. ~ **one's best,** appear to the greatest advantage: 最能显现优点: *She ~s her best in jeans.* 她穿着牛仔裤最漂亮. ~ **black (at),** angrily (at). 而带怒色; 怒目而视. ~ **blue,** appear sad or discontented. 面现忧伤或不满之色. ~ **good, (a)** seem attractive, enticing, etc. 看来可爱, 动人. **(b)** seem to be making satisfactory progress, doing well, etc: 似乎有令人满意的进步; 似乎做得不错: *The horse I put my money on ~ed good until the last hundred metres.* 我赌的那匹马在最后的一百米以前表现不错. Hence, 由此产生, **good-'~ing** adj of fine appearance. 动人的; 可爱的; 好看的. ~ **small,** mean or insignificant: 显得卑鄙或不重要: *We made him ~ small,* exposed him as being insignificant. 我们使他显得不重要了. *L~ alive! Get busy! Make haste!* 赶快! 快些! *L~ here!* often used to call attention to sth; or demand attention. 看这里! (常用以引人注意或要人注意). *L~ sharp! Hurry up!* 赶快! ~ **well, (a)** (of persons) be healthy in appearance. (指人) 看来健康. **(b)** (of things) be attractive, pleasing, satisfactory: (指物)美观; 悦目; 令人满意: *Does this hat ~ well on me?* 我戴上这顶帽子好看吗? **(c)** (of a person wearing sth) ~ attractive: (指穿着某衣物的人)看来动人; 显得漂亮: *He ~ed well in naval uniform.* 他穿着海军制服很漂亮. **3** [VP2C] ~ **like/as if,** seem (to be): 似乎是; 看来象是: *It ~s like salt as if it is salt.* 它看来象盐, 而事实上也是盐. *It ~s like* (= threatens to) *rain.* 天象是要下雨的样子. *It ~s like being* (= promises to be) *a fine day.* 看来会是一个好天. *This ~s to me like a way in.* 在我看来这象是进去的路. *You ~ as if she were about to faint.* 你象是要晕倒的样子. *You ~ as if you slept badly.* 你看来象是睡眠不足. *It doesn't ~ to me as if we shall get there in time.* 我看我们不能及时到达了. **4** [VP8] pay attention; learn by seeing: 注意; 由观看而知晓: *L~ where you're going!* 当心走路! *L~ who's here!* 看谁在这里! *L~ (and see) whether the postman has been yet.* 去看看邮差来过没有. **5** (= ~ at) ~ **sb/sth in the eye(s)/face,** confront calmly and bravely: 镇定勇敢地面对: ~ *death/one's enemy in the face.* 镇定勇敢地面对死亡(敌人). **6** [VP6A] express by one's appearance: 露出…之表情; 用脸色表示: ~ *one's thanks/consent.* 露出感激(同意)的表情. **7** [VP 2C, 3A, 15B] (uses with adverbial particles and preps): (与副词性小品词和介词连用的用法):

look about (for sth), be on the watch, in search of; examine one's surroundings, the state of affairs, etc: 警戒; 看望; 寻找; 审视环境; 查看情况: *Are you still ~ing about for a job?* 你仍在找工作吗? ~ **about one,** examine one's surroundings; give oneself time to make plans: 审视环境; 找时间安排: *We hardly had time to ~ about us before we had to continue our journey.* 我们几乎没有时间安排一下便不得不继续旅行了.

look after sb/sth, (a) take care of; watch over; attend to: 照顾; 照看; 照料: *Who will ~ after the children while their mother is in hospital?* 在他们的母亲住院期间, 谁照顾这些孩子? *He needs a wife to ~ after him.* 他需要一个妻子照顾他. *He's well able to ~ after himself/to ~ after his own interests.* 他很会照顾自己(顾到自己的利益). **(b)** follow with the eyes: 目送: *They ~ed after the train as it left the station.* 他们目送火车离站.

look at sth, (special uses) (特殊用法) **(a)** *not ~ at sth,* (usu with will, would) not consider: (通常与 will 或 would 连用)不考虑: *They wouldn't ~ at my proposal.* 他们不考虑我的建议. **(b)** examine: 检查: *We must ~ at the question from all sides.* 我们必须从各方面检讨此

问题. *Will you please ~ at the battery of my car?* 请你检查一下我车上的电瓶好吗? *Doctor, will you ~ at my ankle?* 医师, 请你检查一下我的脚脖子好吗? **(c)** in polite requests: *Will you please ~ at* (ie read) *this letter?* 请你读一读这封信好吗? **good/bad, etc to ~ at,** of good, etc appearance: 外表美观(不美观等): *The hotel is not much to ~ at,* does not appear to be good from the outside. 这旅馆的外表不太美观. **look away (from sth),** turn the eyes away. (自…)转移目光.

look back (on/to sth), (fig) turn one's thoughts to sth in the past. (喻)追想; 回顾. *never ~ back,* make uninterrupted progress. 不断进步.

look down on sb/sth, despise; consider oneself superior to; show false contempt for: 轻视; 瞧不起; 蔑视: *When she married the boss, she ~ed down on the office girls she had worked with.* 她嫁给老板后, 便瞧不起曾同她在一起办公的女职员了. ~ **down one's nose at sb/sth,** (colloq) regard with displeasure or contempt. (口)对某人不悦或轻视.

look for sb/sth, (a) search for; try to find: 寻找; 寻求: *Are you still ~ing for a job?* 你仍在找工作吗? *That foolish fellow is ~ing for trouble,* is behaving in a way that will get him into trouble. 那个愚蠢的家伙在自找麻烦. **(b)** expect: 期望: *It's too soon yet to ~ for results.* 现在便期望有结果为时尚早.

look forward to sth, anticipate (usu with pleasure): 盼望; 期待 (通常以愉快的心情): *We're ~ing forward to seeing you again.* 我们盼望再见到你.

look in (on sb), make a short (usu casual) visit; pay a call: (顺便)看望; 拜访: *Why don't you ~ in (on me) next time you're in town?* 你下次进城来时请顺便看看我好吗? *The doctor will ~ in again this evening.* 医生今晚将再来. **give sb/get a '~-in,** (colloq, sport, etc) chance (of winning, etc): (口, 运动等)给予某人(获得)(得胜等)的机会: *You won't get a ~-in with such strong competition.* 在这种激烈的竞争下你没有机会获胜.

look into sth, (a) investigate; examine: 调查; 检查: ~ *into a question.* 调查一问题. **(b)** dip into (a book, etc). 浏览(书等). **(c)** ~ *at the inside of, the depths of:* 注视…的内部或深处: *He ~ed into the box/the mirror/her eyes.* 他注视箱底(镜子, 她的眼睛).

look on, be a spectator; watch: 旁观; 观望: *Why don't you play football instead of just ~ing on?* 你为什么不参加踢足球而只是旁观? Hence, 由此产生, **,~er-'on** n person who ~s on. 旁观者. ~ **on/upon sb/sth as,** regard as: 视作: *Do you ~ on him as an authority on the subject?* 你认为他是这问题的权威吗? ~ **on/upon sb/sth with,** regard in the way specified: 以特殊方式看某人: *I have always ~ed on sb with distrust.* 我似乎不信任他. ~ **on to,** (of a place, room, etc) overlook, give a view of: (指地点, 房间等)面对; 濒临: *My bedroom ~s on to the garden.* 我的卧室面对着花园.

look out (of sth) (at sth): *He stood at the window and ~ed out (at the view).* 他站在窗前向外望(观看景色). *They were ~ing out of the window.* 他们正向窗外看. ~ **out on (to)/over,** supply an outlook or view over: 供以瞭望的景色: *Our hotel room here ~s out on the sea front.* 我们的旅馆房间面对海滨. ~ **out (for sb/sth),** be prepared (for); be on the watch (for): 准备; 警戒; 当心; 守候: *L~ out!* Be on the watch, be careful! 当心! 小心! *Will you go to the station and ~ out for Mr Hill?* 请你到车站去等候希尔先生好吗? Hence, 由此产生, **'~-out** n **(a)** keep a good **~-out (for); be on the ~-out (for),** be watchful (for). 注意守望; 严密注意. **(b)** [C] place from which to watch; person who has the duty of watching: 守望处; 守望者: (attrib) (用作定语) a ~ *post;* 监视哨所; send ~outs in advance. 预先派出监视哨. **(c)** (sing only) prospect; what seems likely to come or happen: (仅用单数) 远景; 前途: It's a bad ~out for their children. 他们的孩子们的前途似乎不佳. *That's your own ~out,* sth you yourself must be responsible for. 那是你自己应负责任

的事。~ **sth out (for sb)**, select by making an inspection: 检查以选出; 挑选: ~ *out some books for a friend in hospital.* 为一住院友人挑选几本书。

look over sth, inspect; examine: 检阅;检查: *We must ~ over the house before we decide to rent it.* 在决定租这房子前我们必须先看一下。~ **sth over**, inspect one by one or part by part: 逐一检查; 逐步检阅: *Here's the correspondence; I've ~ed it over.* 这就是那封信,我已检查过。Hence, 由此产生, **'~over** *n:* give something a ~over, examine it. 检查某物。

look round, (a) (fig) examine possibilities before deciding sth: (喻)事前仔细考虑: *Don't make a hurried decision;* ~ *round well first.* 不要急作决定,先好好考虑一下。**(b)** turn the head (to see): 转首(张看): *When I ~ed round for her, she was leaving the hall.* 当我转过头去看她时, 她正离开大厅。~ **round (sth)**, go sightseeing, etc: 观光; 游览: *Have we time to ~ round (the town) before lunch?* 我们在中饭前有时间(在城里)游览一下吗?

look through sth, revise (a lesson, etc); study; examine: 仔细研读(功课等); 温习; 检查: *L~ through your notes before the examination.* 考试前温习你的笔记。*I must ~ through these bills and check them before I pay them.* 我必须在付款前审查和核对一下这些帐单。~ **sth through**, inspect carefully or successively: 仔细检查; 逐项审查: *He ~ed the proposals through before approving them.* 他在核准前仔细审查那些提议。

look to sth, be careful of or about: 注意: *The country must ~ to its defences.* 国家必须注意其防务。*L~ to your manners, my boy, Don't be so rude.* 注意你的态度, 孩子, 别这么无礼。~ **to it** (= Take care) *that this does not happen again.* 注意不要使此事再发生。~ **to sb for sth/to sing**, rely on: 依赖: *They all ~ to you for help.* 他们全仰赖你的帮助。*They're ~ing to you for a solo/to sing to them.* 他们期待着你的独唱(唱给他们听)。~ **to/towards**, face: 面对: *a house ~ing towards the river/to the south.* 面临河的(朝南的)一所房屋。

look up, (a) raise the eyes: 仰视: *Don't ~ up.* 不要向上看。**(b)** improve in price or prosperity: 涨价; 繁荣: *Business is/Oil shares are ~ing up.* 商业(石油股票)呈现起色。~ **sth up**, search for (a word in a dictionary, facts in a reference book, etc): 查(词典中的词, 参考书中的事实等): *Please ~ up a fast train to Leeds, in a railway guide.* 请查一下去里兹的快车(查一下火车时刻表)。~ **sb up**, pay a call on; visit: 拜访; 探访: *Do ~ me up next time you're in London.* 你下次到伦敦时, 务必请来访我。~ **up to sb (as ...)**, respect: 尊敬: *They all ~ up to him as their leader.* 他们都尊他为他们的领袖。~ **sb up and down**, examine him carefully or contemptuously. 上下打量某人; 轻蔑地打量某人。

look² /luk; lʊk/ *n* [C] **1** act of looking: 看; 望; 视: *Let me have a ~ at your new car.* 让我看一看你的新车。**2** facial expression; appearance: 表情; 神色; 外表; 外观: *A ~ of pleasure came to her face.* 她脸上显出愉快的表情。*There were angry ~s from the neighbours.* 邻人们有愠怒之色。*The town has a European ~.* 这城市的外貌有欧洲的风格。*give sth/get a new ~*, a new and more up-to-date appearance: 给予(获得)新面貌: *The High Street has been given a new ~.* 高街的外貌一新。**3** (*pl*) person's appearance: (复)容貌: *She's beginning to lose her ~s*, her beauty. 她的容颜渐老。**~er** *n: a ,good-'~er*, a good-looking person. 美貌之人。

loom¹ /luːm; lum/ *n* machine for weaving cloth. 织布机。

loom² /luːm; lum/ *vi* [VP2C, D] *loom (large)*, appear indistinctly and in a threatening way; (fig) appear great and fill the mind: 隐约地或威胁性地出现; (喻)庞然逼压心头: *The dark outline of another ship ~ed (up) through the fog.* 另一只船的黑影在雾中隐现。*The threat of the H-bomb ~ed large in their minds.* 他们

心中深受氢弹的威胁。

loon¹ /luːn; lun/ *n* large diving-bird that lives on fish and has a loud, wild cry. 潜鸟; 阿比(一种大潜水鸟, 以鱼为食, 鸣声响亮)。

loon² /luːn; lun/ *n* (Scot and archaic) foolish, idle, good-for-nothing person. (苏, 古)愚蠢、懒惰、无用的人。

loony /'luːnɪ; 'lunɪ/ *n, adj* (sl) lunatic. (俚)疯子;疯人;疯狂的。**'~-bin** /-bɪn; -bɪn/ *n* (sl) mental home. (俚)疯人院。

loop /luːp; lup/ *n* **1** (shape produced by a) curve crossing itself as in the letters *l* and *h* in ordinary handwriting). 本身形成环的曲线; 纽形弧; 环形花样(如手写体中写 l 和 h 所形成者)。**2** part of a length of string, wire, ribbon, etc in such a shape, eg as a knot or fastening; curved piece of metal as a handle; (colloq) ~-shaped intra-uterine contraceptive device. (绳, 金属线、丝带等绕成的) 环或圈(例如做结或系物者): 金属环钩; (口)乐普(一种置于子宫内之避孕器)。**3** (also 亦作 **'~-line**) railway or telegraph line that separates from the main line, runs in a curve, and then rejoins the main line farther on. 铁轨或电报线之环状侧线; 回车道; 回线。**4** circuit in which an aviator, motorcyclist, etc is for a time travelling in a ~ or in ~s: 飞机之翻圈飞行; 斤斗; 环飞; 汽车等之环状行驶: *The airman looped the ~ five times, flew the shape of a ~ five times.* 那飞行员翻了五次斤斗飞行。□ *vt, vi* **1** [VP6A, 15B] form or bend into a ~ or ~s; supply with a ~ or ~s: 使成环或圈; 形成环; 围以环或圈: ~ *the curtains up/back;* 卷起窗帘; ~ *things together.* 用环将物系在一起。**2** [VP6A, 2A] perform a ~ (4); make a ~ or ~s. 作环状飞行或驾驶; 斤斗飞行; 环飞。

loop·hole /'luːphəʊl; 'lup,hol/ *n* **1** narrow vertical opening in a wall for shooting or looking through, or to admit light and air (as in old forts, stockades, etc). (墙上供射击, 了望或通光通风用的)枪眼; 窄窗; 窗孔(如古堡垒, 栅栏等中者)。**2** (fig) way of escape from control, esp one provided by careless and inexact wording of a rule: (喻)(因措词欠妥而造成的法规上的)漏洞: *find a ~ in the law.* 找出法律上的漏洞。

loopy /'luːpɪ; 'lupɪ/ *adj* (sl) crazy. (俚)疯狂的。

loose¹ /luːs; lus/ *adj* (**-r, -st**) **1** free; not held, tied up, fastened, packed, or contained in sth: 无约束的; 松开的; 未受束缚的: *Many Englishmen carry their small change (ie coins) ~ in their trouser pocket, not in a purse.* 许多英国人将零钱散置在裤子口袋内, 而不放在钱袋内。*That dog is too dangerous to be left ~.* 那狗太危险, 不可放开。*break/get ~*, escape confinement: 自拘禁中逃出: *One of the tigers in the zoo has broken/got ~*, has escaped from its cage. 动物园中有一支虎自笼中逃出来了。*let sth ~*, allow it to be free from control: 任其自由; 放任: *He let ~ his indignation*, did not control it. 他发泄他的愤慨。**'~ box**, separate compartment in a stable or railway van, in which a horse can move about freely. (马厩或运货火车中之)马匹自由活动间。**,~-'leaf** *attrib adj* (of a notebook) with leaves that may be detached separately and replaced. (指笔记本)活页的。**2** not close-fitting; not tight or tense: 不紧

a hand loom

的；宽松的: *a ~ collar*: 宽松的衣领; *~-fitting clothes.* 宽大的衣服. **3** moving more freely than is right or usual: 不牢的; 松弛的: *a ~ tooth*; 松动的牙齿; *~ bowels*, with a tendency to diarrhoea; 泻肚; *a ~ thread*; 松弛的线; one that shakes or rattles in the wind. 不固定的窗子. *come ~*, (of a fastening, etc) come unfastened or insecure. (指缚系物等)解开; 变松. *have a 'screw ~*, (colloq) be unsound in one's mind. (口)心智不健全. *have a ~ tongue*, be in the habit of talking too freely. 爱多嘴的; 喜欢饶舌的. *ride with a ~ rein*, **(a)** allow the horse freedom. 放松缰绳. **(b)** (fig) manage a person indulgently. (喻)放任; 纵容. *work ~*, (of a bolt, etc) become insecure, no longer tight. (指螺钉等)松动. **4** not firmly or properly tied: 未系牢的: *a ~ knot*; 未系牢的结; *a ~ end of rope*, one that is not fastened. 绳子未系牢的一端. *at a ~ end*, (fig of a person) having nothing to do. (喻, 指人)无事做的. **5** (of talk, behaviour, etc) not sufficiently controlled: (指言行等)不严谨的; 放荡的: *~ conduct*; 放荡的行为; *lead a ~ life*; 过放荡的生活; *a ~ (= immoral) woman*. 放荡的女子. *(be) on the ~*, (colloq) free from the restraints of morality or discipline; dissipated. (口)放荡; 耽于游乐. *play fast and ~ (with sb)*, behave dishonestly or in a deceitful manner. 欺骗; 欺诈. **6** not strict; inexact; indefinite; (of translations) not close to the original: 不严格的; 不精确的; 不确定的; (指翻译)不忠于原著的: *~ thinking*; 不严密的思想; *a ~ thinker*; 思想不严密的人; *a ~ (= badly constructed) argument*. 不严密的论据. **7** not compact; not closely packed: 松散的; 未包装紧的: *~ soil*; 松土; *cloth with a ~ weave*. 织得松的布. **8** (of the human body) not closely knit: (指人体)不结实的: *a ~ frame*; 不结实的体格; *~ limbs*, rather awkward, ungainly in appearance; 笨拙难看的四肢; (of bodily actions) careless, bungling or inaccurate: (指身体动作)随便的; 笨拙的; 不准确的: *~ bowling and fielding* (in cricket). (板球戏中)不准确的抛出与远掷. *~·ly adv* in a ~ manner: 松开地; 宽松地; 松弛地; 不精确地; 不严格地; 放荡地: *words ~ly employed*, ⇨ **1** above; 用得不精确的字(参看上列第 6 义); *rules ~ly enforced*. 未严格执行的法规.

loose² /luːs; lus/ *vt* [VP6A] make free or loose: 使无约束; 使松弛: *Wine ~d his tongue*, made him talk freely (*loosen* is more usu). 酒使他话多 (*loosen* 较常用).

loosen /ˈluːsn; ˈlusn̩/ *vt, vi* [VP6A, 2A, 15B] *~ (up)*, make or become loose or looser: 使松; 放松; 变松; 松弛: *L~ the screw*. 把螺丝钉放松. *The screw has ~ed*. 螺丝钉松了. *This medicine may ~ your cough*, help to get up the phlegm. 此药可减轻你的咳嗽(助你消痰). *I must take some exercise and ~ up my muscles*. 我必须做点运动以放松我的肌肉.

loot /luːt; lut/ *n* [U] goods (esp private property) taken away unlawfully and by force, eg by thieves, or by soldiers in time of war. (盗贼的)赃物; (战时士兵之)掠夺物; 战利品. □ *vt, vi* [VP6A, 2A] carry off ~ from: 抢劫; 劫掠: *The brutal soldiers ~ed and massacred for three weeks*. 那些残忍的士兵劫掠屠杀了三个星期. *~·er n*

lop¹ /lɒp; lɑp/ *vt* (**-pp-**) [VP6A, 15B] *lop (away/off)*, cut off, separate branches, etc from a tree. 砍去(树枝等); 砍掉.

lop² /lɒp; lɑp/ *vi* (**-pp-**) hang down loosely; (chiefly in compounds): 松弛地垂下; (主要用于复合词中): **'lop-ears** *n pl* drooping ears. 下垂的耳朵. **'lop-eared** *adj* having lop-ears: 耳朵下垂的: *a lop-eared rabbit*. 一只垂耳朵的兔子. **lop-'sided** *adj* with one side lower than the other. 一边低于另一边的; 一边高一边低的.

lope /ləʊp; lop/ *vi* [VP2A, C] move along with long, easy steps or strides (as a hare does). 大步慢跑; 缓驰(如野兔所做者). □ *n* step or stride of this kind: 大步慢跑; 缓驰: *The deer went off at an easy ~*. 那鹿轻松地缓驰而去.

lo·qua·cious /ləˈkweɪʃəs; loˈkweʃəs/ *adj* talkative; fond of talking. 多嘴的; 饶舌的. *~·ly adv* *~·ness*, **lo·quac·ity** /ləˈkwæsətɪ; loˈkwæsətɪ/ *nn* [U] being ~. 多嘴; 饶舌; 刺刺不休.

lo·quat /ˈləʊkwɒt; ˈlokwɑt/ *n* [C] (tree, common in China and Japan, with a) yellow or yellowish-red fruit that grows in clusters and has a sharp taste. 枇杷(树). ⇨ the illus at **fruit**. 参看 fruit 之插图.

lor /lɔː(r); lɔr/ *int* (vulg substitute for) Lord! (= God). (鄙)主啊! 天啊!

lord /lɔːd; lɔrd/ *n* **1** supreme male ruler: 最高统治者; 君主: *our sovereign ~ the King*. 我们的君主. **2 the L~**, God; Christ. 上帝; 基督. *L~! L~ God! Good L~! L~ knows! L~ bless us!* exclamations of surprise, etc. 天呀! 哎呀! 哎呀! *Our L~*, Christ. 耶稣基督. **the 'L~'s Day**, Sunday. 主日; 星期日. **the ¦L~'s 'Prayer**, that given by Jesus to his followers. 主祷文. **the 'L~'s 'Supper**, the taking of bread and wine to commemorate the last meal taken by Jesus Christ with his twelve disciples before his death. 圣餐 (吃面包和酒以纪念耶稣及其十二门徒共进最后晚餐之仪式). **3** peer; nobleman: 贵族: *live/treat sb like a ~*, sumptuously. 过奢华的生活(把某人视做王公一般接待). *as drunk as a ~*, excessively drunk. 酩酊大醉. **the House of L~s**, (in GB) the upper division of Parliament, consisting of *the ~s spiritual* (the Archbishops and Bishops) and *the ~s temporal* (hereditary and life peers). (英国之)上议院(议员可包括主教和贵族). **4** (in feudal times) superior. (封建时代之)领主. **the ~ of the manor**, man from whom vassals held land and to whom they owed service. 领主. **5** (joc, also 谑, 亦作 *~ and master*) husband; great leader of industry: 丈夫; 夫君; 工业界领袖; 实业巨子: *the 'cotton ~s*. 棉业界领袖. (cf 参较 *'beer barons*); *the ~s of creation*, mankind (contrasted with the animals). 人类(以别于动物). **6** person in a position of authority: 权要: *the L~s of the Admiralty/Treasury*, the chief members of these Boards: (英)海军部(财政部)的要员; *the First L~ of the Admiralty*, the president of this Board. 海军部长. **7** first word in many official titles: 用作许多官衔的第一字: *the L~ Mayor of London*; 伦敦市长; *the L~ Chamberlain*, etc. 宫务大臣等. **8** title prefixed to names of peers and barons: 对贵族或男爵的尊称: 勋爵: *L~ Derby*. 德贝勋爵. Cf 参较 the *Earl of Derby*. 德贝伯爵. **9** *My ~*, respectful formula for addressing certain noblemen and judges and bishops. 阁下(对某些贵族, 法官及主教的尊称). □ *vt* (chiefly in) (主用于) *~ it over sb*, rule over like a ~: 作威作福; 盛气凌人: 专横霸道: *'I will not be ~ed over,' she said to her husband*. '我不愿受人主宰,' 她向她丈夫说. *~·less adj* without a ~. 无贵族的; 无君王的; 无主的.

lord·ly /ˈlɔːdlɪ; ˈlɔrdlɪ/ *adj* (**-ier, -iest**) **1** haughty; insolent. 傲慢的; 无礼的. **2** like, suitable for, a lord; magnificent. 似贵族的; 适于贵族的; 堂皇的. **lord·li·ness** *n*

lord·ship /ˈlɔːdʃɪp; ˈlɔrdʃɪp/ *n* **1** [U] *~ over*, rule, authority. 统治; 权威. **2** [C] *His/Your L~*, used when speaking of/to a lord. 阁下(对贵族的尊称).

lore /lɔː(r); lɔr/ *n* [U] learning or knowledge, esp handed down from past times, or possessed by a class of people: 学问或知识(尤指自过去传下, 或某一阶级或民族所有者): *'Irish ~*; 爱尔兰人的学问; *'Gypsy ~*; 吉普赛人的学问; or of a special subject: 特殊科目的知识: *'fairy ~/'folk ~*. 神话(飞禽学; 民俗学).

lor·gnette /lɔːˈnjet; lɔrnˈjet/ *n* pair of eye-glasses held to the eyes on a long handle. 长柄眼镜.

lorn /lɔːn; lɔrn/ *adj* (poet or hum) forlorn; desolate: (诗或谐)孤单的; 孤寂的: *a lone, ~ widow*. 寂寞孤单的寡妇.

lorry /ˈlɒrɪ US: ˈlɔːrɪ; ˈlɔrɪ/ *n* (*pl* **-ries**) (US = truck) long, low, open motor-vehicle, for carrying goods by road. 载货卡车.

lose /luːz/ luz/ *vt, vi* (*pt, pp* **lost** /lɒst US: lɔːst; lost/) **1** [VP6A] no longer have; have taken away from one by accident, carelessness, misfortune, death, etc: 失去; 损失; 丧失: ~ *one's money;* 损失金钱; ~ *a leg,* eg in a road accident; 失去一腿(例如在车祸中); ~ *a lot of money at the races* (by betting); 赌赛马输了很多钱; ~ *one's balance,* fall over. 跌倒. *He lost two sons in the war,* They were killed. 他有两个儿子在战争中阵亡. *She lost her husband,* He is dead. 她的丈夫已去世. *He has lost his job,* has been dismissed. 他失业了. *You're losing your hair,* getting bald. 你的头发渐渐脱落了. *She has lost her good looks,* is no longer good-looking. 她已失去她的美貌. *It was so cold that we lost the use of our hands,* could not use them. 天太冷, 我们的手都冻僵了. *He's losing patience,* is becoming impatient. 他失去耐心了. ~ *one's cool,* (colloq) lose one's composure; be no longer calm or composed. (口) 失去镇定; 心情慌乱. ~ *ground,* ⇨ **ground**[1](2). ~ *one's head,* ⇨ **head**[1](19). ~ *heart,* ⇨ **heart**(2). ~ *one's heart to sb,* ⇨ **heart**(2). ~ *interest (in sb/sth),* cease to be interested in, attracted by. (对某人或某物)失去兴趣; 不再引起兴趣. ~ *one's reason/senses,* become insane or wildly excited. 失去理性; 发狂. ~ *one's temper,* become angry. 发怒. ~ *A to B,* have A taken away by B: A 被 B 取而代之: *The little grocery shop is losing all its customers to the new supermarket.* 那个小杂货店的顾客都跑到新开的超级市场去了. ~ *touch (with),* ⇨ **touch**[1](6). **2** (passive) be lost, disappear; die; be dead: (被动语态)失踪; 死: 死去: *The ship and all its crew were lost.* 该船及其所有船员皆失踪了. *Is letter-writing a lost art,* Has the art of writing (social) letters died, eg because of the use of the telephone? 写信这种方法已被淘汰了吗(例如由于电话之采用)? *be lost to sth,* be no longer affected by, be insensible to, eg all sense of shame, decency, honour, duty. 不为(羞耻, 体面, 荣誉心, 责任感等)所动; 对…无感觉. *be lost in sth,* be deeply occupied or filled with, eg thought, wonder, admiration. 沉入(思想, 惊异, 羡慕等)中. **3** [VP6A] (contrasted with *find, recover*) be unable to find: (与 *find, recover* 相对)遗失; 失落; 找不到: *I've lost the keys of my car.* 我的汽车钥匙丢了. *The books seem to be lost/to have been lost.* 那些书好象不见了. *She lost her husband in the crowd.* 她和她丈夫在人群中走散了. ~ *one's place,* (in a book, etc) be unable to find the page, paragraph, etc where one stopped reading. (读书等)忘记上次读到的地方. ~ *oneself/one's way,* be lost, be unable to find the right way, road, etc; not know where one is: 迷路: *The children lost their way in the forest.* 孩子们在森林中迷了路. *We lost our way in the dark.* 我们在黑暗中迷了路. *I hope the children haven't got lost/lost themselves.* 我希望孩子们没有迷路. ~ *sight of sth,* (a) overlook; fail to take account of: 忽视; 忽略: *We mustn't ~ sight of the fact that* .... 我们切不可忽视…之事实. **(b)** no longer be able to see: 看不见: *The early navigators disliked losing sight of land.* 早期的航海探险者不喜欢望不见陆地. *We lost sight of him in the crowd.* 我们在人群里看不见他了. ~ *the thread of sth,* eg an argument, ⇨ **thread.** 失去(例如议论的)条理. ~ *one's tongue,* ⇨ **tongue.** ~ *track of sth,* ⇨ **track. 4** [VP6A] (contrasted with *catch*) be too late for; fail to hear, see, etc: (与 *catch* 相对)未能赶上; 未能听到; 看见等: ~ (more usu 较常用 *miss*) *one's train/the bus;* 未赶上火车(公共汽车); ~ *the post,* get to the post office, etc too late for the collection; 未赶上邮局收信的时间; ~ (= not hear) *the end of a sentence.* 没听见一个句子的末尾. *What he said was lost in the applause that greeted him.* 他的话被淹没了的喝彩声淹没了. **5** [VP12C] cause (sb) the loss of: 使(某人)损失: *Such insolence will ~ you your situation.* 如此无礼的态度将会使你失去你的职位. *This remark lost him our sympathy.* 此话使我们对他失去了同情心. **6** [VP6A, 2A] fail to win, be

defeated: 未能获胜; 输; 失败: ~ *a game/a match/a battle/a war/a lawsuit/a prize;* 比赛输了(赛跑; 打败, 败诉; 未能获奖); ~ *a motion,* fail to carry it in a debate. (辩论中)未能使一项动议获得支持. *a lost cause,* one that has already been defeated or is sure to be defeated. 已失败或注定失败的主义, 运动等. **(play) a losing game,** one in which defeat is likely or certain. (参加)多半或必定会输的比赛. ~ *out (to),* (colloq) be overcome and replaced (by): (口)被取而代之: *Has the cinema lost out to TV?* 电影已被电视取代吗? **7** [VP6A, 15A, 3A] ~ *by/in on sth,* lose or become worse: 受亏损; 蒙损害: *You will ~ nothing by waiting,* will not suffer any loss. 等待不会使你吃亏: *Will the publisher ~ by it,* be worse off because of publishing the book? 出版商会为(出版)这本书受损失吗? *How much did he ~ on the transaction?* 该项交易使他受到多少亏损? *The story does not ~ in the telling,* is not made less interesting, is perhaps exaggerated. 这故事讲起来照样有趣(或许有些夸张). **8** [VP2A, B] (of a watch or clock) go too slowly; fail to keep correct time because of this: (指钟表)走得太慢; 因慢而不准确: *Does your watch gain or ~?* 你的表快了还是慢了? *My watch ~s two minutes a day.* 我的表一天慢两分钟. **9** [VP6A] spend time, opportunity, efforts to no purpose; waste: 浪费(时间, 机会, 努力): *There's not a moment to ~.* 没有时间可浪费了. *I shall ~ no time in doing it,* shall do it at once. 我将即刻做此事. *be lost upon sb,* fail to influence or attract the attention of: 未能影响或引起注意: *My hints were not lost upon him,* They were noted. 我的暗示受到了他的注意. **10** ~ *oneself in sth,* (reflex) become engrossed in it: (反身)专心于某事; 埋头于某事: *She lost herself in a book,* became so deeply interested in it that she was unaware of other things. 她去埋头读一本书. ~*r* n person who ~s or is defeated: 输者; 失败者: *He's a good/bad ~r,* is cheerful/discontented when he ~s. 他是个输得起(不起)的人.

loss /lɒs US: lɔːs; los/ *n* **1** [U] act or fact or process of losing: 损失; 丧失; 遗失: ~ *of blood;* 失血; ~ *of prestige.* 丧失声誉. *L~ of health is more serious than ~ of money.* 健康的丧失较金钱的损失尤为严重. *The ~ of his heavyweight title doesn't seem to worry him.* 重量级拳王头衔的丧失似乎并不使他烦恼. *The ~ of so many ships worried the Admiral.* 这么多艘船只的损失使舰队司令忧愁. **2** [U] (and with *indef art*) failure to keep, maintain or use: (与不定冠词连用)未能保住; 未能持; 未能利用: *a heavy ~;* 严重损失; ~ *of opportunities;* 机会的失去; *without (any) ~ of time.* 未浪费时间. *There was a temporary ~ of power.* 暂时失去势力. **3** [U] failure to win or obtain: 输; 未获得: *the ~ of a contract.* 未获承包. **4** [C] that which is lost: 损失物; 丧失物; 损耗: *sell sth at a ~;* 亏本卖出某物; *suffer heavy ~es in war,* men killed, wounded, captured; ships and aircraft lost. 战争中遭受重大损失(即士兵伤亡或被俘, 战舰和飞机被毁). ⇨ **gain**[1], **profit**[1](2). *a total ~,* from which nothing can be saved: 完全损失: *The ship was wrecked and became a total ~.* 那条船失事, 全部损失了. *,~'leader* n (comm) article, etc sold at a ~ in order to attract customers to buy other goods. (商)为招徕顾客亏本卖出的货物. **5** (*sing* only) disadvantage or deprivation: (仅用单数)不利; 剥夺: *Such a man is no great ~,* We need not regret losing his services. 损失这样一个人并不遗憾. *be a dead ~,* (colloq, of a person) be quite worthless: (口, 指人)毫无用处: *We'd better fire Smith—He's a dead ~.* 我们最好辞退史密斯——他毫无用处. **6 (be)** *at a ~ for sth/to do sth,* be perplexed, uncertain: 困惑; 不知所措: *He was at a ~ for words/to know what to say,* did not know how to express himself. 他不知道说些什么话.

lost /lɒst US: lɔːst; lost/ *pt, pp* of **lose.**

lot[1] /lɒt/ lat/ *n* (colloq) (口) **1** *the lot; the whole lot; all the lot,* the whole number or quantity: 全体; 全部; 总量: *That's the lot,* That's all or everything. 全

都在此。*Take the (whole) lot.* 统统拿去。*Go away, the whole lot of you/all the lot of you,* (emphat for) 'all of you', 'every one of you'. 你们全都走开 (较 'all of you', 及 'every one of you' 语气犹重). *She wants a new car, a fridge, and a colour TV—the lot!* 她要一部新汽车, 一个冰箱, 和一部彩色电视机——全套! **2** *a lot (of); lots (and lots) (of),* a great amount or number (of): 很多; 许多: *What a lot of time you take to dress!* 你穿衣服费的时间真多! *She spends a lot of money on clothes.* 她花很多钱添置衣服。*There were such a lot of people in the shops!* 商店里的人真多! *I want lots.* 我要很多。*I saw quite a lot of her* (= saw her often) *when I was in London last month.* 我上月在伦敦时常常看到她。*We don't see a lot of her nowadays.* 我们现在很少看到她。**3** (used adverbially) very much: (用作副词)很多: *He's feeling a lot better today.* 他今天身体好多了。*A lot 'you care!* (ironic) You don't care at all! (反语)你才不开心哩! Cf 参较 *a good deal, a little.*

lot² /lɒt; lɑt/ *n* [U] **1** (one of a set of objects used in) the making of a selection or decision by methods depending upon chance: 抽签法; 拈阄法; 签; 阄: *divide property by lot.* 用抽签法分财产。 *draw/cast lots,* eg by taking pieces of paper marked in some way from a box: 拈阄; 抽签: *They drew lots as to who should begin.* 他们抽签以决谁应先开始。**2** *the lot,* decision or choice resulting from this; 中签; 抽中: *The lot came to/fell upon me.* 我抽中了。**3** person's fortune or destiny: 命运; 运气: *His lot has been a hard one.* 他的命苦。*Such good fortune falls to the lot of few men.* 这种好运气很少有人获得。*It has fallen to my lot to oppose the President in the election.* 命中注定要我在选举中对抗总统。*cast/throw in one's lot with sb,* decide to share the fortunes of. 与某人祸福相共。**4** item, or number of items, (to be) sold at an auction sale: (拍卖品之)项目; 组: *Lot 46, six chairs.* 第四十六项, 椅子六把。**5** collection of objects of the same kind: 一批(同样的东西): *We have received a new lot of hats from the manufacturers.* 我们从制造商那里收到了一批新帽子。**6** *a bad lot,* (colloq) a bad person. (口)坏人; 恶人。**7** (cinema) studio and surrounding land. (电影)摄影场。**8** plot of land: 一块地; 一块地皮: (esp US) (尤美) a *'parking lot,* for cars; 一块停车场地; *a vacant lot,* a building site. 一块空地皮。

loth /ləʊθ; loθ/ *adj* ⟹ **loath.**

lo·tion /'ləʊʃn; 'loʃən/ *n* [C, U] (kind of) medicinal liquid for use on the skin: (一种)洗剂: *a bottle of cleansing ~ for the face;* 一瓶洗面剂; *soothing ~s for insect bites.* 虫咬镇痛洗剂。

lot·tery /'lɒtərɪ; 'lɑtərɪ/ *n* (pl **-ries**) [C] **1** arrangement to give prizes to holders of numbered tickets previously bought by them and drawn by lot: 发行奖券或彩票的办法: (attrib) (用作定语) *~ tickets.* 奖券; 彩票。**2** (fig) sth considered to be as uncertain as the winning of prizes in a ~: (喻)不定之事 (如奖券之中奖): *Is marriage a ~?* 婚姻是可遇而不可求的吗?

lot·to /'lɒtəʊ; 'lɑto/ *n* [U] game of chance; bingo. 一种赌博性游戏; 宾果游戏。

lo·tus /'ləʊtəs; 'lotəs/ *n* (pl **-es** /-sɪz; -sɪz/) (not often used in the pl; 'lotus' blooms is preferred) (不常用复数形, 复数多由 lotus blooms 表示) **1** (kind of) waterlily, esp Egyptian and Asiatic kinds. 荷(尤指埃及和亚洲所产者)。⟹ the illus at **flower.** 参看 flower 之插图。**2** (in old Gk legends) plant represented as bringing about a distaste for an active life. (古希腊传说)忘忧树(据传可使人厌恶积极进取的生活)。**'~-eater** *n* person who gives himself up to indolent enjoyment. 贪图安逸的人。

loud /laʊd; laʊd/ *adj* (**-er, -est**) **1** not quiet or soft; easily heard: 高声的; 喧闹的; 响亮的: *~ voices/cries/laughs.* 宏亮的嗓音(大声的喊声; 哄然的笑声)。*The bomb exploded with a ~ noise.* 那炸弹一声巨响爆炸了。**,~-'hailer** *n* electronic device that enables a voice

to be magnified and so be audible at a great distance: 强力扬声器: *The naval officer called to the trawler by ~hailer across the water.* 那海军军官以强力扬声器向海面上的拖网渔船呼喊。**,~-'speaker** *n* (often shortened to 常略作 *speaker*) part of a radio receiving apparatus that converts electric impulses into audible sounds. 扩音器; 扬声器。**2** (of a person's behaviour; of colours) of the kind that forces itself on the attention. (指人的)行为; 指颜色)引人注目的; 刺眼的。□ *adv* (after *talk, speak, laugh* etc) in a ~ manner: (用于 talk, speak, laugh 等动词后)高声地; 大声地; 喧噪地: *Don't talk so ~.* 不要如此高声谈话。*They laughed ~ and long.* 他们大声地笑了好一阵子。*Speak ~er!* 讲大声点! *Who laughed ~est?* 谁笑的声音最大? **~·ly** *adv* in a ~ manner: 高声地; 喧噪地; 刺目地: *Someone knocked ~ly at the door.* 有人大声敲门。*What a ~ly dressed girl!* 这女孩子的衣服多么刺眼啊! **~·ness** *n*

lough /lɒk; lɑx/ *n* (in Ireland) lake; arm of the sea. (爱尔兰)湖; 海湾。

lounge /laʊndʒ; laʊndʒ/ *vi* [VP2A, C] sit, stand about (leaning against sth) in a lazy way: 懒洋洋地坐着或站着(倚靠某物): *idlers lounging at street corners;* 在街道转弯处闲散的游民; *lounging over a café table.* 懒洋洋地倚靠着咖啡馆的桌子。**~r** *n* person who ~s. 懒洋洋地坐着或站着的人。□ *n* **1** act of lounging: 懒洋洋地坐着或站着: *have a ~.* 懒坐一会儿。**2** comfortable sitting-room, esp in a club or hotel. 休息处; 休息室(尤指俱乐部或旅馆中者)。**'~-lizard** *n* (dated *sl*) professional dance-partner for women at dances in hotel ~s. (旧时俚语)旅馆休息室中陪妇女跳舞的职业舞伴。**3** '**~-bar** *n* smartest bar in a public house. 酒馆中最好的吧台。'**~-chair** *n* comfortable easy-chair. 安乐椅; 躺椅。'**~-suit** *n* man's ordinary suit of jacket, (waistcoat) and trousers. 男子平常穿的一套衣服(包括上衣, 背心和裤子)。

lour, lower /'laʊə(r); laʊr/ *vi* [VP2A, 3A] ~ *at/on/upon,* frown; look sullen or threatening; (of the sky, clouds) look dark, as if threatening a storm. 皱眉头; (指天气, 云)变阴暗 (好象预示暴风雨)。**~·ing·ly** *adv*

louse /laʊs; laʊs/ *n* (pl **lice** /laɪs; laɪs/) **1** small insect living on the bodies of animals and human beings under dirty conditions; similar insect living on plants. 虱; (植物上的)寄生虫。**2** (sl) contemptible person: (俚)可鄙之人: *He's an absolute ~.* 他是个极为可鄙的人。

lousy /'laʊzɪ; 'laʊzɪ/ *adj* (**-ier, -iest**) infested with lice; (colloq) bad: 多虱的; (口)坏的: *a ~ dinner;* 很坏的一餐; (sl) well provided (with): (俚)有很多的(与 with 连用): *He's ~ with money.* 他有很多钱。

lout /laʊt; laʊt/ *n* clumsy, ill-mannered person. 粗鄙的人。'**litter-~,** ⟹ **litter²**(1). '**~·ish** /-ɪʃ; -ʃ/ *adj* of or like a ~: 粗鄙之人的; 似粗鄙之人的: *~ish behaviour.* 粗鄙的行为。

louvre (also **lou·ver**) /'luːvə(r); 'luvə/ *n* arrangement of fixed or moveable slats (in a door or window) for ventilation (like the slats in a Venetian blind). (通风用)门上百叶板窗; 百叶板窗。**lou·vered** *adj* having ~s: 有百叶板窗的: *a ~ed door.* 有百叶窗的门。

lov·able /'lʌvəbl; 'lʌvəbl/ *adj* deserving of inspiring love; worthy of love: 可爱的; 惹人爱的; 值得爱的: *a ~ child;* 可爱的孩子; *a child's ~ ways.* 孩子可爱的地方。

love¹ /lʌv; lʌv/ *n* **1** [U] warm, kind feeling; fondness; affectionate and tender devotion: 热爱; 喜爱; 挚爱; 钟爱: *a mother's ~ for her children;* 母爱; *a ~ of learning/adventure;* 爱好学问(冒险); *~ of (one's) country,* patriotism; 爱国心; *show ~ towards one's neighbours.* 爱邻居。*give/send sb one's ~,* give or send an affectionate greeting. 向某人致意。*play for ~,* for the pleasure of the game, not for stakes. 为娱乐(非为赌钱)而玩。*not to be had for ~ or money,*

impossible to get by any means. 任何方法都得不到的。 *There's ,no* '∼ *lost between them,* They dislike each other. 他们互相嫌恶。 *a labour of* ∼, **(a)** sth that one enjoys doing for its own sake. 嗜爱的工作。 **(b)** one does for the ∼ of sb. 为他人所做的事。 *for the* ∼ *of,* (in appeals, etc) for the sake of; in the name of: (用于恳求等)为……的缘故; 为了: *Put that gun down, for the* ∼ *of God!* 请看在上帝的面上放下那枝枪吧! ' ∼-**feast** *n* meal taken by early Christians in token of brotherly ∼; religious service imitating this. 爱席(早期基督教徒间表示兄弟爱的聚餐); 教会仿此举行之爱餐)。 **2** [U] warm, kind feeling between two persons; sexual passion or desire; this as a literary subject: 爱情; 恋爱; 性爱; 肉欲; (文学上的)爱情主题: *a* '∼-*story;* 爱情故事; *marry for* ∼, *not for money.* 为爱情而结婚, 非为金钱。 *be in* ∼ *(with sb),* have ∼ and desire (for): (与某人)恋爱; 爱上(某人): *Hero and Leander were in* ∼. 希罗和丽安黛在恋爱。 *Leander was in* ∼ *with Hero.* 丽安黛爱上了希罗。 *fall in* ∼ *(with sb),* come to feel ∼ (for); begin to be in ∼ (with). (与某人)恋爱; 爱上(某人)。 *make* ∼ *(to sb),* show that one is in ∼ with sb; do the things that lovers do, eg kiss, caress, have sexual intercourse: (向某人)示爱; 调情(例如接吻, 抚爱, 性交); 做爱: *Jane thinks it's more fun to make* ∼ *than to make the beds.* 简认为做爱比铺床有趣。 *Make* ∼, *not war!* 相爱, 不要相战! Hence, 由此产生, '∼-**making** *n* '∼-**affair** *n* instance of being in ∼, often with a physical relationship: 恋爱; 韵事: *a girl who had numerous* ∼-*affairs before her marriage.* 婚前曾经多次恋爱的女子。 '∼-**bird** *n* small brightly coloured parrot said to pine away when it loses its mate; *(pl)* lovers very much in ∼. 情鸟(颜色鲜明的小鹦鹉, 据说丧偶后会憔悴); (复)恋爱中的情侣。 '∼-**child** *n* child of unmarried parents. 私生子。 '∼-**knot** *n* bow of ribbon, tied in a special way, formerly given or worn as a pledge of ∼. 相思结(一种丝带结, 昔时赠送或佩带表示爱的誓约)。 '∼-**letter** *n* letter between persons in ∼ and concerned with their ∼. 情书。 '∼-**lorn** /-lɔːn; -ˌlɔːrn/ *adj* unhappy because one's ∼ is not returned; pining with ∼. 失恋的; 害相思病的。 '∼-**match** *n* marriage made for love's sake, not an arranged marriage. 恋爱结婚(纯为爱情而结婚)。 '∼-**philtre**/-**potion** *nn* magic drink supposed to make the person who drinks it fall in ∼ with the person from whom it is received. 春药; 媚药。 '∼-**seat** *n* S-shaped bench with two seats facing in opposite directions. 情人座(一种两人可面对相坐的 S 形座椅)。 '∼-**sick** *adj* languishing because of ∼. 害相思病的。 '∼-**song** *n* song about or expressing ∼. 情歌; 恋歌。 '∼-**story** *n* novel or story of which the main theme is ∼. 爱情小说; 恋爱故事。 '∼-**token** *n* sth given as a symbol of ∼. 象征爱情的赠品。 **3** form of address between lovers, husband and wife, or to a child: 亲爱的(爱人和夫妻间, 或对孩子的称呼): *Come here, my* ∼. 过来, 亲爱的。 **4** (colloq) delightful or lovable person or thing: (口)令人愉快或可爱的人或物: *Isn't she a little* ∼? 她不是娇小可爱吗? *What a* ∼ *of a cottage!* 多么可爱的村舍呀! **5** person who is a sweetheart: 爱人: *She was an old* ∼ *of mine years ago* (*flame* is more usu). 她是我多年前的旧情人 (*flame* 较常用)。 **6** personification of ∼, ie a Cupid. 爱的化身; 爱神。 **7** [U] (in games) no score, nothing, nil: (比赛)零分: ∼ *all,* no score for either side; 零比零; '∼ *game,* one in which the loser did not score. 输方无分的一局比赛。 ∼-**less** *adj* unloving; unloved; without ∼: 无爱情的: *a* ∼*less marriage.* 无爱情的婚姻。

love² /lʌv; lʌv/ *vt* **1** [VP6A] have strong affection or deep tender feelings for: 爱; 深爱; 热爱: ∼ *one's parents*/*one's country*/*one's husband.* 爱父母(国家, 丈夫)。 **2** [VP6A] worship: 敬拜: ∼ *God.* 敬拜神(上帝)。 **3** [VP6A] have kind feelings towards: 以仁爱对待: *The Bible tells us to* ∼ *all men.* 圣经告诉我们

要爱所有的人。 **4** [VP6A, D, 7A, 17] (colloq) be very fond of; like; find pleasure in: (口)喜好; 喜欢: ∼ *comfort*/*mountain-climbing.* 喜好舒适(爬山)。 *She* ∼*s to have*/∼*s having a lot of dogs and young men round her.* 她喜欢 有许多狗和青年男子在她周围。 '*Will you come with me?*'—'*I should* ∼ *to.*' '你跟我一块去好吗?'——'我乐意奉陪。' *I'd* ∼ *you to come with me.* 我喜欢你跟我一起来。

love·ly /'lʌvlɪ; 'lʌvlɪ/ *adj* **1** beautiful; attractive; pleasant: 美丽的; 动人的; 可爱的: *a* ∼ *view;* 可爱的景色; *a* ∼ *woman;* 美丽的女人; ∼ *hair*/*weather.* 美丽的头发(好天气)。 **2** (colloq) enjoyable; amusing: (口)令人愉快的; 有趣的: *We had a* ∼ *holiday.* 我们这个假日过得很快乐。 *What a* ∼ *joke!* 这个笑话多么有趣! *It's* ∼ *and warm here,* ∼ *because warm.* 这儿的天气温暖宜人。 **love·li·ness** *n*

lover /'lʌvə(r); 'lʌvɚ/ *n* **1** person who is fond of or devoted to (sth): 喜爱或专心于某一事物的人; 爱好者: *a* ∼ *of music*/*horses*/*good wine.* 音乐(马匹, 好酒)的爱好者。 **2** person in love with another; regular sexual partner. 爱人; 情人; 经常发生性关系之伴侣。 '∼-**like** *adj* in the manner of a ∼. 象爱人的。

lov·ing /'lʌvɪŋ; 'lʌvɪŋ/ *adj* feeling or showing love: 爱的; 钟情的; 亲爱的: ∼ *a friend.* 亲爱的朋友。 '∼-**cup** *n* large wine-cup passed round from person to person so that everyone may drink from it. 爱杯(供多人轮流饮酒的大杯)。 ∼-**kindness** *n* [U] tender consideration; mercy and kindness coming from love. 慈爱; 出于爱心的怜悯与仁慈。 ∼-**ly** *adv* in a ∼ way: 亲爱地: *Yours* ∼*ly,* formula at the end of a letter, eg from a child to its parents. 你的亲爱的(信末结语, 如子女写给父母亲者)。

low¹ /ləʊ; lo/ *adj* (-**er**, -**est**) **1** not high; not extending far upwards: 低的; 矮的: *a low wall*/*ceiling*/*shelf;* 矮的墙(天花板, 架子); *a low range of hills;* 一列矮山; *low-rise housing,* of houses not many storeys high. 低层(层数不多)房屋。 *The moon was low in the sky.* 月亮低挂在天空。 *The glass is low,* The mercury in the barometer is low. 气压计所显示的度数很低。 *He has a low brow,* short distance between the hair and the eyebrows. 他的前额很低。 *She was wearing a dress low in the neck*/*a 'low-necked dress,* one leaving the neck and (part of) the shoulders and breasts visible. 她穿着一件低领的衣服(开领很低, 露出一部分肩膀和胸部者)。 ,low-re'lief, ⇨ bas-relief. **2** below the usual or normal level or intensity: 低于通常或正常高度或强度的: *low-lying land;* 低地; *low pressure,* eg of the atmosphere, of gas or water from the mains: 低压(例如气压, 煤气或水压); *a low-density housing estate,* with comparatively few houses to the acre. 低密度的宅地(房屋较少)。 *The rivers were low during the dry summer.* 干旱的夏日里河水低浅。 **low gear,** ⇨ gear(1). **low tide**/**water,** time when the tide is out and far from the shore or river bank. 低潮; 低水。 ,low-'water **mark,** lowest points reached at low tide. 低潮点; 低潮线; 低水位线。 *be in low water,* (fig) short of money. (喻)缺少金钱。 **3** (of sounds) not loud; not high in pitch: (指声音)不大的; 不高的; 不尖的; 低的: *speak in a low voice;* 低声说话; *the low notes of a cello.* 大提琴的低调。 *A tenor cannot get so low as a baritone.* 男高音不能唱得象男中音那样低。 ,low-'keyed, (fig) restrained in style or quality. (喻)在式样或性质方面抑制的; 不张扬的。 ,low-'pitched, (mus) low in pitch. (音乐)低调的。 **4** of or in inferior rank or social class: 身份或地位卑下的: *all classes of people, high and low;* 所有上下各阶层的人们; *men of low birth;* 出身微贱的人; *have a low station in life.* 身份卑贱。 *be brought low,* be humbled. 被贬抑; 被屈辱; 败落。 **5** commonplace; coarse; vulgar; little civilized: 平凡的; 粗俗的; 鄙俗的; 鄙野的: *low manners;* 粗鄙的态度; *low company;* 下层社会的朋友; *low life,* of persons who are vulgar, coarse, etc; 下层生活; *low tastes;* 低级趣味; *low cunning,* cunning

typical of sb who is mean or morally degraded. 卑鄙的
狡诈。 *I never fell as low as that*, never let my standard
of behaviour fall so low. 我的行为从未那样恶劣。 **6**
feeble; lacking in strength of body or mind: 虚弱的;无
力的; 没精神的: *in a low state of health*; 健康情形不佳;
feel low/in low spirits, unhappy, depressed. 不高兴
(无精打采)。 Hence, 由此产生, **'low-'spirited** adj **7** of
small amount as measured by a scale or by degrees: 小
量的;低度的: *a low temperature*; 低的温度; *a low pulse*;
慢的脉搏; *low prices/wages/rates of pay*. 低的价格
(工资, 薪给)。 **low latitudes**, near the equator. 低纬
度;靠近赤道地区。 *have a low opinion of sb/sth*,
think very little of him, his work, etc. 对某人(某事)
评价很低。 *at lowest*, at the least possible figure,
quantity, etc. 至少。 **8** (of a supply of anything) (指供
应物品) *be/run low*, be/become nearly exhausted: 几
乎耗尽或用光的: *Our stock of coal is running low*. 我们
的煤炭快烧完了。 *Food supplies were running low in the
besieged town*. 这个被包围的城镇里的粮食供应将尽。 **9**
(of the position of the tongue when speaking) not
raised: (指说话时舌头位置)不抬高的: 舌位低下的: *a
low vowel*, one, eg the vowel /ɑ:/, made with the
tongue low in the mouth. 低元音(例如低低舌部所发出
的元音 /ɑ:/)。 **10** not highly developed: 低度发展的; 低
等的: *low forms of life*. 低等生物。 **11 Low Church**,
party in the Church of England giving a low place to
the authority of bishops and priests, ecclesiastical
organization, ritual, etc. (contrasted with *High Church*).
低派教会(英国国教中的一派,对主教和牧师的权威、教会
组织、仪式等不予重视; 与 High Church 相对)。 Hence,
由此产生, **Low Churchman**, supporter of this. 拥护低
派教会者;低派教会之分子。 **12** (phrases) (短语) *bring/
lay sb/sth low*, make low in health, wealth, position,
etc; defeat; humble. 使健康情形、财富或地位等低落; 挫
败; 贬抑。 *lie low*, (fig) keep quiet or hidden; say
nothing and wait: (喻)隐匿;静待: *The escaped prisoners
had to lie low for months*. 那些逃犯必须隐匿几个月。 **13**
(compounds) (复合词) **,low-'born** adj of humble birth.
出身微贱的。 **,low-'bred** adj having vulgar manners.
教养不良的; 行为粗野的。 **'low-brow** n, adj (person)
showing little interest in or taste for intellectual
things, esp art, music, literature (contrasted with
highbrow). 缺少文化(尤指艺术, 音乐, 文学)素养的(人);
知识程度低的(与 highbrow 相对)。 **lower case**, (in
printing) small letters, not capitals. (印刷)小楷字母;
小写字体。 **Lower Chamber/House**, lower branch of a
legislative assembly, eg the House of Commons in GB,
the House of Representatives in US. 下议院(如英国之
下议院,美国之众议院)。 **low comedian**, person who
acts in **low comedy**, kind of drama bordering on
farce, with laughable actions, comic dialogue, etc.
滑稽剧演员; 丑角 (low comedy 滑稽戏剧——由许多笑
料, 滑稽对话等构成, 近乎闹剧的一种喜剧)。 **the lower
deck**, (in the Navy) the ratings; those who are not
officers. (海军中)全体士兵。 **'low-down** adj (colloq)
caddish; dishonourable: (口)卑鄙的;下贱的;不光荣的:
~down behaviour/tricks. 卑鄙的行为(诡计)。 *give
sb/get the low-down (on sth/sb)*, (colloq) give/
get the true facts, inside information which is not
generally known. (口)给予(获得)实情或内幕消息。
'low-lander /-lǝndǝ(r); -lǝndɚ/ n person who lives in
lowlands, esp (**L~**) one who lives in the Scottish
Lowlands. 低地居民; (大写时尤指)苏格兰低地居民。
'low-lands /-lǝndz; -lǝndɚ/ n pl low level country: 低
地: *the lowlands of Scotland*. 苏格兰的低地。 **Low Latin**,
late, popular Latin (contrasted with classical Latin).
近代之通俗拉丁文(以别于古典拉丁文)。 **Low Mass**,
(formerly) celebration of the Eucharist without a
choir. 平时没有唱诗班的弥撒; 小弥撒。 **Low Sunday**,
Low Week, coming after Easter Day and Easter
Week. 复活节后的星期日,复活节后的下一周。 **'low-er-
most** adj lowest. 最低的。 **low-ness** n

low² /lǝʊ; lo/ adv (**-er**, **-est**) in or to a low position;
in a low manner: 在低下之位置; 向低下之位置; 低; 卑下
地: *aim/shoot low*; 向低处瞄准(射击); *bow low to the
Queen*; 向女王深深一鞠躬; *buy low* (= at low prices)
and sell high; 低价买进高价卖出; 贱买贵卖; *play low*,
(in gambling) for small sums; 赌小钱; *speak low*. 低
声说话。

low³ /lǝʊ; lo/ n sth low; low level or figure: 低的东西;
低的水准或低的数目: *Several industrial shares reached
new lows yesterday*, Their prices went down to a new
low price (on the stock market). 昨天有一些工业股票落
到新的低点。

low⁴ /lǝʊ; lo/ n sound made by cattle. 牛叫声; 牛鸣。
□ vi (of cattle) make this characteristic sound. (指
牛)哞哞叫。

lower¹ /'lǝʊǝ(r); 'loɚ/ vt, vi **1** [VP6A] let or bring
down; cause to be down: 降低; 降下; 使低落: *~ the
sails/a flag*. 将帆(旗)降下。 *~ away*, (naut) lower a
boat, sail, etc. (航海)放下小船, 降下船帆等。 **2** [VP
6A, 15A, 2A] make or become less high: 降低; 减低;
跌落: *the rent of a house*. 减低房租。 *The stocks ~ed
in value*. 股票跌价。 *He ~ed his voice to a whisper*. 他
把声音降到耳语那么低。 *We can't ~ the ceiling*. 我
们不能降低天花板。 **3** [VP15A] *~ oneself*, degrade,
disgrace: 降低品格; 污辱: *He would never ~ himself by
taking bribes*. 他绝不会降低自己的品格去接受贿赂。 **4**
[VP6A] weaken: 使弱; 削弱; 削减: *Poor diet ~s
resistance to illness*. 营养太差的饮食会削弱对于疾病的
抵抗力。

lower² /'laʊǝ(r); 'laʊɚ/ vi = **lour**.

low-ly /'lǝʊlɪ; 'lolɪ/ adj (**-ier**, **-iest**) humble; simple;
modest. 谦卑的;卑微的;谦逊的。 **low-li-ness** n

loyal /'lɔɪǝl; 'lɔɪǝl/ adj true and faithful (*to*): 忠诚
的; (对…)忠贞的(与 to 连用): *~ subjects of the Queen*;
女王的忠贞臣民; *~ supporters*; 忠实的拥护者; *~ to
one's country*. 忠于国家。 忠于国家。 *'~-ist* /-ɪst; -ɪst/ n person
who is ~ to his ruler and government, esp one who
supports the head of an established government during
a revolt: 忠于政府的人;(尤指)暴乱时期护政府元首者:
(attrib) (用作定语) *the ~ist army/troops*. 忠于政府
的军队。 *~ly* /'lɔɪǝlɪ; 'lɔɪǝlɪ/ adv ~ly n (pl -ties) **1**
[U] being ~; conduct. 忠诚; 忠诚的行为。 **2** (pl)
kinds of ~ attachment: (复)忠义: *tribal loyalties*. 对
种族或部落的效忠。

loz-enge /'lɒzɪndʒ; 'lɑzɪndʒ/ n **1** four-sided, diamond-
shaped figure. 棱形;棱形物。 **2** small tablet of flavoured
sugar, esp one containing medicine: 小糖块; (尤指)带
味的小药片: *cough ~s*. 咳嗽药片。

L-plate /'el pleɪt; 'el plet/ n plate with a large capital
L, fixed to a motor-vehicle being driven by a learner
who has not passed his driving test. 学习驾驶牌(上书一
大写 L, 固定于行驶中的车上, 表示驾驶人在学习阶段, 尚
未通过考试);实习车牌。

L S D /,el es 'di:; ,el es 'di/ n [U] odourless, colourless
and tasteless semi-synthetic substance causing hallucinations (often referred to as 'acid'). 迷幻药。 ⇨
App 2. 参看附录二。

£ s d /,el es 'di:; ,el es 'di/ n [U] term used, before
British currency was decimalized, for pounds, shillings
and pence; (colloq) money: 镑, 先令和便士; (口)金钱:
I'm short of £sd just now. 我现在缺钱。 ⇨ **App 5.** 参
看附录五。

lub-ber /'lʌbǝ(r); 'lʌbɚ/ n big, clumsy, stupid fellow.
大而蠢笨的人; 笨汉。 ⇨ *land~* at **land¹(6)**. **~-ly** adj

lu-bri-cate /'lu:brɪkeɪt; 'lubrɪˌket/ vt [VP6A] put
oil or grease into (machine parts) to make (them)
work easily; (fig) do sth that makes action, etc easier.
给(机件)加润滑油使(它们)转动顺畅; 使润滑; 加润滑
油; (喻)做出某事以使行动等顺利进行。 **lu-bri-cant**
/'lu:brɪkǝnt; 'lubrɪkǝnt/ n [U, C] substance that ~s.
润滑剂。 **lu-bri-ca-tion** /,lu:brɪ'keɪʃn; ,lubrɪ'keʃǝn/ n
[U, C] (instance of) lubricating or being ~d. 润滑。

lu·cent /'luːsnt; 'lusn̩t/ adj (liter) shining; translucent. (文)明亮的;半透明的。

lu·cerne /luːˈsɜːn; luˈsɚn/ n [U] (GB) clover-like plant used for feeding animals. (英)紫花苜蓿(供动物食用)。(US 美 = alfalfa).

lu·cid /'luːsɪd; 'lusɪd/ adj 1 clear; easy to understand: 清楚的; 容易了解的; 明白的: a ~ explanation; 明白的解释; a ~ literary style; 明晰的文体; a ~ mind. 清晰的头脑。 2 mentally sound: 神志清醒的: ~ intervals, periods of sanity between periods of insanity. 精神病患者之神志清醒的时期。 3 (poet) bright, clear, transparent. (诗)明亮的; 清澈的; 透明的。 ~·ly adv ~·ity /luːˈsɪdɪtɪ; luˈsɪdɪtɪ/ n [U] quality of being ~. 明白;清澈;透明;神志清醒。

Luci·fer /'luːsɪfə(r); 'lusəfɚ/ n 1 Satan, the chief rebel angel: 撒旦; 魔鬼: as proud as ~. 极其傲慢。 2 (the planet Venus as) the morning star. 金星; 晓星; 启明星。

luck /lʌk; lʌk/ n [U] chance; fortune (good or bad); sth that is considered to come by chance: 机运; (好或坏的)运气; 不期而遇的事物: have good / bad ~ in one's affairs; 事情顺利(不顺利); have hard ~, be unfortunate. 遭遇不幸。 As ~ would have it, ... Fortunately, ... (or Unfortunately, ..., according to context). 幸运的是…; 不幸的是…(视上下文而定)。 It was hard ~ on you that ..., used to show sympathy. 你遭遇…真是不幸(用以表示同情)。 He tried his ~ at the gaming tables, gambled, hoping for success. 他在赌台上碰运气。 What rotten ~! Bad ~! (used to show sympathy). 运气真不好! (用以表示同情)。 Good ~! (used to encourage, express hopes of good fortune, etc). 祝你好运! (用以鼓励, 表示盼望有好运等)。 Just my ~! I am unlucky, as usual. 我总是这样倒霉! My ~'s in / out, I am / am not fortunate. 我是幸运(不幸)的。 I never have any ~. 我从没有走过好运。 I had the ~ (= was fortunate enough) to find him at home. 我幸而在他家里找到他。 be down on one's ~, (colloq) be unfortunate; suffer misfortune. (口)运气不好; 倒霉。 be in / out of ~, have / not have good fortune. 运气好(不好)。 for ~, to bring good fortune: 为了讨吉利; 求福: keep sth for ~. 为了讨吉利而保有某种东西。 worse ~, (used parenthetically) more's the pity; unfortunately. (作插入语用)更不幸地; 不幸地。 ~·less adj unfortunate; turning out badly: 运气不佳的; 不幸的; 结果不好的: a ~less day / attempt. 倒霉的日子(不成功的尝试)。

lucky /'lʌkɪ; 'lʌkɪ/ adj (-ier, -iest) having, bringing, resulting from, good luck: 有好运的; 带来好运的; 由好运所产生的; 运气好的: a ~ escape / guess / man. 侥幸的逃脱(侥幸的猜中; 幸运的人)。 It's my ~ day, one on which I am having good fortune. 今天我很走运。 You are ~ to be alive after being in that accident. 你真幸运, 经过那场灾祸而能生还。 ,~ 'dip n tub, etc containing articles of various values for which a person may dip in (taking the chance of getting sth of value) for a payment: 摸彩袋; 幸运袋(袋中装有价值不等之物,付钱即可摸取): L~ dip, 10 p. 摸彩, 十便士。 **luck·ily** /'lʌkɪlɪ; 'lʌkɪlɪ/ adv in a ~ manner; fortunately: 幸运地;侥幸地;幸亏: Luckily for me the train was late, so I just caught it. 幸而火车误点了,所以我刚好搭上。

lu·cra·tive /'luːkrətɪv; 'lukrətɪv/ adj profitable; bringing in money. 可获利的;赚钱的。

lucre /'luːkə(r); 'lukɚ/ n [U] (in a bad sense) profit or money-making (as a motive for action): (坏的意思)利益或赚钱(作为行为的一种动机): a man who would do anything for ~. 为了赚钱什么都干的人。

Lud·dite /'lʌdaɪt; 'lʌdaɪt/ n member of bands of workers who, in England, 1811—1816, destroyed new machinery which, they thought, would cause unemployment. 一八一一至一八一六年间英国摧毁新机器的工人组织之一员(彼等认为机器将导致失业)。

lu·di·crous /'luːdɪkrəs; 'ludɪkrəs/ adj ridiculous; causing laughter. 荒谬的;可笑的。 ~·ly adv

ludo /'luːdəʊ; 'ludo/ n [U] simple game played by moving counters on a special board after throwing dice. 一种骰子游戏。

luff /lʌf; lʌf/ vt, vi (naut) bring the head of a ship in a direction nearer to that of the wind; turn (the helm) so that this happens. (航海)转船首顺风行驶; 为达到此一目的而转(舵)。

lug¹ /lʌg; lʌg/ vt (-gg-) [VP6A, 15A, B] pull or drag roughly and with much effort: 用力拉或拖: lugging two heavy suitcases up the stairs; 拖着两只重衣箱上楼; lug a handcart along. 拉着一辆手车。 □ n hard or rough pull. 用力拉;强拖。

lug² /lʌg; lʌg/ n projecting part (of a metal casting) by which it is kept securely in place. (金属铸品的)突出部分(为便于稳固放置之用);耳。

luge /luːʒ; luʒ/ n (F) short toboggan for one person, as used in Switzerland. (法)一人乘的短雪橇(如用于瑞士者)。

lug·gage /'lʌgɪdʒ; 'lʌgɪdʒ/ n [U] bags, trunks, etc and their contents taken on a journey: 行李: six pieces of ~; 六件行李; get one's ~ through the Customs. (US 美 = baggage.) 使行李通过海关查验。 '~·carrier n metal frame, eg one fixed behind the saddle of a bicycle, for ~. 行囊架(例如自行车后面放东西的架子)。 '~·rack n rack (above the seats) in a railway carriage, coach, etc, or on the roof of a motor-car, for ~. (火车等内座位上头或汽车顶上的)行囊架。 '~·van n van for ~ on a railway train. (火车的)行李车。

lug·ger /'lʌgə(r); 'lʌgɚ/ n small ship with one or more four-cornered sails set fore and aft. 四角纵帆帆船(有一个或多个四角帆的小船)。

lug·sail /'lʌgseɪl; 'lʌgsel/ n (naut) four-cornered sail. (航海)四角帆;斜桁用纵帆。

lu·gu·bri·ous /lʊˈgjuːbrɪəs; luˈgjubrɪəs/ adj (formal) dismal; mournful. (正式用语)阴郁的; 悲哀的; 阴沉的。 ~·ly adv ~·ness n

luke·warm /ˌluːkˈwɔːm; 'lukˈwɔrm/ adj 1 (of liquids, etc) neither very warm nor cold. (指液体等)微温的; 不很热也不冷的。 2 (fig) not eager either in supporting or opposing: (喻)拥护或反对都不热心的: give only ~ support to a cause; 对某一运动仅予以淡漠的支持; ~ friendship. 淡薄的友谊。 ~·ly adv ~·ness n

lull /lʌl; lʌl/ vt, vi [VP6A, 15A, 2A] make or become quiet or less active: 使安静或缓和; 停息; 平息; 缓和: ~ a baby to sleep, eg by rocking it and singing to it; 哄婴孩入睡(如借轻摇或唱催眠歌); ~ a person's fears / suspicions. 消除一个人的恐惧(猜疑)。 The wind / sea was ~ed. 风(海)已平息。 The wind ~ed. 风已停息。 □ n [C] interval of quiet; period of lessened activity, etc: 间歇; 稍息; 稍止: a ~ in the storm / in the conversation. 暴风雨的间歇(谈话的中断)。

lull·aby /'lʌləbaɪ; 'lʌlə͵baɪ/ n (pl -bies) song for lulling a baby to sleep; gentle, soft sound, eg made by wind in trees or by the running water of a brook. 催眠曲; 摇篮曲; 轻柔的声音(如林间轻风或溪涧流水的声音)。

lum·bago /lʌmˈbeɪgəʊ; lʌmˈbego/ n [U] muscular pain in the lumbar regions. 腰肌痛;腰痛;风湿病。

lum·bar /'lʌmbə(r); 'lʌmbɚ/ adj of the loins: 腰部的: the ~ regions, the lower part of the back. 腰背部位。

lum·ber¹ /'lʌmbə(r); 'lʌmbɚ/ n [U] 1 roughly prepared wood; wood that has been sawn into planks, boards, etc. 木材; 木料; 木条; 木板。 '~·man /-mən; -mən/, '~·jack n man who fells trees; man who saws or transports ~. 伐木工人; 锯木材或运木材的人。 '~·mill n saw-mill. 锯木厂。 '~·yard n place where ~ is stored. 木材堆置场。 2 (chiefly GB) useless or unwanted articles stored away or taking up space (eg old furniture, pictures). (主英)无用的杂物(例如旧家具,图画等)。 '~·room n one in which ~ is stored. 储旧东西

的储存室。 □ vt [VP6A, 14, 15A, B] ~ *sth (up) (with)*, (often in passive) fill with ~; fill space inconveniently; encumber: (常用被动语态)堆满无用之物;零乱堆积;阻碍: *a room ~ed up with useless articles.* 堆满无用物品的房间; (fig) (喻) *a mind that is ~ed (up) with useless bits of information.* 充满无用资料的头脑。

lum·ber² /'lʌmbə(r); 'lʌmbɚ/ vi [VP2C] move in a heavy, clumsy, noisy way: 笨拙地移动; 隆隆地行进: *The heavy army tanks ~ed along by/past.* 重型战车隆隆驶过。 *What a big ~ing cart!* 一辆多么大而笨重的载货马车!

lu·min·ary /'lu:mɪnərɪ US: -nerɪ; 'lumə,nɛrɪ/ n (pl -ries) 1 star; the sun or moon; any light-giving body in the sky. 星; 太阳; 月亮; 天上任何的发光体。 2 (fig) person who, because of his learning, is like a shining light; great moral or intellectual leader. (喻)领导人物;先知先觉者;学识卓越的人;道德或知识上伟大的领袖;泰斗。

lu·mi·nous /'lu:mɪnəs; 'lumənəs/ adj 1 giving out light; bright: 发光的; 明亮的: ~ *paint*, as used on road signs, clocks and watches, visible in the dark. 发光涂料(如用于道路标志, 钟表上, 暗中可见者)。 2 (fig) clear; easily understood: (喻)清楚的;容易了解的: *a ~ speaker/explanation.* 明晰的演说者(明白的解释)。 **lu·min·os·ity** /ˌlu:mɪ'nɒsɪtɪ; ˌlumə'nɑsətɪ/ n [U] quality of being ~. 发光;明亮;光辉;清晰;明白。

lummy, lumme /'lʌmɪ; 'lʌmɪ/ int (dated GB sl) indicating surprise. (过时英俚)表示惊奇的感叹词。

lump¹ /lʌmp; lʌmp/ n [C] 1 hard or compact mass, usu without a regular shape: 堆;块;团(通常没有一定形状): *a ~ of clay;* 一块泥土; *break a piece of coal into small ~s;* 把一块煤打成一些小块; *a ~ of sugar;* 一块糖; *'~ sugar,* sugar cut into cubes. 块糖; 方糖。 *in the ~,* added together; taken as a whole. 总计; 全部; 总括。 *~ sum,* one payment for a number of separate sums that are owed. 一次总付之款;总数; 2 swelling or bump; bruise: 肿; 隆起; 伤痕: *He has a bad ~ on the forehead.* 他的额头伤肿得很厉害。 *have a ~ in one's/the throat,* a feeling of pressure (as caused by strong emotion). 喉咙哽住 (如因情绪激动所致)。 3 (colloq) heavy, dull person: (口)笨拙迟钝的人: *Get out of my way, you big fat ~ of a man!* 滚开,你这大笨猪! □ vt, vi 1 [VP6A, 15B] ~ *(together)*, put together in one ~; include (a number of things) under one heading: 堆成一堆; 合在一起; 概括: *The boys agreed to ~ the expenses of their camping holiday.* 孩子们同意把露营费用合在一起而不分彼此。 *Can we ~ all these items together under the heading 'incidental expenses'?* 我们能不能把所有这些项目归纳在 '临时费' 项下? 2 [VP2A] form into ~s: 结块: *This oatmeal ~s if you don't stir it well.* 假若你不好好搅动,这麦片粥会结块。 ~·**ish** /-ɪʃ; -ɪʃ/ adj (of a person) thickset; clumsy; stupid. (指人)矮胖的; 笨拙的; 愚蠢的。 ~·**y** adj (-ier, -iest) full of, covered with ~s: 多块状的的; 覆有块状物的: *a ~y sauce;* 成团的酱; (of the surface of water) cut up by wind into small waves; choppy. (指水面)波浪起伏的。

lump² /lʌmp; lʌmp/ vt (only in) (仅用于) ~ *it*, (colloq) endure, put up with, sth unpleasant or unwanted: (口)忍受(不愉快或不需要之事物): *If you don't like it you can ~ it.* 即使你不喜欢它, 你也得忍受它。 *Well, you'll just have to ~ it!* 哼,你就得忍受它!

lu·nacy /'lu:nəsɪ; 'lunəsɪ/ n (pl -cies) 1 [U] madness; state of being a lunatic; mad or foolish behaviour: 疯狂; 精神错乱; 疯狂或愚蠢的行为: *It's sheer ~.* 这完全是愚蠢的行为。 2 (pl) mad or very foolish acts. (复)疯狂或愚蠢的行动。

lu·nar /'lu:nə(r); 'lunɚ/ adj of the moon: 月亮的: *a ~ month*, average time between successive new moons, about 29½ days; 恒星月; 朔望月(约为二十九天半)/阴历一个月; *a ~ module*, detachable section of a spacecraft that orbits the moon and may descend to its surface; 登

陆月球之小艇; *a ~ orbit* (by a spacecraft); (太空船)绕行月球之轨道; *a ~ year*, period of 12 ~ months. 阴历一年。

lu·na·tic /'lu:nətɪk; 'lunə,tɪk/ n 1 mad person; mental patient (the preferred term). 疯子; 精神病人 (mental patient 较好)。 '~ **asylum**, hospital (*mental home* and *mental hospital* are the names in present-day use) for the care and treatment of ~s. 疯人院; 精神病院(现今多用 mental home 和 mental hospital)。 2 (attrib) mad; extremely foolish: (用作定语)疯狂的; 极愚蠢的: *a ~ proposal.* 极愚蠢的建议。 '~ **fringe**, minority group with extreme views, or engaged in eccentric activities, eg in politics or literature. 极端分子(例如在政治或文学方面持极端意见或从事怪异活动的少数分子。)

lunch /lʌntʃ; lʌntʃ/ n meal taken in the middle of the day: 午餐; 中饭: *They were at ~ when I called.* 我去看他们的时候他们正在吃中饭。 □ vi, vt eat ~; provide ~ for: 吃中饭; 供给…午餐: *He ~ed me well at the Savoy.* 他在萨伏伊饭店招待我吃丰盛的午餐。 ~**eon** /'lʌntʃən; 'lʌntʃən/ n (formal word for) ~. (正式用语)午餐;午宴。

lung /lʌŋ; lʌŋ/ n 1 either of the two breathing organs in the chest of man and other animals: 肺; 肺脏: *the '~ passages/tissues;* 肺脏通道(组织); ~ *cancer.* 肺癌。 *That opera singer has good ~s*, produces a great volume of sound. 那个歌剧演唱者声音宏亮。 ⇨ the illus at **respiratory**. 参看 respiratory 之插图。 '~ **power** n [U] power of voice. 发声力; 肺活量。 2 (fig) open space in or close to a large city. (喻)大城市内或附近的空旷地方。

lunge /lʌndʒ; lʌndʒ/ n sudden forward movement, eg with a sword, or forward movement of the body (eg when aiming a blow): (身体的)前冲; (以剑等的)冲刺; 戳; 击。 □ vi [VP2A, C] make a ~: 冲刺; 前冲; 戳; 击: *He ~d at his opponent/~d out suddenly.* 他突然向他的对手冲去(突然刺出)。

lu·pin (US = **lu·pine**) /'lu:pɪn; 'lupɪn/ n garden or fodder plant with tall spikes of flowers of various colours. 羽扇豆。

lurch¹ /lɜ:tʃ; lɝtʃ/ n (only in) (仅用于) *leave sb in the ~*, leave him when he is in difficulties and needing help. 在某人危难时离弃不顾。

lurch² /lɜ:tʃ; lɝtʃ/ n sudden change of weight to one side; sudden roll or pitch: 突然倾斜; 倾侧: *The ship gave a ~ to starboard.* 船突然向右侧倾斜。 □ vi [VP2C] move along with a ~ or ~es: 蹒跚而行; 东倒西歪地前进: *The drunken man ~ed across the street.* 那个醉汉蹒跚地穿过街道。

lurcher /'lɜ:tʃə(r); 'lɝtʃɚ/ n dog, a cross between a sheepdog and a greyhound, used for retrieving game (esp by poachers). 一种猎狗(牧羊犬和灵猩交配而生的杂种狗,用以寻回猎物,尤指盗猎之人所用者。)

lure /lʊə(r); lʊr/ n [C] bunch of brightly coloured feathers used to attract and recall a trained hawk; bait or decoy to attract wild animals; (fig) sth that attracts or invites; the attraction or interest that sth has: 用以唤回猎鹰的一束彩色羽毛; 引诱野兽的饵; (喻)诱惑物;某事物所具有的吸引力或趣味: *the ~ of the sea;* 大海的诱惑; *the ~s used by a pretty woman to attract men.* 一个漂亮的女人用以吸引男人的魅力。 □ vt [VP 6A, 15B] attract, tempt: 吸引;诱惑: ~ *sb away from his duty;* 诱人离开职守; *be ~d on to destruction.* 被诱惑而走向毁灭。

lu·rid /'lʊərɪd; 'lʊrɪd/ adj 1 highly coloured, esp suggesting flame and violence: 火红的;鲜红的: *a ~ sky/sunset;* 火红的天空(落霞); ~ *thunderclouds.* 紫红的雷云。 2 (fig) sensational; violent and shocking. (喻)耸人听闻的; 暴烈而骇人的: ~ *details of a railway accident;* 火车失事的惊人详情; *a ~ tale.* 可怖的故事。 ~·**ly** adv ~·**ness** n

lurk /lɜ:k; lɝk/ vi [VP2C] be, keep, out of view,

lying in wait or ready to attack: 潜伏; 埋伏(等待或伺机出击): *a suspicious-looking man ~ing in the shadows.* 一个形迹可疑的人潜伏在暗处。*Some suspicion still ~ed in his mind.* 他的心中仍然潜藏着怀疑。'*~-ing-place* n hiding-place. 隐匿处; 潜伏地点。

luscious /'lʌʃəs; 'lʌʃəs/ adj **1** rich and sweet in taste and smell, attractive: 味道与气味甜美的; 动人的: *~ peaches/lips.* 甜美的桃子(动人的嘴唇)。**2** (of art, music, writing) very rich in ornament; suggesting sensual delights. (指艺术, 音乐, 写作)铺张华丽的; 引起快感的。**~·ly** adv **~·ness** n

lush /lʌʃ; lʌʃ/ adj (esp of grass and vegetation) growing luxuriantly: (尤指草木)茂盛的: *~ meadows;* 青草繁茂的草原; *a ~ growth of vegetation after the rains;* 雨后植物的茂盛生长; (fig) luxuriously comfortable. (喻)豪华舒适的。□ n (US sl) drunkard. (美俚)醉汉; 酒鬼。

lust /lʌst; lʌst/ n [U] violent desire to possess sth, esp strong sexual desire *(for);* passionate enjoyment *(of):* 欲望(尤指强烈的性欲); 色欲; 贪欲: *filled with ~;* 充满欲望; [C] instance of this: 此种欲望的实例: *a ~ for power/gold;* 对权力(金钱)的欲望; *the ~s of the flesh.* 肉体的欲望。□ vi [VP3A] **~ after/for,** have ~ for: 贪求; 渴望: *~ for/after gold;* 贪财; (biblical) (圣经) *~ after a woman,* have strong sexual desire. 贪恋女色。**~·ful** /-fl; -fəl/ adj full of ~. 多贪欲的; 好色的。**~·fully** /-fəlɪ; -fəlɪ/ adv

lustre (US = **lus·ter**) /'lʌstə(r); 'lʌstə/ n **1** [U] quality of being bright, esp of a smooth or polished surface; sheen; soft reflected light: 光辉; 光辉; 光彩: *the ~ of pearls.* 珍珠的光泽。**2** [U] (fig) glory; distinction: (喻)光荣; 出色; 卓越: *add ~ to one's name;* 使其声名增辉; *deeds that shed ~ on an honoured family,* make its reputation more distinguished. 使光荣的家声更为显赫的功业。**3** (glass pendant of a) chandelier. 枝形吊灯; 枝形吊灯之玻璃垂饰。**lus·trous** /'lʌstrəs; 'lʌstrəs/ adj having ~: 有光泽的; 光辉的: *lustrous pearls;* 光亮的珍珠; *her lustrous eyes.* 她明亮的眼睛。

lusty /'lʌstɪ; 'lʌstɪ/ adj healthy and strong; vigorous: 健壮的; 精力充沛的; 有力的: *a ~ girl from the country;* 乡下来的一个健壮的女孩; *~ cheers.* 高声的欢呼。**lust·ily** /-ɪlɪ; -əlɪ/ adv: *work/fight/shout lustily.* 起劲地工作(打斗, 叫喊)。

lute /luːt; luːt/ n stringed musical instrument (14th to 17th cc) associated with poets and poetry. 鲁特琴(十四至十七世纪的一种弦乐器); 琵琶。**lu·tan·ist** /'luːtənɪst; 'lutnɪst/ n player of the ~. 鲁特琴弹奏者。

Lu·theran /'luːθərən; 'luːθərən/ adj, n (follower) of Martin Luther; (member) of the Protestant Church named after Luther. 马丁·路德的(信徒); (起源于德国的)一派基督教, 以马丁·路德之名)路德会的(教友); 信义会的(教友)。

luxe /lʌks; lʌks/ n = **de luxe.**

lux·ur·iant /lʌg'ʒʊərɪənt; lʌg'ʒʊrɪənt/ adj **1** strong in growth; abundant: 繁茂的; 丰富的: *the ~ vegetation of the tropics;* 热带繁盛的草木; (fig) (喻) *a ~ imagination.* 丰富的想象力。**2** (of liter and artistic style) richly ornamented; very elaborate. (指文体及艺术品之风格)华丽的; 绚烂的。**~·ly** adv **lux·ur·iance** /-əns; -əns/ n [U] ~ growth. 茂盛; 丰富。

lux·ur·iate /lʌg'ʒʊərɪeɪt; lʌg'ʒʊrɪ,et/ vi [VP3A] *~ in,* take great delight in: 耽溺于; 尽情享受: *~ in the warm spring sunshine.* 尽情享受春天温暖的阳光。

lux·ur·ious /lʌg'ʒʊərɪəs; lʌg'ʒʊrɪəs/ adj **1** supplied with luxuries; very comfortable: 供有奢侈享受的; 豪华的; 非常舒服的: *live in ~ surroundings;* 生活在奢侈的环境中; *a ~ hotel.* 豪华的旅馆。**2** choice and costly: 精美昂贵的: *~ food.* 精美昂贵的食物。**3** fond of luxuries; self-indulgent: 爱好奢侈的; 放纵的: *~ habits.* 奢侈的

习惯。**~·ly** adv

lux·ury /'lʌkʃərɪ; 'lʌkʃərɪ/ n (pl **-ries**) **1** [U] state of life in which, to an excessive degree, one has and uses things that please the senses (good food and drink, clothes, comfort, beautiful surroundings): 奢侈; 豪华; 奢华: *live in ~ of 奢侈的生活; a life of ~.* 奢侈的生活。**2** (attrib use) enabling people to live this kind of life: (用作定语)豪华的: *a ~ hotel/ocean liner* (perhaps suggesting ostentation rather than real comfort, etc. ⇨ **luxurious**). 豪华旅馆(海轮)(此处可能表示装饰华美而非实际舒适等)。**3** [C]sth not essential but which gives enjoyment and pleasure, esp sth expensive, out of season, etc: 奢侈品: *His salary is low and he gets few luxuries.* 他的薪水微薄, 所以很少买奢侈品。

lycée /'liːseɪ US: liːseɪ; ,li'se/ n state secondary school in France. 法国公立中等学校。

ly·ceum /laɪ'siːəm; laɪ'siəm/ n (US) lecture hall; (building of an) association for organizing lectures, concerts, etc. (美)演讲厅; 举行学术演讲或音乐会等之社团; 此种社团之建筑物; 学园; 文苑。

ly·chee (also **li·chee, li·tchee, li·tchi**) /'laɪtʃiː; 'litʃi/ n fruit-tree, originally from China, widely grown in Bengal; its fruit consisting of a thin brown shell containing a white pulp round a single seed. 荔枝; 荔枝树。⇨ the illus at **fruit.** 参看 fruit 之插图。

lych·gate n = **lichgate.**

lye /laɪ; laɪ/ n alkali obtained by passing water through wood ashes, used in washing; any alkaline solution or detergent. 从木灰中滤出的碱水(供洗涤用); 灰汁; 任何碱水或清洁剂。

ly·ing /'laɪɪŋ; 'laɪɪŋ/ pres p of lie[1], lie[2].

lymph /lɪmf; lɪmf/ n [U] colourless fluid in animal matter, like blood but without colouring matter. 淋巴; 淋巴液。**lym·phatic** /lɪm'fætɪk; lɪm'fætɪk/ adj **1** of or carrying ~: 淋巴的; 输送淋巴的: *the ~atic vessels,* carrying ~ from the tissues with any waste matter. 淋巴管。**2** (of persons) sluggish; slow in thought and action. (指人)迟钝的; 思想和行动迟缓的。

lynch /lɪntʃ; lɪntʃ/ vt [VP6A] put to death (usu by hanging) without a lawful trial (sb believed to be guilty of crime). 不经合法审判而将(被认为有罪之人)处死(通常用绞刑); 施私刑。□ n '~ **law,** procedure of persons who executed a (supposed) criminal in this way. 私刑。

lynch·pin /'lɪntʃpɪn; 'lɪntʃpɪn/ = **linchpin.**

lynx /lɪŋks; lɪŋks/ n short-tailed wild animal of the cat family, noted for its keen sight. 林猄; 大山猫(一种短尾的猫科动物, 视力锐利)。⇨ the illus at **cat.** 参看 cat 之插图。Hence, 由此产生, ,~'eyed adj keen-sighted. 眼光锐利的。

lyre /'laɪə(r); laɪr/ n kind of harp with strings fixed in a U-shaped frame, used by the ancient Greeks. (古希腊人的)一种七弦琴; 竖琴; 抱琴。'~·bird n Australian bird, the male having a long tail, shaped like a ~ when spread out. 澳洲产的琴鸟(雄者生有长尾, 开展时状似七弦琴)。

lyric /'lɪrɪk; 'lɪrɪk/ adj **1** of, composed for, singing. 吟唱的; 供吟唱的。**2** of poetry expressing direct personal feeling. 抒情诗的。□ n [C] ~ poem; (pl) verses of a song, eg in a musical play. 抒情诗; (复)抒情的韵文(如音乐剧中者)。

lyri·cal /'lɪrɪkl; 'lɪrɪkl/ adj **1** = **lyric. 2** full of emotion; enthusiastic: 充满感情的; 热情的: *She became/waxed quite ~ over the news she had brought back from Paris.* 她从巴黎带回来的新衣使她显得兴高采烈。**~·ly** /-klɪ; -klɪ/ adv

ly·sol /'laɪsɒl US: -sɔl; 'laɪsɑl/ n [U] (P) dark oily, liquid used as an antiseptic and disinfectant. (商标)来沙尔(防腐及消毒用的一种黑色油质药水)。

M m

M, m /em; ɛm/ (*pl* **M's, m's** /emz; ɛmz/) the 13th letter of the English alphabet; symbol for the Roman numeral 1000. 英文字母的第十三个字母；罗马数字的 1000。 ⇨ **App 4.** 参看附录四。

ma /mɑː; mɑ/ *n* (colloq, abbr of) **mamma.** (口)为 mamma 之略。

ma'am /mæm; mæm/ *n* madam, used in addressing a Queen. 对女王或皇后之尊称。

mac /mæk; mæk/ *n* (GB colloq, abbr of) **mackintosh.** (英口)为 mackintosh 之略。

ma·cabre /məˈkɑːbrə; məˈkɑbrə/ *adj* gruesome; suggesting death. 可怕的；可怖的；表示死亡的。 **danse** /dɑːns; dɑs/ ~ *n* (F) dance of death. (法)死之舞；骷髅舞。

ma·cadam /məˈkædəm; məˈkædəm/ *n* [U] ~ **road,** road with a surface of several layers of crushed rock or stone, each rolled hard before the next is put down. 碎石路(由几层碎石压成的道路)。 ~**·ize** /-aɪz; -aɪz/ *vt* make or cover with such layers: 铺以碎石；用碎石铺成: ~*ized roads.* 铺碎石的道路。 ⇨ **tarmac.**

maca·roni /ˌmækəˈrəʊni; ˌmækəˈroni/ *n* [U] flour paste made in the form of long tubes (often chopped into short pieces), prepared for eating by being boiled. 通心粉；通心面。

maca·roon /ˌmækəˈruːn; ˌmækəˈrun/ *n* [C] small, hard, flat, sweet cake or biscuit made of sugar, white of egg, and crushed almonds or coconut. 蛋白杏仁饼或椰子饼(由糖、蛋白和杏仁或椰子粉制成的一种小甜饼或饼干)。

ma·caw /məˈkɔː; məˈkɔ/ *n* large, long-tailed parrot of tropical America. 鹦鹉(热带美洲产的一种长尾大鹦鹉)；金刚鹦鹉。

mace[1] /meɪs; mes/ *n* **1** large, heavy club, usu with a metal head covered with spikes, used as a weapon in the Middle Ages. 中古时代用作武器的一种钉头锤；锤矛。 **2** ceremonial rod or staff(often very much ornamented) carried or placed before an official, eg a Mayor. 权杖 (通常装饰得很精美，持于或置于官员，如市长之前)。 **'~-bearer** *n* person who carries an official ~. 持权杖的人。

a ceremonial mace

mace[2] /meɪs; mes/ *n* [U] dried outer covering of nutmegs, used as spice. 作香料用的干豆蔻皮；豆蔻香料。

mac·er·ate /ˈmæsəreɪt; ˈmæsəˌret/ *vt, vi* [VP6A, 2A] make or become soft by soaking in water or caustic potash. 在水或苛性钾中浸软。

Mach /mɑːk; mɑk/ *n* '~ **number,** ratio of the air speed of an aircraft to the speed of sound: 马赫值(飞行速度与音速之比的值): ~ *two,* twice the speed of sound. 二倍于音速。

ma·chete /məˈtʃetɪ US: -ˈʃetɪ; mɑˈtʃete/ *n* cutlass (2); broad, heavy knife used in Latin America and the W Indies as a cutting tool and weapon. 种植可可及干椰子者所用的大刀；拉丁美洲和西印度群岛人当作工具和武器的大刀。

mach·ia·vel·lian /ˌmækɪəˈvelɪən; ˌmækɪəˈvɛlɪən/ *adj* showing or having no scruples in gaining what is wanted; of or like the ideas set out by Machiavelli, Italian statesman, who advocated putting expediency above political morality and the use of deceit in statecraft. 无所顾忌以求取得所想得到之物的；运用权术的；意大利政治家马基雅维里所主张之权术观念的；为政治目的而不择手段的。

machi·na·tion /ˌmækɪˈneɪʃn; ˌmækəˈneʃən/ *n* [C, U] (esp evil) plot/plotting; scheme/scheming. 诡计或阴谋；图谋不轨；设阴谋。

ma·chine /məˈʃiːn; məˈʃin/ *n* [C] **1** appliance or mechanical device with parts working together to apply power, often steam or electric power (*a* '*printing-~*), but also human power (*a* '*sewing-~*). 机器；机械(通常由蒸汽或电力推动，如印刷机等，亦有由人力推动者，如缝纫机等)。 *We live in the ~ age,* the age in which ~s more and more replace hand labour. 我们生活于机器的时代(在这时代里，机器越来越代替了人力)。 '~**-gun** *n* gun that fires continuously while the trigger is pressed. 机关枪；机枪。 ~'s'**made** *adj* made by ~ (contrasted with *handmade*). 机器制的(与 hand-made 相对)。 '~ **tool,** tool, mechanically operated, for cutting or shaping materials. 机械用具；工作母机。 **2** persons organized to control a group: 操纵集团的核心组织: (US) (美) *the Democratic* ~. 民主党核心人物。 □ *vt* [VP6A] operate on, make (sth) with, a ~ (esp of sewing and printing). 用机器制造(尤指用缝纫机和印刷机)。 **ma·chin·ist** /məˈʃiːnɪst; məˈʃinɪst/ *n* one who makes, repairs or controls ~ tools; one who works a ~, esp a sewing-~. 制造机器的人；修理机器的人；管理机器的人；机械师；机械工人；操作机器的人(尤指使用缝纫机者)。

ma·chin·ery /məˈʃiːnəri; məˈʃinɚi/ *n* [U] **1** moving parts of a machine; machines collectively: 机器的转动的部分；机械；机器(集合名词): *How much new ~ has been installed?* 安装了多少新机器了？ (Cf 参较 *How many new machines have been installed?* 安装了多少部新机器？) **2** methods, organization (eg of government). 方法；组织；机构(例如政府的)。

ma·chismo /məˈtʃɪzməʊ; mɑˈtʃɪzmo/ *n* [U] exaggerated male pride; man's need to prove his virility. 夸张的男子气概；证明男子气概的需要。

mack·erel /ˈmækrəl; ˈmækərəl/ *n* (*pl* unchanged) striped seafish used as food. (复数不变)鲭鱼(亦称青花鱼)。 ~ **sky** *n* sky with bars of cloud like the stripes on a ~'s back. 鲭天(云层似鲭鱼鳞之天空)。

mack·in·tosh /ˈmækɪntɒʃ; ˈmækɪnˌtɑʃ/ *n* (GB) rainproof coat made of cloth treated with rubber. (英)雨衣(橡皮布制成的)。

mac·ro·biotic /ˌmækrəʊbaɪˈɒtɪk; ˌmækrobaˈɑtɪk/ *adj* prolonging life. 延长寿命的。 ~ **food,** containing pure vegetable substances grown and prepared without chemical assistance. 延长寿命的食物(生长与调制过程均不借化学助力的纯净蔬菜)。

mac·ro·cosm /ˈmækrəʊkɒzəm; ˈmækrəˌkɑzəm/ *n* the universe; any great whole. 宇宙；任何大而完整的实体。 ⇨ **microcosm.**

mad /mæd; mæd/ *adj* (**-dder, -ddest**) **1** having, resulting from, a diseased mind; mentally ill. 疯狂的；由于疯狂的；精神错乱的。 *drive/send sb mad,* cause him to be mad. 逼人发狂。 *as mad as a March hare/ as a hatter,* very mad. 非常疯狂。 '**mad-house** *n* (colloq) mental hospital. (口)疯人院。 '**mad · man** /-mən; -ˌmæn/, '**mad-woman** *nn* person who is mad. 疯人；疯女人。 **2** (colloq) much excited filled with enthusiasm: (口)非常激动的；充满热情的: *mad about pop music;* 对流行歌曲着迷; (esp US) angry: (尤用于美国)愤怒的: *mad about/at missing the train;* 未赶上火车气得要命; wild: 激动的；狂乱的: *mad with pain.* 痛得发狂。 *The dog was mad for water,* behaving wildly because it needed water; 这狗渴得要命(因为没有水的缘故)。 foolish; foolish: 愚蠢的: *What a mad thing to do!* 多么愚蠢的一件事！ *be/go mad,* be/become wildly excited, angry, upset, etc. 极为激动、愤怒、不安等。 *like mad,* (colloq) with great

energy; much: (口)拼命地; 猛烈地: *work / run / smoke like mad*. 拼命工作(奔跑,吸烟). '**mad·cap** / -kæp; -ˌkæp/ *n* person acting recklessly or on impulse. 行动卤莽的人; 做事冲动的人. **3** (of a dog, etc) rabid. (指狗等)患狂犬病的; 疯的. **mad·ly** *adv* in a mad manner; (colloq) extremely: 疯狂地; 疯的; (口)极其: *madly excited / jealous*. 极其激动(嫉妒). **mad·ness** *n* [U] the state of being mad; mad behaviour: 疯狂; 疯狂的行为: *It would be madness to try to climb the mountain in such a snowstorm*. 想在这样大的暴风雪中去爬山简直是疯狂.

mad·den /'mædn; 'mædn/ *vt* [VP6A] make mad; irritate; annoy: 使疯狂; 激怒; 使苦恼: *maddening delays*. 令人生气的延误.

madam /'mædəm; 'mædəm/ *n* **1** respectful form of address to a woman (whether married or unmarried): 夫人; 女士(对妇女的尊称): *Can I help you, ~?* (eg asked by a shop assistant); 我能为你效劳吗, 夫人? (例如店员所问); used in letters, as *Sir* is used to a man: 用于信件中, 如对男人称 Sir 一样: *Dear M~*. 夫人 (女士) 台鉴. **2** (colloq) woman or girl who likes to order people about: (口)喜欢指使他人的妇女: *She's a bit of a ~*. 她有点儿喜欢指使别人. *Isn't she a little ~!* 她不是个很喜欢指使旁人的女孩吗! **3** (colloq) woman who manages a brothel. (口)妓院女老板; 鸨母.

Mad·ame /mə'dɑːm *US:* 'mædəm/ *n* (abbr 略作 **Mme**) (*pl* **Mesdames** /mer'dɑːm; me'dɑm/) French title before the name of a married woman; also used before names of married women who are not British or American. 夫人(法国对已婚妇女之尊称, 置于姓名之前; 亦用于非英美已婚妇女之姓名前).

mad·der /'mædə(r); 'mædə/ *n* [U] (red dye obtained from the root of a) herbaceous climbing plant with yellowish flowers. 茜草(开黄花的一种草本攀缘植物); 茜草根制成的红色染料.

made /meɪd; med/ *pt, pp* of **make**[1].

Ma·deira /mə'dɪərə; mə'dɪrə/ *n* white dessert wine from ~ (an island in the Atlantic Ocean). (大西洋 Madeira 岛出产的)一种白葡萄酒. '~ *cake* *n* kind of sponge-cake. 一种松软蛋糕.

Mad·emoi·selle /ˌmædmwɑ'zel; ˌmædəmə'zel/ *n* (abbr 略作 **Mlle**) (*pl* **Mesdemoiselles** /ˌmerdmwɑ'zel; ˌmedəmə'zel/) French title used before the name of a young girl or an unmarried woman. 小姐(用于未婚女子姓名前之法语称呼).

Ma·donna /mə'dɒnə; mə'dɑnə/ *n* **the ~**, (picture or statue of) Mary, Mother of Jesus Christ. 圣母(耶稣基督的母亲)玛利亚的画像或雕像. '~ *lily*, kind of pure white lily (as often shown in pictures of the ~). 白百合花(纯白色, 如常见于圣母像中者).

mad·ri·gal /'mædrɪɡl; 'mædrɪɡl/ *n* part-song for several voices without instrumental accompaniment. 牧歌(一种无伴奏的多声部歌谣).

mael·strom /'meɪlstrəm; 'melstrəm/ *n* great whirlpool; (fig) violent or destructive force; whirl of events: 大漩涡; (喻)暴烈的或破坏性的力量; 大动乱: *the ~ of war*. 战争的动乱.

mae·nad /'miːnæd; 'minæd/ *n* priestess of Bacchus, the Greek god of wine; frenzied woman. 希腊酒神巴克斯的女祭司; 狂乱的女人.

maes·tro /'maɪstrəʊ; 'maɪstro/ *n* (*pl* ~**s** or **maestri** /'maɪstriː; 'maɪstrɪ/) (I) eminent musical composer, teacher, or conductor. (意)著名的作曲家、音乐教师或指挥家; 大师.

maf·fick /'mæfɪk; 'mæfɪk/ *vi* go in for wild public merry-making and rejoicing (eg in war, when there is news of a victory). 狂欢庆祝(如战时获悉胜利的消息时).

Ma·fia /'mæfɪə *US:* 'mɑːf-; 'mɑfɪə/ *n* **the ~**, secret organization in Sicily, opposed to legal authority and engaged in crime; similar organization on the mainland of Italy and in US. 黑手党(西西里岛人的秘密组织, 反对合法的当局, 并从事犯罪行为); 意大利本土及美国类似的秘密组织.

mag /mæɡ; mæɡ/ *n* (colloq abbr of) **magazine(3)**. (口)为 magazine 之略: *the colour mags*. 彩色杂志.

maga·zine /ˌmæɡə'ziːn *US:* 'mæɡəziːn; ˌmæɡə'zin/ *n* **1** store for arms, ammunition, explosives, etc. 武器、弹药、炸药等的仓库; 军火库. **2** chamber for holding cartridges to be fed into the breech of a rifle or gun; place for rolls or cartridges of film in a camera. (枪的)子弹夹; 弹仓; (照相机内的)软片盒. ⇨ the illus at **rifle**. 参看 rifle 之插图. **3** paper-covered (usu weekly or monthly, and illustrated) periodical, with stories, articles, etc by various writers. 杂志(通常为周刊或月刊, 有插图).

ma·genta /mə'dʒentə; mə'dʒentə/ *adj, n* bright crimson (substance used as a dye). 洋红色(的); 洋红色染料.

mag·got /'mæɡət; 'mæɡət/ *n* larva or grub, esp of a kind of fly (the bluebottle) that lays its eggs in meat, and of the cheese-fly. 蛆; 蝇的幼虫. *have a '~ in one's head*, have a strange whim or fancy. 想入非非. ~*y adj* having ~s: 有蛆的: *~y cheese*. 生蛆的干酪.

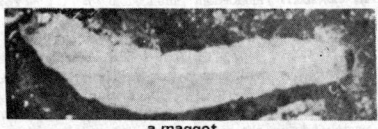

a maggot

Magi /'meɪdʒaɪ; 'medʒaɪ/ *n* *pl* **the M~**, the three wise men from the East who brought offerings to the infant Jesus. 由东方来朝见耶稣的三个贤人(俗称三博士). ⇨ **Matt 2: 1**. 参看新约圣经马太福音第2章第1节.

magic /'mædʒɪk; 'mædʒɪk/ *n* [U] **1** art of controlling events by the pretended use of supernatural forces; witchcraft; primitive superstitious practices based on a belief in supernatural agencies. 魔法; 巫术; 基于相信超自然的力量之原始迷信行为. *like ~; as if by ~*, in a mysterious manner. 象借魔法般地; 不可思议地. *black / white ~*, ~ done with / without the help of devils. 借(不借)助于恶魔的巫术. **2** art of obtaining mysterious results by tricks; 魔术; 戏法: *The conjurer used ~ to produce a rabbit from his hat*. 魔术家用戏法从帽子里变出一只兔子. **3** the identification of a symbol with the thing it stands for, as when the wearing of a lion's skin is thought to give the wearer a lion's courage. 将一标志与其所代表的事物视为同一 (例如穿狮皮被认为使穿者有狮子的勇气). **4** (fig) mysterious charm; quality produced as if by ~: (喻)神秘的魔力; 媚力; 魅力: *the ~ of Shakespeare's poetry / of the woods in autumn*. 莎士比亚诗章(秋林)之美. □ *adj* done by, or as if by, ~; possessing ~; used for ~: 由魔术造成的; (似出于魔术的)有魔力的; 用于魔术的: *~ arts / words*; 魔术的技艺(魔术用语); 具有魔力的言语); *a ~ touch*. 魔术的手法. ~ *eye*, (colloq) name used for various electronic devices which control or indicate sth, eg the automatic opening and closing of doors, exact tuning of a radio set. (口)魔眼(各种用以控制或指示之电子仪器, 例如用于自动门之开关, 收音机之精确调整者). ~ *lantern*, apparatus (now a toy) for throwing a magnified image of a picture, etc from a glass slide on to a white screen (*projector* is the name of the modern apparatus). 幻灯 (现已用做玩具, 现代幻灯称为 projector). ⇨ the illus at **lantern**. 参看 lantern 之插图. ~ *square*, square large divided into smaller squares, each with a number, so that the sum of each row, vertical, horizontal or diagonal is always the same. 魔术方格(将一大方格分成若干小方格, 每格上面均有数字, 每行、每列或对角线上各数之和均相等). **magi·cal** /-kl; -kl/ *adj* of or like ~; (colloq) charming: 魔术的; 似魔术的; 不可思议的; (口)迷人的: *a ~al stage set*. 迷人的舞台布景. **magi·cally** /-klɪ; -klɪ/ *adv* **ma·gician** /mə'dʒɪʃn; mə'dʒɪʃn/

n person skilled in ~ (2); wizard. 精于变法术的人；魔术家；术士。

magis·terial /ˌmædʒɪˈstɪərɪəl; ˌmædʒɪsˈtɪrɪəl/ *adj* of, conducted by, a magistrate; having or showing authority: 地方法官的；由地方法官办的；有权威的；威风的：~ *rank;* 官吏的身份；*a* ~ *manner / opinion.* 威严的态度(权威的意见)。 ~·**ly** /-ɪəlɪ; -ɪəlɪ/ *adv*

magis·trate /ˈmædʒɪstreɪt; ˈmædʒɪsˌtret/ *n* civil officer acting as a judge in the lowest courts; Justice of the Peace. 在地方法庭当法官的文官；地方官吏；地方法官；治安推事。 **magis·tracy** /ˈmædʒɪstrəsɪ; ˈmædʒɪstrəsɪ/ *n* (*pl* **-cies**) position of a ~. 地方法官或官吏的职位。**the magis·tracy,** ~s collectively. 地方法官或官吏的总称。

mag·nani·mous /mæɡˈnænɪməs; mæɡˈnænəməs/ *adj* having, showing, generosity. 宽宏大量的；慷慨的。 ~·**ly** *adv* **mag·nan·im·ity** /ˌmæɡnəˈnɪmətɪ; ˌmæɡnəˈnɪmətɪ/ *n* [U] being ~; [C] (*pl* **-ties**) ~ act, etc. 宽宏大量；雅量；宽宏大量的行为。

mag·nate /ˈmæɡneɪt; ˈmæɡnet/ *n* wealthy leading man of business or industry; person who has power through wealth or position: 工商界大亨；工商界巨头；因财富或地位而有权力的人物：*territorial* ~*s,* influential landowners. 大地主。

mag·nesia /mæɡˈniːʃə; mæɡˈniʃə/ *n* [U] white, tasteless powder (carbonate of magnesium, **MgO**) used medicinally and in industry. 苦土；镁氧(医药和工业用的一种无味的白色粉状碳酸镁，分子式为 MgO)。

mag·nesium /mæɡˈniːzɪəm; mæɡˈniʃɪəm/ *n* [U] silver-white metal (symbol **Mg**) used in the manufacture of aluminium and other alloys, fireworks and flash photography: 镁(银白色金属元素，符号为 Mg，用于制造铝，其他合金及烟火，亦用于镁光灯摄影)：~ *light,* bright light obtained by burning ~ wire. 镁光(燃烧镁线而发的亮光)。

mag·net /ˈmæɡnɪt; ˈmæɡnɪt/ *n* [C] **1** piece of iron, often a horseshoe shape, able to attract iron, either natural (as in lodestone) or by means of an electric current. 磁铁；磁石。**2** (fig) person or thing that attracts. (喻)有吸引力的人或物。~·**ic** / mæɡˈnetɪk; mæɡˈnetɪk/ *adj* **1** having the properties of a ~; able to attract, etc: 有磁性的；能吸引的：~*ic field,* area in all parts of which a ~*ic* force may be detected; 磁场；*a* ~*ic mine,* submarine mine that is detonated when a large mass of iron (eg a ship) approaches it; 磁性水雷；*a* ~*ic needle,* one that points north and south; (指向南北的)磁针；指南针；*the* ~*ic north,* the point indicated by such a needle; 磁针所指之北；磁北；*a* ~*ic smile / personality,* attracting the attention of people. 吸引人的微笑(性格)。~*ic tape,* kind of tape coated with iron oxide used for recording sound and vision. (录音及录像用)磁带；录音带；录像带；录影带。**2** of magnetism. 磁力学的；磁的。**mag·neti·cally** /-klɪ; -klɪ/ *adv*

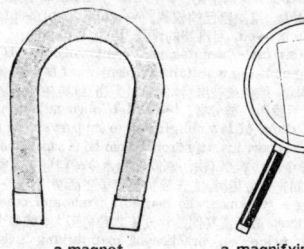

a magnet   a magnifying glass

mag·net·ism /ˈmæɡnɪtɪzəm; ˈmæɡnəˌtɪzəm/ *n* [U] (the science of) magnetic phenomena and properties; (fig) personal charm and attraction. 磁的现象和性质；磁力现象；磁性；磁力学；磁学；(喻)人的魅力和吸引力。

mag·net·ize /ˈmæɡnɪtaɪz; ˈmæɡnəˌtaɪz/ *vt* [VP6A]

give magnetic properties to; (fig) attract as a magnet does, eg by personal charm, moral or intellectual power. 使生磁性；使有磁力；磁化；(喻)吸引(例如以外表魅力、品行或智慧力量等)。

mag·neto /mæɡˈniːtəʊ; mæɡˈnito/ *n* (*pl* **-tos** /-təʊz; -toz/) electric apparatus for producing sparks in the ignition system of an internal combustion engine. (内燃机内用以发生火花的)小型磁石发电机；永磁电机。

Mag·nifi·cat /mæɡˈnɪfɪkæt; mæɡˈnɪfɪˌkæt/ *n* song of the Virgin Mary in Luke 1: 46—55. 玛利亚的赞美诗(指新约圣经路加福音第 1 章 46 到 55 节中，圣母玛利亚对上主的歌赞)。

mag·nifi·cent / mæɡˈnɪfɪsnt; mæɡˈnɪfəsnt/ *adj* splendid; remarkable; important-looking: 壮丽的；不凡的；堂皇的；庄严的；看起来很了不起的：*a* ~ *house;* 华丽的房子；*his* ~ *generosity.* 他的了不起的宽宏大量。 ~·**ly** *adv* **mag·nifi·cence** /-sns; -sns/ *n* [U].

mag·nify /ˈmæɡnɪfaɪ; ˈmæɡnəˌfaɪ/ *vt* (*pt, pp* **-fied**) [VP6A] **1** make (sth) appear larger (as with a lens or microscope): 放大；扩大：*a* ~*ing glass,* lens for this purpose. 放大镜。**2** exaggerate: 夸大：~ *dangers.* 夸大危险。**3** extol; give praise to (God): 歌奖；赞美(上帝)：~ *the Lord.* 赞美上帝。**mag·ni·fier** /-faɪə(r); -faɪə/ *n* instrument, etc, that magnifies. 放大器；放大镜。**mag·ni·fi·ca·tion** /ˌmæɡnɪfɪˈkeɪʃn; ˌmæɡnəfəˈkeʃən/ *n* (esp) power of ~ing, eg of a lens, a pair of binoculars. 放大；(尤指)放大率；倍率(如透镜、双眼望远镜等的)。

mag·nil·oquent /mæɡˈnɪləkwənt; mæɡˈnɪləkwənt/ *adj* (of words, speech) pompous; (of a person) using pompous or high-sounding words. (指文字、言词)夸大的；(指人)使用夸大的言词的。 ~·**ly** *adv* **mag·nil·oquence** /-əns; -əns/ *n*

mag·ni·tude /ˈmæɡnɪtjuːd US: -tuːd; ˈmæɡnəˌtjud/ *n* [U] size; (degree of) importance; comparative brightness of stars. 大小；积；量；重要(的程度)；星的光度。

mag·no·lia /mæɡˈnəʊlɪə; mæɡˈnolɪə/ *n* tree with large, sweet-smelling wax-like flowers. 木兰；木莲。

mag·num /ˈmæɡnəm; ˈmæɡnəm/ *n* (bottle containing) two quarts (of wine or spirit). 两夸脱(酒或酒精)；装两夸脱之瓶。

mag·pie /ˈmæɡpaɪ; ˈmæɡˌpaɪ/ *n* noisy black-and-white bird which is attracted by, and often takes away, small, bright objects; (fig) person who chatters very much; (fig) petty thief. 鹊；(喻)多话的人；(喻)小偷。

Mag·yar /ˈmæɡjɑː(r); ˈmæɡjɑr/ *n, adj* (member, language) of the largest group of people in Hungary. 马扎儿人(匈牙利的主要民族)；马扎儿语；马扎儿人的。

Ma·ha·ra·ja(h) /ˌmɑːhəˈrɑːdʒə; ˌmɑhəˈrɑdʒə/ *n* title of a prince in India, esp a sovereign ruler of one of the indigenous states. 印度某些君主的称呼；大君。**Ma·ha·ra·nee** /ˌmɑːhəˈrɑːniː; ˌmɑhəˈrɑnɪ/ *n* wife of a ~; queen or princess with a position like that of a ~. 大君的妻子；女大君。

Ma·hatma /məˈhætmə; məˈhætmə/ *n* (in India, etc) (title given to) one of a class of persons revered as having great high-mindedness and love of humanity. (印度等地)哲人；伟人；圣贤；圣雄(对某些智慧超群、爱心广被之人的尊称)。

mah·jong /ˌmɑːˈdʒɒŋ; mɑˈdʒɔŋ/ *n* Chinese game for four persons played with 136 (or 144) pieces or tiles of wood, bone or ivory. 麻将(四个人玩的一种中国牌戏，共有 136 或 144 块木、骨或象牙制的牌)。

ma·hog·any /məˈhɒɡənɪ; məˈhɑɡənɪ/ *n* (tropical tree with) dark-brown wood much used for furniture. (做家具用的)桃花心木；红木；红木树(一种热带树)。

maid /meɪd; med/ *n* **1** (liter) girl. (文)少女。**2** (old use) young, unmarried woman. (旧用法)年轻未婚女子。**old** ~, elderly woman who is considered unlikely to marry. 年老未婚女子；老处女。 ~ **of 'honour, (a)** unmarried woman attending a queen or princess. 侍候皇后或公主的未婚女子；宫女。**(b)** principal bridesmaid.

主要女傧相. **3** (usu modern sense) woman servant: (通常为现代含义)女佣人; 女仆: *It's the ~'s day off,* 女佣人今天休假; (in compounds): (用于复合词): *a ~servant,* 女仆, *'house~,* 女管家; 女佣人, *'nurse~,* 保姆.

maiden /'meɪdn; 'medn/ *n* (liter) girl; young unmarried woman. (文)少女; 年轻未婚女子; 处女. □ *adj* (attrib only) (仅用作定语) **1** of a girl or woman. 少女的; 女子的. *'~ name,* family name before marriage. 婚前姓氏. **2** first or earliest: 首次的; 初次的: *a ship's ~ voyage.* 船的处女航. *~ speech,* first speech in Parliament of a new member. (新议员在国会中发表的)首次演说. **3 ~ (over),** (cricket) one in which no runs are scored. (板球) 未得分的投球. **4** (of a woman) unmarried: (指女子)未婚的: *my ~ aunt.* 我未婚的姑姑(阿姨). **5** (compounds) (复合词) *'~hair* n (kinds of) fern with fine stalks and delicate fronds. 过坛龙; 孔雀草(数种生细茎嫩叶的羊齿植物名). *'~head* /-hed; -hed/ *n* [U] the hymen; virginity. 处女膜; 童贞. *'~hood* /-hʊd; -hʊd/ *n* state of being a ~, period when one is a ~. 处女身分; 少女时代. *'~like, ~ly* *adjj* gentle; modest; of or like a ~. 文雅的; 温顺的; 少女的; 象少女的.

mail¹ /meɪl; mel/ *n* [U] body armour of metal rings or plates: 铠甲: *a coat of ~;* 铠甲; *'chain~.* 锁子甲. *~ed* *adj* only in 仅用于 *the ~ed fist,* (threat of) armed force. 武力(的威吓).

mail² /meɪl; mel/ *n* **1** [U] government system of collecting, carrying and delivering letters and parcels: 邮政: *send a letter by air~;* 寄一封航空信; *the '~coach,* (formerly) horse-drawn stage-coach for carrying ~. (昔时)邮件马车; 邮车. *'~bag* n stout bag in which ~ is carried. 邮袋. *'~boat* n one that transports ~. 邮件船. *'~box* n (US) letter-box. (美)邮筒; 信箱. *'~man* /-mæn; -mæn/ n (pl **-men**) (US) postman. (美)邮差. *'~order* n order for goods to be delivered by post; 邮购订货单; 邮购: *a ~order business,* one in which the buying and selling of goods is conducted by correspondence; 邮购业务; 函购商业; *a ~order catalogue,* one with a price-list of goods. 邮购货物价目单. *'~train* n train that carries ~. 邮件火车. **2** [C,U] letters, parcels, etc, sent or delivered by post; the letters, etc, sent, collected or delivered at one time: 信件; 邮寄的包裹; 某一时间内所投寄、收取或送递的邮件: *Is there any ~ this morning?* 今早有邮件吗? *I had a lot of ~ last week.* 上星期我收到好多信. *My secretary usually opens the ~.* 我的秘书通常为我开启信件. *The ship sank and the ~s were lost.* 船沉没, 邮件全遗失了. □ *vt* [VP6A] (chiefly US; in GB post is more usu) send by ~. 邮寄. *'~ing-card,* (US) postcard. (美)明信片. *'~ing-list* n list of names of persons to whom sth, eg announcements of new books from a publisher, is regularly sent: 收邮件人的名单; 邮寄名单(例如出版商经常将新书广告寄给的某些人): *Please add my name to your ~ing-list.* 请将本人姓名列入我人贵处之邮寄名单内.

maim /meɪm; mem/ *vt* [VP6A] wound or injure so that some part of the body is useless: 伤残废; 使受重伤: *He was seriously ~ed in the war.* 他在战争中重伤成残.

main¹ /meɪn; men/ *adj* (attrib only; no comp or superl) (仅用作定语; 无比较级或最高级) **1** chief; most important: 主要的; 最重要的: *the ~ thing to remember;* 所要记的主要东西; *the ~ street of a town;* 市内的主要街道; *the ~ line of a railway;* 铁道的干线; *the ~ point of my argument;* 我的议论的要点; *the ~ current / stream of traffic;* 交通的主线; *the ~ course of a meal.* 一餐的主菜. *'have an eye to the ~ chance,* ⇨ chance¹ (3). **2** exerted to the full. 尽全力的. *do sth by ~ force,* using one's strength to the utmost. 尽最大力量做某事. **3** (compounds) (复合词) *'~ deck* n upper deck. 上层甲板; 主甲板. *'~land* /-lænd; -lænd/ n country, continent or land mass, without its islands. 大陆. *'~mast* n principal mast of a sailing-ship. 帆

船的主桅. *'~spring* n **(a)** principal spring of a clock or watch. 钟表的主发条. **(b)** (fig) driving force or motive. (喻)推动的力量或动机. *'~stay* /-steɪ; -ste/ n rope from the top of the ~mast to the bottom of the foremast; (fig) chief support. 从主桅顶至前桅底的支索; 大桅支索; (喻)主要的支持. *'~stream* n **1** dominant trend, tendency, etc: (潮流、倾向等)主流: *the ~stream of political thought.* 政治思想的主流. **2** style of jazz between traditional and modern. 传统与现代爵士乐间之爵士乐. *'~ly* adv chiefly; for the most part. 主要地; 大部分: *The people in the streets were ~ly tourists.* 街上的人大部分是游客. *You are ~ly to blame.* 你应负大部分责任(应该受责备者是你).

main² /meɪn; men/ n **1** [C] (often 常作 **the ~s**) principal pipe bringing water or gas, principal wire transmitting electric current, from the source of supply into a building (contrasted with pipes from a cistern inside the building, etc); principal sewer to which pipes from a building are connected: (自来水、煤气、电流, 下水道等的)总管; 总线; 干管; 干线(以别于建筑物内的支线): *My new house is not yet connected to the ~s.* 我的新房子的水电)还没有接上干线. *We take our electric current from the ~s.* 我们从总电线接上电流. *'~s set,* radio set to be connected to the ~s for current, not a battery set. 用总线电流的收音机(非用电池的). **2** *in the ~,* for the most part; on the whole. 大体上; 从全体看来; 就一般而论. **3** *with might and ~,* ⇨ might². **4** (poet) sea, esp a wide expanse of sea. (诗)海; (尤指)大海; 沧海. **5 the Spanish M~,** that part of the NE coast of S America and the adjoining part of the Caribbean Sea, visited by the early Spanish navigators. 拉丁美洲大陆(指早年西班牙航海者所到达的南美洲东北海岸及邻近的加勒比海部分海面).

main·tain /meɪn'teɪn; men'ten/ *vt* **1** [VP6A] keep up; retain; continue: 保持; 维持; 继续: *~ friendly relations (with ...);* (与…)保持友好关系; *~ prices,* keep them steady; 保持物价的平稳; *~ law and order;* 维持治安; *~ a speed of 60 miles an hour.* 保持一小时六十英里的速度. *The improvement in his health is being ~ed.* 他的健康正在好转中. *~ an open mind on sth,* be ready to listen to and consider the views of others on a subject. 愿意听取他人对某事的意见. **2** [VP6A] support; provide: 供给; 供养: *~ a son at the university;* 供给一个儿子读大学; *neglect to ~ one's family.* 忽略赡养家属. *Can you ~ my daughter* (ie if you marry her) *in the style she has been accustomed to?* 你能供养我的女儿(如果你娶了她)过她所习惯的那种生活吗? *It's difficult to ~ a family on £30 a week.* 每周三十英镑难以赡养一个家庭. **3** [VP6A, 9, 25] assert as true: 坚持; 主张: *~ one's innocence;* 坚持自己的无辜; *~ that one is innocent of a charge.* 坚持自己对某项罪名是无辜的. **4** [VP6A] keep in good repair or working order: 保养: *~ the roads.* 保养道路. **5** [VP6A] defend: 维护: *~ one's rights.* 维护自己的权利. *~able* /-əbl; -əbl/ *adj* that can be ~ed. 可维持的; 可支持的; 可维护的.

main·ten·ance /'meɪntənəns; 'mentənəns/ n [U] maintaining or being maintained; (esp) what is needed to support life. 维持或被维持; 保养; (尤指)维持生活所需的东西; 生活费用; 赡养费. *'~ order* n (legal) order made by a court of law obliging sb to support sb, eg a husband to support his wife from whom he is separated. (法律)赡养令; 扶养令 (由法庭颁发的命令, 判定某人须赡养某人, 如夫妇分居时, 丈夫应负担妻子生活费用). *'~men / gang* n workmen who maintain roads and other public services. 道路或其他公共设施之维修工人; 维修大队. *,retail ,price ~,* practice of maintaining fixed retail prices. 保持固定零售价格; 维持不二价. ⇨ cut prices at *cut¹* (9).

mai·son·nette /,meɪzə'net; ,mezə'nɛt/ *n* flat¹ on two floors¹ (2). (二层楼)公寓.

maize /meɪz; mez/ *n* [U] (also called 亦称 *Indian corn*) sort of grain plant. 玉蜀黍; 玉米. ⇨ the illus at

685

cereal. 参看 cereal 之插图。

ma·jes·tic /məˈdʒestɪk/ məˈdʒestɪk/ adj having, showing, majesty. 有威严的；庄严的；高贵的；宏大的。 **ma·jes·ti·cally** /-klɪ/ -klɪ/ adv

maj·esty /ˈmædʒəstɪ/ ˈmædʒəstɪ/ n (pl -ties) **1** [U] kingly or queenly appearance, conduct, speech, causing respect; stateliness; royal power. 君王或皇后之令人敬仰的威仪、举止、言词；庄严；威严；王权。**2** His/Her/ Your M~; Their/Your Majesties, form used when speaking of or to a sovereign ruler or rulers. 陛下(对君王的称呼)。

ma·jol·ica /məˈdʒɒlɪkə/ məˈdʒɑlɪkə/ n [U] (kinds of) Italian ornamented pottery, with white or coloured glazes. (数种)意大利的花饰陶器；此类陶器的现代仿制品(涂有白色或彩色的釉)。

ma·jor¹ /ˈmeɪdʒə(r)/ ˈmeɪdʒə/ adj (contrasted with minor) greater or more important: (与 minor 相对)较大的；较重要的；主要的：~ roads; 要道；the ~ portion; 较大的部分；a ~ operation, (surgery) one that may be dangerous to the person's life. (外科)大手术。~ premise n ⇨ premise. ~ scale n (music) scale having two full tones between the key note and the third note. (音乐)大音阶；长音阶。~ suit n (cards, bridge) either spades or hearts. (纸牌、桥牌) 大牌(黑桃或红心心)。**2** (placed after a name) elder or first of two persons of the same name, eg in a school: (置于姓名后)同姓名的二人中较长的(例如在同一学校内)：Smith ~. 较长的史密斯。□ vi [VP3A] ~ in sth, specialize in (a certain subject) at college or university: 主修；专研(大学里某一科目)：Christina ~ed in sye subjects at Keele University. 克里斯蒂娜在基尔大学主修两门科目。Brian ~ed in economics. 布赖恩主修经济学。□ n subject ~ed in. 主修学科。

ma·jor² /ˈmeɪdʒə(r)/ ˈmeɪdʒə/ n army officer between a captain and a colonel. 陆军少校。~·'gen·eral n army officer next above a brigadier and under a lieutenant-general. 陆军少将。

ma·jor-domo /ˌmeɪdʒə ˈdəʊməʊ/ ˌmeɪdʒə ˈdomo/ n (pl ~s /-məʊz; -moz/) head steward in a great household, esp of a prince in Italy or Spain in former times. (尤指昔时意大利或西班牙王公家中的)总管家。

ma·jor·ity /məˈdʒɒrətɪ US: -ˈdʒɔːr-; məˈdʒɔrətɪ/ n (pl -ties) **1** (with sing or pl v) a the ~ (of), the greater number or part (of): (动词可用单数或复数)多数；大半：The ~ of people seem to prefer watching games to playing games. 大部分的人似乎都喜欢看比赛，而不喜欢参加比赛。The ~ were/was in favour of the proposal. 多数人赞成这个建议。**2** [C] number by which votes for one side exceed those for the other side: (投票时)超过对方的票数：He was elected by a large ~/by a ~ of 3749. 他以大多数票(超过对方3,749票)当选。The Government's ~ was a small one. 政府的多数票多得有限。be in the/a ~, have the ~. 拥有多数；占多数。a ~ verdict, verdict of the ~ (of a jury, etc). (陪审团等的)多数判决。**3** one's ~, (a) legal age of reaching manhood or womanhood: 达到成年的法定年龄：He will reach his ~ next month. 下个月他将达到法定年龄。(b) army rank of major: 少校军衔；少校职阶：obtain one's ~. 获得少校军衔。

make¹ /meɪk/ mek/ vt, vi (pt, pp made /meɪd/ med/) (For uses with nn, ⇨ **25,26** below; for uses with adjj, ⇨ **27** below; for uses with adverbial particles and preps, ⇨ **30** below.) (与名词连用，参看下列25、26义；与形容词连用，参看27义；与副词性小品词及介词连用，参看30义。) **1** [VP6A, 14, 12B, 13B] ~ sth from/(out) of sth; ~ sth into sth, construct or produce by combining parts or putting materials together; form or shape from material; bring into existence (esp by effort): 建造；制造；产生(尤指费力而做成)：~ bricks; 造砖；~ bread; 制面包；a ~ coat; 做一件外衣；~ (= manufacture) paper. 造纸。She made (= prepared) coffee for all of us. 她为我们大家煮咖

啡。I made myself a cup of tea. 我为自己泡一杯茶。Cloth is made of cotton, wool, silk and other materials. 衣料是棉、毛、丝和其他原料制成的。Wine is made from grapes. 葡萄酒是葡萄酿成的。We ~ bottles (out) of glass. 我们用玻璃制造瓶子。Glass is made into bottles. 玻璃可以制成瓶子。God made man. (宗教)上帝创造了人。show sb/sb see what one is made of, show sb one's qualities, powers, abilities, etc. 让人知道自己的品格、力量、能力等。be as clever etc as they ~ 'em, be very clever etc. 非常精明等。⇨ come(10). **2**[VP6A] cause to appear by breaking, tearing, removing material: 借打破、撕裂、移去而形成：~ a hole in the ground/a gap in a hedge. 在地上挖一个洞(在树篱上弄一缺口)。~ a hole/dent in one's savings/reserves/finances etc, reduce them by a considerable amount. 用去一大笔储蓄(准备金，资金等)。**3** [VP6A, 16A] enact; establish: 制定；规定：The regulations were made to protect children. 这些规则系为保护儿童而制定的。Who made this ridiculous rule? 这个荒谬的规则是谁定的？**4**[VP6A] draft; draw up: 草拟；起草：Father is making a fresh will. 父亲正重新立遗嘱。A treaty has been made with our former enemies. 与我们过去的敌人间的一项条约业经拟定。I'll get my solicitor to ~ a deed of transfer. 我要找我的律师拟一让渡书。**5** [VP6A] eat, have (a meal): 吃；进(餐)：He made a good breakfast before leaving. 我们在离开前吃了一顿丰富的早餐。He made a hasty lunch. 他匆匆吃了午饭。**6** [VP6A, 13B] cause to be: 引起：Why ~ a disturbance at this time of night? 值此深夜为何如此骚扰？I don't want to ~ any trouble for you. 我不想为你惹麻烦。**7** [VP16A] (passive only) be meant or intended: (仅作被动语态)预定；指定：John and Mary seem to have been made for each other, eg because they get on so well together. 约翰和玛丽似乎是天生的一对。In England we think bacon and eggs are made to be eaten together. 在英国我们认为腌肉和鸡蛋是配在一起食用的。**8** [VP22, 24A] cause to be or become: 使；使成为：The news made her happy. 这消息使她高兴。He made his meaning clear. 他把他的意思说得很明白。He made clear his objections/made it clear that he objected to the proposal. 他明白表示他的异议(反对此项提议)。His actions made him universally respected. 他的行为使他到处受尊敬。He soon made himself understood. 他立刻把他的意思说明白了。Can you easily ~ yourself understood in English? 你能用英语轻易地表明你的意思吗？The full story was never made known/public. 全部情节从未公开过。He couldn't ~ himself/his voice heard above the noise of the traffic. 在交通的喧嚣中他无法使他的声音让别人听到。~ oneself useful (about the house etc), do sth to help: 做有用的事：Don't stand about doing nothing—~ yourself useful! 不要闲站在这里——做点有用的事! ~ it worth sb's while (to do sth), pay or reward him: 使某人(做某事)；酬谢某人：If you'll help me with this job, I'll ~ it worth your while. 如果你愿意帮我做这件工作,我会酬谢你。~ sth good, ⇨ good¹(20). **9** [VP6A] earn; win; gain; acquire: 赚；赢；得；获：~ £5000 a year; 一年赚五千英镑；~ a profit/loss of £100. 获利(损失)一百英镑。He first made his name/reputation as a junior Minister. 他以次长之职崭露头角。He made a name/reputation for himself at the Bar, ie as a barrister. 做为律师他赢得了好名誉。He soon made a fortune on the Stock Exchange. 他不久便买卖股票发了财。~ a pile/packet, (colloq) acquire a great deal of money. (口)赚许多钱；发财。~ one's living (as/at by/from), have as one's work or livelihood: 谋生；(以做…为生：He ~s his living by giving piano lessons. 他以教授钢琴为生。Can you ~ a living from freelance journalism? 你能靠在报上自由写稿为生吗？Does he ~ a living at it? 他以此为生吗？**10** [VP2A,6A] (various uses in card games, eg bridge) (在桥牌等纸牌戏中的各种用法) (a) win (a trick), play to advantage: 赢(一墩牌)；打出能赢的(一张牌)：He made his Queen of Hearts. 他打出红心女王。(b) (of a

card) win a trick: (指纸牌)赢一墩: *Your ace and king won't make until you've drawn trumps.* 非等到你出王牌吊光,你的爱司和老 K 赢不到牌。 **(c)** win (what one has set out to win): 赢得 (所问的分数或墩数); 做成: *Little slam bid and made.* 叫小满贯而做成了。 **(d)** shuffle, mix (the cards): 洗(牌): *Will you ~ the pack?* 请你洗牌好吗? *My turn to ~.* 轮到我洗牌(该我洗牌)。 **11** [VP 6A] score (at cricket): (板球戏中)得分: *~ a century in a test match.* 在决赛中得一百分。 *50 runs were made in the first hour.* 第一小时得五十分。 **12** [VP2A] (of the tide) begin to flow or ebb: (指潮)开始涨或退: *The tide is making fast.* 潮水正在很快地涨。 *The ebb tide was now making,* The ebb tide was flowing. 正在退潮。 **13 ~ or break / mar,** either be successful or be ruined: 成功就是失败; 孤注一掷。 *a made man,* one whose success has been assured: 确定会成功的人: *Get the Minister's help and you'll be a made man.* 去找部长帮忙,你一定会成功。 **14** [VP18B] compel; force; persuade; cause (sb) to do sth; cause (sth) to happen: 迫; 强使; 说服; 使(某人)做某事; 使(某事)发生: *They made me repeat / I was made to repeat the story.* 他们要我重述那个故事。 *Can you ~ this old engine start?* 你能发动这个旧引擎吗? *The children never behave well and no one ever tries to ~ them* (= ~ them behave well). 那些小孩子从不守规矩, 也从没有人要他们守规矩。 *What ~s the grass grow?* 什么东西使得青草生长? *I can't ~ anyone hear,* eg by ringing the doorbell, knocking, calling. 我没法子使任何人听得见 (如按门铃、敲门、叫喊)。 *His jokes made us all laugh.* 他的笑话使我们都笑起来。 *~ one's 'blood boil; ~ one's 'hackles rise,* anger one. 使人大怒。 *~ one's 'hair stand on end,* shock or frighten one: 使人毛发竦然: *His ghost stories made our hair stand on end.* 他的鬼故事令我们毛发竦然。 *~ (sth) do; ~ do with sth,* manage with it although it may not be really adequate or satisfactory: 用某种东西勉强应付; 将就着用; 凑合着用: *You'll have to ~ do with cold meat for dinner.* 晚餐你只好将就一下吃冷肉了。 *There's not much of it but I'll try to ~ (it) do.* 东西不多, 但我会将就着用。 *~ do and mend,* manage without buying new articles, eg clothing, bed linen, household articles, esp by repairing and remaking old ones. (如衣服、床单、家具等)修补好凑合使用。 *~ sth go round,* make it last or be enough: 使某物能维持或足够分配: *I don't know how she ~s the money go round.* 我不知道她如何能靠这笔钱维持。 *~ believe (that ... / to be ...),* pretend: 假装; 假扮: *Let's ~ believe that we're Red Indians.* 我们来假扮红种印第安人。 *The children made believe that they were / made believe to be shipwrecked on a desert island.* 孩子们假装他们在荒岛上遭遇船难。 Hence, 由此产生, **'~believe** *n* [U] pretending; [C] pretence. 假装; 托辞; 口实。 **15** [VP22, 18B, 23] represent as; cause to appear as; allege (to be, to do): 表现; 使显现为; 表示; 断定: *Olivier, in the film, ~s Hamlet a figure of tragic indecision.* 在该影片中, 奥利维尔饰哈姆雷特演成了优柔寡断的悲剧人物。 *Most of the old Chronicles ~ the king die in 1026,* give 1026 as the date of his death. 古史多半认为那个国王死于一〇二六年。 *In the play the author ~s the villain commit suicide,* describe him as doing this. 在这部戏里, 作者让歹徒自杀了。 *You've made my nose too big,* eg in a drawing or painting. 你把我的鼻子画得太大了。 **16** [VP6A,25] estimate or reckon (to be); put (a total, etc) at: 估计; 推断; 算定: *What time do you ~ it?* 你认为现在几点钟了? *What do you ~ the time?* 你认为现在是几点钟? *How large do you ~ the audience?* 你估计观众(听众)有多少? *I ~ the total (to be) about £50.* 我算总数约为五十英镑。 *I ~ the distance about 70 miles.* 我估计那段距离大约有七十英里。 **17**[VP 6A] come to, equal; add up to; constitute; amount to (in significance): 总计; 合计; 等于; 构成: *Twenty shillings used to ~ one pound.* 二十先令过去等于一英镑。 *Twelve inches ~ one foot.* 十二英寸等于一英尺。 *5 and 7 is 12, and 3 is 15, and 4 more ~s 19.* 五加七等

于十二, 再加三等于十五, 再加四等于十九。 *How many members ~ a quorum?* 多少人才构成法定人数? *His adventures ~ excellent reading.* 他的冒险故事是非常好的读物。 *The play ~s an excellent evening's entertainment.* 那剧是一极好的晚间娱乐。 *~ (good / not much) sense,* seem to have (plenty of / little) sense: 有意义(很有意义); 没有什么意义: *His arguments have never made much sense.* 他的论据从来没有什么意义。 *One swallow doesn't ~ a summer,* ⇨ **swallow¹**. **18** [VP6A] (be in a series); count as: 算为: *This ~s the fifth time you've failed this examination.* 这次是你第五度参加这项考试失败。 *Will you ~ a fourth at bridge?* 我们打桥牌还缺一个人, 你要不要参加? (你要不要做第四个打牌的人?) **19** [VP6A, 23] turn into; turn out to be; prove to be: 变为; 结果为; 证明为: *If you train hard, you will ~ a good footballer.* 假若你加紧锻炼, 你会成为一个好的足球员。 *He will ~ an excellent husband.* 他会成为一个非常好的丈夫。 *She will ~ him a good wife,* will be one. 她将成为他的好妻子。 *This length of cloth will ~ me a suit,* can be made up into one. 这块布料够我做一套衣服。 **20** [VP6A] (colloq uses) travel over (a distance); reach, maintain (a speed); be in time to catch or reach; (US) gain the rank or place of: (用作口语)旅行(某一路程); 达到或维持(某一速度); 赶上(火车等); 到达(某地); (美)获…之等级或地位: *We've made 80 miles since noon.* 从中午以来我们赶了八十英里的路。 *We've made good time,* travelled the distance in good time, ie fast. 我们这一路走得够快了。 *The ship was making only nine knots.* 这艘船仅以每小时九海里的速度航行。 *The disabled cruiser was only just able to ~* (= reach) *port.* 那艘损坏的巡洋舰只能够到达港口。 *The train leaves at 7.13; can we ~ it,* reach the station in time? 火车在七点十三分开, 我们能赶得上吗? *He's tired out already—he'll never ~ the summit.* 他已经疲惫了, 他绝对不了山顶。 *His new novel has made the best-seller list,* has sold enough copies to be on this list. 他的新小说被列为畅销书之一。 *He'll never ~* (= win a place on) *the team.* 他永远没有加入那个队的机会。 *Jones made ~* (= reached the rank of) *sergeant in six months.* 琼斯经六个月后当了士官。 **21** [VP23] elect; appoint; nominate; raise to the dignity of: 选举; 被任命; 派定; 获高位显爵: *~ sb King / an earl / a peer.* 拥某人为王(封某人为伯爵; 封某人为贵族)。 *Newton was made President of the Royal Society.* 牛顿被选为皇家学会会长。 *He was made General Manager by the directors.* 他被董事们推选为总经理。 *We ~ you our spokesman.* 我们指定你做我们的发言人。 *He made her his wife,* married her. 他娶她为妻。 **22** [VP12A, 13A] offer, propose, hold out (to sb): 提供; 提出; 出让: *M~ me an offer,* suggest a price! 请开价! *We made them two or three attractive proposals.* 我们向他们提供两个动人的建议。 *The Chairman of British Rail has made a new offer to the men,* eg of a rise in wages during a strike. 英国铁路局主席向工人提出新的建议(例如在罢工时提出增加工资)。 *I made him a bid for the antique table.* 我向他出价购买那张古老的桌子。 *I made her a present of the vase.* 我给她一个花瓶作礼物。 **23 ~ sth of sb / sth; ~ sth / sb sth,** cause sb / sth to be or become sth: 使某人 / 某物成为: *His parents want to ~ a doctor of him,* want him to be educated for the medical profession. 他的父母要他将来做医生。 *We must ~ an example of him,* eg by punishing him as a warning to others. 我们必须惩罚他以儆他人。 *Don't ~ a habit of it / Don't ~ it a habit,* Don't let it become a habit. 不要使它成为习惯。 *Don't ~ a hash / mess / muddle of it,* Don't do the job badly. 不要把事情弄糟了。 *He has made a business of politics,* has made politics his chief concern. 他已经把政治作为他的事业。 *Don't ~ an ass / fool of yourself,* behave foolishly. 不要象驴子那样笨(不要做傻瓜)。 *Don't ~ a practice of cheating at exams.* 不要养成考试作弊的习惯。 *Don't ~ cheating a practice.* 不要养成欺骗的习惯。 ⇨ *n* entries esp in **25** and **26** below for other examples

of this pattern. 参看下列第 25 和 26 义中其他使用此一句型的例句。**24** [VP2C] behave as if about to do sth: 做出…的举动; 好象要: *He made as if to strike me.* 他做出要打我的样子。 *He made to reply* (= seemed to be about to do so) *and then became silent.* 他欲象要回答, 然后又停住了。 **25** [VP6A,14] (used with many *nn* where ~ + *n* have the same meaning as a *v* related in form to the *n*). (与许多名词连用, 其意义和该名词的相关动词的含义相同)。 ~ *allowance(s) (for)*, ⇨ allowance(3). ~ *(an) application (to sb) (for sth)*, apply to sb) (for sth). (向某人) 申请。 ~ *arrangements for*, arrange for. 安排。 ~ *a decision*, decide. 决定。 ~ *a guess (at)*, guess (at). 推测。 ~ *an impression (on)*, impress. 予以印象。 ~ *a request (to sb) (for sth)*, request (sth) (from sb). (向某人)要求。 ~ *a success of sth*, succeed with it/in doing it. 把…做得很成功。 (For other phrases of this kind, ⇨ the *n* entries.) (其他此类短语参看各短语的名词)。 **26** [VP6A, 14] (used with a large number of *nn* in special senses; cf **do²(2)** for *nn* used with do; the examples below are a selection only; ⇨ the *n* entries): (与许多名词连用形成特殊含义的短语; 参较 do² 第 2 义中与 do 连用之名词; 以下各例仅为选出的一部分; 参看各短语中的名词): ~ *much ado (about)*; 大忙一阵; 费尽力气。 ~ advances *(to)*; (向…)表示友好; (向…)献殷勤; ~ amends *(to sb/for sth)*; (为某事)赔偿(某人); ~ *an appointment*; 约会; ~ *an attempt*; 尝试;试图; ~ *the bed(s)*; 铺床; ~ *a bee-line (for)*; 取捷径前往; 迅速前往; ~ *the best of*; 尽量利用; ~ *a bid (for)*; 企图获得; ~ *no bones about*; 毫不犹豫; ~ *a break for it*; 逃脱;逃跑; ~ *a clean breast of*; 坦白供认; ~ *capital (out) of sth*; 利用; ~ *a change*; 改变; ~ *one's day*; 使某人非常快乐地过一天; ~ *a deal (with sb)*; (与某人)做买卖; (与某人)妥协; ~ demands *(of/on)*; 要求; ~ *some /little difference*; 甚为重要(不大重要); ~ *an effort*; 努力; 尽力; ~ *an excuse*; 找借口; ~ *eyes at*; 对…眉目传情; ~ *a face/faces (at)*; 拗鬼脸; 作鬼脸; ~ *a fuss (of)*; 小题大作; 大惊小怪; ~ *a game of*; 嘲弄;取笑; ~ *a gesture*; 作手势; 表示; ~ *a go of sth*; 使某事成功; ~ *hay of*; 使混乱; ~ *head or tail of*; 明白; 了解; ~ *a hit (with)*; 给予…良好印象; ~ inroads *into*; 侵犯;袭击; ~ *a good/poor job of*; 把(某事)做好(弄糟); ~ *a man of*; 使有男子气; 使成男子汉; ~ *one's mark*; 成名; ~ *mincemeat of*; 彻底击败(某人); 完全驳倒(某论点); ~ *mischief*; 搬弄是非; ~ *a mockery of*; 嘲笑; 愚弄; ~ *money*; 赚钱; ~ *the most of*; 充分利用; ~ *a mountain out of a* **molehill**; 小题大做; ~ *much of*; 了解; 重视; 夸张; ~ *a name for oneself*; 成名; ~ *a night of it*; 痛痛快快地玩一个晚上; ~ *nonsense of*; 破坏;使无效; ~ *a pass at*; 向…献殷勤; ~ *one's peace (with)*; (与…)和解; ~ *a point (of)*; 坚持; 决心; ~ *room (for)*; 腾出空间; ~ *a secret of*; 隐瞒; ~ *a shift with*; 尽量设法; ~ *a song and dance about*; 大惊小怪; 小题大做; ~ *war (on)*; (向…)开战; ~ *water*; 小便; (指船)漏水; ~ *one's way in the world*; 有成就; 发迹; ~ *heavy weather of*; 发现某事颇为棘手; ~ *the worst of*. 对…做最坏的打算。 **27** [VP2D] (used with *adjj* in special senses; ⇨ the *adj* entries): (与形容词连用的特殊用法; 参看各短语中之形容词): ~ *so bold (as to)*; 不揣冒昧; ~ *certain (of/that)*; 弄清楚;弄确实; ~ *sth fast*; 系牢; ~ *free with*; 随意使用; 擅用; ~ *sth good*; 补偿; 赔偿; 实现; 证实; 修复; ~ *light of*; 轻视; ~ *merry*; 作乐; 行乐; ~ *sure*. 确信; 查明。 **28** [VP2C,3A] (of arguments, evidence, etc) point; tend: (指辩论、证据等)指向; 趋于: *All the evidence ~s* (points is more usu) *in the same direction.* 所有的证据指向同一方向(point 一词较常用)。 ~ *against*, (rare) be contrary, unfavourable, prejudicial or harmful to: (罕)与…相反; 不利于; 有害于; 有损于: *These dissipations ~ against your chance of success.* 这些不正当的消遣有损你成功的机会。 **29** (compounds) (复合词) '**~-believe** *n* ⇨ **14** above. 参

看上列第 14 义。 '**~-shift** *n* sth used for a time until sth better is obtainable: 暂时的代用品: *use an empty crate as a ~shift for a table/as a ~shift table.* 用一个空箱子做桌子的代用品(代替桌子)。 '**~-up** *n* (⇨ ~ *up* in **30** below)(参看下列第30义之 ~ up) **(a)** arrangement of type, etc on a printed page. (印刷品之字图等的) 编排; 版面。 **(b)** character, temperament: 性格; 气质: *people of that ~up.* 那种性格的人。 **(c)** [C,U] cosmetics, etc as used by actors; result of using these: 化妆品(尤指演员所用者); 使用化妆品的效果: *What a clever ~up!* 多妙的化妆! **(d)** [U] cosmetics as used on the face: 面部用的化妆品: *use too much ~up/the wrong kind of ~up.* 使用太多(不当的)化妆品。 '**~-weight** *n* small quantity added to get the weight required; (fig) sth or sb of small value that fills a gap, supplies a deficiency. 补足重量的小量东西; (喻)填补欠缺的不重要的人或物。 **30** [VP2C, 14, 15B, 3A] (uses with *adverbial particles* and *preps*): (与副词性小品词及介词连用的用法):

make after sb, (formal) pursue; chase: (正式用语)追求;追赶: *She made after him like a mad woman.* 她象个疯女人似地追起他。

make at sb, move aggressively towards: 表击; 攻击: *The angry woman made at me with her umbrella.* 那个愤怒的女人用雨伞表击我。 ⇨ come at at **come(16)**.

make away with oneself, commit suicide: 自杀: *Why did he ~ away with himself?* 他为什么自杀? ~ *away with sth*, destroy or steal it. 摧毁;窃取。

make for sb/sth, **(a)** move in the direction of; head for: 向某方向移动;走向: *The frigate made for the open sea.* 那艘护卫舰开向公海。 *It's late; we'd better turn and ~ for home.* 时间晚了, 我们最好转向回家。 **(b)** charge at, rush towards: 攻击; 表击; 冲向: *The bull made for me and I had to run.* 那只公牛向我冲来, 我不得不逃跑。 *When the interval came everyone made for the bar,* ie to buy drinks. 休息时间一到, 每个人都跑向酒吧。 **(c)** contribute to, tend towards: 有助于; 倾向于: *Does early rising ~ for good health?* 早起对健康有益吗? *The improved lid of this jar ~s for easier opening.* 这个改良过的广口瓶盖子易于开启。

make sth/sb into sth, change or convert to: 使变为; 转变为: *The huts can be made into temporary houses.* 这些简陋的小屋可改装为临时住宅。 *He wasn't always a bully—you made him into one.* 他并不老是个恃强凌弱的人, 是你使他变成那样的。

make sth of sth, understand, interpret: 了解; 解释: *What do you ~ of it all?* 你对这一切作何解释? *What are we to ~ of his behaviour?* 我们怎么解释他的行为? *I can ~ nothing of all this scribble.* 这些潦草的笔迹我一点也看不懂。

make off, hurry away (esp in order to escape): 匆匆离开(尤指逃走): *The get-away car made off at top speed.* 那辆逃走的汽车开动全速慌忙驶去。 ~ *off with sth*, steal and hurry away: 卷逃: *The cashier made off with the firm's money.* 那个出纳带着公司里的款逃走了。

make sth out, **(a)** write out; complete or fill in: 写出; 开出; 填写: ~ *out a cheque for £10;* 开出一张十英镑的支票; ~ *out a list for the grocer;* 把要向杂货商购买的东西列成一张单子; ~ *out a document in duplicate.* 将一文件写成一式两份。 **(b)** manage to see, read (usu implying difficulty): 看出; 读出来; 认出来(通常含示经过困难): *We made out a figure in the darkness.* 我们在黑暗里看出一个人影。 *The outline of the house could just be made out.* 那屋子的轮廓勉强可以看出。 ~ *out that .../~ sb out to be*, claim; assert; maintain: 声称; 断言; 认定: *He made out that he had been badly treated.* 他声称他曾受到虐待。 ~ *himself ~ out to be cleverer than he really is.* 他认为他比实际上更聪明。 *He's not such a good lawyer as some people ~ out,* ie ~ him out to be. 他不是象某人所说的那样的律师。 ~ *sb out*, understand sb's nature: 了解某人的性情: *What a queer fellow he is! I can't ~ him out at all.* 他是多么奇怪的一个人! 我完全不能了解他。 ~ *it out; ~ (it)*

out if /whether, understand: 了解: *I can't ~ out what he wants.* 我不了解他要什么。 *I couldn't ~ it out—did they want our help or not?* 我不了解——他们到底需不需要我们帮忙? *How do you/does he, etc ~ that out?* How do you/does he reach that conclusion, support that contention? 你(他等)怎么会得出那个结论(支持那个论点)? *~ out (with sb),* progress, get on: 进展: *How are things making out?* 一切事情进展如何? *How are you making out with Lucy?* How's your friendship progressing? 你和露西的友谊进展如何? *~ out a case for/against/that...,* argue for/against: 为赞成(反对)而争论: *He has made out a strong case for prison reform.* 他为监狱改革而力争。 *A case could be made out that Smith should be released/for Smith's release.* 有人主张史密斯应被释放。

make sth/sb over, **(a)** change, transform, convert: 改变; 变更; 转变: *The basement has been made over into a workshop.* 那地下室已改作工厂。 *You can't ~ over a personality in one day.* 一个人的个性非一日所能改变。 **(b)** transfer the possession or ownership of: 转让所有权; 移转: *He has made over the whole of his property to the National Trust.* 他把全部财产交托给国立信托局。 *How much did he ~ over?* 他转让多少?

make sth up, **(a)** complete: 完成: 补足: *We still need £5 to ~ up the sum we asked for.* 我们还需要五英镑, 以补足我们所要求的数目。 *They need ten more men to ~ up their full complement.* 他们尚需十个人员以补足。 **(b)** supply; make good: 补充; 弥补: *Our losses have to be made up with more loans.* 我们的损失必须靠更多的贷款来补充。 **(c)** invent; compose (esp to deceive): 捏造: 编造 (尤用指于欺骗): *The whole story is made up.* 整个故事是虚构的。 *It's all a made-up story.* 这完全是捏造的故事。 *Stop making things up!* 不要再编造了! **(d)** arrange type, illustrations, etc in columns or pages for printing: 将铅字、插图等排成栏或页; 排版; 整版: *Who is in charge of making up/the ~-up of the financial pages?* 谁负责排财务版? **(e)** form; compose; constitute: 合成;组成;组织: *Are all animal bodies made up of cells?* 所有动物的身体都是细胞组成的吗? *What are the qualities that ~ up Hamlet's character?* 哈姆雷特的性格是由哪些特质构成的? *I object to the way the committee is made up/to the ~-up of the committee.* 我反对这委员会的组织方式。 **(f)** prepare, eg medicine, a prescription, tonic, by mixing ingredients: 配药: *Ask the chemist to ~ this up for you.* 请药商为你配这服药。 **(g)** put together; shape: 整理; 收拾: *~ up a bundle of old clothes for the church bazaar.* 整理出一包旧衣服供教会义卖。 *The grocer was making up the butter into packages of half a kilo.* 杂货店老板正在把奶油分成半公斤盒装。 *Have you made up Mrs Smith's order yet,* ie collected the items, articles, she ordered? 你把史密斯太太要的货物拾好了没有? **(h)** ~ (material, cloth, etc) into a garment: 把(布料等)缝制成衣服; 裁制: *Customer's own materials made up.* 顾客自备材料, 本店代为缝制衣服。 *Can you ~ up this suit length for me?* 你能用这块料子为我做成一套衣服吗? *This material will ~ up into two dresses.* 这块料子可裁制两件衣服。 **(i)** add fuel to, eg a fire in a fireplace or stove: 加燃料于(火或炉): *The fire needs making up,* needs to have more coal put on it. 这火需要添煤。 *If the stove isn't made up, it will go out.* 如果炉子不加燃料, 火会熄灭。 **(j)** prepare (a bed) not at present in use (as for a new hospital patient); prepare (a new makeshift bed, eg on the floor): 准备(床铺)备用(例如为医院新病人); 准备(临时床铺, 如在地板上): *You can't go into the ward yet; your bed's still to be made up.* 你现在还进不病房, 你的床铺尚未备妥。 *They made up a bed on the sofa for the unexpected visitor.* 他们为那个不速之客在沙发上铺个床铺。 *~ sb/oneself up,* prepare (an actor/oneself) for the stage by applying grease-paint, hair, etc to his/one's face or body; apply cosmetics to the face: 使某演员(自己)装扮好准备登台; 化妆; 打扮: *It takes him more than an*

hour to ~ up/do his ~-up for the part of Othello. 他花费一个多小时化装为奥赛罗。 *Isn't she badly made up!* 她化妆得多难看! Hence, 由此产生, *'~-up n ~ up one's/sb's mind,* come/cause sb to come to a decision: 下决心; 决定: 使某人下决心: *I've made up my mind.* 我已决定了。 *My mind's made up.* 我的心意已定。 *He needs someone to ~ up his mind for him.* 他需要别人替他作决定。 *~ up for sth,* compensate for; outweigh: 补偿; 弥补; 胜过: *Hard work can often ~ up for a lack of intelligence.* 勤能补拙。 *Do you think her beauty could ~ up for her stupidity?* 你认为她的美丽能弥补她的愚蠢吗? *~ up for lost time,* hurry, work hard, etc after losing time, starting late, etc. 加紧努力补回失去或落后的时间。 *~ up to sb for sth,* atone; redress; ~ amends for: 为某事而补偿某人: *How can we ~ it up to them for what they have suffered?* 我们如何能补偿他们所遭受的损害? *~ up to sb,* ~ oneself pleasant to sb, to win favours: 向某人献殷勤; 向某人献媚邀宠: *He's always making up to influential people.* 他经常向有势力的人献媚邀宠。 *He doesn't welcome being made up to.* 他不喜欢别人向他献殷勤。 *~ it up to sb,* compensate sb for sth missed or suffered, or for money etc spent: 补偿某人: *Thanks for buying my ticket—I'll ~ it up to you later,* by refunding you. 谢谢你为我买票—我稍后会还你钱的。 *~ it up (with sb),* end a quarrel, dispute or misunderstanding: (与某人)和解; 和好: *They quarrel every morning and ~ it up every evening.* 他们每天早上吵架, 晚上和好。 *Why don't you ~ it up with her?* 你为什么不跟她和解?

make² /meɪk; mek/ n [C, U] **1** way a thing is made; method or style of manufacture: 制造的方法; 样式: *cars of all ~s;* 各种厂牌的车; *an overcoat of first-class ~.* 第一流货色的外套。 *Is this your own ~,* made by you? 这是你自己做的吗? *on the ~,* (sl) concerned with making a profit, gaining sth. (俚)急求得利; 急求获得某种利益。 **2** (electr) completion of an electric circuit. (电)电路接通。

maker /'meɪkə(r); 'mekə/ n **1** the/our M~, the Creator; God. 创造者; 造物主; 上帝; 神。 **2** (esp in compounds) person or thing that makes: (尤用于复合词中)制造者; 能制造的机器或工具: *'dress-~.* 女裁缝。

mak·ing /'meɪkɪŋ; 'mekɪŋ/ n **1** *be the ~ of,* cause the well-being of; cause to develop well: 为…之成功(发展)的因素: *The two years he served in the Army were the ~ of him,* made him develop well (physically, etc according to context). 两年军中服役使他身心发展良好(体格或心智发展, 视上下文而定)。 **2** *have the ~s of,* have the necessary qualities for becoming: 有成为…所需的性质: *He has in him the ~s of a great man.* 他有成为伟大人物的特质。

ma·lacca /mə'lækə; mə'lækə/ n *~ 'cane,* cane walking-stick. 麻六甲手杖。

mala·chite /'mæləkaɪt; 'mæljə,kaɪt/ n [U] green mineral, a kind of stone used for ornaments, decoration, etc. 孔雀石(一种绿色矿物, 用作首饰、装饰等)。

mal·adjusted /ˌmælə'dʒʌstɪd; ˌmælə'dʒʌstɪd/ adj badly adjusted; (esp of a person) unable to adapt himself properly to his environment, eg social or occupational. 不适应的; 适应情形不良好的; (尤指人)不能适应(社会或职业)环境的。 **mal·adjust·ment** n [U] condition of being ~. 不适应; 适应不良; 失调。

mal·adroit /ˌmælə'drɔɪt; ˌmælə'drɔɪt/ adj not adroit; clumsy; tactless. 不熟练的; 笨拙的; 无机智的。 *~·ly adv ~·ness n*

mal·ady /'mælədɪ; 'mælədɪ/ n (pl -dies) [C] disease; illness: 疾病: 疾病: *a social ~;* 社会的病态(弊端); *spiritual maladies.* 道德败坏; 败德。

mal·aise /mæ'leɪz; mæ'lez/ n [U, C] feeling of bodily discomfort, but without clear signs of a particular illness: 身体不舒服; 小病; 微恙; (fig) (喻) *years of ~ in industrial relations.* 数年来劳资关系上的不愉快。

mala·prop·ism /'mæləprɒpɪzəm; 'mæləprɑp.ɪzəm/ n [C] misuse of a word, esp in mistake for one that resembles it, causing amusement, eg *'Come girls, this gentleman will exhort (for escort) us!'* 文字的错用; 误用文字(尤指因相似而造成可笑的错误,例如将 escort 误作 exhort).

mal·apro·pos /,mæl,æprə'pou; ,mæl,æprə'po/ adj, adv inappropriate(ly); inopportune(ly). 不适当的(地); 不合时宜的(地);不适合的(地).

ma·laria /mə'leərɪə; mə'lerɪə/ n [U] kinds of fever conveyed by mosquitoes, which introduce the germs into the blood. 疟疾. **ma·lar·ial** /-ɪəl; -ɪəl/ adj of ~; having ~: 疟疾的; 患疟疾的: a ~l patient; 疟疾病人; a ~l district. 疟疾地区(疟疾传染病流行地区).

Ma·lay /mə'leɪ; mə'le/ adj, n (language, member) of the people living in the ~ peninsula and adjacent areas. 马来人的;马来的;马来语;马来人.

mal·con·tent /'mælkɒntent; 'mælkən,tɛnt/ adj, n [C] (person who is) discontented and inclined to rebel. 不满的;反叛的;不满者;意图反叛者.

male /meɪl; mel/ adj 1 of the sex that does not give birth to offspring; of or for this sex: 男性的; 公的; 雄的: a ~ voice 'choir, of men and/or boys. 男声唱诗班. 2 (of parts of tools, etc) designed for insertion into a bore or socket, the corresponding female part: (指工具的零件等)阳的: a ~ screw. 阳螺钉. □ n ~ person, animal, etc. 男人;公的动物;雄性动物等.

mal·edic·tion /,mælɪ'dɪkʃn; ,mælə'dɪkʃən/ n [C] curse; prayer to God that sb or sth may be destroyed, hurt, etc. 诅咒.

mal·efac·tor /'mælɪfæktə(r); 'mælə,fæktə/ n wrongdoer; criminal. 作恶者;罪犯.

ma·lefi·cent /mə'lefɪsnt; mæˈlɛfəsn̩t/ adj hurtful (to). (对…)有害的;罪行的(与 to 连用).

ma·levo·lent /mə'levələnt; mə'lɛvələnt/ adj wishing to do evil or cause harm to others; spiteful (to/ towards). 恶意的; 恶毒的; (对…)怀恨的(与 to 或 towards 连用). ~·ly adv **ma·levo·lence** /-əns; -əns/ n [U] ill will. 恶意;敌意;怨恨.

mal·feas·ance /,mæl'fiːzns; ,mæl'fizn̩s/ n [U] (legal) wrongdoing; [C] illegal act, esp an instance of official misconduct. (法律) 恶事; 恶行; (尤指公务员之)不法行为;渎职.

mal·for·ma·tion /,mælfɔː'meɪʃn; ,mælfɔr'meʃən/ n [U] state of being badly formed or shaped; [C] badly formed part: 畸形; 不正常的部分: a ~ of the spine. 脊椎骨的畸形. **mal·formed** /,mæl'fɔːmd; mæl-ˈfɔrmd/ adj badly formed or shaped. 畸形的.

mal·func·tion /,mæl'fʌŋkʃn; mæl'fʌŋkʃən/ vi [VP2A] fail to function in a normal or satisfactory manner. 发生故障; 未起作用. □ n [U, C] failure of this sort. 发生故障.

mal·ice /'mælɪs; 'mælɪs/ n [U] ~ (towards), active ill will; desire to harm others: 恶意; 恶意; 怨恨: *bear sb no ~; 不怀恨某人; with ~ towards none.* 不对任何人怀恶意. **(with) ~ aforethought,** (legal) (with) conscious intention to cause harm, do wrong. (法律)蓄意. **ma·licious** /mə'lɪʃəs; mə'lɪʃəs/ adj feeling, showing, caused by, ~: 怀恶意的; 出于恶意的; 存心不良的: *malicious gossip.* 恶意的闲话. **ma·licious·ly** adv

ma·lign /mə'laɪn; mə'laɪn/ adj (of things) injurious; (指事物)有害的: *exercise a ~ influence.* 运用不良的影响. □ vt [VP6A] speak ill of (sb); tell lies about: 诽谤(某人); 中伤; 诬蔑: *~ an innocent person.* 诋毁一个无辜的人.

ma·lig·nant /mə'lɪgnənt; mə'lɪgnənt/ adj 1 (of persons, their actions) filled with, showing, a desire to hurt (~ is stronger in meaning than *malicious* and *malevolent*): (指人,其行为)恶毒的; 恶意的 (malignant 的含义较 malicious 及 malevolent 强): ~ fairies; 恶毒的妖怪; ~ glances. 凶恶的眼光. 2 (of diseases) harmful to life; violent: (指疾病)致命的; 恶性的: ~ cancer. 恶

性的癌. **~·ly** adv **ma·lig·nancy** /-nənsɪ; -nənsɪ/ n [U] the state of being ~. 恶毒;恶性;恶念.

ma·lig·nity /mə'lɪgnətɪ; mə'lɪgnətɪ/ n (pl **-ties**) 1 [U] deep-rooted ill will; [C] instance of this; act, remark, etc, caused by such ill will. 极深的恶意; 恶意的言行;憎恨. 2 (of diseases) malignant character. (指疾病)恶性.

ma·lin·ger /mə'lɪŋgə(r); mə'lɪŋgɚ/ vi [VP2A] pretend to be ill, protract an illness, in order to escape duty or work. 装病以逃避责任; 诈病. **~er** n person who ~s. 装病以逃避责任的人;诈病者.

mal·lard /'mælɑːd; 'mælɚd; 'mæləd/ n kind of wild duck. 一种野鸭;凫.

mal·leable /'mælɪəbl; 'mælɪəbl/ adj 1 (of metals) that can be hammered or pressed into new shapes. (指金属)可锻的; 可压制的; 可锤薄的; 有展性的. 2 (fig, eg of a person's character) easily trained or adapted. (喻, 如指人的性格)易训练的; 易适应的. **mal·lea·bil·ity** /,mælɪə'bɪlətɪ; ,mælɪə'bɪlətɪ/ n

mal·let /'mælɪt; 'mælɪt/ n 1 hammer with a wooden head, eg for striking the handle of a chisel. 木槌(如用于敲击凿子把柄者). ⇨ the illus at **tool**. 参看 tool 之插图. 2 long-handled wooden-headed hammer for striking a croquet or polo ball. 球槌(玩槌球或马球时用的).

mal·low /'mæləu; 'mælo/ n wild plant with hairy stems and leaves and pink, mauve or white flowers; garden varieties of this. 锦葵;锦葵属植物.

malm·sey /'mɑːmzɪ; 'mɑmzɪ/ n [U] a sweet wine from Greece, Spain, etc. (希腊、西班牙等国出产的)一种甜葡萄酒.

mal·nu·tri·tion /,mælnjuː'trɪʃn US: -nuː-; ,mælnju'trɪʃən/ n [U] condition caused by not getting enough food or (enough of) the right kind(s) of food. 营养不良.

mal·odor·ous /,mæl'əudərəs; mæl'odərəs/ adj (formal) ill-smelling. (正式用语)恶臭的.

mal·prac·tice /,mæl'præktɪs; mæl'præktɪs/ n (legal) [U] wrongdoing; neglect of duty; [C] instance of this, eg the dishonest use of a position of trust for personal gain. (法律)不法行为; 怠忽职守; 利用职位营私舞弊;渎职.

malt /mɔːlt; mɔlt/ n [U] grain (usu barley) allowed to germinate, used for brewing or distilling: 麦芽: (attrib) (用作定语) ~ liquors, eg beer, stout. 麦芽酒 (如啤酒,黑啤酒). □ vt, vi 1 [VP6A] make (grain) into ~; [VP2A] (of grain) come to the condition of ~. 使(麦)发芽;(指麦)发芽. 2 [VP6A] prepare with ~: 以麦芽调制: ~ed milk. 麦芽乳.

Mal·tese /,mɔːl'tiːz; 'mɔl,tiz/ adj, n (pl unchanged) (language, native) of Malta: (复数不变) 马尔他的; 马尔他语;马尔他人: ~ cross, ⇨ the illus at **cross**. 马尔他式十字架(参看 cross 之插图).

Mal·thu·sian /mæl'θjuːzɪən US: -'θuːʒn; mæl'θjuːzɪən/ adj, n (supporter) of the principles of T R Malthus, who declared that the growth of the world's population world, unless checked, lead to a world shortage of food. 马尔萨斯人口论的; 拥护马尔萨斯人口论者(马尔萨斯宣称,世界人口之增加如不加以节制,将导致粮食不足).

mal·treat /,mæl'triːt; mæl'trit/ vt [VP6A] treat roughly or cruelly. 恶待; 虐待. **~·ment** n [U] ~ing or being ~ed. 虐待;被虐待.

malt·ster /'mɔːltstə(r); 'mɔlt,stɚ/ n person who makes malt. 制麦芽者.

mal·ver·sa·tion /,mælvə'seɪʃn; ,mælvɚ'seʃən/ n [U] (formal) corrupt administration (of public money, etc). (正式用语)(公款等的)滥用; 贪污; 盗用(与 of 连用).

mamba /'mæmbə; 'mæmbə/ n black or green poisonous African snake. 非洲黑色或绿色毒蛇. ⇨ the illus at **snake**. 参看 snake 之插图.

mam(m)a /mə'mɑː US: 'mɑːmə; 'mɑmə/ n familiar

word for *mother*. 妈妈.

mam·mal /'mæml; 'mæml/ *n* any of the class of animals which feed their young with milk from the breast. 哺乳类动物. ⇨ the illus at ape, cat, **domestic**, **large**, **small**. 参看 ape, cat, domestic, large, small 各插图.

mam·mon /'mæmən; 'mæmən/ *n* [U] wealth (regarded as an evil influence). 财富(被视为有坏影响). **M~**, the god of greed: 贪欲之神; 财神: *worshippers of M~*. 拜金主义者.

mam·moth /'mæməθ; 'mæməθ/ *n* large hairy kind of elephant now extinct; (attrib) immense: 猛犸(已绝种的古代有毛的大象); (用作定语)巨大的: *~ business enterprises*. 庞大的企业.

tusk

a mammoth

mammy /'mæmɪ; 'mæmɪ/ *n* (*pl* **-mies**) **1** (child's word for) mother. (小儿语)妈咪. **2** (US)(old use, now derog) △ negro nursemaid for white children. (美)(旧用法,现为贬抑语)照顾白人小孩的黑人褓姆.

man¹ /mæn; mæn/ *n* (*pl* **men** /men; men/) **1** adult male human being. 男人; 男子. *one's man of business*, one's agent or solicitor. 某人的经纪人或律师. *a man of letters*, a writer and scholar. 作家; 文学家; 文人. *a man about town*, one who spends much time in society, in clubs, at parties, theatres, etc. 经常出入社交场所的人物. *a man of the world*, one with wide experience of business and society. 饱经世故的人; 熟悉世情的人. *man and boy*, from boyhood onwards: 从小: *He has worked for the firm, man and boy, for thirty years*. 他从小就在这家公司工作, 已有三十年之久. **2** human being; person: 人 (包含男女在内): *All men must die*. 所有人都会死亡. *Growing old is something a man has to accept*. 变老是人必须接受的事实. *be one's own man*, be free to act or do as one pleases; be in full possession of one's own senses. 独立自主; 随心所欲; 神智健全. *every man for himself (and devil take the hindmost)*, all must see to their own safety. 争先恐后. *the man in the street*, person looked upon as representing the interests and opinions of ordinary people. 普通人; 一般人; 世人. *a man to the last man*, all without exception: 毫无例外; 全部: *They answered 'Yes' to a man*. 他们全体答'是'. *They were killed to the last man*. 他们全被杀死, 一个也不留. **3**(*sing* only, no *article*) the human race; all mankind: (仅用单数,不加冠词)人类; 全人类: *Man is mortal*. 人都是会死的. **4** husband (usu in *man and wife*). 丈夫(通常用于 *man and wife* 短语中). **5** male person under the authority of another; manservant or valet: (男性的)下属; 仆人; 佣人: *masters and men*, employers and workers; 主人和仆人; 雇主和雇员; *officers and men*, eg in the army. 官长和士兵. **6** piece used in such games as chess. (国际象棋)一颗棋子. **7** male person having the good qualities associated with men: 男子汉; 大丈夫: *Be a man! Play the man! Be brave!* 做个大丈夫! 要有男子气概! *He's only half a man*, is lacking in spirit,

strength, courage. 他没有男子气概(他缺少精神、力量、勇气). *How can we make a man of him?* 我们怎样使他成为男子汉? **8** (as a vocative, to call attention; used in a lively or impatient way): (作为促使注意的呼喊语;用于兴奋或不耐烦的情况下): *Hurry up, man!* 赶快, 赶快! *Nonsense, man!* 胡说八道! **9** (with *possessive adj*) the person required: (与所有格形容词连用)所需要的人: *If you want to sell your car, I'm your man*, I'll make an offer. 假如你要卖你的车子, 我就是要买的人. *If you want a good music teacher, here's your man*, here's someone suitable. 如果你需要一位良好的音乐教师, 这就是你所需要的人. **10**(as second element in compounds): (用于复合词中的第二部分之后): *'clergyman'; 'postman'; 'fisherman*, etc. 教士; 邮差; 渔夫(等). ⇨ App 3. 参看附录三. **11** (compounds) (复合词) **,man-at·'arms** *n* soldier, esp (in the Middle Ages) a mounted soldier with heavy armour and weapons. 士兵(尤指中古时代的重骑兵). **'man·eater** *n* cannibal; man-eating tiger or shark. 吃人的野蛮人; 吃人的老虎或鲨鱼. **'man·handle** *vt* move by physical strength; handle roughly: 由人力操作; 粗野地对付: *The drunken man was manhandled by the police*. 醉汉被警察以强硬手段制服了. **'man·hole** *n* opening (usu with a lid) through which a man may enter (an underground sewer, boiler, tank, etc) for inspection purposes. 人孔(通常有孔盖,供工人进入检查或修理用, 如下水道、锅炉、槽柜等所设置者). **'man-hour** *n* work done by one man in one hour. 工作时(一个人一小时的工作量). **,man-of-'war** *n* (old use) armed ship belonging to a country's navy. (旧用法)军舰; 战斗舰. **'man·power** *n* number of men available for military service, industrial needs etc: 人力(可供军事、工业等使用的人数): *a shortage of manpower in the coal-mines*. 煤矿坑里缺少人力(人工). **'man·servant** *n* male servant. 男仆; 男佣人. **'man-sized** *adj* of a size or type right for a man; large-scale: 大小适合男人的; 大的; 大规模的: *a man-sized beefsteak*. 大块牛排. **'man·slaughter** *n* [U] act of killing a human being unlawfully but not wilfully. 杀人; 误杀(非法但非故意的杀人); 过失杀人. **'man·trap** *n* trap for catching trespassers, poachers, etc. 捕人的陷阱(用以捕捉侵入私宅、偷猎等之人者).

man² /mæn; mæn/ *vt* **(-nn-)** [VP6A] supply with person(s) for service or defence: 供以人员(用于工作或防卫): *man a fort/a ship*: 部署一个堡垒(给一艘船配置船员); *man a telephone switchboard*. 为一电话总机配备人员.

man·acle /'mænəkl; 'mænəkl/ *n* (usu *pl*) fetter or chain for the hands or feet. (通常用复数)手铐; 足镣. □ *vt* [VP6A] fetter with **~s**; (fig) restrain. 上手铐; 加足镣; (喻)束缚; 妨碍.

man·age /'mænɪdʒ; 'mænɪdʒ/ *vt, vi* **1** [VP6A] control: 控制; 驾驭; 处理; 管理: *~ a horse*; 驾驭一匹马; *~ a sailing-boat*, handle the sails, etc, properly; 驾驭一艘帆船; *~ a business/household*; 开店(管理家务); *~ a naughty child/one's wife*; 驾驭顽童(妻子); *the managing director*, who controls the business operations of a company. 常务董事. *Mrs Hill is a very managing woman*, one who likes to *~* or control other people. 希尔太太是个喜欢管别人的女人. **2** [VP2A, C, 4A, 3A] **~ (to do sth); ~ (with/without sth/sb)**, succeed; contrive: 完成; 设法办到: *I shan't be able to ~ without help*. 没有人协助我将不能办到. *If I can't borrow the money I shall have to ~ without*. 我若是借不到那笔钱, 那就只好撑下去了. *We can't ~ with these poor tools*. 我们无法用这些坏工具做工. *In spite of these insults, she ~d to keep her temper*. 她虽然受尽侮辱, 还是尽量克制自己的怒气. **3** [VP6A] (colloq, with *can*, *could*, *be able to*) make use of; eat: (口,与 can, could, be able to 连用)使用; 吃: *Can you ~ another slice of cake?* 你能不能再吃一块蛋糕? **~·able** /-əbl; -əbl/ *adj* that can be **~d**; easily controlled. 能处理的; 易于管理的. **~·abil·ity** /ˌmænɪdʒə'bɪlɪtɪ; ˌmænɪdʒə'bɪlɪtɪ/ *n*

man·age·ment /'mænɪdʒmənt; 'mænɪdʒmənt/ n
1 [U] managing or being managed: 管理; 处理; 经营;
支配: The failure was caused by bad ~. 这个失败是因
管理不善造成的。The business is under new ~. 这
个商务现在用新的方式经营。2 [U] skilful treatment;
delicate contrivance (and perhaps trickery): 手段; 周
密的策划(或欺诈): It needed a good deal of ~ to
persuade them to give me the job. 要用很多手段才能说服
他们给我那个差事。3 [C, U] (with sing or pl v) all
those concerned in managing an industry, enterprise,
etc: (接单数或复数动词)经理人员; (工业、企业等的)管理
人员; 主管阶层; 资方: joint consultation between workers
and ~. 劳资联席会议。What this department store needs
is a stronger ~. 这家百货公司所需要的是一个较健全的
经理阶层。

man·ager /'mænɪdʒə(r); 'mænɪdʒɚ/ n 1 person who
controls a business, a hotel, etc. 经理。2 (usu with an
adj) one who conducts business, manages household
affairs, etc, in a certain way: (通常与形容词连用)管理
业务者; 管理家务者: My wife is an excellent ~. 我内
人是一个非常好的管家。~·ess /ˌmænɪdʒə'res; 'mænɪ-
dʒərɪs/ n woman ~. 女经理。

mana·gerial /ˌmænɪ'dʒɪərɪəl; ˌmænə'dʒɪrɪəl/ adj of
managers: 经理的: the '~ class, people such as
managers, directors, etc. 经理阶层。

mana·tee /ˌmænə'tiː; ˌmænə'ti/ n large sea mammal
with flippers and a broad, flat tail; sea-cow. 一种巨大
的海洋哺乳动物; 海牛。⇨ **dugong**.

man·da·rin /'mændərɪn; 'mændərɪn/ n 1 (old use)name
for high Chinese government official. (旧用法)(中国清
朝高级的)官员。2 standard spoken Chinese language.
中国官话(普通话的旧称)。3 ~ **duck**, small Chinese
duck with brightly coloured feathers. 鸳鸯。4 ~ **orange**,
tangerine. 柑。5 person whose behaviour and language
seems deliberately remote and difficult: 行为和语言似
乎故作隐秘艰涩的人: (attrib) (用作定语) the ~ prose of
some civil servants. 某些文官之隐秘艰涩的文章。

man·date /'mændeɪt; 'mændet/ n [C] 1 order from
a superior; command given with authority. 命令; 训令。
2 (hist) authority to administer a territory authorized
by the League of Nations after the First World
War. (史) (第一次世界大战后国联所授予的)托管权。
3 authority given to representatives by voters, members of a trade union, etc: 选举人、工会会员等对代表的
授权; 代表所获之权限: the ~ given to us by the electors.
选举人授与我们的权限。□ vt [VP6A] put (a territory)
under a ~(2): 将(某地)委托统治; 托管: the ~d
territories. 托管地。**man·da·tory** /'mændətrɪ US:
-tɔːrɪ; 'mændə,tori/ adj of, conveying, a command;
compulsory, obligatory: 命令的; 含有命令的; 委托的;
强制性的; 义务性的: the mandatory power. 受委托统治的
国家; 托管国。□ n (also 亦作 **-tary** /-tɔrɪ US: -terɪ;
-,terɪ/) person or state to whom a ~ has been given.
受托者; 受委托统治的国家。

man·dible /'mændɪbl; 'mændəbl/ n 1 jaw, esp the
lower jaw in mammals and fishes. 颚(尤指哺乳动物和鱼
的下颚)。2 either part of a bird's beak. 鸟嘴的上部或
下部。3 (in insects) either half of the upper pair of
jaws, used for biting and seizing. (昆虫之)上颚之任一
半; 大颚(用于咬攫)。

man·do·lin /ˌmændə'lɪn; 'mændl,ɪn/ n musical
instrument with 6 or 8 metal strings stretched in pairs
on a rounded body. 曼陀林(一种六弦或八弦的乐器, 每二
弦为一组, 张紧于圆形共鸣箱上)。

man·drag·ora /mæn'drægərə; mæn'drægərə/ n
[U] poisonous plant used in medical preparations (as
an emetic and for causing sleep). 曼德拉草; 曼陀罗华
(可炼制催吐剂及催眠剂的有毒植物)。

man·drake /'mændreɪk; 'mændrɪk/ n = **mandragora**.

man·drill /'mændrɪl; 'mændrɪl/ n large baboon of
West Africa. 山魈(一种大狒狒,产于西非)。

mane /meɪn; men/ n [C] long hair on the neck of a
horse, lion, etc; (colloq or hum) thick hair on a man's
head. (马、狮子等动物颈上的)鬃; (口或谐)浓密的头发。
⇨ the illus at **cat, domestic.** 参看 cat, domestic 之
插图。

manes /'mɑːneɪz; 'meniz/ n pl (Lat) (among the
ancient Romans) spirits of the dead, esp of ancestors
worshipped as guardian influences. (拉) (古罗马人所信
的)阴魂; (尤指被崇奉为守护神的)祖先的灵魂。

ma·neu·ver /mə'nuːvə; mə'nuvɚ/ n, v (US
spelling of) **manoeuvre**. 为 manoeuvre 之美国拼法。

man·ful /'mænfl; 'mænfəl/ adj brave; resolute;
determined. 勇敢的; 果断的; 坚决的。~·ly /-fəlɪ;
-fəlɪ/ adv

man·ga·nese /'mæŋgəniːz; 'mæŋgə,nis/ n [U]
hard, brittle, light-grey metal (symbol **Mn**) used in
making steel, glass, etc. 锰(用以制钢、玻璃等的一种坚
硬易碎的淡灰色金属,符号为 Mn)。

mange /meɪndʒ; mendʒ/ n [U] contagious skin
disease, esp of dogs and cats. (狗猫所患的)皮肤病; 畜
疥。**mangy** /'meɪndʒɪ; 'mendʒɪ/ adj 1 suffering from
~: 生疥癣的: a mangy dog. 生疥的狗。2 squalid;
neglected. 污秽的; 被丢弃的。**mang·ily** /'meɪndʒɪlɪ;
'mendʒəlɪ/ adv

man·gel-wur·zel /'mæŋgl wɜːzl; 'mæŋgl'wɜzl/ n
[C] large round root, a kind of beet, used as cattle
food. 饲料甜菜(一种饲牛用的甜菜)。

manger /'meɪndʒə(r); 'mendʒɚ/ n long open box or
trough for horses or cattle to feed from. 饲牛马用的槽。
dog in the ~, ⇨ **dog¹(2).**

mangle¹ /'mæŋgl; 'mæŋgl/ n [C] machine with
rollers for pressing out water from and for smoothing
clothes, etc, that have been washed. (洗衣用的)轧干
机; 辗压机。□ vt [VP6A] put (clothes, etc) through
a ~. 将(衣服等)用此种机器轧干或轧平。

mangle² /'mæŋgl; 'mæŋgl/ vt [VP6A] 1 cut up,
tear, damage, badly: 切碎; 撕裂; 损坏: He was knocked
down by a lorry and badly ~d. 他被一辆卡车撞倒而皮开
肉绽。2 (fig) spoil by making bad mistakes: (喻)(因重
大错误而)损坏; 毁坏: ~ a piece of music. 损害了一首
乐曲。

mango /'mæŋgəʊ; 'mæŋgo/ n (pl ~es or ~s /-gəʊz;
-goz/) (tropical tree bearing) pear-shaped fruit with
yellow flesh: 芒果; 芒果树: ~ chutney, kind made with
(green) unripe ~es. 芒果酱(用未成熟的芒果制成)。⇨
the illus at **fruit.** 参看 fruit 之插图。

man·go·steen /'mæŋgə,stiːn; 'mæŋgə,stin/ n (E
Indian tree bearing) fruit with thick red rind and
white juicy pulp. (东印度群岛之)山竹果树; 山竹果。

man·grove /'mæŋgrəʊv; 'mæŋgrov/ n [C] tropical
tree growing in swamps and sending down new roots
from its branches. 红树(一种热带树, 生于沼泽地, 自枝上
向下生长树根)。

mangy /'meɪndʒɪ; 'mendʒɪ/ ⇨ **mange.**

man·handle ⇨ **man¹(11).**

man·hat·tan /mæn'hætn; mæn'hætn/ n (US)
cocktail of whisky and vermouth. (美)曼哈坦鸡尾酒(由
威士忌与苦艾酒合成)。

man·hood /'mænhʊd; 'mænhʊd/ n [U] 1 the state
of being a man: (男子之)成年; 成人: reach ~; 到达成
年; ~ suffrage, giving the vote to male citizens. 男性
公民选举权。2 manly qualities; courage; sexual virility.
男人气质; 勇气; 刚毅; 男子气概。3 all the men (collectively, of a country): 男人的总称(指一国之男子,与의
连用): the ~ of Scotland. 苏格兰男儿。

mania /'meɪnɪə; 'menɪə/ n 1 [U] violent madness.
癫狂; 疯狂; 躁狂。2 [C] ~ (for), extreme enthusiasm
(for sth): 热中; 狂热: a ~ for collecting china
ornaments. 收藏瓷器饰物癖。**maniac** /'meɪnɪæk; 'menɪ-
æk/ n raving madman; (fig) extreme enthusiast. 叫
嚣的疯子; (喻)极端狂热者。**ma·niacal** /mə'naɪəkl;
mə'naɪəkl/ adj violently mad; (fig) extremely enthusiastic. 疯狂的; (喻)极端狂热的。**ma·niacally** /mə'naɪəklɪ;

mə'naɪəkl̩ɪ/ *adv*

manic-depressive /ˌmænɪk dɪ'presɪv; ˌmænɪkdɪ-
'presɪv/ *adj, n* (person) suffering from alternating
periods of happy excitement and melancholic depression.
癫狂与抑郁交替发作的(患者); 躁郁性精神病患者.

mani·cure /'mænɪkjʊə(r); 'mænɪˌkjʊr/ *n* [U] care
of the hands and finger-nails: 修指甲: *have a course in
～:* 学修指甲; [C] treatment of this kind: 修指甲: *She
has a ～ once a week.* 她每星期修指甲一次. □ *vt
[VP6A] give ～ treatment to; cut, clean and polish
the finger-nails. 为…修指甲; 修剪, 洗净及涂染(指甲).
'**mani·cur·ist** /-ɪst/ *n* person who practises ～ as
an occupation. 以修指甲为业的人.

mani·fest¹ /'mænɪfest; 'mænəˌfest/ *n* list of a ship's
cargo; list of passengers in an aircraft; list of trucks
of a goods train. (船的)载货单; (飞机的)旅客名单; (运
货火车的)无盖货车清单.

mani·fest² /'mænɪfest; 'mænəˌfest/ *adj* clear and
obvious: 明白的; 明显的: *a ～ truth;* 明显的真理; *sth
that should be ～ to all of you.* 你们全体应该明白的事
情. □ *vt [VP6A]* **1** show clearly: 清楚表
示: ～ *the truth of a statement.* 明白显示一项陈述的真
实性. **2** give signs of: 显露(…的征象): *She doesn't ～
much desire to marry him.* 她没有显露很想嫁给他的样
子. **3** (*reflex*) come to light; appear: (反身)显明; 显
现: *No disease ～ed itself during the long voyage.* 在这
长久的航行中没有发生任何疾病. *Has the ghost ～ed
itself recently?* 最近那个鬼魂出现过了吗? **mani·fes·ta·**
tion /ˌmænɪfe'steɪʃn; ˌmænəfes'teʃən/ *n* [U] ～ing;
making clear; [C] act or utterance that ～s. 显示; 表
明; 明白表示的言行; 发表. **～·ly** *adv* clearly; obviously.
明白地; 显然地.

mani·festo /ˌmænɪ'festəʊ; ˌmænə'festo/ *n* (*pl* **～s**
or **～es** /-təʊz, -toz/) public declaration of principles,
policy, purposes, etc by a ruler, political party, etc or
of the character, qualifications of a person or group.
宣言; 声明; 布告.

mani·fold /'mænɪfəʊld; 'mænəˌfold/ *adj* having or
providing for many (uses, forms, parts etc); many
and various. 多种用途的; 有多种形式的; 多样的; 多
方面的. □ *vt [VP6A]* (now usu *duplicate*) make a
number of copies of (a letter, etc) on a machine. (现
在通常用 duplicate) 用机器复印(信件等). □ *n* pipe or
chamber with several openings, for connections, eg for
leading gases into or out of cylinders. 歧管; 多支管(如
用于使气体通入或流出汽缸者).

mani·kin /'mænɪkɪn; 'mænəkɪn/ *n* **1** small, undersized man; dwarf. 矮人; 侏儒. **2** anatomical model of
the human body; figure of the human body used by
artists, eg for drapery, clothes. 人体解剖模型; 艺术家
用的人体模型(例如用于穿戴织物, 衣服者).

Ma·nilla (US also **Ma·nila**) /məˈnɪlə; məˈnɪlə/ *n* **1 ～**
(hemp), plant fibre used for making ropes, mats, etc.
吕宋麻. **2 ～ paper,** strong, brown wrapping paper
made from ～ hemp. 吕宋纸(吕宋麻制成的强韧的棕色
包装纸). **m～ envelopes,** strong variety. 吕宋纸袋.
3 cheroot made in ～, the capital of the Philippine
Islands. 吕宋烟(菲律宾首都马尼拉制造的雪茄).

ma·nipu·late /məˈnɪpjʊleɪt; məˈnɪpjəˌlet/ *vt* [VP
6A] **1** operate, handle, with skill: 熟练地使用; 操纵:
～ *the gears and levers of a machine.* 操纵机件. **2** manage
or control (sb or sth) skilfully or craftily, esp by using
one's influence or unfair methods: 操纵; 控制; 利用(尤
指使用影响力或不公平手段者): *A clever politician knows
how to ～ his supporters.* / ～ *public opinion.* 一个聪明的
政治家知道如何去操纵他的拥护者(舆论). **ma·nipu·la·tion**
/məˌnɪpjʊ'leɪʃn; məˌnɪpjə'leʃən/ *n* [U] manipulating
or being ～d; [C] instance of this: 操纵; 操纵; 被操
纵: *made a lot of money by clever manipulation of the
Stock Market.* 由于巧妙的操纵股票市场而赚大钱.

man·kind *n* [U] **1** /ˌmæn'kaɪnd; mæn'kaɪnd/ the
human species. 人类. **2** /'mænkaɪnd; 'mænˌkaɪnd/

the male sex (contrasted with '*womankind*). 男性(与
womankind 相对).

man·like /'mænlaɪk; 'mænˌlaɪk/ *adj* having the
qualities (good or bad) of a man. 有男人(好或坏)气质
的; 象男人的.

man·ly /'mænlɪ; 'mænlɪ/ *adj* (**-ier, -iest**) having the
good qualities expected of a man; (of a woman) having
a man's qualities; (of things, qualities, etc) right for
a man. 有男子气概的; (指女人)有男人气质的; 男性化
的; (指物品、性质等)适合于男人的. **man·li·ness** *n*

manna /'mænə; 'mænə/ *n* [U] (in the Bible) food
provided by God for the Israelites during their forty
years in the desert (⇨ **Exod 16);** (fig) sth unexpectedly
supplied or that gives spiritual refreshment. 吗哪(圣
经中以色列人在旷野四十年中所获得的神赐食物; 参看旧
约出埃及记第十六章); (喻)不期而获的东西; 精神食粮.

man·ne·quin /'mænɪkɪn; 'mænəkɪn/ *n* **1** woman
employed to display new clothes for sale by wearing
them (*model* is the usual word today). 时装模特儿(现
在通常多用 model). **2** life-size dummy of a human
body, used by tailors and in shops and shop-windows
for the display of clothes. (裁缝、商店及橱窗中用以展示
衣服的)人体模型.

man·ner /'mænə(r); 'mænə/ *n* [C] **1** way in which
a thing is done or happens: 方式; 方法: *Do it in this ～.*
以这种方式来做. **(as) to the ～ born,** as if knowing
how to deal with a situation, practice, custom, etc
from birth; naturally fitted for a position, duty, etc.
好象生来就知道如何应付某种情况、习俗等; 天生适合于某
种职位的. **2** (*sing* only) person's way of behaving
towards others: (仅用单数)态度: *He has an awkward
～.* 他的举止笨拙. *I don't like his ～.* 我不喜欢他的态
度. **3** (*pl*) habits and customs; social behaviour: (复)
习惯; 风俗; 社交; 行为: *good/bad ～s;* 有礼貌/没
礼貌的; *He has no ～s at all,* is very badly behaved. 他毫
无礼貌. *It is bad ～s to stare at people.* 瞪着眼睛看人
是不礼貌的. *Aren't you forgetting your ～s, Mary?* (对
to a child who forgets to say 'Thank you' for a
present). 玛丽, 你是不是忘记了礼貌?(例如小孩收了礼
物应记说"谢谢", 向他这句话). **comedy of ～s,** play
which is a satire on the customs of (a certain section
of) society. 讽刺(某阶层)社会风俗的喜剧. **4** style in
literature or art: (文学或艺术的)风格; 文体; 作风: *a
painting in the ～ of Raphael.* 一幅模仿斐尔作风的
画. **5** kind, sort: 种类: *What ～ of man is he?* 他是哪
种人? *all ～ of,* every kind of. 各种的. *in a ～,* in a
certain degree; to a certain extent. 有几分; 有点儿; 在
某种意义上. *in a ～ of speaking,* as one might say
(used to weaken or qualify what one says). 可以说; 可
谓. *by 'no ～ of means,* in no circumstances. 绝不; 任
何情况之下均不. **～ed** *adj* **1** (in compounds) (用于复
合词中) *ill-* / *well-* / *rough-'～ed,* having bad /
good / rough ～s(3). 无礼貌的(有礼貌的); 粗鲁的).
2 showing mannerisms. 表现出特殊习惯或奇癖的.

man·ner·ism /'mænərɪzəm; 'mænəˌrɪzəm/ *n* [C]
peculiarity of behaviour, speech, etc, esp one that is
habitual; excessive use of a distinctive manner in art
or literature. (行为、言语等的)特殊习惯; 奇癖(文学或艺
术的)过份强调独特风格.

man·ner·ly /'mænəlɪ; 'mænəlɪ/ *adj* having good
manners; polite. 有礼貌的; 谦恭的; 客气的.

man·nish /'mænɪʃ; 'mænɪʃ/ *adj* **1** (of a woman)
like a man. (指女人)象男人的; 巾帼须眉的. **2** more
suitable for a man than for a woman: 较适合男人的(较
不适合女人的): *a ～ style of dress;* 男式的服装;
characteristic of a man. 男人特质的.

ma·noeuvre (US = **ma·neu·ver**) /məˈnuːvə(r);
məˈnuvə/ *n* **1** planned movement (of armed forces);
(*pl*) series of such movements, eg as training exercises:
(军队的)调遣; 机动(性); (复)演习; 军事; 陆
军(舰队)演习; *troops on ～s.* 调动(或演习)中的部队.
2 movement or plan, made to deceive, or to escape

from sb, or to win or do sth: 用于欺骗、逃避或取胜等的行动或计划; 策略; 巧计: the despicable ~s of some politicians. 政客的卑劣策略. □ vi, vt [VP2A, C, 6A, 15A] (cause to) perform ~s: 调遣; 演习; 计谋; 策划: The fleet is manoeuvring off the east coast. 舰队正在东海岸外演习. Can we ~ the enemy out of their strong position? 我们能不能用计诱骗敌军离开他们坚固的阵地? She ~d her car into a difficult parking space. 她设法把车子开进了一个不方便停车的地方. Can you ~ me into a good job, do you use your influence, etc in order to get a good job for me? 你能不能想办法给我找个好差事? The yachts were manoeuvring for position, moving about to get advantageous positions (in a race). 那些小艇正在移动以取得有利位置. ma·noeuvr·able (US = ma·neu·ver·able) /-vrəbl; -vrəbl/ adj that can be ~d. 能调遣的; 能演习的; 可运用的; 可操纵的. ma·noeuvr·abil·ity (US = -neu·ver-) /mə,nu:vrə'bɪlətɪ; mə,nuvrə'bɪlətɪ/ n ~r (US = ma·neu·verer) n

manor /'mænə(r); 'mænɚ/ n (in England) (在英国) **1** unit of land under the feudal system, part of which was used directly by the lord of the ~ (⇨ **lord**(4)) and the rest occupied and farmed by tenants who paid rent in crops and service. 封建制度下贵族的领地; 采地(此种土地部分为贵族自用, 其余租给佃农耕种). **2** (modern use) area of land with a principal residence (called 称作 the '~-**house**). (现代用法) 大宅邸的庄园. **ma·nor·ial** /mə'nɔ:rɪəl; mə'nɔrɪəl/ adj of a ~. 领地的; 采邑的; 领主田地的; 庄园的.

man·sard /'mænsɑ:d; 'mænsɑrd/ n ~ (**roof**), roof with a double slope, the lower being steeper than the upper. 复折屋顶(下部分坡度比上部分陡).

manse /mæns; mæns/ n church minister's house, esp in Scotland. 牧师住宅(尤指在苏格兰者).

man·sion /'mænʃn; 'mænʃən/ n **1** large and stately house. 大厦; 巨宅; 官邸. the '**M~ House**, the official residence of the Lord Mayor of London. 伦敦市长官邸. **2** (pl, in proper names) block of flats: (复, 用于专有名词中) 公寓大厦: Victoria M~s. 维多利亚公寓.

man·tel /'mæntl; 'mæntl/ n structure of wood, marble, etc above and around a fireplace; (in modern houses, usu '~-piece) shelf projecting from the wall above a fireplace. 壁炉上部及两侧的木石等构造; (现代房屋里, 通常称 mantelpiece) 壁炉台(壁炉上突出的架子); 壁炉前饰.

man·tilla /mæn'tɪlə; mæn'tɪlə/ n large veil or scarf worn by Spanish women to cover the hair and shoulders. (西班牙妇女披盖头发和肩膀的)披肩; 头纱; 头巾.

man·tis /'mæntɪs; 'mæntɪs/ n (**praying**) ~, (kinds of) long-legged insect. 螳螂. ⇨ the illus at **insect**. 参看 insect 之插图.

mantle[1] /'mæntl; 'mæntl/ n **1** loose, sleeveless cloak; (fig) covering: 无袖外套; 斗篷; (喻) 覆盖物: hills with a ~ of snow. 覆着一层雪的山. **2** lace-like cover fixed round the flame of a gas lamp and becoming incandescent, to provide bright light. (装于煤气灯火焰四周使灯光明亮的)白热纱罩; 燃罩.

mantle[2] /'mæntl; 'mæntl/ vt, vi **1** [VP6A] cover in, or as in, a mantle: 覆盖; 套; 罩; 包: an 'ivy-~d wall. 爬满常春藤的墙. **2** [VP6A, 2C] (old use, or liter) (of blood) flow into the blood-vessels of; (of the face) flush: (旧用法或文学用语)(指血液) 流入 … 之血管; (指脸)涨红; 发红: Blushes/Blood ~d (over) her cheeks. 她满脸绯红. Her face ~d with blushes. 她满脸羞红. (fig)(喻) Dawn ~d in the sky. 朝晖抹红了天际.

man·ual /'mænjʊəl; 'mænjʊəl/ adj of, done with, the hands: 手的; 手制的: ~ labour. 手工; 体力劳动; ~ training, eg in schools, training in carpentry, metal work; 手工艺训练(如在学校内学习木工、金工等); ~ exercises, gt drill in handling a rifle. 操枪教练. □ n **1** handbook or textbook: 手册; 教科书: a shorthand ~.

速记手册. **2** keyboard of an organ, played with the hands. (风琴之)手键盘. ~**ly** /-jʊəlɪ; -jʊəlɪ/ adv

manu·fac·ture /,mænjʊ'fæktʃə(r); ,mænjə'fæktʃɚ/ vt [VP6A] **1** make, produce (goods, etc) on a large scale by machinery: 制造; 以机器大量生产(货物等): ~ shoes/cement; 制造鞋子(水泥); manufacturing industries; 制造工业; ~d goods (contrasted with raw materials, hand-made goods, etc). 机器制造物品; 制造品(以别于原料、手工制品等). **2** invent (a story, an excuse, etc). 捏造(故事、托辞等). □ n **1** [U] the making or production of goods and materials: 制造; 生产: firms engaged in the ~ of plastics. 从事制造塑胶的公司; goods of foreign ~. 外国产品. **2** (pl) ~d goods and articles. (复)机器制造物品; 制造品; 产品. **manu·fac·turer** n person, firm, etc that ~s things. 制造者; 制造商; 制造厂; 生产者.

manu·mit /,mænjʊ'mɪt; ,mænjə'mɪt/ vt (-tt-) (in former times) set (a slave) free. (旧时) 释放(奴隶). **manu·mission** /,mænjʊ'mɪʃn; ,mænjə'mɪʃən/ n

ma·nure /mə'njʊə(r); mə'njʊr/ n [U] animal waste, eg from stables and cow barns, or other material, natural or artificial, spread over or mixed with the soil to make it fertile. 肥料(兽类粪便, 或其他天然的及人造的物质, 施于土壤上或混合于土壤中以使之肥沃). ⇨ fertilizer, the usu word for chemical or artificial manure, at **fertilize**. (fertilizer 通常指化学或人造肥料). □ vt [VP6A] put ~ in or on (land/soil). 施肥于(土地、土壤).

manu·script /'mænjʊskrɪpt; 'mænjə,skrɪpt / n (shortened to 简写为 **MS**, pl 复数简写为 **MSS**, both etc as first written out or typed: 手稿; 原稿; 草稿: send a ~ to the printers. 将一份原稿送往印刷商. in ~, not yet printed: 尚未付印的: poems still in ~. 尚未付印的诗稿.

Manx /mæŋks; mæŋks/ adj of the Isle of Man. 曼岛的. '~ **cat**, tailless kind of cat. 曼岛猫(一种无尾的猫). □ n language. 曼岛语.

many /'menɪ; 'mɛnɪ/ adj, n (contrasted with few; 与 few 相对; ⇨ **more, most**) **1** (used with pl nn; 与复数名词连用) **much**; in purely affirm sentences it is often preferable to use 在纯粹的肯定句中, 最好用 a large number (of), numerous, or (colloq) (口) a lot (of), lots (of), plenty (of)): 许多(的): Were there ~ people at the meeting? 有很多人到会吗? I have some, but not ~. 我有一些, 但是不很多. M~ people think so. 很多人这么想. M~ of them were broken. 其中许多是破的. M~ of us left early. 我们有很多人早离开了. How ~ do you want? 你要多少? How ~ of them were absent? 他们当中有多少人缺席呀? You gave me two too ~. 你多给了我两个. Do you need so ~? 你需要这么多吗? He made ten spelling mistakes in as ~ lines, ie in ten lines. 他在十行里拼错了十个字. I have six here and as ~ again (ie six more) at home. 我这里有六个, 在家里还有六个. a great/good ~, a large number (of): 很多(的): I have a good ~ things to do today. 我今天有很多事情要做. one too ~, one more than the correct or needed number: 比正确的或所需要的多个; 多余的: I wish Jane would go away; she's one too ~ here, We don't want her company. 我希望简走开, 她在这儿碍手碍脚. be one too ~ for, be more than a match?(2) for; get the better of; outwit: 比胜; 胜过: He was one too ~ for you that time. 那次他胜过了你. the ~, the masses; the large number of ordinary people: 多数人; 群众: Is it right that the ~ should starve while the few have plenty? 多数人挨饿而少数人富足是应该的吗? **2** ~ a, (used with a sing n; rather liter, usu replaced by ~ and the pl n in ordinary use): (与单数名词连用; 比较有文学意味, 在一般文体中通常由 many 与复数名词所取代): M~ a man (= M~ men) would welcome the opportunity. 许多人会很高兴有这个机会. I've been here ~ a time. 我来

过这儿好多次了。~'s the sth/sb that/who..., it/he has often... 此事曾时常…(他曾时常…)。~'s the time (that) sth/sb..., it/he often... 此事（他）时常…。|~-'sided adj having ~ sides; (fig) having ~ aspects, capabilities, etc: 多边的；(喻)多方面的；多才多艺的：a ~-sided problem. 一个多方面的问题(牵扯很多的问题)。

Maori /'mauri; 'mauri/ n member, language, of the aboriginal race of New Zealand. 新西兰土人；毛利人；毛利语。

map /mæp; mæp/ n representation on paper, etc of the earth's surface or a part of it, showing countries, oceans, rivers, mountains, etc; representation of the sky showing positions of the stars, etc. 地图；天体图。⇨ the illus at **projection.** 参看 projection 之插图。⇨ **chart, plan.** **on the map,** (fig) important, to be reckoned with. (喻)重要的；不可小看的。**off the map,** (colloq, of a place) inaccessible; (fig) unimportant. (口，指地点)不能到达的；(喻)不重要的。**'map-reader** n (with an adj) person able to get information from maps: (与一形容词连用)能利用地图的人：He's a good/poor map-reader. 他是个会(不会)使用地图的人。□ vt (-pp-) [VP6A] make a map of; show on a map; 绘制…的地图；以地图表示；[VP15B] **map out,** plan, arrange; 计划；设计：map out one's time. 支配时间(计划时间的利用)。

maple /'meɪpl; 'mepl/ n 1 [C] (sorts of) tree of the northern hemisphere, grown for timber and ornament. 枫树；槭树。⇨ the illus at **tree.** 参看 tree 之插图。~-sugar/syrup n sugar/syrup obtained from the sap of one kind of ~. 枫糖(枫蜜)。'~-leaf n emblem of Canada. 枫叶(加拿大的象征)。2 [U] wood of this tree. 枫木。

ma·quis /'mæːkɪ: US: 'maːkiː; ˌmaˈki/ n **the ~,** the secret army of French patriots during World War II, fighting in France against the Germans. 第二次世界大战中法国境内抗德游击队。

mar /maːr; mar/ vt (-rr-) [VP6A] injure; spoil; damage; 损伤；毁损；毁坏：Nothing marred the happiness of our outing. 没有任何事物损害我们远足的快乐。**make or mar,** make a great success of or ruin completely. 使大为成功或彻底失败。

mara·bou /'mærəbuː; 'mærə,bu/ n large W African stork; tuft of its soft feathers as trimming, eg for a hat. 产于西非的大鹳/(做帽子等装饰用的)鹳毛。

mar·as·chino /ˌmærə'skiːnəu; ˌmærə'skino/ n (pl ~s /-nəuz; -noz/) sweet liqueur made from a small black kind of cherry. 黑樱桃酒。

mara·thon /'mærəθən US: -θən; 'mærə,θɑn/ n **the M~,** long-distance race on foot (about 26 miles (or 41.8 kilometres) at modern sports meetings); (fig) test of endurance. 马拉松赛跑 (现代比赛全长约 26 英里或 41.8 公里)。(喻)耐力的考验。

ma·raud /məˈrɔːd; məˈrɔd/ vi [VP2A] go about in search of plunder or prey: 到处抢劫；劫夺；掠取：The Roman Empire was attacked by ~ing Goths and Huns. 罗马帝国遭受到处抢劫的哥特人和匈奴人所攻击。~**er** n person or animal that ~s. 劫掠的人或动物。

marble /'maːbl; 'marbl/ n 1 [U] (sorts of) hard limestone used, when cut and polished, for building and sculpture; 大理石；(attrib) (用作定语) a ~ statue/tomb. 大理石像(墓)。2 (pl) works of art in ~; collection of ~ sculptures. (复)大理石艺术品；一批大理石雕刻品。3 small ball of glass, clay or stone used in games played by children. (小孩玩的) 玻璃弹子；泥弹子；石弹子；弹珠。~**s,** game played with these balls: 弹珠戏：Let's have a game of ~s. 我们来打弹珠。4 (attrib) like ~: (用作定语)象大理石的：a ~ brow, smooth and white; 光滑而洁白的前额；a ~ breast, hard and unsympathizing personality. 冷酷无情的个性。~**d** /'maːbld; 'marbld/ adj stained or printed so as to look like variegated ~: (染印成)大理石花纹的：a book with ~d edges. 边缘有大理石花纹的书。

March /maːtʃ; martʃ/ n the third month of the year: 三月：M~ hare, ⇨ **hare.**

march[1] /maːtʃ; martʃ/ vi, vt 1 [VP2A, B, C] walk as soldiers do, with regular and measured steps: 前进；齐步前进：They ~ed thirty miles today. 他们今天已经行走了三十英里。They ~ed into the town. 他们进入那个城镇了。Quick ~! (military command to begin ~ing). 快步走！(军队口令)。The troops ~ed by/past/in/out/off/away. 军队走过(走过，走进，出发，离开，开走)。He ~ed impatiently up and down the station platform. 他在月台上不耐烦地踱来踱去。'~**ing orders,** orders for troops to leave for manoeuvres, for war, etc; (fig) dismissal. 出发令；开拔令；行军命令；(喻)免职令；解雇通知。2 [VP15A,B] cause to ~: 使前进：They ~ed the prisoner away. 他们把犯人押走。He was ~ed off to prison. 他被押去监狱。

march[2] /maːtʃ; martʃ/ n 1 [U] act of marching (by soldiers, etc). (军队)进军；前进。**on the ~,** marching. 在行进中；行军中：a line of ~, a route followed by troops when ~ing: 行军路线：Scouts were sent out to discover the enemy's line of ~. 侦察员被派出去探查敌人行军路线。2 [C] instance of marching; distance travelled: 进军或前进之实例；行程：a ~ of ten miles. 十英里的行程。a ~ past, ie of troops past a saluting point at a review. 分列式。a forced ~, one made more quickly than usual, or for a greater distance, in an emergency. 强行军；兼程行军。steal a '~ on sb, win a position of advantage by doing sth earlier than expected by him. 抢先某人；早某人一步。3 **the ~ of,** progress; onward movement: 进步；进展：the ~ of events/time. 事件的发展(时间的过去)。4 [C] piece of music for marching to: 进行曲：military ~es; 军队进行曲；a dead ~, one in slow time for a funeral. 送葬曲；哀乐。~er n

march[3] /maːtʃ; martʃ/ n (usu pl) (hist) frontier areas (esp between England and Scotland or Wales), esp land that is in dispute: (通常用复数)(史)边界；边境；(尤指英格兰与苏格兰或威尔士之间接壤的地带)；闹纠纷的边界：riding round the ~es. 在英格兰与苏格兰的边界驰车(骑马)。□ vi [VP3A] ~ upon/with, (archaic) (of countries, estates, etc) border upon; have a common frontier with: (古)(指国家、产业等)接邻；毗连：Our territory ~es with theirs. 我们的土地和他们的毗邻。

mar·chion·ess /ˌmaːʃə'nes; 'marʃənɪs/ n wife or widow of a marquis; woman who holds in her own right a position equal to that of a marquis. 侯爵夫人；侯爵未亡人；女侯爵。

Mardi Gras /ˌmaːdi'graː; 'mardi'gra/ n (F) Shrove Tuesday; last day of carnival before Lent, celebrated in some places with parades and merrymaking. (法)忏悔星期二；四旬斋前的狂欢节最后一日(某些地方以游行和狂欢庆祝之)。

mare /meər; mer/ n female horse or donkey. 母马；母驴。a '~'s nest, a hoax; a discovery that turns out to be false or worthless. 戏弄人的事；假的或无价值的发现；一场空欢喜。

mar·gar·ine /ˌmaːdʒə'riːn US: 'maːrdʒərin; 'mar-dʒə,rin/ n [U] food substance, used like butter, made from animal or vegetable fats. 人造奶油(以动物或植物脂肪制成的代用品)。

marge /maːdʒ; mardʒ/ n (colloq abbr for) margarine. (口)为 margarine 之略。

mar·gin /'maːdʒɪn; 'mardʒɪn/ n [C] 1 blank space round the printed or written matter on a page: 空白边；印刷品或书写品每页的空白边缘：wide/narrow ~s; 宽(窄)边；notes written in the ~. 在空白处的注解；眉批。2 edge or border: 边；缘：sit on the ~ of a lake/swimming pool; 坐在湖边(游泳池边)；road ~s. 路边。3 amount (of time, money, etc) above what is estimated as necessary. (钱、时间等超出估计所需要之)余裕；余地。4 condition near the limit or borderline, below or

beyond which sth is impossible: 边际; 极限: *a safety
~.* 安全限度. *He escaped defeat by a narrow ~.* 他差
一点儿失败了. **5** (comm) difference between cost price
and selling price: (商)成本与售价的差额; 盈余; 毛利:
*an increase of a penny a gallon in the dealer's ~ on the
price of petrol.* 在汽油的价格上商人的利润每加仑增加一
便士. **~al** /-nl/ **~l** /-nl/ *adj* **1** of or in a ~(1): 页边的;
空白处的: *~al notes.* 页边的注解. **2** of a ~(4): 边际
的: *The differences between the employers and the
workers are ~al.* 雇主与工人间的不同有限。**~al land**,
land which is not fertile enough for profitable farming
except when prices of farm products are high. 边际土
地(不够肥沃, 耕种无利可获, 非至农产价格高涨时不加利
用). **~al seat ∕ constituency**, one where the MP has
been elected by a small majority. 边际席位(选区)(超
过对方票数很少而当选国会议员的席位或选区)。**~·ally**
/-nl1/ *adv*

Mar·grave /ˈmɑːgreɪv; ˈmɑrgrev/ *n* hereditary
title of certain princes in the Holy Roman Empire. (神
圣罗马帝国之)侯爵.

mar·guer·ite /ˌmɑːgəˈriːt; ˌmɑrgəˈrit/ *n* kinds of
daisy, esp the ox-eye daisy with white petals round a
yellow centre. 延命菊; 雏菊(尤指牛眼菊).

mari·gold /ˈmærɪgəʊld; ˈmærəˌgold/ *n* (kinds of)
plant with orange or yellow flowers. 金盏草.

mari·juana, mari·huana /ˌmærɪˈwɑːnə; ˌmærə-
ˈwɑnə/ *n* (also called 亦称作 *hashish, cannabis, pot*)
dried leaves and flowers of Indian hemp, (esp) smoked
in cigarettes (called *reefers or joints*) to induce
euphoria. 印度大麻; 干的大麻叶和花(尤指混于烟叶当麻
醉剂吸用者); 大麻烟.

mar·imba /məˈrɪmbə; məˈrɪmbə/ *n* musical instrument similar to the xylophone. 原始木琴; 马林巴(一种
类似木琴的乐器).

ma·rina /məˈriːnə; məˈrinə/ *n* harbour designed for
pleasure boats (small yachts, cabin cruisers, etc)
often with hotels, etc. 游艇停泊港(常有旅社等场所).

mari·nade /ˌmærɪˈneɪd; ˌmærəˈned/ *n* [U] pickle
of wine, vinegar and spice; fish or meat pickled in this.
(一种包含酒、醋、香料等的)腌泡汁; 卤汁; 浸在此种卤汁中
的鱼或肉. ▷ *vt* (also 亦作 **mari·nate** /ˈmærɪneɪt;
ˈmærəˌnet/) steep, make tender, in ~. (用此种腌汁)
浸; 使嫩.

mar·ine /məˈriːn; məˈrin/ *adj* **1** of, by, found in,
produced by, the sea: 海的; 近海的; 海中的; 海产的:
~ products; 海产; *a '~ painter,* artist who paints
seascapes. 海景画家. **2** of ships, sea-trade, the navy,
etc: 船只的;海运的;海军的: *~ insurance,* of ships and
cargo; 海上(运)保险; *~ stores,* materials and supplies
for ships. 船用物品. **'~ corps**, body of soldiers
serving on warships and trained for amphibious
warfare. 海军陆战队. □ *n* **1** ,**merchant** ∕**mercantile
'~**, all the merchant ships of a country. 一个国家的
船的总称. **2** [C] soldier of a ~ corps serving on a
warship. 海军陆战队军官或士兵. **the M~s**, country's
general body of such soldiers. 一国之海军陆战队. *Tell
that to the ~s*, (used to express disbelief in an
impossible story): 谁会相信! 没有这回事! (表示不相信一
件不可能的事).

mari·ner /ˈmærɪnə(r); ˈmærənə/ *n* sailor, esp one
who assists in navigating a ship: 水手; 海员: *a ~'s
compass.* 航海罗盘. **master ~,** captain of a merchant
ship. 商船船长.

mari·on·ette /ˌmærɪəˈnet; ˌmærɪəˈnet/ *n* jointed
doll or puppet moved by strings on a small stage. (用
线牵动在小舞台演出的)木偶; 傀儡. ▷ the illus at
puppet. 参看 puppet 之插图.

mari·tal /ˈmærɪtl; ˈmærɪtl/ *adj* of a husband; of
marriage: 丈夫的; 婚姻的: *~ obligations,* eg providing
for one's wife. 丈夫的责任(如供养妻子).

mari·time /ˈmærɪtaɪm; ˈmærəˌtaɪm/ *adj* **1** connected with the sea or navigation: 海上的; 航海的; 海事

的: *~ law;* 海事法; *the great ~ powers.* 海权强国. **2**
situated or found near the sea: 近海的; 靠海的: *the ~
provinces of the USSR.* 苏联的沿海省份.

mar·joram /ˈmɑːdʒərəm; ˈmɑrdʒərəm/ *n* [U] sweet-
smelling herb used as seasoning in cooking and in
medicine. 茉沃刺那(佐料及制药用的唇形科薄荷植物).

mark¹ /mɑːk; mɑrk/ *n* **1** line, scratch, cut, stain,
etc that spoils the appearance of sth: 痕迹; 斑点; 污点:
Who made these dirty ~s on my new book? 谁在我的新书
上弄了这些污迹? **2** noticeable spot on the body by
which a person or animal may be recognized: (人或动
物身上可供识别用的)记号; 标识; 特征: *a horse with a
white ~ on its head;* 头上有个白点的马; *a 'birth~.* 胎
记; 生来就有的特征. **3** visible trace; sign or indication
(of a quality, etc): 形迹; (性质等的)标志; 标示: *~s of
suffering ∕ old age.* 痛苦(年老)的标志. *Please accept
this gift as a ~ of my esteem.* 请接受我这个表示敬意的
礼物. **4** figure, design, line, etc, made as a sign or
indication: 符号; 标志: *punctu'ation ~s;* 标点符号;
'price-~s, on goods; 价目标签; *'trade ~s.* 商标. **5**
numerical or alphabetical symbol, eg β+, to indicate
an award in an examination, or for conduct. 分数; 评
定考试成绩或操行的符号(例如 β+). *give sb ∕ get ∕
gain a good ∕ bad, etc ~, (for sth):* (为某事)给某人
(获得)良好(不好)的成绩: *get 72 ~s out of 100 for
geography ∕ full ~s for science.* 地理科考了72分(自然
科学得了满分). *He got the best ~s of his year.* 他是同
年级中成绩最好的. **6** target; sth aimed at. 目标; 目的
物. *be ∕ fall wide of the ~*, be inaccurate, imprecise:
不准确; 不正确: *Your guess ∕ calculation is wide of
the ~.* 你的猜测(计算)不对. *hit ∕ miss the ~,* (fig)
succeed ∕ fail in an attempt. (喻)尝试成功(失败).
an easy ~, (colloq) person who is easily cheated,
persuaded or ridiculed. (口)易受骗, 被说服或受嘲弄的
人. *beside the ~*, irrelevant. 不中肯; 不切题. **7** [U]
distinction; fame: 显赫; 卓越: *make one's ~,*
become distinguished. 成名. **8** the ~, (a) standard.
标准. *be up to ∕ below the ~*, equal to ∕ below the
required standard. 达到(低于)标准. (b) what is
normal. 常态. *not be ∕ feel (quite) up to the ~*, not
in one's usual health. 健康情形欠佳. **9** cross made on
a document by an illiterate person: (文盲画在文件上当
作签名的)十字画押: *make one's ~.* 画十字押. *John Doe,
his ~*, cross made by John Doe instead of a signature.
某甲, 他的十字画押. **10** (athletics) line indicating the
starting-point of a race: (体育)起点; 起跑线: *On your
~s, get set, go!* (words used by the starter). 各就各
位, 预备, 跑! **11** (with numbers) model or type: (与数
字连用)型; 式: *Meteor M~3,* eg of an aircraft. 流星
三型(如飞机的型式).

mark² /mɑːk; mɑrk/ *vt, vi* **1** [VP6A, 15A, B] ~
sth on ∕ with sth; ~ sth down ∕ up, put or leave a ~
on sth by writing, stamping, etc: 加记号; 加符号; 作标
志; 加标签; 标价格: *~ one's name on one's clothes ∕ ~
one's clothes with one's name.* 把名字写在衣服上(把衣
服写上自己的名字). *All our stock has been ~ed down
for the sales,* reduced in prices. 我们所有的存货都减价
蹇售. *The new tax made it necessary to ~ up all the
goods in the shop,* put higher price ~s on them. 新税
迫使商店所有的货物涨价. Hence, 由此产生, *'~-up n*
amount by which a price is ~ed up: 价格增额: *a
10% ~-up.* 加价百分之十. *'~-ing-ink n* indelible ink
for ~ing linen, etc. 不褪色墨水(在布帛等上标写用的). **2**
(passive) have natural ~s or visible signs: (用于被动
语态)有天然的痕迹或可见的迹象: *A zebra is ~ed with
stripes.* 斑马身上有条纹. *His face is ~ed with smallpox,* has the scars of smallpox. 他的脸有天花疤痕(有
麻子). *Her face is ~ed with grief.* 她面露戚容. **3**
[VP6A] give ~s(5) to: 批分数; 评成绩: ~ *examination papers;* 评阅考卷; 评考试成绩; *have twenty
essays to ~ ∕ to be ~ed.* 有二十份论文要评分数. **4**
[VP22] indicate sth by putting a ~, eg a tick or a

cross, on or against: 作记号以表示(例如以 '✓' 或 '+' 等记号): ~ *sth wrong*; 记下某事有问题; ~ *a pupil absent*. 记下一学生缺席. **5** [VP6A, 8, 10, 2A] pay attention (to): 注意: M~ *carefully how it is done*/ *how to do it*/*how he does it*. 注意这是怎么做的(怎么做, 他怎么做). **(You) ~ my words**, Note what I say (and you will find, later that I am right). 留心听我所说的话(你以后会发现我是对的). **a ~ed man**, one whose conduct is watched with suspicion or enmity. 嫌疑份子. **6** [VP6A] be a distinguishing feature of: 为…的特征: *What are the qualities that ~ a great leader?* 伟大领袖的特质是什么? **7** [VP6A] signal; denote: 表示; 指示: *His death ~ed the end of an era.* 他的逝世表示一时代的结束. *There will be ceremonies to ~ the tenth anniversary of the Queen's accession.* 将有典礼以庆祝女王就位十周年. **8** ~ *time*, stamp the feet as when marching but without moving forward; (fig) wait until further progress becomes possible. 原地踏步; (喻)俟机; 迁延. **9** [VP15B] (uses with *adverbial particles* (与副词性小品词连用) ~ *sth off*, put ~s on to (show boundary lines, measurements, etc). 加标志于某物(以示界线, 测量等): 以界线隔开. ~ *sth out*, put lines on sth to indicate limits, etc: 画线表示界限: ~ *out a tennis-court*. 用线画出一个网球场. ~ *sb out for sth*, decide in advance that sb will receive sth: 事先决定(某人将接受某物): ~ *sb out for promotion*. 内定某人升迁. *Peter was ~ed out for a special management course.* 彼得被选定接受一特别管理课程. ~**ed** /mɑːkt/ *adj* clear; readily seen: 明显的; 显著的: *a ~ed difference*/*improvement*. 显著的不同(改良). *a man of ~ed ability*. 才能显著的人. ~**·ed·ly** /ˈmɑːkɪdlɪ; ˈmɑrkɪdlɪ/ *adv* in a ~ed manner. 显著地; 明显地. ~**ing** *n* (esp) pattern of different colours of feathers, skin, etc. (尤指羽毛, 皮肤等的)斑点; 条纹; 花纹.

mark³ /mɑːk; mɑrk/ *n* unit of German currency. 马克(德国钱币单位).

marker /ˈmɑːkə(r); ˈmɑrkɚ/ *n* **1** person or tool that marks, esp a person who marks the score at games, eg billiards. 作记号的人或器具; (尤指)(撞球等竞赛中之)记分员; 记分器. **2** sth that marks or indicates, eg a flag or post on a playing field, a post showing distances. 作为标志之物(例如操场上的旗帜或标杆, 表示距离的里程碑).

mar·ket¹ /ˈmɑːkɪt; ˈmɑrkɪt/ *n* **1** [C] public place (an open space or a building) where people meet to buy and sell goods; time during which such a meeting takes place: 市场; 市集; 市日: *She went to (the) ~ to buy food for the family.* 她去市场给家人购买食物. *There are numerous small ~s in the town.* 镇里有许多小市场. *The next ~ is on the 15th.* 下一次市日是在十五日. **bring one's eggs**/**hogs to a bad** ~/**to the wrong** ~, fail in one's plans, fail because one goes to the wrong people for help. 计划失败; 找错了求援对象而失败; 失策; 失算. **go to** ~, go there for the purpose of shopping. 去市场购物. **go to a bad**/**good** ~, be (un)successful. 买卖(成功). '~**·day** *n* fixed day on which a ~ is held. 定期的交易日; 市日. ,~**·garden** *n* one where vegetables are grown for ~s. 种植蔬菜出售的菜园. Hence, 由此产生, ,~**·gardening** *n* [U] the practice of doing this. 种植蔬菜出售的行业. '~**·place**/**·square** *n* square or open place in a town where a ~ is held. 市场(指交易的地点); 市集; 商业集中地. '~ **hall**, (usu large) roofed area for a ~. 市场(指建筑物). '~**·town** *n* one where a ~ (esp one for cattle and sheep) is held. 市集(尤指有牛羊买卖的市镇). **2** trade in a class of goods: 买卖某种货物的行业: *the 'corn ~*; 谷物业(市场); *the 'coffee ~*; 咖啡业(市场); state of trade as shown by prices: 市况; 行情; 市价: *a dull*/*lively ~*. 萧条的(繁荣的)市况. *The ~ rose*/*fell*. 价格 rose/fell. *Prices rose*/*fell*/did not change much. 行情上涨(下跌, 平稳). ~ **price**, price for which sth, eg commodities/securities, is sold in the open ~. 市价;出售价格. '**down-**/'**up-**~ *adjj*

(trade use) low/high class. (贸易用语)低(高)级的. **3** demand: 需求: *There's no*/*not much*/*only a poor ~ for these goods.* 这些货品没有销路(销路不好, 销路很差). **4 the** ~, buying and selling. 买卖; 交易. **be on**/**come on (to) the** ~, be offered for sale: 出售: *This house will probably come on the market next month.* 这幢屋子可能下个月要出售. **be in the** ~ **for sth**, be ready to buy or (fig) consider sth. 准备买某物; (喻)准备考虑某事. **play the** ~, speculate (by buying and selling shares, commodities, etc). (买卖股票, 商品等)投机. **put sth on the** ~, offer it for sale. 出售某物. ,~ **re'search**, study of the reasons why people buy, or do not buy, certain goods, how sales are affected by advertising, etc. 市场调查(研究顾客购买或不愿购买某些货品的原因, 以及广告的效果等). **5** [C] area, country, in which goods may be sold: 推销地区; 市场: *We must find new ~s for our products.* 我们必须为我们的产品找新的市场(推销地区). *Which countries are Brazil's best ~s for coffee?* 哪些国家是巴西咖啡的最佳市场? ,**Common 'M~**, ⇨ **common¹**(1).

mar·ket² /ˈmɑːkɪt; ˈmɑrkɪt/ *vi*, *vt* **1** [VP2A] buy or sell in a ~: (在市场内)买; 卖: *go ~ing*. 去市场买或卖东西. **2** [VP6A] take or send to ~; prepare for (a/ the) ~ and offer for sale. 带或送货到市场出售; 销售. ~**·able** /-əbl; -əbl/ *adj* that can be sold; fit to be sold: 可卖的; 适合在市场出售的: ~**able products**. 畅销的产品. ~**·ing** *n* theory and practice of (large-scale) selling. (大规模)推销原理和实务.

marks·man /ˈmɑːksmən; ˈmɑrksmən/ *n* (*pl* **-men** /-mən; -mən/) person skilled in aiming at a mark, esp with a rifle. 善射手; 名射手; (尤指)神枪手. ~**·ship** /-ʃɪp; -ʃɪp/ *n* skill in shooting. 射击术.

marl /mɑːl; mɑrl/ *n* [U] soil consisting of clay and carbonate of lime, used as a fertilizer. 泥灰(用作肥料).

mar·line·spike /ˈmɑːlɪnspaɪk; ˈmɑrlɪn,spaɪk/ *n* pointed iron tool used for separating the strands of a rope which is to be spliced. 解索针; 穿索钻.

mar·ma·lade /ˈmɑːməleɪd; ˈmɑrml,ed/ *n* [U] (bitter) jam made from citrus fruit (usu oranges). (苦味的)柑桔酱.

mar·mor·eal /mɑːˈmɔːrɪəl; mɑrˈmɔrɪəl/ *adj* (poet) white, cold or polished, like marble. (诗)象大理石般洁白, 凉爽或光滑的.

mar·mo·set /ˈmɑːməzet; ˈmɑrmə,zɛt/ *n* small, tropical American monkey with soft, thick hair and a bushy tail. 狨; 绢猴(中南美所产的一种小猴). ⇨ the illus at **ape**. 参看 ape 之插图.

mar·mot /ˈmɑːmət; ˈmɑrmət/ *n* small animal of the squirrel family. 土拨鼠.

ma·ro·cain /ˈmærəkeɪn; ˈmærəken/ *n* [U] thin, fine dress material of silk or wool. 丝或毛的衣料; 一种绉绸.

ma·roon¹ /məˈruːn; məˈrun/ *adj*, *n* brownish-red (colour). 栗色; 褐红色; 栗色的; 褐红色的.

ma·roon² /məˈruːn; məˈrun/ *n* rocket, esp the kind used as a warning signal. 烟火(尤指示警用者).

ma·roon³ /məˈruːn; məˈrun/ *vt* [VP6A] put (sb) on a desert island, uninhabited coast, etc, and abandon him there. 放逐(某人)于荒岛, 无人烟的海边等; 弃(某人)于荒岛.

marque /mɑːk; mɑrk/ *n* **letters of** '~, authority formerly given to private persons to fit out an armed ship and use it to attack, capture, and plunder. 捕拿特许状(昔时颁给私人的特许, 准其装备武装船只并用以攻击, 缉捕和劫掠).

mar·quee /mɑːˈkiː; mɑrˈki/ *n* large tent (as used for flower shows, garden parties, or for a circus). 大帐幕; 大帐篷(如花展, 园游会, 马戏场所用者).

mar·quetry /ˈmɑːkɪtrɪ; ˈmɑrkɪtrɪ/ *n* [U] inlaid work (wood, ivory, etc) used for decorating furniture. (装饰家具的木或象牙等)镶嵌细工.

mar·quis, mar·quess /'mɑːkwɪs; 'mɑrkwɪs/ n (GB) nobleman next in rank above an earl and below a duke; (in other countries) nobleman next in rank above a count. 侯爵(在英国高于 earl 而低于 duke; 在其他国家高于 count). ⇨ **marchioness**.

mar·riage /'mærɪdʒ; 'mærɪdʒ/ n **1** [C, U] (instance of a) legal union of a man and woman as husband and wife; state of being married: 结婚; 婚姻: A ~ has been arranged between … and …. 某人与某人已准备结婚. She has had an offer of ~. 有人向她求婚. **give sb** (esp one's daughter) **in ~ (to sb),** offer her as a wife. 把某人(尤指自己的女儿)嫁出去, **take sb in ~,** take as husband or wife. 嫁给某人; 娶某人为妻. ~ **certificate / licence / settlement,** ⇨ these words. 参看各词条. '~ **lines,** (colloq) ~ certificate. (口)结婚证书. **2** (usu 通常用 wedding) ceremony of being married: 结婚仪式; 婚礼: Was it a civil or a church ~? 是普通婚礼还是在教堂行婚礼? ⇨ civil(1). ~·**able** /-əbl; -əbl/ adj (of a young person) old enough, fit for, ~: (指年轻人)已届适婚年龄的; 适合结婚的: a girl of ~able age. 到达适婚年龄的女子. ~·**abil·ity** /ˌmærɪdʒə'bɪlətɪ; ˌmærɪdʒə'bɪlətɪ/ n

mar·ried /'mærɪd; 'mærɪd/ adj united in marriage; of marriage: 结婚的; 已婚的; 婚姻的: ~ couples; 夫妇; ~ life. 婚姻生活.

mar·row /'mærəʊ; 'mæro/ n **1** [U] soft, fatty substance that fills the hollow parts of bones. 髓; 骨髓. **chilled to the ~,** cold through and through. 寒冷彻骨. '~·**bone** n bone containing edible ~. 髓骨(含有可吃的骨髓). **2** [U] (fig) essence; essential part: (喻)精华; 重要的部分: the pith and ~ of his statement. 他的声明的要点. **3** [C] (**vegetable**) ~, vegetable of the gourd family (US 美 = **squash**, like a large fat cucumber); [U] the flesh of this, eg stuffed with minced meat: 葫芦科蔬菜(西洋南瓜); (食用之)葫芦(如填以碎肉者): stuffed ~ for lunch. 以葫芦盅做午餐. ⇨ the illus at **vegetable**. 参看 vegetable 之插图.

marry /'mærɪ; 'mærɪ/ vt, vi (pt, pp **-ried**) **1** [VP 6A, 2A, D, 4A] take as a husband or wife; have a husband or wife: 结婚; 娶; 嫁: John is going to ~ Jane. 约翰将要和简结婚. Tom and Alice are going to get married. 汤姆和艾丽斯将要结婚. Mary married young. 玛丽早婚. Harry didn't ~ until he was over fifty. 哈里过了五十岁才结婚. She married again six months after the death of her first husband. 她在前夫死后六个月又结婚了. She married to get away from her tyrannical mother. 她为了脱离她那暴虐的母亲而结婚. **2** [VP6A] (of a priest, a civil official) join as husband or wife: (指牧师, 官员)主持…的婚礼; 使结为夫妇: Which priest is going to ~ them? 哪一位牧师将要主持他们的婚礼? **3** [VP6A, 15B] ~ (**off**), give in marriage: 嫁(女): He married both his daughters to rich directors. 他把两个女儿都嫁给富有的董事. She has married off all her daughters, has found husbands for them. 她把她所有的女儿都嫁出去了. **4** [VP6A] obtain by ~ing: 由结婚而获得: money / wealth. 由结婚而得到金钱(财富).

Mars /mɑːz; mɑrz/ n **1** (Roman myth) the god of war. (罗马神话)战神. **2** (astron) planet fourth in order from the sun. (天文)火星. ⇨ the illus at **planet**. 参看 planet 之插图.

Mar·sala /mɑːˈsɑːlə; mɑrˈsɑːlə/ n [U] sweet white wine originally exported from Marsala, Sicily. 马沙拉白葡萄酒(产于西里岛上马沙拉地方).

Mar·seil·laise /ˌmɑːseˈleɪz; ˌmɑrsˈlez/ n French national anthem. 马赛进行曲(法国国歌).

marsh /mɑːʃ; mɑrʃ/ n [C, U] (area of) low-lying, wet land: 沼泽(地带); 湿地: miles and miles of ~; 绵延连连(表示面积甚大的沼泽地带); the Romney ~es. 隆尼沼泽地区. '~ **gas,** fire-damp; methane. 沼气; 甲烷. '~·**mallow** n (**a**) shrubby herb that grows near salt ~es. 药蜀葵. (**b**) soft, spongy sweetmeat. 一种软糖. ~·**y** adj (**-ier, -iest**) of or like a ~. 沼泽的; 像沼泽的;

多沼泽的.

mar·shal¹ /'mɑːʃl; 'mɑrʃl/ n **1** Officer of highest rank: 最高级军官; 元帅: ˌField-'M~, (in the Army); 陆军元帅; ˌAir-'M~, (in the Air Force). 空军中将. **2** official responsible for important public events or ceremonies, eg one who accompanies a High Court judge; an officer of the royal household. 司仪; 司宾官; 典礼官. **3** (US) official with the functions of a sheriff; head of a fire or police department. (美)地方法律执行官; 消防队长; 警长.

mar·shal² /'mɑːʃl; 'mɑrʃəl/ vt (**-ll-, US -l-**) [VP6A, 15A, B] **1** arrange in proper order: 整理; 序列: ~ facts / military forces. 整理事实(军队). **marshalling-yard** n railway yard in which goods trains, etc are assembled. (货运火车)调车场. **2** guide or lead (sb) with ceremony: 按礼仪引导(某人): ~ persons into the presence of the Queen. 引导人们觐见女王.

mar·su·pial /mɑːˈsuːpɪəl; mɑrˈsuprəl/ adj, n (animal) of the class of mammals the females of which have a pouch in which to carry their young, which are born before developing completely, eg kangaroos. 有袋动物的; 有袋动物(如袋鼠等).

mart /mɑːt; mɑrt/ n **1** (liter) market-place; centre of commerce. (文)市场; 商业中心. **2** auction room. 拍卖室.

mar·ten /'mɑːtɪn; 'mɑrtɪn/ n [C] small animal of the weasel family; [U] its fur. 貂; 貂皮.

mar·tial /'mɑːʃl; 'mɑrʃəl/ adj **1** of, associated with, war: 战争的; 军事的: ~ music; 军乐; ~ bearing. 军仪. ~ '**law,** military government, by which ordinary law is suspended, eg during a rebellion: 戒严令: declare ~ law; 宣布戒严令; be under ~ law 戒严期中; 在戒严地区内. **2** brave; fond of fighting: 勇敢的; 好战的: show a ~ spirit, show eagerness for war. 表现尚武精神. ~**ly** /-ʃəlɪ; -ʃəlɪ/ adv

Mar·tian /'mɑːʃn; 'mɑrʃɪən/ n, adj (hypothetical inhabitant) of the planet Mars. 火星的; (假想的)火星人.

mar·tin /'mɑːtɪn US: -tn; 'mɑrtɪn/ n ('**house-**) ~, bird of the swallow family that builds a mud nest on walls, etc. (筑泥巢于墙壁等上的)一种燕子.

mar·ti·net /ˌmɑːtɪˈnet US: -tn'et; ˌmɑrtn'et/ n person who requires and enforces strict discipline. 厉行严格纪律的人.

mar·tini /mɑːˈtiːnɪ; mɑrˈtinɪ/ n cocktail made of gin and dry vermouth. 马丁尼酒(以杜松子酒和苦艾酒混合成的一种鸡尾酒).

mar·tyr /'mɑːtə(r); 'mɑrtɚ/ n person who is put to death or caused to suffer greatly for his religious beliefs or for the sake of a great cause or principle: 烈士; 殉道者: the early Christian ~s in Rome. 在罗马的早期基督教殉道者. He died a ~ in the cause of science, lost his life through his efforts to help forward the cause of science. 他为科学而牺牲. **make a ~ of oneself,** sacrifice one's own wishes or advantage (or pretend to do so) in order to get credit or reputation. 牺牲(或假装牺牲)自己的愿望或利益以博得信用声誉. **be a ~ to sth,** suffer greatly from: 遭受…的极大痛苦: He's a ~ to rheumatism. 他为风湿症所苦. ⇨ vt [VP 6A] put to death, cause to suffer, as a ~. (因其坚守所信而)杀害; 使受苦. ~·**dom** /-dəm; -dəm/ n ~'s suffering or death: 殉道; 牺牲; 成仁; 受难; 受苦: His wife's never-ending complaints made his life one long ~dom. 他妻子无尽期的抱怨使他受罪一辈子.

mar·vel /'mɑːvl; 'mɑrvl/ n [C] **1** wonderful thing; sth causing great surprise, pleased astonishment: 奇妙的事物; 令人惊奇或惊喜的事物: the ~s of modern science. 近代科学的奇迹. It's a ~ to me that he escaped unhurt. 他能安然无恙地逃脱, 在我看来是件奇事. The doctor's pills worked ~s, had wonderful results. 那医生的药丸有神奇的效果. **2** ~ of sth, wonderful example: 奇异的例子; 不凡的例子: She's a ~ of

patience. 她的耐心是罕见的。 *Your room is a ～ of
neatness and order.* 你的房间是出奇的整洁。 □ vi (-ll-,
US -l-) 1 [VP3A] ～ at sth, be greatly surprised at:
(对…)大为惊讶; 惊叹; 惊异: ～ at sb's boldness. 对
某人的勇敢感到惊异。 2 [VP3B] ～ that/why, etc,
wonder: 惊奇; 惊异; 诧异: *I ～ that she should agree to
marry that man ／ why she should want to marry
him.* 我觉得奇怪 她会同意嫁给那个人(为什么她要嫁给
他)。 ～·lous, (US = ～·ous) /'mɑːvələs; 'mɑrvləs/
adj astonishing; wonderful. 惊奇的; 神妙的; 不可思议
的。 ～·lous·ly (US = ～·ous·ly) adv

Marx·ist /'mɑːksɪst; 'mɑrksɪst/ n 马克思主义者:
(attrib) (用作定语) ～ criticism; 马克思主义的批评;
a ～ party. 一个马克思主义的政党。 **Marxism** /'mɑː-
ksɪzəm; 'mɑrksɪzm/ n 马克思主义。

mar·zi·pan /'mɑːzɪpæn; 'mɑrzɪpæn/ n [U] thick
paste of ground almonds, sugar, etc, made up into
small cakes; [C] small cake made of this mixture. 杏
仁粉和糖等所调成用以制小饼的浓膏; 小杏仁饼。

mas·cara /mæ'skɑːrə US: -'skærə; mæs'kærə/ n
[U] cosmetic preparation for darkening the eye-lashes.
染睫毛油; 睫毛膏。

mas·cot /'mæskət; 'mæskət/ n person, animal or
object considered likely to bring good fortune. 吉祥物
人, 动物或东西(被认为会带来好运者)。

mas·cu·line /'mæskjulɪn; 'mæskjəlɪn/ adj 1 of,
like, the male sex: 男性的; 像男性的: a ～ style; 男人
的式样; a ～ woman. 男性化的女人。 2 of male gender:
(语法)阳性的: 'He' and 'him' are ～ pronouns. He 和
him 都是阳性代词。 **mas·cu·lin·ity** /ˌmæskjuˈlɪnətɪ;
ˌmæskjəˈlɪnəti/ n quality of being ～. 男性; 阳性。 ⇨
feminine

ma·ser /'meɪzə(r); 'mezɚ/ n device for producing or
amplifying microwaves. 微波器; 微波放大器。

mash /mæʃ; mæʃ/ n [U] 1 grain, bran, etc cooked
in water for poultry, cattle or pigs. 由谷物、麦麸等
煮成的家禽、牛或猪的饲料。 2 [U, C] any substance
softened and crushed, eg boiled potatoes beaten and
crushed: 任何糊状物(如捣烂的熟马铃薯): a plate of
sausage and ～. 一盘香肠和马铃薯泥。3 mixture of
malt and hot water used in brewing. 麦芽浆(酿啤酒用
的热水泡的麦芽)。 □ vt [VP6A] beat or crush into a
～: 捣碎成糊状: ～ed turnips. 捣烂的萝卜。 '～·er n
cooking utensil for ～ing, eg potatoes. 捣碎机(如捣马铃
薯器);捣碎器。

mask[1] /mɑːsk US: mæsk; mæsk/ n 1 covering for the
face, or part of it, eg a piece of silk or velvet for
hiding the face; replica of the face carved in wood,
ivory, etc; disguise. 面罩; 面具; 假面具; 伪装。 do sth under a ／ the ～
of friendship, while pretending to be a friend. 借友谊
之名(装做朋友)做某事。 throw off one's ～, (fig) show
one's true character and intentions. (喻)揭掉假面具;
现出本来的面目。 2 ('gas) ·～, breathing apparatus, in
some cases for the whole of the head, worn as a
protection against poisonous gas, smoke, etc, eg in
coalmines, or by a fireman in a burning building. 防毒
(火)面具(一种用以防止吸入毒气、烟等的呼吸器具，有时
遮住整个面部，如煤矿坑内工人，或救火员进入火场所用
者)。 3 pad of sterile gauze worn over the mouth and
nose by eg doctors and nurses, eg for a surgical
operation. (医生或护士手术时所戴的纱布)口罩。 4 rep-
lica of the face worn by an actor or actress. (演员所戴
的)假面具。 5 likeness of a face made by taking a
mould in wax, etc. (用蜡等)模制的面像。 'death ～,
one made by taking a mould of the face of a dead
person. 照死人的脸面模制的面像。 6 face or head of a
fox. 狐狸的面或头。

mask[2] /mɑːsk US: mæsk; mæsk/ vt [VP6A] 1 cover
(the face) with a mask: 戴假面具; 戴面罩: a ～ed
woman, one wearing a mask; 戴着面罩的女人; a ～ed
ball, one at which masks are worn. 化装舞会。 2

conceal: 隐蔽; 遮掩: ～ one's enmity under an appearance
of friendliness. 把敌意隐藏在友谊的外表之下; ～ed
guns, hidden from the enemy. 隐蔽的大炮。

maso·chism /'mæsəkɪzəm; 'mæsə,kɪzəm/ n [U] getting satisfaction (esp sexual pleasure) from pain or
humiliation. 受虐狂(以受异性虐待为快的病态色情狂);
(尤指)受虐淫。 ⇨ sadism. **maso·chist** /-kɪst; -kɪst/
n **maso·chis·tic** /ˌmæsəˈkɪstɪk; ˌmæzəˈkɪstɪk/ adj

ma·son /'meɪsn; 'mesn/ n 1 stone-cutter; worker
who builds or works with stone. 石匠; 砖石匠; 泥瓦匠。
2 freemason. 互助会会员。 ～ic /mə'sɒnɪk; mə'sɑnɪk/
adj of freemasons. 互助会的; 互助会会员的。 ～ry
/'meɪsnrɪ; 'mesnri/ n 1 stonework; that part of a
building made of stone and mortar. 石造物; 石工; 建筑
的石造部分。 2 freemasonry. 互助会之制度。

Mason-Dixon line /ˌmeɪsn 'dɪksn lam; 'mesn
'dɪksṇ laɪn/ n (US hist) boundary between Pennsylvania and Maryland, dividing the free and the slave
States before the Civil War. (美史)美国内战前在宾夕
法尼亚州与马里兰州间之界线，用以表示蓄奴州与非蓄奴
州的界线。

masque /mɑːsk US: mæsk; mæsk/ n drama in verse,
often with music, dancing, fine costumes and pageantry,
esp as given in castles and great mansions in England
during the 16th and 17th cc. 假面剧(一种诗剧,常伴以
音乐、舞蹈、美观剧装及壮丽行列,尤指十六、十七世纪在英
国城堡及巨宅中演出者)。

mas·quer·ade /ˌmɑːskəˈreɪd US: ˌmæsk-; ˌmæskə-
'red/ n 1 ball at which masks and other disguises are
worn. 假面具舞会; 化装舞会。 2 (fig) false show or
pretence. (喻)假装; 伪装。 □ vi [VP2A, VP3A] ～ (as),
appear, be, in disguise: 假装; 乔装; 伪装: a prince who
～d as a peasant. 一个乔装为农民的王子。

mass[1] /mæs; mæs/ n 1 [C] ～ (of), lump, quantity
of matter, without regular shape; large number,
quantity or heap: 块; 堆; 大量; 大堆: ～es of dark
clouds in the sky. 天上一朵朵的乌云。 The azaleas made
a ～ of colour in the garden. 杜鹃花给花园里添上一大片
色彩。 A ～ of snow and rock broke away and started an
avalanche. 一大堆雪和岩石裂开了就开始崩前。 The poor
fellow was a ～ of bruises, (colloq) was covered
with bruises. (口)那个可怜的人遍体鳞伤。 2 the ～es,
(manual) workers. 工人; 群众。 in the ～, in the main;
as a whole: 大体而论; 整体上: The nation in the ～ was
not interested in politics. 这个国家的人民大体说来对政
治不感兴趣。 ～ meeting, large meeting, esp of people
wishing, or requested, to express their views (protesting
against sth, urging that sth be done, etc). 群众大会(尤
指发表意见以为请愿等的集会)。 ～ com·munications;
～ media, means (esp newspapers, radio, TV) of
imparting information to, influencing the ideas of,
enormous numbers of people. 大众传播工具(尤指报纸、
无线电、电视等用以向大众传达消息或影响大众意见者)。
～ observation, study of the social customs of ordinary
people. 对群众的社会风俗的研究。～ production, manufacture of large numbers of identical articles by
standardized processes. 大量生产(以标准化方法制造大

death
mask

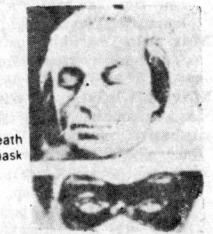

masks

量同样的产品）. Hence, 由此产生, **~-produce** vt **3** [U] (science) quantity of material in a body measured by its resistance to change of motion. (科学)物体的质量. ⇨ **size¹(1)**. □ vt, vi [VP6A, 2A] form or collect into a ~: 集合; 集结: ~ed bands, number of bands(5) playing together. 混合大乐队(集合在一起演奏的数个乐队). Troops are ~ing/are being ~ed on the frontier. 军队正在边境集结. The clouds are ~ing. 云朵密布. **~y** adj solid; massive. 结实的; 巨大的.

Mass /mæs; mæs/ n [C, U] celebration (esp RC church) of the Eucharist: 弥撒(尤指天主教的领圣餐): high/solemn ~, with eg incense, music and considerable ceremony; 大弥撒(有烧香, 奏乐, 而仪式繁多者); go to ~; 去望弥撒; hear ~. 听弥撒. M~es were said for peace in the world. 为世界和平作弥撒.

mass·acre /'mæsəkə(r); 'mæsəkə/ n [C] cruel killing of large numbers of (esp defenceless) people (occasionally used of animals). 大屠杀(尤指屠杀无防卫的人群, 有时亦指兽类). □ vt [VP6A] make a ~ of. 大屠杀.

mass·age /'mæsɑ:ʒ US: mə'sɑ:ʒ; mə'sɑʒ/ n [C, U] (instance of) pressing and rubbing the body, usu with the hands, esp the muscles and joints, in order to lessen pain, stiffness, etc. 按摩; 揉捏(按摩身体上肌肉与关节以减少痛苦, 僵硬等). □ vt [VP6A] apply ~ to. 按摩; 揉捏. **mass·eur** /mæ'sɜ:(r); mæ'sɝ/, **mass·euse** /mæ'sɜ:z; mæ'sɝz/ nn man, woman, who practises ~. 男按摩师; 女按摩师. ⇨ physiotherapist at physiotherapy.

massif /mæ'si:f; 'mæsɪf/ n compact group of mountain heights. 山岳; 山群.

mass·ive /'mæsɪv; 'mæsɪv/ adj **1** large, heavy and solid: 大而重的; 大块的; 巨大的: a ~ monument. 一个巨大的纪念碑. **2** (of the features) heavy-looking: (指容貌) 粗大的: a ~ forehead. 宽大的前额. **3** (fig) substantial; impressive. (喻)结实的; 予人深刻印象的. **~·ly** adv **~·ness** n

mast¹ /mɑ:st US: mæst; mæst/ n **1** upright support (of wood or metal) for a ship's sails. (木制或金属制的)船桅; 樯. ⇨ the illus at **barque, ship**. 参看 barque, ship 之插图. **sail before the ~**, work as an ordinary seaman (with a berth in the forepart of the ship). 做普通海员(铺位在船之前部者). '**~-head** n highest part of a ~, used as a look-out post. 桅顶(供瞭望用). **2** tall pole (for a flag). (挂旗用的)长杆. **3** tall steel structure for aerials of a radio or television transmitter; (also 亦作 '**mooring~**) tall tower to which an airship may be moored. 无线电或电视发射机的天线塔; 飞艇系留塔.

mast² /mɑ:st US: mæst; mæst/ n [U] fruit of beech, oak and other forest trees (as food for pigs). 山毛榉, 橡树等的果实(作猪的饲料).

mas·ter¹ /'mɑ:stə(r) US: mæs-; 'mæstɚ/ n **1** man who has others working for him or under him: 主人; 雇主: ~ and man, employer and workman (or manservant); 雇主与雇工; 主人与仆人; (attrib) skilled workman or one in business on his own account: (作定语)熟练技工; 能手; 独立经营者: a ~ carpenter/builder, etc. 木工能手(独立经营的建筑师或营造商等). be one's own ~, be free and independent. 独立自主. **2** male head of a household: 家里的男主人: the ~ of the house. 家长. be ~ in one's own house, manage one's affairs without interference from others. 处理自己的事务不受他人干涉. **3** captain of a merchant ship: 商船的船长: a ~ mariner; 船长; obtain a ~'s certificate, one that gives the holder the right to be a ship's captain. 取得船长证书. **4** male owner of a dog, horse, etc. 狗, 马等的男主人. **5** male teacher: 男教师: the ˌmathe'matics ~; 数学老师; 'school~; 教师; 校长; 'house~, (house¹(7)) male teacher of subjects taught outside school: 担任校外所授科目的男教师; 教练: a 'dancing/'fencing/'riding~. 舞蹈教练/击剑教练/骑术教练. **6** ~ of, person who has control or who has (sth) at his disposal: 能控制或掌握某事物的人; 能

自由运用某事物的人; 精通某事物的人: He is ~ of the situation, has it under control. 他能控制这个情况. If only I could be ~ of this subject, come to know it thoroughly. 我多么希望能精通这个科目. He has made himself ~ of the language, has learnt it well, so that he can use it freely. 他已经精通这种语言. You cannot be the ~ of your fate, cannot decide your own destiny. 你不能决定你自己的命运. He is ~ of a large fortune, can use it as he wishes. 他能随意处理一大笔财产. **7** the M~, Jesus Christ. 主; 耶稣基督. **M~ of 'Arts/ 'Science, etc**, holder of the second university degree. 文学(理学等)硕士. ⇨ **bachelor**. **8** (with a boy's name) young Mr: (与男孩的姓名连用)小主人; 少爷: M~ Charles Smith, sometimes used when speaking of or to a boy up to about the age of 14. 查尔斯·史密斯少爷(有时用以对十四岁左右的男孩的尊称). **9** title of the heads of certain colleges: 某些学院的院长: the M~ of Balliol, Oxford. 牛津大学巴利奥学院院长. **10** great artists, esp old ~s, the great painters of the 13th to 17th cc; painting by one of these artists. 名家; 大师(尤用于 old masters 中, 指十三至十七世纪间的大画家); 大画家之作品. **11** (attrib) commanding; superior: (用作定语)主要的; 熟练的; 高超的: the work of a ~ hand, superior and skilful artist, etc. 能手的作品; 名家的作品. His ~ passion (= The passion that dominates his thoughts, etc) is motor-racing. 他最大的爱好是赛车. '**~·mind** n person with superior brains (esp one who plans work to be carried out by others). 英才; 老手; 主脑(尤指计划工作由别人执行的人物). Hence, 由此产生, '**~·mind** vt plan, direct, a scheme: 策划: The whole affair was ~-minded by the publicity department. 整个事情是由宣传部门策划的. **12** as title of various officials. 某些官员的头衔. **M~ of the Horse**, official in the royal household. 御马长官. **M~ of foxhounds**, man who controls them. 管猎狐狗的官员. **M~ of Ceremonies**, (abbr 略作 M C) person who superintends the forms to be observed on various social occasions, eg a public banquet. 司礼官; 司仪. **13** (compounds) (复合词), '**~-at-'arms** n police officer in the Navy and in passenger ships of the merchant service. (海军或商船上的)警卫长. '**~-key** n one that will open many different locks, each also opened by a separate key. 万能钥匙(可以开很多不同锁的钥匙). '**~-less** adj having no ~. 无主人的. '**~-piece** n sth made or done with very great skill. 杰作; 名著. '**~-stroke** n surpassingly skilful act or piece (of policy, etc). (政策等)绝妙的行动; 绝招. ⇨ (for senses 1-5) **mistress**.

mas·ter² /'mɑ:stə(r) US: mæs-; 'mæstɚ/ vt [VP6A] become the ~ of; overcome: 成为 … 之主人; 精通; 征服; 控制: ~ one's temper/feelings; 控制脾气(感情); ~ a foreign language/the saxophone. 精通一种外国语(擅于吹奏萨克斯管).

mas·ter·ful /'mɑ:stəfl US: mæs-; 'mæstəfəl/ adj fond of controlling others; dominating: 爱控制别人的; 专横的: speak in a ~ manner. 以专横的态度说话. **~·ly** /-flɪ; -fəlɪ/ adv

mas·ter·ly /'mɑ:stəlɪ US: mæs-; 'mæstəlɪ/ adj worthy of a great master; very skilful: 巧妙的; 精巧的: with a few ~ strokes of the brush. 用巧妙的几笔.

mas·ter·ship /'mɑ:stəʃɪp US: mæs-; 'mæstɚʃɪp/ n **1** [U] dominion; control. 主权; 控制. **2** [C] office, duties, of a (esp school-) master: 教师(尤指校长)的职位, 职务: He was offered an assistant-~ (now usu usu the more common teaching post) in Bolton. 他被邀请担任博尔顿学校的助教.

mas·tery /'mɑ:stərɪ US: mæs-; 'mæstərɪ/ n [U] **1** ~ (of), complete control or knowledge: 控制; 熟练; 精通: his ~ of the violin; 他拉小提琴很熟练; get ~ of a wild horse. 驯服一匹野马. **2** ~ (over), supremacy: 控制权; 优势: Which side will get the ~? 哪一边将要取得控制权?

mas·ti·cate /'mæstɪkeɪt; 'mæstəˌket/ vt [VP6A]

chew; soften, grind up (food) with the teeth. 咀嚼；咬碎(食物)。 **mas·ti·ca·tion** /ˌmæstɪˈkeɪʃn/; ˌmæstəˈkeʃən/ n

mas·tiff /ˈmæstɪf; ˈmæstɪf/ n large, strong dog with drooping ears, much used as a watchdog. 獒(一种大猛犬，两耳下垂，多作看守用)。

mas·to·don /ˈmæstədɒn; ˈmæstəˌdɑn/ n large extinct elephant-like animal. 乳齿象(已绝种的古代像象的巨兽)。

mas·toid /ˈmæstɔɪd; ˈmæstɔɪd/ n bone at the back of the ear. (耳后的)乳突。 ~**·itis** /ˌmæstɔɪˈdaɪtɪs; ˌmæstɔɪˈaɪtɪs/ n inflammation of the ~. 乳突炎。

mas·tur·bate /ˈmæstəbeɪt; ˈmæstəˌbet/ vi, vt [VP2A, 6A] procure or provide sexual excitement by manual or other stimulation of the genital organs. 手淫。 **mas·tur·ba·tion** /ˌmæstəˈbeɪʃn; ˌmæstəˈbeʃən/ n

mat[1] /mæt; mæt/ n 1 piece of material (woven or plaited, of straw, rope, rushes, rags, fibre, etc) used for a floor covering, for sleeping on, or (a 'doormat) for wiping dirty shoes on. 席；垫(草、绳、灯心草、碎布、纤维等制成的织物，用以铺地板、睡觉或擦鞋垫或doormat用)。 2 small piece of material placed under vases, ornaments, etc, or (a 'table-mat of cork, asbestos, etc) under hot dishes on a table (to prevent injury to a varnished surface, etc). (用以垫瓶子、装饰品、热盘子等的)小垫。 3 anything thickly tangled or twisted together: 缠结之物，一丛；一簇；一团: a mat of weeds; 一丛野草; comb the mats out of a dog's thick hair. 梳理一只狗身上缠结的厚毛。 □ vt, vi (-tt-) [VP6A] cover or supply with mats; [VP6A, 15A, 2A, C] (cause to) be or become tangled or knotted: 铺席子；垫垫子；(使)缠结: matted hair. 乱蓬蓬的头发。

mat[2], **matt** (US also **matte**) /mæt; mæt/ adj (of surfaces, eg paper) dull; not shiny or glossy: (指纸等之表面)不光滑的；粗糙的: paint that dries with a ~ finish. 干后表面粗糙的漆。 ⇨ gloss[1](1).

mata·dor /ˈmætədɔː(r); ˈmætəˌdɔr/ n man whose task is to kill the bull in the sport of bull-fighting. 斗牛士。

match[1] /mætʃ; mætʃ/ n short piece of wood, pasteboard, wax taper, etc, with a head made of material that bursts into flame when rubbed on a rough or specially prepared surface (the second kind being called 'safety ~es). 火柴(有的火柴在粗糙表面摩擦即生火，有的须在特制的表面摩擦始能生火，后者称为"安全火柴"): strike a ~; 划火柴; 擦火柴; a box of ~es. 一盒火柴。 '~·box n box for holding ~es. 火柴盒。 '~·wood n (a) wood suitable for making ~es. 适于制造火柴棒的木材。 (b) splinters or fragments of wood: 碎木；细木片: smashed to ~wood, completely broken up. 完全破碎；粉碎。

match[2] /mætʃ; mætʃ/ n 1 contest; game: 比赛；竞赛: a 'football/'wrestling ~; 足球(角力)比赛; a 'boxing ~ of twenty rounds. 二十回合的拳击比赛。 '~'point, final point needed to win a ~, eg tennis. 最后决胜负的一分(如网球赛中)。 2 person able to meet another as his equal in strength, skill, etc: 对手；敌手；在体力、技巧等方面相等的人: find/meet one's ~. 遇到对手。 He is up against more than his ~, has met sb who is his superior (in skill, etc). 他遇到比他高明的对手。 You are no ~ for him, are not strong, clever, etc enough to compete with him. 你不是他的对手(你敌不过他)。 3 marriage: 婚姻；匹配: They decided to make a ~ of it, (of two persons) They decided to marry. 他俩决定结婚。 '~·maker n (esp) person who is fond of arranging ~es(3) for others. 媒人；喜欢做媒的人。 4 person considered from the point of view of marriage: 婚姻对象；配偶: He's a good ~, is considered satisfactory or desirable as a possible husband. 他是个好配偶。 5 person or thing exactly like, or corresponding to, or combining well with, another: 彼此完全相像的人或物；相配的人或物: colours/materials that are a good ~. 很相配的颜色(材料)。 ~·less adj unequalled. 无比的。

双无敌的；无敌的。

match[3] /mætʃ; mætʃ/ vt, vi 1 [VP14] ~ sth/sb against/with, put in competition: 使相竞争；使比赛: I'm ready to ~ my strength with/against yours. 我准备跟你比力气。 2 [VP6A] be equal to; be, obtain, a match(2) for: 和…匹敌；是…的对手；为…找到对手: a well-~ed pair, eg boxers about equal in skill. 旗鼓相当的一对；势均力敌的一对(例如拳击手)。 No one can ~ him in archery. 在箭术方面没有人能够和他相比。 Can you ~ that story, tell one that is equally good, amusing, etc? 你讲出一个同样精彩的故事吗？ 3 [VP6A, 2A] be equal to or corresponding (with) (in quality, colour, design, etc): (在品质、颜色、设计等方面)(与…)相等；相当；相配: The carpets should ~ the curtains. 地毯该和窗帘相配。 The curtains and carpets should ~. 窗帘和地毯应该相配。 She was wearing a brown dress with hat and gloves to ~. 她穿着一件棕色的衣服，并有帽子和手套相配。 ⇨ clash(4). 4 [VP6A, 12B, 13B] find a material, etc that ~es(3) with (another): 给object(另一件)相配的布料等: Can you ~ (me) this silk? 你能替我找到和这块绸子相配的布料吗？

match·et /ˈmætʃɪt; ˈmætʃɪt/ n = machete.

match·lock /ˈmætʃlɒk; ˈmætʃˌlɑk/ n old-fashioned style of musket. 旧式毛瑟枪；火绳枪。

mate[1] /meɪt; met/ n 1 (colloq) friend; companion; fellow-worker (often as a form of address): (口)朋友；伙伴；同事(常作称呼用): Where are you going, ~? 老兄，你去哪儿？ ⇨ class- or class, at class, class, at play[1](1). 2 ship's officer (not an engineer) below the rank of captain: 副船长；大副；副手(低于船长，但非轮机师): the chief ~, below the captain; 大副; the first/second/third ~. 大(二、三)副。 3 helper: 助手: (in titles) (用于称谓) the cook's/gunner's/surgeon's ~; 厨子的(炮手的、外科医生的)助手; a plumber's ~. 铅管工人的助手。 4 one of a pair of birds or animals: 鸟兽之偶: the lioness and her ~. 母狮与其配偶。 5 (colloq) partner in marriage, ie husband or wife: (口)配偶(夫或妻): She has been a faithful ~ to him. 她一直都是他的忠实配偶。

mate[2] /meɪt; met/ vt, vi [VP6A, 14, 2A, 3A] ~ (with), (of birds or animals) (cause to) unite for the purpose of having sexual intercourse, producing young: (指鸟兽)使交配；交配: the 'mating season, spring, when birds make their nests. 交配季节。 The zoo's camels have not ~d this year. 动物园里的骆驼今年还没有交配。

mate[3] /meɪt; met/ n, v (in chess) (下棋) = check-mate.

maté /ˈmɑːteɪ; ˈmɑte/ n (tea made from) dried leaves of a S American evergreen holly shrub. 南美马黛茶树；马黛茶。

ma·terial[1] /məˈtɪərɪəl; məˈtɪrɪəl/ adj 1 (contrasted with mental and spiritual) made of, connected with, matter or substance: (与mental及spiritual相对)物质的；由物质构成的: the ~ world; 物质世界; a '~ noun, naming a material, eg stone, wood, wool. 物质名词(例如石头、木材、毛织品)。 2 of the body; of physical needs: 肉体的；肉体所需的: ~ needs, eg food and warmth; 身体的需要(如食物与温暖); ~ comforts and pleasures; 使肉体得到安适与快乐的事物; a ~ point of view, worldly, considering only the things of the senses. (仅仅考虑感官之事物的)物欲的观点。 3 (legal) important; essential: (法律)重要的；重大的: ~ evidence/testimony. 重要的证据(证言)。 The judge warned the witness not to hold back ~ facts, facts that might influence a decision. 法官警告证人不得隐瞒重要的事实。 Is this point ~ to your argument? 这一点对你的议论很重要吗？ ~·ly /-ɪəlɪ; -ɪəlɪ/ adv in a ~(3) manner; essentially. 重要地；实质地。

ma·terial[2] /məˈtɪərɪəl; məˈtɪrɪəl/ n 1 [C, U] that of which sth is or can be made or with which sth is done: 材料；原料: raw ~s, not yet used in manufacture; 原料; 'dress ~s, cloth: 衣料; fabrics from which dresses may be made: 织物；布料: too much

~ *for one overcoat;* 做一件大衣又太多的料子; *not enough* ~ *for two overcoats.* 做两件大衣又不够的料子。 **'writing** ~**s,** pen, ink, paper, etc. 文具。 **2** [U] (fig) facts, happenings, elements: (喻)事实; 事件; 要素; 资料: ~ *for a newspaper article;* 一篇报纸上的文章所需要的资料; *the* ~ *from which history is made.* 史料。

ma·teri·al·ism /məˈtɪərɪəlɪzəm; məˈtɪrɪəl,mɪzəm/ *n* [U] **1** 唯物主义; 唯物论。 **2** (注重物质利益的)实利主义。 **3** (艺术上的)写实主义。 **ma·teri·al·ist** /-ɪst; -ɪst/ *n* 唯物论(主义)者; 实利主义者。 **ma·teri·al·is·tic** /mə,tɪərɪəˈlɪstɪk; mə,tɪrɪəlˈɪstɪk/ *adj* 唯物主义(者)的; 实利主义(者)的。 **ma·teri·alis·ti·cally** /-klɪ; -klɪ/ *adv*

ma·teri·al·ize /məˈtɪərɪəlaɪz; məˈtɪrɪəl,aɪz/ *vt, vi* [VP6A, 2A] (cause to) take material form; (cause to) become fact: (使)具体化; (使)实现: *Our plans did not* ~, came to nothing, were not carried out. 我们的计划没有实现。 **ma·teri·al·iz·ation** /mə,tɪərɪəlaɪˈzeɪʃn; US: -lɪˈz-; mə,tɪrɪəlˈzeʃən/ *n*

ma·ternal /məˈtɜːnl; məˈtɜrnl/ *adj* of or like a mother: 母亲的; 似母亲的; 慈母的: ~ *care/instincts;* 母爱(母性); *my* ~ *grandfather/aunt, etc,* on my mother's side of the family. 我的外祖父(姨母等)。 ~**·ly** /-nəlɪ; -nlɪ/ *adv*

ma·tern·ity /məˈtɜːnɪtɪ; məˈtɜrnɪtɪ/ *n* [U] being a mother: 母性; 母道: (attrib) (用作定语) '~ *ward/hospital,* for women who are about to become mothers. 产科病房(医院)。

matey /ˈmeɪtɪ; ˈmetɪ/ *adj* ~ *(with),* (colloq) sociable, familiar, friendly. (口)友善的; 亲切的。

mathe·mat·ics /,mæθəˈmætɪks; ,mæθəˈmætɪks/ *n* (with *sing* or *pl v*) science of size and numbers (of which arithmetic, algebra, trigonometry and geometry are branches): (用单数或复数形式)数学 (包括算术, 代数, 三角与几何等科目): *His* ~ *are weak.* 他的数学不好。 *M~ was his weak subject.* 数学是他比较差的科目。 **math·emat·ical** /,mæθəˈmætɪkl; ,mæθəˈmætɪkl/ *adj* of ~. 数学的。 **math·ematically** /-klɪ; -klɪ/ *adv* **math·ema·tician** /,mæθəməˈtɪʃn; ,mæθəməˈtɪʃən/ *n* expert in ~. 数学家。

maths /mæθs/ (US = **math** /mæθ; mæθ/) *n* (colloq abbr of) **mathematics.** (口) 为 mathematics 之略。

mati·née /ˈmætɪneɪ; US: ,mætnˈeɪ; ,mætnˈe/ *n* [C] afternoon performance at a cinema or theatre: 电影院或戏院里的下午演出; 日戏: '~ *idol,* much admired actor. 甚受爱慕的男明星。

mat·ins /ˈmætɪnz; US: -tnz; ˈmætɪnz/ *n pl* service of Morning Prayer in the Church of England; prayers recited at daybreak in the RC Church. 英国教的晨祷; 天主教的黎明祷告。

ma·tri·arch /ˈmeɪtrɪɑːk; ˈmetrɪ,ɑrk/ *n* woman head of a family or tribe. 女家长; 女族长。 **ma·tri·archy** /-ɑːkɪ; -ɑrkɪ/ *n* social organization in which mothers are the heads of families. 母权制; 母系制(以母亲为家长或族长的社会组织)。 **ma·tri·ar·chal** /,meɪtrɪˈɑːkl; ,metrɪˈɑrkl/ *adj*

ma·tric /məˈtrɪk; məˈtrɪk/ *n* (colloq abbr of) **matri·culation.** (口) 为 matriculation 之略。

ma·trices /ˈmeɪtrɪsiːz; ˈmetrɪ,siz/ *pl* of **matrix.**

mat·ri·cide /ˈmætrɪsaɪd; ˈmætrə,saɪd/ *n* [U] killing of one's own mother; [C] instance of this; [C] person guilty of this. 弑母; 弑母者。

ma·tricu·late /məˈtrɪkjuleɪt; məˈtrɪkjə,let/ *vt, vi* **1** [VP6A, 2A] (allow to) enter a university as a student, usu after passing an examination; admit, be admitted, as a member of a university. (准许)进入大学(通常指考试及格之后); 注册入大学。 **2** [VP2A, C] (formerly) pass the final school examination. (昔时)通过学校终考试。 **ma·tricu·la·tion** /mə,trɪkjuˈleɪʃn; mə,trɪkjəˈleʃən/ *n* **1** [U] matriculating or being ~d; [C] instance of this. 准许进入大学; 被准许进入大学; 注

册入学。 **2** [U] (formerly) final school examination (昔时)期终考试; 大考。

mat·ri·mony /ˈmætrɪmənɪ; US: -məʊnɪ; ˈmætrə,monɪ/ *n* [U] state of being married: 婚姻; 婚姻生活: *unite persons in holy* ~. 使人结成神圣的婚姻。 **mat·ri·mo·nial** /,mætrɪˈməʊnɪəl; ,mætrəˈmonɪəl/ *adj* of ~: 婚姻的: *solicitors who help people who have matrimonial troubles,* eg persons wanting divorce. 帮助人们解决婚姻纠纷的律师。

ma·trix /ˈmeɪtrɪks; ˈmetrɪks/ *n* (*pl* **matrices** /-trɪsiːz; ˈmetrɪ,siz/, or ~**es**) **1** mould into which hot metal, or other material in a soft or liquid condition, is poured to be shaped, eg in the printing trade, or for making gramophone records. 铸模; 模型(例如印刷业所用的字模, 纸型; 制造唱片的原模)。 **2** substance in which a mineral, etc is found embedded in the ground. 矿脉; 母岩。 **3** place where sth begins or develops. 创始地; 发祥地。

ma·tron /ˈmeɪtrən; ˈmetrən/ *n* **1** woman housekeeper in a school or other institution. (学校或其他机构的)女舍监; 女总管。 **2** woman who manages the domestic affairs and nursing staff of a hospital. 护士长。 **3** married woman or widow (often used with a suggestion of dignity and social position): 已婚妇女; 寡妇(常用以表示尊严及社会地位): (dressmaking) (女装裁剪) *styles suitable for* ~**s,** for middle-aged women. 适合中年妇女的式样。 ~**·ly** *adj* of, like, suitable for, ~**s:** 女总管(等)的; 似女总管(等)的; 适合女总管(等)或已婚妇女的: ~*ly duties;* 女总管(等)的责任; *a* ~*ly* (ie dignified) *manner.* 庄严的仪态。

matt /mæt; mæt/ *adj* = **matt**[2].

mat·ted /ˈmætɪd; ˈmætɪd/ *adj* ⇒ **mat**[1] *v*.

mat·ter[1] /ˈmætə(r); ˈmætɚ/ *n* **1** [U] substance(s) of which a physical thing is made (contrasted with mind, spirit, etc): 物质(与心、精神等相对): *organic/inorganic* ~. 有机(无机)物。 **2** material for thought or expression; substance of a book, speech, etc contrasted with the form or style: 思想或表达的题材; 书籍、演说等的内容(以别于形式或文体): *The* ~ *in your essay is good but the style is deplorable.* 你文章的内容很好, 但是体裁太糟糕了。 **3** [U] sth printed or written. 印刷或书写之物。 **'reading** ~**,** books, periodicals, etc. 读物(书籍,刊物等)。 **'postal** ~**,** everything sent by post. 邮件。 **'printed** ~**,** (used on sth sent by post, to show that it goes out at a rate cheaper than for ordinary letters, etc). 印刷品(用于邮寄物品上, 表示邮资低于一般函件)。 **4** [C] sth to which attention is given; piece of business; affair: 事务; 事情; 情况: '*money* ~**s.** 金钱方面的事情。 *This is a* ~ *I know little about.* 这件事我不大知道。 *There are several* ~*s to be dealt with at the committee meeting.* 有几件事要在委员会的会议中讨论。 *a* ~ *of course,* sth to be expected in the natural course of events. 理所当然的事。 Hence, 由此产生, ~*-of-'course adj* to be expected. 理所当然的; 意料中的。 *a* ~ *of opinion,* sth about which opinions may differ. 观点问题; 看法不同的问题。 *as a* ~ *of fact,* in reality; although you may not know it or may be surprised. 事实上; 实际上; 其实。 Hence, 由此产生, ~*-of-'fact adj* (of a person, his manner) unimaginative; ordinary; keeping to the facts. (指人, 其态度)缺少想像力的; 实际的; 平凡的; 拘泥事实的。 *for 'that* ~*; for the* ~ *of that,* so far as that is concerned. 就那件事而论; 关于那件事。 *in the* ~ *of,* as regards, in what concerns: 至于; 关于: *He is strict in the* ~ *of discipline.* 在纪律方面他是严格的。 *a 'hanging* ~, a crime for which the penalty may be death by hanging. 可处绞刑的罪。 *no 'laughing* ~, sth serious, sth not to be joked about. 正经的事; 重要的事; 不是开玩笑的事情。 **5** [U] importance. 重要; 要紧。 *(make/be) no* ~, (be) of no importance:

无关紧要；不重要：*If you can't do it, no ~.* 你如果不能做，没有关系。*It's no ~/it makes no ~ whether you arrive early or late.* 不论你早到或晚到都无关紧要。**no ~ who/what/where, etc,** whoever (it is), whatever (happens, etc): 不论谁(什么，在哪里等)：*Don't trust him, no ~ what* (=whatever) *he says.* 不管他说什么，你都不要信任他。*Don't believe the rumour, no ~ who* (= whoever) *repeats it/no ~ how often you hear it.* 不论是谁说的(不论你听到多少次)，都不要相信这谣言。**6 *be the ~ (with),*** be wrong (with): 有了毛病；发生困难：*What's the ~ with it?* (colloq) Surely this is all right, isn't it? (口)这有什么差错吗？(意谓：这不会有什么差错的，是不是？) *Is there anything the ~ with him,* Is he ill, in trouble, etc (according to context)? 他有什么困难吗？(是否生病，或遭遇困难等，视上下文而定)。**7 *a ~ of,*** approximately; only: 大约；仅有：*a ~ of 20 weeks/10 miles/£50;* 大约二十个星期(十英里，五十英镑)；*within a ~ of hours.* 大约数小时内。

mat·ter[2] /'mætə(r); `mætɚ/ *vi* [VP2A, C] (chiefly in interr, neg and conditional sentences) be of importance: (主要用于疑问句，否定句和条件句中)关系重要；要紧：*What does it ~?* 有什么关系？*It doesn't ~ much, does it?* 没什么大关系，是不是？*It hardly ~s at all.* 没什么要紧。*It doesn't ~ to me what you do or where you go.* 你做什么或去什么地方，对我都无关紧要。

mat·ting /'mætɪŋ; `mætɪŋ/ *n* [U] rough woven material used for floor covering and for packing goods: (用以覆盖地板和包装货物的)粗糙织物；草席；席：*coconut-~.* 棕席。

mat·tins /'mætɪnz *US:* -tnz; `mætɪnz/ *n pl*=**matins.**

mat·tock /'mætək; `mætək/ *n* heavy tool with a long handle and an iron head, one end of which is pointed and the other blunt, used for breaking up hard ground, etc. 鹤嘴锄；十字镐。⇨ the illus at **tool.** 参看 tool 之插图。

mat·tress /'mætrɪs; `mætrɪs/ *n* [C] long, thick, flat, oblong pad of wool, hair, feathers, foam rubber, etc on which to sleep. 床垫。**spring ~,** one with coiled wires fitted inside a padded cover of canvas or other frame of strong material. 弹簧床垫。

matu·rate /'mætjʊreɪt; `mætʃʊ,ret/ *vi* [VP2A] become mature. 成熟。**matu·ra·tion** /ˌmætjʊ'reɪʃn; ˌmætʃʊ`reʃən/ *n* [U] process of becoming mature. 成熟的过程。

ma·ture /mə'tjʊə(r) *US:* -'tʊər; mə`tjʊr/ *vt, vi* [VP 6A, 2A] **1** come or bring to full development or to a state ready for use: 成熟；使成熟：*His character ~d during these years.* 在这些年月里他的性格发展成熟了。*These years ~d his character.* 这几年使他的性格成熟了。*This wine has not ~d properly.* 这酒还没有酿熟。**2** (of bills) become due. (指票据)到期。□ *adj* **1** fully grown or developed; ripe with fully developed powers: 完全长成的；成熟的；具有充分发展之能力的：*persons of ~ years.* 成年人。**2** careful; perfected: 慎重的；完善的；周密的：*after ~ deliberation;* 经过慎重考虑之后；*~ plans,* based on ~ deliberation. 周密的计划。**3** (comm, of bills) due for payment. (商，指票据)到期的。**~·ly** *adv* **ma·tur·ity** /mə'tjʊərətɪ *US:* -'tʊə-; mə`tjʊrətɪ/ *n* [U] the state of being ~. 成熟；完成；到期。

ma·tuti·nal /mə'tju:tɪnl *US:* -'tu:tnl; mə`tjutɪnḷ/ *adj* (formal) of, occurring in, the morning. (正式用语)早晨的；发生在早晨的。

maud·lin /'mɔ:dlɪn; `mɔdlɪn/ *adj* sentimental or self-pitying in a silly or tearful way: 易伤感的；爱哭的：*The drunken man began to get ~.* 那个喝醉的人开始伤感落泪。

maul /mɔ:l; mɔl/ *vt* [VP6A, 15B] hurt or injure by rough or brutal handling: 伤害；虐待；殴打：*~ed by a tiger.* 为虎所伤。*Stop ~ing the cat.* 不要再虐待那只猫了。*His latest novel has been ~ed by the critics,* They have written extremely adverse reviews. 他最近的一部小说被批评家挑剔得体无完肤。*Stop ~ing me about!* 不要再虐待我！

maul·stick /'mɔ:lstɪk; `mɔl,stɪk/ *n* light stick held by a painter's (left) hand as a support to the (right) hand that holds the brush. (画家持于左手中以支持右手的)小杖；支手杖。

maun·der /'mɔ:ndə(r); `mɔndɚ/ *vi* [VP2A, C] talk in a rambling way; move or act in a listless way. 唠唠叨叨地讲话；胡言乱语；没精打采地行走或行动。

Maundy Thurs·day /ˌmɔ:ndɪ 'θɜ:zdɪ; `mɔndɪ-`θɝzdɪ/ *n* Thursday before Easter, commemorating the Last Supper. 复活节前的星期四(纪念耶稣最后的晚餐)。⇨ **lord(2); John 13: 14.** 参看 lord 第2义及约翰福音第13章第14节。

mau·so·leum /ˌmɔ:sə'li:əm; ˌmɔsə`liəm/ *n* magnificent and monumental tomb. 壮丽之墓；陵。

mauve /məʊv; mov/ *adj, n* bright but delicate pale purple. 淡紫色的；淡紫色。

mav·er·ick /'mævərɪk; `mævərɪk/ *n* (US) (美) **1** unbranded calf. 未打烙印的小牛。**2** unorthodox person; person who dissents from the ideas, etc of an organized group: 意见等与众不同者；持异议者；特立独行者；自行其是者：*~ politicians.* 自行其是的政客。

ma·vis /'meɪvɪs; `mevɪs/ *n* (poet) song-thrush. (诗)善鸣的画眉鸟。

maw /mɔ:; mɔ/ *n* animal's stomach or throat; (fig) devouring or destructive agency ready to swallow or engulf sth. 动物的胃或咽喉；(喻)随时欲吞噬或毁灭他物之物。

mawk·ish /'mɔ:kɪʃ; `mɔkɪʃ/ *adj* foolishly sentimental. 太容易伤感的；伤感到令人厌恶的。**~·ly** *adv* **~·ness** *n*

maxi- /'mæksɪ; `mæksɪ/ *pref* of a large or long size, length, etc. (表示尺寸，长度等)大或长的。⇨ **mini-.**

maxim /'mæksɪm; `mæksɪm/ *n* widely accepted rule of conduct or general truth briefly expressed, eg *'Waste not, want not'.* 箴言；格言('如不浪费，不穷困')。

maxi·mize /'mæksɪmaɪz; `mæksə,maɪz/ *vt* [VP6A] increase to a maximum: 使达最高限度；增至最大限度：*~ educational opportunities.* 尽量增加受教育机会。**maxi·mi·za·tion** /ˌmæksɪmaɪ'zeɪʃn *US:* -mɪ'z-; ˌmæksəmɪ`zeʃən/ *n*

maxi·mum /'mæksɪməm; `mæksəməm/ *n, adj* (*pl* **~s** or **-ma** /-mə; -mə/) (opposite of *minimum*) (of) greatest possible or recorded degree, quantity, etc: 最大量(的)；最高点(的)；极点(的)；极大(的)(为 minimum 之反义词)：*the ~ temperature recorded in London;* 伦敦的最高温度；*a ~ and minimum thermometer,* made so as to register ~ and minimum temperatures; 可指示最高温与最低温的温度计；*obtain 81 marks out of a ~ of 100.* 得到最高分一百分当中的八十一分。*The ~ load for this lorry is one ton.* 这辆卡车最大载重量是一吨。

may /meɪ; me/ *anom fin* (*pt* **might** /maɪt; maɪt/) (*neg* **may not,** shortened to **mayn't** /'meɪənt; ment/ and **might not** shortened to **mightn't** /'maɪtnt; `maɪtṇt/) [VP5] **1** (used to indicate possibility or probability; as *might* is used to indicate a future condition, the perfect infinitive *might have* is used for past time): (用以表示'可能'，'或许'；might 用来表示未来情况，might have + p.p. 用来表示过去)：*That may or may not be true.* 那可能是真的，也可能不是真的。*He may have* (= Perhaps he has) *missed his train.* 他或许没赶上那班火车。*This medicine may/might cure your cough.* 这种药可能治好你的咳嗽。*This might have cured your cough,* if you had taken it. 这药可能已经治好了你的咳嗽(假如你以前吃过这种药的话)。*You may walk* (= It is possible to walk) *for miles and miles among the hills without meeting anyone.* 你可能在山区走了许多英里路而遇不到任何人。**2** (used to indicate

permission or request for permission; *might* suggests greater hesitation or diffidence. ⇨ **can²(3)**: (用以表示许可或请求许可; might 含有比较迟疑或缺乏自信之意): *May I come in?* 我可以进来吗? *Might I make a suggestion?* 我可以提出一个建议吗? *Well, if I may say so, …*. 嗯, 假如我可以这么说的话, …. *You may come if you wish.* 你要来就来好了。 **3** (used to indicate uncertainty, and asking for information, or expressing wonder): (用以表示不确定, 询问或表露惊愕): *Well, who may you be?* 啊, 你会是谁呢? *How old may/might she be?* 她的年龄会有多大呢? **4** (used with *well* to suggest 'There is good reason'): (与 well 连用表示'有良好的理由'): *You may well say so.* 你很有理由这么说。*Well may/might you be surprised!* 当然你会感到惊讶! *We may as well stay where we are,* It seems reasonable to do so. 我们留在现在的地方倒也不错。*You might just as well go as not,* There is just as much to be said in favour of going as there is against. 你去也好, 不去也好。 ⇨ **well²(4)**. **5** (used to express wishes and hopes): (用以表示愿望和希望): *May you both be happy!* 祝你们两位幸福! *Long may she live to enjoy her good fortune!* 愿她长寿以享幸福! **6** (used to express requests): (用以表示请求): *You might do me a favour,* Please do sth for me. 请你帮我一点忙。*I think you might at least offer to help.* 我想你至少应该表示要帮帮忙。 **7** (in clauses) (used to express purpose, and after *wish, fear, be afraid,* etc): (在从句内) (用以表示目的, 并用于 wish, fear, be afraid 等之后): *He died so that others might live.* 他死了, 为了使旁人可以活下去。*I'll write to him today so that he may know when to expect us.* 今天我要写信给他, 好让他知道我们什么时候会去。*I'm afraid the news may be true.* 我恐怕这个消息可能是真的。

May /meɪ; me/ n **1** the fifth month of the year. 五月。 'May Day, 1st of May, celebrated as a spring festival and also as a day for socialist and labour demonstrations. 五朔节(五月一日, 西方的春节); 劳动节(五月一日)。'May Queen, girl crowned with flowers on May Day. 五朔节花后(五朔节以花冠加冕为后之少女)。'may-beetle, 'may-bug nn cockchafer. 金龟子。'may-fly n short-lived insect that appears in May. 蜉蝣(出现于五月)。'may·pole n flower-decorated pole danced round on May Day. 五月柱(五月柱卉装饰的柱子, 于五朔节日供男女围绕着跳舞者)。**2 m~,** hawthorn (blossom). 山楂花。

may·be /'meɪbi:; 'mebi/ adv perhaps; possibly. 也许; 可能。*as soon as maybe,* as soon as possible. 尽可能地快。

may·day /'meɪdeɪ; 'me,de/ n (radio telephony) (from French m'aider, help me) international signal (used by aircraft and ships) of distress: (无线电话) (飞机或船只所发射的)国际无线电求救讯号(由法文 m'aider '帮助我'而来): *a ~ call from an airliner.* 一架客机发出的求救呼号。

May·fair /'meɪfeə(r); 'me,fɛr/ n fashionable district in the West End of London. 伦敦 西区上流社会住宅区。

may·hem /'meɪhem; 'mehəm/ n **1** (old use, and US) crime of maiming. (旧用法, 美国)伤人肢体罪。**2** state of violent disorder; havoc. 大混乱; 大灾害: *cause/create ~.* 造成大灾害。

may·on·naise /,meɪə'neɪz US: 'meɪəneɪz; ,meə'nez/ n [U] thick dressing of eggs, cream, oil, vinegar, etc used on cold foods, esp salads; dish of food with this dressing: 蛋黄酱(一种调味酱, 用蛋、奶油、植物油、醋等制成, 用于调制凉菜, 尤其是生菜); 美乃滋; 用此种酱汁调味的食物: *salmon ~.* 蛋黄酱鲑鱼。

mayor /meə(r) US: 'meɪər; 'meə/ n head of a municipal corporation of a city or borough. 市长。~·ess /meə'res US: 'meɪərəs; 'meəərɪs/ n wife or female relative of a ~, helping in social duties; woman holding the office of ~. 市长夫人; (帮助市长做社交活动的)市长的女性亲戚; 女市长。~·alty /'meələtɪ

US: 'meɪər-; 'meəəəltɪ/ n ~'s (period of) office. 市长的职位; 市长之任期。

maze /meɪz; mez/ n **1** network of lines, paths, etc; labyrinth. 错综复杂的曲径; 迷宫: *a ~ of narrow alleys.* 错综复杂的窄巷。**2** state of confusion or bewilderment (when faced by a confused mass of facts, etc). (面临纷杂乱事物时所感到的)迷惘; 困惑。*be in a ~,* be puzzled, bewildered. 迷惘; 困惑; 不知所措。**mazed** adj bewildered. 迷惘的; 困惑的。

ma·zurka /mə'zɜ:kə; mə'zɝkə/ n [C] (piece of music for a) lively Polish dance for four or eight couples. 玛祖卡舞(一种轻快活泼的波兰舞, 供四对或八对男女共舞); 玛祖卡舞曲。

Mc·Carthy·ism /mə'kɑ:θɪzəm; mə'kɑrθɪnzɪ̩/ n 麦卡锡主义。

me /mi:; mi/ pron object form for the pronoun *I:* (代词 I 的宾格): *He saw me.* 他看见我。*Give me one.* 给我一个。*It's me* (now usu for 'It is I'). 是我(现在通常用以代替 'It is I')。

mead¹ /mi:d; mid/ n [U] alcoholic drink made from fermented honey and water. 蜂蜜酒。

mead² /mi:d; mid/ n [C] (poet) meadow. (诗)草地。

meadow /'medəʊ; 'medo/ n [C, U] (area, field, of) grassland, esp kept for hay. 草地(尤指生长畜类食用草秣者); 牧场。

meagre (US = **mea·ger**) /'mi:gə(r); 'migɚ/ adj **1** thin; lacking in flesh: 瘦的; 皮包骨的: *a ~ face.* 清瘦的脸。**2** insufficient; poor; scanty: 不足的; 贫乏的; 量少的: *a ~ meal;* 一顿简单或不丰盛的饭食; *a ~ fare;* 简陋的伙食; *a ~ attendance at the council meeting.* 议会会议席上出席人数甚少。~·ly adv ~·ness n

meal¹ /mi:l; mil/ n [C] **1** occasion of eating: 餐; 饭食: *three ~s a day;* 一日三餐; *breakfast, the first ~ of the day.* 早餐。*~-time* n usual time for taking a ~. (平常的)吃饭时间。**2** food that is eaten: 一餐所吃的食物: *have a good ~.* 吃丰富的一餐; 饱餐一顿。

meal² /mi:l; mil/ n [U] grain coarsely ground: 粗略碾磨的谷物: (未经细磨的)粗粉: *'oat~;* 麦片; *'corn ~,* (US) ~ of maize or other grain. (美)玉蜀黍(或其他谷类之)粉。Cf 参较 *flour* for grain finely ground. flour 系碾细的谷粉。

mealie /'mi:lɪ; 'milɪ/ n (S Africa) (pl) maize; [C] an ear of maize. (南非洲) (复)玉蜀黍; 玉米。

mealy /'mi:lɪ; 'milɪ/ adj (-ier, -iest) of, like, containing, covered with, meal; (of potatoes when boiled) dry and powdery. 粗粉的; 粗粉状的; 含粗粉的; 撒有粗粉的; (指煮过后的马铃薯)干而易变成粉状的。'~-bug n insect that infests vines, etc. 水腊虫 (葡萄树等的害虫)。~'-mouthed adj too squeamish in the choice of words; tending to avoid plain speaking. 讲话时选辞用字过于审慎的; 不坦率的; 油嘴滑舌的。

mean¹ /mi:n; min/ adj (-er, -est) **1** poor in appearance; shabby-looking: 粗陋的; 破烂不堪的: *a ~ house in a ~ street.* 陋巷街道上的郦陋房屋。**2** (of behaviour) unworthy; discreditable: (指行为)卑鄙的; 丢脸的; 不名誉的: *That was a ~ trick!* 那是一个卑鄙的诡计! *It was ~ of you to eat all the peaches!* 你把桃子全吃光了, 真不害羞! *He took a ~ advantage of me.* 他用卑鄙的手段欺骗了我。*What a ~ revenge!* 多么卑鄙的报复! **3** (of persons, their character, etc) having or showing a fondness for ~ behaviour: (指人、人格等)卑贱的; 卑鄙的: *a ~ rascal.* 卑鄙的流氓。*Don't be so ~ to your little brother,* Don't tease him, treat him unkindly, etc. 不要那样恶待你的小弟弟(指揶揄他, 或苛待他等)。*He's a ~-minded sort of fellow.* 他是一种心地卑下的人。**4** of low rank or humble birth: 地位卑下的; 出身微贱的。**5** (of the understanding, the natural powers) inferior; poor: (指理解力, 秉赋)低劣的; 不如人的: *This should be clear even to the ~ st intelligence.* 即使智力最低的人对此亦应了如指掌。*He is no ~ scholar,* is a good one. 他是个优秀的学者。**6** lacking in generosity;

selfish: 吝啬的; 自私的: *Her husband is rather ~ over money matters.* 她的丈夫对钱财相当吝啬. **7** (colloq) secretly ashamed: (口)暗自惭愧的; 不好意思的: *feel rather ~ for not helping more.* 因未多帮忙而感到歉疚. **8** (US) nasty; vicious: (美)刻毒的; 邪恶的: *He's a really ~ fellow—he likes to see people suffer.* 他真是个邪恶的人——他喜欢看别人受苦. **~·ly** *adv* **~·ness** *n* **~ie**, **~y** /'miːnɪ; 'minɪ/ *nn* (colloq) **~-minded** person: (口)心地卑鄙的人; 吝啬或自私的人; 吝啬鬼: *What a ~ie you are!* 你真是个吝啬鬼! ⇨ **6** above. 参看上列第 6 义.

mean² /miːn; min/ *adj* occupying the middle position between two extremes; average: (居于二极端之间)中间的; 平均的; 中庸的: *the ~ annual temperature in Malta.* 马尔他岛的每年平均温度. **Greenwich M~ Time,** ⇨ **Greenwich.** ~ **price,** (fin, Stock Exchange) the average between the Stock jobber's buying and selling price; the market price of an investment. (财务, 证券交易)股票经纪人买进卖出的平均价格; 投资的市价.

mean³ /miːn; min/ *n* [C] condition, quality, course of action, etc that is halfway between two extremes. 中间; 居中: *the happy / golden ~,* a moderate course of action. 中庸之道; 折衷办法. **2** (maths) term between the first and the last of a series; an average amount or value: (数学)比例中项; 平均数: 平均值: *In 1:3::3:9, the ~ is 3.* 在 1:3::3:9 中, 比例中项是 3. *The ~ of 3, 5 and 7 is 5* (because $3 + 5 + 7 = 15$ and $15 \div 3 = 5$). 3, 5 和 7 的平均数是 5.

mean⁴ /miːn; min/ *vt* (*pt, pp* **meant** /ment; ment/) **1** [VP6A] (of words, sentences, etc) signify; import: (指词, 句等)表示…的意思; 含…之意: *A dictionary tries to tell you what words ~.* 词典告诉你语词的含意. *The Latin word 'amo' ~s 'I love'.* 拉丁字 'amo' 的意思是 '我爱'. **2** [VP6A, C, 9] be a sign of; be likely to result in; entail: 为…的征兆; 意谓; 可能造成; 使成为必要: *This new frontier incident probably ~s war / that there will be war.* 这个新的边境事件可能带来战争. *These new orders for our manufactures will ~ working overtime.* 这些订购我们产品的新订单意谓着要加班. **3** [VP6A, 9, 14, 16B, 17] ~ (by), have as a purpose; contemplate; intend; refer to: 图谋; 计划; 意欲; 企图; 意指: *What do you ~ by saying that? What have you in mind?* (or if the context allows) *How dare you say that?* 你那样说是什么意思?(你怎敢讲那些话?视上下文而定). *I wasn't serious—I ~t it / It was ~t as a joke.* 我不是认真的——我把它当作玩笑的. *Do you ~* (= refer to) *Miss Elsie Smith or Miss Dora Smith?* 你是指艾尔丝·史密斯小姐还是指多拉·史密斯小姐? *I didn't ~ you to read the letter.* 我并没有打算要你拆阅信信. *Is this figure ~t to be a 1 or a 7?* 这个数字是 1 还是 7? *I'm sorry if I hurt your feelings—I didn't ~ to.* 假如我伤了你的感情, 真对不起——我并不是故意的. *I ~ there to be / that there should be no argument about this,* won't allow any argument. 我的意思是不许对此事有任何争议. *Is this valuable painting ~t for me,* Is the owner thinking of giving it to me? 这幅名贵的画是要送给我的吗? ~ *business,* (colloq) be in earnest, ready to act (not merely talk). (口)认真要办(非仅空谈). ~ *mischief,* have in mind sth evil or injurious. 心存恶意; 意欲伤害; 存心捣乱. **4** [VP7A, 12A, 13A, 14, 17] ~ (for), intend; be determined; destine: 意欲; 决定; 预定: *He ~s to succeed.* 他意欲获致成功. *He ~s his son to succeed.* 他要他的儿子成功. *He ~s you no harm,* does not intend to hurt you. 他无意伤害你. *He ~s no harm to anyone.* 他无意伤害任何人. *I ~t this for my son,* intended to give it to him. 我打算把这个给我的儿子. *He seems obviously ~t for the army / ~t to be a soldier,* seems to be the sort of man destined for the army. 他似乎生来就适于做军人. **5** [VP14] ~ *sth to sb,* be of importance or value to: 对某人重要; 对某人有价值: *Your friendship ~s a great deal to me,* I value it highly. 你的友谊对我极为珍贵. *£20 ~s a lot to her, is*

quite a large sum in her view. 二十英镑对她是个大数目. *I can't tell you what Mary has ~t to me,* what a difference she has made in my life. 我没法告诉你玛丽对我的影响是多么大. *The high cost of living ~s nothing to some people,* They do not worry about it (eg because they are very rich). 对某些人来说, 高昂的生活费用算不得什么. **6** ~ *well,* have good intentions (though perhaps not the will or capacity to carry them out): 怀有善意(虽然不见得有意或有能力实践): *Of course he ~s well.* 当然他是好意. ~ *well by sb,* have kindly intentions towards sb: 对某人怀有善意: *We all know that he ~s well by you.* 我们都知道他对你是好意. ~ *·ing* *n* [C, U] that which is ~t or intended: 意义; 含意; 企图: *a word with many distinct ~ings;* 一个有许多不同意义的字; *a passage without much ~ing.* 一段没有多大意义的文字. *He looked at me with ~ing.* 他意味深长地看着我. *What's the ~ing of this?* (asked, for example, by sb who thinks he has been badly treated, etc). 这是什么意思? (例如某人认为受不平待遇等而发问). □ *adj* full of ~ing: 有意义的; 意味深长的: *a ~ing look;* 意味深长的表情; *well-~ing,* having good intentions. 善意的. ~ *·ing·ful* /-fl; -fl/ *adj* significant; full of ~ing. 富有意义的; 意味深长的. ~ *·ing·fully* /-fəlɪ; -flɪ/ *adv* ~ *·ing·less* *adj* without ~ing or motive. 无意义的, 无目的的. ~ *·ing·ly* *adv* with ~ing. 有意义地; 意味深长地; 故意地.

me·ander /mɪ'ændə(r); mɪ'ændɚ/ *vi* [VP2A, C] wander here and there; (fig) speak in an aimless way; (of a stream) follow a winding course, flowing slowly and gently. 漫游; (喻)漫谈; 闲聊; (指河川)缓缓蜿蜒而流. ~ *·ings* /mɪ'ændrɪŋz; mɪ'ændrɪŋz/ *n pl* winding path, course, etc. 曲折的路, 途程. ~ *·ing·ly* /mɪ'ændrɪŋlɪ; mɪ'ændrɪŋlɪ/ *adv*

means¹ /miːnz; minz/ *n pl* (often treated as a *sing,* as in examples) method, process, by which a result may be obtained: (常作单数用, 如例句中)方法; 手段: *a ~ to an end,* a way of achieving sth. 达到目的的手段. *There is / are no ~ of learning what is happening.* 我们无法知道现在有什么事情发生. *Every ~ has / All possible ~ have been tried.* 每种(所有可能的)方法都尝试过了. *Does the end always justify the ~,* If the aim or purpose is good, may any methods, even if bad, be employed? 目的正当就可不择手段吗? *by ~ of,* through; with the help of: 借; 用: *Thoughts are expressed by ~ of words.* 思想借文字表达出来. *by 'all ~,* certainly. 当然; 必定. *by 'no ~,* not at all: 决不; 一点也不: *These goods are by no ~ satisfactory.* 这些货品一点也不令人满意. *by 'no manner of ~,* in no way. 决不; 任何情况之下均不. *by some ~ or other,* somehow or other; if not in one way, then in another. 用某种方法; 总有办法. *by fair ~ or foul,* by any methods, just or unjust. 用任何方法; 不择手段. *ways and ~,* methods, esp of providing money by taxation for government needs. 方法; 办法; (尤指)政府税收途径.

means² /miːnz; minz/ *n pl* money; wealth; resources: 金钱; 财富; 财源: *a man of ~,* a rich man; 富有的人; *a man of your ~,* with the money, etc you have at your disposal; 像你这样财力的人; *have private ~,* an income from property, investments, etc (not earned as salary, etc). 有来自财产、投资等方面之收入. *live beyond / within one's ~,* spend more / less than one's income. 不能量入出(能量入为出). '~ *test* *n* inquiry into the ~ of sb seeking help from the State or local authorities (eg if unemployed or too old to work). 个人经济状况调查 (如因失业或年老不能工作而向政府申请补助时而作的).

meant /ment; ment/ *pt, pp* of **mean⁴**.

mean·time /'miːntaɪm; 'min,taɪm/ *adv, n (in the)* ~, meanwhile. 其间; 当其时.

mean·while /'miːnwaɪl *US:* -hwaɪl; 'min,hwaɪl/ *adv* in or during the time between. 其时; 此际.

measles /'miːzlz; 'mizlz/ *n* (with *sing v*) [U]

infectious disease, marked by fever and small red spots that cover the whole body. (用单数词)麻疹。

measly /'mi:zlɪ; 'mizlɪ/ adj (colloq) of little value; of poor quality; of small size or amount: (口)无价值的; 劣质的; 微小的; 少量的: What a ~ birthday present! 一件多么没有价值的生日礼物! What a ~ helping of ice-cream! 多么少的一份冰淇淋!

measure[1] /'meʒə(r); 'mɛʒɚ/ n 1 [U] size, quantity, degree, weight, etc as found by a standard or unit. (由一个标准或单位所测定的)大小; 数量; 度量; 重量。give full / short ~, give the full / less than the full amount. 给予足(不足)量。made to ~, (of clothes) specially made for sb after taking ~ments. (指衣服)量尺寸后做的; 定做的。get / take the ~ of sb, (fig) form an estimate of his character, abilities, etc. (喻)估量某人的品格, 能力等。2 [C] unit, standard or system used in stating size, quantity, or degree: 度量的单位, 标准或制度: liquid / dry ~. 液(干)量。~ an inch is a ~ of length. 英寸是长度的单位。Twenty ~s of wheat means twenty bushels. 二十单位的小麦即二十蒲式耳。⇨ App 5. 参看附录五。3 [C] sth with which to test size, quantity, etc: (用以测量大小, 数量等的)量度器: a pint ~. 品脱量器。A yardstick is a ~; so is a foot-rule. 码尺是量长短的器具, 一英尺长的直尺也是。A chain's weakest link is the ~ of its strength. 链条之强度是最弱之环为准。Words cannot always give the ~ of one's feelings, cannot show the depth or strength of one's feelings. 言词不一定总能表示出感情的程度(即不能表示出感情的深度或强度)。'tape-~, ⇨ tape. ,greatest ,common ~, (abbr 略作 GCM) largest number that will divide each of several given numbers exactly. 最大公约数。4 extent. 程度; 范围; 限度。beyond ~, very great(ly): 逾限的; 过度的; 极其: Her joy was beyond ~. 她高兴逾常; 她非常高兴。in 'some / 'any ~, to some / any extent or degree. 达某种(任何)范围或程度; 有几分; 稍许。in great / large ~, to a large extent: 很; 大半; 大部分: Their success was in some ~ / in great ~ the result of thorough preparation. 他们的成功有几分(大部分)是周密准备的结果。set ~s to, limit: 限制; 约束: set ~s to one's ambitions. 约束某人的野心。5 [C] (proposed) law. 议案; 法规。6 [C] proceeding; step: 处置办法; 步骤; 措施: What ~ (= plan) do you propose? 你建议用什么办法? They took strong ~s (= acted vigorously) against dangerous drivers. 他们对危害公众的驾驶采取强硬的措施。7 [U] verse-rhythm; metre; time of a piece of music; [C] (archaic) dance. 诗的韵律; 音乐的拍子; (古)舞蹈。tread a ~ (with sb), dance (with him). (与某人)跳舞。

measure[2] /'meʒə(r); 'mɛʒɚ/ vt, vi 1 [VP6A, 2A] find the size, extent, volume, degree, etc of (sth or sb): 量; 度量; 测量(某物或某人的大小, 范围, 容量, 程度等): ~ a piece of ground / the strength of an electric current / the speed of a car; 测量一块土地/一电流的强度, 一辆汽车的速度); tested for speed over a ~d mile. 在整整一英里的路程上试验过速度的。The tailor ~d me for a suit. 裁缝给我量尺寸做衣服。Can you ~ accurately? 你能准确地量吗? 2 [VP2B] be (a certain length, etc): 为(某长度等): ~ long / wide, high等): This room is 10 metres across. 这个房间有10公尺宽。3 [VP6A, 15A, B] ~ out / off, give a ~d quantity of: 配出…的一定之量: ~ out a dose of medicine; 配出一服药; mark out: 划出; 量好: ~ off 2 metres of cloth. 量好(剪下)两公尺布。4 ~ one's length, fall flat on the ground. 扑倒在地上。~ swords against / with sb, (fig) try out one's strength against him. (喻)与某人较量力; 与人一较长短。~ one's strength (with sb), try or test it. (与某人)比赛力气。meas·ured adj 1 (of language) considered and weighed: (指言词)慎重的; 考虑过的: ~d words. 慎重考虑过的话语。2 in slow and regular rhythm: 缓慢而有韵律的: with a ~d tread. 步伐整齐。measur·able /'meʒərəbl; 'mɛʒrəbl/

adj that can be ~d: 可测量的; 可衡量的: We came within measurable distance of (close to) success. 我们接近成功了。measur·ably /-əblɪ; -əblɪ/ adv ~ly很 adj immeasurable; limitless. 不可测量的; 无限度的。~·ment n 1 [U] measuring: 测量; 衡量: the metric system of ~ment. 十进法度量衡制; 公制。2 (pl) figures about length, breadth, depth, etc: (复)长度; 宽度; 深度; 大小: the ~ments of a room. 房间的大小(长宽高)。

meat /mi:t; mit/ n 1 [U] flesh of animals used as food, excluding fish and birds: 食用的兽肉(不包括鱼类、鸟类之肉): ~-eating animals; 肉食动物; cold ~, meat that has been cooked and has become cold; 凉了的熟肉; 冷肉; chilled / frozen ~, meat chilled / frozen in order to keep it in good condition; 冷冻的肉; fresh ~, from a recently killed animal. 鲜肉。'~-ball n small ball of minced meat or sausage-meat. 肉丸。'~-safe n cupboard for storing ~, usu with sides of wire gauze. 贮肉的橱柜(通常带丝纱的). ~ pie n ~ cooked with a covering of pastry. 肉馅饼; 馅饼。a ~ tea, high tea with some kind of ~ dish included. 有肉类点心的下午茶。⇨ high[1](12). 2 (pl) figures important or substantial part of sth: (喻)重要部分; 重要内容; 实质: There's not much ~ in this argument. 这篇摘要没有什么内容。3 (old use) food in general: (旧用法)食物的总称: ~ and drink. 饮食。One man's ~ is another man's poison, (prov) What one person likes is not necessarily liked by another one. (谚)甲所喜者未必为乙所喜;利于甲者未必利于乙。~·less adj without ~: 没有肉的: ~less days during the war. 战时无肉可吃的日子。~·y adj (-ier, -iest) (fig) full of substance; substantial. (喻)内容丰富的。

Mecca /'mekə; 'mɛkə/ n 1 city in Saudi Arabia, birthplace of Muhammad and the spiritual centre of Islam. 麦加(沙特阿拉伯一城, 为穆罕默德的诞生地及伊斯兰教的精神中心)。2 goal of one's ambitions; place one is anxious to visit: 希望的目标; 渴望前往的地方: Stratford-on-Avon, the ~ of tourists in Britain. 埃文河畔的斯特拉特福——英国的观光胜地。

mech·anic /mɪ'kænɪk; mə'kænɪk/ n skilled workman, esp one who repairs or adjusts machinery and tools: 技工; (尤)修理或调整机器的工人; 机械工人: a 'motor-~. 汽车修理工人。

mech·an·ical /mɪ'kænɪkl; mə'kænɪkl/ adj 1 of, connected with, produced by, machines: 机械的; 与机械有关的; 机械制成的: ~ power / transport / engineering. 机械动力(汽车运输, 机械工程); 2 (of persons, their actions) like machines; automatic; as if done without thought: (指人, 其动作)似机械的; 机械的; 无意识的: ~ movements. 机械般的行动。~·ly /-klɪ; -klɪ/ adv in a ~ way: 机械地; 呆板地; 无意识地: ~ly operated. 用机械操作的。⇨ manual at **manual**.

mech·an·ics /mɪ'kænɪks; mə'kænɪks/ n 1 (usu with sing v) science of motion and force; science of machinery: (通常用单数动词)力学; 机械学: M~ is taught by Mr MacHine. 力学由麦克翰先生执教。2 (with pl v) (method of) construction: (用复数动词)结构; 构成法; 技巧: the ~ of play-writing. 戏剧写作方法。

mech·an·ism /'mekənɪzəm; 'mɛkə,nɪzm/ n [C] 1 working parts of a machine collectively; structure or arrangement of parts that work together as the parts of a machine do: 一部机器之各种机件之总称; 如机械般之结构或装置; 机构: the ~ of the body; 身体结构; the ~ of government. 政府之机构。2 way in which sth works or is constructed. (某物之)机械作用; 结构方式。

mech·an·is·tic /ˌmekə'nɪstɪk; ˌmɛkə'nɪstɪk/ adj the ~ theory, the theory that all changes in the universe and all living creatures are caused by physical and chemical forces only. 机械论(认为宇宙和生物中所有的变化皆由物理和化学作用所造成)。

mech·an·ize /'mekənaɪz; 'mɛkə,naɪz/ vt [VP6A] use machines in or for; give a mechanical character to: 在…中使用机械; 为…而使用机械; 使机械化: ~d

forces, eg in the army, using motor transport instead of horses or mules. 机械化部队(例如陆军中运用汽车运输,而不用马骡等驮兽). **mech·an·iz·ation** /,mekənaɪ'zeɪʃn US: -nɪˈz-; ,mekənə'zeʃən/ n

medal /'medl; 'medl/ n flat piece of metal, usu shaped like a coin, with words and a design stamped on it, given as an award for bravery, to commemorate sth, or for distinction in scholarship. (金属制, 通常为钱币状的)奖章; 勋章; 纪念章. **~·list** (US 美 = **~·ist**) /'medəlɪst; 'medlɪst/ n person who has been awarded a ~, eg for distinction in literature, sport. 得过奖章的人;奖章持有人(例如因文学或运动方面的成就而得奖).

me·dal·lion /mɪ'dæliən; mə'dæljən/ n large medal; large, flat circular ornamental design, eg on a carpet or on a lace curtain. 大奖章; 大而扁平的圆形装饰图案(如在地毯上或纱帘上者).

meddle /'medl; 'medl/ vi [VP2A, 3A] ~ *(in sth)*, busy oneself in sth without being asked to do so: 管闲事; 干预: *Don't ~ in my affairs.* 不要干预我的事. *Don't ~ in politics.* 不要干预政治. ~ *(with sth)*, interfere: 妨碍; 干扰; 玩弄; 乱弄: *Who's been meddling with my papers?* 谁动了我的文件? *You're always meddling.* 你老是多事. **meddler** n person who ~s. 干预者;爱管闲事者. **~·some** /-səm; -səm/ adj fond of, in the habit of, meddling. 爱管闲事的;好干预的.

me·dia /'miːdɪə; 'midɪə/ n **the ~**, (usu with *sing* v) mass communications, eg television, radio, the press. (通常用单数动词)大众传播工具(如电视, 无线电, 报纸). ⇨ **mass(2), medium.**

medi·aeval /,medɪ'iːvl US: ,miːd-; ,mɪdɪ'ivl/ = **medieval.**

me·dial /'miːdɪəl; 'midɪəl/ adj **1** situated in the middle. 中间的; 中央的; 居中的. **2** of average size. 等的; 一般的; 普通的. **~·ly** /-ɪəlɪ; -ɪəlɪ/ adv

me·dian /'miːdɪən; 'midɪən/ adj situated in, passing through, the middle. 在中间的; 通过中间的; 中部的. □ n ~ point, line, part, etc. 中点;中线;中部;中数.

me·di·ate /'miːdɪeɪt; 'midɪ,et/ vi, vt **1** [VP2A, 3A] ~ *(between)*, act as go-between or peacemaker: 居中调停; 斡旋: ~ *between two warring countries/between employers and their workers.* 斡旋于两交战国之间(资方与劳方之间). **2** [VP6A] bring about by doing this: 促成; 促进: ~ *a settlement/a peace.* 居间促成和解(和平). **me·di·ation** /,miːdɪ'eɪʃn; ,midɪ'eʃən/ n [U] mediating: 调停; 调解; 斡旋: *All offers of mediation by a third party were rejected.* 第三方面所提有关调处之建议均遭拒绝. **me·di·ator** /-tə(r); -tɚ/ n one who ~s. 调停者;斡旋者.

medic /'medɪk; 'medɪk/ n (colloq abbr for) medical student. (口) 为 medical student 之略.

medi·cal /'medɪkl; 'medɪkl/ adj **1** of the art of medicine (the treatment of disease): 医学的; 医术的; 医疗的: *a '~ examination*, to ascertain one's state of health; 体格检查; *a practitioner*, a qualified doctor; 合格医生; *a '~ school*; 医学校; *~ students/knowledge*; 医科学生(医学知识); ~ *jurisprudence*, legal knowledge required by a doctor. 法医学. **2** of the art of medicine (contrasted with *surgery*): 内科的: ~, *not surgical, treatment.* 内科而非外科的治疗. *The hospital has a ~ ward and a surgical ward.* 这家医院有一个内科病房和一个外科病房. □ n **1** (colloq) ~ student. 医科学生. **2** ~ examination. 体格检查. **~·ly** /-klɪ; -klɪ/ adv

medi·cament /mɪ'dɪkəmənt; mə'dɪkəmənt/ n substance used in medical treatment, internally or externally. (内服或外用的)药; 药剂. ⇨ **medicine(2).**

Medi·care /'medɪkeə(r); 'medɪ,kɛr/ n [U] (US) government programme providing medical care (esp for old persons). (美)(政府办的)医疗保险制度(尤指给老年人所办者).

medi·cate /'medɪkeɪt; 'medɪ,ket/ vt [VP6A] treat medically; permeate with a medicinal substance: 以药物治疗; 以药物处理; 加以药; 掺以药: *~d soap/gauze.*

药皂(药用纱布). **medi·ca·tion** /,medɪ'keɪʃn; ,medɪ'keʃən/ n [U] process of medicating: 药物治疗;药物处理; mass medication, eg, the addition of fluorine to public water supplies; the supply of vitamin tablets through the social services; 大众药物供应(例如加氟于自来水,经社会服务团体供应维他命丸等); [C] medicine. 药品;药.

medi·ci·nal /mɪ'dɪsɪnəl; mə'dɪsɪnl/ adj having healing or curative properties: 有药性的; 医药的; 治疗的: ~ *preparations for both internal and external use.* 供内服和外用的药剂.

medi·cine /'medsn US: 'medɪsn; 'medəsn/ n **1** [U] the art and science of the prevention and cure of disease: 医学; 医术; 内科学: *study ~ and surgery*; 研究内科与外科; *a Doctor of 'M~.* 医学博士. **2** [C, U] (kind of) substance, esp one taken through the mouth, used in ~: 药; 药剂; (尤指)内服药: *He's always taking ~s.* 他时常吃药. *He takes too much ~.* 他吃药吃得太多. *This is a good (kind of) ~ for a cough.* 这是(一种)治咳良药. (Note: 注意: for remedies not taken through the mouth, 非口服药, ⇨ *injection* at **inject, lotion,** *medicinal preparation* at **medicinal, ointment.**) '**~·ball** n large, heavy ball thrown and caught for physical exercise. (供运动用内有填塞物之)实心皮球. '**~·chest** n chest with a selection of useful medicinal preparations. 药箱;药柜. **3** (fig) deserved punishment. (喻)应受的惩罚. *take one's ~,* (fig) submit to what is unwelcome and unpleasant. (喻)忍受不喜欢或不愉快的事. *get some/a little of one's own ~,* be given the kind of unwelcome treatment that one has given to others. 自食其果. **4** [U] (among primitive peoples) spell; charm; fetish; magic. (原始民族所崇信的)符咒; 咒文;物神(风,石等); 巫术. '**~·man** /-mæn; -mæn/ n (*pl* **-men**) witch-doctor. 巫医.

medi·co /'medɪkəʊ; 'medɪ,ko/ n (*pl* **~s** /-kəʊz; -koz/) (colloq, hum) doctor or medical student. (口, 谐)医生; 医科学生.

medi·eval (also **medi·aeval**) /,medɪ'iːvl US: ,miːd-; ,mɪdɪ'ivl/ adj of the Middle Ages (about AD 1100—1500). 中古的;中世纪的(约在公元一〇〇年至一五〇〇年之间).

me·di·ocre /,miːdɪ'əʊkə(r); 'midɪ,okɚ/ adj not very good; neither very good nor very bad; second-rate. 平庸的;普通的;第二流的;中等的. **me·di·oc·rity** /,miːdɪ'ɒkrətɪ; ,midɪ'akrətɪ/ n (*pl* **-ties**) [U] quality of being ~; [C] person who is ~ (in qualities, abilities, etc): 平庸; 普通; 中等; 平庸的人: *a Government of mediocrities.* 庸才政府.

medi·tate /'medɪteɪt; 'medə,tet/ vt, vi **1** [VP6A] think about; consider: 想; 考虑: ~ *revenge/mischief.* 图谋报复(打算胡闹). **2** [VP2A, 3A] ~ *(up/upon)*, give oneself up to serious (esp religious) thought: (尤指在宗教上)沉思; 冥想: *He sat there meditating upon his misfortunes.* 他坐在那儿沉思他的不幸遭遇.

medi·ta·tion /,medɪ'teɪʃn; ,medə'teʃən/ n **1** [U] meditating: 沉思; 冥想; 考虑: *deep in ~.* 陷于沉思之中. **2** [C] instance of this: 沉思等的实例; 深思探讨某问题之演说或文章: 沉思录: *a ~ on the causes of aggression in man.* 一篇探讨人类侵略的原因的文章. **medi·tat·ive** /'medɪtətɪv US: -teɪt-; 'medə,tetɪv/ adj of ~; fond of ~. 沉思的;默想的;爱沉思的. **medi·tat·ive·ly** adv

Medi·ter·ra·nean /,medɪtə'reɪnɪən; ,medətə'renɪən/ adj of, characteristic of, the M~ Sea or the countries, etc bordering this sea: 地中海的; 地中海沿岸诸国的; 地中海(地区)特有的: ~ *climate.* 地中海的气候.

me·dium /'miːdɪəm; 'midɪəm/ n (*pl* **~s** or **media** /'miːdɪə; 'midɪə/) **1** that by which sth is expressed: 媒介; 方法; 手段: *Commercial television is a ~ for advertising.* 商业电视是一种广告媒介. *Vacant positions can be made known through the ~ of the press,* by putting announcements in newspapers. 职位空缺可借报

纸公诸大众(即在报端刊登广告). *Oil paints and water colours are ~s for the creation of works of art.* 油画颜料和水彩颜料是艺术创作的媒介. ⇨ also **mass(2).** **2** middle quality or degree. 中庸: **the happy ~,** avoidance of extremes, eg by being neither very lax nor very severe in maintaining discipline. 中庸之道(如维持纪律时不宽也不严). **3** (*pl* often 复数常作 **media**) substance, surroundings, in which sth exists or through which sth moves: 借以生存之物或环境; 媒介物; 传导体; 介质: *Air is the ~ of sound.* 空气是传声的媒介物. **4** person who acts as a go-between, esp in spiritualism; person who claims to be able to receive messages from the spirits of the dead. 中间人; (尤指)招魂者; 关亡人; 通灵之人. □ *adj* coming halfway between; not extreme: 中庸的; 中等的; 普通的: *a man of ~ height;* 中等身材的人; *a ~-sized firm,* 中型规模的公司; *~ bonds,* maturing in a period between 15 and 20 years; 十五至二十年到期的债券; *the ~ income group,* those who have incomes between high and low. 中等收入的人们. '~ **wave,** (radio telegraphy) one having a length of from 100 to 1000 metres. (无线电报)中波(波长为 100 至 1000 米).

med·lar /'medlə(r); `mɛdlɚ/ *n* (tree with) fruit like a small brown apple, eaten when it begins to decay. 山楂; 山楂树.

med·ley /'medlɪ; `mɛdlɪ/ *n* (*pl* ~s) [C] mixture of things or persons of different sorts: 混合; 混合物; 杂处的人群: *the ~ of races in Hawaii.* 夏威夷各种族的大杂烩.

meed /miːd; mid/ *n* (poet) deserved portion (*of* praise, etc). (诗)(赞美等的)应得之份(与 *of* 连用).

meek /miːk; mik/ *adj* (**-er, -est**) mild and patient; unprotesting (the contrary of *self-assertive*): 温顺的; 谦和的(与 self-assertive 相反): *She's as ~ as a lamb.* 她像小羊一般的温顺. **~·ly** *adv* **~·ness** *n*

meer·schaum /'mɪəʃəm; `mɪrʃəm/ *n* [U] white clay-like substance; [C] tobacco pipe with a bowl made of this. 海泡石;海泡石所制的烟斗.

meet[1] /miːt; mit/ *vt, vi* (*pt, pp,* **met** /met; mɛt/) **1** [VP6A, 2A, C] come face to face with (sb or sth coming from the opposite or a different direction); come together from different points or directions: 遇见; 碰见; 相逢: ~ *sb in the street.* 在街上遇见某人. *We met (each other) quite by chance.* 我们的相遇十分偶然. *Goodbye till we ~ again.* 珍重再见(道别时的用语). *The two trains* (= pass each other) *at Crewe.* 那两辆火车在克鲁地方相遇(即在该地错车). *We write regularly but seldom ~,* see each other. 我们经常通信但却很少见面. *Can you ~* (= face) *misfortune with a smile?* 你能面对不幸的遭遇而一笑置之吗? *The Debating Society ~s every Friday at 8 pm.* 辩论会每星期五下午八时开会. **(a)** experience: 遭遇; 受到: ~ *with misfortune/an accident/great kindness.* 遭遇不幸(遇到意外; 受到优遇). **(b)** come upon by chance: 偶遇; 碰到: ~ *with obstacles;* 碰到阻碍; ~ *with an old friend at a dinner party.* 在一个宴会上偶然遇到一位老友. **(c)** (US) have a meeting with. (美)和…会面. **2** [VP6A, 2A] make the acquaintance of; be introduced to: 结识; 被介绍: *I know Mrs Hill by sight, but have never met her/we've never met.* 我跟希尔夫人只是面熟, 但并不认识她(从来没人给我们介绍过). (As a form of introduction)(作为一种介绍用语) *M~ my wife.* 这是内子. *Pleased to ~ you.* 高兴见到您; 久仰久仰. **3** [VP 6A] go to a place and await the arrival of: 迎接: *Will you ~ me at the station?* 你要到车站接我吗? *I'll ~ your train.* 我要到车站接你的班车. *The hotel bus ~s all the trains.* 旅馆的汽车在火车站迎接各班车的旅客. **4** [VP 6A] satisfy (a demand, etc): 应付; 满足(要求等): ~ *sb's wishes,* do what he wants. 满足某人的愿望. *Can you ~ their objections/criticisms,* answer them in a satisfactory way? 你能圆满答复他们的抗议(批评)吗? ~ *the case,* be adequate, satisfactory: 适当; 令人满意:

I'm afraid your proposal hardly ~s the case. 我恐怕你的提议不大合适. ~ *sb halfway,* (fig) compromise; give way to some extent in order to satisfy him. (喻)与人妥协; 迁就某人. ~ *all expenses/bills, etc,* pay them. 付全部费用(帐单等). **5** [VP6A, 2A] come into contact; touch: 接触: *Their hands met.* 他们的手相触. *His hand met hers.* 他的手碰到她的手. *My waistcoat won't ~,* is too small to be buttoned. 我的背心太小了, 扣不上. *make (both) ends ~,* make one's income and one's expenditure equal. 使收支相抵; 量入为出. **6** ~ *the eye/ear,* be visible/audible. 看得见(听得到). *There is more to/in sth/sb than ~s the eye,* it/he has qualities, characteristics, etc that are not immediately seen. (喻)某事物(某人)的特性、特质等不是一眼看得出的. ~ *sb's eye,* look in his eyes: 与某人目光相遇: *She was afraid to ~ my eye.* 她怕与我目光相遇.

meet[2] /miːt; mit/ *n* **1** (GB) gathering of riders and hounds at a fixed place (for foxhunting). (英)出发猎狐前骑马的猎者与猎犬的集合. **2** (US) coming together of a number of people for a purpose: (美)集会; 会: *an ath'letic ~;* 运动会; *a 'track/'swimming ~* (*meeting* is the usu word in GB). 田径(游泳)比赛(英国通常用 meeting).

meet[3] /miːt; mit/ *adj* (archaic) right; suitable; proper. (古)对的; 适合的; 适当的.

meet·ing /'miːtɪŋ; `mitɪŋ/ *n* **1** coming together of a number of persons at a certain time and place, esp for discussion: 集会; (尤指)会议: *political ~s.* 政治集会; 政治会议. *Mr Smith will now address the ~.* 史密斯先生现在要对大会演讲. '**~-house** *n* building for ~s, esp those held by Quakers. 聚会所(尤指教友派的聚会所). '**~-place** *n* place fixed for a ~. 集会地点; 集合场所. **2** any coming together: 聚会; 会晤: *a 'race-~;* 赛马会; *a 'sports-~.* 运动会. *The ~ between the two families was a joyful one.* 这两家人的聚会颇为愉快. *She is shy at a first ~, when she meets sb for the first time.* 她与人初次见面时很害羞.

mega·cycle /'megəsaɪkl; `megə͵saɪkl/ *n* [C] one million cycles (of changes of radio current). (无线电频率的)百万周; 兆周.

mega·death /'megədeθ; `megə͵dɛθ/ *n* death of one million people (in nuclear war). 一百万人之死亡(如核战争中).

mega·lith /'megəlɪθ; `megə͵lɪθ/ *n* large stone, esp one used as a monument. 巨石; 大石头(尤指作纪念碑用). **mega·lithic** /͵megə'lɪθɪk; ͵megə'lɪθɪk/ *adj* made of ~s; marked by the use of ~s (esp in very early times). 巨石建造的; 有使用巨石之特征的(尤指远古时代).

megaliths

mega·lo·ma·nia /͵megələ'meɪnɪə; ͵megələ'menɪə/ *n* [U] form of madness in which a person has exaggerated ideas of his importance, power, wealth, etc: 自大狂; 妄自尊大狂. *The dictator was obviously suffering from ~.* 那个独裁者显然有自大狂. **mega·lo·ma·niac** /-nɪæk; -nɪ͵æk/ *n* person suffering from ~. 有自大狂的人.

mega·phone /'megəfəun; `megə͵fon/ *n* [C] horn for speaking through, carrying the voice to a distance. 扩音喇叭; 传声筒.

mega·ton /'megətʌn; `megə͵tʌn/ *n* explosive force equal to one million tons of TNT. 百万吨级(相当于一百万吨黄色炸药之爆炸威力).

me·grim /'miːgrɪm; `migrɪm/ *n* (archaic) (古) **1** migraine. 偏头痛. **2** (*pl*) low spirits. (复)沮丧;忧郁.

mei·osis /maɪˈəʊsɪs; maɪˈosɪs/ n = **litotes**.

mel·an·cholic /ˌmelənˈkɒlɪk; ˌmelənˈkɑlɪk/ adj melancholy; with a tendency to melancholy. 忧郁的; 容易忧郁的。

mel·an·choly /ˈmelənkɒlɪ; ˈmelənˌkɑlɪ/ n [U] sadness; low spirits. 悲哀; 忧郁。□ adj sad; low-spirited; causing sadness or low spirits: 悲哀的; 忧郁的; 引起悲哀或忧郁的: ~ news; 令人忧伤的消息; a ~ occasion, eg a funeral. 令人悲伤的场合 (如葬礼)。 **mel·an·cholia** /ˌmelənˈkəʊlɪə; ˌmelənˈkolɪə/ n [U] mental illness marked by ~. 忧郁症。

mé·lange /meɪˈlɑːnʒ US: meɪˈlɑːnʒ; meˈlɑ̃ʒ/ n (F) mixture; medley. (法)混杂; 混合物。

mê·lée /ˈmeleɪ US: meɪˈleɪ; meˈle/ n (F) confused struggle; confused crowd of people. (法)混战; 乱斗; 混乱的群众。

meli·or·ate /ˈmiːlɪəreɪt; ˈmiljəˌret/ vt, vi [VP6A, 2A] make or become better; improve. 改善; 改良; 变为良好。 **meli·or·ation** /ˌmiːlɪəˈreɪʃn; ˌmiljəˈreʃən/ n process of improving. 改善; 改良。 **meli·or·ism** /ˈmiːlɪərɪzəm; ˈmiljəˌrɪzəm/ n belief that mankind tends to ~, and that conscious human effort may further this tendency. 世界改善论 (相信人类会改善, 人类自觉的努力会加强此一趋势)。

mel·lif·lu·ous /meˈlɪflʊəs; məˈlɪflʊəs/ adj (of a person's voice or words, of music, etc) sweet-sounding; smooth-flowing. (指人的声音, 言语, 音乐等)甜美的; 流畅的。

mel·low /ˈmeləʊ; ˈmelo/ adj (-er, -est) **1** soft and sweet in taste; soft, pure and rich in colour or sound: 软而甜的; 香醇的; (颜色)柔和的; (声音)圆润的: a ~ wine; 醇酒; the ~ colours of the roofs in Dubrovnik. 杜勃罗夫尼克屋顶柔和的色彩。 **2** made wise and sympathetic by age or experience: (因年龄或经验而)成熟的; 老练的: ~ judgement. 成熟的判断。 **3** (colloq) genial; slightly intoxicated. (口)高兴的和善的; 微醺的。□ vt, vi [VP6A, 2A] make or become ~. (使)变香醇; (使)变柔美; (使)变成熟。 **~·ly** adv **~·ness** n

mel·odic /meˈlɒdɪk; meˈlɑdɪk/ adj of melody; melodious. 旋律的; 音调悠扬的; 音调美妙的。

mel·odi·ous /meˈləʊdɪəs; meˈlodɪəs/ adj of, producing, melody; sweet-sounding. 旋律的; 产生旋律的; 声调优美的; 悦耳的: the ~ notes of a thrush. 画眉鸟的美妙歌声。 **~·ly** adv **~·ness** n

melo·drama /ˈmeləˌdrɑːmə; ˈmeləˌdrɑmə/ n **1** [C] exciting and emotional (often sensational, exaggerated) drama, usu with a happy ending; event or series of events, piece of behaviour or writing, which suggests a stage ~. 一种通俗闹剧(刺激观众情感, 常为感人、夸大的, 且通常以欢乐为结局的戏剧); 有此种戏剧性的事件、行为或文章。 **2** [U] language, behaviour, suggestive of plays of this kind. 具有通俗闹剧性质的言语或行为。 **melo·dram·atic** /ˌmelədrəˈmætɪk; ˌmelədrəˈmætɪk/ adj of, like, suitable for, ~. 通俗闹剧的; 通俗闹剧般的; 适于通俗闹剧的。 **melo·dram·ati·cally** /-klɪ; -klɪ/ adv

mel·ody /ˈmelədɪ; ˈmelədɪ/ n (pl **-dies**) **1** [U] sweet music; tunefulness; arrangement of notes in a musically expressive succession. 美妙的音乐; 和谐的音调; 音律。 **2** [C] musical arrangement of words; song or tune: 歌曲; 曲调: old Irish melodies. 古老的爱尔兰歌曲。 **3** [C] principal part or thread in harmonized music: 主调; 旋律: The ~ is next taken up by the flutes. 这主调接着由横笛合奏。

melon /ˈmelən; ˈmelən/ n (kinds of) large, juicy round fruit growing on a plant that trails along the ground: (各种的)瓜: a slice of ~. 一片瓜。 ⇨ the illus at **fruit**. 参看 fruit 之插图。

melt /melt; melt/ vt, vi (pt, pp **~ed**; pp as adj (of metal) 过去分词用作形容词而指金属时作 **molten** /ˈməʊltən; ˈmoltn/) **1** [VP6A, 15B, 2A, C] (cause to) become liquid through heating: (使)融化; (使)熔

化: The ice will ~ when the sun shines on it. 当太阳照到冰的时候, 冰就融化。 The hot sun soon ~ed the ice. 炎热的太阳很快地把冰融化了。 It is easy to ~ butter. 融化奶油很容易。 The snow soon ~ed away when the sun came out. 太阳出来后不久, 雪就融化掉了。 Money seemed to ~ away in Paris. 在巴黎, 她的钱仿佛一会儿就花掉了。 The crowd quickly ~ed away (= dispersed) when the storm broke. 暴风雨来袭, 人群很快地四散了。 ~ sth down, ~ (a metal article) in order to use the metal as raw material. 熔做某物; 熔化 (金属器, 以作铸造之材料)。 **2** [VP2A, C] (of soft food) dissolve, be softened, easily: (指软的食物)易于溶解或软化: This cake/pear ~s in the mouth. 这莲糕(梨)在嘴里就软化了。 **3** [VP2A, 6A] (of a solid in a liquid) dissolve: (指液体中的固体)(使)溶解; 溶于: Sugar ~s in tea/Hot tea ~s sugar. 糖溶于茶(热茶使糖溶化)。 **4** [VP6A, 2C] (of a person, heart, feelings) soften, be softened: (指人、人心、感情)(使)软化; (使)感动: Her heart ~ed with pity. 她的心因怜悯而软化。 Pity ~ed her heart. 怜悯软化了她的心。 She ~ed into tears. 她感动得哭起来了。 **5** [VP2C] fade; go (slowly) away: 褪色; 逐渐消失; 变淡: One colour ~ed into another, eg in the sky at sunset. 一种颜色渐渐变成另一种颜色(如在日落时之天空景色)。 **~·ing** adj (fig) tender; sentimental: (喻)柔情的; 感伤的: in a ~ing voice/mood. 以感伤的声音(情绪)。 **'~ing-point** n temperature at which a solid ~s. (固体的)熔点。 Lead has a lower ~ing-point than iron. 铅的熔点比铁低。 **'~ing-pot** n **(a)** pot in which metals, etc, are ~ed. 熔炉。 **go into the ~ing-pot**, (fig) undergo a radical change. (喻)彻底改变。 **(b)** place, country, eg US, where immigrants from many different countries are assimilated. 各不同种族之移民受同化的地方或国家(如美国); 大熔炉。

mem·ber /ˈmembə(r); ˈmembɚ/ n **1** person belonging to a group, society, etc: (团体、学会等的)一份子; 会员; 成员: a ~ of a club. 俱乐部会员。 Every ~ of her family came to her wedding. 她家里的每一个人都来参加她的婚礼。 **,M~ of 'Parliament,** (abbr 略作 **MP**) elected representative in the House of Commons. (下议院的)国会议员。 **2** part of a human or animal body: 人或动物身体的某一部分; 器官: The tongue is sometimes called 'the unruly ~'. 舌头有时候被称为 '难以控制的器官'。 **~·ship** /-ʃɪp; -ʃɪp/ n **1** [U] the state of being a ~ (of a society, etc). (社团等的)会员的身份、资格。 **2** (no pl) number of ~s: (无复数形式)会员的人数: The society has a large ~ship/a ~ship of 80. 该学会会员很多(有八十个会员)。

mem·brane /ˈmembreɪn; ˈmembren/ n [C] soft, thin, pliable skin-like covering or lining, or connecting part, in an animal or vegetable body: (动植物的)膜; 薄膜; 形成此等薄膜的组织。 **mem·bra·nous** /ˈmembrənəs; ˈmembrənəs/ adj of or like ~. 膜的; 膜状的。

mem·ento /mɪˈmentəʊ; mɪˈmento/ n (pl **~s, ~es** /-təʊz, -toz/) sth that serves to remind one of a person or event. 纪念品; 令人回忆起(某人或某事件)的东西。

memo /ˈmeməʊ; ˈmemo/ n (pl **~s** /-məʊz; -moz/) short for **memorandum**. 为 memorandum 之略。

mem·oir /ˈmemwɑː(r); ˈmemwɑr/ n **1** record of events, esp by someone with first-hand knowledge. 传记 (尤指有第一手资料之人所写者)。 **2** (pl) person's written account of his own life or experiences: (复)自传; 回忆录: the flood of war ~s by generals and politicians. 将军和政治家们所写的多如潮涌的战争回忆录。

mem·or·able /ˈmemərəbl; ˈmemərəbl/ adj deserving to be remembered. 值得纪念的。 **mem·or·ably** /-əblɪ; -əblɪ/ adv

mem·or·an·dum /ˌmeməˈrændəm; ˌmeməˈrændəm/ n (pl **-da** /-də; -də/ or **~s**) (abbr 略作 **memo**) **1** note or record for future use: 备忘录: make a ~ of sth. 记录某事(以免遗忘)。 **2** informal business communication,

usu without a personal signature, on paper headed *M~* (or *Memo*). 非正式的商业文件；便条(通常私人不加签名，纸上端并印有 Memorandum 或 Memo 字样). **3** (legal) record of an agreement that has been reached but not yet formally drawn up and signed. (法律)已经商妥但尚未正式起草签署之协议的报告书；备忘录。

mem·or·ial /mɪˈmɔːrɪəl; məˈmɔrɪəl/ *n* **1** sth made or done to remind people of an event, person, etc: 纪念物；纪念馆；纪念仪式: *a ~ to the dead*; 对死者的纪念仪式; *a 'war ~*, a monument with the names of men killed in wars. 阵亡将士纪念碑. **2** (attrib use) serving to keep in mind: (用作定语)纪念性的: *a ~ tablet*, eg in the wall of a church, in memory of someone; 纪念牌匾(如在教堂墙上，用以纪念某人者); *a ~ service.* 追悼会；追思礼拜。'**M~ Day**, (US) day set aside by law for honouring the memory of members of the armed forces killed in war (30 May in most States). (美)阵亡将士纪念日(在大多数州为五月三十日). **3** (usu *pl*) historical records or chronicles. (通常用复数)历史记录；编年史. **4** (more usu 较常用 *petition*) written statement of facts, views, etc sent to authorities making a request or protest. 请愿书；陈情书；抗议书. ~·**ize** /-aɪz; -ˌaɪz/ *vt* [VP6A] **1** (more usu 较常用 *petition*) present a ~(4) to. 向···上陈情书；向···呈递请愿书. **2** commemorate (which is the more usu word). 纪念(commemorate 为较常用字).

mem·or·ize /ˈmeməraɪz; ˈmeməˌraɪz/ *vt* [VP6A] learn by heart; commit to memory. 熟记；记住.

mem·ory /ˈmeməri; ˈmeməri/ *n* (*pl* **-ries**) **1** [U] power of keeping facts in the conscious mind and of being able to call them back at will; preservation of past experience for future use. 记忆力；记忆. *commit sth to ~*, learn it by heart. 熟记某事物；熟记某事物。*speak from ~*, ie without referring to notes, etc. 凭记忆讲述. *to the best of my ~*, as far as I can remember. 就我记忆所及；凭我所记得的. *in ~ of sb; to the ~ of sb*, serving to recall sb, to keep him fresh in peoples' minds. 以纪念某人；为了纪念某人. **2** [C] this power in an individual (also used, by extension, of the unit of a computer which stores data for future use): 个人的记忆力；记性; (亦可引伸用以指电脑的)储存器. *Some people have better memories than others.* 有些人的记忆力比别人好. *He has a bad ~ for dates.* 他对日期的记忆力很差. **3** [U] period over which the ~ can go back: 记忆的期限: *beyond/within the ~ of men.* 在人类有史以前(以来). *within living ~*, within the years that people now alive can remember. 在活着的人们所能记忆的年月里. **4** [C] sth that is remembered; sth from the past stored in the mind: 记住的事情；留在记忆之中的往事: *memories of childhood.* 童年的回忆. **5** [U] reputation after death (esp of saints, great rulers): 死后的名望(尤指圣人、君王者): *the late king/pope, of blessed ~.* 先王(故教皇)(对已故国王、教皇的敬称)。

mem·sa·hib /ˈmemsaːb; ˈmɛmˌsɑˈɪb/ *n* (In India) (form of address to a) European woman. (在印度)欧洲妇女；太太(印度人对欧洲妇女之称呼)。

men /men; mɛn/ *n pl* of **man**[1].

men·ace /ˈmenəs; ˈmɛnɪs/ *n* [C, U] danger; threat: 危险；威胁: *a ~ to world peace*; 对世界和平的威胁; *in a speech filled with ~.* 在一次满口恫吓的演说中。*That woman is a ~*, is a nuisance, is troublesome! 那女人真讨人厌(真难缠)! □ *vt* [VP6A] threaten; endanger: 恐吓；威胁: *countries ~d by/with war.* 受到战争威胁的国家. **men·ac·ing·ly** *adv* in a threatening manner. 威吓地；胁迫地.

mé·nage /meɪˈnɑːʒ; meˈnɑʒ/ *n* (F) household. (法)家庭管理；家政；家务；家庭。

men·ag·erie /mɪˈnædʒəri; məˈnædʒəri/ *n* collection of wild animals in captivity, esp for a travelling circus. 樊笼等之中的野兽; (尤指)马戏团在各地表演时囚于笼中之兽群；动物展览。

mend /mend; mɛnd/ *vt*, *vi* **1** [VP6A] remake, repair, set right (sth broken, worn out, or torn); restore to good condition: 修补；修理: *~ shoes/a broken window.* 修补鞋子(破窗户). **2** [VP6A, 2A] (= *amend*) free from faults or errors: 修正；改良；改善: *That won't ~* (= improve) *matters.* 那无济于事. *it's never too late to ~*, (prov) reform one's way of living. (谚)改过不嫌迟；改过永远不会太晚。*one's ways*, ⇨ **way**(10). **3** [VP2A] regain health; heal: 恢复健康；痊愈: *The patient is ~ing nicely.* 这病人康复得很快. **4** [VP6A] increase: 增加: *~ one's pace*, quicken it; walk faster; 加快脚步; *~ the fire*, (regional use) put more coal on it. (地方性用语)在火里加煤炭；加添燃料. □ *n* damage or torn part, that has been ~ed: 修补处: *The ~s were almost invisible.* 修补的地方几乎看不出来. *on the ~*, improving in health or condition. 康复中；改进中. ~·**er** *n* (chiefly in compounds) one who ~s: (主用于复合词)修补者；修理者: *'road~er.* 修路工人. '~·**ing** *n* (esp) work of ~ing (clothes, etc): 修补; (尤指衣服等的)补缀: *a basketful of ~ing*, of clothes, etc, to be ~ed; 一篮待修补的衣物; *invisible ~ing.* ⇨ **invisible**. 织补。

men·da·cious /menˈdeɪʃəs; mɛnˈdeʃəs/ *adj* (formal) false; untruthful: (正式用语)假的；虚伪的: ~ *newspaper reports.* 不实的新闻报导. ~·**ly** *adv* **men·dac·ity** /menˈdæsəti; mɛnˈdæsətɪ/ *n* (formal) [U] untruthfulness; [C] (*pl* **-ties**) untrue statement. (正式用语)虚假；虚伪之言语；谎言。

Men·delian /menˈdiːliən; mɛnˈdilɪən/ *adj* of the theory of genetics of Mendel, the Austrian geneticist. (奥地利遗传学家)孟德尔之遗传学说的。

men·di·cant /ˈmendɪkənt; ˈmɛndɪkənt/ *n*, *adj* (person) getting a living by asking for alms, or as a beggar: 靠救济品过活的(人)；行乞的(人): ~ *friars.* 托钵僧(到处化缘的和尚)。

men·folk /ˈmenfəʊk; ˈmɛnˌfok/ *n pl* (colloq) men, esp the men of a family: (口)男人们(尤指一家之中的男人们); *The ~ have all gone out fishing.* 男人们都出去钓鱼了。

me·nial /ˈmiːniəl; ˈminɪəl/ *adj* suitable for, to be done by, a household servant: 适合于佣人的；由佣人做的: *such ~ tasks as washing pots and pans.* 洗锅洗盆这类用人所做的工作. □ *n* (usu derog) servant. (通常含贬抑意味)奴仆；贱仆. ~·**ly** /-iəli; -iəli/ *adv*

men·in·gi·tis /ˌmenɪnˈdʒaɪtɪs; ˌmɛnɪnˈdʒaɪtɪs/ *n* [U] (serious illness caused by) inflammation of any or all of the membranes enclosing the brain and spinal cord. 脑膜炎；脑膜炎症。

meno·pause /ˈmenəpɔːz; ˈmɛnəˌpɔz/ *n* final cessation of the menses at the age of about 50 (colloq called *'change of life'*). 断经；停经；断经期；经绝期(俗称'更年期'妇女之月经停闭约在五十岁左右)。

men·ses /ˈmensiːz; ˈmɛnsiz/ *n pl* monthly bleeding from the uterus. 月经。

men·stru·ate /ˈmenstrueɪt; ˈmɛnstruˌet/ *vi* [VP2A] discharge the menses. 月经来潮；行经. **men·stru·ation** /ˌmenstruˈeɪʃn; ˌmɛnstruˈeʃən/ *n* [U] this process. 月经；行经. **men·strual** /ˈmenstruəl; ˈmɛnstruəl/ *adj* of the menses or menstruation. 月经的。

men·sur·ation /ˌmensjuˈreɪʃn; ˌmɛnʃəˈreʃən/ *n* process of, mathematical rules for, finding length, area and volume. (长度、面积、体积之)测量；测量法；测量术. **men·sur·able** /ˈmensjurəbl; ˈmɛnʃʊrəbl/ *adj* (rare) measurable. (罕)可测量的；可量度的。

men·tal /ˈmentl; ˈmɛntl/ *adj* of or in the mind. 心智的；心理的；智力的；心中的。'~ *age*, person's ~ level measured in terms of the average age of children having the same ~ standard. 心理年龄；心龄. ~ a'rithmetic, done in the mind without using written figures or a mechanical device. 心算. '~ de'ficiency, subnormal development of intellectual powers, preventing a person from learning normally, looking after

himself, etc. 心智缺陷(智力欠正常的发育, 使患者不能正常学习、照料自己等). '~ **home**／**hospital**, one for ~ patients. 精神病院。 '~ **illness**, illness of the mind. 精神病。 '~ **patient**, person suffering an illness of the mind. 精神病人。 ,~ **reser'vation**, one concerning a statement, oath, etc present in the mind but not spoken in words. 心意保留(作一项陈述、誓言等时出现在心中但没有说出的心意). ~**ly** /'mentəlɪ; 'mɛntlɪ/ *adv:* ~*ly deficient*／*defective*, suffering from ~ illness; unable to profit from the ordinary kind of school education; 患精神病的; 智力不足的; 心理有缺陷的; ~*ly deranged*, (colloq □ = **mad**). 精神错乱的; 疯的。

men·tal·ity /men'tælətɪ; mɛn'tælətɪ/ *n* **1** [U] general intellectual character; degree of intellectual power: 心智; 智力: *persons of average* ~. 智力普通的人。 **2** [C] (*pl* **-ties**) characteristic attitude of mind: 心理状态: *a war* ~. 战争心理。

men·thol /'menθɒl; 'mɛnθɔl/ *n* [U] solid white substance obtained from oil of peppermint, used, eg by being rubbed on the skin, to relieve neuralgia, etc and as a flavouring, eg in ~ cigarettes. 薄荷脑(从薄荷油提炼出的一种白色固体, 用于涂擦皮肤以减轻神经痛等, 及用作香料, 如薄荷香烟中所用者). **men·tho·lated** /'menθəleɪtɪd; 'mɛnθə,leɪtɪd/ *adj* containing ~. 含有薄荷脑的。

men·tion /'menʃn; 'mɛnʃən/ *vt* [VP6A, C, 9, 13A] speak or write sth about; say the name of; refer to: 说到; 写到; 提及: *He* ~*ed to me that he had seen you.* 他向我提到曾经见过你。 *I shall* ~ *it to him.* 我将向他提到这件事。 *Did I hear my name* ~*ed*, Was somebody talking about me? 是不是有人提到我的名字; 是否有人在谈论我? *not to* ~; *without* ~*ing*, phrases used either to excuse ~ of sth unimportant or to emphasize sth important: 不用说; 更不必说: *We're too busy to take a long holiday this year, not to* ~ *the fact that we can't afford it.* 我们今年太忙不能去度一个长的假期, 更不必说我们出不起这笔钱。 *Don't* ~ *it*, phrase used to indicate that thanks, an apology, etc are unnecessary. 不必客气, 哪里哪里(对感谢及道歉的答语)。 □ *n* **1** [U] ~*ing* or naming: 提到: *He made no* ~ *of your request.* 他没有提到你的请求。 **2** [C] brief notice or reference: 简要的告示或提述: *Did the concert get a* ~ *in the paper?* 报上报导这次音乐会没有? **men·tioned** *adj* (with an *adv* prefixed): (字前附以副词): *a,bove-*／*be,low-'mentioned*, referred to above／below. 上述的／下述的。

men·tor /'mentɔ(r); 'mɛntə/ *n* wise and trusted adviser and helper (of an inexperienced person). (无经验之人的)明智可靠的顾问和帮助者。

menu /'menju:; 'mɛnju/ *n* list of courses at a meal or of dishes available at a restaurant. 菜单。

Mephi·stoph·elian /,mefistɒ'fi:liən; ,mɛfɪstɔ'filɪən/ *adj* of or like Mephistopheles /,mefi'stɒfəli:z; ,mɛfə'stɑfə,liz/ (the devil in a German legend); fiendish. (德国传奇中之恶魔)麦费斯托费利的; 像麦费斯托费利的; 魔鬼的。

mer·can·tile /'mɜ:kəntaɪl; 'mɝkəntɪl/ *adj* of trade, commerce and merchants. 贸易的; 商业的; 商人的。 ~ **marine**, country's merchant ships and seamen. 一国商船及海员的总称。

Mer·cator's pro·jec·tion /mə,keɪtəz prə'dʒekʃn; mɝ,ketɚ prə'dʒɛkʃən/ *n* method of making maps of the world in which meridians and parallels of latitude cross at right angles (so that areas far from the equator are exaggerated in size). 麦卡托投影法(一种绘制世界地图的方法, 经纬线成直角相交, 使远离赤道的地区被放大)。 ⇨ the illus at **projection**. 参看 projection 之插图。

mer·cen·ary /'mɜ:sɪnərɪ US: -nerɪ; 'mɝsn̩,ɛrɪ/ *adj* working only for money or other reward; inspired by love of money: 仅为工钱或其他报酬而工作的; 爱财所致的; 图利的: ~ *politicians*; 以金钱为目的之政客; *act from* ~ *motives.* 所作所为出自图利的动机。 □ *n* (*pl* **-ries**) soldier hired for pay to serve in a foreign army. 雇佣兵(为金钱而受雇于外国军队中的士兵)。

mer·cer /'mɜ:sə(r); 'mɝsɚ/ *n* (GB) dealer in woven materials, esp silk and other textiles. (英)布商;(尤指)经销绸缎及其他织物之商人。

mer·cer·ize /'mɜ:səraɪz; 'mɝsə,raɪz/ *vt* [VP6A] treat (cotton threads) so that they are better able to take dyes and become glossy like silk: 处理(棉纱)使易于染色且具有丝绸光泽: ~*d cotton.* 丝光棉布;府绸。

mer·chan·dise /'mɜ:tʃəndaɪz; 'mɝtʃən,daɪz/ *n* [U] goods bought and sold; trade goods. 商品;货品。

mer·chant /'mɜ:tʃənt; 'mɝtʃənt/ *n* **1** (usu wholesale) trader, esp one doing business with foreign countries. (通常指批发)商人;(尤指)国际贸易商人。 **2** (chiefly attrib) of commercial shipping: (主用作定语)海运商的: (attrib) (用作定语) ~ *ships.* 商船。 **the** ~ **navy**／**service**／**marine**, the ~ ships and seamen of a country collectively. 一国商船及船员的总称。 ~ **seaman**, sailor in a ~ ship. 商船船员。 **3** (as the second half of a compound *n*) person trading inside a country in the goods indicated: (用于复合词中接另一名词后) 经售某种货品的商人: *a 'coal-*~／*'wine-*~. 煤炭商(酒商). **4** (GB sl) person who is very fond of (sth) or addicted to (sth): (英俚)狂热于从事(某事物)的人;耽于(某事物)的人: *a 'speed* ~, person who likes to drive at high speeds. 好开快车的人。 ~·**man** /-mən; -mən/ *n* (*pl* -men) ~ ship. 商船。

mer·ci·ful /'mɜ:sɪfl; 'mɝsɪfəl/ *adj* ~ **(to)**, having, showing, feeling mercy (to). (对⋯)仁慈的; 慈悲的。 ~·**ly** /-fəlɪ; -fəlɪ/ *adv*

mer·ci·less /'mɜ:sɪlɪs; 'mɝsɪlɪs/ *adj* ~ **(to)**, showing no mercy (to). (对⋯)无慈悲心的; 无怜悯心的。 ~·**ly** *adv*

mer·cur·ial /mɜ:'kjʊərɪəl; mɝ'kjʊrɪəl/ *adj* **1** of, like, caused by, containing, mercury: 水银的; 似水银的; 由水银造成的: *poison*; 含水银的; ~ *ointment*; 含汞药膏; ~ *poisoning*. 水银中毒。 **2** (fig) lively; quick-witted. (喻)活泼的;机智的。 **3** (of persons) changeable; inconstant. (指人)多变的;三心二意的。

mer·cury /'mɜ:kjʊrɪ; 'mɝkjərɪ/ *n* [U] (also called 亦称为 *quicksilver*) heavy, silver-coloured metal (symbol **Hg**) usu liquid, as in thermometers and barometers. 水银; 汞(银白色重金属, 化学符号 Hg, 通常为液态, 如温度表及气压计中所用者)。

Mer·cury /'mɜ:kjʊrɪ; 'mɝkjərɪ/ *n* (Roman myth) messenger of the gods; (astron) planet nearest the sun. (罗神)莫丘利(众神的使者);(天文)水星(最接近太阳)。 ⇨ the illus at **planet**. 参看 planet 之插图。

mercy /'mɜ:sɪ; 'mɝsɪ/ *n* (*pl* **-cies**) **1** [U] (capacity for) holding oneself back from punishing, or from causing suffering to, sb whom one has the right or power to punish: 仁慈; 怜悯; 宽恕; 慈悲心: *They showed little* ~ *to their enemies.* 他们对仇敌毫无怜悯之意。 *We were given no* ~. 我们没有得到宽恕。 *He threw himself on my* ~, begged me to have ~ on him, not to punish him, etc. 他求我宽恕他。 *The jury brought in a verdict of guilty, with a recommendation to* ~, asking that the punishment should not be too severe. 陪审团宣判被告有罪附带建议从轻量刑。 *at the* ~ *of*, in the power of; without defence against: 任由⋯摆布; 在⋯的掌握中; 无法防御中: *The ship was at the* ~ *of the waves*, was out of control, likely to be wrecked, etc. 船在浪涛中随波漂流。 *be left to the tender* ~／*mercies of*, be exposed to the probably unkind, rough or cruel treatment of. 任凭⋯宰割。 **2** [C] piece of good fortune; sth to be thankful for; relief: 幸运; 应感谢的事物; 恩惠; 减轻或解除痛苦之事物: *That's a* ~! 那真幸运! *We must be thankful for small mercies.* 我们对小惠也应感激。 *His death was a* ~, eg of sb with a painful and incurable illness. 他的死亡是一种解脱(例如对一患痛苦而不治之症者)。 '~ **killing** *n* (colloq for) euthanasia. 无痛苦致死术; 安乐死术(使患痛苦不治之症者无痛苦致死亡); 为

euthanasia 之口语). **3** *M~! M~ on us!* exclamations of surprise or (often pretended) terror. (表示惊愕或故作惊怒时的感叹词句)啊呀! 我的天哪!

mere¹ /mɪə(r); mɪr/ *adj* not more than! 仅仅; 只不过: *She's a ~ child.* 她只不过是个小孩而已. *It's a ~/the ~st trifle,* nothing at all important, nothing of any value, etc. 那只不过是件小事. *M~ words (= Words without acts) won't help.* 光说(不做)无济于事. **~·ly** *adv* only; simply: 仅仅; 只不过: *I ~ly asked his name.* 我只问了问他的名字. *I said it ~ly as a joke.* 我只不过把它当做笑话说说而已.

mere² /mɪə(r); mɪr/ *n* pond; small lake. 池塘; 小湖.

mer·etri·cious /ˌmerɪˈtrɪʃəs; ˌmerəˈtrɪʃəs/ *adj* attractive on the surface but of little value: 外表华丽而实际并无价值的; 虚有其表的: ~ *jewellery,* 仅供眩惑的珠宝; *a ~ style,* superficially attractive. 浮华不实的文体. **~·ly** *adv* **~·ness** *n*

merge /mɜːdʒ; mɜrdʒ/ *vt, vi* **1** [VP2A, 3A, 6A, 14] ~ *(in/into/with),* (comm) (of business companies) (cause to) become one: (商)(指两个或数个公司)(使)合并: *We are merging with the company that supplies components for our cars.* 我们即将并入那家供应我们汽车配件的公司. *The small banks ~d/were ~d into one large organization.* 这几家小银行合并成一个大机构. **2** [VP3A] ~ *into,* fade or change gradually into: 逐渐消失而变成…; 逐渐融入: *Twilight ~d into darkness.* 落日余辉逐渐地融入了黑暗之中. *His fear gradually ~d into curiosity to know what was happening.* 他的恐惧逐渐消失而变成欲知何事发生的好奇心. **merger** /ˈmɜːdʒə(r); ˈmɜrdʒər/ *n* [U] merging; [C] instance of this; combining of estates, business companies, etc. 吞并;(产业、公司等的)合并; 联合组织.

me·rid·ian /məˈrɪdɪən; məˈrɪdɪən/ *n* **1** (either half of a) circle round the globe, passing through a given place and the north and south poles: 子午线; 子午圈; 经线: *the ~ of Greenwich,* longitude 0°. 格林威治子午线(地图上的零度经线, 即经度起算处). **2** highest point reached by the sun or other star as viewed from a point on the earth's surface; 12 noon. 从地面观测太阳或其他星球所到达的最高点; 中天; 中午十二时正; 正午. **3** (fig) period of greatest splendour, success, power, etc. (喻)(声望、成就、权力等的)鼎盛时期; 顶点. **4** (attrib) of a ~ (用作定语)子午线(圈)的; 正午的: ~ *line/altitude;* 子午线(中天高度); (fig) (喻) *in his ~ splendour.* 他最辉煌的时期.

mer·idi·onal /məˈrɪdɪənl; məˈrɪdɪənl/ *adj* of the south; of the south of Europe, esp the south of France. 南方的; 南欧的; (尤指)法国南部的.

me·ringue /məˈræŋ; məˈræŋ/ *n* [U, C] whites of egg and sugar baked and used as a covering over pies, tarts, etc; small cake made of this mixture. (将蛋白与糖掺混而烘成、用以包复果馅饼等之)饼皮;(用蛋白与糖混合做成的)蛋白甜饼.

mer·ino /məˈriːnəʊ; məˈrino/ *n* (*pl* ~**s** /-nəʊz; -noz/) **1** (also 亦作 '~**-sheep**) breed of sheep with long, fine wool. 麦利诺羊(一种毛细长的绵羊). **2** [U] yarn or cloth from this wool; soft wool and cotton material. 此种羊毛所制成的毛线或呢绒; 柔软的棉毛料子.

merit /ˈmerɪt; ˈmerɪt/ *n* **1** [U] quality or fact of deserving well; worth; excellence: 功劳; 勋绩; 价值; 优点: *There isn't much ~ in giving away things you don't value or want.* 把你那不上或者不需要的东西给人, 算不了什么功德. *Do men of ~ always win recognition?* 有功劳的人总会受到褒奖吗? *She was awarded a certificate of ~ for her piano playing.* 她得到一张钢琴演奏优异奖状. **2** [C] quality, fact, action, etc, that deserves reward: 应受奖赏的特质、事实、行动等: *We must decide the case on its ~s,* according to the rights and wrongs of the case, without being influenced by personal feelings. 我们必须按照事情的是非曲直来决定这个案件. *make a ~ of sth,* represent it as deserving reward or praise: 夸

称某事值得奖赏或赞美; 夸称某事是件大功: *Don't make a ~ of being punctual—it's only what we expect of you.* 不要认为你准时能有什么了不起——那只是我们预期你应该做到的. □ *vt* [VP6A] deserve; be worthy of: 应受; 值得: ~ *reward/punishment.* 该受奖赏(惩罚).

meri·toc·racy /ˌmerɪˈtɒkrəsɪ; ˌmerəˈtɑkrəsɪ/ *n* (*pl* -**cies**) (system of government or control by) persons of high practical or intellectual ability. 具高度实干能力或智力的人们; 才智卓越的人们; 能人治理; 贤能政治(由才智卓越的人们执政的政治制度).

meri·tori·ous /ˌmerɪˈtɔːrɪəs; ˌmerəˈtorɪəs/ *adj* praiseworthy; deserving reward: 应受称赞的; 配受奖赏的; 有功劳的; 有助绩的: *a prize for ~ conduct.* 优良行为或勋绩之奖赏. **~·ly** *adv*

mer·maid /ˈmɜːmeɪd; ˈmɜːˌmed/ *n* (in children's stories, etc) woman with a fish's tail in place of legs. (童话等中之)美人鱼(人身鱼尾之女人). **mer·man** /ˈmɜːmæn; ˈmɜːˌmæn/ *n* (*pl* -**men**) male ~. 雄人鱼(雄性之人鱼).

merry /ˈmerɪ; ˈmerɪ/ *adj* (-**ier, -iest**) **1** happy; cheerful; bright and gay: 高兴的; 愉快的; 欢乐的: *a ~ laugh;* 愉快的笑; *wish sb a ~ Christmas.* 祝某人圣诞快乐. *make ~,* be gay and cheerful; laugh, talk, sing and feast. 作乐; 行乐; 宴乐. '**~-maker** *n* person who does this. 作乐者; 行乐者. '**~-making** *n* [U] doing this. 作乐;行乐; 欢乐. '**~-go-round** *n* revolving machine with horses, cars, etc on which children ride at fun fairs, etc. 旋转木马(娱乐场所内供儿童乘坐的旋转机械装置, 上有木马, 小车等). **2** (old use) pleasant: (旧用法)令人愉快的; 令人快乐的; 可爱的; 美妙的: *the ~ month of May;* 可爱的五月; 美好的五月; *M~ England.* 可爱的英格兰; 美丽英岛. **mer·rily** /ˈmerɪlɪ; ˈmerɪlɪ/ *adv* **mer·ri·ment** /ˈmerɪmənt; ˈmerɪmənt/ *n* [U].

mé·sal·liance /ˌmeˈzælɪɑːns; meˈzælɪəns/ *n* marriage with a person of lower social position. 与社会地位较自己为低的人所缔结的婚姻; 屈就的婚姻.

mes·cal /ˈmeskl; mesˈkæl/ *n* **1** globe-shaped cactus of Mexico. 墨西哥仙人掌(呈球形). **2** Mexican liquor distilled from the juices of the agave plant. 墨西哥林酒(一种墨西哥烈酒, 由蒸馏龙舌兰液汁而制成). **mes·ca·line** /ˈmeskəlɪn; ˈmeskəlɪn/ *n* [U] hallucinatory drug extracted from the ~ cactus. 麦斯克尔(从墨西哥仙人掌汁中提炼出的一种迷幻药).

Mes·dames /meɪˈdɑːm; meˈdɑm/ *n pl* of **madame**.

Mes·demoi·selles /ˌmeɪdəmwəˈzel; ˌmeɪdmwəˈzel/ *pl* of **mademoiselle**.

me·seems /mɪˈsiːmz; mɪˈsimz/ *vi* (old use) it seems to me. (旧用法)据我看来; 我以为.

mesh /meʃ; meʃ/ *n* **1** one of the spaces in a net or wire screen: 网眼; 筛孔: *a net with half-inch ~es.* 有半英寸网孔的网; spaces in other material. 其他材料上的空格. **2** (*pl*) network: (复)网状组织; 网状物: *the ~es of a spider's web;* 蜘蛛网的网状组织; (fig) (喻) *entangled in the ~es of political intrigue.* 卷入政治阴谋. **3** (mechanics) (机械) *in ~,* (of the geared teeth of wheels) engaged, interlocked. (指齿轮的齿)相咬合. ⇨ also **synchromesh**. □ *vt, vi* **1** [VP6A] catch (eg fish) in a net. 用网捕捉(鱼等). **2** [VP2A, 3A] ~ *(with),* (of toothed wheels) interlock; be engaged (with others): (指有齿的轮)互咬合; (指齿轮)(与其他齿轮)相咬合: (喻)调和; 和谐: *Our ways of looking at these problems don't ~.* 我们对这些问题的看法并不协调一致.

mes·mer·ism /ˈmezmərɪzəm; ˈmesmə,rɪzəm/ *n* [U] (older name for) hypnotism. 催眠; 催眠术 (hypnotism 的较古名称). **mes·meric** /mezˈmerɪk; mesˈmerɪk/ *adj* hypnotic. 催眠的. **mes·mer·ist** /-ɪst; -ɪst/ *n* hypnotist. 催眠者. **mes·mer·ize** /-aɪz; -aɪz/ *vt* [VP6A] hypnotize. 施催眠术于(某人).

me·son /ˈmiːsɒn; ˈmisɑn/ *n* (phys) type of subatomic particle with a mass between that of an electron and a proton. (物理)介子.

mess¹ /mes; mes/ *n* (with *indef art,* but rarely *pl*)

state of confusion, dirt or disorder: (可与不定冠词连用, 但罕用复数)混乱; 污秽; 杂乱: *The workmen cleaned up the ~ before they left.* 工人在离开之前把肮脏东西清理干净了。 *Who's going to clear up the ~ made by the cat?* 谁去把猫弄乱的东西整理一下? *You've made ~ of the job,* you have done it very badly. 你已经把这事弄糟了。 *He has got into another ~,* is in trouble again. 他又遇到麻烦了。 *A nice ~ you've made of it,* You've spoilt it! *I've never seen so much ~ and disorder!* 我从来没有见过这么乱七八糟的样子! □ *vt, vi* 1 [VP6A, 15B] **~ sth (up),** make a ~ of; put into disorder or confusion: 弄脏; 弄乱; 弄糟(某事物): *The late arrival of the train ~ed up all our plans.* 火车误点把我们的计划全弄糟了。 Hence, 由此产生, **'~ up** *n* (colloq) disorder or confusion: (口)紊乱; 混乱: *There's been a bit of a ~-up* (= a misunderstanding, a failure to do what was needed) *about booking seats for that concert.* 音乐会预定座位(即预售门票)的情形有点儿紊乱。 2 [VP2C, 15B] **~ (sth/sb) about, (a)** do things with no very definite plan; behave foolishly. 瞎忙; 乱做。 **(b)** make a ~ or muddle (of sth); treat (sb) roughly or inconsiderately: 弄乱(某物); 粗鲁地对待(某人): *Stop ~ing me about!* 别再对我粗鲁! **~y** *adj* (-ier, -iest) dirty; in a state of disorder: 肮脏的; 杂乱的; 混乱的: *a ~y job,* eg one that makes the hands and clothes dirty. 肮脏的工作(如会把手和衣服弄脏的工作)。

mess[2] /mes/; mes/ *n* [C] company of persons taking meals together (esp in the Armed Forces); these meals; the room, etc in which the meals are eaten. 共餐者; 伙食团(多指军中者); 伙食; (供伙食团用之)餐厅; **'~-jacket** *n* (uniform) jacket worn at ~. 军官开饭时所穿的一种短上衣; 用燕尾服或制服。 **'~-mate** *n* member of the same ~ (esp a ship's ~ in the Navy). 在同一伙食团用饭的人(尤指在海军军舰上者)。 □ *vi* **~ together,** eat meals. 与某人共餐; 会餐。 *The five young men ~ together.* 那五个青年在一起吃饭。 **'~ing allowance** *n* money allowed (in the Armed Forces) for cost of meals in a ~. (军中)伙食津贴。

mess·age /'mesɪdʒ/; 'mesɪdʒ/ *n* 1 piece of news, or a request, sent to sb: 消息; 讯息: *Radio ~s told us that the ship was sinking.* 无线电报告诉我们那艘船在下沉中。 *Will you take this ~ to my brother?* 请把这消息带给我哥哥(弟弟)好吗? *Got the ~?* (sl) Have you understood? (俚)(你)懂了吗? 2 social, moral or religious teaching: 教训; 寓意; 宗教训示: *the ~ of Muhammad to his age.* 穆罕默德对他那个时代的启示。

mess·en·ger /'mesɪndʒə(r)/; 'mesɪndʒə/ *n* person carrying a message. 报信者; 信差。

Mess·iah /mɪ'saɪə/; mə'saɪə/ *n* person expected by the Jews to come and set them free; Jesus Christ considered as this. 弥赛亚(犹太人所期待的救主); 救世主; 耶稣基督。

Mess·ieurs /'mer'sjɜː(r)/; 'mesəz/ *n pl* of **monsieur.**

Messrs /'mesəz/; 'mesəz/ *n* (abbr of *Messieurs*) used as the *pl* of *Mr* before a list of men's names: (为 Messieurs 之略) Mr 的复数(用于一列男子姓名之前): *~ Smith, Brown and Robinson,* 史密斯, 布朗及鲁宾逊诸先生; and before names of business firms: 亦可用于公司行号之前: *~ T Brown & Co.* 布朗公司。

mes·suage /'meswɪdʒ/; 'meswɪdʒ/ *n* (legal) dwelling-house with the outbuildings and land that go with it. (法律)包括附属建筑与基地在内之住宅。

met /met/; met/ *pt, pp* of **meet.**

Met /met/; met/ *adj* (abbr of) Meteorological: 为 Meteorological 之略: *get the latest ~ report,* issued by the 'Met Office on the weather. 获得(气象局发布的)最新气象报告。

me·tab·olism /mɪ'tæbəlɪzəm/; mə'tæbḷɪzəm/ *n* [U] process by which food is built up into living matter or by which living matter is broken down into simple substances. 新陈代谢。 **meta·bolic** /metə'bɒlɪk/; metə-'bɒlɪk/ *adj* of ~. 新陈代谢的。

meta·car·pal /metə'kɑːpl/; metə'kɑrpḷ/ *adj, n* (anat) (of a) bone in the hand. (解剖)掌骨(的)。 ➪ the illus at **skeleton.** 参看 skeleton 之插图。

metal /'metl; 'metḷ/ *n* 1 [C] any of a class of mineral substances such as tin, iron, gold and copper: (某一种)金属(如锡、铁、金及铜等): *a worker in ~s.* 金属工人; 五金工人。 **'~-work** *n* artistic work in ~. 金属工艺; 五金工艺。 **'~-worker** *n* one who shapes objects in ~. 金属工人; 金属匠。 2 [U] one of these (as a material *n*): 金属(作物质名词用): *Is it made of wood or ~?* 它是木头还是金属做的? 3 [U] **('road-) ~,** (GB) broken stone used for making roads or the beds of railways. (英)铺马路或铁路路基所用的碎石。 4 *(pl)* railway-lines: (复)火车轨道: *The train left/jumped the ~s.* 火车离(脱)轨。 □ *vt* **(-ll-; US -l-)** [VP6A] make or repair a road with ~(3): 用碎石铺或修补道路: *~led roads;* 用碎石修补的道路; *a ~led road surface.* 用碎石修补的路面。

me·tal·lic /mɪ'tælɪk; mə'tælɪk/ *adj* of or like metal: 金属的; 似金属的: *a ~ currency,* ie with metal coins; 硬币; 金属钱币; *~ compounds;* 金属化合物; *~ sounds,* eg as made by brass objects struck together. 金属声音(例如铜器互击的声音)。

me·tal·lurgy /mɪ'tælədʒɪ US: 'metələːrdʒɪ; 'metḷ.ɜːdʒɪ/ *n* [U] science and technology of metals, eg of separating metal from ore, purifying it, and of working in metal. 冶金术; 冶金学。 **me·tal·lur·gist** /-dʒɪst; -dʒɪst/ *n* expert in ~. 冶金家。 **me·tal·lur·gi·cal** /metə'lɜːdʒɪkl; metḷ'ɜːdʒɪkḷ/ *adj* of ~. 冶金的; 冶金学的。

meta·mor·phose /metə'mɔːfəuz; metə'mɔrfoz/ *vt, vi* [VP6A, 14, 3A] **~ (sb/sth) (into),** change in form, change the nature of (as by sorcery): 使...变形; 使...变质: *Circe ~d the companions of Odysseus into swine.* 塞西把奥德赛的几个同伴都变成了猪。

meta·mor·pho·sis /metə'mɔːfəsɪs; metə'mɔrfə-sɪs/ *n* (*pl* **-oses** /-əsiːz; -ə,siz/) change of form or character, eg by natural growth or development: 变形; 变态; 变质(如因自然成长或发展者): *the ~ in the life of an insect,* from the egg, etc; 昆虫的蜕变; *social ~.* 社会变化。

meta·phor /'metəfə(r); 'metəfə/ *n* [C, U] (example of) the use of words to indicate sth different from the literal meaning, as in 'I'll make him *eat* his words' or 'He has a heart of *stone*'. 隐喻(之例); 暗喻(之例)(用言词表示与其字面意义不同之某事物, 例如 I'll make him eat his words 中的 eat, 或 He has a heart of stone 中的 of stone)。 Cf 参较 *simile:* 明喻: 'a heart *like stone*'. **~·i·cal** /metə'fɒrɪkl US: -'fɔːr-; metə'fɔrɪkḷ/ *adj* of or like a ~; containing or using ~s. 隐喻的; 似隐喻的; 含有隐喻的; 用隐喻的。 **~·i·cally** /-klɪ; -klɪ/ *adv*

meta·phys·ics /metə'fɪzɪks; metə'fɪzɪks/ *n* (with *sing v*) (用单数动词语) 1 branch of philosophy dealing with the nature of existence, truth and knowledge: 形而上学; 玄学: *M~ deals with abstractions.* 玄学讨论抽象的概念。 *Do we need a new ~?* 我们需要一个新的玄学吗? (Note: on the analogy of French and German, *metaphysic* is sometimes used, meaning 'system of ~'). (注: 依法语及德语类推, 此字有时写作 metaphysic, 意指'玄学体系')。 2 (pop use) speculative philosophy; abstract talk. (通俗用法)思辨哲学; 空泛的理论; 空谈。 **meta·phys·ical** /metə'fɪzɪkl; metə'fɪzɪkḷ/ *adj* of ~; based on abstract reasoning. 玄学的; 形而上学的; 根据抽象推理的。

meta·tar·sal /metə'tɑːsl; metə'tɑrsəl/ *adj, n* (anat) (of a) bone in the foot. (解剖)蹠骨(的)。 ➪ the illus at **skeleton.** 参看 skeleton 之插图。

mete /miːt; miːt/ *vt* [VP15B] **~ out,** portion or measure: 分配; 衡量: *~ out rewards/punishments.* 给予报酬(处以刑罚)。 *Justice was ~d out to them.* 他们受到公平的赏罚。

me·teor /'miːtɪə(r); 'miːtɪə/ *n* [C] small particle of matter that enters the earth's atmosphere from outer

space and becomes bright (as a *'shooting star'* or *'falling star'*) in the night sky as it is burnt up. 流星; 陨星.

me·teor·ic /ˌmiːtɪˈɒrɪk US: -ˈɔːr-; ˌmitiˈɔrik/ *adj* **1** of the atmosphere or of atmospheric conditions; of meteors. 大气的; 大气状况的; 流(陨)星的. **2** (fig) brilliant but brief: (喻)光辉但短暂的: *a ~ career*. 昙花一现的事业.

me·teor·ite /ˈmiːtɪəraɪt; ˈmitiəˌraɪt/ *n* [C] fallen meteor; fragment of rock or metal that has reached the earth's surface from outer space. 陨石.

me·teor·ol·ogy /ˌmiːtɪəˈrɒlədʒɪ; ˌmitiəˈralədʒɪ/ *n* [U] science of the weather; study of the earth's atmosphere and its changes. 气象学. **me·teor·ol·ogist** /ˌmiːtɪəˈrɒlədʒɪst; ˌmitiəˈralədʒɪst/ *n* expert in ~. 气象学家. **me·teoro·logi·cal** /ˌmiːtɪərəˈlɒdʒɪkl US: ˌmiːtɪɔːr-; ˌmitiərəˈladʒɪkl/ *adj* of ~: 气象(学)的: *weather forecasts from the Central Meteorological Office*, 中央气象局的天气预报.

me·ter[1] /ˈmiːtə(r); ˈmitɚ/ *n* [C] apparatus which measures, esp one that records the amount of whatever passes through it, or the distance travelled, fare payable, etc: 计量器; 仪表(尤指记录所通过之物的数量、行走之路程或应付之车费等者): *an ˌelec'tricity-~*, 电表; *a 'gas-~*; 煤气表; *a 'water-~*; (自来水)水表; *an ex'posure-~*, for measuring the time needed for exposure of photographic film, etc; (照相用)曝光表; *a 'parking-~*, one that measures the time during which a car is (for a fee) parked in a public place; 停车计时表(设置于公共场所用以计量停车时间,以收取停车费); *fares mounting up on the ~*, eg of a taxi-cab. (如计程车之)车上累积之费用.

an electricity meter　　　　**a metronome**

me·ter[2] /ˈmiːtə(r); ˈmitɚ/ *n* (US) = metre.

meth·ane /ˈmiːθeɪn; ˈmɛθen/ *n* [U] odourless, colourless inflammable gas (CH₄) that occurs in coalmines (as fire damp, causing explosions) and (as natural gas, marsh gas) on marshy areas. 甲烷; 沼气(煤矿中及沼泽地区之一种无臭、无色、可燃之气体,化学符号为 CH₄).

me·thinks /mɪˈθɪŋks; mɪˈθɪŋks/ *vi* (*pt* **methought** /mɪˈθɔːt; mɪˈθɔt/) (old use) it seems to me. (旧用法)据我看来;我以为.

method /ˈmeθəd; ˈmɛθəd/ *n* **1** [U] system(3), orderliness: 规律;秩序: *He's a man of ~*. 他是个有条理的人. *There's ~ in his madness*, His behaviour, etc is not so unreasonable as it seems. 他表面虽疯狂,实并有理性. **2** [C] way of doing sth: 方法;办法: *modern ~s of teaching arithmetic*; 现代教算术的方法; *~s of payment*, eg cash, cheques, monthly instalments. 付款办法(如现金、支票、按月分期付款等). **~·i·cal** /mɪˈθɒdɪkl; məˈθɑdɪkl/ *adj* **1** done, carried out, with order or ~: 按次序做成的; 有条理的: *~ical work*. 井然有序的工作; 按部就班所完成的工作. **2** doing things with ~; having orderly habits: 做事有条理或有次序的人; having regular habits: 有条不紊的工人. **~·i·cally** /-klɪ; -klɪ/ *adv* **~·ol·ogy** /ˌmeθəˈdɒlədʒɪ; ˌmɛθədˈɑlɑdʒɪ/ *n* [U] science or study of ~; [C] set of ~s used in working at sth. 方法学;研究法;一套方法.

Meth·od·ism /ˈmeθədɪzəm; ˈmɛθədˌɪzm/ *n* teaching,

organization and manner of worship in the Christian denomination deriving from John Wesley. 卫理公会; 美以美会(约翰卫理所创的一种基督教教派); 卫理公会的教义、组织及礼拜方式. **Meth·od·ist** /-ɪst; -ɪst/ *n, adj* (member) of this denomination. 卫理公会的; 卫理公会教友(信徒). ⇨ **Wesleyan**.

me·thought /mɪˈθɔːt; mɪˈθɔt/ *pt* of **methinks**.

meths /meθs; mɛθs/ *n pl* (colloq abbr for) **methylated spirits**. (口)= methylated spirits 之缩.

Me·thuse·lah /mɪˈθjuːzələ; məˈθjuzlə/ *n* (in the Bible) man stated to have lived 969 years; (hence) man who lives to a great age. 玛土撒拉(圣经中所述享年高 969 岁的老人); (由此产生)长寿的人; 人瑞. ⇨ **Gen 5: 27**. 参看旧约圣经创世纪 5 章 27 节.

methyl /ˈmeθɪl; ˈmɛθəl/ *n* ~ **alcohol**, kind of alcohol (also called 亦称作 *wood spirit*) present in many organic compounds. 甲醇. **'~·ated** /-eɪtɪd; -ɛtɪd/ *adj* ~**ated spirit(s)**, [U] form of alcohol (made unfit for drinking) used for lighting and heating. 含甲醇酒精 (不适于饮用,仅用作燃料).

me·ticu·lous /mɪˈtɪkjuləs; məˈtɪkjələs/ *adj* ~ (*in*), giving, showing, great attention to detail; careful and exact. 极注意细节的; 仔细的; 精确的. **~·ly** *adv*

mé·tier /ˈmeɪtɪeɪ; meˈtje/ *n* one's trade, profession or line of business. 职业; 专业; 行业.

metre[1] (US = **me·ter**) /ˈmiːtə(r); ˈmitɚ/ *n* unit of length in the metric system. 公尺; 米. ⇨ **App 5**. 参看附录五.

metre[2] (US = **me·ter**) /ˈmiːtə(r); ˈmitɚ/ *n* [U] verse rhythm; [C] particular form of this; fixed arrangement of accented and unaccented syllables. (诗的)韵律; 某种的韵律形式; 步格(重音节与非重音节之一定的排列方式).

met·ric /ˈmetrɪk; ˈmɛtrɪk/ *adj* of the metre[1]: 公尺的; 米制的: **the '~ system**, the decimal measuring system based on the metre as the unit of length, the kilogram as the unit of mass and the litre as the unit of capacity. 十进制; 公制(十进法的度量衡制,以米为长度单位,公斤为重量单位,公升为容量单位). ~ **ton**, 1000 kilograms. 公吨(等于 1000公斤). **met·ri·cize** /ˈmetrɪsaɪz; ˈmɛtrɪˌsaɪz/ *vt* convert to the ~ system. 将…改为十进制; 使变为公制.

metri·cal /ˈmetrɪkl; ˈmɛtrɪkl/ *adj* **1** of, composed in, metre[2] (contrasted with ordinary prose): 韵律的; 有韵律的; 诗体的(与'普通散文'相对): *a ~ translation of the Iliad*. 伊里亚特的诗体译本. **2** connected with measurement: 测量的: *~ geometry*. 测量几何. **~·ly** /-klɪ; -klɪ/ *adv*

metri·ca·tion /ˌmetrɪˈkeɪʃn; ˌmɛtrɪˈkeʃən/ *n* conversion to the metric system. 十进化; 公制化.

Metro /ˈmetrəʊ; ˈmɛtro/ *n* (**the**) ~, the underground railway system in Paris. 巴黎的地下铁路系统. Cf 参较 in London, 伦敦的 *Underground* or *tube*.

met·ro·nome /ˈmetrənəʊm; ˈmɛtrəˌnom/ *n* (music) graduated inverted pendulum for sounding an adjustable number of beats per minute. (音乐)节拍器; 节奏器(有刻度的倒置的摆杆,摆动而每项分钟的节拍数,节拍数可调整). ⇨ the illus at **meter**. 参看 meter 之插图.

me·trop·olis /məˈtrɒpəlɪs; məˈtrɑplɪs/ *n* (*pl* ~**es**) chief city of a country; capital; 大城市; 大都会; 首府; (in GB) (在英国) *the* ~, London. 伦敦.

metro·poli·tan /ˌmetrəˈpɒlɪtən; ˌmɛtrəˈpɑlətn/ *adj* **1** of or in a capital city: 大城市的; 大都会(市)的; 首府的: *the ~ po'lice*. 首都警察. **2** of an ecclesiastical province. 大主教教区的. ~ **bishop**, one (usu an archbishop) having authority over the bishops in his province. 总主教(在其教区中有权管辖各主教者,通常为大主教). **3** M~ **France**, France itself as distinct from its dependencies overseas. 法国本土(即海外属地). □ *n* **1** person who lives in a metropolis. 大都市之居民. **2** M~, ~ **bishop**. 总主教; 大主教.

mettle /ˈmetl; ˈmɛtl/ *n* [U] quality, eg in persons,

horses, of endurance and courage: (人、马等之)忍耐力;
勇气: *a man of ~*; 有勇气的人; *a horse that is full of
~*; 精力充沛的马; *try sb's ~*, test his quality. 考验
某人的耐力或勇气. *be on one's ~*; *put sb on his ~*,
rouse oneself/him to do one's/his best, put oneself/
him in a position that tests one's/his ~. (使某人)奋发
起来; (使某人)鼓起勇气. '**~·some** /-səm; -səm/ *adj*
high-spirited. 有精神的; 勇敢的.

mew /mjuː; mju/ *n* (also 亦作 *miaow*) sound made by
a cat or a seabird. 猫或海鸟叫的声音; 咪咪; 喵喵. □
vi [VP2A] make this sound: 发此种的声音; 咪咪叫; 喵
喵地叫: *We heard the mewing of a cat.* 我们听到猫在咪
咪叫.

mews /mjuːz; mjuz/ *n* (with *sing v*) (old use) square
or street of stables behind a residential street; (modern
use) such stables rebuilt for use as garages or converted
into flats, etc. (用单数动词)(旧用法)住宅街后面的一圈
或一排马厩; (现代用法)由此类马厩改建而成之车房、公寓
等: *living in a Chelsea ~*. 住在契尔西由马厩改建成的
公寓里.

mezza·nine /'mezəniːn; 'mezə,nin/ *n*, *adj* (floor)
between ground floor and first floor, often in the form
of a balcony. 中楼(介于一楼与二楼之间, 通常为阳台形
式); 中楼的.

mezzo /'metsəu; 'metso/ *adv* (musical direction)
moderately; half: (乐谱说明)适中; 半: *~ forte*, moderately loud. 中强. **~·so·prano** /,metsəusə'prɑːnəu
US: -'præn-; ,metsəsə'præno/ *n* (person with, part for
a) voice between soprano and contralto. 次高音; 女中
音; 唱次高音或女中音的人; 次高音部; 女中音部.

mezzo·tint /'metsəutɪnt; 'metsə,tɪnt/ *n* [C, U]
(print produced by a) method of printing from a metal
plate which has a rough surface of small dots scraped
and polished to produce areas of light and shade. 金属
版印刷术; 金属版所印成之印刷品.

mi, mi /miː; mi/ *n* third note in the musical octave.
全音阶的第三音.

mi·aou, mi·aow /miːˈaʊ; mɪˈaʊ/ *n*, *vi* = **mew**.

mi·asma /mɪˈæzmə; maɪˈæzmə/ *n* unhealthy mist
rising from the ground; (fig) unhealthy environment
or influence. 瘴气(一种有害于健康的雾气); (喻)不健康
的环境或影响.

mica /'maɪkə; 'maɪkə/ *n* [U] transparent mineral
substance easily divided into thin layers, used as an
electrical insulator, etc. 云母(一种易分为薄片的透明矿
物, 用作电器的绝缘体等).

mice /maɪs; maɪs/ *n pl* of **mouse**.

Michael·mas /'mɪklməs; 'mɪklməs/ *n* 29 Sept, the
feast of St Michael. 米迦勒节(九月廿九日, 天使长米迦
勒之节日). ,**~ 'daisy**, perennial aster flowering in
autumn, with blue, white, pink or purple flowers. 紫
菀(多年生的园艺植物, 秋季开蓝、白、粉红或紫色的花).

mickey /'mɪkɪ; 'mɪkɪ/ *n take the ~ (out of sb)*,
(sl) hold (him) up to ridicule; mock or tease (him).
(俚)使某人显得可笑; 嘲笑某人; 揶揄某人.

mickle /'mɪkl; 'mɪkl/ (also 亦作 **muckle** /'mʌkl;
'mʌkl/) *n* (Scot) large amount: (苏)大量: *Many a
little makes a ~*. 积少成多; 聚沙成塔.

microbe /'maɪkrəub; 'maɪkrob/ *n* tiny living creature that can be seen only with the help of a microscope,
esp kinds of bacteria causing diseases and fermentation.
微生物; 细菌; 酵母菌.

micro·bi·ol·ogy /,maɪkrəubaɪˈɒlədʒɪ; ,maɪkrobaɪ-
'ɑlədʒɪ/ *n* [U] study of micro-organisms. 微生物学.

micro·chip /'maɪkrəutʃɪp; 'maɪkrotʃɪp/ *n* chip used
in an integrated circuit. 微集成电路. ⇨ **integrate**(1).

micro·cosm /'maɪkrəukɒzəm; 'maɪkrə,kazəm/ *n*
[C] sth, (esp man, by the ancient philosophers)
considered as representing (on a small scale) mankind
or the universe; miniature representation of a system,
etc). 微观世界; 微观宇宙; (被古哲学家认作)代表人类或
宇宙之缩影的某物(尤指人); (制度, 系统等之)缩图(与

of 连用). ⇨ **macrocosm**.

micro·dot /'maɪkrəudɒt; 'maɪkrədat/ *n* photograph
reduced to the size of a dot. 微粒照片(缩小至微粒大小
的相片).

micro·elec·tron·ics /,maɪkrəuɪˌlekˈtrɒnɪks; ,maɪ-
kroɪˌlekˈtrɑnɪks/ *n* (with *sing v*) design, construction
and use of devices with extremely small (usu solid
state) components. (用单数动词)微电子学.

micro·fiche /'maɪkrəufiːʃ; 'maɪkrofiʃ/ *n* [C, U]
sheet of microfilm. 缩微胶片; 一张缩影胶片.

micro·film /'maɪkrəufɪlm; 'maɪkrə,fɪlm/ *n* [C, U]
(roll, section, of) photographic film for small-scale
reproduction of documentary material, etc. 缩微胶卷;
缩微照片; 缩影胶片(用于缩小摄制文件、书籍等); 一卷或
一段缩影胶片. □ *vt* [VP6A] photograph in this way:
用缩微法摄制; 缩小摄制; 将…摄成缩影胶片: *~ old
historical records/bank accounts*. 将旧日历史纪录(银
行帐目)摄制成缩影胶片.

mi·crom·eter /maɪˈkrɒmɪtə(r); maɪˈkrɑmətə/ *n*
device for measuring very small objects. 测微器(测量
极小物体的仪器); 测微表; 测微计.

mi·cron /'maɪkrɒn; 'maɪkrɑn/ *n* unit of length
(symbol μ) equal to one millionth of a metre. 微米(长
度单位, 符号μ, 等于百万分之一米).

micro·or·gan·ism /,maɪkrəuˈɔːɡənɪzəm; ,maɪkro-
'ɔrɡənˌɪzəm/ *n* organism so small as to be visible only
under a microscope. (仅在显微镜下才看得见的)微生物.

micro·phone /'maɪkrəfəun; 'maɪkrə,fon/ *n* instrument for changing sound waves into electrical current,
as in telephones, radio, etc. 扩音器; 麦克风(将音波化
作电波之器具, 如电话、无线电等所装置者).

a microphone   a microscope

micro·pro·ces·sor /,maɪkrəuˈprəusesə(r); ,maɪkro-
'prɑsɛsɚ/ *n* (comp) type of integrated circuit used
in a computer. (电脑)(电子计算机中之)微处理机. ⇨
integrate(1).

micro·scope /'maɪkrəskəup; 'maɪkrə,skop/ *n* instrument with lenses for making very small near
objects appear larger: 显微镜: *examine sth under
the ~*. 在显微镜下检查某物. **micro·scopic** /,maɪkrə-
'skɒpɪk; ,maɪkrə'skɑpɪk/, **micro·scopi·cal** /-kl; -kl/
adj of the ~; too small to be visible except under a
~. 显微镜的; 须用显微镜方能看见的; 极微小的. **micro·
scopi·cally** /-klɪ; -klɪ/ *adv*

micro·wave /'maɪkrəuweɪv; 'maɪkrə,wev/ *n* very
short wave (as used in radio and radar). 微波(如无线
电与雷达所用者).

mid[1] /mɪd; mɪd/ *adj* **1** in the middle of; 在…中间的:
from mid June to mid August; 从六月中旬到八月中
旬; *in mid winter*, 在仲冬时节; *a collision in mid
Channel/in mid air*. 在英伦海峡中部(在半空中)相撞.
2 (in compounds used attrib): (在作定语的复合词中):
a midwinter day; 仲冬的一日; *mid-morning coffee*. (上
午十时左右的)午前咖啡. **the ,Mid·west**, (also known
as 亦通称为 the ,Middle 'West) that part of the US
which is the Mississippi basin as far south as Kansas,
Missouri and the Ohio River. (美国之)中西部(指包括
密西西比河流域南至堪萨斯州、密苏里州及俄亥俄河之地
区). **3** (cricket) (板球) **mid·'off**, **mid·'on**, fielder near
the bowler on the off, on, side. 在投手左侧右侧的
外场员. ⇨ the illus at **cricket**. 参看 cricket 之插图.

mid·most /'mɪdməʊst; 'mɪd,most/ *adj, adv* (*superl* of **mid**) (that is) in the very middle. (mid 的最高级)正中的(地);正中央的(地)。

mid² /mɪd; mɪd/ *prep* (poet) amid; among. (诗)在…中。

mid·day /,mɪd'deɪ; 'mɪd,de/ *n* noon: 中午: (attrib) (用作定语) *the ~ meal*, ie lunch. 午餐。

mid·den /'mɪdn; 'mɪdn/ *n* heap of dung or rubbish. 粪堆;垃圾堆。

middle /'mɪdl; 'mɪdl/ *n* **1 the ~**, point, position or part, which is at an equal distance from two or more points, etc or between beginning and end: 中间; 中央: *the ~ of a room*; 房间的中央; *in the ~ of the century*; 在这世纪的中叶; *in the very ~ of the night*; 就在午夜的时候; *standing in the ~ of the street*; 站在街的中央; *a pain in the ~ of the back*. 在后背当中部分的疼痛。*They were in the ~ of dinner* (= were having dinner) *when I called*. 我去拜访他们的时候,他们正在吃饭。*I was in the ~ of reading* (= was busy reading) *when she telephoned*. 她打电话来的时候,我正在读书。**,~-of-the-'road,** (attrib) (of policies, etc) avoiding extremes. (用作定语)(指政策等)中间路线的;不走极端的。**2** (colloq) waist: (口)腰部: *seize sb round the ~*; 拦腰抱住某人; *fifty inches round the ~*. 腰围五十英寸。**3** (attrib use) in the ~: (用作定语)在中间的: *the ~ house in the row*. 居于这一排当中的房子。**,~ 'age,** the period of life between youth and old age. 中年。Hence, 由此产生, **,~-'aged** /-'eɪdʒd; -'edʒd/ *adj* of ~ age: 中年的: *a ~-aged woman*. 中年妇人。**,~-age(d) 'spread,** (colloq) corpulence that tends to come with ~ age. (口)中年发胖。**the ,M~ 'Ages,** the period (in European history) from about AD 1100 to 1500. (欧洲史上之)中世纪 (约自公元一〇〇年至一五〇〇年之期间)。**,~ 'class,** class of society between the lower and upper classes (eg shopkeepers, business men, professional workers). 中产阶级 (例如店主、商人、专业人员等)。Hence, 由此产生, **,~-'class** *adj* of this class: 中产阶级的;中层社会的: *a ~-class residential area*. 中层社会住宅区。**(take / follow) a ~ course,** a compromise between two extreme courses of action). (采)中间路线; (取)中庸之道。**the ,~ 'distance,** that part of a landscape, scene, painting, etc between the foreground and the background. 中距离; 中景(风景、场面、绘画等中介于前景与背景间之部分)。**the ,~ 'ear,** hollow space of the central part of the ear, in front of the eardrum. 中耳。⇨ the illus at **ear**. 参看 ear 之插图。**the ,M~ 'East,** ⇨ **East**. **,~ 'finger,** the second. 中指。**'~-man** /-mæn; -mæn/ *n* (*pl* **-men**) any trader through whose hands goods pass between the producer and the consumer. 中间人(货品经其手由生产者传至消费者的中间之人);经纪人。**,~ 'name,** second of two given names, eg *Bernard* in *George Bernard Shaw*. 教名或所取名字中之第二个名字 (如 George Bernard Shaw 中的 Bernard)。**'~ school,** (in some countries) type of school between elementary school and high school. (某些国家的)初中。**the ,~ 'watch,** (on ships) between midnight and 4am. (船上)夜半值班; 夜半更(自午夜至上午四时)。**'~-weight,** (esp) boxer weighing between 147 and 160 lb or (66.6 to 72.5 kg). 中量级; (尤指)中量级拳击手(体重在 147 至 160 磅之间, 或 66.6 至 72.5 公斤之间)。**the ,M~ 'West,** ⇨ *Midwest* at **mid¹(2)**.

mid·dling /'mɪdlɪŋ; 'mɪdlɪŋ/ *adj* of middle or medium size, quality, grade, etc: (大小、品质、等级等)中等的;普通的: *a town of ~ size*. 中型市镇。*He says he's feeling only ~* (often refer **fair to ~**), (colloq) in fairly good but not very good health. (口)他说他的健康还过得去(但并不是顶好)。□ *adv* (colloq) moderately: (口)中等地; 略为; 颇为: *~ tall*. 颇高的。□ *n* (usu *pl*) goods of second or inferior quality, esp coarse-ground wheat flour mixed with bran. (通常用复数)二等货; 次

等货;(尤指)混有麦麸的粗面粉。

middy /'mɪdɪ; 'mɪdɪ/ *n* (*pl* **-dies**) (colloq abbr of) midshipman. (口)= midshipman 之略。**'~ blouse,** loose blouse like that worn by naval seamen. 水兵式的宽外衣。

midge /mɪdʒ; mɪdʒ/ *n* small winged insect like a gnat. 蚊蚋之类的小昆虫; 摇蚊。

midget /'mɪdʒɪt; 'mɪdʒɪt/ *n* extremely small person, eg one exhibited as a curiosity at a circus; (attrib) very small: 侏儒; 矮人(例如马戏班展出者); (用作定语)极小的: *a ~ submarine*. 极小型潜艇。

midi·nette /,mɪdɪ'net; ,mɪdɪ'nɛt/ *n* Parisian shop-assistant, esp a milliner's assistant. 巴黎店员(尤指女帽店的店员)。

mid·land /'mɪdlənd; 'mɪdlənd/ *n* (often attrib) middle part of a country. (常用作定语)一国的中部。**the M~s,** the ~ counties of England. 英格兰中部诸郡。

mid·night /'mɪdnaɪt; 'mɪd,naɪt/ *n* **1** 12 o'clock at night: 午夜; 子夜; 夜半: *at / before / after ~*. 在午夜(在午夜前, 在午夜后)。**2** (attrib) during the middle of the night; at ~: (用作定语)在午夜的; 在夜半的: *the ~ hours*. 午夜时分; 午夜的那几小时。**burn the ~ oil,** sit up and work late at night. 工作到深夜; 焚膏继晷。*the ~ sun,* the sun as seen at ~ in summer within the Arctic or Antarctic Circle. (北极圈及南极圈内夏季所见到的)午夜太阳。

mid·riff /'mɪdrɪf; 'mɪdrɪf/ *n* **1** (anat) diaphragm. (解剖)横隔膜。**2** abdomen, belly: 腹部; 肚子: (boxing) (拳击)对腹部的一击。对腹部的一击。

mid·ship·man /'mɪdʃɪpmæn; 'mɪd,ʃɪpmən/ *n* (*pl* **-men**) non-commissioned officer ranking below a sublieutenant in the Royal Navy; student training to be commissioned as an officer in the US Navy. 英国皇家海军中军阶低于尉官的非委任军官; (美)海军学校见习生。

mid·ships /'mɪdʃɪps; 'mɪd,ʃɪps/ *adv* = **amidships**.

midst /mɪdst; mɪdst/ *n* (liter or archaic) middle part: (文或古)中部; 中间: *in / into / from / out of the ~ (of)*; 在(到, 从, 从)(…的)中间; *in our / your / their ~*, among, with us etc. 在我们(你们, 他们)中间。□ *prep* (liter or archaic) in the middle of; amidst. (文或古)在…中间;在…之间。

mid·stream /,mɪd'striːm; ,mɪd'strɪm/ *n* [U] the part of a stream, river, etc away from both its banks. 中流。*in ~*, in the middle of the action, event, etc. 在进行中。

mid·sum·mer /,mɪd'sʌmə(r); 'mɪd'sʌmɚ/ *n* [U] period about 21 June. 仲夏(六月廿一日左右之期间)。**,M~ 'day,** 24 June. 仲夏结帐日(六月廿四日)。**'~-madness,** the height of madness. 极度疯狂。

mid·way /,mɪd'weɪ; 'mɪd'we/ *adj, adv* (**between**), situated in the middle; halfway. 位于中间的; 在中途的(地)。

mid·wife /'mɪdwaɪf; 'mɪd,waɪf/ *n* (*pl* **midwives** /-waɪvz; -,waɪvz/) woman trained to help women in childbirth. 助产士; 接生婆。**mid·wifery** /'mɪdwɪfrɪ; 'mɪd,waɪfərɪ/ *n* [U] profession and work of a ~; obstetrics: 助产士之职; 助产学; 产科学: *take a course in ~ry*. 选助产学课程。

mien /miːn; min/ *n* (liter) person's appearance or bearing (as showing a mood, etc): (文)仪表; 态度; 风采; 样子; 神态: *with a sorrowful ~*; 带着忧伤的神色; *of pleasing ~*; 有惹人喜欢的仪表的; *the severity of his ~*. 他严肃的态度。

might¹ /maɪt; maɪt/ *pt* of **may**.

might² /maɪt; maɪt/ *n* [U] great power; strength: 强权; 权力; 力气: *work with all one's ~*; 尽全力工作; *'M~ is right', he said,* ie Having power to enforce one's will gives one the right to do so. 他说: '强权即公理.' *with ~ and main,* using all one's physical force. 倾全力;竭尽体力。

mighty /'maɪtɪ ; 'maɪtɪ/ adj (**-ier, -iest**) **1** (liter, biblical) powerful: (文,圣经)强而有力的; 强大的: a ~ nation. 强大的国家. **2** great; massive: 伟大的; 巨大的: the ~ ocean. 浩大的海洋. **high and ~**, very proud. 非常骄傲的. □ adv (colloq) very: (口)很; 非常: think oneself ~ clever. 认为自己很聪明. **'might·ily** /-lɪ; -ɪlɪ/ adv greatly; (dated colloq) extremely: 非常地; (过时口语)极其; 极端地: mightily indignant. 极为气愤的.

mignon·ette /ˌmɪnjə'net; ˌmɪnjən'ɛt/ n [U] garden plant with small, sweet-smelling, greenish-white flowers. 木犀草(园艺植物,开绿白色的芳香小花).

mi·graine /'miːɡreɪn; 'maɪɡren/ n severe, frequently recurring, headache (usu on one side only of the head or face), often accompanied by nausea. 偏头痛.

mi·grant /'maɪɡrənt; 'maɪɡrənt/ n one who migrates, esp a bird: 移居者; (尤指)候鸟: Swallows are ~s. 燕子是候鸟. **~ labour**, that available in a country from (short-term) immigrants. (短期)移民之劳工.

mi·grate /maɪ'ɡreɪt US: 'maɪɡreɪt; 'maɪɡret/ vi [VP2A, 3A] **~ (from/to)**, **1** move from one place to another (to live there). 迁移; 迁居; 移往. **2** (of birds and fishes) come and go with the season; travel regularly from one region to another. (指鸟,鱼)随季节之转换而移栖; 定期移栖. **migra·tion** /maɪ'ɡreɪʃn; maɪ'ɡreʃən/ n [U] migrating; [C] instance of this; [C] number of persons, animals, etc migrating together. 迁移; 移动; 候鸟; 移栖; 成群移栖的人或动物. **mi·gra·tory** /'maɪɡrətrɪ US: -tɔːrɪ; 'maɪɡrə,tɔrɪ/ adj having the habit of migrating: 有迁移习惯的; 流动的; 漂泊的: migratory birds. 候鸟.

mi·kado /mɪ'kɑːdəʊ; mə'kɑdo/ n (name formerly used outside, but not inside, Japan for) Emperor of Japan. 日本天皇(原为外国人给日本天皇所取的名称, 日本人不用这名词).

mike /maɪk; maɪk/ n (colloq abbr for) **microphone**. (口)microphone之略.

mi·lady /mɪ'leɪdɪ; mɪ'ledɪ/ n (pl **-dies**) (dated form of address to a) lady. (过时的称呼)上流妇女; 贵妇; 女士; 夫人. Cf 参较 current use 现今用之 My Lady.

mi·lage /'maɪlɪdʒ; 'maɪlɪdʒ/ n = **mileage**.

milch /mɪltʃ; mɪltʃ/ adj (of domestic mammals) kept for, giving, milk: (指家畜)为取乳而饲养的; 产乳的: '~ cows. 乳牛.

mild /maɪld; maɪld/ adj (**-er, -est**) **1** soft; gentle; not severe: 温和的; 温柔的; 有节制的; 不严厉的: ~ weather; 温和的天气; ~ punishments; 轻微的惩罚; a ~ answer. 温和的回答. I'm the ~est man alive, No one is gentler, than I am. 我是世上最和善的人. **2** (of food, drink, tobacco) not sharp or strong in taste or flavour: (指食物,酒类,烟草)味道或气味不浓的; 不强烈的; 淡的; 酯味的: ~ cheese; 清淡的乳酪; a ~ cigar; 淡而顺口的雪茄; ~ (ale) and bitter, ~ and bitter beer mixed. 淡色啤酒与苦味啤酒混合起来的啤酒. **draw it** ~, ⇨ **draw²(4)**. **3** ~ **steel**, tough and malleable, with a low percentage of carbon. 软钢(坚韧可锻, 含碳之百分比低). **~·ly** adv in a ~ manner. 温和地. **to put it** ~**ly**, to say the least of it, to speak without exaggeration. 稳妥地说; 委婉地说. **~·ness** n

mil·dew /'mɪldjuː US: -duː; 'mɪl,dju/ n [U] (usu destructive) growth of tiny fungi forming on plants, leather, food, etc in warm and damp conditions: (通常指破坏性的)霉; 霉病: roses ruined by ~. 给霉菌弄死了的玫瑰. □ vt, vi [VP6A, 2A] affect, become affected, with ~. 使发霉; 发霉.

mile /maɪl; maɪl/ n measure of distance, 1760 yards: 英里; (合1760码): For ~s and ~s there's nothing but desert. 一连许多英里, 除了沙漠以外, 什么也没有. It's a 30 ~/a 30 ~s' journey. 那是一个长达三十英里的行程. He ran the ~ in 4 minutes/a 4-minute ~. 他

四分钟跑完了一英里. She's feeling ~s better today, (colloq) very much better. (口)她今天觉得好得多了. There's no one within ~s of him as a tennis player, no one who can rival him. 没有人网球打得比他好. ⇨ **nautical**; ⇨ **App 5**. 参看附录五. **~·om·eter** /maɪ'lɒmɪtə(r); maɪ'lɑmɪtɚ/ n device (in a motor-vehicle) recording the number of ~s travelled. (汽车等的)哩程表. **'~·stone** n (a) stone set up at the side of a road showing distances. (立于路边示明路程的)哩程标; 里程碑. (b) (fig) (important) stage or event in history or in human life. (喻)历史上或人生的(重要)阶段或事件.

mile·age /'maɪlɪdʒ; 'maɪlɪdʒ/ n **1** distance travelled, measured in miles: 英里数; 里程: a used car with a small ~, one that has not run many miles. 还没有跑多少英里的旧汽车. **2** allowance for travelling expenses at so much a mile. 按英里计算的旅费津贴.

miler /'maɪlə(r); 'maɪlɚ/ n (colloq) runner specializing in one mile races: (口)专长于一英里赛跑的人(或马): He's our best ~. 他是我们之中最擅长一英里赛跑的人.

mi·lieu /'miːljə US: ˌmiː'ljə; the ə: having no r quality 此 ə: 无 r 音; mi'ljə/ n environment; social surroundings. 环境; 社会环境.

mili·tant /'mɪlɪtənt; 'mɪlətənt/ adj ready for fighting; actively engaged in or supporting the use of force or strong pressure: 好战的; 积极从事使用武力的; 支持武力之使用的; 尚武的: ~ students/workers. 好战的学生(工人). □ n ~ person, eg in trade unionism, politics. 好战者; 好战份子(如在工会主义,政治等方面者). **'mili·tancy** /-tənsɪ; -ənsɪ/ n

mili·tar·ism /'mɪlɪtərɪzəm; 'mɪlətə,rɪzəm/ n [U] belief in, reliance upon, military strength and virtues. 军国主义; 黩武主义; 尚武精神. **mili·tar·ist** /'mɪlɪtərɪst; 'mɪlətərɪst/ n supporter of, believer in ~. 军国主义者; 黩武主义者. **mili·tar·istic** /ˌmɪlɪtə'rɪstɪk; ˌmɪlətə-'rɪstɪk/ adj

mili·tary /'mɪlɪtrɪ US: -terɪ; 'mɪlə,terɪ/ adj of or for soldiers, an army; or for or by all the armed forces: 军人的; 军用的; 陆军的; 军事的; 军队的: in ~ uniform, 穿军服的; ~ government; 军政府; called up for ~ service, eg to train or serve as a soldier. 被征召受军训或服兵役. □ n [U] (with sing or pl v) (与单数或复数动词连用) **the ~**, the soldiers; the army; the armed forces: 军人; 陆军; 军队; 军力: The ~ were called in to deal with the rioting. 军队被调来应付暴乱.

mili·tate /'mɪlɪteɪt; 'mɪlə,tet/ vi [VP3A] **~ against**, (of evidence, facts) have force, power: (指证据,事实)…发生影响; 起作用; 妨碍: Several factors combined to ~ against the success of our plan. 若干因素合在一起妨碍了我们计划的成功.

mil·itia /mɪ'lɪʃə; mə'lɪʃə/ n (usu 通常用 **the ~**) force of civilians trained as soldiers but not part of the regular army. 国民自卫队; 民团. **~·man** /-mən; -mən/ n (pl **-men**) member of the ~. 国民自卫队队员; 民兵.

milk¹ /mɪlk; mɪlk/ n [U] **1** white liquid produced by female mammals as food for their young, esp that of cows, drunk by human beings and made into butter and cheese: 乳; 奶; (尤指)牛奶: ~ fresh from the cow; 刚从母牛挤出来的鲜奶; tinned ~, 罐装牛奶; ~ puddings, eg rice, sago or tapioca baked with ~ in a dish. 牛奶布丁(由牛奶与米, 西米或椰木薯淀粉烤制而成). **the ~ of human kindness**, that should be natural to human beings. 人类本性中的仁慈; 天生的恻隐之心. It's no use crying over spilt ~, over a loss or error for which there is no remedy. 覆水难收, 悔亦无益. ~ **and water**, (fig) feeble discourse or sentiment. (喻)无味的言谈; 脆弱的情感. **2** (compounds) (复合词) **'~-bar** n bar for the sale of drinks made from ~, ice-cream and other light refreshments. 牛奶吧台(售卖牛奶,冰淇淋及其他点心的柜台); 奶类饮食供应处. **'~-churn** n large vessel fitted

with a lid for carrying ~. 有盖的大牛奶罐(此义不用于美国)。 '~ **loaf**, sweet-tasting white bread. 甜味的白面包。 '~**maid** n woman who milks cows and works in a dairy. 挤牛奶的女工。 '~**-man** /-mən; -mən/ n (pl **-men**) man who sells ~; man who goes from house to house delivering ~. 卖牛奶的人; (挨户)送牛奶的人。 '~**-powder** n ~ dehydrated by evaporation. 奶粉。 '~ **round** n ~man's route from house to house, street to street. (从一条街到另一条街挨户的)送牛奶路线。 '~**-shake** n beverage of ~ with ice-cream mixed into it and beaten up. 牛奶加冰淇淋搅打而成的饮料; 泡沫奶。 '~**-sop** /-sɒp; -sɑp/ n man or youth who is lacking in spirit, who is too soft and gentle. 懦弱的人或青年; 懦夫; 柔弱的人; 没骨气的人。 '~**-tooth** n (pl **-teeth**) one of the first (temporary) teeth in young mammals. 乳齿。 ˌ~'**white** adj as white as ~. 乳白的。 **3** ~**like** juice of some plants and trees, eg the juice inside a coconut. 乳状树液或果汁(如椰子所含之液汁)。 '~**-weed** n name used for several kinds of wild plant with a juice like ~. 乳草(有乳液之若干野生植物)。 **4** ~**like** preparation made from herbs, drugs, etc: (由草,药等制成的)乳状药品; 乳剂: ~ of magnesia. 乳剂氧化镁。

milk[2] /mɪlk; mɪlk/ vt, vi **1** [VP6A] draw milk from a cow/ewe/goat, or juice from a plant, or venom from a snake; extract money, information, etc (by guile or dishonesty) from a person or institution. 挤(牛、绵羊、山羊)之奶; 挤(植物)之乳液; 挤(毒蛇)之毒液; (以诈术或不正当的手段)自(某人或某机构)榨取金钱, 情报等; 勒索。 **2** [VP2A] yield milk: 产奶: The cows are ~ing well. 这些牛产奶很多。 '~**ing-machine** n apparatus for ~ing cows mechanically. 挤奶器。

milky /'mɪlkɪ; 'mɪlkɪ/ adj (-**ier**, -**iest**) of or like milk; mixed with milk; (of a liquid) cloudy, not clear. 牛乳的; 乳状的; 搀奶的; (指液体)混浊的; 不清的。 the ˌM~'**Way**, the broad luminous band of stars encircling the sky; the Galaxy (as seen from earth). 银河; 天河。

mill[1] /mɪl; mɪl/ n **1** (building ('flour-~) with) machinery or apparatus for grinding grain into flour (old style, 'water~, 'wind~). 磨粉机(旧式有: watermill 水力磨粉机, windmill 风力磨粉机); 磨粉厂(亦称: flour-mill); 磨坊。 put sb/go through the ~, (cause to) undergo hard training or experience. 经历(使某人经历)磨练; (使)从痛苦经历中学习。 run-of-the-~, ⇨ run[1](10)。 '~**-dam** n dam built across a stream to make water available for a ~. 磨坊水坝(拦溪流所建使磨坊有水可用的水坝)。 '~**-pond** n water retained by a ~dam, to flow to the ~. 磨坊蓄水池(由磨坊水坝所拦取的水而流入磨坊者): like a ~-pond, (of the sea) very calm. (指海洋)象磨坊蓄水池那样平静; 非常平静。 '~**-race** n current of water that turns a ~-wheel. 旋转磨坊水车的水流。 '~**-stone** n one of a pair of circular stones between which grain is ground. 磨; 石磨; 磨石; 两片磨刀石磨中之一片。 a ~**stone round one's neck**, (fig) heavy burden: (喻)沉重的负担; 重担: That mortgage has been like a ~stone round my neck. 那份抵押契据一直象块磨石般压在我的颈项上。 be between the **upper and nether** (= lower) ~**stone**, be subject to irresistible pressure. 被夹在上下两片磨石之间(即受到无法抗拒的重压)。 '~**-wheel** n wheel (esp a water-wheel) that supplies power to drive a ~. (推动磨粉机的)车轮; (尤指)水车车轮。 '~**-wright** n man who builds and repairs water~s and wind~s. 修建水力风力磨粉机的人。 **2** building, factory, workshop, for industry: 工厂; 工场: a 'cotton-/'paper-/'silk-/'steel-~. 纱(纸,丝,钢)铁)厂。 '~**-hand** n factory worker. 工厂工人。 '~**-girl** n girl who works in a ~, esp a cotton-~. 工厂女工; (尤指)纱厂女工。 **3** small machine for grinding: 小型研磨机: a 'coffee-~; 咖啡研磨机; a 'pepper-~. 胡椒研磨机。

mill[2] /mɪl; mɪl/ vt, vi **1** [VP6A] put through a machine for grinding; produce by doing this: 碾碎; 磨

细; 碾磨成: ~ grain; 碾磨谷粒; ~ flour; 磨制面粉; ~ ore, crush it; 碾碎矿石; ~ steel, make it into bars. 碾压钢铁而成钢条。 **2** [VP6A] produce regular markings on the edge of (a coin): 在(硬币)上轧花边: silver coins with a ~ed edge. 轧有花边的银币。 **3** [VP 2C] ~ about/around, (of cattle, crowds of people) move in a confused way; move in a mass. (指牛群,人群)乱动; 骚动; 成群兜圈子。

mill·board /'mɪlbɔːd; 'mɪl,bɔrd/ n [U] stout pasteboard used in binding books. (装订书籍用的)硬纸板。

mil·len·nium /mɪ'lenɪəm; mə'lɛnɪəm/ n (pl -**nia** /-nɪə/, ~**s**) **1** period of 1000 years. 一千年。 **2** (fig) future time of great happiness and prosperity for everyone. (喻)未来的太平盛世。 **mil·len·arian** /ˌmɪlɪ-'neərɪən; ˌmɪlə'nɛrɪən/ n person who believes that the ~(2) will come. 相信太平盛世将会来临的人。

mil·le·pede /'mɪlɪpiːd; 'mɪlə,pid/ n small wormlike creature with very many legs, usu in double pairs at each segment. 马陆(一种多节足的虫)。 ⇨ the illus at **insect**. 参看 insect 之插图。

mil·ler /'mɪlə(r); 'mɪlə/ n owner or tenant of a mill, esp the old-fashioned flour-mill worked by wind or water. 磨坊主人或租用人; 磨粉厂厂主(尤指使用旧式风车或水车磨坊者)。

mil·let /'mɪlɪt; 'mɪlɪt/ n [U] cereal plant growing 3 to 4 feet high and producing a large crop of small seeds (as food). 稷; 黍; 小米。

milli- /'mɪlɪ; 'mɪlɪ/ pref (in the metric system) one-thousandth part of: (米制)千分之一; 毫: '~**-gram**; 千分之一公分; 毫克; 公丝; '~**metre**. 千分之一米; 毫米; 公厘。 ⇨ App 5. 参看附录五。

mil·liard /'mɪlɪɑːd; 'mɪljəd/ n (GB) thousand millions (1 000 000 000) (US am = billion). (英)十万万; 十亿。 ⇨ App 4. 参看附录四。

mil·li·bar /'mɪlɪbɑː(r); 'mɪlɪ,bɑr/ n unit of atmospheric pressure. 毫巴(大气压力的单位)。

mil·liner /'mɪlɪnə(r); 'mɪlənə/ n person who makes and sells women's hats, and sells lace, trimmings, etc for hats. 女帽(及其饰物)商。 ~**y** /-nərɪ US: -nerɪ; -,nɛrɪ/ n [U] (the business of making and selling) women's hats, with lace, ribbons, etc. 女帽(及其饰物)类; 女帽(及其饰物)业。

mil·lion /'mɪljən; 'mɪljən/ n, adj one thousand thousand (1 000 000). (Note: the pl is rarely used after a number): 一百万(注意: 在数字之后罕用其复数形): ~s of pounds; 好几百万英镑; six ~ people. 六百万人。 make a ~, make a ~ pounds/dollars, etc. 赚一百万(英镑、元等)。 ~**-aire** /ˌmɪljə'neə(r); ˌmɪljən'ɛr/ n person who has a ~ dollars, pounds, etc; extremely rich man. 百万富翁; 大财主; 大富豪。 '~**-fold** adv a ~ times. 百万倍。 **mil·lionth** /-lɪənθ; -ljənθ/ n, adj ⇨ App 4. 参看附录四。

mil·li·pede /'mɪlɪpiːd; 'mɪlə,pid/ n = **millepede**.

mil·ometer /maɪ'lɒmɪtə(r); maɪ'lɑmɪtə/ n = **mileometer**. ⇨ **mile**.

mi·lord /mɪ'lɔːd; mɪ'lɔrd/ n (F word formerly used for) English lord; wealthy Englishman. (昔时法语用以称呼)英国士绅; 富有的英国人。

milt /mɪlt; mɪlt/ n [U] (soft) roe of male fish; fish sperm. 雄鱼之精液; 鱼精。

mime /maɪm; maɪm/ n [U] (in the theatre, etc) use of only facial expressions and gestures to tell a story; [C] such a performance; actor in such drama. (在戏剧等中)只用面部表情及手势的讲述故事; 此种戏剧的演出; 滑稽哑剧演员。 □ vi, vt **1** [VP2A] act in a ~. 演滑稽模仿动作剧; 演滑稽哑剧。 **2** [VP6A] express by ~. 以滑稽模仿动作剧表现。

mimeo·graph /'mɪmɪəɡrɑːf US: -ɡræf; 'mɪmɪə,ɡræf/ n apparatus for making copies of written or typed material from a stencil. (蜡纸)油印机。 □ vt [VP6A] make (copies) with a ~. 用油印机油印。

mi·metic /mɪ'metɪk; mɪ'mɛtɪk/ adj of, given to,

imitation or mimicry. 模仿的; 好模拟的。

mimic /'mɪmɪk; 'mɪmɪk/ *attrib adj* imitated or pretended: 模仿的; 假装的: ~ *warfare*, as in peacetime manoeuvres; 模拟战; 军事演习; ~ *colouring*, eg of animals, birds and insects that have the colours of their natural surroundings. (动物、鸟类及昆虫的)保护色。 □ *n* person who is clever at imitating others, esp in order to make fun of their habits, appearance, etc. 善于模仿的人(尤其是模仿他人之习惯、外貌等而戏弄他人者)。 □ *vt* (*pt, pp* **~ked**) [VP6A] 1 ridicule by imitating: 以模仿而取笑; 戏拟: *He was ~king his uncle's voice and clevarly very cleverly.* 他把他叔父的声音和姿态模仿得惟妙惟肖。 2 (of things) resemble closely: (指物品)与...极相似: *wood painted to ~ marble.* 漆成酷似大理石的木料。 **~ry** *n* [U] ~king: 模仿; 戏拟: *protective ~ry*, the resemblance of birds, animals and insects to their natural surroundings, giving some protection from enemies. 保护性的模拟; 拟态; 拟色(鸟类、鸟类、昆虫模拟自然环境的形态或颜色, 可帮助防止外敌之伤害)。

mim·osa /mɪ'məʊzə US: -'məʊsə; mɪ'mosɪ/ *n* [U, C] shrub with clusters of small, ball-shaped, sweet-smelling yellow flowers. 含羞草。

min·aret /ˌmɪnə'ret; ˌmɪnə'rɛt/ *n* tall, slender spire, connected with a mosque, from the balconies of which people are called to prayer by a muezzin (or, often today, by loudspeaker). 伊斯兰教寺院的尖塔(上有阳台, 由报时人站立呼喊伊斯兰教徒作作祈祷, 现今则多在塔顶上装置扩音器)。 ⇨ the illus at **mosque**. 参看 mosque 之插图。

mina·tory /'mɪnətərɪ US: -tɔːrɪ; 'mɪnəˌtorɪ/ *adj* threatening. 恐吓性的。

mince /mɪns; mɪns/ *vt, vi* 1 [VP6A] cut or chop (meat, etc) into small pieces (with a knife, or a machine with revolving blades, called a '*mincing machine* or *mincer*). 将(肉等)切碎; 剁碎(用刀切或用机器绞碎, 此种机器称为 mincing machine 或 mincer)。 *not to '~ matters/~ one's words*, to speak plainly or bluntly in condemnation of sth or sb; not take pains to keep within the bounds of politeness. 直言不讳; 率直地说。 2 [VP6A] say (words) with an affectation of delicacy; [VP2A] put on fine airs when speaking or walking, trying to appear delicate or refined. 故作文雅地说(话); 言行矫饰; 装腔作势。 □ *n* minced meat. 绞碎的肉; 肉末。 '~·meat *n* [U] mixture of currants, raisins, sugar, candied peel, apples, suet, etc for a ~-pie. 百果馅(由葡萄干、糖、蜜饯果皮、苹果、板油等混合而成)。 *make ~meat of*, (colloq) defeat a person/an argument, etc. (口)彻底击败(某人、一论据等)。 '~·pie *n* small round pie containing ~meat. 百果馅饼。 **mincer** *n* device for mincing food. 剁碎食物的机器; 绞肉机。 '**minc·ing** *adj*: *take mincing steps*; take mincing steps. 走; *an affected, mincing young girl*, 一个矫揉造作装腔作势的女孩, ⇨ 2 above. 参看上列第 2 义。 '**minc·ing·ly** *adv*

mind¹ /maɪnd; maɪnd/ *n* 1 [U] memory; remembrance. 记忆; 回忆。 *bear/keep sth in ~*, remember sth. 记住某事物。 *bring/call sth to ~*, recall it to the memory. 回忆某事。 *go/pass from/out of one's ~*, be forgotten. 被忘记; 被遗忘。 *put sb in ~ of sth*, remind sb of, cause sb to think of sth. 提醒某人某事; 使某人想起某事物。 *Out of sight, out of ~*, (prov) What is not seen is soon forgotten. (谚)离久情疏; 看不见的人或东西很快地就会被遗忘。 2 [U] (but with *indef art* or *pl* in some phrases, as shown below) what a person thinks or feels; way of thinking; conscious thoughts; feeling, wishing; opinion; intention; purpose: (但在某些短语中与不定冠词连用, 或用复数形, 如下所列)一个人所思想或感觉者; 思想; 精神; 想法; 心意; 意欲; 感想; 愿望; 意见; 意向; 目的: *Nothing was further from his ~*, his intentions. 那根本不是他的本意。 *absence of ~*, failure to think of one is doing. 心不在焉。 ⇨ *absent-minded* at **absent¹**. *presence of ~*, ability

to act or decide quickly when this is needed. 当需要时能迅速采取行动或作决定的能力; 应变才能; 急智; 镇定。 *be out of one's ~/not in one's right ~*, mad. 发狂的; 精神错乱的。 *be of one ~ (about sth)*, be in agreement; have the same opinion. (关于某事)意见一致; 意见相同。 *be of the same ~*, (a) (of a number of persons) be in agreement. (指许多人)意见一致。 (b) (of one person) be unchanged in an opinion, decision, etc: (指一个人)不改变意见, 决定等: *Is he still of the same ~?* 他仍然不改变初衷吗? *be in two ~s about sth*, feel doubtful, hesitate, about sth. 对某事感到怀疑; 疑忌; 犹豫不决; 三心两意。 *bend one's ~*, influence the ~ so that it is permanently affected (by beliefs, etc). (信仰等)左右某人的思想使其永远受影响。 Hence, 由此产生, *change one's ~*, change one's purpose or intention. 改变主意。 *give one's ~ to sth*, direct one's attention to sth. 注意某事物。 *give sb a piece of one's ~, piece¹(2)*. *have a good ~ to do sth*, be strongly disposed to do sth. 极有意做某事。 *have half a ~ to do sth*, be rather inclined to do sth. 有点想要做某事。 *have sth on one's ~*, be troubled about sth which, one feels, one ought to deal with. (某事该处理而未处理时)为某事耿耿于怀; 为某事操心; 为某事焦虑。 *keep one's ~ on sth*, continue to pay attention to, not be diverted from: 继续注意某事而不分心; 专心于某事; 留意着某件事: *Keep your ~ on what you're doing.* 注意你正在做的事情(勿分心)。 *know one's own ~*, know what one wants, have no doubts: 深知自己的需要: *He never knows his own ~*, often doubts, hesitates, about what to do. 他从不知道自己需要的是什么(对要做什么常迟疑不决)。 *make up one's ~*, (a) come to a decision: 决定; 决心: *I've made up my ~ to be a doctor.* 我已决心当医生。 *Have you made up your ~ about what you'll do?* 你要做什么, 决定了没有? (b) reconcile oneself to sth that cannot be changed, etc: 安于无法变更等的事情: *We're no longer a first-class power; we must make up our ~s to that.* 我们不再是第一等的强国; 我们必须接受那事实。 *read sb's ~*, know what he is thinking. 知道某人在想什么。 Hence, 由此产生, *~ reading*, guessing; knowing by intuition what sb is thinking. 猜测; 测心术(凭直觉知道某人在想什么)。 Hence, 由此产生, '*~·reader n set one's ~ on sth*, want very much; be determined to have: 极想得某物; 决心要有或要做某事物: *We've set our ~s on a holiday in France.* 我们已决定在法国度假一天。 *speak one's ~*, say plainly what one thinks. 坦率说出心中的话。 *take one's/sb's ~ off sth*, turn one's/sb's attention away from sth; distract from. 转移自己(某人)的注意力; 使自己(某人)分心。 *in the ~'s eye*, in imagination; in memory. 在想像中; 在记忆中。 *to 'my ~*, according to my way of thinking: 照我的想法; 依我之见: *To my ~, this is just a nonsense.* 依我看来, 这简直是胡闹。 3 [C, U] (person with) mental ability; intellect: 心智; 智力; 有才智的人: *He has a very good ~.* 他极有才智。 *He has one of the great ~s of the age.* 他是当代最有头脑的人物之一。 *No two ~s think alike.* 没有两个人的想法是完全相同的。

mind² /maɪnd; maɪnd/ *vt, vi* 1 [VP6A, 9] take care of; attend to: 留心; 注意: *Who is ~ing the baby?* 谁在照顾那婴孩? *When Mr Green was called to the phone, his wife had to ~ the shop, to attend to the shop.* 当格林先生去听电话时, 其妻必须照顾店铺。 *M~ the step,* Watch out for it. 小心那阶梯。 *M~ your head*, (as a warning to stoop, eg at a low doorway). 注意不要碰到头(走过矮门等时提醒屈身的警告)。 *M~ the dog,* Beware of it. 注意那条狗。 *M~ that you don't forget.*

注意不要忘记。~ **out (for sth),** be careful (of it): 当心; 小心关注: *M~ out!* (as a warning). 当心! (作为警告). *Could you ~ out, please—I want to pass.* 请留神——要当过去。*When you go into the garden, remember to ~ out for the new seedlings.* 你走进花园时要当心那些幼苗。~ *one's P's and Q's,* be careful and polite about what one says or does. 注意言行。*,M~ your ,own 'business,* Do not interfere in the affairs of others. 注意你自己的事; 少管闲事。~ *'you or~,* used as an *int* meaning 'Please note': 注意; 请注意(用做惊叹语): *I have no objection, ~ (you) but I think it unwise.* 请注意, 我并不反对, 不过我认为那样做并不聪明。**2** [VP 6A, C, 2A, 19C] (usu in interr, neg and conditional sentences, and in affirm sentences that answer a question) be troubled by; feel objection to: (通常用于疑问句、否定句和条件句中, 以及答复询问的肯定句中)介意; 反对: *He doesn't ~ the cold weather at all.* 他对寒冷的天气一点也不在乎。*Do you ~ if I smoke?* 我抽烟你介意吗? *Do you ~ my smoking?* 你介意我抽烟吗? *Would you ~ opening the window,* Will you please do this? 请你打开窗子好不好? *Would you ~ my opening the window,* Would you object if I did this? 我打开窗子你反对吗? *'Do you ~ my leaving this payment until next year?'—'Yes, I do ~',* I object to this. '这笔账我留到明年行吗? 你反对吗?'—'当然反对。' *I shouldn't ~ a glass of iced beer,* I should like one. 来一杯冰啤酒也好(即我想要一杯冰啤酒). *Never ~,* **(a)** It doesn't matter. 没关系。**(b)** Don't worry about it. 不必担心。~**er** *n* person whose duty it is to attend to sth: 看守人; 守护人; 照料者: (in compounds) (用于复合词中) *ma'chine-~er;* 守护机器的人; *'baby-~er.* 照看嬰儿的人。

minded /'maɪndɪd; 'maɪndɪd/ *adj* **1** (*pred* only) (仅用作表语) disposed or inclined: 倾向于做某事; 有意做某事: *He could do it if he were so ~.* 假如他想做, 他就能做。*If she were ~ to help, ...* 如果她有意帮忙, …。**2** having the kind of mind indicated (by an *adj* or *adv* prefixed): (词前附以形容词或副词)有…头脑的; 有…心意的: *a 'strong-~ man;* 意志坚强的人; *'high-~ leaders;* 品格高尚的领袖们; *'evil-~ opponents;* 存心不良的对手; *com'mercially-~ men.* 有商业头脑的人。**3** conscious of the value or importance of (what is indicated by a *n* prefixed): (词前附以名词)认识…的价值或重要性的: *He has become very 'food-~ since his holiday in France,* has become a gourmet. 自从他到法国度假以后; 他就变得非常考究饮食了。

mind·ful /'maɪndfl; 'maɪndfəl/ *adj* ~ **of,** giving thought and attention to: 留意; 注意: ~ *of one's duties/the nation's welfare.* 留意职责(国家的福利)。~**ly** /-fəlɪ; -fəlɪ/ *adv* ~**ness** *n*

mind·less /'maɪndlɪs; 'maɪndlɪs/ *adj* **1** ~ **of,** paying no attention to; forgetful of: 不注意; 忘却: ~ *of danger.* 不注意危险; 忘却危险。**2** quite lacking in or not requiring intelligence: 智慧很差的; 愚蠢的; 不需要智慧的: ~ *drudgery,* 不必花脑筋的讨厌的苦工; ~ *layabouts.* 愚蠢的游荡者。~**·ly** *adv* ~**ness** *n*

mine¹ /maɪn; maɪn/ *poss pron* of or belonging to me: 我的: *Is this book yours or ~?* 这本书是你的还是我的? *He's an old 'friend of ~,* one of my old friends. 他是我的老友(之一)。□ *poss adj* (in poet and biblical style only, before a vowel sound or *h;* sometimes placed after the *n*) my: (仅用于诗与圣经文体中, 置于元音或 h 音之前; 有时置于名词之后)我的(= my): ~ *eyes;* 我的眼睛; ~ *heart;* 我的心; *O mistress ~;* 哦, 我的(女)主人; ~ *enemy.* 我的敌人。

mine² /maɪn; maɪn/ *n* **1** excavation with shafts, galleries, etc made in the earth from which coal, mineral ores, etc, are extracted. ⇨ **quarry** for stone or slate: 矿坑; 坑道; 矿: *'coal~;* 煤矿; *'gold~;* 金矿; (fig) rich or abundant source: (喻)丰富的资源: *A good encyclopedia/My grandmother is a ~ of information.* 一部好的百科全书(我的祖母)是知识的宝库。**2** (tunnel

for) charge of high explosive (as used to destroy enemy fortifications); charge of high explosive buried and exploded, eg electrically, from a distance or laid on or just below the ground, exploded by contact with a vehicle, or a time fuse, etc: 地雷坑; 地雷; 触发地雷; 遥控地雷: *The lorry was destroyed by a buried ~.* 卡车被一枚埋在地下的地雷炸毁。**3** (in war at sea) charge of high explosives in a metal case, placed in the sea, exploded on contact, or electrically, or mechanically. (海战中的)水雷。**4** '~-detector *n* electromagnetic device for finding ~s(2, 3). 测雷器(探测地雷及水雷的电磁装置); 地雷测探器。'~-disposal *n* the making of ~s harmless (by defusing them, etc): 地雷处理(如拆除信管等使地雷不能爆炸): ~-disposal squads. 地雷处理队; 拆雷小组。'~-field *n* **(a)** area of land or sea where ~s(2, 3) have been laid. 雷区(设有地雷之地面区域); 水雷区(布有水雷之水域)。**(b)** area of land where there are many ~s(1). 矿区。'~-layer *n* ship or aircraft used for laying ~s at sea. 布雷艇; 布雷飞机。Hence, 由此产生, '~-laying, 布雷, as in 如用于 ~-laying vessel. 布雷艇。'~-sweeper *n* naval vessel (usu a trawler) employed for clearing the sea of ~s. 扫雷艇(通常为拖捞船)。Hence, 由此产生, '~-sweeping *n*

mine³ /maɪn; maɪn/ *vt, vi* **1** [VP6A, 2A, 3A] ~ **(for),** dig (for coal, ores, etc) from the ground; obtain (coal, etc) from mines: 采掘(煤、矿、砂等); 开矿: 采矿: ~ *(for) coal/gold;* 采煤(金); ~ *the earth for coal.* 挖地取煤。*Gold is ~d from deep under ground.* 金(矿)自地下深处采掘出来。**2** [VP6A] (= *undermine*) make tunnels (in the earth) under: 在…下掘地道; 挖坑: ~ *the enemy's trenches/forts.* 挖掘地道直通敌军战壕(堡垒)之下。**3** [VP6A] lay mines (2, 3) in; destroy by means of these: 布水雷于; 布水雷于; 以地雷(水雷)炸毁: ~ *the entrance to a harbour.* 在进港处布置水雷。*The cruiser was ~d, and sank in five minutes.* 巡洋舰触雷后, 五分钟内即沉没。**4** [VP6A] (fig) weaken; undermine (which is the more usu word). (喻)使变弱; 暗地破坏 (undermine 为较常用词)。

miner /'maɪnə(r); 'maɪnɚ/ *n* **1** man who works in a mine underground: 矿工: *'coal~s.* 煤矿工人。**2** soldier trained to dig tunnels and lay mines under enemy trenches, etc. 地雷工兵; 坑道工兵。

min·eral /'mɪnərəl; 'mɪnərəl/ *n* [C] natural substance (not vegetable or animal) got from the earth by mining, esp one that has a constant chemical composition: 矿物: *Coal and iron ore are ~s.* 煤与铁矿是矿物。□ *adj* of the class of ~s; containing, mixed with, ~s: 矿物的; 含矿物的; 混有矿物质的: ~ *ores.* 矿砂。**the ~ kingdom,** natural substances of inorganic matter. 矿物界。⇨ **animal** and **vegetable.** '~ **oil,** any oil or ~ substance. 矿油(源于矿物的油类)。'~ **pitch,** asphalt. 地沥青; 柏油。'~ **water, (a)** water that naturally contains a ~ substance, esp one said to have medicinal value. 矿泉水(天然含有矿物质的水, 尤指有医药价值者)。**(b)** (GB) non-alcoholic drink (usu bottled, often flavoured) containing soda-water. (英)含苏打水的非酒精性饮料(通常为瓶装, 且常加有香料); 碳酸水。'~ **wool,** inorganic fibrous material (used for insulating, etc). 矿绵(无机物纤维质, 用于绝缘等)。

min·er·al·ogy /,mɪnə'rælədʒɪ; ,mɪnə'ælədʒɪ/ *n* [U] the study and science of minerals. 矿物学。**min·er·al·ogist** /,mɪnə'rælədʒɪst; ,mɪnə'ælədʒɪst/ *n* student of ~. 研究矿物学的人; 矿物学家。

min·estrone /,mɪnɪ'strəʊnɪ; ,mɪnə'stronɪ/ *n* [U] (I) rich soup (of Italian origin) of mixed vegetables, vermicelli and meat broth. (意)(源于意大利的)含蔬菜, 细面条及肉之浓汤。

mingle /'mɪŋgl; 'mɪŋgl/ *vt, vi* [VP6A, 14, 2A, C] ~ **(with),** mix: 混合: *truth ~d with falsehood;* 掺合着虚假的事实; ~ *with* (= go about among) *the crowds;* 混在人群中; *two rivers that join and ~ their waters.*

汇而为一的两条河。

mingy /'mɪndʒɪ; 'mɪŋdʒɪ/ *adj* (**-ier, -iest**) (GB colloq) mean, ungenerous, stingy: (英口)小气的; 不慷慨的; 吝啬的。*a ～ fellow.* 吝啬的家伙; 小气鬼。

mini- /'mɪnɪ; 'mɪnɪ/ *pref* of small size, length, etc. ⇨ **maxi-**: 迷你(表示小、短等之义): '*～bus*; 微型公共汽车; '*～cab*; 微型计程车; '*～skirt*; 超短裙; '*～tour*. 短程旅行。

minia·ture /'mɪnɪtʃə(r) US: -tʃʊər; 'mɪnɪtʃə/ *n* **1** [C] very small painting of a person, esp one on ivory or vellum; [U] this branch of painting. 小型画像(尤指刻于象牙或画于软皮纸上者); 小型画像绘画术。*in ～*, on a small scale. 袖珍的; 小型的; 缩小的。**2** [C] small-scale copy or model of any object. 缩图; 缩影; 缩小之模型。**3** (attrib) on a small scale: (用作定语)小型的; 缩小的: *a ～ railway*; (玩具用)小铁道; *a ～ camera*, one for 35 mm or sub-standard size of film. 小型照相机, (使用 35 毫米或小于标准规格之底片者)。**minia·tur·ist** /'mɪnɪtʃərɪst; 'mɪnɪtʃərɪst/ *n* painter of ～s. 小型画像画家。

minim /'mɪnɪm; 'mɪnɪm/ *n* (music) note half the value of a semibreve. (音乐)二分音符; 半音符。⇨ The illus at **notation**. 参看 notation 之插图。

mini·mal /'mɪnɪml; 'mɪnɪml/ *adj* smallest in amount or degree: 最小量的; 最低程度的: *On these cliffs vegetation is ～.* 在这些峭壁上极少植物生长着。

mini·mize /'mɪnɪmaɪz; 'mɪnɪˌmaɪz/ *vt* [VP6A] reduce to, estimate at, the smallest possible amount or degree: 将…减至最小量或最低程度; 将…作最低估计: *～ an accident*, try to reduce its importance, say that it is not serious. 低估意外事件的严重性。

mini·mum /'mɪnɪməm; 'mɪnəməm/ *n, adj* (*pl* **-ma** /-mə; -mə/, *～s*) (opposite of *maximum*) (of) least possible or recorded amount, degree, etc: (为 maximum 之反义词)最小量(的); 最低额(的); 最低程度(的): *reduce sth to a ～*; 将某项减至最少; *the ～ temperature*; 最低温度; *a maximum and ～ thermometer*; 可记录最高温及最低温之温度计; *a ～ wage*, lowest wage that regulations allow to be paid. (规定的)最低工资。

min·ing /'maɪnɪŋ; 'maɪnɪŋ/ *n* the process of getting minerals, etc from mines: 采矿: *a '～ engineer*; 采矿工程师; *the '～ industry*; 采矿工业; 矿业; *open-cast ～*, getting coal, etc that is near the surface, using mechanical shovels, etc. 露天采矿(法)。

min·ion /'mɪnɪən; 'mɪnjən/ *n* (derog) servant who, in order to win favour, obeys a master slavishly. (贬)宠信之仆人; 唯命是从的奴仆。*the ～s of the law*, police, jailers. 警察; 狱卒。

min·is·ter[1] /'mɪnɪstə(r); 'mɪnɪstə/ *n* **1** person at the head of a Department of State (and often a member of the Cabinet): 部长(通常为内阁阁员): *the M～ of Employment and Productivity*; 劳工生产部部长; *the Prime M～*. 首相。**2** person representing his Government in a foreign country but of lower rank than an ambassador. 公使。**3** Christian priest or clergyman, esp one in the Presbyterian and Nonconformist Churches. 基督教之牧师(尤指长老教会与独立教会的牧师)。Cf *priest* for the RC Church, and *vicar, rector, curate* for the Church of England. 天主教用 priest, 英国国教用 vicar, rector, curate。

min·is·ter[2] /'mɪnɪstə(r); 'mɪnɪstə/ *vi* [VP3A] *～ to*, give help or service: 帮助; 服侍: *～ to the wants of a sick man*; 服侍病人; 随时照应病人之急需; *～ing to her husband's needs*, satisfying them. 满足她丈夫的需要。

min·is·ter·ial /ˌmɪnɪˈstɪərɪəl; ˌmɪnɪsˈtɪrɪəl/ *adj* **1** of a Minister of State, his position, duties, etc: 部长的; 部长之地位, 职责等的: *～ functions/duties*. 部长的权限(职务)。**2** of or for a ministry(1) (or Cabinet): 部的; 内阁的: *the ～ benches*. (英国下议院中的)执政党阁员所坐的席次。*～ly* /-ɪəlɪ; -ɪəlɪ/ *adv*

min·is·trant /'mɪnɪstrənt; 'mɪnɪstrənt/ *attrib adj*

(formal) administering. (正式用语)服侍的; 给予济助的。□ *n* attendant; supporter or helper. 服侍者; 济助者。

min·is·tra·tion /ˌmɪnɪˈstreɪʃn; ˌmɪnəˈstreɪʃən/ *n* [U] ministering or serving, eg in performing a religious service; [C] act of this kind: 帮助; 服侍; 行宗教仪式: *Thanks to the ～s* (= nursing, services) *of my devoted wife, I was restored to health.* 多蒙爱妻的服侍, 我终于恢复了健康。

min·is·try /'mɪnɪstrɪ; 'mɪnɪstrɪ/ *n* (*pl* **-ries**) **1** Department of State under a Minister: 部: *the 'Air M～*; 空军部; *the ,M～ of 'Finance.* 财政部。**2** **the ～**, the ministers of religion as a body: 全体牧师; *He was intended for the ～*, destined to be a minister, eg by his parents. 他注定(他的父母有意让他)以后做牧师。*enter the ～*, become a minister of religion. 做牧师。**3** [C] office, duties, term of service, of a minister of religion. 牧师的职位、职责和任期。

mini·ver /'mɪnɪvə(r); 'mɪnəvə/ *n* [U] ermine fur (as for the ceremonial robes of peers). 白貂皮(如用以制大典时贵族所穿的长袍)。

mink /mɪŋk; mɪŋk/ *n* [C, U] (valuable brown fur skin of a) small stoat-like animal: 貂; (褐色而贵重的)貂皮: (attrib) (用作定语) *a ～ coat.* 貂皮大衣。

min·now /'mɪnəʊ; 'mɪno/ *n* (sorts of) very small freshwater fish. 鲦鱼。

mi·nor /'maɪnə(r); 'maɪnə/ *adj* **1** smaller, less important: 较小的; 次要的: *～ repairs/alteration*; 小修理(修改); *a broken leg and ～ injuries.* 一条腿断了, 还有一些轻伤。**2** comparatively unimportant: 比较不重要的: *the ～ planets*, the asteroids; 小行星; ～ *poets*; 不太重要的诗人; *play only a ～ part in the play*; 仅担任剧中的次要角色; (cards) (牌戏) *a ～ suit*, ie diamonds or clubs. 一副低花牌(指方块或梅花)。**3** (in schools) second or younger of two boys (esp in the same school) with the same surname: (学校中用语, 尤指同学校中之)两同性男生中的老二或年龄较小的: *Smith ～*. (两个史密斯中的)小史密斯。**4** (music) (音乐) *a ～ third*, an interval of three semi-tones; 小三度(即含三个半音的音程); *a ～ key*, in which the scale has a ～ third. 小调(即有小三度之音阶)。*in a ～ key*, (fig) in a melancholy or depressed mood. (喻)带有一种忧郁或颓丧的心情。⇨ **major**. □ *n* (legal) person not yet legally of age. (法律)未成年者。

mi·nor·ity /maɪˈnɒrətɪ US: -'nɔːr-; məˈnɔrətɪ/ *n* (*pl* **-ties**) **1** [U] (legal) the state of being under age (in GB under 18). (法律)未成年(在英国指未满十八岁)。**2** [C] the smaller number or part, esp of a total of votes; small racial, religious, etc group in a community, nation, etc. 少数(尤指投票总数中的少数票); (在一社会、国家等中之)少数民族、少数宗教等。*be in a/the ～*, be in the smaller of two groups: 属于(两个团体中之)较小团体; 是少数派: *We're in the ～*, More people are against us than with us. 我们是少数派(赞成我们的居少数)。*I'm in a ～ of one*, have had support from no one. 赞成我的只有我自己一票(没有人支持我)。'*～ government*, one which has a ～ of the total number of seats in a legislative assembly. 少数党政府(占国会席次较少之党所组成的政府)。'*～ programme*, (TV, radio) one viewed or listened to by a comparatively small proportion of the total viewers or listeners. (电视、无线电)收视(听)率低的节目。'*～ report*, one made (after an official inquiry or investigation) by the ～, giving views, etc, different from those of the majority. (在一次正式调查后)由部分少数人提出的报告(与多数人所持之意见相异)。

Mino·taur /'maɪnətɔː(r); 'mɪnə,tor/ *n* **the ～**, (Gk myth) monster, half man and half bull, fed with human flesh, kept in the labyrinth in Crete. (希神)牛头人身怪物(食人肉, 养于克里特的迷宫中)。

min·ster /'mɪnstə(r); 'mɪnstə/ *n* large or important church, esp one that once belonged to a monastery. 大。

the Minotaur   a centaur

礼拜堂(尤指曾经一度属于修道院者): *York* ~. 约克大教堂.

min·strel /ˈmɪnstrəl; ˈmɪnstrəl/ *n* **1** (in the Middle Ages) travelling composer, player and singer of songs and ballads. (中世纪时周游四方并制作、演奏及演唱歌谣的)吟游诗人. **2** one of a company of public entertainers. 技艺团团员. ~**sy** /ˈmɪnstrəlsɪ; ˈmɪnstrəlsɪ/ *n* [U] the art, songs, etc of ~s(1). 吟游诗人的技艺、歌谣等.

mint[1] /mɪnt; mɪnt/ *n* [U] (sorts of) plant whose leaves are used for flavouring (eg in drinks and in chewing-gum) and in making a sauce: 薄荷: ~ *sauce*, chopped-up ~ leaves, in vinegar and sugar, as eaten with lamb. 薄荷酱(捣烂的薄荷叶, 调以醋和糖, 与羊肉同食).

mint[2] /mɪnt; mɪnt/ *n* **1** place where coins are made, usu under State authority: 造币厂: *coins fresh from the* ~. 刚出厂的硬币. **2** *make / earn a* ~ *(of money)*, (colloq) a large amount. (口)赚大钱. **3** (attrib, of medals, stamps, prints, books, etc) unused. (用作定语, 指奖章、邮票、印刷品、书籍等)未用过的. *in* ~ *condition*, as if new; unsoiled; perfect. 崭新的; 无污损的; 完美的. □ *vt* [VP6A] **1** make (coin) by stamping metal: 铸造 (铸币): ~ *coins of 50 p*. 铸造五十便士的硬币. **2** (fig) invent a word, phrase, etc. (喻)创造(词、短语等).

min·uet /ˌmɪnjuˈet; ˌmɪnjʊˈet/ *n* [C] (piece of music for a) slow, graceful dance for groups of two couples (dating from the middle of the 17th c). 自十七世纪中叶流传下来的一种缓慢而幽雅的双人团体舞; 小步舞; 小步舞曲.

minus /ˈmaɪnəs; ˈmaɪnəs/ *adj* **1** the '~ sign, the sign −. 减号; 负号 (−). ⇨ plus. **2** ⇨ positive. negative: 负的: *a* ~ *quantity*, a quantity less than zero (eg $-2x^2$). 负数(小于零的数, 如 $-2x^2$). □ *prep* less; with the deduction of: 减; 减去: 7 ~ 3 *is 4*; 七减三等于四; (colloq) without: (口)缺少; 无: *He came back from the war* ~ *a leg*. 他作战回来, 少了一条腿. □ *n* ~ sign or quantity. 减号; 负数.

min·us·cule /ˈmɪnəskjuːl; mɪˈnʌskjul/ *adj* tiny; very small. 微小的; 很小的.

min·ute[1] /ˈmɪnɪt; ˈmɪnɪt/ *n* **1** the sixtieth part of one hour: 分(一小时的六十分之一): *seven* ~*s to six*; 五点五十三分(差七分六点); *arrive ten* ~*s early*. 早十分钟到达. ⇨ App 4. 参看附录四. '~-*gun* *n* one fired at intervals of a ~, eg at a grand funeral. 分炮(每隔一分钟放一次炮, 如在一隆重葬礼中施放者). (钟表上的)分针. '~-*hand* *n* hand indicating the ~ on a watch or clock. (钟表上的)分针. '~-*man* /-mən; -mæn/ *n* (*pl* -*men*) (US hist) militiaman ready to fight at a minute's notice. (美史)接获命令立即应召的民兵. *in a* ~, soon: 立刻: *I'll come downstairs in a* ~. 我马上下楼. *to the* ~, exactly: 一分不差; 准确地: *The train arrived at 5 o'clock to the* ~. 那班列车在五点整到站. *the* ~ *(that)*, as soon as: ……就: *I'll give him your message the* ~ *(that) he arrives*. 等他一到, 我就把你的信给他. *up to the* ~, most recent or fashionable. 最近的; 最新的; 时新的. ,*up-to-the-'*~ *attrib adj* most recent or fashionable: 最新的; 时髦的: *up-to-the-*~ *information* /

hairstyles. 最新消息(时髦的发式). **2** the sixtieth part of a degree (in an angle): (角度上)一度的六十分之一; 分: *37°30′*, 37 degrees 30 ~s. 37 度 30 分. **3** [C] official record giving authority, advice or making comments: 正式记录; 备忘录: *make a* ~ *of sth*. 记录某事. **4** (*pl*) summary, records, of what is said and decided at a meeting, esp of a society or committee: (复)会议记录(尤指社团或委员会的会议记录): *read and confirm the* ~*s of the last meeting*. 宣读并追认上次会议记录. '~-*book* *n* book in which ~s are written. 会议记录簿. □ *vt* [VP6A] record (sth) in the ~s(4); make a record of sth in a memorandum. 将(某事)列入会议记录; 将(某事)制成备忘录.

mi·nute[2] /maɪˈnjuːt US: -ˈnuːt; məˈnjut/ *adj* **1** very small: 极小的: ~ *particles of gold dust*. 金粉的细小微粒. **2** giving small details; careful and exact: 详细的; 仔细而准确的: *a* ~ *description*; 细腻的描写; *the* ~*st details*. 最细微的细节. ~·*ly* *adv* ~·*ness* *n*

mi·nu·tiae /maɪˈnjuːʃiː US: mɪˈnuːʃiː; mɪˈnjuʃi,i/ *n pl* precise or trivial details. 细节; 琐事.

minx /mɪŋks; mɪŋks/ *n* sly, impudent girl. 顽皮而冒失的女孩.

mir·acle /ˈmɪrəkl; ˈmɪrəkl/ *n* **1** act or event (sth good or welcome) which does not follow the known laws of nature; remarkable and surprising event: 奇迹(属于好的一方面); 特出而令人惊奇的事: *work / accomplish a* ~. 产生(造成)奇迹. *Her life was saved by a* ~. 她的命是奇迹救活的. *The doctors said that her recovery was a* ~. 医师们说她的康复是件令人惊奇的事. ~ *play*, dramatic representation (in the Middle Ages) based on the life of Jesus or the Christian saints. 奇迹剧; 神迹剧(中世纪的戏剧, 根据耶稣或圣徒的生平事迹而编写). **2** ~ *of*, remarkable example or specimen: (…的)特出事例: *It's a* ~ *of ingenuity*. 这是匠心独运的惊人例子. **mir·acu·lous** /mɪˈrækjʊləs; məˈrækjələs/ *adj* like a ~; contrary to the laws of nature; surprising. 似奇迹的; 违反自然律的; 不可思议的; 令人惊奇的. **mir·acu·lous·ly** *adv*

mi·rage /ˈmɪrɑːʒ US: mɪˈrɑːʒ; məˈrɑʒ/ *n* [C] **1** effect, produced by hot air conditions, causing an optical illusion, esp the illusive appearance of a sheet of water eg in the desert. 海市蜃楼(因热的大气变化而造成的视觉上的幻景, 尤指沙漠中所出现的水景幻象); 蜃景. **2** (fig) any illusion or hope that cannot be realized. (喻)任何不能实现的幻想; 妄想.

mire /ˈmaɪə(r); maɪr/ *n* [U] swampy ground; soft, deep mud. 沼地; 泥泞; 泥坑. *be in the* ~, (fig) be in difficulties. (喻)处于困境中; 陷入困难之中. *drag sb / sb's name through the* ~, bring disgrace on him, expose him to contempt. 使某人(某人之姓名)蒙受羞辱. □ *vt*, *vi* **1** [VP6A] cover with mud; cause to be fast in deep mud. 使蔽满污泥; 使陷入泥坑. **2** [VP2A] sink in mud. 陷入泥中. **3** [VP6A] (fig) involve (sb) in difficulties. (喻)使(某人)陷入困境. **miry** /ˈmaɪərɪ; ˈmaɪrɪ/ *adj* muddy: 泥泞的: *miry roads*. 泥泞的道路.

mir·ror /ˈmɪrə(r); ˈmɪrə/ *n* **1** polished surface that reflects images: 镜子: *a 'driving* ~, ~ in a motor-car to enable the driver to see what is behind him. (汽车之)反光镜(供驾驶者观看车后有无车辆行人之镜). *'image*, reflection or copy of sth with the right and left sides reversed. 镜像(与某物左右两边相反之映像或摹制品); 反像. **2** (fig) sth that reflects or gives a likeness: (喻)反映真象之物: *Pepys's 'Diary' is a* ~ *of the times he lived in*. 英国作家佩皮斯的‘日记’是他那个时代的一面镜子(即反映该时代社会情况的著作). □ *vt* [VP6A] (lit or fig) reflect as in a ~: (字面或喻)象镜子一样)反映: *The still water of the lake* ~*ed the hillside*. 平静的湖水映出山坡.

mirth /mɜːθ; mɝθ/ *n* [U] being merry, happy and bright; laughter. 欢乐; 快乐; 欢笑. ~·*ful* /-fl; -fəl/ *adj* full of ~; merry. 充满欢乐的; 快乐的; 欢笑的. ~·*fully* /-fəlɪ; -fəlɪ/ *adv* ~·*less* *adj* without ~: 没有欢

乐的; 忧愁的: *a ~less laugh*. 苦笑。

mis·ad·ven·ture /ˌmɪsədˈventʃə(r)/; ˌmɪsədˈvɛntʃə/ *n* [C, U] (event caused by) bad luck; misfortune. 恶运; 不幸; 不幸事件; 灾祸。*death by ~*, by accident. 意外死亡; 死于非命。

mis·ad·vise /ˌmɪsədˈvaɪz/; ˌmɪsədˈvaɪz/ *vt* [VP6A] (usu passive) advise wrongly. (通常用被动语态) 谬误地劝告。

mis·al·liance /ˌmɪsəˈlaɪəns/; ˌmɪsəˈlaɪəns/ *n* unsuitable alliance, esp marriage; mésalliance. 不适宜的结合 (尤指结婚); 不相匹配的婚姻。

mis·an·thrope /ˈmɪsənθrəʊp/; ˈmɪsənˌθrop/ *n* person who hates mankind; person who avoids society. 厌恨人类的人; 厌世者。**mis·an·thropic** /ˌmɪsənˈθrɒpɪk/; ˌmɪsənˈθrɑpɪk/ *adj* hating or distrusting mankind or human society. 厌恨人类的; 厌世的。**mis·an·thropy** /mɪsˈænθrəpɪ; mɪsˈænθrəpɪ/ *n* [U] hatred of mankind. 厌恨人类; 厌世。

mis·apply /ˌmɪsəˈplaɪ/; ˌmɪsəˈplaɪ/ *vt* (*pt, pp* **-lied**) [VP6A] apply wrongly; use for a wrong purpose, eg public funds. 误用; 滥用(如公款)。**mis·ap·pli·ca·tion** /ˌmɪsæplɪˈkeɪʃn/; ˌmɪsæpləˈkeʃən/ *n* wrong or unjust use (*of*). 误用; 滥用(与 of 连用)。

mis·ap·pre·hend /ˌmɪsæprɪˈhend/; ˌmɪsæprɪˈhɛnd/ *vt* [VP6A] misunderstand. 误解。**mis·ap·pre·hen·sion** /ˌmɪsæprɪˈhenʃn/; ˌmɪsæprɪˈhɛnʃən/ *n do sth/be under a misapprehension*, do sth because of have a failure to understand correctly. 出于误解而做某事(误解)。

mis·ap·pro·pri·ate /ˌmɪsəˈprəʊprɪeɪt/; ˌmɪsəˈproprɪ,et/ *vt* [VP6A] take and use wrongly; apply (sb else's money) to a wrong (esp one's own) use: 误用; 滥用 (别人之钱, 尤指自己之已用): *The treasurer ~d the society's funds*. 这会计曾盗用该会的公款。**mis·ap·pro·pri·ation** /ˌmɪsəˌprəʊprɪˈeɪʃn/; ˌmɪsəˌproprɪˈeʃən/ *n: misappropriation of public funds*. 盗用公款。

mis·be·got·ten /ˌmɪsbɪˈɡɒtn/; ˌmɪsbɪˈɡɑtn/ *adj* illegitimate; bastard; (colloq, as a term of scorn): 非婚生的; 私生的(口, 作为骂人的用语): *Who's the author of these ~* (= ill-advised, worthless) *plans?* 谁定的这些莫名其妙(愚蠢无用)的计划?

mis·be·have /ˌmɪsbɪˈheɪv/; ˌmɪsbɪˈhev/ *vt, vi* [VP 6B, 2A] behave (oneself) improperly. 行为不端; 做不正当的事。**mis·be·hav·iour** (US = **-ior**) /ˌmɪsbɪˈheɪvɪə(r)/; ˌmɪsbɪˈhevjə/ *n*

mis·cal·cu·late /ˌmɪsˈkælkjuleɪt/; mɪsˈkælkjə,let/ *vt, vi* calculate (amounts. etc) wrongly. 误算(数额等); 计算错误。**mis·cal·cu·la·tion** /ˌmɪskælkjuˈleɪʃn/; ˌmɪskælkjəˈleʃən/ *n*

mis·call /ˌmɪsˈkɔːl/; mɪsˈkɔl/ *vt* call by a wrong name; misname; 误呼; 叫错: *King Robert, ~ed 'the Just'*. 被误称为'公正者'的罗伯特王。

mis·car·riage /ˌmɪsˈkærɪdʒ/; mɪsˈkærɪdʒ/ *n* 1 [U] *~ of justice*, failure of a court to administer justice properly; mistake in judgement or in punishment; [C] instance of this. 误审; 误判; 误罚; 审判不公; 误审的案件; 审判或量刑不公的案件。2 [U] failure to deliver to, or arrive at, the destination: 误送; 未能送达: *~ of goods*; 货物误送; [C] instance of this. 误送的事例。3 [U] premature expulsion of a foetus from the womb; [C] instance of this: 流产; 小产: *have a ~*. 流产; 小产

mis·carry /ˌmɪsˈkærɪ; mɪsˈkærɪ/ *vi* (*pt, pp* **-ried**) [VP2A] 1 (of plans, etc) fail; have a result different from what was hoped for. (指计划等)失败; 不顺利; 未达预期效果。2 (of letters, etc) fail to reach the right destination. (指书信等)误投; 未送达目的地。3 (of a woman) have a miscarriage(3). (指妇人)流产; 小产。

mis·cast /ˌmɪsˈkɑːst US: -ˈkæst/; mɪsˈkæst/ *vt* (*pt, pp* **miscast**) [VP6A] (usu passive) (通常用被动语态) 1 (of an actor) be cast for a role for which he is unfitted: (指演员)被派扮演不适合的角色: *She was badly*

~ as Juliet. 她被派扮演朱丽叶, 这角色对她非常不合适。⇨ **cast**[1](6). 2 (of a play) have the parts badly allocated to the actors and actresses. (指戏剧)角色被不当地分派给男女演员; 乱派角色。

mis·cegen·ation /ˌmɪsɪdʒɪˈneɪʃn/; ˌmɪsɪdʒəˈneʃən/ *n* [U] mixture of races, the production of offspring by the sexual union of two people of different races. 人种混杂; 异族通婚。

mis·cel·lan·eous /ˌmɪsəˈleɪnɪəs/; ˌmɪsˈenɪəs/ *adj* of mixed sorts; having various qualities and characteristics: 各式各样的; 有不同性质与特征的; 多方面的: *a ~ collection of goods*; 一批杂货; *Milton's ~ prose works*. 弥尔顿的各种散文作品。**mis·cel·lany** /mɪˈseləni US: ˈmɪsəleɪni/; ˈmɪsl,enɪ/ *n* (*pl* **-nies**) collection, eg of writings on various subjects by various authors. 杂集(例如不同作者所写不同题目的文集)。**mis·cel·lanea** /ˌmɪsəˈleɪnɪə/; ˌmɪsəˈlenɪə/ *n pl* literary miscellany. (文学的)杂集; 杂录。

mis·chance /ˌmɪsˈtʃɑːns US: -ˈtʃæns; mɪsˈtʃæns/ *n* [C, U] (piece of) bad luck: 不幸; 厄运; 不幸事件; 灾祸: *by ~*; 由于不幸; 不幸地; *through a ~*. 因一不幸事件。

mis·chief /ˈmɪstʃɪf/; ˈmɪstʃɪf/ *n* 1 [U] injury or damage done by a person or other agent, esp on purpose: 伤害; 损害(尤指故意造成者): *a storm that did much ~ to shipping*. 损害航运甚巨的一次暴风雨。*do sb a ~*, hurt him. 伤害某人。2 [U] moral harm or injury: 道德上的损害; 精神上的伤害: *Such wild speeches may work great ~*, eg may rouse evil passions. 这种狂野的言论可能严重地危害人心。*make ~* (*between ...*), cause discord or ill feeling. (在…之间)搬弄是非。Hence, 由此产生, *'~-maker*, *'~-making*. 3 [U] foolish or thoughtless behaviour likely to cause trouble; not very serious wrongdoing: 胡闹; 恶作剧: *Boys are fond of ~*, of playing tricks, etc. 男孩子们喜欢恶作剧。*Tell the children to keep out of ~*. 告诉那些小孩不要胡闹。*He's up to ~ again*, planning some piece of ~. 他又在打算胡闹了。*She's always getting into ~*. 她老爱胡闹。4 light-hearted, innocent desire to tease: 调皮; 淘气; 嬉戏: *Her eyes were full of ~*. 她的两眼充满了调皮捣蛋的神情。5 [C] person who is fond of ~(3, 4): 好嬉戏的人; 调皮捣蛋者: *Those boys are regular ~s*. 那几个男孩子经常爱嬉闹。*Where have you hidden my book, you little ~?* 你这个小淘气, 把我的书藏到哪儿去了?

mis·chiev·ous /ˈmɪstʃɪvəs; ˈmɪstʃɪvəs/ *adj* 1 causing mischief(2); harmful: 为害的; 有害的: *a ~ letter / rumour*. 害人的信(谣言)。2 filled with, fond of, engaged in, mischief(3, 4); showing a spirit of mischief(3, 4): 胡闹的; 恶作剧的; 淘气的; 顽皮的; 爱捣乱的: *~ looks / tricks*; 调皮的样子(恶作剧的花样); *as ~ as a monkey*. 象猴子一样的顽皮。*~·ly adv* *~·ness n*

mis·con·ceive /ˌmɪskənˈsiːv/; ˌmɪskənˈsiv/ *vt, vi* 1 [VP6A] understand wrongly. 误解。2 [VP3A] *~ of*, have a wrong conception of: 对…有错误观念: *~ one's duty*. 误解个人的职责。**mis·con·cep·tion** /ˌmɪskənˈsepʃn/; ˌmɪskənˈsepʃən/ *n* [U] misconceiving; [C] instance of this. 误解; 错误的观念。

mis·con·duct /ˌmɪsˈkɒndʌkt/; mɪsˈkɑndʌkt/ *n* [U] 1 improper behaviour. 不规矩的行为。2 bad management. 不当的处理; 不善的管理。□ *vt* /ˌmɪskənˈdʌkt; ˌmɪskənˈdʌkt/ 1 [VP6B, 14] *~ oneself* (*with sb*), behave badly. 行为不规矩。2 [VP6A] manage badly: 处理不当; 管理不善: *~ one's business affairs*. 对于个人的商务处置不当。

mis·con·struc·tion /ˌmɪskənˈstrʌkʃn/; ˌmɪskənˈstrʌkʃən/ *n* [U] false or inaccurate interpretation or understanding; [C] instance of this: 曲解; 误解: *Your words were open to ~*. 你的话容易被误解。

mis·con·strue /ˌmɪskənˈstruː/; ˌmɪskənˈstru/ *vt* [VP6A] get a wrong idea of (sb's words, acts, etc): 误解; 误会(某人的言语, 行动等): *You have ~d my words*. 你误会了我的话。

mis·count /ˌmɪsˈkaʊnt; ˌmɪsˈkaʊnt/ vt, vi [VP6A, 2A] count wrongly. 误算; 数错。□ n [C] wrong count, esp of votes at an election. 错误的计算(尤指选票的误计)。

mis·cre·ant /ˈmɪskrɪənt; ˈmɪskrɪənt/ n (dated) scoundrel; villain. (过时用语)无赖; 恶徒。

mis·date /ˌmɪsˈdeɪt; ˌmɪsˈdeɪt/ vt [VP6A] give a wrong date to an event, etc; put a wrong date on a letter, cheque, etc. 误记(事件等)的日期; 在(书信、支票等)之上填错日期。

mis·deal /ˌmɪsˈdiːl; ˌmɪsˈdil/ vt, vi (pt, pp -**dealt** /-ˈdelt; -ˈdelt/) [VP6A, 2A] deal (playing-cards) wrongly. 发错(纸牌)。□ n error in dealing cards: 错牌: ~ a letter, by 发牌错误: I've got 14 cards; it's a ~. 我有了十四张牌; 这是发牌的错误。

mis·deed /ˌmɪsˈdiːd; ˌmɪsˈdid/ n wicked act; crime: 恶行; 罪行: be punished for one's ~s. 因恶行而受罚。

mis·de·mean·our (US = -**meanor**) /ˌmɪsdɪˈmiːnə(r); ˌmɪsdɪˈminɚ/ n (legal) offence less serious than a felony. (法律)较轻的犯法行为; 轻罪; 小罪。

mis·di·rect /ˌmɪsdɪˈrekt; ˌmɪsdəˈrekt/ vt [VP6A] direct wrongly: 错误指示; 写错地址: 错用: ~ a letter, by failing to put the full or correct address on it; 写错一信的投递地址; ~ one's energies or abilities, eg by using them for a bad purpose; 错用精力或能力(如用于为非作歹); ~ a jury, (of a judge in a law court) give the jury wrong information on a point of law. (指推事)在法律问题上对陪审团做错误的指示。**mis·di·rec·tion** /ˌmɪsdɪˈrekʃn; ˌmɪsdəˈrekʃən/ n.

mis·doing /ˌmɪsˈduːɪŋ; ˌmɪsˈduɪŋ/ n (usu pl) misdeed. (通常用复数)恶行; 罪行。

mise en scène /ˌmiːz ɒn ˈseɪn; ˌmizɑ̃ˈsɛn/ n scenery and properties of an acted play; (fig) general surroundings of an event. 舞台的布景与道具; (喻)事件周遭之一般情况。

miser /ˈmaɪzə(r); ˈmaɪzɚ/ n person who loves wealth for its own sake and spends as little as possible. 守财奴; 吝啬的人。~·**ly** adj like a ~; stingy. 似守财奴的; 吝啬的; 小气的。~·**li·ness** n.

mis·er·able /ˈmɪzrəbl; ˈmɪzərəbl/ adj 1 wretched; very unhappy: 可怜的; 不幸的; 悲惨的; 愁苦的: ~ from cold and hunger; 因饥寒而痛苦的; the ~ lives of the refugees in Europe after the war. 战后欧洲难民的悲惨生活。He makes her life ~. 他使她的生活苦不堪言。2 causing wretchedness and unhappiness: 造成不幸与痛苦的: ~ weather; 恼人的天气; ~ slums. 令人难过的贫民区。3 poor in quality: 简陋的; 粗劣的: What a ~ meal! 多么粗劣的一顿饭! What a ~ pension after fifty years' hard work! 五十年的辛苦工作只拿到这么可怜的一笔养老金! **mis·er·ably** /-əblɪ; -əblɪ/ adv: die miserably; 悲惨地死去; be miserably poor; 穷得无是可怜; miserably underpaid. 待遇奇薄。

mis·ery /ˈmɪzərɪ; ˈmɪzərɪ/ n (pl -**ries**) 1 [U] state of being miserable; great suffering (of mind or body): 悲惨; 不幸; (心灵或身体上的)痛苦: be in a ~/suffer ~ from the toothache; 受牙痛之苦; living in ~ and want, in wretched conditions and poverty. 生活在贫穷困苦之中。put the animal out of its ~, end its sufferings by killing it. 解除动物的痛苦(杀死它以结束其痛苦)。2 (pl) painful happenings; great misfortunes: (复)痛苦的事; 大不幸: the miseries of mankind. 人类的大不幸。3 (colloq) person who is always miserable and complaining: (口)总是不高兴而抱怨的人: I've had enough of your complaints, you little ~! 我已经听够了你的抱怨, 你这个小唠叨鬼!

mis·fire /ˌmɪsˈfaɪə(r); ˌmɪsˈfaɪr/ vi [VP2A] (of a gun) fail to go off; (of a motor-engine) fail to ignite in a cylinder; (colloq of a joke, etc) fall flat; fail to have the intended result. (指枪炮)不发火; 打不出; (指发动机)不着火; 发不动; (口, 指笑话等)完全失败; 达不到目的。□ n such a failure. 不发火, 不能发动; 未达到目的。

mis·fit /ˈmɪsfɪt; ˈmɪsˌfɪt/ n article of clothing which does not fit well the person it is meant for: (fig) person not well suited to his position or his associates. 不合身的衣服; (喻)不甚称职的人; 不甚适合其地位的人; 与伙伴合不来的人。

mis·for·tune /ˌmɪsˈfɔːtʃuːn; ˌmɪsˈfɔrtʃən/ n 1 [U] bad luck: 不幸: suffer ~; 遭受不幸: companions in ~. 患难中的友伴; 患难之交。2 [C] instance of bad luck; unfortunate accident or happening: 灾祸; 不幸事故: He bore his ~s bravely. 他勇敢地忍受他所遭遇的灾难。

mis·give /ˌmɪsˈgɪv; ˌmɪsˈgɪv/ vt (pt misgave /-ˈgeɪv; -ˈgev/, pp misgiven /-ˈgɪvn; -ˈgɪvən/) (used impersonally; old use) cause to feel doubt, fear or anxiety: (无人称用法; 旧用法)使感到怀疑、恐惧或焦虑: My mind/heart ~s me, I am filled with suspicion or foreboding, I feel doubtful, troubled. 我感到疑虑不安。**mis·giv·ing** /ˌmɪsˈgɪvɪŋ; ˌmɪsˈgɪvɪŋ/ n [C, U] (feeling of) doubt, suspicion, distrust, etc: 怀疑; 疑惑; 担忧: a heart/mind full of misgiving(s). 心中充满疑虑; 心中大感不安。

mis·gov·ern /ˌmɪsˈgʌvn; ˌmɪsˈgʌvən/ vt [VP6A] govern (the State, etc) badly. 治理(国家等)不当。~·**ment** n [U].

mis·guide /ˌmɪsˈgaɪd; ˌmɪsˈgaɪd/ vt [VP6A, 14] give wrong or misleading information or directions to: 给予错误的消息或指导; 使误入歧途: We had been ~d into thinking that .... 我们受到错误的指导, 认为…。**mis·guided** adj foolish and wrong (because of bad or wrong guidance or influence): 愚昧而错误的(因受不良或错误引导所致); 误入歧途的: ~d conduct/zeal; 愚昧的行为(错用的热心); ~d boys. 被导入歧途的男孩们。

mis·handle /ˌmɪsˈhændl; ˌmɪsˈhændl/ vt deal with roughly, rudely or inefficiently. 粗暴地对待; 虐待; 瞎弄; 处理不当。

mis·hap /ˈmɪshæp; ˈmɪsˌhæp/ n [C] unlucky accident: 不幸的意外事故: meet with a slight ~; 遭遇一件小意外事件; arrive home after many ~s; 历经许多事故方才到家; [U] bad luck; accident: 不幸; 意外: arrive without ~. 平安抵达。

mish·mash /ˈmɪʃmæʃ; ˈmɪʃˌmæʃ/ n [U] confused mixture; hotchpotch. 杂乱的一堆; 混杂。

mis·in·form /ˌmɪsɪnˈfɔːm; ˌmɪsɪnˈfɔrm/ vt [VP6A] give wrong information to; mislead: 供给…错误消息; 误传; 误引: You've been ~ed. 你所得到的消息不确。

mis·in·ter·pret /ˌmɪsɪnˈtɜːprɪt; ˌmɪsɪnˈtɝprɪt/ vt [VP6A] give a wrong interpretation to; make a wrong inference from: 误解; 误以为; 误译: He ~ed her silence as giving consent. 他把她的沉默误认为同意。

mis·judge /ˌmɪsˈdʒʌdʒ; ˌmɪsˈdʒʌdʒ/ vt, vi [VP6A, 2A] judge or estimate wrongly; form a wrong opinion of: (把…)判断错误; (把…)估计错误; (将…)论断错误: You have ~d my motives. 你把我的动机判断错了。He ~d the distance and fell into the stream. 他把距离估计错误, 结果跌进小河里去了。

mis·lay /ˌmɪsˈleɪ; ˌmɪsˈle/ vt (pt, pp **mislaid** /-ˈleɪd; -ˈled/) [VP6A] put (sth) by an oversight where it cannot easily be found: 因疏忽而把(某物)放在不容易找到的地方; 误置: I've mislaid my passport. 我忘了把护照放到哪里去了。

mis·lead /ˌmɪsˈliːd; ˌmɪsˈlid/ vt (pt, pp **misled** /-ˈled; -ˈled/) [VP6A] lead wrongly; cause to be or do wrong; give a wrong idea to: 错误引领; 使入歧途; 使…有错误的想法: be misled by a guide, during a journey: 被向导领错了路; misled by bad companions, led into evil ways. 被不良伙伴领入歧途。You misled me as to your intentions. 你使我对于你的意向有错误的想法。This information is rather ~ing, gives a wrong impression. 这个消息容易引起误解。

mis·man·age /ˌmɪsˈmænɪdʒ; ˌmɪsˈmænɪdʒ/ vt [VP6A] manage badly or wrongly. 管理不善; 处理错误。~·**ment** n

mis·name /ˌmɪsˈneɪm; mɪsˈnem/ vt [VP6A] (usu passive) call by a wrong or improper name. (通常用被动语态)误称; 称呼不当; 取名不妥。

mis·nomer /ˌmɪsˈnəʊmə(r); mɪsˈnomə/ n [C] wrong use of a name or word: 错用名称; 用字错误: It's a ~ to call this place a first-class hotel. 把这地方叫做第一流旅馆是不当的。

mis·ogyn·ist /mɪˈsɒdʒɪnɪst; mɪˈsɑdʒənɪst/ n hater of women. 憎恨女人的人。

mis·place /ˌmɪsˈpleɪs; mɪsˈples/ vt [VP6A] 1 put in a wrong place. 错放; 误置。 2 (usu passive) give love, affection wrongly or unwisely: (通常用被动语态)错误或愚昧地付出 (爱情、情感): ~d confidence, given to sb who does not deserve it or who misuses it. 错给予的信任(即对方不值得信任或胡乱利用其既得之信任)。

mis·print /ˌmɪsˈprɪnt; mɪsˈprɪnt/ vt [VP6A] make an error in printing, eg errors and omissions expected for errors and omissions excepted. 误印; 印刷错误 (如 errors and omissions excepted 误印为 errors and omissions expected)。 □ n /ˈmɪsprɪnt; mɪsˈprɪnt/ such an error. 误印; 排印上的错误。

mis·pro·nounce /ˌmɪsprəˈnaʊns; ˌmɪsprəˈnaʊns/ vt [VP6A] pronounce wrongly. 发音错误; 念错。 **mis·pro·nun·ci·ation** /ˌmɪsprəˌnʌnsɪˈeɪʃn; ˌmɪsprəˌnʌnsɪˈeʃən/ n

mis·quote /ˌmɪsˈkwəʊt; mɪsˈkwot/ vt [VP6A] quote wrongly. 引述错误。 **mis·quo·ta·tion** /ˌmɪskwəʊˈteɪʃn; ˌmɪskwoˈteʃən/ n [C, U].

mis·read /ˌmɪsˈriːd; mɪsˈrid/ vt (pt, pp misread /-ˈred; -ˈred/) [VP6A] read or interpret wrongly: 错读; 误读; 将…解释错误: ~ one's instructions. 误解训令。

mis·rep·re·sent /ˌmɪsˌreprɪˈzent; ˌmɪsreprɪˈzent/ vt represent wrongly; give a false account of: 不正确地表达、解释、描述; 不实地报导、叙述: be grossly ~ed by the press. 被报纸作粗鄙不实的报导。 **mis·rep·re·sen·ta·tion** /ˌmɪsˌreprɪzenˈteɪʃn; ˌmɪsreprɪzenˈteʃən/ n [C, U].

mis·rule /ˌmɪsˈruːl; mɪsˈrul/ n [U] bad government; lawlessness; confusion. 苛政; 暴政; 无法无天; 混乱; 紊乱。

miss¹ /mɪs; mɪs/ n [C] failure to hit, catch, reach, etc: 未打中; 未捉到; 没达到; 错过; 避过; 省略: ten hits and one ~. 十次打中, 一次未中。 That was a lucky ~, a fortunate escape. 得免于难, 真是侥幸。 **give sth a ~**, (colloq) omit it, leave it alone: (口)省略掉某物, 不管它: I'll give the fish course a ~. 我不吃那道鱼了。 **A ~ is as good as a mile,** (prov) A narrow escape is the same in effect as an escape by a wide margin. (谚)大错小错终归是错; 死里逃生与轻易逃脱结果相同。

miss² /mɪs; mɪs/ n 1 **M~**, title prefixed to the (first name +) surname of an unmarried woman: (对未婚女子之称呼, 加于姓或姓名前): M~ (Gloria) Kelly. (格洛里亚)凯莉小姐。 **M~ Jamaica**, eg as the title of a beauty queen. 牙买加小姐(选美会上优胜者的头衔)。 2 (small m, usu playful or perhaps derog) young girl, schoolgirl: (小写, 通常含戏弄或轻蔑之意)少女; 小姐; 小女生: She's a saucy ~. 她是个孟浪的小姐。 3 (as a vocative, eg by schoolchildren to a woman teacher, also to shopkeepers, etc): (用作呼唤语, 例如学童对女老师或商店女老板等之称呼): Good morning, ~! 小姐! 您早啊! Two cups of coffee, ~. (美)两杯咖啡, 小姐(或老板娘)。 4 (trade use, pl) young girls: (商业用语, 复数)少女们: shoes, coats, etc for Junior M~es, (today, often replaced by teenagers). 供少女穿的鞋子, 上衣等(此短语中之 Junior Misses 现常以 teenagers 一词代之)。

miss² /mɪs; mɪs/ vt, vi (pt, pp **missed**) 1[VP6A, B, C, 2A] fail to hit, hold, catch, reach, see, etc what it is desired to hit, hold, etc: 未打中; 未抓住; 未捉到; 未达到; 未看见; 未赶上; 错过; 避过: fire at a tiger and ~ (it). 开枪打虎但没有打中(它); ~ one's aim, 没达到目的; ~ the target. 没打中目标。 He ~ed his footing, slipped, eg while climbing on rocks. 他失足滑了一下(如在攀登山石时)。 He ~ed the 9.30 train (= was too late for it, did not catch it), and therefore ~ed (ie luckily escaped) the accident. 他没赶上九时三十分的那班火车, 也正因此而逃过那次车祸。 The house is at the next corner; you can't ~ it, you'll certainly see it. 那房子就在下一个拐弯的地方, 你不会看不见的。 He ~ed (= failed to see) the point of my joke. 他没听懂我的笑话。 I ~ed (=did not hear) the first part of the speech. 我没听到演说的第一部分。 We only just ~ed (= escaped) having a nasty accident. 我们侥幸逃过了一场大难。 We ~ed seeing (= didn't see, failed to see) that film when it was at the local cinema. 那影片在本地电影院上映时我们没去看。 2 [VP6A] realize, learn, feel regret at, the absence of: 发现遗失; 得丢失掉; 惋惜; 怀念: When did you ~ your purse, realize that you no longer had it? 你什么时候发现你的钱包不见了? He's so rich that he wouldn't ~ £100. 他非常有钱, 不会因失掉一百英镑而觉得可惜。 She'd ~ her husband if he died. 假如她丈夫死了她就会怀念他的。 Old Smith won't be ~ed, Nobody will feel regret at his absence, death, retirement, etc. 老史密斯要是不在了(死亡或者退休等), 没有人会感到遗憾。 3 [VP2C] ~ out (on sth), (colloq) lose an opportunity to benefit from sth, enjoy oneself: (口)失去(自某事物)获益的机会; 失去享乐的机会: If I don't go to the party, I shall feel that I'm ~ing out. 如果我不去参加那场舞会, 我将会感到失去享乐的良机。 I ~ed out on his offer of a free holiday in Spain. 他让我免费去西班牙度一次假, 我却坐失良机。 [VP15B] ~ sth out, omit; fail to put in or say: 省掉; 遗漏; 漏述: The printers have ~ed out a word/line. 印刷工人遗漏了一个字(一行)。 I shall ~ out the sweet course, ie at a meal, not take it. 我要省掉那道甜食(即不吃它)。 When we sing this song, ~ out the second and fourth verses, don't sing them. 当我们唱这首歌的时候, 大家省去第二节和第四节(即不唱这两节)。 ~·ing adj not to be found; not in the place where it ought to be: 找不到的; 失去的; 失踪的: a book with two pages ~ing; 掉了两页的一本书; the dead, wounded and ~ing, ie soldiers in war; 伤亡与失踪的官兵; ~ing persons, persons who cannot be traced. 行踪不明的人。 **the ~ing link,** ⇨ link¹(3).

mis·sal /ˈmɪsl; ˈmɪsl/ n book containing the order of service for Mass in the RC Church; book of prayers and devotions. 天主教的弥撒书; 祈祷书。

mis·shapen /ˌmɪsˈʃeɪpən; mɪsˈʃepən/ adj (esp of the body or a limb) deformed; badly shaped. (尤指身体或四肢之一)残废的; 畸形的。

mis·sile /ˈmɪsaɪl US: ˈmɪsl; ˈmɪsl/ n object or weapon that is thrown (eg a stone), shot (eg an arrow) or projected (eg a rocket): 投出的东西或(用以抛掷的)石头、射出的箭矢或发射的火箭); 射体; 导弹; 飞弹: (attrib) (用作定语) ~ sites/bases, for ballistic ~s, etc. 导弹发射场(基地)。 **guided ~,** eg from ground to air, for destroying aircraft, guided by electronic devices. 导向导弹 (如发自地面摧毁空中飞机之地对空电导导弹)。 **inter-continental ballistic ~,** (abbr 略作 **ICBM**), long-range rocket with a warhead. 洲际弹道导弹。

mission /ˈmɪʃn; ˈmɪʃən/ n 1 (the sending out of a) number of persons entrusted with special work, usu abroad: (负有特殊任务通常派往国外的)代表团; 工作团; 使节团; 此等团体之派遣: a trade ~ to S America; 派往南美的商务团(贸易考察团); go/come/send sb on a ~ of inquiry, 去(来, 派遣某人去)担任调查工作; complete one's ~ successfully. 成功地完成任务; 达成任务。 2 (the sending out of) religious teachers (~aries) to convert people by preaching, teaching, etc: 布道团; 布道团之派遣: Foreign M~s; 国外布道团; Home M~s, ie to preach to people in the home country, esp those not usu interested in religion. 国内布道团。 3 place where the work of a ~(2) is carried on; building(s), organization, etc needed for such work; settlement where charitable or medical work is carried on, esp among poor people. 传道地区; 传道机构; 传道会; 布道

所；慈善教育机构；教济所。**4 ~ in life,** that work which a person feels called upon to do: 天职: *She feels her ~ in life is to reform juvenile delinquents.* 她觉得她的天职是改造少年罪犯。**5** (esp US) special task, assigned to an individual or a unit of the armed forces: (美)(指派给某人或部队单位的)特殊任务；作战任务: *The group has flown twenty ~s.* 该小组已完成了二十次的特殊飞行任务。

mis·sion·ary /ˈmɪʃənrɪ US: -nerɪ/, ˈmɪʃən,ɛrɪ/ n (pl **-ries**) person sent to preach his religion, esp among people who are ignorant of it; (attrib) of missions(2) or missionaries: 传教士；(用作定语)传道(团)的；传教士的: *a ~ meeting,* at which a ~ talks about his work or one held to raise funds; 布道会(会中由传教士布道或募集基金); *a ~ box,* in which money is collected for charitable missions. 慈善奉献箱。

mis·sis /ˈmɪsɪz; ˈmɪsɪz/ n ⇨ **missus.**

mis·sive /ˈmɪsɪv; ˈmɪsɪv/ n (used hum for) (esp a long, serious-looking) letter. (诙谐的用法)书信(尤指长篇正式者); 公文; 公函。

mis·spell /ˌmɪsˈspel; ˌmɪsˈspɛl/ vt (pt, pp **misspelled** or **misspelt** /-ˈspelt; -ˈspɛlt/) [VP6A] spell wrongly. 误拼; 拼错。~·**ing** n

mis·spend /ˌmɪsˈspend; ˌmɪsˈspɛnd/ vt (pt, pp **misspent** /-ˈspent; -ˈspɛnt/) [VP6A] spend or use wrongly or foolishly (esp pp): 误用; 浪费; 虚度(尤常用过去分词形式): *a misspent youth,* (used of one who spends or has spent his early years only in foolish pleasures). 一位虚度光阴的青年。

mis·state /ˌmɪsˈsteɪt; ˌmɪsˈstet/ vt [VP6A] state wrongly: 误述; 虚言; 伪述: *He was careful not to ~ his case.* 他很小心, 免得把他的事实讲错。~**ment** n

mis·sus, mis·sis /ˈmɪsɪz; ˈmɪsəz/ n (colloq or sl) (used with *the, my, his, your*) wife: (口或俚)(与 the, my, his, your 连用)妻子: *How's the ~?* 尊夫人好吗? *My ~ won't like that.* 内人不会喜欢那个。

missy /ˈmɪsɪ; ˈmɪsɪ/ n (pl **-sies**) (colloq, familiar) young girl; miss: (口, 亲昵语)小姑娘; 小姐: *Well, ~, what do you want?* 喂, 小姑娘, 你要什么?

mist /mɪst/ n 1 [C, U] (occasion when there is, an area with) water vapour in the air, at or near the earth's surface, less thick than fog and not so light as haze: 雾; 霭; (在地面上或近地面雪之雾, 密度低于 fog 而高于 haze; 气象学上省词 fog = 雾, mist = 霭, haze = 霾, 但一般通称为雾); 有雾之时; 有雾地区: *Hills hidden / shrouded in ~;* 隐在雾中(为雾所笼罩)的小山; (fig) (喻) *lost in the ~s of time;* 消失于时间的薄雾之中(时间久了, 渐被遗忘); such vapour condensed on a surface, eg glass, clouding its appearance. 凝结于物体(如玻璃)表面上的水蒸气; 迷濛。**2** [C] filmy appearance before the eyes (caused by tears, etc); (fig) sth that darkens the mind, makes understanding difficult, etc: (因流泪等而在眼前形成的)朦胧不清; (喻)蒙蔽心思之事物; 使了解困难之事物: *see things through a ~.* 模糊糊地看事物。□ vi, vt [VP2C, 6A] ~ (**over**), cover, be covered, with ~: 笼罩以雾; 被雾所笼罩; 模糊不清: *The scene ~ed over.* 景色被雾笼罩着。*The mirror ~ed over.* 那镜子模糊不清。*Her eyes (were) ~ed with tears.* 她的眼睛给泪迷濛了。~**y** adj (**-ier, -iest**) **1** with ~: 有雾的; 雾的: *a ~y evening;* 有雾的晚上; *~y weather;* 有雾的天气。~**y** ~ **2** not clear: 朦胧不清的; 模糊的: *have only a ~y idea.* 只有一个模糊的观念。~**·ily** /-ɪlɪ; -əlɪ/ adv ~**i·ness** n

mis·take[1] /mɪsˈteɪk; məˈstek/ n [C] wrong opinion, idea or act: (意见、想法或行为上的)错误; 误: *spelling ~s.* 拼字错误。*We all make ~s occasionally.* 我们偶尔都会犯错。*There's some ~!* 有点儿错! *There must be some ~!* 一定有些什么错了! *by ~,* as the result of carelessness, forgetfulness, etc; in error: 由疏忽、健忘等所致; 由于错误; 错: *I took your umbrella by ~.* 我错拿了你的雨伞。*and no ~,* (colloq) without any doubt: (口)毫无疑问; 的确: *It's hot today and no ~!* 今天的确很热!

mis·take[2] /mɪˈsteɪk; məˈstek/ vt, vi (pl **mistook** /mɪˈstʊk; mɪsˈtʊk/, pp **mistaken** /mɪˈsteɪkn; məˈstekən/) **1** [VP6A, 10] be wrong, have a wrong idea, about: 弄错; 误解。~ *sb's meaning.* 误解某人的意思。*We've ~n the house,* come to the wrong house. 我们走错了房子。**There's no mistaking,** no possibility of being wrong about: 不会弄错: *There's no mistaking what ought to be done.* 应该做什么, 是不会弄错的。**2** [VP14] ~ *sb/sth for,* wrongly suppose that sb or sth is (as of sth else): 误认某人或某物为; 错把···当做: *Don Quixote mistook the windmills for giants.* 唐吉诃德错把风车当巨人。*She is often ~n for her twin sister.* 她常常被误认为她的孪生姐姐(妹妹)。**3** (older uses) (较旧用法) *If I ~ not,* unless I am wrong. 假如我没错的话; 除非我错了。*You ~, my dear,* you're wrong. 亲爱的, 你错了。~**·taken** (pp as 过去分词用作) adj **1** in error; wrong in opinion: 错误的; 见解上错误的: *a case of ~n identity;* 认错人的事件; ~*n ideas.* 错误的观念。**be ~n (about sth),** be in error: (对某事)持错误的见解; (把某事)弄错: *If I'm not ~n, there's the man we met on the train.* 如果我没弄错, 那个人就是我们在火车上碰到的。*You're ~.* 你错了。**2** ill-judged: 判断错误的; 不合时宜的: ~*n kindness / zeal.* 用错地方的慈爱(热心)。**mis·tak·en·ly** adv

mis·ter /ˈmɪstə(r); ˈmɪstɚ/ n **1** (always written 总是写成 **Mr**) title prefixed to a man's (first name +) surname when he has no other title: *Mr (Henry) Green,* or to his office: *Mr Secretary.* 先生;(冠于没有特殊衔称的男人姓名或姓之前的称呼, 如 Mr (Henry) Green (亨利)格林先生, 或冠于职务之前, 如 Mr Secretary 秘书先生)。⇨ **Mrs, Ms. 2** (used *without* a person's name; sl, or used by children): (不附带姓名的称呼); 俚, 或孩童所用的称呼)先生: *Listen to me, ~.* 听我说, 先生。*Please, ~, can I have my ball back?* 先生, 请把我的球(给)还给我好吗?

mis·time /ˌmɪsˈtaɪm; mɪsˈtaɪm/ vt (used esp in the pp) say or do sth out of season, at an unsuitable time: (尤用过去分词)说不合时宜的话; 做不合时宜的事: *a ~d (= inopportune) intervention.* 不合时宜的介入。

mistle·toe /ˈmɪsltəʊ; ˈmɪsl,to/ n [U] parasitic evergreen plant (growing on fruit and other trees) with small white sticky berries (used in making bird-lime and as a Christmas decoration): 槲寄生(一种寄生于果树上的的常青植物, 其白色小浆果具粘性, 用以制粘鸟胶, 树或枝则用作圣诞节之装饰)。

mis·took /mɪˈstʊk; mɪsˈtʊk/ pt of **mistake.**

mis·tral /ˈmɪstrəl; ˈmɪstrəl/ n cold, dry wind blowing from the north through the Rhone valley in France. 吹过法国境内罗讷河流域的寒冷而干燥的北风。

mis·trans·late /ˌmɪstrænzˈleɪt; ˌmɪstræns'let/ vt [VP6A] translate wrongly. 误译。**mis·trans·la·tion** /-ˈleɪʃn; -ˈleʃən/ n [C, U].

mis·tress /ˈmɪstrɪs; ˈmɪstrɪs/ n **1** woman at the head of a household or family; woman in authority who gives orders to servants: 主妇; 女主人: *Servants willingly obey a kind ~.* 佣人愿意听从和善的女主人。*Is your ~ at home?* 你家太太在家吗? **2** woman school teacher: 女教师: *the 'French mistress,* teacher of French (but not necessarily a Frenchwoman); 女法语教师(但不一定是法国妇女); *the 'games ~,* in charge of games (hockey, etc). 女体育教员(负责曲棍球等者)。**3** woman with a good knowledge or control of sth: 精通某事的妇女; 能控制某情况的妇女: *a ~ of needlework.* 精于缝纫的妇女。*She is ~ of the situation.* 她能控制这局面。*Venice used to be called the ~ of the Adriatic.* 威尼斯从前称亚得里亚海的门户。**4** (in stories, plays, etc dealing with periods before the 18th c, and still in Scotland by some people) title equivalent to the modern *Mrs* or *Miss:* (用于叙述十八世纪以前之故事, 戏剧等, 且仍为苏格兰某些人民所沿用)相当于现代习用之'夫人' (Mrs) 或'小姐' (Miss) 的称呼。**5** (poet) woman loved and courted by a man: (诗)女爱人; 女

情人: '*O* ~ *mine!*' '哦，我的情人！' **6** woman having regular sexual intercourse with one man to whom she is not married. 情妇。Cf 参较 *paramour* (liter) (文学用语) and *concubine* (dated) (过时用语). ⇨ **master**.

mis·trial /ˌmɪsˈtraɪəl; mɪsˈtraɪəl/ *n* (legal) trial which is made invalid because of some error in the proceedings. (法律) 误审 (因程序错误而宣告无效的审判); 无效审判。

mis·trust /ˌmɪsˈtrʌst; mɪsˈtrʌst/ *vt* [VP6A] feel no confidence in: 不信任; 不相信; 怀疑: ~ *one's own powers*. 不相信自己的智能。□ *n* [U] (also with *indef art*) (亦与不定冠词连用) (a) ~ (*of*), want of confidence or trust (in): 不信任; 疑惑; 怀疑: *She had a strong* ~ *of anything new and strange*. 她对任何新奇的事物都非常不信任。~·ful /-fl; -fl/ *adj* suspicious (*of*). 疑惑的; 疑心的 (*of* 之连用)。~·fully /-fələr; -fələr/ *adv*

misty /ˈmɪstɪ; ˈmɪstɪ/ ⇨ **mist**.

mis·un·der·stand /ˌmɪsˌʌndəˈstænd; ˌmɪsʌndəˈstænd/ *vt* (*pt, pp* **-stood** /-ˈstʊd; -ˈstʊd/) [VP6A] take a wrong meaning from (instructions, messages, etc); form a wrong opinion of (sb or sth): 误会; 误解: *His intentions were misunderstood*. 他的意图被误解了。*She had always felt misunderstood*. 她老是以为被人误解了。~·ing *n* [C, U] failure to understand rightly, esp when this has led or may lead to ill feelings: 误会; 误解: ~*ings between nations that may lead to war*; 可能导致战争的国际间的误会; *clear up a* ~*ing*. 澄清误会。

mis·use /ˌmɪsˈjuːz; mɪsˈjuz/ *vt* [VP6A] use wrongly; use for a wrong purpose; treat badly. 误用; 错用; 滥用; 虐待。□ *n* /ˌmɪsˈjuːs; mɪsˈjus/ [U] using wrongly; [C] instance of this: 误用; 错用; 滥用; 误用之实例: *the* ~ *of power*. 滥用权力。

mite[1] /maɪt; maɪt/ *n* **1** very small or modest contribution or offering: 极少的捐助或贡献: *offer a* ~ *of comfort*; 给予一点安慰; *give one's* ~ *to a good cause*. 对善举聊尽绵薄。**2** tiny object, esp a small child (usu as an object of sympathy): 小东西 (尤指小孩, 通常为可寄予同情之对象): *Poor little* ~! 可怜的小孩儿！*What a* ~ *of a child!* 一个多么小的孩子！

mite[2] /maɪt; maɪt/ *n* [C] small parasitic arachnid that may be found in food, eg '*cheese* ~*s*, and may carry disease. (发现于食物等中, 可传布疾病之) 节肢小寄生虫 (如 cheese mites 乳酪中之虫)。

mi·ter /ˈmaɪtə(r); ˈmaɪtɚ/ *n* (US) = mitre.

miti·gate /ˈmɪtɪgeɪt; ˈmɪtəˌget/ *vt* [VP6A] make less severe, violent or painful. 使缓和; 使减轻; 使减少。**mitigating circumstances**, those that may make a mistake, crime, etc seem less serious. 似乎可减轻错误、犯罪等之严重性的情况; 有缓和作用的情势。**miti·ga·tion** /ˌmɪtɪˈgeɪʃn; ˌmɪtəˈgeʃən/ *n* [U].

mi·tre (US = **mi·ter**) /ˈmaɪtə(r); ˈmaɪtɚ/ *n* **1** tall head-dress worn by bishops at some ceremonies. 主教冠 (主教在某些仪式进行时所戴者)。⇨ the illus at **vestment**. 参看 vestment 之插图。**2** '~(-joint), joint whose line of junction bisects the angle between the two bevelled surfaces it joins. 斜榫; 斜接。

mitt /mɪt; mɪt/ *n* **1** mitten. (拇指分开其他四指连在一起的) 手套。**2** baseball glove; (colloq) boxing-glove. 棒球手套; (口) 拳击手套。**3** (sl) hand; fist. (俚) 手; 拳。

mit·ten /ˈmɪtn; ˈmɪtn/ *n* **1** kind of glove covering four fingers together and the thumb separately. (拇指分开, 其他四指连在一起的) 手套。**2** covering for the back and palm of the hand only, leaving the thumb and fingers bare. 露指手套 (仅套住掌心与手背)。

mix[1] /mɪks; mɪks/ *vt, vi* **1** [VP6A, 12B, 13B, 14, 2A, C] (of different substances, people, etc) put, bring or come together so that the substances, etc are no longer distinct; make or prepare (sth) by doing this: (指不同物质、人等) 混合; 混在一起; 借混合以做成或调制成 (某物): *mix flour and water*. 把面粉和水混合在一起。*The doctor mixed me a bottle of medicine/mixed a bottle of medicine for me*. 医生为我配了一瓶药。*We

can sometimes mix business with pleasure*. 我们有时候能把工作和享乐合在一起。*She was mixing* (= preparing) *a salad*. 她正在调制沙拉 (凉菜)。*Oil and water don't mix*. 油和水不相混合。*You can't mix oil with water*. 你不能使油与水相混合。*Many races are mixed in Hawaii*. 在夏威夷, 许多人种混合在一起。**2** [VP2A, 3A] *mix (with)*, (of persons) come or be together in society: (指人) 交往; 相处: *He doesn't mix well*, doesn't get on well with people, esp people of different social classes or different interests. 他不善与人相处(尤指不善与社会阶层不同或兴趣不同的人相处)。**3** [VP15B] *mix sth/sb up (with sth/sb)*, mix thoroughly (with); confuse in the mind (with); be unable to distinguish (from): 完全混合; 使弄不清楚; 不能分辨: *Mix up the salt with the pepper*. 把盐和胡椒粉调合在一起。*Now you've mixed me up completely/ completely confused me!* 你可把我完全弄糊涂了！*You're always mixing me up with my twin brother*. 你老是分辨不出我和我的孪生哥哥(弟弟)。*be/ get mixed up in/with sth*, be involved in/with: 参与: *Don't get mixed up in politics/mixed up with those politicians*, keep clear of them. 不要参与政治活动(不要和那些政客混杂在一起)。*I don't want to be mixed up in the affair*, I don't want to be connected with it in any way. 我不愿被牵涉到那件事中。'**mix-up** *n* confused state: 混乱; 混杂: *What a mix-up!* 情形多混乱！*There's been a bit of a mix-up about who should be invited to the party*, some confusion and mistakes. 应该请谁参加宴会已经有点儿弄不清楚了, 有误会和错误。'**mixed-up** *adj* mentally confused; mal-adjusted: 糊涂的; 不适应的: *He feels very mixed-up about life*, cannot see clearly what principles, etc to adopt. 他对人生感到很迷惘。*I'm sorry for these mixed-up kids*, children who are confused by social problems. 我为这些无法适应社会的孩子们感到惋惜。

mix[2] /mɪks; mɪks/ *n* (chiefly in trade and comm) ingredients, mixed or to be mixed, for a purpose, eg for plaster, mortar, concrete or kinds of food: (主用于贸易与商业) (为了调制灰泥、混凝土或某些食品等而混好或待混的) 混合成分: *an ice-'cream mix*; 冰淇淋粉; *a 'cake mix*, of flour, egg-powder, sugar, etc to be used in making cakes. 糕饼混合料(面粉、蛋粉、糖等)。

mixed /mɪkst; mɪkst/ *adj* of different sorts: 混合的; 杂样的: ~ *biscuits/pickles*; 什锦饼干(泡菜); *a* ~ *school*, for boys and girls; 男女兼收的学校; *a* ~ *company*, including people of different classes, tastes, etc. 一群形形色色的人。*have* ~ *feelings (about sth)*, feel eg both sorrow and pleasure (about it). 对某事具备混杂的感情(如欢乐悲欢喜); 百感交集。~ '**blessing**, sth that has both advantages and disadvantages. 有利亦有弊之事。~ '**doubles**, (tennis, etc) with two players, one man and one woman, on each side. (网球等)男女混合双打。~ '**farming**, eg dairy farming and cereals. 农业的混合经营(例如兼营牛奶制品与谷物)。~ '**grill**, eg liver, kidney and bacon. 什锦烤肉(例如由肝、腰子、腌肉等混杂而成)。~ '**marriage**, one between persons of different races or religions. 杂婚; 异族通婚; 不同宗教的通婚。~ '**metaphor**, two or more metaphors used inconsistently together, producing a ludicrous effect, eg 'The scourge of tyranny had burnt his fingers'. 混合隐喻(二个或更多的隐喻矛盾地用在一起, 以收可笑之效, 例

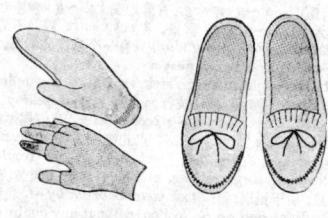

mittens   moccasins

如‘暴虐的鞭笞已烧伤了他的手指’）.

mixer /'mɪksə(r); 'mɪksɚ/ n 1 person or thing that mixes: 使混合的人或物; 混合者; 混合机; 拌合机; 搅拌器: a ce'ment ~; 水泥 (混凝土) 搅拌机; an electric 'food~; 电动食物搅拌机; (TV, films) person or thing that combines shots on to one length of film or video-tape. (电视、电影) (电影胶片或电视录象带的) 剪接者; 剪接器. 2 be a good ~, (colloq) one who is at ease with others on social occasions. (口) 一个善于交际的人(在社交场合上易于与人相处). ⇨ **mix¹(2).**

mix·ture /'mɪkstʃə(r); 'mɪkstʃɚ/ n 1 [U] mixing or being mixed. 混合; 被混合. 2 [C] sth made by mixing: 混合物: a 'smoking ~, made by blending different kinds of tobacco; 混合烟草; a 'cough ~, ~ of several medicines. 咳嗽混合药 (药水). Air is ~, not a compound, of gases. 空气是气体的混合物(而非化合物). the ~ as before, (colloq) the same procedure, treatment, etc as in the past. (口)(手续、疗法等)与以前一样; 照老办法.

miz·zen, mizen /'mɪzn; 'mɪzn̩/ n 1 '~(-mast), mast nearest the stern on a ship with three masts. 第三桅(三桅船上最靠近船尾的桅)前桅. 2'~ (-sail), lowest square sail set on this mast. 后帆(第三桅上最低的方形帆); 最后纵帆. ⇨ the illus at **barque.** 参看 barque 之插图.

mizzle /'mɪzl; 'mɪzl̩/ vi (dial or colloq) [VP2A] rain in fine drops; drizzle. (方或口)下毛毛雨; 下细雨.

mne·monic /nɪ'mɒnɪk; nɪ'mɑnɪk/ adj of, designed to help, the memory: 记忆的; 帮助记忆的: ~ verses, eg for remembering irregular declensions or conjugations. 帮助记忆的歌诀(如帮助记忆不规则名词或动词变化之词尾变化或动词变化). **mne·mon·ics** n pl (with sing v) art of, system for, improving the memory. (与单数动词连用) 增进记忆之术; 记忆法.

mo /məʊ; mo/ n (sl abbr of) **moment:** (俚) moment 之略: half a mo. 一会儿.

moan /məʊn; mon/ n [C] low sound of pain or regret, or one suggesting suffering: 呻吟声; 呜咽声: the ~s of the wounded; 受伤者的呻吟声; the ~ of the wind on a winter evening. 冬夜寒风的呼啸声. □ vi, vt [VP2A, C, 15B] utter ~s; say with ~s: 呻吟; 悲叹: ~ (out) a plea for help. 哀哀求助. What's she ~ing (= complaining) about now? 她在抱怨些什么?

moat /məʊt; mot/ n deep, wide ditch filled with water, round a castle, etc as a defence. (防御城堡等之) 壕沟. ⇨ the illus at **drawbridge.** 参看 drawbridge 之插图. ~ed adj having a ~: 有壕沟的; 围有壕沟的: a ~ed manor house. 围有壕沟的领主邸宅.

mob /mɒb; mɑb/ n [C] disorderly crowd, rabble, esp one that has gathered for mischief or attack: 无秩序之民众; 乌合之众; (尤指) 暴民; 滋事的群众; (attrib) (用作定语) mob law, mob rule, imposed or enforced by a mob. 暴民的法律; 私刑. 2 the mob, the masses: 民众: mob oratory, the kind of speech-making that appeals to the emotions of the masses, not to the intellect. 煽动群众的演讲. 3 gang of criminals. 犯罪集团; 匪帮. □ vt (-bb-) [VP6A] (of people) crowd round in great numbers, either to attack or to admire: (指民众) 包围 (为攻击或赞赏): The pickpocket was mobbed by angry women. 扒手被愤怒的妇女们包围着. The pop singer was mobbed by teenagers. 那个流行歌曲歌手被少年男女包围了. **mob·ster** /'mɒbstə(r); 'mɑbstɚ/ n member of a gang or mob of rowdy persons. 暴徒或流氓集团的一份子.

mob·cap /'mɒbkæp; 'mɑb,kæp/ n (18th c) woman's indoor head-dress covering the whole of the hair. (十八世纪) 室内用头巾式女帽.

mo·bile /'məʊbaɪl US: -bl; 'mɒbl/ adj 1 moving, able to be moved. easily and quickly from place to place: 易动的; 可迅速移动的: ~ troops/artillery. 机动部队 (机动炮兵). 2 easily and often changing: 易变的; 常变的: ~ features, quickly showing changes of

thought and emotion. 迅速显露思想与感情之转变的面容. □ n ornamental structure with parts that move in currents of air. 某些部分迎风转动的装饰性结构.

mo·bil·ity /məʊ'bɪlətɪ; mo'bɪlətɪ/ n [U] being ~. 可动性; 流动性; 移动性; 易变性.

mo·bi·lize /'məʊbɪlaɪz; 'mobl̩,aɪz/ vt, vi [VP6A, 2A] collect together for service or use, esp in war. 动员 (尤指战时人力物力等动员). **mo·bi·liz·ation** /,məʊbɪlaɪ'zeɪʃn US: -lɪ'z-; ,mobl̩ə'zeʃən/ n mobilizing or being ~d: 动员: (attrib) (用作定语) mobilization orders. 动员令.

mob·ster /'mɒbstə(r); 'mɑbstɚ/ ⇨ **mob.**

moc·ca·sin /'mɒkəsɪn; 'mɑkəsɪn/ n [U] soft leather made from deerskin; (pl) shoes made from this, as worn by N American Indians, or in similar style. 鹿皮制的软革; (复) (北美印第安人等所穿的) 鹿皮鞋. ⇨ the illus at **mitten.** 参看 mitten 之插图.

mo·cha /'mɒkə US: 'məʊkə; 'mokə/ n [U] fine quality of coffee, originally shipped from the Arabian port of M~. 摩卡咖啡(一种精良咖啡, 原系自阿拉伯摩卡港输出者).

mock /mɒk; mɑk/ vt, vi 1 [VP6A, 3A] ~ sb; ~ at sb, make fun of; ridicule (esp by copying in a funny or contemptuous way): 愚弄; 嘲弄(尤指以讥笑或侮慢的方式模仿): The naughty boys ~ed the blind man. 那些顽皮的男孩子愚弄那个盲人. They ~ed at my fears. 他们嘲弄我的恐惧. '~·ing bird n American bird of the thrush family that mimics the notes of other birds. 反舌鸟(美洲的一种画眉鸟, 善于模仿其他鸟类的声调). 2 [VP6A] defy contemptuously: 使挫折; 使使泰然无功: The heavy steel doors ~ed the attempts of the thieves to open the safe. 厚重的铁门使盗贼开启保险箱的企图无法得逞. '~·up n (a) full-scale model, eg of an aircraft, made of wood, showing the appearance of a proposed machine (or any part of it). 实体模型(与实物同大小, 如木制之飞机模型等). (b) lay-out of sth to be printed. 待印之某物的图样. □ attrib adj not real or genuine: 假的; 模拟的: a ~ battle; 假想战; ~-turtle soup, made to imitate turtle soup; 充鳖汤(即小牛头汤); ,~-'modesty, pretence of being modest; 假谦逊; ,~-he'roic, making fun of heroic style in literature. 戏拟英雄体的; 模拟英雄诗的. □ n (archaic) derision. (古) 嘲笑. **make a ~ of,** ridicule. 讥笑; 嘲弄. **~er** n person who ~s. 嘲笑者; 作嘲弄的模仿者. **~·ing·ly** adv

mock·ery /'mɒkərɪ; 'mɑkərɪ/ n (pl -ries) 1 [U] mocking; ridicule: 嘲弄; 讥笑: hold a person up to ~. 嘲弄某人. 2 [C] sth that is mocked; occasion when sb or sth is mocked: 被嘲弄之人或事物; 笑柄; 受嘲弄的场合. 3 [C] bad or contemptible example (of sth): (某事的) 恶例; 可蔑视之例: His trial was a ~ of justice. 他所受的审判是蔑视正义之的恶例(他受到不公正的审判). He received only the ~ of a trial. 他只是受到一场不公正的审判.

mod /mɒd; mɑd/ adj (sl) up-to-date and smart (esp in dress). (俚) 最新式的; 时髦的 (尤指服装). □ n **Mod,** (1960's in GB) young person wearing smart clothes and riding on motor-scooters:(二十世纪六十年代用于英国) 马德(指骑低座小摩托车, 穿时髦服装的青年); Mods and Rockers, ⇨ **rock².** 马德与罗克.

mo·dal /'məʊdl; 'modl̩/ adj relating to mode or manner (contrasted with substance); (gram) relating to the mood of a verb: 形式上的; 方式上的(与实质相对); (语法) 动词语气的: ~ auxiliaries, eg can, may. 语气助动词(如 can, may 等是). **mo·dal·ity** /məʊ'dælɪtɪ; mo'dælɪtɪ/ n being ~. 形式. 2 [C] way in which sth is done. 作法; 方式.

mode /məʊd; mod/ n [C] 1 way in which sth is done; way of speaking or behaving: 做事、说话或行为的方式; 方法: a ~ of life/dressing the hair; 一种生活方式 (一种发型的梳理); fashion or style: 样式; 型; 式: the latest ~s (of clothes). (服装的) 最新款式. 2 (music)

one of the two chief scale systems in modern music: (音乐)调式: *the major and the minor* ~s. 大调式及小调式。

model¹ /ˈmɒdl; ˈmɑdl/ *n* [C] **1** small-scale reproduction or representation of sth; design to be copied: 模型; 模样: ~ *of an ocean liner;* 一艘海轮的模型; *a clay or wax* ~ *for a statue,* to be copied in stone or metal; 塑像的泥质或蜡质模型(供制作石像或金属像时模仿用); (attrib) (用作定语) ~ *aircraft / trains.* 模型飞机(火车)。 **2** person or thing to be copied: 供模仿的人或物; 模范: *He's a* ~ *of industry.* 他是勤劳的模范。 *Make yours on the* ~ *of your brother's.* 要以你哥哥(弟弟)为模范。 **3** (colloq) person or thing exactly like another: (口)极相似的人或物: *She's the* ~/*a perfect* ~ *of her mother.* 她(完全)像她的母亲。 **4** person who poses for sculptors, painters or photographers. 模特儿(供雕塑家、画家或摄影家用者)。 **5** person employed to wear clothes, hats, etc so that prospective buyers may see them; mannequin. 时装模特儿(穿着衣帽等以示顾客);木头或蜡制的时装模特儿。 **6** article of clothing, hat, etc shown publicly by ~s(5). 模特儿表演时所穿着的衣帽等;模特儿身上所展示的服饰: *the latest Paris* ~s, clothes, etc from the Paris dressmakers. 最新巴黎时装。 **7** design or structure of which many copies or reproductions are (to be) made: 产品的型式: *the latest* ~s *of Ford cars;* 最新型的福特汽车; *a 'sports* ~, a car designed for fast driving. 跑车型汽车。 **8** (attrib) perfect; deserving to be imitated: (用作定语)完善的; 值得仿效的; 典型的: ~ *behaviour.* 模范行为; *a* ~ *wife.* 模范妻子。

model² /ˈmɒdl; ˈmɑdl/ *vt, vi* (**-ll-,** US **-l-**) **1** [VP6A, 14, 15A] ~ *(in),* shape (in some soft substance): (用某些软物质)制作: 塑造: ~ *sb's head in clay;* 用粘土制作某人头部的塑像; (fig): (喻): *delicately* ~*led features.* 清秀的面貌。 **2** [VP2A, 6A] practise as a model(4, 5): 做模特儿: *She earns a living by* ~*ing clothes / hats.* 她做时装模特儿以谋生(她的职业是时装模特儿)。 **3** [VP14] ~ *oneself on / upon sb,* make from a model; take as a copy or example: 模仿; 仿效: 仿制: ~ *oneself on one's father.* 以父亲为模范而仿效之。 ~**(l)er** *n* person who practises ~ling. 制作模型的人。 ~**(l)ing** *n* [U] art of making ~(5); way in which this is done; working as a ~(5): 模型制作术; 制作模型的方法; 当时装模特儿: *She did some* ~*ling as a student to earn pocket-money.* 她做学生时偶尔当时装模特儿以赚点零用钱。

mod·er·ate¹ /ˈmɒdərət; ˈmɑdərɪt/ *adj* **1** not extreme; limited; having reasonable limits: 适度的; 有节制的; 有合理限度的: *He has a* ~ *appetite.* 他的食欲还可以。 *Prices in this hotel are strictly* ~, not at all high. 这个旅馆里的各种价格都很公道。 *I'd like a* ~*-price room,* eg in a hotel. 我要一间价钱适中的房间(如旅馆中的)。 *We need a* ~*-sized house,* eg with 3 or 4 bedrooms, not 7 or 8. 我们需要一幢大小适中的房子(例如有三四间卧室而非七八间)。 **2** keeping or kept within reasonable limits: 中庸的; 温和的; 稳健的: *a man of* ~ *opinions;* 意见不偏激的人; *a* ~ *political party;* 温和主义的政党; *a* ~ *drinker;* 饮酒不过量的人; *be* ~ *in one's demands.* 需求有度。 □ *n* person who holds ~ opinions, eg in politics. 持温和意见的人(如在政界方面)。 ~**·ly** *adv* to a ~ extent: 适度地; 普通地; 中等地; 适中地: *a* ~*ly large audience.* 人数适度的观(听)众。

mod·er·ate² /ˈmɒdəreɪt; ˈmɑdəˌret/ *vt, vi* [VP6A, 2A] **1** make or become less violent or extreme. 节制; 缓和; 减轻; 稳定: ~ *one's enthusiasm / demands.* 节制个人的热心(需求)。 *The wind is moderating.* 风势渐趋缓和。 *His wife exercises a moderating influence upon him,* is able to restrain him. 他的妻子对他有一种缓和作用(即能约束他)。 **2** act as moderator. 主持宗教会议; 当主考人。

mod·er·ation /ˌmɒdəˈreɪʃn; ˌmɑdəˈreʃən/ *n* **1** [U] quality of being moderate; freedom from excess: 适

度; 温和; 中庸: *My doctor has advised* ~ *in eating and drinking.* 我的医师劝告我节制饮食。 *in* ~, in a moderate manner or degree: 适度地: *Alcoholic drinks are not harmful taken in* ~. 适度饮酒不会有害。 **2** (*pl*) (shortened to 略作 **Mods**) first public examination for a degree in classical studies at Oxford. (复)牛津大学之古典文学研究之学位的初试。

mod·er·ator /ˈmɒdəreɪtə(r); ˈmɑdəˌretə/ *n* **1** Presbyterian minister presiding over a church court. 基督教长老会对宗教会议的议长。 **2** presiding examiner at some university examinations. (某些大学之考试的)主考人。 **3** material in which neutrons are slowed down in an atomic pile. 减速剂; 缓和剂(原子堆中使中子减速的物质)。

mod·ern /ˈmɒdn; ˈmɑdən/ *adj* **1** of the present or recent times: 现代的; 近代的: ~ *history,* eg of Europe, from 1475 onwards; 近代史(如欧洲近代史,自一四七五年起); ~ *languages,* those now spoken and written; 现代语言(现今所说所写的各种语文); *M* ~ *English,* from the 15th c onwards; 近代英语(十五世纪以后的英语); ~ *inventions and discoveries.* 现代的发明与发现。 **,secondary '**~ **school,** (GB; 1950's and 1960's) type of non-academic, semi-technical, secondary school (英; 二十世纪五十年代及二十世纪六十年代)半工业技术中等学校。 ⇨ **secondary.** **2** new and up-to-date: 新近的; 时髦的: ~ *methods and ideas;* 新的方法与观念; *a house with all* ~ *conveniences.* 有全部新式设备的房子。 □ *n* person living in ~ times. 现代人。

mod·ern·ism /ˈmɒdnɪzəm; ˈmɑdənˌɪzəm/ *n* [U] modern views or methods; (theology) subordination of tradition to modern thought. 现代的观点或方法; 现代思潮。 (神学)现代主义。 **mod·ern·ist** /-ɪst; -ɪst/ *n* believer in, supporter of, ~. 现代主义者; 现代思潮者。 **mod·ern·is·tic** /ˌmɒdəˈnɪstɪk; ˌmɑdəˈnɪstɪk/ *adj* of ~. 现代的; 现代主义的。

mo·dern·ity /mɒˈdɜːnətɪ; mɑˈdɝnɪtɪ/ *n* [U] being modern. 现代; 现代性; 现代作风。

mod·ern·ize /ˈmɒdənaɪz; ˈmɑdənˌaɪz/ *vt* [VP6A] make suitable for present-day needs; bring up to date: 使适合现代需要; 使现代化: *Ought we to* ~ *our spelling?* 我们应该把我们的拼字法现代化吗? **mod·ern·iz·ation** /ˌmɒdənaɪˈzeɪʃn US: -nɪˈz-; ˌmɑdənəˈzeʃən/ *n* [U].

mod·est /ˈmɒdɪst; ˈmɑdɪst/ *adj* **1** having, showing, a not too high opinion of one's merits, abilities. etc. 谦逊的; 客气的: *be* ~ *about one's achievements.* 不夸耀一己之成就; *a* ~ *hero.* 一位谦逊的英雄。 **2** moderate; not large in size or amount: 适度的; 适中的; 质朴的: *He lives in a* ~ *little house,* not showy or splendid. 他住在一幢普通的小房子。 *My demands are quite* ~. 我的要求不多。 *He is* ~ *in his requirements.* 他不过份要求。 **3** taking, showing, care not to do or say anything impure or improper: 谨慎的; 庄重的; 有礼貌的: ~ *in speech, dress and behaviour.* 在言语、服装、行为方面谨慎。 ~**·ly** *adv* **mod·esty** /ˈmɒdɪstɪ; ˈmɑdɪstɪ/ *n* [U] state of being ~ (all senses): 谦逊; 适度; 谨慎; 质朴; 有礼貌; 客气: *Her* ~y *prevented her from making her feelings known to him.* 她的谨慎使她不敢向他表露感情。 *in all* ~y, without the least intention of boasting, etc. 一点也没有自夸等的意思。

modi·cum /ˈmɒdɪkəm; ˈmɑdɪkəm/ *n* (*sing only*) small or moderate amount: (仅用单数)小量; 适量: *achieve success with a* ~ *of effort;* 稍微努力就获得成功; *a simple meal with a* ~ *of wine.* 备有少量葡萄酒的一顿简单餐食。

mod·ify /ˈmɒdɪfaɪ; ˈmɑdəˌfaɪ/ *vt* (*pt, pp* **-fied**) [VP6A] **1** make changes in; make different: 修改; 变更: *The industrial revolution modified the whole structure of English society.* 工业革命改变了整个英国社会的结构。 **2** make less severe, violent, etc: 减轻; 缓和: *You'd better* ~ *your tone,* be less rude. 你最好说话文雅一点。 *He won't* ~ *his demands,* reduce them. 他不减少他的要求。 **3** (gram) qualify the sense of

(a word): (语法)修饰; 限制(词)义: *Adjectives ~ nouns.* 形容词修饰名词, **modi·fier** /-faɪə(r); -ˌfaɪəʊ/ *n* (gram) word that modifies, eg an *adj* or *adv.* (语法)修饰语(如形容词或副词). **modi·fi·ca·tion** /ˌmɒdɪfɪˈkeɪʃn; ˌmɑdəfəˈkeʃən/ *n* [U] ~ing or being modified; [C] instance of this; change or alteration. 修改; 修饰; 减轻; 缓和; 变化.

mod·ish /ˈməʊdɪʃ; ˈmodɪʃ/ *adj* fashionable. 流行的; 时髦的。**~·ly** *adv*

mo·diste /məʊˈdiːst; moˈdist/ *n* (formal) milliner; dress-maker. (正式用语)女帽制造者; 女衣缝制者。

modu·late /ˈmɒdjʊleɪt US: -dʒu-; ˈmɑdʒəˌlet/ *vt, vi* **1** [VP6A] regulate; adjust; adapt; (music) make a change in the key of. 调节; 调整; 使适应; (音乐)改变…的调子; 使变音; 使变调. **2** [VP2C] ~ *from / to,* change from one key to another. 由一调变为另一调; 变调; 转调. **3** [VP6A] (radio) vary the frequency, amplitude or phase of a wave. (无线电)改变声波的频率、振幅或相位; 调制; 调变。**⇨ modulation.**

modu·la·tion /ˌmɒdjʊˈleɪʃn US: -dʒuˈl-; ˌmɑdʒəˈleʃən/ *n* **1** [U] process of modulating; state of being modulated; [C] change resulting from this; [U] (music) changing of key; [C] particular change of key. 调节; 调整; 因调节而产生的变化; (音乐)变调; 转调。**2** (radio) variation in the amplitude, frequency or phase of a wave so that it is suitable for radio, eg of the human voice to a wave for radio or the telephone. (无线电)调制; 调变(声波之振幅、频率或相位的改变使适合于无线电, 例如人的声音改变成无线电或电话的电波)。

mod·ule /ˈmɒdjuːl US: -dʒuːl; ˈmɑdʒul/ *n* [C] **1** standard or unit of measurement as used in building. (建筑方面所用的)标准尺寸; 基本单位; 模数。**2** standard uniform component used in the structure of a building or in sectional furniture; unit of electronic components as used in the assembly of a computer: (建筑物之构造或组合家具中之)组件; (电子计算机等之)模组; 单体: *a 'memory ~*, unit of components in a mechanical system. (机械系统中的)记忆单体。**3** independent and self-contained unit of a spacecraft. 舱(太空船中具有一切必需配备的独立单位): **com'mand ~**, for the astronaut in command. 指挥舱(供负责指挥太空探险之太空人乘坐者). **'lunar ~**, to be separated for a moon landing. 登月小艇。**modu·lar** /ˈmɒdjʊlə(r) US: -dʒu-; ˈmɑdʒʊlə/ *adj* based on a ~ or unit: 以组件为基本的; 以模组或单体为基本的: *modular design / construction,* based on a ~ which is repeated throughout the design. 单体设计(构造物)(整个图样或构造物中以一单体之一再重复而成)。

modus op·er·andi /ˌməʊdəs ˌɒpəˈrændiː; ˈmodəsˌɑpəˈrændaɪ/ *n* (Lat) method of dealing with a piece of work; method of being operated. (拉)做法; 方法; 惯技.

modus vi·vendi /ˌməʊdəs vɪˈvendiː; ˈmodəsˌvɪˈvendaɪ/ *n* (Lat) way of living; (way of getting a) temporary agreement (while awaiting the final settlement of a dispute, etc). (拉)生活方式; 生活之道(在等待争执等之最后解决时的)暂时协议; 获得暂时协议之途径.

mo·gul /ˈməʊgl; ˈmogəl/ *n* (colloq) very rich or important person: (口)非常富有或重要的人; 巨子; 大亨: *Hollywood ~s.* 好莱坞大亨.

mo·hair /ˈməʊheə(r); ˈmoˌhɛr/ *n* [U] (thread, cloth, made from the) fine, silky hair of the Angora goat. 安哥拉山羊羊毛(质细而有光泽); 此种羊毛所织成的毛线或毛料; 马海.

Mo·ham·medan /məˈhæmɪdən; moˈhæmədən/ *n* **⇨ Muhammad.**

moi·ety /ˈmɔɪətɪ; ˈmɔɪətɪ/ *n* (*pl* **-ties**) (esp in legal sense) one of two parts into which sth is divided. (尤用于法律意义上)一半; 二分之一.

moil /mɔɪl; mɔɪl/ *vi* (only in) (仅用于) *toil and ~*, work hard. 辛勤工作.

moist /mɔɪst; mɔɪst/ *adj* (esp of surfaces) slightly wet: (尤指表面)潮湿的; 润湿的: *eyes ~ with tears;* 为

泪水所润湿的眼睛; *a ~ wind from the sea.* 从海上吹来的潮湿的风。**~en** /ˈmɔɪsn; ˈmɔɪsn/ *vt, vi* [VP6A, 2A] make or become ~: 使润湿; 使变潮湿, eg by licking them; 舔湿嘴唇; *~en a sponge.* 把海绵沾湿. **~·ure** /ˈmɔɪstʃə(r); ˈmɔɪstʃə/ *n* [U] condensed vapour on a surface; liquid in the form of vapour. 潮湿; 湿气; 水气.

moke /məʊk; mok/ *n* (GB sl) donkey. (英俚)驴.

mo·lar /ˈməʊlə(r); ˈmolə/ *n, adj* (one) of the teeth used for grinding food. 臼齿; 臼齿的。**⇨ the illus at mouth.** 参看 mouth 之插图.

mo·las·ses /məˈlæsɪz; məˈlæsɪz/ *n* [U] thick dark syrup drained from raw sugar during the refining process. 糖蜜; 糖浆.

mold, molder, mold·ing, moldy, **⇨ mould,** etc.

mole¹ /məʊl; mol/ *n* permanent, small, dark spot on the human skin. 痣; 黑痣.

mole² /məʊl; mol/ *n* small, dark-grey, fur-covered animal with tiny eyes, living in tunnels (or burrows) which it makes in the ground. 鼹鼠。**⇨ the illus at small.** 参看 small 之插图. *blind as a ~*, having bad eye-sight. 视力很差的。**'~-skin** *n* fur of a ~, used for making garments and hats. 鼹鼠皮(制衣帽等用). **'~-hill** *n* pile of earth thrown up by a ~ while burrowing. 鼹鼠丘(鼹鼠掘地洞时所堆积的泥土堆)。*make a mountain out of a ~-hill,* make a trivial matter seem important. 小题大做.

mole³ /məʊl; mol/ *n* stone wall built in the sea as a breakwater or causeway. 防波堤; 堤道。**⇨ the illus at breakwater.** 参看 breakwater 之插图.

mol·ecule /ˈmɒlɪkjuːl; ˈmɑləˌkjul/ *n* smallest unit (one or more atoms) into which a substance can be divided without a change in its chemical nature. 分子(物质不改变其化学性质的最小单位, 含一个或数个原子)。**mol·ecu·lar** /məˈlekjʊlə(r); məˈlekjələ/ *adj* of or related to ~s: 分子的; 与分子有关的: *molecular structure.* 分子结构.

mo·lest /məˈlest; məˈlest/ *vt* [VP6A] trouble or annoy intentionally. 故意干扰; 妨害; 作弄; 骚扰. **mol·es·ta·tion** /ˌməʊlesˈteɪʃn; ˌmoləsˈteʃən/ *n* [U].

moll /mɒl; mɑl/ *n* (sl) woman companion of a gangster, vagrant, etc; prostitute. (俚)匪徒、流氓等的情妇; 妓女.

mol·lify /ˈmɒlɪfaɪ; ˈmɑləˌfaɪ/ *vt* (*pt, pp* **-fied**) [VP6A] make (a person, his feelings) calmer or quieter. 使(人、其情绪)平静; 安慰; 抚慰; 缓和。*~ing remarks;* 安慰的话语; *~ sb's anger.* 缓和某人的愤怒. **mol·li·fi·ca·tion** /ˌmɒlɪfɪˈkeɪʃn; ˌmɑləfəˈkeʃən/ *n* [U].

mol·lusc (US also **mol·lusk**) /ˈmɒləsk; ˈmɑləsk/ *n* one of a class of animals with soft bodies (and often hard shells), eg oysters, mussels, cuttlefish, snails, slugs. 软体动物 (常有硬壳, 如牡蛎、贻贝、乌贼、蜗牛、蛞蝓).

molly·coddle /ˈmɒlɪkɒdl; ˈmɑlɪˌkɑdl/ *n* person who takes too much care of his health, who pampers himself and likes others to pamper him. 过分当心自己健康的人; 纵容自己并喜欢被别人纵容的人. □ *vt* [VP6A] (often reflex) pamper (sb, oneself). (常用反身式)溺爱; 纵容(某人、自己).

Mo·loch /ˈməʊlɒk; ˈmolɑk/ *n* (in the Bible) god to whom children were sacrificed; (fig) dreadful thing, eg war, that requires great sacrifice of human life. (圣经中)莫洛克(须以孩子为祭品的神); (喻)需要牺牲人命的恐怖事物(如战争).

molt /məʊlt; molt/ *vi* **⇨ moult.**

mol·ten /ˈməʊltən; ˈmoltn/ *pp* of **melt.** **1** (of metals) in a melted (and therefore very hot) state: (指金属)熔化的; ~ *steel.* 钢水. **2** made of metal that has been melted and cast. 由熔化金属铸造成的: *a ~ image,* eg of a god. 金属铸像(如神像).

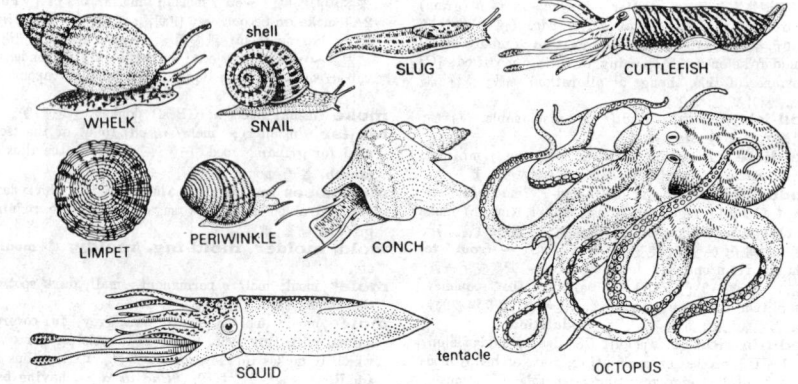

WHELK · SNAIL · shell · SLUG · CUTTLEFISH · LIMPET · PERIWINKLE · CONCH · SQUID · tentacle · OCTOPUS

molluscs

molto /'mɒltəʊ *US:* 'məʊltəʊ ; 'molto/ *adv* (musical direction) very: (乐谱说明) 很; 甚; 颇; 极: ~ *espressivo*, with much expression. 富于表情的; 颇有表情似的.

mo·lyb·denum /mə'lɪbdənəm; mə'lɪbdənəm/ *n* [U] silvery-white brittle metallic element (symbol **Mo**) used in alloys for making high-speed tools. 钼(一种银白色性脆的金属元素, 化学符号为 Mo, 其合金用以制造高速工具).

mo·ment /'məʊmənt ; 'moment/ *n* **1** [C] point or very brief period of time: 瞬间; 片刻: *It was all over in a few ~s.* 没多久就结束了. *Please wait a ~.* 请稍等. *Just a ~, please.* 请等一会儿. *He'll be here (at) any ~, very soon now.* 他立刻就要到了. *It was done in a ~.* 一会儿它便完成了. *He arrived at the last ~,* almost too late. 他在最后一刻才到达. *Study your notes at odd ~s,* whenever you have a few minutes to spare. 抽空研读你的笔记. *I have just this ~ / only this ~ heard the news,* heard it only a ~ ago. 我刚刚听到这消息. *Not for a ~,* never: 从来没有: '*Have you ever thought of making your own dresses?*' — '*Not for a ~!*' '你曾否想到自己缝制衣服?' — '从来没有!' *man of the ~,* man who is important just now. 时下重要的人物. **2** *the ~,* (used as a *conj*) as soon as; at the time when: (作连接词用)一…就…; 一当; 就在那时: *I started the ~ your letter arrived.* 我一收到你的信就动身了. *The ~ I saw you I knew you were angry with me.* 我一看到你, 就知道你在生我的气. **3** [U] *of (great, small, little, no, etc) ~,* of (great, small, etc) importance: (非常, 没什么, 不等)重要的: *an affair of great ~;* 非常重要的事情; *a matter of ~;* 重大的事; *men of ~.* 要人.

mo·men·tary /'məʊməntrɪ *US:* -terɪ ; 'momən,terɪ/ *adj* **1** lasting for, done in, a moment. 短暂的; 瞬息间的; 刹那的. **2** at every moment: 随时的: *with a learner at the wheel, and in ~ expectation of an accident.* 由一个初学的人驾驶, 并且随时都在准备着车祸的发生. **mo·men·tar·i·ly** /'məʊməntrəlɪ *US:* ,məʊmən'terəlɪ; 'momən,terəlɪ/ *adv*

mo·men·tous /mə'mentəs ; mo'mentəs/ *adj* important; serious. 重要的; 严重的. **~·ly** *adv* **~·ness** *n*

mo·men·tum /mə'mentəm ; mo'mentəm/ *n* [U] **1** (science) quantity of motion of a moving body (the product of its mass and velocity): (科学)动量(即物体之质量及速度的乘积): *Do falling objects gain ~?* 下落物体的动量是否增加? **2** (fig, of events) impetus gained by movement: (喻, 指事件)因动作而得到的冲力; 动向; 冲劲: *lose / gain ~.* 失去(获得)推动力; 松弛(扩展).

mon·arch /'mɒnək ; 'manək/ *n* supreme ruler (a king, queen, emperor or empress). 君主(国王、女王、皇帝或女皇). **mon·ar·chic** /mə'nɑːkɪk ; mə'nɑrkɪk/ *adj* of a ~ or a ~y. 君主的; 帝王的; 王朝的; 君主制度的; 君主政体的. ⇨ **absolute**(2). **mon·ar·chism** /-,kɪzəm / *n* [U] system of government by a single ruler or ~. 君主制度. **mon·ar·chist** / -ɪst; -ɪst / *n* supporter of ~ism. 拥护君主制度者. **mon·archy** /'mɒnəkɪ ; 'manəkɪ/ *n* [U] government by a ~; [C] (*pl* **-chies**) state ruled by a ~. 君主政体; 君主国. ⇨ **limit**[2].

mon·as·tery /'mɒnəstrɪ *US:* -sterɪ ; 'manəs,terɪ/ *n* (*pl* **-ries**) place where monks live as a community under religious vows. 修道院.

mon·as·tic /mə'næstɪk ; mə'næstɪk/ *adj* of monks or monasteries: 修道士的; 僧侣的; 修道院的: ~ *vows,* ie of poverty, chastity, and obedience; 修道誓愿(即贫苦、贞洁与服从); ~ *architecture,* of the kind used for monasteries, abbeys, etc. 寺院式建筑. **mon·as·ti·cism** / mə'næstɪsɪzəm ; mə'næstə,sɪzəm / *n* [U] system of living as practised by monks in monasteries. 修道制度; 修道生活.

mon·aural /mɒn'ɔːrəl ; man'ɔrəl/ *adj* for one ear; (with trade abbr *mono;* of sound-reproducing equipment and recordings) not stereophonic. 为一边耳朵的; (商用略作 mono; 指放音设备及录音)非立体音响的.

Mon·day /'mʌndɪ ; 'mʌndɪ/ *n* second day of the week. 星期一.

mon·et·ary /'mʌnɪtrɪ *US:* -terɪ ; 'mʌnə,terɪ/ *adj* of money or a currency: 钱的; 货币的: *a ~ policy,* of control over money; 货币政策; ~ *reform,* eg to create a decimal coinage. 币制改革. *The ~ unit of the US is the dollar.* 美国的货币单位是'元'. **mon·et·ar·ism** / -tərɪzəm , -tə,rɪzəm / *n* [U] policy of control over money as the chief method of managing a country's economy. 货币主义(以控制货币作为管理国家经济之主要方法的政策). **mon·et·ar·ist** / -tərɪst; -tərɪst/ *n* person favouring monetarism. 货币主义者.

mon·et·ize /'mʌnətaɪz ; 'mʌnə,taɪz/ *vt* [VP6A] **1** put (coins, notes) into circulation as money. 使(硬币、钞票)为货币; 定为货币; 发行货币. **2** give (a currency) a fixed value 给予(货币)固定价值.

money /'mʌnɪ ; 'mʌnɪ/ *n* **1** [U] coins stamped from metal (gold, copper, alloys), printed notes, given and accepted when buying and selling, etc: 钱; 货币: *I keep my ~ in the bank.* 我把我的钱存在银行. *I could hear ~ jingling in his pocket.* 我听见他口袋里的钱叮珰地响. *be 'coining / 'minting ~,* be getting rich quickly. 迅速致富; 暴富. *be in the ~,* (sl) be rich. (俚)富有; 有钱. *get one's '~'s worth,* get full value

for ~ spent. 花钱得到应得的价值; 捞回本儿。 **make ~**, earn it. 赚钱。 **marry ~**, marry a rich person. 娶(嫁)富有的人。 **(pay) ~ down**, (pay) in cash (contrasted with *credit*). 付现金(与 credit 相对)。 **put ~ into sth**, invest ~ in an enterprise, etc. 投资于某一企业等。 **,~ of ac'count**, ⇨ account¹(2). **ready ~**, cash (contrasted with *credit*, etc). 现款;现钱(与 credit 等相对)。 **2** (compounds)(复合词) **'~-box** n closed box into which coins are dropped through a slit, used for savings or for collecting contributions (to **charities**, etc). 钱箱(储蓄或收集捐款用);扑满。 **'~-changer** n one whose business is to exchange ~ of one country for that of another country. 以兑换各国货币为业的人; 兑换业者。 **'~-grubber** n person whose chief or only interest in life is making ~. 守财奴; 唯利是图的人。 **'~-lender** n one whose business is to lend ~ at interest. 放债的人。 **the '~-market** n the body of bankers, financiers, etc whose operations decide the rates of interest on borrowed capital. 金融市场。 **'~ order** n order¹(7) bought from a post office for ~ to be paid by another post office to a named person. (邮政)汇票。 **'~-spinner** n (colloq) book, play, etc that makes a lot of ~. (口)赚大钱的书、戏剧等。 **3** (pl, **moneys** or **monies** /'mʌnɪz; 'mʌnɪz/)(legal or archaic) sums of ~: (法律或古)金额: **~s** paid in/out; 收进(付出)的钱款; sundry **~s** owing to the estate. 来自财产的各项收益。 **~ed** /'mʌnɪd; 'mʌnɪd/ adj having (much) ~: 有钱的;富有的: a ~ed man; 富人; the ~ed classes; 有钱阶级; the ~ed interest, the owners of capital. 金融业者; 资本家; 金融界。 **~-less** adj having no ~. 没钱的。

mon·ger /'mʌŋgə(r); 'mʌŋgə/ n (chiefly in compounds) trader, dealer: (主要用于复合词中)商人; 贩子: 'iron~; 五金商; 'fish~; 鱼贩; 'scandal-~. 专事毁谤的人。

mon·gol·ism /'mɒŋgəlɪzəm; 'mɑŋgə,lɪzəm/ n [U] congenital condition in which a child is born with mental deficiency and a flattened broad skull and slanting eyes. 先天愚型;伸舌样白痴(先天性之智力不足,头颅平而宽,斜眼)。 **mon·gol** /'mɒŋgl; 'mɑŋgəl/ n, attrib adj (person) suffering from ~. 伸舌样白痴的(患者): a mongol baby. 患伸舌样白痴的婴儿。

mon·goose /'mɒŋguːs; 'mɑŋgus/ n (pl **~s** -sɪz; -sɪz) small Indian animal clever at destroying venomous snakes. 獴; 猫鼬(善于捕杀毒蛇之小动物, 产于印度)。 ⇨ the illus at **small**. 参看 small 之插图。

mon·grel /'mʌŋgrəl; 'mʌŋgrəl/ n **1** dog of mixed breed. 杂种狗。 **2** any plant or animal of mixed origin. 杂种的动物或植物。 □ attrib adj of mixed breed or origin. 杂种的; 混种的。

mon·ies /'mʌnɪz; 'mʌnɪz/ n pl ⇨ **money(3)**.

moni·tor /'mɒnɪtə(r); 'mɑnɪtə/ n **1** pupil given authority over his fellows. 级长; 班长。 **2** person employed to listen to and report on foreign broadcasts. 受雇监听外国广播的人员。 **3** apparatus for testing transmissions by radio or TV, for detecting radio-activity, for tracing the flight of missiles, etc. 稽查器; 监测器; 无线电或电视传播侦测器;放射性侦察器;火箭追踪器。 **'~ (screen)**, television screen used in a studio to check or select transmissions. 电视台播送室中用以检查或选择播送的电视荧光幕。 □ vt, vi act as ~(2). 监听(外国广播)。

monk /mʌŋk; mʌŋk/ n member of a community of men living together under religious vows in a monastery. 僧侣; 修道士。 **'~-ish** /-ɪʃ; -ɪʃ/ adj of or like ~s. (像)僧侣的;修道士的。

mon·key /'mʌŋkɪ; 'mʌŋkɪ/ n (pl **~s**) **1** member of the group of animals most closely resembling man. 猴; 猿。 ⇨ the illus at **ape**. 参看 ape 之插图。 be/get up to '~ business/tricks, to mischief. 胡闹; 恶作剧; 顽皮。 have a '~ on one's back, (sl)(俚) (a) be a drug addict; 染上毒瘾; (b) bear a grudge. 怀恨。 get one's ~ up, (sl) become angry. (俚)生气; 发怒。 put sb's ~

up, (sl) make him angry. (俚)使某人生气。 **'~-jacket** n short, close-fitting jacket as worn by some sailors. (某些水手等所穿的)紧身短上衣。 **'~-nut** n groundnut. 落花生。 **'~-puzzle** n Chilean pine-tree, 智利松。 **'~-wrench** n wrench (spanner) with a jaw that can be adjusted to various lengths. 活动扳钳; 活口钳。 ⇨ the illus at **tool**. 参看 tool 之插图。 **2** (playfully) person, esp a child, who is mischievous. (戏语)顽皮的人(尤指小孩)。 **3** (sl) £500 or $500. (俚)五百英镑; 五百(美)元。 □ vi [VP2C] **~ about**, fool about. 胡闹。

mono, mono- ⇨ **monaural** and **App 3**. 参看 monaural 和附录三。

mono·chrome /'mɒnəkrəʊm; 'mɑnə,krom/ n painting in (different tints of) one colour. 单色画。 □ adj having one colour. 单色的。

mon·ocle /'mɒnɒkl; 'mɑnɒkl/ n eyeglass for one eye only, kept in position by the muscles round the eye. 单眼镜。

mon·og·amy /məˈnɒgəmɪ; məˈnɑgəmɪ/ n [U] practice of being married to only one person at a time. 一夫一妻制。 ⇨ **polygamy**. **mon·og·amist** /-ɪst; -ɪst/ n person who practises ~. 实行一夫一妻制者。 **mon·og·amous** /məˈnɒgəməs; məˈnɑgəməs/ adj having only one wife or husband at a time. 一夫一妻(制)的。

mono·gram /'mɒnəgræm; 'mɑnə,græm/ n two or more letters (esp a person's initials) combined in one design (used on handkerchiefs, notepaper, etc). 字母组合图案(以二个或更多字母,尤其是姓名的起首字母,编成的图案,用于手帕、私人信纸等上)。

a monogram   a monolith

mono·graph /'mɒnəgrɑːf US: -græf; 'mɑnə,græf/ n detailed learned account, esp a published report on one particular subject. 专论; 专文; 专题研究报告。

mono·lin·gual /ˌmɒnəˈlɪŋgwəl; ˌmɑnəˈlɪŋgwəl/ adj using only one language: 只用一种语言的: The OALDCE is a ~ dictionary. 牛津现代高级英语词典是部只用一种语言的词典。

mono·lith /'mɒnəlɪθ; 'mɑnlˌɪθ/ n single upright block of stone (as a pillar or monument). 巨石; 独立柱或碑。 **~ic** /ˌmɒnəˈlɪθɪk; ˌmɑnlˈɪθɪk/ adj of or like a ~. 独石的;似独石的。

mono·logue /'mɒnəlɒg US: -lɔːg; 'mɑnl,ɔg/ n scene in a play, etc in which only one person speaks; dramatic composition for a single performer; soliloquy. 戏剧等中的独白场景;独演剧本;独脚戏;自言自语;独白。

mono·mania /ˌmɒnəʊˈmeɪnɪə; ˌmɑnəˈmenɪə/ n [U] state of mind, sometimes amounting to madness, caused by the attention being occupied exclusively by one idea or subject; [C] instance of this. 偏执狂; 对一事的狂热; 单狂; 偏癖; 其实例。 ⇨ **paranoia**. **mono·maniac** /ˌmɒnəʊˈmeɪnɪæk; ˌmɑnəˈmenɪ,æk/ n sufferer from ~. 患偏执狂的人;有偏癖的人。

mono·plane /'mɒnəpleɪn; 'mɑnə,plen/ n aircraft with one wing on each side of the fuselage. 单翼飞机。 ⇨ **biplane**.

mon·op·ol·ize /məˈnɒpəlaɪz; məˈnɑpl,aɪz/ vt [VP 6A] get or keep a monopoly of; control the whole of, so that others cannot share: 专利; 垄断; 独占: Don't let me ~ the conversation, 不要光让我一个人讲话。 **mon·op·ol·iz·ation** /məˌnɒpəlaɪˈzeɪʃn US: -lˈɪ-z-; məˌnɑplɪˈzeʃən/ n

mon·op·oly /məˈnɒpəlɪ; məˈnɑplɪ/ n (pl **-lies**) [C]

1 (possession of the) sole right to supply; the supply or service thus controlled. 专利权; 专利权之占有; 专卖; 独占事业. **2** complete possession of trade, talk, etc: 垄断: *In many countries tobacco is a government ~.* 在许多国家中, 烟草是政府的专卖事业. **3** anything over which one person or group has control and which is not or cannot be shared by others. 专利品; 专卖品. **mon·op·ol·ist** /-lɪst ; -lɪst/ *n* person who has a ~. 专利者; 专卖者. **mon·op·ol·is·tic** /mə,nɒpə'lɪstɪk; mə,nɑpə'lɪstɪk/ *adj*

mono·rail /'mɒnəʊreɪl; 'mɑnə,rel/ *n* single rail serving as a track for vehicles; railway system for vehicles using such a rail, or for vehicles suspended from one. (供车辆行驶的)单轨; 单轨铁道; 单轨索道(供吊车行驶者).

mono·syl·lable /'mɒnəsɪləbl; 'mɒnə,sɪləbl/ *n* word of one syllable. 单音节的词. **mono·syl·labic** /,mɒnəsɪ'læbɪk; ,mɑnəsɪ'læbɪk/ *adj* having only one syllable; made up of words of one syllable: 单音节的; 由单音节的词组成的: *monosyllabic answers*, eg 'Yes' or 'No'. 单音词的回答(如答 Yes 或 No).

mono·theism /'mɒnəʊθiːɪzəm ; 'mɑnəθi,ɪzəm/ *n* doctrine that there is only one God (contrasted with *polytheism*). 一神论; 一神教(与 polytheism 相对). **mono·theist** /'mɒnəʊθiːɪst; 'mɑnəθiɪst/ *n* believer in ~. 信一神教(论)者. **mono·the·istic** /,mɒnəʊθiː'ɪstɪk; ,mɑnəθi'ɪstɪk/ *adj*

mono·tone /'mɒnətəʊn; 'mɑnə,ton/ *n* (keeping a) level tone in talking or singing; utterance without change of pitch: 单调; 音调无变化; 平音: *speak in a ~.* 语调无变化地说话.

mon·ot·onous /mə'nɒtənəs; mə'nɑtnəs/ *adj* (uninteresting because) unchanging, without variety: 单调的; 千篇一律的; 单调乏味的: *a ~ voice*, one with little change of pitch; 单调的声音; *~ work.* 单调乏味的工作. **~·ly** *adv* **mon·ot·ony** /mə'nɒtənɪ; mə'nɑtnɪ/ *n* [U] the state of being monotonous; wearisome absence of variety. 单调; 千篇一律.

mono·type /'mɒnətaɪp; 'mɑnə,taɪp/ *n* (**P**) composing machine that casts, sets and assembles type letter by letter. (商标)单式自动铸排机; 自动铸字机.

mon·ox·ide /mɒ'nɒksaɪd; mɑn'ɑksaɪd/ *n* [C, U] oxide containing one oxygen atom in the molecule: 一氧化物: *carbon ~*, (**CO**). 一氧化碳.

Mon·roe /mən'rəʊ; mən'ro/ *n* ~ **doctrine**, (based on statements by James Monroe, US president (1817—1825) in 1823) US policy of opposing any interference by European powers in N and S America. 门罗主义(基于美国总统(一八一七至 一八二五)詹姆士·门罗一八二三年所发表的声明, 反对欧洲强国对南北美洲事务作任何干涉).

Mon·sieur /mə'sjɜː(r) ; mə'sjɜ/ *n* (abbr 略作 **M**) (*pl* **Messieurs** /'mer'sjɜː(r); 'mesjɜ/) French title before the name of a man; Mr, sir, gentleman: (法)先生(冠于男子姓名前): *M~ Hercule Poirot*: 埃居尔·普瓦罗先生; *yes*, ~. 是的, 先生.

Mon·si·gnor /mɒn'siːnjə(r); mɑn'sɪnjə/ *n* (title of honour given to) certain priests in the RC Church. 阁下(对某些天主教教士的尊称).

mon·soon /mɒn'suːn ; mɑn'sun/ *n* seasonal wind blowing in the Indian Ocean from SW from April to October (*wet ~*) and from NE during the other months (*dry ~*); the rainy season that comes with the wet ~, 季风(印度洋上四月至十月期间吹自西南的 '湿季风', 在其他月份中吹自东北的 '干季风'); 湿季风所带来的雨季.

mon·ster /'mɒnstə(r); 'mɑnstə/ *n* **1** abnormally misshapen animal or plant; person or thing of extraordinary size, shape or qualities: (in stories) imaginary creature (eg half animal, half bird): 畸形的动物或植物; 大小、形状或癖性奇特的人或物; (故事中的)怪物; 巨兽; 怪兽(如半兽半鸟之怪物): *Mermaids, griffins and dragons are ~s.* 雌人鱼、鹰头狮身怪兽和龙都是怪物. *A*

five-legged dog is a ~. 五条腿的狗是一只怪兽. **2** person who is remarkable for some bad or evil quality: 恶人; 残忍的人: *a ~ of cruelty/ingratitude;* 极残酷的人(忘恩负义的恶徒); *the Commissioners of Inland Revenue, those ~s of greed.* 国内税务官, 那些贪婪的恶吏. **3** (attrib) huge: (用作定语)巨大的: *a ~ ship.* 大船.

mon·strance /'mɒnstrəns; 'mɑnstrəns/ *n* (in RC Church) vessel in which the Host is exposed for veneration. (天主教)圣饼匣.

mon·strous /'mɒnstrəs; 'mɑnstrəs/ *adj* **1** of or like a monster; of great size. (似)畸形之动物或植物的; (像)怪物的; 巨大的. **2** atrocious; causing horror and disgust: 凶暴的; 恐怖的; 令人厌恶的: *~ crimes.* 恐怖的罪行. **3** (colloq) quite absurd: incredible; scandalous: (口)荒诞的; 难以置信的; 可耻的: *It's perfectly ~ that men should be paid more than women for the same job.* 做相同的工作, 而男人所得报酬比女人多, 这简直是荒谬透顶. **~·ly** *adv* **mon·stros·ity** /mɒn'strɒsətɪ; mɑn'strasətɪ/ *n* (*pl* **-ties**) [U] state of being ~: [C] monster; hideous object, building, etc. 畸形; 怪异; 怪兽; 怪物; 令人恐怖的东西、建筑物等.

mon·tage /'mɒntɑːʒ; *US:* mɒn'tɑːʒ; 'mɑn'taʒ/ *n* (F) [U] selection, cutting and arrangement of photographic film, etc to make a consecutive whole; process of using many pictures, designs, etc sometimes super-imposed, to make a composite picture. (法)蒙太奇(把已经拍好的许多镜头等加以选择、剪接及编排成连贯的影片); 镜头剪辑; 集锦剪辑(用许多图片、图案等, 有时予以重迭, 以拼凑成一幅集锦图片的过程).

month /mʌnθ ; mʌnθ/ *n* **calendar ~**, any of the twelve parts into which the year is divided; period of time from a day in one ~ to the corresponding day in the next ~ (eg 2 Jan to 2 Feb). 历月; 月, 一个月的时间(如自一月二日至二月二日). **lunar ~**, period in which the moon makes a complete revolution round the earth; period of 28 days: 太阴月(月球绕地球一周的期间);二十八天的期间: *a baby of three ~s/a three-~-old baby.* 三个月大的婴孩. *In which ~ were you born?* 你是几月生的? *I shall be back this day ~*, four weeks from today. 我将在下个月的今天回来. *a ~ of Sundays*, a very long time: 很长的一段时间: *Never in a ~ of Sundays!* 决不! 永不! **~·ly** *adj, adv* done, happening, published, etc, once a ~; valid for one ~: 每月一次的; 每月出版一次的(地); 有效一个月的(地): *a ~ly season ticket*, eg for railway travel. 月票(如乘火车用的). □ *n* **1** periodical issued once a ~. 月刊杂志. **2** (*pl* **-lies**) (colloq used) occurrence of menstruation. (口, 过时用语)月经.

monu·ment /'mɒnjʊmənt; 'mɑnjəmənt/ *n* **1** building, column, statue, etc serving to keep alive the memory of a person or event: 纪念馆; 纪念碑; 纪念像; 纪念物: *a ~ to soldiers killed in the war.* 阵亡将士纪念碑. **the M~**, the column in London that commemorates the Great Fire of London in 1666. 伦敦(一六六六年)大火纪念塔. **2 Ancient M~s**, objects, of special historic interest, such as prehistoric fortifications and remains, old buildings and bridges (often preserved by official bodies). 古迹; 名胜(例如史前的防御工事和遗迹, 古老的建筑物和桥梁等, 通常由政府机构保存之). **3** piece of scholarship or research that deserves to be remembered; work of literature or science of lasting value: 值得纪念的学术或研究成就; 有永久价值的文学作品或科学研究成果: *a ~ of learning.* 学术上的不朽成就.

monu·men·tal /,mɒnjʊ'mentl; ,mɑnjə'mɛntl/ *adj* **1** of, serving for, a monument: 纪念物的; 做为纪念的: *a ~ inscription*, 碑铭; *~ masons*, eg making tombstones. 碑匠. **2** (of books, studies, etc) of lasting value: (书籍、研究等)不朽的: *a ~ production*, eg *the Oxford English Dictionary.* 不朽的作品(如牛津英语词典). **3** (of qualities, buildings, tasks) very great: (指性质、建筑物、工作)巨大的: *~ ignorance.* 极度的愚蠢.

moo /muː; mu/ *n* sound made by a cow. 牛鸣声. □ *vi*

(*pt* **mooed**) make the sound moo. 作牛鸣声。'**moo-cow** *n* (child's word for) cow. (儿语) 牛。

mooch /muːtʃ; mutʃ/ *vi* [VP2C] ~ **about,** (colloq) loiter about: (口) 徘徊；闲荡: *out-of-work men* ~*ing about (the streets)* (在街上)闲荡的失业男人。

mood[1] / muːd; mud/ *n* [C] state of mind or spirits: 心境；情绪: *in a merry* ~; 心情快乐; *in the* ~ *for work,* inclined to work; 想工作; *not in the* ~ *for serious music.* 不想听严肃的音乐。*He's a man of* ~*s,* his ~*s change often.* 他是喜怒无常的人。~**y** *adj* (**-ier, -iest**) **1** having ~*s* that often change. 心情变化无定的。**2** gloomy; bad-tempered. 忧郁的；易怒的。~**·ily** /-ɪlɪ; -əlɪ/ *adv* '~**i·ness** *n*

mood[2] /muːd; mud/ *n* (gram) one of the groups of forms that a verb may take to show whether things are regarded as certain, possible, doubtful, etc (语法)语气(表示事物之确实性、可能性或可疑性等的动词形式之一): *the indicative / imperative / subjunctive* ~. 陈述(祈使, 假设)语气。

moon[1] /muːn; mun/ *n* **1 the** ~, the body which moves round the earth once in a month and shines at night by light reflected from the sun: (指绕地球运行, 并在夜间借反射太阳的光而发亮的天体)月球: *Men have explored the surface of the* ~. 人类已经勘测了月球的表面。*The* ~ *shone brightly.* 月光皎洁。*a+adj+* ~, this body regarded as an object distinct from that visible in other times: (指某一时期出现而与其他时间所见有别的)月亮；月: *a new / half / full* ~. 新月(半月; 满月)。 ⇨**new:** ⇨ the illus at **phase.** 参看 illus之插图。*a / no* ~, the ~ visible / invisible: 有 (没有) 月亮: *There was no* ~, It was a night with no ~ visible in the sky. 那晚没有月亮。*Is there a* ~ *tonight?* 今晚有月亮吗? *cry for the* ~, yearn for sth impossible. 渴望不可能的事物。*promise sb the* ~, make extravagant promises. 许下过份的诺言。**2** (compounds) (复合词) '~**·beam** *n* ray of ~*light.* 一道月光。'~**buggy/rover** *n* vehicle for travelling on the ~. 月球车 (行驶于月球上的一种单座车)。 '~**·flower** *n* ox-eye daisy. 牛眼菊。'~**·light** *n* light of the ~; 月光; (often attrib) (常用作定语) *go swimming in the* ~*light / by* ~*light;* 月光下去游泳; *a* ~*light night* 月夜。'~**·lit** *adj* lit by the ~: 被月光照亮的: *a* ~*lit scene / landscape.* 月夜的景色(风景)。'~**·shine** *n* **(a)** light of the ~. 月光。**(b)** foolish or idle talk, ideas, etc. 愚昧的言谈；空谈; 妄想。**(c)** (US) whisky or other spirits illicitly distilled or smuggled. (美)私酒 (私酿或走私的)。'~**·stone** *n* semi-precious felspar. 月长石; 月石。'~**·struck** *adj* wild and wandering in the mind (supposedly as the result of the ~'s influence). 发狂的 (被认为是受月光的影响)。**3** [C] satellite of other planets: 其他行星的卫星: *How many* ~*s has the planet Jupiter?* 木星有几个卫星? **4** [C] (poet) month. (诗)一个月的时间。*once in a blue* ~, (colloq) rarely or never. (口)罕有；永无。~**·less** *adj* without a visible ~: 没有月亮的: *a dark,* ~*less night.* 无月光的黑夜。

moon[2] /muːn; mun/ *vi, vt* **1** [VP2C] ~ *about / around,* move or look listlessly. 闲荡; 茫然注视。**2** [VP15B] ~ *away,* pass (time) listlessly or aimlessly: 闲度(时光): ~ *away the summer holidays.* 无所事事度过暑假。~**y** *adj* (**-ier, -iest**) given to ~*ing* away the time. 迷迷糊糊地过日子的。

moor[1] /muə(r); mur/ *n* [C, U] (area of) open, uncultivated land, esp if covered with heather (and often, in GB, used for preserving game, esp grouse). 荒野; 旷野 (尤指长有石南属植物者, 在英国常被保留作松鸡类猎物之繁殖地区); 松鸡类猎物保留区。'~**·fowl,** **game** *nn* (*pl* unchanged) red grouse. (复数不变)红松鸡。'~**·cock** *n* male of this. 公红松鸡。'~**·hen** *n* **(a)** female of this. 母红松鸡。**(b)** water-hen. 鹬; 水鸡。 ⇨ the illus at **water.** 参看 water之插图。'~**·land** /-lənd; -ˌlænd/ *n* land consisting of open ~ and covered with heather. (长有石南的)荒地。

moor[2] /muə(r); mur/ *vt* [VP6A, 15A] make (a boat, ship, etc) secure (to land or buoys) by means of cables, etc. 使(船)碇泊。'~**·ing-mast** *n* one for ~ing airships. 飞艇系留桅。~**·ings** /'muərɪŋz; 'murɪŋz/ *n pl* **1** cables, anchors and chains, etc, by which a ship or boat is ~ed 系船的缆、锚、链等; 系船具; 系留锚; 碇泊锚。**2** place where a ship is ~ed. 系船处; 停船处。

Moor /muə(r); mur/ *n* member of the Muslim peoples of mixed Arab and Berber blood who now live in NW Africa; one of the Muslim Arabs who invaded Spain in the 8th c: 摩尔人(现居于非洲西北部之伊斯兰教民族, 具有阿拉伯人与柏柏尔人之血统; 八世纪入侵西班牙之阿拉伯伊斯兰教徒): *the conquest of Spain by the* ~*s.* 摩尔人之征服西班牙。

Moor·ish /'muərɪʃ; 'murɪʃ/ *adj* of the Moors and their culture: 摩尔人的; 摩尔文化的: ~ *palaces in Granada.* 在格拉纳达的摩尔式宫殿。

moose /muːs; mus/ *n* (*pl* ~ or ~**s** -sɪz; -sɪz/) large sort of deer with coarse fleece and thick antlers, found in the forests of N America, and (where it is called an *elk*) in northern Europe and Asia. 麋(长有粗毛及厚角的一种大鹿, 产于北美洲森林地带, 北欧及北亚, 在北欧及北亚被称为 elk)。

moot /muːt; mut/ *adj* (only in) (仅用于) **a** ~ *point / question,* one about which there is uncertainty. 未决之点(问题)。 □ *vt* [VP6A] raise or bring forward for discussion: 提出讨论: *This question has been* ~*ed again.* 这问题已再度提出讨论。

mop[1] /mɒp; mɑp/ *n* **1** bundle of coarse strings, cloth, etc fastened to a long handle for cleaning floors, etc; similar material on a short handle for cleaning dishes, etc. (擦地板等用的)拖把; 洗碗刷。**2** mass of thick, untidy hair. 乱蓬蓬的头发。 □ *vt* (**-pp-**) **1** [VP6A] clean with a mop: 用拖把擦拭: *mop the floor.* (用拖把)拖地板; 擦地板。**2** [VP6A, 15B] ~ (*up*), clean (away) with, or as with, a mop: (用拖把等)擦; 揩: *mop one's brow,* wipe away sweat, eg with a handkerchief; (如用手帕)擦额上的汗; *mop up a mess.* 擦掉一堆脏东西。*mop up,* (colloq uses) finish off, make an end of: (口)结束; 做完: *mop up arrears of work;* 把耽误的工作做完; *mopping-up operations* (in a military sense), getting rid of defeated remnants of enemy troops. 扫荡战。*mop the floor with sb,* defeat him completely, eg in a debate. 彻底击败某人 (如在辩论中)。

mop[2] /mɒp; mɑp/ *vi* (**-pp-**) (archaic or liter, only in) (古或文; 仅用于) *mop and mow,* make grimaces. 扮鬼脸。

mope /məup; mop/ *vi* [VP2A, C] pity oneself, give oneself up to sadness or low spirits: 郁郁不乐: ~ (*about*) *in the house all day.* 整天在屋里郁郁不乐。 □ *n* the ~**s,** low spirits: 抑郁; 沮丧: *suffer from the* ~*s;* 抑郁不乐; *have a fit of the* ~*s.* 突然沮丧起来。

mo·ped /'məuped; 'moped/ *n* (GB) motor-cycle with pedals and a petrol engine of low power. (英)(装有小型引擎的)机器脚踏车。

mo·quette /mɒ'ket; US: məu-; mə'kɛt/ *n* [U] synthetic fabric used for carpets and soft furnishings. 毛凯(地毯及柔软家具等用之一种合成纤维织物)。

mo·raine /mɒ'reɪn; US: mo'ren/ *n* heap or mass of earth, gravel, rock, etc carried down and deposited by a glacier. 冰川堆石; 冰碛 (由冰河夹带并堆积的泥土沙石)。 ⇨ the illus at **mountain.** 参看 mountain 之插图。

moral[1] /'mɒrəl; US: 'mɔːrəl; 'mɑːrəl/ *adj* **1** concerning principles of right and wrong: 有关是非之原则的; 道德的: ~ *standards;* 道德标准; *a* ~ *question;* 道德问题; *the* ~ *sense,* the power of distinguishing right and wrong; 是非感(分辨是非的能力); ~ *law;* 道德律; ~ *rights / obligations,* based on ~ law; (基于道德律的)道德上的权利(义务); ~ *philosophy,* ethics, the study of right and wrong in human behaviour. 伦理学; 道德哲学。**2** good and virtuous: 品行端正的: *live a* ~

life; 过规矩的生活; *a ~ man.* 品行端正的人. **3** able to understand the difference between right and wrong: 能辨是非的: *At what age do we become ~ beings?* 我们要到什么年龄才能辨别是非? **4** teaching or illustrating good behaviour: 教导良好品德的; 道德教育的; 有寓意的: *a ~ book/story/talk.* 有寓意的书籍/故事, 言谈). **5** (contrasted with *physical* or *practical*) connected with the sense of what is right and just: (与 physical 或 practical 相对) 精神上的; 道义上的: *a ~ victory,* outcome of a struggle in which the weaker side is comforted because it has established the righteousness of its cause. 精神胜利. *a ~ certainty,* sth so probable that there is little room for doubt. 确实可靠的事; 非常可能的事. *~ courage/cowardice,* strength/lack of strength to face contempt or ridicule rather than do wrong. (缺少)宁受轻蔑或嘲笑而不肯做坏事的勇气; 道德上的勇气(怯弱). *give sb ~ support,* help by saying that he has justice and right on his side. 给某人道义上(或精神上)的支持(如申言正义是在他这一边). *~ly* /-rəlɪ; -rəlɪ/ *adv* in a ~ manner: 道德上: *M~ly he is all that she desired.* 就道德而言, 她对他十分满意.

moral[2] /ˈmɒrəl US: ˈmɔːrəl; ˈmɔrəl/ *n* **1** that which a story, event or experience teaches: 教训; 寓意: *And the ~ of this story is that a young girl should not speak to strange men.* 这个故事的教训是年轻的女子不应和陌生男人谈话. *You may draw your own ~ from this.* 你可以从这个找出对你自己的教训. **2** (pl) moral habits; standards of behaviour; principles of right and wrong: (复)品行;风化;行为的标准; 是非的原则; 道德; 伦理: *a man without ~s;* 没有道德的人; 不讲是非的人; *a man of loose ~s;* 品行不佳的人; *improve the ~s of a country.* 改良一国的风气.

mo·rale /məˈrɑːl US: -ˈræl; məˈræl/ *n* [U] state of discipline and spirit (in a person, an army, a nation, etc); temper, state of mind, as expressed in action: (个人、军队、国家等之)士气; 风气; (表现于行为的)性情; 心境: *The army recovered its ~ and fighting power.* 这军队恢复了士气与战斗力. *The failing ~ of the enemy* (= Their loss of confidence in themselves) *helped to shorten the war.* 敌军士气的衰落使战争缩短.

mor·al·ist /ˈmɒrəlɪst US: ˈmɔːr-; ˈmɔrəlɪst/ *n* person who points out morals(1); person who practises or teaches morality. 训诲师;道德家;德育家.

mor·al·is·tic /ˌmɒrəˈlɪstɪk US: ˌmɔːr-; ˌmɔrəˈlɪstɪk/ *adj* concerned with morals(2). 注重道德的; 说教的.

mor·al·ity /məˈrælətɪ; mɔˈrælɪtɪ/ *n* (pl **-ties**) **1** [U] (standards, principles, of) good behaviour: 美德; 道德; 道义; 伦理: *Have standards of political ~ improved in recent years?* 近年来政治道德标准改进了吗? *Is commercial ~ high in your country?* 贵国商业道德高不高? **2** [C] particular system of morals: 某一伦理体系或道德准则: *Muslim ~.* 伊斯兰教的道德律. **3** [C] '**~(play),** form of drama, popular in the 16th c, teaching good behaviour, the chief characters being personifications of virtues and vices. 道德剧; 寓意剧 (流行于十六世纪, 剧中主角为善与恶之化身, 主旨在于劝善规过).

mor·al·ize /ˈmɒrəlaɪz US: ˈmɔːr-; ˈmɔrəlˌaɪz/ *vt, vi* **1** [VP2A, 3A] *~ (about/on/upon),* deal with moral questions; talk or write on questions of duty, right and wrong, etc: 讨论道德问题; 作有关义务、是非等问题之谈话或写作; 讲道德: *~ upon the failings of the young generation.* 讨论年轻一代品行缺点的问题. *Oh, do stop moralizing! None of your moralizing! Stop preaching at me!* 哦! 不要说教啦! **2** [VP6A] give a moral interpretation of. 对…作道德意义解释.

mo·rass /məˈræs; mɔˈræs/ *n* [C] stretch of low, soft, wet land; marsh; (fig) entanglement. 低而柔软的湿地;沼泽;(喻)困难.

mora·torium /ˌmɒrəˈtɔːrɪəm US: ˌmɔːr-; ˌmɔrəˈtɔrɪəm/ *n* (pl **~s** or **-ria** /-rɪə/) [C] legal authorization to delay payment of debts; agreed

deferment or delay. 延期偿债(令); (经同意的)延期; 延缓.

mor·bid /ˈmɔːbɪd; ˈmɔrbɪd/ *adj* **1** diseased: 疾病的: *a ~ growth,* eg a cancer or tumour. 病态的生长(如癌或瘤); ~ *anatomy,* the study of diseased organs in the body. 病理解剖学. **2** (of sb's mind or ideas) unhealthy: (指人的心思或观念)不健全的;病态的: *~ imagination,* one that dwells on horrible or nasty things. 病态的想象 (只想到恐怖或卑鄙的事物). *~·ly adv ~·ity* /mɔːˈbɪdətɪ; mɔrˈbɪdətɪ/, *~·ness nn* state of being ~. 病态;不健康的状态.

mor·dant /ˈmɔːdnt; ˈmɔrdn̩t/ *adj* biting; sarcastic: 尖酸的; 讽刺的: *~ criticism;* 尖刻的批评; *a ~ wit.* 尖刻的机智.

more /mɔː(r); mɔr/ (contrasted with *less* and *fewer;* 与 less 及 fewer 相对; ⇨ **many, most**[1], **much**[1]) *adj* (independent comp) greater in number, quantity, quality, degree, size, etc; additional: (独立比较级)数目更多的;更大量的;更佳的;程度更高的;更大的;附加的: *We need ~ men/help, etc.* 我们需要更多的 (帮助等). *Instead of fewer helpers, we want ~.* 我们需要更多的助手,而不是更少的助手. *Have you any ~ paper?* 你还有纸吗? *Would you like some/a little ~ soup/a little ~ of this soup?* 你要不要再喝一点汤? □ *n* a greater amount, number, etc; an additional amount: 更大的量,数等; 额外数量: *What ~ do you want?* 你还要什么? *There are still a few ~.* 还有一些. *There is hardly any ~.* 差不多没有了. *That is ~ than enough.* 那是太多了. *May I have one ~?* 我可以再要一个吗? *I should like as many ~,* the same number again. 我愿意照同样的数目再要一些. *I hope to see ~ of you, to see you ~ often.* 我希望以后时常和你见面. □ *adv* **1** (forming the comparative degree of most *adjj* and *advv* of more than two syllables and of some of two syllables, esp if stressed on the first): (构成含有三个或三个以上音节的大多数形容词及副词的比较级;某些两音节的词,尤指重音在前者,亦可用 more): *~ beautiful/useful/interesting/serious (than...);* (比…)更美丽 (更有用,更有趣,更严重); *~ easily/quietly/foolishly (than...).* (比…)更容易地 (更安静地,更愚昧地). *and what is ~,* important, serious, etc (according to context). 更重要者; 更严重者; 再者; 更有甚者 (视上下文而定). **2** to a greater extent; in a greater degree: 更多地;更大地: *You need to sleep ~,* ie ~ than you sleep now. 你需要更多的睡眠. *You must attend to your work ~.* 你必须更专心于你的工作. *He was ~ frightened than hurt,* 他感受的伤害不大, 倒是受惊不小. *He likes summer ~ than autumn.* 他喜欢夏天甚于秋天. **3** again: 再: *Once ~, please.* 请再来一次. *I shall not go there any ~,* ever again. 我再也不去那儿了. *We saw him no ~,* did not see him again. 我们再也没看到他了. **4** *~ and ~,* by ~ stages, degrees, etc: 越来越…: *The story gets ~ and ~ exciting.* 故事越来越越动人. *Life is becoming ~ and ~ expensive.* 生活费用越来越昂贵. *~ or less,* about: 大约;多少有点儿: *It's an hour's journey, ~ or less.* 大约一小时的路程. **5** (with a n, equivalent to an *adj*): (与名词连用, 相当于形容词): *(The) ~ fool you to believe him,* You are, if you believe him, foolish in a higher degree. 你如果相信他, 你就蠢不可言了. *It had ~ the characteristic* (= was ~ characteristic) *of a foolish dream than of a nightmare.* 说它是梦魇还不如说它是个荒谬的梦. *(The)~'s the pity,* It is, to that extent, a greater pity. 那就更可惜了. ⇨ also the *(adv).* *no ~,* neither: 亦不; 都不: *A: 'I can't understand this at all.' B: 'No ~ can I.'* 甲说:'我根本不懂这个.' 乙说:'我也不懂.' *no ~... than:* 和…一样不…; 和…都不:*He's no ~ able to read Chinese than I am,* He is as unable to do so as I am. 他和我一样都不懂中文.

mo·rello /məˈreləʊ; məˈrelo/ *n* (pl **~s** -ləʊz; -loz/) *~(cherry),* bitter kind of cherry (used for jam). 黑樱桃 (味苦, 作果酱用).

more·over /mɔːˈrəʊvə(r); mɔrˈovɚ/ *adv* further;

besides; in addition (to this). 再者; 此外; 而且。

mores /'mɔːreɪz ; 'mɔriz/ *n pl* (formal) customs, usages, conventions, regarded as essential to a social group. (正式用语)某一社会团体的传统习俗。

Mo·resque /mɔː'resk; mə'resk/ *adj* (of style, design, decoration, architecture) Moorish. (指型式、设计、装饰、建筑)摩尔式的。

mor·ga·natic /ˌmɔːgə'nætɪk ; ˌmɔrgə'nætɪk/ *adj* ~ **marriage,** one between a man of high rank (eg a prince) and a woman of lower rank, who remains in her lower social station, the children having no claim to succeed to the property, titles, etc, of their father. 贵贱婚姻(贵族, 如王子, 和身份较低的女子的婚姻, 女方保留原有较低身份, 子女不得继承父亲财产、头衔等)。

morgue /mɔːg; mɔrg/ *n* **1** building in which bodies of persons found dead are kept until they are identified and claimed by members of their families. (待家人认领尸体的)陈尸所。 ⇨**mortuary**. **2** file (in the office of a newspaper or magazine) with obituary notices of famous people still living (ready for use when they die). (报馆或杂志社资料室中的尚活着的)名人档案(收集其生平简传, 准备其死亡时登载讣闻之用)。

mori·bund /'mɒrɪbʌnd US: 'mɔːr-; 'mɔrə,bʌnd/ *adj* at the point of death; about to come to an end: 将死的; 将要消灭的: ~ *civilizations.* 即将消灭的文明。

Mor·mon /'mɔːmən; 'mɔrmən/ *n, adj* (member) of a religious organization founded in the US in 1830, officially called 'The Church of Jesus Christ of Latter-day Saints'. 摩门教派的; 摩门教徒(摩门教是基督教的一个宗派, 一八三〇年创于美国, 正式名称为'末世圣徒基督教会')。 ~**·ism** /-ɪzəm/ *n* [U].

morn /mɔːn; mɔrn/ *n* (poet) morning. (诗)早晨。

morn·ing /'mɔːnɪŋ; 'mɔrnɪŋ/ *n* **1** [C, U] early part of the day between dawn and noon (or, more generally, before the midday meal): 早晨; 上午: *in/during the* ~; 在早晨; 在上午; *this* ~; 今早; 今天上午; *yesterday/tomorrow* ~; 昨天(明天)早上; *every* ~; 每天上午; *on Sunday/Monday, etc* ~; 星期日(星期一等)上午; *the* ~ *of May the 1st;* 五月一日上午; *one* ~ *last week;* 上星期某一天上午; *one summer* ~; 一个夏天的早晨; *a few* ~*s ago;* 几天前上午; *several* ~*s lately.* 最近几个上午。 *When he awoke it was* ~. 当他醒来时, 已经是早晨了。 **2** (attrib) (用作定语): *a* ~ *walk;* 早晨的散步; *an early* ~ *swim.* 清晨的游泳。 '~ **coat,** long black coat with the front cut away. 常礼服上衣。 '~ **dress,** ~ coat with striped trousers. 常 礼服(包含灰色上衣及条纹裤)。 ,M~ 'Prayer, service used in the Church of England at ~ service. (英国国教会的)晨祷。 **the** ~ **star,** Venus, or other bright star seen about dawn. 金星; 晨星; 晓星。 **the** ~ **watch,** (at sea) period of duty, 4am to 8am. (航海)早班(上午4时至8时)。 ,~**·glory** *n* climbing plant of the convolvulus family, with flowers that fade by midday. 牵牛花。 '~**-room** *n* sitting-room for the ~. 上午用的起居间。 '~ **sickness** *n* (feeling of) nausea early in the morning, during the first few months of pregnancy. 孕妇晨吐; 孕妇恶心(妇女怀孕最初几个月期间早晨时的作呕感觉)。

mo·rocco /mə'rɒkəʊ; mə'rako/ *n* [U] soft leather made from goatskins. (山羊皮制成的)鞣皮; 摩洛哥皮。

mo·ron /'mɔːrɒn; 'mɔrɑn/ *n* feeble-minded person (with a mental level not so low as imbeciles or idiots); (colloq) stupid person. 轻度低能者(智能程度高于imbeciles 或 idiots者); (口)笨人; 傻瓜。 ~**ic** /mə'rɒnɪk; mo'rɑnɪk/ *adj*

mo·rose /mə'rəʊs; mə'ros/ *adj* sullen; ill-tempered; unsocial. 抑郁的; 坏脾气的; 不与人来往的; 孤僻的。 ~**·ly** *adv* ~**·ness** *n*

mor·pheme /'mɔːfiːm; 'mɔrfim/ *n* (ling) smallest meaningful part into which a word can be divided: (语言)词素 (一个词可分割成的最小意义单位): *'Run-s' contains two* ~*s and 'un-like-ly' contains three.* runs 一词含两个词素(即 run 和 s), unlikely 一词含三个词素

(即 un, like 及 ly)。

Mor·pheus /'mɔːfiəs; 'mɔrfiəs/ *n* (Gk myth) god of dreams and sleep. (希神)睡梦之神。

Mor·phia /'mɔːfiə; 'mɔrfiə/, **mor·phine** /'mɔːfiːn; 'mɔrfin /*nn* [U] drug, usu in the form of a white powder, made from opium and used for relieving pain. 吗啡(由鸦片制成的一种止痛剂, 通常为白色粉状)。

mor·phol·ogy /mɔː'fɒlədʒɪ; mɔr'fɑlədʒɪ/ *n* [U] **1** (biol) branch of biology dealing with the form and structure of animals and plants. (生物)生物形态学。 **2** (ling) study of the morphemes of a language and of how they are combined to make words. (语言)有关一语言的词素及其组合的研究; 词法; 形态学。 ⇨ **syntax.**

mor·ris dance /'mɒrɪs dɑːns US: 'mɔrɪs dæns; 'mɔrɪs dæns/ *n* old English folk-dance for men. 英国古时一种(男人)舞蹈。

mor·row /'mɒrəʊ US: 'mɔːr-; 'mɔro/ *n* **1** (liter) the next day after the present or after any given day: (文)翌日; 次日: *What had the* ~ *in store for them?* 他们后来的遭遇如何? **2** (archaic) morning: (古)早晨: *Good* ~! 早安!

Morse /mɔːs; mɔrs/ *n* '~**(code),** system of dots and dashes or short and long sounds or flashes of light, representing letters of the alphabet and numbers, to be signalled by lamp, radio, etc: 摩尔斯电码(用点和线或长短的声音、闪光代表字母及数字, 可用灯光、无线电等发送): *a message in* ~; 用摩尔斯电码传达的消息; *the* ~ *alphabet.* 摩尔斯电码。

mor·sel /'mɔːsl ; 'mɔrsl/ *n* [C] tiny piece (esp of food); mouthful: 小块; 一小片(尤指食物); 一口: *I haven't had a* ~ *of food since I left the house.* 我从家里出来到现在还没有吃过一点点东西。 *What a dainty/choice* ~! 多精美的一点食物!

mor·tal /'mɔːtl; 'mɔrtl/ *adj* **1** (contrasted with *im-mortal*) which must die; which cannot live for ever: (与 immortal 相对)必死的; 不能永存的: *Man is* ~, All men must die. 人人必有一死; 人是会死的。 *Here lie the remains of....* (eg on a tombstone) Here is buried what now remains of the body of.... ...葬于此处(刻于墓碑等上的词句)。 **2** causing death: 致命的: *a* ~ *wound.* 致命伤。 *His injuries proved* ~. 他的伤成了致命伤。 ~ **sins,** causing spiritual death. 大罪; (宗教)使灵魂死亡的罪。 **3** lasting until death: 持续到死的: ~ *hatred.* 终身的憎恨。 ~ **combat,** only ended by the death of one of the fighters. 殊死战; 拼命的争斗; 不死不休的战斗。 ~ **enemies,** whose enmity will not end until death. 死敌; 不共戴天的仇敌。 **4** accompanying death: 垂死的; 临终的: *in* ~ *agony.* 临死的痛苦。 **5** (colloq) extreme; very great or long: (口)极端的; 极大的; 极长的: *in* ~ *fear;* 极大的恐惧; *in a* ~ *hurry.* 非常匆促。 □ *n* human being. 人。 ~**·ly** /-təlɪ; -tlɪ/ *adv* **1** so as to cause death: 致命地: ~*ly wounded.* 受了致命伤。 **2** deeply, seriously: 深重地; 严重地: ~*ly offended.* 极为震怒。

mor·tal·ity /mɔː'tælətɪ; mɔr'tælətɪ/ *n* [U] **1** state of being mortal. 必死的状态; 不可免的死亡。 **2** number of deaths caused by sth (eg a disaster or disease): 死亡数目(如灾害或疾病所造成的): *an epidemic with a heavy* ~, a large number of deaths. 造成大量死亡的流行性传染病。 **3** death-rate: 死亡率: '~**tables,** (insurance) tables showing how long people at various ages may expect to live. (保险)死亡率表。

mor·tar[1] /'mɔːtə(r); 'mɔrtə/ *n* [U] mixture of lime, sand and water used to hold bricks, stones, etc together in building. (建筑时用以粘接砖、石等的)砂浆; 灰泥。 '~**-board** *n* **(a)** small, flat board with a short handle on the underside, used for holding a supply of ~ (while laying bricks, plaster, etc). 灰泥板; 镘板(砌砖时盛灰泥用的底面有短把手的小平板)。 **(b)** square cap worn as part of their academic costume by members of a college, etc. (大学生等所戴的)方顶礼帽; 学位帽。 □ *vt* [VP6A] join (bricks, etc) with ~. 用灰泥粘接(砖等)。

mor·tar[2] /'mɔːtə(r); 'mɔrtə/ *n* **1** bowl of hard material

in which substances are crushed with a pestle. 臼; 研钵.
⇨ the illus at **pestle**. 参看 pestle 之插图. **2** (mil)cannon
for firing shells at high angles. (军)曲击炮; 臼炮.

mort·gage /'mɔːgɪdʒ; 'mɔrgɪdʒ/ vt [VP6A, 14] ∼
(to) (for), give sb a claim on (property) as a security
for payment of a debt or loan: 抵押. ∼ a house (to sb
for £20 000); 将一幢房子抵押(给某人, 借款二万英镑);
land that may be ∼d. 可以抵押的土地. □ n act of
mortgaging; agreement about this: 抵押; 抵押单据(契
约): raise a ∼ (on one's house) from a bank. (把房子)
抵押给银行. I can buy the house only if a ∼ for £20 000
is obtainable. 只要能抵押借到二万英镑, 我就能买这幢房
子. We must pay off the ∼ this year. 我们今年必须还清
抵押借款. be ∼d up to the hilt, have the maximum
∼ possible (on property). (财产) 抵押到可能的最高额.
mort·gagee /ˌmɔːgɪ'dʒiː; ˌmɔrgɪ'dʒi/ n person to whom
property is ∼d. 承受抵押者; 贷款人. **mort·gagor**
/ˌmɔːgɪ'dʒɔː(r) US: 'mɔːrgɪdʒər; ˈmɔrgɪdʒɚ/ n person
who gives a ∼ on his property. 抵押人; 借款人.

mor·tice /'mɔːtɪs; 'mɔrtɪs/ n ⇨ **mortise**.

mor·ti·cian /mɔː'tɪʃn; mɔr'tɪʃən/ n (US) funeral
director, undertaker. (美)殡仪业者.

mor·tify /'mɔːtɪfaɪ; 'mɔrtəˌfaɪ/ vt, vi (pt, pp -**fied**)
1 [VP6A] cause (sb) to be ashamed, humiliated, or
hurt in his feelings: 使(某人)蒙羞、或因羞辱或感情受伤
害; mortified by sb's rudeness; 被某人的粗暴所羞辱;
feel mortified at one's failure to pass an examination; 因
考试不及格而感到羞耻; a ∼ing defeat. 屈辱的失败.
2 [VP6A] ∼ the flesh, discipline bodily passions,
overcome bodily desires. 抑制肉体的情欲; 克制肉体的
欲望. **3** [VP2A] (of flesh, eg round a wound) decay,
be affected with gangrene. (指肌肉, 如伤口周围者)溃烂;
生坏疽. **mor·ti·fi·ca·tion** /ˌmɔːtɪfɪ'keɪʃn; ˌmɔrtəfə'keʃən/
n [U] ∼ing or being mortified (all senses). 羞辱; 屈
辱; 制欲; 坏疽.

mor·tise, mor·tice /'mɔːtɪs; 'mɔrtɪs/ n hole (usu
rectangular) cut in a piece of wood, etc to receive
the end of another piece (the tenon). (通常为长方形
的)柄穴; 榫眼. '∼-**lock**, secure lock which is fitted
inside the woodwork (of a door, etc), not screwed on
to the surface. (不在木器如门等表面上螺栓, 而在其内
部的)榫眼接合. □ vt [VP15A, B] join or fasten in
this way: 以榫穴接牢; 上榫: ∼ two beams together; 把
两根梁用榫接在一起; ∼ one beam to/into another. 把
一根梁接榫到另一根梁.

mor·tu·ary /'mɔːtʃərɪ US: -tʃuerɪ; 'mɔrtʃʊˌɛrɪ/ n
(pl -**ries**) room or building (eg part of a hospital) to
which dead bodies are taken to be kept until burial.
停尸处; 太平间; (用作定语)
(attrib) of death or burial: 停尸处; 太平间; (用作定语)
∼ rites. 葬仪; 葬礼.

mo·saic /məʊ'zeɪɪk; mo'zeˌɪk/ n, adj (form or work
of art) in which designs, pictures, etc are made by
fitting together differently coloured bits of stone, etc:
镶嵌细工; 镶嵌的艺术品; 镶嵌细工的: a design in ∼;
镶嵌细工的图案; a ∼ pavement/ceiling. 嵌花的地面
(天花板).

Mo·saic /məʊ'zeɪɪk; mo'zeˌɪk/ adj of Moses. 摩西
(旧约圣经中的先知)的. **(the) ∼ law**, the first five
books of the Old Testament. 摩西的律法(即旧约圣经的
前五卷).

mo·selle /məʊ'zel; mo'zɛl/ n dry, white wine from
the valley of the River M∼ (in W Germany). 摩泽尔
酒(产于西德摩泽尔河流域的无甜味白葡萄酒).

mosey /'məʊzɪ; 'mozɪ/ vi [VP2A, C] ∼ (along),
(sl) amble leisurely. (俚)漫步; 徘徊.

Mos·lem /'mɒzləm; 'mazləm/ n, adj = Muslim.

mosque /mɒsk; mɑsk/ n building in which Muslims
worship Allah. 伊斯兰教寺院; 清真寺.

mos·quito /mə'skiːtəʊ; mə'skito/ n (pl ∼**es** /-təʊz;-toz/)
small, flying, blood-sucking insect, esp the sort that
spreads malaria. 蚊; (尤指)疟蚊. ⇨ the illus at **insect**.
参看 insect 之插图. '∼-**net** n net, hung over a bed,

a mosque

through which ∼es cannot fly. 蚊帐. '∼-**craft** n
(collective pl) small, armed ships with high speed and
able to manoeuvre easily. (集合名词复数)迅速敏捷的小
舰艇; 蚊式艇.

moss /mɒs US: mɔːs; mɔs/ n [U] sorts of small green
or yellow plant growing in thick masses on wet surfaces:
苔; 藓: ∼-covered rocks/roofs/tree-trunks. 生满了青
苔的岩石(屋顶,树干). A rolling stone gathers no ∼,
(prov) A person who too frequently changes his
occupation or who never settles in one place will not
succeed in life. (谚) 滚石不生苔, 转业不聚财(喻人若
不能专心一事, 时常改动, 则难望有成). '∼y adj
covered with growing ∼. 生苔的. '∼y adj (-ier, -iest)
covered with ∼; like ∼: 生苔的; 似苔的: ∼y green.
苔绿色.

most /məʊst; most/ (contrasted with least and fewest;
与 least 和 fewest 相对) ⇨ **many, more, much**[1]) adj,
n **1** (independent superl) greatest in number,
quantity, degree, etc: (独立最高级)最多数的; 最大量的;
最高程度的: Which is ∼, 3, 13 or 30? 哪一个数目最
大, 3, 13, 还是 30? Which of you has made the ∼
mistakes? 你们当中哪一个犯错误最多? Those who have
(the) ∼ money are not always (the) happiest. 最有钱的
人不一定是最快乐的. Do the ∼ you can. 尽你所能去
做. at (the) ∼; at the very ∼, not more than: 至多:
I can pay only £10 at the ∼. 我最多只能付十英镑. There
were only 30 people at the meeting at the very ∼, There
were 30 or fewer. 最多只有三十个人参加那次会议. make
the ∼ of, use to the best advantage: 充分利用; 善为利
用: We have only a few hours so we must make the ∼ of
our time. 我们只有几小时, 所以我们必须善于利用我们
的时间. She's not really beautiful, but she makes the ∼
of her looks. 她并不十分漂亮, 却很会打扮. for the ∼
part, usually; on the whole: 通常地; 大体说来: Japanese
TV sets are, for the ∼ part, of excellent quality. 大体说
来, 日本的电视机品质极优良. **2**(not preceded by def art in
this sense) the majority of; the greater part of: (用作
此义时不加定冠词)大多数; 大部分: M∼ people fear
pain. 大多数人都怕痛. He was ill ∼ of the summer. 那
年夏天他大部分时间都在病中. □ suff (with preps or
adjj of position): (与表示位置的介词或形容词连用):top-
∼, highest; 最高的; in(ner)∼, furthest in. 最内的.

most /məʊst; most/ adv **1** (forming the superlative
degree of nearly all adjj and advv of more than one
syllable): (与绝大部分两音节或多音节的形容词和副词连
用,形成最高级)最: the ∼ beautiful/interesting/useful,
etc; 最美丽的(最有趣的; 最有用的等); ∼ carefully/
accurately, etc. 最小心地(最准确地等). **2** (modifying
vv, but not to be placed between a v and its object): (修
饰动词,但不放在动词和它的宾语之间): What is troubling
you ∼? 什么事情最使你烦恼? What ∼ pleased me/
What pleased me ∼ was that ... 最令我高兴的是 ... .
3 (intensive, modifying an adj; may be preceded by
indef art) very; exceedingly: (用于加强语气; 修饰形容
词; 前面可加不定冠词)非常; 极: This is a ∼ useful book. 这是一
本极其有用的书. He was ∼ polite to me. 他对我非常有

礼貌。*Your news is ~ interesting.* 你的消息非常有趣。**4** (modifying an *adv*) quite: (修饰副词)完全地; 十分: *I shall ~ certainly go.* 我一定去。**5** (dial and US colloq) almost: (方,美口)几乎: *M~ everybody has gone home.* 几乎所有的人都回家去了。**~·ly** *adv* chiefly; almost all; generally: 主要地; 几乎全部; 大概: *The medicine was ~ly sugar and water.* 那种药主要成份是糖和水。*The village is ~ly of mud houses.* 这个村庄里的房子几乎全是泥土造的。*We are ~ly out on Sundays,* are not at home on ~ Sundays. 星期天我们通常都不在家。

mote /məʊt/ *n* particle (of dust, etc): (灰尘等的)微粒: *~s dancing in a sunbeam.* 在阳光中飞扬的尘埃。*the ~ in sb's eye,* the fault that he has committed (trifling if compared to one's own fault). 某人眼中的灰尘 (意谓看见别人的小错而忽视自己的大错)。⇨ **Matt 7:3.** 参看新约圣经马太福音 7 章 3 节。

mo·tel /məʊˈtel/ ; moˈtel/ *n* motorists' hotel (with rooms or cabins, a parking area, service station, etc). 汽车旅馆(供司机停车住宿,备有停车场、汽车修护站的)。

moth /mɒθ US: mɔːθ/ ; mɔθ /*n* sorts of winged insect flying chiefly at night, attracted by lights. 蠹; 蛾。⇨ the illus at **insect.** 参看 insect 之插图。**'~-ball** *n* small ball (of camphor, etc) intended to discourage clothes-~s. 防蠹丸(樟脑等制成的)。⇨ *naphthalene* at **naphtha.** *in ~-balls,* (fig) in storage: (喻)贮存中: *After ten years in ~-balls the ships were sent to be broken up.* 经过十年的封存后, 那些船只被送去拆卸。**'clothes-~** *n* kind which breeds in cloth, fur, etc, its grub feeding on the cloth and making holes. 蠹鱼(蛀衣服的蠹虫)。**'~-eaten** *adj* eaten or destroyed by clothes-~s; (fig) antiquated; out-of-date. 蠹鱼蛀过的; (喻)古旧的; 过时的。**'~-proof** *adj* (of fabrics) treated chemically against damage by clothes-~s. (织织物)防蛀的。□ *vt* make ~proof: 使有防蛀功能: *~-proof carpets.* 把地毯加以防蛀处理。

mother/ ˈmʌðə(r)/ ; ˈmʌðɚ /*n* **1** female parent; woman who has adopted a child; woman (often 常作 *'housemother'*) who is in charge of children in a boarding-school or home¹(2). 母亲; 养母; (寄宿学校或孤儿院中照管孩子们的)保母。**2** quality or condition that gives rise to sth: 根本; 来源: *Misgovernment is often the ~ of revolt.* 治理不善常常是叛乱的根源。*Necessity is the ~ of invention,* (prov). (谚)需要为发明之母。**3** head of a female religious community. 妇女宗教团体的首长。**M~ Superior,** head of a convent. 女修道院院长。**4** (various uses)(各种不同用法) **the '~-country, (a)**one's native land. 祖国。**(b)** a country in relation to colonies, etc. (殖民地等的)母国。**~-in-law** /ˈmʌðər ɪn lɔː; ˈmʌðɚɪn,lɔ /*n* (*pl* **~s-in-law**) ~ of one's wife or one's husband. 岳母; 婆婆。**~-of-'pearl** *n* [U] hard, smooth, shiny, rainbow-coloured material that forms the lining of some shells, esp the pearl-oyster, used for making buttons, ornaments, etc. (贝壳,尤指珍珠贝的)珠母层; 真珠母(贝壳里层坚硬光滑而发亮的彩色物质,可用于制造钮扣、装饰品等)。**~ ship** *n* one from which other ships (eg submarines) get supplies. 母舰(其他舰艇, 如潜艇等, 获取补给的舰只)。**~ tongue** *n* one's native language. 本国语言。**~ wit** *n* common sense; the intelligence with which one is born. 常识; 天赋。**'~-hood** /-hʊd; -,hʊd /*n* [U] state of being a ~. 母性; 母权; 母亲的地位。**~·less** *adj* having no ~. 无母亲的。**'~·like** *adj* in the manner of a ~. 似母亲的。**~·ly** *adj* having, showing, the tender, kind qualities of a ~. 母性的; 母性的; 母爱的; 慈爱的。**~·li·ness** *n* □ *vt* [VP6A] take care of (as a ~ does); protect or adopt (a child) as one's own. 对…尽母职; 保护或收养(小孩)视同己子。

mo·tif /məʊˈtiːf; ˈmoˈtif/ *n* [C] theme in music for treatment and development, often one which recurs; main feature in a work of art. (音乐或艺术品的)主题;主旨。

mo·tion /ˈməʊʃn; ˈmoʃən /*n* **1** [U] (manner of)

moving: 运动; 移动; 动作; 动态: *If a thing is in ~, it is not at rest.* 如果一个物体在运动中, 它就不在静止中。*put /set sth in ~,* cause it to start moving or working. 使某物开始转动或工作。⇨ **picture** *n* cinema film. 电影。Cf 参较 (colloq) (口) *moving pictures; the movies.* **2** [C] gesture; particular movement; way of moving the hand, body, etc: 姿势; 特别的动作; (手、身体等的)摆动方式: *If you watch my ~s carefully you will see how the trick is performed.* 假如你仔细看我的动作, 你就会明白这个技巧是怎么变的。*All her ~s were graceful.* 她的一举一动都很优雅。*go through the ~s,* (colloq) do sth (that one is expected or required to do) in a perfunctory or insincere manner. (口)敷衍塞责。**3** [C] proposal to be discussed and voted on at a meeting: 提议; 动议: *On the ~ of Mr X the committee agreed to...* 由于 X 先生的提议, 委员会同意... *The ~ was adopted / carried / rejected, etc by a majority of six.* 该项提议以六票的多数票获采纳(通过, 否决)。**4**[C]=movement(6). □ *vt, vi* **1** [VP17, 15A, B] direct (sb) by a motion or gesture: 以动作或手势示意: *~ sb in /away /to a seat.* 以手势示意某人进来(离开, 就坐)。*He ~ed me to enter.* 他示意我进去。**2** [VP3A] *~ to sb (to do sth),* indicate by a gesture: 打手势表示; 向某人打手势(请他做某事): *He ~ed to me to come nearer.* 他打手势叫我再走近一些。**~·less** *adj* not moving; still. 不动的;静止的。

mo·ti·vate /ˈməʊtɪveɪt; ˈmotə,vet/ *vt* [VP6A] be the motive of; give a motive or incentive to: act as an incentive. 为…的动机; 引起动机; 给予刺激; 激发; 促使。**mo·tiv·ation** /ˌməʊtɪˈveɪʃn; ˌmotəˈveʃən/ *n*

mo·tive /ˈməʊtɪv; ˈmotɪv/ *adj* (attrib only) causing motion: (仅用作定语)发动的; 起动的: *~ power /force,* eg steam, electricity. 动力(如蒸汽, 电)。□ *n* [C] **1** that which causes sb to act: 动机: *actuated by low and selfish ~s;* 出于卑下而自私的动机也; *do sth from ~s of kindness.* 由于仁慈的动机而做善事。*Hatred was his ~ for attacking me.* 憎恨是他攻击我的动机。**2**=motif. **~·less** *adj* without a ~. 无动机的; 无主旨的; 无目的的。

mot·ley /ˈmɒtlɪ; ˈmɑtlɪ/ *adj* **1** of various colours: 不同颜色的; 杂色的: *a ~ coat,* eg that worn by a jester or fool in olden times. 杂色花衣(如古时弄臣或小丑所穿者)。**2** of varied character or various sorts: 不同性质的; 不同种类的; 混杂的: *a ~ crowd,* eg people of many different occupations, social classes, etc. 混杂的人群(如由许多不同职业、社会阶层等的人们所形成的群众)。□ *n* jester's dress. 弄臣的花衣; 小丑的花衣。*wear the ~,* play the part of a fool or jester. 扮演丑角。

mo·tor /ˈməʊtə(r); ˈmotɚ/ *n* **1** device which imparts or utilizes power (esp electric power) to produce motion, but not used of a steam engine: 发动机, 马达(尤指以电力发动者, 但不用以指蒸汽引擎): *fans driven by electric ~s.* 由电动机转动的电扇。**2** (attrib, and in compounds) having, driven by, an internal combustion engine, a diesel engine, etc which generates mechanical power: (用作定语及用于复合词中)由产生机械动力之内燃机、柴油机等所推动的: *~-vehicles;* 机动车辆; 摩托车辆; *a '~-boat /-coach /-scooter, etc.* 汽艇(公共汽车, 低座小摩托车等)。**~-as'sisted** *adj* (eg of a pedal bicycle) having an engine to help propulsion. (如脚踏车)有发动机辅助推进的。**'~·cade** *n* (US) procession of ~ vehicles. (美)机动车辆行列; (汽)车队。**'~-car** (also **car**) *n* closed road vehicle on four wheels with a ~ engine, with seats usu both front and back, for 2—6 people. 汽车。**'~·cycle** (colloq 口语 **'~-bike**) *n* open road vehicle on two wheels with a ~ engine, with one seat for the driver, and usu with space for a passenger behind the driver. 机车; 摩托车。**pillion. '~·man** /-mæn; -mən/ *n* (*pl* **-men**) driver of an electric vehicle. 电车或电动火车司机。**'~·way** *n* road designed and built especially for continuously moving fast traffic, with dual carriageways and going over or under other roads. 高速公路(供高速车辆行驶的双线车道, 高架于其他道路之上或穿过其他道路之下)。**3** =**~-car** (*car* is more usu) (car 较常

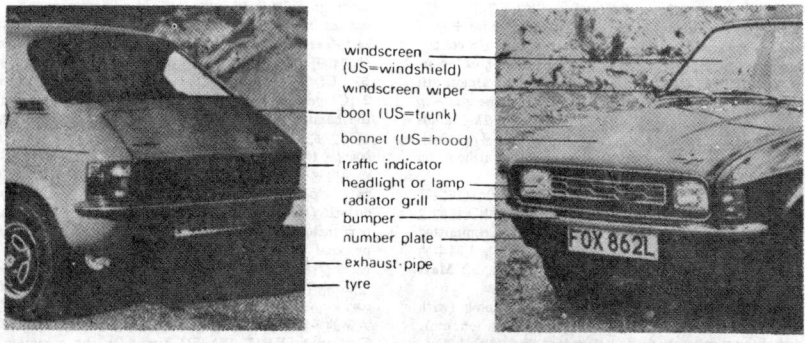

windscreen (US=windshield)
windscreen wiper
boot (US=trunk)
bonnet (US=hood)
traffic indicator
headlight or lamp
radiator grill
bumper
number plate
exhaust-pipe
tyre

FOX 862L

dashboard or fascia
mileometer
speedometer
steering-wheel
ignition switch
gear lever
clutch pedal
brake pedal
accelerator pedal

the motor-car

用): the '~ trade; 汽车业; the 'M~ Show. 汽车展览. **4** muscle able to produce movement of a part of the body: 运动肌: ~ **nerve,** nerve that excites movements of a muscle or muscles. 运动神经. □ vi [VP2A, C] travel by ~-car: 乘汽车旅行: ~ from London to Brighton. 乘汽车从伦敦去布赖顿. ~·**ist** /-ɪst; -ɪst/ n person who drives (and usu owns) a ~-car. 驾驶汽车(通常指自己的汽车)者; 乘汽车旅行者. '~·**ize** /-aɪz; -ˌaɪz/ vt [VP6A] equip (troops, etc) with ~ transport. 摩托化; 以汽车装备(军队等).

mottle /'mɒtl; 'mɑtl/ vt [VP6A] (usu in pp) mark with spots or areas of different colours without a regular pattern: (通常用过去分词)使成杂色; 弄成斑驳: the ~d skin of a snake; 花斑纹的蛇皮; linoleum with a ~d finish. 有花斑纹的油地毯.

motto /'mɒtəʊ; 'mɑto/ n (pl ~es or ~s /-təʊz;-toz/) **1** short sentence or phrase used as a guide or rule of behaviour (eg 'Every man for himself', 'Always merry and bright'). 箴言; 座右铭(如'人人为己各尽所能', '永保喜乐'). **2** short sentence or phrase written or inscribed on an object (eg a coat of arms) expressing a suitable sentiment; quotation prefixed to a book or chapter. (书于或刻于纹章等物品上以表示一适当之感怀的)铭辞; 一本书或书中某章前面的引用句.

mou·jik /'muːʒɪk; 'muʒɪk/ n (esp before the Revolution of 1917) Russian peasant. (尤指一九一七年革命前的)俄国农民.

mould[1](US=**mold**) /məʊld; mold/ n [C] container, hollow form, into which molten metal or a soft substance is poured to cool into a desired shape; the shape or form given by this container; jelly, pudding, etc made in such a container. 铸模; 模子; 由模子压成的形状; 由模子制成的果冻、布丁等. **be cast in one/the same/a different, etc ~,** (fig) have the same, different, etc (eg heroic, stubborn, rugged) character. (喻)由同一(相同、不同等)模子铸出来的; 具有一样(相同、不同等)的性质(如英雄气概, 顽固, 粗鲁). □ vt [VP6A, 14] ~ sth (in/from/out of sth), make sth in, or as

in, a ~, from some material: 造型; (用…)铸造; 塑造: ~ a head out of/in clay; 用粘土塑造一个头; (fig) guide or control the growth of; influence: (喻)指导或控制…的生长; 影响: ~ a person's character. 塑造一个人的性格.

mould[2](US=**mold**) /məʊld; mold/ n woolly or furry growth of fungi appearing upon moist surfaces, eg leather, cheese or on objects left in a moist, warm atmosphere. 霉菌; 霉. ⇨ iron[1] at **iron**[1](3). □ vi [VP2A] (US) become covered with ~: (美)长毛; 发霉: Cheese ~s in warm, wet weather. 干酪在暖和潮湿的天气里会发霉. ~**y** adj (-ier, -iest) **1** covered with ~: 发霉的: ~y bread. 发霉的面包. **2** stale; smelling of ~: 不新鲜的; 发霉味的. **3** (fig) out-of-date; old-fashioned; (sl, of a person) mean and obstructive; worthless. (喻)过时的; 旧式的; (俚, 指人)卑贱而碍事的; 无用的.

mould[3] (US = **mold**) /məʊld; mold/ n [U] soft, fine loose earth, esp from decayed vegetable matter, 松软的泥土; 沃土(尤指由腐败的植物所变成者), eg 'leaf ~, from decayed leaves fallen from trees. 腐叶土(由落叶腐败而成的沃土).

moulder (US = **molder**) /'məʊldə(r); 'moldɚ/ vi [VP2A, C] crumble to dust by natural decay: 由于自然腐烂而崩碎; 腐朽: the ~ing ruins of an old castle. 古堡的腐朽遗迹.

mould·ing (US = **mold-**) /'məʊldɪŋ; 'moldɪŋ/ n **1** [U] act of moulding or shaping; way in which sth is shaped. 铸造; 塑造; 造型; 铸造或塑造方式. **2** line of ornamental plaster, carved woodwork, etc round a wall or window, or in the cornices of a building, or on a pillar. 线脚(筑物之墙或窗户四周, 或檐板上, 或柱上的装饰性之灰泥线或木工嵌线). ⇨ the illus at **column.** 参看 column 之插图.

moult (US = **molt**) /məʊlt; molt/ vt, vi [VP6A, 2A] (of birds) lose (feathers) before a new growth; (more rarely, of dogs and cats) lose hair. (指鸟)脱换(羽毛); (此义较少用, 指狗或猫)脱毛. □ n process or time of ~ing. 脱毛; 换羽; 脱毛(换羽)期.

mound /maʊnd; maʊnd/ n [C] mass of piled up earth;

small hill: 土墩; 土堆; 小山: *a 'burial-~*, of earth over a grave; 墓冢; *~s built for defensive purposes in olden times.* 古代为防御目的而建的掩体。

mount[1] /maʊnt; maʊnt/ *n* (liter except in proper names) mountain, hill: (文, 或用于专有名词中)山; 丘; 峰: *Christ's sermon on the ~;* 基督的山上宝训; (shortened to *Mt* before proper names): (用于专有名词前简写为 Mt): *Mt Etna.* 埃特纳山。

mount[2] /maʊnt; maʊnt/ *vt, vi* 1 [VP6A, 2A] go up (a hill, a ladder, etc); get on to (a horse, etc); supply (sb) with a horse: put (sb) on a horse: 爬上; 走上; 登上 (山, 梯等); 骑上(马等); 供给(某人)马; 使(某人)骑上 马: *He ~ed (his horse) and rode away.* 他骑上马走了。 *The ~ed police were called out to control the crowds.* 骑 警队(骑马的警察)被召来控制那些群众。 ~ *the throne,* become king, etc. 登极(成为国王等)。 2 [VP2A, C] ~ **(up),** become greater in amount: 增加; 上升: *Our living expenses are ~ing up.* 我们的生活费用日渐增高。 *Bills soon ~ up at hotels.* 旅馆里帐单很快地增高。 3 (of blood) rise into the cheeks: (指血液)上升到面颊: *A blush ~ed to (= spread over) the child's face.* 小孩的脸红了。 4 [VP6A] put and fix in position: 装置: ~ *a gun,* on a gun-carriage; 装置一门炮(于炮架上); ~ *pictures,* fix them with backings, margins, etc; 裱装图画; ~ *jewels in gold:* 把珠宝镶在金(制品)上; ~ *specimens,* eg on a slide for a microscope; 固定标本(于显微镜的承物玻璃 片上等); ~ *insects,* eg for display or preservation in a museum. 把昆虫作成标本。 5 (mil uses): (军语): ~ *an offensive/attack,* take the offensive, attack. 发动 攻击; 攻击。 ~ *guard (at/over),* act as a guard or sentinel: 站岗; 守卫: *The House-hold Troops ~ guard at Buckingham Palace.* 近卫骑兵队守卫白金汉宫。 6[VP6A]

put (a play) on the stage: 上演(剧本): *The play was well ~ed,* was provided with good scenery, costumes, etc. 那出戏配有很好的布景, 服装等。 7 (esp of large animals, eg a stallion) get up on (a female animal) in order to copulate. (尤指大的动物, 如长成的牡马)骑 在(雌性动物身上)交配。 ~ *n* [C] that on which a person or thing is or may be ~ed (eg a card for a drawing or photograph, a glass slide for specimens, a horse for riding on, a gun-carriage, the ornamental metal part in which a jewel is fixed). 承载物(如画或相 片的衬板纸, 承载标本的玻璃片, 乘用的马, 炮架, 镶珠宝的 金属托等)。

moun·tain /'maʊntɪn US: -ntn; 'maʊntn/ *n* 1 mass of very high land going up to a peak: 山; 高山: *Qomolangma is the highest ~ in the world.* 珠穆朗玛峰是 世界上最高的山。 ~ **ash,** the rowan tree, with scarlet berries. 山梨; 花楸树。 ~ **chain,** series of ~s. 山脉。 ~ **dew,** (colloq) Scotch whisky. (口)苏格兰威士忌酒。 ~ **range,** series of ~s more or less in a line. (约成直 线延伸的)山脉。 '~ **sickness,** illness caused by rarefied air on high ~s. 高山病(因空气稀薄所致)。 2 (fig uses) sth immense: (比喻用法)巨大之物: *a ~ of debts/difficulties.* 债台高筑(困难重重)。 *The waves were ~ high,* very high. 波浪像山那么高。 ~·**eer** /,maʊntɪ'nɪə(r) US: -ntn]ər; ,maʊntn'ɪr/ *n* person who lives among ~s or is skilled at climbing ~s; 山地居民; 善于爬山 者; hence, 由此产生, ~·**eer·ing** *n* [U] climbing ~s (as a sport). 登山(一种运动)。 ~·**ous** /'maʊntɪnəs US: -ntənəs; 'maʊntnəs/ *adj* having ~s: 有山的; 多山的: ~*ous country;* 多山的地区; huge: 巨大的: ~*ous waves.* 巨浪。

1 valley
2 peak
3 pass
4 shoulder
5 saddle
6 scree
7 crevasses
8 arete
9 chimney
10 plateau
11 glacier
12 moraine
13 col
14 face

mountain features

moun·te·bank /'maʊntɪbæŋk; 'maʊntə,bæŋk/ *n* sb who tries to cheat people by clever talk 巧言惑众之人。

Mountie /'maʊntɪ; 'maʊntɪ/ *n* (colloq) member of the Royal Canadian Mounted Police. (口)加拿大的骑警。

mourn /mɔːn; mɔrn/ *vi, vt* [VP3A, 6A] ~ **(for/over),** feel or show sorrow or regret(for/over); grieve (for/over): 悲悼; 哀悼; 悲叹: ~ *for a dead child;* 悲悼 一个死去的小孩; ~ *over the child's death;* 悲悼小孩的死 亡; ~ *the loss of one's mother.* 哀悼母亲的逝世。 ~**er** *n* person who ~s, esp one who attends a funeral as a relative or friend of the dead person. 哀悼者; 送丧者。

~·**ful** /-fl; -fəl/ *adj* sad; sorrowful. 悲哀的; 凄惨的。 ~**fully** /-fəlɪ; -fəlɪ/ *adv*

mourn·ing /'mɔːnɪŋ; 'mɔrnɪŋ/ *n* [U] 1 grief. 悲 哀; 悲伤。 2 **go into/be in ~,** (start to) wear black clothes as a sign of grief. 穿丧服; 戴孝。 '~·**band** *n* band of black crepe worn round the sleeve. 丧章。 '~·**ring** *n* (formerly) worn as a memorial of a dead person. (昔时)纪念死者的戒指。

mouse /maʊs; maʊs/ *n* (*pl* mice /maɪs; maɪs/) sorts of small rodent (*'house-~, 'field-~, 'harvest-~*); (fig) shy, timid person. 鼠(家鼠, 田鼠, 巢鼠); (喻)羞怯或胆

小的人. '~-**trap** *n* trap for catching mice: 捕鼠器: ~-*trap cheese*, (hum) unpalatable kind of cheese. (谐) 味道不佳的干酪. □ *vi* [VP2A] (of cats) hunt for, catch, mice: (指猫) 捕鼠: *Our cat ~s well*. 我们的猫很会捕鼠. **mouser** /'mauzə(r); 'mauzə/ *n* cat who does this. 会捕鼠之猫. **mousy** /'mausɪ; 'mausɪ/ *adj* (**-ier, -iest**) (esp of hair) dull brown; (of a person) timid, shy. (尤指毛发)暗褐色的; (指人)胆小的; 羞怯的.

mousse /muːs; muːs/ *n* [C, U] (dish of) meat, fish, flavoured cream, etc beaten and served cold: (一盘)肉、鱼、乳脂等搅匀后冷冻之食品; 奶油冻: *chocolate ~*. 巧克力奶油冻.

mous·tache (US = **mus·tache**) /mə'stɑːʃ US: 'mʌstæʃ; 'mʌstæʃ/ *n* [C] hair allowed to grow on the upper lip. 髭(长在嘴唇上面的胡子).

mouth[1] /mauθ; mauθ/ *n* (*pl* ~s /mauðz; mauðz/) **1** opening through which animals take in food; space behind this containing the teeth, tongue, etc. 嘴; 口. ⇨ the illus here. 参看本条之插图. *by word of ~*, (of news, etc) orally (not in writing, etc). (指新闻等)口头的(非书写等的). *down in the ~*, sad, dejected. 悲哀的; 沮丧的. *out of the ~s of babes and sucklings*, (prov) innocent young people may speak wisely. (谚) 黄口孺子也能说出道理名言. *laugh on the wrong side of one's ~*, lament, be disappointed. 悲伤; 失望. *look a gift-horse in the ~*, accept sth ungraciously esp by examining it critically for faults. 接受礼物而不表感谢(尤指检查礼物挑剔缺点). *put words into sb's ~*, (a) tell him what to say. 告诉某人说什么. (b) suggest or claim that he has said something. 暗示或声称某人曾说过什么. *take the words out of sb's ~*, say what he was about to say; anticipate his words. 说某人将要说的话; 抢先说某人要说的话. ~·**ful** /-ful; -ful/ *n* as much as can be put into the ~ comfortably at one time: 一口的量: *swallow sth at a ~ful*; 一口吞下某物; *have only a ~ful of food*. 只有一口的食物. '~-**organ** *n* small musical wind-instrument with metal reeds, played by passing it along the lips and blowing; harmonica. 口琴. '~·**piece** *n* (a) that part of a tobacco pipe, a musical instrument, etc placed at or between the lips. (烟斗的)烟嘴; (乐器的)吹口; 接口(管). (b) person, newspaper, etc that expresses the opinions of others: 代言人; 机关报; 发言人: *Which newspaper is the ~piece of the Socialists?* 哪一家报纸是社会党的机关报? '~-**watering** *adj* ⇨ **water**[2](3). **2** opening or outlet (of a bag, bottle, tunnel, cave, river, etc): (袋、瓶、隧道、洞穴、河流等的)口; 开口处.

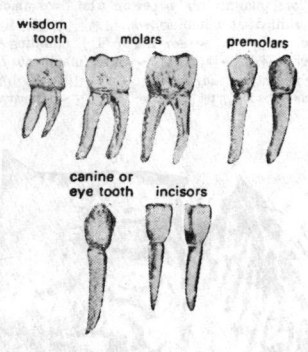

wisdom tooth   molars   premolars

canine or eye tooth   incisors

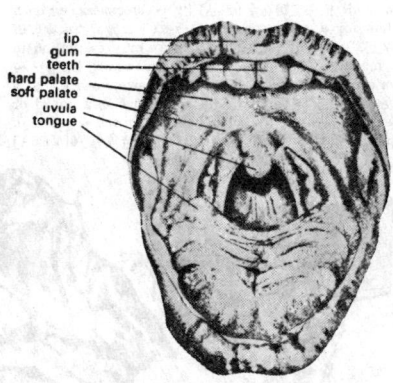

lip
gum
teeth
hard palate
soft palate
uvula
tongue

the mouth

mouth[2] /mauð; mauð/ *vt, vi* [VP6A, 2A] **1** speak with movement of the jaw but no sound. 以嘴唇的动作但不出声地说出. **2** utter pompously: 夸大地说话: *An actor who ~s his words is a poor actor*. 装腔作势背诵台词的演员是不好的演员. □ *vt* take (food) into the ~; touch with the ~. 把(食物)放进口中; 用口接触.

mov·able /'muːvəbl; 'muːvəbl/ *adj* **1** that can be moved; (of property) that can be taken from place to place (eg furniture, contrasted with land and buildings, called *real* property or estate). 可移动的; (指财产)可搬动的 (如家具等, 与土地、房屋等不动产相对): 动产的. ⇨ **portable**. **2** varying in date: 日期变动的: *Christmas is fixed but Easter is a ~ feast*. 圣诞节是固定的, 而复活节是每年变动日期的节日. □ *n* (*pl*) personal property; articles that can be removed from the house (contrasted with *fixtures*). (复)动产; 可搬动的家具(与 fixtures 相对).

move[1] /muːv; muːv/ *n* [C] **1** change of place or position, esp of a piece in chess or other games played on boards; player's turn to do this: 移动位置; (国际象棋或其他盘上游戏之)一步; (下棋等)轮到走: *Do you know all the ~s in chess?* 你知道国际象棋的所有走法吗? *Whose ~ is it?* 该谁走(棋)啦? *The ~ to achieve a purpose*: (为达到目的所采取的)行动; 步骤: *a ~ towards settling the strike*. 解决罢工的一个行动. *What's our next ~?* 我们的下一个步骤是什么? **3** *on the ~*, moving about: 在移动中: *Our planes reported that large enemy forces were on the ~*. 我们的飞机报告说大批敌军在移动中. *make a ~*, (a) ~ to a different place: 迁移: *Shall we make a ~ now?* 我们现在要不要迁移? (b) begin to act: 开始行动: *Unless we make a ~ soon, we shall be in a hopelessly weak position*. 除非我们赶快开始行动, 否则我们将处于劣势. *get a ~ on*, (sl) hurry up. 赶快.

move[2] /muːv; muːv/ *vt, vi* **1** [VP6A, 15A, B, 2A, C] (cause to) change position; put, cause to be, in a different place or attitude; (cause to) be in motion: (使)改变位置; 移动; 搬动; 开动: *M~ your chair nearer to the fire*. 把你的椅子挪近火炉一点. *It was calm and not a leaf ~d*. 平静得连一片叶子也没有动. *It's your turn to ~*, (in chess, etc) to ~ a piece from one square to another. (下棋等)该你走了; 轮到你走(棋)了. *~ heaven and earth*, do one's utmost, use every possible means (*to do* sth). 尽最大力量; 千方百计(与不定式连用). **2** [VP6A, 2C] *~ (house)*, take one's furniture, etc to another house, flat, etc: 搬家; 迁居: *We're moving (house) next week*. 我们下星期搬家. *~ in*, take possession of a new dwelling-place. 搬进; 迁入新居. *~ out*, give up a dwelling-place: 搬出; 迁出: *We ~d out on Monday and the new tenants ~d in on Tuesday*. 我们星期一迁出, 新房客星期二就搬进来. **3** [VP2C, 15B] *~ on*, ~ to another place or position

(eg when ordered to do so by a policeman). 朝前走; 走开(如警察命令行人、车辆等移动). **~ sb on,** cause him to ~ by giving him the order 'M~ on, please'. 命令某人朝前走或走开. **~ along/down/up, ~** farther in the direction indicated so as to make space for others: 往前移动(往下移动; 往上移动; 以让出空间给别人): 'M~ along, please', said the bus conductor. 公共汽车售票员说, '请往前走'. **4** [VP6A, 15A] arouse, work on, the feelings of; affect with pity, etc: 激动; 煽动; 感动: be ~d with pity/compassion; 为怜悯之情所动: be ~d to tears. 感动得流泪. We were all ~d by her entreaties. 我们都被她的恳求所感动. The story of their sufferings ~d us deeply. 他们苦难的经历深深地感动了我们. It was a moving sight. 那是个感人的情景. **5** [VP17] cause (to do sth): Nothing I said ~d him to offer his help. 我说什么都不能使他提供协助. The spirit ~d him to get up and address the meeting, He felt a desire to do this. 他觉得自己有一种愿望, 想要站起来不参加这个会的人们说话. Who was the moving spirit in the enterprise, Who started it and was most active? 谁是这个企业起作用最大的人? **6** [VP6A, 9] put forward for discussion and decision (at a meeting): (开会时)提议: Mr Chairman, I ~ that the money be used for library books. 主席, 我提议把那笔钱用来增购图书馆的藏书. ⇨ **motion**(3). **7** [VP3A] ~ **for,** make formal application for: 正式要求; 请求: The noble Lord ~d for papers, ie in a debate in the House of Lords. (英)这位上议院议员正式要求查看一些文件. **8** [VP2A, C] make progress; go forward: 进步; 前进: Time ~s on. 时光流逝. The work ~s slowly. 工作进展缓慢. Things are not moving as rapidly as we had hoped. 事情进行没有像我们希望的那么快. **9** [VP2A, C] take action: 采取行动: Nobody seems willing to ~ in the matter. 似乎没有人愿意对这件事采取行动. **10** [VP2C] live one's life; pass one's time: 生活; 度日子: They ~ in the highest society. 他们和上流社会人士交往. **11** [VP6A, 2A] cause (the bowels) to act, to empty; (of the bowels) be emptied. 使(肠)通便; (指肠)通便.

move·ment /ˈmuːvmənt; ˈmuvmənt/ n **1** [U] moving or being moved; activity (contrasted with quiet and rest): 移动; 运动; 活动 (与安静及静止相对): He lay there without ~. 他一动也不动地躺在那里. The novel/play lacks ~, ie there is not enough action in it. 那部小说(戏)情节呆滞. **2** [C] act of changing position, esp a military evolution: 移动(尤指军事调动): By a series of rapid ~s the general placed his forces in an advantageous position. 经一连串的迅速调动, 将军把他的军队置于有利的地位. **3** [C] moving part of a machine or mechanism or a particular group of such parts: 机器、机械装置等的运转部分: the ~ of a clock or a watch. 钟或表的运转部分. **4** [C] united actions and efforts of a group of people for a special purpose: (一群人为某种目的而联合起来的)运动: the ~ to abolish slavery. 废除奴役的运动. the **'Labour M~,** organized (2) (manual) workers. 劳工运动; 劳工工会. **5** [C] (music) principal division of a musical work with a distinctive structure of its own: (音乐)乐章: the final ~ of the Ninth Symphony. 第九交响曲的最后乐章. **6** [C] emptying of the bowels. 通便. **7** [U] activity (in a stock market, etc) for some commodity: (股票市场等的)交易活动; 变动: not much ~ in oil shares. 石油股票没有什么大的波动.

mover /ˈmuːvə(r); ˈmuvɚ/ n (esp) person who moves(6) a proposal. (尤指)提议人. the **prime ~,** the person chiefly responsible for starting sth. 主要负责创办某事物的发起人; 创办人.

movie /ˈmuːvi; ˈmuvi/ n (colloq) (口) **1** motion picture. 电影. **2** the **~s,** the cinema; the cinema industry: 电影院; 电影; 电影业: How often do you go to the ~s? 你多久看一次电影?

mow¹ /məʊ; mo/ vt, vi (pt **mowed**, pp **mown** /məʊn; mon/ or **mowed**) **1** [VP6A, 2A] cut (grass, etc) with a scythe or a machine: 用镰刀或刈草机割(草等):

mow the lawn; 修剪草地; new-mown hay; 新割下的干草; mow a field. 割除田里的草. **2** [VP15B] **mow down,** cut down like grass; destroy as if by sweeping movements: (像刈草一样)刈除; 扫除: Our men were mown down by the enemy's machine-gun fire. 我们的士兵被敌人的机枪扫射倒地. **mower** /ˈməʊə(r); ˈmoɚ/ n person or machine that mows: 割草人; 刈草机: a 'lawn-mower. 刈草机.

mow² /məʊ/ ; məʊ/ n [C] heap of hay, straw, etc; place in a barn where hay, etc is stored. 草堆; 禾堆; (谷仓之)禾草堆积处.

mow³ /məʊ/ vi mop and mow, ⇨ **mop²**.

Mr /ˈmɪstə(r); ˈmɪstɚ/ title prefixed to the (first name and) surname of a man: 先生(冠于男子之姓或姓名前的称呼): Mr (John) Brown. (约翰·)布朗先生.

Mrs /ˈmɪsɪz; ˈmɪsɪz/ title prefixed to the (first name and the) surname of a married woman: 夫人; 太太(冠于已婚妇女之姓或姓名前之称呼): Mrs (Jane) Brown; (简·)布朗太太; (formal): (正式用语): Mrs John Brown. 约翰·布朗太太.

Ms /mɪz; mɪz/ title prefixed to the (first name and the) surname of a woman, whether married or unmarried: 女士 (冠于已婚或未婚女子之姓或姓名前之称呼): Ms (Mary) Green. (玛丽·)格林女士.

much¹ /mʌtʃ; mʌtʃ/ (**more, most**. ⇨ **little**) adj, n (~ is used with sing nn, uncountable. Cf **many,** used with pl nn. In purely affirm sentences it is often preferable to use **plenty** (of), **a lot** (of), **a large quantity** (of), **a good/great deal** (of). M~ is often used in affirm sentences when it is (a part of) the subject, and when used with how, too, so, or as): (much 与单数不可数名词连用. 参较 **many,** 与复数名词连用. 纯粹肯定句中最好用 **plenty** (of), **a lot** (of), **a large quantity** (of), **a good** (great) **deal** (of). much 作主词(或其一部份)或与 how, too, so, as 等连用时, 常用于肯定句): There isn't ~ food in the house. 家里食物不多了. He never eats ~ breakfast. 他早餐从来吃得不多. Did you have ~ difficulty in finding the house? 你找那所房子很困难吗? M~ of what you say is true. 你听说的大部份是真实的. We have ~ to be thankful for. 我们有很多应该感谢的. You have given me too ~. 你已经给我太多了. **come to ~,** ⇨ **come**(3). **how ~, (a)** what quantity: 多少: How ~ flour (= What weight) do you want? 你要多少面粉? **(b)** what price: 什么价格: How ~ a kilo is that beef? 那牛肉一公斤多少钱? **be up to ~,** be worth ~: 很有价值: I don't think his work is up to ~, ie it is not good. 我不以为他的作品很有价值. **not ~ of a,** not a good: 不算好的: He's not ~ of a linguist/scholar, etc. 他不是一个很好的语言学家(学者). It wasn't ~ of a dinner. 这顿饭并不怎么好. I'm not ~ of a cinema-goer, I seldom go to the cinema. 我不常去看电影. **this/that ~,** the quantity, extent, etc indicated: 这样(那样)多: Can you let me have this ~? 你能让我拿这样多吗? I will say this ~ in his favour..., I will admit in his favour.... 我要说这些对他有利的话.... This ~ is certain, that he will never try to play that trick on us again. 这一点是有把握的, 他再也不会跟我们要那个把戏了. **be too ~ for, be** more than a match for, too difficult for; be superior in skill, etc, to: 非…能力所及; 对…太难了; (技术等)胜过: The school tennis champion was too ~ for me. 学校的网球冠军非我所能敌. I couldn't finish that philosophy book, it was too ~ for me. 我无法读完那本关于哲学的书, 那本书对我是太难了. **make ~ of,** (a) understand: 了解; 明白: I didn't make ~ of that lecture. 我不了解那篇演讲. **(b)** attach importance to; exaggerate: 重视; 夸张: We mustn't make too ~ of this incident. 我们不必太重视这个事件. He makes (too) ~ of his connections with rich people. 他(过份)夸张他与有钱人的关系. **think ~ of,** have a good opinion of: 认为佳: I don't think ~ of my English teacher. 我觉得我的英语老师不怎么高明. **as ~ (as),** the same (as): 与…相同; 与…同样: Give me as ~ again, the same quantity again. 再给我同样的份量. I thought as ~, That is what I thought. 我也这样

想. *You have always helped me and I will always do as ~ for you,* will always help you. 你总是帮助我，我将要同样地帮助你。 *It is as ~ your responsibility as mine,* You and I are equally responsible. 你和我对这件事都要负责。 *It was as ~ as he could do to* (= He could do no more than) *pay his way.* 他以身出冲过去，连一声"借光"也没说。 *He hadn't so ~ as his fare home.* 他甚至连回家的车费都没有。 ⇨ **also** so ~ *(many),* not so ~ *as,* so ~ *so that,* so ~ *for,* under so[1] (6).

much[2] /mʌtʃ; mʌtʃ/ *adv* **1** (modifying comparatives and superlatives, preceding the *def art*): (修饰比较级与最高级，置于定冠词之前): *He is ~ better today.* 他今天好得多了。 *You must work ~ harder.* 你必须要更加努力。 *This is ~* (= by far) *the best.* 这是最好的了。 *He's not ~ the worse for his fall into the canal.* 他从身陷运河里而受到什么损伤。 *~ more / less,* (used to indicate that what has been stated about sth applies with greater force to the following statement): (用以表示前句含义加强后句含义)更加; 更没有; 遑论; 何况: *It is difficult to understand his books, ~ more his lectures.* 他的书难懂，而他的演讲更难懂。 *I didn't even speak to him, ~ less discuss your problems with him.* 我甚至没有跟他说话，当然更没有与他讨论你的问题。 **2**(modifying passive *participles* and *pred adjj* such as *afraid.* Of *very,* used to modify passive and *present participles* which are true *adjj* as *very frightened*): (修饰被动的分词及 afraid 等表语形容词。用于修饰成为真正形容词的被动与现在分词，如 very frightened): *I am very ~ afraid that...;* 我非常害怕...; *I shall be ~ surprised if he succeeds.* 假如他成功的话，我将极为惊奇。 *I hope you will not be ~ inconvenienced.* 我希望你将不会太不方便。 **3** (When **much** modifies a *v* phrase, it may occur within the *v* phrase or in end position, but may not occur between this *v* phrase and its object): (当 much 修饰一动词短语时，其位置可在动词短语之中及在句末，但不可置于动词短语与其宾语之间): *It doesn't ~ matter.* 不大要紧; 不关重要。 *It doesn't matter very ~.* 没什么大要紧。 *I very ~ enjoyed the concert.* 我非常喜欢那个音乐会。 *I enjoyed it very ~.* 我非常喜欢它。 *I don't like beef ~.* 他不太喜欢吃牛肉。 **4**(in phrases) (用于短语内) *as: M~ as I should* (= Although I should ~) *like to go,...;* 虽然我很想去,...; *M~ as she disliked the idea* (= Although she ~ disliked the idea), ...*.* 虽然她很不喜欢那种意见,...。 *~ the same,* about the same: 差不多一样: *The patient's condition is ~ the same.* 那病人的情况没有什么变化。 *~ to,* greatly to; to one's great...: 大为; 对...大为: *M~ to her surprise / regret, etc.* 她大为惊讶(深感遗憾)...。 *how ~,* to what extent: 何等程度: *How ~ do you really want to marry the man?* 你有几分真意想要嫁给那个人？ ⇨ **much**[1]. *too ~,* too highly: 太高: *He thinks too ~ of himself.* 他自视过高。 *not so ~ X as Y,* Y rather than X: 与其说 X, 不如说 Y: *Oceans don't so ~ divide the world as unite it,* They serve to unite countries rather than to divide them. 与其说海洋分隔了世界，不如说海洋联结了世界。 **~·ness** *n* (only in the colloq phrase) (仅用于口语短语中) *of a ~ness,* the same; almost alike. 相差不多相同; 几乎同样。

mu·ci·lage /'mjuːsɪlɪdʒ; 'mjuːsɪlɪdʒ/ *n* [U] kinds of vegetable glue (obtained from plants, seaweed, etc), used as an adhesive. 植物质胶水; 粘液(从植物、海草等提取者)。

muck /mʌk; mʌk/ *n* [U] **1** dung; farmyard manure (the droppings of animals). 粪; 粪肥。 **'~-heap** *n* heap of farmyard ~. (农家田院内的)粪肥堆。 **'~-raker** *n* (usu *fig*) person who is always looking for scandal, corruption, etc. (通常为喻)经常探听丑闻、贪污等的人。

Hence, 由此产生, **'~-raking** *n* **2** dirt; filth; (colloq) anything disgusting or dirty. 脏物; 污物; (口)任何令人讨厌或不洁的东西。 *make a ~ of sth,* (colloq) make a mess of it; make it dirty; spoil it. (口)把某事弄得一团糟; 弄乱; 弄脏; 弄坏某事物。 □ *vt, vi* **1** [VP6A, 15B] *~ sth (up),* (colloq) make a mess of it; spoil it. (口)弄脏某事物; 弄坏; 弄糟。 **2**[VP2C] *~ about,* (GB sl) do useless or unnecessary things; go about, spend time, aimlessly: (英俚)做无用或无必要之事; 混日子; 虚掷光阴: *'What's he ~ up to?'—'Oh, just ~ing about.'* '他在干什么?'——'哦，不过混日子而已。' **3** [VP2C, 15B] *~ out,* clean out (stables, etc) by removing dung: 扫除粪便以清理(马厩等): *She ~s out (the stables) every morning.* 她每天早晨清扫(马厩)。 **~y** *adj* (-ier, -iest) dirty. 脏的。

muckle /'mʌkl; 'mʌkl/ *n* ⇨ **mickle.**

mu·cous /'mjuːkəs; 'mjuːkəs/ *adj* of, like, covered with, mucus. 粘液的; 似粘液的; 布满粘液的。 *the ~ membrane,* the moist skin that lines the nose, mouth and food canal. 粘膜。

mu·cus /'mjuːkəs; 'mjuːkəs/ *n* [U] sticky, slimy substance produced by the mucous membrane; similar slimy substance: (由粘膜分泌的)粘液; 类似粘液的物质: *Snails and slugs leave a trail of mucus.* 蜗牛和蛞蝓行进中会留下一道粘液。

mud /mʌd; mʌd/ *n* [U] soft, wet earth: 软湿的泥土: *Rain turns dust into mud.* 雨将尘土弄成软泥。 *throw / fling / sling mud at sb,* speak evil of him, try to damage his reputation. 说某人坏话，企图破坏某人名誉。 Hence, 由此产生, **'mud-slinger** *n. sb's name is mud,* he is in disgrace. 某人声名狼藉。 **'mud-bath** *n* bath in mud of mineral springs (eg for treating rheumatism). 泥浴(在含有矿泉的泥中沐浴，如作为治风湿病的一种医疗法)。 **'mud flat** *n* muddy land covered by the sea at high tide and not covered at low tide. 泥滩(高潮时为海水所浸，低潮时不为海水所浸的软泥地)。 **'mud·guard** *n* curved cover over a wheel (of a bicycle, etc). (脚踏车等的弯形)挡泥盖; 挡泥板。 ⇨ the illus at **bicycle.** 参看 bicycle 之插图。 □ *vt* **(-dd-)** [VP6A] cover with mud: 覆以泥; 使弄脏; *He ~ded the carpet.* 你把地毯弄得身子泥巴了。 **muddy** *adj* (-ier ,-iest) **1** full of, covered with, mud: 多泥的; 覆着泥巴的: *muddy roads / shoes.* 泥泞的路 (沾满泥巴的鞋)。 **2** mud-coloured; like mud because thick: 泥色的; (因其浓稠)似泥的; *a muddy stream,* 泥浊的溪流; *a muddy skin;* 泥土色的皮肤; *muddy coffee;* 泥色的咖啡; *muddy* (fig, = confused) *ideas.* (喻)混乱的意念。 □ *vt*(*pt, pp* -died)[VP6A] make muddy. 使多泥; 使覆着软泥。

muddle /'mʌdl; 'mʌdl/ *vt, vi* **1** [VP6A, 15B] *~ (up),* bring into a state of confusion and disorder; make a mess of: 使混乱; 弄成一团糟: *You've ~d the scheme completely.* 你已把这个计划完全弄糟了。 *A glass of whisky soon ~s him.* 一杯威士忌很快就会把他醉得迷迷糊糊。 *Don't ~* (= mix) *things up (together).* 不要把东西弄乱(在一起)。 *~ sth / sb up with sth / sb,* (colloq) be unable to distinguish sth / sb from sth / sb else. (口)不能分辨某两物(人); 把两物(人)弄混。 **2** [VP2C] *~ along / on,* get on in a foolish or helpless way, with no clear purpose or plan: 漫无目的而糊里糊涂地混: *He's still muddling on / along.* 他仍然是糊里糊涂地混日子。 *~ through,* reach the end of an undertaking in spite of inefficiency, obstacles of one's own making, etc. 混过去。 □ *n* (usu 通常作 *a ~*) *~d* state; confusion of ideas: 混乱; 意念的紊乱: *Everything was in a ~ and I couldn't find what I wanted.* 每一件东西都是乱糟糟的，我找不到我所要的东西。 *You have made a ~ of it,* mismanaged it, bungled it. 你已经把它弄糟了。 **'~-headed** *adj* confused in mind; stupid. 头脑不清楚的; 愚笨的。

muesli /'mjuːzlɪ; 'mjuːzlɪ/ *n* [U] breakfast food of a mixture of uncooked cereal, nuts, dried fruit, etc. 一种由未经烹煮的壳类，坚果，干果等混合制成的早餐食品。

mu·ez·zin /muːˈezɪn US: mjuː-; mjuːˈɛzɪn/ *n* man

who proclaims the hours of prayers from the minaret of a mosque. (在伊斯兰教寺院的尖塔上)呼报祈祷时刻的人。

muff¹ /mʌf; mʌf/ n covering, usu a cylindrical padded bag of fur, open at both ends, used to keep the hands warm; similar covering for the foot. (通常为圆筒形、皮制、两端开口的)暖手袋; 皮手筒; (类似皮手筒的)暖足套。

muff² /mʌf; mʌf/ n person who is awkward or clumsy, esp in games (eg by failing to catch the ball at cricket). 笨拙的人 (尤指游戏时笨手笨脚的人，如板球戏中接球失误者)。 □ vt [VP6A] bungle; fail to catch; miss: 笨拙地做; 接不住; 漏接: ~ a ball; 漏接一球; ~ an easy catch. 没接住一个容易接的球。

muf·fin /'mʌfɪn; 'mʌfɪn/ n small, light, flat, round cake, usu eaten hot with butter. 小松饼(通常加奶油趁热吃)。

muffle /'mʌfl; 'mʌfl/ vt 1 [VP6A, 15B] ~ (up), wrap or cover for warmth or protection: 包; 覆; 裹住: ~ oneself up well; 把自己裹得紧紧的; ~ one's throat, eg by putting a scarf round it; 把颈部围起来(如用围巾); ~d up in a heavy overcoat. 裹在厚重的大衣里。 2[VP6A] make the sound of sth (eg a bell or a drum) dull by wrapping it up in cloth, etc: 将某物(如钟或鼓)包住使之声音低沉; 使发闷音; 使消音: ~ the oars of a boat, to deaden the sound of their touching the water; 把船的桨包扎起来(使划船时能清音); ~d voices, eg from persons whose mouths are covered. 闷住的声音(如蒙住口之人所发出者)。

muf·fler /'mʌflə(r); 'mʌflə/ n 1 cloth, scarf, worn round the neck for warmth. 围巾; 领巾。 2 (US) **silencer**. (美)消音器; 灭音器。

mufti /'mʌftɪ; 'mʌftɪ/ n (usu 通常用于 in ~) plain, ordinary clothes worn by someone (eg an official, an army officer) who has the right to wear uniform. 便衣; 便装(指有权穿制服之官员、军官等所穿的普通服装)。

mug¹ /mʌg; mʌg/ n 1 (usu straight-sided) drinking vessel of china or metal with a handle, for use without a saucer; its contents: (通常周边垂直、不用杯托之)有把手的瓷杯或金属杯; (该杯的)一杯容量: a 'beer-mug; 啤酒杯; a mug of milk. 一大杯牛奶。 2 [sl] face; mouth. (俚)脸; 嘴。

mug² /mʌg; mʌg/ n (sl) simpleton; easily deceived person. (俚)愚人; 容易受骗的人。 a 'mug's game, sth unlikely to bring profit or reward. 不大可能获利或得到报酬的事物。

mug³ /mʌg; mʌg/ vt (-gg-) [VP15B] mug sth up, (colloq) (try to) become quite familiar with sth on which one is to be tested. (口)(试图)把要测验的事物读得很熟; 勤习; 苦读。

mug⁴ /mʌg; mʌg/ vt (-gg-) [VP6A] (colloq) attack (sb) violently and rob in a dark street, a lift, an empty corridor, etc). (口)(如在黑暗的街道上，电梯中，空无人的通道中)猛烈袭击并抢劫(某人)。 **mug·ger** n **mug·ging** n [U, C].

mug·gins /'mʌgɪnz; 'mʌgɪnz/ n (colloq) fool. (口)愚人; 傻瓜; 笨蛋。

muggy /'mʌgɪ; 'mʌgɪ/ adj (-ier, -iest) (of the weather, a day, etc) damp and warm; close and sticky: (指天气、某天等)湿而热的; 闷人的; 闷热的: ~ days during the rainy season. 雨季里的闷热日子。 **muggi·ness** n

mug·wump/ 'mʌgwʌmp; 'mʌgwʌmp/ n (US) conceited person; person who has a high opinion of his own importance. (美)自负的人; 自以为了不起的人。

Mu·ham·mad /məˈhæmd; muˈhæməd/ n Prophet and Founder of Islam. 穆罕默德(伊斯兰教的先知及创始者)。 ~an /-ən; -ən/ n, adj Muslim. 回教的; 伊斯兰教徒。 **Mu·ham·ma·dan·ism** /məˈhæmɪdənɪzəm; muˈhæmədn̩ˌɪzəm/ n Islam (the preferred name). 伊斯兰教(Islam 为较为人所喜用之名称)。

mu·latto /mjuːˈlætəʊ US: məˈl-; məˈlæto/ n (pl ~s, ~es /-təʊz; -toz/) person who has one parent of black

race and one of white race. (白人与黑人所生的)黑白混血儿。

mul·berry /'mʌlbrɪ US: 'mʌlberɪ; 'mʌlˌberɪ/ n (pl -ries) [C] tree with broad, dark-green leaves on which silkworms feed; its fruit (dark purple or white). 桑树; 桑葚(桑树所结之深紫色或白色的果实)。

mulch /mʌltʃ; mʌltʃ/ n [C] protective covering of peat, spread over the roots of trees and bushes, to retain moisture, smother weeds, etc. 护根(铺于树木根部之泥炭，有保持潮湿及遏制杂草生长等功用)。 □ vt cover (ground) with a ~. 在(地面)上覆以护根。

mulct /mʌlkt; mʌlkt/ vt [VP12C, 14] ~ (in/of), (rare) punish by means of a fine; take (sth) away from: (罕)处以罚金; 自…夺取(某物): ~ a man £5; 罚某人五英镑; ~ a man in £5; 罚某人五英镑; be ~ed of one's money. 某人的钱被抢去。

mule¹ /mjuːl; mjul/ n 1 animal that is the off-spring of an ass and a mare. 骡。 as obstinate/stubborn as a ~, very obstinate/stubborn. 象骡子一样的固执(顽固); 非常固执(顽固)。 2 (colloq) stubborn person. (口)顽固的人。 3 kind of spinning-machine. 走锭精纺机。 **mu·le·teer** /ˌmjuːlɪˈtɪə(r); ˌmjuləˈtɪr/ n ~-driver. 驭骡者。 **mul·ish** /-ɪʃ; -ɪʃ/ adj stubborn; obstinate. 顽固的; 执拗的。 **mu·lish·ly** adv **mu·lish·ness** n

mule² /mjuːl; mjul/ n heelless slipper. 无后侧鞋帮的便鞋。

mull¹ /mʌl; mʌl/ vt [VP6A] make (wine, beer) into a hot drink with sugar, spices, etc: 加糖、香料等温热(葡萄酒，啤酒): ~ed claret. 加糖、香料等温热的红葡萄酒。

mull² /mʌl; mʌl/ n (Scot) (in place-names) promontory: (苏)(与地名连用)海角; 岬: the M~ of Kintyre. 琴泰岬。

mull³ /mʌl; mʌl/ vt [VP15B] ~ sth over; ~ over sth, ponder over it. 思索; 沉思(某事)。

mul·lah /'mʌlə; 'mʌlə/ n Muslim learned in theology and sacred law. 伊斯兰教的神学家。

mul·lein /'mʌlɪn; 'mʌlɪn/ n kinds of plant with leaves covered with grey hairs, and small yellow flowers. 毛蕊花。

mul·let /'mʌlɪt; 'mʌlɪt/ n kinds of seafish used as food, esp red ~ and grey ~. 刀鱼(数种食用之海鱼，尤指绯鲵鲣与鲻)。

mul·li·ga·tawny /ˌmʌlɪgəˈtɔːnɪ; ˌmʌlɪgəˈtɔnɪ/ n ~ (soup), thick, highly seasoned soup with curry powder in it, often with boiled rice added. 咖哩浓汤(常加有米饭)。咖哩烩饭。

mul·lion /'mʌlɪən; 'mʌljən/ n vertical stone division between parts of a window. (某些窗之)石质中框; 直棂。 ⇨ the illus at **window**. 参看 window 之插图。 ~ed /'mʌlɪənd; 'mʌljənd/ adj having ~s. 有石质中框的; 有直棂的。

multi- /'mʌltɪ; 'mʌltɪ/ pref having many of (eg ~-coloured, of many colours; a ~-ˌmillioˈnaire, person having 2 or more millions of money): 多 (如 multi-coloured 多色的; a multi-millionaire, 数百万富翁); a ~-ˌstage 'rocket, with parts that ignite (and then fall away) in stages; 多节火箭; a ~-ˌracial 'country, with many races of people. 多种族的国家。

mul·ti·far·ious /ˌmʌltɪˈfeərɪəs; ˌmʌltɪˈfɛrɪəs/ adj many and various: 各种各样的; 五花八门的: his ~ duties; 他的各种各样的职责; having great variety. 多样性的。 ~·ly adv

mul·ti·form /'mʌltɪfɔːm; 'mʌltɪˌfɔrm/ adj having many forms or shapes. 各式各样的; 形式繁多的。

mul·ti·lat·eral /ˌmʌltɪˈlætərəl; ˌmʌltɪˈlætərəl/ adj involving two or more participants: 多边的; 多方面的: ~ disarmament, after agreement between two or more countries; 多边裁军; ~ trade, carried on between many or all countries without the need for pairs of countries to balance payment between themselves. 多边贸易; 多国贸易。

mul·tiple /'mʌltɪpl; 'mʌltəpl/ adj having many

parts or elements: 复合的; 多样的; 多数的: *a man of ~ interests*; 有多方面兴趣的人; *a ~ shop/store*, one with many branches, cf *chain store*, the more usu term; 联号商店 (参较比较常用的的 chain store); *a ~-unit train*, made up of several coaches (eg Diesel coaches) each of which can run independently. 联列火车或电车 (例如每节可单独行驶之柴油列车). □ *n* quantity which contains another quantity a number of times without remainder: 倍数: *28 is a ~ of 7. 28 is 7 的倍数. 30 is a common ~ of 2, 3, 5, 6, 10 and 15.* 30 是 2,3,5,6,10 和 15 的公倍数. **least**/**lowest common ~**, (abbr 略作 **LCM**) least quantity that contains two or more given quantities exactly: 最小公倍数: *12 is the LCM of 3 and 4.* 12 是 3 和 4 的最小公倍数. ⇨ **factor(1)**.

mul·ti·plex / 'mʌltɪpleks ; 'mʌltə,plɛks/ *adj* having many parts or forms; of many elements. 有很多部分的; 多种形式的; 多种成分的.

mul·ti·pli·ca·tion /,mʌltɪplɪ'keɪʃn ; ,mʌltəplə'keʃən/ *n* **1** [U] multiplying or being multiplied: 增多; 倍加; 乘; 被乘; 乘法; 繁殖: *The symbol × stands for ~.* 符号×代表乘法. **'~ table**, list of numbers, usu 1 to 12, showing the results of multiplying by the same number successively. 乘法表; 乘数表. **2** [C] instance of this: 相乘之实例; 乘算: *3×11 is an easy ~.* 3×11 是一个容易的乘算.

mul·ti·plic·ity /,mʌltɪ'plɪsətɪ ; ,mʌltə'plɪsətɪ/ *n* [U] being great in number: 多; 多样; 繁多: *the ~ of small city states into which ancient Greece was divided*; 古希腊分割成的许多小城邦; *a ~ of duties.* 繁多的职责.

mul·ti·ply /'mʌltɪplaɪ ; 'mʌltə,plaɪ/ *vt, vi* (*pt, pp* **-lied**) **1** [VP14] *~ sth by sth*, add (a given quantity or number) a given number of times: 乘: *~ 3 by 5*, to make 15. 用 5 来乘 3 以成 15. *6 multiplied by 5 is 30*, *6×5=30.* 6 乘以 5 等于 30. **2** [VP6A] produce a large number of; make greater in number: 提出大量的…; 增多; 增加: *~ instances*, produce a larger number of examples. 举出更多的例证. **3** [VP2A] increase in number by procreation: 繁殖: *Rabbits ~ rapidly.* 兔子繁殖甚快.

mul·ti·tude /'mʌltɪtjuːd *US*: -tuːd ; 'mʌltə,tjud/ *n* **1** [C] great number (esp of people gathered together): 多数; 大批 (尤指集结的人群). **2** *the ~*, the common people; the masses: 群众; 大众: *demagogues who appeal to the ~.* 煽动群众的政客. **3** [U] greatness of number: 大量: *like the stars in ~.* 象繁星 (那么多). **multi·tud·in·ous** /,mʌltɪ'tjuːdɪnəs *US*: -'tuːdənəs ; ,mʌltə'tjudnəs/ *adj* very numerous; great in number. 非常多的; 众多的; 大量的.

mul·tum in parvo /,mʌltəm ɪn 'pɑːvəʊ ; 'mʌltəm ɪn 'parvo/ *n* (Lat) much in a small space. (拉) 形体小而内容多.

mum¹ /mʌm ; mʌm/ *int, n* Silence! 安静! ***Mum's the word!*** Say nothing about this. 别说出去! □ *adj* **keep mum**, silent. 保持安静.

mum² /mʌm ; mʌm/ *n* (colloq) mother. (口) 妈; 母亲.

mumble /'mʌmbl ; 'mʌmbl/ *vt, vi* [VP6A, 2A, C] **1** say sth, speak one's words, indistinctly: 喃喃而言; 言语不清; 咕哝: *The old man was mumbling away to himself.* 那个老人不停地喃喃自语. *Don't ~ your words.* 别喃喃而言. **2** bite or chew as with toothless gums. 如无齿般地咀嚼; 瘪着嘴咀嚼.

mumbo-jumbo /,mʌmbəʊ 'dʒʌmbəʊ ; 'mʌmbo-'dʒʌmbo/ *n* meaningless or obscure ritual; gibberish. 无意义或暧昧难解的宗教仪式; 无意义的声音.

mum·mer /'mʌmə(r) ; 'mʌmə/ *n* actor in an old form of drama without words. 哑剧演员. **~y** *n* (*pl* **-ries**) **1** [C] performance by a ~; 哑剧表演; 哑剧的表演; 哑剧. **2** [U] foolish or unnecessary ceremonial (esp religious); [C] instance of this. 愚昧或无必要的仪式 (尤指宗教的).

mum·mify /'mʌmɪfaɪ ; 'mʌmɪ,faɪ/ *vt* (*pt, pp* **-fied**) [VP6A] preserve (a corpse) by embalming; shrivel.

用香料防腐法保存(尸体); 使皱缩。 **mum·mi·fi·ca·tion** /,mʌmɪfɪ'keɪʃn ; ,mʌmɪfə'keʃən/ *n*

mummy¹ /'mʌmɪ ; 'mʌmɪ/ *n* (*pl* **-mies**) body of a human being or animal embalmed for burial; dried-up body preserved from decay (as in early Egypt). 为埋葬而涂有香料以防腐的人或兽的尸体; (经过防腐处理的) 干尸 (如古埃及所为者); 木乃伊.

a mummy in a sarcophagus

mummy² /'mʌmɪ ; 'mʌmɪ/ *n* (*pl* **-mies**) (chiefly child's word for) mother. (主要为小儿语) 妈咪; 妈妈.

mumps /mʌmps ; mʌmps/ *n* (with *sing v*) contagious disease with painful swellings in the neck. (用单数动词) 耳下腺炎; 腮腺炎.

munch /mʌntʃ ; mʌntʃ/ *vt, vi* [VP6A, 2A, C] chew with much movement of the jaw: 用力咀嚼; 大声咀嚼: *~ing away at a hard apple*; 用力咬硬一个硬苹果; *cattle ~ing their fodder.* 正在大声咀嚼草料的牛群.

mun·dane /mʌn'deɪn ; 'mʌnden/ *adj* **1** worldly (contrasted with *spiritual* or *heavenly*): 世俗的; 尘世的 (与 spiritual 或 heavenly 相对): *When a man is near death he loses interest in ~ affairs.* 人快要死的时候, 对世事都失去兴趣. **2** dull, ordinary: 平凡的: *~ occupations/speeches.* 平凡的职业 (演说). **~·ly** *adv*

mu·nici·pal /mjuː'nɪsɪpl ; mjuˈnɪsəpl/ *adj* of a town or city having self-government: 市的; 市政的; 自治城市的: *~ buildings*, eg the town hall, public library; 市属建筑物 (如市政府, 公共图书馆); *~ undertakings*, eg the supply of water, tram and bus services; 市营事业 (如自来水之供应, 公共电车及公共汽车之营运); *the ~ debt.* 市债. **~·ly** /-pəlɪ; -plɪ/ *adv* **~·ity** /mjuː,nɪsɪˈpæletɪ ; ,mjunɪsəˈpælətɪ/ *n* (*pl* **-ties**) town, city, district, with local self-government; governing body of such a town, etc. 自治市; 自治区; 市政府.

mu·nifi·cent /mjuːˈnɪfɪsnt ; mjuˈnɪfəsnt/ *adj* (formal) extremely generous; (of sth given) large in amount or splendid in quality. (正式用语) 非常慷慨的; 宽厚的; (指给与之物) 大量的; 精美的. **~·ly** *adv* **mu·nifi·cence** /-sns ; -sns/ *n* [U] great generosity. 慷慨; 大度; 宽厚; 宽大.

mu·ni·ments /'mjuːnɪments ; 'mjunəmənts/ *n* (legal) documents kept as evidence of rights or privileges. (法律) 契据; 证书.

mu·ni·tion /mjuːˈnɪʃn ; mjuˈnɪʃən/ *n* (*pl* except when attrib) military supplies, esp guns, shells, bombs, etc: (用复数, 但作定语时用单数) 军火; 军需品 (尤指枪炮, 炮弹, 炸弹等): *The war was lost because of a shortage of ~s/a ~ shortage.* 战事因为缺乏军火而失败. □ *vt* [VP6A] provide with ~s: 供以军火: *~ a fort.* 以军火供应一个堡垒.

mural /'mjʊərəl ; 'mjʊrəl/ *adj* of, like, on, a wall: 墙壁的; 似壁的; 在壁上的: *a ~ painting.* 一幅壁画. □ *n* [C] wall-painting; fresco. 壁画.

mur·der /'mɜːdə(r) ; 'mɝdɚ/ *n* **1** [U] unlawful killing of a human being on purpose; [C] instance of this: 谋杀; 谋杀案: *commit ~*; 犯杀人罪; *be declared guilty of ~*; 被宣判犯杀人罪; *six ~s in one week.* 一星期内有六起杀人案. **cry blue ~**, (colloq) shout loudly and in alarm. (口) 大声而惊慌地喊叫. **,M~ will 'out**, (prov) cannot be hidden (谚) 谋杀案终必败露; 纸包不住火. ⇨ homicide manslaughter, regicide, etc. **2** [U] unjustifiable sacrifice of life (eg in war): (战时等之) 无端杀害; 滥杀无辜; 屠杀: *Nothing could justify the bombing of the town; it was sheer ~.* 实在没有理由要炸这个城市; 这简直是屠杀. □ *vt* [VP6A] **1** kill (a

human being)unlawfully and on purpose. 谋杀。 **2** spoil by lack of skill or knowledge: (因缺乏技术或知识而)糟蹋: ~ *a piece of music*, play it very badly. 把一支曲子演奏得糟透了。 *Do you ever* ~ *the English language?* 你有没有胡乱使用英语? ~**er** *n* person guilty of ~. 谋杀犯; 凶手。 ~**ess** /-ɪs ; -ɪs/ *n* woman ~er. 女谋杀犯; 女凶手。 ~**ous** /'mɜːdərəs ; 'mɜrdərəs/ *adj* planning, suggesting, designed for, ~: 计划、暗示或设计凶杀人的; 谋杀的; 要人命的; 凶残的: *a* ~*ous-looking villain*: 一脸凶杀相的恶棍; *a* ~*ous burst of fire from the enemy's guns*. 敌人枪炮冒出的凶恶火焰。 ~**·ous·ly** *adv*

murk /mɜːk ; mɜrk/ *n* [U] darkness; gloom. 黑暗; 阴暗。 ~**y** *adj* (**-ier, -iest**) dark; gloomy: 暗的; 阴暗的: *a* ~*y night*; 黑夜; (of darkness) thick. (指黑暗)深的; 浓的。 ~**·ily** /-ɪlɪ; -əlɪ/ *adv*

mur·mur /'mɜːmə(r) ; 'mɜrmə/ *n* **1** low, continuous, indistinct sound, rising and falling very little in pitch: 低沉连续而极少高低变化的模糊声: *the* ~ *of bees in the garden*; 花园中蜜蜂的嗡嗡声; *the* ~ *of a distant brook/ of distant traffic*. 远方溪流的潺潺声(远处车辆的隆隆声)。 **2** softly spoken word(s): 低语: 轻语: *a* ~ *of conversation from the next room*. 隔壁房间里传来的轻微的谈话声。 **3** subdued expression of feeling: 表示感情的细语; 怨言: *a* ~ *of delight*. 表示愉快的细语。 *They paid the higher taxes without a* ~, ie without complaining. 他们毫无怨言地付了更高的税。 □ *vi, vt* **1** [VP2A, C] make a ~(1): 发低沉连续的模糊声: *a* ~*ing brook*. 潺潺的小溪。 **2** [VP2A, C 3A] ~ (*at/against*), complain in a ~(3): (对…) 低声抱怨: ~ *at injustice*; 抱怨不公平; ~ *against new taxes*. 抱怨新的税捐。 **3** [VP6A] utter in a low voice: 低声说: ~ *a prayer*. 低声作祷告。

murphy /'mɜːfɪ ; 'mɜrfɪ/ *n* (*pl* **-phies**) (sl) potato. (俚) 马铃薯。

mur·rain /'mʌrɪn ; 'mʌrɪn/ *n* **1** [U] infectious disease of cattle. 牛瘟; 牛疫。 **2** (old use): (旧用法): *A* ~ *on you!* A plague on you! Curse you! 该死的! 天咒你!

mus·ca·tel /ˌmʌskə'tel ; ˌmʌskə'tel/ *n* [U] rich, sweet wine made from musk-flavoured kinds of grape. 麝香葡萄酒。

muscle /'mʌsl ; 'mʌsl/ *n* [C, U] (band or bundle of) elastic substance in an animal body that can be tightened or loosened to produce movement: (一束) 肌肉: *When you walk you exercise your leg* ~*s*. 你走路时就会使你腿上的肌肉行动。 *Physical exercises develop* ~. 运动锻炼肌肉。 *Don't move a* ~, stay perfectly still. 不要动。 '~**-man** /-mæn ; -ˌmæn/ *n* (*pl* **-men**) man of great muscular development. 肌肉发达的人; 力气大的人。 '~**-bound** *adj* having stiff ~s as the result of over-training or excessive exercise. (因过度运动而)肌肉僵硬的。 □ *vi* [VP2C] ~ *in* (*on sth*), (colloq) use force to get a share of sth considered advantageous. (口)强取; 夺取; 用强制手段取得(一份利益)。

Mus·covy /'mʌskəvɪ ; 'mʌskəvɪ/ *n* (old name for) Russia. (旧名称)俄罗斯。 **Mus·co·vite** /'mʌskəvaɪt ; 'mʌskəˌvaɪt/ *n, adj* (citizen) of Moscow. 莫斯科人; 莫斯科的。

mus·cu·lar /'mʌskjʊlə(r) ; 'mʌskjələ/ *adj* **1** of the muscles: 肌肉的: ~ *tissue/rheumatism*. 肌肉组织(肌肉风湿病)。 **2** having strong muscles. 肌肉发达的。

muse¹ /mjuːz ; mjuz/ *n* **1 the M**~**s**, (Gk myth) the nine goddesses, daughters of Zeus, who protected and encouraged poetry, music, dancing, history and other branches of art and learning. (希神)缪斯女神(宙斯的九个女儿,为保护和鼓励诗歌、音乐、舞蹈、历史和其他艺术与学术的女神);文艺女神。 **2** (**the**) **M**~, poet's genius: spirit that inspires a poet. 诗才; 诗人的灵感; 诗兴。

muse² /mjuːz ; mjuz/ *vi* [VP2A, 3A] ~ (*over/on/ upon*), think deeply or dreamily, ignoring what is happening around one: 沉思; 冥想: *musing over memories of the past*. 缅怀往事。 **mus·ing·ly** *adv*

mu·seum /mjuː'zɪəm ; mjuˈzɪəm/ *n* building in

which objects illustrating art, history, science, etc are displayed. 博物馆。 *a* '~ *piece*, fine specimen suitable for a ~; (fig) sth or sb antiquated. 值得陈列于博物馆中的精致标本;(喻)过时的人或物;旧思想的人。

mush /mʌʃ; mʌʃ/ *n* [U] soft, thick mixture or mass; (US) boiled corn meal. 软而浓的混合物或块物;(美)玉蜀黍粥。 ~**y** *adj* like ~; (colloq) weakly sentimental. 浓浆的; 糊状的;(口)多愁善感的。

mush·room *US:* -ruːm; 'mʌʃrʊm/ *n* [C] fast-growing fungus of which some kinds can be eaten: 蕈; 菌; 蘑菇: (attrib)(用作定语) *the* ~ (=rapid) *growth of London suburbs*. 伦敦郊区的迅速发展。 *The* ~ *cloud* (because of its ~ shape) *of a nuclear explosion*. 核爆所生的蕈状云。 ⇨ the illus at **fungus**. 参看 fungus 之插图。 □ *vi* **1** go out into the fields to gather ~s. 采蘑菇去。 **2** [VP2C] spread or grow rapidly: 迅速发展或生长: *English language schools are* ~*ing in Bournemouth*. 英语学校象雨后春笋般纷纷在伯恩茅斯市设立。

mu·sic /'mjuːzɪk ; 'mjuzɪk/ *n* [U] art of making pleasing combinations of sounds in rhythm, harmony and counterpoint; the sounds and composition so made; written or printed signs representing these sounds: 作曲法; 音乐; 乐曲; 乐谱: (attrib)(用作定语) *a* ~ *lesson/ teacher*. 音乐课(老师)。 *face the* ~, face one's critics; face difficulties boldly. 面对批评者; 勇敢地面对困难。 *set/put sth to* ~, provide words, eg of a poem, with ~. 将…配上音乐。 '~**-box** *n* (US) musical-box, = **musical**. (美)音乐匣。 '~**-hall** *n* (GB) hall or theatre used for variety entertainment (eg songs, acrobatic performances, juggling). (英) 杂耍戏院; 歌厅。 ⇨ *concert-hall* at **concert¹**(1). '~**-stand** *n* light (usu folding) framework for holding sheets of printed music. 乐谱架。 '~**-stool** *n* seat without a back (usu adjustable in height) used when playing a piano. 琴凳(弹奏钢琴时用的无靠背凳子, 通常可调节高低)。 ⇨ the illus at **brass, keyboard, notation, percussion, string**. 参看 brass, keyboard, notation, percussion, string 之插图。

mu·si·cal /'mjuːzɪkl ; 'mjuzɪkl/ *adj* of, fond of, skilled in, music: 音乐的; 爱好音乐的; 精于音乐的: ~ *instruments*, eg the violin, piano, harp; 乐器(如小提琴、钢琴、竖琴); *She's not at all* ~, does not enjoy or understand music. 她不喜欢音乐; 她不懂音乐。 '~**-box** *n* box with a mechanical device that produces a tune when the box is opened. 音乐匣(盒内有机械装置, 匣盖开启时即鸣奏简单音乐)。 '~ '**chairs**, game in which players go round a row of chairs one fewer than the number of players. Each time the music stops, the players sit down and the one left without a chair is eliminated. 占椅子游戏(参加游戏者绕着一排椅子而走, 椅子数比游戏人数少一个。每一次音乐停止时, 参加者占一椅子坐下, 占不到椅子的人被淘汰)。 '~ '**comedy**, a light, amusing play with songs and dancing音乐喜剧; 歌舞剧。 □ *n* [C] **1** musical comedy. 音乐喜剧; 歌舞剧。 **2** cinema film in which songs have an essential part. 音乐片(以音乐为主的电影片)。 ~**ly** /-klɪ; -klɪ/ *adv*

mu·si·cian /mjuːˈzɪʃn ; mjuˈzɪʃən/ *n* person skilled in music; composer of music. 精于音乐的人; 乐师; 音乐家; 作曲家。 ~**·ship** *n* [U] art and skill in (performing) music. 音乐的技巧。

musk /mʌsk ; mʌsk/ *n* [U] **1** strong-smelling substance produced in glands by male deer, used in the manufacture of perfumes. 麝香(雄鹿腺体所分泌的物质, 具强烈香味, 用以制香水)。 '~**-deer** *n* small hornless deer of central Asia. 麝; 麝香鹿(产于中亚的一种体小的无角鹿)。 '~**-rat** (or the *musquash*) *n* large rat-like water animal of N America, valuable for its fur. 麝香鼠(北美产的一种似鼠的大水生动物, 其毛皮甚为珍贵)。 **2** kinds of plant with musky smell. 麝香植物。 '~ **melon** *n* sweet juicy kind of melon. 一种香瓜; 甜瓜; 金瓜。 '~**-rose** *n* rambling rose with large, sweet-smelling flowers. 麝香玫瑰。 ~**y** *adj* (**-ier, -iest**)

having the smell of ~. 有麝香味的。

mus·ket /'mʌskɪt; 'mʌskɪt/ *n* firearm used by foot-soldiers (16th to 19th cc) now replaced by the rifle. (十六世纪至十九世纪步兵所用的)旧式步枪; 滑膛枪(今已为火枪所取代)。**~·eer** /ˌmʌskɪ'tɪə(r); ˌmʌskə'tɪr/ *n* foot-soldier armed with a ~. 装备滑膛枪的步兵。**~·ry** /'mʌskɪtrɪ; 'mʌskɪtrɪ/ *n* [U] **1** (science of, instruction in) shooting with rifles. 步枪射击(术); 步枪射击教练。**2** (old use) troops armed with ~s. (旧用法)装备滑膛枪的军队。

Mus·lim /'mʊzlɪm *US:* 'mʌzləm; 'mʌzləm/ *n* one who professes Islam; follower of Muhammad; (attrib) of ~s and Islam: 伊斯兰教徒; (用作定语)伊斯兰教徒的: ~ *historians/holidays.* 伊斯兰教历史家(伊斯兰教节日)。

mus·lin /'mʌzlɪn; 'mʌzlɪn/ *n* [U] thin, fine, cotton cloth, used for dresses, curtains, etc. (做衣服、窗帷等用的)细薄棉布。

mus·quash /'mʌskwɒʃ; 'mʌskwɑʃ/ *n* (fur of the) musk-rat. 麝香鼠; 麝香鼠皮。⇨ **musk**(1).

muss /mʌs; mʌs/ *n* (US) [U] disorder; [C] muddle. (美)混乱: 杂乱。□ *vt* [VP6A, 15B] ~ *(up)*, put into disorder: 使混乱: *Don't ~ up my hair!* 别弄乱我的头发!

mus·sel /'mʌsl; 'mʌsl/ *n* (sorts of) mollusc with a black shell in two parts. 贻贝; 淡菜。⇨ the illus at **bivalve.** 参看 bivalve 之插图。

must[1] /mʌst; mʌst/ *n* [U] grape-juice before fermentation has changed it into wine. 发酵前的葡萄汁。

must[2] /*usual form:* məst; məst; *strong form:* mʌst; mʌst/ *aux* vv, *anom fin* (No infinitive, no participles, no inflected forms; ~ *not* may be contracted to ~n't /'mʌsnt; 'mʌsn̩t/.) (无定式, 无分词, 亦无词形变化; must not 可缩写为 mustn't。) [VP5] **1** (expressing an immediate or future obligation or necessity; ~ *not* expresses a prohibition. Cf the use of *may* to express permission and of *need not* to express non-obligation. Cf the use of *had to* for a past obligation and *shall/will have to* for a future obligation): (表示立即的或将来的义务或必要; must not 表示禁止。参较 may 表示许可, 与 need not 表示无义务的用法。参较 had to 为过去义务, 与 shall 或 will have to 为将来义务的用法): *You ~ do as you're told.* 你必须照着吩咐去做。*Soldiers ~ obey orders.* 军人必须服从命令。*Cars ~ not be parked in front of the entrance.* 车辆不可停在入口处。*You ~n't do that.* 你不可以做那件事。*We ~n't be late, ~ we?* 我们不可以迟到, 是吗? *A:* 'M~ you go so soon?' *B:* 'Yes, I ~.' (or) 'No, I needn't.' 甲: '你必须这么早去吗?' 乙: '是的, 我必须这么早去。'(或) '不, 我不需要这么早去。' **2** (= had to, used to indicate what was necessary or obligatory at a time in the past): (用以表示过去的必要或义务): *She said she ~ have a new hat for Easter.* 她说复活节时她必须要有一顶新帽子。*As he had broken it, he agreed that he ~ buy a new one.* 由于他把它弄破了, 他答应要买一个新的。*On the other side of the wood was a field that he ~ cross.* 森林的另一边有一片他必须穿过的田野。**3** (with less emphasis on necessity; stressing what is desirable or advisable): (不太强调必要; 着重想做或该做之事)应该: *We ~ see what can be done.* 我们应该看看能做些什么。*I ~ ask you not to do that again.* 我应该劝你不要再做那种事情。**4** (expressing certainty): (表示确定)一定: *Don't bet on horse-races, you ~ lose* (= will certainly lose) *in the long run.* 不要赌赛马, 你终久必然输。**5** (expressing strong probability): (表示极大的可能性)必定; 必然: *You ~ be hungry after your long walk.* 你走了远路后必定会饿。*This ~ be* (= very probably is) *the book you want.* 这一定是你要的书。*You ~ have known* (= Surely you knew) *what she wanted.* 你当时一定知道她要什么。*You ~ be joking!* You can't be serious! 你一定是在开玩笑吧! **6** (indicating the occurrence of sth unwelcome, sth contrary to what was wanted): (表示发生不受欢迎或不需要之事): *He ~ come and worry her with questions, just when*

she was busy cooking the dinner! 正当她在忙着做饭的时候, 偏巧他来了, 问一些问题麻烦她! □ *n* (colloq) sth that ~ be done, seen, heard, etc: (口)必须做、看、听等的事物: *Green's new novel is a ~ for all lovers of crime fiction.* 格林新出版的小说是爱好罪犯小说者所必须看的一本书。

mus·tache /'mʌstæʃ; 'mʌstæʃ/ *n* (US) = **moustache.**

mus·tachio /mə'stɑ:ʃɪəʊ *US:* -'stæʃ-; mə'stɑʃo/ *n* (*pl* ~**s** /-ɪəʊz; -oz/) a large (usu long-haired) moustache. 大的(通常长发的)髭。

mus·tang /'mʌstæŋ; 'mʌstæŋ/ *n* small wild or half-wild horse of the American plains. 产于美国平原的小野马或半野马。

mus·tard /'mʌstəd; 'mʌstəd/ *n* [U] **1** plant with yellow flowers and seeds (black or white) in long, slender pods. 芥。**2** fine, yellow powder made from the seeds of this plant; this powder made into hot-tasting sauce. 芥末; 芥粉; 芥子酱。'~ **gas** *n* kind of liquid poison with vapour that burns the skin (used in World War I). 芥子气(第一次世界大战中用的一种糜烂皮肤的毒气)。'~**plaster** *n* poultice made with ~. 芥末硬膏。**as keen as ~,** very keen. 很起劲; 很感兴趣。**grain of** '~ **seed,** sth very small capable of developing into sth very large. 一粒芥菜种 (喻可以长得很大的小东西)。⇨ **Matt 13: 31.** 参看圣经马太福音13章31节。

mus·ter /'mʌstə(r); 'mʌstə/ *n* assembly or gathering of persons, esp for review or inspection. 人员的集合; 集中(尤指为检阅或检查而召集者)。**pass** '~, be considered satisfactory; be good enough for the purpose or occasion. 被认为满意; 合格。□ *vt, vi* [VP6A, 15B, 2A] ~ *(up)*, call, collect or gather together: 召集; 集合; 集中: *Go and ~ all the men you can find.* 去把能找到的人都集合起来。*They ~ed (up) all their courage.* 他们鼓起所有的勇气。

musty /'mʌstɪ; 'mʌstɪ/ *adj* (**-ier, -iest**) **1** stale; smelling or tasting mouldy: 有霉味的; 发霉的: ~ *books;* 发霉的书; a ~ *room.* 有霉味的房间。**2** (fig) stale; out-of-date: (喻)陈旧的; 过时的: *a professor with ~ ideas.* 观念陈旧的教授。**musti·ness** /'mʌstɪnɪs; 'mʌstɪns/ *n*

mu·table /'mjuːtəbl; 'mjutəbl/ *adj* liable to change; likely to change. 可变的; 易变的; 不定的。**mu·ta·bil·ity** /ˌmjuːtə'bɪlətɪ; ˌmjutə'bɪlɪtɪ/ *n*

mu·ta·tion /mjuː'teɪʃn; mjuː'teʃən/ *n* [U] change; alteration; [C] instance of this: 变化; 更换; 转变: *Are ~s in plants caused by cosmic rays?* 植物的变种是宇宙射线所造成的吗?

mu·ta·tis mu·tan·dis /muːˌtɑːtɪs muː'tændɪs; mjuˈtetɪs mjuˈtændɪs/ *adv* (Lat) with necessary alterations or changes (when comparing cases). (拉)(就实际情形)已作必要改变或修正。

mute /mjuːt; mjut/ *adj* **1** silent; making no sound: 沉默的; 无声的: *staring at me in ~ amazement.* 目瞪口呆地凝视着我。**2** (of a person) dumb; unable to speak. (指人)哑吧的; 不能说话的。**3** (of a letter in a word) not sounded= (指词中的字母)不读音的; 不发音的: *The 'b' in 'dumb' is ~.* 'dumb' 词中的 'b' 是不读音的。□ *n* **1** dumb person. 哑子; 哑吧。**2** piece of bone or metal used to soften the sounds produced from a stringed instrument; pad placed in the mouth of a wind instrument for the same purpose. 弱音器(置于乐器上使声音变柔和的装置, 在弦乐器上者为骨片或金属小片; 在管乐器上者为管口的塞头)。□ *vt* [VP6A] deaden or muffle the sound of (esp a musical instrument) 减弱或减低(尤指乐器)的声音。**~·ly** *adv*

mu·ti·late /'mjuːtɪleɪt; 'mjutl̩ˌet/ *vt* [VP6A] damage by breaking, tearing or cutting off a necessary part; destroy the use of (a limb, etc). 使残缺不全; 使残废; 残害; 毁坏; 切断(手足等)。**mu·ti·la·tion** /ˌmjuːtɪ'leɪʃn; ˌmjutl̩'eʃən/ *n* [U] mutilating or being ~d; [C] injury or loss caused by this. 毁伤; 残害; 由此种残害所造成的损伤或损失。

mu·ti·nous /'mjuːtɪnəs; 'mjutɪnəs/ *adj* guilty of

mutiny; rebellious: 反叛的; 叛变的; 反抗的: ~ *sailors*: 叛变的水手; ~ *behaviour*. 背叛的行为。

mu·tiny /'mjuːtɪnɪ; 'mjutn̩ɪ/ *n* (*pl* **-nies**) [U] (esp of soldiers and sailors) open rebellion against lawful authority; [C] instance of this. (尤指军人和水手)哗变;抗命;叛变;兵变。 □ *vi* [VP2A, 3A] ~ (*against*), be guilty of ~; revolt. 哗变; 反抗。 **mu·tin·eer** /ˌmjuːtɪ'nɪə(r); ˌmjutn̩'ɪr/ *n* person guilty of ~, 反叛者;叛兵;反抗者。

mutt /mʌt; mʌt/ *n* (sl) (俚) **1** ignorant blunderer: 笨蛋: *You silly big* ~! 你这大笨蛋! **2** mongrel dog. 杂种狗。

mut·ter /'mʌtə(r); 'mʌtɚ/ *vt, vi* [VP6A, 14, 2A, C] speak, say (sth), in a low voice not meant to be heard; grumble in an indistinct voice: 轻声低语; 喃喃而语; 咕哝地抱怨: *He was ~ing away to himself*. 他不停地喃喃自语。 *Are you ~ing threats at me?* 你是在咕哝咕哝地对我说说威胁话吗? *We heard thunder ~ing in the distance*. 我们听到远处隆隆的雷声。 □ *n* ~ed utterance or sound. 喃喃低语; 呢喃低语声。 **~er** *n* person who ~s. 喃喃低语者。

mut·ton /'mʌtn̩; 'mʌtn̩/ *n* [U] flesh of fully grown sheep: 羊肉: *a leg/shoulder of* ~; 羊腿(羊的肩膀肉); *roast* ~ *chop*, piece of ~ rib. 羊排(带肋骨的一片羊肉)。 *as dead as* ~, quite dead. 死翘翘了。 ~ *dressed as lamb*, used of an elderly person dressed in a style suitable for a young person. (指作年轻人打扮的老年人)老来俏。 '~-**head** *n* (colloq) dull, stupid person. (口)愚人; 笨人。

mu·tual /'mjuːtʃʊəl; 'mjutʃʊəl/ *adj* **1** (of love, friendship, respect, etc) shared; exchanged equally; (of feelings, opinions, etc) held in common with others: (指爱情、友谊、尊敬等)共有的; 相互的;(指感情、意见等)与旁人共同持有的: ~ *suspicion/affection*. 互相猜疑(亲爱)。 **2** each to the other(s): 彼此的;相互的: ~ *enemies/well-wishers*; 互相敌对的人(互相祝福者); ~ *aid*. 互助。 ~ *funds*, (US) (美)=unit trusts. **a** ~ **in'surance company**, one in which some or all of the profits are divided among the policy-holders. 互助保险公司(部分或全部的营利由投保人分享的保险公司)。 **3** common to two or more persons: 为两人或更多人所共有的; 共同的: *our* ~ *friend Smith*, ie Smith, a friend of both of us. 我们共同的朋友史密斯。 ~**ly** /-ʊəlɪ; -ʊəlɪ/ *adv*

muzzle /'mʌzl; 'mʌzl/ *n* **1** nose and mouth of an animal (eg dog or fox); guard of straps or wires placed over this part of an animal's head to prevent it biting, etc. (狗或狐等的)鼻和嘴; 动物的口套; 口络。 ⇨ the illus at **dog.** 参看 dog 之插图。 **2** ⇨ the illus at **cannon.** 参看 cannon. 之插图。 open end or mouth of a fire-arm: 枪口; 炮口: *a* ~*-loading gun*. 前膛装填的枪或炮。 '~-**velocity**, speed of a projectile as it leaves the ~. (弹丸离开枪膛口时的)初速; 枪(炮)口速度。 ⇨ **breech.** □ *vt* [VP6A] put a ~ on (a dog, etc); (fig)prevent (a person, society, newspaper etc) from expressing opinions freely. 戴口络于(狗等)的口部; (喻)禁止(人、会社、报纸等)自由发表意见。

muzzy /'mʌzɪ; 'mʌzɪ/ *adj* (**-ier, -iest**) **1** confused in mind; spiritless; stupid from drinking. 迷糊的; 没精神的; 醉得发昏的。 **2** blurred. 弄污的; 模糊不清的。

my /maɪ; maɪ/ *poss adj* **1** belonging to me: 我的: *Where's my hat?* 我的帽子在哪里? *This car is my own*. 这部汽车是我自己的。 **2** as a part of a form of address: 作为称呼的一部分: *Yes, my dear* 是的, 我亲爱的。 *My dear fellow!* 我亲爱的伙伴! **3** in exclamations: 用于惊叹语中: *My goodness!* 天呀! *Oh, my!* 啊呀!

my·col·ogy /maɪ'kɒlədʒɪ; maɪ'kɑlədʒɪ/ *n* [U] science or study of fungi. 真菌学; 霉菌学。

my·el·itis /ˌmaɪə'laɪtɪs; ˌmaɪə'laɪtɪs/ *n* (path) inflammation of the spinal cord. (病理)脊髓炎。

my·na(h) /'maɪnə; 'maɪnə/ *n* ~ *bird*, (kinds of) starling of SE Asia, known for their ability to mimic human speech. (产于东南亚之能模仿人的) 燕八哥。

⇨ the illus at rare. 参看 rare 之插图。

my·opia /maɪ'əʊpɪə; maɪ'opɪə/ *n* [U] short-sightedness. 近视。 **my·opic** /maɪ'ɒpɪk; maɪ'ɑpɪk/ *adj* short-sighted. 近视的。

myr·iad /'mɪrɪəd; 'mɪrɪəd/ *n* [C] ~ (*of*), very great number. 极大数量。

myr·mi·don /'mɜː mɪdən US: -dɒn; 'mɝmə,dɑn/ *n* (contemptuous or humorous term for a) person who carries out any kind of order without questions: (轻蔑或诙谐用语)不迟疑奉行任何命令的人: ~*s of the law*, eg bailiffs. 法律执行官; 警察。

myrrh /mɜː(r); mɝ/ *n* [U] sweet-smelling, bitter-tasting kind of gum or resin obtained from shrubs, used for making incense and perfumes. 没药(一种有香气、带苦味的树脂,用以制造香料)。

myrtle /'mɜː tl; 'mɝtl/ *n* (kinds of) evergreen shrub with shiny leaves and sweet-smelling white flowers. 桃金孃(数种常绿灌木,叶发亮,开有香味的白花)。

my·self /maɪ'self; maɪ'self/ *pron* (reflex and emphat): (反身及强势语)我自己: *I hurt* ~. 我伤了自己。 *I can do it (all) by* ~, ie without help. 我能独自做。 *I tired* ~ *out*. 我疲倦极了。 *I* ~ *said so*. 我亲口这么说的。 *I said so* ~. 我亲口这么说的。 *I'm not* ~ *today*, am not feeling so well as I usually do. 我今天有点不舒服(或失常)。

mys·teri·ous /mɪ'stɪərɪəs; mɪs'tɪrɪəs/ *adj* full of, suggesting, covered in, mystery. 神秘的; 难解的; 隐秘的: *a* ~ *crime*; 神秘的罪行; *a* ~*-looking parcel*. 一个样子很神秘的包裹。 ~**ly** *adv*

mys·tery /'mɪstərɪ; 'mɪstərɪ/ *n* (*pl* **-ries**) **1** [C] sth of which the cause or origin is hidden or impossible to understand: 神秘的事物; 不可思议的事物; 难解的事物: *The murder remained an unsolved* ~. 那件谋杀案仍然是个解不开的谜。 **2** [U] condition of being secret or obscure: 秘密; 神秘: *The origin of this tribe is lost in* ~, It has been impossible to learn anything about it. 这个种族的来源是个难解的谜。 **3** (*pl*) secret religious rites and ceremonies (of ancient Greeks, Romans, etc). (复)(古希腊、罗马等的)秘密的宗教仪式。 **4** [C] '~ (**play**), medieval drama based on episodes in the life of Jesus. 神秘剧(以耶稣一生事迹为本的中古戏剧)。

mys·tic /'mɪstɪk; 'mɪstɪk/ *adj* of hidden meaning or spiritual power; causing feelings of awe and wonder: 神秘的; 不可思议的; 令人敬畏而惊奇的: ~ *rites and ceremonies*; 神秘的仪式; ~ *teachings*. 神秘的教义。 □ *n* person who seeks union with God and, through that, realization of truth beyond men's understanding. 寻求接近上帝借以了解人类所不能明白的真理的人; 神秘主义者。 **mys·ti·cal** /'mɪstɪkl; 'mɪstɪkl/ *adj*=mystic.

mys·ti·cism /'mɪstɪsɪzəm; 'mɪstə,sɪzəm/ *n* [U] beliefs, experiences, of a mystic; teaching and belief that knowledge of God and of real truth may be obtained through meditation or spiritual insight, independently of the mind and the senses. 神秘主义; 相信不用思考力与感官而借默想与心灵内省可以认识上帝与真理的学说。

mys·tify /'mɪstɪfaɪ; 'mɪstə,faɪ/ *vt* (*pt, pp* **-fied**) [VP6A] puzzle; bewilder. 使迷惑; 使困惑。 **mys·ti·fi·ca·tion** /ˌmɪstɪfɪ'keɪʃn; ˌmɪstəfə'keʃən/ *n* [U] ~ing or being mystified; [C] sth that mystifies. 迷惑; 困惑; 令人迷惑的事物。

mys·tique /mɪ'stiːk; mɪs'tik/ *n* **1** esoteric character of a person, institution, etc caused by mystical devotion and veneration: (由于不可思议的热爱与崇拜所造成的个人、团体等的)神秘性: *the* ~ *of the monarchy in Great Britain*. 英国君主政治的奥秘。 **2** incommunicable quality; skill known only to a few practitioners. 不可言传的性质; 奥妙; 秘诀。

myth /mɪθ; mɪθ/ *n* **1** [C] story, handed down from olden times, esp concepts or beliefs about the early history of a race, explanations of natural events, such as the seasons. 神话(由古相传的故事,尤指有关一民族早期历史的观念或信仰、自然现象如季节等的解释): *ancient Greek*

~s. 古希腊的神话。**2** [U] such stories collectively: 神话(集合用法): *famous in ~ and legend*. 在神话与传奇中有名的。**3** [C] person, thing, etc, that is imaginary, fictitious, or invented: 想像、虚构或创造的人或事物: *That rich uncle of whom he boasts is only a ~*. 他所夸耀的那位阔叔叔不过是个虚构的人物。**~i·cal** /ˈmɪθɪkl; ˋmɪθɪkḷ/ *adj* **1** of ~; existing only in ~: 神话的; 仅存在于神话中的: *~ical heroes;* 神话中的英雄; *~ical literature*. 神话文学。**2** imaginary; fictitious: 想像的; 虚构的: *~ical wealth*. 想像中的财富。

myth·ol·ogy /mɪˈθɒlədʒɪ; mɪˋθɑlədʒɪ/ *n* (*pl* **-gies**) **1** [U] study or science of myths. 神话学。**2** [U] myths collectively: 神话(集合用法): *Greek ~;* 希腊神话; [C] body or collection of myths: 神话集: *the mythologies of primitive races*. 原始民族的神话集。**myth·ol·ogist** /mɪˈθɒlədʒɪst; mɪˋθɑlədʒɪst/ *n* student of ~. 研究神话者; 神话学家。**mytho·logi·cal** /ˌmɪθəˈlɒdʒɪkl; ˌmɪθəˋlɑdʒɪkḷ/ *adj* of ~ or myths; unreal. 神话学的; 神话的; 非真实的; 假的。

myxo·ma·to·sis /ˌmɪksəməˈtəʊsɪs; ˌmɪksəməˋtosɪs/ *n* [U] infectious fatal disease of rabbits. 兔瘟; 兔疫。

Nn

N, n /en; ɛn/ (*pl* **N's, n's** /enz; ɛnz/) the 14th letter of the English alphabet. 英文字母的第十四个字母。

nab /næb; næb/ *vt* **(-bb-)** (colloq) catch in wrong-doing; seize: (口)逮捕; 捉: *The thief was nabbed by the police.* 小偷被警察逮住了。

na·bob /ˈneɪbɒb; ˋnebɑb/ *n* (18th c use) wealthy, luxury-loving person. (十八世纪用语)富有而喜爱奢华的人。

na·celle /næˈsel; nəˋsɛl/ *n* outer casing for an engine of an aircraft or airship. (飞机的)发动机短舱; (飞艇的)吊舱。⇨ the illus at **air**. 参看 air 之插图。

nacre /ˈneɪkə(r); ˋnekɚ/ *n* [U] mother-of-pearl. 珠母层; 真珠母。⇨ **nother** (4).

na·dir /ˈneɪdɪə(r); ˋnedɚ/ *n* point of the heavens directly beneath an observer; (fig) lowest, weakest, point: 天底; (喻)最低点; 最弱点: *at the ~ of one's hopes*. 希望极为渺茫。⇨ **zenith.**

nag[1] /næg; næg/ *n* (colloq) (usu old) horse. (口)(通常指老的)马; 驽马。

nag[2] /næg; næg/ *vt, vi* **(-gg-)** [VP6A, 2A, C, 3A] ***nag (at)(sb),*** find fault with continuously; worry or annoy by scolding: 不断地挑剔(某人); 以责骂来恼人: *She nagged (at) him all day long*. 她整天唠唠叨叨地责骂他。**nag·ger** *n*

naiad /ˈnaɪæd; ˋneæd/ *n* (*pl* **~s, ~es** /-diːz; -ˌdiz/) (Gk myth) water-nymph. (希神)水神。

nail /neɪl; nel/ *n* **1** layer of hard substance over the outer tip of a finger **(ˈfinger-~)** or toe **(ˈtoe-~)**. 指甲(finger-nail 手指甲, toe-nail 脚趾甲)。⇨ the illus at **arm, leg.** 参看 arm, leg 之插图。***fight tooth and ~***, with all one's strength, making every possible effort to win. 尽全力攻击以求胜。**ˈ~·brush** *n* for cleaning the ~s. 指甲刷。⇨ the illus at **brush.** 参看 brush 之插图。**ˈ~-file,** small, flat file for shaping the ~s. 指甲锉。**ˈ~-scissors** *n* for trimming the ~s. 指甲剪刀。**ˈ~-varnish/-polish** *n* for giving a shiny tint to the ~s. 指甲油。**2** piece of metal, pointed at one end and with a head at the other, (to be) hammered into articles to hold them together, or into a wall, etc to hang sth on. 钉; 铁钉; 钢钉。***drive a ~ into sb's coffin,*** ⇨ **coffin.** ***as hard as ~s,*** (of a person) (指人) **(a)** in first-rate physical condition. 身体极为健壮的; 最佳健康状况中的。**(b)** pitiless; unsympathetic. 无情的; 无同情心的; 冷酷的。***hit the ~ on the head,*** pick out the real point at issue; give the true explanation. 一针见血; 说中; 解释正确; 中肯。***right as ~s,*** quite right. 完全对的。***right on the ~,*** at once. 立即; 立刻。□ *vt* [VP15A, B] **1** make fast with a ~ or ~s: 用钉钉牢: *~ a lid on a box*. 把箱盖钉牢。***~ sb down (to sth),*** make him say clearly what he intends to do (about sth). 使某人明白说出他打算做的事; 使某人负责。***~ sth down,*** make (eg a carpet, a cover) secure by using nails. 用钉子钉牢(如地毯、遮盖物等)。***~ sth up,*** make (a door, window, etc) secure with ~s. 用钉子钉住或钉牢(门、窗等)。***~ one's colours to the mast,*** ⇨ **colour**[1]**(8)**. ***~ a lie (to the counter),*** prove that a statement is false. 证实某些话是假的; 拆穿谎言。**2** hold fast, keep fixed (a person, sb's attention, etc): 使固定; 使不动; 捉牢; 吸引(人、某人的注意力等): *He ~ed me in the corridor*. 他在走廊缠住我(不让我走开)。

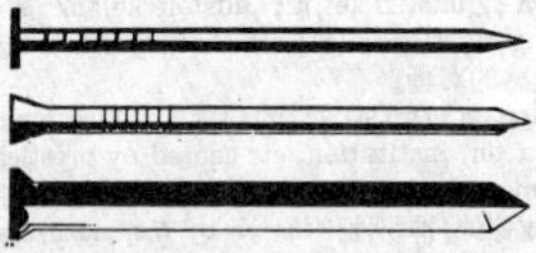

nails

nain·sook /ˈneɪnsʊk; ˋnensʊk/ *n* [U] fine cotton cloth. 细棉布。

naira /ˈnaɪrə; ˋnaɪrə/ *n* [C] unit of Nigerian currency, = 100 kobos. 奈拉(尼日利亚货币单位, 合 100 科博)。

naïve, naive /naɪˈiːv; nɑˋiv/ *adj* natural and innocent in speech and behaviour (eg because young or inexperienced); amusingly simple: 言行自然而天真的(如因年轻或无经验所致); 质朴的: *~ remarks/tourists*. 天真的话(观光客)。**~·ly** *adv* **~té** /-teɪ; -te/, **~ty** /-tɪ; -tɪ/ *n* [U] artlessness; being ~; [C] ~ remark, etc. 天真; 质朴; 天真的话等。

naked /ˈneɪkɪd; ˋnekɪd/ *adj* **1** without clothes on: 裸体的: *as ~ as the day he was born*. 象他初生时那样赤裸裸的。**2** without the usual covering: 没有通常的遮盖物的: *a ~ sword,* without its sheath; 无鞘之剑; *fight with ~ fists,* without boxing-gloves; 不带拳击手套的打斗; *~ trees,* without leaves; 光秃秃(无叶)的树; *a ~ light,* not protected from the wind by glass, without a lampshade. 没有灯罩的灯。***see sth with the ~ eye,*** without using a microscope, telescope or other aid to seeing. 用肉眼看某物(不用显微镜、望远镜或任何其他助视器)。***the ~ truth,*** not disguised, softened, ornamented. 原原本本的事实; 赤裸裸的事实。**~·ly** *adv* **~·ness** *n*

namby-pamby /ˌnæmbɪ ˈpæmbɪ; ˋnæmbɪˋpæmbɪ/ *adj* (of persons, talk) foolishly sentimental. (指人、言谈)感伤得可笑的。□ *n* person of this sort. 感伤得可笑之人。

name[1] /neɪm; nem/ *n* **1** word(s) by which a person, animal, place, thing, etc is known and spoken to or of: 名字; 名称: *A person of the ~ of Smith* (= Someone who is called Smith) *wants to see you*. 有个名叫史密斯的人要见你。*He writes under the ~ of Nimrod,* uses Nimrod instead of his real name. 他用尼蒙洛这个名字发表著作。*I know the man by ~,* only by hearsay, not by personal acquaintance. 我只知道这个人的名字。*The teacher knows all the pupils in his class by ~,* knows them individually. 该教师知道他班上全部学生的名字。***in the ~ of,*** **(a)** with the authority of: 凭…的权威: *Stop! in the Queen's ~*. 停住! 凭女王的名义(命令你)。*In the ~ of the law...* 凭法律…。**(b)** in the cause of (used when making an appeal): 为…的缘故(在提出一项恳求时使用): *In the ~ of common sense, what are you doing?* 你

究竟在干什么? *call sb ~s*, call him insulting ~s (eg liar, coward). 辱骂某人(为说谎者, 懦夫等)。 *enter/put down one's ~ for*, (a school, college, etc), apply for entry (at a future date). 申请(于将来某一日期)入(学校, 大学等)。 *not have a penny to one's ~*, be without money. 没有钱; 一文不名。 *lend one's ~ to*, (an enterprise, etc), allow it to be quoted in support or in favour of (the enterprise, etc). 让自己的名字被列为(一项事业等)的赞助人。 *take sb's ~ in vain*, use a ~ (esp God's) disrespectfully. 滥用某人的名字(尤指上帝之名)。 **'~-day** *n* feast day of the Saint whose ~ one was given at christening. 命名日(本人教名所纪念的圣徒的节日)。 **'~-dropping** *n* the practice of casually mentioning the ~s of important people to impress. 随便地提起重要人物的名字给人印象以提高身份。 Hence, 由此产生, **'~-drop** *vi* [VP2A] talk in this way. 随便提起要人名字以提高身份。 **'~-part** *n* title-role of a play: 戏名角色: *Who will play the ~-part in 'Hamlet'?* 谁将饰演'哈姆雷特'中的哈姆雷特? **'~-plate** *n* plaque(on the door of a building, room, etc) with the ~ of the occupant. 名牌(挂于建筑物、房间等门上的金属板, 上有使用人的姓名)。 **'~-sake** *n* person or thing with the same ~ as another. 同名的人或物。 **2** (*sing* only) reputation; fame. (仅用单数)名誉; 声誉。*make/win a ~ for oneself*, become well-known. 使自己成名; 为自己赢得名声。 *The firm has a ~ for good workmanship*. 这家公司以手艺精良著称。 **3** famous person: 著名的人物: *the great ~s of history*. 历史上的伟人。

name[2] /neɪm; nem/ *vt* **1** [VP6A, 14, 23] ~ *(after/* (US) *for)*, give a ~ to: 命名: *They ~d the child John*. 他们给小孩取名名为约翰。 *The child was ~d after its father*, given its father's first ~. 这个小孩以他父亲的名字为名字。 *Tasmania was ~d after its discoverer, A J Tasman*. 塔斯曼尼亚是以它的发现者塔斯曼为名。 **2** [VP6A] say the ~(s) of: 说出 … 的名字: *Can you ~ all the plants and trees in this garden?* 你能说出这花园里所有花草树木的名称吗? **3** make an offer of (price etc): 提出 (价格等): *N~ your price*, Say what price you want. 开出你的价格。 **4** state (what is desired, etc): 说出; 指定; 订定(所欲求者等): *Please ~ the day*, say on what date you will be willing to (eg marry). 请指定日期。 **5** [VP6A, 14] ~ *(for)*, nominate for, appoint to, a position: 提名; 任命: *Mr X has been ~d for the directorship*. 某先生已经被提名担任董事职务。

name·less /'neɪmlɪs; 'nemləs/ *adj* **1** not having a name; having an unknown name: 无名的; 不知名的: *a ~ grave*; 没有名字的墓; *a well-known person who shall be ~*, whose name I shall not mention. 姑隐其名的某一名人。 **2** too bad to be named: 太恶劣而不宜说明的: *~ vices*. 不堪说明的恶行。 **3** difficult or impossible to name or describe: 难以名状的; 无法描述的: *a ~ longing/horror*. 一种无可名状的渴望(恐惧)。

name·ly /'neɪmlɪ; 'nemlɪ/ *adv* that is to say: 即; 就是: *Only one boy was absent*, ~ *Harry*. 只有一个男孩缺席, 就是哈里。

nan·keen /næn'kiːn; næn'kin/ *n* [U] kind of cotton cloth, originally made of naturally yellow cotton. (一种结实耐穿的) 本色布(原产中国南京)。

nanny /'nænɪ; 'nænɪ/ *n* (*pl* -nies) = nurse[1](1).

nanny-goat /'nænɪ gəʊt; 'nænɪˌgot/ *n* female goat. 母山羊, 牝山羊。 ⇨ **billy-goat**.

nap[1] /næp; næp/ *n* [C] short sleep (esp during the day, not necessarily in bed): 小睡; 打盹(尤指在白天, 不一定要躺在床上上): *have/take a nap after lunch on a hot day*. 热天午饭后小睡片刻。 □ *vi* **(-pp-)** (rare, except in) (罕, 除非用于) *catch sb napping*, find him asleep; catch him unawares (in error, etc). 看到某人在打盹; 乘某人不备而抓到他的过错等。

nap[2] /næp; næp/ *n* [U] surface of cloth, felt, etc, made of soft, short hairs or fibres, smoothed and brushed up. (绒布、呢等上面的一层) 细毛。

nap[3] /næp; næp/ *n* (GB) name of a card-game. (英) 一

种纸牌戏。

na·palm /'neɪpɑːm; 'neˌpɑm/ *n* [U] jellied petroleum used in making fire-bombs. 凝固汽油; 胶化汽油; 纳鲍油(用以制造烧夷弹)。

nape /neɪp; nep/ *n* back (of the neck). 颈背。 ⇨ the illus at **head**. 参看 head 之插图。

na·pery /'neɪpərɪ; 'nepərɪ/ *n* [U] (old use) household linen, esp table linen (tablecloths and napkins). (旧用法) 布巾; (尤指) 桌布; 餐巾。

naph·tha /'næfθə; 'næfθə/ *n* [U] kinds of inflammable oil obtained from coaltar and petroleum 石油精; 石脑油(从煤焦油和石油中提炼出来的可燃油)。 **~·lene** /-liːn; -ˌlin/ *n* [U] strong-smelling substance made from coaltar and petroleum, used in the manufacture of dyes and (in the form of white 'moth balls') to put among clothes. 萘; 臭樟脑; 酵瑙脑; 骈苯(从煤焦油和石油中提炼出来一种气味浓烈的物质, 用以制造染料及防蛀丸等)。

nap·kin /'næpkɪn; 'næpkɪn/ *n* [C] **1** ('table) ~, piece of cloth used at meals for protecting clothing, for wiping the lips, etc. 餐巾。 **'~-ring** *n* ring to hold and distinguish a person's ~. 套餐巾的小环。 ⇨ **serviette**. **2** (US 美 = *diaper*) (*nappy* is more usu) towel folded round a baby's bottom and between its legs, to absorb excreta. 婴孩的尿布(nappy 较常用)。

Na·po·leonic /nəˌpəʊlɪ'ɒnɪk; nəˌpolɪ'ɑnɪk/ *adj* of or like Napoleon Bonaparte, ruler of France. (法国统治者) 拿破仑一世的; 似拿破仑一世的。

nappy /'næpɪ; 'næpɪ/ *n* (*pl* -pies) (GB colloq) (英口) = **napkin**(2).

nar·ciss·ism /'nɑːsɪsɪzəm; nɑr'sɪsˌɪzəm/ *n* [U] (psych) obsessive and exclusive interest in one's own self. (心理) 自体观窥狂; 自恋; 自爱欲。

nar·cissus /nɑː'sɪsəs; nɑr'sɪsəs/ *n* (*pl* -es -səsɪz, -səsɪz or -cissi -sɪsaɪ, -sɪˌsaɪ) sorts of bulb plant (daffodil, jonquil, etc), esp the kind having heavily scented white or yellow flowers in the sprirg. 水仙花。

nar·cotic /nɑː'kɒtɪk; nɑr'kɑtɪk/ *n, adj* (kinds of drug) producing sleep, often blunting the senses and, in large doses, producing complete insensibility: 麻醉剂, 麻醉的; 催眠的: *Opium is a ~ drug*. 鸦片是一种麻醉药。 *The use of ~s by teenagers is a problem in many countries*; 青少年服麻醉药在许多国家中是一个问题; (person) addicted to ~s. 服用麻醉药成瘾的(人); 瘾君子。

nark[1] /nɑːk; nɑrk/ *n* (GB sl) police decoy or spy. (英俚) 协助警察诱捕人犯的人, 密探。

nark[2] /nɑːk; nɑrk/ *vt* (GB sl) annoy: (英俚) 烦扰; 使苦恼: *feel ~ed at unjust criticism*. 对不公正的批评感到苦恼。

nar·rate /nə'reɪt; næ'ret/ *vt* [VP6A] tell (a story); give an account of: 讲(故事); 叙述: ~ *one's adventures*. 叙述奇遇。 **nar·rator** /-tə(r); -tɔ/ *n* person who ~s. 讲述者; 叙述者。 **nar·ra·tion** /nə'reɪʃn; næ'reʃən/ *n* [U] telling of a story, etc; [C] story; account of events. 讲述; 故事; 叙述。

nar·ra·tive /'nærətɪv; 'nærətɪv/ *n* **1** [C] story or tale; orderly account of events; 故事; 叙述; 讲述; [U] (composition that consists of) story-telling. 故事; 叙述; 叙事体。 **2** (attrib) in the form of, concerned with, story-telling: (用作定语) 叙述的: ~ *literature*, stories and novels; 叙事文学(故事及小说); ~ *poems*; 叙事诗; *a writer of great ~ power*, able to describe events well. 富有叙述能力的作家。

nar·row /'nærəʊ; 'næro/ *adj* **(-er, -est)** (opposite of *wide*) (为 wide 之反义词) **1** measuring little across in comparison with length: 窄的: *a ~ bridge*. 窄桥。 *The road was too ~ for cars to pass*. 这条路太窄了, 车辆过不去。 *A ~-gauge railway is one with rails less than 4 ft 8 in apart* 窄轨铁路是轨宽不到四英尺八英寸的铁路。 **2** small, limited; esp in extent: 狭小的; 有限制的: *a ~ circle of friends*; 交游狭小; *living in ~ circumstances*, in poverty. 生活于贫穷中。 **3** with a small margin: 所余不多的; 勉强的: *a*

~ *escape from death*. 勉强逃过死亡; 九死一生. **a ~ squeak,** (colloq) sth barely avoided or escaped from. (口) 幸免于难. *elected by a ~ majority,* eg when voting is 67 to 64. 以差距甚小之多数当选(如以 67 票对 64 票当选). **4** strict; exact: 严格的; 精确的: *a ~ search.* 严密的搜查. *What does the word mean in the ~est sense?* 就最精确含义来说, 这个词是什么意思? **5** limited in outlook; having little sympathy for the ideas, etc, of others. 褊狭的; 度量小的. **,~-'minded** /'maɪndɪd/ 'maɪndɪd/ *adj* not easily seeing or sympathizing with the ideas of others. 胸襟褊狭的; 度量小的. **,~-'minded·ly** *adv* **,~-'minded·ness** *n* □ *vt, vi* [VP6A, 2A] (cause to) become ~. 使窄小; 变窄. □ *n* (usu *pl*) ~ strait or channel between two larger bodies of water; ~ place in a river or pass. (通常用复数)海峡; 江峡; 狭路. **~·ly** *adv* **1** only just; with little to spare: 仅仅; 勉强地: *He ~ly escaped drowning.* 他差一点儿淹死. **2** closely; carefully: 严密地; 仔细地: *Watch that fellow ~ly.* 注意看着那家伙. **~·ness** *n*

nar·whal /'nɑːwəl; 'nɑrhwəl/ *n* Arctic whale with (in the male) a long spiral tusk. 一角鱼; 角獭(一种产于北极的鲸鱼, 雄者有一螺旋形的长牙).

na·sal /'neɪzl; 'nezl/ *adj* of, for, in the nose: 鼻的; 为鼻子的; 在鼻中的: *~ sounds,* eg /m, n, ŋ/; 鼻音(如 /m, n, ŋ/); *~ catarrh;* 鼻粘膜炎; *a ~ douche.* 鼻孔灌洗; 鼻孔灌洗器. □ *n* [C] nasal sound. 鼻音. **~·ize** /'neɪzəlaɪz; 'nezl,aɪz/ *vt* [VP6A] make (a sound) with the air stream, or part of it, passing through the nose. 使鼻音化.

nascent /'næsnt; 'næsn̩t/ *adj* (formal) coming into existence; beginning to exist. (正式用语) 初生的; 初期的.

nas·tur·tium /nə'stɜːʃəm US: næ-; næ'stɜ(r)ʃəm/ *n* [C] garden plant with red, orange or yellow flowers, round-shaped leaves, and seeds that may be pickled and eaten. 藻菜; 金莲花.

nasty /'nɑːstɪ US: 'næ-; 'næstɪ/ *adj* (**-ier, -iest**) **1** dirty; disgusting; unpleasant: 脏的; 令人厌恶的; 令人不快的: *medicine with a ~ smell and a nastier taste.* 既难闻而且更难吃的药. **2** morally dirty and unpleasant: 在道德上令人不快的; 淫猥的; 卑鄙的: *a man with a ~ mind;* 心思卑鄙的人; *~ stories.* 下流的故事. **3** showing ill will and spite: 表示恶意的; 坏心眼的: *a ~ temper.* 坏脾气. **4** dangerous; threatening: 危险的; 带有威胁意味的; 威胁人的: *There was a ~ sea when we got out of the harbour.* 我们离港后, 海上风浪险恶. *There was a ~ look in his eye.* 他的眼中露出威胁的眼光. **5** causing difficulty or danger; awkward: 引起困难或危险的; 难应付的: *That's a ~ corner for a car that's travelling fast.* 那是个开快车不容易通过的街角. **nas·tily** /-ɪlɪ; -əlɪ/ *adv* **nas·ti·ness** *n*

na·tal /'neɪtl; 'netl/ *adj* of, from, one's birth. 诞生的; 初生的; 出生的.

na·tion /'neɪʃn; 'neʃən/ *n* [C] large community of people associated with a particular territory usu speaking a single language and usu having a political character or political aspirations: 国家; 民族: *the ~s of Western Europe;* 西欧诸国; *the United N~s Organization,* UNO. 联合国组织. ⇨ **state¹(2).** ,~'wide *adj, adv* throughout a ~; concerning, expressed by, all citizens. 遍及全国(的), 有关全国公民的; 由全国人民所表示的; 全国性的.

na·tion·al /'næʃnəl; 'næʃənl/ *adj* of a/the nation; common to a/the whole nation; characteristic of a/the nation: 国家的; 国有的; 全国普遍的; 国民的; 民族的; 某国家或民族特有的: *a ~ theatre,* one supported by the State; 国立剧院; 国家剧院; *~ opposition to a government policy,* expressed by all citizens. 全国人民对政府某项政策的普遍反对. **,~ 'anthem,** song or hymn of a nation (eg 'God Save the Queen' in GB). 国歌(如英国国歌'天佑吾王'). **the ,N~ 'Debt,** total money owed by the State to those who have lent it money. 国债; 公债.

,~ 'monument, structure, landmark, site of historic interest (often one maintained by the government). 国家古迹(通常由政府所维护). **,~ 'park,** area of land declared to be public property, for the use and enjoyment of the people 国家公园. **,~ 'service,** period of compulsory service in the armed forces. 国民兵役. **,N~ 'Trust,** (in GB) society founded in 1895 to preserve places of natural beauty or historic interest for the nation. (英) 国家信托社 (创立于一八九五年, 旨国家保护天然风景区或历史古迹). **the ,Grand 'N~,** the chief steeplechase in **GB,** run in March. (每年三月举行的)英国大赛马. □ *n* citizen of a particular nation; (某一国之) 公民; 国民: *One of a consul's duties is to help his own ~s,* his fellow countrymen. 领事职责之一是协助他自己的同胞. **~·ly** /'næʃnəlɪ; 'næʃənlɪ/ *adv*

na·tion·al·ism /'næʃnəlɪzəm; 'næʃənl,ɪzəm/ *n* [U] **1** strong devotion to one's own nation; patriotic feelings, efforts, principles. 爱国心; 国家主义; 民族主义. **2** movement for political/economic, etc independence in a country controlled by another). 政治(经济等)独立运动(指受他国管制的国家内的).

na·tion·al·ist /'næʃnəlɪst; 'næʃənl,ɪst/ *n* supporter of nationalism(2): 政治独立运动的拥护者: *Scottish ~s,* those who want Scotland to have more self-government. 苏格兰自治论者. □ *adj* (also 亦作 **~·ic** /,næʃnə'lɪstɪk; ,næʃən'ɪstɪk/)favouring, supporting, nationalism: 国家主义的; 民族主义的; 政治独立运动的; 拥护国家独立的: *~ movements in Zimbabwe.* 津巴布韦的民族独立运动.

na·tion·al·ity /,næʃə'nælətɪ; ,næʃən'æləti/ *n* (*pl* **-ties**) [C, U] being a member of a nation: 国籍: *What is your ~?* 你是哪一国的人? *There were men of all nationalities in Geneva.* 在日内瓦有各种国籍的人.

na·tion·al·ize /'næʃnəlaɪz; 'næʃənl,aɪz/ *vt* [VP6A] **1** transfer from private to State ownership: 使归为国有; 国有化: *~ the railways/the coal-mines/the steel industry.* 使铁路(煤矿, 钢铁工业)归为国有. **2** make (a person) a national; 使归化为国民; 使归化: *~d Poles and Greeks in the US.* 已归化为美国人的波兰人与希腊人. **3** make into a nation: 使成为国家: *The Poles were ~d after the war of 1914—1918,* They became an independent nation. 在一九一四至一九一八年战争后, 波兰获得独立. **na·tion·ali·zation** /,næʃnəlaɪ'zeɪʃn US: -lɪ'z-;,næʃənl'ɪ'zeʃən/ *n* nationalizing or being ~: 收归国有; 国有化; 归化: *the nationalization of the railways.* 铁路国有化.

na·tive /'neɪtɪv; 'netɪv/ *n* **1** person born in a place, country, etc and associated with it by birth: (生于该地且与该地有渊源的)某地人; 某国人: *a ~ of London/Wales/India/Kenya.* 伦敦(威尔士, 印度, 肯尼亚)人. **2** such a person as distinguished from immigrants, residents, visitors, tourists, etc from other countries, usu when the race to which he belongs is different in culture:(别于从外国来的移民、居民、游客、观光客等的)当地人; 土人(通常指文化迥异者): *the first meetings between Captain Cook and the ~s* (=the aboriginal inhabitants) *of Australia.* 库克船长与澳洲土著最初几次的会面. **3** animal or plant natural to and having its origin in a certain area. 原产于某地域的动物或植物; 土生的动(植)物: *The kangaroo is a ~ of Australia.* 袋鼠是澳大利亚的土产动物. **4** (GB) oyster reared wholly or partly in British waters, esp in artificial beds: (英)全部或部份养殖于英国水域的蚝(尤指生长于人工养殖场的): *Whitstable ~s.* 威兹特布尔土产的蚝. □ *adj* **1** associated with the place and circumstances of one's birth: 出生地的; 与出生地有关联的: *your ~ land/place.* 你的祖国(故乡). **2** of ~s (2 above): 当地的; 土著的: *~ customs.* 土著的风俗. **3** (of qualities) belonging to a person by nature, not acquired through training, by education, etc: (指性质)本性的; 天赋的; 天然的: *~ ability/charm.* 天赋才能(魅力). **4** **~ to,** (of plants, animals, etc) having their origin in: (指动植物等)原属于…的; 源于…的; 土产的; 原产于: *plants ~ to America,* eg tobacco, potatoes. 原产于美洲的

植物(如烟草、马铃薯)。*One of the animals ~ to India is the tiger.* 老虎是印度土产动物之一。**5** (of metals) found in a pure state, uncombined with other substances: (指金属)天然纯净的: ~ *gold.* 原金。

na·tiv·ity /nə'tɪvətɪ; nə'tɪvətɪ/ *n* (*pl* **-ties**) birth, esp **(the N~)** of Jesus Christ; picture of the N~ of Christ. 诞生; (尤指)耶稣基督的诞生; 基督诞生图。**a 'N~ Play,** one about the N~. 基督诞生剧。

nat·ter /'nætə(r); 'nætɚ/ *vi* [VP2A, C] (GB colloq) chatter, grumble (esp to oneself): (英口)(尤指对自己)喋喋不休; 发怨言; 抱怨: *What's she ~ing (on) about now?* 她在抱怨什么？

natty /'nætɪ; 'nætɪ/ *adj* (**-ier, -iest**) (colloq) (口) **1** neat: smart and tidy: 整洁的; 漂亮干净的: *new and ~ uniforms for bus conductresses.* 给公共汽车女售票员穿的整洁的新制服。**2** quick and skilful. 敏捷而灵巧的。**nat·tily** /-ɪlɪ; -əlɪ/ *adv*

nat·u·ral /'nætʃrəl; 'nætʃərəl/ *adj* **1** of concerned with, produced, by nature; by nature: 自然的; 有关自然的; 天然产生的: *animals living in their ~ state,* wild, not domesticated; 生活于自然环境中的动物; *a country's ~ resources,* its minerals, forests, etc: 一国之天然资源; *land in its ~ state.* not used for industry, farming, etc. 未用于工业或未加耕种的土地。,~'**forces/phe'nomena,** the forces of nature, such as storms, thunder and lightning. 自然力量(现象)(如暴风雨,雷电等)。~' **gas,** gas occurring with petroleum deposits, eg North Sea gas. 天然气(蕴藏于石油层中,如北海天然气)。,~'**history,** botany and zoology; (formerly) scientific study of all nature. 动植物学; (昔时)博物学(研究自然界万物的科学)。,~ '**law,** rules for behaviour considered as innate and universal. 自然法则; 被认为是天生且普遍化的行为准则; 天理。,~ **phi'losophy,** (name formerly used for) the science of physics, or physics and dynamics. (旧名称)物理学; 物理学与力学。,~ **re'ligion,** religion and ethics based on reason (contrasted with religion from divine revelation). 自然宗教(基于理性的宗教及伦理,与出自神启的宗教相对)。,~ **se'lection,** evolutionary theory that animals and plants survive or become extinct in accordance with their ability to adapt themselves to their environment. 天择; 自然淘汰(动植物的生存或绝种系视其对环境的适应力而定的进化论)。**2** of, in agreement with, the nature(4) of a living thing: 本性的; 天性的: ~ *gifts/abilities.* 天赋。**3** (of persons) possessing qualities by nature(4); born with qualities or powers: (指人)天生赋有某些性质的; 生而具有某些性质或能力的: *He's a ~ orator,* makes speeches easily. 他是天生的演说家。*She's a ~ linguist,* learns languages easily. 她是个天生的语言学家(善于学习语言)。*It comes ~ to her.* 那事对于她不学自会。⇨ **come(10).** **4** ordinary: normal; to be expected: 普通的; 正常的; 预期的: *die a ~ death,* not as the result of an accident, violence, etc. 自然死亡(非因意外或横死); 寿终正寝。*It is ~ for a bird to fly.* 鸟会飞是自然的。*He was sentenced to prison for the term of his ~ life,* ie until he died. 他被处无期徒刑(终身监禁)。**5** simple; not cultivated or self-conscious: 自然的: 不造作的: ~ *behaviour;* 自然的行为(非故意的); *speak in a ~ voice,* not affected. 用自然(不造作)的声调说话。*It was a ~ piece of acting,* with no exaggeration. 那是自然的演出(毫无夸张的)。**6** (music) neither sharp nor flat: (音乐)本位音的; 自然的: *B ~* (cf 参较 *B sharp, B flat*). 本位 B 调。⇨ the illus at **notation.** 参看 notation 之插图。**7** (of a son or daughter) illegitimate: (指子女)不合法的; 私生的。□ *n* **1** (music) ~ note; musical note that is not a sharp or a flat; the sign (♮) placed before a note in (printed music) to make it ~: (音乐)本位音; 本位音符; 键盘上之白键; (乐谱上之)本位记号(♮)。**2** person born without ordinary intelligence; person feeble-minded from birth. 低能之人; 白痴。**3** (colloq) (口) *a ~ for sth,* person naturally fitted or qualified: 天生适合(作某事)的人: *He's a ~ for the job/the part.* 他是天生适合做那件工作(担任那个职位)的人。

natu·ral·ism /'nætʃrəlɪzəm; 'nætʃərəl,ɪzəm/ *n* [U] **1** adherence to nature in literature and art; drawing and painting things in a way true to nature. (文学及艺术的)自然主义; 写实主义; 写实。**2** (phil) system of thought which rejects the supernatural and divine revelation and holds that natural causes and laws explain all phenomena. (哲学)自然主义(反对超自然或神启,主张天然因素现象及法则解释一切现象)。

natu·ral·ist /'nætʃrəlɪst; 'nætʃərəlɪst/ *n* person who makes a special study of animals or plants. 博物学家; 研究动(植)物的人。

natu·ral·is·tic /ˌnætʃrə'lɪstɪk; ˌnætʃərə'lɪstɪk/ *adj* of naturalism: 自然主义的; 写实派的: *a ~ painter.* 写实派画家。⇨ **abstract¹(1), cubism, surrealism.**

natu·ral·ize /'nætʃrəlaɪz; 'nætʃərəl,aɪz/ *vt, vi* **1** [VP6A] give (sb from another country) rights of citizenship: 予(外国人)公民权; 使归化; 使入籍: *She was ~d in Japan,* was made a Japanese subject. 她入日本国籍。**2** [VP6A] take (a word) from one language into another: 将(某一语言中之字或词)采用于另一种语言: *English sporting terms have been ~d in many languages.* 英语的运动名词已经被许多语言所采用。**3** [VP6A] introduce and acclimatize (an animal or plant) into another country. 移殖(动物); 移植(植物)。**4** [VP6A] plant (bulbs, etc) in woodland areas so that the flowers appear to be growing wild or naturally. 把(鳞茎等)种植于森林地区使其花卉自然生长。**5** [VP2A] become ~d. 归化。**natu·ral·iz·ation** /ˌnætʃrəlaɪ'zeɪʃn US: -lɪ'z-, ˌnætʃərəl'zeʃən/ *n* [U] naturalizing or being ~d: 归化; 入籍; 移置; 移植: *Naturalization papers,* the documents that prove that a person has been admitted to citizenship of another country. 归化证书(证明一个人已取得他国公民权之文件)。

nat·ur·ally /'nætʃrəlɪ; 'nætʃərəlɪ/ *adv* **1** by nature (4): 天性地; 天生地: *She's ~ musical.* 她天性喜爱音乐。**2** of course; as might be expected: 当然; 必然地: '*Did you answer her letter?'—'N~!* '你回了她的信吗?'——'当然啰'。**3** without artificial help, special cultivation, etc: 无人工帮助或特别培植等地; 天然地: *Her hair curls ~.* 她的头发自然卷曲。*Plants grow ~ in such a good climate.* 在这么好的气候里, 植物能自然生长。**4** without artifice: 不用手段地; 自然地: *She speaks and behaves ~.* 她的言谈和举止都很自然。

na·ture /'neɪtʃə(r); 'netʃɚ/ *n* **1** [U] the whole universe and every created thing: 自然; 自然界; 宇宙万物: *Is ~ at its best in spring?* 自然界在春天最美好吗?~ **study,** the study of animals, plants, insects, etc: 动植物、昆虫等的研究; 自然研究。'~ **worship,** the worship of trees, oceans, the winds, etc. 自然崇拜(对树、海洋、风等之自然崇拜)。**2** [U] force(s) controlling the phenomena of the physical world: 自然力; 控制物质世界现象的力量: *Man is engaged in a constant struggle with ~.* 人类不断地与大自然竞争。*Miracles are contrary to ~.* 奇迹是与自然力相反的。~ **cure,** form of therapy relying upon natural remedies (sunlight, diet, exercise). 自然疗法(靠天然治疗物如日光、食物、运动的一种疗法)。*pay the debt of ~; pay one's debt to ~,* die. 死亡。*in the course of ~,* according to the ordinary course of things. 根据事物的常规。**3** [U] simple life without civilization; outdoor, animal-like existence: 自然的生活; 无文明的简单生活; 户外的似兽类的生活: *Some 18th-century writers were in favour of a return to ~,* to the simple and primitive life that people were thought to have led before mankind became civilized. 有些十八世纪作家赞成回返自然的生活(文明前的原始生活)。*be in a state of ~,* be completely naked (as in a nudist camp). 全裸着(如天体营中者)。**4** [C, U] qualities and characteristics, physical, mental and spiritual, which belong to a person or thing: 天性; 性质: *It is the ~ of a dog to bark.* 吠是狗的天性。*Cats and dogs have quite different ~s.* 猫和狗有相当不同的天性。*That man is proud by ~.* 那个人天性骄傲。*Chemists study the*

~ *of gases*. 化学家研究气体的性质. **,human '~**, the qualities possessed by man (in contrast with animals). 人性(与兽性相对). **good ~**, unselfishness; willingness and readiness to help; kind-heartedness. 善良的本性(不私、乐于助人、仁慈等). Hence, 由此产生, **good-/ill-'~ed**, having a good /ill ~. 本性善良(邪恶)的. **5** qualities of non-material things (eg art, knowledge, language). 抽象之物(例如艺术、知识、语言)的性质. **6** sort; kind: 种类: *Things of this ~ do not interest me*. 这类事物不会使我感兴趣. *His request was in the ~ of a command, could not be ignored*. 他的要求就是一命令令.

na·tur·ism /'neɪtʃərɪzəm/ 'netʃərɪzəm/ n nudism. 裸体主义. **na·tur·ist** /-ɪst/ -ɪst/ n nudist. 裸体主义者.

naught /nɔːt/ n = **nought**(1).

naughty /'nɔːtɪ; 'nɔtɪ/ adj (**-ier, -iest**) **1** (of children, their behaviour, etc) bad; wrong; disobedient; causing trouble: (指儿童,其行为等)坏的;错的;不听从的;惹麻烦的;顽皮的;淘气的: *a ~ child*. 顽皮的小孩. *It was ~ of you to pull the cat's tail*. 你拉猫的尾巴太顽皮了. **2** taking pleasure in shocking, intended to shock; people: 以令人震惊或反感为乐的; 企图令人震惊或反感的; 猥亵的: *a ~ novel(ist)*; 猥亵的小说(小说家); ~ *stories*. 猥亵的故事. **naught·ily** /-ɪlɪ; -əlɪ/ adv **naughti·ness** n

nausea /'nɔːsɪə; 'nɔzɪə/ n [U] feeling of sickness (eg as caused by bad food) or disgust; seasickness: 作呕; 恶心; 晕船: *overcome by ~ after eating octopus*; 吃了章鱼后感到恶心; *filled with ~ at the sight of cruelty to animals*. 看到虐待动物心中充满厌恶. **naus·eate** /'nɔːsɪeɪt US: 'nɔːz-; 'nɔzɪˌet/ vt [VP6A] cause ~: 使作呕; 使恶心: *nauseating food*; 令人作呕的食物; *a nauseating sight*. 令人恶心的情景. **naus·eous** /'nɔːsɪəs US: 'nɔːʃəs; 'nɔzəs/ adj disgusting; causing ~. 令人厌恶的; 令人作呕的.

nautch /nɔːtʃ; nɔtʃ/ n performance by a professional dancing-girl ('**~girl**) in India, etc. (印度等之)职业舞女的表演; 印度舞.

nauti·cal /'nɔːtɪkl; 'nɔtɪkl/ adj of ships, sailors or navigation: 船舶的;船员的;航海的: ~ *terms*, used by sailors; 航海用语;航海用语; *a ~ almanac*. with information about the sun, moon, tides, etc; 航海历书(上载日、月、潮水等资料); *a ~ mile*, 1/60 of a degree, 6080 ft (= 1852 metres), 一海里; 一浬(为一纬度的六十分之一, 计 6080 英尺或 1852 公尺).

nauti·lus /'nɔːtɪləs US: 'nɔːtələs; 'nɔtḷəs/ n (pl **~es** /-ləsɪz/, -ləsɪz/) small sea animal of which the female has a very thin shell. 鹦鹉螺(小海生动物, 雌者壳极薄).

na·val /'neɪvl; 'nevḷ/ adj of a navy; of warships; 海军的; 军舰的: ~ *officers/battles*. 海军军官(海战).

nave /neɪv; nev/ n central part of a church where the people sit. 教堂的正厅(会众所坐的部份). ⇨ the illus at **church**. 参看 church 之插图.

na·vel /'neɪvl; 'nevḷ/ n small depression in the middle of the surface of the belly(left by the severance of the umbilical cord). 肚脐. ⇨ the illus at **trunk**. 参看 trunk 之插图. ~ **orange**, large orange with a ~-like formation in the top. 脐柑(顶端形状象肚脐).

navi·gable /'nævɪgəbl; 'nævəgəbḷ/ adj **1** (of rivers, seas, etc) that can be navigated; suitable for ships: (指江河、海洋等)可航行的;适于行船的: *The Rhine is ~ from Strasbourg to the sea*. 莱茵河从斯特拉斯堡到海口是可以通航. **2** (of ships, etc) that can be steered and sailed: (指船等)可驾驶的;可航行的: *not in a ~ condition*. 不能航行. **navi·ga·bil·ity** /ˌnævɪgə'bɪlɪtɪ; ˌnævəgə'bɪlətɪ/ n

navi·gate /'nævɪgeɪt; 'nævəˌget/ vt, vi [VP6A, 2A] **1** plot the course, find the position, etc of a ship or aircraft, etc, using maps and instruments. 利用地图及仪器测定 (船只或飞机等) 的航道、航线及位置等; 测航. **2** steer (a ship); pilot (an aircraft); (fig) direct: 驾驶(船只、飞机); (喻)指导; 使通过: ~ *a Bill through the House of Commons*. 使一个法案在下议院通过. **3** sail over (a sea); sail up or down (a river). 航行于 (海)上; 沿(河)而行.

向上游或下游航行; 的. **navigator** /-tə(r)/; -tɚ/ n **1** person who ~s(1). 测航者. **2** sailor with skill and experience who has taken part in many voyages; (esp) early explorer: 精于航术且富有航海经验的海员;航海者; (尤指)早期的探险者: *the 16th c Spanish and Portuguese navigators*. 十六世纪的西班牙与葡萄牙航海家.

navi·ga·tion /ˌnævɪ'geɪʃn; ˌnævə'geʃən/ n [U] **1** the act of navigating. 航行; 航海; 航空. **2** the art or science of navigating. 航行学; 航海术; 航空术. **3** the making of voyages on water or of journeys through the air: 水路航行; 空中航行: *inland ~*, by river and canal. 内河航行. *There has been an increase in ~ through the Panama Canal*, more ships use it. 通过巴拿马运河的船只一直在增加中.

navvy /'nævɪ; 'nævɪ/ n (pl **-vies**) (GB) unskilled workman. (英)无技术的工人; 粗工; 小工.

navy /'neɪvɪ; 'nevɪ/ n (pl **-vies**) **1** (a/the) ~, (with *sing* or *pl v*) that part of a country's military forces that is organized for fighting at sea: (与单数或复数动词连用)海军: *join the ~*; 参加海军; *an officer/sailor in the Royal N~*. 皇家海军军官(水兵). ~ **'blue**, dark blue as used for naval uniforms. (海军制服用的)深蓝色. **2** a country's warships collectively: (集合用法)海军(指一国之舰艇): *a small ~*. 舰艇为数甚少之海军.

nay /neɪ; ne/ adv (old use) no; (rhet) not only that, but also: (旧用法)不; 否; (修辞)不仅如此, 而且: *I suspect, nay, I am certain, that he is wrong*. 我不仅猜想而且确信他错了.

Nazi /'nɑːtsɪ; 'nɑtsɪ/ n, adj (member) of the German National Socialist Party founded by Hitler. 纳粹党 (希特勒所创的德国国家社会党)的; 纳粹党员. **Nazism** /'nɑːtsɪzəm; 'nɑts,ɪzəm/ n the ideology of the ~s. 纳粹主义.

Ne·an·der·thal /nɪ'ændəta:l; nɪ'ændɚˌtɑl/ adj ~ **man**, extinct type of man of the stone age. 尼安得特人(已绝种的石器时代原始人).

neap /niːp; nip/ n '~(-tide), tide when high water is at its lowest level of the year. 一年中的最低潮; 小潮. ⇨ spring tide at **spring**(3).

Nea·poli·tan /ˌnɪə'pɒlɪtən; ˌnɪə'pɑlətn/ n, adj **1** (inhabitant) of Naples. 那不勒斯的; 那不勒斯人. **2** (small n) with many flavours and colours: (小写)多种味道及颜色的: ~ *ice-cream*. 三色冰淇淋.

near¹ /nɪə(r); nɪr/ adj (**-er, -est**) **1** not far from; close in space or time: 不远的; (空间或时间上)接近的: *The post office is quite ~*. 邮局距离这边很近. *Christmas is ~*. 圣诞节快到了. *Come ~er*. 再走近些. *Can you tell me the ~est* (= shortest) *way to the station?* 你能告诉我去车站最近的路吗? *She was ~ to tears*, was almost crying. 她几乎哭了. *~ the ~ distance*, that part of a scene between the foreground and the background. 近景. *a ~ miss*, eg of a bomb or shell, not a direct hit, but close enough to the target to cause damage. (指弹或炮弹等)近似命中(虽非直接命中,但极接近目标而造成毁坏). *a ~ thing*, a narrow escape. 勉强的逃脱; 九死一生. '*~sighted* adj short-sighted; seeing well only when sth, eg a book, is held close to the eyes. 近视的. **2** close in relation or affection: 近亲的; 亲密的: *a ~ relation*, eg a mother, a son or daughter; 近亲(例如母亲、子或女); *friends who are ~ and dear to us*. 我们所亲近的朋友. **3** (contrasted with off) (of parts of animals and vehicles, or of horses in a team, when on a road, etc)the left side(与 off 相对)(指行走在路上等的动物或车辆或一组马匹)左边的; the '~foreleg; 左前腿; the ~ *front wheel of a car*. 汽车的左前轮. '*~side* n side ~est the kerb: 最靠近人行道的一边; (最)左边: the ~ *side lane of traffic*. 左边的车道. **4** niggardly (contrasted with generous): 悭吝的(与 generous 相对): *He's very ~ with his money*. 他对金钱很吝啬. □ vt, vi [VP6A, 2A] come or draw ~; to; approach: 走近; 靠近; 行近: *The ship was ~ing land*. 那只船正在抛锚. *He's ~ing his end*, is dying. 他快要死了. *The road is ~ing completion*. 那

条路快完成了。 ~·**ness** *n*

near[2] /nɪə(r); nɪr/ *adv* not far; to or at a short distance in space or time: 不远; (空间或时间上)至近距离; 在近距离: *We searched far and* ~ (= everywhere) *for the missing child.* 我们到处寻找那失踪的孩子。 *as* ~ *as*, nearly: 接近地: *As* ~ *as I can guess* (= My ~est or best guess is that) *there were forty people present.* 就我所能猜测, 有四十个人出席。 *He was as* ~ *as could be to* (= only, just escaped, narrowly escaped) *being knocked down by the bus.* 他差点被公共汽车撞倒。 *as* ~ (= nearly) *as makes no difference*, with no difference worth considering: 接近到几乎没什么两样: *They're the same height, or as* ~ *as makes no difference.* 他们身高相同, 或是说接近到几无两样。 ~ *at hand* (a) within easy reach: 在近旁: *Always have your reference books* ~ *at hand.* 要经常把参考书摆在手边。 (b) not far distant in the future: 在不久的将来: *The examinations are* ~ *at hand.* 考试快到了。 ~ *on/upon*, not far in time from; almost: 将近; 几近: *It was near upon midnight.* 将近午夜。 *nowhere* ~, (colloq) (口) *not* ~, far from: 离…很远。 *The concert hall was nowhere* ~ *full.* 那音乐厅离满座还差得远。 她远远不如她丈夫那么老(比她丈夫小得多)。 ~ *by*, not far off. 不远; 在附近。 Hence, 由此产生, '~·*by* *adj*

near[3] /nɪə(r); nɪr/ *prep* (equivalent to *near*[1] with *to*) close to (in space, time, relationship, etc): (等于 *near*[1] 与 *to* 连用之用法)(空间, 时间, 关系等)近于; 靠近: *Come and sit* ~ *me.* 来靠近我坐。 *It's convenient living so* ~ *the station.* 住在离车站这么近实在很方便。

near·ly /'nɪəlɪ; 'nɪrlɪ/ *adv* 1 almost: 几乎; 将近: *It's* ~ *one o'clock / time to start.* 将近一点钟了(差不多是开始的时刻)。 *I'm* ~ *ready.* 我差不多准备好了。 ⇨ **hardly, scarcely.** 2 closely: 密切地; 亲近地: *We're related*, *are near relations.* 我们是近亲。 3 *not* ~, far from: 相差甚远: *I have £20, but that isn't* ~ *enough for my journey, I shall need much more.* 我有二十英镑, 但是远不够我旅行用, 我还需要更多(钱)。

neat /niːt; nit/ *adj* (-er, -est except 5 below 下列第 5 义外) 1 (liking to have everything) tidy; in good order with nothing out of place; done carefully: (喜爱)整洁的; 整齐的; 小心做成的; 精巧的: ~ *work*; 精巧的制作品; *a* ~ *worker*; 灵巧的工人; 干净的工人; *a* ~ *desk*; 整齐的书桌; ~ *writing.* 工整的笔迹。 2 simple and pleasant; in good taste: 简洁的; 雅致的: *a* ~ *dress.* 雅致的衣服。 3 pleasing in shape and appearance: 形态优雅的; 匀称的: *a* ~ *figure.* 匀称的身材。 4 cleverly said or done: 巧妙的: *a* ~ *answer / conjuring trick.* 巧妙的回答(魔术)。 5 (of wines and spirits) unmixed with water; undiluted: (指酒类)没搀水的; 纯的: *drink one's whisky* ~. 喝纯威士忌。 ~·*ly* *adv* ~·*ness* *n*

'neath /niːθ; niθ/ *prep* (poet) beneath. (诗)在…下面。

neb·ula /'nebjʊlə; 'nɛbjələ/ *n* (*pl* ~**e** /-liː; -,li/ or ~**s**) [C] cluster of very distant stars, diffuse mass of gas, seen in the night sky as an indistinct patch of light. 星云; (夜晚天空所见之片状光雾, 系由极遥远之恒星群及散布之气团形成)。 **nebu·lar** /-lə(r); -lə/ *adj* of ~s. 星云的。

nebu·lous /'nebjʊləs; 'nɛbjələs/ *adj* cloud-like; hazy; indistinct; vague. 似云的; 云雾状的; 模糊不清的; 含糊的。

neces·sar·ily /ˌnesə'serəli; 'nɛsə,sɛrəli/ *adv* as a necessary result; inevitably: 必要地; 必然地; 必定地: *Big men are not* ~ *strong men.* 大块头的人不一定就是强壮的人。

neces·sary /'nesəsərɪ US: -serɪ; 'nɛsə,sɛri/ *adj* which has to be done; which must be; which cannot be done without or escaped from: 必须做的; 必要的; 必需的; 必定的; 难以逃避的: *Sleep is* ~ *to health.* 睡眠对于健康是必要的。 *Is war a* ~ *evil in this world?* 战争是世上难以避免的祸害吗? *Is it* ~ *for you to be / Is it* ~ *that you should be so economical?* 你非要如此节省不可吗? □ *n* [C]

(usu *pl*) things ~ (for living). (通常用复数)(生活)必需品。

ne·cessi·tate /nɪ'sesɪteɪt; nə'sɛsə,tet/ *vt* [VP 6 A, C] make necessary: 使成为必要: *Your proposal* ~*s borrowing money.* 你的提议使借款成为必要。 *The increase in population* ~*s a greater food supply.* 人口的增加需要更多的食物供应。

ne·cessi·tous /nɪ'sesɪtəs; nə'sɛsətəs/ *adj* (formal) poor; needy: (正式用语)穷的; 贫困的: *in* ~ *circumstances*, in poverty. 处于贫困之境。

ne·cessi·ty /nɪ'sesɪtɪ; nə'sɛsəti/ *n* (*pl* -**ties**) 1 [U] urgent need; circumstances that compel sb to do sth; natural laws that direct human life and action: 急需; 迫使某人作某事的情况; 支配人类生活与行动的自然律: *He was driven by* ~ *to steal food for his starving children.* 他为了替他饥饿的儿女偷窃食物。 *The doctor asked us not to call him during the night except in case of* ~, eg unless the patient's condition changed very much for the worse. 医生吩咐我们除非必要不要在夜里叫他。 *be under the* ~ *of...*, be compelled by.... 不得已而…。 *bow to* ~, do what one is compelled to do. 做不得已的事。 *make a virtue of* ~, accept credit without protest; claim credit for doing sth that one cannot help doing. 认可而不加抗议: 把不得不做的事当作应当做的事。 *of* ~, as a matter of ~. 必然; 必定; 不得已。 2 [C] sth that is necessary: 必需品: *The necessities of life*, food, clothing and shelter. 生活必需品(食物、衣服及住所)。 3 [C] sth of which the absence or non-occurrence cannot be imagined: 必然的事; 绝不可无的事物: *Is it a logical* ~ *that the cost of living will go up if wages go up?* 假如工资增加, 生活费用也要增加, 这是不是逻辑上必然的结果?

neck /nek; nɛk/ *n* 1 part of the body that connects the head and the shoulders: 颈; 脖子: *wrap a scarf round one's* ~. 在颈上围一条围巾。 ⇨ the illus at **head**. 看看 head 之插图。 *break one's* ~, work extremely hard to achieve sth. 拼命地干以完成某事。 ⇨ **breakneck.** *breathe down sb's* ~, (colloq) be close behind, almost touching, eg in a race; be watching closely. (口)紧跟在某人后头(至几乎能触及的程度, 如在赛跑中); 紧迫地盯住某人。 *get it in the* ~, (sl) suffer a severe or a fatal blow; have a painful experience. (俚)遭受严重的或致命的打击; 有痛苦的经验。 *have the* ~ (more usu 较常用 *nerve*) *to do sth*, (sl) be impudent, cheeky enough to do it. (俚)厚着脸皮做某事。 *save one's* ~, escape hanging; (fig) escape the results of being foolish, etc. 免受绞刑; (喻)免于遭受由愚昧等所造成的结果。 *stick one's* '~ *out*, (sl) do or say sth that may bring severe criticism, or result in a painful experience. (俚)做出(说出)会使自己受到严厉批评或遭受痛苦的事(话); 自找麻烦。 *win / lose by a* ~, (horse-racing) by the length of a horse's ~; (fig) by a narrow margin. (赛马)以一颈之差获胜(失败); (喻)险胜(小败)。 ~ *and crop*, headlong; altogether; bag and baggage: 匆促地; 全部地; 完全地; 带着全部东西: *throw him out* ~ *and crop.* 要他带着全部东西滚蛋。 ~ *and* ~, (of horse-racing, and fig) side by side, with no advantage over the other in a race or struggle. (指赛马, 亦作比喻用法)并驾齐驱; 不分上下。 ~ *or nothing*, taking desperate risks; venturing everything. 冒一切危险; 拼命。 2 flesh of an animal's ~ as used for food, esp ~ of mutton. 作食物用的动物的颈肉; (尤指)羊颈肉。 3 sth like a ~ in shape or position: 形状或部位象颈之物; 颈状物: *the* ~ *of a bottle*; 瓶颈; *a narrow* ~ *of land*, eg an isthmus. 狭窄的地带(如地峡)。 4 (compounds) (复合词) '~·*band* *n* part of a shirt, etc that goes round the ~. (衬衣等的)领圈(装领的部分)。 '~·*cloth* *n* cravat. 旧式领带。 '~·*er·chief* /'nekətʃɪf; 'nɛkətʃɪf/ *n* (old use) cloth or scarf worn round the ~. (旧用法)围于颈项的布或围巾。 '~·*lace* /-lɪs; -lɪs/ *n* string of beads, pearls, etc worn round the ~ as an ornament. 项链。 '~·*let* /-lɪt; -lɪt/ *n* ornament (eg of

beads) for the ~. 颈饰；项珠；小项链。'~·line n (of
fashions for women's clothes) line of a garment at or
near the ~: (指女装的款式)领口；开领: *This year the
~line is up and the hemline is down.* 今年流行的女装款
式领口高下摆低。'~·tie n (now usu 今通常称 tie) band
of material worn round the ~ and knotted in front. 领
带。'~·wear /-weə(r); -,wɛr/ n [U] (term used by
shopkeepers for) collars and ties. (商人所用的名词)
领子和领带。□ vi (sl) (of couples) exchange kisses,
caresses and hugs: (俚)(指一对男女)互相亲吻、抚爱、拥
抱: *sitting on park benches petting and ~ing in the dark.*
坐在公园长凳上在黑暗中互相亲吻、抚爱、拥抱。

nec·ro·mancy /'nekrəmænsɪ; 'nɛkrə,mænsɪ/ n [U]
art or practice of communicating by magic with the
dead in order to learn about the future. 施魔法问未来
于亡魂的法术；巫术；关亡术。 **nec·ro·man·cer** /-sə(r);
-sɚ/ n person who practises ~, 问未来于亡魂的法师；巫
师；行关亡术者。

ne·crop·olis /nɪ'krɒpəlɪs; nɛ'krɑpəlɪs/ n (pl ~es
/-lɪsɪz; -lɪsɪz/) cemetery, esp a large one in an ancient
town. 墓地；公墓；(尤指)(古城市中的)大墓地。

nec·tar /'nektə(r); 'nɛktɚ/ n [U] 1 (in old Gk
stories) the drink of the gods. (古希腊传说) 神的饮
料；琼浆玉液。 ⇨ **ambrosia.** 2 sweet liquid in flowers,
collected by bees; any delicious drink. 花蜜；任何美味的
饮料。

nec·tar·ine /'nektərɪn; 'nɛktə,rin/ n kind of peach
with thin, smooth skin and firm flesh. 油桃(桃的一种，
皮薄而光滑,果肉坚实)。

née /neɪ; ne/ adj (F) born (put after the name of a
married woman and before her father's family name):
(法)本姓; 娘家姓…的(用于已婚妇女姓氏之后，娘家姓氏
之前，表示其娘家的姓氏): *Mrs J Smith, née Brown.* 娘
家姓布朗的史密斯夫人。

need¹ /niːd; nid/ anom fin (no inf, no participles, 3rd
p sing present tense is need, not needs; used in interr
and neg followed by inf without to; need not contracted
to needn't /'niːdnt; 'nidnt/) (无不定式，无分词，第三人
称单数现在式是 need 而非 needs; 用于疑问句及否定句中
后接没有 to 的不定式; need not 缩写为 needn't) [VP5]
1 be obliged; be necessary: 必要; 必须: *N~ you go yet?
No, I ~n't. Yes, I must.* 你一定要去吗？不，我不必去。
是的，我必须去。 *You ~n't go yet, ~ you?* 你不一定要
去，是吗？ *I ~ hardly tell you* (= You must already know
or guess) *that* … 不用我说你也知道…。 2 (followed by
a perfect infinitive, ~ indicates that although sth may
have occurred or been done in the past, it was or may
have been unnecessary); (后接完成式不定式，表示虽然
某事可能在过去曾经发生或已做了，但此事并不需要):
N~ it have happened? 难道当时没法避免吗？ *We ~n't
have hurried,* We hurried but now we see that this was
unnecessary. 我们当时实在不必急着赶路。 Cf 参较 *We
didn't ~ to hurry,* We didn't hurry because it was
unnecessary. 我们当时无须匆忙(我们当时并没忙)。 ⇨
need² (2). ~**ful** /-fl; -fəl/ adj necessary: 需要的；
必须的: *do what is ~ful.* 做你必须做的事。 **do the** ~**ful,**
(colloq) provide the money, perform the action. that
is required. (口)供所需的款；采取必要的行动。 ~**fully**
/-fəlɪ; -fəlɪ/ adv ~**less** adj not ~ed; unnecessary: 不
需要的; 不必要的: *~less work/trouble.* 不必要的工作
(麻烦)。 *N~less to say,* he kept his promise. 不用说，他
信守了他的诺言。 ~**less·ly** adv

need² /niːd; nid/ n 1 [U] ~ (for), circumstances in
which sth is lacking, or necessary, or requiring some
course of action: 困乏之境; 缺乏; 需要; 必须: *There's no
~ (for you) to start yet.* (你)现在还不必动身。 *There's
no/not much ~ for this.* 不必(太)焦虑。 *There's a
great ~ for a book on this subject.* 非常需要有一本关于
这题目的书。 *if ~ be,* if necessary. 如果需要的话。 2
(used in pl) requirement; sth felt to be necessary: (用
复数)要求；需要之物: *He earns enough to satisfy his ~s,*
ie to buy food, clothing, etc. 他赚得的钱足够满足他的需

要。 *My ~s are few.* 我的需求很少。 *£10 will meet my
immediate ~s.* 十英镑足以应付我目前的需要。 3 [U]
poverty; misfortune; adversity: 贫穷；不幸；逆境: *He
helped me in my hour of ~.* 他在我遇难的时候帮助了我。
A friend in ~ is a friend indeed, (prov)A friend who
helps when one is in trouble is a real friend. (谚)患难
之交才是真正的朋友。 ~**y** adj (-ier, -iest) very poor;
lacking the necessities of life: 非常贫穷的; 缺乏生活必
需品的: *a ~y family;* 贫穷家庭; *help the poor and ~y.*
帮助贫穷的人。

need³ /niːd; nid/ vt 1 [VP6A, E] want; require: 需
要; 要: *The garden ~s rain.* 花园需要雨水。 *Does he ~
any help?* 他需要帮助吗？ *It only ~s good will from both
sides.* 它只要双方的善意。 *This chapter ~s rewriting/
~s to be rewritten.* 这一章需要重写。 2 [VP7A] be
a necessity or obligation: 必要; 必须: *He didn't ~
to be reminded about it.* 不必向他提醒那事情。 *Does
he ~ to know?* 他一定要知道吗？ *It ~s to be done
carefully.* 此事必须仔细地做。 *He ~s to be kept informed
about developments.* 他必须随时获知有关发展的情形。 3
[VP6A] deserve; ought to have: 值得; 该有: *What he
~s is a good whipping!* 应该狠狠地给他一顿鞭打！

needle /'niːdl; 'nidl/ n 1 small, thin piece of polished
steel, pointed at one end and with a small hole at
the other end for thread, used in sewing and darning.
针；缝衣针。 *look for a ~ in a haystack,* (prov) engage
in a hopeless search. (谚)从事无希望的搜索；海底捞针。
as sharp as a ~, quickwitted; observant. 非常机警；非
常敏锐。 '~**woman** n (pl **women**) woman who sews.
善缝纫的妇女; 善女红的妇女。 '~**craft, '~·work** nn
[U] sewing, embroidery. 缝纫; 刺绣; 女红。 **pins and
'~s,** ⇨ **pin¹**(1). 2 long, thin piece of polished wood,
bone or metal (without an eye). with a pointed end(for
knitting) or a hook (for crocheting). (木质、骨质或金
属的无针孔的)编织针; 钩针(一端有钩, 钩织用)。 3 thin
steel pointer in a compass, showing the magnetic north;
similar pointer in a telegraphic instrument. 磁针;
指南针; 电报机上之针。 4 sth like a ~ (1) in shape,
appearance or use (eg the thin, pointed leaves of pine-
trees; a sharp, pointed peak or rocky summit; the
sharp, hollow end of a syringe used for giving
injections). 针状物(如松树之针状叶、尖峰、注射针)。 ⇨
the illus at **tree; syringe.** 参看 tree, syringe 之插图。 5
stylus used in recording and playing gramophone
records. (唱机用的)唱针。 Cf 参较 *sapphire and diamond
styluses.* 6 the ~, (sl) nervous excitement: (俚)激动;
兴奋: *give sb the ~,* provoke or excite him; 激怒或刺激
某人; *get the ~,* be provoked. 被激怒。 7 obelisk: 方尖
石碑; 方尖柱碑: *Cleopatra's ~,* in London. (伦
敦的)克利奥佩特拉尖塔。 □ vt 1 [VP6A, 15A] sew,
pierce, operate on, with a ~; thread (one's way)
between or through things. 用针缝、刺穿或施手术; 穿过。
2 (colloq) goad, provoke (sb, esp by making cruel
comments, etc). (口)刺激或激怒(某人,尤指以残酷的批
评等)。

needs /niːdz; nidz/ adv (now used only with must) of
necessity. (现在只与 must 连用)必要地; 一定; 务必。 *N~
must when the devil drives,* (prov) Circumstances
may compel us to act in a certain way. (谚)情势所迫,
只好如此。 (When the adv follows must, as in 'He must
~', the sense is usu sarcastic, as here): (当此副词用于
must 之后时, 例如 'He must needs', 通常含有讽刺之意,
如下例): *He must ~ go away just when I want his help,*
He foolishly or stupidly insisted on going away. 我正
需要他协助的时候, 他偏要走开(他愚昧地坚持要走开)。

ne'er /neə(r); nɛr/ adv (poet) never. (诗)永不; 决不;
从未。 ~**-do-well** /'nɛə du:wel; 'nɛrdu,wɛl/ n useless
or good-for-nothing person. 无用之人。

nefarious /nɪ'feərɪəs; nɪ'fɛrɪəs/ adj (formal) wicked;
unlawful. (正式用语)邪恶的; 不法的。 ~**ly** adv ~**ness** n

ne·gate /nɪ'geɪt; nɪ'get/ vt [VP6A] (formal) deny;
nullify. (正式用语)否定; 使无效。

ne·ga·tion /nɪˈgeɪʃn; nɪˈgeʃən/ n [U] **1** (opp of *affirmation*) (为affirmation 之反义词) act of denying: 否定;否认: *Shaking the head is a sign of* ~. 摇头是否认的表示。 **2** absence of any positive or real quality or meaning: 实质或真义的不存在;虚无: *The life of an evil man is a moral* ~. 恶人的生命毫无道德价值。

nega·tive /ˈnegətɪv; ˈnegətɪv/ adj **1** (opp of *affirmative*) (为 affirmative 之反义词) (of words and answers) indicating *no* or *not*: (指词句及回答)否定的(含'不'之义): *give sb a* ~ *answer*. 给某人一个否定的答复。 **2** (opp of *positive*) (为 positive 之反义词) expressing the absence of any positive character; that stops, hinders or makes powerless: 消极的; 反对的: ~ *criticism*, that does not help by building up, making suggestions; 消极的批评; ~ *praise*, not finding fault; 消极的称赞(即不找碴); ~ *virtue*, doing nothing wrong but doing nothing good or right, either. 消极的美德 (不做好事, 也不做坏事)。 **3** (maths) of number or quantity that has to be subtracted (数学)负的(eg 如 $-x^2y$). **4** of that kind of electricity produced by rubbing wax, vulcanite, etc; of or from the cathode: (电)负的; 阴的; 阴性的: *the* ~ *plate in a battery*, from which electrons will flow to the positive plate. 电池中的阴(极)板。**the** ~ **pole**, (made of zinc) in a cell. 电池中的阴极(锌制成)。 **5** (photo) having lights and shades reversed. (摄影)明暗相反的;底片的。 □ n [C] **1** word or statement that denies: 否定词; 否定; 否认: *'No', 'not' and 'neither' are* ~*s*. no, not 及 neither 都是否定词。 *The answer is in the* ~, is 'No'. 答复是否定的。 **2** (maths) a minus quantity (数学)负数; 负值(eg 如 $-5x$). **3** (photo) developed plate or film on which lights and shades are reversed. (摄影)底片。 □ vt [VP6A] **1** prove (a theory, etc) to be untrue: 否定(理论等)的真实性; 推翻; 驳斥: *Experiments* ~*d his theory*. 实验否定了他的理论。 **2** reject; refuse to accept; neutralize (an effect). 拒绝; 否决; 抵销。 ~**·ly** adv

the negative of the photograph at *ski*

ne·glect /nɪˈglekt; nɪˈglekt/ vt **1** [VP6A] pay no attention to; give no or not enough care to: 疏忽; 忽略: ~ *one's studies/children/health*. 疏忽学业(子女, 健康)。 **2** [VP7A, 6C] omit or fail (*to do* sth); leave undone (what one ought to do): 遗漏(与不应做的事); 漏做; 忘记做(该做的事): *He* ~*ed to write and say 'Thank you'*. 他忘了写信道谢。 *Don't* ~ *writing to your mother*. 不要忘了写信给你母亲。 □ n (of being or being ~ed: 疏忽; 忽略; 遗漏: *He lost his job because of* ~ *of duty*. 他因为疏忽职责而失去工作。 *The garden was in a state of* ~. 那花园疏于整理。~**·ful** /-fl; -fl/ adj in the habit of ~ing things: 疏忽的; 忽视的; 不留心的: *boys who are* ~*ful of their appearance*. 不注意自己仪表的男孩们。 ~**·fully** /-fəlɪ; -fəlɪ/ adv ~**·ful·ness** n: *He has a tendency to* ~*fulness*. 他有疏忽的倾向。

nég·ligé, neg·li·gee /ˈneglɪʒeɪ US: ˌneglɪˈʒeɪ, ˌneglɪˈʒe/ n [C, U] (condition of being in a) loose, free style of informal dress. 宽松的便服; 穿着宽松便服的状态。

neg·li·gence /ˈneglɪdʒəns; ˈneglədʒəns/ n [U] **1** carelessness; failure to take proper care or precautions: 不留心; 疏忽; 不注意; 粗心大意: *The accident was due to* ~. 这次意外是由于疏忽。 **2** neglected condition or

appearance: 随便; 不注意仪表: ~ *of dress*. 衣着随便; 衣冠不整。

neg·li·gent /ˈneglɪdʒənt; ˈneglədʒənt/ adj taking too little care, guilty of neglect: 不注意的; 疏忽的; 随便的: *He was* ~ *in* (= in respect of) *his work*. 他不注意工作。 *He was* ~ *of his duties*. 他疏忽职责。 ~**·ly** adv

neg·li·gible /ˈneglɪdʒəbl; ˈneglədʒəbl/ adj that need not be considered; of little or no importance or size: 不需要加以考虑的; 不重要的; 很小的: *a* ~ *quantity*. 小量; 小数目。

ne·go·ti·able /nɪˈgəʊʃɪəbl; nɪˈgoʃɪəbl/ adj **1** that can be negotiated (2): 可商议的; 可谈判的: *Is the dispute* ~? 那争执可用谈判加以解决吗? **2** that can be changed into cash, or passed from person to person instead of cash: 可兑换现金的; 可转让的; 可流通的: ~ *securities/instruments*, eg cheques, promissory notes. 可转让的证券或票据。 **3** (of roads, rivers, etc) that can be passed over or along. (指道路、河流等)可通行的。

ne·go·ti·ate /nɪˈgəʊʃɪeɪt; nɪˈgoʃɪ,et/ vi, vt **1** [VP2A, 3A] ~ (*with* sb), discuss, confer, in order to come to an agreement: (与某人)商议; 谈判; 磋商: *We've decided to* ~ *with the employers about our wage claims*. 我们已经决定和雇主谈判关于我们的工资要求。 **2** [VP6A, 14] ~ *sth* (*with* sb), arrange by discussion: (以谈判)商议处理某事; 商订: ~ *a sale/a loan/a treaty/peace*. 商订售卖(贷款, 条约, 和约)。 **3** [VP6A] get or give money for (cheques, bonds, etc). 买卖; 让渡(支票, 债券等)。 **4** [VP6A] get past or over: 通过; 越过: *This is a difficult corner for a large car to* ~. 这个拐角大的汽车很难通过。 *My horse* ~*d* (ie jumped over) *the fence very well*. 我的马轻易地跳过了栅栏。 **ne·go·tiator** /-tə(r); -tɔ/ n one who ~s. 谈判者; 商议者。

ne·go·ti·ation /nɪˌgəʊʃɪˈeɪʃn; nɪˌgoʃɪˈeʃən/ n [C, U] negotiating: 商议; 谈判; 让与; 流通: *enter into/open/ start/carry on/resume* ~*s with* sb; 与某人着手(展开, 进行, 恢复)谈判; *be in* ~ *with* sb. 与某人商议。 *The price is a matter of* ~. 价格是可商议的事。

Ne·gress /ˈniːgres; ˈnigrɪs/ n (derog) Negro woman or girl. (贬)女黑人;黑妞。

Ne·gro /ˈniːgrəʊ; ˈnigro/ n (pl ~**es** /-rəʊz; -roz/) member (or, outside Africa, descendant) of one of the black-skinned African peoples south of the Sahara. 黑人(非洲撒哈拉沙漠以南的黑种人, 或在非洲以外此种人的后代)。

Ne·groid /ˈniːgrɔɪd; ˈnigrɔɪd/ adj of or akin to Negroes or the Negro race. 黑人的; 黑种人的; 类似黑种人的。 □ n person of the ~ race. 黑种人; 黑人。

ne·gus /ˈniːgəs; ˈnigəs/ n hot, sweetened wine, lemon juice, nutmeg and water. 尼加斯酒(甜酒、柠檬汁、荳蔻末及水混合成的一种热酒)。

Ne·gus /ˈniːgəs; ˈnigəs/ n (title of the) ruler of Ethiopia. 埃塞俄比亚王(的称号)。

neigh /neɪ; ne/ vi, n (make) cry of a horse. (作)马叫; 马嘶。

neigh·bour (US = **-bor**) /ˈneɪbə(r); ˈnebɚ/ n person living in a house, street, etc near another; person, thing or country that is near(est) another: 邻人; 邻居; 邻近的人或物; 邻国: *We're nextdoor* ~*s*, Our houses are side by side. 我们是隔壁邻居。 *We were* ~*s at dinner*, We sat together at table. 我们在用餐时坐在一起。 *When the big tree fell, it brought down two of its smaller* ~*s*, two smaller trees near it. 当那棵大树倒下来的时候, 它把附近的两棵小树也压倒了。 *Britain's nearest* ~ *is France*. 英国最近的邻国是法国。 □ vt, vi [VP6A, 3A] ~ (*on/ upon*), (chiefly in the form ~*ing*) be near to: (主要用于现在分词形式)邻接; 相邻: ~*ing countries*; 邻国; *an* ~*ing village*. 在邻近的村庄里。 ~**·hood** /-hʊd; -hʊd/ n **1** (people living in a) district; area near the place, etc referred to: 地区; 某一地区的人们; 邻居; 邻近地方: *There's some beautiful scenery in our* ~*hood*. 在我们附近地方有一些美丽的景色。 *He was liked by the whole* ~*hood*. 他为邻近的人们所喜爱。 *He wants to live in the*

~**hood of London.** 他要住在伦敦附近。**2** condition of being near: 邻近；大约：*The ~hood of this noisy airport is a serious disadvantage.* 和这嘈闹的飞机场邻近是一个严重的缺点。*He lost a sum in the ~hood of £500.* 他丢了大约五百英镑的钱。~**·ly** *adj* kind; friendly. 亲切的；友善的。~**·li·ness** *n* [U] friendly feeling, help, that is expected from ~s. (邻人间应有的)友善；和睦；睦邻。

nei·ther /'naɪðə(r) *US:* 'niːðə; 'niðɚ/ *adj, pron* (used with a *sing n* or *pron;* 与单数名词或代词连用；cf 参较 *either*) not one nor the other (of two): (两者)都不：*N~ statement is true.* 两个说法都不是真的。*N~ (one) is satisfactory.* 两个都不令人满意。*I like ~ of them.* 他们两个我都不喜欢。*I can agree in ~ case.* 两种情形我都不能同意。*In ~ case can I agree.* 两种情形我都不能同意。□ *adv, conj* **1** ~... nor..., not... and not...: 既不···也不···; *He ~ knows nor cares what happened.* 他既不知道也不在乎发生了什么。*It's ~ pleasant to eat nor good for you.* 它既不好吃也对你没有好处。*N~ you nor I could do it.* 你和我都不能做这件事。*The cat has not been fed;* ~ has the dog 猫还没喂；狗也没喂(or) (或) *N~ the cat nor the dog has been fed.* 猫和狗都还没喂。**2** (after a negative *if*-clause, etc) (用于否定的 if 从句等之后) and not: 亦不；也不：*If you don't go,* ~ shall I. 假如你不去，我也不去。*As he won't help you,* ~ will I. 既然他不会帮助你，我也不会帮助你。*I haven't been to the Exhibition;* ~ do I (= and I do not) *intend to go.* 我还没去看展览会；我也不想去。A: *'I don't like it'*—B: *'N~ do I'* 甲：'我不喜欢它'——乙：'我也不喜欢' Cf 参较 *Nor do I. No more do I.*

Nelly /'nelɪ; 'nɛlɪ/ *n* (only in) (仅用于) *not on your* ~, (GB sl) certainly not! (英俚)决不!

nem con /,nem 'kɒn; ,nem 'kɑn/ *adv* (abbr Lat) unanimously; without any objection being raised: (略，拉)全体一致地；无异议地：*The resolution was carried* ~. 决议案无异议通过了。

nem·esis /'neməsɪs; 'nɛməsɪs/ *n* (*pl* -eses /-əsiːz; -ə,siz/) (formal) (正式用语) **1** deserved fate; just punishment for wrong-doing. 报应；公正的惩罚。**2** N~, goddess of vengeance. 复仇女神。

neo- /'niːəʊ; ,niə/ *pref* new; modern. 新的；新近的；现代的。⇨ **App 3.** 参看附录三。

neo·col·onial·ism /,niːəʊ kə'ləʊnɪəlɪzəm; ,nɪokə'lonɪə,lɪzəm/ *n*

neo·lithic /,niːəʊ'lɪθɪk; ,niə'lɪθɪk/ *adj* of the new or later stone age: 新石器时代的。~ *man.* 新石器时代的人。

neol·ogism /niː'ɒlədʒɪzəm; niːˈɑlə,dʒɪzəm/ *n* [U] coining or using of new words; [C] newly coined word. 新词的创造或使用；新创的词。

neon /'niːɒn; 'nɪɑn/ *n* [U] colourless gas forming a very small proportion of the earth's atmosphere. 氖(一种无色气体元素，在地球的大气中所占比例极小)。~ **light** *n* coloured light produced when an electric current passes through this gas in a low-pressure bulb or tube. 霓虹光；霓虹灯。~ **sign** *n* advertisement, etc in which ~ light is used. 霓虹灯广告。

neo·phyte /'niːəfaɪt; 'niə,faɪt/ *n* person who has newly been converted to some belief or religion. 刚改奉某种信仰的人；新近改信某一宗教的人；新信徒；新入教者。

neo·plasm /'niːəʊplæzəm; 'niə,plæzəm/ *n* (path) tumor. (病理)赘瘤；赘疣；赘生物。

nephew /'nevjuː; *US:* 'nefjuː; 'nɛfju/ *n* son of one's brother or sister. 侄儿；外甥。

neph·ri·tis /nɪ'fraɪtɪs; nɪ'fraɪtɪs/ *n* [U] inflammation of the kidneys. 肾脏炎。

ne plus ultra /,niː plɑs 'ʌltrə;'niːplʌs'ʌltrə/ *n* (Lat) farthest point attained or attainable; highest point; culmination (of). (拉) (已达到或可达到的)最远点；最高点；至高；至上(与 of 连用)。

nep·ot·ism /'nepətɪzəm; 'nɛpə,tɪzəm/ *n* [U] the giving of special favour (esp employment) by a person

in high position to his relatives. 袒护亲戚；重用亲戚；裙带关系。

Nep·tune /'neptjuːn *US:* -tuːn; 'nɛptjun/ *n* **1** (Roman god of) the sea. (罗马神话中之)海神；海洋。**2** one of the farthest planets of the solar system. 海王星。⇨ the illus at **planet.** 参看 planet 之插图。

ne·reid /'nɪərɪɪd; 'nɪrɪɪd/ *n* (Gk myth) sea-nymph. (希神)海的女神。

nerve /nɜːv; nɝv/ *n* **1** [C] fibre or bundle of fibres carrying feelings and impulses between the brain and all parts of the body. 神经。~**cell** *n* cell that conducts impulses. 神经细胞。~**-centre** *n* group of closely connected ~cells; (fig) centre of control. 神经中枢；(喻)控制中心。**2** (*pl*) condition of being easily excited, worried, irritated: (复)神经过敏；神经紧张：*He is suffering from* ~s, quickly and easily becomes excited, frightened, etc. 他患神经过敏的病。*That man doesn't know what* ~s *are,* is never worried, upset, etc by events. 那个人不知神经紧张为何物(即从不为某些事情而忧虑、不安等)。*He has* ~s *of iron,* is never upset, etc. 他从不紧张。*get on one's* ~s, worry or annoy: 使某人心烦；使烦恼：*That noise gets on my* ~s. 那声音吵得我心烦。*war of* ~s, campaign in which an attempt is made to weaken an opponent by destroying his morale. 神经战；心理战(破坏对方士气以减弱其战力的活动)。~**-racking** *adj* inflicting strain on the ~s. 伤脑筋的；令人紧张的。**3** [U] quality of being bold, self-reliant, etc: 胆量；勇气；自信心：*A test pilot needs plenty of* ~. 飞机的试飞员需要大量勇气。*What a* ~! What cheek! 多无耻啊! 脸皮真厚! *have the* ~ *to do sth,* (a) have the necessary courage, self-reliance: 有足够的勇气(自信心)去做某事：*have the* ~ *to drive a racing car.* 有勇气驾驶竞赛用的汽车。(b) (colloq) be impudent enough: (口)厚颜：鲁莽：*He had the* ~ *to suggest that I was cheating.* 他竟敢说我在欺骗。*have a* ~, (colloq) be self-assured or audacious: (口)自信；大胆：*He's got a* ~, *going to work dressed like that!* 他真大胆，竟敢穿着那样的衣服去工作! *lose/regain one's* ~, lose / recover one's courage and self-assurance. 失去(恢复)勇气及自信。**4** [C] (old use) sinew, tendon. (旧用法)腱。*strain every* ~ *to do sth,* make great efforts. 尽全力做某事。**5** (bot) rib, esp mid-rib, of a leaf. (植物)叶脉；(尤指)叶的中脉。□ *vt* [VP6A, 14, 16A] ~ *oneself for sth/to do sth,* summon up one's strength (physical or moral): 唤起(肉体或精神的)力量去做某事；鼓起勇气：~ *oneself for a task;* 鼓起勇气去做某件工作；~ *oneself ready to face troubles.* 鼓起勇气准备面对困难。~**-less** *adj* (from ~(4)) lacking in vigour or spirit; without energy: (由上列第4义而来)没精神的；没劲儿的；萎靡的：*The knife fell from his* ~*less hand.* 那把刀从他那没气力的手中掉了下来。~**·less·ly** *adv*

nerv·ous /'nɜːvəs; 'nɝvəs/ *adj* **1** of the nerves①: 神经的：*the* ~ *system of the human body.* 人体的神经系统。*a* ~ *breakdown,* neurasthenia. 神经衰弱症。**2** tense; excited: 神经过敏的；激动的：*Are you* ~ *in the dark?* 你在暗处会神经紧张吗? *What's she so* ~ *about?* 她为着什么而神经紧张? **3** having strong sinews; vigorous: 刚健的；有力的：*full of* ~ *energy;* 精力充沛；*a* ~ *style of writing.* 有力的文体。~**·ly** *adv* ~**·ness** *n*

nervy /'nɜːvɪ; 'nɝvɪ/ *adj* **1** (GB colloq) suffering from nervous strain. (英口)神经紧张的。**2** (sl) impudent. (俚)厚脸皮的；鲁莽的。

nes·cience /'nesɪəns; 'nɛʃɪəns/ *n* [U] (formal) absence of knowledge. (正式用语)无知。**nes·cient** /-ənt; -ənt/ *adj* without knowledge. 无知的。

ness /nes; nɛs/ *n* (usu in place names) promontory; headland. (通常用于地名)海角；岬；岬角。

nest /nest; nɛst/ *n* **1** place made or chosen by a bird for its eggs. 鸟巢；鸟窝。⇨ the illus at **prey.** 参看 prey 之插图。*feather one's* ~, ⇨ **feather²(1).** *foul one's own* ~, abuse(2) one's own family, home, etc. 骂自己的家庭等；家丑外扬。~**-egg** *n* (fig) sum of money

saved for future use. (喻)为将来之用而储蓄的钱。**2** place in which certain living things have and keep their young: 某些生物育幼之处: a 'wasps' ~; a 'turtle's ~. 海龟窠。**3** comfortable place: 舒适之处: make oneself a ~ of cushions. 用垫子给自己做个舒适的地方。**4** number of like things (esp boxes, tables) fitting one inside another. 一套相似物(一个比一个小,可以重叠在一起,尤指箱、桌等)。**5** (fig) shelter; hiding-place; secluded retreat: (喻)庇护所; 隐藏处; 隐退处: a ~ of crime / vice / pirates; 罪恶的渊薮(罪恶的隐藏所); 海盗窝; machine-gun ~s, where they are hidden from direct view. 机枪巢(机枪在该处被隐蔽起来,不使看见)。□ vi [VP2A, C] 1 make and use a ~: 做窠; 筑巢: The swallows are ~ing in the woodshed. 燕子正在柴房里做巢。**2 go ~ing,** search for the ~s of wild birds and take the eggs. 找鸟巢(寻找野鸟的巢并取其蛋)。

nestle /'nesl; 'nɛsl/ vt, vi **1** [VP2C] ~ **(down),** settle comfortably and warmly: 舒适而温暖地安顿下来: ~ down among the cushions: 舒适地坐在垫子堆里; ~ down in bed. 舒适地躺卧在床上。**2** [VP2C] ~ up (against / to), press oneself lovingly to: 偎依; 挨靠: The child was nestling closely up to her mother. 小孩紧紧地偎依着她的母亲。**3** [VP15A] cradle: 抱; 怀抱: She ~d the baby in her arms. 她把婴儿抱在怀里。

nest·ling /'nestlɪŋ; 'nɛstlɪŋ/ n [C] bird too young to leave the nest. 雏鸟。

Nes·tor /'nestə(r); 'nɛstə/ n wise, old counsellor (the name of one of the Greeks in Homer's *Iliad*). 贤明的长者; 聪明的老年忠告者(荷马史诗『伊里亚德』中一希腊人的名字)。

net[1] /net; nɛt/ n [U] **1** open-work material of knotted string, hair, wire, etc; [C] such material made up for a special purpose: (绳、毛发、铁丝等编成的)网织品; (为某一特殊目的用的)网织品: a mos'quito-net, for use over a bed; 蚊帐; 'fishing-nets; 鱼网; 'tennis nets, ⇨ the illus at tennis; 网球网(参看 tennis 之插图); 'hair-nets (used by women to keep the hair in place). (女人用以保护头发不乱的)发网。**2** (fig) moral or mental snare. (喻)(精神或心理上的)罗网; 陷阱; 圈套。**3 'net·ball** n girls' game in which a ball has to be thrown so that it falls through a net fastened to a ring on the top of a post. 落网球戏(一种女子球戏,务于柱顶的网圈上,投球进网始能得分)。**the nets,** (cricket) wickets set up inside a net for practice: (板球)(练习用之)张网的三柱门: have an hour at the nets. 在张了网的三柱门前练习一小时。'**net·work** n **(a)** complex system of lines that cross: 网状组织; 网形系统: a network of railways / canals. 铁路网(运河网)。**(b)** connected system: 连接的系统: An intelligence / spy network. 情报(间谍)情报(间谍)系统。A world communications network, eg for radio and TV, using satellites. 世界通讯系统(例如利用人造卫星的无线电及电视通讯网)。□ vt (**-tt-**) [VP6A] **1** catch (fish, animals, etc) with or in a net. 用网捕(鱼、兽等)。**2** cover (eg fruit trees) with a net or nets: 用网覆盖(果树等): net strawberries / currant bushes, against birds. 用网覆盖草莓(红醋栗树)(防鸟啄食)。**3** put nets in place in: 布网于: net a river. 布网于河。

net[2], **nett** /net; nɛt/ adj remaining when nothing more is to be taken away: 净的; 纯净的: net price, off which discount is not to be allowed; (不能再打折扣的)实价; net profit, when working expenses have been deducted; 净利; 纯利; net weight, of the contents only, excluding the weight of packing, the container, etc. (包装重量除外的)实重; 净重。□ vt (**-tt-**) [VP6A] gain as a net profit: 净得; 净赚: He netted £5 from the deal. 该笔买卖他净赚五英镑。

nether /'neðə(r); 'nɛðə/ adj **1** (archaic) lower: (古)下面的; 较下的: the ~ regions / world, the world of the dead; hell. 冥府; 阴间; 地狱。**2** (joking style) (戏谑语) ~ garments, trousers. 裤子。**~·most** /-məust; -,most/ adj

Neth·er·lander /'neðəlændə(r); 'nɛðə,lændə/ n

native of the Netherlands (Holland). 荷兰人。

nett ⇨ **net**[2]

net·ting /'netɪŋ; 'nɛtɪŋ/ n [U] **1** making or using nets. 制网; 用网。**2** netted string, thread or wire: 网状编织物; (由绳、金属线等织成的)网: five yards of wire ~; 五码金属网; windows screened with ~. 装有纱窗或铁网的窗户。

nettle /'netl; 'nɛtl/ n [C] common wild plant which has on its leaves hairs that sting and redden the skin when touched. 荨麻。'**~·rash** n eruption on the skin with red patches like those caused by ~s. 荨麻疹; 风疹块。□ vt [VP6A] sting (oneself) with ~s; (喻)激刺; 使 rather angry; annoy: 用荨麻刺(自己); (喻)激怒; 使烦恼: She looked ~d by my remarks. 她看来被我的话语激恼。

net·work ⇨ **net**[1].

neu·ral /'njuərəl US: 'nuərəl; 'njʊrəl/ adj of the nerves. 神经的。

neu·ral·gia /njuə'rældʒə US: nu-; nju'rældʒə/ n [U] sharp, jumping pain in the nerves, esp of the face and head. 神经痛; (尤指面部及头部的)神经痛。**neural·gic** /njuə'rældʒɪk; nju'rældʒɪk/ adj of ~. 神经痛的。

neur·as·thenia /,njuərəs'θiːnɪə US: ,nur-; ,njʊrəs-'θinɪə/ n [U] exhausted condition of the nervous system; low state of health, general weakness, accompanying this condition. 神经衰弱; (此症所带来的)身体虚弱。**neur·as·thenic** /-'θenɪk; -'θɛnɪk/ adj suffering from, related to, ~. (患)神经衰弱的。□ n person suffering from ~. 患神经衰弱的人。

neur·itis /njuə'raɪtɪs US: nu-; nju'raɪtɪs/ n [U] inflammation of a nerve or nerves. 神经炎。

neur·ol·ogy /njuə'rɒlədʒɪ US: nu-; nju'rɑlədʒɪ/ n [U] branch of medical science that is concerned with nerves. 神经学(医学中有关神经的一门)。**neurol·ogist** /njuə'rɒlədʒɪst US: nu-; nju'rɑlədʒɪst/ n expert in ~. 神经学家。

neur·osis /njuə'rəusɪs US: nu-; nju'rosɪs/ n (pl **-oses** /-əusiːz; -osiz/) functional derangement caused by disorder of the nervous system or by something in the subconscious mind. 神经官能症; 精神神经病。**neur·otic** /njuə'rɒtɪk US: nu-; nju'rɑtɪk/ adj (of a person) suffering from a ~; of abnormal sensitivity; obsessed. (指人)患神经官能症的; 患精神神经敏感的; 神经过敏的; 有强迫观念的。□ n neurotic person. 患神经官能症者; 患精神神经病者。

neu·ter /'njuːtə(r) US: 'nuː-; 'njutə/ adj **1** (gram; of gender) neither feminine nor masculine. (语法; 指性)中性的; 无性的。**2** (of plants) without male or female parts. (指植物)无雌雄之别的; 无性的。**3** (of insects, eg worker ants) sexually undeveloped; sterile. (指昆虫, 如工蚁)性器官发育不完全的; 不能生育的。□ n **1** ~ noun or gender. 中性名词; 中性。**2** sexually undeveloped insect; castrated animal: 性器官发育不完全的昆虫; 经阉割的动物: My cat is an enormous ginger ~, 我的猫是一只阉割过的美黄色的大猫。□ vt castrate: 阉割: a ~ed tomcat. 经阉割过的雄猫。

neu·tral /'njuːtrəl US: 'nuː-; 'njutrəl/ adj **1** helping neither side in a war or quarrel: (他国战争或他人争吵时)中立的; 不助战任何一方的: ~ nations; 中立国; be / remain ~, 守(保持)中立。**2** of a country that remains ~ in war: 中立国的: ~ territory / ships. 中立国的地区(船只)。**3** having no definite characteristics; not clearly one (colour, etc) or another: 无确定性质的; 不属于某一颜色的; 中色的: ~ tints. 不明显的颜色(如浅灰色等)。**4** (chem) neither acid nor alkaline. (化学)非酸非碱的; 中性的。**5** (of gear mechanism) of the position in which no power is transmitted: (指齿轮机械)空档的; 不传动的: leave a car in ~ gear. 让车子放空档。□ n ~ person, country, etc; ~ position of gears: 中立的人; 中立国; (齿轮的)空档位置: slip the gears into ~. 把齿轮推到空档。**~·ity** /njuː'trælətɪ US: nuː-; nju'trælətɪ/ n [U] state of being ~, esp in war: 中性; (尤指战争中的)中

立; armed ~ity, readiness to fight if attacked, but remaining ~ unless or until this happens. 武装中立(保持中立,但如遭攻击而除非打以应战). ~·ize /-aɪz /ˈaɪz/ vt [VP6A] 1 make ~; declare by agreement that (a place) shall be treated as ~ in war; exempt or exclude from hostilities. 使中立; 经协议宣告(某地)为中立; 免除或排除敌对行为。 2 take away the effect or special quality of, by means of sth with an opposite effect or quality: ~ize a poison. 中和~ize a poison. 中和一种毒物。 ~·iz·ation /ˌnjuːtrəlaɪˈzeɪʃn US:-lɪˈz-; ˌnjutrələˈzeʃən/ n

neu·tron /ˈnjuːtrɒn US: ˈnuː-; ˈnjutrɑn/ n particle carrying no electric charge, of about the same mass as a proton, and forming part of the nucleus of an atom. 中子(构成原子核的一份,质量约与质子相同,但不带电荷).

never /ˈnevə(r); ˈnɛvɚ/ adv 1 at no time; on no occasion: 从未; 未曾: She ~ goes to the cinema. 她从来不去看电影。 He has ~ been abroad. 他从未出过国。 They say that he ~ told a lie. 据说他从来没有撒过谎。 I'm tired of listening to your ~-ending complaints. 我听腻了你那永远没完的抱怨.(Front position for emphasis): (never 放在句首表示强调语气): N~ in all my life have I heard such nonsense! 我这辈子从没听过这种废话! (modifying again and before): (修饰 again 与 before): I shall ~ again stay at that hotel. 我绝对不再住那家旅馆。 Such a display has ~ before been seen / has ~ been seen before. 这一种展览以前从未见过。 2 (used as an emphatic substitute for not): (用作 not 的强调代用词): That will ~ do, won't do at all. 那绝对不行。 I ~ slept a wink all night. 我整夜没合过眼(一会儿也没睡)。 He ~ so much as smiled, didn't smile even once. 他甚至连笑也不笑。 3 (phrases) (短语) Well, I'~ (did)! expressing surprise. 我从来不曾听见或看见这此类事(表示惊讶)! 哇,真没想到! N~ mind! Don't worry! Don't trouble about it. 不要紧!不必介意!没关系! the ,N~ 'N~ Land, imaginary land. 想象中的地方。 on the ~ (US: on the hire-purchase system: (俚)以分期付款方式(购买某物): buy sth on the ~~. 分期赊购买某物。 ~·more /ˈnevəˈmɔː(r); ˈnɛvɚˈmor/ adv ~ again. 永不再; 决不再。

never·the·less /ˌnevəðəˈles; ˌnɛvɚðəˈlɛs/ adv, conj however; in spite of that; still: 然而; 虽然如此; 依然: There was no news; ~, she went on hoping. 没有消息;然而她继续存着希望。

new /njuː US: nuː; nju/ adj (-er, -est) 1 not existing before; seen, heard of, introduced, for the first time; of recent origin, growth, manufacture, etc: 从未有过的; 初见到的; 初听到的; 新产的; 新的: a new school /idea/ film /novel /invention; 新学校 (观念,影片,小说,发明); new potatoes, lifted from the soil early in the season; 早收的马铃薯; new clothes /furniture, 新衣服 (家具); new (= freshly baked) bread; 刚出炉的面包; the newest (= latest) fashions; 最新的款式; new members of Parliament, elected to Parliament for the first time. 初次当选的国会议员。 new look, ⇨ look²(2). the New Testament, (abbr 略作 NT) the second part of the Bible. (圣经中的)新约。 2 already in existence, but only now seen, discovered, etc: 已经存在但现在才被看到、发现等的; 初见的; 新发现的: learn new words in a foreign language; 学外国语的生词。 see a new star. 发现一颗新星。 the New World, N and S America. 新大陆; 新世界(指北美洲与南美洲)。 3 new to, unfamiliar with; not yet accustomed to: 对…不熟悉; 尚未习惯于…: I am new to this town. 我不熟悉此城。 They are still new to the work /trade. 他们对这个工作(行业)还没习惯。 new from, freshly or recently arrived from: 新近来自: an office boy new from school; 一个刚出校门的办公室工友; a person new from the provinces. 刚自外地来的人。 4 (with def art) later, modern, having a different character. (与定冠词连用)新近的; 现代的; 与众不同的。 the new poor /rich, those people recently made poor/ rich by social changes, etc. 新形成的穷人(富人)。 the

new woman, (as used in the first half of the 20th c) woman having or claiming independence, social freedom, etc. 新女性(二十世纪前半期的新型女性,指已具有或主张独立、社会自由意义的妇女)。 a new deal, ⇨ deal⁴ (1). 5 beginning again. 再开始的。 lead a new life, give up old habits, etc. (摈弃旧习惯等)过新生活。 a/ the new moon, seen as a thin crescent. 新月。 wish sb a Happy New Year, ie on New Year's Eve, 31 Dec. (在一月一日元旦,或十二月三十一日除夕)祝某人新年快乐。 □ adv (preceding, joined or hyphened to, the word it qualifies) recently: (置于所修饰的词之前,与该词连合,表示"新近"之意,连字符")新近地: a newborn baby; 新生婴孩; new-laid eggs: 刚下的蛋; new-fallen snow; 新降的雪; new-made graves. 新建的坟墓。 'new-comer n person who has recently arrived in a place. 新来者。 new-'fangled /-ˈfæŋgld; -ˈfæŋgld/ adj newly come into use or fashion (and, for this reason, disliked by some): 刚被采用的; 新流行的(因此有些人不喜欢的): newfangled ideas about education. 有关教育的新奇见解。 'new·ly adv 1 recently: 新近地: a newly married couple; 新婚夫妇; her newly awakened curiosity. 她的新近激起的好奇心。 2 in a new, different way: 以一种新方式: newly arranged furniture. 以新方式排列的家具。 new·ness n

newel /ˈnjuːəl US: ˈnuːəl; ˈnjuəl/ n centre pillar of a winding stair; post supporting a hand-rail at the top, bottom or turn of a staircase. (旋梯的)中柱; (楼梯顶部,底部或转弯处的)栏杆柱。

new-fangled /ˌnjuːˈfæŋgld US: ˌnuːˈ; ˌnjuˈfæŋgld/ adj ⇨ new.

New·found·land /ˈnjuːfəndlənd US: ˈnuː-; ˈnjufəndlənd/ n large breed of spaniel, originally from ~, a large island in Canada, noted for its intelligence and swimming powers. 纽芬兰狗(原产于加拿大之大岛纽芬兰,体大,性机敏,善泳)。

New·mar·ket /ˈnjuːmɑːkɪt US: ˈnuː-; ˈnjuˌmɑrkɪt/ n English town noted for horse-races; kind of card-game. 纽马基特(英国一城镇,以赛马闻名); 一种纸牌戏。

news /njuːz US: nuːz; njuz/ n sing [U] new or fresh information; report(s) of what has most recently happened: 新闻; 消息; 新闻报道: What's the news? 有什么最新的消息?(TV and radio): (电视或无线电): Here is the ~. 现在报告新闻。 Here are the ~ headlines. 现在报告新闻标题。 Here is a ~ summary /a summary of the ~. 现在报告新闻提要。 Here are some interesting items /pieces /bits of ~. 现在报告几件有趣的新闻。 That's no ~ to me, I already know that. 我早就知道啦(对我不是新闻)。 Sandra is in the ~, is being written about in the papers. 桑德拉现在是新闻人物(报纸正登载她的消息)。 The ~ that the enemy were near alarmed the citizens. 敌军迫近的消息使市民惊慌。 Have you any ~ of (= concerning) where your brother is staying? 你有没有你哥哥(弟弟)现在在何处的消息? No ~ is good ~, (prov) If there were bad ~ we should hear it. (谚)没有消息就是好消息(如果有坏消息我们就会听到了)。 '~ agency n agency that collects ~ and sells it to the press. 通讯社(收集并卖新闻给报纸的机构)。 '~·agent n shopkeeper who sells ~papers. periodicals. etc. 报纸经售人; 卖报纸杂志等的店商。 '~·boy n boy who sells ~papers in the streets. (沿街的)卖报童; 报童。 '~·cast n broadcast of ~. 新闻广播。 '~·caster n person who does this. 新闻广播员。 '~ cinema /theatre, cinema showing ~reels, cartoons, and other short films. 放映新闻片, 动画片及其他短片之电影院。 '~·dealer, (US) (美) = ~agent。 '~·letter n letter or circular sent out to members of a society, etc. (对一会社之会员等发行的)通讯; 简讯。 '~·monger n person who gossips. 喜欢说闲话的人; 饶舌的人。 '~·paper /ˈnjuːˌspeɪpə(r) US: ˈnuːz-; ˈnjuzˌpepɚ/ n printed publication, usu issued every day, with ~, advertisements, etc. 报纸; 新闻纸。 '~·paper-man /-mæn;-mæn/

-ˌmæn/ n (pl **-men**) journalist. 新闻工作者; 新闻记者。 '**~-print** n [U] paper for printing ~papers on. 白报纸。 '**~-reel** n cinema film of recent events. 新闻影片。 '**~-room** n room (in a library, etc) where ~papers and other periodicals may be read. (图书馆等中之)阅报室(阅读报纸、杂志等的房间)。 '**~-sheet** n simple form of ~paper. 单页报纸; 单张报纸。 '**~-stand** n stall for the sale of ~papers, etc. 报摊; 杂志摊; 书报摊。 '**~-vendor** n seller of ~papers. 卖报者。 '**~-worthy** adj sufficiently interesting for reporting, eg in a newspaper. 有趣而值得在报纸上发表的; 值得报道的; 有报道价值的。 **~-less** adj without ~. 没有消息的; 无新闻的。 **~y** adj (colloq) full of ~ or gossip: (口) 多新闻的; 饶舌的: a ~y letter. 满纸新闻的信。

newt /njuːt US: nuːt/ n (kinds of) small lizard-like animal which spends most of its time in the water. 水蜥; 蝾螈。 ⇨ the illus at **amphibian**, 参看 amphibian 之插图。

New·to·nian /njuːˈtəʊnɪən US: nuː-; njuˈtonɪən/ adj related to Sir Isaac Newton, and his theories, esp his law of gravity. 牛顿的; 牛顿学说的; (尤指)牛顿万有引力律的。 □ n follower of Newton and his system. 牛顿及其学说的信徒。

next /nekst; nɛkst/ adj, n 1 ~ (**to sth/sb**), coming immediately after, in order or space: 仅次的; 其次的; 下一个与···邻接的: What's the ~ thing to do? 其次要做的是什么? Take the ~ turning to the right. 前面向右转弯。 Miss Green was the ~ (person) to arrive. 下一个来到的(人)是格林小姐。 Come and sit down ~ to me. 来坐在我旁边。 Which is the town ~ to London in size? 大小仅次于伦敦的是哪一个城? the ~ best (thing), that which is chosen or accepted if the first choice fails: 第二好的; 次好的事物: There are no tickets left for the Circus; the ~ best thing is the Zoo. 看马戏的票没有了, 次好的去处是动物园。 ~ to nothing, scarcely anything; almost nothing: 几乎没有: No wonder she's ill! She eats ~ to nothing. 怪不得她病了! 她几乎什么都没吃。 ~ door, in the ~ house: 邻家; 隔壁: He lives ~ door (to me). 他住在我(隔壁。 The people ~ door are very noisy. 隔壁的人很吵闹。 ~ door neighbours. 我们是隔壁邻居。 ~ door to, (fig) almost; not far from: (喻)几乎; 近乎; 差不多: Such ideas are ~ door to madness. 这种主意近乎疯狂。 next of kin, ⇨ kin. 2 (of time: def art needed if the reference is to a time that is future in relation to a time already mentioned): (指时间; 假如所指的时间是在已提到的时间的未来, 则须加定冠词): I shall go there ~ Friday/week/year. 下星期五(下星期, 明年)我要到那里去。 We shall be in France by this time ~ week. 下星期这个时候我们将在法国了。 He will spend the first week of his holiday in France and the ~ (week) in Italy. 他将要在法国度他的假期的第一周, 在意大利度第二周。 We arrived in Turin on a Monday; the ~ day we left for Rome. 我们星期一抵达了都灵; 次日我们去罗马。 That summer was very wet; the ~ summer was even wetter. 那年夏天雨很多; 次年夏天雨更多。 Is he coming this weekend (ie the coming weekend) or ~ weekend (ie the following weekend)? 他是本周末要来还是下周末要来? □ adv 1 after this/that; then: 在这(那)以后; 然后: What are you going to do ~? 你接着要做什么? When I ~ saw her she was dressed in green. 我再度看到她时, 她穿着绿色衣服。 come ~, follow: 随着; 跟着: What comes ~, what's the ~ thing (to do, etc)。接下去(要做的等)是什么? 2 used to express surprise or comment: 用于表示惊讶: What will he be saying ~? 他下一步又要说什么呢? A new motor-car! What ~? 一辆新车! 还要什么(含讥刺意味)? □ prep (archaic) (古) =next to.

nexus /ˈneksəs; ˈnɛksəs/ n (pl ~es -səsɪz; -səsɪz/) connection; bond; connected series. 关系; 连结; 连系; 连结的系列。

nib /nɪb; nɪb/ n split pen-point (to be) inserted in a pen-holder. 钢笔尖。

nibble /ˈnɪbl; ˈnɪbl/ vt, vi [VP6A, 2A, 3A] ~ (**at**), 1 take tiny bites: 细咬; 轻咬: fish nibbling (at) the bait. 轻咬鱼饵的鱼。 2 (fig) show some inclination to accept (an offer), agree to (a suggestion, etc), but without being definite. (喻)表示有意(但未确定地)接受(提议), 赞同(建议等)。 □ n [C] act of nibbling: 轻咬; 细咬: I felt a ~ at the bait. 我觉得有鱼轻轻地咬了一下鱼饵。

nice /naɪs; naɪs/ adj (**-r, -st**) 1 (contrary to nasty) pleasant; agreeable; kind; friendly; fine: (与 nasty 相反)令人愉快的; 宜人的; 良好的; 友善的; 优美的: a ~ day; 好天气; 美好的一天; ~ weather; 好天气; a ~ little girl; 可爱的小女孩; ~ to the taste/the feel, etc; 味道佳美(摸起来觉得柔细等); medicine that is not ~ to take. 不好吃的药。 ~ and + adj, because...: 因为···而宜人: ~ and warm by the fire; 在火边温暖而舒适; ~ and cool in the woods. 在森林里很凉快。 2 needing care and exactness; sensitive; subtle: 需要谨慎和精确的; 精微的; 敏感的; 狡黠的: a ~ point of law, one that may be difficult to decide; 法律上难以决定之处; a ~ (= delicate) shades of meaning. 意义的微妙区别。 3 (ironic) difficult; bad: (反语)困难的; 坏的: You've got us into a ~ mess. 你使我们陷入困境了。 4 hard to please; having or showing delicate tastes: 难以取悦的; 难侍候的; 讲究的: too ~ in one's dress. 衣着过份讲究。 5 punctilious; scrupulous: 谨慎的; 多顾虑的: He's not so ~ in his business methods. 他的经营方法不太谨慎。 **~·ly** adv 1 in a ~ manner. 美好地; 宜人地; 精细地; 讲究地; 谨慎地。 2 (colloq) very well; all right: (口)很好; 相宜: That will suit me ~ly. 那会刚好适合我。 The patient is doing ~ly, is making good progress. 那个病人好得很快。 **~·ness** n

nicety /ˈnaɪsətɪ; ˈnaɪsətɪ/ n (pl **-ties**) 1 [U] accuracy; exactness: 准确; 精确。 ~ of judgement; 判断的准确; a point of great ~, one needing most careful and exact consideration. 需要仔细考虑之处。 2 [C] delicate distinction: 细微的区别: the niceties of criticism. 批评的细微之处。 **to a** ~, exactly right: 正确地; 恰好地: He judged the distance to a ~. 他判断那段距离甚为精确。

niche /nɪtʃ; nɪtʃ/ n [C] 1 (usu shallow) recess (often with a shelf) in a wall, eg for a statue or ornament. (通常为浅的)壁龛(常有框架, 用以放置塑像或装饰品等)。 have a ~ in the temple of fame, have achievements that will not be forgotten. 流芳百世。 2 (fig) suitable or fitting position: (喻)适当的位置; 恰当的场所: He found the right ~ for himself, a place where he could do what he wanted to do, comfortably and happily. 他找到了适当的职位。

nick[1] /nɪk; nɪk/ n 1 small V-shaped cut (made in sth), eg as a record. V 形的小刻痕(例如作记录者)。 **2 in the ~ of time,** only just in time; at the critical or opportune time. 刚来得及; 在恰好的时候; 正当危急之际。 **3 in the ~,** (sl) in prison. (俚)在监狱中; 在监禁中。 □ vt make a ~ in: 刻痕于: ~ one's chin, while shaving; (刮胡子时)在下巴处留下一道割痕; cut a notch in. 刻 V 形缺口于。

nick[2] /nɪk; nɪk/ n (sl) (only in) (俚)(仅用于) **in good/poor ~,** in good/poor health or condition: 健康情形良好(不好); 情况良好: feeling in very good ~. 感觉健康情形非常良好。 The house is in pretty poor ~. 那幢房子的情况糟透了。

Nick /nɪk; nɪk/ n short for Nicholas. 为 Nicholas 的简写。 **Old N~,** the devil. 魔鬼。

nickel /ˈnɪkl; ˈnɪkl/ n 1 [U] hard, silver-white metal (symbol **Ni**) used in the form of ~-plating and in alloys (,~-steel, ,~-silver). 镍(一种银白色的坚硬金属, 用于镀镍及镍钢、镍银等合金中)。 2 US coin, value 5 cents. 美国的镍币(值五分钱)。 □ vt (**-ll-**, US = **-l-**) coat with ~. 镀镍于。

nick·nack /ˈnɪknæk; ˈnɪknæk/ n = **knick-knack**.

nick·name /ˈnɪkneɪm; ˈnɪkˌneɪm/ n name given in addition to or altered from or used instead of the real name (eg Fatty for a fat person; Shorty humorously for

a very tall person). 绰号；浑名(例如叫胖的人"胖子"；对非常高的人诙谐地称为"矮子")。 □ vt [VP6A, 23] give a ~ to: 加绰号于; 给…起绰号: They ~d him Hurry. 他们给他起了绰号号"慌张"。

nic·o·tine /'nɪkəti:n; 'nɪkə,tin/ n [U] poisonous, oily substance in tobacco-leaves: 尼古丁(烟叶中所含的有毒的油质成分)： ~-stained fingers: 被尼古丁熏黄的手指; cigarettes with a low ~ content. 含尼古丁成分低的香烟。

niece /ni:s; nis/ n daughter of one's brother (-in-law) or sister (-in-law). 侄女; 甥女。

niff /nɪf; nɪf/ n (GB sl, dial) (unpleasant) smell. (英俚，方)臭味。 ~**y** adj (sl) having a bad smell. (俚)有臭味的。

nifty /'nɪftɪ; 'nɪftɪ/ adj (sl) (俚) **1** smart; stylish. 漂亮的; 时髦的。 **2** having an unpleasant smell. 有臭味的。 **3** quick, efficient: 迅速敏捷的: Look ~! 赶快! (more usu 较常用 Look nippy!)

nig·gard /'nɪgəd; 'nɪgəd/ n mean, stingy person. 小气鬼; 吝啬鬼。 ~·**ly** adj giving, given, unwillingly, in small amounts; miserly: 吝啬的; 小气的: ~ly contributions. 小气的捐助。 ~·**li·ness** n

nig·ger /'nɪgə(r); 'nɪgɚ/ n △ (impolite and offensive word for) Negro. (讳)黑鬼(指黑人，为不礼貌及侮蔑用语)。

niggle /'nɪgl; 'nɪgl/ vi give too much time or attention to unimportant details; complain about trivial matters. 过份为小事费时或操心; 为琐事发牢骚。 **nig·gling** adj trifling; lacking in boldness of effect. 琐碎的; 无关重要的; 微小的; 不显目的。

nigh /naɪ; naɪ/ adv, prep (-er, -est) (archaic and poet) near (to). 近; 靠近。

night /naɪt; naɪt/ n [C, U] **1** dark hours between sunset and sunrise or twilight and dawn: 夜: in/during the ~; 在夜里; on Sunday ~; 在星期日夜里; on the ~ of Friday, the 13th of June; 在六月十三日星期五晚上; a late-~ show at the cinema, one given much later than the usual shows. 夜晚最后一场电影。 He stayed three ~s with us, slept at our house three ~. 他在我们家里住了三夜。 Can you stay over ~, spend the ~ with us? 你能在我们家里过夜吗? What a dirty ~ it has been! 这一夜风雨好大! ~ after ~, for many ~s in succession. 一夜又一夜; 连着几夜。 all ~ (long), throughout the whole ~. 整夜里; 彻夜; 终夜。 ~ and day, continuously: 日以继夜; 不断地: travel ~ and day for a week. 昼夜不停地旅行一星期。 at ~, when ~ comes; during the ~: 夜里: 6 o'clock at ~, 6pm. 下午六时。 by ~, during the ~: 夜间: travel by ~. 夜间旅行。 get/have/take a ~ off, a ~ free from work usually done at ~. 一夜不值(通常在夜间的)工作; 一夜不当班。 have a good/bad ~, sleep well/badly. (夜里)睡得好(不好)。 have a ~ out, spend an evening and ~ in pleasure, eg by having dinner out, followed by a visit to the cinema. 在外头玩一个晚上(如在外面吃饭,接着去看电影等)。 make a ~ of it, spend all ~ in pleasure-making, esp at a party. 痛痛快快地玩一个晚上。 turn ~ into day, do at ~ what is usu done during the day. 以夜作昼(把通常在日间做的工作放在夜里做); 日夜颠倒。 work ~s, work on ~ shift: 上夜班: My husband's working ~s this week. 我丈夫这星期过夜班。 ⇨ shift¹(2). **2** (compounds) (复合词) '~·**bell** n bell (eg on the street door, at a doctor's house) to be used at ~. (医师住宅等大门上所装的)夜间门铃。 '~·**bird** n (a) bird (eg an owl) which is active at ~. 夜鸟(夜间活动的鸟,如猫头鹰)。 (b) person (usu disreputable) who goes about at ~. 夜游人(通常指品行不良之人)。 '~·**cap** n (a) cap (formerly) worn in bed. (昔时睡觉戴的)睡帽。 (b) (usu alcoholic) drink taken before going to bed. 睡前的饮料(通常指酒类); 睡前酒。 '~·**club** n club open until the early hours of the morning to members for dancing, supper, entertainment, etc. 夜总会。 '~·**dress** n long, loose garment worn by a woman or child in bed. (妇女和小孩的)睡袍; 睡衣。

'~·**fall** n [U] the coming of ~; evening. 日暮; 傍晚; 黄昏。 '~·**gown** n = ~dress. '~·**ie**, ~**y** n (colloq) (口) = ~dress. '~·**jar** n ~-flying bird that resembles a swift. 欧夜鹰。 '~·**life**, entertainment, eg cabaret, available in a town late at ~. 夜生活(城市中深夜里的娱乐,如餐饮场所的歌舞表演、夜总会等)。 '~·**light** n light (eg a short, thick candle, or a small electric bulb) kept burning in a bedroom at ~ (esp for a small child or an invalid). 通夜不熄的灯;通宵灯(如组短的蜡烛或小电灯,尤指为小孩或病人而点者)。 '~·**line** n line left in a river, lake, etc with baited hooks, to catch fish by ~. 夜钓绳(夜间放在水中以钓鱼, 绳端装有上了饵的钩)。 '~·**long** adj lasting the whole ~. 通宵的; 彻夜的。 '~·**mare** -mea(r); -mɛr/ n [C] **(a)** terrible. frightening dream. 梦魇; 恶梦。 **(b)** haunting fear; sth dreaded; (memory of a) horrible experience: 萦绕于心的恐惧; 可怕的事物; 可怕经验的(记忆): Travelling on those bad mountain roads was a ~mare. 在那些崎岖山路上旅行是可怕的事。 '~·**porter** n hotel porter on duty during the ~. 旅馆夜间当班的门房。 '~·**safe** n facility or opening like a letter-box in a wall of a bank, so that valuables, money, etc may be deposited after banking hours. 夜间保险箱(装置于银行墙上象信箱的开口, 供客户于银行下班后存放珍贵物品、金钱等)。 '~·**school** n one that gives lessons to persons who are unable to attend classes during the day. 夜校。 '~·**shade** n [U] name of various wild plants with poisonous berries. 龙葵(结有毒浆果的数种野生植物)。 '~**shift**, ⇨ shift¹(2). '~·**shirt** n boy's or man's long shirt for sleeping in. 男睡衣。 '~·**soil** n contents of earth-closets and cesspools, removed during the ~. 粪坑和粪池中的粪便(通常在夜间运走)。 '~·**stop** n, '~·**stop** n break in a journey for a night. 夜间停留过夜。 '~·**time** n time of darkness: 夜间;由夜~time, by ~. 在夜间; 夜里。 '~·**watch** n (person or group of persons keeping) watch by ~. 守夜;守夜者。 **in the ~-watches**, during the wakeful, restless, or anxious periods of ~. 在夜里睡不着,不安或焦急的那几段时间中。 '~·**watchman** /-mən; -mən/ n (pl -men) man employed to keep watch (eg in a factory) at ~. (工厂等所雇用的)守夜者。 '~·**work** n work that is done, or must be done, by ~. 夜间工作; 夜工。 ~·**ly** adj, adv (taking place, happening, existing) in the ~ or every ~: 在夜间: 夜间发生、存在等的;每夜(的): ~ly performances; 夜间演出; 每晚演出; a film show twice ~ly; 每晚放映两次的电影; do something ~ly. 每天晚上都要做的事情。

night·in·gale /'naɪtɪŋgeɪl US: -tŋg-; 'naɪtŋ,gel/ n small, reddish-brown migratory bird that sings sweetly by night as well as by day. 夜莺。 ⇨ the illus at bird. 参看 bird 之插图。

ni·hil·ism /'naɪ ɪlɪzəm; 'naɪəl,ɪzəm/ n [U] total rejection of current political institutions and religious and moral beliefs. 无政府主义;虚无主义。 **ni·hil·ist** /-ɪst; -ɪst/ n believer in ~. 无政府主义者;虚无主义者。 **ni·hil·is·tic** /,naɪ ɪ'lɪstɪk; ,naɪə'lɪstɪk/ adj relating to ~. 无政府主义的;虚无主义的。

nil /nɪl; nɪl/ n nothing: 无; 零: The result of the game was three nil/three goals to nil, ie 3-0. 比赛结果是三比零。

Ni·lotic /naɪ'lɒtɪk; naɪ'lɑtɪk/ adj of the Nile, the Nile region, or its inhabitants. 尼罗河的; 尼罗河流域的;尼罗河流域之居民的。

nimble /'nɪmbl; 'nɪmbl/ adj **1** quick-moving: 敏捷的; 迅速的: as ~ as a goat. 象山羊一样敏捷。 **2** (of the mind) sharp; quick to understand. (指头脑)敏锐的;聪明的。 **nim·bly** /'nɪmblɪ; 'nɪmblɪ/ adv ~·**ness** n

nim·bus /'nɪmbəs; 'nɪmbəs/ n (pl ~es /-bəsɪz; -bəsɪz/, **-bi** /-baɪ; -baɪ/) **1** bright disc round or over the head of a saint (in a painting, etc). (在画等之中,圣者头部四周或上面的)光环; 光轮; 光云。 ⇨ halo. **2** rain-cloud. 雨云。

nim·iny-pim·iny /,nɪmɪnɪ 'pɪmɪnɪ; 'nɪmənɪ'pɪmənɪ/

adj affected; mincing; prim. 做作的; 矫饰的; 拘泥形式的。

Nim·rod /'nɪmrɒd; 'nɪmrɑd/ *n* great hunter. 宁录(大猎人)。 ⇨ Gen 10: 8, 9. 参看创世记 10 章 8 节和 9 节。

nin·com·poop /'nɪŋkəmpuːp; 'nɪŋkəm,pup/ *n* foolish, weak-minded person. 愚人; 傻子。

nine /naɪn; naɪn/ *n*, *adj* the number 9, ⇨ **App 4**. 九; 九个; 九个(的)(参看附录四)。 *a ~-days' wonder*, sth that attracts attention for a few days and is then forgotten. 一时引人注意不久即被遗忘的事物。 *dressed up to the ~s*, (colloq) dressed very elaborately or extravagantly. (口)穿着非常考究或奢侈。 *~ times out of ten*, very often. 十有八九。 **nine·pence** /'naɪnpəns US: -pens; 'naɪnpəns/ *n* 九便士。 **nine·penny** /'naɪnpenɪ US: -penɪ; 'naɪn,penɪ/ *adj* 九便士的。 **~·teen** /,naɪn'tiːn; naɪn'tin/ *n*, *adj* the number 19. 十九; 十九(的)。 *~teen to the dozen*, (talk) continually. 不停地(讲话); 喋喋不休。 **~·teenth** /,naɪn'tiːnθ; naɪn'tinθ/ *n*, *adj* the next after the 18th, one of 19 equal parts. 第十九(的); 十九分之一。 **~·ti·eth** /'naɪntɪɪθ; 'naɪntɪɪθ/ *adj* the next after the 89th; one of 90 equal parts. 第九十(的); 九十分之一。 **~·ty** /'naɪntɪ; 'naɪntɪ/ *n*, *adj* the number 90. 九十(的)。 *~ty-~ times out of a hundred*, almost always. 一百次中有九十九次; 几乎总是如此。 **the ~·ties**, 90—99. 90 至 99 之数。 *'~-fold* /-fəʊld; -fold/ *adj*, *adv* ~ times as many or much. 九重的(地); 九倍的(地)。 **ninth** /naɪnθ; naɪnθ/ *n*, *adj* the next after the 8th; one of 9 equal parts. 第九(的); 九分之一。 **ninth·ly** *adv*

nine·pins /'naɪnpɪnz; 'naɪn,pɪnz/ *n pl* (with *sing v*) (与单数动词连用) **1** game in which a ball is rolled along the floor at nine bottle-shaped pieces of wood. 九柱戏(沿地面滚球撞击九根瓶状木柱的一种游戏)。 ⇨ **tenpins**. **2** (*sing*) one of these pieces. (单)(九柱戏中的一根)摧秧。= 柱。 *go down like a ninepin*, fall heavily. 重重跌倒(象九柱戏中的木柱般跌倒)。

ninny /'nɪnɪ; 'nɪnɪ/ *n* (*pl* **-nies**) fool; simpleton. 愚人; 傻子。

Niobe /'naɪəbɪ; 'naɪəbɪ/ *n* (Gk myth) woman who was changed into a stone fountain while weeping for her children who had been killed; woman who weeps and cannot be comforted. (希神)尼奥比(当哀哭其子女被杀时,被化为石泉之女人); 哀泣而无法安慰的女人。

nip /nɪp; nɪp/ *vt*, *vi* (**-pp-**) **1** [VP6A, 15A, B] pinch; press hard (eg between finger and thumb, or with the claws, as a crab does, or with the teeth, as a dog or horse might do): 捏; 掐; 夹(例如用大拇指与食指, 蟹等用螯, 狗马等用牙): *A crab nipped my toe while I was swimming*. 当我游泳的时候, 一只螃蟹箝住了我的脚指头。 *He nipped his finger in the door*, ie between the door and the door-post. 他的手指给门缝夹了。 *The gardener was nipping off* (= pinching out) *the side shoots from his chrysanthemums*. 园丁正在把菊花的边芽掐掉。 (sewing) alter the size slightly: (缝纫)略为修改: *The dress fits me now that I've nipped in the sides a little*, reduced the width by altering the seams. 这件衣服两边恰为修改后很合我的身。 **2** [VP6A, 15A] (of frost, wind, etc) stop the growth or: damage. (指霜、风等)伤害; 摧残。 *nip sth in the bud*, stop its development. 在萌芽时摘取, 阻止某事物的发展; 防患于未然。 **3** [VP2A] perform the action of biting or pinching. 咬; 夹; 掐。 **4** (colloq) [VP2C] hurry: (口)赶快; 急忙: *nip along*. 急忙赶进。 *He nipped in* (= got in quickly) *just in front of me*. 他就在我前面插进来。 *I'll nip on ahead and open the door*. 我要赶到前面去打开那个门。 □ *n* [C] **1** sharp pinch or bite: 捏; 掐; 夹; 咬: *a cold nip in the air*, a feeling of frost. 空气里的刺骨的寒冷。 **2** small drink (esp of spirits): 少量(尤指烈酒): *a nip of brandy*. 少量的白兰地。 *'nip·ping adj* (of the air or wind) sharp; biting cold. (指空气或风)凛冽的; 刺骨的; 严寒的。 ⇨ **nippy(1)**.

nip·per /'nɪpə(r); 'nɪpɚ/ *n* **1** (*pl*, colloq) pincers,

---

forceps or other tool for gripping. (复)(口)镊子; 钳子; 拔钳; 任何夹东西的工具。 **2** crustacean's claw. 甲壳类动物的螯。 **3** (GB colloq) small child. (英口)小孩。

nipple /'nɪpl; 'nɪpl/ *n* **1** part of the breast through which a baby gets its mother's milk; similar small projection on the breast of a human male. (人类的)乳头; 奶头。 Cf 参较 *teat* for other mammals. 其他哺乳动物的奶头用 *teat*。 **2** (more usu 较常用 *teat*) rubber mouth-piece of a baby's feeding bottle. (奶瓶上的)橡皮奶头。 **3** sth shaped like a *~*: 似奶头之物: *'greasing ~s*, through which grease is injected. 加脂乳头(滑脂经由其灌入)。

Nip·pon·ese /,nɪpə'niːz; ,nɪpɑn'iz/ *adj* of Nippon /'nɪpɒn; 'nɪpɑn/ (= Japan). 日本的。

nippy /'nɪpɪ; 'nɪpɪ/ *adj* (**-ier, -iest**) (colloq) (口) **1** (GB) biting cold. (英)刺骨的; 严寒的。 **2** nimble. 敏捷的; 迅速的。 *look ~*, be quick. 赶快。

nir·vana /nɪə'vɑːnə; nɪr'vænə/ *n* (in Buddhism) state in which individuality becomes extinct by being absorbed into the supreme spirit. (佛教的)涅槃(个体借融入最高之精神体而寂灭之境界)。

nisi /'naɪsaɪ; 'naɪsaɪ/ *conj* (Lat, legal) unless. (拉, 法律)除非。 *decree ~*, decree (of divorce, etc) valid unless cause is shown for rescinding it before the time when it is made absolute. 在指定时日以前不提出反对理由即行生效的(离婚等的)判决。

Nis·sen hut /'nɪsn hʌt; 'nɪsn hʌt/ *n* prefabricated semicircular hut of sheets of corrugated iron, erected over a concrete floor. 尼森式小屋(建于混凝土地面上, 用波状铁皮预造的半圆形小屋)。

nit[1] /nɪt; nɪt/ *n* egg of a louse or other parasitic insect. 虱或其他寄生虫的卵。

nit[2] /nɪt; nɪt/ *n* = **nitwit**.

ni·ter /'naɪtə(r); 'naɪtɚ/ ⇨ **nitre**.

ni·trate /'naɪtreɪt; 'naɪtret/ *n* salt formed by the chemical reaction of nitric acid with an alkali, esp *potassium ~ and sodium ~*, used as fertilizers. 硝酸盐(尤指作肥料用的硝酸钾与硝酸钠)。 (Used in *pl* for 'kinds of ~'). (复数指各类的硝酸盐)。

nitre (US = **niter**) /'naɪtə(r); 'naɪtɚ/ *n* [U] potassium or sodium nitrate (also called 亦称作 *salt-petre*). 硝酸钾(即硝石); 硝酸钠。

ni·tric /'naɪtrɪk; 'naɪtrɪk/ *adj* of, containing, nitrogen. 氮的; 含氮的。 *~ 'acid*, (**HNO₃**), clear colourless, powerful acid that eats into and destroys most substances. 硝酸(无色强酸, 能侵蚀大多数物质, 分子式为 HNO_3)。

ni·tro·chalk /,naɪtrəʊ'tʃɔːk; ,naɪtro'tʃɔk/ *n* [U] fertilizer used in spring to encourage growth of grass. 白垩硝(春季里用以加速青草生长的肥料)。

ni·tro·gen /'naɪtrədʒən; 'naɪtrədʒən/ *n* [U] gas (symbol **N**) without colour, taste or smell, forming about four-fifths of the atmosphere. 氮(化学符号 N, 无色、无味、无臭的气体, 大约占空气的五分之四)。

ni·tro·glycer·ine, -glycerin /,naɪtrəʊ'glɪsəriːn US: -rɪn; ,naɪtro'glɪsrɪn/ *n* [U] powerful explosive made by adding glycerine to a mixture of nitric and sulphuric acids. 硝化甘油; 炸药油。硝化甘油炸药。

ni·trous /'naɪtrəs; 'naɪtrəs/ *adj* of, like, nitre. 硝石的; 似硝石的。 *~ oxide*, ga s**(N₂O)** (also called *laughing-gas*) sometimes used by dental surgeons to make a person unconscious while having a tooth or teeth pulled out. 氧化亚氮(亦称笑气, 分子式为 N_2O, 牙医拔牙时作麻醉剂用)。

nitty-gritty /,nɪtɪ 'ɡrɪtɪ; ,nɪtɪ 'ɡrɪtɪ/ *n* [U] the *~*, (colloq) the basic fact(s) of a matter. (口)事情的基本事实。

nit·wit /'nɪtwɪt; 'nɪt,wɪt/ *n* (colloq) person with very little intelligence. (口)笨人。 Hence, 由此产生, *~·ted* /,nɪt'wɪtɪd; ,nɪt'wɪtɪd/ *adj* unintelligent. 愚昧的。

nix /nɪks; nɪks/ *n* (sl) nothing. (俚)无物。

no /nəʊ; no/ *adj* **1** not one; not any: 无; 没有: *She had no friends*. 她没有朋友。 *The poor boy had no money*. 那

可怜的男孩没有钱。*No words can describe the scene.* 那景色非笔墨所能形容。*There was no end to our troubles,* They were endless. 我们的麻烦是没完的。**no end of,** (colloq) a large number or quantity of; very great: (口) 多的；大量的；极大的: *He spends no end of money on clothes.* 他花大量的钱在衣着上。*We had no end of a good time,* a very enjoyable time. 我们玩得极为愉快。(Note that *no* precedes numerals and *other*): (注意 no 放在数字与 other 之前): *No one man could have done it.* No man could have done it by himself. 没有一个人能单独完成那件事。*No two men think alike.* 没有两个人想法是一样的。*No other man could do the work.* 没有别的人能做那个工作。**2** (implying the opposite of the following word): (表示随在后面那个词的相反的意思): *He's no friend of mine.* 他不是我的朋友。*The task is no easy one.* 那工作是不容易的。*This nightclub is no place for a young and innocent girl.* 这家夜总会不是年轻纯洁的女孩应该去的地方。*Matilda is no beauty,* is not at all beautiful. 马蒂尔达一点也不漂亮。**3** (in the pattern: 用于下列句型: there + be + no + gerund): *There's no saying* (= It is impossible to say) *what he'll be doing next.* 他接下去将要做什么，很难断言。*There's no denying* (= We cannot deny) *that... .* 无可否认的···。**4** (in elliptical constructions): (用于省略结构): *No smoking* (= Smoking is not allowed). 禁止吸烟。*No surrender!* 绝不投降! *It's raining hard and no mistake,* and there can be no doubt about it. 现在正下着大雨; 这是千真万确的。**5** (phrases) (短语) *It's no go,* (colloq) can't be done, won't succeed. (口) 行不通; 不行; 不成。**be no good/use,** useless: 无用; 没有用: *It's no good crying over spilt milk.* 牛奶洒了, 哭也无益。⇨ **milk**[1](1). **be no wonder (that),** not surprising (that). 怪不得(···); (···) 是不足为奇的。**by no means,** ⇨ **means**[1]. **in 'no time,** very soon, very quickly. 立刻。**,no-'ball,** unlawfully delivered ball in cricket. 玩板球时所投的不合规则的球。**,no-'go area,** (colloq) (usu urban) area barricaded to prevent the police or security force from entering. (口) (通常指都市的) 没有障碍物的地区(阻止警察或保安部队进入者)。**'no-man's-land,** (in war) ground between the fronts of two opposing armies. (战争时两军阵前之) 无人地带。**'no one, 'no-one,** *pron*=nobody. □ *adv* **1** (used with comparatives): (与比较级形容词或副词连用): *We went no farther than* (= only as far as) *the bridge.* 我们只走到桥边。*I hope you're feeling no worse this morning.* 我希望你今早不会觉得更不舒服。*I have no more money.* 我没有更多的钱了。**2** (phrases) (短语) *I have no more...than,* ⇨ **more**(5). *no such,* ⇨ **such.** **3** *whether or no,* whether or not: *Whether or no you like it, you've got to do it.* 不论你是否喜欢它, 你都得去做。□ *particle* **1** (opposite of 'Yes'): (Yes 之反义词): *Is it Monday today?—No, it isn't.* 今天是星期一吗? —— 不, 今天不是星期一。*Isn't it Monday today?—No, it isn't.* 今天不是星期一吗? —— 不, 今天不是星期一。*Aren't you busy?—No, I'm not.* 你不忙吗? ——不, 我不忙。**2** (used with *not* or *nor* to emphasize a negative): (与 not 或 nor 连用以加强否定语气): *One man couldn't lift it; no, nor half a dozen.* 这玩意儿一个人举不起来; 就是六个人也不行。□ *n* [C] refusal; denial: 拒绝; 否认: *The noes* /nəʊz; noz/ *have it,* Those voting 'no' are in the majority. 反对的占多数。

Noah's ark /ˌnəʊəz ˈɑːk ; ˌnoəzˈɑrk/ *n* model of the ark in which Noah and his family were saved from the Flood, with small animal and human figures. 挪亚方舟(挪亚及其家人从大洪水中逃生所乘方舟的模型, 上有小动物及人物的形象)。⇨ **Gen, chap 5-9.** 参看旧约圣经创世记第5至9章。

nob[1] /nɒb; nɑb/ *n* (sl) head. (俚)头。

nob[2] /nɒb; nɑb/ *n* (sl) member of the upper classes; person of high rank. (俚)上流社会的人物; 地位高的人。

nobble /'nɒbl; 'nɑbl/ *vt* (GB sl) (英俚) [VP6A] **1** tamper with (a race-horse) to lessen its chance of winning. 暗害(赛跑的马)以减少其获胜机会。**2** (colloq)

get the attention of (in order to gain an advantage, etc); get sth dishonestly or by devious means. 引起···的注意(以期获得好处等); 诈取; 骗取; 以不正当手段取得某物。

Nobel Prize /ˌnəʊbel 'praɪz; ˌno͵bɛl 'praɪz/ *n* any of the prizes awarded each year by the Nobel Foundation for outstanding achievements in literature, science and the promotion of world peace (after A B Nobel, Swedish inventor of dynamite who established the awards). 诺贝尔奖 (每年由诺贝尔基金会颁奖给在文学、科学及促进世界和平方面有卓越成就者; 该奖系由瑞典炸药发明家 A B Nobel 所设立)。

no·bil·ity /nəʊ'bɪlətɪ; no'bɪlətɪ/ *n* [U] **1** quality of being noble; noble character, mind, birth, rank. 高尚; 高贵; 高尚的性格、思想、出身、地位。**2** (usu with *def art*) the nobles as a class: (通常与定冠词连用)贵族: *a member of the ~;* 贵族阶级的人; *marry into the ~.* 嫁给贵族。

noble /'nəʊbl; 'nobl/ *adj* **1** having, showing, high character and qualities: 高尚的; 崇高的; 伟大的: *a ~ leader;* 伟大的领袖; *~ sentiments;* 高尚的情操; *a ~ mind.* 高尚的思想。Hence, 由此产生, *~'minded* /'maɪndɪd; 'maɪndɪd/ *adj.* *~'minded·ness* *n* **2** of high rank, title or birth: 贵族的; 高贵的: *a man of ~ rank /birth.* 身份(出身)高贵的人。**3** splendid; that excites admiration: 卓越的; 辉煌的: *a building planned on a ~ scale;* 设计宏伟的建筑物; *a ~ horse;* 一匹骏马; *~ metals,* eg gold, silver, platinum, that do not easily tarnish in air or water. 贵金属(例如在空气或水中不易失去光泽的金、银、铂)。□ *n* person of ~ birth. 出身高贵的人; 贵族。**'~·man** /-mən; -mən/ *n* (*pl* **-men**) (GB) peer; person of parallel rank in other countries. (英)贵族; 在其他国家内相当于英国贵族身份的人。**nobly** /'nəʊblɪ; 'noblɪ/ *adv* in a ~ manner; splendidly. 高尚地; 高贵地; 华丽地。

no·blesse /nəʊ'bles; no'blɛs/ *n* (F) class of nobles. (法)贵族阶级。**~ o'blige** /ə'bliːʒ; o'bliʒ/ (prov) privilege entails responsibility. (谚)位高任重。

no·body /'nəʊbədɪ; 'no͵bɑdɪ/ *pron* (*pl* **-dies**) **1** not anybody; no person: 没有人; 无人: *We saw ~ we knew.* 我们没有看到我们认识的人。*He said he would marry me or ~.* 他说他要娶我否则就不结婚。*N~ could find their luggage* (colloq for *his or her luggage*). 没有人能找到自己的行李 (本句的 their 为口语用法, 代替 his or her)。*N~ else* (= No other person) *offered to help.* 没有其它的人愿意协助。**2** (used in the *sing* with the *indef art,* and in the *pl*) unimportant or unimpressive person: (单数与不定冠词连用, 且可用复数)不重要的人; 小人物: *Don't marry a ~ like James.* 不要嫁给象 詹姆斯那样毫碌的人。

noc·tam·bu·list /nɒk'tæmbjʊlɪst; nɑk'tæmbjəlɪst/ *n* sleepwalker. 梦游者。

noc·tur·nal /nɒk'tɜːnl; nɑk'tɝnl/ *adj* of or in the night; done, active, or happening, in the night: 夜的; 在夜间的; 在夜间做的; 在夜间活动的; 发生于夜里的: *a man of ~ habits;* 有夜生活习惯的人; *~ birds,* eg owls. 夜鸟(如猫头鹰)。

noc·turne /'nɒktɜːn; 'nɑktɝn/ *n* [C] **1** painting of a scene at night. (画的)夜景。**2** soft, dreamy piece of music. 夜曲; 梦幻曲。

nod /nɒd; nɑd/ *vi, vt* (**-dd-**) **1** [VP2A, 3A, 4A] *nod (to/at),* bow the head slightly and quickly as a sign of agreement or as a familiar greeting: 点头(表示同意或招呼): *He nodded to me as he passed.* 他在过的时候向我点头打招呼。*He nodded to show that he understood.* 他点头表示他明白了。*have a nodding acquaintance with,* ⇨ **acquaintance.** **2** [VP2A, 2C] *nod (off),* let the head fall forward when sleepy or falling asleep; make a mistake as if asleep or half asleep: 垂着头打瞌睡; 打吨; (在类似打瞌睡的状态下)犯错: *She sat nodding by the fire.* 她坐在火炉边打吨。*She often nods off* (= falls asleep) *during the afternoon.* 她下午常常打瞌睡。

The teacher caught one of her pupils nodding, falling asleep, or so sleepy as to make mistakes. 那老师发现她的一个学生在打瞌睡(或因昏昏欲睡而犯错)。*Homer sometimes nods,* (prov) Even the greatest may make a small mistake.(谚) 荷马有时也打瞌睡;最伟大的人也可能犯小错误;智者千虑,必有一失。**3**[VP2C, 6A, 12A, 13A] indicate by nodding; 以点头表示: *He nodded approval/in approval/approvingly.* 他点头表示赞成。*He nodded me a welcome/nodded a welcome to Mary.* 他对我点头表示欢迎(向玛丽点头欢迎)。□ *n* **1** nodding of the head: 点头: *He gave me a nod as he passed.* 他走过时对我点头。**2** *the Land of Nod,* sleep. 睡乡。**3** *on the ~,* (US sl) on credit. (美俚)凭信用(赊购)。

noddle /'nɒdl; 'nɑdl/ *n* (colloq) head. (口)头。

node /nəʊd; nod/ *n* [C] **1** (bot) point on the stem of a plant where a leaf or bud grows out. (植物)茎节(长叶或发芽的部位)。**2** (phys) point or line of rest in a vibrating body. (物理)波节(不受振动之点或线)。**3**(fig) point at which the parts of sth begin or meet. (喻)起点;交点。

nod·ule /'nɒdju:l; US: 'nɒdʒu:l; 'nɑdʒul/ *n* small rounded lump; small knob or swelling. 小圆块;小结节;小瘤。**nod·u·lar** /-lə(r); -lə/, **nod·u·lat·ed** /-leɪtɪd; -leɪtɪd/ *adjj* having ~s. 有小圆块的;有结节的;有瘤块的。

Noel /nəʊ'el; no'ɛl/ *n* Christmas. 圣诞节。

nog·gin /'nɒgɪn; 'nɑgɪn/ *n* small measure, usu ¼ pint, of liquor; (sl) head. 酒类的小量名(通常为 ¼ 品脱);(俚)头。

no·how /'nəʊhaʊ; 'no,haʊ/ *adv* (colloq) in no way; not at all. (口)决不;毫不。

noise /nɔɪz; nɔɪz/ *n* [C, U] loud and unpleasant sound, esp when confused and undesired: 声音;噪音;喧声;闹声: *the ~ of jet aircraft:* 喷气式飞机的噪音; *Don't make so much ~/such a loud ~!* 不要那么吵闹! *What's that ~?* 那是什么声音? *What are those strange ~s?* 那些奇怪的声音是什么声音? **make a ~ (about sth),** talk or complain in order to get attention. (为某事而)高声谈论或抱怨(以引起别人的注意)。**make a '~ in the world,** become famous, be much talked about. 成名;成为人们议论的对象。**a 'big ~,** (sl) important person. (俚)要人。□ *vt ~ sth abroad,* make public: 宣扬;映传;谣传: *It was ~d abroad that he had been arrested.* 盛传他已经被逮捕了。**~·less** *adj* making little or no ~: 无声的;静的: *with ~less footsteps.* 以无声的脚步。**~·less·ly** *adv* **~·less·ness** *n*

noi·some /'nɔɪsəm; 'nɔɪsəm/ *adj* offensive; (esp, of smell) disgusting. 令人不快的; (尤指气味)令人讨厌的;难闻的。

noisy /'nɔɪzɪ; 'nɔɪzɪ/ *adj* (-ier, -iest) **1** making, accompanied by, much noise: 吵闹的;发吵声的: *children;* 吵闹的小孩; *~ games.* 喧闹的游戏。**2** full of noise: 喧哗的; 嘈杂的: *a ~ classroom.* 喧嚣的教室。**nois·ily** /-ɪlɪ; -ɪlɪ/ *adv* **noisi·ness** *n*

no·mad /'nəʊmæd; 'nomæd/ *n* member of a tribe that wanders from place to place, with no fixed home. 游牧部落的人;流浪者。**~ic** /nəʊ'mædɪk; no'mædɪk/ *adj* of ~s: 游牧部落的: *a ~ic society.* 游牧部落的社会。

nom de plume /,nɒm də 'plu:m; 'nɑmdə,plʌm/ *n* (*pl* **noms** /nɒm; nɑm/ **de plume**) (F) pen-name. (法)笔名。

no·men·cla·ture /nə'menklətʃə(r) US: 'nəʊmən-kleɪtʃər; 'nomən,kletʃə/ *n* [C] (formal) system of naming; (正式用语)命名法;专门名词;术语: *botanical ~;* 植物的命名法; *the ~ of chemistry.* 化学的专门名词。

nom·inal /'nɒmɪnl; 'nɑmənl/ *adj* **1** existing, etc in name or word only, not in fact: 名义上的;有名无实的: *the ~ ruler of the country;* 名义上的国家统治者; *the ~ value of the shares.* 股份的面值(股票的票面价值,并非市场价值)。**2** of little importance or value: 不重要或无价值的: *a ~ sum;* 极小的数目; *a ~ rent,* one very much below the actual value of the property. 名义租金(极少

的象征性租金)。**3** (gram) of a noun or nouns. (语法)名词的。**4** of, bearing, a name: 名字的;带有名字的;记名的: *a ~ roll.* 名薄。**~·ly** /-nəlɪ; -nlɪ/ *adv*

nomi·nate /'nɒmɪneɪt; 'nɑmə,net/ *vt* [VP6A, 14, 23] **1** *~ sb (for),* put forward for election to a position: 提名某人(为…候选人): *~ a man for the Presidency;* 提名一个人竞选总统; *~ Mr X for Mayor.* 提名 X 先生为市长候选人。**2** *~ sb (to),* appoint to office: 任命某人(做…);指定;指派: *a committee of five ~d members and eight elected members.* 由五个指派的委员和八个选出的委员组成的委员会。**nomi·nee** /,nɒmɪ'ni:; ,nɑmə'ni/ *n* person who is ~d for an office or appointment. 被提名的候选人;被任命者。

nomi·na·tion /,nɒmɪ'neɪʃn; ,nɑmə'neʃən/ *n* **1** [U] nominating; [C] instance of this: 提名;任命: *How many ~s have there been* (= How many persons have been nominated) *so far?* 到现在有多少人被提名? **2** [U] right of nominating sb for an office or position. 提名权;任命权。

nomi·na·tive /'nɒmɪnətɪv; 'nɑmənətɪv/ *adj, n* (of the) form of a word (eg the pronoun *we*) when it is the grammatical subject: 主格;主格的(例如 we): *the ~ case.* 主格。⇨ case¹(3).

nomi·nee /,nɒmɪ'ni:; ,nɑmə'ni/ *n* ⇨ **nominate.**

non- /,nɒn; nɑn/ *pref* who or which is not, does not, etc: 不;非;无:

,non-ag'gression *n* not attacking; not starting hostilities: 不侵略;不攻击;不挑衅: *a ,non-ag'gression pact.* 不侵略协定。

,non-a'lignment *n* principle or practice of not joining either of the great power blocs. 不结盟(不与世界上大集团任何一方结盟的原则或做法)。

,non-'combatant *n* person (esp in the armed forces, eg a surgeon or chaplain) who does not take part in the fighting. 非战斗人员(尤指军中的医官或牧师等不参与战斗的人员)。

,non-com'missioned *adj* (esp of army officers such as sergeants and corporals) not holding commissions(4). 无委任状的;非受任命的(尤指军中士官)。

,non-com'mittal *adj* not committing oneself to a definite course or to either side (in a dispute, etc): (在争论等中)不表示确定意见或立场的; 不明确的: *give a non-committal answer.* 给一个不明确的回答。

,non-com'pliance *n* refusal to comply (with an order, etc). 不顺从(命令等)。

,non-con'ductor *n* substance that does not conduct heat or electric current. 非导体(不传热或电的物质)。

,non-con'formist *n* **1** person who does not conform to society's standards. 不遵奉社会标准者。**2** (in England) member of a sect that has separated from the Church of England. (在英国)与英国国教分离的教派的教友。

,non-con'formity *n* **1** failure to conform. 不遵从;不适合;不一致。**2** (beliefs and practices of) non-conformists as a body. 非国教教徒(之信仰与惯例)。

,non-con'tentious *adj* not likely to cause contention. 不会引起争论的。

,non-e'vent *n* (colloq) planned event which turns out to be unworthy of what it was expected or hoped to be. (口)经计划但结果却不如当时所预料那样有价值的事件。

,non-'fiction *n* [U] prose books other than writings (eg novels, stories, plays) which deal with fictitious events and persons. 非小说性的散文文学(不象小说,故事,戏剧中之事件与人物均系虚构者)。

,non-'flammable *adj* (in official use, contrary to *inflammable*) having no tendency to burst into flames. (正式用语,与 inflammable 相对)不燃烧的。

,non-inter'ference, ,non-inter'vention *nn* principle or practice, esp in international affairs, of keeping out of other people's disputes. 不干预;不干涉(尤指在国际事务中避免卷入他国争执之原则或做法)。

,non-'moral *adj* that cannot be considered or judged as either moral or immoral. 非道德的(既非有道德的,亦非

不道德的);与道德无关的。

,non-ob'servance n failure to observe (a rule, etc). 不遵从;违反(规则等)。

,non-'payment n failure or neglect to pay (a debt, etc). 不支付;未偿付(债务等)。

,non-'resident adj who does not reside in: 非住在(某地)的: a non-resident priest, not living where he performs his duties. 不住在其执行职务地区的牧师。⇨ n person not staying at a hotel, etc: 非住宿于旅馆等中的人: Meals served to non-residents. 餐食供应非住宿本馆之客人。

,non-'skid adj (of tyres) designed to prevent or reduce the risk of skidding. (指轮胎)防滑的;不打滑的。

,non-'smoker n person who does not smoke tobacco: place, eg a train compartment, where smoking is forbidden. 不抽烟的人;禁烟的场所(例如火车的隔间)。

,non-'starter n horse which, although entered for a race, does not run; (fig) person who has no chance of success in sth he undertakes to do. 虽参加但未出赛的马;(喻)虽从事某工作但无成功机会的人。

,non-'stick adj (eg of a pan) made so that food, etc will not stick to its surface. (指锅等)不粘食物的。

,non-'stop adj, adv without a stop: 中途不停的: a non-stop train from London to Brighton, 从伦敦到布赖顿的直达火车; fly non-stop from New York to Paris. 从纽约直飞巴黎。

,non-'U adj ⇨ App 2. 参看附录二。

,non-'union adj not belonging to a trade union; not observing trade union rules: 没参加工会的;不遵守工会规章的: non-union labour. 没参加工会的工人。

,non-'violence n policy of rejecting violent means (but using peaceful protest, etc) to gain a political or social objective. 反暴力(政策);以不采取暴力手段,而以和平方式的抗议等,以达到政治或社会的目的)。

non-age /'nəʊnɪdʒ; 'nɑnɪdʒ/ n [U] = minority(1); immaturity. 未成年;未成熟。

nona-gen-ar-ian /ˌnəʊnədʒɪ'neərɪən; ˌnɑnədʒə'nɛrɪən/ n, adj (person who is) between 89 and 100 years old. 九十到九十九岁的(人)。

nonce /nɒns; nɑns/ n (old use, or liter; only in) (旧用法,或文义;仅用于) for the ~, for the present time only. 暂时;目前。'~-word n word coined for one occasion. 临时语(为某一场合而临时创造的词语)。

non-cha-lant /'nɒnʃələnt; 'nɑnʃələnt/ adj not having, not showing, interest or enthusiasm; deliberately casual. 不感兴趣的;冷漠的;不热心的;故意漠不关心的。~-ly adv **non-cha-lance** /-ləns; -ləns/ n [U].

non com-pos men-tis /ˌnɒn ˌkɒmpəs 'mentɪs; ˌnɑn,kɑmpəs'mɛntɪs/ (Lat)(legal)not legally responsible because not of sound mind; (colloq) confused in one's mind. (拉)(法律)因精神不正常而不负法律上责任的;心神丧失的;(口)心乱如麻的。

non-de-script /'nɒndɪskrɪpt; 'nɑndɪ,skrɪpt/ n, adj (person or thing) not easily classed, not having a definite character; uninteresting. 不易分类的;没有特征的;难以区别的;难以形容的人或物;难以区别的人或物;无趣味的。

none /nʌn; nʌn/ pron 1 not any, not one: 毫无;一个也没有: I wanted some string but there was ~ in the house. 我需要一些绳子,但家里一根也没有。N~ of this money is mine. 这笔钱没有一点是我的。'Is there any coal left?' 'No, ~ at all.' '还有煤炭吗?' '没有,一点儿也没有'。There are faults from which ~ of us (= not one of us, or not any of us) is / are free. 有一些错误我们任何人均不能避免。N~ of them has / have come back yet. 他们之中还没有一个人回来。He is aware, ~ better than he (ie no one is better aware than he), that... . 没有一个人比他更知道…。~ the less, nevertheless. 然而;虽然如此;依然。~ but, only: 仅;只: They chose none but the best. 他们只挑最好的。~ other than: 就是: The new arrival was ~ other than the President (emph for the President himself). 刚到达的就是总统本人(为 the

President himself 的强调说法)。 2 (in constructions equal to an imperative): (用在相当于祈使句的结构中): N~ of that! Stop that! 不要那样! N~ of your impudence! Don't be impudent! 不得无礼!别那么不要脸! 3 (separated from its n, in liter or rhet style): (在文学或修辞体裁中,与所代表的名词分开使用): They looked down on the plain, but village there was ~. 他们往下看那原野,但是那儿一个村庄也没有。Sounds there were ~ (= There were no sounds) except the murmur of the bees. 除了蜜蜂的嗡嗡声以外,没有别的声音。⇨ adv by no means; in no degree; not at all: 绝不;决不;毫不: I hope you're ~ the worse for that fall from your horse. 你从马上跌下来,我希望你没有受伤。I'm afraid I'm ~ the wiser for your explanation. 我恐怕听了你的解释我还是不明白。The salary they pay me is ~ too high. 他们付给我的薪水一点也不高。There are ,~ so ,deaf as those who will not 'hear, (prov) who refuse to hear. (谚)最聋的莫过于那些不愿意听话的人。

non-en-tity /nɒ'nentətɪ; nɑn'sntətɪ/ n (pl -ties) [C] 1 unimportant person. 不重要的人。2 thing that does not really exist or that exists only in the imagination. 并不真正存在之事物;想象中的事物。

none-such, non-such / 'nʌnsʌtʃ; 'nʌn,sʌtʃ/ n person or thing without equal; paragon. 无双之人或物;绝品;模范。

non-pareil /ˌnɒn pə'reɪl US: -'rel; ˌnɑnpə'rɛl/ adj, n (formal) unique or unrivalled (person or thing). (正式用语)独特的;无匹的;独特的人或物。

non-plus /nɒn'plʌs; nɑn'plʌs/ vt (-ss-, US -s-)[VP6A] (usu passive) surprise or puzzle (sb) so much that he does not know what to do or say: (通常用被动语态)使(某人)惊讶或困窘而不知所措;使狼狈: I was completely ~sed when she said 'No' to my proposal of marriage. 她拒绝我的求婚时,我感到十分狼狈。

non-sense /'nɒnsns US: -sens; 'nɑnsɛns/ n (usu 通常作 [U]) meaningless words; foolish talk, ideas, behaviour: 无意义的话;废话;愚昧的思想;愚蠢的行为: You're talking ~! 你在胡说八道! I want no more of your ~. 我受不了你的胡闹。What (a) ~! 简直是一派胡言! **non-sen-si-cal** /nɒn'sensɪkl; nɑn'sɛnsɪkl/ adj not making sense: 无意义的: nonsensical remarks. 无意义的言词。

non se-qui-tur /ˌnɒn'sekwɪtə(r); nɑn'sɛkwɪtə/ n (Lat) (logic) conclusion which does not follow from the premises; illogical step. (拉)(逻辑)非由前提推演出的结论;与前提不符的结论;不合逻辑的步骤。

non-such ⇨ **nonesuch**.

noodle[1] /'nuːdl; 'nudl/ n fool. 笨人。

noodle[2] /'nuːdl; 'nudl/ n (usu pl)type of paste of flour and water or flour and eggs prepared in long, narrow strips and used in soups, with a sauce, etc. (通常用复数)面条。

nook /nʊk; nʊk/ n out-of-the-way place; inside corner: 偏僻之处; 角落; 内隅: search every ~ and cranny, everywhere. 搜查每个角落和裂隙(搜遍每一个地方)。

noon /nuːn; nun/ n midday; 12 o'clock in the middle of the day: 中午;正午; at ~; in the ~; the ~ gun. 午炮。'~-day /-deɪ; -,de/, '~-tide /-taɪd; -,taɪd/ nn = ~.

no-one, no one /'nəʊ wʌn; 'no,wʌn/ pron = **nobody** (1).

noose /nuːs; nus/ n ⇨ the illus at knot. 参看 knot 之插图。loop of rope (with a running knot) that becomes tighter when the rope is pulled: 索套;活结;套圈: the hangman's ~. 绞刑吏的索套。put one's head in the ~, (fig) allow oneself to be caught. (喻)自投罗网。⇨ vt catch with a ~; make a ~ on a cord, rope, etc. 用索套捕捉;在索,绳等上结成活套。

nope /nəʊp; nop/ int (sl) No! (俚)不! 没!

nor /nɔː(r); nɔr/ conj 1 (after neither or not) and not: (用在 neither 或 not 之后)也不: I have neither time nor money for skiing. 我既没有时间也没有钱去滑雪。Not a flower nor even a blade of grass will grow in this desert.

没有一朵花甚至也没有一片草将会生长在这沙漠里。**2 and ... not**: 而……也不: *He can't do it; nor can I, nor can you, nor can anybody.* 他不能做; 我也不能, 你也不能, 任何人都不能。这不是全部; 仅仅此止。*Nor will I* (= And I will not) *deny that....* 我也不否认….

nor'- /nɔː(r); nor/ *pref* ⇨ **north**.

Nor·dic /'nɔːdɪk; 'nɔrdɪk/ *n, adj* (member) of the European type marked by tall stature, blond hair, and blue eyes, esp in Scandinavia. 北欧人(身材高大、金发蓝眼的种族, 尤指居住于斯堪的纳维亚半岛的人); 北欧人的。

Nor·folk /'nɔːfək; 'nɔrfek/ *n* English county. 诺福克(英国的郡)。⇨ **jacket**, man's loose-fitting jacket with a waistband. 诺福克夹克(宽松有腰带的男上衣)。

norm /nɔːm; norm/ *n* **1** standard; pattern; type (as representative of a group when judging other examples). 标准; 典型; 模范(当评判某类中之其他例子时所用的代表)。**2** (in some industries, etc) amount of work required or expected in a working day: (在某些工业等中)每一工作日所要求或预期的工作量: *set the workers a ~*; 给工人定个标准工作量; *fulfil one's ~.* 达到一个人的标准工作量。

nor·mal /'nɔːml; 'nɔrml/ *adj* in agreement with what is representative, usual, or regular: 正常的; 常态的; 平常的; 正规的: *the ~ temperature of the human body.* 人体的正常温度。*'~ school*, (in some countries, not in GB) one for the training of teachers (usu in elementary grades). (在若干国家, 但不在英国)师范学校(通常指培育小学师资者)。□ *n* [U] usual state, level, standard, etc: 通常情况; 常态; 通常的标准: *above/below ~.* 高于(低于)常态。**~·ly** /'nɔːməlɪ; 'nɔrməlɪ/ *adv* **~·ity** /nɔːˈmælətɪ; nɔrˈmælətɪ/ **~·cy** /'nɔːmlsɪ; 'nɔrmlsɪ/ *nn* [U] the state of being ~. 正常; 常态; 标准。**~·ize** /'nɔːməlaɪz; 'nɔrml̩aɪz/ *vt* make ~. 使正常; 正常化。**~·iz·ation** /,nɔːməlarˈzeɪʃn; ,nɔrml̩əˈzeɪʃən/ *n*

Nor·man /'nɔːmən; 'nɔrmən/ *n* inhabitant or native of Normandy; descendant of the mixed Scandinavian and Frankish race established there in the 9th c. 法国诺曼底人; 第九世纪以来住在诺曼底的斯堪的纳维亚和法兰克混血种族的后代。□ *adj* of the ~, esp those who conquered England in the 11th c: 诺曼底人的; (尤指)第十一世纪征服英格兰之诺曼底人的: *the ~ Conquest*; 诺曼底人的征服(英国); *~ architecture.* 诺曼底式建筑。

nor·ma·tive /'nɔːmətɪv; 'nɔrmətɪv/ *adj* setting a standard: 定标准的: *a ~, prescriptive grammar of the English language.* 英语之标准、合乎惯例的语法; 标准英语惯用法语法。

Norse /nɔːs; nors/ *n* the Norwegian language. 挪威语。□ *adj* of Norway. 挪威的。

north /nɔːθ; norθ/ *n* **1** one of the four cardinal points of the compass, lying to the left of a person facing the sunrise; part of any country lying farther in this direction than other parts: 北; 北方; 北部: *the ~ of England*; 英格兰北部; *cold winds from the ~.* 寒冷的北风。⇨ the illus at **compass**. 参看 compass 之插图。**2** (attrib) situated in, living in, pertaining to, coming from, the ~: (用作定语)位于北部的; 居于北方的; 属于北方的; 来自北方的: *the N~ Star*, the pole-star; 北极星; *the ~ pole*; 北极; *a ~ wind*; 北风; *a ~ light*, from the ~, as usu desired by artists in studios; 从北面来的光线(画家在画室中所希望的光线来源方向); *the 'N~ Country*, ~ part of England; 英格兰的北部; *a 'N~ 'countryman* /-mən; -mən/, a native of the ~ of England. 英格兰北部的人。□ *adv* to or towards the ~: 在北方; 向北方: *sailing ~.* 向北航行。**~'east, ~'west** (abbr 略作 NE, NW) *nn, adjj, advv* (sometimes, esp naut, for 时, 尤指航海用语, *for* **north'east**/nɔrˈiːst; nɔrˈiːst/, **nor'·west**/nɔː nɔː'west; nɔr'west/) (regions) midway between ~ and east, ~ and west. 东北(地区); 西北(地区); 东北的; 西北的(在东北; 向东北; 向西北。**the ,N~·west 'Passage**, the sea route from the Atlantic to the Pacific along the ~ coast of Canada and Alaska.

西北航路(自大西洋至太平洋沿加拿大及阿拉斯加北方海岸之海洋航线)。**,~~'east, ,~~'west** (abbr 略作 NNE, NNW) *nn, adjj, advv* (sometimes, esp naut, for 时作, 尤指航海用语, *for* **nor'·nor·'east**/,nɔː nɔrˈiːst; ,nɔr ˈiːst/, **nor'·nor·'west**/,nɔː nɔː 'west; ,nɔr nɔr 'west/) (regions) midway between ~ and ~east, ~west. 北北东(地区); 北北西(地区); 北北东的; 北北西的; 在北北东; 向北北东; 在北北西; 向北北西。**,~·'easter** *n* strong wind, storm, or gale, from the ~east. 强烈的东北风; 东北风暴。**,~·'easter·ly** *adj* (of wind) blowing from the ~east; (of direction) towards the ~. (指风) 吹自东北的; (指方向) 向东北的。**,~·'wester** *n* strong wind from the ~west. 强烈的西北风。**,~·'wester·ly** *adj* (of wind) from the ~west: (of direction) towards the ~west. (指风) 吹自西北的; (指方向) 向西北的。**,~·'eastern** /-'iːstən; -'istən/ *adj* of, from, situated in, the ~east. 东北的; 来自东北的; 在东北的。**,~·'western** /-'westən; -'wɛstən/ *adj* of, from, situated in the ~west. 西北的; 来自西北的; 在西北的。**'N~·man** /-mən; -mən/ *n* (*pl* -**men**) (hist) Viking; native of Scandinavia. (史)古代北欧人; 八至十世纪北欧之海盗; 斯堪的纳维亚人。**,~·wards** /'nɔːθwədz; 'nɔrθwədz/ *adv* towards the ~. 向北方。

north·er·ly /'nɔːðəlɪ; 'nɔrðəlɪ/ *adj, adv* (of winds) from the north; towards the north; in or to the north. (指风)来自北方; 向北方; 在北方; 往北方。

north·ern /'nɔːðən; 'nɔrðərn/ *adj* in or of the north: 在北方的; 北方的: *the ~ hemisphere.* 北半球。**the ~ lights**, streamers and bands of light appearing in the ~ sky; the aurora borealis. 北极光; 北光。**~·er** /'nɔːðənər/ /'nɔrðənɚ/ *n* person born in or living in the ~ regions of a country. 北方人(出生或居于一国家之北部地区的人)。**'~·most** /-məust; -ˌmost/ *adj* lying farthest north. 最北的; 极北的。

Nor·we·gian /nɔːˈwiːdʒən; nɔrˈwidʒən/ *n, adj* (native, language) of Norway. 挪威人; 挪威语; 挪威的。

nose¹ /nəuz; noz/ *n* **1** part of the face above the mouth, through which breath passes, and serving as the organ of smell: 鼻: *hit a man on the ~* (note *def art*). 打一个人的鼻子(注意用定冠词)。⇨ the illus at **head**. 参看 head 之插图。*bite/snap sb's ~ off*, (head is more usu) *off*, answer him sharply and angrily. 气势汹汹地回答 (head 较常用)。*count/tell ~s*, (heads is more usu) (heads 较常用) count the number of persons (esp supporters, when voting to decide sth). 数人数; 计算人数(尤指投票决定某事时, 计算支持的人数)。*cut off one's ~ to spite one's face*, damage one's own interests in an attempt at revenge on sb. 因企图报复而危害了自己。*follow one's ~*, go straight forward; be guided by instinct. 向前直走; 由本能引导; 凭本能行动。*keep a person's ~ to the grindstone*, make him work hard without rest. 使人劳动不息。*lead sb by the ~*, ⇨ **lead²**(2). *look down one's ~ at sb*, treat haughtily. 傲慢地对待某人。*pay through the ~*, pay an excessive price 付出太多的代价。*poke/stick one's ~ into* (sb else's business), intrude; ask questions without being asked to do so. 干预(他人的事); 问长问短。*put sb's ~ out of joint*, ⇨ **joint²**(2). *turn one's ~ up at*, show disdain for. 瞧不起; 鄙视。*as plain as the ~ on one's face*, obvious; easily seen. 清楚明白的; 显而易见的。**(right)** *under one's very ~*, **(a)** directly in front of one. 就在某人的面前。**(b)** in one's presence, and regardless of one's disapproval. 当着某人的面前, 而不顾其反对。**2** sense of smell: 嗅觉: *a dog with a good ~*; 嗅觉灵敏的狗; (fig) 《喻》*a reporter with a ~ for news/scandal/a story.* 善于采探新闻(丑闻, 故事)的记者。**3** sth like a ~ in shape or position, eg the open end of a pipe, bellows or retort; the forward part of the fuselage of an aircraft. 形状或位置似鼻子的东西; 鼻形物(例如管的开口处、风箱口、蒸馏器的管口); 机身的最前端; 机首。**4** (compounds) (复合词) **'~·bag** *n* bag for food (oats, etc) fastened on a horse's head. 挂在马首的粮秣袋。**'~·bleed** *n* bleeding from the ~. 流

鼻血；鼻出血。'**~·cone** n most forward section of a rocket or guided missile, usu separable. (火箭或导弹最前部的)鼻锥体 (通常可分离)。 ⇨ the illus at **capsule**. 参看 capsule 之插图。'**~·dive** n sharp vertical descent made by an aircraft. 飞机的俯冲。 □ vi (of an aircraft) come down steeply with the ~ pointing to earth. (指飞机)俯冲。'**~·flute** n musical instrument blown with the ~, as used in some Asian countries. 鼻笛 (用鼻子吹的笛子，为亚洲某些国家用的乐器)。'**~·gay** n bunch of cut (esp sweet-scented) flowers. 花束 (尤指有香味的花)。 '**~·ring** n ring fixed in the ~ of a bull, etc, for leading it. 牛的鼻环(供人牵引者)。'**~·wheel**, the front landing-wheel under the fuselage of an aircraft. 鼻轮 (飞机机首下的着陆前轮)。 **-nosed** suff (in compounds) having the kind of ~ indicated: (用于复合词中)有某种鼻子的: red-~d; 红鼻子的; long-~d. 长鼻子的。

nose[2] /nəʊz; noz/ vt, vi **1** [VP15A] go forward carefully, push (one's way): 小心地向前推进; 谨慎地前进; 挺进: The ship ~d its way slowly through the ice. 那艘船缓慢地破冰前进。 **2** [VP15B] ~ sth out, discover by smelling: 嗅出; 嗅到: The dog ~d out a rat. 那只狗嗅到一只老鼠的气味。That man will ~ out a scandal anywhere. 那个人在任何地方都会探听出丑闻。 **3** [VP2C, 3A] ~ about (for sth), smell for; (fig) pry or search for. 嗅寻; (喻)探听; 搜查; 侦查。~ into sth, pry into: 探听; 打听: a man who is always nosing into other people's affairs. 常常打听别人事情的人。

nosey, nosy /'nəʊzɪ; 'nozɪ/ adj (-ier, -iest), n (sl) inquisitive (person). (俚)好打听别人事情的(人); 好管闲事的(人)。 '~ **parker** n (colloq) inquisitive person. (口) 好打听别人事情的人; 好管闲事者。

nosh /nɒʃ; naʃ/ n [U] (GB sl) food. (英俚)食物。'~·**up** n a good meal. 丰盛的一餐。 □ vi (colloq) eat. (口)吃。

nos·tal·gia /nɒ'stældʒə; nɑ'stældʒɪə/ n [U] homesickness; wistful longing for sth one has known in the past. 思乡病; 留恋过去; 怀旧。 **nos·tal·gic** /nɒ-'stældʒɪk; nɑ'stældʒɪk/ adj of, feeling or causing, ~. 思乡病的; 怀旧的; 感到或引起乡愁的。 **nos·tal·gi·cally** /-klɪ; -klɪ/ adv

nos·tril /'nɒstrəl; 'nɑstrəl/ n either of the two external openings into the nose. 鼻孔。 ⇨ the illus at **head**. 参看 head 之插图。

nos·trum/'nɒstrəm;'nɑstrəm/n [C] (usu contemptuous) medicine, etc, prepared by the person who recommends it; quack remedy; scheme for political or social reform (called a ~ by its opponents). (通常为轻蔑语)庸医的药; 江湖郎中的药; 骗人的疗法; 政治或社会改革的方案(被反对者称之为骗人的方案)。

not /nɒt; nɑt/ adv **1** (used to make negative one of the 24 anom fin vv listed in the Introduction under 'Anomalous Verbs': is not; must not; could not; often contracted to -n't /-nt; -ṇt/; hasn't /'hæznt; 'hæzṇt/, needn't /'niːdnt; 'nidṇt/.) (用于使本词典序言中所列之24个变态限定 vv 成为否定: 如 is not; must not; could not; 常缩写为 -n't: 如 hasn't, needn't。) **2** (used with non-finite vv): (与非限定动词连用): He warned me not to be late. 他警告我不要迟到。You were wrong in not making a protest. 你错在没有提出抗议。 **3** (used after certain vv, esp think, suppose, believe, expect, fear, fancy, trust, hope, seem, appear, be afraid, as equivalent to a that-clause): (用于某些动词之后, 尤指 think, suppose, believe, expect, fear, fancy, trust, hope, seem, appear 和 be afraid 之后, 相当于一个由 that 所引导的从句): 'Can you come next week?'—'I'm afraid not.' I'm afraid that I cannot come. '你下星期能来吗?'——'我恐怕不能。' 'Will it rain this afternoon?'—'I hope not.' '今天下午会下雨吗?'——'我希望不会。' **4** (used elliptically in phrases.) (省略地用于短语中)as likely as not, probably: 可能; 也许; 说不定: He'll be at home now, as likely as not. 说不定他现在在家。 as soon as not, ⇨ soon(5). not at all, /nɒt ə'tɔːl; ,nɑt ə'tɔl/ used as a polite response to

thanks, enquiries after sb's health, etc: 别客气; 没关系; 不要紧; 没什么 (回答感谢、问安等客气话): 'Thank you very much.'—'Not at all', No need to mention it. '非常谢谢你。'—'别客气。' 'Are you tired?'—'Not at all', Not in the least. '你累了吗?'——'没什么。' 'not that, it is not suggested that: 并非意指: If he ever said so—not that I ever heard him say so—he told a lie. 假如他是那么说——并不是指我听到他那么说——他就是撒谎。 'not but what, nevertheless; although: 虽然…但是; 虽然: I can't do it; not but what a younger man might be able to do it. 我不能做; 但是一个比较年轻的人也许能做。 **5** (in understatements): (用于谨慎的陈述): not a few, many; 不少; 许多; not seldom, often; 常常; 屡次; not without reason, with good reason; 不无理由; 有充分理由; not half, (sl) exceedingly; (俚)非常地; in the not-so-distant (= recent) past. 久久以前。 **6** (used to indicate the absence, opposite, or negative of sth): (用以指不在, 相反或否定): not here; 不在这里; not anything; 什么也没有; not clean /hot/good; 不清洁(热, 好); not he /John /my son. 不是他(约翰, 我的儿子)。

nota bene /,nəʊtə 'benei; ,notə'bini/ v imper (Lat) (拉) (abbr 略作 **NB, nb** /,en 'biː; ,ɛn 'bi/) observe carefully. 注意。

no·table /'nəʊtəbl; 'notəbl/ adj deserving to be noticed; remarkable; 值得注意的; 显著的; 著名的: ~ events /speakers /artists. 著名的事件 (演说家, 艺术家)。 □ n eminent person. 名人。 **no·tably** /'nəʊtəblɪ; 'notəblɪ/ adv **nota·bil·ity** /,nəʊtə'bɪlətɪ; ,notə'bɪlətɪ/ n (pl -ties) **1** [U] the condition of being ~. 显著; 著名。 **2** [C] ~ person. 名人。

no·tary /'nəʊtərɪ; 'notərɪ/ n (pl -ries) (often 常作 '~ 'public) official with authority to perform certain kinds of legal transactions, esp to record that he has witnessed the signing of legal documents. (法律上的)公证人。

no·ta·tion /nəʊ'teɪʃn; no'teʃən/ n **1** [C] system of signs or symbols representing numbers, amounts. musical notes, etc. (代表数字、数量等的)一套符号; (音乐之)乐谱, 记谱法。 **2** [U] representing of numbers, etc by such signs or symbols. (以此等符号)表记; 记号法; 符号法(法之; 符记。

notch /nɒtʃ; natʃ/ n V-shaped cut (in or on sth); (US) narrow pass through mountains; defile[2]. (在某物上的) V 形切痕(与 in 或 on 连用, 后接某物); (美)山间小径; 隘路。 □ vt **1** [VP6A] make or cut a ~ or ~es in or on, eg a stick, as a way of keeping count. 刻 V 形凹痕于(例如刻在棒上作为记数用)。 **2** [VP15B] ~ up, (colloq) achieve; score: (口)完成; 得分: ~ up a new record. 缔造新记录。

note[1] /nəʊt; not/ n **1** short record (of facts, etc) made to help the memory: 笔记; 摘记: He spoke for an hour without a ~/ without ~s. 他不用草稿演讲了一小时。 '~·**book** n book in which to write ~s. 笔记簿。 **2** short letter: 短信; 短简: a ~ of thanks; 谢函; an exchange of ~s between two governments. 两国政府间的函件往返。'~·**paper** n [U] paper for (esp private) correspondence. 信纸(尤指私人的)。 **3** short comment on or explanation of a word or passage in a book, etc: 评注; 注解: a new edition of 'Hamlet', with copious ~s. 有详细注释的'哈姆雷特'新版本。 ⇨ footnote at **foot**[1](8). **4** observation (not necessarily written): 观察所得; 评论(不一定是书面的): He was comparing ~s with a friend, exchanging views, comparing experiences, etc. 他和一个朋友交换意见。 **5** (US 美 = bill) piece of paper money; bank~: 纸币; 钞票: a £5 ~. 一张五英镑的纸币。'~·**case** n wallet. 皮夹。 **6** single sound of a certain pitch and duration: 单音; 音声; 音调; 调: the blackbird's merry ~; 画眉的轻快鸣声; sign used to represent such a sound in manuscript or printed music ⇨ the illus at **notation**; any one of the keys of a piano, organ, etc. (乐谱上的)音符(参看 notation 之插图); (钢琴, 风琴等的)键。 **sound a ~ of warning (against sth)**, warn against sth. (就某事物) 提出警告。 **strike the right ~**, (fig) speak in such a

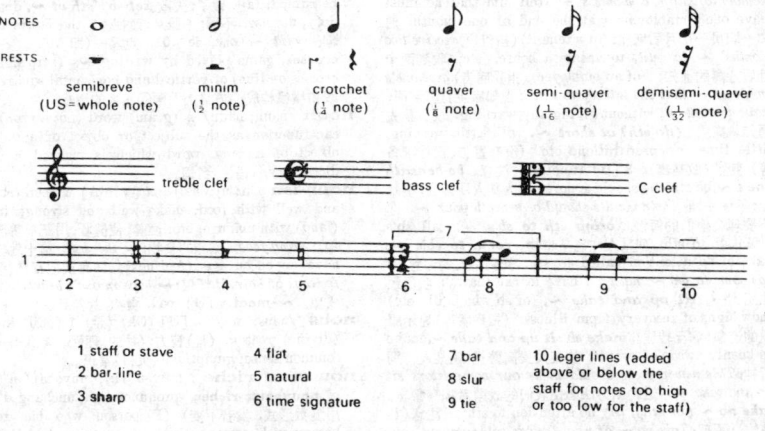

NOTES					
RESTS					
semibreve (US= whole note)	minim (½ note)	crotchet (¼ note)	quaver (⅛ note)	semi-quaver (1/16 note)	demisemi-quaver (1/32 note)

treble clef   bass clef   C clef

1 staff or stave   4 flat   7 bar   10 leger lines (added
2 bar-line   5 natural   8 slur   above or below the
3 sharp   6 time signature   9 tie   staff for notes too high
or too low for the staff)

musical notation

way that one wins the approval or sympathy of one's listeners. (喻)说话使听的人赞同或同情; 说话适当; 说话得体. **strike/sound a false ~,** (fig) do or say sth that causes one to lose sympathy or approval. (喻)说某些话或做某事而致失去他人的同情或赞许; 做错事; 说错话. **7** quality (esp of voice) indicating the nature of sth (usu *sing* with the *indef art*): 声调; 语气; 特征(通常为单数, 与不定冠词连用): *There was a ~ of self-satisfaction in his speech.* 在他的话语中有一种自满的语气. **8** [U] distinction; importance: 著名; 重要: *a singer of ~.* 著名的歌唱家. **9** [U] notice; attention: 注意: *worthy of ~.* 值得注意的. *Take ~ of what he says,* pay attention to it. 注意他所说的.

note² /nəʊt; not/ *vt* **1** [VP6A, 8, 9, 10] notice; pay attention to: 注意; 留心: *Please ~ my words.* 请注意我的话. *N~ how to do it/how I did it.* 注意看怎么做(我是怎么做的). *She ~d that his hands were dirty.* 她注意到他的手是脏的. **2** [VP6A, 15B] **~ sth (down),** make a ~ of; write down in order to remember: 记下(某事)/记录: *The policeman ~d down every word I said.* 警察记下了我所说的每一句话. **noted** *adj* celebrated (*for, as*): 著名的(与 *for, as* 连用): *a town ~d for its pottery/~d as a health resort.* 以出产陶器闻名(以疗养地著名)的城镇. **'~-worthy** *adj* deserving to be ~d; remarkable. 值得注意的; 显著的.

noth·ing /'nʌθɪŋ; 'nʌθɪŋ/ *n* **1** (with *adj, inf,* etc, following) not anything: (后接形容词,不定式等)没什么; 没什么东西; 无物: *There's ~ interesting in the newspaper.* 报纸上没有什么有趣的新闻. *He's had ~ to eat yet.* 他还没有东西吃. *N~ (that) I could say had any influence on her.* 我所说的任何话都不会对她发生任何影响(说什么也没用). *N~ ever pleases her.* 没有任何东西能取悦她. *He's five foot ~,* exactly five foot tall. 他整整五英尺高. *There's little or ~ wrong with him,* very little wrong. 他没有什么不正常. *There's ~ like leather* (= ~ is so good as leather) *for shoes.* 做鞋用皮革再好没有了. **2** (phrases) (短语) **be ~ to,** (a) be a matter of indifference to: 对…无关重要: *She's ~ to him,* He is indifferent to, uninterested in, her. 她在他心目中算不了什么. (b) be as ~ if compared: 假如比较起来等于没有: *My losses are ~ to yours.* 我的损失和你的比起来算不了什么. **come to ~,** fail; be without result. 失败; 无结果. **go for ~,** be without reward, result, value: 没有报酬(没有结果; 没有价值): *Six months' hard work all gone for ~.* 六个月的辛劳工作毫无结果. **have ~ to do with,** (a) avoid; have no dealings with: 避免;不与…来往: *I*

advise you to have ~ to do with that man. 我劝你不要跟那个人来往. (b) not to be the business or concern of: 与…无关: *This has ~ to do with you.* 这跟你没有关系. **make ~ of,** be unable to understand. 不能了解. **mean ~ to, (a)** have no meaning for: 对…没有意义: *These technical words mean ~ to me.* 这些专门术语对我毫无意义. (b) be sth or sb that sb has no concern or interest in: 不为…所关心或感兴趣: *He used to like Jane but she means ~ to him now.* 他以前喜欢过简,但现在对她不感兴趣了. **to say ~ of,** not to mention: 更不用说; 更不待言: *He had his wife and seven children with him in the car, to say ~ of* (= as well as) *two dogs, a cat and a parrot.* 他的车里载着他的太太和七个孩子,更不用说二只狗,一只猫和一只鹦鹉了. **think ~ of,** consider as ordinary, usual or unremarkable: 认为平常; 认为…算不了什么: *He thinks ~ of a twenty-mile walk/of asking me to lend him £20.* 他认为走二十英里(向我借二十英镑)不算一回事. **think ~ 'of it,** friendly reply to sb who offers thanks, an apology, etc: 这算不了什么(对致谢、道歉等的友善的回答): *'You didn't mind my using your typewriter?' — 'Of course not! Think ~ of it!'* '你没介意我用了你的打字机吗?'—'当然没有!这算得了什么!' **for ~, (a)** free; without payment. 免费; 不要钱的. (b) without a reward or result; to no purpose: 没有酬劳; 无结果; 无收获: *It was not for ~ that he spent three years studying the subject.* 他花了三年时间研究这题目并非毫无收获. **next to ~,** ⇨ **next.** **~ but,** merely: 仅仅, 只不过; 只: *N~ but doubts can prevent you from succeeding;* 仅仅是疑虑就会防碍你成功. *Only ~ but a miracle can save him.* 只有奇迹能挽救他. **There's ~ 'for it but to...,** The only thing we can do is to.... 我们唯一能做的是.... **N~ doing!** (colloq) expression used to indicate refusal of a request, etc. (口)(用于表示拒绝请求等)不行! □ *adv* not at all; in no way: 毫不; 决不: *The house is ~ near as large as I expected.* 那幢房屋远不如我预期的那么大. *His new book is ~ like as good as his earlier books.* 他的新作远不如他以前的作品那么好. **~·ness** *n* [U] being ~; the state of non-existence: 空; 无; 不存在: *pass into ~ness.* 化为乌有; 消灭.

no·tice /'nəʊtɪs; 'notɪs/ *n* **1** [C] (written or printed) news of sth about to happen or sth that has happened: (手写的或印刷的)布告; 公告; 告示; 消息: *put up a ~;* 张贴布告; *~s of births, deaths and marriages in the newspapers.* 报纸上出生、死亡和结婚的启事. **'~-board** *n* one provided for ~s to be affixed to. 布告板. **2** [U] warning (of what will happen): 警告; 通知: *give a*

member of staff a month's ~, tell him that he must leave one's employment at the end of one month; 通知一职员一个月后解雇; (of a tenant) (指租户) *receive two months'* ~ *to quit,* to vacate a house, etc; 收到两个月后迁离的通知; (of an employee) (指受雇者) *give one's employer* ~ *that one intends to leave;* 告知雇主打算辞职; *leave without* ~, without giving any warning. 没有预先通知就离去. **(do sth) at short** ~, with little warning, little time for preparation, etc. (没有警告、没作准备等) 突然 (做某事). **3** [U] attention. 注意. *be beneath one's* ~,be sth one should ignore: 不为某人所理会;不足取;不值一顾: *Their insults should be beneath your* ~. 你不要理会他们的侮慢. **bring sth to sb's** ~, call sb's attention to sth. 使某人注意某事物. **come to sb's** ~, have one's attention called to sth: 受到某人的注意:*It has come to my* ~ *that...,* I have learnt that.... 我已经注意到···. *sit up and take* ~, (of sb who is ill, etc) show signs of recovery from illness. (指病者等) 显示康复的征象;病况转佳. *make sb sit up and take* ~, make sb keenly aware of events: 使某人提高警觉;使某人特别留神: *This new process should make our competitors sit up and take* ~. 这种新过程会使我们的竞争者提高警觉. *take no* ~ *(of sth),* pay no attention to sth: 不注意(某事物);不理: *Take no* ~ *of what they're saying about you.* 别理会他们对你的微词. **4** [C] short review of a new book, play, etc in a periodical. (杂志上关于新的书籍、戏剧等的) 短评;评介. □ *vt, vi* 1[VP6A, 8, 9, 10, 18A, 19A, 2A] take ~ (of); observe: 注意(到);看到: *I didn't* ~ *you.* 我没注意到你. *I* ~*d that he left early.* 我注意到他提早离开了. *I wasn't noticing.* 我那时候没有在注意. *Did you* ~ *him pause?* 你有没有注意到他停顿? *Did you* ~ *his hand shaking?* 你有没有注意到他的手发抖? *He was too proud to* ~ *me.* 他太傲慢了,连理都不理我.**2**[VP6A] say or write sth about (a book, play, etc). 评介(书,戏剧等). ~**able** /-əbl; -əbl/ *adj* easily seen or ~d. 易见的;显而易见的. ~**ably** /-əblɪ; -əblɪ/ *adv*

no·ti·fi·able /'nəʊtɪfaɪəbl; 'nətə,faɪəbl/ *adj* that must be notified (esp of certain diseases that must be notified to public health authorities). 应通知的;应报告的 (尤指必须通知卫生当局的某些疾病).

no·tify /'nəʊtɪfaɪ; 'nətə,faɪ/ *vt* (*pt, pp* -**fied**) [VP6A, 14, 11] ~ *sb of sth;* ~ *sth to sb,* give notice of; report: 通知;报告: ~ *the police of a loss;* 向警察局报告损失情形; ~ *a loss to the police;* 向警察局报告损失情形; ~ *a birth;* 公告出生; ~ *the authorities that....* 报告当局···. **no·ti·fi·ca·tion** /ˌnəʊtɪfɪ'keɪʃn; ˌnotəfə'keʃən/ *n* [U] ~ing; [C] instance of this (eg to the authorities, of births, deaths, cases of infectious disease). 通知; 报告 (如向当局报告出生、死亡、传染病例等).

no·tion /'nəʊʃn; 'nʃən/ *n* [C] **1** idea; opinion: 观念;意见: *I have no* ~ *of what he means.* 我不明白他的意思. *Your head is full of silly* ~*s.* 你满脑子都是愚蠢想法. *He has a* ~ *that I'm cheating him.* 他认为我在欺骗他. **2** (*pl*) (US) small miscellaneous goods. (复) (美) 小杂物. ⇨ **novelty(3).** ~**al** /-ʃənl; -ʃənl/ *adj* **1** (of knowledge, etc) speculative; not based on experiment or demonstration. (指知识等) 思辨的; 理论的; 不是根据实验或证明的. **2** nominal; token. 名义上的; 象征的.

no·tori·ous /nəʊ'tɔːrɪəs; no'torɪəs/ *adj* widely known (esp for sth bad): (尤指因坏事) 著名的; 声名狼藉的:*a* ~ *criminal;* 声名狼藉的罪犯; ~ *for his goings-on;* 以其行为不检而著名; ~ *as a rake.* 以浪子的身份闻名. ~·**ly** *adv* **no·tor·iety** /ˌnəʊtə'raɪətɪ; ˌnotə'raɪətɪ/ *n* [U] state of being ~. 狼藉的声名; 恶名. (语义为贬)

not·with·stand·ing /ˌnɒtwɪθ'stændɪŋ; ˌnɑtwɪθ-'stændɪŋ/ *prep* in spite of. 虽然; 尽管. □ *adv* nevertheless; all the same. 仍然; 仍然. □ *conj* although. 虽然.

nou·gat /'nuːɡɑ; US: 'nuːɡət; 'nuɡət/ *n* sort of hard sweet made of sugar, nuts. etc. 一种用糖、核果等制成的坚硬甜点; 杏仁糖.

nought /nɔːt; nɔt/ *n* **1** nothing. 无. **bring sb/sth to** ~, ruin; baffle. 毁灭某人 (某物); 难倒. **come to** ~,

be ruined; fail. 毁了; 失败.**set sb/sth at** ~, disregard; defy; despise. 不顾; 不服从; 蔑视. **2** the figure 0; zero: 零: *point* ~ *one,* ie .01. 点零一(即 .01). ~**s and crosses,** game played by writing ~s (zero signs) and crosses on lines of vertical and horizontal squares. 在直线和横线构成的方格上面画〇和×的游戏.

noun /naʊn; naʊn/ *n* (gram) word (not a *pron*) which can function as the subject or object of a *v,* or the object of a *prep;* word which is marked *n* in this dictionary. (语法) 名词.

nour·ish /'nʌrɪʃ; 'nɝɪʃ/ *vt* [VP6A] **1** keep (sb) alive and well with food; make well and strong; improve (land) with manure, etc: 滋养; 使健壮; 用肥料等改良(土地): ~*ing food;* 滋养的食物; ~ *the soil.* 给土地施肥. **2** have or encourage (feelings): 怀有或抱有(情绪): ~ *feelings of hatred;* 怀恨; ~ *hope in one's heart.* 心中抱着希望. ~·**ment** *n* [U] food. 食物; 营养品.

nous /naʊs; nus/ *n* [U] (Gk) (希) **1** (phil) intellect; (divine) reason. 理智; 智力; (神的) 理性. **2** (GB colloq) common sense; gumption. (英口) 常识.

nou·veau riche /ˌnuːvəʊ'riːʃ; nuvo'riʃ/ *n* (usu in *pl* **nouveaux riches,** pronunciation unchanged) (通常用复数形式, 发音不变) (F) person who has recently become rich, esp one who is ostentatious. (法) 暴发户.

nova /'nəʊvə; 'novə/ *n* (*pl* ~**s, -vae** /-viː; -vi/) (astron) star that suddenly increases its brilliance for a period. (天文) 新星 (在一段时间中突然增强其光度的星).

novel[1] /'nɒvl; 'nɑvl/ *adj* strange; of a kind not previously known: 奇异的; 新奇的: ~ *ideas.* 新奇的想法.

novel[2] /'nɒvl; 'nɑvl/ *n* story in prose, long enough to fill one or more volumes, about either imaginary or historical people: 小说:*the* ~*s of Dickens.* 狄更斯的小说. ~·**ette** /-'et; -'ɛt/ *n* short ~. 中篇小说. ~·**ist** /-ɪst; -ɪst/ *n* writer of ~s. 小说家.

nov·elty /'nɒvltɪ; 'nɑvltɪ/ *n* (*pl* -**ties**) **1** [U] newness; strangeness; quality of being novel: 新鲜; 奇异; 新奇: *The* ~ *of his surroundings soon wore off,* He become accustomed to them. 他对environ环境的新奇不久就觉得平淡了. **2** [C] previously unknown thing, idea, etc; sth strange or unfamiliar. 新奇的事物、观念等; 奇异或不熟悉的事物. **3** (*pl*) miscellaneous manufactured goods of low cost, eg toys, small ornaments. (复) 各种廉价制品 (如玩具、小装饰品等).

No·vem·ber /nəʊ'vembə(r); no'vɛmbə/ *n* the eleventh month of the year, with thirty days. 十一月.

nov·ice /'nɒvɪs; 'nɑvɪs/ *n* person who is still learning and who is without experience, esp a person who is to become a monk or a nun. 生手; 初学者; (尤指) 见习修士或修女. **no·vi·ci·ate, no·vi·ti·ate** /nə'vɪʃɪət; no'vɪʃɪɪt/ *n n* period or state of being a ~. 初学; 做见习修士或修女; 见习期.

now /naʊ; naʊ/ *adv* **1** at the present time; in the present circumstances: 现在: 目前: *Where are you now living/living now?* 你现在住在什么地方?*Now is the best time to visit Devon.* 现在是游览德文最好的时候.*I cannot now* (ie in the circumstances, after what has happened, etc) *ever believe you again.* 我现在不能再相信你了. **2** (used after a *prep*): (用于介词之后): *He will be in London by now.* 他这时将到达伦敦. *Up to/till/until now we have been lucky.* 直到如今我们一直是幸运的. *From now onwards I shall be stricter.* 从今以后我将要更严格. **3**(*phrases*) *(every) now and then* / *again,* occasionally; from time to time: 有时候; 偶尔: *We go to the opera now and then.* 我们有时候去看歌剧. *now... now/then...,* at one time..., at another time...: 时而···时而···: *What mixed weather, now fine, now/then showery!* 多难捉摸的天气, 时而晴朗, 时而阵雨! **4** at once; immediately: 立刻;马上: *Do it now.* 马上做. *Now or never!* 机会难再! *just now,* ⇨ just[2](6). **5** (used without reference to time, to indicate the mood of the speaker,

to explain, warn, comfort, etc): (与时间无关, 系用以表示说话者的语气, 或解释, 警告, 安慰等): *Now what happened was this* (explanatory). 所发生的事情就是这样(解释性的). *Now stop quarrelling and listen to me* (entreaty or reproof). 别吵闹, 听我说(请求或斥责). *No 'nonsense, now* (warning). (警告)别胡扯呢. **now, 'now; 'now then,** (used at the beginning of a sentence, often as a protest or warning, or simply to call attention): (用于句首, 常作抗议或警告, 或仅仅引人注意): *Now then, what's troubling you?* 喂, 你有什么苦恼呀? □ *conj* as a consequence of the fact (that): 既然: *Now* (*that*) *you mention it, I do remember.* 你这样一说, 我想起来了. *Now* (*that*) *you're grown up, you must stop this childish behaviour.* 你既然长大了, 就必须停止这种稚气的行为.

now·a·days /'nauədeiz; 'nauə‚dez/ *adv* at the present time (and often used in contrasts between present day manners, customs, etc, and those of past times): 时下; 现今 (常用于现今与旧时之礼俗、习惯等的对比中): *N~ children prefer TV to reading.* 现今儿童喜欢看电视而不喜欢读书.

no·where /'nəuweə(r) US: -hweər; 'no‚hwer/ *adv* not anywhere: 无处: *The boy was ~ to be found.* 到处都找不到那个男孩. *Such methods will get you ~,* will not produce results. 这些方法将不会产生结果. *~ near enough,* not nearly enough. 五十英镑根本就不够. **come (in)/be ~,** fail to win or get a place (in a competition). (比赛时)输了; 没得到名次.

no·wise /'nəuwaiz; 'no‚waiz/ *adv* (old use) not at all; in no way. (旧用法)决不; 毫不.

noxious /'nɒkʃəs; 'nɑkʃəs/ *adj* harmful: 有害的; 有毒的: *~ gases.* 有毒的气体. **~·ly** *adv* **~·ness** *n*

nozzle /'nɒzl; 'nɑzl/ *n* metal end of a hose or bellows, through which a stream of liquid or air is directed. 管嘴(水管的金属管口); 喷嘴(风箱的金属喷火口). ⇨ the illus at hosepipe. 参看 hosepipe 之插图.

nuance /'nju:ɑ:ns US: 'nu:-; nju'ɑns/ *n* [C] delicate difference in, or shade of, meaning, opinion, colour, etc. 意义, 意见、颜色的细微差异.

nub /nʌb; nʌb/ *n* **1** small lump or knob (eg of coal), (煤等的)小块. **2** (colloq, fig) gist or point (of a story, affair). (口, 喻)(故事, 事情的)要旨; 要点.

nu·bile /'nju:bail US: 'nu:bl; 'njubl/ *adj* (of girls) marriageable; old enough to marry. (指女子)及笄的; 到出嫁年龄的.

nu·clear /'nju:kliə(r) US: 'nu:-; 'njuklɪr/ *adj* of a nucleus, esp of a heavy atom, with release of energy: 核心的; (尤指)原子核的; 核的: *~ energy,* obtained by *~ fission;* 核能 (由核分裂而得); *a ~ power station;* 核能发电厂; *~-powered submarines;* 核动力潜艇; *bombs/missiles;* 核炸弹(导弹); *~ disarmament,* the renunciation of *~* weapons. 放弃核武器的协议.

nu·cleic /nju:'kleiik US: nu:-; nju'klik/ *adj ~* **acid,** one of two complex compounds occurring in all living cells. 核酸.

nu·cleus /'nju:kliəs US: 'nu:-; 'njukliəs/ *n* (*pl* **nuclei** /-kliai; -klɪ‚ai/) central part, round which other parts are grouped or round which other things collect; (esp) central part of an atom, consisting of protons and neutrons. 中心; 核心; (尤指)原子核; 核子(包括质子和中子).

nude /nju:d US: nu:d; njud/ *adj* naked. 裸体的. □ *n* [C] *~* human figure (esp in art). 裸体人像(尤指艺术的). *in the ~,* unclothed: 未穿衣的; 裸露的: *pose in the ~ for an artist.* 裸体摆成姿势供画家作画. **nu·dist** /-ist; -ist/ *n* person who believes that exposure of the naked body to sun and air is good for the health. 裸体主义者(认为曝露裸体于阳光及空气中对健康有益). **'nudist camp/colony,** place where nudists practise their beliefs. 天体营(裸体主义者实行其信念的场所). **nu·dism** /-izəm; -izəm/ *n* the practice of going *~.* 裸体主义. **nu·dity** /'nju:dəti US: 'nu:-; 'njudəti/ *n* nakedness. 裸体; 裸露.

nudge /nʌdʒ; nʌdʒ/ *vt* [VP6A] touch or push slightly with the elbow in order to draw sb's attention privately. 以肘轻碰或轻推, 暗中促人注意. □ *n* push given in this way. 此种轻碰或轻推.

nu·ga·tory /'nju:ɡətəri US: 'nu:ɡətɔ:ri; 'njuɡə‚tori/ *adj* (formal) trifling; worthless; not valid. (正式用语)微小的; 无价值的; 无效的.

nug·get /'nʌɡit; 'nʌɡit/ *n* lump of metal, esp gold, as found in the earth. 矿块(尤指天然的金块); 块金.

nui·sance /'nju:sns US: 'nu:-; 'njusns/ *n* [C] thing, person, act, etc that causes trouble or offence: 讨厌的事物、人、行为: *The mosquitoes are a ~.* 蚊子是讨厌的东西. *What a ~ that child is!* 那个小孩多讨厌!

null /nʌl; nʌl/ *adj* of no effect or force. 无效的; 无力量的. *~ and void,* (legal) without legal effect; invalid. (法律)法律上无效的; 无效的. **nul·lify** /'nʌlifai; 'nʌlə‚fai/ *vt* (*pt, pp* **-fied**) [VP6A] make *~* and void. 使无效. **nul·li·fi·ca·tion** /‚nʌlifi'keiʃn; ‚nʌləfə'keʃən/ *n* [U] making *~.* 使无效. **nul·lity** /'nʌləti; 'nʌləti/ *n* being *~*; invalidity: 无效; 无力: *nullity of marriage;* 婚姻无效; *a 'nullity suit,* one that asks for *~ity* of marriage. 请求宣判婚姻无效的诉讼.

numb /nʌm; nʌm/ *adj* without ability to feel or move: 失去感觉的; 麻木的: *fingers ~ with cold.* 冻僵了的手指. □ *vt* [VP6A] make *~*; deaden: 使麻木; 使失去感觉: *~ed with grief.* 因悲伤而变得麻木的. **~·ly** *adv* **~·ness** *n*

num·ber /'nʌmbə(r); 'nʌmbə/ *n* **1** 3, 13, 33 and 103 are *~*s. 3, 13, 33 和 103 都是数字. ⇨ **App 4.** 参看附录四. **2** quantity or amount: 总数; 总数: *a large ~ of people.* 很多人. *N~s of people* (= Very many people) *came from all parts of the country to see the exhibition.* 许许多多人从国内各地来参观这个展览. *The ~ of books missing from the library is large.* 图书馆遗失的书籍数量很大. *A ~ of books* (= Some books) *are missing from the library.* 图书馆里有一些书找不到了. *His/Your, etc ~ is up,* (colloq) He is/You are, etc ruined, going to die, to pay a penalty, etc. (口)他(你等)完了(要死了, 要受罚了等). *in ~:* 总共: *They were fifteen in ~,* There were fifteen of them. 他们总共是十五个. *to the ~ of,* mounting to. 达到...数目; 总数为. *without ~,* too many to be counted. 无数的; 太多而数不清的. *times without ~,* very often: so often that counting is impossible. 常常; 经常; 无数次地. **'~-plate** *n* plate showing the licence number of motor vehicles, the *~* of a house, etc. (汽车等的)牌照; 门牌; 标示数字编号的牌子. ⇨ the illus at **motor.** 参看 motor 之插图. **3** (attrib use before a definite *~* (1), usu shortened to **No,** *pl* **Nos**): (置于数字之前, 用作定语, 表示号数, 通常缩写为 No, 复数作 Nos): *Room No 145,* eg in a hotel; 145 号房间 (如旅馆中之) living at No 4, house number four. 住在四号房屋. **No 10 (Downing Street),** official residence of the British Prime Minister. (唐宁街)十号(英国首相之官邸). **look after/take care of ~ one,** (colloq) look after oneself and one's own interests. (口)照顾自己和自己的利益. **4** one issue of a periodical, esp for one day, week, etc: 期刊的一期: *the current ~ of 'Punch';* 这一期的 Punch 杂志; *back ~s* (= earlier issues) *of 'Nature'.* 旧版的 Nature 杂志. *a back ~,* (fig) out of date or old-fashioned. (喻)落伍者; 过时者. **5** part of an opera indicated by a *~*; dance, song, etc for the stage. (以号数代表的)歌剧的一段; 舞台演出的舞蹈、歌曲等的一个节目. **6** (gram) variations in the forms of *nn, vv,* etc according to whether only one or more than one is to be indicated: (语法) 数(依据所指者仅是一个或为多个而决定的名词、动词等形式的变化): *Man/men, does/do and I/we illustrate grammatical ~ in English.* Man and men, does 和 do, I 和 we 都是说明英语语法上数的变化. **7** (*pl*) numerical superiority: (复)数量上的优势: *The enemy won by ~s/by force of ~s.* 敌人以人多获胜. **8** (*pl*) arithmetic: (复)算术: *He's not good at ~s.* 他不擅长算术. □ *vt, vi* **1** [VP6A, 14] give a *~* to: 编号: *Let's ~*

them *from 1 to 10.* 给他们从一到十编号。 **2** amount to; add up to: 计有; 总共: *We ~ed 20 in all.* 我们共计二十个人。 **3** [VP14] **~** *sb* / *sth among*, include; place: 包括 (某人或某事物于其中); 置…于…中; 计入; 算为: **~** *sb among one's friends.* 把某人算为一个朋友。 **4** (passive) be restricted in **~**: (被动语态)在数目方面受到限制: *His days are ~ed,* He has not long to live. 他活不久了。 **5** [VP2C] **~** *off,* (mil) call out one's **~** in a rank of soldiers: (军)报数: *The company ~ed off from the right.* 该连士兵从右开始报数。

nu·mer·able /ˈnjuːmərəbl US: ˈnuː-; ˈnjumərəbl/ *adj* that can be numbered or counted. 可数的; 可计算的。

nu·meral /ˈnjuːmərəl US: ˈnuː; ˈnjumrəl/ *n, adj* (word, figure or sign) standing for a number; of number. 代表数目的(字、数字或符号); 数字的。 **Arabic ~s,** 1, 2, 3, etc. 阿拉伯数字 (1, 2, 3, 等)。 **Roman ~s,** I, II ,III, etc. 罗马数字(I, II, III 等)。 ⇨ **App 4.** 参看附录四。

nu·mer·ate /ˈnjuːmərət US: ˈnuː-; ˈnjumrɪt/ *adj* (of a person) having a good basic competence in mathematics and science. (指人)对数学及科学具有良好之基本能力的。 ⇨ **literate. nu·mer·acy** /ˈnjuːmərəsɪ US: ˈnuː-; ˈnjumərəsɪ/ *n*

nu·mer·ation /ˌnjuːməˈreɪʃn US: ˌnuː-; ˌnjuməˈreʃən/ *n* method or process of numbering or calculating; expression in words of numbers written in figures. 计算(法); 命数(法); 读数法。

nu·mer·ator /ˈnjuːməreɪtə(r) US: ˈnuː-; ˈnjuməˌretə/ *n* number above the line in a vulgar fraction, eg 3 in ³/₄. 分数中的分子(如 ³/₄ 中的 3)。 ⇨ **denominator.**

nu·meri·cal /njuːˈmerɪkl US: nuː-; njuˈmɛrɪkl/ *adj* of, in, denoting, numbers: 数字的; 数字上的; 表示数量的: **~** *symbols.* 数字符号。 **~ly** -klɪ; -klɪ/ *adv: The enemy were ~ly superior.* 敌方在数量上占优势。

nu·mer·ous /ˈnjuːmərəs US: ˈnuː-; ˈnjumrəs/ *adj* great in number; very many: 极多的; 甚多的: *her ~ friends.* 她的许多朋友。

nu·min·ous /ˈnjuːmɪnəs US: ˈnuː-; ˈnjumɪnəs/ *adj* awe-inspiring; divine. 令人敬畏的; 神圣的。

nu·mis·mat·ics /ˌnjuːmɪzˈmætɪks US: ˌnuː-; ˌnjumɪzˈmætɪks/ *n* (with *sing v*)the study of coins, coinage and medals. (用单数动词)对钱币、铸币及奖章之研究; 钱币学。 **nu·mis·ma·tist** /njuːˈmɪzmətɪst US: nuː-; njuˈmɪzmətɪst/ *n* expert in **~**; collector of coins and medals. 钱币学家; 钱币及奖章收藏家。

num·skull /ˈnʌmskʌl; ˈnʌmˌskʌl/ *n* stupid person. 笨人。

nun /nʌn; nʌn/ *n* woman who, after taking religious vows, lives, with other women, in a convent, a life in the service of God. 修女; 尼姑。 **nunnery** /ˈnʌnərɪ; ˈnʌnərɪ/ *n* (*pl* **-ries**) home of nuns; convent. 女修道院; 尼姑庵。 ⇨ **monk, monastery.**

nun·cio /ˈnʌnsɪəʊ; ˈnʌnʃɪ,o/ *n* (*pl ~s*) ambassador or representative of the Pope in a foreign country. 罗马教宗的(驻外)使节。

nup·tial /ˈnʌpʃl; ˈnʌpʃəl/ *adj* of marriage or weddings; 婚姻的; 婚礼的: **~** *happiness;* 婚姻的快乐; *the ~ day.* 结婚之日。 **nup·tials** *n pl* wedding. 结婚; 婚礼。

nurse¹ /nɜːs ; nɝs/ *n* **1** ('**~**)**maid,** woman or girl employed to look after babies and small children. 保姆; 照顾小孩的女用人。 **~ nanny.** **2** ('**wet-**)**~,** woman employed to suckle another's infant. 奶妈。 **3** [U] nursing or being nursed: 看护; 受照顾: *put a child to ~.* 把小孩交保姆看护。 **4** person, usu trained, who cares for people who are ill or injured: 护士: *hospital ~s;* 医院护士; *Red Cross ~s;* 红十字会护士; *male ~s,* eg in a mental home for men. 男护士(如精神病院中看护男病人者)。 **5** country, college, institution, etc which protects or encourages a certain quality: 保护或鼓励某一特质的国家、大学、机构等: *Iceland, the ~ of liberty.* 冰岛, 自由的保护者。

nurse² /nɜːs; nɝs/ *vt* [VP6A] **1** take charge of and

look after (persons who are ill, injured, etc) (but not used in the sense of **nurse¹** **(1)**): 看护; 护理(病人、伤患等)(不用以指做保姆照顾小孩): (gerund) (动名词) *the nursing profession;* 护理的职业; *take up nursing as a career.* 以护理为职业。 *Careful nursing will be needed.* 需要细心的看护。 '**nursing-home** *n* building, usu privately owned and smaller than a hospital, where persons who are ill may be cared for, operated on, etc. 疗养院(通常为私立且比医院小, 病人在院中可获得照料、接受手术等)。 **2** feed (a baby) at the breast: suckle. 哺乳; 给(婴孩)喂奶。 **3** hold (a baby, a child, a pet dog) on the knees; clasp caressingly. 抱 (婴孩, 小孩, 爱犬)在膝上; 拥抱。 **4** give special care to: 特别照料; 养育; 保护: **~** *young plants.* 培养幼苗。 ⇨ **nursery(2);** **~** *a constituency,* keep in touch with the voters (to obtain or retain their support). 维护选举区(与选民保持接触, 以获得或保有他们的支持)。 **~** *a cold,* stay at home, keep warm, in order to cure it. 待在家里保持温暖以使伤风痊愈。 **5** have in the mind, think about a great deal: 蓄; 怀: **~** *feelings of revenge.* 蓄意复仇。

nurse·ling, nurs·ling /ˈnɜːslɪŋ; ˈnɝslɪŋ/ *n* infant, esp in relation to its nurse. 婴孩(尤指由保姆或奶妈抚养者)。

nurs·ery /ˈnɜːsərɪ; ˈnɝsrɪ/ *n* (*pl* **-ries**) **1** room for the special use of small children. 幼儿室; 保育室。 '**day ~,** building where mothers who go out to work may leave babies and young children. (日间)托儿所。 '**~ rhymes,** poems or songs (usu traditional) for young children. 儿歌; 童谣。 '**~ school,** for children of 2 to 5; pre-primary school. 托儿所(收纳二至五岁的小孩); 幼儿园。 '**~ slope,** (skiing) slope suitable for learners. (滑雪)适合初学者的坡地。 **2** place where young plants and trees are raised (for transplanting later, and usu for sale). 植物育苗场; 苗圃; 苗床。 '**~·man** /-mən; -mən/ *n* (*pl* **-men**) man who works in a **~**(2)。 苗圃主人; 苗圃工人。

nur·ture /ˈnɜːtʃə(r); ˈnɝtʃɚ/ *n* [U] (formal) care, training; education (of children). (正式用语) (儿童的)养育; 教养; 训练; 教育。 □ *vt* bring up; give **~** to: 养育; 教养; *a delicately ~d girl.* 一个经悉心教养的女孩。

nut /nʌt; nʌt/ *n* **1** fruit consisting of a hard shell enclosing a kernel that can be eaten. 坚果(有硬壳, 内含可吃的果肉)。 *a hard nut to crack,* a problem difficult to solve. 不易解决的难题。 '**nut-brown** *adj* (of ale) coloured like ripe hazel-nuts. (指啤酒等) 栗色的。 '**nut-'butter** *n* butter substitute made from nuts (eg peanut butter). 坚果奶油 (奶油的代用品, 如花生酱)。 '**nut-crackers** *n pl* device for cracking nuts open. 坚果钳; 胡桃钳。 '**nut-shell** *n* hard outside covering of a nut. 坚果壳。 *(put sth) in a nutshell,* (fig) in the fewest possible words. (喻)用最少的几句话 (说明某事物)。 **2** small piece of metal with a threaded hole for screwing on to a bolt. 螺母; 螺帽。 ⇨ the illus at **bolt.** 参看 bolt 之插图。 **3** (sl) head (of a human being). (俚) (人的)头。 *off one's nut,* (sl) insane. (俚)疯狂的。 '**nut house** *n* (sl) mental hospital. (俚)精神病院; 疯人院。 **4**(*pl*) small lumps of coal. (复)小煤块。 □ *vi go nutting,* look for, gather nuts (eg hazel-nuts in the woods and hedges). 采集坚果(例如在树林或树篱中采集橡果)。

nut·meg /ˈnʌtmeg; ˈnʌtmeg/ *n* **1** [C] hard, small, round; sweet-smelling seed of an E Indian evergreen. 豆蔻; 肉豆蔻。 **2** [U] this seed grated to powder, used as a flavouring. 豆蔻末(用作香料)。

nu·tria /ˈnjuːtrɪə US: ˈnuː-; ˈnjutrɪə/ *n* skin or fur of the small S American rodent called coypu. (南美产的)河鼠毛皮。

nu·tri·ent /ˈnjuːtrɪənt US: ˈnuː-; ˈnjutrɪənt/ *adj* (formal) serving as or providing nourishment. (正式用语)营养的; 滋养的。

nu·tri·ment /ˈnjuːtrɪmənt US: ˈnuː-; ˈnjutrəmənt/ *n* (formal) nourishing food. (正式用语)营养品; 营养的食物。

nu·tri·tion /njuːˈtrɪʃn US: nuː-; njuˈtrɪʃən/ *n*

(formal) [U] the process of supplying and receiving nourishment; the science of food values: (正式用语)营养(作用);营养学: *the care and ～ of children.* 儿童的照顾与营养。

nu·tri·tious /'njuː'trɪʃəs *US:* nuː-; nju'trɪʃəs/ *adj* (formal) nourishing; having high value as food. (正式用语)营养的;多滋养的。

nu·tri·tive /'njuːtrɪtɪv *US:* 'nuː-; 'njutrɪtɪv/ *adj* (formal) serving as food; of nutrition. (正式用语)用作食物的;营养的。

nuts/ nʌts; nʌts/ *adj* (sl) crazy; insane. (俚) 疯狂的;发疯的。 *be ～ about/over sb/sth,* be in love with, infatuated with. 迷恋某人(热爱某事物)。

nutty /'nʌtɪ; 'nʌtɪ/ *adj* (-ier, -iest) 1 tasting like nuts. 有坚果味的。 2 (sl) mad; crazy. (俚)疯的;狂的。 3 containing; made up of, nuts(4): 含小块煤的;小块煤构成的: ～ *slack coal.* 小块的松煤。

nuzzle /'nʌzl; 'nʌzl/ *vt, vi* 1 [VP6A] press the nose against: 以鼻推压: *The horse ～d my shoulder.* 那匹马用鼻子摩我的肩膀。 2 [VP2C] ～ *up (against/to),* rub or push with the nose: 用鼻子摩擦或推压: *The horse ～d up against my shoulder.* 那匹马用鼻子摩我的肩膀。

ny·lon /'naɪlɒn; 'naɪlɑn/ *n* 1 [U] synthetic fibre used for hosiery, rope, brushes. etc: 尼龙(一种合成纤维,用以制衣袜、绳索、刷等): ～ *stockings/blouses, etc.* 尼龙袜子(短衫等)。 2 (*pl*) ～ stockings. (复)尼龙长袜。

nymph /nɪmf; nɪmf/ *n* 1 (in old Gk and Roman stories) one of the lesser goddesses, living in rivers, trees, hills, etc; (liter) beautiful young woman. (希腊与罗马神话)居住河上、林中、山上等的仙女;(文)美丽的少女。 2 pupa; chrysalis. 蛹。

nym·phet /nɪm'fet; nɪm'fɛt/ *n* (colloq) young girl looked upon as sexually desirable. (口)性感的少女。

nym·pho /'nɪmfəʊ; 'nɪmfo/ *n* (*pl* ～s /-fəʊz; -foz/) (colloq abbr of) nymphomaniac. (口) nymphomaniac 之略。

nym·pho·mania /ˌnɪmfə'meɪnɪə; ˌnɪmfə'menɪə/ *n* [U] abnormal sexual desire in women. 女子淫狂;女花痴。 **nym·pho·maniac** /-'meɪnɪæk; -'menɪæk/ *n, adj* (woman) suffering from ～. 女子淫狂者;花痴女;女子淫狂的。

O o

O, o /əʊ; o/ (*pl* O's, o's/ əʊz; oz/) the 15th letter of the English alphabet; O-shaped sign or mark; (in quoting telephone numbers) 6033, 'six O double three'. 英文字母的第十五个字母; O 形的符号或标记; (报电话号码)零 (6033 读作 six O double three)。 ⇨ **APP 4.** 参看附录四。

O, oh /əʊ; o/ *int* cry of surprise, fear, pain, sudden pleasure, etc. 啊;呀(表示惊讶、恐惧、痛苦、突然的高兴等的感叹词)。

o' /ə; ə/ (abbr of) *of*, as in *o'clock, man-o'-war*. of 的略写(如 o'clock, man-o'-war 中之 o')。

oaf /əʊf; of/ *n* (*pl* ～s or, rarely 罕作 **oaves** /əʊvz; ovz/) awkward lout. 笨拙的粗人; 蠢汉。 **'oaf·ish** /-ɪʃ; -ɪʃ/ *adj* roughly behaved; loutish. 行为粗野的;粗鄙的。

oak /əʊk; ok/ *n* [C] sorts of large tree with tough, hard wood, common in many parts of the world, ⇨ the illus at **tree;** [U] the wood of this tree: 橡树(参看 tree 之插图);橡木: *a forest of oak(s)/oak-trees;* 橡林; *an oak door;* 橡木门; *oak panels.* 橡木镶板。 **'oak-apple** *n* growth on an oak leaf or stem caused by an insect. 长在橡树叶或茎上的虫瘿;五倍子;没食子。 **the Oaks,** name of a classic horse-race, run at Epsom, near London. 在伦敦附近艾普瑟姆举行的著名的赛马会。 **oaken** /'əʊkən; 'okən/ *adj* made of oak. 橡木做的。

oa·kum /'əʊkəm; 'okəm/ *n* [U] loose fibre or threads obtained by picking old ropes, used for filling up spaces between the boards of a ship. (从旧索中解得的)麻絮;麻丝(用于填塞船缝)。

oar /ɔː(r); or/ *n* pole with a flat blade, pulled by hand against a pin, rowlock or other support on the side of a boat, in order to propel the boat through the water. 桨;橹。 ⇨ the illus at **eight, row.** 参看 eight, row 之插图。 *put a good oar in,* (colloq) interfere. (口)干涉; 干预。 *rest on one's oars,* stop working for a time. 停工休息一会儿。 **oars·man** /-mən; 'ɔːzmən; 'ɔrzmən/ *n* (*pl* -men), **'oars·woman** *n* (*pl* -women) rower. 男划手;女划手。 Hence, 由此产生, **'oars·man·ship** *n*

oasis /əʊ'eɪsɪs; o'esɪs/ *n* (*pl* **oases** /-siːz; -siz/) fertile place, with water and trees, in a desert; (fig) experience, place, etc which is pleasant in the midst of what is dull, unpleasant, etc. 沙漠中的绿洲;(喻)在枯燥、不愉快等情况中的愉快经验,宜人的地方。

oast /əʊst; ost/ *n* kiln for drying hops. 烘乾麻子的炉。 **'～·house** *n* building containing an ～. 蛇麻子烘干所。

oat /əʊt; ot/ *n* (usu *pl*) (通常用复数) 1(grain from a) hardy cereal plant grown in cool climates as food (oats for horses, *oatmeal* for human beings). 燕麦(燕麦供马食用,麦片 oatmeal 供人食用)。 ⇨ the illus at **cereal.** 参看 cereal 之插图。 *feel one's oats,* (colloq) feel gay, lively, ready for activity, active. (口)觉得愉快而精力充沛;轻松活跃。 *sow one's wild oats,* lead a life of pleasure and gaiety while young before settling down seriously. 年轻时纵情玩乐。 **'oat·cake** *n* (esp in Scot and N England) thin, unleavened cake made of oatmeal. 光指在苏格兰及英格兰北部)燕麦饼;麦片饼。 **'oat·meal** *n* meal made from oats, used in porridge and oatcakes. 麦片; 燕麦片(用于煮麦片粥及制麦片饼)。 2 (*pl* with *sing v*) oatmeal porridge: (复数,与单数动词连用)麦片粥;燕麦粥: *Is Scotch ～s on the breakfast menu?* 早餐菜单上有苏格兰燕麦粥吗?

oath /əʊθ; oθ/ *n* (*pl* ～s /əʊðz; oðz/) 1 solemn undertaking with God's help to do sth; solemn declaration that sth is true. 誓约;誓。 *be on/under ～,* (legal) having sworn to tell the truth: (法律)已宣誓说实话;宣誓不作伪证: *The judge reminded the witness that he was still under ～.* 那法官提醒证人他已宣誓不作伪证(其誓言仍然有效)。 *put sb under ～,* (legal) require sb to swear an ～. (法律)使某人宣誓(或立誓)。 *swear/take an ～,* promise solemnly to give (one's loyalty, allegiance, etc). 发誓;宣誓;立誓(忠诚,效忠等)。 *on one's ～,* (nonlegal) used to emphasize that one is telling the truth: (非法律用语) …发誓(用以强调所说的话绝对真实): *I didn't say anything to him about you, on my ～.* 我发誓,我没有对他说任何有关于你的事。 2 wrongful use of God's name or of sacred words to express strong feeling; swear-word; piece of profanity. 表示强烈情绪的咒语;诅咒;亵渎的言语。

ob·bli·gato /ˌɒblɪ'gɑːtəʊ; ˌɑblɪ'gato/ *n* (*pl* ～s /-təʊz; -toz/), *adj* (music) (音乐) 1 (to be) performed without any omissions (opp to *ad libitum*) 全部演奏的 (为 ad libitum 之反义词)。 2 (accompanying part) forming an integral part of a composition. 必须的或不可缺少的(伴奏)。

ob·du·rate /'ɒbdjʊərət *US:* -dər-; 'ɑbdjɪərɪt/ *ad* (formal) stubborn; impenitent. (正式用语)执拗的;顽固的;不悔悟的。 **～·ly** *adv* **ob·du·racy** /'ɒbdjʊərəsɪ; 'ɑbdjɪərəsɪ/ *U*: /-dər-; -dərəsɪ/ *n* [U]。

obedi·ent /ə'biːdɪənt; ə'bidɪənt/ *adj* doing, willing to do, what one is told to do: 服从的; 遵从的; 听话的

~ *children*. 听话的孩子们。 *your* ~ *servant,* formula used at the end of letters of an official or public nature. 正式或公开的书信中所用结尾套语；顿首；敬启。 ~·**ly** *adv* **obedi·ence** /-əns; -əns/ *n* [U] being ~. 服从；遵从；听话: *Soldiers act in obedience to the orders of their superior officers*. 军人服从上级军官的命令而行动。

obeis·ance /əʊˈbeɪsns; oˈbeəsns/ *n* [C] (formal) deep bow (of respect or homage): (正式用语)(表示尊敬或臣服的)深深的鞠躬: *do/pay* ~ *to a ruler*. show respectful homage or submission. 向统治者表示臣服。

ob·elisk /ˈɒbəlɪsk; ˈɑbl͵ɪsk/ *n* tall, pointed, tapering, four-sided stone pillar, set up as a monument or landmark. 方尖形的石碑(作记念碑或路标用)；方尖塔；方尖柱碑。

obese /əʊˈbiːs; oˈbis/ *adj* (of persons) very fat. (指人)非常肥胖的。 **obes·ity** /əʊˈbiːsɪtɪ; oˈbisətɪ/ *n* [U] being ~. 肥胖。

obey /əˈbeɪ; əˈbe/ *vt, vi* [VP6A, 2A] do what one is told to do; carry out (a command): 服从；执行(命令): ~ *an officer*. 服从官长; ~ *orders*. 服从命令。

ob·fus·cate /ˈɒbfəskeɪt; əbˈfʌskeɪt/ *vt* [VP6A] (formal) darken or obscure (the mind); bewilder. (正式用语) 使(心灵)迷惑；使困惑。

obi /ˈəʊbɪ; ˈobɪ/ *n* (*pl* **obis**) (Japanese) broad sash (often ornamental) fastened round the waist so that there is a large bow. (日)(围扎和服,常作装饰用的)宽腰带。

obiter dic·tum /͵ɒbɪtə ˈdɪktəm; ˈɑbɪtɚˈdɪktəm/ *n* (*pl* **dicta** /ˈdɪktə; ˈdɪktə/) (Lat) incidental remark or statement. (拉)附带的陈述；附言。

obitu·ary /əˈbɪtʃʊərɪ US: əˈbɪtʃʊ͵erɪ/ *n* (*pl* -**ries**) printed notice of sb's death, often with a short account of his life; 讣闻(常附有死者的传略)；(attrib) (用作定语) ~ *notices,* eg in a newspaper. 讣闻(如报纸上所刊载者)。

ob·ject[1] /ˈɒbdʒɪkt; ˈɑbdʒɪkt/ *n* 1 sth that can be seen or touched; material thing: 看得见或摸得到的东西；物体；物品: *Tell me the names of the ~s in this room*. 告诉我这屋里各件东西的名称。 '~ **lesson, (a)** one (to be) taught or learnt from an example, or from specimens, etc placed before or shown to the learner. 实物教学。 **(b)** practical illustration of some principle, often given or used as a warning. 用作警戒的某种行为准则的实例；殷鉴。 '~ **glass / lens** *n* = **objective** *n*(2). **2** person or thing to which action or feeling or thought is directed; thing aimed at; end; purpose: 对象；目的物；目标；目的: *an* ~ *of pity / admiration,* sb or sth pitied / admired; 怜悯(钦佩)的对象; *with no* ~ *in life;* 没有生活的目标; *work with the* ~ *of earning fame;* 为了要想成名而工作; *fail / succeed in one's* ~. 未达到(达到)目的。 **no** ~, no hindrance; not important: 无障碍；不重要: *money / time / distance, etc no* ~, (in advertisements, eg for jobs) the person answering may make his own terms about money, time, etc. 待遇(时间,距离远近等)不计(如报纸征聘人员的广告中,可由应征者开列自己所要求的待遇,时间等)。 **3** person or thing of strange appearance, esp if ridiculous, pitiful or contemptible: 样子怪异的人或物(尤指可笑、可怜或可鄙者): *What an* ~ *you look in that old hat!* 你戴着那顶旧帽子显得多么滑稽啊! **4** (gram) *n* or *n* equivalent (eg a clause) towards which the action of the *v* is directed, or to which a preposition indicates some relation, as in (direct object) 'He took *the money*' or 'He took *what he wanted*' or (indirect ~) 'I gave *him the money*' or (prepositional ~) 'I gave the money to *the treasurer*'. (语法)宾语(由名词或名词相等词,如名词从句,所构成,作为动词之动作或介词表示某种关系的对象,如 He took the money 中的 money 或 He took what he wanted 中的 what he wanted 均为直接宾语, I gave him the money 中的 him 为间接宾语, I gave the money to the treasurer 中的 the treasurer 为介词宾语)。

ob·ject[2] /əbˈdʒekt; əbˈdʒɛkt/ *vi, vt* **1** [VP2A, 3A] ~

(to), say that one is not in favour of sth; be opposed (to); make a protest against: 不赞成; 反对: *I* ~ *to all this noise / to being treated like a child*. 我反对所有这种闹声(被当做小孩看待)。 *He stood up and* ~*ed in strong language*. 他站起来以强硬的言词抗议。 **2** [VP9] ~ *(against sb) that,* give as a reason against: 提出…作为反对(某人)的理由: *I* ~ *(against him) that he is too young for the position*. 我反对(他)的理由是他太年轻不适合那个职位。 **ob·jec·tor** /-tə(r); -tə/ *n* person who ~s. 反对者; 抗议者。 **conscientious ~or,** ⇨ **conscientious.**

ob·jec·tion /əbˈdʒekʃn; əbˈdʒɛkʃən/ *n* **1** [C, U] statement or feeling of dislike, disapproval or opposition: 厌恶; 不赞成; 反对: *He has a strong* ~ *to getting up early*. 他强烈地反对早起。 *Is there a / any* ~ *to the plan will be listened to sympathetically*. 对本计划的异议将予以考虑。 **take** ~ *to,* object to. 反对。 **2** [C] that which is objected to; drawback; defect. 被反对的事物; 缺点; 缺陷。 ~·**able** /-əbl; -əbl/ *adj* likely to be objected to; unpleasant: 可能会引起反对的; 令人不愉快的: *an* ~*able smell;* 难闻的味道; ~*able remarks*. 可能会引起反对的言词。 ~·**ably** /-əblɪ; -əblɪ/ *adv*

ob·jec·tive /əbˈdʒektɪv; əbˈdʒɛktɪv/ *adj* **1**(in philosophy) having existence outside the mind; real. (哲学)客观的; 真实的。 ⇨ **subjective. 2** (of persons, writings, pictures) uninfluenced by thought or feeling; dealing with outward things, actual facts, etc uninfluenced by personal feelings or opinions. (指人, 著作, 图画)客观的; 实体的; 不受个人的感情或意见所影响的。 **3** (gram) of the object(4): (语法)宾语的: *the* ~ *case,* in Latin and other inflected languages. (拉丁文及其他有词形变化的文字中)宾格。 □ *n* **1** object aimed at; purpose; (esp mil) point to which armed forces are moving to capture it: 目标; 目的; (尤指军语)进攻目标: *All our* ~*s were won*. 我们所有的目的都达到了。 **2** lens of a microscope or telescope closest to the object being looked at. (显微镜或望远镜最接近目的物的)物镜; 接物镜。 ~·**ly** *adv* in an ~ (2) manner. 客观地。 **ob·jec·tiv·ity** /͵ɒbdʒek-ˈtɪvətɪ; ͵ɑbdʒɛkˈtɪvətɪ/ *n* state of being ~; impartial judgement; ability to free oneself from personal prejudice. 客观; 公平的判断; 大公无私; 无偏见。

ob·jur·gate /ˈɒbdʒəgeɪt; ˈɑbdʒə͵get/ *vt* [VP6A] (liter) scold; rebuke. (文)骂; 叱责。 **ob·jur·ga·tion** /͵ɒbdʒəˈgeɪʃn; ͵ɑbdʒəˈgeʃən/ *n* [C, U] scolding; rebuke. 骂; 叱责。

ob·late /ˈɒbleɪt; ˈɑblet/ *adj* (geom) flattened at the poles: (几何)两极扁平的; 扁圆的: *The earth is an* ~ *sphere*. 地球是一扁圆球体。

ob·la·tion /əˈbleɪʃn; ɑˈbleʃən/ *n* [C] offering made to God or a god. 祭物;献神物;牲礼。

ob·li·gate /ˈɒblɪgeɪt; ˈɑblə͵get/ *vt* [VP17] ~ *sb to do sth,* (formal) bind (a person, esp legally) (usu passive): (正式用语) (通常用被动语态)强制(某人,尤指依法)作某事: *He felt* ~*d to help*. 他觉得有责任去帮助。

ob·li·ga·tion /͵ɒblɪˈgeɪʃn; ͵ɑbləˈgeʃən/ *n* [C] promise, duty or condition that indicates what action ought to be taken (eg the power of the law, duty, a sense of what is right): 义务; 职责; 责任: *the* ~ *s of good citizenship / of conscience;* 好公民的义务 (良心上的责任); *fulfil / repay an* ~, eg by returning hospitality that one has received. 履行义务(报恩)。 **be / place sb under an** ~, be / make sb indebted to another. 受人恩惠; 负有义务(对某人施恩惠; 使某人负有义务)。

ob·li·ga·tory /əˈblɪgətrɪ US: -tɔːrɪ; əˈblɪgə͵torɪ/ *adj* that is required by law, rule or custom: (法律, 规则或习俗上)要求的; 必须的; 必须做的: *Is attendance at school* ~ *or optional in that country?* 在那个国家里, 上学是强制的还是随意的? *It is* ~ *on café owners to take precautions against fire*. 餐馆老板必须作防火的措施。

ob·lige /əˈblaɪdʒ; əˈblaɪdʒ/ *vt* [VP17] **1** ~ *sb to do sth,* require, bind (sb) by a promise, oath, etc: 要求(某人作某事); 以诺言、誓约等束缚(某人): *The law* ~*s*

parents to send their children to school. 法律要求父母送子女入学。 **2** [VP17] (esp in passive) be ~d to do sth, compel: (尤用于被动语态)强迫: *They were ~d to sell their house in order to pay their debts.* 他们被迫出卖他们的房子来还债。 ⇨ have²(1). **3** [VP6A, 14] do sth for sb as a favour or in answer to a request: 施惠; 答应要求而作: *Please ~ me by closing the door.* 请替我关上那个门。 *Can you ~ me with...,* lend or give me...? 能借我(或给我)···吗? *I'm much ~d to you,* I'm grateful for what you've done. 我非常感激你。 **oblig·ing** *adj* willing to help: 愿意协助的: *obliging neighbours.* 热心助人的邻居。 **oblig·ing·ly** *adv*

ob·lique /ə'bliːk; ə'blik/ *adj* **1** sloping; slanting: 歪的; 斜的: *an ~ angle,* any angle that is not a right angle (ie that 90°). 斜角(非九十度的角, 包括锐角和钝角)。 **2** indirect: 间接的: *an ~ reference to sth.* 间接提及某事物。 **~·ly** *adv* **ob·li·quity** /ə'blɪkwətɪ; ə'blɪkwətɪ/ *n* (*pl* **-ties**) **1** [U] state of being ~. 歪; 斜。 **2** [C, U] (instance of) moral perversity. 邪恶的(实例); 不正的行为。

ob·lit·er·ate /ə'blɪtəreɪt; ə'blɪtə,ret/ *vt* [VP6A] rub or blot out; remove all signs of; destroy. 擦掉; 涂掉; 除去; 毁灭。 **ob·lit·er·ation** /ə,blɪtə'reɪʃn; ə,blɪtə'reʃən/ *n* [U].

ob·liv·ion /ə'blɪvɪən; ə'blɪvɪən/ *n* [U] state of forgetting or being quite forgotten: 遗忘或完全被遗忘的状态; 湮没: *sink/fall into ~;* 湮没无闻; (colloq) unconsciousness. (口)失去知觉。

ob·livi·ous /ə'blɪvɪəs; ə'blɪvɪəs/ *adj* ~ of, unaware, having no memory: 不注意的; 忘记的: *~ of one's surroundings/of what was taking place.* 忘了周围的一切(没注意到所发生的事)。

ob·long /'ɒblɒŋ *US:* -lɔːŋ; 'ɑblɔŋ/ *n, adj* (figure) having four straight sides and angles at 90°, longer than it is wide. 长方形; 长方形的。

ob·loquy /'ɒbləkwɪ; 'ɑbləkwi/ *n* [U] public shame or reproach; abuse; discredit. 公开的辱骂; 咒骂; 污辱, 不名誉。

ob·nox·ious /əb'nɒkʃəs; əb'nɑkʃəs/ *adj* nasty; very disagreeable (to). 可憎的; 非常讨厌的(与 to 连用)。 **~·ly** *adv* **~·ness** *n*

oboe /'əʊbəʊ; 'obo/ *n* woodwind instrument of treble pitch with a double-reed mouthpiece. 双簧管; 欧巴管 (一种高音的木管乐器)。 ⇨ the illus at **brass.** 参看 brass 之插图。 **obo·ist** /-ɪst; -ɪst/ *n* player of the ~. 吹奏双簧管的人。

ob·scene /əb'siːn; əb'sin/ *adj* (of words, thoughts, books, pictures, etc) morally disgusting; offensive; likely to corrupt and deprave (esp by regarding or describing sex indecently). (指文字、思想、书籍、图画等)猥亵的; (尤指由于对于性活动的看法或描写不正当而)淫秽的。 **~·ly** *adv* **ob·scen·ity** /əb'senətɪ; əb'sɛnətɪ/ *n* (*pl* **-ties**) [U] being ~; ~ language, etc; [C] instance of this. 猥亵; 淫秽; 猥亵或淫秽的话; 猥亵或淫秽的实例(行为)。

ob·scure /əb'skjʊə(r); əb'skjʊr/ *adj* **1** dark; hidden; not clearly seen or understood: 暗的, 隐藏的; 不清楚的; 含糊难解的: *an ~ view/corner.* 朦胧的景色(隐僻的角落)。 *Is the meaning still ~ to you?* 那意义对你还是含糊难懂吗? **2** not well known: 不著名的: *an ~ village/poet.* 无名的村庄(诗人)。 □ *vt* [VP6A] make ~: 使暗; 使不明显: *The moon was ~d by clouds.* 月亮被云遮暗了。 *Mist ~d the view.* 雾使景色迷濛不清。 **~·ly** *adv* **ob·scur·ity** /əb'skjʊrətɪ; əb'skjʊrətɪ/ *n* (*pl* **-ties**) **1** [U] state of being ~: 含糊; 朦胧; 默默无闻; 不显扬: *content to live in obscurity.* 安于默默无闻的生活。 **2** [C] sth that is ~ or indistinct: 晦涩或不明之事物: *a philosophical essay full of obscurities.* 一篇充满晦涩文字的有关哲学的文章。 **ob·scur·ant·ism** /,ɒbskjʊ'ræntɪzəm; əb'skjʊrən̩t,ɪzəm/ *n* [U] **1** opposition to enlightenment. 反启蒙主义。 **2** deliberate vagueness. 故意含混不明。 **ob·scur·ant·ist** /-ɪst; -ɪst/ *n* person who practises

obscurantism. 反启蒙主义者。

ob·sequies /'ɒbsɪkwɪz; 'ɑbsɪkwɪz/ *n pl* funeral ceremonies. 葬礼。

ob·sequi·ous /əb'siːkwɪəs; əb'sikwɪəs/ *adj* ~ (to/towards), too eager to obey or serve; showing excessive respect (esp from hope of reward or advantage): 逢迎的; 卑躬的(尤指希望借以得到报酬或好处者): *~ to the Manager.* 对经理卑躬屈膝。 **~·ly** *adv* **~·ness** *n*

ob·serv·able /əb'zɜːvəbl; əb'zɜvəbl/ *adj* that can be seen or noticed; deserving to be observed. 看得见的; 值得注意的。 **ob·serv·ably** /-əblɪ; -əblɪ/ *adv*

ob·serv·ance /əb'zɜːvəns; əb'zɜvəns/ *n* **1** [U] the keeping or observing (2) of a law, custom, festival, etc: (法律、习俗、节日等的)遵守; 奉行: *the Lord's Day Observance Society,* ie for seeing that proper respect is paid to Sunday; 守主日会; *the ~ of the Queen's birthday.* 女王诞辰之庆祝。 **2** [C] act performed as part of a ceremony, or as a sign of respect or worship. 庆典仪节; 宗教仪式; 表示尊敬之礼节。

ob·serv·ant /əb'zɜːvənt; əb'zɜvənt/ *adj* **1** quick at noticing things: 善于观察的; 注意的; 机警的: *an ~ boy.* 机警的男孩。 **2** careful to observe(2) laws, customs, etc: 小心尊奉(法律、习俗等)的: *~ of the rules.* 遵守规则。 **~·ly** *adv*

ob·ser·va·tion /,ɒbzə'veɪʃn; ,ɑbzə'veʃən/ *n* **1** [U] observing or being observed: 观察; 注意: *~ of natural phenomena;* 自然现象的观察; *escape ~,* 不为人所注意; 没有被察觉 *come under ~,* be observed. 受到观察中; 被看到。 *keep sb under ~,* watch him carefully (eg a suspected criminal by the police; a hospital patient by the medical staff). 注意观察某人(如警察对可疑的罪犯; 医护人员对医院中的病人)。 *'~ car,* (in a railway train) one with wide windows through 'which to watch the scenery, etc. (火车之)瞭望车(有宽阔的窗户以供观赏风景等者)。 *'~ post,* (mil) post as near to the enemy's lines as possible, from which reports of the enemy's movements may be obtained. (军)观测所; 监视哨; 瞭望哨。 **2** [U] power of taking notice: 观察力: *a man of little ~.* 观察力极差的人。 **3** [U] (usu *pl*) collected and recorded information: (通常用复数)经收集并作记录的资料; 观测报告: *Has he published his ~s on bird life in the Antarctic yet?* 他已经把观察南极鸟类生活的报告出版了吗? **4** *take an ~,* take the altitude of the sun or other heavenly body in order to find the latitude and longitude of one's position. 测天(测量太阳或其他天体的高度, 借以测定本身所处位置的经纬度)。

ob·serv·atory /əb'zɜːvətrɪ *US:* -tɔːrɪ; əb'zɜvə,torɪ/ *n* (*pl* **-ries**) building from which natural phenomena (eg the sun and the stars, volcanic activity, marine life) may be observed. 天文台; 气象台; 瞭望台。

an astronomical observatory

ob·serve /əb'zɜːv; əb'zɜv/ *vt, vi* **1** [VP6A, 8, 9, 10, 25, 2A, and 18'A, 19 A, in passive 用被动语态] see and notice; watch carefully: 看; 观察: *~ the behaviour of birds.* 观察鸟类的行为。 *The accused man was ~d to enter the bank/trying to force the lock of the door.* 被告被看到进入银行(企图撬开门锁)。 *I have never ~d him*

do otherwise. 我从来没有看到他别的做法。*He ~d that it had turned cloudy.* 他发觉天已经转阴。*He ~s keenly but says little.* 他观察敏锐但很少说话。**2** [VP6A] pay attention to (rules, etc); celebrate (festivals, birthdays, anniversaries, etc): 遵守(规则等); 庆祝(节日, 生日, 周年等); 守; 过: *Do they ~ Christmas Day in that country?* 那个国家的人过圣诞节吗? **3** [VP6A, 9] say by way of comment: 评论; 评述; 说: *He ~d that we should probably have rain.* 他说也许会下雨。**~r n 1** one who ~s(1). 观察者: *an ~r of nature.* 自然界的观察者。**2** one who observes(2). 遵行者; 奉行者: *an ~r of the Sabbath.* 守安息日的人。**3** person who attends a conference, etc to listen but who does not otherwise take part. 会议等的观察员(出席会议等, 但仅旁听而不参加)。
ob·serv·ing *adj* quick to notice. 善于观察的; 注意的。
ob·serv·ing·ly *adv*

ob·sess /əb'ses; əb'sɛs/ *vt* [VP6A] (usu passive; **~ed by/with**) (of a fear, a fixed or false idea) occupy the mind of; continually distress: (通常用被动语态)(指恐惧, 固执的或错误的观念)占据心思; 不断地困扰: *~ed by/with fear of unemployment.* 被失业的恐惧所困扰。**~·ion** /əb'seʃn; əb'sɛʃən/ *n* **1** [U] state of being ~ed. 被困扰; 缠绕。**2** [C] *~ion (about/with sth/sb),* sth that ~es; fixed idea that occupies one's mind. 萦绕于心的事物; 成见; 顽念。**~·ive** /əb'sesɪv; əb'sɛsɪv/ *adj* of or like an obsession. 萦绕的; 似萦绕于心之事物的。

ob·sid·ian /əb'sɪdɪən; əb'sɪdɪən/ *n* dark volcanic rock like the glass of which some bottles are made. 黑曜岩。

ob·sol·escent /ˌɒbsə'lesnt; ˌɑbsə'lɛsnt/ *adj* becoming out of date; passing out of use. 过时的; 已废的。 **ob·sol·escence** /-'lesns; -'lɛsns/ *n* [U] being ~. 过时; 作废。

ob·sol·ete /'ɒbsəli:t; 'ɑbsə,lit/ *adj* no longer used; out of date. 作废的; 过时的。

ob·stacle /'ɒbstəkl; 'ɑbstəkl/ *n* sth in the way that stops progress or makes it difficult: 障碍; 妨害物: *~s to world peace.* 世界和平的障碍。**'~ race,** one in which ~s, natural or artificial, eg ditches, hedges, have to be crossed. 障碍赛跑。

ob·stet·ric /əb'stetrɪk; əb'stetrɪk/ (also **ob·stet·ri·cal** /-kl; -kl/) *adj* of obstetrics: 产科的: *the ~ ward* (in a hospital). (医院中之)产科病房。**ob·stet·rics** *n pl* (with *sing v*) branch of medicine and surgery connected with childbirth, its antecedents and sequels. (与单数动词连用)产科医学; 接生术。**ob·ste·trician** /ˌɒbstə'trɪʃn; ˌɑbstə'trɪʃən/ *n* expert in obstetrics. 产科医生。

ob·sti·nate /'ɒbstɪnət; 'ɑbstənɪt/ *adj* **1** not easily giving way to argument or persuasion: 顽固的; 不易说服的; 倔强的: *an ~ character/streak.* 顽固的性格(倔强的性情)。**2** not easily overcome: 不易屈服的; 难克服的: *~ resistance;* 顽强的抵抗; *an ~ disease.* 难治的病。**~·ly** *adv* **ob·sti·nacy** /-nəsɪ; -nəsɪ/ *n* [U] being ~; stubbornness. 顽固; 倔强; 固执。

ob·strep·er·ous /əb'strepərəs; əb'strɛpərəs/ *adj* unruly; noisily resisting control: 难驾驭的, 吵闹不驯管束的; 暴躁的: *~ behaviour/children.* 难驾驭的行为(吵闹不服管束的孩子们)。**~·ly** *adv* **~·ness** *n*

ob·struct /əb'strʌkt; əb'strʌkt/ *vt* [VP6A] **1** be, get, put, sth in the way of; block up (a road, passage, etc): 阻隔; 阻塞; 遮断(道路、通道等): *The mountain roads were ~ed by falls of rock.* 山路被落下的石头所阻塞。*Trees ~ed the view.* 树木遮蔽了视野。**2** make (the development, etc of sth) difficult: 使(事物发展等)困难; 妨碍: *~ the progress of a Bill through the House of Commons.* 阻碍一个法案在下议院中的审议。

ob·struc·tion /əb'strʌkʃn; əb'strʌkʃən/ *n* **1** [U] obstructing or being obstructed: 阻碍; 障碍; 封锁: *The Opposition adopted a policy of ~.* 反对党采取一种阻碍政策。**2** sth that obstructs: 阻碍物; 障碍物: *~s on the*

road, eg trees blown down in a gale. 路上的障碍物(如被强风吹倒的树)。**~·ism** /-ɪzəm; -ˌɪzəm/ *n* systematic ~ of plans, legislation, etc. (对计划、立法等之)有系统的阻碍。**~·ist** /-ɪst; -ɪst/ *n*

ob·struc·tive /əb'strʌktɪv; əb'strʌktɪv/ *adj* causing, likely or intended to cause, obstruction: 阻碍的; 妨害的: *a policy ~ to our plans.* 妨害我们计划的政策。**~·ly** *adv*

ob·tain /əb'teɪn; əb'ten/ *vt, vi* **1** [VP6A] get; secure for oneself; buy; have lent or granted to oneself: 取得; 获得; 买到; 借到: *~ what one wants.* 获得所要的东西。*Where can I ~ the book?* 在什么地方我可以买到这本书? **2** [VP2A] (of rules, customs) be established or in use: (指规则, 习俗)制定; 通行; 流行: *The custom still ~s in districts.* 这种风俗在某些地区仍然流行。**~·able** /-əbl; -əbl/ *adj* that can be ~ed. 可得到的; 能取得的。

ob·trude /əb'tru:d; əb'trud/ *vt, vi* [VP 14, 2A] *~ (upon),* push (oneself, one's opinions, etc) forward, esp when unwanted. 强入; 闯入; 强使(某人)接受(自己, 自己的意见等)。**ob·trus·ive** /əb'tru:sɪv; əb'trusɪv/ *adj* inclined to ~. 强入的; 强人接受己见的; 闯入的。**ob·trus·ive·ly** *adv*

ob·tuse /əb'tju:s US: -'tu:s; əb'tus/ *adj* **1** blunt. 钝的。**2** (of an angle) between 90° and 180°. (指角度)在90度与180度之间的; 钝角的。⇨ *the illus at* **angle.** 参看 angle 之插图。**3** slow in understanding; stupid. 迟钝的; 愚笨的。**~·ly** *adv* **~·ness** *n*

ob·verse /'ɒbvɜ:s; 'ɑbvɝs/ *n* side of a coin or medal having on it the head or principal design, ⇨ **reverse;** face of anything intended to be presented; counterpart: (钱币、奖章等的)正面; 表面; (事实等的)对应部分: (attrib) (用作定语) *the ~ side.* 正面。

ob·vi·ate /'ɒbvɪeɪt; 'ɑbvɪ,et/ *vt* [VP6A] get rid of; clear away; anticipate: 排除; 清除; 预防: *~ dangers/difficulties.* 预防危险(排除困难)。

ob·vi·ous /'ɒbvɪəs; 'ɑbvɪəs/ *adj* easily seen or understood; clear; plain. 显而易见的; 清楚的; 明白的。**~·ly** *adv* **~·ness** *n*

oca·rina /ˌɒkə'ri:nə; ˌɑkə'rinə/ *n* small, egg-shaped musical wind-instrument (with holes for the fingertips) made of porcelain, plastic or metal. 奥卡利那笛; 洋埙(一种陶器、塑胶或金属的卵形吹奏乐器)。

oc·ca·sion /ə'keɪʒn; ə'keʒən/ *n* **1** [C] time at which a particular event takes place; right time (*for sth*): (发生特殊事情的)时机; 机会(与 for 连用, 后接某事物): *on this/that ~...;* 在这个(那个)时机...; *on the present/last ~...;* 在这次(上次)...; *on one ~;* once; 曾经; 有一次; *on rare ~s.* 很少; 不常。*I have met Mr White on several ~s.* 我曾经见过白特先生几次。*This is not an ~* (= a suitable time) *for laughter.* 这不是开玩笑的时候。*He has had few ~s to speak French.* 他很少有机会说法语。**on ~,** now and then; whenever the need arises. 不时地; 必要时。*rise to the ~,* show that one is equal to what needs to be done. 显出有应付特殊事故的能力。*take this/that ~ to say sth,* avail oneself of the opportunity. 利用这(那)机会说某事。**2** [U] reason; cause; need: 理由; 原因; 需要: *I've had no ~ to visit him recently.* 我最近没有必要去看他。*You have no ~ to be angry.* 你没有生气的理由。**3** [C] immediate, subsidiary or incidental cause of sth: 某事的近因, 附带原因或偶因: *The real causes of the strike are not clear, but the ~ was the dismissal of two workmen.* 罢工的真正原因并不清楚, 但近因是由于两个工人的被开除。□ *vt* [VP6A, 12A, 13A] be the cause of: 引起; 惹起: *The boy's behaviour ~ed his parents much anxiety.* 那孩子的行为使他父母大为着急。

oc·ca·sional /ə'keɪʒənl; ə'keʒənl/ *adj* **1** happening, coming, seen, etc from time to time, but not regularly: 偶尔的; 偶然的: *He pays me ~ visits.* 他偶尔来看我。*There will be ~ showers during the day.* 今天将会有阵雨。*the ~ + n,* = an *~ + n: He pays me the ~ visit,* an *~ visit.* 他偶尔来看我。**2** used or meant for a

special event, time, purpose, etc: 应时的;应景的: ~ verses, eg written to celebrate an anniversary. 应景诗 (如庆祝周年纪念会者). ~·ly /-nəlɪ; -nlɪ/ adv now and then; at times: 偶尔地;间或: He visits me ~ly. 他偶尔来看我。

Oc·ci·dent /'ɒksɪdənt; 'ɑksədənt/ n the ~, (liter) the countries of the West, ie Europe and America, contrasted with the Orient. (文)西方(包括欧洲与美洲,与东方 the Orient 相对). **Oc·ci·den·tal** /ˌɒksɪ'dentl; ˌɑksə'dentl/ n, adj (native) of the ~ or a country in the ~. 西方的;西方国家的;西方人。

oc·cult /ə'kʌlt US: ə'kʌlt, 'ɒ'kʌlt/ adj 1 hidden; secret; only for those with special knowledge. 隐密的;秘密的;神秘的;玄奥的。 2 supernatural, magical: 超自然的;神秘的: ~ sciences, eg astrology. 秘术(例如占星术). the ~, that which is ~. 神秘的事物;奥秘。

oc·cu·pant /'ɒkjupənt; 'ɑkjəpənt/ n person who occupies a house, room or position; person in actual possession of land, etc. (房屋、地位等的)占据者;居住者;占有者;(土地等的)实际拥有者。 **oc·cu·pancy** /-pənsɪ; -pənsɪ/ n act, fact, period of occupying a house, land, etc by being in possession. (房屋、土地等的)据有;居住;占有;占有期间;居住期间。

oc·cu·pa·tion /ˌɒkju'peɪʃn; ˌɑkjə'peʃən/ n 1 act of occupying(1); taking and holding possession of: 占有;据有;占领;居住;拥有: the ~ of a house by a family; 某屋为一个家庭所居住; an army of ~, one that occupies conquered territory until peace is made. 占领军。 2 [U] period during which land, a building, etc is occupied. (土地、建筑物等的)占有期间;居用期。 3 [C] business, trade, etc; that which occupies one's time, either permanently or as a hobby, etc: 事业;职业;行业: 工作(永久的或作为娱乐而费时而占据某人之时间的): useful ~s for long winter evenings. 消磨漫长冬夜的有用的工作。他正忙于翻译一本法文小说。 ~·al /-ʃənl; -ʃənl/ adj arising from, connected with, a person's ~. 职业的;因职业而有的;与职业有关的。 ~·al 'hazards, risks that arise from a person's ~ (eg explosions in coalmines). 职业上的危险(如煤矿坑中的爆炸)。 ~·al 'therapy, treatment of illness, etc by activity in creative or productive employment. 职业疗法(由从事创造性或生产性的工作来治疗疾病等)。

oc·cu·pier /'ɒkjupaɪə(r); 'ɑkjə,paɪə/ n occupant; person in (esp temporary or subordinate) possession of land or a building (contrasted with the owner or tenant). 土地或建筑物的占据者(尤指暂时的占有者;与地主、房东、佃户或租户相对)。

oc·cupy /'ɒkjupaɪ; 'ɑkjə,paɪ/ vt (pt, pp -**pied**) [VP 6A] 1 live in, be in possession of (a house, farm, etc). 居住;拥有(房屋、田庄等)。 2 take and keep possession of (towns, countries, etc, in war): 占领(城镇、国家等): ~ the enemy's capital. 占领敌人的首都。 3 take up, fill (space, time, attention, etc): 占;填满;盘据(空间、时间、注意力、心思): The dinner and speeches occupied three hours. 餐宴和演讲占了三小时。 Many anxieties ~ my mind. 许多忧虑盘据我的心头。 He is occupied in translating / occupied with a translation of a French novel. 他正忙于翻译一本法文小说。 4 hold, fill: 占;充任: My sister occupies an important position in the Department of the Environment. 我姐姐在环境处充任要职。

oc·cur /ə'kɜ:(r); ə'kɝ/ vi (-rr-) 1 [VP2A] take place; happen: 发生: Don't let this ~ again. 不要让这件事再发生。 When did the accident ~? 那意外事故是什么时候发生的? 2 [VP3A] ~ to, come into (sb's mind): 想起;想到: An idea has ~red to me. 我想到了一个主意。 Did it ever ~ to you that..., Did you ever have the idea that...? 你有没有想到···? 3 [VP2C] exist; be found: 存在;被发现: Misprints ~ on every page. 每一页都有印刷的错误。

oc·cur·rence /ə'kʌrəns; ə'kɝəns/ n 1 [C] happening; event: 发生;事件: an everyday ~; 每日发生的事件; an unfortunate ~. 不幸的事件。 2 [U] fact or process

of occurring: 发生的事实或过程: of frequent / rare ~, happening frequently / rarely. 经常(极少)发生的。

ocean /'əuʃn; 'oʃən/ n 1 the great body of water that surrounds the land masses of the earth: 海洋; 大海: an ~ voyage. 海洋航行。 ~·going ships, (contrasted with coastal ships), 远洋船只(与近海船只相对)。 2 one of the main divisions of this: 世界上的大洋之一: the Atlantic / Pacific / Indian O~. 大西洋(太平洋;印度洋)。 the ~ lanes, the routes regularly used by ships. 海洋航线;远洋航线。 3 (colloq) great number or quantity: (口)极多的数目或数量;大量: ~s of time / money. 极多的时间(金钱)。 ~·ic /ˌəuʃɪ'ænɪk, ˌoʃɪ'ænɪk/ adj of, like, living in, the ~. 海洋的;似海洋的;生活于海洋中的。

ochre (US also **ocher**) /'əukə(r); 'okɚ/ n [U] sorts of earth used for making pigments varying from light yellow to brown; pale yellowish-brown colour. 赭石; 赭土石(用以制作自浅黄色至棕褐色之颜料);淡黄褐色; 赭石色。

o'clock /ə'klɒk; ə'klɑk/ particle (= of the clock) used in asking and telling the time (to specify an hour): 点钟: He left at five ~ / between five and six ~, 他于五点钟离职(五点钟与六点钟之间离开)。 ⇨ **App 4.** 参见附录四。

oc·ta·gon /'ɒktəgən US: -gɒn; 'ɑktəˌgɑn/ n plane figure with eight sides and angles. 八边形;八角形。 **oc·tag·onal** /ɒk'tægənl; ɑk'tægən/ adj eight-sided. 八边的。

oc·tane /'ɒkteɪn; 'ɑkten/ n paraffin hydro-carbon: 辛烷: high ~, (of fuels used in internal-combustion engines) having good anti-knock properties; (指内燃机用的燃料)高辛烷的;具有良好抗爆性的: '~ rating, measure of these properties, esp of petrol. 辛烷等级 (尤指汽油之抗爆性能数)。 ⇨ **knock²(3).**

oc·tave /'ɒktɪv; 'ɑktev/ n 1 (music) the note that is six whole tones above or below a given note; the interval of five whole tones and two semitones (do, re, mi, fa, so, la, ti, do); note and its ~ sounded together. (音乐) 八度(音);一音阶;第八音阶;第八度音程;八度和音。 ⇨ **scale²(7).** 2 (poetry) first eight lines of a sonnet; stanza of eight lines. (诗)商籁体诗(十四行诗)的起首八行;八行的诗节。

oc·tavo /ɒk'teɪvəu; ɑk'tevo/ n (abbr 略作 **8vo,** or **oct;** pl ~s /-vəuz; -voz/) (size of a) book or page produced by folding sheets of paper three times or into eight leaves. 八开本的书;八开的纸;八开;八开大小。

oc·tet, oc·tette /ɒk'tet; ɑk'tɛt/ n 1 (piece of music for) eight singers or players. 八重唱(曲);八重奏(曲)。 2 = octave(2).

Oc·to·ber /ɒk'təubə(r); ɑk'tobɚ/ n the tenth month of the year, with 31 days. 十月。

oc·to·gen·arian /ˌɒktədʒɪ'neərɪən; ˌɑktədʒə'nɛrɪən/ n, adj (person) of an age from 80 to 89. 八十多岁的(人)。

oc·to·pus /'ɒktəpəs; 'ɑktəpəs/ n (pl ~**es** /-pəsɪz; -pəsɪz/) sea animal with a soft body and eight arms (tentacles) provided with suckers. 章鱼。 ⇨ the illus at **mollusc.** 参看 mollusc 之插图。

oc·troi /'ɒktrwɑ: US: ɒk'trwɑ:; 'ɑktrɔɪ/ n [C] duty levied (in some European countries) on goods brought into a town; place where, officials by whom, the levy is collected. (某些欧洲国家之)货物入市税;入市税征收处;入市税征收吏。

ocu·lar /'ɒkjulə(r); 'ɑkjəlɚ/ adj of, for, by, the eyes; of seeing: 眼睛的;适于眼睛的;用眼睛的;视觉的: ~ proof / demonstration. 目睹的证明。

ocu·list /'ɒkjulɪst; 'ɑkjəlɪst/ n specialist in diseases of the eye. 眼科医生。

oda·lisque /'əudəlɪsk; 'odl,ɪsk/ n Eastern female slave or concubine, eg in a seraglio in olden times. 东方的女双或婢妾(例如古代土耳其其皇宫中的奴婢)。

odd /ɒd; ɑd/ adj 1 (of numbers) not even; not exactly

divisible by two: (指数字)奇数的; 不能用二除尽的: *1, 3, 5 and 7 are odd numbers.* 1, 3, 5 和 7 都是奇数。 **2** of one of a pair when the other is missing: 一双中的单个的: *an odd shoe/boot/glove* 单只鞋子(靴子,手套)。 **3** of one or more of a set or series when not with the rest: 一套中的单个的: *two odd volumes of an encyclopaedia;* 一部百科全书中的两本; *an odd player,* (in a game) an extra player above the number actually needed. (比赛中之)额外选手。 **odd man out, (a)** person or thing left when the others have been arranged in pairs. 无配对的人或物(其他的全已成双配对而剩下的一个); 落单的人或物。 **(b)** (colloq) person who stands aloof from, or cannot fit himself into, the society, community, etc, of which he is a member. (口)社会团体中不能与他人相处的人; 独来独往的人。 **4** with a little extra: 零头的; 少量剩余的: *five 'hundred odd,* a number greater than 500; 五百多; *'thirty-odd, years,* between 30 and 40; 三十几岁; *twelve 'pounds odd,* £12 and some pence extra. 十二英镑多。 **5** not regular, habitual, or fixed; occasional: 非经常的; 非固定的; 临时的: *make a living by doing odd jobs;* 靠做零工生活; *weed the garden at odd times/moments,* at various and irregular times. 在空闲的时候除去花园里的杂草。 *the odd + n,* = an **odd** + *n: The landscape was bare except for the odd cactus.* 那片地上除了零星的仙人掌外什么也没有。 **6(-er, -est)** strange; peculiar: 奇怪的; 古怪的: *He's an odd/odd-looking old man.* 他是一个古怪(样子古怪)的老人。 *How odd!* 好奇怪! **odd·ly** *adv* in an odd manner: 成奇数; 单个地; 零星地; 非经常地; 奇怪地: *oddly enough,* strange to say. 说来奇怪。

odd·ity /'ɒdɪtɪ; 'ɑdətɪ/ *n (pl -ties)* **1** [U] quality of being odd(6); strangeness: 奇怪; 古怪; 怪异: ~ *of behaviour/dress.* 行为(服装)的古怪。 **2** [C] queer act, thing or person: 怪异的行为; 怪事; 怪物: *He's something of an* ~, is unusual in some ways. 他在某些方面异于常人。

odd·ment /'ɒdmənt; 'ɑdmənt/ *n* [C] **1** remnant; sth left over; odd piece: 残余之物; 零头; 零碎: *The chair was sold as an* ~ *at the end of the auction.* 拍卖结束时那把椅子单独卖掉了。 **2** (*pl*) odd pieces. (复)零零碎碎的东西; 零星杂物。 ⇨ *odds and ends* at **odds(5).**

odds /ɒdz; ɑdz/ *n pl* **1** the chances in favour of or against sth happening: 可能的机会; 成败的可能性: *The* ~ *are against us,* We are unlikely to succeed. 我们成功的机会甚小。 *The* ~ *are in your favour,* You are likely to succeed. 你们有成功的可能。 *The* ~ *are that...,* It is probable that...; 可能是…。 *They were fighting against heavy* ~. 他们和优势的敌人作战。 **It makes no** ~, makes no difference, will not influence the outcome. 没有关系; 没有差别。 **What's the** ~? (colloq) What does it matter? (口)有什么关系? *give/receive* ~, give/receive an equalizing allowance (eg a number of strokes in golf, when a player is known to be stronger or weaker than another). 比赛时让与(接受)有利条件(例如高尔夫球比赛中的让杆)。 **2** things that are not even; inequalities: 不平均之事物; 不平等: *make* ~ *even.* 使不平均之事物平均; 使不均衡之事物均衡。 **3** (betting) difference in amount between the money staked on a chance and the money that will be paid if the chance is successful: (打赌)赌注与付款的差额: ~ *of ten to one.* 十赔一(输时付十, 赢时只得一, 即输赢为十与一之比)。 **fixed** ~, (eg football pools) with a promise to pay agreed odds, eg 100—1, regardless of the number of punters, gamblers. (足球赛之赌注等)固定比数(不管下注者的人数, 以允诺的比数付款,如赔百赢一)。 **lay** ~ **of,** offer ~ of: 提出…的差额比数: *I'll lay* ~ *of three to one that....* 我将以三比一(输三赢一)打赌…。 **long** ~, eg 20 to 1. 长差比数(例如二十比一)。 **short** ~, eg 3 to 1. 短差比数(例如三比一)。 ~ **-'on,** better than even (chance). 有一半以上的(成功机会); 有一半以上的胜算。 **be at** ~ **(with sb) (over/on sth),** be quarrelling or disagreeing. (为某事)(与某人)争吵; 论论。 **5** ~ **and**

ends, small articles, bits, and pieces, of various sorts and usu of small value. 零星杂物; 零碎杂物。

ode /əʊd; od/ *n* poem, usu in irregular metre and expressing noble feelings, often in celebration of some special event. 颂; 歌(通常为不规则韵律和表达高尚情感的诗,常常为庆祝某一特殊事情而写的)。

odi·ous /'əʊdɪəs; 'odɪəs/ *adj* hateful; repulsive. 可恨的; 讨厌的。 ~ **·ly** *adv*

odium /'əʊdɪəm; 'odɪəm/ *n* [U] general or widespread hatred; strong feeling against sth: 普遍的憎恨; 讨厌: *behaviour that exposed him to* ~. 使他被人憎恨的行为。

odor·if·er·ous /,əʊdə'rɪfərəs; ,odə'rɪfərəs/ *adj* (formal) fragrant. (正式用语)香的。

odor·ous /'əʊdərəs; 'odərəs/ *adj* (chiefly poet) fragrant. (主要用于诗歌)香的。

odour (US = **odor**) /'əʊdə(r); 'odə/ *n* **1** [C] smell (pleasant or unpleasant). (香或臭的)气味。(古) **(2)** [U] reputation; approval; favour. 名誉; 称赞; 好感。 *be in good/bad* ~ **(with sb),** enjoy/not enjoy his favour or approval. (在某人心目中)有良好(不良)的声誉。 ~ **-less** *adj*

od·ys·sey /'ɒdɪsɪ; 'ɑdəsɪ/ *n* long, adventurous journey, or series of adventures (from the voyage of Odysseus /ə'dɪsɪəs; o'dɪsɪəs/ after the siege of Troy, in Homer's epic). 长久的冒险旅行; 一连串的冒险(源出荷马史诗奥德修斯围攻特洛伊后的航海历程)。

oecu·meni·cal /,iːkju'menɪkl; ,ɛkju'mɛnɪkl/ *adj* = ecumenical.

Oedipus complex /'iːdɪpəs kɒmpleks *US:* 'ed-; 'edəpəs 'kɑmpleks/ *n* (psych) sexual love of an infant for the parent of the opposite sex, with jealousy of the other parent. (心理)恋母情结(儿子对母亲的性爱及对父亲的嫉妒); 恋父情结(女儿对父亲的性爱及对母亲的嫉妒)。

o'er /ɔː(r); or/ *adv, prep* (poet) (诗) =over.

oesoph·agus /iː'sɒfəgəs; ɪ'sɑfəgəs/ *n* = esophagus.

of /*usual form:* əv; əv; *strong form:* ɒv; ɑv/ *prep* **1** (indicating separation in space or time) (表示空间或时间的距离): *five miles south of Leeds;* 里兹以南五英里; *within a hundred yards of the station;* 距车站一百码以内; *within a year of his death;* 他死后一年内; (US) *five minutes/a quarter of* (= before) *two* (GB 英 = 'five minutes/a quarter *to* two'). 差五分(一刻钟)两点。 **2** (indicating origin, authorship) (表示来源, 作者): *a man of humble origin;* 出身低微的人; *of royal descent;* 皇家后裔的; *the works of Shakespeare;* 莎士比亚的著作; *the Iliad of Homer.* 荷马的伊里亚特。 **3**(indicating cause): (表示原因): *die of grief/hunger, etc;* 悲伤(饥饿等)而死; *do sth of necessity/of one's own choice/of one's own accord;* 做必要的(自己选择的, 出于本意的)事; *sick/proud/ashamed/afraid/glad/tired, etc of sth or sb;* 对某事物或某人感到厌恶(骄傲, 羞耻, 害怕, 高兴, 厌倦等); *taste/smell, etc of sth;* 某物的味道(气味等); *because of;* 因为; 由于; *for fear of.* 因为怕…。 *The explosion couldn't have happened of itself,* ie without an external cause. 那爆炸不会无缘无故发生的。 **4** (indicating relief, deprivation, riddance): (表示解除, 剥夺, 免除): *cure sb of a disease/a bad habit, etc;* 治愈某人的病(矫正某人的坏习惯等); *rid a warehouse of rats;* 清除仓库里的老鼠; *be/get rid of sth or sb;* 摆脱某事物(或某人); *rob sb of his money;* 抢某人的钱; *relieve sb of anxiety;* 解除某人的忧虑; *clear oneself of an accusation;* 证明自己无罪; *destitute of sense;* 无感觉的; *trees bare of leaves;* 没有叶子的树; *free of customs duty;* 免关税的; *independent of help;* 不依赖帮助的; *short of money.* 缺钱的。 **5** (indicating material or substance): (表示材料或原料): *a table of wood;* 木桌; *a house of stone;* 石屋; *a dress of silk;* 绸衣; *made of steel and concrete;* 钢筋混凝土造成的; *built of brick.* 砖造的。 **6** (forming *adj* phrases; descriptive genitive): (构成形容词短语; 描述的所有格): *goods of our own*

manufacture; 我们自己制造的货物; *tomatoes of my own growing,* that I have grown myself; 我自己种的番茄; *a girl of ten years,* a girl ten years old, a ten-year-old girl; 十岁的女孩子; *a man of foreign appearance;* 外国人模样的男人; *a man of genius;* 有天才的人; *a man of ability,* an able man; 能干的人; *a woman of no importance,* an unimportant woman; 不重要的女人; *the vice of drunkenness,* the vice that is drunkenness; 酗酒之害; *a coat of many colours,* a many-coloured coat; 一件彩色的上衣; *the city of Dublin;* 都柏林市; *the Isle of Wight.* 怀特岛。 **7** (in the pattern 'noun¹ of noun²' = noun² that is noun¹): (在 'noun¹ of noun²' 的句型中, 表示 noun² 具有 noun¹ 的属性): *They live in a palace of a house,* a house that is a palace, a palatial house. 他们住在一栋宫殿似的房子里。 *He has the devil of a temper,* a devilish temper. 他的脾气非常坏。 *Where's that fool of an assistant,* that foolish assistant? 那个笨助手在哪里? *What a mountain of a wave,* a mountainous wave! 山一般高的浪涛! *She's a fine figure of a woman,* a woman with a fine figure. 她是个身材很美的女人。 *Where's your rascal of a husband,* your rascally husband? 你的流氓丈夫在哪儿? **8** (objective genitive): (宾格的所有格): *a maker of pots,* a man who makes pots; 制锅者; *the love of study;* 爱好研究; *the writing of a letter;* 信件的写作; *loss of power / appetite;* 权力(胃口)的失去; *great eaters of fish,* people who eat much fish; 爱吃鱼的人; *the fear of God,* ie felt by men towards God. 人对上帝的敬畏。 **9**(subjective genitive): (主格的所有格): *the love of God,* God's love for mankind, 上帝对世人的爱, (⇨ **8** above, 参看上列第 8 义 *the fear of God*); *the love of a mother,* a mother's love, the love that a mother has for her children. 母爱。 Cf 参看 *his love of* (ie for) *his mother.* 他对母亲的爱。 **10** (indicating connection, reference or relation): (表示连接、关连或关系): *the cause of the accident;* 意外事件的原因; *the result of the debate;* 辩论的结果; *a topic of conversation;* 话题; *the first day of June;* 六月的第一天; 六月一日; *the manners of the present day;* 时下的习俗; *those of the middle classes;* 那些中产阶级的人; *the master of the house;* 一家之主; *the wall of the garden,* the garden wall; 花园的围墙; *the leg of the table,* the table leg; 桌子的腿; *the opposite of what I intended;* 和我所计划的相反; *Doctor of Medicine;* 医学博士; *Master of Arts;* 文学硕士; *think well of sb;* 重视某人; 对某人印象甚好; *admitting / allowing of no doubt;* 不容怀疑; *accused / suspected / convicted of a crime;* 被控有(涉嫌, 被判有)某一罪状; *speaking / talking / dreaming of sth;* 说(谈, 梦)到某事物, *sure / certain / confident / fond / guilty / innocent, etc of sth;* 确信有把握得到(确定, 深信, 喜欢, 触犯, 没有犯)某事物; *hard of hearing,* deaf; 重听; *blind of* (= in respect of) one eye; 瞎了一只眼睛; *at thirty years of age.* 三十岁。 *What of* (= about) *the risk?* 有什么危险? *Well, what of it?* 嗯, 这有什么关系? **11** (indicating partition, inculsion, measure): (表示区分、包含、分量): **(a)** *a sheet of paper;* 一张纸; *a roll of cloth;* 一匹布; *a pint of milk;* 一品脱牛奶; *a ton of coal;* 一吨煤; *3 acres of land;* 三英亩的土地; *2 yards of cloth;* 二码布; *part of that cake;* 那个蛋糕的一部分; *one / a few / all of us;* 我们当中的一个(我们当中的几个)我们全体); *a lot / a great deal / not much of this stuff;* 这种材料很多(甚多,不多); *no more of that.* 那个没有了; 不要再来那个了。 *The car won't hold the six of us.* 这辆车载不了我们六个人。 **(b)** (after superlatives): (在最高级的形容词后面): *He is the most dangerous of enemies.* 他是仇敌中最凶恶的。 *You have had the best of teachers,* the best of those teachers who were available. 你有了最好的教师。 **(c)** (= out of): *It surprises me that you, of all men, should be so foolish.* 在所有的人之间, 偏偏你那么笨, 真令我惊奇。 *On this day of all days.* 就在这一天。 **(d)** (intensive): (加强语气): *the song of songs;* 歌中之歌; *the Holy of Holies,* best deserving the name. 至圣所。 **12** (in the pattern *n + of + possessive*) (在 n + of + possessive 的句型中):

(a) from among the number of: 其中的一部分; 出自…之中: *a friend of mine;* 我朋友中的一个; 我的一个朋友; *no business of yours;* 没你的事儿; *reading a volume of Ruskin's,* a book, one of a number of which Ruskin was the author; 读一本拉斯金的著作; *a painting of the king's,* one of a number belonging to, or painted by, the king. 国王所有的图画中的一幅。 Cf 参较 *a portrait of the king,* a painting to show the king's appearance. 国王的肖像。 **(b)** (used when the *n* is modified by a demonstrative or other word that cannot be combined with a possessive): (用于当名词被指示词或其他不能与所有格连用的词所修饰时): *that long nose of his;* 他那个长鼻子; *this essay of Green's;* 格林这篇短论; *that foolish young wife of yours;* 你那位年轻无知的太太; *that queer-looking hat of hers.* 她那顶怪模样的帽子。 **13** (in the pattern *adj + of + n / pron*): (用于 adj + of + n / pron 之句型中): *How kind of you to help!* 非常谢谢你的帮助! *It was good of your brother to come.* 谢谢令兄(令弟)的光临。 **14** (indicating time): (表示时间): *in days of old / of yore,* in the past; 以前的日子; *of late,* recently; 近来; *of late years,* during recent years. 最近几年。 *What do you do of a Sunday,* on Sundays? 你星期天都做什么? *He sometimes comes in of an evening,* in the evenings. 他有时候晚上来。 **15** by: 等于 by 的含义: *beloved of all.* 被大家所爱。

off¹ /ɒf US: ɔːf/ *adj* **1** (contrasted with *near*) (of horses, vehicles) on the right-hand side: (与 near 相对)(指马、车)右边的: *the off front wheel;* 右前轮; *the off hind leg of a horse;* 马的右后腿; *the off horse* (of a pair). (一对中的)右边的马。 **2** (remotely) possible or likely. (极少)可能的; 不大可能的。 *on the off chance,* ⇨ **chance¹(2).** **3** inactive; dull: 不活动的; 沉闷的; 清淡的; 萧条的: *the 'off season.* ⇨ **season.**

off² /ɒf US: ɔːf/ *adverbial particle* (For special uses with *off* as an *adverbial particle* such as *go off: turn sth off* ⇨ the *v* entries.) (off 作副词性小品词的特殊用法如 go off, turn sth off, 参看 go, turn 等动词。) **1** (indicating distance in space or time) departure, removal, separation at or to a distance; away: (表示空间或时间的距离)离去; 移去; 除去; 离开; 在远处; 至远处: *The town is five miles off.* 那个城在五英里外。 *We're still some way off,* from our destination. 我们距离目的地还有一些路。 *The holidays are not far off.* 假期不远了。 *Why don't you have that long beard off,* cut off, shaved off? 你为什么不把那么长的胡子剃掉(或剪短)? *He's off to London.* 他到伦敦去了。 *It's time I was off / I must be off now,* I must leave now. 是我该走的时候了(我得走啦)。 *We're off / Off we go!* We've started / We're starting! 我们走啦(我们要走啦)! *They're off!* (in racing) The race has started! (赛跑)比赛已经开始了! 他们已经起跑了! *Off with him!* Take him away! 把他赶走! *Off with his head!* Cut his head off! 砍掉他的头! **2** (contrasted with *on*) indicating the ending of sth arranged, planned, etc: (与 on 相对) 表示经安排、计划等之事的结束: *Their engagement* (ie to marry) *is off / broken off,* ended. 他们的婚约取消了。 *The miners' strike is off,* will not now take place. 矿工罢工已取消了。 **3** (contrasted with *on*) disconnected; no longer available: (与 on 相对)中断的; 没有了: *The water / gas / electricity is off.* 自来水(煤气、电)没有了; 自来水(煤气、电)停了。 *Are the brakes off?* 煞车松开了吗? *The central heating is off.* 集中供暖系统停了。 *That dish is off,* (in a restaurant) no more of that dish is available (even though it is on the menu). (餐馆中)那一样菜没有了(虽然菜单上列有)。 **4** indicating absence or freedom from work or duty: 表示缺席、不在、不工作或责任的免除: *I think I'll take the afternoon off,* not do my usual work, etc. 我想我下午要休假。 *The manager gave the staff a day off,* a day's holiday. 经理放全体职员一天假。 *You mustn't take time off* (= stay away from work) *just because you want to see a football match.* 你不可只是为了想看一场足球赛而休假。 **5** (of food) no longer fresh: (指食物)不新鲜:

This fish has gone slightly off, is beginning to smell or taste rather bad. 这鱼有点不新鲜了。 **6** (in a theatre) behind or at the side(s) of the stage: (戏院中)在舞台后方或两旁: *Noises off, eg* as a stage direction in a printed play. 舞台外发出声音(如剧本中的舞台说明)。 **7** (phrases) (短语) **off off**, (US) (美) = **off** (prep). **on and off; off and on**, from time to time; now and again; irregularly: 不时; 断断续续地; 间歇地; 不规则地: *It rained on and off all day.* 整天断断续续地下着雨。 **badly / comfortably / well off**, ⇨ various adverbs. 参看各副词。 **better / worse off**, ⇨ **better²**(1). **worse** *adv* (1). **right / straight off**, at once; immediately. 立即; 立即。

off³ /ɒf US: ɔ:f/ *prep* **1** not on; down from; away from: 不在…上; 从…下来; 离开: *fall off a ladder / a tree / a horse.* 从梯子(树,马)上跌下来。 *The rain ran off the roof.* 雨水从屋顶流下来。 *The ball rolled off the table.* 球从桌上滚下来。 *Keep off the grass.* 勿践踏草地。 *Cut another slice off the loaf.* 再切一片面包。 *Can you take something off (ie reduce) the price?* 你能减点价钱吗? **2** (of a road or street) extending or branching from: (指路或街道)自…延伸或分叉: *a narrow lane off the main road;* 大路边的一条小巷; *a street off the Strand*, branching from the street called the Strand. 自斯特兰街分叉出的一条街。 **3** at some distance from: 离…一些距离: *a house off the main road;* 离大路不远处的一幢房子; a short distance seaward of: 离…不远的海上: *an island off the Cornish coast;* 康瓦尔海岸外的一个小岛; *a ship anchored off the harbour entrance.* 下碇在港口外的一艘船。 *The battle was fought off Cape Trafalger.* 海战在特拉法加角附近海面上进行。 **4** (colloq) feeling averse to; not taking or indulging in: (口)对…感觉讨厌; 嫌恶; 不吃; 不饮; 不抽; 不耽溺于: *I'm off my food,* have little or no appetite, don't enjoy it. 我没有食欲(胃口不好)。 *She's off smoking / drugs*, does not smoke / take drugs any more. 她不再抽烟(不再服麻醉药)。

off⁴ /ɒf US: ɔ:f/ *pref* (used in numerous compounds) (用于许多复合词中) ⇨ the entries below. 参看下列各条。

of·fal /'ɒfl US: 'ɔ:fl; 'ɔfl/ *n* [U] those parts, eg heart, head, kidneys, which are considered less valuable than the flesh when an animal is cut up for food. 动物屠宰后被认为食用价值较少的部分(如心、头、腰子); 肠肚杂碎。

off-beat /ˌɒf 'bi:t US: ˌɔ:f; 'ɒf,bit/ *adj* (colloq) unusual; unconventional: (口)不平常的; 非传统的: *an ~ TV comedy.* 新奇的电视喜剧。

off-day /'ɒf deɪ US: 'ɔ:f; 'ɒf de/ *n* (colloq) day when one is unlucky, when one does things badly, clumsily, etc: (口)倒霉的日子(运气不佳的一天, 笨手笨脚什么事都做不好等): *I'm afraid this is one of my ~s.* 我恐怕这又是我倒霉的一天。

of·fence (US = **of·fense**) /ə'fens; ə'fɛns/ *n* **1** [C] *an ~ against*, crime, sin, breaking of a rule: 过错; 罪; 犯法: *an ~ against the law / against good manners;* 违犯法律(没有规矩); *be charged with a serious ~.* 被控告犯严重的罪。 **2** [U] the hurting of sb's feelings; condition of being hurt in one's feelings. 伤人感情; 触怒; 不悦。 *give / cause ~ (to sb);* 触怒(某人); *take ~ (at sth);* (因某事物而)发怒: *He is quick to take ~,* is easily offended. 他容易生气。 *No ~!* (phrase used to say) I did not intend to hurt your feelings. 我无意伤你(的)感情? **3** [U] attack: 攻击: *weapons of ~.* 攻击性的武器。 *They say that the most effective defence is ~.* 据说最有效的防御就是攻击。 **4** [C] that which annoys the senses or makes sb angry: 令人讨厌或生气的事物: *That cesspool is an ~ to the neighbourhood.* 那个污水坑是令附近邻居闷的东西。 **~·less** *adj* without ~; not giving ~. 无罪的; 无咎的; 不攻击的; 不触怒的。

of·fend /ə'fend; ə'fɛnd/ *vi, vt* **1** [VP3A] *~ against*, do wrong; commit an offence: 犯法; 犯罪; 违犯: *~*

against good manners / the law / traditions, etc. 违犯礼貌(法律, 传统等)。 **2** [VP6A] hurt the feelings of: give offence to: 伤…的感情; 触怒: *I'm sorry if I've ~ed you.* 假如我冒犯了你, 我很抱歉。 *He was ~ed at / by my remarks.* 他被我的话触怒了。 *She was ~ed by / with her husband.* 她被她丈夫触怒了(她生她丈夫的气)。 **3** [VP6A] displease; annoy: 使不愉快; 烦扰: *sounds that ~ the ear;* 刺耳的声音; *ugly buildings that ~ the eye.* 难看的丑陋建筑物。 **~·er** *n* person who ~s, esp by breaking a law: 冒犯者; (尤指)犯罪者; 犯人: *first ~ers,* found guilty for the first time and not usu treated severely; 初犯; *an old ~er,* one who has often been found guilty. 累犯; 惯犯。

of·fense /ə'fens; ə'fɛns/ ⇨ **offence**.

of·fen·sive /ə'fensɪv; ə'fɛnsɪv/ *adj* **1** causing offence to the mind or senses; disagreeable: 令人不快的; 讨厌的: *fish with an ~ smell;* 有难闻气味的鱼; *~ language.* 无礼的言语。 **2** used for, connected with, attack: 攻击(性)的: *~ weapons / wars.* 攻击性的武器 (攻击战)。 ⇨ **defensive**. □ *n* attack; an attitude of attack. 攻击; 攻势。 *go into / take the ~,* go into attack. 进攻; 采取攻势。 *a peace ~,* (modern jargon) sustained effort the declared aim of which is to lessen the risk of war. (现代术语)和平攻势。 **~·ly** *adv* **~·ness** *n*

of·fer /'ɒfə(r) US: 'ɔ:f-; 'ɔfər/ *vt, vi* **1** [VP6A, 7A, 12A, 13A, 14] *~ sth to sb; ~ sb sth; ~ sth for sth,* hold out, put forward, to be accepted or refused; say what one is willing to pay, give or exchange: 提供; 提出; 出价: *They ~ed a reward for the return of the jewels that had been lost.* 他们悬赏找失去的珠宝。 *I have been ~ed a job in Japan.* 有人提供我一个在日本的工作机会。 *He ~ed to help me.* 他表示要帮助我。 *He ~ed me his help.* 他给我帮助。 *We ~ed him the house for £20000 /* ~ed *him £20000 for the house.* 我们索(出)价二万英镑卖给(买)他那幢房子。 *~ battle,* give the enemy an opportunity of fighting. 给敌人一个作战的机会; 挑战。 *~ one's hand,* hold it out (to shake hands). 伸出手来(准备握手)。 *~ one's hand (in marriage),* make a proposal of marriage to a woman. 向女人求婚。 **2** [VP 6A, 12A, 13A, 15B] *~ sth (up) (to God),* present (to God): (向上帝) 奉献: *~ prayers to God;* 向上帝祈祷; *~ up a sacrifice.* 奉献牺牲; 献祭。 **3** [VP6A, 7A, 14] *~ (to),* attempt; give signs of: 企图; 表示: *~ no resistance to the enemy.* 表示不抵抗敌人。 **4** [VP2A] occur; arise: 发生; 出现: *Take the first opportunity that ~s,* that there is. 抓住第一个出现的机会。 *as occasion ~s,* when there is an opportunity. 有机会时; 机会来到时。 □ *n* [C] statement ~ing to do sth or give sth; that which is ~ed; 提供; 提议; 提出之物; 提供的机会; 出价: *an ~ of help;* 援助的提议; *your kind ~ to help;* 你的援助的好意; *an ~ of marriage,* a proposal. 求婚。 *I've had an ~ of £20000 for the house.* 有人已经出价二万英镑要买我那幢房子。 *Make me an ~.* 给我出个价。 *be open to an ~,* be willing to consider a price to be named by a buyer. 愿意考虑买主所出的价。 *(goods) on ~,* for sale at a certain price. 出售的(货品)。 **~·ing** /'ɒfərɪŋ US: 'ɔ:f-; 'ɔfərɪŋ/ *n* **1** [U] that which is ~ed; 提供; 奉献: *the ~ing of bribes.* 提出贿赂; 行贿。 **2** [C] sth ~ed or presented: 提供之物: *a 'peace ~ing,* sth ~ed in the hope of restoring friendship after a quarrel, etc. 谢罪之礼(争吵等之后为求恢复友谊而奉送之礼物)。

of·fer·tory /'ɒfətrɪ US: -tɔ:rɪ; 'ɔfə,tɔrɪ/ *n* (*pl* -ries) [C] gifts collected in church during, or at the end of, a service. (教堂做礼拜时所收的)奉献金。

off-hand /ˌɒf 'hænd US: ˌɔ:f; 'ɒf'hænd/ *adj* **1** without previous thought or preparation; extempore: 事先未加思索或未作准备的; 临时的; 即席的: *~ remarks.* 随口说出的话。 **2** (of behaviour, etc) casual; curt: (指行为等)随便的; 唐突的: *in an ~ way.* 随便地。 □ *adv* without previous thought: 事先未加思索地; 随便地: *I can't say ~.* 我不能随便说。 **off-'handed(ly)** *adj, adv* = ~.

of·fice /'ɒfɪs US: 'ɔːf-; 'ɔfɪs/ n [C] **1** (often pl) room(s) used as a place of business: (常用复数)办公处;办公室;事务所; 营业所: a lawyer's ~; 律师事务所; working in an ~, in business, eg as a clerk or typist; 做办公室的工作(如当办事员或打字员); our London ~, our branch in London; 我们的伦敦分公司(办事处或分行); (US) surgery. (美)(医师或牙医的)诊所. **'booking ~**, ⇨ **book²(2)**. **'box-~**, ⇨ **box¹(2)**. **'~-block**, (usu large) building containing ~s (often of more than one company or firm). 办公大楼 (通常为高楼大厦,内有许多办公室,常为数家公司者). **'~-boy** n boy employed to do less important duties in an ~. (办公室的)工友. **2** (buildings of a) government department, including the staff, their work and duties: 政府机关,部,局,处等; 其建筑物: the 'Foreign O~. 外交部. **3** the work which it is sb's duty to do, esp in a public position of trust and authority: 职位; 职务; 公职: enter upon/leave/accept/resign ~, esp of positions in the government service. 担任(离开,接受,辞去)公职. Which party will be in ~ after the next general election? 哪一党会在下次大选后执政? The Liberals have been out of ~ for a long time now. 自由党已经很久没有执政了. **'~-bearer** n person who holds an ~. 公务员; 官吏. **4** duty: 职责; 任务: the ~ of host/chairman. 主人(主席)的职责. **5** (pl) attentions, services, help: (复)殷勤; 服务; 帮助: through the good ~s = (kind help) of a friend; 借着一个朋友好意的协助; perform the last ~s for..., conduct the burial service of.... 为...举行葬礼. **Divine O~**, certain forms of worship in the Roman Catholic and Episcopal Churches. (天主教和圣公会的)礼拜仪式.

of·fi·cer /'ɒfɪsə(r) US: 'ɔːf-; 'ɔfəsɚ/ n **1** person appointed to command others in the armed forces, in merchant ships, aircraft, the police force, etc usu wearing special uniform with indications of rank: 军官; 高级船员; 高级航空人员; 警官: commissioned and non-commissioned ~s; 军官与军士; ~s and crew.高级船员与水手. **2** person in a position of authority or trust, engaged in active duties, eg in the government: 官员; 官吏; 公务员: executive/clerical ~s, in the civil service; 行政官员(文书官); a customs ~; 海关人员; ~s of state, ministers in the government; 部长: the ~s of the Debating Society, ie the President, Secretary, Treasurer; 辩论会职员(即主席、秘书、财务); the Medical O~ of Health; 卫生官员; 'Welfare O~s. 福利官员. **3** form of address to a policeman. 警官(对警察的称呼).

of·fi·cial /ə'fɪʃl; ə'fɪʃəl/ adj **1** of a position of trust or authority; said, done, etc with authority: 公务的; 凭职权所说、所做等的;职权上的;官方的;正式的: ~ responsibilities/records; 公务(正式记录); in his ~ uniform; 穿着他的制服; ~ statements. 正式声明. The news is not ~. 这消息不是正式的. **2** characteristic of, suitable for, persons holding office: 官式的; 官腔的: written in ~ style. 用官式体写成的. □ n person holding public office (eg in national or local government): 公务员; 官员: government ~s. 政府官员. **~ly** /-ʃəlɪ; -ʃəlɪ/ adv in an ~ manner; with ~ authority. 正式地; 官方地; 凭职权地. **~·dom** /-dəm; -dəm/ n ~s collectively; the ways of doing business of (government) ~s. (集合名词)官员; 官场; 官僚作风. **~·ese** /ə,fɪʃə'liːz; ə,fɪʃə'liz/ n [U] language characteristic of the writing of some government ~s (considered to be too formal or obscure). (一般认为太正式或含糊难解的)公文术语; 公文用语. ⇨ **journalese** at **journal**.

of·fi·ci·ate /ə'fɪʃɪeɪt; ə'fɪʃɪet/ vi [VP2A, C, 3A] ~ (as) (at), perform the duties of an office or position: 执行职务: ~ as chairman; 担任主席; ~ as host at a dinner party; 作宴会的主人; ~ at a marriage ceremony, (of a priest) perform the ceremony. (指神父)主持结婚仪式.

of·fi·cious /ə'fɪʃəs; ə'fɪʃəs/ adj too eager or ready to help, offer advice, use authority. 过份殷勤的; 好管闲事的; 好用权威的. **~·ly** adv **~·ness** n

off·ing /'ɒfɪŋ US: 'ɔːf-; 'ɔfɪŋ/ n part of the sea distant from the point of observation but visible: 视界范围内的远处海面: a ship in the ~; 在看得见的远处海面上的一艘船; (fig) (喻) a quarrel in the ~, one that appears likely to break out. 即将发生的争吵.

off·ish /'ɒfɪʃ US: 'ɔːf-; 'ɔfɪʃ/ adj (colloq) inclined to aloofness; distant in manner. (口)疏远的; 冷淡的. ⇨ stand-offish at **stand²(10)**.

off·li·cence /'ɒf laɪsns US: 'ɔːf; 'ɔf,laɪsns/ n licence to sell beer and other alcoholic drinks for consumption off the premises; shop, part of a public house, where such drinks may be bought and taken away. (英)卖酒执照 (所卖之酒应携出店外喝); 卖酒店 (为酒馆的一部分, 所卖之酒可携带出外).

off·peak /'ɒf piːk US: 'ɔːf; 'ɔf'pik/ attrib adj ⇨ **peak¹(4)**.

off·print /'ɒf prɪnt US: 'ɔːf; 'ɔf,prɪnt/ n [C] separate printed copy of an article in part of a larger publication. 出版物中单篇印刷的文章; 抽印本; 选刊.

off·put·ting /,ɒf 'pʊtɪŋ US: ,ɔːf; 'ɔf,pʊtɪŋ/ adj (colloq) disconcerting. (口)令人不安的; 使人慌乱的. ⇨ put off at **put¹(11)**.

off·scour·ings /'ɒf skaʊərɪŋz US: 'ɔːf; 'ɔf,skaʊrɪŋz/ n pl (usu fig) refuse; dregs. (通常为喻)垃圾; 渣滓.

off·set vt (-tt-) [VP6A, 14] balance, compensate for: 抵销; 弥补: He has to ~ his small salary by living economically. 他薪水微薄, 不得不节俭度日. □ n **1** ~ (process), method of printing in which the ink is transferred from a plate to a rubber surface and then on to paper. 胶印; 橡皮版印刷术; 透印版印刷术. **2** = offshoot.

off·shoot /'ɒf ʃuːt US: 'ɔːf-; 'ɔf,ʃut/ n [C] stem or branch growing from a main stem (lit or fig): (树木的)旁枝; 分枝(书面或喻): an ~ of a plant/a mountain range/a family. 植物的分枝(山脉的支脉; 家族的旁系).

off·shore /,ɒf 'ʃɔː(r) US: 'ɔːf; 'ɔf'ʃɔr/ adj **1** in a direction away from the shore or land: 自海岸的; 从陆上的: ~ breezes. 吹向海洋的微风. **2** at a short way out to sea: 在近海处的: ~ islands/fisheries. 近海岛屿(渔场). **3** ~ purchases, (US) goods purchased by the US for countries in receipt of economic or military aid, but which do not come from the US directly, eg aluminium shipped from Canada to Europe. (美)国外采购(美国向国外购买以援助他国的经援或军援物资, 例如向加拿大购买铝运往欧洲国家).

off·side /'ɒf saɪd US: 'ɔːf; 'ɔf'saɪd/ attrib adj, adv (football, hockey) (of a player) in a position on the field in relation to the ball which is debarred by the rules: (足球、曲棍球)(指球员)越位的: ~ play; 越位踢球; the ~ rule. 越位的规则.

off·spring /'ɒfsprɪŋ US: 'ɔːf; 'ɔf,sprɪŋ/ n (pl unchanged) child; children; young of animals: (复数不变)子孙; 后代; 后裔;(动物的)幼仔: He is the ~ of a scientific genius and a ballet dancer. 他是一位天才科学家和一位芭蕾舞蹈家的后代. Their ~ are all slightly mad. 他们的子孙都有一点疯狂.

off·street /'ɒf striːt US: 'ɔːf; 'ɔf'strit/ attrib adj not on the main streets: 不在大街上的: ~ parking, of motor vehicles; 不在大街上停车; ~ (un)loading, eg of lorries at the rear entrances of buildings. 不在大街上装货(卸货)(例如载货卡车在建筑物后门的装货或卸货).

off·white /,ɒf 'waɪt US: ,ɔːf 'hwaɪt; 'ɔf'hwaɪt/ adj not pure white, but with a pale greyish or yellowish tinge. 灰白色的; 米色的.

oft /ɒft US: ɔːft; ɔft/ adv (in poetry) often: (诗)时常: an oft-told tale. 常讲的故事; many a time and oft, very often. 常常. **'oft·times** adv (archaic) often. (古)时常.

of·ten /'ɒfn US: 'ɔːfn; 'ɔfən/ adv of frequency (usu occupying mid-position (ie with the v); may occupy front-position or end-position for emphasis (esp when modified by very or quite), or for contrast; comp and sup either ~er, ~est, or more ~, most ~.) (通常置于

句子中间，即与动词连用；亦可置于句首或句末，作加强语气用，尤其被 very 或 quite 所修饰时，或作对比；比较级或最高级可写为 ～er，～est 或 more ～，most ～。) **1** many times; in a large proportion of the instances: 时常；常常: *We ～ go there.* 我们常常去那儿。*We have ～ been there.* 我们时常去那儿。*We've been there quite ～.* 我们经常到那儿去。*It very ～ rains here in April.* 这儿四月间或经常下雨。**2** (in phrases) (在短语中) *how ～:* 多少时候一次；多久一次: *How ～ do the buses run?* 公共汽车多久有一班? *as ～ as,* each time that: 每一次: *As ～ as I tried to ring him the line was engaged.* 每次我想打电话给他, 总是有人在讲话。*as ～ as not; more ～ than not,* very frequently: 常常；极常；屡屡: *During foggy weather the trains are late more ～ than not.* 有雾的时候火车常常误点。*every so ～,* from time to time. 时时。*once too ～,* once more than is wise, safe, etc: 又一次；再一次；次数太多(即超过明智、安全等的限度, 而发生问题): *He exceeded the speed limit once too ～ and was fined £50.* 他又一次超速, 被罚了五十英镑。

ogle /'əʊgl; 'ogl/ *vi, vt* [VP3A, 6A] *～ (at),* look at (suggesting lust or longing): 色迷迷地看；向…送秋波；向…抛媚眼: *ogling all the pretty girls.* 色迷迷地看所有漂亮的女郎。

ogre /'əʊgə(r); 'ogə/ *n* [C] (in fables) cruel man-eating giant. (寓言中)残忍的吃人巨妖。**ogress** /'əʊgres; 'ogrəs/ *n* female ～. 女的吃人巨妖。'**～ish** /-ɪʃ; -ɪʃ/ *adj* like an ～. 似吃人巨妖的；凶暴的；可怕的。

oh /əʊ; o/ *int* exclamation of surprise, fear, etc. 啊；噢；呀(表示惊讶、恐惧等的惊叹词)。

ohm /əʊm; om/ *n* [C] unit of electrical resistance (symbol Ω). 欧姆(电阻的单位, 符号 Ω)。

oho /əʊ'həʊ; o'ho/ *int* exclamation of surprise or triumph. 表示惊奇或得意的感叹词。

oil /ɔɪl; ɔɪl/ *n* [C, U] **1** (sorts of) (usu easily burning) liquid which does not mix with water, obtained from animals (eg *whale-oil*), plants (*coconut oil, olive-'oil, oil of peppermint, essential oils*), or found in rock underground (*mineral oil, petroleum*): (各种)油类；油(通常为易燃的液体, 不与水混合, 取自动物者, 如鲸油 whale-oil. 取自植物者, 如椰子油 coconut oil, 橄榄油 olive-oil, 薄荷油 oil of peppermint, 挥发油 essential oils。或自地下层层中所探得者, 如矿物油 mineral oil, 石油 petroleum): *cod-liver oil; salad oil; hair oil.* 鱼肝油；沙拉油；发油。**2** (phrases) (短语) *burn the midnight oil,* sit up late at night to study, etc. 读书等直到深夜; 开夜车。*paint in oils,* paint with oil-colours (⇨ below). 用油画颜料画(参看下列之 oil-colours)。*pour oil on the flame(s),* make anger more intense, make a quarrel more bitter, etc. 火上加油；煽动。*pour oil on troubled waters,* act or speak in such a way as to end quarrelling, bitterness, etc. 调解争端；劝人息怒。*smell of the midnight oil,* bear marks of study (as if done late at night by the light of an oil-lamp). 有用功的痕迹(似乎曾在油灯旁熬夜用功)。*strike oil,* find petroleum in the ground by sinking a shaft, etc; (fig) become very prosperous or successful. 发现石油；(喻)发大财；极为成功。**3** (compounds) (复合词) '**oil-bearing** *adj* (eg rock strata) containing mineral oil. (例如岩层)含(矿)油的。'**oil-burner** *n* engine, ship, heater, etc that uses oil as fuel. 以油为燃料的发动机、船只、生热器等。'**oil-cake** *n* [U] cattle food made from seeds after the oil has been pressed out. 油渣饼；油粕(植物种子经榨油后制成的家畜饲料)。'**oil-can** *n* can with a long nozzle, used for oiling machinery. 加油壶；加油器。'**oil-cloth** *n* [U]cotton material waterproofed and used as a covering for shelves, etc. (防水)油布。'**oil-colours, oils** *n pl* paints made by mixing colouring matter in oil. 油画颜料。'**oil-field** *n* area where petroleum is found. 油田(发现有石油的地区)。'**oil-fired** *adj* (of a furnace) burning oil as fuel: (指火炉等)以油为燃料的；烧油的: *oil-fired central heating.* 烧油的集中供暖系统。'**oil-painting** *n* [U] art of painting in oil-colours;

[C] picture painted in oil-colours. 油画术；油画。'**oil-palm** *n* tropical palm tree yielding oil. 油棕榈(产油的热带棕榈树)。'**oil-paper** *n* paper made transparent and waterproof by being treated with oil. (用油处理透明而防水的)油纸。'**oil-rig** *n* structure and machinery for drilling (eg in the sea-bed) for oil. 钻油机械装置(如用于海底者)。⇨ **derrick(2).** '**oil-silk** *n* silk cloth treated with oil to make it air-tight and water-tight, used for making rain-coats, etc. 油质绸(上油的绸布, 不透气又不漏水, 用以制雨衣等)。'**oil-skin** *n* [C, U] (coat etc, made of) cloth treated with oil to make it water-proof; (*pl*) suit of clothes made of this material, as worn by sailors, etc. 油衣；防水布；(复)(水手等所穿的)一套油衣衣；防水衣。'**oil-slick,** ⇨ **slick.** '**oil-tanker** *n* ship, large vehicle, for carrying oil (esp petroleum). 油轮；运油车。'**oil-well** *n* well from which petroleum is obtained. 油井。□ *vt* [VP6A] put oil on or into (eg to make a machine run smoothly): 给…加油；上油; 润于: *oil a lock/bicycle;* 给锁(自行车)上油; *oil the wheels/works,* (fig) make things go smoothly by being tactful; (喻)用圆滑手段使事情顺利进展; *oil (more usu grease) sb's palm,* give him a bribe. 贿赂某人。**oiled** *adj* (usu 通常作 *well-oiled*) (sl) rather drunk. (俚)相当醉的。

an oil-tanker

oiler /'ɔɪlə(r); 'ɔɪlɚ/ *n* **1** ship built for carrying oil; oil-tanker. 油轮；运油车。**2** oil-can for oiling machinery. 加油壶；加油器。**3** person who oils machinery, eg in the engine-room of a ship. 为机器加润滑油的人(例如船上轮机室中的油工)。

oily /'ɔɪlɪ; 'ɔɪlɪ/ *adj* (-ier, -iest) **1** of or like oil: 油的；似油的: *an ～ liquid.* 油质液体。**2** covered or soaked with oil: 涂有油的；浸过油的: *～ fingers.* 沾着油的手指。**3** (of speech or manner) too smooth; fawning; trying by fawning to win favour. (指言语或态度)太圆滑的；奉承的；拍马屁讨好的;油腔滑调的。'**oili-ness** *n* also ⇨ **oleaginous.**

oint-ment /'ɔɪntmənt; 'ɔɪntmənt/ *n* [C, U] (sorts of) medicinal paste made from oil or fat and used on the skin (to heal injuries or roughness, or as a cosmetic). (各种)药膏；油膏。

okapi /əʊ'kɑːpɪ; o'kɑpɪ/ *n* rare forest ruminant animal of Central Africa. 奥卡皮(产于非洲中部的一种罕见森林反刍动物)。

okay /əʊ'keɪ; o'ke/ (abbr 略作 **OK**) *adj, adv* (colloq) all right; correct; approved. (口)好；对的；行。□ *vt* [VP6A] agree to; approve of. 同意；赞成；赞同。□ *n* agreement; sanction: 同意；许可: *Have they given you their OK?* 他们同意你吗?

okra /'əʊkrə; 'okrə/ *n* (tropical and semi-tropical plant with) edible green seed pods used as a vegetable. 秋葵(热带及亚热带植物)；秋葵荚(呈绿色, 作蔬菜食用)。

old /əʊld; old/ *adj* (-er, -est) ⇨ also **elder⁴, eldest. 1** (with a period of time, and with *how*) of age: (与一段时间, 或与 how 连用)年岁的: *He's forty years old.* 他四十岁。*At fifteen years old he left home to become a sailor.* 他十五岁时离家去当水手。*How old are you?* 你几岁了? *He is old enough to know better.* 他已经长大了, 应该更懂事些。*Ought a seven-year-old child to be able to read?* 七岁的小孩应该会读书吗? **2** (contrasted with *young*) having lived a long time; no longer young or middle-aged: (与 young 相对)老的；年老的；年长的: *Old people cannot be so active as young people.* 老年人不能象年轻人那么活跃。*He's far too old for a young girl like you to marry.* 他太

老了，象你这样年轻的女孩子不适于嫁给他。*What will he do when he grows /is /gets old?* 当他老了的时候，他要做什么? **the old,** old people. 老人们。 **young and old,** everyone. 每个人; 无论老少。 **old age,** the latter part of life. 晚年; 老年。 **old age pension,** (abbr 略作 **OAP**), (or 或作 *retirement pension*) pension paid by the State to old persons. (国家发给老年人的)养老金。 Hence, 由此产生, **old age pensioner** *n* (or 或作 *senior citizen*). 领养老金者; 领退休金者。 **the old man,** (colloq) (口) **(a)** one's husband or father. 老丈(指丈夫或父亲)。 **(b)** (among sailors) the captain of a ship. (水手间用语)船长。 **the old woman,** (colloq) one's wife. (口)老婆(指妻子)。 **,old-'womanish** *adj* fussy and timid. 大惊小怪而胆怯的。 **an old maid,** ⇨ **maid.** **,old-'maidish** *adj* precise, tidy, fidgety. 严谨、整洁、烦躁的。 **3** (contrasted with *new, modern, up-to-date*) belonging to past times; having been in existence or use for a long time: (与 new, modern, up-to-date 相对) 古老的; 旧的; 用久的: *old customs /families /civilizations;* 古老的习俗(家庭、文明); *old houses /clothes.* 旧房子(衣服)。 **one of the 'old school,** conservative; old-fashioned. 保守的(人等); 旧派的; 守旧的; 老式的。 **the Old World,** Europe, Asia and Africa. 旧世界(指欧、亚、非三洲)。 **,old-'fashioned** *adj* **(a)** out of date. 旧式的; 老式的: *old-fashioned styles /clothes.* 老式的样子(衣服)。 **(b)** keeping to old ways, ideas, customs, etc: 守旧的: *an old-fashioned aunt;* 守旧的姑妈; *an old-fashioned child,* one who behaves like a much older person. 老成的孩子。 **(c)** (of glances) reproving: (指目光)谴责的: *She gave him an old-fashioned look.* 她瞪他一眼。 □ *n* (US) kind of cocktail made with whiskey. (美)用威士忌调成的鸡尾酒。 **old fogey** *n* ⇨ **fogey.** **old hat,** (colloq) out of date. (口)旧式的; 老式的; 过时的。 **'old-time** *adj* belonging to, typical of, past times: 古时的; 往昔的: *old-time dances.* 古时的舞蹈。 **'old-world** *adj* belonging to, typical of, past times; not modern: 古时的; 老式的; 古色古香的: *an old-world cottage /garden.* 老式的小屋(花园)。 **4** long known or familiar: 熟悉的; 亲密的: *an old friend of mine,* one who has been a friend for a long time (but not necessarily old in years). 我的一个老朋友。 **Old Glory,** used by Americans of the flag of the US. 美国国旗(美国人用语)。 **5** former; previous (but not necessarily old in years). 从前的; 早先的; 以前的(不一定是古老的)。 **'old boy /girl,** former member of the school in question. 校友; 毕业生。 **the 'old country,** one's mother country (used esp when one has left it to settle elsewhere). 祖国 (尤为定居于国外者之用语)。 **the /one's old school,** the school one attended as a boy /girl. 幼年时代所上的学校; 母校。 **the /one's old school tie, (a)** tie worn by former pupils. 昔日小学生所结的领带。 **(b)** feeling of solidarity, wish to give mutual help, among former pupils of the same school or similar types of school. (同一小学或同类小学)校友间之团结互助感。 **6** having much experience or practice: 老经验的; 老练的: *a man who is old in diplomacy.* 富有外交经验的人; 外交界元老。 **the old guard,** long-standing faithful supporters. 长期的忠实拥护者。 **old offender,** person who has often been convicted of crime. 累犯; 惯犯。 **an old hand (at sth),** person with long experience. (做某事的)老手; 熟手。 **old-'timer** *n* person who has for many years lived in a place, been associated with (a club, occupation, etc.) 久居一地、久为会员或久任一职的人; 老资格的人; 老前辈。 **come the old soldier (over sb),** (colloq) claim, because of long experience, to have superior knowledge or ability. (口)因有长久经验而(向某人)声称具有较高的学识或能力; (对某人)摆老资格。 **7** (colloq) used in addressing persons, and with names (and nicknames) giving intimacy, or in joking style: (口)用于称呼而与姓名 (或绰号) 连用, 表示亲切或戏谑: *'Good old John!'* '老约翰!' *'Listen, old man.'* '老兄, 请听。' *'Hullo, old thing!'* '喂, 老兄!' **the 'old one; the old gentleman; old Harry /Nick /Scratch,** the devil.

恶魔; 老魔头。 **8** (sl) used as an intensive: (俚)用于加重语气: *We're having a high old time,* a very good time. 我们过得非常愉快。 *Any old thing* (= Anything whatever) *will do.* 什么东西都行。 □ *n* the past: 往昔; 昔时; 古时: *in days of old;* 在往昔的日子里; *the men of old.* 昔时的人。 **old·ish** /-ɪʃ; -ɪʃ/ *adj* rather old. 稍老的; 稍旧的。

olden /'əʊldən; 'oldn/ *adj* (archaic, liter) of a former age: (古, 文)往昔的; 古老的: *in ~ times /days.* 往昔(昔日)。

old·ster /'əʊldstə(r); 'oldstə/ *n* (colloq) (opposite to *youngster*) old person. (口)长者 (为 youngster 之反义词): *Some of us ~s have more energy than the youngsters.* 咱们有些老人比年轻小伙子更有精力。

ole·agi·nous /,əʊlɪ'ædʒɪnəs; ,olɪ'ædʒənəs/ *adj* having properties of oil; producing oil; fatty; greasy. 油质的; 产油的; 多脂肪的; 油腻的。

ole·an·der /,əʊlɪ'ændə(r); ,olɪ'ændə/ *n* [C]evergreen shrub with tough leaves and red, pink or white flowers growing in clusters. 夹竹桃。

ol·fac·tory /ɒl'fæktərɪ; al'fæktərɪ/ *adj* concerned with smelling: 嗅觉的: *the ~ nerves.* 嗅觉神经。

oli·garchy /'ɒlɪgɑːkɪ; 'ɑlɪ,gɑrkɪ/ *n* (*pl* **-chies**) [C, U] (country with) government by a small group of all-powerful persons; such a group. 寡头政治; 行寡头政治的国家; 寡头政治的执政团。 **oli·garch** /'ɒlɪgɑːk; 'ɑlɪ,gɑrk/ *n* member of an ~. 寡头政治的执政者。

ol·ive /'ɒlɪv; 'ɑlɪv/ *n* **1** ⇨ the illus at **tree.** 参看 tree 之插图。 **'~(-tree),** (evergreen tree common in S Europe bearing a) small oval fruit with a hard stone-like seed and a bitter taste, yellowish-green when unripe and bluish-black when ripe; used for pickling, to be eaten as a relish, and for oil, **(,~'oil),** which is used for cooking, dressing salads, etc. 橄榄树(盛产于南欧); 橄榄 (果椭圆形, 果核坚如石, 味苦, 未成熟时为黄绿色, 成熟时呈蓝黑色; 用之腌泡以作佐料, 所制成之橄榄油 olive-oil 用于烹调、调生菜等)。 **2** leaf, branch or wreath of ~ as an emblem of peace. 作为和平象征的橄榄叶、橄榄枝或橄榄枝叶花圈。 **,hold out the '~-branch,** show that one is ready to discuss peace-making. 表示愿意讲和。 □ *adj* the colour of the unripe fruit, yellowish-green or yellowish-brown. 橄榄色的; 黄绿色的; 黄褐色的。

Olym·piad /ə'lɪmpɪæd; o'lɪmpɪ,æd/ *n* period of four years between celebrations of the Olympic Games. 两次奥林匹克运动会之间的四年期间。

Olym·pian /ə'lɪmpɪən; o'lɪmpɪən/ *adj* (of manners, etc) magnificent; god-like: (指仪态等)高贵的; 庄严的; 似神的: *~ calm.* 庄严的静穆。 □ *n* one of the greater gods of ancient Greece; person with god-like qualities. 奥林巴斯神中(古希腊重要神祇之一); 有神性的人。

Olym·pic /ə'lɪmpɪk; o'lɪmpɪk/ *adj* the ~ **Games, (a)** the contests held at Olympia in Greece in ancient times. 古时在希腊奥林比亚举行的竞赛会。 **(b)** the inter-national athletic competitions held in modern times every four years in a different country. (近代每四年在不同国家举行的)世界运动会。

om·buds·man /'ɒmbʊdzmæn; 'ɑmbədzmən/ *n* **the O~,** (in GB officially called 在英国正式名称为 *Parliamentary Commissioner*) experienced person having authority to inquire into and pronounce upon grievances of citizens against public authorities. 国会民间冤情调查员(经验丰富、有权调查并断定人民对政府行政当局的诉愿者)。

omega /'əʊmɪgə *US:* əʊ'megə; o'mɛgə/ *n* the last letter (Ω) of the Greek alphabet, (⇨ **App 4**;) final development. 希腊字母中最末一个字母(Ω)(参看附录四); 终局; 结局。 ***Alpha and O~,** the beginning and the end. 始与终; 首尾; 始末。

om·elette, om·elet /'ɒmlɪt; 'ɑmlɪt/ *n* [C] eggs beaten together and fried, often flavoured with cheese or containing herbs, etc or *(sweet ~)* jam, sugar. 煎蛋

卷(常常以乳酪作调味, 或以香草等作馅; 甜煎蛋卷 sweet omelet 则以果酱, 糖作馅)。

omen /'əʊmen; 'omIn/ n [C, U] (thing, happening, regarded as a) sign of sth good or warning of evil fortune: 征兆; 预兆; 视为预兆之事物: an ~ of success; 成功的预兆; an event of good/bad ~. 一件被视为好(坏)征兆的事。 □ vt [VP6A] be an ~ of. 为…的征兆, 显出…的预兆。

om·in·ous /'ɒmInəs; 'ɑmənəs/ adj of bad omen; threatening: 恶兆的; 不祥的: an ~ silence; 一阵不祥的静寂; ~ of disaster. 预示灾祸的。 ~·ly adv

omission /ə'mIʃn; o'mIʃən/ n 1 [U] act of omitting, leaving out or undone: 省略; 删除; 遗漏: sins of ~, leaving undone those things that ought to be done. 该做的事而未做之过失; 疏忽罪。 2 [C] sth that is omitted. 省略之事物; 删除之事物; 遗漏之事物。

omit /ə'mIt; o'mIt/ vt (-tt-) 1 [VP7A,6C] ~ to do/doing sth, fail: 疏忽; 怠忽: ~ to do/doing a piece of work. 忘记做一件事(漏做一件事)。 2 [VP6A] fail to include; leave out: 遗漏; 省略: This chapter may be ~ted. 这一章可以省掉。

om·ni·bus /'ɒmnIbəs; 'ɑmnə,bʌs/ n (pl ~es /-bəsIz; -bəsIz/) 1 (former name for a) bus; (in names): (以前的名称)公共汽车(用于名称中): The Midland 'O~ Co. 中部公共汽车公司。 2 (attrib) for, including, many purposes: (用作定语)为着许多目的的; 包含多项目标的: an ~ volume, a large book in which a number of books, eg by the same author, are reprinted. 汇编; 选集。

om·nip·otence /ɒm'nIpətəns; ɑm'nIpətəns/ n [U] infinite power: 全能: the ~ of God. 上帝的全能。 **om·nip·otent** /-tənt; -tənt/ adj having infinite power: 全能的: the O~, God. 全能者(上帝)。

om·niscience /ɒm'nIsIəns; ɑm'nIʃəns/ n (formal) infinite knowledge. (正式用语)全知; 无所不知。 **om·niscient** /-sIənt; -ʃənt/ adj having infinite knowledge. 全知的; 无所不知的。

om·niv·or·ous /ɒm'nIvərəs; ɑm'nIvərəs/ adj (formal) eating all kinds of food; (fig) reading all kinds of books, etc: (正式用语)什么都吃的; 杂食的; (喻)无所不读的: an ~ reader. 无所不读的读者。

on[1] /ɒn; ɑn/ adverbial particle (For special uses with on as an adverbial particle such as go on, go on sth, ⇨ the v entries.) (on 作副词性小品词用之特殊用法, 如 go on, go on something 等, 参看各动词。) 1 (expressing the idea of progress, advance, continued activity; ⇨ v entries for special uses): (表示进展、向前、继续活动的观念; 特殊用法参看各动词): Come on! 来呀! They hurried on. 他们匆匆前进。 I will follow on, come after you. 我会跟上来的。 He's getting on in years, growing old. 他渐渐老了。 The war still went on, did not end. 战争仍在进行中。 How can you work on (= continue working) so long without a rest? 你怎么能不休息而继续工作那么久? On with the show! Let the show begin! Let the show continue! 开始表演! 继续表演! **and 'so on**, and other things of the same kind; et cetera. 等等。 **later on**, at, during, a later time. 后来; 过些时。 **on and on**, without stopping: 不停地: We walked on and on. 我们不停地行走。 2 (corresponding in meaning to **on**[2](1)): (相当于 on[2] 第1义): On with your coat, Put it on. 穿上你的外衣。 Your hat is not on straight. 你的帽子没有戴正。 He had nothing on, was naked. 他什么也没穿。 Has he got his spectacles on? Is he wearing them? 他戴眼镜了吗? **on to, onto** prep to a position on: 达于…上; 向而及于: She fainted and fell on to the floor. 她晕倒在地板上。 The actor stepped onto the stage. 那演员走上舞台。 We ran out of the sea and on to the beach. 我们跑出海水, 跑上海滩。 3 (contrasted with **off**[2](3)): (与 off[2] 第3义相对) (a) in action; in use; functioning; flowing, running, etc: 行动中; 使用中; 操作中; 流动中: The lights were all full on, giving their maximum light. 灯光全亮着。 Someone has left the bathroom tap on, running. 有人没关掉洗澡间的水龙头。 I can smell gas — is one of the

taps on, is gas escaping from one of them? 我闻到煤气味——是不是有一个煤气栓开着? Be sure the handbrake is on before you leave the car. 你离开车子前, 务必要拉手煞车。 The performance is on, has begun. 表演已经开始了。 The strike of postal workers is still on, has not ended yet. 邮政工作者的罢工仍在进行中。 (b) available or procurable when or if needed: 需要时可获得的; 可得到的: Is the water on yet? Is a supply available from the mains? 水管接通了吗? 4 (combined with **be** and **have** in various meanings): (与 be 和 have 连用, 表各种含义): What's on? What's the programme? What's happening? 有什么节目? 发生了什么事? What's on (= What films are being shown) at the local cinema this week? 这个星期本地电影院上演什么片子? There's nothing on tomorrow, is there, eg no meeting I ought to attend, no engagement I ought to carry out? 明天没事儿, 是吗? Have you anything on this evening, any engagements, plans, etc? 你今晚有事儿吗? **be 'on about sth**, (colloq) talk or grumble about it: (口)谈论; 抱怨: What's he on about now? 他现在谈些什么? **be 'on at sb**, (colloq) nag or pester him (about or to do sth). (口)唠叨地责骂或纠缠(与 about 或不定式连用)。 **be 'on to sb/sth**, (a) be in contact with: 与…连络: I've been on to the President, and he told me that.... 我曾与总统连络, 他告诉我说…。 (b) be aware of the plans, actions, importance etc of; be in pursuit of: 知晓…的计划, 行动, 重要性等; 追踪: be on to a conspiracy/scandal/murderer. 得悉一阴谋(得悉一丑行; 追踪一凶手)。 **be ,on to a good 'thing**, be lucky or successful. 幸运; 成功。 5 towards: 向着; 朝向: a ship broadside on to the dock gates, with its side facing towards the gates: 舷侧朝向船坞闸门的一条船; end on, ie with the end forward. 末端向前。

on[2] /ɒn; ɑn/ prep 1 supported by; fastened or attached to; covering or forming part of (a surface); lying against; in contact with: 支承在…上; 系于; 附于; 盖在(表面); 构成(表面)一部分; 靠在; 与…接触; 在…上面: a carpet on the floor; 铺在地板上的地毯; the jug on the table; 桌上的水罐; pictures on the wall; 挂在墙上的图画; the words (written) on the blackboard; (写)在黑板上的字; flies on the ceiling; 天花板上的苍蝇; a blister on the sole of my foot; 我脚掌上的一个水泡; put a roof on the shed; 给棚子盖一个顶; sit on the grass; 坐在草地上; floating on the water; 漂在水上; write on paper; 写在纸上; hang sth on a peg/a nail; 挂某物于钉子上; stick a stamp on the envelope; 贴一张邮票于信封上; live on the Continent, 住在欧洲大陆上, Cf 参较 live in Europe; 住在欧洲; have a hat on one's head/a ring on one's finger; 头上戴着一顶帽子/手指上戴着一个戒指; carry a coat on/over one's arm; 手臂上挂着一件外衣; be/go on board a ship; 在船上(上船); have lunch on the train; 在火车上吃午餐; continued on page five, 下接第五页, Cf 参较 in a book, magazine, etc. Have you a match/any money on you, ie in your pockets, etc? 你(口袋里等)带了火柴(钱)没有? 2 (indicating time) (指时间) (a) on Sunday(s); 在星期日; on the 1st of May; 在五月一日; on the evening of May the first, 在五月一日晚上, Cf 参较 in the evening; on New Year's Day/Eve; 在元旦(除夕); on a sunny day in July, ⇨one[1](4); 在七月里一个晴朗的日子; on that day; 在那一天; on this occasion. 在这一次。 (b) at the time of: 在…之时: on the death of his parents, when they died; 在他父母亲逝世的时候; on my arrival home; 在我到家的时候; 当我抵家时; payable on demand; 来取即付的; 见票即付的; (指票据)即期的; on (my) asking for information. 在(我)询问消息时。 (c) on time, on the minute, ie punctually. 准时。 3 about; concerning: 关于; 论及: speak/lecture/write on international affairs; 演说(演讲, 撰写)国际形势; a lecture on Shakespeare; 关于莎士比亚的演讲; be keen/bent/determined/set on sth/on doing sth. 渴望(一心, 决心, 决定)要某物(作某事)。 4 (indicating membership): (表示为…之一份子): He is on the committee/the jury/the staff. 他是委员会(陪审团, 幕僚)中之一员。 He's on 'The

Daily Telegraph', is a member of the staff of this newspaper. 他在'每日电讯报'工作。 **5** (indicating direction) towards: (指方向)向: *marching on the enemy's capital;* 向敌人首都进军; *turn one's back on sb;* 不理睬某人; *smile/frown on sb;* 向某人微笑(皱眉头); *draw a knife on sb,* ie to attack him; 拔刀攻击某人; *a ship drifting on(to) the rocks,* 漂向礁石的船; *hit sb on the head,* (note: not *his* head); 击打某人的头(注意: 此语中不可用 his head); *give sb a box/blow on the ear.* 打某人一个耳光。 **6** (expressing the basis, ground or reason for sth); (表示某事物的根据或理由): *on this/that/no account;* 为了这个缘故(为了那个缘故; 无缘无故); *a story based on fact;* 根据事实写成的故事; *have sth on good authority;* 从可靠方面获悉某事; *act on your lawyer's advice;* 依照你的律师的意见行事; *arrested on a charge of theft;* 被控偷窃而遭逮捕; *retire on a pension;* 领取养老金而退休; *on penalty of death;* 以死刑作为惩罚; *on an average;* 平均算来; *swear sth on the Bible;* 手按圣经发誓; *be on one's oath/one's honour.* 发誓(以人格保证)。 **7** (indicating a charge or imposition): (指费用或征税): *put a tax on tobacco;* 征烟草税; *charge interest on money,* 索取利息; *place a strain on the economy.* 加重经济负担。 **8** (indicating proximity) close to; against: (表示接近)接近; 靠近: *Henley-on-Thames;* 泰晤士河边的恒利城; *a town on the coast;* 海边的一个城市; *a house on the main road;* 大路边的一幢房子; *a village on the frontier;* 在边境内的一个村庄; *on both sides of the river;* 在河的两岸; *on my right/left;* 在我右(左)边; *just on* (= almost) *2 o'clock;* 差不多两点钟; *just on a year ago;* 差不多一年前; *just on £10.* 差不多十英镑。 **9** (followed by a *n*, or *adj*) (indicating an activity, action, manner, state): (后接名词或形容词, 表示活动、行动、态度、情况): *on business,* engaged in business; 因商务; 因公; 有事; *on holiday;* 度假; *on tour,* touring; 在旅行; 在参观; *on an errand;* 办差事; 跑腿; *on the way;* 在途中; *on the sly,* in a sly manner; 秘密地; 暗地地; *buy sth on the cheap,* (colloq) at a low price; (口)廉价买进某物; *on his best behaviour,* behaving very well; 表现他最好的行为; 行为检点; *be on the look-out for sb,* watching for him; 注意某人; *be on fire,* burning; 着火; 失火; *on sale;* 出售; *on loan.* 出借。 **10** added to: 加添: *suffer disaster on disaster/insult on insult.* 遭受一次又一次的灾祸(一次又一次的侮辱)。

once /wʌns; wʌns/ *adv* **1** (usu end position) for one time, on one occasion, only: (通常置于句末)一次: *I have been there* ~. 我到过那儿一次。 *This clock needs winding* ~ *a week.* 这个时钟一星期只需要上一次发条。 *He goes to see his parents in Wales* ~ *(in) every six months.* 他每六个月去威尔士看他父母一次。 *We go to the cinema* ~ *a week/a fortnight, every week/every two weeks.* 我们每星期(每两星期)去看一次电影。 ~ **more,** again; another time. 再一次; 再来一次。 ~ **or twice;** ~ **and again;** ~ **in a while,** now and again; occasionally; a few times. 一两次; 一再; 有时; 偶尔。 **(for) this** ~; **(just) for** ~, on this one occasion only, as an exception. 只此一次(下不为例)。 ~ **for all,** ⇨ **all⁵ (5).** ~ **in a blue moon,** ⇨ **blue¹.** **2** (often mid position) at some indefinite time in the past; formerly: (常置于句子中间)曾经; 从前; 昔时: *He* ~ *lived in Persia.* 他从前住在波斯。 *This novel was* ~ *very popular but nobody reads it today.* 这本小说曾经一度很受人欢迎, 但是现在没有人读它了。 *~ upon a 'time,* (in story-telling style): (讲故事用语): *O~ upon a time there was a giant with two heads.* 从前有个两头巨人。 **3** (in negative, conditional or indefinite clauses) ever; at all; even for one time: (用于否定从句、条件从句或不定从句中)曾; 全然; 一旦: *He didn't* ~ *offer/He never* ~ *offered to help.* 他从没有提供过帮助。 *O~* (= If you ~, As soon as) *you understand this rule, you will have no further difficulty.* 你一旦了解这个规则, 就不会再有困难。 **4** *at* ~, **(a)** without delay; immediately: 立刻; 马上: *I'm leaving for Rome at* ~. 我马上就去罗马。 *Come here at* ~! 立刻到这儿来! **(b)** at the same time:

同时: *Don't all speak at* ~! 不要全体同时说! *I can't do two things at* ~. 我不能同时做两件事。 *The book is at* ~ *interesting and instructive.* 这本书既有趣又有益。 **all at** ~, suddenly: 突然: *All at* ~ *I saw a rabbit dart across the road.* 突然间我看到一只兔子急速越过道路。 **get/give sb/sth the ~-over,** (colloq) get/give sb/sth a rapid inspection or examination. (口)被迅速检查一遍; 将某人(某物)迅速检查一遍。

on·com·ing /'ɒnkʌmɪŋ; 'ɑn,kʌmɪŋ/ *adj* advancing; approaching: 即将来临的; 接近的: *the* ~ *shift,* the shift (of workers) coming on duty (in a factory); (工厂中的)下一班(工人); ~ *traffic.* 迎面而来的行人车辆。 □ *n approach:* 来临: *the* ~ *of winter.* 冬天的来临。

one¹ /wʌn; wʌn/ *numeral adj, pron* **1** the number 1, ⇨ **App 4.** 一; 一个(参看附录四)。 **(a)** as in the series: 如用于一系列数目中: *one pen, two pencils and three books;* 一枝钢笔, 两枝铅笔, 三本书; as in: 如用于下列场合: *one from twenty leaves nineteen;* 二十减一剩下十九; *one is enough;* 一个够了; *one o'clock,* 一点钟; as in: 如用于下列场合: *,twenty-'one, ,thirty-'one,* etc. 二十一、三十一等。 **(b)** as in: 如用于下列场合: *one hundred, one thousand, one million;* 一百, 一千, 一百万; *one half, one third,* etc. 一半, 三分之一等。 (Except in formal, precise or legal style, *a year and a half* or *eighteen months* is preferred to *one and a half years; a million and a half* to *one and a half millions; a pound of tea* to *one pound of tea.*) (除非用于正式的、精确的或法律的文体, *a year and a half* 或 *eighteen months* 较 *one and a half years* 为佳; *a million and a half* 较 *one and a half millions* 为佳; *a pound of tea* 较 *one pound of tea* 为佳) **(c)** as in: 如用于下列场合: *one pound ten, one pound and ten pence.* 一英镑十便士。 **2** (as a *n*, with *pl* **ones**) the symbol or figure 1: (作为名词, 复数用 ones) 表示'一'的符号或数字: *a row of ones,* ie **1111.** 一排的'一'(即 1111)。 **3** as in: 如用于下列场合: *Book One, Chapter One,* the first book, the first chapter. 第一册, 第一章。 **4** as in: 如用于下列场合: *one day/morning/afternoon/evening/night,* 有一天(早上, 下午, 晚上, 夜晚), (similar in function to the *indef art,* but with the difference that the *prep 'on'* is used before the *indef art.* 此种用法其功用与不定冠词相似, 所不同者, 不定冠词前应加介词 on。 ⇨ **on²(2a).** Cf 参较 *one summer, evening* and *on a summer evening; one morning in June* and *on a June morning).* **5** (One is used to indicate a contrast(expressed or implied) with *the other,* or *another,* or *other(s)*): (one 用以表示与 the other, 或 another, 或 other(s) 的对比(表明的或暗示的)): *The two girls are so much alike that it is difficult for strangers to tell (the) one from the other.* 这两个女孩是如此相象, 以致陌生人难以辨别她们。 *He did not know which to admire more, the one's courage or the other's determination.* 他不知道比较钦佩何者, 那个人的勇气呢, 还是另一个人的决心。 *Well, that's one way of doing it, but there are other and better ways.* 不错, 那是做这件事的一种方法, 但是还有其他更好的方法。 *If, for one, don't like the idea,* suggesting 'and there may also be others who do not like it'. 拿我来说, 我就不喜欢这个主意(暗示可能还有其他的人不喜欢它)。 **for 'one thing,** for one reason (out of several or many): 举个理由, 一则: *I can't help you. For one thing, I've no money.* 我不能帮你的忙, 理由之一是我没有钱。 **6** (always stressed; used for emphasis): (永远重读; 用以加强语气): *There's only 'one way to do it.* 做这事只有一个方法。 *That's the 'one thing needed.* 那是唯一需要的东西。 *No 'one of you could lift it,* ie two or more of you would be needed. 你们当中没有人能单独把它举起来(即需要两个或更多的人才能举起)。 *They went forward as one man,* ie all together, in a body. 他们一同前进。 **7** (before a family name, with or without a title: ⇨ **a²(9))** (用在姓氏之前, 可以和或不和称呼连用; 参看 a² 第 9 义) a certain: 某一: *I heard the news from one (Mr) Smith,* (dated formal) from a certain person named Smith. (过时正式用语)我从一位史密斯(先生)那儿听到

这消息。(Note that if *one* is replaced by the *indef art* a title must be used: 注意: 假如以不定冠词代替 one, 则必须用称呼: *A Mr Smith has called to see you* 有位史密斯先生来过, 他要见你。**8** (as *adj*) the same: (作形容词用)同样的: *They all went off in one direction.* 他们都往同一方向去了。**be at 'one (with sb)**, be in agreement: 意见一致: *I'm at one with you on this subject / We are at one on this subject,* Our opinions are the same. 关于这个问题, 我和你的意见是一致的(我们对这个问题的意见是一致的)。**it's all one (to sb),** It's all the same, it makes no difference: (对某人)都一样, 没有什么不同: *It's all one to me whether you go or don't go.* 你去不去, 对我都是一样。**one and the same,** (emph for) the same: 一样的 (the same 的强调用法): *One and the same idea occurred to each of them.* 他们每一个人都想起同样的念头。**become one; be made one,** be united; be married. 团结一致; 结合; 结婚。**9** (phrases) (短语) **one and all,** everyone. 每一个人。**(all) in one,** combined: 合在一起: *He is President, Chairman and Secretary in one.* 他一身兼董事长、主席和秘书三职。**one or two,** a few: 一两个; 一些: *I shall be away only one or two days.* 我只要离开这儿一两天。**by ones and twos,** one or two at a time: 一次一两个; 三三两两: *People began to leave the meeting by ones and twos.* 人们开始三三两两地离开会场。**be one 'up (on sb),** have an advantage over him, be one step ahead of him. (比某人) 占优势; (比某人)领先一步。Hence, 由此产生, **,one-'up-man·ship** /-mənʃɪp; -menˌʃɪp/ *n* technique of being one up. 占优势或领先的技巧。**number 'one,** (colloq) oneself; one's own interests: (口) 自己; 自己的利益: *He's always thinking of 'number one',* of himself, his own welfare. 他总是想到自己(自己的利益)。**10** (with an *of*-adjunct) a single person or thing of the sort indicated or supplied (with *some, any, several,* etc for the *pl*; ⇨ **a²(3)** and **one²(1)**: (与 of 短语连用)表示同类中的一人或物(与 some, any, several 等连用表示多数): *One of my friends (pl 复 some of my friends) arrived late.* 我的朋友有一个迟到了。*If one of them (pl 复 any of them) should need help....* 假如他们当中有一个需要帮助的话⋯⋯。*I borrowed one of your books* (= a book of yours; *pl* 复 *some of your books) last week.* 上个星期我借了你的一本书。(Note the use of *his, her, herself* and *himself* in these examples): (注意下面这些例句中的 his, her, herself, 及 himself 的用法): *One of the boys / girls lost his / her shoe.* 男(女)孩子中有一个丢了一只鞋。*One of the girls / boys has hurt herself / himself.* 女(男)孩子中有一个弄伤了自己。**11** (compounds) (复合词) **,one-armed** *adj* having only one arm. 只有一只手臂的; 独臂的。**,one-armed 'bandit** *n* (colloq) coin-operated gambling machine (also called 亦称 a *fruit-machine*). (口) 吃角子老虎(一种投硬币操作的赌博机器)。**,one-'eyed** *adj* having only one eye. 只有一只眼睛的; 独眼的。**,one-'horse** *adj* **(a)** drawn or worked by a single horse. 由一匹马拖拉或工作的; 单马的。**(b)** (fig, sl) poorly equipped: (喻,俚)简陋的: *a one-horse town,* a small provincial town with few attractions. 一个简陋的小镇。**,one-i'dea'd** *adj* possessed by a single idea. 只有一种思想的; 心目中只有一个观念的; 思想狭隘的。**,one-'sided** *adj* having one side only; occurring on one side only; partial; unfair; prejudiced: 只有一边的; 单方面的; 偏袒的; 不公平的; 偏见的: *a one-sided argument;* 片面的议论; *a one-sided account of a quarrel.* 对于一场纷争的片面之词。**'one-time** *adj* former: 从前的; 昔时的: *a one-time politician.* 一位昔时的从政者。**,one-track 'mind** *n* one dominated by one interest, subject, etc. 偏狭的思想。**,one-way "street** *n* street in which traffic may proceed in one direction only. 单行道。

one² /wʌn; wʌn/ *indef pron* (used in place of a preceding or following *n* standing for a member of a class) (用以代替前述或后述名词, 代表同类中的一个) **1** (with an *of*-adjunct, indicating inclusion; equivalent to *among*; ⇨ **a²(3):** no corresponding *pl* word): (与 of 短语连用, 表示包括在内之意; 此处 of 相当于 among; 此种用法无相当的复数词): *Mr Smith is not one of* (= not numbered or included among) *my customers.* 史密斯先生并不是我的顾客之一。Cf for *pl*: 参较复数用法: *Mr Green and Mr Smith are not customers of mine.* 格林先生和史密斯先生都不是我的顾客。*This problem is one of great difficulty (pl; These problems are of great difficulty.* 这个问题是一个大难题 (复: 这些问题是大难题)。*We have always treated her as one* (= as a member) *of the family (pl: We have always treated them as members of the family).* 我们总是把她当作家中一份子来看待(复: 我们总是把他们当作家里人看待)。*One of my friends was ill (pl: Some of my friends were ill).* 我的一个朋友病了(复: 有我几个朋友病了)。⇨ **one¹(10).** **2** (Cf *one* and *it. One* replaces a *n* modified by the *indef art* or a *pl n* modified by *some* or *any. It* replaces a *n* made definite in some way, eg *a n* modified by *the, this, that*): (参较 one 与 it. one 代替由不定冠词所修饰的名词或由 some 或 any 所修饰的复数名词; it 代替经以某种方式所确定的名词, 例如由 the, this, that 所修饰的名词): *I haven't a pen. Can you lend me one?* 我没有钢笔。你能借我一枝吗？*I haven't any stamps. Will you please give me one?* 我没有邮票。请给我一张好吗？Cf 参较 *I'd like to look at that atlas. May I borrow it?* 我想看那本地图集。我可以借它吗？*Where's the railway timetable? Have you seen it?* 火车时间表在哪儿？你有没有看到它？**3** (the *pron 'one', pl 'ones'* is used, in colloq style, equivalent to *that, those*): (代名词 one, 复数为 ones, 用于口语文体中相当于 that 与 those): *I drew my chair nearer to the one* (= to *that) on which Mary was sitting.* 我把我的椅子拉到玛丽所坐的那把椅子旁边。*It's in that drawer—the one* (=that) *with the key in the lock.* 它是在那个抽屉里 —— 有钥匙插在锁孔的那一个。*The students who do best in examinations are not always the ones* (= those) *with the best brains.* 考试考得最好的学生不一定都是聪明的学生。**4** (when the *pron 'one'* is used after the *def art,* or after an *adj* (or a *n* used as an *adj*), it may be called a 'prop-word'. As an *adj* cannot stand alone for one or more members of a class, *one* is used to support or 'prop up' the *adj*, as in): (当代词 one 用于定冠词之后, 或形容词(或当作形容词的名词)之后, 它可以称为 '垫字'。由于形容词不能单独代表某一类中的一个成分, 故 one 就被用来支助或'支撑'那个形容词, 如下列所用者): *a better one;* 更好的一个; *that one;* 那个; *my old ones.* 我的几个旧的。*Your plan is a good one on paper.* 你的计划在理论上是个好计划。There's a *right answer and a wrong one.* 有一个对的答案和一个错的答案。*Yours may be the right answer and mine the wrong one.* 你的答案可能是对的, 而我的可能是错的。*The chance was too good a one to let pass.* 这是一个不能放过的好机会。*He keeps his postage-stamps—he has some very rare ones—in a fire-proof safe.* 他把他的邮票——他有一些珍贵的邮票——放在防火的保险箱里。**5** (The 'prop-word' *one* is not used, except in colloquial style, after a possessive (eg *your, Mary's)* unless there is also an *adj.* It is not used after *own*): (除用于口语中外, '垫字' one 不可用于所有格如 your, Mary's 之后, 除非还有一个形容词。one 不可用于 own 之后): *This is my hat and that is my brother's.* 这顶帽子是我的, 那顶是我哥哥(弟弟)的。Not: 不可写作: *my brother's one.* *Tom's exercise book is neater than John's.* 汤姆的练习簿比约翰的整洁。Not: 不可写作: *John's one. Do you rent the house or is it your own?* 那幢房子是你租的还是你自己的？Not: 不可写作: *your own one.* (With an *adj)* (与形容词连用): *My cheap camera seems to be just as good as John's expensive one.* 我这架便宜的照相机似乎跟约翰那架昂贵的同样好用。*Your old suit looks as smart as your brother's new one.* 你这套旧衣服看来跟你哥哥(弟弟)那套新衣服同样漂亮。**6** (In formal or written style it is preferable to avoid the use of the 'prop-word' *one,* esp when there are two *adjj* indicating a contrast. The *n* is placed after only one of the *adjj*): (在正式或

写作文体中，最好避免使用'垫字'one，尤其当两个形容词表示相对的意义时。仅在其一个形容词之后放置名词即可）: *If we compare British with American universities* (better than: 不宜写为: *If we compare British universities with American ones*).... 假如我们把英国和美国的大学作一比较…。Cf 参较 *Don't praise the younger child in the presence of the elder.* 不要在大的孩子面前称赞小的孩子。*I put my right arm through Mary's left.* 我把我的右手臂穿过玛丽的左臂弯。*At home Hanako prefers Japanese to European-style clothes.* 花子在家里比较喜欢穿日本式衣服，不大喜欢穿西式衣服。*What the teacher said seemed to go in at one ear and out at the other.* 老师所说的话好象从一边耳朵进去，再从另一边耳朵出来。**7** (*One* is used after *this* and *that*, but is better avoided, in formal or written style. after *these* and *those*): (one 可用于 *this* 和 *that* 之后，但是在正式或写作文体中最好避免用于 *these* 和 *those* 之后): *Will you have this (one) or that (one)?* 你要这(一)个或是那(一)个? *Will you have these or those?* 你要这些或是那些? (With an *adj*, 'one' is necessary): (与形容词连用时，需要 one): *Will you have this green one/these green ones or that blue one/those blue ones?* 你要这(这些)绿色的还是那个(那些)蓝色的? **8** (The 'prop-word' *one* is used with *which*, esp to distinguish *sing* from *pl*): ('垫字' one 可与 which 连用，尤用于分别单数与复数): *Here are some books on European history. Which one(s) do you want?* 这儿有一些关于欧洲历史的书。你要哪一本（哪几本）?

one³ /wʌn; wʌn/ *pers pron* **1** (used, always with a qualifying word or phrase, for a particular person or creature): (总是与修饰词或短语连用，指某某种人或生物): *the 'Holy One*, God; 上帝; *the 'Evil One*, Satan, the Devil; 撒旦; 魔鬼; *the absent one.* eg the absent member of the family; 缺席者; *the little ones*, the children; 小孩子们; *a nest with five young ones*, young birds; 一个有五只小鸟的巢; *my sweet one*, as a term of endearment. 我亲爱的人儿。**2** (used, in liter style, with a following *adj*, phrase or clause): (在文学体裁中，与随后的形容词、短语或从句连用): *He lay there like one dead*, as if he were dead. 他象死人一样躺在那儿。*He worked like one possessed*, like a man possessed by a spirit. 他着了魔一般地工作。*He was one* (= the sort of person) *who never troubled about his personal comfort.* 他是一个从来不为自己舒适而操心的人。*He's not one to be* (= not a man who is) *easily frightened.* 他不是一个轻易被吓倒的人。**3 one another**, (used like *each other*, to indicate mutual action or relation; may be the object of a *v* or a *prep*; possessive form is *one another's*; both words usu unstressed): 彼此; 互相(用法类似 each other，表示彼此的行为或关系;可作动词或介词的宾语;所有格作 one another's; 两字通常都不重读): *They don't like one another.* 他们彼此不喜欢。*They have quarrelled and no longer speak to one another.* 他们吵过架而彼此不再讲话。*They were fighting with cudgels, trying to break one another's heads.* 他们用棍子打架，都想打破对方的头。

one⁴ /wʌn; wʌn/ *impers pron* (standing for any person, including the speaker or writer. 代表任何人，包括说者或写者在内。Cf 参较 French *on*, German *man*. 法文的 on，德文的 man. Possessive: 所有格为: *one's*, reflexive: 反身代词为: *oneself*. ⇨ **one**¹(10)): *One cannot always find time for reading.* 人不一定能常常有时间阅读。*If one wants a thing done well, one had best do it oneself.* 一个人如果要事情做好，最好自己去做。*One doesn't like to have one's word doubted.* 人不喜欢自己的话被别人怀疑。(In colloq style it is more usual to employ *you*, *we*, *people*) Cf 参较 *We live and learn.* (我们)活到老学到老。*You never can tell.* 很难说。*What's a chap/a fellow to do in such a situation?* 一个人在这种情况下应该怎么办? (In American usage, *one* may be followed by *he*, *his*, *him*, *himself* instead of by *one*, *one's*, *oneself*): (美国用法，one 之后可以使用 he, him, his, himself 代替 one, one's, oneself): *One does not*

like to have his word doubted. 谁也不愿让自己的话受到怀疑。

on·er·ous /'ɒnərəs; 'ɑnərəs/ *adj* needing effort; burdensome (*to*): 麻烦的;繁重的: ~ *duties.* 繁重的职务。~·**ly** *adv*

one·self /wʌn'self; wʌn'sɛlf/ *reflex, emphat pron* one's own self: 自己;自身: *wash/dress oneself.* 洗澡(穿衣服)。*One should not live for oneself alone.* 人不应该专为自己而活。

on·go·ing /'ɒn gəʊɪŋ; 'ɑn,goɪŋ/ *adj* ⇨ *go on* at **go**¹(29).

onion /'ʌnɪən; 'ʌnjən/ *n* [C] **1** vegetable plant with a round bulb of many concentric coats, a strong smell and flavour, used in cooking and pickled: 洋葱; *spring-~s*; 春季洋葱; *Spanish ~s*; 西班牙洋葱; [U] this plant as food: (作为食物的)洋葱: *too much ~ in the salad*; 生菜里洋葱太多; *the ~-domed churches of Austria*, having ~-shaped domes. 奥地利的洋葱形屋顶的教堂。⇨ the illus at **vegetable**. 参看 vegetable 之插图。*know one's ~s*, (sl) be clever (because experienced). (俚)(因经验丰富而)聪明; 精明练达。**2** (sl) head. (俚)头。*off his ~*, (sl) mentally unbalanced. (俚)精神错乱; 神智失常。

on·looker /'ɒnlʊkə(r); 'ɑn,lʊkə/ *n* person who looks on at sth happening. 旁观者。*The ~ sees most of the game*, (prov) The spectator is in a better position to judge than those who are taking part. (谚)旁观者清。

only¹ /'əʊnlɪ; 'onlɪ/ *adj* **1** being the one specimen of its class; single: (与单数名词连用)独一的;唯一的: *Smith was the ~ person able to do it.* 史密斯是唯一能做那事的人。*Harry is an ~ child*, has no brothers or sisters. 哈里是个独子。*Her ~ answer was a shrug.* 她唯一的回答是耸一下肩膀。**2** (with a *pl n*) that are all the specimens or examples: (与复数名词连用)仅有的: *We were the ~ people there.* 只有我们在那里。**3** best; most or best worth consideration: 最佳的: 最值得考虑的: *He's the ~ man for the job.* 他是这个职位的最佳人选。*She says holidays in Ireland are the ~ thing these days.* 她说在爱尔兰度假是目前最称心的事。

only² /'əʊnlɪ; 'onlɪ/ *adv* solely; and no one, nothing, more. 单独地; 仅仅; 只。**1** (modifying a single word, and placed, in written or formal style, close to the word it modifies; in speech the stress-pattern may indicate this, so that *only* may have various positions): (修饰一个词，在书写或正式文体中，通常放在被修饰的词紧邻;在说话中，重音型式可表明其所修饰的词，故 only 可置于不同的位置): *I ~ saw 'Mary*, I saw Mary and no one else (= written style, I saw ~ Mary). 我只看到玛丽一个人 (only 与 Mary 重读，表示除了玛丽外我没看到别人;如为书写文体，应作 I saw only Mary). Cf 参较 *I ~ 'saw Mary*, I saw her but didn't speak to her. 我仅仅是看到玛丽而已 (only 与 saw 重读，表示我只是看到她而没有跟她讲过话)。*O~ the teachers are allowed to use this room.* 只有教员可以使用此房间。*O~ five men were seriously hurt in the accident.* 那次意外事件中只有五个人重伤。*We've ~ half an hour to wait now.* 现在我们只要等半个小时。*Ladies ~*, eg on a compartment in a railway carriage. 仅限妇女 (例如指火车车厢中之一隔间)。*We can ~ guess* (= We cannot be certain about) *what happened.* 我们只能猜测发生了什么事。**2** ~ *too*, (with an *adj* or *pp*) very: (与形容词或过去分词连用)极: *I shall be ~ too pleased to get home.* 我回到家里将非常高兴。*The news was ~ too true*, was really true, and not, as might be hoped or expected, untrue. 这消息是极真实的。*if ~*, expressing a wish or assumption. 但愿。⇨ **if**(8).

only³ /'əʊnlɪ; 'onlɪ/ *conj* but then; it must, however, be added that: 但是; 不过; 可是: *The book is likely to be useful, ~ it's rather expensive.* 这本书可能很有用，只是相当贵。*He's always ready to promise help, ~ he never keeps his promises.* 他总是轻易允诺协助，但是他从来不

守诺言. **~ that,** with the exception that; were it not that: 若不是; 若非: *He would probably do well in the examination, ~ that he gets rather nervous.* 若不是他有点紧张, 他可能考得很好。

ono·mato·poeia /ˌɒnəˌmætəˈpiːə; ˌɑnəˌmætəˈpiə/ n [U] formation of words in imitation of the sounds associated with the thing concerned (as *cuckoo* for the bird that utters this cry). 拟声造字法(如 cuckoo 一词即由模拟布谷鸟的鸣声而造成的)。

on·rush /ˈɒnrʌʃ; ˈɑnˌrʌʃ/ n strong, onward rush or flow. 猛冲; 急流.

on·set /ˈɒnset; ˈɑnˌsɛt/ n attack; vigorous start: 进攻; 有力的开始: *at the first ~;* 在最初着手时; *the ~ of a disease.* 疾病的起始; 起病.

on·shore /ˈɒnʃɔː(r); ˈɑnˌʃɔr/ adj, adv toward the shore. 朝着岸(的); 在岸上(的).

on·slaught /ˈɒnslɔːt; ˈɑnˌslɔt/ n [C] furious attack (on). 猛攻; 突击(与 on 连用).

onto /before consonants: ˈɒntə; ˈɑntə; before vowels or finally: ˈɒntu:; ˈɑntu/ prep ⇨ **on**[1](2).

on·tol·ogy /ɒnˈtɒlədʒɪ; ɑnˈtɑlədʒɪ/ n [U] department of metaphysics concerned with the nature of existence; [C] specific theory of this. 实体论; 本体论.

onus /ˈəʊnəs; ˈonəs/ n the ~, responsibility for, burden of, doing sth: 责任; 负担: *The ~ of proof rests with you,* It is for you to supply proof. 提出证据的责任在你.

on·ward /ˈɒnwəd; ˈɑnwəd/ adj forward: 前进的; 向前的: *an ~ march/movement.* 前进(向前移动). □ adv (also 亦作 **~s**) towards the front; forward: 向前; 前进地: *move ~(s).* 向前移动.

onyx /ˈɒnɪks; ˈɑnɪks/ n [U] (sorts of) quartz in layers of different colours, used for ornaments, etc. (各色)截子玛瑙(作装饰品等用).

oodles /ˈuːdlz; ˈudlz/ n pl (sl) **~ of,** great amounts or sums: (俚)大量; 多量: *~ of money.* 大量金钱.

oomph /ʊmf; ʊmf/ n (sl) energy; sex appeal. (俚)精力; 性感.

ooze /uːz; uz/ n [U] soft liquid mud, esp on a river-bed, the bottom of a pond, lake, etc. 泥浆; (指河床, 湖底等的)淤泥; 软泥. □ vi, vt 1 [VP2C] (of moisture, thick liquids) pass slowly through small openings: (指水份, 浓液)慢慢地渗出: *Blood was still oozing from the wound.* 血仍然从伤口徐徐渗出. (fig) (喻) *Their courage was oozing away.* 他们的勇气慢慢地消失. 2 [VP6A] pass out; emit: 流出; 渗出: *He was oozing sweat.* 他出汗. **oozy** adj of or like ~; slimy. 软泥的; 泥浆的; 象软泥的; 象黏泥的.

opac·ity /əʊˈpæsətɪ; oˈpæsəti/ n [U] (quality of) being opaque. 不透明(性); 晦暗; 愚钝.

opal /ˈəʊpl; ˈopl/ n semi-precious stone in which changes of colour are seen, often used as a gem. 蛋白石; 猫眼石. **opal·escent** /ˌəʊpəˈlesnt; ˌoplˈɛsnt/ adj like an ~. 象蛋白石的; 发乳白光的.

opaque /əʊˈpeɪk; oˈpek/ adj not allowing light to pass through; that cannot be seen through; dull. 不透光的; 不透明的; 晦暗的; 愚钝的. **~·ly** adv **~·ness** n

op art /ˈɒp aːt; ˈɑp ɑrt/ n form of modern abstract art using geometrical patterns which produce optical illusions. 光效应绘画艺术; 欧普艺术 (一种现代抽象艺术, 利用几何图案使人产生视觉上的错觉).

open[1] /ˈəʊpən; ˈopən/ adj 1 not closed; allowing (things, persons) to go in, out, through: 开着的; 开放的; 开的: *sleep with ~ windows.* 开着窗户睡觉; *leave the door ~.* 让门开着. **,~-'eyed** adj with ~ eyes; watchful; surprised. 睁着眼睛的; 留心的; 惊讶的. **,~-'mouthed** /-ˈmaʊðd; -ˈmaʊðd/ adj **(a)** showing greed (for food, etc). 贪吃的; 贪婪的. **(b)** showing great surprise or stupidity. 惊讶的; 发呆的. **~ vowel,** one made with the roof of the mouth and the tongue fairly wide apart, eg /ɑː, ɒ; ɑr, ɑ/ 开元音(如 /ɑː, ɒ; ɑr, ɑ/). **'~-work** n [U] pattern (in metal, lace, etc) with

spaces: (金属、花边等)网状细工; 透孔镂刻: *~-work lace;* 透孔花边; *~-work stockings.* 网状长袜. 2 not enclosed, fenced in, barred or blocked: 开阔的; 空旷的: *the ~ country,* land affording wide views, without forests, etc. 空旷之地; 旷野. **the ~ sea,** not a bay or harbour, not closed in by land. 大海; 公海. **an ~ river,** not barred by ice, mudbanks, etc. 畅通的河流. **~ water,** navigable, free from ice. (没有冰的)可航行的水域. **an ~ prison,** one with fewer restrictions than usual, esp one where prisoners with good records come and go freely to work outside. 开放式监狱(比一般监狱较少禁制, 尤指纪录良好之囚犯可自由出外工作者). 3 not covered in or over: 无遮盖的; 敞开的: *an ~ boat,* one without a deck; 无甲板的敞船; *an ~ car,* with no roof, or a roof that is folded back; 无篷或未张篷的汽车: *an ~ drain/sewer,* in the form of a ditch, not in pipes under the ground; 明沟; *an ~ sandwich,* single slice of bread with meat, etc on top; 单片三明治(只用一片面包, 上有肉等); *in the ~ air,* out of doors. 在户外; 在野外. **'~-air** attrib adj taking place out of doors; fond of life in the ~ air: 户外的; 喜欢野外生活的: *an ,~-air 'theatre.* 露天戏院. 4 spread out; unfolded: 开放的; 开自的; 张开的: *The flowers were all ~.* 那些花都开了. *The book lay ~ on the table.* 那本书摊开着摆在桌子上. *His mind was/His thoughts were an ~ book,* It was easy to read his thoughts. 他的思想象一本摊开的书(易于被人了解). **with ~ hands,** generously. 慷慨地. Hence, 由此产生, **,~-'handed** adj generous; giving freely. 慷慨的; 好施舍的. **,~-'hearted** adj sincere; frank. 诚挚的; 坦白的. **with ~ arms,** with affection or enthusiasm. 热诚地. **~ order,** (of troops), with wider space than usual between ranks. (指军队的)散开队形(列与列间之距离较平常为大). 5 public; free to all; not limited to any special persons, but for anyone to enter: 公开的; 公共的; 不限制任何人的: *an ~ competition/championship/scholarship;* 公开竞争(公开竞争的锦标; 公开竞争的奖学金); *tried in ~ court,* of a law case, the public being freely admitted to hear the trial. 在法庭公开审判的. *The position is still ~,* No one has yet been chosen to fill it. 这个职位仍然悬着. **the ~ door,** policy of free trade or freedom from tariffs; admission of foreign traders. 门户开放(自由贸易或免除关税的政策). **~ shop,** workshop, factory, etc where members and non-members of trade unions work on equal terms. 开放工厂(工会会员及非工会会员以平等之条件雇用者). ⇨ *closed shop* at **close**[4](2). **keep ~ house,** offer hospitality to all comers. 对所有来客. 6 not settled or decided: 未解决的; 未决定的: *leave a matter ~.* 留下一件事没解决. **,~-'ended** adj (of a discussion, a subject for debate, etc) having a variety of possible solutions; on which no decision or agreement is reached, expected or required. (指讨论、辩论之主题等) 无固定答案的; 具多种不同之解决办法的; 达不到、不期望有或不必有决定或一致意见的; 可广泛解释的. **an ~ question,** with no decision, answer. 未解决的问题. **an ~ verdict,** jury's verdict of the fact and cause of a death, but not saying whether it is natural, accidental, suicide or murder. 存疑裁决 (陪审团对死亡案件的判决, 但未说明是自然死亡、意外死亡、自杀抑或谋杀). **have/keep an ~ mind (on sth),** be ready to consider sth further, to listen to new evidence, agreements, etc. (对某事)准备再加思考, 听取新的证据、协议等; 虚心研讨(某事). Hence, 由此产生, **,~-'minded** adj unprejudiced. 无偏见的; 虚心的. 7 ready for business or for the admission of the public: 开放营业的; 开着可以进去的; 开放的: *Are the shops ~ yet?* 商店开始营业了吗? *Doors ~ at 7.00pm,* eg of a theatre. 下午七点钟开门或开始营业 (如指戏院). 8 known to all; not secret or disguised; frank: 公开的; 无秘密的; 坦白的: *an ~ quarrel/scandal;* 公开的争吵(丑闻); *an ~ character/countenance.* 坦率的性格(面孔). *Let me be quite ~ (= frank) with you.* 让我坦白对你说. **an ~ letter,** one that is addressed to an individual

or group but sent to and published in a periodical, usu in protest against sth. 公开信（写给某人或某一团体，送往期刊公开登载的信，通常为对某事提出抗议者）. **9** unprotected; unguarded; vulnerable. 不设防的; 未加防护的; 易受攻击的. **be/lay oneself ~ to sth,** behave so that one is vulnerable to sth: 易受（使自己易受）某事物的伤害或攻击的: *Don't lay yourself ~ to ridicule/attack.* 不要使自己易招致嘲笑(攻击). **10** not settled, finished or closed: 未解决的; 未完成的; 未结束的: *keep one's account ~ at a bank;* 在银行里开着一个户头; *be ~ to an offer,* willing to consider one. 愿意考虑某一提议. **11** (phrases) (短语) '**~cast** adj surface: 表面的: *~cast coal;* 地面露天; 表层煤层; *~cast mining,* from strata near the earth's surface (contrasted with production from deep mines). 露天采矿(法); 表层采矿(法)(从靠近地面之矿层采矿，与深坑采矿相对). **an ~ cheque,** one that is not crossed and which may be cashed at the bank on which it is drawn. 普通支票(向银行提示即可兑现的支票，非划线支票). **the '~ season,** (fishing and shooting) when there are no restrictions. (渔猎) 开放季节. ⇨ **close**[1](11). **an ~ secret,** sth supposed to be a secret but in fact known to all people. 公开的秘密(被认为是一秘密，事实上是大家全都知道的事). **the O~ University,** (GB) university (founded in 1971) whose students live at home and get tuition by correspondence, textbooks and special radio and TV programmes. (英)空中大学(创办于 1971 年，学生在家里借函授、教科书和特殊无线电广播及电视节目上课). **~ weather, an ~ winter,** free from severe frost and snow, so that it is possible to get about. 和暖的天气, 和暖的冬天. ⇨ **the ~,** the ~ air. 户外; 野外. ⇨ **3** above. 参看上列第 3 义. **come (out) into the ~,** (fig) come into public view; make one's ideas, plans, etc, known. (喻)成为公开; 现身; 把意见, 计划等公开. **~·ly** adv without secrecy; frankly; publicly: 公然地; 坦白地; 公开地: *speak ~ly;* 公开说; *go ~ly into a place,* eg where one might be expected to go secretly. 公开地进入某一场所 (例如该场所可能被认为宜秘密进入者). **~·ness** n [U].

open[2] /'əʊpən; 'opən/ vt, vi **1** [VP6A, 14, 16A, 12C] make open or cause to be open; unfasten: 打开; 开启: *~ a box.* 打开盒子. *He ~ed the door for me to come in/to let me in.* 他开门让我进去. *O~ the window a fraction/crack/bit, please.* 请稍窗子打开一点点. **~ one's eyes,** express surprise. 睁大眼睛(表示惊讶). **~ (sb's) eyes to sth,** cause him to realize sth, eg how he has been deceived. 使(某人)明白或醒悟某事. **2** [VP6A, 15A, B] cut or make an opening in or a passage through: 开口; 开通: *~ a mine/a well;* 开矿(凿井); *~ a new road through a forest;* 开一条新路穿过森林. *O~ up!* command to ~ a door, etc. 开门! 打开! **~ sth up,** make ~, make accessible; make possible the development of: 打开某物; 打通; 开展: *~ up a wound/a mine/undeveloped land/a new territory to trade.* 打开伤口/开矿/开发未垦土地/开拓新的贸易地区. **3** [VP6 A,15A,B] spread out; unfold: 展开; 解开; 张开: *~ one's hand/a book/a newspaper/a parcel;* 张开手(翻开书; 打开报纸; 解开包裹); *~ out a folding map.* 展开一幅折叠的地图. **~ one's mind/heart to sb,** make known one's ideas/feelings. 对某人吐露心意(真情). **4** [VP6 A] start: 开始: *~ an account at a bank, shop;* (在银行、店铺等)开个户头; *~ a debate/a public meeting.* 开始辩论(会议). **~ the bidding,** make the first bid (at an auction, at bridge). 叫第一次价(拍卖场中叫第一口价; (在桥牌戏中) 作第一次叫牌; 开叫. **~ fire (at/on),** start shooting. (向…)开火. **5**[VP6A] declare, indicate, that business, etc may now start: 开业; 开幕: *~ a shop;* 开一家店铺; *~ Parliament.* 主持国会开幕. **6** [VP 2A, C] become open; be ~ed; allow of being ~ed: 开着; 开启; 展开: *The flowers are ~ing.* 花正开着. *This shop does not ~ on Sundays.* 这家店铺星期天不开门(营业). *The door ~ed and a man came in.* 门开了, 一

个人走进来. *Does this door ~ inwards or outwards?* 这个门朝里还是朝外开? *The two rooms ~ into one another,* have a door between them. 这两个房间有门相通. *This door ~s on to the garden.* 这个门通向花园. **7** [VP3A] **~ with,** start: 开始: *The story ~s with a murder.* 这故事以一个谋杀案件开始. **8** [VP2A, C] **~ (out),** become visible: 展示; 显现: *The view ~ed (out) before our eyes.* 景色显现在我们眼前. **~·er** n person or thing that ~s: 开启的人或工具: (chiefly in compounds) (主要用于复合词中) *'pen-~er;* 教堂中引人入座者; *'tin-~er;* 开罐器; *'bottle-~er.* 开瓶盖工具; 开瓶器. '**eye-opener,** ⇨ **eye**[1](3).

open·ing /'əʊpənɪŋ; 'opənɪŋ/ n **1** open space; way in or out: 口; 穴; 孔; 洞; 通路: *an ~ in a hedge.* 篱笆上的一个洞口. **2** beginning: 开始; 开端: *the ~ of a book/speech.* 书(演讲)的开端. **the ~ night,** eg on which a new play/film is performed/shown for the first time, and to which dramatic critics are invited. (戏剧或电影)上演第一夜; 首映夜. **~ time,** eg at which public houses open and begin to serve drinks. 开放时间; 开始营业时间. **3** process of becoming open: 张开; 开展: *watch the ~ of a flower.* 看一朵花开. **4** position (in a business firm) which is open or vacant; opportunity: (公司行号中职位的)空缺; 机会: *an ~ in an advertising agency.* 广告代理处的空缺. □ adj first: 第一次的; 开头的: *his ~ remarks.* 开场白.

op·era /'ɒprə; 'ɑpərə/ n **1** [C] dramatic composition with music, in which the words are sung. 歌剧. **comic ~,** humorous, with spoken dialogue and a happy ending. 喜歌剧 (有对白及喜剧结尾者). **grand ~,** serious, with no spoken dialogue. 大歌剧; 庄歌剧(无对白者). **light ~,** not serious. 轻歌剧. ⇨ **cantata, oratorio.** **2** [U] dramatic works of this kind as entertainment: 歌剧(作品); 歌剧: *fond of ~;* 喜欢歌剧; *the ~ season.* 歌剧季节. '**~-cloak** n lady's cloak for wearing with evening dress. 配合晚礼服穿的女披风. '**~-glasses** n pl small binoculars for use in a theatre. 看戏用的小型双眼望远镜. '**~-hat** n man's tall, black silk hat, made so that it folds flat. 可折叠的男用高顶丝质黑礼帽. '**~-house** n theatre for performances of ~s. 歌剧院. **op·er·atic** /ˌɒpəˈrætɪk; ˌɑpəˈrætɪk/ adj of or for an ~: 歌剧的: *~tic music/singers.* 歌剧音乐(演唱者).

op·er·ate /'ɒpəreɪt; 'ɑpəˌret/ vt, vi **1** [VP6A, 2A, C, 4A] (cause to) work, be in action, have an effect; manage: (使)运转; 操作; 起作用; 管理; 经营: *a machine;* 操纵一部机器; *machinery that ~s night and day.* 日夜运转的机器. *The company ~s three factories and a coal-mine.* 那家公司经营三个工厂和一个煤矿. *The lift was not operating properly.* 那电梯操纵不灵. *The lift is ~d by electricity.* 那部升降机(电梯)是用电操作的. *This new law ~s (= produces an effect) to our advantage.* 这条新法律对我们有利. *Several causes ~d to bring about the war.* 若干原因引起这次战争. **2** [VP2A, 3A] **~ (on sb) (for sth),** perform a surgical operation: 动手术: *The doctors decided to ~ at once.* 医生们决定立刻动手术. '**operating-table/-theatre** n for use in surgical operations. 手术台(室). **3** [VP2A, C] (of an army) carry out various movements: (指军队)作军事行动: *operating on a large scale.* 作大规模军事行动. **4** [VP2A, C] (of a stockbroker) buy and sell, esp in order to influence prices. (指股票经纪人)买卖以左右股票价格; 做价; 操纵市场. **op·er·able** /'ɒpərəbl; 'ɑpərəbl/ adj that can be treated by means of a surgical operation. 可动手术的.

op·er·ation /ˌɒpəˈreɪʃn; ˌɑpəˈreʃən/ n **1** [U] working; way in which sth works. 运转; 操作; 作用; 运行法. **be in/bring sth into/come into ~,** be/cause to be/become effective: 生效中(使生效;生效): *When does the plan come into ~?* 该计划何时开始生效? *Is this rule in ~ yet?* 这条规则开始生效了吗? **2** [C] piece of work; sth (to be) done: 工作; (待) 完成的事: *begin ~s;* 开始工作; *the ~s of nature,* changes

brought about by natural forces. 自然力量的作用; 大自然之变化。 **3** (usu *pl*; 通常用复数; colloq abbr 口语略作 **ops**) movements of troops, ships, aircraft, etc in warfare or during manoeuvres. (作战或演习中的) 军事行动; 作战行动。 '~s room, from which ~s are controlled; (*sing*) in code names for military campaigns (*O~Overlord*)and, by extension, for planned campaigns in industry, commerce, etc: 作战指挥室; (单)用于代号表示战役或演习名称(如 Operation Overlord); (工商界等的)有计划行动: *building/banking* ~s; 有计划的建屋(存款)行动; ~s *research*, to promote greater efficiency in industry. (提高工业效率的)营运研究; 作业研究。 **4** [C] *an* ~ *(on sb) (for sth)*, act performed by a surgeon on any part of the body, esp by cutting to take away or deal with a diseased part: 手术: *an* ~ *for appendicitis*. 阑尾手术; 割除阑尾。 **5** (maths) addition, subtraction, multiplication, division, etc. (数学)加、减、乘、除等; 运算。 ~al /-fǝnl; -fǝnl/ *adj* **1** of, for, used in, ~s. 操作(等)的; 管理的; 工作的; 军事的; 手术的; 适于操作(等)的; 用于操作(等)的。 ~al *costs/expenditure*, needed for operating (machines, aircraft, etc). 营运成本 (费用)。 ~al *research*, into the best ways of using, improving, etc new weapons, machinery, etc. (新武器、机器等的)更新研究; 营运研究。 **2** ready for use: 即可使用的: *When will the newly designed airliner be* ~*al?* 新设计的客机何时启用?

op·er·at·ive /'ɒpǝrǝtɪv US: -reɪt-; 'ɑpǝ,retɪv/ *adj* **1** operating; having an effect: 操作的; 有效的: *This law became* ~ *on 1 May*. 这条法律五月一日生效。 **2** ~ *words*, those having legal effect in a deed, etc; (loosely) most significant words. 在契约等中有法律效力的文字; (泛指)最重要的文字。 **3** of surgical operations: 外科手术的: ~ *treatment*. 手术治疗。 □ *n* worker; mechanic: 工人; 机械工人; 技工: *cotton* ~s. 棉纺工人。

op·er·ator /'ɒpǝreɪtǝ(r); 'ɑpǝ,retǝ/ *n* **1** person who operates or works sth: 操作者; 工作者: *telephone/telegraphy* ~s; 电话接线生(无线电报报务员); *private* ~s *in civil aviation*, privately owned companies (contrasted with state-owned corporations). 民营航空公司(与国营航空公司相对)。 **2** (sl) confident, efficient man in business, love affairs, etc): (俚)在事业、爱情等方面)自信而又能干的人; 精明的人: *He's a smooth/slick* ~. 他是个精明圆滑的家伙。

op·er·etta /,ɒpǝ'retǝ; ,ɑpǝ'retǝ/ *n* one-act, or short, light musical comedy. (独幕或短而轻松的)小歌剧; 轻歌剧。

oph·thal·mia /ɒf'θælmɪǝ; ɑf'θælmɪǝ/ *n* [U] inflammation of the eye. 眼炎。 **oph·thal·mic** /-mɪk; -mɪk/ *adj* of the eyes; afflicted with ~. 眼睛的; 眼炎的。 **oph·thal·mo·scope** /ɒf'θælmǝskǝʊp; ɑf'θælmǝ,skop/ *n* instrument with a mirror (having a hole in the centre) through which the eye may be examined. 检眼镜。

opi·ate /'ǝʊpɪǝt; 'ɒpɪ,et/ *n* [C] drug containing opium, used to relieve pain or to help sb to sleep. 鸦片剂(用以止痛或安眠)。

opine /ǝ'paɪn; o'paɪn/ *vt* [VP9] ~ *that*, (formal) have or express the opinion. (正式用语)认为; 以为。

opin·ion /ǝ'pɪnjǝn; ǝ'pɪnjǝn/ *n* **1** [C] belief or judgement not founded on complete knowledge: 意见; 看法; 主张: *political* ~s. 政见。 *What's your* ~ (= view) *of the new President?* 你对新总统的看法如何? *Those are my* ~s *about the affair*. 那些就是我对这事的意见。 *in my, your, etc* ~; *in the* ~ *of sb*, it is my, your, etc view that .... 我的(你的等)意见是…; 我(你等)认为…: *In my/In the* ~ *of most people, the scheme is unsound*. 我认为(大部分的人认为)这个计划不完善。 *act up to one's* ~s, act according to them. 按照自己的主张行事。 *be of the* ~ *that*..., feel, believe, that.... 觉得…; 相信…; 认为…。 *have a good/bad/high/low* ~ *of sb/sth*, think well/badly, etc of. 对某人(某事物)的评价很好(坏、高、低)。 **2** [U] views, beliefs, of a group: 团体的意见; 团体的看法; 群众的见

解: *O~ is shifting in favour of stiffer penalties for armed robbery*. 群众的意见趋向于赞成对武装抢劫处以较严厉的刑罚。 *public* ~, what the majority of people think: 大众意见; 舆论: *Public* ~ *is against the proposed change*. 舆论反对拟议中的更动。 '~ *poll*, ⇨ **poll**[1](2). **3** [C] professional estimate or advice: 专业性的鉴定或意见: *get a lawyer's* ~ *on the question*. 听取律师对这个问题的意见。 *You had better have another* ~ *before you let that man take out all your teeth*. 在让那个人拔掉你全部牙齿之前, 你最好先听取其他的意见。 ~·**ated** /-eɪtɪd; -etɪd/, ~·**at·ive** /-ǝtɪv US: -etɪv; -etɪv/ *adj* obstinate in one's ~s; dogmatic. 固执己见的; 武断的。

opium /'ǝʊpɪǝm; 'ɒpɪǝm/ *n* [U] substance prepared from poppy seeds, used to relieve pain, cause sleep, and as a narcotic drug. 鸦片。 '~·**den** *n* place where ~ smokers can obtain and use this drug. 鸦片烟窟。

opos·sum /ǝ'pɒsǝm; ǝ'pɑsǝm/ *n* (also 亦作 **possum** /'pɒsǝm; 'pɑsǝm/) *n* kinds of small American animal that lives in trees. 負鼠; 負鼠。

op·po·nent /ǝ'pǝʊnǝnt; ǝ'ponǝnt/ *n* person against whom one fights, struggles, plays games, or argues. 对手; 敌手; 反对者。

op·por·tune /'ɒpǝtjuːn US: -tuːn; ,ɑpǝ'tjuːn/ *adj* **1** (of time) suitable, favourable; good for a purpose: (指时间)合适的; 恰好的: *arrive at a most* ~ *moment*. 在最适当的时刻到达。 **2** (of an action or event) done, coming, at a favourable time: (指行动或事件)适时的; 及时的: *an* ~ *remark/speech*. 合时宜的话(演说)。 ~·**ly** *adv*

op·por·tun·ism /,ɒpǝ'tjuːnɪzǝm US: -'tuːn-; ,ɑpǝ'tjuːnɪzǝm/ *n* [U] being guided by what seems possible, or by circumstances, in determining policy; preferring what can be done to what should be done. 机会主义; 投机。 **op·por·tun·ist** /-ɪst; -ɪst/ *n* person who acts on this principle; person who is more anxious to gain an advantage for himself than to consider whether he is trying to get it fairly. 机会主义者; 唯利是图的投机者。

op·por·tun·ity /,ɒpǝ'tjuːnǝtɪ US: -'tuːn-; ,ɑpǝ'tjuːnǝtɪ/ *n* (*pl* -ties) [C, U] ~ *(for sth/of doing sth/to do sth)*, favourable time or chance: 机会; 时机: *to make/find/get an* ~; 制造(寻找, 获得)机会; *have few opportunities of meeting interesting people*; 遇见有趣的人的机会并不多; *have no/little/not much* ~ *for hearing good music*. 没有(很少, 没有多少)机会听到好的音乐。 *I had no* ~ *to discuss the matter with her*. 我没有机会和她讨论那件事。 *The* ~ *came early one morning*. 有一天清早机会来了。

op·pose /ǝ'pǝʊz; ǝ'poz/ *vt* **1** [VP6A] set oneself, fight, against (sb or sth): 反对; 反抗(某人或某事物): ~ *the Government*; 反对政府; ~ *a scheme*. 反对某一计划。 *I am very much* ~*d to your going abroad*, I am against the plan. 我非常反对你出国。 **2** [VP14] ~ *(against/to)*, put forward as a contrast or opposite; set up against: 使对立; 使对照; 使对照; 以…对抗: ~ *your will against mine/your views to mine*; 把你的意向与我的意向(你的观点与我的观点)对照一下; ~ *a vigorous resistance to the enemy*. 猛烈抵抗敌人。 *as* ~*d to*, in contrast with. 与…对照; 与…成对比。

op·po·site /'ɒpǝzɪt; 'ɑpǝzɪt/ *adj* **1** ~ *(to)*, facing; front to front or back to back (with): 朝向…的; 与(…)面对面的; (与…)背对背的; 对立的; 相对的: *the house* ~ *(to) mine*; 与我的房子相对的那幢房子; *on the* ~ *side of the road*. 在路的对面。 **2** entirely different; contrary: 完全不同的; 相反的: *in the* ~ *direction*. 朝相反的方向。 **3** similarly placed elsewhere. 对当的。 *one's* ~ *number*, person occupying the same or a similar position in another group, etc: 与其地位相等或相当的人: *The British Foreign Minister is in Washington discussing problems with his* ~ *number*. 英国外相正在华盛顿与其身份相等的人(美国国务卿)讨论问题。 □ *n* word or thing that is ~: 反义词; 相对的事物: *Black and white are* ~*s*. 黑

与白相反。*I thought quite the* ~. 我想的刚好相反。

op·po·si·tion /ˌɒpəˈzɪʃn; ˌɑpəˈzɪʃən/ *n* **1** [U] the state of being opposite or opposed: 反对; 敌对; 相反; 相对: *The Socialist Party was in* ~, formed the O~. 社会党是国会中的反对党。 ⇨ **2** below. 参看下列第 2 义。 *be in* ~ *to*, opposing: 反对;与…相反: *We found ourselves in* ~ *to our friends on this question.* 我们发现我们对于这个问题和我们的朋友意见(立场)相反。 **2** (*sing*) MP's of the political party or parties opposing the Government: (单)国会中的反对党(与执政党敌对的政党): *Her Majesty's O*~; 女王(英国政府)所属反对党; *the leader of the O*~; 反对党的领袖; *the O*~ *benches*. (国会中的)反对党席。 *We need a stronger O*~. 我们需要一个更强大的反对党。 **3** [U] resistance: 抵抗: *Our forces met with strong* ~ *all along the front.* 我军在前线遭遇到全面的强烈抵抗。

op·press /əˈpres; əˈprɛs/ *vt* [VP6A] **1** rule unjustly or cruelly; keep down by unjust or cruel government. 压制; 压制。 **2** (fig) weigh heavily on; cause to feel troubled, uncomfortable: (喻)重压;使烦恼;使难受: ~*ed with anxiety / with a foreboding of misfortune;* 因焦虑(因不幸的预感)而烦恼; *feel* ~*ed with the heat.* 因热难耐。 ~*or* /-sɔ(r); -sɔ/ *n* person who ~es; cruel or unjust ruler. 压迫者; 暴君。 **op·pression** /əˈpreʃn; əˈprɛʃn/ *n* **1** [U] the condition of being ~ed: 压抑; 郁闷: *a feeling of* ~*ion.* 郁闷之感。 **2** [U] ~*ing* or being ~ed: 压迫;被压迫: *victims of* ~*ion;* 受压迫的苦难者; [C] instance of this; cruel or unjust act. 压迫或被压迫的实例; 暴虐或不公平的行为。 **op·press·ive** /əˈpresɪv; əˈprɛsɪv/ *adj* **1** unjust: 不公平的; 暴虐的; 压迫的: ~*ive laws / rules.* 不公平的法律(规则)。 **2** hard to endure; over-powering: 难以忍受的; 压制的: ~*ive weather / heat / taxes.* 难以忍受的天气(闷热, 苛税)。 **op·press·ive·ly** *adv*

op·pro·bri·ous /əˈprəʊbrɪəs; əˈprobrɪəs/ *adj* (formal) (of words, etc) showing scorn or reproach; abusive. (正式用语)(指文字等)辱骂的; 侮辱的。 ~*·ly* *adv* **op·pro·brium** /-brɪəm; -brɪəm/ *n* (formal) [U] scorn; disgrace; public shame. (正式用语)轻蔑; 耻辱; 不名誉。

op·pugn /əˈpjuːn; əˈpjun/ *vt* [VP6A] (formal) call in question; be contrary to. (正式用语)反对; 反驳; 质问。

opt /ɒpt; ɑpt/ *vi* **1** [VP3A] *opt for sth*, choose; decide on: 选择; 挑选: *Fewer students are opting for science courses nowadays.* 时下很多少学生选择科学课程。 **2** *opt out of*, choose to take no part in: 决定不参加;决定退出: *young people who have opted out of society*, chosen not to be conventional members of society. 决定退出现社会的年轻人(不为社会的传统分子)。

op·tat·ive /ˈɒptətɪv; ˈɑptətɪv/ *adj*, *n* (of) verbal form expressing desire: 表愿望的; 祈愿的; 祈愿式: ~ *mood*, eg in Greek, but not in English. 祈愿语气(如希腊语中者, 但英语中无此名称)。

op·tic /ˈɒptɪk; ˈɑptɪk/ *adj* of the eye or the sense of sight: 眼睛的; 视觉的: *the* ~ *nerve*, from the eye to the brain. 视觉神经。 ⇨ the illus at **eye.** 参看 eye 之插图。 ~*s n* (with *sing v*) science of light and the laws of light. (与单数动词连用)光学。

op·tical /ˈɒptɪkl; ˈɑptɪkl/ *adj* **1** of the sense of sight. 视觉的。 **an** ~ **illusion**, sth by which the eye is deceived: 光幻视; 视错觉; 错觉: *A mirage is an* ~ *illusion.* 海市蜃楼是一种视错觉。 **2** for looking through; to help eyesight: 用以看得清楚的; 帮助视力的: ~ *instruments*, eg microscopes, telescopes; 帮助视力的工具;光学仪器(如显微镜、**望远镜**); ~ *glass*, the kind used for ~ instruments, (用于光学仪器的)光学玻璃。 ~*·ly* /-klɪ; -klɪ/ *adv*

op·ti·cian /ɒpˈtɪʃn; ɑpˈtɪʃən/ *n* person who makes or supplies optical instruments, eg lenses and spectacles. 光学仪器(尤指透镜及眼镜)制造者或售卖者;光学仪器商。

op·ti·mism /ˈɒptɪmɪzəm; ˈɑptəˌmɪzəm/ *n* [U] (opp of *pessimism*) belief that in the end good will triumph over evil; tendency to look upon the bright side of things; confidence in success. (为 pessimism 之反义词)乐观; 乐天; 乐观主义; 对成功的信心。 **op·ti·mist** /-mɪst; -mɪst/ *n* person who is always hopeful and looks upon the bright side of things, who believes that all things happen for the best. 乐观的人; 乐观主义者。 **op·ti·mistic** /ˌɒptɪˈmɪstɪk; ˌɑptəˈmɪstɪk/ *adj* expecting the best; confident: 乐观的; 有信心的: *an optimistic view of events.* 对事情乐观的看法。 **op·ti·mis·ti·cally** /-klɪ; -klɪ/ *adv*

op·ti·mum /ˈɒptɪməm; ˈɑptəməm/ *n* (attrib) best or most favourable: (用作定语)最佳的; 最适宜的; 最有利的: *the* ~ *temperature for the growth of plants.* 对植物生长的最佳温度。

op·tion /ˈɒpʃn; ˈɑpʃən/ *n* **1** [U] right or power of choosing. 选择权; 选择力。 *have no / little, etc* ~, have no / little, etc choice: 无选择余地; 不能作选择: *I haven't much* ~ *in the matter*, cannot choose. 对这件事我不能选择。 *I had no* ~, was forced to act as I did. 我没有选择的余地。 *He was given six months' imprisonment without the* ~ *of a fine.* 他被判监禁六个月而不得易以罚金。 *local* ~, right of people (in some towns, districts) to decide, by voting, whether or not to have or allow sth, eg the sale of alcoholic liquor. 地方居民选择权(例如由投票决定是否可卖酒等)。 **2** [C] thing that is or may be chosen: 选择之事物; 可选择之事物: *None of the* ~*s is satisfactory.* 所选之物无一令人满意。 *leave one's* ~*s open*, not commit oneself. 不作选择; 不作承诺。 **3** [C] (comm) right to buy or sell sth at a certain price within a certain period of time: (商)(在某一期间内可以某种价格)买卖某物的权利: *have an* ~ *on a piece of land.* 对某块土地有买卖权。 *~al* /-ʃənl; -ʃənl/ *adj* which may be chosen or not as one wishes; not compulsory: 可选择的; 非强制的; 随意的: *al subjects at school.* 学校的选修课。 ~*·ally* /ˈɒpʃənəlɪ; ˈɑpʃənlɪ/ *adv*

opu·lence /ˈɒpjələns; ˈɑpjələns/ *n* [U] (formal) wealth; abundance. (正式用语)富裕; 丰富。 **opu·lent** /-ənt; -ənt/ *adj* rich; wealthy; luxuriant: 富足的; 富有的; 华丽的; 繁茂的: ~ *vegetation.* 茂盛的草木。 **opu·lent·ly** *adv*

opus /ˈəʊpəs; ˈopəs/ *n* (*pl opera* /ˈɒpərə; ˈɑpərə/, rarely used)separate musical composition (abbr 略作 **op**, used in citing a composition by number, as *Beethoven, Op 112*). (复数作 *opera*, 罕用)乐曲; 作品(用以表示作品编号, 如 Beethoven, Op 112)。 ˌ**magnum** '~, great artistic undertaking, completed or in course of being completed. 巨著; 杰作。

or /ɔː(r); ɔr/ *conj* **1** (introducing an alternative): (引出另一个代替的事物,表示两者居其一) 或;抑: *Is it green or blue?* 它是绿的还是蓝的? *Are you coming or not?* 你来还是不来? *either…*, *or*, ⇨ *either whether … or*: 是…还是…; 不论…或…: *I don't care whether he stays or goes.* 我不在乎他留下来还是离去。 *or else*, otherwise: 否则: *Hurry up or else you'll be late.* 赶快, 否则你会迟到。 *Pay up, or else!* (as a threat). 付款付清, 否则的话! (作为一种威胁)。 **2** (introducing all but the first of a series of alternatives): (引出除首项事物外之一系列的代替者, 表示其中任何一个): *I'd like it to be black, (or) white or grey.* 我希望它是黑的, (或者)白的或者灰的。 **3** (introducing a word that explains, or means the same as, another): (表示一个词可解释另一词的含义或与该词同义)换言之即;也就是: *an English pound, or one hundred pence;* 一个英镑, 也就是一百个便士; *a dugout, or a canoe made by hollowing out a tree trunk;* 独木舟, 也就是挖空树干造成的小舟: *geology, or the science of the earth's crust.* 地质学, 换句话说就是研究地壳的科学。 **4** *or so*, (often equivalent to *about*) suggesting vagueness or uncertainty about quantity: (常等于 about; 表示数量不确定)大约: *There were twenty or so.* 有二十个

左右. **or somebody/something/somewhere; somebody/something/somewhere or other,** (colloq) (口) (expressing uncertainty about who/what/where): (表示不能确定是谁或何事物或是何地方)某人;某事物;某地: *I put it in the cupboard or somewhere,* ie somewhere, perhaps in the cupboard. 我大概是把它放在柜柜里或是其他什么地方了. *'Who told you?'*—*'Oh, somebody or other, I've forgotten who.'* '谁告诉你的?'——'噢, 有个人告诉我的, 我忘记是谁了.'

or·acle /'ɒrəkl US: 'ɔːrəkl/ *n* **1** (in ancient Greece) (answer given at) place where questions about the future were asked of the gods; priest(ess) giving the answers: (古希腊)神谕;祈求神谕的庙;传神谕的祭司(女祭司): *consult the ~.* 询求神谕. **2** person considered able to give reliable guidance. 被认为是能给予可靠指导的人. **oracu·lar** /ə'rækjʊlə(r); ə'rækjələ/ *adj* of or like an ~; with a hidden meaning: 神谕的;象神谕的;有隐意的: *oracular utterances.* 玄奥难解的话.

oral /'ɔːrəl; 'ɔrəl/ *adj* **1** using the spoken, not the written, word: 口说的;口头的: *an ~ examination.* 口试. **2** (anat) of, by, for, the mouth: (解剖)口的; 用口的;适于口的: *~ contraceptives,* 口服避孕药. □ **pill(2).** 口服避孕药. □ *n* (colloq) *~ examination.* (口)口试. **~·ly** /'ɔːrəlɪ; 'ɔrəlɪ/ *adv* by spoken words; by the mouth: 口头上;用口: *not to be taken ~ly,* (eg of medical preparations) not to be swallowed; for external use only. (如指药剂)不可口服;外用的;外敷的.

or·ange /'ɒrɪndʒ US: 'ɔːr-; 'ɔrɪndʒ/ *n, adj* [C] **1** the illus at **fruit.** 参看 fruit 之插图. (evergreen tree with a) round, thick-skinned juicy fruit, green and usu changing to a colour between yellow and red; [U] (of the) usu colour of this fully-ripened fruit. 柑(树)橙(树);橘(树);橙黄色(的). **~·ade** /ˌɒrɪndʒ'eɪd US: ˌɔːr-; ˌɔrɪndʒ'ed/ *n* [U] drink made of ~ juice. 柑汁饮料;橘子水.

Or·ange·man /'ɒrɪndʒmæn US: 'ɔːr-; 'ɔrɪndʒmən/ *n* (*pl* **-men**) member of a Protestant political society in Ulster, Northern Ireland. 奥兰治党员(北爱尔兰阿尔斯特省拥护新教之政治社团中之一员).

orang-outang /ɔːˌræŋ 'uːtæŋ; ə'ræŋ; ə'tæŋ/ (also **-utan, -outan** /-'tæn; -ˌtæn/) *n* large, long-armed ape of Borneo and Sumatra. (产于婆罗洲和苏门答腊的)长臂巨猿;猩猩. □ the illus at **ape.** 参看 ape 之插图.

orate /ɔː'reɪt; 'ɔret/ *vi* [VP2A] speak publicly. 演说;演讲.

ora·tion /ɔː'reɪʃn; ə'reʃən/ *n* [C] formal speech made on a public occasion: 正式演讲;演说: *a funeral ~.* 悼辞.

ora·tor /'ɒrətə(r) US: 'ɔːr-; 'ɔrətə/ *n* person who makes speeches (esp a good speaker). 演说者;(尤指出色的)演说家. **~·i·cal** /ˌɒrə'tɒrɪkl US: ˌɔːrə'tɔːr-; ˌɔrə'tɔrɪkl/ *adj* of speech-making and ~s: 演说的;演说家的: *~ical phrases/gestures;* 演说家的辞令(演讲的手势); *an ~ical contest.* 演讲比赛.

ora·torio /ˌɒrə'tɔːrɪəʊ US: ˌɔːr-; ˌɔrə'torɪo/ *n* (*pl* **~s**) [C] musical composition for solo voices, chorus and orchestra, usu with a religious subject: 圣乐;神剧 (包括独唱、合唱及管弦乐, 通常以宗教为主题): *the ~s of Handel;* 韩德尔的圣乐; [U] musical compositions of this kind collectively: 圣乐的总称: *Do you like ~?* 你喜欢圣乐吗? □ **cantata, opera.**

ora·tory¹ /'ɒrətrɪ US: 'ɔːrətɔːrɪ; 'ɔrəˌtorɪ/ *n* (*pl* **-ries**) [C] small chapel for private worship or prayer. 小礼拜堂;祈祷室.

ora·tory² /'ɒrətrɪ US: 'ɔːrətɔːrɪ; 'ɔrəˌtorɪ/ *n* [U] (art of) making speeches; rhetoric. 演说(术);修辞.

orb /ɔːb; ɔrb/ *n* globe, esp the sun, moon or one of the planets; jewelled globe with a cross on top, part of a sovereign's regalia. 球体;(尤指)星球(太阳、月亮或行星);王权宝球(镶珠宝的球, 球顶有十字架, 为王权标志之一). □ the illus at **regalia.** 参看 regalia 之插图.

or·bit /'ɔːbɪt; 'ɔrbɪt/ *n* path followed by a heavenly body, eg a planet, the moon, or a manmade object, eg a spacecraft, round another body: (天体、如行星、月球或太空船等人造飞行物, 绕行另一天体的)轨道: *the earth's ~ round the sun.* 地球绕行太阳的轨道. *How many satellites have been put in ~ round the earth?* 有多少个人造卫星已被射入环绕地球的轨道? □ *vt, vi* [VP 6A, 2A, C] put into, (cause to) move in, ~ (round): 使进入轨道;(使)循轨道运行: *When was the first manmade satellite ~ed?* 第一颗人造卫星是何时射入轨道的? *How many spacecraft have orbited the moon?* 有多少艘太空船在绕月球轨道运行? **~al** /'ɔːbɪtl; 'ɔrbɪtl/ *adj* of an ~: 行星(卫星)轨道的: *a spacecraft's ~al distance from the earth.* 太空船轨道与地球的距离. **~ velocity,** minimal velocity needed to place sth in ~. 轨道速度(某物进入轨道所需的最低速度).

or·chard /'ɔːtʃəd; 'ɔrtʃəd/ *n* [C] piece of ground (usu enclosed) with fruit-trees: 果园(通常指围起来的): *apple-~s.* 苹果园.

or·ches·tra /'ɔːkɪstrə; 'ɔrkɪstrə/ *n* **1** group of persons playing musical instruments together: 管弦乐队;管弦乐团: *a dance/string/symphony ~.* 舞蹈乐队(弦乐队;交响乐团). □ *brass band* at **brass(3).** **2** ~ **(pit),** place in a theatre for an ~. (剧院里的)乐队席. **~ stalls,** front seats on the floor of a theatre. 剧院正厅的前座. **3** semicircular space in front of the stage of a theatre in ancient Greece, where the chorus sang and danced. 合唱舞蹈席(古希腊剧场中舞台前的半圆场地, 为合唱队歌唱舞蹈之处). **or·ches·tral** /ɔː'kestrəl; ɔr'kestrəl/ *adj* of, for, by, an ~: 管弦乐队的;适于管弦乐队的;管弦乐队所演奏的: *orchestral instruments/performances.* 管弦乐队所用的乐器(管弦乐演奏). **or·ches·trate** /'ɔːkɪstreɪt; 'ɔrkɪsˌtret/ *vt* [VP6A] compose, arrange, score, for orchestral performances. 把…作成管弦乐;把…编成管弦乐;把…谱入管弦乐. **or·ches·tra·tion** /ˌɔːkɪ'streɪʃn; ˌɔrkɪs'treʃən/ *n*.

or·chid /'ɔːkɪd; 'ɔrkɪd/ (also **or·chis** /'ɔːkɪs; 'ɔrkɪs/) *n* [C] sorts of plant of which the English wild kinds (usu *orchis*) have tuberous roots, and the tropical kinds (usu *orchid*) have flowers of brilliant colours and fantastic shapes. 兰花(英国野生兰通常称为 orchis, 有块状根, 热带兰通常称为 orchid, 开绚丽奇状的花). □ the illus at **flower.** 参看 flower 之插图.

or·dain /ɔː'deɪn; ɔr'den/ *vt* **1** [VP6A, 23] make (sb) a priest or minister: 立(某人)为神父或牧师: *He was ~ed priest.* 他被立为神父. **2** [VP9] *~ that,* (of God, law, authority) decide; give orders (that); destine: (指上帝、法律、当局)决定;命令;注定: *God has ~ed that all men shall die.* 上帝注定所有的人终必死亡.

or·deal /ɔː'diːl; ɔr'dil/ *n* severe test of character or endurance: 对于品格或耐力的严酷考验: *pass through terrible ~s.* 经历可怕的考验.

or·der¹ /'ɔːdə(r); 'ɔrdə/ *n* **1** [U] way in which things are placed in relation to one another: 次序; 顺序: *names in alphabetical ~;* 照字母顺序排列的名字; *in chronological ~,* ie according to dates. 按年代顺序. *in ~ of,* arranged according to: 照…排列: *in ~ of size/merit/importance, etc.* 依大小(功绩, 重要性等)次序排列. **2** [U] condition in which everything is carefully arranged; working condition. 有规律的状况;工作状况. *(not) in ~,* (not) as it should be: 处于(不)正常状况中;情况良好(不良): *Is your passport in ~,* Has it all the necessary entries to satisfy the authorities? 你的护照办好了吗? *He put/left his affairs/accounts/papers in ~ before he left the country.* 他出国前把他的事务(帐目, 文件)都整理好了. *Get your ideas into some kind of ~ before beginning to write.* 在动笔之前先把你的概念作一整理. *in good ~,* without any confusion: 整齐;不乱;井然有序;情况良好: *The troops retired in good ~,* Their retreat was orderly, disciplined. 军队秩序井然地撤退. *in good/bad/running/working ~,* (esp of machines) working well/badly/smoothly, etc: (尤指

机器)运转良好(不佳,正常): *The engine has been tuned and is now in perfect running ～.* 发动机已经调整过,现在运转十分良好。 **out of ～,** (of a machine, a bodily organ) not functioning properly: (指机器、身体器官)坏了;有毛病;不能适当地起效用: *The lift/phone is out of ～.* 电梯(电话)坏了。*My stomach is out of ～.* 我的胃有点毛病。**3**[U](condition brought about by) good and firm government, obedience to law, rules, authority: 秩序;良好与稳固的管理;对法律、规则、权威的遵守: *The army restored law and ～.* 军队使法律与秩序恢复。*It is the business of the police to keep ～.* 维持秩序(治安)是警察的事。*Some teachers find it difficult to keep ～ in their classes/to keep their classes in ～.* 有些教师发现很难维持教室秩序。⇨ **disorder. 4**[U] rules usual at a public meeting; rules accepted, eg in Parliament, committee meetings, by members and enforced by a president, chairman, or other officer. 会议规则;(国会、委员会会议等所遵守的)议事规则;会议程序;会场秩序。*call (sb) to ～,* (of the Speaker in the House of Commons, the chairman of a meeting, etc) request (a member, etc) to obey the rules, the usual procedures.(指英国下议院议长、会议主席等)请(某人)遵守会场秩序。*be in ～ to do sth,* be according to the rules, etc: 依照规定等做某事: *Is it in ～ to interrupt?* 打岔(插嘴)合规矩吗? *on a point of ～,* on a point (= question) of procedure. 在程序问题上。*O～! O～!* (used to call attention to a departure from the usual rules of debates or procedures). 守秩序! 守秩序! *the ～ of the day,* programme of business to be discussed. 当日议题。*'～-paper n* written or printed ～ of the day. 当日议程表。**standing ～s,** ⇨ **standing** *adj*(1). **5** [C] command given with authority: 命令: *Soldiers must obey ～s.* 军人必须服从命令。*He gave ～s for the work to be started/that the work should be started at once.* 他下令立刻开始工作。*be under ～s (to do sth),* have received ～s: 奉命(做某事): *He is under ～s to leave for Finland next week.* 他奉命下星期前往芬兰。*by ～ of,* according to directions given by proper authority of: 奉…之命: *by ～ of the Governor.* 奉省(州)长之命。*under the ～s of,* commanded by. 受…指挥。*under starters' ～s,* ⇨ **start².** **6** [C] request to supply goods; the goods (to be) supplied: 定购;定单;定货;(待)交付之货:*an ～ for two tons of coal;* 二吨煤的定单; *give a tradesman an ～ for goods;* 向商人定购货物;*fill an ～,* supply the goods asked for. 交付定货。*The butcher has called for ～s,* to ask what is wanted. 肉商来问需要什么肉。**on ～,** requested but not yet supplied. 定购中。**made to ～,** made according to the customer's special requirements or instructions. 定做的。⇨ *ready*-made at **ready. a large/ tall ～,** (colloq) sth difficult to do or supply. (口)难做的事; 难供应之物。*'～-book n* one in which a tradesman, commercial traveller, manufacturer, etc writes down ～s for goods: 定货簿: *The company has full ～-books,* orders for large quantities of goods. 该公司有多本满满的定货簿(有大量的定货)。*'～-form n* printed form with blank spaces to be filled in by the customer. 定货单。**7** [C] written direction to a bank (**'banker's ～**) or post office (**'postal ～**) to pay money, or giving authority to do sth: (银行或邮局之)汇票; 授权凭证: *an ～ on O'Reilly's Bank;* 欧来利银行汇票; *a postal ～ for £9;* 九英镑的邮政汇票; *an ～ to view,* eg from an estate-agent to inspect a house that is for sale. 察看许可书(例如房地产经纪人所开让人察看出售房屋者)。**8** [U] purpose, intention. 目的;意向。**in ～ to do sth,** with the purpose of doing sth, with a view to doing sth: 欲做某事; 为了做某事: *in ～ (for you) to see clearly.* 为着(使你)看得清楚。**in ～ that,** with the intention that; so that: 为了; 以便: *in ～ that he may/might/ shall/should arrive in time.* 以便他能及时到达。**9** [C] group of people belonging to or appointed to a special class(as an honour or reward): 属于或被列入某一特殊等级(作为一种荣誉或酬报)的一批人:*the O～ of Merit/*

---

of Knights/of the Bath/of the Golden Kite, etc; 获得殊功勋位(爵士勋位, 巴斯勋位, 金鸢勋位等)的一批人; badge, sign, etc worn by members of such an ～: (有此类勋位者所佩带的)勋章; 勋位标志: *wearing all his ～s and decorations.* 佩带着他所有的勋章和奖章。**10** *(pl)* authority given by a bishop to perform church duties. (复)主教所授予以便履行教会职责的权力; 牧师职务。**be in/take (holy) ～s,** be/become a priest. 担任牧师(受圣职; 就任牧师职)。**11** [C] class of persons on whom holy ～s have been conferred: 圣职人员等级: *the O～ of Deacons/Priests/Bishops.* 执事(牧师, 主教)等级。**12** [C] group of persons living under religious rules: 教团; 修道会: *the monastic ～s; 修士会; the ～s of Dominicans.* 圣多明尼克教会之一。**13**[C] method of treating architectural forms, esp of columns (pillars) and capitals, esp the classical ～s (*Doric, Ionic, Corinthian*). (尤指柱子与柱冠的)建筑形式; 柱范; 柱式(尤指古典柱式)(Doric order, 希腊 Doris 地方流行的一种最古朴的柱式; Ionic order, Ionia 地方流行的一种雕刻较精的柱式; Corinthian order, 希腊 Corinth 地方流行雕刻最华丽的柱式)。⇨ the illus at **column.** 参看 column 之插图。**14**(biol)[C] highest division under *class* in the grouping of animals, plants, etc:(生物)目(生物分类中仅次于'纲'的分类):*The rose and the bean families belong to the same ～.* 蔷薇科与豆科属于同一个目。(目)。**15** [C] kind; sort; 种; 类: *intellectual ability of a high～.* 高等的智能。**16** [U] arrangement of military forces: 军队的排列; 队形; 序列: *advance in review ～,* on parade; (阅兵中)以分列式行进; *advance in extended ～,* in battle. (战斗中)以疏开队形前进。*advance in open/close ～,* with wide/ with only slight spaces between the men, etc. 以散开(密集)队形前进。

or·der² /'ɔːdə(r); 'ɔrdɚ/ *vt* **1** [VP 6 A, 9, 12 B, 13 B, 15 A, B, 17] give an order (5, 6, 7) to (sb) or for sth: (对某人或为某事)命令; 指令; 定购; 汇寄; 授权: *The doctor ～ed me to (stay in) bed.* 医生吩咐我卧床休息。*The disobedient boy was ～ed out of the room.* 那个不听话的男孩被赶出房间。*The chairman ～ed silence.* 主席命令保持肃静。*The regiment was ～ed to the front.* 该团奉令开赴前线。*The judge ～ed that the prisoner should be remanded.* 法官谕令被告还押。*The doctor has ～ed me absolute quiet.* 医生嘱我要绝对安静。*She ～ed herself two dozen oysters and a pint of stout.* 她自己点了两打牡蛎和一品脱黑啤酒。*I've ～ed lunch for 1.30.* 我已经下令一点三十分开午饭。*The regiment was ～ed up (to the front).* 该团奉令出发(开赴前线)。**～ sb about,** keep on giving orders to him. 不断驱使某人。**2** [VP 6 A, 15 A] arrange; direct: 安排; 指导; 管理: *～ one's life according to strict rules.* 依严格的规律安排自己的生活。**～ing** *n* (from 2 above)(出自上列第 2 义) arrangement. 安排; 布置。

or·der·ly /'ɔːdəlɪ; 'ɔrdɚlɪ/ *adj* **1** well arranged; in good order; tidy: 有秩序的; 有顺序的; 整齐的: *an ～ room/desk;* 整齐的房间(书桌); methodically inclined: 有条理的: *a man with an ～ mind.* 思想有条不紊的人。**2** well behaved; obedient to discipline: 守秩序的; 守规律的: *an ～ crowd.* 守秩序的群众。**3** (army use, attrib only) concerned with carrying out orders: (军队用语,仅用作定语) 执行命令的: *the ～ officer,* the officer on duty for the day; 值日官; 值勤官; *the '～ room,* room in barracks where the clerical work is done. (营房内之)办公室; 文书室。□ *n* (*pl* -**lies**) (army) officer's messenger. (军语)传令兵。**medical ～,** attendant in a military hospital. 医务兵。**or·der·li·ness** *n*

or·di·nal /'ɔːdɪnl *US:* -dənl; 'ɔrdɪnl/ *n, adj* [C] (number) showing order or position in a series. 序数; 顺序的; 依次的。**～ numbers,** eg *first, second, third.* 序数(例如第一,第二,第三)。⇨ **cardinal; App 4.** 参看 cardinal 及附录四。

or·di·nance /'ɔːdɪnəns; 'ɔrdɪnəns/ *n* [C] order, rule, statute, made by authority or decree: 法令; 条例: *the ～s of the City Council.* 市议会颁布的法令。

or·di·nand /ˌɔːdɪˈnænd *US*: ˈɔːrdənænd; ˌɔrdəˈnænd/ *n* candidate for ordination. 圣职候选人。

or·di·nary /ˈɔːdɪnrɪ *US*: ˈɔːrdənerɪ; ˈɔrdnerɪ/ *adj* normal; usual; average: 正常的; 通常的; 普通的: *an ~ day's work;* 日常的工作; *in ~ dress.* 穿着平常的衣服。 *in an ~ way,* if the circumstances were ~ or usual. 若按常情; 就通常情形。 *in the ~ way,* in the usual or customary way. 通常地; 通例地; 惯常地; 一般。 *in ~,* by permanent appointment, not temporary or extraordinary: 常任的; 非临时的: *physician in ~ to Her Majesty.* 女王的常任医师/御医。 *out of the ~,* unusual. 不平常的。 *~ seaman,* (abbr 略作 **OS**) one who has not yet received the rank of *able seaman* (abbr 略作 *A B*). 二等水兵 (一等水兵为 able seaman)。 **or·di·nar·ily** /ˈɔːdɪnrəlɪ *US*: ˌɔːdnˈerəlɪ; ˌɔrdnˈerəlɪ/ *adv* in an ~ way: 通常地; 正常地; 一般: *behave quite ordinarily.* 行为十分平常。

or·di·na·tion /ˌɔːdɪˈneɪʃn *US*: -dnˈeɪʃn; ˌɔrdnˈeʃən/ *n* [U] ceremony of ordaining (a priest or minister); [C] instance of this. 任命(神父或牧师)的仪式; 圣职的任命。

ord·nance /ˈɔːdnəns; ˈɔrdnəns/ *n* [U] artillery; munitions. 炮; 军火。 **Royal Army 'O~ Corps,** (US 美 = **O~ Corps**), that which is responsible for military supplies. 皇家陆军兵工署(部队)。 **the O~ Survey,** (the preparation of) accurate and detailed maps of GB. 精确详细的英国地图; 此种地图之测绘。

or·dure /ˈɔːdjʊə(r) *US*: -dʒər; ˈɔrdʒɚ/ *n* [U] excrement; dung; filth. 排泄物; 粪; 污物。

ore /ɔː(r); ɔr/ *n* [C, U] (kinds of) rock, earth, mineral, etc from which metal can be mined or extracted: 矿石; 矿沙; 矿块: *iron ore; 铁矿; a district rich in ores.* 矿产丰富的地区。

or·gan /ˈɔːgən; ˈɔrgən/ *n* **1** any part of an animal body or plant serving an essential purpose: (动植物的)器官: *the ~s of speech.* the tongue, teeth, lips, etc; 语言器官(如舌、牙、唇等); 发音器官; the *'nasal ~,* the nose; 鼻器官; *the reproductive ~s.* 生殖器官。 the illus at **alimentary, ear, eye, respire, reproduce.** 参看 alimentary, ear, eye, respire, reproduce 等之插图。 **2** means of getting work done; organization: 工作机关; 组织: *Parliament is the chief ~ of government.* 国会是政府的主要机关。 **3** means for making known what people think: 传播工具; 报纸: *~s of public opinion,* newspapers, radios, TV, etc. 舆论的喉舌(报纸, 无线电广播, 电视等)。 **4** musical instrument from which sounds are produced by air forced through pipes, played by keys pressed with the fingers and pedals pressed with the feet (in US also called 美亦称 a **'pipe~**). ⇨ the illus at **church.** 参看 church 之插图。 **'reed / A'merican ~,** harmonium (with reeds instead of pipes). 簧风琴(以簧代管的风琴)。 **'~-blower** *n* person who works the bellows of an ~. 操作风琴风箱的人。 **'~-grinder** *n* person who plays a barrel-~. 操作筒风琴的人。 ⇨ **barrel.** **'~-loft** *n* gallery (in some churches, etc) where the ~ is placed. (某些教堂等中的)风琴台。 **'~-ist** /-ɪst; -ɪst/ *n* person who plays an ~ (4). 风琴演奏家。

or·gan·die (US also **-dy**) /ˈɔːˈgændɪ; ˈɔrgəndɪ/ *n* [U] kind of fine translucent muslin. 蝉翼纱(一种透明的细棉布)。

or·ganic /ɔːˈgænɪk; ɔrˈgænɪk/ *adj* **1** of an organ or organs of the body: 器官的: *~ diseases,* affecting the structure of these organs, not only their functions. 器官性病; 器质性病。 **2** (opp *inorganic*) having bodily organs: (为 inorganic 之反义词)有机(体)的: *~ life.* 有机的生物。 *~ chemistry,* dealing with carbon compounds. 有机化学。 **3** made of related parts; arranged as a system: 有组织的; 有系统的: *an ~* (ie organized) *whole;* 有组织的整体; *an ~* (ie structural) *part.* 一个组成部分。 **or·gani·cally** /-klɪ; -klɪ/ *adv.*

or·gan·ism /ˈɔːgənɪzəm; ˈɔrgənɪzəm/ *n* [C] living

being with parts which work together; individual animal or plant; any system with parts dependent upon each other: 生物; 个别的动物或植物; 有机体; 组织: *the social ~.* 社会; 社会组织。

or·gan·iz·ation /ˌɔːgənaɪˈzeɪʃn *US*: -nɪˈz-; ˌɔrgənəˈzeʃən/ *n* **1** [U] act of organizing; condition of being organized: 组织的行动; 被组织的状况; 组织: *He is engaged in the ~ of a new club.* 他正忙着组织一个新俱乐部。 *An army without ~ would be useless.* 无组织的军队是没用的。 **2** [C] organized body of persons; organized system: 机构; 组织; 有组织的系统: *The human body has a very complex ~.* 人体有很复杂的组织。

or·gan·ize /ˈɔːgənaɪz; ˈɔrgənˌaɪz/ *vt, vi* [VP6A, 2A] **1** put into working order; arrange in a system; make preparations for: 组合; 组织; 筹划; 筹办; 创办: *~ an army /a government /a political party /an expedition to the South Pole /one's work /oneself.* 编组军队(组织政府; 组织政党; 组织南极探险队; 筹划工作; 使自己心里有准备)。 **2** (of workers, etc) form into, join, a trade union. (指工人等)组成工会; 参加工会。 **or·gan·ized** *adj* **1** ordered; orderly. 有组织的; 有秩序的。 **2** furnished with organs; made into a living organism: 有器官的; 作成生物的: *highly ~d forms of life.* 器官发达的生物。 **3** (of workers) in a trade union. (指工人)加入工会的。 **or·gan·izer** *n* person who ~s things. 组织者; 创办者。

or·gasm /ˈɔːgæzəm; ˈɔrgæzəm/ *n* [C] violent (esp erotic) excitement; the climax of sexual excitement. 激烈的(尤指性的)兴奋; 性欲高潮; 性欲亢进。

or·gi·as·tic /ˌɔːdʒɪˈæstɪk; ˌɔrdʒɪˈæstɪk/ *adj* of the nature of an orgy; frenzied. 狂欢的; 狂乱的。

orgy /ˈɔːdʒɪ; ˈɔrdʒɪ/ *n* [C] (*pl* orgies) **1** occasion of wild merry-making; (*pl*) drunken or licentious revels. 狂欢; (复)醉酒或淫佚的宴乐; 喝花酒。 **2** (colloq) excessive amount: (口)过量; 过多: *an ~ of parties / concerts / spending.* 过多的聚会(音乐会, 花费)。

oriel /ˈɔːrɪəl; ˈɔrɪəl/ *n* **1** part of a room projecting from an upper storey and supported from the ground or on corbels and having a window in it. 楼房悬凸壁外而带窗的部分。 **2** '~ **(window),** window of an ~. 凸窗; 突窗。 ⇨ the illus at **window.** 参看 window 之插图。

orient[1] /ˈɔːrɪənt; ˈɔrɪˌɛnt/ *n* **the O~,** (liter) the countries of the East, ie Asia, contrasted with *the Occident.* (文)东方诸国(即亚洲, 与 the Occident 相对)。 □ *adj* (poet) Eastern; (of the sun) rising: (诗)东方的; (指太阳)上升的: *the ~ sun.* 上升的太阳; 朝阳。

orient[2] /ˈɔːrɪənt; ˈɔrɪˌɛnt/ *vt* = orientate.

orien·tal /ˌɔːrɪˈentl; ˌɔrɪˈɛntl/ *adj* of the Orient: 东方(诸国)的: *~ civilization /art /rugs.* 东方文明(艺术, 地毯)。 □ *n* **O~,** inhabitant of the Orient, esp China and Japan. 东方人(尤指中国人与日本人)。 **~·ist** /-ɪst; -ɪst/ *n* person who studies the languages, arts, etc of ~ countries. 研究东方语言、艺术等的人。

orien·tate /ˈɔːrɪənteɪt; ˈɔrɪənˌtet/ *vt* [VP6A] **1** place (a building, etc) so as to face east; build (a church) with the chancel end due east. 使(建筑物等)朝向东方; 建筑(教堂)使其圣坛在东端。 **2** place or exactly determine the position of (sth) with regard to the points of the compass; (fig) bring into clearly understood relations: 照指南针安置或决定(某物)之位置; (喻)使认清形势: *~ oneself,* make oneself familiar with a situation, determine how one stands in relation to one's surroundings, etc. 认识环境, 确定立场(使自己认识环境, 决定自己在所处环境中的立场, 并使自己能够适应)。 **orien·ta·tion** /ˌɔːrɪenˈteɪʃn; ˌɔrɪənˈteʃən/ *n* [U] orientating or being ~d. 朝向东方; 使在东端; 定方向; 定方位; 朝向; 认识环境。

ori·fice /ˈɒrɪfɪs *US*: ˈɔːr-; ˈɔrəfɪs/ *n* outer opening; mouth (of a cave, etc). 外孔; (洞穴等的)口; 洞口。

ori·gin /ˈɒrɪdʒɪn *US*: ˈɔːr-; ˈɔrədʒɪn/ *n* [C, U] starting-point; 起源: *the ~ of a quarrel;* 争吵的起因; *the ~(s) of civilization;* 文明的起源; *a man of humble ~,* parentage; 出身寒微的人; *words of Latin*

~. 词源出自拉丁文的词。

orig·inal /əˈrɪdʒənl; əˈrɪdʒənl/ *adj* **1** first or earliest: 原先的; 最早的; 最初的: *the ~ inhabitants of the country.* 这个国家最早的居民。*The ~ plan was better than the plan we followed* 原先的计划优于我们所实行的计划。**~ sin,** ⇨ **sin.** **2** newly formed or created; not copied or imitated: 新创的; 创举的; 非抄袭的; 非模仿的: *~ ideas;* 创见; *an ~ design.* 别出心裁的设计。**3** able to produce new ideas, etc; inventive: 能产生新见解的; 有创见的: *an ~ thinker / writer;* 富创见的思想家(作家); *an ~ mind.* 独具卓见的人。□ *n* **1** [C] that from which sth is copied: 原作品; 原物: *This is a copy; the ~ is in the Prado in Madrid.* 这是仿造品, 原作是在马德里的国家美术馆。**2** the **~,** language in which sth was first composed: 原文: *read Homer in the ~,* in ancient Greek; 读原文(即古希腊文)的荷马作品; *study Don Quixote in the ~,* in Spanish. 研读原文(即西班牙文)的唐吉诃德。**3** [C] person with an original(3) mind. 有创见的人。**~·ly** /-nəlɪ; -nlɪ/ *adv* **1** in an ~ manner: 新颖地; 独特地; 别出心裁地: *speak / think / write ~ly.* 别出心裁地说话(思想, 写作)。**2** from or in the beginning: 原先; 起始: *The school was ~ly quite small.* 这个学校原先是相当小的。**~·ity** /ə,rɪdʒəˈnælətɪ; ə,rɪdʒəˈnælətɪ/ *n* [U] state or quality of being ~(2): 创新; 创造性; 创造力; 独特: *work that lacks ~ity,* is copied or imitated. 缺少创造性的作品(抄袭或模仿的作品)。

orig·inate /əˈrɪdʒɪneɪt; əˈrɪdʒə,net/ *vi, vt* **1** [VP2C, 3A] **~** *from / in sth;* **~** *from / with sb,* have as a cause or beginning: 发源; 发起; 发生: *The quarrel ~d in rivalry between two tribes.* 争论是由两个部落之间的竞争而起的。*With whom did the scheme ~?* 这计划是谁发起的? **2** [VP6A] be the author or creator of: 创作; 发明: *~ a new style of dancing.* 创造一种新的舞步。**orig·in·a·tor** /-teɪtə(r); -tə/ *n*

ori·ole /ˈɔːrɪəʊl; ˈɔrɪ,ol/ *n* **(golden) ~,** kinds of bird with black and yellow feathers. 金莺。

ori·son /ˈɔːrɪzn US: ˈɔːr-; ˈɔrɪzn/ *n* [C] (archaic) prayer. (古)祈祷。

or·lop /ˈɔːlɒp; ˈɔrlɑp/ *n* **~ (deck),** lowest deck of a ship with three or more decks. (具有三层或更多层甲板之船的)最下层甲板。

or·molu /ˈɔːməluː; ˈɔrmə,lu/ *n* [U, C] (article made of, or decorated with) gilded bronze or a gold-coloured alloy of copper, zinc and tin: 金色黄铜(镀金的黄铜或金色的铜, 锌, 锡合金); 金色黄铜制品; 用金色黄铜装饰的物品: *an ~ cock.* 金色黄铜时钟。

or·na·ment /ˈɔːnəmənt; ˈɔrnəmənt/ *n* **1** [U] adorning or being adorned; that which is added for decoration: 装饰; 装饰物: *add sth by way of ~;* 加添某物作为装饰; *an altar rich in ~.* 装饰华丽的祭坛。**2** [C] sth designed or used to add beauty to sth else: 装饰品: *a shelf crowded with ~s,* eg small vases, statuettes, pieces of china. 摆满装饰品的架子。**3** [C] person, act, quality, etc that adds beauty, charm, etc: 添加光彩的人; 增添优美或着味的动作, 品质等: *He is an ~ to his profession.* 他是一个为他职业增光的人。□ *vt* /ˈɔːnəment; ˈɔrnə,ment/ [VP6A, 14] be an ~ to; make beautiful: 装饰; 修饰: *~ a dress with lace.* 用花边装饰衣服。**or·na·men·tal** /,ɔːnəˈmentl; ,ɔrnəˈmentl/ *adj* of or for ~. 装饰的; 为着装饰的。**or·na·men·ta·tion** /-menˈteɪʃn; ,ɔrnəmenˈteʃən/ *n* [U] ~ing or being ~ed; that which ~s: 装饰; 被装饰; 装饰物: *a church with no ~ation.* 没有装饰的教堂。

or·nate /ɔːˈneɪt; ɔrˈnet/ *adj* richly ornamented; (of liter style) full of flowery language; not simple in style or vocabulary. 装饰华丽的; (指文学体裁)词藻华美的; 文词繁复的。**~·ly** *adv* **~·ness** *n*

or·nery /ˈɔːnərɪ; ˈɔrnərɪ/ *adj* (US colloq) ill-tempered; perverse and stubborn. (美口)坏脾气的; 偏强顽固的。

or·ni·thol·ogy /,ɔːnɪˈθɒlədʒɪ; ,ɔrnəˈθɑlədʒɪ/ *n* [U] scientific study of birds. 鸟类学。**or·ni·thol·ogist** /-dʒɪst; -dʒɪst/ *n* expert in ~. 鸟类学家。**or·ni·tho-**

logi·cal /,ɔ:nɪθəˈlɒdʒɪkl; ,ɔrnɪθəˈlɑdʒɪkl/ *adj*

oro·tund /ˈɔːrəʊtʌnd; ˈɔrə,tʌnd/ *adj* (formal) (正式用语) **1** imposing; dignified. 宏壮的; 庄严的。**2** pompous; pretentious. 夸大的; 矫饰的。

or·phan /ˈɔːfn; ˈɔrfən/ *n* person (esp a child) who has lost one or both of its parents by death: 父亲, 母亲或双亲死亡的人; (尤指)孤儿: (attrib) (用作定语) *an ~ child.* 孤儿。□ *vt* [VP6A] cause to be an ~: 使成为孤儿: *~ed by war.* 因战争而成为孤儿的。**~·age** /-ɪdʒ; -ɪdʒ/ *n* home for ~s. 孤儿院。

or·ris·root /ˈɒrɪsruːt US: ˈɔːr-; ˈɔrɪs,rut/ *n* fragrant root of some kinds of iris, used in perfumes and cosmetics. 鸢尾根(某些鸢尾属植物之蓝紫色香根, 用以制香水及化妆品)。

or·tho·dox /ˈɔːθədɒks; ˈɔrθə,dɑks/ *adj* (having opinions, beliefs, etc which are) generally accepted or approved: 持有正统或纯正之见解, 信仰等的; 正统的; 纯正的; 公认的; 传统的: *an ~ member of the Church;* 正统教会的教友; *~ beliefs;* 正统的信仰; *~ behaviour.* (公认的)正当的行为。⇨ **heterodox.** the O~ Church, the Eastern Church, recognizing the Patriarch of Constantinople (= *Istanbul*) as chief bishop; the communion of the autonomous churches of the Soviet Union, Romania, Greece, etc. 东正教; 希腊正教。**~·y** /-dɒksɪ; -,dɑksɪ/ *n* (*pl* **~ies**) [U] being ~; [C] ~ belief, character, practice. 正统; 纯正; 正教; 传统的说法; 正统的信仰, 性格, 常规。

or·thog·ra·phy /ɔːˈθɒɡrəfɪ; ɔrˈθɑɡrəfɪ/ *n* [U] (system of) spelling; correct or conventional spelling. 拼字(法); 正确的拼字; 传统的拼字。**or·tho·graphic** /,ɔːθəˈɡræfɪk; ,ɔrθəˈɡræfɪk/ *adj*

or·tho·paedic (also **-pedic**) /,ɔːθəˈpiːdɪk; ,ɔrθəˈpidɪk/ *adj* of the curing of deformities and diseases of bones: 矫形(畸形及骨病之治疗)的: *~ surgery.* 矫形外科; 整形科。**or·tho·paed·ics** (also 亦作 **-ped·ics**) *n* (with *sing* v) branch of surgery dealing with bone deformities and diseases. (用单数动词)矫形学。

or·to·lan /ˈɔːtələn; ˈɔrtələn/ *n* small wild bird valued as a table delicacy. 莺雀(可作美味食品)。

oryx /ˈɒrɪks US: ˈɔːr-; ˈɔrɪks/ *n* African antelope with long, straight or arching horns. 非洲大羚羊(角长而直或弯成拱形)。

Os·car /ˈɒskə(r); ˈɒskə/ *n* the annual US award for what is judged to be a great achievement in cinema: 奥斯卡金像奖(美国每年一度颁给电影艺术之伟大成就奖): *be nominated for / win an ~.* 被提名竞选(获得)奥斯卡金像奖。

os·cil·late /ˈɒsɪleɪt; ˈɑsl,et/ *vi, vt* **1** [VP2A] swing backwards and forwards as the pendulum of a clock does; (fig) waver or change between extremes of opinion, etc 来回摆动; (喻)意见等游移不定; 踌躇。**2** [VP6A] cause to swing to and fro. 使来回摆动; 使动摇。**3** (electr, of current) undergo high frequency alternations; (of radio receivers) radiate electromagnetic waves; experience interference (in reception) from this. (电学, 指电流)振荡; (指无线电接收器)发射电磁波; (接收时由于电磁波而)受干扰; 发杂音。**oscillating current,** current whose direction is periodically reversed. 振荡电流。**os·ci·la·tion** /,ɒsɪˈleɪʃn; ,ɑslˈeʃən/ *n* oscillating or being ~d; [C] one swing of a pendulum or other object or of an electric charge. 来回摆动; 振荡; (钟摆等的)一次摆动。**os·cil·lator** /-teɪtə(r); -tə/ *n* (esp) device for producing electric oscillations (eg for wireless telegraphy). (尤指)使电振荡的工具; 发振器; 振荡器(如无线电报等中所用者)。

os·cillo·graph /əˈsɪləɡrɑːf US: -ɡræf; əˈsɪlə,ɡræf/ *n* (electr) instrument for recording oscillations. (电)示波记录器(记录振荡的仪器)。

os·cillo·scope /əˈsɪləskəʊp; əˈsɪlə,skop/ *n* (electr) instrument which shows on the screen of a cathode ray tube (like a TV screen) variations of current as a wavy line. (电)示波器(在阴极射线管屏幕上, 如电视之

萤光幕, 显出波动曲线以表示电流变动之仪器)。

osier /'əʊzɪə(r) US: 'əʊʒə(r); 'oʒɚ/ n [C] kind of willow-tree, the twigs of which are used in basketwork. 一种柳树(其枝用于编结筐篮)。

os·prey /'ɒsprɪ; 'ɑsprɪ/ n (pl ~s) large kind of hawk that preys on fish. 鹗(一种食鱼的大鹰)。

osseous /'ɒsɪəs; 'ɑsɪəs/ adj consisting of bone; having a bony skeleton. 含骨的; 有骨骼的。

oss·ify /'ɒsɪfaɪ; 'ɑsə,faɪ/ vt, vi (pt, pp **-fied**) [VP 6A, 2A] (formal) make or become hard like bone; change into bone, (fig) make or become rigid, unprogressive, unable to change. (正式用语) (使)硬化如骨; (使)骨化; 成为骨; (使)僵化或不进展; (使)不改变。 **ossi·fi·ca·tion** /,ɒsɪfɪ'keɪʃn; ,ɑsəfə'keʃən/ n [U] ~ing or being ossified; that part of a structure that is ossified. 骨化; 硬化部分。

os·ten·sible /ɒ'stensəbl; ɑs'tɛnsəbl/ adj (of reasons, etc) put forward in an attempt to hide the real reason; apparent. (指理由等) 假装的; 表面的。 **os·ten·sibly** /-əblɪ; -əblɪ/ adv

os·ten·ta·tion /,ɒsten'teɪʃn; ,ɑsten'teʃən/ n [U] display (of wealth, learning, skill, etc) to obtain admiration or envy; (财富、学识、技术等的)夸耀; 虚饰; 卖弄: the ~ of the newly rich. 暴发户的夸耀。 **os·ten·ta·tious** /,ɒsten'teɪʃəs; ,ɑsten'teʃəs/ adj fond of, showing, ostentation: 好夸耀的; 招摇的; 炫耀的; 卖弄的: ~ jewellery; 外观华丽的珠宝; in an ~ manner. 以夸张的态度。 ~·ly adv

os·te·opathy /,ɒstɪ'ɒpəθɪ; ,ɑstɪ'ɑpəθɪ/ n [U] treatment of certain diseases by manipulation of the bones and muscles. 骨疗法(以按摩骨骼与肌肉以治疗某些疾病的方法); 按摩术; 骨疗术。 **os·teo·path** /'ɒstɪəpæθ; 'ɑstɪə,pæθ/ n person who practises ~. 按摩术士; 施行骨疗者。

os·tler /'ɒslə(r); 'ɑslɚ/ n (old use) stableman (man who looks after horses) at an inn. (旧用法)小旅店中的马夫。

os·tra·cize /'ɒstrəsaɪz; 'ɑstrə,saɪz/ vt [VP6A] 1 shut out from society; refuse to meet, talk to, etc: 放逐; 排斥; 摈弃: People who hold very unorthodox opinions are sometimes ~d. 持非正统意见的人有时会遭受排斥。 2 (in ancient Greece) banish by popular vote for ten or five years. (在古希腊)由公民投票放逐十年或五年; 流放。 **os·tra·cism** /-sɪzəm; -sɪzəm/ n [U] ostracizing or being ~d. 放逐; 排斥; 摈弃。

os·trich /'ɒstrɪtʃ; 'ɔstrɪtʃ/ n fast-running bird, the largest in existence, unable to fly, bred for its valuable tail feathers: 鸵鸟: have the digestion of an ~, be able to digest almost anything. 有鸵鸟那样的消化力(几乎能消化任何东西)。 ⇨ the illus at **rare**. 参看 rare 之插图。

other /'ʌðə(r); 'ʌðɚ/ adj, pron (person or thing) not already named or implied. 其他的(人或物); 另外的(人或物); 别的(人或物); 别的(人或物)。 **1 the ~**, (sing) the second of two: (单)(指两者中之第二个)另一(个): The twins are so much alike that people find it difficult to tell (the) one from the ~. 那一对孪生子彼此如此相象, 使人们难以分辨彼此。 One of them is mine; the ~ is my sister's. 两个之中一个是我的, 另一个是我姐姐(妹妹)的。 The post office is on the ~ side of the street. 邮局在街的另一边。 Where are the ~ boys? 其他的男孩子在哪儿? on the '~ hand, used (sometimes, but not always, after on the one hand) to introduce sth in contrast to an earlier statement, etc: (有时用在 on the one hand 之后, 但并非总是如此)另一方面: It's cheap, but on the ~ hand the quality is poor. 它是便宜的, 但在另一方面, 质料很差。 **2 the ~s**, (pl) when the reference is to two or more: (复)其他的(指两个或更多的人、物等); 其余的(人、物): Six of them are mine; they are ~s are John's. 其中六个是我的, 其余是约翰的。 Where are the ~s? 其他的人在哪儿? **3** (with the indef art, written and printed as one word, **an~** /ə'nʌðə(r)/ an additional (one); a different one. (与不定冠词连用, 写成或印成一个字, 即 another) 再一; 又一(个); 另一个。 ⇨ **another**. Will you have

an~ cup of tea? 你再来一杯茶好吗? I won't say an~ word about it. 我不愿再谈这件事。 I don't like this one; can you show me an~? 我不喜欢这一个; 你能给我看另外一个吗? (The pl of an~ is some/any ~s or some/any more): (another 的复数是 some/any others 或 some/any more): I don't like these. Have you any ~s/any more? 我不喜欢这些。你还有没有其他的吗? Please let me see some ~s some more. 请另外拿一些给我看。 **4** (when one member of a group is compared with any ~ member of the group, other is usu used): (当一群中某一分子与该群中其他分子比较时, 通常用 other): Green is far better as a bowler than any ~ member of the team. 身为板球投手, 格林比队里其他队员强得多。 **5** (phrases)(短语) each ~, ⇨ each(4). every ~, ⇨ all the ~s: 所有其他的: John is stupid; every ~ boy in the class knows the answer. 约翰很笨; 班上所有其他的男孩都知道这答案。 **(b)** alternate: 间隔的; 交替的: Write only on every ~ line. 务必隔行书写。 one an~, ⇨ one³ (3). one after the ~; one after an~, in succession, not together. 一个接一个地; 相继地。 ... or ~, used to suggest absence of certainty or precision: 用以表示不肯定或不精确之意: I shall be coming again some day or ~, one of these days. 我大约过几天还会再来。 I'll get there somehow or ~, by one means if not by an~. 我无论如何会到那儿。 Someone or ~ (= Some unknown person) has left the gate open. 有人没关上门。 ~ things being equal, if conditions are/were the same or alike except for the point in question: 如果其他情形都一样: O~ things being equal, Alice would marry Jim, not Tom, but Jim is poor and Tom is rich. 如果其他情形都一样, 爱丽丝会嫁给吉姆, 不会嫁给汤姆, 可是汤姆贫穷而汤姆富有。 the ~ day, a few days ago. 几天前。 **6** different: 不同的: I do not wish her ~ than she is. 我不希望她改变现状。 The question must be decided by quite ~ considerations. 这个问题必须根据完全不同的因素来决定。 ~·worldly /,ʌðə'wɜːldlɪ; 'ʌðɚ'wɝldlɪ/ adj concerned with, thinking of, another world, of sth mystic rather than with this world. 来世的; 凝想来世的; 超脱世俗的。 □ adv (= otherwise) in a different way: 用别的方法; 否则地: I could not do it ~ than hurriedly. 我只好匆忙忙地做那件事。

other·wise /'ʌðəwaɪz; 'ʌðɚ,waɪz/ adv **1** in another or different way: 用其他的方法; 不同地; 另地: You evidently think ~. 你显然有不同的想法。 He should have been working but he was ~ engaged, but he was doing sth different. 他应该已在工作, 但是他却在忙别的事。 **2** in other or different respects; in different conditions: 在其他方面; 在不同方面; 在不同的情况之下: The rent is high, but ~ the house is satisfactory. 租金昂贵, 但在其他方面这屋子还令人满意。 □ conj if not; or else: 否则; 不然: Do what you've been told; ~ you will be punished. 照所吩咐的做, 否则你将受处罚。

oti·ose /'əʊʃɪəʊs; 'oʃɪ,os/ adj (formal) serving no practical purpose; not required; functionless. (正式用语)没用处的; 无用的; 无效的。

ot·ter /'ɒtə(r); 'ɑtɚ/ n [C] fur-covered, fish-eating aquatic animal with four webbed feet and a flat tail; [U] its fur. (水)獭; 獭皮。 ⇨ the illus at **small**. 参看 small 之插图。

ot·to·man /'ɒtəmən; 'ɑtəmən/ n long cushioned seat without back or arms, often used as a box, eg for storing bedding. 无椅背和扶手而有软垫的长椅(常用做放置寝具等的箱子)。

ou·bli·ette /,uːblɪ'et; ,ublɪ'ɛt/ n secret dungeon (underground prison) with an entrance only by a trapdoor in the roof. (只有顶上有孔出入的)地下密牢。

ouch /aʊtʃ; aʊtʃ/ int used to express sudden pain. 哎唷(表示突然疼痛)!

ought /ɔːt; ɔt/ anom fin [VP7B] ~ to, (defective; no infinitive, no participles, no inflected forms; ought not is contracted to **oughtn't** /'ɔːtnt; 'ɔtnt/; for past time, ought is used with a perfect infinitive; in reported

speech, the perfect infinitive is not always necessary; *ought to = should* as found at **shall(3,8,9)).** (变化不完全的动词；无不定式，无分词，无词形变化；ought not 缩写为 oughtn't；表示过去时，ought 与完成时的不定式连用；在间接引语时，完成时的不定式并不一定需要；ought to = should，参看 shall 第 3,8,9 义）。**1** (indicating duty or obligation): *You ～ to start at once.* 你应该立刻开始。*Such things ～ not to be allowed, ～ they?* 这类事不应该准许，是吗？*'O～ I to go?'— 'Yes, I think you ～ (to).'* '我应该去吗？'——'是的，我认为你应该去.' *You ～ to have done that earlier.* 你早就应该做那事了。*I told him (that) he ～ to do it,* ie now, or in future. 我对他说他应该去做。*I told him (that) he ～ to have done it,* ie in the past. 我对他说他早就应该去做了。**2** (indicating what is advisable, desirable or right): (表示适当、合意或应该): *There ～ to be more buses during the rush hours.* 在上下班交通拥挤的时刻，公共汽车应增加班次。*You ～* (ie I advise you) *to see that new film at the Odeon.* 你应该去看在奥登电影院上映的那部新影片。*Coffee ～ to be drunk while it is hot.* 咖啡应该趁热喝。*Your brother ～ to have been a doctor.* 你的哥哥(弟弟)过去应该学医才对。**3** (indicating probability): (表示可能性): *If he started at nine, he ～ to be here now.* 假如他在九点出发的话，现在大概到达这儿了。*That ～ to be enough fish for three people, I think.* 我想大概有够三个人吃的鱼。*Harry ～ to win the race.* 哈里可能会在这场竞赛中获胜。

ouija /'wiːdʒə, 'wiːdʒə/ *n* '～(-board), board lettered with the alphabet, and with other signs, used in seances to obtain messages said to come from the spirits of the dead. 灵应盘（写有字母及其他符号的板，降神会时用作传达所谓来自亡魂的讯息）。

ounce /auns; auns/ *n* one sixteenth of a pound avoirdupois or one twelfth of a pound troy. 盎斯；英两；唡(常衡为 1/16 磅，金衡为 1/12 磅)。⇨ **App 5.** 参看附录五。

our /'aːr), 'auər; auɾ/ *adj* of or belonging to us, that we are concerned with, etc: 我们的；属于我们的: *We have done our share.* 我们已经做完我们那一份。**Our Father,** God, 天父(上帝)。**Our Lady,** the Virgin Mary. 圣母玛利亚。**Our Lord,** Jesus Christ. 我们的主(耶稣基督)。

ours /'aːz, 'auəz; auɾz/ *pron, pred adj*(the one or ones) belonging to us: 我们的(东西)；属于我们的(东西): *This house is ～.* 这幢房子是我们的。*Don't stay at their house; stay at ～.* 不要住在他们家；住在我们家。*O～ is larger than theirs.* 我们的比他们的大。*Let me show you some of ～.* 我给你看一些我们的。*This dog of ～ never wins any prizes.* 我们的这只狗从没有得到任何奖。*The land became ～ by purchase.* 那块地经购买而成为我们的。

our·selves /aːr'selvz, auə'-; auɾ'selvz/ *pron* **1** (reflex): (反身)我们自己: *It's no use worrying ～ about that.* 我们为那件事着急是没用的。*We shall give ～ the pleasure of visiting you soon.* 我们不久将很高兴去拜访你。**2** (emphat): (强势语): *We ～ have often made that mistake / We've often made that mistake ～.* 我们自己常常犯那个错误。*We'd better go and see the house (for) ～,* not be content to rely upon what others say. 我们最好亲自去看一看那幢房子(不要听信别人所说的就认为满意)。**(all) by ～, (a)** without help. 无他人帮助的。**(b)** alone, without company: 单独的；无他人在一起的: *Come in; we're all by ～,* there are no visitors, etc. 进来，我们没有外人。

oust /aust; aust/ *vt* [VP6A, 14] ～ *sb (from),* drive or push (sb) out (from his employment, position, etc): 驱逐(某人)；赶走(某人): *～ a rival from office.* 罢黜政敌对者。

out /aut; aut/ *adv part* (For special uses in combination with *vv,* ⇨ the *v* entries. Specimens only are given here.) (与动词连用的特殊用法，参看各动词。此处仅提

供一些范例)。**1** away from, not in or at, a place, the usual or normal condition, etc: 离去；在外；出外: *go out;* 出外; *run out;* 跑出; *walk out;* 走出; *take sb out;* 带某人出去; *find one's way out;* 想出办法来; *lock sb out;* 把某人锁在外面; *throw sth out.* 把某物丢出。*Out you go!* Go out! 滚出去! *Out with it!* Bring it out! Say it! 把它拿走! 坦白说出! 从实招来! **2** (with *be,* various meanings): (与 be 连用，表不同的含义): *Mrs White is out,* not at home. 怀特太太不在家。*The manager is out,* not in the office. 经理出去了。*The dockers are out again,* on strike. 码头工人又罢工了。*The book I wanted was out,* ie had been borrowed; was not in the library. 我要的那一本书已被借走了。*The tide is out,* low. 潮退了。*The ship was four days out from Lisbon,* had sailed from Lisbon four days earlier. 那艘船已离开里斯本四天了。*The Socialist party was out,* out of office; not in power. 社会党下台了。*Short skirts are out,* not fashionable. 短裙过时了。**be out and about,** (of a person who has been in bed through illness or injury) able to get up, go outdoors, etc. (指因病或受伤卧床的人)能起床走动。**3** (in various phrases to indicate absence from home): (在不同的短语中表示不在家): *We don't go out much.* 我们不常外出。*Let's have an evening out,* eg at a cinema or discotheque, or having dinner at a restaurant, etc. 我们出去玩一个晚上吧（如看电影，去狄斯科科舞厅跳舞或吃馆子等）。**4** (with *advv* and *adv* phrases, to emphasize the idea of distance): (与副词及副词短语连用，强调距离观念): *He lives out in the country.* 他住在很远的乡下。*My brother is out in Australia.* 我的哥哥(弟弟)远在澳大利亚。*He lived out East for many years.* 他远在东方住过许多年。*The fishing boats are all out at sea.* 所有渔船都出海了。*What are you doing out there?* 你在那里做什么? **5** (indicating liberation from confinement or restraint; into the open; exposed; discovered): (表示脱离限制或约束; 公开; 暴露; 被发现): *The secret is out,* discovered, known. 秘密泄露了。*The apple blossom is out,* open. 苹果花开了。*The sun is out,* not hidden by cloud. 太阳出来了。*His new book is out,* published. 他的新书出版了。*There's a warrant out* (ie issued) *against him.* 逮捕他的拘票已经发出。*Out with it!* Tell the news! Explain it! etc, according to context. 说出来呀! 讲讲看! 从实招来! (此等含义视上下文而定)。*It's the best game out,* the best ever invented. 这是最好的策略。**6** (indicating exhaustion extinction): (表示耗尽，消灭): *The fire/gas/candle, etc is out,* not burning. 火(煤气，蜡烛等)熄灭了。*The fire has burnt out.* 火已经烧完了。*The lease/copyright is out,* has reached the end of its term. 租约(著作权)到期了。*The warships steamed towards the enemy with all lights out.* 军舰熄灭全部灯火向敌方驶去。*Put that cigarette out!* 把香烟熄掉! *The wind blew the candles out.* 风把蜡烛吹灭了。*The candle blew out.* 蜡烛吹灭了。**7** (to or at an end; completely) (used with many *vv,* as): (结束; 完全地)(与许多动词连用，如): *hear sb out;* 听完某人的话; *work out a problem;* 解决一个难题; *supplies running out;* 供应品快完了; *fight it out,* settle the dispute by fighting. 决斗以解决争端。*I'm tired out.* 我精疲力竭了。*He'll be here before the week is out.* 本星期内他会来这儿。*Let her have her sleep out,* have all the sleep she needs. 让她睡个够。**cry one's eyes out,** continue crying until this brings relief. 痛哭。**have it out with sb,** ⇨ **have¹(9). out and out,** thoroughly: surpassingly: 完全的(地); 彻底的(地); 超越的(地): *He's a crook out and out /an out-and-out crook.* 他是个十足的恶棍。**out and away,** by far: 远; 甚: *I was out and away the handsomest man in the room.* 我是房间里最漂亮的男人。**8** (indicating error): (表示错误): *I'm out in my calculations/reckoning.* 我的计算错了。*We're ten pounds out in our accounts.* 我们把帐算错了十英镑。*You're not far out,* not much in error; almost right. 你几乎没什么错误。*Your guess was a long way out,* badly in error. 你的猜测差太远了。*You've put me out,* distracted me, upset the thread of my ideas, etc. 你分

散了我的注意力。*My watch is five minutes out* (more usu *five minutes slow or fast*). 我的表差了五分钟(较常用 slow 或 fast 代替 out, 表示慢或快五分钟)。**9** (indicating clearness or loudness): (表示清楚或响亮): *call/cry/shout out;* 大声叫(嚷,喊); *say sth out loud,* in a loud voice; 大声把某事说出来; *speak out,* clearly, or without hesitation; 明白地说; 直截了当地说出; *bring out* (= make clearer) *the meaning of a paragraph by paraphrasing it;* 用意译把一段的意思写出来; *tell sb sth straight out/right out,* without keeping anything back, without ambiguity. 明白而彻底地将某事告诉人。**10** (in phrases) (用于短语中) *be out for,* be engaged in seeking, interested in obtaining: 企求; 想获得: *I'm not out for compliments.* 我并不想得到称赞。*He's out for your blood,* anxious to attack you. 他要打你。*out to+inf,* trying or hoping to: 企图; 希望: *I'm not out* (= It is not my aim) *to reform the world.* 我并不企图改革世界。*The firm is out to* capture the Canadian market. 这公司有意获得加拿大市场。*all out,* exerting the maximum power or effort: 全力地: *His new car does 80 miles an hour when it's going all out.* 他的新车全速行驶时每小时跑八十英里。*What is needed is an all-out effort.* 所需要的是全力以赴。**11** (cricket) (of a batsman) no longer batting; having been bowled, caught, etc: (板球) (指击球员)出局; 退场: *The captain was out for three.* 队长出局三次。*Kent all out, 137,* innings ended for 137 runs. 肯特队赛毕, 获得 137 分。**12 out of,** *prep* (contrasted with *in* and *into*. ⇨ the *n* and *v* entries for special uses, eg *out of date* at **date¹**(3). *out of the way* at **way**(2).) (与 in 及 into 相对。特殊用法参看连用的名词及动词冠条目, 例如 date¹ 第 3 义之 out of date, way 第 2 义之 out of the way。) **(a)** (of place): (指地点): *Fish cannot live out of water.* 鱼离水便不能活。*Mr Green is out of town this week.* 格林先生这星期不在城里。*This plant is not found out of* (= is found only in) *a small area in Central Asia.* 这种植物只在亚洲中部一小片地区才有。**(b)** (of movement): (指动作): *He walked out of the shop.* 他从店铺里走出来。*He jumped out of bed.* 他从床上跳下来。*We pulled the cart out of the ditch.* 我们把车子拖出壕沟。**(c)** (indicating motive or cause): (表示动机或原因): *It was done out of mischief/spite.* 这是由于恶作剧(恶意)所造成的。*They helped us out of pity/kindness.* 他们基于同情(仁慈)而帮助我们。*She asked out of curiosity.* 她只是出于好奇而探问。**(d)** from among: 从⋯中: *Choose one out of these ten.* 从这十个当中挑选一个。*It happens in nine cases out of ten.* 十次有九次如此。*This is only one instance out of several.* 这不过是若干例子中的一个。**(e)** by the use of: 用: 利用: 从: *The hut was made out of old planks.* 这小屋是用旧木板造的。*She made a hat out of bits of old material.* 她用零星旧布料做了一顶帽子。*Can good ever come out of evil?* 恶能生善吗? **(f)** without: 无; 不; 没有: *out of breath,* breathless; 喘不过气来; *out of work,* unemployed; 失业; *out of patience;* 不耐烦; *(born) out of wedlock,* of unmarried parents. 非婚生的; 私生的; 庶出的。*We're out of tea/petrol,* We have no tea/petrol left. 我们没有茶叶(汽油)了。*This book is out of stock,* There are no copies left in the shop. 这本书卖完了(没有存货了)。**(g)** (indicating condition): (表示情况): *out of fashion;* 不流行; *out of control;* 失去控制; *out of order;* 坏了; 发生故障; 出毛病; 弄乱; *out of danger.* 脱离危险。⇨ the *n* entries. 参看各短语中的名词。**(h)** (indicating origin or source): (表示起源或来源): *a scene out of a play;* 剧里的一场(景); *drink out of a cup/a bottle;* 从一只杯(瓶)里喝; *copy sth out of a book;* 从一本书里抄录某些东西; *steps cut out of the solid rock;* 由坚固岩石雕成的梯级; *paid for out of the housekeeping money;* 由家用款项开支的; *a dog and a cat eating out of the same dish.* 一只狗和一只猫同用一个盘子吃东西。**(i)** (indicating result): (表示结果): *talk sb out of doing sth,* talk to him with the result that he does not do it; 劝某人不做某事; *reason sb out of his fears;* 说服某人使他不再恐

惧; *cheat sb out of his money;* 骗走某人的钱; (colloq) (口) *be done* (= cheated) *out of sth;* 被骗去某物; *frighten sb out of his wits.* 吓得某人不知所措。**(j)** at a certain distance from: 距; 离: *The ship sank ten miles out of Singapore.* 该船在距新加坡十英里处沉没了。*out of it,* **(a)** not invited to be a member of a party, etc; sad for this reason: 未被邀请; 因未被邀请而难过: *She felt out of it as she watched the others set off on the picnic.* 当她看着别人出发去野餐时, 因为自己未被邀请而感到难过。**(b)** not concerned with, not involved in, sth: 与某事物无关; 不牵连在内: *It's a dishonest scheme and I'm glad to be out of it.* 那是个阴谋, 我很高兴自己与它无关。**13** (used as *n*) (用作名词) *the ins and (the) outs,* **(a)** those in office and those out of office; the Government and the Opposition. 执政党与在野党; 政府与反对党。**(b)** the details (of procedure, etc). (程序等的)细节。□ *vt* (sl or colloq) eject by force. (俚或口) 驱逐; 赶走。

out·back /'autbæk; 'autbæk/ *adj, n* (eg in Australia) (of) the more remote and sparsely populated areas. (澳大利亚)偏僻而人口稀少的地区(的); 内陆(的); 内地(的)。

out·bal·ance /aut'bæləns; aut'bæləns/ *vt* [VP6A] weigh down; outweigh. 重于; 重量上胜过; 比⋯来得重要。

out·bid /aut'bɪd; aut'bɪd/ *vt* (**-dd-**) (*pt, pp* **-bid**) [VP6A] go beyond in bidding; bid higher than (another person) at an auction, etc. 出价或叫牌超过; (拍卖等中)出价高于(他人)。

out·board /'autbɔːd; 'autˌbɔrd/ *attrib adj* placed on or near the outside of a ship or boat. 在船外的; 舷外的。～ **motor** *n* detachable engine that is mounted at the stern, outside the boat. 装于船尾外的马达。

out·bound /'autbaund; 'autˌbaund/ *adj* (of a ship) outward bound; going away from a home port. (指船)往外地的; 离开船籍港的。

out·brave /aut'breɪv; aut'brev/ *vt* [VP6A] defy: 奋勇抵抗; 以勇气胜过: ～ *the storm.* 勇敢地抵抗暴风雨。

out·break /'autbreɪk; 'autˌbrek/ *n* [C] breaking out: 爆发; 发生: *an ～ of anger/fever/hostilities.* 发怒(发烧; 开战)。

out·build·ing /'autbɪldɪŋ; 'autˌbɪldɪŋ/ *n* building, eg a shed or stable, separate from the main building: (与正屋分开的)附属建筑物(如棚或畜舍): 库房: *a ten-roomed farmhouse, with useful ～s.* 一幢十间房的农舍, 附有若干有用的库房。

out·burst /'autbɜːst; 'autˌbɜst/ *n* [C] bursting out (of steam, energy, laughter, anger, etc). (蒸气、能量、笑声、怒气等的)爆发; 突发。

out·cast /'autkɑːst *US:* -kæst; 'autˌkæst/ *n, adj* (person or animal) driven out from home or society; homeless and friendless. 被逐出家庭或社会的(人或动物); 流浪者; 无家可归且无友的; 被逐出的。

out·caste /'autkɑːst *US:* -kæst; 'autˌkæst/ *n, adj* (eg in India) (person) having lost, or been expelled from, or not belonging to, a caste. (在印度等地)失去阶级的(人); 被驱出阶级的(人); 无种姓的(人)。

out·class /aut'klɑːs *US:* -'klæs; aut'klæs/ *vt* [VP6A] be much better than; surpass: 远胜过; 远超过: *He was ～ed from the start of the race,* His competitors were much better. 比赛一开始他就落后许多。

out·come /'autkʌm; 'autˌkʌm/ *n* [C] effect or result of an event, or of circumstances. 结果; 成果; 结局。

out·crop /'autkrɒp; 'autˌkrɑp/ *n* [C] that part of a layer or vein (of rock, etc) which can be seen above the surface of the ground. (岩石等)露出地面的部分; 露出地面的地层或矿层; 露头。

out·cry /'autkraɪ; 'autˌkraɪ/ *n* (*pl* **-cries**) **1** (恐惧、警告等的)大声喊叫; 尖叫。**2** [C, U] public protest (*against* sth). (指)公开反对(与某事物)。后接某事物)。

out·dated /aut'deɪtɪd; aut'detɪd/ *adj* made out of date (by the passing of time). 过时的; 不流行的。

out·dis·tance /aut'dɪstəns; aut'dɪstəns/ *vt* [VP6A]

travel faster than, and leave behind: 在行进上快过; 超过; 把⋯抛在后头: *Tom ~d all his competitors in the mile race.* 汤姆在一英里赛跑中胜过所有竞争者。

out·do /ˌaʊtˈduː/ *vt* (*3rd person sing pres t* **-does** /-ˈdʌz; -ˈdʌz/, *pt* **-did** /-ˈdɪd; -ˈdɪd/, *pp* **-done** /-ˈdʌn; -ˈdʌn/) [VP6A] do more or better than: 胜过; 优于: *Not to be outdone* (ie not wanting to let someone do better than he himself had done), *he tried again.* 为了不让别人胜过自己, 他再试一次。

out·door /ˈaʊtdɔː(r); ˈaʊtˌdor/ *attrib adj* done, existing, used, outside a house or building: 户外的; 在户外的; 用于户外的: *leading an ~ life,* eg of a person fond of open-air activities and sport; 过着户外的生活 (如指某人喜欢户外活动和运动); *~ dress/clothes,* worn outside the house; 户外服装(衣服); *~ sports* (cf 参较 *indoor games*) 户外运动。

out·doors /ˌaʊtˈdɔːz; ˈaʊtˈdorz/ *adv* in the open air; outside: 在户外; 户外: *It's cold ~.* 屋外寒冷。*In hot countries it's possible to sleep ~.* 在炎热的国家里可以睡在屋外。*Farm workers spend most of their time ~.* 农场工人大部分时间在户外。

outer /ˈaʊtə(r); ˈaʊtə/ *adj* of or for the outside, ⇨ **inner**; farther from the middle or inside: 外的; 外面的; 外部的; 外边的: *~ garments.* 外衣。⇨ **underwear**; *the ~ suburbs,* 郊外; *journeys to ~ space,* eg to the planet Mars; 太空旅行(例如前往火星); *the ~ man,* his personal appearance, dress, etc. 人的外表; 外貌。'**~most** /-məʊst; -most/ *adj* farthest from the inside or centre. 最外的; 离内面或中心最远的。

out·face /ˌaʊtˈfeɪs; aʊtˈfes/ *vt* [VP6A] face boldly; stare at (sb) until he turns his eyes away; cause (sb) to be embarrassed. 大胆地面对; 逼视(某人)直至其眼睛转开; 使(某人)局促不安。

out·fall /ˈaʊtfɔːl; ˈaʊtˌfɔl/ *n* place where water falls or flows out (of a lake, river, etc); outlet; river mouth. (湖泊, 河流等的)出口; 排泄口; 河口。

out·field /ˈaʊtfiːld; ˈaʊtˈfild/ *n* (usu 通常作 **the ~**) (cricket and baseball) part of the field farthest from the batsmen; the fielders there. (板球及棒球)外场; 外野; 外场员; 外野手。**~er** n

out·fight /ˌaʊtˈfaɪt; aʊtˈfaɪt/ *vt* (*pt, pp* **-fought** /-ˈfɔːt; -ˈfɔt/) [VP6A] fight better than: 战胜; 打败: *The champion outfought his opponent.* 那位卫冕者打败了他的对手。

out·fit /ˈaʊtfɪt; ˈaʊtˌfɪt/ *n* [C] all the clothing or articles needed for a purpose: (为某一目的所需要的)服装; 装备; 用具: *a camping ~,* tent, etc; 露营装备; *a boy's ~ for school;* 男孩上学的用具; *a carpenter's ~,* his tools, etc. 木匠的工具。□ *vt* (**-tt-**) fit out (chiefly in the *pp* 主要用过去分词形式 **~ted**). 装备。**~ter** n shopkeeper selling clothes. 售卖服装的商人。

out·flank /ˌaʊtˈflæŋk; aʊtˈflæŋk/ *vt* [VP6A] go or pass round the flank of (the enemy): 包围(敌人)的侧翼; 包抄: *an ~ing movement.* 包围侧翼的调动。

out·flow /ˈaʊtfləʊ; ˈaʊtˌflo/ *n* [C] flowing out: 流出; 外流: *an ~ of water/bad language;* 水的流出(滔滔不绝的粗话); *the ~ of gold bullion.* 金块外流。

out·fox /ˌaʊtˈfɒks; aʊtˈfaks/ *vt* [VP6A] get the better of by being cunning. 以计胜过。

out·go /ˈaʊtgəʊ; ˈaʊtˌgo/ *n* (*pl* **~es** /-gəʊz; -goz/) (opp of *income*) that which goes out or is paid out; expenditure. (为 *income* 之反义词)消耗; 支出; 付出; 开支。

out·go·ing /ˈaʊtgəʊɪŋ; ˈaʊtˌgoɪŋ/ *adj* (attrib only) going out; leaving: (仅用作该词)外出的; 离开的: *the ~ tenant,* the one who is giving up the house, etc; 即将迁出的房客; *an ~ ship/tide.* 离港出航的船(退落的潮水)。**out·go·ings** *n pl* expenditure; outlay. 支出; 开支。

out·grow /ˌaʊtˈgrəʊ; aʊtˈgro/ *vt* (*pt* **-grew** /-ˈgruː; -ˈgru/, *pp* **-grown** /-ˈgrəʊn; -ˈgron/) [VP6A] grow too large or too tall for, eg one's clothes; grow faster or taller than, eg one's brother; leave behind, as one

grows older (bad habits, childish interests, opinions, etc): 长得太大或太高而不适于(原有的衣服); 长得比(本人的哥哥等)更快或更高; 因长大而放弃(坏习惯, 儿时的兴趣, 幼稚的意见等): *~ one's strength,* grow too quickly (during childhood), so that the health suffers. 个子长得太快而体力赶不上。

out·growth /ˈaʊtgrəʊθ; ˈaʊtˌgroθ/ *n* [C] 1 natural development or product. 自然的发展; 自然的产物。2 that which grows out of sth; offshoot: 生出之物; 枝条; 分枝: *an ~ on a tree.* 树的分枝。

out·herod /ˌaʊtˈherəd; aʊtˈherəd/ *vt* [VP6A] *~ Herod,* be more cruel, violent, etc than King Herod (ruler of Palestine when Jesus was born). 比希律王更暴虐(希律是耶稣诞生时巴勒斯坦的统治者)。

out·house /ˈaʊthaʊs; ˈaʊtˌhaʊs/ *n* (*pl* **-houses** /-haʊzɪz; -ˌhaʊzɪz/) small building adjoining the main building (eg a shed, barn, or stable); (US) outdoor lavatory. 附属的建筑物(如棚, 仓, 畜舍); 库房; (美)户外厕所。

out·ing /ˈaʊtɪŋ; ˈaʊtɪŋ/ *n* [C] holiday away from home; pleasure trip: 出外度假; 远足; 旅行: *go for an ~;* 去远足; *an ~ to the seaside.* 到海滨小游。

out·land·ish /aʊtˈlændɪʃ; aʊtˈlændɪʃ/ *adj* looking or sounding odd, strange or foreign: 看起来或听起来怪异的; 古怪的; 异国风格的: *~ dress/behaviour/ideas.* 奇装异服(怪异的行为; 怪主意)。**~·ly** *adv* **~·ness** n

out·last /ˌaʊtˈlɑːst *US:* -ˈlæst; aʊtˈlæst/ *vt* [VP6A] last or live longer than. 比⋯耐久; 比⋯活得长。

out·law /ˈaʊtlɔː; ˈaʊtˌlɔ/ *n* (hist) person punished by being placed outside the protection of the law; criminal. (史)被剥夺法律保障的人; 罪犯; 亡命之徒。□ *vt* [VP6A] make (sb) an ~; drive out from society. 使(某人)失去法律保障; 将(某人)逐出社会。**~·ry** /ˈaʊtlɔːrɪ; ˈaʊtˌlɔrɪ/ *n* [U] being an ~; being **~ed.** 逐出法外; 被放逐; 法律保障的丧失。

out·lay /ˈaʊtleɪ; ˈaʊtˌle/ *n* [U] ~ (**on**), spending; laying out money; [C] sum of money that is spent: 开支; 花费; 费用; 花费数目: *a large ~ on / for scientific research.* 科学研究的大量费用。

out·let /ˈaʊtlet; ˈaʊtˌlet/ *n* ~ (**for**), 1 way out for water, steam, etc: (水流、蒸气等的)出口; 出路: *an ~ for water;* 进水口; *the ~ of a lake.* 湖泊的出水口。2 (fig) means of or occasion for releasing (one's feelings, energies, etc): (喻)发泄(情感, 精力等)的方法或机会: *Children need an ~ for their energies.* 孩子们需要发泄精力的机会。

out·line /ˈaʊtlaɪn; ˈaʊtˌlaɪn/ *n* [C] 1 line(s) showing shape or boundary: 外形; 轮廓: *an ~ map of Great Britain;* 大不列颠的略图; *draw sth in ~.* 画某物的轮廓。2 statement of the chief facts, points, etc: 要点; 大纲; 纲要: *an ~ for an essay/a lecture;* 一篇短论(演讲)的要点; *An O~ of European History,* title of a book with a summary of the chief events, etc. 欧洲史大纲。□ *vt* [VP6A] draw in ~; give an ~ of: 画⋯的轮廓; 叙述⋯的要点: *~ Napoleon's Russian campaign.* 概述拿破仑的征俄战役。

out·live /ˌaʊtˈlɪv; aʊtˈlɪv/ *vt* [VP6A] 1 live longer than: 活得比⋯长久。*~ one's wife.* 比妻子活得久。2 live until sth is forgotten: 时久而淡忘了耻辱: *~ a disgrace.* 时久而淡忘了耻辱。

out·look /ˈaʊtlʊk; ˈaʊtˌlʊk/ *n* 1 view on which one looks out: (所眺望之)景色; 光景: *a pleasant ~ over the valley;* 山谷的宜人景色; *an ~ on to roofs and chimneys.* 看得见屋顶和烟囱的景色。2 what seems likely to happen: 展望; 前途; 远景: *a bright ~ for trade;* 商业的光明远景; (weather forecast): (气象预报): *further ~, dry and sunny.* 未来天气展望, 干燥而晴朗。3 person's way of looking at sth: 对事物的看法: *a man with a narrow ~ on life.* 人生观狭窄的人。

out·lying /ˈaʊtlaɪɪŋ; ˈaʊtˌlaɪɪŋ/ *adj* far from the centre: 远距的; 远离中心的: *~ villages, with poor communications.* 交通不便的边远村庄。

out·man·oeuvre (US = -ma·neu·ver) /ˌautmə-ˈnuːvə(r); ˌautməˈnuvə/ vt [VP 6 A] overcome, get the better of, by being superior in manoeuvring. 以战略取胜；以谋略取胜。

out·march /ˌautˈmaːtʃ; autˈmartʃ/ vt [VP 6 A] surpass by marching faster or longer. 以行进较快或较久而超过；赶过。

out·match /ˌautˈmætʃ; autˈmætʃ/ vt [VP 6 A] be more than a match for; excel: 胜过；超过；优于: be ~ed in skill and endurance. 技术与耐力不如人。

out·moded /ˌautˈməudıd; autˈmodıd/ adj out of fashion. 过时的；不流行的。

out·most /ˈautməust; ˈaut‚most/ adj = outermost.

out·num·ber /ˌautˈnʌmbə(r); autˈnʌmbə/ vt [VP 6 A] be greater in number than. 数量上胜过；比…多。

out-of-date /ˌaut əv deıt; ˈautəvˈdet/ adj not modern; not fashionable: 过时的；不流行的: ~ styles /methods / slang. 过时的式样(方法,俚语)。

out-of-door /ˌaut əv ˈdɔː(r); ˈautəvˈdor/ attrib adj = outdoor.

out-of-doors /ˌaut əv ˈdɔːz; ˈautəvˈdorz/ adv = outdoors.

out-of-the-way /ˌaut əv ðə ˈweı; ˈautəvðəˈwe/ adj 1 remote; secluded: 荒僻的; 对外隔绝的; 人迹罕至的: an ~ cottage. 一个偏远的村舍。 2 not commonly known: 不寻常的; 非一般人所知的: ~ items of knowledge. 一些不寻常的知识。

out·patient /ˈautpeıʃnt; ˈautˌpeʃənt/ n person visiting a hospital for treatment but not staying there. 不住院的病人; 门诊病人。

out·play /ˌautˈpleı; autˈple/ vt [VP 6 A] play better than: (在比赛中) 打败; 胜过: The English team was ~ed by the Brazilians. 英国队给巴西队打败。

out·point /ˌautˈpɔınt; autˈpɔınt/ vt [VP 6 A] (in boxing, etc) score more points than; defeat on points: (拳击等) 得分多于; 以积分胜过; 以点数胜过: The British champion was ~ed by the Mexican. 英国卫冕者以点数输给了墨西哥对手。

out·port /ˈautpɔːt; ˈautˌport/ n port or harbour away from a central custom-house or centre of trade. (离内于主要海关或贸易中心的) 外港。

out·post /ˈautpəust; ˈautˌpost/ n 1 (soldiers in an) observation post at a distance from the main body of troops. 前哨; 哨兵。 2 any distant settlement: 遥远的殖民地; 边远地区: an ~ of the Roman Empire. 罗马帝国的边远地区。

out·pour·ing /ˈautpɔːrıŋ; ˈautˌporıŋ/ n [C] pouring out; (usu pl) expression of feeling: 倾倒; 流出; (通常用复数)感情流露: ~s of the heart. 倾诉衷曲。

out·put /ˈautput; ˈautˌput/ n (sing only) (仅用单数) 1 quantity of goods, etc, produced: 生产量: the ~ of a gold mine /a factory; 金矿(工厂)的产量; the literary ~ of the year, the books, etc published. 本年的出版物数量。 2 power, energy, etc produced; information produced from a computer. 输出的动力、功能等; 输出物; (电子计算机资料的)输出。输出资料。 ⇨ **input.**

out·rage /ˈautreıdʒ; ˈautˌredʒ/ n [U, C] 1 (act of) extreme violence or cruelty: 极度暴烈或残忍; 残暴; 暴行: never safe from ~; 永不能免受迫害; ~s committed by a drunken mob. 一群酒鬼犯的暴行。 Would the use of H-bombs be an ~ against humanity? 使用氢弹是违背人道的暴行吗？ 2 act that shocks public opinion. 使舆论震惊的行为。 □ vt [VP 6 A] treat violently; be guilty of an ~ upon, violate: 虐待; 侵害; 触犯; 违犯: ~ public opinion; 违反民意; ~ one's sense of justice. 违反某人的正义感。

out·rage·ous /autˈreıdʒəs; autˈredʒəs/ adj shocking; very cruel, shameless, immoral: 骇人的; 暴虐的; 无耻的; 不道德的: ~ behaviour; 暴行; an ~ price /remark. 骇人的价格(谈话)。 ~·ly adv

out·range /ˌautˈreındʒ; autˈrendʒ/ vt [VP 6 A] have a greater range than: 射程超过: Our guns were ~d by

those of the enemy's cruisers. 我们大炮的射程不如敌人巡洋舰的炮。

out·rank /ˌautˈræŋk; autˈræŋk/ vt [VP 6 A] rank higher than. 阶级高于; 地位高于。

outré /ˈuːtreı US: uːˈtreı; uˈtre/ adj outside the bounds of what is conventionally correct; contrary to what is decorous: 超出常轨的; 越礼的; 过分的: ~ behaviour. 超出常轨的行为。

out·ride /ˌautˈraıd; autˈraıd/ vt (pt -rode /-ˈrəud; -ˈrod/, pp -ridden /-ˈrıdn; -ˈrıdn/) [VP 6 A] ride better or faster than: 骑得比…好或快: ~ one's pursuers. 骑得比追赶者快。

out·rider /ˈautraıdə(r); ˈautˌraıdə/ n person on horseback, a motor-cycle, etc, accompanying a vehicle, as an attendant or guard. (随护车辆的)骑马的侍从; 驾机车的马夫。

out·rig·ger /ˈautrıgə(r); ˈautˌrıgə/ n (boating) beam, spar or structure projecting from or over the side of a boat for various purposes (eg for the rowlock in a racing shell, or to give stability to a canoe or yacht). (驾舟)舷外木(铁)杆(装在舷外的梁架,帆桨或其他装置,例如赛艇上的桨架或独木舟、游艇的稳定装置);又架。 **out·rigged** /ˈautrıgd; ˈautˌrıgd/ adj (of a boat) having an ~ or ~s. (指船)有舷外装置的; 有又架的。

out·right /ˈautraıt; ˈautˌraıt/ adj 1 thorough; positive: 完全的; 确实的; 断然的: an ~ denial: 断然否认; 明白的拒绝; ~ wickedness; 十足的邪恶; an ~ manner, ie thoroughly frank. 彻底坦白的态度。 2 clear; unmistakable: 明白的; 显然的; 无疑的: On the voting for secretary, Smith was the ~ winner. 关于投票选干事, 史密斯是无疑的当选者。 □ adv 1 openly, with nothing held back: 公然地; 率直地: tell a man ~ what one thinks of his behaviour. 坦白告诉某人自己对他的行为的看法。 2 completely; at one time: 完全地; 一次: 即: buy a house ~, ie not by instalments; 一次付款买下房屋; be killed ~ by a blow. 当场一击致命。

out·rival /ˌautˈraıvl; autˈraıvl/ vt (-ll-, US also -l-) [VP 6 A] be or do better than (sb) as a rival. 竞争中胜过(某人)。

out·run /ˌautˈrʌn; autˈrʌn/ vt (pt -ran /-ˈræn; -ˈræn/, pp -run; -nn-) [VP 6 A] run faster or better than; go beyond: 跑得比…快; 跑得比…好; 超过: His ambition outran his ability, He was ambitious to do more than he was able to do. 他的野心超过了他的才能(他眼高手低)。

out·sail /ˌautˈseıl; autˈsel/ vt [VP 6 A] sail faster than. 航行得比…快。

out·set /ˈautset; ˈautˌset/ n start. 开始。 at /from the ~, at /from the beginning: 在(从)开始时: at the ~ of his career. 在他事业的初期。

out·shine /ˌautˈʃaın; autˈʃaın/ vt (pt, pp -shone /-ˈʃɒn; -ˈʃon/) [VP 6 A] shine more brightly than. 照得比…更亮。

out·side /ˌautˈsaıd; ˈautˌsaıd/ n (contrasted with inside; 与inside 相对) 1 the outer side or surface; the outer part(s): 外面; 外部: The ~ of the house needs painting. 房子外部需要油漆。 Don't judge a thing from the ~, from the external appearance. 不可凭外表判断事物。 2 at the (very) ~, at the most; at the highest reckoning: 至多; 充其量: There were only fifty people there at the ~, certainly not more than fifty. 那儿最多不过五十个人。 He earns £10000 a year at the ~. 他一年至多赚一万英镑。 □ /ˈautsaıd; ˈautˌsaıd/ adj (or attrib use of n) (或名词用作定语) 1 of or on, nearer, the ~: 外面的; 在外面的; 外头的; 外部的: ~ repairs, ie to the ~ of a building; (建筑物的)外部修理; ~ measurements, eg of a box; (盒子等的)外部尺寸; an ~ broadcast, from a place ~ the studios. 室外广播(非在播音室中所作者)。 2 greatest possible or probable: 可能性最大的; 最可能的: an ~ estimate /price. 最高的估计(价格)。 3 not connected with or included in a group, organization, etc: 局外的; 外界的:

We shall need ~ help (= extra workers) *for this job.* 我们这项工作需要外界的协助。*She doesn't like meeting the ~ world*, people not belonging to the close circle of her family and friends. 她不喜欢与外人结识。□ *adv* on or to the ~: 在外面;在外头;在外部: *The house is painted green ~.* 那幢房子外面漆成绿色。*The car is waiting ~.* 车子在外面等着。□ *prep* **1** at or on the outer side of: 在…的外面;在…的外边: ~ *the house*; 在屋子外面; *a ship moored ~ the harbour.* 一艘停泊在港外的船。**2** beyond the limits of: 超出…的范围: *We cannot go ~ the evidence.* 我们不能超出证据的范围。*He has no occupation ~ his office work.* 除了上班以外,他没有别的工作。

out·sider /ˌaʊtˈsaɪdə(r); ˌaʊtˈsaɪdɚ/ *n* **1** person who is not, or who is not considered to be, a member of a group, society, etc; (colloq) ill-mannered person not socially acceptable. 非会员;局外人;(口)社交上不受欢迎的粗俗人。**2** (racing) horse that is thought to have little chance of winning a race. (赛马)获胜机会甚微的马;冷门马。

out·size /ˈaʊtsaɪz; ˈaʊtˌsaɪz/ *adj* (esp of articles of clothing, etc) larger than the usual size. (尤指衣服等)大于通常尺码的;特大的。

out·skirts /ˈaʊtskɜːts; ˈaʊtˌskɝts/ *n pl* borders or outlying parts (esp of a town): 边界;(尤指)市郊: *on the ~ of Lille.* 在里尔的郊区。

out·smart /ˌaʊtˈsmɑːt; aʊtˈsmɑrt/ *vt* [VP 6 A] (colloq) be smarter (= cleverer, more cunning) than. (口)比…更聪明;以机智胜过。

out·span /ˌaʊtˈspæn; aʊtˈspæn/ *vi, vt* (**-nn-**) [VP 6A, 2A] (S Africa) unyoke; unharness. (南非)解除牛轭;卸下马具。

out·spoken /ˌaʊtˈspəʊkən; ˈaʊtˈspokən/ *adj* saying freely what one thinks; frank: 直言的;坦白的: ~ *comments;* 坦率的批评; *be ~ in one's remarks.* 说话直率。~**·ly** *adv* ~**·ness** *n*

out·spread /ˌaʊtˈspred; aʊtˈspred/ *adj* spread or stretched out: 张开的;伸开的: *with ~ 'arms;* 伸开双臂地; *with arms ~.* 两臂伸开着。

out·stand·ing /ˌaʊtˈstændɪŋ; ˈaʊtˈstændɪŋ/ *adj* **1** in a position to be easily noticed; attracting notice: 杰出的;显著的;引人注意的: *the ~ features of the landscape;* 风景特别引人注意之处; *an ~ landmark.* 显著的陆标。*The girl who won the scholarship was quite ~.* 那个获得奖学金的女孩是相当杰出的。**2** (of problem, work, payments, etc) still to be attended to: (指问题,工作,债务等)尚未解决的: ~ *debts / liabilities;* 未偿的债务; *a good deal of work still ~.* 尚待完成的一大堆工作。**3** /ˈaʊtstændɪŋ; ˈaʊtˈstændɪŋ/ sticking out: 突出的;伸出的: *a boy with big, ~ ears.* 两耳大而突出的男孩。~**·ly** *adv* to a high degree: 高度地: ~*ly intelligent.* 非常聪明。

out·station /ˈaʊtsteɪʃn; ˈaʊtˌsteʃən/ *n* remote station (2). 远方的驻所;远方支部。

out·stay /ˌaʊtˈsteɪ; aʊtˈste/ *vt* [VP 6 A] stay longer than: 居留比…长久;停留较…长久: ~ *the other guests.* 停留的时间比其他客人长久。~ *one's welcome*, stay too long, until one is no longer a welcome guest. 停留太久而令主人生厌。

out·stretched /ˌaʊtˈstretʃt; aʊtˈstrɛtʃt/ *adj* stretched or spread out: 伸开的;展开的: *with ~ arms;* 伸开双臂地; *lie ~ on the grass.* 手脚伸开地躺卧草地上。

out·strip /ˌaʊtˈstrɪp; aʊtˈstrɪp/ *vt* (**-pp-**) [VP 6 A] do better than; pass (sb) in a race, etc: 做得比…好;(在赛跑中)超过(某人): *The hare was ~ped by the tortoise.* 兔子被乌龟超过了。

out·vie /ˌaʊtˈvaɪ; aʊtˈvaɪ/ *vt* [VP6A] do better than in competition. (在竞赛中)胜过;击败。

out·vote /ˌaʊtˈvəʊt; aʊtˈvot/ *vt* [VP6A] win, obtain, more votes than. 比…得票多;票数超过。

out·ward /ˈaʊtwəd; ˈaʊtwəd/ *adj* **1** of or on the outside: 外面的;在外面的: *the ~ appearance of things;* 东西的外表; *the ~ man* (contrasted with the spiritual nature, the soul). 人的躯壳;肉体(与精神,灵魂相对)。**2** going out: 出去的;外出的: *during the ~ voyage.* 在出航期间。□ *adv* (also *adv* **out·wards** /-wədz; -wədz/) towards the outside; away from home or the centre: 向外;在外: *The two ends must be bent ~s.* 两端必须向外弯。*The ship is ~ bound,* sailing away from its home port. 这艘船是开往外埠的。~**·ly** *adv* on the surface; apparently: 表面上;外表上: *Though badly frightened she appeared ~ly calm.* 虽然大受惊吓,她外表上还是显得很镇静。

out·wear /ˌaʊtˈweə(r); aʊtˈwɛr/ *vt* (*pt* **-wore** /-ˈwɔː(r); -ˈwor/ *pp* **-worn** /-ˈwɔːn; -ˈwɔrn/) [VP6A] **1** last longer than: 比…耐穿;比…经久: *Well-made leather shoes will ~ two pairs of these cheap rubber shoes.* 做得好的皮鞋比两双这种便宜的胶鞋还耐穿。**2** wear out; use up; exhaust (esp in the *pp* when attrib): 穿破;用尽;用完;使无力或疲惫(过去分词用作定语时,尤作此解): *outworn quotations,* used so often that they no longer strike the listener or reader; 陈旧的引语; *outworn* (= out-of-date) *practices in industry.* 工业界落伍的惯例。

out·weigh /ˌaʊtˈweɪ; aʊtˈwe/ *vt* [VP6A] be greater in weight, value or importance than: 比…更重;比…更有价值;比…更重要;重量、价值或重要性超过…: *Do the disadvantages ~ the advantages?* 弊多于利吗?

out·wit /ˌaʊtˈwɪt; aʊtˈwɪt/ *vt* (**-tt-**) [VP6A] get the better of by being cleverer or more cunning than: 以机智胜过;以狡计击败: *The thief ~ted the police and got away with his loot.* 小偷以狡计骗过警察带着赃物逃跑了。

out·wore /ˌaʊtˈwɔː(r); aʊtˈwor/, **out·worn** /ˌaʊtˈwɔːn; aʊtˈwɔrn/ ⇨ **outwear**.

out·work /ˈaʊtwɜːk; ˈaʊtˌwɝk/ *n* part of a military defence system away from the centre: 军事的外围防御工事;外堡;外垒: *the ~s of a castle.* 城堡的外垒。

ouzel /ˈuːzl; ˈuzl/ *n* kinds of small bird of the thrush family. 黑鸫。

ouzo /ˈuːzəʊ; ˈuzo/ *n* [U] aniseed-flavoured Greek liqueur, drunk with water. 茴香烈酒(产于希腊,与水掺饮)。

ova /ˈəʊvə; ˈovə/ *n pl of* **ovum**.

oval /ˈəʊvl; ˈovl/ *n, adj* (plane figure or outline that is) egg-shaped; shaped like an ellipse. 卵形的;椭圆的;椭圆形。

ovary /ˈəʊvərɪ; ˈovərɪ/ *n* (*pl* **-ries**) either of the two reproductive organs in which ova are produced in female animals; seed-vessel in a plant. (雌性动物的)卵巢;(植物的)子房。⇨ **ovum**. ⇨ the illus at **flower, reproduce.** 参看 flower, reproduce 之插图。

ova·tion /əʊˈveɪʃn; oˈveʃən/ *n* [C] enthusiastic expression of welcome or approval: 热烈欢迎;大鼓掌: *The leader was given a standing ~,* The audience stood to clap, etc. 那队长指挥受到听众的起立欢呼。

oven /ˈʌvn; ˈʌvən/ *n* **1** enclosed box-like space which is heated for cooking food: 烤炉;烤箱: *Bread is baked in an ~.* 面包是在烤炉里烘成的。**2** small furnace or kiln used in chemistry, etc. (化学等方面所用的)小烘炉;小窑。'~·ware /-weə(r); -wɛr/ *n* heat-proof dishes for use in an ~: (经得起在烤箱中烘烤的)耐热盘碗。~*ware pottery.* 耐热陶器。

over[1] /ˈəʊvə(r); ˈovɚ/ *adv* (⇨ the *v* entries for special combinations, eg *give over.* Specimens only are given here.) (与动词连用的特殊用法,例如 give over,参看各动词条。本条中仅提供举例句。) **1** (indicating movement from an upright position, from one side to the other side, or so that a different view is seen, etc): (表示从直立位置倒下,从一边到另一边,或使不同之一边被看见的动作): *He fell ~ on the ice.* 他跌倒在冰上。*Don't knock that vase ~.* 不要把那只花瓶碰倒。*A slight push would send it ~.* 轻轻一推会把它弄倒。*He gave me a push and ~ I went,* I fell. 他推我一下,我就跌倒了。*Turn the patient ~ on his face and rub his back.* 把病人翻过去俯卧,按摩他的背部。*Turn ~ the page.* 把这一页翻过去。

It rolled ~ and ~, made a series of revolutions. 它一再滚动。 *He turned ~ in bed.* 他在床上翻身。 **2** (indicating motion upwards and outwards): (表示向上及向外的动作): *The milk boiled ~.* 牛奶沸腾出来了。 *He was boiling ~ with rage.* 他正在发怒。 **3** from beginning to end; through: 自始至终; 遍及: *I'll look the papers ~,* look or read through them. 我要把这些文件全部看过。 *You should think it ~,* consider the matter carefully. 你应该把它仔细考虑一下。 **4** (indicating repetition) again: (表示重复)再: *Count them ~,* a second time. 再把它们数一数。 **(all) ~ again,** a second time (from the beginning): 再一次: *He did the work so badly that I had to do it all ~ again myself.* 他把那项工作做得那么糟我自己还得再做一次。 **~ and ~ again,** repeatedly; many times: 一再地; 许多次: *I've warned you ~ and ~ again not to do that.* 我一再警告你不要做那件事。 **5** across (a street, an open space, a distance, etc): 越过(街道, 空地, 一段距离等): *Take these letters ~ to the post office.* 把这些信送到邮局去。 *Let me row you ~ to the other side of the lake.* 让我把你划到湖的那一边去。 *Ask him ~,* Ask him to come here／to pay a visit. 请他到这里来。 *He's ~ in／has gone ~ to France.* 他到法国去了。 **Come ~ and see me some time,** Come to visit me some time. 哪一天请过来看看我。 *Some wild geese have just flown ~.* 有几只雁刚刚飞过。 **~ against,** (lit or fig) (字面或喻) **(a)** opposite to. 与…相对; 在…对面。 **(b)** in contrast with. 与…相比。 **6** remaining; not used after part has been taken or used: 剩余; 余下: *Seven into thirty goes four times and two ~.* 三十除以七得四余二。 *If there's any meat (left) ~,* give it to the dog. 如果有肉剩下的话, 把它喂狗。 *I've paid all my debts and have £15 ~.* 我把欠债都还清了还剩下十五镑。 **7** in addition; in excess; more: 加之; 超过; 更多: *children of fourteen and ~;* 十四岁以上的孩子们; *10 metres and a bit ~.* 十米多一点。 **8** ended; finished; done with: 结束; 完毕; 完成: *The meeting will be ~ before we arrive if we don't hurry.* 假如我们不赶快的话, 会议在我们到达, 就已经散会了。 *The storm is ~.* 风暴已经过去了。 *His sufferings will soon be ~.* 他的痛苦不久就要过去了。 *It's all ~ with him,* He's ruined, sure to die soon, etc, according to context. 他一切都完了(垮了, 即将死亡等, 其意义视上下文而定)。 **9** more than is right, usual, wise, etc: 太过; 过份: *~ anxious;* 太焦急的; 过于忧虑的; *~ polite.* 太多礼的; 过份客气的。 *If she grieves ~ much, she may fall ill.* 假如她过度悲伤, 她可能会生病。 *He's not ~ strong,* not so strong as is desirable. 他并不太强壮。 *He has done it ~ well,* He has done it rather badly. 他做得不太好。 ⇨ **over-** below. 参看下列之 over-。 **10** (indicating transference or change from one person, party, etc to another): (表示移转或更换): *He has gone ~ to the enemy,* joined them. 他已经投向敌人。 *He made his business ~ to his son.* 他已经把事业移转给他的儿子。 *Hand that weapon to me.* 把那武器交给我。 *Over (to you)!* (in radio telegraphy, etc) It is now your turn to speak. 请回话到到! **11** on the whole surface; in all parts: 遍布; 到处: *He was aching all ~.* 他全身都痛。 *This pianist is famous all the world ~.* 这位钢琴家闻名全世界。 *Your clothes are all ~ dust／are dusty all ~.* 你的衣服到处都是灰尘。 *Paint the old name ~,* cover it with paint. 把旧名字全部用油漆涂盖起来。 *That's Smith all ~,* It's characteristic of him, what he might be expected to do. 史密斯就是这么一个人。

over² /'əuvə(r); 'ovɚ/ *prep* **1** resting on the surface of and covering, partly or completely (not, in this sense, replaceable by *above*): 在…上面(部分或全部盖着)(用在此义时, 不能以 above 代替): *He spread his handkerchief ~ his face to keep the flies off.* 他把手帕盖在脸上阻挡苍蝇。 *Spread a cloth ~ the table.* 铺一块布在桌上。 *Tie a piece of paper firmly ~ the top of the jar.* 在瓶口紧紧地扎上一张纸。 *I knocked the man's hat ~ his eyes,* so that he couldn't see. 我把那人的帽子碰到他脸上, 遮住了他的

眼睛。 **2** at or to a level higher than, but not touching (in this sense often replaceable by *above*): 在…之上(但未接触)(用作此义, 常可被 above 代替): *Attendants held a large umbrella ~／above the chief's head.* 随从们把一支大伞撑在首领的头顶上。 *The sky is ~／above our heads.* 天在我们的头顶上。 *These telegraph wires ~ the streets are ugly.* 街道上空这些电报线很难看。 *The balcony juts out ~ the street.* 阳台向大街伸展出去。 *There was a lamp ~ the table.* 桌子上方有一盏灯。 **3** (indicating superiority in rank, authority, etc): (表示等级高, 权力大等): *He reigns ~ a great empire.* 他统治一个大帝国。 *He has jurisdiction ~ three provinces.* 他管辖三个省。 *These people need a firm ruler ~ them.* 这些人民需要一个坚定的统治者管理他们。 *He has no command ~ himself／~ his passions.* 他控制不了(自己的情感)。 *Mr White is ~ me in the office.* 怀特先生在我的职位比我高。 **4** in or across every part of: 在…的各部分; 遍及…的各部分: *Snow is falling ~ the north of England.* 英格兰北部到处都在下雪。 *He is famous all ~ the world.* 他闻名全世界。 ⇨ **over¹**(11). *He has travelled all ~ Europe.* 他已经游遍欧洲。 **5** from one side to the other of; to or at the other side of: 从…一边到…的另一边; 到或在…的另一边: *He escaped ~ the frontier.* 他逃过边界了。 *She spoke to me ~ her shoulder.* 她转过头对我说话。 *Look ~ the hedge.* 看围篱的那一边。 *We heard voices from ~ the fence.* 我们听到从篱笆那一边传来的声音。 *Who lives in that house ~ the way,* on the opposite side of the road or street? 谁住在路对面的那一幢屋子里? **6** (of time): (指时间): *Can you stay ~ Sunday,* until Monday? 你能够停留在这里过了星期日再走吗? **7** so as to be ~ and on the other side of: 越过; 过到…的另一边: *climb ~ a wall;* 爬过一道墙; *jump ~ a brook.* 跳过一条小溪。 **8** (opp of *under*) more than: (为 under 之反义词) 超过: *He spoke for ~ an hour.* 他说过了一个多钟头。 *He stayed in London (for) ~ a month.* 他在伦敦停留一个多月。 *She is ~ 40 inches round the waist.* 她的腰围四十八英寸。 *The river is ~ fifty miles long.* 这条河长五十多英里。 *He's ~ fifty.* 他五十多岁了。 **~ and above,** besides; in addition to: 除…之外: *The waiters get good tips ~ and above their wages.* 侍者们除了工资外, 还有可观的小费。 **9** in connection with; while engaged in; concerning: 与…有关; 从事…之际; 关于: *He went to sleep ~ his work,* while doing it. 他在工作时睡着了。 *How long will he be ~ it?* How long will it take him to do it, get there, etc? 他要多久才会做完(到达等)? *We had a pleasant chat ~ a cup of tea,* while drinking tea. 我们一边喝茶, 一边愉快地聊天。 *We all laughed ~ the affair.* 我们都为那件事情而发笑。

over³ /'əuvə(r); 'ovɚ/ *n* (cricket) number of balls bowled in succession by each bowler in turn. (板球)每个投手一次连续所投出的球数。

over- /ˌəuvə(r), ˌovɚ/ *pref* too (much): 太(多): *~-po'lite;* 太多礼的; 太拘礼的; *~-'tired;* 太疲倦的; *~-'heated.* 加热过度的; 过度激昂的。 (Note: compounds not entered below have the same stress pattern as the examples below.) (注意: 未列在下面的复合词, 其重音型式一如以下各例。) The meanings of the *adjj* below may be obtained by putting *too* in place of *over.* 下列形容词的含义可以 too 代替 over 来表示, 即 '太过…' 之意。

ˌ~-a'bundant	ˌ~-'eager
ˌ~-'active	ˌ~-e'motional
ˌ~-am'bitious	ˌ~-en,thusi'astic
ˌ~-'anxious	ˌ~-ex'cited
ˌ~-'bold	ˌ~-fa'miliar
ˌ~-'busy	ˌ~-'fond
ˌ~-'careful	ˌ~-'full
ˌ~-'cautious	ˌ~-'generous
ˌ~-'confident	ˌ~-'greedy
ˌ~-'credulous	ˌ~-'hasty
ˌ~-'critical	ˌ~-'jealous
ˌ~-'curious	ˌ~-'modest
ˌ~-'delicate	ˌ~-'nervous

ˌ~-'proud　　　　　　ˌ~-'serious
ˌ~-'ripe　　　　　　　ˌ~-sus'picious
ˌ~-'sensitive　　　　　ˌ~-'zealous

The meanings of the *nn* below may be obtained by putting *too much* in place of *over*. 下列名词的含义可以 *too much* 代替 over 来表示,即 "太多…" 之意。

ˌ~-a'bundance　　　　ˌ~-in'dulgence
ˌ~-an'xiety　　　　　ˌ~-'payment
ˌ~-'confidence　　　　ˌ~-ˌpopu'lation
ˌ~-cre'dulity　　　　ˌ~-pro'duction
ˌ~-ex'ertion　　　　　ˌ~-'strain
ˌ~-ex'posure　　　　　ˌ~-'tolerance

The meaning of the *vv* below may be obtained by putting *too much* after the *v* in place of *over*. 下列动词 的含义可以 too much 接该动词之后代替 over 来表示, 即 "…得太过" 或 "…得太多" 之意。

ˌ~-'burden　　　　　ˌ~-'heat
ˌ~-'cook　　　　　　ˌ~-in'dulge
ˌ~-'eat　　　　　　　ˌ~-'praise
ˌ~-'emphasize　　　　ˌ~-pro'duce
ˌ~-'estimate　　　　　ˌ~-'simplify
ˌ~-ex'ert　　　　　　ˌ~-'strain
ˌ~-ex'pose　　　　　　ˌ~-'value

over·act /ˌəʊvər'ækt; 'ovɚˈækt/ *vi, vt* [VP2A, 6A] **act²(4)** in an exaggerated way: 演得过火;演得太夸张: ~*ing (in) his part.* 把他的角色演得太夸张。

over·all¹ /ˌəʊvər'ɔːl; 'ovɚˌɔl/ *adj* including every-thing; containing all: 包含一切的: *the ~ measurements of a room*; 一个房间的全部面积; *coal burnt at an ~ efficiency of only 18 per cent.* 只用百分之 十八的全效能燃烧的煤。

over·all² /'əʊvərɔːl; 'ovɚˌɔl/ *n* **1** (GB) loose-fitting garment that covers other garments (eg as worn by small children during play). (英)罩衫;罩衣(如小孩游 戏时所穿的)。 **2** (*pl*) loose-fitting trousers, with the front extended above the waist, with shoulder straps, and made of heavy, strong material, worn over other clothes to protect them from dirt, etc. (复)工作裤;工 装裤。

over·arch /ˌəʊvər'ɑːtʃ; ˌovɚ'ɑrtʃ/ *vt,vi* [VP6A,2A] form an arch (over): (在…上面)形成拱形: *Trees ~ed the road.* 树木在道路上方形成拱形。

over·arm /ˌəʊvər'ɑːm; 'ovɚˌɑrm/ *adj, adv* (sport, eg cricket) with the arm swung over the shoulder: (运动, 如板球)举臂过肩的(地): *bowling ~*; 举臂过肩地投球; *an ~ bowler.* 举臂过肩的投手。

over·awe /ˌəʊvər'ɔː; ˌovɚ'ɔ/ *vt* [VP6A] awe complete-ly; awe through great respect, etc: 使畏缩;使敬畏;威 压;威吓: ~ *sb into submission.* 使某人敬畏而屈服。

over·bal·ance /ˌəʊvə'bæləns; ˌovɚ'bæləns/ *vt, vi* **1** [VP6A, 2A] (cause to) lose balance; fall over: (使)失 去平衡;跌倒: *He ~d and fell into the water.* 他失去平衡 跌入水中。 *Don't ~ the canoe.* 不要使独木舟失去平衡。 **2** [VP6A] outweigh: 重于;价值超过;超过: *The gains ~ the losses.* 利润多于亏损。

over·bear /ˌəʊvə'beə(r); ˌovɚ'bɛr/ *vt* (*pt* **-bore** /-'bɔː(r); -'bor/, *pp* **-borne** /-'bɔːn; -'born/) [VP6A] overcome (by forcible arguments, strong force, or authority): (以有力的论据,强力,权威)压服;克服;镇服: *My objections were overborne in the argument.* 我的异 议都在辩论中被压服。 **~·ing** *adj* masterful; forcing others to one's will: 专横的;强人所从的;压倒的: *an ~ing manner.* 盛气凌人的态度。 **~·ing·ly** *adv*

over·bid /ˌəʊvə'bɪd; ˌovɚ'bɪd/ *vi, vt* (*pt, pp* **-bid**; **-dd-**) **1** [VP6A] (at an auction) bid higher than (another person). (拍卖时)出价高过(他人)。 **2** [VP6A, 2A] bid more than the value of (sth offered for sale). 出价高过(待售之物)的价值;出价过高。 **3** [VP6A, 2A] (bridge) make a higher bid than (one's partner) or than one's hand is worth, (桥牌戏)叫牌过高于(伙伴的叫 牌,或自己手上的牌力);叫牌过高。 □ *n* /'əʊvəbɪd; 'ovɚ-ˌbɪd/ act of ~ding. 出价过高;叫牌过高。

over·blown /ˌəʊvə'bləʊn; ˌovɚ'blon/ *adj* (of flowers) too fully open; past their best. (指花)开得过盛的;盛开 期已过的。

over·board /'əʊvəbɔːd; 'ovɚˌbord/ *adv* over the side of a ship or boat into the water: 越过船边落入水中: *fall/jump ~*; 从船上跌(跳)入水中; *throw sb ~*, (fig) get rid of him, stop supporting him, etc. (喻)摆脱某 人;停止支持某人;抛弃某人。

over·bore /ˌəʊvə'bɔː(r); ˌovɚ'bor/, **over·borne** /ˌəʊvə'bɔːn; ˌovɚ'born/ ⇨ **overbear**.

over·bur·den /ˌəʊvə'bɜːdn; ˌovɚˌbɚdn/ *n* surface soil, etc which must be moved away to get at coal, etc underneath. 地层表土(采矿时必须挖去的地表土石层)。 □ *vt* [VP6A] burden too heavily: 使负担过重;使装载 太多: ~*ed with grief.* 悲伤过度。

over·call /ˌəʊvə'kɔːl; ˌovɚ'kɔl/ *vt, vi* = **overbid(3)**.

over·capi·tal·ize /ˌəʊvə'kæpɪtəlaɪz; 'ovɚ'kæpətl-ˌaɪz/ *vt* fix or estimate the capital of (a company) too high. 将(某一公司)的资本定得或估计过高。 **over·capi-tal·iz·ation** /ˌəʊvəˌkæpɪtəlaɪ'zeɪʃn US: -lɪ'z-; 'ovɚ-ˌkæpətlɪ'zeʃən/ *n*

over·cast /ˌəʊvə'kɑːst US: -'kæst; 'ovɚˌkæst/ *adj* (of the sky) darkened (as) by clouds; (fig) gloomy; sad. (指天空)因多云而阴暗的;多云的; 阴沉的; (喻)忧郁 的;悲哀的。 □ *n* (*sing only*) cloud-covered sky: (仅作 单数)多云的天;密云: *Breaks in the ~ will give sunny periods.* 密云中,偶尔出现阳光;阴偶晴。

over·charge /ˌəʊvə'tʃɑːdʒ; 'ovɚ'tʃɑrdʒ/ *vt, vi* **1** [VP6A, 2A] charge (sb) too high a price: (向某人)索 价太高: *We were ~d for the eggs.* 我们的鸡蛋买贵了。 *That grocer never ~s.* 那个杂货商从来不乱索价。 **2** [VP 6A] fill or load too heavily: 使装填过多; 使装载过多; 使超载: ~ *a gun;* 使枪炮弹药装填过多; ~ *an electric circuit.* 使电路荷电太多。 □ *n* /'əʊvətʃɑːdʒ; 'ovɚ'tʃɑrdʒ/ [C] charge that is too high or great, eg of electric current, explosive or for a purchase. 荷电太多;超载;索 价太高;装填太多的货物。

over·cloud /ˌəʊvə'klaʊd; ˌovɚ'klaʊd/ *vt, vi* [VP6A, 2A] cover, become covered, with clouds or shadows; (fig) make or become gloomy. 以(云)遮蔽物; 以(被)阴 影遮住;(使)变阴暗;(喻)使忧郁;变为忧郁。

over·coat /'əʊvəkəʊt; 'ovɚˌkot/ *n* long coat worn out of doors over ordinary clothes in cold weather. 大衣。

over·come /ˌəʊvə'kʌm; ˌovɚ'kʌm/ *vt* (*pt* **-came** /-'keɪm; -'kem/, *pp* **-come**) [VP6A] **1** get the better of; be too strong for: 胜过;击倒;克服: ~ *the enemy;* 击败敌人; ~ *a bad habit;* 克服一种恶习; ~ *temptation.* 克制诱惑。 **2** make weak: 使弱;使无能力: *be ~ by fatigue/emotion/liquor/fumes.* 筋疲力竭(不胜感触; 酒醉;被烟熏倒)。

over·crop /ˌəʊvə'krɒp; ˌovɚ'krɑp/ *vt* (**-pp-**) [VP 6A] take too many crops from (land) (so that it loses fertility). 把(农地)使用过度;耕种过多以致使(地)变 贫瘠。

over·crowd /ˌəʊvə'kraʊd; ˌovɚ'kraʊd/ *vt* [VP6A] crowd too much: 使过度拥挤: ~*ed buses/trains;* 拥挤 不堪的公共汽车(火车); *the ~ing of large cities.* 大城市 的拥挤。

over·do /ˌəʊvə'duː; 'ovɚ'du/ *vt* (*pt* **-did** /-'dɪd; -'dɪd/, *pp* **-done** /-'dʌn; -'dʌn/) [VP6A] **1** do too much; exaggerate; overact: 做太多或过份;出力夸张;搞 得过火: *The comic scenes in the play were overdone.* 这戏 的滑稽场面太夸张了。 *He overdid his part in the play.* 在 那出戏里他把他的角色演得太过火了。 ~ *it,* (a) work, etc too hard: 太用功;努力过度: *You should work hard, but don't ~ it and make yourself ill.* 你应该努力工作,但 不可过度把自己累病了。 **(b)** exaggerate; go too far in order to achieve one's object: 夸张;过火: *He showed sympathy for us, but didn't he rather ~ it?* 他对我们表 同情,但是否稍嫌过火? **2** cook too much: 煮过度; 烧太 久: *overdone beef.* 煮太久的牛肉。

over·dose /'əʊvədəʊs; 'ovɚ,dos/ *n* too great an

amount (of a drug) taken at one time: (指药物)过度剂量;过量: take an ~; 服药过量; die of an ~ of morphine. 死于服用过量吗啡. □ /ˌəuvəˈdəus; ˈovəˈdos/ vt [VP 6A, 14] ~ sb (with sth), give him an ~ (of sth). 使服用过量(某物).

over·draft /ˈəuvədrɑːft US: -dræft; ˈovəˌdræft/ n amount of money by which a bank account is overdrawn. 超支银行存款的金额;透支.

over·draw /ˌəuvəˈdrɔː; ˈovəˈdro/ vt, vi (pt -drew /-ˈdruː; -ˈdru/, pp -drawn /-ˈdrɔːn; -ˈdron/) [VP6A, 2A] 1 draw a cheque for a sum in excess of (one's credit balance in a bank): 开支票超过(在银行之存款额);透支;超支: an ~n account. 透支了的帐户. 2 exaggerate: 夸张: The characters in this novel are rather ~n, are not true to life. 这部小说中的人物有点夸张(不够逼真真).

over·dress /ˌəuvəˈdres; ˈovəˈdrɛs/ vt,vi [VP6A, 2A] dress (oneself, etc) too richly or more showily than is suitable for the occasion. 打扮(自己等)太考究;过度装饰(不适于某场合).

over·drive /ˈəuvədraiv; ˈovəˌdraiv/ n mechanism fitted into the normal gear-box of a motor vehicle to reduce the power output while maintaining the driving speed. 加速传动装置(加装于汽车齿轮箱中的装置,用以减低动力输出量而又能维持行车速度).

over·due /ˌəuvəˈdjuː US: -ˈduː; ˈovəˈdju/ adj beyond the time fixed (for arrival, payment, etc): 过时(到达,付款等)的;迟到的;过期的: The train is ~, is late. 火车误点了. These bills are all ~, ought to have been paid before now. 这些帐单过期了还没付. The baby is two weeks ~, still not born two weeks after the expected date of birth. 那胎儿已超过预产期两个星期了.

over·flow /ˌəuvəˈfləu; ˈovəˈflo/ vt, vi (pt, pp ~ed) 1 [VP6A, 2A] flow over; flow over the edges or limits; flood; spread beyond the ordinary or usual area: 淹没;泛滥;溢出;漫出: The river ~ed its banks. 河水淹没两岸. The lake is ~ing. 湖水正在泛滥. The crowds were so big that they ~ed the barriers. 人太多了,以致挤出栅栏. 2 [VP3A] ~ with, be more than filled: 充溢;洋溢: a heart ~ing with gratitude; 充满着感激的心; a friend ~ing with kindness. 洋溢着慈爱的朋友. □ n /ˈəuvəfləu; ˈovəˌflo/ [C] flowing over of liquid; flood; that which flows over or is too much for the space, area, etc available: 溢流;泛滥;洪水;无法容纳而溢出或过多之物: new suburbs for the ~ of population; 为着人口过剩而辟的新郊区; an ~ meeting, one held for those unable to find room in the hall, etc where the principal meeting is held. 增设之会场(因主要会场人满而加设者).

over·grown /ˌəuvəˈgrəun; ˈovəˈgron/ adj 1 having grown too fast: 长得太快的: an ~ boy. 长得太快的男孩. 2 covered with sth that has grown over: 覆着蔓生之物的;长满的: a garden ~ with weeds; 长满野草的花园; walls ~ with ivy. 爬满着常春藤的墙.

over·growth /ˈəuvəgrəuθ; ˈovəˌgroθ/ n 1 [U, C] that which has grown over: 蔓生或滋蔓之物: the ~ of weeds. 蔓生的野草. 2 [U] growth that is too fast or excessive: 生长过速;生长过度; weakness due to ~. 由于生长过速所致的虚弱.

over·hand /ˈəuvəhænd; ˈovəˈhænd/ adj (cricket, etc) overarm; (in swimming) with the hand and arm raised out of the water: (板球等)举臂过肩的; (游泳)手和胳膊伸出水面的; the ~ stroke. 两手交扣水面的泳法.

over·hang /ˌəuvəˈhæŋ; ˌovəˈhæŋ/ vt, vi (pt, pp -hung /-ˈhʌŋ; -ˈhʌŋ/) [VP6A, 2A] 1 hang over; be over; project over, like a shelf: 悬于…之上;悬垂;伸出;突出于…之上: The cliffs ~ the stream. 那些峭壁悬在溪流之上. The ledge ~s several feet. 这个突出部分伸出好几英尺. 2 threaten; be likely to happen: 威胁;逼近;可能来到: ~ing dangers. 逼近的危险. □ n /ˈəuvəhæŋ; ˈovəˌhæŋ/ part that ~s: 突出部分;悬垂部分: the ~ of a roof/cliff. 屋顶(峭壁)的悬垂部分.

over·haul /ˌəuvəˈhɔːl; ˌovəˈhol/ vt [VP6A] 1 examine thoroughly in order to learn about the condition of: 细密检查;彻底检查以期了解…之状况;检修: have the engine of a car ~ed; 将汽车引擎彻底检修; (colloq) (口) go to one's doctor to be ~ed, physically examined. 到医生那里去彻底检查身体. 2 overtake; catch up with: 追上;超上: The fast cruiser soon ~ed the old cargo boat. 那艘快速的巡洋舰不久就赶上了那老旧的货轮. □ n /ˈəuvəhɔːl; ˈovəˌhol/ [C] examination for the purpose of repairing, cleaning, etc. (为修理、清洁等而作的)彻底检查;检修.

over·head /ˌəuvəˈhed; ˈovəˈhɛd/ adv above one's head; in the sky: 在头顶上;在上空: the people in the room ~; 在头顶上那个房间里的人; the stars ~. 天上的星星. □ adj /ˈəuvəhed; ˈovəˌhed/ 1 raised above the ground: 离地面的;凌空的;高架的: ~ wires/cables; 飞线;架空线(缆); an ~ railway, built at a level higher than that of the streets. 高架铁道. 2 (business): (贸): ~ expenses/charges (or, n pl, 或作复数名词 ~s), those expenses, etc needed for carrying on a business, eg rent, advertising, salaries, light, heating, not manufacturing costs. 经常费; 营业费用(维持商业所需要的费用,如租金,广告,薪水,照明,暖气等,非指制造成本).

over·hear /ˌəuvəˈhiə(r); ˈovəˈhɪr/ vt (pt, pp -heard /-ˈhɜːd; -ˈhɜd/) [VP6A, 18A, 19A] hear without the knowledge of the speaker(s); hear what one is not intended to hear; hear by chance. 偷听;无意中听到;偶然听到.

over·joyed /ˌəuvəˈdʒɔid; ˈovəˈdʒɔid/ adj greatly delighted (at one's success, etc). 大为高兴的;极开心的(与at连用,后接成功等事).

over·kill /ˈəuvəkil; ˈovəˌkɪl/ n capacity exceeding what is needed to destroy. 超出所需的杀伤威力.

over·land adj /ˈəuvəlænd/, adv /ˌəuvəˈlænd; ˈovəˌlænd/ across the land (contrasted with the sea): 经过陆地的;陆上的;经陆路(与海路相对): the ~ route used by Marco Polo; 马可波罗所走的陆上路线; travel ~. 作陆上旅行.

over·lap /ˌəuvəˈlæp; ˌovəˈlæp/ vt, vi (-pp-) [VP6A, 2A] 1 partly cover by extending beyond one edge: 部分重迭: tiles that ~ one another; 彼此部分重迭的瓦片; ~ping shingles; 部分重迭的屋顶板; ~ping boards. 部分重迭的墙板; 鱼鳞板. 2 (fig) partly coincide; involve duplication: (喻)部分相同;重复: His duties/authority and mine ~. 他的职责(权力)和我的有一部分相同. His visit and mine ~ped. 他的访问和我的正好在同一时间. □ n /ˈəuvəlæp; ˈovəˌlæp/ [C] ~ping part; [U] fact or process of ~ping. 重迭或重复的部分;重迭;重复.

over·lay /ˌəuvəˈlei; ˈovəˈle/ vt (pt, pp -laid /-ˈleid; -ˈled/) put a coating over the surface of: 覆盖; 包;镀: wood overlaid with gold. 包一层金的木料. □ n /ˈəuvəleɪ; ˈovəˌle/ thing laid over sth. 覆盖之物.

over·leaf /ˌəuvəˈliːf; ˈovəˈlif/ adv on the other side of the leaf (of a book, etc). 在(书等的)某面的背面;在反面.

over·leap /ˌəuvəˈliːp; ˌovəˈlip/ vt (pt, pp ~ed or -leapt /-ˈlept; -ˈlɛpt/) [VP6A] leap over; (fig) go too far, attempt too much: 跳过; (喻)做得过份;企图太多: Ambition often ~s itself. 野心太大常招致失败.

over·load /ˌəuvəˈləud; ˌovəˈlod/ vt [VP6A] put too great a load on; (electr) put too great a charge into. 使过量载重;使超载; (电)使超量负载;使过量负荷.

over·look /ˌəuvəˈluk; ˈovəˈluk/ vt [VP6A] 1 have a view of from above: 俯视;俯瞰: From my study window I ~ the bay and the headlands. 从我书房的窗口,我可以俯瞰海湾和海岬. Our garden is ~ed from the neighbours' windows, They can look down on to our garden from their windows. 从邻居的窗口可以看到我们的花园. 2 fail to see or notice; pay no attention to: 忽视;忽略;没注意到: ~ a printer's error. 看漏了一个印刷错误. His services have been ~ed by his employers, They have not properly rewarded him. 他的服务一直未

得到他雇主的重视(即未获得适当的报酬)。**3** pass over without punishing: 宽恕: ~ *a fault.* 宽恕一个过失。**4** superintend; supervise. 监督; 指导。

over·lord /'əʊvəlɔːd; 'ovɚ,lord/ *n* (in feudal times) nobleman in relation to his vassals; superior from whom men held land and to whom they owed service. (在封建时代)大封主; 大地主。

over·ly /'əʊvəlɪ; 'ovɚlɪ/ *adv* to an excessive degree: 过度地; 极度: ~ *cautious.* 极度小心。Cf 参较 *over-cautious.*

over·man·tel /'əʊvəmæntl; 'ovɚ,mæntl/ *n* structure (wood or stone, carved or decorated) over a mantle-piece. 壁炉上的饰架(木质或石质, 刻有花纹或加有其他装饰)。

over·mas·ter /,əʊvə'mɑːstə(r) *US:* -mæs-; ,ovɚ'mæstɚ/ *vt* [VP6A] overcome, overpower; 胜过;压服: *an ~ing passion,* a passion so strong that it is difficult to subdue it. 一种难以压制的强烈情感。

over·much /,əʊvə'mʌtʃ; 'ovɚ'mʌtʃ/ *adj, adv* too great(ly): 太多: *give children ~ homework;* 给儿童太多的作业; *an author who has been praised ~.* 受到过份赞扬的作者。

over·night /,əʊvə'naɪt; 'ovɚ'naɪt/ *adv* **1** on the night before: 在前一夜: *get everything ready for the journey ~;* 为旅行的前一夜把一切都准备好; *make preparations ~.* 前一夜做准备。**2** for, during the night: 一夜(间): *stay ~ at a friend's house,* sleep there for the night. 在朋友家里过夜。*The situation changed ~.* 一夜之间情况改变了。□ /'əʊvənaɪt; 'ovɚ'naɪt/ *adj* during or for the night: 晚上的; 夜间的: *an ~ journey;* 夜间旅行; *an ~ stop at Rome.* 在罗马停留过夜。

over·pass /'əʊvəpɑːs *US:* -pæs; 'ovɚ,pæs/ *n* bridge or road that carries a road over a highway or motorway. (架设于公路或快车道之上的)天桥; 陆桥; 高架道路。⇨ **flyover, underpass.**

over·pay /,əʊvə'peɪ; 'ovɚ'pe/ *vt* (*pt, pp* **-paid** /-'peɪd; -'ped/) [VP6A, 14] pay too much or too highly: 多付; 给付过高: *Has Jack been overpaid for his work?* 杰克的工作报酬是否过高?

over·play /,əʊvə'pleɪ; 'ovɚ'ple/ *vt* ~ *one's hand,* (gambling, cards) take risks that are not justified (by over-estimating one's own strength). (赌博, 牌戏)(由于高估自己手中的牌力而)冒不应当冒的险。

over·plus /'əʊvəplʌs; 'ovɚ,plʌs/ *n* [C] amount which is surplus or in excess. 剩余数量; 超过的数量。

over·power /,əʊvə'paʊə(r); ,ovɚ'paʊɚ/ *vt* [VP6A] overcome; be too strong for; defeat by greater strength or numbers: 克服; 压服; 以力量或数目胜过: *The criminals were easily ~ed by the police.* 那些犯人轻易地被警察镇压住。*He was ~ed by the heat.* 他受不住热。~·**ing** *adj* very powerful; very powerful of this: 强烈的; 难抗拒的: *an ~ing stink,* 强烈的恶臭; *~ing grief.* 难以抑制的悲伤。

over·print /,əʊvə'prɪnt; ,ovɚ'prɪnt/ *vt* [VP6A] print additional matter on (an already printed surface, eg of postage stamps). 在(印刷品, 如邮票)上加印; 复印。□ *n* /'əʊvəprɪnt; 'ovɚ,prɪnt/ thing ~ed. 加印之物; 复印之物。

over·rate /,əʊvə'reɪt; 'ovɚ'ret/ *vt* [VP6A] put too high a value on: 高估; 估计…过高: ~ *sb's abilities;* 高估某人的能力; *an ~d book.* 一本评价太高的书。

over·reach /,əʊvə'riːtʃ; 'ovɚ'ritʃ/ *vt* [VP6A] **1** get the better of (by trickery). (以诡计)胜过。**2** ~ *oneself,* fail in one's object, damage one's own interests, by being too ambitious. 因野心太大而失败; 因操之过急而蒙受损失。

over·ride /,əʊvə'raɪd; ,ovɚ'raɪd/ *vt* (*pt* **-rode** /-'rəʊd; -'rod/, *pp* **-ridden** /-'rɪdn; -'rɪdn/) [VP6A] prevail over (sb's opinions, decisions, wishes, claims, etc): 不顾; 蔑视; 不理(某人的意见, 决定, 愿望, 要求等): *They overrode my wishes,* set them aside without consideration. 他们不顾我的愿望。

over·rule /,əʊvə'ruːl; 'ovɚ'rul/ *vt* [VP6A] decide

against (esp by using one's higher authority): 反对; 拒绝; (尤指利用较高职权)否决; 驳回: ~ *a claim or objection.* 不准某项要求或异议。*The judge ~d the previous decision.* 法官宣布撤销原判。*We were ~d by the majority.* 我们被多数所否决。

over·run /,əʊvə'rʌn; ,ovɚ'rʌn/ *vt* (*pt* **-ran** /-'ræn; -'ræn/, *pp* **-run**) [VP6A] **1** spread over and occupy or injure: 蔓延; 占领; 侵害: *a country ~ by enemy troops;* 被敌军占据的国家; *warehouses ~ with rats;* 老鼠猖獗的货栈; *a garden ~ with weeds.* 杂草蔓生的花园。**2** go beyond (a limit): 超过; 超出(某一范围): *speakers who ~ the time allowed them.* 讲话超过规定时间的演讲者。*The broadcast overran the allotted time.* 广播超过了排定的时间。

over·sea(s) /,əʊvə'siː(z); 'ovɚ'si(z)/ *adj* (at, to, from, for, places) across the sea: (在, 到, 来自, 为)海外的: ~(*s*) *trade;* 海外贸易; *an ~(s) broadcast programme.* 国外广播节目。□ *adv:* *go/live ~(s),* across the sea; abroad. 到海外去(住在国外)。

over·see /,əʊvə'siː; ,ovɚ'si/ *vt* (*pt* **-saw** /-'sɔː; -'sɔ/, *pp* **-seen** /-'siːn; -'sin/) [VP6A] look after, control (work, workmen). 监察; 监督(工作, 工人)。**over·seer** /'əʊvəsɪə(r); 'ovɚ,sɪɚ/ *n* foreman; person whose duty it is to take charge of work and see that it is properly done. 工头; 监工(管理工作并负责该工作妥善完成的人)。

over·sexed /,əʊvə'sekst; ,ovɚ'sekst/ *adj* having sexual desire in excess of what is normal; obsessed by sex. 性欲过强的; 好色的; 淫荡的。

over·shadow /,əʊvə'ʃædəʊ; ,ovɚ'ʃædo/ *vt* [VP6A] throw a shade over; (fig) render less conspicuous; cause to seem less important. 遮蔽; 使蒙上阴影; (喻)使不显著; 使显得较不重要。

over·shoe /'əʊvəʃuː; 'ovɚ,ʃu/ *n* [C] rubber shoe worn over an ordinary one for protection against wet and mud. 套鞋(套在普通鞋上的橡皮鞋, 以防雨水及泥土)。⇨ **galoshes.**

over·shoot /,əʊvə'ʃuːt; ,ovɚ'ʃut/ *vt* (*pt, pp* **-shot** /-'ʃɒt; -'ʃɑt/) [VP6A] shoot over or beyond (a mark); (lit, fig) go too far: 射击高过或超过(标的); (字面, 喻)超过; 把…做得过份: *The aircraft overshot the runway.* 那架飞机降落时超出了跑道(滑行过头)。

over·shot /,əʊvə'ʃɒt; ,ovɚ'ʃɑt/ *adj* ~ *wheel,* water wheel driven by the pressure of water falling on to it from above. 上射式水车(水由上冲下而推动者)。

over·side /'əʊvəsaɪd; 'ovɚ,saɪd/ *adv* over the side (of a ship, etc): 越过(船只等之)边缘地; 从船边: *discharge cargo ~,* eg into lighters, and on to the quay. 从船边卸货(如卸货于驳船而非卸于码头上)。

over·sight /'əʊvəsaɪt; 'ovɚ,saɪt/ *n* **1** [U] failure to notice sth; [C] instance of this: 失察; 疏忽: *Through an unfortunate ~ your letter was left unanswered.* 由于令人遗憾的疏忽, 没有给你回信。**2** [U] watchful care: 小心照料: *under the ~ of a nurse.* 在护士小心照顾之下。

over·sim·plify /,əʊvə'sɪmplɪfaɪ; ,ovɚ'sɪmplə,faɪ/ *vt, vi* [VP6A, 2A] state (problem, facts) too imply for the truth to be fully told. 过于简单地陈述(问题, 事实等)。**over·sim·pli·fi·cation** /,əʊvə,sɪmplɪfɪ'keɪʃn; ,ovɚ,sɪmpləfə'keʃən/ *n* [U, C] (instance of) over-simplifying. 过于简单的陈述。

over·skirt /'əʊvəskɜːt; 'ovɚ,skɝt/ *n* one worn over a skirt. (穿在裙子外面的)外裙; 上裙。

over·sleep /,əʊvə'sliːp; ,ovɚ'slip/ *vi* (*pt, pp* **-slept** /-'slept; -'slɛpt/) [VP2A] sleep too long; continue sleeping after the proper time for waking: 睡得太久; 睡过头醒得过迟: *He overslept and was late for work.* 他睡过了头而上班迟到了。

over·spill /'əʊvəspɪl; 'ovɚ,spɪl/ *n* sth that spreads into surrounding areas; (esp) excess population: 溢出之物; 溢出物; (尤指)过剩的人口: *build new towns for London's ~.* 为伦敦过剩的人口设置新市镇。

over·state /,əʊvə'steɪt; 'ovɚ'stet/ *vt* [VP6A]

express or state too strongly; state more than is true about: 夸大叙述; 言过其实: *Don't ~ your case.* 不要夸张你的实情. **~·ment** /'əʊvəˈsteɪtmənt; 'ovɚ'stetmənt/ n [U] exaggeration; [C] exaggerated statement. 夸张; 夸张的叙述.

over·stay /ˌəʊvəˈsteɪ; 'ovɚ'ste/ vt [VP6A] stay too long. 停留太久而超过…之期限. **~ one's welcome,** stay until one is no longer a welcome guest. 停留过久而令人生厌.

over·step /ˌəʊvəˈstep; 'ovɚ'stɛp/ vt (-pp-) [VP6A] go beyond: 逾越; 越过: **~** *one's authority.* 越权.

over·stock /ˌəʊvəˈstɒk; 'ovɚ'stɑk/ vt [VP6A] supply with too large a stock: 供以过多的存货; 供给过多; 使过剩: **~** *a farm with cattle,* with more cattle than there is food or space for. 供给某一农场过多的牛.

over·strung /ˌəʊvəˈstrʌŋ; 'ovɚ'strʌŋ/ adj 1 (of a person, his nerves) intensely strained; easily excited; too sensitive. (指人, 人的神经)过度紧张的; 容易激动的; 过敏的. 2 (of a piano) with strings crossing obliquely to save space. (指钢琴)为节省空间把琴弦斜向交叉装置的.

over·stuffed /ˌəʊvəˈstʌft; 'ovɚ'stʌft/ adj (of seats, etc) made soft and comfortable by very thick padding. (指座位等)因用厚垫而柔软舒适的.

over·sub·scribed /ˌəʊvəsəbˈskraɪbd; 'ovɚsəb'skraɪbd/ adj (fin) (of an issue of shares, etc) with applications in excess of what is offered. (财政)(指股份等之发行)认购逾额的; 求过于供的.

overt /'əʊvɜːt US: əʊ'vɜːrt; o'vɝt/ adj done or shown openly, publicly: 公然的; 公开的: **~** *hostility.* 公然的敌意. **~·ly** adv ⇨ **covert.**

over·take /ˌəʊvəˈteɪk; 'ovɚ'tek/ vt (pt **-took** /-'tʊk; -'tʊk/, pp **-taken** /-'teɪkən; -'tekən/) [VP6A] 1 come or catch up with; outstrip: 赶上; 追上; 超过: **~** *other cars on the road;* 追过路上的其他车辆; **~** *arrears of work.* 赶补耽搁的工作. 2 (of storms, troubles, etc) come upon (sb) suddenly, by surprise: (指暴风雨, 麻烦等)突然降临(某人); 意外地临到(某人): *be ~n by/with fear/surprise/events;* 突然感到恐惧(惊喜或感到惊愕, 突然节外生枝); *be ~n by a storm.* 突然受到暴风雨的袭击.

over·tax /ˌəʊvəˈtæks; 'ovɚ'tæks/ vt [VP6A] tax too heavily; put too heavy a burden or strain on: 课税过重; 加过重负担担于: **~** *one's strength/sb's patience.* 过于用力(使某人失去耐心).

over·throw /ˌəʊvəˈθrəʊ; 'ovɚ'θro/ vt (pt **-threw** /-'θruː; -'θru/, pp **-thrown** /-'θrəʊn; -'θron/) [VP6A] defeat; put an end to; cause to fall or fail: 击败; 使覆灭; 倾覆; 推翻; 打倒: **~** *the government.* 推翻政府. □ n /'əʊvəθrəʊ; 'ovɚθro/ ruin; defeat; fall. 毁灭; 击败; 打倒; 推翻; 倾覆.

over·time /'əʊvətaɪm; 'ovɚtaɪm/ n [U], adv (time spent at work) after the usual hours: 超出的时间; 额外的时间; 加班的时间; 超出时间地: *working* **~**; 加班工作; *be paid extra for* **~**; 因加班而得到额外给付; *be on* **~**, ie working; 在加班工作中; **~** *pay.* 加班费.

over·tone /'əʊvətəʊn; 'ovɚ,ton/ n (music) higher note more faintly heard than the main note produced from a string, pipe, etc; (often pl) (fig) implication. (音乐)泛音(高于而较弱于主音的音); (常用复数)(喻)含意; 暗示.

over·top /ˌəʊvəˈtɒp; 'ovɚ'tɑp/ vt (-pp-) [VP6A] be higher than; rise above: 高于; 高过; 高于…之上: **~ped** *by the new skyscraper.* 在新建的摩天楼之下.

over·trump /ˌəʊvəˈtrʌmp; 'ovɚ'trʌmp/ vt [VP6A] (whist, bridge) play a higher trump than. (惠斯特牌戏, 桥牌戏)以更大的王牌取胜.

over·ture /'əʊvətjʊə(r); 'ovɚtʃɚ/ n 1 (often pl) approach made (to sb) with the aim of starting discussions: (常用复数)提议; 建议(与 to 连用, 后接某人): *peace* **~**s; 和平建议; *make* **~**s *to sb.* 向某人提议. 2 musical composition played as an introduction to an opera, or as a separate item at a concert. (音乐的)序乐; 序曲.

over·turn /ˌəʊvəˈtɜːn; 'ovɚ'tɝn/ vt, vi [VP 6A, 2A] (cause to) turn over; upset: 使倾覆; 颠覆; 翻倒; 推翻: *He ~ed the boat.* 他弄翻了那只船. *The boat ~ed.* 船翻了.

over·ween·ing /ˌəʊvəˈwiːnɪŋ; 'ovɚ'winɪŋ/ adj having, marked by, excessive self-confidence or conceit: 过份自信的; 傲慢的: **~** *ambition/vanity.* 自负的雄心(虚荣心).

over·weight /ˌəʊvəwert; 'ovɚ,wet/ n excess of weight above what is usual or legal: 过重; 超重: *Shopkeepers rarely give* **~**. 店家很少给超过应得的重量. □ adj /ˌəʊvəˈwert; 'ovɚ'wet/ exceeding the weight allowed or normal: 超重的; 超重的: *an* **~** *bag.* 过重的袋子. *If your luggage is* **~** *you'll have to pay extra.* 假如你的行李过重, 你得付额外的运费. *Your suitcase is five kilograms* **~**. 你的小提箱超重五公斤. ⇨ **under·weight.** **~ed** /ˌəʊvəˈweɪtɪd; 'ovɚ'wetɪd/ part adj carrying too much weight: 超载的; 载重过多的: **~ed** *with packages.* 包裹装载过多的.

over·whelm /ˌəʊvəˈwelm US: -'hwelm; ˌovɚ'hwɛlm/ vt [VP6A] weigh down; submerge, cover completely by flowing over or pouring down on; crush; destroy; cause to feel confused or embarrassed: 压制; 浸没; 淹没; 使粉碎; 击溃; 使不安; 使困窘: *be ~ed by the enemy/by superior forces;* 被敌军(被优势兵力)所击溃; *an* **~ing** *victory;* 势如破竹的胜利; 压倒性的胜利; **~ing** *sorrow;* 极度的悲哀; *be ~ed by a flood;* 被洪水淹没; *be ~ed with grief/gratitude.* 不胜悲哀(感激).

over·work /ˌəʊvəˈwɜːk; 'ovɚ'wɝk/ vt, vi [VP6A, 2A] (cause to) work too hard or too long: (使)工作过劳或太久; 过度工作: **~** *oneself;* 操劳过度; **~** *a horse.* 使马疲劳过度. *It's foolish to* **~**. 工作过度是愚蠢的. □ n /'əʊvəwɜːk; 'ovɚ'wɝk/ [U] working too much or too long: 过多或过久的工作; 过度工作; 过劳: *ill through* **~**. 因过劳而生病.

over·wrought /ˌəʊvəˈrɔːt; 'ovɚ'rɔt/ adj tired out by too much work or excitement; in a state of nervous excitement. 过劳的; 过份紧张而疲倦的; 神经紧张的.

ovi·duct /'əʊvɪdʌkt; 'ovɪ,dʌkt/ n (also called 亦称作 *Fallopian tube*) either of two tubes through which ova pass from the ovary to the uterus. 输卵管. ⇨ the illus at **reproduce.** 参看 reproduce 之插图.

ovip·ar·ous /əʊˈvɪpərəs; o'vɪpərəs/ adj producing young from eggs which hatch outside the body. 卵生的.

ovoid /'əʊvɔɪd; 'ovɔɪd/ adj, n egg-shaped (object). 卵形的; 卵形物.

ovum /'əʊvəm; 'ovəm/ n (pl ova /'əʊvə; 'ovə/) female germ or sex cell in animals, capable of developing into a new individual when fertilized by male sperm. 卵; 卵子; 卵细胞.

owe /əʊ; o/ vt, vi 1 [VP6A, 12A, 13A, 2A, 3A] *owe sb sth; owe sth to sb; owe for sth,* be in debt to (sb) (for sth): 欠; 负(某人)债: *He owes his father £50.* 他欠他父亲五十英镑. *He owes £50 to his father.* 他欠他父亲五十英镑. *I have paid all that was owing.* 我已经把所有的欠债还清. *He still owes for the goods he had last month.* 他仍然欠上个月买东西的帐. 2 [VP12A, 13A] be under an obligation to, feel the necessity of gratitude to: 受到…的恩惠; 感激: *I owe a great deal to my parents and teachers.* 我深受父母及师长之恩. *I owe it to you that I am still alive.* 我感激你的救命之恩. 3 [VP12A, 13A] be bound to give as a duty: 按责任或义务须给: 应尽; 负有: *We owe reverence and obedience to the Pope.* 应该尊敬并服从教皇. 4 [VP14] *owe sth to sth,* be indebted to as the source of: 应该把…归功于: *He owes his success to good luck more than to ability.* 他的成功与其靠幸运, 较少靠能力. *To whom do we owe the discovery of penicillin?* 盘尼西林的发现该归功于谁?

ow·ing /'əʊɪŋ; 'o·ɪŋ/ adj still to be paid: 未付的; 欠着

的: *large sums still* ~. 尚未偿付的大批款项。 ~ *to* prep because of; on account of: 因为; 由于: *O~ to the rain the match was cancelled.* 因为下雨, 比赛取消了。

owl /aʊl/ aʊl/ *n* night-flying bird that lives on small birds and animals, eg mice. 猫头鹰; 枭。 ⇨ the illus at **prey.** 参看 prey 之插图。 **owl·et** /'aʊlɪt/ ˈaʊlɪt/ *n* young owl. 小猫头鹰。 **owl·ish** /'aʊlɪʃ/ ˈaʊlɪʃ/ *adj* of or like an owl; looking, or trying to look, solemn and wise. 猫头鹰的; 似猫头鹰的; 显得严肃而聪明的; 装着严肃而聪明的。 **owl·ish·ly** *adv*

own¹ /əʊn/ əʊn/ *adj, pron* **1** (used with possessives, either attributively or predicatively, to give emphasis to the idea of personal possession, to the peculiar or individual character of sth): (与所有格连用, 可作定语或表语, 强调个人所有或某事物的特性)自己的: *I saw it with my own eyes.* 我亲眼看到它。 *It was her own idea.* 那是她自己的意思。 *This is my own house / This house is my own,* belongs to me, is not rented. 这是我自己的房子。 *This fruit has a flavour all its own,* is not to be compared to the flavour of any other fruit. 这种水果有它特有的味道。 *May I have it for my very own,* Are you willing to let me be the sole owner, so that I need not share it? 我可以把它据为己有吗? *My time is my own,* I can spend it as I wish. 我的时间是我自己的(我可以自由支配)。 *For reasons of his own* (= For particular reasons, reasons perhaps only known to him), *he refused to join the club.* 为了个人的理由, 他拒绝参加那俱乐部。 **(be) (all) on one's own, (a)** alone: 单独; 独自: *I'm all on my own today.* 今天就只有我一个人。 *She lives on her own,* alone, not with family or friends. 她独自一个人住(没和家人或朋友同住)。 **(b)** independently of an employer; without supervision: 独立地; 不受雇于人地; 不受监督地: *He's (working) on his own.* 他现在独立工作。 *He can be left to work on his own.* 可以让他独立工作。 **(c)** outstanding; excellent: 杰出的; 优异的: *For craftsmanship, Smith is on his own,* has no equal. 论到手艺, 史密斯是杰出无匹的。 **own brother / sister,** with both parents the same, not a half-brother / sister. 亲兄弟(姐妹); 胞兄弟(姐妹)。 **be one's own man / master,** be independent; be self-employed. 独立自主; 自己做老板。 **come into one's own,** receive what rightly belongs to one, the credit, fame, etc that one deserves: 得到自己应得之物; 获得应得的信誉等: *Along unpaved and rutted tracks, this sturdy car really comes into its own,* shows what it is capable of. 在这些未经铺设而且崎岖坎坷的路上, 这部结实的车真正表现了它独到的性能。 **get one's own back,** have one's revenge. 报仇。 **hold one's own (against sb / sth), (a)** maintain one's position against attack; not be defeated. (对某人或某事物)固守立场; 不为所败。 **(b)** not lose strength: 支撑; 硬挺: *The patient is holding her own.* 这个女病人还在支撑着。 **2** (used to indicate the idea of personal activity; done or produced by and for oneself): (用以表示个人的行动; 自己做的; 为自己而做的): *She makes all her own clothes.* 她身上穿的衣服都是自己缝制的。 *I can cook my own meals.* 我能够自己煮饭。 *It's unwise to try to be your own lawyer.* 你想当你自己的律师是不智的。

own² /əʊn/ əʊn/ *vt, vi* **1** [VP6A] possess; have as property: 据有; 拥有: *This house is mine; I own it.* 这屋子是我的; 我拥有它。 *Who owns this land,* To whom does it belong? 这块地为谁所有? **2** [VP6A, 9, 2C, 3A, 25] ~ *(to),* agree; confess; recognize: 同意; 坦承; 承认: *own that a claim is justified;* 同意某一要求是正当的; *own to having told a lie;* 承认曾撒一次谎; *own one's faults;* 坦承错误; *own oneself (to be) defeated;* 承认失败; *own the force of an argument.* 承认一项论据令令人折服。 *The man refused to own the child,* would not admit that he was its father. 那个人拒绝承认自己是那小孩的父亲。 *I must own myself no* (= confess that I am not a) *supporter of reform.* 我必须坦白承认我不是拥护改革者。 **own up (to sth),** confess fully and frankly. 完完

全全地坦白供认。

owner /'əʊnə(r)/ ˈonɚ/ *n* person who owns sth: 所有者; 拥有人: *Who's the* ~ *of this house?* 谁是这房子的房主? **,~·'driven** *adj* (of a vehicle) driven regularly by the ~. (指车辆)车主经常驾驶的。 **,~·'driver** *n* motorist who drives a car which he owns. 开自己车子的驾驶人。 **~·less** *adj* without an ~; not known to belong to anyone: 无主的; 不知属于谁的: ~*less dogs.* 无主的狗。 **,~·'occupied** *adj* (of a house, etc) lived in by the ~ (not rented to sb else). (指房子等)主人自己住的; 自用的。 **,~·'occupier** *n* one who owns the house he lives in. 住自己房子的居住人。 **'~·ship** /-ʃɪp; -ʃɪp/ *n* state of being an ~; right of possessing: 物主; 主权; 所有权: *land of uncertain* ~*ship.* 所有权不详的土地。

ox /ɒks; ɑks/ *n* (*pl* **oxen** /'ɒksn; ˈɑksn̩/) **1** general name for domestic cattle. 牛(家畜的牛的通称)。 ⇨ **bull¹(1), bullock, cow¹.** ⇨ the illus at **domestic.** 参看 domestic 之插图。 **2** (esp) fully grown castrated bullock, used as a draught animal. (尤指作驮兽用而去势的)大公牛。 **'ox-eye** *n* name (often used *attrib*) of several kinds of plants (daisies, wild chrysanthemums, etc). (常用作定语)牛眼菊。 **,ox-'eyed** *adj* with large, round eyes like those of an ox. 长着象牛眼一般大而圆的眼睛的。 **'ox-tail** *n* tail of ox, much used for soup, etc. 牛尾 (常用以作羹汤等)。

Ox·bridge /'ɒksbrɪdʒ; ˈɑks,brɪdʒ/ *n* (invented name for) Oxford and/or Cambridge (contrasted with *Redbrick,* ⇨ **red(3)**). (创造的名词)牛桥(指"牛津"及(或)"剑桥")与 Redbrick 相对)。

Ox·ford /'ɒksfəd; ˈɑksfɚd/ *n* (university city in England). 牛津(英格兰的一个大学城)。 ~ **bags,** trousers with very wide legs. 牛津袋裤(裤腿特别宽大的裤子)。 ~ **blue,** dark, purplish blue. 略带紫色的深蓝色。 **the** ~ **Movement,** religious movement (19th c) advocating the revival of Catholicism within the Anglican Church. 牛津运动(十九世纪的宗教运动, 主张在英国国教内恢复天主教教义与仪式)。 ~ **shoes,** low shoes lacing over the instep. 牛津鞋(在鞋面系带的浅口低跟鞋)。

ox·ide /'ɒksaɪd; ˈɑksaɪd/ *n* [C, U] compound of oxygen: 氧化物: *iron* ~; 氧化铁; ~ *of tin.* 氧化锡。 **oxi·dize** /'ɒksɪdaɪz; ˈɑksə,daɪz/ *vt, vi* [VP6A, 2A] (cause to) combine with oxygen; make or become rusty. (使)氧化; (使)生锈。 **oxi·diz·ation** /,ɒksɪdaɪ-'zeɪʃn *US:* -dɪz-; ,ɑksədɪ'zeʃən/ *n*

Ox·on·ian /ɒks'əʊnɪən/ *n, adj* (member) of the University of Oxford. 牛津大学的(学生或教师)。

oxy·acety·lene /,ɒksɪə'setɪliːn; ,ɑksɪə'sɛtl,in/ *adj, n* (of a) mixture of oxygen and acetylene: 氧乙炔(的): ~ *torch / blowpipe,* tool burning ~; 氧炔焰喷灯(氧炔吹管); ~ *welding,* by means of a hot flame of ~. 汽焊; 氧乙炔焊接。

oxyacetylene welding

oxy·gen /'ɒksɪdʒən; ˈɑksədʒən/ *n* [U] chemical element (symbol **O**), gas without colour, taste, or smell, present in the air and necessary to the existence of all forms of life. 氧; 氧气(符号为 O)。 **'~ mask,** mask placed over the mouth and nose to supply ~, eg in an aircraft at a great altitude. 氧气面具(戴于口鼻上以供给氧气, 高空飞行等人员用之)。 **'~ tent,** small tent or canopy placed over the head and shoulders of a patient who needs an extra supply of ~. 氧气帐(罩于需要加量氧气之病人身上的小帐幕)。 **'~·ate** /-ert; -,et/,

'**·ize** /-aɪz/; -ˌaɪz/ vt supply, treat, or mix, with ~. 给…氧;用氧处理;使与氧混合。

oyez /əʊˈjez; ˈoʊjez/ (also **oyes** /əʊˈjes; ˈoʊjes/) int cry meaning 'Listen', repeated three times by (hist) a town-crier, or (in a law court) by an usher to demand silence and attention. '听','静听';'肃静'(昔时由街头公告员或在法庭上由法警呼喊三次,促人安静并注意)。

oy·ster /ˈɔɪstə(r); ˈɔɪstɚ/ n kinds of shellfish much used as food, usu eaten uncooked. 蚝;牡蛎。 ⇨ the illus at **bivalve.** 参看 bivalve 之插图。 '~**-bar** n counter (in a restaurant, etc) where ~s are served. (菜馆等内的)供应蚝肉的柜台。 '~**-bed**, '~**-bank** nn part of the seabottom where ~s breed or are bred. 养蚝场。 '~**-catcher** n wading seabird. 蛎鹬。

ozone /ˈəʊzəʊn; ˈozon/ n [U] form of oxygen with a sharp and refreshing smell; (fig) exhilarating influence; (colloq) pure refreshing air as at the seaside. 臭氧;(喻)使人高兴的力量;(口)(海边等的)新鲜空气。

P p

P, p /piː; piː/ (pl **P's, p's** /piːz; piːz/) the 16th letter of the English alphabet. 英文字母的第十六个字母。 **mind one's p's and q's,** be careful not to offend against propriety. 谨慎行事;留心言行。

pa /pɑː; pɑ/ n (colloq) short for papa. (口) papa 之略。

pabu·lum /ˈpæbjʊləm; ˈpæbjələm/ n [U] food (usu fig): 食物(通常作喻):mental ~, food for thought. 精神食粮。

pace /peɪs; pes/ n [C] 1 (distance covered by the foot in a) single step in walking or running. (走或跑的)一步;一步的距离。 2 rate of walking or running, or (fig) progress. 走或跑的速度;(喻)进步的速度。 **go at a good ~,** go fast. 快速地行走。 **go the ~, (a)** go at great speed. 飞快地行进。 **(b)** (fig) spend money freely (esp on pleasure or in dissipated ways). (喻)随便花钱(尤指花在享乐或放荡方面)。 **keep ~ (with sb/sth),** (lit or fig) go forward at the same rate: (字面或喻)同速前进;(与某人)并驾齐驱:He finds it hard to keep ~ with all the developments in nuclear physics. 他发现要赶上核物理学上所有的发展很难。 **set the ~ (for sb),** set a speed for sb. 定速度(让某人跟从)。 '~**-maker** n **(a)** (also 亦作 '~**-setter)** rider, runner, etc who sets the ~ for another in a race. 竞赛时为别人定速度的人;带步人。 **(b)** electronic device (with radioactive core) to correct weak or irregular heart beats. 电子心脏定调器(用以纠正微弱或不规则之心跳)。 3 (esp of horses) way of walking, running, etc. (尤指马的)步态;步法。 **put a person through his ~s,** test his abilities, etc. 试验某人之本领等。 □ vi, vt 1 [VP2A, C] walk with slow or regular steps: 缓慢而行; 以规律的步伐行走; 踱:~ up and down; 来回走动; (of a horse) amble; go at an easy, unhurried ~. (指马)溜蹄; 缓蹄。 2 [VP6A] move across in this way: 以缓慢或规律的步伐走过:~ a room; 在房间里踱来踱去; pacing the station platform. 在火车站月台上踱着。 3 [VP15B] ~ sth off/out, measure it by taking ~s: 以走步测量:~ off a distance of 30 metres; 用走步测一段三十米的距离;~ out a room. 用走步测一房间之大小。 4 [VP6A] set the ~ for (a rider or runner in a race). 为(骑士或赛跑者)定步调;定步速。

pachy·derm /ˈpækɪdɜːm; ˈpækə,dɝm/ n (kinds of) thick-skinned, four-footed animal, eg an elephant. 厚皮四足动物(如象);厚皮类。

pa·ci·fic /pəˈsɪfɪk; pəˈsɪfɪk/ adj peaceful; making or loving peace. 和平的; 和解的; 爱好和平的。 **pa·ci·fically** /-klɪ; -klɪ/ adv

paci·fi·ca·tion /ˌpæsɪfɪˈkeɪʃn; ˌpæsəfəˈkeʃən/ n [U] making or becoming peaceful; bringing about a state of peace. 媾和;和平;平定。

·**paci·fism** /ˈpæsɪfɪzəm; ˈpæsəˌfɪzəm/ n [U] principle that war should and could be abolished. 和平主义;绥靖主义;反战主义。 **paci·fist** /-ɪst; -ɪst/ n believer in ~. 和平主义者;反战论者。

pac·ify /ˈpæsɪfaɪ; ˈpæsə,faɪ/ vt (pt, pp **-fied)** [VP6A] calm and quieten; end violence in. 使平静;抚慰;平定;绥靖。

pack[1] /pæk; pæk/ n 1 bundle of things tied or wrapped up together for carrying; (US) packet: 捆; 包裹; (美)小包:a ~ of cigarettes. 一包香烟。 '~**-horse,** '~**-animal** nn one used for carrying ~s. 驮马; 驮兽。 '~**-saddle** n one with straps for supporting ~s. 驮鞍。 '~**-thread** n [U] strong thread for sewing or tying up ~s or canvas bags. 包裹绳; 包装线; 包扎绳。 2 number of dogs kept for hunting (a ~ of hounds) or of wild animals that go about together: (猎狗或野兽)一群(a ~ of hounds 一群猎犬): Wolves hunt in ~s. 狼成群猎食。 3 (usu contemptuous) number of things or persons: (通常为轻蔑用语)(人或事物的)群; 集团; 套; 帮:a ~ of thieves/liars/lies. 一群贼(一群骗子、一套谎言)。 4 complete set (usu 52) of playing-cards. 一副纸牌(通常为52张)。 5 (Rugby football) a side's forwards. (橄榄球)(一队之)全体前卫。 6 '~**-ice** n [U] mass of large pieces of floating ice in the sea. 海上大堆浮冰。 7 quantity of fish, meat, fruit, etc packed in a season: 一季中装成罐头的鱼、肉、水果等的数量:this year's ~ of salmon. 今年鲑鱼的装罐量。 ⇨ **pack**[2](5).

pack[2] /pæk; pæk/ vt, vi 1 [VP6A, 14, 15A, B, 2A, C] ~ (up)(in/into), put (things) into a box, bundle, bag, etc; fill (a bag, box, etc) with things; get ready for a journey by doing this: 包扎; 捆扎; 包装(东西); 装(袋、盒等); 整理行装:~ clothes into a trunk; 把衣服装进衣箱内;~ a trunk with clothes. 把衣服装进衣箱内。 Have you ~ed (up) your things? 你把行李收拾好了没有? You must begin ~ing at once. 你必须立刻动手整理行装。 These books ~ easily, It is easy to ~ them. 这些书很容易包装。 Her husband takes a ~ed lunch (eg sandwiches, etc ~ed into a box or other container) to work every day. 她的丈夫每天带装盒的午餐(如装在盒子或其他容器中的三明治等)去工作。 ~ one's bags, (lit or fig) prepare to leave. (字面或喻)准备离开。 ~ it in, (sl) give up doing sth; end it. (俚)放弃做某事; 结束某事。 ~ up, (colloq) put one's tools, etc away; stop working: (口)收拾工具; 停止工作; 收工:It's time to ~ up. 是收工的时候了。 One of the aircraft's engines ~ed up, (sl) failed. (俚)飞机的一个引擎坏了。 2 [VP14, 3A] ~ into, crush or crowd together (into a place or period of time): 挤进;挤进(某一地方或某一段时间):~ ing people into an already overcrowded bus; 使人们挤进已经太拥挤的公共汽车; crowds ~ing into the cinemas on a wet day. 在雨天挤进电影院的大群人。 She managed to ~ a lot of sightseeing into the short time she had in London. 她在伦敦逗留的短短时间中, 紧凑地安排了一连串的观光活动。 3 [VP6A, 15A] put soft material into or round (sth) to keep it safe, or to prevent loss or leakage: (用柔软材料)塞; 包垫(以保护物品, 或防止损失或破漏):glass ~ed in straw; 包扎于稻草中的玻璃器皿;~ a leaking joint. 填塞破裂的接头。 4 ~ sb off; send sb ~ing, send him away quickly and unceremoniously (because he is troublesome, etc): 迅急而唐突地打发某人走; 辞退某人:I wish you'd ~ yourself off, go away. 我真希望你快点离开这儿。 5 [VP6A] prepare and put (meat, fruit, etc) in tins for preservation. 把

(肉类、水果等)装罐; 制成罐头. ⇨ **pack**[1](7). **6** [VP6A] choose (the members of a committee, etc) so that their decisions are likely to be in one's favour. 挑选(委员会的委员等)以使他们的决定对自己有利; 笼络; 纠集. ~**er** *n* person or machine that ~s; (esp, usu *pl*) person who ~s meat, fruit etc for market. 包装者; 包装机;(尤指, 通常用复数)罐头食品工人.

pack·age /'pækɪdʒ; 'pækɪdʒ/ *n* [C] parcel of things, packed together; (fig, colloq) detailed plan. 捆; 束; 包; 裹; (喻、口) 详细的计划. ~ **deal** / **offer** *n* (colloq) number of proposals for discussion or acceptance. (口) 整批交易(指必须同时讨论或接受之若干提议). ~ **tour**, (colloq) holiday tour with many details arranged in advance by travel agents and sold at a fixed price. (口) 一切由旅行社代办且费用固定的假日旅游. □ *vt* place in a ~; make a ~ of. 包装; 打包; 捆扎.

packet /'pækɪt; 'pækɪt/ *n* **1** small parcel or bundle: 小包; 小捆: *a* ~ *of letters*; 一捆信件。*a* ~ *of postal* ~; 邮政包裹; *a* ~ *of 20 cigarettes*. 二十支装的一包香烟. **2** '~(-boat), mailboat. 邮船. **3** (sl) considerable sum of money: (俚)大笔款项: *make/cost a* ~. 赚(花)很多. **4** (army sl) trouble of some sort: (军俚)麻烦; 不幸的事; 困难: *catch / stop / get a* ~, (esp) be severely wounded. 惹上麻烦;(尤指)受了重伤.

pack·ing /'pækɪŋ; 'pækɪŋ/ *n* [U] process of packing (goods); materials used in packing(3), eg for closing a leaking joint. 包装(货物的过程); 填塞或包扎的材料(如填塞裂漏之接头用者). '~-**case** *n* one of rough boards in which goods are packed for shipment. 装运货物的粗木箱. '~-**needle** *n* large needle used for sewing up canvas packages, etc. 缝包装袋的粗针.

pact /pækt; pækt/ *n* compact; agreement: 协定; 公约: *the P~ of Locarno*; 罗迦诺协定; *a new Peace P~*. 新的和平公约.

pad[1] /pæd; pæd/ *n* **1** mass of, container filled with, soft material, used to prevent damage, give comfort or improve the shape of sth. (用以防止损坏, 增加舒适或改进物品形状的)垫塞物; 垫子. **2** guard for the leg or other parts of the body (in cricket and other games). (打板球或做其他运动时)保护腿部或身体其他部分的垫子; 护胫; 护胸; 护膝(等). ⇨ the illus at **cricket**. 参看 cricket 之插图. **3** number of sheets of writing-paper fastened together along one edge. 拍纸簿. **4** (also 亦作 '**ink-pad**) absorbent material (usu in an oblong box) used for inking rubber stamps. 橡皮图章用的印色(通常装于长方形的盒子中); 印色盒; 打印台. **5** soft, fleshy underpart of the foot (of a dog, fox, etc). (狗、狐等的)肉趾; 爪掌(足底的软肉部分). **6** (usu 通常作 '**launching-pad**) platform from which missiles are launched into outer space. 飞弹(火箭)发射台. ⇨ the illus at **rocket**. 参看 rocket 之插图. **7** (sl) bed; room to sleep in; apartment. (俚)床; 卧室; 房间. □ *vt* (-dd-) **1** [VP6A] put pads(1) in or on (to prevent injury, to give comfort, or to fill out hollow spaces, etc): 加垫子于; 塞填料于(以防受伤、增加舒适或填补凹部分缝): *a jacket with padded shoulders*; 有垫肩的上装; *a padded cell*, one with padded walls (in a mental hospital). (精神病院里的)墙壁装有护垫的小房间. **2** [VP6A, 15B] *pad sth out*, make (a sentence, essay, book, etc) longer by using unnecessary material: (以不必要的材料)拉长(句子、文章、书等)添凑; 过事铺陈: *an essay padded out with numerous quotations*. 用许多引语添凑起来的短论. **pad·ding** /'pædɪŋ; 'pædɪŋ/ *n* [U] material used for making pads(1) or for padding (*v*, 2). 填塞的材料; 添凑语; 补白.

pad[2] /pæd; pæd/ *vi*, *vt* (-dd-) [VP2A, C] travel on foot: 步行; 走路: *padding along*; 向前走去; [VP6A] tramp (the roads) on foot: 走(路): *He lost all his money and had to pad it home*. 他的钱都丢了, 而只好步行回家.

paddle[1] /'pædl; 'pædl/ *n* **1** short oar with a broad blade at one or (*double* ~) at both ends, used (without a rowlock) to propel a canoe through the water. (一端

或两端有宽阔桨叶而不用桨架的)短桨. ⇨ the illus at **canoe**. 参看 canoe 之插图. **2** (in rowing) act or period of propelling a boat with light, easy strokes. (划船时的)划桨; 荡桨. **3** '~-**box** *n* wooden covering for the upper part of a ~-wheel. 明轮壳(明轮上部的盖). '~-**steamer** *n* steam vessel propelled by ~-wheels. 明轮船 (用明轮推进的船). '~-**wheel** *n* one of a pair of wheels, each with boards round the circumference which press backwards against the water and propel a ~-steamer (装有翼板用以击水推进轮船的)明轮; 踱轮. **4** ~-shaped instrument (eg one used for beating, stirring or mixing things). 桨形工具(如用于击打、搅拌或混合物品者); 桨形板. □ *vt*, *vi* [VP6A, 2A] send (a canoe) through the water by using a ~ or ~s; row with light, easy strokes. 以桨划动(小船); 荡桨. ~ **one's own canoe**, (colloq) depend on oneself alone. (口) 靠自己; 自立; 自力更生.

paddle[2] /'pædl; 'pædl/ *vi* [VP2A] walk with bare feet in shallow water (as children do at the seaside): 涉水; 玩水: *a 'paddling pool*, shallow pool (eg in a public park) where children ~. 浅水池(如公园内供儿童玩水的小池子). □ *n* act or period of paddling. 涉水; 玩水.

pad·dock /'pædək; 'pædək/ *n* **1** small grass field, esp one used for exercising horses. 小牧场(尤指用来溜马的草地). **2** (at a race-course) enclosed area of grassland where horses are assembled and paraded before a race. (赛马场中)比赛前供马匹聚集及受检阅的围场.

paddy[1] /'pædɪ; 'pædɪ/ *n* [U] rice that is still growing; rice in the husk. (生长中的)稻;(未碾磨的)壳. '~-**field** *n* rice-field. 稻田.

paddy[2] /'pædɪ; 'pædɪ/ *n* (*pl* -**dies**) (colloq) rage; fit of bad temper: (口) 愤怒; 发脾气: *She's in one of her paddies*, one of the fits of bad temper to which she is subject. 她在发脾气.

Paddy /'pædɪ; 'pædɪ/ *n* (nickname for an) Irishman. 爱尔兰人(绰号). '~-**wagon**, (US sl) police van for taking persons suspected of crime into custody. (美俚)逮捕嫌疑犯用的警车.

pad·lock /'pædlɒk; 'pæd,lak/ *n* lock of the kind shown here. 挂锁; 扣锁. □ *vt* [VP6A] fasten with a ~: 锁以挂锁: *The gate was ~ed*. 那门有挂锁锁着.

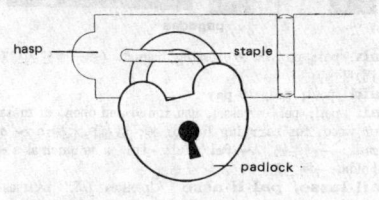

a padlock

padre /'pɑːdreɪ; 'pɑdrɪ/ *n* (army and navy colloq) chaplain; (GB colloq) priest; parson. (陆海军口语)随军牧师;(英口)传教士; 牧师.

paean, (US) **pean** /'piːən; 'piən/ *n* song of thanks-giving, praise or triumph. 感恩歌; 赞美歌; 凯歌.

paed·er·asty / 'pedəræstɪ ; 'pedə,ræstɪ / *n* = pederasty.

paedi·at·rics /,piːdɪ'ætrɪks; ,pidɪ'ætrɪks/ *n* = pediatrics.

pae·ony /'piːənɪ; 'piənɪ/ *n* = peony.

pa·gan /'peɪɡən; 'peɡən/ *n*, *adj* (person who is) not a believer in any of the chief religions of the world. 不是世界上任一主要宗教之教徒的; 异教徒的; 异教徒: ~·**ism** /-ɪzəm; -,ɪzəm/ *n* [U] beliefs, practices, of ~s. 异教徒的信仰与习俗.

page[1] /peɪdʒ; pedʒ/ *n* one side of a leaf of paper in a book, periodical, etc; entire leaf of a book, etc: (书籍、

期刊等的)一面;页;(书等的)一张(两页):*Several ~s have been torn out.* 好几页被撕掉了。 □ *vt* number the ~s of. 标明…的页数。

page² /peɪdʒ; pedʒ/ *n* **1** (also 亦作 '~ **boy**) boy servant, usu in uniform, in a hotel, club, etc. 僮仆 (指旅馆、俱乐部等内通常穿制服的男侍)。 **2** (in the Middle Ages) boy in training for knighthood and living in a knight's household. (中古)住在骑士家中的学习骑士。 □ *vt* [VP6A] call by name, by means of, or as if by means of (eg over a loudspeaker), a page(1). (派僮仆或以扩音器等)在公共场所呼喊(某人)名字以寻找。

pag·eant /'pædʒənt; 'pædʒənt/ *n* **1** public entertainment, usu outdoors, in which historical events are acted in the costume of the period. 历史事迹之表演(通常在户外举行,着古装演出)。 **2** public celebration, esp one in which there is a procession of persons in fine costumes (eg a coronation). 庆典(尤指含有盛装行列者,如加冕典礼)。 **~ry** /'pædʒəntrɪ; 'pædʒəntrɪ/ *n* [U] rich and splendid display. 华丽的展示;盛观。

pagi·na·tion /ˌpædʒɪ'neɪʃn; ˌpædʒə'neʃən/ *n* [U] (figures used for the) numbering of the pages of a book. 标记页数的(数字)。

pa·goda /pə'gəʊdə; pə'godə/ *n* (in India, Nepal, Sri Lanka, Burma, China, Japan, etc) religious building, typically a sacred tower of pyramidal form (Hindu temple), or of several storeys (Buddhist tower). (印度、尼泊尔、斯里兰卡、缅甸、中国、日本等地的)宝塔;浮屠。

pagodas

pah /pɑː; pɑ/ *int* expressing disgust. (表示憎恶的感叹词)呸! 哼!

paid /peɪd; ped/ ⇨ **pay²**.

pail /peɪl; pel/ *n* vessel, usu like round and open, of metal or wood, for carrying liquid; 桶;铁桶;木桶:*a ~ of milk.* 一桶牛奶。 '~·**ful** /-ful; -fʊl/ *n* as much as a ~ holds. 一桶之量。

pail·lasse, **pal·li·asse** /'pælɪæs US: ˌpælɪ'æs; ˌpælɪ'æs/ *nn* mattress filled with straw. 草褥;草荐。

pain /peɪn; pen/ *n* **1** [U] suffering of mind or body: (心或身的)痛苦; 痛; 疼:*be in (great) ~;* (深为)痛苦; *cry with ~;* 痛得大叫; *feel some / no / not much / a great deal of ~.* 觉得有点痛(不痛,非常痛)。 '~·**killer** *n* medicine for lessening ~. 止痛药。 **2** [C] particular or localized kind of bodily suffering: 身体某部分的痛: *a ~ in the knee;* 膝盖痛; *~s in the back;* 背痛; *stomach ~s.* 胃痛。 *a ~ in the neck,* (sl) irritating person. (俚)令人感到不舒服的人; 讨厌的家伙。 **3** [U, C] (old use) punishment; penalty: (旧用法)罚; 刑罚: *~s and penalties.* 刑罚。 *on / under ~ of death,* at the risk of being sentenced to death. 冒着被处死刑的危险。 □ *vt* [VP6A] cause ~ to: 使痛苦: *Doesn't your laziness ~ your parents?* 你的懒惰不会使你父母亲难过吗? *My foot is still ~ing me.* 我的脚还在痛。 *~ed* adj distressed: 痛苦的: *She looked ~ed when I refused to help.* 当我拒绝帮助她时,她显得很痛苦。 *She had a ~ed look.* 她的表情悲痛。 '~·**ful** /-fl; -fəl/ *adj* causing ~: 痛的;使痛苦的;会痛的:

This duty is ~ful to me. 这责任使我很痛苦。 '~·**fully** /-fəlɪ; -fəlɪ/ *adv* ~·**less** *adj* without ~; causing no ~: 无痛的;不会痛的: *~less extractions,* (of teeth). 无痛的拔牙。 ~·**less·ly** *adv*

pains /peɪnz; penz/ *n pl* trouble; effort: 劳苦; 辛劳; 烦劳: *work hard and get very little for all one's ~.* 辛勤工作而所得极微。 *be at ~ to do sth,* make a great effort, work hard, to do it. 努力做某事; 费尽心机做某事。 *spare no ~,* do everything possible. 不辞劳苦。 *take (great) ~ (over sth / to do sth),* take great trouble: 煞费苦心(做某事);(为某事)费尽心机: *take great ~ to please one's lover.* 煞费苦心使爱人高兴; 费尽心机取悦爱人。 '~·**taking** *adj* careful; industrious. 小心的;辛勤的。

paint /peɪnt; pent/ *n* **1** [U] solid colouring matter (to be) mixed with oil or other liquid and used to give colour to a surface: 油漆; 涂料: *give the doors two coats of ~.* 把门涂上两层油漆。 **2** [U] material used to colour the face. 香粉; 脂胭。 **3** (*pl*) collection of tubes or cakes of colouring materials. (复)(管装或块状的一组)颜料。 '~·**box** *n* box with such a collection. (装有一组颜料的)颜料盒。 '~·**brush** *n* brush for applying ~. 画笔; 油漆刷。 ⇨ the illus at **palette.** 参看 palette 之插图。 □ *vt, vi* **1** [VP6A, 22] coat with paint: 油漆; 漆: *~ a door;* 漆一扇门; *~ the gate green.* 把大门油漆成绿色。 *~ the town red,* (colloq) go out and have a lively, exciting time esp when celebrating sth. (口)逛游寻欢作乐(尤指当庆贺某事时)。 **2** [VP6A, 15A, B, 2A, C] make a picture (of) with paint: (用颜料)画; 绘画: *~ flowers / a landscape;* 画花卉(风景); *~ in oils / in water-colours.* 画油画(水彩画)。 *~ sth in,* add to a picture: 画某物于图中: *~ in the foreground.* 画出前景。 *~ sth out,* cover up or hide by using paint. 用颜料或油漆涂去。 **3** [VP6A, 22] (fig) describe vividly in words. (喻)逼真地描述; 生动地描写。 *not so black as one is ~ed,* not so bad as one is represented to be. 并不象所形容的那样坏。

painter¹ /'peɪntə(r); 'pentɚ/ *n* **1** person who paints pictures; artist. 图画者; 画家。 **2** workman who paints woodwork, walls, buildings, ships, etc. 油漆工人; 油漆匠。

painter² /'peɪntə(r); 'pentɚ/ *n* rope fastened to the bow of a boat by which it may be tied to a ship, pier, etc. 艇头索; 系索(连于小艇首部的缆索,用以连系他船、码头等)。 ⇨ the illus at **sail.** 参看 sail 之插图。 *cut the ~,* (a) set (a boat, etc) adrift. 使(船等)漂流。 (b) (fig), effect a separation; become independent. (喻)和…脱离关系; 独立。

paint·ing /'peɪntɪŋ; 'pentɪŋ/ *n* **1** [U] using paint; occupation of a painter. 油漆; 绘画; 油漆业; 绘画业。 **2** [C] painted picture. 图画; 油画。

pair /peə(r); per/ *n* **1** two things of the same kind (to be) used together: 一双; 一对: *a ~ of shoes / gloves;* 一双鞋(手套); *two ~s of socks.* 两双短袜。 **2** single article with two parts always joined: 由两部分合在一起的单件物品: *a ~ of trousers / tights / scissors / tongs.* 一条裤子(一件紧身衣; 一把剪刀; 一把钳子)。 **3** two persons closely associated, eg an engaged or married couple: 两个关系密切的人(如已订婚的男女或夫妻): *the happy ~,* eg two newly married persons. 快乐的一对(如新婚夫妇)。 *in ~s,* in twos. 成双的; 成对的。 **4** two animals of opposite sex; two horses harnessed together. 雌雄一对的动物; 套在同一马具上的两匹马。 **5** (in Parliament) two persons of opposite political parties who absent themselves from a division(6) by mutual agreement; one member willing to do this: (国会中)分属两敌对政党而约好对某项表决放弃投票权的两个人; 约好愿意放弃投票权的一方: *The member for Lewisham couldn't find a ~.* 路易萨姆的议员找不到对方比愿意放弃投票的人。 □ *vt, vi* [VP6A, 15B, 2A, C] form a ~ or ~s; join in ~s; (of animals) mate. (使)成对; 配合; (指动物)交配。 *~ off,* put in ~s; go off in ~s; (in Parliament) make a ~(5). 配成对; 成双; (国会中)敌对双方同意放弃投票。

pais·ley /ˈpeɪzlɪ; ˈpezlɪ/ n (soft wool fabric with) curved patterns in bright colours: 帕斯力图案(色彩鲜明的弧曲图案): 帕斯力毛料(上有此种图案的柔软毛织品):a ~ shawl. 帕斯力披肩.

pa·ja·mas /pəˈdʒɑːməz; pəˈdʒæməz/ n pl ⇨ pyjamas.

pal /pæl; pæl/ n (colloq) comrade; friend. (口)同志; 朋友. □ vi (-ll-) pal up (with sb), become friendly. (与某人)要好起来; (与某人)结交. **pally** /ˈpælɪ; ˈpælɪ/ adj (colloq) friendly. (口)亲密的; 友好的.

pal·ace /ˈpælɪs; ˈpælɪs/ n **1** official residence of a sovereign, archbishop or bishop; any large and splendid house; large, splendid building for entertainment. 皇宫; 官殿; (大主教或主教的)官邸; 豪华大厦; 豪华的娱乐大厦. **2 the ~**, influential persons at the ~ of a sovereign ruler. 官廷权贵. **~ revolution**, overthrow of sb in a position of great power, eg a President, by high-ranking colleagues or close subordinates. 官廷革命(揽大权者, 如总统, 被其高级同僚或亲信属僚所推翻的革命).

pala·din /ˈpælədɪn; ˈpælədn/ n any of the twelve Peers of the court of Emperor Charlemagne; knight errant; notable champion. 查理曼大帝的十二武士之一; 游侠; 著名的斗士.

palaeo- /ˈpælɪəu- US: ˈpeɪlɪəu-; ˈpeɪlɪo-/ pref (in compounds, etc) (用在复合词等中) = paleo-.

palan·quin, palan·keen /ˌpælənˈkiːn; ˌpælənˈkin/ nn covered litter for one person, carried on poles by two or more men, as formerly used in India and other Eastern countries. (印度及其他东方国家昔时所用的由二人或更多人抬的)单座轿子.

pal·at·able /ˈpælətəbl; ˈpælətəbl/ adj agreeable to the taste or (fig) to the mind. 可口的; 美味的; (喻)怡人的.

pala·tal /ˈpælətl; ˈpælətl/ n, adj (sound) made by placing the tongue against or near (usu the hard) palate (eg /j, ʒ, ʃ, dʒ/); of the palate. 舌头接触口盖所发的(音); 颚音(如/j, ʒ, ʃ, dʒ/ 等音); 上颚的.

pal·ate /ˈpælɪt; ˈpælɪt/ n **1** roof of the mouth: 上颚; 口盖:the hard/soft ~, its front/back part. 硬(软)颚, ~ cleft '~, ⇨ cleave'(3). ⇨ the illus at mouth. 参看 mouth 之插图. **2** sense of taste: 味觉:have a good ~ for fine wines. 精于品评上等酒类.

pa·la·tial /pəˈleɪʃl; pəˈleʃəl/ adj of or like a palace; magnificent: 官殿的; 象官殿的; 堂皇的; 庄严的:a ~ residence. 富丽堂皇的居所.

pal·at·in·ate /pəˈlætɪnət US: -tənət; pəˈlætɪn‚et/ n territory ruled over by an earl or count having some royal privileges. 有王权伯爵的领地.

pal·aver /pəˈlɑːvə(r) US: -ˈlæv-; pəˈlævə/ n [C] (hist) talk or conference, esp one between traders or explorers and the people of the country; [U] idle talk; [U, C] (colloq) bother. (史)商谈; 交涉; 谈判(尤指与外来商旅与当地人之间所作者); 闲谈; 空话. □ vi [VP2A] talk idly for a long time. 长时间闲谈; 闲聊.

pale¹ /peɪl; pel/ adj (-r, -st) **1** (of a person's face) having little colour; bloodless: (指脸色)苍白的; 没有血色的:He turned ~ at the news. 他听到那消息面容失色. You're looking ~ today. 你今天脸色苍白. '~-face n name said to have been used by N American Indians for a European white person. 白脸人(据说北美印第安人从前用此名称指欧洲的白种人). **2** (of colours) not bright; faintly coloured: (指颜色)暗淡的; 浅淡的:~ blue. 淡蓝色. □ vi [VP2A, C] grow ~; lose colour. 变淡; 变暗淡; 失色. ~ before/by the side of, (fig) be far outshone by; appear weak when seen with. (喻)远逊于; (与...在一起) 相形见绌; 黯然失色. ~·ly adv /ˈpeɪllɪ; ˈpellɪ/ ~·ness n

pale² /peɪl; pel/ n pointed piece of wood used for fences; stake. 围篱用的尖木条; 桩. ⇨ paling.

pale³ /peɪl; pel/ n (hist) area around Dublin (in Ireland) controlled by the English. (史)爱尔兰都柏林

周围的英属地域. Now, only in: 今仅用于:beyond / outside the ~, socially unacceptable or unreasonable: 社交上不为人所接受的或不当的:His remarks put him quite outside the ~. 他所说的话使他被远拒于社交圈子外.

paleo·lithic (also palaeo-) /ˌpælɪəuˈlɪθɪk US: ‚perl-; ˌpeɪlɪ·ˈlɪθɪk/ adj of the period marked by the use of primitive stone implements. 旧石器时代的.

pale·on·tol·ogy (also palae-) /ˌpælɪɒnˈtɒlədʒɪ US: ‚perl-; ‚pelɪɑnˈtɑlədʒɪ/ n [U] study of fossils as a guide to the history of life on earth. 古生物学; 化石学. **pale·on·tol·ogist** (also palae-) /-ədʒɪst; -ədʒɪst/ n

pal·ette /ˈpælɪt; ˈpælɪt/ n board (with a hole for the thumb) on which an artist mixes his colours. (画家用的)调色板. '~-knife n thin steel blade with a handle, used (by artists) for mixing (and sometimes spreading) oil colours, (by potters) for moulding clay, and in cookery. (调油画用的)调色刀; (陶工用的)塑陶土刀; (烹饪用的)烹饪刀.

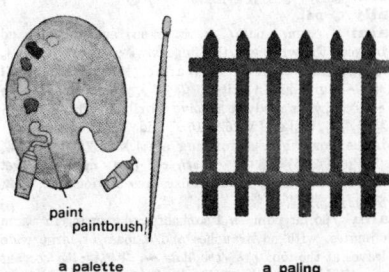

paint
paintbrush

a palette   a paling

pal·frey /ˈpɔːlfrɪ; ˈpɔlfrɪ/ n (pl -freys) (old use, and in poetry) saddle-horse for riding, esp one for a woman. (旧用语及诗中用语)供乘骑的马(尤指供妇女乘用者).

pal·imp·sest /ˈpælɪmpsest; ˈpælɪmp‚sɛst/ n [C] piece of parchment or other writing material from which the original writing has been erased to make room for new writing, esp as a source for lost works of the remote past. 刮去旧字以供书写新字的羊皮纸及其他书写材料(尤指作为古代佚失作品之来源者).

pal·in·drome /ˈpælɪndrəum; ˈpælɪnˌdrom/ n word, verse, etc that reads the same, backwards as forwards, eg madam. 回文(正读反读都一样的字、诗句等, 如 madam).

pal·ing /ˈpeɪlɪŋ; ˈpelɪŋ/ n fence made of pales². 用桩围成的栅; 木栅; 围篱.

pali·sade /ˌpælɪˈseɪd; ‚pæləˈsed/ n **1** fence of strong, pointed wooded stakes (eg as used to defend a building in former times). 木栅(用坚固的尖木桩围成, 如昔时用于防卫建筑物者). **2** (pl) (US) line of high, steep cliffs (esp along a river). (复)(美)一列高耸的峭壁(尤指沿河者). □ vt [VP6A] enclose or fortify with a ~(1). 用栅围绕, 用栅防卫.

pal·ish /ˈpeɪlɪʃ; ˈpelɪʃ/ adj somewhat pale. 略带苍白的.

pall¹ /pɔːl; pɔl/ n **1** heavy cloth spread over a coffin. 枢衣. '~-bearer n person who helps to carry, or who walks alongside, a coffin at a funeral. (出殡时)扶枢者; 护枢者. **2** (fig) any dark, heavy covering: (喻)任何深色而厚重的覆盖物:a ~ of smoke. 一片浓烟.

pall² /pɔːl; pɔl/ vi [VP2A, 3A] ~ (on/upon), become distasteful or boring because done, used, etc for too long a time: (久而)乏味; 令人生厌; 扫兴: pleasures that ~ after a time; 久而令人生厌的娱乐; a long lecture that ~ed upon most of the listeners. 令大多数听众生厌的长篇演讲.

pal·let /ˈpælɪt; ˈpælɪt/ n **1** straw-filled mattress for

sleeping on. 稻草床垫; 草荐. **2** large tray or platform for moving loads (by means of slings, etc), eg from a lorry in a train or on to a ship, and so save handling of separate items. (利用吊索等从货车上运货至火车或船上的)输送台.

pal·li·asse /'pælɪæs US: ˌpælɪ'æs; ˌpælɪˈæs/ n = **paillasse**.

pal·li·ate /'pælɪeɪt; ˈpælɪˌet/ vt [VP6A] (formal) lessen the severity of (pain, disease); excuse the seriousness of (a crime, etc). (正式用语)减轻; 缓和(痛、病), 掩饰(罪等). **pal·li·ation** /ˌpælɪˈeɪʃn; ˌpælɪˈeʃən/ n [U] the act of palliating; the state of being ~ed; [C] that which ~s; excuse. 减轻; 缓和; 掩饰; 使减轻或缓和之物; 辩解; 掩饰之词; 托辞; 借口. **pal·li·ative** /'pælɪətɪv; ˈpælɪˌetɪv/ n, adj (sth) serving to ~. 减轻的; 缓和的; 掩饰的; 用以减轻、缓和或掩饰之物.

pal·lid /'pælɪd; ˈpælɪd/ adj pale; ill-looking. 苍白的; 有病容的. ~**·ly** adv ~**·ness** n

pal·lor /'pælə(r); ˈpælɚ/ n [U] paleness, esp of the face. 苍白; (尤指)脸色苍白.

pally ⇨ **pal**.

palm¹ /pɑːm; pɑm/ n inner surface of the hand between the wrist and the fingers. 掌; 手掌; 掌心; 手心. ⇨ the illus at **arm**. 参看 arm 之插图. **grease/oil sb's ~**, give him a bribe. 贿赂某人. **have an itching ~**, be always ready to receive a bribe. 贪贿; 随时准备接受贿赂. □ vt [VP6A, 15B] hide (a coin, card, etc) in the hand when performing a trick. (表演魔术时)藏(硬币、纸牌等)于掌中. ~ **sth off (on/upon sb)**, get him to accept it by fraud, misrepresentation, etc. 以欺骗的方式使(某人)接受某物; 骗卖.

palm² /pɑːm; pɑm/ n **1** sorts of tree growing in warm climates, with no branches and a mass of large wide leaves at the top: 棕榈:the 'date-~; 枣椰树; the 'coconut ~. 椰子树. '~-**oil** n [U] oil obtained from the nuts of a W African ~. 棕榈油. '~ **wine** n [U] W African alcoholic drink, the sap of ~ trees. 棕榈酒(非洲西部由

COCONUT PALM

DATE PALM

coconut

date

palms

棕榈树液制成的一种酒). ˌP~-ˈSunday, the Sunday before Easter. 棕榈主日(复活节前的礼拜天). **2** leaf of a ~ as a symbol of victory. (象征胜利的)棕榈叶. **bear/carry off the ~**, be victorious. 得胜. **yield the ~ (to sb)**, admit defeat (by sb). 承认(被某人)打败; (向某人)认输. ~**y** adj (-ier, -iest) flourishing; prosperous: 繁盛的; 兴盛的: in my ~y days. 我的全盛时代. ~**er** n (formerly) pilgrim returning from the Holy Land with a ~-leaf. (昔时)带着棕榈叶自圣地归来的朝圣者.

pal·metto /pælˈmetəʊ; pælˈmɛto/ n (pl ~s or ~es /-təʊz; -toz/) kinds of small palm with fan-shaped leaves, common in the West Indies and the S E coast of the US. (产于西印度群岛及美国东南沿海一带, 有扇形叶的)小棕榈.

palm·ist /'pɑːmɪst; ˈpɑmɪst/ n person who claims to tell a person's future by examining the lines on his palm. 手相家. **palm·is·try** /'pɑːmɪstrɪ; ˈpɑmɪstrɪ/ n art of doing this. 手相术.

pal·pable /'pælpəbl; ˈpælpəbl/ adj that can be felt

or touched; clear to the mind: 可触知的; 摸得出的; 明显的; 明白的: a ~ error. 一个明显的错误. **pal·pably** /-əblɪ; -əblɪ/ adv

pal·pi·tate /'pælpɪteɪt; ˈpælpəˌtet/ vi [VP2A, C] (of the heart) beat rapidly and irregularly; (of a person, his body) tremble (with terror, etc). (指心脏)急速而不规则地跳动; 悸动; (指人、人体)(因恐惧等)发抖. **pal·pi·ta·tion** /ˌpælpɪˈteɪʃn; ˌpælpəˈteʃən/ n palpitating of the heart (from disease, great efforts, etc). (由于疾病, 用力等所致的)心脏急跳; 心悸; 悸动; 忐忑.

palsy /'pɔːlzɪ; ˈpɔlzɪ/ n [U] paralysis: 麻痹; 瘫痪; 中风: suffering from cerebral ~. 患大脑性瘫痪. **spastic**. □ vt paralyse. 使麻痹; 使瘫痪.

pal·ter /'pɔːltə(r); ˈpɔltɚ/ vi [VP3A] ~ **with**, be insincere when dealing with; trifle with: 不诚恳地对待或处理; 敷衍; 马马虎虎应付: Don't ~ with the question, Do treat it seriously. 不要马马虎虎处理这个问题.

pal·try /'pɔːltrɪ; ˈpɔltrɪ/ adj (-ier, -iest) worthless; of no importance; contemptible. 无价值的; 不重要的; 微不足道的; 可鄙的.

pam·pas /'pæmpəs US: -əz; ˈpæmpəz/ n pl extensive, flat, grassy, treeless plains of S America. 南美的大草原. ⇨ **prairie, savanna, steppe, veld**. '~-**grass** n [U] tall grass with sharp-edged blades and a silvery plume-like flower. 一种茎高大, 叶片锐利, 生银色羽状花的草; 银茅.

pam·per /'pæmpə(r); ˈpæmpɚ/ vt [VP6A] indulge too much; be unduly kind to: 纵容; 娇养: a ~ed poodle. 一只娇生惯养的狮子狗. She sometimes ~s herself and has a day in bed. 她有时纵容自己, 一整天躺在床上.

pamph·let /'pæmflɪt; ˈpæmflɪt/ n [C] small paper-covered book, esp on a question of current interest. 小册子(尤指有关于时事问题者). ~**·eer** /ˌpæmfləˈtɪə(r); ˌpæmfləˈtɪr/ n writer of ~s. 小册子作者.

pan¹ /pæn; pæn/ n **1** flat dish, usu shallow and without a cover, used for cooking and other domestic purposes. (烹饪及其他家务用途的)无盖浅锅; 平底锅; 盘子; 盆子. 'pan-**cake** n **(a)** batter cooked on both sides until brown and (usu) eaten hot. 薄煎饼. 'Pancake **Day**, = Shrove Tuesday. **(b)** pancake **landing**, emergency landing in which the aircraft drops flat to the ground. 平坠着陆(飞机平落地面之紧急降落). **(c)** cosmetic face-powder pressed into a flat cake, used without a foundation cream. (化妆用的)粉饼. **2** receptacle with various uses: (各种用途的)容器:the pan (= bowl) of a lavatory; (盥洗室中的)洗脸盆. a 'bedpan, ⇨ **bed¹(6)**. **3** (natural or artificial) depression in the ground: (地面上天然或人工的)凹穴; 坑:a 'salt-pan, where salt water is evaporated. 晒盐池. **4** 'brain-pan, upper part of the skull, enclosing the brain. 头盖. **5** either of the dishes on a pair of scales. (天平的)秤盘. ⇨ the illus at **balance**. 参看 balance 之插图. **6** open dish for washing gravel, etc to separate gold ore or other metals. 汰锅; 淘金盘(用以将金或其他金属与砂石分开). **7** (in flintlock guns) cavity in the lock that holds the gunpowder. (旧式燧发枪中的)火药池. a **flash in the pan**, ⇨ **flash¹(1)**. **8** [U] ('hard-)pan, hard subsoil. 硬的底土; 磐; 硬磐. **9** (sl) face. (俚)脸; 面. □ vt, vi (-nn-) **1** [VP15B, 3A, 2C] pan **sth off/out**, wash (gold-bearing gravel, etc) in a pan. 淘洗金(矿砂等). pan **for**, wash gravel, etc for eg gold. 淘洗金砂等以取(金). ~ **out**, **(a)** yield gold. 产金. **(b)** (fig) succeed; turn out: (喻)成功; 结果:How did things pan out? 事情的结果如何? The scheme panned out well. 那计划结果甚佳. **2** [VP6A] (colloq) criticize harshly. (口)严厉批评; 苛评.

pan² /pæn; pæn/ vi, vt (cinema and TV) turn a camera right or left to follow a moving object or get a panoramic effect. (电影及电视)左右转动摄影机使镜头能对着移动的目的物或收到摄取全景的效果; 转动(镜头). ⇨ **zoom(2)**.

pan- pref ⇨ **App 3**. 参看附录三.

pana·cea /ˌpænəˈsɪə; ˌpænəˈsiə/ n remedy for all troubles, diseases, etc. 解决一切弊病的方法;万灵药。

pa·nache /pæˈnæʃ US: pə-; pəˈnæʃ/ n [U] confident and flamboyant manner: 自信, 浮华的态度: 夸耀: *There was an air of ~ about everything he did.* 他做每一件事都带着浮夸的态度。

pa·nama /pəˈnɑːmɑː; ˈpænəˌmɑ/ n ~ **(hat)**, hat made from fine pliant straw-like material from the leaves of a plant of S and Central America. 巴拿马草帽。

pana·tella /ˌpænəˈtelə; ˌpænəˈtɛlə/ n [C] long slender cigar. 细长的雪茄烟。

pan·chro·matic /ˌpænkrəˈmætɪk; ˌpænkroˈmætɪk/ adj (photo) equally sensitive to all colours: (摄影)对所有颜色都同样感应的;全色的;泛色的: ~ *film.* 全色软片。

pan·creas /ˈpæŋkrɪəs; ˈpæŋkrɪəs/ n [C] gland near the stomach, discharging a juice which helps digestion. 胰;胰腺。⇨ the illus at **alimentary**. 参看 alimentary 之插图。**pan·cre·atic** /ˌpæŋkrɪˈætɪk; ˌpæŋkrɪˈætɪk/ adj of the ~. 胰(腺)的。

panda /ˈpændə; ˈpændə/ n bear-like mammal of China, with black legs and a black and white body. 熊猫(产于中国, 似熊, 脚黑色, 身体为黑白色)。'**P~ car** n (GB) police patrol car. (英)警察巡逻车。'**P~ crossing** n (GB) road crossing controlled by flashing lights, operated by pedestrians who press a button on a post. (英)(由行人按钮控制红绿灯的)行人穿越道。

pan·demic /pænˈdemɪk; pænˈdɛmɪk/ n, adj (disease) prevalent over the whole of a country or continent. 流行全国或全洲的(疾病);流行性的;大流行病。

pan·de·mo·nium /ˌpændɪˈməʊnɪəm; ˌpændɪˈmonɪəm/ n [C, U] (scene of) wild and noisy disorder. 大混乱;嘈杂;骚动(的场面)。

pan·der /ˈpændə(r); ˈpændə/ vi [VP3A] ~ **to**, 1 give help or encouragement (to sb, to his base passions and desires): 帮助;鼓动;煽动(与 to 连用, 后接某人卑鄙的情欲): *newspapers that ~ to the public interest in crime*; 煽动读者对犯罪感兴趣的报纸。~ *to low tastes.* 迎合低级趣味。2 act as a go-between (eg to sb's sexual desires): 作淫媒;拉皮条。⇨ **procure(3)**, the more usu word now. (今较常用 procure)。□ n person who ~s(2). 淫媒;拉皮条者。

pane /peɪn; pen/ n single sheet of glass in (a division of) a window. 窗上的单块玻璃;窗玻璃片。⇨ the illus at **window**. 参看 window 之插图。

pan·egyric /ˌpænɪˈdʒɪrɪk; ˌpænəˈdʒɪrɪk/ n [C] speech, piece of writing, praising a person or event. 颂词;颂文;褒词。

panel /ˈpænl; ˈpænl/ n 1 separate part of the surface of a door, wall, ceiling, etc usu raised above or sunk below the surrounding area. 门,墙,天花板等的镶板;嵌板;方格 (通常高出或低于其周围部分)。2 piece of material of a different kind or colour inserted in a dress. 衣服上所缝缀的不同质料或颜色的布块;饰块。3 board or other surface for controls and instruments: 装有控制开关及仪器的板或面;仪表板: '*instrument ~*, of an aircraft or motor-vehicle; (飞机或汽车的)仪表板; *con'trol ~*, on a radio or TV set. (收音机或电视机上的)控制板。4 list of names, eg of men who may be summoned to serve on a jury. 名单(例如陪审员名单)。5 group of speakers, esp one chosen to speak, answer questions, take part in a game, before an audience, eg of listeners to a broadcast: (广播等中的)座谈小组; 咨问小组; 游戏小组: (attrib) (用作定语) *a '~ discussion / game.* 小组讨论 / 小组游戏。□ vi (-ll-, US -l-) furnish or decorate with ~s(1, 2): 镶板于…为…装饰板; 饰以嵌板; 缝饰块于…: *a ~led room / wall / wainscot.* 嵌板房间(格子墙, 护壁板)。~·**ling** n [U] series of ~s on a wall, etc. 墙壁等的镶板。

pang /pæŋ; pæŋ/ n sharp, sudden feeling of pain, remorse, etc. 突然的剧痛, 懊悔等;悲痛。

panga /ˈpæŋɡə; ˈpɑŋɡə/ n large chopping knife used by African workers. (非洲工人用的)大斧头;大砍刀。

pan·handle /ˈpænhændl; ˈpænˌhændl/ n (US) narrow strip of land projecting from a larger area. (美)锅柄地带(突出于一块大地域的狭长地带)。□ vi (US colloq) beg, esp on the streets. (美口)行乞;(尤指)在街上行乞。

panic /ˈpænɪk; ˈpænɪk/ n [C, U] 1 unreasoning, uncontrolled, quickly spreading fear: 惊慌; 恐慌: *There is always danger of (a) ~ when a cinema catches fire.* 电影院着火时总是有引起惊慌的危险。'~**-stricken** adj terrified; overcome by ~: 为惊慌所袭的; 极度受惊的; 惊慌失措的: *The crowd was ~-stricken,* filled with ~. 群众极为惊慌。2 (attrib) unreasoning: (用作定语)没理由的: ~ *fear.* 没理由的恐惧。□ vi (-ck-) be affected with ~: 受惊; 惊慌: *Don't ~! There's no danger!* 不要惊慌! 没有危险! **pan·icky** /ˈpænɪkɪ; ˈpænɪkɪ/ adj (colloq) easily affected by ~; in a state of ~. (口)容易受惊的; 惊慌的。

pan·jan·drum /pænˈdʒændrəm; pænˈdʒændrəm/ n name applied jokingly to an exalted personage or to a pompous official. 大老爷(戏谑地加诸大人物或自大的官员的称谓)。

pan·nier /ˈpænɪə(r); ˈpænjə/ n one of a pair of baskets placed across the back of a horse or donkey; one of a pair of bags on either side of the back of a (motor-)cycle. (挂在驮马或驮驴两侧的)驮篮; (挂在脚踏车或机车后座两旁的)载物袋。

cycle panniers   donkey panniers

pan·ni·kin /ˈpænɪkɪn; ˈpænəkɪn/ n (GB) small metal cup; its contents. (英)小金属杯;一小杯之量。

pan·oply /ˈpænəplɪ; ˈpænəplɪ/ n (pl **-plies**) complete suit of armour; (fig) splendid array. 全副甲胄; (喻)华丽的衣服。Hence, 由此产生, **pan·oplied** /ˈpænəplɪd; ˈpænəplɪd/ adj provided with a ~. 披甲胄的; 全身披甲的; 盛装的。

pan·op·tic /pænˈɒptɪk; pæˈnɑptɪk/ adj giving a complete view, eg by diagram, illustration, of sth. (以图解、插图等)表示某物全貌的。

pan·orama /ˌpænəˈrɑːmə US: -ˈræmə; ˌpænəˈræmə/ n wide, uninterrupted view; constantly changing scene: 全景;全图;活动画景;连续转换之景: *the ~ of London life.* 伦敦生活的形形色色。**pan·or·amic** /ˌpænəˈræmɪk; ˌpænəˈræmɪk/ adj

pan-pipes /ˈpæn paɪps; ˈpænˌpaɪps/ n pl musical instrument made of a series of reeds or pipes, played by blowing across the open ends. 排箫; 潘神箫(芦杆制的乐器)。

pansy /ˈpænzɪ; ˈpænzɪ/ n (pl **-sies**) 1 flowering herbaceous plant. 三色紫罗兰。2 △ (derog, offensive term for) effeminate man; homosexual. (讳)(贬抑及侮蔑语)女性化的男子;同性恋的男人。

pant /pænt; pænt/ vi, vt 1 [VP2A, C] take short, quick breaths; gasp: 喘气; 喘息: *The dog ~ed along behind its master's horse.* 那只狗喘着气跟在主人的马后。2 [VP6A, 15B] say while ~ing: 喘着气说: *He ~ed out his message.* 他气喘吁吁地说出他的口信。3 [VP3A] ~ **for**, (old use) have a strong wish for. (旧用法)切望; 渴望。□ n short, quick breath; gasp. 喘气; 喘息。~·**ing·ly** adv

pan·ta·loon /ˌpæntəˈluːn; ˌpæntlˈun/ n 1 (in pantomime) foolish character upon whom the clown

plays tricks. (哑剧中) 为丑角取笑对象的愚蠢角色。 **2** (*pl*) (now hum, or US) = **pants**. (复)(谐,美)裤子。

pan·tech·ni·con /ˈpænˈteknɪkən; ˌpænˈtɛknɪˌkɑn/ *n* (GB) large van for removing furniture. (英)家具搬运车。

pan·the·ism /ˈpænθiɪzəm; ˈpænθiˌɪzəm/ *n* [U] belief that God is in everything and that everything is God; belief in and worship of all gods. 宇宙即神论; 泛神论; 多神崇拜。 **pan·the·ist** /-ɪst; -ɪst/ *n* believer in ~. 宇宙即神论者; 泛神论者; 多神崇拜者。 **pan·the·is·tic** /ˌpænθiˈɪstɪk; ˌpænθiˈɪstɪk/ *adj* of ~. 宇宙即神论的; 泛神论的; 崇拜多神的。

pan·theon /ˈpænθiən US: -ɒn; ˈpænθiən/ *n* temple dedicated to all the gods: 万神殿; 万神祠: *the P~ in Rome*; 罗马万神殿; all the gods of a nation collectively: 一国的众神: *the (ancient) Egyptian ~*; (古代)埃及的众神; building in which the illustrious dead are buried or have memorials. 伟人祠; 先贤祠(内有名人坟墓或纪念碑的建筑物)。

pan·ther /ˈpænθə(r); ˈpænθɚ/ *n* black leopard; (US) puma. 黑豹; (美)山豹。 ⇨ the illus at **cat**. 参看 cat 之插图。

pan·ties /ˈpæntɪz; ˈpæntɪz/ *n pl* **1** short trousers worn by children. 儿童所穿的短裤。 **2** (woman's or girl's) close-fitting short drawers. (妇人或少女的)内裤。

pan·tile /ˈpæntaɪl; ˈpænˌtaɪl/ *n* curved roof tile: 波形瓦: (attrib) (用作定语) *a ~ roof*. 波形瓦屋顶。

panto /ˈpæntəʊ; ˈpæntəʊ/ *n* (colloq abbr of) **pantomime**. (口) pantomime 之略。

pan·to·graph /ˈpæntəgrɑːf US: -græf; ˈpæntəˌgræf/ *n* **1** device for copying a plan, etc on a different scale. 比例尺; 放大尺; 伸缩绘图器; 缩放绘图器。 **2** device for carrying electric current to a vehicle from overhead wires. (电车顶之)电杆架。

pan·to·mime /ˈpæntəmaɪm; ˈpæntəˌmaɪm/ *n* **1** [C, U] (example of a) kind of English drama based on a fairy tale or traditional story, with music, dancing and clowning. 取材于童话或传说, 有音乐、舞蹈及滑稽表演的一种英国戏剧; 哑剧。 **2** [C] acting without words: 表意动作; 手势。

pan·try /ˈpæntrɪ; ˈpæntrɪ/ *n* (*pl* **-tries**) **1** room (in a large house, hotel, ship, etc) in which silver, glass, table-linen, etc are kept. (大房子、旅馆、船等的)餐具室。 **'~·man** /-mən; -mən/ *n* (*pl* **-men**) butler or his assistant. 饭厅管理员; 饭厅管理员的助手。 **2** larder; room (in a house) in which food is kept. 食品室; 备餐室。

pants /pænts; pænts/ *n pl* (GB) underpants; (US) trousers. (英)内裤; (美)裤子。 *bore/scare/talk, etc the '~ off one*, bore, etc one extremely. 极端令人厌烦(极为使人惊吓; 谈话使人极为厌烦等)。 *catch sb with his '~ down*, find him in an unprepared state. 出其不意; 乘其不备。

panty-hose /ˈpæntɪ həʊz; ˈpæntɪ hoz/ *n* = **tights**.

pan·zer /ˈpæntsə(r); ˈpænzɚ/ *attrib adj* (G) armoured. (德) 装甲的; 配有装甲车辆及武器的: *'~ divisions/troops*. 装甲师(装甲部队)。

pap /pæp; pæp/ *n* [U] soft or semi-liquid food for very young children or invalids; (fig) easy, trivial reading matter. (婴儿或病人食用的)柔软或半流质食物; (喻)浅易娱乐性读物。

papa /pəˈpɑː; ˈpɑːpə/ *n* (child's word for) father. (儿语)父亲; 爸爸。

pa·pacy /ˈpeɪpəsɪ; ˈpepəsɪ/ *n* (*pl* **-cies**) position of, authority of, the Pope; system of government by Popes. 罗马教皇的职位或权柄; 教皇治理的制度; 教皇政治。 **pa·pal** /ˈpeɪpl; ˈpepl/ *adj* of the Pope or the ~. 罗马教皇之职位、权柄或政治的, 权柄或制度的。

pa·paw, paw·paw /pəˈpɔː; US: ˈpɔːpɔː; ˈpɔpɔ/ *n* **1** tropical tree with a straight trunk like that of a palm; its large edible fruit with yellow pulp inside. 木瓜树; 木瓜。 ⇨ the illus at **fruit**. 参看 fruit 之插图。 **2** small N American evergreen tree with small fleshy edible

fruit (also called 亦称作 *custard apple*). 蕃荔枝; 释迦果。

pa·paya /pəˈpaɪə; pəˈpaɪə/ *n* = **papaw**.

pa·per /ˈpeɪpə(r); ˈpepɚ/ *n* **1** [U] substance manufactured from wood fibre, rags, etc in the form of sheets, used for writing, printing, drawing, wrapping, packing, etc: 纸: *a sheet of ~*; 一张纸; *a bag*. 一个纸袋。 *(be/look) good on ~*, (be/look) good when judged from written or printed evidence, eg plans, proposals, diplomas, testimonials: 照书面的情形看来很多(如计划, 提议, 文凭,证明书): *a good scheme on ~* (but not yet tested). 好的书面计划(但尚未经过实验)。 *This applicant looks good on ~*, has good ~ qualifications. 照书面资料来看, 这个申请人的资历很不错。 *put pen to ~*, (dated for) begin to write, eg a letter. (过时用语)开始写(信等)。 *'~·backed adj* (of books) bound in paper covers. (指书)以纸作书面的; 平装的。 Hence, 由此产生, *'~·back n* such a book and such a form: 平装书; 平装: *Has the book appeared in ~back?* 此书的平装本出来了吗? *'~·chase n hare and hounds*, at hare. *'~·clip n = clip¹(1)*. *'~·hanger n* man whose trade is to paste ~ on the walls of rooms. 贴壁纸的工人。 *'~·knife n* one for cutting open the leaves of books, opening envelopes, etc. (用于割开书页,信封等的)裁纸刀; 拆信刀。 *'~·mill n* one where ~ is made. 造纸厂。 *'~·tiger n* person, group of persons, etc which seems to be, but is not, powerful. 外强中干的人; 纸老虎。 *'~·weight n* weight placed on loose ~s to prevent them from being blown away. 纸压; 书镇。 *'~·work n* [U] written work (in an office, etc, eg filling in forms, correspondence, contrasted with practical affairs, dealing with people): 文书业务; 文书工作: *He's good at ~work*. 他擅长文书工作。 **2** [C] newspaper: 报纸: *today's ~s*; 今天的报纸; *the evening ~*. 晚报。 **3** [U] ~ (money), banknotes, etc used as currency. 钞票; 纸币。 **4** (*pl*) documents showing who sb is, what authority he has, etc: (复)身份证明文件; 证件: *send in one's ~s*, (mil) resign. (军)辞职; 退伍。 **5** [C] set of printed examination questions on a given subject: 试卷; 试题: *The biology ~ was difficult*. 生物学试题很难。 **6** [C] essay, paper one is to read to a learned society: 论文(尤指在学会宣读者): *a ~ on currency reform*. 一篇关于通货改革的论文。 □ *vt* [VP6A, 15B] paste ~ on (walls, etc): 贴纸于(墙上等): *~ the dining-room*; 用纸表糊餐厅; *cover with ~*. 用纸覆盖; 用纸包。 *~ over the cracks*, (fig) cover up, conceal, faults, etc. (喻)隐瞒、掩饰过错等。 *~ the house*, (fig) issue free tickets for a theatre, etc (to give the impression of success). (喻)戏院等发行招待券(以显示其成功)。

pa·pier-mâché /ˌpæpɪeɪ ˈmæʃeɪ US: ˌpeɪpɚ məˈʃeɪ; ˈpepɚˌʃe/ *n* [U] paper pulped and used as a plastic material for making trays, boxes, etc. 混凝纸(用于制造盘、盒等的可塑纸料)。

pa·pist /ˈpeɪpɪst; ˈpepɪst/ *n, adj* (unfriendly word, as used by some Protestants) (member) of the Roman Catholic Church. (某些基督教教徒等所用的不友善用语)天主教的; 天主教徒。

pa·poose /pəˈpuːs US: pæˈpuːs; pæˈpus/ *n* (word used by Indians of N America for a) baby; framed bag (like a rucksack) for carrying a young baby on sb's back. (北美印地安人用语)婴孩; (背婴儿用的)背囊。

pap·rika /ˈpæprɪkə US: pæˈpriːkə; pæˈprikə/ *n* [U] sweet red pepper used in cooking. (烹调用的)辣椒。 ⇨ the illus at **vegetable**. 参看 vegetable 之插图。

pa·py·rus /pəˈpaɪərəs; pəˈpaɪrəs/ *n* **1** [U] (kind of paper made in ancient Egypt from) tall water plant or reed. 纸草; (古埃及用纸草制成的)纸草纸。 **2** [C] (*pl* **papyri** /pəˈpaɪəraɪ; pəˈpaɪraɪ/) manuscript written on this paper. 写在此种纸上的文稿。

par¹ /pɑː(r); pɑr/ *n* [U] **1** average or normal amount, degree, value, etc. 平均数量; 正常数量; 一般程度; 常态。 *above/below/at par*, (of shares, bonds, etc), above/below/at the original price or face value. (指

股票、证券等)高于(低于, 照)原价或票面价值。*on a par*
(with), equal (to). 等于。*up to par*, (colloq) as
good / well as usual. (口) 达到正常标准。**par of**
exchange, normal rate of exchange between two
currencies, eg the £ and the US $. 汇兑平价(如英镑和
美元之汇率)。**par value**, nominal or face value of
a share. 面值: 股票的面值。**2** (golf) number of
strokes considered necessary for a good player to complete a
hole or course. (高尔夫球)(一洞或一场球的)标准杆数。

par² /pɑ:(r); pɑr/ ⇨ **parr**.

par·able /'pærəbl; 'pærəbl/ *n* simple story designed
to teach a moral lesson: 寓言; 比喻:*speak in ～s*. 以比
喻来说。*Jesus taught in ～s*. 耶稣以比喻讲道。**para-**
boli·cal /,pærə'bɒlɪkl; ,pærə'bɑlɪkl/ *adj* of, expressed
in, ～s. 寓言的; 以比喻说明的。

par·ab·ola /pə'ræbələ; pə'ræbələ/ *n* plane curve
formed by cutting a cone on a plane parallel to its side,
so that the two arms get farther away from one
another. 抛物线。**para·bolic** /,pærə'bɒlɪk; ,pærə'bɑlɪk/
adj of, like, a ～. 抛物线的; 似抛物线的。

para·chute /'pærəʃu:t; 'pærə,ʃut/ *n* apparatus used
for a jump from an aircraft or for dropping supplies,
etc: 降落伞: (attrib) (用作定语) '～ *troops / flares /*
mines. 伞兵部队(附伞照明弹; 伞投水雷)。□ *vt, vi* [VP
2A, C, 6A, 15A, B] drop, descend, from an aircraft by
means of a ～: (用降落伞) 空降; 空投: *men ～d behind*
the enemy lines. 空降敌后的部队。**para·chut·ist** /-ɪst;
-ɪst/ *n* person who jumps with a ～. 跳伞人; 伞兵。

par·ade /pə'reɪd; pə'red/ *vt, vi* **1** [VP6A, 2A] (of
troops) (cause to) gather together for drilling, inspection,
etc; march in procession. (指部队) (为训练、检阅等而)
集结; 列队行进: (指人群) 游行。**2** [VP6A] make a
display of; try to attract attention to: 表示; 炫耀:
one's abilities. 炫耀个人的能力。□ *n* **1** [U] parading
of troops: 阅兵: (军队的) 分列式; 游行: *be on ～*, 在游
行; [C] instance of this. 阅兵或游行之实例。**2** [C]
'～-ground, area of ground on which ～s are held. 阅
兵场; 游行地区。**3** [C] display or exhibition. 陈列; 展
览。*make a ～ of one's virtues*, try to impress people
by showing them. 夸示个人的优点。**4** public promenade;
wide, often ornamented pathway, esp on a seafront. 公
共散步所; (尤指海边之)宽阔且常有装饰物的人行道。

para·digm /'pærədaɪm; 'pærə,daɪm/ *n* example or
pattern, esp of the declension of a noun, the conjugation
of a verb, etc. (名词、动词等的) 变化例; 变化表。

para·dise /'pærədaɪs; 'pærə,daɪs/ *n* **1** the Garden of
Eden, home of Adam and Eve. 伊甸园; (亚当和夏娃之)
乐园。,bird of '～, bird (of New Guinea) with
beautiful feathers. (新几内亚产的) 极乐鸟; 风鸟。**2**
heaven. 天堂; 天国。**3** [C] any place of perfect
happiness; place of perfect happiness. 乐土; 极乐的地方;
极乐; 至福。*a fool's ～*, ⇨ **fool¹(1)**.
para·dis·iac /,pærə'dɪzɪæk; ,pærə'dɪsɪ,æk/, **para-**
disia·cal /,pærədɪ'zaɪəkl; ,pærədɪ'saɪəkl/ *adj* of or
like ～: (似) 乐园的; 天堂的; 极乐的: *Adam and Eve in*
their paradisiac state, in their pristine innocence. 乐园
中天真无邪的亚当和夏娃。

para·dox /'pærədɒks; 'pærə,dɑks/ *n* [C] statement
that seems to say sth opposite to common sense or the
truth, but which may contain a truth (eg 'More haste,
less speed'). 似非而是的隽语(如'欲速则不达'); 反论。
～i·cal /,pærə'dɒksɪkl; ,pærə'dɑksɪkl/ *adj* **～i·cally**
/-klɪ; -klɪ/ *adv*

par·af·fin /'pærəfɪn; 'pærə,fɪn/ *n* [U] **1** '～ (oil),
(GB) oil obtained from petroleum, coal, etc used as a
fuel (in lamps, heating and cooking-stoves). (英)(从石
油、煤等提炼出来的)煤油; 石蜡油(作燃料用; 煤灯或炉灶
的燃料)。(US 美 = *kerosene*). **2** ～ **(wax)**, wax-like
substance used for making candles. (制造蜡烛用的)石
蜡。**3** (,liquid) '～, odourless, tasteless form of ～ used
as a laxative. (无臭无味, 作通便剂用的)液状石蜡。

para·gon /'pærəgən *US:* -gɒn; 'pærə,gɑn/ *n* model

---

of excellence; apparently perfect person or thing: 模
范; 完美的人或物: *I make no claim to be a ～ of virtue*.
我并不认为自己是个美德的典范。

para·graph /'pærəgrɑ:f *US:* -græf; 'pærə,græf/ *n*
[C] **1** division (usu a group of several sentences dealing
with one main idea) of a piece of writing, started on a
new line (and usu indented); the mark (¶) used to
show where a new ～ is to begin, and as a mark of
reference. 段; 节(文章的段, 通常包含若干句子表达某一
要旨, 每段都另起一行且通常缩进若干字母); 表示新段落或
参看某一附注之符号(¶)。**2** small item of news in a
newspaper. (报纸上新闻的)小节。□ *vt* divide into ～s.
将…分段。

para·keet /'pærəki:t; 'pærə,kit/ *n* small, long-tailed
parrot of various kinds. 长尾小鹦鹉。⇨ the illus at
rare. 参看 rare 之插图。

par·al·lel /'pærəlel; 'pærə,lɛl/ *adj* (of lines) continuing at the same distance from one another; (of one
line) having this relation (*to* or *with* another): (指线
条)彼此间保持等距离的; 平行的: (指一线)与他线相平行
的(后接 to 或 with): *a road running ～ to / with the*
railway; 与铁路平行的道路; *in a ～ direction (with...)*.
朝着(与…)平行的方向。,～ 'bars, pair of ～ bars on
posts for gymnastic exercises. (运动用的) 双杠。□ *n*
1 ～ of latitude, line on a map ～ to, and passing
through all places the same distance north or south of,
the equator. 纬线; 纬圈。⇨ the illus at **projection**. 参
看 projection 之插图。*in ～*, (of the components of an
electrical circuit) with the supply of current taken to
each component independently, not in series. (指电路
结构)并联的。**～ series. 2** [U, C] person, event, etc
precisely similar: 极相似的人或物: *a brilliant career*
without (a) ～ in modern times. 近世无匹的辉煌事迹。
3 comparison: 比较; 对比: *draw a ～ between....* 在～之
间作一比较。□ *vt* **(-l-** or (GB) **-ll-)** [VP6A] **1** quote,
produce or mention sth ～ or comparable. 比较。**2** be
～ to: 与…相似; 与…相比: *His experiences ～ mine in*
many instances. 他的经历在许多方面与我的相似。*The*
street ～s the railway. 这条街与铁路平行。**～·ism**
/-ɪzəm; -ɪzəm/ *n* (lit or fig) being ～. (字面或喻)平
行; 相似; 相类; 类似。**～o·gram** /,pærə'leləgræm; ,pærə-
'lelə,græm/ *n* four-sided plane figure whose opposite
sides are ～. 平行四边形。⇨ the illus at **quadrilateral**.
参看 quadrilateral 之插图。

par·al·ysis /pə'ræləsɪs; pə'ræləsɪs/ *n* [U] loss of
feeling or power to move in any or every part of the
body; (fig) state of utter powerlessness. 麻痹; 瘫痪; (喻)
毫无力量; 无能力。**para·lyt·ic** /,pærə'lɪtɪk; ,pærə'lɪtɪk/
n, adj **1** (person) suffering from ～: 麻痹的; 瘫痪的; 麻
痹患者:*a paralytic stroke*; 中风; (fig)helpless: (喻)无助
的; 无用的; 无能为力的:*paralytic laughter*. 不能自已的
笑声。**2** (person who is) very drunk. 烂醉如泥的; 酩酊大
醉之人。**para·lyse** (US=**-lyze**) /'pærəlaɪz; 'pærə,laɪz/
vt [VP6A] **1** affect with ～. 使麻痹; 使瘫痪。**2** make
helpless: 使无助, 使无能为力: *paralysed with fear*. 吓得
瘫软。

par·ameter /pə'ræmɪtə(r); pə'ræmətə/ *n* characteristic
or determining feature. 特色; 特点。

para·mili·tary /,pærə'mɪlɪtrɪ *US:* -terɪ; ,pærə'mɪlɪ-
,terɪ/ *adj* having a status or function ancillary or
similar to that of regular military forces: 有辅助正规
军之地位或功能的; 准军事性的: ～ *organizations*. 准军事
性的组织。

para·mount /'pærəmaʊnt; 'pærə,maʊnt/ *adj* (formal) supreme, superior in power: (正式用语) 最高的;
至上的: ～ *chiefs*: 最高首领; pre-eminent: 超越其他的;
卓越的:*of ～ importance*; 最重要的; superior. 优于; 胜
过。**～cy** /-tsɪ; -tsɪ/ *n*

para·mour /'pærəmʊə(r); 'pærə,mʊr/ *n* (archaic)
illicit partner of a married man or woman. (古)情夫;
情妇。

para·noia /,pærə'nɔɪə; ,pærə'nɔɪə/ *n* [U] menta

disorder (usu incurable), marked by fixed delusions, eg of persecution or grandeur. 妄想狂(一种精神病,通常无法医治)。 **para·noiac** /ˌpærəˈnɔɪæk/, ˌpærəˈnɔɪæk/, **para·noid** /ˈpærəˌnɔɪd/ nn, adjj (person) suffering from ~. 妄想狂患者;患妄想狂的。

para·pet /ˈpærəpɪt/; ˈpærəpɪt/ n 1 (usu low) protective wall at the edge of a flat roof, side of a bridge, etc. (平屋顶之边缘、桥之侧旁等处之) 扶墙; 栏杆; 矮垣。 2 defensive bank of earth, stone, etc along the front edge of a trench (in war). (战壕的)前墙; 护墙; 胸墙。

para·pher·nalia /ˌpærəfəˈneɪlɪə/; ˌpærəfəˈneɪlɪə/ n [U] numerous small possessions, tools, instruments, etc esp concerning sb's hobby or technical work. 个人财物; 工具; 行头(尤指与某人之嗜好或技术性工作有关者)。

para·phrase /ˈpærəfreɪz/; ˈpærəˌfreɪz/ vt [VP6A], n (give a) restatement of the meaning of (a piece of writing) in other words. 释义; 意译; 解述(一作品)之意义。

para·ple·gia /ˌpærəˈpliːdʒə/; ˌpærəˈplɪdʒɪə/ n [U] (path) paralysis of the lower part of the body, including both legs, caused by injury to the spinal cord. (病理)下身瘫痪; 截瘫(因脊髓受伤所致)。 **para·plegic** /ˌpærəˈpliːdʒɪk/; ˌpærəˈplɛdʒɪk/ n, adj (person) suffering from ~. 下身瘫痪患者; 下身瘫痪的。

para·site /ˈpærəsaɪt/; ˈpærəˌsaɪt/ n 1 animal (eg louse, hookworm) or plant (eg mistletoe) living on or in another and getting its food from it. 寄生动物; 寄生虫; 寄生植物。 2 person supported by another and giving him nothing in return. 靠他人为生的人; 食客。 **para·sitic** /ˌpærəˈsɪtɪk/, ˌpærəˈsɪtɪk/, **para·siti·cal** /ˌpærəˈsɪtɪkl/, ˌpærəˈsɪtɪkl/ adjj caused by, living as, a ~. 寄生物引起的; 寄生的; 靠他人为生的。

para·sol /ˈpærəsɒl/ US: -sɔːl/; ˈpærəˌsɔl/ n umbrella used to give shade from the sun. 阳伞。

para·troops /ˈpærətruːps/; ˈpærəˌtrups/ n pl troops trained for being dropped by parachute. 伞兵部队。 **para·trooper** /ˈpærətruːpə(r)/; ˈpærəˌtrupə/ n one of these. 伞兵。

para·typhoid /ˌpærəˈtaɪfɔɪd/; ˌpærəˈtaɪfɔɪd/ n [U] kind of fever in some ways like typhoid but milder and caused by a different bacterium. 副伤寒。

par·boil /ˈpɑːbɔɪl/; ˈpɑrˌbɔɪl/ vt [VP6A] boil (food) until partially cooked; (fig) make uncomfortably hot. 将(食物)煮到半熟; (喻)使过热; 使热得难受。

par·cel /ˈpɑːsl/; ˈpɑrsl/ n [C] 1 thing or things wrapped and tied up for carrying, sending by post, etc: 包裹; 小包; 邮包: She left the shop with an armful of ~s. 她抱着一抱小包离开店铺。 '~ post n [U] system, method, etc of carrying ~s by post. 包裹邮递(制度、方法等); 包裹邮寄部; 包裹邮件。 2 part and ~ of, an essential part of. …的主要部分。 a ~ of land, an area of land (esp part of an estate). 一块地(尤指产业之一部分)。 □ vt (-ll-, US also -l-) [VP6A, 15B] ~ out, divide into portions. 分为数份; 分配。 ~ up, make (books, etc) into a ~. 将(书等)捆扎成包裹; 打包。

parch /pɑːtʃ/; pɑrtʃ/ vt [VP6A] 1 (of heat, the sun, etc) make hot and dry: (指热、阳光等)使焦干: the ~ed deserts of N Africa. 北非的干燥沙漠。 2 dry or roast by heating: 烤干; 烘干: ~ed peas. 干炒豌豆。

parch·ment /ˈpɑːtʃmənt/; ˈpɑrtʃmənt/ n 1 [C, U] (manuscript on) writing material prepared from the skin of a sheep or goat. 羊皮纸; 写在羊皮纸上的文件或手稿。 2 [U] kind of paper resembling ~. 类似羊皮纸的纸。

par·don /ˈpɑːdn/; ˈpɑrdn/ n 1 [U] forgiveness: 宽恕; 赦免: ask for ~; 恳求宽恕; [C] instance of this. 宽恕或赦免的实例。 2 [U] indulgence; forbearance. 原谅; 宽容。 beg sb's ~, excuse oneself, eg for disagreeing with what sb says, or apologize, eg for not hearing or understanding what sb says: 请原谅, 不敢苟同(对不起请再说一遍): I beg your ~! 对不起请再说一遍! ⇨ excuse²(3); sorry(2). 3 (archaic) indulgence(4). (古)

赦罪; 免罪符。 □ vt [VP6A, 12B, 13B] ~ sb for sth! ~ sb sth, forgive; excuse; overlook: 饶恕; 宽恕; 原谅: ~ sb for doing wrong; 宽恕某人犯了过错; ~ sb an offence. 原谅某人的罪过。 P~ me for/P~ my contradicting you. 原谅我反驳你。 ~able /ˈpɑːdnəbl; ˈpɑrdnəbl/ adj that can be ~ed. 可宽恕的; 可原谅的。 ~ably /-əblɪ; -əblɪ/ adv (formal) in a way that can be ~ed: (正式用语)可原谅地; 难怪地: She was ~ably proud of her wonderful cooking. 她的烹调讲得当高明, 难怪她会那么骄傲。 ~er n (in the Middle Ages) person who had been licensed to sell papal indulgences(4). (中古时代)获准售卖天主教免罪符的人。

pare /peə(r)/; pær/ vt [VP6A, 15B] cut away the outer part, edge or skin of: 剥; 削; 切去…的外部、外边或外皮: ~ the (finger-)nails; 剪指甲; ~ the claws of an animal; 切掉兽爪; ~ (= peel) an apple; 削苹果皮; (fig) (喻) ~ down (= reduce) one's expenses. 削减开支。 **par·ings** /ˈpeərɪŋz; ˈpɛrɪŋz/ n pl that which is ~d off: 削去之物; 剥去之物; 切去之物: 'nail-parings. 剪下的指甲。

par·egoric /ˌpærɪˈɡɒrɪk US: -ˈɡɔːr-; ˌpærəˈɡɔrɪk/ n [U] soothing medicine containing opium and flavoured with aniseed. (含有鸦片而带茴香味的)镇痛剂; 缓和剂。

par·ent /ˈpeərənt; ˈpɛrənt/ n father or mother; ancestor: 父; 母; 祖先: the ~ birds; 亲鸟; the ~ plant. 母树。 May I introduce you to my ~s? ie to my father and mother. 我把你介绍给我的父母好吗? ~ company, (comm) one that controls another, eg by owning more than half its shares or because of the composition of its Board of Directors. (商)母公司(因拥有较多股份或因董事会的结构而控制另一公司者)。 '~age /-ɪdʒ; -ɪdʒ/ n [U] fatherhood or motherhood; origin; birth: 父亲的身份; 母亲的身份; 根本; 出身: of unknown ~age, having unknown ~s. 身世不明的。 ~al /pəˈrentl; pəˈrɛntl/ adj of ~s: 父的; 母的: ~al anxieties; 父母的忧虑; children who lack ~al care. 缺乏父母照顾的孩子们。 ~ally /-təlɪ; -tlɪ/ adv

par·enth·esis /pəˈrenθəsɪs; pəˈrɛnθəsɪs/ n (pl -eses /-əsiːz; -ə,siz/) sentence within another sentence, marked off by commas, dashes or brackets; (sing or pl) round brackets ( ) for this. 插句(用逗点、破折号或括弧加以分开); (用单数或复数)圆括弧。 ⇨ bracket². App 9. 参看附录九。 in ~, between parentheses; (fig) taking (sth) separately. 括在括弧里; (喻)顺带。 **par·en·thetic** /ˌpærənˈθetɪk; ˌpærənˈθɛtɪk/, **par·en·theti·cal** /-ɪkl; -ɪkl/ adjj of, relating to, used as, a ~. 插句的; 括弧的; 作为插句的。 **par·en·theti·cally** /-klɪ; -klɪ/ adv

par ex·cel·lence /ˌpɑːr ˈeksəlɑːns US: ˌɛksəˈlɑns; pɑrˈɛksəˌlɑns/ adv (F) by virtue of special excellence; in the highest degree. (法)由类拔萃地; 卓越地。

pa·riah /pəˈraɪə; pəˈraɪə/ n (India) person of low caste or of no caste; (fig) social outcast. (印度)低等级或不列级的人; (喻)流浪者; 无赖汉。 '~-dog n (India) ownerless dog of mixed breed. (印度)无主的杂种狗。

pari-mu·tuel /ˌpærɪ ˈmjuːtjʊəl US: ˈmjuːtʃʊəl; ˈmjuːtʃʊəl/ n (F) form of betting (on races) in which the winners divide the stakes of the losers, less a percentage for management expenses. (法)赛马赌博的一种分注法(获胜者除去付出百分之一的手续费外将所有输者的赌注平分)。

pari passu /ˌpærɪ ˈpæsuː; ˌpærɪˈpæsju/ adv (Lat) simultaneously and equally; at an equal rate of progress. (拉)同时而同等地; 同一步调地; 并行地。

par·ish /ˈpærɪʃ; ˈpærɪʃ/ n (GB) division of a county with its own church and priest: (英)教区(郡以下的区分, 有属于本区的教堂和牧师): the ~ church; 教区礼拜堂; the ~ council. 教区会议。 ~ clerk, official with various duties connected with the ~. 教区执事。 ,~'pump, (used attrib) of local interest only: (用作定语)地域性的; 地区性的: ~-pump affairs/politics. 地区性的事务(政治)。 ~ register, book with records of christenings, marriages and burials. 教区记事录(记录

本区居民之洗礼、命名以及婚丧等事). **civil** ～, division of a county for local government. 郡以下的地方行政区。～**ioner** /pə'rɪʃənə; pəˈrɪʃənə/ n inhabitant of a ～. 一教区内的居民。

Pa·ris·ian /pəˈrɪzɪən US: -ɪʒn; pəˈrɪʒən/ n, adj (native, inhabitant) of Paris. 巴黎人; 巴黎居民; 巴黎的。

par·ity /ˈpærətɪ; ˈpærətɪ/ n [U] equality; being equal; being at par: 同等; 平等; 等价: *Should teachers in secondary schools and teachers in primary schools receive ～ of pay?* 中学教师和小学教师应否接受同等的薪水？ *The two currencies have now reached ～,* are at par. 这两种货币现在已达到同等价值。 ～ **of ex'change,** rates of currency exchange officially determined by Governments. (政府所订定之)汇率。

park[1] /pɑːk; pɑrk/ n 1 public garden or public recreation ground in a town. 公园。 '**ball** ～, (US) playing-field. (美)球场; 运动场; 儿童游戏场。 2 area of grassland (usu with trees) round a large country house or mansion. 庭园; 邸园(乡村巨宅或大厦周围之草地,通常有树木)。 3 '**car-～,** place where motor-vehicles may be left for a time. 停车场。 4 ,**national** '～, area of natural beauty, eg mountains, forests, lakes, set apart by the State for public enjoyment, and where industrial and urban development is forbidden or limited. 国家公园; 国立公园。 5 place used by the military for artillery, stores, etc. 军队的枪炮、军需品等的放置场。

park[2] /pɑːk; pɑrk/ vt, vi 1 [VP6A, 2A] put (a motor-vehicle) for a time, unattended: 停(车等): *Where can we ～ (the car)?* 我们可以在哪里停车？ 2 [VP6A, 15A] (colloq) put (sth or sb) somewhere: (口) 将(某人或某物) 放置在某处: *Where can I ～ my luggage?* 我可以在哪里放行李？ *～ yourself in that chair while I make you a cup of tea.* 请在那张椅子上坐, 我去给你泡茶。

parka /ˈpɑːkə; ˈpɑrkə/ n (US) waterproof jacket with a hood attached (as worn for skiing, mountain-climbing, etc). (美)带兜帽的防水短外套(如滑雪, 爬山等所穿着者)。 (GB 英 = anorak).

parking /ˈpɑːkɪŋ; ˈpɑrkɪŋ/ n [U] (area for the) ～ of motor-vehicles: 停车; 停车区; 停车场: *No ～ between 9am and 6pm.* 上午九时至下午六时不准停车。 '～ **lot,** (US) area for the ～ of motor-vehicles. (美)停车场。 '～ **meter,** coin-operated meter beside which a car may be parked in a public place, eg a street. 停车计时器。 '～ **orbit,** temporary orbit for a spacecraft. (太空船的)驻留轨道。

Parkinson's /ˈpɑːkɪnsnz; ˈpɑrkɪnsənz/ adj '～ **disease,** (path) chronic progressive disease of old people, with muscular tremors, muscular rigidity and general weakness. (病理)帕金森氏病; 震颤麻痹(老年人因肌肉僵硬或身体衰弱而引起的慢性震颤症)。 '～ **law,** (hum) suggestion that work will always last as long as the time available for it. (谐)帕金森氏定律(只要时间许可, 工作总会拖到最后)。

parky /ˈpɑːkɪ; ˈpɑrkɪ/ adj (sl) (of the air, weather) chilly. (俚)(指空气、天气)寒冷的。

par·lance /ˈpɑːləns; ˈpɑrləns/ n use or choice of words; way of speaking: 用语; 说法: *common/legal ～.* 一般说法(法律用语)。

par·ley /ˈpɑːlɪ; ˈpɑrlɪ/ n (pl -leys) [C] conference, esp between leaders of two opposed forces. 会谈; 谈判(尤指敌对两军领袖所作者)。 □ vi [VP2A, 3A] ～ (**with sb**), discuss terms, hold a conference. (与某人)谈判; 讨论。

par·lia·ment /ˈpɑːləmənt; ˈpɑrləmənt/ n (in countries with representative government) supreme law-making council or assembly, esp of GB, formed of the House of Commons and the House of Lords: (在代议政体的国家内)国会; 议会(尤指英国由上议院及下议院所构成者); *enter P～.* 成为国会议员; ,*Members of*

'*P～*; 国会议员; *summon/adjourn P～*; 召开国会(宣布国会休会); *P～ sits/rises*; 国会开会(休会); *open P～*, (of the Sovereign) declare it open with traditional ceremonial. (指君王) 宣布议会开会。 **par·lia·men·tarian** /ˌpɑːləmənˈteərɪən; ˌpɑrləmənˈtɛrɪən/ n person skilled in the rules and procedures of ～, who is a good debater, etc. 精于议会法规与程序的人; 议会中的雄辩家。 **par·lia·men·tary** /ˌpɑːləˈmentrɪ; ˌpɑrləˈmɛntərɪ/ adj of ～: 议会的; 国会的: ～*ary debates;* 议会辩论; ～*ary language,* polite, civil language, as required in ～*ary* debates. (如议会辩论时所用的)慎重有礼的言语。

par·lour (US = **-lor**) /ˈpɑːlə(r); ˈpɑrlə/ n 1 ordinary sitting-room for the family in a private house (now more usu called sitting-room or living-room). 起居室(现多称作 sitting-room 或 living-room)。 '～ **games,** games played in the home (competitions, guessing, etc). 室内游戏或比赛(如竞争、猜测等)。 2 official room for the reception of visitors: 会客室; 接待室: *the Mayor's* ～, in a town hall, etc. 市长的会客室。 3 (esp US) room for customers and clients: (尤美)接待顾客的房间: *a 'beauty ～;* 美容院; *a 'hairdresser's ～.* 女子美发店。 '～-**car** n (US) luxurious railway coach with individual reserved seats. (美)豪华的铁路客车。

par·lous /ˈpɑːləs; ˈpɑrləs/ adj (formal) perilous. (正式用语)危险的。

Par·me·san /ˈpɑːmɪzæn; ˌpɑrməˈzæn/ n kind of cheese made at Parma and elsewhere in N Italy. (意大利北部帕尔马等地所制的)帕尔马干酪。

par·ochial /pəˈrəʊkɪəl; pəˈrokɪəl/ adj of a parish; (fig) limited, narrow: 教区的; (喻)有限的; 狭小的: *a ～ outlook/mind/point of view.* 狭隘的见地(思想,观点)。 ～**ly** /-kɪəlɪ; -kɪəlɪ/ adv ～**ism** /-ɪzəm; -ɪzəm/ n.

par·ody /ˈpærədɪ; ˈpærədɪ/ n (pl -**dies**) 1 [C, U] (piece of) writing intended to amuse by imitating the style of writing used by sb else. (模仿他人文体所作的)游戏诗文; 讽刺诗文。 2 [C] weak imitation. 拙劣的仿造物。 □ vt [VP6A] make a ～ of: 借模仿…而作游戏诗文; 歪改; 拙劣地模仿: ～ *an author/a poem.* 模仿某作家而作成一篇游戏文字; 歪改某一首诗。 **par·odist** /-ɪst; -ɪst/ n person who writes parodies. 借模仿而作游戏诗文的人。

pa·role /pəˈrəʊl; pəˈrol/ n [U] prisoner's solemn promise, on being given certain privileges, that he will not try to escape. 囚犯为获得某些特许而作的不企图逃脱的誓言。 **on** ～, liberated after making such a promise. 发誓后而假释的。 **break one's** ～, (try to) escape while on ～. 违誓; 发誓获释后(企图)逃脱。 □ vt [VP6A] set (a prisoner) free on ～. 使 (囚犯) 宣誓后假释。

paro·quet /ˈpærəkiːt; ˈpærəˌkɛt/ n = **parakeet.**

par·ox·ysm /ˈpærəksɪzəm; ˈpærəksˌɪzəm/ n [C] sudden attack or outburst (of pain, anger, laughter, etc). (痛苦、愤怒、笑等之)突然发作。

par·quet /ˈpɑːkeɪ US: pɑrˈkeɪ; pɑrˈke/ n flooring of wooden blocks fitted together to make a pattern. 木块拼花地板; 嵌木地板。

parr, par /pɑː(r); pɑr/ n young salmon. 幼鲑。

par·ri·cide /ˈpærɪsaɪd; ˈpærəˌsaɪd/ n [C, U] (person guilty of the) murder of one's father or near relation. 弑父; 弑亲; 弑君者; 弑君者。

par·rot /ˈpærət; ˈpærət/ n 1 sorts of bird with a hooked bill and (usu) brightly coloured feathers, some kinds of which can be trained to imitate human speech. 鹦鹉。 ⇨ the illus at **rare.** 参看 rare 之插图。 ～ **fever, = psittacosis.** 2 person who repeats, often without understanding, what others say. 重复他人之言而毫不解其义的人。

parry /ˈpærɪ; ˈpærɪ/ vt (pt, pp -**ried**) [VP6A] turn aside (a blow); (fig) evade (a question). 挡开或闪避(打击); (喻)避开(问题)。 □ n [C] act of ～ing, esp in fencing and boxing. 挡开; 闪避(尤指击剑与拳击时的动作)。

parse /pɑːz US: pɑrs; pɑrs/ vt [VP6A] describe

(a word) grammatically; point out how the words of a sentence are related. 将(某词)作语法上的分析; 指出句中各词的关系。

Par·see /pɑːˈsiː; parˈsi/ *n* member of a religious group in India, the members being descended from Persians who settled in India in the 8th c. (印度的)袄教徒(为第八世纪定居印度的波斯人的后裔)。

par·si·mony /ˈpɑːsɪmənɪ *US:* -məunɪ; ˈparsəˌmonɪ/ *n* [U] (formal) (usu as a bad quality) excessive carefulness in using money or (fig) immaterial things. (正式用语)吝啬; 小气; 过份节省; (喻)过于节约的非物质之物。**par·si·moni·ous** /ˌpɑːsɪˈməunɪəs; ˌparsəˈmonɪəs/ *adj* too economical or miserly. 太节省的; 吝啬的; 小气的。

pars·ley /ˈpɑːslɪ; ˈparslɪ/ *n* [U] garden plant with crinkled green leaves, used in seasoning and sauces and for garnishing food. 芫荽菜; 香菜。

pars·nip /ˈpɑːsnɪp; ˈparsnəp/ *n* [C] long, white or pale-yellow root, cooked as a vegetable. (可煮食的)防风草根。

par·son /ˈpɑːsn; ˈparsṇ/ *n* parish priest; (colloq) any clergyman. 教区长; (口)牧师。**～'s nose,** (colloq) rump of a cooked fowl. (口)烹调过的禽类的尾部; 鸡鸭等的屁股。**'～·age** /-ɪdʒ; -ɪdʒ/ *n* ～'s house. 教区长住宅。

part¹ /pɑːt; part/ *n* [C] **1** (often *sing* without *indef art*) some but not all of a thing or a number of things; something less than the whole: (常为单数, 不用不定冠词)部分: *We spent (a) ～ of our holiday in France/in a ～ of the country we had never visited before.* 我们假期的一部分是在法国(以前没去过的地方)度过。*P～s of the book are interesting.* 这本书有些部分很有趣。*The greater ～ of what you heard is only rumour.* 你所听到的大部分不过是谣言而已。**for the 'most ～,** in most cases; mostly. 一般地; 大抵; 大半。**in ～,** in some degree. 一部分; 有几分。**,～'owner** *n* person who owns sth in common with others. (财物之)共有人。**,～'time** *adj, adv* for only a ～ of the working day or week: 部分时间的(地); 一天或一周中工作一部分时间的(地); 兼任的(地): *be employed ～-time;* 受雇从事部分时间的工作; ～*-time teaching,* eg two days a week. 部分时间的教学; 兼任教学(如每周两天)。Hence, 由此产生, **part-'timer** *n.* 部分时间工作者; 兼任者; 兼差者。**2** (*pl*) region; district: (复数地区); 区域: *in these/those ～s.* 在这些(那些)地区。**3** any one of a number of equal divisions: 若干等分之一; …分之一: *A minute is the sixtieth ～ of an hour.* 一分钟是一小时的六十分之一。**4** person's share in some activity; his duty or responsibility; what an actor in a play, film, etc says and does: (某人在某一活动中所担任的)职份; 职责: 本分; (戏剧、电影等中之)角色, 台词及动作: *a man with a ～ in a play/in a conference.* 剧中扮演一个角色的人(参加某一会议的人)。*He spoke/acted his ～ very well.* 他的台词会得(他的戏演得)很好。*Do the actors all know their ～s?* 演员们都熟悉他们的台词及动作吗? *I had only a small ～ in these events.* 在这些事件中我只尽了一小部分力量。**play a (big, small, etc) ～ (in sth),** be concerned in sth, make a contribution: 与(某事)有(极大或一点)关系; 对(某事)有(极大一点)贡献: *He had an important ～ to play in ensuring the success of the scheme.* 为确保该计划的成功他作过重大贡献。**take ～ (in),** have a share (in); help: 参加; 协助: *Are you going to take ～ in the discussion,* Do you intend to speak? 你要参加讨论吗? **5** side in a dispute, transaction, agreement, mutual arrangement, etc. (辩论、交易、合约、双方协议等之)一方。**take sb's ～; take the ～ of sb,** support sb: 支持某人; 祖护某人: *He always takes his brother's ～.* 他总是祖护他哥哥(弟弟)。**for 'my ～,** as far as I am concerned: 就我而论: *For my ～ I am quite happy about the division of the money.* 就我来说, 我对于那笔钱的分配感到相当满意。**on 'my/'his/'your, etc;** on the ～ of (Mr A, etc), proceeding from, done by, me/him/you/Mr A, etc: 在我(他、你等)来说; 在(A 先生等)来说; 在我(他、你等)的方面。

(A 先生等)的方面: *There was no objection on his ～/on the ～ of the owner of the land,* He did not object. 在他(地主)来说, 不表示反对。*The agreement has been kept on my ～ but not on his.* 我遵守了协议, 而他却没有。**6 take sth in good ～,** not be offended at it. 乐意接受某事。**7** division of a book; each issue of a work published in instalments: (书的)部; 篇; 卷; (连续出版物的)部分: *a new encyclopaedia to be issued in monthly ～s.* 将按月分期出版的一套新百科全书。**8** essential piece or section of sth. 重要部分。**(spare) ～,** extra piece, etc to be used when needed, when sth breaks or wears: (机器的)备件; 备用器材: *When can I get a ～ for my pump?* 我何时才能获得我的唧筒的零件? **9** (music) each of the melodies that make up a harmony; the melody for a particular voice or instrument: (音乐)乐曲的一部分; 适于某一人声演唱或某一乐器演奏的部分; 声部: *orchestra ～s;* 管弦乐部分; *sing in three ～s.* 三部合唱。**'～-singing, '～-song** *n* singing, song, with three or more voice ～s. (三部或三部以上的)无伴奏合唱; 合唱曲。**10** (gram) **～ of 'speech,** one of the classes of words, eg noun, verb, adjective. (语法)词类(如名词、动词、形容词)。**11** *a man/woman of (many) ～s,* of (many) abilities; talented. 有(极有)才干的男人(女人)。□ *adv* (usu ～…～…) in some degree: 部分地; 有几分: *made of iron and ～ of wood.* 部分用铁部分用木材造成的。**～·ly** *adv* in some degree. 部分地; 有几分。

part² /pɑːt; part/ *vt, vi* **1** [VP6A, 2A, 2] (cause to) separate or divide: (使)分离; 分开: *The policemen ～ed the crowd.* 警察排开群众。*We tried to ～ the two fighters.* 我们试图把两个打架的人拉开。*Let us ～ friends,* leave each other with no feeling of enmity. 让我们和和气气地分手。*The crowd ～ed and let us through.* 人群分开来让我们通过。**～ company (with sb),** (a) end a relationship. (与…)断绝关系。**(b)** leave; separate from. 各自东西; 各奔前程。**(c)** disagree: 意见不合: *On that question I am afraid I must ～ company with you.* 关于那个问题, 我恐怕要和你分道扬镳了。**2** [VP3A] **～ with,** give up, give away: 放弃; 舍弃: *He hates to ～ with his money,* doesn't like to spend it or give it away. 他极不喜欢花钱。**3** [VP6A] **～ one's 'hair,** make a dividing line by combing the hair in opposite ways. 梳分头(把头发梳向两边)。**～·ing** *n* **1** [C] line where the hair is combed in opposite ways. 头发的分梳线。**2** [C, U] departure; leave-taking: 离开; 分别: (attrib) (用作定语) *his ～ing injunctions,* those given on taking leave. 他的临别训谕。**at the ～ing of the ways,** at the point where the road divides or forks; (fig) when one has to choose between courses of action. 在岔路口; (喻)到了必须抉择的时候。**～·ing shot =** *Parthian shot,* ⇨ **Parthian.**

par·take /pɑːˈteɪk; parˈtek/ *vi* (*pt* **-took** /-ˈtuk; -ˈtuk/, *pp* **-taken** /-ˈteɪkən; -ˈtekən/) [VP3A] **～ of sth,** (dated formal) (过时的正式用语) **1** take a share in: 分享; 分担; 参与: *They partook of our triumph.* 他们分享我们的胜利。*They were partaking of our simple meal.* 他们跟我们一起吃便饭。**2** have some of (the nature or characteristics of): 带有几分(…的性质或特性): *His manner ～s of insolence.* 他的态度带有几分倨慢。

par·terre /pɑːˈteə(r); parˈtɛr/ *n* **1** (in a garden) level space with lawns and flower-beds. (庭园之)花坛。**2** (in a theatre) part of the auditorium behind the orchestra. (戏院之)楼下正厅。

par·theno·gen·esis /ˌpɑːθɪnəuˈdʒenəsɪs; ˌparθəno-ˈdʒenəsɪs/ *n* [U] reproduction of offspring without fertilization by sexual union. 孤雌生殖; 单性生殖。

Par·thian /ˈpɑːθɪən; ˈparθən/ *adj* of Parthia, ancient country of N E Iran conquered by the Persians in AD 226. 帕提亚, 即安息 (古伊朗东北一古国) 的。**～ shot/shaft,** (fig) sth said or done as a final reply, argument, etc at the moment of parting. (喻)临去时所说的话或所做的事; 回马枪; 回马箭。

par·tial /ˈpɑːʃl; ˈpɑrʃəl/ adj 1 forming only a part; not complete: 部分的; 不完全的: a ~ success; 部分的成功; a ~ eclipse of the sun. 日偏蚀。 2 ~ (towards), showing too much favour to one person or side: 偏袒的; 偏袒的: examiners who are ~ towards pretty women students. 偏袒漂亮女生的主考人员。 3 ~ to, having a liking for: 对…偏爱的: ~ to French cuisine. 偏爱法国菜调。 ~ly /ˈpɑːʃəlɪ; ˈpɑrʃəlɪ/ adv 1 partly; not completely. 部分地; 不完全地。 2 in a ~(2) manner. 偏袒地。 ~ity /ˌpɑːʃɪˈælɪtɪ; ˌpɑrʃæˈlætɪ/ n 1 [U] being ~(2) in treatment of people, etc; bias; favouritism. 偏袒; 偏心; 偏见; 徇私。 2 ~ity for, [C] fondness: 喜爱: a ~ity for moonlight walks. 喜欢在月光下散步。

par·tici·pate /pɑːˈtɪsɪpeɪt; pəˈtɪsə.peɪt/ vi [VP2A, 3A] ~ (in), have a share, take part (in): 分享; 参与: ~ in sb's suffering/in a plot. 分担某人的痛苦(参与某一图谋)。 **par·tici·pant** /pɑːˈtɪsɪpənt; pəˈtɪsəpənt/ n person who ~s (in sth). 分享者; 参与者(与 in 连用后接某事物)。 **par·tici·pa·tion** /pɑːˌtɪsɪˈpeɪʃn; pɑrˌtɪsəˈpeʃən/ n [U] act of participating. 分享; 参与。

par·ti·ciple /ˈpɑːtɪsɪpl; ˈpɑrtəsəpl/ n (gram) verbal adj qualifying nn but retaining some properties of a v: (语法)分词(动词变成的形容词, 可修饰名词, 但尚保有动词的某些特性): 'Hurrying' and 'hurried' are the present and past ~s of 'hurry'. hurrying and hurried 是 hurry 的现在分词和过去分词。 **par·ti·cip·ial** /ˌpɑːtɪˈsɪpɪəl; ˌpɑrtəˈsɪpɪəl/ adj of a ~: 分词的: a participial adjective, eg 'loving' in 'a loving mother'. 分词形容词(如 a loving mother 中的 loving)。

par·ticle /ˈpɑːtɪkl; ˈpɑrtɪkl/ n 1 very small bit: 极小之物; 粒子; 微粒; 质点: ~s of dust; 尘埃; smallest possible quantity: 极小量: She hasn't a ~ of sense. 她一点儿脑筋也没有。 **elementary ~**, (phys) one of the constituents of an atom, not yet known to be composed of simpler ~s, eg an electron. (物)基本粒子。 2 (gram) minor part of speech, eg an article (a, an, the), a preposition or adverb (up, in, out), a conjunction (or), an affix (un-, in-, -ness, -ly). (语法)虚词, 不变词(如冠词 a, an, the; 介词或副词 up, in, out; 连接词 or); 词缀 (前缀或后缀 un-, in-, -ness, -ly)(如 yes, no)。

parti·col·oured, (US = -col·ored) /ˈpɑːtɪ kələd; ˈpɑrtɪ.kʌləd/ adj differently coloured in different parts. 杂色的; 斑驳的。

par·ticu·lar /pəˈtɪkjʊlə(r); pəˈtɪkjələr/ adj 1 relating to one as distinct from others: 单独的; 特殊的: in this ~ case. 在这种特殊情况下。 2 special; worth notice; outstanding: 特别的; 值得注意的; 突出的: for no ~ reason. 没有特别理由。 He took ~ trouble to get it right. 他特别费力把它弄好。 in ~, especially: 特别地; 尤其: I remember one of them in ~. 我特别记得其中一个。 3 very exact; scrupulous: 极精确的; 严谨的: a full and ~ account of what we saw. 对于我们所见情形完整而精确的记述。 4 ~ (about/over), hard to satisfy; fastidious: 难以满足的; 挑剔的; 吹毛求疵的: She's ~ about what she wears. 她对于穿着很讲究。 He's too ~ over what he will eat and drink. 他对于吃喝太讲究了。 □ n detail. 细节; 琐碎; 细项。 go into ~s, give details. 详细列出。 ~ly adv in a ~ manner: 特别地; 显著地: His good humour was ~ly noticeable. 他的好脾气是显而易见的。 I ~ly mentioned that point. 我特地提到那一点。 ~ity /pəˌtɪkjʊˈlærətɪ; pərˌtɪkjəˈlærətɪ/ n [U] exactness; attention to detail. 精确; 考究; 详创; 特质。 ~·ize /-aɪz; -ˌaɪz/ vt, vi [VP6A, 2A] name specially or one by one. 逐一列举; 特别提出。

part·ing /ˈpɑːtɪŋ; ˈpɑrtɪŋ/ ⇨ part².

par·ti·san /ˌpɑːtɪˈzæn US: ˈpɑːrtɪzn; ˈpɑrtəzn/ n 1 person devoted to a party, group or cause. 死党; 帮伙; 党羽。 2 (esp) member of an armed resistance movement in a country occupied by enemy forces: (尤指)沦陷区的抗敌分子; 游击队员: ~ troops. 游击队。 □ adj uncritically devoted to a cause: 致忠的; 献身的; 盲目推崇的: His loyalties are too ~. 他的忠诚太盲目了。 ~·

ship /-ʃɪp; -ˌʃɪp/ n

par·ti·tion /pɑːˈtɪʃn; pɑrˈtɪʃən/ n 1 [U] division into parts: 分割; 划分; 分配; 瓜分: the ~ of India in 1947. 一九四七年印度的分割。 2 [C] that which divides, esp a thin wall between rooms, etc. 分隔物; 隔墙。 3 [C] part formed by dividing; section. 分割的部分; 区分。 □ vt [VP6A, 15B] ~ (sth off), divide into sections, etc; separate by means of a ~(2). 分割; 瓜分; 区分; 隔开。

par·ti·tive /ˈpɑːtɪtɪv; ˈpɑrtɪtɪv/ n, adj (word) denoting part of a collective whole: 表示部分的词; 表示部分的: 'Some' and 'any' are ~s. some 和 any 都是表示部分的词。

part·ner /ˈpɑːtnə(r); ˈpɑrtnər/ n 1 person who takes part with another or others in some activity, esp one of the owners of a business: 伙伴; 合作者; 合伙(指经商之)合伙人: ~s in crime; 共犯; profits shared equally among all the ~s; 合伙人平均分享的利润; active ~, one taking part in the affairs of the business. 参与业务的合伙人。 sleeping ~, ⇨ sleep²(2). 2 one of two persons dancing together, playing tennis, cards, etc together; husband or wife. 舞伴; (打网球、玩纸牌等的)同业者; 搭档; 夫或妻。 □ vt [VP6A, 15A] be a ~ to; bring (people) together as ~s. 做…的伙伴; 使(人们)成为伙伴。 ~·ship /-ʃɪp; -ˌʃɪp/ n 1 [U] state of being a ~; [C] joint business: 合伙; 合股; 合股经营的生意: enter into ~ship (with sb); 与(某人)合伙; be in ~ship. 入伙; 合伙。

par·took /pɑːˈtʊk; pɑrˈtʊk/ ⇨ **partake**.

par·tridge /ˈpɑːtrɪdʒ; ˈpɑrtrɪdʒ/ n [C] sorts of bird of the same family as the pheasant; [U] its flesh as food. 鹧鸪; 鹌鹑; 松鸡; 雉肉。 ⇨ the illus at **fowl**. 参看 fowl 之插图。

par·tur·ition /ˌpɑːtjʊˈrɪʃn US: -tʃʊ-; ˌpɑrtʃʊˈrɪʃən/ n [U] childbirth. 分娩。

party /ˈpɑːtɪ; ˈpɑrtɪ/ n (pl -ties) 1 [C] group of persons united in policy and opinion, in support of a cause, esp in politics: 党派; 政党: the Conservative, Liberal and Socialist parties. 保守党、自由党和社会党。 2 [U] (esp attrib use) government based on political parties: (尤用作定语)政党政治: the '~' system; 政党制度; ~ politics, politics of and within a ~, eg manoeuvres designed to win influence or power; 政党策略(如意在争取影响力或权力的策略): Should a politician put public interest before ~ interest? 政治家应该把公共利益放在政党利益之前吗? follow the ~ line; ~ line, ⇨ line¹(11). ~ machine, ⇨ machine(2). ~-spirited adj 热衷(政)党的; 党性强的。 3 one of the persons or sides in a legal agreement or dispute. (契约或争论的)一方; 当事人。 ~-wall, one that divides two properties and is the joint responsibility of the owners of these properties. 共有隔墙; 界墙。 4 group of persons travelling or working together, or on duty together: 同行的一群人; 共同工作的人; 一同值班的人: a 'firing-~, of soldiers, at a military funeral or execution. (军事葬礼之)鸣枪班; (执行死刑之)行刑班。 5 gathering of persons, by invitation, for pleasure: 集会; 聚会: a 'dinner/'birthday ~; 宴会; 庆祝生日的集会: give a ~, arrange one and be the host(ess); 举办集会; 请客; (attrib)(用作定语) a ~ dress. 宴会服装。 lack the ~ spirit, be without enthusiasm for a ~. 对宴会不热心; 对宴会不起劲。 make up a ~, join together to form a ~. 聚会; 参加聚会。 6 person taking part in and approving of or being aware of what is going on: 参与人; 赞同人; 关系人: a ~ to a conspiracy; 参与阴谋的人; an innocent ~. 无辜的关系人。 7 (hum) person: (谐)人: Who's the old ~ in blue, the old person dressed in blue? 穿蓝衣服的那个老头儿是谁? 8 '~-coloured, = parti-coloured.

par·venu /ˈpɑːvənjuː US: -nu; ˈpɑrvə.nju/ n person who has suddenly reached higher economic or social status from a lower status. 暴发户; 崛起者。

pas·chal /'pæskl; 'pæskl/ adj 1 of the Jewish Passover. (犹太人之)逾越节的。 2 of Easter. 复活节的。

pasha /'pɑːʃə US: 'pæʃə; 'pɑːʃə/ n (hist) title of honour placed after the name of a Turkish officer of high rank or the governor of a province. (史)帕夏(从前土耳其高级官员或省长的头衔或尊称,通常置于人名之后)。

pass¹ /pɑːs; pæs; pæs/ n 1 success in an examination, esp (in university degree examinations) success in satisfying the examiners but without distinction or honours¹ (7): 考试及格; 考试通过(尤指大学学位考试达到及格标准,但并无特别优异的成绩):*get a ~*; 及格; *a '~ degree.* 达到及格标准的学位。 2 *come to/reach a pretty / sad / strange, etc ~*, reach such a state or condition. 遭遇困难; 陷入困境。 3 *bring to ~*, accomplish, carry out. 完成;实行。 *come to ~*, happen: 发生: *How exactly did that come to ~?* 那事到底是怎么发生的呀? 4 (paper, ticket, etc giving) permission or authority to travel, enter a building, occupy a seat in a cinema, etc: 通行证及出入许可证。通行证:入场券: *a free ~*, ticket giving free travel on the railways, etc. (如火车之)免费乘车证;免票证。 *All ~es to be shown at the barrier*, eg in a station. 所有通行证都要在(车站等的)栅口出示。 *No admittance without a ~.* 没有通行证不准进入。 ⇨ **~-book** below. 参看下列之 pass-book。 5 act of kicking, throwing, or hitting the ball from one player to another player (of the same team): 传球(给本队的队员): *a clever ~ to the forward.* 给前锋的一个妙传。 6 movement of the hand over or in front of sth (as in conjuring or juggling, or in mesmerism): 手在某物东西上面或前面的动作(如玩魔术、变戏法或催眠术时手的动作)。 7 forward movement, blow (in fencing, etc). (击剑等之)刺;戳。 *make a ~ at sb*, (sl) make (possibly unwelcome) amorous advances. (俚)向(某人)做出非礼的举动。 8 narrow way over or through mountains, such a way viewed as the entrance to a country. 山间隘路; 狭路; 进入一个国家的通路。 ⇨ the illus at **mountain.** 参看 mountain 之插图。 *hold the ~*, (fig) defend a cause. (喻)捍卫某一目标(主义或运动)。 *sell the ~*, (fig) betray a cause; yield up a position. (喻)背叛某一目标(主义或运动); 放弃立场。 9 (card games) act of passing. (纸牌戏)放弃出牌或叫牌。 ⇨ **pass**²(15). 10 (compounds) (复合词) '~·**book** n **(a)** book supplied by a bank to a customer with records of his account. 银行往折。 **(b)** (S Africa) booklet, document, allowing a black African person to be in a certain area. (南非)(准许非洲黑人在某地居留的)小册子,证明文件。 '~·**key** n private key to a gate, etc; key which opens a number of locks; master key. 大门钥匙; (能开启若干锁的)总钥匙;万能钥匙。 '~·**word** n secret word or phrase which enables a person to be recognized as a friend by sentries: (哨兵等借以辨别敌友的)口令;密语: *give / demand the ~word.* 答(问)口令。

pass² /pɑːs US: pæs; pæs/ vi, vt (pp ~ed, or, as adj past /pɑːst US: pæst; pæst/) (For special uses with adv and preps, ⇨ 19 below.) (与副词及介词连用的特殊用法参看下列第 19 义。) 1 [VP2A, C] move towards and beyond, proceed (along, through, down, etc): 前进; 通过; 穿过(往 along, through, down 等连用): *The two ships ~ed each other during the night.* 那两艘船在夜间错过了。 *I glanced at her and ~ed on.* 我看了她一眼,继续往前走。 *He ~ed in front of/behind me.* 他从我前面/后面通过。 *They ~ed by, went past.* 他们走过去了。 Hence, 由此产生, '~**er-'by** n (pl **passers-by**) person who ~es sb or sth: 过路人; 偶然经过的人: *The purse was picked up by a ~er-by.* 钱包被路人捡到了。 2 [VP6A] leave (a person, place, object, etc) on one side or behind as one goes forward: 经过: *Turn right after ~ing the Post Office.* 经过邮局后右转。 *I ~ed Miss Green in the street.* 我在街上遇见格林小姐。 3 [VP6A] go through, across, over or between: 通过;

The ship ~ed the channel. 船驶过海峡。 *No complaints ~ed her lips.* 她毫无怨言。 4 [VP2A] (of time) go by; be spent: (指时间)过去; 消逝:*Six months ~ed and still we had no news of them.* 六个月过去了,而我们还没有他们的消息。 *The time ~ed pleasantly.* 很愉快地度过了那一段时间。 5 [VP6A] spend (time): 消磨(时间):*How shall we ~ the evening?* 我们如何消磨今晚的时间? *What can we do to ~ the time?* 我们能做什么来消磨时间? 6 [VP3A] *~ (from...)(to/into...)*, change from one state of things to another; change into another state of things: 改变事物的状况; 变成另一种状况: *Water ~es from a liquid to a solid state when it freezes.* 水冻结时由液体变成固体。 *When water boils it ~es into steam.* 水煮沸时变为蒸气。 7 [VP6A, 15B, 12A, 13A] give by handing: 传递: *Please ~ (me) the butter.* 请把奶油递过来(给我)。 *The letter was ~ed on / round to all the members of the family.* 那封信给全家人传阅。 *The note was ~ed round the table.* 那字条由桌子周围的人传阅。 8 [VP6A] utter: 说出: *~ a remark*, say sth. 说一些话。 *~ the time of day with sb*, engage them in light conversation, 跟某人寒暄或打招呼。 9 [VP6A, 2A, C] (cause to) circulate; 传布: *He was imprisoned for ~ing forged banknotes.* 他因使用伪钞而被监禁。 *He ~es under the name of Mr Green, is known and accepted as Mr Green.* 他用格林先生这个名字; 已经通过被人接受。 10 [VP 6A, 2A] examine and accept; be examined and accepted: 审查通过; 考试及格: *Parliament ~ed the Bill.* 国会通过那个法案。 *The Bill ~ed and became law.* 那个法案已经通过成为法律。 *The examiners ~ed most of the candidates.* 主考人让大部分参加考试的人及格。 *The candidates ~ed (the examination).* 参加考试的人都及格了。 *Will the play ~ the censor?* 那个剧本会通过检查吗? *We have to ~ the Customs before we leave.* 我们在离开以前,得先通过海关检查。 11 [VP2A, C] take place; be said or done (between persons): 发生; (在人们之间)说出或做出:*Did you see/hear what was ~ing?* 你有没有看见(听到)所发生的事情? *Tell me everything that ~ed between you.* 把你们之间的一切情形告诉我。 12 [VP6A] be beyond the range of: 超过; 超出…之范围:*a story that ~es my belief.* 无法令人相信的故事。 *It ~es my comprehension.* 那是我所不能了解的。 13 [VP14] *~ sth on sth/sb*, give (an opinion, judgement, sentence on sth or sb): (对某事物或某人)表示(意见); 作(判断); 处(刑): *~ sentence on an accused man.* 给被告判刑。*I can't ~ an opinion on your work without seeing it.* 我没有看到你的作品,不能发表意见。 14 [VP2A] be accepted without rebuke or blame; go unnoticed or unreproved: 不受非难而被接受; 被宽大的放过; 不被注意或不被谴责: *His rude remarks ~ed without comment.* 他那些粗鲁的话没有引起批评。 *I don't like it, but I'll let it ~*, will not make objections, etc. 我不喜欢它, 但我并不会表示反对。 *Such conduct may ~ in certain circles but cannot be tolerated here.* 这种行为在某些圈子里也许没有问题, 在此地却不允许。 *~ muster*, ⇨ **muster.** 15 [VP2A] (card games) let one's turn go by without playing a card or making a bid. (纸牌戏)放弃出牌或叫牌。 16 [VP15A] move; cause to go: 使移动; 使进行:*He ~ed his hand across his forehead / his fingers through his hair.* 他用手抚摸额头(用手梳理头发)。 *I ~ed a rope round the barrel.* 我把一根绳子绕在桶上。 *Will you please ~ your eye (= glance) over this note.* 这张条子请你过目一下。 17 (in football, hockey, etc) kick, hand or hit (the ball) to a player of one's own side. (足球、曲棍球等)传(球)给本队的球员。18 [VP6A, 15A] cause (troops) to go by: 使(部队)走过: *~ troops in review.* 检阅时使部队成分列式走过。 19 [VP2C, 15B] (special uses with adverbial particles and preps): (与副词性小品词及介词连用的特殊用法):

pass away, (euphem) die: (委婉语)逝世; 去世; 过世:*He ~ed away peacefully.* 他安详地逝世了。

pass sb/sth by, pay no attention to; disregard: 不注

意; 忽视: I can't ~ the matter by without a protest. 我不能忽视此事而不提出抗议。

pass for sb / sth, be accepted as: 被认为; 被当做: In this small village, he ~ed for a learned man. 在这个小村子里, 他被视为学识丰富的人。Do I speak French well enough to ~ for a Frenchman? 我的法文能说得好到让人把我当成法国人吗?

pass in; pass into sth, gain admission (to): 获准入学; 获准进入: He ~ed into the Military College with no difficulty. 他毫无困难地获准就读军事学院。

pass off, (a) (of events) take place, be carried through: (指事件)发生; 进行: The meeting of the strikers ~ed off quietly. 罢工者的会议进行得很平稳。**(b)** (of pain, a crisis) end: (指痛苦、危机)结束: Has your toothache ~ed off yet? 你的牙疼好了没有? **~ sth off,** turn attention from: 不注意; 把注意力从…移到他处: ~ off an awkward situation. 不去注意一个尴尬的处境。**~ sth/sb off as sth/sb,** represent falsely to be: 把某事物或某人假装为; 冒充: He tried to ~ himself off as a qualified doctor. 他试图冒充合格医生。

pass on, (euphem) die: (委婉语)逝世; 去世: I'm grieved to learn that your dear mother has ~ed on. 听说令堂去世我非常难过。**~ sth on,** hand or give it (to sb else, to others). 将(某物)交给(别人)。

pass out, (colloq) faint; lose consciousness. (口)昏厥; 失去知觉。**~ out (of sth),** leave college, etc having ~ed one's examinations. 毕业; 通过考试。Hence, 由此产生, ,**~ing·out (ceremony/parade),** rite for cadets who have completed their training. 毕业(典礼, 游行) (尤指为已完成训练的军校学生所举行者)。

pass sb over, overlook; fail to notice: 忽视; 不注意: They ~ed me over (eg failed to promote me) in favour of young Hill. 他们忽视我(例如未提升我), 而看重年轻的希尔。

pass through sth, experience it. 经历; 体验。

pass sth up, (colloq) neglect it; not take advantage of it: (口)忽略; 放过(某事物): ~ up an opportunity. 放过一次机会。

pass·able /'pɑːsəbl US: 'pæs-; 'pæsəbl/ adj **1** (of roads, etc) that can be passed over or crossed: (指道路等)可通过的: Are the Alpine roads ~ yet? 阿尔卑斯山上的路畅通了吗? **2** that can be accepted as fairly good but not excellent: 还好的; 尚可的; 过得去的: a ~ knowledge of German. 粗通德文。**pass·ably** /-əbli; -əblɪ/ adv

pass·age /'pæsɪdʒ; 'pæsɪdʒ/ n **1** [U] passing; act of going past, through or across; right to go through: 通过;经过;穿过;通过权: the ~ of time. 时光的流逝。**bird of** ~, **(a)** migratory bird. 候鸟。**(b)** person who passes through a place without staying there long. 到处漂泊的人。**2** [C] voyage; journey from point to point by sea or air: 航行; (从一地到他地之间乘船或乘飞机的)旅行: book one's ~ to New York. 定去纽约的船(飞机)票。**work one's** ~, ⇨ **work**[2](4). **3** [C] way through: 通路: force a ~ through a crowd. 在人群中挤出一条通路。**4** [C] '~·(way),** corridor in a house. (屋内之)通道; 走廊。**5** [C] short extract from a speech or piece of writing, quoted or considered separately. (演讲词或文章)的一段; 一节。**6** passing of a Bill so that it becomes law. 法案的通过。**7** (pl) what passes between two persons in conversation: (复)(两个人谈话中)彼此所说的话: have angry ~s with an opponent during a debate. 在辩论过程中与对方恶言相向。**8** ~ of '**arms,** (lit, fig) combat; dispute. (字面,喻)交战; 争论。

pass·book n ⇨ **pass**[1](10).

passé /'pæseɪ US: pæ'seɪ; pæ'se/ adj (fem 阴性作 **passée**) (F) past his/her/its best; no longer current; out of date. (法)已过盛年的; 过时的。

pas·sen·ger /'pæsɪndʒə(r); 'pæsndʒə/ n **1** person being conveyed by bus, taxi, tram, train, ship, aircraft, etc. (公共汽车、计程车、电车、火车、船、飞机等的)乘客。**2** (colloq) member of a team, crew, etc who does no effective work. (口)(一队、一组等单位中)工作表现不佳

的人, 无能的选手。

passe·par·tout /ˌpæspɑː'tuː; ˌpæspɑr'tu/ n **1** master-key. 万能钥匙。**2** kind of adhesive tape used eg as a mounting for a picture, etc (to form a frame). (镶照片等用的)胶(纸)带。

passer-by /ˌpɑːsə'baɪ US: 'pæsər-; 'pæsə'baɪ/ ⇨ **pass**[2](1).

pas·sim /'pæsɪm; 'pæsɪm/ adv (Lat) (of allusions, phrases, etc to be found in a book or author) frequently; in every part: (拉)(指出现在某书或某作者的作品中的引述或词句等)时常; 到处: This occurs in Milton ~. 这个在米尔顿的作品中到处可见。

pas·sing /'pɑːsɪŋ US: 'pæs-; 'pæsɪŋ/ adj going by; not lasting: 经过的; 目前的; 短暂的: the ~ years. 目前的几年。□ adv (old use) very: (旧用法)极其; 很: ~ rich. 极其富有。□ n [U] the act of going by: 逝去;过去: the ~ of the old year, ie on New Year's Eve. 旧年的逝去(即在除夕)。

passion /'pæʃn; 'pæʃən/ n **1** [U, C] strong feeling or enthusiasm, esp of love, hate or anger: 热情; 激情; 强烈的感情(尤指爱、恨或怒): be filled with ~ (ie love) for sb; choking with ~, ie anger or hate. 因生气或愤恨而说不出话来。P~s were running high, People were filled with strong feeling. 群情激昂。**2 a** ~, outburst of strong feeling: 强烈感情的突发: fly into a ~, become very angry; 勃然大怒; be in a ~. 在生气; 发怒。**3 the P~,** the suffering and death of Jesus. 耶稣的受难。'P~ 'Sunday, the fifth Sunday in Lent. 受难主日(封斋期中的第五个星期日, 亦即复活节前第二个星期日)。'P~ Week, the week between P~ Sunday and Palm Sunday. 受难周(复活节前第二周)。'P~ play, drama dealing with the P~. 受难剧(描写耶稣受难的戏剧)。'~-flower n kinds of (usu climbing) plants with flowers that are thought to resemble the crown of thorns placed on the head of Jesus. 西番莲 (此花被认为与耶稣受难时所戴的荆棘冠冕相似)。'~ fruit, edible fruit of the ~-flower. 西番莲果实(可食用)。**~·less** adj

passion·ate /'pæʃənət; 'pæʃənɪt/ adj easily moved by passion; filled with, showing, passion: 易动情的; 热情的; 多情的: a ~ nature; 热情的天性; ~ language. 热情的言语。**~·ly** adv in a ~ manner: 热情地; 深情地: She is ~ly fond of tennis. 她热爱网球。

pass·ive /'pæsɪv; 'pæsɪv/ adj **1** acted upon but not acting; not offering active resistance: 被动的; 消极的: ~ obedience. 消极的服从。In spite of my efforts the boy remained ~, showed no signs of interest, activity, etc. 尽管我费了很多力, 那男孩还是不起劲。'~ re'sistance, resistance that takes the form of not obeying orders, the law, etc but without active measures of opposition. 消极抵抗。'~ re'sister, persons who practise this. 消极抵抗者。**2** the ~ (voice), (gram) the form in italic type in the sentence 'The letter was written yesterday.' ie the verb phrase containing be + pp. (语法)被动语态 (如 The letter was written yesterday 一句中的 was written 就是被动语态, 亦即 be + 过去分词)。⇨ **active.** □ n ~ voice. 被动语态。**~·ly** adv **~·ness, pass·iv·ity** /pæ'sɪvətɪ; pæ'sɪvɪtɪ/ n [U] the state or quality of being ~. 被动; 被动性; 消极; 不抵抗。

pass·key ⇨ **pass**[1](10).

Pass·over /'pɑːsəʊvə(r) US: 'pæs-; 'pæs,ovə/ n Jewish religious festival commemorating the liberation of the Jews from slavery in Egypt. ⇨ Exod 12. 逾越节(犹太人的宗教节日, 纪念其祖先在埃及为奴获释放); 参看旧约出埃及记第 12 章)。

pass·port /'pɑːspɔːt US: 'pæs-; 'pæs,port/ n government document to be carried by a traveller abroad, giving personal particulars; (fig) sth that enables one to win or obtain sth: 护照 (往外国旅行者所持的政府证明文件, 载明持用人的个人资料); (喻)使人获得某物之物; 达到某一目的之手段: Is flattery a ~ to success? 阿谀是成功的手段吗?

pass·word ⇨ **pass**[1](10).

past¹ /pɑːst US: pæst; pæst/ *adj* (Cf 参较 passed, pp of **pass²**) of the time before the present; gone by in time: 过去的; 已过的: *for the ~ few days / weeks, etc:* 过去的几天 (几周等); *during the ~ week;* 在过去的一周里; *in times ~;* 在过去; 好久以前; *for a long time ~;* 在过去的一段长时间中; *~ generations;* 过去的几代; *the ~ tense;* (动词的) 过去式; *a ~ participle,* eg passed, taken, gone. 过去分词 (如 passed, taken, gone)。□ *n* 1 **the ~, ~ time:** 往时; 昔时; 过去: *We cannot change the ~.* 我们不能改变过去。*Memories of the ~ filled her mind.* 她的脑海里充满了过去的回忆。**2** person's ~ life or experiences, esp when these are not reputable: 过去的生活或经验 (尤指不名誉者): *We know nothing of his ~.* 我们不知道他过去的生活情形。*She's a woman with a ~.* 她过去是个生活放荡的女人。

past² /pɑːst US: pæst; pæst/ *prep* **1** beyond in time; after: 在时间上超过; 在…之后: *half ~ two;* 两点半; *ten (minutes) ~ six;* 六点十分; *buses every twenty minutes ~ the hour,* ie at 1.20, 2.20, 3.20, etc; 公共汽车每小时二十分开一班 (即一点二十分、两点二十分、三点二十分等各一班); *stay out until ~ 11 o'clock;* 留在外面到十一点过后 (才回来); *an old man ~ seventy;* 七十多岁的老人; *a woman ~ middle age.* 过了中年的妇人。**2** beyond in space; up to and farther than: 在空间上超过; 经过; 经由: *He walked ~ the house.* 他走过那房子。*He hurried ~ me without stopping to speak.* 他匆忙地从我身旁走过, 没有停下来说话。*The driver took the bus ~ the traffic signal.* 司机开着公共汽车通过交通信号。**3** beyond the limits, power or range of: 超出…之限制、权力或范围: *The old man is ~ work,* too old, weak, etc to work. 这老人再也不能工作了。*She's ~ child-bearing,* too old to bear a child. 她不能再生育了。*The pain was almost ~ bearing,* too severe to be endured. 这种痛苦实在是叫人受不了。*He's ~ praying for,* There's no hope of cure, improvement, etc. 他已经没救了。*She's ~ caring what happens,* has reached the stage of complete indifference, is quite resigned to ill fortune, etc. 她对一切都不在乎了。**be / get ~ it,** (colloq) be no longer able to do the things one could formerly do: (口) 再也不能做过去所能做的事了: *My gardener is over seventy-five and I'm afraid he's getting ~ it.* 我的园丁已超过七十五岁, 恐怕已力不从心了。**wouldn't put sth '~ sb,** consider him capable of doing sth disreputable, unusual, etc: 认为某人会做出不名誉或不寻常的事来: *You may say that he is honest but I wouldn't put it ~ him to run off with the money.* 你可以说他很诚实, 但我认为他会携款潜逃。□ *adv* (in the sense of 2 above): (照上例第 2 义): *walk / march / go / run / hurry ~.* 走过 (齐步走过; 经过; 跑过; 匆匆走过)。

pasta /'pæstə US: 'pɑːstə; 'pɑːstə/ *n* [U] (I) (dish of food prepared from a dough of) flour, eggs and water mixed and dried, eg macaroni, spaghetti, ravioli. (意) 面食 (如通心面、细面条、馄饨等)。

paste /peɪst; pest/ *n* [U] **1** soft mixture of flour, fat, etc for making pastry. (做点心用的) 面团; 面糊。**2** preparation of food-stuffs, cut up and pounded to a soft, moist mass: (食物捣烂的) 糊; 酱: *'anchovy ~* 鳀鱼酱; *'fish~.* 鱼糊。**3** mixture of flour and water used for sticking things together, esp paper on walls and boards: 浆糊: *a bottle of ~.* 一瓶浆糊。**'~ board** *n* [U] stiff board-like material made by pasting sheets of paper together; cardboard. 硬纸板; 纸板。**4** substance (a glass-like material) used in making artificial diamonds, etc. 制造假钻石等的原料 (一种似玻璃的物质)。□ *vt* **1** [VP6A, 15A, B] stick with ~(3). (用浆糊) 粘贴。**~ sth down,** fasten down with ~. 粘贴某物。**sth up, (a)** fasten with ~ to a surface: 把某物粘贴在平面上; 把某物贴起来: *~ up a notice.* 张贴告示。**(b)** seal or cover using ~: 用浆糊封闭或遮盖: *~ up*

cracks with paper. 用纸贴补裂缝。**(c)** fasten sheets or strips of paper on larger sheets, eg to design pages for a magazine, book, etc. 把小张条贴在较大的纸上 (如设计杂志、书籍等的版页)。Hence, 由此产生, **'~-up** *n.* **2** [VP6A] (colloq) thrash; beat. (口) 痛打; 打。Hence, 由此产生, **past·ing** *n* (colloq) severe beating: (口) 痛打; 毒打: *Get / Give sb a pasting.* 把某人痛打一顿。

pas·tel /'pæstl US: pæ'stel; pæs'tel/ *n* **1** (picture drawn with) coloured chalk made into crayons. 彩色粉笔; 蜡笔; 彩色粉笔画; 蜡笔画。**2** (attrib) (用作定语) *~ shades,* soft, light, delicate shades of colour. 轻淡柔和的色彩。

pas·tern /'pæstən; 'pæstən/ *n* part of a horse's foot between the fetlock and the hoof. (马足部的) 骹。⇨ the illus at **domestic.** 参看 domestic 之插图。

pas·teur·ize /'pæstʃəraɪz; 'pæstə,raɪz/ *vt* [VP6A] rid (milk, etc) of disease-producing bacteria by using the heating method of Louis Pasteur. 以巴斯德法除去 (牛奶等的) 病菌。**pas·teur·iz·ation** /ˌpæstʃəraɪ'zeɪʃn US: -rɪ'z-; ˌpæstərə'zeɪʃən/ *n*

pas·tiche /pæ'stiːʃ; pæs'tiʃ/ *n* [C] literary or other work of art composed in the style of another author, etc; musical composition made up from various sources. (文学或艺术的) 模仿作品; (音乐的) 混成曲。

pas·tille /'pæstl US: pæ'stiːl; pæs'til/ *n* [C] small flavoured tablet to be sucked, eg one containing medicine for the throat. (含治喉疾药物等的) 锭剂; 喉片。

pas·time /'pɑːstaɪm US: 'pæs-; 'pæs,taɪm/ *n* [C] anything done to pass time pleasantly; game: 消遣; 娱乐; 游戏: *Photography is her favourite ~.* 摄影是她最喜欢的消遣。

pas·tor /'pɑːstə(r) US: 'pæs-; 'pæstə/ *n* minister (3), esp of a nonconformist church. 牧师 (尤指非英国国教的牧师)。

pas·toral /'pɑːstərəl US: 'pæs-; 'pæstərəl/ *adj* **1** of shepherds and country life: 牧人及田园生活的: *~ poetry.* 田园诗。**2** of a pastor; (esp) of a bishop: 牧师的; (尤指主教的): *a ~ letter,* one to the members of a bishop's diocese: 主教给教区教友的书信; *~ staff,* bishop's emblem, like a shepherd's crook, carried by or before bishops ceremonially. 主教的权杖 (牧杖)。**3** of (duties towards) a priest's or a minister's flock: 传教士或牧师之教徒的; 牧师对教徒之职责的: *~ care / responsibilities.* 牧师对教徒的照顾 (责任)。□ *n* poem, play, letter. etc. 田园诗; 牧歌; 田园剧; 主教给教友的书信 (等)。

pas·tor·ate /'pɑːstərət US: 'pæs-; 'pæstərɪt/ *n* **1** office of a pastor; time during which he holds it. 牧师职务; 牧师任期。**2** body of pastors. 牧师团。

pas·try /'peɪstrɪ; 'pestrɪ/ *n* (*pl* -ries) **1** [U] paste of flour, fat, etc baked in an oven; pie-crust. 用面粉和油脂等做成的面团所烤成的点心; 馅饼皮。**2** [C] article of food made wholly or partly of this, eg a pie or tart: [U] such articles collectively: 全部或部分此种原料制成的食物 (如饼干或果糕); 此种食物之总称; 面制糕饼: *eat less ~.* 少吃糕饼。**'~-cook** *n* person who makes ~, esp for public sale. 糕饼点心制造人 (尤指制造以供出售者)。

pas·ture /'pɑːstʃə(r) US: 'pæs-; 'pæstʃə/ *n* [U] grassland for cattle; grass on such land, ⇨ **meadow;** [C] piece of land of this kind. 牧场; 草原; 草地; 牧草; 牧场。□ *vt, vi* **1** [VP6A] (of persons) put (cattle, sheep, etc) to graze: (指人) 放牧; 牧 (牛、羊等): *~ one's sheep on the village common;* 在村民的公地上放羊; (of cattle, etc) eat down grassland. (指牛等) 在牧场上吃草。**2** [VP2A] graze. 吃草。**pas·tur·age** /-ɪdʒ; -ɪdʒ/ *n* [U] (right to graze cattle on) ~ land. 牧场; 放牧权。

pasty¹ /'peɪstɪ; 'pestɪ/ *adj* (-ier, -iest) like paste(1), 如面团的: *a ~ complexion,* white and unhealthy. 苍白的脸色。

pasty² /'pæstɪ; 'pæstɪ/ *n* (*pl* -ties) pie of meat, jam, etc enclosed in paste and baked without a dish: 肉馅饼;

饹饼: *a Cornish* ~. 康瓦尔饹饼.

pat[1] /pæt; pæt/ *adv* at the right moment; at once and without hesitation: 适时地(的); 不犹豫地: *The answer came pat.* 那个回答适时答出(来得正好). *He had his excuse pat.* 他正好有个借口. **stand pat,** stick to one's decision; refuse to change. 坚持自己的决定; 拒绝改变.

pat[2] /pæt; pæt/ *vt, vi* (**-tt-**) **1** tap gently with the open hand or with sth flat: (用掌或扁平物)轻拍: *pat a dog;* 轻拍一只狗; *pat a ball,* 轻拍球; sth that bounces up and down. 拍球(使其上下跳动). *pat sb/oneself on the back,* (fig) express approval, congratulate, etc. (喻)表示赞成、恭贺等. **2** [VP2A] carry out the action of patting. 拍; 轻拍. □ *n* [C] **1** tap with the open hand, eg as a caress or to show sympathy. 轻拍(如作为爱抚动作或表示同情). **2** small mass of sth, esp butter, formed by patting. 一小团东西(尤指拍成的奶油). **3** light sound made by striking sth with a flat object. 轻拍声.

patch[1] /pætʃ; pætʃ/ *n* **1** small piece of material put on over a hole or a damaged or worn place: 补钉; 补片: *a coat with* ~*es on the elbows;* 肘部有补钉的上衣; *a* ~ *on the inner tube of a tyre.* 车内胎的一块补片. ~**-pocket** *n* one made by sewing a piece of cloth on to the outside of a garment. 缝在衣服外面的口袋. **2** piece of plaster put over a cut or wound. 贴伤口的膏药(胶带). **3** pad worn to protect an injured eye. 保护受伤眼睛的眼罩. **4** small, irregular, differently coloured part of a surface: 表面上颜色不同的小斑块: *a dog with a white* ~ *on its neck.* 一头颈上有一块白斑的狗. **5** small area (of ground, esp for garden vegetables): 小块土地(尤指作菜园用的): *the 'cabbage* ~; 卷心菜菜圃; small area of anything: 任何小片的东西: ~*es of fog;* 几片浓雾; *small* ~*es of blue in a cloudy sky.* 云天中的几片的蓝天. **6** *not a* ~ *on,* not nearly so good as. 远不如; 比…差得远. **7** *go through/hit/strike a bad* ~, be in/reach a period of bad luck, difficulty, unhappiness. 遭遇不幸、困难或不愉快; 倒霉. '~**-work** *n* [U] **1** piece of material made up of bits of cloth of various colours, shapes and colours: 各形各色小布片缝缀而成的材料; 补缀品: (attrib) (用作定语) *a* ~*work quilt.* 补缀布面的棉被. **2** (fig) piece of work made up of odds and ends. (喻)拼凑之物; 杂凑之物.

patch[2] /pætʃ; pætʃ/ *vt* [VP6A] **1** put a patch on; (of material) serve as a patch for. 补缀; 缝补; (指布料等)作为…的补片. **2** [VP15B] ~ *up,* repair; make roughly ready for use: 修理; 草率做成: *an old,* ~*ed-up motor-cycle;* 一辆修好的旧机器脚踏车; (fig)(喻) ~ *up a quarrel,* settle it for a time. 暂时止息口角. ~*y adj* (**-ier, -iest**) made up of ~*es;* not regular or uniform; of uneven quality: 补缀的; 不规律的; 不划一的; 质地不均的: ~*y work/knowledge.* 零星的工作(零碎的知识). *The fog was* ~*y.* 雾散落各处. ~**-ily** /-ɪlɪ; -əlɪ/ *adv* ~**-iness** *n* **-ness** *n*

patch·ouli /'pætʃulɪ; 'pætʃulɪ/ *n* [U] (perfume derived from an) Asiatic plant. 亚洲产的一种薄荷;薄荷香水.

pate /peɪt; pet/ *n* (colloq) head: (口)头: *a bald* ~. 秃头.

pâté /'pæteɪ US: pɑ:'teɪ; pɑ:'te/ *n* **1** [C] paste; patty. 饹饼; 小面饼. **2** paste. 制饹饼的面团. ~ **de foie gras** /, -də fwɑ: 'grɑ:; -,də,fwɑ'grɑ/, (F) (patty of) goose-liver paste. (法)制鹅肝饼的面团; 鹅肝饼.

pa·tella /pə'telə; pə'telə/ *n* (anat) kneecap. (解剖)膝盖骨.

pat·ent[1] /'peɪtnt US: 'pætnt; 'petnt/ *adj* **1** evident, easily seen: 显著的; 明显的: *It was* ~ *to everyone that he disliked the idea.* 每个人都看得出他不喜欢这个主意. **2** (letters ~) /'peɪtnt US: 'pætnt/, government authority to manufacture sth invented and protect it from imitation. 专利权状; 专利证. **3** protected by letters ~: 有专利的; 受专利权保护的: ~ *medicines,* made by one firm or person only. 专利药品. **4** ~ **leather,** leather with a hard, smooth, shiny surface. 漆皮(通常为黑色). ~**·ly** *adv* clearly; obviously. 清晰地; 显然地.

pat·ent[2] /'peɪtnt US: 'pætnt; 'petnt/ *n* [C] **1** (privilege granted by) letters patent: 专利证; 专利权: *take out a* ~ *to protect a new invention.* 取得专利权以保护一项新发明. **P~** (usu 通常读 /'peɪtnt; 'petnt/) **Office,** government department which issues ~s. 专利局 (政府中主管颁发专利权状, 注册商标等事务的机构). **2** that which is protected by letters ~; invention or process. 受到专利证保护之物; 发明或方法. □ *vt* [VP6A] obtain a ~ for (an invention or process). 取得(发明物或方法)之专利权. ~**·ee** /,peɪtn'ti: US: ,pætn-; ,peɪtn'ti/ *n* person to whom a ~ is issued. 获有专利权者.

pater·fa·mil·ias /,peɪtəfə'mɪlɪæs US: ,pæt-; 'petəfə-'mɪlɪ,æs/ *n* (hum) father or head of a family. (谐)父亲或家长.

pa·ter·nal /pə'tɜ:nl; pə'tɜrnl/ *adj* **1** of or like a father: 父亲的; 似父亲的: ~ *care.* 父亲的照顾. **2** related through the father: 父系的: *my* ~ *grandfather.* 我的祖父. ~**·ly** /-nəlɪ; -nəlɪ/ *adv* ~**·ism** /-ɪzəm; -,ɪzəm/ *n* [U] (practice of) governing or controlling people in a ~ way (providing for their needs but giving them no responsibility). 仁慈的专制政治; 家长政治(供给人民所需而不赋予任何义务).

pa·ter·nity /pə'tɜ:nətɪ; pə'tɜrnətɪ/ *n* [U] fatherhood; being a father; origin on the father's side: 父性; 父道; 父职; 父系: *of unknown* ~. 生父不明.

pater·nos·ter /,pætə'nɒstə(r); 'pætə'nɑstə/ *n* (Lat 拉丁文为 'Our Father') **1** (recital of) the Lord's Prayer. 主祷文(的诵读). **2** bend in a rosary at which the Lord's Prayer is repeated. 念珠串上主祷文重复之处. **3** lift(2) with a series of doorless cars(3) moving on a continuous belt so that passengers can step on or off at each floor. 连锁式电梯(有一串无门的梯箱, 由一条转动的链带牵动, 使乘客在每一楼上下).

path /pɑ:θ US: pæθ; pæθ/ *n* (*pl* ~**s** /pɑ:ðz US: pæðz;* pæðz/) **1** ~**·(·way),** ('foot') ~, way track made (across fields, through woods, etc) by or for people walking: 小路; 小径(田野、林中等由行人踩成者): *Keep to the* ~ *or you may lose your way.* 沿着这小路走, 否则你可能会迷路. '~**-finder** *n* explorer; sb sent on ahead to find a route, etc; pioneer. 探路者;探险者;开拓者;先驱. **2** track specially made for foot or cycle racing (usu 通常作 *cinder track*). (竞走或脚踏车比赛的)跑道. **3** line along which sth or sb moves: 轨道; 路线: *the moon's* ~ *round the earth;* 月亮绕行地球的轨道; *the 'flight* ~ *of a spacecraft;* 太空船飞行的轨道; *the* ~ *of a tornado.* 飓风经过的路线. ~**·less** *adj* having no ~s: 无路的: ~*less jungles.* 无路可走的丛林.

pa·thetic /pə'θetɪk; pə'θetɪk/ *adj* **1** able to be considered sad, pitiful, or (colloq) contemptible: 悲哀的; 可怜的; 可鄙的: *a* ~ *sight;* 悲惨的景象; ~ *ignorance.* 可怜的无知. **2** *the* ~ **fallacy,** the error of imaginatively endowing inanimate objects with life, human feelings, etc. 感情的谬误; 在想象中把生命、感情等赋予无生命的东西. **pa·theti·cally** /-klɪ; -klɪ/ *adv*

pa·thol·ogy /pə'θɒlədʒɪ; pæ'θɑlədʒɪ/ *n* [U] science of diseases. 病理学. **path·ol·ogist** /pə'θɒlədʒɪst; pæ'θɑlədʒɪst/ *n* student of, expert in, ~. 研究病理学者; 病理学家. **path·o·logi·cal** /,pæθə'lɒdʒɪkl; ,pæθə-'lɑdʒɪkl/ *adj* of ~; of the nature of disease. 病理学的; 与疾病有关的; 由疾病引起的. **path·o·logi·cally** /-klɪ; -klɪ/ *adv*

pa·thos /'peɪθɒs; 'peθɑs/ *n* [U] quality in speech, writing, etc which arouses a feeling of pity, sympathy or tenderness. (演讲、文章等)哀婉动人的性质.

pa·tience /'peɪʃns; 'peʃəns/ *n* [U] **1** (power of) enduring trouble, suffering, inconvenience, without complaining; ability to wait for results, to deal with problems calmly and without haste: 容忍; 忍耐; 耐心; 耐性; 忍耐力: *I haven't the* ~ *to hear your complaints again.* 我没有耐心再听你的抱怨. *She has no* ~ *with people who are always grumbling,* cannot endure them.

她不能容忍那些常常发牢骚的人. **be out of ~ (with)**, be unable to endure further. 对…忍无可忍. **the ~ of Job**, very great ~: 极度的忍耐: *His behaviour would try (= test) the ~ of Job*. 他的行为考验最有耐性的人 (意即: 连最有耐性的人也无法忍受). **2** (GB) kind of card game, usu for one player (US 美 = *solitaire*). (英)一种一个人玩的纸牌游戏.

pa·tient[1] /'peɪʃnt; 'peʃənt/ *adj* ~ **(with sb)**, having or showing patience (with him): 有耐性的; 忍耐的; 容忍的: *be ~ with a tired child*. 对疲倦的小孩要有耐性. **be ~ of sth**, (archaic) (古) **(a)** be able to endure it ~ly. 能忍受. **(b)** admit(5). 容有. ~**ly** *adv: wait/sit/listen* ~*ly*. 耐心地等(坐,听).

pa·tient[2] /'peɪʃnt; 'peʃənt/ *n* [C] person who has received, is receiving, or is on a doctor's list for, medical treatment: 病人: *The Smiths are ~s of Dr Quack*. 库瓦瓦克医生替史密斯全家人看病. ~**ly** *adv*

pat·ina /'pætɪnə; 'pætɪnə/ *n* (usu) green, glossy surface formed on old bronze or copper; glossiness of old woodwork, etc. 古铜上所生的(通常为)绿色光滑的表面; 铜绿; 古老木器等的光泽; 古色.

patio /'pætɪəʊ; 'pɑti,o/ *n* (*pl* ~**s** /-əʊz; -oz/) **1** courtyard, open to the sky, within the walls of a Spanish or Spanish American house. (西班牙或使用西班牙语之美洲各国的)屋内庭院; 天井. **2** (modern use) paved area near a house, used for recreation. (现代用法)房屋附近用砖石等铺平的游乐场地.

pa·tis·serie /pə'tiːsərɪ; pə'tisərɪ/ *n* (F) shop, bakery, specializing in (French) pastry and cakes. (法)(专门制售法国点心的)面包店.

pat·ois /'pætwɑː; 'pætwɑ/ *n* dialect of the common people of a district, differing from the standard language of the country. 方言; 土话.

pa·trial /'peɪtrɪəl; 'peɪtrɪəl/ *n* person who has qualifications which give him the right to be considered legally a British citizen. 有英国公民资格的人.

patri·arch /'peɪtrɪɑːk; 'peɪt-, -ɑrk/ *n* **1** venerable old man. 年高德劭的人. **2** male head of a family or tribe. (男性)家长; 族长. **3** bishop among the early Christians; (in the RC Church) high-ranking bishop; (in Eastern Churches) bishop of highest honour: 早期基督教徒中的监督; (罗马天主教的)高级主教; (东正教的)大主教: *the P~ of Antioch/Jerusalem*. 安提阿(耶路撒冷)的大主教. ~**al** /,peɪtrɪ'ɑːkl US: ,peɪt-, ,petrɪ'ɑrkl/ *adj* of or like a ~. (似)家长的; (似)族长的; (似)监督的. ~**ate** /-ert; -rɪt/ *n* position, see[2], residence, of a Church = 主教的职位、辖区、住所.

pa·tri·cian /pə'trɪʃn; pə'trɪʃən/ *n, adj* (person) of noble birth (esp in ancient Rome); aristocrat(ic). 出身高贵的; (尤指古罗马时)出身高贵的人; 贵族; 贵族的.

pat·ri·cide /'pætrɪsaɪd; 'pætrɪ,saɪd/ *n* [U] killing of one's own father; [C] instance of this; [C] person guilty of this. 弑父; 此种行为之实例; 弑父者.

pat·ri·mony /'pætrɪmənɪ US: -məʊnɪ; 'pætrə,monɪ/ *n* (*pl* -**nies**) [C] property inherited from one's father or ancestors; endowment. 世袭的财产; 祖传的产业; 捐赠的财产. **pat·ri·mo·nial** /,pætrɪ'məʊnɪəl; ,pætrə'monɪəl/ *adj* of a ~. 世袭财产的; 祖传产业的; 捐赠财产的.

pa·triot /'pætrɪət US: 'peɪt-; 'petrɪət/ *n* person who strongly supports his country. 爱国者. ~**·ism** /-ɪzəm; -,ɪzəm/ *n* [U] the feelings and qualities of a ~. 爱国心; 爱国精神. ~**·ic** /,pætrɪ'ɒtɪk US: ,peɪt-; ,petrɪ'ɑtɪk/ *adj* having, showing, the qualities of a ~. 爱国的; 有爱国心的. ~**·i·cally** /-klɪ; -klɪ/ *adv*

pa·trol /pə'trəʊl; pə'trol/ *vt, vi* (-**ll**-) [VP6A, 2A] go round (a camp, town, the streets, roads, etc) to see that all is well, to look out (for wrongdoers, persons in need of help, the enemy, etc). 巡逻; 巡查. □ *n* **1** [U] the act of ~ing: 巡逻: *soldiers on* ~; 巡逻中的士兵; *maintain a constant sea and air* ~, eg looking for submarines during a war; 维持不断的海空巡逻(如

在战时搜索潜水艇); (attrib) (用作定语) *a police '~ car*, eg on a motorway. 警察巡逻车(如在公路上者). **2** [C] person(s), ship(s) or aircraft on ~ duties: 巡逻者; 巡逻员; 巡逻船; 巡逻机: *We were helped by an AA (= Automobile Association)* ~ *(man)*, scout. 我们受到汽车协会巡逻员的协助. **3** (US) (美) '~ **wagon** *n* one used by the police for conveying prisoners or persons who have been arrested. (运送犯人用的)警车; 囚车. '~**·man** /-mən; -mən/ *n* (*pl* -**men**) (esp) policeman who ~s an area. (尤指)巡警.

pa·tron /'peɪtrən; 'petrən/ *n* **1** person who gives encouragement, moral or financial support, to a person, cause, the arts, etc: (对某人, 某种目标, 艺术等之)赞助人; 资助人: *Modern artists have difficulty in finding wealthy* ~*s*. 现代艺术家们难以找到富有的赞助人. '**saint**, saint regarded as the special protector (*of a* church, town, travellers, etc). (教堂, 城镇, 旅行者等的)守护神. **2** regular customer at a shop. 主顾. '~**·ess** /-ɪs; -ɪs/ *n* woman ~. 女赞助人; 女主顾.

pa·tron·age /'pætrənɪdʒ US: 'peɪt-; 'petrənɪdʒ/ *n* [C] **1** support, encouragement, given by a patron: 支持; 赞助; 资助: *with/under the* ~ *of the Duke of X*. 在某公爵的赞助之下. **2** right of appointing sb to a benefice or office, to grant privileges, etc: 任命圣职之权; 委派职务之权; 给予权力之权: *He's an influential man, with a great deal of* ~ *in his hands*. 他是个有影响力的人, 握有任免大权. **3** customer's support (to a shopkeeper, etc): (顾客的)惠顾: *take away one's* ~ *because of poor service*. 因服务欠佳, 不再惠顾. **4** patronizing manner. 施恩的态度. ⇨ **patronize(2)**.

pa·tron·ize /'pætrənaɪz US: 'peɪt-; 'petrən,aɪz/ *vt* [VP6A] **1** act as patron towards: 光顾; 惠顾; 照顾; 赞助: ~ *a young musician/a dressmaker*. 赞助一个年轻的音乐家(光顾一个裁缝师). **2** treat (sb whom one is helping, talking to, etc) as if he were an inferior person; be condescending towards. 以恩赐的态度对待(所赞助的人或谈话的对象); 对…表现屈尊的样子. **pat·ron·iz·ing** *adj* **pat·ron·iz·ing·ly** *adv*

pat·ro·nymic /,pætrə'nɪmɪk; ,pætrə'nɪmɪk/ *n, adj* (name) derived from that of a father or ancestor, eg *Robertson; MacNeil; O'Neil*. 取自父亲或祖上名字的(姓); 取自父亲或祖上名字的姓 (如: Robertson 意即 son of Robert; MacNeil 意即 son of Neil; O'Neil 意即 son of Neil).

pat·ten /'pætn; 'pætn/ *n* clog, wooden shoe, mounted on a metal framework to keep the wearer's foot above the mud. (防泥用的)木套鞋.

pat·ter[1] /'pætə(r); 'pætɚ/ *n* [U] **1** kind of talk used by a particular class of people: 行话; 切口; 暗语: *thieves'* ~; 小偷们的暗语; *the* ~ *of an auctioneer*. 拍卖人的行话. **2** rapid talk of a conjuror or comedian; rapid speech introduced into a song (*a '*~ *song*). 魔术家或喜剧演员的喋喋快语; 歌(快调滑稽歌)中的快调插词. □ *vt, vi* [VP6A] recite, say, repeat (prayers, etc) rapidly or in a mechanical way; [VP2A] talk fast or glibly. 喋喋背诵; 喋喋地说; 喋喋地重复(祈祷等); 快速或敏捷地讲.

pat·ter[2] /'pætə(r); 'pætɚ/ *n* [U] sound of quick, light taps or footsteps: 急速的轻拍声; 轻快的脚步声: *the* ~ *of rain on a roof*; 雨打屋顶的滴答声; *the* ~ *of footsteps*. 脚步的啪哒啪哒声. □ *vi* [VP2A, C] make this sound: 发出急速轻拍声; 滴答地响; 啪哒地响: *rain* ~*ing on the window-panes*. 雨点啪哒地打在玻璃窗上.

pat·tern /'pætn; 'pætən/ *n* [C] **1** excellent example; sb or sth serving as a model: 模范; 典型; 作为典范的某人或某事物: *She's a* ~ *of all the virtues*. 她是一切美德的典范. (attrib) (用作定语) *He has a* ~ *(model* is the usu word) *wife*. 他有个模范的妻子(本义通常用 model). **2** sth serving as a model, esp shape of a garment, cut out in paper, used as a guide in dressmaking, etc; model from which sth is to be cast and from which a mould is made (in a foundry, etc): (做衣服等用的)纸

样; 式样; (铸造工厂等用的)模子; 模型: '~-maker; 制模工人; '~-shop, in a foundry. (铸造工厂中的)制模房。 **3** sample, esp a small piece of cloth: 样品; (尤指)布样: *a bunch of ~s from the tailor.* 裁缝给的一束布样。 **4** ornamental design, eg on a carpet, on wallpaper, curtain material: (地毯、壁纸、窗帘布等的)图案; 花样; 式样: *a ~ of roses;* 玫瑰的图案; *geometrical ~s.* 几何图案。 **5** way in which sth happens, develops, is arranged, etc: 方式: *new ~s of family life,* eg when married women, instead of keeping house, go out to work and add to the family income. 家庭生活的新方式(例如已婚妇女不做家事而外出工作, 以增加家庭收入)。 □ *vt* 1 [VP14] **~** *sth/oneself upon/after sth/sb,* model: 仿造; 模仿: *a dress ~ed upon a Paris model.* 照巴黎式样的衣服。 *He ~s himself upon his father.* 他仿效他的父亲。 **2** decorate with a ~. 以图案装饰; 加花样。

patty /ˈpætɪ; ˈpætɪ/ *n* (*pl* **-ties**) little pie or pasty: 小馅饼; 小面饼: *oyster patties.* 牡蛎饼。 '~**-pan** *n* pan for baking a ~. 焙饼锅。

pau·city /ˈpɔːsətɪ; ˈpɔsətɪ/ *n* [U] (formal) smallness of number or quantity. (正式用语)少数; 少量。

Paul /pɔːl; pɔl/ *n* **rob Peter to pay** ~, ⇨ **Peter.** ~ **Pry,** an inquisitive person. 爱管闲事的人。

paunch /pɔːntʃ; pɔntʃ/ *n* belly, esp if fat: 腹(尤指肥大的肚子): *a ~ like that of Falstaff.* 象孚斯塔夫那样的大肚子。 *He was getting quite a ~,* getting wide round the waist. 他的腰围越来越粗了。 ~**y** *adj* having a large ~. 肚子大的; 大腹便便的。 ~**i·ness** *n*

pau·per /ˈpɔːpə(r); ˈpɔpɚ/ *n* person with no means of livelihood, esp one who is supported by charity. 穷人; 贫民(尤指靠施舍度日者)。 '~**·ism** /-ɪzəm; -ɪzəm/ *n* [U] state of being a ~; existence of ~s: 贫穷; 穷困: *abolish ~ism.* 消除贫穷。 '~**·ize** /-aɪz; -aɪz/ *vt* [VP 6A] bring to the state of being a ~. 使贫穷; 使成为穷人。 ~**·iz·ation** /ˌpɔːpəraɪˈzeɪʃn US: -rɪˈz-; ˌpɔpərə-ˈzeʃən/ *n*

pause /pɔːz; pɔz/ *n* **1** short interval or stop (while doing or saying sth): 中止; 暂停: *during a ~ in the conversation;* 在会谈中停顿的时候; *a ~ to take breath.* 停下来喘口气。 **give ~ to,** cause (a person) to hesitate, to stop and think. 使(人)踌躇。 **2** (music) sign (◠ or ◡) over or under a note or rest to show that it is to be prolonged. (音乐)延长记号(◠或◡), 置于音符或休止符上或下, 以示该符号应予延长。 □ *vi* [VP2A, 4A] make a ~: 暂停; 中止: ~ *to look round.* 停下来看看四周。

pave /peɪv; pev/ *vt* [VP6A] put flat stones, bricks, etc on (a path, etc): 铺石板、砖等于(道路等): *a path ~d with brick;* 铺砖的小路; (fig)(喻) *a career ~d with* (= full of) *good intentions.* 充满善意的生涯。 ~ **the way for,** make conditions easy or ready for. ~ 作准备; 使…容易进行; 为…铺路。 '**paving-stone** *n* slab of stone for paving. 铺路用的石板。

pave·ment /ˈpeɪvmənt; ˈpevmənt/ *n* **1** (GB) paved way at the side of a street for people on foot (US 美 = *sidewalk*). (英)(街边的)人行道。 '~ **artist,** one who draws pictures on a ~ with coloured chalks (to get money from passers-by). 马路画家(用彩色粉笔在人行道上画图向行人讨钱者)。 **2** (US) hard surface for streets, roads, etc. (美)(街道,道路等的)硬路面。 **crazy** ~, ⇨ **crazy(4).**

pa·vil·ion /pəˈvɪlɪən; pəˈvɪljən/ *n* **1** building on a sports ground for the use of players, spectators, etc. 运动场上供运动员、观众等使用的建筑物。 **2** ornamental building for concerts, dancing, etc. 供音乐会、舞蹈等使用的装饰华美的建筑物。 **3** large tent, as used for a flower exhibition. 大帐篷(如供花展使用的)。

paw /pɔː; pɔ/ *n* animal's foot that has claws or nails (contrasted with *hoof*): (动物有爪的)脚掌; 脚爪(异于 hoof): *a dog's paw,* ⇨ the illus at **dog;** 狗掌; 狗爪(参看图之插图); (colloq; hum) hand. (口, 谑)手。 □ *vt* [VP6A, 15B] **1** (of animals) feel or scratch with the paw(s); (of a horse) strike (the ground) with a hoof.

(指动物)以掌摸或抓; (指马)以蹄扒(地)。 **2** (of persons) touch with the hands, awkwardly, rudely or with improper familiarity. (指人)用手粗笨地摸; 毛手毛脚地摸。

pawky /ˈpɔːkɪ; ˈpɔkɪ/ *adj* (Scot) sly; arch: (苏)狡猾的; 顽皮的: ~ *humour.* 俏皮的幽默。 **pawk·ily** /ˈpɔːkɪlɪ; ˈpɔkɪlɪ/ *adv*

pawl /pɔːl; pɔl/ *n* **1** lever with a catch for the teeth of a ratchet wheel or rod, to prevent slipping or movement in the opposite direction. (防止棘齿轮逆转的)掣手; 倒齿; 爪。 **2** short bar used to prevent a capstan or windlass from recoiling. (防止绞盘退转的)掣耳杆。

pawn[1] /pɔːn; pɔn/ *n* least valuable piece in the game of chess; person made use of by others for their own advantage. (国际象棋中的)兵; 卒(国际象棋中最不重要的棋子); 被别人利用的人。 ⇨ the illus at **chess.** 参看 chess 之插图。

pawn[2] /pɔːn; pɔn/ *vt* [VP6A] **1** deposit (clothing, jewellery, etc) as a pledge for money borrowed: 典当; 质押 (衣物、珠宝等): *The medical student ~ed his microscope to pay his rent.* 那个医学院学生典当他的显微镜付房租。 **2** (fig) pledge: (喻) 以 … 为赌注: ~ *one's life/honour.* 以生命(荣誉)担保。 □ *n* [U] **in** ~, in a state of being ~ed: 当掉; 押掉: *My watch is in* ~. 我的表当掉了。 '~**·broker** *n* person licensed to lend money at interest on the security of goods left with him. 开当铺者; 当铺老板。 '~**·shop** *n* ~broker's place of business. 当铺。 '~**·ticket** *n* ~broker's receipt for goods pledged with him. 当票; 质押单据。

paw·paw /pəˈpɔː US: ˈpɔːpɔː; ˈpɔpɔ/ *n* = **papaw.**

pax /pæks; pæks/ *n* (in church) kiss or sign of peace. (教会) 表示和平之吻或圣号。 **Pax Romana** /ˌpæks rəʊˈmɑːnə; ˌpæks roˈmɑnə/, peace enforced on states in the ancient Roman Empire. 罗马帝国统治下的和平。

pay[1] /peɪ; pe/ *n* [U] money paid for regular work or services, esp in the armed forces (*Pay* is used instead of *wages* and *salary* in the Navy, Army and Air Force): 工资; 薪饷(在海、陆、空军中用 pay 而不用 wages 与 salary): *draw one's pay;* 领薪饷; *get an increase in pay.* 获得加薪。 **in the pay of,** employed by (often with a suggestion of dishonour, eg *in the pay of the enemy*). 受雇于 (常指不名誉者, 如被敌方收买)。 '**pay-claim** = *wage-claim.* '**pay-day** *n* **(a)** day on which wages, salaries, etc are (to be) paid. 发薪日。 **(b)** day (on the Stock Exchange) on which transfer of stock has to be paid for. (证券市场的)交割日。 '**pay-dirt** [U] (US) earth in which there is of a grade high enough to make mining profitable. (美)(含量具有开采价值的)矿土; 矿苗。 '**pay·load** *n* **(a)** that part of the load (of a ship, aircraft, etc) for which payment is received, eg passengers and cargo, but not fuel. (船、飞机等)收费的载重; 酬载(如旅客与货物, 但便用的燃料不计在内)。 **(b)** bomb in a missile. 飞弹所载之炸弹。 **(c)** crew and instruments of a spacecraft. 太空船中的人员和仪器。 '**pay·master** *n* official responsible for paying troops, workers, etc. (负责发放薪饷的)军需官; 出纳员; 发款员。 '**pay·master 'general,** officer at the head of a department of the Treasury. (英国财政部的)会计长。 '**pay-off** *n* (colloq) (time of) full and final settlement of accounts or of final retribution or revenge. (口) 总结算 (的时刻); 报复(的时刻); 报应(的时刻)。 '**pay-packet** *n* envelope or packet containing pay. 薪水袋。 '**pay-phone** / **-station** *nn* (US) coinoperated telephone / call-box. (美)(投硬币的)公共电话(亭)。 '**pay-roll** / **-sheet** *nn* **(a)** list of persons to be paid and the amounts due to each. 薪饷表; 工资单(载明每人应得的薪额)。 **(b)** total amount of wages, salaries, etc to be paid to them. 所有员工薪给的总数。 '**pay-slip** *n* slip of paper included in a pay-packet, showing how pay has been calculated, deductions for tax, etc. (放在薪水袋内注明薪资核算方法、扣税额等的)薪资核算单。

pay[2] /peɪ; pe/ *vt, vi* (*pt, pp* **paid** /peɪd; ped/) (For

special uses with *adverbial particles* and *preps*, ⇨ **6** below.) (与副词性小品词及介词连用的特殊用法，参看下列第 6 义。) **1** [VP6A, 12A, 13A, 14, 3A] *pay sb; pay for sth; pay sb for sth; pay sth; pay sth (to sb) (for sth)*, give (sb) money for goods, services, etc: 付给; 付款; 付还; 偿付(某人): *You must pay me what you owe.* 你必须把你所欠我的付给我。*You must pay for what you eat and drink.* 你必须付你吃喝的费用。*Have you paid the milkman this month?* 你这个月付钱给卖牛奶的人了吗？ *I paid you the money last week.* 我上星期把钱还(付)给你了。*He paid £600 to a dealer for that car.* 他花了六百镑向汽车商人买了那辆车子。*I pay £5 a week for guitar lessons.* 我每周为吉他课付五英镑学费。**2** [VP 2A, 14, 12A, 13A] give (sb) reward or recompense: 给(某人)报酬; 报偿; 补偿: *He says that sheep farming doesn't pay,* but it isn't profitable. 他说养羊不赚钱。*He has been amply paid for his trouble.* 他的辛劳已经获得丰富的报酬。*They say it pays to advertise.* 他们说登广告很有利。**3** [VP6A] settle (debts, etc): 偿还; 付清(债务等): *Have you paid all your debts yet?* 你偿还你全部的债了吗？ *He has paid his bills / dues / subscriptions / taxes.* 他已付清帐单(应付之款，订阅费，税金)。 *put 'paid to sth*, (colloq) settle it; end it so that it gives no more trouble. (口)解决某事物; 结束某事物以免再有麻烦。**4** [VP6A, 12A, 13A] ～ *(to)*, give, eg attention, respect, etc to: 给予; 付出(如注意力、敬意等): *Please pay more attention to your work.* 请更加注意你的工作。*He has called to pay* (= offer) *his respects.* 他曾经前来拜访致敬。*He seldom pays his wife any compliments,* seldom compliments her. 他很少称赞他的太太。*I look forward to paying you a visit* (= visiting you) *next week.* 我期待着下星期去拜访你。**5** (phrases) (短语) *pay one's way,* not get into debt. 不负债。*pay through the nose,* ⇨ *nose[1](1)*. *pay-as-you-'earn,* (abbr 略作 **PAYE**), method of collecting income tax (in GB) by requiring employers to deduct it from earnings. 预扣所得税(英国的一种征收所得税的方法，要求雇主在发薪时就扣缴所得税)。*pay·able* /'peɪəbl; 'peəbl/ *adj* which must or may be paid. 应付的; 可付的。*payee* /peɪ'iː; pe'i/ *n* person to whom sth is (to be) paid. 受款人; 受款人。*payer n* person who pays or who is to pay. 付款人; 付给者。**6** [VP15B, 3A, 2C] (special uses with *adverbial particles* and *preps*): (与副词性小品词及介词连用的特殊用法):

pay sth back, return (money, etc) that has been borrowed. 归还; 偿还。*pay sb back / out (for sth),* punish him; have one's revenge: 惩罚某人; 向某人报复: *I've paid him out for the trick he played on me.* 我已经报复他对我的愚弄。

pay for, (a) ⇨ **1** above. 参看上列第1义。*(b)* suffer pain or punishment for: 为…受痛苦或惩罚: *He'll have to pay for this foolish behaviour.* 他将为这种愚蠢行为而得到报应。

pay sth in; pay sth into sth, deposit (money) with a bank, to one's own or another's account: 将钱存入(自己或他人的)银行帐户: *Please pay this sum into my / my wife's account.* 请把这笔钱存入我的(我太太的)帐户。

pay sb off, (a) pay sb his wages and discharge him. 给薪解雇; 遣散。*(b)* pay in full and be free from obligation: 全部还清: *pay off one's creditors;* 把所有债权人的债都还清; *pay off the crew of a ship.* 发清全船船员的薪水。⇨ *pay-off* at *pay[1]*.

pay sth out, (a) give money, eg in settlement of expenses: 付钱(如付清费用): *When you move into a new house you really have to start paying out (money).* 当你迁入新居，你就得开始付钱了。*(b)* (naut) allow (rope) to run out freely through the hands; slacken (rope) so that it runs freely. (航海)放松(绳子)使其顺利滑出。

pay up, pay in full what is owing: 付清; 交清: *If you don't pay up,* I'll take you to court. 如果你不还清欠款，我就送到法院告你。

pay·ment /'peɪmənt; 'peəmənt/ *n* **1** [U] paying or being paid: 支付; 缴纳; 报酬: *demand prompt ～;* 要求即时付款; *a cheque in ～ for services rendered.* 偿付所作服务的支票。**2** [C] sum of money (to be) paid: 付出的款额; (应)支付的款额: *£50 cash down and ten monthly ～s of £5.* (交货时)先付五十英镑现款，然后分十个月摊付，每月五英镑。**3** [C, U] (fig) reward; punishment. (喻)报偿; 惩罚。

pay·nim /'peɪnɪm; 'penɪm/ *n* (archaic) pagan; heathen; (esp during the Crusades to the Holy Land) Saracen. (古)异教徒; 不信基督教者; (尤指十字军东征时的)穆斯林。

pea /piː; pi/ *n* [C] plant with seeds in pods, used for food. 豌豆。⇨ the illus at **vegetable**. 参看 vegetable 之插图。*as like as two peas (in a pod),* exactly alike. 完全相似; 一模一样。'**pea-chick, 'pea-fowl, 'pea-hen** *nn* ⇨ **peacock**. '**pea-flour** *n* [U] meal made from dried peas. 豌豆粉。'**pea-green** *adj, n* bright light-green colour of young peas. 青豆色(的); 浅绿色(的)。'**pea-shooter** *n* (toy) tube from which dried peas are shot by blowing through the tube. (玩具)豆子枪(由管中吹出吃豌豆的一种玩具)。'**pea-soup** *n* thick soup made from dried peas. 豌豆汤。'**pea-'souper** *n* (colloq) thick yellow fog. (口)黄色浓雾。

peace /piːs; pis/ *n* [U] (not used in *pl*, but see examples for use of *indef art*) (不用作复数，但与不定冠词连用者见以下例句) **1** state of freedom from war: 和平: *be at ～ with neighbouring countries.* 与邻国和平相处。*After a brief ～* (= a brief period of ～) *war broke out again.* 经过短暂的和平，战争又爆发了。*make ～ (with),* bring ～ (with): (跟…)讲和; (与…)重新和好。**2** (often 常作 P～) treaty of ～; 和约: *P～/ A P～ was signed between the two countries.* 两国签订了和约。**3** freedom from civil disorder. (社会的)安定; 安宁; 治安。*break the ～,* cause civil disorder, rioting, etc. 破坏治安; 妨害安宁。*keep the ～,* obey the laws and refrain from disorder and strife. 维持治安; 遵守法纪。*breach of the ～,* a disturbance or riot. 妨害治安; 骚乱; 暴动。*the King's / Queen's ～,* the general ～ of the country, as secured by law. (某王国的)社会安宁; 治安。*Justice of the P～,* (abbr 略作 **JP**) a magistrate. 保安官; 地方执法官。**4** rest; quiet; calm: 安稳; 安静; 宁静: *the ～ of the countryside;* 乡间的宁静; *～ of mind.* 心境的安宁。*at ～ (with),* in a state of friendship or harmony: (与…)保持友好、和谐; 平静: *He's never at ～ with himself,* is always restless. 他总是坐立不安。*in ～,* peacefully: 平安地; 和平地: *live in ～ with one's neighbours.* 与邻居和睦相处。*hold one's ～,* keep silence; stop talking or arguing. 保持缄默; 停止说话或争论。*make one's ～ (with sb),* settle a quarrel. (与某人)和解。'*～-maker* *n* person who restores friendly relations. 调停人; 和事佬。'*～-offering n* sth offered to show that one is willing to make ～. 表示愿意和解而献出的东西。

peace·able /'piːsəbl; 'pisəbl/ *adj* not quarrelsome; free from fighting or uproar. 温和的; 和平的; 平静的。**peace·ably** /-əblɪ; -əblɪ/ *adv*

peace·ful /'piːsfl; 'pisfəl/ *adj* **1** loving peace: 爱好和平的: *～ nations.* 爱好和平的国家。**2** calm; quiet: 安详的; 宁静的; 和平的: *a ～ evening;* 宁静的夜晚: *a ～ death.* 安详的死亡。*～ly* /-fəlɪ; -fəlɪ/ *adv* *～ness n*

peach[1] /piːtʃ; pitʃ/ *n* **1** (tree with) juicy, round fruit with delicate yellowish-red skin and a rough stone-like seed; yellowish-red. 桃; 桃树; 桃色。⇨ the illus at **fruit**. 参看 fruit 之插图。**2** (sl) person or thing greatly admired. (俚)极受爱慕的人或物。

peach[2] /piːtʃ; pitʃ/ *vi, vt* [VP2A, 3A, 6A] ～ *(against / on / upon) (sb),* (sl) inform (against); betray. (俚)告密; 告发; 出卖。

pea·cock /'piːkɒk; 'pi,kɑk/ *n* large male bird noted for its fine tail feathers. 雄孔雀。⇨ the illus at **rare**. 参看 rare 之插图。'*～-'blue* *adj, n* bright blue (colour)

孔雀蓝(的); 鲜蓝色(的)。'**pea-chick** n young pea-fowl. 小孔雀。'**pea-fowl** n ～ or pea-hen. 孔雀。'**pea-hen** n female of the ～. 雌孔雀。

pea-jacket /'piːdʒækɪt/ n short double-breasted overcoat of thick woollen cloth, as worn by sailors. 粗呢短外衣(如水手所穿着者)。

peak[1] /piːk/ n **1** pointed top, esp of a mountain; point, eg of a beard. 尖顶; (尤指)山峰; (胡须等的)尖端。⇨ the illus at **mountain**. 参看 mountain 之插图。'**P～ District**, area in Derbyshire, England having many ～s. (英国德贝郡的)山峦地区。**2** pointed front part of a cap; projecting brim (to shade the eyes). 帽舌; 帽檐。**3** narrow part of a ship's hold at the bow ('**fore～**) or stern ('**after～**). 船首舱 (forepeak); 船尾舱 (afterpeak)。**4** highest point in a record of figures that fluctuate (升降不定之数字记录的) 最高点: ～ hours of traffic, times when the traffic is heaviest; 交通最频繁的高峰时刻; industry's ～ hours, when consumption of electric current, etc is highest; 工业用电等最多的高峰时刻; off-～ periods, when traffic, consumption of current, etc is light; 非高峰时刻(指交通量较小、用电量较小等的时间); off-～ flights to Rome, during the less busy times, eg during hours of darkness. 飞往罗马的不拥挤班次(如夜间班次)。**peaked** adj having a ～: 有尖顶的; 有帽檐的: ～ed cap/roof. 有檐的帽子(尖的屋顶)。

peak[2] /piːk/ pik/ vi [VP2A] **1** reach the highest point, value, etc: 达于顶点: Property prices have ～ed. 房地产价格已达最高点。**2** ～ and pine, waste away. 消瘦; 憔悴。**peaked** pp sharp-featured; thin, pale and weak-looking. 消瘦的; 憔悴的。**peaky** adj = peaked.

peal /piːl/ pil/ n [C] **1** loud ringing of a bell or of a set of bells with different notes; changes rung upon a set of bells; set of bells tuned to each other. 响亮的钟声; 一组钟的变奏法; 彼此谐音的一组钟。**2** loud echoing noise: 宏亮的回响声; 隆隆声: a ～ of thunder; 雷声隆隆; ～s of laughter. 一阵大笑声; 哄堂大笑。□ vi, vt **1** [VP 2A, C] sound forth in a ～; ring out loudly. 隆隆地响; 大声鸣响。**2** [VP6A] cause to ring or sound loudly. 使大声鸣响。

pean /piːn/ 'piən/ (US) (美) = **paean**.

pea-nut /'piːnʌt/ 'piˌnʌt/ n groundnut. 花生; 落花生; 花生米。,～ '**butter**, paste of ground ～s. 花生酱。,～ '**oil**, oil pressed from ～s, used in cooking, etc. 花生油。～**s**, (sl, derog) small amount of money. (俚,贬)少数的钱; 很少的钱。

pear /peə(r); pɛr/ n [C] (tree with) sweet, juicy fruit, usu tapering towards the stalk. 梨; 梨树。⇨ the illus at **fruit**. 参看 fruit 之插图。

pearl /pɜːl; pɝl/ n **1** silvery-white or bluish-white spherical formation found inside the shells of some oysters, valued as a gem: 珍珠; 蚌珠: a necklace of ～s; 珍珠项链; a ～ necklace. 珍珠项链。'～-**diver** n one who dives for ～-oysters. 潜水采珍珠贝的人。'～-**fishery** n place where ～-oysters are fished up. 珍珠贝采集场; 养珠场。'～-**oyster** n kind in which ～s are found. 珍珠贝。**2** = mother-of-～: 贝壳之珠母层: ～ buttons. 贝壳纽扣。⇨ **mother**. **3** small round fragment of various substances. 小圆形物。,～-'**barley**/-'**sago** nn barley/sago rubbed into small ～-like grains. 珍珠麦(西米); 被揉搓得象球粒的大麦(西米)。**4** sth that looks like a ～, eg a dew-drop; sb or sth very precious: 象珍珠之物(如露珠); 极重要之人; 极珍贵之物: She's a ～ among women. 她是妇女中的杰出者。cast ～s before swine, (prov) offer sth valuable or beautiful to those who cannot appreciate it. (谚)把珍美之物献给不能赏识者; 对牛弹琴。□ vi fish for ～s: 采珠: go ～ing. 去采珠。'～y adj of, like, ornamented with, ～s. 珠的; 似珠的; 以珍珠装饰的。**P～y King**/**Queen**, costermonger wearing pearlies. 穿着饰有贝壳纽扣衣服的小贩。～**-ies** n pl (the now festive) dress of some London costermongers, ornamented with many mother-of-～ buttons. (目前节日时)伦敦某些小贩所穿的衣服(上面饰有许多贝壳纽扣)。

pear·main /'peəmeɪn; 'pɜrmen/ n variety of apple. 一种苹果。

peas·ant /'peznt; 'peznt/ n (not GB or US) country-man working on the land, either for wages or on a very small farm which he either rents or owns: (不用于英国或美国)小农; 佃农; 农民: (attrib)(用作定语) ～ labour, ⇨ for GB, smallholder, at **small** and, for US, sharecropper at **share**[1](1). 农工。～**ry** /'pezntrɪ; 'pezntrɪ/ n the ～s of a country; ～s as a class. 一国的农民; 农民阶级。

pease /piːz; piz/ n ～-**pudding** n pudding of boiled peas. 豌豆布丁。

peat /piːt; pit/ n [U] plant material partly decomposed by the action of water, found in bogs, used in horticul-ture, and as a fuel: 泥炭(用于园艺、并用作燃料): a bag/bale of ～; 一袋(包)泥炭; a '～-**bog**, a marshy place where ～ is found; 泥炭田; a ～ fire, one on which cut pieces of ～ are burnt as fuel. 泥炭火。～**y** adj of, like, smelling of, ～. 泥炭的; 似泥炭的; 有泥炭味的。

pebble /'pebl; 'pebl/ n small stone made smooth and round by the action of water, eg in a stream or on the seashore. (河里或海边的)小圆石; 卵石。**peb·bly** /'peblɪ; 'peblɪ/ adj covered with ～s: 覆有小圆石的: a pebbly beach. 遍布小圆石的海滩。

pe·can /pɪˈkæn US: pɪˈkɑːn; pɪˈkɑn/ n [C] (nut of a) kind of hickory tree growing in the Mississippi region of the USA. (产于美国密西西比河流域的)山核桃; 山核桃树。

pec·cable /'pekəbl; 'pekəbl/ adj (formal) liable to sin. (正式用语)易犯罪的。

pec·ca·dillo /ˌpekəˈdɪləʊ; ˌpekəˈdɪlo/ n (pl ～es or ～s -ləuz; -loz/) small weakness in a person's character; small sin or fault. 性格上的小缺点; 小过失。

pec·cary /'pekərɪ; 'pekərɪ/ n (pl -ries) kind of wild pig found in America. 美洲的一种野猪。

peck[1] /pek; pek/ n measure of capacity for dry goods (=2 gallons or approx 9 litres): 配克(干货容量单位, 等于两加仑或者约九公升): a ～ of beans; 一配克的豆; (fig) a lot: 许多: a ～ of troubles. 许多麻烦。⇨ **App 5**. 参看附录五。

peck[2] /pek; pek/ vi, vt **1** [VP2A, C, 3A, 6A] ～ (at), (try) to strike with the beak: 以啄啄: hens ～ing at the corn; 啄食谷粒的母鸡; cocks ～ing (at) the hens; 啄母鸡的公鸡; (colloq) (口)～ at one's food, (of a person) eat only small bits of food; eat without appetite. (指人)只吃少量食物; 吃东西没有胃口。'～-**ing order**, order(within a flock of poultry) in which each bird submits to ～ing and domination by stronger birds and itself ～s and dominates weaker birds; any similar arrangement in a group of human beings: (一群家禽中, 强者啄欺弱者的)强弱顺序; (一群人中)强弱的顺序: Poor Tom! He's at the bottom of the ～ing order, is dominated by all the members of his group. 可怜的汤姆! 他是他们那群人中最受气的一个。**2** [VP6A] get or make by striking with the beak: 啄食; 啄到; 啄成: ～ corn. 啄食谷粒。The hens ～ed a hole in the sack. 母鸡在袋上啄了一个洞。**3** (colloq) kiss hurriedly from habit or a sense of duty rather than from affection. (口)匆忙而敷衍地吻。□ n **1** stroke with the beak; mark made by this. 啄击; 啄痕。**2** (colloq) hurried, unemotional kiss. (口)匆忙而敷衍的吻。～**er** n (GB sl) human nose; (fig) courage; spirits. (英俚)(人的)鼻子; (喻)勇气; 精神。,keep your ～**er up**, stay cheerful; don't let your spirits droop. 保持愉快; 打起精神来。'～**ish** /-ɪʃ; -ɪʃ/ adj (colloq) hungry. (口)饥饿的。

pec·tin /'pektɪn; 'pektɪn/ n [U] (chem) compound similar to sugar, formed in fruits by ripening process and by heating, eg that becomes jam when made into jam. (化学)果胶(由水果由成熟过程或加热制酱等时所产生的一种似糖的粘胶质)。**pec·tic** /'pektɪk; 'pektɪk/ adj of ～; producing ～: 果胶的; 产生果胶的: pectic acid. 果胶酸。

pec·toral /ˈpektərəl; ˈpɛktərəl/ adj 1 of, for, the chest or breast: 胸的; 为着胸部的: a ~ muscle/fin. 胸肌(胸鳍). 2 worn on the chest or breast: 佩于胸前的: a ~ cross, as worn by a bishop. 佩于胸前的十字架(如主教所佩者).

pecu·late /ˈpekjuleɪt; ˈpɛkjəˌlet/ vi, vt embezzle. 侵吞; 盗用; 挪用(公款). **pecu·la·tion** /ˌpekjuˈleɪʃn; ˌpɛkjəˈleʃən/ n [U] peculating; [C] instance of this. 侵吞; 盗用; 挪用(公款).

pe·cu·liar /prˈkjuːlɪə(r); prˈkjuljə/ adj 1 ~ (to), belonging exclusively; used, adopted, practised, only by: 特有的; 独特的; 仅由…使用、采纳、实行的: customs ~ to these tribes, 这些部落所特有的习俗; a style ~ to the 18th century. 十八世纪特有的风格。2 strange; unusual; odd. 奇怪的; 罕有的; 奇异的。3 particular; special: 特殊的; 特别的: a matter of ~ interest. 特别有趣的事。~·ly adv in a ~ manner: 独地地; 特别地; 奇异地: ~ly annoying, more than usually annoying. 特别恼人的。~·ity /prˌkjuːlɪˈærɪtɪ; prˌkjuljɪˈærɪtɪ/ n (pl -ties) 1 [U] the quality of being ~. 独特性; 特质; 特色。2 [C] sth distinctive or characteristic. 独特之处; 特征; 特点。3 [C] sth odd or strange: 奇异之事物; 怪癖: ~ities of speech/dress/behaviour. 言语(服装, 行为)的怪异。

pe·cuni·ary /prˈkjuːnɪərɪ US: -erɪ; prˈkjunɪˌerɪ/ adj (formal) of money: (正式用语)钱的: ~ aid; 金钱援助; work without ~ reward. 没有金钱报酬的工作。

peda·gogue (US also **-gog**) /ˈpedəgɒg; ˈpɛdəˌgɑg/ n (formal) schoolmaster; (colloq) pedantic teacher. (正式用语)教师; (口)卖弄学问的教师。**peda·gogy** /ˈpedəgɒdʒɪ; ˈpɛdəˌgodʒɪ/ n [U] science of teaching. 教学法。**peda·gog·ic** /ˌpedəˈgɒdʒɪk ; ˌpedəˈgodʒɪk / , **peda·gogi·cal** /-ɪkl; -ɪkl/ adjj of pedagogy. 教学法的。

pedal[1] /ˈpedl; ˈpɛdl/ n lever (eg on a bicycle, sewing-machine, organ or piano) worked by the foot or feet: (如脚踏车、缝纫机、风琴或钢琴的)踏板: (attrib) (用作定语) ~ cyclist; 骑脚踏车者: ~ boat, propelled by ~s. 用脚踏动的船。⇨ the illus at **bicycle, church, key.** 参看 bicycle, church, key 之插图。□ vi, vt (**-ll-**, US also **-l-**) [VP2A, C, 6A] use a ~ or ~s (for playing an organ, riding a bicycle, etc); move or work by the use of a ~ or ~s: 踩踏板; 踩踏板转动或操作(如弹风琴、骑脚踏车等): The boy ~led away on his tricycle. 那男孩踩着他的三轮脚踏车走了。

pedal[2] /ˈpedl; ˈpɛdl/ adj (zool) of the foot or feet. (动物)脚的。

ped·ant /ˈpednt; ˈpɛdn̩t/ n person who lays too much stress on book-learning, technical knowledge, rules and adherence to rules. 太过强调书本学问、专门知识、规则等的人; 拘泥于规则的人; 迂腐的人; 书呆子; 学究。~ry /ˈpedntrɪ; ˈpɛdn̩trɪ/ n [U] tiresome and unnecessary display of learning; too much insistence upon formal rules; [C] instance of this. 卖弄学问; 拘泥于拘泥形式上的规则。**pe·dan·tic** / prˈdæntɪk; prˈdæntɪk / adj of or like a ~. 学究的; 迂腐的。**pe·dan·ti·cally** /-klɪ; -klɪ/ adv

peddle /ˈpedl; ˈpɛdl/ vi, vt 1 [VP2A] be a pedlar; go from house to house trying to sell small articles. 做小贩; 沿街叫卖。2 [VP6A] deal out in small quantities: 零售; 散播: She loves to ~ gossip round the village. 她喜欢在村里到处说闲话。**ped·dler** n = pedlar. **ped·dling** adj petty; trivial: 细小的; 琐碎的: peddling details. 琐碎的细节。

ped·er·asty /ˈpedəræstɪ; ˈpɛdəˌræstɪ/ n [U] amorous or sexual relations between a man and a boy. 鸡奸; 男色(指男人与男童之间的色情或性关系)。**ped·er·ast** n man who practices ~. 鸡奸者; 男色者。

ped·estal /ˈpedɪstl; ˈpɛdɪstl/ n base of a column; base for a statue or other work of art; each of the two supports of a knee-hole writing-desk. 柱基; (塑像或艺术品的)座座; 基座(式书桌的踏脚板。Hence, 由此产生, '~ desk. 基座式书桌。**knock sb off his ~,** show that he is no longer highly regarded. 不再推崇某人; 不再看重某人。**set sb on a ~,** make him an object of high regard. 把某人当做偶像崇拜; 把某人理想化。

pe·des·trian /prˈdestrɪən; pəˈdɛstrɪən/ n person walking in a street, etc: 行人; 走路的人: ~s killed in traffic accidents. 车祸中死亡的行人。~ **crossing,** street crossing specially marked, where ~s have priority over traffic. 行人穿越道。⇨ **precinct,** ⇨ **precinct.** □ adj 1 connected with walking. 步行的。2 (of writing, a person's way of making speeches, etc) prosaic; dull; uninspired. (指文章、演说的方式等)平淡的; 单调的; 沉闷的。

pedi·at·rics /ˌpiːdɪˈætrɪks; ˌpidrˈætrɪks/ n (with sing v) branch of medicine concerned with children and their illnesses. (用单数动词)小儿科; 儿科学。**pedia·tric·ian** /ˌpiːdɪəˈtrɪʃn; ˌpidɪəˈtrɪʃən/ n physician who specializes in ~. 小儿科医师。

pedi·cab /ˈpedɪkæb; ˈpɛdɪˌkæb/ n (in some Asian countries) tricycle with one seat for the man in charge and a seat behind for two passengers, used as a form of public transport. (在某些亚洲国家内用的)三轮车; 三轮人力车。

pedi·cure /ˈpedɪkjʊə(r); ˈpɛdɪˌkjur/ n treatment of the feet, esp toe-nails, corns, bunions, etc. 修脚指甲; 脚上鸡眼、踇囊炎肿等的治疗; 脚病的治疗。

pedi·gree /ˈpedɪgriː; ˈpɛdəˌgri/ n 1 [C] line of ancestors: 家系; 家谱: proud of their long ~s; 为他们长远的家系而骄傲; [U] ancestry, esp ancient descent. 世系; 门第; 出身。2 (attrib) having a line of descent that has been recorded: (用作定语)有血统记录的: ~ cattle; 纯种牛; a ~ poodle. 有血统书的贵宾狗。

pedi·ment /ˈpedɪmənt; ˈpɛdəmənt/ n (in Gk architecture) triangular part over the front of a building; similar part over the portico of a building in other styles of architecture. (希腊建筑)正面上方的三角墙; 门廊上方的三角墙。⇨ the illus at **column.** 参看 column 之插图。

ped·lar, ped·dler /ˈpedlə(r); ˈpɛdlə/ n person who travels about selling small articles. 小贩。

ped·ometer /prˈdɒmɪtə(r); prˈdɑmətə/ n device which measures the number of steps taken by a walker, and the approximate distance he walks. (步行者计步数及距离的)计步表; 步程计; 万步表。

pee /piː/ vi [VP2A] (colloq) urinate: (口)解小便: Do you want to pee? 你要解小便吗? □ n [U] urine: 尿: a puddle of pee; 一滩尿; [C] act of urinating: 解小便: I must go for/must have a pee. 我必须解小便。

peek /piːk; pik/ vi ~ at, peep at. 窥视; 偷看。□ n quick look: 一瞥; 匆忙看过: have a quick ~ over the fence. 匆匆地看了篱笆那边一眼。

peek-a-boo /ˌpiːk ə ˈbuː; ˈpikəˌbu/ n game for amusing a small child, in which one covers and then uncovers the face, repeatedly, saying '~!' as one does this. 躲躲猫(面孔一隐一现以逗小孩之游戏)。

peel /piːl; pil/ vt, vi ~ (off), 1 [VP6A, 15B] take the skin off (fruit, etc): 剥; 削(水果等的)皮: ~ a banana; 剥一根香蕉的皮; ~ potatoes. 削马铃薯的皮。2 [VP2A, C] come off in strips or flakes: 剥落; 脱皮: These potatoes ~ easily, the skin comes off them easily. 这些马铃薯容易脱皮。The wall-paper is ~ing off. 壁纸开始脱落了。After a day in the hot sun my skin began to ~/my face ~ed. 晒了一天炎热的太阳后, 我的皮肤开始脱皮了(我的脸脱皮了)。The bark of plane-trees ~s off regularly. 法国梧桐的树皮会定时脱落。It was so hot that we all ~ed off (= undressed) and jumped into the lake. 天气太热, 我们全都脱光了衣服跳入湖中。□ n [U] skin of fruit, some vegetables, young shoots, etc. (水果、蔬菜、嫩枝等的)皮。⇨ the illus at **fruit.** 参看 fruit 之插图。**candied ~, ⇨ candy.** 蜜饯果皮。~**er** n (in compounds) device used for ~ing, eg potatoes. (用于复合词中)(用来削马铃薯皮等的)刨刀; 削皮刀。~**ings** n pl parts ~ed off (esp of potatoes). 削下的皮(尤指马铃薯皮)。

peep¹ /piːp; pip/ n **1** short, quick look, often one taken secretly or inquisitively; incomplete view: 偷看; 瞥见; 窥视; 不完全的景象: ~ *through the window*. 从窗口偷看我们。 **'~-hole** n small opening in a wall, partition, etc through which one can have a ~. 窥孔。 **'~-show** n exhibition of small pictures to be seen through a magnifying lens in a small opening. 西洋镜(从装有放大镜的小孔看箱中的小图片)。 **2** the first light (of day): (一天的)破晓: ~ *of day*, dawn. 黎明。 □ vi [VP2A, C] **1** ~ *(at)*, take a ~ (at); look slyly or cautiously: 窥视; 偷看: ~ *through a keyhole at sth*; 从钥匙孔偷看某事物; *neighbours* ~*ing at us from behind curtains*. 邻人从窗帘后偷看我们。 **~ing 'Tom**, name used of a prurient person who spies on people who think they are alone; voyeur. 爱偷看别人的好色男子(含淫猥狂者)。 **2** come slowly or partly into view: 微现; 慢慢露出: *The moon* ~*ed out from behind the clouds*. 月亮从云后慢慢露出。 **1** person who ~s. 窥视者; 偷看者。 **2** (sl) eye. (俚)眼睛。

peep² /piːp; pip/ n [C] weak, shrill sound made by mice, young birds, etc. (鼠、小鸟等的)吱吱声; 啾啾声。 □ vi make this sound. 吱吱地叫; 啾啾地叫。

pee·pul, pi·pal /'piːpəl; `pipəl/ n large Indian figtree. (印度产的)菩提树。

peer¹ /pɪə(r); pɪr/ n **1** equal in rank, merit or quality: 同辈; 同等之人; 同侪; 匹敌: *It will not be very easy to find his* ~. 不太容易找到与他匹敌的人。 **2** (in GB) member of one of the degrees of nobility, eg duke, marquis, earl, viscount, baron. (英)贵族; 公侯伯子男(爵)中之任一个。 ~ **of the realm**, person with the right to sit in the House of Lords. 可成为上议院议员的贵族。 **'life** ~, one elected to the House of Lords for life only (contrasted with a **he'reditary** ~). 终身任职上议院议员(此等被选为上议院议员者只能任职一生、而不能传后; 与hereditary peer '世袭上议院议员'相对)。 ~·**ess** /'pɪərɛs; `pɪrɪs/ n woman ~; wife of a ~ (2). 女贵族; 女上议院议员; 贵族夫人; 上议院议员夫人。 ~·**less** adj without a ~ (1); without equal. 无匹敌的; 无双的。

peer² /pɪə(r); pɪr/ vi [VP2A, 3A] ~ *(at /into)*, look closely, as if unable to see well: 凝视; 盯着看; 眯着眼看: ~ *into dark corners*, 凝视黑暗的角落; ~*ing at her over his spectacles*. 从他的眼镜上方盯着看。

peer·age /'pɪərɪdʒ; `pɪrɪdʒ/ n **1** the whole body of peers; rank of peer (2). 全体贵族; 贵族爵位; 上议院议员的地位,身分。 *raise sb to the* ~, elect sb to the ~. 封一个人为贵族。 **2** book containing a list of peers (2) with their ancestry. 贵族名鉴(记载所有贵族及其世系)。

peeve /piːv; piv/ vt (colloq) vex; annoy. (口)使气恼; 使恼怒。 ~**d** adj (colloq) annoyed. (口)气恼的; 恼怒的。

pee·vish /'piːvɪʃ; `pivɪʃ/ adj irritable. 易怒的; 脾气乖张的。 ~·**ly** adv ~·**ness** n

pee·wit /'piːwɪt; `piwɪt/ n = **pewit**.

peg¹ /peg; peg/ n **1** wooden or metal pin or bolt, usu pointed at one end, used to fasten parts of woodwork together. 木(或金属的)栓; 钉。 *a square peg in a round hole*, a person unsuited to the position he fills. 不称职的人。 **2** pin driven into the ground to hold a rope (*a 'tent-peg*), or fastened to a wall or door (*'hat and 'coat pegs*), or to mark a position or boundary. 系帐篷的桩; 挂衣帽的钉; 定位置或界限的桩。 *(buy sth) off the peg*, (colloq) (buy clothes) ready-made (as if off a peg in a shop). (口)(买)现成的(衣服); (好象从店里的衣服钉上取下来的一样)。 **3** **'clothes-peg**, device for holding laundered clothes in place on a line. 晒衣服的夹子。 **4** (fig) theme, pretext or excuse: (喻)主题; 题词; 借口: *a peg on which to hang a speech*. 演说的主题。 **5** wooden screw for tightening or loosening the string of a violin, etc. (提琴等用于调整弦线松紧的)轸; 木栓。 ⇨ the illus at **string**. 参看 string 之插图。 **,take sb 'down a peg (or two)**, humble him. 抑某人的傲气; 挫某人的锐气; 煞某人的威风。 **6** piece of wood for stopping the vent of a cask, etc. (塞桶孔等的)木塞。 **7** (colloq)

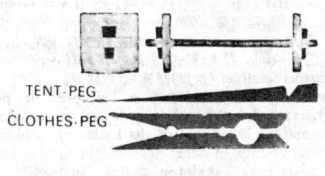

TENT·PEG

CLOTHES·PEG

pegs

wooden leg. (口)木腿; 义腿。

peg² /peg; peg/ vt,vi (**-gg-**) **1** [VP6A, 15B] *peg sth (down)*, fasten with pegs: 以栓、钉、桩等钉牢或系紧: *peg a tent down*. 把帐篷用木桩系牢在地上。 *peg sb down*, (fig) make him keep to a certain line of action, restrict him to the rules, etc. (喻)约束某人; 管住某人。 **2** [VP15B] *peg sth out*, mark by means of pegs fixed in the ground; show (a score, esp at cribbage) by means of pegs. 以木桩钉在地上标出; 以木桩划分; (尤指一种纸牌戏中)以木钉在有孔的木板上记(分)。 *level pegging*, (often fig) making progress at the same rate. (常作比喻用法)以相同比率进展; 以同样速度进步。 **3** [VP6A, 15B] (comm) keep (prices, etc) steady by buying and selling (stocks) freely at fixed prices; keep (wages) steady: (商)以固定价格随时买卖股票以稳定(价格等); 使(工资)稳定: *wage-pegging efforts that failed*. 业已失败的稳定工资的努力。 **4** [VP2C] *peg away at*, keep on working at. 继续做。 *peg out*, (colloq) die. (口)死亡。

pei·gnoir /'peɪnwɑː(r); pen'wɑr/ n woman's loose dressing gown. 妇女梳妆时所着的宽袍; 女用浴袍; 女用宽大便服。

pe·jor·at·ive /pɪ'dʒɒrətɪv US: -'dʒɔːr-; `pidʒə,retɪv/ adj depreciatory; disparaging; deteriorating in use or meaning. 轻视的; 蔑视的; (意义或用法)有贬抑意味的。 ~·**ly** adv

peke /piːk; pik/ n short for *pekinese (dog)*. 哈巴狗(简称)。

pe·kin·ese /ˌpiːkɪ'niːz; ˌpikɪn'iz/ n small Chinese dog with long, silky hair. 哈巴狗。 ⇨ the illus at **dog**. 参看 dog 之插图。

pe·koe /'piːkəʊ; `piko/ n [U] high grade of black tea. 白毫(一种上等红茶)。

pelf /pelf; pelf/ n [U] (usu contemptuous use) money. (通常为轻蔑用语)钱。

peli·can /'pelɪkən; `pelɪkən/ n large water-bird with a large bill under which hangs a pouch for storing food. 塘鹅; 鹈鹕。 ⇨ the illus at **water**. 参看 water 之插图。

pe·lisse /pe'liːs; pə'lis/ n mantle. 无袖外套; 斗篷。

pel·let /'pelɪt; `pelɪt/ n **1** small ball of sth soft, eg wet paper, bread, made, for example, by rolling between the fingers. (用手指将湿的纸或面包等捻成的)小团; 小球; 小丸。 **2** slug of small shot, eg as used from an air-gun. 小弹丸(如气枪所用者)。 **3** pill. 药丸。

pell-mell /ˌpel'mel; `pel'mel/ adv in a hurrying, disorderly manner. 匆忙杂乱地; 混乱地; 乱七八糟地。

pel·lu·cid /pe'luːsɪd; pə'lusɪd/ adj (lit, fig) very clear. (字面,喻)清晰的; 清晰的。 ~·**ly** adv

pel·met /'pelmɪt; `pelmɪt/ n strip (of wood, cloth, etc) above a window or door to conceal a curtain rod. (窗帘或门帘于上方用以遮蔽帘子拉杆的)窗帘盒; 短帷幔等。

pe·lota /pə'ləʊtə; pə'lotə/ n [U] ball game popular in Spain, Latin America, and the Phillippines, the players using a long basket strapped to the wrist to hit the ball against a wall. 回力球(西班牙、拉丁美洲和菲律宾风行之一种球戏)。

pelt¹ /pelt; pelt/ n animal's skin with the fur or hair on it. 带毛的兽皮; 毛皮。

pelt² /pelt; pelt/ vt, vi **1** [VP6A, 14] ~ *sth (at sb)*; ~ *sb (with sth)*, attack by throwing things at: 投掷; 投击: ~ *sb with stones / snowballs / mud*. 以石头(雪球、泥巴)掷向某人。 **2** [VP2C] (of rain, etc) beat down;

fall heavily: (指雨等)急降;下得很大: *It was ~ing with rain.* 大雨倾盆而降。*The rain was ~ing down.* 大雨倾盆。*The hail was ~ing against the roof.* 冰雹猛打着屋顶。□ *n ~ing.* 投掷;投击;急降。**at full ~,** (running) as fast as possible. (跑步)尽速地;尽快地。

pel·vis /'pelvɪs; 'pɛlvɪs/ *n* (*pl* ~**es** or **pelves** /'pelviz; 'pɛlviz/) (anat) bony frame within the hipbones and the lower part of the backbone, holding the kidneys, rectum, bladder, etc. (解剖)(人体的)骨盆。⇨ the illus at **skeleton.** 参看 skeleton 之插图。**pelvic** /'pelvɪk; 'pɛlvɪk/ *adj* of the ~. 骨盆的;骨盆的。

pem·mi·can /'pemɪkən; 'pɛmɪkən/ *n* [U] dried lean meat beaten and mixed into cakes (as by N American Indians). 干肉饼(如北美洲印地安人所制者)。

pen[1] / pen; pɛn / *n* 1 (formerly) quill-feather, pointed and split at the end, for writing with ink; (mod use) instrument with a pointed piece of split metal ('*pen-nib*') fixed into a holder ('*pen-holder*') of wood or other material; ballpoint-pen; fountain-pen, ⇨ **ball** (*point*)-*pen* at **ball**[1](1) *and fountain-pen* at **fountain.** (昔时之)鹅毛笔(用翎羽削尖剪裂为笔,蘸墨水书写);(现在之)蘸水笔(用金属笔尖 'pen-nib, 固定于木制或其他材料制成之笔管 'pen-holder 而成);圆珠笔;钢笔。2 (style of) writing: 写作;文体: *make a living with one's pen.* 靠写作为生。3 ,**pen-and-'ink,** (attrib) drawn with these: (用作定语)用钢笔墨水画出的: *a pen-and-ink sketch.* 钢笔画素描。'**pen·friend** *n* person (eg in another country) with whom one has a friendship through exchanges of letters. 笔友。'**pen·knife** *n* small folding knife, usu carried in the pocket. (可以折起来放在口袋里携带的)小刀;削铅笔刀。**pen·man·ship** /'penmənʃɪp; 'pɛnmənʃɪp/ *n* [U] art or style of handwriting. 书法;笔迹。'**pen-name** *n* name used by a writer instead of his real name. 笔名。'**pen-pusher** *n* (derog) clerk. (贬)书记;抄写员。□ *vt* (**-nn-**) write (a letter, etc). 写(信等)。

pen[2] / pen; pɛn / *n* 1 small enclosure for cattle, sheep, poultry, etc or other purposes. (牛、羊、家禽等的)圈;围栏;槛。2 ('**play**)-**pen,** portable enclosure for a very small child to play in safety. (供幼儿游玩于其中的)安全围栏。3 bomb-proof shelter for submarines. (供潜水艇停泊的)防弹掩体(如修理潜水艇之船坞、上有厚混凝土顶盖者)。□ *vt* (**-nn-**) ~ (in), **pen up/in,** shut up in, or as in, a pen. 关入栏中;把…关起来。

penal /'pi:nl; 'pinl/ *adj* connected with punishment: 刑罚的; 刑事的: ~ *laws;* 刑法; *a* ~ *offence,* one for which there is legal punishment. 刑事罪。'~ '**servitude,** imprisonment with hard labour. 劳役监禁。'~ **settle-ment/colony,** one used as a place of punishment. 监禁地;充军地。~**ly** /'pi:nəlɪ; 'pinlɪ/ *adv*

pe·nal·ize /'pi:nəlaɪz; 'pinl,aɪz/ *vt* 1 [VP6A] make (sth) punishable; declare to be punishable by law. 规定(某事物)应罚;宣告有罪应罚。2 [VP6A, 14] ~ **sb (for sth),** place at a disadvantage; give a penalty(2) to (a player, competitor, etc). 使不利; 处罚(运动员、比赛者等)。**pe·nal·iz·ation** /,pi:nəlaɪ'zeɪʃn US: -lɪ'z-; ,pinl'zeʃən/ *n*

pen·alty /'penltɪ; 'pɛnltɪ/ *n* (*pl* -**ties**) 1 [U] punishment for wrongdoing, for failure to obey rules or keep an agreement; [C] what is imposed (imprisonment, payment of a fine, etc) as punishment; (fig) suffering which a wrongdoer brings upon himself or others: 惩罚; 刑罚; 处罚 (如服刑、罚款等); (喻)报应: *Spitting forbidden:* ~ £5. 禁止吐痰;违者罚款五英镑。*The* ~ (eg in a business agreement) *for non-performance of contract is heavy.* 不履行契约的罚款很重。'~ **clause,** (comm) clause in a contract requiring payment for breaking it. (商)合约中违约罚款之条款;罚款规定。**on/under** ~ **of (death, etc),** with (death, etc) as the ~: 违者处(死刑等):*forbidden under* ~ *of death.* 违者处以死刑的;以死刑严禁的。2 (in sport, competitions, etc) disadvantage to which a player or team must submit for breaking a rule: (运动、竞赛等)犯规的处罚: *The referee awarded a*

~. 裁判员判罚球。'~ **area,** (football) part of the ground in front of the goal where a breach of the rules by defenders gives the opposing team the right to a free kick *(a '~ kick)* at the goal. (足球)罚球区(如守方球员在此区内犯规、则应由对方罚十二码球 a penalty kick)。3 handicap imposed upon a player or team for winning a previous contest. (对上次比赛中获胜者或获胜队给予的)困难;障碍。

pen·ance /'penəns; 'pɛnəns/ *n* [U] 1 punishment which one imposes upon oneself to show repentance, eg upon the advice of a priest. (表示忏悔的)自我惩罚;(赎罪的)苦行。**do** ~ **(for sth),** perform an act of ~ (for sth). (为…)苦行赎罪。2 (RC Church) name for the sacrament that includes contrition, confession and penance. (天主教)告解。

pence /pens; pɛns/ *n* pl ⇨ **penny.**

pen·chant /'pɑ:nʃɑ:n US: 'pentʃənt; 'pɛntʃənt/ *n* (F) *a* ~ **(for),** taste, liking, inclination: (法)嗜爱;爱好;倾向: *have a* ~ *for marshmallows.* 喜爱药蜀葵根制成的甜食。

pen·cil /'pensl; 'pɛnsl/ *n* instrument for drawing or writing with, esp of graphite or coloured chalk enclosed in wood or fixed in a metal holder; stick of cosmetic material: 铅笔; 彩色画笔; 眉笔: *an 'eyebrow* ~. 一枝眉笔。□ *vt* (**-ll-,** US also **-l-**) [VP6A] write, draw, mark, with a ~: 用铅笔画、写、作记号: ~*led eyebrows.* 画过的眉毛。

pen·dant /'pendənt; 'pɛndənt/ *n* 1 ornament which hangs down, esp one attached to a necklace, bracelet, etc; lustre attached to a chandelier, etc. (项链、手镯、枝形吊灯架等的)坠子;垂环;垂饰。2 (naut) (航海) = **pennant.**

pen·dent /'pendənt; 'pɛndənt/ *adj* (formal) (正式用语) 1 hanging; overhanging: 下垂的; 悬挂的; 吊着的: ~ *rocks.* 悬岩。2 = pending.

pend·ing /'pendɪŋ; 'pɛndɪŋ/ *adj* waiting to be decided or settled: 待决的;未决的: *The lawsuit was then* ~. 那件诉讼那时尚未解决。□ *prep* 1 during: 当…的时候;在…期间: ~ *these discussions.* 在讨论期间。2 until: 直到…;在…之前: ~ *his decision.* 在他决定之前。

pen·du·lous /'pendjuləs US: -dʒuləs; 'pɛndʒələs/ *adj* (formal) hanging down loosely so as to swing freely: (正式用语)下垂的;悬垂而摇摆不定的: *the* ~ *nests of the weaver-birds.* 莺鸟的垂巢。

pen·du·lum /'pendjuləm US: -dʒuləm; 'pɛndʒələm/ *n* weighted rod hung from a fixed point so that it swings freely, esp one to regulate the movement of a clock. 摆;摆锤;(尤指)钟摆。*the swing of the* ~. (fig) the movement of public opinion from one extreme to the other. (喻)舆论之自一个极端转变到另一个极端。

pen·etrable /'penɪtrəbl; 'pɛnɪtrəbl/ *adj* (formal) that can be penetrated. (正式用语)能被穿入的; 能渗透的; 能透过的。**pen·etra·bil·ity** /,penɪtrə'bɪlətɪ; ,pɛnɪtrə'bɪlətɪ/ *n*

pen·etrate /'penɪtreɪt; 'pɛnə,tret/ *vt, vi* 1 [VP6A, 3A] ~ **(into/to/through),** make a way into, etc. (fig) see into, etc: 进入;贯穿;(喻)看穿;透视: *The cat's sharp claws* ~*d my skin.* 猫的尖爪刺入我的皮肤。*The mist* ~*d (into) the room.* 雾渗入房间。*He* ~*d their thoughts.* 他看穿了他们的心思。*Our eyes could not* ~ *the darkness.* 我们的眼睛在黑暗里看不到。*We soon* ~*d his disguise,* saw through it, knew who he really was. 我们很快地看穿了他的伪装。2 **be** ~**d with,** be filled with: 充满: *be* ~*d with a desire for mystical experiences.* 充满了要获得神秘经验的欲望。**pen·etrat·ing** *adj* 1 (of a person, his mind) able to see and understand quickly and deeply. (指人、其思想)聪敏的、有眼光的;敏锐的。2 (voices, cries, etc) piercing; loud and clear. (指声音、喊叫等)尖锐的;响亮的。**pen·etrat·ing·ly** *adv*

pen·etra·tion /,penɪ'treɪʃn; ,pɛnə'treʃən/ *n* [U] 1 penetrating: 穿入;浸入;渗透;贯穿: *peaceful* ~, acquiring influence, control, etc without the use of force, eg by trade, supplying a country with capital. 和平的

渗透。**2** mental quickness; ability to grasp ideas. (心智的) 敏锐; 洞察力。

pen·etra·tive /'penɪtrətɪv US: -treɪtɪv; 'pɛnə,tretɪv/ adj able to penetrate; intelligent. 能穿入的; 能渗透的; 能贯穿的/敏锐的; 有眼光的; 聪慧的。

pen-friend /'pen frend; 'pɛn,frɛnd/ ⇨ **pen¹(3).**

pen·guin /'pengwɪn; 'pɛngwɪn/ n seabird of the Antarctic with wings used for swimming. 企鹅(南极产海鸟, 有用于游泳之翼)。 ⇨ the illus at **water.** 参看 water 之插图。

peni·cil·lin /,penɪ'sɪlɪn; ,pɛnɪ'sɪlɪn/ n [C] antibiotic drug that, by changing the chemical environment of germs, prevents them from surviving or multiplying. 盘尼西林; 青霉素(一种抗生素)。

pen·in·sula /pə'nɪnsjʊlə US: -nsələ; pə'nɪnsələ/ n area of land, eg Italy, almost surrounded by sea and projecting far into the sea. 半岛。 **pen·in·su·lar** /-lə(r); -lɚ/ adj of or like a ~.半岛的; 似半岛的; 半岛形的。

pe·nis /'piːnɪs; 'pinɪs/ n organ of urination and copulation of a male animal. (雄性动物的)生殖器; 阴茎。

peni·tence /'penɪtəns; 'pɛnətəns/ n [U] ~ (for), sorrow and regret (for wrongdoing, sin). 忏悔; 悔罪; 后悔(所犯之错、所犯之罪)。

peni·tent /'penɪtənt; 'pɛnətənt/ adj feeling regret; showing regret or remorse. 忏悔的; 悔罪的; 后悔的。 ~·ly adv

peni·ten·tial /,penɪ'tenʃl; ,pɛnə'tenʃəl/ adj of penitence or penance. 悔悟的; 后悔的; 赎罪苦行的。~·ly /-ʃəlɪ; -ʃəlɪ/ adv

peni·ten·tiary /,penɪ'tenʃərɪ; ,pɛnə'tenʃərɪ/ n (pl -ries) (US) prison for persons guilty of serious crimes, esp one in which reform of the prisoners is the main aim. (美) 监狱(尤指以感化犯人为主要目的的监狱); 感化院。 □ adj of reformatory treatment. 感化的。

pen-name /'pen neɪm; 'pɛn,nem/ ⇨ **pen¹(3).**

pen·nant /'penənt; 'pɛnənt/ n flag (usu long and narrow) used on a ship for signalling, identification, etc. (船上用的)信号旗; 小旗(通常为狭长者)。 ⇨ the illus at **barque.** 参看 barque 之插图。

pen·ni·less /'penɪlɪs; 'pɛnlɪs/ adj without any money: 一文不名的; 分文没有的; 贫穷的: *I'm ~ until pay-day.* 在发薪日以前我分文没有。

pen·non /'penən; 'pɛnən/ n **1** long, narrow (usu triangular) flag, as used by a knight on his lance, by soldiers in lancer regiments, and on ships, eg in signalling. (骑士矛上的)小三角旗; (枪骑兵士兵所用的)小三角旗; (船上用的)小旗(如做信号所用者)。 **2** (US) flag of this shape as a school banner, with the school's name or initials on it. (美)长三角形校旗。

penn'orth /'penəθ; 'pɛnəθ/ n = pennyworth. ⇨ **penny(5).**

penny /'penɪ; 'pɛnɪ/ n (pl **pence** /pens; pɛns/ when combined with numbers, as in *'sixpence, 'tenpence, ,eighteen'pence*; pl **pennies** /'penɪz; 'pɛnɪz/ when used of individual coins: 与数目字连用时, 复数为 pence, 如 sixpence 六便士, tenpence 十便士, eighteenpence 十八便士; 指硬币的复数的时候, 复数为 pennies: *Please give me ten pennies for this tenpence piece.* 请把这个十便士的铜币换成十个便士。) ⇨ **App 5.** 参看附录五。 **1** (until 1971) British bronze coin (abbr 略作 **d**) worth one twelfth of a shilling. (到 1971 年为止)便士(价值十二分之一先令的英国铜币)。 **2** (since decimal coinage was introduced, 1971) British bronze coin (abbr 略作 **p**) worth one hundredth of a pound: (一九七一年采用十进位币制之后)(新)便士(价值百分之一英镑): *These cigarettes are 70 pence a packet.* 这些香烟卖七十便士一包。 **3** (US colloq) cent. (美口)一分(等于 cent)。 **4**(phrases, all pre-1971 in origin)(用作短语, 全部沿用一九七一年以前用法)*(cost) a pretty* ~, a large sum of money. (值)很多钱。 *in for a* ~*, in for a pound,* sth that one has begun must be finished, whatever the cost may be. 一不做, 二不休; 一

且开始, 无论如何必须完成。 *~ wise and pound foolish,* careful in small matters and wasteful in large matters. 小处节省, 大处浪费; 小处聪明, 大处糊涂; 明于小事而昧于大事。 正正当当地赚一点钱。 **5** (compounds) (复合词)。 '~ 'dreadful, (colloq) cheap, sensational, popular novel, etc. (口)耸人听闻而且很流行的廉价小说等。 '~ **pincher,** (colloq) miser. (口)守财奴; 吝啬鬼。 '~ **pinching** adj mean; miserly. 吝啬的。 '~·**weight** n 24 grains, one-twentieth of an ounce Troy. (英国金衡制)英钱(二十四英厘或二十分之一英两重)。 ⇨ **App 5.** 参看附录五。 '~ **whistle,** simple, cheap musical pipe. 一种简单、便宜的小笛。'~·**worth** (also 亦作 **penn'orth** /'penəθ; 'pɛnəθ/) n as much as can be bought for a ~ 一便士之值; 值一便士之物。 *a good/bad ~worth,* a good/bad bargain. 合算(不合算)的交易。 **6**(from the use of pennies in coin-operated machines, locks on doors, etc) (下列用法源出于投便士开转的机器, 门锁等)。 *spend a* ~, (colloq) urinate. (口)小便。 *The ~ dropped,* The desired result was achieved, the meaning of a remark, etc was understood. 目的已达到; 话已听明白。

pe·nol·ogy /piː'nɒlədʒɪ; pi'nɑlədʒɪ/ n [U] study of the problems of legal punishment and prison management. 刑罚学; 监狱管理学。

pen·sion¹ /'penʃn; 'pɛnʃən/ n [C] regular payment made by the State to sb old (*Re'tirement P~*, or old-'age ~), disabled (eg 'war ~) or widowed, or by a former employer to an employee after long serivce. (国家定期付给老年人的)养老金(亦作 Retirement Pension 或 old-age pension); (国家定期付给残废者或寡妇的)抚恤金(如 war pension); (原雇主给予长久服务后之人员的)退休金; 年金。 *draw a/one's* ~, receive it on one occasion or regularly. 领退休金。 *on (a)* ~, receiving a ~: 领退休金; 领养老金: *be/go/retire on (a)* ~. 领养老金; 退休。 □ vt [VP15B] ~ *sb off,* grant or pay a ~ to; dismiss or allow to retire with a ~. 发给(某人)养老金、退休金、抚恤金; 发给(某人)养老金而令其退休。 ~·**able** /-əbl; -əbl/ adj (of services, posts, age, work, etc) entitling one to a ~. (指服务、职位、年龄、工作等)有资格领退休金的。 ~·**er** n person who is receiving a ~. 领养老金者; 领抚恤金者; 领退休金者。

pen·sion² /'pɒnsɪɒn; 'pɑnsɪ,ɑn/ n (in Europe, but not GB) boarding-house at which fixed rates are charged (by the week or month). (在欧洲但英国除外, 按周或按月付固定之食宿费的)公寓; 供膳的宿舍。 *en* ~ /ɒn 'pɒnsɪɒn; ɑn 'pɑnsɪ,ɑn/, as a boarder. 在公寓寄宿。

pen·sive /'pensɪv; 'pɛnsɪv/ adj deep in thought; seriously thoughtful: 沉思的; 愁眉苦脸的: *a ~ look;* 沉思状; *look* ~. 显得愁眉苦脸。 ~·**ly** adv ~·**ness** n

pen·stock /'penstɒk; 'pɛn,stak/ n flood-gate; sluice. 洪水闸门; 水门。

pen·ta·gon /'pentəgən US: -gɒn; 'pɛntə,gan/ n plane figure with five sides and five angles. 五角形; 五边形。 **the P~,** building in Arlington, Virginia, headquarters of the US Armed Forces. 五角大楼(美国国防部办公处; 位于弗吉尼亚州的阿灵顿郡)。**pen·tag·onal**/pen'tægənl; pɛn'tægənl/ adj

pen·tam·eter /pen'tæmɪtə(r); pɛn'tæmətɚ/ n (in English verse) line of five iambic feet. (英诗中之)五音步诗行(为抑扬格)。

Pen·ta·teuch /'pentətjuːk; 'pɛntə,tjuk/ n **the ~,** the first five books of the Bible. 圣经的首五卷; 摩西五经。

pen·tath·lon /pen'tæθlən; pɛn'tæθlən/ n (modern Olympic Games) contest in which each competitor takes part in five events (running, horseback riding, swimming, fencing and shooting with a pistol). (现代奥林匹克运动会中)五项运动(赛跑、骑马、游泳、击剑和手枪射击)。

Pente·cost /'pentɪkɒst US: -kɔːst; 'pɛntɪ,kɔst/ n [U] **1** Jewish harvest festival, fifty days after the Passover.

(犹太人的)五旬节(逾越节后五十天)。**2** (esp US) Whit Sunday, the seventh Sunday after Easter. (尤美)圣灵降临节 (复活节后第七个星期日)。~**al** /ˌpentɪˈkɒstl US: -ˈkɔːstl/ ˌpentɪˈkɒstl/

pent·house /ˈpenthaʊs/ ˈpɛntˌhaʊs/ n **1** sloping roof supported against a wall, esp one for a shelter or shed. 庇檐；披屋(靠墙壁的斜屋顶，尤指用于避雨棚或棚舍者)。**2** apartment built on the roof of a tall building. (建于大厦屋顶的)楼顶房屋。

pent·up /ˌpent ˈʌp/ ˈpɛntˈʌp/ adj repressed: 被幽禁的；被抑制的: ~ feelings/fury. 被抑制的情绪(愤怒)。

pen·ul·ti·mate /penˈʌltɪmət/ prɪˈnʌltɪmɪt/ n, adj (word, syllable, event, etc which is) the one before the last one. (指词、音节、事件等)倒数第二个(的)。

pen·um·bra /prɪˈnʌmbrə/ prɪˈnʌmbrə/ n partly shaded region around the shadow of an opaque body (esp round the total shadow of the moon or earth in eclipse). 黑影周围的半明影(尤指日月蚀周围的半明影)。

pen·uri·ous /prɪˈnjʊərɪəs US: -ˈnʊr-/ pəˈnʊrɪəs/ adj (formal) poor; grudging; stingy: (正式用语)贫穷的；缺乏的；吝啬的: a man who is ~ in his habits. 吝啬成性的人。~**ly** adv ~**ness** n **pen·ury** /ˈpenjʊərɪ/ ˈpɛnjərɪ/ n [U] (formal) poverty: (正式用语)贫穷: living in penury; 过着贫穷的生活; reduced to penury. 陷于贫困。

peon /ˈpiːən/ ˈpiən/ n **1** (in Latin America) unskilled farm worker, esp one who is not wholly free. (拉丁美洲的)不熟练的农场工人(尤指不太自由者)；被迫为劳役偿债的工人。**2** (in India and Pakistan) office messenger; orderly. (印度及巴基斯坦的)(机关的)信差；传令兵。'~**age** /-ɪdʒ/ -ɪdʒ/ n [U] system of employing ~s(1); (legal) use of indebtedness to compel sb to work. 劳役偿债制度；(法律)劳役偿债。

peony /ˈpiːənɪ/ ˈpiənɪ/ n (pl -**nies**) [C] garden plant with large round pink, red or white flowers. 牡丹；芍药。

people /ˈpiːpl/ ˈpipl/ n [U] (collective, with pl v. Note that for one human being, it is preferable to use man, woman, boy, girl and not person, which, although useful in definitions, may be derogatory or formal). (集合名词,与复数动词连用。注意:当指一个人的时候,最好用 man, woman, boy, girl, 而不用 person; person 虽可用于定义中, 但可能是贬抑或正式的用法)。**1** persons in general: 人; 一般的人: streets crowded with ~. 挤满人的街道。Some ~ are very inquisitive. 有些人很爱管闲事。**2** those persons belonging to a place, or forming a social class: 某地区的人; 某阶层的人: The ~ in the village like the new doctor. 村里的人喜欢那位新来的医生。Some ~ spend a lot of money on clothes. 有些人花很多钱在衣着上。**3** all the persons forming a State: 全国的人; 人民: government of the ~, by the ~, for the ~. 民有,民治,民享的政府。**4** those persons who are not nobles, not high in rank, position, etc. 平民; 黎民; 庶民。**5** (colloq) one's near relations: (口)家人; 亲属: You must come home with me and meet my ~, darling. 亲爱的,你一定要跟我一起回家会见我的家人。**6** [C] (not collective) race, tribe, nation: (非集合用法)种族;民族: the ~s of Asia; 亚洲各民族; a brave and intelligent ~. 勇敢而有智慧的民族。vt [VP6A] fill with ~; put ~ in: 供以人民;使人民居于: a thickly ~d district. 人口稠密的地区。

pep /pep/ pɛp/ n [U] (sl) vigour; spirit. (俚)精力;精神。'**pep pill**, one that stimulates the nervous system (usu one containing amphetamine). 兴奋药丸; 提神药丸(通常含有刺激中枢神经的安非他明(氨基丙素))。'**pep talk**, one intended to fill the listener(s) with spirit and energy. 鼓励的话;精神训话。□ vt (**-pp-**) [VP15B] **pep up**, give energy to; liven up. 激励; 鼓舞;使有活力。

pep·per /ˈpepə(r)/ ˈpɛpə/ n **1** [U] hot-tasting powder made from the dried berries of certain plants, used to season food. 胡椒粉。'~**-and-salt** n (colour of) cloth of dark and light wools woven together, with small dark and light dots. (杂有深色和浅色斑点的)椒盐色;椒

盐色的毛料。'~**-corn** n the dried, black berry of the plant; (fig) this as a nominal rent. 干胡椒子; (喻)空有其名的象征性租金。'~**-mill** n container in which ~corns are ground to powder and sprinkled on food. 碾胡椒子的小罐。'~**-mint** n **(a)** [U] kind of mint grown for its essential oil, used in medicine and confectionery. (一种制药与作糖果香料用的)薄荷。**(b)** [C] sweet of boiled sugar flavoured with ~mint. 薄荷糖。'~**-pot** n small container with a perforated top from which ~ is sprinkled on food. 胡椒盒;胡椒罐;胡椒瓶。**2** (garden plant with a) red or green seed pod (eg capsicum) which is used as a vegetable. 辣椒;生辣椒之植物: stuffed ~s. 内有填塞物的辣椒。□ vt [VP6A] **1** put ~ on (food). 洒胡椒粉于(食物)上。**2** pelt (sb) (with stones, shot, questions, etc). (以石头)投掷(某人); (以子弹)射击(某人); (以问题)质问(某人)。~**y** adj tasting of ~; (fig) hot-tempered: 胡椒味的; (喻)暴躁的; 易怒的; 性子急的: a ~y old colonel. 暴躁的老上校。

pep·sin /ˈpepsɪn/ ˈpɛpsɪn/ n [U] liquid (an enzyme) produced in the stomach for helping to digest food. 胃液素; 胃蛋白酶。**pep·tic** /ˈpeptɪk/ ˈpɛptɪk/ adj digestive; of digestion or the digestive system: 消化的; 消化系统的: a peptic ulcer. 胃溃疡; 消化性溃疡。

per /pɜː(r)/ pɝ/ weak form pə(r)/ pɚ/ prep **1** (when comparing two amounts; when quoting a rate¹(1)) for each: (比较两种数量或引述一种比率时)每一; 每: per annum /ˈænəm/ ˈænəm/, for each year; 每年; per diem /ˈdiːem/ ˈdiəm/, for each day; 每天; per pound; 每磅: 15 rounds of ammunition per man; 每人十五发子弹; interest at 6 per cent, (6%); 百分之六的利息; 30 miles per gallon, (abbr 略作 **m p g**). 每加仑(油)跑三十英里。⇨ **to¹**(12). **2** by means of: 由; 经; 靠: per post/rail. 由邮寄(铁路)。as per, (colloq) following: (口)按照; 根据: as per instructions. 按照指示。as per usual, (colloq) as usual. (口)照常。

per·ad·ven·ture /ˌpɜːrədˈventʃə(r)/ ˌpɝədˈvɛntʃə/ adv (archaic) **1** perhaps. 也许。**2** (after if and lest) by chance! (用在 if 及 lest 之后)偶尔; 万一: If ~ you fail. 万一你失败了。

per·am·bu·late /pəˈræmbjʊleɪt/ pəˈæmbjəˌlet/ vi, vt [VP6A, 2A] (liter) walk through or over; walk up and down. (文)巡行; 回回; 漫步; 徘徊。**per·am·bu·la·tion** /pəˌræmbjʊˈleɪʃn/ pəˌæmbjəˈleʃən/ n

per·am·bu·la·tor /pəˈræmbjʊleɪtə(r)/ pəˈæmbjəˌletɚ/ n (common colloq abbr 口语用法常略作 **pram** /præm/; præm/) four-wheeled carriage, pushed by hand, for a baby; baby-carriage (the usu word in US). 四轮婴儿车; 婴儿车(美国通常用 baby-carriage)。

per·ceive /pəˈsiːv/ pəˈsiv/ vt [VP6A, 8, 9, 10, 18A, 19A, 25] (formal) become aware of, esp through the eyes or the mind: (正式用语)感觉; 察觉; 看出: On entering his house, she at once ~d him to be a man of taste. 我们一进他的房子, 立刻感觉到他是个高雅的人。**per·ceiv·able** /-əbl/ -əbl/ adj

per·cen·tage /pəˈsentɪdʒ/ pəˈsɛntɪdʒ/ n **1** rate or number per cent (= for each hundred). 百分比; 百分率。**2** proportion: 部分; 比率: What ~ of his income is paid in income tax? 他所缴的所得税占他的收入的百分之几;

per·cep·tible /pəˈseptəbl/ pəˈsɛptəbl/ adj (formal) that can be perceived. (正式用语)能感觉到的; 看得出的; 可察觉的; 显而易见的。**per·cep·tibly** /-əbl/ -əblɪ/ adv **per·cep·ti·bil·ity** /pəˌseptəˈbɪlətɪ/ pəˌsɛptəˈbɪlətɪ/ n

per·cep·tion /pəˈsepʃn/ pəˈsɛpʃən/ n [U] (formal) process by which we become aware of changes (through the senses of sight, hearing, etc); act or power of perceiving. (正式用语)感觉; 知觉; 了解; 领悟力; 理解力。

per·cep·tive /pəˈseptɪv/ pəˈsɛptɪv/ adj (formal) having, connected with, perception; able to perceive; discerning. (正式用语)有知觉的; 与感觉有关的; 有理解力的; 有悟性的。~**ly** adv

perch¹ /pɜːtʃ/ pɝtʃ/ n (pl unchanged) kinds of

freshwater fish with spiny fins, used as food. (复数不变) 鲈鱼.

perch² /pɜːtʃ; pɝtʃ/ *n* **1** bird's resting-place, eg a branch; bar or rod provided, eg in a bird-cage, a hen-roost, for this purpose. 鸟的栖息之所(如树枝); (鸟笼或鸡笼中的)栖木. **2** (colloq) high position occupied by a person; elevated and secure position: (口) 某人所居的高位; 高而安全的地位; *come off your* ~, (colloq) stop being so superior (in manner, etc); (口)别趾高气扬; *knock sb off his* ~, stop sb being too confident and superior. 打败某人; 挫某人锐气. **3** (also 亦作 *pole, rod*) measure of length, esp for land, 5½ yds; 杆(长度单位, 尤用于丈量土地, 等于 5½ 码); *square* ~, 30¼ sq yds. 平方杆(等于 30¼ 平方码). ⇨ **App 5.** 参看附录五. □ *vi, vt* **1** [VP2C] alight: 栖息; 栖止; 停歇: *The birds* ~*ed upon the television aerial.* 鸟栖在电视天线上. **2** [VP2C] (of a person) take up a position (usu on sth high): (指人)就位(于高处): ~*ed on stools at the bar.* 坐在酒吧间里的凳子上. **3** (chiefly in *pp*) (of buildings) be situated (on sth high): (主要用过去分词)(指建筑物)位于(高处): *a castle* ~*ed on a rock.* 位于岩上的堡垒.

per·chance /pəˈtʃɑːns US: -ˈtʃæns; pɚˈtʃæns/ *adv* (archaic) by chance; possibly. (古)偶然; 可能地.

per·cipi·ent /pəˈsɪpɪənt; pɚˈsɪpɪənt/ *adj* (formal) perceiving (quickly and keenly). (正式用语)知觉的; 感觉的; 感觉敏锐的.

per·co·late /ˈpɜːkəleɪt; ˈpɝkəˌlet/ *vi, vt* [VP6A, 2A, 3A] ~ **(through),** (of liquid) (cause to) pass slowly; filter: (指液体)(使)渗透过; 滤; 滤过: *Water* ~*s through sand.* 水由沙中渗过; 水渗入沙中. *I make coffee by percolating boiling water through ground coffee.* 我借滚水滤过磨碎的咖啡来煮咖啡. *I'll* ~ *some coffee.* 我将用过滤法煮一点咖啡. **per·co·la·tor** /-tə(r); -tɚ/ *n* (esp) kind of coffee pot in which boiling water ~s through coffee (in a container near the top). (尤指)(滚水过滤咖啡的)煮咖啡壶.

per·cussion /pəˈkʌʃn; pɚˈkʌʃən/ *n* the striking together of two (usu hard) objects; sound or shock produced by this. 撞击; 碰撞; 震动; 撞击声. **the** '~ **(section),** musical instruments played by ~, eg drums, cymbals. 打击乐器(例如鼓、铜钹). '~ **cap,** ⇨ **cap** *n* (4). ~·**ist** /-ɪst; -ɪst/ *n* player of ~ instruments. 打击乐器演奏者.

per·di·tion /pəˈdɪʃn; pɚˈdɪʃən/ *n* [U] (formal) complete ruin; everlasting damnation. (正式用语)全毁; 永死; 万劫不复.

per·egri·na·tion /ˌperɪgrɪˈneɪʃn; ˌpɝrəgrɪˈneʃən/ *n* [U] (formal) travelling; [C] journey. (正式用语)旅行; 旅程.

per·emp·tory /pəˈremptərɪ US: ˈperəmptɔːrɪ; pəˈrɛmptərɪ/ *adj* (formal) (of commands) not to be disobeyed or questioned; (of a person, his manner) (too) commanding; insisting upon obedience. (正式用语)(指命令)不许违反的; 不容疑问的; (指人、态度)威风凛凛的; 专横的. ~ **writ,** (legal) one that compels a defendant to appear in court. (法律)强制令状(强迫被告出庭之传票). **per·emp·torily** /-trəlɪ US: -tɔːrəlɪ; -tərəlɪ/ *adv*

per·en·nial /pəˈrenɪəl; pəˈrɛnɪəl/ *adj* **1** continuing throughout the whole year. 终年的; 一年到头的; 四季不断的. **2** lasting for a very long time. 长久的; 持久的. **3** (of plants) living for more than two years. (指植物)多年生的(超过两年的). □ *n* ~ plant: 多年生植物: *hardy*(1) ~*s.* 耐寒的多年生植物. ~**ly** /-nɪəlɪ; -nɪəlɪ/ *adv*

per·fect¹ /ˈpɜːfɪkt; ˈpɝfɪkt/ *adj* **1** complete with everything needed. 完全的; 完备的. **2** without fault; excellent: 完美的; 无瑕的; 极佳的: *a* ~ *performance of a play.* 一个剧的完美的演出. **3** exact; accurate: 正确的; 准确的: *a* ~ *circle.* 一个正圆. **4** having reached the highest point in training, skill, etc: 技术精湛的; 熟练的: ~ *in the performance of one's duties.* 克尽自己的责任. **5** ~ **tenses,** those composed of *have* + *pp*, eg 'He has / had / will have written the letter' (present, past, future ~). 完成时(由 have + pp 形成的时态, 如 'He

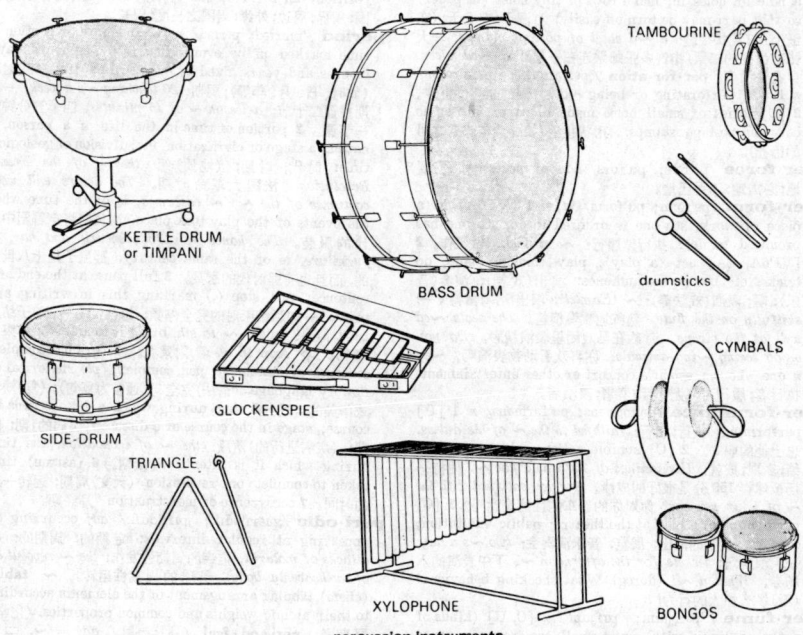

KETTLE DRUM or TIMPANI

TAMBOURINE

BASS DRUM

drumsticks

GLOCKENSPIEL

SIDE-DRUM

TRIANGLE

CYMBALS

XYLOPHONE

BONGOS

percussion instruments

has /had /will have written the letter' 中的斜体字就是现在、过去、未来三种完成时). **6** (attrib only) complete; utter; unqualified: (仅用作定语)完全的; 全然的; 绝对的: a ~ stranger /fool; 完全陌生的人(十足的笨蛋); ~ nonsense. 完全胡说八道; 一派胡言。~·ly adv 1 quite; quite well; completely; 十分地; 美好地; 完全地: ~ly happy /satisfied. 十分快乐(满意)。**2** in a ~ way: 完美地; 极佳地: Your trousers fit ~ly. 你的裤子极为合身。

per·fect² /pə'fekt; pɚ'fɛkt/ vt [VP6A] make ~: 使完美; 使完善; 改善: She's ~ing her Arabic before taking up her job in Cairo. 她去开罗上任之前，一直在提高她的阿拉伯语。~·i·ble /-əbl; -əbl/ adj that can be ~ed. 可使之完美的; 可臻完善的; 可改善的。~·i·bil·ity /pə,fektə-'bɪlətɪ; pɚ,fɛktə'bɪlətɪ/ n

per·fec·tion /pə'fekʃn; pɚ'fɛkʃən/ n [U] **1** perfecting or being perfected: 完成: busy with the ~ of detail. 忙于细节的完成。**2** perfect quality or example: 完善之性质或典型: It was the very ~ of beauty. 它是美的极致。**3** best possible state; highest point attainable: 完美; 十全十美; 尽善尽美: bring something to ~. 使某事物达到十全十美。**4** (with pl) accomplishment(3). (用复数)成就; 才艺;优点。~·ist /-ɪst; -ɪst/ n **1** person who believes that moral ~ can be attained, that it is possible to live without sinning. 至善论者(认为道德上的十全十美可以达到，无过错的生活乃属可能)。**2** (colloq) person who is satisfied with nothing less than what he thinks to be perfect. (口)凡事求其完美的人。

per·fer·vid /pə'fɜːvɪd; pɚ'fɝvɪd/ adj (formal) extremely zealous or eager. (正式用语)非常热心的; 热烈的。

per·fid·i·ous /pə'fɪdɪəs; pɚ'fɪdɪəs/ adj (formal) treacherous; faithless (to). (正式用语)不义的; (对…)不忠心的(与to连用)。~·ly adv ~·ness n

per·fidy /'pɜːfɪdɪ; 'pɝfədɪ/ n [U] (pl -dies) (formal) treachery; breaking of faith; [C] instance of this. (正式用语)不义;不忠;背信;不义、不忠、背信之实例。

per·for·ate /'pɜːfəreɪt; 'pɝfə,ret/ vt [VP6A] make a hole or holes in; make rows of tiny holes (in paper) so that part may be torn off easily: 打洞于; 穿孔于; (在纸上)打孔状接缝: a ~d sheet of postage stamps; 一大张有齿孔的邮票(指许多张邮票连在一起); a ~d ulcer. 穿孔性溃疡。**per·for·ation** /,pɜːfə'reɪʃn; ,pɝfə'reʃən/ n **1** [U] perforating or being ~d. 打洞; 穿孔; 贯穿。**2** [C] series of small holes made in paper, etc eg as between postage stamps. 孔状接缝(如邮票与邮票之间的齿孔)。

per·force /pə'fɔːs; pɚ'fɔrs/ adv of necessity. 必要地; 必需地; 不得已地。

per·form /pə'fɔːm; pɚ'fɔrm/ vt, vi **1** [VP6A] do (a piece of work, sth one is ordered to do, sth one has promised to do): 执行; 履行: ~ a task. 做工作。**2** [VP6A, 2A] act (a play); play (music); sing, do tricks, etc before an audience: 演出(戏剧); 演奏(音乐); 唱; 表演(戏法等): ~ 'Hamlet'; 演出'哈姆雷特'; ~ skilfully on the flute. 熟练地吹奏横笛。The seals ~ed well at the circus. 海豹在马戏团里表演精彩。Do you enjoy seeing ~ing animals? 你喜欢看动物表演吗? ~·er n one who ~s, esp at a concert or other entertainment. 执行者; 履行者; (尤指)演奏者; 表演者。

per·form·ance /pə'fɔːməns; pɚ'fɔrməns/ n **1** [U] performing: 执行; 履行: faithful in the ~ of his duties. 忠于他的职守。**2** [C] notable action; achievement: 成绩;表现;成就: His innings of 150 was a fine ~. 他打一场板球得150分是很好的成绩。Are you satisfied with the ~ of your new car? 你对你的新车的性能满意吗? **3** [C] performing of a play at the theatre; public exhibition; concert: 戏剧的演出; 展览; 音乐演奏会: two ~s a day; 一天演两场; tickets for the afternoon ~. 下午表演的入场券。What a ~! (derog) What shocking behaviour! (贬)多么惊人的行为!

per·fume /'pɜːfjuːm; 'pɝfjum/ n [C, U] (kinds of prepared liquid with) sweet smell, esp from an essence

of flowers. 香味; 香水。 □ vt /pə'fjuːm; pɚ'fjum/ [VP 6A] give a ~ to; put ~ on. 使有香味; 加香味于; 洒香水于。~·r n person who makes and sells ~s. 香水制造商;香料商。

per·func·tory /pə'fʌŋktərɪ; pɚ'fʌŋktərɪ/ adj **1** done as a duty or routine but without care or interest: 敷衍的; 塞责的; 马虎的: a ~ inspection. 马虎的观察。**2** (of persons) doing things in this way. (指人)做事敷衍塞责的。**per·func·torily** /-trəlɪ US: -tɔːrəlɪ; -tərəlɪ/ adv

per·gola /'pɜːgələ; 'pɝgələ/ n structure of posts (forming an arbour, or over a garden path) for climbing plants. (构成凉亭，或架于花园通道上的)蔓藤花棚;藤架。

per·haps /pə'hæps; pɚ'hæps/ adv possibly; maybe. 也许;可能。

peri /'pɪərɪ; 'pɪrɪ/ n (in Persian myth) beautiful girl or woman; fairy; elf. (波斯神话中的)美女; 小仙子; 精灵。

peri·gee /'perɪdʒiː; 'perə,dʒi/ n point in an orbit of a planet or spacecraft at which it is closest to the earth. 近地点(行星或太空船的轨道上最接近地球之点)。

peri·helion /,perɪ'hiːlɪən; ,perɪ'hiljən/ n point in a planet's orbit at which it is nearest to the sun. 近日点(行星轨道上最接近太阳之点)。

peril /'perəl; 'perəl/ n **1** [U] serious danger: 危险: in ~ of one's life; 冒着生命的危险; do sth at one's ~, at one's own risk. 冒险做某事。**2** [C] sth that causes danger: 危险的事物: the ~s of the ocean, storm, shipwreck, etc. 海洋上的危险(如暴风雨,海难等)。 □ vt (-ll-, US also -l-) (liter, poet) (= imperil, which is more usu) put or bring into danger. (文学, 诗)(等于imperil, 但imperil 较为常用)置于危险。~·ous /'perələs; 'perələs/ adj dangerous; full of risk. 危险的,多险的。~·ous·ly adv

per·imeter /pə'rɪmɪtə(r); pə'rɪmətɚ/ n [C] (length of the) outer boundary of a closed figure, a military position, an airfield, etc. (封闭图形,阵地,机场等的)周围;周界;周边;外缘;周围之长度;周长。

period /'pɪərɪəd; 'pɪrɪəd/ n [C] **1** length or portion of time marked off by events that recur, eg hours, days, months and years, fixed by events in nature: 一段时间(如时、日、月、年等); 周期: 20 teaching ~s a week; 一星期授课二十节; a lesson ~ of 45 minutes. 四十五分钟的一节课。**2** portion of time in the life of a person, a nation, a stage of civilization, etc; division of geological time: 时代; 时期; (地质)纪: the ~ of the French Revolution. 法国大革命时期。The actors will wear costumes of the ~/~ costumes, ie of the time when costumes of the ~/~ costumes, ie of the time when the actors wore costumes of the play took place. 演员们将穿着剧中时代的服装。The house is 18th century and has ~ furniture, ie of the same century. 那屋子是十八世纪的, 而且也有那时代的家具。**3** full pause at the end of a sentence; full stop (.) marking this in writing and print: 一句话结束时的完全停顿; 句点(.)(一个句子结束时的标点): put a ~ to sth, bring it to an end. 结束某事物。 ⇨ App 9. 参看 附录九。**4** (gram) complete sentence or statement, usu complex; (pl) rhetorical or flowery language. (语法)完全句(通常为复句); (复)矫饰或华美的言词。**5** time during which a disease runs its course; stage in the course of a disease: (疾病的)期; 时期: (疾病进行的)阶段: the ~ of incubation, the time during which it is latent. 潜伏期。**6** (astron) time taken to complete one revolution. (天文)周期; 运转一周的时间。**7** occurrence of menstruation. 月经期。

peri·od·ic /,pɪərɪ'ɒdɪk; ,pɪrɪ'adɪk/ adj occurring or appearing at regular intervals: 定期的; 周期的: ~ attacks of malaria. 周期性的疟疾发作。the ~ revolution of a heavenly body. 星球的周期性运转。, ~ 'table, (chem) tabular arrangement of the elements according to their atomic weights and common properties. (化学)周期表。**peri·od·ical** /-kl; -kl/ adj = ~. □ n

magazine or other publication which appears at regular intervals, eg monthly, quarterly. 期刊(定期如每月或每季出版的杂志或其他他刊物)。 **peri·od·ically** /-klɪ; -klɪ/ adv

peri·pa·tetic /ˌperɪpəˈtetɪk; ˌperəpəˈtetɪk/ adj going about from place to place; wandering: 走来走去的; 徘徊的; 漫游的; 巡游的: the ~ religious teachers of India. 印度的游方宗教教师。

pe·riph·ery /pəˈrɪfərɪ; pəˈrɪfərɪ/ n (pl -ries) external boundary or surface. 外围; 表面。 **pe·riph·eral** /-ərəl; -ərəl/ adj of, on, forming, a ~. 外围的; 表面的;在外围上的;形成外围的。

peri·phra·sis /pəˈrɪfrəsɪs; pəˈrɪfrəsɪs/ n (pl -ases /-əsiːz; -əˌsiz/) roundabout way of speaking; circumlocution; (gram) using an auxiliary word in place of an inflected form, eg 'It does work' for 'It works', 'the word of God' for 'God's word'. 迂回的说法; 绕圈子的陈述; (语法)迂说法(用助动词代替词尾的说法, 如用 'It does work' 代替 'It works', 'the word of God' 代替 'God's word')。 **peri·phras·tic** /ˌperɪˈfræstɪk; ˌperəˈfræstɪk/ adj of ~. 迂回的; 转弯抹角的; 用迂说法表示的。

peri·scope /ˈperɪskəʊp; ˈperəˌskop/ n instrument with mirrors and lenses arranged to reflect a view down a tube, etc so that the viewer may get a view as from a level above that of his eyes; used in submarines, trenches, etc. (潜水艇、战壕等中所用的)潜望镜。

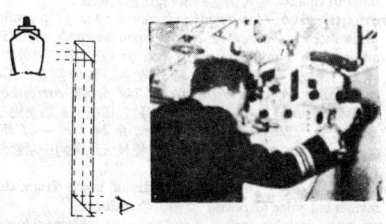

a submarine periscope

per·ish /ˈperɪʃ; ˈperɪʃ/ vi, vt 1 [VP2A, C] (liter or journalism) be destroyed, come to an end, die: (文或新闻学) 毁灭; 死亡: Hundreds of people ~ed in the earthquake. 数以百计的人死于那次地震。 I shall do it or ~ in the attempt. 我要拼死一试。 P~ the thought! May even the thought die! 死了这条心吧! 千万不要存这种念头! 2 [VP6A] (of cold or exposure; usu passive) reduce to distress or inefficiency: (指寒冷或暴露; 通常用被动语态) 使陷于痛苦或无能: We were ~ed with cold/hunger. 我们冻(饿)得要死。 3 [VP2A] (cause to) lose natural qualities; decay: (使)失去本质; (使)损坏: The rubber belt on this machine has ~ed, has lost its elasticity. 这机器上的橡皮带已失去弹性。 Oil on your car tyres will ~ them. 在你车胎上的油将会使车胎损坏。 **~·able** /-əbl; -əbl/ adj (esp of food) quickly or easily going bad. (尤指食物) 易坏的。 **~·ables** n pl (esp) goods that go bad if delayed in transit, eg fish, fresh fruit. (尤指)易坏的物品(如鱼、新鲜水果)。 **~er** n (sl) person who is unpleasant and disliked; naughty child. (俚)讨厌鬼; 顽皮的孩子。

peri·style /ˈperɪstaɪl; ˈperəˌstaɪl/ n (archit) row of columns surrounding a temple, court, etc; space so surrounded. (建筑) (寺庙、宫殿等的)周围列柱; 列柱廊; 列柱中庭。

per·ito·ni·tis /ˌperɪtəˈnaɪtɪs; ˌperətəˈnaɪtɪs/ n [U] inflammation of the membrane lining the walls of the abdomen. 腹膜炎。

peri·wig /ˈperɪwɪg; ˈperəˌwɪg/ n = wig.

peri·winkle¹ /ˈperɪwɪŋkl; ˈperəˌwɪŋkl/ n creeping, evergreen plant with light-blue flowers. 长春花(一种开淡蓝色花的常绿蔓生植物)。

peri·winkle² /ˈperɪwɪŋkl; ˈperəˌwɪŋkl/ n [C] edible sea snail with a spiral shell. 玉黍螺(一种可食海螺)。 ⇨ the illus at mollusc. 参看 mollusc 之插图。

per·jure /ˈpɜːdʒə(r); ˈpɜːdʒə/ vt [VP6A] (reflex) ~ oneself, knowingly make a false statement after taking an oath to tell the truth. (反身)作伪证。 **~r** /ˈpɜːdʒərə(r); ˈpɜːdʒərə/ n person who has ~d himself. 作伪证者。 **per·jury** /ˈpɜːdʒərɪ; ˈpɜːdʒərɪ/ n [U] act of perjuring oneself; [C] (pl -ries) wilful false statement. 作伪证; 伪证罪; 伪证。

perk¹ /pɜːk; pɜːk/ vi, vt [VP2C] ~ up, (of a person) become more lively and active (after depression, illness, etc). (指人) (在愁苦、疾病等之后)活泼起来; 振作起来。 2 [VP15B] ~ sb/sth up, smarten; raise (head); make (sb) lively: 打扮起来; 举(首); 使(某人)活泼: ~ oneself up. 把自己打扮起来。 The horse ~ed up its head, lifted its head as a sign of interest. 那匹马兴致勃勃地昂起头来。 **~y** adj (-ier, -iest) 1 lively; showing interest or confidence. 活泼生动的; 有兴趣或有信心的。 2 self-assertive; impudent. 坚持己见的; 卤莽的。 **~·ily** /-ɪlɪ; -əlɪ/ adv **~·i·ness** n

perk² /pɜːk; pɜːk/ vi, vt (colloq) percolate (coffee): (口)过滤(咖啡); (指咖啡)渗滤: Is the coffee ~ing yet? 咖啡还在渗滤吗? We ~ed some coffee. 我们用过滤法煮了些咖啡。

perk³ /pɜːk; pɜːk/ n (colloq; usu pl) perquisite: (口; 通常用复数) 额外津贴; 小帐; 奖金; 赏钱; 额外利益: an executive's salary with the usual ~s. 一位总经理的薪水及津贴。

perm /pɜːm; pɜːm/ n (colloq abbr for) (口, 为下列各词的略称) 1 permanent wave: 电烫的头发: go to the hairdresser's for a ~. 到美容院去烫头发。 2 permutation (in football pools): (足球赛赌注)选择若干足球队名所做成之任一组合。 □ vt give a ~ to. 电烫(头发); 选择并组合(足球队名)。

per·ma·frost /ˈpɜːməfrɒst US: -frɔːst; ˈpɜːməˌfrɔst/ n permanently frozen subsoil (in the polar regions). (在南、北极地区的)永久冻土; 永冻层。

per·ma·nence /ˈpɜːmənəns; ˈpɜːmənəns/ n [U] state of being permanent. 永久; 恒久。 **per·ma·nency** /-nənsɪ; -nənsɪ/ n (pl -cies) 1 (U) permanence. 2 permanent thing, person or position: 永久性的事物、人或职位: Is your new job a permanency or merely temporary? 你的新工作是永久性的, 还是暂时性的?

per·ma·nent /ˈpɜːmənənt; ˈpɜːmənənt/ adj not expected to change; going on for a long time; intended to last: 长久的; 永久的; 恒久的: my ~ address; 我的永久地址; a ~ position in the Civil Service. 一个永久性的文官职位。 ⇨ temporary. ~ wave, style of hairdressing in which artificial waves or curls are put in the hair so that they last several months. 电烫头发。 **~·ly** adv

per·manga·nate /pəˈmæŋgəneɪt; pəˈmæŋgəˌnet/ n ~ of potash, potassium ~, (KMnO₄) dark-purple crystalline salt which is used, dissolved in water, as an antiseptic and disinfectant. 高锰酸钾(深紫色结晶盐, 溶于水中可用作防腐剂及消毒剂)。

per·meate /ˈpɜːmɪeɪt; ˈpɜːmɪˌet/ vt, vi [VP6A, 3A] ~ (through/among), pass, flow or spread into every part of: 弥漫; 散布; 普及; 渗透: water permeating (through) the soil; 水渗透到泥土里面; new ideas that have ~d (through/among) the people. 已普及民间的新观念。 The smell of cooking ~d (through) the flat. 烹饪的气味弥漫整层公寓。 **per·meation** /ˌpɜːmɪˈeɪʃn; ˌpɜːmɪˈeʃən/ n [U] permeating or being ~d. 弥漫; 普及; 散布; 渗透。 **per·meable** /ˈpɜːmɪəbl; ˈpɜːmɪəbl/ adj that can be ~d by fluids; porous. 可渗透的; 可透过的。 **per·mea·bil·ity** /ˌpɜːmɪəˈbɪlətɪ; ˌpɜːmɪəˈbɪlətɪ/ n

per·mis·sible /pəˈmɪsəbl; pəˈmɪsəbl/ adj that may be permitted. 可允许的。 **per·mis·sibly** /-əblɪ; -əblɪ/ adv

per·mission /pəˈmɪʃn; pəˈmɪʃən/ n [U] act of

allowing or permitting; consent: 许可; 准许; 允许; 同意: *with your ～, if you will allow me;* 如果你许可的话: *give sb ～ to do sth.* 允许某人做某事. *You have my ～ to leave.* 我准许你离开; 你可以走了. *By whose ～ did you enter this building?* 是谁准许你进入这建筑物的?

per·miss·ive /pə'mɪsɪv/ *adj* giving permission: 许可的; 准许的; 允许的: ～ *legislation,* that gives powers to do sth but does not require that it shall be done. 伸缩性立法(赋予权力可做某事但非必须完成该事). **the ～ society,** (in GB, 1967 onwards) term used for social changes, including greater sexual freedom, homosexual law reform, abolition of censorship in the theatre, frank discussion of hitherto taboo subjects, etc. 宽容的社会(指英国自一九六七年以后社会的变迁, 包括更多的性自由, 改革同性恋法律, 废止对影剧院的检查, 自由谈论避讳的事等). ～**ness** *n*

per·mit /pə'mɪt/ *vt, vi* (**-tt-**) **1** [VP6A, C, 17, 19C] allow: 允许; 许可: *weather ～ting.* 如果天气好的话; 要是天气许可的话. *Smoking not ～ted in this cinema.* 本电影院禁止吸烟. *Circumstances do not ～ me to help you/do not ～ my helping you.* 情况不许可我帮助你. **2** [VP3A] ～ *of,* (formal) admit of: (正式用语) 容许: *The situation does not ～ of any delay,* There must be no delay. 这种情况不容许有任何耽搁. □ *n* /'pɜ:mɪt; 'pɜrmɪt/ [C] written authority to go somewhere, do sth, etc: 通行证; 许可证: *You won't get into the atomic research station without a ～.* 你一定要有通行证才能进入原子研究站.

per·mu·ta·tion /ˌpɜ:mju:'teɪʃn; ˌpɜrmjə'teʃən/ *n* (maths) [U] change in the order of a set of things arranged in a group; [C] any one such arrangement: (数学)排列; 置换; 排列之一: 一组: *The ～s of x, y and z are xyz, xzy, yxz, yzx, zxy, zyx.* x, y 和 z 的排列是 xyz, xzy, yxz, yzx, zxy, zyx.

per·mute /pə'mju:t; pə'mjut/ *vt* [VP6A] change the order of. 改变…的序列; 排列.

per·ni·cious /pə'nɪʃəs; pə'nɪʃəs/ *adj* ～ (**to**), harmful, injurious: (对…)有害的; 伤害性的: ～ *habits;* 有害的习惯; ～ *to the welfare of society;* 对社会福利有害的; ～ *anaemia,* a severe kind, often fatal. 恶性贫血. ～**ly** *adv* ～**ness** *n*

per·nick·ety /pə'nɪkətɪ; pə'nɪkɪtɪ/ *adj* (colloq) fussy; worrying about trifles. (口)好挑剔的; 过于顾虑琐事的; 吹毛求疵的.

per·or·ation /ˌperə'reɪʃn; ˌpero'reʃən/ *n* (formal) last part of a speech; summing up. (正式用语)(演说的)结尾; 总结; 结论.

per·ox·ide /pə'rɒksaɪd; pə'rɑksaɪd/ *n* (hydrogen ～; ～ of hydrogen (**H₂O₂**)) colourless liquid used as an antiseptic and to bleach hair. 过氧化氢 (H_2O_2, 无色液体, 用作防腐剂及漂染头发). ～ **blonde,** person with hair bleached with ～. 头发染为金黄色的人.

per·pen·dic·u·lar /ˌpɜ:pən'dɪkjʊlə(r); ˌpɜrpən'dɪkjələ/ *adj* **1** ～ (**to**), at an angle of 90° (to another line or surface). (与另一线或面)成直角的; 正交的. **2** upright; crossing the horizontal at an angle of 90°; (archit; **P～**) of the style of English Gothic architecture of the 14th and 15th cc, marked by vertical lines in the tracery of its windows. 垂直的; 与水平线成直角的; (建筑)垂直式的(指十四、十五世纪英国哥德式建筑, 其特征为窗上用垂直纹饰花图案). □ *n* [C] ～ **line;** [U] ～ position: 垂直线; 垂直位置: *The wall is a little out of the ～.* 这墙有点倾斜. ～**ly** *adv*

per·pe·trate /'pɜ:pɪtreɪt; 'pɜrpəˌtret/ *vt* [VP6A] commit (a crime, an error); be guilty of (sth wrong or sth considered outrageous): 做(错事、错误、残暴或不道德之事): ～ *a crime/a blunder/a frightful pun.* 犯罪(犯错; 乱讲恶劣的双关语). **per·pe·tra·tor** /-tə(r); -tɚ/ *n* **per·pe·tra·tion** /ˌpɜ:pɪ'treɪʃn; ˌpɜrpə'treʃən/ *n*

per·pet·ual /pə'petʃʊəl; pə'petʃuəl/ *adj* **1** never-ending; going on for a long time or without stopping: 永久的; 持久的。～ **'motion,** the motion of a machine, if such could be invented, which would go on for ever without an external source of energy, 永久运动(一种假想的机械运动, 虽无持续的能源亦能永远运转). **2** continual; often repeated: 不断的; 一再重复的: *She's tired of their ～ chatter.* 她对他们没完没了的闲谈感到厌倦. ～**ly** /-tʃʊəlɪ; -tʃuəlɪ/ *adv*

per·petu·ate /pə'petʃʊeɪt; pə'petʃu,et/ *vt* [VP6A] preserve from being forgotten or from going out of use: 使永存; 使不被遗忘; 使不朽: ～ *the memory of a great statesman by erecting a statue of him.* 借建造一座塑像来纪念一位伟大的政治家. **per·petu·ation** /pə,petʃʊ'eɪʃn; pə,petʃu'eʃən/ *n*

per·petu·ity /ˌpɜ:pɪ'tju:ɪtɪ US: -'tu:-; ˌpɜrpə'tjuətɪ/ *n* (*pl* **-ties**) **1** [U] state of being perpetual. 永恒; 永存; 不朽. *in ～,* for ever. 永远. **2** [C] (legal) perpetual annuity or possession. (法律)终身年金; 永久产业.

per·plex /pə'pleks; pə'pleks/ *vt* [VP6A, 14] ～ (**with**), **1** puzzle; bewilder: 使困惑; 使迷惑: ～ *sb with questions.* 以问题使某人困惑. **2** make more complex or intricate: 使更复杂: *Don't ～ the issue.* 不要把这问题弄得更复杂. ～**ed** *adj* puzzled; complicated. 困惑的; 复杂的. ～**ed·ly** /-ɪdlɪ; -ɪdlɪ/ *adv* ～**ity** /-ətɪ; -ətɪ/ *n* (*pl* **-ties**) **1** [U] state of being ～ed: 困惑: *He looked at us in ～ity.* 他困惑地看着我们. **2** [C] perplexing thing; cause of bewilderment. 令人困惑的事物; 迷惑的原因.

per·qui·site /'pɜ:kwɪzɪt; 'pɜrkwəzɪt/ *n* [C] profit, allowance, etc given or looked upon as one's right in addition to regular wages or salary: (正式薪资以外的)津贴; 赏钱; 小帐; 奖金; 额外收入; 额外利益: *The salesman's ～s include the use of his firm's car out of business hours.* 这推销员的额外津贴包括在下班后使用公司的车子. *Politics in Britain used to be the ～ of the great landowners.* 在英国, 参政曾经是大地主的一项额外利益. ⇨ **perk³.**

perry /'perɪ; 'perɪ/ *n* [U] drink made from the fermented juice of pears, 梨酒. ⇨ **cider.**

per·se /ˌpɜ:'seɪ; 'pɜ'si/ *adv* (Lat) (of sth) considered alone. (拉)(指事物)本身; 本质上.

per·se·cute /'pɜ:sɪkju:t; 'pɜrsɪ,kjut/ *vt* **1** [VP6A] punish, treat cruelly, esp because of religious beliefs. (尤指因宗教信仰不同而)迫害; 惩罚. **2** allow no peace to; worry: 烦扰; 困扰: ～ *a man with questions.* 以问题困扰一个人. **per·se·cu·tor** /-tə(r); -tɚ/ *n* **per·se·cu·tion** /ˌpɜ:sɪ'kju:ʃn; ˌpɜrsɪ'kjuʃən/ *n* **1** [C] persecuting or being ～d: 迫害; 烦扰: *suffer persecution for one's religious beliefs.* 为了宗教信仰而遭受迫害. **2** [C]instance of this (in history, etc): (历史等中的)迫害事件: *the numerous persecutions of the Jews.* 对犹太人的许多迫害.

per·se·vere /ˌpɜ:sɪ'vɪə(r); ˌpɜ'sə'vɪr/ *vi* [VP2A, 3A] ～ (**at/in/with**), keep on steadily, continue (esp sth difficult or tiring): 坚忍; 坚持; 固守(尤指困难或令人厌倦的事): ～ *in one's studies.* 孜孜不倦地研读. **per·se·ver·ing** *adj* **per·se·ver·ing·ly** *adv* **per·se·ver·ance** /-rəns; -rəns/ *n* [U] constant effort to achieve sth; steadfastness. 毅力; 坚忍; 不屈不挠.

Per·sian /'pɜ:ʃn US: 'pɜ:rʒn; 'pɜʒən/ *n adj* (inhabitant) of Persia (now Iran); language of the people of Persia (now Iran): 波斯的; 波斯人; 波斯语(波斯即现在的伊朗): ～ *carpets;* 波斯地毯; ～ *cats,* with long, silky hair. 波斯猫.

per·si·flage /'pɜ:sɪflɑ:ʒ; 'pɜrsɪ,flɑʒ/ *n* [U] banter; light, good-humoured teasing. 嘲弄; 戏谑; 挖苦.

per·sim·mon /pə'sɪmən; pə'sɪmən/ *n* (tree bearing) soft yellow fruit which becomes sweet when completely ripe, esp when softened by frost. 柿子; 柿子树.

per·sist /pə'sɪst; pə'sɪst/ *vi* **1** [VP3A] ～ *in sth/in doing sth,* refuse, in spite of argument, opposition, failure, etc to make any change in (what one is doing, one's beliefs, etc): 坚持; 固执(所为、所信等): *She ～s in*

wearing that old-fashioned hat. 她坚持要戴那顶旧式的帽子。 **~ with,** continue to work hard at. 继续努力。 **2** [VP2A] continue to exist: 持续; 存留: *The fog is likely to ~ in most areas.* 可能大部分地区还有雾。 **~ence** /-əns; -əns/ *n* [U] **~ing** or being **~ent**: 坚持; 固执; 持续; 存留: *The ~ence of a high temperature in the patient puzzled the doctor.* 这病人一直发烧使医生困惑。 **~·ent** /-ənt/ -ənt/ *adj* **~ing**; continuing; occurring again and again; 坚持的; 固执的; 持续的; 一再发生的: *~ent attacks of malaria.* 疟疾的持续发作。 **~·ent·ly** *adv*

per·son /'pɜːsn; 'pɜsn/ *n* **1** man, woman (which are the preferred words; *people* is preferred to **~s** for the *pl*; **~** is often derog except when official or impersonal): 人(指一个人时, man 或 woman 比 person 更常用; 指许多人时 people 比 persons 更常用; 除了用于公务或非特指某一个人以外, person 常有轻蔑之意): *Who is this ~?* 这家伙是谁? *There's a young ~ to see you.* 有个年轻人来看你。 *Any ~* (= Anyone) *leaving litter in the park will be prosecuted.* 任何人在公园里丢垃圾将被告发。 **in the ~ of,** in the man / woman who is. 在…人那里; 在…人身上: *She found a good friend in the ~ of her landlady,* Her landlady became her good friend. 她的女房东变成了她的好朋友。 **,~-to-'~ call,** (of a telephone call) made (via the operator) to a particular ~ and charged for only from the time that ~ answers the phone. 叫人电话(自接话人答话时开始计算费用者)。 **2** living body of a human being: 人身: *Offences against the ~* (eg assaults, bodily attacks) *are punished severely.* 对人身的攻击处罚很重。 **in ~,** physically present: 亲身; 亲自: *I shall be present at the meeting in ~,* I shall be there myself (instead of sending sb to represent me). 我将亲自出席那个会议。 *Will you apply for the position by letter or in ~?* 你要亲自去申请那个工作, 还是写信去申请? **3** (gram) each of three classes of personal pronouns: (语法)人称; 身: *the first* ~ (I, we), *the second* ~ (you) *and the third* ~ (he, she, it, they). 第一人称 (I, we), 第二人称 (you), 和第三人称 (he, she, it, they)。

per·sona /pɜː'səʊnə; pɜ'sonə/ *n* (psych) role that a person assumes to show his conscious intentions to himself and others. (心理)(一个人为了对自己及他人表示自己的意向而扮演的)人物角色。 **~ 'grata** /'ɡrɑːtə; 'ɡretə/ , (Lat) person who is acceptable, esp a diplomat who is acceptable to a foreign government. (拉)受欢迎的人; 被接受的人(尤指被外国政府所接受的外交官)。 **~ ,non 'grata** /,nɒn'ɡrɑːtə; ,nɑn'ɡretə/ , one who is not acceptable in this way. 不受欢迎的人; 不被接受的人(外交官)。

per·son·able /'pɜːsənəbl; 'pɜsnəbl/ *adj* handsome; pleasing in manner. 英俊的; 美貌的; 风度好的。

per·son·age /'pɜːsənɪdʒ; 'pɜsnɪdʒ/ *n* (important) person; person of distinction. (要)人; 名士; 显要。

per·son·al /'pɜːsənl; 'pɜsnḷ/ *adj* **1** private; individual; of a particular person: 私人的; 个人的; 某一个人的: *my ~ affairs/needs/opinions;* 我个人的事(需要, 意见); *your ~ rights.* 你个人的权利(你的人权)。 *I have something ~ to discuss with you,* either my own or your intimate affairs. 我有点私事和你商量(有关我个人的事或与你切身的事)。 **'~ column,** (in a newspaper, etc) column in which private messages or advertisements appear. (报纸等的)人事广告栏。 **2** done or made by a person himself: 本人所做的; 亲身的: *a ~ interview.* 亲自晤谈。 *The Prime Minister made a ~ appearance at the meeting,* appeared himself, instead of sending one of his colleagues. 首相亲自参加会议。 **3** done or made for a particular person: 为了某人的; 某一人所做的: *provide a ~ service for sb;* 为某人提供服务; *give sb one's ~ attention.* 给某人以关注。 *He did me a ~ favour,* one directed to me and to him only. 他亲自帮了我一个忙。 **~** **as'sistant** (abbr 略作 **PA**), one who helps an official, etc in an office, government department, etc usu doing more than a secretary, eg by making travel ar-

rangements interviewing people. 私人助理(在办公室, 政府机关等中协助官员等之人, 其职务通常超过一般秘书, 如安排旅行、接见访客等)。 **4** of the body: 人身的; 身体的: *P~ cleanliness is important to health as well as to appearance.* 个人清洁对健康及仪表同样重要。 **5** of the nature of a human being: 人性的: *Do you believe in a ~ God?* 你相信有人性的神吗? **6** of or about a person in a critical or hostile way: 涉及私人的; 攻击个人的: *I object to such highly ~ remarks.* 我反对这种纯粹是攻击个人的批评。 *Let's not be too ~.* 我们别过于涉及私人。 **7** , ~ 'property/e'state,** (legal) temporal or movable property, not land. (法律)动产。 ⇨ *real estate* at **real¹** (2). **8** , ~ 'pronoun,** pronoun for the three persons(3): 人称代词: *I, we; you; he, she, it; they.* 我、我们; 你(你们); 他、她、它; 他们。 □ *n* [C] short newspaper item about a particular person. 有关个人的短闻。 **~ly** /-ənəlɪ; -ənḷɪ/ *adv* **1** in one's own person, not through an agent: 本人; 亲自: *He conducted me ~ly through the mansion.* 他亲自带我到大厦各处参观。 *~ly conducted tours,* holiday tours with a courier or guide who accompanies those making the tour. 她喜欢有人向导的旅行。 **2** speaking for oneself; for one's own part: 就自己而言; 为自己地: *P~ly I see no objection to your joining us.* 就我个人而言, 我不反对你加入我们。

per·son·al·ity /,pɜːsə'nælətɪ; ,pɜsṇ'ælətɪ/ *n* (*pl* **-ties**) **1** [U] state of being a person; existence as an individual: 人格; 个人的存在: *respect the ~ of a child.* 尊重儿童的人格。 **2** [C, U] qualities that make up a person's character: 个性: *a man with little ~;* 没有什么个性的人; *a woman with a strong ~.* 个性强的女人。 They both have striking personalities. 他们两人都有突出的个性。 **3** [C] (mod use) person, esp one who is well known in certain circles (though perhaps quite unknown in other circles): (现代用法)人物; (某圈子里)名人: *personalities of the stage and screen;* 影剧界名人; *a TV ~,* sb known to television viewers. 电视明星。 **'~ cult,** practice of giving fervent admiration, devotion, etc to a ~, esp a political leader. 人物崇拜(尤指对政治领袖的崇拜)。 **4** (*pl*) impolite remarks about sb's looks, habits, etc: (复)对某人的容貌、习惯等的不客气批评; 对某人的攻击: *indulge in personalities,* utter such remarks. 任意讲谤他人。

per·son·al·ize /'pɜːsənəlaɪz; 'pɜsṇḷ,aɪz/ *vt* [VP6A] have (sth) printed with one's address (*~d stationery*) or given a monogram with one's initials) (*~d shirts, handkerchiefs*). 印个人地址于(信纸等上); 印个人姓名的第一个字母于(衬衫、手帕等上)。

per·son·alty /'pɜːsənltɪ; 'pɜsn̩ltɪ/ *n* [U] (legal) personal estate. (法律)动产。

per·son·ate /'pɜːsəneɪt; 'pɜsṇ,et/ *vt* [VP6A] **1** play the part of (a character in a drama). 扮演; 饰演(戏中某一角色)。 **2** = impersonate (the more usu word). (impersonate 较为常用)。 **per·son·ation** /,pɜːsə'neɪʃn; ,pɜsṇ'eʃən/ *n*

per·son·ify /pə'sɒnɪfaɪ; pə'sɑnə,faɪ/ *vt* (*pt, pp* **-fied**) [VP6A] **1** regard or represent (sth) as a person: 拟(某物)为人; 视(某物)为人: *~ the sun and moon,* by using 'he' and 'she'. 把太阳和月亮看作人(以‘他’和‘她’称呼之)。 **2** be an example of (a quality): 为(某性质)的实例; 为…的化身: *That man personifies avarice/is avarice personified.* 那个人是贪婪的化身。

per·soni·fi·ca·tion /pə,sɒnɪfɪ'keɪʃn; pə,sɑnəfə'keʃən/ *n* **1** [U] **~ing** or being personified; [C] instance of this. 拟人; 人格化。 **2** *the ~ of,* a striking example of a quality of: 典型; 化身; 活例: *He's the personification of selfishness.* 他是自私的化身。

per·son·nel /,pɜːsə'nel; ,pɜsṇ'ɛl/ *n* (with *sing* or *pl v*) staff; persons employed in any work, esp public undertakings and the armed forces: (与单数或复数动词连用)职员; 人员(尤指公职和军职人员): *There were five airline ~ on the plane that crashed.* 失事的飞机上有五位工作人员。 **'~ officer/manager,** one employed to deal

with relationships between individual employees, their problems, grievances, etc. 人事官(人事主任)。

per·spec·tive /pəˈspektɪv; pəˈspɛktɪv/ *n* **1** [U] the art of drawing solid objects on a flat surface so as to give the right impression of their relative height, width, depth, distance, etc; [C] drawing so made. 透视法; 透视绘图法; 透视图. *in/out of ~*, drawn/not drawn according to the rules of ~. 按照(未按照)透视法画的. **2** [U] apparent relation between different

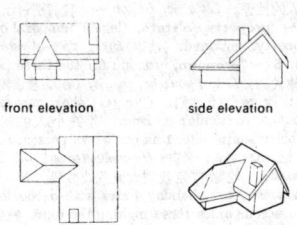

front elevation   side elevation

top elevation   perspective drawing

aspects of a problem. (问题之不同方面的)明显关系. *in the/its right/wrong ~*, in the right/wrong relationship; with/without exaggeration or neglect of any aspects: 正确地(不正确地): *You must get the story in (its right) ~.* 你必须正确地了解这故事. *He sees things in their right ~.* 他正确地察觉事物; 他对事物有正确的观点. **3** [C] (lit, fig) view; prospect: (字面, 喻)景色; 远景; 看法; 前途: *a distorted ~ of the nation's history.* 对过国家历史的歪曲看法.

per·spex /ˈpɜːspeks; ˈpɝˌspɛks/ *n* [U] (P) tough plastic material that will not splinter, used as a substitute for glass (eg in the windscreens of cars). (商标)不碎透明塑胶(如汽车的挡风屏).

per·spi·ca·cious /ˌpɜːspɪˈkeɪʃəs; ˌpɝspɪˈkeʃəs/ *adj* (formal) quick to judge and understand. (正式用语)敏于判断与了解的; 敏锐的; 聪明的. **per·spi·cac·ity** /ˌpɜːspɪˈkæsɪtɪ; ˌpɝspɪˈkæsɪtɪ/ *n* [U].

per·spic·u·ous /pəˈspɪkjʊəs; pɚˈspɪkjʊəs/ *adj* (formal) expressed clearly; expressing things clearly. (正式用语)意思明白的; 说明清楚的; 明晰的. **~·ly** *adv* **~·ness** *n* **per·spi·cu·ity** /ˌpɜːspɪˈkjuːɪtɪ; ˌpɝspɪˈkjuɪtɪ/ *n*

per·spire /pəˈspaɪə(r); pɚˈspaɪr/ *vi* [VP2A] sweat. 出汗; 流汗. **per·spir·ation** /ˌpɜːspəˈreɪʃn; ˌpɝspəˈreʃən/ *n* [U] sweat; sweating. 汗; 流汗.

per·suade /pəˈsweɪd; pɚˈswed/ *vt* **1** [VP11, 14] *~ sb that...*; *~ sb of sth*, convince (sb): 使(某人)相信: *How can I ~ you of my sincerity/that I am sincere?* 我如何能够使你相信我的诚意(我是诚意的)? **2** [VP17] cause (sb) by reasoning (to do sth): 说服; 劝诱: *We ~d him/He was ~d to try again.* 我们劝他(他被人劝说)再度尝试. **3** [VP14] *~ sb into/out of (doing) sth*, cause sb to do/stop doing sth: 劝某人做(不做)某事: *Can you ~ her out of her foolish plans?* 你能劝她放弃那些愚蠢的计划吗? *Who ~d you into writing that letter?* 谁劝你写那封信? **per·suad·able** /-əbl; -əbl/ *adj*

per·sua·sion /pəˈsweɪʒn; pɚˈsweʒən/ *n* **1** [U] persuading or being persuaded; power of persuading. 说服; 劝说; 被说服; 说服力. **2** [U] conviction; belief (the usu word): 确信; 信念(较为常用词): *It is my ~ that...*. 我相信...; 我认为...。 **3** [C] group or set holding a particular belief: 持某信仰的宗派: *men of various (religious) ~s*. 持各种不同(宗教)信仰的人们.

per·sua·sive /pəˈsweɪsɪv; pɚˈswesɪv/ *adj* able to persuade; convincing: 有说服力的; 能劝说的; 令人信服的: *She has a ~ manner.* 她有令人信服的态度. **~·ly** *adv* **~·ness** *n*

pert /pɜːt; pɝt/ *adj* **1** saucy; not showing proper respect: 鲁莽的; 无礼的: *a ~ child/answer.* 无礼的小

孩(回答). **2** (US) lively; sprightly. (美)活泼的; 轻快的. **~·ly** *adv* **~·ness** *n*

per·tain /pəˈteɪn; pɚˈten/ *vi* [VP3A] *~ to*, (formal) belong as a part or accessory; have reference; be appropriate:(正式用语)属于; 关于; 适合于: *the enthusiasm ~ing to youth*; 属于年轻人的热情; *the mansion and the lands ~ing to it.* 大厦及所附属的土地.

per·ti·na·cious /ˌpɜːtɪˈneɪʃəs *US*: -tnˈeɪʃəs; ˌpɝtnˈeʃəs/ *adj* (formal) not easily giving up (what has been started); determined. (正式用语)顽固的; 执拗的; 固执的; 坚决的. **~·ly** *adv* **per·ti·nac·ity** /ˌpɜːtɪˈnæsɪtɪ; *US*: -tnˈæ-; ˌpɝtnˈæsɪtɪ/ *n* [U].

per·ti·nent /ˈpɜːtɪnənt *US*: -tənent; ˈpɝtnənt/ *adj* *~ (to)*, (formal) referring directly; relevant: (正式用语)有关的; 中肯的: *remarks not ~ to the subject under discussion*; 与讨论中的题目无关的谈话; *a ~ reply.* 恰当的回答. **~·ly** *adv* **per·ti·nence** /-əns; -əns/ *n* [U].

per·turb /pəˈtɜːb; pɚˈtɝb/ *vt* [VP6A] (formal) trouble; make anxious: (正式用语)烦扰; 使焦急: *~ing rumours*; 令人不安的谣言; *a man who is never ~ed*. 从来不烦恼的人. **per·tur·ba·tion** /ˌpɜːtəˈbeɪʃn; ˌpɝtɚˈbeʃən/ *n* [U] ~ing or being ~ed. 扰乱;不安;焦虑;烦恼.

pe·ruke /pəˈruːk; pəˈruk/ *n* long wig. 长假发.

pe·ruse /pəˈruːz; pəˈruz/ *vt* [VP6A] (formal) read carefully. (正式用语)细读;细读. **pe·rusal** /pəˈruːzl; pəˈruzl/ *n* [C, U] act of reading carefully. 细读.

Peru·vian /pəˈruːvɪən; pəˈruvɪən/ *adj* of Peru: 秘鲁的: *~ bark*, of the cinchona tree, the source of quinine. 金鸡纳皮(为制奎宁的原料). □ *n* native of Peru. 秘鲁人.

per·vade /pəˈveɪd; pɚˈved/ *vt* [VP6A] spread through every part of: 蔓延; 遍及; 弥漫; 渗透; 充满: *The subversive ideas that ~ all these periodicals may do great harm.* 遍布所有这些杂志中的颠覆思想可能造成很大的危险. **per·va·sion** /pəˈveɪʒn; pɚˈveʒən/ *n* [U] pervading or being ~d. 蔓延;遍布;弥漫;渗透.

per·va·sive /pəˈveɪsɪv; pɚˈvesɪv/ *adj* tending to pervade: 蔓延的; 遍布的; 弥漫的; 渗透的: *~ influences.* 普遍性的影响;深入各处的影响. **~·ly** *adv* **~·ness** *n*

per·verse /pəˈvɜːs; pɚˈvɝs/ *adj* **1** (of persons) wilfully continuing in wrongdoing; wilfully choosing a wrong course. (指人)刚愎的; 故意作恶的; 怙恶不悛的; 邪恶的. **2** (of circumstances) contrary (to one's wishes). (指环境)与意愿相违的. **3** (of behaviour) contrary to reason. (指行为)背理的; 悖谬的. **~·ly** *adv* **~·ness** *n*

per·ver·sion /pəˈvɜːʃn *US*: -ʒn; pɚˈvɝʒən/ *n* **1** [U] perverting or being perverted. 误用; 滥用; 堕落. **2** [C] turning from right to wrong; change to sth abnormal, unnatural, etc: 歪曲; 曲解; 倒错; 颠倒; 反常: *a ~ of justice*; 歪曲正义; *a ~ of the appetite*, eg a desire to eat grass, as Nebuchadnezzar had; 食欲反常(如古代巴比伦国王尼布加尼撒之吃草欲); *sexual ~s.* 性欲倒错;性变态.

per·ver·sity /pəˈvɜːsɪtɪ; pɚˈvɝsɪtɪ/ *n* (pl -ties) [U] being perverse; [C] perverse act. 刚愎; 怙恶不悛; 邪恶; 背理; 荒谬; 反常的行为.

per·vert /pəˈvɜːt; pɚˈvɝt/ *vt* [VP6A] **1** turn (sth) to a wrong use. 误用; 滥用(某事物). **2** cause (a person, his mind) to turn away from right behaviour, beliefs, etc; 使(人、心智)堕落; 诱(人)入邪道: *~ (the mind of) a child.* 使小孩(的心智)走上邪道. *Did Socrates really ~ the youth of Athens?* 苏格拉底真的使雅典的青年误入歧途吗? *Do pornographic books ~ those who read them?* 色情书籍会使读者堕落吗? □ *n* /ˈpɜːvɜːt; ˈpɝvɝt/ ~ed person; person whose behaviour deviates from what is normal, eg in sexual practices. 堕落的人; 入邪道的人; 行为反常的人; 乖癖者; 性欲倒错者; 性变态者.

pe·seta /pəˈseɪtə; pəˈsetə/ *n* (pl ~s) unit of currency in Spain. 比塞塔(西班牙的货币单位).

pesky /ˈpeskɪ; ˈpɛskɪ/ *adj* (colloq) troublesome; annoying. (口)麻烦的; 恼人的.

peso /'peɪsəʊ; 'peso/ n (pl ~s) unit of currency in many Latin American countries and the Philippines. 比索(拉丁美洲许多国家及菲律宾的货币单位).

pes·sary /'pesərɪ; 'pesɛrɪ/ n (pl -ries) (med) any of various devices placed and left in the vagina to support the uterus or prevent conception. (医)子宫压定器; 子宫托; 子宫套; 通经器.

pes·si·mism /'pesɪmɪzəm; 'pesə,mɪzəm/ n [U] (opp of optimism) tendency to believe that the worst thing is most likely to happen, that everything is essentially evil. (为 optimism 之反义词)悲观; 悲观主义。 **pes·si·mist** /-ɪst; -ɪst/ n person subject to ~. 悲观者。 **pes·si·mis·tic** /,pesɪ'mɪstɪk; ,pesə'mɪstɪk/ adj **pes·si·mis·ti·cally** /-klɪ; -klɪ/ adv

pest /pest; pest/ n troublesome or destructive thing, animal, etc; (colloq) person who is a nuisance: 令人讨厌或有害之物、动物等; (口)惹人讨厌的人; 讨厌鬼: garden ~s, eg insects, mice, snails; 园中害物(如昆虫、老鼠、蜗牛); ▷ ~ control, the use of various methods to get rid of ~s. 害物控制。 **pest·i·cide** /'pestɪsaɪd; 'pestɪ,saɪd/ n substance used to destroy ~s, esp insects. 除虫药; 杀虫剂; 灭鼠药。

pes·ter /'pestə(r); 'pestɚ/ vt [VP6A, 17, 14] ~ sb (with sth/for sth/to do sth), annoy; trouble; 使困恼; 使苦恼; 烦扰: be ~ed with flies/with requests for help; 为苍蝇(为求助)所扰; ~ sb for money; 缠着某人要钱; ~sb to help. 麻烦某人去帮助。

pes·tif·er·ous /pe'stɪfərəs; pes'tɪfərəs/ adj causing disease; morally dangerous. 引起疾病的; 邪恶的; 伤风败俗的。

pes·ti·lence /'pestɪləns; 'pestɪləns/ n [C, U] (any kind of) fatal epidemic disease, esp bubonic plague. (任何一种)瘟疫; 恶疫(尤指腺鼠疫)。 **pes·ti·lent** /-ənt; -ənt/, **pes·ti·len·tial** /,pestɪ'lenʃl; ,pestɪ'ɛnʃəl/ adjj **1** like a ~; carrying infection. 似瘟疫的; 似恶疫的; 传染的。 (口)extremely annoying or objectionable: (口)极其恼人的; 极讨厌的; 最可恶的: These pestilential flies/children give me no peace. 这些可恶的苍蝇(小孩子)使我不得安宁。

pestle /'pesl; 'pesl/ n stick with a thick end used in a mortar for pounding or crushing things. (捣研用的)杵。 ▢ vt crush in (or as in) a mortar. (在臼等中)以杵捣; 研碎。

pet¹ /pet; pet/ n **1** (often attrib) animal, etc kept as a companion, treated with care and affection, eg a cat or a dog: (常用作定语)宠爱的动物; 爱物; 宠物(如猫或狗): a 'pet shop, one where pets, eg dogs, canaries, tortoises are sold. 宠物店(如出售狗、金丝雀、乌龟等者)。 **2** person treated as a favourite: 受宠爱的人: Mary is the teacher's pet. 玛丽是老师宠爱的学生。 **3** sb specially loved or lovable: 特别受爱护的人; 可爱的人: make a pet of a child. 宠爱小孩。 She's a perfect pet, (colloq) has very winning ways, is very lovable. (口)她是最可爱的人儿。 **pet aversion**, sth or sb most disliked: 最令人厌恶的物或人: Cowboy films are her pet aversion. 她最讨厌看西部牛仔片。 'pet name, name other than the real name, used affectionately. 爱称; 昵称。 ▢ vt (-tt-) fondle; kiss and caress: 抚弄; 爱抚; 亲吻: silly women petting their poodles. 爱抚着卷毛狗的愚蠢妇人。

pet² /pet; pet/ n fit of ill temper, esp about sth trifling: 发怒; 发脾气(尤指为着小事生气): in one of her pets. 在她某次发脾气时。

petal /'petl; 'petl/ n one of the leaf-like divisions of a flower: 花瓣: 'rose ~s. 玫瑰花瓣。 ▷ the illus at flower. 参看 flower 之插图。 **pet·alled** (US **pet·aled**) /'petld; 'petld/ adj having ~s. 有花瓣的。

pe·tard /pe'tɑːd; pɪ'tɑrd/ n kind of bomb used in former times to break down doors, gates, walls, etc. (昔时用以爆破城门、围墙等的)炸药筒。 hoist with one's own ~, (prov) caught or injured by what one intended as a snare for others. (谚)作法自毙; 害人反害己。

peter /'piːtə(r); 'pitɚ/ vi [VP2C] ~ out, (of supplies, etc) come gradually to an end. (指供应品等)渐渐耗尽; 渐渐消失。

Peter /'piːtə(r); 'pitɚ/ n rob ,~ to pay 'Paul, take from one to give to another. 取诸甲偿诸乙; 借债还债; 剜肉补疮。 ,blue 'peter, blue flag with a white square, flown by a ship before leaving port. 开船旗(船离港时所悬的蓝底白方格旗)。

pe·tit bour·geois /,petiː 'bʊəʒwɑː; ,petɪ'bʊrʒwɑ/ n (F) member of the lower middle class: (法)小资产阶级; 中下层阶级一份子: (attrib) (用作定语) ~ habits/opinions. 小资产阶级的习惯(思想)。 ▷ middle class at **middle(3)**; ▷ **bourgeois**.

pe·tite /pə'tiːt; pə'tit/ adj (of a person) small, slender, neat and dainty. (指人)娇小玲珑的。

pe·ti·tion /pɪ'tɪʃn; pə'tɪʃən/ n [C] **1** prayer; earnest request; appeal (esp a written document signed by a large number of people): 祈祷; 恳求; 请愿; (尤指有多人签名的)请愿书; 陈情书。 **2** formal application made to a court of law. (向法庭呈出的)诉状。 ▢ vt, vi **1** [VP6A, 17, 11, 14] ~ sb (for sth/to do sth/that...), make a ~ to, eg the authorities; 向(当局等)请求: Parliament to redress grievances. 向国会请求解除疾苦。 **2** [VP3A] ~ for, ask earnestly or humbly: 祈求; 恳求; 请求: ~ for a retrial. 请求再审。 ~er n one who ~s, esp the plaintiff in a divorce suit. 请求人; 请愿人; 原告(尤指离婚诉讼的原告)。

pet·rel /'petrəl; 'petrəl/ n long-winged black and white seabird. 海燕。 ▷ the illus at water. 参看 water 之插图。 stormy ~, (fig) person whose coming causes (eg social or industrial) unrest. (喻)一来就造成(社会或工业等)不安的人。

pet·rify /'petrɪfaɪ; 'petrə,faɪ/ vt, vi (pt, pp -fied) [VP6A, 2A] (cause) to change into stone; (fig) take away power to think, feel, act, etc (through terror, surprise, etc): (使)变为石头; (使)石化; (喻)使无思考、感觉、行动等能力; 使发呆(因恐惧、惊吓等之故): petrified with terror. 被吓呆了。 **pet·ri·fac·tion** /,petrɪ'fækʃn; ,petrə'fækʃən/ n ~ing or being petrified; petrified substance. 石化; 吓呆; 化石。

petro- /,petrəʊ-; 'petrə-/ pref of rocks or of petroleum. 表示'岩石'或'石油'。 ~-chemical chemical substance derived from petroleum or natural gas. 石油化学产品。

pet·rol /'petrəl; 'petrəl/ n [U] refined petroleum used as a fuel in internal combustion engines (US 美 = gasoline): 汽油: fill up with ~; 灌满汽油; stop at the next '~ station; 停在下一个加油站; the '~ tank. (汽)油箱。

pe·tro·leum /pɪ'trəʊlɪəm; pə'trolɪəm/ n [U] mineral oil (vegetable in origin, from forests in prehistoric times) found underground and obtained from wells; used in various forms (petrol, paraffin, etc) for lighting, heating and driving machines. 石油。 ,~ 'jelly n [U] semi-solid substance obtained from ~, used as a lubricant and in ointments. 矿脂; 凡士林。

pe·trol·ogy /pɪ'trɒlədʒɪ; pɪ'trɑlədʒɪ/ n [U] the study of rocks. 岩石学。

pet·ti·coat /'petɪkəʊt; 'pɛtɪ,kot/ n woman's underskirt. (妇女的)衬裙。

pet·ti·fog·ging /'petɪfɒgɪŋ; 'pɛtɪ,fagɪŋ/ adj (of a person) worrying about small and unimportant details; (of a method) unnecessarily concerned with small matters. (指人)为不重要小节而烦恼的; (指方法)小题大作的; 不必要地注意小事的。

pet·tish /'petɪʃ; 'pɛtɪʃ/ adj **1** (of a person) having short and often repeated fits of ill temper, like a spoiled child. (指人)易怒的; 使性子的; 爱闹脾气的。 **2** (of a remark, act) said or done in a fit of ill temper. (指言语、行为)发怒时说出的; 发脾气做的。 ~·ly adv ~·ness n

petty /'petɪ; 'pɛtɪ/ adj (-ier, -iest) **1** small; unimportant: 小的; 不重要的: ~ troubles/details; 小毛病

(琐碎细节); ~ *regulations enforced by* ~ *officials*. 小公务员执行的琐细的法规。 **2** on a small scale: 小规模的; 小型的: ~ *farmers/shopkeepers*. 小农(小店主)。 **3** having or showing a narrow mind; mean: 小器的; 卑鄙的: ~ *spite*. 卑鄙的恶念。 **4** ~ **cash**, (business) money for or from small payments. (商)小额收支的现金; 零用现金。 ~ **larceny**, theft of articles of little value. 轻窃盗罪。 ~ **officer**, highest rank of non-commissioned officer in the navy. 海军上士。 **pet·tily** /'petɪlɪ; 'petɪlɪ/ *adv* **pet·ti·ness** *n*

petu·lant /'petjulənt US: -tʃu-; 'petʃələnt/ *adj* unreasonably impatient or irritable. 性急的; 暴躁的。 ~·**ly** *adv* **petu·lance** /-əns; -əns/ *n* [U].

pe·tu·nia /pɪ'tjuːnɪə US: -'tuː-; pə'tjunjə/ *n* [C] garden plant with funnel-shaped flowers of various colours. 矮牵牛属; 毡子花; 牵牛花(一种园艺植物, 开各色漏斗状花)。

pew /pjuː; pju/ *n* bench with a back, usu fixed to the floor, in a church: (教堂里)有靠背的长椅: *empty pews at morning service;* 早晨礼拜时空的长椅; (colloq) seat: (口)座位: *Take a pew!* 请坐! ⇨ the illus at **church**. 参看 church 之插图。 '**pew-opener** *n* person who conducted persons to their seats when, in former times, family pews were enclosed and had doors. (从前教堂里的)领座人(当时教堂里的家族席位是隔开的, 有门的门扇)。

pe·wit, pee·wit /'piːwɪt; 'piwɪt/ *n* lapwing; kind of mountain plover, named after its cry. 田凫; 京燕(一种山鹬, 英文名字得自其鸣声)。

pew·ter /'pjuːtə(r); 'pjutɚ/ *n* [U] grey alloy of lead and tin; kitchen vessels made of this: 白镴(铅与锡的合金); 白镴所制成的容器: *a good collection of* ~; 可观的白镴器皿收藏; (attrib) (用作定语) ~ *mugs/dishes*. 白镴制成的杯(盘子)。

pe·yote /peɪ'əʊtɪ; pe'otɪ/ *n* Mexican cactus from which is derived a drug *(mescaline)* which causes hallucinations. 一种墨西哥产仙人掌(此种仙人掌所制成之毒碱能使人产生幻觉)。

pfen·nig /'fenɪɡ; 'fenɪɡ/ *n* German copper coin, one hundredth of a mark. 芬尼(德国铜币, 值百分之一马克)。

phae·ton /'feɪtn US: 'feɪətən; 'fetn/ *n* (hist) light, four-wheeled open carriage, usu drawn by a pair of horses. (史)轻快四轮敞篷马车(通常由两匹马拉之)。

phago·cyte /'fæɡəsaɪt; 'fæɡə,saɪt/ *n* sort of leucocyte (blood cell) capable of guarding the system against infection by absorbing microbes. 吞噬细胞(借吞噬微生物而能保护身体以抵抗疾病的一种白血球)。

phal·anx /'fælæŋks; 'fælæŋks/ *n* (*pl* ~**es** or **phalanges** /fə'lændʒiːz; fə'lændʒɪz/) **1** (in ancient Greece) body of soldiers in close formation for fighting. (古希腊)排成作战的密集队形的军队; 方阵。 **2** number of persons banded together for a common purpose. 为共同目标而结合的一群人。 **3** (anat) bone in a finger or toe. (解剖)指骨; 趾骨。 ⇨ the illus at **skeleton**. 参看 skeleton 之插图。

phal·lus /'fæləs; 'fæləs/ *n* image of the erect penis, as a symbol of generative power. 阴茎像(作为生殖力的象征)。 **phal·lic** /'fælɪk; 'fælɪk/ *adj* of a ~: 阴茎像的: *phallic symbols/emblems*. 阴茎象征。

phan·tasm /'fæntæzəm; 'fæntæzəm/ *n* 幻影; 幻像; 幽灵; 空想。 **phan·tas·mal** /fæn'tæzməl; fæn'tæzməl/ *adj* of or like a ~. 幻影的; 似幻影的; 幻觉的; 幽灵的; 非真实的。 **phan·tas·ma·goria** /ˌfæntæzmə'ɡɔːrɪə US: -'ɡɔːrɪə; ˌfæntæzmə'ɡorɪə/ *n* changing group of images, real or imagined figures, etc eg as seen in a dream: 变幻不定的成群影像; 变幻不定的许多真实的或幻想的人物(如梦中所见者)。

phan·tasy /'fæntəsɪ; 'fæntəsɪ/ *n* = fantasy.

phan·tom /'fæntəm; 'fæntəm/ *n* 幽灵的东西; 幻想; sth without [reality, as seen in a dream or vision: 幽灵; 幻像; 幻影; 梦幻: (attrib) (用作定语) ~ *ships*. 鬼船。

Phar·aoh /'feərəʊ; 'fɛro/ *n* title of the kings of

ancient Egypt. 法老(古埃及国王的称谓)。

Phari·see /'færɪsaɪ; 'færəˌsaɪ/ *n* member of an ancient Jewish sect known for strict obedience to written laws and for pretensions to sanctity; (small p) hypocritical and self-righteous person. 法利赛人(古犹太人中的一派, 以严格遵守成文法律及自命圣洁见称); (小写 p)自以为正直的伪善者。 **phari·saic**, /ˌfærɪ'seɪɪk; ˌfærə'se·ɪk/, **phari·sai·cal** /-kl; -kl/ *adj* of or like a ~ or the ~s. (似)法利赛人的; 自以为正直的; 伪善的。

phar·ma·ceuti·cal /ˌfɑːmə'sjuːtɪkl US: -'suː-; ˌfɑrmə'sjutɪk/ *adj* of, engaged in, pharmacy of medicinal drugs: 制药的; 配药的; 药物的; 医药的: *the* ~ *industry*. 制药业; 制药工业。

phar·ma·cist /'fɑːməsɪst; 'fɑrməsɪst/ *n* person professionally qualified to prepare medicines. 药剂师。 ⇨ **chemist, druggist**.

phar·ma·col·ogy /ˌfɑːmə'kɒlədʒɪ; ˌfɑrmə'kɑlədʒɪ/ *n* [U] science of pharmacy. 药物学; 药理学。 **phar·ma·col·ogist** /-ədʒɪst; -ədʒɪst/ *n* expert in, student of, ~. 药物学家; 研习药物学的人。

phar·ma·co·poeia /ˌfɑːməkə'piːə; ˌfɑrməkə'piə/ *n* (officially published) book with list of medicinal preparations and directions for their use. (官方出版的)药典; 药方书。

phar·macy /'fɑːməsɪ; 'fɑrməsɪ/ *n* (*pl* -**cies**) **1** [U] preparation and dispensing of medicines and drugs. 制药; 配药。 **2** [C] dispensary; (part of a) shop where medical goods are sold. (US 美 = *drugstore*). 药房; 药店。

pharos /'feərɒs; 'fɛrɑs/ *n* lighthouse; beacon for sailors. 灯塔; 航线标灯。

phar·ynx /'færɪŋks; 'færɪŋks/ *n* cavity (with the muscles, etc ˌthat enclose it) at the back of the mouth, where the passages to the nose, mouth and larynx begin. 咽。 ⇨ the illus at **head**. 参看 head 之插图。 **phar·yn·gi·tis** /ˌfærɪn'dʒaɪtɪs; ˌfærɪn'dʒaɪtɪs/ *n* [U] inflammation of the mucous membrane of the ~. 咽炎。

phase /feɪz; fez/ *n* [C] **1** stage of development: 阶段; 时期; 局面: *a* ~ *of history;* 历史的一个阶段; *the critical* ~ *of an illness;* 疾病的危险期; *enter upon a new* ~ *of one's career;* 开始自己事业的新局面; stage in a cycle. 相; 周相。 *in/out of* ~, having/not having the same ~ at the same time; in/out of harmony. 同(异)相; 和(不和)谐。 **2** (of the moon) amount of bright surface visible from the earth (new moon, full moon, etc). (指月亮)位相; 盈亏(新月、满月等)。 ⇨ [VP6A, 15B] plan, carry out, by ~s: 分期计划; 按阶段执行: *a* ~*d withdrawal*, one made by stages. 分期撤出。 ~ *in*, introduce, one stage at a time. 逐步采用; 逐步实施。 ~ *out*, withdraw, one stage at a time. 逐步结束; 逐步撤出。

crescent   half moon   gibbous   full moon

the phases of the moon

pheas·ant /'feznt; 'fɛznt/ *n* [C] long-tailed game bird; [U] its flesh as food. 雉; 雉肉。 ⇨ the illus at **fowl**. 参看 fowl 之插图。

pheno·bar·bi·tone /ˌfiːnəʊ'bɑːbɪtəʊn; ˌfino'bɑrbɪˌton/ *n* [U] drug used to calm the nerves and induce sleep. 苯巴比妥(一种镇静剂及安眠药)。

phe·nol /'fiːnɒl; 'finɒl/ *n* [U] (comm, science) carbolic acid (as used in disinfectants). (商, 科学)石碳酸; 酚(用作消毒剂)。

phe·nom·enal /fɪ'nɒmɪnl; fə'nɑmənl/ *adj* **1** perceptible to the senses. 感觉得到的。 **2** concerned with

phenomena. 关于现象的。**3** prodigious; extraordinary. 奇异的；非常的。**~ly** /-nəlɪ; -n̩lɪ/ *adv*

phe·nom·enon /fɪ'nɒmɪnən US: -nɒn; fə'namə-ˌnɑn/ *n* (*pl* **-ena** /-ɪnə; -ənə/) **1** thing that appears to or is perceived by the senses: 现象: *the phenomena of nature.* 自然的现象。**2** remarkable or unusual person, thing, happening, etc. 非凡的或特殊的人、物、事件等。

phew /fju:; fju *or a less precise puffing noise* 或是一种不太清楚的吹气声/ *int* natural cry indicating astonishment, impatience, discomfort, disgust, etc according to context. 呸! 啐! (表示惊讶、不耐烦、不舒服、憎厌等的感叹声,其意义视上下文而定)。

phial /'faɪəl; 'faɪəl/ *n* small bottle, esp one for liquid medicine; vial. 小瓶; (尤指)小药水瓶。

phil·an·der /fɪ'lændə(r); fə'lændə/ *vi* [VP2A] be in the habit of making love without serious intentions; flirt. 用情不专; 调情。**~er** *n* person who does this. 用情不专者; 调情者。

phil·an·thropy /fɪ'lænθrəpɪ; fə'lænθrəpɪ/ *n* [U] love of mankind; practical sympathy and benevolence. 博爱; 慈善; 同情; 仁慈。**phil·an·thro·pist** /-ɪst; -ɪst/ *n* person who helps others, esp those who are poor or in trouble. 博爱者; 慈善家。**phil·an·thropic** /ˌfɪlən'θrɒpɪk; ˌfɪlən'θrɑpɪk/ *adj* of **~**; benevolent; kind and helpful: 博爱的; 慈善的; 助人的: *philanthropic institutions,* eg for blind people or orphans. (为盲人或孤儿等所设设立的)慈善机构。**phil·an·thropi·cally** /-klɪ; -klɪ/ *adv*

phil·at·ely /fɪ'lætəlɪ; fə'lætl̩ɪ/ *n* postage-stamp collecting. 集邮。**phil·at·el·ist** /-ɪst; -ɪst/ *n* person who collects postage-stamps; person with expert knowledge of them. 集邮者; 集邮专家。

phil·hel·lene /fɪl'heliːn; fɪl'helin/ *n, adj* (person) friendly to the Greeks. 对希腊人友善的; 希腊之友。**phil·hel·lenic** /ˌfɪlhe'liːnɪk US: -'lenɪk; ˌfɪlhe'lenɪk/ *adj*

Phi·lis·tine /'fɪlɪstaɪn US: -stiːn; fə'lɪstɪn/ *n* **1** (Biblical) one of the warlike people in Palestine who were the enemies of the Israelites. (圣经)非利士人(古以色列人的仇敌, 居于巴勒斯坦, 好战)。**2** (mod use; small **p**) uncultured person; person whose interests are material and commonplace: (现代用法, 小写 p) 没教养的人; 庸俗的人: (attrib) (用作定语) **~** *neighbours.* 缺乏教养的邻居。

phil·ol·ogy /fɪ'lɒlədʒɪ; fɪ'lɑlədʒɪ/ *n* [U] study of the development of language, or of particular languages. 语文学; (旧用法)语言学。⇨ **linguistics. phil·ol·ogist** /fɪ'lɒlədʒɪst; fɪ'lɑlədʒɪst/ *n* student of, expert in, **~**. 语文学家; 语言学家; 研究语文学的人。**philo·logi·cal** /ˌfɪlə'lɒdʒɪkl; ˌfɪlə'lɑdʒɪkl̩/ *adj* of **~**. 语文学的。

phil·os·opher /fɪ'lɒsəfə(r); fə'lɑsəfə/ *n* **1** person studying or teaching philosophy, or having a system of philosophy. 哲学家; 研究或教授哲学的人。**2** person whose mind is untroubled by passions and hardships; person who lets reason govern his life. 豁达的人; 重理性的人。**~'s stone,** substance which, alchemists believed, could change any metal into gold; elixir. 点金石; 仙石(从前的炼金术士认为能使金属变成黄金的物质)。

phil·os·ophy /fɪ'lɒsəfɪ; fə'lɑsəfɪ/ *n* (*pl* **-phies**) **1** [U] the search for knowledge, esp the nature and meaning of existence. 哲学; 学问的研究(尤指对存在之性质及意义所作之探讨)。**moral ~,** the study of the principles underlying the actions and behaviour of men; ethics. 伦理学。**natural ~,** (old use) physics. (旧用法)物理学。**2** [C] system of thought resulting from such a search for knowledge: (由此研究所得之)思想体系; 原理; 原则; 人生观: *conflicting philosophies;* 互相矛盾的思想体系; *a man without a ~,* with no views upon the problems of life. 没有人生观的人。**3** [U] calm, quiet attitude towards life, even in the face of unhappiness, danger, difficulty, etc. 达观; 冷静; 沉着。**philo·sophi·cal** /ˌfɪlə'sɒfɪkl; ˌfɪlə'safɪkl̩/ *adj* **1** of, devoted to,

guided by, **~**. 哲学的; 专心于哲学的; 以哲学为准则的。逆**2** resigned; of or like a philosopher: 忍从的; 豁达的: 逆来顺受的; 豁达的。**philo·sophi·cally** /-klɪ; -klɪ/ *adv* **phil·os·ophize** /fɪ'lɒsəfaɪz; fə'lɑsəˌfaɪz/ *vi* [VP2A] think or argue like a philosopher; discuss, speculate about, a theory in **~**. 象哲学家那样思考或辩论; 讨论哲理; 默想哲理。

philtre (US = **phil·ter**) /'fɪltə(r); 'fɪltə/ *n* [C] love-potion. 春药; 媚药。

phleb·itis /flɪ'baɪtɪs; flɪ'baɪtɪs/ *n* inflammation of a vein. 静脉炎。

phlegm /flem; flɛm/ *n* [U] **1** thick, semi-fluid substance forming abnormally in the respiratory passages, and brought up by coughing. 痰。**2** quality of being slow to act, or to feel and show emotion or interest. 迟钝; 冷漠; 冷静。**phleg·matic** /fleg'mætɪk; flɛg'mætɪk/ *adj* having the quality of **~**(2): 迟钝的; 冷漠的; 冷静的: *Not all English people are ~atic.* 并非所有英国人都是冷漠的。**phleg·mat·i·cally** /-klɪ; -klɪ/ *adv*

phlox /flɒks; flɑks/ *n* [U] kinds of garden plant with clusters of flowers in various colours. 草夹竹桃。

pho·bia /'fəubɪə; 'fobɪə/ *n* morbid or pathological fear and dislike; aversion. (病态的)恐惧; 憎恶; 恐怖症。

phoe·nix /'fiːnɪks; 'finɪks/ *n* mythical bird which, after living hundreds of years in the Arabian desert, burnt itself on a funeral pile and rose from the ashes young again, to live for another cycle. 长生鸟(神话中的鸟, 在阿拉伯沙漠活了数百年后, 自焚于火葬柴堆, 复自灰中新生, 再开始另一循环)。

phone[1] /fəun; fon/ *n, vt, vi* (colloq abbr for) telephone. (口) telephone 之略。**'~·booth** *n* telephone kiosk; call-box. 电话亭; 公共电话间。**'~·call** *n* telephone call. 打电话。**'~-in** *n* radio/television programme in which listeners/viewers participate by telephone. 由听(观)众借电话参与的广播(电视)节目。

phone[2] /fəun; fon/ *n* (ling) single speech-sound (vowel or consonant). (语言)单音(元音或辅音)。

pho·neme /'fəuniːm; 'fonim/ *n* [C] (ling) unit of the system of sounds of a language: (语言)音位; 音素(某一语言的语音系统中的一个单元): *English has 24 consonant ~s.* 英语中有二十四个辅音音素。**pho·nemic** /fə'niːmɪk; fo'nimɪk/ *adj* (of transcriptions) providing one symbol for each **~** of the language transcribed (as with the pronunciations in this dictionary). (指标音)音位的(只用一个符号表示一个音素的, 如本词典所用的音标)。**pho·nem·ics** *n* (with *sing v*) study and description of the phonemic systems of languages. (用单数动词)音位学; 音素学。

pho·netic /fə'netɪk; fo'netɪk/ *adj* (ling) (语言) **1** concerned with the sounds of human speech. 语音学的; 语音的。**2** (of transcriptions) providing not only a symbol for each phoneme of the language transcribed but with additional symbols for differences between variations of the same phoneme in different situations. (指标音)表实际语音的(不仅以一个符号表示一个音素, 而且用附加符号表示此音素在不同情况下之不同发音的)。**3** (of a language) having a system of spelling that approximates closely to the sounds represented by the letters used: 拼音的(指语言)拼字与发音相似的: *Spanish spelling is ~.* 西班牙语的拼字与发音相似。**pho·net·ics** *n* (with *sing v*) study and science of speech sounds, their production, and the signs used to represent them. (用单数动词)语音学。**pho·neti·cally** /-klɪ; -klɪ/ *adv* **pho·neti·cian** /ˌfəunɪ'tɪʃn; ˌfonə'tɪʃən/ *n* expert in **~s**. 语音学家。

pho·ney, phony /'fəunɪ; 'fonɪ/ *adj* (colloq) sham; unreal; not genuine. (口)假的; 假冒的; 不真实的。□ *n* **~** person: 虚假的人; 冒充的人; 骗子: *He's a complete ~.* 他是个十足的骗子。

pho·nic /'fɒnɪk; 'fɑnɪk/ *adj* of sound; of vocal sounds. 声音的; 语音的。**~s** *n* (with *sing v*) the use of elementary phonetics in the teaching of reading. (用单数动词)看词

读音法(一种教初学者按照字母及音节的基本语音读出单词的方法)。

pho·no·graph /ˈfəʊnəɡrɑːf US: -ɡræf; ˈfonəˌɡræf/ n (US) record player. (美)唱机;留声机。

pho·nol·ogy /fəˈnɒlədʒɪ; foˈnɑlədʒɪ/ n [U] (ling) scientific study of the organization of speech sounds (including phonemes), esp in particular languages. (语言)音韵学(对某些语言的语音结构之研究)。 **pho·no·logi·cal** /ˌfəʊnəˈlɒdʒɪkl; ˌfonəˈlɑdʒɪkl/ adj

phooey /ˈfuːɪ; ˈfuɪ/ int exclamation of contempt, disbelief or displeasure. 呸! 啐! (表示轻视、不信或失望的感叹词)。

phos·gene /ˈfɒzdʒiːn; ˈfɑsdʒin/ n [U] colourless gas (COCl₂), used as a poison gas and in industry. 氯化碳酰;二氯化碳;氯代碳化甲醯;光气(一种毒气)。

phos·phate /ˈfɒsfeɪt; ˈfɑsfet/ n any salt of phosphoric acid, esp one of the numerous artificial fertilizers containing or composed of various salts of this kind, used widely in agriculture. 磷酸盐;(尤指)含有磷酸盐的肥料;磷肥。

phos·pho·res·cence /ˌfɒsfəˈresns; ˌfɑsfəˈresns/ n [U] the giving out of light without burning, or by gentle burning without heat that can be felt. 发磷光;磷光性;磷光;磷火;鬼火。 **phos·pho·res·cent** /-snt; -snt/ adj giving out light without burning. 发磷光的;磷光性的。

phos·phorus /ˈfɒsfərəs; ˈfɑsfərəs/ n [U] yellowish, nonmetallic, poisonous wax-like element (symbol P) which catches fire easily and gives out a faint light in the dark; red, non-poisonous form used in the manufacture of safety matches. 磷;黄磷;赤磷。 **phos·phoric** /fɒsˈfɒrɪk US: -ˈfɔːr-; fɑsˈfɔrɪk/, **phos·phor·ous** /ˈfɒsfərəs; ˈfɑsfərəs/ adjj relating to or containing ~. 磷的;含磷的。

photo /ˈfəʊtəʊ; ˈfoto/ n (pl ~s /-təʊz; -toz/) (colloq abbr for) photograph. (口) n photograph 之略。

photo- /ˈfəʊtəʊ; ˈfoto/ pref of light or of photography. 表示'光'或'摄影'。 '**~·copy** vt, n [VP6A] (make a) copy of (a document, etc) by a photographic method. (用照相法)影印(文件等);影印本。 Hence, 由此产生, '**~·copier** n (用照相法之)影印机;复印机。 **~·e'lectric** adj: 光电的: ~electric cell, cell or device which emits an electric current when light falls on it, used for many purposes, eg to measure light for photography, to cause a door to open when someone approaches it, to count objects passing before it. 光电管;光电仪(遇到光线即产生电流的装置,用途甚广,如照相时测光,使门在有人接近时自动开启,计算通过该门的物体等)。 ~ '**finish** n (horse-racing) finish so close that only a photograph of the horses as they pass the winning-post can decide the winner. (赛马)摄影终局(指比赛的马匹到达终点时,先后非常接近,唯有从马匹跑过终点标杆时所摄的照片,才能判断获胜者)。 '**~·'genic** /-ˈdʒenɪk; -ˈdʒenɪk/ adj suitable for being photographed; photographing well or effectively. 适于拍照的;可照得好的;上像的。 '**~·sensitize** vt make (sth) sensitive to light. 使(某物)感光灵敏。

photo·graph /ˈfəʊtəɡrɑːf US: -ɡræf; ˈfotəˌɡræf/ n [C] picture recorded by means of the chemical action of light on a specially prepared glass plate or film in a camera, transferred to specially prepared paper. 照片;相片。 □ vt, vi 1 [VP6A] take a ~ of. 拍…的照片;摄影。 2 ~ well /badly, come out well /badly when ~ed. 上(不上)像;照相照得好(不好)。 **photo·grapher** /fəˈtɒɡrəfə(r); fəˈtɑɡrəfə/ n person who takes ~s: 摄影者: amateur and professional ~s. 业余的和职业的摄影者。 Cf 参较 camera man, for cinema and TV. 电影及电视的摄影师。 **photo·gra·phy** /fəˈtɒɡrəfɪ; fəˈtɑɡrəfɪ/ n [U] art or process of taking ~s. 摄影术;摄影。 **photo·graphic** /ˌfəʊtəˈɡræfɪk; ˌfotəˈɡræfɪk/ adj of, related to, used in, taking ~s: 摄影的;摄影用的;与摄影有关的: photographic apparatus /goods /periodicals,

etc. 摄影的器械(器材,杂志等)。 **photo·graphi·cally** /-klɪ; -klɪ/ adv

photo·gra·vure /ˌfəʊtəɡrəˈvjʊə(r); ˌfotəɡrəˈvjʊr/ n [U] process of producing a picture on a metal plate from a photographic negative so that the plate can be used in printing; [C] picture printed from such a plate. 照相制版法;照相版印成的图画。

photo·li·tho·gra·phy /ˌfəʊtəʊlɪˈθɒɡrəfɪ; ˌfotəlɪˈθɑɡrəfɪ/ n [U] process of reproducing on plates (stone or zinc) by means of photography. 照相石(锌)版法;照相石(锌)版术;照相平版印刷术。

photo·meter /fəʊˈtɒmɪtə(r); foˈtɑmətə/ n device for measuring the intensity of light. 测光表;曝光表。

photon /ˈfəʊtɒn; ˈfotɑn/ n (phys) unit of quantity of energy in light. (物理)光量子;光子。

photo·stat /ˈfəʊtəstæt; ˈfotəˌstæt/ vt, n (P) (商标) = photocopy.

photo·syn·thesis /ˌfəʊtəʊˈsɪnθəsɪs; ˌfotəˈsɪnθəsɪs/ n [U] process by which the energy of sunlight is used by a green plant to keep it growing. 光合作用。

phrase /freɪz; frez/ n [C] 1 group of words (often without a finite v) forming part of a sentence, eg in the garden, in order to. 短语(常无限定动词,构成句的一部分,如 in the garden, in order to)。 '**~·book** n one containing and explaining (or giving equivalents of in another language) ~s of a language: 短语集(收集短语并加以解释,或与其他语言中的短语对照): an English-Polish ~book. 英波短语集。 2 striking, clever way of saying sth. (简明的)警句。 3 (music) short, independent passage forming part of a longer passage. (音乐)乐句;分句。 □ vt [VP6A] express in words: 用语表示;措词: a neatly ~d compliment. 措辞简洁的赞语。 **phrasal** /ˈfreɪzl; ˈfrezl/ adj in the form of a ~: 短语的;短语形式的: phrasal verbs, eg go in for, fall over, blow up. 短语形式的动词(如 go in for, fall over, blow up)。 **phras·eol·ogy** /ˌfreɪzɪˈɒlədʒɪ; ˌfrezɪˈɑlədʒɪ/ n [U] choice of words; wording.措辞;用词;用语。

phren·etic /frəˈnetɪk; frɪˈnetɪk/ adj = frenetic.

phren·ol·ogy /frəˈnɒlədʒɪ; frəˈnɑlədʒɪ/ n [U] the judging of a person's character, capabilities, etc from an examination of the shape of his skull. 颅相学(由熟骨的形状判断一个人的性格,能力等)。 **phren·ol·o·gist** /-ɪst; -ɪst/ n person who practises ~.颅相学家。

phthi·sis /ˈθaɪsɪs; ˈθaɪsɪs/ n [C] tuberculosis of the lungs. 肺痨;肺结核。

phut /fʌt; fʌt/ adv go ~, (lit or fig) (colloq) collapse; break down: (字面或喻)(口)崩溃;破裂;坏掉: My record player has /holiday plans have gone ~. 我的唱机坏了(度假计划泡汤了)。

phylum /ˈfaɪləm; ˈfaɪləm/ n (biol) highest division in the animal kingdom. (生物)门(为动物之最高分类)。

physic /ˈfɪzɪk; ˈfɪzɪk/ n 1 (archaic) medicine. (古)药。 2 (pl) (复) = physics.

physi·cal /ˈfɪzɪkl; ˈfɪzɪkl/ adj 1 of material (contrasted with moral and spiritual) things: 物质的(与道德及精神相对): the ~ world /universe; 外界; 物质世界; ~ force. 物质的力量。 2 of the body; bodily: 身体的; 肉体的: ~ exercise, eg walking, playing football; 运动(如散步、踢足球); ~ education. 体育。 3 of the laws of nature: 自然律的: It's a ~ impossibility to be in two places at once. 同时在两地是自然律上不可能的事。 4 of the natural features of the world: 地球之自然特征的: ~ geography, of the earth's structure. 地文学; 自然地理。 **~·ly** /-klɪ; -klɪ/ adv

phys·ician /fɪˈzɪʃn; fəˈzɪʃən/ n person qualified to practise both medicine and surgery. 医生。

physi·cist /ˈfɪzɪsɪst; ˈfɪzəsɪst/ n expert in, student of, physics. 物理学家;研究物理学之人。

phys·ics /ˈfɪzɪks; ˈfɪzɪks/ n (with sing v) group of sciences dealing with matter and energy (eg heat, light, sound), but usu excluding chemistry and biology: (用单数动词)物理学: P~ is taught by Professor Molecule.

物理学是莫立逑尔教授教的。

physi·og·nomy /ˌfɪzɪ'ɒnəmɪ *US:* -'ɒgnəʊmɪ; ˌfɪzɪ'ɑgnəmɪ/ *n* (*pl* **-mies**) [C, U] (art of judging character from the features of) the face; general features of a country. 相面术; 相貌; 脸; 国家的地势。

physi·ol·ogy /ˌfɪzɪ'ɒlədʒɪ; fɪzɪ'ɑlədʒɪ/ *n* [U] science of the normal functions of living things, esp animals. 生理学; (尤指)动物生理学。**physi·ol·ogist** /-ɪst; -ɪst/ *n* expert in, student of, ~. 生理学家; 研究生理学的人。**physio·logi·cal** /ˌfɪzɪə'lɒdʒɪkl; ˌfɪzɪə'lɑdʒɪkl/ *adj*

physio·ther·apy /ˌfɪzɪəʊ'θerəpɪ; ˌfɪzɪo'θɛrəpɪ/ *n* [U] treatment of disease by means of exercise, massage, the use of light, heat, electricity and other natural forces. 物理治疗法(借运动、按摩或使用光、热、电及其他自然力量治疗疾病之法)。**physio·thera·pist** *n* person trained to give such treatment. 物理治疗师; 物理治疗家。

phy·sique /fɪ'zi:k; fɪ'zik/ *n* [U, C] structure and development of the body: 体格; 身体的构造与发育: *a man of strong* ~. 体格强壮的人。

pi /paɪ; paɪ/ *n* the Greek letter p (π), esp (maths) as a symbol of the ratio of the circumference of a circle to its diameter (ie 3.14159). 希腊字母 p (π); (尤指)(数学)圆周率(为圆周与直径之比, 其值为 3.14159) 的符号。⇨ **App 4.** 参看附录四。

pi·ano[1] /'pjɑ:nəʊ; pɪ'ɑno/ *adv, adj* (music) soft(ly). (音乐)弱; 轻; 柔和; 温和。**pia·nis·simo** /pjæ'nɪsɪməʊ; ˌpiə'nɪsəˌmo/ *adv, adj* very soft(ly). 最轻; 最弱。

pi·ano[2] /pɪ'ænəʊ; pɪ'æno/ *n* (*pl* ~**s** /-nəʊz; -noz/) musical instrument in which stretched metal strings are struck by hammers operated by keys. 钢琴。⇨ the illus at **keyboard.** 参看 keyboard 之插图。**cottage ~,** small upright ~. 竖式小钢琴。**grand ~, ~** with horizontal strings. 大钢琴(即平台钢琴)。**upright ~,** one with vertical strings. 竖式钢琴。**pia·nist** /'pɪənɪst; pɪ'ænɪst/ *n* person who plays the ~. 钢琴弹奏者; 钢琴家。**piano·forte** /pɪˌænəʊ'fɔ:tɪ *US:* pɪ'ænəfɔ:rt; pɪ'ænəˌfort/ *n* (full name, now formal, for) ~. 钢琴(钢琴的全名, 现在为钢琴的正式名称)。**pia·nola** /pɪə'nəʊlə; ˌpiə'nolə/ *n* (P) ~ operated mechanically. (商标)一种附有自奏机的钢琴; 自动钢琴。

pi·astre (US = **pi·as·ter**) /pɪ'æstə(r); pɪ'æstə/ *n* unit of currency in some countries in the Middle East. 中东某些国家的货币单位。

pi·azza /pɪ'ætsə; pɪ'æzə/ *n* **1** public square or market-place, esp in an Italian town. (尤指意大利城市内的)公共广场; 市场。**2** (US) veranda. (美)走廊。

pi·broch /'pi:brɒk; 'pibrɑk/ *n* piece of martial music for the bagpipes. 风笛变奏曲。

pica /'paɪkə; 'paɪkə/ *n* printer's unit for the size of type[1](3). 派卡(印刷商计算活字大小的单位, 等于 12 point); 十二磅大的活字。

pica·dor /'pɪkədɔ:(r); 'pɪkəˌdɔr/ *n* man (mounted on a horse) who uses a lance to incite and weaken bulls in the sport of bull-fighting. (以矛刺牛使之激怒及衰弱的)骑马的斗牛士。

pic·ar·esque /ˌpɪkə'resk; ˌpɪkə'rɛsk/ *adj* (of a style of fiction) dealing with the adventures of rogues and vagabonds. (指小说文体) 以恶徒及流浪者之冒险事迹为题材的。

pic·ca·lilli /ˌpɪkə'lɪlɪ; ˌpɪkə'lɪlɪ/ *n* [U] kind of hot-tasting pickle made of chopped vegetables, spices in mustard, vinegar, etc. 辛辣的泡菜(以切碎的蔬菜、香料、芥末、醋等制成)。

pic·ca·ninny /ˌpɪkə'nɪnɪ *US:* 'pɪkənɪnɪ; 'pɪkəˌnɪnɪ/ *n* (*pl* **-nies**) (old use) small child, esp a Negro baby. (旧用法)小孩; (尤指)黑人小孩。

pic·colo /'pɪkələʊ; 'pɪkəˌlo/ *n* (*pl* ~**s** /-ləʊz; -loz/) small flute producing notes an octave higher than those of the ordinary flute. 短笛(其音度较长笛高出一倍)。⇨ the illus at **brass.** 参看 brass 之插图。

pick[1] /pɪk; pɪk/ *n* picking; selection. 挑选; 选择。***the ~ of,*** the best (part) of a collection of things or people. 最优部份; 最优秀的份子。

pick[2] /pɪk; pɪk/ *n* **1** **'~(-axe),** heavy tool with an iron head having two pointed ends, used for breaking up hard surfaces. 镐; 尖锄; 鹤嘴锄。⇨ the illus at **tool.** 参看 tool 之插图。**2** small, sharp-pointed instrument: 尖锐的小工具: *an 'ice-~;* 冰凿子; *a 'tooth~.* 牙签。

pick[3] /pɪk; pɪk/ *vt, vi* (For special uses with *adverbial particles* and *preps,* ⇨ 7 below.) (与副词性小品词及介词连用的特殊用法参看下列第 7 义。) **1** [VP6A] take up, remove, pull away, with the fingers: (以手指)采; 摘; 取去: ~ *flowers,* gather flowers; 摘花; 采花; ~ *fruit,* take fruit from the bush or tree; 摘水果; ~ *a thread from one's coat;* 从外套上拔下一根线; ~ *one's nose,* remove bits of dried mucus from the nostrils. 挖鼻孔。***~ sb's brains,*** get ideas and information from sb. 剽窃某人的思想。***~ sb's pocket,*** steel sth from it. 窃取某人口袋内的东西; 扒某人的口袋。Hence, 由此产生, **'~·pocket** *n* person who ~s pockets. 扒手。***~ and steal,*** pilfer. 扒窃。**2** [VP6A] tear or separate; use a pointed instrument to clean, etc: 撕; 扯; 剔; 挖: ~ *rags,* tear them to small pieces; 撕破布; ~ *one's teeth,* get bits of food from the spaces between them, etc by using a pointed stick of wood *(a 'toothpick);* (以牙签 toothpick) 剔牙; ~ *a lock.* use a pointed tool, a piece of wire, etc to unlock it without a key; 撬开锁; ~ *a bone,* get all the meat from it. 啃骨头(啃食骨头上的肉)。***have a 'bone to ~ with sb,*** ⇨ **bone(1).** **3** [VP6A] choose; select: 挑选; 选择: ~ *only the best;* 只挑最好的; ~ *one's words,* choose those words that express one's meaning best, that will not cause offence etc (according to context); 慎选最适当的字眼; 注意措词; ~ *one's way along a muddy road;* 在泥泞的路上选择可走的路; ~ *sides,* choose players for the two teams in a game (of football, cricket, etc) or competition; (足球、板球等比赛或竞赛时)挑选两队选手; ~ *the winning horse/~ the winner,* make a successful guess at the winner (before the race). (赛马之前)挑中获胜的马(获胜者)。***~ a quarrel with sb,*** bring about a quarrel intentionally. 向某人挑衅; 故意和某人争吵。**4** [VP6A] make by ~ing: 剔成; 挖成; 凿成: ~ *holes in sth.* 在某物上凿洞。***~ holes in an argument,*** (fig) find its weak points. (喻)在辩论中找漏洞。**5** [VP6A] (of birds) take up (grain, etc) in the bill; peck; (of persons) eat (food, etc) in small amounts; (指鸟)啄食(谷物等); (指人)一点一点地吃(食物等)。[VP3A] ***~ at,*** eat without interest or appetite: 不感兴趣或没食欲地吃: *She only ~ed at 'her food.* 她只吃了一点点食物。**6** (US) pluck (the strings of): (美)弹奏; 拨奏(琴弦): ~ *a banjo/the strings of a banjo.* 弹奏五弦琴。**7** [VP3A, 15B] (special uses with *adverbial particles* and *preps*): (与副词性小品词及介词连用的特殊用法):

pick at sb, (colloq) nag at; find fault with: (口)挑剔; 找毛病: *Why are you always ~ing at the poor child?* 你为什么总是找那个可怜的小孩的毛病?

pick sth off, take or pluck off. 摘去。***~ sb off,*** shoot him with deliberate aim: 瞄准射死某人: *A sniper behind the bushes ~ed off three of our men.* 藏在树丛后面的一个狙击手射死了我方三个人。

pick on sb, single out, esp for sth unpleasant: 挑选某人(尤指挑选去做不愉快的事): *Why should you ~ on me to do the chores?* 你为什么要挑我去做那些杂务?

pick sb/sth out, **(a)** choose. 选择; 选拔。**(b)** distinguish from surrounding persons, objects, etc: 分辨出: ~ *out one's friends in a crowd.* 在人群中辨出自己的朋友。***~ sth out,*** **(a)** make out, see, (the meaning of a passage, etc) by careful study. 了解; 领会(一段文字的含义等)。**(b)** play (a tune) by ear on a piano, etc. 凭听过后的记忆而弹奏(曲子)。**(c)** relieve (one colour, the ground colour) with touches of a different colour: 衬托; 使(一种颜色、底色)明显: *green panels ~ed out with brown.* 以褐色衬托的绿镶板。

pick sth over, examine and make a selection from: 检

查并从中挑选: ～ *over a basket of strawberries*, eg to throw out any that are bad. 拣选一篮草莓(把坏的挑掉)。

pick sth up, (a) break up (ground) with a pick-axe. 用尖锄掘(地)。 **(b)** take hold of and lift: 拾起; 捡起: ～ *up one's hat / parcels, etc.* 拾起帽子(包裹等)。 **(c)** gain; acquire: 得到; 获得: ～ *up a foreign language*, learn it without taking lessons or studying; 自学学得一种外语; ～ *up a livelihood by selling things from door to door;* 挨家售卖东西谋生; ～ *up bits of information;* 得到一些消息; 获得点滴的资料; ～ *up a bargain at an auction sale.* 在拍卖时买到便宜货。 *The locomotive ～s up current from a third rail.* 火车机车从第三轨获得电力。 **(d)** succeed in seeing or hearing (by means of apparatus): (借着仪器)看到; 听到; 侦得: *enemy planes ～ed up by our searchlights / radar installations, etc.* 被我们的探照灯照到(雷达测得等)的敌机。 **(e)** recover; regain: 恢复; 重获: *You'll soon ～ up health when you get to the seaside.* 你到了海滨, 就会很快地恢复健康。 ～ *sb up, (a)* take the acquaintance of casually: 偶然结识: *a girl he ～ed up on the street.* 他在街上邂逅的女孩子。 **(b)** take (persons) along with one: 搭载(人); 带(人)走: *He stopped the car to ～ up a young girl who was hitch-hiking across Europe.* 他停下车来搭载一个乘便车旅行欧洲的年轻女郎。 *The escaped prisoner was ～ed up* (= seen and arrested) *by the police at Hull.* 逃犯在赫尔被警察逮到了。 ～ *oneself up*, raise (oneself) after a fall: 跌倒后自己站起来: *She slipped and fell but quickly ～ed herself up.* 她滑了一跤, 但是很快地站了起来。 ～ *up (health)*, recover health; improve: 恢复健康; 健康进步: *He's beginning to ～ up now.* 他现在已经在好起来了。 ～ *up speed*, gain speed. 加速。 ～ *up with sb*, make acquaintance with: 结识; 与…交朋友: *Where did you ～ up with that queer fellow?* 你在什么地方结识那个怪家伙的?' '～-**up** *n* (*pl* ～-**ups**) **(a)** that part of a record-player that holds the stylus. 唱头(电唱机之装置唱针的部分)。 **(b)** small general-purpose van or truck, open and with low sides, (eg as used by builders, farmers, etc, for carrying merchandise). 小型轻载汽车(如建筑商、农夫等用于载货的车子)。 **(c)** (sl) person whose acquaintance is made casually. (俚)偶然认识的人。 **(d)** acceleration: 加速: *an engine / car with a good ～-up.* 加速效能良好的引擎(车子)。 '～-**me-up** /'pɪk mi ʌp; 'pɪkmɪʌp/ *n* sth, eg a drink, that gives new strength and cheerfulness. 增加精力或使人愉快之物(如饮料); 提神酒。

picka·back /'pɪkəbæk; 'pɪkə,bæk/ *adv* (eg of the way a child is carried) on the shoulders or back like a bundle. 在肩上; 在背上(如背小孩的方式)。

picker /'pɪkə(r); 'pɪkɚ/ *n* person or thing that picks (chiefly in compounds): 采摘者; 捡拾器(主要用于复合词中): '*hop~s;* 蛇麻子采集人(机); '*rag~s.* 拾荒者; 捡破烂的人。

pick·erel /'pɪkərəl; 'pɪkərəl/ *n* (*pl* unchanged) young pike. (复数不变)小梭鱼。

picket /'pɪkɪt; 'pɪkɪt/ *n* **1** pointed stake, etc set upright in the ground (as part of a fence, or to tether a horse to). (篱笆间或系马用的)尖桩。 **2** small group of men on police duty, or sent out to watch the enemy. 哨; 哨兵。 **3** worker, or group of workers, stationed at the gates of a factory, dock-yard, etc during a strike, to try to persuade others not to go to work: 罢工时守在工厂等门口劝阻他人上班的工人; 罢工纠察员: *a '～ line*, line of ～s, eg outside a factory. 罢工时在工厂外面等劝阻他人上班的一排工人; 一排罢工纠察员。 *flying ～*, formed of workers who do not work at the place where the ～ is stationed. 由他处工人组织的罢工纠察队。 □ *vt, vi* [VP6A, 2A] **1** guard with ～s: 用～守卫: *～ a factory.* 派纠察员守卫工厂。 ～-*vt* **1** round; tether (a horse) to a ～ (1). 围以尖桩; 系(马)于尖桩。 **2** place ～s(2) in or round; station (men) as ～s. 配置哨兵; 放哨; 派(人)为哨兵。 **3** place ～s(3) at: 配置罢工纠察员于: *～ a factory.* 在一家工厂配置罢工纠察员; act as a ～(3). 担任罢工纠察员。

pick·ing /'pɪkɪŋ; 'pɪkɪŋ/ *n* **1** [U] act of picking. 采摘; 窃取; 选择; 凿掘。 ～ *and stealing*, stealing cheap things. 扒窃(廉价物品); 偷窃。 **2** (*pl*) things left over from which profits may be made; these profits; profits made from stealing cheap things. (复)尚可获得利益的剩余物; 从剩余物所获得之利益; 由扒窃所得的利益。

pickle /'pɪkl; 'pɪkl/ *n* **1** [U] salt water, vinegar, etc for keeping meat, vegetables, etc, in good condition. (腌肉、泡菜等的)腌汁; 泡菜水。 *have a rod in ～ for sb*, ⇨ **rod**. **2** (usu *pl*) vegetables kept in ～: (通常用复数)泡菜: *onion ～s.* 泡洋葱。 **3** *in a sad / sorry / nice ～*, in a sad, etc plight. 处于困难的境地; 处境困难。 □ *vt* [VP6A] **1** preserve in ～: 腌; 泡: ～*d onions / walnuts.* 腌泡的洋葱(胡桃)。 **2** ～*d pp* (sl) drunk. (俚)醉的。

pic·nic /'pɪknɪk; 'pɪknɪk/ *n* **1** pleasure trip on which food is carried to be eaten outdoors: 野餐: *have / go for a ～;* 举行(去)野餐; (attrib) (用作定语) *a '～ hamper*, one for holding food, dishes, etc. 野餐用的篮子。 **2** (colloq) sth easy and enjoyable: (口)轻松而愉快的事物: *It's no ～, is not an easy job.* 那不是容易的工作。 □ *vi* (**-ck-**) take part in a ～: 参加野餐; 去野餐: ～ *in the woods.* 在森林中野餐。 **pic·nicker** *n* person who ～s. 野餐者。

pic·ric /'pɪkrɪk; 'pɪkrɪk/ *adj* ～ *acid*, acid used in dyeing, explosives and antiseptics. 苦味酸(用于染物、制造炸药、防腐等)。

pic·tor·ial /pɪk'tɔːrɪəl; pɪk'tɔrɪəl/ *adj* of, having, represented in, pictures: 图画的; 有图的; 以图画表示的: *a ～ record of the wedding.* 婚礼的图片记录。 □ *n* periodical in which pictures are the main feature. 画刊; 图画杂志。

pic·ture /'pɪktʃə(r); 'pɪktʃɚ/ *n* **1** painting, drawing, sketch, of sth, esp as a work of art. 画; 图画(尤指艺术作品)。 '～-**book** *n* book consisting mainly of ～s, esp one for children. 图画书(尤指供儿童阅读者)。 '～-**card** *n* (in playing cards) court-card; one with a king, queen or knave on it. (纸牌中)花牌(上面有 king, queen 或 knave 之牌)。 '～-**gallery** *n* room or building in which ～s are exhibited. 图画陈列室; 画廊。 '～ *hat*, woman's hat with a very wide brim. (女人戴的)宽边帽。 **2** beautiful scene, object, person, etc. 美丽的景色、物品、人等。 **3** type or embodiment. 典型; 化身。 *be the ～ of health*, appear to have it in a high degree. 健康良好。 **4** (fig) account or description that enables sb to see in his mind an event, etc. (喻)(使人明白某事件等的)陈述; 描写。 *be / put sb in the ～*, be / cause sb to be well informed, aware of all the facts of a situation. (使某人)了解实情。 **5** film (to be) shown in a cinema. 影片; 电影。 *the ～s*, the cinema: 电影: *We don't often go to the ～s,* 我们不常去看电影。 **6** what is seen on a television screen: 电视图像: *a set free from ～ distortion.* 画面不会失真的电视机。 □ *vt* **1** [VP6A] make a ～ of; paint. 绘画。 **2** [VP14] ～ *sth to oneself*, imagine: 想象: *He to himself what it might be like to live in Java.* 他想象生活在爪哇的情况。

pic·tur·esque /ˌpɪktʃə'resk; ˌpɪktʃə'rɛsk/ *adj* **1** having the quality of being like, or of being fit to be, the subject of a painting: 如画的; 可入画的: *a ～ village.* 风景如画的村庄。 **2** quaint; vivid; graphic: 有趣的; 逼真的: ～ *language.* 生动的言词。 **3** (of a person, his character) striking; original. (指人、性格)引人注意的; 独特的。 ～·**ly** *adv* ～·**ness** *n*

piddle /'pɪdl; 'pɪdl/ *vi, n* (colloq) (pass) urine. (口)(解)小便。

pid·dling /'pɪdlɪŋ; 'pɪdlɪŋ/ *adj* trifling; insignificant: 微小的; 不重要的: ～ *jobs.* 小差事; 琐碎的工作。

pidgin /'pɪdʒɪn; 'pɪdʒɪn/ *n* **1** any of several languages resulting from contact between European traders and local peoples, eg in West Africa and the Far East, containing elements of the local language(s) and English, French or Dutch, still used for internal communication.

洋泾浜语；不纯正的英、法或荷兰语(原为西非及远东地区的人与欧洲商人交谈时用的不纯正英语、法语或荷兰语，现仍用于其国内)。**2** 'one's **~**, (colloq) one's job or concern: (口)自己的事；与自己有关的事: *Don't ask me; that's 'your ~.* 别问我，那是你的事。

pie /paɪ; paɪ/ n [C, U] meat or fruit covered with pastry and baked in a deep dish: 以肉或水果为馅的烤饼；馅饼: *fruit pies;* 水果馅饼; *a meat pie;* 肉馅饼; *eat too much pie.* 吃太多馅饼。 ⇨ **flan, tart**[2]. *have a finger in the/every pie,* be concerned in the/every matter (esp in an officious way). 干预某事；参与某事；管闲事。 *as easy as pie,* (sl) very easy. (俚)极容易。 *pie in the sky,* happiness in Heaven; unrealistic hopes. 天堂之乐；不切合实际的希望；空头支票。 '**pie-crust** n [U] baked paste of a pie. 馅饼皮。

pie·bald /'paɪbɔːld; 'paɪˌbɔld/ adj (of a horse) having white and dark patches of irregular shape. (指马)黑白斑驳的。

piece[1] /piːs; pis/ n **1** part or bit of a solid substance (complete in itself, but broken, separated or made from a larger portion): 块；片；段；断片；部分: *a ~ of paper/wood/glass/chalk.* 一张纸／一块木头／一片玻璃／一支粉笔。 *Will you have another ~* (= slice) *of cake?* 你要不要再吃一块蛋糕? *This ~ of string is too short.* 这根绳子太短。 *(be) in ~s,* broken; dismantled: 破碎了；拆散了: *The vase is in ~s.* 这花瓶破了。 *break (sth) to ~s,* be in ~s as the result of an accident: 打裂；打碎: *The teapot fell and was broken to ~s.* 茶壶掉在地上打碎了。 *come/take (sth) to ~s,* divide (sth) into the parts which make it up: 拆开；分散: *Does this machine come/take to ~s?* 这部机器能拆开吗? *go (all) to ~s,* (colloq) (of a person) break up physically, mentally or morally. (口)(指人的)身体、精神或道德)崩溃。 *a ~ of cake,* (sl) sth very easy. (俚)容易的事。 *~ by ~,* one at a time. 一块一块地；一片一片地。 *of a ~ (with sth),* (fig) of the same character (as); consistent (with); in keeping (with). (喻)(与…)同性质的；(与…)一致的。 **2** separate instance or example: 个别的事例: *a ~ of news/luck/advice/information, etc;* 一条新闻／一件幸事／一项忠告／一项消息等)；single article: 一件东西: *a ~ of furniture.* 一件家具。 *give sb a ~ of one's mind,* tell him candidly what one thinks of him. 坦白告诉某人对他的看法。 *say one's ~,* say what one has to say, sth one has learnt to say, eg a poem to be recited. 说出自己准备说的话(如讲读一首诗)。 **3** standard length or quantity in which goods are prepared for distribution: (指物品长度或数量标准的)件；个；份；块: *a ~ of wallpaper* (usu 12 yds); 一张壁纸(通常为十二码); *a ~ of cloth;* 一块布; *sold only by the ~.* 只论个或件实卖的。 '**~-goods** n pl textile fabrics (esp cotton and silk) made in standard lengths. (标准长度的)布匹(尤指棉布和丝的布匹)。 **4** single composition (in art, music, etc): (艺术品、音乐等的)幅；篇；首: *a fine ~ of work/music/poetry,* 一件完美的作品／一支优美的乐曲／一首好诗; *a dramatic ~.* 一部剧本。 **5** single thing out of a set: (一套中的)件；个: *a dinner service of 50 ~s;* 一套五十件的餐具; one of the wooden, metal, etc objects moved on a board in such games as chess. (棋类等的)棋子。 **6** coin: 硬币: *a ten-pence ~;* 十便士的硬币; *a five cent ~;* 五分的硬币; *a ~ of eight,* an old Spanish silver coin. 西班牙昔时的一种银币(等于8 reals)。 **7** gun: 枪炮: *a fixed-~,* field-gun; 野战炮; a 'fowling-~,* for shooting game. 鸟枪。 **8** (fixed or agreed) amount of work to be done: (工作的)件: *pay a workman by the ~,* according to the work produced (not by the time taken). 按件计酬。 Hence, 由此产生, '**~-work** ⇨ *time-work* at **time**[1](13). **9** (in compounds) (用于复合词中) **(a)** (player of a) musical instrument: 乐器(的演奏者): *a six-~ jazz group.* 六人组成的爵士乐队。 **(b)** item in collection: 一套: *a 25-piece dinner service,* ⇨ **service**(7).

piece[2] /piːs; pis/ vt [VP6A, 15A, B] **~ (together).** put (parts, etc) together; make by joining or adding (pieces) together: 凑合；凑成: *~ together odds and ends of cloth;* 把零碎的布拼凑在一起; *a quilt;* make one by putting ~s together; 将零碎布头而缝成一床棉被; *one thing to another.* 把一件东西拼合到另一件东西上。 *~ sth out,* make (a story, theory etc) complete by connecting the parts. 借凑连各部分而完成(故事、理论等)。

piece·meal /'piːsmiːl; 'pisˌmil/ adv piece by piece; a part at a time: 一件一件地; 零碎地: *work done by ~.* 零碎做成的工作。 □ adj coming, done, etc piece by piece. 一件一件的; 零碎的。

pied /paɪd; paɪd/ adj of mixed colours, of black and white, of birds. (指鸟等)杂色的; 黑白的。

pied-à-terre /ˌpjeɪd ɑː 'teə(r); ˌpjedɑˈtɛr/ n (F) extra room(s) or house which one keeps for use when needed: (法)备用的房屋; 临时休息处: *He lives in the country, and has a ~ in London.* 他住在乡间，而在伦敦有个临时的住所。

pier /pɪə(r); pɪr/ n **1** structure of wood, iron, etc built out into the sea as a landing-stage; similar structure for walking on for pleasure (with a pavilion, restaurant, etc). 码头(供旅客、货物上下或供人散步游乐用，常附有帐篷、餐馆等)。 **2** pillar supporting a span of a bridge, etc. 桥墩; 桥台。 **3** wall between windows or other openings. 窗间壁; 户间壁。 '**~-glass** n large, long mirror in which one can see the whole of oneself. 可照全身的长镜; 穿衣镜。

a pier

pierce /pɪəs; pɪrs/ vt, vi **1** [VP6A] (of sharp-pointed instruments) go into or through; make (a hole) by doing this: (指尖锐工具)戳入; 刺穿; 穿(洞); 穿(孔): *The arrow ~d his shoulder.* 箭射入他的肩膀。 *She had her ears ~d in order to be able to wear earrings.* 她为了能戴耳环而把耳朵穿孔。 **2** [VP6A] (fig, of cold, pain, sounds, etc) force a way into or through; affect deeply: (喻, 指寒冷、痛苦、声音等)刺入; 穿透; 响彻; 深深感动: *Her shrieks ~d the air.* 她的尖叫声响彻长空。 *A ray of light ~d the darkness.* 一道光线穿透黑暗。 **3** [VP2C] penetrate (through, into, etc): 进入; 穿入; 突破(与through, into 等连用): *Our forces ~d through the enemy's lines.* 我军突破了敌人的防线。 **~·ing** adj (esp of cold, voices) sharp; penetrating: (尤指寒冷、声音)刺骨的; 尖锐的: *a piercing wind.* 刺骨的寒风。 **~·ing·ly** adv: *a piercingly cold wind.* 刺骨的寒风。

pier·rot /'pɪərəʊ; ˌpjɛˈro/ n **1** character in French pantomime. (法国哑剧中的)丑角。 **2** member of a group of entertainers (esp at seaside resorts), dressed in loose white clothes and with a whitened face. 穿宽松白衣而涂白色的表演者(尤指在海滨游乐场所献艺者)。

pietà /ˌpiːeɪˈtɑː; pjeˈtɑ/ n (I) painting or sculpture of the Virgin Mary holding the dead body of Jesus in her lap. (意)圣母玛利亚抱耶稣尸体于膝上的画像或雕像。

piety /'paɪətɪ; 'paɪətɪ/ n **1** [U] devotion to God and good works; being pious. 虔敬; 虔诚。 **filial ~,** correct behaviour towards a parent. 孝道; 孝顺。 **2** [C] (pl -ties) act, etc that shows ~. 虔诚的行为; 孝行。

piffle /'pɪfl; 'pɪfl/ n [U] (colloq) nonsense. (口)废话; 无聊的话; 胡说八道。 □ vi talk ~. 胡说; 胡扯。

pif·fling /'pɪflɪŋ; 'pɪflɪŋ/ adj trivial; worthless. 琐屑的; 无价值的; 无聊的。

pig /pɪg; pɪg/ n **1** [C] domestic and wild animal, ⇨ the illus at **domestic;** 猪(参看 domestic 之插图); ⇨

boar, hog, sow¹, swine; [U] its flesh (esp *roast pig*) as meat. 猪肉(尤指烤猪肉). ⇨ **bacon, ham, pork, bring one's pigs to the wrong market,** fail in an undertaking (to sell sth). 卖东西吃亏。*buy a pig in a poke,* buy sth without seeing it or knowing its value, which turns out to be worth less than one paid for it. 乱买；瞎买。*pigs might fly,* (expressing disbelief) wonders might happen. (表示不相信)奇迹很少发生；不可能的. '**pig‧boat** *n* (US sl) submarine. (美俚) 潜水艇. ,**pig‧'headed** *adj* stubborn. 顽固的；固执的. ,**pig‧'headedly** *adv* ,**pig‧'headedness** '**pig‧skin** *n* [U] (leather made of a) pig's skin; (sl) saddle. 猪皮；猪革；(俚)马鞍. '**pig‧sticking** *n* [U] the sport of hunting wild boars with spears. 用矛猎野猪。'**pig‧sty** -*sty;* -*staɪ/ n* (a) small building for pigs. 小猪舍；猪栏；猪圈. (b) dirty hovel. 肮脏的住处. '**pig‧tail** *n* plait of hair hanging down over the back of the neck and shoulders. 发辫；辫子. '**pig‧wash, pig‧swill** *nn* [U] waste food (from a brewery or kitchen) given to pigs as food. (给猪吃的)残食；泔脚；猪食. **2** (colloq) dirty, greedy or ill-mannered person. (口)肮脏的人；贪婪的人；粗野的人. *make a 'pig of oneself,* eat or drink to excess. 过分地吃喝。**3** '**pig‧iron** *n* [U] oblong mass of iron extracted from ore and shaped in a mould. 生铁块. □ *vi* (-gg-) *pig it; pig together,* live or herd together in dirty conditions. 住在肮脏的环境里；群居于肮脏的地方. '**pig‧gish** -*ɪʃ/;* -*ɪʃ/ adj* like a pig; dirty, greedy. 象猪的；脏的；贪婪的. **pig‧gish‧ly** *adv* **pig‧gish‧ness** *n* **pig‧gery** /'pɪɡərɪ; 'pɪɡərɪ/ *n*(*pl* -ries)pig-breeding establishment; pig-farm. 养猪的地方；养猪场. **piggy** /'pɪɡɪ; 'pɪɡɪ/ *n* little pig. 小猪. □ *adj* (colloq) greedy. (口)贪婪的. '**piggy‧back,** (US) (美)= **pickaback.** '**piggy bank** *n* model (of a pig) with a slot for coins, used by a child for saving coin money. (储蓄钱用的)扑满.

pigeon /'pɪdʒɪn; 'pɪdʒən/ *n* **1** bird, wild or tame, of the dove family: 鸽子: '*carrier-~,* '*homing-~,* kind trained to carry messages or bred for sport. 传信鸽；⇨ the illus at **bird.** 参看 bird 之插图. '**~-breasted** *adj* (of a person) having a bulging, convex chest. (指人)有鸽胸的；有鸡胸的. '**~-toed** *adj* (of a person) having the toes turned inwards. (指人)脚趾向内弯的；足内翻的. '**~‧hole** *n* one of a set of small open boxes for keeping papers in. 文件架的格架. □ *vt* put (papers, etc) in a ~-hole and ignore or forget them; postpone consideration of: 将(文件)放在架中并置之不理；搁置: *The scheme was ~holed.* 那计划被搁置了. **2** clay thrown up into the air as a mark for shooting. 飞靶(抛到空中作射击目标的泥饼). **3** simpleton; easily deceived person. 愚人；容易受骗的人. *one's ~,* = *one's pidgin,* ⇨ **pidgin**(2).

pig‧iron /'pɪɡ aɪən; 'pɪɡaɪən/ *n* ⇨ **pig**(3).

pig‧let /'pɪɡlɪt; 'pɪɡlɪt/ *n* young pig. 小猪.

pig‧ment /'pɪɡmənt; 'pɪɡmənt/ *n* **1** [U] colouring matter for making dyes, paint, etc; [C] particular substance used for this. (用于制造染料、油漆等用的)颜料. **2** [U] the natural colouring matter in the skin, hair, etc of living beings. (生物之皮、毛发等的)色素. **pig‧men‧ta‧tion** /,pɪɡmen'teɪʃn/ *n* [U] colouring of tissues by ~. 染色；着色；色素形成.

pigmy /'pɪɡmɪ; 'pɪɡmɪ/ *n* = **pygmy**.

pike¹ /paɪk; paɪk/ *n* long wooden shaft with a spearhead, formerly used by soldiers fighting on foot. 矛；枪(昔时步兵用的武器). '**~‧staff** *n* wooden shaft of a ~. 矛杆；矛柄. *as plain as a ~staff,* quite plain; easy to see or understand. 非常明显的；显而易见的.

pike² /paɪk; paɪk/ *n* (*pl* unchanged) large, fierce, freshwater fish. (复数不变)梭子鱼(一种凶猛的大淡水鱼).

pike³ /paɪk; paɪk/ *n* **1** turnpike road. 收费的公路. **2** toll-bar; toll. 收通行费的关卡；通行费.

pike⁴ /paɪk; paɪk/ *n* (dialect, N of England) peaked top of a hill: (方，英国北部)山峰；尖峰: *Langdale P~.*

兰德尔峰.

pi‧laf(f) /pɪ'læf US: -'lɑːf; pə'lɑf/ = **pilau.**

pi‧las‧ter /pɪ'læstə(r); pə'læstə/ *n* rectangular column, esp an ornamental one that projects from a wall into which it is set. 方形柱；(尤指一半嵌在墙里的)壁柱；半柱.

pi‧lau /pɪ'laʊ; pɪ'laʊ/ (also **pi‧laf(f)** /pɪ'læf US: -'lɑːf; pə'lɑf/) *n* [U] oriental dish of steamed rice with meat, etc. 肉饭.

pil‧chard /'pɪltʃəd; 'pɪltʃəd/ *n* small sea-fish resembling the herring. 类似鲱鱼的一种小海鱼.

pile¹ /paɪl; paɪl/ *n* [C] heavy beam of timber, steel, concrete, etc driven into the ground, esp under water, as a foundation for a building, a support for a bridge, etc. (作墙基、桥基等的)木桩、铁桩、水泥桩等. '**~-driver** *n* machine for driving ~s into the ground. 打桩机. '**~-dwelling** *n* (also called 亦称作 *lake-dwelling*) house resting on ~s, esp at the side of a lake. 建于桩上的房屋(尤指建于湖边者). □ *vt* [VP6A] supply with ~s. 供以桩；打桩于.

pile² /paɪl; paɪl/ *n* **1** number of things lying one upon another: 堆；排；叠: *a ~ of books.* 一堆书. **2** funeral ~, heap of wood, etc on which a corpse is burnt. 火葬的柴堆. **3** (colloq) large amount of money. (口)大量的钱. *make a / one's ~,* earn a lot of money. 发财；赚大钱. **4** large high building or group of buildings. 高大的建筑物；一堆建筑物. **5** dry battery for producing electric current. 一种干电池；电堆. atomic ~, apparatus for the controlled release of atomic energy; nuclear reactor. 核反应器；原子炉.

pile³ /paɪl; paɪl/ *vt, vi* **1** [VP6A, 15A, B] make into ~: put on or in a ~: 堆起；堆叠: ~ *logs;* 堆木头; ~ *up dishes on a table;* 将盘子堆在桌上; ~ *a table with dishes;* 将盘子堆满在桌子上; ~ *more coal on (the fire).* 将煤于(火炉)…. ~ *arms,* place (usu four) rifles together with butts on the ground and muzzles touching. 架枪(通常为四支步枪，枪托触地，枪口靠在一起). ~ *it on,* (colloq) exaggerate. (口)夸张. ~ *on the agony,* (colloq) make a description of a painful event more agonizing than is necessary. (口)把一件惨事描写得格外悲惨. **2** [VP2C] ~ *up,* (a) accumulate: 累积: *My work keeps piling up,* There is more and more work for me to do. 我的工作越来越多. (b) (of a number of vehicles) crash into each other, forming a ~. (指若干车辆)碰撞在一起. Hence, 由此产生, '**~-up** *n* another bad ~-up on the motorway during thick fog. 浓雾中高速公路上又发生了一件严重的连环车祸. **3** ~ *into / out of sth,* enter / leave in a disorderly way: 蜂涌而入(出): *They all ~d into / out of the car / cinema.* 他们一窝蜂地涌进(出)汽车(电影院).

pile⁴ /paɪl; paɪl/ *n* [U] soft, thick, hair-like surface of velvet, some carpets, etc. (天鹅绒，某些地毯等的)绒面；软绒.

piles /paɪlz; paɪlz/ *n* [U] hemorrhoids. 痔疮.

pil‧fer /'pɪlfə(r); 'pɪlfə/ *vt, vi* [VP6A, 2A] steal, esp in small quantities: (尤指小量地)偷窃: ~*ed during transit by rail.* 在火车输送时被窃. ~**er** *n* ~**‧age**/-ɪdʒ; -ɪdʒ/ *n* [U] act of ~ing; loss by ~ing. 偷窃；失窃.

pil‧grim /'pɪlɡrɪm; 'pɪlɡrɪm/ *n* person who travels to a sacred place as an act of religious devotion: 往圣地朝拜者; 朝山进香者: ~*s to Mecca;* 去麦加圣地朝拜者; *the Canterbury ~s,* in England, during the Middle Ages. (英国中古时)往坎特伯雷的朝圣者. **the P~ Fathers,** English Puritans who went to America in 1620 and founded the colony of Plymouth, Massachusetts. 一六二〇年往美洲建立普利茅斯殖民地的英国清教徒. ~**‧age** /-ɪdʒ; -ɪdʒ/ *n* journey of a ~: 朝圣者的旅程: *go on a ~age to Benares.* 往贝拿勒斯朝圣.

pill /pɪl; pɪl/ *n* **1** small ball or tablet of medicine for swallowing whole. 药丸. *a bitter ~ (to swallow),* ⇨ **bitter.** *sugar / sweeten the ~,* make sth disagreeable seem less so. 使令人不愉快之事物较易为人接受. '**~‧box**

n **(a)** small cylindrical box for holding ~s. 装药丸的小圆筒。**(b)** (army use) small (often partly underground) concrete fort. (陆军用语)枪堡(常为部分建于地下者); 掩体。**2 the** ~, oral contraceptive. 口服避孕药。*be* / *go on the* ~, be taking /start to take such ~s regularly. 按时服用(开始服用)避孕药丸。

pil·lage /'pɪlɪdʒ; 'pɪlɪdʒ/ *n, vt* plunder, esp in war 掠夺; (尤指在战争中)抢劫。**pil·lager** /-ɪdʒə(r); -ɪdʒə/ *n* one who ~s. 掠夺者; 抢劫者。

pil·lar /'pɪlə(r); 'pɪlə/ *n* **1** upright column, of stone, wood, metal, etc as a support or ornament. 柱子(作支持或装饰用的石柱、木柱、金属柱等)。⇨ the illus at **church, column.** 参看 church, column 之插图。*from* ~ *to post,* (fig) from one resource to another, to and fro. (喻)从一个地方到另一个地方; 走投无路。**2** (fig) ~ *of,* strong and important supporter: (喻)坚强而重要的支持者; 支柱; 栋梁: *a* ~ *of the establishment.* 这组织的一位强力支持者。**3** '~**-box** *n* cylindrical container (in GB, scarlet) about 5 feet high, standing in a public place, in which letters are posted. 邮筒(英, 深红色)。**4** sth in the shape of a ~, eg a column of fire, smoke, cloud or, in a coalmine, of coal left to support the roof. 柱形物(如火柱、烟柱、云柱或煤矿中留着支持矿顶的煤柱)。

pil·lion /'pɪljən; 'pɪljən/ *n* seat for a second rider behind the rider of a horse; saddle for a passenger behind the driver of a motor-bike: 马鞍后附加的座位; 机器脚踏车的后座; 后座的乘客。*riding* ~; 骑在后座; *the* ~ *passenger.*

pil·lory /'pɪlərɪ; 'pɪlərɪ/ *n* (*pl* **-ries**) wooden framework in which the head and hands of wrongdoers were, in olden times, secured whilst they were ridiculed. 枷(古代的刑具, 系木材制成, 可将犯人的头手夹在其中)。

pil·low /'pɪləʊ; 'pɪlo/ *n* soft cushion for the head, esp when lying in bed. 枕头。'~**-case** / '~**-slip** *n* washable cover for a ~. 枕套。'~**-fight** *n* child's game of fighting with ~s. 枕头战 (儿童互掷枕头的游戏)。□ *vt* [VP6A] rest, support, on or as on a ~; serve as a ~ for. 搁在枕头上; 枕于; 作为…的枕头。

pi·lot /'paɪlət; 'paɪlət/ *n* **1** person trained and licensed to take ships into or out of a harbour, along a river, through a canal, etc. 领港员; 领航员。*drop the* ~, (fig) dismiss a trusted adviser. (喻)开革可信的顾问; 不听忠告。**2** person trained to operate the controls of an aircraft. 飞机驾驶员。**P~ Officer,** lowest commissioned rank in the Royal Air Force, below that of Flying Officer. 英国皇家空军少尉。**3** (attrib) experimental; used to test how sth on a larger scale will work, how it may be improved, etc: 以小规模作试验的: *a* '~ *census* / *survey* / *scheme;* 实验性的人口调查 (测量, 计划); *a* '~ *plant,* for a manufacturing process: 小规模实验的工厂: *a* '~ *tunnel.* 试验性的隧道。**4** (compounds) (复合词) '~**-boat** *n* one which takes ~s to ships. 领港船; 运送领航员到船上的小船。'~**-cloth** *n* [U] blue woollen cloth used for overcoats, etc. (制大衣等的)蓝色呢绒。'~**-engine** *n* railway engine that goes in advance (eg to check for safety). (铁道上作安全检查等而先行的)清路机车; 前导机车。'~**-fish** *n* small fish which often swims in company with larger fish, eg sharks, or sometimes ships. (常伴随鲨鱼或船只等游动的)鲭类海鱼。'~**-light** / '~**-burner** *n* small flame in a gas cooker or lamp, kept burning continuously, which lights large burners, etc when the gas is turned on. (煤气炉或灯中之)点火苗(为着准备点燃大的灯头而不停地燃着的小火种)。□ *vt* [VP6A, 15A] act as a ~ to: 领航; 驾驶: ~ *ships through the Panama Canal.* 引领船只通过巴拿马运河。

pi·mento /pɪ'mentəʊ; pɪ'mɛnto/ *n* (*pl* ~**s** /-təʊz/; -toz/) **1** [U] dried aromatic berries of a West Indian tree, also called *Jamaica pepper* and *all-spice.* 产于西印度群岛的一种胡椒(亦称 Jamaica pepper 与 all-spice)。牙买加胡椒; 甘椒。**2** [C] tree that produces the berries.

牙买加胡椒树; 甘椒树。

pimp /pɪmp; pɪmp/ *n* pander (2). 淫媒; 拉皮条者; 妓院老板。□ *vi* [VP2A, 3A] ~ *(for sb),* act as a ~. 作淫媒; 拉皮条。

pim·per·nel /'pɪmpənel; 'pɪmpə,nɛl/ *n* small annual plant growing wild in wheatfields and on waste land, with scarlet, blue or white flowers. 海绿属植物; 紫繁篓。

pimple /'pɪmpl; 'pɪmpl/ *n* small, hard, inflamed spot on the skin. 丘疹; 粉刺; 面疱。**pim·pled** *adj* having ~s. 有丘疹的; 长面疱的; 长粉刺的。**pim·ply** /'pɪmplɪ; 'pɪmplɪ/ *adj* (**-ier, -iest**) having ~s: 有丘疹的; 长粉刺的: *a pimply boy* / *face.* 长丘疹的男孩(脸)。

pin¹ /pɪn; pɪn/ *n* **1** short, thin piece of stiff wire with a sharp point and a round head, used for fastening together parts of a dress, papers, etc. 大头针。*don't care a pin,* don't care at all. 一点也不在乎。*as a new pin,* very neat. 非常整洁。*pins and needles,* tingling sensation in a part of the body caused by blood flowing again after its circulation has been checked for a time. (身体某部血液受阻一段时间后, 再行流动时所感到的)发麻; 刺麻。**2** similar piece of wire with an ornamental head for special purposes: 饰针; 别针: *a* '*tie-pin;* 领带别针; *a* '*hat-pin.* 帽子饰针。'**safety-pin,** pin bent with a guard at one end to protect and hold fast the point at the other end. 安全别针。⇨ the illus at **safety.** 参看 safety 之插图。**3** peg of wood or metal for various purposes. (木制的或金属的)栓; 钉; 针。⇨ *drawing-pin* at **drawing,** *hairpin* at **hair (2),** *ninepins, rolling-pin* at **roll² (10);** peg round which a string of a musical instrument is fastened. (乐器上系弦的)木栓。'**pin-ball** *n* game played with a small ball which has to be electrically struck against one of several upright knobs, and guided into one of several numbered holes on a sloping board. 弹球戏 (斜板上置若干和数的洞, 电动弹球进洞时需触及钉于板上的钉头)。'**pin-table** *n* table used in pin-ball. 弹球台。**4** (*pl*) (sl) legs: (复)(俚)腿: *He's quick on his* ~*s.* 他走(跑)得快。**5** (compounds) (复合词) '**pin-cushion** *n* pad into which (a dressmaker's) pins are stuck. (裁缝插针用的)针垫。'**pin-head** *n* (colloq) very stupid person. (口)非常愚蠢之人; 傻瓜。'**pin-money** *n* [U] money allowance to, or money earned by, a woman for dress, small personal necessities, etc. (给妇女的)零用钱; (妇女的)私房钱。'**pin-point** *n* sth very small; (attrib; of targets) requiring accurate and precise bombing or shelling. 极小之物; (用作定语, 指目标)需要精确轰击的。□ *vt* find, hit, such a target with the required accuracy: 精确地找到(目标); 精确地轰击(目标): *Our planes pin-pointed the target.* 我们的飞机精确地炸中目标。'**pin-prick** *n* (fig) small act, remark, etc causing annoyance. (喻)令人气恼的小动作、话语等。'**pin-stripe** *adj* (of dress material) with many very narrow stripes. (指衣料)带有许多细窄条纹的。

pin² /pɪn; pɪn/ *vt* (**-nn-**) [VP15A, B] **1** fasten (things *together, up, to* sth, etc) with a pin or pins: (用针)别住; 钉住(东西, 后接 together, up, to 等): *pin papers together;* 将文件用针别起来; *pin up a notice* eg with drawing-pins on a notice-board. 钉上一张告示(如用图钉钉在布告板上)。*pin sth on sb,* make him appear responsible; place the blame for sth on sb. 让某人对某事负责; 将责任推到某人身上。*pin one's hopes on sb,* have strong hope that he will help; rely on him unquestioningly. 将希望寄托在某人身上; 毫不怀疑地依赖某人。'**pin-up** *n* picture of a favourite or much admired person, pinned up on a wall: 钉在墙上的最令人喜欢或十分令人爱慕的人的照片: (attrib) (用作定语) *a* '*pin-up girl.* 其照片常被人钉在墙上的漂亮女孩子。**2** make unable to move: 阻止; 扣牢; 止住: *He was pinned under the wreckage* / *the wrecked car.* 他被压在残骸(破车子)底下。*He pinned his assailant against the wall,* held him there and prevented his from moving. 他把攻击他的人按在墙上。*The troops were pinned down by accurate fire,* were unable to advance or

withdraw. 部队被准确的炮火所困(无法前进或后退).**pin sb down**, (fig) get him to commit himself, to state his intentions, etc: (喻)使某人履行其义务(说明其意图等): *He's a difficult man to pin down.* 他是个不易说服的人。 **pin sb down to sth**, get him to agree to keep, eg a promise, an agreement. 使某人信守诺言(遵守合约)。

pina·fore /'pɪnəfɔ:(r)/ n loose article of clothing worn over a dress to keep it clean. 围裙; 围兜; 涎布。

pince-nez /'pæns neɪ; 'pæns,ne/ n pair of spectacles with a spring to clip the nose (instead of a frame that fits round the ears).夹鼻眼镜(不用钩住耳朵者)。

pin·cers /'pɪnsəz; 'pɪnsəz/ n pl (pair of) ~, 1 instrument for gripping things, pulling nails out of wood, etc. 钳子; 手钳。⇨ the illus at **tool**. 参看 tool 之插图。 '**pincer movement**, (mil) attack by two converging forces. (军)钳形攻势。 2 pincershaped claws of certain shellfish. (蟹、虾等的)螯。⇨ the illus at **crustacean**. 参看 crustacean 之插图。

pinch /pɪntʃ/ vt, vi 1 [VP6A, 15A, B] take in a tight grip between the thumb and finger; have in a tight grip between two hard things which are pressed together: 捏; 掐; 夹; 挤: *He ~ed the boy's cheek.* 他捏拍男孩的面颊。 *He ~ed the top of the plants off /~ed out the side shoots.* 他把植物的顶端掐掉(把旁边的新芽掐掉)。 *I ~ed my finger in the doorway.* 我在门口夹到了手指头。 2 [VP6A, 2A] be too tight; hurt by being too tight: 紧压; 挤痛: *These shoes ~ (me).* 这双鞋子会夹脚。 **(see, etc) where the shoe ~es,** (fig) where the difficulty or hardship lies. (喻)(找出)困难所在。 3 (in passive) suffer; feel the effects of: (用于被动语态)遭受; 尝到: *be ~ed with cold/poverty.* 遭受寒冷(贫穷)的苦。 **be ~ed for money,** be short of money. 缺少钱; 经济拮据。 4 [VP6A] (colloq) steal; take without permission: (口)偷; 窃; 未经许可而取用: *Who's ~ed my dictionary?* 谁拿了我的字典? 5 [VP2A] be niggardly; be very mean; live sparingly or economically: 小气; 吝啬; 节省: *parents who have to ~ and scrape in order to save money for a child's clothes.* 必须格外节俭以便为孩子买衣服的父母。 6 (sl) (of the police) take into custody: arrest: (俚)(指警察)逮捕; 捉住: *You'll be ~ed if you're not careful.* 你如果不小心, 将会被逮捕。 □ n 1 act of ~ing; painful squeeze: 捏; 掐; 夹: *He gave her a spiteful ~.* 他狠狠地把她掐一下。 2 (fig) stress: (喻)重压; 压迫: *feel the ~ of poverty.* 感到贫穷的痛苦。 3 amount which can be taken up with the thumb and finger: 一撮或一捏之量: *a ~ of salt/snuff.* 一撮盐(鼻烟)。 **take sth with a ~ of salt,** ⇨ **salt.** 4 **at a ~; if it comes to the ~,** if there is need and if there is no other way: 必要时: *We can get six people round the table at a ~.* 必要时我们可以使六个人坐在一桌。

pinch·beck /'pɪntʃbek; 'pɪntʃbek/ n alloy of copper and zinc, simulating gold, used in cheap jewellery, etc. 用于廉价珠宝等的合金; 金色铜。 □ adv sham. 假的。

pine¹ /paɪn; paɪn/ n [C] kinds of evergreen tree with needle-shaped leaves ('~-needles) and cones ('~-cones); [U] the wood of this tree. 松树; 松木。⇨ the illus at **tree**. 参看 tree 之插图。

pine² /paɪn; paɪn/ vi 1 [VP2A, C] waste away through sorrow or illness: 消瘦; 憔悴: *pining from hunger.* 饿瘦了。 2 [VP3A, 4C] ~ **for sth; ~ to do sth,** have a strong desire: 渴望: 渴慕: *exiles pining for home/to return home.* 渴望回家的流亡者。

pin·eal /'paɪnɪəl; 'pɪnɪəl/ adj shaped like a pinecone: 松果形的: ~ **gland**, gland in the brain. 松果腺。

pine·apple /'paɪnæpl; 'paɪn,æpl/ n [C] (tropical plant with sweet; juicy fruit; (U) this as food: 凤梨(亦名波罗): ~ **juice**; 凤梨汁; tinned ~. 罐头凤梨。⇨ the illus at **fruit.** 参看 fruit 之插图。

ping /pɪŋ; pɪŋ/ n short, sharp, ringing sound as of elastic being stretched and released or a rifle bullet in the air or striking a hard substance. 砰(短促尖锐

的响声, 如枪弹在空中的响声, 或击中硬物的响声)。□ vi make this sound. 发出砰声。

ping·pong /'pɪŋpɒŋ; 'pɪŋ,pɑŋ/ n (colloq) table tennis. (口)乒乓球; 桌球。

pin·ion¹ /'pɪnɪən; 'pɪnjən/ n 1 bird's wing, esp the outer joint; flight-feather of a bird. 鸟翼(尤指末端的一段); 翮。 2 (poet) wing: (诗)翼: *an eagle's ~s.* 鹰的翅膀。 □ vt [VP6A] 1 cut off a ~ of (a wing or bird) to hamper flight. 剪掉(翼)之尖端或(鸟)之羽翼使不能飞。 2 [VP15A, B] ~ **(to/together),** bind the arms of (a person); bind (sb's arms); bind (sb) fast (to sth). 绑住(一人)的手臂; 绑住(某人的手臂); 将(某人)绑在(某物)上。

pin·ion² /'pɪnɪən; 'pɪnjən/ n small cogwheel with teeth fitting into those of a larger cogwheel. (接合大齿轮的)小齿轮; 蜗轮; 副齿轮。⇨ the illus at **gear.** 参看 gear 之插图。

pink¹ /pɪŋk; pɪŋk/ n 1 [U] pale red colour of various kinds (rose ~, salmon ~). 淡红色; 粉红色(玫瑰红、浅红)。 ~ **gin**, portion of gin with angostura. 苦味杜松子酒。 2 [C] garden plant with sweet-smelling white, ~, crimson or variegated flowers. 石竹; 石竹花。 **3 in the ~ (of health),** (colloq) very well. (口)(健康)良好; 甚佳。 □ adj 1 of pale red colour. 淡红的; 粉红的。 2(colloq) inclined to be rather left-wing in politics. (政治上)左倾的。 ⇨ **red.** ~·**ish** /-ɪʃ/; -ɪʃ/ adj rather ~. 略带淡红色的。

pink² /pɪŋk; pɪŋk/ vt 1 [VP6A] pierce with a sword. 以剑刺。 2 [VP6A, 15B] ~ **(out),** decorate (leather, cloth) with small holes, etc. 以小孔等装饰(皮革、布)。 '~**·ing scissors/shears** n pl sewing scissors with serrated edges, used to prevent edges of cloth from fraying. 有锯齿形刃的剪刀(用以剪布边以防其脱散)。

pink³ /pɪŋk; pɪŋk/ vi(of an internal combustion engine) make high-pitched, explosive sounds; knock(3). (指内燃机)发响爆声; 发格达格达的响声。

pin·nace /'pɪnɪs; 'pɪnɪs/ n big ship's small motorboat. 附属于大船的小汽艇。

pin·nacle /'pɪnəkl; 'pɪnəkl/ n 1 tall, pointed ornament built on to a roof or buttress. (屋顶上的)尖顶; 尖塔。⇨ the illus at **church.** 参看 church 之插图。 2 high, slender mountain peak, 尖峰; 高峰。 3(fig) highest point: (喻)最高点; 顶点: *at the ~ of his fame.* 在他声誉最高的时候。 ~ (set as (on a ~; supply with ~s. 置于尖顶上; 筑尖顶于; 建尖塔于。

pin·nate /'pɪnet; 'pɪnet/ adj (bot) (of a leaf) formed of small leaves on opposite sides of a stem. (植物)(指叶)由外柄两旁对称的小叶构成的; 羽状的。

pinny /'pɪnɪ; 'pɪnɪ/ n (pl -nies) (child's name for a) pinafore. (儿语)围兜; 涎布。

pint /paɪnt; paɪnt/ n unit of measure for liquids and certain dry goods, one-eighth of a gallon or about .57 of a litre: 品脱 (容量单位, 等于八分之一加仑或约0. 57公升): *a ~ of milk/beer/lentils.* 一品脱的牛奶(啤酒, 扁豆)。 ⇨ **App 5.** 参看附录5。

pion·eer /ˌpaɪə'nɪə(r); ˌpaɪə'nɪr/ n 1 person who goes into a new or undeveloped country to settle or work there; first student of a new branch of study, etc; explorer. 拓荒者; 开辟者; (新学科等的)先驱; 探险者。 2 (mil) one of an advance party of soldiers (eg clearing or making roads). (军)先遣兵; 工兵(担任清除道路障碍或开通道路等任务)。 □ vi, vt [VP2A] act as a ~; [VP6A] open up (a way, etc); show (new methods, etc) to others. 作先驱; 作拓荒者; 开辟(道路等); 提倡(新法等)。

pious /'paɪəs; 'paɪəs/ adj 1 having, showing, deep devotion to religion. 虔诚的; 虔敬的。 2 (old use)dutiful to parents. (旧用法)孝顺的。 ~·**ly** adv

pip¹ /pɪp; pɪp/ n seed, esp of a lemon, orange, apple or pear. 种子(尤指柠檬、柑、苹果或梨的种子)。⇨ the illus at **fruit.** 参看 fruit 之插图。

pip² /pɪp; pɪp/ n **the pip,** disease of poultry; (sl) fit

of depression or irritation. 家禽的舌病; (俚)沮丧; 厌烦。 **have/get/give sb the pip:** 感到 (使某人感到) 厌烦: *That man gives me the pip.* 那人使我感到厌烦。

pip³ /pɪp; pɪp/ *n* note of a time-signal on the telephone or radio; (电话或收音机的) 报时响声: *The last of the six pips gives the time to the second.* 六个响声的最后一响表示准确的时刻。

pip⁴ /pɪp; pɪp/ *n* **1** each spot on playing-cards, dice and dominoes. (纸牌、骰子、骨牌上的) 点。 **2** (GB colloq) star (1 to 3 according to rank) on an army officer's shoulder-strap. (英口) 陆军军官肩章上的星 (一至三颗, 视军阶而定)。

pip⁵ /pɪp; pɪp/ *vt* **(-pp-)** [VP6A] (GB colloq) hit with a gunshot. (英口) 以子弹射击。 **pipped at the post,** defeated at the last moment. 于最后时刻被击败; 功败垂成。

pi·pal /ˈpiːpəl; ˈpipəl/ ⟹ **peepul.**

pipe¹ /paɪp; paɪp/ *n* **1** tube through which liquids or gases can flow: (供液体或气体流动的) 管: 'water~s; 水管; 'gas~s; 煤气管; 'drain~s. 排水管。 '~line *n* line of connected ~s, often underground, for conveying eg petroleum to distant places. (通常埋设于地下用以输送石油等的) 管道; 管线。 **in the ~line,** (of any kind of goods or proposals) on the way; about to be delivered in a schedule, list, etc to receive attention. (指任何货物或提议) 运输中; 递送中; 即将递送。 **2** musical wind-instrument (a single tube with holes stopped by the fingers); each of the tubes from which sound is produced in an organ; (pl) bag~s. 管乐器(如笛、箫等); (风琴中的) 音管; (复) 风笛。 **3** (sound of the) whistle used by a boatswain. (水手长用的) 笛子(水手长的笛声。 **4** song or note of a bird. (鸟的) 鸣声。 **5** tubular organ in the body: (身体内的) 管状器官: 'wind~s. 气管。 **6** (to'bacco) ~, tube with a bowl, used for smoking tobacco; quantity of tobacco held in the bowl: 烟斗; 一烟斗的烟丝: smoke a ~. 抽烟斗。 Give me a ~ of tobacco, please. 请给我一烟斗的烟丝。 **Put 'that in your ~ and smoke it,** (colloq) That is sth for you to reflect upon and accept if you can. (口) 你好好考虑一下吧。 '~-clay *n* [U] fine, white clay formerly used for making tobacco ~s, and (by soldiers) for whitening leather belts and other pieces of equipment. 烟斗泥; 陶土。 (昔时用以制烟斗及士兵用来擦皮带等装备的上等白粘土)。 '~-dream *n* plan, idea, etc that is fantastic and impracticable. 狂想; 幻想; 不切实际的计划、观念等。 '~-rack *n* rack for tobacco ~s. 烟斗架。 **7** cask for wine (equal to about 105 gallons). 大酒桶(约合 105 加仑)。 '~-ful /-ful; -ˌful/ *n* as much as a ~(6) holds. 一烟斗的量。

pipe² /paɪp; paɪp/ *vi, vt* **1** [VP6A, 15A] convey (water, etc) through pipes; 以管输送 (水等): ~ water into a house. 以管输送水到屋里。 **2** [VP6A, 2A] play (a tune) on a pipe; whistle; utter or sing in a thin, treble voice. 用管乐器吹奏(曲调); 吹哨子; (以尖细的声音) 说或唱。 [VP2C] ~ up, (colloq) begin to play, sing or speak. (口)开始奏, 开始唱; 开始说。 ~ down (colloq) be quiet; be less noisy or cocksure. (口)安静下来; 压低过高的声音; 不再过于自信。 **3** [VP15A] (naut) summon (sailors) by blowing a boatswain's pipe: (航海) 吹水手长的笛子召集(水手): ~ all hands on deck; 吹笛子召集所有的水手到甲板上; lead or welcome (sb) by the sound of a boatswain's pipe: 以水手长的笛引领或欢迎 (某人): ~ the captain on board. 以笛声欢迎船长登船。 **4** [VP6A] trim (a dress), ornament (a cake, etc) with piping. 以管状窄条装饰(衣服); 以糖边装饰(蛋糕等)。 ⟹ **piping(2).**

piper /ˈpaɪpə(r); ˈpaɪpə/ *n* one who plays on a pipe, esp a player of the bagpipes. 吹奏乐器者; (尤指)吹风笛者。 **pay the ~ (and call the tune),** bear the cost of an undertaking (and have control of what is done). 负担费用(而取得控制权)。

pip·ette /pɪˈpet; pɪˈpɛt/ *n* slender tube for transfer-

ring small quantities of liquid, esp in chemistry. 吸量管(用以输送小量液体的细管, 尤指作化学实验时所用者); 球吸管; 移液管。

pip·ing /ˈpaɪpɪŋ; ˈpaɪpɪŋ/ *n* [U] **1** length of pipes(1), esp for water and drains: 管道; 管系(尤指水管和排水管); 某管系的总长: ten feet of lead ~. 十英尺长的铅管。 **2** narrow cord-like material used to ornament the edges of some garments; cord-like lines of icing-sugar used to decorate cakes, etc. (装饰衣服边的)管状窄条; (装饰糕饼等的)糖线。 **3** action of playing on a pipe; sound produced from a pipe. 吹笛; 笛声。 □ *adj* like the sound from a pipe(2): 似笛声的; 尖声的: a ~ voice. 尖叫声。 **the ~ time(s) of peace,** time(s) when there is peaceful music instead of martial music. 承平的时代。 □ *adv* ~ hot, (of liquids, food) hissing or steaming hot. (指液体、食物)滚烫的。

pip·pin /ˈpɪpɪn; ˈpɪpɪn/ *n* kinds of apple. 数种苹果的统称。

pip·squeak /ˈpɪpskwiːk; ˈpɪpskwik/ *n* (sl) insignificant or contemptible person or thing. (俚)不重要的人或物; 可轻视的人或物。

pi·quant /ˈpiːkənt; ˈpikənt/ *adj* pleasantly sharp to the taste: 辛辣而开胃的: a ~ sauce; 辣酱; (fig) pleasantly exciting to the mind: (喻)刺激的, 令人兴奋的: a ~ bit of gossip. 有趣的闲话。 ~·ly *adv* **piquancy** /-ənsɪ; -ənsi/ *n* the quality of being ~. 辛辣; 刺激; 兴奋。

pique /piːk; pik/ *vt* [VP6A] **1** hurt the pride or self-respect of. 伤害…的自尊心; 激怒; 使生气。 **2** stir (the curiosity); stir the curiosity of (sb). 激起(好奇心); 激起(某人的)好奇心。 **3** ~ oneself on sth, pride oneself on; feel proud about: (以…自豪; 对…感到自傲: He ~d himself on being punctual. 他以能准时自傲。 □ *n* [U, C] pride; feeling one has when one's curiosity is unsatisfied; resentment: 骄傲; (好奇心未能满足时的)不高兴; 愤恨: go away in a fit of ~; 不高兴地走开; take a ~ against sb 生某人的气。

pi·quet /pɪˈket; pɪˈkɛt/ *n* card game for two players with a pack of 32 cards. 两人玩的一种纸牌戏(用 32 张纸牌)。

pi·ranha /pɪˈrɑːnjə; pɪˈrɑnjə/ *n* (kinds of) tropical American freshwater fish, noted for attacking and eating live animals. 产于南美洲的一种淡水鱼, 会攻击并吞食活的动物。

pi·rate /ˈpaɪərət; ˈpaɪrət/ *n* **1** sea-robber; sea-robber's ship. 海盗; 海盗船。 **2** person who infringes another's copyright, who broadcasts without a licence, usurps trading rights, etc. (不顾著作权的)盗印者; 无照设立广播电台者; 侵犯专利权者。 □ *vt* [VP6A] use, reproduce (a book, a recording, another's work, etc) without authority and for one's own profit. 盗印(书籍); 盗制(唱片、录音带等)。 **pi·rati·cal** /paɪˈrætɪkl; paɪˈrætɪkl/ *adj* of, in the manner of, a ~. 海盗的; 海盗作风的; 盗印的; 盗制的。 **pi·rati·cally** /-klɪ; -kli/ *adv* **pi·racy** /ˈpaɪərəsɪ; ˈpaɪrəsi/ *n* (pl -cies) [U] robbery by ~s; pirating of books, etc; [C] instance of either of these. 海上抢劫; 盗印书籍; 盗制唱片、录音带等。

pir·ou·ette /ˌpɪruˈet; ˌpɪruˈɛt/ *n* [C] ballet-dancer's rapid turn on the ball of the foot or on the point of the toe. (芭蕾舞蹈者的)单足旋转; 趾尖旋转。 □ *vi* dance a ~ or ~s. (跳芭蕾舞时)用单足旋转; 用趾尖旋转。

pis al·ler /ˌpiːz ˈæleɪ *US*: ˌpiːz æˈleɪ; ˌpizaˈle/ *n* (F) the last resort; course of action taken because there seems to be nothing better. (法)最后的手段。

pis·ca·tor·ial /ˌpɪskəˈtɔːrɪəl; ˌpɪskəˈtoriəl/ *adj* of fishing; addicted to fishing. 捕鱼的; 嗜好钓鱼的。

Pis·ces /ˈpaɪsiːz; ˈpaɪsiz/ *n* twelfth sign of the zodiac (also called 亦称作 the fish). (十二宫中的)双鱼宫。 ⟹ the illus at **zodiac.** 参看 zodiac 之插图。

piss /pɪs; pɪs/ *vi, vi* ⚠ (not in polite use) pass urine; discharge (blood) with urine; wet with urine. (讳)(不雅的用法)小便; 排尿带血; 尿湿。 **P~ off!** (vulg) Go away! (鄙)走开! 滚蛋! **~ed** *adj* (vulg) very drunk.

(鄙)大醉的。 **~ed off**, (vulg) annoyed. (鄙)厌烦的。 □
n urine. 尿。

pis·ta·chio /pɪˈstɑːtʃɪəʊ US: -ˈtæʃɪəʊ; pɪsˈtɑːʃɪˌo / *n*
(*pl* **~s** /-tʃɪəʊz; -ʃɪoz/) (tree yielding) nut with a green
edible kernel; colour of this kernel. 阿月浑子树; 阿月浑
子(其绿色果仁可吃); 其果仁的绿色。

pis·til /ˈpɪstl; ˈpɪstl/ *n* seed-producing part of a flower.
雌蕊。 ⇨ the illus at **flower**. 参看 flower 之插图。

pis·tol /ˈpɪstl; ˈpɪstl/ *n* [C] small firearm held and
fired in one hand. 手枪。 **hold a ~ to sb's head**, try,
by using threats, to make him do what one wants. 以恐
吓方式使某人从命。

pis·ton /ˈpɪstən; ˈpɪstn/ *n* round plate or short
cylinder of wood or metal, fitting closely inside another
cylinder or tube in which it moves up and down or
backwards and forwards, used in engines, pumps, etc
to impart or receive motion by means of a rod, called a
'**~-rod**. (引擎、抽水机等中的)活塞(借活塞杆 piston-rod,
以传递或承受运动)。 ⇨ the illus at **motor**. 参看 motor
之插图。 '**~ engined**, (of aircraft) having engines with
~s (contrasted with jet engines). (指飞机)装活塞引擎
的(与喷射引擎相对)。 '**~ ring** *n* split metal ring used
in a **~** to make a gastight joint. 活塞胀圈; 活塞环。

pit¹ /pɪt; pɪt/ *n* **1** hole in the earth, usu with steep
sides, esp one from which material is dug out (a
'*chalk-pit; a 'clay-pit; a 'coal-pit*) or for industrial
purposes (a '*saw-pit*). 坑(尤指挖掘后所留的坑), 如 chalk-
pit 白垩坑, clay-pit 粘土坑, coal-pit 煤坑; 或为着工业目
的所掘成的坑, 如 saw-pit 锯木坑)。 '**pit·head** *n* entrance
of a coalmine: 煤矿坑入口: *pithead baths*. 坑矿坑口的
浴室。 '**pit·man** /-mən; -mən/ *n* (*pl*-**men**)collier; worker
in a coal-pit. 矿工; 煤矿工。 '**pit pony** *n* pony kept
underground in coalmines. 煤矿坑里运输用的小驴。
'**pit-prop** *n* prop used to support the roof of a gallery in
a mine pit. 用以支持坑道顶部的支柱。 '**pit·saw** *n* saw
used in a saw-pit. 锯木坑内用的锯。 **~saw².2** covered
hole as a trap for wild animals,etc. (捕兽等的)陷阱,
pit·fall *n* covered pit as a trap for animals; (more usu,
fig) unsuspected snare or danger. 陷坑; (更常作比喻用)
诱惑物; 圈套; 暗伏的危险。 **3** hollow in an animal or
plant body. 动物或植物体的凹陷处。 *the pit of the
stomach*, the depression in the belly between the ribs.
心窝。 ⇨ also *armpit* at **arm¹(1)**. **4** scar left on the body
after smallpox. 生天花后的疤痕; 麻子。 **5** (GB, not US)
seats on the ground floor of a theatre behind the stalls;
people occupying these seats. (英, 不用于美国)(戏院中
之)正厅后座; 正厅后座的观众。 **6** (US) part of the floor
of an exchange used for a special commodity: (美)交易
所供特定货品交易的地方: *the 'wheat-pit*. 小麦交易处。 **7**
the pit, (rhet, biblical) hell. (修辞, 圣经用语)地狱。 **8**
hole in the floor (of a garage, workshop) from which
the underside of a motor-vehicle can be examined and
repaired; place (at a race-course) at which racing cars
stop for fuel, new tyres, etc, during a race. (修车场
内)检修汽车底部的地上凹坑;(赛车场内)比赛中供汽车加
油或换车胎等的地方。 **9 = cockpit**. □ *vt* **1** [VP6A]
mark with pits(or with hollows in the ground): make
痘痕; 使有麻子; 使有凹陷: *a face pitted with smallpox;
the surface of the moon, pitted with craters.* 布满
岩坑的月球表面。 **2** [VP14] **~against**, cause to
struggle against: 使与…相对: *pit one's wits against the
Income Tax Office*. 以智力对抗所得税务局。

pit² /pɪt; pɪt/ *n* (US) hard, stone-like seed of such
fruits as cherries, plums, peaches, dates). (美)樱桃、
李、桃、枣等水果的核。 □ *vt* (-**tt**-) (US) remove pits
from. (美)除去…之核。

pit-a-pat /ˌpɪtə ˈpæt; ˈpɪtəˌpæt/ *adv* with quick
beating, with the sound of light, quick taps or steps: 毕
毕卜卜地; 有轻快之拍击声或步伐声地: *Her heart/feet went
~.* 她的心卜卜地跳(她的脚噼啪噼啪地走)。

pitch¹ /pɪtʃ; pɪtʃ/ *n* **1** place where sb (esp a street
trader) usu does business, where a street entertainer

usu performs. (街上零售商的)售货摊; (街上卖艺人的)路
边表演场。 *queer sb's ~*, upset his plans; thwart him.
破坏某人的计划; 阻挠某人。 **2** (cricket) part of the
ground between the wickets; manner in which the ball
is delivered in bowling; (baseball) manner or act of
pitching the ball; (football) ground, field (the usual
words) on which the game is played. (板球)柱与柱间的
场地; 投球式; (棒球)投球式; 投球; (足球)足球场(ground,
field 较常用)。 **3** act of pitching or throwing anything;
distance to which sth is thrown. 投掷; 所投的距离。 **4**
(music and speech) degree of highness or lowness;
quality of sound. (音乐与说话)音调; 音质。 **5** degree:
程度: *at the lowest ~ of his (ill) fortune.* 在他最不幸的时
候。 *Excitement rose to fever ~.* 兴奋达到极点。 **6**
amount of slope (esp of a roof). 斜度(尤指屋顶的斜
度)。 **7** (of a ship) process of pitching(5). (指船)上下
颠簸。

pitch² /pɪtʃ; pɪtʃ/ *n* [U] black substance made from
coal-tar, turpentine or petroleum, sticky and semi-
liquid when hot, hard when cold, used to fill cracks or
spaces, eg between planks forming a floor or ship's deck,
make roofs waterproof, etc. 沥青(由煤焦油或松节油提
炼的黑粘物), 遇热成粘性半液体, 遇冷变硬, 用以填塞板面
等之间的裂缝或使屋顶防水等)。 *as black/dark as ~*,
completely black/dark. 漆黑的; 极暗的。 **~-'black**
-'dark *adj* completely black/dark. 漆黑的; 极暗的。
'**~-blende** *n* [U] black, shining mineral ore (oxide of
uranium) yielding radium. 沥青铀矿。 '**~ pine** *n*
specially resinous kinds of pine-tree or its wood. 脂松;
脂肪木。

pitch³ /pɪtʃ; pɪtʃ/ *vt, vi* **1** [VP6A] set up, erect (a
tent, camp); [VP2A] set up one's tent or camp. 搭架
(帐幕); 扎(营); 搭帐篷; 扎营。 **2** [VP6A, 15A, B] throw
(a ball, etc); throw (sb or sth out, aside, etc), esp with
impatience or energetic dislike: 投; 掷(球等); 抛; 丢弃
(某人或某物, 以致 away, aside 等): *Let's ~ the drunkard
out.* 我们来把那个醉鬼撵出去。 *The men were ~ing hay,
lifting it, eg into a wagon, with forks.* 那些人正在用
叉把干草(干草)叉到车上)。 '**~-fork** *n* long-handled fork with
sharp prongs for lifting hay, etc. (叉干草等用的)长柄
叉。 □ *vt* lift or move with a fork; (fig) thrust (a
person) forcibly (into a position, etc). 以叉叉起(以叉
去;(喻)强插(某人)(于某一位置等, 与 into 连用)。 **3** [VP
15A] (music) set in a certain pitch(4) or key: (音乐)
定为某调: *~ a tune too high/in a lower key.* 把一曲的
调子定得太高(较低)。 *This song is ~ed too low for
me.* 这支歌的调子对我是太低了。 **4** [VP2C, 15A, B]
(cause to) fall heavily forwards or outwards: (使)向前
倾跌; (使)向外摔: *He ~ed on his head.* 他头朝地跌倒
了。 *The carriage overturned and the passengers were
~ed out.* 车子翻了, 乘客都被摔出来。 **5** [VP2A, C] (of
a ship) move up and down as the bows rise and fall.
(指船)上下颠簸。 ⇨ **roll²(6).6 ~ in**, set to work with
energy. 开始努力工作。 **~ into**, (a) attack violently:
猛烈攻击: *They ~ed into him.* 他们猛烈攻击他。 **(b)** get
busy with: 着手; 忙于做某事: *We ~ed into the work.* 我
们开始忙于干那件工作。 *The hungry boy ~ed into the
meatpie*, began to eat it. 那个饥饿的男孩开始大吃肉馅
饼。 **~ upon**, select by chance; light or pick upon: 偶
然选中; 偶然发现: *~ upon the most suitable man for
the job.* 碰巧选到最合适的人做那件工作。 **7 ~ed battle**,
one that is fought with troops arranged in prepared
positions, not a casual encounter. 阵地战(并非偶然的遭
遇战)。 **8** [VP15B, 22] (cricket)cause(the ball)to strike
the ground near or around the wicket: (板球)使(球)碰
到三柱门附近的地面: *~ the ball short;* 击短球; *~ the
ball up a bit;* 球投得高一点; (baseball) throw (the ball)
to the batter. (棒球)将(球)投向打击手。 **~ wickets**,
(cricket) fix the stumps in the ground with the bails in
place. (板球)固定三柱门于地上。 **9** (sl) tell (a yarn, a
story). (俚)讲(故事)。 **10** ,**~-and-'toss** *n* game of skill
and chance in which coins are **~ed** at a mark. 一种向

pitcher¹ /'pɪtʃə(r); 'pɪtʃɚ/ n large (usu earthenware) vessel with a handle and lip for holding liquids; large jug. 大水罐(通常为陶制品,有柄和嘴);大壶;盂。

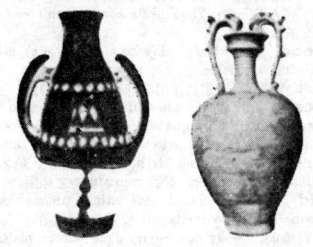

pitchers

pitcher² /'pɪtʃə(r); 'pɪtʃɚ/ n (baseball) player who throws the ball. (棒球)投手。 ⟹ the illus at **baseball**. 参看 baseball 之插图。

pit·eous /'pɪtɪəs; 'pɪtɪəs/ adj arousing pity. 令人同情的;可怜的。 **~·ly** adv

pit·fall /'pɪtfɔːl; 'pɪt,fɔl/ ⟹**pit¹(2)**.

pith /pɪθ; pɪθ/ n [U] 1 soft substance that fills the stems of some plants (eg reeds); similar substance lining the rind of oranges, etc. (某些植物茎中的)木髓;(柑橘等果皮内)类似木髓的柔软组织。 '~ **hat/helmet**, light sun hat made of dried ~. 木髓制的轻便遮阳帽。 2 (fig) essential part: (喻)重要部分: the ~ of his argument / speech, etc. 他的辩论(演讲等)的重点。 3 vigour; force. 精力;力量。 **~·y** adj (**-ier, -iest**) 1 of, like, full of, ~. 木髓的;似木髓的;多木髓的。 2 forcible; full of meaning: 有力的;简洁的: **~y** sayings. 简洁的谚语。 **~·ily** /-ɪlɪ; -ɪlɪ/ adv

piti·able /'pɪtɪəbl; 'pɪtɪəbl/ adj exciting pity; deserving only contempt: 令人怜悯的;可怜的;可怜又可鄙的: a ~ attempt. 可怜又可鄙的企图。 **piti·ably** /-əblɪ; -əblɪ/ adv

piti·ful /'pɪtɪfl; 'pɪtɪfəl/ adj 1 feeling pity; compassionate. 怜悯的;慈悲的。 2 causing pity: 令人同情的;可怜的: a ~ sight. 可怜的景象。 3 arousing contempt. 可鄙的。 **~·ly** /-fəlɪ; -flɪ/ adv

piti·less /'pɪtɪlɪs; 'pɪtɪlɪs/ adj showing no pity. 无怜悯心的;无情的。 **~·ly** adv

pi·ton /'piːtɒn; 'pitɑn/ n metal spike driven into rock, with a hole for rope, used as a hold in mountain climbing. (一头有孔可穿绳, 尖端可钉入岩石, 爬山时用以抓握之)长钉;岩钉。

pit·tance /'pɪtns; 'pɪtns/ n low, insufficient payment or allowance (for work, etc): 微薄的薪资或津贴: work all day for a mere ~. 为着一点薄酬而整天工作。

pitter-patter /'pɪtə pætə(r); 'pɪtə,pætɚ/ n patter: 啪哒声(轻拍声、脚步声等): the ~ of rain on the roof. 雨落在屋顶上的啪哒声。

pi·tu·itary /pɪ'tjuːɪtərɪ US: -'tuːɪterɪ; pɪ'tjuə,tɛrɪ/ adv ~ **gland**, small ductless gland at the base of the brain, secreting hormones that influence growth, etc. 脑垂体;脑下腺。 □ n ~ gland. 脑垂体;脑下腺。

pity /'pɪtɪ; 'pɪtɪ/ n (pl **-ties**) 1 [U] feeling of sorrow for the troubles, sufferings, etc of another person: 同情;怜悯: be filled with / feel ~ for sb. 同情某人。 **for ~'s sake**, (used as a form of entreaty): 发发慈悲 (作恳求的用语): For ~'s sake try to stop this persecution. 发发慈悲停止这种迫害吧。 **out of ~**, because of a feeling of ~: 出于同情; 因为觉得可怜: give a beggar a few coins out of ~. 出于同情而给乞丐几个硬币。 2 (with indef art, but not in pl except as below) (event which gives) cause for regret or sorrow: (与不定

冠词连用, 但除了下面例句的用法外不用复数)令人遗憾的事;可悲的事: What a ~ (= How unfortunate) (that) you can't come with us! 你不能跟我们一起去,真可惜! It's a ~ (that) he can't swim. 真遗憾,他不会游泳。 The ~ is that..., The thing to be regretted is that.... 遗憾的是...;可惜...。 It's a thousand pities that..., is most unfortunate that.... 最不幸的是...。 □ vt (pt, pp **-tied**) [VP6A] feel genuine ~ for; feel contemptuous ~ for: 同情;怜悯;对...觉得可怜又可鄙: He is much to be pitied. 他很可怜;他值得给予同情。 I ~ you if you think that you deserve to be helped. 如果你以为你配接受帮助, 我会觉得你可怜。 **~·ing** adv expressing ~. 表示同情的。 **~·ing·ly** adv

pivot /'pɪvət; 'pɪvət/ n 1 central pin or point on which sth turns, ⟹ the illus at **balance**; (fig) sth on which an argument or discussion depends. 轴;枢轴;支点(参看 balance 之插图); (喻)辩论或讨论的要点;中心点。 2 (mil) man or unit on whom a body of troops turns or wheels when changing front or direction. (军)基准兵;标兵;标轴单位。 □ vt, vi 1 [VP3A] **~ on**, turn as on a ~. (以某事物为轴心而)旋转;以...为转移;由...而定。 2 [VP6A] place on a ~; supply with a ~. 放在轴上;装置枢轴。 **~·al** /-tl; -tl/ adj of, forming, a ~; (fig) of great importance because other things depend upon it. 轴的;作为枢轴的; (喻)(因被其他事物所依靠而)非常重要的;关键的。

pixi·lated /'pɪksɪleɪtɪd; 'pɪksə,letɪd/ adj (dial) slightly crazy. (方)有点疯狂的;疯疯癫癫的。

pixy, pixie /'pɪksɪ; 'pɪksɪ/ n (pl **-xies**) small elf or fairy. 小精灵;小仙子。

pizza /'piːtsə; 'pitsə/ n (I) dish of food made by baking a layer of dough covered with a mixture of tomatoes, cheese, etc. (意)(上面覆有番茄酱及乳酪等的)煎饼。

piz·zi·cato /ˌpɪtsɪ'kɑːtəʊ; ˌpɪtsɪ'kɑto/ adj, adv (I) (music) (played) by plucking the strings (of a violin, etc) instead of using the bow. (意)(音乐)用指弹拨(提琴等)的(地);拨奏的(地)。

plac·ard /'plækɑːd; 'plækɑrd/ n written or printed announcement or advertisement; poster. 公告;布告;招贴;海报。 □ vt [VP6A] put ~s on (walls, etc); make known by means of ~s. 贴公告于(墙上等); (以布告)宣布;招贴)公告。

pla·cate /plə'keɪt US: 'pleɪkeɪt; 'pleket/ vt [VP6A] soothe; pacify. 安慰;抚慰。

place¹ /pleɪs; ples/ n 1 particular part of space occupied by sb or sth: 地方;所在地: I can't be in two ~s at once. 我不能同时在两个地方。 2 city, town, village, etc: 城市;镇;村: visit ~s and see things, travel as a tourist. 到各地旅行观光。 '**go ~s**, (colloq) have increasing success. (口)成功;胜利;表演精彩。 '**~-name** n name of a city, town, village, hill, lake, etc: 地名 (城镇、村庄、山、湖等之名称): an expert on the origin of ~-names. 详识地名起源之专家。 3 building or area of land used for some particular purpose that is specified: (用作某种特殊目的)建筑物; 场所: a ~ of worship, a church, etc; 礼拜的场所(如教堂等); ~s of amusement, theatres, discotheques, cinemas, etc. 娱乐场所; a 'market-~; 市场; a ~ of business. 营业处。 4 particular ~ on a surface: 表面上的某部分: a sore ~ on my neck. 我脖子上痛的地方。 5 passage, part, in a book, etc: 书籍等中的段落或部分: I've lost my ~, can't find the ~ where I stopped reading. 我找不到原来读的地方了。 Use a book-mark to keep your ~ instead of turning down the corner of the page. 用一个书签指明你所读到的地方, 而不要把书页折角。 6 rank or station (in society, etc): 地位; (社会上的)阶级: keep / know one's ~. 保持(了解)自己的身分或地位。 7 (in a race) position among those competitors who are winners: (竞赛时)获胜者的名次: Whose horse got the first ~? 谁的马获得第一名? I shall back (= bet some money on) the favourite for a ~, ie to be one of the first three past the winning-post. 我要赌那

匹最有希望获得前三名的马。Hence, 由此产生, **'~-bet** n 8 (maths) position of a figure in a series as indicating its value in decimal or other notation:(数)位:*calculated to five ~s of decimals/to five decimal ~s*, eg 6.57132. 计算到小数点后五位(如 6.57132)。**9** single step or stage in an argument, etc. (议论等的)步骤;层次。*in the first /second, etc ~*, firstly/secondly, etc. 第一(第二等)点;首先(其次等)。**10** proper or natural position: 适当的位置; 天然的位置: *A tidy person likes to have a ~ for everything and everything in its ~*. 一个整洁的人喜欢每一样东西都有其位置, 而每一样东西都在其应在的位置。*Please take your ~s*, eg ready for a dance. 请就位(如准备跳舞)。*Go back to your ~*, eg your seat. 回到你的位子去。*There's always a ~ for you around our table*, You will always be a welcome guest. 我们的餐桌总是有你的位子(随时欢迎你来)。*in ~*, **(a)** in the right or proper ~: 在对的位置; 在适当的位置: *I like to have everything in ~*. 我喜欢一切都在其适当的位置。**(b)** (fig) suitable; appropriate: (喻) 适合的; 适当的: *The proposal is not quite in ~*. 那提议并不十分适当。*out of ~*, **(a)** not in the right or proper ~. 不在应在的位置; 不在适当的位置。**(b)** (fig) unsuitable; inappropriate: (喻)不适合的; 不适当的: *Your remarks were rather out of ~*. 你的话有点不恰当。*in ~ of*, instead of. 代替。*give ~*, yield. 屈服; 让步。*give ~ to*, be succeeded by. 让位于。*make ~ for*, **(a)** make room (which is the more usu word) for. 腾出空位给…(room 较常用)。**(b)** yield precedence to. 让…在先。**(c)** be superseded by. 被…所取代。*put sb in his (proper) ~; put oneself in sb's/sb else's ~*, ⇨ put¹(2). *take the ~ of*, be substituted for: 代替; 取代: *Who will take the ~ of Mr X/take Mr X's ~?* 谁将要代替某先生? *Plastics have taken the ~ of many materials.* 塑胶已经取代了许多材料。*take ~*, happen: 发生; 举行: *The wedding/party/celebration took place yesterday.* 婚礼(宴会, 庆祝会)在昨日举行。*pride of ~*, position, of superiority. 高位; 尊位。**11** office, employment, esp a government appointment; duties of an office-holder: 职位,(尤指公职); 职责: *It's your ~ to see that the junior members of the staff do not arrive late.* 你的职责是使下级职员不迟到。*He will get a ~ in the Oxford boat*, will be chosen to be a member of the crew. 他将被选为牛津校船上的一名划手。**'~-man, '~-seekers**, man looking for favoured positions, eg in government. 钻营职位的人(尤指官吏)。**12** estate; house; home: 地产; 房屋; 住所: *He has a nice little ~ in the country.* 他在乡间有所漂亮的小房屋。*Come round to my ~ one evening.* 随便那天晚上请到舍下来。**13** (in proper names) alternative name for *Street, Square*, etc in a town: (专有名词连用)城市之 Street, Square 等的代称: *St James's P~*. 圣詹姆斯街。**14** **'~-kick** n (Rugby football) kick made when the ball is previously placed for that purpose on the ground. (橄榄球)定位踢(由另外球员预先将球置于地上然后踢出)。

place² /pleɪs; ples/ vt [VP6A, 15A, B] **1** put (sth) in a certain place; arrange (things) in their proper places: 放(某物)于某一位置; 放置; 安排(各物)于适当的位置; 安置: *P~ them in the right order.* 把它们按顺序放好。**2** appoint (sb) to a post; put in office or authority: 任命(某人); 给予职务或职权: *He was ~d in command of the Second Army.* 他被任命指挥第二军团。**3** put, invest (money): 存(款); 投(资): *~ £500 in Saving Bonds*, 买了五百英镑的储蓄公债; *~ £100 to sb's credit in the bank.* 将一百英镑存入某人在银行的户头。**4** put (an order for goods, etc) with a business firm: 发出(订单): *~ an order for books with Blackwell's.* 向布莱克韦尔公司订购书籍。**5** dispose of (goods) to a customer: 售出(货物): *How can we ~ all this surplus stock?* 我们怎样才能够卖出全部剩余存货? **6** have, fix, repose: 寄托; 信赖: *~ confidence in a leader.* 信赖一个领袖。**7** recognize or estimate (sb) by connecting him with past experience; fully identify: 认出或估计(某人); 完全认定: *I know*

that man's face, but I can't ~ him. 我认得那人的面孔, 但我认不出来他是谁。*He's a difficult man to ~.* 难以判断他是何许人物。**8** (racing) state the position of runners(in a race), contestants(in an athletic contest). (赛跑等)定出(选手的)名次。*be ~d*, be among the first three: 列入前三名: *The Duke's horse wasn't ~d.* 公爵的马没进入前三名。

pla·cebo /pləˈsiːbəu; pləˈsibo/ n (pl ~s) sth not containing medicine given to soothe, not to cure, a patient. 安慰剂(安慰病患用之非药剂性物品)。宽心丸。

pla·centa /pləˈsentə; pləˈsɛntə/ n (zool) organ lining the womb during pregnancy, by which the foetus is nourished. It is expelled with the foetus and the umbilical cord following birth. (动物) 胎盘; 胎衣。⇨ the illus at **reproduce**. 参看 reproduce 之插图。

pla·cid /ˈplæsɪd; ˈplæsɪd/ adj calm; untroubled; (of a person) not easily irritated. 安静的; 平静的;(指人)温和的; 沉着的。*~·ly* adv *~·ity* /pləˈsɪdətɪ; pləˈsɪdətɪ/ n [U].

placket /ˈplækɪt; ˈplækɪt/ n opening in a woman's skirt to make it easier to put on and take off; pocket inside this. 女裙的开口; 此种开口内的口袋。

plage /plɑːʒ; plɑʒ/ n (F) sea beach (esp at a fashionable seaside resort). (法)海滩(尤指在时髦人物常去的海滨游乐地)。

pla·giar·ize /ˈpleɪdʒəraɪz; ˈpledʒɪəˌraɪz/ vt, vi [VP 2A, 6A] take and use (sb else's ideas, words, etc) as one's own. 抄袭(他人的思想、文字等); 剽窃。**pla·giar·ism** /-ɪzəm; -ɪzəm/ n [U] plagiarizing; [C] instance of this. 抄袭; 剽窃。**pla·giar·ist** /-ɪst; -ɪst/ n person who ~s. 抄袭者; 剽窃者。

plague /pleɪg; pleg/ n **1 the ~**, = bubonic plague. ⇨ **bubonic**. **'~-spot** n **(a)** spot on the skin characteristic of ~. 疫斑。**(b)** district infected with ~. 瘟疫区。**(c)** centre, source or symptom of moral evil. 罪恶的中心, 根源或征兆。**2** cause of trouble, annoyance or disaster: 麻烦、讨厌或灾祸的原因; 祸患: *a ~ of locusts/flies.* 蝗虫(苍蝇)的灾祸。*What a ~ that boy is!* What a nuisance he is! 那小孩多么讨厌! □ vt [VP6A,14] *~ (with)*, annoy (esp with repeated requests or questions). 烦扰(尤指以一再请求或询问来困扰)。**plaguy** /ˈpleɪgɪ; ˈplegɪ/ adj (colloq) annoying. (口)烦扰的; 麻烦的。**pla·guily** /-ɪlɪ; -əlɪ/ adv annoyingly; provokingly. 烦扰地; 恼人地。

plaice /pleɪs; ples/ n (pl unchanged) edible flatfish. (复数不变)鲽(一种可食的比目鱼)。⇨ the illus at **fish**. 参看 fish 之插图。

plaid /plæd; plæd/ n **1** [C] long piece of woollen cloth worn over the shoulders by Scottish Highlanders. (苏格兰高地人所披的)肩巾。**2** [U] cloth, usu with a chequered or tartan pattern, used for this article of dress. (用作肩巾的)方格呢; 格子花呢。

plain¹ /pleɪn; plen/ adj (-er, -est) **1** easy to see, hear or understand: 明白的; 清楚的; 易了解的: *~ English;* 简明英语; *in ~ speech;* 以明白的言词; *~ language*, (of telegrams, etc) not in code. (指电报等)明码。*The meaning is quite ~.* 这意义十分清楚。*~ 'sailing*, (fig) course of action that is simple and free from difficulties: (喻)一帆风顺: *After we engaged a guide, everything was ~ sailing.* 我们雇到一个向导之后, 一切都顺利了。**2** simple; ordinary; without luxury or ornament: 简单的; 平凡的; 朴素的: *a ~ blue dress*, of blue material without a design on it, or without trimmings, etc; 一件纯蓝的衣裳; *in ~ clothes*, (esp of policemen) in ordinary clothes, not in uniform; (尤指警察)穿便服的; *~ food/cooking;* 简单的食物(烹饪); *a ~ cook*, one who can prepare ~ meals. 能烹调简单餐食的厨子。**3** (of persons, their thoughts, actions, etc) straightforward; frank: (指人、思想、行为等)直截了当的; 坦白的: *in ~ words*, frankly; 坦白地说; *in ~ dealing*, honesty, sincerity. 诚实; 真挚。*to be '~ with you*, to speak openly. 坦白对你说。**~·'spoken** adj frank in speech.

说话坦白的; 直言的。 **4** (of a person's appearance) not pretty or handsome. (指人的容貌)不漂亮的; 不美的。 **5** '**~-song/-chant** *n* music for a number of voices in unison, used in the Anglican and Roman Catholic Church services. (英国国教及天主教礼拜式中所唱的) 齐唱的歌曲; 素歌。 □ *adv* clearly: 清楚地; 明白地: *learn to speak ~*; 学习说清楚; 明白地; entirely: 完全地: *You are ~ wrong.* 你完全错了。 **~·ly** *adv* clearly: 清楚地: *The rock stuck out ~ly*; 那岩石清楚地突了出来; obviously: 显然地: *You are ~ly wrong.* 你显然错了。 **~·ness** *n*

plain² /pleɪn; plen/ *n* area of level country: 平原; 平地: *the wide ~s of Canada.* 加拿大的广大平原。'**~s·man** /-zmən; -zmən/ *n* (*pl* **-men**) inhabitant of a ~. 平原居民。

plain³ /pleɪn; plen/ *n* simple stitch in knitting. (编织时的)正编; 上针。 ⇨ **purl¹**. □ *vt, vi* knit this stitch. 正编; 用上针织。

plaint /pleɪnt; plent/ *n* **1** (legal) charge; accusation. (法律) 告诉; 控诉。 **2** (poet) complaint; lamentation. (诗)诉怨; 悲叹。

plain·tiff /'pleɪntɪf; 'plentɪf/ *n* person who brings an action at law. 原告。 ⇨ **defendant**.

plain·tive /'pleɪntɪv; 'plentɪv/ *adj* sounding sad; sorrowful. 哀伤的; 悲哀的。 **~·ly** *adv* **~·ness** *n*

plait /plæt; plet/ *vt* [VP6A] weave or twist (three or more lengths of hair, straw, etc) under and over one another into one rope-like length. 编(头发)成辫; (草)成绳。 **~** *n* sth made by **~**ing; 发辫; 发辫; 辫子; 缠: *wearing her hair in a ~.* 将她的头发编成一条辫子。

plan /plæn; plæn/ *n* **1** outline drawing (of or for a building) showing the relative size, positions, etc of the parts, esp as if seen from above: (建筑物的)设计图; 图面; 平面图: *~s for a new school.* 一所新学校的平面图。 ⇨ **elevation(5)**; ⇨ the illus at **perspective**. 参看 perspective 之插图。 **2** diagram (of the parts of a machine). (机器各部的) 图解; 说明图。 **3** diagram showing how a garden, park, town or other area of land has been, or is to be, laid out. (花园、公园、城镇或其他地区的)详图; 计划图。 Cf *map* for a large area of land. (参较 map 表示大地区的地图)。 **4** arrangement for doing or using sth, considered in advance: 计划; 策略; 方案: *make ~s for the holidays*; 作度假的计划; *a ~ to encourage saving*; 鼓励储蓄的方案; *a five-year ~*, eg for a country's economic and industrial development. 五年计划(例如为国家的经济和工业发展而拟订者)。 (**go**) *according to ~*, (happen) as planned. 照计划进行。 □ *vt* (**-nn-**) **1** [VP6A] make a ~ of or for: 设计; 作…的计划; 绘…的设计图: *~ a house/garden.* 设计一座房子(花园)。 **2** [VP7A] *~ to do sth*, make ~s: 计划(做某

事): *We're ~ning to visit Europe this summer.* 我们正计划今年夏天去欧洲旅行。 **3** [VP6A, 15B] **~** (*out*), consider and arrange in advance: 策划; 筹划: *~ (out) a military campaign.* 策划一个战役。 **a ~ned economy**, economic system ~ned by government authorities. 计划经济。 ⇨ **town(2)**. **~·ner** *n* one who makes ~s. 设计者; 策划者。 **~·less** *adj* without a ~. 没有计划的。

plan·chette /plɑːnˈʃet *US*: plænˈʃet; plænˈʃɛt/ *n* small board supported by two castors, with a vertical pencil said to trace marks on paper at spiritualistic seances without conscious direction by hand. 扶乩写字板; 乩板。

plane¹ /pleɪn; plen/ *n* '**~(-tree)**, one of several kinds of tree with spreading branches, broad leaves and thin bark, which comes off in flakes. 法国梧桐。

plane² /pleɪn; plen/ *n* tool for trimming the surface of wood by taking shavings from it. 刨刀; 刨子。 ⇨ the illus at **tool**. 参看 tool 之插图。 □ *vt, vi* [VP2A, 15B, 2D, 22] use a ~; make smooth with a ~: 用刨子; 用刨刨平: *~ sth smooth.* 将某物刨平滑。 **~ away/down**, remove irregularities with a ~. 刨去不平之处。

plane³ /pleɪn; plen/ *n* **1** flat or level surface; surface such that the straight line joining any points on it is touching it at all points; imaginary surface of this kind: 平面; 几何平面; 想象中的绝对平面; (attrib) (用作定语), '**~ ge'ometry**, geometry of figures on a ~. 平面几何学。 '**~ 'sailing**, the art of determining a ship's position on the theory that the ship is moving on a ~. 平面航行术 (依据船只在一平面上航行之理论以决定一船的位置)。 ⇨ *plain sailing* at **plain¹(1)**. **2** main supporting surface of an aeroplane. 机翼。 **3** (fig) level or stage (*of* development, etc): (喻)(发展等)水准; 阶段: *on the same ~ as a savage*; 跟野蛮人同样阶段; *on a higher social ~.* 在更高的社会水准。 □ *vi* (**down**), (of aeroplanes) travel, glide. (指飞机)航行; 下滑。

plane⁴ /pleɪn; plen/ *n* (colloq abbr for) **aeroplane**. (口)为 aeroplane 之略。

planet /'plænɪt; 'plænɪt/ *n* one of the heavenly bodies (eg *Mars, Venus*) which moves round a star such as the sun and is illuminated by it. 行星 (如火星、金星)。 **plan·et·ary** /'plænɪtrɪ *US*: -terɪ; 'plænəˌterɪ/ *adj* relating to, moving like, a ~. 行星的; 有关行星的; 运行象行星的。 **plan·et·ar·ium** /ˌplænɪ'teərɪəm; ˌplænə'tɛrɪəm/ *n*(building with a) device for representing the movements of the stars and ~s by projecting spots of light on the inner surface of a large dome that represents the sky. 行星运行仪; 太阳系仪(将光点投射于代表天空的大圆顶内面以表示星球运行的仪器); 装有此种仪器的建筑物; 假天; 天文馆。

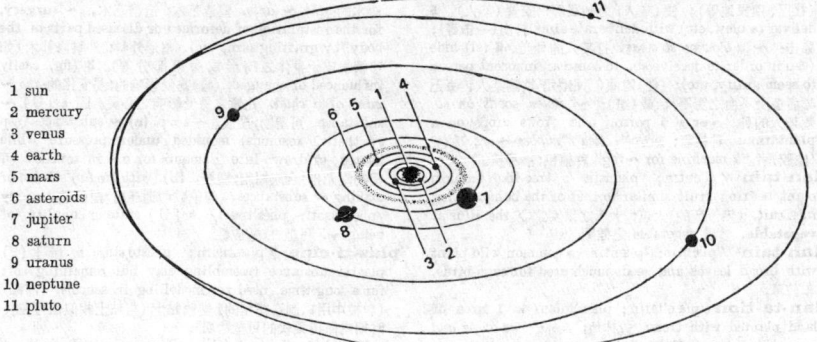

1	sun
2	mercury
3	venus
4	earth
5	mars
6	asteroids
7	jupiter
8	saturn
9	uranus
10	neptune
11	pluto

the planets of our solar system

plan·gent /'plændʒənt; 'plændʒənt/ adj (formal) (of sounds) resounding; vibrating. (正式用语) (指声音) 回响的; 震颤的。

plank /plæŋk; plæŋk/ n 1 long, flat piece of timber, 2 to 6 inches thick, 9 or more inches wide; board. 厚木板 (厚二英寸到六英寸，宽九英寸以上); 板。 '~-**bed** n one of boards, without mattresses. 木板床。 **walk the ~,** ⇨ **walk²(4).** 2 basic principle in a political platform. 政纲的准则; 政纲的基本条款。 □ vt 1 [VP6A] furnish with ~s; cover (a floor, etc) with ~s. 供以厚板; 以厚板铺 (地面等)。 2 [VP15B] ~ sth down, (colloq) put down (esp money); pay at once. (口) 放下 (尤指钱); 立刻付款。 ~·**ing** n [U] ~s put down to form a floor. (用以铺地板之) 板材; 铺板。

plank·ton /'plæŋktən; 'plæŋktən/ n [U] the (chiefly microscopic) forms of organic life that drift in or float on the water of the oceans, lakes, rivers, etc. 浮游生物 (主要为微生物)。

plant¹ /plɑːnt; US: plænt; plænt/ n 1 living organism which is not an animal, esp the kind smaller than trees and shrubs: 植物; (尤指小于乔木及灌木的) 花草; 苗木: garden ~; 庭园中的花木; 园艺植物; a tobacco ~. 一株烟草。 '~-**louse** n kinds of insect pest that attack ~s, esp aphis. 危害植物的昆虫; (尤指) 蚜虫。 2 [U] apparatus, fixtures, machinery, etc used in an industrial or manufacturing process: 用于工业生产中之仪器、设备、机器等: We get our tractors and bulldozers from a ~-hire firm. 我们向一家机器出租公司租用牵引机和推土机。 The farm has its own lighting ~, eg a generator for producing electric current. 这农场有自己的发电设备。 3 [U] (US) factory; buildings and equipment of an institution. (美) 工厂; 一个机构的建筑物与设备。 4 (sl) planned swindle; hoax; person who joins a gang of criminals to get evidence against them. (俚) 骗局; 诈; 参加犯罪集团以套取可资控告之证据的人。

plant² /plɑːnt; US: plænt; plænt/ vt [VP6A, 15A, B] 1 put ~s, bushes, trees, etc in (a garden, etc): 栽植花木、灌木、乔木等于 (庭园等) 中: ~ a garden with rose bushes; 在花园里栽植玫瑰花; 栽 set up a monument and ~ it round with trees / ~ trees round it. 设立纪念碑并在其四周栽种树木。 2 put (plants, trees etc in the ground to grow; (fig) cause (an idea) to take root in sb's mind: 种植 (花木、树等); (喻) 灌输 (观念) 于某人心中: ~ (out) strawberry runners / pansies. 种植草莓的藤蔓 (三色紫罗兰)。 ⇨ **sow²**. 3 place firmly in position; take up a position or attitude: 安置; 处于某一位置; 取某一姿势: He ~ed his feet firmly on the ground. 他把脚稳踏在地上。 He ~ed himself in front of the fire. 他站在炉火的前面。 He ~ed his feet wide apart. 他两脚跨得很开地站着。 4 establish, found (a community, colony, etc); settle (a person) in a place as a colonist, etc. 建立; 设立 (社区、殖民地等); 使 (某人) 为殖民者; 安置 (某人)。 5 deliver (a blow, etc) with deliberate aim: 打出 (一击等); 瞄击: ~ a blow on sb's ear. 打某人的耳光。 6 (sl) hide (esp in order to deceive sb, to cause an innocent person to seem guilty, etc): (俚) 隐藏 (尤指为了欺骗某人、使无辜者蒙受不白之冤等); 栽 (赃): ~ stolen goods on sb. 栽某人的赃。 ~·**er** n 1 person who grows crops on a plantation: 种植者; 栽培者: 'tea / 'rubber-~ers. 茶客 (橡胶) 者。 2 machine for ~ing. 种植机; 播种机。

plan·tain¹ /'plæntin; 'plæntin/ n tree-like tropical plant bearing fruit similar to that of the banana palm; its fruit. (热带产的) 大蕉; 大蕉之果实。 ⇨ the illus at **vegetable**. 参看 vegetable 之插图。

plan·tain² /'plæntin; 'plæntin/ n common wild plant with broad leaves and seeds much used for cage-birds. 车前草。

plan·ta·tion /plæn'teiʃn; plæn'teʃən/ n 1 area of land planted with trees: 造林地; 森林: ~s of fir and pine. 杉树及松树的森林。 2 large estate on which tea, cotton, sugar, tobacco or other commercial crop is cultivated: 大农场; 大种植园: '~ songs, songs sung by

Negroes who formerly worked as slaves on cotton ~s in N America. 昔时北美洲棉花农场上黑奴所唱的歌。

plaque /plɑːk; US: plæk; plæk/ n flat metal or porcelain plate fixed on a wall as an ornament or memorial. 装在墙上作装饰或纪念用的薄金属板或瓷片; 饰板。

plash /plæʃ; plæʃ/ n (sing only) light splashing sound: (仅用单数) 轻轻的拍水声: the ~ of oars in water. 桨拍在水上的激溅声。 □ vt, vi [VP6A, 2A] strike the surface of (water) gently; splash. 轻拍 (水) 面; 激溅。

plasm /'plæzəm; 'plæzəm/ n [U] genetic material of a cell. (细胞的) 原浆; 原生质; 胞浆。

plasma /'plæzmə; 'plæzmə/ n (blood) ~, [U] clear, yellowish fluid in which the blood-cells are carried. 血浆。

plas·ter /'plɑːstə(r); US: 'plæs-; 'plæstɚ/ n 1 [U] soft mixture of lime, sand, water, etc used for coating walls and ceilings. 灰泥 (用于涂墙及天花板)。 '~ of 'Paris n [U] white paste made from gypsum, that becomes very hard when dry, used for making moulds, etc. 烧石膏; 熟石膏。 '~ cast n (a) mould made with gauze and ~ of Paris to hold a broken or dislocated bone in place. (用于固定折骨或脱臼之骨的) 石膏绷带; 石膏夹。 (b) mould (eg for a small statue) made of ~ of Paris. 石膏模型 (如制小雕像者)。 '~ board n [U] board made of gypsum and thick paper or cardboard, used for inside walls and ceilings instead of plastering. 石膏厚纸板 (用作内墙及天花板而无需涂灰泥)。 2 [C] piece of fabric spread with a medicinal substance, for application to part of the body, to relieve pain, cover a wound, etc. 膏药。 3 ('sticking-)~, [U, C] material treated with some substance so that it will stick to the skin, used for covering a cut, blister, burn, for holding a bandage in position, etc. 橡皮膏; 绊创膏 (用于包覆轻伤、固定绷带等)。 □ vt [VP6A, 14] 1 cover (a wall, etc) with ~(1); put a ~(2) on (the body). 涂灰泥于 (墙等); 敷膏药于 (身体)。 2 ~ sth with sth; ~ sth on sth, cover thickly: 厚厚地涂盖: hair ~ed with oil; 油涂得很厚的头发; an old suitcase ~ed with hotel labels. 贴满了旅馆标签的一只旧手提箱。 ~·**ed** adj (colloq) drunk. (口) 醉的。 ~·**er** n workman who ~s walls and ceilings. 涂灰泥于墙壁及天花板的工人; 泥水匠。

plas·tic /'plæstik; 'plæstik/ adj 1 (of materials) easily shaped or moulded: (指物质) 易做成各种形态的; 易塑的: Clay is a ~ substance. 粘土是易塑的物质; (of goods) made of such materials, esp synthetic resinous substances; (指货物) 由易塑物质做成的; (尤指) 合成树脂做成的; 塑胶做成的: ~ raincoats / flowers / cups / spoons. 塑胶雨衣 (花, 杯, 匙)。 ~ ex'plosive, kind that is easily moulded around the object it is to destroy. 可塑炸药。 '~·**bomb**, one made of such explosive. 可塑炸药制成的炸弹; 塑胶炸弹。 2 of the art of modelling: 塑造术的: the ~ arts. 塑造艺术; 造型艺术。 ~ 'surgery, for the restoration of deformed or diseased parts of the body (by grafting skin, etc). 整形术; 外科修补术 (如移植表皮于身体之畸形或病患部分等)。 3 (fig) easily influenced or changed: (喻) 易受影响的; 易变化的: the ~ mind of a child. 儿童之易受影响之心灵。 □ n [C] ~ substance. 可塑物; 塑胶。 ~s n pl (a) ~ substances (esp synthetic, resinous) moulded under pressure while heated, or drawn into filaments for use in textiles. 可塑物; (尤指) 合成树脂; 塑胶。 (b) (with sing v) science of making ~ substances. (与单数动词连用) 塑胶学。 ~·**ity** /plæ'stisəti; plæ'stisəti/ n [U] state or quality of being ~. 可塑性; 适应性。

plas·ti·cine /'plæstisi:n; 'plæstəsin/ n [U] (P) plastic substance resembling clay but remaining soft for a long time, used for modelling in schools. (商标) (学校中用以制造模型的) 塑胶粘土 (与粘土相似但可在长时期内保持柔软的可塑物质)。

plate¹ /pleit; plet/ n 1 [C] shallow, usu circular, almost flat dish, made (usu) of earthenware or china, from which food is served or eaten: 盘; 碟: a dinner / soup /

dessert ~; 餐(汤, 水果或甜点)盘; contents of this: 盘或碟所盛之物: *a ~ of beef and vegetables.* 一盘牛肉和青菜. **hand／give sb sth on a ~,** (colloq) give sb to have, sth without his having to make any effort. (口)使某人轻易得到某物; 给人送上门去. **on one's ~,** to occupy one's time: 占据时间: *He has enough／a lot／too much on his ~.* 他的时间排了够多(很多, 太多)的活动或工作. **'~-rack** n rack in which ~s are kept or placed to drain after being washed. 餐具架(放置盘碟或盘具洗过后晾干用的架子). **2** [C] similar vessel or dish (usu of metal) used for collection of money in churches: (教会中的)奉献盘(通常为金属制): *put only a dime in the ~.* 只放一角钱在奉献盘上. **3** [U] (collective) gold or silver articles, eg spoons, dishes bowls, for use at meals: (集合名词)金质或银质的餐具(如匙, 碟, 碗): *a fine piece of ~,* one of these articles. 一件精致的金质或银质餐具. ⇨ plate² (2). **'~-powder** n [U] powder for cleaning and polishing ~. 擦亮金属餐具之粉; 擦银粉. **4** [C] flat, thin sheet of metal, glass, etc eg steel ~s for building ships: 金属、玻璃等薄片(如用以造船的薄钢板): *'boiler ~s.* 锅炉钢板. **'~-'glass** n [U] thick and very clear glass in sheets for windows, mirrors, doors, etc. 平板玻璃(透明的厚玻璃板, 用以做窗玻璃、镜子、门等). **5** [U, C] sheet of glass coated with sensitive film for photography: (照相用的玻璃质)感光板; 底片: *'whole-~,* 全张感光板, *'half-~,* 对开感光板, *'quarter-~,* the usual sizes. 四开感光板(通常用的尺码). **6** [C] oblong piece of metal (usu brass) with a person's name, etc on it, fixed to the door or gate (as used by doctors, solicitors and other professional persons): 名牌; 招牌(长方形的金属板, 通常为铜制, 上有姓名, 悬于门旁, 医生、律师等专业人员多用之). **7** sheet of metal, plastic, rubber, etc from which the pages of a book are printed; book illustration (usu photographic) printed separately from the text. (印刷之)金属、塑胶或橡皮版; 书中插图(与书之本文分开印刷, 通常为照相者). **8** '**dental** ~, (also called 亦称作 a *denture*) thin piece of plastic material, moulded to the shape of the gums, with artificial teeth attached to it. 假牙床. **9** [C] silver or gold cup as a prize for a horse-race; the race. (作为赛马奖品之)金杯; 银杯; (以金杯或银杯作奖品之)赛马. **10** (in baseball) (also 亦作 **home** ~) home base of the batting area. (棒球)本垒. **'~-ful** /-ful; -,ful/ n amount that a ~ holds. 一盘或一碟之量.

plate² /pleɪt; plet/ vt [VP6A, 14] ~ *(with),* **1** cover (esp a ship) with metal plates (4). 以薄金属板覆盖(尤指)以薄钢板包被(船). **2** cover (another metal) with gold, silver or tin: 以金、银、铜或锡镀(另一金属): *gold-~d dishes;* 镀金的碟子; *silver-~d spoons.* 镀银的匙.

pla·teau /'plætəʊ US: plæ'təʊ; plæ'to/ n (pl ~s or ~x /-təʊz; -'toz/) expanse of level land high above sea-level. 高地; 高原. ⇨ the illus at mountain. 参看 mountain 之插图.

plate-layer /'pleɪtleɪə(r); 'plet,leɪ/ n workman who lays and repairs railway tracks. (铁路之)路工.

plat·form /'plætfɔːm; 'plæt,fɔrm/ n **1** flat surface built at a higher level than the track in a railway station, used by travellers: (火车站之)月台: *Which ~ does the Bournemouth train leave from?* 往伯恩茅斯的火车由哪个月台开出? **2** flat structure raised above floor-level for speakers in a hall or in the open air, teachers in a classroom, etc; space at the entrance of a bus or tram (for the conductor): 讲台; (公共汽车或电车入口处剪票员站立之)平台. **3** programme of a political party, esp as stated before an election. (政党之)政纲; 党纲(尤指在选举前所列的纲领).

plat·ing /'pleɪtɪŋ; 'pletɪŋ/ n [U] (esp) thin coating of gold, silver, etc. (尤指)一层极薄之金属(如金、银等)镀层; 镀银; 镀铬. ⇨ plate² (2).

plati·num /'plætɪnəm; 'plætɪnəm/ n [U] grey untarnishable metal (symbol **Pt**) used for jewellery and alloyed with other metals for use in industry. 铂; 白金

(符号为 **Pt**). **,~ 'blonde,** (colloq) woman with silvery-white hair (but not used of a hair that has turned white with age). (白)银白色头发的女人(非指因年老而头发变白者).

plati·tude /'plætɪtjuːd US: -tuːd; 'plætə,tjud/ n **1** [C] statement that is obviously true, esp one often heard before, but uttered as if it were new. 平凡陈腐的话; 陈腔滥调. **2** [U] quality of being commonplace. 平凡; 陈腐. **plati·tudi·nous** /,plætɪ'tjuːdɪnəs US: -'tuːdənəs; ,plætə'tjudnəs/ adj commonplace: 平凡的; 陈腐的: *platitudinous remarks.* 平凡的话.

Pla·tonic /plə'tɒnɪk; plə'tɑnɪk/ adj of Plato or his teachings: 柏拉图的; 柏拉图哲学的: ~ *love／friendship,* between two people without a desire for physical love. 柏拉图式的爱情(友谊)(即两人之间不掺杂色情或肉欲成分的爱情或友谊); 精神恋爱; 纯洁友谊.

pla·toon /plə'tuːn; plə'tun/ n body of soldiers, subdivision of a company, acting as a unit and commanded by a lieutenant. 排(军队中连以下的单位).

plat·ter /'plætə(r); 'plætə/ n **1** (US) large, shallow dish for serving food, esp meat and fish. (美)(盛食物, 特别是盛肉及鱼的)大浅盘. **2** (archaic in GB) flat dish, often of wood. (古英)扁平之盘碟(常为木制).

platy·pus /'plætɪpəs; 'plætəpəs/ n (pl ~es /-pəsɪz; -pəsɪz/)(,**duck-'billed**) ~, (also called 亦称作 *duckbill*) small Australian animal which suckles its young but lays eggs (called *duckbill* because it has a bill like that of a duck). 鸭嘴兽(产于澳洲的小兽, 哺乳但卵生, 因其嘴似鸭, 故名). ⇨ the illus at small. 参看 small 之插图.

plau·dit /'plɔːdɪt; 'plɔdɪt/ n (usu pl) cry, clapping or other sign of approval: (通常用复数)喝采; 鼓掌; 称赞: *gratified at the ~s of the audience.* 因观众之喝采而感到满意.

plaus·ible /'plɔːzəbl; 'plɔzəbl/ adj **1** seeming to be right or reasonable: 似真实的; 似合理的: *a ~ excuse／explanation.* 似乎合理的理由(解释). **2** (of persons) clever at producing convincing arguments, etc: (指人)能言善辩的; 嘴巧的; 花言巧语的: *a ~ rogue.* 花言巧语的歹徒. **plaus·ibly** /-əblɪ; -əblɪ/ adv **plausi·bil·ity** /,plɔːzə'bɪlɪtɪ; ,plɔzə'bɪlɪtɪ/ n [C] state of being ~; [C] (pl **-ties**) ~ excuse, argument, etc. 似真; 似合理; 似真实的借口、议论等.

play¹ /pleɪ; ple/ n **1** [U] (what is done for) amusement; recreation: 游玩; 游戏; 娱乐: *the children are at* ~, engaged in playing. 孩子们在游戏. *What I said was only in* ~, not intended to be taken seriously. 我所说的话不过是开玩笑而已. *a ~ on words,* a pun. 双关语; 俏皮话. **'child's-~** n [U] sth simple and easy. 简单之事. **'~-box** n box to hold toys. 玩具箱; 玩具盒. **'~-boy** n rich young man chiefly interested in enjoying himself. 花花公子, 主要兴趣在享乐的年轻人. **'~-fellow／mate** n companion in ~. 玩伴. **'~-ground** n piece of ground used for ~, eg one at a school or in a public park (cf 参较 *playing-field* below). (学校或公园内之)运动场. **'~-group** n = ~school. **'~-pen** n portable enclosure in which a baby or small child may be left to ~. (可将小孩放在里面玩的)轻便围栏. **'~-room** n one in a house for children to ~ in. (儿童的)游戏室; 娱乐间. **'~-school** a group of young children who play together regularly under supervision. 幼稚园; 托儿所. **'~-suit** n loose garment(s) to be worn (eg on a beach) by a child while playing. (幼儿在海滨等地游戏时所穿着之)运动装; 运动衫. **'~-thing** n toy; (fig)sb treated as a mere toy. 玩具; 玩物; (喻)被玩弄取乐的人; 玩物. **'~-time** n period for ~. 游戏时间; 休闲时间. **2** [U] the playing of a game; manner of playing: 竞赛; 运动; 游戏或竞赛的方式: *There was a lot of rough ~ in the football match yesterday.* 昨天的足球比赛很粗野. *That was expert ~／an expert bit of ~!* 那场竞赛漂亮极了! *in／out of ~,* (of the ball in football, cricket, etc) in／not in a position where the rules of the game allow it to be played. (指足球、板球等比赛中的球)位(未位)于比赛规则允许之

处;(不是)死球。**fair ~**, (fig) justice, equal conditions and treatment for all: (喻)公正; 公平; 平等对待; 公平处理: *I will see fair ~*, I will ensure that both sides are treated justly. 我将公平处理的。**foul ~**, ~ contrary to the rules; (fig) treachery; violence: 犯规; (喻)奸诈; 暴力: *Do the police suspect foul ~?* 警方怀疑其中有奸诈吗? **3** [U] turn or move in a game (eg chess): (下棋等之)轮到; 移动; 走棋: *It's your ~*, You are to make the next move. 该你了。**4** [U] gaming; gambling; 赌; 赌博: *lose £50 in one evening's ~*, 一晚上赌博输掉五十镑; *high ~*, ie for high stakes. 输赢很大的赌博。**5** [C] drama for the stage: 剧本; 戏剧: *the ~s of Shakespeare.* 莎士比亚的剧本。*Let's go to a ~* (= theatre) *this evening.* 我们今晚去看戏吧。**as good as a ~**, amusing, interesting. 很好玩的; 有趣的。**'~-acting** [U] n performance of ~s; (fig) pretence. 戏剧的演出; 表演; (喻)假装; 矫饰。**'~-actor** n (old use) actor. (旧用法)演员; 伶人。**'~-bill** n bill announcing the performance of a ~. 戏单; 戏码。**'~-goer** /-gəʊə(r)/; -goə/ n person who often goes to the theatre. 常去看戏的人。**'~-house** n theatre. 戏院。**'~-wright** n dramatist. 剧作家。**6** [U] light, quick, fitful movement: 轻快而断续的动作: *the ~ of sunlight upon water.* 阳光在水面上的闪烁。**7** [U] (space for) free and easy movement; scope for activity: 自由活动; 自由活动的空间; 活动的范围: *allow full ~ to one's curiosity;* 让好奇心自由发展; *give free ~ to one's fancy/emotions;* 纵情想象(任感情泛滥); *a knot with too much ~*, one that is not tight enough. 不够紧的结。*Give the rope more ~*, keep it less taut. 把绳子放松一些。**8** [U] activity; operation: 活动; 运转; 作用: *the ~ of forces.* 力的作用。**be in full ~**, be fully operating or active. 在全力运转(活动)中。**bring sth into ~**, make use of it; bring it into action. 利用某物; 使某物发生作用。**come into ~**, begin to operate or be active. 开始活动。

play² /pleɪ/; ple/ vt, vi (pt, pp ~ed /pleɪd/; pled/) (For special uses with adverbial particles and preps, ⇨ **15** below.) (与副词性小品词及介词连用的特殊用法，参看下列第15义。) **1** [VP2A, B, C] (contrasted with *work*) have fun; do things to pass the time pleasantly, as children do: (与 work 相对)玩耍; 游乐: *The children are ~ing in the park.* 孩子们正在公园里玩耍。*Let's go out and ~.* 我们出去玩吧。*~ with*, amuse oneself with: 以…自娱: *~ with the kitten.* 以逗小猫自娱。**2** [VP3A, 6A] ~ (*at doing sth*), pretend, for fun, to be sth or do sth: 假装; 假扮: *Let's ~ (at being) pirates.* 我们来假扮海盗吧。*The children were ~ing at keeping shop.* 孩子们在假装开店铺。**3** [VP6A, 14, 12C] ~ *a joke/prank/trick (on sb)* trick him. 开玩笑; 戏谑某人。**4** [VP6A, 14, 2A, C, 3A] (be able to) take part in a game, eg of cricket, football, golf, cards: 参加(板球、足球、高尔夫球、纸牌等)游戏; 打(球); 玩(游戏): *Do you ~ cricket?* 你打板球吗? *He ~s (football) for Stoke/England.* 他参加斯多克市队(英国队)(踢足球)。*On Saturday France ~s (Rugby) against Wales/~s Wales at Rugby.* 星期六法国队和威尔士队比赛橄榄球。*They were ~ing bridge.* 他们在玩桥牌。*Will you ~ me at chess/~ chess with me?* 你愿意和下棋吗? *He went on ~ing* (= gambling) *until he had lost everything.* 他继续赌博直到输得精光。**5** [VP2C, 3A, 6A] ~ (*as/at*), fill a particular position in a team: 在队中担任某一职务: *I've never ~ed (as/at) centre-forward before.* 我从来没有担任过中锋。*Who's ~ing in goal/as goalkeeper?* 谁做守门员? [VP6A, 15A, 16B] ~ *sb* (*as/at*), include in a team: 起用某人参加比赛; 使包括在队中: *I think we should ~ Smith in the next match.* 我认为我们应该起用史密斯参加下场比赛。*Who shall we ~ as goalkeeper?* 我们将派谁担任守门员? **6** [VP15A, B] (cricket, football, etc) strike (the ball) in a specified manner: (板球、足球等)按一定方式打出球: ~ *the ball to mid-on;* 把球打到投手右侧外场员的附近; *~ (the ball) on to one's own wicket* (and so put oneself out). 将(球)打到自己的三柱门(而使自己出局)。*In soccer only*

the goalkeeper may ~ the ball with his hands. 踢足球时，只有守门员可以用手拿球。~ *ball (with)*, (fig, colloq) be ready to act in partnership; co-operate: (喻，口)(和…)合伙; 合作: *The French President refused to ~ ball, eg to co-operate with the leader of another country.* 法国总统拒绝合作。[VP2C] (cricket, of the ground) be in good, poor, etc condition for ~ing: (指球场)适合(不适合)打球: *The pitch is ~ing well/badly.* 柱间的场地适合(不适合)打球。**7** [VP6A] move (a piece) in chess: 移动; 走(棋子): ~ *a pawn;* 移动小卒; take (a playing-card) from one's hand (in whist, bridge, etc) and lay it down face upwards when one's turn comes: (在惠斯特、桥牌等中)出(牌): ~ *one's ace of hearts/a trump.* 出红心么点牌(一张王牌)。~ *one's cards well/badly*, (fig) make good/bad use of opportunities. (喻)善(不善)于利用机会。**8** ~ *fair*, fairly; in accordance with the rules. 公平地玩; 规规矩矩地玩。~ *hard*, (of a player) ~ vigorously. (指球员、比赛者)实力地比赛(打球等)。~ *the ball, not the man*, kick the ball, not one's opponent. 踢球而非踢人(对手)。~ *the game*, observe the rules of the game; (fig) be fair and honest; observe the code of honour. 遵守这场规则; (喻)公正诚实; 遵守社会礼法。**9** [VP 6A, 2A, 12B, 13B] perform on (a musical instrument), perform (music); cause (music) to be heard (by operating a record-player or taperecorder): 演奏(乐器); 弹; 拉; 吹; 演奏(乐曲); (用唱机或录音机)放出: ~ *the piano/flute/violin, etc;* 弹钢琴(吹笛子; 拉小提琴等); ~ *a Beethoven sonata.* 演奏贝多芬的奏鸣曲。*Won't you please ~ me some Chopin/some Chopin for me?* 请你为我演奏一些萧邦的作品好吗? *He was ~ing an old tune on his guitar.* 他用吉他弹奏一首老曲子。*We ~ed a lot of reggae at our party.* 我们在宴会上放了很多西印度群岛的流行音乐。*P~ me Pat Simon's latest disc.* 给我放些派特·赛门最近灌制的唱片。[VP15B] ~ *sth back*, reproduce (music, speech, etc) from a tape or disc after it has been recorded: 播放(录下的音乐、演讲等): *The discussion was recorded on tape and then ~ed back.* 讨论的内容被录音，然后再播放出来。Hence, 由此产生, **'~-back** n (a) the device on a taperecorder which ~s back recorded material. (录音机上的)放音装置。(b) occasion when this is done. 放音。~ *second fiddle (to sb)*, ⇨ **fiddle**. ~ *sth by ear/at sight*, ⇨ **ear¹(2)**, *at/on sight* at **sight¹(2)**. ~ *it cool*, ⇨ **cool¹(5)**. **10** [VP6A, 2A] perform (a drama on the stage); act (a part in a drama); (of a drama) be performed: 演(戏); 扮演(角色); (指戏剧)上演: ~ *'Twelfth Night';* 演出'第十二夜'; ~ *Shylock;* 扮演'威尼斯商人'中的夏洛克; *~ the National Theatre, where 'Hamlet' is now ~ing,* ~ being ~ed. 正在上演'哈姆雷特'的国家戏院。~ *the fool*, act foolishly. 行为愚蠢; 干傻事。~ *the man*, act like a man; be manly. 行为象男人; 有男子气概。~ *a (big/small, etc) part (in sth)*, ⇨ **part¹(4)**. **11** [VP2A, C, 15A] move about in a light or capricious manner; direct (light) (on, over, along, etc sth): 轻快或不定地活动; 投射(光线)(到某处上): *sunlight ~ing on the water.* 在水面闪烁的阳光。*They ~ed coloured lights over the dance floor.* 他们把彩色灯光投射到舞池上。*A smile ~ed on her lips.* 她的唇上露出一丝微笑。*His fancy ~ed round the idea of entering a monastery.* 他一心想着进修道院。*They ~ed searchlights on the clouds/along the road.* 他们用探照灯照射云(沿路照射)。**12** [VP2A, 6A, 15A] operate continuously; discharge in a steady stream: 继续或持续地操作; 规律地放出; 发射: *The fountains in the park ~ on Sundays.* 公园里的喷泉星期天才喷水。*The firemen ~ed their hoses on the burning building.* 消防队员用水管向着火的建筑物喷水。**13** [VP14, 3A] ~ (*sth*) *on/upon sth, fire:* 射击; 开火: *We ~ed our guns on the enemy's lines.* 我们对着敌人的炮线射击。*Their guns ~ed on the fort.* 他们的炮朝着城堡发射。**14** ~ *a fish*, (when angling with a rod and line) allow a fish to exhaust itself by pulling against the line. 让鱼拉动钓线以致疲乏。**15** [VP2C,

3A, 15B] (special uses with *adverbial particles* and *preps*): (与副词性小品词及介词连用的特殊用法):

play at sth, (a) ⇨ **2, 5** above. 参看上列第 2, 5 义。 **(b)** engage in sth in a trivial or half-hearted way, or merely for pleasure: 不轻心地做某事; 纯粹为了好玩而做某事: *Go for him properly—you're only ~ing at boxing!* 好好地和他打——你简直是在玩弄拳击!

play sth back, ⇨ **9** above. 参看上列第 9 义。

play down to sb, deliberately talk to or behave towards sb so that he does not feel inferior, in order to win support or favour. (为了免得对方觉得自卑, 或是为了赢得支持或好感而)和善地与某人讲话; 和善地对待某人。~ **sth down,** deliberately minimize its importance. 故意减低某事物的重要性。

play sb in; play sb into a place, ~ music while he is entering (the place). 在某人进入(某地)时奏乐; 奏乐欢迎某人。

play into sb's hands/the hands of sb, act so as to give him an advantage or benefit: 为某人造福; 有利于某人: *My opponent ~ed into my hands.* 我的对手做出了有利于我的行动。

play one person off against another, oppose him against another, esp for one's own advantage; stimulate rivalry between them. 挑拨离间; 使双方面翻以坐收渔利。~ **(sth) off,** ~ again (eg a football match that was drawn): (足球等比赛结束双方积分相等时) 延长比赛; 加赛: ~ *off a draw/tie.* 打成平手后延长比赛以决胜负。*Leeds and Liverpool ~ off (their tie) tomorrow.* 里兹队和利物浦队明天将加赛一场以决胜负。Hence, 由此产生, **'~-off** n such a match. 延长比赛; 加赛。

play on/upon sth, try to rouse or make use of (sb's feelings, incredulity, etc): 激起或利用(某人的感情, 不信任等): *He tried to ~ on her sympathies.* 他想利用她的同情心。~ **on/upon words,** make puns. 说双关语; 说俏皮话。

play sth out, ~ it to the end (usu fig): 结束(通常作比喻用法): *The long struggle between the strikers and their employers is not yet ~ed out.* 罢工者和雇主间的长期斗争尚未结束。**be ~ed out,** be exhausted of energy or usefulness; be out of date: 衰竭; 无用; 过时: *His horse was ~ed out when the day's hunting was over.* 打了一天猎之后, 他的马筋疲力竭了。*Is that theory ~ed out,* no longer worth considering? 那种理论已经陈旧了吗?

play up, (a) (esp in the imper) (sport) ~ vigorously, energetically. (尤用于祈使句中)(运动) 使劲参加比赛, 加油。**(b)** (colloq) behave mischievously: (口)行为顽皮; 恶作剧: *Don't let the children ~ up.* 别让孩子们淘气。~ **sth up,** give excessive importance to: 特别重视; 过度重视: *Don't let him ~ up his illness, eg making it an excuse for doing nothing.* 别让他过于重视他的病(如以病为借口而无所事事)。~ **(sb) up,** (colloq) give trouble (to): (口)给某人麻烦: *This sciatica has been ~ing me up again.* 我这坐骨神经痛又使我烦恼了。~ **up to sb, (a)** act in a drama so as to support another actor. 担任另一演员的配角。(b) (口)(colloq) flatter (to win favour for oneself): (口)谄媚; 拍马屁: *He always ~s up to his political bosses.* 他老是拍他政界上司的马屁。

play with sb, (a) ⇨ **1** and **4** above. 参看上列第 1 义及第 4 义。**(b)** trifle with; consider lightly: 轻视; 忽略(待某人): *It's wrong for a man to ~ with a woman's affections.* 男子玩弄女子的情感是不对的。*He's ~ing with the idea of emigrating to Canada.* 他目前不太重视移民到加拿大的想法。

player /'pleɪə(r); `pleə/ n **1** one who plays a game. 游戏者; 运动者。**2** actor. 演员; 伶人。**3** person who plays a musical instrument; mechanical device for producing musical sounds: 演奏乐器者; 产生乐声之机器: *a 'record-~.* 电唱机。**'~-piano** n piano fitted with a mechanism which enables the piano to be played automatically. 自奏钢琴; 自动钢琴。

play·ful /'pleɪfl; `pleɪfəl/ adj full of fun; in a mood

for play; not serious: 十分有趣的; 爱游戏的; 嬉戏的; 顽皮的: *as ~ as a kitten;* 象小猫一样顽皮; *a ~ manner;* 嬉戏的态度。**~ly** /-fəlɪ; -flɪ/ adv **~ness** n

play·ing /'pleɪɪŋ; `pleɪŋ/ n **~-card,** ⇨ **card¹(3).** **'~-field** n field for such games as football and cricket. field for children's games. (足球、板球游戏等的)球场; 操场; 儿童游戏场。

play·let /'pleɪlɪt; `pleɪlɪt/ n short dramatic piece. 短剧。

plaza /'plɑːzə US: `plæzə; `plæzə/ n market-place; open square (esp in a Spanish town). 市场; (尤指西班牙城市的)广场。

plea /pliː; pli/ n [C] **1** (legal) statement made by or for a person charged in a law court. (法律)(法庭中被告之)答辩; 抗辩; 辩护。**2** request: 恳求; 请求: ~*s for mercy.* 恳求慈悲。**3** reason or excuse offered for wrongdoing or failure to do sth, etc: (为做错事或未能某事所做的)辩解; 借口: *on the ~ of ill health.* 以健康不良为理由。

pleach /pliːtʃ; plitʃ/ vt [VP6A] interlace: 交错; 编结: ~*ed hedges,* made by intertwining growing branches. 交错的树篱。

plead /pliːd; plid/ vt, vi (pt, pp ~ed, or, US **pled,** /pled; plɛd/) **1** [VP3A] (legal) ~ **for/against st,** address a court of law as an advocate on behalf of either the plaintiff or the defendant. (法律)为某人辩护(反驳某人); 抗辩; 答辩。~ **guilty/not guilty,** admit/ deny that one is guilty: 承(否)认有罪; 服(不服)罪: '*How do you ~?*'—'*Not guilty, my Lord.*' '你服罪吗'?——'不服罪, 法官'。**2** [VP6A] (legal) (of a lawyer) present the case (to a court of law); put forward as a plea: (法律)(指律师)(向法庭)提出抗辩; 辩护: *You should get a lawyer to ~ your case.* 你该请一位律师为你的案子辩护。*Her counsel ~ed insanity,* declared that his client was insane, and therefore not legally responsible for her actions. 她的律师辩护说她的精神不健全(故对她的行为不负法律责任)。**3** [VP3A] ~ **(with sb) (for sth/to do sth),** ask earnestly: 恳求; 祈求: ~ *(with sb) for mercy.* (向某人)祈求宽恕。*He ~ed with his son to be less trouble to his mother.* 他求他的儿子少给他母亲添麻烦。**4** [VP6A] offer as an explanation or excuse: 以…为口实; 以…为托词: *The thief ~ed poverty.* 那贼以贫穷为托词。*She ~ed ignorance of the law.* 她以不谙法律为借口。**5** [VP6A] argue in favour of; advance reasons for (a cause, etc): 主张; 为…辩护; 提出 (运动等) 的理由: ~ *the cause of the political prisoners.* 为政治囚犯辩护。**~·ings** n pl (legal) formal (usu written) statements, replies to accusations, etc, made by the parties in a legal action. (法律)(原告的)诉状; (被告的)答辩状。**~·ing·ly** adv

pleas·ance /'plezns; `pleznz/ n [C] (archaic) pleasure. pleasure-ground. (古)游乐; 游乐园。

pleas·ant /'pleznt; `pleznt/ adj giving pleasure; agreeable; friendly: 可喜的; 愉快的; 适意的; 友爱的: *a ~ afternoon/taste/wine/surprise/companion;* 愉快的下午(合意的味道); 美味的葡萄酒; 惊喜; 友爱的伴侣: *make oneself ~ to visitors;* 亲切周到地待客; ~ *to the taste.* 好吃; 可口。**~·ly** adv **~·ness** n [U].

pleas·ant·ry /'plezntrɪ; `plezntrɪ/ n (pl **-ries**) **1** [U] being jocular; humour. 诙谐; 幽默。**2** [C] humorous or joking remark: 诙谐的笑话; 幽默话: *The girls smiled dutifully at the headmistress's pleasantries.* 女生们对于女校长所说的笑话发出应付的微笑。

please /pliːz; pliz/ vt, vi **1** (imper) (abbr of *if you ~*) (used as a polite form of request): (祈使用法)(if you ~之略)(用作请求的客套话): *Come in, ~* 请进来。*P~ come in.* 请进来。*Two coffees, ~* 请来两杯咖啡。*P~ don't do that.* 请别做那件事。**2** [VP6A] give satisfaction to; be agreeable to: 使愉快; 使满意; 使惬意: *That will ~ you.* 那将会合你的意。*It's difficult to ~ everybody.* 很难使每人满意。*Are you ~d with your new clothes?* 你对你的新衣服满意吗? *We're very ~d to see*

you here. 我们很高兴在这里见到你。 I shall be ~d to come. 我将乐意来。 ,P~ your'self, Do as you like. 随你的意思，随便你。 3 [VP2A] think fit; choose: 认为合适；选择： I shall do as I ~. 我将随我的意思去做。 Take as many as you ~. 你要取多少就取多少。 You may do as you ~. 你可以照你的意思做。 4 if you ~, (used with the ironical implication that nothing could be more reasonable): (用作反语)真是怪事，竟然： 'And now, if you ~, I'm to get nothing for all my work!' 真是怪事，我做了这么多工作，却将一无所获！ ~ God, if it be pleasing to God: 如果上帝愿意；如果幸运： War may be abolished one day, ~ God. 如果幸运，战争将有一天会被废止。 ~d adj glad; feeling or showing satisfaction: 欣喜的；愉快的；感到或表示满足的： He looked ~d with himself. 他看起来对自己感到满足(怡然自得)。 I'm very (much) ~d with what he has done. 我对他所做的事感到高兴。 pleas·ing adj affording pleasure (to); agreeable. 令人喜爱的(与to连用)；合意的。 pleas·ing·ly adv

pleas·ure /'pleʒə(r)/ n 1 [U] feeling of being happy or satisfied: 快乐；享乐；愉快；满足： It gave me much ~ to hear ~ of your success. 听到你成功我很快乐。 Is this a ~-seeking age? 这是寻欢作乐的时代吗？ Has he gone abroad for ~ or on business? 他出国是为游乐，还是为业务？ May we have the ~ of your company for lunch? 请和我们共进午餐好吗？ 'Will you join us?'—'Thank you, with ~'. '你愿和我们一起吗？'——'谢谢，非常愿意。' His life is given to ~, to sensuous enjoyments. 他耽于逸乐。 take (no/great, etc) ~ in sth, experience (no, etc) enjoyment: 对…感到乐趣(对…不感乐趣；对…感到极大乐趣等)： Some boys take great ~ in teasing their little sisters. 有些男孩很喜欢逗弄他们的小妹妹。 '~-boat/~craft n one used for ~ only. 游艇(专供游乐用的飞机)。 '~-ground n amusement park; recreation ground. 游乐场；娱乐场。 2 [U] will; desire: 意志；愿望： We await your ~. 我们听候你的意思。 We needn't consult his ~. 我们不必徵他的意思。 You may go or stay at your ~, as you wish. 去留悉听尊便。 3 [C] thing that gives happiness: 使人愉快的事物；乐趣： the ~s of friendship. 友谊的乐趣。 pleas·ur·able /'pleʒərəbl/ adj giving ~. 悦人的；愉快的。 pleas·ur·ably /-əblɪ; -əblɪ/ adv

pleat /pliːt; pliːt/ n fold made by doubling cloth on itself. (衣服上的)褶。 □ vt [VP6A] make ~s in: 打褶于： a ~ed shirt. 褶裙。

pleb /pleb; plɛb/ n (colloq abbr for) plebeian. (口)为plebeian之略。

pleb·eian /plɪˈbiːən; plɪˈbiən/ n, adj (person who is) of the lower social classes (originally in ancient Rome); coarse; ignoble. (源自古罗马)下层社会的(人)；平民(的)；粗俗的；鄙贱的。

plebi·scite /'plebɪsɪt US: -saɪt; 'plɛbə,saɪt/ n [C] (decision made upon a political question by) the votes of all qualified citizens. 公民投票；公民投票对政治问题所作的决定。

plec·trum /'plektrəm; 'plɛktrəm/ n small piece of metal, bone or ivory attached to the finger for plucking the strings of some stringed instruments, eg the mandolin, guitar. (戴于手指以拨动曼陀林、吉他等弦乐器之弦的)拨子；琴拨。

pled /pled; plɛd/ pt ~ plead.

pledge /pledʒ; plɛdʒ/ n 1 [C] sth left with sb to be kept by him until the giver has done sth which he is under an obligation to do; article left with a pawn-broker. 抵押品；典当品。 2 [U] state of being left with sb on these conditions: 抵押；典当： goods lying in ~; 作抵押的货物； put/hold sth in ~; 以(收下)某物作抵押； take sth out of ~. 赎出某物。 3 [C] sth given as a sign of love, approval, etc: (表示爱、赞许等的)信物；保证物： a ~ of friendship, 友谊的信物； (fig) (喻) the ~ of their youthful love, their child. 他们年轻时爱情的信物(即他们的孩子)。 4 [U] agreement; promise: 信约；誓

约；承诺： under ~ of secrecy. 在誓守秘密之下。 take/sign the ~, (esp) make a written promise to abstain from alcoholic drink. (尤指)作书面保证戒酒；立誓戒酒。 □ vt [VP6A] 1 give as security; put in pawn. 以…作担保；抵押；典当。 2 give; engage; make an undertaking (to do sth): 提出；誓言；保证： be ~d to secrecy; 誓守秘密； ~ one's word/honour. 保证；发誓。 3 drink the health of: 举杯祝…健康： ~ the bride and bridegroom. 举杯祝新娘和新郎健康。

ple·nary /'pliːnərɪ; 'plinərɪ/ adj 1 (of powers, authority) unlimited; absolute. (指权力、权威)无限制的；绝对的。 2 (of meetings) attended by all who have a right to attend: (指会议)全体出席的： a ~ session. 一项全体出席的会议。 plen·ar·ily /'pliːnərəlɪ; 'plinərəlɪ/ adv

pleni·po·ten·tiary /,plenɪpəˈtenʃərɪ; ,plɛnəpəˈtɛnʃərɪ/ n (pl -ries), adj (person, eg a representative, an ambassador) having full power to act, make decisions, etc (on behalf of his government, etc). (代表其政府等之)全权代表(大使等)；有全权的。

pleni·tude /'plenɪtjuːd US: -tuːd; 'plɛnə,tjud/ n (sing only) (formal) fullness; abundance: (仅用单数)(正式用语)充足；丰饶： in the ~ of his powers. 在他权力的最高峰。

plen·teous /'plentɪəs; 'plɛntɪəs/ adj (chiefly poet) plentiful. (主要用于诗中)充足的；丰富的。 ~·ly adv

plen·ti·ful /'plentɪfl; 'plɛntɪfəl/ adj in large quantities or numbers; abundant. 大量的；丰富的。 ~·ly /-fəlɪ; -flɪ/ adv

plenty /'plentɪ; 'plɛntɪ/ n [U] ~ (of), as much as or more than is needed or desired; a large number or quantity: 富足；充裕；大量： There are ~ of eggs in the house. 家里有很多蛋。 There's ~ more (of it). (这东西)尚有许多。 We must get to the station in ~ of time. 我们必须及早动身以便从容抵达车站。 Six will be ~, as many as I need. 六个足够了。 I've had ~, thank you. 我已经够了，谢谢你。 ~ in a large quantity: 大量的；许多： There was food and drink in ~. 有许多食物和饮料。 □ adv (colloq) quite: (口)十分；充分地： It's big enough. 够大的了。

pleo·nasm /'plɪənæzəm; 'pliə,næzəm/ n [C, U] (instance of the) use of more words than are needed to express the meaning, eg 'each of the two twins'; 'divide sth into four quarters'. 冗言或赘言之使用；冗言或赘言使用之实例；冗言；赘言(如twins之前加two, quarters之前加four)。

pleth·ora /'pleθərə; 'plɛθərə/ n (formal) (正式用语) 1 glut; (over-)abundance. 过量供应；过剩；充斥。 2 (med) unhealthy condition of the body marked by an excess of red corpuscles in the blood. (医)多血症；红血球过多症。

pleur·isy /'pluərəsɪ; 'plurəsɪ/ n [U] serious illness with inflammation of the delicate membrane of the thorax and the lungs, marked by pain in the chest or sides. (医)肋膜炎；胸膜炎。

plexus /'pleksəs; 'plɛksəs/ n (pl ~es -səsɪz; -səsɪz/ or ~) (anat) network of fibres or vessels in the body: (解剖)(纤维或血管之)丛： the solar ~, in the abdomen. 腹腔丛；太阳神经丛。

pli·able /'plaɪəbl; 'plaɪəbl/ adj easily bent, shaped or twisted; (of the mind) easily influenced; open to suggestions. 易曲折的；柔顺的；(指思想)易受影响的；能接受意见的。 pli·abil·ity /,plaɪəˈbɪlətɪ; ,plaɪəˈbɪlətɪ/ n [U].

pli·ant /'plaɪənt; 'plaɪənt/ adj = pliable. ~·ly adv pli·ancy /'plaɪənsɪ; 'plaɪənsɪ/ n

pli·ers /'plaɪəz; 'plaɪəz/ n pl (pair of), kind of pincers with long, flat jaws, used for holding, bending, twisting or cutting wire, etc. (钳钢丝等的)钳子；老虎钳。 ⇒ the illus at tool. 参看tool之插图。

plight[1] /plaɪt; plaɪt/ n serious and difficult condition: 严重和困难的情况；困境；苦境： His affairs were in a

terrible ∼. 他的事情陷入严重的情况。*What a ∼ to be in!* 处境多坏啊!

plight² /plaɪt; plaɪt/ *vt* [VP6A] (archaic) (古) **1** pledge, promise: 保证; 誓约: *one's ∼ed word.* 某人的誓言。 **2** ∼ *one's troth;* ∼ *oneself*, engage oneself to be married. 订婚。

Plim·soll /'plɪmsəl; 'plɪmsl/ *n* '∼ *line ⁄ mark*, line on the hull of a ship to mark how far it may legally go down in the water when loaded. (船身上的)法定载货吃水线; 普绍索标; 装载水线标。

plim·solls /'plɪmsəlz; 'plɪmslz/ *n pl* rubber-soled canvas shoes (US 美 = *sneakers*). (轻便的)橡皮底帆布鞋。

plinth /plɪnθ; plɪnθ/ *n* square base or block on which a column or statue stands. (柱或雕像的)基脚; 基础; 基座。 ⇨ the illus at **column**. 参看 column 之插图。

plod / plɒd; plɑd/ *vi, vt* (**-dd-**) [VP2C] continue walking, working, etc slowly and wearily but without resting: 缓慢、疲倦但不休息地继续步行, 工作等: ∼ *on one's way;* 缓慢而不停地行走; ∼ *away at a dull task.* 孜孜不息地做着沉闷的工作。 ∼**·der** *n* person who ∼s; slow but earnest person. 缓慢而不休息的步行者、工作者; 动作缓慢而有热忱者; 孜孜从事者。 ∼**·ding** *adj* ∼**·ding·ly** *adv*

plonk¹ /plɒŋk; plɑŋk/ *n* sound of sth dropping (esp into liquid). 坠落声; (尤指某物落入水中的)扑通声。 □ *adv* with a ∼. 扑通一声。 □ *vt* ∼ (*down*), drop sth with a ∼ing sound: 扑通一声坠落; 发出落水声: ∼ *the fish down on the table.* 啪当一声把鱼丢在桌子上。

plonk² /plɒŋk; plɑŋk/ *n* [U] (sl) cheap wine. (俚)便宜的酒。

plop /plɒp; plɑp/ *n* [C] sound (as) of a small smooth object dropping into water without a splash. (光滑的小物体落入水中而未溅泼的)落水声; 扑通声。 □ *adv* with a ∼. 扑通一声地。 □ *vi* (**-pp-**) make a ∼; fall with a ∼. 发出落水声; 扑通地坠落。

plo·sive /'pləʊsɪv; 'plosɪv/ *n, adj* (phon) (consonant sound) with a complete closing of the air passage followed by an audible release of the air compressed behind the closure, eg /t/ and /p/ in *top*. (语音)爆破的; 爆裂音(使气流全部阻塞然后再清晰可闻地吐气所发的辅音,如 top 中的 /t/ 及 /p/)。

plot¹ /plɒt; plɑt/ *n* piece of ground (usu small): (通常指小的)一块地: *a building* ∼; 建地; *a* ∼ *of vegetables.* 一块做菜园用的地。 □ *vt* (**-tt-**) **1** [VP6A] make a plan, map or diagram of; mark (the position of sth) on a diagram by connecting points on a graph: 制…之图、绘图或图解; 在图解上标明(某物之位置): *a temperature curve;* 绘制温度曲线; *aircraft movements by radar.* 借雷达标示飞机的动向。 **2** [VP6A, 15B] ∼ (*out*), divide into ∼s. 分成小块地。

plot² /plɒt; plɑt/ *n* [C] **1** secret plan (good or bad); conspiracy: 密谋(好的或坏的); 阴谋: *a* ∼ *to overthrow the government.* 推翻政府的阴谋。 **2** plan or outline (of the events of a story, esp of a novel or drama). (指小说或戏剧之故事的)情节; 结构。 □ *vt, vi* (**-tt-**) [VP2A, 3A, 4A, 6A, 8, 10] make secret plans; form, take part in, a ∼: 密谋; 计划; 参与阴谋: ∼ *with sb against the government.* 与某人密谋反对政府。 ∼**·ter** *n* person who ∼s; conspirator. 密谋者; 阴谋者。

plough (US = **plow**) /plaʊ; plaʊ/ *n* **1** implement for cutting furrows in soil and turning it up, drawn by animals or (more usually) a tractor. 犁(由兽力或曳引机拖动)。 *put one's hand to the* ∼, (fig) undertake a task. (喻)着手工作。 '∼**·boy** *n* boy who leads the horses that pull a ∼. 牵引犁田之马的孩子; 耕童。 '∼**·man** /-mən; -mən/ *n* (*pl* **-men**) man who guides a ∼. 以犁耕田者; 农夫。 '∼**·share** *n* broad blade of a ∼. 犁铧。 **2** kinds of implement resembling a ∼. 犁形器具。 '**snow**∼ *n* one for clearing away snow from roads and railways. 除雪机; 排除道路上及铁道上积雪的器具。 **3** [U] ploughed land: 耕地; 耕过的地: *100 acres of* ∼.

一百英亩耕地。 **4 the P**∼, (astron) the group of stars called *Charles's Wain, the Big Dipper* or *the Great Bear.* (天文)北斗七星(又称为 Charles's Wain, the Big Dipper 或 the Great Bear)。 □ *vt, vi* **1** [VP6A, 15B] ∼ (*back*), break up (land) with a ∼: 犁(地); 耕(田): ∼ *a field;* 耕田; (fig) (喻) ∼ *back the profits of a business,* reinvest them. 以利润作为资本投资; 再投资。 ∼ *a lonely furrow,* (fig) work without help or support. (喻)孤独地无援地工作。 ∼ *the sand,* (fig) do useless work. (喻)做无用之事; 徒劳无功。 **2** [VP3A] ∼ *through,* force a way through; advance laboriously: 费力穿过; 艰苦前进: *a ship* ∼*ing through the heavy waves;* 冒着大浪前进的一条船; ∼ (*one's way*) *through the mud;* 在泥泞中费力前行; ∼ *through a dull textbook.* 很费力地阅读一本枯燥的教科书。 **3** [VP6A] (sl) reject (a candidate) in an examination: (俚)在考试中淘汰(应试者); 当掉(应试者): *The examiners* ∼*ed half the candidates.* 主考人员刷掉了一半的应试者。

tractor

plough

furrows

a plough

plover /'plʌvə(r); 'plʌvə/ *n* sorts of long-legged, short-tailed land bird that frequents marshy ground near the sea, esp (in England) the golden ∼, the green ∼, and the lapwing or peewit. 千鸟; 鹬; 睢鸠(长足短尾之陆上禽类, 常见于靠近海洋的沼泽地带, 在英格兰尤指黄鹬、绿鹬及田凫)。

plow /plaʊ; plaʊ/ (US) = **plough.**

ploy /plɔɪ; plɔɪ/ *n* [C] manoeuvre; sth said or done, eg in a game, to win an advantage over one's opponent. 策略; 手法(例如在比赛时为了战胜对方而采取的)。

pluck /plʌk; plʌk/ *vt, vi* **1** [VP6A] pull the feathers off (a hen, goose, etc): 拔去(鸡、鹅等)的毛: *Has this goose been* ∼*ed?* 这只鹅的毛拔过了吗? **2** [VP6A] pick (flowers, fruit, etc). 摘(花、果等)。 [VP15B] ∼ *sth out ⁄ up*, pull (weeds, etc, up or out). 拔(野草等)。 **3** [VP3A] ∼ *at*, snatch at; take hold of and pull: 拉; 拽; 抓住: *The child was* ∼*ing at its mother's skirt.* 那孩子抓住母亲的裙子。 **4** ∼ *up courage*, summon one's courage; overcome one's fears. 鼓起勇气; 克服恐惧。 **5** [VP6A] (sl) swindle (esp a young or inexperienced person, eg in gambling). (俚)诈欺(尤指年轻或无经验之人, 如在赌博中)。 □ *n* **1** [C] courage; spirit. 勇气; 精神。 **2** [U] that which is ∼ed out, esp the heart, liver and lungs of an animal that has been killed. 被摘除或拔除之物; (尤指从被杀死之动物所取出之)心、肝和肺; 内脏。 **3** [C] short, sharp pull. 短急的拉; 拽。 ∼**·y** *adj* (**-ier, -iest**) brave; having ∼ (1). 勇敢的; 有胆量的。 ∼**·ily** /-ɪlɪ; -ɪlɪ/ *adv*

plug /plʌg; plʌg/ *n* **1** piece of wood, metal, rubber etc used to stop up a hole (eg in a barrel, wash-basin, bath, cistern, etc) (US 美 = *stopper*). (用于塞大桶、脸盆、浴盆等之洞的)栓; 塞子。 '∼**·hole**, hole for a ∼ (US 美 = *drain*). 排水洞。 **2** device for making a connection with a supply of electric current: 电插头; 插头: *a three-⁄two-pin* ∼; (三/二)脚的电插头; *put the* ∼ *in the socket ⁄ outlet.* 把插头插在插座内。 ⇨ also *sparking-*∼ at **spark¹.** **3** cake of pressed or twisted tobacco; piece of this cut off for chewing. 烟饼; 板烟; 口嚼烟(切开之烟饼供咀嚼者)。 **4** (sl) piece of favourable publicity

(eg in a radio or TV programme) for commercial product. (俚) (广播或电视的) 一则商业广告。 ⇨ **5** below. 参看下列第5义。 □ *vt, vi* (**-gg-**) **1** [VP6A, 15B] ~ **(up),** stop or fill (up) with a ~: 以塞子塞住: ~ *a leak.* 塞住漏洞。 **2** [VP2C] (colloq) (口) ~ *away at,* work hard at. 孜孜从事。 **3** [VP2C, 15B] ~ **(sth) in,** make a connection with a ~(2): 插上 (某物的) 插头通电: ~ *in the TV set.* 插上电视机的插头。 **4** [VP6A] (US, sl) hit; shoot. (美, 俚) 打; 射击。 **5** [VP6A] (sl) cause (sth) to be widely known by giving repeated publicity: (俚) 借反复宣传使 (某事物) 为大众所知; 大事宣传: ~ *a new song,* eg on radio or TV. 宣传一首新歌 (如借无线电广播或电视反复播放)。

plum /plʌm; plʌm/ *n* **1** (tree having) soft round, smooth-skinned fruit with a stone-like seed. 梅子 (树); 李子 (树)。 ⇨ the illus at **fruit.** 参看 fruit 之插图。 **2** ,~ **'cake,** kind containing dried raisins, currants, etc. 葡萄干糕饼。 ~ **'duff,** boiled pudding containing dried raisins, currants, etc. 葡萄干布丁。 ~**'pudding,** boiled pudding containing dried fruits and spices, part of traditional Christmas food. 干果布丁 (相当为圣诞节食品之一部分)。 **3** (colloq) sth considered good and desirable, esp a well-paid position. (口) 被认为是理想之事物 (尤指待遇好的职务); 肥缺, 好差事。

plum·age /'pluːmɪdʒ; 'pluːmɪdʒ/ *n* [U] bird's feathers; 鸟羽; 羽毛: *tropical birds in their brightly coloured* ~. 羽毛鲜艳的热带鸟。

plumb /plʌm; plʌm/ *n* ball or piece of lead tied to the end of a cord or rope (**a '~-line**) for finding the depth of water or testing whether a wall is vertical. 垂球; 铅垂; 测锤 (固定于铅垂线 'plumb-line 之一端, 以测定水深或墙是否垂直的铅球或铅块)。 *out of* ~, not vertical. 不垂直的。 □ *adv* **1** exactly. 正确地; 精确地。 **2** (US, colloq) quite: (美, 口) 完全; 全然: ~ *crazy.* 非常疯狂。 □ *vt* [VP6A] (fig) get to the root of: (喻) 追根究底; 查明: ~ *the depths of a mystery.* 查明某项神秘事物的底细。

plum·bago¹ /plʌm'beɪgəʊ; plʌm'bego/ *n* [U] black substance, graphite, used for pencils, etc and mixed with clay for making crucibles. 黑铅; 石墨 (用于制铅笔等, 与粘土混合可制坩埚)。

plum·bago² /plʌm'beɪgəʊ; plʌm'bego/ *n* (*pl* ~**s** /-gəʊz, -goz/) blue-flowered plant. **1.** 石墨。 **2.** 矾松属植物 (一种琉璃茉莉, 开蓝花)。

plumber /'plʌmə(r); 'plʌmə/ *n* workman who fits and repairs water-pipes, water-tanks, cisterns, etc in a building. 装修水管的工人; 铅管工人。

plumb·ing /'plʌmɪŋ; 'plʌmɪŋ/ *n* [U] **1** the work of a plumber. 铅管工; 装修水管业。 **2** the water-pipes, water-tanks, cisterns, etc in a building: (建筑物之) 水管装置 (水管、水槽等): *The* ~ *is out of order.* 水管装置出了毛病。

plume /pluːm; plum/ *n* feather, esp a large one used as a decoration; ornament of feathers; sth suggesting a feather by its shape: 羽毛 (尤指作装饰用的大羽毛); 羽毛饰; 羽毛状的东西: *a* ~ *of smoke/steam.* 一缕烟 (水气)。 ⇨ the illus at **rare.** 参看 rare 之插图。 *borrowed* ~**s,** (fig) finery displayed as one's own but borrowed from someone. (喻) 穿着借来的华美衣服而夸为己有。 □ *vt* [VP6A] (of a bird) smooth (its feathers); preen (itself, its wings). (指鸟) 整刷 (其羽毛), 以喙整理 (自己, 其翅膀)。 ~ *oneself (on sth),* (fig) congratulate oneself. (喻) (为某事) 自庆; 自鸣得意。

plum·met /'plʌmɪt; 'plʌmɪt/ *n* weight attached to a) plumb-line; weight attached to a fishing-line to keep the float upright. 铅垂线; 铅锤; 钓丝上的坠子 (能使浮子垂直)。 □ *vi* (**-tt-**) [VP2A] fall, plunge, steeply: 骤降; 笔直下坠: *Share prices have* ~*ted.* 股票价格直线下跌。

plummy /'plʌmɪ; 'plʌmɪ/ *adj* (**-ier, -iest**) (colloq) good; desirable: (口) 好的; 理想的: ~ *jobs;* 理想的工作; affected, snobbish: 矫揉造作的; 势利的: *a* ~ *voice.* 矫揉造作的声音。

plump¹ /plʌmp; plʌmp/ *adj* (esp of an animal, a person, parts of the body) rounded; fat in a pleasant-looking way: (尤指动物、人、身体之各部分) 圆胖的; 丰满的: *a baby with* ~ *cheeks.* 面庞肥肥胖胖的婴儿。 □ *vt, vi* [VP6A, 2A, 15B, 2C] ~ **(out/up),** make or become rounded: 使圆胖; 使膨胀; 变圆胖; 变膨胀: *His cheeks are beginning to* ~ *up/out.* 他的面颊胖起来了。 *She* ~*ed up the pillows.* 她把枕头填得鼓鼓的。

plump² /plʌmp; plʌmp/ *vi, vt* [VP2C, 15B] ~ **(sb/oneself/sth) down,** (cause to) fall or drop, suddenly and heavily: (使) 突然而沉重地落下: ~ **(oneself) down in a chair,** 猛一下子坐在椅子上; ~ *down a heavy bag.* 扑通一声把一只沉重的袋子放下。 **2** [VP3A] ~ *for,* vote for, choose, with confidence: 充满信心地支持或选择; 投力支持; 衷心拥护: ~ *for the Liberal candidate.* 极力支持自由党候选人。 □ *n* abrupt, heavy fall. 突然而沉重的落下。 □ *adv* **1** suddenly; abruptly: 突然地; 蓦地: *fall* ~ *into the hole.* 突然落入洞中。 **2** bluntly: 率直地: *I told him* ~ *that....* 我率直地告诉他....。 □ *adj* unqualified; direct: 绝对的; 直接的: *give sb a* ~ *'No' for an answer.* 直截了当地以 '不' 回答某人。

plun·der /'plʌndə(r); 'plʌndə/ *vt, vi* [VP6A, 14, 2A] ~ **(of),** rob (people), esp during war or civil disorder; take goods from (places) by force: (尤指在作战或内乱时) 抢劫 (人); 抢夺 (某地) 的东西: ~ *a palace of its treasures;* 劫掠宫廷的财宝; ~ *the citizens of a conquered town.* 抢劫沦陷市镇的市民。 □ *n* [U] ~*ing;* goods taken: 抢劫; 抢夺; 抢夺物; 战利品: *live by* ~; 以抢劫为生; *wagon-loads of* ~. 一车车的赃物。 ~**er** *n*

plunge /plʌndʒ; plʌndʒ/ *vt, vi* **1** [VP6A, 14, 2A, C] ~ **(into),** put (sth), or go suddenly and with force, into: 投入 (某物) 使陷入; 突入: ~ *one's hand into cold water/a hole;* 将手伸入冷水 (洞) 中; ~ *a country into war;* 使一国陷入战争; ~ *a room into darkness,* eg by cutting off the current; 使一房间陷入黑暗中 (如切断电源); ~ *into a swimming-pool;* 跳入游泳池; ~ *into an argument;* 突然开始争论; *be* ~*d into grief.* 陷入悲哀的境地。 **2** [VP2A, U] (of a horse) move forward and downward quickly; (of a ship) thrust its bows into the water; (sl) gamble deeply; run into debt. (指马) 颠跃; (指船) 颠簸; (俚) 狂赌; 负债。 □ *n* act of plunging (eg from a diving-board into water); violent thrust or other movement. 投入; 陷入; 跳入 (如从跳台跳水); 突进。 *take the* ~, (fig) take a critical step; do sth decisive. (喻) 采取重大步骤, 做决定性的事。 **plunger** *n* (esp) part of a mechanism that moves with a plunging motion, eg the piston of a pump; suction device for clearing a blocked pipe. (尤指机器之) 活柱顶塞 (如唧筒的活塞); 柱塞。

plunk /plʌŋk; plʌŋk/ = **plonk¹.**

plu·per·fect /,pluː'pɜːfɪkt; ,plu'pɜːfɪkt/ *n, adj* (gram) (tense) expressing action completed before some past time stated or implied (and in English conveyed by *had* and a *pp,* as in 'As he *had not received* my letter, he did not come'). (语法) 过去完成的; 过去完成时 (在英语中以 had 及过去分词表示之, 如 As he had not received my letter, he did not come 中的 had received)。

plu·ral /'plʊərəl; 'plʊrəl/ *n, adj* (form of word) used with reference to more than one: 复数 (式); 复数的; 多于一个的: 'The ~ *of child is children.'* 'child 的复数是 children。' ~ *society,* one with more than one race, eg Kenya, with Africans, Asians and Europeans. 复社会 (多数人种组成的社会, 如肯尼亚有非洲人、亚洲人和欧洲人)。 ~ *voter,* person who has a vote in more than one constituency. 有权利在一个以上的选区投票的人; 有复投票权者。

plu·ral·ism /'plʊərəlɪzəm; 'plʊrəlɪzm/ *n* [U] the quality of being plural; the holding of more than one office at one time. 复数性; 多元性; 兼职。 **plu·ral·ist** /-ɪst; -ɪst/ *n* supporter of ~. 赞成兼职者。

plu·ral·ity /pluə'ræləti; plu'ræləti/ *n* (*pl* **-ties**) **1** [U] state of being plural; [C] large number; majority (*of* votes, etc). 复性; 众多的状态; 大量; 多数: (选票等的)过半数(与 *of* 连用). **2** [U] holding of more than one office at a time; [C] office held with another. 兼职, 所兼之职位.

plus /plʌs; plʌs/ *prep* with the addition of: 加; 加上: *Two ~ five is seven,* 2+5=7. 二加五等于七. **,~-'fours** *n pl* wide, loose knickerbockers. 一种宽松的灯笼裤. □ *adj* positive: 正的: *a ~ quantity,* one greater than zero. 正数. ⇨ **minus**. □ *n* the sign +; (colloq, fig) positive quality. 加号; 正号(+); (口, 喻)利益; 优点.

plush /plʌʃ; plʌʃ/ *n* [U] kind of silk or cotton cloth with a soft nap. 一种有软绒的棉布或绸布. □ *adj* (also **~y (-ier, -iest)**) (sl) smart; sumptuous: (俚)漂亮的; 豪华餐馆. 豪华餐馆.

Pluto /'pluːtəu; 'pluto/ *n* **1** (Roman myth) god of the underworld. (罗神)冥府之神; 阎罗王. **2** (astron) planet farthest from the sun. (天文)冥王星. ⇨ the illus at **planet**. 参看 planet 之插图.

plu·toc·racy /pluː'tɒkrəsi; plu'tɑkrəsi/ *n* (*pl* **-cies**) [C, U] (government by a) rich and powerful class. 富豪阶级; 财阀阶级; 富豪政治; 财阀政治. **plu·to·crat** /'pluːtəkræt; 'plutə,kræt/ *n* person who is powerful because of his wealth. 有权有势的人; 富豪; 财阀. **plu·to·cratic** /,pluːtə'krætɪk; ,plutə'krætɪk/ *adj* of ~ or a plutocrat. 富豪阶级的; 富豪政治的; 富豪的.

plu·to·nium /pluː'təunɪəm; plu'tonɪəm/ *n* [U] (artificially produced) radioactive element (symbol **Pu**) derived from uranium, used in nuclear reactors and weapons. 钚(以人工方法由铀形成的放射性元素, 符号 Pu, 用于核反应堆及核武器中).

ply¹ /plaɪ; plaɪ/ *n* [C] **1** layer of wood or thickness of cloth: (木的)板层; (布的)厚度: *three-ply wood,* made by sticking together three layers with the grain of each at a right angle to that of the next. 三夹板. **'ply·wood** *n* [U] board(s) made by gluing together thin layers of wood. 合板; 夹板. **2** one strand in wool, rope, etc: (毛线、绳等的)绺; 股; 缕: *four-ply wool for knitting socks.* 织袜子的四股毛线.

ply² /plaɪ; plaɪ/ *vt, vi* (*pt, pp* **plied** /plaɪd; plaɪd/) **1** [VP6A] (formal) work with (an instrument): (正式用语)使用(器具): *ply one's needle,* work busily with it. 忙于针黹. **2** [VP2C] (of ships, buses, etc) go regularly to and fro: (船舶、公共汽车等)定期往来; 定时往来: *ships that ply between Glasgow and New York;* 在格拉斯哥与纽约之间定期往来的班船; *ferry-boats plying across the Channel.* 定时往来英吉利海峡的渡船. **3** *ply a trade,* work at it. 经营一商业; 从事一行业. ~ *sb with sth,* keep him constantly supplied with (food and drink); attack him constantly with (questions, arguments, etc). 经常以(食物和饮料)供给某人; 经常以(问题、议论等)攻击某人.

pneu·matic /njuː'mætɪk *US:* nuː-; nju'mætɪk/ *adj* worked or driven by compressed air: 由压缩空气操作或推动的: ~ *drills,* 气钻; 风钻; filled with compressed air: 充气的; 装有压缩空气的: ~ *tyres.* 充气的轮胎. **pneu·mati·cally** /-klɪ; -klɪ/ *adv*

pneu·monia /njuː'məunɪə *US:* nuː-; nju'monjə/ *n* [U] serious illness with inflammation of one or both lungs. 肺炎.

poach¹ /pəutʃ; potʃ/ *vt* [VP6A] cook (an egg) by cracking the shell and dropping the contents into boiling water; simmer (eg fish) in liquid (eg wine). 煮(荷包蛋); 在液体(如酒)中炖(如鱼).

poach² /pəutʃ; potʃ/ *vt, vi* [VP6A, 2A, 3A] ~ *on/ for,* **1** (go on sb else's property and) take (hares, pheasants, salmon, etc) illegally: (侵入他人之土地)非法猎取或捕取(野兔、野鸡、鲑等); 盗猎; 盗捕: ~ *hares;* 非法猎野兔; ~ *for salmon;* 非法猎鲑; go out ~ing; 出外偷猎; ~ *on a neighbour's land.* 侵入他人的土地非法行猎. **2** (fig) be active in some kind of work that properly

belongs to another (or that he considers to be his preserve): (喻)在他人的领域内活动; 侵害他人的领域: *Don't ~ on my preserves.* 不要侵入我的领域. **~er** *n*

pock /pɒk; pɑk/ *n* spot on the skin caused by smallpox. 痘疱; 痘痕; 麻子. **'~-marked,** with marks left after smallpox. 有痘痕的; 麻脸的. **~ed** *adj* be ~**ed with,** have holes or depressions in: 有凹洞的: *The moon's surface is ~ed with craters.* 月球的表面布满了陨石坑.

pocket /'pɒkɪt; 'pɑkɪt/ *n* **1** small bag sewn into and forming part of an article of clothing, for carrying things in: 口袋; 衣袋: *trouser/waistcoat, etc ~.* 裤(背心等)口袋. *put one's hand in one's ~,* be ready to spend or give money. 愿意花钱; 愿出钱. **'~-book** *n* **(a)** notebook. 小记事簿; 袖珍记事册. **(b)** (US) leather case for paper money (GB 英 = *wallet*). (美)钱包; 皮夹子. **(c)** (US) woman's purse or handbag. (美)(女人的)手提包; 钱袋. **'~-'handkerchief** *n* one to be carried in the ~; (attrib) of small size: 手巾; 手绢; (用作定语)小型的: *a ~-handkerchief rug.* 小块地毯. **'~-knife** *n* small knife with one or more folding blades. (可折合的)小刀. **'~-money** *n* [U] money for small needs, esp money given to children. 零用钱 (尤指给与小孩者). **2** money resources; money: 财源; 钱: *He will suffer in his ~,* will lose financially. 他将在钱财方面有所损失. *in/out of ~,* having gained/lost money as the result of doing sth: 因做某事而赚(亏)钱的: *The deal left him hundreds of dollars out of ~.* 那笔生意使他亏了好几百元. **out-of-~ expenses,** actual outlay incurred; what one has actually spent. 实际花费; 现金支出. **3** bag, hollow, cavity, eg a string pouch at the corner of a billiard or pool table; small cavity in the ground or in rock, containing gold or ore; partial vacuum in the atmosphere (*an 'air-~*) affecting the flight of an aircraft; cavity of air (*an 'air-~*) in a mine²(1), eg when a shaft is flooded; isolated area: 袋; (如撞球台角的网)网袋; (地面或岩石中的)矿穴; 矿脉袋; 空中陷阱; 气潭(大气中部分真空之现象, 影响飞机飞行, 亦称作 'air-~); 矿穴里的气坑(亦称做 'air-~); 孤立地区: *enemy ~s,* eg occupied by enemy forces; 孤立的敌人占领区; ~*s of resistance;* 孤军抵抗地区; ~*s of unemployment in the Midlands.* 英格兰中部诸郡的失业地区. **4** (attrib) of a size suitable for a ~: (用作定语)袖珍的; 小型的: *a ~ guide/dictionary/edition;* 袖珍指南(字典, 版本); *a ~-size camera.* 袖珍照相机. **'~-ful** /-ful; -ful/ *n* amount which a ~ holds. 一袋之量; 满袋. □ *vt* [VP6A] **1** put into one's ~: 放入袋中; 纳入袋中: *He ~ed the money.* 他把钱纳入口袋. ~ *an insult,* endure it without protest. 忍受侮辱. ~ *one's pride,* suppress or hide one's feelings of mortification. 压抑或掩饰自己的屈辱感觉. **2** appropriate for oneself (usu but not necessarily dishonestly): 据为己有; (通常指)侵吞; 僭取: *He ~ed half the profits.* 他把一半的利润据为己有. *He was given £5 for expenses, but ~ed most of it.* 他得到五英镑的经费, 但侵吞了大部分. **3** send (a ball) into a ~ on a billiard or pool table. (撞球)把(球)打进网袋中.

pod /pɒd; pɑd/ *n* [C] long seed-vessel of various plants, esp peas and beans. 荚; 荚; (尤指)豆荚. ⇨ the illus at **vegetable.** 参看 vegetable 之插图. □ *vt, vi* (**-dd-**) **1** [VP6A] take (peas, etc) out of pods. 剥掉(豌豆等)之荚. **2** [VP2A, C] ~ (*up*), form pods: 结荚; 生荚: *The peas are podding (up) well.* 豌豆结荚良好.

podgy /'pɒdʒi; 'pɑdʒi/ *adj* (**-ier, -iest**) (of a person) short and fat. (指人)矮胖的.

podi·atry /pə'daɪətri; po'daɪətri/ *n* [U] (US) (美) = **chiropody.**

po·dium /'pəudɪəm; 'podɪəm/ *n* platform, eg for the conductor of an orchestra, a lecturer, etc. 高台; (乐队的)指挥台; 讲台.

poem /'pəʊɪm; 'poʊ·ɪm/ n [C] piece of creative writing in verse form, esp one expressing deep feeling or noble thought in beautiful language, composed with the desire to communicate an experience; piece of prose writing in elevated style: (一篇或一首)诗; 韵文; 风格高尚的散文: a 'prose ~. 散文诗.

po·esy /'pəʊɪzɪ; 'poʊ·ɪsɪ/ n [U] (archaic) poetry. (古) 诗.

poet /'pəʊɪt; 'poʊ·ɪt/ n writer of poems. 诗人. ~ **laureate**, ⇨ **laureate**. '**poet·ess** /-es; -əs/ n woman ~. 女诗人.

po·etic /pəʊ'etɪk; poʊ'etɪk/ adj of poets and poetry: 诗人的; 诗的; 韵文的; 诗意的: in ~ form; 以诗的形式; ~ genius. 诗才. ~ '**justice**, ideal justice, with proper distribution of rewards and punishments. 理想的因果报应; 诗的正义. ~ '**licence**, **licence**. **po·eti·cal** /-kl; -kl/ adj = ~: ~al works of Keats, his poetry. 济慈的诗. **po·eti·cally** /-klɪ; -klɪ/ adv

po·etry /'pəʊɪtrɪ; 'poʊ·ɪtrɪ/ n [U] 1 the art of a poet; poems. 作诗法; 诗(总称). 2 quality that produces feelings as produced by poems: 诗情; 诗意; 诗或似诗的性质: the ~ of motion, eg in ballet or some kinds of athletics. (如芭蕾舞或若干其他运动之)动作的韵律.

po·grom /'pɒgrəm US: pə'grɒm; 'poʊgrəm/ n [C] organized persecution or killing and plunder (of a group or class of people). (对某一团体或阶层之人的)有组织的屠杀或劫掠; 集体迫害.

poign·ant /'pɔɪnjənt; 'poʊnənt/ adj distressing to the feelings; deeply moving; keen: 痛切的; 伤心的; 深刻的: ~ sorrow/regret/memories. 深切的悲哀(痛悔; 伤心的回忆). ~·**ly** adv **poign·ancy** /-ənsɪ; -ənsɪ/ n [U] state or quality of being ~. 痛切; 伤心; 深刻.

point·set·tia /pɔɪn'setɪə; pɔɪn'setɪə/ n tropical plant with small, greenish-yellow flowers surrounded by large scarlet leaves. 猩猩木; 圣诞红(热带植物, 有鲜红的大叶, 开绿黄色的小花).

point¹ /pɔɪnt; pɔɪnt/ n 1 [C] sharp tip (of a pin, pencil, knife, etc). (针、铅笔、刀等的)尖. **not to put too fine a ~ on it**, to speak bluntly, to tell the plain truth. 坦白地说; 老实说. 2 [C] tapering end; tip: 尖端: the ~ of the jaw, eg as the place for a knockout in boxing; 颚端(拳赛中击倒对方之处); headland or promontory; piece of land that stretches out into the sea, a lake, etc: 崎; 岬; (伸入海、湖等之)地角: a ~ of land; 陆地的海角; Pagoda P~, in Burma. 宝塔角(在缅甸). 3 dot made by or as with the ~ of a pen, etc: (用笔尖等画的或类似的)点: a decimal ~; 小数点; four ~ six (4.6); 四点六; a full ~, a full stop, the sign. 句点. 4 [C] real or imaginary mark of position, in space or time: (在空间或时间真实的或想象的)要点: a ~ of departure. 起点. a/the ~ of no return, ⇨ return¹(1). ~ of view, position from which sth is viewed; (fig) way of looking at a question. 观察点; 着眼点; (喻)观点. ~ **angle**¹(2) (US). **at 'this ~**, at this place or moment. 在此地; 在此刻. **be at the ~ of death**, be dying. 弥留时刻. **be on the ~ of doing sth**, be about to do sth. 正要做某事. **if/when it comes to the ~**, if/when the moment for action or decision comes: 如果(当)时机到来(时): When it come to the ~ he refused to help. 到了需要他帮忙的时候, 他却拒绝帮忙. '~-**duty** n [U] duty of a policeman stationed at a particular ~ to control traffic. (警察指挥交通的)值勤; 站岗. '**turning-~**, ⇨ **turning**. '~-**to-'~ race**, race (by persons riding horses) across country, from one ~ to another (these being recognized by certain landmarks). (骑马者所作之)越野赛马(途中各点借各种界标指明). 5 [U] (printing) unit of measurement for type: (印刷)磅(计算活字大小的单位): 6-~ is small and 18-~ is large. 六磅的活字小而十八磅的活字大的. Is this sentence printed in 8-~? 这个句子是8磅的活字印的吗? 6 [C] mark on a scale; unit of measuring; degree: 量器等上之刻度; 点; 度: the 'boiling-~ of water; 水的沸点; the 'melting-~ of lead. 铅的熔点. The cost of living went up several ~s last month, eg from 105 to 110, with 100 as a standard fixed earlier. 上个月的生活物价指数上升了好几点 (如以过去某时的生活费用为标准, 定为 100, 而从 105 涨到 110). Oil shares rose several ~s (ie on the Stock Exchange) yesterday. 昨天石油股票涨了数点 (即证券交易所). **Possession is nine ~s** (= nine-tenths) **of the law**, is strong evidence in favour of the person in possession of sth. 现实占有之物主在法律上占有九分道理(终必继续占用). 7 [C] unit of scoring in some games and sports, in measuring the quality, etc of exhibits in a show: (运动及比赛, 评量展览物品之品质时的)分; 点: score twenty ~s. 获得二十分. **give sb ~s; give ~s to sb**, be able to offer him advantages and still win: 让(某人)分数而仍然获胜: He can give me ~s at golf, give me odds; is a better player. 打高尔夫球他让我分数仍然能赢(打得比我好). **score a ~ (against/off/over sb)**, ⇨ **score²** (3). **win/be beaten on ~s**, (boxing) win/be beaten by the ~s awarded, there being no knockout. (拳赛)由积分获胜(被击败)(并非由于击倒). 8 [C] one of the thirty-two marks on the circumference of a compass; one of the divisions (11°15') between two such consecutive marks. 罗盘上三十二个刻度之一; 方位(相连二刻度间的区划之一, 等于 11¹/₄ 度). the illus at **compass**. 参看 compass 之插图. 9 [C] chief idea of sth said, done or planned; single item, detail or particular: (所说、所做、所计划之某事物的)要点; 论点; 主旨: There are ~s on which we've agreed to differ. 有几个论点我们已经同意保持异议. Let me explain the theory ~ by ~. 让我一点一点地说明这理论吧. What was the first ~ in his argument? 他所争论的第一点是什么? **carry/gain one's ~**, persuade sb to agree to one's objective. 说服别人同意自己的目标; 达到目的. **come to/get to/reach the ~**, give the essential fact or part of what one is trying to say, ignoring what is irrelevant. 说明重点. **get/see/miss the ~ of sth**, see/fail to see what sb is trying to make clear, etc: 明白(不明白)重点; 抓得(不)到要点: I don't quite get the ~. 我抓不到要点. She missed the ~ of the story/joke. 她没有听懂故事或笑话的重点. **make one's ~**, win acceptance for an argument, establish what one is proposing. 论点获得认可; 立论成立. **make a ~ of doing sth**, regard or treat as important or necessary. 认为(做)某事是必要的; 坚持(做)某事. **stretch a ~**, go beyond what is normally allowable on a question of principle, etc: 通融; 变通: Can't you stretch a ~ in my favour? 你不能为我通融一下吗? **take sb's ~**, (during a discussion) understand, appreciate what sb is proposing, etc. (在讨论中)明白或喜欢某人的建议. **(get/wander) away from/off the ~**, (say sth) not relevant to what is being discussed. 离题. **a case in ~**, one connected with the subject being discussed: 与讨论有关的事例; 适当的例子: Let me give you a case in ~, an example that illustrates my argument. 让我给你一个适当的例子. **a ~ of fact**, in reality; indeed. 事实上; 实际上. **a ~ of honour/conscience**, sth of great importance to one's honour/conscience. 关系荣誉(良心)之事. **on a ~ of order**, ⇨ **order¹(4)**. 10 [U] reason. 理由. **no/not much ~ in doing sth**, no good reason, little reason, for doing it: 没有做某事的理由: There's very little ~ in protesting, 抗议没有什么用处. It won't help much. 抗议没有什么用处. **What's the ~?** Why bother? (It's irrelevant, useless, etc). 有什么关系? 别管它! 11 [C] marked quality; characteristic: 特征; 特点: What are her best ~s as a secretary? 作为一个秘书, 她的长处是什么? He has many good ~s and few bad ~s. 他有许多优点而很少缺点. Singing is not my best ~, I don't sing well. 唱歌非我所擅长. 12 [C](GB) socket or outlet for electric current. (英)电插座. 13 (pl) tapering movable rails by which a train can move from one track to another. (复)(铁路上之)转辙器; 路闸(一端尖细的活动轨道, 火车可借此换轨). '~s·**man** /-smən; -smən/ n (pl -**men**) worker in charge of ~s

on a railway, to keep them in order, see that they are moved as needed, etc. (铁路之)转辙手; 搬闸工. **14** [U] effectiveness; urgency: 有效; 有力; 锋利: *His remarks lack ~.* 他的评语不够犀利.

point² /pɔɪnt; pɔɪnt/ *vt, vi* **1** [VP2A, 3A] ~ *(to).* direct attention to; show the position or direction of; be a sign of: 指向; 显示…之位置或方向; 表明; 表示: *The needle of a compass ~s to the north.* 罗盘针指向北方. *He ~ed to the door.* 他指着门. *It's rude to ~.* 用手指人是不礼貌的. *Both the hour hand and the minute hand ~ed to twelve,* It was noon. 时针和分针都指着十二; 是正午的时候. *All the evidence ~s to his guilt.* 一切证据均去表明他有罪. **2** [VP14] ~ *sth at / towards,* aim or direct (at, towards): 瞄准; 对着: ~ *a gun at sb;* 以枪瞄准某人; ~ *a telescope at the moon;* 以望远镜对着月亮; *~ing his forefinger at me reprovingly.* 他谴责地用食指指着我. **3** [VP15B] ~ *sth out,* show; call or direct attention to: 指出; 使注意: ~ *out a mistake;* 指出错误; ~ *out to sb the stupidity of his behaviour.* 促使某人注意其愚行. *Can you ~ (me) out the man you suspect?* 你能把你怀疑的那个人指出来吗? *He ~ed out the finest pictures to me.* 他把最好的图画指给我看. *I must ~ out that delay is unwise.* 我必须指出, 拖延是不智的. **4** [VP6A] make a point on (pg a pencil); (fig) give force to (advice, a moral). 削尖(铅笔); (喻)增强(忠言, 教训)之力量; 强调. **5** [VP6A] fill in the joints of (brickwork, etc) with mortar or cement, using a trowel to smooth the material. 以灰泥或水泥填塞(砌砖工程等)的接合处; 用泥刀抹平. **6** (of a dog) take up a position with the body steady and the head ~ing in the direction of game. (指犬)站住以头指向猎物. ⇨ **pointer(3).** ~ed *adj* **1** (fig) directed clearly against a particular person or his behaviour: (喻)明指某人或其行为的; 直截了当的; 率直的: *a ~ed reproof.* 率直的责备. *Jack was showing ~ed attentions to the glamorous film star.* 杰克特别对那位迷人的电影明星献殷勤. **2** (of wit) incisive. (指机智)锐敏的; 犀利的. ~**ed·ly** *adv*

point-blank /ˌpɔɪnt ˈblæŋk; ˈpɔɪntˈblæŋk/ *adj* **1** (of a shot) aimed, fired, at very close range: (指弹丸)极近距离瞄准、射出的; 零距离的; 零分画的: *fired at ~ range.* 在最近距离内射击的. **2** (fig, of sth said) in a manner that leaves no room for doubt: (喻, 指所说的话)无疑虑之余地的; 坦白的; 率直的: ~ *refusal.* 率直的拒绝. □ *adv* in a ~ manner: 近射地; 坦白地; 率直地: *fire ~ at sb;* 对着某人近射; *ask sb ~ whether he intends to help;* 率直地问某人是否有意帮助; *refuse ~ to help.* 坦白地拒绝帮助.

pointer /ˈpɔɪntə(r); ˈpɔɪntɚ/ *n* **1** stick used to point to things on a map, etc. (指示地图等的)指示棒; 指示物; 教鞭. **2** indicator on a dial or balance. (标度盘或天平上的)指针. **3** large, short-haired hunting dog trained to stand still with its nose pointing in the direction of game it scents. 一种短毛大猎犬(训练后可站住以鼻指向所嗅出之猎物的方向).

point·less /ˈpɔɪntlɪs; ˈpɔɪntlɪs/ *adj* **1** (fig) with little or no sense, aim or purpose: (喻)无意义的; 无目标的; 无方针的: *It seemed ~ to go on until they were certain of being on the right road.* 在他们确定未走错路以前, 继续前进似乎漫无目标. **2** without points scored: 未得分的: *a ~ draw.* 双方均未得分之平手(即零比零). ~·**ly** *adv*

poise /pɔɪz; pɔɪz/ *vt, vi* **1** [VP6A] be balanced; (fig) be ready: 均衡; 保持平衡; (喻)准备好: ~*d in mid-air / on the brink / poised for action.* 在半空中保持平衡(在峭壁顶端的边缘保持平衡; 准备好行动). **2** [VP6A, 15A] balance; support in a particular place or manner: 使平衡; 在某处方以某种姿式支持: *He ~d himself on his toes.* 他用脚尖站立使自己保持平衡. *Note the way he ~s his head.* 注意他使头部保持平衡的方式. □ *n* **1** [U] balance, equilibrium; [C] way in which one carries oneself, holds one's head, etc. 平衡; 均衡; (身体、头部等的)姿态. **2** [U] quiet self-confidence; self-possession. 泰然自若; 镇静.

poi·son /ˈpɔɪzn; ˈpɔɪzn/ *n* [C, U] **1** substance causing death or harm if absorbed by a living thing (animal or plant): 毒药; 毒物 (动植物吸收后可能致死或受害): *'rat-~;* 毒老鼠药; ~ *for killing weeds on gravel paths;* 除去碎石路上野草的药物; *commit suicide by taking ~.* 服毒自杀. *,~-'gas* n deadly gas used in warfare. (战时用的)毒气. *,~-'ivy* n N American shrub or vine which causes painful spots if brought into contact with a person's skin. 野葛(一种北美灌木或攀爬植物, 如与人的肌肤接触, 会造成使人觉得疼痛之斑点). *'~ pen,* person who writes anonymous letters full of malice, slander, etc. 写匿名诽谤信者. *,~ 'pen letter,* letter of this kind. 匿名诽谤信. **2** (fig) evil principle, teaching, etc considered harmful to society. (喻)败坏社会之有害的主义、教训等. □ *vt* [VP6A] **1** give ~ to; put ~ on or in; kill with ~; infect: 使中毒; 放毒于; 毒杀; 毒害; 使感染: ~ *a cat;* 将猫毒死; ~ *the wells;* 置毒物于井中; *a ~ed hand,* inflamed because of an infected cut, etc. (因切伤等感染病菌而)发炎的手. **2** injure morally: (在道德上)败坏; 沾污: ~ *a person's mind against sb;* 使对某人发生恶感; *an experience which ~ed his whole life,* which spoilt or ruined his life. 一种毁了他一生的经验. ~**er** *n* (esp) person who murders by means of ~. (尤指)毒杀者; 放毒者. ~·**ous** /ˈpɔɪzənəs; ˈpɔɪznəs/ *adj* **1** acting as ~; causing death or injury if taken into the system: 有毒的; 进入身体组织内会造成死亡或伤害的: ~*ous plants.* 有毒的植物. **2** morally injurious: 败德的; ~*ous play / novel / doctrine;* 败德的戏剧(小说、教条); *a man with a ~ous tongue,* one who spreads evil reports, wicked scandal, etc. 口舌恶毒之人. ~·**ous·ly** *adv*

poke¹ /pəʊk; pok/ *vt, vi* **1** [VP6A, 15A, B] push sharply, jab (with a stick, one's finger, etc): (以棍、手指等)拨; 推: ~ *a man in the ribs,* nudge him in a friendly way: 友善地轻触一个人的肋骨(以便其注意); ~ *the fire,* move the coals, to make the fire burn up. 拨火(拨动煤块使火燃烧旺). **2** [VP15A] put, move (sth) in a given direction, with a sharp push: 戳; 刺(洞); 穿; 塞: *Don't ~ your umbrella through the bars of the lion's cage.* 别把伞伸进栏中去. *She ~d a toffee into my mouth.* 她把一块太妃糖塞进我的口中. *Don't let your boy ~ his head out of the (train) window—it's dangerous!* 别让你的男孩子把头伸出(火车)窗外——太危险了! ~ *fun at sb,* ridicule him. 嘲弄某人. ~ *one's nose into sth,* (colloq) interfere in (sb's business, affairs). (口)干预(别人的事). **3** [VP2C] ~ *(about),* search, feel about: 到处拨动; 寻求: *He was poking (about) at the rubbish.* 他拨动垃圾. *Who's that poking about in the attic?* 谁在小阁楼上翻动东西? **4** [VP6A, 15A] make (a hole) by poking: 刺(洞); 穿(洞): ~ *a hole in a paper screen.* 在纸屏上戳一个洞. □ *n* act of poking; nudge: 拨; 推; 戳; 刺: *give the fire a ~;* 拨一拨火; *give sb a ~ in the ribs.* 轻触某人的肋骨(以促其注意).

poke² /pəʊk; pok/ *n* sack 袋; 囊 (now dial, except in 现为方言), *buy a pig in a ~,* ⇨ **pig.**

poke-bonnet /ˌpəʊk ˈbɒnɪt; ˌpokˈbanɪt/ *n* bonnet with a broad projecting brim. 有宽撑边的女帽.

poker¹ /ˈpəʊkə(r); ˈpokɚ/ *n* strong metal rod or bar for stirring or breaking up the coal in the fire. 拨火铁棒; 火钩.

poker² /ˈpəʊkə(r); ˈpokɚ/ *n* [U] card game for two or more persons in which the players bet on the value of the cards they hold. 扑克牌(供二人或多人玩的一种纸牌游戏). *'~-face* n (colloq) (person with a) face that betrays no emotion. (口)无表情的面孔; 面无表情的人.

poky /ˈpəʊkɪ; ˈpokɪ/ *adj* (**-ier, -iest**) (of a place) small; limited in space: (指地方)窄小的; 有限的: *a ~ little room.* 窄小的房间.

po·lar /ˈpəʊlə(r); ˈpolɚ/ *adj* **1** of or near the North or South Pole: 北极的; 南极的; 近北极或南极的: *the ~ circles,* the Arctic and Antarctic Circles. 北极圈和南

极圈。'~ **bear,** the white kind living in the north ~ regions. 北极熊。⇨ the illus at **bear.** 参看 bear 之插图。**2** directly opposite. 正相反的。 ⇨**·ity** /pə'lærəti; pɔ'lærəti/ *n* [U, C] state in which there are two opposite, conflicting or contrasting qualities, principles or tendencies. (性质, 原则或倾向之)正相反。

po·lar·ize /'pəʊləraɪz; 'poləˌraɪz/ *vt* [VP6A] cause to concentrate about two opposite, conflicting or contrasting positions. 赋与极性; 使极化。**po·lar·iz·ation** /ˌpəʊləraɪ'zeɪʃn US: -rɪ'z-; ˌpolərə'zeʃən/ *n* act of polarizing; state of being ~d. 生极性; 得极性; 极化; 成极作用。

po·lar·oid /'pəʊlərɔɪd; 'poləˌrɔɪd/ *n* [U] (P) thin transparent film used in sun-glasses, car windows, etc to lessen sun glare: (商标)(太阳眼镜、汽车窗子等的)偏光玻; 偏光片: ~ *camera,* one able to produce positive prints within seconds after the picture has been taken. 拍立得(立即显影)照相机。

pole¹ /pəʊl; pol/ *n* **1 North/South P~,** either of the two ends of the earth's axis. 北极(南极)。**2 North/South Magnetic P~,** either of the two points near the North P~ or South P~ to which the compass needle points. 北磁极; 南磁极 (磁针所指接近南北极之点)。**3 North/South P~,** (astron) either of the two points in the celestial sphere about which the stars appear to turn. (天文)天球北极; 天球南极(假想之地轴延伸线与天球所交之两点, 众星似绕此两极转动)。'~-**star** *n* the North Star or **Polaris** /pəʊ'læɪɪs; po'lɛɪɪs/, almost coinciding with the true north of the celestial sphere. 北极星(几与天球之正北相合)。**4** either of the two ends of a magnet or the terminal points of an electric battery: 磁极; 电极: *the negative/positive ~.* 阴(阳)极。**5** (fig) each of two opposite, conflicting or contrasting principles, etc. (喻)二相反原则等之一; 二极端之一。**be ~s apart,** be widely separated: 相距甚远: *The employers and the trade union leaders are still ~s apart,* are far from reaching an agreement or compromise, eg about wages. 雇主们与工会领袖们的意见仍然相差太远(如有关工资问题)。

pole² /pəʊl; pol/ *n* **1** long, slender, rounded piece of wood or metal, esp as a support for a tent, telegraph wires, etc or for flying a flag. 细长的圆木棒或金属棒(尤指用于支撑帐篷、电线等、或张悬旗帜者); 柱; 杆; 竿。*under bare ~s,* (naut) with all sails furled. (航海)不张帆。*up the ~,* (sl) **(a)** in a difficulty. (俚)在困难中。**(b)** slightly mad; eccentric. 微狂的; 古怪的。'~-**jumping** n (athletic contest) jumping with the help of a long ~ held in the hands. 撑竿跳。'~-**vault** *n* jump of this kind over a bar which can be raised or lowered. (越过可升降之横竿的)撑竿跳高。**2** measure of length (also called 亦称作 *rod* or *perch),* 5½ yds or about 5 metres. 杆(长度单位名, 合 5½ 码或 5 公尺左右)。 ⇨ **App 5.** 参看附录五。

Pole /pəʊl; pol/ *n* native of Poland. 波兰人。

pole-axe, pole-ax /'pəʊl æks; 'pol̩æks/ *n* **1** (hist) axe for use in war, with a long handle. (史)长柄战斧; 钺。**2** butcher's implement for slaughtering cattle. (杀牲畜用的)屠斧。□ *vt* [VP6A] strike down with a ~; (fig) slaughter; destroy. 以斧砍倒; (喻)屠杀; 摧毁。

pole·cat /'pəʊlkæt; 'pol̩kæt/ *n* small, dark-brown, fur-covered animal of the weasel family which gives off an unpleasant smell, native of Europe. 鸡貂—一种臭猫, 覆有深褐色毛皮之颇小类动物; 发臭气, 原产于欧洲。

pol·emic /pə'lemɪk; pə'lɛmɪk/ *n* [C] (formal) dispute; argument; (pl) art or practice of carrying on arguments. (正式用语)争论; 辩论; (复)辩论法。□ *adj* of ~s. 引起争论的; 好辩论的; 辩论法的。**pol·emi·cally** /-klɪ; -klɪ/ *adv*

po·lice /pə'liːs; pə'lis/ *n* (collective *n,* always *sing* in form, used with *pl v*) **(the) ~,** men and women belonging to a department of government concerned with the keeping of public order: (集合名词, 形式上

永远是单数, 与复数动词连用) 警察当局; 警察: *Several hundred ~ were on duty at the demonstration.* 在示威运动中有数百名警察值勤。*Extra ~ are needed here.* 这里需要加派警察。*The ~ have not made any arrests.* 警方尚未逮捕人。,~ '**constable** *n* ~-officer of ordinary rank. 普通警员。'~ **dog** *n* dog trained to track or attack suspected criminals. 警犬。'~ **force** *n* body of ~-officers of a country, district or town. (一个国家、地区或城镇所有的)警察; 警察力量。'~-**man** /-mən; -mən/ *n* (pl -**men**) male member of the ~. 警员; 警察。'~-**office** *n* headquarters of the ~ in a city or town. (市、镇)警察局。'~-**officer** *n* ~man or ~woman. 警官; 警员。'~ **state** *n* one controlled by political ~, eg a totalitarian state. 警察国家 (通常 为极权国家)。'~-**station** *n* office of a local ~ force: (当地的)警察分局; 派出所: *The drunken driver was taken to the ~-station.* 酒醉驾车者被带进派出所。'~-**woman** *n* (pl -**women**) female member of the ~ force. 女警员。□ *vt* [VP6A] keep order in (a place) with ~ or as with ~; control: 以警察管治(一地方); 统治: *United Nations forces ~d the Gaza strip for a long period.* 联合国军队在加沙走廊管辖一段很长的时期。

pol·icy¹ /'pɒlɪsɪ; 'pɑləsɪ/ *n* (pl -**cies**) **1** [U, C] plan of action, statement of aims and ideals, esp one made by a government, political party, business company, etc: (尤指政府、政党、公司等的)方针; 政策: *British foreign ~,* official relations between the British government and other governments. 英国的外交政策。*Is honesty the best ~?* 诚实为最上策吗? **2** [U] wise, sensible conduct; art of government. 明智的行为; 治术; 权谋。

pol·icy² /'pɒlɪsɪ; 'pɑləsɪ/ *n* written statement of the terms of a contract of insurance: 保险单: *a 'fire-insurance ~;* 火险保险单; *a '~-holder.* 投保人; 保险客户。

po·lio /'pəʊlɪəʊ; 'polɪo/ *n* [U] (colloq abbr for) poliomyelitis: (口) 脊髓灰白质炎 (为 poliomyelitis 之略): '~ *victims;* 小儿麻痹症患者; *anti-'~ injections.* 预防小儿麻痹症的注射。

polio·my·eli·tis /ˌpəʊlɪəʊˌmaɪə'laɪtɪs; ˌpolɪoˌmaɪə'laɪtɪs/ *n* [U] infectious, virus-caused disease with inflammation of the grey matter of the spinal cord, often resulting in physical disablement; formerly called 'infantile paralysis'. 脊髓灰白质炎(由滤过毒引起的一种传染病, 常导致身体的残废); (昔时称为)小儿麻痹症。

polish /'pɒlɪʃ; 'pɑlɪʃ/ *vt, vi* **1** [VP6A, 15B, 2A] ~ (**up**), make or become smooth and shiny by rubbing (with or without a chemical substance): 磨光; 擦光; 使光滑; 变光滑: ~ *furniture/shoes;* 擦光家具(擦鞋); ~ *sth up.* 将某物擦亮。*This wood won't ~.* 这种木材无法磨光。**2** [VP6A] (usu in *pp)* improve in behaviour, intellectual interests, etc; make refined or elegant: (通常用过去分词)在行为, 雅趣各方面改进; 使优雅; 文饰: ~*ed speech/performance.* 优雅的演说(演奏)。**3** [VP15B] ~ **sth off,** finish quickly: 很快做好: ~ *off a large plateful of pie;* 很快吃完一大盘馅饼; ~ *off arrears of correspondence.* 尽快赶完积欠的回信。□ *n* **1** [U, C] (shiny surface, etc obtained by) ~ing: 磨光; 擦光; 光滑的表面等: *shoes/tables with a good ~.* 擦亮的鞋(桌)。**2** [U, C] substance used for ~ing: 擦亮剂; 上光剂: *'shoe/'furniture/'floor ~;* 鞋油(家具擦光油; 地板蜡); *a tin of metal ~.* 一罐金属擦亮剂。**3** [U] (fig) refinement; elegance. (喻)优雅; 精良。~**er** *n* workman skilled in ~ing wood or metal. 精于磨光木器或金属器的工人; 磨擦匠。

Pol·ish /'pəʊlɪʃ; 'polɪʃ/ *adj* of Poland or the Poles. 波兰的; 波兰人的。□ *n* [U] language of the Poles. 波兰语。

pol·it·buro /'pɒlɪtbjʊərəʊ; 'pɑlɪtbjʊro/ *n* (pl -**ros;** -rəʊz; -ro) chief executive committee of a political (esp the Communist) party. 政党(尤指共产党)的执行委员会; 政治局。

pol·ite /pə'laɪt; pə'laɪt/ *adj* **1** having, showing the possession of, good manners and consideration for other people: 有礼貌的; 客气的: *a ~ boy*; 有礼貌的男孩; *a ~ remark*. 客气话。 **2** refined; polished; elegant: ~ *society*; 上流社会; ~ *literature*. 纯文雅的。 ~·**ly** *adv* ~·**ness** *n*

pol·i·tic /'pɒlɪtɪk; 'pɑlə,tɪk/ *adj* **1** (of persons) acting or judging wisely; prudent: (指人) 有智虑的; 明达的; 精明的。 **2** (of actions) well judged; prudent: (指行为) 权策略的; 得当的; 审慎的: *follow a ~ course*; 采取审慎的方针; *make a ~ retreat*. 作策略上的退却。 **3 the ,body** '~, the state as an organized group of citizens. 国家。

pol·iti·cal /pə'lɪtɪkl; pə'lɪtɪkl/ *adj* **1** of the State; of government; of public affairs in general: 政府的; 政治的; 行政的: ~ *liberties*; 政治自由; *for ~ reasons*. 为了政治上的理由。 ~ **a'sylum**, protection given by a State to sb who has left his own country for ~ reasons: 政治庇护: *a sailor who deserted his ship and asked for ~ asylum*. 一个弃船要求政治庇护的水手。 ,~ **e'conomy**, study of the ~ problems of government. 政治经济学。 ,~ **ge'ography**, dealing with boundaries, communications, etc. Cf 参较 *physical* and *economic geography*. 地文地理学及经济地理学。 ,~ **'prisoner**, one who is imprisoned because he opposes the (system of) government. 政治犯。 **2** of politics: 政治学的; 政治上的: *a ~ crisis*. 政治上的危机。 ~·**ly** /-klɪ; -klɪ/ *adv*

poli·ti·cian /,pɒlɪ'tɪʃn; ,pɑlə'tɪʃən/ *n* person taking part in politics or much interested in politics; (in a bad sense) person who follows politics as a career, regardless of principle: 从政者; 热心政治者; (贬义)政客: *party ~s*. 政党的政客。 *Is your leader a ~ or a statesman?* 你的首领是个政客还是位政治家?

pol·iti·cize /pə'lɪtɪsaɪz; pə'lɪtə,saɪz/ *vt, vi* [VP6A, 2A] become or cause to become politically conscious or organized. (使)具有政治意义; (使)政治化。

poli·tick /'pɒlɪtɪk; 'pɑlə,tɪk/ *vi* [VP2A] engage in politics. 从事政治活动。

poli·tics /'pɒlɪtɪks; 'pɑlə,tɪks/ *n pl* (with *sing* or *pl* v) the science or art of government; political views, affairs, questions, etc: (用单数或复数动词)政治学; 政治; 政治策略; 政见; 政务; 政治问题等: *party ~*; 政党政治; *local ~*. 地方行政。 *What are your ~?* 你的政见是什么? *'P~ is much more difficult than physics,' said Einstein*. 爱因斯坦说: '政治比物理难得多。'

pol·ity /'pɒlətɪ; 'pɑlətɪ/ *n* (*pl* **-ties**) [U] form or process of government; [C] society as an organized State. 政府; 国家; 政体; 行政; 国体。

polka /'pɒlkə US: 'pəʊlkə; 'polkə/ *n* [C] (piece of music, of E European origin, for a) lively kind of dance. 波尔卡舞(源自东欧的一种轻快舞蹈); 波尔卡舞曲。 '~ **dots**, regular pattern of large dots on cloth: (布料上的)圆点花样: (attrib) (用作定语) *a ~-dot scarf*. 有圆点花样的围巾。

poll[1] /pəʊl; pol/ *n* **1** voting at an election; list of voters; counting of the votes; place where voting takes place: 选举之投票; 投票者之名册; 投票之计算; 投票处: *a light/heavy ~*, voting by a small/large proportion of the voters; 很(高)的投票率; *awaiting the result of the ~*; 等候开票的结果; *go to the ~s* (= *~ing-booths*), vote; 到投票处去; 前往投票; *exclude people from the ~*; 不许人们投票; *be successful at the ~*; 竞选获胜; 当选; *head the ~*, have the largest number of votes; 得票最多; *declare the ~*, announce the result. 宣布选举结果。 **2** survey of public opinion by putting questions to a representative selection of persons: 民意调查: *a public opinion ~*; 民意调查或测验; *the Gallup ~*. 盖洛普民意测验。 ⇨ *straw vote* at **straw**. **3** (old use) head: (旧用法)头: (hum) (谐) *a grey ~*, a grey-haired person. 白发人。 '~-**tax** *n* tax levied on every person in a community. 人头税。

poll[2] /pəʊl; pol/ *vt, vi* **1** [VP2A, C] vote at an election; [VP6A] receive (a certain number of) votes;

take the votes of electors in (a constituency): (在选举时)投票; 获得(某数之)选票; 得到(一选区之)选举人票: *Mr Hill ~ed over 3000 votes*. 希尔先生获得三千多选票。 *The constituency was ~ed thoroughly*. 这选区的选举人票尽被得去。 '~-**ing-booth** *n* place where voters go to record votes. 投票处; 投票所。 '~-**ing-day** *n* day appointed for a ~. 投票日。 **2** [VP6A] cut off the top of (the horns of cattle): 切短 (牛角): *~ed cattle*; 角被切短的牛; cut off the top of (a tree) (= pollard). 剪去(树)梢。

poll[3] /pɒl; pal/ *n* (also 亦作 '~-*parrot*) conventional name for a parrot. 鹦鹉的俗称。

pol·lard /'pɒləd; 'paləd/ *vt* [VP6A] cut off the top of (a tree) so that a thick head of new branches grows out. 剪去 (树) 梢; 使成截头树。 □ *n* ~ed tree. 截头树。

pol·len /'pɒlən; 'palən/ *n* [U] fine powder (usu yellow) formed on flowers which fertilizes other flowers when carried to them by the wind, insects etc. 花粉(通常为黄色, 结于花上, 由风、昆虫等带至其他花上使之受精)。 '~ **count**, figure of the ~ in the atmosphere in a given volume of air during 24 hours, from deposits on slides, as a guide to possible attacks of hay fever, etc. 花粉数量(在定量空气中, 二十四小时之内, 可能引起花粉热等症的花粉数量)。

pol·lin·ate /'pɒlɪneɪt; 'palə,net/ *vt* [VP6A] make fertile with pollen. 授以花粉; 使受精。 **pol·li·na·tion** /,pɒlɪ'neɪʃn; ,palə'neʃən/ *n* [U].

poll·ster /'pəʊlstə(r); 'polstə/ *n* (colloq) person who conducts public opinion polls. (口)民意测验者; 民意调查者。

pol·lute /pə'luːt; pə'lut/ *vt* [VP6A] make dirty; destroy the purity or sanctity of: 使脏; 污染; 亵渎: *rivers ~d with filthy waste from factories*; 为工厂污秽废物所污染的河流; *~d water*, unfit to drink. 污水(不宜饮用)。 **pol·lu·tant** /-ənt; -ənt/ *n* anything that ~s, eg exhaust fumes from motor-vehicles. 污染物(如机动车辆排出之废气)。 **pol·lu·tion** /pə'luːʃn; pə'luʃən/ *n* [U] polluting or being ~d; that which ~s. 弄脏; 亵渎; 污染; 污秽物。

polo /'pəʊləʊ; 'polo/ *n* [U] ball game played on horseback with mallets. (用球棍在马上玩的)马球。 '**water-** ~ *n* game played by swimmers with a large ball. 水球。 '~-**neck**, *adj* = *turtle-neck*(*ed*). ⇨ **turtle**[1].

pol·on·aise /,pɒlə'neɪz; ,palə'nez/ *n* (piece of music for a) slow processional dance of Polish origin. 波罗奈斯舞(一种起源于波兰的慢步舞); 波罗奈斯舞曲。

po·lony /pə'ləʊnɪ; pə'loni/ *n* [U] sausage of partly cooked pork. (由半熟猪肉做成的)腊肠。

pol·ter·geist /'pɒltəgaɪst; 'poltə,gaɪst/ *n* [C] (in folklore, etc) noisy, mischievous spirit(2). (民间传说等中的)吵闹顽皮的鬼。

pol·troon /pɒl'truːn; pal'trun/ *n* coward. 卑怯者; 懦夫。 ~·**ery** /-ərɪ; -ərɪ/ *n* cowardice. 卑怯; 懦弱。

poly /'pɒlɪ; 'palɪ/ *n* (colloq abbr for) polytechnic. (口)polytechnic 之略。

poly·an·dry /'pɒlɪændrɪ; 'palɪ,ændrɪ/ *n*[U] custom of having more than one husband at the same time. 一妻多夫; 一妻多夫制。 **poly·an·drous** /,pɒlɪ'ændrəs; ,palɪ'ændrəs/ *adj* **1** of, practising, ~. 一妻多夫的; 实行一妻多夫制的。 **2** (bot) (of plants) having numerous stamens. (植物)(指植物)多雄蕊的。

poly·an·thus /,pɒlɪ'ænθəs; ,palɪ'ænθəs/ *n* (*pl* **~es** /-əsɪz/ -ˈθəsɪz/ for individual plants) (复数指个别的植物) kinds of cultivated primrose with several flowers on one stalk. 种种在同一茎上开数朵花的栽培樱草; 黄花九轮草; 夜香兰。

poly·gamy /pə'lɪgəmɪ; pə'lɪgəmɪ/ *n* [U] custom of having more than one wife at the same time. 一夫多妻; 一夫多妻制。 **poly·ga·mist** /-ɪst; -ɪst/ *n* man who practises ~. 有多妻的人; 实行一夫多妻制的人。 **poly·ga·mous** /pə'lɪgəməs; pə'lɪgəməs/ *adj* of,

practising. ~. 一夫多妻的; 实行一夫多妻制的。

poly·glot /'pɒlɪglɒt; 'pɑlɪˌglɑt/ *adj* knowing, using, written in, many languages. 通晓或使用多种语言的; 用多种语言写成的。□ *n* ~ person or book. 通晓多种语言的人, 用多种语言写成的书。

poly·gon /'pɒlɪgən US: -gɒn; 'pɑlɪˌgɑn/ *n* plane figure with many (usu five or more) straight sides. (有五边或多于五边的)平面多边形; 多角形。

poly·mor·phous /ˌpɒlɪ'mɔːfəs; ˌpɑlɪ'mɔrfəs/, (also 亦作 **poly·mor·phic** /-fɪk; -fɪk/) *adj* having, passing through, many stages (of development, growth, etc). 多形的; 多态的; 复式的。

polyp /'pɒlɪp; 'pɑlɪp/ *n* (zool) very simple form of animal life found in water; polypus. (动物)水螅; (病)粘膜瘤; 息肉。

poly·ph·ony /pə'lɪfənɪ; pə'lɪfənɪ/ *n* [U] (music) counterpoint. (音乐)多音曲; 复调音乐; 对位法。 **poly·phonic** /ˌpɒlɪ'fɒnɪk; ˌpɑlɪ'fɑnɪk/ *adj* (music) contrapuntal. (音乐)复调的; 对位法的。

poly·pus /'pɒlɪpəs; 'pɑləpəs/ *n* (*pl* ~es -pəsɪz; -pəsɪz, **-pi** -paɪ; -paɪ/) (path) kinds of tumour (eg in the nose) usu with many stems like tentacles, extending down into the tissue. (病)息肉; 粘膜瘤(生于鼻子等中, 通常有许多似触须之茎, 伸入组织内)。

poly·sty·rene /ˌpɒlɪ'staɪriːn; ˌpɑlɪ'staɪrin/ *n* [U] type of light, firm plastic material (a good insulator), used esp for making boxes etc. 聚苯乙烯(一种又轻又硬的塑胶物质, 也是一种良好的绝缘体, 特别用于制造箱匣等)。

poly·syl·lable /'pɒlɪsɪləbl; 'pɑləˌsɪləbl/ *n* word of several (usu more than three) syllables. 多音节字(通常多于三个音节)。 **poly·syl·labic** /ˌpɒlɪsɪ'læbɪk; ˌpɑləsɪ'læbɪk/ *adj* 多音节的。

poly·tech·nic /ˌpɒlɪ'teknɪk; ˌpɑlə'teknɪk/ *n* (colloq abbr 口略作 **poly** /'pɒlɪ; 'pɑlɪ/) institution for advanced full-time and part-time education, esp in scientific and technical subjects. 工艺学校。

poly·theism /'pɒlɪθiːɪzəm; 'pɑləθiˌɪzəm/ *n* [U] belief in, worship of, more than one god. 多神论; 多神教; 多神崇拜。 **poly·theis·tic** /ˌpɒlɪθiː'ɪstɪk; ˌpɑləθi-'ɪstɪk/ *adj* 多神论的; 多神教的; 信多神教的。

poly·thene /'pɒlɪθiːn; 'pɑləθin/ *n* [U] plastic material widely used for waterproof packaging, insulation, etc. (普遍用于防水包装, 绝缘等的)塑胶。

pom /pɒm; pɑm/ *n* (abbr) (略) = **pommy**.

po·made /pə'mɑːd US: pəʊ'meɪd; pə'med / *n* [U] perfumed ointment for use on the hair. (香的)发油; 发膏。□ *vt* put ~ on. 涂发油于……上。

pom·egran·ate /'pɒmɪˌgrænɪt; 'pʌmˌgrænɪt/ *n* (tree with) thick-skinned round fruit which, when ripe, has a reddish centre full of seeds. 石榴; 石榴树。

pom·elo /'pɒmɪləʊ; 'pʌmələ/ *n* (*pl* ~s /-ləʊz; -loz/) kind of large grapefruit; shaddock. 柚子; 朱栾。

pom·mel /'pɒml; 'pʌml/ *n* 1 the rounded part of a saddle which sticks up at the front. 鞍头, 前鞍(鞍最前端向上突起之圆形部分)。 ⇨ the illus at **harness.** 参看 harness 之插图。 2 rounded knob on the hilt of a sword. (剑柄之)圆头; 欄头。□ /'pʌml; 'pʌml/ *vt* (**-ll-,** US also **-l-**) = **pummel.**

pommy /'pɒmɪ; 'pɑmɪ/ *n* (*pl* **-mies**) (sl) British immigrant in Australia or New Zealand; British person. (俚)(澳大利亚或新西兰之)英国移民; 英国人。

pomp /pɒmp; pɑmp/ *n* [U] splendid display, magnificence, esp at a public event: 壮观; 壮丽; 盛况(尤指公开之盛大事件): *the* ~ *and ceremony of the State Opening of Parliament.* 国会正式揭幕的盛况。

pom·pon /'pɒmpɒn; 'pɑmpɑn/ *n* ornamental tuft or bunch of feathers, silk, ribbon, etc worn on a hat or dress or shoes; ball of wool worn on eg a soldier's cap. (帽、女装或鞋上所缀之装饰性)绒球; 丝球; (军帽的)毛球。

pom·pous /'pɒmpəs; 'pɑmpəs/ *adj* full of, showing,

self-importance: 自大的; 夸大的; 虚夸的; 华而不实的: *a* ~ *official;* 自大的官员; *language,* full of high-sounding words. 浮夸不实的言词。 **pom·pos·ity** /pɒm'pɒsətɪ; pɑm'pɑsətɪ/ *n* [U] being ~; [C] (*pl* **-ties**) instance of this. 自大; 夸大; 虚夸; 自大或夸大的实例。

ponce /pɒns; pɑns/ *n* man who lives with a prostitute and lives on her earnings. 与妓女同居且靠其收入为生的男子。

pon·cho /'pɒntʃəʊ; 'pɑntʃo/ *n* (*pl* ~**s** -tʃəʊz; -tʃoz/) large piece of cloth with a slit in the middle for the head, worn as a cloak; similar garment in waterproof material used by hikers, cyclists, etc. 一种斗篷(一块长布, 中央开缝以伸出头部); (徒步, 骑自行车的人所穿之)斗篷式雨衣。

pond /pɒnd; pɑnd/ *n* small area of still water, esp one used or made as a drinking place for cattle. 池塘 (尤指供家畜饮水者)。

pon·der /'pɒndə(r); 'pɑndə/ *vt, vi* [VP6A, 2A, 8, 10, 3A] ~ **(over),** consider; think over: 考虑; 沉思: *We* ~*ed many things.* 我们考虑了许多事情。 *He* ~*ed over the incident.* 他沉思那事件。

pon·der·able /'pɒndərəbl; 'pɑndərəbl/ *adj* (phys) that can be weighed or measured. (物)可衡量的; 能估计的。□ *n* (*pl*) events, conditions, etc that can be taken into account and estimated. (复)可予考虑及估计的事件, 情况等。

pon·der·ous /'pɒndərəs; 'pɑndərəs/ *adj* 1 heavy; bulky; unwieldy: 沉重的; 庞大的; 笨重的: ~ *movements,* eg of a heavy man. 笨重的动作(如鲁钝的人所表现者)。 2 (of style) dull; laboured. (指文体)沉闷的; 艰涩的。 ~·**ly** *adv*

pone /pəʊn; pon/ *n* (also 亦作 **'corn** ~) maize bread, esp as made by N American Indians. 玉米面包(尤指北美印第安人做的)。

pon·gee /pɒn'dʒiː; pɑn'dʒi/ *n* [U] kind of soft silk cloth, usu unbleached so that it has the natural colour (brownish yellow). 茧绸; 府绸(通常未漂白, 故为天然的淡褐黄色)。

pon·iard /'pɒnjəd; 'pɑnjəd/ *n* (archaic or poet) dagger. (古或诗)匕首; 短剑。

pon·tiff /'pɒntɪf; 'pɑntɪf/ *n* 1 the Pope. 教皇; 教宗。 2 (old use) bishop; high priest; chief priest. (旧用法)主教; 高僧; 教长; 大祭司。

pon·tifi·cal /pɒn'tɪfɪkl; pɑn'tɪfɪkl/ *adj* 1 of or relating to the Pope or a bishop. 教皇的; 教宗的; 有关教皇的; 主教的。 2 authoritative (in a pompous way). 权威的; 傲慢武断的。□ *n* (*pl*) vestments and insignia used by bishops and cardinals at some church functions and ceremonies. (复)(主教及红衣主教在教会的若干仪典中所用的)法衣及徽章。

pon·tifi·cate /pɒn'tɪfɪkət; pɑn'tɪfɪkɪt/ *n* office of a pontiff, esp of the Pope; period of this. 主教, 高僧, 大祭司, (尤指)教皇的职位; 其任期。□ *vi* /-keɪt; -ket/ [VP2A] assume airs of infallibility. 装作绝无错误的样子; 武断。

pon·toon[1] /pɒn'tuːn; pɑn'tun/ *n* flat-bottomed boat; one of a number of such boats, or a floating hollow metal structure, supporting a roadway over a river: 平底船; 趸船; 用以支撑桥的平底船或金属浮筒: *a* ~ *bridge.* 浮桥。 ⇨ the illus at **bridge.** 参看 bridge 之插图。

pon·toon[2] /pɒn'tuːn; pɑn'tun/ *n* [U] kind of card game. 一种纸牌戏。

pony /'pəʊnɪ; 'ponɪ/ *n* (*pl* **-nies**) 1 horse of small breed. 小马; 驹。 '~-**tail** *n* style of girls' hairdressing which became popular in the 1950's with long hair tied in a bunch at the back of the head. (女孩的发型)马尾 (流行于二十世纪五十年代)。 '~-**trekking** *n* [U] the making of a journey for pleasure by riding on ponies. (以玩乐为目的的)骑小马旅游。 2 (GB sl) £25. (英俚)二十五英镑。 3 (US sl) (美俚) = **crib**[2]**(2).**

poodle /'puːdl; 'pudl/ n kind of dog with thick curling hair, often clipped and shaved into fantastic patterns. 一种有鬈曲厚毛之狮子狗; 贵宾狗(其厚毛常剪成各种花样). ⇨ the illus at **dog**. 参看 dog 之插图.

poof /puːf; puf/ n = pouf(2).

pooh /puː; pu/ int expressing impatience or contempt or disgust at a bad smell. 呸! 啐! (表示不耐烦、轻蔑或厌恶臭味).

pooh-pooh /ˌpuː'puː; ˌpu'pu/ vt [VP6A] treat (an idea, etc) with contempt. 藐视(意见等).

pool¹ /puːl; pul/ n **1** small area of still water; esp one naturally formed or made: (尤指自然形成的)小池; 水塘; 水坑: After the rainstorm there were ~s on the roads. 骤雨后路上有水坑. **2** quantity of water or other liquid lying on a surface: 一滩水或其他液体: The corpse was lying in a ~ of blood. 尸体躺在血泊中. **3** ('swimming-)~, large paved hole filled with water to swim in. 游泳池. **4** part of a river where the water is quiet and deep. 河水静止而且很深的地方; 渊; 潭.

pool² /puːl; pul/ n **1** (gambling) total of money staked by a number of gamblers. (赌博)(参与赌博者所下的)全部赌金; 总赌注. **the** ('football) **~s,** organized gambling on the results of football matches: 以足球比赛之输赢赌博: hoping to win a fortune on the ~s. 希望在足球比赛的赌博中赢一大笔钱. **2** arrangement by business firms to share business and divide profits, to avoid competition and agree on prices. 企业行号为避免竞争而协议价格并共同经营且分享利润的措施; 联营. **3** common fund, supply or service, provided by or shared among many: (由众人出资或共有的)共同的基金, 供应物或服务: a 'typing ~, arrangement by which many persons share the services of typists instead of each having the services of his or her own typist. 联合打字服务(许多人共用打字员, 而非各人有其打字员的措施). **4** [U] (US) game for several players played on a billiard-table with six pockets (GB 英 = snooker): (美)撞球; 弹子: to shoot (= play) ~. 打撞球; 打弹子. **'~-room** n place, room, in which the game of ~ is played. 撞球场. □ vt [VP6A] share in common; put (money, resources, etc) together for the use of all who contribute: 共有; 分享; 集中(钱, 资源等)共同使用; 联营: They ~ed their savings and bought a used car. 他们用他们的积蓄合资买了一部旧汽车.

poop /puːp; pup/ n (raised deck at the) stern of a ship. 船尾; 船尾高甲板; 船尾楼. ⇨ the illus at **barque.** 参看 barque 之插图.

poor /pʊə(r); pur/ adj (-er, -est) **1** having little money; not having and not able to get the necessaries of life. 无钱的; 贫穷的; 衣食不足的. **the** ~ n pl 穷人. **'~-box** n (formerly, in a church) box in which money may be placed to be given to the ~. (昔时教堂的)济贫捐款箱; 慈善箱. **'~-house** n (formerly) building where ~ people were maintained at the public expense. (昔时)公立贫民院; 救济院. **'~ law** n (formerly) group of laws relating to the relief and care of the ~ (now replaced by Social Security Services). 济贫法(昔时英国之法律, 现由社会救济服务法取代之). **'~-rate** n (formerly) rate (= local tax) for the relief of the ~. (昔时)济贫税. **~ 'white,** (in southern US and S Africa) one of a class of socially inferior white people. (美国南方及南非之)社会地位低的白人. **2** deserving or needing help or sympathy: 值得或需要帮助或同情的: The ~ little puppy had been abandoned. 那可怜的小狗已被遗弃了. **3** (often hum or ironic) humble; of little value: (常为诙谐或反语)不足道的; 无价值的: in my ~ opinion. 依愚见以为. **4** small in quantity: 少量的; 稀少的: a ~ supply of well-qualified science teachers; 资格好的自然科学教师的缺乏; a country ~ in minerals. 缺乏矿产的国家. **5** low in quality: 质劣的; 坏的: ~ soil; 贫瘠的土地; ~ food; 差的食物; ~ health. 健康不佳. **,~-'spirited** adj lacking in courage; timid. 无勇气的; 胆怯的.

poor·ly /'pʊəlɪ; 'purlɪ/ pred adj (colloq) unwell: (口)身体不适的; 不舒服的: He's rather ~ this morning. 他今晨颇感不适. □ adv **1** in a poor manner, badly; with little success: 贫乏地; 拙劣地; 结果不佳地: ~ lighted streets; 灯光不足的街道; ~ dressed. 穿得不好的. **2 ~ off,** having very little money: 无钱的; 贫困的: She's been ~ off since her husband died. 丈夫死后她一直是贫困的.

poor·ness /'pʊənɪs; 'purnɪs/ n [U] lack of some desirable quality or element (note that poverty is usu for being poor(1)): 贫乏; 不足; 可怜; 拙劣(注意: poverty 通常是指无钱或贫穷): the ~ of the soil. 土壤的贫瘠.

pop¹ /pɒp; pɑp/ n **1** short, sharp, explosive sound: 短而尖锐的爆裂声; 砰的一声: the pop of a cork. 瓶塞的砰然声. **2** [U] (sl) bottled drink with gas in it: (俚)加有气体的瓶装饮料; 汽水; 啤酒; 香槟酒: ginger pap, ginger beer; 姜汁啤酒; a bottle of pop. 一瓶汽水. **3** (sl) **in pop,** in pawn. (俚)被典当; 在质押中. □ adv with the sound of popping: 砰然; 发爆裂声地: I heard it go pop. 我听到它砰然一响. Pop went the cork! 瓶塞砰地一声跳出来!

pop² /pɒp; pɑp/ n (US abbr for) **poppa.** (美)为 poppa. 之略.

pop³ /pɒp; pɑp/ adj (colloq abbr for) popular: (口, popular 之略)通俗的; 流行的; 大众的: 'pop music; 流行音乐; 通俗音乐; 热门音乐; 'pop singers; 流行歌曲歌手; 热门歌曲歌手; 红歌星; 'pop groups, (singers and players) (esp) those whose records sell in large numbers and who are most popular on radio, TV and in discotheques. 热门音乐团; 流行歌曲合唱团. **'pop art,** the depiction of scenes of everyday life, using comic strips, commercial technique, etc. 以漫画或广告技巧描绘现实生活的艺术; 流行艺术. **'pop concert,** of popular music. 大众音乐会; 流行音乐会; 热门音乐会. **'pop festival,** large, usu outdoor, gathering of people to hear pop singers and musicians. (通常在室外举行的)大众音乐欣赏会; 热门音乐会. □ n [U] (colloq) pop music, pop art, etc; [C] pop song: (口)流行音乐; 流行艺术等; 流行歌曲: top of the pops, disc, etc which (calculated by sales) is most popular during a given period of time. (某一段时期内)最畅销的唱片; 冠军歌曲; 金唱片.

pop⁴ /pɒp; pɑp/ vt, vi (-pp-) **1** [VP6A, 15B, 2C] (cause to) make a sharp, quick sound (as when a cork comes out of a bottle): (使)发出短促的砰声(如软木塞拔出瓶子时所发出者); 发爆裂声: Champagne corks were popping (away) on all sides. 到处都是打开香槟酒塞子的砰声. **pop the question,** (sl) propose marriage. (俚)求婚. **'pop-eyed** adj having bulging eyes or eyes very wide open (with surprise, etc). (因惊奇等)眼睛睁大的; 眼球突出的. **'pop·gun** n child's toy gun which fires a cork with a popping sound. 玩具气枪. **2** [VP15A, B, 2A, C] (uses with adverbial particles and preps) (与副词性小品词及介词连用) pop across to, ⇨ pop over below. 参看下列之 pop over. **pop in/out (of),** (cause to) go or come in/out quickly (giving the idea of rapid or unexpected movement or activity): (使)突然地进出; 突然地活动: He popped his head in at the door. 他突然将头伸进门内. Pop in and see me some time. 找一个时候来看我. The neighbours' children are always popping in and out, are very frequent visitors. 邻居的孩子们总是走进走出的,(是走动很勤的常客). His eyes almost popped out (of his head) in surprise. 他因惊讶而睁大着眼睛(他的眼睛因惊讶而几乎跟眶而出). **pop sth into sth,** quickly put it there: 将某物很快地放于某处: She popped the gin bottle into the cupboard as the vicar entered the room. 牧师进入房间时, 她很快地把杜松子酒瓶放进橱柜. **pop off,** (a) go away. 忽然离去. (b) (sl) die: (俚)死掉: I don't intend to pop off yet. 我还不想死呢. **pop over/across to,** make a quick, short visit to: 突然造访; 匆促前往: She has just popped over/across to the grocer's. 她刚刚匆促地往杂货店去了. **3** (sl) [VP2C] shoot: (俚)射杀; 开枪: They

were popping away at the pigeons. 他们用枪打鸽子。**4** (sl) pawn: (俚) 典当: *I'll pop my watch and take you to the cinema.* 我要把手表当掉, 请你看电影。**5** (US) parch (maize) until it bursts open and puffs out. (美) 爆玉米花。'**pop·corn** *n* maize treated in this way. 玉米花。

Pope /pəʊp; pop /n (often 常作 **the ~**) the Bishop of Rome as chief bishop of the Roman Catholic Church. (天主教的)教宗; 教皇。**pop·ery** /'pəʊpərɪ; 'popərɪ/ n [U] (in hostile use) Roman Catholicism; papal system. (含有敬意的用法)天主教之教义; 教皇制度。**pop·ish** /'pəʊpɪʃ; 'popɪʃ/ adj (in hostile use) of popery. (含有敬意的用法)天主教之教义之或教皇制度的。**pop·ish·ly** adv

pop·in·jay /'pɒpɪndʒeɪ; 'papɪnˌdʒe/ n conceited person, esp one who is vain about clothes. 自大者; (尤指)讲究衣着者; 纨绔子弟。

pop·lar /'pɒplə(r); 'paplə/ n [C] tall, straight, fast-growing tree; [U] its wood. 白杨; 白杨树; 白杨木。

pop·lin /'pɒplɪn; 'paplɪn/ n [U] (formerly) cloth of silk and wool with a ribbed surface; (now, usu) kind of strong, shiny cotton cloth used for shirts, etc. (昔时之)毛葛(丝与羊毛合织的一种起皱的布料); (现在通常指)一种用于制衬衣等之坚实发光的棉布。

poppa /'pɒpə; 'papə/ n (US) = **papa**.

pop·pet /'pɒpɪt; 'papɪt/ n (GB) used as a term of endearment (usu to a child): (英) 小乖乖; 小宝贝(通常用做对小孩的昵称): *Isn't she a ~?* 她不是一位可爱的人儿吗? *And how's my little ~ this morning?* 我的小宝贝今天早上好吗?

poppy /'pɒpɪ; 'papɪ/ n (pl **-pies**) sorts of plant, wild and cultivated, with large flowers, esp red, and a milky juice: 罂粟(野生或栽培的植物, 开大花, 尤多红色, 果含浆汁): '*opium ~,* kind from which opium is obtained. 产鸦片的罂粟。

poppy·cock /'pɒpɪkɒk; 'papɪˌkak/ n [U] (sl) nonsense. (俚)胡说; 废话。

popu·lace /'pɒpjʊləs; 'papjələs/ n (formal) the common people; the general public; the masses. (正式用语)平民; 大众; 民众; 老百姓。

popu·lar /'pɒpjʊlə(r); 'papjələ/ adj **1** of or for the people: 人民的; 民众的; 为了人民的: *~ government,* by the elected majority of all those who have votes. 民治的政府。**,~ 'front,** (in politics) coalition of parties opposed to reaction and fascism. (政治)(反对保守派及法西斯主义的)联合阵线; 民众阵线。**2** suited to the tastes, needs, educational level, etc of the general public: 适于大众之爱好, 需要, 教育水准等的; 一般的; 通俗的: *~ science;* 大众科学; 通俗科学; *meals at ~* (= low) *prices.* 廉价膳食。**3** liked and admired: 受爱慕的; 被拥戴的; 有名气人望的: *a ~ hero;* 一般民众崇拜的英雄; *~ film stars;* 有名气的影星; *a man who is ~ with his neighbours.* 一位受邻居欢迎的人。⇨ **pop**[3]. **~·ly** adv

popu·lar·ity /ˌpɒpjʊ'lærɪtɪ; ˌpapjə'lærətɪ/ n [U] quality of being popular(**3**): 受爱慕; 被拥戴; 声望; 普遍: *win ~;* 得人心; 得名望; the *~ of baseball in Japan.* 日本人对棒球的普遍爱好。

popu·lar·ize /'pɒpjʊləraɪz; 'papjələˌraɪz/ vt [VP 6A] make popular: 使普及; 使通俗; 使得人心: *~ a new method of teaching spelling.* 推广一种教拼字的新方法。**popu·lar·iz·ation** /ˌpɒpjʊləraɪ'zeɪʃn US: -rɪ'z; ˌpapjə-ləraɪ'zeʃən/ n

popu·late /'pɒpjʊleɪt; 'papjəˌlet/ vt [VP6A] supply with people; inhabit; form the population of: 殖民于; 居住于; 构成…之人口: *thinly ~d;* 人口稀少的; *the densely ~d parts of India.* 印度人口稠密的地方。

popu·la·tion /ˌpɒpjʊ'leɪʃn; ˌpapjə'leʃən/ n (number of) people living in a place, country, etc or a special section of them: (地方, 国家等之全部或一部分的)人口(人口数): *a fall/rise in ~;* 人口的减少(增加); *the ~ of London;* 伦敦的人口; *the working-class ~.* 工人阶级的人口数。

popu·lism /'pɒpjʊlɪzəm; 'papjəlɪzm/ n [U] govern-

ment or politics based on an appeal to popular sentiments or fears. 民粹主义。**popu·list** /-ɪst; -ɪst/ n supporter or promoter of ~. 民粹党党员; 拥护或提倡民粹主义者。

popu·lous /'pɒpjʊləs; 'papjələs/ adj thickly populated. 人口稠密的。

por·ce·lain /'pɔːsəlɪn; 'pɔrslɪn/ n [U] (articles, eg cups and plates, made of a) fine china with a coating of translucent material called *glaze.* 瓷(其表面涂有透明的釉); 瓷器(如杯盘)。

porch /pɔːtʃ; pɔrtʃ/ n **1** built-out roofed doorway or entrance to a building. 门廊。**2** (US, also) veranda. (美国亦指)走廊。

por·cine /'pɔːsaɪn; 'pɔrsaɪn/ adj of or like a pig. 猪的; 似猪的。

por·cu·pine /'pɔːkjʊpaɪn; 'pɔrkjəˌpaɪn/ n small rat-like animal covered with spines that the animal can stick out if attacked. 豪猪(又名箭猪, 似鼠之小动物, 体生硬刺毛, 遇敌时可竖立以自卫)。

pore[1] /pɔː(r); pɔr/ n tiny opening (esp in the skin of an animal body) through which fluids (eg sweat) may pass: 小孔; (尤指动物身体上的)毛孔: *He was sweating at every ~.* 他的每一个毛孔都在出汗。

pore[2] /pɔː(r); pɔr/ vi [VP3A] **~ over sth,** study it with close attention: 仔细研读某物; 熟读: *~ over a letter/book.* 仔细研读一信(书)。

pork /pɔːk; pɔrk/ n [U] flesh of a pig (usu fresh, not salted or cured) used as food: 猪肉(通常指未加盐或熏腌的鲜肉): *a leg of ~;* 猪腿; *a ~ chop;* 猪排; *roast ~.* 烤猪肉。⇨ **bacon, ham**(**1**). '**~-barrel** n (US, sl) money from State or Federal taxes, etc spent to confer local benefits for political reasons. (美俚)为了政治因素由州或联邦的赋税等中拨出而花费于地方福利的经费; 政治分肥。'**~-butcher** n one who kills pigs for sale as food, makes ~ sausages, ~ pies, etc. 屠户; 猪肉商。,**~ 'pie** n minced ~, highly seasoned, in a container of piecrust. 猪肉饼。**~er** n pig raised for food, esp one fattened for killing. 猪; (尤指养肥后宰食之)肉猪。

porn /pɔːn; pɔrn/ n (colloq abbr of) pornography. (口)= pornography 之略。'**~ shop** n shop where pornographic books etc are sold. 色情书报店。

por·nogra·phy /pɔː'nɒgrəfɪ; pɔr'nagrəfɪ/ n [U] treatment of obscene subjects, in writing, pictures, etc; such writings, etc. (写作、图画等中之)淫秽题材的处理; 海淫; 色情文学; 色情画; 春画; 春宫。**por·nogra·pher** /pɔː'nɒgrəfə(r); pɔr'nagrəfə/ n person who makes or deals in ~. 撰写色情文学者; 制作色情书画者; 推销色情书画者。**por·no·graphic** /ˌpɔːnə'græfɪk; ˌpɔrnə'græfɪk/ adj

po·rous /'pɔːrəs; 'pɔrəs/ adj **1** full of pores. 多孔的。**2** allowing liquid to pass through: 能浸透的; 可渗水的: *Sandy soil is ~.* 沙土会渗水。**~·ness, po·ros·ity** /pɔː'rɒsətɪ; pɔ'rasətɪ/ nn quality or condition of being ~. 孔; 多孔; 多孔性; 渗水性。

por·phyry /'pɔːfɪrɪ; 'pɔrfərɪ/ n [U] hard, red kind of rock with red and white crystals bedded in it, polished and made into ornaments. 斑岩(有红色和白色结晶嵌于其中的一种坚硬的红岩石, 磨光后可做成装饰品); 细纹硬石。

por·poise /'pɔːpəs; 'pɔrpəs/ n sea animal rather like a dolphin or small whale. 海豚。⇨ the illus at **sea.** 参看 sea 之插图。

por·ridge /'pɒrɪdʒ US: 'pɔːr-; 'pɔrɪdʒ/ n [U] soft food made by boiling a cereal, eg oatmeal, in water or milk: (用麦片等谷类加水或牛奶煮成的)粥; 麦片粥: *a bowl/plate of ~.* 一碗(盘)麦片粥。

por·rin·ger /'pɒrɪndʒə(r) US: 'pɔːr-; 'pɔrɪndʒə/ n small bowl with a handle (for a child) from which porridge, soup, etc is eaten. (小孩用的、有柄的)小汤碗; 粥碗。

port[1] /pɔːt; pɔrt/ n **1** harbour: 港; 港口: *a naval ~;* 军港; *reach ~.* 靠港。**2** town or city with a harbour,

esp one where customs officers are stationed. 港市(尤指有海关官员驻征关税者)。 **free ~,** one open for the merchandise of all countries to load and unload in; one where there is exemption of duties for imports or exports. 自由港（各国商品皆可装卸而无进出口税之港口）。 **3** (fig) refuge. (喻)避难所；休息处。 *any ~ in a storm,* in time of difficulty help or safety may be sought anywhere. 危难时可寻求帮助或安全的任何处所。 *~ after stormy seas,* rest after struggles. 挣扎后的休息。

port[2] /pɔːt; pɔrt/ *n* (naut) opening in the side of a ship for entrance, or for loading and unloading cargo; ~hole(b). (航海)(船的)舱门；上下货口；舷窗。 '**~·hole** *n* **(a)** opening in a ship's side for admission of light and air. 船侧供采光通气的窗孔。 **(b)** small glass window in the side of a ship or aircraft. 舷侧或机侧之小玻璃窗；舷窗。

port[3] /pɔːt; pɔrt/ *n* left-hand side of a ship or aircraft as one faces forward: (船的)左舷；(飞机的)左侧: *put the helm to ~;* 把舵朝向左舷(使船首向右转)；(attrib) (用作定语) *on the ~ bow/quarter.* 在左舷船首(船尾)。 ⇨ **starboard;** ⇨ the illus at **ship.** 参看 ship 之插图。 □ *vt* [VP6A] turn (the ship's helm) to ~. 把(船舵)转向左舷。

port[4] /pɔːt; pɔrt/ *n* [U] strong, sweet, dark-red or white wine of Portugal. (葡萄牙产的)暗红色或白色浓而甜的葡萄酒。

port[5] /pɔːt; pɔrt/ *n at the ~,* (mil) position of a rifle on porting arms. (军)作端枪的姿势。 □ *vt* carry (a rifle or other weapon) diagonally across and close to the body ready for inspection by an officer: 握持(枪)使枪管斜交于身体，以备检查；端枪: *P~ arms!* command for this to be done. (军队口令)端枪!

port·able /'pɔːtəbl; 'pɔrtəbl/ *adj* that can be carried about; not fixed: 可携带的；手提式的；能移动的: *~ radios/typewriters.* 手提收音机(打字机)。 **port·abil·ity** /ˌpɔːtə'bɪlətɪ; ˌpɔrtə'bɪlətɪ/ *n* [U] being ~ (可携带；能移动；轻便: *The portability of my tape-recorder is exaggerated.* 我这录音机的轻便性是夸大其词的。

port·age /'pɔːtɪdʒ; 'pɔrtɪdʒ/ *n* [C, U] (cost of) carrying goods, esp when (eg in forest country in Canada) goods have to be carried overland from two rivers or parts of a river; place where this is done. 货物搬运；搬运费；(尤指)两河之间或一河的两部分之间的陆上运送(如在加拿大的林区)；两水路之间的陆上运送地点。

por·tal /'pɔːtl; 'pɔrtl/ *n* doorway, esp an imposing one of a large building. 入口；大门；(尤指大建筑物的)正门。

port·cul·lis /ˌpɔːt'kʌlɪs; pɔrt'kʌlɪs/ *n* (hist) iron grating that could be raised or lowered to protect the gateway of a castle. (史)(保护城堡入口之可升降的)铁门；城堡吊门。 ⇨ the illus at **drawbridge.** 参看 drawbridge 之插图。

porte-cochère /ˌpɔːt kə'ʃeə(r); ˌpɔrtkə'ʃɛr/ *n* (F) gateway at the entrance to a building to give shelter to persons entering or leaving cars, etc. (法)(建筑物大门前供人进入或下车等)有顶盖的通道。

por·tend /pɔː'tend; pɔr'tend/ *vt* [VP6A] (formal) be a sign or warning of (a future event, etc): (正式用语)预示；为(未来事件等)之征兆: *This ~s war.* 这是战争的预兆。

por·tent /'pɔːtent; 'pɔrtent/ *n* thing, esp sth marvellous or mysterious, that portends sth; omen. (尤指奇特或神秘的)预兆；征兆。 **por·ten·tous** /pɔː'tentəs; pɔr'tɛntəs/ *adj* **1** ominous; threatening. 预示的；不祥的。 **2** marvellous; extraordinary. 奇特的；可惊的；非常的。 **por·ten·tous·ly** *adv*

por·ter[1] /'pɔːtə(r); 'pɔrtə/ *n* **1** person whose work is to carry luggage, etc at railway stations, airports, hotels, etc. (火车站，飞机场，旅馆等处搬运行李之)脚夫。 **2** person carrying a load on his back or head (usu in

country where there are no roads for motor-vehicles). (在无汽车道路地区以背或头负物之)挑夫；驮夫。 **3** (US) attendant on a sleeping-car or parlour-car on a train. (美)(铁路之卧车或特等客车上的)侍者；服务员。 '**~·age** /-ɪdʒ; -ɪdʒ/ *n* [U] (the charge for) carrying of luggage, etc by a ~. 搬运行李；行李搬运费。

por·ter[2] /'pɔːtə(r); 'pɔrtə/ *n* doorkeeper (at a hotel, public building, etc) (US 美 = *doorman*): (旅馆、公共建筑等之)门房；守门者: *The hotel ~ will call a taxi for you.* 旅馆的门房将为你叫一部计程车。 *~'s lodge,* ⇨ **lodge**[1](3).

por·ter[3] /'pɔːtə(r); 'pɔrtə/ *n* [U] dark-brown bitter beer. 一种黑褐色的苦啤酒。

por·ter·house /'pɔːtəhaus; 'pɔrtə,haus/ *n ~* **(steak),** choice cut of beefsteak. 上等牛排。

port·folio /pɔːt'fəuljəu; pɔrt'folɪ,o/ *n* (*pl ~s* /-lɪəuz; -lɪoz/) **1** flat case (usu leather) for keeping loose papers, documents, drawings, etc. 公事包(通常为皮制)。 **2** position and duties of a minister of state: 大臣(部长)的职位和职责: *He resigned his ~.* 他辞去部长职务。 *Mr X is minister without ~,* not in charge of any particular department. 某先生是不管部大臣(部长)。 **3** list of securities and investments (stocks, shares, etc) owned by an individual, a bank, etc. 有价证券类。

port·hole *n* ⇨ **port**[2].

port·ico /'pɔːtɪkəu; 'pɔrtɪ,ko/ *n* (*pl ~es or ~s* /-kəuz; -koz/) roof supported by columns, esp at the entrance of a building. 柱廊；(尤指)有圆柱的门廊。

a portico

port·ière /ˌpɔːtɪ'eə(r); ˌpɔrtɪ'ɛr/ *n* (F) heavy curtain hung over a door(way). (法)门帷；门帘。

por·tion /'pɔːʃn; 'pɔrʃən/ *n* **1** part, esp a share, (to be) given when sth is distributed: 部份；(尤指某物被分配时之)一份: (of a railway ticket) *this ~ to be given up;* (指火车票)此联须缴回; (of a railway train) *the through ~ for Liverpool,* the coaches for Liverpool (passengers in which will not need to change trains); (指火车)直达利物浦的一部份车厢; *a marriage ~,* dowry. 嫁资；妆奁。 **2** quantity of any kind of food served in a restaurant: (餐馆食物的)一份: *a generous ~ of roast duck.* 一大份烤鸭。 **3** (sing) one's lot or fate: (单)命运: *Brief life is here our ~.* 短暂的人生是我们今世的命运。 □ *vt* **1** [VP15B] *~ sth out (among/between),* divide into *~s,* share. 分配。 **2** [VP14] *~ sth to sb,* provide a *~* of (sth to sb). 把(某物)之一份给某人。

Port·land /'pɔːtlənd; 'pɔrtlənd/ *n ~* **stone,** yellowish-white limestone (quarried near *~,* Dorset), used for building. 一种微黄色石灰石（建筑用，产于英国 Dorset 郡的 Portland）；波特兰石。 *~ cement,* cement used for concrete that resembles *~* stone in colour. 波特兰水泥（用此种水泥和成之混凝土，其颜色似波特兰石）。

port·ly /'pɔːtlɪ; 'pɔrtlɪ/ *adj* (usu of elderly persons) stout; round and fat: (通常指长者)壮硕的；肥胖的: *a ~ city councillor.* 一位肥胖的市议员。

port·man·teau /pɔːt'mæntəu; pɔrt'mæntо/ *n* (*pl ~s or ~x* /-təuz; -toz/) oblong, square-shouldered leather case for clothes, opening on a hinge into two equal parts. 一种装衣服的皮箱(长方形，肩部平正，以铰

链连合，打开时成为相同的两部分）。 **~ word,** one made by using two or more words and combining their meanings, eg *shamateur* (from *sham* and *amateur*). 用两个以上的词并结合其意义所造成的词(如 shamateur, 系由 sham 及 amateur 所构成)。

por·trait /'pɔːtrɪt; 'portret/ n **1** painted picture, drawing, photograph, of a person or animal. 人或动物之图像或照片；肖像；人像。 **2** vivid description in words. 生动之文字描写。 **'~·ist** /-ɪst; -ɪst/ n maker of ~s. 人像画家；人像摄影师。 **'~·ure** /-tʃə(r) US: -tʃʊə(r), -tʃə/ n [U] art of making ~s; ~. 人像或肖像画法；人像摄影；人像；肖像；描写。

por·tray /pɔː'treɪ/ vt [VP6A] **1** make a picture of. 作…之画像；描画。 **2** describe vividly in words. (以文字生动地)描写。 **3** act the part of (in a play). 扮演；饰演…之角色。 **~al** /pɔː'treɪəl; pɔr'treəl/ n [U] ~ing; [C] description. 画像；描画；描写。

pose /pəʊz; poz/ vt, vi **1** [VP6A] put (sb) in a desired position before making a portrait, taking a photograph, etc: (在画作、摄影等之前)使(某人)摆成所要求之姿势: *The artist ~d his model carefully.* 那画家仔细地把他的模特儿的姿势摆好。 *All the subjects are well ~d.* 所有的人都摆好了姿势。 **2** [VP2A, 3A] ~ (for), take up a position (for a portrait, etc): (为画像等)摆姿势: *Are you willing to ~ for me?* 你愿意摆个姿势让我为你拍照(画像)吗？ **3** [VP6A] put forward for discussion; create; give rise to: 提出讨论；造成；引起: *The increase in student numbers ~s many problems for the universities.* 学生人数增加给大学带来许多问题。 **4** [VP2C] ~ as, set oneself up as, claim to be: 使自己成为；以…身份出现；佯装: *~ as an expert on old coins.* 佯装为古钱币专家。 **5** [VP2A] behave in an affected way, hoping to impress people: 态度做作(以使人印象深刻)；矫揉造作: *She's always posing,* is never natural in her behaviour. 她总是矫揉造作。 □ n **1** position taken up for a portrait, photograph, etc: (为绘画、照相等所取的)姿势: *a striking and unusual ~.* 显眼而不寻常的姿势。 **2** attitude, unnatural way of behaving, intended to impress people; affectation: 姿态；不自然的态度；装腔作势(为使人印象深刻所做者): *That rich man's socialism is a mere ~.* 那位富人标榜的社会主义只是一种姿态。 **poser** n awkward or difficult question. 难题。

po·seur /pəʊ'zɜː(r); po'zɝ/ (fem) (阴) **po·seuse** /pəʊ'zɜːz; po'zɝz/ n person who poses(5); affected person. 态度做作的人；装腔作势的人。

posh /pɒʃ; paʃ/ adj (colloq) smart; first-class: (口)漂亮的；头等的: *a ~ hotel;* 头等旅馆; *~ clothes;* 华服; *her ~ friends.* 她的出众的朋友。 □ vt [VP15B] **~ up,** make ~: 打扮: *We must ~ ourselves up for the party.* 我们必须打扮得漂亮一点去参加宴会。

posit /'pɒzɪt; 'pazɪt/ vt [VP6A] postulate. 假设；假定。

po·si·tion /pə'zɪʃn; pə'zɪʃən/ n **1** [C] place where sth or sb is or stands, esp in relation to others: 位置(尤指在相关位置中)： *fix a ship's ~,* eg by observation of the sun or stars; (借观察太阳或星球)确定船只的位置: *secure a ~ where one will get a good view of the procession;* 找一个能看清楚游行的位置; *storm the enemy's ~s,* the places they occupy. 猛攻敌军的阵地。 *in/out of ~,* in/not in the right place. 在(不在)适当位置。 **2** [C] state of being advantageously placed (in war or any kind of struggle): (在战争或任何斗争中之)有利之地位或阵势: *They were manoeuvring for ~.* 他们在用策略以取得有利之阵势。 **3** [C] way in which sb or sth is placed; attitude or posture: 某人或某物被安置的方式；姿势: *sit/lie in a comfortable ~.* 舒适地坐(躺)着。 **4** [C] person's place or rank in relation to others, in employment, in society, etc: 阶级；地位: *a pupil's ~ in class,* 一个学生在班上的名次; *a high/low ~ in society.* 高(低)的社会地位。 **5** [C] job; employment: 工作；职位: *apply for the ~ of assistant manager.* 申请副经理的职位。 **6** [C] condition; circumstance: 状况；环境: *placed in an awkward ~.* 处于困窘之境地。 *I regret I am not in a ~* (= am unable) *to help you.* 我很抱歉无力帮助你。 **7** [C] attitude; opinion: 态度；见解；主张: *What's your ~ on this problem?* 你对这个问题的意见如何？ □ vt [VP6A] place (sth or sb) in ~; determine the ~ of. 安置(某物或某人)在适当的位置；决定…之位置。

posi·tive /'pɒzətɪv; 'pazətɪv/ adj **1** definite; sure; leaving no room for doubt: 确定的；确实的；无疑的: *give a man ~ orders/instructions;* 给某人明确的命令(指示); *~ knowledge.* 确定的知识。 **2** (of persons) quite certain, esp about opinions: (指人)极有把握的；确信的 (尤指在某方面): *Are you ~ (that) it was after midnight?* 你能断定是在午夜后(发生的)吗？ *Can you be ~ about what you saw?* 你能确定你所见到的是真的吗？ **3** practical and constructive; that definitely helps: 实际而有建设性的；确有助益的: *a ~ suggestion;* 积极的建议; *~ help;* 实际的帮助; *~ criticism.* 建设性的批评。 **4** (colloq) down-right; out and out: (口)安全的；彻底的: *That man is a ~ fool/nuisance.* 那家伙是一个彻头彻尾的傻瓜(讨厌鬼)。 *It's a ~ crime to drink and drive.* 醉酒驾车绝对有罪。 **5** (maths) greater than zero: (数学)正的；正数的: *the ~ sign* (+). 正号。 **6** (of electricity) of the sort caused by rubbing glass with silk; of the sort caused by deficiency of electrons: (指电)阳的；正: *a ~ charge.* 阳电荷; 正电荷。 *~ pole,* anode. 阳极。 **7** (photo) showing light and shadows as in nature, not reversed (as in a *negative*). (摄影)正片的。 **8** (gram, of *adjj* and *advv*) of the simple form, not the comparative or superlative. (语法,指形容词及副词)原级的(非比较级或最高级的)。 □ n ~ degree, adjective, quantity, etc; photograph printed from a (negative) plate or film. 原级；原级形容词；正量；正数；(照相之)正片。 **~·ly** adv definitely; certainly. 明确地；断然地；绝对地。 **~·ness** n [U] confidence. 确实；确信。

posi·tiv·ism /'pɒzɪtɪvɪzəm; 'pazətɪv,ɪzəm/ n philosophical system of Auguste Comte, based on observable phenomena and positive facts rather than speculation. 实证主义；实证论(为法国哲学家孔德所倡，其体系基于可观察之现象及实在之事实)。 **logical ~,** modern (20th c) development of this philosophy mainly concerned with linguistic analysis and verification of empirical statements by observation. 逻辑实证论；论理实证法。 **posi·tiv·ist** /-ɪst; ɪst/ n

posse /'pɒsɪ; 'pasɪ/ n (chiefly US) body of constables or other men having authority who can be summoned by a sheriff to help him in maintaining order, etc. (主美)武装队；地方团队(郡执行官可召集以维持治安等)。

pos·sess /pə'zes; pə'zɛs/ vt [VP6A] **1** own, have: 有；具有: *~ nothing,* 一无所有; 身无长物; *lose all that one ~es.* 失去一个人所拥有的全部财物。 **2** keep control over: 控制；抑制；克制: *~ one's soul in patience,* be patient. 竭力忍耐。 *~ self-~ed at* self-. **3** ~ *oneself of,* (old use) become the owner of. (旧用法)持有；为…之主人。 *be ~ed of,* have: 有；握有；据有: *He is ~ed of great natural ability.* 他很有天才。 **4** *be ~ed,* be mad, be controlled by an evil spirit: 疯狂；着魔: *She is surely ~ed.* 她确是发疯了。 *He fought like one ~ed,* like a person having a devil inside him. 他象着了魔似地打斗。 **5** occupy (the mind); dominate: 占据(心)；摆布；支配: *What ~ed you to do that?* What influenced or dominated your mind and caused you to do that? 什么使你做出那种事的？ *He is ~ed with the idea that someone is persecuting him.* 他心里老想着有人要加害于他。 **~or** /-sə; -sɚ/ n owner; person who ~es sth. 持有者；所有人。

pos·session /pə'zeʃn; pə'zɛʃən/ n **1** [U] possessing; ownership; the act or state of having: 有；有权; *come into ~ of a large estate;* 获得一大笔地产; *get ~ of sth,* succeed in getting ~ of it. 拿到; 占有; 占领。 *The players fought for/won ~ of the ball.* 球员们争夺(抢到)球。 *Who is in ~ of the property?* 谁持有那财产？ *The information in my ~ is strictly confidential.* 我握有的情报是极度机密的。 *You can't take ~ of the house* (= move into it) *until all the*

papers have been signed. 在各项证件签字以前，你不能住进那房屋。*Is the woman in full ~ of her senses? Is she quite sane?* 那女人神志健全吗？ **2** [C] (often *pl*) sth possessed; property: (常用复数)所有物; 财产: *lose all one's ~s;* 失去所有的财产; *a man of great ~s.* 富人。*Most of Britain's ~s overseas* (= her former colonies, etc) *are now independent countries.* 英国昔日的海外属地如今大部分已成为独立的国家。

pos·sess·ive /pə'zesɪv; pə'zɛsɪv/ *adj* **1** of possession or ownership: 所有的; 所有权的: *He has a ~ manner,* *seems to assert, claims, eg to the attention of people.* 他有一种想要慑服人的态度(如想引起旁人注意)。*She has a ~ nature,* is eager to acquire things or wants the whole of (someone's) love or attention. 她有一种爱占有的天性。所有格的: *the ~ case, eg Tom's, the boy's;* 所有格(如 Tom's, the boy's, the boys'); *~ pronouns,* eg *yours, his.* 所有格代词(如 yours, his)。*~·ly adv*

pos·set /'pɒsɪt; 'pɑsɪt/ *n* drink of warm milk with ale or wine and spices in it, formerly much used as a remedy for colds. 牛奶酒(热牛奶加淡啤酒或葡萄酒及香料而成之饮料,昔时多用以治疗受寒)。

pos·si·bil·ity /ˌpɒsə'bɪlətɪ; ˌpɑsə'bɪlətɪ/ *n* (*pl* -ties) **1** [U] state of being possible; (degree of) likelihood: 可能; 可能性; 可能的程度: *Is there any ̸ much ~ of your getting to London this week?* 本周你(很)有可能到伦敦去吗? *I admit the ~ of your being right.* 我承认你可能是对的。*Help is still within the bounds of ~.* 援助的可能性仍然存在。**2** [C] sth that is possible: 可能之事; 可能发生之事物: *I see great possibilities in this scheme,* It can have great success in many ways. 我看这计划很可能成功。*Don't neglect the ~ that his train has been delayed ̸ the ~ of an accident.* 不要忽略他所搭的火车有误点的可能(可能发生意外事故)。

poss·ible /'pɒsəbl; 'pɑsəbl/ *adj* **1** that can be done; that can exist or happen: 可能的; 可能存在或发生的: *Come as quickly as ~.* 尽快来。*Frost is ~, though not probable, even at the end of May.* 即使在五月底，下霜也是可能的，虽然可能性不大。*Are you insured against all ~ risks?* 你投保了一切可能发生的危险吗? **2** that is reasonable or satisfactory: 合理的; 令人满意的: *a ~ answer to a problem,* one that may be accepted, though not, perhaps, the best. 对于一个问题较合理的解答。*He is the only ~ man for the position.* 他是该职位唯一合适的人选。□ *n* ~ person or thing: 可能的人或物: *A trial game was arranged between ~s and probables.* 预备队员之间安排了一次预赛。**poss·ibly** /-əblɪ; -əblɪ/ *adv* **1** in accordance with what is ~: 可能地: *I will come as soon as I possibly can.* 我尽可能早来。*Can you possibly lend me £5?* 你可能借我五英镑钱吗? **2** perhaps: 或者; 或许: *'Will they cut your salary up?'—'Possibly.'* '他们会提高你的薪水吗?'—'也许会。'

pos·sum /'pɒsəm; 'pɑsəm/ *n* (colloq abbr of) opossum. (口)o opossum 之略。*play ~,* pretend to be asleep, unaware, etc so as to deceive sb (from the ~'s habit of feigning death when attacked). 装睡; 装病; 装迷糊(由鼷鼠被袭击时装死之习惯而来)。

post¹ /pəʊst; post/ *n* [C] **1** place where a soldier is on watch; place of duty: 哨所; 岗位: *The sentries are all at their ~s.* 哨兵们都在岗位上。**2** place occupied by soldiers, esp a frontier fort; the soldiers there: 军队驻扎地; 营区; (尤指)边疆堡垒; 屯兵。⇨ **outpost.** **3** trading station, esp one in a country where law and order are not yet firmly established: (尤指法治尚未充分建立之国家的)贸易站: *trading ~s in northern Canada a hundred years ago.* 一百年前在加拿大北部的贸易站。**4** position or appointment; job: 职位; 工作: *get a better ~;* 得到一个更好的工作; *be given a ~ as general manager.* 获得总经理之职位。□ *vt* [VP6A, 15A] **1** put at a ~(1): 配置于哨站: *~ sentries at the gates of the camp.* 在军营的大门口布置哨兵。**2** send to a ~(1, 2, 4): 派往哨站或驻扎地; 指派: *~ an officer to a unit.* 指派一军官至某单位。

I hope to be ~ed to Damascus next year. 我希望明年被派往大马士革。

post² /pəʊst; post/ *n* (mil) bugle-call sounded at sunset: (军)日落时所吹之号音: (esp) (尤指) **the first ̸ last ~,** (The last ~ is also sounded at military funerals.) 就寝或熄灯预备号(熄灯号)(熄灯号在军队葬礼中亦吹之。)

post³ /pəʊst; post/ *n* **1** (hist) one of a number of men placed with horses at intervals, the duty of each being to ride with letters, etc to the next stage; letter-carrier; mail-cart. (史)骑驿马送信件者之人; 信差; 邮车。,~·'chaise *n* (hist) travelling carriage hired from stage to stage or drawn by ~-horses hired from stage to stage. (史)驿车。**'~-horse** *n* (hist) horse kept at inns, etc for the use of men carrying letters, etc and for other travellers. (史)驿马。**2** (GB) transport and delivery of letters, etc; one collection of letters, etc; one delivery or distribution of letters, etc (US 美 = *mail*): (英)邮政; 邮务; 一批邮件; 一次投递或分送的邮件: *miss ̸ catch the ~,* be too late ̸ in time for one of the regular clearances of letters. 未赶上(赶上)邮局收信的时间。*Has the ~ come yet?* 邮件来过没有? *I will send you the book by ~.* 我将把这本书邮寄给你。*Please reply by return of ~,* by the next ~ (from your town, etc to mine). 回信请交下一班邮递。**the P~ (Office),** public corporation set up to perform these duties, responsible to the Ministry of ~s and Telecommunications. 邮政总局。**3** the ~, ~ box or ~ office: 邮筒; 邮局: *take letters to the ~.* 把信邮寄出去。**4** (compounds) (复合词) **'~·bag** = mailbag. 邮包。**'~·box,** box into which letters are dropped for collection. 邮筒; 邮箱。**'~·card** *n* card, one side of which is usu a photograph or picture, used instead of a letter. 明信片。**'~·code,** (US 美 = *zipcode*) group of letters and numbers, eg W1X4AH, used to make the sorting and delivery of letters easier (by use of a computer). 邮递区号(用字母和数字表示，如 W1X4AH，借电脑处理，以便于邮件之分类及递送)。**,~·'free** *adj,* mail carried free of charge by ~, or with postage prepaid; (of a price) including the charge for postage. 免付邮费(的); 邮资已预付(的); (指价格)邮费已包括在内(的)。**'~·man** /-mən; -mən/ *n* (*pl* -men) man employed to deliver letters, etc (US 美 = *mailman*). 邮差; 信差。**'~·mark** *n* official mark stamped on letters, cancelling postage stamp(s) and giving the place, date, and time of collection. 邮戳。□ *vt* mark (an envelope, etc) with this. 以邮戳盖于(信封等)。**'~·master, '~·mistress** *nn* official in charge of a ~ office. 邮政局长; 女邮政局长。**'~ office** *n* office, building, etc where ~al business is carried on, together with the business of telegraphs and telephones, payment of state pensions, etc. (包含电报、电话等业务的)邮局。**'~ office** (abbr 略作 **PO**) **box** *n* numbered box in a ~ office for ~ addressed to an individual or company. (在邮局内为私人或公司所开的)邮政信箱。**,~·'paid** *adj, adv* with postage already paid. 邮资已付(的)。

post⁴ /pəʊst; post/ *vt, vi* **1** [VP6A] put (letters, etc) into a postbox or take (them) to a post office to be forwarded (US 美 = *mail*). 邮寄(信件等); 投寄。**2** [VP3A] (hist) travel (*from ̸ to*) by stages, using relays of horses. (史)骑驿马旅行(与to 或 from 连用)。⇨ **post³(1).** ~ *~·haste adv* in great haste. 急速地; 火速地。**3** [VP6A, 15B] *~ (up),* (book-keeping) write items in (a ledger); transfer (items) from a day-book to a ledger: (簿记)登录于(分类帐); 从日记簿过(帐)于分类帐: *~ (up) export sales;* 过销帐于分类帐; *~ up a ledger.* 记入分类帐。*keep sb ~ed,* (fig) keep him supplied with news. (喻)不断供给某人消息。

post⁵ /pəʊst; post/ *n* upright piece of wood, metal, etc supporting or marking sth: (木、金属等的)柱; 支柱; 标竿: *'gate~s;* 门柱; *the 'starting ̸ 'winning~,*

marking the starting and finishing points in a race; (赛跑用之)起(终)点标; *'bed~s* (in the old-fashioned kind of bed which had curtains round it); (旧式床用以支撑帐幕之)床柱; *'lamp-~s*, poles in towns, etc with electric lamps for street-lighting. (市镇等之)灯柱: 电灯杆. □ *vt* [VP6A, 15A, B] 1 ~ *(up)*, display publicly in a public place by means of a paper, placard, etc: (以纸报、招贴等在公共地方)公布: *P~ no bills* (warning that notices, advertisements, etc, must not be pasted on the wall, etc). 禁止招贴(警告不得在墙壁等处张贴告示、广告等). *The announcement was ~ed up on the wall of the town hall*. 该通告公布在市政厅的墙上. **2 ~ *(over)***, cover with bills, placards, etc: (以告示、招贴等)张贴于: ~ *a wall (over) with placards*. 贴招贴纸于墙上. **3** make known by means of a ~ed notice: 告示; 揭示: *a ship ~ed as missing*. 公告失踪的一只船.

post- /pəust; post/ *pref* after. 在后. ⇨ App 3. 参看附录三.

post·age /'pəustɪdʒ; 'postɪdʒ/ *n* [U] payment for the carrying of letters, etc: 邮费; 邮资: *What is the ~ for an air-letter?* 寄一封航空邮筒的邮费要多少? '~ **stamp** *n* stamp (to be) stuck on letters, etc with a specified value, showing the amount of ~ paid. 邮票.

postal /'pəustl; 'postl/ *adj* of the post[3](2): 邮政的; 邮局的: '~ *rates*; 邮费; '~ *workers*; 邮政人员; *a ~ vote*, sent by post to decide a ballot; 通讯选票; 通讯选举; '~ *union*, agreement by governments of most countries for the regulation of international postal business. 万国邮政协会. '~ **order**, 邮政汇票. ⇨ **order[1](7).

post·date /,pəust'deɪt; ,post'det/ *vt* [VP6A] **1** put (on a letter, cheque, etc) a date later than the date of writing. (在信件、支票等上)填迟日期; 预填日期. **2** give (to an event) a date later than its actual date. 把(一事件)的日期填迟; 写迟日期.

poster /'pəustə(r); 'postə/ *n* **1** placard displayed in a public place (announcing or advertising sth); large printed picture. (张贴于公共场所的)海报; 告示; 广告; 印成的大照片. **2** ('bill-)~, person who posts bills or placards on walls, hoardings, etc. 张贴告示或广告的人.

poste res·tante /,pəust 'resta:nt *US*: re'stænt; ,postres'tant/ *n* [U] (F) post office department to whose care letters may be addressed, to be kept until called for. (法)(邮局之)待领邮件部.

pos·terior /pɒ'stɪərɪə(r); pɑs'tɪrɪɚ/ *adj* **1 ~ *(to)***, later in time or order. (时间或顺序上)在后的; 较迟的; 较晚的. ⇨ **prior[1]**. **2** placed behind. 位于后部的; 后面的. □ *n* (hum) buttocks: (谐)屁股; 臀部: *kick his ~*. 踢他的屁股.

pos·ter·ity /pɒ'sterɪtɪ; pɑs'terɪtɪ/ *n* [U] **1** person's descendants (his children, their children, etc). (某人之)后裔; 子孙. **2** future generations: 后代; 后世: *plant trees for the benefit of ~*. 为谋后代之利益而种树.

pos·tern /'pɒstən; 'postɚn/ *n* side way or entrance; (esp, in former times) concealed entrance to a castle or fortress: 旁门; 后门; 便门; 便道; 边道; (尤指昔时通往城堡的)暗道. (attrib) (用作定语) *door/gate*. 后门.

Post Exchange /,pəust ɪk'stʃeɪndʒ; ,postɪk'stʃendʒ/ *n* (abbr 略作 **PX**) (US) store at a military base where personnel and their families may buy services and tax-free goods. (美)(在军事基地所设立的免税)福利社; 营地服务商店.

post·gradu·ate /,pəust'grædʒuət; post'grædʒuɪt/ *adj* (of studies, etc) done after taking a first academic degree. (指学科研究等)大学毕业后所做的; 研究院的. □ *n* person engaged in ~ studies. (大学毕业后的)研究生.

post·hum·ous /'pɒstjuməs; 'postʃuməs/ *adj* **1** (of a child) born after the death of its father. (指小孩)父死后出生的; 遗腹的. **2** coming or happening after death: 死后出现或发生的; 身后的: ~ *fame*; 死后的声

誉; *a ~ novel*, published after the author's death; 作者死后出版的小说; *the ~ award of a Victoria Cross*. 死后颁赠的维多利亚十字勋章. ~·**ly** *adv*

pos·til·ion (also **pos·til·lion**) /pə'stɪljən; po'stɪljən/ *n* man riding on one of the two or more horses pulling a carriage or coach. 马车骑手(骑在拉曳马车左之两匹或多匹马中的一马上面者); 骑在左马上的御者.

post·mas·ter /'pəustmɑːstə(r) *US*: -mæs-; 'post,mæstɚ/ *n* ,**P~ 'General**, the Minister at the head of a country's Post Office Department. 邮政总长. ⇨ **post[3](4).

post meri·diem /,pəust mə'rɪdɪəm; ,postmə'rɪdɪ,ɛm/ *adv* (abbr 略作 **pm**) time between noon and midnight: 午后;下午: *7.30 pm*. 午后七时半. ⇨ *am* at **ante meridiem**; ⇨ **App 4(6).** 参看附录四之六.

post-mor·tem /,pəust 'mɔːtəm; ,post'mɔrtəm/ *n*, *adj* **1** (medical examination) made after death: 死后所做的(医学检验): *A ~ showed that the man had been poisoned*. 验尸显示那人是被毒死的. **2** (colloq) review of an event, etc in the past. (口)(对过去事件的)检查; 检讨.

post·pone /pə'spəun; post'pon/ *vt* [VP6A, C] put off until another time: 展缓; 延搁: ~ *a meeting*; 展缓会期; ~ *sending an answer to a request*. 延搁对一请求的答复. ~·**ment** *n* [U] postponing; [C] instance of this: 展缓; 延搁: *after numerous ~ments*. 在无数次的延搁之后.

post·pran·dial /,pəust'prændɪəl; post'prændɪəl/ *adj* (usu hum) after dinner: (通常为诙谐用法)饭后的; 餐后的: ~ *oratory*. 餐后演说.

post·script /'pəustskrɪpt; 'postskrɪpt/ *n* **1** (abbr 略作 **PS**) sentence(s) added (*to a* letter) after the signature. (信件的)附笔; 又及; 再启(与句通用). **2** additional or final information. 附加或最后的消息.

pos·tu·lant /'pɒstjulənt *US*: -tʃu-; 'postʃələnt/ *n* candidate, esp for admission to a religious order. 志愿人; 候选人; (尤指)(尤)(职)志愿人; 牧师志愿人. ⇨ **novice**.

pos·tu·late /'pɒstjuleɪt *US*: -tʃu-; 'postʃə,let/ *vt* [VP6A] demand, put forward, take for granted, as a necessary fact, as a basis for reasoning. (认作必然的事实或推理的基础而)要求; 假设; 假定; 公设; 以…为前提. □ *n* sth ~d; sth that may be considered axiomatic: 要求事项; 基本要求; 假设; 公设; 公理: *the ~s of Euclidean geometry*, eg the possibility of drawing a straight line between any two points. 欧几里德几何学的假设(如任何二点之间可作一直线的可能性).

pos·ture /'pɒstʃə(r); 'postʃɚ/ *n* **1** [C] attitude of, way of holding, the body: (身体的)姿势; 体态: *The artist asked his model to take a reclining ~*. 艺术家要求他的模特儿作斜躺的姿势. *Good ~ helps you to keep well*. 好的姿势帮助你保持健康. **2** [U] state or condition: 状态; 情况: *in the present ~ of public affairs*. 在目前的公共事务情况之下. **3** frame of mind; attitude: 心境; 态度: *Will the Government alter its ~ over aid to the railways?* 政府会改变其对补助铁路方面的态度吗? □ *vt, vi* **1** [VP6A] put or arrange in a ~: 令采某种姿势: ~ *a model*. 令模特儿摆某种姿势. **2** [VP2A] adopt a vain, pretentious ~: 摆姿势; 装模作样: *The vain girl was posturing before a tall mirror*. 那个虚荣的女郎对着大镜子摆姿势. **pos·tur·ing** *n* [U, C] (from the *v*(2)): (由动词第 2 义转变而来): *All this posturing must stop!* 所有这些装模作样都必须停止!

posy /'pəuzɪ; 'pozɪ/ *n* (*pl* **-sies**) small bunch of cut flowers. 小花束.

pot[1] /pɒt; pat/ *n* **1** round vessel of earthenware, metal or glass, for holding liquids or solids, for cooking things in, etc; contents of such a vessel: 罐; 壶; 盆; 瓶; 锅(作容器、烹调等用); 一罐(锅等)之物: 一罐(锅等)之量: *a 'jam-pot*; 果酱罐; *eat a whole pot of jam*; 吃整罐的果酱; *a 'teapot*; 茶壶; *a 'coffee-pot*; 咖啡壶; *a 'flower-pot*; 花盆; *a 'chamber-pot*. 便盆; 夜壶. ⇨ the *nn* forming the first element of such compounds.

参看构成上列复合词前一部分的名词。**2** (phrases and provs) (短语与谚语) **go to pot,** (sl) be ruined or destroyed. (俚)毁灭；毁坏。**keep the 'pot boiling,** earn enough money to buy one's food, etc; keep sth, eg a children's game, going briskly. 糊口；谋生；使事情 (如儿童游戏)保持生气勃勃。*take 'luck,* whatever is available (without choice); whatever is being prepared for a meal: 有什么吃什么；吃便饭: *Come home with me and take pot luck.* 跟我回家吃便饭吧。*the ,pot calling the ,kettle 'black,* the accuser having the same fault as the accused. 五十步笑百步；一丘之貉。**3** (colloq) large sum: (口)巨款: *make a pot / pots of money.* 赚大钱。**4 a big pot,** (colloq) an important person. (口)大人物。**5** (colloq) prize in an athletic contest, esp a silver cup: (运动会的)奖品;(尤指)银杯: *all the pots he won when he was young.* 他年轻时所赢得的全部奖品。**6** (sl) marijuana. (俚)大麻烟。**7** (compounds) (复合词) **'pot-belly** n (person with a) large, prominent belly. 大腹；有大腹之人。**pot·'bellied** adj (of a person) having a potbelly; (of a stove) having a rounded container in which fuel, eg wood, burns. (指人)大腹的；(指炉灶)有燃烧燃料之圆肚的。**'pot-boiler** n book, picture, etc produced merely to bring in money. 仅为赚钱而作的书、图画等。**'pot-bound** adj (of a plant) having roots that have filled its pot. (指植物)根生满一花盆的。**'pot-boy, 'pot-man** /-mæn; -mən/ (pl -men) nn (hist) one who helps in a public house by filling pots with beer, etc. (史)酒馆侍役(帮助斟啤酒等)。**'pot hat** n (sl) bowler hat. (俚)高顶礼帽。**'pot-head** n (sl) habitual marijuana user. (俚)吸食大麻烟上瘾者。**'pot-herb** n plant, etc whose leaves or stems, or whose roots or tubers, are used in cooking. 蔬菜类植物(其叶、茎或根块茎用于烹饪);调味用之植物。**'pot-hole** n (a) hole in a road made by rain and traffic. (道路因雨及行车形成的)坑；穴。(b) deep cylindrical hole worn in rock (eg in limestone caves) by water. 地壶(石灰岩洞穴等内之岩石上为水侵蚀成的圆筒状深洞)。**'pot-holer** n person who explores pot-holes in caves. (在岩穴内)探勘地壶之人。**'pot-hook** n (a) hook, often S-shaped, which can be raised or lowered on a metal bar, for holding pots, etc over a fireplace. 锅钩；挂钩(可上下挪动,用以悬挂壶火炉上之锅,壶等)。(b) curved or wavy stroke made by children when learning to write their letters. (儿童学写字母时所作之)弯形笔画。**'pot-house** n (old use) low-class public house; ale-house: (旧用法)低级酒店；啤酒店: *pot-house manners,* vulgar manners. 粗鄙之举止。**'pot-hunter** n (a) sportsman who shoots anything he comes across, thinking only of food for the pot or profit. (只想打猎取食物或牟利的)乱猎者。(b) person who takes part in contests merely for the sake of the prizes. (只为获奖品而参加竞赛的人。⇨ **5** above. 参看上列第5义。**'pot roast** n beef, etc browned in a pot and cooked slowly with very little water. 焖炖牛肉等。**'pot-shot** n shot aimed at a bird or animal that is near, so that careful aim is not needed; random shot. (鸟兽距离甚近无需仔细瞄准的)近距离射击；乱射。**'pot-trained** adj (of a small child) trained to use a chamber-pot. (指小孩)会使用便壶便溺的。

pot² /pɒt; pɑt/ vt, vi (-tt-) **1** [VP6A] put (meat, fish paste, etc) in a pot to preserve it: 装(肉、鱼酱等)于罐内以保存之: *potted shrimps / ham.* 罐装小虾(火腿)。**2** [VP6A, 15B] pot (up), plant in a flower-pot: 种在花盆内: *pot (up) chrysanthemum cuttings.* 把菊花的插枝种在花盆内。**3** [VP6A] kill with a pot-shot: 近距离射击: *pot a rabbit; pot at a hare.* 射兔子；射野兔。*pot at,* shoot at: 射击；射杀: ~ *at a hare.* 射野兔。**4** (billiards) drive a ball into a pocket. (撞球)击球入袋。**5** (colloq) put (a baby) on a chamber-pot. (口)置(婴儿)于便壶上便溺。

pot·able /'pəutəbl; 'potəbl/ adj fit to drink. 可以喝的。

pot·ash /'pɒtæʃ; 'pɑt,æʃ/ n [U] common name for various potassium salts, used in the manufacture of fertilizers, soap, and various chemicals. 钾碱(数种钾盐学品之通用名称),用以制造肥料、肥皂及各种化学品)。

po·tass·ium /pə'tæsiəm; pə'tæsiəm/ n [U] soft, shining, white metallic element (symbol K), vital to all living matter, occurring in the form of mineral salts and in rocks. (化)钾(柔软而有光泽的白色金属元素,为一切生物所必需,存在于矿盐及岩石中;符号为K)。

po·ta·tion /pəu'teiʃn; po'teʃən/ n (liter) drink. (文)饮料。

po·tato /pə'teitəu; pə'teto/ n (pl ~es /-təuz; -toz/) plant with rounded tubers eaten as a vegetable; one of the tubers: 马铃薯(一种植物,其圆形块茎可作蔬菜): baked ~es; 烤马铃薯; mashed ~ (es); 马铃薯泥; ~ soup; 马铃薯汤; (US) (美) ~ chips (= GB 英 crisps). 炸马铃薯片。⇨ the illus at **vegetable.** 参看 vegetable 之插图。*,sweet '~,* tropical plant with long tuberous roots used for food. 红薯；甘薯。*'~ beetle,* beetle that destroys the leaves of ~ plants. 薯虫(伤害马铃薯叶的昆虫)。

po·teen /pɒ'ti:n; po'tin/ n [U] Irish whisky from an illicit still. (爱尔兰的)私造威士忌酒。

po·tent /'pəutnt; 'potnt/ adj (not of persons or machines) powerful: (不指人或机器)有力的；有效的: ~ reasons / arguments / charms / drugs / remedies; 有力的理由(有力的论点)；有效的符咒；有效的药物；有效的治疗法; (of males) not sexually impotent. (指男人)有性交能力的。 ~·ly adv **po·tency** /-nsi; -nsi/ n

po·ten·tate /'pəutnteit; 'potn,tet/ n powerful person; monarch; ruler. 有权威的人；君王；统治者。

po·ten·tial /pə'tenʃl; pə'tɛnʃəl/ adj **1** that can or may come into existence or action: 可能的；潜在的: ~ wealth / resources; 潜在的财富(资源); ~ energy (waiting to be released); (物理)位能；势能(待放出之能); the ~ sales of a new book. 一本新书的可能销售量。**2** ~ mood, (gram) indicating possibility. (语法)可能语气。□ n **1** [C] that which is ~; possibility; [U] what sb or sth is capable of: 可能之事物；可能；可能性；潜力；潜势；潜能: He hasn't realized his full ~ yet. 他尚未了解他的最大潜力。**2** (gram) ~ mood. (语法)可能语气。**3** (electr) energy of an electric charge, expressed in volts: (电)电势；电位(以电压之实用单位伏特表示之): a current of high ~. 高压电。 ~·ly /-ʃəli; -ʃəli/ adv a ~ly rich country, eg one with but undeveloped natural resources. 具开发潜力的国家(蕴藏丰富资源的国家)。 ~·ity /pə,tenʃi'æləti; pə,tɛnʃi'ælɛti/ n (pl -ties) power or quality which is ~, and needs development; latent capacity: 可能性；潜能；潜力: a situation / a country with great potentialities. 大有发展的情况(潜力大的国家)。

pother /'pɒðə(r); 'pɑðə/ n trouble; commotion. 骚动；喧扰。

po·tion /'pəuʃn; 'poʃən/ n [C] dose of liquid medicine or poison, or of sth used in magic: (液体药物或毒物的)一剂；一服；(魔术中所用之某物的)一份: a 'love ~. 可以引起爱情的魔药；春药；媚药。

pot-pourri /,pəu 'puəri; US: pə'ri:; pɑt'puri/ n **1** mixture of dried rose-petals and spices, kept in a jar for its perfume. 干玫瑰花瓣及香料的混合物(置于瓶中以闻其香味)。**2** musical or literary medley. (音乐之)杂曲；混成曲；(文学作品之)杂集。

pot·sherd /'pɒtʃɜːd; 'pɑt,ʃɑd/ n broken piece of pottery (esp in archaeology). (尤指考古学上的)陶器碎片。

pot·tage /'pɒtidʒ; 'pɑtidʒ/ n (old use) thick soup. (旧用法)浓汤。

potted /'pɒtid; 'pɑtid/ adj **1** ⇨ **pot².** **2** (of a book, etc) inadequately summarized: (指书等)摘要的；简略的: a ~ version of a classical novel. 一本古典小说的简易本。

pot·ter¹ /'pɒtə(r); 'pɑtə/ (US = **put·ter** /'pʌtər;

ˈpɒtə/) vi, vt **1** [VP2A, C] work with little energy; move about from one little job to another: 懒散地工作; 各处走动做些琐碎事情: ~ing about in the garden. 在花园各处做些琐碎的工作。 **2** [VP15B] waste (time) in ~ing: 虚度(时间): ~ away a whole afternoon. 浪费整个下午。 ~**er** n person who ~s. 懒散的工作者; 各处走动做些琐屑工作者; 虚掷光阴者。

pot·ter² /ˈpɒtə(r); ˈpɑtɚ/ n maker of pots. 制陶工人; 陶工。 ~**'s wheel**, horizontal revolving disc on which pots are shaped. (制陶器用之) 模式转盘; 拉坯轮车。

pot·tery n (pl **-ries**) [U] earthenware; pots; [C] ~'s workshop. 陶器; 瓦器; 陶器场所。 **the Potteries**, district in Staffordshire, England where ~y is the chief industry. 帕特利斯(英国斯塔福郡之陶器出产地)。

a potter's wheel

potty¹ /ˈpɒtɪ; ˈpɑtɪ/ adj (**-ier, -iest**) (GB dated colloq) (英国过时口语) **1** petty; unimportant; insignificant: 细小的; 不重要的; 琐碎的: ~ little details / jobs. 琐碎的细节(工作)。 **2** ~ (**about sb/sth**), (of a person) foolish, crazy: (指人) 胡涂的; 疯癫的; 着迷的: She's quite ~, mad. 她疯了。 He's ~ about his new gramophone. 他迷上了他新买的唱机。

potty² /ˈpɒtɪ; ˈpɑtɪ/ n (pl **-ties**) child's chamberpot. (小孩的) 便壶。

pouch /paʊtʃ; paʊtʃ/ n **1** small bag carried in the pocket (a to'bacco-~) or fastened to the belt (a soldier's ˌammu'nition-~). 小袋; 小包 (或携带于口袋中, 如烟草袋; 或固定于束带上, 如兵士的弹药包)。 **2** baglike formation, eg that in which a female kangaroo carries her young. 袋状物 (如雌袋鼠装幼仔的肚袋)。 ⇨ the illus at **large**. 参看 large 之插图。 **3** puffy area of skin, eg under the eyes of a sick or old person. 皮肤之肿胀处 (如病人或老人眼下之眼包)。 □ vt **1** [VP6A] put into a ~. 装入袋中。 **2** [VP6A] make (part of a dress, etc) like a ~; [VP2A] hang like a ~. 把 (衣服等之一部分) 做成袋状; 似袋般悬挂; 悬垂如袋。

pouf, pouffe /puːf; puf/ n **1** large, thick cushion used as a seat. 大而厚的坐垫; 蒲团。 **2** /puːf; puf/ △ (derog sl) male homosexual. (讳) (贬抑俚语) 男同性恋者。

poul·terer /ˈpəʊltərə(r); ˈpoltɚɚ/ n (GB) dealer in poultry and game, eg hares. (英) 家禽贩; 鸡贩; 猎物贩 (如卖野兔者)。

poul·tice /ˈpəʊltɪs; ˈpoltɪs/ n [C] soft heated mass of eg linseed, mustard, spread on a cloth, and put on the skin to relieve pain, etc. 糊剂; 膏药 (以亚麻子、芥子末等做成的软糊而敷于布上者, 加热软化后贴于皮肤以减痛等)。 □ vt [VP6A] put a ~ on. 敷糊药于。

poul·try /ˈpəʊltrɪ; ˈpoltrɪ/ n (collective n) (集合名词) **1** (with pl v) large domestic fowl (eg hens, ducks, geese, turkeys) kept for eating or for egg-laying: (用复数动词)(养来吃或下蛋之) 家禽 (如鸡、鸭、鹅、火鸡等): The ~ are being fed. 家禽正在吃饲料。 **2** (with sing v) these considered as food: (用单数动词)鸡肉; 鸭肉; 鹅肉; 家禽肉: P~ is expensive this Christmas. 今年圣诞节的禽肉很贵。 ⇨ the illus at **fowl**. 参看 fowl 之插图。

pounce /paʊns; paʊns/ vi [VP3A] ~ **on/at**, make a sudden attack or downward swoop on: 突袭; 猛扑: The hawk ~d on its prey. 鹰向着它的捕食对象猛扑。 The tiger ~d savagely on the goat. 那虎凶猛地突袭那只山羊。 (fig) (喻) He ~d at (= seized) the first

opportunity to inform against his colleague. 他抓住第一个机会去密告他的同事。 □ n such an attack. 突袭; 猛扑。

pound¹ /paʊnd; paʊnd/ n (⇨ **App 5**) (参看附录五) **1** unit of weight, 16 ounces avoirdupois, 12 ounces troy. 磅(重量单位, 常衡时等于 16 盎斯, 金衡时等于 12 盎斯)。 **2** ~ (**sterling**), British unit of money: 英镑 (英国货币单位): five ~s, written £5; 五英镑(书作 £5); a five~ note, banknote for £5. 五英镑之纸币。 penny wise, ~ foolish; in for a penny, in for a ~, ⇨ **penny**. **3** monetary unit of various other countries. 镑(许多其他国家之币制单位)。

pound² /paʊnd; paʊnd/ n **1** enclosed area in a village where, in olden times, cattle that had strayed were kept until claimed by their owners. (昔时乡村中)收留迷失牲畜以待失主认领的兽栏。 **2** (mod use) place where stray dogs and cats, and motor-vehicles left in unauthorized places, are kept until claimed. (现代用法)收留迷失之犬猫及随意放置之摩托车以待认领的地方。

pound³ /paʊnd; paʊnd/ vt, vi [VP6A, 15A, 2C, 3A] ~ (**away**) (**at/on**), **1** strike heavily and repeatedly; thump: 连续重击; 重击发声; 砰砰地打: Our heavy guns ~ed (away at) the walls of the fort. 我们的大炮轰击保垒的墙(对着堡垒的墙轰击)。 Who is ~ing (on) the piano? 谁在用力弹钢琴? Someone was ~ing at the door with a heavy stick. 有人在用粗棍敲门。 I could hear feet ~ing on the stairs. 我听到楼梯上的沉重脚步声。 She could feel her heart ~ing as she finished the 100 metres race. 结束一百米的赛跑后, 她感到心脏跳动得很厉害。 **2** crush to powder; break to pieces: 捣成粉; 击碎: ~ crystals in a mortar; 捣碎研钵中的结晶体; a ship ~ing/being ~ed to pieces on the rocks. 在岩石上撞碎的一只船。 **3** ride, run, walk, heavily: 沉重地骑马、跑、走: He ~ed along the road. 他沿着大路沉重地跑。

pound·age /ˈpaʊndɪdʒ; ˈpaʊndɪdʒ/ n [U] commission or fee of so much (eg 5p) per pound sterling (£1) or payment of so much (eg 3 oz) per pound weight (1 lb). 按每英镑五便士等所抽取的佣金或费用; 按每磅三盎司等所付之佣金。

pounder /ˈpaʊndə(r); ˈpaʊndɚ/ n (usu in compounds) sth weighing so many pounds: (通常用于复合词中)有…磅重之物: a three-~; a fish weighing 3 lb; 一件三磅重之物(如鱼); gun that fires a shot of so many pounds: 发射…磅炮弹的炮: an eighteen-~. 发射十八磅炮弹的大炮。

pour /pɔː(r); pɔr/ vt, vi **1** [VP6A, 12B, 13B, 15A, B, 14] cause (a liquid or a substance that flows like a liquid) to flow in a continuous stream: 使(液体或流动似液体之物)流动; 灌; 浇; 注; 倒: P~ yourself another cup of tea. 你再倒杯茶喝吧。 Please ~ a cup of tea for me, too. 请你也为我倒一杯茶。 He ~ed the coffee out of the saucepan into the jug. 他把咖啡从深平底锅倒进壶中。 (fig) (喻) He ~ed out his tale of misfortunes. 他倾诉自己的不幸遭遇。 The underground stations ~ thousands of workers into the streets between 8 and 9.30 each morning. 每日早晨八时至九时半之间, 成千成万的工人从地下火车站涌到各街道去。 ~ cold water on sth, discourage (a person's plan, zeal or enthusiasm). 使沮丧; (对某人之计划或热心)浇冷水。 ~ oil on troubled waters, try to calm a disturbance or quarrel with soothing words. 调解争端。 **2** [VP2C] flow in a continuous stream; come freely (out/off, etc): 流; 泻; 涌入; 涌出 (out/off, off 等连用): The sweat was ~ing off him. 他汗流浃背。 Tourists ~ into London during the summer months. 在夏季游客涌入伦敦。 The crowds were ~ing out of the football ground. 群众正自足球场蜂涌而出。 Letters of complaint ~ed in. 抱怨的信件源源而来。 **3** (of rain) come down heavily: (指雨)倾注: The rain ~ed down. 大雨倾盆而下。 It was a ~ing wet day. 那是一个大雨天。 It never rains but it ~s, a saying used when (usu unwelcome) things come or events happen in quick succession. 事情(通常指不利的事)不发生则已, 一

发生就接二连三地来; 祸不单行。

pout /paut/ *vt, vi* [VP6A, 2A] (as a sign of displeasure) push out (the lips). (作为不悦之表示)噘(嘴)。□ *n* such a pushing out of the lips. (不悦时的)噘嘴。 **~·ing·ly** *adv* sulkily. 绷着脸地; 不悦地。

pov·erty /'pɒvətɪ/ *n* [U] state of being poor: 贫穷: *live in ~;* 过穷日子; *fall into ~;* 变穷; lack, inferiority: 缺乏; 低劣: *an essay which shows ~ of ideas.* 缺乏思想的一篇文章。 **~-stricken** *adj* affected by ~: 穷困的; 贫穷的; 为贫穷所苦恼的: *~-stricken homes.* 贫苦的家庭。

pow·der /'paudə(r)/ *n* 1 [C, U] (kind of) substance that has been crushed, rubbed or worn to dust; special kind of this, eg for use on the skin (*a tin of* '*talcum-~*), or as a medicine (*take a ~ every morning*), for cleaning things ('*soap-~,* '*bleaching-~*), or for cooking ('*baking-~*). 粉; 细粉; 粉末; 特别调制的粉末(如 a tin of talcum-~, 一罐搽皮肤用的爽身粉); take a ~ every morning, 每天早晨服用药粉; soap-~, 肥皂粉; bleaching-~, 漂白粉; baking-~, 烹调用的团粉)。 '**~-puff** *n* soft pad used for applying cosmetic ~ to the skin. 粉扑。 '**~-room** *n* ladies' room in a hotel, restaurant, cinema, etc with wash-basins and lavatories. (旅馆、餐馆、电影院等的)女用盥洗室; 化妆室。 2 = gunpowder. 火药。 ◇ **gun. not worth ~ and shot,** not worth fighting for. 不值得浪费弹药(一战)。 '**~-flask/-horn** *n* (hist) for carrying gun~. (史)火药筒(角制火药筒)。 '**~-magazine** *n* place where gun~ is stored. 火药库。 □ *vt, vi* 1 [VP6A] put ~ on (the face, etc). 搽粉于(脸等)。 2 [VP2A] use face-powder. 搽粉。 **~ed** *adj* reduced to ~; dehydrated: 弄成粉的; 脱水的: *~ed milk/eggs.* 奶(蛋)粉。 **~y** *adj* of, like, covered with, ~: 粉的; 粉状的; 敷粉的: *~y snow;* 粉状的雪; *a ~y nose.* 敷着粉的鼻子。

power /'paʊə(r)/ *n* 1 [U] (in living things, persons) ability to do or act: (生物或人之)做事或行动的能力: *It is not within/It is beyond/outside my ~ to help you,* I am unable, or am not in a position, to do so. 我没有能力帮助你。 *This animal, the chameleon, has the ~ of changing its colour.* 变色蜥蜴这种动物能变更自体的颜色。 *I will do everything in my ~ to help.* 我愿(就我的能力范围内)尽量协助。 2 (pl) faculty of the body or mind: (复)体力; 智力; 精力: *His ~s are failing,* He is becoming weak. 他的体力在衰退中。 *You are taxing your ~s too much.* 你耗费太多的精力。 *He's a man of great intellectual ~s.* 他是一位大智者。 3 [U] strength; force: 力; 力气: *the ~ of a blow.* 一击之力。 **More ~ to your elbow!** (phrase used to encourage sb.) 努力做! 祝你成功(用以鼓励人的短语)。 4 [U] energy of force that can be used to do work: 动力; 力power: '*water ~;* 水力; *e'lectric ~.* 电力。 '**horse-~,** ◇ **horse.** (attrib) (用作定语) '**~-lathe/-loom/-mill** operated by mechanical ~, not by hand labour. 动力车床(布机, 磨坊)。 '**~-boat,** one with an engine; motorboat (esp one used for racing; or towing water-skiers). 汽艇(尤指比赛或拖曳滑水者所用之汽艇)。 '**~-dive** *vt, n* (put an aircraft into a) steep dive with the engines working. (使飞机)动力俯冲; 开油门俯冲。 '**~-house/-station,** building where electric ~ is generated for distribution. 发电所。 '**~-point,** socket on a wall, etc for a plug to connect an electric circuit. 电插座。 5 [U] right; control; authority: 权; 权力; 势力: *the ~ of the law;* 法律的力量; *the ~ of Congress,* 国会的权力; *have a person in one's ~,* be able to do what one wishes with him; 能左右一个人; *have ~ over sb;* 对某人有控制力; *Spain at the height of her ~;* 全盛时期的西班牙; *fall into sb's ~.* 落入某人的控制中。 **in ~,** (of a person or political party) in office. (指人或政党)当权; 秉政。 ◇ **politics,** diplomacy backed by force. 以武力为后盾的外交; 权力政治; 强权政治。 6 [C] right possessed by, or granted to, a person or group of persons: (个人或团体所拥有的)权限; 职权: *Are the ~s*

of the Prime Minister defined by law? 首相的权限法律有明文规定吗? *The President has exceeded his ~s,* has done more than he has authority to do. 总统已逾越他的职权。 7 [C] person or organization having great authority or influence: 很有权力的人或组织; 当权者: *Is the press a great ~ in your country?* Are the newspapers influential, etc? 贵国的报界有很大的影响力吗? *the ~s that be,* (hum) those who are in authority. (谐)当局。 8 [C] State having great authority and influence in international affairs. 强国。 **the Great P~s,** the largest and strongest ·States. 列强。 9 [C] (maths) result obtained by multiplying a number or quantity by itself a certain number of times: (数学)乘方; 乘幂; 幂: *the second, third, fourth, etc ~ of x* (= x^2, x^3, x^4, etc) x 的二次, 三次, 四次等幂; *the fourth ~ of 3* (= $3 \times 3 \times 3 \times 3 = 81$). 三的四次幂 (= 81)。 10 [U] capacity to magnify: 放大力: *the ~ of a lens;* 透镜的放大力; *a telescope of high ~.* 高倍望远镜。 11 (colloq) large number or amount: (口)许多; 大量: *This brandy is doing me a ~ of good!* 这种白兰地酒对我助益甚大。 12 [C] god, spirit, etc: 神; 幽灵; 鬼怪: *Preserve us from the ~s of darkness.* 保佑我们不受魔鬼的侵害。 **pow·ered** *adj* having, able to exert or produce, mechanical energy: 有动力的; 能产生机械力的: *an aircraft ~ed by Rolls Royce engines;* 一架以劳斯莱斯引擎为动力的新飞机; *a high-~ed car;* 一部大马力引擎的汽车; (fig) (喻) *a high-~ed salesman,* one with great ~s of persuasion. 很有说服力的推销员。

power·ful /'paʊəfl/ 'paʊəfəl/ *adj* having· or producing great power: 有力的; 强的: *a ~ blow/enemy;* 强有力的一击(敌人); *a ~ remedy for constipation.* 便秘的特效药。 **~ly** /-fəlɪ; -fəlɪ/ *adv*

power·less /'paʊəlɪs; 'paʊəlɪs/ *adj* without power; unable (*to do* sth): 无力的; 无权的; 不能(做某事)的: *render sb ~;* 使某人无能为力; *be ~ to resist.* 无力抵抗。 **~·ly** *adv*

pow·wow /'paʊwaʊ/ 'paʊ,waʊ/ *n* conference of N American Indians; (colloq) any other kind of conference. 北美印第安人的会议; (口)任何集会。 □ *vi* hold a conference (*about* sth). (为某事)举行会议(与 *about* 连用)。

pox /pɒks; pɑks/ *n* (colloq, usu *the ~*) syphilis: 梅毒: *catch/give sb the pox.* 染上梅毒(把梅毒传染给某人)。

prac·ti·cable /'præktɪkəbl; 'præktɪkəbl/ *adj* that can be done or used or put into practice: 可做的; 可用的; 可实行的: *methods that are not ~;* 不可实行的措施; *a mountain pass that is ~ only in summer.* 只在夏季可通行的山路。 **prac·ti·cably** /-əblɪ; -əblɪ/ *adv* **prac·ti·ca·bil·ity** /ˌpræktɪkə'bɪlətɪ; ˌpræktɪkə'bɪlətɪ/ *n*

prac·ti·cal /'præktɪkl; 'præktɪkl/ *adj* 1 concerned with practice (contrasted with *theoretical*): 实际的; 实行上的(与 theoretical 相对): *overcome the ~ difficulties of a scheme;* 克服某计划的实际困难; *a suggestion/proposal with little ~ value;* 甚少实际价值的建议; *a ~ joke,* ◇ **joke.** 2 (of persons, their character, etc) clever at doing and making things; preferring activity and action to theorizing: (指人, 其性格等)做事灵敏的; 喜实际工作的; 不好理论的: *a ~ young wife;* 做事灵敏的年轻妻子; *ideas that appeal to ~ minds.* 合乎实事求是者的主意(切合实际的想法)。 3 useful; doing well what it is intended to do: 有用的; 实用的: *Your invention is ingenious, but not very ~.* 你的发明物很精巧, 但是不很实用。 **~·ly** /-klɪ; -klɪ/ *adv* 1 in a ~ manner. 实际地; 实用地。 2 almost: 几乎: *We've had ~ly no fine weather this month.* 这个月份以这种天气。 *He says he is ~ly ruined.* 他说他几乎破产了。 **~·ity** /ˌpræktɪ'kælɪtɪ; ˌpræktɪ'kælətɪ/ *n* (*pl* **-ties**): *Let's get down to ~ities,* to considering ~ proposals. 我们来考虑实际的问题吧。

prac·tice /'præktɪs; 'præktɪs/ *n* 1 [U] performance; the doing of sth (contrasted with *theory*): 实施;

实行;应用(与 theory 相对): put a plan into ~, carry it out, do what has been planned. 实行某计划. The idea would never work in ~, may seem good theoretically, but would be useless if carried out. 那主意不能实现(理论上或许是好的). **2** [C] way of doing sth that is common or habitual; sth done regularly: 习惯; 常例: the ~ of closing shops on Sundays; 星期日休业的惯例; Christian / Protestant / Catholic ~s, ceremonies or observances; 基督教(新教, 天主教)的教规或仪式; an aperitif before dinner, as is my usual ~; 饭前喝一杯酒, 那是我的习惯. **make a ~ of (sth),** do it habitually: 养成…之习惯; 惯常做(某事): boys who make a ~ of cheating at examinations. 以考试作弊为常事的男孩子们. **3** [U] frequent or systematic repetition, repeated exercise, in doing sth (esp an art or craft): 经常或有系统的重复; 练习(尤指在艺术或手艺方面): Piano-playing needs a lot of ~. 弹钢琴需要多练习. That is a stroke, eg in golf, that needs a lot of ~. 那是需要经常练习的打法(如打高尔夫球时). It takes years of ~ to acquire the skill of an expert. 要想获得专家的技术, 需要多年的练习. (attrib) (用作定语) Let's have a ~ game. 我们一场练习赛吧. **in / out of ~,** having/not having given enough time recently to ~: 近来勤(疏)于练习; 练习充足(不足): Please don't ask me to play the piano for you: I'm out of ~. 请勿要我为你弹钢琴: 我近来疏于练习. **4** [U] work of a doctor or lawyer: (医生或律师之)业务: retire from ~; 从业务中退休; no longer in ~; 不再执业; (C) (collective) (number of) persons who regularly consult a doctor or lawyer: (集合名词)医生或律师之经常主顾; 此种主顾之数目: a doctor with a large ~; 求诊者很多的一位医生; sell one's ~, sell (to another doctor) the connection one has (of regular patients); 转让主顾(如把经常求医的病人转让给另一医生); a doctor in general ~, ⇨ general practitioner at **practitioner. 5 sharp ~,** [U] not strictly honest or legal ways of doing business. 做生意不很规矩的方法.

prac·ti·cian /præk'tɪʃn; præk'tɪʃən/ n = **practitioner.**

prac·tise (US = **-tice**) /'præktɪs; 'præktɪs/ vt, vi [VP6A, C, 2A, B] **1** do sth repeatedly or regularly in order to become skilful: 练习; 实习: ~ the piano; 练习弹钢琴; ~ making a new vowel sound; 练习一个新母音的发音; ~ (for) two hours every day. 每日练习两小时. **2** make a habit of: 惯做; 常为; 养成…的习惯: early rising. 养成早起的习惯. ~ **what one preaches,** make a habit of doing what one advises others to do. 教诲他人之事必先自己实践; 躬行己说. **3** exercise or follow (a profession, etc): 操持(专业等): ~ medicine / the law, work as a doctor / lawyer. 执业为医生(律师); 开业做律师(医师). **4** [VP3A, 4A] **~ on / upon; ~ to do sth,** (old use) take advantage of (sb's credulity, etc); set oneself: (旧用法)利用(某人之轻信等); 竭力想: ~ to deceive. 竭力想行骗. **~d** (US = **-ticed**) adj skilled; having had much practice. 熟练的; 练习充分的.

prac·ti·tioner /præk'tɪʃnə(r); præk'tɪʃənə/ n **1** one who practises a skill or art. 实习者; 练习者; 操持者. **2** professional man, esp in medicine and the law. 从业者; (专指)开业医生; 律师. **general** '~ (abbr 略作 **GP**), doctor who is qualified in both medicine and minor surgery (also called 亦称作 a family doctor) who sees patients either in his surgery or in their homes. 全科医生 (在其诊所或出诊者病者).

prae·sid·ium /prɪ'sɪdɪəm; prɪ'sɪdɪəm/ n = **presidium.**

prae·tor (also **pre·tor**) /'priːtə(r); 'priːtə/ n annually elected magistrate in ancient Rome. 古罗马每年选出的执政官. **prae·tor·ian** /prɪ'tɔːrɪən; prɪ'tɔːrɪən/ adj of, having the rank of, a ~; of the bodyguard of a Roman commander or Emperor. 古罗马之执政官之地位的; 古罗马统帅或皇帝之卫队的.

prag·matic /præg'mætɪk; præg'mætɪk/ adj concerned with practical results and values; treating things in a matter-of-fact or practical way. 关心实际之效果或价值的; 实事求是的; 实用主义的; 重效验的. **prag·mati·cally** /-klɪ; -klɪ/ adv

prag·ma·tism /'prægmətɪzəm; 'prægmə,tɪzəm/ n [U] **1** (phil) belief or theory that the truth or value of a conception or assertion depends upon its practical bearing upon human interests. (哲)实用主义(认为一概念或主张之真理或价值, 系以其对人生利益之实效为依归). **2** dogmatism; officiousness; pedantry. 独断; 好管闲事; 装腔作势. **prag·ma·tist** /-tɪst; -tɪst/ n believer in ~ (1). 实用主义者.

prairie /'preərɪ; 'prerɪ/ n wide area of level land with grass but no trees, esp in N America. (尤指北美洲无树木的)大草原. ⇨ **pampas, savanna, steppe, veld.**

praise /preɪz; prez/ vt [VP6A] **1** speak with approval of; say that one admires: 称赞; 赞美: ~ a man for his courage. 赞美一个人的英勇. Our guests ~d the meal as the best they had had for years. 来宾们都称赞说, 这是他们多年来所吃过的最好的一顿饭. **2** give honour and glory to (God). 赞颂(神). □ n **1** [U] act of praising: 称赞; 赞美: His heroism is worthy of great ~ / is beyond (= too great for) ~. 他的英勇值得大大赞扬(是赞美不尽的). The leader spoke in ~ of the man who had given his life for the cause. 领袖称赞那位为主义捐躯的人. **2** (pl) (复) sing sb's / one's own ~s, ~ him / oneself enthusiastically. 热烈颂扬某人(自己). **3** [U] worship; glory: 崇拜; 荣耀: P~ be to God. 荣耀归于上帝. P~ be! Thank goodness! 谢天谢地! '~·worthy /-wɜːðɪ; -,wɜːðɪ/ adj deserving ~. 值得称赞的; 值得赞美的. '~·worth·ily /-ɪlɪ; -əlɪ/ adv '~·worthi·ness n

pram /præm; præm/ n (GB) (short for, and the usu word for) **perambulator.** (英) perambulator 之常用略语.

prance /praːns US: præns; præns/ vi [VP2A, C] **~ (about), 1** (of a horse) move forwards jerkily, by raising the forelegs and springing from the hind legs. (指马)(前足离地而以后足向前)腾跃. **2** (fig) move, carry oneself, in an arrogant manner; dance or jump happily and gaily. (喻)昂然而行; 举止骄傲; 欢跳. □ n prancing movement. (马的)腾跃; (喻)昂然而行; 欢跃.

prank /præŋk; præŋk/ n [C] playful or mischievous trick: 开玩笑; 恶作剧: play ~s on sb. 戏弄某人.

prate /preɪt; pret/ vi [VP2A, C] talk (foolishly); talk too much: 谈; 空谈; 瞎谈; 喋喋不休): a silly young fellow prating about a subject of which he knows nothing. 对自己一无所知的题目大谈特谈的一位愚昧的年轻人.

prattle /'prætl; 'prætl/ vi [VP2A, C] (of a child) talk in a simple, artless way; (of adults) talk in a childish, simple way; chatter. (指小孩)自然而天真地谈话; (指成人)谈话一般天真地谈话; 喋喋不休. □ n [U] such talk. 自然而天真的谈话; 孩子气的话. **prat·tler** /'prætlə(r); 'prætlə/ n one who ~s. 谈话天真者; 喋喋不休者.

prawn /prɔːn; prɔn/ n [C] edible shellfish like a large shrimp: 大虾; 斑节虾: a dish of curried ~s. 一盘咖哩大虾. □ vi fish for ~s: 捕大虾: go ~ing. 去捕大虾.

pray /preɪ; pre/ vt, vi **1** [VP2A, 3A] **~ (to God) (for sth),** commune with God; offer thanks, make requests known: 祈祷; 祷告; 感恩; 祈求: ~ to God for help. 祈求神赐予援助. They knelt down and ~ed. 他们跪下祈祷. The farmers are ~ing for rain. 农民正在求雨. He's past ~ing for, There now seems to be little hope for his recovery, eg from illness, or from some fault, etc. 他已无药可救了(为他祷告是无用的, 如已病入膏肓, 或积重难返等). **2** [VP17, 14, 11] **~ sb for sth / to do sth,** (liter, rhet) ask sb as a favour: (文, 修辞)乞求; 恳求(某人)帮忙做(某事): I ~ you to think

again. 我求你再想一想。*We ~ you for mercy/to show mercy.* 我们恳求你发慈悲。*We ~ you that the prisoner may be set free.* 我们恳求你释放犯人。**3** (formal request equivalent to) please: (正式的请求，相当于 please) 请: *P~ don't speak so loud.* 请勿大声说话。

prayer /preə(r); `prɛr/ n **1** [U] act of praying to God: 祈祷; 祷告: *He knelt down in ~.* 他跪下祷告。**2** [U] form of church worship: 教堂之祈祷式: *Morning/Evening P~.* 早(晚)祷。**3** [C] form of words used in praying: 祈祷文: *the Lord's P~.* 主祷文。⇨ **lord**; request or petition (spoken or unspoken) to God: 对上帝之恳求或祈祷(包括说出或未说出的): *say one's ~s*; 祈祷; 祷告; 家庭祷告; *a ~ for rain.* 求雨。**'~book** n book containing ~s for use in church services, etc. 祈祷书。**the 'P~ Book,** (also called 亦称作 *Book of Common P~*) the one used in Church of England services. (英国国教的)祈祷书。**'~meeting** n meeting at which those present offer up ~s to God in turn. 祈祷会(参加者轮流向神祈祷)。**'~rug/-mat** n small rug used by Muslims to kneel on when they pray. 伊斯兰教徒跪下祈祷时所用的小块毡子(垫子)。**'~wheel** n revolving cylinder inscribed with or containing ~s, used by the Buddhists of Tibet. (西藏喇嘛教徒所用的)祈祷轮; 地藏车。

pre- /pri:; pri/ pref before; beforehand: 在…之先; 前; 预先: *pre-war;* 战前的; *a pre-amplifier;* 前置放大器; *pre-natal;* 出生前的; 胎儿期的; *pre-arrange.* 预先安排。⇨ **App 3.** 参看附录三。

preach /pri:tʃ; pritʃ/ vt, vi **1** [VP6A 2A, B, C, 3A] ~ (to), deliver (a sermon); make known (a religious doctrine, etc); give a talk (esp in church) about religion or morals: 讲(道); 传布(教旨等); (尤指在教堂)布道; 传教: ~ *the gospel,* 传布福音; (尤指 *Buddhism;* 宣扬佛教; ~ *against covetousness;* 讲道指摘贪婪; ~ *for two hours.* 讲道达二小时。**2** [VP3A, 12A, 13A] ~ (to), give moral advice: 劝诫; 说教: *the headmaster ~ing to his pupils.* 对学童们谆谆劝诫的校长。*Don't ~ me a sermon about being lazy now, please.* 请勿现在对我讲有关懒惰的大道理。**3** [VP6A] urge; recommend (as right or desirable): (认为正当或有价值而) 鼓吹; 倡导: *The Dictator ~ed war as a means of making the country great.* 那位独裁者鼓吹战争为强国的一种手段。~**er** n one who ~s (esp sermons). 鼓吹者; 鼓吹者; (尤指)传教者; 讲道者。~**·ify** /-ɪfaɪ; -ə‚faɪ/ vi (pt, pp **-fied**) ~, esp(2); moralize in a tedious way. 讲道; (尤指)劝诫; 说教;唠叨地教诲。

pre·am·ble /pri:'æmbl; `priæmbl/ n introduction or preliminary statement (esp to a formal document). 序言; (尤指法律文件的)序文。

pre·ar·range /‚pri:ə'reɪndʒ; ‚priə'rendʒ/ vt arrange in advance. 事前安排。~**·ment** n

preb·end /'prebənd; `prɛbənd/ n (eccles) part of the revenue of a church granted as a stipend to a priest. (教会) 教会之收入中拨为牧师或神父薪俸之部分。**preb·en·dary** /'prebəndrɪ US: -deri; `prɛbənd‚ɛrɪ/ n (pl **-ries**) priest who receives a ~. 受俸牧师或神父。

pre·cari·ous /prɪ'keərɪəs; prɪ'kɛrɪəs/ adj (formal) uncertain; unsafe; depending upon chance: (正式用语) 不稳定的; 不确定的; 危险的; 随机会而定的: *make a ~ living as an author.* 当一名作家，维持着不稳定的生计。~**·ly** adv

pre·cast /‚pri:'kɑːst US: -'kæst; prɪ'kæst/ adj (of concrete) cast into blocks ready for use in building. (指水泥)预凝成块的; 预铸的。

pre·caution /prɪ'kɔːʃn; prɪ'kɔʃən/ n [U] care taken in advance to avoid a risk; [C] instance of this: 预防; 防备; 预防或防备的实例: *take an umbrella as a ~;* 带伞以为防备; *take ~s against fire;* 采取防火的措施; *insure one's house as a measure of ~.* 给房屋保险作为预防的措施。~**·ary** /prɪ'kɔːʃənrɪ US: -nerɪ; prɪ'kɔʃən‚ɛrɪ/ adj for the sake of ~. 为了预防的; 防备的。

pre·cede /prɪ'siːd; prɪ'sid/ vt, vi [VP6A, 2A] come or go before (in time, place or order): (在时间、位置或顺序上)在前; 居先; 先于: *the calm that ~d the storm;* 暴风雨前的平静; *the Mayor, ~d by the mace-bearer;* 市长，由执权杖者前导; *in the preceding paragraph/the paragraph that ~s.* 在前一段里; 在上一段里。**pre·ced·ing** adj existing or coming before. 在前的; 在先的。

pre·ced·ence /'presɪdəns; prɪ'sidns/ n [U] (right to a) priority, or to a senior place. 居前; 居先; (优越)优先权。**have/take ~ (over):** 在…之上; 优于: *questions which take ~ over all others,* which must be considered first. 必须在所有其他问题之先加以考虑的一些问题(必须优先考虑的问题)。

pre·ced·ent /'presɪdənt; `prɛsədənt/ n earlier happening, decision, etc taken as an example or rule for what comes later. 先例; 前例。**set/create/establish a ~ (for sth):** 开创(某事的)先例: *Is there a ~ for what you want me to do?* 你要我做的事有前例可援吗? ~**ed** adj having, supported by, a ~. 有先例的; 有前例可援的。

pre·cen·tor /prɪ'sentə(r); prɪ'sɛntɚ/ n (eccles) person in general control of the singing. (教会)领唱之人。

pre·cept /'pri:sept; `prisɛpt/ n **1** [U] moral instruction: 道德上的箴言; 告诫; 教训: *Example is better than ~.* 以身作则胜于口头告诫(言教不如身教)。**2** [C] rule or guide, esp for behaviour. (尤指行为的)规范; 教训; 戒律; 格言。

pre·cep·tor /prɪ'septə(r); prɪ'sɛptɚ/ n (formal) teacher; instructor. (正式用语)教师; 导师。

pre·cession /prɪ'seʃn; prɪ'sɛʃən/ n ~ of the equinoxes, change by which the equinoxes occur earlier in each successive year. 岁差(每年二分点提早发生之变化)。

pre·cinct /'pri:sɪŋkt; `prisɪŋkt/ n [C] **1** space enclosed by outer walls or boundaries, esp of a cathedral or church: (尤指教堂的)界域; 境域: *within the sacred ~s.* 在(教堂之)神圣的境域内。**2** (US) subdivision of a county or city or ward: (美)郡、市或区的次级区分; 辖区: *an election ~;* 选举区; *a police ~.* 警察的辖区。**3** (pl) neighbourhood or environs (of a town). (复) (城市的) 附近; 周围; 邻域。**4** boundary: 界限; 范围: *within the city ~s.* 在市区范围内。**5** area of which the use is in some way restricted. 使用上受限制的地区。**pedestrian ~,** where vehicles are not allowed. 行人区;不准车辆行驶之地区。**'shopping ~,** for shops only. 商店区。

pre·ci·os·ity /‚preʃɪ'ɒsətɪ; ‚prɛʃɪ'asətɪ/ n [U] over-refinement; being precious(4); [C] (pl **-ties**) instance of this. (言语, 手艺等之) 过于讲究; 过于细心; 过于细腻; 矫揉造作。

precious /'preʃəs; `prɛʃəs/ adj **1** of great value and beauty: 贵重的; 宝贵的: *the ~ metals,* gold, platinum; 贵金属(金、铂等); ~ *stones,* diamonds, rubies, etc. 宝石(钻石、红宝石等)。**2** highly valued; dear: 珍爱的; 可爱的: *Her children are very ~ to her.* 她极珍爱她的孩子。**3** (colloq) (as in intensive) complete: (口) (用于加强语气)完全的; 彻底的: *a ~ fool.* 大傻瓜。*It cost a ~ sight more than I could afford,* very much more. 它的价格远超出我所能负担的。**4** (of language, workmanship, etc) over-refined; affected. (指言语, 手艺等)讲究的; 过于细心的; 矫揉造作的。□ adv (colloq) very: (口)很; 甚: *~ little* (= hardly any) *money left.* 我没剩下什么钱了。~**·ly** adv。~**·ness** n

preci·pice /'presɪpɪs; `prɛsəpɪs/ n vertical or very steep face of a rock, cliff or mountain. 悬崖; 绝壁。

pre·cipi·tate /prɪ'sɪpɪteɪt; prɪ'sɪpə‚tet/ vt [VP6A, 14] **1** throw or send (sb or sth) violently down from a height. (自高处)将(某物)猛然掷下, 猛投。~ *sb/sth into sth,* thrust violently into (a condition): 使突然陷入某种状态: ~ *the country into war.* 使国家

突然陷入战争。**2** cause (an event) to happen suddenly, quickly, or in haste: 使(事件)突然, 迅速或急促地发生: ~ *a crisis*; 突然引起危机; *events that* ~*d his ruin.* 使其突然破产的事件。**3** (chem) separate (solid matter) from a solution. (化学) 使 (固体) 沉淀。**4** condense (vapour) into drops which fall as rain, dew, etc. 使 (水气) 凝为雨, 露等。 □ *n* that which is ~d as solid matter, rainfall, etc. 沉淀物; 凝结物 (如雨等)。 □ *adj* /prɪˈsɪpɪtət; prɪˈsɪpəˌtet/ violently hurried; hasty; (doing things, done) without enough thought. 急促的; 卤莽的; 未多加思考的。 **~·ly** *adv*

pre·cipi·ta·tion /prɪˌsɪpɪˈteɪʃn; prɪˌsɪpəˈteʃən/ *n* **1** (esp) fall of rain, sleet, snow or hail; amount of this: (尤指)雨, 霰, 雪或雹之下降; 其降量; 雨量: *the annual* ~ *in the Lake District*; 大湖区每年的雨量; *a heavy* ~. 一阵大雨。**2** [U] violent haste or being violently hurried: 急促; 卤莽: *act with* ~, without enough thought or consideration of the consequences. 卤莽行事。**3** act of precipitating. 猛掷; 猛投; 加速; 促进; 沉淀; 凝结。

pre·cipi·tous /prɪˈsɪpɪtəs; prɪˈsɪpətəs/ *adj* (formal) like a precipice; very steep. (正式用语) 似悬崖的; 陡峭的; 险峻的。 **~·ly** *adv*

pré·cis /ˈpreɪsiː US: preɪˈsiː; preˈsi/ *n* (*pl* unchanged in spelling, pronunciation /-iːz, -iz/) restatement in shortened form of the chief ideas, points, etc of a speech or piece of writing. (复数的拼法不变, 读作 /ˈpreɪsiːz; preˈsiz/) (演说或文章之)摘要; 大纲; 梗概。 □ *vt* make a ~ of. 写大纲; 摘要。

pre·cise /prɪˈsaɪs; prɪˈsaɪs/ *adj* **1** exact; correctly and clearly stated; free from error: 精确的; 叙述正确的; 明白的; 无误的: ~ *measurements*; 精确的尺寸; ~ *orders*; 严格的命令; *at the* ~ *moment when I lifted the receiver*. 正好在我拿起听筒的时刻。**2** taking care to be exact, not to make errors; 小心谨慎的; 注意不犯错的; *a very* ~ *man*; 非常严谨的人; *too careful, fussy, about details*: 对细节过于小心或挑剔的; 斤斤计较的: *prim and* ~ *in his manner.* 他在态度上拘泥而斤斤计较。 **~·ly** *adv* **1** in a ~ manner; exactly: 精确地; 明白地; 谨慎地; 无错误地; 斤斤计较地: *state the facts* ~*ly*; 明白地叙述事实; *at 2 o'clock* ~*ly.* 恰好在两点钟。**2** (as a response, agreeing with sb) quite so. (用作同意某人之答语)对; 正是如此; 一点不错。 **~·ness** *n*

pre·ci·sion /prɪˈsɪʒn; prɪˈsɪʒən/ *n* [U] accuracy; freedom from error: 精确(度); 正确: (attrib) (用作定语) ~ *instruments/tools*, those, used in technical work, that are very precise (for measuring, etc): 精密仪器(工具): ~ *bombing.* 正确轰炸; 精密轰炸。

pre·clude /prɪˈkluːd; prɪˈklud/ *vt* [VP6A, C, 14] ~ *sb from doing sth*, prevent; make impossible: 阻止某人做某事; 使不可能: ~ *all doubts/misunderstanding.* 排除所有疑虑(误解)。 **pre·clu·sion** /prɪˈkluːʒn; prɪˈkluʒən/ *n*

pre·co·cious /prɪˈkəʊʃəs; prɪˈkoʃəs/ *adj* **1** (of a person) having developed certain faculties earlier than is normal: (指人)早熟的: *a* ~ *child*, eg one who reads well at the age of three. 早熟的孩子(如三岁时即能阅读书籍)。**2** (of actions, knowledge, etc) marked by such development. (指行为, 知识等)早熟的; 象大人的; 过早的。 **~·ly** *adv* **~·ness, pre·coc·ity** /prɪˈkɒsətɪ; prɪˈkɑsətɪ/ *nn* [U] being ~. 早熟。

pre·cog·ni·tion /ˌpriːkɒɡˈnɪʃn; ˌprikɑɡˈnɪʃən/ *n* [U] knowledge of sth before it occurs. 预知; 先知。

pre·con·ceive /ˌpriːkənˈsiːv; ˌprikənˈsiv/ *vt* [VP 6A] form (ideas, opinions) in advance (before getting knowledge or experience): 预想; (在未获得对某事物之知识或经验前)预先形成 (概念, 意见): *visit a foreign country with* ~*d ideas.* 怀着成见访问外国。 **pre·con·cep·tion** /ˌpriːkənˈsepʃn; ˌprikənˈsepʃən/ *n* [U, C] ~d idea. 预想; 先入之见; 成见。

pre·con·certed /ˌpriːkənˈsɜːtɪd; ˌprikənˈsɝtɪd/ *adj* (formal) agreed in advance: (正式用语)事先同意的; 预定的: *following* ~ *plans.* 依照预定的计划。

pre·con·di·tion /ˌpriːkənˈdɪʃn; ˌprikɑnˈdɪʃən/ *n* = prerequisite.

pre·cur·sor /priːˈkɜːsə(r); prɪˈkɝsɚ/ *n* [C] (formal) person or thing coming before, as a sign of what is to follow. (正式用语)先驱; 先兆。 **pre·cur·sory** /-sərɪ; -sərɪ/ *adj* preliminary; anticipating. 前驱的; 先锋的; 预先的; 前兆的。

preda·tory /ˈpredətrɪ US: -tɔːrɪ; ˈprɛdəˌtɔrɪ/ *adj* (formal) (正式用语) **1** (of people) plundering and robbing; 掠夺人抢劫的; 掠夺的: ~ *tribesmen/habits*; 以掠夺为生的部族(掠夺的习惯); ~ *incursions*, raids made for plunder. 掠夺性的侵袭。**2** (of animals) preying upon others. (指动物)食肉的。 **predator** /-tə(r); -tɚ/ *n* animal. 食肉动物。

pre·de·cease /ˌpriːdɪˈsiːs; ˌpridɪˈsis/ *vt* (legal) die before (another person). (法律)死于(某人)之先。

pre·de·cessor /ˈpriːdɪsesə(r) US: ˈpredɪ-; ˈprɛdɪˌsɛsɚ/ *n* **1** former holder of any office or position: (某职位的)前任: *Mr Green's* ~; 格林先生所任职位的前任。**2** thing to which another has succeeded: 原有的事物: *Is the new proposal any better than its* ~? 新提议比原提议好吗?

pre·des·ti·nate /priːˈdestɪneɪt; prɪˈdɛstənɪt/ *adj* foreordained by God; fated. 神预先安排的; 命中注定的。 □ *vt* = **predestine**(1).

pre·des·ti·na·tion /ˌpriːdestɪˈneɪʃn; prɪˌdɛstəˈneʃən/ *n* **1** theory or doctrine that God has decreed from eternity that part of mankind shall have eternal bliss and part eternal punishment. 命定论; 宿命论(认为神早已预定某部分人类将得永远幸福, 某部分人类将万劫不复)。**2** destiny; doctrine that God has decreed everything that comes to pass. 命运; 一切事物均已由神定说。

pre·des·tine /priːˈdestɪn; prɪˈdɛstɪn/ *vt* **1** [VP14, 17] (often passive) (常用被动语态) ~ *sb to sth/to do sth*, (of God, fate) decide, ordain, before-hand; cause (sb) to behave, etc in a certain way. (指神, 命运)注定某人做某事; 预定。**2** [VP17] ~ *sb to do sth*, decide or make inevitable: 注定某人做某事: *Everything took place as if he was* ~*d to succeed.* 他一切顺利, 似乎注定该成功。*These events were clearly* ~*d (to happen).* 这些事件显然是注定(要发生)的。

pre·de·ter·mine /ˌpriːdɪˈtɜːmɪn; ˌpridɪˈtɝmɪn/ *vt* (formal) (正式用语) **1** [VP6A] decide in advance: 预先决定: *The social class into which a child is born often seems to* ~ *his later career.* 婴儿所出生的社会阶层往往能决定他以后的事业。**2** [VP17] ~ *sb to do sth*, persuade or impel sb in advance to do sth: 预先说服或驱使某人做某事: *Did an unhappy childhood* ~ *him to behave as he did?* 是否系不愉快的童年驱使他这么做? **pre·de·ter·mi·na·tion** /ˌpriːdɪˌtɜːmɪˈneɪʃn; ˌpridɪˌtɝməˈneʃən/ *n*

pre·dica·ment /prɪˈdɪkəmənt; prɪˈdɪkəmənt/ *n* difficult or unpleasant situation from which escape seems difficult: 苦境; 困境; 穷境; 险境: *be in an awkward* ~. 处于困境。

predi·cate¹ /ˈpredɪkət; ˈprɛdɪkɪt/ *n* (gram) part of a statement which says sth about the subject, eg '*is short*' in '*Life is short*'. (语法)谓语; 谓词(如 'Life is short' 中之 'is short' 即为谓语)。

predi·cate² /ˈpredɪkeɪt; ˈprɛdɪˌket/ *vt* (formal) (正式用语) **1** [VP6A, 17, 9] declare to be true or real: 宣称…为真实; 断言: ~ *of a motive that it is good*; 断言某动机是好的; ~ *a motive to be good.* 断言某动机是好的。**2** [VP6A] make necessary as a consequence: 使成为必然的结果: *These policies were* ~*d by Britain's decision to join the Common Market.* 这些措施是英国决定加入共同市场的必然结果。

pre·di·ca·tive /prɪˈdɪkətɪv US: ˈpredɪkeɪtɪv; ˈprɛdɪˌketɪv/ *adj* (gram, of an *adj* or *n*, opposed to *attrib*) forming part or the whole of the predicate. (语法, 指形容词或名词, 与 attributive 相反)用作表语的; 表语的。 ~

adjective, one used only in the predicate, eg *asleep, alive*. (仅用于谓语中的)表语形容词(如 asleep, alive)。

pre·dict /prɪ'dɪkt; prɪ'dɪkt/ vt [VP6A, 9, 10] say, tell in advance: 预言;预测;预示: ~ *that there will be an earthquake*. 预测将有地震。 **pre·dic·tion** /prɪ'dɪkʃn; prɪ'dɪkʃən/ n [U] ~ing; [C] instance ~ed; prophecy. 预言;预测;预示或预测将要发生之事物。 ~·**able** /-əbl; -əbl/ adj that can be ~ed. 可预言的;可预测的;可预示的。 ~**or** /-tə(r); -tə/ n instrument or device that ~s, eg one used in war to determine when to open anti-aircraft fire. 测位器; 位置预测器(如战时用的高射瞄准器)。 ~**a·bil·ity** /prɪ,dɪktə'bɪlətɪ/ n

pre·di·gest /,priːdaɪ'dʒest; ,priːdə'dʒest/ vt treat (food) so that it is easily digested: 处理(食物)以便容易消化: ~ed food for babies. 经过处理而容易消化的婴儿食物。

pre·di·lec·tion /,priːdɪ'lekʃn US: ,predl'ek-; ,prɪdl'ekʃən/ n [C] a ~ for, special liking, mental preference. 偏爱;偏好。

pre·dis·pose /,priːdɪ'spəuz; ,priːdɪs'poz/ vt [VP14, 17] ~ sb to sth/to do sth, (formal) cause (sb) to be inclined or liable before the event: (正式用语)使先倾向于;使先偏向于;使偏爱;易易罹染: *His early training ~d him to a life of adventure/to travel widely*. 他早年所受的教养使他偏爱冒险生活(到处旅行)。 *I find myself ~d in his favour*, inclined to favour him. 我发现自己对他有所偏爱。 **pre·dis·po·si·tion** /,priːdɪspə'zɪʃn; ,priːdɪspə'zɪʃən/ n [C] ~ to sth/to do sth, state of mind or body favourable to: (身心的)倾向;爱好;偏好;癖性;易…之体质: *a ~ to arthritis*; 易罹关节炎的体质; *a ~ to find fault*. 吹毛求疵的癖性。

pre·domi·nant /prɪ'dɒmɪnənt; prɪ'dɑmənənt/ adj ~ (over), (formal) having more power or influence than others; prevailing, conspicuous: (正式用语)有势力的;优势的;主要的;卓越的;流行的;显著的: *The ~ feature of his character was pride*. 他的性格的主要特色是骄傲。 ~·**ly** adv in a ~ manner: 有较大之力量或影响地: 主要地;显著地: *a ~ly brown-eyed race*. 棕色眼睛占大多数的民族。 **pre·domi·nance** /-əns; -əns/ n [U] superiority in strength, numbers, etc; state of being ~. (力量, 数量等的)优越; 卓越; 支配;显著。

pre·domi·nate /prɪ'dɒmɪneɪt; prɪ'dɑmə,net/ vi [VP2A, 3A] ~ (over), (formal) have or exert control (over); be superior in numbers, strength, influence, etc: (正式用语)统治;支配; (在数量,力量,势力等上)占优势: *a forest in which oak-trees ~*. 橡树为主的森林。

pre·emi·nent /,priː'emɪnənt; prɪ'ɛmənənt/ adj excelling others; best of; 最好的; 优秀的; 卓越的: ~ *above all his rivals*. 超越他所有的敌手。 ~·**ly** adv **pre·emi·nence** /-əns; -əns/ n [U].

pre·empt /,priː 'empt; prɪ'ɛmpt/ vt [VP6A] (formal) (正式用语) 1 obtain by pre-emption. 以优先购买权取得。 2 (US) occupy (public land) so as to have the right of pre-emption. (美)占用(公地)以取得优先购买权。 **pre·emp·tion** /,priː 'empʃn; prɪ'ɛmpʃən/ n [U] (formal) purchase by one person, etc before others are offered the chance to buy; right to purchase in this way; the obtaining of sth in advance. (正式用语)先买(权); 优先购买(权); 抢先取得。 **pre·emp·tive** /-tɪv; -tɪv/ adj relating to pre-emption: 先买(权)的; 先买的: *a ~ bid*, (in bridge) one intended to be high enough to prevent further bidding; (桥牌)为吃住对方尽量叫大声; *a ~ 'air strike*, by bombing, against forces considered likely to attack. 先发制人之空袭(为预防敌人攻击而先向敌人实施的袭击等)。

preen /priːn; prin/ vt 1 (of a bird) smooth (itself, its feathers) with its beak. (指鸟)以喙整理(羽毛)。 2 [VP6A, 14] (of a person) tidy (oneself). (指

人)打扮(自己)。 ~ *oneself on*, (fig) pride oneself (on); show self-satisfaction. (喻)以…自负;显出自满。

pre·exist /,priːɪg'zɪst; ,priːɪg'zɪst/ vi [VP2A] exist beforehand; live a life before this life. 先存;先在;存在于前世。 ~·**ence** /-əns; -əns/ n lIfe of the soul before entering its present body or this world. 前生; 前世(灵魂进入今生前的生命)。 ~·**ent** /-ənt; -ənt/ adj existing in a former life or previously. 在前世存在的; 以前存在的。

pre·fab /'priː,fæb; 'priː,fæb; ,priː'fæb/ n [C] (colloq abbr of) prefabricated house. (口)活动房屋; 预铸房屋(为 prefabricated house 之略)。

pre·fab·ri·cate /,priː'fæbrɪkeɪt; prɪ'fæbrə,ket/ vt [VP6A] manufacture the parts, eg roofs, walls, fitments, of a building, a ship, etc before they are put together on the site, in the yards, etc: 预先建造(房屋,船等的)组成部分(如房顶,墙,镶造部分)以便在基地,工场等处装架: ~d houses; 活动房屋; 预铸房屋; *a ~d school*. 活动校舍。 **pre·fab·ri·ca·tion** /,priː,fæbrɪ'keɪʃn; ,priː,fæbrɪ'keʃən/ n.

pref·ace /'prefɪs; 'prɛfɪs/ n [C] author's explanatory remarks at the beginning of a book; preliminary part of a speech: (书籍之)序言; 序文; (演讲之)开场白; 开端: *write a ~ to a book*. 写一本书的序言。 □ vt [VP14] ~ *sth with sth/by doing sth*, provide with a ~; begin (a talk, etc) with a ~: 给…作序; 以…作(讲话等的)开端: *The chairman ~d his remarks with some sharp raps on the table*. 主席重重地敲了几下桌子, 然后开始讲话。 **prefa·tory** /'prefətərɪ US: -tɔːrɪ; 'prɛfə,torɪ/ adj of or in the nature of a ~: 序言的; 开端的;序言或开端性质的: *after a few prefatory remarks*. 在几句开场白之后。

pre·fect /'priːfekt; 'priːfɛkt/ n 1 (in ancient Rome) title of various civil and military officers; governor. (古罗马)某些文武官员的头衔; 行政长官; 司令官。 2 (in France, Japan) title of the chief administrative officer of a department; head of the Paris police. (法国及日本之)最高行政长官; 首长; 巴黎的警察局长。 3 (in some English schools) one of a number of senior pupils given responsibility, eg for keeping order. (英国若干学校之)级长;(负责维持纪律等的)高年级生。

pre·fec·ture /'priːfektjʊə(r) US: -tʃər; 'priːfɛktʃə/ n 1 administrative area in some countries, eg France, Japan. (法,日等国之)省; 郡; 州(最大的地方行政区划)。 ⇨ **county** (in GB). 2 (in France) place or office where a prefect(2) works; his official residence. (法国)省长或巴黎警察局长之官署; 其官邸。 3 position of a prefect(1); period of office. (古罗马)行政长官或司令官之任期。 **pre·fec·tural** /priː'fektʃərəl; prɪ'fɛktʃərəl/ adj of a ~: 省(州)的; 省长(或巴黎警察局长)之官署或官邸的;古罗马地方行政长官之职位或任期的: *the prefectural offices*. 地方官署。

pre·fer /prɪ'fɜː(r); prɪ'fɚ/ vt (-rr-) 1 [VP6A, D, 7A, 9, 14, 17] ~ (to), choose rather; like better: 较喜欢; 宁取: *Which would you ~, tea or coffee?* 你比较喜欢喝茶, 还是喝咖啡? *I ~ walking to cycling*. 我喜爱步行胜过骑单车。 *He ~s to write his letters rather than dictate them*. 他喜欢自己写信, 不愿口授自己的信。 *I should ~ to wait until evening*. 我愿意等到天晚。 *I should ~ you not to go/that you did not go there alone*. 我剖希望你不要单独前往。 2 [VP6A, 14] ~ *a charge/charges (against sb)*, put forward, submit: 提出控告; 告发(某人): ~ *a charge against a motorist*, ie accuse him of sth. 控告驾驶汽车者。 3 [VP6A, 14] ~ *sb (to sth)*, appoint (sb) (to a higher position). 擢升(某人)(至较高之职位)。 ~·**able** /'prefrəbl; 'prefrəbl/ adj (not used with more) ~ (to), superior; to be ~red. (不可与 more 连用)优越的; 较好的; 较合人意的。 ~·**ably** /'prefrəblɪ; 'prefrəblɪ/ adv

pref·er·ence /'prefrəns; 'prefərəns/ n 1 [C, U] act of preferring: 较喜欢; 宁愿; 喜爱: *have a ~ for French novels*. 喜读法国小说。 *I should choose this in ~*

to any other. 我宁愿选择这个而不要其他的。**2** [C] that which is preferred: 喜爱物；嗜好物: *What are your ~s?* 你喜爱些什么？**3** [U] the favouring of one person, country, etc more than another (in business relations, etc esp by admitting imports at a lower import duty); [C] instance of this: (在商务关系上给予某人、某国等的)优先权；优待; (尤指推许课以较低之进口税的)特惠；优待或特惠的实例: *give sb ~ (over others).* 给某人(较他人)优待。**4** 'P~ **Stock**, stock on which dividend payments must be made before profits are distributed to holders of Ordinary Stock. 优先股(对股利之分配较普通股享有优先权)。

pref·er·en·tial /ˌprefəˈrenʃl; ˌprefəˈrɛnʃəl/ adj of, giving, receiving preference; (eg of import duties, etc) favouring particular countries: 优先的；给予优先的; (指进口税等之)特惠的: *get ~ treatment.* 享受优先的待遇。

pre·fer·ment /prɪˈfɜːmənt; prɪˈfɝmənt/ n [U] act of preferring(3); promotion or advancement: 擢升；晋级: *~ to a directorship.* 擢升为董事。

pre·fig·ure /ˌpriːˈfɪɡə(r) US: -ɡjər; priˈfɪɡjə/ vt (formal) (正式用语) **1** [VP6A] represent before-hand; show (what is coming). 预表；预示。**2** [VP6A, 9, 10] imagine, picture to oneself, before-hand. 预想。

pre·fix /ˈpriːfɪks; ˈprifɪks/ n **1** (abbr *pref* in this dictionary) word or syllable, eg *pre-, co-,* placed in front of a word to add to or change its meaning. (本词典略为 pref) 前缀(加于一词之前，以增加或改变其意义的字或音节，如 pre-, co-)。⇨ **App 3.** 参看附录三。**2** word used before a person's name, eg Mr, Dr. 人名前用的尊称(如 Mr, Dr)。□ vt /ˌpriːˈfɪks; priˈfɪks/ [VP6A, 14] *~ sth (to sth),* add a ~ to or in front of; add at the beginning: 置前缀或尊称于…之前；加在前头: *~ a new paragraph to Chapter Ten.* 在第十章的前头新加一段。

preg·nant /ˈpreɡnənt; ˈprɛɡnənt/ adj **1** (of a woman or female animal) having in the uterus offspring in a stage of development before birth. (指女人或雌性动物)怀孕的；有胎的。**2** (of words, actions) significant; full of promise. (指文字，行动)重要的；富有意义的；可望成功的。*~ with,* filled with: 充满着: *words ~ with meaning;* 富有意义之言词; certain or likely to have: 一定或可能的: *political events ~ with consequences.* 可能会产生重大后果的政治事件。**preg·nancy** /-nənsɪ; -nənsɪ/ n [U] the state of being ~; (fig) fullness; depth; significance; [C] instance of being ~: 怀孕; (喻)丰富；深刻；重大；富有意义; 此等之实例: *She's had six pregnancies in six years.* 她在六年中怀孕六次。

pre·hen·sile /prɪˈhensaɪl US: -sl; prɪˈhɛnsl/ adj (of a foot or tail, as a monkey's) able to seize and hold. (指猴等的足或尾)能捉住的；适于卷缠的。

pre·his·toric /ˌpriːhɪˈstɒrɪk US: -ˈtɔːrɪk, ˌpriːhɪˈstɔrɪk, -tɑrɪk/, **-tori·cal**/-kl; kl/ adjj of the time before recorded history. 史前的。**pre·his·tory** /ˌpriːˈhɪstrɪ; priˈhɪstrɪ/ n

pre·judge /ˌpriːˈdʒʌdʒ; priˈdʒʌdʒ/ vt [VP6A] make up one's mind about a person, cause, action, etc before hearing the evidence, making a proper inquiry, etc. 未经详细研究而对(某人，主张，行动等)作判断；未获充分证据而作判断；预断。*~·ment* n

preju·dice /ˈpredʒədɪs; ˈprɛdʒədɪs/ n **1** [U] opinion, like or dislike, formed before one has adequate knowledge or experience; [C] instance of this: 偏见；成见; 偏见或成见的实例: *have a ~ against/in favour of modern jazz;* 对现代爵士乐有偏见(偏爱); *listen to new poems without ~;* 未存成见地聆听新诗; *racial ~,* against members of other races. 种族偏见；种族歧视。**2** [U] (legal) injury that may or does arise from some action or judgement: (法律)伤害；损害；不利(由某种行为或判断所造成或可能造成者): *to the ~ of sb's rights,* with (possible) injury to them. 损及(或可能损及)某人的权利。*without ~ (to),* without injury to any existing

right or claim. (对任何现有的权益)无损害。□ vt [VP6A, 15A] *~ sb (against/in favour of sb/sth),* **1** cause sb to have a ~(1). 使某人(对某人或某物)有偏见；损害(某人之利益等): *He ~d his claim by asking too much.* 他因需索过度而影响到他所作的要求。**preju·di·cial** /ˌpredʒʊˈdɪʃl; ˌprɛdʒəˈdɪʃəl/ adj *~ (to),* causing *~* or injury. 造成偏见或损害的。

prel·acy /ˈpreləsɪ; ˈprɛləsɪ/ n (pl **-cies**) **1** office, rank, see, of a prelate. 主教或高级教士之职位，等级或教区。**2** the ~, the whole body of prelates. 主教或高级教士团；主教或高级教士(集合用法)。

prel·ate /ˈprelət; ˈprɛlɪt/ n bishop or other churchman of equal or higher rank. 主教；高级教士(与主教平行或高于主教)。

pre·lim /prɪˈlɪm; prɪˈlɪm/ n (colloq abbr for preliminary) (口，为 preliminary 之略) **1** preliminary examination. 初试。**2** (pl) /ˈpriːlɪmz; ˈprɪlɪmz/ pages (with title, contents, etc) preceding the actual text (in a book). (复)(书中)正文前的几页(包括书名，目录等)。

pre·limi·nary /prɪˈlɪmɪnərɪ US: -nerɪ; prɪˈlɪmə,nɛrɪ/ adj coming first and preparing for what follows: 初步的；开始的: *a ~ examination;* 初试; *after a few ~ remarks.* 在几句开场白之后。□ n (pl **-ries**) (usu pl) *~* actions, measures, etc: (通常用复数)初步的行动，措施等: *the usual preliminaries to a Geneva conference,* eg the wrangling about procedures and agenda. 日内瓦会议之预备会(如对程序和议程的折冲)。

prel·ude /ˈpreljuːd; ˈprɛljud/ n [C] *~ to,* action, event, etc that serves as an introduction to (another); (music) introductory movement (to a fugue or as part of a suite). 先驱；前奏；序幕; (音乐)序曲；前奏曲。□ vt [VP6A] serve as, be, a ~ to. 作为…之前奏，序幕，先驱。

pre·mari·tal /ˌpriːˈmærɪtl; priˈmærətl/ adj before marriage. 婚前的。

pre·ma·ture /ˈprematjʊə(r) US: ˌpriːməˈtʊər; ˌprɪmeˈtjʊr/ adj done, happening, doing sth, before the right or usual time: 太早的；未成熟的: *~ decay of the teeth;* 牙齿之过早龋腐; *~ birth;* 早产; *a ~ baby,* one born at less than 38 weeks of pregnancy. 早产的婴儿(怀孕不到 38 周而产下之婴儿)。**~·ly** adv

pre·medi·tate /ˌpriːˈmedɪteɪt; priˈmɛdə,tet/ vt [VP6A] consider, plan, (sth) in advance: 预谋；预先考虑或计划(某事): *a ~d murder.* 预谋的凶杀。**pre·medi·ta·tion** /ˌpriːmedɪˈteɪʃn; ˌprimɛdəˈteʃən/ n [U].

pre·mier /ˈpremɪə(r) US: ˈpriːm-; ˈprimɪə/ adj first in position, importance, etc. 第一的；首要的。□ n prime minister; head of the government. 首相；内阁总理。**'~·ship** /-ʃɪp; -,ʃɪp/ n

pre·mière /ˈpremɪeə(r) US: prɪˈmɪər; prɪˈmɪr/ n first performance of a play or ('*film~*) first public showing of a cinema film. (戏剧之)首次公演; (影片之)首次放映(亦作 film-première)。

prem·ise, prem·iss /ˈpremɪs; ˈprɛmɪs/ n **1** statement on which reasoning is based. (为推理之根据的)前提。**2** each of the two first parts of a syllogism: (三段论法的)前提: *the major ~,* eg 'Boys like fruit'; *the minor ~,* eg 'You are a boy'; the conclusion being 'Therefore you like fruit'. 大前提(如'男孩喜欢水果')；小前提(如'你是男孩')；结论是'所以你喜欢水果'。**3** (pl) house or building with its outbuildings, land, etc: (复)房屋连同附属建筑，土地等; 房产: *business ~s,* the building(s), offices, etc where a business is carried on; 事务所；办公室; *to be consumed on the ~s,* eg of alcoholic drinks in a public house or hotel which has no 'off-licence'. 限在店内喝完(如指某些酒店或旅馆中出售的酒不得携出饮用)。**4** (pl) (legal) details of property, names of persons, etc in the first part of a legal agreement. (复)(法律)契约之缘起或要件(契约的开头部分记述让渡财产之详情、当事人姓名等)。□ vt [VP6A,

9] ~ *(sth/that ...)*, state by way of introduction. 提论;预述;立前提.

pre·mium /'pri:mɪəm/ 'priːmɪəm/ *n (pl ~s)* **1** amount or instalment paid for an insurance policy. 保险费(总额或分期摊付之额). **2** reward; bonus: 报酬;奖金: *a ~ for good conduct.* 品行优良奖. **'P~ Bond,** (GB) government bond that offers the chance of prizes (in a draw) instead of the more usual interest¹(6). (英)以抽奖代替一般利息的公债. *put a ~ on sth,* make it advantageous for sb (to behave in a certain way, to do sth): 诱发;鼓励(某种行为,行动): *Does high taxation put a ~ on business dishonesty?* 重税会诱使人做生意不规矩吗? **3** addition to ordinary charges, wages, rent, etc; bonus: (一般费用,工资,租金等之外的)额外费用;赏金: *He had to pay the agent a ~ before he could rent the house,* an extra sum above the rent. 租用那幢房子以前,他须先付代理人一笔佣金. **4** fee (to be) paid by a pupil to a professional man, eg an accountant or architect, for instruction and training. (学生付给会计师或建筑师等专业人员的)学费; 束脩. **5** (of stocks and shares) amount above par value: 指(公债及股票)超过票面的价值;溢价: *The shares are selling at a ~.* 这些股票溢价出售. *at a ~,* (fig) highly valued or esteemed. (喻)非常宝贵的;甚受尊敬的.

pre·mon·ition /,pri:mə'nɪʃn/ ,priːmə'nɪʃən/ *n [C]* feeling of uneasiness considered as a warning (of approaching danger, etc): (对于即将来到之危险等的)预感;前兆: *have a ~ of failure.* 有失败之预感. **pre·moni·tory** /prɪ'mɒnɪtərɪ US: -tɔːrɪ/ prɪ'mɑnə,tɔrɪ/ *adj*

pre·natal /,pri:'neɪtl/ priː'netl/ *adj* preceding birth. 出生前的; 胎儿期的.

pren·tice /'prentɪs/ 'prentɪs/ *n* (old use, short for *apprentice*) (旧用法,为 apprentice 之略) *try his ~ hand,* make an unskilled or novice's attempt. 初次尝试.

pre·oc·cu·pa·tion /,pri:ɒkju'peɪʃn/ prɪ,akjə'peʃən/ *n [U]* state of mind in which sth takes up all a person's thoughts; [C] the subject, etc that takes up all his thoughts: 全神贯注; 出神; 使人全神贯注的事物; 急务: *His greatest ~ was how to find money for a holiday in Europe.* 他的首务之务是如何筹钱去欧洲度假.

pre·oc·cupy /pri:'ɒkjupaɪ/ prɪ'akjə,paɪ/ *vt (pt, pp -pied)* [VP6A] take all the attention of (sb, his mind) so that attention is not given to other matters: 使全神贯注; 盘据(心头); 迷住: *preoccupied by family troubles;* 心神被家庭纠纷盘据着; *preoccupied with thoughts of the coming holidays.* 一心一意想着即将来临之假期.

pre·or·dain /,pri:ɔ:'deɪn/ ,priɔr'den/ *vt* [VP6A, 9] decree or determine in advance. 预先注定;预定.

prep /prep/ prɛp/ *n* (schoolboy slang for) (学童俚语) **1** preparation(3). 课外作业. **2** preparatory school. 预备学校;预科.

pre·pack·aged /,pri:'pækɪdʒd/ priː'pækɪdʒd/, **packed** /,pri:'pækt/ priː'pækt/ *adj* (of products) wrapped, packed, before being supplied to shops, etc where they are to be sold. (指产品)(在送往商店等出售前)预先包装好的.

prep·ara·tion /,prepə'reɪʃn/ ,prɛpə'reʃən/ *n* **1** [U] preparing or being prepared: 准备; 预备: *The meal is in ~.* 饭菜在预备中. *We're getting things together in ~ for the journey.* 我们正在收拾东西准备旅行. *Don't try to do it without ~.* 没准备就不要试着去做. **2** [C] (usu *pl*) things done to get ready for sth: (通常用复数)准备之事务: ~*s for war;* 战备; *make ~s for a voyage.* 做航海之准备. **3** [U] (school abbr *prep*) homework. (口略作 prep) 课外作业. **4** [C] kind of medicine, food, etc specially prepared: (特别调制的)药剂,食物等;配制品: *pharmaceutical ~s.* 药剂.

pre·para·tory /prɪ'pærətrɪ US: -tɔːrɪ/ prɪ'pærə,tɔrɪ/ *adj* introductory; needed for preparing: 初步的;

备的;准备上需要的: ~ *measures/training.* 初步的措施(训练). ~ *to,* in readiness for; before. 作为…之准备; 在…之先. '~ **school,** (esp in England) private school where pupils are prepared for entry to a higher school (esp a public school); (US) (usu private) school where pupils are prepared for college. (英国之)预备学校;预科(尤指使学生准备升入公立学校的私立学校);(美)预科(通常为私立).

pre·pare /prɪ'peə(r)/ prɪ'pɛr/ *vt, vi* **1** [VP6A, 7A, 14, 3A] ~ *(for),* get or make ready: 预备;准备: ~ *a meal/one's lessons/a sermon;* 预备饭(功课,讲道); ~ *pupils for an examination,* coach them; 指导学生准备考试; ~ *for an attack,* get ready to repel an attack; 准备应付攻击; ~ *to attack,* get ready to make an attack; 准备攻击; *be ~d for anything to happen.* 准备好对付任何可能发生的事件. **2** *be ~d to,* be able and willing to: 有能力而且愿意: *We are ~d to supply the goods you ask for.* 我们能够而且愿意供应你要的货物. ~**d·ness** /prɪ'peədnɪs/ prɪ'pɛrdnɪs/ *n* [U] being ~d: 预备; 准备: *Everything was in a state of ~dness.* 一切都准备好了.

pre·pay /,pri:'peɪ/ priː'pe/ *vt (pt, pp -paid* /-'peɪd/ -'ped/) [VP6A] pay in advance: 预付;先付: *send a telegram with reply prepaid.* 发一电报并预付回电费用.

pre·pon·der·ant /prɪ'pɒndərənt/ prɪ'pɑndərənt/ *adj* (formal) greater in weight, number, strength, etc. (正式用语)(在重量,数量,力量等上)占优势的. ~**·ly** *adv* **pre·pon·der·ance** /-əns; -əns/ *n*

pre·pon·der·ate /prɪ'pɒndəreɪt/ prɪ'pɑndə,ret/ *vi* [VP2A, C] (formal) be greater in weight, number, strength, influence, etc: (正式用语)(在重量, 数量, 力量, 影响等上)超过; 胜过; 压倒: *reasons that ~ over other considerations.* 需要优先考虑的理由.

prep·osi·tion /,prepə'zɪʃn/ ,prɛpə'zɪʃən/ *n* word or group of words (eg *in, from, to, out of, on behalf of*) often placed before a *n* or *pron* to indicate place, direction, source, method, etc. 介词; 前置词(置于名词或代词之前,以表示位置,方向,来源,方法等,如 in, from, to, out of, on behalf of). ~**al** /-ʃənl/ -ʃənl/ *adj* of, containing, a ~. 介词的;含有介词的. ~**al phrase,** (a) phrase made up of a group of words used as a ~, (用作介词的)介词短语, eg 如 *in front of, on top of.* (b) ~ + the *n* or *phrase* following it, (用作形容词或副词之)介词短语, eg 如 *in the night, on the beach.*

pre·pos·sess /,pri:pə'zes/ ,priːpə'zɛs/ *vt* [VP6A, 15A] (formal) give (a person) a feeling (about sth), usu favourable; fill (a person *with* or *by* an idea, a feeling): (正式用语)使有好感;使(某人)充满(某种思想,感情): *I was ~ed by his appearance and manners,* They made a favourable impression upon me. 他的仪表与举止给我留下了好印象. ~**·ing** *adj* attractive; making a good impression: 吸引人的; 给人良好印象的: *a girl of ~ing appearance.* 仪表动人的女郎. **pre·pos·session** /,pri:pə'zeʃn/ ,priːpə'zɛʃən/ *n* [C] favourable feeling experienced in advance. 预先怀有的好感;偏爱.

pre·pos·ter·ous /prɪ'pɒstərəs/ prɪ'pɑstərəs/ *adj* completely contrary to reason or sense; absurd. 完全与理性或常识相反的;荒谬的;反常的. ~**·ly** *adv*

pre·puce /'pri:pju:s/ 'priːpjus/ *n* (anat) foreskin. (解剖)包皮.

pre·re·cord /,pri:rɪ'kɔ:d/ ,priːrɪ'kɔrd/ *vt* [VP6A] record, eg a radio or TV programme, in advance on tape or discs. 预先录音或录像(如广播或电视节目).

pre·requi·site /,pri:'rekwɪzɪt/ priː'rɛkwəzɪt/ *n, adj* (thing) required as a condition for sth else: 首要的(事物); 必备的(事物); 先决条件: *Three passes at 'A' level are a ~ for university entrance/are ~ for university entrance.* 必须有三个科目达到 A 的标准才能进大学.

pre·roga·tive /prɪ'rɒgətɪv/ prɪ'rɑgətɪv/ *n [C]* special right(s) or privilege(s), esp of a ruler: 特权; (尤指)统治者的特权: *the ~ of pardon,* eg to pardon a

condemned criminal. 赦免(罪犯)权。 **the Royal P~**, (GB) the (theoretical) right of the sovereign to act independently of Parliament. (英)皇室的特权。

pre·sage /ˈpresɪdʒ; ˈprɛsɪdʒ/ n [C] (formal) presentiment; sign looked upon as a warning. (正式用语) 预知；预感；预示；预兆。 □ vt /prɪˈseɪdʒ; prɪˈsedʒ/ [VP6A] foretell; be a sign of: 预言；预示: *The clouds ~ a storm*. 密云为暴风雨的先兆。

pres·by·ter /ˈprezbɪtə(r); ˈprɛzbɪtə/ n elder (person in authority) in some Protestant churches, esp the Presbyterian Church. (若干新教，尤指长老会中的)长老；教会监督人。

Pres·by·terian /ˌprezbɪˈtɪərɪən; ˌprɛzbəˈtɪrɪən/ adj **~ Church**, one governed by elders, all of equal rank (in England, since 1972, united with the Congregational Church to form the United Reformed Church) (⇨ **episcopal**, governed by bishops). 基督教长老会(由长老监督之，在英国自一九七二年起与公理会合并成联合改革教会)(参看 episcopal, 由主教监督之英国国教)。 □ n member of the ~ Church. 长老会教友。 **~ism** /-ɪzəm; -ˌɪzəm/ n the ~ system of church government; the beliefs of ~s. 长老会制；长老会之教义。

pres·by·tery /ˈprezbɪtrɪ US: -terɪ; ˈprɛzbəˌterɪ/ n (pl **-ries**) [C] **1** (in a church) eastern part of the chancel beyond the choir; sanctuary. (教堂中之)祭司席；内殿。 **2** (regional) administrative court of the Presbyterian Church. 长老会之(地区性的)教务评议会。 **3** residence of a Roman Catholic parish priest. 天主教神父的居所。

pre·sci·ent /ˈpresɪənt; ˈprɛʃɪənt/ adj (formal) knowing about, able to see into, the future. (正式用语)预知的；有先见的。 **~·ly** adv **pre·sci·ence** /-əns; -əns/ n

pre·scribe /prɪˈskraɪb; prɪˈskraɪb/ vt, vi **1** [VP6A, 14] **~ sth (for sth)**, advise or order the use of: 劝告或吩咐使用；开(药方): *~d textbooks*, books which pupils are required to use. 指定的教科书。 *The doctor ~d a long rest.* 医生吩咐作长期的休息。 *What do you ~ for this illness?* 你对此病开什么方子呢? **2** [VP6A, 8, 10, 21; 2A, 3A] say, with authority, what course of action is to be followed: 指示所应遵循的行动方针；指挥；规定: *penalties ~d by the law.* 法律规定的惩罚。 *Complete the ~d form.* 填好规定的表格。

pre·script /ˈpriːskrɪpt; ˈpriskrɪpt/ n ordinance; command. 规定；法律；命令。

pre·scrip·tion /prɪˈskrɪpʃn; prɪˈskrɪpʃən/ n [U] act of prescribing; [C] that which is prescribed; (esp) doctor's written order or direction for the making up and use of a medicine; the medicine itself: 吩咐；指定；指示；规定；所规定之事物；(尤指)医生开的处方；处方上的药: *~ charges*, (in GB) charges made under National Health Service requirements for ~s. 处方收费(英国国民保健制度规定之处方统一收费标准)。

pre·scrip·tive /prɪˈskrɪptɪv; prɪˈskrɪptɪv/ adj giving orders or directions; authorized; prescribed by custom: 规定的；指示的；惯例的: *a ~ grammar of the English language*, one telling the reader how he ought to use the language. 说明如何使用英语之语法书。 ⇨ **descriptive**.

pres·ence /ˈprezns; ˈprɛzns/ n [U] **1** being present in a place, etc: 出席；在场: *in the ~ of his friends*, with his friends there. 在他朋友的面前。 *Your ~ is requested at the annual general meeting*, Please be there. 敬请光临一年一度的大会。 *He was calm in the ~ of danger.* 危急当前，他镇定自若。 **~ of mind**, ⇨ **mind**[1](2). **2** bearing; person's way of carrying himself: 仪容；态度: *a man of noble ~.* 仪态高贵的人。

pres·ent[1] /ˈpreznt; ˈprɛznt/ adj **1** being in the place in question: 出席的；在场的: *the Smiths, and other people ~* (= who were ~), the Smiths and other people in the place. 史密斯夫妇以及其他在场的人。 *Were you ~ at the ceremony?* 你参加了典礼吗? **~ company excepted**, (colloq) used to show that one's

remarks do not apply to anyone who is ~. (口)在场的人不算；在座的诸位除外。 ⇨ **absent**[1](1). **2** being discussed or dealt with; now being considered: 在讨论或处理中的；正在考虑中的: *in the ~ case*, this case. 在这件事中；此际；当下。 **3** existing now: 现在的；现存的: *the ~ government.* 现在的政府。现在之政府。 **4** **~ to**, felt, remembered by: 由…所感觉或记忆的: *~ to the mind / imagination.* 记忆犹新(呈现于想像中)。 **5** (archaic) ready at hand: (古)在手边的；应急的；随时的: *'a very ~ help in trouble'.* '在患难中随时的帮助'。 □ n **1 the ~**, the ~ time, the time now passing: 现在；目前: *the past, the ~, and the future;* 过去，现在和未来； (gram) (语法) *the ~ tense.* 现在时。 *We don't need any more at ~.* 我们现在不需要更多的了。 **for the ~**, for the time being, as far as the ~ is concerned: 目前；暂且: *That will be enough for the ~.* 暂且够用。 **2 by these ~s**, (legal) by this document. (法律)根据本文件。

pres·ent[2] /ˈpreznt; ˈprɛznt/ n gift: 礼物；赠品: *'birthday ~s;* 生日礼物； *I'm buying it for a ~* (= as a gift), so please wrap it up nicely. 我买这东西作礼物，请好好地包装。 **make sb a ~ of sth**, give sb sth: 把某物赠送某人: *I'll make you a ~ of my old car.* 我将把我的旧车送给你。

pre·sent[3] /prɪˈzent; prɪˈzent/ vt **1** [VP14, 15A] **sth to sb; ~ sb with sth**, give; offer; put forward; submit: 给；赠；交出；提出；呈递: *~ the village with a bus-shelter / ~ a bus-shelter to the village*: 赠送一座公共汽车候车亭给该村庄； *the clock that was ~ed to me when I retired;* 我退休时赠给我的钟； *~ a petition to the Governor;* 向总督呈递请愿书； *~ a cheque at the bank*, ie for payment; 向银行兑支票； *~ one's compliments / greetings, etc to sb*, (polite phrases). (客套语)恭维(问候)某人。 **2** [VP6A, 14, 15A] **~ sb to sb**, introduce formally. 引见；介绍。 **3** [VP15A] (reflex) appear; attend: (反身式)出现；出席: *~ oneself at a friend's house;* 到朋友家来； *~ oneself for trial / for examination.* 出席受审(参加考试)。 **4** [VP6A] show; reveal: 呈现；显示；显出: *He ~ed a bold front to the world*, showed that he was facing his difficulties, etc bravely. 他勇敢地面对困难来。 *This case ~s some interesting features.* 这事件显出若干有趣的特色。 *A good opportunity has ~ed itself for doing what you suggested.* 照你的建议去做的好机会已经到了。 **5** [VP6A] (of a theatrical manager or company) produce (a play); cause (an actor) to take part in a play: (指戏院经理或剧团)演出(戏剧)；使(演员)参加演出: *The Mermaid Company will ~ 'Hamlet' next week / will ~ Tom Hill as Brutus in 'Julius Caesar'.* 美人鱼剧团将于下周演出'哈姆雷特'(将由汤姆·希尔演出'朱利阿斯·西撒'中的布鲁塔斯)。 **6** [VP14] **~ sth at sb**, aim (a weapon) at him; hold out (a weapon) in position for aiming at him: 以(武器)瞄准；举枪瞄准: *The intruder ~ed a pistol at me.* 闯人者用手枪对准我。 **7** [VP6A] hold (a rifle, etc) vertically in front of the body as a salute, etc. 举(枪等)敬礼。 **P~ arms!** (the order to do this). (口令)举枪敬礼! □ n position of a weapon in a salute: 敬礼时枪的位置: *at the ~*, with the weapon held in a perpendicular position. 枪直举着。

pre·sent·able /prɪˈzentəbl; prɪˈzɛntəbl/ adj fit to appear, be shown, in public: 适于公然出现或展示的: *Is this old suit still ~?* 这套旧衣服还穿得出去吗? *Is the girl he wants to marry ~*, the sort of girl he can introduce to his friends and family? 他要娶的那个女孩能见得人吗(即教养，出身等良好吗)? **pre·sent·ably** /-əblɪ; -əblɪ/ adv

pres·en·ta·tion /ˌprezn̩ˈteɪʃn US: ˌpriːzen-; ˌprɛzn̩ˈteʃən/ n sth presented: 赠送；提出；引见；介绍；出席；呈现；演出；被赠送、提出等之物: *the ~ of a new play;* 新剧的演出； *a ~ copy*, a book given as a present, esp by the author. (尤指作者送的)赠阅本。 *The cheque is payable on ~*, ie at

the bank. 此支票交银行即可兑现。

pre·sen·ti·ment /prɪˈzentɪmənt; prɪˈzentəmənt/ *n* [C] (formal) vague feeling that sth (esp unpleasant or undesirable) is about to happen. (正式用语)预感(尤指感觉坏事即将发生)。

pres·ent·ly /ˈprezntlɪ; ˈprɛzntlɪ/ *adv* 1 soon: 不久; 即刻: *I'll be with you ~.* 我不久就可同你~。2 (US) at the present time: (美)现在: *The Secretary of State is ~ in Africa.* 国务卿目前正在非洲。

pres·er·va·tion /ˌprezəˈveɪʃn; ˌprɛzəˈveʃən/ *n* [U] 1 act of preserving: 保护; 贮藏; 维持; 留存: *the ~ of food/one's health;* 食物的保存(健康的维护); *the ~ of peace;* 和平的维持; *the ~ of wild life.* 保护野生动物。2 condition of sth preserved: 某物被保存的状况: *old paintings in an excellent state of ~.* 保存得很好的古画。

pre·ser·va·tive /prɪˈzɜːvətɪv; prɪˈzɝvətɪv/ *n, adj* (substance) used for preserving: 保护的; 保存的; 防腐的;保护物;防腐剂: *fresh cream free from ~s,* with no substances added to preserve the cream. 未加防腐剂的新鲜奶油。

pre·serve /prɪˈzɜːv; prɪˈzɝv/ *vt* [VP6A, 14] ~ *(from),* 1 keep safe from harm or danger: 保护; 防护: *social activities preserving old people from the loneliness of old age.* 防止老年人寂寞的社交活动。*God ~ us all!* 上帝保佑我们全体! 2 keep from decay, risk of going bad, etc (by pickling, making into jam, etc): (借腌渍、制成果酱等而)保藏; 贮存: ~ *fruit/eggs, etc.* 保藏水果(蛋等)(即制成果酱, 贿成成瓶等)。3 keep from loss; retain (qualities, etc): 使不损失; 维持(品质等): ~ *one's eyesight;* 保护视力; *a well-~d old man,* one who shows few signs of the usual weaknesses of old age. 保养得好的老人。4 care for and protect land, rivers, lakes, etc with the animals, birds and fish, esp to prevent these from being taken by poachers: 禁止渔猎并保护土地, 河, 湖等: *The fishing in this stream is strictly ~d.* 此河严禁捕鱼。5 keep alive (sb's name or memory): 使(某人的名字或名声)流传; 使留存: *Few of his early poems are ~d.* 他早期的诗很少保存下来。 □ *n* 1 (usu *pl*) jam. (通常用复数)果酱: 蜜饯。2 woods, streams, etc where animals, birds and fish are ~d: 渔猎禁地: *a 'game ~.* 禁猎地。*poach on another's ~,* (fig) take a share in activities, interests, etc looked upon as associated especially with sb else. (喻)侵害他人的活动, 利益等的领域。**pre·serv·able** /-əbl; -əbl/ *adj* that can be ~d. 可保护的; 可贮藏的; 可维持的;可保存的。~**r** *n* person or thing that ~s. 保护之人或物;贮藏食品者;禁猎地管理者。

pre·side /prɪˈzaɪd; prɪˈzaɪd/ *vi* [VP2A, C, 3A] ~ *at,* be chairman: 作主席: *The Prime Minister ~s at meetings of the Cabinet.* 首相在内阁会议中当主席。~ *over,* be the head or director of: 主持; 管理: *The city council is ~d over by the mayor.* 市政会议由市长主持。

presi·dency /ˈprezɪdənsɪ; ˈprɛzədənsɪ/ *n* (*pl* **-cies**) 1 **the ~,** the office of president. 总统, 部会首长, 董事长, 总经理, 院长, 校长, 社长, 主席, 会长等的职位。2 term of office as a president: 上述各职位的任期: *during the ~ of Lincoln.* 在林肯当总统的期间。

presi·dent /ˈprezɪdənt; ˈprɛzədənt/ *n* 1 (elected) head of the government in the US and other modern republics. (美国及其他现代共和国民选的)总统。2 head of some government departments (*P~ of the Board of Trade*), of some business companies, colleges, societies, etc. 若干政府机关的首长(如商务部长); 若干商行, 大学, 会社等的首长; 董事长; 院长; 校长; 社长; 会长; 主席。**presi·den·tial** /ˌprezɪˈdenʃl; ˌprɛzəˈdɛnʃəl/ *adj* of a ~ or his duties: 总统的; 首长(等)的; 其职务的: *the ~ial election;* 总统选举; *the ~ial year,* (in US) the year of the ~ial elections. (美国的)总统选举年; 大选年。

pre·sid·ium /prɪˈsɪdɪəm; prɪˈsɪdɪəm/ *n* executive committee of the administration, and of various organisations, in some socialist countries; group of presiding persons. (某些社会主义国家的政府及其各种组织的)常务委员会;主席团。

press[1] /pres; pres/ *n* 1 act of pressing: 压;按;挤;榨;紧握; 拥抱: *a ~ of the hand;* 紧握手; *give sth a light ~.* 轻按某物。2 machine or apparatus for pressing: 压榨机; 压力机; 夹具; (网球拍等的)夹子: *a 'wine-~;* (榨汁机用的)榨葡萄机; *a 'cider-~;* 苹果汁榨取器; *keep one's (tennis) racket in a ~;* 把(网球)球拍放在球拍夹子中; *a hydraulic ~.* 水压机。3 (usu 常作 **the ~**), printed periodicals; newspapers generally; journalists: 定期刊物; 杂志; 报纸(集合称);新闻记者;新闻界: *The book was favourably noticed by the ~/had a good ~,* was favourably reviewed by the literary critics. 这书曾得报章杂志的好评。*There was a ~ campaign against him,* He was attacked in the newspapers. 各报对他发动了一场攻击。*The liberty/freedom of the ~* (= The right of newspapers to report events, express opinions, etc freely) *is a feature of democratic countries.* 出版自由是民主国家的特征。'~**-agent** *n* person employed by a theatre, actor, musician, etc to arrange for publicity in the newspapers. (戏院、演员, 音乐家等雇来设计散播宣传的)宣传员; 公共关系人员。Hence, 由此产生, '~**-agency** *n* '~**-box** *n* place reserved for reporters at a football or cricket match, etc. (足球或板球比赛等的)新闻记者席。'~ **conference** *n* one of newspaper reporters, convened by a minister, government official, etc who talks about policy, achievements, etc. 记者招待会。'~**-cutting /-clipping** *nn* paragraph, article, etc cut out from a newspaper or other periodical. 从报纸杂志剪下的资料; 剪报。'~**-gallery** *n* gallery reserved for reporters, esp in the House of Commons. (尤指英国下议院的)新闻记者席。'~**-lord** *n* powerful newspaper proprietor. 报业巨子。'~**-photographer** *n* newspaper photographer. 摄影记者。4 business for printing (and sometimes publishing) books or periodicals: 印刷业; 出版业; 出版社: *Oxford University P~;* 牛津大学出版社; (also 亦作 '**printing-~**) machine for printing: 印刷机: *in the ~,* being printed; 印刷中; *send a manuscript to the ~,* send it to be printed; 把原稿付印; *go to ~,* start printing; 付印;开始印刷; *correct the ~,* correct errors in printing, be a proof-reader. 校对印刷稿。5 crowd: 群众; 人丛: *lost in the ~;* 在人群中走失; *fight one's way through the ~.* 拼命挤过人丛。6 pressure: 紧迫; 压力: *the ~ of modern life;* 现代生活的压力; *because of the ~ of business.* 由于事忙(事情之急待处理)。7 cupboard with shelves for clothes, books, etc usu in a recess in a wall. (放衣服、书籍等之)橱(通常为嵌入墙壁的凹处者)。'~**-mark** *n* mark or number in a book showing its place in a library shelf. (书本上表示其在图书馆位置的)书架号码。8 ~ *of sail/canvas,* (naut) as much sail as the wind will allow. (航海)吃满风的帆;满帆。

press[2] /pres; pres/ *vt, vi* 1 [VP6A, 15B] push steadily against: 压;按;扣: ~ *the trigger of a gun;* 扣枪的扳机; ~ *(down) the accelerator pedal* (of a car); 踩(下)(汽车的)加速器踏板; ~ *the button,* eg of an electric bell. 按钮(如按电铃)。'~**-up** *n* (*pl* ~**-ups**) exercise in which one stretches out face down on the floor, the arms being straightened and bent by ~ing against the floor with the palms of one's hands to raise and lower one's body. 伏地挺身(运动)。'~**-stud** = snap(5). 2 [VP6A, 15B, 22] use force or weight to get sth smooth or flat, to get sth into a smaller, space, to get juice out of fruit, etc: 压平; 熨平; 塞进较小的空间; 压榨; 榨出果汁(等): ~ *a suit/skirt, etc,* with an iron, to remove creases, etc; (用熨斗)熨平一套衣服(一条裙子等); ~ *grapes,* when making wine; (制酒时)压榨葡萄; ~ *the juice out of an orange;* 挤出橘子汁; ~*ed beef,* beef that has been boiled and pressed into shape for packing in tin boxes. (煮熟并压成某形状以便装罐的)罐头牛肉; 牛肉干。3 [VP6A, 15A, B] keep close to and attack; bear heavily on: 接近而攻击;进逼:

~ *the enemy hard*, attack with determination; 进逼敌人; 果敢袭击敌人; ~ *(home) an attack*, carry it out with determination; 强袭; 紧攻; ~ *a point* (in an argument, debate) *home*, (fig) obtain support, agreement, etc by a determined, articulate, speech; (喻)(在辩论中)因坚决清晰的言辞而获得支持或赞成; *be hard ~ed*, be under determined attack. 被猛攻; 被逼表。 **4** ~ *for*, make repeated requests for; demand urgently: 反复请求; 紧急要求: ~ *for an inquiry into a question.* 反复要求调查某一问题。 **5** *be ~ed for*, have barely enough of: 缺少; 缺乏: ~*ed for time/money/space.* 缺少足够的时间(金钱, 空间)。 **6** [VP2C] push, crowd, with weight or force: 用力推; 推进; 拥挤: *crowds ~ing against the barriers/~ing round the royal visitors.* 向栅栏推挤(拥挤在王室宾客周围)的群众。 **7** [VP3A, 4A, 14, 17] ~ *(sb) for sth*; ~ *(sb) to do sth*, urge; insist on: 敦促; 催促; 力劝; 坚持: ~ *(sb) for an answer*, 敦促(某人)作答; ~ *sb for a debt/to pay a debt.* 催促某人还债。 *He did not need much ~ing.* 他并不需要多加催逼。 *They are ~ing for a decision to be made.* 他们坚持要作一决定。 ~ *sth on/upon sb*, insist that sb takes it: 坚持要某人接受某事物: *He ~ed the money on me*, insisted on my accepting it. 他坚持要我接受那笔钱。 *Don't ~ your opinions upon her*, Don't insist that she should accept them. 不要逼她接受你的意见。 **8** [VP2A] demand action or attention: 急迫; 需要行动或注意: *The matter is ~ing*, is urgent. 事情紧急。 **9** *Time ~es*, There is no time to lose. 时间紧迫。 **10** [VP6A, 15A] squeeze (sb's hand, arm, etc) as a sign of affection or sympathy; draw (sb) to oneself in an embrace: 紧握(某人之手、臂等, 表示关切或同情); 拥抱: *He ~ed her to his side.* 他把她拥向身边。 **11** [VP2C] ~ *(down) on/upon sb*, weigh; oppress: 使负重担; 压迫: *His responsibilities ~ heavily upon him.* 他的责任沉重地压在他身上。 *The new taxes ~ed down heavily on the people.* 新税使人民不胜负荷。 **12** [VP2C] ~ *on/forward (with sth)*, hurry, continue in a determined way: 加紧; 奋勇继续进行: ~ *on with one's work.* 加紧自己的工作。 *It was getting dark, so the travellers ~ed forward.* 天快黑了, 因此旅客们尽快赶路。 ~*ing n* one of many identical gramophone records made from the same matrix: 同一模型做出来的许多唱片之一; 唱片: *make and sell 10,000 ~ings of a symphony.* 制造并销售一万张某交响乐的唱片。 □ *adj* **1** urgent; requiring immediate attention: 紧急的; 急迫的; 需要立刻处理的: ~*ing business.* 急事。 **2** (of persons, their requests, etc) insistent: (指人, 其要求等)坚持的; 执拗的: *a ~ing invitation*; 恳切的邀请: *as you are so ~ing.* 你既然这样坚持。 ~*ing·ly adv*

press³ /pres; pres/ *vt* [VP15A] **1** (hist) force (a man) to serve in the navy or army. (史)强迫(人)服从役。 '~*gang n* (hist) body of men employed to ~ men. (史)兵士强募队(强拉他人服役之)拉伕队。 **2** take (sth) for public use; requisition. 征用(某物); 征发。 ~ *into service*, make use of because of urgent need: 因急需而使用: *Even my thirty-year-old car was ~ed into service to take voters to the polling-station.* 甚至我那那三十年的老爷车也用来载送选民前往投票所。

press·ure /'preʃə(r); 'preʃɚ/ *n* [C, U] **1** pressing; (the amount of) force exerted continuously on or against sth by sth which touches it: 压; 压力; 施诸某物的压力之量: *a ~ of 6 lb to the square inch*; 每平方英寸上的六磅的压力; *see that the tyre ~ is right*; 注意要使轮胎的压力正常; *atmospheric ~/the ~ of the atmosphere*, the ~ of weight of air, as measured by a barometer. 大气的压力(如气压计所测量者)。 '**blood·~** *n* tension of the blood-vessels. 血压。 '~ *cabin n* cabin (in an aircraft) that is pressurized. (飞机上的)压力舱。 '~*cooker n* airtight container for cooking quickly with steam under ~. 快锅;压力锅(利用蒸气在其压力下快速烹煮的紧密的容器)。 '~*gauge n* apparatus or device for measuring the ~ of a liquid or gas at

a given point. (测量液体或气体在某一点上压力的)压力计。 **2** compelling force or influence: 强制力; 影响力: *He pleaded ~ of work/family ~s and resigned his place on the committee.* 他以工作繁重(家庭负担)为由而辞掉在委员会的职位。 *be/come under ~*, feel/be caused to feel strongly compelled (to act): 受到压力;在压力之下: *He's under strong ~ to vote with the government on this issue.* 他受到强大的压力而投票赞成政府的这项主张。 *He always works best under ~*, when he has to. 他总是在迫不得已时工作成绩才最好。 *bring ~ to bear on sb (to do sth)*; *put ~ on sb/put sb under ~ (to do sth)*, use force or influence on sb. 压迫某人; 对某人施压力。 '~ *group*, organized group, eg an association of manufacturers such as brewers, farmers, which tries to exert influence or lobby for the benefit of its members. 压力集团(为其会员谋取福利的集团, 如造酒公会、农会)。 **3** sth that oppresses or weighs down: 压迫物; 困苦; 艰难; 重荷: *the ~ of taxation*; 税的重负; *under the ~ of poverty/necessity.* 在贫困(需要)的压迫下。 **4** *(at) high ~*, (with) great energy and speed: 拼命(地);很有冲劲(的): *work at high ~*; 拼命地工作; *a high-~ salesman.* 很有冲劲的推销员。 □ *vt* = **pressurize**.

press·ur·ize /'preʃəraɪz; 'preʃɚ,raɪz/ *vt* **1** [VP6A] apply pressure to. 加压力于。 **2** [VP6A, 14, 17] ~ *sb (into doing sth/to do sth)*, use force (of persuasion, influence, etc) to make him do it: 迫使某人(做某事): ~ *the President into resigning/to resign.* 迫使总统辞职。 **3** (usu *pp*) (of an aircraft, a submarine, etc) construct so that the internal air pressure can be controlled and kept normal: (通常用过去分词)使(飞机、潜艇等之内部)增压: *a ~d cabin.* 增压舱。

presti·digi·ta·tor /,prestɪ'dɪdʒɪteɪtə(r); ,prestɪ'dɪdʒɪ,tetɚ/ *n* juggler; conjuror. 变戏法者; 演幻术者。 **pres·ti·digi·ta·tion** /,prestɪ,dɪdʒɪ'teɪʃn; ,prestɪ,dɪdʒɪ'teʃən/ *n*

pres·tige /pre'stiːʒ; 'prestɪdʒ/ *n* [U] **1** respect that results from the good reputation (of a person, nation, etc); power or influence coming from this: (指人、国家等的)声望; 威望; 威力: *behaviour that would mean loss of ~.* 可能会降低声望的行为。 **2** distinction, glamour, that comes from achievements, success, possessions, etc: (由于成就、成功、财富等而产生的)显赫; 魅力; 烜赫: (attrib) (用作定语) *the ~ value of living in a fashionable district/of owning a Rolls-Royce.* 居住于高级住宅区(拥有劳斯莱斯汽车)之显赫价值。 **pres·tig·ious** /pre'stɪdʒəs; pres'tɪdʒɪəs/ *adj* bringing ~. 带来声望的; 有声望的。

pres·tis·simo /pre'stɪsɪməʊ; pres'tɪsə,mo/ *adj, adv* (I; music) very quickly; as quickly as possible. (意; 音乐)极快的(地); 尽快地。

presto /'prestəʊ; 'presto/ *adj, adv* (I; music) quickly. (意; 音乐)急速的; 急速地。 *Hey ~!* words used by a conjuror when performing a trick. 快, 快! 变!(变戏法时用语)。

pre·stressed /,priː'strest; priː'strest/ *adj* (of concrete) strengthened by having stretched cables inserted. (指凝土)预力的; 借嵌入拉紧的钢筋以加固。

pre·sum·able /prɪ'zjuːməbl US: -'zuː-; prɪ'zjuməbl/ *adj* that may be presumed. 可假定的; 可能的。 **pre·sum·ably** /-əblɪ; -əblɪ/ *adv*

pre·sume /prɪ'zjuːm US: -'zuːm; prɪ'zjum/ *vt, vi* **1** [VP6A, 9, 25] take for granted; suppose (to be true): 以为; 认定; 推测; 假定(为真实): *In Britain an accused man is ~d (to be) innocent until he is proved guilty.* 在英国被告在未证实有罪以前, 仍被认作是无辜的。 *Let us ~ that … Dr Livingstone, I ~.* 我想, 你是利文斯通博士。 **2** [VP7A] venture; take the liberty: 敢于; 擅敢; 冒昧: *I won't ~ to disturb you.* 我不敢打扰你。 *May I ~ to advise you?* 我可以冒你进一言吗? **3** [VP3A] ~ *upon sth*, (formal) make a wrong use of, take an unfair advantage of: (正式用语)

错用；不当地利用: ~ *upon sb's good nature*, take advantage of it by asking for help, etc; 利用某人性情好(而要求帮助等); ~ *upon a short acquaintance*, treat sb familiarly even though one has known him for only a short time. 凭着一面之交就和人亲热起来。 **pre·sum·ing** *adj* having, showing, a tendency to ~, to take liberties. 冒昧的；不客气的；僭越的。

pre·sump·tion /prɪˈzʌmpʃn; prɪˈzʌmpʃən/ *n* 1 [C] sth presumed(1); sth which seems likely although there is no proof: 被认定之理由；假定之理由；推测；假定；推定: *on the false ~ that the firm was bankrupt;* 基于该公司破产之谬误的推测; *the ~ that he was drowned.* 他被淹死的假定。 2 [U] arrogance; behaviour that is too bold: 傲慢；僭越；过于大胆的行为；冒昧: *If you will excuse my ~, I should like to contradict what you have just said.* 请恕我冒昧，我要反驳你刚才说的话。

pre·sump·tive /prɪˈzʌmptɪv; prɪˈzʌmptɪv/ *adj* based on presumption(1): 基于推测的；假定的；推定的: ~ *evidence;* 推定的证据; *the ~ heir/the heir ~,* person who is heir (to the throne, etc) until sb with a stronger claim is born. (王位等之)推定继承人(在更具有继承权的人诞生以前的继承者)。 ~·**ly** *adv*

pre·sump·tu·ous /prɪˈzʌmptʃʊəs; prɪˈzʌmptʃʊəs/ *adj* (formal) (of behaviour, etc) too bold or self-confident. (正式用语)(指行为等)胆大妄为的；僭越的；夸大的；专擅的。 ~·**ly** *adv*

pre·sup·pose /ˌpriːsəˈpəʊz; ˌprisəˈpoz/ *vt* [VP6A, 9] 1 assume beforehand. 预想；预先假定；事先推测。 2 imply; require as a condition: 含示；以…为先决条件: *Sound sleep ~s a mind at ease.* 心情舒畅才能酣睡。 **pre·sup·po·si·tion** /ˌpriːsʌpəˈzɪʃn; ˌprisʌpəˈzɪʃən/ *n* [C] sth ~d; [U] presupposing. 预想之事；预先假定之事；先决条件；推测；含示。

pre·tence (US = -**tense**) /prɪˈtens; prɪˈtens/ *n* 1 [U] pretending; make-believe: 虚假；伪装；掩饰: *do sth under the ~ of friendship/religion/patriotism.* 以友谊(宗教,爱国)为掩饰而做某事。 *It's all ~.* 那全是虚假。 2 [C] pretext or excuse; false claim or reason: 借口；托辞；口实；伪称: *He calls for the night porter on the slightest ~.* 他有一点点借口就把夜班侍者召来。 *It is only a ~, of friendship.* 那不过是以友谊为口实罢了。 *false ~s,* (legal) acts intended to deceive: (法律)诈欺: *obtain money by/on/under false ~s.* 借诈骗敛钱。 3 [C] claim (to merit, etc); [U] ostentation: 自称(有优点,功绩等)；夸耀；虚饰: *a man without ~.* 实事求是的人。

pre·tend /prɪˈtend; prɪˈtend/ *vt, vi* 1 [VP7A, 9] make oneself appear (to be sth, to be doing sth), either in play or to deceive others: 伪装；伪装(为某身份,正做某事,或出于嬉戏,或欲欺骗他人): ~ *to be asleep;* 假装睡着; *boys ~ing that they are pirates.* 伴装海盗的男孩们。 *Let's ~ we are cow-boys.* 我们假装牛仔好吧。 *They ~ed not to see us.* 他们伴装没看见我们。 2 [VP6A] say falsely that one has (as an excuse or reason, or to avoid danger, difficulty, etc): (作为借口或理由, 或想避免危险、困难等而)伪称；伴称有: ~ *sickness.* 伴称有病。 *He ~ed ignorance, hoping to avoid being fined for breaking the law.* 他伴装不知情以避免违法罚锾。 3 [VP3A] ~ *to,* put forward a claim to: 自称；自认；觊觎；争: *There are not many persons who ~ to an exact knowledge of the subject.* 自认对那题目有透彻了解的人不多。 *Surely he does not ~ to intelligence!* 当然他不会自以为聪明！ *The young man ~ed to the throne,* claimed it(falsely). 那青年觊觎王位。~·**ed·ly** *adv* ~**er** *n* person whose claim (to a throne, a title, etc) is disputed. 觊觎(王位、爵位、名份等)者；伴称者；伪称者。

pre·tense /prɪˈtens; prɪˈtens/ *n* **pretence**.

pre·ten·sion /prɪˈtenʃn; prɪˈtenʃən/ *n* 1 [C] (often *pl*) (statement of a) claim: (常用复数)要求；主张；权利: *He makes no ~ to expert knowledge of the subject.* 他不自诩对那问题具有专家的学识。 *Has he any ~s to being considered a scholar?* 他有被认为是学者的资格吗？ *She*

has some social ~s, claims some place in high society. 她自称在上流社会颇有地位。 2 [U] being pretentious. 自负；骄傲。

pre·ten·tious /prɪˈtenʃəs; prɪˈtenʃəs/ *adj* claiming (without justification) great merit or importance: (无正当理由)自命不凡的；自负的；骄傲的: *a ~ author/book/speech;* 自夸的作者(书,演说); *use ~ language.* 使用骄傲的言词。 ~·**ly** *adv* ~·**ness** *n*

pret·er·ite (also -**erit**) /ˈpretərɪt; ˈpretərɪt/ *n, adj* ~ (tense), (gram) (tense) expressing a past action or state. (语法)过去的；过去式；过去时态。

pre·ter·natu·ral /ˌpriːtəˈnætʃrəl; ˌpritəˈnætʃərəl/ *adj* out of the regular course of things; not normal or usual. 越出事物之常轨的；异常的；奇特的；不可思议的。 ~·**ly** *adv*: ~*ly solemn.* 异常肃穆的。

pre·text /ˈpriːtekst; ˈpritekst/ *n* [C] false reason (for an action, etc): (行动等的)借口；托辞: *On/Under the ~ of asking for my advice, he called and borrowed £10 from me.* 以向我讨教为借口,他来我处借去十英镑。 *Can we find a ~ for refusal/refusing the invitation?* 我们能找到拒绝(不接受邀请)的托辞吗？

pre·tor /ˈpriːtə(r); ˈpritɔ/ *n* ⇨ **praetor**.

pret·tify /ˈprɪtɪfaɪ; ˈprɪtɪˌfaɪ/ *vt* (*pt, pp* -**fied**) [VP 6A] make pretty, esp in an insipid way. 使美；美化；(尤指)平淡无奇地装饰。

pretty /ˈprɪtɪ; ˈprɪtɪ/ *adj* (-**ier, -iest**) 1 pleasing and attractive without being beautiful or magnificent: 悦人的；可爱的；漂亮的；精致的(非华丽或堂皇的): *a ~ girl/garden/picture/piece of music.* 漂亮的女郎(漂亮的花园；美丽的图画；优美的乐曲)。 '~-~ *adj* (colloq) superficially ~ or charming. (口)装饰过分的；打扮得俗气的；娇揉造作的。 2 fine; good: 好的；优良的: *a ~ wit.* 一个有才气的人。 (ironic) (反语) *A ~ mess you've made of it!* 你把它弄得多糟糕？ 3 (colloq) considerable in amount or extent. (口)相当多的；相当大的。 *a ~ penny,* quite a lot: 很多钱；相当多的钱: *It will cost you a ~ penny.* 它会花费你不少钱。 *come to/reach a ~ pass,* reach a difficult position. 陷入困境。 *a ~ kettle of fish,* ⇨ **fish**[1](1). □ *adv* fairly, moderately: 相当地；颇: *The situation seems ~ hopeless.* 这情况似乎没有多大希望了。 *It's ~ cold outdoors today.* 今天户外颇冷。 ~ *much,* very nearly: 几乎；差不多: *The result of the ballot is ~ much what we expected.* 投票的结果和我们预料的差不多。 ~ *nearly,* almost. 几乎；差不多: *The car is new, or ~ nearly so,* almost new. 这汽车是新的,或近乎新的。 ~ *well,* almost: 几乎: *We've ~ well finished the work.* 我们已经差不多完成这工作。 *sitting ~,* (colloq) well off; favourably placed for future developments, etc. (口)小康; 所处地位有利于未来发展等。 □ *n* (*pl* -**ties**) *my ~, my ~* one (used of a child). 我的好孩子。 **pret·tily** /ˈprɪtɪlɪ; ˈprɪtlɪ/ *adv* in a ~ or charming way. 悦人地；可爱地。 **pret·ti·ness** *n*

pret·zel /ˈpretsl; ˈpretsl/ *n* (G) crisp, salt-flavoured biscuit, made in the shape of a knot or stick. (德)松脆的椒盐饼干(做成组结状或棒状)。

pre·vail /prɪˈveɪl; prɪˈvel/ *vi* 1 [VP2A, 3A] ~ (*over/against*), gain victory (over); fight successfully (against): 获胜; 战胜: *Truth will ~.* 真理将获胜。 *We ~ed over our enemies.* 我们胜过敌人。 2 [VP2A] be widespread; be generally seen, done, etc: 盛行；流行: *the conditions now ~ing in Africa.* 非洲目前普遍的状况。 *The use of opium still ~s in the south.* 吸鸦片在南方仍甚盛行。 3 [VP3A] ~ *on/upon sb to do sth,* persuade: 劝导: ~ *upon a friend to lend you £10.* 劝朋友借给你十英镑钱。 ~·**ing** *adj* most frequent or usual: 最常有的；最普通的: *the ~ing winds/fashions in dress.* 最常刮的风(流行的服式)。

preva·lent /ˈprevələnt; ˈprevələnt/ *adj* (formal) common, seen or done everywhere at the time in question: (正式用语)在谈论之时)普遍的；流行的: *the ~ fashions;* 流行的服装式样; *the ~ opinion on the*

proposed reforms. 对于提议中的改革一般意见。*Is malaria still ~ in that country?* 疟疾在那个国家仍然流行吗? **preva·lence** /-əns; -əns/ *n* [U] being ~: 普遍; 流行: *I'm shocked at the prevalence of bribery among these officials.* 这些官员普遍的受贿使我深感惊愕。

pre·vari·cate /prɪ'værɪkeɪt; prɪ'værə,ket/ *vi* [VP 2A] (formal) make untrue or partly untrue statements; try to evade telling the (whole) truth. (正式用语)作不实或部分不实之言; 支吾; 搪塞。 **pre·vari·ca·tion** /prɪ,værɪ'keɪʃn; ,prɪværə'keʃən/ *n* [U] prevaricating; [C] instance of this. 支吾; 搪塞; 其实例。

pre·vent /prɪ'vent; prɪ'vɛnt/ *vt* 1 [VP6A, 14, 19C] ~ *sb (from doing sth);* ~ *sth (from happening),* stop or hinder: 阻止; 妨碍; 预防: ~ *a disease from spreading.* 防止一疾病蔓延。 *Who can ~ us from getting married /* ~ *our getting married now that you are of age?* 既然你已成年, 谁能阻止我们结婚呢? *Your prompt action* ~*ed a serious accident.* 你及时的行动防止了一次严重的事故。 **2** (old use) go before as a guide: (旧用法) 前行而引导; 带领: '*P~ us, O Lord, in all our doings.*' '主啊, 求您带领我们的所做所为。' ~·**able** /-əbl; -əbl/ *adj* that can be ~ed. 可阻止的; 能防止的。

pre·ven·ta·tive /prɪ'ventətɪv; prɪ'vɛntətɪv/ *adj,* *n* = **preventive.**

pre·ven·tion /prɪ'venʃn; prɪ'vɛnʃən/ *n* [U] act of preventing: 阻止; 妨碍; 预防: *the Society for the P~ of Cruelty to Animals.* 防止虐待动物协会。 *P~ is better than cure.* 预防胜于治疗。

pre·ven·tive /prɪ'ventɪv; prɪ'vɛntɪv/ *adj* serving or designed to prevent; precautionary. 阻止性的; 预防的。 ~ **custody,** imprisonment of sb considered unlikely to be reformed, so that he may not commit further crimes. 防范性的监禁(施于被认为无法改过之罪犯, 以防止其再犯罪)。 ~ **detention,** detention without trial because a person is thought likely to commit crime or (in some countries) oppose the government. 预防羁押(未经审判而拘留以防止其犯罪或(在某些国家)反抗政府)。 ~ **medicine,** research into means of warding off disease, illness, eg hygiene, working

conditions. 预防医学。 □ *n* sth (eg medicine) to prevent or ward off sth. 预防物; 预防剂; 预防药。

pre·view /'priːvjuː; 'priˌvju/ *n* [C] view of a film, play, etc before it is shown to the general public. (电影之)预映; 试映; (戏剧等之)预演; 试演。 □ *vt* have/give a ~ of. 预映; 预演。

pre·vi·ous /'priːvɪəs; 'priviəs/ *adj* **1** coming earlier in time or order: (时间或顺序上) 在前的; 早先的: *on a ~ occasion;* 在早先的一个场合; ~ *convictions,* convictions for earlier offences, taken into account by a judge when passing sentence upon sb convicted of a further offence. 先前的判罪; 前科(法官对某人再犯罪时作为量刑的参考)。 *I regret that a ~ engagement prevents me from accepting your kind invitation.* 我有约在先, 故不能接受你好意的邀请, 实在很遗憾。 **2** too hasty: 过急的; 太快的: *Aren't you rather ~ in supposing that I will marry you?* 你以为我会嫁给你, 那不是言之过早吗? **3** ~ *to,* before. 在…以前。 ~·**ly** *adv*

pre·vi·sion /,prɪ'vɪʒn; priˈvɪʒən/ *n* [U] foresight; [C] instance of this: 预见; 预知; 其实例: *have a ~ of danger.* 预知危险。

prey /preɪ; pre/ *n* (*sing* only) animal, bird, etc hunted for food: (仅用单数) 被捕食之动物(兽、禽等): *The eagle was devouring its ~.* 鹰在吞食捕获物。 **be/fall a ~ to,** (a) be seized, caught by: 被…捕获; 被…捕食: *The zebra fell a ~ to the lion.* 那斑马被狮子所捕食。 **(b)** be greatly troubled by: 深为…所苦; 深为…所折磨: *be a ~ to anxiety and fears.* 深为忧虑和恐惧所折磨。 ,**beast/bird of '~,** one that kills and eats others, eg tigers, eagles. 食肉兽(鸟); 猛兽(禽)(如虎、鹰)。 □ *vi* [VP3A] ~ **on/upon, 1** take, hunt, as ~(1): 捕食; 攫食: *hawks ~ing on small birds.* 捕食小鸟的老鹰。 **2** steal from; plunder: 掠夺; 劫掠: *Our coasts were* ~*ed upon by Viking pirates.* 我们的海岸曾被威金族的海盗劫掠。 **3** (of fears, etc) trouble greatly: (指恐惧等)使苦恼: *anxieties/losses that ~ upon my mind.* 使我心中苦恼的忧虑(损失)。

price /praɪs; praɪs/ *n* **1** [C] sum of money for which sth is (to be) sold or bought; that which must be done,

birds of prey

given or experienced to obtain or keep sth: 价格; 价钱; 代价: *What ~ are you asking?* 你要价多少? *P~s are rising/falling/going up/going down.* 物价正上涨(下跌). *I won't buy it at that ~.* 我不会以那价钱买它的. *He sold the house at a good ~.* 他以高价卖了那房子。 *Loss of independence was a high ~ to pay for peace.* 丧失独立来换取和平是一项重大的代价。 **at a ~,** at a fairly high price: 以高价: *There's fresh asparagus in the shops—at a ~!* 店里有新鲜的芦笋, 价钱很贵呢! **Every man has his ~,** can be bribed. 人人都可能受到利诱。 **put a '~ on sb's head,** offer a reward for his capture (dead or alive). 悬赏缉拿某人(无论死活)。 **'asking ~,** (for a house, etc) price stated by the vendor: 开价; 初价: *accept an offer of £200 below the asking ~.* 接受低于初价二百英镑的交易。 **'~-control** n control or fixing of ~s by authorities, manufacturers, etc. (由当局、厂商等所定的)物价管制; 定价。 Hence, 由此产生, **'~-controlled** adj. 限价的。 **'~-list** n list of current ~s of goods for sale. 定价表; 价目表。 **'list-** n ~ recommended by the manufacturer, etc but not always compulsory. 厂商等提供之价格; 报价; 定价。 **2** [U] value; worth: 价值: *a pearl of great ~.* 极贵重的珍珠。 **beyond/above/without ~,** so valuable that buying is impossible. 非任何价钱所能购买的; 无价的; 极贵重的。 **3** [C] (betting) odds. (赌博)赌注与赢款的差额。 **What ~ ...?** (sl) (俚) **(a)** What is the chance of ...? …的胜算如何? …的机会如何? **(b)** (used to sneer at the failure of sth): (用以嘲笑某事物的失败): *What ~ peace now?* 和平现在有什么用? **'starting ~,** odds offered by bookmakers as the race is about to start. 赛马将开始时赌业者所开出的赔钱的价码。 □ vt 1 [VP6A] fix, ask about, the ~ of sth; mark (goods) with a ~: 定…之价; 问…之价; 以价格标明(货物): *All our goods are clearly ~d.* 我们所有的货品都标明了价格。 **2 ~ oneself/one's goods out of the market,** (of manufacturers, producers) fix ~s so high that sales decline or stop. (指厂商、制造者)定价过高以致销路减少或停顿。 **~·y** /'praisi, 'praisi/ adj (sl) expensive. (俚)贵的; 昂贵的。 **~·less** adj 1 too valuable to be ~. 无价的; 极贵重的。**2** (sl) absurd: (俚)荒谬的: *a ~less old fellow;* 不象话的老家伙; very amusing: 非常有趣的: *a ~less joke.* 极有趣的笑话。

prick¹ /prik; prik/ n 1 small mark or hole caused by the act of pricking: (穿刺之)小洞; 刺痕: *~s made by a needle.* 以针穿刺的小孔。**2** pain caused by pricking: 刺痛; 扎痛: *I can still feel the ~.* 我仍能感到那刺痛。*He feels the ~ of conscience/remorse,* mental uneasiness. 他感到良心不安。**'pin-~,** (fig) sth small that irritates. (喻)小刺激; 小烦恼。**3** (old use) goad for oxen. (旧用法) 驱牛之刺棒。**kick against the ~s,** (fig) hurt oneself by useless resistance. (喻)作无谓之抵抗徒使自己受到损害; 螳臂挡车。**4** △ (vulg) penis; (vulg) term of abuse: (诽)(鄙)阳物; 阴茎; 辱骂人的话: *He's a stupid ~!* 他是个蠢货!

prick² /prik; prik/ vt, vi 1 [VP6A] make a hole or a mark in (sth) with a sharp point: 以尖物在(某物)上刺洞或作记号; 穿; 刺: *~ a toy balloon;* 在玩具气球上刺洞; *~ a blister,* on the skin; 穿刺(皮肤上的)水泡; *~ holes in paper.* 在纸上穿洞。**2** [VP6A] hurt, cause pain to, with a sharp point or points: 以尖物刺伤; 刺痛: *~ one's finger with/on a needle.* 用针刺伤手指。 *The thorns on these roses ~ed my fingers.* 这些玫瑰上的刺刺痛了我的手指。(fig) (喻) *His conscience ~ed him.* 他的良心使他不安。**3** [VP2A] feel sharp pain: 感到剧痛: *My fingers are ~ing.* 我的手指感到刺痛。**4** [VP15B] **~ sth out/off,** put (seedlings) in the earth (in holes made with a pointed stick, etc): 移植(幼苗)(于以尖棒等所挖的地洞中): *~ out young cabbage plants.* 移植甘蓝菜的幼苗。**5** [VP15B] **~ up one's ears,** (of dogs, horses) raise the ears; (fig, of persons) pay sharp attention to sth being said. (尤指犬、马)竖起耳朵; (喻, 指人)竖耳静听。**~·er** n person who, thing

which, ~s; instrument for piercing holes, eg a bradawl. 刺者(人或物); 刺洞之用具(如打眼钻)。**~·ing** n act of ~ing; ~ing sensation. 刺; 刺伤; 刺痛。

prickle /'prikl; 'prikl/ n [C] (usu small) pointed growth on the stem, etc of a plant, or on the skin of some animals, eg hedgehogs; thorn. (植物之茎等上, 或猬等动物之皮上的)尖刺; 小刺; 荆棘。□ vt, vi give or have a pricking sensation. 刺痛; 感觉刺痛。**prick·ly** /'prikli; 'prikli/ adj 1 covered with ~s. 多刺的。**prickly pear,** cactus covered with ~s and having pear-shaped fruit. 霸王树(一种多刺的仙人掌, 结梨形之果实)。**2 prickly heat,** inflammation of the sweat glands, marked by a pricking sensation, common in the tropics during the hot-weather season. 痱子(汗腺之发炎, 有刺痛感, 常见于热带之炎热季节)。**3** (colloq) easily irritated or angered: (口)易生气的; 易发脾气的: *You're a bit prickly today.* 你今天很容易发脾气

pride /praid; praid/ n 1 [U] feeling of satisfaction arising from what one has done, or from persons, things, etc one is concerned with: (因曾做某事, 或因某些人、物等与自己有关而生的)得意之感; 自豪: *look with ~ at one's garden.* 得意地看着自己的花园。**take (a) ~ in sb/sth; take no/little, etc ~ in sb/sth,** have some/no/little, etc ~ in doing sth/about sth/in sb/sth/about sth: 对…感到(不感, 很少感到)自豪: *take (a) great ~ in one's achievements/in the success of one's children.* 对自己的成就(孩子的成功)感到自豪。**2 of place,** a position of superiority. 高位; 优越的位置。**2** [U] (also 亦作) **proper ~,** self-respect; knowledge of one's worth and character: 自尊; 自尊心: *He has no ~.* 他没有自尊心。 *His ~ prevents him from doing anything dishonourable.* 他的自尊使他未做出任何不名誉的事。*Don't say anything that may wound his ~.* 不要说任何可能伤他自尊心的话。**false ~,** mistaken feeling of this kind; vanity. 妄自尊大; 虚荣心。**3** [U] object of ~(1): 引以自豪的对象: *a girl who is her mother's ~ and joy.* 一位使她的母亲感到自豪与欣喜的女孩。**4** [U] too high an opinion of oneself, one's position, possessions, etc; arrogance: 自大; 傲慢: *the sin of ~;* 傲慢罪(宗教或道德方面者); *be puffed up with ~.* 充满傲气。**P~ goes before a fall,** (prov) ⇨ go before at go¹(29). (谚)骄者必败。**5 the ~ of,** the prime, flower, etc of 全盛; 精华: *in the full ~ of youth.* 正值少壮时期。**6** [C] group: 群: (esp) (尤用于) *a ~ of lions/peacocks.* 一群狮子(孔雀)。□ vt (reflex) **~ oneself on/upon sth,** take ~ in; be pleased and satisfied about: (反身式)以…自豪; 自负; 自傲: 得意于: *He ~s himself upon his skill as a pianist.* 他对于自己的钢琴技巧感到很得意。

prie-dieu /'pri: djə:; pri'djə/ n small piece of furniture at which to kneel when praying to God. 祷告台; 祷告椅。

priest /pri:st; prist/ n 1 ordained minister of a Christian Church, esp one who is between a deacon and a bishop in the Anglican, Orthodox or Roman Catholic Church. 基督教的教士; 牧师; 神父; (尤指英国国教, 东正教或天主教级位于执事与主教之间的)僧侣。⇨ the illus at vestment. 参看 vestment 之插图。*Clergyman* is usu in the Anglican Church, except in official use, *minister* in the non-conformist Churches. 在英国国教中, 除正式用法外, clergyman 是此义的通用词, 不遵奉英国国教的基督新教中用 minister 一词。**~-ridden** adj ruled by, under the subjection of, ~s. 受教士支配的; 僧侣统治的。**2** (of non-Christian religions) person trained to perform special acts of religion, to serve the deity, give advice, etc. (指基督教以外之宗教)训练来担任宗教之特别活动、伺奉神等的祭司; 术士; 和尚。**~·ess** /'pri:stes; 'pristis/ n woman ~(2). 女祭司; 女术士; 尼姑。**'~·craft** n [U] ambitious or worldly policy of ~s. 僧侣之谋略(谋求遂行野心或干预俗务者)。**'~·hood** /-hud; -hud/ n the whole body of a Church: 教会之全体教士, 牧师或僧侣: *the Irish ~hood.* 爱尔兰的教士们。**~·ly, ~·like** adjj of or for a ~; like a ~.

教士的; 适于教士的; 似教士的。

prig /prɪg; prɪg/ n [C] smug, self-satisfied, self-righteous person. 自满的人; 沾沾自喜的人; 自以为正直的人。~·**gish** /-ɪʃ; -ɪʃ/ adj behaving like, typical of, a ~; full of self-satisfaction. 一本正经的; 沾沾自喜的。~·**gish·ly** adv ~·**gish·ness** n

prim /prɪm; prɪm/ adj (**-mmer, -mmest**) neat; formal: 整洁的; 整齐的: a ~ garden; 整齐的花圃; (of persons, their manner, speech, etc) disliking, showing a dislike of, anything rough, rude, improper: (指人、其仪态、言词等)不喜欢或厌恶粗鲁、无礼或不规矩之事物的; 拘谨的; 规矩的; 正经的: a very ~ and proper old gentleman. 一位非常规矩有礼的老绅士。□ vt (**-mm-**) put (the face, lips) into a ~ expression. 使(面部、唇)作出正经的表情。~·**ly** adv ~·**ness** n

prima /'priːmə; 'primə/ adj (I) first. (意)第一的; 主要的。~，**balle·ri·na** /ˌbæləˈriːnə; ˌbæləˈrinə/, leading woman performer in ballet. 芭蕾舞之首席女演员。~ **'donna** /'dɒnə; 'dɑnə/, leading woman singer in opera; (colloq) arrogant, temperamental person. 歌剧中的首席女歌手; 首席女声; (口)傲慢和性情多变的人。

pri·macy /'praɪməsɪ; 'praɪməsɪ/ n (pl **-cies**) 1 pre-eminence. 首要; 首位。2 position of an archbishop. 大主教之职位。

pri·mae·val /praɪˈmiːvl; praɪˈmivl/ adj ⇨ **primeval**.

prima facie /ˌpraɪmə ˈfeɪʃiː; ˈpraɪməˈfeʃɪ/ adv, adj (Lat) (based) on the first impression: (法)乍看起来; 据初次印象: have a good case. 遇到初看起来似乎真实的事件; (法律)遇到乍看起来证据充分的案件。~ **evidence**, (legal) sufficient to prove something (unless refuted). (法律)初步的证据。

pri·mal /'praɪml; 'praɪml/ adj (formal) primeval; chief; first in importance. (正式用语)最初的; 原始的; 主要的; 首要的。

pri·mary /'praɪmərɪ US: -merɪ; 'praɪˌmɛrɪ/ adj 1 leading in time, order or development: 在时间、次序或发展上领先的; 第一的; 基本的; 主要的: of ~ (= chief) importance; 首要的; a '~ school, (GB) for junior pupils (5 to 11 years); 小学(英国, 五岁至十一岁儿童就读的学校); ~ rocks, of the lowest series of strata; 原成岩(最下层的岩石); the ~ meaning of a word, the earliest and original meaning. 一个词的原义(本义)。2 ~ colours, red, blue and yellow, from which all other colours can be obtained by mixing two or more. 原色(即红、蓝、黄三色, 由混合二种或二种以上之原色可得所有其他的颜色)。□ n (pl **-ries**) (US) meeting of electors to name candidates for a coming election. (美)提名候选人的预选会。 **pri·mar·ily** /'praɪmərəlɪ US: praɪˈmerəlɪ; 'praɪˌmɛrəlɪ/ adv in the first place; essentially. 首先; 主要地; 基本地。

pri·mate[1] /'praɪmeɪt; 'praɪmɪt/ n archbishop. 大主教。

pri·mate[2] /'praɪmeɪt; 'praɪmɪt/ n one of the highest order of mammals (including men, apes, monkeys and lemurs). 灵长类动物(最高级之哺乳动物, 包括人、猿、猴及狐猴)。

prime[1] /praɪm; praɪm/ adj 1 chief; most important: 主要的; 最重要的: his ~ motive. 他的主要动机。P~ **Minister**, chief minister of a Government. 首相; 内阁总理。2 excellent; first-rate: 第一流的; 上等: (cuts of) beef. 上等牛肉(片)。3 fundamental; primary. 基本的; 根本的。~ **cost**, cost of production not including overhead charges, margin for profit, etc. 主要成本(不包含间接费用、赚头等的制造成本)。~ **meridian**, the zero meridian, that of Greenwich. 本初子午线。~ **mover**, primary source of motive power, eg wind, water; (fig) person who initiates a plan, action, etc. 主动力; 原动力(如风、水等); (喻)发起人; 发动者。~ **number**, (maths) one which cannot be divided exactly except by itself and the number 1 (eg 7, 17, 41). (数学)质数; 素数(除本身和1以外, 不能被其他数目除尽的数, 如7, 17, 41等)。

prime[2] /praɪm; praɪm/ n [U] 1 state of highest perfection; the best part: 最完美的状态; 最佳部分: in the ~ of youth; 正值少壮时期; in the ~ of life. 在壮年。When is a man in his ~? 何时是一个人的盛年? He is past his ~. 他已过了盛年。2 first or earliest part: 第一部分; 最初部分: the ~ of the year, spring. 春季。3 church service at 6 am or sunrise. (教堂在早晨六时或日出时举行的)早课; 晨祷。

prime[3] /praɪm; praɪm/ vt [VP6A] 1 get ready for use or action: 把…准备好以便使用或行动: ~ a gun, (hist) put in gunpowder, etc; (史)装火药等于枪炮; ~ a pump, wet it, pour in water, to get it started. 倒水于抽水机(使能发生吸力开始抽水)。~ the pump, (fig) put money into an inactive industry, etc or into the economy, to stimulate it to growth. (喻)将钱投入不景气的工业等, 或作经济投资, 以刺激其成长。2 supply with facts, etc: 供以事实等: The witness had been ~d by a lawyer. 这证人曾经受到律师的指点。The Socialist candidate had been well ~d with facts by Party headquarters. 社会党的候选人已由该党总部供给各种事实。3 (colloq) fill (a person) with food or drink: (口)以食物或饮料塞饱(某人): well ~d with liquor. 喝足了酒。4 cover (a surface) with the first coat of paint, oil, varnish, etc. 以头道油漆等涂(表面)。

primer[1] /'praɪmə(r); 'prɪmə/ n first school textbook: 儿童的启蒙读物; 初级读本; 入门书: a Latin ~. 拉丁文入门。

primer[2] /'praɪmə(r); 'praɪmə/ n [C] 1 small quantity of explosive, contained in a cap or cylinder, for igniting the powder in a cartridge, bomb, etc. 底火; 火帽; 雷管; 起爆剂(装在帽形或棒形容器内的少量炸药, 用以引发弹药筒、炸弹等)。⇨ the illus at **cartridge**. 参看cartridge之插图。2 priming (of paint). (油漆的)底涂; 底层漆。

pri·me·val (also **-mae·val**) /praɪˈmiːvl; praɪˈmivl/ adj 1 of the earliest time in the world's history. 世界史之最初期的; 太古的。2 very ancient: 古老的; 原始的: ~ forests, natural forests in which no trees have ever been felled. (从未加以砍伐的)原始森林; 原生林。

prim·ing /'praɪmɪŋ; 'praɪmɪŋ/ n 1 gunpowder used to fire the charge of a gun, bomb, mine, etc. 点火药; 起爆剂。2 mixture used by painters for a first coat. 油漆底子; 底漆。

primi·tive /'prɪmɪtɪv; 'prɪmətɪv/ adj 1 of the earliest times; of an early stage of social development: 上古的; 原始的; 社会发展之早期的: ~ man; 原始人; 初民; ~ culture. 原始文化。2 simple; old-fashioned; having undergone little development: 简单的; 原始性的; 不发达的: ~ weapons, eg bows and arrows, spears. 原始性的武器(如弓、箭、矛)。□ n painter or sculptor of the period before the Renaissance; example of his work. 文艺复兴以前之画家或雕刻家; 其作品。~·**ly** adv ~·**ness** n

pri·mo·geni·ture /ˌpraɪməˈdʒenɪtʃə(r) US: -tʃʊər; ˌpraɪməˈdʒenətʃə/ n fact of being the firstborn of the children of the same parents. 长子身份。**right of** ~, (legal) system by which all real estate passes on from a father to the eldest son. (法律)长子继权(所有不动产由父亲传给长子之制度)。

pri·mor·dial /praɪˈmɔːdɪəl; praɪˈmɔrdɪəl/ adj in existence at or from the beginning; primeval. 原生的; 原始的; 最初的。

primp /prɪmp; prɪmp/ vt = **prink**.

prim·rose /'prɪmrəʊz; 'prɪmˌroz/ n [C] common wild plant with pale yellow flowers; the flower; its colour. 樱草(开淡黄色花); 樱草花; 樱草色; 淡黄色。**the ~ way/path**, (fig) the pursuit of reckless pleasure. (喻)追求使人堕落的享乐。

prim·ula /'prɪmjʊlə; 'prɪmjʊlə/ n kinds of perennial herbaceous plants with flowers of various colours and sizes (including the primrose and polyanthus). 樱草属

(多年生的草本植物,其花之颜色及大小各不相同,包括樱草及黄花九轮草)。

pri·mus /ˈpraɪməs; ˈpraɪməs/ n (pl ~es /-məsɪz; -məsɪz/) (P) kind of cooking stove that burns vaporized oil. (商标)一种燃烧汽化油油的炉子。

prince /prɪns; prɪns/ n **1** ruler, esp of a small state. (尤指小国的)君主;诸侯。**2** male member of a royal family, esp (in GB) a son or grandson of the Sovereign. 太子;王子(在英国尤指君主的儿子或孙子)。**3** the ~ of **darkness**, Satan. 撒旦;魔鬼。the **P~** of **Peace**, Jesus. 和平之君(耶稣)。**P~ Consort**, husband of a reigning queen. 女王之夫。~·**dom** /-dəm; -dəm/ n rank or dignity of, or area ruled by, a ~ (1). 小国君主的地位,领地。~·**ly** adj (-ier, -iest) (worthy) of a ~; splendid; generous: 君主的;王侯的;与王侯相称的;壮丽的;慷慨的: a ~ly gift. 丰厚的礼物。**prin·cess** /prɪnˈses; ˈprɪnsɪs/ n wife of a ~; daughter or granddaughter of a sovereign. 王妃;公主。

prin·ci·pal /ˈprɪnsəpl; ˈprɪnsəpl/ adj highest in order of importance: 主要的;首要的;重要的: the ~ rivers of Europe; 欧洲的主要河流; the ~ food of the people of Java. 爪哇人的主食。~ **boy**, person (traditionally, in GB, an actress, not an actor) who takes the leading part in a pantomime. 哑剧里的主角(在英国,一向由女演员而非男演员担任)。□ n **1** title of some heads of colleges and of some other organizations. (学校或机关之主管的称谓)校长;首长。**2** person for whom another acts as agent in business: (代理人所代表的)本人;委托人: I must consult my ~. 我必须跟我的委托人商量。**3** main girder or rafter in a roof. (屋顶的)主梁;主椽。**4** (fin) money lent, put into a business, etc on which interest is payable. (财政)(生息之)本金;资本。**5** (legal) person directly responsible for a crime (distinguished from an abetter or accessory). (法律)主犯(有别于教唆犯或从犯)。~·**ly** /-plɪ; -plɪ/ adv for the most part; chiefly. 大抵;主要地。

prin·ci·pal·ity /ˌprɪnsɪˈpælətɪ; ˌprɪnsəˈpælətɪ/ n (pl -ties) country ruled by a prince. 公国;侯国。the **P~**, Wales. 英国威尔士之别名。

prin·ciple /ˈprɪnsəpl; ˈprɪnsəpl/ n [C] **1** basic truth; general law of cause and effect: 原理;原则;一般因果律: the (first) ~s of geometry /political economy / navigation. 几何学(政治经济学,航海学)的(首要)原理。**2** guiding rule for behaviour: 行为的准则: moral ~s; 道义;道德规范; 节操; ~s of conduct; 行为的准则; live up to one's ~s; 照自己的标准行事; (collective sing) (集合数数) a man of high ~. 操守好的人。in ~, (contrasted with in detail) in general. 大体上(与in detail 相对)。on ~, from conviction, from a settled moral motive: 根据信念,由于一种固定的道德上的动机: He refused on ~ to understate his income for taxation purposes. 他由于一种道德上的动机,拒绝为了少纳税而少报收入。**3** general law shown in the working of a machine, etc: 机器等的运转原理: These machines work on the same ~. 这些机器按照相同的原理运转。~·**d** adj (in compounds) following, having, the kind of ~ (2) indicated: (用于复合词中)遵守行为准则的,有节操的: a most high-~d woman, unhappily married to a low-~d man. 一位很有节操的女子,不幸与一位没有节操的男人结婚。⇨ **unprincipled**.

prink /prɪŋk; prɪŋk/ vt ~ oneself (up), make oneself look smart or spruce. 把自己打扮得漂亮。

print¹ /prɪnt; prɪnt/ n **1** [U] mark(s), letters, etc in printed form: 印刷符号;字母等;印刷体;版: clear ~; 清晰的印刷; in large /small ~. 用大(小)铅字;以大(小)字体印刷。in ~, (of a book) printed and on sale. (指书)已出版; 出售中; 在销印。out of ~, (of a book) no more printed copies available from the publisher. (指书)绝版。rush into ~, (of an author) hasten to publish sth he has written. (指作者)急于把作品付印。**2** [C] (usu in compounds) mark left on a surface preserving the form left by the pressure of sth: (通

常用于复合词中)印迹;痕迹。ˈfinger-~s; 指纹;指印: ˈfoot-~s. 足迹;足印。**3** [U] printed cotton fabric: 印花棉布: (attrib) (用作定语) a ~ dress. 印花布的衣服。**4** [C] picture, design, etc made by ~ing from a block, plate, etc: (由印模,感光版等)印成的画片,图案等;版画;印画: old Japanese ~s; 古老的日本版画; photograph ~ed from a negative. 印出之照片。ˈblue-~, ⇨ **blue²(7)**. ˈ~-**seller** n man who sells engravings, etchings, etc. 版画售卖者。ˈ~-**shop** n shop of a ~-seller. 版画店。**5** [C] (now chiefly US) ~ed publication, esp a newspaper (现在主要用于美)印刷物;出版物;(尤指)报纸。

print² /prɪnt; prɪnt/ vt, vi **1** [VP6A] make marks on (paper), etc by pressing it with inked type, etc; make books /pictures, etc in this way; (of a publisher, an editor, an author) cause to be ~ed: 印符号于(纸等上);印刷(书,图画等);(指出版者,编辑,作者)出版;编印;刊行: ~ 6000 copies of a novel. 印刷某小说六千册。Do you intend to ~ your lectures /have your lectures ~ed? 你有意把你的讲稿印行吗? (fig) (喻) The incidents ~ed themselves on her memory. 那些小事深深地印在她的记忆中。ˈ~ed **matter /papers**, (as on envelopes, wrappers, etc) circulars, prospectuses, etc to be charged for postage at a reduced rate. 印刷品(注于邮件上以获得邮资之优待)。ˈ~-**out** n the ~ed output of a computer. (电子计算机之)输出资料。**2** [VP6A] shape (one's letters), write (words), in imitation of ~ed characters (instead of ordinary joined handwriting). 照印刷体写(字母,字)。**3** [VP6A, 15B] ~ (off), make (a photograph) on paper, etc from a negative film or plate: 用底片(相片)于纸上等: How many copies shall I ~ (off) for you from this negative? 你要我用这张底片洗出多少张相片? **4** [VP2A] (of a plate or film) produce a picture; be produced as the result of ~ing(3): (指感光板或底片)印相片; 被印出来: This film /plate /picture hasn't ~ed very well. 这胶卷(感光板,照片)印出来不清楚。**5** [VP6A] mark (a textile fabric) with a coloured design. 印彩色图案于(织物)。~·**able** /-əbl; -əbl/ adj that can be ~ed, or ~ed from; fit to be ~ed. 可印刷的;可供印出的;适于印行的。~·**er** n workman who ~s books, etc; owner of a ~ing business. 印刷工人;印刷业者。~·**ing** n (in verbal senses): (按动词各义): ˈ~ing-ink, kind of ink used for ~ing books, etc. 印刷用油墨。ˈ~ing-**machine**, ˈ~ing-**press** nn machine for ~ing books, etc. 印刷机。ˈ~ing **office** n place where ~ing is done. 印刷厂。

prior¹ /ˈpraɪə(r); ˈpraɪə/ adj ~ (to), earlier in time, order or importance: 较早的;顺序在先的;更重要的: have a ~ claim to sth. 对某事物有优先权。~ **to**, prep (formal) before: (正式用语)在…之前: ~ to any discussion of this matter. 在讨论这事之前。The house was sold ~ to auction, before the day of the auction. 这房子在拍卖日之前业已售出。

prior² /ˈpraɪə(r); ˈpraɪə/ n head of a religious order or house; (in an abbey) next below an abbot. 教派的首长; 小修道院院长; (大修道院的)副院长; 副主持。~·**ess** /ˈpraɪərɪs; ˈpraɪərɪs/ n woman: ~·**y** /ˈpraɪərɪ; ˈpraɪərɪ/ n religious house governed by a ~ or ~ess. 小修道院或女修道院。

pri·or·ity /praɪˈɒrətɪ US: -ˈɔːr-; praɪˈɔrətɪ/ n (pl -ties) **1** [U] ~ (over), being prior; right to have or do sth before others: 较早; 顺序在先; 优先权: I have ~ over you in my claim. 我的请求比你优先。The proceeds of the sale (eg of the property of a bankrupt) will be distributed according to ~. 售卖所得(如出卖破产者之财产)将按优先顺序分配。**2** [C] claim to consideration; high place among competing claims: 被考虑的权利; 占优先的位置; 需要优先考虑的事物: Road building is a first ~ (or, colloq, 口, a top ~). 筑路为第一优先。The Government gave a ~ to housing after the War. 政府在战后优先考虑房屋问题。

prise /praɪz; praɪz/ vt = **prize³**.

prism /'prɪzəm; 'prɪzəm/ n 1 solid figure with similar, equal and parallel ends, and with sides which are parallelograms. 墙; 棱柱 (各对应边均平行, 各面为平行四边形之立体图形). 2 body of this form, usu triangular and made of glass, which breaks up white light into the colours of the rainbow. 棱柱体; (通常指) 三棱镜; 棱镜.

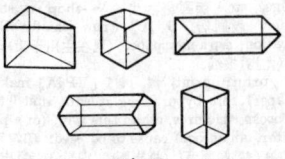

prisms

pris·matic /prɪz'mætɪk; prɪz'mætɪk/ adj 1 like, having the shape of, a prism. 似棱柱或三棱镜的; 棱柱或三棱镜形的. 2 (of colours) brilliant and varied. (指颜色)光彩夺目的; 五光十色的.

prison /'prɪzn; 'prɪzn/ n [C] building in which wrongdoers are kept locked up; place where a person is shut up against his will; [U] confinement in such a building: 监狱; 牢房; 监禁; 禁锢: escape/be released from ~; 逃出(被放出)监狱; be in/go to/send sb to ~. 坐牢(入狱; 把某人关进监狱). **~-breaking** n the illegal act of escaping from ~. 越狱. **~er** n person kept in ~ for crime or until tried in a law court; person, animal or bird kept in confinement: 囚犯; 犯人; 刑事被告; 被禁闭的人, 动物或鸟: a bird kept ~er in a cage. 被关在笼中的鸟. **,~er of 'conscience**, political ~er, 政治(囚)犯, ⇨ **political(1)**. **,~er of 'war**, person captured in war and (usu) kept in a camp for the duration of the war. 战俘; 俘虏.

pris·tine /'prɪstiːn; 'prɪstin/ adj (formal) primitive; of early times; unchanged by later developments; fresh as if new: (正式用语)原始的; 初期的; 未受后来发展之影响的; 象新的一般鲜明的: Who would want to get back to the ~ simplicity of Anglo-Saxon days? 谁会想要回复盎格鲁撒克逊时代原始的质朴呢?

prithee /'prɪðiː; 'prɪðɪ/ int (archaic) I pray thee; please: (古)请你; 请: P~, keep silent. 请君保持安静. Tell me, ~, ... 请告诉我….

priv·acy /'prɪvəsɪ US: 'praɪv-; 'praɪvəsɪ/ n [U] 1 state of being away from others, alone and undisturbed: 隐退; 静居; 独处而不受干扰: the invasion of ~ by the press and TV. 报纸和电视对静居的侵扰. I should hate to live in a household where ~ was impossible. 我讨厌住在没法静居的家中. I don't want my ~ disturbed. 我不愿私生活受干扰. 2 secrecy (opp to publicity): 秘密(与 publicity 相反): They were married in strict ~. 他们在极度秘密下结婚.

pri·vate /'praɪvɪt; 'praɪvɪt/ adj 1 (opp of public) of, for the use of, concerning, one person or group of persons, not people in general: (为 public 之反义词)私人的; 私用的; 私有的: a ~ letter, about personal matters; 私人信件; for ~ reasons, not to be explained to everybody. 为了私人的理由. ,~ 'enterprise, the management of industry, etc by ~ individuals, companies, etc (contrasted with State ownership or control). 私人企业(与国营企业相对). ,~ 'means, income not earned as a salary, etc but coming from personal property, investments, etc. 私产所得(指来自个人之财产, 投资等, 而非来自薪金之收入). ,~ 'school, one at which fees are paid (contrasted with a school financially supported by the State, etc). 私立学校(与公立学校相对). 2 secret; kept secret: 秘密的; 保持秘密的: a letter marked 'P~'. 标有'密'字的信件; have ~ information about sth. 得到有关某事的秘密消息. **parts**, external sex organs. 私处; 阴部. 3 having no

official position; not holding any public office: 无官职的; 平民的: do sth in one's ~ capacity, not as an official, etc; 以平民资格做某事; his ~ life, the life he leads away from business or public affairs. 他的私生活(与业务或公务无关者). retire into ~ life, retire after a public career. 退休(从公职退休). ~ member (of the House of Commons), one who is not a member of the Government. 未担任公职的下议院议员. 4 ~ (soldier), ordinary soldier without rank: 兵; 兵士: P~ Dodd. 兵士陶德. □ n 1 ~ soldier. 兵; 兵士. 2 in ~, 私下; ~ly, not in public. 私下地; 秘密地. ~·ly adv

pri·va·teer /ˌpraɪvə'tɪə(r); ˌpraɪvə'tɪr/ n (formerly) armed vessel under private ownership, allowed to attack enemy shipping in time of war; commander or member of the crew of such a vessel. 私掠船(昔时一种私有的武装船, 在战时可攻击敌船); 私掠船的指挥官或船员.

pri·va·tion /praɪ'veɪʃn; praɪ'veʃən/ n 1 [U, C] lack of the necessaries of life; destitution: 生活必需品的缺乏; 穷困: fall ill through ~; 因缺乏生活必需品而生病; 贫病交加; suffering many ~s. 备尝艰辛. 2 [C] state of being deprived of sth (not necessarily sth essential): 被剥夺某物(不一定为必需品); 丧失; 不便: He found it a great ~ not being allowed to smoke in prison. 他觉得在监狱中禁止吸烟是一件很大的不便.

privet /'prɪvɪt; 'prɪvɪt/ n [U] evergreen shrub, bearing small white flowers, much used for garden hedges: 水蜡树; 女贞(一种常绿灌木, 开小白花, 多用作园篱): clipping the ~ hedges. 修剪水蜡树树篱.

pri·vi·lege /'prɪvɪlɪdʒ; 'prɪvlɪdʒ/ n 1 [C] right or advantage available only to a person, class or rank, or the holder of a certain position, etc: (某人, 某阶级或地位, 或担任某职位者等的)特权; 特惠: the ~s of birth, eg that come because one is born into a wealthy family. 与生俱来的特权(例如因为生于富家). 2 [C] special favour or benefit: 特殊的荣幸, 恩惠或利益: grant sb the ~ of fishing in a privately owned trout stream. 给予某人在私有的产鳟鱼的河中捕鱼. It was a ~ to hear her sing. 听她唱歌是一桩很荣幸的事. 3 [C, U] right to do or say things without risk of punishment, etc (as when Members of Parliament may say things in the House of Commons which might result in a libel case if said outside Parliament). 做或说某事而不致受罚的权利; 特权(例如国会议员可在下议院内发表的某些言论, 如在国会以外说出可能招致毁谤罪). ~d /'prɪvɪlɪdʒd; 'prɪvlɪdʒd/ adj having, granted, a ~ or ~s. 有特权的; 获得特殊利益的. **the ~d classes**, those who enjoy the advantages of the best education, of wealth, and secure social position. 特权阶级. ,**under-'~d**, suffering from poverty. 贫苦的.

privy /'prɪvɪ; 'prɪvɪ/ adj 1 (old use, except legal) secret; private. (除法律用语外为旧用法)秘密的; 私有的. ~ **to**, having secret knowledge of: 与闻…之机密: charged with having been ~ to the plot against the prince. 被控密谋与背叛王子的阴谋. 2 the **P~ Council**, committee of persons appointed by the Sovereign, advising on some State affairs, but membership now being chiefly a personal dignity. 英国枢密院(英国国君任命之组织, 咨议国事, 但枢密顾问之身份现在主要为个人的一种尊荣而已). **P~ Councillor/Counsellor**, member of the P~ Council. 枢密顾问官. **P~ Purse**, allowance of money from the public revenue for the Sovereign's private expenses. 国家岁收中拨为君主私用的钱财. **P~ Seal**, State seal affixed to documents of minor importance. (英)御玺. □ n (pl **-vies**) (old use) water-closet. (旧用法)旧式厕所; 茅坑. **priv·ily** /-ɪlɪ; -ɪlɪ/ adv privately; secretly. 私下地; 秘密地.

prize¹ /praɪz; praɪz/ n 1 sth (to be) awarded to one who succeeds in a competition, lottery, etc: 奖品; 赠品; 奖金: be awarded a ~ for good conduct; 因品行优良获奖; draw a ~-winning ticket in a lottery; 抽到一张得奖的彩票; 中奖; carry off most of the ~s at the village

flower show; 夺得该村花展的大部分奖品; *win first ~ on the pools,* 赢得总赌注的头奖; *consolation ~s,* given to console those who do not win the good *~s;* 精神奖(安慰奖)(以安慰未获大奖者); *a ~ cattle,* cattle that have been awarded *~s;* 获奖的牛; *a ~ scholarship,* one awarded as a *~.* 成绩优良奖学金。**2** (fig) anything struggled for or worth struggling for: (喻)奋斗争取的东西;值得奋斗争取的东西: *the ~s of life.* 人生之目的。**3** '**~-fight** n boxing match for money. (以营利为目的之)职业性拳赛。Hence, '**~-fighter**, '**~-fighting** nn '**~-ring** n the enclosed area (now usu a square) in which boxing-matches are fought; the sport of *~-fighting.* 职业性拳击(现在通常为方形);职业性拳击。**4** '**~-man** /-mən; -mən/ n (pl **-men**) winner of a *~* (usu with the name of the *~* or scholarship prefixed): 得奖者;得奖学金者(通常其前冠以奖品或奖学金之名称)。□ vt value highly; 珍视; 重视: *my most ~d possessions.* 我最珍视的财产。

prize² /praɪz; praɪz/ n [C] sth, esp a ship or its cargo, captured at sea during a war. 战时在海上捕获之物(尤指船或船货);海上战利品。'**~-money** n money realized by the sale of a *~* (and divided up among those who captured it). 捕获赏金(出售海上捕获物所得之钱,由捕获者分享之)。

prize³ (also **prise**) /praɪz; praɪz/ vt [VP15A, B] use force to get sth, eg a box, lid, *open/up/off.* 撬开;撑起(如箱,盖)(与 open, up, off 连用)。

pro¹ /prəʊ; pro/ n [C] (usu only in) (通常仅用于) *the ~s and cons (of sth),* the arguments for and against (sth). 赞成论与反对论;正反双方的理由。□ adv **pro and con,** for and against: *argue pro and con.* 从正反两方辩论。

pro² /prəʊ; pro/ n (pl **pros**) (colloq) (short for) professional (player): (口)为 professional (player) 之略: *a golf pro.* 高尔夫球职业选手。

pro- /prəʊ; pro/ pref supporting; favouring: 支持的;赞成的; 亲善的: *pro-British;* 亲英的; acting for: 代理的: *pro-consul;* 代理领事; 副领事; *pro-vice-chancellor.* 代理副校长。⇨ **App 3.** 参看附录三。

prob·abil·ity /ˌprɒbəˈbɪlətɪ; ˌprɑbəˈbɪlətɪ/ n (pl **-ties**) **1** [U] quality of being probable. 或然; 大概。*in all ~,* most probably. 大概; 多半; 十之八九。**2** [U] likelihood: 可能性: *There is no/little/not much ~ of his succeeding/that he will succeed.* 他不(很少,不大)可能会成功。**3** [C] (most) probable event or outcome: (最)可能发生的事件或结果: *What are the probabilities?* 成算怎样?

prob·able /ˈprɒbəbl; ˈprɑbəbl/ adj likely to happen or to prove true or correct: 可能发生或证实的; 或然的; 大概的: *the ~ result;* 可能的结果; *a ~ winner.* 有希望的得胜者。*Rain is possible but not ~ before evening.* 在傍晚前下雨是可能的,但是不大可能会下。*It seems ~ that ....* 很可能是; 恐怕要...。□ n person who will most likely be chosen, eg for a team, or do sth; 候选人,winner, etc. 最可能被选出(参加球队)的人; 有希望的候选人、得胜者等。**prob·ably** /-əblɪ; -əblɪ/ adv most likely: 或许; 大概: *Jim's late—he's probably stuck in a traffic jam.* 吉姆晚了——他大概被交通阻塞困住了。

pro·bate /ˈprəʊbeɪt; ˈprobet/ n **1** [U] the official process of proving the validity of a will: 遗嘱之认证: *take out ~ of a will;* 取得某遗嘱的认证; *grant ~ of a will.* 通过某遗嘱的认证。**2** [C] copy of a will with a certificate that it is correct. 经认证的遗嘱。□ vt (US) establish the validity of a will (GB 英 = **prove**). (美)认证遗嘱的效力。

pro·ba·tion /prəˈbeɪʃn US: proʊ-; proˈbeʃən/ n [U] **1** testing of a person's conduct, abilities, qualities, etc before he is finally accepted for a position, admitted into a society, etc: (在决定给予某人一职位,准许某人加入某会社等之前的)试验;试用;见习: *two years on ~,* ie undergoing such testing; 试用两年; *an officer on ~.*

见习官。**2** the '**~ system,** (legal) that by which (esp young) offenders are allowed to go unpunished for their first offence while they continue to live without further breaking of the law: (法律)缓刑; 缓刑制: *three years' ~ under suspended sentence of one year's imprisonment.* 判刑一年, 缓刑三年。'**~ officer,** one who watches over the behaviour of offenders who are on *~.* 缓刑监视官(对缓刑期间犯人之行为加以监视者)。**~·ary** /prəˈbeɪʃnrɪ US: proʊˈbeɪʃənerɪ; proˈbeʃənˌerɪ/ adj relating to *~.* 试验的; 缓刑的。**~·er** n **1** hospital nurse receiving training and still on *~* (1). (医院中的)见习护士。**2** wrongdoer who has been released on *~* (2). 缓刑期中的罪犯。

probe /prəʊb; prob/ n **1** slender instrument with a blunt end, used by doctors for learning about the depth and direction of a wound, etc. 探针(一种钝头之细长工具,医生用以探测伤处的深度及方向者)。**2** (journalism) investigation (*into* a scandal, etc). (新闻用语)刺探; 侦察(丑闻等,与 into 连用)。□ vt [VP6A] **1** examine with a *~.* 用探针检查;探查。**2** investigate or examine thoroughly (sb's thought, the causes of sth). 侦察; 细察(某人的思想,某事的原由)。

prob·ity /ˈprəʊbətɪ; ˈprobətɪ/ n [U] (formal) uprightness of character; integrity. (正式用语)性格之刚直; 诚正。

prob·lem /ˈprɒbləm; ˈprɑbləm/ n [C] question to be solved or decided, esp sth difficult: 问题; 难题: *mathematical ~s;* 数学问题; *the ~s of youth.* 青少年的问题。'**~ child,** one whose behaviour offers a difficult *~* to his parents, teachers, etc. 问题儿童。**~ picture,** one in which the artist's intention is obscure. (艺术家意向不明的)问题图画。**~ play/novel,** one dealing with a social or moral *~.* (处理社会或道德问题的)问题剧(小说)。**~·atic** /ˌprɒbləˈmætɪk; ˌprɑbləˈmætɪk/ adj (esp of a result) doubtful; that cannot be seen or foretold. (尤指结果)有疑问的; 不能看出或预知的。**~·atically** /-klɪ; -klɪ/ adv

pro·bos·cis /prəˈbɒsɪs; proˈbɑsɪs/ n (pl **~es** -sɪsɪz; -sɪsɪz/) n **1** elephant's trunk. 象鼻。**2** elongated part of the mouth of some insects. (某于昆虫的)长喙; 吻部。

pro·cedure /prəˈsiːdʒə(r); proˈsidʒɚ/ n [C, U] (the regular) order of doing things, esp legal and political: 做事的(一般)手续; (尤指)诉讼程序; 议事程序: *the usual ~ at committee meetings;* 委员会会议的一般程序; *stop arguing about (questions of) ~ and get down to business.* 停止争辩程序(问题)而致力于议事。**pro·cedural** /prəˈsiːdʒərəl; proˈsidʒərəl/ adj of *~.* 手续的; 诉讼程序的; 议事程序的。

pro·ceed /prəˈsiːd; proˈsid/ vi **1** [VP2A, 3A, 4C] *~ to sth/to do sth,* go forward; go on: 前进; 着手; 继续进行: *Let us ~ to business/to the next item on the agenda.* 我们着手工作吧(我们继续进行议程上的下一个项目吧)。*He ~ed to inform me that ....* 他开始告诉我...。*They ~ed* (more usu 较常用 went) *from London to Leeds.* 他们由伦敦前往里兹。*~ with sth,* start or continue with it: 开始; 继续: *Please ~ with your explanation.* 请继续解释。**2** [VP3A] *~ from sth,* come, arise from: 来到; 发生: *famine, plague and other evils that ~ from war.* 因战争引起的饥馑, 瘟疫及其他弊害。**3** [VP3A] *~ against sb,* take legal action. 控诉; 起诉。**4** [VP3A] *~ to sth,* go on from a lower university degree: (在获得较低的大学学位后)继续攻读: *~ to the degree of M A.* 攻读文学硕士学位。

pro·ceed·ing /prəˈsiːdɪŋ; proˈsidɪŋ/ n **1** [C] course of action; (way of) behaving: 动作之过程; 进行; 举止; 行径: *What is our best way of ~?* 我们最好的进行方式是什么? **2** [C] sth done; piece of conduct: 已做之事; 行为; 行动; 处置: *What he did was a rather high-handed ~.* 他的所做所为是一种相当专横的行为。*The ~s at the meeting were rather disorderly.* 会议的进展颇为紊乱。*There have been suspicious ~s in committee meetings.* 委员会会议中有可疑的处置。**3** (pl) (复) **take/start**

legal ~**s (against sb)**, take legal action. (对某人)提起诉讼; 控诉。 **4** (pl) records (of the activities of a society, etc); minutes: (复)(会社等活动的)记录; 议事录; the ~s of the Kent Archaeological Society. 肯特考古学会的活动记录。

pro·ceeds /'prəʊsiːdz; 'prosidz/ n pl financial results, profits, of an undertaking: 所得; 赢利; 收入: hold a bazaar and give the ~ to local charities. 举行义卖, 所得捐给当地的慈善机构。

pro·cess¹ /'prəʊses US: 'prɒses; 'prɑsɛs/ n **1** [C] connected series of actions, changes, etc esp such as are involuntary or unconscious: 相互关联的一系列的活动、变化等(尤指不随意的或不自觉的); 进行; 经过; 过程: the ~es of digestion, reproduction and growth. 消化、生殖及生长的过程。 **2** [C] series of operations deliberately undertaken: 一系列审慎采取的步骤; 手续; 程序: Unloading the cargo was a slow ~. 卸船货的程序是缓慢的。 **3** [C] method, esp one used in manufacture or industry: (尤指用于生产或实业中的)方法; 制法: the 'Bessemer ~, in steel manufacture. 英人 Henry Bessemer 的制钢法。 **4** [U] forward movement; progress: 前进; 进展: The glasses were broken during the ~ of removal. 在拆除的过程中眼镜片破了。 **in** ~ **of**, during: 在…期间: a building in ~ of construction; 建造中的房屋; **in** ~ **of** time, as time goes on. 随着时间的进展; 逐渐地。 **in** ~, in course of being done. 进行中。 **5** [C] (legal) action at law; formal commencement of this; summons or writ ordering a person to appear in a law court. (法律)诉讼; 正式提起诉讼; 诉讼程序; 传票。 **'~·server** n sheriff's officer who delivers writs. 送达传票的司法人员。 □ vt [VP6A] treat (material) in order to preserve it: 处理(原料)以保存之: ~ leather; 鞣制皮革; put (esp food) through a special ~(3): 特别处理(尤指食物); 加工: ~ed cheese; 加工奶酪; (photo) (摄影) ~ film, develop it, etc; 冲洗软片; (computers) (电脑) ~ tape/information, put it through the system in order to obtain the required information. 处理资料带(资讯)。

pro·cess² /prə'ses; prɒ'sɛs/ vi walk in or as if in procession. 列队队之进行。

pro·ces·sion /prə'seʃn; prə'sɛʃən/ n [C] number of persons, vehicles, etc moving forward and following each other in an orderly way: (人、车辆等的)进行行列; 队伍: a 'funeral ~; 送葬行列; **1** act of moving forward in this way: 列队进行: walking in ~ through the streets. 排成队伍走过街道。 ~**al** /-ʃənl; -ʃənl/ adj of, for, used in, ~s: 行列的; 队伍的; 适于行列或队伍的; 用于行列或队伍的: a ~al chant, sung by persons taking part in a religious ~. 行列圣歌(在宗教的游行队伍中由参加者唱之)。

pro·claim /prə'kleɪm; proˈklem/ vt [VP6A, 9, 23, 25] **1** make known publicly or officially: 宣告; 公布; 正式宣布; (= declare) war/peace, 宣战(宣告和平); ~ a public holiday; 宣布节日; 宣布公定假日; ~ a republic; 宣布一共和国的成立; ~ a man (to be) a traitor / ~ that he is a traitor. 宣布某人为叛徒。 He ~ed Anne his heir. 他的口谕显示他是苏格兰人。 **2** reveal, show: 显示; 显露: His accent ~ed him a Scot/that he was a Scot. 他的口音显示他是苏格兰人。 **proc·la·ma·tion** /ˌprɒkləˈmeɪʃn; ˌprɑkləˈmeʃən/ n [U] act of ~ing; 宣告; 公布: by public proclamation; 公开宣告; [C] that which is ~ed: 宣言; 布告; 文告: issue/make a proclamation. 发表文告。

pro·cliv·ity /prəˈklɪvəti; proˈklɪvətɪ/ n (pl **-ties**) [C] ~ (**to / towards sth / to do sth**), (formal) tendency, inclination. (正式用语)倾向; 癖性。

pro·con·sul /ˌprəʊˈkɒnsl; proˈkɑnsl/ n (in ancient Rome) governor of a Roman province; (rhet, mod use) governor of a colony or dominion. (古罗马之)地方总督; (修辞, 现代用法)殖民地或自治领的总督。 **pro·con·su·lar** /ˌprəʊˈkɒnsjʊlə(r) US: -səl-; proˈkɑnslə/ adj **pro·con·su·late** /-lət; -lɪt/ n position of a ~; his

pro·cras·ti·nate /prəʊˈkræstɪneɪt; proˈkræstəˌnet/ vi [VP2A] (formal) delay action; keep on putting off: (正式用语)耽搁; 拖延; 迟滞: He ~d until it was too late. 他拖延得太迟了。 **pro·cras·ti·na·tion** /prəʊˌkræstɪˈneɪʃn; proˌkræstəˈneʃən/ n [U]: Procrastination is the thief of time, (prov) procrastinating wastes time. (谚)拖延乃时间之贼。

pro·create /ˈprəʊkrɪeɪt; ˈprokrɪˌet/ vt [VP6A] beget, generate (offspring). 生育; 生殖; 产(子)。 **pro·cre·ation** /ˌprəʊkrɪˈeɪʃn; ˌprokrɪˈeʃən/ n

proc·tor /ˈprɒktə(r); ˈprɑktə/ n **1** (at Oxford and Cambridge) university official with various duties, including the maintenance of discipline among students. (牛津及剑桥大学的)学监; 训导员(其职务包括维持学生的纪律)。 **2** Queen's/King's P~, official whose duty is to watch the parties in certain kinds of legal cases, eg divorce, and to intervene if there are irregularities, eg collusion or suppression of facts. 王室的讼监(在某些法律案件如离婚等中, 监视诉讼当事人, 不使有串骗或隐匿事实等情者)。

procu·ra·tor /ˈprɒkjʊreɪtə(r); ˈprɑkjəˌretə/ n **1** agent, esp one who has a power of attorney. 代理人; (尤指)诉讼代理人; 代诉人。 **2** ~ **fiscal**, public prosecutor of a district in Scotland. 苏格兰的地方检察官。

pro·cure /prəˈkjʊə(r); proˈkjʊr/ vt [VP6A, 12B, 13B] **1** obtain, esp with care or effort: 获得; (尤指用心或费力)取得: Can you ~ me some specimens? 你可以为我取得一些标本吗? The book is out of print and difficult to ~. 那书已绝版, 难于获得。 **2** (old use) bring about; cause: (旧用法)促成; 引致: ~ sb's death by poison. 毒死某人。 **3** obtain clients for a prostitute. 介绍媚妓; 为…拉皮条。 **pro·cur·able** /-əbl; -əbl/ adj obtainable. 可获得的。 ~**·ment** n procuring; 获得; 得到: the ~ment of military supplies. 获得军用物资; 获得补给。 ~**r** n (esp) pander. (尤指)淫媒; 拉皮条者。 **pro·cur·ess** /-rɪs; -rɪs/ n woman ~r. 老鸨; 鸨母。

prod /prɒd; prad/ vt, vi (**-dd-**) [VP6A, 3A] ~ **(at)**, push or poke with sth pointed; (fig) urge (to action): 以尖物推或戳; (喻)促(采取行动); 激起: The cruel boys were ~ding (at) the bear through the bars of the cage. 那些残忍的孩子们隔着笼子的栏杆以尖物刺那只熊。 □ n poke or thrust: 刺; 戳: She gave the man a ~ with her umbrella. 她用伞戳了那男人一下。

prodi·gal /ˈprɒdɪɡl; ˈprɑdɪɡl/ adj ~ **(of)**, wasteful; spending or using too much: 浪费的; 挥霍的; 不吝惜的: a ~ administration, spending public funds too freely. 浪费(公帑)的政府。 Nature is ~ of her gifts. 大自然不吝惜其赐品。 **the** ~ **son**, wasteful and improvident man (in one of the parables of Jesus) who repents of his actions. 浪子(见于耶稣的寓言之一)。 ⇨ Luke 15:11. 参看路加福音第15章第11节。 □ n [C] person who is wasteful. 浪费之人; 浪子。 ~**·ly** /-ɡəli; -ɡlɪ/ adv in a manner: 浪费地; 挥霍地; 不吝惜地: a man who gives ~ly to charities. 不吝捐赠慈善事业的人。 ~**·ity** /ˌprɒdɪˈɡælɪti; ˌprɑdrˈɡælɪtɪ/ n [U] (in a good sense) being ~: (好的意思)不吝惜; 慷慨: the ~ity of the sea, ie in supplying fish; 海洋的慷慨(即大量供应鱼产); (in a bad sense) extravagance; wasteful spending. (坏的意思)浪费; 挥霍。

pro·di·gious /prəˈdɪdʒəs; prəˈdɪdʒəs/ adj enormous; surprisingly great; wonderful: 巨大的; 大得惊人的; 奇异的: a ~ sum of money. 巨款。 ~**·ly** adv

prod·igy /ˈprɒdɪdʒɪ; ˈprɑdədʒɪ/ n (pl **-gies**) sth wonderful because it seems to be contrary to the laws of nature; person who has unusual or remarkable abilities or who is a remarkable example of sth: 似乎与自然律相抵触的奇怪事物; 了不起的事物; 不凡之人; 典型人物: a ~ of learning; 饱学之士; prodigies of nature. 大自然的珍宝。 **infant** ~, extremely talented child, eg one who plays the piano well at six. 神童(具有非常才智之

儿童，如六岁即善弹钢琴）。

pro·duce /prə'djuːs US: -'duːs; prə'djus/ vt, vi [VP6A, 2A] **1** put or bring forward to be looked at or examined: 提出；呈出: ~ *proofs of a statement*: 提出说明的证据; ~ *one's railway ticket when asked to do so*. 缴验火车票. *The conjuror ~d a rabbit from his hat*. 魔术师从帽中取出一只兔子. **2** manufacture; make; grow; create: 制造; 生产; 出产; 生长; 创造: ~ *woollen goods*; 生产毛织品; *fields which ~ heavy crops*. 产量丰富的田地. *We must ~ more food for ourselves and import less*. 我们必须增产粮食减少进口. *This artist ~s very little*. 这位艺术家作品甚少. **3** give birth to; lay (eggs). 生; 产(卵). **4** cause; bring about: 引起; 导致: *success ~d by hard work and enthusiasm*; 由努力工作及热忱导致的成功; *a film that ~d a sensation*. 轰动一时的影片. **5** (maths) make (a line) longer (*to a point*). (数学)引长(线段至某点). **6** bring before the public: 演出; 出版: ~ *a new play*, organize it and put it on the stage; 演出新剧; *a well-~d book*, one that is well printed, bound, etc. 印刷、装订等都很好的书. □ n /'prɒdjuːs US: -duːs; 'prɑdjus/ [U] that which is ~d, esp by farming: 生产品; 出产品; (尤指)农产品: *garden/farm/agricultural ~*. 农圃(农场, 农业)的产品.

pro·ducer /prə'djuːsə(r) US: -'duː-; prə'djusɚ/ n **1** person who produces goods (contrasted with *consumer*). 生产者(与 consumer 相对). **2** person responsible for presenting a play in the theatre or for the production of a film (apart from the directing of the actors); person in charge of a broadcast programme (radio or TV). (戏剧)演出人; (影片)制片人; (广播或电视节目的)制作人. ⇨ **director**. **3** '~ **gas**, gas obtained by passing air through red-hot carbon or air and steam through hot coal or coke. 发生炉煤气(使空气通过炽热之碳, 或使空气与水气通过炽热之煤或焦炭所得者).

prod·uct /'prɒdʌkt; 'prɑdʌkt/ n [C] **1** sth produced (by nature or by man): (天然或人造的)产品; 生产物: '*farm ~s*; 农产品; *the chief ~s of Scotland*; 苏格兰的主要产物; *the ~s of genius*, eg great works of art. 天才的产品(如伟大的艺术作品). **2** (maths) quantity obtained by multiplication; (chem) substance obtained by chemical reaction. (数学)积; 乘积; (化学)生成物.

pro·duc·tion /prə'dʌkʃn; prə'dʌkʃən/ n **1** [U] process of producing: 制造; 生产: *the ~ of crops/manufactured goods*, etc. 农作物(工业品等)的生产. **mass ~**, ⇨ **mass**. **2** [U] quantity produced: 产量: *increase ~ by using better methods and tools*; 利用更好的方法及工具增加生产; *a fall/increase in ~*. 产量的减少(增加). **3** [C] thing produced: 制造品; 生产品: *epic ~s at the cinema*; 以英雄事迹为题材的影片; *his early ~s as a writer*, his first novels, plays, etc. 他的早期作品(小说, 戏剧等).

pro·duc·tive /prə'dʌktɪv; prə'dʌktɪv/ adj **1** able to produce; fertile: 能生产的; 肥沃的: ~ *land*. 肥沃的土地. **2** ~ *of*, tending to produce; resulting in: 有生产或导致…之倾向的; 可能产生…的: ~ *of happiness*; 可产生幸福的; *discussions that are ~ of only quarrels*. 似乎只会导致口角的讨论. **3** producing things of economic value: 生产有经济价值之东西的: ~ *labour*. 有生产作用的劳动. ~**·ly** adv

pro·duc·tiv·ity /ˌprɒdʌk'tɪvətɪ; ˌprɑdʌk'tɪvətɪ/ n [U] being productive; power of being productive: 能生产; 生产力; 生产力: *increase ~*, increase efficiency and the rate at which goods are produced; 增加生产力; *a ~ bonus for workers*. 工人的增产红利. '~ **agreement**, (as part of a wage settlement) better pay and conditions for an increased output. 增产协议(生产增加时则提高工人的薪资或改善工作环境).

pro·fane /prə'feɪn US: prəʊ-; prə'fen/ adj **1** (contrasted with *sacred*, *holy*) worldly: 凡俗的; 世俗的(与 sacred, holy 相对): ~ *literature*, (opp *biblical*). 世俗文学(为 biblical 之反义词). **2** having or showing contempt for God and sacred things: 渎神的; 亵渎的; 不敬神的: ~ *language/words/practices*; 亵渎神的言语(话, 习惯); *a ~ man*. 不敬神的人. □ vt [VP6A] treat (sacred or holy places, things) with contempt, without proper reverence: 亵渎; 玷污(圣地, 圣物): ~ *the name of God*. 亵渎上帝之名. ~**·ly** adv ~**·ness** n **pro·fa·na·tion** /ˌprɒfə'neɪʃn; ˌprɑfə'neʃən/ n [C, U] instance of profaning. 亵渎神圣; 亵渎之事例. **pro·fan·ity** /prə'fænətɪ US: prəʊ-; prə'fænɪtɪ/ n (pl **-ties**) **1** [U] ~ conduct or speech; use of ~ language. 亵渎行为或言语; 亵渎神圣; 不敬语的使用. **2** (pl) ~ phrases, utterances: (复)亵渎的词句、话: *A string of profanities came from his lips*. 从他的口里说出了一连串亵渎的话.

pro·fess /prə'fes; prə'fɛs/ vt, vi **1** [VP6A] declare that one has (beliefs, likes, ignorance, interests, etc). 公开承认; 公言; 明言具有(信念, 喜好, 愚昧, 兴趣等): *He ~es a distaste for modern music*. 他声言不喜欢现代音乐. *He ~ed a great interest in my welfare*. 他明白表示非常关心我的幸福. **2** [VP6A] affirm one's faith in, allegiance to, (a religion, Christ): 表白信仰(某宗教, 基督): ~ *Islam*. 表白信仰伊斯兰教. **3** [VP6A] (formal) have as one's profession or business: (正式用语)以…为业; 执业: ~ *law/medicine*; 做律师(医生); teach as a professor: 教; 教授: ~ *history/modern languages*. 教授历史(现代语). **4** [VP6A, 7A, 9, 25] claim; represent oneself: 声称; 自称: *I don't ~ to be an expert on that subject*. 我不自认为是那问题的专家. *He ~ed himself satisfied*. 他声称感到满意. *She ~ed that she could do nothing unaided*. 她自称无法独力做任何事. ~**ed** adj **1** self-acknowledged: 自认的; 明言的: a ~ *atheist*. 自认的无神论者. **2** falsely claiming to be: 声称的; 自称的: a ~*ed friend*. 表面上的朋友. **3** having taken religious vows: 已立誓俗行的; 已受戒的: a ~*ed nun*. 已受戒的女尼. ~**·ed·ly** /-ɪdlɪ; -ɪdlɪ/ adv according to one's own claims or admissions: 根据其声言或承认; 公言地; 诈称地: *He is ~edly a Communist*. 他自称是共产党员.

pro·fes·sion /prə'feʃn; prə'fɛʃən/ n [C] **1** occupation, esp one requiring advanced education and special training, eg the law, architecture, medicine, accountancy: 职业; (尤指需接受高深教育及特殊训练的)专门职业(例如律师, 建筑师, 医师, 会计师的职业): *He is a lawyer by ~*. 他的职业是律师. ~ *of*, statement or declaration of belief, feeling, etc: (信念, 感情等的)表白; 宣示: ~ *of faith/loyalty*. 信仰(忠诚)的表白. *She does not believe in his ~s of passionate love*. 她不相信他所表白的热爱. **3** **the ~**, the body of persons engaged in a particular ~ (1). 某专业的团体(同义). **pro·fes·sional** /prə'feʃənl; prə'fɛʃənl/ adj **1** of a profession (1): 专门职业的; 职业上的: ~ *skill*; 专门职业上的技术; ~ *etiquette*, the special conventions, forms of politeness, etc associated with a certain profession; 某行业特有的礼仪; 行规; ~ *men*, eg doctors, lawyers. 从事专门职业的人(如医生, 律师). **2** doing or practising sth as a full-time occupation or for payment or to make a living (opp of *amateur*): 职业性的; 专业的(与 amateur 相对): ~ *football*; 职业足球赛; ~ *tennis-players*; 职业网球选手; a ~ *politician*. 以从政为职业的人. □ n (contrasted with *amateur*) (与 amateur 相对) **1** (often abbr to 常略作 *pro* /prəʊ; pro/) person who teaches or engages in some kind of sport for money. 为赚钱而从事某种活动的人; 职业教练; 职业选手. **2** person who does sth for payment that others do (without payment) for pleasure: 为赚钱而从事某种游戏的人; 职业艺人; *musicians*. 职业乐师; 职业乐手; 职业音乐家. **turn ~**, become a ~. 成为职业的(选手, 演员等). ~**·ly** /-nəlɪ; -nlɪ/ adv in a ~ manner or capacity. 专业地; 在职业上. ~**·ism** /-elɪzəm; -əlɪzm/ n **1** mark or qualities of a profession (1). 某专门职业的标记或特性. **2** the practice of employing ~s to play games. 雇用职业选手参加比赛.

pro·fes·sor /prə'fesə(r); prə'fɛsɚ/ n **1** university

teacher of the highest grade, holding a chair of some branch of learning (in US, also) teacher or instructor. (大学)教授; (在美国, 亦作)教师; 讲师。**2** title assumed by instructors of various subjects: 若干科目之教师的称谓; 专家; 教授: *P~ Pate, the renowned phrenologist.* 培德教授, 著名的颅相学家。**3** one who makes a public profession(2): 公开表白其信仰等之人: *a ~ of pacifism/Catholicism.* 信守和平主义(信奉天主教义)之人。**prof·es·sorial** /ˌprɒfɪˈsɔːrɪəl; ˌprɑfəˈsɔrɪəl/ *adj* relating to a ~: (大学)教授的, 有关教授的: *his ~ial duties.* 他的教授职务。**~·ship** /-ʃɪp; -ʃɪp/ *n* ~'s post at a university: (大学的)教授职位: *be appointed to a ~ship.* 被聘为大学教授。

prof·fer /ˈprɒfə(r); ˈprɑfɚ/ *vt* [VP6A, 7A] offer. 提供; 提出。□ *n* offer. 提供; 提出。

pro·fi·cient /prəˈfɪʃnt; prəˈfɪʃənt/ *adj* ~ (in), skilled; expert. 熟练的; 精通的。**~·ly** *adv* **pro·fi·ciency** /-nsɪ; -nsɪ/ *n* **proficiency (in)**, [U] being ~: 熟练; 精通: *a certificate of proficiency in English.* 熟谙英语的证书。

pro·file /ˈprəʊfaɪl; ˈprofaɪl/ *n* **1** [U, C] side view, esp of the head: 侧面; 侧面像: *a portrait drawn in ~.* 侧面画像。**2** edge or outline of sth seen against a background. (背景衬出之)轮廓; 外形。**3** brief biography, as given in an article in a periodical or a broadcast talk. 对于人物之简短的描述; 人物素描(如杂志或广播中所作者)。□ *vt* draw, show, in ~: 作…之侧面像; 描绘…之轮廓: *a line of hills ~d against the night sky.* 以夜空为背景的群山的轮廓。

profit[1] /ˈprɒfɪt; ˈprɑfɪt/ *n* **1** [U] advantage or good obtained from sth: 利益; 裨益: *gain ~ from one's studies;* 从读书获得益处; *study sth to one's ~.* 学习某事以获益。**2** [C, U] money gained in business, etc: 利润; 赢利: *make a ~ of ten pence on every article sold;* 每卖一物获利十便士; *sell sth at a ~;* 赚钱卖出某物; *do sth for ~.* 为赢利做某事。'**~ and loss account**, (book-keeping) one that shows the trading ~ or loss for a definite period. (簿记)损益帐。'**~-margin** *n* difference between cost of purchase or production and selling price. 盈余; 成本与售价之差额。'**~-sharing** *n* [U] the sharing of ~s between employers and employees: (雇主与雇员间的)分红; 分红制: *start a ~-sharing scheme.* 开始实行一项分红制。**~·less** *adj* **~·less·ly** *adv*

profit[2] /ˈprɒfɪt; ˈprɑfɪt/ *vt, vi* **1** [VP3A] ~ **from**/ **by**, (of persons) be benefited or helped: (指人)获益; 获利: *Have you ~ed by the experience?* 你是否从该经验中获益? *I ~ed from your advice.* 你的劝告使我得到好处。**2** [VP6A, 13A] (old use) (of things) be of advantage to: (旧用法)(指事物)有利; 对…有益: *What can it ~ him?* 对他有什么利益呢? *It ~ed him nothing.* 此事对他毫无益处。

prof·it·able /ˈprɒfɪtəbl; ˈprɑfɪtəbl/ *adj* bringing profit; beneficial: 赚钱的; 获利的; 有益的: *~ investments;* 有利的投资; *a deal that was ~ to all of us.* 对大家有利的一桩买卖。**prof·it·ably** /-əblɪ; -əblɪ/ *adv*

profi·teer /ˌprɒfɪˈtɪə(r); ˌprɑfəˈtɪr/ *vi* [VP2A] make large profits, esp by taking advantage of times of difficulty or scarcity, eg in war. 获暴利; 赚大钱 (尤指利用局势困难或物资缺乏之时机, 如在战时)。□ *n* person who does this. 获暴利者, 投机商人。

prof·li·gate /ˈprɒflɪgət; ˈprɑflɪgɪt/ *adj* **1** (of a person, his behaviour) shamelessly immoral. (指人或其行为)放荡的; 淫佚的。**2** (of the spending of money) reckless; very extravagant: (指花钱)恣意的; 极其浪费的: *~ of one's inheritance.* 挥霍遗产。□ *n* ~(1) person. 放荡的人; 淫佚者。**prof·li·gacy** /ˈprɒflɪgəsɪ; ˈprɑfləgəsɪ/ *n* [U] being ~. 放荡; 淫佚; 恣意浪费。

pro forma /ˌprəʊ ˈfɔːmə; ˌpro ˈfɔrmə/ *adj* (Lat) as a formality only. (拉)仅为形式之故; 仅为样式文章。**~ invoice**, one that notifies the value of goods dispatched but does not ask for payment. 估价单。

pro·found /prəˈfaʊnd; prəˈfaʊnd/ *adj* **1** deep: 深的, 极度的: *a ~ sleep/sigh/bow;* 熟睡 (深长的叹息, 深深的鞠躬); *take a ~ interest in sth;* 对某事物深感兴趣; *listen with ~ interest.* 深感兴趣地聆听。**2** needing, showing, having, great knowledge: 需要、显示或具有渊博知识的(读者): *~ books/authors/thinkers;* 深奥的书(著作者, 思想家); *a man of ~ learning.* 博学的人。**3** needing much thought or study to understand: 需要多加思索或研究才能了解的; 奥妙的: *~ mysteries.* 奥秘。**~·ly** *adv* in a ~ manner: 深深地; 深奥地; 奥妙地: *~ly* (= deeply) *grateful/disturbing.* 深为感激的(极为扰人的)。**pro·fun·dity** /prəˈfʌndətɪ; prəˈfʌndətɪ/ *n* (*pl* **-ties**) [U] depth: 深; 精深: *the profundity of his knowledge;* 他的学问的精深; [C] (chiefly in non-material senses) that which is deep or abstruse; (*pl*) depths of thought or meaning. (主要用作非物质的意思)有深度的东西; 深奥之事物; (复)思想或意义的深奥。

pro·fuse /prəˈfjuːs; prəˈfjuːs/ *adj* **1** very plentiful or abundant: 非常丰富的; 大量的: *~ gratitude.* 千恩万谢。**2** ~ **in**, lavish or extravagant: 浪费的; 奢侈的: *He was ~ in his apologies,* apologized almost to excess. 他一再道歉(几达过分程度)。**~·ly** *adv* **~·ness** *n* **pro·fu·sion** /prəˈfjuːʒn; prəˈfjuʒən/ *n* [U] abundance; great supply: 丰富; 大量: *roses growing in profusion:* 大量盛开的玫瑰; *make promises in profusion.* 作过多的允诺。

pro·geni·tor /prəʊˈdʒenɪtə(r); proˈdʒenətɚ/ *n* (formal) ancestor (of a person, animal or plant); (fig) political or intellectual predecessor. (正式用语)(人、动植物的)祖先; (喻)政治上或学术上的前辈。

prog·eny /ˈprɒdʒənɪ; ˈprɑdʒənɪ/ *n* (formal) (collective *sing*) offspring; descendants, children. (正式用语)(集合名词单数)子孙; 后裔; 小孩。

prog·no·sis /prɒgˈnəʊsɪs; prɑgˈnosɪs/ *n* (*pl* **-noses** /-nəʊsiːz; -nosɪz/) (med) forecast of the probable course of a disease or illness. (医)病状之预断; 预后。 ⇨ **diagnosis**.

prog·nos·tic /prɒgˈnɒstɪk; prɑgˈnɑstɪk/ *adj* (formal) predictive (*of*). (正式用语)预测的; 病状预断的(与 of 连用)。□ *n* pre-indication (*of*): 预兆(与 of 连用): *a ~ of failure.* 失败的预兆。

prog·nos·ti·cate /prɒgˈnɒstɪkeɪt; prɑgˈnɑstɪˌket/ *vt* [VP6A, 9] (formal) foretell; predict: (正式用语)预言; 预示; 预测: *~ trouble.* 预示困难。**prog·nos·ti·ca·tion** /prɒgˌnɒstɪˈkeɪʃn; prɑgˌnɑstɪˈkeʃən/ *n* [U] prognosticating; [C] sth which ~s. 预言; 预示; 预测; 前兆; 征候。

pro·gramme (also **-gram**) /ˈprəʊgræm; ˈprogræm/ *n* **1** list of items, events, etc, eg for a concert, or to be broadcast for radio or TV, or for a sports meeting; list of names of actors in a play, singers in an opera, etc. 节目单(例如音乐会、广播、电视或运动会中者); 程序表; (戏剧或歌剧等中之)演员名单。'**~ music**, music designed, in sound, to suggest to the listener a known story, picture, etc. 效果音乐; 背景音乐; 标题音乐。'**~ note**, short account, in a ~, eg of a musical work, a performer, etc. (对乐曲、表演者等的)简短介绍。**2** plan of what is to be done: 工作计划; 行动预定表: *a political ~.* 政治纲领。*What's the ~ for tomorrow?* What are we/you going to do? 明天要做什么? **3** coded collection of information, data, etc fed into an electronic computer. (电脑)程序。□ *vt* [VP6A] make a ~ of or for; supply (a computer) with a ~; plan. 编制…之节目单; 拟…之计划; 以一批相关的资料供给(电脑)作为计算资料; 设计。**~d course**, (education) one in which the material to be learnt is presented (in books or a machine) in small, carefully graded amounts. (教育)编序课程。**~d learning**, self-instruction using such courses. 编序教学; 程序学习。**pro·gram·mer** *n* person who prepares a computer ~. 电脑程序设计人; 程序师。

prog·ress /ˈprəʊgres US: ˈprɒg-; ˈprɑgres/ *n* **1** [U] forward movement; advance; development: 进步; 进

展; 改进; 发展: *making fast* ~; 进步神速: *make* ~ *in one's studies*; 学业有进步; ~ *in civilization*. 文明的进展. *An inquiry is now in* ~, *being made*. 一项调查目前正在进行中. *The patient is making good* ~, *is improving*. 这个病人的病情大有起色. **2** [C] (old use) state journey: (旧用法)王侯的视察; 巡行: *a royal* ~ *through Cornwall*. 国王巡行康沃尔. □ *vi* /prə'gres; prə'grɛs/ [VP2A, C] make ~: 进步; 进行: *The work is* ~*ing steadily*. 工作正在稳定地进行中. *She is* ~*ing in her studies*. 她在学业上有进步.

pro·gres·sion /prə'greʃn; prə'grɛʃən/ *n* **1** [U] progress; moving forward: 进步; 前进; 行进: *modes of* ~, eg crawling, walking. 行进的方式(如爬、步行). **2** (maths) (数学) ⇨ **arithmetic, geometry**.

pro·gres·sive /prə'gresɪv; prə'grɛsɪv/ *adj* **1** making continuous forward movement. 前进的. **the** ~ **tenses**, (gram) forms of the verb (using the ending *-ing*) that express action that continues over a period of time, as in 'I am/was/will be/have been writing, (Also called 亦称作 *continuous tenses*.) (语法)进行时(be + -ing 之形式, 表示动作持续一段时间, 如 I am/was/will be/have been writing). **2** increasing by regular degrees or advancing in successive stages: 累进的; 递增的: ~ *education/schools*; 循序渐进的教育(学校); ~ *taxation*, with an increase of the rate of tax as the incomes increase; 累进课税; ~ *cancer*, becoming steadily worse. 继续恶化的癌; 扩散性癌. **3** undergoing improvement; getting better, eg in civilization; supporting or favouring progress: 改进的; 上进的; 进步的(如在文明方面): supports or approves of 支持或赞成进步的: a ~ *policy*; 进步的政策; a ~ *political party*. 提倡改革的政党. □ *n* person supporting a ~ policy. 支持进步政策者; 进步论者. ~·**ly** *adv* ~·**ness** *n*

pro·hibit /prə'hɪbɪt US: proʊ-; pro'hɪbɪt/ *vt* [VP 6A, 14] ~ *sb* (**from doing sth**), forbid (esp by rules or regulations); say that sth must not be done, that sb must not do sth: 禁止; 阻止: *Smoking strictly* ~*ed*. 严禁吸烟. *Children are* ~*ed from buying cigarettes*. 禁止儿童购买香烟.

pro·hib·ition /ˌprəʊɪ'bɪʃn; ˌproə'bɪʃən/ *n* **1** [U] prohibiting; (esp) prohibiting by law the making or sale of alcoholic drinks (esp, US, the period 1920–1933): 禁止; (尤指美国 一九二〇至一九三三 年期间)禁止造酒或卖酒: *the* ~ *law(s)*; 禁酒法; *in favour of/opposed to* ~. 赞成(反对)禁酒. **2** [C] edict or order that forbids: 禁令; 禁律: a ~ *against the sale of cigarettes to children*. 禁止售卖香烟给儿童之命令. ~·**ist** /-ɪst; -ɪst/ *n* person who favours the ~ of sth, esp the sale of alcoholic drink. 赞成禁止某物者; (尤指)赞成禁酒者.

pro·hibi·tive /prə'hɪbətɪv US: proʊ-; pro'hɪbɪtɪv/ *adj* tending to, intended to, prevent the use or abuse or purchase of sth: 禁止的; 意欲阻止使用, 滥用或购买某物的: a ~ *tax*; 寓禁税; *books published at* ~ *prices*. 以高至令人不敢问津的价格所发行的书.

pro·hibi·tory /prə'hɪbətrɪ US: proʊ'hɪbɪtɔːrɪ; pro'hɪbə,tori/ *adj* designed to prohibit sth: 有禁止之意的: 为禁止某物而设计的: ~ *laws*. 查禁的法令.

pro·ject¹ /'prɒdʒekt; 'prɑdʒɛkt/ *n* [C] (plan for a) scheme or undertaking: 计划; 计划; 事业; 企业: a ~ to *establish a new national park*; 建立一座新的国家公园的计划; *form/carry out/fail in a* ~. 拟订一计划(执行一计划; 计划失败).

pro·ject² /prə'dʒekt; prə'dʒɛkt/ *vt*, *vi* **1** [VP6A] make plans for: 计划; 设计: ~ *a new dam/waterworks*. 设计新水坝(自来水厂). **2** [VP6A, 14] ~ *sth* (**on** (**to**) *sth*), cause a shadow, an outline, a picture from a film, slide, etc to fall on a surface, etc: 使(影子、轮廓、影片、幻灯片等之图像)投落在某物表面等上; 投射; 放映: ~ *a picture on a screen*; 将影片放映在银幕上; ~ *a beam of light on to sth*. 投射一道光线在某物上. **3** [VP14] ~ *sth on to sb*, attribute unconsciously (usu

unpleasant feelings such as guilt, inferiority) to other people (often as a means of self-justification or self-defence): 归咎; 将某事归罪某人; (心理)投射: *She always* ~*s her own neuroses on to her colleagues*, describes them as suffering from them. 她有神经病, 总是对她的同事疑神疑鬼. **4** [VP6A] make known the characteristics of: 使…之特色为人所知; 表达…的特色: *Do the B B C External Services adequately* ~ *Great Britain*, give listeners right ideas about British life, etc? 英国广播公司的海外广播部能使听众对英国生活有正确认识吗? **5** [VP6A, 15A] throw; hurl: 抛; 投; 射: *an apparatus to* ~ *missiles into space*. 发射导弹进入太空的装置. **6** [VP6A] represent (a solid thing) on a plane surface by drawing straight lines through every point of it from a centre; make (a map) in this way. 借投影图表示(某立体物); 以投影法制作(地图). **7** [VP2A, C] stick out; stand out beyond the surface nearby: 突出; 伸出附近之平面: ~*ing eyebrows*; 突出的眉毛; *a balcony that* ~*s over the street*. 伸到街上的阳台.

pro·jec·tile /prə'dʒektaɪl US: -tl; prə'dʒɛktḷ/ *n* sth (to be) shot forward, esp from a gun; self-propelling missile, eg a rocket. 抛射物; 投射物; (尤指)弹丸; 火箭; 导弹. □ *adj* able to send sth, or be sent, forward through air, water, etc: 能(被)抛射或送入空气、水等的: 抛射的; 发射的: a ~ *missile/torpedo*. 抛射导弹(鱼雷).

pro·jec·tion /prə'dʒekʃn; prə'dʒɛkʃən/ *n* **1** [U] the act of projecting (all senses); [C] sth that projects or has been projected; prominence. 计划; 投射; 抛掷; 投影; 突出; 投射作用; 所计划, 投射, 投掷, 投影之物; 突出部分. '~ **room**, (in a cinema) room from which pictures are projected on to the screen. (电影院)放映室. ⇨ **Mercator's projection**. ~·**ist** /-ɪst; -ɪst/ *n* (in a cinema) person who projects the pictures on to the screen. (电影院)放映电影者; 放映技师.

pro·jec·tor /prə'dʒektə(r); prə'dʒɛktɚ/ *n* [C] apparatus for projecting pictures by rays of light on to a screen: 影像放映机: a '*cinema*/'*slide* ~. 电影(幻灯片)放映机.

pro·lapse /'prəʊlæps; prə'læps/ *vi* (med, eg of the bowel or uterus) slip forward or down out of place. (医, 如指肠或子宫)脱出; 脱垂. □ *n* /'prəʊlæps; 'proʊlæps/ such a movement. 脱出, 脱垂.

prole /prəʊl; prol/ *n* (colloq) member of the proletariat. (口)无产者.

pro·let·ariat /ˌprəʊlɪ'teərɪət; ˌprolɪ'tɛrɪət/ *n* **1** the whole body of wage-earners (esp manual workers) contrasted with the owners of industry (the bourgeoisie): 无产阶级; 劳动阶级: *the dictatorship of the* ~, as a Communist aim or ideal. 无产阶级专政. **2** (in ancient Rome) the lowest class of the community. (古罗马)社会之最下层阶级. **pro·let·arian** /-ɪən; -ɪən/ *n*, *adj* (member) of the ~. 无产者; 无产阶级的.

pro·lif·er·ate /prə'lɪfəreɪt US: proʊ-; pro'lɪfə,ret/ *vi*, *vt* **1** [VP2A] grow, reproduce, by rapid multiplication of cells, new parts, etc. 增生或繁殖(细胞等). **2** [VP6A] reproduce (cells, etc). 增生或繁殖(细胞等). **pro·lif·er·ation** /prəˌlɪfə'reɪʃn US: proʊ-; pro,lɪfə'reʃən/ *n*. **non-proliferation treaty**, eg one for controlling the spread of nuclear weapons to States not having them. 禁止扩散条约(如防止无核武器国家拥有此种武器).

pro·lific /prə'lɪfɪk; prə'lɪfɪk/ *adj* (formal) producing much or many: (正式用语)多产的; 大量生产的: a ~ *author*, one who writes many books, etc; 多产作家; *as* ~ *as rabbits*, producing numerous offspring. 多产如兔; 生殖力特强的.

pro·lix /'prəʊlɪks US: prə'lɪks; pro'lɪks/ *adj* (formal) (of a speaker, writer, speech, etc) tedious; tiring because too long. (正式用语)(指演说者、作家、演说等)啰嗦的; 冗长令人生厌的. **pro·lix·ity** /prəʊ'lɪksətɪ; pro'lɪksəti/

pro·logue /'prəʊlɒg US: -lɔːg; 'prolɔg/ *n* **1** introductory part of a poem; poem recited at the beginning

map projection | Lines of Latitude run in the same direction as the equator

Lines of Longitude run from Pole to Pole

CONICAL PROJECTION

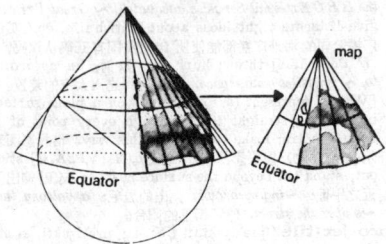

Equator / map / Equator

MERCATOR'S PROJECTION

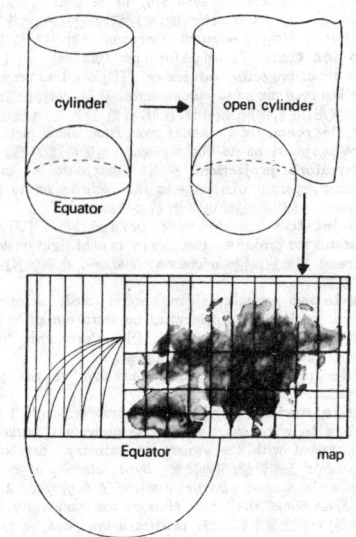

cylinder → open cylinder

Equator

Equator / map

ZENITHAL PROJECTION

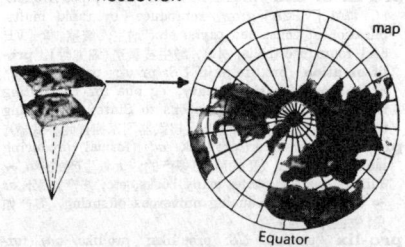

map

Equator

of a play: (诗之)序词; 序诗(诗的介绍部分); (戏剧的)开场白; 开场诗: *the 'P~' to the 'Canterbury Tales'*. 《坎特伯雷故事集》的'序诗'. **2** (fig) first of a series of events. (喻)一连串事件的开端; 序幕性事件.
pro·long /prə'lɒŋ *US:* -'lɔːŋ; prə'lɔŋ/ *vt* [VP6A] make longer: 延长; 拖延: *~ a visit / a line.* 延长访问

(一条线). **~ed** *adj* continuing for a long time: 持续很久的; 长时期的: *after ~ed questioning.* 在长时间的质询之后. **pro·lon·ga·tion** /ˌprəʊlɒŋ'geɪʃn *US:* -lɔːŋ-; ˌprolɔŋ'geʃən/ *n* [U] making longer; the state of being made longer; [C] that which is added in order to ~. 延长; 拖延; 延长或附加之部分.
prom /prɒm/ *n* (colloq abbr of) (口, 以下各义之略) **1** (GB) seaside promenade; promenade concert. (英)海滨胜地临水的大路; 逍遥音乐会. **2** (US) promenade(2). (美)(高中或大学某班学生的)正式舞会.
prom·en·ade /ˌprɒmə'nɑːd *US:* -'neɪd; ˌprɑmə'ned/ *n* **1** (place suitable for, specially made for, a) walk or ride taken in public, for exercise or pleasure, esp a broad road along the water-front at a seaside resort, or a part of a theatre where people may walk about during the intervals, etc. (为运动或散心所作的)散步; 骑马; 散步或骑马的地方; (尤指)海滨胜地临水的大道; 戏院供人们在幕间休息时走动的场所. '~ concert, one at which parts of the concert hall have no seats and are used by listeners who stand. 逍遥音乐会(部分场所无座位; 以容纳站定的听众). '~ deck, upper deck of a liner, where passengers may walk. 客轮的上层甲板(旅客可在上面散步); 散步甲板. **2** (US) formal dance or ball (for a class in a high-school or college). (美)(高中或大学某班学生的)正式舞会. □ *vi, vt* [VP2A, C] go up and down a ~; [VP6A, 15A] take (sb) up and down a ~: 在散步场、海滨大道等处来回走动; 带着(某人)在此等场所散步, 骑马等. *~ one's children / one's husband along the sea-front.* 带着孩子(丈夫)在海滨大道散步.
promi·nent /'prɒmɪnənt; 'prɑmənənt/ *adj* **1** standing out; easily seen: 突出的; 显着的: *~ cheek-bones;* 突出的颧骨; *the most ~ feature in the landscape.* 那风景中最显着的特色. **2** (of persons) distinguished; eminent: (指人)卓越的; 杰出的: *~ politicians / scientists.* 卓越的政治家(科学家). **3** important; conspicuous: 重要的; 引人注目的: *occupy a ~ position;* 居高位; 居显职; *play a ~ part in civic life.* 在市民生活中扮演重要的角色. **~·ly** *adv* **promi·nence** /-əns; -əns/ *n* **1** [U] the state of being ~. 突出; 显着; 卓越; 重要. *bring sth / come into prominence,* (cause to) become ~. (使某物)变得显着, 重要. **2** [C] ~ part or place: 突出的部分或地方: *a ~ in the middle of a plain.* 平原中央突起的部分.
pro·mis·cu·ous /prə'mɪskjʊəs; prə'mɪskjʊəs/ *adj* **1** confused and disorderly; unsorted: 杂乱的; 混淆的; 一团糟的: *in a ~ heap.* 成为杂乱的一堆. **2** indiscriminate; casual: 不加选择的; 随便的: *~ friendships,* made without careful choice; 交友不加选择; *~ sexual intercourse.* 乱交; 杂交. **~·ly** *adv* **prom·is·cu·ity** /ˌprɒmɪ'skjuːətɪ; ˌprɑmɪs'kjuətɪ/ *n* (state of) being ~; confusion caused by being ~. 杂乱; 不加选择; 杂交; 混乱.
prom·ise¹ /'prɒmɪs; 'prɑmɪs/ *n* **1** [C] written or spoken undertaking to do, or not to do, sth: 诺言; 约定: *~s of help;* 给予帮助的诺言; *make / give / keep / carry out / break a ~;* 许下(提出, 信守, 履行, 违背)诺言; *under a ~ of secrecy.* 在保守秘密的承诺之下. **2** [C] that which one undertakes to do: 约定或承诺要做的事: *I claim your ~,* require you to do what you said you would do. 我要求你履行诺言. **3** [U] (sth that gives) hope of success or good results: (有成功或良好结果的)希望; 有希望的事物: *boys who don't show much ~,* do not seem likely to succeed; 没有多大出息的男孩们; *a writer of ~;* 有希望的作家; *the land of ~.* 想望之福地.
prom·ise² /'prɒmɪs; 'prɑmɪs/ *vt, vi* **1** [VP6A, 7A, 9, 11, 12A, 13A, 17] make a promise(1) to: 答应; 允诺; 约定: *They ~d an immediate reply.* 他们答应即刻回复. *He ~d me to be here / that he would be here at 6 o'clock.* 他和我约好(六点钟)到此. *I ~d myself a quiet weekend.* 我决定要过一个平静的周末. *'Will you*

come?'—'Yes, I ~.' '你会来吗?'——'是的, 我会的。' **the P~d Land,** the land of promise: **(a)** the fertile country ~d to the Israelites by God; Canaan. 上帝答应给以色列人的肥沃土地; 迦南。**(b)** any state of future happiness. 未来的幸福境界。**2** [VP6A, 2A] give cause for expecting: 有…希望; 预示: *The clouds ~ rain.* 阴云预示有雨。*It ~s to be warm this afternoon.* 今天下午可望转暖。**~ well,** show signs of success. 大有希望; 显示成功的迹象。**prom·is·ing** *adj* full of promise(3); seeming likely to succeed, have good results, etc. 有希望的; 有前途的; 大有可为的。

prom·iss·ory /'prɒmɪsərɪ *US:* -sɔːrɪ; 'prɑməˌsorɪ/ *adj* conveying a promise. 约定的; 应许的。**'~ note,** signed promise to pay a stated sum of money to a specified person or to the bearer on a specified date or on demand. 期票; 本票。

prom·on·tory /'prɒməntrɪ *US:* -tɔːrɪ; 'prɑmənˌtorɪ/ *n* [C] headland; high point of land standing out from the coastline. 岬; 海角。

pro·mote /prə'məʊt; prə'mot/ *vt* **1** [VP6A, 14] **~ (to),** give (sb) a higher position or rank: 擢升: *He was ~d sergeant/to sergeant/to the rank of sergeant.* 他被升做士官。**2** [VP6A] help to organize and start; help the progress of; help to found or organize: 协办; 筹设; 提倡; 促进; 创设: *~ a new business company;* 筹设一家新的商行; *~ a bill in Parliament;* 促使议案在国会通过; *try to ~ good feelings (between ...).* 设法促进(…彼此间的)好感。**pro·mo·ter** *n* (esp) person who ~s new trading companies, professional sports, etc. (尤指)新公司的发起人; 筹设者; 职业性运动的倡导人; 赞助人。

pro·mo·tion /prə'məʊʃn; prə'moʃən/ *n* **1** [U] promoting or being promoted: 擢升; 晋级; 协办; 筹设: *win/gain ~.* 获得晋级。*Ought ~ to go by seniority or by merit and abilities?* 擢升应以年资, 还是以功绩和能力为准? **2** [C] instance of promoting or being promoted: 擢升、协办等的实例: *He resigned from the firm because ~s were few and far between.* 他辞去那家公司的差事, 因为升迁少, 而每升一级又要隔很长时间。**3** encouragement by publicity, etc: 以广告推销; 促销: *the ~ of a new commercial product/a new book;* 一种新商品(一本新书)的推销; *sales ~,* advertising, publicising one's products. 以广告推销; 宣传产品。

prompt[1] /prɒmpt; prɑmpt/ *adj* acting, done, sent, given, without delay: 迅速的; 敏捷的; 即时的: *a ~ reply;* 迅速的回答; *~ payment;* 即时付钱; *men who are ~ to volunteer;* 敏于自告奋勇的人; *at 6 pm ~* (=~ly). 下午六时正。**~·ly** *adv* **~·ness** *n*

prompt[2] /prɒmpt; prɑmpt/ *vt* **1** [VP6A, 17A] be the reason causing (sb to do sth): 促使(某人做某事); 激励; 鼓励; 唤起; 驱使: *He was ~ed by patriotism.* 他为爱国心所激励。*What ~ed him to be so generous?* 是什么使得他如此大方? **2** [VP6A] follow the text of a play and, when an actor forgets his words, say quietly some of these to him. 提示台词给(演员); 提词。□ *n* action of ~ing (an actor): 提词: *wait for a ~.* 等候提词。**'~-box** *n* place where the ~er sits. 提词者的座位。**'~-copy** *n* text of a play, used by a ~er. 提词者用的剧本。**~er** *n* person who ~s actors. 提词者。

promp·ti·tude /'prɒmptɪtjuːd *US:* -tuːd; 'prɑmptəˌtjud/ *n* [U] promptness; readiness to act. 迅速; 敏捷; 机敏行事。

prom·ul·gate /'prɒmlgeɪt; prə'mʌlget/ *vt* [VP6A] **1** make public, announce officially (a decree, a new law, etc). 宣布; 公布; 颁布(命令、新法律等)。**2** spread widely beliefs, knowledge, opinions, etc. 传播; 散播(信念、知识、意见等)。**prom·ul·ga·tion** /ˌprɒml'geɪʃn; ˌpromʌl'geʃən/ *n* [U].

prone /prəʊn; pron/ *adj* **1** (stretched out, lying) face downwards; prostrate: 面向下的; 俯伏的; 俯卧的: *in a ~ position;* 成俯伏的姿势; 卧姿地; *fall ~.* 面朝下跌倒。**2 ~ to,** liable, inclined: 易于…的; 有…之倾向的: *~ to accidents/error/anger/idleness/superstition* (and other generally undesirable things). 容易发生意外事故(犯错、发怒、偷懒、迷信以及其他令人不快的事物)的。**'accident-~** *adj* often experiencing accidents: 时常发生意外事故的: *Some people seem to be accident-~.* 有些人似乎时常发生意外事故。**~·ness** *n*

prong /prɒŋ *US:* prɔːŋ; prɔŋ/ *n* each one of the long, pointed parts of a fork. 叉(之一)股; 叉尖; 叉头。**~ed** *adj* (in compounds) having the kind or number of ~s indicated: (用于复合词中)有某种或某数量之叉股的: *a ˌthree-~ed 'fork;* 一把三股叉; *a ˌthree-~ed at'tack,* (mil) one made by three attacking forces. (军)三路进攻。

pro·nomi·nal /prəʊ'nɒmɪnl; prə'nɑmənl/ *adj* of (the nature of) a pronoun. 代词的; 有代词性质的。

pro·noun /'prəʊnaʊn; 'pronaʊn/ *n* word used in place of a *n* or *n phrase*, eg *he, it, hers, me, them.* 代词(如 he, it, hers, me, them)。

pro·nounce /prə'naʊns; prə'naʊns/ *vt, vi* **1** [VP 6A, 9, 22, 25] declare, announce (esp formally, solemnly or officially): 宣称; 宣布(尤指正式, 严肃或官方地): *The doctors ~d him to be/~d that he was out of danger.* 医生们宣称他已脱离危险。*Has judgement been ~d yet?* 判决已宣布了吗? **2** [VP9, 25] declare as one's opinion: 断言; 声言: *The wine was tasted and ~d excellent.* 那葡萄酒已被尝过并被认定为好酒。*He ~d himself in favour of the plan.* 他声言赞成那计划。**3** [VP3A] **~ for/against sb,** (legal) pass judgement (in a law court). (法律)(在法院)判决有利(不利)某人。**~ on/upon,** give one's opinion on, eg a proposal. 对(如某提议)表示意见。**4** [VP6A, 2A] utter, make the sound of (a word, etc): 发出(字等的)声音; 发音: *He ~s badly.* 他发音不好。*How do you ~ p-h-l-e-g-m?* 你怎样读 p-h-l-e-g-m 这字? *The 'b' in 'debt' is not ~d.* debt 中的 b 不发音。**~·able** /-əbl; -əbl̩/ *adj* (of sounds, words) that can be ~d. (指声音, 字)可发音的。**~d** *adj* definite; strongly marked: 确切的; 明白表示的: *a man of ~d opinions.* 有坚定意见的人。**~·ment** *n* [C] formal statement or declaration. 公告; 文告; 声明。

pronto /'prɒntəʊ; 'prɑnto/ *adv* (sl) quickly; at once. (俚)很快地; 立刻; 马上。

pro·nun·cia·mento /prəˌnʌnsɪə'mentəʊ; prəˌnʌnsɪə'mɛnto/ *n* (*pl* **~s** /-təʊz; -toz/) manifesto or proclamation. 宣言; 檄文; 布告。

pro·nun·ci·ation /prəˌnʌnsɪ'eɪʃn; prəˌnʌnsɪ'eʃən/ *n* **1** [U] way in which a language is spoken: (一种语言的)发音; 发音法: *lessons in ~;* 发音课程; *study the ~ of English.* 研究英语的发音法。**2** [U] person's way of speaking a language, or words of a language: (一个人的)发音; 发音方式: *His ~ is improving.* 他的发音在进步中。**3** [C] way in which a word is pronounced: (一字的)读法: *Which of these three ~s do you recommend?* 这三种读法你认为哪一种好?

proof[1] /pruːf; pruf/ *n* **1** [U] evidence (in general), or [C] a particular piece of evidence, that is sufficient to show, or helps to show, that sth is a fact: (一般的)证据; 证明文件; 证言; 物证: *We shall require ~(s) of that statement.* 我们将需要那项声明之证据。*Is there any ~ that the accused man was at the scene of the crime?* 有没有证据证明被告在犯罪的现场? *They gave him a gold watch as (a) ~ of their regard.* 他们送他一个金表, 以表示敬意。*Can you give ~ of your nationality/~ that you are British?* 你能证明你的国籍(你是英国人)吗? **2** [U] demonstrating; testing of whether sth is true, a fact, etc: 证明; 验证: *Is life on the planet Mars capable of ~?* 火星上有生物存在的说法能验证吗? *He produced documents in ~ of his claim.* 他提出文件以证明他的所有权。**3** [C] test, trial, examination: 考验; 试验; 测验: *put sth to the ~,* test it. 试验某事物。*It has stood the ~,* has passed the test. 经得起考验(已通过了试验)。***The ~ of the pudding is in the eating,*** (prov) The real test is practical, not theoretical. (谚)

布丁之美味吃时方知; 空言不如实验。 **4** [C] trial copy of sth printed or engraved, for approval before other copies are printed: (印刷物的)校样; 校稿: *pass the ~s for press,* approve them, approve that printing may be begun. 看完校样同意付印。 **'~-read** *vi, vt* [VP2A, 6A] read and correct ~s. 校对。 **'~-reader** *n* person employed to read and correct ~s. 校对员; 改正校稿者。 **5** [U] standard of strength of distilled alcoholic liquors: (酒的)标准酒精度: *This rum is 30 per cent below ~.* 这种朗姆酒的酒精度低于标准百分之三十。 ⇨ **spirit,** alcoholic mixture which is up to standard. 标准强度的酒; 合酒精。

proof² /pruːf; pruf/ *adj* **~ (against),** giving safety or protection; able to resist or withstand: 防止的; 耐…的; 有耐力的; 不能透入的; 坚固的: *~ against bullets;* 防弹的; *'bullet-~;* 防弹的; *'water ~;* 防水的; *'sound~;* 隔音的; *'splinter-~;* 防弹片的; 防碎片的; *'shatter-~;* 防破碎的; 不碎的; (fig) (喻) *~ against temptation.* 能抵抗诱惑的。 **'fool-~** *adj* incapable of failure; involving no risk. 永不会失败的, 安全无比的; 万无一失的。 □ *vt* [VP6A] make (sth) ~ (esp make a fabric *water~*). 使(某物)禁得住…; (尤指)使(布)防水。

prop¹ /prɒp; prɑp/ *n* **1** support used to keep sth up: 支持物; 支柱; 撑材: *'pit-~s,* supporting the roof in a coalmine; 煤矿的坑道支柱; *a 'clothes-~,* holding up a line on which laundered clothes are drying. 晾衣绳支柱。 **2** person who supports sth or sb: 支持者; 后援者; 倚靠人: *He is the ~ of his parents in their old age.* 他是父母年老时的奉养者。 □ *vt* (-pp-) [VP6A, 15A, B, 22] *~ sth (up),* support; keep in position: 支持; 维持; 使…倚靠某一位置: *Use this box to ~ the door open.* 用这箱子撑门, 让它开着。 *The nurse ~ped her patient (up) on the pillows.* 护士使病人倚靠在枕头上。 *I ~ped the ladder against the wall.* 我把梯子靠着墙放。 (fig) (喻) *He can't always expect his colleagues to ~ him up.* 他不能老期望他的同事们支持他。

prop² /prɒp; prɑp/ *n* (colloq abbr of) **propeller.** (口) 为 propeller 之略。 ⇨ **turboprop.**

prop³ /prɒp; prɑp/ *n* (colloq abbr of) (stage) property: (口) 为 (stage) property 之略: *Who's in charge of the ~s?* 谁负责管理道具? ⇨ **property(5).**

propa·ganda /ˌprɒpə'gændə; ˌprɑpə'gændə/ *n* [U] information; (derog) doctrines, opinions, official statements: 宣传资料; (贬) 宣传(指教条、言论、官方声明): *~ by government departments for public health, better driving, etc;* 政府机构为公共卫生、驾驶安全等所作的宣传; *political ~;* 政治宣传; (attrib) (用作定语) *~ plays / films.* 宣传剧(电影)。 **the Congregation / College of the P~,** a committee of RC cardinals in charge of foreign missions. 天主教的传道总会(负责海外传教由红衣主教组成的委员会)。 **propa·gan·dist** /-dɪst; -dɪst/ *n* person who spreads ~. 宣传者; 宣传家。 **propa·gan·dize** /-daɪz; -daɪz/ *vi* spread ~; 宣传; 传播; 传教。

propa·gate /'prɒpəgeɪt; 'prɑpəget/ *vt, vi* (formal) (正式用语) **1** [VP6A] increase the number of (plants, animals, diseases) by natural process from the parent stock: 繁殖; 增值; 繁衍; 使(疾病)蔓延: *~ plants by taking cuttings.* 借插枝繁殖植物。 *Trees ~ themselves by seeds.* 树木借种子繁殖。 **2** [VP6A] spread more widely: 传播: *~ news / knowledge.* 传播消息(知识)。 **3** [VP6A] transmit; extend the operation of: 传导; 传送: *vibrations ~d through rock.* 由岩石传导的震动。 **4** [VP2A] (of animals and plants) reproduce; multiply. (指动植物)繁殖; 增殖。 **propa·ga·tor** /-tə(r); -tɚ/ *n* **propa·ga·tion** /ˌprɒpə'geɪʃn; ˌprɑpə'geʃən/ *n* [U] propagating: 繁殖; 增殖; 传播; 传导: *the propagation of disease by insects / of plants by cuttings.* 由昆虫传播疾病(借插枝繁殖植物)。

pro·pane /'prəupeɪn; 'propen/ *n* [U] colourless gas (C_3H_8) (in natural gas and petroleum) used as a fuel. 丙烷(取自天然煤气和石油的无色气体, 用作燃料)。

pro·pel /prə'pel; prə'pɛl/ *vt* (-ll-) [VP6A, 15A] drive forward: 推进; 推动: *mechanically ~led vehicles;* 机械力推动的车辆; *a boat ~led by oars;* 以桨操作的船; *a ~ling pencil,* with lead that is ~led forward as the outer case is turned. 自动铅笔(转动笔杆, 铅心即向前推进)。 **~·lant, ~·lent** /-ənt; -ənt/ *adj, n* ~ling (agent); explosive substance that ~s a bullet from a fire-arm; fuel that burns to ~ a rocket, etc. 推进的; 推动的; 推进者; 推动物; 发射弹丸的火药; 发射火箭的燃料。 **~·ler** *n* two or more spiral blades, fixed to a revolving shaft, for driving a ship or aircraft. 推进器; 螺旋桨。 ⇨ *air-screw* and the illus at **air¹.** 参看 air¹ 之 air-screw 及插图。

pro·pen·sity /prə'pensətɪ; prə'pɛnsəti/ *n* [C] (pl -ties) ~ *to / towards sth / to do sth / for doing sth,* natural tendency: 倾向; 习性; 嗜好: *a ~ to exaggerate;* 夸大的习性; *a ~ for getting into debt.* 好欠债的习性。

proper /'prɒpə(r); 'prɑpɚ/ *adj* **1** right, correct, fitting, suitable: 正当的; 正确的; 适当的; 适合的: *clothes ~ for such an occasion;* 适合此种场合的衣服; *not a ~ time for merrymaking.* 不是作乐的适当时候。 *Are you doing it the ~ way?* 你是在用正确的方法做那事吗? *Is this the ~ tool for the job?* 这是做那工作的适当工具吗? *We must do the ~ thing by him,* treat him in the right way, be fair or loyal to him. 我们必须合理对待他(对他公平或忠实)。 **2** in conformity with, paying regard to, the conventions of society; respectable: 遵守或注重社会习尚的; 可敬的; 高尚的: *~ behaviour.* 高尚的行为。 *He's not at all a ~ person for a young girl to know.* 他根本不是适于少女结识的男子。 *That's not a ~ thing to do in the public park.* 那是不适于在公园中做的事。 **3** ~ *to,* (formal) belonging especially; relating distinctively: (正式用语)专属的; 独特的; 专述的; 专为…的: *the books ~ to this subject;* 专论本题的书; *the psalms ~ to this Sunday.* 这个礼拜天专用的圣诗。 **4** (placed after the *n*) strictly so called; genuine: (置于名词之后)严格所言的; 真正的; 本来的: *architecture ~,* excluding, for example, the question of water-supply, electric current, etc. 建筑物的本身(例如不包括水电装置等)。 **5** (colloq) great; thorough: (口语的) 彻底的: *We're in a ~ mess.* 我们真是一团糟。 *He gave the burglar a ~ hiding,* beat him thoroughly. 他痛殴那窃贼。 **~ fraction,** (eg $\frac{1}{2}$, $\frac{3}{4}$) one in which the number above the line is smaller than that below the line. (数学)真分数(如 $\frac{1}{2}$, $\frac{3}{4}$)。 **~ noun / name,** (gram) name used for an individual person, town, etc eg *Mary, Prague.* (语法)专有名词(如 *Mary, Prague*)。 **~·ly** *adv* **1** in a ~ manner: 正当地; 适合地; 可敬地; 专属地; 真正地: *behave ~ly.* 行为正当。 *Do it ~ly or not at all.* 好好地做, 否则就别做。 *He is not ~ly (= strictly) speaking a chemist.* 严格地说, 他不是一位化学家。 **2** (colloq) thoroughly: (口)彻底地: *The American boxer was ~ly beaten by the new world champion.* 那位美国拳击手被本届世界冠军打得惨败。

prop·erty /'prɒpətɪ; 'prɑpɚti/ *n* (pl -ties) **1** [U] (collectively) things owned; possessions: (总称)财产; 资产; 拥有之物: *Don't interfere with these tools— they're not your ~.* 不要乱弄这些工具—它们不是你的东西。 **man of ~,** wealthy man. 富人; 财主。 **common ~,** known to, possessed by, many people. 公物; 人所共知之事。 **personal ~,** movable belongings. 动产。 **real ~,** land, buildings. 不动产。 **2** [C] estate; area of land or land and buildings: 地产; 房地产: *He has a small ~ (a house and a house) in Kent.* 他在肯特有一笔小小的房地产。 **3** [U] ownership; the fact of owning or being owned: 所有权; 所有: *There is no ~ in the sea-shore,* it cannot be privately owned. 海岸不能据为私有。 **4** [C] special quality that belongs to sth: 特性; 属性; 性质: *the chemical properties of iron;* 铁的化学性质; *herbs with healing properties.* 有治疗性能的药草。 **5** (theatre) (abbr 略作 prop) article of dress or furniture or other thing (except scenery) used on the stage in

the performance of a play. (戏剧)服装或道具(布景以外的一切舞台用具). '**~-man/-master,** (also 亦以 *props-man / -master*), *n* man in charge of stage properties. (舞台的)道具、服装等之管理人。 **prop·er·tied** /'prɒpətɪd; 'prɑpətɪd/ *adj* owning ~, esp land: 有财产的; (尤指)有地产的: *the propertied classes*, the landowners. 地主阶级。

proph·ecy /'prɒfɪsɪ; 'prɑfəsɪ/ *n* (*pl* **-cies**) **1** [U] power of telling what will happen in the future: 预言能力: *have the gift of* ~. 有预言的天才。 **2** [C] statement that tells what will happen: 预言: *His ~ was fulfilled*. 他的预言应验了。

proph·esy /'prɒfɪsaɪ; 'prɑfə,saɪ/ *vt, vi* (*pt, pp* **-sied**) **1** [VP6A, 9, 10] foretell; say (what will happen in the future): 预言; 预言(未来将发生之事): ~ *war / that war will break out*. 预言战争将爆发。 **2** [VP2A, C] speak as a prophet: 预言;预告: *He prophesied of strange things to come*. 他预言有怪事要发生。 *Does he ever ~ right?* 他的预言应验吗?

prophet /'prɒfɪt; 'prɑfɪt/ *n* **1** person who teaches religion and claims that his teaching comes to him directly from God: 先知;代神发言者: *the ~ Isaiah*; 先知以赛亚; *Muhammad, the P~ of Islam*. 伊斯兰教先知穆罕默德。 **the P~s**, the prophetical books of the Old Testament. 旧约圣经中的预言书。 **2** pioneer of a new theory, cause, etc; advocate: 新理论、主义等的鼓吹者; 提倡者: *William Morris, one of the early ~s of socialism*. 威廉·莫里斯, 社会主义早期的鼓吹者之一。 **3** person who tells, or claims to tell, what will happen in the future: 预言者: *I'm not a good weather-~*. 我不大会预测天气。 **~·ess** /-es; -ɪs/ *n* woman ~. 女先知; 女预言者;女预言者。

pro·phet·ic /prə'fetɪk; prə'fɛtɪk/ *adj* of a prophet or prophecy; containing a prophecy: 先知的;预言者的;预言的; 预示的: *accomplishments which were ~ of her future greatness*. 预示她来日之伟大的成就。 **pro·pheti·cal** /-kl; -kl/ *adj* = ~. **pro·pheti·cally** /-klɪ; -klɪ/ *adv*

pro·phy·lac·tic /ˌprɒfɪ'læktɪk; ˌprofə'læktɪk/ *n, adj* [C] (substance, treatment, action) serving or tending to protect from disease or misfortune. 预防疾病的; 预防药(剂); 预防处理; 预防灾祸之行动; 预防法。 **pro·phy·lax·is** /-'læksɪs; -'læksɪs/ *n* [U] preventive treatment of disease. 疾病之预防处理;疾病之预防法。

pro·pin·quity /prə'pɪŋkwɪtɪ; prə'pɪŋkwɪtɪ/ *n* [U] (formal) nearness (in time, place, relationship); similarity (of ideas). (正式用语)(时间,地点,关系上之)接近; (观念之)相近; 类似。

pro·pi·ti·ate /prə'pɪʃɪ,et; prə'pɪʃɪ,et/ *vt* [VP6A] (formal) do sth to take away the anger of: (正式用语)劝解; 慰解。 **pro·pi·ti·ation** /prəˌpɪʃɪ'eɪʃn; prəˌpɪʃɪ'eʃən/ *n* [U] propitiating; atoning. 劝解; 慰解; 赎罪。 **pro·pi·ti·atory** /prə'pɪʃɪətrɪ US: -ˌtɔːrɪ; prə'pɪʃɪə,tɔrɪ/ *adj* serving to, intended to, ~: 劝解的, 慰解的; 意欲慰解的: *With a propitiatory smile he offered her a large bunch of roses*. 他带着歉意的微笑, 送给她一大束玫瑰。

pro·pi·tious /prə'pɪʃəs; prə'pɪʃəs/ *adj* ~ *to sb/for sth*, favourable; well-disposed: 顺遂的; 有利的; 善意的; 慈悲的: ~ *omens*; 吉兆; *weather that was ~ for our enterprise*. 有利于我们事业的天气。 **~·ly** *adv*

pro·pon·ent /prə'pəʊnənt; prə'ponənt/ *n* person who proposes sth: 提议者; 建议者: *a ~ of a theory/a course of action*. 一项理论(行动)之提出者。

pro·por·tion /prə'pɔːʃn; prə'porʃən/ *n* **1** [U] relation of one thing to another in quantity, size, etc; relation of a part to the whole: (一物与他物在量、大小等方面的)比例; 比率; 部分与整体的关系: *The ~ of imports to exports* (= *The excess of imports over exports*) *is worrying the government*. 进出口的比率(入超)令政府担忧。 *in ~ to*, relative to: 按着…的比例; 与…成比例: *wide in ~ to the height*; 就其高度的比例而言是很宽的; *payment in ~ to work done, not in ~ to the*

time taken to do it. 薪资与工作量成比例,并非与花费的时间成比例。 *get sth/be out of (all/any) ~ (to),* (make sth) bear no relation (to): (使)与…不相称; (使)与…不成比例: *His earnings are out of all ~ to his skill and ability,* He earns much more than is right for his skill and ability. 他的收入和他的技术能力不相称(收入多,本事小)。 *When you're angry, you may get things out of ~,* have an exaggerated or distorted view of things. 你在气愤时可能会歪曲事实。 **2** (often *pl*) the correct relation of parts or of the sizes of the several parts: (常用复数)均衡; 相称: *a room of good ~s*. 各方面很相称的房间。 *The two windows are in admirable ~*. 两扇窗子非常相称。 **3** (*pl*) size; measurements: (复)大小; 面积; 体积: *a ship of majestic ~s*; 一艘巨船; *build up an export trade of substantial ~s*. 建立相当规模的输出贸易。 **4** [C] part; share: 部分; 份: *You have not done your ~ of the work*. 你没做完你的那份工作。 **5** (maths) equality of relationship between two sets of numbers; statement that two ratios are equal (eg 4 is to 8 as 6 is to 12, $^5/_8$ and $^{10}/_{16}$ are in ~). (数学)比例; 二比相等之叙述(如 4 比 8 等于 6 比 12, $^5/_8$ 和 $^{10}/_{16}$ 成比例)。 □ *vt* [VP6A] ~ *(to),* put into ~ or right relationship: 使均衡; 使相称; 使成比例: *Do you ~ your expenditure to your income?* 你量入为出吗? *What a well-~ed room!* 多么相称调和的房间! **~·able** /-fənəbl; -fənəbl/ *adj* = ~al.

pro·por·tional /prə'pɔːʃənl; prə'porʃənl/ *adj* ~ *(to),* (formal) in proper proportion; corresponding in degree or amount: (正式用语)成适当比例的; 相称的: *payment ~ to the work done*; 和所做之工作相称的薪资; *compensation ~ to his injuries*. 与他所受伤害相称的赔偿。 *,~ ,represen'tation,* ⇨ *representation* at *represent[1]*. **~·ly** /-ənəlɪ; -ənlɪ/ *adv*

pro·por·tion·ate /prə'pɔːʃənət; prə'porʃənɪt/ *adj* (formal) (正式用语) = proportional. **~·ly** *adv*

pro·po·sal /prə'pəʊzl; prə'pozl/ *n* **1** [U] proposing. 提议; 建议。 **2** [C] sth proposed; plan or scheme: 所提议之事; 计划: *a ~ for peace*; 和平建议; *~s for increasing trade between two countries*. 促进两国间贸易的计划。 **3** (esp of marriage): 求婚: *a girl who had five ~s in one week*. 一星期中受到五次求婚的女郎。

pro·pose /prə'pəʊz; prə'poz/ *vt, vi* **1** [VP6A, D, 7A, 9] offer or put forward for consideration, as a suggestion, plan or purpose: 提议; 建议: *I ~ starting early/an early start/to start early/that we should start early*. 我建议(我们)早些动身。 *We ~ leaving at noon*. 我们提议中午离开。 *The motion was ~d by Mr X and seconded by Mr Y*. 那动议由 X 先生提出, Y 先生附议。 *~ a toast/sb's health*, ask persons to drink sb's health or happiness. 提议为某人干杯(以祝福某人健康或快乐)。 **2** [VP6A, 2A] ~ *(marriage) (to sb),* offer marriage. (向某人)求婚。 **3** [VP6A, 14] ~ *sb (for sth),* put forward (sb's name) for an office/for membership of a club, etc: 提出(某人之名)(充任某职或成为俱乐部会员); 推荐: *I ~ Mr Smith for chairman*. 我提名史密斯先生做主席。 *Will you please ~ me for your club?* 请推荐我加入你们的俱乐部好吗? **pro·poser** *n*

pro·pos·i·tion /ˌprɒpə'zɪʃn; ˌprɑpə'zɪʃən/ *n* [C] **1** statement; assertion: 声明; 主张: *a ~ so clear that it needs no explanation*. 非常清楚而无需解释的主张。 **2** question or problem (with or without the answer or solution): (已有解答或尚无解答的)问题; (能解决或未能解决的)难题; 命题; 定理: *a ~ in Euclid*. 欧几里得几何学中的一项定理。 *Tunnelling under the English Channel is a big ~*. 在英吉利海峡海底凿通道是一个大问题。 **3** proposal; suggestion. 提议; 建议。 **4** (colloq) matter to be dealt with. (口)要处理的人或事物。 *a tough ~,* sb or sth difficult to deal with. (口)难对付的人或事物。 □ *vt* [VP6A] (colloq) make a (esp illegal or immoral) ~ (3) to: (口)向…提议; (尤指)向…作不合法或不道德的要求: *She was ~ed by her boss*. 她的老板向她作非分的要求。

pro·pound /prəˈpaʊnd; prəˈpaʊnd/ vt [VP6A] (formal) put forward or offer for consideration or solution: (正式用语)提出以供考虑或解决: ~ a theory/a riddle. 提出一学理(谜语).

pro·pri·etary /prəˈpraɪətrɪ US: -terɪ; prəˈpraɪɛˌtɛrɪ/ adj 1 (abbr (P) used in this dictionary) owned or controlled by sb; held as property: (本字典略为 P)独占的; 专利的; 所有的: ~ medicine, patented; 专卖药品; ~ rights; 所有权; a ~ name, eg Kodak for cameras and films. 专利商标名(如柯达照相机及软片). 2 of or like a proprietor or owner: 所有人的.

pro·pri·etor /prəˈpraɪətə(r); prəˈpraɪɛtə/ n owner, esp of a hotel, store, land or patent: 业主; (尤指旅馆、商店、土地或专利的)所有人: the ~s of the hotel/this patent medicine. 旅馆的所有人(此种药品的专利所有人). **pro·pri·e·tress** /prəˈpraɪətrɪs; prəˈpraɪɛtrɪs/ n woman ~. 女业主; 女性所有人.

pro·pri·ety /prəˈpraɪətɪ; prəˈpraɪɛtɪ/ n (pl -ties) (formal) (正式用语) 1 [U] state of being correct in behaviour and morals: 行为和道德之正当; 礼; 礼貌: a breach of ~; 失礼; (pl) details of correct social behaviour: (复)礼节; 礼仪; 规矩: observe the proprieties; 遵守礼仪; offend against the proprieties. 违反礼节. 2 [U] reasonableness; fitness: 合理; 适当: I question the ~ of granting such a request, doubt whether it is right to do so. 我怀疑答应这项请求是否适当.

pro·pul·sion /prəˈpʌlʃn; prəˈpʌlʃən/ n [U] propelling force. 推进力. **jet ~**, by means of jet engines. 喷气发动机推进. **pro·pul·sive** /prəˈpʌlsɪv; prəˈpʌlsɪv/ adj propelling; serving to propel. 推进的; 有推进功能的.

pro rata /ˌprəʊ ˈrɑːtə; prəʊˈretə/ adv (Lat) in proportion; according to the share, etc of each. (拉)成比例; 按比例.

pro·rogue /prəʊˈrəʊg; prəʊˈrog/ vt [VP6A] bring (a session of Parliament) to an end without dissolving it (so that unfinished business may be taken up again in the next session). 使(国会会期)休会; 闭会. **pro·ro·ga·tion** /ˌprəʊrəˈgeɪʃn; ˌprorəˈgeʃən/ n

pro·saic /prəˈzeɪɪk; proˈzeɪk/ adj dull; uninteresting; ommonplace: 无聊的; 没趣的; 平凡的: a lively woman with a ~ husband; 一个嫁了平凡丈夫的活跃女人; the ~ life of the ordinary housewife. 一般家庭主妇的枯燥无味的生活. **pro·sai·cally** /-klɪ; -klɪ/ adv

pro·scenium /prəˈsiːnɪəm; proˈsɪnɪəm/ n (in a theatre) that part of the stage between the curtain and the orchestra. (戏院中之)舞台前部(指幕及乐队之间的部分); 前台. **~ arch**, arch above this space. 支承幕布的拱架.

pro·scribe /prəˈskraɪb US: prəʊ-; proˈskraɪb/ vt [VP6A] 1 (old use) publicly put (a person) out of the protection of the law. (旧用法)公然摒弃(某人)于法律保护之外; 褫夺(某人)公权. 2 denounce (a person, practice, etc) as dangerous. 指摘(某人, 惯例等)为危险; 排斥. **pro·scrip·tion** /prəˈskrɪpʃn US: prəʊ-; proˈskrɪpʃən/ n [U] proscribing or being ~d; [C] instance of this. 剥夺公权; 排斥; 此等之实例.

prose /prəʊz; proz/ n [U] language not in verse form: 散文: (attrib) (用作定语) the ~ writers of the 19th century. 十九世纪的散文作家. ⇨ **poetry**.

pros·ecute /ˈprɒsɪkjuːt; ˈprɑsɪˌkjut/ vt 1 [VP6A] (formal) continue with: (正式用语)继续从事; 进行: ~ a war/one's studies/an inquiry. 进行作战(研究学问, 查询). 2 [VP6A, 14] ~ sb (for sth), start legal proceedings against: 告发; 检举; 起诉: ~d for exceeding the speed limit. 因行车超速而被控告. Trespassers will be ~d. 闯人免进, 违者法办. **pros·ecu·tor** /-tə(r); ˈprɒsɪˌkjutə/ ˈprɑsɪˌkjutə/ n person who ~s(2). 检举人; 告发人; 起诉人. **Public 'Pros·ecutor**, legal official who ~s criminal cases on behalf of the State or the public. 检察官; 检控官.

pros·ecu·tion /ˌprɒsɪˈkjuːʃn; ˌprɑsɪˈkjuʃən/ n 1 [U] act of prosecuting(1): 继续从事; 进行: In the ~ of his duties he had to interview people of all classes. 在执行职务时他必须接见各阶层的人. 2 [U] prosecuting or being prosecuted(2): 告发; 检举; 起诉; 被告发(等): make oneself liable to ~; 使自己可能遭受控告; [C] instance of this: 告发或检举等的实例: start a ~ against sb. 对某人起诉. **the Director of Public P~s**, Public Prosecutor. 检察官. ⇨ **prosecute**. 3 (collective) person who prosecutes(2), together with his advisers: (总称)原告; 告发人及其律师: the case for the ~. 对原告有利的案子. ⇨ **defence(3)**.

pros·elyte /ˈprɒsɪlaɪt; ˈprɑsɪˌlaɪt/ n person who has been converted from his religious, political or other opinions or beliefs to different ones. 改变宗教、政治或其他信仰者; 改宗者; 改入他党者. **pros·elyt·ize** /ˈprɒsɪlɪtaɪz; ˈprɑsɪlɪˌtaɪz/ vt, vi [VP6A, 2A] make, try to make, converts to a religion or cause; make a ~ of (sb). 使皈依另一宗教或教义; 使(某人)改变宗教信仰或改入他党.

pros·ody /ˈprɒsədɪ; ˈprɑsədɪ/ n [U] science of verse rhythms or metres; (of a language) rhythm, pause, tempo, stress and pitch features. 诗体学; 韵律学; 作诗法;(语言的)抑扬顿挫等特性.

pros·pect¹ /ˈprɒspekt; ˈprɑspekt/ n 1 [C] wide view over land or sea or (fig) before the mind, in the imagination. (陆或海之)景色; (喻)(心灵或想象中的)景象; 概观; 纵览. 2 (pl) sth expected, hoped for, looked forward to: (复)期望, 希望, 盼望之事物: The ~s for the wine harvest are poor this year. 今年的葡萄收成不会好. The manager held out bright ~s to me if I would accept the position. 如果我愿意接受那个职位, 经理答应我光明的前途. 3 [U] expectation; hope: 期望; 希望: I see no little/not much ~ of his recovery. 我看他没有(甚少)痊愈的希望. Is there no ~ of your visiting us soon? 你不可能马上来看我们吗? He is out of work and has nothing in ~ (= no expectation of finding work) at present. 他已失业, 现在也没有找到工作的希望. 4 [C] possible customer or client; sb from whom one hopes to gain something: 可能的主顾或委托人; 可能从中获得利益之人: He's a good/bad ~. 他可能是个有油水(没什么油水)的顾客.

pros·pect² /prəˈspekt US: ˈprɒspekt; ˈprɑspekt/ vi [VP2A, 3A] ~ (for), search (for): 寻找; 探勘: ~ing for gold. 探勘金矿. **pros·pec·tor** /-tə(r); -tə/ n person who explores a region looking for gold or other valuable ores, etc. 探勘矿藏的人; 探矿者.

pros·pec·tive /prəˈspektɪv; prəˈspektɪv/ adj hoped for; looked forward to; which or who will or may be: 有望的; 预期的; 未来的: ~ advantages/wealth; 预期的利益(财富); a ~ buyer; 可能的买主; my ~ bride; 我未来的新娘; the ~ Labour candidate. 未来的工党候选人.

pros·pec·tus /prəˈspektəs; prəˈspɛktəs/ n (pl ~es /-təsɪz; -təsɪz/) printed account giving details of and advertising sth, eg a university, a new business enterprise, a book about to be published. (创办大学、新企业等的)计划书; 发起书; 募股书; (即将出版之书的)内容说明; 大纲.

pros·per /ˈprɒspə(r); ˈprɑspə/ vi, vt 1 [VP2A] succeed; do well: 成功; 兴隆; 昌盛: The business ~ed. 生意兴隆. Is your son ~ing? 你的儿子诸事顺遂吗? 2 [VP6A] (liter or rhet) (of God) cause to ~: (文或修辞)(指上帝)使成功; 使昌隆: May God ~ you! 愿上帝使你成功!

pros·per·ity /prɒˈsperətɪ; prɑsˈperətɪ/ n [U] state of being successful; good fortune: 成功; 幸运; 昌盛; 繁荣: a life of happiness and ~; 幸福而成功的一生; live in ~. 过着富足的生活. The ~ of this industry depends upon a full order book. 这种工业的繁荣要依靠大批的订货.

pros·per·ous /ˈprɒspərəs; ˈprɑspərəs/ adj successful; flourishing: 成功的; 繁荣的; 昌隆的: a ~ business;

兴隆的生意；～ years. 繁荣的年代。～·ly adv

pros·tate /'prɒsteɪt; 'prɑsteɪt/ n **(gland)**, (anat) gland in male mammals at the neck of the bladder. (解剖)前列腺。

pros·ti·tute /'prɒstɪtjuːt US: -tuːt; 'prɑstə,tjut/ n person who offers herself/himself for sexual intercourse for payment. 娼妓; 妓女; 男娼。□ vt **1** [VP6A] (reflex) make a ～ of (oneself). (反身)使(自己)卖淫; 卖身。**2** [VP6A] put to wrong or unworthy uses: 滥用: ～ one's energies/abilities; 滥用精力(才能); ～ one's honour, lose it for money basely gained. 图利而出卖名誉。□ **pros·ti·tu·tion** /,prɒstɪ'tjuːʃn US: -'tuːʃn; ,prɑstə'tjuʃən/ n [U] practice of prostituting oneself, one's talents etc. 卖淫; 操淫业; 滥用才能。

pros·trate /'prɒstreɪt; 'prɑstret/ adj **1** lying stretched out on the ground, usu face downward, eg because exhausted, or to show submission, deep respect. 平卧的; 俯卧的; 卧倒的; 卧拜的(如出于疲乏, 或表示顺从, 深挚的敬意)。**2** (fig) overcome (with grief, etc); conquered; overthrown. (喻)为(悲伤等)征服的; 降伏的; 瓦解的; 沮丧的。□ vt (also US: /prɒ'streɪt; prɑ'stret/) **1** [VP6A] cause to be ～: 使卧; 弄倒: trees ～d by the gale. 被大风吹倒的树。**2** [VP6A] (reflex) make (oneself) ～: (反身)使(自己)平卧; 俯伏: The wretched man ～d himself before his conqueror. 那可怜的家伙拜倒在他的征服者面前。**3** (usu passive) overcome; render helpless: (通常用被动语态)克服; 使无能为力: Several of the competitors were ～d by the heat. 数位竞争者热得昏倒了。She is ～d with grief. 她悲伤不已。**pros·tra·tion** /prɒ'streɪʃn; prɑ'streʃən/ n [U] **1** state of extreme physical weakness; complete exhaustion: 身体极度虚弱; 筋疲力尽; 虚脱; 衰竭: Two of the runners in the Marathon race collapsed and were carried off in a state of prostration. 两位马拉松赛跑的选手倒下, 并在虚脱的状态中被抬走。**2** [C] act of bowing or lying face downwards to show submission or humility. 拜倒; 俯身致敬。

prosy /'prəʊzɪ; 'prozɪ/ adj **(-ier, -iest)** (of authors, speakers, books, speeches, style, etc) dull; tedious; unimaginative. (指作者, 演说者, 书, 演说, 文体等)单调的; 乏味的; 啰嗦的; 缺乏想象的。**pros·ily** /-əlɪ; -əlɪ/ adv **prosi·ness** n

pro·tag·on·ist /prə'tægənɪst; pro'tægənɪst/ n (formal) chief person in a drama; (by extension) chief person in a story or factual event. (正式用语)戏剧中之主角; (广义)故事或实事中的主角。

pro·tean /'prəʊtɪən; 'protɪən/ adj versatile; easily and quickly changing (like Proteus /'prəʊtɪəs; 'protjus/, the Greek sea-god who took various shapes). 变化自如的; 易变的; 多变的(似希腊神话中之海神 Proteus 能变多种形态的)。

pro·tect /prə'tekt; prə'tekt/ vt [VP6A, 14] ～ sb/ sth (from/against), **1** keep safe (from danger, enemies; against attack); guard: 防卫(危险, 敌人, 与 from 连用); 表去, 与 against 连用); 保护; 警戒: well ～ed from the cold/against the weather. 防护良好而不受冻(不被恶劣气候侵袭)。**2** guard (home industry) against competition by taxing imports. (以进口税)保护(国内工业)。

pro·tec·tion /prə'tekʃən; prə'tekʃən/ n [U] **1** protecting or being protected: 防御; 保护; 警戒: travel under the ～ of a number of soldiers. 在一些兵士的保护下旅行。These tender plants need ～ against the weather. 这些幼小的植物需要保护, 以免受恶劣气候的侵害。'～ (money), money demanded by or paid to, gangsters for ～ against acts of violence, etc. 为免受暴力侵害, 付给歹徒或向其索取的保护费。**2** [U] system of protecting home industry against foreign competition. 保护国内工业之制度。**3** [C] person or thing that protects: 保护者; 保护物: wearing a heavy overcoat as a ～ against the cold. 穿着厚大衣御寒。～·ism /-ɪzəm; -ɪzm/ n [U] system of giving ～(2) to home industry.

保护国内工业之制度; 保护贸易主义。～·ist /-ɪst; -ɪst/ n supporter of, believer in, ～ism. 保护贸易主义者。

pro·tec·tive /prə'tektɪv; prə'tektɪv/ adj **1** giving protection: 给予保护的; 防护的: a ～ covering; 保护性的覆盖物; a ～ tariff, ie on imported goods; (加于进口货物之)保护关税; 保护税。～ sheath, ～ **sheath**. ～ **'clothing**, clothes that safeguard the wearer against such risks as burns, contamination and radiation. 防护衣(保护穿着者不灼伤、污染、放射线等)。～ **'colouring**, ie of animals, birds, insects, causing them to be seen with difficulty in their natural surroundings, thus protecting them from their enemies. (鸟, 禽, 昆虫的)保护色(使其在所处的自然环境中难以辨认, 俾防敌袭击)。～ **'foods**, foods that safeguard health, eg kinds with a good supply of essential vitamins. 保健的食物(如含有充分主要维生素者)。**2** ～ (towards), (of persons) with a wish to protect: (指人)有保护意愿的: A mother usually feels ～ towards her children. 一位做母亲的自然会保护她的孩子。～·ly adv

pro·tec·tor /prə'tektə(r); prə'tektə/ n **1** person who protects; sth made or designed to give protection. 保护者; 防御者; 保护物; 保护装置。**2** (GB hist) the P～, official title of Oliver and Richard Cromwell. (英史)护国公(英国共和政治时奥立弗·克伦威尔及其子理查·克伦威尔的称号)。

pro·tec·tor·ate /prə'tektərət; prə'tektərɪt/ n **1** country under the protection of another. 保护国(受他国保护的国家); 保护领地。**2** the P～, period (1653—1659) of rule of Oliver and Richard Cromwell. 摄政时期(奥立弗·克伦威尔和理查·克伦威尔摄政之时期, 一六五三至一六五九)。

pro·tégé (fem **-gée**) /'prɒtɪʒeɪ US: ,prəʊtɪ'ʒeɪ; 'protə,ʒe/ n (F) person to whom another gives encouragement and help (usu over a long period). (法)被保护者; 被提拔者(通常指一段长时期内如此受惠者)。

pro·tein /'prəʊtiːn; 'protin/ n [U, C] body-building substance essential to good health, in such foods as milk, eggs, meat. 蛋白质(促进身体发育之物质, 为健康所必需, 见于牛奶、蛋类、肉类等食物中)。

pro tem·pore /,prəʊ 'tempəri; pro'tempə,ri/ adv (Lat) (often shortened to 常略作 **pro tem**) for the time being; for the present only: (拉)暂时; 目前: I'm in charge of the office pro tem. 我暂时任此职务。

pro·test¹ /'prəʊtest; 'protest/ n [C, U] (statement of) disapproval or objection: 抗议; 反对: make / lodge / enter a ～ (against sth). 对某事)提出抗议。The Government's policy gave rise to vigorous ～s. 政府的政策引起了强烈的反对。He paid the tax demand under ～, unwillingly and after declaring that what he was doing was not right or just. 他抗议着, 满心不服地照税额缴付了。He gave way without ～, without making any objection. 他无异议地让步。**2** (attrib) expressing ～: (用作定语)表示抗议: a '～ movement; 抗议运动; a '～ march, eg by persons objecting to official policy. 抗议游行(如反对官方政策之人所举行者)。

pro·test² /prə'test; prə'test/ vt, vi **1** [VP6A, 9] affirm strongly; assert against opposition: 坚决声明; 力言: He ～ed that he had never been near the scene of the crime. 他坚持说他从未在犯罪现场附近。He ～ed his innocence, asserted his innocence by ～ing. 他力言无罪。**2** [VP2A, 3A] ～ (against), raise an objection, say sth (against): 抗议; 反对: I ～ against being called an old fool. 我抗议被称为老傻瓜。The children ～ed loudly (= cried out in disapproval) when they were told to go to bed early. 当孩子们被吩咐早睡觉的时候, 他们大声抗议。～·er n ～·ing·ly adv

Prot·es·tant /'prɒtɪstənt; 'prɑtɪstənt/ n, adj (member) of any of the Christian bodies that separated from the Church of Rome at the time of the Reformation (16th c), or their later branches. 新教(十六世纪宗教改革时脱离天主教, 或其后来另行分出教派)的; 基督教的; 新教徒; 基督教徒。～·ism /-ɪzəm; -,ɪzm/ n [U]

systems, beliefs, teaching, etc of the ~s; ~s as a body. 新教徒的制度,信仰,教义等;基督教(教会)/新教。

prot·es·ta·tion /ˌprɒtes'teɪʃn; ˌprɑtəs'teʃən/ n [C] (formal)solemn declaration: (正式用语)郑重声明;力言: ~s of innocence/friendship. 郑重声明无罪(友好)。

pro·to·col /'prəʊtəkɒl US: -kɔːl; 'protə,kɑl/ n 1 [C] first or original draft of an agreement (esp between States), signed by those making it, in preparation for a treaty. (尤指国与国间的)条约草案;草约;议定书。 2 [U] code of behaviour; etiquette as practised on diplomatic occasions: 礼规;外交礼仪: Were the seating arrangements for the dinner party according to ~, Were rules of precedence, etc properly observed? 宴会座位的安排合乎礼仪吗?

pro·ton /'prəʊtɒn; 'protɑn/ n positively charged particle forming part of an atomic nucleus. 质子(构成原子之一部分而带有阳电荷的单位)。 ⇨ electron.

pro·to·plasm /'prəʊtəplæzəm; 'protə,plæzəm/ n [C] colourless, jelly-like substance which is the material basis of life in animals and plants. 原生质;原浆;细胞质(无色之胶状物,为动植物生命之物质基础)。

pro·to·type /'prəʊtətaɪp; 'protə,taɪp/ n [C] first or original example, eg of an aircraft, from which others have been or will be copied or developed. 原型(其他同类物从此模仿或发展而来,例如飞机的原始样式)。

pro·to·zoa /ˌprəʊtə'zəʊə; ˌprotə'zoə/ n pl (division of the animal kingdom consisting of) animals of the simplest type formed of a single cell (and usu microscopic). 原生动物(由单细胞组成的最简单之动物,通常为微生物);原生动物门。

pro·tract /prə'trækt US: prəʊ-; pro'trækt/ vt [VP 6A] prolong; lengthen the time taken by: 延长;拖延时间: a ~ed visit/argument. 延长的访问(辩论)。 **pro·trac·tion** /prə'trækʃn US: prəʊ-; pro'trækʃən/ n lengthening out. 延长;拖延; (动)伸展。

pro·trac·tor /prə'træktə(r) US: prəʊ-; pro'træktə/ n instrument, usu in the form of a semicircle, and graduated (0° to 180°), for measuring and drawing angles. 量角器;分度规;分度器;半圆规。

pro·trude /prə'truːd US: prəʊ-; pro'trud/ vi, vt [VP2A, 6A] (cause to) stick out or project: (使)伸出;突出: a shelf that ~s from a wall; 自墙壁伸出的架子; protruding eyes/teeth. 凸眼(暴牙)。 **pro·tru·sion** /prə'truːʒn US: prəʊ-; pro'truʒən/ n [U] protruding; [C] sth that ~s. 伸出;突出;伸出(突出)之物;隆起物。 **pro·trus·ive** /prə'truːsɪv US: prəʊ-; pro'trusɪv/ adj protruding. 伸出的;突出的。

pro·tu·ber·ant /prə'tjuːbərənt US: prəʊ'tuː-; pro'tjubərənt/ adj (formal) curving or swelling outwards; bulging. (正式用语)突出的;隆起的。 **pro·tu·ber·ance** /-əns; -əns/ n [U] being ~; [C] sth that is ~; bulge or swelling. 突出;隆起;突出之物;隆起之物。

proud /praʊd; praʊd/ adj (-er, -est) 1 (in a good sense) having or showing a proper pride or dignity: (好的意义)具有或显出适度骄傲或尊严的; 自重的; 自尊的; 感到光荣或得意的: ~ of their success/of being so successful; 对于他们的成功(如此的成功)感到骄傲; to belong/that they belonged to such a fine team. 对隶属(他们隶属)这么好的一个队感到光荣。 2 (in a bad sense) arrogant; having or showing too much pride: (坏的意义)傲慢的;过于骄傲的: He was too ~ to join our party. 他太骄傲,不屑参加我们的集会。 3 arousing justifiable pride; of which one is or may be properly ~; splendid; imposing: 引以夸耀的;令人感到得意的;壮丽的;堂皇的: soldiers in ~ array. 排成壮丽阵式的兵士。 It was a ~ day for the country when its team won the championship. 该国的球队获得冠军的那一天,全国都感到光荣。 His rose garden was a ~ sight. 他的玫瑰园壮观极了。 4 ~ flesh, overgrown flesh round a healing wound. (伤口长好后所结的)赘肉;疤;浮肉。 5 (compounds) (复合词) **'house-~**, of one's house, of the care with which it is looked after, cleaned, etc. 夸耀自己的家的; 以用心料理家务、

把家收拾整洁等为荣的。 **'purse-~**, arrogant because of one's wealth. 以富骄人的。 6 (adv use; colloq) do sb ~, honour greatly, entertain splendidly. (副词用法;口)十分礼遇(某人);厚待(某人);给而厚。 ~·ly adv in a ~ manner; splendidly. 自重地;骄傲地;傲慢地;壮丽地;光采地。

prove /pruːv; pruv/ vt, vi (pp ~d, or, as 1 below, 第一义并作 ~n /'pruːvn; 'pruvən/) 1 [VP6A, 9, 14, 25] ~ (to), supply proof of; show beyond doubt to be true: 证明; 证实: ~ sb's guilt/that he is guilty. 证明某人有罪。 His guilt was clearly ~d. 他的罪明确地证实了。 I shall ~ to you that the witness is quite unreliable. 我将向你证明,证人十分不可靠。 Can you ~ it to me? 你能对我证实吗? **The exception ~s the rule**, shows that the rule is valid in most cases. 例外证明了本规则的适用性。 **not ~n**, (in a criminal trial in Scotland) jury's decision that as the charge cannot be ~d, the accused may be released (although he may not be innocent). 证据不足(苏格兰的刑事审判中,陪审团对不能证明的指控所作的一种裁决,被告纵然有罪,亦可被开释)。 2 [VP6A] establish the genuineness of: 确定…之真实性; 查验: ~ a will; 查验遗嘱; test the quality or accuracy of: 检验品质或正确性; ~ a man's worth. 考验一个人的价值。 3 [VP4D, 25] ~ (oneself) (to be), be seen or found in the end (to be): 终被发现(是);表现出: The new typist ~d (to be) useless. 那位新打字员终于被发现是不能干的。 He ~d (himself) to be a coward. 他表现出是一个懦夫。 Our wood supply ~d (to be) insufficient. 我们的木材供应显得不够。 **prov·able** /-əbl; -əbl/ adj that can be ~d. 可证明的;可查验的。

prov·enance /'prɒvənəns; 'prɑvənəns/ n [U] (place of) origin: 起源; 出处: antique furniture of doubtful ~, eg that may not be genuinely antique. 出处不明的古董家具(如可能并非真为古代所制)。

prov·en·der /'prɒvɪndə(r); 'prɑvəndə/ n [U] food, eg hay, oats, for horses and cattle; (colloq) food of any kind. 牛和马的饲料;粮草;秣料;(口)任何食物。

prov·erb /'prɒvɜːb; 'prɑvɜb/ n 1 popular short saying, with words of advice or warning, eg 'It takes two to make a quarrel'. 谚语; 格言(如一个巴掌拍不响')。 2 **(the Book of) P~s**, one of the books of the Old Testament. (旧约的)箴言(书)。 3 sb or sth so well known that he/it has become notorious: 恶名远扬的人或事; 话柄; 笑柄: He is a ~ for meanness. 他因卑鄙而恶名远扬。 His meanness is a ~. 他的卑鄙尽人皆知。 ~·ial /prə'vɜːbɪəl; prə'vɜbɪəl/ adj 1 of or expressed in a ~. 谚语的; 格言的; 用谚语表达的: ~ sayings/wisdom. 谚语(格言所表示的智慧)。 2 widely known and talked about; admitted by everyone: 众所周知的; 大家公认的: His stupidity is ~ial. 他的愚蠢是众所周知的。 ~·ial·ly adv he is ~ially stupid. 他是出名的愚蠢。

pro·vide /prə'vaɪd; prə'vaɪd/ vi, vt 1 [VP3A] ~ for sb/sth, make ready, do what is necessary, for: 准备;筹备;(为…)做必须之事;扶养: He has a large family to ~ for. 他要养一大家子。 We must ~ for our visitors, get in supplies of food, etc. 我们要准备好东西款待客人。 He died without providing for his widow, leaving nothing for her to live on. 他死了,没有为他的寡妻留下任何东西维生。 ~ against sth, take steps to guard against: 防备;预防: Have you ~d against a coal shortage next winter? 对于下一个冬季的煤荒你已有防备了吗? 2 [VP6A, 14] ~ sth (for sb); ~ sb with sth, give, supply (what is needed, esp what a person needs in order to live): 供给; 供应; 备办(所需物,尤指生活必需品): ~ one's children with food and clothes; 供应孩子们的衣食; ~ food and clothes for one's family. 供应一家人的衣食。 3 [VP9] stipulate: 约定;规定: A clause in the agreement ~s that the tenant shall bear the cost of all repairs to the building. 协议中有一条规定,房客将负担修理房屋的一切费用。 ~r n person who provides. 准备者;筹备者;供应者;备办者。

pro·vid·ed /prəˈvaɪdɪd; prəˈvaɪdɪd/ *conj* ~ **(that)**, on condition (that). 假若; 倘使。

provi·dence /ˈprɒvɪdəns; ˈprɑvədəns/ *n* 1 [U] (old use) thrift; being provident or prudent (about future needs, etc). (旧用法)节约; 慎重; 深谋远虑。2 **P~**, God; God's care for human beings and all he has created; (small *p*) particular instance of this care: 上帝; 天佑; (小写 p) 天佑的特殊实例。

provi·dent /ˈprɒvɪdənt; ˈprɑvədənt/ *adj* (careful in) providing for future needs or events, esp in old age: (小心)为未来的需要或事件而预做准备的; 顾及未来的; (尤指)为老年的需要而储蓄的: *Our firm has a ~ fund for the staff.* 我们的公司设有员工福利基金。~**·ly** *adv*

provi·den·tial /ˌprɒvɪˈdenʃl; ˌprɑvəˈdenʃəl/ *adj* of, by, through, coming from, Providence(2): 神的; 由神做出的; 借神力做出的; 由神而来的; 天佑的; 幸运的: *a ~ escape.* 一次幸运的逃脱。~**·ly** /-ʃəlɪ; -ʃlɪ/ *adv*

pro·vid·ing /prəˈvaɪdɪŋ; prəˈvaɪdɪŋ/ *conj* ~ **(that)**, = provided (that): *I will go ~ (that) my expenses are paid.* 要是我的费用有人代付我就去。

prov·ince /ˈprɒvɪns; ˈprɑvɪns/ *n* 1 large administrative division of a country. 省(一个国家的大行政区)。2 **the ~s**, all the country outside the capital: 地方(首都以外的全部地区): *people from the ~s visiting London.* 自全国各地到伦敦来游玩的人。*The pop group is now touring the ~s.* 流行乐团正在各省旅行表演。3 district under an archbishop. 大主教辖区; 总主教区。4 area of learning or knowledge: department of activity: 学问中之部门; 范围; 知识范畴: *That is outside my ~,* not sth with which I can or need deal. 那是我研究范围以外的东西。*Doesn't your question fall outside the ~ of science?* 你的问题不是超出科学范围了吗?

prov·in·cial /prəˈvɪnʃl; prəˈvɪnʃəl/ *adj* 1 of a province(1): 省的: ~ *taxes;* 省的税收; ~ *government.* 省政府。2 of the provinces(2): 外省的; 地方的: ~ *roads.* 地方道路。3 narrow in outlook; having, typical of, the speech, manners, views, etc of a person living in the provinces (esp in former times when communications were poor): 见解偏狭的; 地方居民所特有的(尤指以前交通不便时); *a ~ accent.* 地方口音。□ *n* person from the provinces; countrified person. 地方居民; 乡下人。~**·ly** /-ʃəlɪ; -ʃlɪ/ *adv* ~**·ism** /-əm; -ɪzəm/ *n* [C] example of ~ manners, speech, behaviour, etc; [U] attachment to one's province and its customs, etc rather than to one's country. 地方居民特有的态度、语言、行为等之实例; 对于本乡及其习俗的浓厚情感; 乡土观念。

pro·vi·sion /prəˈvɪʒn; prəˈvɪʒən/ *n* 1 [U] providing, preparation (esp for future needs): 准备; 防备 (尤指为未来的需要者); 供应: *the ~ (= supply) of water and gas to domestic consumers;* 为家庭用户供应水和煤气; *make ~ for one's old age,* eg by saving money; 为老年预做准备(如储蓄钱); *make ~ against sth,* guard against it. 防备某事。2 [C] amount (of sth) provided: 准备之量; 供应品: *issue a ~ of meat to the troops.* 拨发肉类供应品给军队。3 (*pl*) food; food supplies: (复)食物; 食物供应: *lay in a store of ~s;* 贮存大量的食物; (attrib, *sing*) (用作定语, 单数) *a ~ merchant,* a grocer; 杂货商; *a wholesale ~ business.* 食品批发店。4 [C] condition in a legal document, eg a clause in a will: (法律文件中之)规定; 条款(如遗嘱中之某一条): *if there is no ~ to the contrary.* 如无相反之条款。□ *vt* [VP6A] supply with ~s(3) and stores: 供以食物及必需品: ~ *a ship for a voyage to the Antarctic.* 供应开往南极的船所需的食物及必需品。

pro·vi·sional /prəˈvɪʒənl; prəˈvɪʒənl/ *adj* of the present time only, and to be confirmed or changed or replaced later; 临时的; 暂时性的: *a ~ government/contract, etc.* 临时政府(草约等)。~**·ly** /-nəlɪ; -nlɪ/ *adv*

pro·viso /prəˈvaɪzəʊ; prəˈvaɪzo/ *n* (*pl* ~**s**, US also

~**es** /-zəʊz; -zoz/) (clause containing a) limitation, esp in a legal document: 附文; 条件; 但书; 限制条款(尤指法律文件中者): *with the ~ that,* on condition that; 以⋯为条件; 但须⋯; *subject to this ~,* with this limitation. 附有此一条件。**pro·vi·sory** /prəˈvaɪzərɪ; prəˈvaɪzərɪ/ *adj* depending upon a ~. 有附文的; 附有条件的。

Provo /ˈprəʊvəʊ; ˈprovo/ *n* (*pl* ~**s** /-əʊz; -oz/) (colloq) member of a group (the Provisional IRA) fighting for the political unification of Ireland. (口) (为争取爱尔兰统一之)爱尔兰共和军之一员。

provo·ca·tion /ˌprɒvəˈkeɪʃn; ˌprɑvəˈkeʃən/ *n* 1 [U] provoking or being provoked: 激怒; 被激怒; 刺激; 被刺激; *wilful ~ of public disorder:* 故意激起公众的骚动; *do sth under ~,* when provoked. 在愤怒下做某事。*Very little things make her anger break out.* 一点点小事都会使她突然发怒。2 [C] sth that provokes or annoys. 激怒之原因; 令人发怒之事。

pro·voca·tive /prəˈvɒkətɪv; prəˈvɑkətɪv/ *adj* causing, likely to cause, anger, argument, interest, etc: 激发的; 引起议论, 兴趣等的; 激起的; 刺激的: ~ *remarks,* 煽动性的言论; 使人恼怒的谈话。~**·ly** *adv*

pro·voke /prəˈvəʊk; prəˈvok/ *vt* 1 [VP6A] make angry; vex: 使⋯发怒; 激怒: ~ *sb beyond endurance.* 他怒不可遏。*If you ~ the dog, it will attack you.* 如果你去招惹那只狗, 它会咬你。2 [VP6A] cause; arouse: 致使; 引起: ~ *laughter/a smile/a riot.* 引起大笑(微笑, 一场骚乱)。3 [VP17, 14] ~ *sb to do sth/into doing sth,* cause or compel them: 驱使; 迫使(某人做某事): *His impudence ~d her into slapping his face.* 他的放肆惹得她打他耳光。*He was ~d to answer rudely.* 他受激料而无礼地回答。**pro·vok·ing** *adj* annoying: 恼人的; 气人的; 叫人烦恼的: *provoking of sb to be late.* 因为某人晚到而气恼。**pro·vok·ing·ly** *adv*

pro·vost /ˈprɒvəst US: ˈprəʊ-; ˈprɑvəst/ *n* 1 title of some heads of university colleges, etc. (大学中某些学院的)院长。2 (in Scotland) head of a municipal corporation or burgh (= mayor). (苏格兰)市长。3 ~ **marshal** /prəˈvəʊ ˈmɑːʃl US: ˌprəʊvəʊ; ˈprovoˈmɑrʃəl/, head of the military police. 宪兵司令。

prow /praʊ; praʊ/ *n* pointed front of a ship or boat. 船首。⇨ the illus at barque. 参看 barque 之插图。

prow·ess /ˈpraʊɪs; ˈpraʊɪs/ *n* [U] bravery; valour; unusual skill or ability. 勇敢; 英勇; 超凡的技术或能力。

prowl /praʊl; praʊl/ *vi, vt* 1 [VP2A, C] go about cautiously looking for a chance to get food (as wild animals do), or to steal, etc. 悄悄潜行以寻找食物 (如野兽所做者), 或偷窃等。2 [VP6A] go about (the streets) in this way. 逡巡于(街上)。□ *n* **be on the ~,** ~**ing.** 在逡巡或徘徊中。'~ **car,** (US) (美) ⇨ **squad** *car* at **squad.** ~**er** *n* animal or person that ~s. 潜行者; 徘徊者; 逡巡者。

prox /prɒks; prɑks/ ⇨ **proximo.**

proxi·mate /ˈprɒksɪmət; ˈprɑksəmɪt/ *adj* (formal) nearest, before or after. (正式用语)最接近的; 前后的。

prox·im·ity /prɒkˈsɪmətɪ; prɑkˈsɪmətɪ/ *n* [U] (formal) nearness: (正式用语)接近: *in (close) ~ to,* (very) near to (which is usu preferable). 非常接近于(通常较常用 very near to)。~ **fuse,** one that explodes the shell to which it is fitted when near the target, eg an enemy aircraft. 近发引信(使炮弹在接近敌机等目标时爆炸者)。

prox·imo /ˈprɒksɪməʊ; ˈprɑksɪmo/ *adj* (abbr 略作 **prox**) (comm or official style, better avoided) of next month: (商业或公务上的文体, 最好不用)下月的; 次月的: *on the 22nd prox.* 下月二十二日。

proxy /ˈprɒksɪ; ˈprɑksɪ/ *n* (*pl* -**ies**) [C] (document giving) [U] authority to represent or act for another (esp in voting at an election): 代理权; 代表权(尤指在选举中代表他人投票): *person given a ~:* 代理权; 代表权(尤指在选举中代表他人投票): 委托书; 委托投票书; 代理人; 代表者: *vote by ~,* 由代理人投票;

make one's wife one's ~. 以妻为自己的代表。

prude /pruːd; prud/ *n* person of extreme or exaggerated propriety (often affected) in behaviour or speech. 极端或过份拘礼的人; 装得规规矩矩的人。**pru·dery** /'pruːdərɪ; 'prudərɪ/ *n* (*pl* -ries) [U] extreme propriety; [C] prudish act or remark. 过份的礼仪; 极端拘谨的行动或言词。**prud·ish** /'pruːdɪʃ; 'prudɪʃ/ *adj* of or like a ~; excessively modest; easily shocked. 过份拘礼者的; 象过份拘礼者的; 过于谦逊的; 装模作样的; 易于惊恐的。**pru·dish·ly** *adv*

pru·dent /'pruːdnt; 'prudn̩t/ *adj* careful; acting only after careful thought or planning: 审慎的; 三思而后行的: *a* ~ *housekeeper*. 一位谨慎的女管家。**~·ly** *adv* **pru·dence** /-dns; -dn̩s/ *n* [U] being a ~; careful forethought. 审慎; 事先仔细的考虑。

pru·den·tial /pruː'denʃl; pru'denʃəl/ *adj* relating to, marked by, prudence. 审慎的; 有智虑的。

prune[1] /pruːn; prun/ *n* dried plum; (colloq) silly person. 梅干; 梅干; (口)傻瓜。

prune[2] /pruːn; prun/ *vt* [VP6A, 14, 15B] ~ *sth from sth;* ~ *sth off sth;* ~ *sth away,* cut away parts of (trees, bushes, etc) in order to control growth or shape; (fig) take out unnecessary parts from: 修剪(树,灌木等); (喻)自…删除不必要的部分: ~ *the rose-bushes;* 修剪玫瑰树丛; ~ *away unwanted growth;* 剪掉不要的枝叶等; ~ *an essay of superfluous matter;* 删去文章中多余的部分; ~ *away unnecessary adjectives.* 删去不必要的形容词。**prun·ing** *n* [U]: *The roses need pruning,* ought to be ~. 这些玫瑰需要修剪了。'**pruning-knife** **-hook** **-saw** **-scissors** **-shears,** kinds of tool used for pruning. 修剪用的刀(弯刀,锯,剪,大剪)。**pruners** *n pl* pruning-scissors. 修枝刀刀。

pru·ri·ent /'pruərɪənt; 'pruriənt/ *adj* having, showing, an excessive and unhealthy interest in matters of sex. 好色的; 贪淫的; 对淫秽之事特别感兴趣的。**~·ly** *adv* **pru·ri·ence** /-əns; -əns/, **pru·ri·ency** /-ənsɪ; -ənsɪ/ *n* state of being a ~; 好色。

Prus·sian /'prʌʃn; 'prʌʃən/ *n*, *adj* (inhabitant, native) of Prussia. 普鲁士居民; 普鲁士人; 普鲁士的。~ **blue,** deep blue colour. 深蓝色; 普鲁士蓝。

prus·sic /'prʌsɪk; 'prʌsɪk/ *adj* ~ '**acid,** violent and deadly poison. 氢氰酸; 普鲁士酸(烈性毒物)。

pry[1] /praɪ; praɪ/ *vi* (*pt, pp* **pried** /praɪd; praɪd/) [VP2A, 3A] **pry (into),** inquire too curiously (into other people's affairs); 侦察; 刺探; 打听(别人之事); [VP2C] **pry about,** look or peer (about) inquisitively. 到处窥探。**pry·ing·ly** *adv*

pry[2] /praɪ; praɪ/ *vt* [VP22, 15A, B] (= *prize*[3]) get (sth open) (eg with a lever); lift (sth up): (以杠杆等)撬开(与 open 连用); 举起(某物,与 up 连用); (fig) (喻) *pry a secret out of sb.* 探知某人之秘密。

psalm /sɑːm; sɑm/ *n* sacred song or hymn, esp **(the P~s)** those in the Bible. 圣歌; 圣诗; 赞美诗; (尤指圣经之)诗篇 (the Psalms)。**~·ist** /-ɪst; -ɪst/ *n* person who writes ~s, esp **the P~ist,** David, said to be the author of ~s in the Bible. 圣歌作者; (尤指)大卫王(据说为圣经诗篇之作者)。**~·ody** /'sɑːmədɪ; 'sɑmədɪ/ (*pl* -dies) 1 [U] practice or art of singing ~s. 唱赞美诗; 唱赞美诗之技巧。2 [C] arrangement of ~s for singing; book of ~s with their musical settings. (附乐谱之)赞美诗集。

psal·ter /'sɔːltə(r); 'sɔltə/ *n* Book of Psalms; copy of the Psalms, esp one designed for use in public worship. (圣经之)诗篇; (尤指做礼拜时所用之)诗篇集。

psal·tery /'sɔːltərɪ; 'sɔltrɪ/ *n* (*pl* -ries) musical instrument (ancient and medieval times) with strings over a sound-board, played by plucking the strings. 萨泰里琴(古代和中世纪的一种弦乐器)。

pse·phol·ogy /se'fɒlədʒɪ; US: siː-; sɪ'fɑlədʒɪ/ *n* scientific study of elections, trends, etc by means of opinion polls. (利用民意测验等研究选举趋势的)选举学。**pse·phol·ogist** /-ɪst; -ɪst/

pseud /sjuːd; US: suːd; sud/ *n* (colloq) (口) = **pseudo(***n***).**

pseudo /'sjuːdəu; US: 'suː-; 'sjudo/ *adj* (colloq) sham; insincere: (口)冒充的; 骗人的; 虚假的; 伪善的: *I've always found him very* ~. 我一直觉得他很虚伪。□ *n* sham person. 虚伪之人。

pseudo- /sjuːdəu; US: ˌsuː-; ˌsjudo /pref* false; spurious: 伪的; 假的: ~*-scientific.* 假科学的。⇨ **App 3.** 参看附录三。

pseu·do·nym /'sjuːdənɪm; US: 'suː-; 'sjudn̩ɪm/ *n* name taken, esp by an author, instead of his real name. 假名; (尤指)笔名。**pseud·ony·mous** /sjuː-'dɒnəməs; US: suː-; sju'dɑnəməs/ *adj* writing, written, under an assumed name. 以笔名写作的; 用笔名的。

pshaw /pʃɔː; ʃɔ or similar *'burst'* of noise 或类似之 '突发' 声/ *int* exclamation to indicate contempt or impatience. (表示不耐烦及轻蔑等之感叹声)呸! 啐!

psit·ta·co·sis /ˌsɪtə'kəusɪs; ˌsɪtə'kosɪs/ *n* [U] (also called 亦称作 *'parrot fever'*) contagious virus disease (caught from parrots and related birds) producing fever and other complications (as in pneumonia). 鹦鹉热; 鹦鹉病。

psyche /'saɪkɪ; 'saɪkɪ/ *n* **1** human soul or spirit. 人之灵魂或精神。**2** human mind; mentality. 人之心灵; 心智。

psyche·delic /ˌsaɪkɪ'delɪk; ˌsaɪkɪ'dɛlɪk/ *adj* **1** (of drugs) hallucinatory: (指药)使人产生幻觉的: *Mescalin and LSD are* ~ *drugs.* Mescalin 和 LSD 是迷幻药。**2** (of visual and sound effects) acting on the mind like ~ drugs: (指视觉和声音效果)引起心神涣散的; 引起幻觉的: ~ *music.* 迷魂音乐。

psy·chia·try /saɪ'kaɪətrɪ; US: sɪ-; saɪ'kaɪətrɪ/ *n* [U] the study and treatment of mental illness. 精神病学; 精神病治疗法。**psy·chia·trist** /-ɪst; -ɪst/ *n* expert in ~. 精神病专家; 精神病医师。**psy·chi·atric** /ˌsaɪkɪ'ætrɪk; ˌsaɪkɪ'ætrɪk/ *adj* of ~: 精神病学的; 精神病治疗的: *a psychiatric clinic.* 精神病医疗诊所。

psy·chic[1] /'saɪkɪk; 'saɪkɪk/ *n* [C] person apparently, or claiming to be, responsive to occult powers; (popular term for a) medium(4). 通灵之人; 巫师; (自称能与鬼魂通讯息的)关心人。

psy·chic[2] /'saɪkɪk; 'saɪkɪk/, **psy·chi·cal** /'saɪkɪkl; 'saɪkɪkl/ *adj* **1** of the soul or mind. 灵魂的; 心灵的。**2** of phenomena and conditions which appear to be outside physical or natural laws: 超自然的; 与通灵有关的: ~ *research,* the study and investigation of such phenomena, eg telepathy, second sight. 心灵研究(对心灵感应、千里眼等现象的研究)。

psy·cho·anal·y·sis /ˌsaɪkəu ə'næləsɪs; ˌsaɪkoə'næləsɪs/ *n* [U] **1** method of healing mental illnesses by tracing them, through interviews, to events in the patient's early life, and bringing those events to his consciousness. 精神分析(一种治疗精神病的方法, 借谈话以追溯患者早年生活中的事件, 并使之重现在他的意识之中)。**2** body of doctrine based on this method concerned with the investigation and treatment of emotional disturbances. 精神分析学。**psy·cho·ana·lyst** /ˌsaɪkəu'ænəlɪst; ˌsaɪko'ænl̩ɪst/ *n* person who practises ~. 从事精神分析的人; 精神分析家。**psy·cho·ana·lytic(al)** /ˌsaɪkəu ˌænə'lɪtɪk(l); ˌsaɪko ˌænl̩'ɪtɪk(l)/ *adj* relating to ~. 精神分析的; 精神分析学的。**psy·cho·ana·lyse** (= **-lyze**) /ˌsaɪkəu 'ænəlaɪz; ˌsaɪko'ænl̩ˌaɪz/ *vt* treat (sb) by ~. 用精神分析法治疗(某人)。

psy·chol·ogy /saɪ'kɒlədʒɪ; saɪ'kɑlədʒɪ/ *n* [U] **1** science, study of the mind and its processes: 心理学: *abnormal/animal/child/industrial* ~, branches of this science. 变态(动物, 儿童, 工业)心理学。**2** [C] (colloq, unscientific use) mental nature, processes, etc of a person: (口, 但非科学的用法)心理(指一个人的心理状态、过程等): *She understands her husband's* ~ *very well.* 她非常了解她丈夫的心理。**psy·chol·ogist** /-ɪst; -ɪst/ *n* student of, expert in, ~. 研究心理学者;

psy·cho·logi·cal /ˌsaɪkəˈlɒdʒɪkl; ˌsaɪkə-ˈladʒɪkl/ *adj* of ~; of the mind. 心理学的; 心理的。 **the psychological moment**, the most appropriate time; the time when one is most likely to achieve the desired end. 最适当的时机; 最能获得所期望之目的的时刻。 **psychological warfare**, waged by trying to influence people's ideas and beliefs. 心理战(用以影响人们的思想和信仰者)。 **psy·cho·logi·cally** /-klɪ; -klɪ/ *adv*

psy·cho·path /ˈsaɪkəupæθ; ˈsaɪkəˌpæθ/ *n* person suffering from severe emotional derangement, esp one who is aggressive and antisocial, with little or no moral sense. 精神变态者; 精神病患者(尤指性好争吵殴斗,反社会,无道德感的人)。 **~ic** /ˌsaɪkəuˈpæθɪk; ˌsaɪkə-ˈpæθɪk/ *adj* of, suffering from, severe emotional or mental disorder. 精神变态的; 患精神病的。

psy·cho·sis /saɪˈkəusɪs; saɪˈkosɪs/ *n* (*pl* **-choses** /-ˈkəusiːz; -ˈkosiːz/) severely abnormal or diseased mental state. 精神变态; 精神病。

psy·cho·so·matic /ˌsaɪkəusəˈmætɪk; ˌsaɪkosoˈmæ-tɪk/ *adj* (of disease) caused by mental stress; (of medicine) concerned with such disease. (指疾病)由心理压力引起的; (指医学)研究由心理压力引起之疾病的; 心身性的。

psy·cho·therapy /ˌsaɪkəuˈθerəpɪ; ˌsaɪkoˈθerəpɪ/ *n* [U] treatment by psychological methods of mental, emotional and nervous disorders. 心理疗法; 精神疗法。

ptar·mi·gan /ˈtɑːmɪgən; ˈtɑrməgən/ *n* bird of the grouse family with black or grey feathers in summer and white in winter. 雷鸟(松鸡类禽鸟,夏季羽毛为黑或灰色,冬季则为白色)。

ptero·dac·tyl /ˌterəˈdæktɪl; ˌterəˈdæktɪl/ *n* extinct flying reptile. 翼手龙(一种已绝迹的会飞的爬虫)。

pto·maine /ˈtəumeɪn; ˈtomen/ *n* (sorts of) poison which is found in decaying food: 尸毒(腐败食物上所产生的各种毒素): *ill with ~ poisoning*. 因中尸毒而生病。

pub /pʌb; pʌb/ *n* (abbr for) public house: 为 public house 之略: *go round to the pub for a drink*. 到酒馆去喝酒。 **'pub-crawl**, ⇨ **crawl** *n*(1).

pu·berty /ˈpjuːbətɪ; ˈpjubətɪ/ *n* [U] stage at which a person becomes physically able to become a parent; maturing of the sexual functions: 青春期; 发情期; 性官能的成熟: *reach the age of ~*. 已届青春期。

pu·bic /ˈpjuːbɪk; ˈpjubɪk/ *adj* of the lower part of the abdomen: 阴部的: *~ hair*. 阴毛。

pub·lic /ˈpʌblɪk; ˈpʌblɪk/ *adj* (opp of *private*) of, for, connected with, owned by, done for or done by, known to, people in general: (为 private 之反意词)公众的; 为公众的; 与公众有关的; 由公众所有或由公众所做的; 为公众所知的: *a ~ library/park*; 公共图书馆(公园); *a matter of ~ knowledge*, sth known to everyone; 人人皆知的事; *enter ~ life*, engage in the affairs or service of the people, eg in government; 从事公务; *elementary and secondary schools*, govern-ment-controlled schools providing free education. 公立小学和中学。 **~·ad'dress system** *n* (abbr 略作 **PA system**) system of microphones and loud speakers for broadcasting in ~ areas. 扩音系统(包括麦克风和扬声喇叭等)。 **~ 'bar**, ordinary bar in a ~ house or hotel. (酒馆或旅馆内的)卖酒柜台; 普通酒吧。 ⇨ *saloon bar* at **saloon**. **~ corpo'ration**, (legal) corporation provid-ing services for the public, eg in GB *the British Broadcasting Corporation*, *the BBC*. (法律)服务大众的公司(如英国广播公司 BBC)。 **~ 'enemy**, person thought to be a danger to the ~, to the whole community. 社会公敌。 **~ 'house** *n* (GB) (formal) (colloq abbr 口语略作 **pub** /pʌb; pʌb/) house (not a club, hotel, etc) licensed to sell alcoholic drinks to be consumed on the premises but not offering accom-modation. (英)(正式用语)酒馆。 **~ 'nuisance**, (legal) illegal act harmful to people in general rather than to an individual; (colloq) sb who is a nuisance to

a community. (法律)对公众的妨害; 公害; (口)对公众造成妨害之人。 **~ o'pinion poll**, ⇨ **poll**[1](2). **~ 'ownership**, ownership by the State, eg of the railways. 国有(如铁路国有)。 **P~ 'Prosecutor**, ⇨ *prosecutor* at **prosecute**. **~ re'lations** (abbr 略作 **PR**) *n pl* (esp) relations between a government department or auth-ority, business organization, etc with the general ~, usu through the distribution of information. 公共关系 (尤指政府各部门或当局,商业机构等透过消息发布而与公众建立的关系)。 **~ re'lations officer** (abbr 略作 **PRO**) person employed in ~ relations. 公共关系人员。 **'~ school**, **(a)** (GB) private school for older fee-paying pupils, usu a boarding school, supported partly by endowments and managed by a board of governors. (英国)私立学校。 公学(为年龄较大且缴付学费的学生设立,通常为寄宿学校,部分经费来自基金,而由董事会管理之)。 ⇨ *preparatory school* (for younger pupils) at **preparatory**. **(b)** (US and Scot) school providing free education, supported by ~ funds. (美国及苏格兰)公立学校。 **~ 'spirit**, readiness to do things that are for the good of the community. 热心公益; 为公众服务的精神。 Hence, 由此产生, **~·'spirited** *adj* **~ 'transport**, transport systems (road and rail) owned by ~ corpora-tions, eg city and town authorities: 公共交通系统; 公共交通设施(如公路,铁路等): *travel by ~ transport*, contrasted with privately owned systems, one's own car, etc. 搭乘公共交通工具旅行。 **~ trustee**, ⇨ **trustee**. **~ u'tilities**, organizations which supply services and commodities, eg water, gas, electricity, transport, communications, to the general ~. 公用事业(如水、煤气、电、交通设施、电信等)。 **go ~**, (of a business organization) offer shares for purchase (on the Stock Exchange) by the ~: (指商业机构)公开发售股票; 股票上市: *Rolls-Royce, after its bankruptcy in 1971, went ~ in 1972*. 罗尔斯-罗伊斯公司在一九七一年破产之后,于一九七二年公开发售股票。 □ *n* **1** the ~, members of the community in general: 公众; 民众: *the British ~*. 英国民众; 一般英国人。 *The ~ are not admitted*. 一般公众不得擅自进入。 *The ~ is/are requested to leave litter in the park*. 公众请勿在公园中抛弃废物。 *in ~*, openly, not in private. 公开地; 公然地。 **2** particular section of the community: 社会上的某一部分人: *the theatre-going ~*, those who attend theatres; 爱看戏的人; *the reading ~*, those who read books, etc; 读者群; 读者群: *a book that will appeal to a large ~*, to many readers. 会吸引很多读者的书。 **~·ly** /-klɪ; -klɪ/ *adv*

pub·li·can /ˈpʌblɪkən; ˈpʌblɪkən/ *n* **1** (GB) keeper of a public house. (英)酒馆老板。 **2** (in Roman times and in the New Testament) tax-gatherer. (在罗马帝国时代和在新约圣经中指)收税员; 税吏。

pub·li·ca·tion /ˌpʌblɪˈkeɪʃn; ˌpʌblɪˈkeʃən/ *n* **1** [U] act of making known to the public, of publishing sth: 发布; 出版: *the ~ of a report*; 一篇报告的公布; *date of ~*. 出版日期。 **2** [C] sth published, eg a book or a periodical. 出版物(如书或期刊)。

pub·li·cist /ˈpʌblɪsɪst; ˈpʌblɪsɪst/ *n* newspaper man who writes on current topics of public interest, eg a political journalist; person who publicizes. (报纸或通讯社等之)时事评论家; 政论作家; 宣扬者; 宣传者。

pub·lic·ity /pʌbˈlɪsətɪ; pʌbˈlɪsɪtɪ/ *n* [U] **1** the state of being known to, seen by, everyone: 为人所知所见之情况; 出风头: *an actress who seeks/avoids ~*; 一位想出风头(避免出风头)的女演员; *heads of state who live their lives in the full blaze of ~*. 在众目睽睽之下过生活的国家元首们。 **2** (business of) providing information to win public interest: 广告; 宣传; 宣传业务: *give a new book/play, etc wide ~*; 对新书(剧本)广事宣传; *conduct a ~ campaign*. 从事一项宣传运动。 **~ agent**, person employed to keep the name of a person, eg an actor, or product constantly before the public. 宣传员(其工作在于使某人, 如某演员, 或某产品的名字经常出现

于大众之前)。

pub·li·cize /'pʌblɪsaɪz; 'pʌblɪ,saɪz/ vt [VP6A] give publicity to bring to the attention of the public. 宣扬; 引起大众注意; 宣传。

pub·lish /'pʌblɪʃ; 'pʌblɪʃ/ vt [VP6A] **1** have (a book, periodical, etc) printed and announce that it is for sale. 出版(书、期刊等)。 **2** make known to the public: 公布; 宣布: ~ *the news*; 发布消息; ~ *the banns of marriage*, announce formally in a church the names of persons shortly to be married. (在教堂中)公布结婚预告。 **~er** n person whose business is the ~ing of books. 出版商; 出版家。

puce /pjuːs; pjus/ n [U] purple-brown. 紫褐色。

puck¹ /pʌk; pʌk/ n (in folklore) mischievous sprite or goblin. (民间传说中之)受恶作剧的精灵或恶鬼。 **~·ish** /-ɪʃ; -ɪʃ/ adj mischievous: 恶作剧的: *a ~ish smile*. 淘气的微笑。 **~·ish·ly** adv

puck² /pʌk; pʌk/ n hard rubber disc used instead of a ball in ice-hockey. (冰球运动中用以代替球的)橡皮圆盘; 冰球。⇨ the illus at **hockey.** 参看 hockey 之插图。

pucker /'pʌkə(r); 'pʌkə/ vt, vi [VP6A, 15B, 2A, C] ~ (*up*), draw or come together into small folds or wrinkles: 折叠; 皱起; 缩拢: ~ *up one's brows/lips.* 皱起眉头(双唇)。 *This coat ~s (up) at the shoulders.* 这件外衣的肩部皱了。 □ n wrinkle. 皱纹。

pud /pʊd; pʊd/ n [U] (sl) pudding. (俚)布丁。

pud·den /'pʊdn; 'pʊdn/ n (colloq) only in (口)(仅用于) **'~-head** n slow, stupid person. 笨人; 愚钝者。

pudding /'pʊdɪŋ; 'pʊdɪŋ/ n [C, U] **1** (dish of) food, usu a soft, sweet mixture, served as part of a meal, generally eaten after the meat course: 布丁(一种松软的甜食, 为正餐之一部分, 通常在主菜后食用); *milk ~s*, of some kind of grain, eg rice, cooked with milk and flavourings. 牛奶布丁(米等同牛奶和香料制成者)。 '~**face**, large fat face. 大而胖的脸。 **2** kind of sausage. 一种腊肠。 '**black** ~, intestine of pig stuffed with oatmeal, blood, etc. 黑腊肠(由燕麦片、血等塞入猪肠中制成)。 **3** sth like a ~ in appearance. 外貌若布丁之物。 **4** '~ **stone**, rock composed of rounded pebbles in a kind of stone like concrete. 圆砾岩(由小卵石组成, 形似混凝土)。

puddle /'pʌdl; 'pʌdl/ n **1** [C] small pool of water. 小水潭。 **2** [U] wet clay and sand mixed to a paste, used as a watertight covering for embankments, etc. (湿黏土与沙混拌成泥浆, 用以涂塞堤防等以免漏水的)胶土; 胶泥。 □ vt **1** mix (wet clay and sand) into a thick paste. 混拌(湿黏土与沙)而成厚泥浆。 **2** stir (molten iron) to produce wrought iron by expelling carbon. 搅动(熔铁)以排除碳而炼出熟铁。 **pud·dler** /'pʌdlə(r); 'pʌdlə/ n worker who ~s clay, etc or molten iron. 混拌泥浆者; 搅炼熔铁者。

pu·denda /pjuː'dendə; pju'dɛndə/ n pl (formal) external genital organs, esp of the female. (正式用语)阴部; (尤指)女阴。

pudgy /'pʌdʒɪ; 'pʌdʒɪ/ adj (-ier, -iest) short, thick and fat: 矮胖的; 短而粗的: ~ *fingers*. 短而粗的手指。

pueblo /'pweblə⊍; 'pwɛblo/ n (pl ~s /-ləʊz; -loz/) communal village dwelling of adobe and stone, as built by American Indians in Mexico and the south-western US. (墨西哥和美国西南部之印第安人)用泥砖和石块建的村落; 印第安人村落。

puer·ile /'pjʊəraɪl US: -rəl; 'pjʊə,raɪl/ adj trivial; suitable only for a child: 琐屑的; 只适合小孩的; 幼稚的: *ask ~ questions*. 问些幼稚的问题。 **puer·il·ity** /,pjʊə'rɪlətɪ; ,pjʊə'rɪlətɪ/ n [U] childishness; foolishness; [C] childish or foolish act, idea, utterance, etc. 幼稚; 愚蠢; 幼稚或愚蠢的言行思想等。

pu·er·peral /pjuː'ɜːpərəl; pju'ɜpərəl/ adj of, due to, childbirth: 分娩的; 因分娩而起的: ~ *fever*. 产褥热。

puff¹ /pʌf; pʌf/ n [C] **1** (sound of a) short, quick sending out of breath, air, etc; amount of steam,

smoke, etc sent out at one time: (呼吸、空气等)短而快的喷送; 喷送声; 一次喷出之(蒸汽、烟等的)量: ~*s from a steam-engine*; 蒸汽机喷出之气; *have a ~ at a pipe*, 吸一口烟斗。 **2** (**'powder-**) ~, piece or ball of soft material, for putting powder on the face. 粉扑。 **3** round, soft mass of material used on an article of dress as an ornament: (衣服上用做装饰的)圆而松的叠结; 褶裥: ~ *sleeves*, swelling out like balloons. (宽松而鼓起的)灯笼袖。 **4** ~ **pastry**, light, flaky pastry. 多层酥饼, 千层饼。 **5** quantity of ~ pastry filled with jam, whipped cream, etc: (包有果酱、奶油等的)酥皮点心: *jam ~s*. 果酱酥皮点心。 **6** review of a book, play, etc, praising it extravagantly. (对书、戏剧等之)过份夸奖的评论; 吹嘘。 **7** '~-**adder** n poisonous African viper which inflates the upper part of its body when excited. 鼓腹蝰(非洲产的一种毒蛇, 受到刺激时身体上半部即胀大)。 '~-**ball** n kind of fungus shaped like a ball which when ripe breaks open and sends out ~s of dust-like spores. 尘菌; 马勃菌(形如球, 成熟时即裂开, 并喷散出尘土状孢子)。 **~·y** adj (-ier, -iest) short of breath; easily made short of breath (by running, climbing, etc); swollen: 喘息的, 易喘息的; 膨胀的: *a red face, ~y under the eyes*. 一张红红的脸, 眼睛下面肿胀的。 **~·i·ness** n [U] state of being ~y. 喘息; 易喘息或膨胀的状态。

puff² /pʌf; pʌf/ vi, vt **1** [VP2A, C] move along with puffs(1); breathe quickly (as after running): (of smoke, steam, etc) come out in puffs: 喷送着气(蒸汽、烟等)而行进; 喘息(如跑后); (指烟、蒸汽等)阵阵喷出: *The old steam-engine ~ed out of the station*. 那辆旧的蒸汽机车喷着阵阵的烟驶出了车站。 *He was ~ing hard when he jumped on to the bus*. 他跳上公共汽车时喘息不已。 *He was ~ing (away) at his cigar*. 他一口一口地喷着雪茄烟。 *Smoke ~ed up from the crater of the volcano*. 烟从火山口一阵阵地喷出。 **2** [VP15A, B] send out in puffs: 阵阵喷出: *He ~ed smoke into my face*. 他向着我的脸喷烟。 *He managed to ~ out a few words*. 他喘息着说出几句话。 *He was rather ~ed* (= out of breath) *after running to the bus stop*. 跑到公共汽车站后, 他喘息不已。 **~ up**, filled with pride; conceited: 洋洋得意的; 自负的。 **3** [VP15B] ~ **sth out**, **(a)** blow out: 吹熄: *He ~ed out the candle*. 他吹熄蜡烛。 **(b)** cause to swell with air: 使胀(使因有空气而胀起): *He ~ed out his chest with pride*. 他傲气十足地挺起胸膛。 **4** [VP6A] praise (a book, etc) in an advertisement or review, esp in an exaggerated way. 在广告或书评中(尤指过分)称赞(某书等); 吹捧。

puf·fin /'pʌfɪn; 'pʌfɪn/ n N Atlantic seabird with a large bill. 善知鸟; 海鹦(产于北大西洋的一种大嘴海鸟)。 ⇨ the illus at **water.** 参看 water 之插图。

pug /pʌg; pʌg/ n (also 亦作 '**pug-dog**) small breed of pug-nosed dog. 哈巴狗。 '**pug-nose(d)** adj, n (with a) short, squat or snub nose. 狮子鼻(短、扁、微向上翻的鼻子); 有狮子鼻的。

pu·gil·ist /'pjuːdʒɪlɪst; 'pjudʒəlɪst/ n (formal) boxer. (正式用语)拳击家。 **pu·gil·ism** /-ɪzəm; -ɪzəm/ n [U] boxing. 拳击。 **pu·gil·is·tic** /,pjuːdʒɪ'lɪstɪk; ,pjudʒə-'lɪstɪk/ adj of ~s or pugilism. 拳击家的; 拳击的。

pug·na·cious /pʌg'neɪʃəs; pʌg'neʃəs/ adj (formal) fond of, in the habit of, fighting. (正式用语)好战的; 好斗的。 **~·ly** adv **pug·nac·ity** /pʌg'næsətɪ; pʌg'næsətɪ/ n [U].

puis·sant /'pjuːɪsnt; 'pjuɪsn̩t/ adj (archaic) having great power or influence. (古)具有极大力量或影响的。 **puis·sance** /-sns; -sn̩s/ n [U] strength. 力量。

puke /pjuːk; pjuk/ vi, vt, n [U] (sl) vomit. (俚)呕吐。

pukka /'pʌkə; 'pʌkə/ adj (dated sl) genuine; authentic; superior. (过时俚语)真正的; 可靠的; 优良的。

pul·chri·tude /'pʌlkrɪtjuːd US: -tuːd; 'pʌlkrɪ,tjud/ n [U] (formal) physical beauty. (正式用语)美丽; 漂亮; 外在美。 **pul·chri·tudi·nous** /,pʌlkrɪ'tjuːdɪnəs US -'tuːdənəs; ,pʌlkrɪ'tjudn̩əs/ adj

pule /pjuːl/ pjul/ *vi* [VP2A] (eg of a baby) cry feebly; whimper. (指嬰兒等)微弱地哭泣; 低泣; 嗚咽.

pull¹ /pul/ pul/ *n* **1** [C] act of pulling: 拖; 拉; 扯; 曳; 吸: *give a ~ at a rope*: 拉繩子; [C] act of deep drinking: 大口喝一大口. *take a ~ at a bottle*, drink deeply from it. 從瓶中喝一大口。**2** [C] attraction: 吸引力: *the ~ of the life of a sailor/singer/tramp*. 船員(歌星, 流浪者)生活的吸引力. **3** [C] effort of moving: 費力; 奮力: *a hard ~ up the hill*. 吃力的(漫長而費力的)爬山. **4** [C, U] (colloq) power to get help or attention through influence, eg with people in high positions: (口)勢力; 影響力: *He has a strong ~ with the Managing Director*. 他對總經理頗有影響力. **5** handle, etc which is to be pulled. 拉手; 把手. **6** (printing) proof; single impression. (印刷)校樣; 校稿.

pull² /pul/ pul/ *vt, vi* (For special uses with *adverbial particles* and *preps*, ⇨ below). (與副詞性小品詞及介詞連用的特殊用法, 參看下列第 **7** 義.) **1** [VP6A, 15A, B, 22, 2A] (contrasted with *push*) use force upon (sth or sb) so as to draw towards or after one, or in the direction indicated: (與 push 相對)拉; 扯; 拖: *The horse was ~ing a heavy cart*. 馬在拉重車. *How many coaches can that locomotive ~*? 那列火車頭能拉多少節客車? *Would you rather push the barrow or ~ it*? 你寧推還是愿拉手推車? *The baby was ~ing its father's beard*. 那嬰兒在扯他父親的鬍子. *P~ your chair up to the table*. 把你的椅子拖近桌去. *She ~ed her tights/gloves on/off*. 她把她的緊身衣(手套)穿(戴)上(脫)下. *He ~ed my ears/~ed me by the ears*. 他拉我的耳朵. *I'm going to the dentist to have a bad tooth ~ed out*. 我要到牙醫那里拔掉一顆壞牙. *Stop ~ing, please*! 請別拉了! ⟹ *~ sth to pieces*, use force to separate its parts or to break it up into parts; (fig) criticize severely by pointing out the weak points or faults: 用力將某物扯成碎片或拆散; (喻)指出缺點或錯誤而加以嚴厲地批評: *He ~ed my proposals / theory to pieces*. 他把我的建議(理論)批評得体無完膚. **2** [VP6A, 15A, B, 2A, C] move (a boat) by ~ing an oar or a pair of oars; (of a boat) be rowed (by): 划(船); (指船)被划動: *Now, all ~ together, please*! 現在請大家一起划! *The men/boat ~ed for the shore*. 那些人(船)划向岸邊. ⟹ *~ together*, (fig) work together; co-operate. (喻)一起工作; 合作. ⟹ *~ one's weight*, exert oneself so as to do a fair share of the work: 盡力做好自己的一份工作: *Either you ~ your weight or we replace you*. 你要是不盡力做好你的工作, 我們便換人做你的事. **3** [VP3A] *~ at/on sth*, (a) give a tug: 拉: *~ at/on a rope*. 拖曳繩子. **(b)** draw or suck: 吸; 吮: *~ing at his pipe*, drawing in breath and smoke through his (tobacco) pipe; 吸他的煙斗; *~ at a bottle*, have a drink from one. 從瓶中喝一口.

pull¹(1). **4** ⟹ *a 'fast one*, (colloq) deceive sb. (口)欺騙某人; 欺詐. ⟹ *a muscle*, strain it. 拉傷肌肉. ⟹ *a proof*, take an impression (from type); print a proof. 印制校樣. For other uses with *nn*, ⟹ the *n* entries, eg 與名詞連用的其他用法參看各名詞, 如 ⟹ *a face/faces*; *sb's leg*; *~ one's punches*; *~ strings*; *~ the 'wool over sb's eyes*. **5** (in games, sport) (用于游戲, 運動) (golf) hit (the ball) wrongly to the left, Cf 參較 *slice*(4); (高爾夫球)擊(球)偏向左方; (cricket) strike (the ball) forward and to the left of the wicket, by striking across the ball's path; (板球)擊(球)向前至三柱門的左方; (horse-racing) ~ in the reins (of a horse) to prevent it .from winning. (賽馬)(故意要輸而)勒住馬. **6** (sl) raid; rob: (俚)突擊; 搶劫: *~ a bank*; 搶劫銀行; *steal*: *a few thousand quid*. 偷竊幾千鎊. **7** [VP15B, 2C] (special uses with *adverbial particles* and *preps*): (與副詞性小品詞和介詞連用的特殊用法):

pull sb/sth about, ~ in different directions; treat roughly. 拖曳某人或某物到處跑; 拖來拖去; 虐待某人或某物.

pull sth apart, tear or ~ into its parts. 扯斷; 拆開; 撕開.

pull sth down, destroy or demolish, eg an old building. 摧毀; 拆除(如舊的建筑物). *pull sb down*, (of illness, etc) weaken; lower the spirits of: (指疾病等)使虛弱; 使精神不振: *An attack of influenza ~ed me down*. 害一次流行性感冒很快就使你虛弱下來.

pull in, **(a)** (of a train) enter a station: (指火車)進站: *The express from Rome ~ed in on time*. 從羅馬來的快車準時進站. **(b)** (of a motor-vehicle or boat) move in towards: (指車輛或船)移向; 駛向: *The boat ~ed in to the bank/shore*. 該船向岸邊駛近. *The lorry driver ~ed in to the side of the road*. 卡車司機把車子駛向路邊. Hence, 由此產生, '*~-in n* place at which to ~ in 可停車之處 (also ⇨ *~-up* below). (亦參看下列之 *~-up*). ⟹ *sb in*, **(a)** attract, draw: 吸引: *The new play at the National Theatre is ~ing in large audiences*. 在國家戲院上演的新劇吸引了大批觀眾. **(b)** (colloq, of the police) detain; arrest: (口, 指警察)拘留; 逮捕: *He was ~ed in for questioning/loitering*. 他被逮捕審問(他因游蕩而遭拘留). ⟹ *sth in*, (colloq) earn: (口)賺進: *How much money is he ~ing in, do you think*? 你認為他賺進多少錢? ⟹ *oneself in*, draw in the stomach muscles (so as to be upright, less flabby). 收縮腹肌 (保持身材正直, 減少腹肌松弛).

pull sth off, **(a)** drive a motor-vehicle into a layby or hard shoulder. 將車開入大路旁的停車站. Hence, 由此產生, '*~-off n* (US) (美) = *layby*. **(b)** succeed in a plan, in winning sth: (某項計划)獲得成功; 得到某物: *~ off a good speculation*: 在一宗投机生意中大獲成功; *~ off some good wins at the races*, make successful bets. 在賽馬中贏了可觀的賭注.

pull out, draw or row out: 駛出; 划出: *The boat ~ed out into midstream*. 該船划出而進入中流. *The driver of the car ~ed out from behind the lorry*. 該車的司机把車子開出由行駛的行列以便超越那輛卡車. **(b)** detach, eg from a periodical: 分開; 分離(如從一期刊中): (attrib) (用作定語) *a '~-out supplement*, part of a magazine, etc which can be ~ed out and kept separately. (雜志等之可取下單獨保存的)增刊. Hence, 由此產生, '*~-out n = out of sth*, leave: 離開; 離去; 脫離: *The train ~ed out of Euston right on time*. 火車準時離開尤斯頓. *Sam ~ed out of the scheme at the last moment*. 薩姆于最后一刻退出那項計划. ⟹ *(sb) out (of sth)*, (cause to) leave a place or situation which is too difficult to manage: (使某人)脫離困境: *Troops are being ~ed out/are ~ing out of these troubled areas*. 軍隊被調離(正离开纷乱地区). Hence, 由此產生, '*~-out n*: *The ~-out was planned to spread over a month*. 撤離的工作計划在一個月的時間內進行.

pull (sth) over, (cause a vehicle, boat, etc to) move or steer to one side, eg to let another vehicle or boat pass: (將車、船等)開向一邊讓其他車、船超越: *P~ (your car) over and let me pass*! (將你的車子)開到一邊讓我超越!

pull (sb) round, (help to) recover from illness, weakness, a faint, etc: 康複; 復元; 協助某人使康復; 醒等: *You'll soon ~ round here in the country*. 住在這乡間你不久即可康復. *Have this brandy; it will ~ you round*. 把這点白兰地喝下; 它会使你(从晕眩等中)復元. *pull through*, **(a)** = *~ round*. **(b)** succeed in avoiding difficulties, dangers, etc; avoid failure. 在逃避困難, 危險等方面成功; 免于失敗. ⟹ *sb through*, (a) help to recover from illness, etc: 幫助(某人)恢复健康等: *The doctors ~ed me through*. 医生们帮助我恢复了健康. **(b)** help to avoid failure, help to pass an examination, etc: 协助(某人)免于失败; 帮助(某人)通过考试等: *David's tutor did what he could to ~ him through*. 大卫的家庭教师尽力帮助他通过考试. '*~-through n* oily rag attached to a cord, ~ed through the barrel of a rifle, etc to clean it. 枪镗清扫布(结于绳上之油布, 用以拉过枪筒而擦净之).

pull together, ⇨ **2** above. 参看上列第2义。**~ oneself together**, get control of oneself, of one's feelings, etc. 控制自己、自己的感情等。

pull (sth) up, bring or come to a stop: 使停止; 停止: *The driver ~ed up when he came to the traffic lights.* 司机遇到交通灯时将车停下来。*He ~ed up his car at the entrance.* 他把他的汽车停在大门口。Hence, 由此产生, '**~-up** n place at which to ~ up: (路旁)饮食店等(可停车于附近者): 'Good ~-up for lorry-drivers', eg as a sign outside a roadside café (also ⇨ ~-in above). '货车司机的理想饮食处'(如路边饮食店所挂的招牌)(亦参看上列之 pull-in above)。 ~ **sb up**, check; reprimand: 阻止; 申斥: *He was ~ed up by the chairman.* 他为主席所阻止。 ~ **up to / with sb / sth**, improve one's relative position (in a race, etc). 改善相对的地位 (如在赛马等中; 在竞赛方面): *The favourite soon ~ed up with the other horses.* 那匹有希望赢得竞赛的马很快追上了别的马。

pul·let /ˈpʊlɪt; ˈpʊlɪt/ n young hen, esp at the time she begins to lay eggs. 小母鸡 (尤指开始生蛋者)。

pul·ley /ˈpʊlɪ; ˈpʊlɪ/ n (pl ~s) grooved wheel(s) for ropes or chains, used for lifting things. 滑轮; 滑车。 '**~-block** wooden block in which a ~ is fixed. 滑车组。

Pull·man /ˈpʊlmən; ˈpʊlmən/ n **1** (also 亦作 '**~ car**) sleeping-car on a railway train. (火车上的)卧车。 **2** especially comfortable railway carriage. (特别舒适的)火车厢。

pull·over /ˈpʊləʊvə(r); ˈpʊlˌovɚ/ n knitted outer garment, with or without sleeves, pulled on over the head. 套头毛衣; 套头毛背心。⇨ **jersey, jumper, sweater**.

pul·lu·late /ˈpʌljʊleɪt; ˈpʌljəˌlet/ vi breed, multiply, rapidly; swarm. 繁殖; 增殖; 充满; 群集。

pul·mon·ary /ˈpʌlmənərɪ US: -nerɪ; ˈpʌlmə,nɛrɪ/ adj of, in, connected with, the lungs: 肺的; 肺部的; 与肺有关的: ~ *diseases*; 肺病; *the ~ arteries*, conveying blood to the lungs. 肺动脉。

pulp /pʌlp; pʌlp/ n **1** [U] soft, fleshy part of fruit: 果肉: *'apple ~.* 苹果的果肉。 **2** [U, C] soft mass of other material, esp of wood fibre as used for making paper: 柔软的材料; (尤指用于造纸, 由木材纤维制成的)木浆; 纸浆。 *reduce to (a) ~*, destroy the shape of by beating up and making soft. 把…打得稀烂如浆。 *magazines / literature*, (term applied disparagingly to) cheap, popular periodicals, etc. (轻蔑语, 指)廉价的低级杂志(作品)。□ vt, vi [VP6A, 2A] make into, become like, ~; remove ~ from: 制成浆; 变成如浆之物; 取出…的浆: *~ old books.* 把旧书化成造纸的纸浆。 **~y** adj (-ier, -iest) like or consisting of ~. 象果肉或浆的; 有果肉或浆的。

pul·pit /ˈpʊlpɪt; ˈpʊlpɪt/ n (usu small) raised and enclosed structure in a church, used by a clergyman, esp when preaching. 教堂中布道的讲坛 (通常指小者)。 **the ~**, the clergy. 教士职; 圣职; 教士(总称)。⇨ the illus at **church**. 参看 church 之插图。

pul·que /ˈpʊlkeɪ; ˈpʊlkɪ/ n [U] fermented milky drink made in Mexico from some kinds of agave. (墨西哥产的)龙舌兰酒。

pul·sar /ˈpʌlsɑː(r); ˈpʌlsɑr/ n star (in a galaxy) detected by pulsating radio signals only. 仅能由脉冲无线电信号测出的银河系星球; 脉冲星。

pul·sate /pʌlˈseɪt US: ˈpʌlseɪt; ˈpʌlset/ vt, vi **1** [VP2A] beat or throb; expand and contract rhythmically; vibrate; quiver. 搏动; 悸动; 有节奏地扩张与收缩; 震动; 震颤; 脉动。 **2** [VP6A] cause to vibrate; agitate. 使震动; 激动。 **pul·sa·tion** /pʌlˈseɪʃn; pʌlˈseʃən/ n **1** [C] single beat or throb; heartbeat. 一次跳动; 悸动; 心脏跳动。 **2** [U] pulsating; throbbing. 震动; 有韵律的悸动; 脉动。

pulse[1] /pʌls; pʌls/ n **1** the regular beat of the arteries, eg as felt at the wrist, as the blood is pumped through them by the heart: 脉搏: *The patient has a weak / strong / low / irregular ~.* 这位病人脉搏很弱 (强, 低, 不规律)。 *feel sb's ~*, feel the artery at the wrist and count the number of beats per minute. 诊脉 (按触脉部动脉, 并计算其每分钟跳动次数)。 **2** (fig) throb or thrill cf life or emotion: (喻)生命或感情的激动: *an event that stirred my ~s*, roused my emotion, excited me. 一件使我感情激动的事件。□ vi [VP2C] beat; throb: 跳动; 震动: *the life pulsing through a great city,* 大城市中紧张纷乱的生活; *news that sent the blood pulsing through his veins.* 使他的血液沸腾的消息。

pulse[2] /pʌls; pʌls/ n [U] (collective sing, sometimes with pl v) seeds growing in pods, eg peas, beans and lentils, used as food. (集合单数, 有时用复数动词)用作食物的豆; 豆类(如豌豆、蚕豆、扁豆)。

pul·ver·ize /ˈpʌlvəraɪz; ˈpʌlvəˌraɪz/ vt, vi **1** [VP 6A] grind to powder; smash completely: 研磨成粉; 彻底摧毁; (fig) (喻) ~ *an opponent's arguments.* 彻底粉碎对方的论点。 **2** [VP2A] become powder or dust. 变成粉状或尘埃。

puma /ˈpjuːmə; ˈpjumə/ n large brown American animal of the cat family 美洲狮 (also 亦称作 a cougar and mountain lion). ⇨ the illus at **cat**. 参看 cat 之插图。

pum·ice /ˈpʌmɪs; ˈpʌmɪs/ n [U] '**~(-stone)**, light, porous stone (lava) used for cleaning and polishing. (轻而多孔的)浮石(可用以擦净或磨光东西)。

pum·mel /ˈpʌml; ˈpʌml/ vt (-ll-, US also -l-) [VP 6A, 15B] beat repeatedly with the fists: 以拳连击: *give sb a good ~ling.* 把某人好好揍一顿。

pump[1] /pʌmp; pʌmp/ n machine or device for forcing liquid, gas or air into, out of or through sth, eg water from a well, petrol from a storage tank, air into a tyre, oil through a pipe-line: 唧筒; 抽水机; 抽油机; 打气筒: *a row of 'petrol ~s*, 一排汽油泵; *a 'bicycle ~.* 自行车打气筒。⇨ the illus at **bicycle**. 参看 bicycle 之插图。 ⇨ also **parish-pump** at **parish**. '**~-room** n (at a spa) room where medicinal water is dispensed. (有矿泉水之疗养地的)药用水调制室。□ vt, vi **1** [VP6A, 15A, B, 22] force, eg water, etc out (up) *into / through* sth, by using a ~: 以唧筒打(水等)(出 out, up, into, through 连用, 后接某物): ~ *water up / out*; 用唧筒把水抽上(出)来; ~ *a well dry*, ~ until there is no water left in the well; 把井中的水抽干; ~ *air into a tyre*, 为轮胎打气; ~ *up the tyres*, 把轮胎打足气; (fig) (喻) ~ *information out of sb*; (经盘问而)从某人口中获得消息; ~ *facts into the heads of dull pupils*; 把事实塞进笨学生的脑子里; *a '~ing station*, eg on a pipe-line for forcing petroleum. (如输油线上的)供油泵; 抽水站。 **2** [VP2A, C] use a ~. 使用唧筒或打气筒: *He was ~ing away.* 他正用唧筒抽水。

pump[2] /pʌmp; pʌmp/ n kind of light, soft shoe worn for sport, dancing, etc; (US) woman's low-heeled shoe without a fastening. 一种轻软的运动鞋或舞蹈鞋; (美)无系带(扣)的低跟女鞋。

pum·per·nickel /ˈpʌmpənɪkl; ˈpʌmpɚˌnɪkl/ n [U] wholemeal rye bread. 裸麦粗面包。

pump·kin /ˈpʌmpkɪn; ˈpʌmpkɪn/ n large, round orange-yellow fruit with many seeds in it, used as a vegetable and (US) as a filling for pies. 南瓜。

pun /pʌn; pʌn/ n [C] humorous use of different words which sound the same or of two meanings of the same word, 双关语(即用同音异义或一词二义之语以为诙谐之用), eg 'A cannon-ball took off his legs, so he laid down his arms.' '一炮弹打断他的腿, 所以他放下他的武器。'□ vi (-nn-) [VP2A, 3A] ~ *(on / upon)*, make a pun or puns (on / upon a word). 用双关谐语; 将(某词)用作双关谐语。

punch[1] /pʌntʃ; pʌntʃ/ n **1** tool or machine for cutting holes in leather, metal, paper, etc; tool for forcing nails beneath a surface, or bolts out of holes. 打洞器; 钻孔机, (压或起)钉器, 钉铳。 **2** tool for stamping designs on surfaces. 打印器。□ vt **1** [VP6A] make a hole (in

sth) with a **~**: 用打洞器打洞(于某物): **~** *holes in a sheet of metal;* 在金属板上钻孔; **~** *a train-ticket;* 轧洞于火车票上; **~***ed cards*, as used in filing systems or computers; 打孔卡片(如用于档案或电脑处理中者); **~***d (paper) tape*, used by computer programmers. (电脑程序师所用的)打孔(纸)带。**2** [VP15B] **~** ***sth in/out,*** drive sth in or out with a **~**. 以钉铳打进或起出。

punch[2] /pʌntʃ; pʌntʃ/ *n* [U] drink made of wine or spirits mixed with hot water, sugar, lemons, spice, etc: 五味酒(用酒同热水,糖,柠檬,香料等混合成的饮料); 潘趣酒: *rum* **~**. 朗姆五味酒。**'~-bowl** *n* bowl in which **~** is mixed. 五味酒钵; 潘趣酒钵。

punch[3] /pʌntʃ; pʌntʃ/ *vt* [VP6A, 15A] strike hard with the fist: 以拳重击: **~** *a man on the chin.* 以拳重击某人之下颚。*He has a face I'd like to* **~**. 他有一张我很想饱以老拳的脸。□ *n* **1** [C] blow given with the fist: 用拳的一击: *give sb a* **~** *on the nose;* 用拳击某人的鼻子; *a boxer with a strong* **~**, the ability to deliver strong **~**es. 出拳很重的拳击手。***pull one's ~es,*** attack less vigorously than one is able to. 没有用尽力气打; 故意不用力打。**'~-ball, '~·ing-ball** *nn* inflated or stuffed ball hung up and **~**ed with the fists for exercise. 拳球; 梨形球(练习拳击的吊球)。**,~-'drunk** *adj* (in boxing) dazed by **~**es received in a fight; (fig) confused. (在拳击中)因受拳击而晕眩的; (喻)惶惑的。**'~ line** *n* climax of a story (where the point is made, where laughter comes). 故事的高潮; 滑稽故事中使人发笑的地方; 妙语。**'~-up** *n* (colloq) fight with the fists: (口)用拳头打斗: *The quarrel ended in a* **~***-up.* 争论酿成了拳斗。**2** [U] (fig) energy: (喻)力量; 精力; 效果; 魄力: *a speech with plenty of* **~** *in it.* 有力的演说。

Punch /pʌntʃ; pʌntʃ/ *n* grotesque hump-backed figure in the traditional puppet-show called **P~ and Judy.** (传统傀儡戏 Punch and Judy 中)滑稽的驼背木偶。***as pleased/proud as P~,*** greatly pleased/very proud. 非常快乐(骄傲)。

punc·tilio /pʌŋk'tɪlɪəʊ; pʌŋk'tɪlɪ,o/ *n* (*pl* **~s** /-lɪəʊz; -lɪoz/) **1** [C] particular point of good conduct, ceremony, honour. (良好行为、仪式、荣誉的)细节。**2** [U, C] formality; (point of) etiquette (esp when it is not really important): 拘泥形式; 礼仪(的细节); (尤指)无谓的礼仪(的细节): *stand upon* **~***s*, insist too much upon protocol(2). 过份拘泥于礼仪。

punc·tili·ous /pʌŋk'tɪlɪəs; pʌŋk'tɪlɪəs/ *adj* (formal) very careful to carry out correctly details of conduct and ceremony; careful in performing duties. (正式用语)留心细节的; 小心执行任务的: **~·ly** *adv* **~·ness** *n*

punc·tual /'pʌŋktʃʊəl; 'pʌŋktʃʊəl/ *adj* neither early nor late; coming, doing sth, at the time fixed: 准时的; 守时的: *be* **~** *for the appointment/in payment of one's rent.* 准时赴约(准时付租金)。**~ly** /-ʊəlɪ; -ʊəlɪ/ *adv* in a **~** manner: 准时地; 守时地: *The train arrived* **~***ly.* 火车准时到站。**~·ity** /,pʌŋktʃʊ'ælətɪ; ,pʌŋktʃʊ'ælətɪ/ *n* [U] being **~**. 准时; 守时。

punc·tu·ate /'pʌŋktʃʊeɪt; 'pʌŋktʃʊ,et/ *vt* **1** [VP6A] put full-stops, commas, etc, (eg. , ; : ? !) into a piece of writing. 加标点于。**2** [VP15A] interrupt from time to time: 不时打断; 不时介入: *a speech* **~***d with cheers;* 不时被欢呼声打断的演讲; **~** *one's remarks with thumps on the table.* 谈话中不时以拳头击桌。**punc·tu·ation** /,pʌŋktʃʊ'eɪʃn; ,pʌŋktʃʊ'eʃən/ *n* [U] punctuating; art or practice of punctuating. 标点; 标点使用法。⇨ **App 9.** 参看附录九。

punc·ture /'pʌŋktʃə(r); 'pʌŋktʃə/ *n* [C] small hole made by sth sharp, esp one made accidentally in a pneumatic tyre. 小洞; 小孔(尤指充气车胎偶然被刺穿者)。□ *vt, vi* **1** [VP6A] make a **~** in: 穿孔于; 刺穿: **~** *an abscess/a motor-car tyre;* 刺破脓肿(汽车胎); (fig) deflate: (喻)减低; 挫…之锐气: *She likes to* **~** *her husband's ego,* lessen his selfconceit. 她喜欢煞她丈夫的威风。**2** [VP2A] experience a **~**: 被刺孔: *Two of my tyres* **~***ed while I was on that stony road.* 我在那碎石路上开车时,有两个轮胎被刺破了。

pun·dit /'pʌndɪt; 'pʌndɪt/ *n* very learned Hindu; authority on a subject; (hum) learned teacher; pedant. 极有学问的印度人; 某一学科之权威; (谐)有学问的教师; 腐儒。

pun·gent /'pʌndʒənt; 'pʌndʒənt/ *adj* (of smells, tastes; fig of remarks) sharp; biting; stinging: (指气味、味道)刺鼻的; 辛辣的; (喻, 指批评)尖刻的: *a* **~** *sauce;* 辣酱油; **~** *remarks/satire/criticism.* 尖刻的评语(讽刺, 批评)。**~·ly** *adv* **pun·gency** /-nsɪ; -nsɪ/ *n* [U] **~** quality. 辛辣; 尖刻。

Pu·nic /'pju:nɪk; 'pjunɪk/ *adj* of ancient Carthage and its people. 古迦太基及其人民的。**the ~ Wars,** the wars between Rome and Carthage. 布匿战争(罗马与迦太基间之三次战争)。**~ faith,** treachery. 背信; 背叛。

pun·ish /'pʌnɪʃ; 'pʌnɪʃ/ *vt* [VP6A, 14] **~*sb (with/by sth) (for sth),*** **1** cause (sb) suffering or discomfort for wrongdoing; cause suffering or discomfort to sb (for wrongdoing): 处罚; 惩罚: **~** *a man with/by a fine.* 处某人以罚金。*How would you* **~** *stealing/sb for stealing/sb who steals?* 你如何处罚偷窃(惩罚偷窃的人)? **2** treat roughly; knock about: 粗鲁地对待; 痛击: *The champion* **~***ed his opponent severely,* (boxing) gave him severe blows. (拳击)那位冠军痛击他的对手。*Chapman* **~***ed the bowling,* (cricket) scored freely (from poor or weak bowling). (板球)(因对方投球失误)查普曼连连得分。**3** (colloq) eat, drink, use up, deal with, etc, much of: (口)猛吃; 猛喝; 大量消耗: **~** *the cold beef/the cider cask.* 猛吃冷牛肉(猛喝苹果酒)。**~·able** /-əbl; -əbl̩/ *adj* that can be **~**ed (by law). 能(由法律)惩罚的。**~·ment** *n* [U] **~**ing or being **~**ed: 处罚; 被处罚: *escape without* **~***ment;* 免受惩罚; [C] penalty inflicted for wrongdoing: 因犯罪而受的惩罚: *make the* **~***ment fit the crime;* 使某种处罚适用于某种罪行; 因罪量刑; *inflict severe* **~***ments on criminals.* 对罪犯施以严厉处罚。

pu·ni·tive /'pju:nɪtɪv; 'pjunətɪv/ *adj* (intended for) punishing: (用以)处罚的; 惩罚性的: *a* **~** *expedition,* a military expedition with the purpose of punishing rebels, etc. 惩罚叛逆者的征伐; 讨逆。

punk /pʌŋk; pʌŋk/ *n* **1** [U] (US) partly decayed wood; rotten wood used as tinder. (美)半朽之木; (做引火物用的)朽木。**2** [U] (colloq) worthless stuff; rubbish: (口)废物; 无意义的话: *He talked a lot of* **~**. 他说了许多废话。**~ rock** *n* [U] (late 1970's) loud, fast, violent style of rock[3] music. (二十世纪七十年代末期之)一种喧嚣热烈的摇滚乐。**3** [C] (sl) worthless person. (俚)无用的人; 不中用的人。**4** [C] (late 1970's) fan[3] (of bizarre appearance) of **~** rock music. (二十世纪七十年代末期)(打扮古怪的)摇滚乐迷。

pun·kah /'pʌŋkə; 'pʌŋkə/ *n* (India) large piece of cloth on a frame, kept moving by means of a cord and pulley, used to keep the air in movement (as an electric fan does). (印度)布风扇(系系于架上的大块布, 由绳索及滑车使之摆动, 以使空气保持流通, 如电扇所为者)。

pun·net /'pʌnɪt; 'pʌnɪt/ *n* small basket, made of very thin wood, plastic, etc esp as a measure for fruit: (用薄木片等所做之)小篮(尤指用以计量水果者): *strawberries, 20p a* **~**. 草莓每篮二十便士。

pun·ster /'pʌnstə(r); 'pʌnstə/ *n* person who has the habit of making puns. 好做双关语者。

punt[1] /pʌnt; pʌnt/ *n* flat-bottomed, shallow boat with square ends, moved by pushing the end of a long pole against the river-bed. 方头平底浅船(以长篙撑之使前进)。□ *vt, vi* [VP6A, 2A] move (a **~**) in this way; carry (sb or sth) in a **~**; go in a **~**. 以长篙撑之使(方头平底浅船)前进; 以此等船载运(人或物); 乘此等船。**punter** *n*

punt[2] /pʌnt; pʌnt/ *vt* [VP6A] kick (a football) after it has dropped from the hands and before it reaches the ground. 踢(从手中扔下而未着地之足球)。□ *n* such a

kick. 踢悬空球。

punt³ /pʌnt; pʌnt/ *vi* [VP2A] (in some card-games) lay a stake against the bank; bet on a horse, etc. (在某些牌戏中)对庄家下赌注; 对一赛马等下赌注。 **~** *n* person who ~s or bets. 下赌注的人。

puny /'pju:nɪ; 'pjunɪ/ *adj* (**-ier, -iest**) small and weak: 小而弱的: *What a ~ little creature!* 一个多么小而弱的人啊! *My ~ efforts are not worth much.* 我这小小的努力算不得什么。 **pun·ily** /'pju:nɪlɪ; 'pjunɪlɪ/ *adv*

pup /pʌp; pʌp/ *n* 1 young dog; young of some other animals, eg the seal. 小狗; 幼犬; 其他动物(如海豹)的幼子. *sell sb a pup,* (colloq) swindle him, esp by selling him sth which, he is made to believe, may have greatly increased value in the future. (口)欺骗某人; (尤指)卖给人某种使他相信价值将会大增的东西。 2 conceited young man. 自负的年轻人。

pupa /'pju:pə; 'pjupə/ *n* (*pl* **~s,** or **~e** /-pi:; -pi/) chrysalis. 蛹。 ⇨ the illus at **butterfly.** 参看 butterfly 之插图。

pu·pil¹ /'pju:pl; 'pjupl/ *n* young person who is learning in school or from a private teacher. 学生(中小学生)。

pu·pil² /'pju:pl; 'pjupl/ *n* (anat) circular opening in the centre of the iris of the eye, regulating the passage of light. (解剖)瞳孔; 瞳人。 ⇨ the illus at **eye.** 参看 eye 之插图。

pup·pet /'pʌpɪt; 'pʌpɪt/ *n* 1 doll, small figure of an animal, etc with jointed limbs moved by wires or strings, used in plays or shows called '~-plays/-shows; marionette; ('glove-~') doll of which the body can be put on the hand like a glove, the arms and head being moved by the fingers of the operator. 木偶戏 ('~-plays 或 '~-shows) 中的木偶; 傀儡; 以手牵动线而使做各种动作之木偶; 牵动木偶; 布袋戏中的木偶; 指动木偶。 2 person, group of persons, whose acts are completely controlled by another: 行动完全受他人控制之人或团体; 傀儡: (attrib) (用作定语) *a ~ government/State.* 一个傀儡政府(国家)。

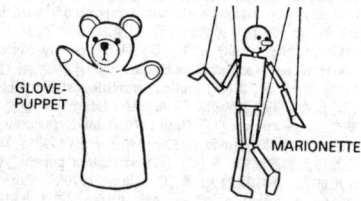

GLOVE-PUPPET

MARIONETTE

puppets

puppy /'pʌpɪ; 'pʌpɪ/ *n* (*pl* **-pies**) 1 young dog. 小狗; 幼犬. '~ *fat n* [U] the kind of fat that boys and girls sometimes have before adolescence. 男女孩子在青春期前所显现的肥胖. '~ *love n* [U] first love affair(s). 初恋。 2 conceited young man. 自负的年轻人。

pur·blind /'pɜ:blaɪnd; 'pɜ,blaɪnd/ *adj* partly or nearly blind; (fig) stupid. 半盲的; 几乎全瞎的; (喻)愚蠢的。

pur·chase¹ /'pɜ:tʃəs; 'pɜtʃəs/ *n* 1 [U] buying: 购买: '~-*money,* price (to be) paid. 买价。 '~ *tax n* (US 美 = *sales tax*) tax on the retail price of goods, collected by the retailer and paid by him to the State (GB since 1973 replaced by value-added tax.) 购物税; 货物税 (由零售商在顾客购物时收缴政府) (英国自一九七三年起由增值税 value-added tax 取代)。 ⇨ **value.** 2 [C] sth bought: 购买之物: *He filled the car with his ~s.* 他把买的东西装满一车。 *I have some ~s to make.* 我要买些东西。 3 (*sing* only) firm hold or grip (for pulling or raising sth, or to prevent sth from slipping): (仅用单数)紧握; 紧抓(以便拉或举某物, 或防止其落下): *get a/any/some ~ on sth.* 紧抓住某物。 4

[U] value or worth, esp as reckoned in annual yield or return: 价值(尤指以每年之收益为准所计算者): *sold at thirty years' ~,* (of land, etc) sold for the equivalent of thirty years' rent. (指土地等)相当于三十年租金的价格卖出. *His life is not worth a day's ~,* He is on the point of death. 他命在旦夕。

pur·chase² /'pɜ:tʃəs; 'pɜtʃəs/ *vt* [VP6A] buy (which is much more usu): 购买 (buy 更为常用): *a dearly ~d victory,* eg a battle in which many lives are lost. 代价甚高(如在战争中伤亡惨重)的胜利。 **pur·chas·able** /-əbl; -əbl/ *adj* that can be ~d. 可购买的。 **~r** *n* buyer. 购买者; 买主。

pur·dah /'pɜ:də; 'pɜdə/ *n* [U] (esp in Muslim communities) curtain for, convention of, keeping women from the sight of strangers, esp men: (尤指穆斯林社会中)使妇女不被男人看见的帘或帏幔; 深闺的习俗: *live/be in ~.* 生活于深闺中。

pure /pjʊə(r); pjʊr/ *adj* (-r, -st except 5, 6 below) (下列第 5, 6 两义无比较级和最高级) 1 unmixed with any other substance, etc: 未同其他物质等混合的; 纯净的: ~ *water/milk/gold;* 纯水(牛奶, 金); ~ *air,* free from smoke, fumes, etc. 纯净的空气。 2 of unmixed race: 血统纯的; 未与他族混血的: ~ *blood;* 纯的血统; a ~ *Negro;* 纯黑人; *a ~bred (= thoroughbred,* which is more usu) *Alsatian dog.* 纯种的亚尔撒森狗(德国牧羊犬) (thoroughbred 较常用)。 3 clean; without evil or sin: 纯洁的; 无恶之罪的: ~ *in body and mind;* 身心纯洁; ~ *thoughts;* 纯洁的思想; *the ~ in heart.* 心地纯洁的人。 4 (of sounds) clear and distinct: (指声音)清亮的: *a ~ note.* 一个清亮的鸣声。 5 dealing with, studied for the sake of, theory only (not *applied*): 纯理论的(非实用的): ~ *mathematics/science.* 理论数学(纯科学)。 6 mere; nothing but: 纯粹的; 完全的: ~ *mischief;* 纯粹的恶作剧; *a ~ waste of time;* 纯粹浪费时间; *spread unkind gossip out of ~ malice.* 纯属恶意地散布刻薄的闲话。 *sth ~ and simple,* it alone: 完全的; 纯粹的; 十足的: *laziness ~ and simple,* sheer laziness. 十足的懒惰。 ~·*ly adv* (esp) entirely; completely; merely: (尤指)全然地; 彻底地; 仅仅地: ~*ly by accident;* 完全出于偶然; *a ~ly formal request.* 一个非常正式的请求。 ~·*ness n = purity* (which is more usu). (purity 较常用)。

pu·rée /'pjʊəreɪ US: pjʊə'reɪ; pjʊ're/ *n* thick liquid made of vegetables, etc boiled to a pulp and pressed through a sieve; fruit similarly treated. (蔬菜等煮成浆状并由筛压榨出的)浓菜汁; 浓果汁。

pur·ga·tion /pɜ:'geɪʃn; pɜ'geʃən/ *n* [U] (formal) purging or purification. (正式用语)涤净; 洗净。

pur·ga·tive /'pɜ:gətɪv; 'pɜgətɪv/ *n, adj* (substance) having the power to purge or cleanse the bowels. (物质)能洗泻或净肠的; 泻药。

pur·ga·tory /'pɜ:gətrɪ US: -tɔ:rɪ; 'pɜgə,torɪ/ *n* (*pl* **-ries**) 1 (esp in RC doctrine) condition after death in which the soul is purified in preparation for heaven; place where souls are so purified. (尤指天主教教义中)死后灵魂需要受涤净以备上天堂的情况; 涤罪; 涤罪所; 炼狱。 2 any place of temporary suffering or expiation. 暂时受苦或赎罪之所。 **pur·ga·torial** /ˌpɜ:gə'tɔ:rɪəl; ˌpɜgə'torɪəl/ *adj* of ~. 涤罪的; 炼狱的。

purge /pɜ:dʒ; pɜdʒ/ *vt* [VP6A, 14, 15A, B] ~ *sb (of/from sth); ~ sth (away) (from sb),* 1 make clean or free (of physical or moral impurity): 使洁净或免于(身体或道德上)的不洁; 清除; 洗涤: *be ~ of/from sin;* 罪被涤除; ~ *away one's sins.* 洗除罪恶。 2 empty (the bowels) of waste matter by means of medicine. 以药物洗净(肠); 泻。 3 clear (oneself, a person of a charge, of suspicion); (legal) atone for (an offence, etc) by submission. 洗雪(自己或某人的罪名, 嫌疑); (法律)借认错或接受刑罚而补偿(一项犯罪等)。 ~ *one's contempt,* (legal) do what is right after showing contempt of court. 于藐视法庭后表示认错或接受改正。 4 rid (a political party, etc) of members who are considered undesirable. 整肃; 排除(政

党等中的）异己份子。□ *n* [C] **1** purging, clearing out or away: 整肃；清除: *the political ~s that followed the overthrow of the government.* 继推翻政府后之政治上的整肃。**2** medicine used for purging(2). 泻药。

pu·ri·fy /'pjʊərɪfaɪ; 'pjʊrə,faɪ/ *vt* (*pt, pp* **-fied**) [VP 6A, 14] **~ sth (of)**, make pure; cleanse: 使纯净；净化: *an air-~ing plant* (eg for providing pure air in a factory). 净化空气的设备（如在工厂中用以使空气清新者）。**pu·ri·fi·ca·tion** /ˌpjʊərɪfɪ'keɪʃn; ˌpjʊrəfə'keʃən/ *n* [U] **~ing**, eg as a religious ceremony. 洗净；涤洗。

pu·rist /'pjʊərɪst; 'pjʊrɪst/ *n* person who pays great attention to correct procedures (eg in the arts). （在艺术等方面）力求纯正之人。

puri·tan /'pjʊərɪtən; 'pjʊrətṇ/ *n* **1 P~**, (16th and 17th cc, in England) member of a division of the Protestant Church which wanted simpler forms of church ceremony. （十六世纪和十七世纪在英国的）清教徒（为基督新教之一派，主张较单纯之宗教仪式）。**2** person who is strict in morals and religion, who looks upon fun and pleasure as sinful, and who believes that all people should work hard always. 道德与宗教观念严格者（视享乐为罪恶，并主张人类应永远辛苦工作）。□ *adj* of or like a P~ or a ~. 清教徒的；似清教徒的；道德及宗教观念严格（之人）的。**~·ism** /-ɪzəm; -ɪzəm/ *n* practices and beliefs of a P~ or a ~. 清教徒之习俗及教义；严格的道德及宗教观念。**puri·tani·cal** /ˌpjʊərɪ'tænɪkl; ˌpjʊrə'tænɪkl/ *adj* very strict and severe, like a P~ in morals and religion. 在道德及宗教方面严格的；严谨的。**puri·tani·cally** /-klɪ; -klɪ/ *adv*

pu·rity /'pjʊərətɪ; 'pjʊrətɪ/ *n* [U] state or quality of being pure. 纯净；纯正；纯粹。

purl¹ /pɜːl; pɝl/ *n* (knitting) inverted stitch, which produces a ribbed appearance (the opp of *plain*). （编织）反针法；倒织（可织出棱纹形状，为plain之反意词）。□ *vt, vi* invert (stitches); invert stitches of (sth being knitted). 反（针）；倒织；以反针织（所织之物）。

purl² /pɜːl; pɝl/ *vi* (poet) (of a small stream) flow with a murmuring sound. （诗）（指小溪）潺潺而流。□ *n* this sound. 潺潺流水声。

pur·lieus /'pɜːljuːz; 'pɝluz/ *n pl* outskirts; outlying parts: 郊区；外缘部分: *the ~ of the camp.* 营地之外缘。

pur·loin /pɜː'lɔɪn; pɝ'lɔɪn/ *vt* [VP6A] (formal) steal. （正式用语）偷窃。

purple /'pɜːpl; 'pɝpl/ *n, adj* (colour) of red and blue mixed together: 紫色；紫色的: *a ~ sunset;* 紫色的落霞; *become ~ with rage.* 气愤脸色发紫。**the ~,** the robes of a Roman emperor or a cardinal. 罗马皇帝或罗马天主教枢机主教所着之紫袍。**a member of a royal family.** 生于王室。**raise sb to the ~,** make him a cardinal. 升某人为枢机主教。**~ 'heart** *n* **(a)** (GB) heart-shaped tablet containing amphetamine, used as a stimulant. （英）一种心形的兴奋剂药片。**(b)** (US 美 **P~ Heart**) medal awarded to a soldier wounded in battle. 紫心章（颁给作战负伤之军人）。**pur·plish** /'pɜːpəlɪʃ; 'pɝplɪʃ/ *adj* somewhat purple. 略带紫色的。

pur·port /'pɜːpət; 'pɝport/ *n* [U] (formal) general meaning or intention of sth said or written; likely explanation of a person's actions: （正式用语）主旨；意义；一个人的行动之可能解释: 所说过的话的含意。□ *vt* /pə'pɔːt; pɝ'port/ **1** [VP6A, 9] seem to mean: 似乎意思是；意谓: *The statement ~s that ....* 这一声明主旨系谓 .... **2** [VP7A] claim: 声称；声言: *The book ~s to be an original work but is really a compilation.* 该书声称是本有独创见解的著作，但实际上是一本编撰的书。

pur·pose /'pɜːpəs; 'pɝpəs/ *n* **1** [C] that which one means to do, get, be, etc; plan; design; intention: 目的；计划；意图；意向: *For what ~ do you want to go to Canada?* 你要去加拿大的目的何在？*I wouldn't go to London for/with the mere ~ of buying a new tie.* 我不

会只为买一条新领带而去伦敦。*This van is used for various ~s.* 这货车可用于不同的目的。*This is a novel with a ~,* one written eg to explain or defend a doctrine, not merely to amuse. 这是一本为阐释或辩护某种理论等而写的小说（并非仅供消遣）。**,~·built** *adj* made to serve a particular function. 为了达成某种目的而设计的。**2** [U] determination; power of forming plans and keeping to them: 决心；形成与坚守计划的力量: *weak of ~;* 没有决心; *wanting in ~.* 缺乏果断力。**3** (phrases)（短语）**on ~,** by intention, not by chance: 故意地；不是偶然地: *You sometimes hurt yourself by accident but you don't hurt yourself on ~.* 有时会偶然伤害自己，但你不会故意伤害自己。*He has left the book here on ~ for you to read.* 他有意把这本书留在这儿让你读。*He came here on ~ to borrow money from you.* 他特地来此向你借钱。*She sometimes does things on ~ just to annoy me.* 她有时故意做些事真气人。**of set ~,** deliberately; not accidentally. 有意地；蓄意地；非偶然地。**to the ~,** useful for one's ~; relevant: 合乎目的；中肯的；切题的: *The reply was so little to the ~ that it was not worth our consideration.* 这答复一点也不中肯，所以不值得我们考虑。**to little/no/some ~,** with little/no/some result or effect. 有很少（毫无，有一些）结果或效果。**serve/answer one's ~,** be satisfactory; do what is required. 令人满意；适合目的。□ *vt* [VP6A, D, 7, 9] (liter) have as one's ~: （文）意欲；意图: *They ~ (making/to make) a further attempt.* 他们意图做进一步的尝试。**~·ful** /-fl; -ful/ *adj* having a conscious ~; full of meaning. 蓄意的；有意义的。**~·fully** /-fəlɪ; -fulɪ/ *adv* **~·less** *adj* lacking ~; having no object in view. 缺乏意义的；没有目的的。**~·less·ly** *adv.* **~·ly** *adv* on ~; intentionally. 故意地；蓄意地。**pur·pos·ive** /'pɜːpəsɪv; 'pɝpəsɪv/ *adj* having, serving, done with, a ~: 有目的的；合于目的的；故意而为的: *purposive movements;* 有目的的行动；(of a person, his conduct) having, showing, ~ and determination. （指人、其行为）有决心的；表现决心的；果断的。

purr /pɜː(r); pɝ/ *vi, vt* **1** [VP2A, C] (of a cat) make a low, continuous vibrating sound expressing pleasure; (of a car engine) make a vibrating sound; (fig, of a person) indicate contentment by using a pleasant tone: （指猫）发出低的连续颤动的呜呜声（表示满意）；（指汽车引擎）发出震颤的声音；（喻，指人）以愉快声调表示满意: *Mrs Black ~ed with delight on receiving the invitation to dine with the duchess.* 布拉克太太接到与公爵夫人共餐的约请时，发出愉快满足的声音。**2** [VP6A] express (contentment, etc) thus: 以愉快声调表示（满足等）: *She ~ed her approval of the suggestion.* 她很高兴地表示赞同此一建议。□ *n* ~ing sound. 满足而低沉的声音。

purse /pɜːs; pɝs/ *n* **1** small bag for money (originally closed by drawing strings together, now usu closed with a clasp): 小钱袋；小钱夹（原来多用拉索合起，现在通常用按扣）: *That big car is beyond my ~,* costs more than I can afford. 那辆大轿车非我财力所能负担得起。**'~-proud** *adj* ⇨ **proud**(5). **hold the '~-strings,** have control of expenditure. 控制钱袋；控制开支。**tighten/loosen the '~-strings,** reduce/increase expenditure; be economical/generous. 紧缩（增加）开支；节省用钱（随便花钱）。**2** money; funds. 金钱；基金。**Privy P~,** ⇨ **privy. the public ~,** the national treasury. 国库。**3** sum of money collected or offered as a prize, gift, etc: 捐赠之款项（作为奖金、赏金等）: *make up a ~;* （为慈善事业）募捐; *give sb a ~,* eg for the winner of a boxing match. 捐赠奖金（如捐给拳击比赛优胜者）。**4** (US) handbag. （美）女用手提包。□ *vi, vt* [VP2A, C, 6A, 15B] **~ (up); ~ (up) the lips,** draw the lips together in tiny folds or wrinkles. 皱起嘴唇；撅嘴。

purser /'pɜːsə(r); 'pɝsɝ/ *n* officer responsible for a ship's accounts and stores, esp in a passenger liner. 船（尤指客轮）上的事务长。

pur·su·ance /pə'sjuːəns US: -'suː-; pɝ'suəns/ *n* in

~ **of,** (formal) in the carrying out of or the performance of (one's duties, a plan, etc). (正式用语)在实施或执行(一个人的职务、计划等)时。 **pur·su·ant** /-ənt; -ənt/ *adj* **pursuant to,** (formal) in accordance with; in agreement with: (正式用语)依照; 遵循: *pursuant to your instructions.* 依随您的指示。

pur·sue /pə'sjuː; pɚ'su/ *vt* [VP6A] **1** go after in order to catch up with, capture or kill: 追赶; 追逐; 追捕; 追杀: *pursuing a robber / a bear;* 追捕盗贼(熊); *make sure that you are not being ~d.* 弄清楚没有人在追捕你。 **2** (fig) (of consequences, penalties, etc) persistently follow: (喻)(指后果、处罚等)永远跟随; 一再伴随: *His record as a criminal ~d him wherever he went.* 不论他到哪里,他的犯罪档案即随之而至。 *He has been ~d by misfortune.* 不幸一直尾随着他(他连遭不幸)。 **3** go on with; work at: 继续做; 做: ~ *one's studies after leaving school.* 离开学校后仍继续研究。 **4** have as an aim or purpose: 以…为目的或目标; 追求: ~ *pleasure.* 追求享乐。 ~**r** *n* person who ~s(1). 追捕者。

pur·suit /pə'sjuːt US: -'suːt; pɚ'sut/ *n* **1** [U] *(in)* ~ *(of),* act of pursuing: 追逐; 追赶; 追求: *a dog in ~ of rabbits;* 一只追逐兔子的狗; *a fox with the hounds in hot ~;* 一只被猎犬穷追的狐狸; *in his ~ of happiness;* 在他追求幸福方面; (attrib) *a ~ plane,* one that pursues and fights enemy planes. 驱逐机。 **2** [C] sth at which one works or to which one gives one's time: 职业; 工作; 消遣: *engaged in scientific/literary ~s.* 从事科学(文学)的研究。

pursy¹ /'pɜːsɪ; 'pɝsɪ/ *adj* (old use) (of a person) fat and short-winded. (旧用法)(指人)肥胖而喘息的。

pursy² /'pɜːsɪ; 'pɝsɪ/ *adj* (old use) puckered: (旧用法)皱起的; 有皱纹的: ~ *eyes.* 皱起的眼睛。 ⇨ **purse,** v.

puru·lent /'pjʊərələnt; 'pjʊrələnt/ *adj* of, containing, discharging, pus. 脓的; 含有脓的; 流脓的。 **puru·lence** /-əns; -əns/ *n*

pur·vey /pə'veɪ; pɚ'veɪ/ *vt, vi* **1** [VP6A, 14] ~ *(to),* (formal) provide, supply (food, as a trader): (正式用语)(商人等)供给; 供应(食物): *A butcher ~s meat to his customers.* 肉商供应顾客肉类。 **2** [VP3A] ~ *for,* supply provisions for: 为…供应食物等: *a firm that ~s for the Navy.* 一负责供应海军粮食的公司。 ~**or** /-ə(r); -ɚ/ *n* person whose business is to supply provisions on a large scale, eg for the Army or Navy, for large public dinners. 大量供应粮食者; 承办公众伙食者。 ~**ance** /-əns; -əns/ *n*

pur·view /'pɜːvjuː; 'pɝvju/ *n* (formal) range of operation or activity; scope; extent: (正式用语)工作或活动的范围; 视界; 范围: *These are questions that lie outside / that do not come within the ~ of our inquiry.* 这些问题是在我们的调查范围之外的。

pus /pʌs; pʌs/ *n* [U] thick yellowish-white liquid formed in and coming out from a poisoned place in the body: 脓(在身体受感染的部位形成后流出之黄白色浓液): *It is unwise to squeeze a boil to force the pus out.* 硬把疖子的脓挤出是不智之举。

push¹ /pʊʃ; pʊʃ/ *n* **1** [C] act of pushing: 推; 推动: *Give the door a hard ~.* He opened the gate *with / at one ~.* 他一下子就把门推开了。 **2** [U] vigorous effort: 奋力: *We must make a ~ to finish the job this week.* 我们必须奋力把这件事本周内做完。 *The enemy made a ~ (= an attack in force) to capture the city.* 敌人对该城发动猛攻。 **3** *get the ~,* (sl) be dismissed (from one's employment, etc). (俚)被解雇。 *give sb the ~,* (sl) dismiss him. (俚)解雇某人。 **4** [U] determination to make one's way in life, to attract attention, etc: 努力上进, 吸引注意等之决心; 毅力: *He hasn't enough ~ to succeed as a salesman.* 他没有做成功的推销员所需要的毅力。 **5** *at a ~,* if compelled by need or circumstances: 若为需要或环境之所迫: 不得已时: *We can sleep seven or eight people in the house at a ~.* 不得已的时候,我们能让七个或八个人住在此屋内。 *if / when / until it comes to the ~,* if / when / until one is compelled by need or circumstances, when an effort is needed: 假如(在, 直到)情势紧急为需要或环境所迫而不能不奋力时; 在(直到)情势紧急之际: *He seemed a satisfactory man until it came to the ~; then he failed us.* 在陷入紧急情势之前, 他似乎一直是个令人满意的人; 到情势紧急时他却令我们甚为失望。

push² /pʊʃ; pʊʃ/ *vt, vi* (For special uses with *adverbial particles* and *preps,* ⇨ 9 below.) (与副词性小品词及介词连用的特殊用法参看下列第9义。) **1** [VP6A, 15A, B, 22, 2A, C] (contrasted with *pull*) use force on (sth / sb) to cause forward movement; exert pressure against: (与 pull 相对)推(某人或某物); 推(某人或某物)使之移动; 挤: *Please ~ the table nearer to the wall.* 请把这桌子推得靠墙一点。 *If you'll ~ the car, I'll steer it.* 如果你来推车, 我就来驾车。 *You can pull a rope, but you can't ~ it!* 你可以拉绳子, 但不能推绳子! *We had to ~ our way (= go forward by ~ing) through the crowd.* 我们必须从人群中挤过去。 *Stop ~ing at the back!* 别在后面推! *He ~ed the door open.* 他把门推开。 *The football crowds ~ed past me.* 看足球的观众从我旁边挤过去。 **2** [VP6A] persuade others to recognize, eg claims, or buy, eg goods: 劝使他人承认(某要求等)或购买(商品等): *Unless you ~ your claims you'll get no satisfaction.* 如果你不努力争取, 你就得不到赔偿。 *You must ~ your wares if you want better sales.* 如果你想要销路好, 你必须大力推销你的商品。 *Haven't you a friend who can ~ you,* use his influence to help you? 你难道没有一个能够提拔你的朋友吗? ~ *oneself,* show energy, etc to win recognition: 驱策自己; 发愤: *You'll never get anywhere if you don't ~ yourself.* 你如果不策励自己, 将永远没有成就。 ⇨ also ~ *oneself forward* in 9 below. 参看下列第9义之 *oneself forward.* **3** [VP6A] sell (illicit drugs) by acting as a link between large suppliers and the drug addicts. (做中间人)贩卖(毒品)。 ⇨ **pusher below.** 参看下列之 **pusher.** **4** [VP14] ~ *sb for sth,* press sb to (get sth): 催迫某人(以获得某物): *We're ~ing them for payment / an answer to our request.* 我们正催促他们付款(答复我们的请求)。 *be ~ed for sth,* have difficulty in finding: 困于…; 为…所迫; 短少: *I'm rather ~ed for money / time just now.* 我目前颇拮据(时间迫促)。 **5** [VP14, 17] ~ *sb / oneself to sth / to do sth,* drive or urge: 驱策某人(自己)做某事: *Tony had to ~ himself to go on doing such dull work.* 托尼不得不驱策自己继续做这种单调无趣的事。 *She'll ~ him to the verge of suicide.* 她将会把他逼到自杀的地步。 **6** [VP6A] press: 按: ~ *a button,* eg to ring a bell; 按电钮(如按电铃); ~*button warfare,* war in which missiles, eg with atomic warheads, are fired by pressing buttons. 按电钮战争(按电钮即可发射带导弹头等的导弹之战争)。 **7** *be ~ing thirty / forty, etc,* (colloq) be nearing the age indicated: (口)接近三十岁(四十岁等)。 *She wouldn't like you to think so, but she's ~ing thirty.* 她不愿让你知道, 其实她已快三十岁了。 **8** (compounds) (复合词) '~*bike n* one that is worked by pedalling (not a *moped* or *motor-bike*). 自行车(以脚踏动而非用发动机者)。 '~*cart n* small cart ~ed by a man. 手推车。 '~*chair n* carriage for a child, like a chair on wheels (used when a child is old enough to sit up). 婴儿推车(在婴儿会坐时使用)。 ~*er n* **1** (colloq) person who ~s himself / herself forward: (口)进取的人; 钻营的人; *Isn't she a ~er!* (said of someone who takes every opportunity of gaining an advantage for herself). 她真是个善于钻营的人! **2** (sl) pedlar of illicit drugs. (俚)贩毒者。 ⇨ **3** above. 参看上列第3义。 ~*ful /-fl; -fl/, ~*ing *adj* having a tendency to ~ oneself: 有进取心的; 爱出风头的: *He's too ~ing with strangers,* tries too much to force himself upon their attention. 他太爱在陌生人面前出风头。 **9** [VP15A, B, 2C] (special uses with *adverbial particles* and *preps*): (与副词性小品词及介词连用的特殊用法): **push along,** (colloq) leave sb / a place: (口)离开某人

(某地): *I'm afraid it's time I was ~ing along*, time for me to go. 恐怕是我该走的时候了。
push sb around, (colloq) bully him; order him about: (口)威胁某人; 驱使某人; 摆布某人: *I'm not going to be ~ed around by you or anybody!* 我将不受你或任何人摆布!

push forward/on (to a place), go on resolutely with a journey, one's work, etc: 坚决地继续旅行,工作等: *It's getting dark; we must ~ on to our destination.* 天渐渐黑了,我们必须赶到目的地。*We must ~ on with our work*, hurry and finish it. 我们必须赶快做完我们的工作。*~ oneself forward*, ambitiously draw attention to oneself, eg at work, in society: 极力表现自己(如在工作上或社交上); 强出风头: *He never ~es himself forward*, is modest, doesn't try to attract attention. 他从不强出风头(他是一个谦逊的人)。

push off, (colloq) leave; go away: (口)离去; 走开: *Tell that rude fellow to ~ off!* 叫那个无礼的家伙走开! *It's time we ~ed off.* 是我们离去的时候了。*~ (a boat, etc) off*, (of sb in a boat) ~ against the bank, etc, eg with an oar or pole, to get the boat moving in the current, etc. (指船中的人)以浆或篙顶岸等使(船)进入水流中等。

push (a boat, etc) out, ~ ⇨ **off**.

push sb/sth over, cause to fall; overturn: 推倒; 使倾覆: *Don't ~ me over!* 不要把我推倒。*Several children were ~ed over in the stampede.* 有几个小孩在惊慌逃奔中绊倒了。'*~-over* n (sl) sth very easy to do; person who is easily overcome or controlled. (俚)容易做的事; 易于征服或控制的人。

push sb through (sth), enable sb (esp sb needing help) to succeed in sth: 促使某人(尤指需要帮助者)成功: *~ a weak student through an exam*. 帮助一个成绩差的学生通过考试。*~ sth through*, bring sth to the final stage by special efforts: 努力完成某事: *~ legislation through*, get it passed. 使之通过。*We must ~ the matter through.* 我们必须把这件事办妥。

push sth up, force, eg prices, to rise. 强使(物价等)上升。*~ up the daisies*, (sl) be buried in a grave. (俚)被埋葬。

pu·sil·lan·i·mous /ˌpjuːsɪ'lænɪməs, ˌpjuslˈænəməs/ adj (formal) timid; easily frightened. (正式用语)胆怯的; 易受惊的。**pu·sil·la·nim·ity** /ˌpjuːsɪlə'nɪmətɪ, ˌpjusləˈnɪmətɪ/ n [U].

puss /pus/ n 1 cat; word used to call a cat. 猫; 用以唤猫的词。2 (colloq) girl: (口)女孩: *She's a sly ~.* 她是个狡猾的女孩。*~y* /'pusɪ, 'pusɪ/ n (pl *-sies*) (also 亦作 '*~y-cat*) (child's word for a) cat. (小儿语)猫。'*~y-foot* vi [VP2A, C] (colloq) move about in a quiet, stealthy way (as a cat does): (口)轻轻地, 偷偷地(如猫所为者): *Why ~y-footing about in the corridor last night?* 昨晚是你蹑手蹑脚地在走廊上走动吗? (fig) act too cautiously or timidly. (喻)过于谨慎或胆小地行事。'*~y willow* n tree with soft silky catkins. 一种生有绒球花的柳树。

pus·tule /'pʌstjuːl US: -tʃuːl; 'pʌstʃul/ n (med) pimple or blister, esp one filled with pus. (医)小脓疱。

put[1] /put/ vt, vt (pt, pp **put**, pres part **-tt-**) (For special uses with *adverbial particles* and *preps*, ⇨ 11 below.) (与副词性小品词及介词连用的特殊用法,参看下列第11义。) 1 [VP6A, 15A] move (sth) so as to be in a certain place or position: 置放于某处; 使处于某种位置: *He put the book on the table.* 他把书放在桌子上。*He put his hands (in) to his pockets.* 他把手放在口袋中。*He put the corpse down the well.* 他把尸体抛进井中。*Did you put milk in my tea?* 你在我的茶中加了牛奶吗? *It's time to put the baby to bed.* 是让婴儿睡觉的时候了。*Will you please put (= sew) a patch on these trousers?* 请为这条裤子补缀一块布好吗? *He put (= fastened) a new handle to the knife.* 他给刀子装上新柄。*He put (= pushed) a knife into me/between my ribs.* 他把刀刺进我的身体(刺进我的肋骨间)。*I'll put a bullet through your head*, kill you. 我将以子弹射穿你的脑袋。*They've put a satellite into orbit round Mars.* 他们已将一人造卫星射进围绕火星的轨道。*They've put men on the moon.* 他们已把人类送上月球。*He put (= pushed) his fist through the window*, broke it by doing this. 他用拳头击破窗子。*He put his pen through the word*, struck the word out. 他用钢笔删掉那个词。*put pen to paper*, start writing. 开始写。*put one's foot in it*, ⇨ **foot**[1](1). 2 [VP15A] cause (sb/oneself) to be in some relationship, eg as an employee, client, with sb. 使(某人, 自己)与某人有某种关系(如成为雇员, 雇客等): *put oneself sth in/into sb's hands*, let him deal with one's problems, etc: 把自己(某事)交给某人处理; 托付: *I put myself entirely in your hands.* 我把自己完全托付给你。*I shall put the matter into the hands of my solicitors.* 我将把此事交给几位律师去处理。*put sb in his (proper) place*, make him humble. 使某人谦卑。*put oneself in sb's/sb 'else's position*, imagine oneself in his position: 设身处地; 站在他人的立场设想: *How would you feel (about the matter)?—Just put yourself in my/her position!* 你(对这事)作何感想?——只要站在我(她)的立场设想就行了! 3 [VP14] make sb bear (the particular nervous or moral strain indicated). 使某人承受(精神或道德的压力)。*put the blame on sb*, blame him: 归咎于某人: *Don't put all the blame on me.* 不要完全归咎于我。*put pressure on sb (to do sth)*, strongly urge him: 对某人施压力迫使: *They're putting great pressure on him (= pressing him hard) to resign.* 他们对他大施压力迫他辞职。*put (a) strain on sb/sth*, make him/it suffer from hard work or use: 使某人(某物)不胜负担: *All this work is putting (a) great strain on him.* 所有这些工作使他不胜负担。4 [VP15A] affect the progress of. 影响…的进展。*put an end/a stop to sth*, end or abolish it. 结束或废除某事物。*put an end to one's life*, commit suicide. 自杀。*put the brake(s) on sth*, (fig, colloq) slow it down. (喻, 口)使缓慢。5 [VP15A] cause to pass into or suffer the emotional, physical etc state indicated by the phrase that follows. 使成为…状态; 使遭受感情或身体上的某种情况。*put oneself to death*, commit suicide. 自杀。*put sb to death*, kill him. 杀死或处死某人。*put sb at his ease*, cause him to feel relaxed, free from anxiety, etc. 使某人感到自在, 不紧张; 使放心。*put sb to (great) expense*, cause him to spend (a lot). 使某人花(很多)钱。*put sb to (great) inconvenience*, cause him (great) inconvenience. 使某人感到(极为)不便。*put sb to the indignity of doing sth*, cause him to do sth involving loss of dignity. 使某人忍辱做某事。*put sb in mind of sb/sth*, recall or remind him of sb/sth. 使某人想起(某人或某事物)。*put sb/sth out of his/its misery*, relieve him/it of anxiety, pain, etc; kill (an animal in pain). 解除某人(某动物)的焦虑, 痛苦等; 使解脱; 杀死(痛苦的动物等)。*put sb on (his) oath*, make sb swear on oath; bind him to tell the truth. 使某人立誓或说实话。*put sb/sth to the test*, test him/it. 考验某人(某事物)。*put sb in the wrong*, cause him to appear to be wrong. 嫁祸于某人; 归咎于某人。6 [VP22] cause sb/sth to become (what is indicated by the *adj*): 使某人(某事物)成…样子(根据下面所接形容词所表示的状态): *That picture on the wall is crooked—I must put it straight.* 墙上那幅画挂歪了——我必须把它摆正。*put sth right*, correct it: 纠正某事: *A short note put the matter right*, ended any misunderstanding. 一封短函把这件事解释清楚了。*put sb right/straight*, correct an error he has made; give him correct information: 改正某人的错误; 告诉某人正确的消息: *We had taken a wrong turning, but a policeman put us right*, told us which way to go. 我们转错了弯, 但一位警察指示了我们正确的方向。7 [VP15A] write; indicate; mark: 写; 指出; 标明: *put a tick against a name/a price on an article/one's signature to a will.* 在名字旁边勾一下(在一件物品上标明价格; 在

遭嘱上签字)。**8** [VP14] *put sth to sb; put it to sb (that),* submit; propound; express: 呈交; 提出; 表示: *put a proposal to the Board of Directors;* 向董事会提出一建议; *put a question to the vote / a resolution to the meeting.* 将问题付诸表决 (将议案提交会议讨论)。*I put it to you that ...,* invite you to agree with me that .... 我请你同意…。*You have put the case very clearly.* 你把事情解释得很清楚。*Put it* (= submit the matter) *to her so as not to offend her.* 把这事情交给她以免使她不快。*How can I put it,* express it? 我该怎样说才好呢? *How would you put* (= express, translate) *this in Danish?* 这个意思在丹麦语里怎么说? *That can all be put in a few words.* 那件事可以用简单几句话说明白。*Please put all questions to the chairman.* 请向主席提出所有的问题。*put the question,* ⇨ **question**[1](2). **9** [VP14] *put a price / value / valuation on sth,* state or estimate the value: 估出某物的价格(价值, 评价): *The experts refused to put a price on the Rubens painting.* 专家们拒绝估计鲁本斯的画的价值。*What value do you put on her advice?* 你对她的建议做何评价? *put sth at (a figure),* say that, eg sb's age, sth's value, weight, is: 估计作(后接数目字, 如表示年龄, 价值, 重量): *I would put her age at about sixty.* 我猜测她的年龄大约是六十岁。*I put her fur coat at £200.* 我估计她的皮外衣值二百英镑。**10** [VP6A] throw with an upward and outward movement of the arm.: 以胳臂向上并向前抛掷。*put the shot,* ⇨ **shot**[1](3). Hence, 由此产生, '**shot-put** *n* this as an event at an athletic meeting. 推铅球(为运动会的项目之一)。**11**[VP15B, 2C, 14] (special uses with *adverbial particles* and *preps*): (与副词性小品词及介词连用的特殊用法):

put (a ship) about, (cause to) change direction: (使)(船)改变方向: *The captain put the ship about.* 船长改变了船的航行方向。*put oneself about,* (chiefly Scots) trouble, distress, oneself: (主要用于苏格兰)自烦恼, 痛苦: *He was very much put about by these false allegations.* 他甚为这些伪辞所苦恼。*put sth about,* spread, eg rumours: 散布(如谣言): *Don't believe all these stories that are being put about.* 不要相信所有这些谣传。

put sth across (to sb), (a) communicate sth successfully: 使(某人)了解或接受某事物; 沟通: *a teacher who quickly puts his ideas across to his students.* 很快和学生沟通观念的教师。(b) (colloq) make a success of: (口)使获得成功: *Put a business deal across* (more usu *through*). 使一桩交易成功 (through 比 across 常用)。*put sth across sb,* (colloq) deceive; trick: (口)欺骗; 欺诈: *You can't put that across me,* make me believe or accept it. 你不能骗我接受(相信)那件事。

put sth aside, (a) lay down: 放下: *put aside one's book;* 把书放下; *put one's work aside.* 把工作搁下。(b) save: 储蓄: *He has put aside a good sum of money.* 他已经储蓄了很多钱。(c) disregard; ignore: 不顾; 忽视: *Put aside for a moment the fact that the man has been in prison.* 暂时先别管那人曾坐牢的事。

put sth away, (a) put in the usual place of storage, eg a drawer, box: 将某物放置于惯常保存之处(如抽屉, 盒子): *Put your books / toys away.* 把你的书(玩具)收起。(b) save: 储存; 储蓄: *put money away for one's old age.* 为防老而储蓄。(c) (colloq) eat or drink (to excess): (口)(过度地)吃或喝: *How can that boy put away so much pie and ice-cream?* 那个男孩如何能吃那么多馅饼和冰淇淋呢? (d) give up; renounce: 放弃; 弃绝: *He's had to put away all ideas of becoming a concert pianist.* 他只好放弃做钢琴演奏家的一切念头。*put sth away,* (a) (colloq) put into confinement, eg in a mental home: (口)囚禁; 监禁(如囚于精神病院): *He was acting so strangely that he had to be put away.* 他的行为十分怪异, 所以不得不被禁锢起来。(b) (colloq, of pets) put to death (because of age, illness): (口, 指宠爱的动物)(因年老或疾病而被)弄死: *The dog was so old and weak that it had to be put away.* 这只狗既老且病, 所以不得不把它弄死。

put back, (naut) return: (航海)归来: *The ship / We put*

back to harbour. 该船(我们)回到港内。*put sth back,* (a) replace: 放回原处: *Put the reference books back on the shelf when you've finished with them.* 参考书看完后放回原来的书架。(b) move backwards: 向后移; 拨回: *That clock is fast; I'd better put it back five minutes,* move the minute hand back. 那钟太快了, 我最好拨回五分钟。(c) (fig) check the advance of, cause delay to: (喻)阻碍; 阻止; 使延滞: *put back the efforts of the reformers.* 阻碍改革家们的努力。*The strike at the car factory put back production badly.* 汽车制造厂的罢工大大妨碍了生产。

put sth by, save for future use: 为将来而储蓄: *Has any money put by?* 她有没有存钱?

put (sth) down, (a) land: (使)着陆: *He put down (his glider) in a field.* 他在原野中降落(他的滑翔机)。(b) set or place down: 放下: *Put down that gun!* 把枪放下! (c) press down: 按下; 压下; 踩下: *When you get on the motorway, you can really put your foot down,* press the accelerator pedal down. 当你到了高速公路上时, 就可真正地踩下油门。*put one's foot down,* ⇨ **foot**[1](1). (d) place in storage: 储藏: *put down eggs,* eg by packing in isinglass. 把蛋储藏起来(如放于鱼胶中)。*He has put down a good supply of port and claret.* 他已经储藏了很多紫葡萄酒和红葡萄酒。(e) suppress by force or authority: 镇压; 平定; 消除; 扑灭: *put down a rebellion;* 敉平叛乱; *put down gambling and prostitution.* 消除赌博与娼妓。(f) write down; make a note of: 写下; 记下: *Here's my address——put it down before you forget it.* 这是我的地址——写下来, 免得忘了。*put sb down,* (a) allow to alight: 让(某人)下车: *The bus stopped to put down passengers.* 公共汽车停下来让乘客下车。(b) snub; reduce to silence: 轻待; 奚落; 制止; 使沉默: *put down hecklers at a political meeting.* 制止政治会议上诘难的人。Hence, 由此产生, '**put-down** *n* snub. 轻待; 奚落。(c) make humble: 使卑微; 贬抑; 挫: (biblical) (圣经) *put down the mighty from their seats.* 降低强者的地位; 使强者谦恭。*put sb down as,* consider that sb is: 认为某人是: *They put me down as a fool.* 他们认为我是个傻瓜。*put sb down for,* write his name on a list as willing to give, eg to a charity or other fund: 登记名字认捐: *You can put me down for £5;* 你可以写上我认捐五镑; *put sb's name down as an applicant, participant, etc:* 登记姓名(如成为申请者, 参与者等): *They put him down for Eton / the school football team.* 他们为他登记进入伊顿公学(参加学校足球队)。*put sth down to sb,* (a) charge to an account: 记在…帐上: *Put the shoes down to my account.* 把这双鞋子记在我的帐上。*You can put the cost of the petrol down to business expenses.* 你买汽油的费用记在业务费用的帐上。(b) attribute to: 归于; 诿于: *The cholera outbreak was put down to bad drinking water.* 那次霍乱的发生归因于不洁的饮水。*Can we put it down to his ignorance?* 我们能把此事归因于他的无知吗?

put sth forth, (formal) send out: (正式用语)发出; 长出: *The trees are putting forth new leaves.* 这些树正在长出新叶子。

put sth forward, (a) advance; put before people for consideration: 提出; 建议: *put forward a new theory.* 提出一新理论。(b) move on: 拨快: *put forward the hands of a clock,* eg when it is stopped or slow. (如时钟停或慢时)拨快钟针。*put sb forward,* propose: 推荐: *put oneself / a friend forward as a candidate.* 推荐自己(一位朋友)为候选人。*put in,* exclaim (often as an interruption): 喊出(常作为打岔); 插嘴: '*But what about us?*' *he put in.*'可是我们怎么办?'他喊道。*put in / into,* (naut) (of a boat, its crew) enter: (航海)(指船或水手)进入; 驶进入港: *The boat put in at Malta / put into Malta for repairs.* 该船驶到马尔他修理。*put in for sth,* apply formally for: 正式申请: *put in for the position of manager.* 申请经理之职位。*put in for leave,* request permission to be absent from duty, work, etc. 请假。*put sth in,* (a) cause to be in: 使在内: *He put his head in at the window.* 他从窗口把头伸进来。(b) submit; present formally: 提

出;正式提呈:*put in a claim for damages*; 提出赔偿损失之要求;*put in a document* (in a law case); (在法律案件中)提出证明文件;*put in a plea of not guilty*. 提出无罪之抗辩。 **(c)** manage to strike or utter: 击出或说出:*put in a blow/word*. 加以打击(说出一句话)。 **put sth in/into sth**, devote; give: 献身于;付出;花费:*put a lot of work into improving one's French*. 下很大的工夫进修法语。*put sb in for sth*, recommend sb for promotion, an award, etc: 推荐某人晋升、得奖等: *The commanding officer is putting Sergeant Green in for the Victoria Cross*. 指挥官推荐格林士官得维多利亚十字勋章。 **put in a good word for sb**, say sth on his behalf, to help him. 为某人说好话。 **(d)** spend, do; perform: 做;履行:*put in an hour's work before breakfast*; 早餐之前做一小时的工作; *put in an hour's piano practice*. 练习弹钢琴一小时。 **(e)** pass(time): 消磨;度过(时间): *There's still an hour to put in before the pubs open*. 酒馆再过一小时才开门。 **put sb in, (a)** give duties to: 任命;使就任:*put in a caretaker/bailiff*. 任用一管理员(一监守官)。 **(b)** elect to office: 选为执事;选为执政: *Which party will be put in at the next general election?* 下一次大选中那一党会当选执政?*put sb in mind of sb/sth*, ⇨ **5** above. 参看上列第 5 义。 **put** n entries for 参看下列各短语中之名词 *put in an appearance*; *put the boot in*; *put one's oar in*; *put a sock in it*. *put off*, (of a boat or crew) leave: (指船或船员)离岸: *We put off from the pier*. 我们驶离码头。 **put sth off, (a)** postpone: 延期:*put off a meeting*; 把会议延期; *put off going to the dentist*. 延期去看牙医。 **(b)** (usu of nonmaterial things, *take off* being usual for clothes) get rid of: (通常指非物质的东西;脱衣服通常多用 *take off*) 消除;祛除:*You must put off your doubts and fears*. 你必须消除疑惧。 **put sb off, (a)** put to a later date an arrangement, etc: 把约会等延后: *We shall have to put the Smiths off till next week*. 我们须把同史密斯夫妇之约会延到下星期。 **(b)** make excuses and try to avoid, eg sth one has promised to do, a duty: 闪避;敷衍;推诿(已答应做的事,责任): *He tried to put me off with vague promises*. 他企图以含混的允诺来敷衍我。 *I won't be put off with such flimsy excuses*, won't accept them. 我不会被这些薄弱的借口敷衍过去的。 **put sb off (sth)**, hinder or distract him (from sth): 妨碍或劝阻:*put sb off his game*, eg distract him when he is about to strike the ball at golf. 妨碍一个人比赛(如在他将出球时分散他的注意力)。 *The mere smell of garlic put him off his supper*, caused him not to want supper. 他一闻到蒜味就对晚餐倒了胃口。 **put sb off his stroke**, distract him; cause him to pause. 使某人分心;使某人停止。 **put sth on, (a)** (contrasted with *take off*) clothe oneself with: (与 *take off* 相对)穿; 戴:*put one's hat/shoes, etc on*. 戴上帽子(穿上鞋子等)。 **(b)** assume; pretend to have: 假装;伪称有:*put on an air of innocence*. 装出一派天真纯朴的样子。 *Her modesty is all put on*, she's only pretending to be modest, eg about her ability or skill. 她的谦逊只是装出来的。 **(c)** increase; add: 增加;添上: *put on more steam/pressure*; 添加更多蒸气(压力); *put on speed*. 增加速度。 *He's putting on weight/flesh*, is getting heavier/fatter. 他的体重在增加(他愈来愈胖)。 *Marks and Sparks put on sixty runs*, (cricket) together added sixty to the score. (板球戏)马克斯和斯帕克斯合起来多得了 60 分。 **(d)** add to: 增添;增加:*This policy will put pounds on the cost of living*, will make it much higher. 这项措施将使生活费用增高。 **(e)** arrange for; make available: 安排;准备;使可利用: *put on extra trains during the rush hours*; 在乘客拥挤时加开火车; *put a play on*, arrange for to be shown at a theatre. 安排一戏剧的演出。 **(f)** advance: 拨快:*put the clock on one hour*, move the hands forward, eg for Summer Time. 把钟拨快一小时(如夏令时间)。 **put sb on**, (colloq) deceive him: (口)欺骗:*He's not really interested; he's putting you on*. 他不是真有兴趣;他只是在欺骗你。 Hence, 由此产生, **'put-on** n deception: 欺骗: *What a put-on!* 好一个骗局! **put it on**, (colloq) (口) **(a)** exaggerate a

show of feeling; pretend to be more important, etc than is justified or warranted; talk or behave in a pretentious way. 夸张感情的表现; 装得过分重要; 装模作样地讲话或行动。 **(b)** overcharge: 索价过高: *Some of the hotels put it on during the holiday season*. 在度假季节有些旅馆提高收费。 **put sb on (to bowl)**, (cricket) arrange for him to bowl at least one over. (板球戏)安排某人至少投球一次。 **put money on sb/sth**, stake (horse-racing, etc): 赌(赛马等): *I've put a pound on the favourite*. 我在有获胜希望的马身上赌一镑。

put over (from), (naut) (of a boat or crew) move out, leave, eg from harbour. (航海)(指船或船员)(从港口)驶出。 **put sth out, (a)** extinguish; cause to stop burning: 扑灭;熄灭;使停止燃烧:*put out the candle/the gas/the gas-fire*. 熄灭灯(烛,煤气,煤气炉)。 *The fireman soon put the fire out*. 消防队员不久即扑灭那场火。 **(b)** cause to be out of joint; dislocate: 使脱开节; 使脱臼: *She fell off a horse and put her shoulder out*. 她从马上跌下,肩膀脱臼了。 **(c)** give (sth) to be done off the premises: 把(某事物)送到外面去做: *All repairs are done on the premises and not by us*. 全部修缮都在家里进行,不送到外面去做。 *We put out the washing*, send it to a laundry instead of having it done at home. 我们把要洗的衣服送到洗衣店去洗。 **(d)** lend (money) at interest: 放利息;放帐: *He has £1000 put out at 5 per cent*. 他以百分之五的利息放款一千英镑。 **(e)** produce: 生产: *The firm puts out 1 000 bales of cotton sheeting every week*. 这家公司每周出产一千包棉质被单布。 ⇨ **output**. **(f)** issue; broadcast: 发布; 广播: *The Health Department has put out a warning about dangerous drugs*. 卫生部就危险药品发布警告。 **put one's 'hand out**, hold it out in welcome, for caning as a punishment, etc 伸出手(以示欢迎,罚打手心等)。 **put one's 'tongue out**, show it, eg for a doctor, or at sb. as a rude act. (向医生,或不雅地向某人)伸出舌头。 **put sb out, (a)** disconcert: cause to be confused or worried: 使困惑不安;使迷惑或忧烦:*The least thing puts him out, he is easily upset*. 一点儿小事就会使他不安。 *She was very much put out by your rudeness*. 你的鲁莽使她感受窘。 **(b)** inconvenience: 使感不便: *Would it put you out to lend me £5 until Friday?* 借给我五镑,(下)星期五归还,对你有什么不方便吗? *He was very much put out by the late arrival of his guests*. 他的客人们姗姗来迟使他大感不便。 **put sb out (of)**, expel; drive out. 驱逐;赶出。

put over, (naut) (of a boat or crew) move over: (航海)(指船或船员)驶过:*put over to the other side of the harbour*. 驶向港的对面。 **put sth over to sb**, (colloq) = put sth across to sb.

put sth through, carry it out: 实行;完成:*put through a business deal*. 完成一桩交易。 **put sb/sth through**, connect (by telephone): 接通(电话): *Please put me/this call through to the Manager*. 请替我接经理。 **put sb through sth**, cause him to undergo, eg an ordeal, a test: 使受(考验,试验): *The police put him through a severe examination*. 警方对他严加询问。 *The trainees were put through an assault course*. 受训人员接受突击训练课程。 *put a person through his paces*, ⇨ **pace** n (3). **put sb 'through it**, (colloq) test or examine him thoroughly, eg by givng him a medical examination, or by inflicting suffering on him to get a confession. (口)彻底地检查或审讯某人。

put sth to sb, ⇨ **8** above. 参看上列第 8 义。 **be hard 'put to it to do sth**, find difficulty in doing sth: 非常为难:*I'd be hard put to it to say exactly why I disliked him*. 我很难启齿说明我到底为什么不喜欢他。 *He was hard put to it to satisfy his creditors*. 他为偿清对债主之欠款感到为难。 **put sth together**, construct (a whole) by combining parts: 结合各部分而构成(一整体); 装配: *It's easier to take a machine to pieces than to put it together again*. 拆卸一台机器比重新装起来容易。 *I must put my thoughts/ideas together before I go on the*

platform, collect my ideas, etc before I give my ad-dress, speech, etc. 在踏上讲台讲演之前，我必须把我的思绪整理一下。*put our/your/their 'heads together*, consult one another. 彼此商量；共同商讨。*put two and two together*, ⇨ **two**.

put up (at), obtain lodging and food. 获得食宿：*put up (at an inn) for the night*. (在客栈)过夜。*put up (for sth)*, offer oneself for election: 竞选：*Are you going to put up for Finchley again*, ie as a prospective member of Parliament? 你还要竞选代表芬契利市的国会议员吗? *put sth up*, **(a)** raise; hold up: 举起；抬起：*put up one's hands*; eg over one's head, as a sign that one is ready to surrender, or with fists clenched, ready to fight; 举起手(如举过头以示投降，或握紧拳头准备打架)；*put up a flag/a sail*. 升旗(张帆)。*put one's 'hair up*, (of long hair) wear it coiled on the head instead of letting it fall over the neck and shoulders. 把头发挽于头上。**(b)** build, erect: 建立；竖立：*put up a shed/a tent*. 搭起一小棚(一帐篷)。**(c)** publish (banns); place so as to be seen: 公布(结婚预告)；公告：*put up a notice*. 公布一通知。**(d)** raise, increase: 提高；增加：*put up the rent by 50p (a week)*. 将房租(每周)提高五十便士。**(e)** pack (in parcels, boxes, etc): 包装(于小包，盒等)：*herrings put up in barrels*. 装于桶中的鲱鱼。*The hotel will put us up some sandwiches*, prepare and pack some for us. 旅馆将为我们准备一些三明治并且包好。**(f)** offer, make: 给予；施以：*put up a stout resistance/a good fight*. 予以顽强的抵抗(挺身奋战)。**(g)** supply (a sum of money for an undertaking): 提供(一笔钱做一事业)：*I will supply the skill and knowledge if you will put up the £ 2000 capital*. 如果你提供两千英镑的资本，我愿贡献技术与知识。**(h)** (old use) sheathe (a sword). (旧用法)插(刀)入鞘。**(i)** cause (wild birds or animals) to leave shelter or cover: 使(野禽野兽)离巢穴：*put up a partridge*. 把一只鹧鸪赶出巢。*put sb's back up*, ⇨ **back**[1](1). *put sth up for auction/sale*, offer it to be auctioned/sold: 提出以供拍卖(出售)：*Has the house been put up for auction?* 那房子是否要拍卖? *a ,put-up 'job*, sth done in order to give a false impression, to swindle sb, etc. 意图蒙混之事(为了给人错误印象或欺骗他人而为者)。*put sb up*, provide lodging and food (for): 供以食宿(与 ... 住宿)：*We can put you up for the weekend*. 周末我们能供你食宿。*put sb up (for sth)*, propose, nominate sb for a position:推荐或提名某人就任某职务: *She was put up for the position of secretary*, eg of a society; 她被推荐担任秘书职务;*put sb up for a club*. 推荐(提名)某人为一俱乐部之会员。*put sb 'up to sth*, suggest sth to sb, esp urge him to do sth mischievous or wrong: 向某人建议做某事(尤指促其做坏事或错事)；教唆:*Who put you up to all these tricks?* 谁教唆你做这些骗人的事? *put 'up with sb/sth*, endure without protest; bear patiently: 容忍;忍受: *There are many inconveniences that have to be put up with when you are camping*. 在你露营时，有很多不方便处必须忍受。

put[2] /pʌt; pʌt/ *n, vi, vt = ***putt**.

pu·ta·tive /'pjuːtətɪv; 'pjutətɪv/ *adj* commonly reputed to be: 一般公认的;推定的: *his ~ father*. 他那位一般公认的父亲。

pu·trefy /'pjuːtrɪfaɪ; 'pjutrə,faɪ/ *vt, vi (pt, pp ***-fied**) [VP6A, 2A] (cause to) become putrid. (使) 腐败。**pu·tre·fac·tion** /,pjuːtrɪ'fækʃn; ,pjutrɪ'fækʃən/ *n ~ing*; sth which has putrefied. 腐败;腐败物。

pu·tres·cent /pjuː'tresnt; pju'trɛsṇt/ *adj* becoming putrid; in the process of rotting. 变为腐败的;正在腐败的。**pu·tres·cence** /-sns; -sṇs/ *n*

pu·trid /'pjuːtrɪd; 'pjutrɪd/ *adj* **1** having become rotten; decomposed and ill-smelling: 已变为腐烂的;腐烂且有臭味的: *~ fish*. 腐烂的臭鱼。**2** (sl) very distasteful or unpleasant: (俚)非常令人不快的: *~ weather*. 很坏的天气。*~·ity* /pjuː'trɪdətɪ; pju'trɪdətɪ/ *n* [U] decomposed matter; *~ state*. 腐烂物;腐败。

putsch /pʊtʃ; pʊtʃ/ *n* (G) revolutionary attempt; insurrection. (德)革命的企图;起义;暴动。

putt /pʌt; pʌt/ *vi, vt* [VP2A, 6A] strike (a golfball) gently with a club so that it rolls across the ground towards or into a hole: 以球棍小心轻击(高尔夫球)使滚过场地滑向或滚进一洞: *spend an hour practising ~ing*. 花一小时练习轻击高尔夫球。'*~·ing-green n* smooth area of lawn around a hole. 高尔夫球穴周围的草地;穴周之平坦的轻打区域。'*~·ing·iorn n* club for *~ing*. 轻击高尔夫球之球棍。□ *n* stroke as described above. 上述的一击;轻击。

put·tee /'pʌtɪ; 'pʌtɪ/ *n* long band of cloth wound round the leg from ankle to knee, for protection and support. 裹腿;绑腿。

put·ter /'pʌtə(r); 'pʌtə/ *vt, vi = ***potter**.

putty /'pʌtɪ; 'pʌtɪ/ *n* [U] soft paste of white powder and oil used for fixing glass in window frames, etc. 白灰同油混合的柔软糊状物;油灰(用以粘玻璃于窗框等者)。□ *vt* [VP6A, 15B] fill or make fast with *~*: 以油灰填塞或粘牢: *~ up a hole*. 以油灰补塞一个洞。

puzzle /'pʌzl; 'pʌzl/ *n* [C] **1** question or problem difficult to understand or answer. 难理解或回答之问题。**2** problem (eg a '*crossword-~*) or toy (eg a '*jigsaw-~*) designed to test a person's knowledge, skill, patience or temper. 用以测验人之知识,技术,耐心或脾气而设计的问题(如纵横字谜)或玩具(如拼图板);谜。**3** (*sing* only)state of bewilderment or perplexity: (仅用单数)迷惑;困惑: *be in a ~ about sth*. 对某事物深感迷惑不解。□ *vt, vi* **1** [VP6A] cause (sb) to be perplexed; make hard thought necessary to (sb): 使(某人)困惑;使苦思: *This letter ~s me*. 这封信使我困惑不解。*He was ~d what to do next/ how to answer the letter*. 他不知道下一步怎么办(如何回这封信)。*He ~d his brains* (= thought hard) *to find the answer*. 他绞尽脑汁以寻求答案。**2** [VP3A] *~ over sth*, think deeply about it. 深思(某事)。**3** [VP15B] *~ sth out*, (try to) find the answer or solution by hard thought. 苦思而找出答案或解决某问题。*~·ment n* state of being *~d*. 困惑;苦思。**puzz·ler** *n* puzzling question: 难解之问题: *ask sb a few ~rs*. 问某人一些难题。*That's a real ~r!* 那真是个难题!

pygmy, pigmy /'pɪgmɪ; 'pɪgmɪ/ *n (pl ***-mies**) **1** P*~*, member of a dwarf people in Equatorial Africa. 赤道非洲等地身体矮小的种族。**2** very small person; dwarf. 十分矮小的人;侏儒。**3** (attrib) very small. (用作定语)非常小的。

py·ja·mas (US = **pa·ja·mas**) /pə'dʒɑːməz US: -'dʒæm-; pə'dʒæməz/ *n pl* **1** (also 亦作 **a pair of ~**) loose-fitting jacket and trousers for sleeping in (*sing* when attrib): 宽松之睡衣裤(用作定语时用单数): *pyjama top/jacket/bottom/trousers*. 睡衣上身(上衣,下身,裤子)。*cat's~=cat's whiskers*, ⇨ **whisker(2)**. **2** loose trousers tied round the waist, worn by Muslims of both sexes in India and Pakistan. (印度与巴基斯坦穆斯林穿的一种围腰而系的)宽松的裤子。

py·lon /'paɪlən; 'paɪlən/ *n* **1** tower (steel framework) for, carrying overhead high-voltage electric cables. 架高压电缆之铁塔。**2** gateway to an ancient Egyptian temple; tall structure erected as a support, boundary or decoration. 古埃及庙宇的大门;作为支柱,界线或装饰用之高大建筑。

pylons

py·or·rhoea (also **-rhea**) /,paɪə'rɪə; ,paɪə'riə/ *n* [U]

inflammation of the gums causing them to shrink, with loosening of the teeth. 齿槽脓溢;牙周病(牙龈发炎,能使牙龈萎缩,牙齿松动)。

pyra·mid /'pɪrəmɪd; 'pɪrəmɪd/ *n* structure with a triangular or square base and sloping sides meeting at a point, esp one of those built of stone in ancient Egypt; pile of objects in the shape of a ~. 角锥;锥体;(尤指古埃及之)金字塔;角锥形之一堆东西。⇨ the illus at **Sphinx.** 参看 Sphinx 之插图。**~ selling,** (comm) method of selling goods whereby distributors pay a premium for the right to sell a company's goods and then sell part of those to other distributors. (由)分层销售(销售商品的方法,即由经销商付权利金取得某商品之经销权,再将部分经销权转卖给其他经销商)。

pyre /'paɪə(r); paɪr/ *n* large pile of wood for burning, esp a funeral pile for a corpse. 大堆供燃烧之木料;(尤指)火葬用之柴堆。

py·rites /ˌpaɪə'raɪtiːz US: pɪ'r-; pə'raɪtiːz/ *n* [U] **copper ~,** sulphide of copper and iron. 黄铜矿(铜与铁

之硫化物)。**iron ~,** either of two sulphides of iron, gold in colour. 黄铁矿(铁之两种硫化物之任一种,色金黄)。

pyro·tech·nics /ˌpaɪrə'teknɪks; ˌpaɪrə'teknɪks/ *n pl* art of making or using fireworks; public display of fireworks;(fig, often ironic) brilliant display of oratory, wit, etc. 烟火制造术或使用法;放烟火;(喻,常作反语)辩才,机智等之炫耀。**py·ro·tech·nic** *adj* of ~. 烟火制造术或使用法的;放烟火的;夸大炫耀的。

Pyr·rhic /'pɪrɪk; 'pɪrɪk/ *adj* ~ **victory,** one gained at too great a cost. 付出过大代价而获取之胜利。

py·thon /'paɪθn; 'paɪθɑn/ *n* large snake that kills its prey by twisting itself round it and crushing it. 一种大蟒(将身体盘绕捕获物,将其绞死)。⇨ the illus at **snake.** 参看 snake 之插图。

pyx /pɪks; pɪks/ *n* (eccles) vessel in which consecrated bread used at Holy Communion is kept. (教会)圣体容器;圣饼盒。

Qq

Q, q /kjuː; kju/ (*pl* **Q's, q's** /kjuːz; kjuz/) the seventeenth letter of the English alphabet. 英文字母之第十七个字母。**mind one's p's and q's,** ⇨ **P, p. on the qt,** ⇨ **quiet(5).**

qua /kweɪ; kwe/ *conj* (Lat) as; in the character or capacity of. (拉)作为;以…之身份或资格。

quack¹ /kwæk; kwæk/ *vi, n* [UP2A] (make the) cry of a duck. (作出)鸭叫声;(指鸭)呷呷地叫。**'~~ n** (child's name for a) duck. (儿语)鸭。

quack² /kwæk; kwæk/ *n* person dishonestly claiming to have knowledge and skill (esp in medicine); (attrib) of, used by, sold by, such persons: 伪称具有知识与技能的人;冒充内行的人;(尤指)庸医;江湖郎中;(用作定语)冒充内行者的,所用的,所售的: a ~ *doctor,* 庸医;江湖郎中;~ *remedies.* 江湖郎中的药物。**'~·ery** /-ərɪ; -ərɪ/ *n* [U] methods, practices, etc of ~s; (*pl*) instances of the use of such methods, etc. 庸医的医术、治疗等;(复) 使用上述医术等之实例。

quad /kwɒd; kwad/ *n* (colloq abbr of) (口,为下列二字之略) **1** quadrangle. **2** quadruplet.

quad·rangle /'kwɒdræŋgl; 'kwɑdræŋgl/ *n* **1** plane figure with four sides, esp a square or a rectangle. 四边形(尤指正方形或长方形)。**2** (abbr 略作 *quad*) space in the form of a ~, wholly or nearly surrounded by buildings, esp in a college, eg at Oxford. (四边有建筑物围着的)四方院, 内院; 方庭(尤指牛津大学等之学院中者)。Cf 参较 *court* at Cambridge. **quad·ran·gu·lar** /kwɒ'dræŋgjulə(r); kwɑd'ræŋgjulə/ *adj* in the form of a ~. 四边形的。

quad·rant /'kwɒdrənt; 'kwɑdrənt/ *n* **1** fourth part of a circle or its circumference. 象限;圆或其圆周的四分之一。⇨ the illus at **circle.** 参看 circle 之插图。**2** graduated strip of metal, etc shaped like a quarter-circle, for use in measuring angles (of altitude) in astronomy and navigation. 象限仪;四分仪。

quad·ratic /kwɒ'drætɪk; kwɑd'rætɪk/ *adj* (maths) ~ **equation,** one in which the second and no higher power of an unknown quantity is used, eg $x^2+2x-8=0$. (数学)二次方程式(如 $x^2+2x-8=0$)。

quad·ri·lat·eral /ˌkwɒdrɪ'lætərəl; ˌkwɑdrə'lætərəl/ *adj, n* four-sided (plane figure). 四边形。

qua·drille /kwə'drɪl; kwə'drɪl/ *n* [C] (music for an) old-fashioned square dance for four couples. 瓜德利尔舞(一种旧式的由四对组成之方块舞);其舞曲。

quad·ril·lion /kwɒ'drɪljən; kwɑd'rɪljən/ *n* **1** (GB) fourth power of one million (1 followed by 24 ciphers). (英)一百万之四次乘方;1 后加 24 个零之数。**2** (US) fifth power of one thousand (1 followed by 15 ciphers).

(美)一千之五次乘方;1 后加 15 个零之数。⇨ **App 4.** 参看附录四。

quad·ro·phony /kwɒ'drɒfənɪ; kwɑ'drɑfənɪ/ *n* [U] recording or reproduction of sound using four channels. 四声道录音或放音。**quad·ro·phonic** /ˌkwɒdrə'fɒnɪk; ˌkwɑdrə'fɑnɪk/ *adj*

quad·ru·ped /'kwɒdruped; 'kwɑdrəˌped/ *n* four-footed animal. 四足兽。

quad·ru·ple /'kwɒdruːpl US: kwɒ'druːpl; 'kwɑdrupl/ *adj* **1** made up of four parts. 由四部分组成的。**2** agreed to by four persons, parties, etc: 由四个人或四方面同意的: a ~ *alliance,* of four Powers. 四国联盟。□ *n* number or amount four times as great as another: 四倍: *20 is the ~ of 5.* 20 为 5 之 4 倍。□ *vt, vi* /kwɒ'druːpl;kwɑd'rupl/ [VP6A, 2A] multiply by 4: 以 4 乘之;四倍之: *He has ~d his income / His income has ~d in the last four years.* 他的收入在过去四年中增加了四倍。

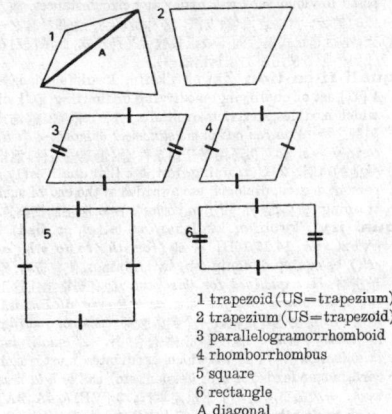

1 trapezoid (US=trapezium)
2 trapezium (US=trapezoid)
3 parallelogram or rhomboid
4 rhombor rhombus
5 square
6 rectangle
A diagonal

quadrilaterals

quad·ru·plet /'kwɒdruːplət US: kwɒ'druːp-; 'kwɑdru,plɪt/ *n* (common abbr 常略作 *quad*) one of four babies at a birth (usu *pl*: *one of the ~s* is commoner than *one ~*). 一胎四婴中之一个(通常用复数: one of the quadruplets 较 one quadruplet 常用)。

quad·ru·pli·cate /kwɒ'druːplɪkət; kwɑd'ruplikɪt/

adj four times repeated or copied. 重复四次的;抄写四份的。 □ *n in ~*, in four exactly similar examples or copies. 以四个同样之例证;以四份同样之文件;一式四份地。 □ *vt* /ˈkwɒˈdruːplɪˌkeɪt/ kwɑdˈrʊplɪˌket/ [VP6A] make four specimens of. 四次重复之;作成…之四个范例或四份文件;把…作成一式四份。

quaff /kwɒf US: kwæf; kwæf/ *vt*, *vi* [VP6A, 15B, 2A] (liter) drink deeply: (文)痛饮;畅饮: *~ (off) a glass of wine.* 饮尽一杯酒。

quagga /ˈkwæɡə; ˈkwæɡə/ *n* (now extinct) S African quadruped related to the ass and the zebra. 泥驴(南非产的一种四足兽,与驴及斑马同属,现已绝种)。

quag·mire /ˈkwæɡmaɪə(r); ˈkwæɡˌmaɪr/ *n* [C] area of soft, wet land; bog; marsh. 沼泽;泥地。

Quai d'Or·say /ˌkeɪ dɔːˈseɪ; ˌkedɔrˈse/ *n* (F) (used for) French Foreign Office; French foreign policy. (法) (用以指)法国外交部;法国外交政策。

quail[1] /kweɪl; kwel/ *n* small bird, similar to a partridge, valued as food: 鹌: (unchanged in the collective *pl*) (集合名词复数不变) *shoot ~ and duck.* 射鹌与野鸭。 ⇨ the illus at **fowl**. 参看 fowl 之插图。

quail[2] /kweɪl; kwel/ *vi* [VP2A, 3A] *~ (at/before)*, feel or show fear: 感到或显露恐惧;胆怯;畏缩: *His heart ~ed.* 他心里感到恐慌。 *He ~ed at the prospect before him.* 他对自己的前途感到惶恐。 *His eyes ~ed before her angry looks.* 在她的怒容之前,他的眼睛里显出畏惧的神情。

quaint /kweɪnt; kwent/ *adj* (**-er, -est**) attractive or pleasing because unusual or old-fashioned; whimsical: (因奇特或老式而)诱人或悦人的;古怪的: *American visitors to England admire our ~ villages/customs.* 来英国的美国游客对于我们的古老乡村(风俗)甚为称赏。 *~·ly adv ~·ness n*

quake /kweɪk; kwek/ *vi* [VP2A, C] 1 (of the earth) shake: (指地)颤动;震动: *The ground ~d under his feet.* 地在他脚下震动。 2 (of persons) tremble: (指人)战栗;颤抖: *quaking with fear/cold.* 因恐惧(寒冷)而战栗。 □ *n* (colloq abbr for) earthquake. (口)为 earthquake 之略。

Quaker /ˈkweɪkə(r); ˈkwekɚ/ *n* member of the Society of Friends, a Christian group that holds informal meetings instead of formal church services and is opposed to violence or war under any circumstances. 教友派的信徒;贵格会员(教友派会,亦称贵格会,为基督教之一支,举行非正式集会而不做正式教会礼拜仪式,此派反对在任何情形下使用暴力或诉诸战争)。

quali·fi·ca·tion /ˌkwɒlɪfɪˈkeɪʃn; ˌkwɑləfəˈkeʃən/ *n* 1 [U] act of qualifying, modifying or limiting; [C] sth which modifies, restricts or limits: 修饰; 限制: 修饰或限制之物: *You can accept his statement without ~/with certain ~s.* 你可以不附带任何条件(附带某些条件)地接受他的声明。 2 [C] training, test, etc that qualifies(1) a person; degree, diploma, etc awarded at the end of such training: 资格;条件;资历: *a doctor's ~.* 医生的资格。

qual·ify /ˈkwɒlɪfaɪ; ˈkwɑləˌfaɪ/ *vt*, *vi* (*pt*, *pp* **-fied**) 1 [VP2C, 6A, 14,17,16B] *~ sb (for sth/to do sth/as sth)*, be equipped, equip (sb) by training: 使有资格;给予资格: *He's qualified for this post.* 他有资格担任这工作。 *His training qualifies him as a teacher of English.* 他受的训练使他有资格做一个英语教师。 *He's not qualified to teach French.* 他没有资格教法语。 *A qualifying examination* (= one at which candidates must reach certain standards for a profession, etc) *will be held next week.* 一次甄审考试将于下星期举行。 2 [VP17, 4A, 3A] *~ sb to do sth*, entitle: 使某人有资格做某事: *He's the manager's son but that does not ~ him to criticize my work.* 他是经理的儿子,但这并不足以使他有资格批评我的工作。 *~ for sth*, be entitled to: 有…的资格: *Do you ~ for the vote/to vote?* 你有投票的资格吗? 3 [VP6A] limit; make less inclusive, less definite; 限制;使包括较少;使较不笼统: *The statement 'Boys are lazy' needs to be qualified*, eg by saying 'Some boys' or 'Many boys'. '男

孩子懒惰' 这句话需要斟酌 (例如改说 '某些男孩' 或 '很多男孩')。 4 [VP6A] (gram) limit the meaning of; name the qualities of: (语法)限制…之意义; 指明…之性质; 修饰; 形容: *Adjectives ~ nouns.* 形容词修饰名词。 5 [VP16B] *~ sb as*, describe: 描写; 将…描述为: *~ a man as an ambitious self-seeker.* 把一个人描述成有野心的自私自利者。 **quali·fied** *adj* 1 having the necessary qualifications: 具必需条件的; 合格的: *a qualified doctor.* 一位合格的医生。 2 limited: 限制的; 有限度的: *give one's qualified approval.* 对一计划给予有限度的赞同。 **quali·fier** /-faɪə(r); -ˌfaɪɚ/ *n* (gram) *~ing* word, eg an adjective or adverb. (语法)修饰词(如形容词或副词)。

quali·ta·tive /ˈkwɒlɪtətɪv US: -teɪt-; ˈkwɑləˌtetɪv/ *adj* relating to quality: 与性质有关的; 定性的: *~ analysis.* 定性分析。 ⇨ **quantitative**.

qual·ity /ˈkwɒlɪtɪ; ˈkwɑlətɪ/ *n* (*pl* **-ties**) 1 [C, U] (degree, esp high degree, of) goodness or worth: 质; 品质;<品级或品质>优良品质: *goods of first-rate ~.* 第一等品质的货物。 *Poor ~ goods won't sell easily.* 品质差的货物不易卖出。 *We aim at ~ rather than quantity*, aim to produce superior goods, not large quantities. 我们的目标是重质不重量。 *We manufacture goods of various qualities.* 我们制造各种不同品质的货物。 *He is a man with many good qualities.* 他是一位有很多优点的人。 *Give us a taste of your ~*, show us what accomplishments you have. 让我们瞧瞧你的才艺吧。 2 [C] sth that is special in, or that distinguishes, a person or thing: 性质;特质: *One ~ of pine-wood is that it can be sawn easily.* 松木的一种特质是它容易被锯开。 *He has the ~ of inspiring confidence.* 他有激发别人对他信任的特质。 3 [U] (archaic) high social position: (古)很高的社会地位: *a lady of ~.* 一位贵妇。

qualm /kwɑːm; kwɑm/ *n* [C] 1 feeling of doubt (esp about whether one is doing or has done right); misgiving: 疑虑(尤指对所做或已做的事是否正确所感觉者); 疑惑; 不安: *He felt no ~s about borrowing money from friends.* 他对于向朋友们借钱未感到丝毫不安。 2 temporary feeling of sickness in the stomach: 胃中暂时之不适: 噁心: *~s which spoilt his appetite during the first few days of the voyage.* 在航海的头几天使他没有食欲的噁心。

quan·dary /ˈkwɒndərɪ; ˈkwɑndrɪ/ *n* [C] (*pl* **-ries**) state of doubt or perplexity: 疑惑;困惑: *be in a ~ about what to do next.* 对下一步该怎么办感到困惑。

quango /ˈkwæŋɡəʊ; ˈkwæŋɡo/ *n* quasi-autonomous non-governmental organisation. 半自治的非政府组织(此字系由 quasi-autonomous non-governmental organisation 一词中每字起首字母组成)。

quan·tify /ˈkwɒntɪfaɪ; ˈkwɑntəˌfaɪ/ *vt* [VP6A] express or measure the quantity of. 表示或测定…之量。

quan·ti·ta·tive /ˈkwɒntɪtətɪv US: -teɪt-; ˈkwɑntəˌtetɪv/ *adj* relating to quantity: 与量有关的; 定量的: *~ analysis.* 定量分析。 ⇨ **qualitative**.

quan·tity /ˈkwɒntɪtɪ; ˈkwɑntətɪ/ *n* (*pl* **-ties**) 1 [U] the property of things which can be measured, eg size, weight, number: 物之能衡量之属性(如大小、重量、数量);量: *I prefer quality to ~.* 我重质不重量。 *Mathematics is the science of pure ~.* 数学是研究纯量之科学。 2 [C] amount, sum or number: 量;数: *There's only a small ~* (ie not much or not many) *left.* 剩下数量很小。 *What ~ do you want?* 你要多少? 3 (often *pl*) large amount or number: (常用复数)大量: *We've had quantities of rain this summer.* 今年夏天雨下得很多。 *He buys things in ~/in large quantities.* 他总是大宗采购东西。 *an unknown ~*, (maths) symbol (usu *x*) representing an unknown ~ in an equation; (fig) person or thing whose action, ability etc cannot be foreseen. (数学)在一个方程式中代表一未知数的符号(通常用 x 表示); 未知数; (喻)其行动、能力等难以预测的人或事物。 *~ survey-or*, expert who estimates quantities of materials needed in building, their cost, etc. 建筑估算师;建筑估料师。 *bill of ~*, one prepared by a *~* surveyor. 建筑工程清单。

quan·tum /'kwɒntəm; 'kwɑntəm/ n (pl **quanta** /-tə; -tə/) amount required or desired. (所需或所欲之)量; 額。 '~ **theory,** (phys) the hypothesis that in radiation the energy of electrons is discharged not continuously but in certain fixed amounts (or *quanta*). (物理)量子论 (物理学上的一个假说,即在辐射中,电子的能量不是接续不断而是以某固定之量 'quanta' 放出的)。

quar·an·tine /'kwɒrəntiːn US: 'kwɔːr-; 'kwɔrən,tin/ n [U] (med) (period of) separation from others until it is known that there is no danger of spreading disease: (医)(防止疾病传染所施行的)隔离; 检疫; 检疫期:*be in ~ for a week,* 隔离一周;*be out of ~;* 解除检疫; (attrib) of the system of ~: (用作定语)隔离制度的:*the ~ regulations.* 隔离管制条例。*How long will my dog be kept in ~?* 我的狗要被隔离多久?□ vt [VP6A] put in ~: 使受隔离:~*d because of yellow fever.* 因黄热病而被隔离。

quark /kwɑːk, kwɑrk/ n (phys) kind of elementary particle. (物理)夸克(一种最基本的粒子)。

quar·rel /'kwɒrəl US: 'kwɔːrəl; 'kwɔrəl/ n [C] 1 angry argument; violent disagreement: 口角; 争论:*have a ~ with sb about sth.* 为某事同某人争论。*They made up their ~,* ended it and became friendly. 他们于争吵后言归于好。*He's always fighting other people's ~s,* helping them, eg to get social justice. 他总是帮着别的人吵架(例如为主持公道)。2 cause for being angry; reason for protest or complaint: 口角的原因; 抗议或抱怨之理由:*I have no ~ with/against him.* 我没有跟他争吵的理由。*pick a ~ (with sb),* find or invent some occasion or excuse for disagreement, etc. (向某人)寻争衅。□ vi (-ll-, US also -l-) 1 [VP2A, C, 3A] ~ *(with sb) (about sth),* have, take part in, a ~: 争论; 争吵:*The thieves ~led with one another about how to divide the loot.* 盗贼们为了如何分赃而彼此争吵起来。2 [VP3A] ~ *with,* disagree with; refuse to accept; complain about: 不同意; 拒绝接受; 抱怨:*It's not the fact of examinations I'm ~ling with; it's the way they're conducted.* 我并非对考试这件事本身有异议,而是不赞成考试的方式。 '~·**some** /-səm; -səm/ adj quick-tempered; fond of ~s. 急躁的; 爱争吵的。

quarry¹ /'kwɒrɪ US: 'kwɔːrɪ; 'kwɔːrɪ/ n (pl -**ries**) (usu sing) animal, bird, etc which is hunted; anything eagerly pursued. (通常用单数)被追猎的兽、禽鸟等; 猎物; 任何被热烈追求之物。

quarry² /'kwɒrɪ US: 'kwɔːrɪ; 'kwɔrɪ/ n [C] (pl -**ries**) place (not underground like a mine) where stone, slate, etc is obtained (for building, road-making, etc). 采石场 (非如在地下之矿坑)。□ vt, vi 1 [VP6A, 15A, B] get from a ~: 从采石场开采:~ *limestones;* 开采石灰石;~ *(out) a block of marble;* 挖出一大块大理石; (fig) search for (facts, etc) in old books, records, etc. (喻)在旧书、记录等中探索(事实等)。2 [VP2A, C] engage in work of this kind: 从事寻找资料之工作:~ *in old manuscripts.* 在旧手稿中寻找资料。 '~·**man** /-mæn; -mən/ n (pl -**men**) man who works in a ~. 采石工人。

quart /kwɔːt; kwɔrt/ n measure of capacity equal to two pints or about 1.14 litre. 夸(脱)(容量之单位,等于二品脱或约 1.14 公升)。 ⇨ **App 5:** 参看附录五:*drink a ~ of beer.* 喝一夸脱的啤酒。*put a ~ into a pint pot,* make the less contain the greater; attempt the impossible. 欲使较小者装较大者; 大脚穿小鞋; 做不可能之事。

quar·ter /'kwɔːtə(r); 'kwɔrtə/ n 1 fourth part (¹/₄); one of four equal or corresponding parts: 四分之一; 四等分或四相关部分之一:*a ~ of a mile;* 四分之一英里;*a mile and a ~;* 一又四分之一英里;*a ~ of an hour,* 15 minutes; 一刻钟;*fifteen minutes;* 十五分钟;*a ~ of this century,* ie 1901-25. 本世纪的前二十五年。*We've come a ~ of the distance now.* 我们现在已走了全程的四分之一。*Divide the apples into ~s.* 把这些苹果分为四份。*a bad ~ of an hour,* a short but unpleasant experience (eg in a dentist's chair). 一段短暂而不愉快的经验(如坐在牙医的椅上)。2 point of time

15 minutes before or after any hour: (任何小时之前或后的)一刻钟:*a ~ to* (US 美 = *of*) *two;* 差一刻两点; *a ~ past six.* 六点一刻。*It isn't the ~.* 还不到一刻钟。*This clock strikes the hours, the half-hours, and the ~s.* 这时钟每逢走了一点钟、半点钟和一刻钟均鸣响。3 three months, esp as a period for which rent and other payments are made: 三个月; 一季(尤指房地租或其他款项偿付之时期):*owe several ~s' rent;* 欠好几季的房(地)租;*pay one's rent at the end of each ~.* 在每季之末交付房(地)租。 '~-**day** n first day of a legal ~ of the year, on which rents and other three-monthly accounts are paid (in England, 25 Mar; 24 June; 29 Sept; 25 Dec). 季结帐日(即一年中各法定季的第一日,为付房地租及其他按季付款之日,在英国为三月二十五日; 六月二十四日; 九月二十九日; 十二月二十五日)。 '~ **sessions,** ⇨ *court of* ~ *sessions* at **court¹**(1). 4 (US) 25 cents; a ~ of a dollar. (美)两角五分; 四分之一元; 两角五分的硬币。5 joint of meat including a leg: 包括一条腿在内的一大块肉:*a ~ of beef;* 有条腿在内的一大块牛肉; also used of the living animal (usu in compounds, as '*fore-~s;* 'hind-~s). 也用以指活的动物(通常用于复合词中,如 fore-~s 前半身; hind-~s 后半身)。6 direction; district; source of supply, help, information, etc: 方向; 区域; 供应、援助、消息等之来源:*men running from all ~s/from every ~;* 从四面八方(从各方)跑来的人们; *travel in every ~ of the globe,* everywhere. 在世界各地旅行。*As his father was penniless, he could expect no help from that ~.* 因为他父亲身无分文,他不能希望从他父亲那里得到援助。*The suggestion did not find favour in the highest ~s,* was not welcomed by those at the head of affairs. 这建议没有得到最高阶层的赞同。7 division of a town, eg one of a special class of people, etc: 一城市中的一区(尤指属于某一特殊阶层者):*the Chinese ~ of San Francisco;* 旧金山的华人区;*the manufacturing/residential ~.*工厂(住宅)区。8 one-fourth of a lunar month; the moon's phase at the end of the first or third week: 阴历一个月的四分之一; 在第一或第三周末月亮之位相:*the moon at the first ~/in its last ~.* 上弦(下弦)月。⇨ the illus at **phase.** 参看 phase 之插图。9 (pl) lodging; (mil) place where soldiers, etc are lodged or stationed: (复)住所; 寓所; (军)营房; 军营:*take up ~s, lodge;* 住宿;*return to ~s.* 回到住所。 '~ **headquarters** at **head¹**(20). **married ~s,** place where soldiers, etc lodge with their families. 军眷区, 军人家属区。**single ~s,** place where unmarried soldiers, etc lodge. (未婚官兵住宿之)单身营房。10 *at close ~s,* (seen) from very near. 非常接近: 从很近的地方(看的)。11(pl) positions taken up by sailors on duty on a ship, esp for fighting: (复)(海员在船上于担任职务时,尤指海军在作战时,所占之)岗位:*Officers and men at once took up their ~s.* 官兵立即各就其岗位。12[U] *ask for/give ~,* mercy to an enemy; life granted to a defeated enemy who is willing to surrender: 请求(给予)饶恕; 宽恕敌人; 给自愿投降之敌人活路:*No ~ was asked for and none given,* There were no prisoners. 无人求饶, 未予饶恕(未留俘虏)。13 (naut) rear part of a ship's side: (航海)船舷之后部; 船尾:*on the port/starboard ~,* 在左(右)舷后部。 '~-**deck** n part of the upper deck between the stern and the aftermast of a warship, reserved for officers; officers of a warship or navy. 军舰上船尾与后樯间的上甲板部分; 后甲板(系供军官所用者); 战舰上或海军之全体军官。 ⇨ lower deck at **low¹**(13), forecastle. 14 (GB) fourth part of a hundredweight, 28 lb; (US)25 lb; grain-measure of eight bushels. 夸特(英为 28 磅; 美为 25 磅; 谷量单位为 8 浦式耳)。 ⇨ **App 5.** 参看附录五。15 one of the four parts of a shield used in armorial bearings. 纹章中所用的盾形的四分之一。16(compounds) (复合词) ,~·**final** n (sport) one of four competitions or matches, the winners of which play in the semi-finals. (运动)四分之一决赛(其获胜者参加半决赛的四场竞赛之一)。 '~-**light** n triangular section at the front or

back window of a car, opened to admit air. (车辆的)边窗. **'~-master** n **(a)** (army) (abbr 略作 **QM**) officer in charge of the stores, etc of a battalion. (陆军)军需官. **(b)** (navy) petty officer in charge of steering the ship, signals, etc. (海军)航信士官. **~-master-'general** n (abbr 略作 **QMG**) staff officer in charge of supplies for a whole army. 军需司令,军需局长. **'~-plate** n photographic plate $3^1/_4$ inches × $4^1/_2$ inches; photograph made from it. $3^1/_4$ 英寸 × $4^1/_2$ 英寸大的照相感光板;由此种感光板照的相片. **'~-staff** n strong pole, 6 to 8 ft long, formerly used as a weapon and in a rough kind of fencing. 长六英尺到八英尺的坚实木棒(以前用作一种武器,并用于一种粗野的击剑术中). □ vt 1 [VP6A] divide into ~s: 分…为四份;四分之: ~ an apple; 把一苹果分为四份; (in former times) divide (a traitor's body) into ~s: (昔时)将(叛国贼之尸体)肢解: condemned to be hanged, drawn =disembowelled)and ~ed. 被判决处以绞刑,取出肠子,并肢解之. 2[VP6A, 15A] find lodgings for (troops); place (troops) in lodgings: 为(军队)找驻屯处; 安置(军队)于驻扎地: ~ troops in the villages. 安置军队驻屯于村中. **~-ing** n method of arranging two or more coats of arms, to show alliances with or descent from various families; coat of arms resulting from this. 排列两个或两个以上的纹章以示与不同家族之联姻或为不同家族之后代的方法;由此种方法排列成之纹章.

quar·ter·ly /'kwɔːtəlɪ; 'kwɔrtəlɪ/ adj, adv (happening) once in each three months; 每三个月(发生)一次的(地); 按季的(地): ~ payments/subscriptions; 按季付款(订阅费); to be paid ~. 按季付款. □ n (pl -lies) periodical published ~. 季刊(每三个月出版一次的期刊).

quar·tet /kwɔː'tet; kwɔr'tɛt/ n (piece of music for) four players or singers: 四个演奏者或歌唱者组成一组;四重奏;四重唱;四部合奏(曲)曲: a string ~, for (usu) two violins, viola and cello; 弦乐四重奏(通常为二小提琴,一中音提琴和一大提琴): a piano ~, for piano and three stringed instruments. 钢琴四重奏(由钢琴和三件弦乐器合奏).

quarto /'kwɔːtəʊ; 'kwɔrto/ n (pl ~s -təʊz; -toz/) (also written 亦书作 **4to**) size given by folding a sheet of paper twice (making four leaves or eight pages); book made of sheets so folded (usu about 9 by 12 in): 四开(将一张纸折两次,折成四张八页); 四开本的书(通常为9×12英寸): the first ~ of 'Hamlet'. 哈姆雷特的第一四开本.

quartz /kwɔːts; kwɔrts/ n [U] sorts of hard mineral (esp crystallized silica), including agate and other semi-precious stones. 石英(尤指结晶之硅石,包括玛瑙及其他次等宝石). **~ clock,** one of very great accuracy, with ~ oscillators. (一种装有石英晶体振荡器的非常准确的)石英钟.

quasar /'kweɪzɑː(r); 'kweɪzɑr/ n (astron) very distant source of radio or light waves. (天文)类星体(极远的无线电波或光波来源).

quash /kwɒʃ; kwɑʃ/ vt [VP6A] put an end to, annul, reject as not valid (by legal procedure): (以法律程序)停止;废止;宣告无效: ~ a verdict/decision. 宣告一判决(决定)无效.

quasi- /'kweɪsaɪ; 'kweɪsaɪ/ pref (with a n or adj) to a certain extent; seemingly: (与名词或形容词连用)有相当程度的;类似的;半官似的: ~ official position. 一个半官方的职位. ➭ **App 3.** 参看附录三.

quas·sia /'kwɒʃə; 'kwɑʃɪə/ n [U] (bitter drug used medicinally and obtained from) wood or bark of a S American tree; the tree. 南美所产一种苦木科植物的木材与树皮;苦木;从苦木中提炼出的一种苦味药;苦木树.

quat·er·cen·ten·ary /ˌkwætəsen'tiːnərɪ, US: -'sen-tənerɪ; ˌkwɑtə'sɛntɪˌnɛrɪ/ n 400th anniversary: 四百周年纪念: the ~ celebrations in 1964 of Shakespeare's birth. 在 1964 年举行的莎士比亚诞生四百周年纪念之庆祝活动.

quat·rain /'kwɒtreɪn; 'kwɑtren/ n verse of four lines, usu rhyming a b a b. 四行诗(其韵脚通常是 a b a b).

quat·tro·cento /ˌkwætrəʊ'tʃentəʊ; ˌkwɑtro'tʃɛnto/ n (I) the 15th century as a period of Italian art and literature. (意)(作为意大利艺术与文学一个时代的)第十五世纪.

qua·ver /'kweɪvə(r); 'kwevə/ vt, vi 1 [VP2A] (of the voice or a sound) shake; tremble: (指声音)颤抖;震颤: in a ~ing voice; 以一种震颤的声音; in a voice that ~ed. 以一种震颤的声音. 2 [VP6A, 15B] say or sing in a shaking voice: 以震颤的声音说出或唱出: She ~ed (out/forth) her little song. 她以震颤的声音唱出她的小调. □ n [C] 1 ~ing sound. 震颤的声音. 2 musical note with one-half the time value of a crotchet. 八分音符. ➭ the illus at **notation**. 参看 notation 之插图.

quay /kiː; kiː/ n solid, stationary landing-place usu built of stone or iron, alongside which ships can be tied up for loading and unloading. 码头;横码头.

queasy /'kwiːzɪ; 'kwizɪ/ adj (-ier, -iest) 1 (of food) causing a feeling of sickness in the stomach. (指食物)令人作呕的. 2 (of the stomach) easily upset. (指胃)易呕吐的. 3 (of a person) easily made sick; feeling sick. (指人)容易不舒服的;感觉不舒服的. 4 (fig, of a person or his conscience) over-scrupulous, tender or delicate. (喻,指人或其良心)过于小心的; 善感的;敏感的. **queas·ily** /-ɪlɪ; -əlɪ/ adv **queasi·ness** n

queen /kwiːn; kwin/ n 1 woman ruler in her own right: 女王: the Q~ of England; 英国女王: Q~ Elizabeth II. 女王伊利莎白二世. 2 wife of a king: 皇后: King George VI and Q~ Elizabeth. 英王乔治六世与伊利莎白白皇后. 3 ~ dowager, widow of a king. 孀居之皇后;太后. ~ mother, dowager who is the mother of a reigning Sovereign. 皇太后;母后. 4 woman regarded as first of a group: 一群妇女中之第一名;美女;佳丽: the ~ of the May; 五月皇后; 'May Q~, girl chosen as ~ in old-time May Day ceremonies; 五月皇后(旧时在 May Day 庆祝时节选出的一个女王); town or place regarded as occupying a leading position: 居于首要地位的城市或地方;首邑: Venice, the ~ of the Adriatic. 威尼斯,亚得里亚海沿岸的首要都市. **'beauty ~,** winner of a beauty contest. "选美比赛"中的第一名;选美皇后. 5 ~ ant/bee/wasp, fertile, egg-producing ant etc. 蚁王(蜂王,黄蜂王). 6 (chess) most powerful piece for attack or defence, ➭ the illus at **chess**. (棋) 攻守最有力的棋子; 后棋(参看 chess 之插图); (cards) one with the picture of a ~: (纸牌)后牌: the ~ of spades/hearts. 黑桃(红心)后牌. 7 △ (GB derog sl) effeminate male homosexual. (讳)(英俚,贬)女性化的男子同性恋者. □ vt ~ it (over sb), act like a ~; assume the leadership. 行动若一女王; 担起领导责任. 行动若一女王;担起领导责任. **~·ly** adj like a ~; fit for a ~; majestic; generous: 象女王的; 适于女王的; 威严的; 谦慨的: ~ly robes; 女王穿的袍; her ~ly duties. 她作为女王的职责.

queer /kwɪə(r); kwɪr/ adj 1 strange; unusual: 奇怪的;不平常的: a ~ way of talking. 一种古怪的讲话方式. 2 causing doubt or suspicion: 引起疑虑或怀疑的: a ~ character; 一个可疑的人; ~ noises in the attic. 顶楼中可疑的响声. 3 (colloq) unwell; faint: (口)不适的;眩晕的: feel very ~. 感觉非常不适. 4 △ (derog sl) homosexual. (讳)(贬俚)同性恋者. 5 in 'Q~ Street, (GB sl) in debt; in trouble. (英俚)负债; 在困难中. □ vt [VP6A] (sl) put out of order; cause to go wrong, (俚)破坏; 使失败, esp 尤用于 ~ sb's pitch, ➭ **pitch**[1](1). **~·ly** adv ~ness n

quell /kwel; kwel/ vt [VP6A] (poet and rhet) suppress; subdue (a rebellion, rebels, opposition). (诗,修辞)镇压; 压制(叛乱,叛徒,反对).

quench /kwentʃ; kwentʃ/ vt [VP6A] 1 put out (flames, fire). 熄灭(焰,火). 2 satisfy (thirst). 解除(口渴). 3 put an end to (hope). 结束; 灭绝(希望). 4 cool in water: 使在水中变冷;淬火;冷浸: ~ steel. 淬钢. **~·less** adj (liter) that cannot be, or is never, ~ed: (文)无法或永不熄灭,解除,结束的: a ~less flame. 一个无法熄灭的火焰.

quern /kwɜːn; kwɝn/ n hand-mill for grinding corn; small hand-mill for pepper, etc. (磨谷粉之)手磨; (研磨椒等之)小型手磨.

queru·lous /ˈkwerʊləs; ˈkwɛrələs/ adj full of complaints; fretful: 多牢骚的; 爱抱怨的; 易怒的: in a ~ tone. 以抱怨的语调. **~·ly** adv **~·ness** n

query /ˈkwɪərɪ; ˈkwɪrɪ/ n [C] (pl **-ries**) **1** question, esp one raising a doubt about the truth of sth: 疑问(尤指对某事物的真实性发生怀疑者): raise a ~. 发问. **2** the mark (?) put against sth, eg in the margin of a document, as a sign of doubt. (画于某物旁边表示怀疑之)问号(?)(例如画于一文件的边上者). □ vt **1** [VP10] ~ whether/if, inquire: 询问; 探问: I ~ whether his word can be relied on. 我怀疑他的话是否可靠. **2** [VP6A] express doubt about: 对…表示怀疑: ~ a person's instructions. 怀疑一个人的指示. **3** [VP6A] put the mark(?) against. 画问号(?)于.

quest /kwest; kwɛst/ n [C] (rhet) search or pursuit: (修辞)寻求; 追求: the ~ for gold. 寻找金子. in ~ of, (old or liter use) seeking for, trying to find: (旧用法或文学用法)寻找; 设法找到: He went off in ~ of food. 他出去找食物. □ vi [VP3A] ~ for, (esp of dogs) look for; (rhet) go about in ~ of: (尤指狗)寻找; (修辞)到处寻找: ~ing for further evidence. 到处寻找更多的证据.

ques·tion¹ /ˈkwestʃən; ˈkwɛstʃən/ n **1** sentence which by word-order, use of interrogative words (who, why, etc) or intonation, requests information, an answer, etc: 疑问句; 问题; 询问; 质问: ask a lot of ~s; 询问很多问题; put a ~ to sb. 向某人提一疑问. '~-mark n the mark (?). 问号(?). ⇨ **App 9**. 参看附录九. '~-master n (in panel games) chairman. (广播或电视等中之)答问节目主持人. '~ time, (in the House of Commons) period of time during which ministers answer ~s put to them by members. 质询时间; 质询期间(英国内阁阁员答复下议院议员之质询时间). **2** sth about which there is discussion; sth which needs to be decided; inquiry; problem; affair: 讨论中之事物; 需要决定之事物; 查询; 问题; 事件: a difficult/vexed ~; 一个困难的 (争论不休的) 问题; economic ~s. 经济问题. Success is only a ~ of time, will certainly come sooner or later. 成功仅系时间问题(迟早会成功). The ~ is..., What we want to know, what we must decide, is... 问题是…我们要知道的是…; 我们必须决定的是…. That's not the ~, not the matter being discussed. 那不在讨论范围之内. in ~, being talked about: 正被谈论的: Where's the man in ~? 我们谈论的那个人在哪里? out of the ~, impossible; not to be discussed at all: 不可能; 根本不必讨论: We can't go out in this weather; it's out of the ~. 我们不能在这种天气下出去, 这事免谈了. be some/no, etc ~ of, some/no, etc discussion of: 对…有些(没有等)讨论: There was no ~ of my being invited to become Chairman, that was not discussed or proposed. 我被邀请担任主席这件事并未被讨论或提出. beg the ~, ⇨ **beg**(2). come into ~, be discussed, become of practical importance: 被讨论; 变为有实际重要性: If sending me in a spacecraft to the moon ever comes into ~, I shall refuse without hesitation. 如果提出以太空船送我到月球的话, 我将毫不犹豫地拒绝. Q~! (at a public meeting) used to warn a speaker that he is not keeping to the subject being discussed, or (less correctly) to express doubt about the truth of sth he has said. (在公共集会上用以警告发言者说话离题)不要扯到题目外去! (较不精确用用法; 对发言者所说的话的真实性表示疑问)有问题! put the ~, (at a meeting) ask those present to record their votes for or against the proposal. (在集会上)要求出席者投票决定; 提付表决. **3** [U](the putting forward of) doubt, objection: 怀疑; 反对; 怀疑或反对之提出: There is no ~ about/some ~ as to his honesty. 他的诚实毫无(有些)问题. There is no ~ but that he will (= He will undoubtedly) succeed. 他会成功是确然无疑的事. beyond (all)/without ~, certainly (无疑地); without doubt: 毫无疑问: His integrity is beyond all ~. 他的廉正是毋庸置疑的. Without ~, he's the best man for the job. 毫无疑问的, 他是做这工作的最佳人选. call sth in ~, raise objections to, express doubt about, it: 对…提出反对, 对…表示怀疑: No one has ever called my honesty in ~. 没有人对我的诚实有所怀疑. His conduct was called in ~. 他的行为被人怀疑.

ques·tion² /ˈkwestʃən; ˈkwɛstʃən/ vt **1** [VP6A] ask a ~ or ~s of; examine: 询问; 审问: a two-hour ~ing session. 两小时的审问庭期. He was ~ed by the police. 他被警方审问. They ~ed the Conservative candidate on his views. 他们询问保守党候选人的意见. **2** [VP6A, 10] ~ (whether/if), express or feel doubt about: 对…表示或感到怀疑: ~sb's veracity; 怀疑某人的诚实; ~ the value (or importance) of compulsory games at school. 怀疑学校中实行强迫学生参加体育运动的价值 (重要性). I ~ whether his proposal will be approved. 我怀疑他的提议是否会被批准. ~·able /-əbl; -əbl/ adj which may be ~ed (2): 可疑的; 有问题的; 引起争论的: a ~able assertion. 一个颇有问题的主张. ~·ably /-əblɪ; -əblɪ/ adv ~er n person who ~s(1). 询问者; 审问者. ~·ing·ly adv in a ~ing manner. 询问地; 表示疑问地.

ques·tion·naire /ˌkwestʃəˈneə(r); ˌkwɛstʃənˈɛr/ n list of (usu printed) questions to be answered by a group of people, esp to get facts or information, or for a survey. 调查表; 问题单; 问卷(由一些人来回答, 以获得资料或进行全面的调查).

quet·zal /ˈkwetsl; US: ket'sæl; ket'sɑl/ n beautiful bird of Central America; monetary unit of Guatemala. 中美产的一种美丽的鸟; 危地马拉的货币单位.

queue /kjuː; kju/ n **1** line of people waiting for their turn (eg to enter a cinema, get on a bus, buy sth): 一排等待(进入电影院, 上公共汽车、购物等)的人; 长队: form a ~; 排长队; stand in a ~. 排队. jump the ~, ⇨ **jump²** (6). **2** line of vehicles waiting to proceed: 等待前进的一列车辆: a ~ of cars held up by the traffic lights. 为交通灯所拦住的一长列汽车. **3** plait of hair hanging down over the back of the neck (eg part of a wig, as worn by men in Europe in former times). 辫子(如从前欧洲男人所戴假发的一部分). □ vi [VP2A, C, 3A] ~ (up)(for sth), get into, be in, a ~: 排成长队: ~ing for a bus; 排长队等公共汽车; ~ up to buy tickets for the film. 排队买电影票.

quibble /ˈkwɪbl; ˈkwɪbl/ n [C] evasion of the main point of an argument, attempt to escape giving an honest answer, by using a secondary or doubtful meaning of a word or phrase. 避开议论之重点; 避重就轻的回答; 支吾; 遁辞. □ vi ~ (over), use a ~s; argue about small points or differences: 用遁辞; 争辩不重要之点或异见: ~ over trivialities. 争辩琐屑之事. **quib·bler** n **quib·bling** adj

quiche /kiːʃ; kiʃ/ n open tart with savoury filling; flan. 一种蛋饼.

quick /kwɪk; kwɪk/ adj (-er, -est) **1** moving fast; able to move fast and do things in a short time; done in a short time: 快的; 迅速的; 动作敏捷的; 在短时间内能动作的: a ~ train/worker; 行驶快速的; 动作敏捷的工人); walking at a ~ pace; 快步行走; have a ~ meal; 吃一顿快餐; find ~ ways of doing sth/getting somewhere. 发现做某事(到某地)之捷径. Be ~ about it! Hurry up! 赶快! Try to be a little ~er. 想办法快一点儿. She's as ~ as lightning. 她迅如闪电. The flashes of lightning came in ~ succession, at very short intervals of time. 闪电频频接连而来. We just have time for a ~ one, (usu = a ~ (alcoholic) drink). 我们时间不多, 只能快饮. (in) ~ time, (of the ordinary rate of marching for soldiers (about four miles an hour). (以)齐步(行军的普通速度, 约每小时四英里). ~ march marching in ~ time. 齐步走. '~-change attrib adj (of an actor, etc) ~ly changing his appearance, costume, etc to play another part: (指演员等)迅速换装以演另一脚色的: a ~'-change artist. 一个换装迅速的艺人. '~-freeze vt freeze (food) very ~ly so as to keep the natural flavours unchanged: 快速冷冻(食物)以保持其原有味道. ~-frozen foods. 速冻的食

物.'~·**step** *n* ballroom dance with both quick and slow steps. 社交舞中的活泼舞步. **2** lively; bright; active, prompt: 活泼的; 伶俐的; 机敏的; 立即的: ~ **to understand;** 敏于领悟的; *a ~ ear for music;* 对音乐感受灵敏的耳朵; ~ **to make up one's mind/to seize an opportunity;** 敏于下决心(抓住机会)的; ~ *at figures;* 敏于计算数字的; *a ~ (= intelligent) child;* 一个聪颖的小孩; *not very ~,* (colloq, of a child) rather dull or stupid;(口, 指儿童)相当迟钝或笨的; *a ~ temper,* soon aroused. 性情急躁, ~·**eared**/ -'**eyed**/-'**sighted**/-'**tempered**/-'**witted** *adjj* having ~ ears/eyes/sight, etc. 听觉灵敏的(眼力敏锐的)眼快的; 性情急躁的/才思敏捷的). **3** (old use) living. (旧用法)活的. **the ~ and the dead.** 生者与死者. □ *n* [U] tender or sensitive flesh below the nails, esp the nails: 皮下(尤指指甲下)细嫩或敏感的肉; 活肉: *bite one's nails to the ~.* 咬指甲直咬到下面的活肉; *cut/touch sb to the ~,* hurt his feelings deeply. 深深伤害某人的感情. □ *adv* (-**er,** -**est**) **1** (common in colloq use for *quickly,* always placed after the *v*): (在口语中常用以代替 quickly, 总是放在动词后面): *You're walking too ~ for me.* 你走得太快了, 我赶不上. *Can't you run ~er?* 你不能跑快一点儿吗? *He wants to get rich ~.* 他想很快地发财. *I don't know any get-rich-~ methods.* 我不知道任何迅速致富的方法. **2** (in compounds, for ~*ly*): (在复合词中, 代替 *quickly*): *a ~-firing gun.* 速射枪. ~·**ly** *adv* in a ~ manner; 迅速地; 快地: *You speak too ~ly.* 你说得太快. *He ~ly changed his clothes.* 他迅速地换衣服. ~·**ness** *n*

quicken /'kwɪkən; 'kwɪkən/ *vt, vi* [VP6A, 2A] **1** make or become quick(er): 使(较)快; 变为(较)快: *We ~ed our pace.* 我们加快脚步. *Our pace ~ed.* 我们的脚步加快了. **2** make or become more lively, vigorous or active: 使或变为更活泼, 有力或敏捷: *Good literature ~s the imagination.* 好的文学作品能激发想象力. *His pulse ~ed.* 他的脉搏加快. *The child ~ed in her womb,* She felt its movement for the first time. 她第一次感到胎儿在她的子宫中动.

quickie /'kwɪkɪ; 'kwɪkɪ/ *n* (colloq) sth made or done very quickly. (口) 仓促制成的物品.

quick·lime /'kwɪklaɪm; 'kwɪk,laɪm/ *n* unslaked lime. 生石灰. ⇨ **lime**[1](1).

quick·sand /'kwɪksænd; 'kwɪk,sænd/ *n* [C] (area of) loose, wet, deep sand which sucks down men, animals, vehicles, etc that try to cross it. 流沙(区).

quick·set /'kwɪkset; 'kwɪk,set/ *adj* (of hedges) formed of living plants, esp hawthorn, set in the ground to grow. (指树篱)插树做成的(尤指)插山楂树做成的.

quick·sil·ver /'kwɪksɪlvə(r); 'kwɪk,sɪlvə/ *n* [U] mercury. 水银; 汞.

quick·step /'kwɪkstep; 'kwɪk,step/ *n* ⇨ **quick**(1).

quid[1] /kwɪd; kwɪd/ *n* lump of chewing tobacco. 含在口中咀嚼的烟草块.

quid[2] /kwɪd; kwɪd/ *n* (GB, sl; *pl* unchanged) pound: (英俚, 复数不变)镑: *earning fifty quid (= £50) a week.* 每周赚五十镑.

quid pro quo /ˌkwɪd prəʊ 'kwəʊ; ˌkwɪdpro'kwo/ *n* (Lat) sth given or returned as the equivalent of sth else. (拉丁补偿物)交换物.

qui·esc·ent /kwaɪ'esnt; kwaɪ'esṇt/ *adj* at rest; motionless; passive. 安静的; 静止的; 不活动的. ~·**ly** *adv* **qui·esc·ence** /-sns; -sṇs/ *n*

quiet /'kwaɪət; 'kwaɪət/ *adj* (-**er,** -**est**) **1** with little or no movement or sound: 静止的; 宁静的: *a ~ sea;* 一片平静无浪的海; *a ~ evening;* 一个宁静的傍晚; ~ *footsteps.* 轻轻的脚步. **2** free from excitement, trouble, anxiety: 没有激动, 烦恼, 忧虑的; 心情宁静的: *live a ~ life in the country;* 在乡间过一种悠然自在的生活; *have a ~ mind;* 有宁静心境; ~ *times.* 平静的时代. **3** gentle; not rough (in disposition, etc): 温柔的; 娴静的: ~ *children;* 文静的孩子; *a ~ old lady.* 一位娴静的老妇. **4** (of colours) not bright. (指颜色)朴素的. **5** not open or revealed: 未予公开或泄露的; 隐密的: *harbouring ~ resentment.* 暗含愤懑. *keep sth ~,* keep it secret. 对某事保密. *on the ~,* (or, sl, 或俚, *on the qt* /ˌkjuː'tiː; ˌkjuˈtɪ/), secretly: 秘密地; 偷偷地: *have a drink on the ~;* 偷偷地喝杯酒; *tell sb sth on the ~,* in confidence. 秘密地将某事告诉某人. □ *n* [U] state of being ~ (all senses): 静止, 宁静, 娴静, 朴素, 隐密等的状态: *in the ~ of the night;* 在夜阑人静时; *have an hour's ~,* an hour free from activity, disturbance, etc; 享受一小时的清静; *live in peace and ~;* 生活于和平宁静中; *a period of ~ after an election,* free from all the activity, etc that usu accompanies an election. 选举后一段平静的日子. □ *vt, vi* (more usu often 常用 ~**en** /'kwaɪ ətn; 'kwaɪ ətṇ/) [VP6A, 15B, 2C] make or become ~: 使或变为平静: ~ *(en) a fretful child;* 让一个急躁的孩子平静下来; ~ *(en) sb's fears/suspicions.* 消除某人的恐惧(疑虑). *The city ~ed/~ened down after the political disturbances.* 在政治骚乱后这个城市平静下来. ~·**ly** *adv* ~·**ness** *n*

quiet·ism /'kwaɪ ɪtɪzəm; 'kwaɪətɪzṃ/ *n* [U] (as a form of religious mysticism) the abandoning of all desire, with a passive acceptance of whatever comes. 寂静主义(弃绝一切欲望, 消极接受发生的一切, 为一种神秘的宗教运动). **quiet·ist** /-ɪst; -ɪst/ *n* person who follows this principle. 寂静主义者.

quiet·ude /'kwaɪ ɪtjuːd US: -tuːd; 'kwaɪə,tjud/ *n* (liter) stillness; tranquillity. (文)寂静; 平静; 宁静.

qui·etus /kwaɪ'iːtəs; kwaɪ'itəs/ *n* (formal) final settlement (eg of a debt); release from life; extinction: (正式用语)解除; 清除(例如债务); 根绝生命; 灭绝; 死: *give sb his ~,* put an end to his life. 结束某人的生命.

quiff /kwɪf; kwɪf/ *n* lock of hair brushed up above the forehead. 梳在额上的鬈发.

quill /kwɪl; kwɪl/ *n* **1** ~ **(-feather),** large wing or tail feather; (hollow stem of) such a feather as formerly used for writing with: 翼或尾上的大羽毛, 羽茎; 翮; (昔时)此等羽茎做的笔: *a ~ pen.* 羽笔. **2** long, sharp, stiff spine of a porcupine. 豪猪的长而尖硬的刺.

quilt /kwɪlt; kwɪlt/ *n* thick bed-covering of two layers of cloth padded with soft material kept in place by crossed lines of stitches. 被; 棉袄. ⇨ **duvet.** □ *vt* make in the form of a ~, ie with soft material between layers of cloth: 制成被状 (即在两层布间加衬而软的东西): *a ~ed dressing-gown.* 中间衬有轻软之物的晨衣.

quin /kwɪn; kwɪn/ *n* (colloq abbr of) quintuplet. (口) 为 quintuplet 之略.

quince /kwɪns; kwɪns/ *n* (tree with) hard, acid, pear-shaped fruit, deep yellow when ripe, used in jams and jellies. 榅桲(为一种硬, 酸, 梨形水果, 成熟后为深黄色, 用于制果酱与冻子); 榅桲树.

quin·cen·tenary /ˌkwɪnsen'tiːnərɪ US: -'sentənerɪ; kwɪn'sɛntɪ,nɛrɪ/ *adj, n* (of the) 500th anniversary. 五百周年纪念(的).

quin·ine /kwɪ'niːn US: 'kwaɪnaɪn; 'kwaɪnaɪn/ *n* [U] bitter liquid made from the bark of a tree and used as a medicine for fevers and a flavouring in drinks. 奎宁; 金鸡纳(从一种树皮中提炼的苦味液体, 用为治疗发烧的药物及饮料中的调味物).

Quin·qua·ges·ima /ˌkwɪŋkwə'dʒesɪmə; ˌkwɪŋkwə'dʒɛsəmə/ *n* the Sunday before Lent. 四旬斋前的星期日.

quinsy /'kwɪnzɪ; 'kwɪnzɪ/ *n* [U] inflammation of the throat with discharge of pus from the tonsils. 扁桃腺炎; (脓性)咽门炎.

quin·tal /'kwɪntl; 'kwɪntḷ/ *n* unit of weight, 100 or 112 lb or 100 kilograms. 重量单位(100 或 112 磅, 或 100 公斤).

quin·tes·sence /kwɪn'tesns; kwɪn'tesṇs/ *n* **1** perfect example: 最完美的榜样: *the ~of virtue/politeness.* 美德(礼貌)的最佳榜样. **2** essential part. 精华; 本质.

quin·tet /kwɪn'tet; kwɪn'tet/ *n* (piece of music for) group of five players or singers: 五位演奏者或歌唱者组成之一组; 五重唱(曲); 五重奏(曲): *piano ~,* piano quartet and piano; 钢琴五重奏 (弦乐四重奏和钢琴合奏); *string ~,* string quartet and an additional cello or

viola; 弦乐五重奏 (弦乐四重奏再加上一大提琴或中音提琴); *wind ~*, bassoon, clarinet, flute, horn and oboe. 管乐 (巴松管、单簧管、长笛、喇叭和双簧管) 五重奏.

quin·tu·plet /ˈkwɪntjuːplet *US*: kwɪnˈtuːplɪt; ˈkwɪntəplɪt/ *n* (common abbr 通常略作 *quin*) one of five children at a birth. (usu *pl: two of the ~s* is commoner than *two ~s*). 五胞胎中之一个 (常用复数: two of the ~s 比 two ~s 常用).

quip /kwɪp; kwɪp/ *n* clever, witty or sarcastic remark or saying; quibble. 妙语; 警语; 讽刺语; 双关语; 遁辞. □ *vi* (**-pp-**) make ~s. 讥讽; 作妙语、警语、遁辞.

quire /ˈkwaɪə(r); kwaɪr/ *n* twenty-four sheets of writing-paper. 二十四张为一帖的写字纸: *buy/sell paper by the ~/in ~s.* 成帖 (二十四张) 买 (卖) 纸.

quirk /kwɜːk; kwɝk/ *n* habit or action peculiar to sb/ sth; foible: 特有的习性或行为; 怪癖: *One of his ~s is sleeping with his socks on.* 他的怪癖之一是穿着袜子睡觉.

quis·ling /ˈkwɪzlɪŋ; ˈkwɪzlɪŋ/ *n* person who co-operates with the authorities of an enemy country who are occupying his country. (与占领本国之敌人当局合作的) 卖国贼; 通敌者.

quit[1] /kwɪt; kwɪt/ *pred adj* free, clear: 免除的; 清除的: *We are well ~ of him*, fortunate to be rid of him. 我们幸而把他摆脱了.

quit[2] /kwɪt; kwɪt/ *vt, vi* (**-tt-**, *US* also **-t-**; *pt, pp* **~ted** or **~**) 1 [VP6A, 2A] go away from; leave: 离开; 离去; *I ~ted him in disgust.* 我怀着嫌恶离开了他. *We've had notice to ~*, a warning that we must give up the house we rent. 我们已得到必须搬家的通知. *I've given my secretary notice to ~*, told her that she must leave my service. 我已通知我的秘书离职. 2 [VP6A, 2] stop: 停止: *~ work when the siren sounds;* 汽笛响时停止工作; *grumbling.* 停止抱怨. *Q~ that!* Stop doing that! 停止做那事! 3 (old use: reflex) acquit: (旧用法) 尽(身)行动; 处己: *They ~ted themselves like heroes.* 他们的行动象英雄. **~·ter** *n* (colloq) person who does not finish what he has started, esp sth undertaken as a duty. (口) 半途而废之人; 虎头蛇尾之人; (尤指) 放弃职责者.

quite /kwaɪt; kwaɪt/ *adv* 1 completely; altogether: 完全地; 彻底地: *He has ~ recovered from his illness.* 他已完全康复. *I ~ agree/understand.* 我十分同意 (了解). *She was ~ alone.* 她非常孤独. *See that your watch is ~* (=exactly) *right*. 务必要把你的表对得非常准确. *That man is not ~ acceptable.* 那个人不大受欢迎. *It was ~* (= at least) *six weeks ago.* 至少是六周以前. *That's ~ another* (ie a completely different) *story.* 那完全是另外一回事. *~ the thing*, (colloq) what is considered correct, fashionable, etc: (口) 被认为是正确、流行等的东西: *These Italian dress materials are ~ the thing this summer.* 这些意大利衣料今夏很流行. 2 to a certain extent; more or less; in some degree: 到某种范围; 或多或少; 在某种程度内; 相当地: (preceding articles and *adj*) (放在冠词和形容词之前) *~ a good player.* 一个相当不错的运动员. *It's ~ warm today.* 今天的天气相当暖和. *He was ~ polite, but he wasn't ready to help me.* 他相当客气, 但他并不愿意帮助我. *She ~ likes him, but not enough to marry him.* 她相当喜欢他, 但还不到跟他结婚的程度. 3 really; truly: 真正地; 真实地: *They are both ~ young.* 他们俩都很年轻. *She's ~ a beauty.* 她真是个美人. *I believe they're ~ happy together.* 我认为他们在一起的确很幸福. 4 (used to indicate agreement, understanding, polite acquiescence): (用以表示同意、了解、礼貌的默许): A: *'It's a difficult situation.'* B: *'Q~ (so)!'* 甲: '那是个很棘手的局面.' 乙: '的确如此!' A: *'I'm so sorry; I'm afraid I've taken your seat.'* B: *'Oh, that's ~ all right.'* 甲: '真抱歉, 我恐怕坐在你的座位上了.' 乙: '哦, 没关系.'

quits /kwɪts; kwɪts/ *pred adj* **be ~ (with sb)**, be on even terms (by repaying a debt of money, punishment, etc): (在偿付债务、给予处罚等而) 与某人处于平等的关系; 不分胜负; 两相抵消: *We're ~ now.* 我们现在两不相欠, 不分胜负. *I'll be ~ with him*, will have my revenge. 我要向他报复. *call it ~*, agree that things are even,

that a dispute or quarrel may cease. 同意不分胜负而使争论或争吵结束. *double or ~*, ⇨ **double**[3](1).

quit·tance /ˈkwɪtns; ˈkwɪtn̩s/ *n* (document giving) release from an obligation or debt. 免除义务或债务 (之文件).

quiver[1] /ˈkwɪvə(r); ˈkwɪvɚ/ *n* archer's sheath for carrying arrows. 箭囊.

quiver[2] /ˈkwɪvə(r); ˈkwɪvɚ/ *vt, vi* [VP6A, 2A] (cause to) tremble slightly or vibrate: (使) 微震; 震颤: *a ~ing leaf.* 一片颤动的叶子. *The moth ~ed its wings.* 蛾颤动其翼. □ *n ~ing* sound or movement. 震颤的声音或动作.

qui vive /ˌkiː ˈviːv; ˌki ˈviv/ *n* (only in) (仅用于) **on the ~**, on the alert; watchful. 警戒中; 警觉的.

quix·otic /kwɪkˈsɒtɪk; kwɪkˈsɑtɪk/ *adj* generous, unselfish, imaginative, in a way that disregards one's own welfare. (不顾自己利益地) 慷慨, 不自私或富于幻想的. **quix·oti·cally** /-klɪ; -klɪ/ *adv*

quiz /kwɪz; kwɪz/ *vt* (**-zz-**) 1 [VP6A] ask questions of, as a test of knowledge. (对知识等之) 测验; 小考. 2 (archaic) make fun of; tease; stare at. (古) 戏弄; 嘲弄; 注视. □ *n* 1 general knowledge test; (broadcasting) game in which members of a panel undergo such a test. 一般知识测验; 小考; (广播) 猜谜或答问节目; 益智节目. *'~-master*, = question-master. 2 (archaic) amused, supercilious look. (古) 高兴而又傲慢的样子.

quiz·zi·cal /ˈkwɪzɪkl; ˈkwɪzɪkl/ *adj* questioning and teasing; mocking; 嘲弄的; 揶揄的: *a ~ smile.* 一种嘲弄的微笑. **~ly** /-klɪ; -klɪ/ *adv*

quoin /kɔɪn; kɔɪn/ *n* exterior angle in the brickwork or stonework of a building; cornerstone. (砖石等建筑物之) 突角; 外角; 角石; 隅石.

quoit /kɔɪt *US*: kwɔɪt; kwɔɪt/ *n* ring (of metal, rubber, rope) to be thrown at a peg so as to encircle it; *(pl)* this game (as often played on the deck of a ship). (掷环套桩游戏等中用之) 铁圈; 橡皮圈; 绳圈; (复) (在甲板等上玩的) 掷环套桩游戏; 套地圈.

Quonset /ˈkwɒnsɪt ˈkwɑnsɪt/ *n* **'~ (hut)**, (US) (P) large prefabricated hut, usu of corrugated iron, semicircular at each end and with a rounded roof, similar to, but much larger than, a Nissen hut. (美) (商标) 活动房屋 (一种很大的简单房屋, 通常用波状铁皮做成, 每端均呈半圆形, 有一圆形屋顶, 同 Nissen hut 形式相似, 但大得多).

quo·rum /ˈkwɔːrəm; ˈkwɔrəm/ *n* (*pl* **~s**) number of persons who must, by the rules, be present at a meeting (of a committee, etc) before its proceedings can have authority: 法定人数: *have/form a ~.* 够 (构成) 法定人数.

quota /ˈkwəʊtə; ˈkwotə/ *n* (*pl* **~s**) limited share, amount or number, esp a quantity of goods allowed to be manufactured, sold, etc or number, eg of immigrants allowed to enter a country: 配额; 限额 (尤指货物之制造、出售或移民入境之定额): *The village was unable to raise its ~ of men for the army.* 该村无法征集到所分配的壮丁额. *The ~ of immigrants for this year has already been filled.* 本年的移民额已满.

quo·ta·tion /kwəʊˈteɪʃn; kwoˈteʃən/ *n* 1 [U] quoting(1). 引述; 引用. 2 [C] sth quoted(1): 引用文; 引用语: *~s from Shakespeare.* 引自莎士比亚作品中的文句. *'~ marks*, the marks '''' or '' enclosing words quoted. 引号. ⇨ **App 8**. 参看附录八. 3 [C] statement of the current price of an article, etc: 物品等的时价; 行市; 行情表: *the latest ~s from the Stock Exchange.* 来自证券交易所的最近的行情. 4 [C] estimate of the cost of a piece of work: 报价单: *Can you give me a ~ for building a garage?* 你能不能给我一张建造一汽车房的报价单?

quote /kwəʊt; kwot/ *vt* 1 [VP6A, 14] **~ (from)**, repeat, write (words used by another); repeat or write words (from a book, an author, etc): 引述 (他人的话); 引用 (一书, 作者等): *~ a verse from the Bible.* 引用圣经中的一节; *~ the Bible.* 引述圣经. *Is Shakespeare the*

author most frequently ~d from? 莎士比亚是最常被引用的作家吗？ He is ~d as having said that there will be an election this autumn. 有人引述他的话说今秋将举行选举。 **2** [VP6A, 13A] give (a reference, etc) to support a statement: 提供(引证等)以支持一陈述: Can you ~ (me) a recent instance? 你能举出一个最近的例证吗？ **3** [VP6A] name, mention (a price): 提出(价格);报(价): This is the best price I can ~ you. 这是我能向你提出的最好的价钱了。 The shares are ~d on the Stock Exchange at 80p. 证券交易所公布的这些股票的价格是八十便士。 □n(colloq) sth ~d, esp sth witty, unusual, etc; quotation (2, 3, 4). (口)引述的话 (尤指富有机智、不平常者); 引用文; 行情

表;报价单。 **quot·able** /-əbl; -əbl/ adj that can be, or deserves to be, ~d. 能够或值得引用，引证，报价的。 **quo·ta·bil·ity** /ˌkwəʊtəˈbɪlətɪ; ˌkwotəˈbɪlɪtɪ/ n [U].

quoth /kwəʊθ; kwoθ/ vt (1st and 3rd person sing, pt only) (archaic) said: (古) 说(仅用于第一和第三人称, 单数, 过去式): ~ I/he/she. 我(他, 她)说过说。 Q~ the raven, 'Nevermore!' 大乌鸦说, '永远不再！'

quo·tid·ian /kwɒˈtɪdɪən; kwoˈtɪdɪən/ adj (of a fever) recurring every day. (指热病)每日发作的。

quo·tient /ˈkwəʊʃnt; ˈkwoʃənt/ n (maths) number obtained by dividing one number by another. (数学)商数;商。

R r

R, r /ɑː(r); ɑr/ (pl R's, r's) the eighteenth letter of the English alphabet. 英文字母之第十八个字母。 **the three R's**, reading, (w)riting and (a)rithmetic as the basis of an elementary education. 读、写、算(为初等教育之基础)。

rabbi /ˈræbaɪ; ˈræbaɪ/ n teacher of the Jewish law; (title of a) spiritual leader of a Jewish congregation. 犹太法学专家; 犹太教教士(的头衔);犹太人的)先生; 老师。 **rab·bini·cal** /rəˈbɪnɪkl; ræˈbɪnɪkl/ adj of ~s, their learning, writings, etc. 犹太法学专家的; 犹太法学专家之学问、著作等的。

rab·bit /ˈræbɪt; ˈræbɪt/ n **1** small burrowing animal of the hare family, brownish-grey in its natural state, black or white or bluish-grey in domestic varieties. 兔。 ⇨ the illus at small. 参看 small 之插图。 '~-hole /-burrow nn hole in which ~s live. 野兔洞; 野兔穴。 '~-hutch n wooden cage for domestic ~s. 兔笼; 兔栏。'~-punch n punch on the back of the neck. 打在颈背的一拳。 '~-warren n area of land full of ~-burrows; (fig) area of narrow, winding streets or rooms and passages. 野兔繁殖区; (喻)有很多狭窄弯曲街道之地区;有很多房间及走道之地区。 Welsh ~, = rarebit. **2** (colloq) poor performer at any game, esp tennis. (口)技术拙劣的运动员(尤指网球员)。 □ vi (-tt-) hunt ~s: 猎兔: go ~ting. 去猎兔。

rabble /ˈræbl; ˈræbl/ n **1** disorderly crowd; mob. 乌合之众; 暴民。'~-rousing adj inciting, designed to rouse, the passions of the mob: 激发或煽动暴民之情绪的: ~-rousing speeches / speakers. 煽动暴民之演说 (演说者)。 **2 the ~,** (contemptuous) the lower classes of the populace. (轻蔑语)下层民众。

Rab·elais·ian /ˌræbəˈleɪzɪən US: -ɪʒn; ˌræblˈeɪzɪən/ adj of or like the writings, marked by coarse humour and satire, of Rabelais, French writer. 法国幽默讽刺作家拉伯雷及其作品的; 拉伯雷式的; 作品粗俗幽默而又讽刺的。

rabid /ˈræbɪd; ˈræbɪd/ adj **1** affected with rabies; mad. 患恐水症的; 患狂犬病的; 疯狂的。 **2** furious; fanatical; violent: 狂怒的; 狂热的; 狂暴的: ~ hate; 痛恨; a ~ Conservative, one with extreme views, violently expressed. 一个思想偏激的保守主义者。

ra·bies /ˈreɪbiːz; ˈrebɪz/ n [U] infectious disease causing madness in wolves, dogs and other animals; hydrophobia. 恐水症; 狂犬病。

rac·coon = racoon.

race[1] /reɪs; res/ n [C] **1** contest or competition in speed, eg in running, swimming or to see who can finish a piece of work, or get to a certain place, first: 速度竞赛;比赛;赛跑: a 'horse-~; 赛马; a 'boat-~; 赛舟; a half-'mile ~! 半英里赛跑; run a ~ with sb; 同某人赛跑; a ~ for a train, an effort to catch it. 赶火车。 a ~ against time, an effort to do sth before a certain time or possible event. 努力在某特定时间或可能事件前做某事;争取时间。 '~-card n programme of a ~-meeting with a list of ~s and names of horses. (赛马大会中的)

赛马节目单。 '~-course n ground where horse-~s are run. 赛马场。 '~-horse n horse specially bred for running ~s. 供赛马用的马。'~-meeting n occasion when a number of horse-~s are held on a certain ~-course on a certain day, or a number of successive days: 赛马会: the Epsom ~-meeting. 在英国埃普瑟姆每年一度的赛马会。 **the ~,** n ~-meeting. 赛马大会。 **2** strong, fast current of water in the sea, a river, etc: (海、河等中的)急流: a 'mill-~, the channel carrying water to the wheel of a water-mill. 向水力磨坊之水车的水渠。 **3** (liter) course of the sun or moon, or (fig) of life: (文)太阳或月亮的运行;(喻)人生之路程: His ~ is nearly run, He is near the end of his life. 他的人生路程快走完了 (他快走到生命尽头了)。 □ vi, vt **1** [VP2A, C, 3A, 4A] ~ (with/against sb), compete in speed, have a ~; move at full speed: 竞赛速度; 赛跑; 全速行进: ~ along; 快步前行; ~ over the course; 在跑道中赛跑; boys racing home from school; 从学校跑回家的孩子们; ~ to see what is happening; 跑着去看发生了什么事情; ~ against time; 争取时间; ~ with sb for a prize. 为一奖品同某人竞赛。 I'll ~ you home, (colloq) ~ against you to get home first. (口) 我要和你比赛谁先到家。 **2** [VP2A, 6A] own or train horses for racing and take part in ~-meetings; cause (a horse) to compete in ~s: 拥有或训练赛马用之马, 并参加赛马大会; 以赛马为业; 使(马)参加赛: He ~s at all the big meetings. 他参加所有大规模的赛马会。 Are you going to ~ your horse at Newmarket next week? 你要让你的马参加下周在纽马基特的赛马会吗？ **3** [VP6A, 15A] cause (sth or sb) to move at full speed: 使(某物或某人)全速行进: He ~d me to the station in his car. 他用他的车子全速把我送到车站。 The Government ~d the bill through the House, pushed it through the House of Commons at great speed. 政府使该法案在下议院很快地通过。 Don't ~ your engine, cause the engine to run very fast when it is not doing any work. 不要快速空转引擎。 [VP2A] Don't let the engine ~. 不要让这引擎空转太快。 **rac·ing** n [U] (esp) the hobby, sport or profession of running horses or motor-cars in races: (尤指)赛马或赛车的嗜好、运动或职业: a 'racing man; 赛马 (车)迷; keep a racing stable; 养有一群比赛用的马; a 'racing car/yacht, designed for racing. 竞赛用的跑车(快艇)。 a 'racing horse, boat, car, etc designed for racing. 比赛用之马、舟、汽车等。

race[2] /reɪs; res/ n **1** [C, U] any of several subdivisions of mankind sharing certain physical characteristics, esp colour of skin, colour and type of hair, shape of eyes and nose: 种族; 人种: the Caucasian / Mongolian / Negroid ~; 高加索(蒙古、黑色)人种; people of mixed ~; 具有混血种的人; people of the same ~ but different culture. 种族相同而文化不同的人们。 **2** [C] (used loosely for) group of people having a common culture, history and / or language: (泛指)一群有共同文化、历史和(或)语言的人; 民族: the ˌAnglo-'Saxon ~; 盎格鲁·撒克逊人; the 'German ~. 日耳曼民族。 **3** (attrib) of, between,

~s(1, 2): (用作定语)种族的; 种族之间的: *Can ~ relations be improved by legislation?* 立法能改善种族关系吗? **4** [U] ancestry; descent: 祖先; 祖籍; 世系: *a man of ancient and noble ~.* 一个古老贵族的后代。**5** [C] main division of any living creatures: 任何生物的种类; 族类: *the human ~;* mankind; 人类; *the 'feathered ~,* (joc) birds; (谑)鸟类; *the 'finny ~,* (joc) fish. (谑)鱼类。

ra·ceme /'ræsi:m *US:* reɪ-; reˈsim/ *n* (botany) flower cluster with the separate flowers on short equal stalks springing from a main central stem, the lowest flowers opening first. (植物)串状花; 总状花序。

ra·cial /'reɪʃl; 'reʃəl/ *adj* relating to **race**(1, 2): 种族的; 人种上的: ~ *conflict / hatred / pride;* 种族的冲突(仇恨, 自尊心); ~ *minorities;* 少数民族; 少数种族: ~ *discrimination.* 种族歧视。**~·ly** /-ʃlɪ; -ʃəlɪ/ *adv* **~·ism** /-ʃəlɪzəm; -ʃəl,ɪzəm/ *n* [U] tendency to ~ conflict; antagonism between different races; belief that one's own race is superior. 种族的冲突; 种族仇视; 种族偏见; 种族主义: 种族优越感。**~·ist** /-ɪst;-ɪst/ *n* person who stirs up ~ism. 煽动种族冲突者; 种族主义者。

rac·ily, raci·ness ⇨ **racy.**

rac·ism /'reɪsɪzəm; 'resɪzəm/ *n* racialism; belief that human abilities are determined by race. 种族主义; 种族偏见; 种族优越感。**rac·ist** /-ɪst; -ɪst/ *n* racialist; believer in racialism or racism. 种族主义者; 种族偏见者。

rack¹ /ræk; ræk/ *n* **1** wooden or metal framework for holding food (esp hay) for animals (in a stable or in the fields). 在马厩或田野中)盛动物饲料(尤指干草)的木质或金属架; 饲草架。**2** framework with bars, pegs, etc for holding things, hanging things on, etc: 挂物架; 放物架: *a 'plate~;* 盘碟架; *a 'hat~;* 帽架; *a 'tool~.* 工具架。**3** shelf over the seats of a railway-carriage, air-liner, bus, etc for light luggage: (火车, 客机, 公共汽车等座位上放轻便行李之)行李架: *a 'luggage~.* 行李架。**4** rod, bar or rail with teeth or cogs into which the teeth on a wheel (or pinion) fit (as used on special railways up a steep hillside): 齿条; 齿轨 (伸轮上或小齿轮上之齿嵌于其中, 如爬陡山坡的特殊铁轨上使用者): ⇨ the illus at **gear**. 参看 gear 之插图。**'~-railway** *n* one with a third rail with cogs between the two rails on which the wheels of trains are supported. 齿轨铁道 (在承载火车轮的两铁轨间设有齿的第三条铁轨。)

rack² /ræk; ræk/ *n* (usu 通常作 **the ~**) instrument of torture consisting of a frame with rollers to which a person's wrists and ankles were tied so that his joints were stretched when the rollers were turned. 拷问台 (一种刑具, 架上有滚轮, 受刑者之腕与踝缚于滚轮上, 轮转动时, 其关节即被拉扯)。**on the ~,** undergoing severe suffering (physical or mental). 受(身心的)极端痛苦。□ *vt* [VP6A, 15A] **1** torture by placing on the ~; (of a disease or of mental agony) inflict torture on: 置于拷问台上折磨; 指疾病或精神痛苦)使痛苦: ~*ed with pain;* 痛苦难忍; *a ~ing headache;* 剧烈的头疼; ~*ed with a bad cough;* 为很厉害的咳嗽所苦; ~*ed by remorse.* 悔恨交加。**2** ~ *one's brains (for),* make great mental efforts (for, in order to find, an answer, method, etc). (为一答案、方法等) 绞尽脑汁。**3** oppress (tenants) with excessive rent. 向(租户)索取过高的租金。Hence, 由此产生, **'~-rent** *n* exorbitant rent. 过高的租金。

rack³ /ræk; ræk/ *n* [U] (liter) drifting cloud. (文)流云; 飞云; 浮云。

rack⁴ /ræk; ræk/ *n* (only in) (仅用于) *go to ~ and ruin,* fall into a ruined state. 毁坏; 朽坏; 衰败。

racket¹ /'rækɪt; 'rækɪt/ *n* **1** (*sing* only, with *indef art* or [U]) uproar, loud noise: (仅用单数, 与不定冠词连用, 或为不可数名词) 喧嚣; 闹声: *What a ~!* 多么大的吵闹声! *The drunken men in the street kicked up no end of a ~,* were very noisy and boisterous. 那些醉汉在街上大鬧大闹。**2** [U] (time of) great social activity, hurry and bustle: 繁忙的社交活动; 繁忙; 繁忙的社交: *the ~ of a politician's life.* 从政者生活的繁忙。**3** [C] (colloq) dishonest way of getting money (by deceiving or threa-

tening people, selling worthless goods, etc): (口) 诈骗勒索: *be in on a ~,* have a share in it, be one of those who make money from it. 参与诈骗勒索。**4** [C] ordeal or trying experience. 严格的考验; 痛苦或难熬的经验。**stand the ~, (a)** come successfully through a test (of sth). 成功地通过(某事物)的考验。**(b)** accept, be responsible for, the consequences (of sth); take the blame: pay the costs. 接受(某事的)后果; 对(某事物)负责; 承担过错; 付帐。□ *vi* [VP2A, C] ~ about; make a ~(1, 2). 喧闹; 过繁忙的社交生活: **~·eer** /,rækə'tɪə(r); ,rækɪt'ɪr/ *n* person who is engaged in a ~(3). 诈骗者; 勒索者。**~·eer·ing** *n* [U] the actions of ~eers. 诈骗、勒索者的行为。

racket², rac·quet /'rækɪt; 'rækɪt/ *n* **1** light bat used for hitting the ball in tennis, badminton, etc. (网球、羽毛球等之)球拍。⇨ the illus at **badminton, tennis.** 参看 badminton, tennis 之插图。**2** (*pl*) ball-game for two or four players in a court with four walls. (复)二或四人在四面有围墙的球场玩的一种网球戏。

rac·on·teur /,rækɒn'tɜ:(r); ,rækɑn'tɝ/ *n* person who tells anecdotes or stories with skill and wit: 善于讲逸事或故事的人: *a good ~.* 一个说故事的高手。

rac·oon, rac·coon /rə'ku:n *US:* ræ-; ræ'kun/ *n* small, flesh-eating animal of N America with a bushy, ringed tail; (US) its fur. 浣熊 (北美产, 食肉, 有多毛而呈环状花纹之尾巴); (美)浣熊之毛皮。

rac·quet = racket².

racy /'reɪsɪ; 'resɪ/ *adj* (**-ier, -iest**) **1** (of speech or writing) vivid; spirited; vigorous: (指言词或写作)生动的; 活泼的; 有力的: *a ~ style.* 活泼而流畅的风格。**2** having strongly marked qualities: 有显著特征的; 道地的: *a ~ flavour.* 道地的口味。~ *of the soil,* showing traces of origin; direct, lively and stimulating. 显出原有之特征的; 活泼而富刺激的。**rac·ily** /-ɪlɪ; -ɪlɪ/ *adv* **raci·ness** *n*

radar /'reɪdɑ:(r); 'redɑr/ *n* [U] (the use of) apparatus that indicates on a screen (by means of radio echoes) solid objects that come within its range, used (eg by pilots of ships, aircraft or spacecraft) in fog or darkness and which gives information about their position, movement, speed, etc: 雷达 (一种无线电装置, 借无线电回波而在一荧光屏上显示出其探测范围的物体; 船、飞机或太空船之驾驶员在大雾或黑夜中使用, 借以测知方位、动向、速度等)雷达之使用: *follow the flight of an aircraft by ~;* 借雷达追踪一飞机之飞行; (attrib)(用作定语) *~ installation;* 雷达装置; *on the '~ screen.* 在雷达荧幕上。

radial /'reɪdɪəl; 'redɪəl/ *adj* relating to a ray, rays or a radius; (of spokes in a bicycle wheel, etc) from a centre; arranged like rays or radii. 光线的; 半径的; (指自行车轮子的辐条)辐射状的; 象光线或半径般排列的。□ *adj* (**tyre**), tyre designed (by having the material inside the tyre wrapped in a direction ~ to the hub of the wheel) to give more grip on road surfaces, esp when cornering or when roads are wet. 防滑轮胎; 加力轮胎。**~·ly** /-ɪəlɪ; -ɪəlɪ/ *adv*

radi·ant /'reɪdɪənt; 'redɪənt/ *adj* **1** sending out rays of light; shining: 光芒四射的; 光辉灿烂的: *the ~ sun.* 光辉灿烂的太阳。**2** (of a person, his looks, eyes) bright; showing joy or love: (指人、其面容、眼睛)明亮的; 流露喜悦或热情的: *a ~ face;* 一张容光焕发的脸; *the ~ figures in the paintings of Renoir.* 雷诺瓦绘画上喜气洋洋的人物。**3** (phys) transmitted by radiation: (物理)辐射的: ~ *heat / energy.* 辐射热(能)。**~·ly** *adv* **radi·ance** /-əns; -əns/ *n* [U] ~ quality. 发光; 闪耀; 辐射。

radi·ate /'reɪdɪeɪt; 'redɪ,et/ *vt, vi* **1** [VP6A] send out rays of (light or heat): 发射(光或热): *a stove that ~s warmth;* 一个发射热力的火炉; (fig) spread abroad, send out: (喻)散发; 发出: *a woman who ~s happiness;* 一个洋溢着快乐的妇人; *an orator who ~s enthusiasm for the cause he supports.* 一个对其所支持的主义满怀激情的演

说家。**2** [VP2A, 3A] ~ *(from)*, come or go out in rays; show: 射出; 表现: *heat that ~s from a stove / a fireplace*; 从火炉(壁炉)散发出来的热; *the happiness that ~s from her eyes*. 从她眼睛里流露出来的快乐。**3** [VP2A, 3A] ~ *(from)*, spread out like radii: 辐射; 向各方伸展: *the avenues that ~ from the Arc de Triomphe in Paris.* 在巴黎以凯旋门为中心向四方伸展的街道。

radi·ation /ˌreɪdɪ'eɪʃn; ˌredɪ'eʃən/ *n* [U] radiating; the sending out of energy, heat, etc in rays. 发射; 放射: 能、热等之辐射。 '~ **sickness**, illness caused by gamma rays or rays from radioactive dust (as from nuclear weapons). 辐射症(由伽马射线或核武器等之辐射尘所引起的病症)。**2** [C] sth radiated: 放射出之物; 辐射线; 辐射能: *~s emitted by an X-ray apparatus.* X 光装置所放射出来的辐射线。

radi·ator /'reɪdɪeɪtə(r); 'redɪˌetɚ/ *n* [C] **1** apparatus for radiating heat, esp heat from steam or hot water supplied through pipes or from electric current. 暖气炉; 散热器。**2** device for cooling the cylinders of the engine of a motor-vehicle: 汽车引擎的冷却器; 水箱: *This car has a fan-cooled ~.* 这部汽车有一个由风扇散热的冷却器。⇨ the illus at **motor**. 参看 motor 之插图。

rad·ical /'rædɪkl; 'rædɪkl/ *adj* **1** of or from the root or base; fundamental: 根本的; 基本的: ~ (= thorough and complete) *reforms*; 彻底而完全的改革; *make ~ changes in a scheme.* 对一个计划做彻底的改变。**2** (politics) favouring fundamental reforms; advanced in opinions and policies: (政治)赞成根本改革的; 激进的; 意见和政策上急进的: *a member of the R~ Party.* 激进党党员。**3** (maths) relating to the root of a number or quantity: (数学)根的: *the ~ sign* (√). 根号(√)。□ *n* **1** person with ~ (2) opinions; member of the R~ Party. 激进份子; 激进党党员。**2** (maths) the ~ quantity expressed as the root of another. (数学)根号; 根数; 根。~**ly** /-klɪ; -klɪ/ *adv* ~**ism** /-kəlɪzəm; -kl,ɪzm/ *n* beliefs and policies of ~ (2) people. 激进主义。~**ize** /-kəlaɪz; -kl,aɪz/ *vt* [VP6A] cause to become ~ (2). 使激进。

rad·icle /'rædɪkl; 'rædɪkl/ *n* embryo root (eg of a pea or bean). (豌豆或豆子的)幼根; 胚根。

radii /'reɪdiaɪ; 'redɪˌaɪ/ ⇨ **radius**.

radio /'reɪdɪəʊ; 'redɪˌo/ *n* (pl ~**s** /-dɪəʊz; -dɪˌoz/) **1** [U] (communication by) use of electromagnetic waves without a connecting wire: 无线电: *send a message by ~.* 以无线电传递消息。**2** [U] broadcasting by this means: 无线电广播: *hear something on the ~*; 在无线电广播中听到某消息; *talk over the ~*; 在无线电广播中讲话; (attrib) (用作定语) *the ~ programme.* 无线电广播节目。**3** [C] (~**-(set)**, apparatus, eg on ships, aircraft, for transmitting and receiving ~ messages or (as in the home) for receiving sound broadcast programmes: (船、飞机等的)无线电收发报机; (家庭等的)收音机: *a portable ~*; 手提式收音机; *the latest types of ~s / ~-sets.* 最新型的收音机。**4** '~ **beacon**, station for transmitting signals to help aircraft pilots. 无线电导航信标(发信号以协助飞机驾驶员)。'~ **beam**, beam of ~ signals from a ~ beacon. 无线电领航信号, 无线电射束。'~ **frequency**, frequency between 10 kilocycles per second to 300,000 megacycles per second. 射(电)频(率)(自每秒十千周至每秒三十万兆周)。'~ **link**, (sound broadcasting) programme in which speakers in widely separated towns are linked by the same programme. (广播)相距甚远城市的不同演讲者, 在同一节目中以无线电联系起来的一种节目, 联播讲演。

radio- /'reɪdɪəʊ; ˌredɪo/ *pref* of rays or radium. 光的; 镭的。'~ **'ac·tive** *adj* (of such metals as radium and uranium) having atoms that break up and, in so doing, send out rays in the form of electrically charged particles capable of penetrating opaque bodies and of producing electrical effects: (指镭和铀等金属)有放射性的; 有辐射能的 (此等金属之原子具分裂性, 在分裂时射出带电微粒之射线,能穿透不透明体,并产生电效应):~*active*

carbon; 放射性碳; 辐射碳; ~*active dust*, dust (eg as carried by winds) from explosions of nuclear bombs, etc; 放射尘 (由核弹等爆炸所产生之尘 由风带往他处); ~*active waste*, waste material from nuclear power stations, etc. (由核能发电厂等排出的) 放射性废料。Hence, 由此产生, '~·**ac'tiv·ity** *n* [U]. '~·**gram** *n* [U] (abbr of) ~-gramophone. 为 ~-gramophone 之略。**2** X-ray photograph. X 光照片。'~·**gramophone** *n* combined ~ receiver and record-player. 收音电唱两用机。'~·**graph** *n* X-ray photograph. X 光照片。ˌ**radi·'ogra·phy** *n* [U] production of X-ray photographs. X 光摄影。ˌ**radi·'ogra·pher** *n* person trained to take ~graphs. X 光摄影师。'~·**'iso·tope** *n* ~active form of an element, used in medicine, industry, etc to study the path and speed of substances through bodies and objects. 放射性同位素 (一元素的放射性之形式, 用于医学, 工业等方面, 以研究物质穿过人体及物体的途径与速度)。'~·**lo'cation** *n* radar. 无线电定位; 雷达。ˌ**radi·ol·ogy** /ˌreɪdɪ'ɒlədʒɪ; ˌredɪ'ɑlədʒɪ/ *n* [U] scientific study of X-rays and other radiation (esp as used in medicine).放射学 (尤指医学中) 放射科科。ˌ**radi'ologist** *n* expert in ~logy. 放射线专家。'~·**'telescope** *n* apparatus that detects stars by means of ~ waves from outer space and tracks spacecraft. (借太空无线电波侦察星球和追踪太空船的)无线电望远镜。'~·**'therapy** *n* treatment of disease by means of X-rays or other forms of radiation, eg of heat. X 光治疗法; 放射疗法。'~·**'therapist** *n* expert in ~-therapy. 放射疗法专家。

a radio telescope

rad·ish /'rædɪʃ; 'rædɪʃ/ *n* salad plant with a white or red edible root. (一种做生菜的)小萝卜。

radium /'reɪdɪəm; 'redɪəm/ *n* [U] radioactive metallic element (symbol **Ra**) used in the treatment of some diseases, eg cancer. 镭(放射性金属元素, 符号为 Ra, 用以治疗某些疾病, 如癌)。

radius /'reɪdɪəs; 'redɪəs/ *n* (pl ~**dii** /-dɪaɪ; -dɪˌaɪ/) **1** (length of a) straight line from the centre of a circle or sphere to any point on the circumference or surface. 半径。⇨ the illus at **circle**. 参看 circle 之插图。**2** circular area measured by its ~: 以半径度量之圆形面积: *The police searched all the fields and woods within a ~ of two miles.* 警方搜查半径两英里范围内所有的田野和森林。**3** (anat) outer of the two bones in the forearm. (解剖)桡骨。⇨ the illus at **skeleton**. 参看 skeleton 之插图。

raf·fia /'ræfɪə; 'ræfɪə/ *n* [U] fibre from the leaf-stalks of a kind of palm-tree, used for making baskets, hats, mats, etc. 酒椰纤维 (由酒椰之叶柄做成, 用于制篮子, 帽子, 席子等)。

raff·ish /'ræfɪʃ; 'ræfɪʃ/ *adj* disreputable; dissipated; 声名狼藉的; 放荡的: *a ~ young man*; 一个声名狼藉的年轻人; *an ~ air.* 有一副放荡的样子。~**ly** *adv*

raffle /'ræfl; 'ræfl/ *n* [C] sale of an article by a lottery, often for a charitable purpose: (常为慈善目的之)抽签售卖: *buy '~ tickets / tickets for a ~.* 购买抽签售物的

彩券。□ vt [VP6A, 15B] ~ sth (off), sell in a ~: 以抽签法售卖: ~ (off) a motor-scooter. 以抽签法卖一部低座小摩托车。

raft /rɑːft US: ræft; ræft/ n **1** number of tree trunks fastened together to be floated down a river. (绑在一起伸顺流漂下的)一排树干; 木排。**2** ('life-)~, flat, floating structure of rough timber, barrels, etc as a substitute for a boat or for the use of swimmers: (用原木、木桶等做成的)筏; 救生筏: The sailors got away from the wrecked ship on a ~. 水手们乘救生筏离开失事的船。□ vt, vi **1** [VP6A, 15A, B] carry on a ~; cross (a stream) on a ~. 以筏送过; 乘筏过(河)。**2** [VP2C] go on a ~: 乘筏航行: ~ down the stream. 乘筏顺流而下。~**er**, **'rafts·man** /-mən; -mən/ (pl -men) nn man who ~s timber. 送筏木排者, 放排工。

rafter /'rɑːftə(r) US: 'ræf-; 'ræftər/ n one of the sloping beams of the framework on which the tiles or slates of a roof are supported. 椽。**raft·ered** /'rɑːftəd US: ræf-; 'ræftəd/ adj provided with ~s; 装有椽的。a ~ed roof, (esp) one of which the ~s are visible from beneath, eg in a hall that has no ceiling. 椽架屋顶(尤指屋子有天花板, 从内部可以望见椽木者)。

rag¹ /ræg; ræg/ n [C] **1** odd bit of cloth: 零头布; 碎布: a rag to polish the car with. 用来擦车的碎布。**2** piece of old and torn cloth; (pl) old and torn clothes: 破布; (复)破旧衣服: dressed in rags; 穿着破衣; My coat was worn to rags. 我的外套破烂不堪了。the **'rag trade**, (sl) the business of making and selling clothes. (俚)制造及售卖成衣。**'glad rags**, ⇨ **glad.** **3** scrap; irregular piece. 碎屑, 一点点; 不规则的碎片。**'rag-bag** n **(a)** bag in which scraps of fabric are stored. 储放碎布或破布的袋子。**(b)** motley collection; confused mass. 杂乱的一堆; 杂凑。**(c)** (sl) untidily dressed person. (俚)衣着不整之人。**4** (pl) old, waste pieces of cloth from which a good quality of paper ('rag paper) is made. (复)做纸浆用的旧布片(可制成上等纸, 称为 rag paper)。**5** (used contemptuously for a) newspaper: (含轻蔑意义)报纸: Why do you read that worthless rag? 你为什么看那种没有价值的报纸?

rag² /ræg; ræg/ vt (-gg-) [VP6A] (colloq) tease; play practical jokes on; be noisy and boisterous. (口)揶揄; 戏弄; 喧闹。□ n (colloq) rough, noisy disturbance; carnival with side-shows, a procession of amusing floats¹(3), etc, eg as held by college students. (口) 粗鲁而喧闹的滋扰; (包括杂耍、花车游行等的)狂欢会(例如大学生所举行者)。**'rag-day**, day (usu annually) on which students hold a rag, and often collect money for charity. (通常一年一度的)学生狂欢会(通常为了募集慈善基金)。

raga·muf·fin /'rægəmʌfɪn; 'rægə,mʌfɪn/ n dirty, disreputable person, esp a small boy dressed in rags. 肮脏而名誉不佳的人; (尤指)衣着褴褛的小男孩。

rage /reɪdʒ; redʒ/ n **1** [C, U] (outburst of) furious anger; violence: 盛怒(之暴发); 狂暴: livid with ~; 气得脸色发青; the ~ of the sea, its violence during a storm 怒海澎湃, 勃然大怒。**2** [C] ~ (for), strong desire: (对某事物之)强烈欲望: He has a ~ for collecting butterflies. 他极好搜集蝴蝶。**be (all) the ~**, (colloq) wish for which there is a widespread but temporary enthusiasm; sth very fashionable: (口)风靡一时之物; 极为流行之物: The new musical comedy at Drury Lane is all the ~. 特鲁利街戏院新推出的喜歌剧风靡一时。These white handbags from Italy are (all) the ~ this summer. 这些由意大利进口的白色手提包今年夏季甚为风行。□ vi [VP 2A, C] be violently angry (of storms, etc) be violent: 发怒; (指暴风雨等)狂暴: He ~d and fumed against me for not letting him have his own way. 他对我竟怒因为我没有让他自行其道。The storm ~d all day. 暴风雨竟日肆虐不已。The wind ~d round the house. 风在房屋四周狂吹。Flu ~d through the country. 流行性感冒在全国各地猖獗。

rag·ged /'rægɪd; 'rægɪd/ adj **1** (with clothes) badly

torn or in rags: 衣服破烂的; 衣衫褴褛的: a ~ coat; 一件破旧外套; a ~ old man. 衣衫褴褛的老人。**2** having rough or irregular edges or outlines or surfaces: 边缘、外形或表面不平滑或参差不齐的: a dog with a ~ coat of hair: 一身毛长短不齐的狗; a sleeve with ~ edges / which is ~ at the cuff; 袖口破烂不齐的袖子; ~ rocks; 嶙峋之石; ~ clouds driven by the gale. 被狂风吹飘的残云。**3** (of work, etc) imperfect; lacking smoothness or uniformity: (指工作等)不完美的; 不流畅的; 不一致的: a ~ performance, eg of a theatrical rôle, a piece of music. 杂乱的表演; 不流畅的音乐演奏。~**·ly** adv ~**·ness** n

rag·lan /'ræglən; 'ræglən/ n (usu attrib) sweater or coat without shoulder seams (so that the seams of the sleeves go up from the armpit to the neckline). (通常用作定语)一种无肩缝的毛线衫或大衣(两袖连到颈部)。

ra·gout /'ræguː US: ræ'guː; ræ'gu/ n (dish of) meat and vegetable stew. (一道)浓味蔬菜炖肉。

rag·tag /'rægtæg; 'ræg,tæg/ n (the) , ~ and 'bobtail, the riff-raff; disreputable people. 流氓; 贱民; 声名狼藉之辈。

rag·time /'rægtaɪm; 'ræg,taɪm/ n [U] (1920's) popular music and dance of US Negro origin, the accent of the melody falling just before the regular beat of the accompaniment. 繁音拍子(起源于美国黑人的一种流行音乐和舞蹈, 旋律中的重音落在伴奏的规则拍子前, 流行于二十世纪二十年代); 一种早期的爵士乐。

rah /rɑː; rɑ/ int hurrah (as used, in US) in cheers at a sports meeting, etc: 呀! (运动会等中的)欢呼声: Rah, rah, rah! 加油! 加油! 加油!

raid /reɪd; red/ n **1** surprise attack made by troops, ship(s) or aircraft: (部队、舰艇或飞机所作之)袭击; 突袭: make a ~ upon the enemy's camp; 突出敌军军营; killed in an 'air-~ (attack by aircraft). 在空袭中丧生。**2** sudden visit by police to make arrests: (警察的)突然搜查: 搜捕: a ~ on a gambling den. 警察搜查赌窟。**3** sudden attack or inroad for the purpose of taking money: 抢劫: 盗用: a ~ on a bank by armed men; 持械暴徒抢劫银行; a ~ on the bank's reserves, when they are to be used by the directors for expansion, etc. 盗用银行之储备金(如董事们为扩张业务等等所作之用)。□ vt, vi [VP6A, 2A] make a ~ on or into; carry out a ~: 表击; 侵入; 抢劫: Boys have been ~ing my orchard, visiting it to steal fruit. 孩子们老跑到我的果园偷果子。~**er** n person, ship, aircraft, etc that makes a ~. 表击之人, 舰艇, 飞机等; 侵入者。

rail¹ /reɪl; rel/ n **1** horizontal or sloping bar or rod or continuous series of bars or rods, of wood or metal, as part of a fence, as a protection against contact or falling over: 横杆; 横栏: wooden ~s round a field; 围着一块地的木栏杆; metal ~s round a monument; 围绕一纪念碑的铁栏杆; build a ~ fence. 装一围栏。He was leaning on the ~s, looking over the water. 他斜倚着船的栏杆眺望水面。One of the horses was forced to the ~s, (in a horse-race) pressed so close to the ~s of the race-course that it was at a disadvantage. (赛马中)一匹马被挤近围栏而无法快跑。**2** similar bar or rod placed for things to hang on: 挂东西用的横杆: a 'towel-~, eg at the side of a wash-basin. 挂毛巾的杆子。**3** steel bar or continuous line of such bars, laid on the ground as one side of a track for trains or trams: 铁轨; (复)铁路: a ~ strike, of railway workers. 铁路工人罢工。**off the ~s**, (of a train) off the track; (fig) out of order, out of control; disorganized; (colloq) eccentric; neurotic mad. (指火车)出轨; (喻)失灵的; 失常的; 失去控制的; 杂乱无章的; (口)怪诞的; 神经过敏的; 疯狂的。**'~·road** n (US)(美)= ~way。~ ~ it, (colloq) [VP15A, B] rush (sb or sth) unfairly (to, into, through, etc): (口)使(某人或某事物)草草了事; 使(议案等)草草通过(与 to, into, through 等连用): ~road a bill through Congress. 仓促将一议案在国会中草草通过。**'~·way** n **1** road or track laid with ~s on which trains run: 铁路: build a new ~way.

修筑一条新铁路。**2** system of such tracks, with the locomotives, cars, wagons, etc and the organization controlling the system: 铁路系统(包括铁路、机车、车厢、货车等,以及管理铁路之机构): *work on the ~way.* 在铁路局工作。*The ~ways in many countries are owned by the State.* 在许多国家,铁路为国有。**3** (attrib) (用作定语) '~*way station / bridge / carriage / engineer / contractors / transport, etc.* 火车站(铁路桥梁; 火车车厢; 铁路工程师; 铁路承建者; 铁路运输等)。'~-*car* n single coach or car, with its own motive power, used on a ~way. (由本身动力在铁轨上行驶的)单节机动车。'~·**head** n farthest point reached by a ~way under construction. 修筑中的铁路的最远点。[VP6A, 15B]~ *off / in,* put ~s(1) round; shut(in, off) separate, by means of ~s(1): 以栏杆围起来, 以栏杆隔开: ~ *off a piece of ground;* 以栏杆围起一块地; *fields that are ~ed off from the road.* 以栏杆同道路隔离的田地。~·**ing** n [C] (often *pl*) fence made with ~s, eg as a protection at the side of a series of steps. (常用复数)(楼梯等的)栏杆;扶手;围栏。

rail[2] /reɪl; rel/ *vi* [VP2A, 3A] ~ *(at/against),* (liter) find fault; utter reproaches: (文)挑剔;抱怨;责骂: *It's no use our ~ing at fate.* 抱怨命运没有用。~·**ing** n [U] act of finding fault, complaining, protesting, etc; (*pl*) utterances of this kind. 挑剔;抱怨;抗议(等);(复)挑剔,抱怨,抗议之言辞。

rail·lery /'reɪlərɪ; 'relərɪ/ n [U] (liter) good-humoured teasing; [C] (*pl* -**ries**) instance of this. (文)善意的嘲弄;此种嘲弄之实例。

rai·ment /'reɪmənt; 'remənt/ n [U] (liter) clothing. (文)衣服。

rain[1] /reɪn; ren/ n **1** [U] condensed moisture of the atmosphere falling in separate drops; fall of such drops: 雨;下雨: *It looks like ~, as if there will be a fall of ~.* 好象要下雨的样子。*Don't go out in the ~.* 不要冒着雨出去。*Come in out of the ~.* 快进来,不要在外面淋雨。*The farmers want ~.* 农民需要雨。~ *or shine,* whether the weather is wet or sunny. 无论晴雨;晴雨无阻。'~·**bow** /'reɪnbəʊ; 'ren,bo/ n arch containing the colours of the spectrum, formed in the sky opposite the sun when ~ is falling or when the sun shines on mist or spray. 虹。'~-**bow trout,** food fish with reddish bands and black spots. 虹鳟鱼。'~-**coat** n light coat of waterproof or tightly-woven material. 雨衣。'~-**drop** n single drop of ~. 雨点。'~·**fall** n amount of ~ falling within a given area in a given time, (eg measured in cm of depth per annum). 雨量 (指某一地区在某一期间内的降雨量目, 例如以每年多少公分深量测之)。'~·**forest** n hot, wet forest in tropical areas, where ~fall is heavy and there is no dry season. (热带的)雨林。'~-**gauge** n instrument for measuring ~fall. 雨量器; 雨量计。'~-**proof** adj able to keep ~ out. 防雨的。'~-**water** n water that has fallen as ~ and has been collected as ~ (contrasted with *well-water,* etc); soft water. 雨水 (与well-water等相对); 软水。~ *a* + *adj* + ~, fall or shower of ~: 落雨; 阵雨: *There was a heavy ~ last night.* 昨晚下过一场大雨。**the ~s,** the season in tropical countries when there is heavy and continuous ~. (热带地区之)雨季。**3** (use 通常用 **a ~**) descent of sth that comes like ~: 如雨般之降落: *a ~ of arrows / bullets;* 箭(弹)如雨下; *a ~ of ashes,* eg from a volcano: (来自火山等之)阵降落尘,(fig)(喻) *a ~ of congratulations.* 一连串的祝贺。

rain[2] /reɪn; ren/ *vi, vt* **1** (impers): (无人称): *It was ~ing, ~ was falling.* 正在下雨。*It has ~ed itself out, has stopped ~ing.* 雨停了。~ *cats and dogs,* ~ *very hard.* 降倾盆大雨。*It never ~s but it pours,* (prov) Things, usu unwelcome, do not come singly but in numbers, eg if one disaster happens, another will follow. (谚)雨不下则已, 一下倾盆; 灾祸接踵而至; 祸不单行。**2** [VP2C] fall in a stream: 洒落: *Tears ~ed down her cheeks.* 她泪珠满面。*Misfortunes have ~ed heavily upon*

the old man. 那老人接连遭遇不幸。**3** [VP14] ~ *sth on/ upon,* send or come down on: 使降下; 落下: *He ~ed blows / Blows ~ed on the door.* 他(有人)连连敲门。*The people ~ed gifts upon the heroes returning from the war.* 人们纷纷送礼物给那些战罢归来的英雄。

rainy /'reɪnɪ; 'renɪ/ *adj* (-**ier, -iest**) having much rain: 多雨的; ~ *weather;* 多雨的天气; *a ~ day / climate;* 雨天(多雨的气候); *the ~ season.* 雨季。**save / provide / put away / keep sth for a ~ day,** save (esp money) for a time when one may need it. 储蓄以备未来之需; 未雨绸缪。

raise /reɪz; rez/ *vt* [VP6A, 15A, B] **1** lift up; move from a low(er) to a high(er) level; cause to rise: 举起; 升起: ~ *a sunken ship to the surface of the sea;* 把一艘沉船吊到海面上来; ~ *one's hat to sb,* as a sign of respect; 向某人举帽致敬; ~ *one's glass to one's lips;* 举杯到唇边; ~ *prices;* 抬高物价; ~ (= build, erect) *a monument.* 建一纪念碑。~ *one's glass to sb,* drink his health. 向某人举杯祝贺健康; 向某人敬酒。~ *one's hand to sb,* move as if to give him a blow. 向某人伸拳(好象要打他的样子)。~ *sb's hopes,* make him more hopeful. 燃起某人的希望。~ *a man to the peerage,* make him a peer. 封某人为贵族。~ *the temperature,* **(a)** make a place warmer. 使温度升高。**(b)** (fig) increase tension, eg by losing one's temper. (喻)使气氛紧张(如因发脾气所致)。~ *one's voice,* speak more loudly or in a higher tone: 提高声音; 提高嗓子: *voices ~d in anger.* 咆哮的声音。**2** cause to be upright; make erect: 使直立; 扶直: ~ *a man from his knees;* 扶起一跪着的人; ~ *the standard of revolt.* 揭竿而起。~ *sb from the dead,* restore him to life. 使某人复生。**3** cause to rise or appear: 引起; 掀起; 惹起: ~ *a cloud of dust;* 扬起一片尘土; *shoes that ~ blisters on my feet;* 把我的脚磨起水泡的鞋; *a story that might ~ a blush on a young girl's cheeks;* 可能使少女听了脸红的故事; *a long, hot walk that ~d a good thirst,* caused the walker to be thirsty. 使人口渴的又长又热的步行。~ *a dust / commotion,* (fig) cause a disturbance. (喻)惹起一场纷扰; 引起骚动。~ *a laugh,* do sth to cause laughter. 惹起一阵大笑。~ *Cain/ hell / the devil / the roof,* (sl) cause an uproar; start a big row or disturbance. (俚)兴风作浪; 惹起骚乱; 闹出问题。**4** bring up for discussion or attention: 提出(以便讨论或引起注意): ~ *a new point / a question / a protest / an objection.* 提出一新论点(问题, 抗议, 异议)。**5** grow or produce (crops); breed (sheep, etc), rear, bring up (a family), 种植或出产(作物); 饲养(羊等); 养(家); 抚育(子女)。**6** get or bring together; manage to get: 集结; 召集; 筹措: ~ *an army;* 召募一支军队; ~ *a loan;* 借款; ~ *money for a new undertaking;* 为一新事业筹款; ~ *funds for a holiday,* eg by pawning one's jewels. 筹集度假费用(例如典当珠宝首饰等)。**7** ~ *a siege / blockade,* end it. 解除包围(封锁)。~ *an embargo,* remove it. 解除禁运。**8** ~ *land,* (naut) come in sight of land that appears to rise above the horizon: (航海)看见陆地: *The ship ~d land the next morning.* 翌晨该船即望见陆地。**9** (esp US, cf GB, *rise*) increase in salary, etc. (尤美, 参较英国用法之 *rise*) 薪资等之提高; 加薪。~**r** n (in compounds) one who, that which, ~s(in various senses): (用于复合词)举起者; 扶直者; 升起者; 提出者; 种植者; 养育者; 募集者; 解除者: '*cattle-~rs;* 养牛业者; '*curtain-~r,* short introductory play; 开台戏 (正戏前之配戏); '*fire-~rs,* arsonists. 纵火者; 放火者。

raisin /'reɪzn; 'rezn/ n [C] dried sweet grape, as used in cakes, etc. 葡萄干。

raison d'être /ˌreɪzɒn 'detrə; 'rezɔn'dɛt/ n (sing only) (F) reason for, purpose of, a thing's existence. (仅作单数) (法) 存在之理由或目的。

raj /rɑːdʒ; rɑdʒ/ n sovereignty: 统治; 主权: *the ending of the British raj in India.* 英国统治印度之结束。

ra·jah /'rɑːdʒə; 'rɑdʒə/ n Indian prince; Malayan chief. 印度王公; 马来亚之酋长。

rake[1] /reɪk; rek/ n **1** long-handled tool with prongs

used for drawing together straw, dead leaves, etc or
for smoothing soil or gravel, ⇨ the illus at **tool**:similar
kinds of tool on wheels, drawn by a horse or tractor.
耙子(参看 tool 之插图); (由马或拖拉机牵的)耙机。 **2**
implement used by a croupier for drawing in money
or chips at a gaming-table. 在赌桌上负责收取或偿付赌
注者用以把取取金或筹码的小耙子。 □ *vt, vi* **1** [VP6A,
22] use a ~ (on); make smooth with a ~: 以耙子耙; 以
耙子耙平: ~ *garden paths*; 以耙子耙花园的小路; ~ *the
soil smooth for a seedbed.* 耙平土壤设一苗圃。 **2** [VP6A,
15A, B, 14] get (sth *together, up, out, etc*) with or as
with a ~: 用耙子等耙(某物)(与 together, up, out 等连
用): ~ *together dead leaves*; 把枯叶耙在一起; ~ *out a
fire*, get the ashes or cinders out from the bottom of a
grate, etc; 把灰或炭渣从炉底耙出; ~ *up hay*; 把干草耙
在一起; ~ *the dead leaves of the lawn.* 把枯叶从草地上
耙除。 ~ *sth in*, (fig) earn, make, much money: (喻)赚
大钱; 发财: *The firm is very successful—they're raking
it in/raking in the money.* 这公司非常成功——他们赚
了很多钱。 '~-off *n* (sl) (usu suggesting dishonesty)
commission; share of profits: (俚) (通常暗示不正当之)
佣金; 回扣; 赢利之一份: *If I put this bit of business in
your way, I expect a ~-off.* 如果我把这笔生意交给你
做, 我希望能得到一些回扣。 ~ *sth up*, (esp) bring to
people's knowledge (sth forgotten, esp sth which it is
better not to recall to memory): (尤指)重新提起(某件被
遗忘的事, 尤指最好不要记起的事): ~ *up old quarrels/
accusations/slanders/grievances.* 重新提起旧日的争吵
(控诉, 诽谤, 冤情)。 *Don't ~ up the past.* 不要把过去的
事都翻出来。 **3** [VP6A, 15A, B, 2C, 3A] ~ *(over/
through) sth*, search for facts, etc: 在…搜寻事实等:
~ *through old manuscripts for information;* 在旧原稿中搜
求资料; ~ *one's memory;* 从记忆中搜觅; ~ *about among
old documents.* 在旧文件中寻找。 **4**[VP6A, 15A]fire with
guns at, from end to end: 扫射; 纵射: ~ *a ship;* 纵射一
船; ~ *a trench with machine-gun fire.* 以机关枪向一战壕
扫射。

rake[2] /reɪk/ rek/ *n* dissolute man. 浪子;放荡的人。

rake[3] /reɪk/ rek/ *vi, vt* [VP2A, 6A] (of a ship, or its
bow or stern) project beyond the keel; (of the funnel,
masts) (cause to) slope towards the stern; (of the stage
of a theatre) slope down (towards the audience). (指船、
船首或船尾)突出于龙骨之外; 倾斜; (指烟囱、桅)向后向船
尾倾斜; (指剧院中之舞台)(向观众)倾斜。 □ *n* degree of
slope: 倾斜度: *the ~ of a ship's masts/of the stage of
a theatre.* 船桅(戏院舞台)的倾斜度。

rak·ish[1] /'reɪkɪʃ; 'rekɪʃ/ *adj* **1** of or like a rake[2];
dissolute: 浪子的; 象浪子的; 放荡的; 淫荡的: *a ~
appearance.* 放荡的样子。 **2** jaunty: 自信和自满的; 扬扬
得意的; 俏皮的: set one's hat at a ~ angle (from *rake*[2]).
俏皮地歪戴帽子。 ~·**ly** *adv* in a ~ manner: 放荡地; 扬
扬得意地; 俏皮地: *with his hat tilted ~ly.* 俏皮地歪戴着
他的帽子。 ~·**ness** *n*

rak·ish[2] /'reɪkɪʃ; 'rekɪʃ/ *adj* (of a ship) looking smart
and as if built for speed (and therefore, in olden times,
suggesting that she might be a pirate ship). (指船)外
形灵巧, 速度似乎很快的(因此在昔时含示这船可能是海盗
船)。

ral·len·tando /ˌrælen'tændəʊ; ˌrælen'tændo/ *adj,
adv* (music) gradually slower. (音乐)逐渐缓慢(的),
渐慢(的)。 ⇨ **accelerando.**

rally[1] /'rælɪ; 'rælɪ/ *vt, vi* (*pt, pp* -**lied**) [VP6A, 15A,
2A, C] **1** (cause to) come together, esp after defeat or
confusion, or in the face of threats or danger, to make
new efforts: (使)重新集结成一起做新的努力(尤指在失败
或混乱后或是面对威胁或危险时); 重整旗鼓: *The troops
rallied round their leader.* 军队重新集结在他们的指挥官
左右。 *The leader rallied his men.* 指挥官重整其部属。 *My
supporters are ~ing round me again.* 拥护我的人再度
集合起来帮助我。 *They rallied to the support of the Prime
Minister.* 他们协力支持首相。 **2** give new strength
to;(cause to) recover health, strength, firmness: 给予新

力量; (使) 恢复健康, 力量, 决心: ~ *one's strength/
spirits;* 恢复一个人的力量(快乐心境); ~ *from an illness.*
从疾病中复元。 *The boy rallied his wits.* 这男孩恢复了
理智。 *The market rallied,* eg of the Stock Exchange,
prices stopped dropping and became firm. (指股票市场
等)价格止跌回稳。 □ *n* (*pl* -**lies**) [C] **1** act or process
of ~ing; coming together after being dispersed;
recovery of strength; improvement during illness. 集结
或重整的行动或过程; 被击溃后之再集结; 力量之恢复; 疾
病之复元。 **2**(tennis) exchange of several strokes before
a point is scored. (网球得分前的)连续对打。 **3** gathering
or assembly, esp to encourage fresh effort: 集会(尤指鼓
舞斗志的努力分子): *a po'litical* ~;政党集会;*a 'peace* ~, one
to urge the necessity of ending or avoiding war. 和平集
会(为力陈结束或避免战争之必要而举行者)。 **4** competi-
tion of motor vehicles over public roads. 汽车竞赛会; 公
路赛车。

rally[2] /'rælɪ; 'rælɪ/ *vt* (*pt, pp* -**lied**) [VP6A] tease;
chaff good-humouredly. 揶揄; 善意地戏弄。

ram /ræm; ræm/ *n* **1** uncastrated male sheep. (未去势
之)公羊; 牡羊。 **2** one of various implements or devices
for striking or pushing with great force, eg the falling
weight of a pile-driving machine; form of water-pump
in which a heavy fall of water is used to force a smaller
quantity to a higher level. 各种撞击工具或装置之一(如
打桩机的下落重锤); 水力泵; 水力扬水机(抽水机的一种,
利用水之大量下降而压使较少量之水达于一较高平面上)。
3 ⇨ *batteringram* at **batter**[1]. **4** metal projection on a
warship's bow for piercing the side of an enemy ship.
(用以撞穿敌人舰舰的)舰首金属撞角。 □ *vt* (-**mm-**) **1**
[VP6A, 15A, B] strike and push heavily: 力击; 夯击;
力冲, 撞: *ram down the soil,* eg when building roads or
embankments; (在筑路建堤时)把土捣固; *ram piles into
a river bed;* 把桩打入河床; *ram a charge home/into a
gun;* 把火药填好(填入一枪膛); (colloq) (口) *ram one's
clothes into a suitcase.* 把衣服塞进衣箱中。 *ram sth
down sb's throat,* (fig) say sth repeatedly so as to
impress it upon sb, get him to learn it or recognize its
truth. (喻)一再叙述某事以使某人获得深刻印象, 使之学
会或认识其真相; 向某人灌输某事。 **2** [VP6A](of a ship)
strike with a ram(4): (指船)以撞角撞击: *ram and sink
a submarine.* 以撞角撞沉一潜水艇。 **3** '**ram·jet** *n* jet
engine in which the air is rammed or forced through
the engine and compressed by the speed of flight. 冲压
式喷气发动机(由飞行速度逼使空气由发动机流过并产生
压缩之喷气)。 '**ram·rod** *n* iron rod for ramming the
charge into old (muzzle-loading) guns. 枪杆; 搠仗; 推弹
杆(旧式枪炮装火药时用的铁棒)。

Rama·dan /ˌræmə'dæn US: -'dæn; ˌræmə'dæn/ *n*
ninth month of the Muslim year, when Muslims fast
between sunrise and sunset. 拉马丹月(伊斯兰教历的第
九个月, 这期间伊斯兰教徒在日出之后到日落之前斋戒);
斋月。

ramble /'ræmbl; 'ræmbl/ *vi* [VP2A, C] **1** walk for
pleasure, with no special destination; (fig) wander in
one's talk, not keeping to the subject. 漫步; 漫游; (喻)
漫谈。 **2** (of plants) grow with long shoots that trail or
straggle. (指植物)蔓生。 *n* rambling walk: 漫步:*go
for a country* ~. 去乡间漫游。 **ram·bler** *n* person or
thing that ~s: 漫步者; 漫谈者; 蔓生植物: (attrib)(用
作定语) ~*r roses.* 攀缘蔷薇。 **ram·bling** *adj* **1** (esp
of buildings, streets, towns), extending in various
directions irregularly, as if built without planning.
(尤指建筑物、街道、城市)排列凌乱无序的(向各方延
伸, 好象建筑时一无计划)。 **2** (of a speech, essay, etc)
disconnected. (指演讲词、文章等)芜杂散漫的。

ram·bunc·tious /ræm'bʌŋkʃəs; ræm'bʌŋkʃəs/ *adj*
boisterous. 狂暴的; 猛烈的; (指人或其行为)喧闹的; 粗
野的。

ram·ify /'ræmɪfaɪ; 'ræmə‚faɪ/ *vi, vt* (*pt, pp* -**fied**)
[VP2A, 6A] form or produce branches; make or
become a network: (使)形成枝节; (使)分出枝节; (使)组

织或形成一网状系统: a *ramified system*. 一种网状系统。
rami·fi·ca·tion /ˌræmɪfɪˈkeɪʃn; ˌræməfəˈkeʃən/ n [C] subdivision of sth complex or like a network: 分枝；分支；支脉；支流；支线；枝节；细节: *the widespread ramifications of trade/a plot/an argument*. 广布各处的商业分支机构(一计划之细节，一论据之枝节)。

ram·jet ⇨ **ram(3)**.

ramp¹ /ræmp; ræmp/ n sloping way from one level to another, eg instead of, or in addition to, stairs or steps in a hospital, so that beds can be wheeled from one floor to another, or, at a kerb in a many-storeyed garage, so that cars can be driven up and down; change of level during road repairs. 坡道；斜坡；滑行道；匝道(从一水平面到另一水平面的斜路或坡道，如医院中代替楼梯或除楼梯外另设的盘道，使病床能从建筑物之一层推到另一层；或如立体停车场中所用者，汽车可以直接开上驶下；或如修路所设者)。

ramp² /ræmp; ræmp/ n (GB, sl) dishonest attempt to obtain an exorbitant price; swindle. (英，俚)诈取过高的价钱；敲诈。

ramp³ /ræmp; ræmp/ vi [VP2C] ~ *about*, (now usu joc) storm, rage or rush. (现通常为谑)暴跳；狂怒；猛冲。

ram·page /ræmˈpeɪdʒ; ræmˈpedʒ/ vi [VP2A] rush about in excitement or rage. 雀跃不已；暴跳如雷。□ n /ˈræmpeɪdʒ; ˈræmpedʒ/ *be/go on the* ~, be/go rampaging. 乱冲乱跳；暴怒。 **ram·pa·geous** /ræmˈpeɪdʒəs; ræmˈpedʒəs/ adj excited and noisy. 兴奋而喧闹的。

ram·pant /ˈræmpənt; ˈræmpənt/ adj 1 (of plants, etc) rank; luxuriant: (指植物等)蔓延的；繁茂的: *Rich soil makes some plants too ~*, causes them to spread too thickly, to have too much foliage, etc. 肥沃的土壤使某些植物过于繁茂。 2 (of diseases, social evils, etc) unchecked; beyond control: (指疾病、社会弊端等)不能制止的；猖獗的；不能控制的: *Cholera was ~ among them.* 他们之中很多人都得了霍乱。 3 (of animals, esp of a lion in heraldry) on the hind legs. (指动物，尤指纹章学上的狮子)举前肢以后腿站立的。 ~**·ly** adv

ram·part /ˈræmpɑːt; ˈræmpɑrt/ n [C] 1 wide bank of earth, often with a wall, built to defend a fort or other defensive work. 壁垒(保护堡垒或其他防御物的厚土墙)。 2 (fig) defence; protection. (喻)防御；保护。

ram·rod /ˈræmrɒd; ˈræmˌrɑd/ ⇨ **ram(3)**.

ram·shackle /ˈræmʃækl; ˈræmˌʃækl/ adj almost collapsing; nearly at breaking-point: 要倒塌的；近于崩溃的: *a ~ house*; 一座摇摇欲倒的房子; *a ~ old bus*; 一辆快报废的公共汽车; *their ~ empire*. 他们那即将解体的帝国。

ran /ræn; ræn/ pt of **run²**.

ranch /rɑːntʃ US: ræn-; ræntʃ/ n (US) large farm, esp one with extensive lands for cattle, but also for fruit, chickens, etc. (美)大农场；农场；(尤指兼种果树养鸡等的)大牧场。 '~ **house**, (US) rectangular bungalow type of house. (美)长方形的平房。 '~ **wagon**, (US) (美)=station-wagon. ~**er** n person who owns, manages or works on a ~. 大农(牧)场的主人，管理人或工人。

ran·cid /ˈrænsɪd; ˈrænsɪd/ adj with the smell or taste of stale, decaying fat or butter; (of fat) having gone bad; ill smelling: 有腐臭脂肪或奶油的气味或味道的；(指脂肪)败坏的；恶臭的: *This butter smells/has gone ~*. 这奶油有臭味(已变臭)。

ran·cour (US =**-cor**) /ˈræŋkə(r); ˈræŋkɚ/ n [U] deep and long-lasting feeling of bitterness; spitefulness: 怨恨；积怨；怀恨: *full of ~ (against sb)*. (对某人)怀恨在心。 **ran·cor·ous** /ˈræŋkərəs; ˈræŋkərəs/ adj

rand /rænd; rænd/ n monetary unit of S Africa, divided into 100 cents. 兰特(南非货币单位)。

ran·dom /ˈrændəm; ˈrændəm/ n 1 *at* ~, without aim or purpose: 无目的或目标: *shooting/dropping bombs at* ~; 胡乱射击(投弹)；乱扔出去; *Hit out at* ~. 随便攻击。胡乱做。 2 (attrib) done, made, taken, at ~: (用作定语)随便做的，造的，选取的: ~ *remarks*; 随便说的话; *a* ~ *sample*, (用

selection; 随意抽取的样品(随意选择之物)； ~ *sampling*. 随意抽样。

randy /ˈrændɪ; ˈrændɪ/ adj (-**ier**, -**iest**) 1 (Scot) boisterous; aggressively noisy. (苏)吵闹的；喧嚣的。 2 full of sexual lust. 淫荡的；好色的。

ranee, rani /ˈrɑːniː; ˈrɑnɪ/ n Hindu queen or princess; wife of a rajah. (印度之)女王；王妃；(王公之)妻室。

rang /ræŋ; ræŋ/ pt of **ring²**.

range¹ /reɪndʒ; rendʒ/ n [C] 1 row, line or series of things: (指物)排；行；系列；山脉之类: *a magnificent* ~ *of mountains*; 魏峨壮丽的山脉; *a 'mountain-*~; 山脉; *a long* ~ *of cliffs*. 一长列绝壁。 2 area of ground with targets for shooting at: 靶场；射击场: *a 'rifle-*~; 步枪靶场; area in which rockets and missiles are fired. (火箭及导弹之)发射场。 3 distance to which a gun will shoot or to which a shell, etc can be fired: 射程: *at a ~ of five miles*; 五英里的射程; *in/within/out of/beyond* ~; 在射程之内(外); distance between a gun, etc and the target: 枪炮等与靶间的距离: *fire at short/long* ~. 短(长)程距离射击。 '~-**finder** n (**a**) instrument for finding the distance of sth to be fired at. 测距仪(用于测定被射击目标之距离之仪器)。 (**b**) device fitted in some cameras for measuring distances. (摄影机中的)测距仪。 4 distance at which one can see or hear, or to which sound will carry. 视域；听域；声音可及的距离。 5 extent; distance between limits: 范围；幅度；差距: *the annual* ~ *of temperature*, eg from −10°C to 40°C; 每年之温度差距(如从摄氏 −10° 到 40°); *a long-*~ *weather forecast*, for a long period; 长期天气预报; *a narrow* ~ *of prices*; 价格差距很小; *cotton fabrics in a wide* ~ *of colours*; 颜色种类很多的棉织物; *the* ~ *of her voice*, in between her top and bottom notes; 她的音域(她能唱出的最高音与最低音间之差距); (fig)(喻) *a subject that is outside my* ~, one that I have not studied; 在我研究范围之外的题目; *a wide* ~ *of interests*. 广泛的兴趣。 6 (US) area of grazing or hunting ground. (美)放牧区；狩猎区。 7 area over which plants are found growing or in which animals are found living: 动植物生长之地区: *What is the* ~ *of the nightingale in this country?* 在这个国家什么地方有夜莺? 8 cooking-stove, usu with ovens, a boiler, and a surface with openings or hot-plates for pans, kettles, etc: 炉灶: *a kitchen* ~. 厨房内的炉灶。

range² /reɪndʒ; rendʒ/ vt, vi [VP6A, 15A] place or arrange in a row or rows; put, take one's place, in a specified situation, order, class or group: 排列成行；安置或列于某一特定的位置，次序，类或组: *The general* ~*d his men along the river bank*. 将军令其士兵沿河岸排队。 *They were* ~*d against us/among the rebels*. 他们站在反对我们的一边(加入了叛徒之列)。 *The spectators* ~*d themselves along the route of the procession*. 观众沿游行行列的路线列队伫立。 2 [VP2C, 3A, 6A] ~ (*through/over*), go, move; wander: (在…)漫游; (在…)徘徊: *animals ranging through the forests*; 在森林中漫游的动物; ~ *over the hills*; 在小山上漫游; ~ *the seas/hills, etc*; 漫游于海洋(山丘等); (fig)(喻) *researches that* ~*d over a wide field*; 涉及范围很广的研究; *a speaker who* ~*d far and wide*, spoke on many topics; 一位讲辞包罗万象的演说者; *a wide-ranging discussion*. 广泛的讨论。 3 [VP2C] extend, run in a line: 延伸；绵延: *a boundary that* ~*s north and south/from A to B*. 南北延展(从 A 延伸到 B)的界限。 4 [VP2C] vary between limits: (在某一范围内)变化；变动；造成差异: *prices ranging from £7 to £10/between £7 and £10*. 从七英镑到十英镑(在七英镑与十英镑间)的各种价格。 5 (of guns, projectiles) carry: (指枪炮，弹丸)射程为: *This gun* ~*s over six miles*, can fire to this distance. 这炮射程超过六英里。

ranger /ˈreɪndʒə(r); ˈrendʒɚ/ n 1 (US) forest guard. (美)森林看守人。 2 (US) one of a body of mounted troops employed as police (eg in thinly populated areas). (美)(在人口稀少等地区担任警察的)骑兵巡逻队队员(骑兵)。 3 (US) commando. (美)突击队员。 4 (GB) keeper of a royal park, who sees that the forest laws are

observed. (英)(皇家森林公园的)守卫员(负责森林法之执行)。

rani /'rɑːniː; 'rɑːnɪ/ ⇨ ranee.

rank¹ /ræŋk; ræŋk/ *n* 1 [C] line of persons or things: (指人或物)一列; 一排; 一行: a '*cab-~*. 一长列出租汽车的 line. 乘坐排在前头的那部计程车。2 number of soldiers placed side by side (on parade, usu in three lines, called the *front*, *centre* and the *rear ~s*). 士兵列成之横排(检阅时, 通常为三排, 称为 '前排'、'中排' 及 '后排')。*keep/break ~*, remain/fail to remain in line. 保持队形(出列; 掉队)。3 the *~s*; the *~ and file*; other *~s*, ordinary soldiers, ie contrasted with officers. 士兵(与军官相对)。*be reduced to the ~s*, (of a non-commissioned officer, eg a sergeant) made an ordinary private soldier (as a punishment). (指士官)降级为士兵(作为一种处罚)。*rise from the ~s*, (of an ordinary soldier) be given a commission as an officer. (指普通士兵)被任命为军官。4 [C, U] position in a scale; distinct grade in the armed forces; category or class: 等级; 军队中的官阶; 种属; 阶层: *be promoted to the ~ of captain*; 擢升到上等军阶; *above/below a major in ~*; 在军阶上高于(低于)少校; *officers of high ~*; 高级军官; *hold the ~ of colonel*; 保有上校军阶; *persons of high ~*, of high social position; 社会地位甚高的人; *people of all ~s and classes*; 各阶层的人; *be in the ~s of the unemployed*; 属于失业者群; *a painter of the first ~*; 第一流的画家; *a second~* (more usu 较常用 *second-rate*) *dancer*. 第二流的舞蹈家。*pull ~ on sb*, use one's superior position to gain an advantage over him. 利用职权压制某人。□ *vt*, *vi* 1 [VP6A, 15A, 16B] put or arrange in a row; put in a class: 排列成一行; 列属某类: *Where/How do you ~ Addison as an essayist?* 你把艾迪生列为那一流的散文家? *Would you ~ him among the world's great statesmen?* 你会把他列为世界上伟大政治家之一吗? 2 [VP3A] have a place: 占有一地位: *Does he ~ among/with the failures?* 他这算是一个失败者吗? *A major ~s above a captain*. 少校军阶高于上尉。*Will my shares ~ for the next dividend?* 我的股份可以享到下次的股息吗? 3 *~ing officer*, (US) the officer of highest ~ present. (美)在场的最高级军官。

rank² /ræŋk; ræŋk/ *adj* 1 (of plants, etc) growing too luxuriantly with too much leaf: (指植物等)繁茂的; 过于茂盛的: *~ grass*; 丛生的杂草; *roses that grow ~*; 过于茂盛的玫瑰; (of land) choked with weeds or likely to produce a lot of weeds: (指土地)长满杂草的; 可能生长很多杂草的: *~ soil*; 杂草丛生的土壤; *a field that is ~ with nettles and thistles*. 一块长满荨麻和蓟的田地。2 smelling or tasting bad; offensive: 气味或味道不好的; 令人不快的: *~tobacco*. 气味可厌的烟草。3 unmistakably bad; possessing a bad quality to an extreme degree: 显然很坏的; 坏到极点的: *a ~ traitor*; 罪大恶极的叛国者; *~ injustice*. 极端的不公正。*These fungi are ~ poison*. 这些菌类是最烈性的毒物。*~·ly adv ~·ness n*

ranker /'ræŋkə(r); 'ræŋkɚ/ *n* commissioned officer who has risen from the ranks. 出身行伍的军官。⇨ rank¹(3).

rankle /'ræŋkl; 'ræŋkl/ *vi* [VP2A] continue to be a painful or bitter memory: 继续成为痛苦或伤心的回忆; 使人痛心: *The insult ~d in his mind*. 那次受辱使他痛心。

ran·sack /'rænsæk US: ræn'sæk; 'rænsæk/ *vt* 1 [VP 6A, 14, 16A] *~ sth (for sth/to do sth)*, search (a place) thoroughly (for sth): 遍搜(某地)(找某物): *~ a drawer*; 搜抽屉; *~ a dictionary to find just the right word*. 遍查词典找寻合适的词。2 [VP6A, 14] *~ sth (of sth)*, rob; plunder: 抢劫; 掠夺: *The house had been ~ed of all that was worth anything*. 屋里一切有点儿价值的东西都被抢去了。

ran·som /'rænsəm; 'rænsəm/ *n* [U] freeing of a captive on payment; [C] sum of money, etc, paid for this. 付赎金赎救; 赎金。*hold a man to ~*, keep him as a captive and ask for *~*. 掳人待赎; 绑票。*worth a king's ~*, worth a very large sum of money. 值一笔巨

额的金钱。□ *vt* [VP6A] obtain the freedom of (sb), set (sb) free, in exchange for *~*: 赎回; 赎出(某人); 取赎金而释放(某人): *~ a kidnapped diplomat*. 赎回遭绑架的外交官。

rant /rænt; rænt/ *vi*, *vt* [VP2A, 6A] use extravagant, boasting language; say or recite (sth) noisily and theatrically: 用狂言壮语; 喧嚣而夸大地说出或背诵(某事物): *an actor who ~s his part*. 一个过份夸夸其脚色的演员。□ *n* piece of ~ing talk. 狂言; 壮语。*~er n* person who ~s. 说狂言壮语者; 说话过份夸张者。

rap¹ /ræp; ræp/ *n* [C] 1 (sound of a) light, quick blow: 轻敲(声); 急拍(声): *I heard a rap on the door*. 我听见敲门声。*give sb a rap on/over the knuckles*, reprove him. 谴责某人。2 (colloq) blame; consequences. (口)责备; 后果。*take the rap (for sth)*, be reproved or reprimanded (esp when innocent). (因某事而)受责备; (尤指)背黑锅。3 (US sl) conversation; discussion. (美俚)谈话; 讨论。□ *vt*, *vi* (-pp-) [VP6A, 15B, 2A, C] 1 give a rap to; make the sound of a rap: 轻敲; 做出轻敲声: *rap (on) the table*; 敲桌子; *rap (at) the door*. 敲门。2 *rap sth out*, **(a)** say sth suddenly or sharply: 突然或厉声说出某事事。厉声发誓。**(b)** (of spirits at a seance) express by means of raps: (指所谓"降神会"上的"鬼魂")以轻敲的动作表达; *rap out a message*. 以轻敲的方式"表达出"所谓鬼魂之意。3 (US sl) talk; discuss. (美俚)谈话; 讨论。

rap² /ræp; ræp/ *n not care/give a rap*, not care at all. 全然不介意。

ra·pa·cious /rə'peɪʃəs; rə'peʃəs/ *adj* (formal) greedy (esp for money). (正式用语)贪婪的(尤指贪钱)。*~·ly adv* **ra·pac·ity** /rə'pæsətɪ; rə'pæsətɪ/ *n* [U] greed; avarice. 贪婪; 贪心。

rape¹ /reɪp; rep/ *n* [U] plant grown as food for sheep and pigs; plant grown for the oil obtained from its seeds. 芸薹; 油菜(作为羊与猪之饲料, 或从其种子榨油)。

rape² /reɪp; rep/ *vt* [VP6A] 1 seize and carry off by force. 强夺; 抢劫。2 commit the crime of forcing sexual intercourse on (a woman or girl). 强奸(妇女)。□ *n* act of raping. 强夺; 抢劫, 强奸。*rap·ist* /'reɪpɪst; 'repɪst/ *n*

rapid /'ræpɪd; 'ræpɪd/ *adj* 1 quick; moving, occurring with great speed: 迅速的; 敏捷的; 快速的: *a ~ decline in sales*; 销售量急速下降; *a ~ pulse/river/worker*; 跳动很快的脉搏(水流湍急的河; 敏捷的工人); (of action) done quickly: (指动作)很快完成的: *~-fire questions*, in ~ succession. 连珠炮似的问题。2 (of a slope) steep; descending steeply. (指斜坡)急陡的; 陡峭下斜的。□ *n* (usu *pl*) part of a river where a steep slope causes the water to flow fast. (通常用复数)急滩; 湍流。*~·ly adv* **rap·id·ity** /rə'pɪdətɪ; rə'pɪdətɪ/ *n* [U].

rapier /'reɪpɪə(r); 'repɪɚ/ *n* light sword used for thrusting in duels and the sport of fencing. 在决斗中或剑术中所用的一种轻剑。*'~-thrust*, (fig) a delicate or witty retort. (喻)灵敏或机智的反驳。

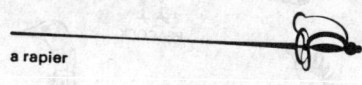

a rapier

rap·ine /'ræpaɪn US: 'ræpɪn; 'ræpɪn/ *n* (liter or rhet) [U] plundering. (文或修辞)抢劫; 强夺。

rap·port /ræ'pɔː(r) US: -'pɔːrt; ræ'pɔrt/ *n* [U, C] sympathetic relationship. 密切、融洽、和谐的关系。*be in ~ (with)*, (or, as in French, 法文作 *en* /ɑːn-, ɑn-/ ~), in close relationship or sympathy (with). (与⋯)关系密切或融洽。

rap·proche·ment /ræ'prɒʃmɒŋ US: ˌræprəʊʃ'mɒŋ; raproʃ'mɑ̃/ *n* [C] coming together again (of persons, parties, States) in friendly relations; renewal of friendship. (人、党派、国家)重建友谊关系; 重归旧好; 恢复友谊; 复交。

rap·scal·lion /ræp'skælɪən; ræp'skæljən/ *n* (old use) rascal; rogue. (旧用法)流氓;恶徒.

rapt /ræpt; ræpt/ *adj* so deep in thought, so carried away by feelings, that one is unaware of other things; enraptured: 全神贯注的; 心移神驰的; 着迷的; 狂喜的: *listening to the orchestra with ~ attention*; 聚精会神地听管弦乐队演奏; *in contemplation of the scenery*; 出神地欣赏风景; *~ in a book.* 潜心于一书. **rap·ture** /'ræptʃə(r); 'ræptʃɚ/ *n* **1** [U] state of being rapt; ecstatic delight: 精神贯注;着迷;狂喜: *gazing with ~ at the face of the girl he loved.* 痴痴地望着他喜爱的那个女孩的脸. **2** (*pl*)(复) **be in**/**go into**/**be sent into** ~**s (over**/**about)**, be/become extremely happy, full of joy and enthusiasm: 极度喜爱; 狂喜; 充满喜悦与热忱: *She went into ~s over the dresses they showed her.* 她对他们给她看的衣服喜爱若狂. **rap·tur·ous** /'ræptʃərəs; 'ræptʃərəs/ *adj* inspiring or expressing ~. 引起或表示狂喜的. **rap·tur·ous·ly** *adv*

rare¹ /reə(r); rɛr/ *adj* (**-r, -st**) **1** unusual; uncommon; not often happening, seen, etc: 罕有的; 稀罕的;不常发生或看见的: *a ~ occurrence*; 罕有的事件; *a ~ book*, one of which few copies are obtainable. 善本书; 珍本书. *It is very ~ for her to arrive late.* 她是很难得迟到的. **2** (dated *colloq*) unusually good: (过时口语)非常好的: *We had a ~ time*/*~ fun.* 我们玩得非常开心. **3** (of a substance, esp the atmosphere) thin; not dense: (指物质,尤指大气)稀薄的,不密的: *the ~ air of the mountains in the Himalayas.* 喜马拉雅山上稀薄的空气. ~**·ly** *adv* **1** seldom: 罕有地;不常地: *I ~ly eat in restaurants.* 我很少在饭馆吃饭. *He visits us only ~ly nowadays.* 如今他很少来看望我们. **2** excellently. 极;非常地. ~**·ness** *n*

rare² /reə(r); rɛr/ *adj* (of meat) underdone; cooked so that the redness and juices are retained: (指肉) 未煮熟的;半熟的: *~ steak.* 煎成半生的牛排.

rare·bit /'reəbɪt; 'rɛr,bɪt/ *n* [C] Welsh ~ (also,

colloq, 口语亦作 *rabbit*), melted or toasted cheese on toasted bread. 涂于烤过的面包上的溶化的或烘烤过的乳酪.

rarefy /'reərɪfaɪ; 'rɛrə,faɪ/ *vt, vi* (*pt, pp* **-fied**) [VP6 A, 2A] make or become less dense; purify: 使或变为稀薄; 使纯净; 使纯: *the rarefied air of the mountain tops*; 山顶上变稀薄的空气; refine; make subtle: 净化;精炼: *rarefied ideas*/*theories.* 千锤百炼的思想(理论). **rare·fac·tion** /,reərɪ'fækʃn; ,rɛrə'fækʃən/ *n* [U] ~ing. 使或变为稀薄;使纯净;精炼.

rar·ing /'reərɪŋ; 'rɛrɪŋ/ *adj* (colloq) full of eagerness: (口)兴致勃勃的; 十分渴望的: *They're ~ to go.* 他们亟欲前往.

rar·ity /'reərətɪ; 'rɛrətɪ/ *n* (*pl* **-ties**) **1** [U] rareness. 罕有; 稀薄. **2** [C] sth rare, uncommon or unusual; sth valued because rare: 罕见之物; 珍贵之物: *Rain is a ~ in Upper Egypt.* 在上埃及雨是罕见的.

ras·cal /'rɑːskl *US*: 'ræskl; 'ræskl/ *n* **1** dishonest person. 不忠实的人;流氓. **2** (playfully) mischievous person (esp a child), fond of playing tricks. 好恶作剧的人;喜欢开玩笑的人;(尤指)小淘气. ~**·ly** /-kəlɪ; -klɪ/ *adj of* or like a ~; mean; dishonest: 流氓的;象流氓的;卑鄙的;欺诈的: *a ~ly trick.* 一个卑鄙的骗局.

rase /reɪz; rez/ *vt* ⇨ **raze**.

rash¹ /ræʃ; ræʃ/ *n* (breaking out of, patch of) tiny red spots on the skin: 疹子; 发疹; 一片红疹: *a 'heat~*; 热疹; *'nettle-~*; 荨麻疹; (fig) (喻) *a ~ of new red brick bungalows on a country road.* 乡间大道旁一片新的红砖平房. *If a ~ appears, the child may have (the) measles.* 如果身上有一片红疹出现,这孩子可能是出麻疹.

rash² /ræʃ; ræʃ/ *adj* too hasty; overbold; done, doing things, without enough thought of the consequences: 太匆忙的; 太鲁莽的; 轻率而未想及后果的: *a ~ act*/*statement*; 一个轻率的行动(声明); *a ~ young man.* 一个鲁莽的年轻人. ~**·ly** *adv* ~**·ness** *n*

rare or exotic birds

rasher /'ræʃ(ə)r/; 'ræʃø/ n slice of bacon or ham (to be) fried: (煎的或待煎的)咸肉片; 火腿片: *eat three ~s and two fried eggs for breakfast.* 早餐吃三片咸肉和两个煎蛋.

rasp /rɑːsp US: ræsp; ræsp/ n [C] metal tool like a coarse file with a surface or surfaces having sharp points, used for scraping; rough, grating sound produced by this tool. 粗锉刀; 锉磨的粗厉刺耳声. □ vt, vi 1 [VP 6A, 15A, B, 22] ~ sth (away / off), scrape with a ~; scrape. 用粗锉刀锉; 锉掉. 2 [VP6A] (fig) grate upon, have an irritating effect upon: (喻)激怒;刺激: ~ sb's feelings/nerves. 刺激某人的感情 (神经). 3 [VP15B] ~ out, utter in a way that grates or sounds like the noise of a ~: 以使人不快或刺耳的声音说出: ~ out orders / insults. 厉声发出命令 (侮辱的话). 4 [VP 2A, C] make a harsh, grating sound: 发出粗厉刺耳之声: a learner ~ing (away) on his violin; 在提琴上拉出刺耳之音的初学者; a ~ing voice. 粗厉刺耳的声音. ~·ing·ly adv

rasp·ber·ry /'rɑːzbrɪ US: 'ræzberɪ; 'ræz‚berɪ/ n (pl -ries) 1 bush with small, sweet, yellow or red berries, wild or cultivated: 悬钩子;木莓;山莓(野生或栽种灌木,其浆果小而甜,呈黄或红色):(attrib)(用作定语)~ jam/canes; 木莓果酱(悬钩子的枝); one of these berries. 悬钩子之果实;木莓. 2 (sl) contemptubus noise made with the tongue and lips, or a gesture indicating dislike, derision or disapproval: (俚)(表示憎恶、嘲弄或不赞成的)咂舌声或姿态: give/blow sb a ~; 咂舌嘲弄某人; get a ~. 受人咂舌嘲弄.

rat /ræt/ ræt/ n 1 animal like, but larger than, a mouse; person who deserts a cause that he thinks is about to fail (from the belief that rats desert a ship that will sink or be wrecked). 鼠(较 mouse 大者);叛变转舵的人;变节者(出自鼠会舍弃将沉没或遇难的船之说法). ⇨ the illus at **small**. 参看 small 之插图. *smell a rat,* suspect that sth wrong is being done. 怀疑其中有诡诈. *(look) like a drowned rat,* wet and miserable; soaked to the skin. (显得)湿而可怜的;全身湿透的. *the 'rat race,* ceaseless and undignified competition for success in one's career. social status, etc as among office workers, etc. 激烈竞争. 2 (fig) cowardly traitor; strike-breaker. (喻) 懦弱的叛逆者; 破坏罢工者. *Rats!* (dated sl, as an exclamation) Nonsense! (过时俚语, 作叹词) 胡说! □ vi (-tt-) 1 [VP2A] hunt rats: 捕鼠; go ratting. 去捕鼠. 2 [VP2A, 3A] ~ (on sb), break a promise, withdraw from an undertaking. 背叛(某人)(如不履行诺言或退出一事业). **rat·ter** n man, dog or cat that catches rats: 捕鼠之人、狗或猫: *Are terriers good ratters?* 㹴是善捕鼠的狗吗? **rat·ty** adj (-ier, -iest) (colloq) irritable; snappish. (口)易怒的;暴躁的.

rat·able, rate·able /'reɪtəbl; 'reɪtəbl/ adj liable to payment of municipal rates: 应征地方税的: ~ property; 应征地方税的财产; the ~ value of a house, its value as assessed for the levying of rates. 一栋房屋之课税现值. **rat·abil·ity, rate·abil·ity** /‚reɪtə'bɪlətɪ/ ‚reɪtə'bɪlɪtɪ/ n [U].

rat·an /ræ'tæn; ræ'tæn/ ⇨ **rattan**.

rat-a-tat-tat /‚ræt‚ə‚tæt 'tæt; ‚ræt‚ə‚tæt'tæt/ ⇨ **rat-tat**.

ratch /rætʃ; rætʃ/ n = ratchet.

ratch·et /'rætʃɪt; 'rætʃɪt/ n toothed wheel provided with a catch (pawl) that prevents, the wheel from slipping back and allows it to move in only one direction. 棘轮; 棘轮机(一种有齿之轮; 装有一棘爪, 用以防止轮子退回, 而只允许向一个方向移动).

rate¹ /reɪt; reɪt/ n 1 [C] standard of reckoning, obtained by bringing two numbers or amounts into relationship: 比率; 率: walk at the ~ of 3 miles an hour; 以每小时三英里的速度走路; a train travelling at a / the ~ of 50 miles an hour; 以时速五十英里行驶的火车; an aircraft with a good ~ of climb: 一种爬升速率甚高的飞机; at a great / fearful, etc ~, at great speed; 以高速度; buy things at the ~ of 55p a hundred. 以每一百个五十五

便士的价格买东西. *What is the airmail letter ~ to Peru?* 寄航空信件到秘鲁的邮资是多少? ⇨ per; to¹(12). **'birth** / **'marriage** / **'death, etc ~,** the number of births, etc in relationship to a period of time and a number of people: 出生 (结婚, 死亡等) 率: a death-~ of 2.3 per 1000 (per year). (每年) 千分之 2.3 的死亡率. ~ of exchange, relationship between two currencies (eg US dollars and F francs). 两种货币间的兑换率. the 'discount ~, the 'bank ~, the officially announced percentage at which a country's central bank is prepared to discount Bills. 贴现率 (银行准备处期票贴现的官方公布之百分率). 2 (phrases)(短语)at 'this / 'that ~, if this / that is true, if we may assume that this / that is the case; if this / that state of affairs continues. 如果此 (彼) 种情形是真实的话; 如果我们可以假定情形如此 (彼); 如此 (彼) 种情形继续下去. at 'any ~, in any case; whatever happens. 在任何情形下; 无论如何. 3 (the) ~s, (GB) tax on property (land and buildings), paid to local authorities for local purposes: (英) 地方征收之财产 (土地与建筑物) 税: an extra penny on the ~s for the public library, ie a charge of one penny on each pound of the assessment. 为建公立图书馆而在财产税上每镑中附征的一便士. ~s and taxes, payments to local authorities and taxes levied by the national government. 地方税与中央税. '~-payer n person liable to have ~s exacted from him. (地方税之) 纳税人. ⇨ also water~ at water¹(7). 4 (with ordinal numbers) class or grade: (与序数连用) 等级: first ~, excellent; 第一等; 最好的; second ~, fairly good; 第二等; 尚好; third ~, (rather) poor; 第三等; (颇) 差; (attrib, with a hyphen) (用作定语, 加连字符号) a first-~ teacher. 第一流的教师. Hence, 由此产生, first-'rater, second-'rater, etc. 一流, 二流等的人或物.

rate² /reɪt; reɪt/ vt, vi 1 [VP6A, 14, 15A, 16B] ~ (at), judge or estimate the value or qualities of: 估价; 评价; 评估: What do you ~ his fortune at? 你估计他的财产有多少? He was a man whom all his friends ~d as kind and hospitable. 所有他的朋友都认为他是一个仁慈而好客的人. Do you ~ (= consider) Mr X among your friends? 你把 X 先生算作你的朋友吗? 2 [VP6A, 14] ~ sth (at), (GB) value (property) for the purpose of assessing rates(3) on: (英) 评估 (财产之) 课税现值: My property was ~d at £100 per annum. 我的财产估计每年应缴税一百英镑. Should private houses be more heavily ~d than factories? 私人房产应该比工厂课更重的税吗? 3 [VP16B] ~ sb as, (naut) place in a certain class: (航海) 定出等级: He was ~d as a midshipman. 他被定为海军学校见习生的等级. 4 [VP2D, C] (colloq) be ~ed: (口) 被定出等级: He ~s high / as a midshipman. 他的等级很高 (被定为海军学校见习生).

rate·able /'reɪtəbl; 'reɪtəbl/ adj ⇨ **ratable**.

rather /'rɑːðər/ US: 'ræ‚; 'ræðø/ adv 1 more willingly; by preference or choice (usu 通常作 would / had ... than; also with inversion 也可颠倒作: than ... would): 更为情愿地; 宁愿: I would ~ you came tomorrow than today. 我宁愿你明天来, 不要今天来. She would ~ have the small one than the large one. 她宁愿要小的一个而不要大的. Wouldn't you ~ be liked than feared? 你不是宁愿受人爱戴, 不肯让人惧怕吗? He resigned ~ than take part in such a dishonest transaction. 他宁愿辞职也不愿参与这种欺诈的交易. A: 'Will you join us in a game of cards?'——B: 'Thank you, but I'd ~ not.' 甲: '你要和我们一起玩牌吗?'——乙: '谢谢, 我不想玩.' 2 more truly, accurately or precisely: 更真实、正确或精密地: He arrived very late last night or ~ in the early hours this morning. 他昨晚深夜到达, 或者更精确地说, 在今天凌晨到达. 3 (to be distinguished from fairly²; note that fairly is not used with comparatives, too, nn, and vv) (应与 fairly² 区分; 按注: fairly² 不与比较级, too, 名词和动词连用) in a certain degree or measure; more (so) than not; somewhat: 相当地; 多多少少; 有一点; (a)(with adjj, preceding or following the indef art, following

the *def art*): (与形容词连用): 放在不定冠词之前或后, 放在定冠词之后: *a ~ surprising result* / ~ *a surprising result*; 一个相当惊人的结果; *the ~ tall boy in the corner.* 在墙角那个相当高的男孩子。 **(b)** (with comparatives): (与比较级的形容词或副词连用): *My brother is ~ better today.* 我哥哥(弟弟) 今天好得多。 *This hat is ~ more expensive than that.* 这顶帽子比那一顶贵得多。 **(c)** (with *too*): (与 too 连用): *This book is ~ too difficult for the juniors and ~ too easy for the seniors.* 这本书对低年级学生太难, 对高年级学生又太容易。 **(d)** (with *nn*): (与名词连用): *It's ~ a pity, ~ regrettable.* 令人相当惋惜。 *She's ~ a dear, ~ lovable.* 她是个相当可爱的人。 *£100 is ~ a lot to pay for a dress, isn't it?* 一百镑买一件女装太贵了点, 不是吗? **(e)** (with *vv* and *pp*): (与动词过及去分词连用): *I ~ think you may be mistaken.* 我倒认为你可能错了。 *The rain ~ spoiled our holiday.* 我们的假日适逢下雨, 颇为扫兴。 *We were all ~ exhausted when we got to the top of the mountain.* 我们到达山顶时, 都相当疲倦了。 **(f)** (with *advv*): (与副词连用): *You've done ~ well / ~ better than I had expected.* 你做得很好 (比我预期的要好得多)。 **4**(colloq; GB /ˌrɑːˈðɜː(r); ˌrɑðə/) (in answers) most certainly. (口)(用于回答中) 确实如此; 当然; 一定。

rat·ify /ˈrætɪfaɪ; ˈrætəˌfaɪ/ *vt* (*pt, pp* **-fied**) [VP 6A] confirm (an agreement) by signature or other formality. 批准。 **rati·fi·ca·tion** /ˌrætɪfɪˈkeɪʃən; ˌrætəfəˈkeʃən/ *n* ~ing or being ratified. 批准; 被批准。

rat·ing /ˈreɪtɪŋ; ˈretɪŋ/ *n* **1** [C] act of valuing property for the purpose of assessing rates, ⇨ rate²(2); amount or sum fixed as the municipal rate. 评估财产之课税现值; 地方税额。 **2** [C] class, classification, eg of yachts by tonnage, motor-cars by engine capacity or horse-power; popularity of radio or TV programmes as estimated by asking a selected group. 等级; 类别; 分类(例如游艇按吨数分类, 汽车按马力分类); (根据抽样调查所得广播或电视节目的) 收视(听)率。 **3** (navy) person's position or class as recorded in the ship's books; non-commissioned sailor: (海军) 舰艇记录上所记载的职别或等级; 兵卒:*officers and ~s.* 海军官兵。

ra·tio /ˈreɪʃɪəʊ; ˈreʃo/ *n* (*pl* ~**s** /-ʃɪəʊz; -ʃoz/) [C] relation between two amounts determined by the number of times one contains the other: 比; 比率: *The ~s of 1 to 5 and 20 to 100 are the same.* 1 与 5 和 20 与 100 的比率是相同的。

rati·oc·in·ation /ˌrætɪˌɒsɪˈneɪʃn US: ˌræʃɪ-; ˌræʃɪˌɑsnˈeʃən/ *n* [U] the process of methodical reasoning, esp by the use of syllogisms. 推论(尤指使用三段论法者)。

ration /ˈræʃn; ˈræʃən/ *n* fixed quantity, esp of food, allowed to one person; *(pl)* fixed allowance served out to, eg members of the armed forces: 定量(尤指配给个人之食物的定额); (复) 口粮; (复)配给三军人员的: *go and draw ~s.* 去领取配给。 '*~ card/book,* one that entitles the holder to ~s, eg for a civilian when there is a food shortage during or immediately after a war. 配给卡(簿)。 **be on short ~s,** be allowed or able to have less than the usual quantity of food. 粮食配给不足; 粮食缺乏。 □ *vt* **1** [VP6A] limit (sb) to a ration of: 配给(某人)。 **2** [VP6A, 15B] ~ (*out*), limit (food, water, etc): 限制使用(食物, 水等): *We'll have to ~ the water.* 我们将限制用水。 *He ~ed out* (= distributed ~s of) *the bread.* 他分发面包。

ra·tional /ˈræʃnəl; ˈræʃənl/ *adj* **1** of reason or reasoning. 理性的; 推理的。 **2** able to reason, having the faculty of reasoning. 能推理的; 有推理能力的。 **3** sensible; that can be tested by reasoning: 明达的; 合理的: ~ *conduct / explanations.* 合理的行为(解释)。 ~**ly** /-ʃnəlɪ;-ʃənlɪ/ *adv* ~**·ity** /ˌræʃəˈnælətɪ; ˌræʃəˈnælətɪ/ *n* quality of being ~; reasonableness. 理性; 明达; 推理能力。

ration·ale /ˌræʃəˈnɑːl; ˌræʃəˈnæl/ *n* fundamental reason, logical basis (of sth). (某事物的)基本理由; 理论基础。

ration·al·ism /ˈræʃnəlɪzəm; ˈræʃənlˌɪzəm/ *n* [U]the practice of treating reason as the ultimate authority in religion as in other subjects of study. 理性主义; 唯理主义。 **ration·al·ist** /-ɪst; -ɪst/ *n* person who accepts reason as the ultimate authority in religion, ethics, etc. 理性主义者; 唯理论者。 **ration·al·is·tic** /ˌræʃnəˈlɪstɪk; ˌræʃənlˈɪstɪk/ *adj* of ~ or rationalists.理性主义的; 理性主义者的。

ration·al·ize /ˈræʃnəlaɪz; ˈræʃənlˌaɪz/ *vt* **1** [VP6 A] bring into conformity with reason; (attempt to) treat or explain in a rational manner: 使合理; (试图以) 合理态度处理或解释: ~ *one's fears / behaviour.* 合理解释自己的恐惧(行为)。 **2** [VP 6A] reorganize (an industry, etc)so as to lessen or get rid of waste(in time, labour, materials, etc). 改组(工业等)以减少或消除(时间、人工、材料等之)浪费; 使合理化。 **ration·al·iz·ation** /ˌræʃnəlaɪˈzeɪʃn US: -lɪˈz-; ˌræʃənlɪˈzeʃən/ *n*

rat·lin, rat·line /ˈrætlɪn; ˈrætlɪn/ *n* (usu *pl*) small rope fixed across the shrouds of a ship (like a rung on a ladder) used as a step by a sailor climbing up or down. (通常用复数)绳梯横索(船上横着固定在护桅索上的细绳, 类似梯阶, 供船员爬上爬下之用)。

rat·tan, ratan /ræˈtæn; ræˈtæn/ *n* **1** [C] (East Indian palm-tree with a) cane-like stem. 白藤 (东印度所产之棕榈树); 藤。**2**[C]walking-stick or cane made from a stem. 藤杖。 **3** [U] ~ stems (collectively), as used for building, basketwork, furniture, etc: (总称)用于建筑、篮状编制品、家具等之藤条: *a chair with a ~ seat.* 一把有藤座的椅子。

rat-tat /ræ ˈtæt; ˌræt·tæt/ *n* (*also* 亦作 **rat-a-tat-tat** /ˌræt ə ˌtæt; ˈtæt; ˌrætəˌtætˈtæt/) *n* sound of a rapping or knocking, esp on a door. 砰砰敲击声; (尤指)敲门声。

rattle /ˈrætl; ˈrætl/ *vt, vi* **1** [VP6A, 15A, 2A, C] (cause to) make short, sharp sounds quickly, one after the other: (使)急速、连续地发出短促尖锐的声音; 发嘎嘎声:*The wind ~d the windows.* 风吹得窗子嘎嘎作响。*The windows were rattling in the wind.* 窗子在风中嘎嘎作响。 *The hailstones ~d on the tin roof.* 冰雹砰砰地落在洋铁皮屋顶上。 *The bus ~d along over the stony road.* 那辆老爷公共汽车在石子路上嘎嘎地往前行驶。 **2** [VP2C, 15B] ~ *away; ~ sth off,* talk, say or repeat (sth) quickly and in a thoughtless or lively way: 疾速而又不加思索地谈, 说或重述(某事物): 喋喋而言:*The boy ~d off the poem he had learnt.* 那男孩将他学到的那首诗背诵得滚瓜烂熟。*The children ~d away merrily.* 这些孩子欢快地喋喋不休地说话。 □ *n* **1** [U] rattling sound: 嘎嘎声; 喋喋声:*the ~ of bottles from a milkman's van;* 送牛奶者的货车里发出的小瓶碰撞击声;*the ~ of hail on the window-panes.* 冰雹打在玻璃窗上的砰砰声。 **2** [C] baby's toy for producing a rattling sound; similar device whirled (eg by spectators at a football match) to make a noisy clatter. 拨浪鼓(能发出嘎嘎声的玩具); 发出嘎嘎声的手摇物 (如足球观众所持者)。 **3** [U] lively flow of talk; chatter . 喋喋不休的谈话; 饶舌。 **4** [C] series of horny rings in a ~snake's tail. (响尾蛇尾部的)一列响环。 '*~·snake n* poisonous American snake that makes a rattling noise with its tail. 响尾蛇 (美洲产的一种毒蛇, 其尾常发出声响)。 ⇨ the illus of **snake.** 参看 snake 之插图。 **5** ('*death*-) ~, rattling sound sometimes produced in the throat immediately before death. 死前喉间有时发出的咯咯声。 **6** '*~-brain, '~-pate nn* person with an empty head; silly chatterer. 没有思想的蠢人; 愚蠢而又唠叨的人。 Hence, 由此产生, '*~-brained, '~-pated adj*j **rat·tler** /ˈrætlə(r); ˈrætlə/ *n* person or thing that ~s, esp a ~snake. 发出嘎嘎、喋喋等声的人或物; (尤指)响尾蛇。 **rat·tling** /ˈrætlɪŋ; ˈrætlɪŋ/ *adj* **1** quick (-moving); first-rate; excellent: (俚)(行动)很快的; 第一流的; 卓越的: *travelling at a rattling rate;* 以极快速度旅行; *a rattling breeze;* 飒飒之微风; *have a rattling* (= enjoyable) *time.* 度过一段非常愉快的时光。 □ *adv* (sl) very: (俚) 非常: *a rattling good speech.* 一篇极好的演说。

ratty /ˈrætɪ; ˈrætɪ/ *adj* ⇨ **rat.**

rau·cous /ˈrɔːkəs; ˈrɔkəs/ *adj* (of sounds) harsh; rough; hoarse: (指声音)粗厉的;沙哑的: *the ~ cries of the crows*; 乌鸦粗哑的叫声; *a ~ voice*; 沙哑的声音; *~ laughter*. 沙哑的笑声。 ~·**ly** *adv*

rav·age /ˈrævɪdʒ; ˈrævɪdʒ/ *vt* [VP6A] **1** destroy; damage badly: 毁坏; 严重损坏: *forests ~d by fire*; 被大火损毁的森林; *a face ~d by disease*, eg covered with marks after smallpox. 为病所毁的面容(如患天花后留有麻子). **2** (of armies, etc) rob, plunder, with violence: (指军队等)抢劫; 掠夺: *They laid ~ the countryside*. 他们已把乡间洗劫一空。 □ *n* **1** [U] destruction; devastation. 破坏; 蹂躏。 **2** (*pl*) (复) *~s of*, destructive effects: 破坏的结果: *the ~s of time*, eg on a woman's looks; 时间的摧残 (如在妇女之容貌上所造成者); *the ~s of torrential rains*. 暴雨造成的灾情。

rave /reɪv; rev/ *vi, vt* **1** [VP2A, C, 3A] *~ (at / against / about sth)*, talk wildly, violently, angrily: 狂野地、粗暴地、愤怒地讲; 发狂言或谵语: *The patient* (eg someone with a high fever) *began to ~*. 病人(如发高烧者)开始胡言乱语. *When he was accused of stealing he ~d wildly against me*. 当他被控犯偷窃罪时, 他气呼呼地把我臭骂一顿. **2** [VP3A] *~ about sb / sth*, talk or act with (often) excessive enthusiasm: 过分热心地谈或做: *She ~d about the food she had had in France*. 她过分夸张地谈她在法国吃过的食物. **3** [VP15B] *~ it up*, (sl) take part in a very noisy, enjoyable party. (俚)参加一热闹愉快的聚会. Hence, 由此产生, '~**-up** *n* lively party. 热闹的聚会. □ *n* **1** (colloq) enthusiastic praise: (口, 常用作定语)热烈的夸奖; 大捧特捧的评论. *a ~ review*, eg of a book. (对一本书等之) 大捧特捧的评论. **2** (sl) wild, exciting party, dance, outing, etc. (俚)狂热的宴会、舞会、远足等. **3** (sl) great enthusiasm: (俚)极端的热心: *be in a ~ about sb*. 对某人极端的热心。 **raver** *n* (colloq) sb who ~s(3). (口)过分热心地说或做的人. **rav·ing** *adj* talking wildly: 发狂言谵语的: *a raving lunatic*. 一个说狂话的疯子. □ *adv* to the point of talking wildly: 近乎放肆地发狂言: *You're raving mad!* 你简直在说疯话! **rav·ings** *n pl* foolish or wild talk: 愚蠢或狂野的谈话: *the ravings of a madman*. 狂人的呓语。

ravel /ˈrævl; ˈrævl/ *vt, vi* (**-ll**, US also **-l-**) **1** [VP 2A, C] (of knitted or woven things) separate into threads; become untwisted; fray: (指编织物)绽线; 绽裂; 散开; 磨散: *Bind the edge of the rug so that it won't ~*. 把地毯边镶好以免它绽线。 **2** [VP6A] cause (threads, hair, etc) to be twisted together, knotted, etc; (fig) make confused. 使(线、发等)纠结一起; (喻)使混乱. **3** [VP6A, 15B] *~ (out)*, disentangle: 解开; 清理: *~ (out) a rope's end*. 解开编头. ⇨ **unravel**.

raven /ˈreɪvn; ˈrevən/ *n* **1** large, black bird like a crow, popularly regarded as a bird of ill omen. 渡鸦(一种大乌鸦, 一般视为不吉之鸟). **2** (attrib) glossy, shining black: (用作定语)乌溜溜的: *~ locks*, black hair. 乌溜溜的头发。

rav·en·ing /ˈrævənɪŋ; ˈrævənɪŋ/ *adj* fierce; savage; crazy for food: 凶猛的; 野蛮的; 贪吃的: *a ~ wolf*. 一只凶猛的饿狼。

rav·en·ous /ˈrævənəs; ˈrævənəs/ *adj* **1** very hungry. 很饿的. **2** greedy: 贪婪的: *a ~ appetite*, 贪婪的食欲; *~ hunger*; 极度饥饿; *~ for power*. 贪图权力。 ~·**ly** *adv* hungrily; greedily: 饥饿地; 贪婪地: *eat ~ly*. 贪婪地吃。

ra·vine /rəˈviːn; rəˈvin/ *n* deep, narrow valley. 深而狭的谷; 峡谷。

ravi·oli /ˌrævɪˈəʊli; ˌrævɪˈolɪ/ *n* (I) dish of small cases of pasta containing chopped meat, etc usu served with a sauce. (意)一种类似饺子的点心。

rav·ish /ˈrævɪʃ; ˈrævɪʃ/ *vt* [VP6A] **1** fill with delight; enchant: 使狂喜; 使陶醉: *a ~ing view*; 醉人的景色; *~ed by the view*; 为美景所陶醉; *~ed with her beauty*. 为她的美所倾倒. ~·**ing·ly** *adv* ~·**ment** *n* ~ing or being ~. 狂喜; 陶醉. **2** (archaic or poet) seize and carry off: (古或诗)攫夺; 掠劫: *~ed from the world by death*. 被死亡劫去; 死. **3** (archaic) rape (a woman or girl). (古)强奸(妇女)。

raw /rɔː; rɔ/ *adj* **1** uncooked: 未煮过的: *raw meat*; 生肉; *eat oysters raw*. 吃生蚝. **2** in the natural state, not manufactured or prepared for use: 天然状态的; 未经制造或加工的: *raw hides*, not yet tanned; 生毛皮(未硝的); *raw sugar*, not yet refined; 粗糖(未精炼过的); *the raw materials of industry*, eg coal, ores; 工业用的原料(如煤,原矿); *raw spirit*, undiluted alcohol. 未稀释之酒精. *in the raw*, unrefined; in the natural state; (fig) naked. 纯真的; 天然的; (喻)裸体的。 '**raw-hide** *adj* made of untanned hide: 生牛皮做的: *rawhide boots*. 生牛皮做的皮靴。 **3** (of persons) untrained; unskilled; inexperienced: (指人)未受训练的; 不熟练的; 无经验的: *raw recruits*, for the army, etc. 新兵. **4** (of the weather) damp and cold: (指天气)潮湿而冷的: *a raw February morning*; 一个阴冷的二月的早晨; *raw winds*. 阴寒的风. **5** (of wounds) unhealed; bloody: (of a place on the flesh) with the skin rubbed off; sore and painful. (指伤)未愈的; 流血的; (指肉上一处)擦掉皮的; 疼痛的。 '**raw-boned** *adj* having little flesh on the bones: 骨瘦如柴的: *a raw-boned horse*. 一匹瘦马. **6** artistically crude: 技艺上不成熟的: *His literary style is still rather raw*. 他的文学风格还相当不成熟. **7** (colloq) harsh; unjust: (口)严苛的; 不公的; (esp) (尤用于) *a raw deal*, harsh or cruel treatment. 严苛或残酷的对待。 □ *n* raw place on the skin, esp on a horse's skin. 皮肤(尤指马的皮肤)上的擦伤之处. *touch sb on the raw*, (fig) wound a person's feelings, wound him on the question, topic, etc on which he is most sensitive. (喻)伤害到某人的感情; 触及某人的痛处。

ray[1] /reɪ; re/ *n* [C] **1** line, beam, of radiant light, heat, energy: (辐射的光、热、能的)线; 射线: *the rays of the sun*; 太阳的光线; '*X-rays*; X 射线; '*heat-rays*; 热射线; (fig) (喻) *a ray of hope*. 一线希望. **2** any one of a number of lines coming out from a centre. 从一中心射出之许多线中之一. □ *vi, vt* send out or come out in rays. 呈线状射出。

ray[2] /reɪ; re/ *n* kinds of large sea-fish with a broad, flat body, eg *skate*. 缸鱼; 鳐鱼(数种大海鱼,身体宽而扁,如鯯虹等)。

rayon /ˈreɪɒn; ˈreɑn/ *n* [U] silk-like material made from cellulose: 嫘萦; 人造丝: (attrib) (用作定语) *~ shirts*. 人造丝做的衬衫。

raze, rase /reɪz; rez/ *vt* [VP6A] destroy (towns, buildings) completely, esp by making them level with the ground: 彻底破坏(城市、建筑物); (尤指)夷为平地: *a city ~d by an earthquake*. 一座被地震摧毁的城市。

razor /ˈreɪzə(r); ˈrezɚ/ *n* instrument with a sharp blade or cutters (some electrically driven) used for shaving hair from the skin. (电动)刮胡刀; 剃刀。 '**safety ~** *n* kind in which a thin blade is fitted between metal guards. 安全剃刀。 '**~-back** *n* kind of whale. 剃刀鲸。 '**~-backed** *adj* having a thin, sharp back: 有尖突脊背的: *a ~-backed pig*. 一只背脊尖突的瘦猪. '**~-blade** *n* disposable blade for a safety ~. 刮胡刀片。 '**~-edge** *n* sharp line of division; critical situation. 明显的分界线; 危险的情势; 危机. □ *vt* (rare, except in *pp*): (罕, 仅用过去分词): *a well-~ed chin*, well shaved. 剃得很光的下巴。

razors

razor-blade   electric shaver

razzle /'ræzl; 'ræzl/ *n* (also 亦作 ‸**~-'dazzle**) *be/go on the ~*, (sl) *be/go* on a spree. (俚) 狂饮. ⇨ **spree**.

re¹ /ri:; ri/ *prep* (in legal style) in the matter of; concerning. (法律用语)关于.

re² /reɪ; re/ *n* second note in the musical octave. 八度音程中之第二音.

re- /ri:; ri:/ *pref* **1** again: 再;重: *reappear*, *refloat*, *replay*. 再出现;再浮起;重赛. **2** in a different way: 以不同之方式: *rearrange*. 重新安排. ⇨ **App 3**. 参看附录三.

reach /ri:tʃ; ritʃ/ *vt, vi* **1** [VP2C, 3C, 15B] ~ *(out)* *(for)*, stretch out: 伸出: *He ~ed out his hand for the knife, but it was too far away*. 他伸出手取那刀子, 但太远了, 够不着. *He ~ed (out) for the dictionary*. 他伸出手拿字典. **2** [VP6A, 15B, 12B, 13B] stretch out the hand for and take (sth); get and give (sth) to: 伸手取(某物); 把(某物)递给: *Can you ~ that book for your brother?* 你能把那本书递给你哥哥(弟弟)吗? *Please ~ me that book*. 请把那本书递给我. *He ~ed down the atlas from the top shelf*. 他从书架的顶层取下地图集来. **3** [VP 6A] (lit or fig) get to, go as far as: (字面或喻)抵达;到: ~ *London*; 抵达伦敦; ~ *the end of the chapter*. 看到这章的末尾. *Can you ~ the branch with those red apples?* 你能够到那根结有红苹果的枝子吗? *Not a sound ~ed our ears*. 我们没有听到任何声音. **4** [VP2C] extend; go; pass: 延伸; 通过; 传达: *The land ~es as far as the river*. 那块地一直延伸到河边. *The speaker's voice did not ~ to the back of the hall*. 讲演者的声音不能传到大厅的后边. *I haven't been able to reach Kate for days*. ie get into contact with her, eg by telephone. 我已好些天没有和联络到凯蒂了 (如以电话联络). *as far as the eye can ~*, to the horizon. 目力之所及, 到达地平线; 极目. **5** '~-**me-downs** *n pl* (sl) second-hand clothes. (俚) 估衣. □ *n* **1** (*sing* only) act of ~ing or stretching out (a hand, etc): (仅用单数)(手等之)伸出; 延伸: *get sth by a long ~*. 把手伸长取某物. **2** [U] extent to which a hand, etc can be ~ed out, a movement carried out or one's mental powers extended or used: (手、活动、心力等所及的)范围: *This boxer has a long ~*. 这位拳击手的手够得很远. *within/out of/beyond ~: I like to have my reference books within my ~/within easy ~*, so near that I can get them quickly and easily. 我喜欢把参考书放在我伸手可取的范围内(顺手可取的地方). *Put that bottle of weed-killer out of the children's ~/out of ~ of the children*. 把那瓶除草药放在孩子们拿不到的地方. *The hotel is within easy ~ of the beach*. 这家旅馆距离海滨很近. *The village is within ~ of London*. 该村庄就在伦敦附近. *He was beyond ~ of human aid*, No one could do anything to help him. 任何人都帮不上他的忙. **3** [C] continuous extent, esp of a river or canal, that can be seen between two bends or locks. 连续不断的地区; (尤指河或运河的两弯间可见的)河段. ⇨ **lock²(3)**: *one of the most beautiful ~es of the Thames*. 泰晤士河最美丽的河段之一.

re·act /rɪ'ækt; rɪ'ækt/ *vi* **1** [VP2A, 3A] ~ *on/upon*, have an effect (on the person or thing acting): 对(行动中的人或进行中的事)有影响: *Applause ~s upon a speaker*, eg has the effect of giving him confidence. 鼓掌对一个演说者有影响 (例如给他信心). **2** [VP3A] ~ *to*, respond; behave differently, be changed, as the result of being acted upon: 反应; 因受影响而改变行动: *An orator ~s to applause*. 一个演说家对于鼓掌有反应. *Do children ~ to kind treatment by becoming more self-confident?* 对孩子们和善是否会使他们更有自信? **3** [VP3A] ~ *against*, respond to sth with a feeling: 反抗;反对: *Will the people ~ against the aggressor?* 人们会反抗侵略者吗? **4** [VP3A] ~ *on*, (chem) (of one substance applied to another) have an effect: (化学)(应用于他种物质之某种物质)(对…)起反应: *How do acids ~ on metals?* 酸对金属会引起怎样的化学反应?

re·ac·tion /rɪ'ækʃn; rɪ'ækʃən/ *n* [C, U] **1** action or state resulting from, in response to, sth, esp a return to an earlier condition after a period of the opposite

condition: 反应;反动;反作用: *action and ~*. 作用与反作用. *After these days of excitement there was a ~*, eg a period when life seemed dull. 经过这些天的兴奋之后又有一段沉闷生活. *Higher wages affect costs of production and then comes the ~ of costs on prices*. 较高的工资会影响生产成本, 而生产成本又会影响售价. **2** retrograde tendency, esp in politics; opposition to progress: 倒退之倾向 (尤指政治方面);反动;进步: *The forces of ~ made reform difficult*. 反动力量使改革困难. **3** responsive feeling: 反应: *What was his ~ to your proposal?* 你对你的建议有何反应? **4** (science) action set up by one substance in another; change within the nucleus of an atom. (科学)化学反应;核反应. *~·ary* /rɪ'ækʃənrɪ US: -neri; rɪ'ækʃən,ɛrɪ/ *n* (*pl* -ries), *adj* (person) opposing progress or reform. 反对进步或改革的(人);反动的(人).

re·ac·tor /rɪ'æktə(r); rɪ'æktə/ *n* nuclear ~, apparatus for the controlled production of nuclear energy; atomic pile. 核反应堆(一种控制核能生产的装置);原子反应堆.

read /ri:d; rid/ *vt, vi* (*pt, pp* read /red; red/) **1** [VP 6A, 2A] (used in the simple tenses or with *can/be able*) look at and (be able to) understand (sth written or printed): (用作简单时态或与 can, be able 连用时)读;看懂: *Can you ~ Chinese characters/French/a musical score?* 你能看懂中文字 (法文, 乐谱)吗? *A motorist must be able to ~ traffic signs*. 驾驶者必须能看懂交通标志. *Can the child ~ the time/the clock yet?* 这孩子会看时间(钟)吗? *I can't ~ your shorthand notes*. 我看不懂你的速记符号. *The boy can neither ~ nor write*. 这男孩既不会读也不会写. **2** [VP6A, 12A, 13A, 15B, 2A, C] (simple or continuous tenses) reproduce mentally or vocally the words of (an author, book, etc). (用于简单时或进行时)阅读;默读;朗诵: *R~ the letter aloud, please*. 请大声念这封信. *She was ~ing the letter silently/to herself*. 她正在默读那封信. *She was ~ing a story to the children*. 她正在念一篇故事给孩子们听. *I haven't enough time to ~/for ~ing*. 我没有足够的时间阅读. *He ~ the letter through six times*. 他把那封信从头到尾看了六次. *Please ~ me the letter*. 请把那封信念给我听. *She ~ out the letter to all of us*. 她向我们大家朗诵那封信. *The old man ~ me a lesson/~ me a severe lecture*, reproved me. 那老人教训了我一番. *The play was ~* (ie each actor ~ his part aloud) *before the cast went on the stage*. 剧本在上演之前先(由演员)诵读台词. **3** [VP6A, 15A, B] study (a subject, esp at a university): 研究;攻读(一学科, 尤指大学中者): *He's ~ing physics/~ing for a degree in physics/~ing for a physics degree at Cambridge*. 他在剑桥大学攻读物理(攻读物理学位). *He's ~ing for the Bar*, studying law in order to become a barrister. 他在攻读法律准备当律师. *You had better ~ the subject up*, make a special study of it. 你最好对这科目作深入的研究. **4** [VP6A] interpret mentally; learn the significance of: 解释;解答;领会…的意义: *~ a riddle/dream*; 解谜(详梦); *~ sb's thoughts*. 了解某人之思想. *The gipsy offered to ~ my hand/palm*, tell me about myself and the future by examining the lines on the palm of my hand. 那个吉卜赛人要为我看手相. **5** [VP2C] give a certain impression; seem (good, etc) when ~: 给予某种印象;读起来似乎(不错等): *The play ~s better than it acts*, is better for ~ing than for performance on the stage. 这个剧本读起来要比上演好得多. **6** [VP16B] assume, find implications in (what is read, etc): 假定或找出(所读之物等中)的含意: *Silence mustn't always be ~ as consent*, We must not always assume that a person means 'Yes' when no answer is given to a request, etc. 沉默并不总是被假定为同意. *~ into*, add more than is justified: 加上某种含意, 且以为有实在的含意: *You have ~ into her letter more sympathy than she probably feels*. 你自以为她信中的同情比她可能感觉到的要多. *~ between the lines*, look for or discover meanings that are not actually expressed. 找出字里行间的言外之意. **7** [VP2 B] (of instruments) indicate: (指仪器)指示: *What does*

the thermometer ~? 温度计指多少度? **8** [VP15A] bring into a specified state by ~ing: 由阅读而进入某种状态: *She ~ herself to sleep.* 她看书看得睡着了. **9** (*pp* with an *adv*) having knowledge gained from books, etc: (过去分词与副词连用)有从书中得来的知识的;有书本知识的: *a well-~ man;* 学问渊博的人;*deeply ~ in the classics.* 精通古典文学. □ *n* period of time given to ~ing: 专注阅读的一段时间: *have a good ~ in the train;* 在火车上好好看一会书;*have a quiet ~.* 静静地看一会儿. ~·**able** /'ri:dəbl; 'ridəbl/ *adj* **1** that is easy or pleasant to ~. 易读的;读来令人愉快的. **2** that can be ~. 能够被读的;可读的;清楚的. *legible, the more usu word.* (legible 较常用). ~·**abil·ity** /ˌri:də'bɪlətɪ; ˌridə'bɪlətɪ/ *n*

re-ad·dress /ˌri:ə'dres; ˈriəˈdrɛs/ *vt* [VP6A] change the address on (a letter, etc). 改写(信等)上的地址.

reader /'ri:də(r); 'ridɚ/ *n* **1** person who reads, esp one who spends much time in reading; (*publisher's* ~) person employed to read MSS offered for publication and say whether they are good, etc; printer's proof-corrector; (*lay* ~) person appointed to read aloud parts of a service in church. 读者;阅读者(指花很多时间于阅读者); (出版者雇用的)审阅原稿的人; 校对员;(在教堂仪式中被指定)朗诵经文者. **2** (GB) university teacher of a rank immediately below a professor: (英)阶级低于教授的大学教师;讲师: *R~ in English Literature.* 英国文学讲师. **3** textbook for reading in class; book with selections for reading by students of a language: 教科书;(学习语言者的)读本:*a Latin R~.* 拉丁文读本. **4** person who can interpret what is hidden or obscure, 释疑者;解答者;阐明者,esp 尤指 a *mind-/'thought-~*. 测心术者;读心术者. '~·**ship** ~/-ʃɪp, -ʃɪp/ *n* **1** position of a ~ (2). 大学讲师之职位. **2** (of a periodical) number of persons who read it (which may be larger than its circulation). (指期刊)读者群(读者人数可能大于发行数量).

read·ily, readi·ness ⇨ ready.

read·ing /'ri:dɪŋ; 'ridɪŋ/ *n* **1** [U] act of one who reads. 阅读或朗诵的动作. '~ **desk,** lectern. (教堂中的)读经台. '~-**glasses** *n* glasses for ~ (contrasted with glasses for long-distance use). 读书时戴用之眼镜(与看远距离所用者相对). '~-**lamp** *n* shaded table-lamp used to read by. (阅读用的)有罩台灯. '~-**room** *n* room (eg in a club or public library) set apart for ~. 阅览室. **2** [U] knowledge, esp of books: 知识(尤指书本知识):*a man of wide ~.* 学识渊博的人. **3** [C] way in which sth is interpreted or understood: 将事物解释解说理解之方式: *my solicitor's ~ of this clause in the agreement,* what he says it means. 我的律师对该契约中这一条文之解释. **4** [C] figure of measurement, as shown on a dial, scale, etc: 读数(刻度盘,尺等上所指出的度数): *The ~s on my thermometer last month were well above the average.* 上月我的温度计所指示出的度数远超过平均温度. **5** [C] variant reading of a text that occurs in copying or printing from time to time: 出现于不同抄本或版本行文稿有出入的同一篇文字: *The ~ of the First Folio is the true one.* 第一对开本的文字是真正的原文. **6** [C] entertainment in which sth is read to an audience; passage so read: (向听众朗诵某东西的)朗诵会;朗诵的章节:*R~s from Dickens.* 狄更斯作品朗诵会;狄更斯朗诵选. '**play-~,** recital of the text of a play by a group. 剧本诵读. **7** [C] (in Parliament) one of the three stages through which a Bill must pass before it is ready for royal assent. (在议会中)一法案三读过程中之任何一次.

re·ad·just /ˌri:ə'dʒʌst; ˌriəˈdʒʌst/ *vt, vi* [VP6A, 3A, 15A] ~ (*oneself*) (*to*), adjust again: 再整理;再调整;重新适应: *It's sometimes difficult to ~ (oneself) to life in Britain after working abroad.* 在国外工作过之后,有时很难再适应英国的生活方式. ~·**ment** *n* ~ing or being ~ed; [C] instance of this. 再整理;再调整;重新适应;被再整理或再调整;再整理、再调整、重新适应之实例.

ready /'redɪ; 'rɛdɪ/ *adj* (-**ier,** -**iest**) **1** (*pred* only) (仅用作表语) ~ (*for sth / to do sth*), in the condition

needed for use; in the condition for doing sth; willing: 在准备使用之状态的;在准备做某事之状态的;自愿(做某事)的;准备妥当的;准备就绪的: ~ *for work;* 为工作作准备就绪;准备妥了,可以工作了;*get ~ for a journey;* 作好旅行准备;*be ~ to start.* 准备出发. *He's always ~ to help his friends.* 他总是乐意帮助朋友. **make** ~, prepare. 预备;准备. **2** quick; prompt: 迅速的;立即的: *Don't be so ~ to find fault.* 不要动不动就吹毛求疵. *He always has a ~ answer.* 他永远有现成的答案. *You are too ~ with excuses.* 你总是有借口. *He has a ~ wit.* 他有机智. **3** within reach; easily procured: 在可及之范围内的;易于取得的: *keep a revolver ~,* near at hand. 把一支手枪放于身边. ~ **money,** money in the form of coins or notes, which can be used for payment at the time when goods are bought (contrasted with *credit*). 现款;现钱(与 credit 相对). ~ **reckoner,** book of answers to various common calculations needed in business, etc. 计算便览; 算术表. **4** (*adv* use, with *pp*) prepared beforehand: (作副词用,与过去分词连用)事先准备好的: *buy food ~ cooked.* 买做好的食品. '~-**made** *adj* (**a**) ~ to wear or use: 现成的;现成的: ~-*made clothes,* made in standard sizes, not to measurements of customers. 成衣(按标准尺码做成者). (**b**) (fig) not original; of standard pattern, etc: (喻)非独创的; 陈腐的; 老套的: *come to a subject with ~-made ideas.* 以陈腐的想法来对待一件事. □ *n* (only in) (仅用于) *at the ~,* (of a rifle) in the position for aiming and firing. (指步枪)准备射击;瞄准. **read·ily** ~/-ɪlɪ; -ɪlɪ/ *adv* **1** without showing hesitation or unwillingness, 毫不迟疑地;欣然. **2** without difficulty. 容易地;无困难地. **readi·ness** /'redɪnɪs; 'rɛdɪnɪs/ *n* [U] **1** *in readiness* (*for*), in a ready or prepared state: 准备好的状态: *have everything in readiness for an early start.* 为及早出发而把一切准备好了. **2** willingness; 情愿: *a surprising readiness to accept the proposal.* 出奇爽快地接受该项提议. **3** promptness; quickness: 敏捷;迅速: *readiness of wit.* 机智;机敏.

re·af·firm /ˌri:ə'fɜ:m; ˌriəˈfɝm/ *vt* [VP6A, 9] affirm again; repeat an affirmation: 重申;再肯定;再断定;再证实: ~ *one's loyalty.* 再申个人的忠诚.

re·af·for·est /ˌri:ə'fɒrɪst *US:* -'fɔ:r-; ˌriəˈfɔrɛst/, (US = **re·for·est** /ˌri:'fɒrɪst *US:* -'fɔ:r-; riˈfɔrɪst/) *vt* replant (an area of land) with forest trees. 再植树;再造林. **re·af·for·est·ation** /ˌri:əˌfɒrɪ'steɪʃn *US:* -ˌfɔ:r-; ˌriəˌfɔrɛsˈteʃən/, (US = **re·for·est·ation** /ˌri:ˌfɒrɪ'steɪʃn *US:* -ˌfɔ:r-; riˌfɔrɪsˈteʃən/) *n*

re·agent /ri:'eɪdʒənt; riˈedʒənt/ *n* [C] (chem) substance used to detect the presence of another by reaction; reactive substance or force. (化学)试剂;试药;反应物;反应剂;反应力.

real[1] /rɪəl; 'riəl/ *adj* **1** existing in fact; not imagined or supposed; not made up or artificial: 事实上存在的; 非想象或假设的; 非虚构的; 真实的: *Is this ~ gold or pinchbeck?* 这是真金还是合金(金色铜)? *Is this ~ silk or rayon?* 这是真丝还是人造丝? *The doctors could not effect a ~* (= genuine, complete) *cure.* 这些医生都不能予以根治. *Things that happen in ~ life are sometimes stranger than things that occur in fiction.* 发生于现实生活中的事有时比小说中虚构的事还要离奇. *Who is the ~ manager of the firm?* 谁是这家商号真正的经理? *Tell me the ~* (= true) *reason.* 把真正理由告诉我. ~ **ale,** (GB 1970s)ale that is made, stored and served in traditional, careful ways. 真正淡色啤酒(英国廿世纪七十年代,以传统而又细心的方式酿制、储存及饮用之淡色啤酒). **2** '~ **estate,** (legal) immovable property consisting of land, any natural resources, and buildings (contrasted with *personal estate*, (法律)房地产; 不动产(与 personal estate 相对). **3** (US colloq as *adv*) really, very: (美口,作副词用)真正地; 非常地: *We had a ~ good time.* 我们玩得非常尽兴. *I'm ~ sorry.* 我的确很抱歉. ~·**ly** /'rɪəlɪ; 'riəlɪ/ *adv* **1** in fact; without doubt; truly: 事实上; 无疑地; 真正地: *What do you ~ly think about it?* 你对那件事到底做何想法? *It was ~ly not my fault.* 那的确不是我的

错。*I'm ~ly sorry.* 我确实很抱歉。**2** (as an expression of interest, surprise, mild protest, doubt, etc according to context): (用以表示兴趣、惊讶、温和的抗议、怀疑等, 其意义依上下文而定): '*We're going to Mexico next month.*'—'*Oh, ~ly!*' (or) '*Not ~ly!*' '我们下个月要去墨西哥'。——'啊! 真的呀! '(或 '不是真的吧? ')*You ~ly shouldn't say that about her!* 你真不该说她那种话!

real² /'reɪɑːl; 'rɪəl/ *n* [C] silver coin and unit of currency formerly used in Spanish-speaking countries. 里亚尔(昔时西班牙语国家所使用之银币和货币单位)。

real·ism /'rɪəlɪzəm; 'rɪəl,ɪzəm/ *n* [U] **1** (in art and literature) showing of real life, facts, etc in a true way, omitting nothing that is ugly or painful, and idealizing nothing. (艺术与文学)写实主义; 现实主义(以忠实的方式表现真实生活、事实等, 不略去丑恶或痛苦的事, 亦不理想化任何事。**2** behaviour based on the facing of facts and disregard of sentiment and convention. 就事论事或面对事实的态度。**3** (phil) theory that matter has real existence apart from our mental perception of it. (哲学)实在论; 唯物论(认为物质真正存在, 不受我们对它认知的影响)。 ⇨ **idealism, realist** /-ɪst; -ɪst/ *n* person who believes in ~ in art, philosophy, social problems, etc; person who believes himself to be without illusions. 写实主义者; 现实主义者; 实在论者; 脚踏实地的人。**real·is·tic** /ˌrɪə'lɪstɪk; ˌrɪə'lɪstɪk/ *adj* **1** marked by, relating to, ~ in philosophy or art. 实在论的; 写实主义的, 现实主义的。**2** practical; not moved by sentiment; 实际的; 现实的; 不为感情所动的: *realistic politics,* 现实的政治。**real·is·ti·cally** /-klɪ; -klɪ/ *adv*

re·al·ity /rɪ'ælətɪ; rɪ'ælətɪ/ *n* (*pl* -ties) **1** [U] the quality of being real; real existence; that which underlies appearance: 真实; 实存; 现实; 真相: *belief in the ~ of miracles,* 相信奇迹之真实性; *the search after God and ~.* 追求上帝与真实。**bring sb back to ~,** get him to stop dreaming, being sentimental, etc. 使某人面对现实。**in ~,** really, in actual fact. 实际上; 事实上。**2** [C] sth real; sth actually seen or experienced: 真实之物; 真正被看到或经验过的事物: *the grim realities of war,* contrasted with romantic ideas, etc. 战争的冷酷事实, 与战争的幻想相对)。**3** [U] realism(1). 写实主义, 现实主义。

real·ize /'rɪəlaɪz; 'rɪə,laɪz/ *vt* **1** [VP6A, 9, 10] be fully conscious of; understand: 完全认知; 了解: *Does he ~ his error yet / ~ that you must have help?* 他知道他的错(你需要帮忙)吗? **2** [VP6A] convert (a hope, plan, etc) into a fact: 实现 (希望、计划等) 实现: ~ *one's hopes /ambitions.* 实现一个人的希望(野心)。**3** [VP 6A] exchange (property, business shares, etc) for money: 变卖(财产、股票等): *these shares/bonds, etc, be ~d at short notice?* 这些股票(债券等)能随时变卖成现款吗? **4** [VP6A, 14] ~ (*on*), (of property, etc) obtain as a price for or as a profit: (指财产等)作为价值或收益而获得; 卖得(若干钱): *The furniture ~d a high price at the sale.* 在拍卖时家具卖到很高的价钱。*How much did you ~ on the paintings you sent to the sale?* 你送去卖的画卖了多少钱? **real·iz·able** /-əbl; -əbl/ *adj* that can be ~d. 可认知的; 可实现的; 可实行的; 可变卖的。**real·iz·ation** /ˌrɪəlaɪ'zeɪʃn *US:* -lɪ'z-; ˌrɪələ'zeɪʃən/ *n* [U] realizing (of a plan, one's ambitions or hopes); act of exchanging property for money. (计划、野心或希望的)实现; 变卖。

realm /relm; relm/ *n* **1** (poet, rhet or legal use) kingdom: (诗, 修辞, 法律用语)王国: *the defence of the R~;* 保卫国家; *a Peer of the R~.* 国家的贵族。**2** region (fig): (喻)区域; 领域: *the ~ of the imagination;* 想象的领域; *in the ~s of fancy.* 在幻想的领域中。

Re·al·tor /'rɪəltə(r); 'rɪəltə/ *n* (US) person engaged in real estate business who is a member of the National Association of Real Estate Boards and subscribes to its standards of ethical conduct (GB *US = estate agent*). (美)房地产经纪人(全国房地产委员会之会员)。

re·alty /'rɪəltɪ; 'rɪəltɪ/ *n* (*pl* -ties) (legal) real estate. (法律)房地产; 不动产。

ream /riːm; rim/ *n* measure for paper, 480 (or US 500) sheets or 20 quires; (colloq, *pl*) great quantity (of writing); 令(量纸的单位, 480 张(美 500 张)或 20 帖)(口, 复)大量(的写作): *She has written ~s of verse.* 她写了无数的诗。

re·ani·mate /riː'ænɪmeɪt; ri'ænə,met/ *vt* [VP6A] fill with new strength, courage or energy. 使充满新力量, 勇气或活力。

reap /riːp; rip/ *vt, vi* [VP6A, 2A] cut (grain, etc), gather in a crop of grain from (a field, etc): 收割; 收获:~ *a field of barley;* 收割田中大麦;~ *the corn,* 割取谷物; (fig) (喻) ~ *the reward of virtue;* 得到美德的报酬; ~ *where one has not sown,* profit from work done by others. 不劳而获。(**sow the wind and) ~ the whirlwind,** (prov) suffer for one's foolish conduct. (谚)因做出愚蠢行为而自食其恶果。'**~ing-hook** *n* sickle. 镰刀。~**er** *n* **1** person who ~s. 收割者。**2** ~ing-machine for cutting grain (and in some cases binding it into sheaves). 收割机。

re·appear /ˌriːə'pɪə(r); ˌriə'pɪr/ *vi* [VP2A] appear again (esp after disappearing). 再出现(尤指消失后再出现)。~**·ance** /-rəns; -rəns/ *n*

re·apprais·al /ˌriːə'preɪzl; ˌriə'prezl/ *n* new examination and judgement: 再评价; 再鉴定; 再估计: *a ~ of our relations with Japan.* 我们同日本的关系的再估计。

rear¹ /rɪə(r); rɪr/ *n* **1** back part: 后部; 背面: *The kitchen is in the ~ of the house.* 厨房在房子的后部。*The garage is at the ~ of* (US 美 *in the ~ of*) *the house.* 车房在房子的后边。**2** (attrib) in or at the ~: (用作定语)在后部的: *the ~ wheels/lamps, of a car, etc;* (汽车的)后轮/(尾灯): *leave the bus by the ~ entrance;* 从后门下公共汽车; *a ~-view mirror,* driving mirror (in a motor-vehicle) for seeing out of the back window. (汽车之)后视镜。**3** last part of any army, fleet, etc: (军队、舰队等的)后阵; 后尾: *attack the enemy in the ~.* 从背后攻击敌人。**bring up the ~,** come the last. 殿后。**4** ,~·**admiral** /'ædmərəl; ˌrɪr'ædmərəl/ *n* naval officer below a vice-admiral. 海军少将。'**~·guard** *n* body of soldiers given the duty of guarding the ~ of an army. 后卫。**a ~guard action,** fight between an army in retreat and the enemy. 后卫战斗。~**·most** /'rɪəməust; 'rɪr,most/ *adj* farthest back. 最后面的。~**·ward** /'rɪəwəd; 'rɪrwəd/ *n*: *to ~ward of,* some distance behind; 遥遥在后的; *in the ~ward, at the back.* 在后面。~**·wards** /'rɪəwədz; 'rɪrwədz/ *adv* towards the ~. 向后面地。

rear² /rɪə(r); rɪr/ *vt, vi* **1** [VP6A] cause or help to grow; bring up: 使或助之生长; 养育; 饲养:~ *poultry/cattle;* 饲养家禽(家畜);~ *a family* (US 美通常作 *raise a family*). 养育子女。**2** [VP2A, C] (esp of a horse) rise on the hind legs. (尤指马)用后腿站立。**3** [VP6A, 15 B] raise; lift up: 抬起; 举起: *The snake ~ed its head.* 蛇抬起了头。*The horse ~ed itself up.* 马用后腿直立。**4** [VP6A] set up: 建立; 竖立:~ *a monument.* 建一纪念碑。

re·arm /ˌriː'ɑːm; ri'ɑrm/ *vt, vi* [VP6A, 2A] supply (an army, etc) with weapons again, or with weapons of new types, etc. 再武装; 重整军备; 重新装备; 配以新式武器。**re·arma·ment** /riː'ɑːməmənt; ri'ɑrməmənt/ *n*

rea·son¹ /'riːzn; 'rizn/ *n* **1** [C, U] (fact put forward as) cause of or justification for sth: 理由; 原因; 缘故: *There is ~ to believe that he is dishonest.* 有理由相信他不诚实。*Is there any ~ why you should not help?* 你有什么理由不帮忙? *He complains with ~* (= rightly) *that he has been punished unfairly.* 他抱怨所受处罚不公平是有理由的。*Give me your ~s for doing it.* 告诉我你做那件事的理由。*My ~ is that the cost will be too high.* 我的理由是费用太高。*The ~ why he's late is that/because there was a breakdown on the railway.* 他迟到的原因是铁路出了毛病。**by ~ of,** because of: 因为; 由于: *He was excused by ~ of his age.* 他因为年龄的关系而被原谅。**2** [U] power of the mind to understand, form opinions, etc: 理解; 理智; 理性: *Only man has ~.* 只有人

类有理性。*lose one's ~*, go mad: 发疯:*The poor old fellow has lost his ~.* 那个可怜的老人疯了。**3** [U] what is right or practicable; common sense; sensible conduct: 正确或可行之事; 道理; 常识; 明智的行为: *He's not amenable to ~.* 他不讲理。*bring sb to ~*, persuade him to give up foolish activities, useless resistance, etc. 说服某人放弃愚蠢的活动, 无用的抵抗等; 使明白道理。*do anything in / within ~*, anything sensible or reasonable: 做任何合理明智的事:*I'm willing to do anything in ~.* 我愿做任何合理的事。*listen to / hear ~*, allow oneself to be persuaded; pay attention to common-sense, advice, etc. 听人道理, 接受劝告。*lose all ~*, become irrational, illogical. 失去理智的; 不合常理的。*without rhyme or ~*, ⇨ **rhyme(1)**. *It stands to ~ (that...)*, is obvious to sensible people (that...); most people will agree (that...). 明眼人一望而知; 大多数人会同意…; 合于道理; 按照常情。*~·less* adj lacking ~. 缺乏理性的; 没有理智的; 不合道理的。

rea·son² /'riːzn; 'rizṇ/ vi, vt **1** [VP2A] make use of one's reason(2); exercise the power of thought: 推理; 思考:*Man's ability to ~ makes him different from the animals.* 人的思考能力使人异于禽兽。**2** [VP3A] *~ with sb*, argue in order to convince him: (为说服某人而) 与某人辩论:*She ~ed with me for an hour about the folly of my plans.* 她同我争辩了一小时, 想使我明白我的计划多荒唐。**3** [VP9] *~ that...*, say by way of argument: 争辩着说:*He ~ed that if we began early enough, we could arrive before noon.* 他争辩着说如果我们黎明即出发, 中午之前就能抵达。**4** [VP6A] express logically or in the form of an argument: 合逻辑地或以议论形式表达:*a well-~ed statement / manifesto.* 一个非常合逻辑的陈述 (宣言)。*~ sth out*, find an answer by considering successive arguments, etc: 推论出某事物的答案:*~ out the answer to a question.* 推论出某问题的答案。**5** [VP14] *~ sb into / out of sth*, persuade by argument to do / not to do sth: 说服某人做(不做)某事:*~ a person out of his fears*, show him that his fears are groundless; 说服某人使消除其恐惧; *~ sb out of a false belief*; 说服某人放弃一错误信仰; *~ sb into a sensible course of action.* 劝某人采取合理的行动。*~·ing* n [U] process of reaching conclusions by using one's reason: 推理的过程:*He surpasses most of us in power of ~ing*, is better at drawing conclusions from facts, etc. 他的推理能力超过我们大多数人。*There's no ~ing with that woman*, She won't listen to reason. 那个女人不可理喻。

rea·son·able /'riːznəbl; 'riznəbḷ/ adj **1** having ordinary common sense; able to reason; acting, done, in accordance with reason; willing to listen to reason: 有普通常识的; 能推理的; 行为或做事合于道理的; 服理的; 讲理的:*You're not very ~ if you expect a child to understand sarcasm*, 你如果希望一个小孩子能懂得讽刺, 那就太不明理了。*Is the accused guilty beyond ~ doubt?* 被告是毫无疑问地有罪吗? **2** moderate; neither more nor less than seems right or acceptable: 适度的; 不多不少的; 公道的: *a ~ price / offer.* 公道的价格 (出价)。**3** fair; just; not absurd: 公平的; 正常的; 不荒谬的:*a ~ excuse*; 一个合理的借口; *be ~ in one's demands.* 要求合理。*~·ness* n **rea·son·ably** /-əblɪ; -əblɪ/ adv

re·as·sure /ˌriːə'ʃʊə(r); ˌriə'ʃur/ vt [VP6A] remove the fears or doubts of: 消除对…之恐惧或疑虑; 使安心:*She felt ~d after the police had told her that her children were safe.* 警察告诉她她的孩子们很安全后, 她就安心了。*re·as·sur·ance* /-rəns; -rəns/ n [U, C]. *re·as·sur·ing* adj comforting: 安慰的; 令人安心的: *a reassuring glance / word / pat.* 令人安心的一瞥 (话, 轻拍)。*re·as·sur·ing·ly* adv

re·bar·ba·tive /rɪ'bɑːbətɪv; rɪ'bɑrbətɪv/ adj (formal) stern; repellent. (正式用语)严厉的; 讨人厌的。

re·bate /'riːbeɪt; 'ribet/ n [C] sum of money by which a debt, tax, etc may be reduced; discount: 债务、租税等可获减免的款额; 宽减额; 折扣; 折让; 议减:*There is a ~ of £1.50 if the account is settled before 31 Dec.* 如果帐目

在十二月三十一日前结清, 可减收一英镑半。

rebel¹ /'rebl; 'rebḷ/ n **1** person who takes up arms against, or refuses allegiance to, the established government; person who resists authority or control: 武装反抗或不服从政府的反叛者; 抗拒权威或控制的人: *a ~ in the home*, eg a child who resists the authority of its parents. 家庭的叛逆(如不服从父母权威的孩子)。**2** (attrib) relating to ~s; of the nature of a rebellion: (用作定语)反叛的; 反叛者的:*the ~ forces.* 叛军。

re·bel² /rɪ'bel; rɪ'bɛl/ vi (-ll-) [VP2A, 3A] *~ (against)*, **1** take up arms to fight (against the government). 武装反抗(政府); 造反; 反叛。**2** show resistance; protest strongly: 抵抗; 强烈抗议:*The prisoners ~led against having no physical exercise.* 囚犯们抗议没有运动的机会。*Such treatment would make anyone ~.* 这样的对待会使任何人起而反抗。

re·bel·lion /rɪ'beljən; rɪ'bɛljən/ n [U] *~ (against)*, rebelling, esp against a government: 反叛(尤指反叛政府):*rise in ~*, 群起反叛; 揭竿而起; [C] instance of this: 反叛之实例; 叛乱:*five ~s in two years*; 两年之内五次叛乱;*a ~ against the dictator.* 对独裁者的反叛。

re·bel·li·ous /rɪ'beljəs; rɪ'bɛljəs/ adj **1** acting like a rebel; taking part in a rebellion: 反叛的; 参与反叛的: *~ subjects*; 反叛的臣民; *~ behaviour.* 反叛行为。**2** not easily controlled: 不易控制的: *a child with a ~ temper.* 一个脾气倔强的孩子。*~·ly* adv *~·ness* n

re·bind /ˌriː'baɪnd; ri'baɪnd/ vt (pt, pp **-bound** /-'baʊnd; -'baʊnd/) [VP6A] put a new binding on (a book, etc). 重新装订(书等)。

re·birth /ˌriː'bɜːθ; ri'bɝθ/ n **1** spiritual change, eg by conversion or enlightenment, causing a person to lead a new kind of life. (由信仰之改变或启蒙等而使人过一种新生活的)精神改变; 再生。**2** revival: 复生; 复兴: *the ~ of learning.* 文艺复兴。

re·born /ˌriː'bɔːn; ri'bɔrn/ adj (fig) born again, ie spiritually. (喻)再生的; 新生的。

re·bound /rɪ'baʊnd; rɪ'baʊnd/ vi [VP2A, 3A] **1** *~ (from)*, spring or bounce back after hitting sth: 跃回; 弹回:*The ball ~ed from the wall into the lily pond.* 球从墙上弹回掉到莲花池中。**2** *~ on / upon*, (fig) come back upon the agent; happen as the consequence of one's own action: (喻) 自食其果; 报应:*The evil you do may ~ upon yourselves.* 你们所做的恶可能回报到你们自己之的身上; 你们会自食恶果。**3** pt, pp of **rebind**. □ n /'riːbaʊnd; 'ribaʊnd/ return; *on the ~*, (a) while bouncing back: 弹回时:*hit a ball on the ~.* 击中弹回之球。(b) (fig) while still reacting to depression or disappointment: (喻)沮丧或失望之余:*She quarrelled with Paul and then married Peter on the ~.* 她和保罗争吵之后旋而嫁给彼得。

re·buff /rɪ'bʌf; rɪ'bʌf/ n [C] *meet with / suffer a ~ (from sb)*, unkind or contemptuous refusal of, or show of indifference to (an offer of or request for help, friendship, etc); snub. (对提供或要求援助、友谊等表示的)严峻或轻蔑的拒绝; 轻待; 冷落。□ vt [VP6A] give a ~ to. 严拒。

re·build /ˌriː'bɪld; ri'bɪld/ vt (pt, pp **-built** /-'bɪlt; -'bɪlt/) [VP6A] build or put together again: 再建; 重新装组:*a rebuilt typewriter.* 一架重装的打字机。

re·buke /rɪ'bjuːk; rɪ'bjuk/ vt [VP6A, 14] *~ sb (for sth)*, reprove, speak severely to (officially or otherwise): 指责; 非难: *~ a subordinate for being impudent.* 指责一属下的卤莽。□ n [C] reproof: 指责; 非难:*administer ~s to sb.* 予某人以指责(责难某人)。*re·buk·ing·ly* adv

re·bus /'riːbəs; 'ribəs/ n puzzle in which a word or phrase has to be guessed from pictures or diagrams that suggest the syllables that make it. 画谜; 字谜。

re·but /rɪ'bʌt; rɪ'bʌt/ vt (-tt-) [VP6A] prove (a charge, piece of evidence, etc) to be false; refute. 证明(控诉、证据等)的为伪; 反驳。*~·tal* /-tl; -tl/ n act of ~ting; evidence that ~s a charge, etc. 反驳; 反证。

re·cal·ci·trant /rɪ'kælsɪtrənt; rɪ'kælsɪtrənt/ adj disobedient; resisting authority or discipline. 不服从

的;反抗权威或纪律的。 **re·cal·ci·trance** /-əns, -ɒns/, **re·cal·ci·trancy** /-ənsɪ; -ɒnsɪ/ *nn* [U] being ~. 不服从;反抗。

re·call /rɪ'kɔːl; rɪ'kɔl/ *vt* 1 [VP6A, 14] ~ *sb (from/ to)*, summon back: 召回: ~ *an ambassador (from his post/to his own country)*. (从其驻在地)召回大使(返国)。 2 [VP6A, C, 8, 9, 10, 19C] bring back to the mind; recollect: 记起;忆起: *I don't ~ his name/face/ meeting him/where I met him*. 我不记得他的名字(他的脸, 见过他, 在什么地方见过他)。 *Can you ~ your schooldays?* 你能忆起学生时代的情形吗? 3 [VP 6A] take back; revoke (an order, a decision). 撤销;取消(订单、决定)。 □ *n* 1 summons to return; (esp) summons to an ambassador to return to his own country: 召回;唤回;(尤指)召回大使: *letters of ~*. 召回大使之函件;解任状。 2 [U] ability to remember: 回忆; 回想: *a man gifted with instant ~*. 一个天生有敏捷记忆力的人。 3 [U] possibility of recalling. 召回, 记起或撤销的可能。 *beyond/past ~*, that cannot be brought back or revoked. 不能召回; 记不起的; 不能撤销的。 4 [C] signal, eg a bugle call, to troops, etc to return: 军队等的召回讯号; 收操(工)号; *sound the ~*. 吹收操(工)号。

re·cant /rɪ'kænt; rɪ'kænt/ *vt, vi* [VP6A, 2A] give up (an opinion, a belief); take back (a statement) as being false: 放弃(意见, 信仰); (因其不实而)撤销(一声明): *The torturers could not make the man ~*, give up his beliefs, eg religious or political. 施酷刑者不能使那个人放弃其(宗教或政治)信仰。 **re·can·ta·tion** /ˌriːkæn'teɪʃn; ˌrikæn'teʃən/ *n* [U] ~ing; [C] instance of this; statement disavowing former beliefs. 放弃信仰或意见;撤销声明;放弃或撤销之实例;放弃原信仰的声明。

re·cap /'riːkæp; 'rɪkæp/ *vt, vi, n* (colloq abbr of) recapitulate, recapitulation. (口) 为 recapitulate, recapitulation 之略。

re·cap² /riː'kæp; rɪ'kæp/ *vt* (-**pp**-) (US) retread (a tyre). (美)翻新(轮胎)。

re·cap·itu·late /ˌriːkə'pɪtʃuleɪt; ˌrikə'pɪtʃəˌlet/ *vt, vi* [VP6A, 2A] repeat, go through again, the chief points of (sth that has been said, discussed, argued about, etc). 对 (已说过, 讨论过, 辩论过的东西等) 做一扼要说明或重述; 摘要重述。 **re·cap·itu·la·tion** /ˌriːkəˌpɪtʃu'leɪʃn; ˌrikəˌpɪtʃə'leʃən/ *n* [U] recapitulating; [C] instance of this. 扼要说明;重述要点。

re·cap·ture /ˌriː'kæptʃə(r); 'riːˈkæptʃə/ *vt* [VP6A] 1 capture again. 再捕获。 2 recall: 回忆: *try to ~ the past*. 试着回忆过去。

re·cast /ˌriː'kɑːst US: -'kæst; riː'kæst/ *vt* [VP6A] 1 cast or fashion anew: 重铸;再铸: ~ *a gun/a bell;* 重新铸造一炮(一钟)。 ~ (= rewrite) *a sentence/para-graph/chapter*. 重写一个句子(一段, 一章)。 2 change the cast of a play, ie find different actors or give actors different parts. 改变一出戏的演员阵容(即另找演员或让演员另演脚色)。

recce /'reki; 'rɛki/ *n* (mil; colloq abbr of) reconnaissance. (军;口)为 reconnaissance 之略。

re·cede /rɪ'siːd; rɪ'sid/ *vi* [VP2A, 3A] ~ *(from)*, 1 (appear to) go back from the observer or from an earlier position: (显得)后退: *As the tide ~d we were able to explore the rocky pools on the beach*. 潮退的时候, 我们得以探察海滩上的石水潭。 *As our ship sailed out to sea the coast slowly ~d*. 我们的船驶向大海时, 海岸离我们越来越远。 2 slope away from the front or from the observer: 向后倾斜: *a receding chin/forehead*. 向后倾斜的下颚(额头)。

re·ceipt /rɪ'siːt; rɪ'sit/ *n* 1 [U] receiving or being received: 收到; 被收到: *on ~ of the news*. 收到消息时。 *I am in ~ of your letter of the 3rd*, (pompous for) I have received…. 我已收到你三日写的信(是 I have received… 的浮夸说法)。 2 (*pl*) money received (in a business, etc, contrasted with *expenditure*). (复)收到之款;进款;收入, (与 expenditure 相对)。 3 [C] written statement that sth (money or goods) has been received: 收据;收条: *get*

---

a ~ for money spent: 收到一张开支收据; *sign a ~*; 在收据上签名; *a '~ book*, one with forms and counterfoil for writing out ~s. 收据簿。 □ *vt* [VP6A] write out and sign and stamp a ~(3): 写并签署或盖章于一收据; 立收据: *a hotel bill*, put 'Paid' or 'Received with thanks' on it. 在旅馆帐单上签字或盖章表示该款业已付清。

re·ceiv·able /rɪ'siːvəbl; rɪ'sivəbl/ *adj* 1 that can be received; fit to be received. 可接收的; 适于接收的。 2 (comm; of bills, accounts, etc) on which money is to be received. (商; 指票据,帐款等)待收款的; 应收的。 *bills ~*, contrasted with *bills payable*. 应收票据(与 bills payable 相对)。

re·ceive /rɪ'siːv; rɪ'siv/ *vt, vi* [VP6A, 2A] 1 accept, take, get (sth offered, sent, etc): 接受; 接收; 领取: *When did you ~ the letter/news/telegram, etc?* 你何时接到那封信(消息, 电报等)? *He ~d a good education*. 他受过良好教育。 *We ~d nothing but insults*. 我们什么也没有得到, 只受到侮辱。 *You will ~ a warm welcome when you come to England*. 你到英国时会受到热烈欢迎。 *He was caught receiving* (ie taking possession of stolen property) *soon after his release from prison*. 他被释出狱不久即因收受赃物而被捕。 **re'ceiving-set** *n* radio receiver. 接收机。 2 allow to enter; (formally) see, welcome or entertain (friends, guests, etc): 准予进入; (正式)接待;招待;款待(朋友、客人等): *The hotel is now open to ~ guests*. 该旅馆现在已开业招待客人。 *He was ~d into the Church*, admitted as a member. 他被准许入教。 *Lady Snooks ~s on Monday afternoons*, is at home to her friends and acquaintances then. 斯努克斯夫人每星期一下午在家见客。 □ *adj* widely accepted as correct: 被认为正确而普遍接受的; 公认为正确的: *the ~d version/ text/view/opinion/pronunciation*. 公认为正确之译本(正文, 看法, 意见, 读音)。

re·ceiver /rɪ'siːvə(r); rɪ'sivɚ/ *n* 1 person who receives, esp who knowingly receives stolen goods. 接受者; (指)收受赃者。 2 (**Official**) **R~**, official appointed to take charge of the property and affairs of a bankrupt, or to administer property in dispute. 破产管理官 (被指派负责清理破产财务或有争议之财产者)。 3 part of an apparatus for receiving sth, eg that part of a telephone that is held to the ear; apparatus for receiving broad-cast signals: 一装置中能接收某种东西的部分; 接收器(如电话之听筒); 收音机: *a 'radio~*. 无线电接收机。 ~**·ship** /-ʃɪp; -ˌʃɪp/ *n* office of a ~(2): his period of office. 破产管理官之职务或任期。

re·cent /'riːsnt; 'risn̩t/ *adj* (having existed, been made, happened) not long before; begun or made not long ago: 不久前(才存在, 才做成, 才发生)的; 不久前开始的; 最近的; 新近的: *~ news*. 最近的消息; *a ~ event*. 不久前发生的事件; *within ~ memory*. 在最近的记忆之中。 *Ours is a ~ acquaintance*, We have been acquainted for only a short time. 我们是最近才认识的。 ~**·ly** *adv* lately; not long ago: 最近地; 不久之前地: *until quite ~ly*. 直到最近。

re·cep·tacle /rɪ'septəkl; rɪ'sɛptək̩l/ *n* container or holder in which things may be put away or out of sight. 容器。

re·cep·tion /rɪ'sepʃn; rɪ'sɛpʃən/ *n* 1 [U] receiving or being received: 接待; 被接待: *prepare rooms for the ~ of guests*. 准备房间以接待嘉宾; *'~ area/camp/ centre*, one where persons, eg evacuees, refugees are received and accommodated: (撤退者,难民等的)接待区 (营,中心); *a '~ committee*. 接待委员会。 *The house has two ~ rooms* (rooms for the ~ of guests, but this usu means living-rooms, *a kitchen, and three bedrooms*. 这座房子有两间接待室(通常指于起居室), 一间厨房, 三间卧房。 *'~ desk* (in a hotel) counter where guests are received, where they ask for rooms, etc. (旅馆中的)接待处(即接待客人, 客人询问房间等事务的柜台)。 *'~ clerk* (US) person at a ~ desk, who attends to inquiries from guests. (美)在接待处负责复客人询问的接待人员。 2 [C] formal party or welcome: 正式招待会或欢迎会: *Mrs X holds a ~ every Monday*. 某太太每星期

一都接见宾客(或举行一个招待会). *There was a ~ after the wedding ceremony.* 结婚典礼之后有宴会. **3** [C] welcome or greeting of a specified kind; demonstration of feeling toward sb or sth: 某种的欢迎或招呼; 对某人或某事物表示的感情: *The new book had a favourable ~,* was welcomed by the critics, the public, etc. 这本新书颇受欢迎. *The President was given an enthusiastic ~.* 总统受到热烈的接待. **4** [U] receiving of radio, etc signals; degree of efficiency of this: (无线电等信号的)接收; 接收力: *Is radio ~ good in your district?* 在你们那一区收音机听得清楚吗? *R~ of TV programmes is unsatisfactory here.* 这里电视节目的接收情形不佳.
~·ist /-ist; -ist/ *n* person employed in a hotel, or by a hair-dresser, dentist or other professional person, to receive clients. 接待员(旅馆, 美容师, 牙医或其他专业人员雇用以招待客人者).
re·cep·tive /rɪˈseptɪv; rɪˈsɛptɪv/ *adj* quick or ready to receive suggestions, new ideas, etc: 敏于接受建议, 新思想等的: *a ~ mind;* 易于接受新思想的头脑; *~ to new ideas.* 易于接受新的观念. **~·ly** *adv* **re·cep·tiv·ity** /ˌriːsepˈtɪvətɪ; rɪˌsepˈtɪvətɪ/ *n*
re·cess /rɪˈses US: ˈriːses; rɪˈsɛs/ *n* **1** (US 美 = *vacation*) period of time when work or business is stopped, eg when Parliament, the law courts, are not in session. 暂歇时期; 休业期; 休会期(例如议会之休会期, 法庭之休庭期). **2** part of a room where the wall is set back from the main part; alcove or niche: 室内墙壁之凹处; 凹室; 壁龛: *a ~ with a writing-desk and a chair in it.* 一个置有一书桌和一椅的凹室. **3** secret place place difficult of access: 隐密地方; 难进入的地方: *the dark ~es of a cave;* 洞穴中隐密的暗处; *a mountain ~;* 山之深处; 山陬; (fig) (喻) *in the innermost ~es of the heart / mind.* 心之最深处. □ *vt* [VP6A] **1** place in a ~; set back: 置于凹室或壁龛内; 置于隐密处; 做成凹处: *~ a wall /a ~ed wall.* 在墙上做一壁龛(有壁龛的墙). **2** provide with ~es. 供以隐处.
re·ces·sion /rɪˈseʃn; rɪˈsɛʃən/ *n* **1** [U] withdrawal; act of receding. 撤回; 退回; 退后. **2** [C] slackening of business and industrial activity: 工商业之衰退; 不景气: *The ~ caused a lot of unemployment.* 不景气造成了大量的失业.
re·ces·sional /rɪˈseʃənl; rɪˈsɛʃənəl/ *n* ~ (hymn), hymn sung while the clergy and choir withdraw after a church service. (礼拜仪式完毕后在牧师和唱诗班退出时唱的)退场赞美诗. □ *adj* ~ of a recession: 撤回的; 退出的: *'~ music.* (礼拜仪式结束时所奏之)退场乐. **2** relating to a Parliamentary recess. 议会休会期的.
re·ces·sive /rɪˈsesɪv/ *adj* **1** having a tendency to recede or go back. 退后的; 倒退的; 有倒退之倾向的. **2** (biol) exhibiting weak characteristics, (the stronger ones are called *dominant*) which are passed on by means of genes to later generations, eg blue eyes and blond hair, (生物)隐性的; 潜性的.
ré·chauffé /reɪˈʃəʊfeɪ US: ˌreɪʃəʊˈfeɪ; ˌreˌʃoˈfe/ *n* dish of food warmed up again; rehash. 再煮热的(剩)菜; 改成新形式的旧材料.
re·cher·ché /rəˈʃeəʃeɪ; rəˈʃɛrʃe/ *adj* devised or selected with (too much) care; too studied or far-fetched. 精心设计的; 精选的; 用心推敲的; 过于造作牵强的; 不自然的.
re·cidi·vist /rɪˈsɪdɪvɪst; rɪˈsɪdɪvɪst/ *n* person who habitually relapses into crime; one who apparently cannot be cured of criminal tendencies; persistent offender, 常犯罪的人; 无法改正犯罪倾向的人; 累犯. **re·cidi·vism** /-ɪzəm; -ɪzəm/ *n*
recipe /ˈresəpɪ; ˈrɛsəpɪ/ *n* [C] ~ (for), direction for preparing (a cake, a dish of food, a medical remedy) or for getting (any result): 烹饪法; 食谱; 处方; 秘诀: *a ~ for a fruit cake.* 水果饼制法. *Have you a ~ for happiness?* 对于幸福快乐你有什么秘诀吗?
re·cipi·ent /rɪˈsɪpɪənt; rɪˈsɪpɪənt/ *n* person who receives sth. 接受者.
re·cip·ro·cal /rɪˈsɪprəkl; rɪˈsɪprəkl/ *adj* **1** given and

received in return; mutual: 互惠的; 交互的; 相互的; *~ affection / help.* 相互的喜爱(帮助). **2** corresponding, but the other way round: 相对的; 彼此相反的: *a ~ mistake, eg I thought he was a waiter and he thought I was a guest, but I was a waiter and he was a guest.* 彼此相反的错误(例如我以为他是侍者, 他想我是客人, 但事实上我是侍者而他是客人). **3** (gram) ~ *pronouns,* those expressing mutual action or relation, eg *each other,* *one another.* (语法)相互代词(表示相互行动或关系者, 例如 *each other, one another*). **~·ly** /-klɪ; -klɪ/ *adv*
re·cip·ro·cate /rɪˈsɪprəkeɪt; rɪˈsɪprəˌket/ *vt, vi* [VP 6A, 2A] **1** give in return; give and receive, each to and from each: 回报; 报答; 互惠: *I ~ your good wishes.* 我也同样祝福您. *He ~d by wishing her a pleasant journey.* 他祝福她旅途愉快, 以为回报. **2** (of parts of a machine). (cause to) move backwards and forwards in a straight line (eg the piston of an engine): (指机件)(使)沿直线来回移动(如引擎的活塞): *a reciprocating engine / saw.* 往复式引擎(锯子). ⇨ **rotatory.** **re·cip·ro·ca·tion** /rɪˌsɪprəˈkeɪʃn; rɪˌsɪprəˈkeʃən/ *n* [U]
reci·proc·ity /ˌresɪˈprɒsətɪ; ˌrɛsəˈprɑsətɪ/ *n* [U] principle or practice of give and take, of making mutual concessions; the granting of privileges in return for similar privileges: 互让与取; 相互让步之原则或实施; 互惠: *~ in trade (between two countries).* (两国间之)贸易互惠.
re·cital /rɪˈsaɪtl; rɪˈsaɪtl/ *n* [C] **1** detailed account of a number of connected events, etc: 一连串相关连事件的)详述: *We were bored by the long ~ of his adventures.* 我们对于他的冒险经历的长篇叙述感到厌烦了. **2** performance of music by a soloist or small group, or of the works of one composer: 音乐演奏会; 独奏会; 独唱会; 个人作品发表会: *a pi'ano ~;* 钢琴独奏会; *a ~ of songs.* 歌曲演唱会.
reci·ta·tion /ˌresɪˈteɪʃn; ˌrɛsəˈteʃən/ *n* **1** [U] the act of reciting (2): 列举; 详述: *the ~ of his grievances.* 详述其苦衷. **2** [U] public delivery of passages of prose or poetry learnt by heart; [C] instance of this: 背诵; 当众吟诵; 背诵之实例: *a 'Dickens ~,* 以诗文片段为内容的朗诵; 狄更斯小说中若干精采段落的朗诵. **3** [C] piece of poetry or prose (to be) learnt by heart and recited, 背诵(用)的诗文. **4** [US] (US) repetition of a prepared lesson by a pupil to his teacher; [C] instance of this. (美)学生向老师背书; 其实例.
reci·ta·tive /ˌresɪtəˈtiːv; ˌrɛsətəˈtiv/ *n* **1** [U] style of music between singing and talking, many words being spoken or sung on the same note, used for the narrative and dialogue parts of some operas. 朗诵调; 宣叙调(介于唱与说话之间的一种音乐体裁, 许多字句以同样调子说或唱, 用于某些歌剧中之叙述或对白部分). **2** [C] passage (in an opera or oratorio) (to be) rendered thus. (歌剧或神剧中的)宣叙部.
re·cite /rɪˈsaɪt; rɪˈsaɪt/ *vt, vi* [VP6A, 15A, 2A] **1** say (esp poems) aloud from memory: 背诵; 吟诵; (尤指)吟诗: *The mayor ~d to the Queen a long and tedious speech of welcome.* 市长向女王背了一篇又长又臭的欢迎词. **2** give a list of, tell one by one (names, facts, etc): 列举一连串(名字、事实等); 详述: *~ one's grievances.* 详述一个人的苦难; *~ the names of all the capital cities of Europe.* 列举欧洲各国首都的名字.
reck·less /ˈreklɪs; ˈrɛklɪs/ *adj* ~ (of), rash; not thinking of the consequences: 鲁莽的; 不考虑后果的: *a ~ spender;* 乱花钱者; *~ of danger / the consequences,* 不管危险(后果); *fined £10 for ~ (=dangerous) driving.* 因卤莽驾驶而被罚款十镑. **~·ly** *adv* **~·ness** *n*
reckon /ˈrekən; ˈrɛkən/ *vt, vi* **1** [VP6A, 15B, 2A] calculate; find out (the quantity, number, cost, etc) by working with numbers: 计算; 计算(量、数、成本等): *~ the cost of a holiday.* 计算假期费用. *Hire charges are ~ed from the date of delivery.* 租金是从交货日开始计算的. *The child can't ~ yet.* 这孩子还不会计算.

~ **sth in**, include, take into account, when ~ing: 把…计算在内: *Did you* ~ *in the cost of a taxi across London?* 你把穿过伦敦的出租汽车车资计算在内了吗? ~ **sth up**, find the total of: 总计; 结算: ~ *up the bill.* 把帐单上各个项目加起来。 **2** ~ **with sb**, (a) deal with; settle accounts with: 处理; 清算: *When the fighting is over, we'll* ~ *with the enemy's sympathizers.* 战争结束之后, 我们就要处理通敌的人。 (b) take into account; consider: 考虑: *He is certainly a man to be* ~ed *with*, a man who cannot be ignored, who may be a serious competitor, opponent, etc (according to context). 他确实是个有力的人物(是个有力的竞争者、对手等, 意义视上下文而定)。 ~ **without sb**, not take into account; not consider. 未将某人算在内; 未在考虑之中。 **3** ~ **on/upon sb/sth**, depend on, base one's hopes on. 依赖; 寄望于: *I* ~ *on your help.* 我寄望于你的帮助。 *The proprietors of the Casino* ~ *on human foolishness and greed*, can depend, for making profit, on the foolishness and greed of those who gamble. 赌场老板全靠人类的愚蠢和贪婪(而获利)。 *He's the sort of man you can* ~ *on in a crisis.* 他是那种在危急时你能信赖的人。 **4** [VP9, 16B, 25, 7A] ~ **sb/sth as/to be**; ~ **that...**, be of the opinion, suppose; consider: 以为; 认定; 认为: *One-quarter of the country is* ~ed *as unproductive.* 该国四分之一的土地被认为是荒瘠不毛的。 *She was* ~ed (to be) *the prettiest girl in the village.* 她被认为是那村子里最漂亮的女孩。 *Do you still* ~ *him among/as one of your friends?* 你还认为他是你的朋友吗? *I* ~ *he is rather too old to marry again.* 我认为他年龄太大, 不适于再婚。 **5** [VP9, 7A] estimate; calculate: 估计: *I* ~ *to arrive in Delhi at noon.* 我估计正午抵达德里。 **6** [VP9] (US colloq) assume: (美口)假定; 以为: *I* ~ *we'll go next week.* 我以为我们下星期会去。 ~**er** /'rekonǝ(r); 'rɛkǝnɚ/ *n* person or thing that counts. 计算者; 计算表。 **ready** ~**er**, ⇨ **ready.** ~**ing** /'rekoniŋ; 'rɛkǝniŋ/ *n* (esp) (尤指) **1** [C] (totalled) account of items to be paid for, eg at a hotel or restaurant: (结算)总帐(旅社或饭店等的费用): *pay the* ~*ing.* 付帐。 *There'll be a heavy* ~*ing to pay if he continues this wild life*, He will have to suffer for it. 如果他仍继续过这种荒唐的生活, 他就得付出一大笔帐(就要自食恶果)。 **day of** ~*ing*, time when sth must be atoned for. 报应来到的日子; 清算日。 **2** [U] calculation, eg of a ship's position by observation of the sun, stars, etc. (由观测太阳、星辰等而对船的位置所做的)推算。 **dead** ~*ing*, method of calculating the position of a ship or aircraft from a known earlier position, and later course and distance, when observations of the sun, etc are impossible. 推算航行法(在不可能观测太阳或星辰时, 仅凭船只或飞机早先的位置以及后来的航向和距离所做的推算)。 **out in one's** ~*ing*, mistaken in one's calculations. 计算不确; 估计错误。

re·claim /rɪ'kleɪm; rɪ'klem/ *vt* [VP6A] **1** bring back (waste land, etc) to a useful condition, a state of cultivation, etc. 开垦(荒地等使之成为可耕植之状态); 垦殖。 **2** reform (a person): 改正; 矫正(人): ~ *a man from error/vice.* 纠正某人之错误(邪恶); *a* ~ed *drunkard.* 一个改邪归正的酒鬼。 **3** demand that sth be given back. 要求归还。 **rec·la·ma·tion** /ˌreklə'meɪʃn; ˌrɛklə'meʃǝn/ *n* [U].

re·cline /rɪ'klaɪn; rɪ'klaɪn/ *vi*, *vt* [VP2A, C, 15A] place oneself, be, in a position of rest; put (one's arms, etc) in a resting position; lie back or down: 处于休息位置; 置(手臂等)于休息位置; 躺倒; 斜倚: ~ *on a couch*, 斜卧榻上; ~ *one's arms on the table*; 把胳膊靠在桌上; *a reclining chair*, one with a back that tilts. 躺椅; 卧椅。

re·cluse /rɪ'kluːs; 'rɛklus/ *n* person who lives alone and avoids other people: 遁世者; 隐士: *live the life of a* ~, live like a hermit, avoiding meeting people. 过隐居的生活。

rec·og·ni·tion /ˌrekəg'nɪʃn; ˌrɛkəɡ'nɪʃǝn/ *n* [U] recognizing or being recognized: 认出; 被认出; 承认; 认识; 识别: ~ *signals*: 识别信号; *aircraft* ~. 飞

行识别。 *He was given a cheque for £25 in* ~ *of his services.* 他得到一张二十五英镑的支票作为对他服务的报酬。 *R*~ *of the new State is unlikely*, It is unlikely that diplomatic relations will be established with it. 那个新国家不大可能获得承认。 *alter/change beyond/out of (all)* ~, change so much that ~ is impossible: 改变得使人认不出: *The town has changed out of all* ~ *since I was there ten years ago.* 自从十年前我离开之后, 这城镇变得认不得了。

re·cog·ni·zance /rɪ'kɒgnɪzns; rɪ'kɑgnɪzǝns/ *n* [C] (legal) (法律) **1** bond by which a person is bound to appear before a court of law at a certain time, or to observe certain conditions, and to forfeit a certain sum if he fails to do so. 保证书; 具结。 *enter into* ~**s**, sign such a bond. 具结。 **2** sum of money (to be) paid as surety for observing such a bond. (交付法院的)保证金; 抵押金; 保释金。

rec·og·nize /'rekəgnaɪz; 'rɛkəɡ,naɪz/ *vt* **1** [VP6A, 16A] know, (be able to) identify again (sb or sth) that one has seen, heard, etc before: 认识; 认出; (能)认明(某人或某物)系曾见过、听到过等: ~ *a tune/an old acquaintance.* 认出一听过的歌曲(旧相识)。 **2** [VP6A] be willing to accept (sb or sth) as what he or it claims to be or has been in the past: 承认; 认可: *refuse to* ~ *a new government/* ~ *sb as lawful heir.* 拒绝承认一新政府(某人为合法继承人)。 **3** [VP6A, 9] be prepared to admit; be aware: 自认; 知道: *He* ~d *that he was not qualified for the post/* ~d *his lack of qualifications.* 他承认他没有资格担任那职位(承认缺乏资格)。 **4** [VP6A, 9, 25] acknowledge: 公认; 赏识: *Everyone* ~d *him to be the greatest living authority on ancient Roman coins.* 大家公认他是当今古罗马钱币的最杰出的行家。 *His services to the State were* ~d, eg he was made a knight. 他对国家的贡献获得赏识(如被封为爵士)。 **rec·og·niz·able** /'rekəgnaɪzəbl; 'rɛkəɡ,naɪzəbl/ *adj* that can be ~d 可认出的; 可辨识的; 可承认的。 **rec·og·niz·ably** / -əblɪ; -əblɪ/ *adv*

re·coil /rɪ'kɔɪl; rɪ'kɔɪl/ *vi* **1** [VP2A, 3A] ~ *(from)*, draw or jump back; shrink: 撤回; 跳回; 退缩: ~ *from doing sth* (in fear, horror, disgust, etc). (因恐惧, 恐惧, 厌恶等)做某事畏缩不前。 **2** [VP2A] (of a gun) kick back (when fired). (指枪炮)(射击时)弹回; 反冲; 后坐。 **3** [VP3A] ~ *on/upon*, (fig) rebound; react: (喻)报应; 反应: *His meanness* ~ed *upon his own head.* 他的卑鄙回报到他自己头上。 *Revenge may* ~ *upon the person who takes it.* 报复者常身受其报。 □ *n* act of ~ing. 退缩; 弹回; 报应; 反应。

rec·ol·lect /ˌrekə'lekt; ˌrɛkə'lɛkt/ *vt*, *vi* [VP6A, C, 8, 10, 9, 2A] call back to, the mind; succeed in remembering: 记起; 忆起; 记得: ~ *childhood days*; 记起童年时代的日子; ~ *meeting the King*; 记起会见国王的事; ~ *how to do sth/how sth was done.* 记得如何做某事(某事是如何做的)。 *As far as I* ~, ...就我所能记忆, ...。

rec·ol·lec·tion /ˌrekə'lekʃn; ˌrɛkə'lɛkʃǝn/ *n* **1** [U] act or power of recollecting: 回忆力; 记忆力: *scenes which arise in quiet* ~ *of the past*; 在对往事静静回忆中出现的情景; *to the best of my* ~, so far as I can recollect; if I remember correctly. 就我所能记忆; 如我记得不错。 **2** [U] time over which the memory goes back: 记忆所及的时间: *Such a problem has never arisen within my* ~. 这样的一个问题从来不曾在我记忆中出现过。 **3** [C] sth recollected; that which is remembered: 回忆的事物; 记起的事物: *The old letters brought many* ~*s to my mind.* 这些旧信使我想起许多往事。

rec·om·mend /ˌrekə'mend; ˌrɛkə'mɛnd/ *vt* **1** [VP6A, 14, 12A, 13A, 16A] ~ *sth (to sb) (for sth)*; ~ *sb sth*; ~ *sb (for sth/as sth)*, speak favourably of; say that one thinks sth is good (for a purpose) or that sb is fitted (for a post, etc as...): 推荐; 介绍: *I can* ~ *this soap.* 我可以推荐这种肥皂。 *He has been* ~ed *for first class honours.* 他被推荐为优

等。 *What would you ~ for getting ink stains from my blouse?* 你看用什么可以洗掉我上衣上的墨水污痕呢？ *Can you ~ me a good novel?* 你能介绍一本好的小说给我吗？ *Can you ~ Miss Hill as a good typist?* 你能推荐希尔小姐说她是个好打字员吗？ **2** [VP17, 6C, 9] suggest as wise or suitable; advise; 建议; 劝告: *I have been ~ed to try these pills for sea-sickness.* 有人建议我试服这些药丸来治晕船。 *I ~ you not to/that you do not disobey your officers.* 我劝你不要反抗你的上司。 *Do you ~ raising the school-leaving age?* 你建议提高离校年龄吗？ **3** [VP6A, 14] *~ sb (to sb),* (of a quality, etc)cause to be or appear pleasing, satisfactory; make acceptable: (指某种性质、特质等)使之或使看来可爱、令人满意; 使受欢迎: *Behaviour of that sort will not ~ you.* 那样的行为不会使别人对你有好感。 **4** [VP14] *~ sb to sb,* commend (the more usu word): 托付; 交付 (commend 较常用): *~ oneself/one's fate to God;* 把自己(自己的命运)交给上帝; *~ a child to sb's care.* 把一个孩子托付某人看顾。 **rec·om·men·da·tion** /ˌrekəmen'deɪʃən/ *n* **1** [U] *~ing:* 推荐; 介绍; 建议; 劝告; 托付: *speak in ~ation of sb or sth;* 推荐某人或某物; *buy sth on the ~ation of a friend, because he has ~ed it.* 由一位朋友的推荐而买某物。 **2** [C] statement that *~*s sb or sth: 推荐书; 介绍信: *My bank manager has sent me a list of ~ations,* eg names of stocks which he *~*s me to buy. 我的银行经理给了我一张推荐单子(例如他建议我买的股票名称)。 *The jury brought in a verdict of guilty, with a ~ation to mercy.* 陪审团宣判被告有罪, 附带建议从轻量刑。 **3** [C] sth which causes a person to be well thought of: (指品质、才能等) 可取之处: *Is a sweet disposition a ~ation in a wife?* 温和的性情是作妻子的可取之处吗？

rec·om·pense /'rekəmpens; 'rɛkən,pɛns/ *vt* [VP6A, 14] *~ sb (for sth),* reward or punish; make payment to: 赏或罚; 报偿: *~ sb for his trouble;* 酬答某人之烦劳; *~ sb with evil;* 以怨报德; *~ sb for a loss.* 赔偿某人的损失。 *□ n* [C, U] reward; payment; satisfaction given for injury: 报偿; 报偿金; 赔偿: *receive a ~ for one's services;* 接受服务; *work hard without ~;* 没有报酬地辛苦工作; *in ~ for your help.* 为报偿你的帮助。

rec·on·cile /'rekənsaɪl; 'rɛkən,saɪl/ *vt* 1 [VP6A,14] *~ sb(with sb),* cause (persons) to become friends after they have quarrelled: 使(人)在争吵后再和好; 使和解; 使复交: *We became ~d.* 我们已言归于好。 *He refused to become ~d with his brother.* 他拒绝同他的兄弟和解。 **2**[VP6A]settle, arrange (a quarrel, difference of opinion, etc), 调解; 调停(口角、歧见等)。 **3** [VP6A, 14] *~ sth (with sth),* bring into harmony with; cause to agree with: 使和谐; 使一致: *How can this decision be ~d with justice?* 这个决定如何能符合公道呢？ *I can't ~ what you say with the facts of the case.* 我看不出你所说的与该案件诸事实相符合。 **4** [VP14] *~ oneself to sth; be ~d to sth,* overcome one's objections to; resign oneself to: 安于; 顺从(于); 听从 (于): *~ oneself to a life of hardship and poverty.* 安于艰苦贫穷的生活。 **rec·on·cil·able** /'rekənsaɪl-; -əbl/; -əbl/ *adj* **rec·on·cili·ation** /ˌrekən-ˌsɪlɪ'eɪʃn; ˌrɛkən,sɪlɪ'eʃən/ *n* [U] reconciling or being *~*d; [C] instance of this: 和解; 复交; 调停; 调解; 和谐; 一致; 顺从; 听从: *bring about a reconciliation between friends who have quarrelled.* 使争吵的朋友重复旧好。

rec·on·dite /'rekəndaɪt; 'rɛkən,daɪt/ *adj* **1** (of subjects of knowledge) out of the way; little known; abstruse: (指知识的学科)深奥的; 鲜为人知的: *~ studies.* 深奥的学问。 **2** (of an author) having *~* knowledge. (指作者)有深奥学问的。

re·con·di·tion /ˌriːkən'dɪʃn; ˌrikən'dɪʃən/ *vt* [VP6A] put into good condition again: 使恢复良好状态; 修复: *a car with a ~ed engine.* 一辆整修过引擎的汽车。

re·con·nais·sance /rɪ'kɒnɪsns; rɪ'kɑnəsəns/ *n* 1 [U] act of reconnoitring: 侦察; 搜索: *~ in force,*

made with sufficient troops to resist any enemy forces that may be encountered. 威力侦察; 威力搜索。 **2** [C] instance of reconnoitring; survey, made by troops or a group of scouting vessels or aircraft, of an enemy's position or whereabouts; (fig) survey of any kind of work before it is started: 侦察或搜索的实例; 由部队或侦察舰或侦察机对敌人位置所做的观测; (喻)任何一件工作开始前所做之通盘考虑或考查; 勘查: *make a ~ of the work to be done.* 在工作开始前做一番考查。

re·con·noitre (US: **-ter**) /ˌrekə'nɔɪtə(r); ˌrikə-'nɔɪtɚ/ *vt, vi* [VP6A, 2A] go to or near (a place or area occupied by enemy forces) to learn about their position, strength, etc: 进至或接近(敌人占据之地方或地区)以探究其阵地、兵力等; 侦察; 搜索: *~ the ground.* 侦察地形。

re·con·struct /ˌriːkən'strʌkt; ˌrikən'strʌkt/ *vt* [VP6A] **1** construct again. 重建; 再建。 **2** build up a complete structure or description (of sth of which one has only a few parts or only partial evidence): 将(只有几部分或部分证据的事物)组成完整的结构或叙述; 重整: *~ a ruined abbey.* 重建一被毁之寺院。 *The detective tried to ~ the crime,* picture to himself how it had been committed. 那侦探试图根据该案之已知事实, 设想出完整的犯罪经过。 **re·con·struc·tion** /ˌriːkən'strʌkʃn; ˌrikən-'strʌkʃən/ *n*

rec·ord[1] /'rekɔːd *US:* 'rekərd; 'rɛkəd/ *n* **1** [C] written account of facts, events, etc: 记录; 记载: *~ of school attendances/of road accidents;* 学生考勤(车祸)记录; *the (ˌPublic) 'E~ Office,* one in London where public documents with accounts of events, official acts, etc written down at the time they occur, are stored. (公共)档案局(在伦敦, 该局保存事件及官方行动等发生时所记录之文件)。 **2** [U] state of being *~*ed or preserved in writing, esp as authentic evidence of sth: 记载; 存证: *a matter of ~,* sth that is established as fact by being *~*ed. 有记录之事物。 *be/go/put sb on ~,* 有记录; 列入记录; 将…列入记录: *It is on ~ that the summer was the wettest for 50 years.* 根据记录今(该)夏是五十年来雨量最多的季节。 *I don't want to go on ~/don't want you to put me on ~ as saying that I think the Prime Minister a fool.* 我不愿你把我所说「我认为首相是傻瓜」之事列入记录。 *off the ~,* (colloq) not for publication or for recording: (口)不公开的; 不发表的; 不记载的; 非正式的: *What the President said at his press conference was off the ~,* not to be repeated by the newspaper-men there, and not to be used in their reports or articles. 总统在记者招待会上所说的话是不准报纸引述或刊登的。 **3** [C] facts known about the past of sb or sth: 有关某人或某事物的过去的已知事实; 履历: 档案记录: *He has an honourable ~ of service/a good ~.* 他有光荣的服务记录(良好的记录)。 *Your ~ is in your favour.* What we know about your past is favourable to you. 你的履历对你有利。 *That airline has a bad ~,* eg has had many accidents to its aircraft. 那家航空公司记录不佳(如曾有多次飞机失事)。 **4** [C] sth that provides evidence or information: 供给证据或资料的东西: *Our museums are full of ~s of past history.* 我们的博物馆有很多过去历史的资料。 *R~s of ancient civilizations are still being excavated.* 古代文明的遗迹仍在不断出土。 **5** [C] disc on which sound has been registered; sth *~*ed on such a disc: 唱片: *'gramophone ~s.* 留声唱片。 ⇨ *recording.* '**~-player** *n* instrument for reproducing sound from discs (often one connected to an external loud-speaker). (电)唱机。 **6** [C] limit, score, point, attainment, mark, etc (high or low), not reached before; (esp in sport) the best yet bone: 以前未达到的(高或低)限制、得分、点、成就、分数等; (尤指运动方面)最高记录: *Which country holds the ~ for the marathon?* 哪一个国家保持马拉松赛跑的最快记录？ *Two ~s fell during the sports meeting at Oslo last week* 上星期在奥斯陆举行的运动会上有两项记录被打破了。 (attrib) (用作定语) *Hill made a ~ score in the match against Kent,* (cricket) scored a total that

was a ~. 在对抗肯特的板球比赛中, 希尔得到刷新记录的得分. *There was a ~ rice crop in Thailand that year.* 那一年泰国的稻谷收成创下了最高记录. **break**/**beat the ~**, do better than has been done before. 打破记录. Hence, 由此产生, '**~breaking** adj

re·cord² /rɪˈkɔːd; rɪˈkɔrd/ vt [VP6A] **1** set down in writing for reference; preserve for use, by writing or in other ways, eg on a disc, magnetic tape, video-tape, film, etc: 写下或以其他方式, 记录: (以书写或其他方式, 如图片、磁带、录影带、影片等)记录: *This volume ~s the history of the regiment.* 这部书记录了该团的历史. *The programme was ~ed.* 该节目被录下来了. Cf 参较 a 'live' broadcast. 实况广播. *The tape-recorder has ~ed his voice and the camera has ~ed his features.* 录音机录下了他的声音, 摄影机留下了他的面貌. **~ing angel**, angel who, it is said, ~s men's good and bad actions. 传说中负责记录人之善恶的天使. **2** (of an instrument) mark or indicate on a scale: (指仪器)标明或表示: *The thermometer ~ed 40°C.* 寒暑表上指明是摄氏 40°.

re·cord·er /rɪˈkɔːdə(r); rɪˈkɔrdə/ n **1** (GB) judge with a certain criminal and civil jurisdiction. (英)民刑推事. **2** apparatus that records. 记录器. '**tape-~**, one that records sound on magnetic tape. 录音机. '**video tape-~**, one that records vision and sound on magnetic tape. 录像机. **3** wooden musical instrument with finger holes, played by blowing it at one end. 八孔直笛(一种木管乐器). ⇨ the illus at **brass**. 参看 brass 之插图.

re·cord·ing /rɪˈkɔːdɪŋ; rɪˈkɔrdɪŋ/ n (esp in sound or TV broadcasting, and for record-players, etc) programme, piece of music, etc registered on a disc, magnetic tape, film, etc for reproduction: 录制(尤指广播、电视、录音等)节目: *It wasn't a 'live' performance but a B B C~.* 那不是现场播出而是英国国家广播公司的录音节目. *I have a good ~ of this opera on three discs.* 我有这出歌剧的三张录制得很好的唱片. ⇨ the illus at **tape**. 参看 tape 之插图.

re·count /rɪˈkaʊnt; rɪˈkaʊnt/ vt [VP6A] give an account of; tell: 叙述; 讲述: *He ~ed to them the story of his adventures in Mexico.* 他向他们讲述他在墨西哥的冒险经过.

re·count /ˌriːˈkaʊnt; ˌriˈkaʊnt/ vt [VP6A] count again: 再算; 重计: *~ the votes.* 重新计票. □ /ˈriːkaʊnt; ˈriˌkaʊnt/ another count; 重新计算; 第二次计算: *One of the candidates demanded a ~.* 候选人中有一位要求重计票数.

re·coup /rɪˈkuːp; rɪˈkup/ vt [VP6A, 14] **~ (for)**, compensate (sb, oneself, for a loss, etc); make up for: 赔偿; 补偿(某人、自己之损失等); 补偿个人的损失: *~ oneself for one's losses.* 补偿个人之损失.

re·course /rɪˈkɔːs; rɪˈkors/ n [U] **1** **have ~ to**, turn to for help; seek help from: 求助于; 求援于: *I don't advise you to have ~ to the money-lenders.* 我劝你不要求援于放利者. **2** sth turned to for help: 求助之事物: *Your only ~ is legal action against them.* 你只有借助法律行动对付他们.

re·cover /rɪˈkʌvə(r); rɪˈkʌvə/ vt, vi **1** [VP6A] get back (sth lost, etc); get back the use of: 寻回(遗失之物等); 恢复: *~ what was lost;* 寻回失去的东西; *~ consciousness* (after fainting); (昏倒后)恢复知觉; *~ one's sight/hearing.* 恢复视力(听力). *I am ~ing my strength,* getting well (after an illness). 我(病后)正在复元. *We soon ~ed lost time.* 我们很快就弥补了浪费的时间. *They have ~ed their losses.* 他们已经补偿了他们的损失. **2** [VP2A, 3A] **~ (from)**, become well; get back to a former position of prosperity, state of health, mental condition, etc: 病后复元; 恢复以前的繁荣、健康、心理状况等: *He is slowly ~ing from his illness.* 他正慢慢从病中复元. *I doubt whether he will ~.* 我不知道他是否会康复. *I haven't yet ~ed from my astonishment.* 我还惊魂未定. *Has the country ~ed from the effects of the war yet?* 那个国家已从战争的影响中复过来了吗? **3** [VP6A] regain control of oneself; become

calm or normal: 重新控制自己; 变得平静或正常; 恢复正常: *He almost fell, but quickly ~ed* (himself). 他几乎跌倒, 但很快又站稳了. *He ~ed his balance/composure.* 他恢复了平衡(平静). **~·able** /-əbl; -əbl/ adj that can be ~ed(1): 能寻回的; 能取回的; 能恢复的: *Is the deposit I've paid ~able?* 我所付的定金能取回吗? **re·cov·ery** n [U] ~ing or being ~ed: 寻回; 被寻回; 恢复; 复元; 痊愈: *make a quick ~y,* get well again quickly or quickly regain one's position after losing for a time in a game, athletic match, etc; 很快康复; 很快赶上(比赛中失去的分数等); *~y' from influenza;* 患流行性感冒后复元; the *~y of a lost article,* getting it back again. 寻回失掉的物件.

re·cover /ˌriːˈkʌvə(r); ˌriˈkʌvə/ vt [VP6A] supply with a new cover: 装以新的盖或封面: *This cushion/quilt needs to be ~ed.* 这个垫子需要换套子(这床棉被需要换被面).

rec·re·ant /ˈrekrɪənt; ˈrɛkrɪənt/ adj, n (liter) cowardly, unfaithful or traitorous (person): (文)懦弱的; 不忠的; 叛逆的; 懦弱者; 叛徒: *a ~ lover.* 一个不忠的爱人.

rec·re·ation /ˌrekrɪˈeɪʃn; ˌrɛkrɪˈeʃən/ n [C, U] (form of) play or amusement; refreshment of body and mind; sth that pleasantly occupies one's time after work is done: (一种)游戏或娱乐; 身心的休闲; 工作之余的消遣活动: *walk and climb mountains for ~.* 为消遣而走路和爬山. *Is gardening a ~ or a form of hard work?* 园艺是一种休闲活动呢, 还是一种劳苦的工作? *Dancing is an innocent ~.* 跳舞是一种无害的娱乐. '**~ ground,** land, eg in a public park, set aside for games, etc. 供游戏活动的场地; 游乐场. **~·al** /-ʃənl; -ʃənl/ adj of ~: 游戏或娱乐的; 休闲的; 消遣的: *provide more ~al facilities,* eg sports grounds, swimming pools. 提供更多消遣活动的设备(如运动场, 游泳池).

re·crimi·na·tion /rɪˌkrɪmɪˈneɪʃn; rɪˌkrɪməˈneʃən/ n [C, U] accusation made in return for one already made; countercharge: 反控诉; 反诉; 反责: *indulge in ~(s).* 热中于互相责备对方; 反诉罪状. **re·crimi·nate** /rɪˈkrɪmɪneɪt; rɪˈkrɪməˌnet/ vi [VP2A, 3A] **~ (against sb)**, accuse(sb)in return. 反控诉; 反责(某人). **re·crimi·na·tory** /rɪˈkrɪmɪnətrɪ US: -tɔːrɪ; rɪˈkrɪmənəˌtɔrɪ/ adj of ~; 反控诉的; 反责的.

re·cru·des·ence /ˌriːkruːˈdesns; ˌrikruˈdɛsns/ n (of disease, violence, etc) new outbreak; breaking out again: (指疾病、暴行等)新发作; 再发作: *a ~ of civil disorder;* 内乱的再爆发; *the ~ of influenza.* 流行性感冒的再发生.

re·cruit /rɪˈkruːt; rɪˈkrut/ n new member of a society, group, etc, esp a soldier in the early days of his training: (会社、团体等中之)新份子; 新会员; 新党员; (尤指)新兵: *gain a new ~ to one's party,* eg in politics; 吸收几个新党员(如在政治方面); *~s being drilled on the parade ground.* 正在检阅场操练的新兵. □ vt, vi **1** [VP6A] get ~s for; enlist (persons) as ~s (for the army, a cause, etc): 为…吸收新份子; (为军队、某一目标)招募(人员)做新份子; 征募新兵: *a ~ing officer;* 征募新兵之军官; *a new political party than the middle classes.* 从中层阶级中的政党吸收新份子. *Were men for the Navy ~ed from men on merchant ships?* 海军的人员是从商船的人员中征募的吗? **2** [VP6A] get a sufficient quantity or store of; bring back to what is usual or normal: 获得…的足量; 补充; 使恢复平常或正常的状态: *~ supplies;* 补充供应品; *~ one's health/strength.* 恢复健康(体力). **~·ment** n

rec·tal /ˈrektəl; ˈrɛktl/ adj of the rectum. 直肠的.

rec·tangle /ˈrektæŋgl; ˈrɛktæŋgl/ n [C] plane foursided figure with four right angles, esp one with adjacent sides unequal. 方形; (尤指)长方形; 矩形. ⇨ the illus at **quadrilateral**. 参看 quadrilateral 之插图. **rec·tangu·lar** /rekˈtæŋgjulə(r); rɛkˈtæŋgjələ/ adj in the shape of a ~. 长方形的.

rec·tify /ˈrektɪfaɪ; ˈrɛktəˌfaɪ/ vt (pt, pp **-fied**) [VP6

A] **1** put right; take out mistakes from: 改正; 矫正: ~ *abuses*; 改正恶习或弊端; *mistakes that cannot be rectified*. 无法改正的错误. **2** purify or refine by repeated distillation or other process: 以连续蒸馏或其他过程净化或精炼; 精馏: *rectified spirits*. 精馏酒精. **rec·ti·fier** n person or thing that rectifies; (electr) device which converts alternating current to direct current. 改正者; 矫正器; 精馏器; (电) 整流器. **rec·tifi·ca·tion** /ˌrektɪfɪˈkeɪʃn; ˌrektəfəˈkeʃən/ n [U] ~ing or being rectified: 改正; 被改正; 精馏; 被精馏: *the rectification of errors/alcohol*; 错误之改正(酒精之精馏); [C] instance of this; sth that has been rectified. 改正或精馏之实例; 被改正或精馏过之物.

rec·ti·lin·ear /ˌrektɪˈlɪnɪə(r); ˌrektəˈlɪnɪə/ adj in or forming a straight line; bounded by, characterized by, straight lines. 直线的; 形成直线的; 由直线围起的; 有直线特征的.

rec·ti·tude /ˈrektɪtjuːd US: -tuːd; ˈrektəˌtjud/ n [U] honesty; upright or straightforward behaviour. 忠实; 正直或坦率的行为.

recto /ˈrektəʊ; ˈrekto/ n (pl ~s /-təʊz; -toz/) any right-hand page of a book. 书的右页. ⇨ **verso**.

rec·tor /ˈrektə(r); ˈrektɚ/ n **1** (C of E) clergyman in charge of a parish, the tithes of which were not withdrawn (eg to a college), at or after the time when the English Church separated from the Church of Rome. (英国教会)仍保留什一税的教区之教区长. ⇨ **vicar**. **2** head of certain universities, colleges, schools or religious institutions. 某些大学、学院、学校、宗教机构之首长; 校长; 院长. ~**y** /ˈrektərɪ; ˈrektərɪ/ n (pl **-ries**) ~'s residence. 教区长、某些学校校长等之住宅.

rec·tum /ˈrektəm; ˈrektəm/ n lower and final part of the large intestine. 直肠. ⇨ the illus at **alimentary**. 参看 alimentary 之插图.

re·cum·bent /rɪˈkʌmbənt; rɪˈkʌmbənt/ adj (esp of a person) lying down: (尤指人)卧倒的; 躺卧的: a ~ figure on a tomb, statue or carving in a ~ position. 坟墓上的一个横卧雕像.

re·cu·per·ate /rɪˈkuːpəreɪt; rɪˈkjupəˌret/ vt, vi [VP6A, 2A] make or become strong again after illness, exhaustion or loss: (使)于病后或疲倦后恢复体力; 休养: 弥补损失: ~ *one's health*; 恢复健康; *go to the seaside to* ~. 到海滨去休养. **re·cu·per·a·tion** /rɪˌkuːpəˈreɪʃn; rɪˌkjupəˈreʃən/ n recuperating. 复元; 休养; 恢复. **re·cu·per·at·ive** /rɪˈkuːpərətɪv; rɪˈkjupəˌretɪv/ adj helping, relating to, recuperation. 有助于或关于休养、恢复的.

re·cur /rɪˈkɜː(r); rɪˈkɝ/ vi (-rr-) **1** [VP2A] come, happen, again; be repeated: 再来; 再发生; 重复: a problem which ~s periodically; 一个定期发生的问题; ~ring decimals, figures in decimal fractions that ~ in the same order, as 3.999... (written 3.9̇), 4.014014... (written 4.01̇4̇). 循环小数, 如 3.999... (写作 4.01̇4̇)... 2 [VP3A] ~ to, go back (to sth) in words or thought: 在谈话或思想中重回(到某事物): ~ing to what you said yesterday; 回到你昨天所说的话题上; if I may ~ to your idea. 如果我可以再谈谈你的意见. **3** [VP3A] ~ to, (of ideas, events etc) come back: (指思想、事件等)重现: My first meeting with her often ~s to my memory. 我同她首次会面的情景时常重现在我的记忆中. **re·cur·rence** /rɪˈkʌrəns; rɪˈkɝəns/ n [C, U] ~ring; repetition: 再发生; 再回到; 重现; 重复: Let there be no ~rence of this error. 不要再有这种错误发生. The frequent ~rence of these headaches made her life miserable. 头痛经常复发使她生活十分痛苦. **re·cur·rent** /-ənt; -ənt/ adj (of events, fevers etc) ~ring frequently or regularly: (指事件、发烧等)经常发生的; 周期性发生的: allow £35 a month for ~rent expenses, eg rent, lighting and heating. 每月留三十五镑作为经常的费用(如房租, 照明, 暖气).

re·curve /riːˈkɜːv; riˈkɝv/ vt, vi curve or bend backwards or downwards. (使)向后或向下弯曲; 折回.

recu·sant /ˈrekjuznt; ˈrɛkjuznt/ n, adj (person) refusing to submit to authority or to comply with regulations, esp (hist) a Roman Catholic who refused to attend Church of England services. 拒绝向权威屈服或遵从规则的(人); (尤指, 史)拒绝参与英国国教礼拜式的天主教徒. **recu·sancy** /-znsɪ; -znsɪ/ n [U].

re·cycle /ˌriːˈsaɪkl; rɪˈsaɪk/ vt [VP6A] treat (substances already used for industry, etc) so that further use is possible: 处理(废物)使成为有用之物: ~ *old newspapers*, by de-inking and pulping then. 以除墨和化成纸浆等方式处理旧报纸.

red /red; red/ adj (-der, -dest) **1** of the colour of fresh blood, rubies, human lips, the tongue, maple leaves in autumn, post-office pillar boxes in GB; of shades varying from crimson to bright brown (as of iron rust): 红色的(如鲜血、红宝石、唇、舌、秋日枫叶、英国邮筒等之颜色); 从深红到鲜褐(如铁锈色)间之不同色调的: *red with anger/embarrassment*, flushed in the face; 气(窘)得满脸通红; *with red hands*, with hands stained with blood; 双手染有血迹; *with red eyes*, eyes red with weeping. 哭得眼睛发红. ~ '**carpet**, one laid out for the reception of an important visitor. (接待贵宾所铺设的)红地毯. *paint the town red*, go on a spree and indulge in noisy, rough behaviour. 狂欢作乐. *see red*, lose control of oneself through anger, or indignation. 怒不可遏. **2** Russian; Soviet; Communist: 俄国的; 苏维埃的; 共产党的: *The Red Army*. 红军. **3** (various uses in compounds, etc): (在复合词等中的各种用法): '**red·breast** n (also 亦作 robin redbreast) bird called the robin. 知更鸟; 红襟鸟. '**Red·brick** adj (GB) name applied to the English universities founded near the end of the 19th c (contrasted chiefly with Oxford and Cambridge——known as Oxbridge). (英)(十九世纪末设立之)大学(主要以别于牛津和剑桥——合称'牛桥')大学. '**redcap** n (GB) member of the military police; (US) railroad porter. (英)宪兵; (美)(火车站的)搬运工. '**red·coat** n (old name for) British soldier. (旧名称)英国兵. ,**Red** '**Crescent** n (emblem of an) organization in Muslim countries corresponding to the Red Cross. 红新月会(穆斯林国家相当于红十字会的组织); 其标记. ,**Red** '**Cross** n (emblem of the) international organization concerned with the relief of suffering caused by natural disasters, etc and for helping the sick and wounded and those taken prisoner in war. 红十字会; 红十字会的标记(红十字会系一国际组织, 办理医院天灾等造成的灾民救济工作, 以及协助战争中之伤患及战俘). ,**red deer** n kind of deer native to the forests of Europe and Asia. (欧洲和亚洲森林中产的)赤鹿. ,**red ensign** (or colloq, ,**red duster**) n red flag with the Union Jack in one corner, used by British merchant ships. (英国商船上悬挂的在一角有英国国旗之)商船旗. ,**red flag** n **(a)** flag used as a symbol of danger (eg on railways, by workers on the roads). (铁路上、道路工人等所用的)作为危险信号的红旗. **(b)** symbol of revolution. (作为革命象征的)红旗. **(c)** the **Red Flag**, revolutionary socialist song. 《红旗歌》(某些左翼团体唱之). (catch sb) ,**red'handed** adj in the act of committing a crime. 趁其犯罪时(逮捕某人); 当场(逮捕某人). ,**red 'hat** n cardinal's hat. 枢机主教之帽子. '**red·head** n person having red hair. 有红发的人. ,**red 'herring** n **(a)** smoke-cured herring. 熏青鱼. **(b)** (fig) irrelevant matter introduced to distract attention from the subject being discussed. (喻)用以分散对本题之注意力的不相干的东西: *neither fish, flesh, nor good red herring*, of a doubtful or ambiguous nature, which cannot be defined. 性质可疑或不明的东西; 非驴非马. *draw a red herring across the trail*, introduce irrelevant matter to distract attention from the subject being discussed. 提出不相干的问题去分散对本题的注意力. ,**red-'hot** adj (of a metal) heated until it is red; (fig) highly excited, furious: (指金属)炽热的; (喻)极端兴奋的; 猛烈的: *red-hot enthusiasm*. 非常的热心. ,**Red 'Indian** n (old use, now impolite) American Indian. (旧用法, 现为不礼貌用语)美洲印第安

人。 **,red 'lead** n [U] pigment made from red oxide of lead. 铅丹(一种颜料)。 **,red-'letter day,** important or memorable day. 重要或值得纪念的日子。 **,red 'light** n **(a)** danger signal on railways, etc; 'stop' signal on roads. 铁路等上的危险信号;道路上'停'的标志。 *see the red light,* realize the nearness of danger or disaster. 看到了红灯(知道危险或灾难之将临)。 **(b)** **red-light district,** part of a town where there are brothels. (城市中之)红灯区;下流场所很多的地区。 **,red 'meat** n [U] beef and mutton (contrasted with *white* meat, ie veal, pork, poultry). 牛羊肉(与 white meat,即小牛肉,猪肉,家禽肉相对)。 **,red 'pepper** n red fruit of the capsicum plant. 红辣椒。 **,red 'rag** n *like a red rag to a bull,* sth that excites a person's anger or passion. (如刺激公牛发怒之红布)能激起愤怒或强烈感情之事物。 **'red-skin** n (old use, now impolite) American Indian. (旧用法,现为不礼貌用语)美洲印第安人。 **the ,Red 'Star,** symbol of the USSR and other Socialist States. 红星(苏联和其他社会主义国家的标志)。 **,red 'tape** n [U] (fig) excessive use of formalities in public business; too much attention to rules and regulations: (喻)繁文缛节;官样文章;官僚习气: *red tape in government offices.* 政府机关中的官僚习气。 **'red-wing** n name used of kinds of thrush and other birds with red wing-feathers. 画眉鸟;红翼鸫。 **'red-wood** n name used of kinds of tree with reddish wood, esp an evergreen Californian tree, some of which are of great height. 红杉(各种有红色木质之树,尤指美国加州产的一种常青树, 有些红杉长得极高)。 □ n 1 [C, U] (shade of) red colour: (深浅程度不同的)红色: *too much red in the painting;* 这画中用的红色太多; *the reds and browns of the woods in autumn,* the red and brown shades of the leaves. 秋林中各种红色和褐色树叶。 2 red clothes: 红衣服: *dressed in red.* 穿红衣。 3 (colloq) person favouring or supporting Communism or the Soviet system. (口)赞成或支持共产主义或苏维埃制度的人。 4 the red, debit side of business accounts. 赤字;亏空。 *be in/get into the red,* have/get liabilities that exceed assets. 负债。 *be/get out of the red,* reach the position when one is no longer in the red. 不再亏空。 ⇨ black n(5)。

re-dact /rɪˈdækt; rɪˈdækt/ vt [VP6A] (formal) edit. (正式用语)编辑。 **re-dac-tion** /rɪˈdækʃn; rɪˈdækʃən/ n [U,C]。

red-den /ˈredn; ˈrɛdn/ vt, vi [VP6A, 2A] make or become red; blush. 使红;变红;脸色变红;赧颜。

red-dish /ˈredɪʃ; ˈrɛdɪʃ/ adj rather red. 微红的;略带红色的。

re-deem /rɪˈdiːm; rɪˈdim/ vt [VP6A, 14] **~ (from),** 1 get (sth) back by payment or by doing sth: 赎回;换回: *~ a pawned watch/a mortgage;* 赎回一典当的表(抵押品);*~ one's honour.* 挽回一个人的名誉。 2 perform (a promise or obligation). 践约;实践(义务)。 3 set free by payment; rescue: 赎救;拯救: *~ a slave/prisoner;* 赎出一奴隶(囚犯);(by Jesus) make free from sin. (由耶稣)赎罪。 4 compensate; make amends for: 赔偿;补救: *his ~ing feature,* the feature or quality that balances his faults, etc. 能弥补他的缺点的特质。 *The acting barely ~s the play,* The play is poor and the acting not very good. 该剧的演出未能补救剧本的缺点(剧本差劲,演得也不好)。 **~-able** /-əbl/ adj that can be ~ed. 可赎回的;可实践的;可拯救的;可补偿的。 **(the) Re-deemer** n Jesus Christ. 救世主(耶稣基督)。

re-demp-tion /rɪˈdempʃn; rɪˈdɛmpʃən/ n [U] redeeming or being redeemed: 赎回;被赎回;实践;被实践;补偿;被补偿: *the ~ of a promise;* 诺言的实践; deliverance or rescue (esp from evil ways): 救出;赎救(尤指从罪恶中救出): *past/beyond ~,* too bad to be redeemed. 无可救药。

re-demp-tive /rɪˈdemptɪv; rɪˈdɛmptɪv/ adj serving to redeem; relating to redemption. 适合于或关于赎回等的;挽回的;实践的;拯救的;补偿的。

re-de-ploy /ˌriːdɪˈplɔɪ; ˌrɪdɪˈplɔɪ/ vt [VP6A] (of

troops, workers in industry, etc) withdraw and rearrange so as to use more efficiently. (指军队,产业工人等)重新部署;转用;调动。 **~-ment** n [U, C] **~-ing:** *the ~ment of labour.* 劳工的调配。

re-dif-fu-sion /ˌriːdɪˈfjuːʒn; ˌrɪdɪˈfjuʒən/ n [U] system of using broadcast programmes (sound and television) in public places (eg cinemas). 在公共场所(如电影院)播放(广播电台及电视)广播节目之系统。

re-do /ˌriːˈduː; rɪˈdu/ vt (pt -did /-ˈdɪd; -ˈdɪd/, pp -done /-ˈdʌn; -ˈdʌn/)[VP6A] do again: 再做: *We must have the walls redone,* repapered, recoloured, etc according to context. 我们必须把这些墙再整理一番(例如重새糊纸、改换颜色等,其意义视上下文而定)。

redo-lent /ˈredələnt; ˈrɛdlənt/ adj **~ of,** (formal) having a strong smell, esp one that is reminiscent of sth: (正式用语)有浓烈气味的;(指)具有使想起某种东西之强烈气味的: *bed sheets ~ of lavender;* 有薰衣草芳香气味的床单;(fig) (喻) *a town ~ of age and romance.* 使人想起古代和奇的一个城市。 **redo-lence** /-əns; -əns/n

re-double /rɪˈdʌbl; rɪˈdʌbl/ vt, vi [VP6A, 2A] 1 make or become greater or stronger: 使或变得更大或更强;增添: *They ~d their efforts.* 他们加倍努力。 *Her zeal ~d.* 她的热心倍增。 2 (bridge) double again a bid already doubled by an opponent. (桥牌)再加倍(把已由对方加倍过的叫牌再予加倍)。 ⇨ double⁴(6).

re-doubt /rɪˈdaʊt; rɪˈdaʊt/ n [C] strong point in a system of fortifications: 棱堡;角面堡;安全退避处;防守据点: *attack and capture a ~.* 攻击并占领一防守重点。

re-doubt-able /rɪˈdaʊtəbl; rɪˈdaʊtəbl/ adj (liter) to be feared; formidable: (文)可怕的;令人畏惧的: *those ~ ladies,* the suffragettes. 那些最强的女士们, 指二十世纪初叶鼓吹英国妇女有参政权的妇女。

re-dound /rɪˈdaʊnd; rɪˈdaʊnd/ vi [VP3A] **~ to,** (formal) contribute greatly to sth; promote: (正式用语)有助于;促进: *Your success will ~ to the fame of the college.* 你的成功将提高该大学的声誉。 *It ~s to your honour.* 这事提高你的荣誉。

re-dress /rɪˈdres; rɪˈdrɛs/ vt [VP6A] 1 set (a wrong) right again; make up for, do sth that compensates for (a wrong): 改正;修正;矫正;补救: *You should confess and ~ your errors.* 你应该忏悔并改正你的错误。 2 **~ the balance,** make things equal again. 使再平衡。 □ n [U] act of ~ing or correcting (abuses, etc); sth that ~es: 改正或矫正(恶习等);有改正或补偿等作用的事物; 赔偿: *seek ~;* 求赔偿; 革除恶习; *go to a lawyer to get legal ~.* 找律师以期获得合法赔偿。

re-duce /rɪˈdjuːs; *US:* -ˈduːs; rɪˈdjus/ vt, vi [VP6A, 14] **~ (to),** 1 make smaller in size, number, degree, price, etc: 使减少;使(体积)变小;减少(数目);降低(程度);减低(价格)等: *~ speed/pressure/costs,* 减低速度(压力,成本);*~ one's expenses,* 减缩开支; *~ one's weight by ten pounds/from X pounds to Y pounds.* 减轻体重十磅(自 X 磅减为 Y 磅)。 *He is ~d almost to a skeleton,* has become very thin. 他瘦得几乎变成了一个骨头架子。 [VP2A, B] (colloq): (口): *She has been reducing for the last few weeks,* has been dieting (or trying other methods) in order to ~ her weight. 最近几个星期她一直在节食(或以其他方法)减轻体重。 2 bring or get to a certain condition, way of living, etc: 使成或达到某种情况、生活方式等: *~ a class of noisy children to order;* (使一群吵闹的孩子恢复秩序; *~ sb to silence,* cause him to stop talking; 使某人不再讲话; *~ sth to order;* 使某事物有秩序; *~ the rebels to submission;* 使叛乱者屈服; *~ a sergeant to the ranks.* 将一士官贬为士兵。 *They were ~d to begging or starving.* They became so poor that they had either to beg or go hungry. 他们穷得不行乞便挨饿。 *They are living in ~d circumstances,* in (comparative) poverty. 他们过着(相当)贫困的生活。 3 change (to another form): 改变(成另一形式,与 to 连用): *~ an equation/argument/statement to its simplest form;* 把一方程式(论据,陈述)化成最简单形式; *~ water by electrolysis,* separate it into oxygen and hydrogen;

以电解法分解水(即部分分解为氧与氢);～ *(sth) to an absurdity,* make, eg a scheme or argument, appear absurd by removing whatever hides its real nature; (揭露其真实性质)使(某一计划或论据等)显得荒谬可笑; ～ *wood logs to pulp.* 把木材化成纸浆. **re·duc·ible** /-əbl; -əbl/ *adj* that can be ～d. 能减低或减小的; 能变形的; 能化简的; 能分解的.

reductio ad absurdum /rɪˌdʌktɪoʊ ˌæd əb'sɜːdəm; rɪˈdʌkʃɪoˌædəb'sədəm/ (Lat) the disproof of a proposition by showing that its conclusion can only be absurd. (拉丁)归谬法; 反证论法(指出某一命题结论之荒谬, 以证明该命题为误之方法).

re·duc·tion /rɪ'dʌkʃn; rɪ'dʌkʃən/ *n* **1** [U] reducing or being reduced; [C] instance of this: 减少; 减低; 使变形; 被减少; 被减低; 变形: *a ～ in/of numbers;* 数目方面的减少; *great ～s in prices; price ～s.* 大减价. **2** [C] copy, on a smaller scale, of a picture, map, etc. (图画、地图等之)缩版; 缩图.

re·dun·dant /rɪ'dʌndənt; rɪ'dʌndənt/ *adj* superfluous; not needed: 过多的; 多余的; 不需要的: *a paragraph without a ～ word;* 没有一个废字的一段文章; ～ *labour,* unneeded or surplus workers. 过剩的劳工. *With the decreasing demand for coal many thousands of miners may become ～.* 由于煤的需要量减少, 成千上万的矿工可能成为过剩的劳工. **re·dun·dance** /-əns/, **re·dun·dancy** /-ənsɪ; -ənsɪ/ *nn* [U] being ～: 过多; 过剩: *redundancy among clerks caused by the increasing use of computers;* 因电子计算机的使用日渐增加而造成职员的过剩. [C] (*pl* **-cies**) instance of this: 过多或过剩之实例: *more redundancies in the docks.* 船坞中有过多的船. **re'dundancy pay,** money paid by an employer to a ～ worker, the sum depending upon age and length of service. 遣散费.

re·dupli·cate /rɪ'djuːplɪkeɪt *US:* -'duː-; rɪ'djuːpləˌket/ *vt* [VP6A] double; repeat. 加倍; 重复. **re·dupli·ca·tion** /rɪˌdjuːplɪ'keɪʃn *US:* -ˌduː-; rɪˌdjupləˈkeʃən/ *n*.

re-echo /riː 'ekoʊ; ri'ɛko/ *vi* [VP2A] echo again and again. 回响; 再发回声. □ *n* (*pl* **-es** /-əʊz; -oz/) echo of an echo. 回声之回响; 再回声.

reed /riːd; rid/ *n* [C] **1** (tall, firm stem or stalk of) kinds of coarse, firm-stemmed, jointed grasses growing in or near water; [U] (collective) mass of such grasses growing together; (*pl*) dried stalks used for thatching. 芦苇(杆); (集合用法)芦苇丛; (复)干芦杆(用于盖屋顶). *a broken ～,* (fig) an unreliable person or thing. (喻)不可靠的人或物. **2** (in some wind-instruments, eg the oboe, bassoon, clarinet and in some organ-pipes) strip of metal, etc that vibrates to produce sound. (某些管乐器, 如双簧管、低音管、竖笛、某些风琴管中之)颤动以发出声音的部分; 簧. **the ～s, ～** instruments of this sort. 簧乐器. **～·y** *adj* **1** abounding in ～s(1). 多芦苇的. **2** (of sounds, voices) shrill; piping. (指声音)细而尖的; 尖锐的.

reef[1] /riːf; rif/ *n* that part of a sail which can be rolled up or folded so as to reduce its area: 缩折帆叶(帆的能卷起或折起以减少面积的部分): *take in a ～,* shorten sail; (fig) go forward more cautiously. 卷叠一部分帆; (喻)加倍小心前进. **'～-knot** *n* ordinary double knot (US = *square knot*) 平结; 方结; 拱结. ⇨ the illus at **knot.** 参看 knot 之插图. □ *vt* [VP6A] reduce the area of (a sail) by rolling up or folding a part. 缩(帆) (由卷起或折叠而减少帆的面积).

reef[2] /riːf; rif/ *n* ridge of rock, shingle etc just below or above the surface of the sea: 礁; 暗礁: *wrecked on a coral ～.* 撞及珊瑚礁而破船的. ⇨ the illus at **atoll.** 看 atoll 之插图.

reefer /'riːfə(r); 'rifə/ *n* **1** close-fitting double-breasted jacket of thick cloth, as worn by sailors. 一种紧身、双排扣的粗布外衣(如海员等所穿者). **2** (sl) kind of cigarette containing marijuana. (俚)含有印度大麻的香烟.

reek /riːk; rik/ *n* [U] **1** strong, bad smell: 浓烈的臭味: *the ～ of stale tobacco smoke.* 发霉烟草的臭味味. **2**

(liter and Scot use) thick smoke or vapour: (文学及苏格兰用语)浓烟或蒸汽: *the ～ of a peat fire.* 泥炭火的浓烟. □ *vi* [VP3A] ～ *of,* smell unpleasantly of: 有臭味: *He ～s of whisky/garlic.* 他有威士忌(大蒜)的臭味. *The room ～ed of stale cigar smoke.* 这房里弥漫着发霉雪茄的臭味味. **2** ～ *with,* be covered (with sweat, blood, etc); show signs or traces of: 为(汗、血等)浸染; 有…迹象: *a horse ～ing with sweat;* 一匹混身汗水的马; *a murderer whose hands still ～ed with blood.* 手上仍然血迹斑斑的一个杀人犯.

reel[1] /riːl; ril/ *n* **1** cylinder, roller or similar device on which cotton, thread, wire, photographic film, magnetic tape, hose (for water, etc), a fishing line, is wound. 线轴; 卷筒; 卷轴; 卷盘. **(straight) off the ～,** (colloq) without a hitch or pause, in rapid succession. (口)迅速不停地. **2** (cinema) length of positive film rolled on one ～: (电影)(影片的)一卷、一盘: *a six-～ film,* a complete film on six ～s. 一部有六大盘的电影片. ⇨ **spool.** □ *vt* [VP6A, 15A, B] roll or wind (thread, a fishing line, etc) on to, or with the help of, a ～; wind (thread, etc) *off:* 卷或缠(线、钓丝等)于轴上; 借轴而卷或缠; 抽出(线等, 与 off 连用): ～ *in the line;* 卷线; ～ *up a fish;* 收钓丝拉鱼; ～ *the silk thread off cocoons.* 从茧中抽出丝. ～ *sth off,* tell, say or repeat sth without pause or apparent effort: 滔滔不绝地说出或背出: ～ *off the verses of a long poem;* 滔滔不绝地背出一首长诗的各节; ～ *off a list of names.* 连续地讲出一串人名.

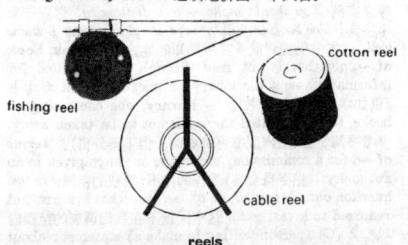

fishing reel   cotton reel   cable reel

reels

reel[2] /riːl; ril/ *vi* [VP2A, C] **1** be shaken (physically or mentally) by a blow, a shock, rough treatment, etc: (身体或心理方面)因打击或惊讶或粗鲁对待等而震颤: *His mind ～ed when he heard the news.* 他听到那消息时, 内心感到一阵震颤. **2** walk or stand unsteadily, moving from side to side; sway: 不稳地走或站; 来回地摇摆; 摇晃: *He ～ed like a drunken man.* 他摇摇晃晃, 象个酩汉. *He went ～ing down the road.* 他摇摇摆摆地沿大路走去. **3** seem to sway; appear to move or shake: 似乎摇晃; 看来摇动或震颤: *The street ～ed before his eyes.* 街道似乎在他眼前摇动起来.

reel[3] /riːl; ril/ *n* [C] (music for a) lively Scottish dance, usu for two couples. 利尔舞(一种轻快的苏格兰舞, 通常由两对共舞); 利尔舞曲.

re-en·try /ˌriː 'entrɪ; ri'ɛntri/ *n* (*pl* **-ries**) act of re-entering; return of a spacecraft into the earth's atmosphere. 再进入; 再登记; (太空船)重回大气层.

reeve /riːv; riv/ *n* **1** (hist) chief magistrate of a town or district. (史)市邑长官; 地方官. **2** (Canada) president of a village or town council. (加拿大)(乡镇议会之)议长.

re-face /riː 'feɪs; ri'fes/ *vt* put a new surface on. 重装新面; 重修表面.

re·fec·tion /rɪ'fekʃn; rɪ'fɛkʃən/ *n* [U] refreshment in the form of food and drink; [C] light meal. 茶点; 点心; 便餐; 小吃.

re·fec·tory /rɪ'fektərɪ; rɪ'fɛktəri/ *n* (*pl* **-ries**) dining-hall (in a monastery, convent or college). (修道)院、尼庵或大学中的)餐厅.

re·fer /rɪ'fɜː(r); rɪ'fɚ/ *vt, vi* (**-rr-**) **1** [VP14, 15B] ～ *sb/sth (back) (to sb/sth),* send, take, hand over (to,

back to) to be dealt with, decided, etc: 送交；呈交；提交(某人或某机构)处理或决定：*The dispute was ~red to the United Nations.* 该项争执已提交联合国处理。*I was ~red to the Manager/to the Inquiry Office.* 我被吩咐去向经理(问讯处)接洽。*The question was ~red back,* was deferred. 该问题被搁置。**2** [VP3A] *~ to,* (of a speaker, what is said, etc) speak of, allude to; apply to: (指讲话者，所谈之事等)谈及；提及；应用于：*When I said that some people are stupid I wasn't ~ring to you.* 当我说某些人很愚蠢的时候，我并不是指你。*Don't ~ to this matter again, please.* 请不要再提这件事了。*What I have to say ~ to all of you.* 我要说的这一切和你们大家有关。*Does that remark ~ to me?* 那批评的话是指我说的吗？ **3** [VP3A] *~ to,* turn to, go to, for information, etc: 参考；咨询：*The speaker often ~red to his notes.* 那位讲演者一再参考他的大纲。**ref·er·able** /ri'fɜːrəbl; 'refrəbl/ adj that can be ~red. 可归因于…的。

ref·er·ee /ˌrefə'riː; ˌrɛfə'ri/ n **1** person to whom disputes, eg in industry, between workers and employers, are referred for decision. 纠纷的仲裁者；调停者(如调停劳资双方间的纠纷者)。**2** (in football, boxing, etc) person who controls matches, judges points in dispute, etc. (足球、拳击等的)裁判员。⇨ **umpire.** □ vt, vi [VP6A, 2] act as ~: 裁判：*~ a football match.* 为足球比赛做裁判。

ref·er·ence /'refrəns; 'rɛfrəns/ n **1** [C, U] (instance of) referring: 送交；交付；谈到；提及；参考；咨询；提及等之实例：*You should make ~ to a dictionary.* 你应该参考字典。*The book is full of ~s to places that I know well.* 这本书里提到很多我所熟知的地方。**'~ book, book of ~,** one that is not read through but consulted for information, eg a dictionary or encyclopaedia. 参考书(例如字典或百科全书)。**'~ library,** one containing ~ books, to be consulted there but not to be taken away. 参考书阅览室(室内藏书可供参阅，但不得外借)。**terms of ~,** (of a commission, etc) scope or range given to an authority: (指委员会等)委任的范围；授权的范围：*Is this question outside our terms of ~,* one that we are not required to investigate? 这个问题不在我们调查的范围内吗？ **2** [C] (person willing to make a) statement about a person's character or abilities: (有关一个人的品格或能力的)证明书；介绍信；(愿提供证明书的)证明人；介绍人：*excellent ~s from former employers.* 以前雇主们给的很好的证明书。*The shop will open a credit account for you if you supply a banker's ~,* a note from your bank stating that your financial position is sound. 如果你提出银行给你的证明书，这家商店就会为你开一个信用帐户。**3** [C] note, direction, etc telling where certain information may be found: 旁注；参照；参照注：*He dislikes history books that are crowded with ~s to other books.* 他不喜欢有很多参看其他书籍的附注的历史书。**'~ marks,** marks, eg *, †, ‡, §, used to refer the reader to the place, eg a footnote, where information may be found. 参照符号(用以指示读者参看资料来源的符号)。**,cross-reference,** ⇨ **cross-~. 4** [U] *in/with ~ to,*concerning; about. 关于；有关。*without ~ to,* irrespective of; having no connection with. 不顾；无关。**ref·er·en·tial** /ˌrefə'renʃl; ˌrɛfə'rɛnʃəl/ adj having ~ to. 参考的；参看的；咨询的；有关的。

ref·er·en·dum /ˌrefə'rendəm; ˌrɛfə'rɛndəm/ n (pl ~s; -da /-də; -də/) [C] the referring of a political question to a direct vote of the electorate. 复决权；复决投票；公民投票。

re·fill /ˌriː'fɪl; ri'fɪl/ vt fill again. 再充满；再注满。□ n /'riːfɪl; 'ri,fɪl/ that which is used to ~; a container: 用以再注满之物；新补充物；容器：*two ~s for a ball-point pen.* 原子笔的两支替换笔心。

re·fine /rɪ'faɪn; rɪ'faɪn/ vt, vi **1** [VP6A, 2A] free from other substances; make or become pure: 净化；使纯净；变纯净；精炼：*~ sugar/oil/ores.* 精炼糖(石油，矿石)。**2** [VP6A] cause to become more cultured, polished in manners; get rid of what is coarse or vulgar: 使文雅

高尚；袪除粗俗的行为，言谈等：*~ a language:* 使一语言纯净纯雅；*~d language/manners/speech/taste.* 高雅的言语(态度，言谈，趣味)。**3** *~ upon,* improve by giving great attention to details: 由特别注意细节而改良；精益求精：*~ upon one's methods.* 改进个人的工作方法。

re·fine·ment /rɪ'faɪnmənt; rɪ'faɪnmənt/ n **1** [U] refining or being refined. 精炼；改良；被精炼；被改良。**2** [U] purity of feeling, taste, language, etc; delicacy of manners: (感情，趣味，语言等的)纯洁；高尚；(态度的)娴雅：*a lady of ~;* 一位娴雅的女士；*lack of ~,* ie vulgarity; 缺乏教养；*aim at acquiring ~.* 以达到高尚娴雅为目的。**3** [C] ingenious or remarkable example of such purity of tastes, etc; delicate or clever development of sth: (趣味等)纯洁高尚之巧妙的或显著的例子；某事物之细致的或巧妙的发展：*~s of meaning/cruelty;* 意义的精微巧妙处(残酷虐待的妙法)；*all the ~s of the age.* 这个时代所有高尚的事物。

re·finer /rɪ'faɪnə(r); rɪ'faɪnə/ n **1** person whose business is to refine sth. 精炼者；精制者：*sugar ~s.* 精炼糖者。**2** machine for refining metals, sugar, etc. (金属，糖等之)精炼机。**~y** /-nəri; -nəri/ n place, building, etc where sth is refined: 精炼厂；精制厂：*a 'sugar ~y;* 炼糖厂；*an 'oil ~y.* 炼油厂。

re·fit /ˌriː'fɪt; ri'fɪt/ vt, vi (-tt-) [VP6A] make (a ship, etc) ready for use again by renewing or repairing parts; [VP2A] (of a ship) be made fit for further voyages: 重新装配或修理(船等)；改装；整修；(指船)被修理或装配：*The ship put into Cardiff to ~.* 该船驶入加地夫修理。□ n /'riːfɪt; ri'fɪt/ refitting. 再装配；修理。

re·flate /ˌriː'fleɪt; ri'flet/ vt [VP6A] restore to a previous economic or currency state: 使(通货)再膨胀；使(经济或货币)恢复原先状态：*plans to ~ the economy.* 计划恢复经济。

re·fla·tion /ˌriː'fleɪʃn; ri'fleʃən/ n [U] inflation of currency after a deflation, to restore the system to its previous condition. 通货再膨胀(使通货恢复原先状态)。

re·flect /rɪ'flekt; rɪ'flɛkt/ vt, vi **1** [VP6A] (of a surface) throw back (light, heat, sound); (of a mirror) send back an image of: (指表面)反射(光、热、声)；(指镜)反映…之像：*The sunlight was ~ed from the water.* 阳光由水面反射出来。*Look at the trees ~ed in the lake.* 看湖中倒映的树影。*The moon shines with ~ed light.* 月以反射之光照耀。*The sight of my face ~ed in the mirror never pleases me.* 我永远不喜欢看自己在镜中反映的面孔。**'~·ing telescope,** one in which the image is ~ed in a mirror and magnified. 反射望远镜。**2** [VP6A] express; show the nature of: 表达；表现…之性质：*Her sad looks ~ed the thoughts passing through her mind.* 她忧戚的面容反映出她内心的思想。*Does the literature of a nation ~ its politics?* 一个国家的文学反映出它的政治吗？**3** [VP14] *~ sth on/upon sb,* (of actions, results) bring (credit or discredit upon): (指行动，结果)带来(荣誉或玷辱)：*The results ~ the greatest credit upon all concerned.* 这些成绩带给所有有关人员最大的荣誉。*Such behaviour can only ~ discredit upon you.* 这样的行为只能给你带来耻辱。**4** [VP3A] *~ on/upon,* bring discredit upon; hurt the good reputation of: 不信任；玷辱名誉：*I do not wish to ~ upon your sincerity,* suggest that you are not sincere. 我不希望怀疑你的诚意。*Your rude behaviour ~s only upon yourself,* You are the only person whose reputation is hurt by it. 你的粗鲁行为只会损及你自己的名誉。**5** [VP2A, 3A, 9, 8, 10] *~ (on/upon),* consider; think on: 考虑；思考：*I must ~ upon what answer to give/how to answer that question.* 我必须思考一下如何答复(如何答复那个问题)。*He ~ed how difficult it would be to escape.* 他在想逃走会有多么困难。

re·flec·tion (GB also **re·flexion**) /rɪ'flekʃn; rɪ'flɛkʃən/ n **1** [U] reflecting or being reflected: 反射；反射；反映：*the ~ of heat.* 热之反射。**2** [C] sth reflected, esp an image reflected in a mirror or surface: 被反射或反映之物；(尤指)镜中或静水中之映像：*see one's ~ in a mirror;* 看自己在镜中的映像；*the ~ of trees in (the*

water of) a lake. 湖(水)中树的倒影。**3** [U] thought; (re)consideration: 思想; 沉思; (再)考虑: *lost in ~*, 陷于沉思中; *do sth without sufficient ~*. 未经过深思熟虑即做某事。*on ~*, after reconsidering the matter. 经再三考虑。**4** [C] expression of a thought in speech or writing; idea arising in the mind: (在言谈或写作中的)思想之表达; 心中产生的意念: *~s on the pleasures of being idle*. 对闲散生活之乐趣的看法。**5** [C] expression of blame: 非难; 责备: *I intended no ~ on your character*, did not want to suggest that you are blameworthy. 我无意对你的品格有可责难。*How dare you cast ~s on my motives?* 你怎敢责难我的动机? **6** [C] sth that brings discredit: 带来耻辱之事物: *This is a ~ upon your honour*. 这对你的名誉是一种损害。

re·flec·tive /rɪ'flektɪv; rɪ'flɛktɪv/ *adj* thoughtful, in the habit of reflection(3). 沉思的; 时常思考的。**~·ly** *adv*

re·flec·tor /rɪ'flektə(r); rɪ'flɛktɚ/ *n* sth that reflects heat, light or sound, esp a piece of glass or metal for reflecting light, etc in a required direction. 反射热、光、声的东西 (尤指向一指定方向反射光等之玻璃或金属面); 反射器; 反射镜; 反射体。**'~ studs,** (GB) studs inserted in a road surface to help drivers by reflecting light from headlamps (= colloq □ *cat's eyes*). (英)反光钉(铺于路面,借反射车辆前灯之灯光以帮助驾驶人员)。⇨ the illus at **bicycle**. 参看 bicycle 之插图。

re·flex /'riːfleks; 'riflɛks/ *adj* **1** '**~ action**, action that is independent of the will, being an involuntary response to a stimulation of the nerves, eg shivering, sneezing. 反射动作(不受意志力所控制, 系对神经感受刺激的自动反应, 如发抖、打喷嚏等)。**2** '**~ camera**, hand camera in which, by means of a mirror, the reflected image of the object or scene to be photographed can be seen and focused up to the moment of exposure. 反射式照相机(一种手提照相机, 借一镜之助, 待拍摄之景物的反射映像可在曝光前被看见并集中在焦点上)。□ *n* **~ action**. 反射动作; 反射。

re·flexion /rɪ'flekʃn; rɪ'flɛkʃən/ *n* = **reflection**.

re·flex·ive /rɪ'fleksɪv; rɪ'flɛksɪv/ *n, adj* (word or form) showing that the agent's action is upon himself, 反身的(词或形式)。**~ verb,** eg He cut himself. 反身动词(如 He cut himself in cut)。**~ pronoun,** eg *myself, themselves*, 反身代词(如 myself, themselves)。

re·float /ˌriː'fləʊt; ri'flot/ *vt, vi* [VP6A, 2A] cause (sth) to float again after it has gone aground, been sunk, etc; float again. 使(某物)在搁浅或沉没后再浮起; 再浮起。

re·flux /'riːflʌks; 'riflʌks/ *n* flowing back; ebb: 回流; 倒流; 退潮: *flux and ~*. 潮之涨落; 事之荣枯。

re·for·est /ˌriː'fɒrɪst US: -'fɔːrɪst; ri'fɔrɪst/ *vt* > **reafforest**. **re·for·es·ta·tion** /ˌriːfɒrɪ'steɪʃn US: -ˌfɔːr-; ˌrifɔrɪs'teʃən/ *n*

re·form /rɪ'fɔːm; rɪ'fɔrm/ *vt, vi* [VP6A, 2A] make or become better by removing or putting right what is bad or wrong: 改革; 改进; 改造; 改善: *a sinner / one's character / the world*: 改造一罪人(一个人的品格, 世界); *~ oneself*; 改过自新; *a ~ed man*, one who has given up his bad ways and is now living a good life. 一个改过自新的人。□ *n* **1** [U] ~ing; removal of vices, imperfections, etc: 改革; 改造; 改进; 改善; 革除恶习, 缺点等: *agitate for social or political ~*; 鼓吹社会或政治的革新; *the Re'form Bill of 1832*, (GB) that which extended the franchise and improved parliamentary representation. 1832 年英国的改革法案(扩大投票权及改革议会代表选举方式的法案)。**2** [C] instance of ~ing; change made in order to remove imperfections: 改革之实例; 为革除缺点所作的改变: *a ~ in teaching methods*. 教学法之改进。**~er** *n* person actively engaged in advocating or carrying out ~s. 从事改革运动者; 改革家。

re-form /ˌriː'fɔːm; ˌri'fɔrm/ *vt, vi* form again; (of soldiers) get into ranks, etc again. 再形成; (指士兵)重编队。**re-for·ma·tion** /ˌriː fɔː'meɪʃn; ˌrifɔr'meʃən/ *n*

ref·or·ma·tion /ˌrefə'meɪʃn; ˌrɛfə'meʃən/ *n* **1** [U]

reforming or being reformed; [C] radical change for the better in social, political or religious affairs. 改革; 被改革; (社会、政治或宗教事务上的)革新。**2 the R~** the 16th-century movement for reform of the Roman Catholic Church, resulting in the establishment of the Reformed or Protestant Churches. 宗教改革(十六世纪改革罗马天主教会的运动, 结果产生了新教)。

re·for·ma·tory /rɪ'fɔːmətrɪ US: -tɔːrɪ; rɪ'fɔrmə,tɔrɪ/ *adj* tending or intending to produce reform. 趋于或意欲改革的; 改善的; 改进的。□ *n* (*pl* **-ties**) (formerly) school or institution for reforming young offenders against the law by means of special training, mental, moral and physical (usu, in GB, called in 英国通常称为 an *approved school* or *community house*). (昔时)少年感化院。

re·fract /rɪ'frækt; rɪ'frækt/ *vt* [VP6A] cause (a ray of light) to bend aside where it enters, eg water, glass, obliquely: 使(光线)在斜进(水, 玻璃等)的地方屈折; 使折射: *Light is ~ed when it passes through a prism*. 光经过棱镜便折射了。**re·frac·tion** /rɪ'frækʃn; rɪ'frækʃən/ *n* ~ing or being ~ed. 折射; 被折射。

re·frac·tory /rɪ'fræktərɪ; rɪ'fræktərɪ/ *adj* **1** resisting control, discipline, etc; wilful: 难控制的; 难驾御的; 任性的; 刚愎的: *as ~ as a mule*; 倔强得象匹骡子; (of diseases) not yielding to treatment. (指疾病)难医治的。**2** (of substances, esp metals) hard to melt, fuse or work. (指物质, 尤指金属)难熔的; 不易处理的。

re·frain¹ /rɪ'freɪn; rɪ'fren/ *n* [C] lines of a song which are repeated, esp at the end of each verse: (歌曲的)重叠句(尤指每节收尾的叠句); 副歌: *Will you all join in singing the ~, please?* 请大家一齐来唱副歌好吗?

re·frain² /rɪ'freɪn; rɪ'fren/ *vi* [VP2A, 3A] **~ (from)**, hold oneself back: 抑制; 克制: *Please ~ from spitting in public places*. 请勿在公共场所吐痰。*Let's hope they will ~ from hostile action*. 希望他们不采取敌对行动。

re·fresh /rɪ'freʃ; rɪ'frɛʃ/ *vt* [VP6A] **1** give new strength to; make fresh: 给…力量的; 使精神爽快的: *~ oneself with a cup of tea / a warm bath*. 喝杯茶(洗个热水澡)提神。**2 ~ one's memory**, call things back to the memory by referring to notes, etc. 唤起记忆。**3** take sth to eat or drink: 吃东西; 喝饮料: *They stopped at a pub to ~ themselves*. 他们在酒馆停下来, 喝几杯酒。*They felt much ~ed*. 他们觉得喝够(吃饱)了。**~ing** *adj* **1** strengthening; giving rest and relief: 给人力量的; 使人恢复体力的; 使人精神爽快的: *a ~ing breeze / sleep*. 使人心旷神怡的微风(使人恢复体力的睡眠)。**2** welcome and interesting because rare or unexpected: (因稀罕或出乎意料而)令人欣喜的; 新奇的: *~ing innocence*, eg of children to older, sophisticated persons. 令人喜爱的天真。**~ing·ly** *adv*

re·fresher /rɪ'freʃə(r); rɪ'frɛʃɚ/ *n* **1** (legal) extra fee paid to counsel[3] while a case is proceeding in the law courts. (法律)(诉讼进行中)律师之额外诉讼费。**2** (colloq) drink. (口)饮料。**3** (attrib) (用作定语) '**~ course**, course providing instuctions, eg to teachers already in service, on modern methods, newer professional techniques, etc. 进修课程(如对在职教师提供有关现代方法、较新的专门技术等的课程)。

re·fresh·ment /rɪ'freʃmənt; rɪ'frɛʃmənt/ *n* **1** [U] refreshing or being refreshed: 精神爽快; 心旷神怡: *feel ~ of mind and body*. 身心均感爽快。**2** [U] (often *pl*) that which refreshes, esp food and drink: (常用复数)提神的东西 (尤指食物和饮料): *order some light ~*(s), snacks; 叫一些点心; '**~ room**, one where one can buy food and drink, eg at a railway station. (火车站等处的)饮食店; 餐室。*R~s were provided during the interval*. 在休息时间有点心供应。

re·frig·er·ate /rɪ'frɪdʒəreɪt; rɪ'frɪdʒə,ret/ *vt* [VP6A] make cool or cold; keep (food) in good condition by making and keeping it cold. 使凉或冷; 冷藏(食物)。**re·frig·er·ant** /-ənt; -ənt/ *n, adj* (substance) serving to ~, eg liquid carbon dioxide. 冷冻的; 清凉剂; 冷却剂; 冰

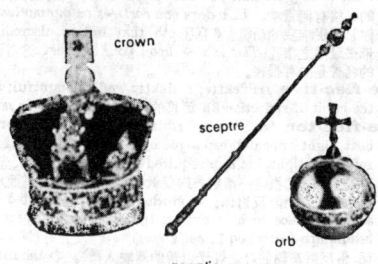

regalia

冻剂。**re·frig·er·ation** /rɪˌfrɪdʒəˈreɪʃn; rɪˌfrɪdʒəˈreʃən/ *n* (esp) the cooling or freezing of food in order to preserve it: (尤指)食物之冷藏: *the refrigeration industry.* 冷藏工业。 **re·frig·er·ator** /rɪˈfrɪdʒəreɪtə(r); rɪˈfrɪdʒəˌretə/ *n* [C] (colloq abbr 口语略作 *fridge*) cabinet or room in which food is kept cold. (电)冰箱; 冷冻库。

reft /reft; reft/ *pp* = **bereft**.

re·fuel /ˌriːˈfjuːəl; rɪˈfjuəl/ *vt, vi* (-ll-; US also -l-) [VP6A, 2A] supply with, take on, a fresh quantity of fuel: 供以或取得新燃料; 加添燃料: *The plane came down to* ~. 飞机降落加油。

ref·uge /ˈrefjuːdʒ; ˈrefjudʒ/ *n* [C, U] (place giving) shelter or protection from trouble, danger, pursuit, etc: 庇护; 避难; 避难所: *seek* ~ *from the floods;* 躲避洪水; *take* ~ *in the cellar;* 在地下室避难; (fig) (喻) *take* ~ *in silence,* eg to avoid answering impertinent questions. 以沉默来逃避(回答无礼或不相干的问题等)。 *Books are a* ~ *of the lonely.* 书籍乃孤独者的慰藉物。

refu·gee /ˌrefjuːˈdʒiː; US: ˈrefjudʒiː; ˌrefjuˈdʒi/ *n* person who has been forced to flee from danger, eg from floods, war, political persecution: 避难者; 难民: (attrib)(用作定语) ˌrefu·gee *camps.* 难民营。

re·ful·gent /rɪˈfʌldʒənt; rɪˈfʌldʒənt/ *adj* (formal) shining; brilliant. (正式用语)光亮的; 灿丽的。 **re·ful·gence** /-əns; əns/ *n* [U].

re·fund /rɪˈfʌnd; rɪˈfʌnd/ *vt* [VP6A] pay back (money to sb): 退还(钱给某人): ~ *the cost of postage.* 退还邮费。 □ *n* /ˈriːfʌnd; ˈriːˌfʌnd/ /ˈriːfʌnd; ˈriːˌfʌnd/ [C, U] repayment: 退还; 退款: *obtain a* ~ *of a deposit.* 得到保证金之退款。

re·fur·bish /ˌriːˈfɜːbɪʃ; rɪˈfɜbɪʃ/ *vt* [VP6A] make clean or bright again; make (as if) like new. 弄新; 刷新; 革新; 翻修; 使清洁。

re·fusal /rɪˈfjuːzl; rɪˈfjuzl/ *n* 1 [U] act of refusing; [C] instance of this: 拒绝; 不愿; 固辞; 推却: *the* ~ *of an invitation;* 对邀请的谢绝; *his* ~ *to do what I asked.* 他之拒绝做我所请求之事。 **2 (the)** ~, right of deciding whether to accept or refuse sth before it is offered to others: 优先决定权; 取舍权; 先买权: *If you ever decide to sell your car, please give me (the) first* ~. 如果你决定把汽车卖掉, 请给我优先购买权。

ref·use¹ /ˈrefjuːs; ˈrefjus/ *n* [U] waste or worthless material: 弃物; 垃圾; 废物: *a '*~ *dump,* eg place where town* ~ (collected from houses, etc) is dumped. 垃圾场; 垃圾堆。 '~-**collector** *n* dustman. 清除垃圾工人。

re·fuse² /rɪˈfjuːz; rɪˈfjuz/ *vt, vi* [VP6A, 7A, 12C, 2A] say 'no' to (a request or offer); show unwillingness to accept (sth offered), to do (sth that one is asked to do): 拒绝(一项请求或提供); 不愿接受(所提供之某物)或做(被请求之事); 固辞; 推却: ~ *a gift;* 拒受礼物; ~ *one's consent;* 不同意; 不 承认; ~ *to help.* 不愿帮助。 *They* ~*d me permission.* 他们拒绝答应我的要求。 *I was* ~*d admittance.* 我未获准进入。

re·fute /rɪˈfjuːt; rɪˈfjut/ *vt* [VP6A] prove (statements, opinions, etc) to be wrong or mistaken; prove (sb) wrong in his opinions: 证明(陈述、意见等)为误; 证明(某人)看法不对; 驳斥; 驳倒; 反驳: ~ *an argument / an opponent.* 驳斥一论据(对手)。 **re·fut·able** /-əbl; əbl/ *adj* that can be ~d. 可驳斥的; 可辩驳的。 **refu·ta·tion** /ˌrefjuːˈteɪʃn; ˌrefjuˈteʃən/ *n* [U] refuting; [C] counter-argument. 驳斥; 驳倒; 反驳。

re·gain /rɪˈɡeɪn; rɪˈɡen/ *vt* [VP6A] 1 get possession of again: 恢复; 复得: ~ *consciousness;* 恢复知觉; 苏醒; ~ *one's freedom.* 重获自由。 2 get back to (a place or position): 重回; 复返(某地方或位置): ~ *one's footing,* recover one's balance after slipping or falling. (滑跤或跌倒后)恢复身体的平衡; 重拾起来。

re·gal /ˈriːɡl; ˈriːɡl/ *adj* of, for, fit for, by, a monarch; royal: 君王的; 适于君王的; 由于君王的; 王室的: ~ *dignity / splendour / power.* 帝王的庄严(豪华, 权力)。 ~**ly** /-ɡli; -ɡlɪ/ *adv*

re·gale /rɪˈɡeɪl; rɪˈɡel/ *vt* [VP6A, 14] ~ *oneself / sb (with / on sth),* give pleasure or delight to: 使喜悦;

娱乐; 款待: ~ *oneself with a cigar;* 享用雪茄; *regaling themselves and their friends on caviar and champagne.* 以鱼子酱及香槟酒供他们自己及朋友们享用。

re·galia /rɪˈɡeɪliə; rɪˈɡeliə/ *n pl* [C] (often with a *sing v*) (常用单数动词) 1 emblems (crown, orb, sceptre, etc) of royalty, as used at coronations. 王权的标志(王冠、宝球、王杖等, 如用于加冕礼)。 2 emblems or decorations of an order(9), eg of the Freemasons. 任何团体(如共济会)之标志或徽章。

re·gard¹ /rɪˈɡɑːd; rɪˈɡɑrd/ *n* 1 (liter or old use) long, steady or significant look. (文或旧用法)注视; 凝视。 2 [U] point attended to; relation. 注意之点; 关系。 *in* '*this* ~, in respect of (= regarding) this point. 在这一点上; 关于此事。 *in / with* ~ *to,* with respect to; concerning. 关于。 3 [U] attention; concern; consideration: 注意; 关心; 顾虑: *You'll get into trouble if you continue to behave without* ~ *to decency.* 如果你继续不顾礼法行事, 你会招来麻烦的。 *He has very little* ~ *for the feelings of others.* 他不大顾虑别人的感情。 *More* ~ *must be paid to safety on the roads.* 应多注意道路安全。 4 [U] esteem; consideration; respect: 敬重; 敬意; 尊敬: *hold sb in high / low* ~; 极为(不大)尊敬某人; *have a high / low* ~ *for sb's judgement.* 非常(不大)尊重某人的判断。 5 (pl) kindly thoughts and wishes: (复)问候; 致意: (at the end of a letter)(用于信尾) *with kind* ~*s, yours sincerely, ...* 谨致问候之意, ~ 敬启。 *Please give my kind* ~*s to your brother.* 请代我向你令兄(令弟)致意。 ~**ful** /-fl; -fəl/ *adj* ~*ful (of),* full of (~): 注意的; 关心的: *Be more* ~*ful of your own interests.* 须多注意你自己的利益。 ~**less** *adj* ~*less of,* paying no attention to: 不顾; 不注意: ~*less of the consequences;* 不顾后果; ~*less of expense.* 不考虑费用。

re·gard² /rɪˈɡɑːd; rɪˈɡɑrd/ *vt* 1 [VP6A] (liter or old use) look closely at. (文或旧用法)注视; 凝视。 2 [VP16B] ~ *sb / sth as,* consider: 视为; 认作: ~ *sb as a hero;* 认为某人是英雄; ~ *sth as a crime.* 把某事认作一种罪行。 *He's* ~*ed as the best dentist in town.* 他被认为是城内最好的牙医师。 3 [VP6A, 14] ~ *(with),* look upon mentally: 在心理上以...看待; 对待: *I* ~ *his behaviour with suspicion / horror.* 我对他的行为感到怀疑(恐惧)。 *How is he* ~*ed locally?* 当地的人对他看法如何? *He is* ~*ed with disfavour / unfavourably.* 他不受喜爱。 4 [VP6A] pay attention to (chiefly neg and interr): 注意; 尊敬(主要用于否定句及疑问句中): *He seldom* ~*s my advice.* 他不大尊重我的忠告。 *Why do you so seldom* ~ *my wishes?* 你为何老是不尊重我的愿望呢? *as* ~*s,* ~**ing** *prep* with reference to; concerning. 关于; 有关。

re·gatta /rɪˈɡætə; rɪˈɡætə/ *n* meeting for boat races (rowing boats or yachts). 赛船会; 赛艇会。

re·gency /ˈriːdʒənsɪ; ˈriːdʒənsɪ/ *n* (pl -cies) the office of a regent; regent's period of office. 摄政职位; 摄政期间。 **the R~,** (in GB) the period 1810—20. (英国之)摄政时期(自 1810 年至 1820 年)。

re·gen·er·ate /rɪˈdʒenəreɪt; rɪˈdʒenəˌret/ *vt, vi* [VP6A, 2A] 1 reform spiritually; raise morally. 在精神上改造; 在道德上提高; 改过自新。 2 give new strength or life

to; restore lost qualities to. 赋与新力量或生命; 恢复…所丧失的性质。 **3** grow again. 重生; 再生。 □ adj /rɪˈdʒenə-rət; rɪˈdʒenərɪt/ spiritually reborn: 精神重生的; 更生的; 革新的: a ~ society. 革新的社会。 **re·gen·er·ation** /rɪˌdʒenəˈreɪʃn; rɪˌdʒenəˈreʃən/ n [U] being ~d. 精神重生; 更生; 更新; 革新。

re·gent /ˈriːdʒənt; ˈridʒənt/ n **1** person appointed to perform the duties of a ruler who is too young, old, ill, etc or who is absent. 摄政者。 **2** (US) member of a governing board (eg of a State university). (美)董事; 评议员(如州立大学者)。 □ adj (following the n) performing the duties of a ~: (置于名词之后)摄政的: the Prince R~. 摄政王。

reg·gae /ˈreɡeɪ; ˈreɡe/ n [U] West Indian popular music and dance with strong rhythms. 西印度群岛的一种节奏强劲的流行音乐和舞蹈。

regi·cide /ˈredʒɪsaɪd; ˈredʒəˌsaɪd/ n [U] crime of killing a king; [C] person who kills, or takes part in the killing of, a king. 弑君; (参与)弑君者。

ré·gime, re·gime /reɪˈʒiːm; rɪˈʒim/ n [C] **1** method or system of government or of administration; prevailing system of things: 政制; 政体; 制度: under the old ~, before the changes were made, etc (according to context). 在旧的制度下(依据上下文而决定其意义)。 **2** = regimen.

regi·men /ˈredʒɪmən; ˈredʒəˌmɛn/ n [C] set of rules for diet, exercise, etc for promoting one's health and physical well-being. 养生之道; 摄生法。

regi·ment /ˈredʒɪmənt; ˈredʒəmənt/ n [C] (cavalry and artillery) unit divided into squadrons or batteries and commanded by a colonel; (GB infantry) organization usu based on a city or county, with special traditions and dress, represented in the field by battalions: (骑兵和炮兵)团; (英国步兵)通常根据城市或郡所构成的军事组织, 以营为单位, 各有其独特的传统和服装: the 1st battalion of the Manchester R~. 曼彻斯特步兵团的第一营。 ~ of, large number: 多数; 大群: whole ~s of starlings. 一群群的欧椋鸟。 □ vt [VP6A] organize; discipline: 组织; 控制: ~ the workers of a country. 组织一国的工人。 **reg·i·men·ta·tion** /ˌredʒɪmenˈteɪʃn; ˌredʒəmənˈteʃən/ n [U] subjection to control; strict political discipline. 统制; 严格管制。

regi·men·tal /ˌredʒɪˈmentl; ˌredʒəˈmɛntl/ adj of a regiment: 团的: the ~ tie, in the colours of the regiment. 团服之领带。 □ n (pl) dress worn by the men of a regiment; military uniform: (复)团服; 军服: in full ~s, in full dress. 着全副戎装。

Re·gina /rɪˈdʒaɪnə; rɪˈdʒaɪnə/ n (abbr 略作 **R**)reigning queen: 女王: (used in signatures to proclamations) (用于宣言或布告之签字中) Elizabeth ~; 伊利莎白女王; (legal) (used in titles of lawsuits): (法律)(用于讼案的名称中): ~ v Hay, the Crown against Hay. 女王对黑伊的讼案。 ⇨**Rex**.

re·gion /ˈriːdʒən; ˈridʒən/ n [C] area or division with or without definite boundaries or characteristics: 地方; 区域; 地区: the Arctic ~s; 北极地区; the forest ~; 林区; the lower ~s, hell; 地狱; the ~ of metaphysics; 玄学的领域; the abdominal ~. 腹部。 ~·al /-nl; -nl/ adj of a ~: 地方的; 区域的; 地区的: the ~al wines of France; 法国各地区产的不同种类的葡萄酒; a ~al geography. 区域地理。 ~·al·ly /-nəlɪ; -nlɪ/ adv

reg·is·ter[1] /ˈredʒɪstə(r); ˈredʒɪstə/ n [C] **1** (book containing a)record or list: 记录; 名册; 登记簿; 名薄: a parish ~, one with records of baptisms, marriages and funerals; 教区记事薄(包括受洗、结婚及丧葬记录); Lloyd's ~, of shipping; 劳依德船舶协会出版的年鉴; the R~ of voters, the Parliamentary R~, of persons qualified to vote at elections. 选举人名簿; 大选名薄。 **2** range of the human voice or of a musical instrument; part of this range: (人声或乐器的)音域; 音域的一部分: the upper/middle ~; 上(中)音域; the lower ~ of the clarinet. 单簧管的下音域。 **3** mechanical

device for indicating and recording speed, force, numbers, etc. (表示速度、力量、数目等的)记录器。 '**cash** ~, as used for recording cash payments in shops, etc. (商店等中所用的)现金出纳机。 ⇨ the illus at **cash**. 参看 cash 之插图。 **4** adjustable metal plate or grating for widening or narrowing the size of an opening and so regulating the passage of air, etc through it: 调节气流等的金属片或格栅装置: a hot-air ~, one controlling the flow of hot air, eg in a building heated from a basement furnace. 调节暖气的装置。 **5** = **registry**. **6** (linguistics) vocabulary, grammar, etc used by speakers in particular circumstances or contexts, eg legal, commercial. (语言学)(说话者在法律、商业等特别的情况或语境中所用之)语法与词汇。

reg·is·ter[2] /ˈredʒɪstə(r); ˈredʒɪstə/ vt, vi [VP2A, 3A, 6A, 14] ~ (sth/oneself)(with sth/sb)(for sth), **1** make a written and formal record of, in a list: 记录; 登记; 注册: ~ one's car/the birth of a child/a new trade-mark; 登记汽车(小孩的出生, 新的商标); a State R~ed Nurse, one who is officially ~ed. 已向政府登记的护士; 正式护士。 I am a foreigner here; must I ~ (myself) with the police? 我在此地是外国人; 我必须向警方登记吗? Where can I ~ for the Arabic course? 我选阿拉伯文一科到哪里注册? **2** put or get (sb's name, one's own name) on a register. 登记(姓名)。 **3** (of instruments) indicate; record: (指仪器)指示; 记出: The thermometer ~ed only two degrees above freezing-point. 寒暑表显示仅高于冰点两度。 **4** (of sb's face) show (emotion, etc): (指人的面孔)显出; 表示(某种情绪等): Her face ~ed surprise. 她的脸上现出惊讶之色。 **5** send (a letter or parcel) by special post, paying an extra charge which ensures compensation if it is lost: 以挂号寄送(信或包裹): It's wise to ~ letters containing cheque. 用挂号信邮寄附有支票的信是明智的。

reg·is·trar /ˌredʒɪˈstrɑː(r); ˈredʒɪˌstrɑr/ n person whose duty is to keep records or registers, eg for a town council or a university. 记录员; 登记员; 主管注册者(如市镇议会的记录官或大学的注册主管人)。

reg·is·tra·tion /ˌredʒɪˈstreɪʃn; ˌredʒɪˈstreʃən/ n **1** [U] registering; recording: 登记; 挂号; 注册: ~ of letters/luggage; 信件(行李)之挂号; ~ of students for an examination/an academic course; 学生之考试报名(选课报名); the '~ number (eg of a car). (汽车等之)登记号码。 **2** [C] entry; record of facts. 登记之项目; 事实之记录。

reg·is·try /ˈredʒɪstrɪ; ˈredʒɪstrɪ/ n (pl **-tries**) **1** (sometimes 有时作 **register**) place where registers are kept: 登记处; 注册处: a ship's port of ~; 某船之船籍港; married at a '~ office, before a registrar (without a religious ceremony). 在婚姻登记处结婚(不举行宗教仪式)。 **2** [U] = registration.

reg·nant /ˈreɡnənt; ˈrɛɡnənt/ adj reigning: 统治的: Queen ~, one who is ruling in her own right and not as a consort. 执政女王; 当朝女王。

re·gress /rɪˈɡres; rɪˈɡrɛs/ vi [VP2A] return to an earlier or more primitive form or state. 退步; 退化; 退回; 倒退; 复归; 回归。 **re·gres·sion** /rɪˈɡreʃn; rɪˈɡrɛʃən/ n ~ing. 退步; 退化; 退回; 倒退; 复归; 回归。 **re·gressive** adj tending to ~. 回归的; 退行的; 退化的; 退步的。

re·gret[1] /rɪˈɡret; rɪˈɡrɛt/ n **1** [U] feeling of sadness at the loss of sth, or of annoyance or disappointment because sth has or has not been done: 悲悔; 惋惜; 懊悔; 抱憾: express ~ at not being able to help; 为帮不上忙而表示抱歉; hear with ~ that a friend is ill. 遗憾地听到一位朋友生病了。 Much to my ~ I am unable to accept your kind invitation. 我不能接受你盛意的邀请, 深感抱歉。 **2** (pl) (in polite expressions of refusal, etc): (复)(用礼貌的谢绝语等): Please accept my ~s at having to refuse. 务希见谅, 诸致歉意。 He refused with many ~s/with much ~. 他非常客气地拒绝了。 I have no ~s, do not feel sorry (about what I did, etc). 我不感到遗憾; 我毫不后悔。 ~·ful /-fl; -fl/ adj sad; sorry. 哀惜的;

遗憾的; 抱歉的。 ～·**fully** /-fəlɪ; -fḷɪ/ adv sadly; with ～. 哀惜地; 遗憾地; 抱歉地。

re·gret² /rɪ'gret; rɪ'grɛt/ vt (-tt-) [VP6A, D, 7A,9] **1** be sorry for the loss of; wish to have again: 以丧失…为憾; 悲悼; 惋惜: ～ lost opportunities. 惋惜失去的机会。 He died ～ted by all. 他死了, 大家深感痛惜。 **2** feel sorry for; be sorry (to say, etc, that...): 为…感到遗憾; 懊悔: 抱歉; 抱歉(后接 to say 等, 或 that...): I ～ being unable to help/～ that I cannot help. 我帮不上忙甚为抱歉。 to say that... 我很抱歉…。 It is to be ～ted that.... is a pity that.... 真可惜…; …为一憾事。 I ～ my child's ignorance. 我为孩子的无知感到遗憾。 ～·**table** /-əbl; -əbḷ/ adj to be: 令人遗憾的; 可惜的; 可悲的; 不幸的: ～table failures. 不幸的失败。 ～·**tably** /-əblɪ; -əblɪ/ adv: a ～tably small attendance. 出席者少得可怜。

re·group /ˌriː'gruːp; 'ri'grup/ vt, vi [VP6A, 2A] form again into groups; form into new groups. 重行编制; 重新编组; 整编; 重新组合。

regu·lar /'regjʊlə(r); 'rɛgjələ/ adj **1** evenly arranged; symmetrical; systematic: 整齐的; 端正的; 对称的; 有系统的: ～ teeth; 整齐的牙齿; ～ features, eg of the face: 端正的面貌; a ～ figure; 匀称的身材; a ～ nomenclature. 有系统的命名法。 **2** coming, happening, done, again and again at even intervals: 习惯性的; 有规律的; 不变的; 经常的; 定期的: a man with ～ habits, doing the same things at the same times every day; 生活习惯有规律的人; keep ～ hours, eg leaving and returning home, getting up and going to bed, at the same times every day; 按时作息; 过规律生活; ～ breathing; 均匀的呼吸; have a ～ pulse; 脉搏跳动正常; walking up and down with ～ steps. 以规律的步子走来走去。 He has no ～ work, no continuous occupation. 他没有固定的工作。 **3** properly qualified; recognized; trained; full-time or professional: 合格的; 认可的; 有训练的; 专任的; 职业性的: ～ soldiers, not volunteers or militia; 常备兵; 正规兵; the ～ army, made up of ～ soldiers. 常备军; 正规军。 **4** conforming to a standard of etiquette; in agreement with what is considered correct procedure or behaviour: 合于礼仪标准的; 合于正确之手续或行为的: I doubt whether your procedure would be considered ～ by the authorities. 我怀疑当局是否会认为你的手续合乎规定。 **5** (gram, of vv, nn, etc) having normal inflections: (语法; 指动词, 名词等) 变化有规则的: The verb 'go' is not ～. 动词 go 的变化不规则。 **6** (eccles) bound by, living under, religious rule (opp of secular): (教会)受教规约束的; 按教规生活的; 属于教团的(为 secular 之反义词): the ～ clergy, eg monks but not parish priests. 属于教团的教士(但并非教区教士)。 **7** (colloq) thorough; complete: (口)彻底的; 完全的: He's a ～ hero/rascal. 他是十足的英雄(流氓)。 **8** ordinary; normal: 普通的; 一般的: Do you want king size cigarettes or ～ size? 你要长枝的还是一般长短的香烟? **9** (colloq) likeable; good: (口)可爱的; 好的: He's a ～ guy. 他是个好人。 □ n **1** soldier of the ～ army. 常备兵; 正规军。 **2** (colloq) ～ customer or client, eg at a hairdresser's or a pub. (口)常客; 老主顾(如美容院或酒馆中者)。 ～·**ly** adv in a ～ manner; at ～ intervals or times: 整齐地; 端正地; 有规律地; 经常地; 定期地: a garden ～ly laid out; 设计得很整齐的花园; as ～ly as clockwork. (象钟表装置一般)非常规律地。 ～·**ity** /ˌregjʊ'lærətɪ; ˌrɛgjə'lærətɪ/ n [U] state of being ～: 整齐; 端正; 规律; 经常; 定期: win a prize for ～ity of attendance. 因全勤而获奖。

regu·lar·ize /'regjʊləraɪz; 'rɛgjələˌraɪz/ vt [VP6A] make lawful or correct: 使合法化; 调整; 整理; 使有组织; 使有秩序: ～ the proceedings. 调整程序。 **regu·lar·iz·ation** /ˌregjʊlərɪ'zeɪʃn; ˌrɛglˌ, ˌrɛgjələraɪ'zeʃən/ n

regu·late /'regjʊleɪt; 'rɛgjəˌlet/ vt [VP6A] **1** control systematically; cause to obey a rule or standard: 有系统地管理; 节制; 调整; 使遵守规则或合标准: ～ one's conduct/expenditure; 节制行为(或花费); ～ the traffic. 管理交通。 Accidents happen even in the best ～d families. 即使在管理最好的家庭中也会发生事故。 **2** adjust (an apparatus,

mechanism) to get the desired result: 调节; 校准(仪器, 机械): ～ a clock; 对钟; ～ the speed of a machine. 调节机器的速度。 **regu·la·tor** /-tə(r); -tɚ/ n person or thing that ～s, eg a device that ～s a mechanical movement, esp in a clock. 调整之人或物; 调节器; (尤指校准钟表的)校时器。

regu·la·tion /ˌregjʊ'leɪʃn; ˌregjə'leʃən/ n **1** [U] regulating or being regulated: 管理; 节制; 调节; 校准: the ～ of affairs/of a clock. 事务的管理(时钟的校准)。 **2** [C] rule; order; authoritative direction: 规则; 规定; 法令; 命令: 'safety ～s, eg in factories; (工厂等中之)安全条例; 'traffic ～s, made by the police for drivers of vehicles; 交通规则; contrary to ～s; 违反规定; Queen's/King's ～s, those governing the conduct of the armed forces. (英国女王或国王颁布之)三军行为条例。 **3** (attrib) as required by rules; correct: (用作定语)规定的; 正规的: ～ dress/uniform; 正式的衣服(制服); application forms of the ～ size. 合于规定大小的申请表格。

re·gur·gi·tate /rɪ'gɜːdʒɪteɪt; ri'gɝdʒəˌtet/ vi, vt [VP2A, 6A] (of liquid, etc) gush back; bring (swallowed food) up again to the mouth. (指液体等)涌回; 流回; 把(吃下的食物)吐出; 反胃。

re·ha·bili·tate /ˌriːhə'bɪlɪteɪt; ˌrihə'bɪləˌtet/ vt [VP6A] **1** restore (eg old buildings) to a good condition. 恢复; 修复(旧房屋等)。 **2** restore (sb) to former rank, position or reputation: 恢复(某人)原有的地位, 职位或名誉: He has been ～d in public esteem. 公众已恢复了对他的敬重。 **3** bring back (sb who is physically disabled or delinquent) to a normal life by special treatment. 借特殊的方法使(身体有缺陷或犯过的人)恢复正常生活。 **re·ha·bili·ta·tion** /ˌriːhəˌbɪlɪ'teɪʃn; ˌriəˌbɪlə'teʃən/ n rehabilitating: 恢复; 修复; 恢复原有地位, 正常生活等: a rehabilitation centre, place where persons are ～d(3). 伤残重建中心。

re·hash /ˌriː'hæʃ; ri'hæʃ/ vt take (eg old literary material) and use again in a new form: 以新的形式改写(旧文稿等); 改作; 重讲: ～ last term's lectures for the coming term. 改编上学期的讲稿在下学期用。 □ n /'riːhæʃ; 'ri,hæʃ/ [C] ～ed material. 改编过的材料; 改作的文稿。

re·hear /ˌriː'hɪə(r); ri'hɪr/ vt [VP6A] hear, consider, again (a case, plea etc in a law court). 再审; 复审。 **re·hear·ing** n instance of this. 再审之案件。

re·hearse /rɪ'hɜːs; rɪ'hɝs/ vt, vi [VP6A, 2A] **1** practise (a play, music, programme, etc) for public performance: 演习; 预演; 排演; 演练(戏、乐曲、节目等): ～ the parts in a play; 排演一出戏的各个角色; an ～ opera 排演一歌剧。 **2** say over again; give an account of: 复述; 详述: ～ the events of the day; 详述当日的诸事件; ～ one's grievances. 反复述说苦情。 **re·hearsal** /-sl; sḷ/ n **1** [U] rehearsing: 演习; 排演; 复述; 详述: put a play into rehearsal. 排演一部戏。 **2** [C] trial performance of a play or other entertainment: 排演; 预演; 试演: a 'dress rehearsal, one in which the actors wear the costumes and use the props as for public performances. (演员穿着演出时之服装的)彩排。

re·house /ˌriː'haʊz; ri'haʊz/ vt [VP6A] provide with a new house (esp in place of one officially condemned): 供以新房屋(尤指代替被官方认为不适于居住者): The people in these slums will have to be ～d. 在这些贫民窟里居住的人们势需供以新房屋。

Reich /raɪk; raɪk/ n the German Commonwealth as a whole. 德国; (德意志)帝国。 the First R～, the Holy Roman Empire, 9th c to 1806. 第一帝国(九世纪至1806年之神圣罗马帝国)。 the Second R～, 1871—1918. 第二帝国(1871年至1918年之德意志帝国)。 the Third R～, the Nazi regime, 1933—45. 第三帝国(1933年至1945年之纳粹德国)。

reign /reɪn; ren/ n [C] (period of) sovereignty, rule; dominance: 主权; 统治; 统治时代; 朝代; 王朝: during five successive ～s; 在接连五个朝代的期间; in the ～ of King Alfred; 在艾尔弗雷德王统治时期; the ～ of law/reason; 法治(以理性治理); the R～ of Terror, (in France,

1793—94, during the Revolution). 恐怖时代(指法国大革命时期 1793 年至 1794 年的一段时间). □ *vi* [VP2A, 3A] ~ (*over*), **1** hold office as a monarch: 为王; 为君; 当朝; 统治: *The king ~ed but he did not rule or govern.* 那国王当朝, 但并不治理国事. *He ~ed over the country for ten years.* 他统治该国有十年之久。 **2** be influential; prevail: 有势力;占优势; 盛行: *the ~ing beauty*, woman acknowledged to be most beautiful for the time in question. 当时的第一美人; 绝代佳人. *Silence ~ed everywhere.* 到处寂静无声。

re·im·burse /ˌriːɪmˈbəːs; ˌriɪmˈbɚs/ *vt* [VP6A, 12A, 13A, 14] ~ *sth* (*to sb*): ~ *sb* (*for*) *sth*, pay back (sb who has spent money, the money spent): 偿还; 补偿(花钱之人, 所花之钱): *We must ~ him the costs of the journey.* 我们必须把旅费偿还给他. *You will be ~d (for) your expenses.* 你的花费将得到偿还. ~·**ment** *n* [C, U] repayment (of expenses). (费用的)偿还; 补偿.

rein /reɪn; ren/ *n* (often *pl* in the same sense as the *sing*) long, narrow strap fastened to the bit of a bridle for controlling a horse. (常用复数, 与单数同义) 缰绳. ⇨ the illus at **harness**. 参看 harness 之插图. *assume / drop the ~s of government*, enter upon/give up office. 掌握(放弃)政权. *draw ~*, (lit and fig) pull up; go slower. (书面与喻)勒缰; 缓行. *give free ~ / the ~s to sb / sth*, (lit and fig) allow freedom to: (字面或喻)放松缰绳; 给予自由; 放任: *give a horse the ~s*; 让马自由奔驰; *give the ~(s) to one's imagination*, allow it great freedom. 任想象驰骋. *hold / take the ~s*, (lit and fig) have / take control: (字面或喻)握着缰绳; 统驭; 支配; 控制; 执掌: *hold the ~s of government*. 执掌政权. *keep a tight ~ on sb / sth*, (lit and fig) let (sb) have / allow little freedom to. (字面或喻)勒紧缰绳; 严格要求; 抑制(某人或某事物). □ *vt* [VP6A, 15B] control with, or as with, ~s: 驾驭; 控制: ~ *in a horse*, restrain it; check it; 勒住马; 控制马; ~ *up / back a horse*, pull it up or back with the ~s. 勒马跃起(后退).

re·in·car·nate /ˌriːɪnˈkɑːneɪt; ˌriɪnˈkɑrnet/ *vt* give a new body to (a soul). 赋予(灵魂)新肉体; 使再生. □ *adj* /ˌriːɪnˈkɑːnɪt; ˌriɪnˈkɑrnet/ born again in a new body. 赋予新肉体而再生的. **re·in·car·na·tion** /ˌriːɪnkɑːˈneɪʃn; ˌriɪnkɑrˈneʃən/ *n* [U] religious doctrine that the soul enters, after death, into another (human or animal) body; [C] instance of this; new body inhabited by the soul. 认为人死后灵魂投入另一(人或动物)躯体的宗教学说; 再生说; 转世说; 再生的实例; 灵魂附着的新躯体; 化身.

rein·deer /ˈreɪndɪə(r); ˈren͵dɪr/ *n* (*pl* unchanged) kind of large deer with branched antlers, used in Lapland for transport and kept in herds for its milk, flesh and hide. (复数不变) 驯鹿. ⇨ the illus at **large**. 参看 large 之插图.

re·in·force /ˌriːɪnˈfɔːs; ˌriɪnˈfors/ *vt* [VP6A] make stronger by adding or supplying more men or material; increase the size, thickness, of sth so that it supports more weight, etc: 增援; 加强; 增加…之大小, 厚度等: ~ *an army / a fleet*; 增援一支军队(舰队); ~ *a garment*, by adding an extra thickness of cloth in places; 加厚一件衣服; ~ *a bridge*. 加强一座桥. ~**d concrete**, concrete strengthened with steel bars or metal netting embedded in it. 钢筋混凝土. ~·**ment** *n* [U] reinforcing or being ~d; (esp *pl*) that which ~s; (esp) men, ships, etc sent to ~. 增援; 加强; (常用复数)增援或加强之物; (尤指)援兵; 援舰等.

re·in·state /ˌriːɪnˈsteɪt; ˌriɪnˈstet/ *vt* [VP6A, 14] ~ *sb* (*in*), replace (sb) (in a former position or condition): 使(某人)恢复(原位或原状): ~ *sb in his former office*. 使某人复职. ~·**ment** *n*

re·in·sure /ˌriːɪnˈʃʊə(r); ˌriɪnˈʃʊr/ *vt* [VP6A] insure again (esp of an underwriter who relieves himself of some or all of a risk by taking out an insurance with another underwriter or insurance company). 再保险; (尤指某保险商为了减轻部分或全部风险而与另一保险商

或保险公司共同承保的) 转保险. **re·in·sur·ance** /-rəns; -rəns/ *n*

re·is·sue /ˌriːˈɪʃuː; riˈɪʃu/ *vt* [VP6A] issue again after temporary discontinuance: 再发行: ~ *stamps / books*. 再发行邮票(书). □ *n* sth ~d, esp a reprint of a book with a change of format or price. 再发行之物; (尤指形式或价格改变的)再版图书. Cf 参较 *new edition*, in which changes are made in the text. 修订版.

re·iter·ate /riːˈɪtəreɪt; riˈɪtə͵ret/ *vt* [VP6A] say or do again several times: 反复地说或做: ~ *a command*. 重申一项命令. **re·iter·ation** /riːˌɪtəˈreɪʃn; riˌɪtəˈreʃən/ *n* [U] act of reiterating; [C] instance of this; repetition. 反复的说或做; 反复的话或动作; 重复.

re·ject[1] /ˈriːdʒekt; ˈrɪdʒɛkt/ *n* sth ~ed: 被弃之物: *export* ~*s*, articles made for export but ~ed because of a flaw or imperfection. 因有瑕疵而被打回的输出品.

re·ject[2] /rɪˈdʒekt; rɪˈdʒɛkt/ *vt* [VP6A] **1** put aside, throw away, as not good enough to be kept: 丢弃; 抛弃: ~ *fruit that is over-ripe.* 抛弃过熟的水果. **2** refuse to accept: 拒绝; 不接受: ~ *an offer of help*; 拒绝别人提供的帮助; ~ *a heart transplant*, (of the body) fail to adapt to the new heart; (指身体)排斥新移植的心脏; *a ~ed suitor*. 未被接受的求婚者. *The army doctors ~ed him*, would not accept him as medically fit. 军医们并未接受他(认为他身体不合格). **re·jec·tion** /rɪˈdʒekʃn; rɪˈdʒɛkʃən/ *n* [U] ~ing or being ~ed; [C] instance of this; sth ~ed: 抛弃; 被弃; 拒绝; 抛弃或拒绝的实例; 被抛弃或拒绝之物: ~*ion slip*, printed or written note from an editor or publisher ~ing an offered article, novel etc. 退稿附条(由编辑或出版人所发之印制或书写的说明).

re·jig /riːˈdʒɪg; ˈriˌdʒɪg/ *vt* (**-gg-**) [VP6A] supply (a factory, etc) with new mechanical equipment. 以新的机械设备供应(工厂等).

re·joice /rɪˈdʒɔɪs; rɪˈdʒɔɪs/ *vt, vi* [VP6A] make glad; cause to be happy: 使喜; 使乐: *The boy's success ~d his mother's heart.* 这男孩的成功使他母亲喜悦心花怒放. **2** [VP2A, C, 3A, B, 4C] ~ (*at / over*), feel great joy; show signs of great happiness: 欣喜; 高兴; 快乐: ~ *over a victory*; 为胜利而欣喜; ~ *at sb's success.* 为某人的成功而高兴. ~ *to hear that you are well again / ~ that you have recovered so quickly.* 听到你已痊愈(你已很快复元)我很高兴. *He ~s in the name of Bloggs*, humorous for 'His name is Bloggs'. (诙谐语)他的大名叫布洛格斯. Note: in colloq style 'be glad' and 'be pleased' are commoner than 'rejoice'. 注意: 在口语中, be glad 及 be pleased 比 rejoice 更为通用. **re·joic·ing** *n* [U] happiness; joy (*pl*) celebrations; merry-making. 快乐; 欣喜; 高兴; (复)庆祝; 欢宴.

re·join[1] /rɪˈdʒɔɪn; rɪˈdʒɔɪn/ *vt, vi* [VP6A, 2A] answer; reply; (legal) answer a charge or plea. 回答; 应答; (法律)答辩. ~·**der** /-də(r); -dɚ/ *n* [C] what is said in reply; retort. 答语; 回答; 还口; 反驳.

re·join[2] /ˌriːˈdʒɔɪn; ˌriˈdʒɔɪn/ *vt* [VP6A] join the company of again: 重返; 再加入: ~ *one's regiment / ship.* 重新回到团里(船上).

re·join /ˌriːˈdʒɔɪn; ˌriˈdʒɔɪn/ *vt* [VP6A] join (together) again. 再接; 再结合.

re·ju·ven·ate /rɪˈdʒuːvəneɪt; rɪˈdʒuvə͵net/ *vt, vi* [VP6A, 2A] make or become young or vigorous again in nature or appearance. (使) 变得年轻; (使) 恢复活力. **re·ju·ven·ation** /rɪˌdʒuːvəˈneɪʃn; rɪˌdʒuvəˈneʃən/ *n*

re·kindle /ˌriːˈkɪndl; riˈkɪndl/ *vt, vi* [VP6A, 2A] kindle again: 再燃; 再点火: ~ *a fire*. 再把火点起来. *Our hopes ~d.* 我们的希望之火又燃起来了.

re·laid /ˌriːˈleɪd; riˈled/ *pt, pp* of **relay**[2].

re·lapse /rɪˈlæps; rɪˈlæps/ *vi* [VP2A, 3A] ~ (*into*), fall back again (into bad ways, error, illness, silence etc): 故态复萌; 重犯(坏习惯、错误); (疾病)复发; 恢复(沉静等): ~ *into smoking twenty cigarettes a day.* 他又每天吸二十支香烟了. □ *n* [C] falling back, esp after recovering from illness: 故态复萌; 重犯; (尤指疾病之)复发: *The patient has had a ~.* 病人旧疾复发.

re·late /rɪ'leɪt; rɪ'let/ *vt, vi* **1** [VP6A, 14] ~ **(to)**, (formal) tell (a story, etc to sb); give an account of (facts, adventures etc): (正式用语)(对某人)讲(故事等); 叙述(事实、奇遇等): *He ~d to his wife some amusing stories about his employer.* 他对妻子讲述有关他雇主的一些趣事。 *Strange to say, I once met Christopher in Katmandu.* 说来奇怪，有一次我在加德满都碰见了克里斯多夫。 **2** [VP14] ~ *to/with*, connect in thought or meaning: 在思想或意义上使有关联: *It is difficult to ~these results with/to any known cause.* 这些结果很难与任何已知的原因相关联。 **3** [VP3A] ~ *to*, have reference(to): 与…有关系: *She is a girl who notices nothing except what ~s to herself.* 她是一个只注意与她有关的事的女孩。 **4** *be ~d (to)*, be connected by family (to): (与…)有亲戚关系: *I am not ~d to him in any way.* 我和他无任何亲戚关系。 *He and I are not ~d.* 他和我无亲戚关系。 *She says she is ~d to the royal family.* 她说她与王室有亲戚关系。

re·la·tion /rɪ'leɪʃn; rɪ'leʃən/ *n* **1** [U] the act of relating(1), narrating or telling: 讲；说；叙述: *the ~ of his adventures;* 叙述他的奇遇; [C] that which is narrated; tale or narrative. 所述说之事物;故事。 **2**[U] (= ~ship) connection; what there is between one thing, person, idea, etc and another or others:关联; (物、人、念念等与他者的)关系: *the ~ between mother and child/between weather and the crops.* 母亲与子女(天气与作物)间的关系。 *The effort and expense needed for this project bore no ~/were out of all ~ to the results,* were not proportional to the results. 此计划所需付出的努力和费用，与其成果(完全)不称(即花费过多)。 *in/with ~ to,* as regards; concerning. 关于;有关。 **3**(usu pl) dealings; affairs; what one person, group, country etc, has to do with another: (通常用复数)交往;事务;(人、团体、国家等与他者的）关系;利害关系; 外交关系: *He has business ~s with a firm in Stockholm;* 与斯德哥尔摩的一家商号有生意上的来往; *the friendly ~s between my country and yours;* 贵我两国间的友好关系; *diplomatic ~s.* 外交关系。 *I have broken off all ~s with that fellow,* have nothing to do with him now. 我已和那家伙断绝一切关系。 **public re'lations officer,** ⇨ **public,** *adj.* **4** [U] kinship (by marriage); [C] kinsman or kinswoman; relative(2): 亲戚关系(现在通常用 ~ship); 男女亲戚；亲属: *He's a near ~ of mine.* 他是我的一位近亲。 *She's a ~ by marriage.* 她是一位姻亲。 ~ship /-ʃɪp; -ʃɪp/ *n* **1** ~ (2): 关系: *He admitted his affair with Susan could never develop into a lasting ~ship.* 他承认和苏珊的爱情绝不会发展成持久的关系。 **2** [U] (= ~(4)) condition of belonging to the same family; being connected by birth or marriage. 属于同一家族之关系;血亲或姻亲关系。 **3**[C]instance of being related; particular connection or ~ *(between/to/with)*. 有关系之实例;某种关系(与 between, to, with连用)。

rela·tive /'relətɪv; 'relətɪv/ *adj* **1** comparative: 比较的；相对的: *the ~ advantages of two methods/of gas and electricity for heating.* 两种方法(煤气取暖及电气取暖)相对的优点。 *They are living in ~ comfort,* ie compared with other people or with themselves at an earlier time. 他们现在生活得比较舒服。 **2** ~ *to,* referring to; having a connection with: 关于…的；与…有关的事: *the facts ~ to this problem;* 与此问题有关的事实; *the papers ~ to the case.* 关于此案件的文件。 **3** (gram) (语法) ~ **adverb** (eg *where* in 'the place where the accident occurred'). 关系副词(例如 the place where the accident occurred 中的 where)。 ~ **clause,** one joined by a ~ **pron** or **adv** to the antecedent of the ~ word. 关系从句(借关系代词或副词与其先行词相连接的从句)。 ~ **pronoun** (eg *whom* in 'the man whom we saw'). 关系代名词(例如 the man whom we saw 中的 whom)。 □ *n* [C] **1** ~ word, esp a ~ pronoun.关系词;(尤指)关系代名词。 **2** person to whom one is related (eg an uncle or aunt, a cousin, a nephew or niece). 亲戚；亲属(如叔、姊、表亲、侄子、侄女等)。 ~ly *adv* comparatively; in proportion to: 比较地;成比例地; (与…)相对而言: *In spite of her dull husband she is ~ly happy.* 尽管她的丈夫迟钝，她还算颇快乐。 *The matter is*

unimportant, ~ly speaking, if we think of this matter in proportion to other matters. 比较地说,此事不重要。

rela·tiv·ity /,relə'tɪvətɪ; ,rɛlə'tɪvətɪ/ *n* [U] (esp) Einstein's theory of the universe, based on the principle that measures of motion, space and time are relative. (尤指)相对论(爱因斯坦对宇宙的理论,系以'运动、时、空之度量乃相对的'原理为基础)。

re·lax /rɪ'læks; rɪ'læks/ *vt, vi* **1** [VP6A] cause or allow to become less tight, stiff, strict or rigid: 使松弛; 放松; 松懈: ~ *one's grip/hold on sth;* 放松对某物的执握; ~ *the muscles;* 松弛肌肉; ~ *discipline;* 松懈纪律; *a ~ing throat,* a form of sore throat; 一种咽喉炎; *a ~ing climate,* (opp of *bracing*) one that causes an inclination to feel sluggish, lacking in energy. (为 bracing 之反意词)使人懒洋洋的气候。 **2** [VP2A, C] become less tense, rigid, energetic, strict: 松驰;放松; 松懈: *His severity ~ed.* 他的严肃缓和了。 *His face ~ed in a smile.* 他的表情在一笑中变轻松了。 *Let's stop working and ~ for an hour.* 我们停工休息一小时吧。*He's feeling ~ed now,* free from nervous anxiety, disturbing tensions etc. 他现在觉得轻松多了。 ~ **·ation** /,riːlæk'seɪʃn; ,rilæks'eʃən/ *n* **1** [U] ~ing or being ~ed: 松驰; 放松: ~ *ation of the muscles.* 肌肉的放松。 **2**[U] recreation; [C] sth done for recreation: 消遣; 娱乐: *Fishing and mountain-climbing are his favourite ~ations.* 垂钓和爬山是他最喜爱的消遣。

re·lay¹ /'riːleɪ; 'rile/ *n* [C] **1** supply of fresh horses to take the place of tired horses; gang or group of men, supply of material, similarly used: 替换马的一批新马;人员、物资等之类似的补充;替班；接力: *working in/by ~s.* 轮班工作。 '~ **race** *n* one between teams, each member of the team running, swimming, etc one section of the total distance. (赛跑、游泳等的)接力赛。 **2** (telegraphy, broadcasting) device which receives messages, radio programmes, etc and transmits them with greater strength, thus increasing the distance over which they are carried. (电报,无线电广播)替续器;继电器。 '~ **station,** place from which radio programmes are broadcast after being received from another station. 转播站；中继站。 **3** (short for) ~ race; ~ed broadcast programme. (简称)接力赛；转播的无线电广播节目。 □ *vt* /rɪ'leɪ; rɪ'le/ *(pt, pp* ~**ed***)* send out (a broadcast programme received from another station). 转播(自另一台收到的广播节目)。

re·lay² /,riː'leɪ; ,riː'le/ *vt* *(pt, pp* -**laid** /-'leɪd; -'led/*)* lay (a cable, carpet, etc) again. 重新放置；再铺设(电缆、地毯等)。

re·lease /rɪ'liːs; rɪ'lis/ *vt* [VP6A, 14] ~ *(from),* **1** allow to go; set free; unfasten: 放行；释放; 免除;解开; 解放: ~ *one's hold of sth;* 松开对某物之执握; ~ *a man from prison/from a promise;* 释放某人出狱(不要求某人履行诺言); ~ *a bomb (from an aircraft),* allow it to fall; (自飞机)投炸弹; ~ *a monk from his vows;* 准许一僧侣还俗; ~ *sb from his suffering;* 解除某人的痛苦; ~ *the handbrake (of a car).* 放开(汽车的)手煞车。 **2** allow (news) to be known or published; allow (a film) to be exhibited or (goods) to be placed on sale: 发布(新闻); 发行(影片);发售(货物): *recently ~d films/discs.* 最近推出之影片(唱片)。 **3** (legal) give up or surrender (a right, debt, property) to another. (法律)放弃;让与(权利、债务、财产)。 □ *n* **1** [U] releasing or being freed; [C] instance of this: 放行;释放; 免除; 发布; 发行; 放弃; 让与; 其实例: *obtain (a) ~ from an obligation;* 获准免除某义务; *an order for sb's ~ from prison;* 释放某人出狱的命令; *the ~ of a film for public exhibition;* 一影片之发行; *a 'press ~,* ie to the newspapers; 发布新闻(给各报纸); *a feeling of ~,* ie of freedom; 解脱的感觉; *the newest ~s,* eg films/discs; 最新的发行物(如影片、唱片); *on general ~,* (of cinema films) available for seeing at the usual network of local cinemas. (影片)普遍发行。 **2** [C] handle, lever, catch, etc that ~s part of a machine: (松开某机件的)把手、杠杆、棘爪等; 松放柄; 放

杆; 脱扣器: the '*carriage* ~ (on a typewriter); (打字机的) 机头水平行放松钮; (attrib) (用作定语) '~ *gear*; 释放装置; the '~ *button/knob*. 脱扣按钮(开关按钮).

rel·e·gate /'religeit; 'rɛlə,get/ vt [VP14] ~ *sth/sb to sth*, 1 delegate². 委托; 付托; 移送. **2** dismiss to a lower position or condition: 贬调; 贬黜; 使归属于低较的地位或状况: *He* ~ *his wife to the position of a mere housekeeper.* 他把妻子贬低到管家婆的地位。(League football) (足球联赛) *Will our team be* ~*d to the second division?* 我们的球队会落入第二组吗? **rel·e·ga·tion** /,reli'geiʃən; ,rɛlə'geʃən/ n [U].

re·lent /rɪ'lent; rɪ'lɛnt/ vi [VP2A] become less severe; give up unkind or cruel intentions: 变温和; 变宽厚; 怜悯恻: *At last their mother* ~*ed and allowed the children to stay up and watch TV.* 最后母亲发了慈悲, 准许孩子们不睡觉看电视节目。~·**less** *adj* without pity: 无慈悲的; 不怜悯的: ~*less persecution.* 残忍的迫害。~·**less·ly** *adv*

rel·evant /'relivənt; 'rɛləvənt/ *adj* ~ *(to),* (closely) connected with what is happening, being discussed, done, etc: (与…)有关的; 切题的; 中肯的: *have all the* ~ *documents ready;* 把所有有关的文件准备妥当; *supply the facts* ~ *to the case.* 提供与该案件相关的资料。~·**ly** *adv* **rel·evance** /-əns; -əns/, **rel·evancy** /-ənsɪ; -ənsɪ/ *nn*

re·liable /rɪ'laiəbl; rɪ'laɪəbl/ *adj* that may be relied or depended upon: 可靠的; 可信赖的: ~ *tools/assistants/ information/witnesses.* 可靠的工具(助手、消息、证人)。**re·li·ably** /-əblɪ; -əblɪ/ *adv* **re·lia·bil·ity** /rɪ,laɪə'bɪlɪtɪ; rɪ,laɪə'bɪlətɪ/ *n* [U] state or quality of being ~. 可靠; 可信赖。

re·li·ance /rɪ'laiəns; rɪ'laɪəns/ *n* [U] ~ *on, upon,* trust; confidence: 信任; 信赖; 信心: *Do you place much* ~ *on your doctor?* 你很信任你的医生吗? *There is little* ~ *to be placed on his promises.* 他的诺言不甚可靠。**2** person or thing depended upon: 所信赖的人或物。**re·li·ant** /-ənt; -ənt/ *adj* having ~; trusting. 有信心的; 信任的。

relic /'relik; 'rɛlɪk/ *n* [C] **1** part of the body, dress, etc of a saint or sth that belonged to him or was connected with him, kept after his death, as an object of reverence, and in some cases said to have miraculous powers. 圣徒的部分遗骸、衣物等 (在其死后保存以作为崇敬的东西, 据说在某些情况下具有神奇的力量); 圣物。**2** sth that has survived from the past and that serves to keep memories alive: 纪念物; 遗物: *a* ~ *of early civilization,* eg a stone implement; 早期文明的遗物(如石器等); ~*s of superstition.* 迷信的遗风。**3** (*pl*) person's dead body or bones; what has survived destruction or decay. (复)遗骸; 遗迹; 废墟。

re·lict /'relikt; 'rɛlɪkt/ *n* (legal) widow: (法律)寡妇: *Alice,* ~ *of Arthur Williams.* 爱丽丝, 亚瑟·威廉斯的未亡人。

re·lief¹ /rɪ'li:f; rɪ'lif/ *n* [U] (used with the *indef art* as in examples, but not normally in the *pl*) (如例句所示与不定冠词连用, 唯一般都不用复数) **1** lessening or ending or removal of pain, distress, anxiety, etc: (痛苦、困苦、忧虑等的)减轻;解除: *The doctor's treatment gave/ brought some/not much* ~. 医生的治疗使(稍使、未能使)病情减轻。*A doctor's task is to work for the* ~ *of suffering.* 医生的工作是解除病痛。*She heaved a sigh of* ~ *when she was told that the child's life was not in danger.* 当她听到孩子无生命危险时, 才松了一口气。*To my great* ~ *the difficulties were all overcome.* 使我大为欣慰, 困难全都克服了。*It was a great* ~ *to find the children safe.* 发现孩子们平安无事, 觉得很放心。**2** that which brings ~ (1); help given to those in need; food, clothes, money, etc for persons in trouble: 减轻或解除痛苦之事物; 给予贫者或需要者的帮助; 救济物 (食品、衣服、金钱等); *send* ~ *to people made homeless by floods;* 送救济品给那些因水灾而变为无家可归的人们; *provide* ~ *for refugees;* 赈济难民; *a* '~ *fund;* 救济基金; 赈款; *a* '~ *road,* alternative road for one that has heavy traffic. 为减轻原来道路之

拥挤交通而设的另一道路; 间道。**3** sth that makes a change from monotony or that relaxes tension: (冲淡单调或松弛紧张的)调剂: *We crossed wide stretches of moorland without* ~, with no change of scenery. 我们走过一大片景色单调的荒野。*Shakespeare introduced comic scenes into his tragedies by way of* ~. 莎士比亚把喜剧的情节穿插于悲剧中, 使观众的心情放松。**4** ~ *(of),* reinforcement of a besieged town; raising (of a siege): (围城的)救援; 解围: *The general hastened to the* ~ *of the fortress.* 将军火速前往救援该要塞。**5** (replacing of a person, persons, on duty by a) person or persons, appointed to go on duty: 换班; 接替; 换接者; 接替者: *on duty from 8am to 8pm with only two hours'* ~; 从上午八时到晚上八时值班, 中间只有两小时的替换; *happy to know that the* ~ *is on the way:* 听到接替者要来了很高兴; (attrib) (用作定语) *a* '~ *driver.* 轮替的驾驶员。

re·lief² /rɪ'li:f; rɪ'lif/ *n* ⇨ **bas-**~. **1** [U] method of carving or moulding in which a design stands out from a flat surface: 凸雕法; 浮雕: *a profile of Julius Caesar in* ~; 凯撒之侧面浮雕; *in high/low* ~, with the background cut out to a deep/shallow degree. 高(薄)浮雕的。**2** [C] design or carving made in this way. 浮雕品。**3** [U] (in drawing, etc) appearance of being done in ~ by the use of shading, colour, etc. (绘画等)用明暗法、色彩等使人或物凸现。'~ *map,* one showing hills, valleys, etc by shading or other means, not only by contour lines. (除了用等高线, 并用阴暗度或其他方法显示丘陵、盆地等的)地形图; 立体地图。**4** [U] (lit and fig) vividness; distinctness of outline. (字面及喻)生动; 轮廓显著。*be/stand out in* ~ *against,* be in contrast to: 与…成为强烈的对照: *The hills stood out in sharp* ~ *against the morning sky.* 在晨空的映衬之下, 群山的轮廓极为明显。*His behaviour stood out in strong* ~ *against his declared principles.* 他的行为与他所标榜的原则成了强烈的对照。

re·lieve /rɪ'li:v; rɪ'liv/ vt [VP6A] **1** give or bring relief¹ to; lessen or remove (pain or distress): 给予救济; 援助; 减轻或解除(痛苦或困难): *We were* ~*d to hear that you had arrived safely.* 听到你已安全到达, 我们安心了。*The fund is for relieving distress among the flood victims.* 这基金是用于赈济水灾灾民的。~ *one's feelings,* provide an outlet for them (eg by shedding tears, or by using strong language, behaving violently). 发泄感情; 泄愤(如借流泪、口出大骂、行为粗暴等)。~ *oneself,* empty the bladder or bowels. 大便; 小便。⇨ **relief¹**(3). **2** take one's turn on duty: 换班; 接替: ~ *the guard/the watch/a sentry.* 接替守卫(看守者、哨兵)。*You will be* ~*d at noon.* 中午会有人来换你的班。⇨ **relief¹**(5). **3** ~ *sb of sth,* **(a)** take it from him: 从某人手中接取某物: *Let me* ~ *you of your suitcase,* carry it for you (which is more usu). 让我替你拿手提箱。**(b)** (joc) steal from: (谑)偷; 窃去: *The thief* ~*d him of his watch.* 那贼偷去他的手表。**(c)** dismiss from: 开除; 解除: *He was* ~*d of his post.* 他被解除职务。**4** bring into relief²; make (sth) stand out more clearly (against a dark background, etc). 使凸起; 使(某物)更清晰地显出(借黑暗的背景衬托等, 与against连用)。

re·li·gion /rɪ'lidʒən; rɪ'lɪdʒən/ *n* **1** [U] belief in the existence of a supernatural ruling power, the creator and controller of the universe, who has given to man a spiritual nature which continues to exist after the death of the body. 宗教信仰。**2** [C] one of the various systems of faith and worship based on such belief: 宗教: *the great* ~*s of the world,* eg Christianity, Islam, Buddhism. 世界之大宗教(如基督教、伊斯兰教、佛教)。**3** [U] life as lived under the rules of a monastic order: 修道生活: *Her name in* ~ *is Sister Mary,* This is her name as a nun. 她的道名是玛莉修女。**4** matter of conscience; sth that one considers oneself bound to do: 良心所安之事; 自认须做之事: *She makes a* ~ *of keeping her house clean and tidy.* 她认为保持房子整洁是她分内的事。

re·lig·ious /rɪ'lɪdʒəs; rɪ'lɪdʒəs/ adj **1** of religion. 宗教的; 宗教信仰的。 **2** (of a person) devout; God-fearing. (指人)虔诚的; 敬畏神的。 **3** of a monastic order: 教团的; 修道的: a ~ house, a monastery or convent. 修道院; 僧院。 **4** scrupulous; conscientious: 谨慎的; 凭良心的: do one's work with ~ care/exactitude. 严谨地做事。 □ n a ~, person bound by monastic vows; monk or nun; 僧侣; 尼姑; 修士; 修女; (pl, unchanged in form) (复数, 字形不变) the/some/several ~, persons bound by monastic vows. 全体(若干, 几位)僧尼。 ~·ly adv

re·line /ˌriː'laɪn; rɪ'laɪn/ vt put a new lining in, eg a garment. 加新衬里于(衣服上等)。

re·lin·quish /rɪ'lɪŋkwɪʃ; rɪ'lɪŋkwɪʃ/ vt **1** [VP6A] give up: 放弃: ~ a hope/a habit/a belief. 放弃希望(习惯, 信仰)。 ~ one's hold of/over sb/sth, give up control. 放手不管(某人, 某事物)。 **2** [VP14] ~ sth (to sb), surrender: 将某事物让与(某人): ~ one's rights/shares to a partner. 把权利(股份)让给合伙人。

reli·quary /'relɪkwərɪ US: -kwerɪ; 'rɛlə,kwɛrɪ/ n (pl **-ries**) box, casket, or other receptacle for a relic or relics. 圣骨箱(匣、盒); 圣物箱(匣、盒); 遗物箱(匣、盒)。

rel·ish /'relɪʃ; 'rɛlɪʃ/ n **1** [C, U] (sth used to give, or which has, a) special flavour or attractive quality: 特别风味; 美味; 吸引力; 调味品; 作料; 引起兴趣之事物: Hunger is the best ~ for food. 肚子饿的时候什么都好吃。 Some pastimes lose their ~ when one grows old. 一个人年纪大了, 对某些娱乐就会不感兴趣。 **2** [U] liking (for); zest: 喜好(与 for 连用); 热心; 兴趣: I have no further ~ for active pursuits now that I am 90. 我已经九十岁了, 对于积极的工作或活动没有多大兴趣了。 □ vt [VP6A, D] enjoy; get pleasure out of: 享受; 爱好: ~ a walk/~ a lobster and a bottle of wine. 我想吃一只龙虾和一瓶酒。 She won't ~ having to get up before dawn to catch that train. 在黎明前须起床赶那班火车, 她不会喜欢的。

re·live /ˌriː'lɪv; rɪ'lɪv/ vt live through, undergo, again: 再经验; 再体验: That was an experience I should not like to ~. 那种经验我不愿再领略了。

re·lo·cate /ˌriː'ləʊ'keɪt US: ˌriː'ləʊkeɪt; rɪ'loket/ vt, vi establish, become established, in a new place or area. 重置于新的地方; 建造于新的地方; 迁建; 迁徙。 **re·lo·ca·tion** /ˌriːləʊ'keɪʃn; ˌrilo'keʃən/ n [U] putting in, moving to, a new place or area: 置于新的地方; 迁徙于新的地方: the relocation of industry; 工业区之迁徙; the relocation of population; 人口之迁移; compulsory evacuation of persons from military areas during a war, with resettlement in a new area. 战时之强迫人们撤离军事地区(另定居于新的地方)。

re·luc·tant /rɪ'lʌktənt; rɪ'lʌktənt/ adj ~ (to do sth), (slow to act because) unwilling or disinclined; offering resistance: 不愿(做某事)的; 因不愿而迟疑的; 勉强的; 顽抗的; 难驾驭的: ~ helpers; 不情愿的帮助者; a ~ recruit into the army. 勉强入伍的新兵。 He seemed ~ to help us. 他似乎不愿帮助我们。 ~·ly adv **re·luc·tance** /-əns; -əns/ n [U].

rely /rɪ'laɪ; rɪ'laɪ/ vi (pt, pp **-lied**) [VP3A] ~ on/upon, depend upon with confidence, look to for help: 信赖; 依赖: He can always be relied upon for help. 他的帮助是永远可依赖的。 You may ~ upon my early arrival. 你放心好了, 我会早到的。 You may ~ upon it that he will be early. 你放心好了, 他一定会早到的。

re·main /rɪ'meɪn; rɪ'men/ vi **1** [VP2A] be still present after a part has gone or has been taken away: 剩下; 遗留: After the fire, very little ~ed of my house. 火烧后, 寒舍所剩无几。 If you take 3 from 8, 5 ~s. 八减三剩五。 Much ~s to be settled. 待解决的事尚多。 **2** [VP2A, B, C, 4A] continue in some place or condition; continue to be: 停留; 保持; 保持某状态存在: How many weeks shall you ~ (=stay) here? 你将在此地停留几个星期? Let things ~ as they are. 一切听其自然吧。 He ~ed silent. 他仍然缄默。 I shall ~ (stay is more usu) to see the end of the game. 我将留下来看比赛的结果 (stay 较常用)。 Man ~ed a hunter for thousands of years, ie before

beginning to cultivate crops, etc. 人类的狩猎时期有数千年之久。

re·main·der /rɪ'meɪndə(r); rɪ'mendɚ/ n that which remains; persons or things that are left over: 剩余物; 剩下的人或物: Twenty people came in and the ~ (= the rest, the others) stayed outside. 二十余人进来, 其余的留在外面。

re·mains /rɪ'meɪnz; rɪ'menz/ n pl **1** what is left: 所剩下或遗留者: the ~ of a meal; 残羹剩饭; the ~ (= ruins) of an old abbey/of ancient Rome. 古寺院(古罗马)的遗迹。 **2** dead body; corpse: 尸体; 遗骸: His mortal ~ are buried in the churchyard. 他的尸体埋葬于教堂的墓地。

re·make /ˌriː'meɪk; rɪ'mek/ vt (pt, pp **-made** -'meɪd; -'med/) make again. 再做; 重做; 改做; 再制; 重造。 □ n /'riːmeɪk; 'ri,mek/ sth made again: 重做之物; 再制品: a ~ of a film. 影片的再摄制。

re·mand /rɪ'mɑːnd US: -'mænd; rɪ'mænd/ vt [VP6A] send (an accused person) back (from a court of law) into custody so that more evidence can be obtained: 还押(将被告自法庭送回监禁以待更多证据): ~ed for a week. 在押一星期。 □ n [U] ~ing or being ~ed: 在押; 还押: detention on ~. 在押; 还押。 **'~ centre/home**, institution to which law-breaking children and adolescents are sent while inquiries are being made, or until the courts have decided their future treatment. 青少年拘留所(在进行调查中, 或法院判决前, 犯法之儿童或青少年被送往拘留的机构)。

re·mark /rɪ'mɑːk; rɪ'mark/ vt, vi **1** [VP6A, 9] say (that): 谈起; 述及(后接名词从句): He ~ed that he would be absent the next day. 他谈到他次日不能出席。 'I thought it was curious,' he ~ed. '我认为这很稀奇,'他说。 **2** [VP3A] ~ on/upon, say sth by way of comment. 谈论; 评论: It would be rude to ~ upon her appearance. 谈论她的容貌是不礼貌的。 **3** [VP26A, 9, 10] (formal, old use) notice; see: (正式用语, 旧用法)注意; 留意; 看: Did you ~ the similarity between them? 你注意到他们之间的相似之处吗? □ n **1** [C] comment; sth said: 评论; 谈话: pass rude ~s about sb; 用粗鲁的话批评某人; make a few ~s, give a short talk. 说几句话; 作短评。 **2**[U] notice; looking at: 注意; 留意; 看: There was nothing worthy of ~ at the Flower Show. 花展中没有值得一看的东西。 ~·able /-əbl; -əbl/ adj out of the ordinary; deserving or attracting attention: 非常的; 值得注意的: a ~able event; 不平常的事件; a boy who is ~able for his stupidity. 笨得惊人的男孩。 ~·ably /-əblɪ; -əblɪ/ adv

re·marry /ˌriː'mærɪ; rɪ'mærɪ/ vt, vi (pt, pp **-ried**) marry again. 再婚; 再与…结婚。 **re·mar·riage** /ˌriː-'mærɪdʒ; rɪ'mærɪdʒ/ n

rem·edy /'remədɪ; 'rɛmədɪ/ n (pl **-dies**) ~ (for), cure(for a disease, evil, etc); method of, sth used for, putting right sth that is wrong: (疾病之)治疗; (坏事等之)矫正; 补救; 治疗法; 药物; 补救物: a good ~ for colds. 治伤风的良药。 The ~ seems to be worse than the disease. 服用这种药物无异于饮鸩止渴。 Your only ~ (= way to get redress) is to go to law. 你唯一的补救办法是诉诸法律。 The evil is past/beyond ~, cannot be cured. 这弊害无药可治。 □ vt [VP6A] put right; provide a ~ for (evils, defects): 矫正(坏事, 缺点): Your faults of pronunciation can be remedied. 你的发音毛病是可以矫正的。 **re·medial** /rɪ'miːdɪəl; rɪ'midɪəl/ adj providing, or intended to provide, a ~: 治疗的; 矫正的; 用于治疗或矫正的: remedial measures; 补救办法; remedial education/classes, eg for children suffering disadvantages. 矫治教育(班)。 **re·medi·able** /rɪ'miːdɪəbl; rɪ'midɪəbl/ adj that can be remedied. 可治疗或矫正的; 可补救的。

re·mem·ber /rɪ'membə(r); rɪ'membɚ/ vt, vi **1** [VP 6A, C, 7A, 8, 9, 10, 14, 16B, 19C] have or keep in the memory; call back to mind the memory of: 记得; 忆及: I can't ~ his name. 我记不起他的名字。 Did I (did not forget) to post your letters. 我(那时)未忘记寄与你寄信。 I ~ posting your letters (= have the memory of

that act in my mind). 我记得为你寄过信。*I ~ having heard you speak on that subject.* 我记得曾听你谈论那题目。*Do you ~ where you put the key?* 你记得把钥匙放在何处吗？*I ~ her* (= picture her in my mind) *as a slim young girl.* 我想起她那时还是个纤弱的小女孩。*Please don't ~ this unfortunate affair against me,* don't bear it in mind and, for that reason, be unfriendly to me. 请不要把这不幸的事记在心里恨恨我。*'Have you ever met my brother?'—'Not that I ~.'* I don't ~ having met him. '你见过我哥哥(弟弟)吗？'—'我不记得曾见过他。' **2** [VP6A] make a present to: 赠与: *Please ~ the waiter,* don't forget to tip him. 别忘了给服务员小费。*I hope you'll ~ me in your will,* leave me sth. 我希望你在遗嘱中对我有所遗赠。**3**[VP14] *~ sb to sb,* convey greetings: 问候; 致意: *Please ~ me to your brother.* 请代向令兄(弟)问候。

re·mem·brance /rɪ'membrəns; rɪ'mɛmbrəns/ *n* **1** [C] remembering or being remembered; memory: 回想; 记忆; 记忆力: *to the best of my ~;* 就我记忆所及; *have no ~ of sth;* 不记得某事物; *a service in ~ of those killed in the war.* 纪念阵亡者的仪式。**R~ Day／Sunday,** (GB) Nov 11th, or the nearest Sunday, on which those killed in the two World Wars are commemorated. (英)阵亡将士纪念日(纪念在两次世界大战中的死难者,在十一月十一日或最近该日的星期天)。**2** [C] sth given or kept in memory of sb or sth: 纪念品: *He sent us a small ~ of his visit.* 他送给我们一个他造访的小纪念品。**3** (pl) regards; greetings ⇨ **regard**¹**(5)**): (复)问候; 致意: *Give my kind ~s to your parents.* 请为我向令尊令堂致意。

re·mili·tar·ize /ˌriː'mɪlɪtəraɪz; rɪ'mɪletəˌraɪz/ *vt* [VP6A] provide, occupy, again with armed forces and military equipment. 使重整军备; 使重新武装。**re·mili·tar·iz·ation** /ˌriː'mɪlɪtəraɪ'zeɪʃn US: -rɪ'z-; ˌrɪmɪletərɪ'zeʃən/ *n*

re·mind /rɪ'maɪnd; rɪ'maɪnd/ *vt* [VP6A, 11, 14, 17, 20, 21] *~ sb (to do sth／that...); ~ sb of sth/sb,* cause (sb) to remember (to do sth, etc); cause (sb) to think (of sth): 提醒(某人)(做某事等, 与不定式或名词从句连用);使(某人)想起(某事物或某人, 与 of 连用): *Please ~ me to answer that letter.* 请提醒我回复那封信。*Travellers are ~ed that* inoculation against yellow fever is advisable. 旅客们被提醒, 注射黄热病预防针是明智的。*He ~s me of his brother.* 他使我想起他哥哥(弟弟)。*This ~s me of what we did together during our holidays.* 这使我想起我们在假日一同做的事。*That ~s me,...,* What you have just said ~s me..., I've just remembered..., etc. 这使我想起...。*~er n* sth (eg a letter) that helps sb to remember sth: 使人记起某事之事物(例如信函): *He hasn't paid me that money yet—I must send him a ~er,* ie a letter to ~ him about it. 他还未付我那笔钱—我必须写一封信提醒他。

remi·nisce /ˌremɪ'nɪs; ˌrɛmə'nɪs/ *vi* [VP2A, 3A] *~ (about),* think or talk about past events and experiences. 回忆; 话旧; 缅怀往事。

remi·nis·cence /ˌremɪ'nɪsns; ˌrɛmə'nɪsn̩s/ *n ~ (of),* **1** [U] reminiscing; recalling of past experiences. 回忆; 话旧; 怀旧。**2** (pl) remembered experiences; narrative, spoken or written, of what sb remembers: (复)所追怀的经验; 旧事; 回忆录; 经验谈: *~s of my days in the Navy.* 我在海军那一段日子的回忆。**3** sth that is suggestive (of sth else): 令人联想(其他事物)的东西(与 of 连用): *There is a ~ of his father in the way he walks.* 他走路的样子使人联想到他的父亲。

remi·nis·cent /ˌremɪ'nɪsnt; ˌrɛmə'nɪsn̩t/ *adj ~ (of),* **1** reminding one of; suggestive of: 使人想起的; 暗示的: *Your face is ~ of your mother's.* 你的面孔使人想起你母亲的面孔。**2** recalling past experiences: 回忆的; 怀旧的: *become ~.* 开始怀旧。*~·ly adv*

re·miss /rɪ'mɪs; rɪ'mɪs/ *adj ~ in,* careless of duty: 疏忽职守的; 不注意的: *to be ~ in your duties.* 不注意你的职守。*~ of,* negligent, lax: 松懈的; 怠慢的; 随便的: *That was very ~ of you.* 你对那件事太疏忽了。*~·ness n*[U].

re·mis·sion /rɪ'mɪʃn; rɪ'mɪʃən/ *n* **1** [U] pardon or forgiveness (of sins; by God). (指上帝对罪过的)赦免; 宽恕。**2** [U] freeing (from debt, punishment, etc): (债务、处分等之)免除; 放弃: *~ of a claim;* 对一项要求权利之放弃; [C] instance of this: 免除或放弃之实例: *(from a prison sentence) for good conduct;* 因行为良好而减免徒刑; *No ~s of examination fees are allowed.* 检查费不减免。**3** [U] lessening or weakening (of pain, efforts, etc): (痛苦、努力等之)缓和; 减轻: *~ of a fever.* 热度之减退。

re·mit /rɪ'mɪt; rɪ'mɪt/ *vt, vi* (-tt-) **1** [VP6A] (of God) forgive (sins). (指上帝)赦(罪)。**2** [VP6A] excuse (sb) payment (of a debt, punishment): 免除(某人之债); 赦免(某人之刑罚): *The taxes have been ~ted.* 税已免除了。*Your fees cannot be ~ted.* 你的费用不能豁免。**3**[VP12A, 13A, 2D] send (money, etc) by post: 汇(钱等): *When can you ~ me the money?* 你何时能汇钱给我? *Kindly ~ by cheque,* send a cheque for the sum owing. 祈惠寄支票付款。**4** [VP6A] make or become less: 缓和; 减轻: *~ one's efforts.* 松懈努力。**5** [VP14] *~ sth to sb,* take or send (a question to be decided) (to some authority): 将 (待决之问题)送呈(有关当局): *The matter has been ~ted to a higher tribunal.* 那事件已送呈上一级法院裁决。*~·tance/-ns; -ns̩/ n* [U] the ~ting, of money; [C] sum of money sent. 汇款; 所汇款额。

re·mit·tent /rɪ'mɪtnt; rɪ'mɪtn̩t/ *adj* (esp of a fever) that abates in severity at intervals. (尤指热病)忽轻忽重的; 间歇性的。

rem·nant /'remnənt; 'rɛmnənt/ *n* [C] **1** small part that remains: 剩下之小部分; 残余; 剩余: *the ~s of a banquet;* 筵席之剩菜; *~s of former glory.* 往昔光荣之遗迹。**2** (esp) length of cloth offered at a reduced price after the greater part has been sold: (尤指减价出售的)零头布; *a ~ sale.* 零头布的减价出售。

re·mon·strance /rɪ'mɒnstrəns; rɪ'mɑnstrəns/ *n* [U] remonstrating (with); [C] protest (against). 抗辩; 规谏(与 with 连用); 抗议(与 against 连用)。

re·mon·strate /'remənstreɪt; rɪ'mɑnstret/ *vi* [VP2A, 3A] *~ with sb (about sth／that...),* make a protest; argue in protest: 抗议; 抗辩; 规谏: *~ with sb about his foolish behaviour;* 就其愚行规谏某人; *~ against cruelty to children.* 抗议对孩子的虐待。

re·morse /rɪ'mɔːs; rɪ'mɔrs/ *n* [U] **1** *~ (for),* deep, bitter regret for wrongdoing: 懊悔; 悔恨: *feel/be filled with ~ for one's failure to help sb;* 因未能帮助某人而感到懊悔; *in a fit of ~.* 在一阵懊悔中。**2** compunction: 良心的不安: *without ~,* merciless(ly). 无情的(地)。*~·ful /-fl; -fəl/ adj* feeling ~. 懊悔的; 良心不安的。*~·fully /-fəlɪ; -fəlɪ/ adv ~·less adj* without ~. 不知懊悔的。*~·less·ly adv*

re·mote /rɪ'məʊt; rɪ'mot/ *adj* (-r, -st) *~ (from),* **1** far away in space or time: 遥远的(在空间或时间上)遥远的: *in the ~st parts of Asia;* 在亚洲的遥远地区; *live in a house ~ from any town or village;* 居住于远离任何城镇或村庄的房子; *in the ~ past/future.* 在遥远的过去(未来)。*~ control,* control of apparatus, eg in an aircraft, a rocket, from a distance by means of radio signals. 遥控(在远处用无线电波对飞机、火箭之控制)。**2** widely separated (in feeling, interests, etc *from*): (在感情、兴趣等方面)距离很大的; 关系甚远的(与 from 连用): *Some of your statements are rather ~ from the subject we are discussing.* 你有一些话与我们所谈论的问题关系不甚密切。**3** distant in manner; aloof. 疏远的; 冷淡的。**4** (esp in the superl) slight: (尤用于最高级)些微的; 轻的: *a ~ possibility;* 极小的可能性; *have not the ~st idea of what sth means.* 一点不知道某事物的含义。*~·ly adv* in a ~ manner: 遥远地: 关系甚远地: *Gillian and I are ~ly related.* 吉利安和我是远亲。*~·ness n*

re·mount¹ /ˌriː'maʊnt; rɪ'maʊnt/ *vt, vi* [VP6A, 2A] get on (a horse, bicycle, etc) again; go up (a ladder, hill, etc) again. 再骑上(马、自行车等); 再爬(梯、山等)。

re·mount² /ˌriː'maʊnt; rɪ'maʊnt/ *vt* [VP6A] **1**

supply (a man, a regiment) with a fresh horse or horses. 以新马供给(某人、某团). **2** put (a photograph, etc) on a new mount. 放(照片等)于新衬纸上; 重新安装. □ *n* /'ri:maunt/ 'ri,maunt/ fresh horse; supply of fresh horses. 新马; 新补充之马.

re·move[1] /rɪ'mu:v; rɪ'muv/ *vt, vi* **1** [VP6A, 14] ~ *(from)*, take off or away from the place occupied: take to another place: 自原来位置拿开; 取去; 移动: ~ *one's hat/coat;* 脱帽(上衣); ~ *one's hand from sb's shoulder;* 把放在某人肩上的手移开; ~ *the cloth from the table;* 把桌上的桌布拿掉; ~ *a boy from school,* eg because of ill health. 使一男孩休学(如因健康不佳). **2** [VP6A, 14] ~ *(from)*, get rid of: 除去; 排除: ~ *doubts/fears.* 消除疑虑(恐惧). *What do you advise for removing grease/ink stains etc from clothes?* 你有什么好办法除去衣服上的油渍(墨水斑等)? **3** [VP6A, 14] ~ *(from)*, dismiss: 免职; 开除: ~ *a man from office;* 免除一人之职务; ~ *a Civil Servant.* 将一公务员革职. **4** [VP2A, C] go to live in another place (move is more usu): 移居 (move 比 remove 常用): *We're removing into the country next week/removing from London to the country.* 我们将于下周迁到乡下(从伦敦迁到乡下). **5** ~*d from*, distant or remote from: 远离的; 关系甚远的: *a dialect equally* ~*d from French and Spanish;* 与法语和西班牙语关系同样疏远的一种方言; *an explanation far* ~*d from the truth.* 与事实相距甚远的一种解释. **6** ~*d,* (of cousins) different by a generation: (指堂、表亲)相隔一代的: *first cousin once* ~*d,* first cousin's child. 堂侄; 表侄. **re·mov·able** /-əbl; -əbl/ *adj* that can be ~*d* (esp of a magistrate or other official who can be ~*d* from office at any time). 可移动的; 可除去的; (尤指官员)可撤任的; 可免职的. □ ~**r** *n* **1** (esp) person who follows the business of moving furniture when people ~ (4). (尤指)搬场业者; 搬迁家具者. **2** (in compounds) that which ~s: 用以除去或排除之物: *superfluous hair* ~*r.* 除去多余毛发的药剂. **re·mov·al** /rɪ'mu:vl; rɪ'muvl/ *n* [U] act of removing: 移动; 搬家; 免职: *the removal of furniture;* 家具之搬运; (attrib)(用作定语) *a re'moval van* (for furniture); 搬运车; *the removal of dissatisfaction;* 不满情绪之排除; [C] instance of removal. 移动、除去、移居、搬家、免职等之实例.

re·move[2] /rɪ'mu:v; rɪ'muv/ *n* stage or degree: 阶段; 程度: *only a few* ~*s from....* 与...仅差少许.

re·mun·er·ate /rɪ'mju:nəreɪt; rɪ'mjunə,ret/ *vt* [VP6A, 14] ~ *sb (for sth)*, pay (sb) (for work or services); reward. (因工作或服务而)酬劳(某人); 报酬. **re·mun·er·ation** /rɪ,mju:nə'reɪʃn; rɪ,mjunə'reʃən/ *n* [U] payment; reward. 酬劳; 报酬. **re·mun·er·ative** /rɪ'mju:nərətɪv US: -nəreɪtɪv; rɪ'mjunə,retɪv/ *adj* profitable. 有酬劳的; 有利益的.

re·nais·sance /rɪ'neɪsns; rɪ'nesṇs; rɪ'nesṇs/ *n* **1** the R~, (period of) revival of literature, painting, etc in Europe in the 14th, 15th and 16th cc, based on ancient Greek learning: (欧洲十四、十五及十六世纪之)文艺复兴; 文艺复兴时期: (attrib)(用作定语) ~ *art.* 文艺复兴时期的艺术. **2** [C] any similar revival. 任何类似的复兴; 再生.

re·nal /'ri:nl; 'rinl/ *adj* (anat) of or in the (region of the) kidneys: (解剖)肾脏的; 肾脏中的; 肾的: ~ *artery.* 肾动脉.

re·name /ˌri:'neɪm; rɪ'nem/ *vt* [VP6A] give a new name to; name again. 予以新名; 再命名.

re·nas·cence /rɪ'næsns; rɪ'næsṇs/ *n* = renaissance(2). **re·nas·cent** /-snt; -sṇt/ *adj* springing up anew; reviving; being reborn. 再生的; 复活的; 重生的.

rend /rend; rend/ *vt* (*pt, pp* rent/rent; rent/) [VP6A, 14, 15A] (liter) (文) **1** pull or divide forcibly; penetrate: 用力拉或分开; 分裂; 刺破: *a country rent (in two) by civil war.* 因内战而分裂(为二)的国家. *Loud cries rent the air.* 吼声震云霄. **2** tear or pull (off, away) violently: 扯裂; 强使分离(与 off, away 连用). *Children were rent from their mothers' arms by the brutal soldiers.* 凶暴的兵士强

使孩子离开母亲的怀抱.

ren·der /'rendə(r); 'rendɚ/ *vt* **1** [VP6A, 14, 12A, 13A, 15A, B] ~ *sth (to sb)*, give in return or exchange, or as sth due: 报答; 回报; 归还; 给予: ~ *thanks to a friend;* 答谢友人; ~ *good for evil;* 以德报怨; ~ *help to those in need;* 予贫困者以帮助; ~ *a service to sb/~ sb a service;* 为某人服务(助某人一忙); ~ *up* (=surrender) *a fort to the enemy;* 把堡垒放弃给敌人; *a reward for services* ~*ed.* 酬谢服务的奖金. **2** [VP6A] present; offer; send in (an account for payment): 呈递; 提供; 开出(帐单催促付款): *an account* ~*ed,* previously presented but not yet paid. 已开来而尚未付款的帐单; 交验帐; 付款催单. *You will have to* ~ *an account of your expenditure.* 你的开支必须报帐. ~ *an account of oneself/one's behaviour,* explain, justify oneself/it. 为自己(自己的行为)辩护; 说明. **3** [VP22] cause to be (in some condition): 使成; 致使(处于某状况): ~*ed helpless by an accident.* 因意外而束手无策. **4** [VP6A, 14] give a performance of (eg a drama, a character in a drama); express in another language: 演出(戏剧, 剧中之角色等); 扮演; 演奏; 翻译: *The piano solo was well* ~*ed.* 那支钢琴独奏曲弹奏得很好. *'Othello' was* ~*ed rather poorly.* '奥赛罗'一剧演出欠佳. *There are many English idioms that cannot be* ~*ed into other languages.* 有许多英文习语无法翻译成其他文字. **5** [VP6A, 15B] ~ *sth (down)*, melt and make clear: 煎熬(脂肪): ~ *down fat/lard.* 熬脂肪(猪油). **6** [VP6A] cover (stone, brick) with the first layer of plaster. 涂第一层灰泥于(石, 砖). ~·**ing** /'rendərɪŋ; 'rendɚɪŋ/ *n* **1** [C] way of performing, playing, translating, sth, ⇨ ~(4): 演出, 演奏, 翻译之方式, ⇨ ~(4): *an* ~ *of the Bible.* 圣经的翻译. **2** [U] first layer of plaster, ⇨ ~(6). 第一层灰泥.

ren·dez·vous /'rɒndɪvu:; 'rɑnde,vu/ *n* (*pl* ~ /-z; -z/) [C] **1** (place decided upon for a) meeting at a time agreed upon. 约会; 集会; 约会地点; 集会地点; 会合点. **2** place where people often meet: 人们常聚会之处: *This café is a* ~ *for writers and artists.* 这家咖啡馆是作家和艺术家们经常聚会的地方. □ *vi* [VP2A, C] meet at a ~: 约见; 聚会; 在约好的地方相见: ~ *in a café/beside a lake.* 约好在一咖啡馆(湖滨)相见.

ren·di·tion /ren'dɪʃn; rɛn'dɪʃən/ *n* [C] interpretation or rendering (of a song, etc). (歌曲等的)解释; 演唱; 演出; 翻译.

ren·egade /'renɪgeɪd; 'rɛnɪ,ged/ *n* [C] person who changes his religious beliefs; person who deserts his political party; traitor: 背教者; 叛党者; 叛徒: (attrib)(用作定语) *a* ~ *priest.* 一位背教的传教士. □ *vi* turn ~. 成为背教者, 叛党者或叛徒.

re·nege, re·negue /rɪ'ni:g; rɪ'nig/ *vi* **1** (in card games) revoke(2). (纸牌戏)手中有可跟之牌而违例不跟. **2** [VP3A] ~ *on,* fail to keep (one's word). 违背(诺言); 背信.

re·new /rɪ'nju: US: -'nu:; rɪ'nju/ *vt* [VP6A] **1** make (as good as) new; put new life and vigour into; restore to the original condition: 使新; 更新; 注入新生命力; 使恢复: ~ *one's youth;* 恢复青春; *with* ~*ed enthusiasm.* 以重新燃起的热情. **2** get, make, say or give, again: 再借; 再做; 再给; 再说: ~ *a lease/contract;* 续订租约(契约); ~ *one's subscription to a periodical;* 续订一期刊; ~ *an attack;* 再行攻击; ~ *one's complaints.* 再次投诉; 再度抱怨. **3** replace (with the same sort of thing, etc): 换新; 补充: *We must* ~ *our supplies of coal.* 我们必须补充煤的储藏. *Snakes cast off and* ~ *their skins.* 蛇蜕皮复长新皮. ~·**able** /-əbl; -əbl/ *adj* that can be ~*ed.* 可更新的; 可重新开始的; 可换新的. ~**al** /-'nju:əl US: -'nu:əl; -'nuəl/ *n* [U] ~ing or being ~*ed:* 更新; 重新开始; 换新; *delighted at the* ~ *of negotiations;* 对恢复谈判感到高兴的; *urban* ~*al,* eg slum clearance for the provision of better housing: 都市更新; 都市改建; [C] *sth* ~*ed.* 更新, 重新开始, 换新等之事物.

ren·net /'renɪt; 'rɛnɪt/ *n* [U] preparation used in curdling milk for making cheese, etc. 凝乳素(用于制干

酪等用)。

re·nounce /rɪˈnauns; rɪˈnaʊns/ vt [VP6A] 1 declare formally that one will no longer have anything to do with, that one no longer recognizes (sb or sth having a claim to one's care, affection, etc): 正式宣称 (与某人或某事物)断绝关系;弃绝: ～ one's faith/religion; 弃绝信仰(宗教); ～ the world, give up meeting people socially, begin to lead the life of a hermit, etc. 脱离社会; 遁世。 2 consent formally to give up (a claim, right, possession): 正式同意放弃(要求, 权利, 财产): ～ one's claim to the throne/a peerage. 放弃王位的继承权 (贵族的地位)。 3 disown; refuse to recognize: 否认; 拒绝承认: He ～d his sons because they were criminals. 他拒绝承认他们是他的儿子, 因为他们是罪犯。

reno·vate /ˈrenəveɪt; ˈrɛnəˌvet/ vt [VP6A] restore, eg old buildings, oil paintings, to good or strong condition. 修理; 恢复(旧房屋, 油画)至良好状况。 **reno·va·tor** /-tə(r); -tɚ/ n person who ～s. 修理者; 使旧房屋、油画等恢复至良好状况者。 **reno·va·tion** /ˌrenəˈveɪʃn; ˌrɛnəˈveʃən/ n [U] renovating; [C] instance of this: 修理; 恢复; 修理或恢复之实例: costly renovations of old college buildings at Oxford. 花费很大的牛津大学旧校舍修复工程。

re·nown /rɪˈnaun; rɪˈnaʊn/ n [U] fame: 名望; 声誉: win～; 赢得声誉; a man of high ～. 极有名望的人。 ～ed adj famous; celebrated: 有名的; 著名的: ～ed as a portrait painter; 是个著名的人像画家; ～ed for his skill. 以其技巧而著名的。

rent[1] /rent; rɛnt/ n [C, U] regular payment for the use of land, a building, a room or rooms, machinery, etc; sum of money paid in this way: (土地,建筑物、房舍、机器等之)定期的租金; 租金总额: owe three weeks' ～ for one's house; 欠三星期的房租; live in a house free of ～, without paying ～; 居住不收租金的房屋; pay a heavy/high ～ for farming land; 缴付农地之昂贵租金; collect the ～s. 收租。 '～-collector n person who goes from house to house to collect ～s for the owner(s). (为房地主挨户)收租者。 ,~-free adj, adv: a ～-free house, for which no ～ is charged to the tenant; 不收租金的房子; occupy a house ～-free. 居住不收租金的房屋。 ~-'rebate n rebate, based on earnings and the amount of ～ payable, given by a local government authority on ～ paid, esp by council tenants. 租金宽减额; 房租之宽减。 '~-roll n (a) register of a person's land and buildings with the ～s due from them. 租折; 房地租帐。 (b) total income from ～s. 房地租总收入。 □ vt, vi 1 [VP6A, 14] ～ (from/to), occupy or use (land, buildings, etc) for ～; allow (land, buildings, etc) to be used or occupied in return for ～: 租用; 出租(土地、建筑物等): We don't own our house, we ～ it from Mr Gay. 我们住的房子不是自己的, 是向盖伊先生租的。 Mr Hill ～s this land to us at £50 a year. 希尔先生把这块地租给我们, 每年五十镑。 2 [VP2A, C] be ～ed: 出租: The building ～s at £150 a year. 这建筑物每年以一百五十镑出租。 ~·able adj that may be ～ed; 可出租的; 可以收益的。 ～ed adj to yield a ～. 可租金的。 ~·al /ˈrentl; ˈrɛntl/ n [C] amount of ～ paid or received; income from ～s. 租金额; 租金收入。

rent[2] /rent; rɛnt/ n 1 torn place in cloth, etc; split: (布等之)破裂处; 裂缝: a ～ in his shirt. 他衬衫上的裂缝。 2 (fig) division or split (in a political party, etc). (政党等的)分裂; 分歧。

rent[3] /rent; rɛnt/ pt, pp of **rend**.

rent·ier /ˈrɒntɪeɪ; ˈrɑntje/ n person whose income comes from investments and/or rents from property. 靠投资收入和(或)房地产租金度日者。

re·nunci·ation /rɪˌnʌnsɪˈeɪʃn; rɪˌnʌnsɪˈeʃən/ n [U] renouncing, self-denial. 放弃; 放弃; 自制; 自制; 舍弃。

re·open /riːˈəʊpən; riˈopn/ vt, vi [VP6A, 2A] open again after closing or being closed: 重开; 再开始: ～ a shop; 重新开一商店; ～ a discussion. 再予讨论。 School ～s on Monday. 星期一恢复上课。

re·or·gan·ize /riːˈɔːɡənaɪz; riˈɔrgəˌnaɪz/ vt, vi

organize again or in a new way. 重新组织; 改组; 整顿。

re·orien·tate /riːˈɔːrɪenteɪt; riˈɔrɪenˌtet/ (also 亦作 **re·orient** /riːˈɔːrɪent; riˈɔrɪˌɛnt/) vt, vi orient(ate) again or anew. 再使朝向东方; 再使在东端; 再予定方位。

rep[1], **repp** /rep; rɛp/, **reps** /reps; rɛps/ n [U] textile fabric used in upholstery. (室内装饰品用的)一种织物。

rep[2] /rep; rɛp/ n (colloq abbr of) representative (n(2)) of a commercial firm; commercial traveler. (口) 公司代表 (为 representative of a commercial firm 之略); 旅行推销员。

rep[3] /rep; rɛp/ n (colloq abbr of) repertory company or theatre: (口) 时常换演员或戏目的剧团或戏院 (为 repertory company 或 theatre 之略): act in rep. 在时常换演员或戏目的剧团或戏院演戏。

re·pair[1] /rɪˈpeə(r); rɪˈpɛr/ vt [VP6A] 1 restore (sth worn or damaged) to good condition: 修补; 修理(破旧或损坏之物): ～ the roads/a puncture/a watch/a shirt. 修路(补胎); 修表; 补衬衣。 2 put right again: 补救; 纠正: ～ an error. 纠正一错误。 □ n 1 [U] ～ing or being ～ed: 修理; 修缮: road under ～. 在修补中的道路。 2 (pl) work or process of ～ing: (复)修理、补救等的工作或过程: The shop will be closed during ～s. 整修期间该店将暂停营业。 The ～s needed before we can occupy the house will be considerable. 那幢房子在我们搬进之前需要大事整修一番。 3 [U] relative condition for using or being used: 使用中的相对状况: The machine is in a bad state of ～/in good ～. 这机器情况不佳 (情况良好)。 ~·able /-əbl; -əbl/ adj that can be ～ed. 可修理的; 可修补的。 ～ n one who ～s things; 修补者: boot and shoe ～ers. 修鞋匠。

re·pair[2] /rɪˈpeə(r); rɪˈpɛr/ vi [VP3A] ～ to, (formal) go to (esp go frequently, go in large numbers to): (正式用语)(尤指)常去; 众多人去: ～ to the seaside resorts for the summer. 大伙去海滨胜地避暑。

rep·ar·able /ˈrepərəbl; ˈrɛpərəbl/ adj (of a loss, etc) that can be made good. (指损失等)能补救的; 可补偿的。

rep·ar·ation /ˌrepəˈreɪʃn; ˌrɛpəˈreʃən/ n [U] act of compensating for loss or damage; (pl) compensation for war damages, demanded from a defeated enemy. 补偿; (复)战败者之赔偿; 赔款。

rep·ar·tee /ˌrepɑːˈtiː; ˌrɛpɑˈti/ n [C] witty, clever retort; [U] the making of such retorts: 巧妙的应答或反驳; 作巧妙的应答或反驳: He's good at ～. 他善作巧妙的应答。

re·past /rɪˈpɑːst US: -ˈpæst; rɪˈpæst/ n (formal) meal: (正式用语)餐; 食事: The guests partook of a luxurious ～ in the banqueting hall. 宾客们在大餐厅参加一次盛宴。

re·pat·ri·ate /riːˈpætrɪeɪt US: -ˈpert-; rɪˈpetrɪˌet/ vt [VP6A] send or bring (sb) back to their own country: 遣返; 遣送(某人)回国: ～ refugees after a war. 战后遣送难民回国。 □ n ～d person. 被遣返者。 **re·pat·ri·ation** /ˌriːpætrɪˈeɪʃn US: -ˌpert-; ˌripetrɪˈeʃən/ n.

re·pay /rɪˈpeɪ; rɪˈpe/ vt, vi (pt, pp **-paid** /-ˈpeɪd; -ˈped/) 1 [VP6A] pay back (money): 付还(钱): If you'll lend me 75p, I'll ～ you next week. 你借给我七十五便士, 我下星期就还你。 2 [VP6A, 14] ～ sth; ～ sb (for sth), give in return: 报答; 回报: ～ sb's kindness; 报答某人的恩惠; ～ sb for his kindness. 报答某人的恩惠。 I have been repaid (for the help I gave) only with ingratitude. (对于我给予的帮助)我只得到忘恩负义的报答。 3 [VP2A] give equal favour (or justice) in return: 报应; 报复: God will ～. eg will punish injustice. 上天会给予报应的。 ~·able /-əbl; -əbl/ adj that can or must be repaid. 可付还或回报的; 必须付还或回报的。 ~·ment n [U] ～ing; [C] instance of this:付还; 回报: bonds due for ～. 到期该偿还的债券。

re·peal /rɪˈpiːl; rɪˈpil/ vt [VP6A] revoke, annul (a law, etc). 撤销; 废止(法令等)。 □ n ～ing. 撤销; 废止。

re·peat /rɪ'piːt; rɪ'pit/ vt, vi **1** [VP6A, 9] say or do again: 重说; 重放; 重复: ~ a word/a mistake. 重复一字（错误）. I ~ that I cannot undertake the task. 我再说一遍, 我不能担任这工作。Don't ~ yourself, say or do the same thing more than once (usu without being aware of doing so). 不要重复(勿说或做同样的事)。Does history ~ itself, Do similar events or situations recur? 历史会重演吗? '~ing rifle, ⇨ **repeater** below. 参看下列之 repeater. **2** [VP6A] say (what sb else has said or what one learnt by heart): 转述; 背诵: You must not ~ what I've told you; it's very confidential. 你切不可转述我告诉你的事, 那是很机密的。His language won't bear ~ing, eg contained too many curses, swear words, etc. 他的话不堪重述（例如含有太多的脏话、粗话等）。**3** [VP2A] (of food) continue to be tasted after being eaten: 你发现吃过洋葱后口里仍留有味道吗? **4** [VP2A] (of numbers, eg decimals) recur: (指数字, 如小数)循环: The last two figures ~. 最后二位数字循环。**5** [VP6A] (comm) supply a further consignment of: (商)再供应(托售之物): We regret that we cannot ~ this article. 很抱歉我们无法再供应此物。▢ n **1** [C] ~ing (eg of an item in a programme) of a performance: 动作或行为的重复；(节目等的)重复表演: (attrib) (用作定语) a ~ performance; 重复的表演; a ~ order, (comm) an order for a further consignment of goods similar to an earlier one. (商)再供给同样货品的订单。There will be a ~ (= another broadcast) of this talk on Friday. 星期五将重播此次的谈话。**2** (music) mark indicating a passage intended to be repeated. (音乐)反复符号。**~ed** part adj: ~ed questioning/banging. 再三询问（猛击）。**~·ed·ly** adv again and again. 反复地；再三地。**~er** n revolver or rifle which can be fired a number of times without being reloaded (now usu a (semi-)automatic or self-loading rifle). 转轮手枪；连发步枪(现在通常为(半)自动或自动装弹步枪)。

re·pel /rɪ'pel; rɪ'pɛl/ vt (-ll-) [VP6A] **1** drive back or away; refuse to accept: 逐退; 驱开; 拒绝: ~ the enemy /temptation; 击退敌人(拒绝诱惑); ~ a young man's advances, discourage him. 拒绝一位年轻人的友谊或求爱。**2** cause a feeling of dislike in: 使厌恶; 使不愉快: His long, rough beard ~led her. 他的长而粗的胡子使她厌恶。**~·lent** /-ənt; -ənt/ adj tending to ~; unattractive; uninviting: 逐退的; 驱开的; 讨人嫌的; 讨厌的: ~lent work/food. 讨厌的工作(食物). His manner is rather ~lent. 他的态度颇令人厌恶。▢ n [C] sth that ~s, esp a preparation that ~s insects: 令人厌恶之物; (尤指)驱虫剂: Smear some of this mosquito ~lent on your legs. 搽一些驱蚊剂在你的腿上。

re·pent /rɪ'pent; rɪ'pɛnt/ vi, vt [VP2A, 3A, 6A, D] ~ (of), think with regret or sorrow of; be full of regret (about); wish one had not done (sth): 悔悟; 懊悔; 痛悔; 后悔曾做(某事): He ~ed of what he had done. 他懊悔他的所作为。Don't you ~ (of) having wasted your money so foolishly? 你不后悔如此糊涂乱花钱吗? He has bitterly ~ed his folly. 他痛悔他的愚行。Have you nothing to ~ of? 你没有可懊悔的事吗? **~·ance** /-əns; -əns/ n [U] regret for wrongdoing: 悔悟; 懊悔; 痛悔; 后悔: show ~ance (for sth). 对(某事)表示悔悟。**~·ant** /-ənt; -ənt/ adj feeling or showing ~ance: 悔悟的; 懊悔的: a ~ sinner; 悔悟的罪人; ~ant of his folly; 懊悔其愚行; the righteous and the ~ant. 正直者与悔悟者。**~·ant·ly** adv

re·per·cussion /ˌriːpə'kʌʃn; ˌripɚ'kʌʃən/ n **1** [U] springing back; driving or throwing back; [C] sth thrown or driven back; echoing sound: 弹回; 逐回; 击退; 反响; 反射; 逐回或击退之声响: the ~ of the waves from the rocks. 从岩石上击回的逆浪。**2** [C] (usu pl) far-reaching and indirect effect (of an event, etc): (通常用复数, 指事件等之)久远而间接的影响; 反应: The assassination of the President was followed by ~s throughout the whole country. 总统被暗杀之后, 全国均有反应。

rep·er·toire /'repətwɑː(r); 'rɛpɚˌtwɑr/ n [C] all the plays, songs, pieces, etc which a company, actor, musician, etc, is prepared to perform, etc: (剧团、演员、音乐家等所预备表演的)全部戏、歌、节目等; 戏目; 曲目: She has a large ~ of songs. 她能演唱很多歌。

rep·er·tory /'repətɔːrɪ US: -tɔːrɪ; 'rɛpɚˌtɔrɪ/ n (pl -ries) [C] **1** = repertoire. '~ **company** / **theatre**, (common abbr 常略作 rep) one in which the actors/plays are changed regularly (instead of having long runs as in most London theatres). 时常换演员或戏目的剧团(非如伦敦的大多数戏院作长期连续的演出)。**2** store or collection, esp of facts, information, etc: (尤指事实、知识等之)搜集; 贮积: My father is a ~ of useful information. 家父是实用知识的宝库。

rep·e·ti·tion /ˌrepɪ'tɪʃn; ˌrɛpɪ'tɪʃən/ n **1** [U] repeating or being repeated; [C] instance of this: 重说; 重做; 重复; 复诵; 背诵; 循环: after numerous ~s. 在无数次的重复后。**2** [C] further recurrence: 复现; 再发生: Let there be no ~ of this, Don't do it again. 不要再做这种事。**3** [C] piece (of poetry, etc) set to be learnt by heart and repeated. 背诵文(诗等). **rep·e·ti·tious** /ˌrepɪ'tɪʃəs; ˌrɛpɪ'tɪʃəs/, **re·peti·tive** /rɪ'petətɪv; rɪ'pɛtɪtɪv/ adjj characterized by ~: 重复的; 反复的: the repetitive work of a factory's production line. 工厂生产线之反复性的工作。

re·pine /rɪ'paɪn; rɪ'paɪn/ vi [VP2A, 3A] ~ (at), (formal) be discontented with: (正式用语)(对…)不满: ~ at misfortune. 对不幸的遭遇怨愤不平。~ against, fret against: 抱怨: ~ against Providence. 怨天。

re·place /rɪ'pleɪs; rɪ'ples/ vt **1** [VP6A, 15A] put back in its place: 放回; 置于原处: ~ a dictionary on the shelf; 把词典放回架上; ~ the receiver, ie after telephoning. (打电话后)置听筒于原处。**2** [VP6A] take the place of: 代替; 取代: Have buses ~d trams in your town? 在你居住的城市里, 公共汽车已取代电车了吗? Can anything ~ a mother's love and care? 有什么东西能取代母亲的爱和关怀吗? **3** [VP14] ~ sb/sth by/with, supply as a substitute for: 以…代替: ~ coal by/with oil. 以油替换煤。**~·able** /-əbl; -əbl/ adj that can be ~d. 可放回原处的; 可替换的。**~·ment** n [U] replacing or being ~d: 放回; 代替; 替换: the ~ment of worn-out parts; 磨损零件的替换; [C] sb or sth that ~s: 替换之人或物: get a ~ment (ie sb to do one's work) while one is away on holiday. 外出度假时找一位代理工作的人。

re·play /ˌriː'pleɪ; rɪ'ple/ vt [VP6A] play (eg a football match that was drawn) again. 重赛(如赛成平手的足球赛); 再播放。▢ n /'riːpleɪ; 'ri,ple/ ~ed match; ~ing of a record, etc. 重赛; (唱片等的)重放。

re·plen·ish /rɪ'plenɪʃ; rɪ'plɛnɪʃ/ vt [VP6A, 14] ~ (with), fill up (sth) again; get a new supply of or for: 再装满; 补充: I must ~ my wardrobe. 我必须添置衣服。**~·ment** n

re·plete /rɪ'pliːt; rɪ'plit/ adj ~ (with), (formal) filled with; holding as much as possible: (正式用语)装满的; 充盈的; 饱足的: ~ with food; 吃得饱饱的; feeling ~; 觉得饱; a home ~ with every modern convenience. 有各种现代设备的家庭。**re·ple·tion** /rɪ'pliːʃn; rɪ'pliʃən/ n [U] (formal) state of being ~: (正式用语)装满; 充盈; 饱足: Is it wrong to eat to repletion? 吃得过饱是不是不好?

rep·lica /'replɪkə; 'rɛplɪkə/ n [C] exact copy (esp one made by an artist of one of his own pictures): 复制品; 摹写品(尤指艺术家对自己作品的复制): make a ~ of a painting. 制作一幅画临摹一次。

re·ply /rɪ'plaɪ; rɪ'plaɪ/ vi, vt (pt, pp -plied) [VP2A, 3A, B, 9] ~ (to), give as an answer to, in words or action: (以话语或行动)回答; 答复: He failed to ~ (to my question). 他无法回答(我的问题)。'Certainly not,' he replied. '当然不会啦,'他回答。He replied that

I could please myself. 他回答说我可以随我自己的意思。 *The enemy replied to our fire, fired in return.* 敌人向我们还击。 *David Jones rose to ~ for* (= speak on behalf of) *the guests.* 大卫·琼斯站起来代表来宾致答词。 □ *n* act of ~*ing*; what is replied: 回答; 答复: *He made no ~.* 他没有回答。 *What did he say in ~?* 他如何答复? *,~-'paid,* (of a telegram, letter, etc) with the cost of the ~ prepaid by the sender. (指电报等)回电费用(回邮等)已付。

e·point /ri:'pɔint/ *vt* [VP6A] point (brickwork, etc) again. 将(建筑物的砌砖部分等之)接缝处再度用水泥或灰泥填塞起来。 ⇨ **point**²(5).

e·port¹ /ri'pɔ:t; rɪ'pɔrt/ *n* 1 [C] account of, statement about, sth heard, seen, done, etc: (对所闻、所见、所做等的)报导; 报告; 记事: ~*s on the state of the roads,* eg from an automobile association; 关于路况的报告: *the annual ~ of a business company;* 一商号的年度报告; *the chairman's ~,* ⇨ **chairman** at **chair**; *'law ~s,* ie of trials, etc, in the law courts; 判决录 (报导法庭审理案件的情形等); *a school ~,* eg by teachers about a pupil, with his examination marks, etc; 学生成绩报告单; *newspaper ~s.* 新闻报导。 2 [U] common talk; rumour; [C] piece of gossip: 传闻; 谣言; 闲话: *R~ has it that...,* People are saying that.... 据说…。 *We have only ~(s)* (ie no reliable news) *to go on.* 我们只有一些传闻可资依据。 *Don't listen to idle ~s.* 勿听信闲话。 3 [U] (formal) repute; way a person or thing is spoken about: (正式用语)名誉; 名声: *of good/evil ~.* 名誉好(坏)的。 4 [C] sound of an explosion: 爆炸声: *the ~ of a gun.* 枪炮声。 *It went off with a loud ~.* 它砰地一声爆炸了。

re·port² /rɪ'pɔ:t; rɪ'pɔrt/ *vt, vi* 1 [VP6A, D, 9, 25, 3A, 15B] give an account of (sth seen, heard, done, etc); give as news: 报导(所见、所闻、所做等的事物); 当作新闻报道: *The discovery of a new planet has been ~ed.* 据报导已发现一颗新行星。 *It is ~ed that another earth satellite has been put into orbit.* 据报导另一地球卫星已被射入轨道。 *They ~ed the enemy to be ten miles away.* 他们说敌人在十英里外。 *He ~ed having seen the escaped convict.* 他称述曾看见那个逃犯。 *~ on sth,* give news about or comment on it: 报导某事; 评论某事: *Jim's been sent to Hong Kong to ~ on the situation there.* 吉姆已被派往香港报导该地之情形。 *~ sth out,* (US) return it with comment: (美) 送回并附审查意见: *The committee ~ed the proposal out in record time.* 委员会以无比的快速送回该提案并附加审查意见。 *~ progress,* state what has been done so far. 报告经过或进展情形。 *~ed·ly adv* according to report(s). 据报导; 据说。 2 [VP6A, 2A] take down (eg in shorthand) the words of speeches, etc for newspapers, etc: 为报馆等记录(如用速记)演讲词等: *~ a speech/a Parliamentary debate;* 写新闻稿报导演说(国会辩论); *~ for 'The Times',* be a correspondent on its staff. 担任'泰晤士报'的记者。 *~ed speech,* = indirect speech. ⇨ **indirect.** 3 [VP3A, 14, 15A] *~ (oneself) (to sb/sth) (for sth),* go (somewhere), and announce that one has come, that one is ready for work, duty, etc: (向某处)报到; 到差; 复命: *~ for duty at the office;* 到办公室报到; *~ to the Manager.* 向经理复命。 *The officer was told to ~ (himself) to headquarters.* 那军官奉命前往司令部报到。 4 [VP6A, 14] *~ sb (to sb) (for sth),* make a complaint against sb (to authorities): (向当局)告发; 检举: *~ an official for insolence.* 告发一官员无礼。 *I shall have to ~ your unpunctuality to the Manager.* 我势将向经理举发你不守时。 *~·age* /,repɔ'tɑ:ʒ; rɪ'pɔrtɪdʒ/ *n* [U] (typical style of) ~*ing* events for newspapers. 新闻报导; 新闻报导式的文体。 *~·er n* person who ~s for a newspaper, for radio or TV. 记者; 通讯员。

re·pose¹ /rɪ'pəʊz; rɪ'poz/ *vt* [VP14] *~ sth in sth/sb,* (formal) place (trust, confidence, etc) in: (正式用语)把(信用, 信心等)寄托于: *Don't ~ too much*

confidence in that man/his honesty/his promises, etc. 不要对那人(他的诚实, 他的诺言等)过于信赖。

re·pose² /rɪ'pəʊz; rɪ'poz/ *vt, vi* (formal) (正式用语) 1 [VP6A, 15A, 2A, C] rest; give rest or support to: 休息; 使休息或依靠: *a girl reposing in a hammock;* 在吊床上休息的女郎; *~ one's head on a cushion;* 将头靠在垫子上; *~ oneself.* 休息; 歇息。 *Below this stone ~ the mortal remains of....* 在此石块下长眠的是…的遗骸。 2 [VP3A] *~ on,* be based on, supported on. 依靠。 □ *n* [U] (formal) (正式用语) 1 rest; sleep: 休息; 睡眠: *earn a night's ~;* 获得一夜的睡眠; *disturb sb's ~.* 打扰某人的安眠。 *Her face is beautiful in ~.* 她的面貌在睡眠中很美。 2 peaceful, restful or quiet behaviour or appearance: 安静的行为或外表: *His attitude lacked ~,* ease of manner. 他的态度不安详。 *~·ful /-fl; -fl/ adj* calm; quiet. 安静的; 沉静的。

re·posi·tory /rɪ'pɒzɪtrɪ US: -tɔːrɪ; rɪ'pazə,tɔrɪ/ *n* [C] (*pl* -ries) place where things are or may be stored. 贮藏物的地方; 仓库; 栈房: *The drawers in my desk are repositories for all sorts of useless papers.* 我书桌的抽屉是各种无用之文件的贮存处。 *My grandfather is a ~ of interesting facts.* 我祖父的肚子里装满了有趣的事实。

re·pot /ri:'pɒt; ri'pɑt/ *vt* transfer (a plant) from one pot to another (usu larger) pot. 将(植物)自一盆移植到另一(较大的)盆。

rep·re·hend /,reprɪ'hend; ,reprɪ'hɛnd/ *vt* [VP6A] rebuke, reprove: 责难; 谴责: *~ sb's conduct.* 指责某人的行为。 **rep·re·hen·sible** /,reprɪ'hensəbl; ,reprɪ'hɛnsəbl/ *adj* deserving to be ~ed. 应受责难的; 该当谴责的。

rep·re·sent¹ /,reprɪ'zent; ,reprɪ'zɛnt/ *vt* 1 [VP6A] be, give, make, a picture, sign, symbol or example of: 表示; 表现; 象征: *Phonetic symbols ~ sounds.* 音标表示声音。 *This painting ~s a hunting scene.* 这是一幅出猎图。 *The new ambassador ~s the best traditions of his country.* 这位新大使表现了其国家最好的传统。 2 [VP16A, 25, 9] declare to be; describe *(as);* allege (that...): 声称; 宣称(与当连用): *He ~ed himself as an expert.* 他声言自己是一位专家。 *I am not what you have ~ed me to be.* 我并不是象你所说的那种人。 3 [VP6A, 9, 14] *~ sth (to sb),* explain; make clear: 说明; 使明白: *Let me try to ~ my ideas to you in another way/in different terms.* 让我试用另外一种方式(不同的说法)向你说明我的想法。 4 [VP6A, 14, 9] *~ sth (to sb),* convey; express: 传达; 表达: *They ~ed their grievances to the Governor.* 他们向总督陈情。 *I will ~ to him the risks he is running.* 我将向他说明他所冒的危险。 *He ~ed to the magistrates that the offender was only a child.* 他向地方法官说明犯罪者仅是个小孩子。 5 [VP6A] act or speak for; be MP for; be agent for: 代表; 为…国会议员; 代理: 霍尔先生; 代表(ie MP's) ~*ing Welsh constituencies.* 代表威尔士各选区的国会议员们。 *Many countries were ~ed by their ambassadors at the Independence Day celebrations.* 庆祝美国独立纪念日时, 许多国家都派其大使代表参加。 *Our firm is ~ed in India and Pakistan by Mr Hall.* 本商号在印度和巴基斯坦的代表是霍尔先生。 6 [VP6A] (of a play, etc); play the part of, on the stage. 演出(戏等); 扮演…角色。 *~·a·tion* /,reprɪzen'teɪʃn; ,reprɪzɛn'teʃən/ *n* 1 [U] ~*ing* or being ~ed; [C] that which is ~ed: 表示; 象征; 声言; 陈述; 说明; 代表; 演出; 扮演; 所表示、声言、说明、代表、扮演等之事物: *no taxation without ~ation,* ie citizens should not be taxed without being ~ed (in Parliament, etc); 议会中无代表者不应纳税; *an unusual ~ation of 'Hamlet'.* 一次不同凡响的'哈姆雷特'的演出。 **proportional ~ation,** an electoral system designed so that minority parties, etc are ~ed (in a legislative assembly) in proportion to their strength. 比例代制 (少数党按其实力之大小推选代表的一种选举制度)。 5 (esp) polite protest or remonstrance: (尤指) 有礼貌的抗议: 陈情: *make ~ations to the Inspector of Taxes about an*

excessive assessment. 就过高估税向税务稽查官陈情。

re·pre·sent² /ˌriːprɪˈzent; ˌriprɪˈzɛnt/ *vt* submit again: 再送; 再提出: *Your cheque has been returned; please ~ it when you have funds in your account.* 你的支票被退回了, 请在你的帐户内有存款时再开一张。

rep·re·sen·ta·tive /ˌreprɪˈzentətɪv; ˌrɛprɪˈzɛntətɪv/ *adj* 1 **~ (of)**, serving to portray or show; serving as an example of a class or group; containing examples of a number of classes or groups: 表明的; 象征的; 代表的: *manuscripts ~ of monastic life;* 说明寺院生活的文稿; *a ~ collection of domestic utensils of the Middle Ages.* 所收藏的一批具有代表性的中世纪家庭用具。 2 consisting of elected deputies; based on representation by such elected deputies: 由选出之代表组成的; 代议制的: *~ government/institutions.* 代议制政府(制度)。□ *n* [C] **~** example; typical specimen (of a group or class). 例子; (一群或一类的)典型。 2 person elected or appointed to represent or act for others: 代表: *send a ~ to a conference;* 派代表参加会议; *sole ~s of the XYZ Petrol Company in Cardiff;* XYZ 石油公司派驻加的夫的总代理; *~s of the press,* newspaper reporters; 新闻记者; *our ~ (= MP) in the House of Commons.* 我们在下议院的代表(国会议员)。 **the House of R~s,** the lower house of the US Congress or of a state legislature. (美)(国会之)众议院; (州议会之)下院。

re·press /rɪˈpres; rɪˈprɛs/ *vt* [VP6A] keep or put down or under; prevent from finding an outlet: 镇压; 抑制; 阻止: *~ a revolt;* 镇压暴动; *~ sedition;* 消弭叛变; *~ a sneeze;* 抑止喷嚏; *~ an impulse;* 抑制冲动; *~ed emotions.* 压抑的情绪。 *~ed adj,* suffering from repression(2).受压制的; 被抑制的。 **re·pres·sion**/rɪˈpreʃn; rɪˈprɛʃən/ *n* 1 [U] ~ing or being ~ed. 镇压; 抑制。 2 [U] (psych) forcing into the unconscious of impulses and desires, esp those in conflict with accepted standards of conduct, often resulting in abnormal behaviour; [C] impulse or instinct ~ed in this way. (心理)压抑(把本能的冲动和欲望, 尤其是与一般公认的行为标准相冲突的, 压抑于非意识中, 往往因而导致行为异常); 被压抑的行为或本能。 **re·pres·sive**/rɪˈpresɪv; rɪˈprɛsɪv/ *adj* serving or tending to ~: 镇压性的; 抑制的; 压抑的: *~ive legislation.* 镇压性的立法。 *The ~ive measures taken by the police were condemned in Parliament.* 警方所采取的镇压措施在国会中受到抨击。

re·prieve /rɪˈpriːv; rɪˈprɪv/ *vt* [VP6A] postpone or delay punishment (esp the execution of sb condemned to death); (fig) give relief for a short time (from danger, trouble, etc). 暂缓处决 (被判死刑的人); (喻)暂时减轻 (危急、困难等)。□ *n* [C] (order giving authority for) postponement or remission of punishment (esp by death); (fig) delay or respite: 暂缓处决; 暂缓处决的命令; (喻)暂缓; 暂止: *grant (sb) a ~.* 准许(某人)暂缓受处决。

re·pri·mand /ˈreprɪmɑːnd US: -mænd; ˈrɛprəˌmænd/ *vt* [VP6A] rebuke (sb) severely and officially (for a fault, etc). 申斥; 惩戒(某人)。□ *n* [C] official rebuke. (当局的)申斥; 惩戒。

re·print /ˌriːˈprɪnt; rɪˈprɪnt/ *vt* [VP6A] print again; print a new impression of: 重印;再版: *The book is ~ing, being ~ed.* 该书在重印中。□ *n* /ˈriːprɪnt; ˈriˌprɪnt/ [C] new impression of sth printed (usu without alterations). 再版;再版本(通常未加修订)。 ⇨ **edition.**

re·pris·al /rɪˈpraɪzl; rɪˈpraɪzl/ *n* 1 [U] paying back injury with injury: 以牙还牙; 报复: *do sth by way of ~.* 出于报复而做某事。 2 (*pl*) acts of retaliation, esp of one country on another during a war. (复)报复行为为(尤指在战时一国对他国所做者)。

re·proach /rɪˈprəʊtʃ; rɪˈprotʃ/ *vt* [VP6A, 14] **~ *sb* (for/with sth),** find fault with (sb, usu with a feeling of sorrow, or suggesting the need for sorrow): 责备(某人, 通常带着难过的心情, 或含示需要感到难过): *~ sb with extravagance/for being late.* 责备某人浪费(迟到)。 *We have nothing to ~ ourselves with,* have done nothing

we need regret. 我们没有值得自责的事。□ *n* 1 [U] ~ing: 责备: *a term/look of ~.* 责备的话(眼光)。 2[C] instance of ~ing; word, phrase, etc that ~es: 责备之实例; 责备的词句等: *She heaped ~es upon her sister.* 她狠狠地责备她的妹妹。 3 [U] state of disgrace or discredit: 耻辱; 不名誉: *bring ~ upon oneself.* 自取其辱。 *above/beyond ~,* perfect; blameless. 无可訾议的; 无瑕疵的。 4 [C] **~ (to),** sth that brings disgrace or discredit 以于: 带来不光彩的事物: *slums that are a ~ to the city council.* 给市议会带来不光彩的贫民窟。 **~·ful** /-fl; -fl/ *adj* full of ~; expressing ~: 责备的; 表示责的: *a ~ful look.* 责备的眼光。 **~·fully** /-fəlɪ; -fəlɪ/ *adv*

rep·ro·bate /ˈreprəbeɪt; ˈrɛprəˌbet/ *vt* [VP6A] express or feel strong disapproval of. 非难; 责备; 拒绝; 反对。□ *n* depraved person; person with no respect for moral behaviour. 堕落的人; 恶棍; 无赖。 **rep·ro·ba·tion** /ˌreprəˈbeɪʃn; ˌrɛprəˈbeʃən/ *n* [U] .

re·pro·duce /ˌriːprəˈdjuːs US: -ˈduːs; ˌriprəˈdjus/ *vi* 1 [VP6A] cause to be seen, heard, etc again: 使再被见到, 听到等; 使重现; 播放; 放映; 复制: *~ music from magnetic tape.* 播放录音带上的音乐。 *This record/record-player ~s every sound perfectly.* 这唱片(电唱机)完美地放出声音。 *The artist has ~d your features very well in this portrait.* 艺术家在此画像中把你的容貌表现得维妙维肖。 2 [VP6A, 2A] bring forth as offspring; bring about a natural increase: 生殖; 繁殖: *~ one's kind;* 生殖; 生殖; *plants that ~ by spores,* eg ferns. 由芽胞繁殖的植物(如羊齿植物)。 3 [VP6A] grow anew (a part that is lost, etc): 再生(已损失的部分等): *Can lizards ~ their tails?* 蜥蜴的尾巴断了以后能再生吗? *Human beings cannot ~ lost limbs.* 人类的肢体断掉以后不能再生。 **~·r** n one who, that which, ~s. 复制者; 复制器; 有再生能力的动物。 **re·pro·duc·ible** /-əbl; -əbl/ *adj* that can be ~d. 可复制的; 可再生的; 可重现的。 **re·pro·duc·tion** /ˌriːprəˈdʌkʃn; ˌriprəˈdʌkʃən/ *n* [U] process of reproducing; [C] sth ~d; copy of sth, esp a work of art. 复制; 再生; 重现; 生殖; 复制或再生之物; (尤指艺术作品的)复制品。 **re·pro·duc·tive** /ˌriːprəˈdʌktɪv; ˌriprəˈdʌktɪv/ *adj* reproducing; for, relating to, reproduction: 复制的; 再生的; 生殖的; 适于, 有关复制或再生的: *reproductive organs.* 生殖器官。

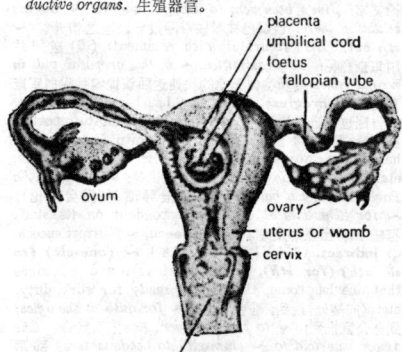

placenta
umbilical cord
foetus
fallopian tube
ovum
ovary
uterus or womb
cervix
vagina or birth canal

the female reproductive organs in early pregnancy

re·proof¹ /rɪˈpruːf; rɪˈpruf/ *n* 1 [U] blame; finding fault: 谴责; 非难: *a glance of ~;* 谴责的一瞥; *conduct deserving of ~.* 该受责备的行为。 2 [C] expression of blame or disapproval: 谴责之词: *administer sharp ~s.* 作严厉的谴责。

re·proof² /ˌriːˈpruːf; ˌriˈpruf/ *vt* [VP6A] make (a coat, etc) waterproof again. 使(外衣等)再能防水。

re·prove /rɪˈpruːv ; rɪˈpruv/ vt [VP6A, 14] ~ sb (for sth), find fault with; say sharp words to: 非难;责骂; 谴责: The priest ~d the people for not attending church services. 牧师责备那些人不上教堂做礼拜. **re·prov·ing·ly** adv

rep·tile /ˈreptaɪl US: -tl; ˈreptl/ n cold-blooded egg-laying animal that creeps or crawls, eg a lizard, tortoise, crocodile, snake. (冷血的卵生)爬行动物; 爬虫(如蜥蜴,龟,鳄鱼,蛇). ⇨ the illus here and at **snake**. 参看 snake 之插图. **rep·til·ian** /repˈtɪlɪən; repˈtɪlɪən/ adj of, or like a ~. 爬虫类的;似爬虫类的.

re·pub·lic /rɪˈpʌblɪk; rɪˈpʌblɪk/ n 1 (country with a) system of government in which the elected representatives of the people are supreme, with an elected head (the President), as eg in the US, France, India. 共和国; 共和政体. (in France) (法国) **the First R~**, 1789-1804; 第一共和国, 1789-1804; **the Second R~**, 1848-1852; 第二共和国, 1848-1852; **the Third R~**, 1871-1940; 第三共和国, 1871-1940; **the Fourth R~**, 1947-1958; 第四共和国, 1947-1958; **the Fifth R~**, from 1958. 第五共和国, 1958-。 2 any society in which the members have equal rights and privileges: (组成分子享有平等权利的)任何社团: the ~ of letters, literary men as a class. 文学界;文坛.

re·pub·li·can /rɪˈpʌblɪkən; rɪˈpʌblɪkən/ adj of, relating to, supporting the principles of, a republic. 共和国的, 共和政体的; 有关共和的; 赞成共和的。□ n 1 person who favours ~ government. 拥护共和政体者. 2 **R~**, member of one of the two main political parties in the US (the other is Democrat). (美国两大政党中之)共和党员(另一为'民主党员'). ~·**ism** /-ɪzəm; -ɪzəm/ n [U] (adherence to) ~ principles. 共和主义; 对共和主义的拥护.

re·pudi·ate /rɪˈpjuːdɪeɪt; rɪˈpjudɪˌet/ vt [VP6A] 1 disown; say that one will have nothing more to do with: 不承认与…有关系; 与…断绝关系: an old friend/a wicked son. 弃绝一位老友(一个败家子). 2 refuse to accept or acknowledge: 拒绝接受或承认; 否认: ~ the authorship of an article, declare that one did not write it. 否认为某篇文章的作者. 3 refuse to pay (an obligation or debt). 拒偿(债务). **re·pudi·ation** /rɪˌpjuːdɪˈeɪʃn; rɪˌpjudɪˈeʃən/ n

re·pug·nant /rɪˈpʌgnənt; rɪˈpʌgnənt/ adj ~ (to), distasteful; causing a feeling of dislike or opposition: 讨厌的; 令人不悦或起反感的: I find his views/proposals ~. 我发觉他的观点(提议)令人起反感. All food was ~ to me during my illness. 生病时所有的食物都使我感到厌恶. **re·pug·nance** /-nəns; -nəns/ n [U] ~ (to), strong dislike or distaste: 嫌弃; 讨厌: a great repugnance to accept charity; 对接受救济的厌恶; the repugnance she has to writing letters. 他对写信的厌恶.

re·pulse /rɪˈpʌls; rɪˈpʌls/ vt [VP6A] 1 repel; drive back (the enemy); resist (an attack) successfully. 驱逐;逐退(敌人);击退(攻击). 2 (not replaceable by repel) refuse to accept (sb's help, friendly offers, etc); discourage (a person) by unfriendly treatment. (不可用 repel 代替)拒绝接受(某人的帮助,友好的建议等);排斥(某人). □ n repulsing or being ~d. 击退;被击退; 拒绝; 排斥. **re·pul·sion** /rɪˈpʌlʃn; rɪˈpʌlʃən/ n [U] 1 feeling of dislike or distaste: 厌恶;嫌恶; feel repulsion for sb. 厌恶某人. 2 (phys) (opp of attraction) tendency of bodies to repel each other. (物理)推斥, 斥力(为 attraction 之反义词).

re·pul·sive /rɪˈpʌlsɪv; rɪˈpʌlsɪv/ adj 1 causing a feeling of disgust: 令人厌恶的;讨厌的: a ~ sight; 使人厌恶的景象: a ~-looking beggar. 样子令人讨厌的乞丐. 2 (phys) repelling; exercising repulsion(2): (物理)拒斥的;推斥的: ~ forces. 斥力;推力. ~·**ly** adv in a ~ manner: 讨厌地;拒斥地: ~ly ugly. 丑得令人厌恶.

repu·table /ˈrepjutəbl; ˈrepjətəbl/ adj respected; of good repute: 受尊敬的;名誉好的: ~ occupations; 高尚的职业; a ~ wine merchant. 名誉好的酒商. **repu·tably** /-əblɪ; -əblɪ/ adv

repu·ta·tion /ˌrepjuˈteɪʃn; ˌrepjəˈteʃən/ n [U, C] the general opinion about the character, qualities, etc of sb or sth: 名声; 名誉: a man of high ~; 名誉很好的人; have a good ~ as a doctor; 是个很有名望的医生; have a ~ for courage; 以勇敢著称; make a ~ for oneself; 为自己博得名声; have the ~ of being a miser. 有守财奴之称. live up to one's ~, live in the way that people expect (because of one's ~). 行为与声誉相符;不负众望.

re·pute /rɪˈpjuːt; rɪˈpjut/ vt [VP25] (usu passive) (通常用被动语态) be ~d as/to be, be generally considered or reported (to be), be thought of as: 被认为;被当作: He is ~ed (to be) very wealthy. 他被认为很富有. He is ~d (as/to be) the best surgeon in Paris. 一般认为他是巴黎最好的外科医生. He is well/ill/highly ~d, thought or spoken of. 他的名誉好(不好, 很好).

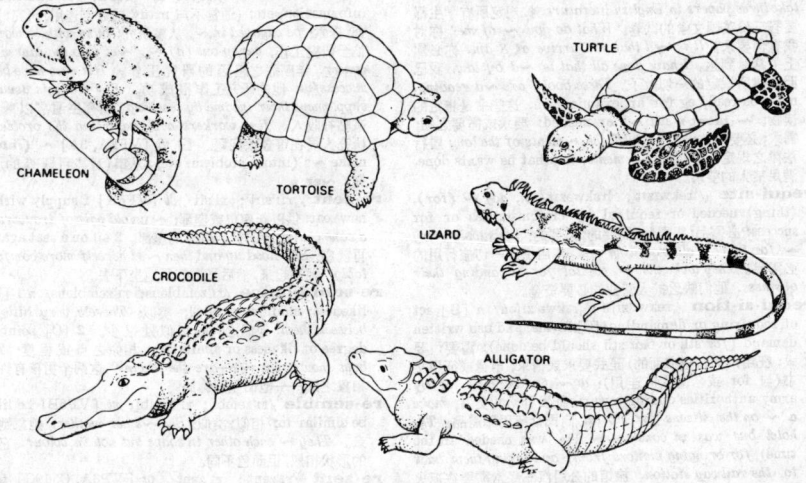

reptiles

~d *attrib adj* generally considered to be (but with some element of doubt): 一般认为的; 号称的(带有若干怀疑的成分): *the ~d father of the child;* 据说是那孩子的父亲的人; *his ~d learning.* 他那被公认的学问。**re·put·ed·ly** *adv* □ *n* [U] **1** reputation (good or bad): (好的或坏的)名声; 名誉: *know a man by ~;* 由某人的名声而知其人; *be held in high ~;* 享有好名声; *be in bad ~ with sb.* 对某人丧失信誉。**2** good reputation: 美名;声望: *wines of ~;* 名酒; *a doctor of ~.* 名医。

re·quest /rɪˈkwest; rɪˋkwɛst/ *n* **1** [U] asking or being asked: 请求; 被求: *We came at your ~/at the ~ of Mr X.* 我们应你(X 先生)的请求而来。*Buses stop here by ~,* if signalled to do so. 有人招呼, 公共汽车才在这里停车。*This is a ~ stop.* 这是个招呼站。*Catalogues of our books will be sent on ~.* 我们的书目函索即寄。**2** [C] expression of desire for sth: 请求;请求书: *repeated ~s for help;* 一再请求帮助; *make a ~ for quiet;* 请求安静; *your ~ that I should lecture on Pakistan.* 你要我以巴基斯坦为题作演讲的要求。**3** [C] thing asked for: 所请求之事物: *You shall have your ~.* 你就会得到你所要的东西。*All my ~s were granted.* 我所请求之事全被允准了。**4** [U] state of being in demand, sought after. 需要。***in ~,*** often asked for. 有必要; 受欢迎。□ *vt* [VP6A, 9, 17] ***~ sth (from/of sb); ~ sb to do sth,*** make a ~: (向某人) 请求某事物; 请求 (某人做某事): *Visitors are ~ed not to touch the exhibits,* as a notice in a museum, etc. 来宾请勿动展览品(如博物馆等中之告示)。*All I ~ of you is that you should be early.* 我对你的唯一请求是要你早点到。*I ~ed him to use/~ed that he (should) use his influence on my behalf.* 我请求他为我施用他的影响力。

requiem /ˈrekwɪəm; ˋrikwɪəm/ *n* [C] (musical setting for a) special mass for the repose of the soul of a dead person. (为死者举行的)追思弥撒;安灵弥撒; 安魂曲; 镇魂曲;奠祭曲。

re·quire /rɪˈkwaɪə(r); rɪˋkwaɪr/ *vt* **1** [VP6A, D, 9] need; depend on for success, fulfilment, etc: 需要; 依靠…而成功、完成等: *We ~ extra help.* 我们需要额外的帮助。*Does this machine ~ much attention?* 这机器需要经常照料吗? *The situation there ~s that I should be present.* 那边的情况需要我到场。**2** [VP6A, 9, 14, 17] ***~ sth (of sb); ~ sb to do sth; ~ that...,*** (often passive) (formal) order; demand; insist upon as a right or by authority: (常用被动语态)(正式用语)命令; 要求;(作为权利或依据权利而)坚持: *Students are ~d to take three papers in English literature.* 按规定所有学生都要答三份英国文学的试卷。*What do you ~ of me?* 你对我有何要求? *It is ~d that you arrive at 8 am.* 你必须上午八时到达。*I have done all that is ~d by law.* 我已照法律所规定的一切做了。*These books are ~d reading,* must be read, eg for an examination. 这些书是指定的读物。**~·ment** *n* sth ~d or needed: 要求或需要之物; 需求;必要条件;规定: *fulfil the ~ments of the law;* 履行法律之规定; *meet sb's ~ments,* do what he wants done. 满足某人的要求。

requi·site /ˈrekwɪzɪt; ˋrɛkwəzɪt/ *n, adj* ***~ (for),*** (thing) needed or required by circumstances or for success: 必需品;需要物;需要的;必要的: *We supply every ~ for travel/all travelling ~s.* 本店供应一切旅行用的必需品。*They lack the ~ capital for expanding their business.* 他们缺乏扩大营业的必要资金。

requi·si·tion /ˌrekwɪˈzɪʃn; ˌrɛkwəˋzɪʃən/ *n* [U] act of requiring or demanding; [C] formal and usu written demand (*for* sth or *that* sth should be done): 需要; 要求; 征用; (通常指书面的) 正式要求或请求; 申请或征用文书(与 for 或名词从句连用): *a ~ for supplies,* eg by army authorities during a war; 征发补给的文书; *make a ~ on the citizens for stores.* 向民众征用军需品。*The hotel bus was in constant ~* (= was needed all the time) *for bringing visitors from, and taking them back to, the railway station.* 旅馆的公用汽车经常需要往返火车站接运旅客。□ *vt* [VP6A, 14] ***~ (for),*** make a ~ for: 要求;征用;征发: *~ food for the troops;* 征发供应部队的食物; *~ sb's services;* 征调某人服务; *~ a town for supplies/lodgings,* eg during a war. 向一城市征用补给品(住处)(例如在战时)。

re·quite /rɪˈkwaɪt; rɪˋkwaɪt/ *vt* [VP6A, 14] ***~ sth/sb (with sth),*** (formal) (正式用语) **1** repay; give in return: 付还;回报; 酬谢: *~ kindness with ingratitude;* 以怨报德; *~ an obligation.* 报恩;还人情债。*Will she ever ~ my love?* 她会回报我对她的爱吗? **2** take vengeance on. 报复;报仇。**re·qui·tal** /-tl; -tl/ *n* [U] repayment: 付还;回报;报仇: *receive food and lodging in requital for/of one's services;* 得到食宿以为服务之报酬; *make full requital.* 给予充分的酬答。

rere·dos /ˈrɪədɒs *US:* ˈrerədɒs; ˋrɪrdɑs/ *n* (*pl* **~es** /-dɒsɪz; -dɑsɪz/) [C] ornamental screen covering the wall at the back of a church altar. (教堂祭坛后部遮覆墙壁的)装饰屏风。

re·run /ˈriːrʌn; riˋrʌn/ *n* (cinema and TV) reshowing of a film or recorded programme. (电影及电视) 重播; 重放。□ *vt* **(-nn-)** show a film, etc again. 重放(影片等)。

re·scind /rɪˈsɪnd; rɪˋsɪnd/ *vt* [VP6A] (legal) repeal, annul, cancel (a law, contract, etc). (法律) 废止; 撤销(法规、合约等)。

re·script /ˈriːskrɪpt; ˋriskrɪpt/ *n* [C] **1** official announcement, esp an edict or decree issued by a ruler or government. 正式公告; (尤指由统治者或政府所颁行的)布告; 敕令; 政令; 法令。**2** decision made by a Pope (esp in reply to a question on matters of law or morality). (教皇对法律或道德问题所作之)敕答;答复书。

res·cue /ˈreskjuː; ˋrɛskju/ *vt* [VP6A, 14] ***~ sb from sth/sb,*** deliver, make safe (from danger, etc); set free: (从危险等中)救出; 解救; 使免于: *~ a child from drowning;* 救出一小孩免于溺毙; *~ a man from captivity;* 营救一人免于被俘: *~ a drunkard,* persuade him to give up drinking; 劝服一醉汉不再酗酒; *~ sb's name from oblivion,* prevent his name from being quite forgotten. 使某人的名声不致湮没。□ *n* [U] rescuing or being ~d. 救出; 解救。***come/go to the ~/to sb's ~,*** help him; [C] instance of this: 援救(救助某人); 救出或解救的实例: *three ~s from drowning in one afternoon.* 在一个下午三人获救而免于溺毙。**res·cuer** *n*

re·search /rɪˈsɜːtʃ *US:* ˈriːsɜːtʃ; ˋrisɜtʃ/ *n* [U, C] (not usu with *many* or numerals) investigation undertaken in order to discover new facts, get additional information, etc: (通常不与 many 或数字连用)研究; 调查;探索: *be engaged in ~;* 从事研究; *busy with ~ work;* 忙于研究工作; *carry out (a) ~/~es into the causes of cancer.* 作癌症之起因的研究工作。*His ~es have been successful.* 他的研究工作很成功。*R~ students usually supplement their income by teaching.* 研究生通常以兼课来贴补收入。*R~ workers are examining the problem.* 研究人员在审查该问题。□ *vi* [VP2A, 3A] ***~ (into),*** make ~s (into a problem, etc). 从事(对某问题等的)研究。**~er** *n*

re·seat /ˌriːˈsiːt; riˋsit/ *vt* [VP6A] **1** supply with a new seat: 供以新座位或座部: *~ an old pair of trousers/a cane chair.* 换旧裤(藤椅)的座部。**2** sit on a seat again: 再就座: *She stood up and then ~ed herself more comfortably.* 她站起来,然后又更舒服地坐下去。

re·sem·blance /rɪˈzembləns; rɪˋzɛmbləns/ *n* **1** [U] likeness; similarity: 相似; 类似: *There's very little ~ between them.* 他们之间的相似处很少。**2** [C] point or degree of likeness or similarity: 相似之点或程度: *The boys show great ~s—are they twins?* 这两个男孩有许多相象之处——他们是双胞胎吗?

re·semble /rɪˈzembl; rɪˋzɛmbl̩/ *vt* [VP6B] be like; be similar to: 相似;类似: *She ~s her mother.* 她象她母亲。*They ~ each other in shape but not in colour.* 它们的形状相似, 但颜色不同。

re·sent /rɪˈzent; rɪˋzɛnt/ *vt* [VP6A, C, 19C] feel bitter, indignant or angry at: 对…感觉不愉快;愤恨;怨

恨: ~ *criticism.* 怨恨批评。*Does he* ~ *my being here?* 我在此地他感觉不愉快吗? ~**·ful** /-fl; -fl/ *adj* feeling or showing ~ment; inclined to ~. 愤恨的; 怨恨的; 易起怨恨的。 ~**·fully** /-fəlɪ; -fəlɪ/ *adv* ~**·ment** *n* [U] feeling that one has when insulted, ignored, injured, etc: 愤恨; 怨恨: *bear/feel no* ~*ment against anyone;* 不对任何人抱怨恨; *walk away in* ~*ment.* 愤恨地走开。

res·er·va·tion /ˌrezəˈveɪʃn; ˌrɛzəˈveʃən/ *n* 1 [U] keeping or holding back; failure or refusal to express sth that is in one's mind; [C] that which is kept or held back: 隐藏; 保留; 隐藏或保留之事物: *accept sth without* ~, wholeheartedly, completely; 无保留地接受某事物; *accept a plan with* ~s, with limiting conditions; 有条件地接受一计划; *the central* ~ *of a motorway,* land dividing the two carriageways. 高速公路双向车道间的分隔地带。 2 [C] (US) area of land reserved for a special purpose. (美) 留待专用之土地; 保留地。 **reserve**[1](5). 3 [C] (esp US) travel arrangement to keep sth for sb, eg a seat in a train or aircraft, a passage on a ship, a room in a hotel: (美国) 预定; 保留 (如火车或班机之座位、轮船之舱位、旅馆之房间): *My travel agents have made all the* ~*s for my journey.* 我的旅行经纪人已为我把行程中的一切安排好了。 ⇨**book**[2](2), for GB usages. 4 R~ **of the Sacrament,** practice of keeping back part of the bread used in the Eucharist for later use, eg at the home of a sick person. 在圣餐礼中保留部分面包以备在病人家中等食用的习俗。

re·serve[1] /rɪˈzɜːv; rɪˈzɚv/ *n* 1 [C] sth that is being or has been stored for later use: 贮以待用之物: *a* ~ *of food;* 存粮; *the bank's* ~s, of money; 银行的储备金; *the company's* ~s, its undivided profits; 商行之公积金 (未分派之利润); the 'gold ~, ie to cover the issue of notes; (银行发行钞票之) 黄金准备; (attrib) (用作定语) *a'* ~ *fund;* 准备金; 预备金; *have* ~s ~ *strength.* 他所储存的气力。 2 (mil) military forces kept back for use when needed. (军) 预备队; 后备军。 **the R~,** forces outside the regular Navy, Army and Air Force, liable to be called out if needed. (正规之海陆空军以外的) 后备海军、陆军及空军; 预备役。 4 [U] in ~, kept back unused, but available if needed: 储藏; 保留: *have/hold a little money in* ~. 储存一些钱。 5 [C] place or area reserved for some special use or purpose: 留待专用的地方或区域: *a 'game* ~, eg in Africa, for the preservation of wild animals; 猎物保留地;禁猎区 (如非洲之野生动物保护区); *a 'forest* ~. 森林保留地; 保留林。 6 [C, U] (instance of) limitation or restriction; condition that limits or restricts: 限制; 节制; 限制或节制的实例、状况: *We accept your statement without* ~, believe it completely. 我们完全相信你的陈述。 *He has put a* ~ *price on his house,* has fixed a price less than which will not be accepted. 他已替他的房子定下最低售价。 *He has placed a* ~ *on the painting,* ie a ~ price. 他已定下那张画的最低售价。 7 [U] self-control in speech and behaviour; keeping silent or saying little; not showing one's feelings: 言行之自制; 缄默; 含蓄; 冷淡: ~ *of manner;* 态度之冷淡; *break through sb's* ~, get him to talk and be sociable. 打破某人之缄默(使之说话而随和)。 **re·serv·ist** /rɪˈzɜːvɪst; rɪˈzɚvɪst/ soldier or sailor belonging to the Army or Navy R~. (后备陆海军之) 后备兵; 预备人员。 ⇨ above. 参看上列第 3 义。

re·serve[2] /rɪˈzɜːv; rɪˈzɚv/ *vt* [VP6A, 14] 1 store, keep back, for a later occasion: 贮备; 保留; 延迟: *R~ your strength for the climb.* 留点力气爬山吧。 *The judge* ~*d his judgement,* deferred announcing it until a future time. 法官延期宣判。 2 keep for the special use of, or for a special purpose: 留作专用: *The first three rows of the hall are* ~*d for special guests.* 大厅的前三排留给特别来宾。 3 secure possession of, or the right to use, eg by advance payment: 预定(例如以先付钱之方式): ~ *rooms at a hotel.* 预定旅馆的房间。 *All seats* ~*d,* ie the seats (in a theatre, concert hall, etc) can be obtained only by booking them in advance. 所有座位必须预定。

All rights ~*d,* (legal) secured or kept (for the owners of property, etc). (法律) 拥有全部权利; 保障所有权利。 4 set apart, destine: 拨出; 留给: *A great future is* ~*d for you.* 光明的前程正等待着你。 ~**d** *adj* (of a person, his character) slow to reveal feelings or opinions; uncommunicative: (指人、其性格) 有所保留的; 含蓄的; 缄默的: *He is too* ~*d to be popular.* 他太沉默寡言, 不会受人欢迎。 ~**d·ly** /rɪˈzɜːvɪdlɪ; rɪˈzɚvɪdlɪ/ *adv*

res·er·voir /ˈrezəvwɑː(r); ˈrɛzɚˌvwɔr/ *n* [C] 1 place (often an artificial lake) where water is stored, eg for supplying a town; anything for holding a liquid: 贮水池; 水库(常为人工的, 如用于供应一城市); 任何贮存液体的东西: *the* ~ *of a fountain-pen/an oil lamp.* 钢笔的蓄水管(油灯的盛油壶)。 2 (fig) supply (of facts, knowledge, etc). (喻) (事实、知识等的) 贮积。

re·set /ˌriːˈset; riˈsɛt/ *vt* (*pt, pp* **reset; -tt-**) [VP6A] 1 sharpen again: 再磨快: ~ *a saw.* 再把锯子磨快。 2 place in position again: 重新放置; 重嵌: ~ *a diamond in a ring,* 重镶钻石于戒指中; ~ *a broken bone.* 重接断骨。 3 (printing) set the type again. (印刷) 重新排版; 重排。 ⇨ **set**[2](9).

re·settle /ˌriːˈsetl; riˈsɛtl/ *vt, vi* [VP6A, 2A] (esp of refugees) (help to) settle again in a new country: (尤指难民) 在新国家再定居下来: ~ *war refugees in Canada.* 将战时的难民安顿在加拿大。 ~**·ment** *n*

re·shuffle /ˌriːˈʃʌfl; riˈʃʌfl/ *vt* [VP6A] shuffle again: 重新洗(牌); 转变; 改组: ~ *the cards.* 重洗纸牌。 □ *n* shuffling again: 重新洗牌; 转变; 改组: *a Cabinet* ~, a redistribution of Cabinet posts among the same persons. 内阁改组。

re·side /rɪˈzaɪd; rɪˈzaɪd/ *vi* 1 [VP2C, 3A] ~ *(in/ at),* live (the more usu word) where one's home is: 住; 居留(~ *abroad;* 居于国外; ~ *at 10 Railway Terrace.* 住在铁路街10号。 2 [VP3A] ~ *in,* (of power, rights, etc) be the property of, be present in: (指权力、权利等) 为…所有; 存在于: *The supreme authority* ~*s in the President.* 最高权力掌握于总统手中。

resi·dence /ˈrezɪdəns; ˈrɛzədəns/ *n* 1 [U] residing; 住; 居留: *take up one's* ~ *in a new house,* go and live in it. 迁入新居。 **in** ~, **(a)** (of an official, etc) living in the house officially provided for him. (指官员等) 住公家宿舍的; 驻于任所的。 **(b)** (of students, etc) residing in a college, etc: (指大学等的学生) 住校的: *The students are not yet in* ~. 学生尚未住校。 2 place where one resides; house (esp a large or dignified one): 住处; 住宅(尤指大的或堂皇的): (as used by house-agents) (房屋经纪人用语) *town and country* ~s; 城市及乡村住宅; *this desirable family* ~ *for sale.* 吉屋出售。

resi·dency /ˈrezɪdənsɪ; ˈrɛzədənsɪ/ *n* [C] (*pl* **-cies**) official residence of a Resident(2). 驻扎官的官邸。

resi·dent /ˈrezɪdənt; ˈrɛzədənt/ *adj* residing: 居住的; 居留的: *the* ~ *population of the town* (contrasted with visitors, tourists, etc); 该城的居民人口(与 visitor, tourist 等相对); *a* ~ *tutor,* one who lives in the household as a member of the family; 住家家庭教师; *a* ~ *physician,* one who lives in the hospital, etc where he works. 住院医师。 □ *n* 1 person who resides in a place (contrasted with a visitor). 居民(与 visitor 相对)。 2 R~, official sent to another country to act as adviser to the administration, etc. (派驻外国充当行政顾问之) 驻扎官。

resi·den·tial /ˌrezɪˈdenʃl; ˌrɛzəˈdenʃəl/ *adj* 1 of residence; 居住的; 居留的: *the* ~ *qualifications for voters,* ie requiring that they should reside in the constituency. 选民之居住资格(即选民必须居住于该选区之规定)。 2 of, with, private houses: 住宅的; 私宅的; 有住宅的: *a* ~ *suburb;* 有住宅的郊区; ~ *parts of the town* (contrasted with business or industrial parts). 该城之住宅区(与商业区或工业区相对)。

re·sid·ual /rɪˈzɪdjʊəl US: -dʒu-; rɪˈzɪdʒʊəl/ *adj* remaining; of, forming, a residue. 剩余的; 残余的; 构成剩余物的。

re·sidu·ary /rɪˈzɪdjuərɪ US: -dʒuerɪ; rɪˈzɪdʒʊˌsrɪ/ *adj* of a residue; (legal) relating to the residue of an estate: 剩余的; 残余的; (法律)剩余财产的; 余产的: *the ~ legatee*, the person to whom the residue of an estate is left. 余产受赠者; 剩余遗产继承人.

resi·due /ˈrezɪdju: US: -du:; ˈrɛzɪdju/ *n* [C] that which remains after a part is taken or used; (legal) that part of an estate which is left after all particular bequests, debts, etc have been settled. 剩余物; 残余; (法律)剩余财产; 余产.

re·sign /rɪˈzaɪn; rɪˈzaɪn/ *vt, vi* 1 [VP6A, 2A, 3A] ~ (from), give up (a post, claim, etc): 辞(职); 放弃(要求等): ~ *one's job*; 辞去工作; ~ *one's position as secretary of the club*; 辞去俱乐部秘书之职位; ~ *from the Cabinet*. 辞去阁员之职; *The Minister of Education has ~ed*. 教育部长已辞职. 2 [VP14] ~ *sb/oneself to sb/sth*, hand over: 委托; 交给: *I ~ my children to your care/myself to your guidance*. 我把我的孩子委托你照顾(我听从你的指导). 3 [VP14] ~ *oneself to sth/be ~ed to sth*, be ready to accept or endure uncomplainingly: 听任; 顺从: *be ~ed to one's fate*. 听天由命. *We must ~ ourselves to leaving the country*. 我们只好离开国家了. ~**ed** *adj* having or showing patient acceptance of sth: 听任的; 顺从的: *with a ~ed look*. 带着顺从的脸色. ~·**ed·ly** /-ɪdlɪ, -ɪdlɪ/ *adv* in a ~ed manner. 听任地; 顺从地.

res·ig·na·tion /ˌrezɪgˈneɪʃn; ˌrɛzɪgˈneʃən/ *n* 1 [U] resigning(1); [C] instance of this; letter (to one's employers, superior, etc) stating this: 辞职; 放弃; 辞职或放弃的实例; (给雇主, 上级等的)辞呈: *offer/send in/hand in one's ~*. 提出(递)辞呈. 2 [U] state of being resigned to conditions, etc; uncomplaining acceptance or endurance: 听任; 顺从: *accept failure with ~*. 顺从地接受失败.

re·sil·ience /rɪˈzɪlɪəns; rɪˈzɪlɪəns/, **re·sil·iency** /-nsɪ/ *nn* [U] quality or property of quickly recovering the original shape or condition after being pulled, pressed, crushed, etc: 弹性(能); 弹力; 回弹; 回复: *the ~ of rubber*; 橡皮的弹性; (fig) power of recuperating quickly; buoyancy: (喻)迅速恢复的力量; 复元力; 愉快: *the ~ of the human body*. 人体的复元力. **re·sil·ient** /-nt ; -nt/ *adj* having or showing ~; (of persons) buoyant in disposition. 有或显出弹性的; (指人)性情开朗的.

resin /ˈrezɪn US: ˈrezn; ˈrɛzɪn/ *n* [C, U] sticky substance that flows out from most plants when cut, or injured, esp from fir and pine trees, hardening in air, used in making varnish, lacquer, etc; kind of similar substance (plastics) made chemically, widely used in industry. 树脂(为指枞脂与松香); 合成树脂; 塑胶. ⇨ **rosin**. ~·**ated** /ˈrezɪnetɪd US: -zən-; ˈrɛzɪnˌetɪd/ *adj* flavoured, permeated, with ~. 加树脂香料的; 掺入树脂的. ~·**ous** /ˈrezɪnəs US: ˈrezənəs ; ˈrɛzɪnəs/ *adj* of or like ~. 树脂的; 似树脂的.

re·sist /rɪˈzɪst; rɪˈzɪst/ *vt, vi* [VP6A, C, 2A] 1 oppose; use force against in order to prevent the advance of: 抵抗; 对抗: 用武力阻止…之前进: ~ *the enemy/an attack/authority/the police*. 抵抗敌人(攻击, 权力, 警察). *He could ~ no longer*. 他再也无法抗拒了. 2 be undamaged or unaffected by: 未受…之损害或影响; 耐得住: *a kind of glass dish that ~s heat, that does not break or crack in a hot oven*. 一种耐热的玻璃盘. 3 try not to yield to; keep oneself back from: 不屈服于; 忍住: ~ *temptation*. 抗拒诱惑. *She can't ~ chocolates*. 她一看见巧克力糖就忍不住要吃. *She couldn't ~ making jokes about his baldness*. 她忍不住拿他的秃头开玩笑. ~·**er** *n* person who ~s: 抵抗者; 不屈服者: *passive ~ers*. 消极抵抗者. ~·**less** *adj* that cannot be ~ed; inevitable: 不可抵抗的; 不可避免的: *a ~less impulse*. 不可抗拒的冲动.

re·sis·tance /rɪˈzɪstəns; rɪˈzɪstəns/ *n* ~ (to), 1 [U] (power of) resisting: 抵抗; 抵抗力: *break down the*

enemy's ~; 粉碎敌人的抵抗; *make/offer no/not much ~ to the enemy's advance*; 对于敌人的前进未作(未作多少)抵抗(drug ~; 抗药性; passive ~, ⇨ **passive**. 消极抵抗). '~ **movement**, (in an enemy-occupied country) effort made by groups of unconquered people to resist the invaders. 在敌人占领的国家中(的)抵抗运动, 反抗侵略者运动. 2 [U] opposing force: 阻力: *An aircraft has to overcome the ~ of the air*. 飞机须克服空气的阻力. *line of least ~*, direction in which a force meets least opposition; (fig) easiest way or method. 阻力最小的方向; 最弱的抵抗力; (喻)最容易的方法. 3 [C, U] antagonism; desire to oppose: 敌对; 反对; 反对之意志: *'sales/con'sumer ~*, unwillingness of the public to buy goods offered for sale. 抵制购买. *A good advertisement should not arouse ~ in the public*. 好的广告应该不会招致公众的反感.

re·sis·tant /rɪˈzɪstənt; rɪˈzɪstənt/ *adj* ~ (to), offering resistance. 抵抗的; 抗拒的: *insects that have become ~ to DDT*; 对 DDT 已有抵抗力的昆虫; ~ *strains of mosquitoes*. 有抵抗力之若干种蚊虫.

re·sis·tor /rɪˈzɪstə(r); rɪˈzɪstɚ/ *n* device to provide resistance in an electric circuit. 电阻器.

re·sole /ˌriːˈsəʊl; riˈsol/ *vt* [VP6A] put a new sole on (a shoe). 装新鞋底于(鞋).

res·ol·ute /ˈrezəluːt; ˈrɛzəˌlut/ *adj* fixed in determination or purpose; firm: 坚决的; 刚毅的: *a ~ man*; 有决心的人; ~ *for peace*. 贯彻和平的. ~·**ly** *adv* ~·**ness** *n*

res·ol·ution /ˌrezəˈluːʃn; ˌrɛzəˈluʃən/ *n* 1 [U] quality of being resolute; fixity or boldness of determination: 坚决; 刚毅: *show great/not much ~*; 表现得很(不够)果断; *a man who lacks ~*. 缺乏毅力的人. 2 [C] sth that is resolved(1); formal expression of opinion by a legislative body or a public meeting; proposal for this: 已决定之事物; 决议; 提案: *pass/carry/adopt/reject a ~ (for/against/in favour of/that...)*. (获得通过、采纳、驳回)(有关、反对、赞成、某…的)提案. ⇨ **resolve**; sth one makes up one's mind to do: 决心; 决心要做之事: *make good ~s*; 下定决心做好事; *her ~ never to marry*; 她永远不嫁的决心; *a New Year ~* (sth one resolves to do in a new year, eg to give up smoking). 在新年下决心要做的事(例如戒烟). 4 [U] resolving, solution of a doubt, question, discord, etc). (疑惑、问题、不和等的)解决. ⇨ **resolve(3)**. 5 process of separating into constituents: 分解: the ~ of white light into the colours of the spectrum. 将白色的光分解成光谱的各种颜色.

re·solve /rɪˈzɒlv; rɪˈzɑlv/ *vt, vi* [VP7A, 9, 3A] ~ *to do sth*; ~ *that...*; ~ *on/upon (doing) sth*, decide; determine: 决定; 决心: *He ~d that nothing should hold him back/~d to be held back by nothing*. 他决心不为任何阻碍所挫.*He ~d on making an early start*. 他决定早日着手. *He ~d to succeed*. 他决定要成功. 2 [VP9] (of a committee, public meeting, legislative body) pass by formal vote the decision *(that)*: (指委员会、集会、议会)议决(与 that 连用): *The House of Commons ~d that...*. 下议院决议…. *R~d, that this meeting is in favour of ~/opposed to ~/views with alarm, etc*. 兹决议, 本会赞成…(反对…、看到…极感惊等). 3 [VP6A] put an end to (doubts, difficulties, etc) by supplying an answer. 解决(疑问、困难等). 4 [VP6A, 14] ~ *sth (into sth)*, break up, separate (into parts); convert; be converted: 分析; 分解(为部分); 转变; 化成: ~ *a problem into its elements*. 分析一个问题之诸因素. *The House of Commons ~d itself into a committee*. 下议院改组为一全院委员会. *A powerful telescope can ~ a nebula into stars*. 一架高性能的望远镜能从星云中分辨出星球来. □ *n* 1 [C] sth that has been determined on; mental resolution(3): 已决定的事物; 决心: *make a ~ to do sth*; 决心做某事; *keep one's ~*. 保持决心, 不改变决心. 2 (liter) resolution(1): (文)坚决; 刚毅: *deeds of high ~*. 极为坚决的行为. **re·solv·able** /-əbl/

-əbl/ *adj* that may be ~d. 可决定的; 可议决的; 可分解的; 可溶解的; 可解决的; 可改变的。

res·on·ant /'rezənənt; 'rɛzənənt/ *adj* **1** (of sound) resounding; continuing to resound: (指声音)反响的; 共鸣的: ~ *notes*; 反响的音调; *a deep,* ~ *voice.* 深沉而宏亮的声音。 **2** (of rooms, etc) tending to prolong sounds by vibration: (指房间等)起共鸣的: ~ *walls which echo and re-echo sound*; 起共鸣的墙壁; *a* ~ *hall.* 起共鸣的大厅。 **3** (of places) resounding: (指地方)回响的; 共鸣的: *Alpine valleys* ~ *with the sound of church bells.* 回响着教堂钟声的阿尔卑斯山谷。 **res·on·ance** /-əns; -əns/ *n* [U] quality of being ~. 回响; 回响; 共鸣; 共振。 **res·on·ate** /'rezəneɪt; 'rɛzə,net/ *vt, vi* produce or show resonance. 造成或产生共鸣; 反响。 **res·ona·tor** /-tə(r); -tɚ/ *n* appliance or system for increasing sound by resonance. 共鸣器; 共振器。

re·sort /rɪ'zɔːt; rɪ'zɔrt/ *vi* [VP3A] ~ *to,* **1** make use of for help or to gain one's purpose, etc: 凭借; 求助; 依赖; 诉诸: *If other means fail, we shall* ~ *to force.* 如果其他手段均失败, 我们将诉诸武力。 *I'm sorry you have*~*ed to deception.* 我很遗憾你竟会用欺骗手段。 **2** frequently visit: 常去: *The police watched the cafés where the wanted man was known to* ~. 警察监视着那些通缉犯常去的各咖啡馆。 □ *n* **1** [U] recourse: ~ing(1): 凭借: *Can we do it without* ~ *to compulsion/force?* 我们能够不靠强制(武力)做那件事吗? *in the last* ~; *as a last* ~, when all else has 'failed, as a last means of finding help or relief. (一切均失败后)作为最后的凭借; 作为最后的依靠。 **2** *sb or sth that is* ~*ed*(1) *to:* 所凭借的人或物: *An old taxi was the only* ~ *left.* 一部旧计程车是唯一留下的可资利用之物。 **3** [C] place ~*ed to:* 常去之处: *'seaside/ 'summer/ 'health* ~*s.* 海滨(避暑、休养)胜地。

re·sound /rɪ'zaʊnd; rɪ'zaʊnd/ *vi, vt* [VP2A, 3A] ~ *(with),* (of a voice, instrument, sound) echo and re-echo; fill a place with sound; send back sound; (of a place) ring or echo: (指人声、乐器、声音)反响; 回荡; 鸣响; 使一地方充满声音; 使声(地地方)回响: *The organ* ~*ed.* 风琴的声音回荡着。 *The hall* ~*ed with cries of dissent.* 大厅里充满反对的叫声。 **2** [VP2C] (fig, of fame, an event) be much talked of; spread far and wide: (喻, 指名誉、事件)被称颂; 哀传; 驰名: *His success* ~*ed through all Asia.* 他的成功传遍整个亚洲。 *The film was a* ~*ing success.* 那影片是驰名的成功之片。 ~·**ing·ly** *adv*

re·source /rɪ'sɔːs US: 'riːsɔːrs; rɪ'sɔrs/ *n* **1** (*pl*) wealth, supplies of goods, raw materials, etc which a person, country, etc has or can use: (复)资源; 富源: *Our* ~*s in men and ammunition were inadequate for the defence of the town.* 我们在人力和弹药方面的来源都不够保卫这座城市。 *We must exploit the natural* ~*s of our country,* its mineral wealth, potential water, power, the productivity of the soil, etc. 我们必须开发本国的天然资源。 *I am at the end of my* ~*s,* have nothing left to use. 我已到了山穷水尽(罗掘俱穷)的地步。 *We must make the most of our* ~*s,* use what we have to the best advantage. 我们必须善加利用我们的富源。 **2** [C] sth which helps in doing sth, that can be turned to for support, help, consolation: 有助于做某事的办法; 给予支持、帮助、安慰的凭借: *He has no inner* ~ *of character/no inner* ~*s to fall back on.* 他没有内在的精神凭借。 *Leave him to his own* ~, Leave him to amuse himself, find his own way of passing the time. 让他独自找消遣打发时间吧! **3** [U] skill in finding ~*s*(2); quick wit: 应变的能力; 机智: *a man of* ~. 有机智的人。 ~·**ful** /-fl; -fəl/ *adj* good or quick at finding ~*s* (2). 善于随机应变的; 机智的。 ~·**fully** /-fəlɪ; -fəlɪ/ *adv*.

re·spect[1] /rɪ'spekt; rɪ'spɛkt/ *n* **1** [U] ~ *(for),* honour; high opinion or regard; esteem for a person or quality: 尊敬; 敬重; 尊重: *The prime minister is held in the greatest* ~. 首相备受拥戴。 *Children should show* ~ *for their teachers.* 学童对老师应表示尊敬。 *He has no* ~ *for his promises,* does not think it necessary to keep them. 他不重视他的诺言。 **2** [U] ~ *(for),* consideration; attention: 考虑; 关心: *We must have* ~ *for the needs of the general reader,* think about his requirements or preferences. 我们须考虑到一般读者之需要。 *pay* ~ *to,* (a) consider. 考虑。 (b) honour. 尊敬。 ~ *for persons,* unfair discrimination, on the basis of wealth, social position, etc. (基于财富、社会地位等而产生之)歧视。 **3** [U] reference; relation. 关系; 有关。 *with* ~ *to,* concerning. 关于。 *without* ~ *to,* paying no attention to, leaving out of the question. 不管; 不考虑。 **4** [C] detail; particular aspect. 细节; 方面。 *in* ~ *of,* as regards. 关于; 方面。 *Your essay is admirable in* ~ *of style but unsatisfactory in other* ~*s.* 你的文章在文体方面非常好, 但在其他方面不够好。 *in some/ any/ no, etc* ~*s,* with regard to some aspect(s), detail(s): 在有些方面(在任何方面; 绝不等): *They resemble one another in some/all/no/a few* ~*s.* 他们在某些(在所有、没有、有些)方面彼此相象。 **5** (*pl*) regards; polite greetings: (复)敬意; 问候: *Give him my* ~*s.* 请代我向他致意。 *My father sends you his* ~*s.* 家父向你候你。 *pay one's* ~*s to sb,* visit, etc sb as a sign of ~ for him. 拜访某人以示敬意。

re·spect[2] /rɪ'spekt; rɪ'spɛkt/ *vt* [VP6A] have ~ for; treat with consideration: 尊敬; 敬重; 尊重: *He is* ~*ed by everyone.* 他受到每个人的尊敬。 *We must* ~ *his wishes.* 我们必须尊重他的意愿。 *I* ~ *your opinions.* 我尊重你的意见。 *I wish people would* ~ *my (desire for) privacy.* 我希望人们尊重我的私生活(保有私生活的意愿)。 *Do you* ~ *the laws of your country?* 你们尊重贵国的法律吗? ~ *oneself,* have proper ~ for one's own character and conduct: 自重; 尊重自己: *If you don't* ~ *yourself, how can you expect others to* ~ *you?* 如果你不尊重自己, 怎能期望别人尊重你? ~*er n* (only in) (仅用在) *no* ~*er of persons,* person or thing paying little no attention to wealth, social rank, etc: 不分财富、社会地位等的人或事物: 一视同仁者: *Death is no* ~*er of persons.* 死亡是不分贫富贵贱的。 ~·**ing** *prep* relating to; concerned with: 关于; 说到: *legislation* ~*ing property.* 关于财产的立法。

re·spect·able /rɪ'spektəbl; rɪ'spɛktəbl/ *adj* **1** (of persons) of good character and good social position; having the qualities associated with such social position; (of clothes, appearance, behaviour, etc) suitable for such persons: (指人)品格高尚而有社会地位的; 品行端正的; 体面的: (指衣服、外表、行为等)适于高尚人士的; 文雅的; 体面的: *Are these clothes* ~ *enough for Mrs Whitehouse's party?* 穿这种衣服参加怀特豪斯太太家的宴会够体面吗? *It is not considered* ~ *in this country to spit in public.* 当众吐痰在这个国家被认为是不雅的。 **2** (ironic use) (of behaviour, appearances, etc) conventional; likely to satisfy conventional people: (反语用法)(指举止、外表等)合乎习俗的; 保守的; 拘泥形式的; 可能使保守人士感到满意的: *Need we worry quite so much about being* ~? 我们需要如此拘泥形式吗? **3** of some size, merit, importance, etc; deserving respect: 相当大的; 相当优秀的; 相当重要的; 值得尊敬的: *do sth from* ~ *motives.* 出于值得尊敬的动机做某事。 *He has quite* ~ *talents.* 他很有才干。 *There was a* ~ *attendance at the meeting this morning.* 今天上午去开会的人相当多。 *He earns a* ~ *income.* 他的收入颇可观。 **re·spect·ably** /-əblɪ; -əblɪ/ *adv in a* ~ *manner:* 可尊重地; 端庄地; 适当地; 体面地: *Go and get respectably dressed.* 去好好地打扮一下。 **re·spect·abil·ity** /rɪˌspektə'bɪlətɪ; rɪ,spɛktə'bɪlətɪ/ *n* [U] quality of being socially ~ (1, 2). 品格高尚, 有社会地位; 体面。

re·spect·ful /rɪ'spektfl; rɪ'spɛktfəl/ *adj* ~ *(to),* showing respect: 表示尊敬的; 有礼貌的: *They stood at a* ~ *distance from the President.* 他们有礼貌地离开总统一些距离站着。 ~·**ly** /-flɪ; -fəlɪ/ *adv*

re·spect·ive /rɪ'spektɪv; rɪ'spɛktɪv/ *adj* for, belonging to, each of those in question: 个别的; 各个的: *The three men were given work according to their* ~

abilities. 那三人各按其才能被分派了工作。*The party ended and we all went off to our ~ rooms, each of us went to his or her own room*. 聚会结束了，我们各自回到自己的房间。**~·ly** *adv* separately or in turn, and in the order mentioned: 分别地；各自地：*Training colleges for miners and fishermen are to be built at Leeds and Hull ~ly*, ie for miners at Leeds and for fishermen at Hull. 矿工训练学院和渔夫训练学院将分别设在里兹和赫尔。

res·pir·ation /ˌrespəˈreɪʃn ; ˌrɛspəˈreʃən/ *n* [U] breathing; [C] single act of breathing, ie breathing in and breathing out. 呼吸；一次呼吸。

res·pir·ator /ˈrespəreɪtə(r) ; ˈrɛspəˌretə/ *n* [C] apparatus for breathing through, eg by aviators at high altitudes to warm the air inhaled, by firemen, to filter the air of smoke and fumes. 呼吸保护器；防毒罩；呼吸器 (如飞行员在高空用以提高所吸入空气之温度者，救火员用以过滤空气之烟气者)。

re·spire /rɪˈspaɪə(r) ; rɪˈspaɪr/ *vi* [VP2A] (formal) breathe; breathe in and out. (正式用语)呼吸；吸入和呼出。**re·spir·atory** /rɪˈspaɪərətrɪ US: ˈrespɪrətɔːrɪ ; rɪˈspaɪrəˌtɔrɪ/ *adj* of breathing: 呼吸的：*the respiratory organs / system*; 呼吸器官 (系统)；*respiratory diseases*, eg bronchitis, asthma. 呼吸器官疾病(如支气管炎、哮喘)。

res·pite /ˈrespaɪt US: ˈrespɪt ; ˈrɛspɪt/ *n* 1 [C, U] ~ *(from)*, time of relief or rest (from toil, suffering, anything unpleasant): 暂止；休息(与 from 连用，后接辛苦、痛苦、任何不愉快之事物)：*work without (a) ~*. 不断地工作。**2** [C] postponement or delay permitted in the suffering of a penalty or the discharge of an obligation; reprieve. (刑罚或义务之)展延；暂缓；暂缓行刑。□ *vt* [VP6A] give a ~ to: 给予展延；缓期处决：~ *a murderer*. 暂缓处决一杀人犯。

re·splen·dent /rɪˈsplendənt ; rɪˈsplɛndənt/ *adj* very bright; splendid: 灿烂的；辉煌的：~ *in coronation robes*. 穿着灿丽夺目的加冕礼服。**~·ly** *adv* **re·splen·dence** /-əns; -əns/, **re·splen·dency** /-ənsɪ; -ənsɪ/ *nn* [U].

re·spond /rɪˈspɒnd ; rɪˈspɑnd/ *vi* **1** [VP2A, 3A, B] ~ *(to)*, (of people at a church service) make the usual answers or responses to the priest. (指做礼拜的人) 对牧师例行行应答。**2** [VP2C] act in answer to, or because of, the action of another: 回报：*When Jack insulted Jill, she ~ed with a kick*. 当杰克侮辱吉尔时，她踢他一脚以为回报。**3** [VP3A] ~ *to*, react to; be affected by: 有反应；有效果；有影响：~ *to kindness*. 对好意有反应。*The illness quickly ~ed to treatment*. 病经过治疗后很快就有起色。*The plane ~s well to the controls*. 这架飞机对一切操纵反应良好。

re·spon·dent /rɪˈspɒndənt ; rɪˈspɑndənt/ *n* (legal) defendant (esp in a divorce case). (法律)被告(尤指离婚案件中者)。

re·sponse /rɪˈspɒns ; rɪˈspɑns/ *n* **1** [C] answer: 回答：*My letter of inquiry brought no ~*. 我的询问信始终未得回音。*She made no ~*. 她没有回答。*In ~ to your inquiry...*. 谨复阁下询问…。**2** [C] (in a church service) part of the liturgy said or sung by the congregation alternately with the priest. (礼拜仪式中)会众同牧师交互应答或吟唱之祈祷文。**3** [C, U] reaction: 反应：*My appeal to her pity met with no / little / some ~*. 我向她求情，她没有(很少，有些)反应。

re·spon·si·bil·ity /rɪˌspɒnsəˈbɪlətɪ; rɪˌspɑnsəˈbɪlətɪ/ *n* (*pl* -ties) **1** [U] being responsible; being accountable: 责任；负责：*You did it on your own ~*, without being told or ordered to do it. 你那么做是出于自己的责任感。*You have a post of great ~*. 你担任的职位责任很大。*I will lend you my camera if you will assume full ~ for it*, pay me the cost of any damage or loss. 如果你能负全责(即任何损坏或遗失均要负责赔偿)，我就把我的照相机借给你。**2** [C] sth for which a person is responsible; duty: 职责；任务：*the heavy responsibilities of the President*. 总统的繁重职责。

re·spon·sible /rɪˈspɒnsəbl ; rɪˈspɑnsəbl/ *adj* **1** ~ *(to sb) (for sb / sth)*, (of a person) legally or morally liable for carrying out a duty, for the care of sth or sb, in a position where one may be blamed for loss, failure, etc: (指人)在道义上负有施行某种义务的；所处地位需照顾某人或某事并对损失、失败等负责的；有责任的；应负责的：*The pilot of an airliner is ~ for the safety of the passengers*. 飞机驾驶员对乘客的安全负有责任。*You are ~ to the Manager for the petty cash*. 小宗的现金收支你要对经理负责。~ *government*, one which is answerable to the electors for its actions. 责任政府(作为能对选民负责的政府)。**2** ~ *(for sth)*, involving the obligation to make decisions for others and bear the blame for their mistakes: (对…)负责的；(对…)有责任的；责任重大的：*The President has a ~ position*. 总统的职责非常重大。*I've made you ~ for the travel arrangements and you must decide what to do*. 我已将旅行的准备事宜交由你负责，你必须决定如何去进行。*Isn't he too young for such a ~ job?* 他担任责任如此重大的工作是不是太年轻了吗? **3** trustworthy; to be relied upon: 可信赖的；可靠的：*Give the task to a ~ man*. 把这工作交给一个可靠的人做。**4** *be ~ for sth*, be the cause or source of: 成为…的原因或根源；对…有责任：*Bad workmanship was ~ for the collapse of the block of flats*. 这排公寓倒塌归咎于施工拙劣。*Who's ~ for this mess in the kitchen?* 是谁把厨

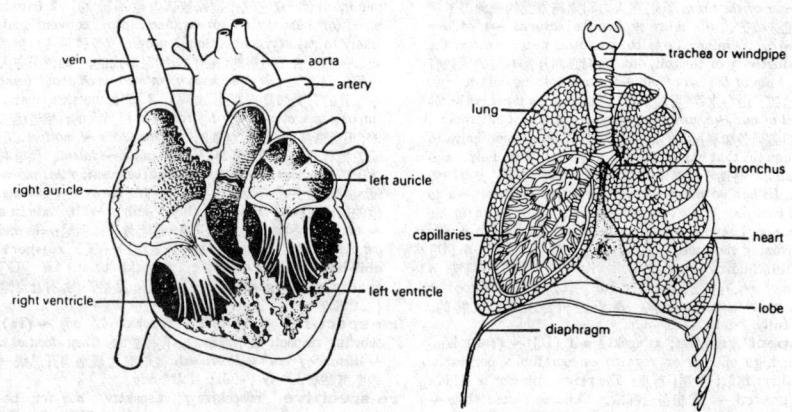

the respiratory system: the heart and the lungs

房里的东西弄得一团糟的? **re·spon·sibly** /-əblɪ; -əblɪ/ adv

re·spon·sive /rɪ'spɒnsɪv; rɪ'spɑnsɪv/ adj 1 answering: 回答的; 应答的: a ~ gesture; 应答的手势; ~ sympathy. 同情的同情。 2 ~ (to), answering easily or quickly: (对…)易于或迅速反应的: a ~ nature; 反应灵敏的天性; ~ to affection/treatment. 易为情爱所动的(对治疗易起反应的)。

rest¹ /rest; rest/ n 1 [U] condition of being free from activity, movement, disturbance; quiet; sleep: 休息;宁静;睡眠: R~ is necessary after hard work. 劳苦工作后,休息是必要的。 She had a good night's ~, sleep. 她好好地睡了一夜。 We had several ~s/stops for ~ on the way up the mountain. 我们在上山途中休息了几次。 Sunday is a day of ~ for many people. 星期日是许多人的休息日。 Let's stop and take/have a ~. 让我们停下来休息一下。 at ~, (a) still; not troubled; free from movement or agitation. 安静的; 宁静的; 静止的。 (b) dead. 死的。 be laid to ~, be buried. 被埋葬。 come to ~, (of a moving body) stop moving. (指活动体)停止移动。 set sb's mind/fears at ~, calm him; relieve him of doubt, anxiety, etc. 使某人平静;使某人免除怀疑、焦虑等;使某人安心。'~-cure n course of treatment for persons suffering from nervous disorders. (精神错乱者的)宁静治疗法; 静养法。 '~-day n day spent in rest. ~ 休息日; 安息日。'~-home n place where old or convalescent people are cared for. 养老院;疗养院。 '~-house n house or bungalow for the use of travellers (esp in areas where there are no hotels). 供旅客休息之房舍 (尤指在没有旅馆的地区)。 '~ room, (US) public lavatory; cloak-room. (美)公用盥洗室;衣帽间。 2 [C] that on which sth is supported: 支撑物; 支架物: a ~ for a billiard cue/a telescope; 台球球杆 (望远镜) 的支架; an 'arm-~; 扶手; a 'neck-~. 枕头。 3 [C] (music) (sign marking an) interval of silence. (音乐)休止; 休止符。 **~·ful** /-fl; -fl/ adj quiet; peaceful; giving ~ or a feeling of ~: 宁静的; 平静的; 给予平静的; 予人以平静感的: a ~ful scene; 宁静的景色; colours that are ~ful to the eyes. 使眼睛感到舒适的颜色。 **~·fully** /-fəlɪ; -fəlɪ/ adv **~·ful·ness** n **~·less** adj never still or quiet; unable to rest: 永不安静或宁静的: the ~less waves; 汹涌的波浪: spend a ~less night. 一夜未眠。 The audience was growing ~less, showing signs of impatience, wishing to leave, etc. 观众渐渐不安起来 (表现出不耐烦、欲离去的样子等)。 **~·less·ly** adv **~·less·ness** n

rest² /rest; rest/ n the ~, 1 what remains; the remainder: 余留者;其余: Take what you want and throw the ~ away. 把你所要的拿去, 把剩下的丢掉。 Her hat was red, like the ~ of her clothes. 她的帽子是红色的, 象她其余的衣着一样。 and (all) the ~ (of it), and everything else that might be mentioned. 以及其他可能提到的一切。 for the ~, as regards other matters. 至于其他。 2 (with pl v) the others: 他们(人): 他其他(人): John and I are going to play tennis; what are the ~ of you going to do? 约翰和我要去打网球;你们其余的人要做什么呢?

rest³ /rest; rest/ vi, vt 1 [VP2A, B, C] be still or quiet; be free from activity, movement, disturbance, etc: 静止; 静止; 休息: We ~ed (for) an hour after lunch. 午饭后我们休息一小时。 He ~s (= is buried) in the churchyard. 他被葬于教堂墓地中。 His last ~ing-place (= place of burial) is on the hillside there. 他的最后安息处 (埋葬处) 在那边的山坡上。 He will not ~ (= will have no peace of mind) until he knows the truth. 在没有获得真相之前, 他是不会安心的。 The matter cannot ~ here, We must investigate it further. 事情不能就此罢了 (我们必须再做进一步调查)。 We shall let this field ~ for a year, let it lie fallow. 我们要让这块地休耕一年。 2 [VP6A] give rest or relief to: 使休息; 使宁静; 使减缓: He stopped to ~ his horse. 他停下来让马休息。 These dark glasses ~ my eyes. 这副墨镜使我的眼睛感觉舒适。 May God ~ his soul, give repose to his soul. 愿上帝

使其灵魂安息。 3 [VP14, 3A] ~ (sth) on/upon/against, (cause to) be supported (on or against sth): (使)被支撑; (使)倚靠; 安放: She ~ed her elbows/Her elbows were ~ing on the table. 她将肘靠在桌上。 R~ the ladder against the wall. 把梯子靠在墙上。 The roof ~s upon eight columns. 这屋顶由八根圆柱支撑。 ~ on one's oars, (a) stop rowing for a time. 暂停划船。 (b) (fig) have a period of rest after any kind of work or effort. (喻)在工作或努力之后小憩休息。 4 [VP14, 3A] ~ (sth) on/upon, lie, spread out, depend or rely (on): (of sight, etc) fall (on), be steadily directed (on): 停卧(于);伸展(于);依赖;凝视: Look at those clouds ~ing upon the mountain top. 请看那些笼罩在山顶上的云。 Her eyes/gaze ~ed on me. 她的眼睛凝视着我。 She, let her glance ~ on me. 她注视着我。

rest⁴ /rest; rest/ vi 1 [VP2D] continue to be in a specified state: 继续保持某种状态; 依然是: You may ~ assured that everything possible will be done. 你尽可放心, 所有能做到的事均将做到。 The affair ~s (=remains, the usu word) a mystery. 那件事仍然是一个谜 (remain 较常用)。 2 [VP3A] ~ with, be left in the hands or charge of: 在于; 取决于: It ~s with you to decide, It is your responsibility. 全由你来决定 (那是你的责任)。 3 [VP3A] ~ on/upon, depend, rely: 依赖;依靠: His fame ~s upon his plays more than upon his novels. 他的名声主要是建立在他的戏剧上, 不是在他的小说上。

re·state /ˌriː'steɪt; rɪ'stet/ vt [VP6A] state again or in a different way. 再陈述或声明; 以不同方式陈述或声明。 **~·ment** n

res·tau·rant /'restrɒnt US: -tərənt; 'rɛstərənt/ n place where meals can be bought and eaten. 饭店; 餐馆。 **res·taur·a·teur** /ˌrestərə'tɜ:(r); ˌrɛstətə'tɜ, res·taur·an·teur** /ˌrestrɒn'tɜ:(r) US: -tərən'tɜ; ˌrɛstərən'tɜ/ n manager of a ~. 饭店或餐馆的经理。

res·ti·tu·tion /ˌrestɪ'tjuːʃn US: -'tuː-; ˌrɛstə'tjuʃən/ n [U] 1 restoring (of sth stolen, etc) to its owner: (赃物等之)归还原主: make ~ of sth to sb; 将某物归还某人; ~ of property. 财产之归还。 2 = reparation.

res·tive /'restɪv; 'rɛstɪv/ adj 1 (of a horse or other animal) refusing to move forward; moving backwards or sideways. (指马或其他动物) 不肯前进的; 向后或向侧移动的。 2 (of a person) reluctant to be controlled or disciplined. (指人) 不愿受控制或管束的; 不安分的; 不受羁束的。 **~·ly** adv **~·ness** n

re·stock /ˌriː'stɒk; rɪ'stɑk/ vt [VP6A] put fresh stock into: 再储存; 再补充; 将新物品置于; 重新进货: a lake with trout. 在湖中补放鳟鱼。

res·to·ra·tion /ˌrestə'reɪʃn; ˌrɛstə'reʃən/ n 1 [U] restoring or being restored: 恢复; 复元; 归还: ~ to health and strength; 健康与体力之复元; ~ of stolen property. 赃物之归还。 2 the R~, (the period of) the re-establishment of the monarchy in England in 1660, when Charles II became king: 1660 年的英国王权复兴; 英王查理二世的复辟; 复辟时代: R~ poetry/comedy. 复辟时代的诗 (喜剧)。 3 [C] model representing the supposed original form of an extinct animal, ruined building, etc; building formerly ruined and now rebuilt: 模拟已灭绝动物、已毁建筑物等之模型; 原先已毁而今重建之建筑物: The castle is a mere ~, ie there is very little of the original left. 这座城堡只不过是重建之物 (原有建筑物的遗迹所留很少)。 Closed during ~s, ie while rebuilding is in progress. 重建期间暂予关闭。

re·stora·tive /rɪ'stɔːrətɪv; rɪ'storetɪv/ adj tending to restore health and strength. 有恢复健康与力量之倾向的, 有助于恢复健康与体力的。 □ n [C, U] ~ food, medicine, etc. 有益于恢复健康与体力的食物, 药物等; 恢复剂。

re·store /rɪ'stɔː(r); rɪ'stor/ vt [VP6A, 14] ~ (to), 1 give back: 归还; 交还: ~ stolen property/borrowed books. 归还赃物 (借的书)。 2 bring back into use; reintroduce: 再使用; 再采用: ~ old customs. 恢复古老风俗。 3 make well or normal again; bring back (to a former

condition): 使恢复健康或正常; 使恢复(以前的情况): *quite* ~*d to health;* 健康完全恢复; *feel completely* ~*d.* 感觉已完全复元。**4** repair; rebuild as before; reconstruct (sth) so that it is like the original: 修复; 重建; 重制(某物)使象原形: ~ *a ruined abbey;* 修复一座毁坏之寺院; ~ *a text,* try to make it as it was originally by supplying missing words and phrases, getting rid of errors made by copyists, etc. 校勘原文(设法补上遗漏字词、改正抄写者之笔误等,使之同原文一样)。**5** place in or bring back to the former position, etc: 使复职; 使复位: ~ *an employee to his old post / an officer to his command.* 使一职员复职(使一军官恢复原指挥权)。~**r** n one who, that which, ~s, eg an expert who cleans old oil paintings: 使恢复原状之人或物(例如使旧油画恢复其鲜明原貌之专家): *'hair~r,* preparation that, it is claimed, will ~ hair to a bald head. 生发油; 生发剂。

re·strain /rɪ'streɪn/ *vt* [VP6A, 14] ~ **(from),** hold back; keep under control; prevent (sb or sth from doing sth): 克制; 管制; 抑制; 阻止(某人或某物做某事): ~ *a child from* (*doing*) *mischief;* 阻止孩子恶作剧; ~ *one's anger / laughter.* 克制一个人的愤怒(忍住不笑)。~**ed** *adj* (esp) not emotional or wild; kept under control. (尤指)不激动的; 不粗野的; 抑制的; 受控制的。~**t** /rɪ'streɪnt/ *n* 1 [U] ~ing or being ~ed: 克制; 遏制; 抑制; 约束; 阻止: *submit to* ~*t;* 遵守约束; *break loose from all* ~*t.* 挣脱出打破一切束缚。*be put under* ~*t,*(esp of a mentally ill person)be placed in a mental home. (尤指精神病患者)被置于精神病院。*without* ~*t,* freely; without control. 自由地; 无拘无束地; 放纵地。**2** [U] (in art, literature, etc) avoidance of excess or exaggeration. (在艺术、文学等方面)适中; 适度(避免过度或夸张)。**3** [C] that which ~s; check; controlling influence: 遏制的东西; 制止者; 约束力: *the* ~*ts of poverty.* 贫穷带来的种种束缚。

re·strict /rɪ'strɪkt/ *vt* [VP6A,14] ~ **(to),** limit; keep within limits: 限制; 约束; 使在限度内: *Discussion at the meeting was* ~*ed to the agenda.* 这次会议上的讨论仅限于议程上的项目。*We are* ~*ed to a speed of 30 miles an hour in built-up areas.* 在房屋林立的地区, 车速限制为每小时三十英里。*The trees* ~ *our vision.* 树木限制了我们的视野。*Is the consumption of alcohol* ~*ed by law in your country?* 在贵国酒的消耗量是否受法律限制? **re·stric·tion** /rɪ'strɪkʃn/ *n* 1 [U] ~ing or being ~ed: 限制; 被限制: ~*ion of expenditure.* 经费开支之限制。**2** [C] instance of this; sth that ~s: 限制之实例; 有限制作用之事物; 限制者: *place* ~*ions on foreign trade / on the sale of alcohol;* 管制对外贸易(酒之售卖); *currency* ~*ions,* eg on the sums that a person may use for foreign travel. 货币管制。~**·ive** /rɪ'strɪktɪv/ *adj* ~ing; tending to ~. 限制的; 限制性的。~**ive practices,** (in industry) practices that hinder the most effective use of labour, technical resources, etc and tend to damage productive efficiency. (工业方面的)限制性常例(妨碍劳力、技术资源等的最有效使用, 因之损及生产效率者)。~**·ive·ly** *adv*

re·struc·ture /ˌriː'strʌktʃə(r)/ ,ˌriː'strʌktʃə/ *vt* [VP6A] give new structure or arrangement to: 改组; 调整; 重新安排: ~ *an organization / a proposal / the plot of a novel.* 改组一机构(调整一计划;重新安排一部小说的情节)。

re·sult /rɪ'zʌlt/ rɪ'zʌlt/ *vi* 1 [VP2A, 3A] ~ **(from),** come about, happen, as a natural consequence: (作为自然结果的)发生; 因…引起; 起因于: *Any damage* ~*ing from negligence must be paid for by the borrower.* 因疏忽引起的任何损坏应由借用者负责赔偿。**2** [VP3A] ~ *in,* bring about; have as a consequence: 致使; 造成…结果;导致: *Their dispute* ~*ed in war.* 他们的争论终于造成战争。**3** end in a specified manner: 终归…; 结果: *Their efforts* ~*ed badly.* 他们的努力结果不佳。□ *n* 1 [C, U] that which is produced by an activity or cause; outcome; effect: 结果; 效果; 成绩: *work without* (*much*) ~; 没有(多大)效果的工作; *obtain good* ~*s;* 得到好的结果; *announce the* ~*s of a competition,* the names of prize-

winners, etc; 宣布竞赛之结果(即宣布优胜者之姓名等); *'football* ~*s,* the scores. 足球赛之结果(积分)。*His limp is the* ~ *of a car accident last year.* 他的腿变瘸是去年一次车祸的不幸结果。**2** [C] sth found by calculation; answer(to a mathematical problem, etc) 由计算得到的某项结果; (数学问题等的)答案。~**·ant** / -ənt; -ənt/ *adj* coming as a ~, esp as the total outcome of forces or tendencies from different directions. 结果的; (尤指来自不同方向的力量或趋势而成的)总结果的。□ *n* [C] product or outcome (*of* sth). (某种事物的)结果。

re·sume /rɪ'zjuːm US: -'zuːm; rɪ'zum/ *vt* 1 [VP6A, D] go on after stopping for a time: 停顿一段时间后再继续; 重新开始; 恢复: ~ *one's work / a story;* 恢复工作(继续一故事); ~ *the thread of one's discourse,* take up an interrupted discourse. 重续打断的谈话。**2** [VP6A] take or occupy again: 再取得; 再占有: ~ *one's seat.* 重回原位。

ré·sumé /'rezjuːmeɪ US: ˌrezʊ'meɪ; ˌrezʊ'me/ *n* [C] summary; abstract(3); (US) = *curriculum vitae,* ⇨ **curriculum.** 摘要; 概略; (美)履历。

re·sump·tion /rɪ'zʌmpʃn; rɪ'zʌmpʃən/ *n* [U] resuming; [C] instance of this. 重新开始; 恢复; 再取得; 再占有。

re·sur·face /ˌriː's9ːfɪs; rɪ'sɜ'fɪs/ *vt, vi* 1 [VP6A] put a new surface on (a road, etc). 再铺(路等)之表面; 换裝新面。**2** [VP2A] (of a submarine) come to the surface again. (指潜水艇)重新露出水面。

re·sur·gent /rɪ's3ːdʒənt; rɪ'sɜdʒənt/ *adj* reviving; coming back to activity, vigour, etc (after defeat, destruction, etc): 复活的; 复苏的; 恢复活力的; 恢复活力的: ~ *nationalism;* 复活的民族主义; ~ *hopes.* 复苏的希望。**re·sur·gence** /-əns; -əns/ *n*

res·ur·rect /ˌrezə'rekt; ˌrezə'rɛkt/ *vt, vi* 1 [VP6A] bring back into use; revive the practice of: 恢复使用; 恢复…之实行; 再流行; 复兴: ~ *an old word / custom.* 恢复使用一个古字(风俗)。**2** [VP6A] take from the grave; (colloq) dig up: 从坟墓中掘出; (口)掘起: *My dog* ~*ed an old bone in the garden.* 我的狗在花园中挖出一根老骨头。**3** [VP6A, 2A] (rare) bring or come back to life again. (罕)(使)复苏; (使)复活。

res·ur·rec·tion /ˌrezə'rekʃn; ˌrezə'rɛkʃən/ *n* [U] 1 **the R~,** (a) the rising of Jesus from the tomb; anniversary of this. 耶稣复活; 耶稣复活的周年纪念日; (b) the rising of all the dead on the Last Day. 最后审判日所有死者之复活。**2** revival from disuse, inactivity, etc: 复兴; 恢复使用; 恢复活力等: *the* ~ *of hope.* 希望之复苏。

re·sus·ci·tate /rɪ'sʌsɪteɪt; rɪ'sʌsə,tet/ *vt,vi* [VP6A, 2A] bring or come back to consciousness: 使恢复知觉; 恢复知觉; 再苏醒: ~ *a person who has been nearly drowned.* 使一个快溺死的人复苏。**re·sus·ci·ta·tion** /rɪ,sʌsɪ'teɪʃn; rɪ,sʌsə'teʃən/ *n* [U].

ret /ret; ret/ *vt* (*-tt-*) [VP6A] soften (flax, hemp, etc) by soaking or exposing to moisture: 将(亚麻、大麻等)浸水或暴露在湿气中使之变软: *Coconut shells are buried in wet sea-sand to ret the coir fibre.* 椰子壳被埋在潮湿的海沙中以使其纤维变软。

re·tail /'riːteɪl; 'ritel/ *n* [C] sale of goods (usu in small quantities) to the general public, but for resale: 货物(通常系少量)之直接售给用户; 零售: *sell goods* (*by*) ~; 零售货物; (attrib)(用作定语) ~ *dealers / prices;* 零售商(价格); ~ *department.* 零售部。⇨ **wholesale.** □ *adv* by ~: 零售地: *Do you buy wholesale or* ~? 你是整批买还是零买? □ *vt, vi* 1 [VP6A, 3A] ~ (*at*), sell (goods) by ~; (of goods) be sold ~: 零售(货物); (指货物)被零售: *an article that is* ~*ed at / that* ~*s at seventy pence.* 一件零售价格七十便士的物品。**2** [VP6A] repeat (what one has heard, esp gossip) bit by bit or to several persons in turn: 一点一点地或一个接一个地向一些人重述; 转述(所听到的话, 尤指闲言): ~ *a slander.* 转述诽谤之言。~**er** *n* tradesman who sells by ~. 零售商。

re·tain /rɪ'teɪn ; rɪ'ten/ vt [VP6A] **1** keep; continue to have or hold; keep in place: 保持; 保有; 保留; 挡住: *This vessel won't ~ water.* 这个容器不能盛水. *This dyke was built to ~ the flood waters.* 这堤是建来挡洪水的. *The ~ing wall* (ie one built to support and confine a mass of earth or water) *collapsed.* 挡土墙(或拥墙)倒塌了. *He is 90 but still ~s the use of all his faculties.* 他已九十高龄, 但各种官能仍未衰退. *She ~s a clear memory of her schooldays.* 她对求学时代仍旧记得很清楚. **2** get the services of (esp a barrister) by payment *(a ~ing fee).* 雇用; 聘请(尤指律师)(聘请费用称作 a retaining fee). ~**er** *n* **1** (legal) fee paid to ~ the services of, eg a barrister. (法律)(律师等之)聘请费. **2** (old use) servant. (旧用法)仆人.

re·take /,riː'teɪk ; rɪ'tek/ vt *(pt -took* /-'tuk; -'tuk/, *pp -taken* /-'teɪkn ; -'tekən/) [VP6A] take, capture, photograph, again. 再夺取; 再攫获; 再拍摄. □ *n* /'riːteɪk; 'ri,tek/ (esp, cinema, TV) rephotographed scene. (尤指电影, 电视)重拍之景; 补拍之镜头.

re·tali·ate /rɪ'tælɪeɪt; rɪ'tælɪet/ vi [VP2A, 3A] ~ *(against/on/upon),* return the same sort of ill treatment that one has received: 报复; 报仇: ~ *upon one's enemy.* 向敌人报仇. *He ~d by kicking the other boy on the ankle.* 他踢另一个男孩的脚踝骨以为报复. *If we raise our import duties on their goods, they may ~ against us.* 如果我们提高他们货物的进口税, 他们可能向我们报复. **re·tali·ation** /rɪ,tælɪ'eɪʃn; rɪ,tælɪ'eʃən/ *n* [U] retaliating: 报复; 报仇: *in retaliation for.* 为…而报复. **re·tali·at·ive** /rɪ'tælɪətɪv US: -ˈlɪeɪt-; rɪ-'tælɪetɪv/, **re·tali·at·ory** /rɪ'tælɪətrɪ US: -tɔːrɪ ; rɪ-'tælɪə,tɔrɪ/ *adj* returning ill treatment for ill treatment; of or for retaliation: 报复的; 回报的; 为报复的: *retaliatory measures.* 报复的手段.

re·tard /rɪ'taːd; rɪ'tɑrd/ vt [VP6A] check; hinder. 阻止; 妨碍: ~ *progress/development;* 阻碍进步(发展); *a mentally ~ed child,* one whose mental or emotional development has been checked. 一个在智能或情绪方面有障碍的孩子. **re·tar·da·tion** /,riːtɑː'deɪʃn /,riˌtɑr'deʃən/ *n*

retch /retʃ ; retʃ/ vi [VP2A] make (involuntarily) the sound and physical movements of vomiting but without bringing up anything from the stomach. 干呕(不自觉地作呕吐之声音及动作, 但并未吐出胃中任何东西).

re·tell /,riː'tel ; rɪ'tel/ vt *(pt, pp -told* /-'təʊld; -'told/) [VP6A] tell again; tell in a different way or in a different language: 再讲; (以不同的方式或不同的语言)重述; 改写: *old Greek tales retold for children.* 为孩子们改写的古希腊故事.

re·ten·tion /rɪ'tenʃn; rɪ'tɛnʃən/ *n* [U] retaining or being retained: 保持; 保留; 被保持; 被保留: *suffering from ~ of urine,* inability to pass it out from the bladder. 患尿闭症.

re·ten·tive /rɪ'tentɪv; rɪ'tɛntɪv/ *adj* ~ *(of),* having the power of retaining(1) things: 有保持之能力的: *a memory that is ~ of details;* 能记得详情细节的记忆力; *a ~ soil,* one that retains water, does not dry out quickly. 能保持水份的土壤. ~**·ly** *adv* ~·**ness** *n*

re·think /,riː'θɪŋk ; rɪ'θɪŋk/ vt, vi *(pt, pp -thought* /-'θɔːt; -'θɔt/) [VP6A, 2A] think about again; reconsider: 再想; 重予考虑: *They will have to ~ their policy towards Japan.* 他们必须重新考虑对日政策. *A good deal of ~ing is needed on this question.* 这个问题需要多加考虑. □ *n* /'riːθɪŋk; 'riθɪŋk/ (colloq) thinking again: (口)再想; 再考虑: *If that's your decision, you'd better have a ~.* 如果那是你的决定, 你最好再考虑一下.

reti·cent /'retɪsnt; 'rɛtəsnt/ *adj* in the habit of saying little; not saying all that is known or felt; reserved: 沉默寡言的; 言不尽意的; 保留的: *She was ~ about/on what Tom had said to her.* 她对汤姆告诉她的话保持沉默. ~**·ly** *adv* **reti·cence** /-sns; -sns/ *n* [U] being ~; [C] instance of this: 沉默寡言; 保留: *His reticences are often more revealing than what he says.* 他的沉默常

比他所说的话显示更多的意思.

re·ticu·late /rɪ'tɪkjuleɪt; rɪ'tɪkjə,let/ vt, vi [VP4A, 2A] divide, be divided, in fact or in appearance into a network of small squares or intersecting lines. 使呈网状; 呈网状. □ *adj* /rɪ'tɪkjulət; rɪ'tɪkjəlɪt/ covered with such a network. 覆以网状物的. **re·ticu·la·tion** /rɪ,tɪkju'leɪʃn ; rɪ,tɪkjə'leʃən/ *n* (often *pl)* net-like mark or structure. (常用复数)网状图案; 网状结构.

reti·cule /'retɪkjuːl; 'rɛtɪ,kjul/ *n* (archaic) woman's small handbag. (古)女用小手提包.

ret·ina /'retɪnə US: 'retənə; 'rɛtnə/ *n (pl* ~**s** or **-nae** /-niː; -,nɪ/) [C] layer of membrane at the back of the eyeball, sensitive to light. 视网膜(在眼球后部之网膜, 对光线敏感). ⇨ the illus at eye. 参看 eye 之插图.

reti·nue /'retɪnjuː US: 'retənu; 'rɛtn,ju/ *n* [C] number of persons (servants, officers, etc) travelling with a person of high rank. 随员(与高级官员等同行的侍从、官员等).

re·tire /rɪ'taɪə(r); rɪ'taɪr/ vi, vt **1** [VP2A, 3A] ~ *(from) (to),* withdraw; go away: 退下; 离开: *He ~d to his bedroom.* 他回到他的卧室. *The batsman ~d hurt,* left the pitch and went back to the pavilion, because hurt. 击球员因受伤退场. **2** ~ *(to bed)* (formal for) go to bed: (正式用语)就寝: *My wife usually ~s at 10 o'clock.* 内人通常十时就寝. **3** [VP2A, C] (of an army) withdraw; go back: (指军队)撤退; 退却: *Our forces ~d to prepared positions.* 我们的部队撤回到既设阵地. Cf 参较 The enemy retreated. 敌人败退. **4** [VP2A,C] give up one's work, position, business etc: 退休; 退职; 退役: *reach retiring age;* 届退休年龄; *a retiring allowance,* one given to a person when he ~s. 退休金. *He will ~ on a pension at 65.* 他将在 65 岁领养老金退休. **5** [VP6A] cause (sb) to ~ to (3, 4): 使(某人)撤退或退休: ~ *the head clerk.* 使主任秘书退休. **6** ~ *from the world,* enter a monastery or become a hermit; become a recluse. 遁世隐居(如进修道院或隐居)成为隐士; 成为隐士. ~ *into oneself,* become unsociable because one is wrapped up in one's own thoughts. (因沉缅于自己的思想而)不和人交际; 苦思不语. □ *n* signal to troops to ~; signal to ~: sound *the ~,* ie on the bugle. 吹撤退号. ~**d** *adj* **1** having ~d(4): 退职的; 退休的; 退役的: *a ~d civil servant;* 一个退休的公务员; *the '~d list,* of officers (of the Army, etc) who have ~d; 退役军官名册; *'~d pay,* pension. 退休金. **2** secluded; quiet: 隐居的; 宁静的: *a ~d valley,* 宁静的山谷; *live a ~d life in a small village.* 在小村中过隐居生活. **re·tir·ing** *adj* (of persons, their way of life, etc) inclined to avoid society; reserved: (指人, 其生活方式等)有隐居倾向的; 孤独缄默的: *a girl of a retiring disposition.* 一个性情孤独的女孩. ~**·ment** *n* **1** [U] retiring or being ~d; seclusion: 隐退; 退休; 隐居: ~*ment from the world,* eg in a convent. 遁世隐居(如遁入女修道院). **2** [U] condition of being ~d: 隐退之状况: *be/live in ~ment.* 过隐居生活. *go into ~ment,* retire (esp 4 and 6 above). 退休(尤指上列第4及第6义). **3** [C] instance of retiring or being ~d: 退隐或退休之实例: *There have been several ~ments in my office recently.* 最近我那办公室有几个人退休了. '~*ment pension,* =old-age pension. 养老金. ⇨ pension.

re·tool /,riː'tuːl; ri'tul/ vt [VP6A] equip (a factory, etc) with new machine tools. 给(工厂等)装备新的工作母机.

re·tort[1] /rɪ'tɔːt; rɪ'tɔrt/ *n* [C] **1** vessel with a long narrow neck turned downwards, used for distilling liquids. 曲颈甑; 曲颈瓶(颈部细长而朝下, 用于蒸溜液体者). **2** receptacle used in the purification of mercury, and in the making of gas. 蒸溜器(用于净化水银及制造气体的容器).

re·tort[2] /rɪ'tɔːt; rɪ'tɔrt/ vt, vi **1** [VP6A, 9, 2A] answer back quickly, wittily or angrily with an accusation or challenge): (尤指对控诉或挑战)立即机智地或愤怒地反驳: *'It's entirely your fault,' he ~ed.* '那全是

你的错，'他又驳说。 **2** [VP14] (formal, rare) get equal with sb by returning (what has been received) in kind: (正式用语, 罕)反击; 回报: ~ *insult for insult*; 以牙还牙; ~ *an argument/affront.* 反驳一论据(回报一侮辱)。 □ *n* [U] ~ing: 反驳; 反击: *say sth in* ~; 反唇相讥; [C] ~ing answer: 反驳的回答: *make an insolent* ~. 作侮慢的反击。

re·touch /ˌriːˈtʌtʃ; ˌriˈtʌtʃ/ *vt* [VP6A] improve (a photograph, painting, etc) by a few touches of a brush, etc. 修描(照片, 图画 等)。

re·trace /riːˈtreɪs; riˈtres/ *vt* [VP6A] **1** go back over or along: 顺…折回; 折返: ~ *one's steps.* 顺原路返回。 **2** go over (past actions, etc) in the mind. 回想; 回顾(过去的活动等)。

re·tract /rɪˈtrækt; rɪˈtrækt/ *vt, vi* **1** [VP6A, 2A] take back or withdraw (a statement, offer, opinion, etc); take back a statement: 收回; 撤回(声明、提议、意见等); 撤回声明: *The prisoner of war* ~*ed his parole.* 该战俘违拒誓脱逃。 *Even when confronted with proof the accused man refused to* ~, would not acknowledge the error of what he had said. 甚至在面对证据的时候, 被告仍拒绝改正其供述。 **2** [VP6A, 2A] draw in or back; move back or in; be capable of doing this: 缩进; 缩回; 移回; 移进; 能缩回或移进: *A cat can* ~ *its claws and a snail its horns.* 猫能缩进其爪, 蜗牛能缩回其触角。 *A cat's claws can* ~. 猫的爪能缩回。 ~·**able** /-əbl; -əbl/ *adj* that can be ~ed: 能收回或撤回的; 能缩进或缩回的: *a* ~*able undercarriage,* (in an aircraft) wheels, etc which can be drawn up into the body of the aircraft during flight. 伸缩式起落架(飞机的轮等, 在飞行时能够拉进机身中)。 **re·trac·tile** /rɪˈtræktaɪl US: -tl; rɪˈtræktl/ *adj* that can be drawn in: 能缩回的; 能缩进的: *the retractile claws of a cat.* 能缩进的猫爪子。 **re·trac·tion** /rɪˈtrækʃn; rɪˈtrækʃən/ *n* [U] ~ing; [C] instance of this. 撤回; 撤消; 缩进; 移回; 撤回, 缩进等之实例。

re·tread /ˌriːˈtred; ˌriˈtred/ *vt* (*pt, pp* ~**ed**) furnish (an old tyre) with a new tread 供(旧轮胎)以新的胎面; 翻新(旧轮胎)。 ⇨ **tread,** *n*(3). □ *n* /ˈriːtred; ˈriˌtred/ tyre that has been ~ed (US 美 = *recap*). 经过翻新的轮胎。

re·treat /rɪˈtriːt; rɪˈtrit/ *vi* **1** [VP2A, C, 3A] ~ (*from*) (*to*), (esp of an army) go back; withdraw: (尤指军队)撤退; 退却: *force the enemy to* ~; 迫使敌人退却; ~ *on* (ie towards) *the capital.* 向首都撤退。 **2** recede (which is more usu): 向后倾 (recede 较常用): *a* ~*ing forehead.* 向后倾斜的额头。 □ *n* **1** [U] act of ~ing: 撤退或后退的行动: *The army was in full* ~. 全军在总撤退。 *We made good our* ~, ~*ed safely.* 我们安全撤退。 **2** [U] signal for ~ing: 退军号; 撤退号; 鸣金收军(例如击军鼓或吹退军号)。 **3** [C] instance of ~ing: 撤退或后退之实例: *after many advances and* ~*s.* 经过许多次的推进与撤退。 *beat a (hasty)* ~, (fig) withdraw from, abandon, an undertaking. (喻)放弃一事业; 打退堂鼓。 **4** [C, U] (place for a) period of quiet and rest: 一段安静和休息的地方; 宁静的休息处所: *a quiet country* ~. 乡间宁静处。 **go into** ~, eg temporary retirement for religious exercises. 避静(如为宗教活动所作之暂时性隐居)。

re·trench /rɪˈtrentʃ; rɪˈtrentʃ/ *vt, vi* [VP6A, 2A] cut down (expenses); make economies: 节省(开支); 缩减支出; 节省: *We must* ~ *this year in order to have a good holiday next year.* 为了明年有个愉快的假日, 我们今年必须节省。 ~·**ment** *n* [U] ~ing; [C] instance of this. 节省; 节省之实例。

re·trial /ˌriːˈtraɪəl; ˌriˈtraɪəl/ *n* act of trying again in a law court; new trial. (法院的)再审; 复审。

ret·ri·bu·tion /ˌretrɪˈbjuːʃn; ˌretrəˈbjuʃən/ *n* [U] deserved punishment: 应得的惩罚; 报应: *R~ for evil will come sooner or later.* 邪恶或迟或早总会得到报应。 *There will be a day of* ~. 总有一天会遭到报应。 **re·tri·bu·tive** /rɪˈtrɪbjʊtɪv; rɪˈtrɪbjətɪv/ *adj* coming as ~; inflicted or coming as a penalty for wrongdoing. 报应的; 惩罚的。

re·trieve /rɪˈtriːv; rɪˈtriv/ *vt, vi* **1** [VP6A] get possession of again: 再获得; 找回: ~ *a lost piece of luggage.* 找回一件遗失的行李。 **2** [VP6A] put or set right; make amends for: 修整; 修理; 补偿: ~ *an error/a loss/disaster/defeat.* 补救一错误(损失, 灾难, 失败)。 **3** [VP6A, 14] ~ (*from*), rescue from; restore to a flourishing state: 解救; 使恢复繁盛情况: ~ *sb from ruin*; 拯救某人免于沉沦; ~ *one's honour/fortunes*; 挽回荣誉(财产); ~ *oneself.* 拯救自己。 **4** [VP6A, 2A] (of specially trained dogs) find and bring in (killed or wounded birds, etc). (指经过特殊训练的狗)找到并带回(被杀死或受伤的鸟等)。 **re·triev·able** /-əbl; -əbl/ *adj* **re·trieval** /-vl; -vl/ *n* [U] **1** act of retrieving: 寻回, 补偿, 挽救之行动: *the retrieval of one's fortunes.* 个人的财产的恢复。 **2** possibility of recovery: 恢复之可能: *beyond/past retrieval.* 不可恢复的; 不可挽救的。 **re·triever** *n* breed of dog used for retrieving(4). 一种用以寻回猎物之猎犬。 ⇨ the illus at **dog.** 参看 dog 之插图。

retro·ac·tive /ˌretrəʊˈæktɪv; ˌretroˈæktɪv/ *adj* (of laws, etc) (指法律等) = retrospective(2). ~·**ly** *adv*

retro·grade /ˈretrəɡreɪd; ˈretrəˌɡred/ *adj* **1** directed backwards: 向后的; 后退的: ~ *motion.* 逆行; 后退的动作。 **2** deteriorating; likely to cause worse conditions: 退化的; 败坏的, 可能使情况变坏的: *a* ~ *policy.* 一种可能使情况变坏的政策。 □ *vi* [VP2A] decline; revert; grow worse. 衰落; 退步; 变坏。

retro·gress /ˌretrəˈɡres; ˈretrəˌɡres/ *vi* [VP2A] go or move backwards. 倒退; 退步; 衰退。 **retro·gression** /ˌretrəˈɡreʃn; ˌretrəˈɡreʃən/ *n* return to a less advanced state; decline. 退步; 退化; 衰微。 **retro·gres·sive** /ˌretrəˈɡresɪv; ˌretrəˈɡresɪv/ *adj* returning, tending to return, to a less advanced state; becoming worse. 退步的; 退化的; 变坏的。

retro·rocket /ˈretrəʊˌrɒkɪt; ˈretroˌrɑkɪt/ *n* jet engine fired to slow down or alter the course of a missile, spacecraft, etc. (使导弹、太空船等减慢或改变航程而发射的)减速火箭; 推后火箭。

retro·spect /ˈretrəspekt; ˈretrəˌspɛkt/ *n* [U] view of past events. 回顾; 回溯。 *in* ~, looking back at past events etc 回顾。 **retro·spec·tion** /ˌretrəˈspekʃn; ˌretrəˈspɛkʃən/ *n* [U] action of looking back at past events, scenes, etc; [C] instance of this. 回顾; 回顾之实例。 **retro·spec·tive** /ˌretrəˈspektɪv; ˌretrəˈspɛktɪv/ *adj* **1** relating to retrospection; looking back on past events, etc: 回顾的; 回溯往事的: *a* ~*ive exhibition of a painter's work,* one that traces his development from his early to his latest work. 一画家作品的回顾展(展示其早期作品直至后期的演变)。 **2** (of laws, payments, etc) applying to the past; not restricted to the future: (指法律、付款等)溯及既往的; 非仅限于未来的: *a* ~*ive legislation*; 追溯既往的法律; 溯及法; *a* ~*ive* (=backdated) *wage increase.* 从过去某一天开始计算的增加薪资。 **retro·spec·tive·ly** *adv*

re·troussé /rəˈtruːseɪ US: ˌretruˈse; ˌretruˈse/ *adj* (of a nose) turned up at the end. (指鼻子)上翘的; 朝上的。

ret·ro·ver·sion /ˌretrəʊˈvɜːʃn US: -ʒn; ˌretrəˈvɜʒən/ *n* state of being turned backwards; turning or tilting backward. 退转; 后转; 后倾; 后屈。

ret·sina /ˈretsiːnə US: ˈretsɪnə; ˈrɛtsɪnə/ *n* [U] resinated Greek wine. 一种有松香味的希腊葡萄酒。

re·turn¹ /rɪˈtɜːn; rɪˈtɜn/ *n* **1** [C, U] ~ing or being ~ed; coming, going, giving, sending, putting, back: 回来; 归去; 归还; 送回; 放回: *a* ~ *home*; 归家; *on my* ~, when I got/get back; 在我归来时; *a poor* ~ *for kindness,* (eg) ungrateful behaviour; 对于他的忘恩负义(如忘恩负义的行为); *the* ~ *of spring*; 春之归来; *have a* ~ *of the symptoms* (of an illness). (疾病的)征候复发。 *by* ~, by the next post 由最近邮班递寄: *Please send a reply by* ~. 请即回示(由原班邮递寄复)。 *in* ~ *(for),* as repayment (for). 以为报答; 回报; 回礼。 *Many*

happy ~s (of the day), phrase used as a greeting on sb's birthday. (生日贺辞)祝你长命百岁. **on sale or ~,** (of goods in commerce) supplied (to retailers) on the understanding that they may be ~ed to the wholesaler or manufacturer if not sold. 卖不掉时可退货的(指供给零售商之货物,经双方协议,未售出之货物可退给批发商或厂商). **a/the point of no ~,** (on a long voyage, flight across an ocean, etc) point at which fuel supplies, etc are insufficient for a ~ to the starting-point, so that continuation of the voyage, etc is essential; (fig) stage of negotiations at which no further progress seems possible. 不能回转点(在横越海洋等的长途航行或飞行中, 届储燃料等供应不足以维持返回原地故必须继续前行之地点); (喻)谈判时无任何进展之阶段. **2** (attrib) involving going back or coming back etc: (用作定语)归去的;回来的: the ~ voyage. 回航. ~ fare, needed for the journey both there and back. (车、船等之)来回费用. ~ half, the half of a ~ ticket for the journey back. 回程票. ~ match, one played between teams which have already played one match. (已经比赛过一次的两队间的)再次比赛. '~ ticket, one giving a traveller the right to go to a place and back to his starting-point (US 美 = two-way ticket). 来回票. ,day-'~, ~ ticket available only for the day of issue: 当天来回票: Two day-~s to London, please. 请卖给我两张去伦敦的当天来回票. **3** (often pl) profit on an investment or undertaking: (常用复数)利润;赢利: get a good ~ on an investment; 在一投资上获得优厚的利润; small profits and quick ~s, motto for shops that rely on large sales and quick turnover. 薄利多销. **4** [C] official report or statement, esp one that is compiled by order: 正式的报告或陈述(尤指受命而为者): make one's ~ of income (to the Inspector of Taxes for purposes of income tax); 向纳所得税向税务稽查)申报所得; the e'lection ~s, figures of the voting at an election. 选举报告(选票,数字之报告).

re·turn[2] /rɪ'tɜːn; rɪ'tɚn/ vi, vt **1** [VP2A, C, 3A, 4A] ~ (to) (from), come or go back: 回来; 归去: ~ home; 回家; ~ to London, 回伦敦; ~ from journey; 旅行回来; ~ to Paris from London. 从伦敦回到巴黎. He ~ed to collect his money. 他回来收取他的钱. I shall ~ to this point later in my lecture. 我稍后将在讲演中回头讨论这一点. **2** [VP3A] ~ to, pass or go back to a former state: 回复到以前状态: He has ~ed to his old habits. 他又恢复了他的旧习惯. After death animal bodies ~ (= change) to dust. 动物死后尸体又化为尘土. **3** [VP6A] (rare) reply; retort: (罕)回答; 反驳: 'Not this time', he ~ed. '这次不行', 他回答说. **4** [VP6A, 12A,13A] give, put, send, pay, carry, back: 归还;放回;送回;偿还;带回: When will you ~ (me) the book I lent you? 你什么时候把我借给你的那本书还我呢? In case of non-delivery, ~ to (the) sender, often written on letters sent by post. 无法投递时,退回原处. All books are to be ~ed to the library before Friday. 星期五前所有借阅书籍必须归还图书馆. He ~ed the blow (ie hit back) smartly. 他猛猛地还击一拳. She ~ed the compliment, said sth pleasant after a compliment had been paid to her. 她答谢别人对她表示的敬意. ~ thanks, express thanks, esp by saying grace before a meal, or in response to a toast. 致谢;感谢(尤用于饭前祷告或回答举杯祝贺). ~ed empties, empty bottles, crates, etc ~ed to the sender for re-use. 归还送来者(以便再使用)的空瓶、空篮等. **5** [VP6A, 16A] (of a constituency) send (sb) as representative to Parliament. (指一选区之选民)选出(某人)为国会议员. '~·ing officer n official in charge of a Parliamentary election and announcing the name of the person elected. 负责国会议员选举及公布当选人名单之官员. **6** [VP6A, 15A] state or describe officially, esp in answer to a demand: 正式宣布或说明(尤指应一项要求而做出者): ~ the details of one's income (for taxation purposes); 申报个人综合所得(为了纳税); liabilities ~ed at £2000. 宣布为两千镑之债务. The prisoner was ~ed guilty. 该囚犯被宣告有

罪. The jury ~ed a verdict of guilty. 陪审团作出有罪宣判. **7** [VP6A] give as a profit: 生(利): an investment that ~s a good interest. 有很好利润的投资. ~·able /-əbl; -əbl/ adj that can be, or is to be, ~ed. 可退还的;必须送还的.

re·un·ion /ˌriː'juːnɪən; ˌri'junjən/ n [U] reuniting or being reunited; [C] (esp) meeting of old friends, former colleagues, etc after separation: 再结合;重行结合;(尤指老友、旧日同僚等离别后之)重聚: a family ~ at Christmas. 圣诞节的合家团聚.

re·unite /ˌriːjuː'naɪt; ˌrijʊ'naɪt/ vt, vi [VP6A, 2A] bring or come together again: 使再结合; 再结合; 使重聚; 重聚: ~d after long years of separation. 多年别离后重聚.

rev /rev; rɛv/ vt, vi (-vv-) [VP2A, 6A, 2C, 15B] **rev (up),** (colloq) increase the speed of revolutions in (an internal-combustion engine): (口) 增加(内燃机)的旋转速度: Don't rev (up) (the engine) so hard. 别让(引擎)转动得太快. □ n revolution = (发动机的) 旋转: You're driving at maximum revs. 你在全速行驶.

re·value /ˌriː'væljuː; ri'vælju/ vt [VP6A] value again or anew; (esp) increase the value of a currency. 再估价; 重新估价; (尤指)增加(货币)的价值. **re·valu·ation** /ˌriːvæljʊ'eɪʃn; ˌrivælju'eʃən/ n revaluing: 再估价;重新估价;(货币的)升值: revaluation of the German mark. 德国马克的升值.

re·vamp /ˌriː'væmp; ˌri'væmp/ vt (colloq) patch up; reconstruct; renew: (口)修补; 重建; 修改: an old comedy; 修改一个旧喜剧; ~ agriculture in a backward country, try to improve it. 改良一落后国家之农业.

re·veal /rɪ'viːl; rɪ'vil/ vt [VP6A, 14, 9,25] ~ (to), **1** allow or cause to be seen; display: 显示; 显出: His worn jacket ~ed his elbows. 他的破短上衣使他露出了肘部. **2** make known: 泄露; 透露: ~ a secret. 泄露一秘密. One day the truth about these events will be ~ed. 这些事件总有一天会真相大白的. The doctor did not ~ to him his hopeless condition. 医生未向他透露他那已无希望的病况. Research has ~ed him to be the father of twelve children. 调查结果显示了他是一个有十二个孩子的父亲. ~ed religion, religion believed to be taught to mankind directly by God. 默示教; 天启教(被认为是系直接由上帝启示于人类的宗教).

re·veille /rɪ'vælɪ US: 'revəlɪ; 'rɛvl̩i/ n (in the armed forces) bugle signal to men to get up in the morning: (部队中的)起床号: sound the ~. 吹起床号.

revel /'revl; 'rɛvl/ vi, vt (-ll-; US -l-) **1** [VP2A, B, C, 15B] make merry; have a gay, lively time: 作乐; 狂欢享乐: They ~led until dawn. 他们通宵作乐. They ~led away the time. 他们狂欢作乐虚掷光阴. **2** [VP3A] ~ in, take great delight in: 深爱; 酷爱; 以…为乐: ~ in one's freedom; 深爱自由; people who ~ in gossip. 好讲闲话的人. □ n [C, U] (occasion of) lively, happy festivity: 作乐; 作乐的时际; 作乐的筵宴: Our ~s now are ended. 我的欢宴现在结束了. ~·ler, (US = ~er) /'revələr; 'rɛvlɚ/ n person who ~s. 纵情享乐的人.

rev·el·ation /ˌrevə'leɪʃn; ˌrɛvl̩'eʃən/ n **1** [U] revealing; making known of sth secret or hidden; [C] that which is revealed, esp sth that causes surprise: 显示; 泄露; 显示或泄露的东西(尤指引起惊愕者): It was a ~ to John when Mary said she had married him only for his money. 当玛丽向约翰说她只是为了他的钱才嫁他时, 使他大为吃惊. **2 R~,** the last book of the New Testament, called The R~ of St John the Divine, or (less correctly) R~s. 约翰启示录; (较不正确的说法)启示录(为新约最后一书).

rev·elry /'revlrɪ; 'rɛvlrɪ/ n [U] (or pl; -ries) noisy, joyous festivity and merrymaking: 吵闹作乐的筵宴; 狂欢作乐: when the ~/revelries ended. 当狂欢作乐结束时.

re·venge /rɪ'vendʒ; rɪ'vɛndʒ/ vt **1** [VP6A] do sth to get satisfaction for (an offence, etc to oneself or another): 报仇; 报复: ~ an injustice/insult; 对不公(侮

辱)采取报复; ~ one's friend, inflict injury (deliberately) on the person who injured one's friend. 为朋友报仇。 **2 be ~d on sb; ~ oneself on sb,** get satisfaction by deliberately inflicting injury in return for injury inflicted on oneself. 向某人报仇。 ⇨ avenge。 □ n [U] **1** deliberate infliction of injury upon the person(s) from whom injury has been received: 报仇; 报复: thirsting for ~; 渴望报仇雪恨; nurse thoughts of ~. 蓄意报仇。 get/take sb his ~; take ~ on sb (for sth); have/get one's ~ (on sb) (for sth); (为某事) 向 (某人) 报仇; do sth in/out of ~ (for sth). (为…) 报复地做某事(出于报复的目的)。 **2** [U] vindictiveness. 报复心; 报仇之欲望。 **3** (in sport) opportunity given for reversing an earlier result by a return match, etc. (运动中)由再次比赛等而获得转败为胜的机会; 雪恨的机会。 give sb his ~; 给某人雪耻的机会; get/take one's ~. 尽雪前耻。 ~ful /-fl, -fl/ adj feeling or showing a desire for ~. 复仇心的; 表现复仇心的。 ~fully /-fəlɪ; -fəlɪ/ adv

rev·enue /'revənjuː US: -ənuː; 'revə,nju/ n 1 [U] income, esp the total annual income of the State; government department which collects money for public funds: 收入; (尤指)国家的岁入; 税务署; 国税局: a '~ officer, a customs and excise officer; 税务官员; a '~ cutter, boat used to detect and prevent smuggling. 缉私船。 **Inland R~,** income from taxation, etc. 国内税收。 '~ tax, one designed to produce ~ (contrasted with taxes designed to protect a country's trade and commerce). 敛政税(为谋政府岁入所课之税, 别于以保护一国工商业所课者)。 **2** (pl) separate items of ~ put together: (复)收入之总额: the ~s of the City Council. 市议会的总收入。

re·ver·ber·ate /rɪ'vɜːbəreɪt; rɪ'vɝbəˌret/ vt, vi [VP6A, 2A] (esp of sound) send or throw back be sent back, again and again: (尤指声音)反复送或掷回; 被反复送回(的声音); 屈折; 反射; 反射: The roar of the train ~d/was ~d in the tunnel. 隧道中回响着火车鸣声。 His voice ~d from the walls of the cave. 他的声音从洞穴的墙壁上反折回来。 **re·ver·ber·ant** /-ənt; -ənt/ adj resounding. 反响的; 回响的。 **re·ver·ber·ation** /rɪ,vɜːbə'reɪʃn; rɪ,vɝbə'reʃən/ n [U] reverberating or being ~d; (pl) echoes; repercussions. 回响; 反射; (复)回声; 反响。

re·vere /rɪ'vɪə(r); rɪ'vɪr/ vt [VP6A] have deep respect for; regard as sacred, with great respect: 崇敬; 敬畏; 视为神圣: ~ virtue; 崇敬美德; my ~ grandfather. 我所崇敬的祖父。

rev·er·ence /'revərəns; 'revrəns/ n [U] deep respect; feeling of wonder and awe: 尊敬; 敬畏之情: hold sb/sth in ~; 尊敬某人或某物; have/show ~ for sb/sth. 对某人或某事物怀有(表示)敬仰。 □ vt [VP 6A] treat with ~. 尊敬; 崇敬。

rev·er·end /'revərənd; 'revrənd/ adj 1 deserving to be treated with respect (because of age, character, etc). (因年龄、品德等)应受尊敬的。 **2 the R~,** (usu shortened in writing to the Rev or Revd), used as a title of a clergyman: (通常缩写为为 the Rev 或 Revd) 牧师(或神父等)之尊称: the Rev John Smith 或 写作 the Rev J Smith (but not the Rev Smith); 约翰·史密斯牧师(注意写可写作 the Rev Smith); the Very R~ (of a dean); 住持或主持牧师; the Right R~ (of a bishop); 主教; the Most R~ (of an archbishop); 大主教; the R~ Father (of a R C priest); 神父。 **R~ Mother,** Mother Superior of a convent. 女修道院院长。 □ n (usu pl) clergyman: (通常用复数)牧师: a crowd of ~s and right ~s at the Lambeth Conference. 出席兰贝斯会议的一群牧师和主教。

rev·er·ent /'revərənt; 'revrənt/ adj feeling or showing reverence. 感觉虔敬的; 表现尊敬的。 ~ly adv

rev·er·en·tial /,revə'renʃl; ,revə'renʃəl/ adj caused or marked by reverence. 出于尊敬的。 ~ly /-fəlɪ; -ʃəlɪ/ adv

rev·erie /'revərɪ; 'revərɪ/ n 1 [C, U] (instance/occasion of a) condition of being lost in dreamy, pleasant thoughts: 沉湎于梦幻或快乐的思想的情况; 幻想; 幻想的实例; 幻想的时机: lost in ~s about the future. 沉醉于对未来的幻想中。 **2** [C] piece of dreamy music. 幻想曲。

re·vers /rɪ'vɪə(r); rə'vɪr/ n (pl ~ /-ɪəz; -ɪrz/) turned-back edge of a coat, etc showing the reverse side, as on a lapel. 外衣等衣里翻折在外面的边(如西服上衣的翻领)。

re·ver·sal /rɪ'vɜːsl; rɪ'vɝsl/ n 1 [U] reversing or being reversed: 反转; 倒退; 废弃; 被反转; 被倒退; 被废弃: the ~ of the seasons in the two hemispheres. 南北半球季节的颠倒。 **2** [C] instance of this: 反转等的实例: a ~ of procedure. 程序的颠倒。

re·verse¹ /rɪ'vɜːs; rɪ'vɝs/ adj ~ (to/of), contrary or opposite in character or order; inverted: 在性质上或顺序上相反的; 相对的; 颠倒的: this is the ~ direction to that; 这是与同那个相反的方向; the ~ side of a length of cloth; 一段布的反面; the ~ side of a coin or disc. 钱币或唱片的反面。 **in ~ order,** from the end to the start, or in the opposite order; in the ~ direction. 以颠倒的次序; 方向相反的。 ~ly adv

re·verse² /rɪ'vɜːs; rɪ'vɝs/ n 1 [U] the ~ (of), opposite; contrary: 相对; 相反: do the ~ of what one is expected to do. 做违背旁人期望的事。 Your remarks were the ~ of polite, were impolite. 你的评论是不礼貌的。 **2** [C] the ~ (of), (sth on the) reverse side of a coin, medal, disc, etc): (钱币、徽章、唱片等的)反面; 反面上的东西: On the ~ of this 50p coin there is a design showing a lion wearing a crown. 这枚五十便士硬币的反面有个戴皇冠的狮子的图案。 ⇨ reverse¹. **3** [U, C] mechanism or device that reverses: 倒退或换向的装置: Most typewriters have an automatic ribbon ~. 大部分打字机有一个自动的色带换向装置。 Most cars have three forward gears and (a) ~. 大多数的汽车都有三个前进档和(一个)倒档。 Put the car into ~. 把车子倒档。 **4** [C] defeat; change to bad for tune: 失败; 挫折; 不幸; 逆运: Our forces have suffered a slight ~. 我们的军队遭到轻微失败。 These financial ~s will prevent my taking a holiday. 这些经济上的挫折使我不能去度假了。

re·verse³ /rɪ'vɜːs; rɪ'vɝs/ vt, vi 1 [VP6A] turn (sth) the other way round or up or inside out: 反转; 颠倒; 翻转: ~ a procedure; 颠倒一程序; ~ one's policy. 完全改变自己的政策; 采取与原定政策相反之政策。 a ~d charge, charge for a telephone call (to be) paid by the person to whom the call is made instead of by the person who makes it. 由受话人缴纳之电话费。 ~ arms, (mil) hold the rifle with the muzzle pointing down (as at military funerals). (军)倒枪(如在军人葬礼中枪口向下致敬)。 **2** [VP6A, 2A] (cause to) go in the opposite direction: (使)向相反方向行进; (使)倒退: ~ one's car into the garage (back is the more usu word). 把车倒进车库(back 为较常用的字)。 **3** [VP6A] change the order, position, etc of: 改变…的次序或地位等: Their conditions are now ~d: A is poor and B is rich. 他们的状况现在改变了: A 穷, B 富有。 **4** [VP6A] revoke, annul: 废除; 取消: ~ the decision of a lower court; 撤消下级法院的判决; ~ a decree. 撤消一法令。 **re·vers·ible** /-əbl; -əbl/ adj that can be ~d, eg of cloth, either side of which can be used on the outside. 可反转、倒退、废弃的; 两面都可用的(例如布)。 **re·versi·bil·ity** /rɪ,vɜːsə'bɪlətɪ; rɪ,vɝsə'bɪlətɪ/ n

re·ver·sion /rɪ'vɜːʃn US: -ʒn; rɪ'vɝʒən/ n ⇨ revert.

re·vert /rɪ'vɜːt; rɪ'vɝt/ vi [VP2A, 3A] ~ (to), 1 return to a former state, condition, topic, etc): 恢复 (至以前的状态、情况、话题等): The fields have ~ed to moorland, have gone out of cultivation, etc. 这些田地又恢复成荒地。 R~ing to your original statement, I think…. 重回到你原来的叙述, 我认为…。 Garden plants sometimes ~ to type, go back to the wild kind from which they were developed. 园艺植物有时会恢复其原来

的野生形态。 *Mental patients sometimes ~*, ie to their condition before treatment started. 治疗中的精神病患者有时会回复到治疗前的状态。 **2** (legal) (of property, rights, etc) return at some named time or under certain conditions (to the original owner, the State, etc): (法律) (指财产、权利等) 在某指定时间或在某些情况下复归(原主、国家等): *If he dies without an heir, his property will ~ to the state*. 如果他死后无继承人, 他的财产即归国家。 **~·ible** /-əbl; -əbl/ *adj* that may ~. 可恢复原状的; 可复归观的; 可复归的。 **re·ver·sion** /rɪˈvɜːʃn *US*: -ʒn; rɪˈvɜʒən/ *n* **1** [U] ~ing (of property, etc). (财产等之)归属; 复归原主。 ⇨ **2** above. 参看上列第 2 义。 **2** [C] right to possess property in certain circumstances; land, property, etc to which one has such a right. 在某些情况下具有的财产权; 将来享有权; 继承权; 对之有此等权利的土地、财产等。 **3** [U] ~ing(1): 恢复; 倒转; 返祖: *reversion of plants, etc* (ie to ancestral types). 植物等之返祖(即恢复其生物形态)。 **re·ver·sion·ary** /rɪˈvɜːʃənərɪ *US*: -ʒəneri; rɪˈvɜʒən-,erɪ/ *adj* of reversion (2). 将来可享有的; 继承的。

re·vet·ment /rɪˈvetmənt; rɪˈvetmənt/ *n* retaining wall; facing of masonry, concrete, etc on an embankment, etc. 护土墙; 护堤壁; 拥壁; 护岸; 土堡。

re·view /rɪˈvjuː; rɪˈvju/ *vt*, *vi* **1** [VP6A] consider or examine again; go over again in the mind: 再考虑; 再检查; 检讨; 回顾; 复习: *~ the past*; 回顾过去; *~ last week's lesson*. 温习上礼拜的功课。 **2** [VP6A] inspect formally (troops, a fleet, etc). 正式考察; 检阅(部队、舰队等)。 **3** [VP6A,2A, C] write an account of (new books, etc) for newspapers and other periodicals: (为报纸或期刊) 写 (新书等)之评论: *His new novel has been favourably ~ed*. 他新写的小说已得到有利的批评。 *Mr Hay ~s for 'The Spectator'*. 海伊先生为'观察报'写书评。 ▭ *n* **1** [U] act of ~ing(1). 检讨; 回顾; 温习。 **come under ~**, be considered or examined. 被考虑或受检查。 [C] instance of such ~ing: 检讨、回顾、温习的实例: *a ~ of the year's sporting events*. 回顾一年中的运动项目。 **2** [C] inspection of military, naval, etc forces: 军事检阅: *hold a ~*. 举行军事检阅。 **3** [C] article that critically examines a new book, etc: 书评文章; 评论: *write ~s for the monthly magazines*; 为月刊写书评; *a copy of a book*, one presented by the publishers to the editor of a periodical for ~. 出版商送给杂志编辑以供写书评之用的书。 **4** [C] periodical with articles on current events, etc; new books, etc. 评论性杂志(刊载时事、新书等之评论文章的杂志)。 **~er** *n* person who writes ~s (of books, etc). 评论家; 书评家。

re·vile /rɪˈvaɪl; rɪˈvaɪl/ *vt*, *vi* [VP6A, 3A] ~ *at/against*, swear at; abuse: 向…咒骂; 辱骂; 谩骂: ~ *at/ against corruption*, 痛斥贪污舞弊; ~ *one's persecutors*. 辱骂虐待者。

re·vise /rɪˈvaɪz; rɪˈvaɪz/ *vt* [VP6A] reconsider; read carefully through, esp in order to correct and improve: 再考虑; (尤指)为改正或修订而仔细阅读; 校订: ~ *one's estimates*; 修订自己的估计; ~ *one's opinion of sb*. 改正对某人的看法。 *She's revising her notes for the exams*, going through them in preparation for them. 她为了准备考试而仔细阅读她的笔记。 **the R~d Version**, the Version of the Bible made in 1870—84 as a Revision of the translation published in 1611, known as the *Authorized Version*. 圣经修订本(在一八七○至一八八四年间, 由修订一六一一年出版的圣经钦定英译本而成)。 ▭ *n* [C] (printing) proof-sheet in which errors marked in an earlier proof have been corrected. (印刷)再校样; 再校稿。 **re·viser** *n* person who ~s. 校订者; 修订者; 再校者。 **re·vi·sion** /rɪˈvɪʒn; rɪˈvɪʒən/ *n* [U] revising or being ~d; [C] instance of this: 修订; 校订; 被修订; 被校订: *after two revisions*; 经两次修改或改正; [C] that which has been ~d; corrected version. 业经修订或改正之物; 改正之校样或版本之一。 **re·vi·sion·ist** /rɪˈvɪʒənɪst; rɪˈvɪʒənɪst/ *n* person who supports a review of the fundamental tenets of a political ideology. 修正主义者。 **re·vi·sion·ism** /-ɪzəm; -,ɪzəm/ *n* 修正主义; (对条约等的)主张修改论。

re·vital·ize /riːˈvaɪtəlaɪz; rɪˈvaɪtl,aɪz/ *vt* put new life into; restore vitality. 使新生; 使恢复活力。 **re·vital·iz·ation** /,riːˌvaɪtəlaɪˈzeɪʃn *US*: -lɪˈz-; ,rivaɪtl-ˈzeʃən/ *n*

re·vival /rɪˈvaɪvl; rɪˈvaɪvl/ *n* **1** [U] reviving or being revived; bringing or coming back into use or knowledge; [C] instance of this: 复活; 复苏; 复兴; 再兴; 复活等的实例: *the ~ of an old custom*; 一种古老风俗的再兴; *a ~ of a play by Maugham*; 毛姆的一个剧本的重新演出; *a ~ of trade*. 贸易之复兴。 **the R~ of Learning**, the Renaissance. 文艺复兴。 **2** [C] (series of meetings intended to produce an) increase of interest in religion: 宗教的奋兴; 信仰恢复: (用以提高大众信教兴趣的)奋兴大会: *a religious ~*; 宗教的奋兴; *~ meetings*. 宗教的奋兴大会。 **~·ist** /-vəlɪst; -vlɪst/ *n* person who organizes or conducts religious ~ meetings. 组织或领导宗教奋兴大会者; 信仰复兴运动(论)者。

re·vive /rɪˈvaɪv; rɪˈvaɪv/ *vi*, *vt* [VP6A, 2A] **1** come or bring back to consciousness, strength, health or an earlier state: 恢复或使恢复知觉、力量、健康或较早的情况; (使)复活; (使)复苏; (使)复兴: ~ *a person who has fainted*; 使一个晕厥的人复苏; ~ *an old play*, produce it for the theatre after many years. 重演一个老剧本。 *The flowers will ~ in water*. 这些花在水中会再活。 *Our hopes ~d*. 我们的希望复活了。 **2** come or bring into use again; 复用; 再兴; 使复用; 使再兴: *customs which ~/are ~d*. 再兴的风俗。

re·viv·ify /riːˈvɪvɪfaɪ; rɪˈvɪvə,faɪ/ *vt* (*pt*, *pp* **-fied**) restore to animation; give new life or liveliness to. 使苏醒; 使复活; 使有生气, 活力。

revo·cable /ˈrevəkəbl; ˈrevəkəbl/ *adj* that can be revoked. 可废止的; 可撤销的。 **revo·ca·tion** /,revə-ˈkeɪʃn; ,revəˈkeʃən/ *n* [U] revoking or being revoked; [C] instance of this. 废止; 撤销; 取消; 宣告无效等及其实例。

re·voke /rɪˈvəʊk; rɪˈvok/ *vt*, *vi* **1** [VP6A] repeal; cancel; withdraw (a decree, consent, permission, etc): 废止; 撤销; 取消; 宣告(命令、同意、允许等)无效: ~ *an order /a driving licence*. 撤销一命令(吊销一驾驶执照)。 **2** [VP 2A] (of a player at such card games as whist and bridge) fail to follow suit (ie not play a card of the same suit as that led by another player although he could do so). (指玩惠斯特和桥牌者)有牌不跟。 ▭ *n* failure of this kind. 有牌不跟。

re·volt /rɪˈvəʊlt; rɪˈvolt/ *vi*, *vt* **1** [VP2A, 3A] ~ (*against*), rise in rebellion: 反叛; 反抗: *The people ~ed against their oppressors*. 人民反抗其压迫者。 **2** [VP3A] ~ *against/at/from*, be filled with disgust or horror: 嫌恶; 厌恶: *Human nature ~s at/from/against such a crime*. 人性厌恶这样的罪行。 *This is a doctrine from which sensitive persons must ~*. 这是一种必为敏感的人所厌恶的教条。 **3** [VP6A] fill with disgust or horror: 使充满厌恶: *scenes that ~ed all who saw them*. 见者无不厌恶的景象。 ▭ *n* [U] act of ~ing; state of having ~ed(1): 反抗的行为; 厌恶的情况: *a period of ~*; 叛乱时期; *break out in ~*; 爆发叛乱; *stir sb to ~*; 鼓动某人反抗; [C] instance of this; rebellion or rising: 反抗的实例; 反叛; 暴动: *~s against oppression*. 对压迫的反抗。

re·volt·ing /rɪˈvəʊltɪŋ; rɪˈvoltɪŋ/ *adj* disgusting: 令人厌恶的: ~ *behaviour*; 令人厌恶的行为; ~ *to our ideas of morality*. 违反我们的道德观念。 **~·ly** *adv* in a way that disgusts: 令人厌恶地: *a ~ly dirty room*. 一个脏得令人讨厌的房间。

rev·ol·ution /,revəˈluːʃn; ,revəˈluʃən/ *n* **1** [C] act of revolving or journeying round: 旋转; 环绕: *the ~ of the earth round the sun*; 地球绕太阳的公转; [C] complete turn of a wheel, etc: (轮等的)旋转一周: *sixty-five ~s* (or, colloq ▭ *revs*) *a minute*. 每分钟旋转六十五次。 **2** [C, U] (instance of) complete change (in

conditions, ways of doing things, esp in methods of government when caused by the overthrow of one system by force): (情况、做事之方式, 尤指武力推翻一种制度引起的统治方法的)彻底改变; 革命: *the French R~* (in 1789); (1789年的)法国大革命; *~s in our ideas of time and space;* 我们对时空观念的大改变; *~s in our ways of travelling,* eg as the result of travel by air. 我们旅行方式的大改变(例如坐飞机旅行)。 **~·ary** /-ʃənərɪ US: -nerɪ; -ʃən,erɪ/ *adj* of a ~(2); bringing, causing, favouring, great (and perhaps violent) changes: 革命的; 带来、造成、赞成大(并可能是激烈的)改变的: *~ary ideas;* 革命的思想; *a ~ary society;* 革命性的社会; *imprisoned for advocating ~ary principles.* 为赞成革命的主义被监禁。 □ *n* supporter of a (political) ~. (政治)革命的支持者; 革命份子。 **~·ize** /-naɪz; -n,aɪz/ *vt* [VP6A] 1 fill with ~ary principles. 使有革命信仰。 2 make a complete change in; cause to be entirely different: 对…造成彻底改革; 使完全不同: *The use of atomic energy will ~ize the lives of coming generations.* 原子能的使用将使未来人类的生活有巨大改变。

re·volve /rɪˈvɒlv; rɪˈvɑlv/ *vt, vi* 1 [VP6A, 2A, 3A] ~ *(about/around),* (cause to) go round in a circle: (使)旋转: *A wheel ~s about/round its axis.* 轮子绕轴旋转。 *The earth ~s round/about the sun.* 地球绕太阳旋转。 *This theatre has a revolving stage.* 这家戏院有个旋转式舞台。 2 [VP6A] turn over in the mind; think about all sides of (a problem, etc): 考虑; 熟思(一问题等): *~ a problem in one's mind.* 熟思一个问题。

re·volver /rɪˈvɒlvə(r); rɪˈvɑlvɚ/ *n* pistol with a revolving mechanism that makes it possible to fire it a number of times without reloading. 转轮手枪; 左轮。

re·vue /rɪˈvjuː; rɪˈvju/ *n* [C] theatrical entertainment which consists of a medley of dialogue, dance and song, usu holding up current events, fashions, etc, to satire; [U] this form of entertainment: 时事讽刺剧(包括对话、舞蹈、歌唱, 通常多对时事、风尚等加以讽刺); 此种形式之表演: *to appear/perform in ~.* 演出(表演)时事讽刺剧。

re·vul·sion /rɪˈvʌlʃn; rɪˈvʌlʃən/ *n* [U] (no *pl*) 1 sudden and complete change of feeling: 心情的突然改变: *There was a ~ of public feeling in favour of the accused woman.* 舆论突然转而同情那个被指控的妇女了。 2 ~ *(against/from),* feeling of reaction. 厌恶; 嫌弃。

re·ward /rɪˈwɔːd; rɪˈwɔrd/ *n* 1 [U] recompense for service or merit: 报酬; 报答: *work without hope of ~;* 没有希望得到报酬的工作; *the ~ of virtue;* 美德的报酬; *get very little in ~ for one's hard work.* 虽辛苦工作, 得到的报酬却很少。 2 [C] that which is offered, given or obtained in return for work or services, or the restoration of lost or stolen property, the capture of a criminal, etc: (为工作或服务, 或寻回遗失或被偷的财物, 或捉住一罪犯等而给予或得到的)酬劳金; 赏金: *offer a ~ of £100 for information about a stolen painting.* 悬赏一百镑寻找失窃的画。 □ *vt* [VP6A, 14] ~ *sb (for sth),* give a ~ to (sb for sth): (为某事)给(某人)报酬或奖赏: *Is that how you ~ me for my help?* 那就是你为了我的帮忙而给予我的报酬吗?

re·wire /ˌriːˈwaɪə(r); rɪˈwaɪɚ/ *vt* provide, eg a building, with new wiring (for electric current). 装设新电线; 改装(电)线路。

re·word /ˌriːˈwɜːd; rɪˈwɚd/ *vt* [VP6A] express again in different words: 再以不同的词句表示; 改写; 改说: *If we ~ the telegram we can save one-third of the cost.* 我们如果把这电报改写一下, 就能省下三分之一的费用。

re·write /ˌriːˈraɪt; rɪˈraɪt/ *vt* [VP6A] write again in a different style, etc. 重写; 再写; 改写。 □ /ˈriːraɪt; ˈriˌraɪt/ *n* (colloq) sth rewritten: (口)改写的作品: (attrib) (用作定语) *a ~ man,* one employed to ~ articles, books, etc in a form suitable for publication. 受雇从事改写文章、书籍等的作家。

Rex /reks; reks/ *n* (abbr 略作 **R**) reigning king (used as **Regina** is used). 君; 王(用法如 Regina)。

rhap·sody /ˈræpsədɪ; ˈræpsədɪ/ *n* [C] (*pl* **-dies**) 1 enthusiastic expression of delight (in speech, poetry, etc): (在言论或诗等中)狂热欣喜的表现: *Everyone went into rhapsodies over Helen's wedding dress.* 大家热烈赞扬海伦的结婚礼服。 2 (music) composition in irregular form: (音乐)狂想曲: *Liszt's Hungarian Rhapsodies.* 李斯特的匈牙利狂想曲。 **rhap·so·dize** /ˈræpsədaɪz; ˈræpsəˌdaɪz/ *vi* [VP2A, 3A] *rhapsodize (about/over/on),* talk or write with great enthusiasm. 极热烈地说或写。

rhea /rɪə; ˈriə/ *n* three-toed ostrich of S America. 鹲鶓; 美洲鸵(南美洲产三趾鸵鸟)。

Rhen·ish /ˈrenɪʃ; ˈrenɪʃ/ *adj* of the River Rhine and the districts on its banks: 莱茵河及其流域的: *~ wine, hock.* 莱茵酒。

rheo·stat /ˈriːəstæt; ˈriəˌstæt/ *n* instrument for regulating the strength of an electric current by means of different resistances in the circuit, eg as in the volume control of a radio receiver. 变阻器(在电路中以不同的电阻控制电流强度的器具, 如无线电接收机的音量控制器内所用者)。

rhe·sus /ˈriːsəs; ˈrisəs/ *n* small monkey with a short tail, common in N India, often used in biological experiments. 印度北部常见的一种短尾小猴; 罗猴; 恒河猴(常被用来做生物学方面的试验)。 ⇨ the illus at **ape.** 参看 ape 之插图。

rhet·oric /ˈretərɪk; ˈretərɪk/ *n* [U] 1 (art of) using words impressively in speech and writing. 修辞; 修辞学。 2 language with much display and ornamentation (often with the implication of insincerity and exaggeration): 辞藻华丽的语言(常含浮夸的意味): *the ~ of that speaker.* 那个演讲人的花言巧语。

rhe·tori·cal /rɪˈtɒrɪkl US: -ˈtɔːr-; rɪˈtɔrɪkl/ *adj* in, using, a style designed to impress or persuade; artificial or exaggerated in language: 修辞的; 辞藻华丽或夸张的: *a ~ speech.* 夸张的演说。 *a ~ question,* one asked for the sake of effect, to impress people, no answer being needed or expected. (修辞学上的)反问; 反诘(为获取效果或加强别人印象, 而非需要或预期有答案的问题)。 **~·ly** /-klɪ; -klɪ/ *adv*

rhet·or·ician /ˌretəˈrɪʃn; ˌretəˈrɪʃən/ *n* person skilled in rhetoric or fond of rhetorical language. 修辞学家; 雄辩家; 好用华丽词藻的人。

rheum /ruːm; rum/ *n* [U] watery discharge from the nose or eyes. 鼻或眼所分泌之稀粘液; 鼻涕; 眼泪。

rheu·matic /ruːˈmætɪk; ruˈmætɪk/ *adj* relating to, causing, caused by, rheumatism; suffering from, liable to have, rheumatism: 风湿症的; 引起风湿症的; 由风湿症引起的; 患风湿症的; 易罹风湿症的: *~ joints.* 患风湿症的关节。 *~ fever,* serious fever with inflammation of joints, chiefly in children. 风湿病。 □ *n* 1 person who suffers from rheumatism. 风湿症患者。 2 (*pl* colloq) *~ pains.* (复, 口)风湿痛。

rheu·ma·tism /ˈruːmətɪzəm; ˈrumə,tɪzəm/ *n* [U] (kinds of) painful disease with stiffness and inflammation of the muscles and joints. 风湿症。

rheu·ma·toid /ˈruːmətɔɪd; ˈrumə,tɔɪd/ *adj* of rheumatism. 风湿样的; 风湿症的。 *~ arthritis,* chronic form of arthritis. 风湿样关节炎; 风湿性关节炎。

rhinal /ˈraɪnl; ˈraɪnl/ *adj* (anat) of the nose or nostrils. 解剖)鼻的; 鼻腔的。

Rhine /raɪn; raɪn/ *n* German river: (德国之)莱茵河: *~ wine,* = **hock.** 莱茵石。 '**~·stone** *n* kind of rock-crystal; paste gem made in imitation of a diamond. 莱茵石(一种水晶); 假金钢钻。

rhino /ˈraɪnəʊ; ˈraɪno/ *n* (*pl* **~s** /-nəʊz; -noz/) (colloq abbr of) rhinoceros. 为 rhinoceros 之略。

rhi·noc·eros /raɪˈnɒsərəs; raɪˈnɑsərəs/ *n* (*pl* **~es** /-əsɪz; -əsɪz/ or, collectively, **~**) thick-skinned, heavily built animal of Africa and Asia with one or

two horns on the snout. 犀牛(非洲与亚洲产的一种动物，皮厚体重，鼻上有一角或两角)。⇨ the illus at **large**. 参看 large 之插图。

rhi·zome /'raɪzəʊm; 'raɪzom/ n [C] (bot) thick, horizontal stem of some plants, eg iris, on or just below the ground, from which new roots grow. (植物)(鸢尾等植物长于地面上或刚好在地面下的)根茎；根茎。

rho·do·den·dron /ˌrəʊdə'dendrən; ˌrodə'dɛndrən/ n [C] kinds of evergreen shrub with large flowers growing in clusters. 杜鹃花属；山杜鹃。

rhomb /rɒm; ramb/, **rhom·bus** /'rɒmbəs; 'rambəs/ nn four-sided figure with equal sides, and angles which are not right angles (eg diamond or lozenge shape). 菱形。⇨ the illus at **quadrilateral**. 参看 quadrilateral 之插图。 **rhom·boid** /'rɒmbɔɪd; 'rambɔɪd/ adj of the shape of a ~. 菱形的。 rhombus with only its opposite sides equal. 平行四边形。⇨ the illus at **quadrilateral**. 参看 quadrilateral 之插图。

rhu·barb /'ruːbɑːb; 'rubɑrb/ n [U] 1 (garden plant with) thick, juicy stalks which are cooked and eaten like fruit. 大黄；大黄茎(粗大而多汁，可如水果般煮食之)。 2 (colloq) nonsense; (US) angry disagreement. (口) 胡说；(美) 争吵。

rhyme (US also **rime**) /raɪm; raɪm/ n 1 [U] sameness of sound of the endings of two or more words at the ends of lines of verse, eg say, day, play; measure, pleasure; puff, rough. 韵；韵脚(诗行末尾两字以上之尾音彼此相同，如 say, day, play 同韵; measure, pleasure 同韵; puff, rough 同韵)。 **without ~ or reason**, without meaning; nonsensically. 无意义的(地)。 2 [C] ~ (for/to), word which provides a ~: 押韵的字: Is there a ~ to/for 'hiccups'? 有什么字和 hiccups 押韵吗？ 3 [C] verse or verses with ~. 有韵的诗。 '**nursery ~**, verse for small children. 摇篮歌；儿歌；童谣。 4 [VP2A] write verse(s) with ~. 写押韵的诗。 **rhyming slang**, eg 'trouble and strife' for 'wife'. 押韵的俚语(如用 trouble and strife 表示 wife)。 3 [VP2A] write verse(s) with ~. 写押韵的诗。 ~d adj having ~s: 有韵的: ~d verse. 有韵的诗。 ~·ster /'raɪmstə(r); 'raɪmstɚ/ n (usu contemptuous) person who writes ~s or verses. (通常有轻蔑之意)写诗的人；打油诗人。

rhythm /'rɪðəm; 'rɪðəm/ n 1 [U] regular succession of weak and strong stresses, accents, sounds or movements (in speech, music, dancing, etc); regular recurrence of events, processes, etc: (说话、音乐、舞蹈等的)韵律；节奏；(事件、过程等的)有规律的重复: the ~ of the tides, their regular rise and fall. 潮汐的涨落。 2 [C] particular kind of such regular succession or recurrence. 某种有规律的连续或重复。 **rhyth·mic** /'rɪðmɪk; 'rɪðmɪk/, **rhyth·mi·cal** /'rɪðmɪkl; 'rɪðmɪkl/ adjj, marked by ~; having ~: 有节奏的；有韵律的妙处: the ~ical tread of marching soldiers. 行军中之士兵有节奏的步伐。

rib /rɪb; rɪb/ n [C] 1 any one of the 12 pairs of curved bones extending from the backbone round the chest to the front of the body in man, ⇨ the illus at **skeleton**; corresponding bone in an animal. 肋骨(参看 skeleton 之插图)；动物之肋骨。 **dig/poke sb in the ribs**, poke him to draw his attention (good-naturedly) to sth or to show enjoyment of a joke. (善意地) 触某人之肋骨(使其注意某事物，或表示欣赏一种有趣的笑话)。 2 (of various things like ribs) vein of a leaf; mark left on sand on the sea-shore by waves; (in a wooden boat) one of the curved pieces of timber to which planks are secured; raised line in a piece of knitting; long, narrow, raised ridge on cloth;

hinged rod of an umbrella-frame. (指许多类似肋骨的东西)叶脉；波浪留于海岸沙滩上的痕迹；(船的)肋材；织物的棱线；布上狭长高起的棱条；伞架之骨。 □ vt (-bb-) [VP 6A] supply with, mark off in, ribs: 供以肋骨状物; 以肋骨状物标示: ribbed cloth, having rib-like marks. 有棱条的布。 2 (US, colloq or sl) tease. (美，口或俚) 戏弄；嘲笑。

rib·ald /'rɪbld; 'rɪbld/ adj (of a person) using indecent or irreverent language or humour; (of language, laughter, etc) coarse; mocking: (指人) 使用猥亵或不敬的言语的; (指言语、笑声) 粗野的; (指言语、笑声) 粗鄙的: ~ jests/songs. 下流的戏谑(歌)。 □ n person who uses ~ language. 说脏话的人。 ~·ry /-drɪ; -drɪ/ n [U] ~ language; coarse jesting. 猥亵的言语，脏话；粗鄙的戏弄。

rib·and /'rɪbənd; 'rɪbənd/ n (old use) ribbon. (旧法) 丝带。

rib·bon /'rɪbən; 'rɪbən/ n 1 [C, U] (piece or length of) silk or other material woven in a long, narrow strip or band, used for ornamenting, for tying things, etc: 丝质或其他质料的狭长带子 (供装饰或绑东西等用): Her hair was tied up with a ~. 她的头发用一条丝带扎着。 Typewriter ~s may be all black or black and red. 打字带可以是全部黑色或黑红两色。 2 [C] piece of ~ of a special design, colour, etc worn to indicate membership of an order, as a symbol of a military decoration (when medals are not worn). (表示勋位，或作为军事勋章之象征的)勋表；奖表。 3 [C] long, narrow strip: 狭长之条: His clothes were hanging in ~s, were torn or worn to strips. 他的衣服褴褛不堪(破成一条一条的)。 The shirts were torn to ~s in the washing machine. 这些衬衣在洗衣机中被绞成了许多长条。 4 '~de'velopment n (the building of) long lines of houses along main roads leading out of a large town (considered to spoil the countryside). 带状发展 (大城市通往郊区的大路旁的建筑，被认为是会破坏乡村)。

ri·bo·fla·vin /ˌraɪbəʊ'fleɪvɪn; ˌraɪbə'flevɪn/ n [U] growth-producing factor in the vitamin B$_2$ complex, found in meat, milk, some vegetables, and produced synthetically. 核黄素(复合维生素 B$_2$ 中促进生长之要素，肉类、牛奶和某些蔬菜均含有此种成分，并可由人工合成)。

rice /raɪs; raɪs/ n [U] (plant with) pearl-white grain used as a staple food everywhere: 稻；米；大米: polished ~, with the husks removed; 精米; brown ~, unpolished ~; 糙米; ground ~, ~ ground to a fine powder. 米磨成之粉。⇨ the illus at **cereal**. 参看 cereal 之插图。 '~-paper n kind of thin paper used by Chinese artists for painting on; edible kind used in cooking and for packing cakes, sweets, etc. 宣纸(中国画家绘画所用者)；糯米纸(一种可食之纸，用于烹饪及包装糖果等)。

rich /rɪtʃ; rɪtʃ/ adj (-er, -est) 1 having much money or property: 富有的: the ~ and the poor, ~ people and poor people. 富人和穷人。 2 costly; splendid; luxurious: 昂贵的；华丽的；豪华的: ~ clothes/jewels/furniture. 华丽的衣服(昂贵的珠宝；豪华的家具)。 3 ~ in, producing or having much or many; abundant: 多的；富于…的；丰饶的: ~ in minerals; 矿藏丰饶的; an art gallery ~ in paintings by the Dutch masters. 一个收藏了很多荷兰大师绘画作品的画廊。 4 (of food) containing a large proportion of fat, oil, butter, eggs, etc: (指食物) 含大量脂肪、油、牛油、蛋类等的; 油腻的: a ~ fruit cake; 含大量油脂的水果蛋糕; a ~ diet. 油腻的食物。 5 (of colours, sounds, etc) full; deep; mellow; strong: (指颜色、声音等)宏亮清晰的；深沉的；柔和的；浓厚的: the ~ colours of the begonias, 秋海棠的鲜丽颜色; ~ tones; 宏亮的声调; the ~ voice of the baritone. 男中音宏亮的声音。 6 (colloq) highly entertaining; giving opportunities for humour: (口) 非常有趣的；很好笑的: a ~ joke; 一个非常有趣的笑话; a ~ incident. 一件很好笑的事。 That's ~! (often ironic). 真好笑！真有趣！(通常含有讽刺意味)。 ~·ly adj 1 in a ~ manner: 华丽地；富丽地；丰饶地；浓郁地: ~ly dressed. 衣着富丽。 2 (esp) (尤用于) ~ly deserved, thoroughly; fully: 彻底

地;充分地: *He ~ly deserved the punishment he received.* 他所受到的处罚实在是罪有应得。 **~·ness** *n* [U] quality or state of being ~ (but not usu in sense of 1 above). 富丽、肥沃、丰饶、柔和、低沉、浓郁等的性质或状况。

riches /ˈrɪtʃɪz; ˋrɪtʃɪz/ *n pl* wealth; being rich: 财富; 财宝; 富有: *the enjoyment of ~;* 财富之享受; *amass great ~.* 积聚大财富。

rick[1] /rɪk; rɪk/ *n* [C] mass of hay, straw, corn, etc regularly built up (and usu thatched or otherwise covered to protect it from the rain). 干草堆;禾堆。 □ *vt* [VP6A] make (hay, etc) into a ~. 堆(干草等)成禾堆。

rick[2] /rɪk; rɪk/ = **wrick.**

rick·ets /ˈrɪkɪts; ˋrɪkɪts/ *n* (with *sing* or *pl v*) disease of childhood, marked by softening and malformation of the bones, caused by deficiency of vitamin D as found in fresh food, eg milk, butter. (与单数或复数动词连用)佝偻病; 软骨病(小儿因缺乏新鲜食物如奶、牛油中的维生素 D 所致)。

rick·ety /ˈrɪkətɪ; ˋrɪkətɪ/ *adj* weak, esp in the joints; likely to break and collapse: 连接处不坚牢的; 易于破碎或倒塌的; 摇晃的: *~ furniture;* 摇动不牢的家具; *a ~ old car.* 一辆摇摇晃晃的旧汽车。

rick·shaw /ˈrɪkʃɔː; ˋrɪkʃɔ/ *n* two-wheeled covered vehicle for one or two passengers, pulled by a man. 人力车; 黄包车。 ˈ**cycle ~,** three-wheeled bicycle with ~ seating attached behind the driver. 三轮车。

rico·chet /ˈrɪkəʃeɪ *US:* ˌrɪkəˈʃeɪ; ˌrɪkəˋʃe/ *n* [U] jumping or skipping movement (of a stone, bullet, etc) after hitting the ground, a solid substance or the surface of water; [C] hit made by sth after such a jumping or skipping movement. (石头、子弹等击中地面、坚固物体或水面后的)跳飞; 回跃; 漂掠; 跳飞、回跃或漂掠后的一击。 □ *vi, vt* **(-t-** or **-tt-)** (*pt, pp* **-che(t)ted** /-ʃeɪd; -ˋʃed/) [VP6A, 2A] (of a shot, etc) (cause to) rebound, skip or bound off: (指弹丸等)(使)跳飞; 回跃; 漂掠: *The bullet ~ed off the wall.* 子弹自墙上跳飞。

rid /rɪd; rɪd/ *vt* (*pt, pp* **rid**) [VP14] ***rid of,*** make free: 使获自由; 解除; 免除: *rid oneself of debt/lice;* 还清债务(清除虱子); *rid a country of criminals ists/a house of mice.* 清除一个国家内的犯罪份子(一屋内的老鼠)。 ***be/get rid of,*** be/become free of: 摆脱; 解脱; 除去: *We were glad to be rid of our overcoats.* 我们很高兴脱掉了外套。 *These shoes are difficult to get rid of,* (eg of articles in a shop) difficult to sell. 这些鞋子很难卖掉。 *How can we get rid of this unwelcome visitor;* How can we manage to make him leave? 我们怎样才能摆脱这位不受欢迎的客人?

rid·dance /ˈrɪdns; ˋrɪdn̩s/ *n* [U] (usu 通常作 ***good ~***) welcome clearing away; state of being rid of sth unwanted or undesirable: 清除; 解除; 摆脱不需要或讨厌的事物的状态: *Their departure was a good ~,* it brought satisfaction because we wanted to be rid of them. 他们的离去真是一大快事。

rid·den /ˈrɪdn; ˋrɪdn̩/ (*pp* of **ride**[2]) (esp in compounds) oppressed or dominated by: (尤用于复合词中)受…压迫的; 受…控制的: ˈ*priest-~;* 教士嚣张的; 被教士压迫或控制的; ˈ*crisis-~;* 充满危机的。

riddle[1] /ˈrɪdl; ˋrɪdl̩/ *n* [C] **1** puzzling question, statement or description, intended to make a person use his wits: 谜(难解的问题、陈述或叙述, 目的在使一个人运用他的机智): *ask sb a ~;* 出一个谜给某人猜; *know the answer to a ~.* 知道一个谜的解答。 **2** puzzling person, thing, situation, etc: 难理解的人、事物、情况等: *the ~ of the universe/of existence.* 宇宙(存在)之谜。 □ *vt* ***~ me this,*** solve this ~ (as a challenge). 为我解决这个问题; 请你猜这个谜(作为一项挑战)。

riddle[2] /ˈrɪdl; ˋrɪdl̩/ *n* [C] coarse sieve (for stones, earth, gravel, cinders etc). (筛石、土、砂、煤渣等用的)粗筛。 □ *vt* **1** [VP6A] pass (soil, ashes, corn etc) through a ~; agitate (a grate, eg in a stove) in order to force ashes, small cinders, etc, through. 筛(土、灰、谷物等); 掏通(火炉等的铁架)以使灰、小煤渣落下。 **2** [VP6A, 14] ***~ (with),*** make many holes in (sth), eg by firing bullets into it: 打许多洞在(某物)上(如向之发射子弹): *~ a ship with shot;* 用炮弹把一条船打许多洞; *~ a man with bullets;* 用子弹把一人打得满是窟窿; *~ an argument,* refute it by bringing many facts, etc against it. 列举事实等反驳一议论。 ***be ~d with,*** be filled or permeated with: 充满; 弥漫: *a murder ~d with puzzles.* 迷离不解的凶杀案。

ride[1] /raɪd; raɪd/ *n* [C] **1** period of riding; journey on horseback, on a bicycle, etc or in a public conveyance: 骑乘的一段时间; 骑马、骑脚踏车或乘坐公共交通工具旅行 (cf 参较 *go for a drive* in a privately owned car, etc 驾自用汽车等出游): *go for a ~ before breakfast.* 早饭前骑一会儿马(或脚踏车)。 *'Give me a ~ on your shoulders, Daddy.'* '爹爹, 让我在你肩上骑一会儿。' *It's a fivepenny ~ on a bus.* 乘公共汽车去要五便士。 ***take sb for a ~,*** (colloq) deceive, swindle, or humiliate him. (口)欺骗或羞辱某人。 **2** road or track (use unpaved), esp one through a wood or forest for the use of persons on horseback and not normally used by vehicles. 供骑马用而在正常情形下不能行车的林间道路(通常为未铺路面者); 骑径。

ride[2] /raɪd; raɪd/ *vi, vt* (*pt* **rode** /rəʊd; rod/, *pp* **ridden** /ˈrɪdn; ˋrɪdn̩/) **1** [VP2A, B, C, 4A] sit on a horse, etc and be carried along; sit on a bicycle, etc and cause it to go forward: 骑马(等); 骑脚踏车(等): *He jumped on his horse and rode off/away.* 他跃上马背弛骋而去。 *He was riding fast.* 他骑马急驰(或骑脚踏车等飞奔)。 ***~ for a fall,*** ride recklessly; (fig) act in such a way that failure or disaster is probable. 骑马横冲直撞; (喻)卤莽行事。 **2** [VP6A] sit on and control: 骑(马等); 乘(车等): *~ a horse/pony/bicycle.* 骑马(小马、脚踏车)。 **3** [VP2A, C, 4A] be in, and be carried in, a cart, bus or other vehicle: 乘坐车辆或其他陆上交通工具: *~ in a bus;* 乘公共汽车; *~ in/on a cart.* 乘二轮马车。 **4** [VP6A] compete in, on horseback, etc: 比赛骑马或驾车: *~ a race.* 赛马; 赛车。 **5** [VP2C, 3A] ***~ on,*** sit or go or be on sth, esp astride, as if on a horse: 如骑马般跨坐或行进: *The boy was riding on his father's shoulders.* 那男孩正跨坐在他父亲的肩上。 **6** [VP15A] allow (sb) to ~(**5**): 让(某人)骑坐: *Shall I ~ you on my shoulders/knees?* 你跨坐在我的肩(膝)上好吗? **7** [VP2A] go out regularly on horseback (as a pastime, for exercise, etc): 经常骑马外出(作为娱乐或运动等): *I've given up riding.* 我已放弃骑马。 ***~ to hounds,*** go fox-hunting. 去猎狐。 **8** [VP6A] go through or over on horseback, etc: 骑马等穿越或跃过: *~ the prairies/the desert.* 骑马穿过大草原(大沙漠)。 **9** [VP2B] (of a jockey or other person) weigh when ready for riding: (指骑师或其他人)出赛前量体重: *He ~s 9 stone, 6 pounds.* 他出赛前重九呎六磅。 **10** [VP2D] (of ground, etc) be in a specified condition for riding on (usu on horseback): (指地面等)成某种供骑乘(通常指骑马)的特殊状况: *The heavy rain made the course ~ soft.* 大雨使那跑马场变得松软(骑起马来觉得地面很松软)。 *The ground rode hard after the frost.* 降霜后的地面骑起马来很坚硬。 **11** [VP6A, 2C] float on: 漂浮于; 漂行; 航行: *a ship riding the waves;* 一艘乘风破浪的船; float on water: 停泊水上: *a ship riding at anchor;* 一艘抛锚停泊的船; be supported by: 被…所支撑: *an albatross riding (on) the wind.* 一只御风飞行的信天翁。 *The moon was riding high,* appeared high as if floating. 月亮高悬天空。 ***~ out a storm,*** (of a ship) come safely through it; (fig) come safely through trouble, attack, controversy, etc. (指船)安然度过狂风暴雨; (喻)平安度过困难、攻击、争辩等。 ***let sth ~,*** (colloq) take no action on it; leave things to take their natural course. (口)听其自然。 **12** ***~ sb down,*** **(a)** chase (on horseback) and catch up with. 骑马追上。 **(b)** direct one's horse at sb so as to let the horse knock him down: 策马撞倒: *~ down a fugitive.* 策马撞倒一逃犯。 **13** [VP2C] ***~ up,*** eg of an article of clothing, shift or move upwards,

out of place. (如衣服等)往上滑而离开了原来的位置。**14 ridden** pp tyrannized, dominated: 受…压迫的;受…控制的: *ridden by fears/prejudices;* 充满恐惧(偏见)的; *'pest-ridden.* 满是害虫的。

rider /'raɪdə(r); 'raɪdɚ/ n **1** person who rides, esp one who rides a horse: 骑乘者; (尤指)骑马者: *Miss White is no ~.* 怀特小姐不善骑马。⇨ also di'spatch¹ at **dispatch**¹(2). **2** additional observation following a statement, verdict, etc: 供述、判决文等后面附加的评论; 附文: *The jury added a ~ to their verdict recommending mercy.* 陪审团在他们的判决文后面添加了一段建议,请求从轻量刑。~**less** adj without a ~: 无骑乘者的: *a ~less horse careering round the race-course.* 一匹无人骑坐的马在赛马场上奔驰。

ridge /rɪdʒ; rɪdʒ/ n [C] **1** raised line where two sloping surfaces meet: 脊: *the ~ of a roof.* 屋脊。'~**pole** n horizontal pole of a long tent; strong horizontal main beam at the apex of a roof. (长形帐篷的)横梁; (屋脊之)梁木。'~**tile** n tile for the ~ of a roof. 屋脊瓦。**2** long, narrow stretch of high land along the tops of a line of hills; long mountain range or watershed. 沿一列小山顶上的狭长高地; 山脊; 山脉; 分水岭。**3** (in ploughed land) raised part between two furrows. (耕地之)两畦间隆起部分; 畦背。□ vt [VP6A] make into cover with, ~s. 使成脊状。

ridi·cule /'rɪdɪkjuːl; 'rɪdɪkjul/ n [U] making or being made fun of; derision; mockery: 嘲笑; 被嘲弄; 嘲弄: *pour ~ on a scheme;* 对一计划加以讥笑; *an object of ~.* 被嘲弄之目标。*hold a man up to ~,* make fun of him. 嘲笑某人。*lay oneself open to ~,* behave so that people are likely to make fun of one. 使自己易受嘲笑。□ vt [VP6A] make fun of; cause (sb or sth) to appear foolish: 嘲弄; 使(某人或某事物)显出蠢相: *Why do you ~ my proposal?* 你为什么嘲笑我的提议?

rid·icu·lous /rɪ'dɪkjuləs; rɪ'dɪkjələs/ adj deserving to be laughed at; absurd: 可笑的; 荒谬的: *You look ~ in those tight jeans.* 你穿上那条紧身牛仔裤样子很可笑。*What a ~ idea!* 一个多么荒谬的想法。~**ly** adv

rid·ing¹ /'raɪdɪŋ; 'raɪdɪŋ/ n [U] (from **ride**²) (由 **ride**² 变来) '~**breeches** n pl used for riding on horseback. 马裤。'~**habit** n woman's long skirt and tight-fitting coat (worn when riding a horse). 女用骑装(长裙和紧身外衣)。'~**light/lamp** n light in the rigging of a ship which is at anchor. (船抛锚时缆索上挂的)碇泊灯。'~**master** n man who teaches horse-~. 骑术师。'~**school** n one for teaching and practising horse-~. 骑术学校。

rid·ing² /'raɪdɪŋ; 'raɪdɪŋ/ n (GB until 1974) one of the three administrative divisions of Yorkshire: (英, 1974 年以前) 约克郡的三个行政区之一: *the North/East/West R~* (约克郡北(东、西)行政区 (自 1974 年起改为亨伯赛德郡及北(南、西)约克郡)。

Ries·ling /'riːslɪŋ; 'rislɪŋ/ n dry, white wine. 一种无甜味的白葡萄酒。

rife /raɪf; raɪf/ adj (pred only) (仅作叙述用法) **1** widespread; common: 流行的;普遍的: *Is superstition still ~ in the country?* 迷信仍盛行于乡间吗? **2** ~ **with,** full of: 充斥的: *The country was ~ with rumours of war.* 这个国家充斥着战争的谣言。

riff /rɪf; rɪf/ n repeated phrase in jazz or pop music. (爵士乐或流行音乐中之)重叠句。

riffle /'rɪfl; 'rɪfl/ vt, vi **1** [VP6A] shuffle playing cards by holding part of the pack in each hand and releasing the edges so that they fall haphazardly into one pack again. 洗纸牌(两手各拿一些纸牌,并将牌的一端松开,使牌交错混在一堆)。**2** [VP6A] turn over (the pages of a book, periodical, etc) quickly. 迅速翻动 (书页)。[VP3A] ~ **through sth,** shuffle (a pack of cards); turn over quickly or casually (the pages of a newspaper, a periodical, etc). 洗(牌); 迅速或随意地翻

动(报纸、杂志书页等)。

riff-raff /'rɪf ræf; 'rɪf,ræf/ n **the ~,** ill-behaved people of the lowest class; the rabble; disreputable persons: 下层社会; 乌合之众; 声名狼藉的人。

rifle¹ /'raɪfl; 'raɪfl/ vt [VP6A] cut spiral grooves in (a gun, its barrel or bore). 在(枪,枪管或枪膛)内刻出螺旋形凹线;加膛线或来复线于。□ n gun with a long ~d barrel, to be fired from the shoulder; large gun with such spiral grooves; (pl) troops armed with ~s: 长枪管刻有螺旋形凹线的枪; 来复枪; 步枪; (复)步枪队: *the Royal Irish R~s.* 英国爱尔兰皇家步枪队。'~**range** n (a) place where men practise shooting with ~s. 步枪射击场。(b) distance that a ~bullet will carry: 步枪射程: *within/out of ~range.* 在步枪的射程内(外)。'~**shot** n (a) distance a ~ will carry. 步枪射程。(b) good marksman with a ~. 优秀的步枪射击手。'~**man** /-mən; -mən/ n (pl **-men**) soldier of a ~ regiment. (步兵团之)步枪兵。

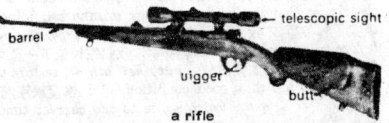
a rifle

rifle² /'raɪfl; 'raɪfl/ vt [VP6A] search thoroughly in order to steal from: 为偷窃而仔细搜查: *The thief ~d every drawer in the room/~d the drawers of their contents.* 那贼把屋里每个抽屉都搜遍了(搜寻抽屉里的东西)。

rift /rɪft; rɪft/ n [C] **1** split or crack: 裂缝; 裂隙: *a ~ in the clouds.* 云间之缝; 云缝。'~**valley** n steep-sided valley caused by subsidence of the earth's crust. 因地壳下沉而成的险峻之谷。**2** (fig) dissension (eg between two friends, friendly groups, parties, etc). (喻) (两个朋友、友好团体等之间的)失和。

rig /rɪg; rɪg/ vt, vi (-gg-) **1** [VP6A, 14, 2 A, C] **rig (with),** supply (a ship) with masts, spars, rigging, sails, etc; (of a ship) be supplied with these things; prepare for sea in this way: 将樯橹、帆桅、索具、帆等装备(船);(指船)装备有此等物件;准备出航: *rig a ship with new sails.* 给一船装新帆。*The schooner is rigging for another voyage.* 这艘纵帆式帆船正准备另一次航行。**2** [VP14, 15 B] **rig sb (out) (in/with sth),** (a) provide with necessary clothes, equipment, etc. 供以必需之衣物,装备等。(b) (colloq) dress up: (口)装束: *She was rigged out in her best clothes.* 她穿上她最漂亮的衣裳。*He rigged himself out as a sailor/tramp.* 他把自己装扮得象个水手(流浪汉)。'**rig-out** n (colloq) person's clothes, etc: (口)一个人的衣物等: *What a queer rig-out!* 一套多么奇特的衣服! *rig sth up,* (a) assemble or adjust parts of. 装配或校准各部分。(b) make, put together, quickly or with any materials that may be available: 匆匆地或用任何可用的材料拼凑: *The climbers rigged up a shelter for the night on a narrow ledge.* 爬山者在一个突出的狭窄岩石上,匆匆地架起一个帐篷过夜。*They rigged up some scaffolding for the workmen.* 他们为工人们搭了脚手架。(c) = rig sth out. □ n [C] **1** way in which a ship's masts, sails, etc, are arranged: 船具装置方法: *the fore-and-aft rig of a schooner.* 大帆船的纵帆装置法。**2** equipment put together for a special purpose: 有特殊用途的一套器材或装置: *an 'oil-rig/'drilling-rig,* ⇨ **oil**; *a test-rig,* on which motor-vehicles are tested for fitness. 试车装置。**3** (colloq) style of dress: (口)衣服的式样: *a bizarre rig.* 奇特的衣服式样。**rig·ging** n [U] all the ropes, etc which support a ship's masts and sails. 支撑船桅和帆的全部绳索;索具。**rig·ger** n person who rigs, etc; (esp) one whose work is to assemble and adjust the parts of aircraft. 装配(船等之)索具者,索具工;坞工; (尤指)装配飞机之人。

rig² /rɪg; rɪg/ vt (-gg-) [VP 6 A] manage or control fraudulently, eg for private profit: 以欺诈手段为私利而管理或控制, eg *rig the market, cause prices (of stocks, shares, etc) to go up (or down) by trickery*: 垄断市场(以欺诈手段使股票等之价格上涨或下跌); *a rigged election.* 有舞弊的选举。

right¹ /raɪt; raɪt/ adj (contrasted with *wrong*) (与 wrong 相对) 1 (of conduct, etc) morally good; required by law or duty: (指行为等) 正当的; 合法的; 应该的: *Always do what is ～ and honourable.* 永远做光明正大的事。 *It seems only ～ to tell you that....* 似乎应该告诉你···。 *You were quite ～ to refuse.* 你拒绝是很对的。 *You were ～ in deciding not to go/were ～ in your decision.* 你决定不去(你的决定)是很正当的。 2 true; correct; satisfactory; true; 对的; 令人满意的: *What's the ～ time?* 现在正确的时间是几点? *Your account of what happened is not quite ～.* 你对于发生的事情所作的叙述不太正确。 *Have you got the ～ (= exact) fare?* 你有恰好的钱付车资吗? *get sth ～*, understand sth clearly, so that there is no error or misunderstanding: 确实了解某事, 不致有错误或误解: *Now let's get this ～ before we pass on to the next point.* 我们在讨论下一点之前, 先把这一点彻底搞清楚。 *put/set sth ～*, restore to order, good health, a good condition, etc: 恢复秩序, 健康, 良好情况等: *put a watch ～*, ie to the correct time. 把表对准确。 *It is not your business to put me ～*, to correct my errors. 用不着你来纠正我的错误。 *This medicine will soon put you ～.* 这要不久就会使你恢复健康。 *,R～ you 'are!/,R～'o!/R～!* int (colloq) used to indicate agreement to an order, request, proposal, etc. (口)对极了! 好极了! (用以表示同意一项命令, 请求, 建议等)。 *All '～!/Alright!* /,ɔːl'raɪt; ɔl'raɪt/ int used to indicate agreement, approval, etc. 对! 好! (用以表示同意, 赞同等)。 *～-'minded* adj having opinions or principles based on what is ～: 见解正确的; 公正的: *All ～-minded people will agree with me when I say....* 当我说···时, 所有见解正确的人都会同意我的看法。 3 most suitable; best in view of the circumstances, etc; preferable: 最合适的; 就情况等而言最好的; 可取的: *Are we on the ～ road?* 我们走的路对吗? *Which is the ～ way to Exeter?* 到爱克塞特去走哪条路? *He is the ～ man for the job.* 他是担任这份工作最适当的人选。 *Which is the ～ side* (ie the side meant to be seen or used) *of this cloth?* 这块布的正面是哪一边? *Have you got it the ～ side up?* 你是否使正面朝上了呢? *He's still on the ～ side of fifty*, is still under 50 years old. 他还不到五十岁; 受某人器重。*get on the ～ side of sb*, win his favour. 获某人赏识; 受某人器重。 4 (all) ～, in good or normal condition; sound; sane: 健康的; 健全的; 神智清楚的: *Do you feel all ～?* 你没什么地方不对劲吧? *not (quite) ～ in the/one's head*, (colloq) not sane; foolish. (口)神智不(太)健全; 愚笨。 *not in one's ～ mind*, in an abnormal mental state. 心理不正常。 *～ as rain/as a trivet*, (colloq) perfectly sound or healthy. (口)十分健全; 十分健康。 5 (of an angle) of 90° (ie neither acute nor obtuse). (指角)九十度的; 直角的。 *at '～ angles/at a ～ angle (to)*, at an angle of 90° (to). (与···)成直角。 the illus at **angle**. 参看 angle 之插图。 *'～-angled* adj having a ～ angle: 成直角的: *a ～-angled triangle.* 一个直角三角形。 □ adv justly; justifiably; correctly; truly: 公正地; 有理由地; 正确地; 确实地: *act ～ly.* 行为正当。 *R～ly or wrongly, I think the man should not be punished.* 对也好, 错也好, 我认为这个人不应该受处罚。 *She has been sacked, and ～ly so.* 她被解雇了, 一点也不冤枉。 *Am I ～ly informed?* 我所知道的消息正确吗? *～ness* n

right² /raɪt; raɪt/ adv 1 straight; directly: 一直地; 直接地: *Put it ～ in the middle.* 把它放在正中间。 *The wind was ～ in our faces.* 风迎面刮来。 *～ away/off*, at once, without any delay. 立刻。 *～ now*, at this very moment. 在此刻; 此时。 *～ on!* int (colloq) used to indicate approval or encouragement. (口)好! (表示同意

或鼓励)。 2 all the way (to/round, etc); completely (off/out, etc): 全程地(与 to, round 等连用); 完全地; 彻底地(与 off, out 等连用): *Go ～ to the end of this winding road, and then turn left.* 走完这条弯弯曲曲的路, 再向左转。 *He slipped ～ to the bottom of the icy slope.* 他一直滑落到盖着冰的斜坡脚下。 *There's a veranda ～ round the building.* 这座建筑物的四周有个阳台。 *The pear was rotten ～ through.* 这个梨烂透了。 *The prisoner got ～ away.* 犯人逃得无影无踪。 *He turned ～ round.* 他转过身来。 3 justly; correctly; satisfactorily; properly: 公正地; 正确地; 令人满意地; 适当地: *if I remember ～* 如果我记得不错 (cf 参较 *if I am ～ly informed* 如果我知道的消息不错)。 *Have I guessed ～ or wrong?* 我猜得对还是错? *Nothing seems to go ～ with him*, Everything he does is a failure. 他似乎没有一件事是顺遂的。 *It serves sb ～*, It is what he deserves, he has been ～ly punished, etc. 某人罪有应得; 某人受罚不冤枉。 4 (old or dial use) to the full; very: (旧用法或方言用法)极度地; 很: *We were ～ glad to hear that....* 我们非常高兴听到···。 *He knew ～ well that....* 他十分了解···。 *'～-down* adj, adv (dial; more usu 较常用 *downright*) thoroughly(ly). (方)彻底的(地)。 5 *R～ Honourable*, ⇨ **honourable**. *R～ Reverend*, ⇨ **reverend**.

right³ /raɪt; raɪt/ n 1 [U] that which is right¹(1), good, just, honourable, true, etc: 公正; 正义; 公义; 道理: *know the difference between ～ and wrong.* 明辨是非。 *May God defend the ～.* 愿上帝维护正义。 *be in the ～*, have justice and truth on one's side. 站在正义与真理的一边。 2 [U] proper authority or claim; the state of being justly entitled to sth; [C] sth to which one has a just claim; sth one may do or have by law: 权利; 对某物有正当权利之状态; 有权利要求的东西; 可依法去做或具有的东西: *He has a ～/no ～/not much ～ to do that.* 他有权利(没有权利, 不大有权利)做那件事。 *What gives you the ～ to say that?* 你有什么权利说这话? *by ～(s)*, if justice were done; justly; correctly: 正当地: *The property is not mine by ～(s).* 这财产不是我的。 *by ～ of*, because of: 因为; 由于: *The Normans ruled England by ～ of conquest.* 诺曼第人统治英格兰, 因为他们征服了英格兰。 *in one's own ～*, because of a personal claim, qualification, etc not depending upon another person: 凭本人的权利, 资格等; 而非依赖他人: *She's a peeress in her own ～*, ie not only by marriage. 她出身贵族(并非靠婚姻关系)。 *～ of way, (a)* ～ of the general public to use a path, road, etc esp a ～ which has existed from ancient times through land that is privately owned: 道路的公众通行权(尤指自古即已存在之通过私有土地间之道路的权利): *Is there a ～ of way across these fields?* 公众有权通过这些田地吗? *(b)* (in road traffic) ～ to use the carriageway before others; precedence: (在交通中)优先使用车道之权; 优先通行权: *It's my ～ of way, so that lorry must stop or slow down until I've passed it.* 我有优先通行权, 所以那卡车必须停驶或减慢车速直到我走过去为止。 *human ～s*, those ～s that all people are or should be entitled to, eg a fair trial in a court of law, access to medical care and education, freedom of religion. 人权(人民有权享受的权利, 例如公平审判, 接受医疗及教育, 宗教信仰自由)。 ⇨ *the four freedoms* at **freedom**. *women's ～s*, (esp) of equality with men (in political, economic, social, etc affairs). 女权(尤指在政治, 经济, 社会等事务上同男人平等之权)。 ⇨ lib. *stand on/assert one's ～s*, say what one's ～s are and declare that they will not be surrendered. 坚持自己的权利。 3 (pl) true state. (复)真实的状态; 真相。 *put/set things to ～s*, put them in order. 使一切就绪。 *～s and wrongs*, true facts: 事实; 真相: *What are ～s and wrongs of the case?* 这案件的真相为何? ⇨ **right¹**(2).

right⁴ /raɪt; raɪt/ vt [VP 6 A] put, bring or come back, into the right or an upright position; make sth right again: 改正; 纠正; 使恢复直立: *The ship ～ed herself after the big wave had passed.* 大浪过去后, 船就

平稳下来了。*That fault will ~ itself,* will be corrected without help. 那错误会自行改正。*The driver quickly ~ed the car after it skidded.* 汽车滑向一侧，司机迅速加以控制。*~ the helm,* put it amidships, is neither to port nor to starboard. 把舵拨正(使不偏左舷，也不偏右舷)。

right⁵ /raɪt; raɪt/ adj (contrasted with *left*) of the side of the body which is toward the east when a person faces north: (与 left 相对)右面的;右方的: *my ~ hand/leg.* 我的右手(腿)。*In Great Britain traffic keeps to the left, not the ~, side of the road.* 在英国，车辆行人靠路的左边而非右边走。*The ~ bank of a river is on the ~ side as you look in the direction it is flowing.* 当你朝着顺流方向看去时，河的右岸就在你的右边。*one's ~ hand/arm,* (fig) one's most reliable helper. (喻)一个人的得力助手。*one's ~ hand,* all one's energy: 一个人所有的精力: *put one's ~ hand to the work,* work hard. 努力工作(全力以赴)。'**~hand** adj (to be) placed on the ~ hand: (要)放于右手的: *a ~hand glove.* 右手的手套。,**~'handed** adj **(a)** (of a person) using the ~ hand more, or with more ease, than the left. (指人)用右手较多或较灵敏的。**(b)** (of a blow, etc) given with the ~ hand. (指打击等)用右手击出的。,**~'hander** n **(a)** ~-handed person. 惯用右手的人。**(b)** ~-handed blow. 用右手击出之拳。,**~'turn** n turn to the ~ into a position at ~ angles (90°) with the original one. 向右转。,**~·about 'turn/'face,** ~ turn continued until one is faced in the opposite direction. 向后转。□ adv to the ~ hand or side: 向右方地;向右手边地: *He looked neither ~ nor left.* 他既不向右看也不向左看。*Eyes ~!* as a military command. 向右看—(齐)! *The crowd divided ~ and left.* 群众向左右两边分开。*~ and left,* everywhere: 到处;四处: *He owes money ~ and left,* owes money everywhere. 他到处欠债。□ n [U] **1** side or direction on one's ~ hand: 右边;右方;右面: *Take the first turning to the ~.* 在第一个拐弯处向右转。*Our troops attacked the enemy's ~,* wing or flank. 我们的军队攻击敌人右翼。**2** (politics; usu **R~**) conservative or reactionary party or parties: (政治; 通常大写)保守的或反动的党派;右翼;右派: *members of the R~.* 保守份子;右翼份子。**~·ist** /-ɪst; -ɪst/ n member of a ~ wing political party. 右翼份子;保守份子。□ adj of such a party: 保守党的;右派的: *~ist sympathizers.* 保守党的同情者;保守党的支持者。

right·eous /'raɪtʃəs; 'raɪtʃəs/ adj **1** doing what is morally right; obeying the law: 正直的;守法的: *the ~ and the wicked,* good and bad people. 正直的人和邪恶的人。**2** morally justifiable: 正当的;正义的: *~ anger.* 义愤。**~·ly** adv **~·ness** n

right·ful /'raɪtfl; 'raɪtfəl/ adj **1** according to law and justice: 依据法律和正义的;合法的: *the ~ king;* 合法的国王; *the ~ owner of the land.* 土地的合法所有人。**2** (of actions, etc) fair; justifiable. (指行动等)公正的;有理由的。**~·ly** /-fəlɪ; -fəlɪ/ adv **~·ness** n

rigid /'rɪdʒɪd; 'rɪdʒɪd/ adj **1** stiff; unbending; that cannot be bent: 僵硬的;坚挺的;不能弯曲的: *a ~ support for a tent.* 一个帐篷的坚挺的支柱。**2** firm; strict; not changing; not to be changed: 坚强的;严厉的;严格的;不变的;不能改变的: *a ~ disciplinarian,* 一个严格维持纪律的人; *practise ~ economy.* 厉行节约。**~·ly** adv **ri·gid·ity** /rɪ'dʒɪdətɪ; rɪ'dʒɪdətɪ/ n [U] **1** stiffness; inflexibility: 僵硬;不变; 刚性; 刚度: *the ~ity of his political beliefs.* 他的政治信仰坚定不移。**2** strictness; sternness. 严厉;严格。

rig·ma·role /'rɪɡmərəʊl; 'rɪɡmə,rol/ n [U] **1** long, wandering story or statement that does not mean much; incoherent account or description. 冗长、散漫而无多大意义的故事或陈述; 散漫无章的说明或描述。**2** confusing and tiring procedure. 纷乱烦杂的手续。

rigor mor·tis /,rɪɡə 'mɔːtɪs; 'raɪɡər'mɔrtɪs/ n (Lat) the stiffening of the muscles after death. (拉)死后肌肉之僵硬;尸僵。

rig·or·ous /'rɪɡərəs; 'rɪɡərəs/ adj **1** stern; strict; severe: 严格的;严厉的: *~ discipline;* 严格的训练; *a ~ search for dutiable goods.* 严格搜查应纳税货物。**2** harsh; severe: 严酷的;剧烈的: *a ~ climate.* 严寒或酷热的气候。**~·ly** adv

rig·our (US = **rigor**) /'rɪɡə(r); 'rɪɡə/ n **1** [U] sternness; strictness; strict enforcement of rules, etc): 严格;严厉;(规则等的)严厉执行: *punish sb with the utmost ~ of the law.* 以最严厉的法律处罚某人。**2** (often *pl*) severe conditions: (常用复数)严酷;艰苦: *the ~s of prison life;* 监狱生活的艰苦; *the ~(s) of the winter in Canada,* the severe climatic conditions. 加拿大冬季的酷寒。

rile /raɪl; raɪl/ vt [VP6A] (colloq) annoy; rouse anger in: (口)惹恼;激怒: *It ~d him that no one would believe his story.* 没有人相信他的故事使他很恼火。

rill /rɪl; rɪl/ n small stream; rivulet. 小溪;小川。

rim /rɪm; rɪm/ n [C] circular edge of the framework of a wheel, on which the tyre is fitted, ⇨ the illus at **bicycle;** border (of steel, gold, etc) round the lenses of spectacles (hence *rimless spectacles,* having lenses without rims); edge, border or margin of sth circular: 轮缘;轮辋(参看 bicycle 之插图);(钢、金等的)眼镜框(由此产生 rimless spectacles,'无框眼镜'一词);任何圆形物体的缘、周或边: *the rim of a cup/bowl;* 杯(碗)之边缘; *frame of a sieve.* 筛框。,**red-'rimmed** adj (of eyes) having red rims, eg from weeping. (指眼)(因哭泣等而)眼圈红红的。□ vt (-mm-) [VP6A] provide with a rim; be a rim for. 镶以边;为…之边。

rime¹ /raɪm; raɪm/ n (liter) hoarfrost. (文)白霜。⇨ **hoar.** □ vt [VP6A] cover with or as with ~. 覆以霜或似霜之物。

rime² /raɪm; raɪm/ n = **rhyme.**

rind /raɪnd; raɪnd/ n [U] hard, outside skin or covering (of some fruits, eg melons, or of bacon and cheese); [C] piece or strip of this skin; tough covering of one fruit. (某些水果如瓜类或腌肉与奶酪的)外皮;此等外皮的一片或一条;一个水果的坚硬外皮。

rin·der·pest /'rɪndəpest; 'rɪndɚ,pest/ n [U] contagious virus disease of cattle. 牛瘟。

ring¹ /rɪŋ; rɪŋ/ n [C] **1** circular band (often of gold or platinum, and set with a gem or gems) worn round a finger as an ornament, or as a token: 戴于指上作装饰物或信物的金属环(常用黄金或白金制成,并常镶有珠宝);指环: *an en'gagement ~;* 订婚戒指; *a 'wedding ~;* 结婚戒指;similar band for other parts of the body: 身体其他部分所戴的类似之环: *an 'ear~,* a 'nose~. 耳环,鼻环。'**~-finger** n third of the left hand. 左手的无名指。**2** circular band of any kind of material, eg metal, wood, ivory: 任何材料(如金属、木、象牙)制的环状物: *a 'napkin ~;* 束餐巾用的小环; *a 'key-~,* one of split metal, for carrying keys on. 锁子铠。⇨ '**~-mail** / **armour** nn = chain-armour. 锁子铠。⇨ **chain(4). 3** circle: 圆圈;圆环: *a ~ of light round the moon;* 月亮的晕轮; *the ~s of a tree,* seen in concentric circles of wood when the trunk is cut across, showing the tree's age: 树的年轮(横切树干时所见到的许多同心圆,可显示树木之年龄); *puff out 'smoke~s* (of cigarette smoke). (抽香烟时)喷出烟圈儿。*The men were standing in a ~.* 那些人站成一个圆圈。*make/run '~s round sb,* move, do things, much faster than he does. 行动或做事比某人快得多。**4** combination of persons working together for their own advantage: (为私利而结合在一起的)集团: *a ~ of smugglers.* 走私集团。**5** ('circus~), circular enclosure or space for circus-riding. 马戏场。'**~·mas·ter** n man who directs performances in a circus-~. 马戏团演出指导。**6** space for the showing of cattle, dogs, etc (at farming exhibitions), etc). (农业展览会等中)家畜展览场。**7** betting at race meetings. 赌赛马。**the ~,** book-makers collectively. (集合用法)以赌赛马为业者。⇨ **book¹(8). 8 the 'prize-~,** ⇨ **prize¹(3). 9** (compounds) (复合词) '**~-leader** n person who leads a group

of criminals, etc (罪犯等之) 首领; 头目. '∼-**road**
n road round and through the outskirts of a town,
for the use of through traffic and designed to avoid
congestion in the centre. 环城公路(围绕城市并穿过市郊
的环状道路,为捷运及避免市区拥塞而建). Cf by-pass, a
new road specially constructed. (参较 by-pass, 系特别
铺筑之新道路). '∼-**side** n place near to the ring of a
circus, prize-fight, etc: 贴近马戏场、拳击场等之处: *have
a* ∼*side seat*, be favourably placed for seeing an event,
etc. 获一场边座位; 位于可以看清楚的地方. '∼-**worm** n
[U] contagious disease of the skin, esp of children,
causing round, red patches. 癣; 金钱癣. □ *vt, vi* (*pt,
pp* ∼ed) 1 [VP6A, 15B] surround: 围绕; 环绕: *be
* ∼ed about with enemies; 为敌人所包围; ∼ *cattle*, hem
them into one place. 把牲口围于一处. 2 [VP6A] put
a ∼ in the nose of (a bull, etc) or on the leg of (a
bird, eg a homing pigeon). 给(牛等)带鼻圈; 给(鸟, 如传
信鸽)腿上系一金属环. 3 [VP6A] (in games) toss or
throw a ring or a horseshoe round, eg a mark, peg,
etc; make a ring round (sth), eg with a pencil, or by
shooting holes round a target. (游戏中)掷环或蹄形铁于
(标的或椿)上; 绕(某物)形成一圆圈(例如用铅笔画); 用弹
绕一靶子用子弹射成一圈). 4 [VP2A] (of a hunted
fox) take a circular course. (指被猎之狐)绕圈跑.

ring[2] /rɪŋ/ rɪŋ/ *vt, vi* (*pt* **rang** /ræŋ/; ræŋ/, *pp* **rung**
/rʌŋ/; rʌŋ/) 1 [VP2A, B, C] give out a clear, musical
sound as when metal vibrates: 发出如金属震动时清晰悦
耳之声音, 鸣; 响: *How long has that telephone* (*bell*) *been
* ∼*ing*? 电话(铃)响了多久啦? *Start work when the bell
* ∼*s*. 铃响时即开始工作. *A shot rang out*, The noise of
a shot was heard. 听到一声枪响. 2 [VP2D] produce a
certain effect when heard: 听起来…: *His words rang
hollow*, What he said seemed insincere. 他的话听起来似
乎不诚恳. *His words rang true*. 他的话听起来似乎是真
的. *The coin rang true/false*, seemed, when tested by
being thrown down, to be genuine/counterfeit. 这硬
币听声音是真的(假的). 3 [VP2A, 3A] ∼ (*for sb/
sth*), cause a bell to sound, as a summons, warning,
etc: 鸣铃召唤, 警告等: *She rang for the porter*. 她按铃叫
门房. *Did you* ∼, *sir*? 是你按铃叫我吗, 先生? *Someone
is* ∼*ing at the door*, ∼ing for admittance or attention.
有人在按门铃. *The cyclist didn't* ∼. 那个骑脚踏车的人
没有按铃. 4 [VP6A] cause sth, esp a bell, to ∼: 使
鸣; 使响; (尤指)使铃、铃响: ∼ *the bells*; 鸣钟; ∼ *the
bell for the steward*; 按铃唤侍者; ∼ *a coin*, test its
genuineness by throwing it down on sth and listening
to the sound. 掷硬币于某物之上, 以听其声音, 辨其真伪.
∼ *a bell*, (colloq) bring sth vaguely back to mind:
(口)模糊忆起某事物: *Ah! That* ∼*s a bell*! 啊! 我好象记
起来了! ∼ *the bell*, (colloq) be successful in sth. (口)
做某事成功. 5[VP3A] ∼ (*with sth*), resound; re-echo:
回响; 回声: *The children's playground rang with happy
shouts*. 孩子们的游戏场上回响着快乐的呼喊声. *The
village rang with the praises of the brave girl*. 村子里人
皆称道那个勇敢的女孩子. 6 [VP2C] linger in one's
hearing or memory: 萦绕于耳际或记忆中: *His last
words are still* ∼*ing in my ears*. 他的遗言仍留在我耳
际. 7 [VP2A, 3A] ∼ (*with*), (of the ears) be filled
with a ringing or humming sound: (指耳)充满着鸣声或
嗡嗡声: *My ears are still* ∼*ing*. 我的耳中仍有鸣声(我
仍耳鸣). 8 ∼ *sb* (*up*), get into communication with sb
by telephone: 打电话找某人: *I'll* ∼ *you* (*up*) *this
evening*. 我今晚将给你电话. (US 美 = *call sb* (*up*).)
∼ *off*, end a telephone conversation. 挂断电话. 9 [VP
6A] (of a chime of bells) announce (the hour, etc);
strike the hours: (指一套钟)报(钟点等); 敲出钟点: *The
bell* ∼*s the hours, but not the quarters*. 那钟是每小时
响, 不是每刻钟响. 10 [VP6A, 15B] give a signal by
∼ing a bell, etc: 鸣铃铃等作信号: ∼ *the knell of sth*,
announce its end or downfall; 宣布某事之结束或崩溃;
∼ *an alarm*, give one by ∼ing bells. 鸣钟示警. ∼ *the
curtain up/down*, (in a theatre) give the signal for

it to be raised/lowered. (剧院中)鸣铃以示升幕(落幕).
11 [VP6A] sound (a peal, etc with a bell or bells).
(以钟)鸣响(钟乐等). ∼ *the changes* (*on*), (of church
bells) ring the bells in the different orders which are
possible; (fig)put or arrange things, do things, in as many
different ways as possible. (指教堂的钟)以各种不同次
序鸣钟; (喻)以各种不同方式安排或做事. 12 [VP15B]
announce or celebrate the beginning or end of sth by
∼ing bells. 以鸣铃宣告以庆祝某事之开始或结束. ∼
out the Old (*Year*) *and* ∼ *in the New*. 鸣钟送旧岁迎
新年. □ n 1 (*sing only*) resonant sound produced by
a bell or piece of metal when it is struck: (仅用单数)钟
或金属所被敲击时发出之共鸣音: *This coin has a good
* ∼. 这硬币声音很悦耳. 2 (*sing only*) loud and clear
sound: (仅用单数)宏亮而清晰的声音: *the* ∼ *of happy
voices*. 欢声响亮. *There was a* ∼ *of sincerity in his
promise*. 他的允诺听起来颇为真诚. 3 [C] act of ∼ing:
There was a ∼ *at the door*. 有人按门铃. *I'll give you
a* ∼ *this evening*, call you up (by telephone). 我今
晚给你电话. ∼*er* n bell-ringer. 摇铃者; 鸣钟(铃)者.

ring·let /'rɪŋlɪt; 'rɪŋlɪt/ n [C] small curl of hair:
小发卷: *Her hair hung down in* ∼*s*. 她的头发呈许多小
发鬈下垂着.

rink /rɪŋk; rɪŋk/ n [C] specially prepared sheet of
ice for skating or hockey, or floor for roller-skating.
溜冰场; 冰球场; 轮式溜冰场.

rinse /rɪns; rɪns/ *vt* [VP6A, 15A, B] 1 ∼ *sth* (*out*);
∼ *sth out of sth*, wash with clean water in order to
remove unwanted substances, etc: 以清水冲洗(以除去不
要之物): ∼ *soap out of the clothes*; 以清水冲去衣服上的
肥皂; ∼ *the clothes*, to get soapy water out; 以清水冲去
衣服上的肥皂水; ∼ (*out*) *the teapot*; 以清水冲洗茶壶; ∼
the tea-leaves out of the pot; 以清水冲去茶壶里的茶叶; ∼
(*out*) *the mouth*, eg while being treated by a dentist.
漱口(如在牙医处接受治疗时). 2 ∼ *sth down*, help
(food) down with a drink: 以水或其他液体吞下(食物):
R∼ *it down with a glass of beer*. 用一杯啤酒把它吞下.
□ n 1 act of rinsing: 冲洗之动作; 洗涤; 清洗: *Give your
hair a good* ∼ *after you've shampooed it*. 头发用过洗发
剂后, 要用清水冲洗干净. 2 solution for tinting the
hair: 染发液: *the blue* ∼ *used by some elderly women*.
某些年长的妇女所用的蓝色染发液.

riot /'raɪət; 'raɪət/ n 1 [C] violent outburst of
lawlessness by the people in a district: 暴动; 骚动: *put
down a* ∼ *by force*. 以武力镇压一场暴动. *R∼s during
the election were dealt with by the police*. 选举时之骚动
被警察制止了. *the* '*R∼ Act*, act dealing with the
prevention of ∼s and the breaking up of disorderly
crowds. 暴乱取缔法. *read the* '*R∼ Act*, (a) read part
of this Act officially to disorderly persons after which,
if they do not disperse, they can be arrested for felony.
宣读暴乱取缔法(向骚扰份子宣读本法案之一部分条文, 如
群众不自动散去, 即以重罪予以逮捕); 下令禁止骚动. (b)
(joc, eg of parents) give a warning that noisy and
unruly behaviour must stop. (谑, 指父母等)警告吵闹和
捣乱行为必须停止. 2 [U] noisy, uncontrolled behaviour
(not lawless). 欢闹, 放肆(但并不违法)的行为. *run* ∼,
throw off all discipline; (of plants) be out of control
by growing fast and luxuriantly. 放肆, 滋闹; (指植物)
蔓延滋长. 3 *a riot* (*of*), profusion; luxuriance: 繁多;
茂盛; 丰盛: *The flower-beds were a* ∼ *of colour*. 花坛里
一片彩色缤纷. 4 *a* ∼ (*of*), unrestrained indulgence
in or display of sth: 无节制的放纵或展示: *a* ∼ *of
emotion*. 感情泛滥. 5 *a* ∼, (colloq) occasion of wild
enthusiasm (as indicating great success): (口)轰动之场
合(如指大的成功): *His latest play was a* ∼ *when it was
produced in New York*. 他最近写的剧本在纽约演出时极
为轰动. □ *vi* 1 [VP2A, B, C] take part in a ∼ (1, 2):
参与骚扰或欢闹: *The voters were* ∼*ing all night after
the election*. 选民们于选举之后终宵狂欢. 2 [VP3A]
∼ *in*, indulge or revel in: 放纵; 恣情: *The tyrant* ∼*ed
in cruely*. 那暴君残暴无度. ∼*er* n person who ∼s. 骚

动者；欢闹者；放纵者。 ~·ous /-əs; -əs/ adj likely to
cause a ~; unruly; disorderly; running wild: 可能引起
暴动的；骚扰的；暴乱的；放荡的: a ~ous assembly; 一个
可能引起骚动的集会; charged with ~ous behaviour. 被
控有骚扰之行为。 ~·ous·ly adv

rip /rɪp; rɪp/ vt, vi (-pp-) **1** [VP 6 A, 15 A, B, 22]
pull, tear or cut (sth) quickly and with force (to get
it off, out, open, etc): 迅速地用力地将(某物)拉开；撕开；
割开: rip open a letter; 撕开一信; rip the cover off; 把
盖子扯开; rip the seams of a garment; 拆开衣缝; rip a
piece of cloth in two; 把一块布撕为两段; make a long
cut or tear in: 割裂；撕裂: rip a tyre, etc on a rocky
road. 把一轮胎刮破(在多石的路上)。 My poor cat
had its ear ripped open by a dog. 我那可怜的猫的耳朵被
一只狗撕裂了。 **rip sth/sb off**, (sl) steal (it); defraud
(him). (俚)偷窃(某物)；诈骗(某人)。 Hence, 由此产生,
'**rip-off** n sth stolen; instance of stealing or defrauding.
被窃之物；偷窃；诈骗。 '**rip-cord** n cord which, when
pulled during a descent, releases a parachute from
its pack; cord pulled to release gas from a balloon. 开伞
索(拉动后使降落伞脱离伞包之绳索)；放气索(拉动后使气
球放气之绳索)。 **2** [VP 6 A] saw (wood, etc) with the
grain. 沿纹理锯(木材等)；纵锯。 '**rip-saw** n saw used
for this. 纵割锯；粗齿大锯。 **3** [VP 2 A] (of material)
tear; be ripped. (衣料)破裂；裂开。 **4** [VP 2 A, C]
go forward, rush along. 向前行；向前冲。 **Let her/it
rip**, (colloq) (of a boat, car, machine, etc) allow it to
go at its maximum speed. 让它全速(指船、车、机器
等, 勿限制其速度)。 **let things rip**, cease to exercise
control; let things take their natural course. 任其自由
发展而不予以控制。 □ n [C] torn place; long cut:
裂开之处；长裂痕: The rips in my tent were made by the
horns of that angry bull. 我帐篷上的裂缝是被那只愤怒
的公牛的角撕破的。

ri·par·ian /raɪˈpeərɪən; rɪˈperɪən/ adj of, on, the
bank(s) of a river or lake: 河岸或湖岸的；在河岸或湖岸
上的: ~ rights, eg to catch fish in the river; 河岸权(例
如在该河中捕鱼之权); ~ property. 河岸财产。

ripe /raɪp; raɪp/ adj **1** (of fruit, grain, etc) ready
to be gathered and used: (指水果、谷物等)成熟的:
~ fruit; 成熟的水果; cherries not ~ enough to eat;
还未熟得能吃的樱桃; ~ corn; 已熟的谷物; ~ lips,
red and soft like ~ fruit. 红润的唇。 **2** matured and
ready to be eaten or drunk: 已做成而可食或可饮的: ~
cheese/wine. 已制成的干酪(酿好的酒)。 **3** fully developed: 充分发展的: ~ judgement/scholarship; 成熟的
判断力(丰富的学识); a person of ~ age, a mature and
experienced person; 成熟而富经验的人; a person of
~(r) years, past the stage of youth. 成年之人。 **4** ~
for, ready, fit, prepared: 准备就绪；时机成熟的: 适于…
的: ~ for mischief/revolt; 恶作剧(起事)的时机已成熟;
land that is ~ for development, eg for building
houses or factories. 已适于发展(如建住宅或工厂)的土
地。~·ly adv ~·ness n

ripen /ˈraɪpən; ˈraɪpən/ vt, vi [VP 6 A, 2 A] make
or become ripe. 使成熟；成熟。

ri·poste /rɪˈpɒst; rɪˈpost/ n **1** quick return thrust
in fencing (after parrying). (剑术中在挡开后之)迅速
还刺。 **2** quick, sharp reply or retort. 迅速犀利的回
答或反驳。 □ vi deliver a ~. 迅速还刺；机敏的答辩或
反驳。

ripple /ˈrɪpl; ˈrɪpl/ n [C] (sound of) small move-
ment(s) on the surface of water, etc, eg made by a
gentle wind; (sound of) the rise and fall of voices
or laughter: 水面上如被微风吹起的微波; 涟漪; 微波
激荡之声音；起伏之声音或笑声; 声浪: A long ~ of
laughter passed through the audience. 听众间响起一阵轻
快的笑声。 □ vt, vi [VP 6 A, 2 A] (cause to) move in
~s; (cause to) rise and fall gently: (使)起微波; (使)轻
轻起伏: The wheat ~d in the breeze. 微风轻拂中小麦
起伏如波。 The breeze ~d the cornfields. 微风使麦田起
浪。 The tide ~d the sand, caused a wavy surface on the

sand. 潮在沙上留下波状沙纹。

rip-tide /ˈrɪp taɪd; ˈrɪpˌtaɪd/ n tide causing strong
currents and rough water. 巨潮(引起巨浪的潮水)。

rise[1] /raɪz; raɪz/ n **1** small hill; upward slope: 小山;
向上的斜坡: a ~ in the ground; 一个向上的斜坡; a
cottage situated on a ~. 在小山上的一座茅屋。 **2** upward
progress; increase (in value, temperature, etc): 向上的
进展；(价值、温度等之)增高: a ~ in prices/social
position, etc; 物价(社会地位等)之升高; have a ~ in
wages (US 美 = raise); 工资提高; the ~ and fall of
the tide. 潮之涨落。 **3** (liter) coming up (of the sun,
etc): (文)(太阳等之)升起: at ~ of sun/day, (more
usu sunrise). 在日出之时 (sunrise 较常用)。 **4** movement
of fish to the surface of water: 鱼之游到水面: not a
sign of a ~. 没有鱼上来的迹象。 I fished two hours
without getting a ~. 我垂钓两小时, 没有一条鱼上来吃
饵。 **get/take a/the ~ out of sb**, cause him to show
petulance or weakness (often by good-natured teasing).
(常指以善意的戏弄)使某人变得暴躁或暴露弱点; 招惹某
人。 **5** origin; start: 起源: The river has/takes its ~
among the hills. 这条河发源于那些小山中。 **give ~ to**,
cause; suggest: 引起; 招致: Such conduct might give ~
to misunderstandings. 这种行为可能导致误解。 ~ n **1**
early/late ~r, person who gets up early/late. 早
(晚)起之人。 **2** vertical part of a step, connecting two
treads of a staircase. 梯级间之竖板。

rise[2] /raɪz; raɪz/ vi (pt rose /rəʊz; roz/, pp risen
/ˈrɪzn; ˈrɪzn/) [VP 2 A, B, C, 3 A, 4 A] ~ (up), **1** (of
the sun, moon, stars) appear above the horizon: (指
日, 月, 星)升起: The sun ~s in the East. 太阳在东方升
起。 Has the moon ~n yet? 月已升起否? ⇨ set[2](1). **2**
get up from a lying, sitting or kneeling position: 从躺、
坐、跪之姿势起身: He rose to welcome me. 他起身欢迎我。
The wounded man fell and was too weak to ~. 那受伤的
人跌倒, 无力爬起。 The horse rose on its hind legs. 那马用
后腿站起。 On rising from table..., leaving the table at
the end of the meal.... 餐后离桌时…。 Parliament will
~ on Thursday next, cease to sit for business, start the
recess. 国会下星期四休会。 The House rose at 10pm,
ended its discussions, etc. 议院下午十时停止议事。 **3**
get out of bed; get up (which is commoner): 起床 (get
up 较常用): He ~s very early. 他起床甚早。 **4** come
to life (again, from the dead): 复活; 复苏: ~ (again)
from the dead. 死后复活。 Christ is ~n (as an Easter
greeting). 基督复活了(用作复活节之祝贺词)。 He looks
as though he had ~n from the grave. 他的样子好象是刚
从坟墓中爬出来。 **5** go, come, up or higher; reach a
high(er) level or position: 上升; 上涨: The smoke from
our fire rose straight up in the still air. 我们所生的火冒
出的烟在无风的空气中袅袅上升。 The river/flood, etc
has ~n two feet. 河水(洪水等)上涨两英尺。 His voice
rose in anger/excitement, etc, became high, shrill. 在
愤怒(兴奋等)中他的声音提高了。 Sugar has ~n a penny
a pound. 糖价每磅涨了一便士。 Prices continue to ~.
物价继续上涨。 The mercury in the barometer is rising.
气压计的水银柱正在上升。 The bread won't ~, The
dough will not swell with the yeast. 面包发不起来(面团
面发不起来)。 New office blocks are rising in our town.
新的办公大楼在我们镇上建造起来了。 '**high-~** attrib
adj having many storeys: 有许多层的: high-~ flats/
office-blocks. 有许多层的公寓(办公大楼)。 ⇨ skyscraper
at **sky(1)**. **the rising generation**, young people who
are growing up. 正在成长的)年轻的一代。 **rising
twelve, etc**, (of a person) nearing the age of twelve,
etc, (指人)近十二岁等。 **6** develop greater intensity or
energy: 发展成较大的强度或能量: The wind is rising.
风势正增强。 His colour rose, He became flushed. 他脸红
了。 **7** come to the surface: 升到表面: The fish were
rising, coming to the surface for food. 鱼正游上水面觅
食。 They say a drowning man ~s three times. 据说一
个将淹死的人会浮上水面三次。 Bubbles rose from the
bottom of the lake. 水泡从湖底冒到湖面来。 **8** become or

be visible above the surroundings: 因高出周围环境而变得可见或能看见; 突出: *A range of hills rose on our left.* 一列小山在我们左方出现。 **9** reach a higher position in society; make progress (in one's profession, etc): 社会地位提高; 升级; 晋升;(在事业等中)进步: ~ *in the world;* 发迹; 出头; ~ *to greatness;* 成为伟大人物; ~ *from the ranks,* ie to be an officer; 从行伍升为军官; *a rising young politician/lawyer.* 一位事业蒸蒸日上的年轻从政者(律师)。 **10** ~ *to,* develop powers equal to. 有应付…之能力。 ~ *to the occasion/challenge/task, etc,* prove oneself able to deal with an unexpected problem, a difficult task, etc. 有随机应变(接受挑战,完成艰难任务等)之能力。 **11** slope upwards: 渐渐高起: *rising ground.* 渐渐高起之地。 **12** have as a starting-point: 以…为起源;源于: *Where does the Nile* ~? 尼罗河发源何处? *The quarrel rose from a mere trifle.* 争吵起于琐事。 **13** ~ *against,* rebel (against the government, etc). 反抗(政府等)。 **ris·ing** *n* (esp) armed outbreak; rebellion. (尤指)武装暴动;起事。

ris·ible /ˈrɪzəbl; ˈrɪzəbl/ *adj* of laughing and laughter; inclined to laugh; causing laughter, ludicrous. 笑的; 欲笑的; 爱笑的; 引人笑的; 可笑的。 **risi·bil·ity** /ˌrɪzəˈbɪlətɪ; ˌrɪzəˈbɪlətɪ/ *n* [U] disposition to laugh. 会笑;爱笑。

risk /rɪsk; rɪsk/ *n* **1** [C, U] (instance of) possibility or chance of meeting danger, suffering loss, injury, etc: 遭遇危难,受损失或伤害等之可能或机会; 危险; 风险: *There's no/not much* ~ *of your catching cold if you wrap up well.* 你如果把衣服穿好妥当,就不会有伤风的危险。 *run/take* ~*s/a* ~, put oneself in a position where there is ~: 冒险: *She's too sensible to take a* ~ *when she's driving.* 她在开车时很有判断力而不致冒险。 *To succeed in business one must be prepared to run* ~*s.* 一个人想在商业上成功,必须做冒险的打算。 *run/take the* ~ *of doing sth,* do sth which may involve ~: 冒险做某事; 冒…之险: *We'll take the* ~ *of being late.* 我们将冒迟到之险。 *He was ready to run the* ~ *of being taken prisoner by the enemy.* 心愿意冒被敌人俘虏的危险。 *at the* ~ *of/at* ~ *to,* with the possibility of (loss, etc): 冒…之险; 不顾…之危险: *He was determined to get there even at the* ~ *of his life.* 他决心到那里,虽冒生命危险在所不惜。 *at* ~, threatened by uncertainties (such as failure, loss, etc): 可能遭到失败; 损失等: *Is the Government's income policy seriously at* ~? 政府的税收政策可能遭到严重失败吗? *at one's own* ~, accepting responsibility, agreeing to make no claims, for loss, injury, etc. 自己负责,同意对损失或伤害等不要求赔偿。 *at owner's* ~, (of goods sent by rail, etc) the owner to bear any loss there may be. (指由火车等所运之货物)由物主负担一切损失。 **2** [C] (insurance) amount for which sb or sth is insured; the person or thing insured. (保险)保险金额; 保险对象(被保险之人或物)。 *He's a good/poor* ~. 他是个条件很好(风险很大)的保险对象。 ⇨ also *security* ⇨ *at security.* □ *vt* **1** [VP6A] expose to ~: 暴于危险; 使置危险: ~ *one's health/fortune/neck* (ie life), *etc.* 冒健康(财富,生命等)之险。 **2** [VP6A, C] take the chances of: 冒…之险: ~ *failure.* 冒失败之险。 *We must* ~ *getting caught in a storm.* 我们必须冒为暴风雨所阻之险。 **risky** *adj* (-ier, -iest) **1** full of ~: 充满危险的; 多风险的: *a* ~*y undertaking.* 一件多风险的事业。 **2** = risqué. **·ily** *adv* **-i·ness** *n*

ri·sotto /rɪˈzɒtəʊ; rɪˈsɔto/ *n* [C] dish of rice cooked with butter, cheese, onions, etc. 一种加奶油、干酪、洋葱等做成的烩饭。

ris·qué /ˈriːskeɪ US: rɪˈskeɪ; rɪsˈke/ *adj* (of a story, remark, situation in a drama, etc) likely to offend against propriety; on the borderline of indecency. (指故事、谈话、剧中场面等)很可能违反礼仪的; 近乎猥亵的。

ris·sole /ˈrɪsəʊl; ˈrɪsol/ *n* [C] small ball of minced meat, fish, etc mixed with potato, eggs, bread-crumbs, etc and fried. 碎肉或碎鱼肉同马铃薯、蛋、面包屑等混合

以油炸成的丸子。

rite /raɪt; raɪt/ *n* [C] act or ceremony (esp in religious services): 典礼; 仪式; (尤指)宗教仪式: 'burial ~*s;* 葬仪; ~*s of baptism;* 洗礼式; i,nitiation ~s. 入会仪式。 *He died after receiving the* ~*s of the church,* eg the sacraments of Penance, the Eucharist, and Extreme Unction. 他作过宗教仪式(如临终忏悔、领圣餐及临终涂油礼等)之后就去世了。

rit·ual /ˈrɪtʃʊəl; ˈrɪtʃuəl/ *n* [U] all the rites or forms connected with a ceremony; way of conducting a religious service: (典礼之)仪式; 宗教仪式: *the* ~ *of the Catholic Church;* 天主教之仪式; [C] particular form of ~; any procedure regularly followed, as if it were a ~: 特别的方式;固定的程序: *He went through the* ~ *of rolling his own cigarette slowly and carefully.* 他按照固定的程序缓慢而小心地卷他自己的香烟。 (pl) ceremonial observances: (复)正式的礼仪: *initiation* ~s. 入会仪式。 □ *adj* of religious rites; done as a rite: 宗教仪式的; 按照仪式的: ~ *laws;* 仪式法典; *the* ~ *dances of an African tribe.* 非洲某部落的祭神舞蹈。 ~·**ism** /-ɪzəm; -ˌɪzəm/ *n* [U] fondness for insistence upon, ~; study of ~. 喜欢仪式; 拘泥仪式; 仪式主义; 仪式研究。 ~·**ist** /-ɪst; -ɪst/ *n* person who has expert knowledge of ~ practices and religious rites; person who supports strict observance of ~. 对礼仪及宗教仪式有专门知识者; 仪式专家; 支持严格进行仪式的人; 拘泥仪式者; 仪式主义者。 ~·**is·tic** /ˌrɪtʃuˈɪstɪk; ˌrɪtʃuəˈɪstɪk/ *adj* relating to ~ism and ~ists. 喜欢仪式的; 拘泥仪式的; 仪式研究的; 仪式专家的; 拘泥仪式者的。

ritzy /ˈrɪtsɪ; ˈrɪtsɪ/ *adj* (sl) luxurious, elegant. (俚)豪华的; 优美的。

ri·val /ˈraɪvl; ˈraɪvl/ *n* person who competes with another (because he wants the same thing, or to be or do better than the other): 竞争者; 对手: 'business ~*s;* 商业上的竞争者; ~*s in love;* 情敌; (attrib) (用作定语) ~ *business firms.* 互相竞争的商行。 □ *vt* (-ll-, US also -l-) [VP6A, 14] ~ (*in*), be a ~ of; claim or seem to be (almost) as good as: 为…之竞争者; 象是或声言(几乎)与…之竞争者; *Cricket cannot* ~ *football in excitement.* 板球远不如足球够刺激。 ~·**ry** /ˈraɪvlrɪ; ˈraɪvlrɪ/ *n* [C, U] (*pl* -ries) (instance or) being ~s; competition: 敌对(之实例); 竞争: *enter into* ~*ry with other shops;* 与其他商店竞争; ~*ry between two schools,* eg in sport; 两学校间之竞争(例如在运动方面); *the rivalries between political parties.* 两政党间的相互竞争。

rive /raɪv; raɪv/ *vt, vi* (*pt* ~**d,** *pp* **riven** /ˈrɪvn; ˈrɪvən/) [VP6A, 15A, B] (archaic or poet) break or tear away violently; split: (古或诗)猛烈地劈开或撕开; 分裂: *trees riven by lightning;* 被闪电劈开的树; (fig)(喻) *a heart riven by grief.* 因忧伤而破碎的心。

river /ˈrɪvə(r); ˈrɪvə/ *n* [C] **1** natural stream of water flowing in a channel to the sea or to a lake, etc or joining another ~: 河; 江: *the R~ Thames.* (英国的)泰晤士河。 *sell sb down the* ~, (fig) betray him. (喻)出卖某人。 **2** (attrib) (用作定语) '~-**basin** *n* area drained by a ~ and its tributaries. 江河流域。 '~-**bed** *n* ground over which a ~ flows in its channel. 河床。 '~-**side** *n* ground along a ~ bank: 河岸: *a* ~*side villa.* 河边别墅。 **3** great flow: 巨流: *a* ~ *of lava;* 滚滚的熔岩; ~*s of blood,* great bloodshed (in war). (战争中之)血流成果。

rivet /ˈrɪvɪt; ˈrɪvɪt/ *n* [C] metal pin or bolt for fastening metal plates (eg in a ship's sides), the plain end being hammered flat to prevent slipping. 铆钉; 包头钉。 □ *vt* [VP6A, 15A, B] **1** fasten with a ~ or ~s; flatten (the end of a bolt) to make it secure. 以铆钉固结; 打平(螺钉之一端)使牢。 **2** fix or concentrate (one's eyes attention) on: 固定或集中(眼睛、注意力)于: *He* ~*ed his eyes on the scene.* 他的眼睛凝视那风景。 **3** take up, secure (attention, etc): 获得; 吸引(注意等): *The scene* ~*ed our attention.* 那风景吸引了我们的注意。

Rivi·era /ˌrɪvɪˈeərə; ˌrɪvɪˈɛrə/ *n* **the** ~, stretch of

the Mediterranean coast (of SE France and NW Italy), used as a holiday resort. 地中海度假区(法国东南部与意大利西北境内地中海沿岸的一带地方，为度假胜地)。

rivu·let /'rɪvjʊlɪt; 'rɪvjəlɪt/ n small stream. 小溪；小川。

roach[1] /rəʊtʃ; rotʃ/ n (pl unchanged) fresh-water fish of the carp family. (复数不变)斜齿鳊(一种鲤科淡水鱼)。

roach[2] /rəʊtʃ; rotʃ/ n (pl **~es**) (colloq (口) = **cockroach**.

road /rəʊd; rod/ n [C] **1** specially prepared way, publicly or privately owned, between places for the use of pedestrians, riders, vehicles, etc: 公路;道路: main and minor ~s; 主要道路和辅道路(attrib) (用作定语) '~ junctions; 道路交叉处; a '~-map of Great Britain (Cf a street-map of London); 大不列颠道路交通图(参校:伦敦街道图); '~ accidents; 交通事件;车祸; ~s works in progress, ~s under construction or repair. 修筑中之道路。 **on the ~**, travelling: 在途中;旅行中: How long were you on the road? 你在路上走了多久? How long did your journey take? 你走这段路程要花多少时间? **rule of the ~**, custom which regulates the side to be taken by vehicles, ships, etc when meeting or passing each other. 交通规则。 **take the ~**, start a journey. 出发;启程。 **take to the ~**, become a tramp. 成为流浪者。 '~ **safety**, safety from traffic dangers: 交通安全: a campaign for ~ safety, for preventing ~ accidents. 交通安全运动。 **2** (compounds) (复合词) '~-**bed** n foundation of rock, stones, etc on which the surface of a ~ is laid. (以石头等铺筑之)路基。 '~-**block** n barricade built across a ~ to stop or slow down traffic (eg by police to catch an escaped prisoner or by military authorities during a period of political disturbances). 路障(例如警方为逮捕逃犯或在政治骚动期间军事当局在道路上拦阻之障碍物,以拦截车辆或使之减低车速)。 '~-**book** n book describing the ~s of a country, with itineraries (for tourists etc). 道路指南(简介一个国家内的道路的书籍,有为观光者等列出的旅行路线)。 '~-**hog** n (colloq) motorist who is reckless and inconsiderate of others. (口)鲁莽而不顾他人的汽车驾驶者。 '~-**house** n building(s) on a main ~, often one with facilities for meals, dancing, etc used by people who travel by car. 公路上供好汽车旅行者休息之客栈(通常供餐饮、跳舞等)。 '~-**man** /-mæn;-mən/, '~-**mender** n man who repairs a ~. 修路工人。 '~-**metal** n stone used for making and repairing ~s. 铺路碎石。 '~-**sense** n capacity for intelligent behaviour on ~s, eg the avoidance of accidents: 在路上安全开车之能力;避免在路上发生意外之能力: Harry/Harry's dog has no ~ sense. 哈利(哈利的狗)没有在道路上避免发生意外的能力。 '~ **show** n (US) theatrical performance by a touring company. (美) 旅行剧团之演出。 '~-**side** n bordering of a ~: 路边;路旁: (attrib) (用作定语) ~side flowers / inns. 路旁的花(客店)。 '~-**way** n (usu with def art) central part used by wheeled traffic (contrasted with the footpath, etc): (通常与定冠词连用)车道(与 footpath, 等相对): Dogs should be kept off the ~way. 狗应该远离车道。 '~-**worthy** adj (of a motor-vehicle, etc) fit for use on the ~s. (指车辆等)适合在道路上使用的。 **3** one's way or route: 途径;路线: You're in the/my ~, in my way, obstructing me. 你挡住了我的路(你妨碍了我)。 **4 ~ to**, (fig) way of getting to: (喻) (导致…之)途径: Is excessive drinking the ~ to ruin? 过度饮酒会使人趋于堕落吗? There's no royal ~ to wisdom, no easy way, ⇨ **royal**. 学识无捷径。 **5** (in proper names) (用于专有名称中) **(a)the ... R~**, name of a ~ leading to the town, etc named: 通往所指出名称之城市等的路名: the Oxford R~, leading to Oxford; 牛津大道(通往牛津之路); the Great West R~, from London to the West of England. 西部大道(从伦敦通往英格兰西部的公路)。 **(b)... R~/Rd**, street of buildings: 街;路: 35 York Rd, London, SW 16. 伦敦西南十六区约

克路三十五号。 **6** (usu pl) stretch of water near the shore in which ships can ride at anchor: (通常用复数) 近岸可供船只停泊的水域;锚地;停泊区域: anchored in the ~s. 在停泊处下锚。 **7** (US) (美) = railway. '~-**less** adj having no ~s. 没有路的。 '~-**stead** /-sted; -stɛd/ n = road(**6**).

road·ster /'rəʊdstə(r); 'rodstɚ/ n [C] open motorcar, usu for two persons. (通常供两人乘坐的)敞篷汽车。

roam /rəʊm; rom/ vi, vt [VP2A, C, 6A] walk or travel without any definite aim or destination over or through (a country, etc): 无目标或目的地漫游; 闲逛: go ~ing; 出去闲逛; ~ about the world; 漫游世界; ~ the seas; 漫游海上; settle down after years of ~ing. 漂泊数年后定居下来。

roan[1] /rəʊn; ron/ adj (of animals) with a coat of a mixed colour, esp brown with white or grey hairs in it. (指动物)杂色的;杂毛的;(尤指)杂有白色或灰色褐色毛皮的。 □ n ~ horse or cow. 杂色马或牛。

roan[2] /rəʊn; ron/ n [U] soft sheepskin leather sometimes used for binding books. 柔软羊皮(有时用来装订书)。

roar /rɔː(r); ror/ n [C] loud, deep sound as of a lion, of thunder, of a person in pain, etc: (狮、雷、痛苦之人等的)吼叫;咆哮;隆隆声;哀号声: the ~s of a tiger; 虎啸; the ~ of the sea / of waves breaking on the rocks; 海浪(大浪冲击岩石)之轰轰声; the ~ of London's traffic; 伦敦车辆之隆隆声; with a ~ of rage; 怒吼地; ~s of laughter; 狂笑声; set the table / room in a ~, cause everyone to laugh loudly. 使全桌(房间)的人捧腹大笑。 □ vt, vi [VP2A, C, 3A] make such loud, deep sounds: 发出如雷大而深沉的声音; 吼叫; 咆哮: lions ~ing in the distance; 在远处吼叫的狮子; ~ with laughter / pain / rage; 高声大笑(痛苦地吼叫;怒吼); ~ for mercy. 高喊请发慈悲。 Several lorries ~ed past. 数辆载货卡车隆隆而过。 **2** [VP6A, 15B] ~ sth out, say, sing, loudly: 大声地说;唱: ~ out an order; 高声发出命令; ~ out a drinking song. 大声唱出饮酒歌。 **3** [VP 22, 15B] ~ oneself hoarse, etc, make oneself hoarse, etc by ~ing. 喊得声音变哑等。 ~ sb down, in order to drown the words of a speaker so that he has to give up. 大声叫喊使某人停止说话。 '~-**ing** adj **1** noisy; rough. 喧嚣的;粗鲁的。 **2** stormy: 有暴风雨的: a ~ing night; 狂风暴雨之夜; the ~ing forties, part of the Atlantic between 40° and 50° N latitude, often very stormy.(北纬四十度至五十度间)大西洋之风暴带。 **3** brisk; healthy: 活泼的;健康的: do a ~ing trade; 经营一门兴隆的生意; be in ~ing health. 甚为健康。 □ adv extremely: 极端地;十分地;非常地: ~ing drunk. 酩酊大醉。

roast /rəʊst; rost/ vt, vi [VP6A, 2A] **1** (of meat, potatoes, etc) cook, be cooked, in a hot oven, or over or in front of a hot fire, eg on a spit, the meat, etc being basted periodically with the fat and juices that come out:(指肉、马铃薯等)烤;炙: ~ a joint. 烤一大块肉。 The meat was ~ing in the oven. 肉在烤炉里烤着。 You've made a fire fit to ~ an ox, a very large, hot fire. 你生的火足以烤一只牛。 **2** heat, be heated: 加热;烘;焙;被烘或焙: ~ coffee-beans. 焙咖啡豆。 **3** expose for warmth to heat of some kind: 暴露于某种热力下以得温暖;取暖: ~ oneself in front of the fire; 炉前取暖; lie in the sun and ~. 躺在太阳下取暖。 □ attrib adj that has been ~ed: 烤炙过的;烘烤过的: ~ beef / pork. 烤牛肉(猪肉)。 □ n **1** [C] joint of ~ed meat; [U] slices from such a joint: 烤炙过的一大块肉;从烤好的肉块切成之肉片: cold ~ on Monday. 星期一吃冷冻烤肉。 **2** operation of ~ing: 烤;炙;烘;焙: give sth a good ~. 好好烘烤某物。 ~**er** n kind of oven for ~ing; apparatus for ~ing coffee-beans; article of food, eg a chicken, sucking pig, suitable for ~ing. 烘烤炉; 焙咖啡豆之器具; 适于烤食之食物(如鸡,乳猪)。 ~**ing** n (from the dated use of ~ meaning criticize harshly). (沿自 ~ 的过时用法,指严厉地批评)。 give sb a good ~ing, (fig) scold or ridicule him harshly: (喻)严厉地责骂或嘲弄某人。

rob /rɒb; rab/ *vt* **(-bb-)** [VP6A, 14] **rob sb/sth (of sth)**, **1** deprive (sb) of his property; take property from (a place) unlawfully (and often by force): 抢夺(某人)之财物; (常以暴力)非法地从(某地)劫去财物: *I was robbed of my watch.* 我的手表被抢走了。 Cf 参较 I had my watch *stolen.* 我的手表被偷了。 *The bank was robbed last night.* 昨晚那银行被劫。 *The village boys rob my orchard.* 村中的男孩子们强摘我的果园中的果子。 Cf 参较 They *steal* apples from my orchard. 他们偷去我果园中的苹果。 **2** deprive a person of (what is due to him, etc): 剥夺某人(有权享有的东西等): *be robbed of the rewards of one's labour.* 被剥夺其劳力应得之报酬。 **rob·ber** *n* person who robs; thief. 强盗; 贼。 **rob·bery** /'rɒbərɪ; 'rɑbərɪ/ *n* [C, U] (*pl* **-ries**) (instance of) robbing; *robbery with violence;* 暴力抢劫; *three robberies in one week.* 一周之内三次抢案。 **daylight 'robbery**, (colloq) charging of excessive prices: (口)讨价过高; 漫天要价: *50p for a cup of coffee is daylight robbery!* 一杯咖啡要五十便士真是敲竹杠!

robe /rəʊb; rob/ *n* [C] **1** long, loose outer garment. 宽松长袍。 **'bath-~** (US) dressing-gown. (美)浴衣; 晨衣。 **2** (often *pl*) long, loose garment worn as a sign of rank or office: (常用复数)表示等级或职位的长袍: *the ˌCoro'nation ~s,* of a king or queen; (国王或女王的)登极时所着之礼服; *magistrates/judges in their black ~s.* 穿黑袍之法官。 □ *vt, vi* [VP6A, 14, 2A] **~ (in),** put a ~ or ~s on: (使)穿着长袍: *professors ~d in their bright-coloured gowns;* 穿着鲜丽长袍的教授们; *~d in the scarlet of a cardinal.* 穿着枢机主教那穿那种红袍。

robin /'rɒbɪn; 'rɑbɪn/ *n* **1** small, brownish bird with red breast-feathers (also called 亦称作 ,**~ 'redbreast**). 红胸鸟; 知更鸟。 ⇨ the illus at **bird**. 参看 bird 之插图。 **2** (name given to kinds of) small bird outside the British Isles (eg the American ~, a redbreasted thrush). 不列颠群岛外某些种 小鸟(之名称)(如 American robin, 一种红褐的画眉鸟)。 ,**R~ 'Goodfellow** *n* type of mischievous but good-natured goblin or elf in English folklore (also called 亦称作 *Puck*). 英国民间故事中好恶作剧但善良的鬼怪或精灵。

ro·bot /'rəʊbɒt; 'robɑt/ *n* [C] machine made to act like a man; machine-like person. 机器人; 行动象机械般的人。

ro·bust /rəʊ'bʌst; ro'bʌst/ *adj* vigorous; healthy: 有活力的; 健康的: *a ~ young man;* 一个精力旺盛的青年; *a ~ appetite.* 好胃口。 **~·ly** *adv* **~·ness** *n*

roc /rɒk; rak/ *n* gigantic bird of Eastern tales. (东方故事中之)巨鸟; 大鹏。

rock¹ /rɒk; rak/ *n* **1** [U] solid stony part of the earth's crust: 地壳之坚硬石质部分; 岩层; 岩: *a house built upon ~.* 建筑于岩石上的一座房屋。 ⇨ *bedrock* at **bed¹(4)**. ⇨ the illus at **stratify**. 参看 stratify 之插图。 **2** [C, U] mass of ~ standing out from the earth's surface or from the sea. (从地球表面或海中突出之)岩石; 礁石。 *as firm/solid as a ~,* immovable; (fig) (of persons) sound; dependable. 安如磐石; (喻)(指人)稳健的; 可靠的。 *on the ~s,* (of a ship) wrecked on ~s; (fig, of a person) very short of money; (of a marriage) likely to end in divorce or separation. (指船)毁于石上; 触礁而破; (喻, 指人)极缺钱; (指婚姻)可能离婚或分居。 *see ~s ahead,* see danger of shipwreck (or fig, any kind of danger). 看到前面的岩礁; 看到船将触礁的危险; (喻)看到任何危险。 *the R~ of Ages,* Jesus Christ. 万世磐石(耶稣基督)。 **3** [C] large, detached stone or boulder: 大石块或大圆石: *~s rolling down the side of a mountain;* 从一山坡滚下之巨石; (US)(美) = **stone¹(2)**. **4** [U](GB) kind of hard, sticky sweet, usu made in long cylindrical pieces: (英)一种硬而粘之糖果(通常制成长圆柱形); 硬糖: *a stick of ~;* 一条硬糖; *almond ~.* 杏仁硬糖。 **5** *on the ~s,* (US) (of whisky) served on ice-cubes without water. (美)(指威士忌酒)加冰块饮用。 **6** (compounds) (复合词) **~·'bottom** *n* [U]

lowest point: 最低点; 最低限度: *Prices have reached ~-bottom;* 价钱已到最低限度; (attrib) (用作定语) *bottom prices.* 最低的价钱。 **'~-cake** *n* [C] small cake or bun with a hard, rough surface. 表面粗糙的小甜饼。 **'~-climbing** *n* the climbing of masses of ~ on mountain-sides (with the help of ropes, etc).(借绳索等之助)攀登岩壁。 **'~-crystal** *n* pure natural transparent quartz. 天然的透明石英石, 水晶。 **'~-garden** *n* artificial or natural bank or mound with ~s and stones and ~-plants growing among them. 岩石庭园(人工筑造之假山或自然之石丘, 并有植物生长于岩石间之)。 **'~-plant** *n* kinds of plant found growing among ~s, esp on mountains and cultivated in ~-gardens, etc. 岩间植物 (尤指长于岩石间, 或栽植于岩石庭园等中者名称)。 **'~-salmon** *n* (trade name for) dogfish. (商用名称)角鲨。 **'~-salt** *n* common salt as found in mines in crystal form. 岩盐; 石盐(在矿中掘得之结晶形食盐)。 **'~-ery** /'rɒkərɪ; 'rɑkərɪ/ *n* [C] (*pl* **-ies**) = ~-garden.

rock² /rɒk; rak/ *vt, vi* [VP6A, 15A, 2A] (cause to) sway or swing backwards and forwards, or from side to side: (使)摆动, 摇动: *~ a baby to sleep;* 摇一婴儿入睡; *~ a baby in its cradle.* 摇摇篮中之婴儿。 *The town was ~ed by an earthquake.* 该镇为地震所摇动。 *He sat ~ing (himself) in his chair.* 他坐在椅中前后摆动着。 *Our boat was ~ed by/was ~ed on the waves.* 我们的船被浪所摇动(在浪上颠簸摇动)。 ~ *the boat,* (fig) do sth that upsets the smooth progress of an undertaking, etc. (喻)扰乱事件等的顺利进行。 **'~-ing-chair** *n* one fitted with rockers on which it rests. 摇椅。 **'~-ing-horse** *n* wooden horse with rockers for a child to ride on. (小孩骑乘的)摇动木马。 **~·er** *n* **1** one of the curved pieces of wood on which a ~ing-chair or ~ing-horse rests. (摇椅或摇动木马下面的)摇板。 **2** (US) ~ing-chair. (美)摇椅。 **3** R~er, (GB, 1960's) member of a teenage gang, wearing leather jackets and riding motor-bikes (英, 二十世纪六十年代)一种喜欢穿皮夹克, 骑摩托车的少年帮派的一份子。 **4** *off one's ~er,* (sl) crazy; out of one's mind. (俚)发疯。

rock³ /rɒk; rak/ *n* (also 亦作 **~·'n-roll** /ˌrɒk ən 'rəʊl; ˌrɑkən'rol/) [U] highly rhythmic popular music for dancing, played on electric guitars, etc. 摇摆乐(极富节奏, 适于跳舞之流行音乐, 用电吉他等演奏。 □ *vi* dance to this music. 跳摇摆舞。

rocket /'rɒkɪt; 'rɑkɪt/ *n* **1** [C] tube-shaped case filled with fast-burning material, which launches itself

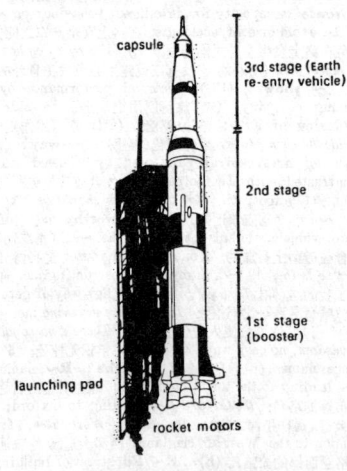

capsule
3rd stage (Earth re-entry vehicle)
2nd stage
1st stage (booster)
launching pad
rocket motors

a rocket launching a spacecraft

into the air (as a firework, as a signal of distress, or as a self-propelled projectile or missile; also used to launch an aircraft or spacecraft or, attached to an aircraft, to give it higher speed and range): (用作烟火、紧急信号等之)冲天炮;(用以发射飞机或太空船，或用以增加飞机速度及航程之)火箭: ~ *propulsion*; 火箭推进; ~*-propelled*. 火箭推动的。 ⇨ also retro⁻. '~**-base** *n* military base for ~ missiles. 火箭基地;导弹基地。 '~**-range** area used for experiments with missiles propelled by ~s. 导弹试验场。 **2** (colloq) severe scolding: (口)严厉的责骂: *get/give sb a* ~. 受到严厉的责骂(严厉地责骂某人)。 □ *vi* [VP2A] go up fast like a ~: 如火箭般迅速上升: (colloq) (口) *Prices* ~*ed after the war.* 战后物价飞涨。 ~**ry** /-trɪ; trɪ/ *n* [U] (art or science of) using ~s for projectiles space missiles, etc. 利用火箭推送抛射体及太空飞船等;火箭术;火箭学。

rock-'n-roll /ˌrɒk ən ˈrəʊl; ˌrɑkənˈrol/ *n* ⇨ rock². **rocky** /ˈrɒkɪ; ˈrɑkɪ/ *adj* (**-ier, -iest**) **1** of rock full of or abounding in rocks; hard like rock: 岩石的;充满或多石的;硬如石的: *a* ~ *road*; 一条多石之路; ~ *soil.* 多石之土壤。 **2** (colloq) shaky; unsteady: (口)动摇的;不稳的: *The table is rather* ~. 桌子相当不稳。*His business is very* ~. 他的生意很不稳定(时赚时赔)。

ro·coco /rəˈkəʊkəʊ; rəˈkoko/ *adj* (of furniture, architecture, etc) with much elaborate ornament (with scrolls, foliage, etc) as in Europe in the late 18th c. (指家具，建筑等)洛可可式的(有很多精美漩涡形、叶形等装饰，如十八世纪末欧洲所用者)。

rod /rɒd; rɑd/ *n* **1** thin, straight piece of wood or metal: 木质或金属的细而直之杆;竿: '*curtain-rods*; 吊挂帐幕之杆; *a* '*fishing-rod*; 钓鱼竿; *fishing with rod and line.* 用钓竿和钓丝钓鱼。 **2** stick used for punishing. 笞鞭;教鞭。 **make a rod for one's own back**, prepare trouble for oneself. 给自己的背做笞鞭;自讨苦吃;自找麻烦。 ,**spare the** '**rod and** ,**spoil the** '**child**, (prov) A child who is not punished will become undisciplined and unruly. (谚)孩子不打不成器。 **have a rod in** '**pickle for sb**, be saving up severe punishment for him when the opportunity comes. 有机会再严惩某人。 **3** (US, sl) revolver. (美，俚)手枪。 **4** measure of length equal to 5¹⁄₂ yds or 5.03 metres (also called 亦称作 *pole* or 或 *perch*). 竿(长度单位，等于 5¹⁄₂ 码或 5.03 公尺)。 **5** metal bar; shaft, etc: 金属条;轴等: '*piston-rods*. 活塞杆。

rode /rəʊd; rod/ *pt of* ride².

ro·dent /ˈrəʊdnt; ˈrodnt/ *n* animal, eg a *rat, rabbit, squirrel* or *beaver*, which gnaws things with its strong teeth specially adapted for this purpose. 啮齿类动物(如鼠、兔、松鼠或海狸等)。

ro·deo /rəʊˈdeɪəʊ US: ˈrəʊdɪəʊ; ˈrodɪ,o/ *n* (*pl* ~**s** /-əʊz; -oz/) [C] **1** (on the plains of Western US) rounding up of cattle. (在美国西部平原)将牛马等聚集到一起。 **2** contest of skill in lassoing cattle, riding untamed horses, etc. 掷索套牛，骑野马等之竞技。

rodo·mon·tade /ˌrɒdəmɒnˈteɪd; ˌrɑdəmənˈted/ *n* [U] (formal) boastful, bragging talk. (正式用语)狂言;大话;吹嘘。

roe¹ /rəʊ; ro/ *n* [C, U] (mass of) eggs or sperm in a fish: 鱼子;鱼精: *salted cod's-roe for Friday's supper.* 为星期五晚餐准备的腌鳕鱼子。

roe² /rəʊ; ro/ *n* (*pl* **roes** or, collectively, **roe**) small kind of European and Asiatic deer. 欧洲和亚洲产的一种小鹿; '**roe·buck** *n* male roe. 雄鹿。

Roent·gen /ˈrɒntjən US: ˈrentɡən; ˈrɛntɡən/ = Rontgen.

ro·ga·tion /rəʊˈɡeɪʃn; roˈɡeʃən/ *n* (usu *pl*) litany of the saints chanted on the three days before Ascension Day: (通常用复数)(耶稣升天节前三天所唱之)圣徒祈祷文: R~ *week*, the week including these days; (包括耶稣升天节前三天在内之)祈祷周; R~ *Sunday*, the Sunday before Ascension Day. 耶稣升天之前的星期日。

roger /ˈrɒdʒə(r); ˈrɑdʒɚ/ *int* (in radio communication) message heard and understood. (用于无线电通讯)收到了! 听懂了!

Rog·er /ˈrɒdʒə(r); ˈrɑdʒɚ/ *n* **the Jolly** ~, pirates' black flag. 海盗用的黑旗。 **Sir** ~ **de Coverley** /sə ˌrɒdʒə də ˈkʌvəlɪ; sɚˈrɑdʒədəˈkʌvɚlɪ/, country-dance and tune. 一种乡村舞蹈及其舞曲。

rogue /rəʊɡ; roɡ/ *n* [C] **1** scoundrel; rascal. 恶徒;流氓。 ~**s' gallery**, collection of photographs of known criminals. 罪犯像片陈列室。 **2** (playfully or humorously) person fond of playing tricks, teasing people. (戏谑或诙谐用法)爱好捉弄人者。 **3** wild animal (esp, ~'**ele·phant**) driven or living apart from the herd and of a savage temper. 离群之猛兽;(尤指)离群之猛象。 **ro·guery** /ˈrəʊɡərɪ; ˈroɡərɪ/ *n* (*pl* **-ries**) **1** [C, U] (instance or example of the) conduct of a ~. 流氓行为(之实例或例子)。 **2** [U] playful mischief; (*pl*) mischievous acts. 嬉戏之恶作剧;(复)恶作剧之行为。

ro·guish /ˈrəʊɡɪʃ; ˈroɡɪʃ/ *adj* **1** dishonest; of the nature of a rogue. 不诚实的;有流氓习性的。 **2** mischievous: 嬉戏的;恶作剧的: ~ *eyes*. 一双调皮的眼睛。 ~**·ly** *adv* ~**·ness** *n*

roist·erer /ˈrɔɪstərə(r); ˈrɔɪstərə/ *n* rough, noisy merry-maker. 粗鲁喧闹的作乐者。

role, rôle /rəʊl; rol/ *n* [C] actor's part in a play; person's task or duty in an undertaking: (剧中演员之)角色;(一个人在某事业中之)职分;责任: *play the* '*title*~ *in* '*Hamlet*', play the part of Hamlet. 在'哈姆雷特'一剧中演主角哈姆雷特。

roll¹ /rəʊl; rol/ *n* **1** sth made into the shape of a cylinder by being rolled: 被做成卷形之物;一卷: *a* ~ *of cloth/newsprint/carpet/photographic film, etc*; 一卷布(白报纸、地毯、胶卷等); sth in this shape, made by rolling or otherwise: 呈卷形之物: *a man with* ~*s of fat on his neck*; 脖子上有层层肥肉的人; *a bread* ~, a small quantity of bread baked in the shape of a ball; 小圆面包; ~*s of butter*; 奶油团; *a sausage* ~, a sausage rolled in pastry and then baked. 卷在面皮中再烤的香肠;香肠卷。 ~'-top 'desk *n* desk with a flexible cover that slides back into a compartment at the top. 有活动顶盖可以推入顶部隔层中的书桌;附有滑动式顶盖的写字台。 **2** turned-back edge: 折回之边: *a* ,~'*collar*, large collar made by turning back the edge of the material. 大翻领。 **3** rolling movement: 滚转;摇晃;摆动: *The slow, steady* ~ *of the ship made us sick.* 船缓慢持续的摇晃使我们晕眩。 *He walks with a nautical* ~, like a sailor. 他走起路来象海员一样摇摇晃晃。 *The young foal was enjoying a* ~ *on the grass.* 小马正在草地上尽情地打滚。 **4** official list or record, esp of names. 正式的表册或记录;(尤指)名册;名簿。 *call the* ~, read the names (to check who is present and who absent). 点名。 Hence, 由此产生, '~*-call n* calling of names. 点名。 ~ *of* '**honour**, list of those who have died for their country in war. 阵亡烈士名册。 *strike off the* ~*s*, take (a solicitor's name) off the list of those who have the right to practise, eg when a solicitor has been proved guilty of dishonesty. 从开业律师名册上除去(例如被证明有欺诈等罪之律师的名字)。 **5** rolling sound: 隆隆之声: *the distant* ~ *of thunder/drums*. 远方隆隆的雷(鼓)声。

roll² /rəʊl; rol/ *vt, vi* (For special uses with *adverbial particles* and *preps*, ⇨ 11 below.) (与副词性小品词及介词连用的特殊用法,参看下列第 11 义。) **1** [VP6A, 15A, 2A, C] (cause to) move along on wheels or by turning over and over: (使)滚动;转动: *The man* ~*ed the barrel into the yard.* 那个人把圆桶滚进院内。 *Rocks and stones were* ~*ing down the hillside.* 岩石与碎石正从山坡滚下。 *The coin fell and* ~*ed under the table.* 铜钱掉落,滚往桌下。 *The bicycle hit me and sent me* ~*ing/* ~*ed me over.* 脚踏车撞到我,使我滚落在地上。 *The child was* ~*ing a hoop.* 孩子正在滚铁环。 *heads will roll*, (colloq) some people will be dismissed or disgraced. (口)某些人将要

被解职或失宠。 **2** [VP6A, 12B, 13B, 15B] **~ *(up),*** cause to revolve between two surfaces; make (sth) by doing this; make into the shape of a ball or a cylinder: 搓;卷;搓或卷制(某物);将…绕成球形或圆柱形: *Please ~ me a cigarette/~ a cigarette for me.* 请给我卷一支香烟。 *R~ the string/wool (up) into a ball.* 把细绳(毛线)绕成线球。 *R~ up the carpet/that map on the wall.* 把地毯(挂在墙上的地图)卷起来。 *He ~ed up* (= furled) *his umbrella.* 他把伞收拢。 *He ~ed* (= wrapped by turning over) *himself (up) in the blanket.* 他把自己裹在毛毯里。 ⇨ **sleeve.** **3** [VP2C] come or go in some direction: 自某方向来;向某方向去: *The clouds ~ed away as the sun rose higher.* 太阳升高时,云散去了。*The years ~ed on/by,* passed. 岁月匆匆逝去。 *The tears were ~ing* (= flowing) *down her cheeks.* 眼泪自她双颊流下。**4** [VP2A, C] turn about in various directions: 向不同方向旋转: *a porpoise ~ing in the water.* 在水中翻滚的海豚。**5** [VP6A, 22] make or become flat, level or smooth by pressing with a ~ing cylinder of wood, metal, etc or by passing between two such cylinders: 以木质或金属等滚筒或在两个此种滚筒间将(某物)压平,辗平,辗光;被压平,辗平,辗光: *~ a lawn/a road surface;* 将草地(路面)压平; *~ sth flat.* 把某物辗平。 *This dough ~s well,* is of the sort that one can ~ easily. 这种面团容易辗压。 **~ed gold,** thin coating of gold on the surface of another metal, applied by ~ing. (砑贴于另一金属上的)金箔。 **6** [VP2A, B, C] (cause to) sway or move from side to side; walk with a side-to-side movement: (使)摇晃或摇动;摇晃而行: *The ship was ~ing heavily.* 船摇晃得很厉害。 *We ~ed and pitched for two days after leaving Lisbon.* 离开里斯本后,我们的船在海上摇晃颠簸了两天。 *Some sailors have a ~ing gait.* 有些水手走起路来摇摇晃晃。 *The drunken man ~ed up to me.* 那醉汉向我蹒跚走来。 **7** [VP2A] (of surfaces) have long slopes that rise and fall: (指表面)绵延起伏: *miles and miles of ~ing country;* 连绵很多英里的起伏地区; *a ~ing plain.* 绵延起伏的平原。 **8** [VP2A, C] move with a rise and fall; be carried with rise-and-fall motion: 起伏地移动;被起伏的动作所带: *The waves ~ed in to the beach.* 海浪起伏地涌向海滩。 **9** [VP2A, C, 6A, 15A, B] make, utter, be uttered with, long, deep, vibrating or echoing sounds: 发出长长的、深沉的、颤动的或回响的声音;发隆隆声;以隆隆声说出: *The thunder ~ed in the distance.* 远处雷声隆隆。 *The drums ~ed.* 鼓声隆隆。 *He ~ed out his words/song, etc.* 他以低沉的声音说话(唱歌等)。 ***~ one's r's,*** utter them with the tongue making a rapid succession of taps against the palate. 把 r 发成舌尖颤音。 **10** [VP2A, C, 14] **~ *(at),*** (of the eyes) (cause to) move from side to side, change direction: (指眼睛)(使)左右转动;溜转: *His eyes ~ed strangely at me.* 他的眼睛奇怪地对着我打转。 *Don't ~ your eyes at me!* 你的睛眼别朝着我打转! **~·ing** *n* (compounds) (复合词) **'~ing-mill** *n* mill where metal is ~ed out into sheets, bars, etc. 辗压机;辗压工厂(把金属辗压成薄片,条块等)。 **'~ing-pin** *n* cylinder of wood, glass, etc usu about a foot long, for ~ing out dough, etc. 面棍;擀面杖。 **'~ing-stock** *n* railway's coaches, wagons, etc; all the stock that is on wheels. 铁路之客车、货车等;全部车辆。 **11** [VP2C, 15B] (special uses with *adverbial particles* and *preps*): (与副词性小品词及介词连用的特殊用法):

roll sth back, turn or force back, eg enemy forces. 把(敌军等)逼回去;把(敌军等)赶回去。

roll in, come, arrive, in large numbers or quantities: 蜂拥而至;大量涌进: *Offers of help are ~ing in.* 大量的援助源源而来。 ***be '~ing in sth,*** have a large quantity of it: 拥有大量的: *He's ~ing in money/property.* 他拥有大量的钱(财产)。

roll on, **(a)** be capable of being put on by ~ing. (指衣物)能卷过肢体而穿上。 **(b)** (of time) pass steadily: (指时间)不断地消逝;流逝: *Time ~ed on.* 光阴荏苒。**(c)** (of time, chiefly *imper*) come soon: (指时间,主要用于祈使句)快点到来: *R~ on the day when I retire from this dull work!* 但愿我退休的日子早日到来,以脱离这种枯燥的工作! ***~ sth on,*** put on by ~ing, eg over a part of the body: 卷过肢体而穿上(衣物): *She ~ed her stockings on.* 她穿上她的长袜。 **'~-on** *n* (woman's) elastic foundation garment ~ed on to the hips. (妇女)束腹(穿着于臀部之一种有弹性的紧身衣)。

roll sth out, **(a)** cause it (ie sth that is ~ed up) to become flat, level or smooth, by opening it out: 展开(卷起之物): *~ out a map/carpet.* 展开一地图(地毯)。 ***~ out the red carpet,*** (fig) give an important visitor a special welcome. (喻)隆重地欢迎嘉宾。 ⇨ *red carpet* at **red(1).** **(b)** flatten it by ~ing: 搓平;擀平: *~ out pastry.* 擀馅饼皮。 ⇨ *~ing-pin* at **10** above. 参看上列第 10 义之 ~ing-pin。

roll up, (of a vehicle) arrive and stop; (of a person) arrive: (指车辆)到达并停下;(指人)到达: *Raymond always ~s up late.* 雷蒙德老是迟到。 ***R~ up! R~ up!,*** used as an invitation to join others, eg possible customers at a street stall. 请光顾! 请光顾! (如街上之货摊请人光顾时所用)。 ***~ sth up,*** **(a)** ⇨ **2** above. 参看上列第 2 义。 **(b)** (mil) drive the flank of (an enemy line) back and round. (军)迫使(敌军阵线)之侧翼向后弯退;席卷;合卷。

roller /'rəʊlə(r); 'rolə/ *n* [C] **1** cylinder-shaped object of wood, metal, rubber, etc, usu part of a machine, for pressing, smoothing, crushing, printing, etc: 滚子;滚轮;滚筒;滚转机: *a 'garden-~,* for use on a lawn; 辗草坪机; *the ~s of a mangle,* (between which articles are passed to press out water); 轧干机的滚筒; *a 'road-~,* used for making roads level, by crushing rock, etc. 轧路机。 **2** cylinder of wood, metal, etc placed beneath an object to make movement easy, or round which sth may be rolled easily: 置于物下使移动容易,或用以卷物之木质或金属等之圆柱;滚柱;卷轴: *a 'blind-~,* on which a window blind (US 美 = *shade*) is rolled; 窗户遮阳上的卷轴; *a '~-towel,* an endless towel on a ~. (两端连结套在轴上之)环状毛巾。 **'~-skate** (often 常作 ***pair of ~-skates***), *n, vi* (use a) skate[1] with small wheels for use on a smooth surface. 有轮溜冰鞋;用有轮溜冰鞋溜冰。 **3 '~ bandage,** long surgical bandage rolled up for convenience before being applied to a limb, etc. 绷带卷。**4** long, swelling wave. 起伏之大浪。

rol·lick·ing /'rɒlɪkɪŋ; 'rɑlɪkɪŋ/ *adj* noisy, jolly and gay: 喧闹而快乐的;欢乐的: *have a ~ time.* 尽情欢乐。

roly-poly /ˌrəʊlɪ 'pəʊlɪ; 'rolɪˌpolɪ/ *n* **1** (GB) (also 亦作 *~ pudding*) pudding made of paste spread with jam, etc formed into a roll and boiled. (英)(含有果酱等的)布丁卷。 **2** (colloq) short, plump child. (口)矮胖的小孩。

Ro·maic /rəʊ'meɪɪk; ro'me·ɪk/ *adj, n* (of, in) modern vernacular Greek (more usu called 通常称作 *demotic*). 现代希腊语;现代希腊语的。

Ro·man /'rəʊmən; 'romən/ *adj* **1** of Rome /rəʊm; rom/, esp ancient Rome: 罗马的;(尤指)古罗马的: *the ~ Empire.* 古罗马帝国。 **the ~ alphabet,** the ABC. 罗马字母。 **~ letters/type,** the plain, upright kind, not italic. 罗马体铅字;正体字(无虚饰,直体)。 **~ numerals,** ⇨ **App 4(1).** 罗马数字(参看附录四之一)。 **2** of the Rome of the Popes, esp = Roman Catholic: 天主教的: *the ~ rite* (contrasted eg with Greek or Russian Orthodox). 天主教之仪式(与希腊或俄国东正教之仪式相对)。 ⇨ **catholic(2); pope; Protestant.** □ *n* **1** citizen of ancient Rome; *(pl)* Christians of ancient Rome: 古罗马市民;(复)古罗马之基督教徒: *the Epistle to the ~s* (in the NT). (新约中的)罗马书。 **2** Roman Catholic. 天主教徒。

ro·mance /rəʊ'mæns; ro'mæns/ *n* **1** [C] story or novel of adventure; love story, esp one in which the events are quite unlike real life; [U] class of literature consisting of such stories. 冒险故事;爱情故事(尤指所述事件与现实生活颇为不同的传奇故事); 传奇文学。 **2** [C] **R~,** medieval story, usu in verse, relating the

adventures of some hero of chivalry. 中世纪的骑士故事 (通常用前文写成，叙述骑士的冒险事迹)。**3** [C] real experience, esp a love-affair, considered to be remarkable or worth description; (colloq) any love-affair. 被认为不平凡或值得叙述的真实经验(尤指风流韵事)；爱情史；(口)恋爱。**4** [U] state of mind which welcomes stories of the marvellous, etc; the qualities characteristic of stories of love and adventure: 喜欢不平凡故事的心理倾向；爱情与冒险故事具有之特质: *travel abroad in search of* ~. 旅行外国以寻找不平凡的经验。*There was an air of* ~ *about the old castle.* 这座古堡颇富浪漫气氛。**5** [C, U] exaggerated description; picturesque falsehood. 夸大的描述；生动的虚构。□ *vi* [VP2A] (more usu 较常用 *romanticize*) exaggerate by adding interesting or attractive details when telling a story, recounting events, etc. (讲故事，重述发生的事件等时)增加有趣味或惊人的细节而夸张说出。

Ro·mance /rəʊˈmæns; roˈmæns/ *adj* ~ **languages**, French, Italian, Spanish, Portuguese, Rumanian and others developed from Latin. 罗曼语(由拉丁语演变而成之法语、意大利语、西班牙语、葡萄牙语、罗马尼亚语及其他语言)；拉丁语系诸语言。

Ro·man·esque /ˌrəʊməˈnesk; ˌromənˈɛsk/ *n* [U] style of architecture, with round arches and thick walls (in Europe between the ancient classical and the Gothic periods). 罗马式建筑(在古典时期与哥德式时期流行欧洲的一种建筑式，以使用圆拱及厚墙为其特色)。

ro·man·tic /rəʊˈmæntɪk; roˈmæntɪk/ *adj* **1** (of persons) having ideas, feelings, etc remote from experience and real life; given to romance(4); visionary. (指人)有浪漫思想、感情等的；富于憧憬故事及不平凡经验的；幻想的。**2** of, like, suggesting, romance: 传奇故事的；象传奇故事的；使人联想到浪漫故事的；浪漫的: ~ *scenes* / *adventures* / *tales* / *situations*; 富有传奇色彩的景色(冒险，故事，情势)；*a* ~ *old castle.* 一个具有传奇性的古堡。**3** (in art, literature and music) marked by feeling rather than by intellect; preferring grandeur, passion, informal beauty, to order and proportion (opp of *classic* and *classical*): (艺术、文学和音乐)浪漫主义的(为 classic 及 classical 之反义词): *the* ~ *poets*, eg Shelley, Keats. 浪漫派诗人(如雪莱, 济慈)。□ *n* **1** person with ~(3) ideals. (文学、音乐、艺术之)浪漫主义者。**2** (pl) ~ ideas; extravagantly visionary feelings, expressions, etc. (复)浪漫的思想；过于幻想的感情、言词等。**ro·man·ti·cally** /-klɪ; -klɪ/ *adv* **ro·man·ti·cism** /-tɪsɪzəm; -təˌsɪzəm/ *n* [U] ~ tendency in literature, art and music (contrasted with *realism* and *classicism*); ~ spirit; quality of allowing full play to the imagination. (文学、艺术、音乐上之)浪漫主义(与 realism 及 classicism 相对)；浪漫精神；充分发挥想象之特质。**ro·man·ti·cist** /-tɪsɪst; -təsɪst/ *n* follower of romanticism in literature or art, eg Wordsworth. 文学或艺术方面的浪漫主义者(如华兹华斯)。**ro·man·ti·cize** /-tɪsaɪz; -təˌsaɪz/ *vt*, *vi* [VP6A, 2A] treat in a ~ way; make ~; use a ~ style in writing, etc; be ~. 以浪漫的方式处理；使浪漫化；以浪漫的风格写作；有浪漫的思想或感情。

Rom·any /ˈrɒmənɪ; ˈrɑmənɪ/ *n* (pl **-nies**) **1** [C] Gypsy. 吉卜赛人。**2** [U] language of the Gypsies. 吉卜赛语。□ *adj* Gypsy. 吉卜赛人的；吉卜赛语的。

Rom·ish /ˈrəʊmɪʃ; ˈromɪʃ/ *adj* (usu disparaging) of the Roman Catholic Church. (通常有轻蔑之意)天主教的。

romp /rɒmp; ramp/ *vi* [VP2A, C] **1** (esp of children) play about, esp running, jumping and being rather rough. (尤指儿童)嬉闹玩耍；(尤指)跑，跳且相当粗鲁地玩。**2** win, succeed, quickly or without apparent effort: 迅速或轻易地获胜，成功: (in a horse-race) (在赛马中) *The favourite* ~*ed home*, won easily. 这匹热门马轻而易举地获胜。*John just* ~*s through his examinations*, passes them easily. 约翰轻而易举地通过考试。□ *n* [C] child fond of ~ing; period of ~ing: 喜欢喧闹嬉戏的孩

子；喧闹嬉戏的一段时间: *have a* ~; 喧闹嬉戏; *a game of* ~*s.* 喧嚣的游戏。~**er** *n* (sing or pl) loose-fitting garment worn by a child: (单数或复数)宽松的连裤童装: *a pair of* ~*ers*; 一套连裤童装; *a* '~*er suit.* 一套连裤童装。

ron·deau /ˈrɒndəʊ; ˈrɑndo/, **ron·del** /ˈrɒndl; ˈrɑndl/ *nn* poem of thirteen or ten lines with two rhymes throughout and the opening words used twice as a refrain. 一种十三行或十行诗(全诗押两韵，以首行开始的字句在两处作为叠句)。

rondo /ˈrɒndəʊ; ˈrɑndo/ *n* (pl ~**s** /-dəʊz; -doz/) piece of music in which the principal theme returns from time to time. (音乐)回旋曲(主题时时重复)。

Ro·neo /ˈrəʊnɪəʊ; ˈronɪo/ *n* (P) machine that duplicates letters, circulars, etc. (商标)一种油印机。□ *vt* duplicate on a ~ machine. 以此种油印机复印。

Rönt·gen /ˈrɒntjən US: ˈrentgən; ˈrɛntgən/ ~ **rays** *n pl* = X-rays.

rood /ruːd; rud/ *n* **1** (old use) (旧用法) '~(-tree) cross on which Jesus was put to death. 耶稣被处死之十字架。**2** crucifix, esp one raised on the middle of a wooden or stone carved screen (*a* '~*-screen*) separating the nave and choir of a church. 基督受难(十字架上的耶稣像，尤指教堂内隔开本堂和唱诗班席位的木质或石头屏风上面突起的雕像)。**3** (GB) measure of land, onefourth of an acre. (英)路得(丈量土地之单位，为 1/4 英亩)。

roof /ruːf; ruf/ *n* **1** top covering of a building, tent, bus, car, etc: (建筑物、帐篷、公共汽车、车辆等之)顶: *How can you live under the same* ~ *as that woman*, in the same building? 你怎么能够同那个女人住在一起？*raise the* ~, (colloq) create an up-roar; make a great noise (indoors). (口)喧嚣不休; (在室内)吵翻了天。'~*-garden n* garden on the flat ~ of a building. 屋顶花园。'~*-tree n* strong horizontal main beam at the apex of a ~. 屋顶之栋梁; 屋脊梁。**2** highest part: 最高点: *the* ~ *of heaven*, the sky; 天顶; 天空; *the* ~ *of the world*, a high mountain range; 世界屋脊; 高的山脉; *the* ~ *of the mouth*, the palate. 上颚。□ *vt* (pt, pp ~**ed** /ruːft; ruft/) [VP6A, 15A, B] supply with a ~; be a ~ for: 给…盖顶; 为…之顶: *a shed* ~*ed over with strips of bark.* 以一片一片狭长的树皮为顶的小屋。~**less** *adj* having no ~; (fig, of persons) homeless; lacking shelter. 没有屋顶的; (喻, 指人)无家可归的; 没有住处的。~**ing** *n* (also 亦作 '~*ing material*) material used for ~s (eg slates, shingles). 做屋顶的材料(如石板瓦，木瓦等)。

rook¹ /rʊk; rʊk/ *n* large black bird like a crow. 一种类似乌鸦的大黑鸟; 白嘴鸦; 山乌。~**ery** /-ərɪ; -ərɪ/ *n* (pl **-ries**) **1** place (a group of trees) where many ~s have their nests; colony of ~s. 白嘴鸦结巢之处(丛林); 白嘴鸦之群。**2** colony of penguins or seals. 企鹅或海豹之群。

rook² /rʊk; rʊk/ *n* person who makes money by cheating at dice and cards, playing with inexperienced gamblers. 以赌博赚取金钱的骗子。□ *vt* [VP6A] win money from (sb) at cards, etc by cheating; swindle; charge (a customer) a ridiculously high price. 以赌博骗取(某人)金钱; 诈取; 向(顾客)索过高之价钱; 敲诈。

rook³ /rʊk; rʊk/ *n* chess piece (also called a 亦称作 *castle*). (国际象棋中之)城形棋子, 车。⇨ the illus at **chess.** 参看 chess 之插图。

rookie /ˈrʊkɪ; ˈrʊkɪ/ *n* (army sl) inexperienced recruit. (军俚)新兵。

room /ruːm; rʊm/ *n* **1** [C] part of a house or other building enclosed by walls or partitions, floor and ceiling. 室; 房间。~**ed** /ruːmd; rumd/ *adj*: *a ten-*~*ed house*, one having ten ~s. 一栋有十个房间的房子。**2** (pl) set of ~s occupied by a person or family; apartments; (pl) 一个人或一家人住的一组房间; 套房: *Come and see me in my* ~*s one evening.* 哪天晚上请到我家来看我。'~*-mate n* one of two or more persons

sharing a ~. 同住一室者; 室友。 **3** [U] ~ *(for sb/sth)*; ~ *(to do sth)*, space that is or might be occupied, or that is enough for a purpose: 被占或可能被占之空间; 足够某一目的所需之空间: *Is there ~ for me in the car?* 车里还有我坐的空位吗? *This table takes up too much ~.* 这张桌子占的地方太多。 *There was ~ in the bus to stand but not to sit.* 公共汽车上仍有站位的地方, 但没有座位了。 *Standing ~ only!* eg in a bus, theatre. (公共汽车或戏院中, 座位票已卖完) 仅有站位! *Can you make ~ on that shelf for some more books?* 你能在那个架子上腾出些地方再放些书吗? *There's no ~ for doubt,* We can be quite certain about it. 没有怀疑之余地。 **4** [U] scope; opportunity: 范围; 机会: *There's ~ for improvement in your work,* It is not as good as it could be. 你的工作还有改进之余地。 □ *vi* [VP2C] ~ *(US)* lodge; occupy a ~ or ~s: (美)居住; 占一个或一套房间: *He's ~ing with my friend Rodney.* 他和我的朋友罗德尼同住。 '~ing house, (US) building where a number of independent ~s can be rented (usu without service). (美) 公寓 (有单独房间可出租之建筑, 通常没有人服务)。 ~er *n* (US) person who lives in a rented ~ in sb else's house; lodger. (美)房客; 寄宿者。 ~·ful /-ful; -ful/ *n* amount (of furniture, etc), number of persons, that fills a ~. 一室所能容纳之 (家具等) 量或人数。 ~y *adj* (-ier, -iest) having plenty of space: 有很多空间的: *a ~y cabin;* 宽敞的客舱; *a ~y raincoat,* one that is loose-fitting. 宽松的雨衣。 ~·ily /-ɪlɪ; -əlɪ/ *adv*

roost /ruːst; rust/ *n* [C] branch, pole, etc on which a bird rests, esp one for hens to sleep or rest on; hen-house, or that part of it, where fowls rest at night: 鸟栖居的树枝、竿等 (尤指供鸡睡眠或栖止者); 鸡舍; 鸡舍内家禽过夜栖息之部分: *at* ~, on a ~. 栖息。 **come home to** ~, (of words) take effect upon the one who utters them. (指言语) 对说出者产生效果。 **rule the** ~, be the leader or master. 做首领; 当主人。 □ *vi* [VP2A] (of birds) settle down for the night's sleep. (指鸟) 栖息。

rooster /ˈruːstə(r); ˈrustə/ *n* domestic cock. 公鸡。

root¹ /ruːt; rut/ *n* [C] **1** that part of a plant, tree, etc which is normally in the soil and which takes water and food from it: (植物之)根: *pull up a plant by the ~s.* 将一植物连根拔起。 *He has no ~s in society,* (fig) is not settled, does not belong to any particular group or place. (喻)他在社会上没有根基。 *pull up one's ~s,* (fig) move from a settled home, job, etc to start a new life elsewhere. (喻)离开固定的居所、工作等而在别处开始新的生活。 *put down new ~s,* (fig) establish oneself in another place after leaving a place where one has been established. (喻)建立新的居所、居所等; 另起炉灶。 *take/strike ~,* **(a)** (eg of a cutting) send out a ~ or ~s; begin to grow. (指插枝等) 扎根; 开始生长。 **(b)** (fig) become established. (喻)固定; 确立。 ~ **and branch,** (fig) thoroughly; completely: (喻)彻底地; 完全地: *This tyrant and his henchmen must be destroyed ~ and branch.* 这暴君及其亲信必须彻底铲除。 **2** ~s, '~-crop, plant with a ~ that is used as food, eg *carrots, turnips, parsnips.* 根菜作物 (例如胡萝卜、萝卜、防风草根等。 '~-beer, (US) non-alcoholic drink made from the ~s of various plants. (美)菜根汽水(一种由多种菜根制成, 不含酒精的饮料)。 **3** that part of a hair, tooth, the tongue, a fingernail, etc that is like a ~ in position, function, etc. 发根、齿根、舌根、指甲根等; 位置、作用等似根之部分。 **4** (fig) that from which sth grows; basis; source; essential substance: (喻)根源; 基础; 泉源; 主要实质: *the ~ of the trouble.* 苦恼的根源。 *Is money the ~ of all evil?* 金钱果真为万恶之源吗? **get at/to the ~ of sth,** tackle at its ~. 深究一事之根源。 *the ~ cause,* the fundamental cause. 基本原因。 **5** (gram) (also 亦作 *base form*) form of a word on which other forms of that word are said to be based:(语法)词根: *'Walk'* is the ~ of *'walks', 'walked', 'walking',* and *'walker'.* walk 为 walks, walked, walking 及 walker 的词根。 **6**

(arith) quantity which, when multiplied by itself a certain number of times, produces another quantity: (算术)根: *4* is the square (= second) ~ of *16* (√/16 = 4), the cube (= third) ~ of *64* (∛/64 = 4), the fourth ~ of *256* (∜/256 = 4). 4 为 16 之平方根, 64 之立方根, 256 之四次方根。

root² /ruːt; rut/ *vt, vi* **1** [VP6A, 2A] (of plants, cuttings, etc) (cause to) send out ~s and begin to grow: (指植物; 插枝等)(使)生根并开始生长: *chrysanthemum cuttings in sand and peat.* 使菊花的插枝生长于沙与泥炭中生根。 *Some cuttings ~ easily.* 有些插枝易于生根。 **2** [VP6A, 15A] cause to stand fixed and unmoving: 使之定不动; 使确立; 使固定: *Fear ~ed him to the ground.* 恐惧使他呆在那里不动。 *He stood there ~ed to the spot.* 他站在该处不动。 **3** (of ideas, principles, etc) (cause to) establish firmly (chiefly in *pp*): (指观念、原则等)使根深蒂固; 使坚定不移(主要用过去分词形式): *She has a ~ed objection to cold baths.* 她坚决反对冷水浴。 *Her affection for him is deeply ~ed.* 她对他的爱是坚定不移的。 **4** [VP15B] ~ **sth out,** get rid of, exterminate (an evil, etc). 根绝; 根除(祸害等)。 ~ **sth up,** dig or pull up with the ~s. 连根拔起。 ~·**less** *adj* having no ~s; (of a person) without ~s in society. 无根的; (指人)无社会基础的; 没有生根的。 ⇔ **root¹(1).**

root³ /ruːt; rut/ *vi, vt* **1** [VP2C, 15B] ~ **about (for),** (of pigs) turn up the ground with the snout in search of food; (of persons) search for; turn things over when searching: (指猪)以鼻拱掘土觅食; (指人)寻觅; 翻找: *~ing about among piles of papers for a missing document.* 在一堆废文件中找一件失掉的文件。 ~ **sth out,** find by searching: 搜出; 找到: *I managed to ~ out a copy of the document.* 我设法找到该文件的一份副本。 **2** [VP2A, 3A] ~ **(for),** (US sl) cheer: (美俚)鼓掌: *~ing for the college baseball team.* 为大学棒球队加油。

rootle /ˈruːtl; ˈrutl/ *vi* [VP2C] ~ **about for,** (of pigs, etc) dig about (with the snout) for food, etc. (指猪等)(以鼻)掘土觅食等。

rope /rəup; rop/ *n* **1** [C, U] (piece or length of) thick strong cord or wire cable made by twisting finer cords or wires together: (一根或一段)坚牢的粗绳; 金属缆; 索: *tie sb's arms behind his back with (a) ~.* 用绳将某人的双臂反绑在背后。 *The climbers were on the ~,* fastened together with a ~ (while climbing on a difficult and dangerous surface). 攀登者(在爬一困难而危险之表面时)用绳联系在一起。 **the** ~, noose for hanging a condemned person. (绞首用的)索套。 **the ~s,** those that enclose the prize-ring or other place used for sport or games. (围在拳击场或其他竞赛场地四周之)栏索; 圈绳。 **show sb/know/learn the ~s,** the conditions, the rules, the procedure (in some sphere of action). 向某人指出(知道, 学知)某行业的情况、规则、手续等。 **give sb (plenty of) ~,** freedom of action. 给某人(充分)行动自由。 *Give sb enough ~ and he'll hang himself,* (prov) Let a fool follow his own devices and he will come to ruin. (谚)任凭愚人为所欲为, 彼将自取灭亡。 **2** (compounds) (复合词) '~-**dancer** *n* performer on a tight-~. 走绳索者。 ,~-'**ladder** *n* ladder made of two long ~s connected by rungs of ~. 绳梯。 '~-**walk**/-**yard** *n* long piece of ground or long, low shed where ~s is made. 做绳索之狭长走道(狭长低矮小屋)。 '~-**walker** *n* = ~-dancer. 走绳索者。 '~-**way** *n* means of carrying goods in buckets, etc suspended from overhead steel cables: (运送装于桶等内的货物之) 绳路; 索道: *'~way buckets.* 索道运输桶。 (attrib) (用作定语) '~**way buckets.** '~-**yarn** *n* [U] material (esp when unpicked) of which ~s are made. 用以制绳索之股线(尤指未拆开者)。 **3** [C] number of things twisted, strung or threaded together: 被扭在、穿在或串在一起的东西: *a ~ of onions.* 一串洋葱。 □ *vt* [VP15A, B] **1** fasten or bind with ~: 以绳缚系: *~ a man to a tree;* 把一个人捆在一棵树上; *~ climbers together,* connect them at intervals with a ~ for safety. 把爬山者系联于一根绳索上。 **2** ~ **sth off,**

enclose or mark off with a ~: 以绳围起或界出: *Part of the field was ~d off.* 一部分土地用绳隔开了. **3** ~ *sb in,* persuade him to help in some activity. 说服某人参与一项活动. **~y** /'rəupɪ; 'ropɪ/ *adj* (sl) very inferior in quality. (俚)品质极差的.

Roque·fort /'rɒkfɔː(r) *US:* 'rəukfərt; 'rokfət/ *n* [U] kind of French cheese made of goats' and ewes' milk. 一种法国制的羊乳酪.

ro·sary /'rəuzərɪ; 'rozərɪ/ *n* (*pl* -**ries**) **1** form of prayer used in the RC Church; book containing this. 念珠祈祷(天主教奉行的一种祈祷式); (收有此种祷文的)玫瑰经. **2** string of beads for keeping count of these prayers, which are said while meditating; such beads used by a person of another religion. (此种祈祷用之)念珠; 其他宗教用之念珠. **3** rose-garden. 玫瑰园.

rose¹ /rəuz; roz/ *pt* ⇨ **rise**².

rose² /rəuz; roz/ *n* **1** (shrub or bush with prickles or thorns on its stems and bearing a) beautiful and usu sweet-smelling flower (red, pink, white, cream, yellow), ⇨ the illus at **flower**; one of various flowering plants: 蔷薇科植物; 蔷薇花; 玫瑰花(参看 flower 之插图): *the 'rock~;* 岩蔷薇; *Christmas ~.* 圣诞蔷薇(欧洲产的一种草本植物, 开白色或紫色花, 开花期在冬天). *a bed of ~s,* a pleasant, easy condition of life. 愉快舒适的生活状况. *not all ~s,* not perfect; having some discomfort and disadvantages. 不完美; 有某种困苦和不利. *no ~ without a thorn,* complete, pure happiness cannot be found. 没有尽美尽善的快乐. *gather life's ~s,* seek the pleasures of life. 寻欢作乐. **2** [U] pinkish-red colour. 粉红色. *see things through ~-coloured / -tinted spectacles,* take an optimistic view of them (perhaps without good reason). 以乐观态度(或许并无充分的理由)看事物. **3** (of various things thought to resemble a ~ in shape) (指形状上被认为象玫瑰花的各种东西) **(a)** sprinkling nozzle of a watering can or hose: 喷水壶或水管的洒水嘴: *Use a fine~d can* (one fitted with such a nozzle) *for watering seedlings.* 用细孔喷水壶浇幼苗. **(b)** bunch of ribbons; rosette. 丝带束; 蔷薇花形丝带结. **(c)** ~-shaped conventional design, the national emblem of England (as the shamrock is used for Ireland). 英国的玫瑰花形国徽(爱尔兰用酢浆草). **4** (compounds) (复合词) *'~-bed* n bed in which ~ bushes are grown. 玫瑰花丛. *'~-bud* n bud of a ~; 玫瑰花苞; (attrib) (用作定语) *a ~-bud mouth,* having this shape. 如玫瑰花苞样的小嘴. *'~-leaf* n petal from a ~ flower. 玫瑰花瓣. *'~-'red* red as a ~. 玫瑰红的. *'~-water* n perfume made from ~s. 玫瑰香水. *,~ 'window* n ornamental circular window (usu in a church, esp one with a pattern of small sections radiating from the centre). 蔷薇形窗; 圆花窗(装饰性的圆形窗, 通常教堂建筑物上用之, 尤指一种具有从中心向外辐射之小瓣型式者). ⇨ the illus at **window**. *'~-wood* n [U] hard, dark red wood obtained from several varieties of tropical tree (so named for their fragrance). 青龙木, 花梨木(木质有玫瑰香味, 因而得名): *a ~-wood piano.* 一架花梨木钢琴.

ro·seate /'rəuzɪeɪt; 'rozɪɪt/ *adj* rose-coloured; pinkish-red. 玫瑰色的; 粉红色的.

rose·mary /'rəuzmərɪ *US:* -merɪ; 'roz,merɪ/ *n* [U] evergreen shrub with fragrant leaves used in making perfumes. 迷迭香(一种常青灌木, 其叶有香味, 可制香水).

ro·sette /rəu'zet; ro'zɛt/ *n* [C] small rose-shaped badge or ornament, eg of silk or ribbon; carved rose on stonework. 小的玫瑰形徽章或饰物; 蔷薇形缎带结; 石上刻的玫瑰花饰.

rosin /'rɒzɪn; 'razɪn/ *n* [U] resin, esp in solid form, as used on the strings of violins, etc and on the bow with which violins are played. 松香(不溶固体, 如小提琴等之弦及弓上所用者). □ *vt* [VP6A] rub with ~. 以松香涂擦.

ros·ter /'rɒstə(r); 'rastə/ *n* list of names of persons showing duties to be performed by each in turn. 名册; 值勤簿.

ros·trum /'rɒstrəm; 'rastrəm/ *n* (*pl* ~**s** or -**tra** /-trə; -trə/) platform or pulpit for public speaking. 讲台; 讲坛.

rosy /'rəuzɪ; 'rozɪ/ *adj* (-**ier**, -**iest**) **1** of the colour of red roses: 玫瑰红的; 淡红色的: ~ *cheeks,* indicating good health. 红润的脸颊. **2** (fig) causing optimism; encouraging:(喻)令人乐观的; 鼓励的: ~ *prospects.* 光明的前途.

rot /rɒt; rat/ *vi, vt* (-**tt**-) **1** [VP2A, C] decay by processes of nature: 腐烂; 腐朽: *A fallen tree soon rots.* 倒在地上的树不久就会腐烂. *The shed had fallen in, and the wood was rotting away.* 小屋塌陷, 木料腐烂了. *One of the branches had rotted off, decayed and broken off.* 其中一根树枝已经枯朽而断落. **2** [VP2A, C] (fig, of a society, etc) gradually perish from lack of vigour or activity; (of prisoners, etc) waste away: (喻, 指一社团等)因缺乏活力或活动而逐渐衰败; (指囚犯等)消瘦; 衰弱: *left to rot in a deep dungeon.* 被弃于深深的地牢中日趋衰弱. **3** [VP6A] cause to decay or become useless: 使腐烂; 使变为无用: *Oil and grease will rot the rubber of your tyres.* 汽油和润滑脂会腐蚀你的轮胎. *'rotgut* n [U] strong alcoholic liquor, esp inferior spirit, that is harmful to the stomach. 伤胃的烈酒; (尤指)劣质烈酒. □ *n* [U] **1** decay; rotting; condition of being bad: 腐烂; 腐朽; 腐败; 堕落: *a tree affected by rot.* 已染枯朽的树. *Rot has set in,* decay has begun. 开始腐烂了. *We have dry rot in the floor.* 我们的地板有朽坏的现象. ⇨ **dry**¹(13). **2** (usu 通常用 **the rot**) liver disease of sheep. 羊肝蛭病. *'foot-rot,* foot disease of sheep. 羊之足病. **3** (,many=)'rot, (sl) nonsense; foolishness; rubbish: (俚)无意义的话; 愚蠢; 胡说: *Don't talk rot!* 不要胡说! *His speech was all rot.* 他的讲演全是胡扯. **4** succession of failures: 一连串的失败: *A rot set in.* 开始节节挫败. *How can we stop the rot?* 我们如何才能止住这一连串的失败?

rota /'rəutə; 'rotə/ *n* (*pl* ~**s**) (GB) list of persons who are to do things in turn; list of duties to be performed in turn. (英)轮流执行职务者的名册; 须轮流执行之任务的表册; 勤务轮值表.

ro·tary /'rəutərɪ; 'rotərɪ/ *adj* **1** (of motion) moving round a central point. (指运动)旋转的. **2** (of an engine) worked by ~ motion: (指机器)由旋转而工作的; 转动的: *a ~ printing machine / press,* that prints from curved metal plates on to a continuous roll of paper. 轮转印刷机. **3** 'R~ **Club,** (branch of an) international association of professional and business men in a town. 扶轮社(各地专业人员及商人所组织之国际性团体); 国际扶轮社. **Ro·tarian** /rəu'teərɪən; ro-'terɪən/ *n* member of a R~ Club. 扶轮社社员. □ *n* (US) (美) = roundabout(2).

ro·tate /rəu'teɪt *US:* 'rəuteɪt; 'rotet/ *vi, vt* [VP6A, 2A] (cause to) move round a central point; (cause to) take turns or come in succession: (使)旋转; (使)轮流; 更迭: ~ *crops,* ⇨ **rotation**(2). 轮种作物. *The office of Chairman ~s.* 主席一职是轮流担任的.

ro·ta·tion /rəu'teɪʃn; ro'teʃən/ *n* **1** [U] rotating or being rotated: 旋转; 转动: *the ~ of the earth;* 地球的自转; [C] complete turning: 一次完全的旋转: *five ~s an hour.* 每小时转五次. **2** [C, U] the regular coming round of things or events in succession: 轮流: '*crop-~,* ~ *of crops,* varying the crops grown each year on the same land to avoid exhausting the soil. 农作物之轮作(在同一块地上每一年换种农作物, 以免耗尽土壤的生产力). *in ~,* in turn; in regular succession. 轮流地; 交替地.

ro·ta·tory /'rəutətərɪ *US:* -tɔːrɪ; 'rotə,torɪ/ *adj* relating to, causing, moving in, rotation: 旋转的; 轮流的; 使旋转或轮流的; 在旋转中移动的: ~ *movement.* 旋转运动.

rote /rəut; rot/ *n* (only in) (仅用于) *by ~,* by heart, from memory without thinking: 熟记地; 由记忆而不必

想地; 死记地: *do/say/know/learn sth by* ~, 由熟记而做(说, 知道, 学)某事物。

ro·tis·se·rie /rəʊˈtiːsəri; roˈtɪsəri/ *n* cooking device with a rotating spit on which meat, etc is roasted; shop or restaurant providing food cooked in this way. 转动的烤肉铁叉; 卖此种烤肉的商店或饭店。

roto·gra·vure /ˌrəʊtəʊɡrəˈvjʊə(r); ˌrotəgrəˈvjʊr/ *n* **1** [U] process of printing from an engraved copper cylinder on which illustrations, etc have been etched. 凹版印刷术。 **2** [C] illustration, etc printed by this process. 以凹版印刷之图画等。

ro·tor /ˈrəʊtə(r); ˈrotɚ/ *n* [C] rotary part of a machine; (esp) assembly of horizontally rotating blades of a helicopter propeller. 机器之旋转部分; (尤指直升飞机的)水平旋翼。

rot·ten /ˈrɒtn; ˈrɑtn/ *adj* **1** decayed; having gone bad: 腐烂的; 已变坏的: ~ *eggs.* 已坏的蛋。 *The sails were* ~ *and so were the ropes.* 帆烂了, 绳索也烂了。 **2** (*sl*) disagreeable; very unpleasant or undesirable: (俚) 讨厌的; 极令人不快或嫌恶的: *What* ~ *luck!* 真倒霉! *I'm feeling* ~ *today,* unwell, tired. 我今天觉得不舒服(疲倦)。 ~·**ly** *adv* ~·**ness** *n*

rot·ter /ˈrɒtə(r); ˈrɑtɚ/ *n* (dated *sl*) worthless, objectionable person. (过时俚语)无用的、讨厌的人。

ro·tund /rəʊˈtʌnd; roˈtʌnd/ *adj* **1** (of a person, his face) round and plump; (of the voice) full-sounding; rich and deep. (指人, 其脸)圆而胖的; (指声音)洪亮的; 圆润而深沉的。 **2** (of speech, liter style) grandiloquent. (指言辞、文体)华丽的; 浮夸的。 ~·**ly** *adv* ~·**ity** /-əti; -əti/ *n* [U] state of being ~. 圆胖; 洪亮; 华丽。

ro·tunda /rəʊˈtʌndə; roˈtʌndə/ *n* round building, esp one with a domed roof. 圆形建筑物(尤指有圆屋顶者)。

rouble /ˈruːbl; ˈrubl/ *n* unit of currency in the USSR (100 kopecks). 卢布(苏联货币单位)。

roué /ˈruːeɪ *US:* ruːˈeɪ; ruˈe/ *n* (esp elderly) dissolute man; rake². 放荡的人; 浪子; (尤指)放荡的老人; 酒色之徒。

rouge /ruːʒ; ruʒ/ *n* [U] fine red powder or other cosmetic substance for colouring the cheeks; powder for cleaning silver plate. 红粉; 胭脂; 擦银器的粉末。 □ *vt, vi* [VP6A, 2A] use ~ on (the face); use ~. 在 (脸)上擦胭脂; 用红粉化妆; 用粉末擦银器。

rough¹ /rʌf; rʌf/ *adj* (**-er, -est**) **1** (of surfaces) not level, smooth or polished; (of roads) of irregular surface, not easy to walk or ride on: (指表面)不平的; 不光的; 未擦亮的; (指路)崎岖不平的; 难行的: ~ *paper.* 糙纸。 *a fruit with a* ~ *skin.* 有粗皮的水果; *cloth that is* ~ *to the touch.* 摸起来很粗的布。 **2** not calm or gentle; moving or acting violently or roughly; 粗鲁的; 粗暴的; 剧烈的: ~ *children;* 举止粗野的孩子; ~ *behaviour;* 粗鲁的行为; *a* ~ (= stormy) *sea;* 风大浪急的海; *have a* ~ *crossing from Dover to Calais.* 从多佛渡到加莱港间一次艰辛的横渡。 *Keep away from the* ~ *quarter of the town,* the part where disorderly and violent people live. 远离城市中暴乱之徒聚居的地区。 *This suitcase has had some* ~ *handling,* has been treated violently, thrown about, etc. 这只小提箱曾被乱抛乱丢。 *He has a* ~ *tongue,* a habit of speaking rudely or sharply. 他讲话粗鲁(尖刻)。 *be* ~ *on sb,* be unpleasant or unlucky for: 使某人不愉快或倒霉: *It's rather* ~ *on her, having to live in a caravan.* 她很倒霉, 不得不住在篷车里。 *give sb the* ~ *side of one's tongue,* speak to sb rudely and/or severely. 粗鲁无礼地(严厉地)对人讲话。 *give sb/have a* ~ *time,* (cause sb to) experience hardship, be treated severely, etc (according to context). (使某人)受苦(受到严苛的待遇)。 '~ *house,* (colloq) noisy quarrelling with exchange of blows, etc. (口)大吵大闹; 大打出手。 '~**-house** *vt, vi* [VP6A, 2A] handle (sb) violently; act violently. 粗鲁地对待(某人); 行为粗暴。 ~ *luck,* worse luck than is deserved. 坏运气。 **3** made or done without attention to detail, esp as a first attempt: 约略的; 概略的: *a* ~ *sketch/translation;* 草图(概

略的翻译); lacking refinement, delicacy or finish: 草率的; 简陋的; 未经润饰的: *a* ~ *draft,* eg of a letter; 草稿; ~ *accommodation at a small country inn;* 乡村小客栈的简陋设备; 简陋设备; *lead a* ~ *life away from civilisation.* 过一种远离文明的简陋生活。 *a* ~ *diamond,* (fig) an uneducated or uncouth person, lacking social graces, but good-hearted and good-natured. (喻)未受教育、举止粗鲁、但心地善良之人。 ~ *and ready,* good enough for ordinary purposes, occasions, etc; not particularly efficient, etc: 粗略而尚能用的; 将就的: ~ *and ready methods.* 粗略而尚能用的方法。 **4** (of sounds) harsh; discordant: (指声音)粗厉的; 沙哑的; 不悦耳的: *a* ~ *voice.* 粗厉的声音。 **5** (compounds) (复合词) '~**-neck** *n* (US colloq)rowdy person; hooligan. (美口)粗暴的人; 流氓。 '~**-rider** *n* person who is expert at breaking in untamed horses. 驯马师; 善骑野马者。 ~·**ly** *adv* **1** in a ~ manner: 粗糙地; 粗暴地; 粗鲁地; 草率地; 简陋地: *treat sb* ~*ly;* 粗暴地对待某人; ~*ly made table,* not finely finished. 草草做成的桌子; **2** approximately: 约略地; 大约: *at a cost of* ~*ly £5;* 约值五镑; **5** (*fig*) ~*ly speaking,* with no claim to accuracy. 约略地说。 ~·**ness** *n* quality or state of being ~. 粗糙; 粗暴; 粗鲁; 约略; 草率; 简陋; 粗哑。

rough² /rʌf; rʌf/ *adv* **1** in a rough manner: 粗鲁地; 严厉地: *play* ~, be (rather) violent (in games, etc); 玩得相当粗野; *treat sb* ~. 严厉地对待某人。 *cut up* ~, (colloq) become angry. (口)发怒。 *live rough,* live in the open (as a vagrant may do). 餐风宿露(如流浪者之生活)。 *sleep* ~, (of homeless persons) sleep out of doors or wherever there is some shelter, eg under a bridge, in the open air. (指无家可归之人)在户外露宿; 随处栖身。 **2** (compounds) (复合词) '~**-cast** *n* coarse plaster containing gravel or pebbles for the surfaces of outside walls. (含有沙石及卵石的)粗灰泥。 □ *vt* coat (a wall) with this mixture. 以粗灰泥涂(墙)。 '~**-dry** *vt* dry (laundered clothes) without ironing them. 晒干(洗过的衣服)而不烫。 '~**-hewn** *adj* shaped or carved ~ly: 粗粗地形成或雕成的: *a* ~*hewn statue.* 粗粗雕成的雕像。 '~**-shod** *adj* (of a horse) having shoes with the heads of the nails projecting to prevent slipping. (指马)钉有防滑钉之铁蹄的。 *ride '~shod over sb,* treat him harshly, inconsiderately or contemptuously. 傲慢某人; 粗暴而轻蔑地对待某人。 '~**-'spoken** *adj* addicted to, using, unrefined or harsh language. 言语粗鲁的。

rough³ /rʌf; rʌf/ *n* **1** [U] rough state; rough ground; rough surface; unpleasantness; hardship. 粗劣的状况; 崎岖的土地; 粗糙的表面; 不愉快; 艰辛。 *take the* ~ *with the smooth,* (fig) accept what is unpleasant with what is pleasant. (喻)不愉快的和愉快的事一起接受; 逆来顺受。 **2** [U] *the* ~, unfinished state: 未加工或未完成之情况: *I've seen his new statue only in the* ~. 我曾看到过他的新雕像的粗坯。 *in* ~, (eg of sth written) as a rough draft. (如文稿)草拟的。 **3** [U] *the* ~, (golf) part of a course (not the fairway or a green) where the ground is uneven and the grass uncut: (高尔夫球)(崎岖不平而且草长得很高的)障碍区域: *lose one's ball in the* ~. 在障碍区失落一球。 **4** man or boy ready for lawless violence; hooligan: 粗暴而不守法纪的男人或男孩; 流氓; 阿飞; 不良少年: *He was set on by a gang of* ~*s who knocked him down and took all his money.* 他被一群流氓攻击, 他们把他击倒并且拿走他所有的钱。

rough⁴ /rʌf; rʌf/ *vt* **1** [VP6A, 15B] ~ *sth (up),* make untidy or rough: 使粗糙或不平; 弄乱: *Don't* ~ *(up) my hair!* 不要弄乱我的头发! ~ *sb up,* (sl) treat him roughly, with physical violence: (俚)以暴力对付某人; 向某人动粗: *He was* ~*ed up by hooligans.* 他被流氓殴打。 ~ (more usu 较常用 *rub*) *sb up the wrong way,* ⇨ rub(3). **2** [VP15B] ~ *sth in,* make a first rough sketch of; sketch in outline. 起草; 草拟; 粗略地绘出草图。 **3** ~ *it,* live without the usual comforts and conveniences of life: 过简陋的生活: *The explorers had to* ~ *it*

when they got into the jungle. 那些探险家进入丛林后，不得不过简陋的生活。

rough·age /ˈrʌfɪdʒ; ˈrʌfɪdʒ/ n [U] coarse, rough foodstuff, esp bran of cereals, supplying bulk, not nourishment, and taken to stimulate bowel movements. 粗糙食物(大指谷物的糠皮之类，无营养，食之可通便)。

roughen /ˈrʌfn; ˈrʌfən/ vt, vi make or become rough. 使粗糙；变粗糙；使成崎岖不平；变得崎岖不平。

rou·lette /ruːˈlet; ruˈlet/ n [U] gambling game in which a small ball falls by chance into one of the compartments of a revolving wheel or disc. 轮盘赌。 **Russian ~,** stunt in which a person holds to his head a revolver, of which only one (unknown) chamber contains a bullet, and then pulls the trigger. 一种惊险的技艺表演(一人拿起左轮对准自己的头部开枪)。

round¹ /raʊnd; raʊnd/ adj 1 shaped like a circle or a ball: 圆的；球状的：*a ~ plate/window/table;* 圆盘(窗,桌)；*a ~-table conference,* at which there is no position of importance at the head of the table, everyone being apparently of equal importance; 圆桌会议(参与会议的人是平等的,议席无主次之分)； *~ cheeks/arms/limbs,* plump and curved. 圆胖的脸(臂,肢)。 **a '~ game,** one in which there are no teams or partners and in which the number of players is not fixed. 不分队或边,人数亦不固定的游戏。 **the R~ Table,** the order of knighthood founded by King Arthur. 由亚瑟王创设的武士勋位；圆桌武士。 2 done with, involving, a circular motion. 旋转的；回旋的。 **~ brackets,** parentheses. 圆括弧。 **'~ dance,** one in which the dancers form a circle, with revolving movements. 圆舞(跳舞者形成圆圈转动)。 **~ robin,** petition with signatures in a circle to conceal the order in which they were written. 圆形签名陈情书(签署者之签字列为圆形,使无法看出签字的前后次序)。 **~ trip,** (GB) circular trip or tour; (US) journey to a place and back again over the same route. (英)环行;环游；(美)双程旅行；来回旅行。 3 entire; continuous; full: 整个的；继续的；完全的：*a ~ dozen/score,* that number and not less; 整整一打(整整二十个)；*a good, ~ sum,* a considerable sum. 相当大的数目。 **in ~ figures/numbers,** given in 10's, 100's, 1000's, etc; not troubling about smaller denominations; (hence) roughly correct. 以十、百、千等整数表示的；不计较较小单位的；(由此产生)约略正确的。 4 full; plain: 充满的；明白的：*at a ~ pace/trot,* vigorous; 以快速的步伐；*a ~ oath,* unmistakably an oath; 确实无疑的誓言；*a ~ voice,* full-toned and mellow; 宏亮圆润的声音；*scold sb in good, ~ terms,* outspokenly; 直率无隐地责备某人；*a ~ unvarnished tale,* the plain truth. 实话。 5 (compounds) (复合词) **'~-arm** adj, adv (cricket) with the arm swung ~ at the height of the shoulder: (板球)臂挥到齐肩高度的(地)；手臂齐肩的(地)：*~-arm bowling;* 手臂齐肩的投球；*bowl ~-arm.* 手臂齐肩地投球。 **,~-backed** adj having the back curved or humped. 驼背的。 **,~-eyed** adj with the eyes wide open: 睁圆眼睛的：*staring/listening in ~-eyed wonder.* 睁大着眼睛惊奇地凝视(聆听)。 **'~-hand** n [U] (a) style of handwriting with the letters well rounded and clearly written. 圆而清楚的书写字体。 (b) *~-arm* (bowling). 手臂齐肩的投球。 **'R~-head** n member of the Parliament side in the Civil War in the 17th c in England, so called from his close-cut hair. 圆颅党人(十七世纪英国内战时期的国会派份子,因发齐头剪短,故有此称)。 **'~-house** n (a) cabin or set of cabins on the after part of the quarter deck (of old sailing ships). (旧式帆船之)后甲板后部的房舱；后甲板室。 (b) building (with a turn-table in the middle) where locomotives are stored and repaired. 圆形机车库(储放及修理机车之建筑物,内有转车台)。 (c) (in former times) place where people were locked up as prisoners. (昔时)囚禁犯人的地方。 **'~-shot** n cannon ball (contrasted with a shell). 炮弹；弹丸(与 shell 相

对)。 **,~-'shouldered** adj having the shoulders bent forward. 圆肩的；削肩的。 **~-ish** /-ɪʃ; -ɪʃ/ adj rather ~. 略圆的。 **~-ly** adv in a thorough-going way; pointedly; 彻底的；率直地：*tell sb ~ly that he is not wanted;* 率直地告诉某人说不需要他；*be ~ly cursed.* 被痛骂。 **~-ness** n

round² /raʊnd; raʊnd/ adv part (may be replaced by *around,* except in special idiomatic uses; for special uses with *vv,* ⇨ the *v* entries; specimens only are given here) (除特殊习惯用法外,可用 around 代替；与动词连用之特殊用法,请参看各动词；此处仅提供少数例子) 1 in a circle or curve to face the opposite way: 成圆形或曲线地；周转地：*Turn your chair ~ and face me.* 把你的椅子转过来对着我。 2 with a return to the starting-point: 周而复始地；循环地：*The hour hand of a clock goes right ~ in twelve hours.* 钟的时针十二小时转一圈。 *Christmas will soon be ~ again.* 圣诞节又快到了。 *I shall be glad when spring comes ~ again.* 春天再来我将很高兴。 **~ and ~,** with repeated revolutions. 旋转不息地。 **all ~; right ~,** completely ~: 从头到尾循环一周地；处处；各处：*We walked right ~ the lake.* 我们环湖走了一周。 **all (the) year ~,** at all seasons of the year. 整年。 3 in circumference: 周围：*Her waist is only twenty-four inches ~.* 她的腰围只有二十四英寸。 4 (so as to be) in a circle: (形成)圆形地：*A crowd soon gathered ~.* 不久就聚集了一群人。 *The garden has a high wall all ~.* 花园有一圈高墙围起。 5 from one place, point, person, etc) to another: 从一(地点、人等)到另一；逐一地：*Please hand these papers ~,* ie distribute them. 请把这些文件分发给大家。 *The news soon passed ~.* 消息不久即传开了。 *Tea was served/handed ~.* 每个人都奉了茶。 **go ~,** supply everybody: 供给每个人：*Have we enough food to go ~?* 我们有足够的食物供给大家吗？ *Will the meat go ~,* ie be enough for everybody? 肉够大家吃吗？ **look ~,** visit, and look at: 参观游览：*Let's go into the town and look ~/have a look ~,* ie see the places of interest, etc. 让我们进城去游览一番。 **taking it all ~,** considering the matter from all points of view. 从各方面考虑之。 6 by a longer way or route; not by the direct route: 绕道地；迂回地；非由近路地：*If you can't jump over the stream, you'll have to go ~ by the bridge.* 你如果不能跳过这条小河,就必须绕道由桥上过河。 *The taxi-driver brought us a long way ~.* 计程车司机带我们绕远路走。 7 to a place where sb is or will be: 到某人所在或将在的地方：*Come ~ and see me this evening.* 今天晚上来看我。 *The Whites have asked me to go ~ this evening,* ie to visit them. 怀特夫妇约我今天晚上去看他们。 8 **~(about),** in the neighbourhood: 在附近地；近处地：*all the country ~;* 在附近一带的乡间；*everybody for a mile ~;* 一英里之内的每个人；*in all the villages ~ about.* 在附近所有的村庄内。

round³ /raʊnd; raʊnd/ n 1 sth round; a slice made by a complete cut across the end of a loaf: 圆的东西；面包片：*two ~s (= sandwiches) of ham and one of beef:* 两片火腿三明治和一片牛肉三明治；*a ~ of toast.* 一片吐司。 2 [U] (sculpture) solid form, enabling an object to be viewed from all sides (contrasted with *relief*). (雕刻)圆雕(能从各面观看的立体形式,与 relief 相对)；立体雕刻。 **in the ~,** (arts) made so that it can be viewed from all sides: (艺术)立体的(能从各面观看的)：*a statue in the ~.* 一个立体雕像。 **theatre in the ~,** with the audience on (nearly) all sides of the stage. 观众围绕在舞台四周观赏的剧院；立体剧场。 3 regular series or succession or distribution: 规则性的系列或连续(或分配)：*the daily ~,* the ordinary occupations of the day; 日常的例行工作；*the earth's yearly ~,* the cycle of the four seasons; 地球每年四季的循环；*the doctor's ~ of visits* (to the homes of his patients): 医生的巡回探视病人(到病人家里)；*a ~ of pleasures/gaiety,* a succession of parties, gay events, etc; 一连串的宴会,游乐节目等；*the postman's ~,* the route he takes to deliver letters. 邮递员的送信路线。 **go the ~s; make one's**

~s, make one's usual visits, esp of inspection: 例行巡视或检查: *The night watchman makes his ~s every hour.* 守夜者每小时巡回一次。 **go the ~ of,** be passed on (to): 传遍: *The news quickly went the ~ of the village.* 这消息很快传遍全村。 **4** (in games, contests, etc) one stage: (在游戏、比赛等中)一回合; 一回合: *a boxing-match of ten ~s;* 十回合的一场拳击比赛; *knocked out in the third ~;* 在第三回合中被击倒; *the semi-final ~ of the League Championship;* 棒球联盟锦标赛的半决赛; *the sixth ~ of the FA Cup,* the quarter-finals of this soccer contest; 英国足球协会杯复赛。 **have a ~ of cards;** 玩一局牌; *a ~ of golf,* to all the 9 or 18 holes of the course. 一局高尔夫球 (把球打进高尔夫球场中所有的九或十八个穴内)。 **5** allowance of sth distributed or measured out; one of a set or series: (分配或量出的某种东西的)一份; (一套或一组中的)一份: *pay for a ~ of drinks,* drinks for every member of the company; 付出每一同伴喝酒的钱; *another ~ of wage claims,* by trade unions for higher wages for their members; 再次要求提高工资; *~ after ~ of cheers,* successive bursts of cheering; 一次连一次的欢呼; *have only three ~s of ammunition left,* enough to fire three times. 只剩下三发弹药。 **6** song for several persons or groups, the second singing the first line while the first is singing the second line, etc. 轮唱曲。 **7** dance in which the dancers move in a circle. 圆舞。

round⁴ /raund; raʊnd/ *prep* (may be replaced by *around,* except in special idiomatic uses) (除特殊习惯用法外, 可由 around 代替) **1** (expressing movement) in a path that passes on all sides of and comes back to the starting-point: (表示动作)环; 绕: *The earth moves ~ the sun.* 地球环绕太阳运行。 *Drake sailed ~ the world.* 德雷克驾船航行世界一周。 *(sleep/work) ~ the clock,* all day and all night. (睡觉, 工作)一昼夜。 *~-the-clock attrib adj* kept up continuously for 24 hours: 持续二十四小时的: *~-the-clock dancing.* 昼夜不停的跳舞。 **2** (expressing movement) in a path changing direction, from one side to another side of: (表示动作)围绕而进; 从…之一边至他边: *follow sb/walk ~ a corner.* 随某人(步行)绕过转弯处。 *~ the bend,* (sl) mad. (俚)疯狂的。 **3** (expressing position) so as to be on all sides of: (表示位置)围绕: *They were sitting ~ the table.* 他们正在桌而坐。 *He had a scarf ~ his neck.* 他的脖子上围着一条围巾。 **4** in various or all directions: 在各处或到处: *He looked ~ the room.* 他在室内四处环顾。 *Shall I show you ~ the house,* ie take you to the various rooms, etc? 要我领你参观这座房子吗? **5** to or at various points away from the centre: 至离开中心之各点: *The captain stationed his fielders ~ the pitch.* 队长把他的外场员配置在三柱门四周之各点。 *We haven't time to go ~* (= to visit) *the museums and art galleries.* 我们没有时间去参观博物馆和美术陈列馆了。 **6** ~ *(about),* (of time, cost, etc) approximately: (喻)大约(地): *Come ~ about 2 o'clock,* 在两点钟左右来。 *He's ready to pay somewhere ~ £1000 for a car.* 他准备以一千镑左右买一部车。

round⁵ /raund; raʊnd/ *vt, vi* **1** [VP6A, 2A] make or become round: (使)成为圆形: *~ the lips,* eg when making the sound /uː; u/; 使嘴唇成圆形(如发 /uː; u/ 音时); *stones ~ed by the action of water.* 被水冲成圆形的石块。 **2** [VP6A] go round: 绕行: *~ a corner.* 绕拐角而行。 **3** [VP15B, 2C, 3A] *~ sth off,* bring it to a satisfactory conclusion, add a suitable finish: 使圆满结束; 使更为完美: *~ off a sentence;* 修饰一个句子使其完美; *~ off one's career by being made a Minister.* 由于被任命为部长而使事业达到顶峰。 *~ out,* (cause to) become round: (使)成为圆形: *Her figure is beginning to ~ out.* 她的身材正开始发胖。 *~ sb/sth up,* drive, bring or collect, together: 驱赶; 聚拢; 逮捕: *The courier ~ed up the tourists and hurried them back into the coach.* 旅行服务员使观光客集合一起, 催他们回到车上。 *The cowboy ~ed up the cattle.* 牧人把牛群驱赶到一起。 Hence, 由此产生, '*~-up* n a driving or bringing together: 驱集; 聚拢: *a ~-up of criminals* (by police);

围捕罪犯; *a ~-up of cattle.* 把牛群驱集到一起。 *~ up (a figure/price),* bring it to a whole number: 将(数目、价格)调整为整数: *The price had been ~ed up from £647.50 to £650.* 该价格从 647.50 镑调整为 650 镑整。 *~ upon sb,* turn on him and attack him (in words or action). (以言词或行动)攻击某人。

round·about /'raundəbaut; 'raundə,baut/ *attrib adj* not going or coming by, or using, the shortest or most direct route: 绕远道的; 间接的: *I heard the news in a ~ way.* 这消息是间接听来的。 *We came by a ~ route.* 我们绕远路而来。 *What a ~ way of doing things!* 这真是一种绕圈子的做法! □ *n* [C] **1** (= *merry-go-round*) revolving circular platform with wooden horses, etc on which children ride for fun (at fairs, etc). 旋转木马 (一种装有木马等的圆形台供儿童乘坐玩乐)。 *You lose on the swings what you make on the ~s,* (prov) have losses and profits which are about equal. (谚)失之东隅, 收之桑榆。 **2** circular road junction causing traffic to go round instead of directly across (US ~ = *traffic circle* or *rotary*). 道路交叉处之圆环(使交通车辆绕行而不直接驶过)。

roun·del /'raundl; 'raundl/ *n* small disc, esp a decorative medallion; small circular panel (eg as used on military aircraft to indicate the country they belong to). 小圆形牌; (尤指)装饰用的圆牌; 小圆形标帜(如用于军用飞机以示国别者)。

roun·de·lay /'raundɪleɪ; 'raundə,le/ *n* short, simple song with a refrain. 一种有叠句的简单歌曲, 回旋曲。

roun·ders /'raundəz; 'raundəz/ *n pl* game for two teams, played with bat and ball, the players running through a number of bases arranged in a square, similar to baseball. 圆场棒球 (一种由两队参与的游戏, 用棒及球玩之, 击球员跑过方形球场边上的几个垒与棒球相似)。

Round·head /'raundhed; 'raund,hed/ ⇨ round¹(5).

rounds·man /'raundzmən; 'raundzmən/ *n* (*pl* -men) tradesman or his employee going round to ask for orders and deliver goods. 巡行各处请人订货或送货之商人或其伙计; 推销员; 送货员; 跑街。

rouse /rauz; rauz/ *vt, vi* **1** [VP 6 A] wake up: 唤醒: *I was ~ed by the ringing of a bell.* 钟声将我吵醒。 **2** [VP6A, 15 A] *~ sb (from sth/to sth),* cause (sb) to be more active, interested, etc (from inactivity, lack of confidence, etc): 激励; 激动: *~ sb/oneself to action,* 激励某人(自己)行动: *~ sb from indolence;* 激励某人从怠惰中奋起; *~d to anger by insults;* 被侮辱所激怒; *rousing cheers.* 令人鼓舞的欢呼。 *He's terrifying when he's ~d,* when his passions have been stirred. 他激动的时候很可怕。 **3** [VP2A] (= *~ oneself*) wake; become active again. 变得活跃。

rout¹ /raut; raut/ *n* **1** utter defeat and disorderly retreat: 彻底失败与溃退: *The defeat became a ~.* 那次失败变成溃退。 *put to ~,* defeat completely. 彻底击溃。 **2** (old use) large festive gathering of people; large evening party or reception. (旧用法)一大帮欢乐的人群; 大规模之晚会或招待会。 **3** (old use, or legal) disorderly, noisy crowd. (旧用法, 或法律)乌合之众; 骚动。 □ *vt* [VP6A] defeat completely; put to ~: 彻底击溃; ~ *the enemy.* 击溃敌人。

rout² /raut; raut/ *vt* [VP15A, B] *~ sb out (of),* get or fetch him up, out of bed, etc: 找出, 唤出, 驱使起床等: *We were ~ed out of our cabins before breakfast for passport examination.* 我们在吃早饭前被唤出房舱以检查护照。

route /ruːt; rut/ *n* **1** way taken or planned from one place to another: 路途; 路线; 路程; 航线: *The climbers tried to find a new ~ to the top of the mountain.* 攀登者试图寻出一条通到山顶的新路。 *He flew from Europe to Tokyo by the ~ across the Pole.* 他从欧洲经北极航线飞到东京。 *en ~* /ˌɒn 'ruːt; ˌɑn'rut/, on the way. 在途中。 **2** [U] (mil) *column of ~,* marching formation. (军)行军纵队。 *'~-march,* long march made

by soldiers in training. (部队在训练中所作之)长途行军。 □ *vt* plan a ~ for; send by a specified ~: 为…设计路线; 经由某特定路线将…送达: *We were ~d to France by way of Dover*. 我们被安排经过多佛港到达国。

rou·tine /ru:'ti:n; ru'tin/ *n* [C, U] fixed and regular way of doing things: 例行公事; 例行手续; 常规: *business ~*; 业务的例行手续: *a question of ~*. 例行手续的问题。 □ *adj* usual; ordinary: 通常的; 普通的: *the ~ procedure*; 普通程序; *my ~ duties*, those performed regularly, as if by rule. 例行职责。

rove /rəʊv; rov/ *vi*, *vt* 1 [VP2C, 6A] roam (the more usu word); wander: 漫游 (roam 较常用); 漂泊; 流浪: ~ *over sea and land*; 在海上陆上漂泊; *the moors*. 在荒野间漫游。 *a roving commission*, duties that take one from one place to another frequently. 巡回性任务。 2 [VP2A] (of the eyes, one's affections) be directed first one way, then another. (指眼睛, 一个人的感情)转来转去; 飘忽不定。 ~**r** *n* 1 wanderer. 漂泊者; 流浪者。 2 (old use) (旧用法) 'sea-~r, pirate. 海盗。 3 (formerly) Venture Scout. (昔时)高年级童子军。

row¹ /rəʊ; ro/ *n* [C] number of persons or things in a line: 一行; 一列; 一排: *a row of books/houses/desks*; 一排书(房子; 书桌); *plant a row of cabbages*; 栽种一排卷心菜; *sitting in a row/in rows*; 坐成一排(数排); *a front-row seat*, eg in a theatre. (戏院等中之)前排座位。 *a hard row to hoe*, a difficult task. 一件困难的工作。

row² /rəʊ; ro/ *vt*, *vi* [VP6A, 2A, B, C, 15A, B] propel (a boat) by using oars; carry or take (sb or sth) in a boat with oars; be an oarsman in a boat: 以桨划(船); 以划艇载(人或物); 在船上为划桨者: *Can you row (a boat)?* 你会划(船)吗? *Shall I row you up/down/across the river?* 要我划你到河的上游(下游, 对岸)去吗? *They rowed forty (strokes) to the minute*. 他们恰好划了四十下。 *He rows No 5 (= has this position) in the Oxford crew*. 他是牛津大学划船队第五桨桨手。 *Let's row a race*. 让我们比赛划船。 *The crew were rowed out (= exhausted by rowing) at the end of the race*. 比赛终了时划船队队员都累了。 'row-boat *n* (US) rowing boat. (美)划艇。 □ *n* journey or outing in a boat moved by oars; period of this; distance rowed: 以划艇所作的旅行或小游; 此种旅行或小游的期间; 划行的路程: *go for a row*; 去划船; *a long and tiring row*. 一段漫长而累人的划艇旅行。 'row·ing *n* (compounds) (复合词) 'rowing-boat *n* one moved by the use of oars. 以桨划动的船; 划艇。 'rowing-club *n* one for persons who row. 赛艇俱乐部。 ~**er** *n* person who rows a boat. 划船者。

a rowing-boat

row³ /raʊ; rau/ *n* 1 [U] uproar; noisy disturbance: 叫闹; 吵闹: *How can I study with all this row going on outside my windows?* 窗外这样的吵闹, 我怎能读书呢? 2 [C] noisy or violent argument or quarrel: 喧闹或激烈的争论或吵架: *have a row with the neighbours*. 同邻居吵架。 *That man is always ready for a row*, he has a quarrelsome nature. 那人性好争吵。 *kick up/make a row*, start a noisy quarrel or scene. 制造吵闹的场面; 争吵。 3 [C] instance of being in trouble, scolded, etc: 受责备; 挨罚: *get into a row for being late at the office*. 因为上班迟到而挨训。 □ *vt*, *vi* 1 [VP6A] scold; reprimand. 责备; 斥责。 2 [VP2A, 3A] row (with), quarrel noisily (with): 大声争吵: *He's always rowing with his neighbours*. 他总是同邻居争吵。

rowan /'rəʊən US: 'raʊən; 'roən/ *n* '~(-tree), small tree of the rose family, also called 亦称作 *mountain ash*. 欧亚花楸树(一种蔷薇科的小树)。 '~(-berry), one of the scarlet berries of this tree. 这种树的深红色浆果; 花楸果。

rowdy /'raʊdɪ; 'raʊdɪ/ *adj* (-ier, -iest) rough and noisy: 粗暴而吵闹的: *The ~ element in the audience continually interrupted the speaker*. 听众间的吵闹分子连续地打断演讲者。 *There were ~ scenes at the elections*. 选举中时有吵闹。 □ *n* (*pl* -dies) ~ person. 粗暴而爱吵闹的人。 **row·dily** /-ɪlɪ; -əlɪ/ *adv* **row·di·ness**, ~**ism** /-ɪzəm; -,ɪzəm/ *nn* [U] ~ behaviour. 粗暴而喧闹的行为。

rowel /'raʊəl; 'raʊəl/ *n* [C] revolving disc with sharp teeth at the end of a spur. 马刺上的小齿轮; 距轮。

row·lock /'rɒlək US: 'rəʊlɒk; 'ro,lɑk/ *n* [C] pivot for an oar or scull on the side (gunwale) of a boat (US 美 = *oarlock*). 桨架; 桨架。 ⇨ the illus at row. 参看 row 之插图。

royal /'rɔɪəl; 'rɔɪəl/ *adj* of, like, suitable for, supported by, belonging to the family of, a king or queen (女)王的; 象王的; 适于王的; 由王支持的; 王室的; 属于王室的; 威严的; 高贵的; 盛大的: *His R~ Highness*; 殿下; *the ~ family*; 王室; 皇族; *the R~ Society*; (英国)皇家学会; *the R~ Navy/Air Force*; 皇家海军(空军); a ~ *welcome*, one fit for a king, etc; splendid. 盛大的欢迎。 ~ *road to*, (fig) easiest way of getting (to): (喻)捷径: *Practice is the ~ road to success when learning a language*. 练习是学习语言的捷径。 **R~ Commission**, one officially appointed to hold an enquiry and issue a report. (由英国皇室正式指派的)调查委员会。 ~**ly** /'rɔɪəlɪ; 'rɔɪəlɪ/ *adv* in a ~ or splendid manner: 威严地; 高贵地; 盛大地: *We were ~ly entertained*. 我们受到盛大地招待。 ~**·ist** /'rɔɪəlɪst; 'rɔɪəlɪst/ *n* supporter of a king or queen or of a ~ government; supporter of the ~ side in a civil war. 保皇者; 保皇党员。

roy·alty /'rɔɪəltɪ; 'rɔɪəltɪ/ *n* (*pl* -ties) 1 [U] royal persons: 皇室; 王族: *The play was performed in the presence of ~*. 这个戏曾在御前演出。 *The hotel was patronized by ~*. 这家旅馆曾有皇族光顾过。 2 [U] position, rank, dignity, power, etc of a royal person. 皇室成员的地位、等级、尊严、权力等。 3 [C] sum paid by a mining or oil company to the owner of the land: (开矿或石油公司付给土地所有者的)矿区使用费: *oil royalties*; 石油产地使用费; sum paid to the owner of a copyright or patent: 版税; 专利权使用费: *a ~ of 10 per cent of the price of the book on all copies sold*. 实售册数每本抽百分之十的版税。

rub¹ /rʌb; rʌb/ *n* 1 period of rubbing: 摩擦的时间: *give the spoons/table, etc a good rub*. 把羹匙(桌子等)好好擦一擦。 2 (esp in the phrase 尤用于短语 *There's the rub*) difficulty; point at which doubt or difficulty arises. 困难; 引起疑惑或困难之点。

rub² /rʌb; rʌb/ *vt*, *vi* (-bb-) (For special uses with *adverbial particles* and *preps*, ⇨ 3 below.) (与副词性小品词及介词连用的特殊用法,参看下列第 3 义。) 1 [VP6A, 15A, 22] move (one thing) backwards and forwards on the surface of (another); make (sth *clean*, *dry*, etc) by doing this: 擦; 搓; 擦净; 擦干: *He was rubbing his hands together*. 他搓着两手。 *Rub this oil on your skin*. 把这油擦在你的皮肤上。 *He rubbed his hands with the soap*. 他在双手上涂擦肥皂。 *You've rubbed your coat against some wet paint*. 你的外套蹭上未干的油漆了。 *Rub the surface dry*. 把表面擦干。 **rub shoulders with**, meet and mix with (people). 同(人们)来往。 2 [VP2A, C] come into, or be in, contact with, by a sliding or up and down movement: 由滑动或上下之动作而接触; 摩擦: *What is the wheel rubbing on/against?* 这轮子擦到什么了? 3 [VP2C, 15B] (special uses with *adverbial particles* and *preps*): (与副词性小品词及介词连用的特殊用法): **rub along**, (colloq) (of a person) manage to exist, pass one's time, without too much difficulty. (口, 指人)无太

大困难地过活，消磨时间。*rub along with sb/together,*
(of two or more persons) live without quarrelling, etc:
(指两个或两个以上的人)和睦相处: *I manage to rub
along with her.* 我和她相处得很不错。*We manage to
rub along together.* 我们相处得很不错。**rubber** ⇨
rubber¹(4).

rub sb/oneself/a horse down, rub thoroughly,
vigorously, eg with a towel, to make dry and clean: (用
毛巾等)用力搓干擦净: *He rubbed himself down after
his bath.* 他洗澡之后用力擦干了身子。*rub sth down,*
make sth smooth or level by rubbing: 磨平: *Rub the
walls down well before applying new paint.* 在涂上新油漆
之前先将墙磨平。 Hence, 由此产生, **'rub-down** n: *Give
the horse/the walls a good rub-down.* 把这匹马好好擦洗
一番(把这些墙好好擦平)。

rub sth in; rub sth into sth, (a) force (ointment, etc)
into sth, eg the skin, by rubbing: 用力擦(药膏等)使渗
进某物(如皮肤): *Rub the ointment well in/into the
skin.* 把这药膏用力擦, 使渗入皮肤。 (b) force (a lesson,
a humiliating or unpleasant fact) into sb's mind: 强使
接受(教训、屈辱或不愉快事件等): *The moral needs to be
well rubbed in.* 这个教训需要好好记住。*rub it in,* (esp)
remind sb repeatedly of a fault, failure, etc: (尤
指)不断地提起某人的错误、失败等: *I know I behaved
foolishly but you needn't rub it in.* 我知道我的行为很愚
蠢, 但你不必老提这件事。

rub sth off, remove sth (from a surface) by rubbing:
擦掉: *How did you rub the skin off your knees?* 你怎么
把膝盖上的皮擦破了? *The nap of this cloth has been
rubbed off.* 这布上的细毛被磨掉了。

rub sth out, remove (marks, writing, etc) by rubbing:
把(记号、笔迹等)擦掉: *rub out a word/pencil marks/
mistakes.* 擦掉一个字(铅笔记号, 错误)。 *The stains
won't rub out,* can't be rubbed, out. 这些污点擦不掉。
rub sb out, (US sl) murder him. (美俚)谋杀某人。

rub sth up, polish by rubbing: 擦光亮: *rub up the
silver spoons.* 把银匙擦亮。 Hence, 由此产生, **'rub-up** n.
rub sb (up) the right/wrong way, placate/irritate
him. 安抚(激怒)某人。

rub-a-dub /ˌrʌb ə ˈdʌb; ˈrʌbəˌdʌb/ n [U] sound
made by beating a drum. 鼓之咚咚声。

rub·ber¹ /ˈrʌbə(r); ˈrʌbɚ/ n **1** [U] tough elastic
substance made from the milky liquid that flows from
certain trees when the bark is cut, used for making
tyres, tennis balls, etc: 橡皮: (attrib) (用作定语)
'~ *trees;* 橡胶树; the '~ *plantations of Malaysia;* 马来
西亚的橡胶园; ~ *bands,* elastic bands for keeping
things together; 橡皮筋; 橡皮圈; a ~ *stamp.* 橡皮图章。
,~'**stamp** vt (colloq) approve or endorse (a proposal,
etc) without giving it proper consideration. (口)不
加适当考虑即赞同或认可(一建议等)。 '~'**neck** n (US
colloq) tourist or sightseer of the kind which constantly
turns his head to see as much as possible. (美口)频
频转头想尽量多看一些的观光客或游客。 □ *vi* look at
sights in this way. 频频转头观看景象。 **2** [C] piece
of ~ material for rubbing out pencil marks, etc: 〔擦
铅笔痕迹等的)橡皮: *a pencil with a ~ at one end.* 一端
带橡皮的铅笔。 **3** (pl) overshoes (galoshes) made of ~.
(复)橡皮套鞋。 **4** [C] person or thing that rubs, eg a
part of a machine that applies friction. 擦者; 搓者; 摩
擦之人或物; 摩擦器。 □ *vt* [VP6A] cover or coat
with ~. 覆以橡皮; 包以橡皮。 ~**ize** /-aɪz; -ˌaɪz/ vt
[VP6A] cover or treat with ~. 覆以橡皮; 以橡皮处理。
~**y** adj made of ~. 橡皮做的。

rub·ber² /ˈrʌbə(r); ˈrʌbɚ/ n [C] (in such card
games as whist and bridge) (在惠斯特和桥牌类的牌戏
中) **1** three successive games between the same sides or
persons: (相同的组或人之间的)连续三盘比赛: *Let's play
another ~.* 让我们再连赛三盘。 **2** the winning of two
games out of three; the third game when each side has
won one: 三盘比赛中的连胜两盘; 双方各胜一盘后以决定
胜负的第三盘比赛: *game and ~,* (We have won) the

third game and (therefore) the ~. (我们赢了)第三盘和
这一局。

rub·bing /ˈrʌbɪŋ; ˈrʌbɪŋ/ n impression of sth, eg a
brass over a grave, by rubbing paper laid over, it with
wax, chalk or charcoal. 摹拓; 拓印(碑文等)。

rub·bish /ˈrʌbɪʃ; ˈrʌbɪʃ/ n [U] **1** waste material;
that which is, or is to be, thrown away as worthless;
refuse. 废物; 垃圾。 **2** nonsense; worthless ideas: 无意
的话; 无意义的思想: *This book is all ~.* 这本书全是一派
胡言乱语。 **3** (as an exclamation) Nonsense! (用作惊叹
词)胡说! ~**y** adj worthless. 无价值的。

rubble /ˈrʌbl; ˈrʌbl/ n [U] bits of broken stone,
rock or brickwork: 碎石; 碎砖瓦砾: *buildings reduced
to ~ by bombing;* 因轰炸而毁成碎砖瓦砾的建筑物; *build
roads with a foundation of ~.* 修筑以碎石为路基的道路。

Ru·bi·con /ˈruːbɪkən US: -kɑn; ˈrubɪˌkɑn/ n *cross
the ~,* commit oneself to an enterprise from which
one cannot turn back. 破釜沉舟; 采断然手段。

ru·bi·cund /ˈruːbɪkənd; ˈrubəˌkʌnd/ adj (of a
person's face or complexion) ruddy; high-coloured. (指
人的脸或面色)红润的; 有血色的。

ru·bric /ˈruːbrɪk; ˈrubrɪk/ n [C] **1** title or heading
printed in red or special type. 红字标题; 以特殊字体
印的标题。 **2** rule; direction; explanation. 规则; 指示;
说明。

ruby /ˈruːbɪ; ˈrubɪ/ n [C] (pl **-bies**) red jewel. 红宝
石; 红玉。 □ adj, n deep red (colour). 深红色的(的)。

ruck¹ /rʌk; rʌk/ n *the ~,* the common ~, ordinary
commonplace things or persons: 普通的事物或人: *He
was ambitious to get out of the ~,* to escape from being
thought of as ordinary, commonplace, etc. 他野心勃勃
想出人头地。

ruck² /rʌk; rʌk/ n [C] irregular fold or crease (esp
in cloth). 皱褶(尤指布上者)。 □ *vi, vt* [VP2A, C, 6 A,
15 B] ~ *(up),* be pulled into ~s; make into ~s: 扯成
皱褶; 使成皱褶: *The sheets on my bed have ~ed up.* 我床
上的床单已经皱起来了。

ruck·sack /ˈrʌksæk; ˈrʌkˌsæk/ n [C] canvas bag
strapped on the back from the shoulders, used by
people on a walking holiday, etc; haversack, knapsack.
一种帆布背囊(步行度假者等用之)。

ruc·tions /ˈrʌkʃnz; ˈrʌkʃənz/ n pl angry words or
protests; noisy argument: 愤怒的话或抗议; 吵闹的争辩:
There'll be ~ if you don't do what you're told. 你如果不
照吩咐去做, 一定会挨骂。

rud·der /ˈrʌdə(r); ˈrʌdɚ/ n [C] **1** flat, broad piece
of wood or metal hinged vertically at the stern of a
boat or ship for steering. (船上的)舵。 **2** similar
structure on an aircraft. (飞机上的)方向舵。 ⇨ the
illus at **air.** 参看 air 之插图。

ruddle /ˈrʌdl; ˈrʌdl/ n [U] red ochre, esp the kind
used for marking ownership of sheep. 红土; 代赭石(尤
指在羊身上做记号用所用者)。 □ *vt* put ~ on (sheep). 在
(羊身)上涂红土。

ruddy /ˈrʌdɪ; ˈrʌdɪ/ adj (**-ier, -iest**) **1** (of the face)
red, as showing good health: (指脸)红润的(表示很健
康): ~ *cheeks;* 红润的脸颊; *in ~ health,* having ~
cheeks indicating good health. 有着表示健康的红润脸色
的。 **2** red or reddish: 红色的; 淡红色的: *a ~ glow in
the sky.* 天空中红色的光辉。 **3** (sl; euphem for) bloody
(3): (俚; bloody 第 3 义之委婉语)用于表示强烈感情的
无意义的话: *What the ~ hell are you doing?* 你在搞
什么鬼呀?

rude /ruːd; rud/ adj (**-r, -st**) **1** (of a person, his
speech, behaviour) impolite; not showing respect or
consideration: (指人、其语言、行为)粗鲁无礼的; 不表示
尊敬或体谅的: *to interrupt/to point at people.* 打断
插嘴(用手指人)是不礼貌的。 *What a ~ reply!* 多么粗鲁
无礼的答复! *Would it be ~ to ask when you are likely
to leave?* 要向一位客人询问他何时动身, 这会是无礼吗?请
问你大概什么时候告辞? (如向一位逗留过久的客人)。 **2**
startling; violent; rough: 骇人听闻的; 狂暴的; 粗野的:

get a ~ *shock.* 受到剧烈的震惊。 *a* ~ *awakening,* a sudden realization of sth unpleasant. 突然的觉醒。 **3** primitive; without refinement: 原始的；粗鄙的： *our* ~ *forefathers.* 我们未开化的祖先。 **4** roughly made; simple: 粗制的；简单的： *a* ~ *wooden plough.* 一具简陋的木犁。 **5** vigorous: 有活力的： *in* ~ *health.* 十分健壮的。 **6** in the natural state; crude, raw (the more usu words): 天然状态的；原质的；粗陋的；生的 (crude, raw 等字较常用)： *cotton in its* ~ *state.* 原棉。 ~ *ore/produce:* 原矿(天然产品)： *cotton in its* ~ *state.* 原棉。 ~**ly** *adv* in a ~ manner: 无礼地；粗暴地；突然地；原始地；简单地；有力地： *a* ~*ly* (ie in a primitive manner) *fashioned craft;* 原始风格的手艺； *be* ~*ly awakened.* 突然觉醒。 ⇨ **2** above. 参看上列第二义。 ~**·ness** *n* [U].

ru·di·ment /'ru:dɪmənt; 'rudəmənt/ *n* **1** (*pl*) first steps or stages (of an art or science): (复)(艺术或科学的)初步；初阶；基础： *learn the* ~*s of chemistry/grammar.* 学习化学(语法)的初阶。 **2** earliest form on which a later development is or might have developed; imperfectly developed part: 可进一步发展的最初的形式；发育不完全的部分；雏型： *Certain fossils reveal the* ~ *of a thumb.* 某些化石显示出拇指的雏型。 *A new-born chicken has only the* ~*s of wings.* 一只新孵出的小鸡仅有翅膀的雏型。 **ru·di·men·tary** /,ru:dɪ'mentrɪ; ,rudə'mentərɪ/ *adj* **1** elementary: 初步的；基础的： *a* ~*ary knowledge of mechanics.* 力学的初步知识。 **2** undeveloped; existing in an imperfect or undeveloped form. 发育未完全的；以不完全或未发展成熟的形式存在的。

rue¹ /ru:; ru/ *n* [U] small evergreen plant with bitter-tasting leaves formerly used in medicine. 芸香 (一种长绿小灌木, 叶味苦, 以前用以制药)。

rue² /ru:; ru/ *vt* [VP6A] (dated or liter) repent of; think of with sadness or regret: 悔恨；悔恨： *You'll live to rue it,* will one day regret it. 总有一天你会后悔的。 *You'll rue the day when....* 你会后悔那一天曾.... **rue·ful** /'ru:fl; 'rufl/ *adj* showing, feeling, expressing regret: 表现、感觉、表示懊悔的： *a rueful smile.* (充满懊悔的)苦笑。 **rue·fully** /'ru:fəlɪ; 'ruflɪ/ *adv*

ruff¹ /rʌf; rʌf/ *n* **1** ring of differently coloured or marked feathers round a bird's neck, or of hair round an animal's neck, 鸟颈的彩羽；兽颈之毛；颈毛。 **2** wide, stiff frill worn as a collar in the 16th c. 十六世纪时所带的宽而硬的绉领。 ⇨ the illus at **doublet**. 参看 doublet 之插图。

ruff² /rʌf; rʌf/ *vi, vt* trump (in a card game). (在牌戏中)出王牌以取胜；切牌。 □ *n* act of trumping. 出王牌以取胜；切牌。

ruf·fian /'rʌfɪən; 'rʌfɪən/ *n* violent, cruel man. 残暴的人；恶棍；暴徒。 ~**·ly** *adj* like a ~; lawless. 象恶棍的；残暴的；无法纪的。 ~**·ism** /-ɪzəm; -ɪzəm/ *n* [U] rough, brutal conduct. 粗野残酷的行为。

ruffle /'rʌfl; 'rʌfl/ *vt, vi* **1** [VP6A, 15B] ~ (*up*), disturb the peace, calm or smoothness of: 扰乱…之和平、宁静或平滑；弄皱；弄乱： *The bird* ~*d up its feathers.* 那鸟竖起了羽毛。 *A sudden breeze* ~*d the surface of the lake.* 一阵突然的微风吹绉了湖水。 *Who's been ruffling your hair?* 谁弄乱了你的头发？ *Anne is easily* ~*d,* easily annoyed, put out of temper. 安易生气。 **2** [VP2A] become ~d: 生气；起绉： *You* ~ *too easily.* 你太容易发脾气了。 □ *n* [C] **1** strip of material gathered into folds; frill used to ornament a garment at the wrist, neck or breast. 绉褶；衣袋等上做饰物用的绉边。 **2** ruffling or being ~d(1). 扰乱；被扰乱。

rug /rʌg; rʌg/ *n* **1** floor mat of thick material (usu smaller than a carpet): 地毯(通常指较 carpet 小者)： *= a 'hearth-rug.* **2** thick, usu woollen, covering or wrap: 厚(毛)毯： *a 'travelling-rug* (for putting round one's knees in a car, etc). 旅行毯(坐汽车等时围着膝部者)。

Rugby /'rʌgbɪ; 'rʌgbɪ/ *n* ~ (**football**), (GB) kind of football using an oval-shaped ball which may be

handled: (英) 橄榄球戏(球为椭圆形, 可使用手)： ~ League, form of ~ with thirteen players and allowing professionalism: 联盟制橄榄球(每队十三名球员, 准许职业球队参加)。 ~ Union, with fifteen players and having amateur teams only. 同盟制橄榄球(每队十五名球员, 限业余球队参加)。

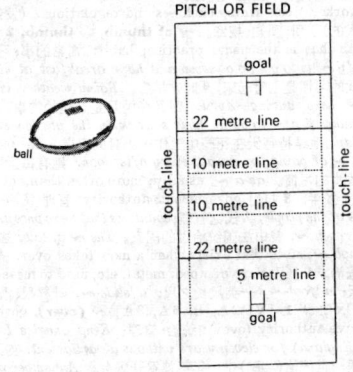

PITCH OR FIELD

Rugby Union football (rugger)

rug·ged /'rʌgɪd; 'rʌgɪd/ *adj* **1** rough; uneven; rocky: 粗糙的；不平的；崎岖的；多岩石的： *a* ~ *coast;* 多岩石的海岸； ~ *country.* 地势起伏的地区。 **2** having furrows or wrinkles: 有皱纹的；多皱纹的： *a* ~ *face;* 多皱纹的脸； ~ *features.* 不平整的面貌。 **3** not refined or gentle: 粗野的；不雅的： *a* ~ *character;* 粗鲁的人； ~ *manners.* 粗野的态度。 ~**·ly** *adv* ~**·ness** *n*

rug·ger /'rʌgə(r); 'rʌgɚ/ *n* [U] (colloq) Rugby football. (口)橄榄球戏。

ruin /'ru:ɪn; 'ruɪn/ *n* **1** [U] destruction; overthrow; serious damage: 毁灭；瓦解；推翻；严重的损坏： *the* ~ *of her hopes;* 她的希望的幻灭； *the impulse that led to my* ~; 使我身败名裂的冲动； *brought to* ~ *by gambling and drink.* 因赌博与酗酒而堕落。 **2** [U] state of being decayed, destroyed, collapsed: 败坏、毁坏、崩溃的状态： *The castle has fallen into* ~. 那城堡已破败不堪。 *go to rack and* ~, ⇨ **rack**⁴. [C] sth which has decayed, been destroyed, etc: 已败坏、被毁坏等之物： *The building is in* ~s. 那建筑物已成断壁残垣。 *The abbey is now a* ~. 该修道院现已成废墟。 **3** [U] cause of ~: 毁灭、败坏等的原因： *Gambling was his* ~ (= was the ~ of him). 赌博是使他堕落的原因。 □ *vt* [VP6A] cause the ~ of: 使毁灭；使败坏： *You will* ~ *your prospects if you continue to be so foolish.* 如果你继续此种愚行, 你将自毁前程。 *The storm* ~*ed the crops.* 暴风雨摧毁了农作物。 *He's bankrupt and* ~*ed,* has lost all his money, property, etc. 他完全破产了。 ~**·ation** /,ru:ɪ'neɪʃn; ,ruɪ'neɪʃən/ *n* [U] being ~ed; bringing to ~: 毁灭；毁坏；导致毁灭或败坏： *These late frosts mean* ~*ation to the fruit farmers.* 春寒意味着对果农之重大破坏。 ~**ous** /-əs; -əs/ *adj* **1** causing ~: 招致毁灭的： *~ous expenditure/folly.* 使人破产的花费(毁人的愚行)。 **2** in ~s: 毁坏的；破落不堪的： *live in a* ~*ous old house.* 住在一所破烂不堪的老屋中。 ~**·ous·ly** *adv*

rule /ru:l; rul/ *n* **1** [C] law or custom which guides or controls behaviour or action; decision made by an organization, etc about what must or must not be done: 指导或控制行为或行动的条规或惯例；一组织等对何者必须做或绝不能做所做之决定；规则；法规： *obey the* ~*s of the game.* 遵守游戏(比赛)规则。 *There is a* ~ *that....* 有一条规定…。 *It's against the* ~*s to handle the ball in soccer.* 在足球赛中以手触球即犯规。 ~(**s**) *of the road,* ⇨ **road**(1). *by/according to* ~, according to

~s and regulations: 依順規則: *He does everything by ~*, never uses his own judgement. 他事事墨守成規(從不用自己的判斷力). **work to ~,** pay exaggerated attention (deliberately) to ~s and regulations and so slow down output: (故意地)過于遵守規則而減低生產; 怠工: *Instead of coming out on strike, the men decided to work to ~.* 工人們決定不罷工而怠工. '**~ book,** book (issued to workers) containing such ~s and regulations. (發給工人的)手册; 須知; 規章. **~ of thumb,** ⇨ **thumb. 2** [C] sth that is the usual practice; habit: 慣常的事; 習慣: *My ~ is to get up at seven and have breakfast at eight.* 我的習慣是七時起床, 八時吃早餐. *Rainy weather is the ~ here during April.* 四月多雨乃是這里的常事. *He makes it a ~ to do an hour's work in the garden every day.* 他維持每天在花園中工作一小時的習慣. *She makes a ~ of going for a walk every afternoon.* 她每天下午散步的習慣. **as a ~,** usually; more often than not. 通常; 多半. **3** [U] government; authority: 管理; 統治: *the ~ of the people;* 人民之管理; *countries that were once under French ~.* 曾由法國統治的國家. *The ~ of law;* 法治; *mob ~,* state that exists when a mob takes over. 暴民統治. **4** [C] strip of wood, metal, etc, used to measure: 尺: *a 'foot-~;* 一英尺長之尺; *a 'slide-~.* 計算尺; 滑尺. □ *vi, vt* **1** [VP2A, B, 6A, 3A] ~ **(over),** govern; have authority (over): 統治; 管理: *King Charles I ~d (England) for eleven years without a parliament.* 英王查理一世統治(英國)十一年不曾召開國會. *An emperor is a monarch who ~s over an empire.* 皇帝是統治一個帝國的君主. **2** (usu in the *passive*) be guided or influenced by; have power or influence over: (通常用被動語態)被引導或被影響; 對…有控制或影響力: *Don't be ~d by your passions/by hatred.* 不要被強烈的情感(仇恨)所支配. **3** [VP6A, 9, 15A, B, 25] give as a decision: 裁決: *The chairman ~d the motion out of order/that the motion was out of order.* 主席裁决該動議不合程序. ~ *sth out,* declare that it cannot be considered, that it is out of the question: 拒絕考慮某事; 宣布某事不可能: *That's a possibility that can't be ~d out,* It is something we must bear in mind. 那種可能性我們不能不加以考慮. **4** [VP6A, 15A, B] make (a line or lines) on paper (with a ruler); make parallel lines on (paper): (用尺)在紙上畫(線); 畫平行線于(紙上): ~ *d notepaper;* 畫格的信紙; ~ *a line across the sheet.* 畫一條橫過全紙的線. ~ *sth off,* separate it by ruling a line: 畫一線而隔開: ~ *off a column of figures.* 畫一線把一欄數字隔開. **5** [VP2C] (comm, of prices) have a certain general level: (商, 指價格)保持某一水准: *Prices ~d high,* were, for the most part, high. 一般物價偏高.

ruler /'ru:lə(r); 'rulɚ/ n **1** person who rules or governs. 統治者. **2** straight length of wood, plastic, metal, etc usu flat, used in drawing straight lines, or, if graduated, for measuring. 尺; 直尺.

rul·ing /'ru:lɪŋ; 'rulɪŋ/ *adj* that rules; predominating; prevalent: 統治的; 支配的; 流行的: *his ruling passion,* that which governs his actions. 支配着他的行動的激情. □ *n* [C] (esp) decision made by sb in authority, eg a judge. (尤指)裁决; 判决.

rum¹ /rʌm; rʌm/ *n* [U] alcoholic drink made from sugar-cane juice; (US) (any kind of) alcoholic liquor. 甘蔗汁制的糖酒; 朗姆酒; (美)(任何種类的)酒. '**rum-runner** *n* (US) person or ship engaged in the illegal importation of alcoholic liquor. (美)輸入私酒之人或船.

rum² /rʌm; rʌm/ *adj* (**rummer, rummest**) (colloq) queer; odd: (口)古怪的; 奇特的: *What a rum fellow he is!* 他是個多么古怪的家伙! **rummy** *adj* = rum².

rumba /'rʌmbə; 'rʌmbə/ n [C] (music for a) ballroom dance that originated in Cuba. 倫巴舞(源于古巴的一种交際舞); 倫巴舞曲.

rumble /'rʌmbl; 'rʌmbl/ *vi, vt* **1** [VP2A, C] make a deep, heavy, continuous sound: 發出隆隆聲或轆轆聲: *thunder/gun-fire rumbling in the distance;* 遠方發出的隆隆雷(炮火)聲; move with such a sound: 隆隆地行進;

轆轆地行進: *heavy carts rumbling along the street;* 在街上轆轆前行的重馬車; (of the bowels) make sounds as gas moves through them. (指肠子)發咕咕声. **2** [VP15B] ~ **out,** utter, say, in a deep voice: 以低沉声音说出: ~ *out a few remarks.* 以低沉的声音说出几句话. □ *n* **1** [U] deep, heavy, continuous sound: 隆隆声; 轆轆声: *the ~ of thunder.* 雷声隆隆. **2** [C] (old use) place at the back of a carriage for a person or for luggage, etc; (= dickey-seat; US, also 美亦作 '~*-seat*) extra, open seat at the back of an (old-fashioned) automobile. (旧用法)马车尾部供人乘坐或載行李之部位; (旧式)汽车后边外加之无蓬座位; 主座.

rum·bus·tious /rʌm'bʌstɪəs; rʌm'bʌstʃəs/ *adj* boisterous. 吵閙的; 喧嚷的.

ru·mi·nant /'ru:mɪnənt; 'rumənənt/ *n, adj* (animal) which chews the cud, eg cows, deer. 反刍的; 反刍动物(如牛、鹿).

ru·mi·nate /'ru:mɪneɪt; 'rumə,net/ *vi* [VP2A, B, C] meditate; turn over in the mind: 沉思; 反复思索: ~ *over/about/on recent events;* 反复思索最近发生的事; (of animals) chew the cud. (指动物)反刍. **ru·mi·na·tive** /'ru:mɪnətɪv US: -neɪtɪv/ *adj* inclined to meditate. 愛沉思的. **ru·mi·na·tion** /ˌru:mɪ'neɪʃn; ˌrumə'neʃən/ *n* [U].

rum·mage /'rʌmɪdʒ; 'rʌmɪdʒ/ *vi, vt* **1** [VP2A, B, C, 3A] ~ **(among/in/through),** turn things over, move things about, while looking for sth: 翻寻; 搜寻: ~ *in/through a desk drawer,* 在书桌抽屉里翻寻东西; ~ *about among old papers.* 在旧报纸中翻找东西. **2** [VP6A, 15B] ~ **(through),** search thoroughly: 彻底搜查: ~ *a ship,* eg by Customs officers who suspect that there is contraband. 彻底搜查一船(如因怀疑走私而由海关官员检查). □ *n* **1** [U] search (esp of a ship by Customs officers). 搜寻(尤指海关官员对一船之搜查). **2** things found by rummaging; miscellaneous old clothes, old stock, etc. 搜寻出来的东西; 杂乱的旧衣物等等. '~ **sale,** = jumble (the more usu word) sale. 旧衣物拍卖(jumble sale 较常用).

rummy¹ /'rʌmɪ; 'rʌmɪ/ *adj* ⇨ rum².

rummy² /'rʌmɪ; 'rʌmɪ/ *n* [U] card game for two or more players, using one or two packs of cards. 用一副或两副纸牌供二人或多人玩的一种牌戏.

ru·mour (US = **ru·mor**) /'ru:mə(r); 'rumɚ/ *n* [U] general talk, gossip, hearsay, [C] (statement, report, story) which cannot be verified and is of doubtful accuracy: (不能证实且正确性可疑的)一般性谈话; 传闻; 传闻; 谣言; 传说: *R~ has it/There is a ~ that there will be a General Election in the autumn.* 据传闻今秋将举行普选. *All sorts of ~s are going round.* 各种谣言正四处流传. *There is a ~ of the Loch. Ness monster having been seen/a ~ that the... has been seen.* 据说奈斯湖中的怪物曾被人看见过. '~**monger** *n* person who spreads ~s. 散布谣言者; 造谣者. □ *vt* (usu passive) report by way of ~: (通常用被动语态)谣传: *It is ~ed that....* 据谣传~. *He is ~ed to have escaped to Dublin.* 据传他已逃往都柏林.

rump /rʌmp; rʌmp/ *n* [C] **1** animal's buttocks; tail-end of a bird; (joc, of a human being) bottom. (动物的)臀部; (鸟的)尾梢; (谑, 人的)臀部. ˌ~'**steak** *n* beefsteak cut from near the ~. 臀部附近的牛排. **2** contemptible remnant of a larger group. 可鄙的残余分子; 余党.

rumple /'rʌmpl; 'rʌmpl/ *vt* [VP6A] crease; crumple; make rough: 弄绉; 压绉; 使乱: *Don't play too violently or you'll ~ your dresses.* 不要玩得太野, 否则你会弄绉衣裳的. *You've just done my hair, so please don't ~ it.* 我刚做好头发, 请不要把它弄乱.

rum·pus /'rʌmpəs; 'rʌmpəs/ *n* (*sing* only; colloq) disturbance; noise; uproar: (用单数; 口)骚乱; 喧哗; 喧嚣: *have a ~ with sb.* 同某人乱吵一阵. *What's all this ~ about?* 什么事情乱哄哄的? *kick up/make a ~,* cause a ~. 引起一场骚乱(掀起一阵喧哗).

run[1] /rʌn; rʌn/ n **1** act of running on foot: 跑: *go for a short run across the fields*; 横过田野做一次短跑; (in fox-hunting) period of chasing a fox. (在猎狐中)追赶狐狸的一段时间。*at a run*, running: 跑: *He started off at a run but soon tired and began to walk.* 他跑步出发, 但不久便累了, 于是改成步行。*on the run*, (a)in flight: 奔逃: *He's on the run from the police.* 他正在逃避警察的追缉。*We have the enemy on the run*, We have caused them to run away. 我们迫使敌人逃窜。(b) continuously active and moving about: 继续忙个不停: *I've been on the run ever since I got up.* 我起床后一直忙个不停。*give sb/get a (good) run for his/one's money*, (a) return (sth) in return for his efforts, expenditure. 给与某人(获得)应得的报酬或享受。(b) provide him with strong competition: 使某人做激烈的竞争: *We must give him a good run for his money.* 我们必须和他做激烈的竞争。**2** [C] excursion or visit: 远足; 游览: *a run to Paris*; 到巴黎去游览; *have a run in the country,* eg by car; 到乡间一游(如乘车游览); outing or journey in a car, train, etc: 乘汽车、火车等的出游或旅行: *How many hours' run is Leeds from London by train?* 从伦敦到里兹乘火车有几小时行程? *Can we have a trial run in the new car?* 我们可以试乘这部新汽车吗? **3** [C] distance travelled by a ship in a specified time: (船的)航程: *make bets on the day's run,* on the distance travelled in 24 hours. 打赌一天的航程。**4** route taken by vehicles, ships, etc: 车、船等走的路线: *The boat was taken off its usual run.* 该船不再航行原有航线。**5** quick fall: 急剧下跌: *Prices/The temperature came down in/with a run.* 物价(温度)急剧下降。**6** series of performances: 连续的演出: *The play had a long run/a run of six months.* 这个戏已连演甚久(连演六个月)。**7** period; succession: 一段时间; 连续: *a run of bad luck,* a series of misfortunes. 一连串的不幸。*a run on sth,* sudden demand by many people for it: 许多人之突然需求某物: *a run on the bank,* a demand by many customers together for immediate repayment. 纷纷到银行提款; 挤兑。*in the 'long run,* ultimately: 最终地; 终极地: *It pays in the long run to buy goods of high quality.* 买质料好的东西究是上算的。**8** (usu large, enclosed) space for domestic animals, fowls, etc: 家畜或家禽的(大)围场: *a 'chicken-run*; 鸡场; *a 'sheep-run,* area of pasture for sheep. 牧羊场。**9** (cricket and baseball) unit of scoring, made by running over a certain course. (板球及棒球)分数单位; 一分。**10** common, average or ordinary type or class: 普通的型式或种类: *the common run of mankind,* ordinary, average people; 普通人; *an hotel out of the common run,* different from, and better than, the kind one usually finds. 与众不同的旅馆。**,run-of-the-'mill,** ordinary; average. 普通的; 一般的。**11** (colloq) permission to make free use (of). (口)准许自由使用。*give sb/get the run of sth,* the permission to use it: 允许某人自由使用某物: *I have the run of his library.* 我可以自由使用他的书房。**12** way in which things tend to move; general direction or trend: 事物进展的方式; 趋势; 趋向: *The run of events is rather puzzling.* 事情发展之趋势令人费解。*The run of the cards* (= The cards that were dealt to me during the evening) *favoured me.* (那晚)我的牌风很顺。**13** (music) series of notes sung or played quickly and in the order of the scale. (音乐)急唱; 急奏。**14** shoal of fish in motion: 一群游动中的鱼: *a run of salmon,* eg on their way upstream. 一群鲑鱼(如正逆流而上者)。**15** (US) ladder(2). (美)袜子脱针处; 抽丝。

run[2] /rʌn; rʌn/ vi, vt (pt **ran** /ræn; ræn/, pp **run; -nn-**) (For special uses with *adverbial particles* and *preps,* ⇨ **26** below; for special uses of *running, part adj,* ⇨ **running.**) (与副词性小品词及介词连用的特殊用法, 参看下列第 26 义; running 用作形容词, 参看 running.) **1** [VP2A, B, C, E, 4A] (of men and animals) move with quick steps, faster than when walking: (指人及动物)跑: *run three miles*; 跑三英里; *run fast*; 跑得快;

run (out) to see what's happening; 跑(出)去看发生了什么事; *run upstairs.* 跑上楼。*She came running to meet me.* 她跑着来接我。*She ran to meet us.* 她跑跑着来接我。*We ran to his aid/ran to help him.* 我们跑去协助他。*The dog was running behind its master.* 这只狗在它主人后面跑着。⇨ **run after** in **26** below. Don't run across the road until you're sure it's safe. 在确定是安全之前, 不要跑过街。*take a running jump,* run up to the point where one starts a jump; (sl, imper) go away, you are being foolish. etc. 跑至起跳点起跳; 作急行跳; (俚, 祈使)滚开, 你这个笨蛋…。**2** [VP2A, B, C] escape or avoid by running away; take to flight: 逃走; 逃走: *As soon as we appeared the boys ran off.* 我们一出现, 孩子们便逃走了。*Run for your lives!* ie run if you want to save your life. 快逃命! *run for it,* avoid sth, eg getting wet in a storm, by running. 赶快躲避(如避免在暴风雨中淋湿而快跑)。*cut and run,* (sl) escape by taking to flight. (俚)奔逃; 逃脱。*a running fight,* a fight between a retreating ship/fleet, etc and those in pursuit. 一场(海上的)追逐战。**3** [VP2A, B, C] practice running for exercise or as a sport; compete in races on foot: 练习跑步; 赛跑: *He used to run when he was at college.* 他在大学时常参加赛跑。*Is he running in the 100 metres?* 他将参加一百米赛跑吗? *Is your horse likely to run in the Derby?* 你的马可能参加大赛马吗? *'also ran,* used of a horse not among the first three past the winning post: (用以指赛马中)非前三名的马; 落选的马: *Hyperion also ran.* 玄伯龙神号马未得前三名。Hence, 由此产生, **'also-ran** n [C] person or animal unsuccessful in a race or other form of competition. 在赛跑或其他竞赛中未成功的人或动物。**4** [VP3A] **~ for,** (esp US) compete for (an elected office). (尤美)竞选。Cf 参较 *stand for,* the more usu GB usage: stand for 为英国比较通行的用法: *run for President/for mayor.* 竞选总统(市长)。**5** [VP6A, 15A] cause to compete (in a race); present or nominate (for an office): 使参加赛跑; 使参加竞选(公职): *run two horses in the Derby.* 让两匹马参加大赛马。*How many candidates is the Liberal Party running in the General Election?* 在这次普选中自由党有多少候选人竞选了? **6** [VP2D, 15A] (cause to) reach a certain condition or place as the result of running: (使)达到某一地位或得到某一名次: *He ran second in the race.* 他赛跑得到第二名。*run oneself out (of breath),* ⇨ **run out** in **26** below. 参看下列第 26 义。*run out,* run out, *run sb (clean) off his feet/legs,* (colloq) keep him going until he is exhausted. (口)使人走得筋疲力竭。*run oneself/sb into the ground,* exhaust oneself/sb by hard work or exercise. 因辛苦工作或运动而(使某人)筋疲力竭。**7** [VP6A] make one's way quickly to the end of, or through or over (sth). 匆匆跑过或通过。*run its course,* develop in the usual or normal way: 依其通常或正常的情形发展下去: *The disease ran its course.* 这病依其通常的情形发展下去。*run a race,* take part in one. 参加赛跑。*run the rapids,* (of a boat, men in a boat) move rapidly over or through them. (指船、船上的人)迅速通过急流。⇨ **shoot**[2]**(4),** the more usu word. *run the streets,* (of children) spend time playing (esp without supervision) in the streets. (指儿童)在街头嬉戏。**8** [VP6A] expose oneself to; be open to. 使遭受; 招惹; 易受; 易接受。*run the chance/danger of sth:* 有…之可能; 有…之危险: *You run the chance of being suspected of theft.* 你将不免被疑偷窃。*run risks/a risk/the risk of sth,* ⇨ **risk.** **9** [VP15A] chase; compete with. 追逐; 与…赛跑。*sb/sth to earth,* pursue until caught or found: 追逐某人(某物)直到捉到或找到为止; 追踪到底: *run a fox to earth,* chase it until it goes to its earth(4); 追踪一狐至其洞穴; (fig)(喻) run a quotation to earth, find, after searching, where it occurs. 追查到一引用句的出处。*run sb/sth close/hard,* be almost equal to, as good as, in merit, etc: 与某人(某事物)不相上下; 平分秋色: *We run*

our competitors close for price and quality. 在价格和品质上，我们和竞争者不相上下。*It was a close run thing,* (of competition, etc) The result was very close. (指竞争等)结果不相上下。**10** [VP2A, C] (of ships, etc) sail or steer; (of fish) swim: (指船等)行驶; (指鱼)游水: *The ship was running before the wind.* 该船正顺风航行。*Our ship ran aground/on the rocks/ashore.* 我们的船搁浅(触礁, 搁浅)。*We ran into port for supplies.* 我们驶进港口装补给品。*The two ships ran foul of each other,* collided. 两船彼此相撞。*The salmon are running,* swimming upstream from the sea. 鲑鱼从海中逆流游到河里。**11** [VP2C] go forward with a sliding, smooth or continuous motion; advance on, or as if on, wheels: 以一种滑动、平稳或继续的行动前行; (在轮上等)滚动: *Trams run on rails; buses don't run on rails.* 电车在轨道上行驶; 公共汽车不在铁轨上行驶。*Sledges run well over frozen snow.* 雪橇适于在冰冻的雪上滑行。*The train ran past the signal.* 那火车已从信号旁边行驶过去了。**12** [VP2A, C] be in action; work freely; be in working order: 在活动中; 自由地转动; 处于正常之运行状态: *Don't leave the engine of your car running.* 不要让你汽车的引擎空转。*The sewing-machine doesn't run properly.* 这缝纫机操作不灵。*The works have ceased running,* The factory has closed, is no longer producing goods. 该工厂已停工。*His life has run smoothly up to now.* 他的生活一直过得平稳无事。**13** [VP2A, C] (of public conveyances, eg buses, ferry-boats) ply; journey to and fro: (指公共运输工具, 如公共汽车、渡船)经常来回; 往来行驶: *The buses run every ten minutes.* 这些公共汽车每隔十分钟开一班。*The 9.05 train is not running today.* 九点零五分的火车今天不开了。*There are frequent trains running between London and Brighton.* 伦敦与布赖顿间火车行驶班次频繁。**14** [VP6A] organize; manage; cause to be in operation: 组织; 管理; 使运转: *run a business/a theatre/a bus company;* 经营一商店(剧院, 公共汽车公司); 将汽车开进汽车间: *run extra trains during the rush hours.* 在拥挤时刻增开加班火车。*Can I run (= operate) my electric sewing-machine off the light circuit?* 我能在电灯电路上接电使用电动缝纫机吗？*I can't afford to run a car (= own and use one) on my small salary.* 以我微薄的薪俸不足以拥有一部自用汽车。*Mr Green is run by his secretary,* She is the dominant personality and tells him what to do, etc. 格林先生受他的秘书控制。**run the show,** (colloq) be boss in an undertaking; have control. (口)当家; 负责指挥。**15** [VP6A, 15A, B] convey; transport: 运送; 运输: *I'll run you up to town/run you back home,* drive you there in my car. 我用车子送你进城(回家)。**run errands/messages (for sb)**, make journeys to do things, carry messages, etc. (为某人)跑腿(送信)。**run arms/guns,** convey them into a country unlawfully. 私运军火去。Hence, 由此产生, **'arms/~ner** n person who does this. 私运军火者。**run liquor/contraband,** smuggle it into a country; get it past the coastguards secretly. 偷运私酒(私货)。**16** [VP14, 15A] cause to move quickly (in a certain direction or into a certain place): 使快速移动或伸展(沿某方向或至某地方): *run a car into a garage;* 将汽车开进汽车间; *run one's fingers/a comb through one's hair;* 以手指(梳子)拢头发; *run one's eyes over a page;* 浏览一页; *run one's fingers over the keys of a piano.* 以手指在钢琴的键上弹。**17** [VP2C] (of thoughts, feelings, eyes, exciting news, etc) pass or move briefly or quickly: (指意念、感情、眼睛、好消息等)匆匆而过; 掠过: *The thought kept running through my head.* 这意念一再掠过我的脑海。*Mary's eyes ran critically over her friend's new dress.* 玛丽吹毛求疵地打量她的朋友的新服。*The pain ran up my arm.* 疼痛已经遍及我的胳臂。*A shiver ran down his spine.* 他不禁全身战栗。*The news ran like wildfire.* 那消息如野火般传开。*A whisper ran through the crowd.* 耳语传遍了人群。**18** [VP15A] cause (sth) to penetrate (intentionally or by accident) or come into contact with; penetrate or pierce (sb/

sth) with sth: (故意地或偶然地)使穿透; 使与…接触; 刺穿: *run a sword through a man/run a man through with a sword;* 以剑刺穿一人; *run a splinter into one's finger;* 手指扎了一根刺; *run one's head against a glass door in a dark corridor.* 在黑暗的走廊上一头撞在玻璃门上。*The drunken driver ran his car into a tree.* 喝醉酒的驾驶员开车撞到树上。**19** [VP2A, B, C] (of liquids, grain, sand, etc) flow, drip; (of surfaces) be wet (with); (of colours, etc) flow and spread: (指液体, 谷粒, 砂等)流; 滴; (指表面)弄湿; (指颜色, 如染料)扩散: *Rivers run into the sea.* 河水流入海中。*The tears ran down my cheeks.* 泪从我的颊旁流下。*Who has left the tap/water running?* 谁忘了关水龙头？*The tide was running strong.* 潮涨甚急。*The beggar's legs were covered with running sores.* 那乞丐的腿上全是流脓的疮。*Your nose is running—use your hanky,* ie wipe your nose clean. 你流鼻涕了——快用手帕擦擦。*Water was running all over the bathroom floor.* 洗澡间地上全是水。*The floor was running with water.* 地板上全是水。*Will the colours run if the dress is washed?* 这衣服洗起来会不会掉颜色？**20** [VP6A, 15A, B] cause (a liquid, molten metal, etc) to flow: 使(液体、熔化的金属等)流动: *Run some hot water into the bowl.* 倒些热水到这碗里。*Run the water off,* (= let it flow out) *when you've had your bath.* 洗过澡后要把水放掉。*The molten metal was run into a mould.* 熔化的金属被倒进模内。**21** [VP2D] become; pass into (a specified condition): 变成; 进入(某指明的情况): *The rivers are running dry,* ceasing to flow. 河流干涸了。*Supplies are running short/low.* 供应品快用完了。*I am run short of money.* 我正缺钱用。*Feelings/Passions ran high,* became stormy or violent. 群情激昂。*My blood ran cold,* I was filled with horror. 吓得我血都凉了。**run riot, (a)** behave in a wild and lawless way. 放荡滋事。**(b)** (of plants, etc) grow unchecked. (指植物等)蔓延。**run wild,** be without control, restraint, discipline, etc: 放任不加管束: 限制, 纪律等: *The garden is running wild.* 园中野草丛生。*She lets her children run wild.* 她纵容孩子, 不加管束。**run a temperature,** (colloq) become feverish. (口)发热。**22** [VP2A, B, C] extend; have a certain course or order; be continued or continuous: 扩延; 有某种途径或次序; 连续: *shelves running round the walls;* 绕墙的架子; *a scar that runs across his left cheek;* 横过他左颊的疤痕; *a road that runs across the plain;* 穿越那平原的一条路; *a fence running round the property.* 环绕那块地产的一道篱。*It happened several days running,* several days in succession. 那事连续发生了好几天。*He hit the target seven times running.* 他连续七次射中目标。*The play ran (for) six months,* was kept on the stage, was performed, during this period of time. 这个剧演了六个月。*The lease of my house has only a year to run.* 我的房子的租约期限只有一年了。**a running commentary,** account of an event as it occurs by a broadcaster: 实况转播; 现场报道: *a running commentary of a football match.* 足球比赛的实况转播。**'running costs,** continuous costs for producing goods, etc (as opposed to costs of original manufacture): 继续成本。这位作家说过，这位作家说过，**23** [VP2C, D] have a tendency or common characteristic; have an average price or level: 有某种倾向或共同特色; 有某种之平均价格或水准: *This author runs to sentiment.* 这位作家好尚于伤感。*Blue eyes run in the family.* 这一家人均是蓝眼睛。*Our apples run rather small this year.* 今年我们的苹果结得很小。*Prices for fruit are running high this season.* 这个季节水果的价格偏高。**24** [VP2A] be told or written: 被说; 被写: *So the story ran,* That is what was told or said. 传说如此。*The story runs that...,* It is said that.... 据说...。*The agreement runs in these words,* 协议上的文字就是这样写的。*I forget how the next verse runs,* how the words or notes follow one another. 我忘记下一节诗了。**25** [VP2A] (of woven or knitted material) become unwoven or unravelled; drop stitches through several rows: (指编织物)脱线; 脱针:

Nylon tights sometimes run. 尼龙紧身衣有时会脱丝。 ⇨
ladder. the more usu word with reference to stockings. (指袜子时 ladder 较常用)。 **26** [VP2C, 3A, 15B] (special uses with *adverbial particles and preps*): (与副词性小品词及介词连用的特殊用法):

run across, pay a short informal visit: 作短暂非正式拜访: *run across to a neighbour's flat to borrow some sugar.* 到邻居公寓去借些糖。 *run across sb / sth,* meet or find by chance: 不期而遇(某人或某物): *I ran across my old friend Jean in Paris last week.* 上星期我在巴黎遇见老友吉恩。

run after sb / sth, **(a)** try to catch: 追逐: *The dog was running after a rabbit.* 狗正在追逐一只兔子。 **(b)** seek the society of; go after in order to get the attention of: 设法和…交际; 追求: *She runs after every good-looking man in the village.* 她追求村中每个漂亮男人。

run against sb, compete with him by running in a race; (esp US) compete with him (for an elected office). 和某人赛跑; (尤美)和某人竞选。

run along, (colloq) go away; be off: (口)走开; 离开: *Now, children, run along!* 孩子们, 走开!

run away, leave rapidly; flee; escape: 迅速离开; 逃走; 逃跑: *Don't run away—I want your advice.* 请不要走——我需要你的意见。 *The boy ran away and went to sea,* left home and became a sailor. 那孩子离家出走, 当海员去了。 Hence, 由此产生, **run·away** /ˈrʌnəweɪ/ n person who has run away. 逃走者; 出走者。 □ adj *runaway success,* great, immediate success, etc. 即时获得的大成功等。 *run away with sb,* **(a)** elope with: 私奔: *The butler ran away with the duke's daughter.* 仆役长和公爵的女儿私奔了。 **(b)** go at a speed too high for control: 行进速度过快而不易控制: *Don't let your horse / car run away with you.* 不要让你的马(汽车)跑得太快而不易控制。 **(c)** destroy the self-control of: 失去自我控制; 无法自制: *Don't let your temper run away with you.* 别让你的脾气失去控制。 *run away with sth,* **(a)** use up: 用尽: *This new scheme will run away with a lot of the ratepayers' money.* 这项新计划将用去纳税人的许多钱。 **(b)** carry off; steal: 拐走; 卷逃; 偷: *The maid ran away with the duchess's jewels.* 女仆带了公爵夫人的珠宝潜逃。 **(c)** get a clear win over: 获全胜: *The girl from Peru ran away with the first set,* eg in a tennis tournament. 来自秘鲁的那个女孩第一局(例如在网球联赛中)获得全胜。 *run away with the idea / notion that,* assume too hastily that sth is the case: 贸然假定; 贸然接受; 轻易相信: *Don't run away with the idea that I can lend you money every time you need help.* 不要认为每当你需要帮助时我就能借钱给你。

run back over sth, review past events, etc: 回忆过去; 重温旧事: *run back over the past.* 回忆往事。 *I'll run back over the procedure again.* 我将再查看一下这个程序。 *run sth back,* rewind (film, tape, etc) (after it has been looked at, listened to): (在看过或听过之后)倒回(影片、录音带等)。

run down, **(a)** (of a clock or other mechanism worked by weights) stop because it needs winding up. (指钟或其他借锤摆而工作之机械装置)因未上弦而停摆。 **(b)** (of a battery) become weak or exhausted: (指电池)变弱; 耗尽: *The battery is / has run down; it needs recharging.* 这电池已变弱; 需要再充电。 *(be / feel / look) run down,* (of a person, his health) exhausted or weak from over-work, mental strain, etc. (指人、其健康)因过度工作, 精神紧张等而疲惫或虚弱。 *run sb / sth down,* knock down or collide with: 撞倒: *The liner ran down a fishing-boat during the dense fog.* 那艘轮在浓雾中撞及一渔船。 *The cyclist was run down by a big lorry.* 那骑脚踏车者被一辆大卡车撞倒了。 *run sb down,* **(a)** say unkind things about; disparage: 诽谤; 诋毁: *That man doesn't like me; he's always running me down.* 那个人不喜欢我; 他总是贬我的坏话。 **(b)** pursue and overtake: 追获: *run down an escaped prisoner.* 追获一越狱的逃犯。 *run sth down,* allow to become less active or occupied: 容许

变得较不活动或忙碌: *run down the ship's boilers;* 减少船上锅炉的负荷; *run down a naval dockyard,* do less work and employ fewer workers. 裁减海军造船所的工作人员。 Hence, 由此产生, **'run-down** *of sth,* **(a)** reduction: 减少; 缩减: *the run-down of the coal industry.* 煤矿工业的萎缩。 **(b)** (colloq) detailed explanation or listing. (口)详细说明或列举。 □ adj (of a place) decayed; dilapidated; not cared for. (指地方)破烂的; 残破的; 未照料的。

run for sth, **(a)** ⇨ **2** above. 参看上列第 2 义。 **(b)** ⇨ **4** above. 参看上列第 4 义。

run in, = run below. *run sb in,* (colloq, of the police) arrest and take to a police station: (口, 指警察)逮捕并送往派出所: *The drunken man was run in for creating a public disturbance.* 那醉汉因扰乱公共秩序被拘到派出所。 *run sth in,* bring (new machinery, esp the engine of a car) into good condition by running it carefully for a time or distance: 小心使用一段时间或行驶一段距离而使(新机器, 尤指汽车引擎)达于良好状况: *He's still running in his new car and doesn't exceed fifty miles an hour.* 他仍在小心试开他的新车, 车速每小时不超过五十英里。

run into sb, meet unexpectedly: 偶遇: *run into an old friend in a pub.* 在酒馆偶遇一老友。 *run into sth,* **(a)** collide with: 撞及: *The bus got out of control and ran into a wall.* 公共汽车失去控制而撞到墙上。 **(b)** fall into: 陷入: *run into debt / danger / difficulties.* 陷于债务(危险, 困难)中。 **(c)** reach (a level or figure): 到达(某一标准或数目): *a book that has run into six editions.* 一本已经销六版的书。 *His income runs into five figures,* is now ten thousand (pounds, dollars, etc) or more. 他的收入已达五位数字。 *run sb into sth,* cause (sb) to fall into (a certain state): 使(某人)陷于(某种情况): *My wife has run me into despair.* 我的太太使我绝望。 *run sth into sth,* cause sth to collide or connect with sth: 使某物与另一物碰撞或衔接: *run one's car into a wall.* 开车撞及一墙。

run off with sb / sth, **(a)** steal and take away: 带着…潜逃; 窃走: *The treasurer has run off with all the club's funds.* 会计带着俱乐部的全部款子潜逃了。 **(b)** elope with: 与…私奔: *My mother has run off with her bank manager.* 我母亲与她的银行经理私奔了。 *run sth off,* **(a)** cause to flow away: 使流走: *run off the water from a tank,* empty the tank. 使桶中的水流尽。 **(b)** write or recite fluently, eg a list of names: 流利地写或背出(名单等): *run off an article for the local (news) paper.* 为地方报纸写一篇文章。 **(c)** print; produce: 印刷; 生产: *run off a hundred copies on the duplicating machine.* 在复印机上印出一百份。 **(d)** decide (a race) after a tie, or trial heats; cause to be run or played: 在得分相同或初赛后再作(比赛)以定胜负; 举行比赛: *run off a heat.* 进行决赛。 *When will the race be run off?* 该项比赛何时举行? Hence, 由此产生, **'run-off** n deciding race, etc after a dead heat or tie. 决赛。 ⇨ **dead.** *run off sb (like water off a duck's back),* have no effect on him: 对(某人)毫无影响(如水流过鸭背): *Her warnings ran off him like water off a duck's back.* 她的警告对他毫无影响, 如同水流过鸭背。

run on, **(a)** talk continuously: 继续谈: *He will run on for an hour if you don't stop him.* 你如不阻止他, 他会一连说上一个小时。 **(b)** elapse: 流逝: *Time ran on.* 时光流逝。 **(c)** (of a disease) continue its course. (指疾病)继续发展。 *run (sth) on,* **(a)** (of written letters of the alphabet) join, be joined, together: (指书写之字母)连缀起来: *When children are learning to write, they should let the letters run on,* not write them separately. 小孩学习写字的时候, 应该把字母连着写, 不能分开写。 *They should run the letters on.* 他们应该把字母连起来写。 *run on / upon sth,* **(a)** (of thoughts, etc) be concerned with: (指思想等)涉及; 关于: *That boy's thoughts are always running on food.* 那孩子脑子里总是想着食物。 *His thoughts were running upon the past / on recent events in India.* 他在回想过去(最近发生在印度的事)。 **(b)** (of ship) strike: (指

船)撞及: *The ship ran upon the rocks.* 该船撞到礁石上。
run out, (a) go out: 消退: *The tide is running out.* 潮正退去。 **(b)** (of a period of time) come to an end: (指一段时间)到期限: *When does the lease of the house run out?* 房子的租约什么时候到期? **(c)** (of stocks, supplies) come to an end, be exhausted; (of persons) become short of (supplies, etc): (指贮存物、供应品等)用尽;(指人)缺乏(供应品等): *Our provisions are running out.* 我们的粮食快吃完了。 *Her patience is running out.* 她渐渐失去耐心。 *The sands are running out,* (with reference to the sand in an hour-glass) the time allowed to us (before something unwelcome ends) is coming to an end. (指更漏中之沙将流尽)期限将届。 **(d)** jut out; project: 伸出; 突伸: *a pier running out into the sea.* 突伸到海中的码头。 **run (rope/string) out,** pass (it) out; be passed out: 抽出(绳);被拉出: *The rope ran out smoothly.* 绳子顺利地拉出来了。 *The sailor ran the rope out neatly.* 水手利落地把绳子拉出。 **run out of sth,** reach an end of (stocks, supplies): 用尽(贮物、供应品): *We're fast running out of beer/cigarettes.* 我们的啤酒(香烟)很快就用完了。 **be run out,** (cricket, of a batsman) have his innings ended because, while trying to make a run, he fails to reach his crease before the wicket-keeper or one of the fielders returns the ball and removes the bails or stump(s): (板球击球员)被杀出局(击球员未能在守门员或外场员将球投回和移走门柱之前得分而被杀出局): *Smith was run out before he had scored.* 史密斯未能得分就被杀出局。 **run oneself out (of breath),** exhaust oneself: 筋疲力竭: *He's completely run out.* 他已疲惫不堪。 **run out on sb,** (sl) abandon, desert: (俚)放弃;背弃: *Poor Jane! Her husband has run out on her.* 可怜的简! 她的丈夫遗弃了她。

run over, (a) (of a vessel or its contents) overflow. (指容器或容器内盛的东西) 流出;溢出。 **(b)** = *run across.* **run over sth, (a)** review; recapitulate: 温习; 简要要旨: *Let's run over our parts again,* eg when learning and rehearsing parts in a play. 我们再把我们的台词温习一遍。 **(b)** read through quickly: 匆匆读一遍: *He ran over his notes before starting his lecture.* 在开始讲演前他把大纲匆匆看了一遍。 **run over sb; run sb over,** (of a vehicle) (knock down and) pass over (sb or sth lying on the ground): (指车辆)(撞倒并)辗过(在地上的某人或某物): *The bus ran over his legs.* 公共汽车辗过他的腿。*He was run over and had to be taken to hospital.* 他被车辗伤, 必须送往医院。
run round, = *run across.*

run sth through sth, draw a line, one's pen, through sth. 画掉。 **run sb through,** pierce with a sword, bayonet, etc. 刺穿。 **run through sth, (a)** use up (a fortune, etc) esp by foolish of reckless spending: 耗尽; 浪费(财产等): *He soon ran through the money he had won at poker.* 不久他就把从赌扑克牌赢来的钱花光了。 **(b)** examine quickly; deal with in rapid succession: 匆匆检查; 连续很快地处理: *run through one's mail during breakfast.* 吃早饭时匆匆阅读信件或邮件。 Hence, 由此产生, **'run-through** n quick examination or discussion: 迅速检查或讨论: *give sth a quick run-through.* 迅速检查或讨论某事物。 **(c)** rehearse. 预演;排演。 Hence, 由此产生, **'run-through** n rehearsal. 排演。

run to sth, (a) reach (an amount, number, etc): 达及(某量、数等): *That will run to a pretty penny,* will cost a lot of money. 那要花很多钱的。 **(b)** have money for; (of money) be enough for: 有用于…之钱; (指钱)数目足够做…: *We can't/Our funds won't run to a holiday abroad this year.* 今年我们没有足够的钱(我们的钱不够)到外国去度假。 *I can't run to that,* can't afford it. 我没有钱做那个。 **(c)** extend to: 扩展到: *His new novel runs for 900 pages/has already run to three impressions.* 他的新小说已经写了九百页了(出了三版了)。 **run to fat,** (of persons) tend to put on too much fat. 有发胖的趋势。 **run to ruin,** fall into ruin. 成为废墟。 **run to seed,** (of plants) tend to develop chiefly seed

instead of new growth of leaves, etc. (指植物)有只结子而不长新叶等之倾向。 **run to waste,** (eg of water) be wasted. (指水等)被浪费。

run up, (cricket of a bowler) gather speed by running, before releasing the ball; (of athletes in some field events) gather speed before jumping, throwing a javelin, etc. (板球: 指投球手) 在投球前跑步以增加速度;(其他运动项目中)在跳或掷标枪等前跑步以增加速度。 Hence, 由此产生, **'run-up** n **(a)** (length or manner of a) bowler's or athlete's approach: 投球员(运动员)在投球或运动前跑步(的长度或方式): *a long/short run-up.* 程(短程)加速跑步。 **(b)** period leading up (to sth): (某事物的)前导时期: *the run-up to the General Election,* the period when candidates are busy seeking support, etc. 普选前的竞选时期。 **run sth up, (a)** raise; hoist: 提高; 升起: *run up a flag on the mast.* 在旗杆上升起一面旗。 **(b)** erect, make or construct quickly or in an unsubstantial way: 匆匆或不坚实地竖起, 制或或建造: *run up a dress/a garden shed.* 草草做套女服(盖一花园小棚)。 **(c)** add up (a column of figures). 加起(一栏数字)。 **(d)** cause to grow quickly in amount: 使疾速增加: *run up a big bill at a hotel;* 迅速积欠一大笔旅馆的帐; *run up the bidding at an auction,* force others to bid higher, force up prices. 在公开拍卖中抬价。 **run up against sth,** meet by chance or unexpectedly: 偶遇: *run up against difficulties.* 遭遇困难。 **run up to,** amount, extend to (a figure): 达及(某数): *Prices ran up to £5 a ton.* 价格达五英镑一吨。

run·a·way /'rʌnəweɪ; 'rʌnə,we/ n, adj ⇨ run away at **run(26).**

rune /ruːn; run/ n any letter of an old alphabet used in N Europe, esp the Scandinavians and Anglo-Saxons (from AD 200); similar mark of a mysterious or magic sort. 古代北欧人用的字母(尤指斯堪的那维亚人和盎格鲁撒克逊人从第二世纪起所用者);相似的神秘符号。 **runic** /'ruːnɪk; 'runɪk/ adj of ~s; written in, inscribed with, ~s. 北欧古文字的;以北欧古文字写或刻的。

rung¹ /rʌŋ; rʌŋ/ n [C] 1 crosspiece forming a step in a ladder: 梯子横木; 梯级: *start on the lowest/reach the highest ~ (of the ladder),* (fig) a particular level in society, one's employment, etc. 从(梯子)的最低一级开始(达到最高一级); (喻)(在社会或职务上等)从某一阶层开始(达到某一阶段)。 2 crosspiece joining the legs of a chair to strengthen it. 椅子腿间之横撑。

rung² /rʌŋ; rʌŋ/ *pp of* **ring².**

run·nel /'rʌnl; 'rʌnl/ n 1 brook. 小河; 小溪。 2 open gutter (for rainwater) at a roadside, etc. (路边等的)明沟。

run·ner /'rʌnə(r); 'rʌnɚ/ n 1 person, animal, etc that runs: 奔跑之人, 兽等: *How many ~s were there in the Derby?* 赛马大会中有多少马出赛呢? ,~**'up** n person or team taking the second place in a competition. 竞赛中之第二名; 亚军。 2 messenger, scout, collector, etc: 信差, 侦察兵, 收税员等: *Bow Street ~,* (hist) police-officer. (史)警官。 3 (in compounds) smuggler: (用于复合词中)私运者: *'gun-~;* 私运军火者; *'rum-~s.* 偷运私酒者。 **blo'ckade-~,** person who tries to get through the forces that are blockading a port, etc. 图突破港口等之封锁线者。 4 part on which sth slides or moves along: 滑行或移动的部分: *the ~s of a sledge.* 雪橇的滑行板。 5 long piece of cloth (for a table, etc); long piece of carpet, eg for stairs. 铺在桌子等上的)长条饰布; (铺在楼梯等上的)长地毯。 6 stem coming from a strawberry plant and taking root; kinds of twining bean-plant: 匐枝; 匐匍茎; 盘绕而生的豆类植物: *scarlet ~s;* ~ *beans.* 红花菜豆。 ⇨ the illus at **vegetable.** ⇨ 看 vegetable 之插图。

run·ning /'rʌnɪŋ; 'rʌnɪŋ/ n [U] 1 act of a person or animal that runs, esp in racing. 跑; 赛跑。 **make the ~,** set the pace (lit or fig). 领跑; 领先; 领头(字面或喻)。 **take up the ~,** take the lead. 领先; 领导。 *in/*

out of the ~, (of competitors) having some/no chance of winning. (指竞赛者)有(无)获胜机会。**'~-board** *n* (now old-fashioned) footboard on either side of a car. (旧式汽车两旁的)踏脚板。**'~ mate, (a)** horse used to set the pace for another horse in a race. (赛马中)领路的马。**(b)** candidate for the lesser of two associated political offices, eg for the Vice-Presidency of the US. 竞选伙伴(如美国的副总统)。□ *adj* 1 done, made, carried on, while or immediately after running: 跑时或刚刚跑过后所为,为,所做,所进行的: *a ~ kick/ jump/fight.* 跑着踢(急行跳;追逐战)。⇨ **run²(1, 2)**. 2 continuous; uninterrupted: 连续的;不断的: *a ~ fire of questions,* coming in a continuous stream; 一连串的问题; *a ~ hand,* (of handwriting) with the letters joined. 连写字体;草书。*a ~ commentary,* ⇨ **run²(22)**. 3 (after a *pl n*) in succession: (在复数名词后)接连的: *win three times ~.* 连胜三次。*a ~* (of water) flowing; coming from a mains supply: (指水)流动的;来自总管的: *All bedrooms in this hotel have hot and cold ~ water,* coming when taps are turned. 这家旅馆中每间卧房都有热的和冷的自来水。*a ~* (of sores, etc) with liquid or pus coming out. (指伤口等)有脓水流出的。**6** *a ~ knot,* one that slips along a rope and is able to make the noose larger or smaller. (随绳滑动使结环可大可小的)活结。⇨ the illus at **knot**. 参看 knot 之插图。

runny /'rʌnɪ; 'rʌnɪ/ *adj* (colloq) semi-liquid; tending to run (口)半液体的或有流动倾向的: *a ~ nose.* 流鼻涕的鼻子。*The jam is rather ~; you'd better boil it again.* 这果酱较稀;你最好再煮一次。

runt /rʌnt; rʌnt/ *n* (colloq) undersized or stunted plant, animal (esp the smallest of a litter); or (derog) person. (口)矮小或发育受阻的植物、动物(尤指一窝中之最小者);(贬)矮小之人。

run·way /'rʌnweɪ; 'rʌn,we/ *n* 1 specially prepared surface along which aircraft take off and land. 飞机跑道。2 way made for rolling felled trees and logs down a hillside. (供砍伐之树木沿山坡滚下的)滑路。

ru·pee /ruːˈpiː; ruˈpi/ *n* [C] monetary unit of India, Pakistan, Sri Lanka, Nepal, Mauritius, etc. 卢比(印度、巴基斯坦、斯里兰卡、尼泊尔、毛里求斯等地的货币单位)。

ru·piah /ruːˈpiːə; ruˈpiɑ/ *n* monetary unit of Indonesia. 卢比;盾(印尼的货币单位)。

rup·ture /'rʌptʃə(r); 'rʌptʃɚ/ *n* 1 [U] breaking apart or bursting; [C] instance of this. 破裂;破裂之实例。2 [C, U] (instance of) ending of friendly relations. 绝交(之实例)。3 [C] swelling in the abdomen caused by the breaking of some organ or tissue through the wall of its retaining cavity. 脱肛;腹疝。⇨ **hernia**. □ *vt, vi* [VP6A, 2A] break or burst, eg a blood-vessel or membrane; end (a connection, etc). 破裂(如血管或薄膜等);断绝(关系等)。

ru·ral /'rʊərəl; 'rʊrəl/ *adj* in, of, characteristic of, suitable for, the countryside (opp of *urban*): 在乡村的;乡村的;有乡村之特色的;适于乡村的(为 urban 之反义词): *~ scenery;* 乡村风光; *live in ~ seclusion.* 过着乡村隐居生活。

Ru·ri·tan·ian /ˌrʊərɪ'teɪnɪən; ˌrʊrə'tenɪən/ *adj* (of a State, its politics) full of plots and intrigues (as in a melodramatic story about an imaginary country called Ruritania). (指一个国家、其政治)充满了阴谋诡计的(如由通俗闹剧中假想国 Ruritania 内所发生的情形)。

ruse /ruːz; ruz/ *n* [C] deceitful way of doing sth, getting sth, etc; trick; stratagem. 欺诈;诈术;计谋。

rush¹ /rʌʃ; rʌʃ/ *n* 1 [U] rapid, headlong movement; sudden swift advance: 急促的动作;突进;冲进;此等动作的实例;急流: *I don't like the ~ of city life.* 我不喜欢终日纷忙的都市生活。*He was swept away by the ~ of the current and drowned.* 他被激流冲走而淹死了。*Why all this ~,* this hurry and excitement? 为什么这样忙乱呢? *There were several ~es to the refreshment tent during the afternoon.* 下午点心摊上有几阵生意很忙的时候。*There was the usual*

Easter ~, ie of traffic to the holiday resorts, etc. 象往常一样复活节时又是人车汹涌。'**gold ~,** ⇨ **gold.** 2 [C] sudden demand: 急需: *a ~ for raincoats,* eg when there is heavy rain; 急需大量的雨衣(如下大雨时); sudden or intense activity: 突然或紧张的活动: *the Christmas ~,* the period before Christmas when crowds of people go shopping. 圣诞节前的抢购。**the '~-hour,** when crowds of people are travelling to or from work in a large town; (大城市上下班时的)拥挤时刻;高峰时刻: (attrib) (用作定语) *We were caught in the ~-hour traffic.* 我们碰上了交通的拥挤时刻。3 (cinema, often *pl*) first print of a film before cutting and editing. (电影,通常用复数)毛片(未经剪接者)。

rush² /rʌʃ; rʌʃ/ *n* [C] (tall stem of one of numerous varieties of) marsh plant with slender leafless stems containing pith, often dried and used for making seats or chairs, for weaving into baskets, etc, and, in olden times, for strewing floors. 灯心草;灯心草之茎。'**~-light** *n* kind of candle made by dipping the pith of a ~ into tallow. 灯心草蜡烛。**rushy** *adj* full of, abounding with, ~es: 多灯心草的;灯心草丛生的: *a ~y ditch.* 一条长满灯心草的沟。

rush³ /rʌʃ; rʌʃ/ *vi, vt* 1 [VP6A, 15A, B, 2A, C, 3A, 4A] ~ *(away/off/out),* (cause to) go or come, do sth, with violence or speed: (使)猛烈或匆匆地去,来,做某事: *The children ~ed out of the school gates.* 孩子们争先恐后地跑出学校大门。*They ~ed (away/off/out) to see the procession.* 他们冲出去看游行的行列。*The bull ~ed at me.* 那牛向我冲来。*They ~ed more troops to the front.* 他们赶调更多部队到前线去。~ *to conclusions,* form them hastily. 仓促下结论。~ *into print,* publish sth without proper care, consideration, etc. 急急忙忙付印。~ *sth through,* do sth at high speed: 匆忙处理: *The order for furniture was ~ed through* (= The goods were packed and sent off) *in two days.* 所订家具已于两天之内送出。*The new Bill was ~ed through Parliament.* 新的议案很快地在国会中通过。2 [VP6A] capture by a sudden attack; get through, over, into, etc by pressing eagerly or violently forward: 突击攻占;突破;攻进;冲进;冲进: ~ *the enemy's trenches;* 突破敌人的战壕; ~ *the gates of the football ground.* 挤进足球场的大门。*The panic-stricken passengers tried to ~ the life-boats,* crowd into them to save their lives quickly. 惊慌的旅客争先恐后,想挤进救生艇。3 [VP6A, 15A] force into hasty action: 使仓促行动: *I must think things over, so don't ~ me.* 我必须把事情考虑一下,不要催我。~ *sb off his feet,* succeed in forcing him into hasty action with no time for thought; exhaust him. 迫使某人无时间思索而急速行动;使某人疲于奔命。4 ~ *(for)*, (sl) charge an exorbitant price: (俚)索高价;敲诈: *How much did they ~ you for this?* 这个东西他们敲了你多少钱?

rusk /rʌsk; rʌsk/ *n* [C] piece of bread baked hard and crisp; kind of crisp biscuit: 烘烤硬而脆的面包片;面包干;脆饼干: *'teething ~s.* (婴儿出牙期)磨牙的饼干。

rus·set /'rʌsɪt; 'rʌsɪt/ *n* 1 [U] yellowish or reddish brown. 黄褐色;赤褐色。2 [C] kind of rough-skinned ~-coloured apple. 一种粗皮的赤褐色苹果。□ *adj* of the colour of ~. 黄褐色的;赤褐色的。

Rus·sian /'rʌʃn; 'rʌʃən/ *adj* of or from Russia. (来自)俄国的。**R~ roulette,** ⇨ **roulette.** □ *n* 1 native of Russia. 俄国人。2 the principal language of the Soviet Union. 俄语(苏联的主要语言)。

rust /rʌst; rʌst/ *n* [U] 1 reddish-brown coating formed on iron by the action of water and air; similar coating on other metals: (铁或其他金属表面因潮湿与空气作用而生的)锈。~*-covered machinery.* 生了锈的机器; *rub the ~ off sth.* 从某物表面把锈擦去。2 (plant-disease with ~-coloured spots caused by) kinds of fungus; mildew; blight. (植物之)锈病;(使植物发生锈病之)各种霉菌;霉;锈霉。□ *vt, vi* [VP6A, 2A, C] (cause to) become covered with ~; (fig) become poor in quality because not used: (使)覆有锈;生锈;(喻)因不用而变坏: *Don't leave the lawn-mower out in the garden*

to ~. 不要把剪草机丢在花园里生锈。*It's better to wear out than to ~ out*, to become worn through use than to lose value by ~ing. 用坏总比不用而放着生锈好。 **~less** *adj* that does not ~: 不生锈的: *~less steel*, used for stainless cutlery, etc. 不锈钢。 **~y** *adj* (**-ier, -iest**) 1 covered with ~: 生锈的: *~y needles*. 生锈的针。 2 in need of practice; out-of-date: 需要练习的; 过时的: *My German is rather ~y*, hasn't been used for a long time and needs to be practised. 我的德文(因经年不用)需要多加练习了。 3 (of black cloth) discoloured by age; dingy or shabby. (指黑布)因太久而褪色的; 脏旧的; 破旧的。 **~i‧ness** *n* [U].

rus‧tic /'rʌstɪk; 'rʌstɪk/ *adj* 1 (in a good sense) characteristic of country people; simple; unaffected: (在好的意义方面)有乡村居民特色的; 纯朴的; 朴素的: *~ simplicity*. 质朴。 2 rough; unrefined: 粗野的; 不雅的: *~ speech/manners*, contrasted with the speech, etc of smart, city people. 粗俗的语言(态度)。 3 of rough workmanship: 手工粗糙的: *a ~ bench/bridge*, made of rough, unplaned timber and untrimmed branches. 用木制的长板凳(桥)。 □ *n* countryman; peasant. 庄稼人; 农民。 **~‧ity** /rʌ'stɪsəti; rʌs'tɪsətɪ/ *n* [U] being ~ in appearance or character. (外表或性格的)纯朴; 朴实; 粗野; 不雅。

rus‧ti‧cate /'rʌstɪkeɪt; 'rʌstɪ,ket/ *vi*, *vt* 1 [VP2A] lead a rural life. 过乡间生活。 2 [VP6A] (GB) send (a student) temporarily away from the university as a punishment. (英)勒令(大学生)暂时停学以为处罚。

rustle /'rʌsl; 'rʌsl/ *vi*, *vt* 1 [VP2A, C] make a gentle, light sound (like dry leaves blown by the wind, or of silk clothes in motion); move along making such a sound: 发出瑟瑟声(如风吹枯叶, 或绸衣动时相擦); 瑟瑟移动: *Did you hear something rustling through the undergrowth?* 你听见有东西在矮树丛中瑟瑟移动吗? 2 [VP6A] cause to make this sound: 使发出瑟瑟声: *I*

wish people wouldn't ~ their programmes while the orchestra is playing. 我希望乐队在演奏时人们不要沙沙地翻弄他们的节目单。 3 [VP6A] (US, colloq) steal (cattle or horses). (美, 口)偷(牛马)。 4 [VP15B] ~ *sth up*, get together, provide: 凑集; 供应: *~ up some food for an unexpected guest*. 给一位不速之客弄点吃的东西。 □ *n* [U] gentle light sound as or dry leaves blown by the wind, of silk clothes, etc: 瑟瑟声; 沙沙声: *the ~ of paper*. 纸张的瑟瑟声。 **rust‧ler** /'rʌslə(r); 'rʌslə/ *n* (US, colloq) cattle thief. (美, 口)偷牛贼。 **rust‧ling** /'rʌslɪŋ; 'rʌslɪŋ/ *n* [U] sound made by sth that ~s: 瑟瑟声; 沙沙声: *the rustling of dry leaves/of sweet wrappings*; 枯叶(糖果纸)的沙沙声; (*pl*) repetitions of such sounds: 连续不断的瑟瑟声: *mysterious rustlings at night*. 夜晚的神秘瑟瑟声。

rut¹ /rʌt; rʌt/ *n* [C] 1 line or track made by wheel(s) in soft ground. 辙迹; 车辙。 2 (fig) way of doing sth, behaving, living, etc that has become established. (喻)常规; 常习。*be in/get into a rut*, a fixed (and boring) way of living so that it becomes difficult to change. 陷入固定(而又乏味)的生活方式; 墨守成规。 □ *vt* (usu in *pp*) mark with ruts: (通常用过去分词)使留有辙迹: *a deeply rutted road*. 留有很深辙迹的路。

rut² /rʌt; rʌt/ *n* [U] periodic sexual excitement of male animals, esp deer. 雄性动物(尤指鹿)之周期性的春情发动; 发情。 □ *vi* [VP2A] be affected with this: 春情发动; 发情: *the rutting season*. 发情期。

ruth‧less /'ruːθlɪs; 'ruθlɪs/ *adj* cruel; without pity; showing no mercy. 残忍的; 无情的; 无怜悯心的。 **~‧ly** *adv* **~‧ness** *n*

rye /raɪ; raɪ/ *n* [U] 1 (plant with) grain used for making flour, and as a food for cattle. 裸麦; 黑麦; 裸麦粒。 ⇨ the illus at **cereal**. 参看 cereal 之插图。 **'rye-bread** *n* bread made with flour from rye. 黑面包。 2 kind of whisky made from rye. 裸麦酒。

S s

S, s /es; es/ (*pl* **S's, s's** /'esiz; 'esiz/) the nineteenth letter of the English alphabet. 英文字母的第十九个字母。

sab‧ba‧tarian /ˌsæbə'teəriən; ˌsæbə'tɛriən/ *n* Christian who advocates strict observance of Sunday (eg by opposing the opening of places of entertainment, the playing of games, etc on Sundays). 主张严守星期日为安息日的基督徒 (例如反对在星期日开放娱乐场所, 举行比赛等); 严守安息日的基督徒。 ⇨ **Sabbath**. □ *adj* of the principles of ~s. 此派基督徒之教义的; 严守星期日为安息日的。

Sab‧bath /'sæbəθ; 'sæbəθ/ *n* day of rest, Saturday for Jews, Sunday for Christians: 安息日(犹太教徒是星期六, 基督徒是星期日): *break the ~*, work or play on the ~; 不守安息日(在安息日工作或游乐); *keep the ~*, spend it in worship of God and in rest. 守安息日(在安息日崇拜神和休息)。

sab‧bati‧cal /sə'bætɪkl; sə'bætɪkl/ *adj* of or like the Sabbath: 安息日的; 似安息日的: *After this uproar there came a ~ calm*. 这阵喧嚣之后, 一切变得非常安静。 *~ (year)*, year of freedom from routine duties given to some university teachers to enable them to travel or undertake special studies. 休假年(给予大学教师, 使能旅行或从事专门研究)。

sa‧ber /'seɪbə(r); 'sebə/ ⇨ **sabre**.

sable /'seɪbl; 'sebl/ *n* [C] 1 small animal valued for its beautiful dark fur; [U] fur of this animal: 黑貂; 黑貂皮: *a ~ coat/stole*. 黑貂皮大衣(披肩)。 2 antelope, large, horned, dark African antelope. 非洲产的一种羚羊(大而有角, 毛皮为浅黑色)。 □ *adj* (liter) black; gloomy. (文)黑色的; 阴惨的。

sa‧bot /'sæbəʊ *US*: sæ'bəʊ; 'sæbo/ *n* [C] shoe hollowed

out of a single piece of wood; wooden-soled shoe with a band of leather across the instep. 木鞋 (由整块木头挖空而成); (有一条皮革横过足背的)木底鞋; 木屐。

sab‧otage /'sæbətɑːʒ; 'sæbə,tɑʒ/ *n* [U] the wilful damaging of machinery, materials, etc or the hindering of an opponent's activity, during an industrial or political dispute, or during war. 阴谋破坏(在产业或政治纠纷中, 或在战争中, 故意损坏机器, 原料等, 或阻碍对方之活动)。 □ *vt* [VP6A] perform an act of ~ against. 对...采取破坏行动。 **sab‧oteur** /ˌsæbəˈtɜː(r); ˌsæbə'tɜ/ *n* person who commits ~. 阴谋破坏者。

sabre (US = **sa‧ber**) /'seɪbə(r); 'sebə/ *n* heavy cavalry sword with a curved blade. (骑兵所用之弯刀)军刀; 马刀。 **'~-rattling** *n* aggressive display of military strength. 炫耀军力; 以武力威胁。 **'~-toothed** *adj* having (usu two) ~-like teeth: 有(通常为两颗)尖长犬齿的: *a ~-toothed tiger* (now extinct). 剑齿虎(现已绝种)。 □ *vt* strike with a ~. 以军刀斩或砍。

sac /sæk; sæk/ *n* bag-like membrane enclosing a cavity in an animal or plant. (动植物组织中的)囊; 液囊。 ⇨ the illus at **flower**. 参看 flower 之插图。

sac‧char‧in /'sækərɪn; 'sækərɪn/ *n* [U] very sweet substance made from coal-tar, used in place of sugar. 糖精 (由煤焦油提取之极甜物质, 为糖的代用品)。 **sac‧char‧ine** /-riːn; -,raɪn/ *adj* resembling sugar; very sweet; too sweet. 似糖的; 极甜的; 太甜的。

sac‧er‧do‧tal /ˌsæsəˈdəʊtl; ˌsæsəˈdotl/ *adj* connected with priests. 僧侣的; 祭司的。 **~‧ism** /-ɪzəm; -,ɪzəm/ *n* [U] system of government in which priests (claiming to be mediators between God and mankind) have a great part or exercise great power. 祭司制度; 僧侣当权

制度；僧侣政治。

sachet /'sæʃeɪ US: sæ'ʃeɪ; sæ'ʃe/ n 1 small perfumed bag. 香囊；小香袋。2 [C, U] (packet of) sweet-smelling dried lavender or other substance for laying among clothes, etc. (放置于衣服等之间的)香粉；香包。3 small packet, containing eg shampoo. 小封袋(例如装洗发粉者)。

sack[1] /sæk; sæk/ n 1 (quantity held by a) large bag of strong material (eg coarse flax, hemp, stiffened paper) for storing and carrying heavy goods, eg cement, coal, flour, potatoes: 大袋(用粗麻、硬纸等做成，以放置和运输水泥、煤、面粉、马铃薯等重物)；大袋之量: coal £3 a ~; 煤三英镑一包；two ~s of potatoes. 二袋马铃薯。'~-race n one between competitors each of whom has his legs tied into a sack and moves by short jumps. 袋鼠竞走(参加者把两腿套入袋内之竞走)。'~·cloth n [U] coarse material made of flax or hemp. 麻袋布；粗麻布。**~cloth and ashes, (a)** regret for wrongdoing; penitence. 悔恨；忏悔。(b) mourning. 悲悼；悲苦。2 short loose dress. (女用)短而松的袍装；布袋装。~·ing n = ~cloth.

sack[2] /sæk; sæk/ n give sb/get the ~, (colloq) dismiss sb/be dismissed from employment. (口)解雇；被解雇: He got the ~ for petty thieving. 他因轻盗窃罪而被解雇。□ vt [VP6A] dismiss from employment. 解雇。

sack[3] /sæk; sæk/ vt [VP6A] (of a victorious army) plunder violently (a captured city, etc). (指得胜的军队)劫掠；掠夺(被攻陷之城市等)。□ n the ~, ~ing of a captured town, etc. 被攻陷之城市等的劫掠；掠夺。

sack[4] /sæk; sæk/ n (sl) bed. (俚)床。hit the ~, go to bed. 就寝。

sack[5] /sæk; sæk/ n [U] (hist) kinds of white wine imported from Spain and the Canary Islands. (史)从西班牙和加那利群岛输入的白葡萄酒。

sack·but /'sækbʌt; 'sæk,bʌt/ n medieval musical wind instrument with a slide like that of a trombone 中古时代似伸缩喇叭的一种管乐器；赛克布特。

sac·ra·ment /'sækrəmənt; 'sækrəmənt/ n [C] solemn religious ceremony in the Christian Church, eg Baptism, Confirmation, Matrimony, believed to be accompanied by great spiritual benefits; (基督教会之)圣礼；圣事(如洗礼，坚信礼，婚礼)；(esp) (尤指) the Blessed/Holy S~, Holy Communion, the Eucharist. 圣餐式；圣餐。**sac·ra·men·tal** /ˌsækrə'mentl; ˌsækrə-'mentl/ adj of, connected with, ~s: 圣礼的；圣餐的: ~al wine. 圣餐中用的葡萄酒。

sacred /'seɪkrɪd; 'seɪkrɪd/ adj 1 of God; connected with religion: 神圣的；宗教上的: a ~ building, eg a church, mosque, synagogue or temple; 宗教建筑物(如教堂，伊斯兰教寺院，犹太教会堂或寺庙)；~ music, for use in religious services; 圣乐；宗教仪式中所用的音乐；~ writings, eg the Koran, the Bible; 宗教经典(如可兰经、圣经)；~ to the memory of ..., phrase seen on tombstones and memorials to the dead. 献给…(用于死者的墓碑及纪念碑上)。2 solemn: 严肃的；郑重的: a ~ promise: 郑重的诺言；hold a promise ~; 信守诺言；regard sth as a ~ duty. 视某事为神圣的职责。3 (to be) treated with great respect or reverence: (须)敬谨处理的；不可冒犯的: In India the cow is a ~ animal. 在印度，牛是神圣(不可冒犯)的动物。Nothing is ~ to these wild youths, They respect nothing. 这些狂野的年轻人什么都不尊敬。~ cow, (colloq) sth to be regarded with reverence, and as immune from reasonable criticism. (口)神圣之事物；不容批评之事物。~·ly adv ~·ness n

sac·ri·fice /'sækrɪfaɪs; 'sækrə,faɪs/ n 1 [U] the offering of sth precious to a god; [C] instance of this; [C] the thing offered: 供奉；献祭；祭礼；祭品；牺牲: the ~ of an ox to Jupiter; 以牛祭祀古罗马主神；kill a sheep as a ~. 宰羊作为牺牲。2 [C, U] the giving up of sth of great value to oneself for a special purpose, or to benefit sb else; [C] sth given up in this way: 牺牲(自

己利益)；献身；所牺牲之物: He gave his life as a ~ for his country, eg of a soldier killed in war. 他为国牺牲了。Parents often make ~s (eg go without things) in order to educate their children. 父母为了教育子女常自我牺牲(例如自己吃俭用)。Is the ~ of one's health to money-making worth while? 牺牲健康去赚钱值得吗？□ vt, vi [VP6A, 14, 3A, 16A] ~ (sth) (to), 1 make a ~ (1): 供奉；献祭；祭祀: ~ a lamb to the gods; 以羔羊祭祀众神；~ to idols. 祭奉偶像。2 give up as a ~ (2): 牺牲利益,生命或享乐: He ~d his life to save the drowning child. 他牺牲性命去拯救快要溺死的孩子。Do you approve of sacrificing comfort to appearance, eg by wearing formal clothes during hot weather? 你赞成牺牲舒适以讲求仪表吗(例如热天穿正式服装)？She has ~d herself/her life/her pleasures and pastimes to her husband's interests and welfare. 她为了丈夫的利益和幸福，牺牲了她自己(她的生命，她的娱乐和消遣)。**sac·ri·fi·cial** /ˌsækrɪ'fɪʃl; ˌsækrə'fɪʃəl/ adj of or like a ~. 供奉的；祭祀的；牺牲的；奉献的。

sac·ri·lege /'sækrɪlɪdʒ; 'sækrəlɪdʒ/ n [U] disrespectful treatment of, injury to, what should be sacred: 亵渎神圣；破坏圣物: It would be ~ to steal a crucifix from a church altar. 从教堂的圣坛窃取耶稣受难像便是亵渎神圣。**sac·ri·legious** /ˌsækrɪ'lɪdʒəs; ˌsækrɪ'lɪdʒəs/ adj

sac·ris·tan /'sækrɪstən; 'sækrɪstən/ n (RC Church) sexton. (天主教)教堂司事。

sac·risty /'sækrɪstɪ; 'sækrɪstɪ/ n (pl -ties) (RC Church) room in a church where vestments and articles used in church worship are kept; vestry. (天主教)(教堂里)圣器收藏室。

sac·ro·sanct /'sækrəʊsæŋkt; 'sækro,sæŋkt/ adj (to be) protected from all harm, because sacred or holy; (fig, often ironic) not to be violated: 神圣不可侵犯的；(喻，常有讥讽之意)不可冒犯的: He regards his privileges as ~. 他认为他的特权是不可侵犯的。

sad /sæd; sæd/ adj (-der, -dest) 1 unhappy; causing unhappy feelings: 悲哀的；忧愁的；凄惨的；使人悲哀的: John is sad because his dog has died. 约翰因他的狗死了而悲伤。It was a sad day for John when her mother died. 玛丽母亲死的那一天，她悲哀极了。Why is he looking so sad? 为什么他愁容满面呢？2 shameful; deplorably bad: 可耻的；非常坏的: a sad case of total callousness. 一个十分无情的可耻事例。**sad·ly** adv **sadness** n **sad·den** /'sædn; sædn/ vt, vi [VP6A, 2A] make or become sad. (使)悲哀；(使)忧愁。

saddle /'sædl; 'sædl/ n 1 leather seat for a rider on a horse, donkey or bicycle; part of a horse's back on which the seat is placed. 鞍；鞍座；(脚踏车)的车座；(马背的)鞍部。⇨ the illus at **bicycle, harness**. 参看 bicycle, harness 之插图。in the ~, on horseback; (fig) in a position of control or power. 骑着马；(喻)处于统驭或当权的地位。'~-bag n (a) one of a pair of bags laid over the back of a horse or donkey. 鞍囊。(b) small bag hung behind a bicycle ~. (挂于脚踏车车座后面的)小袋。'~-sore adj (of a rider) having sores caused by chafing from the ~. (骑马者因马鞍之磨擦所产生之)鞍疮。~ of mutton/venison, joint of meat from the back of the animal, together with part of the backbone and ribs. 带脊骨与肋骨的羊肉(鹿肉)。2 line or ridge of high land rising at each end to a high point. 两峰间的凹下部分；鞍状山脊。⇨ the illus at **mountain**. 参看 mountain 之插图。□ vt [VP6A] put a ~ on (a horse). 装鞍于(马)。2 [VP14] ~ sb with sth, put a heavy responsibility on him; put a burden, etc, on him: 使负重责；加重担等于: be ~d with a wife and ten children; 担负一妻和十个子女的重担；~ sb with heavy tasks. 使某人做吃重工作。**sad·dler** /'sædlə(r); 'sædlə/ n maker of ~s and leather goods for horses. 鞍工；马具师。**sad·dlery** /'sædlərɪ; 'sædlərɪ/ n [U] goods made by a saddler; [C] (pl -ries) saddler's business. 马具；马具业。

sadhu /'saːduː; 'sɑdu/ n Hindu holy man who leads an ascetic life. (印度)圣人。

sa·dism /'seɪdɪzəm; 'sædɪzəm/ n [C] 1 getting sexual pleasure from cruelty to one's partner. 性虐待狂; 施虐淫。 2 (loosely) (delight in) excessive cruelty. (泛指)虐待狂; 极端残酷。 **sa·dist** /-ɪst; -ɪst/ n person displaying ～. 性虐待狂者; 虐待狂者。 **sa·dis·tic** /sə'dɪstɪk; sæ'dɪstɪk/ adj of ～. 性虐待狂的; 淫虐狂的; 虐待狂的。

sado·maso·chism /ˌseɪdəʊˈmæsəkɪzəm; ˌseɪdoˈmæsəkɪzm/ n [U] sadism and masochism found or treated together. 施虐受虐狂(性施虐狂与受虐狂混合者)。 **sado'masochist** /-kɪst; -kɪst/ n person displaying ～. 施虐受虐狂者。

sa·fari /sə'fɑːrɪ; sə'fɑrɪ/ n [C, U] hunting expedition, overland journey, esp in E and Central Africa: (尤指在东非和中非所作的)狩猎远征; 陆地旅行: on ～; 在狩猎旅行中; return from ～; 狩猎远征归来; (by extension) organized tour (for people on holiday) to game reserves, etc. (引申)(假日赴猎物保护区等之)旅行团。

safe[1] /seɪf; sef/ adj (-r, -st) 1 ～ (from), free from, protected from, danger: 安全的; 无危险的: ～ from attack. 免受攻击。 2 unhurt and undamaged. 未受伤害的; 平安的。 ～ and sound, secure and unharmed: 平安无恙: return ～ and sound from a dangerous expedition. 从危险的远征平安无恙地回来。 3 not causing or likely to cause harm or damage: 不致引起危险的; 稳妥的: Is 120 kilometres an hour ～ on this wide road? 在这条宽路上一小时 120 公里的速度安全吗? Is your dog ～? 你的狗不会咬人吗? Are these toys ～ for small children? 这些玩具对于小孩是安全的吗? 4 (of a place, etc) giving security: (指地方等)给予安全的; 不会有危险的: Keep it in a ～ place. 把它放在一个安全的地方。 Is this beach ～ for bathing? 这海滩是个安全的游泳地方吗? Is the bathing ～ here? 在这里游泳安全吗? Is this a ～ seat for the Tories, Is it certain that the Tory candidate will be elected? 这是保守党稳稳的席次吗? 5 cautious; not taking risks: 小心的; 不冒险的: a ～ statesman. 稳健的政治家。 They appointed a ～ man as Headmaster. 他们派一个稳健的人做校长。 **be on the ～ side**, take more precautions than may be necessary: 妥加准备以防万一: Although the sun was shining he took his raincoat and umbrella to be on the ～ side. 虽然出太阳, 他仍带雨衣和雨伞以防万一。 6 certain (to do, be, become): 必定(做, 是, 变为…)的: Mr Hill is ～ to win the seat, will certainly be elected. 希尔先生必定会当选为议员。 7 (compounds) (复合词) '～-conduct n (document giving the) right to visit or pass through a district without the risk of being arrested or harmed (esp in time of war). (尤指战时之)安全通行权; 安全通行证。 '～-deposit (US = ～-de'posit) n building containing strong-rooms and safes which persons may rent separately for storing valuables. 保险仓库; 贵重物品保管处(其保险室与保险箱柜可由私人租用)。 '～·guard n object, condition, circumstance, etc that tends to prevent harm, give protection (against): 有保护作用的物品, 状况, 环境等; 安全设备或措施: smear one's skin with sun-tan lotion as a ～guard against sun-burn. 将皮肤搽上防晒剂以免晒黑。 □ vt [VP6A, 14] ～guard (against), protect, guard: 保护; 防卫: ～guard one's house against burglars, eg with a burglar-alarm. 在家装置防盗警铃等以防窃贼。 '～'keeping n [U] care; custody: 保护; 保管: Leave your jewels in the bank for ～keeping while you are on holiday. 度假时把你的珠宝交给银行保管。 ～·ly adv ～·ness n: a feeling of ～ness. 安全感。

safe[2] /seɪf; sef/ n 1 fireproof and burglar-proof box in which money and other valuables are kept. 保险箱。 2 cool, airy cupboard in which food is kept to protect it from flies, etc: (能防苍蝇等之)饭橱; 菜橱; 纱橱; 冷藏柜: a 'meat-～. 肉类冷藏柜。

safety /'seɪftɪ; 'seftɪ/ n [U] 1 being safe; freedom

from danger: 安全; 平安; 稳妥: do nothing that might endanger the ～ of other people; 不做可能危及他人安全的事; seek ～ in flight; 溜之大吉; 避难; ensure sb's ～; 确保某人的安全; play for ～, avoid taking risks in a game (or fig). (在比赛中或喻)稳扎稳打; 不冒险。 S～ First, motto used to warn that ～ is important. 安全第一(箴言, 以示安全之重要)。 road ～, from traffic dangers. 道路安全(不会发生交通事故)。 2 (compounds) (复合词) '～-belt, = seatbelt. 安全带。 '～-bolt -catch/-lock, device that gives ～ against a possible danger (eg to prevent a gun from being fired by accident or a door being opened without the proper key). 保险销(掣子, 锁)(防止枪炮走火或门户家人开启等)。 '～-curtain n fireproof curtain that can be lowered between the stage and auditorium of a theatre. (可在戏院之舞台及观众席之间降落的)防火幕。 '～-glass n glass that does not shatter or splinter. 安全玻璃; 不碎玻璃。 '～-lamp n miner's lamp in which the flame is protected so as not to ignite dangerous gases. (矿坑用的)安全灯。 '～-match n one that lights only when rubbed on a special surface (on the side of the box). 安全火柴。 '～-pin n one with a guard for the point. 安全别针。 '～-razor n razor with a guard to prevent the blade from cutting the skin. 安全剃刀; 保险剃刀。 '～-valve n (a) valve which releases pressure (in a steam boiler, etc) when it becomes too great. 安全阀(使锅炉等过大之压力泄出的活门)。 (b) (fig) way of releasing feelings of anger, excitement, etc harmlessly. (喻)以无害的方式发泄怒气, 激动等的方法。 sit on the ～valve, follow a policy of repression. 采取压制手段; 竭力抑制激动的情感等。

a safety-pin

saf·fron /'sæfrən; 'sæfrən/ n orange powder obtained from flowers of the autumn crocus, used as a dye and for flavouring; colour of this (bright orange-yellow). 一种取自番红花的橘黄色粉(用于着色及调味); 橘黄色; 鲜黄色。

sag /sæg; sæg/ vi (-gg-) [VP2A] 1 sink or curve down in the middle under weight or pressure: 中间下坠; 压陷: a sagging roof. 下陷的屋顶。 Prices are sagging, falling. 物价在下跌。 2 hang down unevenly; hang sideways: 不整齐地下垂; 松垂: His cheeks are beginning to sag. 他的双颊开始松垂。 □ n [C] (degree of) sagging: 压陷; 松垂; 弛垂; 弛度; 垂度: There is a bad sag in the seat of this chair. 这椅子的座部有很深的陷坑。

saga /'sɑːgə; 'sɑgə/ n [C] 1 mediaeval story of heroic deeds of Icelandic or Norwegian heroes. 英勇故事; (有关中世纪冰岛或挪威的) 北欧英勇传说。 2 long narrative, eg a number of connected books (esp novels) about a family, social group, etc: (有关某家族, 社会团体等的)长篇故事; (尤指)家世小说: the Forsyte S～. 叙述福赛特家族历代事迹的长篇小说。 3 (colloq) long description of an eventful experience: (口)(有关重要经历的)长篇记叙: the ～ of Caroline's trip up the Amazon. 加罗琳的亚马逊河行记。

sa·gacious /sə'geɪʃəs; sə'geʃəs/ adj showing good judgement, common sense or (of animals) intelligence. 睿智的; 精明的; 有判断力的; (指动物)伶俐的; 有灵性的。 ～·ly adv

sa·gac·ity /sə'gæsətɪ; sə'gæsətɪ/ n [U] sound judgement; wisdom of a practical kind: 睿智; 精明: S～, unlike cleverness, may increase with age. 与聪明不同的是: 睿智可能随年龄俱增。

sage[1] /seɪdʒ; sedʒ/ n wise man; man who is believed to be wise. 智者; 哲人; 贤人。 □ adj wise; having the

wisdom of experience; (often ironic) wise-looking. 明智的; 贤明的; (常用作反语) 貌似聪明的。 ~·**ly** adv

sage² /seɪdʒ; sedʒ/ n [U] herb with dull greyish-green leaves, used to flavour food: 鼠尾草(草本植物,有淡灰绿色叶子用于调味): ~ *and onions*, stuffing used for a goose, duck, etc. 鼠尾草和洋葱(用做烹调鹅,鸭等的填料)。 '~·**green** n, adj the colour of ~ leaves. 灰绿色(的); 鼠尾草色的。

Sag·it·ta·rius /ˌsædʒɪˈteərɪəs; ˌsædʒɪˈtɛrɪəs/ n ninth sign of the zodiac. 人马宫; 射手座(黄道带之第九宫)。 ⇨ the illus at **zodiac**. 参看 zodiac 之插图。

sago /ˈseɪɡəʊ; ˈseɡo/ n [U] starchy food, in the form of hard, white grains, from the pith of certain palm-trees ('~ *palms*). 西米; 西谷米(由棕榈之木髓制成的一种白色硬粒状的淀粉质食物)。

Sa·hib US: 'saːb; 'saːɪb/ n (old use, in India and Pakistan, used *after* a title or name) sir: (旧用法, 印度及巴基斯坦,用于称号或名字之后)先生: *Colonel* ~; 上校先生; *Churchill* ~. 邱吉尔先生。

said /sed; sed/ 1 pt, pp of **say**. 2 = *aforesaid*, ⇨ **afore**.

sail¹ /seɪl; sel/ n 1 [C, U] sheet of canvas spread to catch the wind and move a boat or ship forward: 帆: *hoist/lower the* ~s; 扬(下)帆; *in full* ~, with all the ~s spread or set. 张满帆。 *under* ~, (moving) with ~s spread. 张帆地; 在航行中。 *set* ~ *(from/to/for)*, begin a voyage. 启航; 开船。 *take in* ~, reduce the area of sails spread; (fig) become less ambitious or active. 减少船帆张开之面积; 减帆; (喻)减低雄心; 减少活动。 *take the wind out of sb's* ~*s*, ⇨ **wind¹**(1). '~·**cloth** n [U] canvas for ~s. 帆布。 2 [C] set of boards attached to the arm of a windmill to catch the wind. 风车的翼。 3 (*pl* unchanged) ship: (复数不变)船: *a fleet of twenty* ~. 二十艘船的舰队(船)队。 *There wasn't a* ~ *in sight*. 一只船也没有看见。 *S*~ *ho!* (cry announcing that a ship is in sight). 看见船了! (宣布看见船的喊声)。 4 (rarely pl) voyage or excursion on water for pleasure: (罕用复数)航行; 水上游览: *go for a* ~, 去坐船玩; voyage of a specified duration: 航程; 持航时间: *How many days'* ~ *is it from Hull to Oslo?* 从赫尔到奥斯陆有几天的航程?

sail² /seɪl; sel/ vi, vt 1 [VP2A, B, C] move forward across the sea, a lake, etc by using ~s or engine-power; move forward (in sport) across ice or a sandy beach by means of a sail or sails: 张帆或借引擎动力横渡海、湖等;(运动)张帆滑行于冰或沙滩上: ~ *up/along the coast*; 张帆沿海岸行驶; ~ *into harbour*; 驶入海港; *go* ~*ing*. 坐帆船去。 ~ *close/near to the wind*, **(a)** (naut) sail near to the direction in which the wind is blowing. (航海)顶风航行。 **(b)** (fig) nearly, but not quite, break a law or offend against a moral principle. (喻)几乎犯法或违反道德准则。 '~·**ing-boat** /-**ship**/-**vessel**, n boat, etc moved by sails. 帆船。 2 [VP2A, C, 3A] ~ *(for/from/to)*, (of a ship or persons on board) begin a voyage; travel on water by use of sails or engines: (指船或乘客)启航; 坐船旅行: *When does the ship* ~? 船何时启航? *He has* ~*ed for New York*. 他已乘船去纽约了。 *Here is a list of* ~*ings* (= ships that ~, with dates) *from London*. 这是自伦敦开出的船期表。 *The captain has received his* ~*ing orders*, instructions concerning the voyage. 船长已收到有关航行的训令(开航命令)。 3 [VP6A] voyage across or on: 航行越过; 航行于: ~ *the sea/the Pacific*. 航行于海洋(太平洋)。 4 [VP6A, 2A] (be able to) control (a boat): (会)驾驶(船): *He has his own yacht*. 他驾驶自用游艇。 *Do you* ~? 你会驾驶帆船吗? '~·**ing-master** n officer who navigates a yacht. 游艇驾驶员。 5 [VP2C] move smoothly like a ship with sails: 船地行动: *The moon/clouds* ~*ed across the sky*. 月亮(云)平稳地穿(飘)过天空。 *The duchess* ~*ed into the room*, entered in a stately manner. 公爵夫人雍容华贵地步入房间。 6 ~ *in*, begin with energy and confidence. 卖力而有信心地开始做某事。 ~ *into sb*,

scold; attack. 斥责; 攻击(某人)。

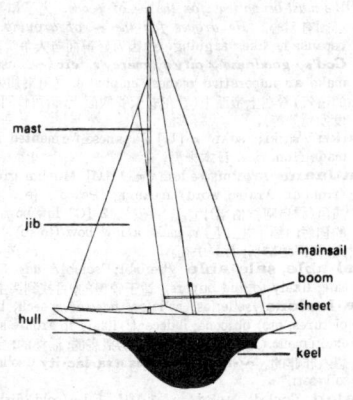

a sailing-boat

sailor /ˈseɪlə(r); ˈselɚ/ n 1 seaman; member of a ship's crew. 海员; 水手。 '~ *hat/blouse/suit*, hat, etc eg to be worn by a child, made in imitation of the kind worn by a ~. 水手帽(衫、装)(如仿照水手所穿戴之衣帽等所制的童装)。 2 *good /bad* ~, person seldom/often seasick in rough weather. (风浪大时)不大(常会)晕船的人。

saint /seɪnt; sent; GB weak form immediately before names: 英国读音在人名前读轻音: snt/ n 1 holy person. 圣人; 道德高尚的人。 2 person who, having died, is among the blessed in Heaven. 已进天国之人; 死者。 3 (abbr 略作 **St**) person who has been declared by the Church to have won by holy living on earth a place in Heaven and veneration on earth. 圣者; 圣徒。 4 unselfish or patient person. 无私心而能容忍之人。 5 '~'**s-day** n Church festival in memory of a ~. 圣徒纪念日。 *St 'Andrew's Day*, 30th November (patron ~ of Scotland). 圣安德鲁日(十一月三十日,圣安德鲁为苏格兰之守护圣徒)。 *St 'David's Day*, 1st March (patron ~ of Wales). 圣大卫日(三月一日,圣大卫为威尔士之守护圣徒)。 *St 'George's Day*, 23rd April (patron ~ of England). 圣乔治日(四月二十三日,圣乔治为英格兰之守护圣徒)。 *St 'Patrick's Day*, 17th March (patron ~ of Ireland). 圣帕特里克日(三月十七日,圣帕特里克为爱尔兰之守护圣徒)。 *St 'Valentine's Day*, ⇨ **Valentine**. 6 *St Bernard* /snt 'bɜːnəd US: ˌseɪnt bɜːˈnɑːd; sent bəˈnɑːrd/ n large, powerful breed of dog, originally bred by monks in the Swiss Alps, trained to rescue travellers lost in snowstorms. 圣伯纳狗(一种大而强壮的狗,最初由瑞士境内阿尔卑斯山的僧人所饲养,训练后用以寻救在暴风雪中迷失的旅客)。 *St 'Vitus's* /ˌvaɪtəsɪz; 'vaɪtəsɪz/ '*dance* n nervous disorder with convulsive, involuntary movements. 舞蹈病(带有抽搐,不随意之动作的神经错乱)。 ~*ed* adj declared to be, regarded as, a ~. 宣为圣者的; 被视为圣人的; 神圣的。 '~·**hood** /-hʊd; -hʊd/ n[U]. ~·**like**, ~·**ly** adj very holy or good; like a ~; of a ~: 神圣的; 崇高的; 似圣者或圣人的; 圣者的; 圣人的: *a* ~*ly expression on his face*. 他脸上神圣的表情。 ~·**li·ness** n [U] holiness of life; condition of being ~*ly*. 生活神圣; 道德崇高。

saith /seθ; seθ/ old form of *says*, ⇨ **say**. says 的古体。

sake /seɪk; sek/ n *for the* ~ *of sb/sth; for sb's/sth's* ~, for the welfare or benefit of; because of an interest in or desire for: 为了…之好处; 出于对…之兴趣: *do sth for the* ~ *of one's family*. 为家庭做某事。 *I'll help you for your sister's* ~, because I want to save your sister

trouble, help her, etc. 为了你姐姐(妹妹)我将帮助你。 *We must be patient for the ~ of peace.* 为了和平我们必须有耐心。 *He argues for the ~ of arguing,* only because he likes arguing. 他因为好辩而与人争辩。 **for God's/goodness'/pity's/mercy's, etc ~,** used to make an imperative request emphatic. (用来加强祈求的语气)看在上帝面上(看在老天爷的面上;请可怜可怜;请发发慈悲等)。

sa·ké /'sɑːkɪ; 'sɑkɪ/ n [U] Japanese fermented liquor made from rice. 日本米酒。

sa·laam /sə'lɑːm; sə'lɑm/ n [C] Muslim greeting (from an Arabic word) meaning 'Peace'. 伊斯兰教问候语(源自阿拉伯字),意指"平安"。 **2** [C] low bow. 深深的鞠躬; 额手礼。 □ vi make a low bow (to sb). (向某人)深深地鞠躬; 行额手礼。

sal·able, sale·able /'seɪləbl; 'seləbl/ adj fit for sale; likely to find buyers. 适于销售的; 可找到买主的。

sa·lacious /sə'leɪʃəs; sə'leʃəs/ adj (of speech, books, pictures, etc) obscene; indecent; likely to arouse sexual excitement.(指言词, 书籍, 图书等)猥亵的; 淫秽的; 会使人想入非非的。 ~·ly adv ~·ness n **sa·lac·ity** /sə'læsətɪ; sə'læsətɪ/

salad /'sæled; 'sæled/ n **1** [C, U] (cold dish of) sliced (and usu uncooked) vegetables such as lettuce, endive, cucumber, tomatoes, seasoned with oil, vinegar, etc eaten with, or including, cheese, cold meat, fish, etc: 生菜; (一道)凉拌食品; 沙拉: *prepare/mix a ~;* 调配(拌)沙拉; *a chicken/lobster ~;* 一道凉拌鸡肉(龙虾); *cold beef and ~.* 牛肉和生菜冷盘。 '**~days** n pl period of inexperienced youth. 少不更事的时期。 '**~-dressing** n mixture of oil, vinegar, herbs, etc used with ~. 生菜之调味酱汁(油, 醋, 奶油等的混合物)。 '**~-oil** n oil used for ~-dressing. 生菜油。 **2 fruit ~,** mixture of fruits, sliced or cut up, eaten cold. 什锦水果。 **3** [U] lettuce, endive or other green vegetable suitable for eating raw. 适于生吃的莴苣, 菊苣或其他蔬菜。

sala·man·der /'sæləmændə(r); 'sælə,mændə/ n lizard-like animal once supposed to be capable of living in fire. 昔时被认为是生活于火中的似蜥蜴的动物; 火龙。

sa·lami /sə'lɑːmɪ; sə'lɑmɪ/ n [U] Italian sausage salted and flavoured with garlic. 意大利腊肠(经腌制并以大蒜调味)。

sal·ary /'sælərɪ; 'sælərɪ/ n [C] (pl -ries) (usu monthly) payment for regular employment on a yearly basis: 薪水; 薪俸(通常由物主或月发给): *a ~ of £8000 per annum.* 年薪两千镑。 Cf 参较 a weekly wage. **sal·ar·ied** adj receiving a ~; (of employment) paid for by means of a ~: 领薪水的; (指职业)支薪水的: *the salaried classes;* 薪水阶层; *salaried posts.* 有薪职务。

sale /seɪl; sel/ n **1** [U] exchange of goods or property for money; act of selling: 出售; 卖出: *The ~ of his old home made him sad.* 出售老宅使他很难过。 **(up) for ~,** intended to be sold (usu by or on behalf of the owners): 待售(通常由物主或物主人经手): *Is the house for ~?* 此屋出售否? *I shall put these goods up for ~,* announce that they may be bought. 我将把这些货物公开出售。 **on ~,** (of goods in shops, etc) offered for purchase. (指商店的货物等)出售的。 **on ~ or return,** (of goods sent to a retailer) either to be sold or, if unsold or unsatisfactory, to be returned. (指批给零售商的货物)可售出或(卖不掉或有瑕疵时)退还。 **bill of ~,** (comm) document which transfers the title(3) of personal chattels, etc to another person although the goods remain with the person making the transfer (used as a method of borrowing money). (商)卖据; 抵押证券。 **2** [C] instance of selling sth: 卖物之实例: *I haven't made a ~ all week.* 我整个星期没有卖出货品。 *He finds a ready ~ for the strawberries he grows.* 他所种植的草莓很有销路。 *His strawberries find a ready ~,* are quickly sold. 他的草莓很快就卖掉了。 *S~s are up/down this month,* more/fewer goods have been

sold. 本月销售量增加(减少)。 '**~s clerk,** (US) shop assistant. (美)售货员; 店员。 '**~s department,** that part of a business company that is concerned with selling goods (contrasted with manufacture, dispatch, etc). 营业部(与公司之生产, 发货等部门相对)。 '**~s resistance,** reluctance of the public to buy goods. 公众之不愿购物; 销货阻力。 '**~s talk,** (colloq □ '~s chat), talk (to a prospective customer) to boost the ~s of goods. 向顾客推销货品时吹嘘的话。 '**~s tax,** tax payable on the sum received for articles sold by retail. 营业税; 销售税。 **3** [C] the offering of goods at low prices for a period (to get rid of old stock, etc): 廉售; 贱卖(以清除旧货等): *the winter/summer ~s;* 冬季(夏季)大贱卖; *buy goods at the ~s;* 廉价期间购物; '~ price, low price at a ~. 廉售价。 **4** [C] occasion when goods, property, etc are put up for ~ by auction: 拍卖: *get bargains by attending ~s.* 参加拍卖会获得廉价品。 '**~-room,** room where goods, etc are sold by public auction. 售卖处; 拍卖处。 **5** ~ of work, of articles (eg clothing) made by members of a church, etc for charity. 教友等为慈善事业所做物品(如衣服)的拍卖。 ⇨ jumble. '**~s·man** /-zmən; -zmən/, '**~s·woman** /-zwʊmən; -z,wʊmən/ nn person selling goods in a shop or (on behalf of wholesalers) to shopkeepers. 店员(女店员); 营货员(女营货员)。 '**~s·man·ship** /-zmənʃɪp; -zmən,ʃɪp/ n [U] skill in selling goods. 销货术; 推销术。 ~·able /-əbl; -əbl/ adj = salable.

sa·li·ent /'seɪlɪənt; 'selɪənt/ adj **1** outstanding; prominent; easily noticed: 显著的; 突出的; 易见的: *the ~ points of a speech.* 一篇演讲之要点。 *Honesty is his most ~ characteristic.* 诚实是他最显著的特点。 **2** (of an angle) pointing outwards. (指角)凸出的。 □ n ~ angle; forward wedge driven into the enemy's battle front. 凸角; (深入敌阵之)突出部。

sa·line /'seɪlaɪn US: -liːn; 'seleɪn/ adj containing salt; salty: 含盐的; 咸的: *a ~ solution,* eg as used for gargling; 食盐水(如用于嗽喉等); ~ springs. 盐泉。 □ n **1** [U] solution of salt and water. 盐水。 **2** [C] lake, marsh, well, spring, etc. 盐湖; 盐沼; 盐井; 盐泉等。 **sa·lin·ity** /sə'lɪnətɪ; sə'lɪnətɪ/ n [U] quality of being ~. 咸; 盐性; 咸度; 盐度。

sal·iva /sə'laɪvə; sə'laɪvə/ n [U] the natural liquid present in the mouth; spittle. 口水; 唾液。 **sali·vary** /'sælɪvərɪ US: -verɪ; 'sælə,vɛrɪ/ adj of in producing ~: 唾液的; 分泌唾液的: *the '~ry glands.* 唾液腺。 ⇨ the illus at **alimentary.** 参看 alimentary 之插图。 **sali·vate** /'sælɪveɪt; 'sælə,vet/ vi secrete too much ~. 分泌过多唾液; 大量流口水。

sal·low /'sæləʊ; 'sælo/ adj (-er, -est) (of the human skin or complexion) of an unhealthy yellow colour. (指人的皮肤或面色)病黄色的。 □ vt, vi make or become ~: (使)发病黄色: *a face ~ed by years of residence in the tropics.* 多年住在热带所致之蜡黄色的面孔。

sally /'sælɪ; 'sælɪ/ n (pl -lies) [C] **1** sudden breaking out by soldiers who are surrounded by the enemy: (被敌人包围之兵士的)突围; 出击: *make a successful ~.* 做一次成功的突围。 **2** lively, witty remark, esp one that is a good-humoured attack on sb or sth. 俏皮话(尤指善意地批评某人或某事所说者)。 □ vi [VP2A, C] **1** make a ~(1): 突围; 出击: ~ *out against the besiegers.* 出击围攻者。 **2** ~ *out/forth,* go out on a journey or for a walk. 出发旅行; 出外散步。

salmon /'sæmən; 'sæmən/ n [C] (pl unchanged) large fish, valued for food and the sport of catching it with rod and line; [U] its flesh as food; the colour of its flesh, orange-pink. (复数不变)鲑; 鲑肉; 橙红色。 ~ **trout,** kinds of fish like ~, esp kinds of) trout. 类似鲑鱼的鱼; (尤指)(各种)鳟鱼。

salon /'sælɒn US: sə'lɑːn; sə'lō/ n **1** assembly, as a regular event, of notable persons at the house of a lady of fashion (esp in Paris); reception room used for this purpose. (尤指巴黎)名流在上流妇女家中之例

行聚会; 名流聚会的客厅; 沙龙。 **2 the S~,** annual exhibition of pictures by living artists in a French town. (在法国城市举行的)当代画家作品年展; 沙龙画展。 **3** establishment offering services connected with fashion, etc: 提供时装或美容服务等的公司行号: *a 'beauty-~.* 美容院。

sa·loon /sə'lu:n; sə'lun/ *n* **1** room for social use in a ship, hotel, etc: (轮船,旅馆等之)交谊厅; 大厅: *the ship's 'dining-~.* 轮船的餐厅。 ⇨ **bar,** most comfortable bar in a public house or inn. 酒店或客栈中最舒适之酒吧; 高级酒吧。 ⇨ *public bar* at **public. 2** public room or rooms for a specified purpose: 供特殊用途的公共大厅或场所: *a 'billiards /'hairdressing ~.* 撞球场(美容院)。 **3** (US) place where alcoholic drinks may be bought and drunk (GB 英 = *pub*); bar. (美)酒店,酒吧。 **4** ('~)- **car,** (GB) motor-car with wholly enclosed seating space for 4—7 passengers (US 美 = *sedan*). (英)(可供四至七人乘坐之)大轿车。

sal·sify /'sælsɪfaɪ; 'sælsəfɪ/ *n* [U] (plant with a) long, fleshy root cooked as a vegetable. 婆罗门参; 婆罗门参根(长而多肉,可作蔬菜)。

salt /sɔ:lt; sɔlt/ *n* **1** [U] (often 常作 *common ~*) white substance obtained from mines, present in sea-water and obtained from it by evaporation, used to flavour and preserve food; sodium chloride **(NaCl):** 盐; 食盐; 氯化钠: *too much ~ in the soup;* 汤里盐太多; *'table ~,* powdered for convenient use at table. 餐桌上用的精盐。 *not /hardly worth one's ~,* not deserving one's pay. 不称职。 *take (a statement, etc) with a grain /pinch of ~,* feel some doubt whether it is altogether true. 对(某一陈述等)有所怀疑或采取保留态度。 *the ~ of the earth,* the finest citizens; persons with very high qualities. 社会中坚份子。 **2** (chem) chemical compound of a metal and an acid. (化学)金属和酸的化合物; 盐。 **3 a ~, an old ~,** an experienced sailor. 有经验的水手。 **4** (*pl*) medicine used to empty the bowels: (复)泻盐: *take a dose of (Epsom) ~s.* 服一剂泻盐。 *like a dose of ~s,* (sl) very fast. (俚)很快。 ⇨ also *smelling ~s* at **smell²(4). 5** (fig) sth that gives flavour or zest: (喻)增加风味或妙趣之物; 刺激物: *Adventure is the ~ of life to some men.* 对于某些人而言, 冒险是生活中的趣味。 **6** (compounds) (复合词) **'~-cellar** *n* small container (open, or with a hole or holes at the top) for ~ at table. (餐桌上开着或顶端有孔的)盐瓶。 **'~-lick** *n* place where animals come to lick earth with ~ in it. 动物来舐食咸味的含盐地。 **'~- pan** *n* hollow place (natural or artificial) near the sea where ~ is obtained by evaporation of sea-water. (近海处由蒸发海水而得盐之天然或人工)盐田。 **'~-shaker** *n* (US) small container (with a hole or holes at the top for sprinkling) for ~ at table. (美)(餐桌上用的)盐瓶。 **'~-water** *adj* of the sea. 海水的; 咸水的。 **'~-works** *n* (*sing* or *pl*) place where ~ is manufactured. (单或复)制盐场; 盐厂。 ⇨ *vt* [VP6A, 15B] put ~ on or in (food) to season it; [VP6A, 15B] ~ *sth (down),* preserve (food) with ~: 加盐于(食物)以调味; 用盐腌(食物): ~ (*down*) *cod;* 腌鳕鱼; ~ed *meat.* 腌肉。 ~ *sth away,* (colloq) put money away for the future: (口)积蓄钱: *He's got quite a bit ~ed away.* 他积蓄了不少钱。 ⇨ *adj* **1** containing, tasting of, preserved with, ~: 有咸味的; 咸的; 腌的: ~ *beef;* 腌牛肉; ~ *water.* 咸水。 **2** (of land) impregnated with ~: (指土地)盐渍的; 多盐的: ~ *marshes;* 盐泽; 盐沼; *the ~ flats of Utah.* 犹他州的盐地。 **~·y** *adj* **(-ier, -iest)** containing, tasting of, ~. 含盐的; 有咸味的; 咸的。 **~·i·ness** *n*

salt·petre (US = **-peter**) /ˌsɔ:lt'pi:tə(r); 'sɔlt'pitɚ/ *n* salty white powder (Potassium nitrate, nitre) used in making gunpowder, for preserving food and as medicine. 硝酸钾; 硝石(有咸味的白色粉末,用于制火药,腌藏食物并用作药物)。

sa·lu·bri·ous /sə'lu:brɪəs; sə'lubrɪəs/ *adj* (esp of climate) health-giving: (尤指气候)有益健康的: *the ~*

mountain air of Switzerland. 瑞士之有益于健康的山地空气。 **sa·lu·brity** /sə'lu:brətɪ; sə'lubrətɪ/ *n*

salu·tary /'sæljʊtrɪ US: -terɪ; 'sæljə'tɛʃən/ *adj* having a good effect (on body or mind): (对身心)有益的: ~ *exercise /advice.* 有益的运动(忠告)。

salu·ta·tion /ˌsæljuː'teɪʃn; ˌsæljə'teʃən/ *n* [C, U] (act or expression of) greeting or goodwill (eg a bow or a kiss): 问候; 欢迎; 敬礼; 招呼; 致意: *He raised his hat in* ~; 他举帽致意; (in a letter, etc) introductory phrase, eg *Dear Sir.* (信函开头之)称呼(如'敬启者')。

sa·lute /sə'lu:t; sə'lut/ *n* **1** sth done to welcome sb or to show respect or honour, esp (eg in the armed forces) the raising of the hand to the forehead, the firing of guns, the lowering and raising of a flag: 欢迎或致敬所行之事; 敬礼; 致敬: *give a* ~; 敬礼; *fire a* ~ *of ten guns;* 鸣礼炮十响; *stand at the* ~, stand with the right hand raised to the forehead. 立正敬礼。 *take the* ~, acknowledge the ~s of a body of soldiers who march past and give ~s. (整队士兵通过并敬礼时)接受敬礼; 还礼。 **2** friendly greeting such as a bow, raising of the hat (by a man). 致意; 招呼(如鞠躬,男子举帽)。 ⇨ *vt, vi* [VP6A, 2A] greet; give a ~ (to): 行礼; (向…)致敬或致意: *The soldier ~d smartly.* 那兵士行礼很有精神。

sal·vage /'sælvɪdʒ; 'sælvɪdʒ/ *n* [U] **1** the saving of property from loss (by fire or other disaster, eg a wrecked ship): (从火灾或其他灾难,如船难等中)抢救财货: *a ~ company,* one whose business is to bring wrecked ships to port, raise valuables from a ship that has sunk, etc; 海难救援公司; 沉船打捞公司; *a ~ tug,* for towing a disabled ship to port. 拖船; 救难船。 **2** property so saved. 获救的财货。 **3** payment given to those who save property. (付予抢救财货者的)救难奖金。 **4** (saving of) waste material that can be used again after being processed: (加工后可再用的)废物; 废物收集利用: *collect old newspapers and magazines for* ~. 收藏旧报纸杂志以便利用。 ⇨ *vt* [VP6A] save from loss, fire, wreck, etc. (在损失,火灾,船难等中)抢救; 援救。

sal·va·tion /sæl'veɪʃn; sæl'veʃən/ *n* [U] **1** the act of saving, the state of having been saved, from sin and its consequences. (免除原罪及其后果之)超度; 拯救; 救世; 得救。 **S~ 'Army,** religious and missionary Christian organization on a semi-military model. 救世军(半军事形式之基督教传教组织)。 **2** that which saves sb from loss, disaster, etc: 救助; 救助者: *Government loans have been the* ~ *of several shaky business companies.* 政府的贷款挽救了几家濒临倒闭的公司。 *work out one's own* ~, find, by one's own efforts, how to save oneself. 谋求自救之道。

salve /sælv US: sæv; sæv/ *n* **1** [C, U] (kinds of) oily medicinal substance used on wounds, sores or burns: 药膏; 软膏: *'lip-~.* 口唇裂痛时所用之药膏。 **2** (fig) sth that comforts wounded feelings or soothes an uneasy conscience. (喻)安慰情感受伤及良心不安之物; 缓和剂; 慰藉。 ⇨ *vt* [VP6A] soothe; be a ~ to; put a ~ on: 安慰; 缓和; 敉以药膏: ~ *one's conscience by giving stolen money to charity.* 把偷来的钱用于慈善救济以减轻良心之不安。

sal·ver /'sælvə(r); 'sælvɚ/ *n* metal household tray. (金属的)托盘; 盘子。

salvo /'sælvəʊ; 'sælvo/ *n* (*pl* **~s, ~es** /-vəʊz; -voz/) **1** the firing of a number of guns together as a salute. 齐发礼炮。 **2** round of applause. 一阵喝彩; 齐声欢呼。

sal vol·atile /ˌsæl vəˈlætəlɪ; 'sælvoˈlætl̩i/ *n* [U] solution of ammonium carbonate (smelling salts) used medically when a person feels faint or becomes unconscious. 碳酸铵水; 挥发盐(用作提神药)。

Sa·mari·tan /sə'mærɪtən; sə'mærətn/ *n* **Good** ~, person who pities and gives practical help to persons in trouble. 同情并援助苦难者的善人。 ⇨ *Luke* 10: 33. 参看新约圣经路加福音第10章第33节。

samba /'sæmbə; 'sæmbə/ *n* (music for a) ballroom dance that originated in Brazil. 桑巴舞(一种始自巴西的交际舞);桑巴舞曲。

same /seim/ *sem*/ *adj, pron* (always the ~, except as noted in **6** below) (除了下列第 6 义所说明的情形外,总是与定冠词连用) **1** not different; unchanged: 同一的;相同的;无变化的: *He is the ~ age as his wife.* 他与妻同年。*We have lived in the ~ house for fifty years.* 我们五十年来一直住在这幢房子里。*We are all going the ~ way.* 我们将走同一条路。**2 the ~ ... that; the ~ ... as:** *She uses the ~ scent that you do/the ~ scent as you.* 她用的香水和你的一样。⇨ **as²(13). 3** (with a relative clause introduced by *that, where, who*, etc. *As* replaces *that* if the *v* is omitted): (后接用 that, where, who 等所引导的关系从句; 如关系从句中之动词省略, 则以 as 代替that): *Put the book back in the ~ place where you found it.* 把书放回原位。*Our eggs are sold the ~ day that/as they come in.* 我们的鸡蛋在进货的当天就卖掉了。*The price is the ~ as last year.* 这价格与去年相同。*Are these the ~ people (whom) we saw here last week?* 这些就是我们上周在此地看到的那些人吗? **4** (as *pron*) the same thing: (用作代词)同样之事物: *We must all say the ~.* 我们大家必须说相同的话。*I would do the ~ again.* 我愿重做一次。**be all/just the ~ to,** make no difference to; be a matter of indifference to: 对…一样; 对…无关紧要: *You can do it now or leave it till later; it's all the ~ to me.* 你现在做或留待以后做, 对我都一样。**5** (in phrases) (用于短语中) **come/amount to the ~ thing,** have the ~ result, meaning, etc: 具有相同的结果、意义等: *You may pay in cash or cheque; it comes to the ~ thing.* 你付现款或支票, 结果是一样的。**the very ~,** (emph): (强势语): *You've made the very ~ mistake again!* 你又犯了一模一样的错误! **one and the ~,** absolutely the ~: 完全相同的: *Dr Jekyll and Mr Hyde were one and the ~ person.* 吉柯医生和海德先生是同一人。**at the ~ time, (a)** together: 共同地; 同时: *Don't all speak at the ~ time.* 不要同时说话。*She was laughing and crying at the ~ time.* 她一面笑一面哭。**(b)** (introducing a fact, etc that is to be borne in mind) yet; still; nevertheless: (引导一项须予记住的事实等)然而; 可是: *At the ~ time you must not forget that….* 可是, 你切不可忘记…。**6** (with this, that, these, those) already thought of, mentioned or referred to: (与 this, that, these, those 连用)已想到、谈到或提到的; 上述的: *I stayed at home on Monday, and on that ~ day, the office was wrecked by a bomb.* 星期一我在家里, 就在那天, 办公室被一枚炸弹毁坏了。**7** (as *pron*, often without the *def art*; comm use only): (用作代词, 常无定冠词, 仅作商业用语): *To dry-cleaning suit, £3; to repairing ~, £2.* 干洗一套衣服, 三镑; 修补一套衣服, 二镑。□ *adv* in the ~ way: 相同地; 相同地: *Old people do not feel the ~ about these things as the younger generation.* 对于这些事情, 老年人和年轻的一代持不同的看法。**all the ~,** nevertheless: 仍然; 然而: *He's not very reliable, but I like him all the ~.* 他不很可靠, 但我仍然喜欢他。**~·ness** *n* [U] the condition of being the ~, of being uninteresting through lack of variety. 同一; 相同; 单调乏味。

samo·var /'sæməvɑː(r); 'sæmə,vɑr/ *n* metal urn

a samovar

with an interior tube, used in Russia for boiling water for tea. 俄国式茶炊(有一内管, 用以煮开水泡茶)。

sam·pan /'sæmpæn; 'sæmpæn/ *n* small, flat-bottomed boat used along the coasts and rivers of China. (中国沿海及内河用的)舢板。

a sampan

sample /'sɑːmpl US: 'sæmpl; 'sæmpl/ *n* [C] specimen; one of a number, part of a whole, taken to show what the rest is like (esp as offered by a dealer in goods sold by weight or measure) 标本; 样品; (尤指按重量或大小售物时商人提出的)货样。**up to ~,** (comm) (of goods) equal in quality to the ~ offered. (商)(指货物)和样品相符。□ *vt* take a ~ of sth or sb; test a part of: 取…的样品; 试验…的一部分: *spend an hour at the wineshop, sampling* (= making a random sampling of) *the wines.* 在酒店内花费一小时抽验各种酒。

sam·pler /'sɑːmplə(r) US: 'sæm-; 'sæmplə/ *n* piece of cloth embroidered to show skill in needlework, often displayed on a wall. 刺绣样品(用以表示刺绣技艺, 常贴于墙上)。

sam·urai /'sæmurai; 'sæmu,rai/ *n* **1** the ~, the military caste in feudal Japan. (日本封建时代之)武士阶级。**2** member of this caste. (日本封建时代之)武士。

sana·tor·ium /,sænə'tɔːrɪəm; ,sænə'torɪəm/ (US also **sana·tar·ium** /,sænə'teərɪəm; ,sænə'tærɪəm/) *n* establishment for the treatment of invalid or convalescent people. 疗养院; 休养地。

sanc·tify /'sæŋktɪfaɪ; 'sæŋktə,faɪ/ *vt* (*pt, pp* **-fied**) [VP6A] make holy; set apart as sacred. 使神圣; 尊祀。**sanc·ti·fi·ca·tion** /,sæŋktɪfɪ'keɪʃn; ,sæŋktəfə'keʃən/ *n*

sanc·ti·moni·ous /,sæŋktɪ'məunɪəs; ,sæŋktə'monɪəs/ *adj* making a show of being devout. 伪装虔诚的。**~·ly** *adv*

sanc·tion /'sæŋkʃn; 'sæŋkʃən/ *n* **1** [U] right or permission given by authority to do sth: (做某事的)权利或许可; 批准: *a book that was translated without the ~ of the author and publisher.* 未经作者及出版商认可而翻译的一本书。**2** [U] approval, encouragement (of behaviour, etc), by general custom or tradition. 一般习俗或传统(对行为等)的赞许, 支持。**3** [C] penalty intended to maintain or restore respect for law or authority, esp as adopted by several States together against a country violating international law: (为维持或恢复法律或权威的尊严所作的)处罚; 制裁(尤指几国联合对某一违反国际法的国家之制裁): *apply arms/economic ~s against an aggressor country.* 对侵略国禁供武器(作经济制裁)。**4** [C] reason for obeying a rule, etc: 遵守规则等的原因; 维护道德的约束力: *The best moral ~ is that of conscience; the worst ~ is the fear of punishment.* 最好的道德约束力是良心的约束力; 最坏的约束力是对惩罚的恐惧。□ *vt* [VP6A] give a ~ to; agree to: 批准; 认可: *Would you ~ flogging as a punishment for crimes of violence?* 你同意以鞭打作为对暴行的一种处罚吗?

sanc·tity /'sæŋktətɪ; 'sæŋktətɪ/ *n* (*pl* **-ties**) **1** [U] holiness; sacredness; saintliness: 神圣; 庄严; 圣洁: *violate the ~ of an oath.* 违背誓言的神圣。**2** (*pl*) sacred

obligations, feelings, etc: (复)神圣的义务,感情等: *the sanctities of the home.* 对家庭的神圣义务。

sanc·tu·ary /'sæŋktʃʊərɪ *US:* -ʊerɪ; 'sæŋktʃʊˌɛrɪ/ *n* (*pl* **-ries**) **1** holy or sacred place, esp a church, temple or mosque. 圣所;圣地;(尤指)教堂;庙;伊斯兰教寺院。 **2** chancel of a church. 圣坛。 **3** sacred place (eg the altar of a church) where, in former times, a person running away from the law or his creditors was secure, by Church law, against arrest or violence. 至圣所(如教堂内之祭坛、内殿,按昔时之教会法,逃犯或逃债者在此处可获安全)。 **4** [U] (right of offering) freedom from arrest: 不受拘捕之权;庇护;庇护权: *to seek/take/be offered* ~. 寻求(受到)庇护。 **5** place of refuge: 庇护所;避难所: *Great Britain has always been a ~ of political refugees from many parts of the world.* 英国一直是世界许多地方政治犯的庇护所。 **6** area where by law it is forbidden to kill birds, rob their nests, etc, or to shoot animals, etc: 禁猎区: *a 'bird-~.* 鸟类禁猎区。

sanc·tum /'sæŋktəm/ *n* **1** holy place. 圣地;圣所。 **2** (colloq) person's private room or study. (口)私室;书房。

sand /sænd; sænd/ *n* **1** [U] (mass of) finely crushed rock as seen on the seashore, in river-beds, deserts, etc: 沙: *mix ~ and cement to make concrete.* 将沙和水泥混合造成混凝土。 **2** (often *pl*) expanse of ~ (on the seashore or a desert): (常用复数)(海滩上或沙漠中的)沙地: *children playing on the ~(s).* 在沙地玩耍的小孩们。 **3** (*pl*) (复) **The ~s are running out,** (with reference to the ~ running through an hour-glass, etc) There is not much time left; time is passing. (源自沙漏等中流下的沙)余时不多了。 **4** (compounds) (复合字) '~·bag *n* bag filled with ~ used as a defence (in war, against rising flood-water, etc). 沙袋;沙包(用于作战,防洪等)。 '~·bank *n* bank or shoal of ~ in a river or the sea. (河或海的)沙洲;沙滩;浅滩。 '~·bar *n* bank of ~ at the mouth of a river or harbour. (河口或港口的)沙洲。 '~·blast *vt* [VP6A] send a jet of ~ against sth, eg stonework, to clean it, or against metal or glass to cut or make a design on it. (用压缩空气等喷出以清洗石造物,或割切金属、玻璃等之)喷沙。 '~·boy *n* (now used only in) (现仅用于) **as happy as a ~boy,** very happy. 极快乐。 '~·dune *n* mound of ~, formed by the wind. 沙丘。 '~·fly *n* (*pl* **-flies**) kind of midge common on seashores. 白蛉;蚋。 '~·glass *n* glass with two connected bulbs containing enough ~ to take a definite time, eg five minutes, one hour, in passing from one bulb to the other. (计时)沙漏。 '~·paper *n* [U] strong paper with ~ glued to it, used for rubbing rough surfaces smooth. 沙纸。 □ *vt* [VP6A] make smooth with ~ paper. 用沙纸磨光。 '~·piper *n* small bird living in wet, sandy places near streams. 矶鹬(栖于溪流附近之湿沙地中的一种小鸟)。 ⇨ the illus at **water.** 参看 water 之插图。 '~·pit *n* unroofed enclosure filled with ~, for children to play in. 沙坑(供儿童游戏用)。 '~·shoes *n pl* canvas shoes with rubber or hemp soles for wearing on sandy seashores. (沙滩上穿之)橡皮或大麻底的帆布鞋。 '~·stone *n* rock formed of compressed ~. 砂岩。 '~·storm *n* storm in a sandy desert with clouds of ~ raised by the wind. 大风沙;沙暴。 □ *vt* [VP6A] cover, sprinkle or scrub with ~. 覆以沙; 撒以沙; 用沙或沙纸磨擦。 **sandy** *adj* (**-ier, -iest**) **1** covered with or consisting of ~: 覆有沙的; 沙质的: *a ~y bottom,* eg of part of the sea. 沙质的(海)底。 **2** (of hair, etc) yellowish-red: (指毛发等)浅的;浅茶色的。 □ *n* (colloq) nickname given to a person with yellowish-red hair. (口)发呈沙色之人的绰号。

san·dal /'sændl; 'sændl/ *n* kind of open shoe made of a sole and heel with straps to hold it on the foot. (系以条带的)草鞋;凉鞋;便鞋。 **~led** /'sændld; 'sændld/ *adj* wearing ~s. 穿草鞋、凉鞋或便鞋的。

san·dal·wood /'sændlwʊd; 'sændlˌwʊd/ *n* [U] hard, sweet-smelling wood used for making fans,

caskets, etc. 檀香木(坚硬楠香的木材,用于制扇,盒子等)。

sand·wich /'sænwɪdʒ *US:* -wɪtʃ; 'sændwɪtʃ/ *n* [C] two slices of buttered bread with meat, etc between: 中间夹肉等并涂有牛油的两片面包;三明治: *ham/chicken/cheese, etc ~es.* 火腿(鸡肉,乳酪等)三明治。 '~·man /-mæn; -ˌmæn/ *n* (*pl* **-men**) man who walks about the streets with two advertisement boards, one hanging over his chest and the other over his back. 胸前及背后均挂一广告牌沿街的人; 夹板广告员。 '~·board *n* one of such boards. 夹板广告员背后或胸前所挂的广告牌。 ~ course, course of training with alternating periods of theoretical and practical study. 理论与实习交替配合之课程。 □ *vt* [VP6A, 14] ~ (**between**), put (one thing or person) between two others, esp when there is little space: 将(一物或一人)夹在(两物或两人)中间;插入: *I was ~ed between two very fat men on the bus.* 我在公共汽车上被夹在两个非常肥胖的人之间。

sane /seɪn; sen/ *adj* (**-r, -st**) **1** healthy in mind; not mad. 心智健全的;神志清楚的。 **2** sensible; balanced: 明智的;稳健的: *a ~ policy;* 稳健的政策; *~ views/judgement.* 明智的看法(判断)。 ~·ly *adv*

sang /sæŋ; sæŋ/ *pt* of **sing.**

sang froid /ˌsɑːŋ'frwɑː; ˌsɑˈfrwɑ/ *n* [U] (F) calmness in face of danger or in an emergency; composure. (法)(面临危险或危急时之)镇定;冷静;从容。

san·gui·nary /'sæŋgwɪnərɪ *US:* -nerɪ; 'sæŋgwɪnˌɛrɪ/ *adj* (formal, old use) (正式用语,旧用法) **1** with much bloodshed: 血腥的; 杀伤甚多的: *a ~ battle.* 血战。 **2** fond of bloodshed; delighting in cruel acts: 嗜杀的; 残暴的: *a ~ ruler.* 残暴的统治者。

san·guine /'sæŋgwɪn; 'sæŋgwɪn/ *adj* (formal) (正式用语) **1** hopeful; optimistic: 有望的; 乐天的: *~ of success;* 对成功抱乐观; *~ that we shall succeed.* 自信我们将成功。 **2** having a red complexion. 面色红润的。

sani·tarium /ˌsænɪˈteərɪəm; ˌsænəˈtɛrɪəm/ *n* (US) sanatorium; health resort. (美)疗养院;休养地。

sani·tary /'sænɪtərɪ *US:* -terɪ; 'sænəˌtɛrɪ/ *adj* **1** clean; free from dirt which might cause disease: 清洁的;无致病之污秽的: *poor ~ conditions in a camp.* 露营地的环境不清洁。 **2** of, concerned with, the protection of health: 保健的,有关保健的,卫生的: *a ~ inspector,* official whose duty it is to see that regulations for the protection of health are obeyed. 卫生检查员。 '~ towel/napkin, absorbent pad used during menstruation. 月经带。

sani·ta·tion /ˌsænɪˈteɪʃn; ˌsænəˈteʃən/ *n* [U] arrangements to protect public health, esp for the efficient disposal of sewage. 卫生;卫生设备(尤指下水道设备)。

san·ity /'sænɪtɪ; 'sænətɪ/ *n* [U] **1** health of mind. 心智健全;神智清明。 **2** soundness of judgement. 判断正确;明达。

sank /sæŋk; sæŋk/ *pt* of **sink**[2].

sans /sænz; sænz/ *prep* (colloq) without: (口)无; 缺乏: *S~ teeth, ~ eyes, ~ taste, ~ everything.* 无齿,无眼,无味,无一切。

San·skrit /'sænskrɪt; 'sænskrɪt/ *n* the ancient language of India; the literary language of Hinduism. 梵语;梵文(印度古语)。

Santa Claus /'sæntə klɔːz; 'sæntɪˌklɔz/ *n* (also 亦称 *Father Christmas*) person who, small children are told, puts toys in their stockings by night at Christmas. 圣诞老人(儿童们常听说,他会在圣诞夜放置玩具于他们的长统袜中)。

sap[1] /sæp; sæp/ *vt* (**-pp-**) [VP6A] weaken; drain away the life and strength of: 削弱; 使逐渐损坏; 耗竭⋯的生命和力量: *sapped by disease/an unhealthy climate.* 因疾病(有害健康之气候)而逐渐衰弱的。

sap[2] /sæp; sæp/ *n* [C] tunnel or covered trench made to get nearer to the enemy (eg in a military strongpoint or, formerly, a besieged town). (接近敌人之军事据点或昔时被围之城池的)地道;对壕。 'sap·head *n* end of a sap nearest to the enemy. (地道之最接近敌人的一

端)。 □ *vt, vi* (**-pp-**) [VP6A, 2A] make a sap or saps; weaken (a wall, etc) by digging under it; (fig) destroy or weaken (sb's faith, confidence, etc). 挖地道;在(墙等)下面挖掘而损坏之;(喻)打击或削弱(某人的信心,自信等)。 **sap·per** *n* soldier engaged in making saps or (mod use) in engineering, eg road and bridge building. 挖地道之士兵;(现代用法)工兵(如从事筑路造桥者)。

sap³ /sæp; sæp/ *n* (dated sl) silly person. (过时俚语)笨人;傻子。

sap⁴ /sæp; sæp/ *n* [U] **1** liquid in a plant, carrying food to all its parts: 树液(将养料输至各部分者): *The sap is beginning to rise in the maple-trees.* 树液开始在枫树中上升了。 **sap·wood** /'sæpwʊd; 'sæp,wʊd/ *n* soft, outer layers of wood. 边材(木之柔软的外层)。 **2** (fig) (anything that provides) vigour or energy. (喻)元气;精力;供给元气或精力之任何事物。 **sap·less** *adj* without sap; dry; lacking vigour. 无树液的;枯萎的;无精力的。 **sap·ling** /'sæplɪŋ; 'sæplɪŋ/ *n* young tree; (fig) young man. 幼树;(喻)青年人。 **sappy** *adj* (**-ier, -iest**) full of sap; young and vigorous. 多树液的;年富力强的。

sa·pi·ent /'seɪpɪənt; 'sepɪənt/ *adj* (liter) wise. (文)有智慧的。 **~·ly** *adv* **sa·pi·ence** /-əns; əns/ *n* (often ironic) wisdom. (常为反语)智慧。

Sap·phic /'sæfɪk; 'sæfɪk/ *adj* of the Greek lesbian poetess Sappho. (希腊女诗人)莎孚的;莎孚式的。 **~ verse/stanza/ode**, (prosody) with three lines that rhyme and one short line. (韵律学)莎孚式诗(诗节,赋)(三行押韵及一短行)。

sap·phire /'sæfaɪə(r); 'sæfaɪr/ *n* **1** [U] clear, bright blue jewel. 青玉;蓝宝石。 **2** [U] bright blue colour. 青玉色;蔚蓝色。

sara·band /'særəbænd; 'særə,bænd/ *n* [C] (piece of music for a) stately old Spanish dance. 莎拉邦舞(一种庄重的旧式西班牙舞);莎拉邦舞曲。

Sara·cen /'særəsn; 'særəsṇ/ *n* (name used by later Greeks and Romans for) Arab or Muslim of the time of the Crusades. 撒拉逊人;(后世希腊人和罗马人用以指十字军东征时之)阿拉伯人或伊斯兰教徒。

sar·casm /'sɑːkæzəm; 'sɑrkæzəm/ *n* [U] (use of) bitter remarks intended to wound the feelings; [C] such a remark; taunt that is ironically worded. 有意伤人感情的恶言;讥讽;讽刺之使用;讥讽;语含讽刺的嘲弄。 **sar·cas·tic** /sɑː'kæstɪk; sɑr'kæstɪk/ *adj* of, using, ~. 讥讽的;使用讥讽的。 **sar·cas·ti·cally** /-klɪ; -klɪ/ *adv*

sar·copha·gus /sɑː'kɒfəgəs; sɑr'kɒfəgəs/ *n* (*pl* -**gi** /-gaɪ; -dʒaɪ/, ~**es** /-gəsɪz; -gəsɪz/) stone coffin (esp as used in ancient times). 石棺(尤指古代所用者)。 ⇨ the illus at **mummy**. 参看 mummy 之插图。

sar·dine /sɑː'diːn; sɑr'din/ *n* small fish (a young pilchard), usu preserved and tinned in oil or tomato sauce. 沙丁鱼 (通常浸于油中或蕃茄酱装罐保藏之)。 *packed like ~s*, closely crowded together. 拥挤不堪。

sar·donic /sɑː'dɒnɪk; sɑr'dɑnɪk/ *adj* mocking; scornful: 讽刺的;讥诮的: *a ~ smile/laugh/expression.* 嘲弄的微笑(大笑,表情)。 **sar·doni·cally** /-klɪ; -klɪ/ *adv*

sari /'sɑːrɪ; 'sɑrɪ/ *n* (*pl* ~**s**) length of cotton or silk cloth draped round the body, worn by Hindu women. 莎丽服(印度女人披裹身上的一段棉布或绸布)。

sa·rong /sə'rɒŋ US: -'rɔːŋ; sə'rɔŋ/ *n* long strip of cotton or silk material worn as a skirt round the middle of the body, tucked round the waist, the national garment of Malays and Indonesians (men and women). 沙龙(裹于身体中部之长条棉布或绸布,在腰际折入,是马来人和印尼人的民族服装);马来围裙。

sar·sa·pa·rilla /ˌsɑːspə'rɪlə; ˌsɑrspə'rɪlə/ *n* [U] (tonic drink made from the roots of a) tropical American plant. 撒尔沙,摈榔(一种热带美洲产的植物);(用撒尔沙根做成之)清凉汽水;沙士。

sar·tor·ial /sɑː'tɔːrɪəl; sɑr'tɔrɪəl/ *adj* concerned

a sari   a sarong   a kimono

with (the making of) men's clothes: 男装;缝制男装的: *~ elegance.* 男性服装的优雅。

sash¹ /sæʃ; sæʃ/ *n* [C] long strip of cloth worn round the waist or over one shoulder for ornament or as part of a uniform. 腰带;肩带(用作装饰或作为制服的一部分)。

sash² /sæʃ; sæʃ/ *n* ~ **window**, one that slides up and down (instead of opening outwards like a casement). 上下拉动的窗子(非如一般开阖窗户之向外推开)。 ⇨ the illus at **window**. 参看 window 之插图。 **'~-cord/-line** *n* strong cord (with a weight at one end) running over a pulley to keep the window balanced in any desired position. 曳窗绳(用以上下拉动窗户,一端有坠子的结实的绳子,滚动滑车以使该窗户在任何所希望的位置保持平衡)。

Sas·sen·ach /'sæsənæk; 'sæsn,æk/ *n* (derog or hum) (name used by the Scots for an) English person. (贬或谐)撒克逊人(为苏格兰人对英格兰人之称呼)。

sassy /'sæsɪ; 'sæsɪ/ *adj* (US colloq) lively; stylish. (美口)有生气的;漂亮的。

sat /sæt; sæt/ *pt, pp* of **sit**.

Satan /'seɪtn; 'setṇ/ *n* the Evil One, the Devil. 撒旦;恶魔。 **~·ic** /sə'tænɪk US: seɪ-; se'tænɪk/ *adj* **1** of ~: 撒旦的;恶魔的: *His ~ic Majesty*, (hum) Satan. (谐)撒旦。 **2** (small **s**) wicked; evil. (小写 s) 邪恶的;如恶魔的。

satchel /'sætʃl; 'sætʃəl/ *n* small bag for carrying light articles, esp school books. 小皮包;小帆布袋(用于携带经便东西,尤用于上下学携带书籍);书包。

sate /seɪt; set/ *vt* [VP6A] =**satiate**.

sat·el·lite /'sætəlaɪt; 'sætḷ,aɪt/ *n* **1** comparatively small body moving in orbit round a planet; moon; artificial object, eg a spacecraft, put in orbit round a celestial body: 卫星;人造卫星: *com,muni'cations ~*, for relaying back to the earth telephone messages, radio and TV signals. 通信卫星。 **2** (fig, often attrib) person, state, depending upon and taking the lead from another. (喻,常用作定语)追随者;附庸国。 **'~ town**, one built to take the excess population of another. 卫星城镇(用以疏散大城市之人口过剩者)。

sati·able /'seɪʃəbl; 'seʃɪəbl/ *adj* (formal) that can be fully satisfied. (正式用语)可使满足的;可使饱的。

sati·ate /'seɪʃɪeɪt; 'seʃɪ,et/ *vt* [VP6A] (formal) satisfy fully; cloy; weary (oneself) with too much: (正式用语)使满足;使饱;(因过多而)使(自己)厌腻: *be ~ed with food/pleasure.* 因过多食物(享乐)而厌腻。

sat·iety /sə'taɪətɪ; sə'taɪətɪ/ *n* [U] (formal) condition or feeling of being satiated: (正式用语)满足;饱足;厌腻: *indulge in pleasure to the point of ~.* 耽于享乐而达厌腻的程度。

satin /'sætɪn US: sætn; 'sætɪn/ *n* [U] silk material smooth and shiny on one side: 缎(一面光滑的丝织品): (attrib) (用作定语): *~ dresses/ribbons.* 缎子衣服(缎带)。 □ *adj* smooth like ~. 光泽如缎的。

sat·in·wood /'sætɪnwʊd US: 'sætṇ-; 'sætṇ,wʊd/ *n* [U] smooth, hard wood of a tropical tree, used for furniture. 缎木(一种热带树的光滑硬木材,用以做家具)。

sat·ire /'sætaɪə(r); 'sætaɪr/ n 1 [U] form of writing holding up a person or society to ridicule, or showing the foolishness or wickedness of an idea, customs, etc. 讽刺文体(讥笑个人或社会, 或揭露观念、习俗等的愚昧)。 2 [C] piece of writing that does this; sth that exposes false pretensions: 讽刺作品; 讽刺诗; 讽刺: *Are our lives sometimes a ~ upon our religious beliefs?* 我们的生命有时是我们宗教信仰的一种讽刺吗? **sa·tiri·cal** /sə'tɪrɪkl; sə'tɪrɪkl/ adj containing, fond of, using, ~; mocking. 含有讽刺的; 喜好讽刺的; 嘲弄的。 **sa·tiri·cally** /-klɪ; -klɪ/ adv **sat·ir·ist** /'sætərɪst; 'sætərɪst/ n person who writes ~s. 讽刺作家。 **sat·ir·ize** /'sætəraɪz; 'sætəraɪz/ vt [VP6A] attack with ~(s); describe satirically. 以讽刺文或作品攻击; 讽刺地描写。

sat·is·fac·tion /ˌsætɪs'fækʃn; ˌsætɪs'fækʃən/ n 1 [U] the state of being satisfied, pleased or contented; act of satisfying: 满意; 满足; 令人满意的举动: *feel ~ at having one's ability recognized;* 由于自己的才能得到赏识而感得满足; *have the ~ of being successful in life;* 一生成功觉得心满意足; *pass an examination to one's own ~ and to the ~ of one's friends;* 通过考试使自己和友人都感到满意; *the ~ of one's hopes/desires/ambitions.* 希望(欲望, 野心)的实现。 2 (with indef art, but rarely pl) sth that satisfies: (与不定冠词连用, 但罕用复数)令人满意之事物: *Your success will be a great ~ to your parents.* 你的成功将使你的父母极感满意。 *It is a ~ to know that he is well again.* 得悉他已痊愈, 深感欣慰。 3 [U] (opportunity of getting) revenge or compensation for an injury or insult: 报复; 补偿; 报复或补偿的机会: *give ~s/demand/obtain ~.* 给予某人(要求, 获得)补偿。 *The angry man demanded ~ but the other refused it,* would neither apologize nor fight. 那愤怒的人要求决斗, 但对方拒绝了(既不肯道歉也不肯决斗)。

sat·is·fac·tory /ˌsætɪs'fæktərɪ; ˌsætɪs'fæktrɪ/ adj giving pleasure or satisfaction; satisfying a need or desire; good enough for a purpose: 令人满意的; 满足需要或欲望的; 圆满的; 良好的: *The result of the experiment was ~.* 实验的结果令人满意。 *We want ~ reasons for your failure to help.* 我们要知道你未能协助的充分理由。 **sat·is·fac·tor·ily** /-tərəlɪ; -trəlɪ/ adv in a ~ manner: 令人满意地; 圆满地: *The patient is getting on satisfactorily.* 病人康复得令人满意。

sat·isfy /'sætɪsfaɪ; 'sætɪs,faɪ/ vt, vi (pt, pp -**fied**) 1 [VP6A, 2A] make contented; give (sb) what he wants or needs: 使满足; 使(某人)的需求: *Nothing satisfies him; he's always complaining.* 任何事物都不能使他满足; 他总是抱怨。 *Riches do not always ~.* 财富并不能永远使人满足。 ~ *the examiners,* just reach the lowest standard needed for passing an examination. 刚好达到及格的最低标准; 考及格。 2 [VP6A, 2A] be enough for (one's needs); be equal to (what one hopes for or desires): 足够(自己的需要); 达到(所期望或欲求者): ~ *one's hunger.* 充饥。 3 [VP6A, 11, 14] ~ *sb (that.../of sth),* convince; make free from doubt: 使确信; 使消除疑虑: *He satisfied me that he could do the work well.* 他使我确信他能把工作做好。 *Have you satisfied yourself of the truth of the report?* 你确信那报告的真实性吗? ~*·ing adj* giving satisfaction: 使满意的; 令人满足的: *a ~ing meal.* 令人满意的一顿饭。 ~*·ing·ly adv*

sa·trap /'sætræp; 'seɪtræp/ n governor of a province in the ancient Persian empire. (古波斯帝国的)省长。

sat·suma /'sæt'su:mə; ˌsæt'sumə/ n tangerine. 小蜜柑; 红橘。

satu·rate /'sætʃəreɪt; 'sætʃə,ret/ vt [VP6A, 14] ~ (*with/in*), 1 make thoroughly wet; soak with moisture; cause to take in as much as possible of sth: 浸; 浸透; 浸湿; 使吸收最饱和物: *We were caught in the rain and came home ~d.* 我们途中遇雨, 回到家全身都湿透了。 *They lay on the beach and were ~d with sunshine.* 他们躺在沙滩上, 沐浴在阳光里。 *He is ~d with Greek*

history. 他精通希腊史。 2 be unable to take any more: 饱和; 饱和状态: *The market for used cars is ~d.* 旧车买卖市场已趋饱和。 3 (chem) cause (one substance) to absorb the greatest possible amount of another: (化学)使(一物质)吸收他物达于饱和: *a ~d solution of salt.* 饱和的食盐溶液。 **satu·ra·tion** /ˌsætʃə'reɪʃn; ˌsætʃə'reʃən/ n [U] state of being ~d. 浸渍, 饱和状态。

saturation bombing, bombing so that everything in the target area is totally destroyed. 饱和轰炸(完全炸毁)。 **satu'ration point,** (chem) the stage at which, if more of one substance is added to another, they will not unite completely: (化学)饱和点(过此阶段时, 再加某一物质于另一物质, 这两种物质就不能完全混合): *The saturation point of a hot liquid is higher than that of a cold one,* eg more sugar can be dissolved in hot tea than in cold tea; (fig) stage at which no more can be absorbed or accepted. 热液的饱和点高于冷液(例如热茶比冷茶能溶解更多的糖); (喻)饱和阶段。

Sat·ur·day /'sætədɪ; 'sætədɪ/ n the seventh and last day of the week. 星期六; 土曜日。

Sat·urn /'sætən; 'sætən/ n 1 (astron) large planet encircled by rings. (天文)土星。 ⇔ the illus at **planet.** 参看 planet 之插图。 2 (myth) ancient Roman god of agriculture. (神话)(古罗马之)农神。

satu·rna·lia /ˌsætə'neɪlɪə; ˌsætə'nelɪə/ n pl 1 S~, yearly festival of the god Saturn, held in ancient Rome in December, a time of wild merry-making. (大写 S)农神节(古罗马于十二月庆祝者, 为一年一度之狂欢期)。 2 [C] time of wild revelry or disorder. 狂欢或喧嚣之时节。

sat·ur·nine /'sætənaɪn; 'sætə,naɪn/ adj (liter) gloomy. (文)忧郁的; 阴沉的。

satyr /'sætə(r); 'sætə/ n 1 (Gk and Roman myth) god of the woods, half man and half animal. (希腊及罗马神话)半人半兽的森林之神。 2 man with uncontrolled sexual desires. 性欲无度之男人。 **sa·tyric** /sə'tɪrɪk; sə'tɪrɪk/ adj of or like ~. 色情狂的; 淫欲的。

sauce /sɔ:s; sɔs/ n 1 [C, U] (kind of) liquid or semi-liquid preparation served with some kinds of food to give a relish or flavour: (一种)调味汁; 酱汁: *spaghetti and tomato ~;* 意大利面条和蕃茄酱; *fruit pudding and brandy ~.* 水果布丁和白兰地调味汁。 *What is ~ for the goose is ~ for the gander.* (prov) what applies in one case must apply in an identical or similar case. (谚)适用于某种情况者, 亦必适用于类似情况。 '~**-boat** n vessel in which ~ is served at table. 餐桌上盛调味汁的器皿。 2 [U] (colloq) impudence (usu amusing rather than annoying): (口)无礼; 莽撞(通常为有趣而非令人恼怒者): *None of your ~! Don't be impertinent.* 不可莽撞! 放规矩点! 别无礼! *How impudent!* 多么无礼! 真没规矩! □ vt [VP6A] (colloq) be impudent to: (口)对…无礼或莽撞: *How dare you ~ your mother?* 你怎敢对令堂无礼? **saucy** adj (-ier, -iest) 1 impudent. 无礼的; 莽撞的。 2 (colloq) smart-looking: (口)时髦的; 漂亮的; 俏俏的: *a saucy little hat.* 一顶漂亮的小帽。 **sauc·ily** adv **sauci·ness** n

sauce·pan /'sɔ:spən US: -pæn; 'sɔs,pæn/ n deep metal cooking pot, usu round and with a lid and a handle. 深金属锅(通常为圆形, 有盖及柄)。

saucer /'sɔ:sə(r); 'sɔsə/ n 1 small curved dish on which a cup stands. 茶杯碟; 茶托。 '~**-eyed** adj with large, round, wide-opened eyes, eg as the result of surprise. 眼睛睁得大而圆的 (例如由于惊讶的缘故)。 ,**flying** '~, ⇔ flying. 2 ~-shaped disc (also called a *dish*) of a radio telescope. (无线电望远镜之)碟形盘。 3 depression in the ground. 凹洼; 洼地。

sauer·kraut /'sauəkraut; 'saur,kraut/ n [U] (G) cabbage cut up, salted and allowed to ferment until sour. (德)泡菜(包心菜切细, 加盐使发酵变酸)。

sauna /'saunə; 'saunə/ n steam bath or bath-house as in Finland. (芬兰等地之)蒸气浴; 蒸气浴室。

saun·ter /'sɔːntə(r); 'sɔntɚ/ vi [VP2A, C] walk in a leisurely way: 闲逛; 漫步: ~ along Oxford Street window-shopping. 沿牛津街漫步浏览商店橱窗. □ n quiet, unhurried walk or pace: 漫步; 闲逛: come at a ~. 漫步走来. ~er n person who ~s. 漫步者; 闲逛者.

saur·ian /'sɔːrɪən; 'sɔrɪən/ n, adj (one) of the order of lizards including crocodiles, lizards and some extinct kinds. 蜥蜴类动物(包括鳄鱼, 蜥蜴及若干已绝种的爬虫动物); 蜥蜴类动物的.

saus·age /'sɔsɪdʒ US: 'sɔːs-; 'sɔsɪdʒ/ n [U] chopped up meat, etc flavoured and stuffed into a casing or tube of thin skin; some kinds sliced and eaten raw, others cooked and eaten hot; [C] one section of such a tube. 腊肠; 香肠; 一段腊肠或香肠. '~-dog, (GB colloq) dachshund. (英口)腊肠狗(一种短腿长身的小狗); 猎腊狗. '~-meat n meat for making ~. 用来做腊肠的碎肉. ~-'roll n ~ in minced a covering of pastry. 腊肠卷(一种用面皮包腊肠馅做成的点心).

sauté /'sɔuteɪ US: sɔu'teɪ; so'te/ adj (F) (of food) quickly fried in a little fat: (法)(指食物, 用少量的油)炒的; 嫩煎的: ~ potatoes. 煎马铃薯. □ vt fry food in this way. 炒; 嫩煎.

sav·age /'sævɪdʒ; 'sævɪdʒ/ adj 1 in a primitive or uncivilized state: 野蛮的; 未开化的: ~ customs. 野蛮的风俗. 2 fierce; cruel: 凶猛的; 残酷的: a ~ dog. 恶犬; make a ~ attack on sb: 猛烈攻击某人. ~ criticism. 猛烈的批评. 3 (colloq) very angry. (口)愤怒的. □ n ~ person, esp a member of a primitive tribe living by hunting and fishing. 野人; 野蛮人(尤指靠渔猎为生之蛮族). □ vt [VP6A] attack, bite, trample on: 表击; 乱咬; 乱踏: The man was badly ~d by his mare. 那人被他的母马伤得很严重. ~·ly adv ~·ness n ~ry /'sævɪdʒrɪ; 'sævɪdʒrɪ/ n [U] the state of being ~; behaviour: 野蛮状态; 未开化; 凶恶; 残酷; 野蛮或残酷的行为: living in ~ry; 生活在野蛮状态中; treat conquered enemies with great ~ry. 残忍酷地对待被征服的敌人.

sa·van·na(h) /sə'vænə; sə'vænə/ n [C] treeless, grassy plain, in tropical and subtropical America and E and W Africa. (热带和亚热带美洲及东西非洲地区之)无树的平原; 热带草原. ⇨ pampas, prairie, steppe, veld.

sa·vant /'sævənt US: sæ'vɑːnt; sə'vɑnt/ n person of great learning. 博学之士; 学者; 专家.

save[1] /seɪv; sev/ vt, vi 1 [VP6A, 14] ~ (from), make or keep safe (from loss, injury, etc): 援救; 拯救; 保全(以免损失, 伤害等): ~ sb from drowning; 救人于溺; ~ sb's life; 救某人的性命; ~ a person from himself, from the results of his own foolishness. 救某人免于自食恶果. ~ one's bacon, ⇨ bacon. ~ one's face, ~ face[1](4). ~ one's skin, avoid, often by cowardice, the risk of loss, injury, etc. 避免损失, 伤害等之危险(常出于胆怯). ~ the situation, deal successfully with a situation which seems hopeless. 挽回局势; 度过难关. 2 [VP2A, C, 3A, 6A, 12B, 13B, 14, 15B] ~ (up)(for sth); ~ sth (up) (for sth), keep for future use: 储存; 贮蓄: ~ (up) money for a holiday; 储钱度假; ~ part of one's salary each month; 贮蓄每月薪水的一部分; ~ some of the meat for tomorrow; 留下一些肉明天吃; ~ me some ice-cream/~ some ice-cream for me; 给我留点冰淇淋; ~ for one's old age. 存钱防老. He has never ~d, never put money by for the future. 他从不储蓄. He is saving himself/saving his strength for the heavy work he'll have to do this afternoon. 他在养精蓄锐以应付今日下午他必须做的繁重工作. ~ for a rainy day, ⇨ rainy. 3 [VP6A, D, 12C] make unnecessary; relieve (sb) from the need of using: 省去; 节省: If you walk to the office every morning, you'll ~ spending money on bus fares. 每天早上步行上班; 可省去公共汽车费. That will ~ you 50 pence a week. 那将可使你每星期节省五十便士. That will ~ us a lot of trouble. 那将可免除我们许多麻烦. We've been ~d a lot of expense by doing the work ourselves. 我们自己做那工作, 节省了一大笔开销. Do

you use modern labour-saving devices in your home? ie machines that make work (eg cleaning, cooking) in the home quicker and easier. 贵府使用节省劳力的现代化设备吗? 4 [VP6A, 14, 2A] ~ sb (from sth), (in the Christian religion) set free from the power of (or the eternal punishment for) sin: (基督教)拯救; 赦罪: Jesus Christ came into the world to ~ sinners from their sins. 耶稣基督来到这世界拯救罪人. 5 [VP6A] make a reservation concerning (sth): 作有关(某事物)之保留: a saving clause, one that stipulates an exemption, etc. 保留条款(规定免除事项等). □ n (in football, etc) act of preventing the scoring of a goal: (足球等)阻碍对方得分之动作; 救球: Banks made a brilliant ~. 班克斯漂亮地救了一球. ~r n person who ~s: 救助者; 拯救者; 俭省人; ~r of souls, eg a priest; 灵魂的拯救者(例如牧师); means of saving: 节省…的器具: This device is a useful 'time-~r. 这是个有用的省时装置. Some machines are ~rs of labour. 有些机器是节省劳力的工具. **sav·ing** adj (esp) that redeems or compensates. (尤指)弥补的; 补偿的. **saving grace**, good quality that redeems a person whose other qualities are not all good: 可弥补个人缺点的优良天性: He has the saving grace of humour. 他有幽默的长处. □ n 1 way of saving; amount ~d: 节省; 储存; 节省或储蓄的金钱: a useful saving of time and money. 一种有益的节省时间和金钱. 2 (pl) money ~d up: (复)储金; 储蓄: keep one's savings in the Post Office. 把储蓄的钱存在邮政局. **'savings account** n (with a bank) on which interest is paid. 储蓄存款; 储蓄帐户. **'savings-bank** n bank which holds, and gives interest on, small savings. 储蓄银行.

save[2] /seɪv; sev/ (also **sav·ing** /'seɪvɪŋ; 'sevɪŋ/) preps except: 除…外: all save him. 除他以外全体. We know nothing about him save that he was in the army during the war. 我们除了知道他在战时曾在陆军服务以外, 其他一无所知.

sav·eloy /'sævəlɔɪ; 'sævə,lɔɪ/ n [C] kind of highly-seasoned pork sausage. 一种味道很浓的猪肉腊肠.

sav·ing /'seɪvɪŋ; 'sevɪŋ/ prep = save[2].

sav·iour (US = -ior) /'seɪvɪə(r); 'sevjɚ/ n person who rescues or saves sb from danger. 拯救者; 救助者. **The S~, Our S~,** Jesus Christ. 救世主(耶稣基督)

savoir-faire /,sævwɑː 'feə(r); ,sævwɑr'fɛr/ n [U] (F) social tact; knowledge of how to behave in any situation. (法)社交手腕; 机敏; 圆滑.

sa·vory /'seɪvərɪ; 'sevərɪ/ n [U] herb of the mint family used in cooking; (US) (美) = savoury. (一种用于烹饪的)香薄荷.

sa·vour (US = -vor) /'seɪvə(r); 'sevɚ/ n [C, U] ~ of, taste or flavour (of sth); suggestion (of a quality): (某物的)味道; 滋味; 风味; (某种性质的)迹象; 意味: soup with a ~ of garlic. 有大蒜味道的汤. His political views have a ~ of fanaticism. 他的政治见解带有狂热的意味. □ vt, vi 1 [VP6A] (lit or fig) appreciate the taste or flavour or character of: (字面或喻)欣赏…的味道或风味: He ~ed the wine/the joke. 他品嗜酒的味道(咀嚼一笑话的妙处). 2 [VP3A] ~ of, suggest the presence of: 具有…的意味: Such a proposal ~s of impertinence. 这样的建议带有莽撞的意味.

sa·voury (US = -vory) /'seɪvərɪ; 'sevərɪ/ adj having an appetizing taste or smell; (of food dishes) having a salt or sharp, not a sweet, taste: 开胃的; 可口的; 香喷喷的; (指菜肴)咸的; 辛辣的: a ~ omelette. 可口的蛋卷. □ n [C] (pl -ries) ~ dish, esp one taken at the start or end of a meal. 开胃或助消化的菜(尤指餐前或餐后所吃者).

sa·voy /sə'vɔɪ; sə'vɔɪ/ n [C, U] (kind of) winter cabbage with wrinkled leaves. (一种)皱叶甘蓝; 皱叶卷心菜.

savvy /'sævɪ; 'sævɪ/ vi (sl) know, understand. (俚)知道; 了解. **no ~**, I do not know/understand. 我不知道; 不懂. □ n [U] (sl) wits; understanding: (俚)机智; 头脑; 理解: Where's your ~? 你的头脑到那里去了?

saw¹ /sɔː/; sɔ/ pt of **see¹**.

saw² /sɔː/; sɔ/ n [C] (kinds of) tool with a sharp-toothed edge, for cutting wood, metal, stone, etc worked by hand or mechanically. 锯. **'saw·dust** n [U] tiny bits of wood falling off when wood is being sawn. 锯屑; 木屑. **'saw·horse** n frame of wood for supporting wood that is being sawn. 锯木架. **'saw·mill** n mill with power operated saws. 锯木厂; 制材厂. **'saw·pit** n pit in which a man stands guiding the lower part of a large hand-saw (= *pit-saw*) for sawing logs, the upper part being guided by another man at an upper level. 锯木坑 (人立其中操作一锯较低之一端, 较高之另一端由另外一人操作). □ vt, vi (pt **sawed** /sɔːd; sɔd/ pp **sawn** /sɔːn; sɔn/ and (US) **sawed**) 1 [VP6A, 15A, B, 2A] cut with a saw; make (boards, etc) with a saw; use a saw: 锯; 锯成 (木板等); 用锯: *saw wood*; 锯木材; *saw a log into planks*, 把圆木锯成厚板; *saw a log in two*. 把木头锯成两截. *saw sth off*, cut off with a saw: 锯掉(某物): *saw a branch of a tree*; 锯掉树枝; *a sawn-off shotgun*, one with (most of) the barrel sawn off (as used by criminals for ease of concealment and carrying). 枪管锯短的枪(例如罪犯为便于隐藏或携带所用者). *saw sth up*, cut into pieces with a saw: 把某物锯成小块: *sawn-up timber*, timber that has been sawn into planks (contrasted with logs). 已锯成厚板的木材(与圆木相对). 2 [VP2A, C, 6A] move backward and forward: 往复移动: *sawing at his fiddle*, using his bow as if it were a saw. 往复地拉提琴. 3 [VP2A] capable of being sawn: 可被锯开: *This wood saws easily*. 此木材容易锯开. **saw·yer** /'sɔːjə(r); 'sɔjɚ/ 'sɔjɚ/ n man whose work is sawing wood. 锯木匠.

saw³ /sɔː/; sɔ/ n [C] proverbial saying. 格言; 谚语.

sax /sæks; sæks/ n (abbr of) saxophone. 为 saxophone 之略.

sax·horn /'sækshɔːn; 'sæks,hɔrn/ n musical instrument made of brass, like a bugle, made in various sizes. 萨克斯号(铜制的喇叭, 有多种尺寸).

saxi·frage /'sæksɪfrɪdʒ; 'sæksəfrɪdʒ/ n [U] kinds of Alpine or rock plant with white, yellow or red flowers. 虎耳草(生于高山或岩石间, 开白、黄或红花).

Saxon /'sæksn; 'sæksən/ n, adj (member, language) of a people once living in NW Germany, some of whom conquered and settled in Britain in the 5th and 6th cc. (昔时居住于德国西北部, 其中部分人于五至六世纪时征服并定居英国)萨克逊人(的); 萨克逊语(的).

saxo·phone /'sæksəfəʊn; 'sæksə,fon/ n (colloq abbr 口语作 *sax*) musical wind instrument with a reed in the mouthpiece and keys for the fingers, made of brass. 萨克斯管(一种铜管乐器). ⇨ the illus at **brass**. 参看 brass 之插图. **sax·ophon·ist** /sæk'sɒfənɪst US: 'sæksəfəʊnɪst; 'sæksə,fonɪst/ n ~ player. 萨克斯管吹奏者.

say /seɪ; se/ vt, vi (3rd pers, pres t **says** /sez; sɛz/, pt, pp **said** /sed; sɛd/) [VP6A, 14, 9, 10] 1 **say sth (to sb)**, utter, make (a specified word or remark); use one's voice to produce (words, sentences): 言; 说(某字或话); 讲(辞, 句): *Be polite and say 'Please' and 'Thank you'*. 要有礼貌, 并且要说'请'和'谢谢你'. *Did you say anything?* 你说了什么话吗? *He said that his friend's name was Sam*. 他说他朋友的名字叫山姆. *Everyone was saying what a handsome couple they made*. 大家都说他们是郎才女貌的一对. *Everyone said how well I was looking*. 人人都说我气色非常好. *I've something to say to you*, to tell you. 我有话要对你说. *I wouldn't say no to a glass of beer*, would accept one willingly. 我愿意喝杯啤酒. *You may well say so*, you are right. 你那样说很对(你说得对). *So you say* (implying that the speaker may be mistaken). 你是那么说的(暗示对方可能有错). *go without saying*, be obvious: 不用说; 不待言: *It goes without saying that country life is healthier than town life*. 乡村生活比城市生活更有益于健康, 自不待言. *have nothing/anything to say for oneself*, ie in one's own

defence: 无可辩白(需要辩白): *Well, what have you to say for yourself*, What can you say to explain or defend your conduct? 你还有何话说? *say the word*, express agreement: 表示同意: *You've only to say the word* (eg say 'Yes') *and the money's yours*, ie I will let you have it. 只要你说声同意, 那笔钱就是你的了. *say a good word for sb/sth*, commend; praise: 推荐; 夸奖某人或某事物: *He hasn't a good word to say for anybody*. 他从不称赞任何人. *say what one has to say*, finish what one has to say: 说完所要说的话: *Have you said your say yet?* 你要说的话说完了吗? *that is to say*, in other words: 换言之; 即: *three weeks tomorrow, that's to say, the 10th of May*. 三个星期后的明天, 也就是说, 五月十日. *What do you say (to sth/doing sth)?* What do you think (about...)? 你想不想...; 你认为...如何? *What do you say to a walk/to going round to my mother's?* 你想不想去散散步(到我母亲那里去走走)? *I say*, exclamation used to draw attention, open a conversation or express surprise. 我说: 哎呀(用于引起注意, 开始谈话或表示惊讶的感叹语). *They say; It's said*, forms used to introduce reports, rumours, etc: 据说(用以引述传闻谣言等的语辞): *They say/It's said that he's a miser*. 据说他是小气鬼. 2 (also [VP10] esp neg and interr) suppose; estimate; form and give an opinion concerning: (亦用作VP10, 尤用于否定及疑问句中)假定; 估计; 姑且说; 形成并说出有关...的意见: *There is no saying when this war will end*. 天晓得这场战争何时会结束. *And so say all of us*, that is the opinion of all of us. 我们全体抱那种看法. *You may learn to play the violin in, let's say, three years*. 你大概要三年才可以学会拉小提琴. □ n (only in the following) (仅用于下列各短语中) *have/say one's say*, express one's opinion; state one's views: 表达意见; 陈述观点: *Let him have his say*. 让他表达他的意见吧. *have a/no/not much, etc 'say in the matter*, have some/no/not much right or opportunity to share in a discussion, decision, express one's opinions, etc: 在该事件中有若干(没有, 不大有)权利或机会参加讨论、决定、表示自己的意见等: *He didn't have much say in deciding where they should spend their holidays*. 对于他们去哪里度假, 他没多少决定的权利. **say·ing** /'seɪɪŋ; 'seɪŋ/ n remark commonly made; well-known phrase, proverb, etc: 谚语; 格言; 名言: *'More haste, less speed'*, *as the saying goes*. 谚云, '欲速则不达'

scab /skæb; skæb/ n 1 [C] dry crust formed over a wound or sore. (创口上结的)疤; 痂. 2 [U] (=*scabies*) skin disease (esp of sheep). 癣; (尤指羊的)疥癣. 3 [C] (colloq) workman who refuses to join a strike, or his trade union, or who takes a striker's place; blackleg. (口)不参加罢工的工人; 不加入工会的工人; 取代罢工者之职位的工人; 破坏罢工者. **scabby** adj covered with scabs(1) 结痂的.

scab·bard /'skæbəd; 'skæbəd/ n sheath for the blade of a sword, dagger or bayonet. (剑、匕首或刺刀的)鞘. ⇨ the illus at **sword**. 参看 sword 之插图.

sca·bies /'skeɪbiːz; 'skeɪbi,iz/ n [U] kind of skin disease causing itching. 疥疮(引起发痒的一种皮肤病).

sca·bi·ous /'skeɪbɪəs; 'skeɪbɪəs/ n kinds of wild and cultivated plant with delicately coloured flowers. 山萝卜; 轮峰菊(花色优美的多种野生和栽培植物).

scab·rous /'skeɪbrəs US: 'skæb-; 'skebrəs/ adj 1 (of animals, plants, etc) having a rough surface. (指动植物等)表面粗糙的; 不平滑的. 2 (of subjects) difficult to write delicately about. (指题目)难以写得委婉的. 3 indelicate; salacious: 粗鄙的; 猥亵的: *a ~ novel*. 一本猥亵的小说.

scads /skædz; skædz/ n pl (sing or pl) (单或复) **~ (of)**, (US colloq) large quantity (of): (美口)大量; 许多: *~ of money/people*. 许多钱(人).

scaf·fold /'skæfəʊld; 'skæfld/ n [C] 1 structure put up for workmen and materials around a building which is being erected or repaired. (建筑或修缮房屋时四周所搭的)施工架; 鹰架. 2 platform on which criminals

are executed: 断头台; 绞台: *go to the* ~, be executed. 上绞台; 被处死。 ~*ing* /'skæfəldɪŋ; 'skæfḷdɪŋ/ *n* [U] (materials for a) ~ (1) (eg poles and planks, or *tubular* ~*ing*, metal tubes to be bolted together). 施工架; 鹰架; 搭施工架或鹰架用的材料(例如长竿和厚板,或用螺栓结合在一起的金属管)。

scal·a·wag /'skæləwæg; 'skæləˌwæg/ *n* (US) (美)= **scallywag**.

scald /skɔːld; skɔld/ *vt* [VP6A] **1** burn with hot liquid or steam: 烫伤; ~ *one's hand with hot fat*. 被热油烫伤手。 *He was* ~*ed to death when the boiler exploded.* 汽锅爆炸时,他被烫死了。 ~*ing tears*, tears of deep and bitter grief. 热泪; 血泪。 **2** clean (dishes, etc) with boiling water or steam. 以沸水或蒸气清洗(碟子等)。 **3** heat (milk) almost to boiling-point. 煮热(牛奶)几达沸点。 □ *n* injury to the skin from hot liquid or steam: 烫伤: *an ointment for burns and* ~*s.* 治疗烫伤的油膏。

scale[1] /skeɪl; skel/ *n* **1** [C] one of the thin overlapping plates of hard material that cover the skin of many fish and reptiles: (鱼及爬虫的)鳞: *scrape the* ~ *off a herring.* 刮去一条青鱼的鳞。 ⇨ the illus at **fish**. 参看 fish 之插图。 **2** [C] scale-like outer piece on an organic or other object, eg a flake of skin that loosens and comes off the body in some diseases; a flake of rust on iron. 鳞状物(例如在某些疾病中自身体脱下的皮屑); 鳞屑; 铁锈屑。 *remove the* ~*s from sb's eyes*, (fig) enable sb who has been deceived to realize the true state of affairs. (喻)使已受骗者认清真相。 **3** [U] chalky deposit inside boilers, kettles, waterpipes, etc (from the lime in hard water); deposit of tartar on teeth. 水垢; 锈皮; 水锈(为硬水中之石灰积存于锅, 壶, 水管等的内壁上的白垩质沉淀物); 齿垢。 □ *vt, vi* **1** [VP6A, 15A, B] cut or scrape ~s from (eg fish) (but *de*~ a boiler or kettle). 刮除(鱼等)之鳞(但除去锅或壶之水垢则用 descale)。 **2** [VP2C] ~ *off*, come off in flakes: 一片片剥落: *paint / plaster scaling off a wall.* 自墙上剥落的油漆(灰泥)。 **scaly** *adj* covered with ~ or ~s; coming off in ~s: 覆有鳞; 鳞状物的; 剥落如鳞的: *a kettle scaly with rust.* 生有锈皮的水壶。

scale[2] /skeɪl; skel/ *n* [C] **1** series of marks at regular intervals for the purpose of measuring (as on a ruler or a thermometer): 尺度; 分度; 刻度(例如尺或温度计上者): *This ruler has one* ~ *in centimetres and another in inches.* 这把尺有厘米的刻度和英寸的刻度。 **2** ruler or other tool or instrument marked in this way. 有刻度之尺或度量器。 **3** system of units for measuring: 度量制; 记数法: *the 'decimal* ~. 十进度量制。 **4** arrangement in steps or degrees: 阶段; 等级: *a* ~ *of wages*; 工资之等级; *a person who is high in the social* ~; 一位社会地位高的人; *sink in the* ~, fall to a lower level. 降至下级。 **sliding** ~, ⇨ **slide**[2](4). **5** proportion between the size of sth and the map, diagram, etc which represents it: (实物与地图,图解等代表实物间的比例); 比例尺; 缩尺: *a map on the* ~ *of ten kilometres to the centimetre*; 按照一厘米代表十公里之比例绘成的一张地图; *drawn to* ~, with a uniform reduction or enlargement. 按比例缩小或放大的。 **6** relative size, extent, etc. 规模; 相对的大小, 程度等。 *on a large / small, etc* ~, to a large, etc extent / degree: 大(小等)规模地: *They are preparing for war on a large* ~. 他们正在大规模地准备战争。 **7** (music) series of tones arranged in order of pitch, esp a series of eight starting on a keynote: (音乐)音阶(按照音调之高低度所组成之一系列的声音, 尤指以某主音起始的一连串八个音): *the* ~ *of F*, beginning with F as the keynote: F 音阶(以 F 为主音而起始); *practise* ~*s on the piano*. 在钢琴上练习音阶。 ⇨ **octave**. □ *vt* **1** [VP6A] make a copy or representation of, according to a certain ~: 按照某比例绘制地图: *a map / building.* 按照比例而绘制地图(建筑物)。 **2** [VP15B] ~ *up / down*, increase / decrease by a certain proportion: 按比例增加(减少): *All wages / marks were* ~*d up to*

10 *per cent.* 所有工资(分数)都按照百分之十增加。

scale[3] /skeɪl; skel/ *n* [C] **1** one of the two pans on a balance: 天平盘; (**pair of**) ~**s**, simple balance or instrument for weighing. 天平; ⇨ the illus at **balance**. 参看 balance 之插图。 *hold the* ~*s even*, judge fairly (between). (在…之间)公平裁判, *turn the* ~(*s*), decide the result of sth which is in doubt: 决定一项尚未确定的事情的结果; 改变情势: *The arrival of reinforcements turned the* ~(*s*) *in our favour.* 援兵的到达改变了情势而对我们有利。 *turn the* ~(*s*) *at*, (colloq) weigh: (口)重(若干): *The jockey turned the* ~(*s*) *at 80 lb*. 那骑师重八十磅。 **2** any machine for weighing: 任何称重量的机器: *bathroom* ~*s*, for measuring one's weight. 家用量体重机; 家用磅秤。 □ *vi* [VP2B] weigh: 重(若干): ~ *10 lb*. 重十磅。

scale[4] /skeɪl; skel/ *vt* [VP6A] climb up (a wall, cliff etc). 攀登(墙, 悬崖等)。 **'scaling-ladder** *n* one used for scaling high walls, eg of a fortified town in former times. (古代攻城用之)云梯; 爬城梯。

scal·lop /'skɒləp; 'skaləp/ *n* **1** kind of bivalve mollusc with a shell divided into grooves. 扇贝(双壳贝类, 其贝壳分裂为许多细槽); 干贝。 ⇨ the illus at **bivalve**. 参看 bivalve 之插图。 '~**-shell** *n* one half of this shell, used as a utensil in which a savoury dish is cooked and served. 扇贝壳之一扇; 贝皿(用以烹煮及装盛一道可口的菜肴)。 **2** (*pl*) ornamental edging of ~-shaped projections cut in pastry, cloth, etc. (复)(糕饼, 布料等之)扇形饰边。 □ *vt* [VP6A] **1** cook (eg oysters) in a ~-shell. 在海扇壳中烹煮(蚝等)。 **2** decorate the edge of (sth) with ~s. 以扇形皱褶装饰(某物)之边缘。

scally·wag /'skæliwæg; 'skæliˌwæg/, (US = **scalawag** /'skæləwæg; 'skæləˌwæg/) *n* (hum) scamp; rascal. (谐)无赖; 恶棍。

scalp /skælp; skælp/ *n* [C] skin and hair of the head, excluding the face; this skin, etc from an enemy's head as a trophy of victory (a former practice of some American Indians). 头皮及头发(面部不包括在内); (昔时北美印第安人取来) 作为战利品之敌人的头皮等。 *out for* ~*s*, (fig) making efforts to win trophies of victory over opponents. (喻)决心击败对手。 *have the* ~ *off*. 剥去…的头皮。 □ *vt* [VP6A] scalp the ~ off.

scal·pel /'skælpəl; 'skælpəl/ *n* small, light knife used by surgeons. (外科医生用的)轻便小刀; 解剖刀。

scamp[1] /skæmp; skæmp/ *n* (often used playfully) rascal; worthless person. (常用作义谑语)恶汉; 无用之人。

scamp[2] /skæmp; skæmp/ *vt* [VP6A] do (work, etc), make sth, carelessly, hastily or without interest. 粗心, 急速或无心地做(工作等); 草率从事。

scam·per /'skæmpə(r); 'skæmpɚ/ *vi* [VP2A, C] (esp of small animals, eg mice, rabbits, when frightened, or of children and dogs at play) run quickly. 快速地惊之小动物, 如鼠, 兔等, 或指在玩耍的小孩和狗)疾走; 奔窜。 □ *n* short, quick run: 疾走; 奔窜: *take the dog for a* ~. 领着狗快走一阵。

scampi /'skæmpɪ; 'skæmpɪ/ *n pl* large prawns. 大虾。

scan /skæn; skæn/ *vt, vi* (**-nn-**) **1** [VP6A] look at attentively; run the eyes over every part of: 细察; 审视: *The shipwrecked sailor* ~*ned the horizon anxiously every morning.* 这位遭船难的水手每晨焦急地审视着海天相接之处。 **2** [VP6A] glance at quickly but not very thoroughly: 匆促地略看; 扫视: *He* ~*ned the newspaper while having his breakfast.* 他在吃早餐的时候把报纸大略地翻阅了一下。 **3** [VP6A] test the metre of (a line of verse) by noting the division into feet, as in: 借分划音步以测定(诗句)之韵律; 按节奏吟诵, 例如:

'Never /'seek to /'tell thy /'love
'Love that /'never /'told can /'be.
切勿试图说出你的爱
爱是无法明言的。

4 [VP2A] (of verse) fit a metrical pattern; be composed so that it can be ~ned: (指诗)合韵律; 可吟

诵: *This line does not /will not* ~. 这诗行不合韵律. *The verses* ~ *well.* 这些诗读起合韵律. 5 [VP6A] (TV) resolve (a picture) into its elements of light and shade for transmission; (radar) traverse an area with electronic beams in search of sth. (电视)分解(图象)为明暗单元以便播出; 扫描; (雷达)以电子(波)束扫描一区域以搜寻某物. ~·**sion** /'skænʃn; 'skænʃən/ *n* [U] the ~ning of verse; the way verse ~s. 诗的节奏分析; 诗的韵律法.

scan·dal /'skændl; 'skændl̩/ *n* **1** [C, U] (action, piece of behaviour, that causes a) general feeling of indignation; [C] shameful or disgraceful action: 公愤; 普遍的反感; 物议; 引起公愤或反感的行动, 行为等; 丑行; 可耻的行动: *cause* (*a*) ~. 引起公愤. *A series of* ~*s caused the Government to fall.* 一连串引起公愤的行动使得政府垮台. *It is a* ~ *that the accused man was declared innocent.* 那被告被宣告无罪实在叫人愤愤不平. *If she leaves her husband she will certainly create* (*a*) ~ *in the village.* 她如果抛弃丈夫, 一定会招村人物议. **2** [U] harmful gossip; careless or unkind talk which damages sb's reputation: 有害的闲话; (无心或恶意的)诽谤; 诋毁: *Don't talk /listen to* ~. 不要诽谤人(听诽谤话). *Most of us enjoy a bit of* ~. 我们大多数人都喜欢听一点闲话. '~·**monger** /-mʌŋgə(r); -mʌŋg/ *n* person who spreads ~s(2). 诽谤者. ~·**monger·ing** /-mʌŋgərɪŋ; -mʌŋgərɪŋ/ *n* [U] the spreading of ~s(2). 散布诽谤. ~·**ize** /'skændəlaɪz; 'skændl̩ˌaɪz/ *vt* [VP6A] shock; offend the moral feelings or the ideas of etiquette of: 使惊骇; 使起反感; 诽谤: ~*ize the neighbours by sunbathing on the lawn in the nude.* 在草地上作裸体日光浴使邻居们骇异. ~·**ous** /'skændələs; 'skændl̩əs/ *adj* **1** disgraceful; shocking. 可耻的; 令人惊骇的. **2** (of reports, rumours) containing ~. (指传闻, 谣言)含有诽谤性的. **3** (of persons) fond of spreading ~. (指人)喜欢讲诽谤的. ~·**ous·ly** *adv*

Scan·di·na·vian /ˌskændɪ'neɪvɪən; ˌskændə'neviən/ *n, adj* (native) of Scandinavia (Denmark, Norway, Sweden, Iceland). 斯堪的纳维亚(包括丹麦、挪威、瑞典、冰岛)的; 北欧的; 斯堪的纳维亚人; 北欧人.

scan·sion /'skænʃn; 'skænʃən/ ⇨ scan.

scant /skænt; skænt/ *adj* ~ (*of*), (having) hardly enough: 不足的; 欠缺的: ~ *of breath;* 上气不接下气; *pay* ~ *attention to sb's advice.* 忽略某人的忠告. □ *vt* [VP6A] skimp; make ~; cut down: 吝啬; 使减少: *Don't* ~ *the butter when you make a cake.* 做糕饼时不要吝惜奶油. ~·**y** *adj* (**-ier**, **-iest**) (opp of *ample*) small in size or amount; barely large enough: (为ample之反义词)(大小或数量)不足的; 刚刚够大的; 恰足够的: *a* ~*y rice crop;* 歉收的稻子; *a* ~*y bikini.* 刚刚够大的比基尼泳装. ~·**i·ly** /-ɪlɪ; -ɪlɪ/ *adv* in a ~y manner: 不足地; 刚刚够地: ~*ily dressed.* 衣着单薄. ~·**i·ness** *n*

scant·ling /'skæntlɪŋ; 'skæntlɪŋ/ *n* small beam or piece of timber; board not more than 5 inches wide. 小木材; 不超过五英寸宽的木材; 制材.

scape·goat /'skeɪpgəʊt; 'skeɪpˌgot/ *n* person blamed or punished for the mistake(s) or wrongdoing of another or others. 代人受过者; 替罪羊.

scape·grace /'skeɪpgreɪs; 'skeɪpˌgres/ *n* (often used playfully) person who constantly gets into trouble. (常用作戏谑语)经常惹是非的人.

scap·ula /'skæpjʊlə; 'skæpjələ/ *n* (anat) shoulder-blade. (解剖)肩胛骨. ⇨ the illus at **skeleton.** 参看skeleton之插图.

scar /skɑː(r); skɑr/ *n* mark remaining on the surface (of skin, furniture, etc) as the result of injury or damage: (皮肤, 家具等的)伤痕; 痕迹; 疤: *a long* ~ *across his cheek;* 横过他面颊的长疤; (fig) (喻) *grief that left a* ~ (*on the heart*). 在心头留下创伤的悲哀. □ *vt, vi* (**-rr-**) **1** [VP6A] mark with a ~ or ~s: 使有伤痕或痕迹: *a face* ~*red by smallpox;* 麻脸(有天花疤痕的脸); *war-* ~*red towns.* 受战争损害的城镇. **2** [VP2C]

heal over (with a ~); form ~s: 痊愈(留下疤痕); 结疤: *The cut on his forehead* ~*red over.* 他的额上的刀伤已结疤痊愈了.

scarab /'skærəb; 'skærəb/ *n* kinds of beetle, esp one regarded as sacred in ancient Egypt; carving in the shape of a ~ (as an ornament or charm). 甲虫(尤指古埃及人奉为神圣的)蜣螂; 蜣螂的雕像(作为装饰或护符).

scarce /skeəs; skɛrs/ *adj* **1** (opp of *plentiful*) not available in sufficient quantity; not equal to the demand: (为plentiful之反义词)不充足的; 缺乏的; 供不应求的: *Eggs are* ~ *and expensive this month.* 本月蛋缺货且价昂. **2** rare; seldom met with: 稀罕的; 难得的: *a* ~ *book.* 珍本; 难得之书. **make oneself** ~, (colloq) keep out of the way, go away. (口)隐退; 离去. **scarc·ity** /'skeəsətɪ; 'skɛrsətɪ/ *n* state of being ~; smallness of supply compared with demand: 不充足; 缺乏; 供不应求: *The scarcity of fruit was caused by the drought.* 水果的供不应求系由干旱所致. [C] (*pl* **-ties**) instance or occasion of scarcity. 不充足, 缺乏, 供不应求之实例.

scarce·ly /'skeəslɪ; 'skɛrslɪ/ *adv* barely; not quite; almost not: 仅仅; 刚刚; 不充分地; 殆不; 几乎没有: *There were* ~ *a hundred people present.* 到场的不足一百人. *I* ~ *know him.* 我不大认识他. *S* ~ *had he entered the room when the phone rang.* 他一进房间电话就响了.

scare /skeə(r); skɛr/ *vt, vi* [VP6A, 15A, B, 2A] frighten; become frightened: 恐吓; 惊吓: *He was* ~*d by the thunder.* 他为雷声所惊吓. *They* ~*d at the strange noise.* 他们听到奇怪的声音觉得害怕. *The dogs* ~*d the thief away.* 那些狗把贼吓跑了. *He* ~*s easily/ is easily* ~*d.* 他容易受惊. ~ *sb stiff,* (colloq) alarm sb, make sb nervous: (口)使某人害怕或神经紧张: *He's* ~*d stiff of women.* 女人使他害怕或神经紧张. ~ *sb out of his wits,* make him extremely frightened: 使某人吓得不知所措; 使某人吓呆: *The sound of footsteps outside* ~*d her out of her wits.* 外面的脚步声把她吓得半了. □ *n* [C] feeling of alarm; state of widespread fear: 惊恐; 恐慌: *The news caused a war* ~, a fear that war might break out. 这消息引起了战争可能会爆发的恐慌. *You did give me a* ~, did frighten me. 你真吓了我一跳. '~·**crow** *n* figure of a man dressed in old clothes, set up to ~ birds away from crops. (置于农作物中用来吓走鸟类的)着破衣的人形; 稻草人. '~·**headline** *n* sensational newspaper headline in heavy black print. 耸人听闻的报纸大标题. '~·**monger** /-mʌŋgə(r); -mʌŋgə/ *n* person who spreads alarming news and starts a ~. 散布骇人新闻以引起恐慌的人. **scary** /'skeərɪ; 'skɛrɪ/ *adj* (colloq) causing alarm. (口)令人惊慌的.

scarf /skɑːf; skɑrf/ *n* (*pl* ~**s** /skɑːfs; skɑrfs/ **scarves** /skɑːvz; skɑrvz/) long strip of material (silk, wool, etc) worn over the shoulders, round the neck or (by women) over the hair. (丝, 毛等的)围巾; 披肩; 围巾; 颈巾; (女人之)头巾. '~·**pin** *n* ornamental pin worn on a ~. 围巾上的装饰别针.

scar·ify /'skærɪfaɪ; 'skærəˌfaɪ/ *vt* (*pt, pp* **-fied**) [VP6A] **1** (in surgery) make small cuts in, cut off skin from. (外科)在…上划痕; 自…割去皮肤. **2** (fig) hurt by severe criticism. (喻)借严厉批评以伤害. **3** loosen (the surface of the soil or a road) by using an agricultural tool or a machine with prongs. 用叉具或耙机弄松(土壤或道路的表面); 松(土).

scar·let /'skɑːlət; 'skɑrlɪt/ *n, adj* bright red: 鲜红; 猩红: *the* ~ *pillarboxes in Great Britain.* 英国的鲜红色邮筒. '~ **fever,** infectious disease with ~ marks on the skin. 猩红热(一种在皮肤上生猩红斑点的传染病). '~ **hat,** cardinal's hat. 红衣主教的帽子. ~-'**flowered** kind of bean plant. 红花菜豆(一种开红花的豆类植物). '~ '**woman,** (old use) prostitute. (旧用法)娼妓.

scarp /skɑːp; skɑrp/ *n* steep slope; escarpment. 陡坡; 急斜面.

scat /skæt; skæt/ *int* (sl) Go away! (俚)走开!

scath·ing /'skeɪðɪŋ; 'skeðɪŋ/ *adj* (of criticism, ridicule, etc) severe; harsh: (指control诉, 嘲笑等)严苛的: *a ~ retort*; 尖刻的反驳; *a ~ review of a new book*. 对一本新书的苛刻评论. **~·ly** *adv*

scat·ter /'skætə(r); 'skætə/ *vt, vi* **1** [VP6A, 15A, B, 2A, C] send, go, in different directions: 驱散; 离散: *The police ~ed the crowd*. 警察驱走群众. *The crowd ~ed*. 群众散去了. **2** [VP6A, 15A] throw or put in various directions, or here and there: 散播; 撒布: *~ seed*; 播种; *~ gravel on an icy road*. 撒布砂石于结冰的路面. **'~-brain** *n* person who cannot keep his thoughts on one subject for long. 注意力不持久的人; 浮躁的人. Hence, 由此产生, **'~-brained** *adj*. □ *n* that which is ~ed; sprinkling: 散布着的东西; 稀疏的少量或少数: *a ~ of hailstones*. 一阵稀疏的冰雹. *~ed* (*pp* as an *adj*) lying in different directions; not situated together; wide apart:(过去分词用作形容词)散布各方的; 离散的; 分散的: *a few ~ed fishing villages*; 一些疏疏落落的渔村; *a thinly ~ed population*. 稀疏的人口.

scatty /'skætɪ; 'skætɪ/ *adj* (*-ier, -iest*) (colloq) (口) **1** mad; feeble-minded: 疯狂的; 低能的: *That man would drive any woman ~!* 那男子会使任何女人为之疯狂! **2** scatter-brained; absent-minded. 思想不集中的; 心不在焉的.

scav·en·ger /'skævɪndʒə(r); 'skævɪndʒə/ *n* **1** animal or bird, eg a vulture, that lives on decaying flesh. 以腐尸为食之禽兽(如兀鹰). **2** person who searches among discarded or refuse material. 在废物或垃圾堆中搜寻有用之物者; 拾荒者. **scav·enge** /'skævɪndʒ; 'skævɪndʒ/ *vi* [VP2A, 3A] *~ (for)*, act as a *~*. 吃腐肉; 在废物或垃圾堆中搜寻.

scen·ario /sɪ'nɑ:rɪəʊ US:ꟼ'nær-; sɪ'nɛrɪ,o/ *n* (*pl ~s* /-rɪəʊz; -rɪ,oz/) written outline of a play, an opera, a film, with details of the scenes, etc; imagined sequence of future events. 电影脚本; 剧情概要; 歌剧概要; 想象中未来事件的顺序. **scen·arist** /sɪ'nɑ:rɪst US: -'nær-; sɪ'nɛrɪst/ *n* writer of ~s. 电影脚本作者.

scene /si:n; sin/ *n* [C] **1** place of an actual or imagined event: (实际或想象中的)事发地点; 场景: *the ~ of a great battle*. 大战场. *The ~ of the novel is laid/set in Scotland*. 该小说的故事发生在苏格兰. **2** description of an incident, or of part of a person's life; incident in real life suitable for such a description: 事件或生活片段的描述; 现实生活中适于描述的事件; 情景; 实况: *'S~s of Clerical Life'*, tales by George Eliot. '教士生活记实'(英国小说家 George Eliot 所著的一本小说集). *There were distressing ~s when the earthquake occurred*. 地震发生时有很多悲惨的情景. **3** (incident characterized by an) emotional outburst: 发脾气; 吵闹; 吵闹的事件: *She made a ~/We had a ~ when I criticized her*. 当我批评她的时候; 她大吵大闹(我们吵闹了一阵). **4** view; sth seen; sth spread out to view (indoors or outdoors, in a town or in the country, with or without action; cf *scenery*, which is used of natural features on land): 风景; 所见之物; 景象(户内或户外的, 城市的或乡村的, 活动的或静态的; 参较地面上自然景色的 *scenery*): *The boats in the harbour make a beautiful ~*. 港中的船只构成美丽的景色. *They went abroad for a change of ~*. 他们出国换换环境. **5** (abbr 略作 **Sc**) one of the parts, shorter than an act, into which some plays and operas are divided; episode within such a part. (戏剧及歌剧之短于一幕的)一场; 一景; 一场或一幕中的一段情节: *'Macbeth', Act II, Sc 1*; '麦克白', 第二幕第一场; *the 'duel' in 'Hamlet'*. '哈姆雷特'中决斗的一场. **6** place represented on the stage of a theatre; the painted background, woodwork, canvas, etc representing such a place: (舞台上的)景; 布景; 道具布置: *The first ~ of 'Lotus Blossom' is a tropical garden*. '荷花' 的第一幕的一景是一热带花园. *The ~s are changed during the intervals*. 休息时间换景. **behind the ~s**, **(a)** out of sight of the audience; behind the stage. 观众看不见地;

在幕后; 秘密地; 暗中. **(b)** (fig, of a person) influencing events secretly; (of an event) in secret, not known to the public. (喻, 指人)秘密左右事件的; (指事件)未公开的. *be/come on the ~*, (fig) be present/appear. (喻)在场; 到场; 出现. **'~-painter** *n* (theatre) person who paints scenery(2). (戏剧)绘制布景者. **'~-shifter** *n* (theatre) person who changes the ~s. (戏剧)更换布景者. **7** (colloq) area of what is currently fashionable or notable: (口)时髦或著名的地区: *the ,enter'tainment ~ in the West End of London*; 伦敦西区的娱乐场所; *the 'drug ~ in our big cities*. 我们大城市中著名的毒证. *be on/make the ~*, (colloq) be part of/present in such a ~. (口)参与时髦地区的活动(出现在时髦地区的活动中).

scen·ery /'si:nərɪ; 'sinərɪ/ *n* [U] **1** general natural festures of a district, eg mountains, plains, valleys, forests: 一地区之天然景色; 风景; 景致(例如高山, 平原, 溪谷, 森林): *mountain ~*; 山景; *stop to admire the ~*. 停下来欣赏风景. Cf 参较 *town scenes*. **2** the furnishings, painted canvas, woodwork, etc used on the stage of a theatre. (舞台上之)布景; 道具布景.

scenic /'si:nɪk; 'sinɪk/ *adj* having fine natural scenery: 天然景色的; 风景优美的: *the ~ splendours of the Rocky Mountains*; 落基山脉壮丽的风景; *a ~ highway across the Alps*. 越过阿尔卑斯山脉的景色优美的公路. **sceni·cally** /-klɪ; -klɪ/ *adv*

scent /sent; sɛnt/ **1** [U] smell, esp of sth pleasant coming from or belonging to sth: 气味; (尤指)香味: *the ~ of new-mown hay*; 新刈干草的气味; *a rose that has no ~*; 无香味的玫瑰; [C] particular kind of smell: 某种气味: *~s of lavender and rosemary*. 薰衣草和迷迭香的气味. **2** [U] (usu liquid) preparation distilled from flowers, etc; perfume: (通常为液体)香精; 香水: *a bottle of ~*; 一瓶香水; *a '~-bottle*. 香水瓶. *She uses too much ~*. 她用了过多的香水. **3** (usu *sing*) smell left by an animal; the track of an animal: (通常用单数)野兽的遗臭; 兽迹: *follow up/lose/recover the ~*. 追踪(失去, 重新发现)兽迹. *The ~ was strong*, easy for the hounds to follow. 那野兽的臭迹是强烈的, 猎犬易于追踪. *on the ~*, having, following, a clue. 获得或追寻⋯的线索. *off the ~*, having, following, no clue'or the wrong clue. 无线索或追寻错误的线索. *put/throw sb off the ~*, (fig) mislead him by giving false information. (喻)以不实的情报或资料)使某人失去线索. **4** [U] sense of smell (in dogs): (犬的)嗅觉: *hunt by ~*. 借嗅觉行猎; 循臭迹猎物. □ *vt* [VP6A] **1** learn the presence of by smell: 嗅出⋯的存在; 闻到: *The dog ~ed a rat*. 那狗嗅出有一只老鼠. **2** begin to suspect the presence or existence of: 开始发觉到⋯的存在或存在; 觉察; 看破; 疑有: *~ a crime*; 识破一项罪行; *~ treachery/trouble*. 疑有阴诈(麻烦). **3** put ~ on; make fragrant: 洒香水; 使⋯香: *a handkerchief*; 洒香水于手帕上; *roses that ~ the air*. 使空气芬香的玫瑰. **~·less** *adj* having no ~: 无气味的; 无香味; 无嗅觉的: *~less flowers*. 无香味的花.

scep·ter /'septə(r); 'sɛptə/ *n* = **sceptre**.

scep·tic (US = **skep·tic**) /'skeptɪk; 'skɛptɪk/ *n* person who doubts the truth of a particular claim, theory, etc; person who doubts the truth of the Christian religion or of all religions. 怀疑者; 怀疑论者; 怀疑基督教或一切宗教之真实者. 张、学说等之真实性者; 怀疑基督教或一切宗教之真理者. **scep·ti·cal** (US = **skep-**) /-kl; -kl/ *adj* inclined not to believe; in the habit of questioning the truth of claims, statements, etc. 怀疑的; 惯于怀疑主张、陈述等之真实性的. **scep·ti·cally** (US = **skep-**) /-klɪ; -klɪ/ *adv* **scep·ti·cism** (US = **skep-**) /'skeptɪsɪzəm; 'skɛptə,sɪzəm/ *n* [U] doubting state of mind; ~al attitude of mind. 怀疑; 怀疑态度; 怀疑主义.

sceptre (US = **scep·ter**) /'septə(r); 'sɛptə/ *n* rod or staff carried by a ruler as a sign of power or authority. 王节; 王权. **scep·tred** (US = **-tered**) *adj* having a ~. 有王权的. ⇨ the illus at **regalia**. 参看 regalia 之插图.

sched·ule /ˈʃedjuːl *US:* ˈskedʒul; ˈskɛdʒul/ *n* [C] list or statement of details, esp of times for doing things; programme or timetable for work: 表；目录；(尤指)时间表；进度表；预定计划表：*a production ~*, eg in a factory; (工厂等中之)生产进度表；生产计划表；*a full ~*, a busy programme. 排得很满的日程表。**on/behind ~**, on/not on time: 准时(迟延)；照进度进行(进度落后)：*The train arrived on ~*, on time, punctually. 火车准时到达。**(according to) ~**, as planned. 按照计划的。 □ *vt* [VP6A, 7A, 14] **~ (for)**, make a ~ of; put in a ~; (esp US)enter in a list of arrangements: 作…之表或目录；列入时间表或进度表；(尤美)排定；安排：*~d services*, (eg of aircraft) flying according to announced timetables. 固定的班机。(Cf 参较 *charter flights.*) *The President is ~d to make a speech tomorrow.* 总统定于明日发表演说。*His arrival is ~d for Thursday.* 他预定于星期四到达。

sche·matic /skɪˈmætɪk; skiˈmætɪk/ *adj* of the nature of a scheme or plan; (shown) in a diagram or chart. 纲要的；图解(式)的。**sche·mati·cally** /-klɪ; -klɪ/ *adv*

scheme /skiːm; skim/ *n* [C] **1** arrangement; ordered system: 安排；配置；系统；体制：*a 'colour ~*, eg for a room, so that colours of walls, rugs, curtains, etc are in harmony. 色彩之调配(如为房间所设计者, 俾使墙壁、地毯、窗帘等之色彩调和。 **2** plan or design (for work or activity): (工作或活动的)计划；设计：*a ~ for manufacturing paper from straw;* 用稻草造纸的计划；*a ~ (= syllabus) for the term's work.* 该学期之课程进度表。 **3** secret and dishonest plan: 阴谋；诡计：*a ~ to defraud a widow.* 意图欺骗一寡妇的阴谋。 □ *vi*, *vt* **1** [VP2A, 3A, 4A] **~ for sth/to do sth**, make a (esp dishonest) ~ or ~s: 设计；策划；图谋(尤指不轨之事)：*He ~d to keep his rivals in ignorance of his plans.* 他图谋不让他的对手们知道他的计划。*They ~d for the overthrow of the government.* 他们谋求推翻政府。 **2** [VP6A] make plans for (esp sth dishonest): 设计；策划；图谋(尤指不轨之事)：*a scheming (= crafty) thief.* 诡诈的窃贼。**~r** *n* person who ~s or intrigues. 设计者；阴谋者。

scherzo /ˈskeətsəʊ; ˈskɛrtso/ *n* (*pl* ~**s** /-səʊz; -soz/) (I) lively, vigorous passage in music. (意)轻快有力的乐节；诙谐曲。

schism /ˈsɪzəm; ˈsɪzəm/ *n* [U] (offence of causing the) division of an organization (esp a Church) into two or more groups, usu through difference of opinion; [C] instance of such separation. 组织分裂(通常由于意见不同而分为两个或多个的小派系)；(尤指)教会分裂；导致组织或教会分裂的冒犯行为；分裂之实例。**schis·matic** /sɪzˈmætɪk; sɪzˈmætɪk/ *adj* tending to or inclined to ~; guilty of ~. 分裂的；有分立趋向的；有使组织或教会分裂(之冒犯行为)的。

schist /ʃɪst; ʃɪst/ *n* kinds of rock which splits easily into thin plates. (结晶)片岩；片麻岩。

schizo·phrenia /ˌskɪtsəʊˈfriːnɪə; ˌskɪzəˈfrinɪə/ *n* type of mental disorder (colloq □ *split personality*) marked by lack of connection between thoughts, feelings, and actions. 精神分裂症；早发性痴呆。**schizo·phrenic** /ˌskɪtsəʊˈfrenɪk; ˌskɪzəˈfrɛnɪk/ *adj* of ~. 精神分裂症的。 □ *n* (colloq abbr 口语略作 *schizo*) person suffering from ~. 精神分裂症患者。

schmal(t)z /ʃmɔːlts; ʃmɑlts/ *n* (colloq) sickly sentimentality. (口) 过份的多愁善感；过份的伤感。**schmal(t)zy** *adj*

schnapps /ʃnæps; ʃnæps/ *n* [U] strong alcoholic spirit distilled from grain. 豆类酿制的烈酒。

schnit·zel /ˈʃnɪtsl; ˈʃnɪtsl/ *n* veal cutlet covered with breadcrumbs and fried in butter. (覆以面包屑, 再用牛油炸的)炸牛肉片。

schnor·kel /ˈʃnɔːkl; ˈʃnɔrkl/ *n* = **snorkel**.

scholar /ˈskɒlə(r); ˈskɑlə/ *n* **1** (dated use) boy or girl at school. (过时用语)学生。 **2** student who, after a competitive examination or other means of selection, is awarded money or other help so that he may attend

school or college, or pursue further education: 领奖学金或津贴的学生：*British Council ~s.* 领英国文化协会奖学金的学生。 **3** person with much knowledge (usu of a particular subject, and esp one who gives careful attention to evidence, method, etc). 学者(通常指某一学科的, 尤指注重证据和方法的)。**schol·ar·ly** *adj* having or showing much learning; of, suitable, or right for a ~(3); fond of learning: 有学问的；博学的；学者派头的；适于做学者的；好学的：*a ~ly translation*, 博学的翻译；*a ~ly woman.* 好学的女青年。

schol·ar·ship /ˈskɒləʃɪp; ˈskɑləˌʃɪp/ *n* **1** [U] learning or knowledge obtained by study; proper concern for scholarly methods. 学识；学问；学术上的成就；做学问的方法。 **2** [C] payment of money, eg a yearly grant to a scholar(2) so that he may continue his studies: 奖学金：*win a ~ to the university.* 获得该大学的奖学金。

schol·as·tic /skəˈlæstɪk; skoˈlæstɪk/ *adj* **1** of schools and education: 学校的；教育的：*the '~ profession*, that of teaching; 教书的职业；*a '~ post*, a position as a teacher; 教书的职位；*a '~ agency*, private one that finds positions for teachers and teachers for schools. 教员职业介绍所。 **2** connected with the learning of the Middle Ages, esp when men argued over small points of dogma. 中世纪之学术研究的；烦琐学派的；学究的。**schol·as·ti·cism** /skəˈlæstɪsɪzəm; skoˈlæstəˌsɪzəm/ *n* [U] the system of philosophy taught in the universities in the Middle Ages. 中世纪之经院哲学；烦琐哲学。

school¹ /skuːl; skul/ *n* **1** [C] institution for educating children: 学校：*'primary and 'secondary ~s*; 小学和中学；*'evening ~s*; 夜校；*'Sunday ~s*; 主日学校；*~ doctors*, medical officers responsible for the health of school children; 校医；(US) college, university. (美)学院；大学。**'~·board** *n* (US) local education authority. (美)(地方上的)教育委员会。**'~·book** *n* book used in ~s; textbook. 课本；教科书。**'~·boy** *n* boy at ~: 学童；男学生。(attrib) (用作定语)*~boy slang.* 学生俚语。**'~·days** *n pl* time of being at ~: 求学时代：*look back upon one's ~·days.* 回顾求学时代。**'~·fellow** *n* member, past or present, of the same ~. 同学；校友。**'~·girl** *n* girl at ~. 女学生。**'~·house** *n* building of a ~ esp a small one in a village. 校舍(尤指乡间之小校舍)。**'~·man** /-mən; -mən/ *n* (*pl* **-men**) teacher in a European university in the Middle Ages; theologian dealing with religious teachings by the use of Aristotle's logic. (中世纪欧洲大学的)教授；烦琐派之神学家(用亚里斯多德之逻辑研究神学者)。**'~·master**, **·mistress** *n* school teacher. 男(女)教师。**'~·mate** *n* = ~fellow. '~·time *n* lesson time at ~. 上课时间。 **2** [U] (not with *def art*) process of being educated in a ~: (不用定冠词)在学校受教育的过程；上学：*'~ age*, between the ages of starting and finishing ~; 学龄；*~·leaving age*, age at which children leave ~. 学童结束义务教育的年龄。*The ~·leaving age has been raised to 16.* 国民义务教育的年龄已经提高到十六岁。*Is he old enough for ~/to go to ~?* 他的年龄大得可以上学了吗？*He left ~ when he was fifteen.* 他十五岁时离开学校。*My boys are still at ~.* 我的孩子们仍在上学。 **3** [U] (not with *def art*) time when teaching is given; lessons: (不用定冠词)上课时间；上课：*S~ begins at 9am.* 上午九时开始上课。*There will be no ~ (= no lessons) tomorrow.* 明天学校放假。*Will you come for a walk after ~?* 放学后你愿来散散步吗？ **4** (with *def art*) all the pupils in a ~: (或定冠词连用)全校学生：*The whole ~ hopes that its football team will win the match.* 全校学生都希望该校的足球队赢得那场比赛。 **5** department or division of a university for the study of a particular subject: 大学的院、系、研究所：*The S~ of Oriental and African Studies*, in the University of London; (伦敦大学的)东方学与非洲学学院；*the 'Law/'Medical S~;* (医学)学院；*the S~ of Dentistry;* 牙医学系；(GB) branch of study for which separate examinations are given in a

university: (英)大学的学位考试科目: the 'History ~; 历史科; hall in which these examinations are held; 举行学位考试的试场; (pl) these examinations. (复)学位考试。 **6** [C] (fig) circumstances or occupation that provides discipline or instruction: (喻)提供训练或教导的环境或工作: the hard ~ of experience/adversity. 经验(逆境)的磨练。 **7** (pl) **the ~s,** medieval universities, their professors, teaching, and arguments. (复)中世纪之大学,其教授,教学,及论据。 ⇨ also ~man in **1** above. 亦参看上列第 1 义之 ~man。 **8** [C] group of persons who are followers or imitators of an artist, a philosopher, etc, or of persons having the same principles or characteristics: (艺术家,哲学家等的)门生; 弟子; 学派; 门派: the Dutch/Venetian, etc ~ of painting; 荷兰(威尼斯等)画派; the Hegelian ~, of philosophers; 黑格尔学派; a gentleman of the old ~, who retains the traditions, manners, etc of older times. 旧派的绅士。 ~ of thought, way of thinking shared by a group of persons. 学派。 □ vt [VP 6 A, 15 B, 16 A] ~ sb (in sth/to do sth), train; control; discipline: 训练; 控制; 教导: ~ a horse; 训练马; ~ oneself in patience/to be patient. 养成自己的耐性。 ~ing n [U] education: 教育: He had very little ~ing. 他受的教育很少。 Who's paying for her ~ing? 谁在付她的教育费用?

school² /sku:l; skul/ n [C] large number (of fish) swimming together; shoal. 鱼群。

schoo·ner /'sku:nə(r); 'skunɚ/ n **1** kind of sailing-ship with two or more masts and fore and aft sails. (有二或更多桅杆的)纵帆式帆船; 斯库纳船。 **2** tall drinking-glass. 大酒杯。

schot·tische /ʃɒ'ti:ʃ; ʃɑ'tiʃ/ n (music for a) kind of polka. 一种波尔卡类的旋舞; 此种舞曲。

schwa /ʃwɑ:; ʃwɑ/ n the symbol /ə; ə/ used in phonetic notation for central vowels or diphthong elements as in /ə'gəʊ; ə'go/ for ago. 轻声元音之发音符号(在国际音标中用/ə/表示); 中性元音。

sci·atic /saɪ'ætɪk; saɪ'ætɪk/ adj of the hip: 臀的;坐骨的: the ~ nerve, nerve extending through the hip and thigh. 坐骨神经。 **sci·atica** /saɪ'ætɪkə; saɪ'ætɪkə/ n [U] neuralgia of the ~ nerve. 坐骨神经痛。

science /'saɪəns; 'saɪəns/ n **1** [U] knowledge arranged in an orderly manner, esp knowledge obtained by observation and testing of facts; pursuit of such knowledge. 科学;科学研究。 S~ is an exact discipline. 科学是一种精确的学科。 **2** [C, U] branch of such knowledge. 某门科学。 ⇨ art¹(2). the natural ~s, eg botany, zoology. 自然科学(如植物学,动物学)。 the physical ~s, eg physics, chemistry. 自然科学(如物理,化学)。 social ~(s), eg psychology, politics. 社会科学(如心理学,政治学)。 the applied ~s, eg engineering. 应用科学(如工程学)。 ~ 'fic·tion, fiction dealing with recent or imagined scientific discoveries and advances (usu fantasies). 科幻小说(以最近或想象中的科学发现及进展为主题者, 通常为怪异的幻想)。 **3** [U] expert's skill (opp of strength): 专门技术或技巧(与「力气」相反): In judo ~ is more important than strength. 在柔道中, 技巧比力气更为重要。 **scien·tist** /'saɪəntɪst; 'saɪəntɪst/ n person expert in one or more of the natural or physical ~s. 科学家; 自然科学家。

scien·tific /ˌsaɪən'tɪfɪk; ˌsaɪən'tɪfɪk/ adj **1** of, for, connected with, used in, science; guided by the rules of science: 科学的;适于科学的;关于科学的;用于科学的; 合乎科学原则的: ~ methods; 科学方法; ~ farming; 科学耕作; ~ instruments. 科学仪器。 **2** having, using, needing, skill or expert knowledge: 有技术或专门知识的; 利用技术或专门知识的; 需要技术或专门知识的: a ~ boxer. 有技术的拳击手。 **scien·tifi·cally** /-klɪ; -klɪ/ adv

scimi·tar /'sɪmɪtə(r); 'sɪmətɚ/ n short, curved, single-edged sword, formerly used by Arabs, Persians, Turks. (阿拉伯人, 波斯人, 土耳其人昔时用的)短弯刀; 偃月刀。

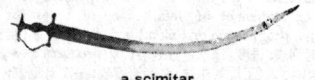

a scimitar

scin·tilla /sɪn'tɪlə; sɪn'tɪlə/ n [C] spark; atom; shred; iota: 火花; 微量; 碎片; 一点: not a ~ of truth in the story; 故事中没有一点真实性; not a ~ of evidence, none at all. 一点证据也没有。

scin·til·late /'sɪntɪleɪt US: -təleɪt; 'sɪntl̩ˌet/ vi [VP 2A] sparkle; be brilliant: 放出火花; 闪烁: scintillating with wit. 才智横溢的。 **scin·til·la·tion** /ˌsɪntɪ'leɪʃn; ˌsɪntl̩'eʃən/ n

scion /'saɪən; 'saɪən/ n **1** young member of a (esp old or noble) family. (尤指世家或贵族的)年幼后裔或子孙。 **2** shoot of a plant, esp one cut for grafting or planting. 幼枝(尤指为接枝或栽植而剪下者); 接穗。

scis·sors /'sɪzəz; 'sɪzɚz/ n pl (pair of) ~, cutting instrument with two blades which cut as they come together: 剪刀; 剪子: Where are my ~? 我的剪刀在哪里? ~ and paste, (of articles, books, etc) compiled from parts of others: (指文章,书籍等)自其他文章或书籍剪辑拼凑而成的: This article's a ~ and paste job. 这篇文章是剪辑拼凑而成。

scler·osis /sklə'rəʊsɪs; sklɪ'rosɪs/ n [U] diseased condition in which soft tissue (eg walls of the arteries) hardens. 硬化症(如血管硬化)。

scoff¹ /skɒf US: skɔ:f; skɑf/ vi [VP2A, 3A] ~ (at), speak contemptuously, mock (at): 轻蔑地说; 嘲弄; 嘲笑: ~ at dangers; 蔑视危险; ~ at religion. 嘲弄宗教。 □ n **1** taunt; mocking remark. 嘲笑; 嘲弄的话。 **2** object of ridicule. 嘲弄的对象; 笑柄。 ~er n person who ~s. 嘲弄者; 嘲笑者。 ~·ing·ly adv

scoff² /skɒf US: skɔ:f; skɑf/ vt (sl) eat greedily: (俚)狼吞虎咽地吃: Who has ~ed all the pastries? 是谁把糕饼全部吃掉了? □ n **1** act of ~ing: 狼吞虎咽: have a good ~. 大吃一顿。 **2** [U] (sl) food: (口)食物; 食品: Where's all the ~ gone? 全部的食物到哪里去了?

scold /skəʊld; skold/ vt, vi [VP2A, 6A, 14] ~ (sb) (for sth), blame with angry words; find fault noisily: 骂; 叱责; 责备: ~ a child for being lazy. 责备孩子懒惰。 □ n person who ~s. 好叱责或骂人的人。 ~·ing n severe rebuke: 骂; 叱责: give sb/get a ~ing for being late. 责备某人迟到(因迟到而挨骂)。

scol·lop /'skɒləp; 'skɑləp/ n, vt = scallop.

sconce /skɒns; skɑns/ n bracket fixed to a wall for a candle (or, today, any other form of light). 装于墙上的蜡烛台或灯台。

scone /skɒn US: skəʊn; skon/ n [C] soft, flat cake of barley meal or wheat flour baked quickly. 一种快烤的扁平软面饼。

scoop /sku:p; skup/ n [C] **1** (sorts of) deep, shovel-like, short-handled tool for taking up and moving quantities of grain, flour, sugar, etc; long-handled, ladle-shaped tool for dipping out liquid. 挖谷粒、面粉、糖等用的深边短柄的)铲子; (舀水等用的长柄)杓子; 戽斗。 **2** motion of, or as of, using a ~: 一铲或一舀地: at one ~, in one single movement of a ~: 一铲; 一舀: at one ~, in one single movement of a ~: 一铲一舀地: He won £50 at one ~. 他一下子赚了五十镑。 **3** (colloq) piece of news obtained and published by one newspaper before its competitors; (comm) large profit made by anticipating competitors. (口)独家新闻; (商)抢先赚得的暴利。 □ vt [VP15B] ~ sth out/up, lift with, or as with, a ~: 以一~铲起; 汲取; 舀出。 **2** [VP6A, 15B] ~ (out), make (a hole, groove, etc) with, or as with, a ~: 掘; 挖; 用或似用铲挖成(洞, 沟等): ~ out a hole in the sand. 在沙中挖洞。 **3** [VP6A] (colloq) get (news, a profit, etc) as a ~(3). (口)抢先获得(新闻, 利润等)。 ~·ful /-ful; -fʊl/ n as much as a ~ holds. 一铲的量。

scoot /sku:t; skut/ vi (either imper or inf) (colloq,

hum) run away quickly: (用于祈使句或不定式)(口,谐) 赶快跑: *S~!* 赶快跑! *Tell him to ~.* 叫他赶快跑。 ⇨ **scram.**

scooter /ˈskuːtə(r); ˈskutɚ/ *n* **1** (ˈmotor-)~, light motor-cycle with small wheels and a low seat. 速克达机车(一种低座小轮轻型摩托车)。 **2** child's toy, an L-shaped vehicle with small wheels, one foot being used to move it by pushing against the ground. 滑行车; 踏板车(供小孩游戏用)。

scooters

scope /skəʊp; skop/ *n* [U] **1** opportunity; outlet: 机会; 出路: *work that gives ~ for one's abilities.* 有机会发挥个人才能的工作。 **2** range of action or observation: 活动或观察的范围; 眼界; 见识: *Ought politics to be within the ~ of a trade union's activities?* 工会的活动应当包括政治吗? *Economics is a subject beyond the ~ of my mind.* 经济学不是我所能了解的学科。

scor·bu·tic /skɔːˈbjuːtɪk; skɔrˈbjutɪk/ *adj* of, affected with, scurvy. 坏血症的; 患坏血症的。

scorch /skɔːtʃ; skɔrtʃ/ *vt, vi* **1** [VP6A] burn or discolour the surface of (sth) by dry heat; cause to dry up or wither: 烘焦; 烧焦(某物)之表面; 使萎; 使枯: *The long, hot summer ~ed the grass.* 炎热的长夏晒枯了青草。 *I've ~ed my shirt when you ironed it.* 你烫我的衬衫时把它烫焦了。 **~ed 'earth policy,** policy of burning crops, and destroying buildings, etc that might be useful to enemy forces occupying a district. 焦土政策(烧毁或破坏可能对于占领某一地区之敌军有用的农作物及建筑物等的政策)。 **2** [VP2A] become discoloured, etc with heat. 焦; 萎; 枯。 **3** [VP2A, C] (colloq, of cyclists, motorists, etc) travel at very high speed. (口, 指骑自行车, 开汽车等者)高速行驶。 □ *n* [C] mark on the surface of sth (esp cloth) made by dry heat. 焦痕(尤指布上者)。 **~er** *n* sth or sb that ~es: 灼热之物; 高速驾车之人: *Yesterday was a ~er,* a very hot day. 昨天热极了。 **~ing** *adj* very hot. 灼热的。 □ *adv:* ~*ing hot,* extremely hot. 极热的。

score¹ /skɔː(r); skor/ *n* [C] **1** cut, scratch or notch made on a surface: 斫痕; 截痕; 刻痕; 记号: *~s on rock,* eg made during the Ice Age: 岩石上的痕迹(如冰河时期所留下的蚀痕): *~s on a slave's back* (made by whipping). 奴隶背上的鞭痕。 **2** (from the old custom of chalking lines on a board in inns, to record what a customer owed for drinks, etc) account or record of money owing: (沿自旧时旅店习俗, 用粉笔在木板上画线以记录顾客所欠之酒帐等)帐; 帐目: *run up a ~,* get into debt. 负债。 *pay/settle/wipe off old ~s,* (fig) get even with sb for past offences; have one's revenge: (喻)算老帐; 报仇雪恨: *I have some old ~s to settle with that fellow.* 我要跟那家伙算一些老帐。 **3** (record of) points, goals, runs, etc made by a player or team in sport: (竞技之)得分; 分数; 得分记录: *The ~ in the tennis final was 6—4, 3—6, 7—5.* 网球决赛的得分记录是六比四, 三比六, 七比五。 *The half-time ~* (at football) *was 2—1.* 上半场(如足球比赛)的记录为二比一。 *keep the ~,* keep a record of the ~ as it is made. (比赛时)记录; 记录。 **~-board/-book/-card,** one on which the ~ (eg in cricket) is recorded (during play). (如板球赛之)记分板(簿, 卡片)。 **4** reason; account. 理由; 原因。 *on the ~ of,* on account of, in consideration of:

rejected on the ~ *(grounds* is more usu) *of ill health.* 因健康不佳而被拒绝 (on the grounds 较常用)。 *on more ~s than one,* for more than one reason. 为了种种理由。 *on 'that ~,* as far as that point is concerned: 在那一点上; 因那理由; 就那一点而言: *You need have no anxiety on ~.* 你无需为那个担忧。 **5** copy of orchestral, etc music showing what each instrument is to play, each voice to sing: 总谱(表明每一乐器部所该演奏, 每一声部所该演唱的管弦乐谱等): *follow the ~ while listening to music.* 照谱聆听音乐。 **6** twenty; set of twenty: 二十; 二十之组: *a ~ of people;* 二十人; *three ~ and ten, 70,* the normal length of human life according to the Bible. 七十(根据圣经是人类的正常寿命)。 *I've been there ~s of times,* very often. 我常去该处。 **7** (sl) remark or act by which a person gains an advantage for himself in an argument, etc: (俚)在辩论等中对自己有利的话或动作: *a politician who is clever at making ~s off hecklers at public meetings,* clever at making them appear foolish. 擅于在公共集会中使诘问者闹笑话的政客。 ⇨ **score²(4).**

score² /skɔː(r); skor/ *vt, vi* **1** [VP6A, 15A, B] mark with cuts, scratches, lines, etc: 加斫痕, 截痕, 刻痕, 记号, 线等: *The mountain side is ~d by torrents,* shows where torrents of water have washed away soil, etc. 山坡留有因被急流冲刷的痕迹。 *Don't ~ the floor by pushing heavy furniture about.* 不要推移笨重家具以免损坏地板。 *The composition was ~d with corrections in red ink.* 这篇作文用红笔批改过。 *~ out,* draw a line or lines through: 划掉; 删去: *Three words had been ~d out.* 三个字已被画掉了。 ⇨ **score¹(1).** **2** [VP6A, 2A, 15B] ~ *(up),* make or keep a record (esp for games): 记录; (尤指)记录比赛分数: *~ up runs,* in cricket. (板球赛)记分。 *Who's going to ~?* 谁担任记分? **3** [VP6A, 2A] make as points in a game: 得分; 获分: *~ a goal,* 进一球; *a century,* 100 runs at cricket; (板球赛)得一百分; *a batsman who failed to ~,* who made no runs; 未得分的击球员; *~ no tricks,* ie whist or bridge. (如惠斯特或桥牌戏中)未赢得一磴牌。 *~ an advantage / a success,* win one; have food fortune. 获得利益 (成功)。 *~ a point (against/off/over sb) / off sb.* **4** [VP3A] ~ *off sb,* (colloq) humiliate him; defeat him in an argument; make a clever retort to sth he says. (口)羞辱某人; 在辩论中击败之; 驳倒其议论。 **5** [VP15B] ~ *sth up (against sb),* enter as a record: 记下; 记住; 计算: *That remark will be ~d up against you,* will be remembered (and, perhaps, be revenged). 我会记住那句话, 将来再跟你算帐。 **6** [VP6A] orchestrate; write instrumental or vocal parts for a musical composition: 作成管弦乐; 写下一乐曲之乐器或歌唱部分; 记入总谱: *~d for violin, viola and cello.* 为小提琴, 中提琴及大提琴配谱。 ⇨ **score¹(5).** **~r** *n* **1** person who keeps a record of points, goals, runs, etc ~d in a game (竞技之)记分员。 **2** player who ~s runs, goals, etc. 得分之运动员。

scorn /skɔːn; skɔrn/ *n* [U] **1** contempt; feeling that sb or sth deserves no respect: 轻蔑; 蔑视: *be filled with ~ for a proposal;* 对一提议深表蔑视; *dismiss a suggestion with ~.* 轻蔑地驳回一建议。 *laugh sb/sth to ~,* treat with contemptuous laughter. 嘲笑某人(某事)。 **2** object of contempt: 轻蔑的对象: *He was the ~ of the village.* 他是全村嘲笑的对象。 □ *vt* [VP6A, D, 7A] feel or show contempt for; refuse (to do sth as being unworthy): 轻蔑; 蔑视; 不屑(做某事): *We ~ a liar.* 我们瞧不起说谎者。 *He ~ed my advice.* 他蔑视我的忠告。 *She ~s lying/telling lies/to tell a lie.* 她不屑说谎。 **~·ful** /-fl; -fəl/ *adj* showing or feeling ~: 轻蔑的; 蔑视的: *a ~ful smile;* 轻蔑的笑; *~ful of material things.* 蔑视物质方面的享受。 **~·fully** /-fəlɪ; -fəlɪ/ *adv*

Scor·pio /ˈskɔːpɪəʊ; ˈskɔrpɪˌo/ *n* eighth sign of the zodiac. 天蝎座; 天蝎宫(黄道带中的第八宫)。 ⇨ the illus at **zodiac.** 参看 zodiac 之插图。

scor·pion /ˈskɔːpɪən; ˈskɔrpɪən/ *n* small animal of the spider group with a poisonous sting in its long,

jointed tail. 蝎. ⇨ the illus at **arachnid**. 参看 arachnid 之插图.

scot /skɒt; skɑt/ n (only in) (仅用于) *pay ~ and lot*, share financial burdens. 分摊财政负担. *get off/escape ,~-'free*, unharmed, unpunished. 安然逃脱; 未受害; 未受罚.

Scot /skɒt; skɑt/ n native of Scotland. 苏格兰人.

Scotch /skɒtʃ; skɑtʃ/ adj of Scotland or its people: 苏格兰的; 苏格兰人的: ~ *whisky*, the kind distilled in Scotland. 苏格兰威士忌酒. ,~ 'terrier, small, rough-haired, short-legged kind of terrier. 苏格兰㹴 (一种粗毛腿短的小狗). □ n **1 the** ~, *n pl* natives of Scotland. 苏格兰人. **2** [U] ~ whisky. 苏格兰威士忌酒. '~·man /-mən; -mən/, '~·woman *nn* = Scotsman, Scotswoman (which are the preferred terms). 苏格兰男人, 苏格兰女人 (Scotsman 和 Scotswoman 较常用).

scotch /skɒtʃ; skɑtʃ/ vt [VP6A] **1** (archaic) wound without killing: (古) 使受伤; 伤害: ~ *a snake*. 打一条蛇弄得半死. **2** put an end to; frustrate (a plan, idea, etc). 阻止; 破坏 (计划, 计策等).

Scot·land Yard /,skɒtlənd 'jɑːd; 'skɑtlənd'jɑrd/ n (now *New S~ Y~*) (used for) the London police; headquarters of the Criminal Investigation Department: (现称 New Scotland Yard) (用以指伦敦警察厅) 伦敦警察厅刑事部: *They called in* ~, asked for the help of this Department. 他们向伦敦警察厅刑事部报警.

Scots /skɒts; skɑts/ adj = Scotch. the ~ *n pl* natives of Scotland. 苏格兰人. '~·man /-mən; -mən/, '~·woman /-wumən; -wumən/ *nn* natives of Scotland. 苏格兰男人, 苏格兰女人.

Scot·tish /'skɒtɪʃ; 'skɑtɪʃ/ adj = Scotch.

scoun·drel /'skaundrəl; 'skaundrəl/ n wicked person with no principles or scruples; villain; rascal. 寡廉鲜耻的坏人; 无赖; 恶棍. ~·ly /-rəlr; -rəlr/ adj of or like a ~. 无赖的; 似恶棍的.

scour[1] /skauə(r); skaur/ vt, vi **1** [VP6A, 15A, B] make a (dirty surface) clean or bright by friction: 刷净; 擦亮 (肮脏的外表): ~ *the pots and pans*; 刷净锅和盘; ~ *out a saucepan*, clean the inside (with a ~er). (用刷刷) 刷净煮锅的内部. **2** [VP6A, 15B] ~ *sth (away/off)*, get rid of (rust, marks, etc) by rubbing or with a strong jet of water: 刷掉; 冲掉 (锈, 污点等): ~ *the rust off*. 刷掉锈迹. **3** [VP6A, 15A] clear out (a channel, etc) by flowing over or through it: 冲刷成; 冲出 (河床等): *The torrent* ~*ed a channel down the hillside*. 急流沿着山坡冲成了一条沟. □ n act of ~ing: 刷; 擦; 冲: *give a dirty saucepan a good* ~. 把肮脏的煮锅好好地刷刷. ~*er* n (esp) pad of stiff nylon or wire for ~ing pots and pans. (尤指) 刷锅用之尼龙或金属网垫.

scour[2] /'skauə(r); skaur/ vt, vi **1** [VP6A] go rapidly into every part of (a place) looking for: 急速走遍 (一地方) 而搜寻: ~ *the woods*. 急速地在树林中搜寻. *The police* ~*ed London for the thief*. 警察当局在伦敦搜捕那贼. **2** [VP2C] ~ *about after/for sb/sth*, go quickly in search or pursuit of. 搜索; 追寻.

scourge /skɜːdʒ; skɝdʒ/ n **1** (old use) whip for flogging persons. (旧用法) 鞭; 笞. **2** cause of suffering; person regarded as an instrument of vengeance or punishment: 痛苦的原因; 被视为报复或惩罚之工具的人: *After the* ~ *of war came the* ~ *of disease*. 战乱之后瘟疫接踵而至. □ vt [VP6A] **1** (old use) use a ~ on. (旧用法) 鞭笞. **2** (fig) cause suffering to: (喻) 使受痛苦.

scout[1] /skaut; skaut/ n **1** person (not a spy), ship or small, fast aircraft, sent out to get information of the enemy's movements, strength, etc. 斥候; 侦察员; 侦察舰; 侦察机. **2** (Boy) S~, member of an organization (the S~ Association) intended to develop character and teach self-reliance, discipline and public spirit. 童子军. Cf 参较 *Girl Guides* (US 美 = *Girl S~*). '~·master n officer who leads a troop of Boy S~s. 童子军团团长或教练. **3** patrol-man on the roads, helping

motorists who are members of the Automobile Association or Royal Automobile Club. (帮助身为汽车协会或皇家汽车俱乐部会员之驾车者的) 公路巡逻人员. **4** person employed to look out for talented performers (in sport, the theatre, etc) and recruit them for his employer(s): 受雇物色运动员或演员之人; 球探; 影星探: *a 'talent* ~. 物色人才之人. **5** (at Oxford) college servant. (牛津大学的) 校工. □ vi [VP2C] ~ *about/around (for sb/sth)*, go about as a ~(1, 4): 侦察; 到处寻找: ~ *about/around for...*, go about looking for.... 往各处寻找….

scout[2] /skaut; skaut/ vt [VP6A] dismiss (an idea, suggestion, etc) as worthless or ridiculous. 认为无用或可笑而驳斥 (意见, 提议等).

scow /skau; skau/ n large flat-bottomed boat used for carrying sand, rock, rubbish, etc. (用于装运沙、石、垃圾等的) 平底船.

scowl /skaul; skaul/ n [C] bad-tempered look (on the face). (脸上的) 不豫之色. □ vi [VP2A, 3A] ~ *(at)*, look in a bad-tempered way: (对…) 作不豫之色; 怒目而视: *The prisoner* ~*ed at the judge*. 那囚犯满面怒容地看着法官.

scrabble[1] /'skræbl; 'skræbl/ n [U] (P) game in which words are built up on a board (marked with squares) from letters printed on counters or blocks (商标) 一种拼字游戏.

scrabble[2] /'skræbl; 'skræbl/ vi **1** [VP2A] scrawl, scribble. 乱写; 乱涂. **2** [VP2C] ~ *about (for sth)*, grope about to find or collect sth: 摸索着找; 爬寻; 抓挠: ~ *about for sth dropped under the table*. 爬寻掉在桌下的某物. □ n act of scrabbling. 乱写; 乱涂; 摸索着找; 爬寻.

scrag /skræg; skræg/ n **1** lean, skinny person or animal. 瘦瘠的人或动物. **2** ,~-('end), bony part of a sheep's neck, used for making soup and stews. 羊颈部的多骨部分 (用于做汤和炖菜). □ vt (-gg-) put to death by strangling; twist the neck of. 掐死; 勒死; 扭杀; 绞一之颈. **scraggy** adj (-ier, -iest) thin and bony: 瘦瘠的: *a long, ~gy neck*. 瘦长的颈子.

scram /skræm; skræm/ vi (either *imper* or *inf*) (sl) go away: (用于祈使句或不定式) (俚) 走开; 滚开: *I told him to* ~. 我叫他走开.

scramble /'skræmbl; 'skræmbl/ vi, vt **1** [VP2A, C, 4A] climb, clamber or crawl (over steep or rough ground): 爬; 攀缘; 爬行 (于陡峭或不平之地): ~ *up the side of a cliff/over a rocky hillside*. 爬上峭壁 (攀登多石的山坡). **2** [VP3A, 4A] ~ *(for)*, struggle with others to get sth, or as much or as many as possible of sth, from competitors: 争取; 争夺: *The players* ~*d for/* ~*d to get possession of the ball*. 球员们抢球. *The children* ~*d for the coins that were thrown to them*. 孩子们争夺扔给他们的硬币. **3** [VP6A] cook (eggs) by beating them and then heating them in a saucepan with butter and milk. (用奶油和牛奶) 炒 (蛋). **4** [VP6A] make a message sent by telephone, etc unintelligible (by changing the wave frequency) without a special receiver. 改变频率使电讯不致被窃听. □ n [C] **1** climb, walk, motor-bike competition or trial, over or through obstacles, rough ground, etc. 爬过障碍或崎岖之地等; 攀缘; 爬行; (摩托车之) 越野比赛; 越野试车. **2** rough struggle: 抢; 争取; 争夺: *There was a* ~ *for the best seats*. 大家都在抢最好的座位. **scrambler** /'skræmblə(r); 'skræmblə/ n device for scrambling telephone messages. 改变电讯频率之装置; 扰频器; 倒频器. ⇨ **4** above.

scrap[1] /skræp; skræp/ n **1** [C] small (usu unwanted) piece: 小片; 碎屑 (通常为不需要者): ~*s of paper/broken porcelain*; 纸 (破瓷) 片; (fig) small amount: (喻) 小量: *not a* ~ *of evidence to support the charge*; 没有一点证据可以支持该控诉; *not even a* ~ *of comfort in the news*. 该消息毫无令人安慰之处. **2** [U] waste or unwanted articles, esp those of value only for the material

they contain: 废料; 报废之物件(尤指仅因其所含之物质而有价值者): *A man comes round regularly collecting* ~. 有个男人定时前来收破烂。 '**~-heap** *n* pile of waste or unwanted material or articles. 废料堆; 废物堆。 '**~-iron** *n* [U] articles made of iron, to be melted down for re-use. 废铁。 **throw** *sth/sb* **on the ~-heap,** discard sth, dismiss sb, as no longer wanted. 丢弃无用之物(淘汰不再需要之人)。 **3** (*pl*) odds and ends; bits of uneaten food: *Give the ~s to the dog.* 把残食喂狗。 **4** [C] picture or paragraph cut out from a periodical, etc for a collection. (从刊物等剪下以供收集的图片; 文章; 残篇。 '**~-book** *n* book of blank pages on which to paste these. 剪贴簿。 □ *vt* (**-pp-**) [VP6A] throw away as useless or worn-out: 废弃: *You ought to ~ that old bicycle and buy a new one.* 你应该丢掉那辆旧自行车, 再买一辆新的。 **~·py** *adj* (**-ier, -iest**) made up of bits or ~s; not complete or properly arranged. 由零碎物件组成的; 不连贯的; 片断的。 **~·ily** *adv* /-ɪlɪ; -ɪlɪ/ *adv* **~·i·ness** *n.*

scrap² /skræp; skræp/ *n* (colloq) fight, quarrel, esp one that is not planned or premeditated: (口)口角; 口角(尤指非出于预谋者): *He had a bit of a ~ with his brother.* 他和他哥哥(弟弟)发生过一次小小的争执。 □ *vi* (**-pp-**) fight; quarrel: 打架; 争吵: *Tell those boys to stop ~ping.* 叫那些男孩子不要再打架。

scrape /skreɪp; skrep/ *vt, vi* **1** [VP6A, 14, 15A, B, 22] ~ *sth* (*from/off sth*); ~ *sth* (*away/off*), make clean, smooth or level by drawing or pushing the hard edge of a tool, or sth rough, along the surface; remove (mud, grease, paint, etc) in this way: (用刀)削, 刮, 擦; 刮落; 擦去(泥, 油脂, 油漆等): ~ *out a sticky saucepan;* 擦净粘糊糊的煮锅; ~ *the rust off sth;* 擦掉某物上的锈; ~ *paint from a door;* 刮去门上的油漆; ~ *a dish clean.* 把盘子擦净。 *The ship's bottom needs to be ~d,* eg in order to remove barnacles. 船底需要刮了(如除去藤壶)。 **2** [VP6A, 14] ~ *sth* (*from/off sth*), injure or damage by harsh rubbing, etc: 刮伤; 擦伤: *The boy fell and ~d his knee/~d the skin off his knee.* 那男孩跌倒, 擦伤了膝盖(擦破了膝盖的皮)。 *He ~d the side of his car/~d the paintwork of his car.* 他刮坏了他的汽车的侧边(油漆)。 **3** [VP6A, 15B] ~ *sth* (*out*), make by scraping: 刮成; 挖空: ~ (*out*) *a hole.* 挖洞。 **4** [VP2C, 3A] go, get, pass along, touching or almost touching: 擦过; 勉强通过: ~ *along a wall;* 擦墙而过; *branches that ~ against the window panes.* 擦到窗玻璃的树枝。 ~ *along,* (fig) manage to live in spite of difficulties. (喻)勉强维持生活。 ~ *through (sth),* only just pass: 勉强通过: *The boy just ~d through(his exams).* 那男孩勉强通过了考试。 **bow and ~,** bow awkwardly while drawing one foot along the floor; (fig) behave with exaggerated respect. (将一只脚往后退)笨拙地打躬作揖; (喻)过分奉承; 巴结。 **5** [VP6A, 15B] ~ *sth/sb together,* obtain by being careful, or with effort: 设法得到; 凑聚积累: *We managed to ~ together an audience of fifty people/enough money for a short holiday.* 我们设法聚集了五十名听众(足够的钱做短期度假)。 ~ (*up*) *an acquaintance with sb,* force one's acquaintance upon sb; push oneself into a person's company in order to get acquainted with him. 硬要与某人结交; 极力与某人接近以结识之。 ~ *a living,* with difficulty make enough money for a living. 勉强够维持生活。 □ *n* **1** act or sound of scraping: 刮; 削; 擦; 刮削声; 磨擦声: *the ~ of sb's pen on paper/of the teacher's fingernail on the blackboard.* 笔在纸上的沙沙声(教师的指甲在黑板上的磨擦声)。 **2** place that is cut; abraded: 擦伤: *a bad ~ on the elbow,* eg as the result of a fall. 肘上的严重擦伤。 **3** awkward situation resulting from foolish or thoughtless behaviour: (由于愚笨或欠考虑之行为所造成的)困境; 困难: *That boy is always getting into ~s.* 那男孩老是陷入困境。 *Don't expect me to get you out of your ~s.* 不要指望我能帮助你脱离困境。 **~r** *n* tool used for scraping, eg for scraping mud from one's shoes at the

entrance to a building, or for scraping paint from woodwork. 刮具; 擦器(例如进门处之除去鞋底的刮具, 或擦掉木器之油漆的刮刀)。 **scrap·ing** *n* (esp *pl*) small bits produced by scraping: (尤用复数)被刮削下的碎屑: *scrapings from the bottom of the barrel.* 从桶底刮下来的碎屑。

scrappy /'skræpɪ; 'skræpɪ/ *adj* ⇨ **scrap¹.**

scratch¹ /skrætʃ; skrætʃ/ *vt, vi* **1** [VP6A, 2A] make lines on or in a surface with sharp point or edge, eg fingernails, claws: (用指甲、爪等)抓; 搔: *The cat ~ed me.* 猫抓了我。 *Does your cat ~?* 你的猫会抓人吗? *Who has ~ed the paint?* 谁抓坏了油漆? ~ *the surface,* (fig) deal with a subject without being thorough, without getting deeply into it: (喻)讨论一题目未能彻底深入: *The lecturer merely ~ed the surface of the subject.* 那演讲者仅抓到该题目的皮毛。 **2** [VP6A] get (oneself, a part of the body) ~ed by accident: 意外地使(自己, 身体的一部分)刮伤: *He ~ed his hands badly while pruning the rosebushes.* 他修剪玫瑰时双手刮伤得很厉害。 **3** [VP15B] ~ *sth out,* draw a line or lines through a word or words, a name, etc: 勾掉; 划去(字, 名字等): ~ *out Smith/his name from the list.* 把史密斯(他的名字)从名单上划去。 *The essay contained a lot of scratched-out words/~ings-out.* 这篇论文有许多划掉的字。 **4** [VP6A, 2A] withdraw (a horse, a candidate, oneself) from a competition; take out (the name of a horse, a candidate) from a list of entries for a race or competition: 使(马, 侯选人, 自己)退出比赛; 自比赛的名单中划去(马, 候选人的名字): *The horse was ~ed,* Its name was withdrawn. 那匹马退出比赛了。 *I hope you're not going to ~* (= withdraw, decline) *at the last moment.* 我希望你不会在最后一刻退出比赛。 **5** [VP6A, 2A] scrape or rub (the skin), esp to relieve itching: (尤指为止痒而)搔(皮肤): ~ *mosquito bites.* 搔蚊子咬处。 *Stop ~ing (yourself).* 停止搔痒皮肤。 ~ *one's head,* show signs of being perplexed. 搔头(显出困惑的样子)。 *If you'll ~ ,my back, I'll ~ 'yours,* (fig) If you'll help, flatter, etc me, I'll do the same for you. (喻)如果你帮我的忙(奉承我), 我也会帮助你(奉承你); 投桃报李。 **6** [VP6A, 15B] ~ *sth (out),* make by ~ing: (用指甲、爪等)抓: ~ (*out*) *a hole.* 挖出一个洞。 **7** [VP6A] write hurriedly; scribble: 匆促地写; 乱写: ~ *a few lines to a friend.* 匆促地写几句话给一位朋友。 ~-**pad** *n* scribbling pad. 拍纸簿; 便笺簿。 **8** [VP2A] make a scraping noise: 发刮擦声: *This pen ~es.* 这钢笔号字时发刮擦声。 **9** [VP2C, 15B] ~ *about (for sth);* ~ *sth up,* tear or dig with the claws, fingernails, etc in search of sth: (以爪, 指甲等)挖寻; 搜寻: *The chickens were ~ing about in the yard.* 鸡正在院子里四处觅食。 *The dog ~ed up a bone.* 那狗挖出一根骨头。 **10** [VP15B] scrape(5): 搔; 凑拢: ~ *up/together a few pounds.* 积攒数英镑钱。

scratch² /skrætʃ; skrætʃ/ *n* **1** [C] mark, cut, injury, sound, made by scratching(1): 抓痕; 搔痕; 抓伤; 搔伤; 抓搔声: *Her· hands were covered with ~es after she had pruned her rose-bushes.* 她修剪过玫瑰丛以后, 双手有是刮痕。 *It's only a ~,* a very slight injury. (它)不过是微伤罢了。 *He escaped without a ~,* quite unhurt. 他安然逃脱。 *a ~ of the pen,* a few words quickly and easily written; a signature. 匆促而随便写的几个字; 签名。 **2** (*sing* only) act or period of scratching(5): (仅用单数)搔; 搔痒的期间: *The dog enjoys having a good ~.* 那狗喜欢搔痒。 **3** (*sing* only; no article) starting line for a race. (仅用单数; 无冠词)(竞赛之)起跑线。 *start from ~,* start from this line; (fig) start without being allowed any advantage(s); (fig) begin (sth) without preparation. 从起跑线出发; (喻)从头做起; 白手起家; (喻)未经准备而做(某事)。 *be/come/bring sb up to ~,* (fig) be ready/get sb ready to do what is expected or required: (喻)准备好(使某人准备好)做期望或要求之事: *Will your teachers manage to bring you up to ~ before you take the examination,* get you ready for it? 你们的老师能使你们在参加考试之前有充分准备

吗? **4** (attrib) (sport) without a handicap: (用作定语) (运动)对参赛条件优者无限制的; 无让分优待的: ~ *player*. 在同样条件下比赛的运动员。'~*race* one in which all competitors start from ~, on equal terms. 在同等的条件下的比赛; 无让分优待的比赛。 **5** (attrib) collected by chance; brought together, done, made, with whatever is available: (用作定语)偶然凑成的, 东拼西凑的; 利用手头材料做成或制成的: *a ~ crew/team*; 临时凑成的一船水手(一个球队); *a ~ dinner*, prepared from what happens to be in the house. (就家中现有食物凑成的)便饭。 ~**y** *adj* **1** (of writing, drawings) done carelessly or unskilfully. (指写作; 图画)草率的; 潦草的。 **2** (of a pen) making a scratching noise. (指钢笔)发沙沙声的。

scrawl /skrɔːl; skrɔl/ *vi*, *vt* [VP6A, 2A, C] write or draw quickly or carelessly; make meaningless or illegible marks: 潦草地写或画; 乱涂: *Who has ~ed all over this wall?* 谁在这墙上乱涂? *He ~ed a few words on a postcard to his wife.* 他潦草地在一张明信片上写了几句话给他的妻子。 □ *n* **1** [C] piece of bad writing; hurried note of letter. 拙劣的写作; 潦草写成的便条或信。 **2** (*sing* only) shapeless, untidy handwriting: (仅用单数)潦草的笔迹; 涂鸦: *What a ~!* 多潦草的字迹! *His signature was an illegible ~.* 他的签名是难以辨认的涂鸦。

scrawny /ˈskrɔːnɪ; ˈskrɔnɪ/ *adj* (-ier, -iest) bony, scraggy: 瘦瘠的: *the ~ neck of a turkey.* 火鸡细而瘦的颈子。

scream /skriːm; skrim/ *vi*, *vt* **1** [VP2A, C, 6A, 15A, B, 22] ~ (*out*), (of human beings, birds, animals) give a loud, sharp cry or cries of, or as of, fear or pain; cry (sth) in a loud shrill voice: (指人、鸟、兽) 发出(如如)恐惧或痛苦的尖叫声; 尖叫着说(某事物): *She ~ed in anger.* 她愤怒地尖声叫喊。 *The baby has been ~ing for an hour.* 那婴儿已经哭了一小时。 *This parrot ~s but does not talk.* 这鹦鹉会尖叫, 但不会说话。 *The child ~ed itself red in the face.* 这孩子尖叫得脸都红了。 *She ~ed out that there was a burglar under the bed.* 她尖叫说床下有贼。 *We all ~ed with laughter,* laughed noisily. 我们都纵声大笑。 ~ **one's head off**, ~ very loudly (and for a long time). 大声喊叫; 拼命喊叫。 **2** [VP2A, C] (of the wind, machines, etc) make a loud, shrill noise: (指风, 机器等)呼啸; 发尖啸声: *The wind ~ through the trees.* 风从林间呼啸而过。 □ *n* [C] **1** loud, shrill, piercing cry or noise: 尖叫声: *the ~ of a peacock*; 孔雀的尖叫声; ~*s of pain/laughter.* 痛苦的尖叫(纵声大笑)。 **2** (colloq) sb or sth that causes ~s of laughter: (口) 非常可笑的滑稽人物或事件: *He/It was a perfect ~.* 他(它)是极其可笑的。 ~**·ing·ly** *adv* (esp): (尤用于): *laughingly funny,* so funny as to cause ~s of laughter. 非常可笑的; 非常有趣的。

scree /skriː; skri/ *n* [C, U] (part of a mountainside covered with) small loose stones which slide down when trodden on. 山坡上的碎石; 覆有碎石的山坡。 ⇨ the illus at **mountain**. 参看 mountain 之插图。

screech /skriːtʃ; skritʃ/ *vi*, *vt* [VP2A, C, 6A, 15A, B] ~ (*out*), **1** make a harsh, piercing sound: 发尖声; 发出尖锐刺耳的声音: *jet planes ~ing over the house-tops.* 在屋顶上呼啸而过的喷射机。 *The brakes ~ed as the car stopped.* 汽车停下时煞车发尖啸声。 **2** scream in anger or pain; cry out in high tones: 愤怒或痛苦地尖叫; 高声喊叫: *monkeys ~ing in the trees.* 在树上尖叫的猴子。 *She ~es out her top notes instead of singing them.* 她尖声叫出高音符, 并非唱出它们。 □ *n* [C] ~*ing* cry or noise: 尖叫; 尖啸声: *the ~ of tyres,* eg when a car is cornering fast. (汽车急转弯等之时)轮胎摩擦的尖啸声。 '~**-owl** kind of owl that ~es instead of hooting. 叫枭(一种叫声很尖而不作咕咕声的枭)。

screed /skriːd; skrid/ *n* [C] long (and usu uninteresting) piece of writing; long monotonous speech. 冗长(且通常枯燥乏味)的文章; 冗长乏味的演讲。

screen /skriːn; skrin/ *n* [C] **1** (often movable) upright framework (some made so as to fold), used to hide sb or sth from view, or to protect from draughts or from too much heat, light, etc. 屏; 幕; 帘; 帐; 隔板 (常为可移动的直立构架, 有的并可折叠, 用于遮蔽某人或某物, 或使不受风吹, 过度受热, 受光等)。 **2** (in a church) structure of wood or stone separating (but not completely) the main part of the church and the altar, or the nave of a cathedral and the choir. 祭坛屏饰(使教堂的中部与祭坛, 或大教堂的正厅与唱诗班席位部分隔开的木造或石造建筑物)。 **3** anything that is or can be used to give shelter or protection from observation, the weather, etc: 可用以防止观察, 躲避风雨等之遮蔽物: *a ~ of trees,* hiding a house from the road; 一列树篱(使房子与大路隔开); *a 'smoke-~,* used in war to hide ships, etc from the enemy; 烟幕(战时用以掩护船只等, 以免被敌人发现); *a ~ of indifference,* an appearance of indifference that hides interest. (掩饰关心之)故示冷淡的外表。 **4** white or silver surface on to which slides, film transparencies, cinema films, TV pictures, etc are projected; surface upon which an image is seen on a cathode ray tube. (电影)、幻灯片)的银幕; (电视的)荧光屏。 Hence, 由此产生, (attrib, = cinema) (用作定语) *a ~ play,* the script of a film; 电影或电视脚本; ~ *actors/stars;* 电影或电视演员(明星); *a '~ test,* test of a person's suitability for acting in films. 试镜(测验一个人是否适于演电影)。 **5** frame with fine wire netting ('*window ~,* '*door ~*) to keep out flies, mosquitoes, etc. 纱窗; 纱门(用以阻挡苍蝇、蚊虫等)。 **6** large sieve or riddle used for separating coal, gravel, etc into different sizes. 大筛; 粗筛(用以按颗粒大小区分煤、砂石等)。 **7** (cricket) one of two large movable erections of white wood or canvas placed near the boundary line to help batsmen to see the ball. (板球)白色木材或帆布活动大屏风(置于球场两端, 使击球员能看见球)。 □ *vt*, *vi* **1** [VP6A, 14, 15A, B] ~ (*off*) (*from*), shelter, hide, protect from view, with a ~: (用屏、幕等)遮蔽; 隐藏; 保护: *The trees ~ our house from public view.* 这些树遮蔽了我们的房屋, 使别人看不见。 *One corner of the room was ~ed off.* 房间的一角被隔开了。 *You should ~ the lens of your camera from direct sunlight.* 你应该使照相机的镜头不直接受到阳光的照射。 *We have ~ed our house* (ie doors and windows) *against mosquitoes.* 我们的房子已装了纱窗纱窗以避蚊虫。 **2** [VP6A, 14] ~ (*from*), (fig) protect from blame, discovery, punishment: (喻)包庇; 庇护: *I'm not willing to ~ your faults/~ you from blame.* 我不愿包庇你。 **3** [VP6A] separate (coal, etc) into different sizes by passing through a ~ (6): 用大筛或粗筛分(煤等); 筛选: ~*ed coal,* from which dust has been removed. 筛去沙土的煤。 **4** [VP6A] investigate (sb's) past history, eg the political antecedents of a refugee or displaced person, sb applying for a position in government service, in order to judge his loyalty, dependability, etc; examine (sb) to judge his qualifications for a post, etc. 调查(某人)的过去历史(例如难民或寻求政治庇护者, 申请公职者的政治背景)以判断其忠诚、可靠性等; 考查(某人)以判断其任职等的资格; 甄别。 **5** [VP6A] show (an object, a scene) on a ~(4); make a cinema film of. 放映(物体、场景)于银幕或屏幕上; 摄制…的电影。 [VP2C] ~ *well/badly,* (of a stage play, an actor, etc) be suitable/unsuitable for filming. (指舞台剧、演员等)适于(不适于)拍电影。

screw /skruː; skru/ *n* **1** metal peg with slotted head and a spiral groove cut round its length, driven into wood, metal, etc by twisting under pressure, for fastening and holding things together. 螺丝; 螺丝钉; 螺旋钉。 *a '~ loose,* (fig) sth wrong or out of order: (喻)毛病; 故障: *There's a ~ loose somewhere.* 某个地方发生故障了。 *He has a ~ loose,* is a little stupid. 他有点笨。 '~-**driver** *n* tool for turning ~s. 螺丝刀; 起子(旋转螺丝钉的工具)。 ⇨ the illus at **tool**. 参看 tool 之插图。 '~-**topped** *adj* (of jars, etc) having a top or lid with a spiral groove, put on or taken off by twisting. (指瓶

thread   types of head

screws

等)有螺线之口或盖的(由拧转以盖上或取下)。 **'~-ball**
n, adj (US, sl) crazy (person). (美,俚)疯狂的(人)。
2 sth that is turned like a screw and is used for exerting
pressure, tightening, etc 螺旋状物;功用似螺丝之物。
put the ~(s) on sb; give (sb) another turn of the ~,
use one's power, a threat of force, etc to force him to
do sth. 施压力逼迫某人做某事。 ⇒ **thumb.**
3 action of turning; turn: 螺旋式的转动;拧转: *This
isn't tight enough yet; give it another ~.* 这个还
不够牢,把它再转一下。 **4** '~(-propeller) propeller of
a ship: 船的螺旋桨或推进器;暗轮: *a twin-~ ship.* 双
螺旋桨的船。 **('air)~,** propeller of an aircraft. 飞机的
螺旋桨或推进器。 ⇒ the illus at **air.** 参看 air 之插图。 **5**
[C, U] (in games, eg billiards) spin given to a ball to
make it curve or change direction. (撞球等游戏)转球;
拧(用球作曲线运动或使之改变方向者)。 **6** small, twisted
piece of paper and its contents: 小卷之纸及卷在纸中之
物;纸包: *a ~ of tea/tobacco.* 一包茶叶(烟草)。 **7**
(colloq) miser. (口)吝啬鬼;守财奴。 **8** (GB, sl) amount
of salary or wages: (英,俚)薪水或工资的数额: *He's
paid a good ~.* 他拿的薪水不少。 **9** (GB, sl) (= turnkey)
prison warder. (英,俚)典狱官;狱吏。 **10** △ act of or
partner in sexual intercourse. (讳)性交;与人性交者。
□ vt, vi **1** [VP6A, 15A, B] fasten or tighten with a ~
or ~s: 用螺旋钉钉住或拧紧: ~ *a lock on a door:*
用螺旋钉把锁钉在门上; ~ *down the lid of a coffin;* 用
螺丝拧紧棺材盖; ~ *up a door,* so that it cannot be
opened. 将门钉死。 *have one's head ~ed on (the right
way),* be sensible, have good judgement. 通达事理;有
良好判断。 **2** [VP6A, 15A] twist round; make tight,
tense or more efficient: 拧转;使紧;使有效率: ~ *a
lid on/off a jar;* 拧上(开)瓶盖; ~ *one's head round,*
in order to look over one's shoulder; (为了回顾)转头;
~ *up one's face/features/eyes,* contract the muscles,
eg when going out into bright sunshine from a dark
room. 皱着脸(皱起面孔;眯着眼睛)(如刚从黑暗的房间走
入强烈的阳光时)。 ~ *up one's courage,* overcome one's
fears. 鼓起勇气。 **3** [VP6A, 15A, B] exert pressure on;
force (out of): 加压力于;压榨;强迫;挤出: ~ *water out
of a sponge/more taxes out of the people.* 自海绵中将水
挤出(向人民榨取更多的税)。 **4** (sl) *be ~ed,* be drunk.
(俚)喝醉的。 **5** [VP6A, 2A] △ have sexual intercourse
with. (讳)与…性交。 ~**y** adj (GB colloq) eccentric:
crazy; (US colloq) ludicrously odd; absurd. (英口)怪
癖的; 疯癫的;(美口)荒谬的;可笑的。

scribble /'skrɪbl; 'skrɪbl/ vt, vi [VP6A, 2A] write
hastily or carelessly; make meaningless marks on paper,
etc. 潦草书写;胡写;乱画。 **'scribbling-block** n pad of
cheap paper making notes. 拍纸簿;便条纸。 □ n **1**
hasty, careless handwriting; [C] sth ~d. 潦草书写;
潦草之字迹; 胡乱写成之物。 **scrib·bler** /'skrɪblə(r);
'skrɪblə/ n person who is; (colloq) inferior author.
潦草书写的人;(口)蓝写的作家;拙劣之作家。

scribe /skraɪb; skraɪb/ n **1** professional letter-writer;
person who, before the invention of printing, made
copies of writings, eg in monasteries. 书记;抄写者(例
如印刷术发明前在寺院中抄写书籍者)。 **2** (Jewish hist)
maker and keeper of records; teacher of Jewish law (at
the time of Jesus Christ). (犹太史)文牍;书记;(耶稣基
督时代的)犹太法学者;律法师。

scrim·mage /'skrɪmɪdʒ; 'skrɪmɪdʒ/ n **1** [C]
confused struggle or fight. 扭打;混战。 **2** (US football)

the play that takes place when two teams are lined up
for the players to begin or resume play. (美式足球)并
列争球(开赛或继续比赛时两队队员排成横队,对面而立,
争取控球)。 **3** = scrum(mage). □ vi, vt engage in a
~(1); put (the ball) in a ~. 参与混战;置(球)于并列争
夺的位置;并列争(球)。

scrimp /skrɪmp; skrɪmp/ vt, vi = **skimp** (which is
more usu). (skimp 较常用)。

scrip /skrɪp; skrɪp/ n [C] document, the possession
of which entitles the holder to a formal certificate of
ownership of stock in a business company, etc on
completion of formalities; [U] such documents collectively. 临时凭单; 股票临时收据(持有者在完成手续后有
权获得公司之正式股票者);代价券(总称)。

script /skrɪpt; skrɪpt/ n **1** [U] (opp of *print*)
handwriting; printed cursive characters in imitation
of handwriting. (为 print 之反义词)手迹;笔迹;草书体
铅字。 **2** [C] (short for) manuscript or typescript (esp
of an actor's part in a play, a talk, discussion, drama,
etc to be broadcast, etc). (为 manuscript 或 typescript
之略)手稿;打字原稿; (尤指)戏剧脚本原稿;广播原稿。
'~-writer n person who writes ~s for films or
broadcast programmes. 电影或广播节目之撰稿人。 ~**ed**
adj read from a ~: 照原稿念出的: *Un~ed discussions
are usually livelier than ~ed discussions,* eg in a
broadcast programme. (在广播节目等中)不用稿的讨论
通常比读稿的讨论更为生动。

scrip·ture /'skrɪptʃə(r); 'skrɪptʃə/ n **1 (Holy) S~,
The (Holy) S~s,** the Bible; (attrib) taken from,
relating to, the Bible: 圣经;(用作定语)引自或有关圣
经的: *a '~ lesson.* 圣经课。 其他宗教的)经典;经文。 **scrip·
tural** /'skrɪptʃərəl; 'skrɪptʃərəl/ adj based on the
Bible. 根据圣经的。

scrof·ula /'skrɒfjulə; 'skrɒfjələ/ n [U] tuberculous
disease in which there are swellings of the lymphatic
glands. 斯科夫拉; 瘰疬; 淋巴腺结核病。 **scrofu·lous**
/'skrɒfjuləs; 'skrɒfjələs/ adj

scroll /skrəul; skrol/ n **1** roll of paper or parchment
for writing on; ancient book written on a ~. 纸卷;卷
轴;成卷轴的古书。 **2** ornamental design cut in stone;
flourish in writing, suggesting by its curves a ~ of
parchment. 石刻上的涡卷形装饰图案;涡卷形字体。

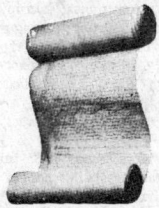

a scroll

Scrooge /skruːdʒ; skrudʒ/ n mean-spirited miser.
度量狭小的吝啬鬼。

scro·tum /'skrəutəm; 'skrotəm/ n pouch of skin
enclosing the testicles in mammals. 阴囊。

scrounge /skraundʒ; skraundʒ/ vt, vi [VP2A, 6A]
(colloq) get what one wants by taking it without
permission or by trickery. (口)偷;擅取;骗取。 ~**r** n
person who ~s. 偷者;擅取者;骗其来者。

scrub¹ /skrʌb; skrʌb/ n **1** [U] (land covered with)
trees and bushes or copse; stunted forest growth:
拙劣的杂树丛;长有杂树丛之地;矮树; (attrib) 用作定
语)'~-pine, '~-oak, dwarf or stunted kinds. 矮松,矮橡
树。 **2** [C] anything below the usual size. 任何矮小之物。
~**by** /'skrʌbɪ; 'skrʌbɪ/ adj (-ier, -iest) **1** small,
stunted; mean. 小的;矮的;卑劣的。 **2** rough and bristly:

粗糙而有刺毛的: *a ~by chin.* 粗糙而刺人的下巴。

scrub² /skrʌb; skrʌb/ *vt, vi* (**-bb-**) [VP6A, 15B, 22, 2A, C] ~ (**out**), clean by rubbing hard, esp with a stiff brush, soap and water: 用力擦洗; 擦净(尤指用硬刷、肥皂和水): ~ *the floor;* 擦洗地板; ~ *out a pan;* 擦净平锅; ~ *the walls clean;* 把墙刷洗干净; cancel; ignore: 取消;不理会。~ (*out*) *an order.* 取消命令。'~**bing-brush** *n* stiff brush for ~bing floors, etc. 硬毛刷子(刷洗地板等所用者)。⇨ the illus at **brush.** 参看 brush 之插图。□ *n* act of ~bing: 擦净; 擦洗: *The floor needs a good ~.* 这地板需要好好刷洗一番。

scruff /skrʌf; skrʌf/ *n* (only in) (仅用于) *the ~ of the neck,* the back of the neck, the nape, when used for grasping or lifting: 颈背(攫握或提起时用之): *seize/take an animal by the ~ of the neck.* 抓住一动物的颈背。

scruffy /'skrʌfɪ; 'skrʌfɪ/ *adj* (**-ier, -iest**) (colloq) dirty, untended and untidy looking. (口)肮脏的;不整洁的;样子邋遢的。

scrum /skrʌm; skrʌm/ *n* (abbr of) **scrummage.** 为 scrummage 之略。**scrum half,** the half-back who puts the ball into the ~. 拿球放在并列争球位置的前卫。

scrum·mage /'skrʌmɪdʒ; 'skrʌmɪdʒ/ *n* the play in Rugby football when the forwards of both sides pack together with their heads down while the ball is thrown into the middle of them and they then try to kick the ball back to their own team; all those forwards when such play occurs. 并列争球(橄榄球赛中双方前锋低着头密集排列,抢夺抛入两队之间的球);参加并列争球的前锋。

scrump·tious /'skrʌmpʃəs; 'skrʌmpʃəs/ *adj* (colloq, chiefly of food) delightful: (口,主要指食物)极好的: ~ *food.* 美食。

scrunch /skrʌntʃ; skrʌntʃ/ *n, vt* = **crunch(2).**

scruple /'skruːpl; 'skrupl/ *n* 1 weight-unit of 20 grains. 衡量单位(等于二十喱)。'⇨ **App 5.** 参看附录五。**2** [C, U] (hesitation caused by) uneasiness of conscience: 良心不安;自责;(由于良心不安引起的)踌躇;犹豫; 顾忌: *Have you no ~ about borrowing things without permission?* 你对于不经允许而借用务人东西无所顾忌吗? *He will tell lies without ~.* 他会肆无忌惮地说谎。□ *vi* [VP4C] ~ *to do sth,* hesitate owing to ~: 踌躇;有所顾忌。(usu neg) (通常为否定句) *He doesn't ~ to tell a lie if he thinks it useful.* 如果他认为说谎有用,他会无所顾忌地说谎。

scru·pu·lous /'skruːpjʊləs; 'skrupjələs/ *adj* careful to do nothing morally wrong; paying great attention to small points (esp of conscience): 多顾虑的; 小心翼翼的; (尤指对良心之所安)审慎的: *He is not ~ in his business dealings.* 他做生意不审慎。*A solicitor must act with ~ honesty.* 一个律师必须审慎正直。~·**ly** *adv* in a ~ manner: 多顾虑地;审慎地: ~*ly exact/careful.* 十分精确(小心)的。

scru·ti·neer /ˌskruːtɪ'nɪə(r) US: -tn'ɪər; ˌskrutə'nɪr/ *n* official who examines ballot papers to see that they are not filled in irregularly. 选票检查员;监票官。

scru·ti·nize /'skruːtɪnaɪz US: -tənaɪz; 'skrutn̩ˌaɪz/ *vt* [VP6A] make a detailed examination of. 细察;详审。

scru·tiny /'skruːtɪnɪ US: -tənɪ; 'skrutn̩ɪ/ *n* (*pl* **-nies**) **1** [U] thorough and detailed examination; [C] instance of this. 细察;详审;细察或详审的实例。**2** [U] official examination of votes, esp a recount of votes at an election when the result of the first count is very close: 核算选票; (尤指第一次计算后结果非常接近之)选票再计算; demand a ~. 要求再计票重点。

scud /skʌd; skʌd/ *vi* (**-dd-**) [VP2A, C] go straight and fast, with smooth motion: (平稳地)疾行;飞驰: *The clouds ~ded across the sky.* 云从天空飞过。*The yacht was ~ding along before the wind.* 那游艇正乘风向前疾行。□ *n* [C] act of ~ding; [U] vapoury clouds driven by the wind. 疾行;飞驰;飞雪;碎雨云。

scuff /skʌf; skʌf/ *vi, vt* **1** [VP2A, C] walk without

properly lifting the feet from the ground; shuffle. 拖足而行; 曳足而行。**2** [VP6A, 15A, B] wear out or injure (shoes, etc) by walking in this way: 曳足而磨损(鞋等): ~ *one's shoes.* 把鞋磨坏。

scuffle /'skʌfl; 'skʌfl/ *vi* [VP2A, C], *n* (take part in a) rough, confused fight or struggle: 混战;乱打;参加混战或乱打: *There was a ~ between the police and some demonstrators.* 警察和一些示威的人发生了一场混战。

scull /skʌl; skʌl/ *n* **1** one of a pair of oars used together by a single rower, one in each hand. (每手各执其一由单人操作的)双桨中之一叶; 短桨。**2** oar worked at the stern of a boat with twisting strokes. 船之尾橹;艄橹。□ *vt, vi* [VP6A, 2A] propel (a boat) with a ~; row (a boat) with ~s; use a ~ or ~s. 以尾橹推进(船)(以短桨划(船);用尾橹或短桨。~**er** *n* person who ~s. 用短桨或尾橹摇舟者。

scul·lery /'skʌlərɪ; 'skʌlərɪ/ *n* (*pl* **-ries**) room usu in a large house next to the kitchen, where dishes, pots, etc are washed up. 碗碟洗涤室(通常在厨房旁)。

scul·lion /'skʌlɪən; 'skʌljən/ *n* (hist) boy or man who did rough work in the kitchen of a large house, etc. (史)在大宅之厨房做粗重工作的帮手。

sculpt /skʌlpt; skʌlpt/ *vt, vi* = **sculpture.**

sculp·tor /'skʌlptə(r); 'skʌlptə/ *n* artist who sculptures. 雕刻家;雕刻师。**sculp·tress** /'skʌlptrɪs; 'skʌlptrɪs/ *n* woman ~. 女雕刻师。

sculp·ture /'skʌlptʃə(r); 'skʌlptʃə/ *n* **1** [U] art of making representations in stone, wood, metal, etc by carving or modelling. 雕刻术;雕塑术;雕刻;雕塑。**2** [C, U] (piece of) such work. (一件)雕刻品;雕塑品。□ *vt, vi* **1** [VP6A] represent in ~; decorate with ~: 雕刻(塑); 用雕刻(塑)物装饰: ~ *a statue out of stone;* 从石块雕出一座雕塑像; ~*d columns.* 雕刻的柱子。**2** [VP 2A] be a sculptor; do ~. 做雕刻(塑)师;干雕刻(塑)行业。**sculp·tural** /'skʌlptʃərəl; 'skʌlptʃərəl/ *adj* of, like, connected with, ~; made by sculpture. 雕刻(塑)的;有关雕刻(塑)的: *the sculptural arts.* 雕刻(塑)技艺。

scum /skʌm; skʌm/ *n* [U] **1** froth which forms on the surface of some boiling liquids; dirt on the surface of a pond or other area of still water. (某些煮沸液体之表面的)泡沫;(池塘或其他静水上的)浮垢;浮渣。**2** *the ~ (of)*, (fig) worthless person(s) (of a place). (喻)(某地的)无用之人;渣滓。*the ~ of the Earth,* worthless person(s). 无价值之人。~**my** *adj* of, like, having or containing, ~. 泡沫的;浮渣的;渣滓的;似浮渣的;有浮渣的。

scup·per /'skʌpə(r); 'skʌpə/ *n* opening in a ship's side to allow water to run off the deck. 船舷上之排水孔(排除甲板上的水)。□ *vt* sink a ship deliberately; (colloq, usu passive) ruin; disable: 故意使(船)沉没;(口,通常用被动语态)摧毁;使我疲: *We're ~ed!* 我们完蛋了!

scurf /skɜːf; skɜf/ *n* [U] small bits of dead skin, esp on the scalp, loosened as new skin grows; dandruff: 皮屑;皮垢;头皮屑;头垢: *monkeys searching each other's fur for ~.* 猴子们彼此搜找皮毛中的皮屑。~**y** *adj* having, covered with, ~. 有皮屑的;有头垢的。

scur·ri·lous /'skʌrɪləs; 'skʌrələs/ *adj* using, full of, violent and taunting words of abuse: 用骂人话的;满口骂人话的;谩骂的;下流的: ~ *attacks upon the Prime Minister.* 对首相作谩骂的攻击。**scur·ril·ity** /skʌ'rɪlətɪ; skə'rɪlətɪ/ *n* [U] ~ language; (*pl;* **-ties**) ~ remarks: 谩骂;下流; (复)骂人话: *indulge in scurrilities.* 肆意谩骂。

scurry /'skʌrɪ; 'skɜɪ/ *vi* (*pt, pp* **-ried**) [VP2A, 3A] ~ (*about*) (*for/through*), run with short, quick steps; hurry: 急忙奔跑; 疾行; 趱赶: *The rain sent everyone ~ing for shelter.* 雨使大家急忙找地方躲避。*Don't ~ through your work.* 不要赶急做你的工作。□ *n* **1** [U] act or sound of ~ing; anxious or excited bustle and movement: 急忙奔跑;疾行;疾行声;赶急;奔忙: *the ~ and scramble of town life.* 城市生活的匆促急忙。

There was a ~ towards the refreshments. 大家一窝蜂涌去吃点心。 **2** [C] **~ (of)**, windy shower (of snow); cloud (of dust). (雪片的)飞散; 一阵风雪; (灰沙的)弥漫; 飞扬的尘土。

scurvy /'skɜːvɪ; 'skɝvɪ/ n [U] diseased state of the blood caused (esp among sailors in former times) by eating too much salt meat and not enough fresh vegetables and fruit. 坏血症(由食咸肉过多, 食新鲜蔬菜及水果不足所致, 从前患此症者尤以水手居多)。 □ adj (sl) dishonourable, contemptuous: (俚)卑鄙的; 可耻的: That was a ~ trick to play on an old lady. 对一位老妇人施这样的诡计是太卑鄙了。 **scurv·ily** /-ɪlɪ; -əlɪ/ adv

scut /skʌt; skʌt/ n [C] short, erect tail, esp of a rabbit, hare or deer. (尤指家兔、野兔或鹿之)短尾。

scutch·eon /'skʌtʃən; 'skʌtʃən/ n = escutcheon.

scuttle[1] /'skʌtl; 'skʌtl/ n ('coal-)~, container for a supply of coal at the fireside. 煤斗; 煤桶(在火炉旁贮放煤者)。

scuttle[2] /'skʌtl; 'skʌtl/ vi [VP2A, C] ~ (off/away), scurry. 急促地跑; 赶急。 □ n hurried flight or departure; cowardly avoidance of, or running away from, difficulties and dangers: 急速的逃走或离去; 胆怯的避开困难和危险: The Opposition leader accused the Government of a policy of ~. 反对党领袖指责政府采取逃避政策。

scuttle[3] /'skʌtl; 'skʌtl/ n small opening with a lid, in a ship's side or on deck, or in a building's roof or wall. 舷窗; 舱室小孔; 天窗; 气窗。 □ vt [VP6A] cut holes in, open valves in, a ship's sides or bottom to sink it: 沉(船); 凿沉: The captain ~d his ship to avoid its being captured by the enemy. 船长把船凿沉以避免被敌人俘获。

Scylla /'sɪlə; 'sɪlə/ n (myth) (six-headed monster living on) a dangerous rock opposite a whirlpool (called Charybdis /kə'rɪbdɪs; kə'rɪbdɪs/) (in the Strait of Messina, S Italy). (神话) Charybdis 涡流对面的一块危险的岩石(位于意大利南方的墨西拿海峡); 居于此石上的六头妖怪。 **between ~ and Charybdis**, between two great dangers. 在两大危险中; 腹背受敌。

scythe /saɪð; saɪð/ n tool with a slightly curved blade on a long wooden pole with two short handles, for cutting long grass, grain, etc. 大镰刀(刃微弯, 装于有二把手之长木柄上,用于割牧草, 谷类等)。 □ vt [VP6A, 15A] cut with a ~. 用大镰刀割。

scything

sea /siː; si/ n **1 the sea,** expanse of salt water that covers most of the earth's surface and encloses its continents and islands; any part of this (in contrast to areas of fresh water and dry land): 海洋(遮覆地球表面大部分地方, 围绕诸大陆及岛屿等之咸水区域); 海洋的任何部分: Ships sail on the sea. 船只在海上航行。 Fish swim in the sea. 鱼在海中游。 The sea covers nearly three-fourths of the world's surface. 海洋约占地球表面的四分之三。 Let's go for a swim in the sea. 我们去海边游水吧! **follow the sea**, be a sailor. 当海员; 做水手。 **on the sea**, (of a place) on the coast: 在海边; 临海: Brighton is on the sea. 布赖顿城濒海。 **2 seas**, same sense, as 1 above. 海洋(与上列第 1 义同)。 **beyond/over the sea(s)**, abroad; to or in countries separated by the sea (note that overseas is more usu). 在海外; 往或

在被海洋所隔开的国家 (overseas 较常用)。 **the high seas**, parts which are not near the land, esp outside the territorial limits over which the nearest country has or claims jurisdiction. 外海; 远洋(海洋不临近陆地的部分); (专指)公海(领海以外之海洋)。 **the freedom of the seas**, the right to carry on sea-trade without interference. 海上贸易权; 商船在海上之自由航行权。 **3** (in proper names) particular area of sea which is smaller than an ocean: (用于专有名词中)海(海洋之某一特定区域, 较洋为小者)。 the Mediterranean Sea; 地中海; the Caribbean Sea; 加勒比海; the South China Sea; 南海; inland body of water; lake: 内海; 湖: the Caspian Sea; 里海; the Sea of Galilee. 加利利海。 **the Seven Seas**, (liter or poet) the Arctic, the Antarctic, the N and S Pacific, the N and S Atlantic and the Indian Oceans: (文或诗)七大洋(指北冰洋, 南冰洋, 北太平洋, 南太平洋, 北大西洋, 南大西洋及印度洋): He has sailed the Seven Seas. 他曾航行七大洋。 **all** (various phrases without articles) (用于无冠词的各短语中) **at sea**, away from, out of sight of, land: 离开陆地; 不见陆地; 在海上: He was buried at sea. 他葬身海中。 **all/completely at sea**, (fig) puzzled; at a loss: (喻)茫然; 迷惑; 不知所措: He was all at sea when he began his new job. 他开始新工作时, 茫然不知所措。 **by sea,** in a ship: 乘船; 由海路: travel by sea and land. 经海路及陆路旅行。 **go to sea**, become a sailor. 做水手。 **put to sea**, leave port or land. 出港; 出海。 **5** [C] local state of the sea; swell of the ocean; big wave or billow: 海洋之局部状态; 海洋之汹涌波浪; 大浪: There was a heavy sea, large waves. 海上波涛汹涌。 The ship was struck by a heavy sea, a large wave. 该船被巨浪冲击。 The seas were mountains high. 海浪高如山。 **half seas over**, having drunk too much; intoxicated. 喝酒太多; 醉了。 **6** [C] large quantity or expanse (of): 大量; 广阔(与 of 连用): a sea of up-turned faces, eg crowds of people looking upwards; 无数朝上的脸; a sea of flame. 巨大火焰; 一片火海。 **7** (attrib and in compounds): (用作定语, 用于复合词中): ,sea 'air at the seaside, considered to be good for health: 海边的空气(被认为有益于健康): enjoy the sea air. 享受海边的空气。 'sea-anemone n ⇨ the illus at anemone. 海葵(参看 anemone 之插图)。 'sea-animal n animal inhabiting the sea, eg fish, mammals, molluscs, etc. 海生动物(居于海中的动物, 如鱼类、哺乳动物、软体动物等)。 'sea-bathing n bathing in the sea. 海水浴。 'sea-bed n floor of the sea. 海床; 海底。 'sea-bird n any of several species of bird which live close to the sea, ie on cliffs, islands, etc. 海鸟。 ⇨ the illus at water. 参看 water 之插图。 'sea-board n coast region; line of coast. 沿海地区; 海滨; 海岸; 海岸线。 'sea-boat n ship with the sea-going qualities specified: 具备航行海洋之条件的船; 远洋船; 海船: a good/bad sea-boat, one that sails well/badly. 适于(不适于)航行海洋的船只。 'sea-borne adj (of trade) carried in ships: (指贸易)以船装运的; 海运的: sea-borne commerce / goods. 海运的贸易(船来的货物)。 'sea-breeze n breeze blowing landward from the sea, esp during the day in alternation with a land-breeze at night. 海风(尤指白天由海洋吹向陆地的和风, 与夜晚由陆地吹向海洋的风相互交替)。 Cf 参较 a ,sea 'breeze, any kind of breeze at sea. 指任何海上的微风。 'sea-coal n (hist) coal brought from Newcastle to London by sea (opp of charcoal). (史)煤(由纽卡斯尔海运至伦敦的煤)(为 charcoal 之反义词)。 'sea-cow n kind of warm-blooded creature living in the sea and feeding its young with milk. 海牛; 海象(一种海生温血哺乳动物)。 'sea-dog n (a) old sailor, esp the captains of English ships during the reign of Elizabeth I. 老练水手; (尤指)伊丽莎白一世时代英国船的船长。 (b) seal. 海豹。 (c) seal. 海豹。 'sea-faring /-feərɪŋ; -fɛrɪŋ/ adj of work or voyages on the sea: 海上工作的; 航海的: a 'seafaring man, a sailor. 海员; 水手。 'sea-fish n fish living in the sea (opp to freshwater-fish). 海鱼(为 freshwater-fish 之反义词)。 'sea fog n

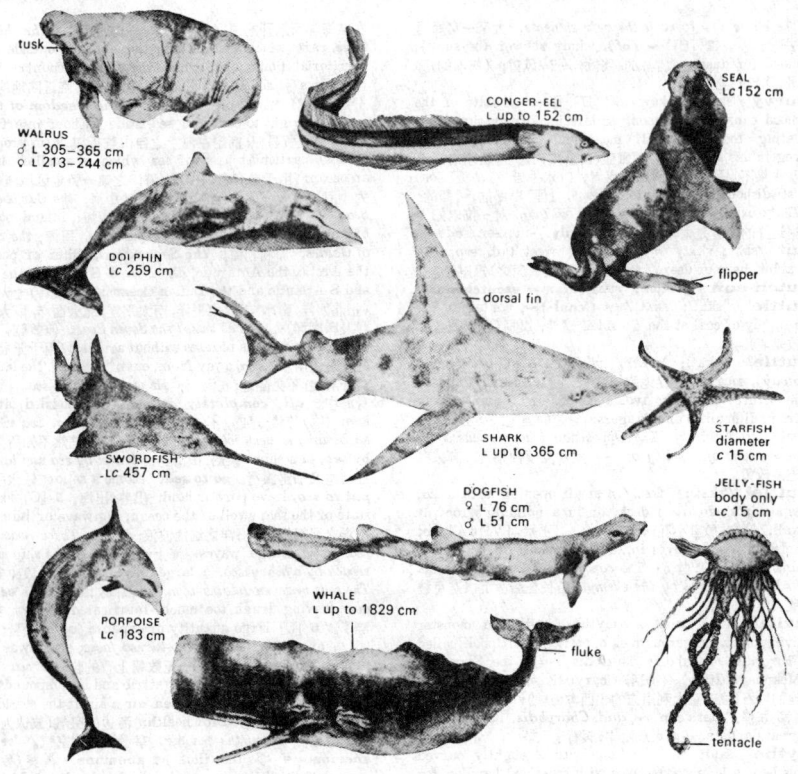

tusk

WALRUS
♂ L 305–365 cm
♀ L 213–244 cm

CONGER-EEL
L up to 152 cm

SEAL
Lc 152 cm

flipper

DOLPHIN
Lc 259 cm

dorsal fin

SWORDFISH
Lc 457 cm

SHARK
L up to 365 cm

STARFISH
diameter
c 15 cm

DOGFISH
♀ L 76 cm
♂ L 51 cm

JELLY-FISH
body only
Lc 15 cm

PORPOISE
Lc 183 cm

WHALE
L up to 1829 cm

fluke

tentacle

sea-animals

fog along the coast, caused by difference between land and sea temperatures. 海雾(沿海岸所起之雾,因陆地及海洋气温不同所致)。 **'sea·food** n edible fish or shellfish from the sea. 海鲜(可食用的海产鱼类或贝类): a '*seafood restaurant; a seafood cocktail.* 海鲜鸡尾酒。 **'sea·front** n part of a town facing the sea: 城镇之面海部分;滨海区: *The best hotels are on the sea-front.* 最好的旅馆在滨海地区。 **'sea·girt** adj (poet) surrounded by the sea. (诗)为海所环绕的。 **'sea·god** n god living in or having power over the sea, eg *Neptune.* 海神。 **'sea·going** adj (of ships) built for crossing the sea, not for coastal voyages only; (of a person) seafaring. (指船)适于越洋的(不仅用作沿海岸航行者);(指人)在海上工作的;航海的。 **,sea·green** adj, n bluish-green as of the sea. 海绿色(的)。 **'sea·gull** n = gull. **'sea·horse** n kind of small fish. 龙落子(一名海马,亦名马头鱼,为一种似马的小鱼)。 **,sea-island 'cotton** n fine quality of long-stapled cotton. 海岛棉(有长纤维而质地优良之一种棉花)。 **'sea·kale** n plant whose young white shoots are used as a vegetable. 宿根草(其白色幼芽用作蔬菜)。 **'sea-legs** n pl ability to walk on the deck of a rolling ship: 能在颠簸之海船甲板上行走而且不会晕船的能力: *get/find one's sea-legs.* 不晕船;有适应船上生活的能力。 **'sea level** n level of sea half-way between high and low tide as the basis for measuring height of land and depth of sea: 海(平)面(高低潮间之平均海面,用作测量地高及海深的基准者): *100 metres above/below sea level.* 海拔(低于海平面)一百公尺。 **'sea·lion** n large seal of the N Pacific Ocean. (北太平洋所产之)海狮。 **'Sea Lord** n one of four naval members of the Board of Admiralty

(London). (伦敦)海军本部四位海军首长之一。 **'sea·man** /-mən; -mən/ n (pl -men) (a) (in the Navy) sailor who is not an officer. (海军)水兵。 (b) person expert in nautical matters. 精于航海事务之人;水手;海员。 Hence, 由此产生, **'sea·man·like** /-mənlaik; -mən͵aik/ adj **'sea·man·ship** /-mənʃɪp; -mən͵ʃɪp/ n skill in managing a boat or ship. 驾船术;航海技术。 **'sea mile** n nautical mile. 海里;浬。 **'sea·plane** n aircraft constructed so that it can come down on and rise from water. 水上飞机(可在水上升降者)。 **'sea·port** n town with a harbour used by sea-going ships. 海埠;海港(具有可供海船使用之港口的城镇)。 **'sea-power** n ability to control and use the seas (by means of naval strength). (凭借海军力量之)制海权。 **'sea-rover** n pirate; pirate's ship. 海盗;海盗船。 **'sea·scape** n picture of a scene at sea. 海景;海画。 ⇨ landscape. **'sea·shell** n shell of any mollusc inhabiting the sea. 贝壳;螺壳。 **'sea·shore** n land bordering on the sea; beach: 海滨;海岸;海边: *children playing on the seashore:* 在海边游戏的儿童; (legal) between high and low-water marks. (法律)前滩(高潮线与低潮线之间的地方)。 **'sea·sick** adj sick, inclined to vomit, from the motion of a ship. 因船之颠簸而感不适或想呕吐的;晕船的。 **'sea·sick·ness** n **'sea·side** n (often attrib) place, town, etc by the sea, esp a holiday resort: (常用作定语)海边的地区, 城镇等(尤指假日游憩胜地): *go to the seaside for one's summer holidays;* 去海滨度暑假; *own a house by the seaside;* 在海滨有一栋房子; *a seaside town.* 海边的市镇。 **'sea·snake** n (kinds of) (usu venomous) snake living in the sea. (各种)海蛇(通常

有毒). **'sea-urchin** n small sea-animal with a shell covered with sharp points. 海胆(外壳覆有尖刺的细小海生动物). **,sea·'wall** n wall built to break the encroachment of the sea on the land. 防波堤; 海堤(用以阻止海水侵入陆地者). **'sea·ward** /-wəd; -wəd/ adj towards the sea; in the direction of the sea. 向海的; 朝海的. **'sea·wards** /-wədz; -wədz/ adv towards the sea. 海水. **'sea·way** n **(a)** progress of a ship through the water. 船舶之航行. **(b)** inland waterway, eg a river, series of lakes, joined by canals and locks, used by sea-going ships: 船舶之内陆航路(如以运河及水闸所连接之河,湖等): *the St Lawrence S~way* (connecting the Atlantic and the Great Lakes between Canada and the US). 圣劳伦斯内陆航路(连接大西洋与美加间的大湖区者). **'sea·weed** n [C, U] kinds of plant growing in the sea, esp on rocks washed by the sea. 海草(生长于海中, 尤指生长于被海水冲刷之岩石上的植物). **'sea·worthy** adj (of a ship) fit for a voyage; well built and in good repair. (指船)适于航海的; 建造与保养良好的.

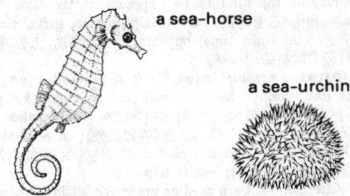

a sea-horse

a sea-urchin

seal¹ /siːl; sil/ n kinds of fish-eating sea-animal hunted for its oil and skin and the fur of some species. 海豹(数种食鱼之海洋动物, 猎取其油脂及皮毛, 种类繁多). ⇨ the illus at **sea**. 参看 sea 之插图. **'~·skin** n skin of a fur-seal; garment made of this. 海豹皮; 海豹皮所制之衣服. □ vi [VP2A] hunt ~s: 猎海豹; go ~ing; 去猎海豹; a ~ing expedition. 海豹狩猎队. **~·er** n person to ship engaged in hunting ~s. 从事猎海豹的人或船.

seal² /siːl; sil/ n **1** piece of wax, lead, etc stamped with a design, attached to a document to show that it is genuine, or to a letter, packet, box, bottle, door, etc to guard against its being opened by unauthorized persons. 封缄用的蜡片、铅片等(盖有图记, 用于公文以证明其为真实, 或用于信函、包裹、盒、瓶、门等, 以防止他人开启); 封蜡; 封铅; 火漆. *given under my hand and ~*, (legal) signed and sealed by me (法律)经我签名封缄发出的. *under ~ of secrecy*, (fig) what has been said must be kept secret because secrecy has been stipulated or is obligatory. (喻)必须保守秘密. **2** sth used instead of a ~(1), eg a plastic disc stuck to, or an impression stamped on, a document. 用以代替封缄, 封铅等的东西(如用于公文上之圆形封签或盖于公文上之印记). **3** piece of metal, etc on which is a design and which is used to stamp the ~ on wax, etc. 印章; 图章(上有图样, 用以在封蜡片等上面盖印). **'~·ring**, finger-ring with a ~ (often with the design cut on a gem). 印章戒指(其印章常刻于戒指的宝石上). **4** ~ *of*, (fig) act, event, etc regarded as a confirmation or guarantee (of sth) or giving approval (of sth): (喻)被认为是证实、批准、保证或赞许(某事物)的行为, 事件等: *By visiting Drake's ship, Queen Elizabeth I put/set the ~ of approval on his piratical voyages.* 伊丽莎白一世驾临德雷克的船只并表赞许他的海盗行径. □ vt **1** [VP6A, 15A, B] ~ *(up)*, put a ~(1) on: 加封蜡, 封铅等于…之上; 封缄: ~ *a letter*; 封缄一封信; fasten or close tightly: 密闭; 密封; 封闭: ~ *up a drawer so that it cannot be opened*; 封闭抽屉使无法打开; ~ *a jar of fruit*, make it air-tight so that the fruit will keep; (使不透气, 使果类易久藏); ~ *up a window*, eg by pasting paper over all the crevices. 密封窗户(如以纸糊起所有

的缝隙). ~ *sth in*, keep it in by ~ing: 密封使不外泄: *Our special canning process ~s the flavour in.* 我们的特殊装罐方法能保存味道. ~ *sth off*, block it: 封闭: ~ *off an area of land*, block all means of entering it, eg one where, after military use, there may be unexploded shells, etc. 封闭某地区(如经军事使用后, 可能留有未爆炸之炮弹等之地区). *One's lips are ~ed*, One must not speak; the matter must be kept secret. 不能讲; 必须保守秘密. *~ed orders*, instructions given to a ship's captain (or other person in authority), esp in wartime, in a ~ed envelope to be opened only at a certain time or place. 密令(尤指战时给予船长或其他当权人士的指令, 密封着, 只可在某时或某地拆开). **'~·ing-wax** n kind of wax that melts quickly when heated and quickly hardens when cooled, used to ~ letters, etc. 封蜡; 火漆(加热易溶, 冷却后甚快变硬的一种蜡, 用于密封信函等). **2** [VP6A] settle; decide: 解决; 决定: ~ *a bargain*; 决定某项买卖; 成交; *His fate is ~ed.* 他的命运已经决定.

seal·skin /'siːlskɪn; 'sil,skɪn/ ⇨ **seal¹**.

Sealy·ham /'siːlɪəm US: -lhæm; 'silɪ,hæm/ n kind of terrier with a long body and short legs. 㹴之一种(体长腿短).

seam /siːm; sim/ n [C] **1** line where two edges, esp of cloth or leather, are turned back and sewn together: 缝; 接缝(尤指布或皮革两边缘反转缝合之处): *searching for a lost coin in the ~s of his trousers.* 在他长裤的接缝处寻找一枚遗失的钱币. **2** line where two edges, eg of boards forming a ship's deck, meet. 两边缘(如构成甲板之木板的边缘)之接合线; 缝合处. **3** layer of coal, etc between layers of other materials, eg rock, clay. 在其他两层物质(如岩石, 粘土)间的煤层等; 层. **4** line or mark like a ~(1) (eg a wrinkle on the face). 似接缝的线或痕迹(如脸上之皱纹). □ vt (esp in the pp, of the face) *~ed with*, marked with (lines, scars, etc). (尤用其过去分词, 指脸)留有(线纹, 疤等)之痕迹的. **~·less** adj without a ~; made in a single piece. 无缝的; 整幅布制成的.

seam·stress /'siːmstrɪs; 'simstrɪs/, **semp·stress** /'sempstrɪs; 'sempstrɪs/ nn woman who makes a living by sewing. 女裁缝; 缝纫女.

seamy /'siːmɪ; 'simɪ/ adj **(-ier, -iest)** (chiefly fig, esp in) (主喻,尤用于) *the '~ side (of life)*, the less attractive aspects of life; poverty, crime, etc. 人生的黑暗面; 贫困、罪恶等.

sé·ance /'seɪɑːns; 'seɑns/ n meeting for the study of spiritualistic phenomena, eg communicating with the spirits of the dead through a medium. 研究招魂现象(如借关亡人与死者之灵魂交谈)之集会; 降神会.

seals

sear¹ /sɪə(r); sɪr/ vt [VP6A] **1** burn or scorch the surface of, esp with a heated iron; cauterize. (尤指用灼热之烙铁)烧…之表面; 烧灼; 炙. **'~·ing-iron** n one used for cauterizing. 烙铁. **2** (fig) make (sb's heart, conscience, etc) hard and without feeling: (喻)使(某人的心肠、良心等)冷酷、麻木而无情: *His soul had been ~ed by injustice.* 不仁不义已经使他的心灵变得冷酷无情.

sear², **sere** /sɪə(r); sɪr/ adj (liter) dried up; withered (esp of flowers, leaves). (文)枯干的; 枯萎的(尤指花、叶).

search /səːtʃ; sɜtʃ/ vt, vi **1** [VP6A, 14, 15A, B, 2A, 3A] ~ *(sb/sth) (for sb/sth)*; ~ *sb/sth out*,

examine, look carefully at, through, or into (in order to find sth or sb): 搜寻; 查究; 查查; 探查: ~ *a criminal to see what he has in his pockets.* 搜查犯人, 看他口袋中有何物。 *He ~ed and ~ed through all the drawers for the missing papers.* 他将所有的抽屉搜了又搜, 寻找遗失的文件。 *I've ~ed my memory but can't remember that man's name.* 我苦思良久, 仍旧记不起那人的名字。 *Do you spend much time ~ing through dictionaries for words to use?* 你花费许多时间在查字典中寻找要用的字吗? ~ **out,** look for: 寻找: ~ *out an old friend.* 寻找一位故友。 ~ **one's heart / conscience,** examine carefully one's own beliefs and conduct. 仔细检讨自己的信仰与行为; 自我反省。 ,S~ 'me! (colloq) I have no idea, no knowledge (of what you are asking about)! (口)我不知道(你所问的事)! **2** [VP6A] (liter) go deeply into; go into every part of: (文)深入; 进入…之每一部分: *The cold wind ~ed the streets.* 寒风吹遍各街道。 □ *n* [C, U] **1** act of ~ing: 搜寻; 查究; 搜查; 探查; 深入: *go in ~ of a missing child;* 寻找失踪的小孩; *a ~ for a missing aircraft;* 搜寻失踪的飞机; *make a ~ for contraband.* 搜查违禁品。 **right of ~,** right of the warships of a country at war to stop and examine a neutral ship (for contraband, etc). 搜索权(交战国之军舰检查审中立国的船只是否有违禁品的权利)。 '~·light *n* powerful light with a beam that can be turned in any direction, as used for discovering enemy movements, etc in war. 探照灯(可照向任何方向的强烈光柱, 战时用以发现敌人的活动等)。 '~·party *n* number of persons looking for sb or sth that is lost. 搜索队(找寻迷失之人或遗失之物者)。 '~·warrant *n* official authority to enter and ~ a building (eg for stolen property). 搜索票(准许搜查住宅, 以寻找赃物等的令状)。 **2** (legal) investigation (eg by lawyers, from local authorities) into possible reasons (eg planned demolition) why one should not buy land or property. (法律)调查不宜置产的原因(如属于拆除计划等)。 '~·er *n* person who ~es. 搜寻者; 探究者; 调查者。 '~·ing *adj* (of a look) taking in all details; (of a test, etc) thorough. (指目光)看到所有细节的; 锐利的; (指考验等)彻底的。 '~·ing·ly *adv*

sea·son /'siːzn/ 'siːzṇ/ *n* [C] **1** one of the divisions of the year according to the weather, eg spring, summer, etc: 季(依天气将年所作之划分,如春、夏等): *the 'dry ~,* 旱季; *the 'rainy ~.* 雨季。 **2** period suitable or normal for sth, or closely associated with sth: 适于某种事物的时期; 某事物惯常发生或与其有密切关联的时期; 季节; 时节: *the 'football ~;* 足球季节; *the 'nesting ~,* when birds build nests and lay eggs; 鸟类筑巢产卵之季节; *the 'dead ~, the 'off ~,* (in hotels at holiday resorts, etc) the time when there are very few guests; (度假胜地之旅馆等)游客稀少时期; 淡季; *the 'holiday/'tourist ~;* 度假的季节(观光的季节); *Christmas, the ~ of goodwill.* 圣诞节, 互示亲善的时节。 **the ~'s greetings,** (as written on a Christmas card). 节日的祝福(如书于圣诞卡上者)。 **in/out of ~, (a)** (of food) normally available / not available: (指食物)正当盛产(已过盛产)季节; 正当时令(不令令): *Oysters / Strawberries are out of ~ now.* 蚝(草莓)的盛产季节已过。 **(b)** at the time when most people take / do not take their holidays: (大多数人出外度假的)旺季; (大多数人不出外度假的)淡季: *Hotel charges are lower out of ~.* 在淡季旅馆收费较低。 **in (~) and 'out of ~,** at all times. 在所有的时间, 不拘任何时间。 **a word in ~,** advice at a time when it is likely to be useful. 适时的忠言。 '**close/the 'open ~,** ⟹ close¹(11), open¹(11). '~·ticket *n* **(a)** one that gives the owner the right to travel between places over a specified route as often as he wishes during a stated period of time: (持有者于一定时期可随意旅行于两地之)季票; 定期车票: *a three-month ~ (-ticket).* 三个月的定期车票。 Cf 参较 US 美 commutation ticket. **(b)** ticket that gives the owner the right to attend a place of amusement, etc, eg a concert hall, as often as he wishes (for the concerts, etc specified on the ticket)

during a certain period. (在一定时期内持有者可随意进入某娱乐场所,如音乐厅等之)长期票; 定期票。 □ *vt, vi* **1** [VP6A, 2A] make or become suitable for use; cause to be acclimatized, etc: 使适用; 使适应; 变为适用: *Has this wood been well ~ed,* dried and hardened? 这木材已干燥可用吗? *The soldiers were not yet ~ed to the rigorous climate.* 士兵们尚未能适应此种酷寒的气候。 **2** [VP6A, 14] ~ **(with),** flavour (food) (with salt, pepper, etc): 调味; 为(食物)加味道(用盐, 胡椒等): *mutton ~ed with garlic;* 用大蒜调味的羊肉; *highly ~ed dishes;* 调味甚浓的菜; (fig) (喻) *conversation ~ed with wit.* 风趣(逸趣横生)的谈话。 **3** [VP6A] (liter) soften; moderate: (文)使温和; 缓和: *'when mercy ~s justice',* ⟹ **Mer of Ven,** Act, IV, Sc 1. '以仁慈调剂峻法的时候' (参看莎士比亚戏剧 '威尼斯商人' 第四幕第一场)。 ~·**ing** *n* [C, U] sth used to ~ food: 调味品; 作料: *There's not enough ~ing in the sausage.* 腊肠中放的作料不够。 *Salt and pepper are ~ings.* 盐和胡椒是调味品。

sea·son·able /'siːznəbl/ 'siːzṇbl/ *adj* **1** (of the weather) of the kind to be expected at the time of year. (指天气)合时的。 **2** (of help, advice, gifts, etc) coming at the right time; opportune. (指帮助, 忠告, 礼物等)适合时机的。

sea·sonal /'siːzənl/ 'siːzṇl/ *adj* dependent upon a particular season; changing with the seasons: 依赖季节而存在的; 随季节而变化的; 季节性的: ~ *occupations,* eg fruit-picking; 季节性的职业(列如采果); *a ~ trade,* eg the selling of Christmas cards. 季节性的生意(如销售圣诞卡)。 ~·**ly** /-nəlɪ; -ṇəlɪ/ *adv*

seat /siːt/ *sit/ n* **1** sth used or made for sitting on, eg a chair, box, bench, the floor: 用以坐着的东西(如椅子, 箱子, 长凳, 地板等); 座; 座位: *There are no more chairs; you'll have to use that box for a ~.* 椅子都有人坐了, 你只好以那个箱子代为座垫。 *The back ~ of the car is wide enough for three people.* 车子的后座足够三个人坐。 **keep one's ~,** remain in one's ~: 坐在自己的座位上不动: *There's no danger — keep your ~s, please,* le don't panic. 没有危险——请坐在自己的座位上不要动。 **lose one's ~,** have one's ~ taken by someone else. 座位被别人占去。 ⟹ **4** below. 参看下列第 4 义。 **take a ~,** sit down: 坐下: *Won't you take a ~?* 请坐。 **take one's ~,** sit down in one's place, eg in a hall or theatre. 就座(如在会场或剧院中)。 **take aback ~,** ⟹ **back⁴(3).** '~·**belt** *n* safety strap (worn as a belt) fastened to the sides of a ~ in a passenger vehicle or aircraft. 安全带; 保险带(车辆或飞机上系于座位两侧的带子)。 ⟹ the illus at **motor.** 参看 motor 之插图。 **2** that part of a chair, stool, bench, etc on which one sits (contrasted with the back, legs, etc): 座部(与背, 腿等相对): *a 'chair~.* 椅子的座部。 **3** part of the body (the buttocks) on which one sits; part of a garment covering this: (人体或衣服上的)臀部: *a hole in the ~ of one's trousers.* 裤子后裆上的一个洞。 **4** place in which one has a right to sit: 某人有权就座之席位; 席次: *I have four ~s* (ie tickets for them) *for 'Swan Lake' at Covent Garden.* 考文特园(英国皇家歌剧院)上演的 '天鹅湖', 我已订下四个座位。 *Mr Smith has a ~ in the House of Commons,* is a member. 史密斯先生是下议院的议员。 **take one's ~,** assume one's membership (in the House of Commons). 担任下议院议员。 **win a ~; lose one's ~,** win/be defeated in a Parliamentary election. 当选(未当选)国会议员。 **5** place where sth is, or where sth is carried on: 所在地; 中心; 场所: *In the US, Washington is the ~ of government and New York City is the chief ~ of commerce.* 在美国, 华盛顿是政治中心, 纽约是主要商业中心。 *A university is a ~ of learning.* 大学乃求学研究之地。 **6** (country-)~, large house in the country, usu the centre of a large estate: 乡间之邸宅; 别庄(通常为大片地产的中心): *He is rich enough to have a country-~/a ~ in the country as well as a large house in London.* 他的财富, 使他在乡间拥有一座别墅, 并且在伦敦拥有一座大房子。 **7** manner of sitting, esp on a horse;

坐姿;(尤指)骑马的姿势或方式: *That rider has a good* ~, *rides his horse well.* 那位骑马者坐姿良好。 □ *vt* [VP6A] 1 ~ *oneself, te ~ed,* (formal) sit down: (正式用语)坐下: *Please be ~ed, ladies and gentlemen.* 请坐下, 各位女士和先生。 2 have ~s for: 有…座位; 可容纳…的座位: *a hall that ~s 500.* 有五百座位的会场。 *Are the ~ing arrangements* (= the arrangements for providing and placing ~s) *in the hall satisfactory?* 大厅里座位的安排还满意吗? ~**·ing·room** *n* [U] seats: 座位: *We have ~ing-room for thirty pupils in this classroom.* 在这教室中, 我们有容纳三十位学生的座位。 3 (usu 通常用 re~) repair the ~ or bottom of: 修理…之座部或底部: ~ *a chair* 修理椅子 *an old pair of trousers.* 修理椅子的座部(修补旧裤子的后裆)。

sec /sek; sɛk/ *n* (sl abbr of) second³(2). ⇨ **mo.** (俚) 为 second³ 第 2 义之略。

seca·teurs /ˈsekətɜːz; ˌsɛkəˈtʒz/ *n pl* pair of clippers used by gardeners for pruning bushes, etc. 剪枝刀; 修枝钳。

se·cede /sɪˈsiːd; sɪˈsid/ *vi* [VP2A, 3A] ~ *(from)*, (of a group) withdraw (from membership of a state, federation, organization, etc). (指团体)脱离; 退出(联盟、组织等之会籍)。

se·cession /sɪˈseʃn; sɪˈsɛʃən/ *n* [U] seceding; [C] instance of this (as in the US when eleven Southern States withdrew from the Federal Union in 1860–1861). 脱离; 退出; 其实例(如 1860—1861 年美国南部十一个州之脱离联邦)。~·**ist** /-ʃənɪst; -ʃənɪst/ *n* supporter of ~. 脱离论者; 主张退盟者。

se·clude /sɪˈkluːd; sɪˈklud/ *vt* [VP6A, 14, 15A] ~ *sb/oneself (from),* keep (a person, oneself) apart from the company of others: 使(人, 自己)与他人隔离, 使隐居: ~ *oneself from society;* 与世隔离; *keep women* ~*d in the harem.* 使妇女们深居于闺阁中。~*d adj* (esp of a place) quiet; solitary. (尤指地方)安静的; 幽僻的。 **se·clu·sion** /sɪˈkluːʒn; sɪˈkluʒən/ *n* [U] secluding or being ~d; ~d place; retirement: 隔离; 隐居; 幽僻之地; 隐退: *live in seclusion;* 隐居; *in the seclusion of one's own home.* 深居简出。

sec·ond¹ /ˈsekənd; ˈsɛkənd/ *adj* 1 (abbr 略作 **2nd**) next after the first (in place, time, order, importance, etc): 第二的(在地位, 时间, 次序, 重要性等方面): *February is the ~ month of the year.* 二月是一年中的第二个月。*Tom is the ~ son—he has an elder brother.* 汤姆是次男—他有一位长兄。*Osaka is the ~ city/the ~ largest city in Japan.* 大阪是日本的第二大城市。~**·'best** *adj* next after the best: 次好的; 第二好的: *my ~best suit.* 我的次好的衣服。□ *n, adv:* I won't accept/put up with ~best. 我不愿接受父(不能忍受)次好的东西。**come off** ~**best,** get the worst of sth. 输了; 被击败。~**·'class** *adj, n* **(a)** (of the) class next after the first: 二等(的); 次等(的): *a ~class hotel;* 二等旅馆; ~*class compartments,* in a railway carriage, etc; 二等车厢; ~*-class mail,* sent at a cheaper rate. (英)平信;(美)印刷品邮件。 **(b)** class below the first in examination results: (考试结果)第二等: *take a ~class (degree) in law.* 法律科考试获得第二等优良成绩。 **(c)** (regarded or treated as) inferior: 明显次等的或较低的: ~*-class citizens.* 社会地位低的市民; 次等公民。 □ *adv:* go/travel ~*class.* 乘二等车旅行。~ **floor** *n* the one above the first (in GB two floors, in US one floor, above the ground): (英)三楼;(美)二楼; (attrib) (用作定语) *a ~-floor apartment.* 三(二)楼的公寓。~**·'hand** *adj* **(a)** previously owned by someone else: 用过的; 旧的; 曾属于他人的: ~*-hand furniture/books:* 旧家具(书); *a ~-hand bookshop,* shop for ~*-hand books.* 旧书店。Cf 参较 *used cars.* **(b)** (from knowledge) obtained from others, not based on personal observation, etc: (指新闻,知识)得自他人的; 非根据亲身观察所得: *get news ~-hand.* 获得转述的消息。~ **lieutenant** *n* lowest commissioned rank in the Army. 陆军少尉。

平庸的: *a man with ~-rate brains.* 头脑平庸的人。 Hence, 由此产生; ~**·'rater** *n* person with ~-rate intelligence or abilities. 中智之人; 平庸之士: *a Cabinet made up mainly of ~-raters.* 由第二流人士组成的内阁。~ **'sight** *n* power to see future events, or events happening at a distance, as if present, 预见力; 千里眼。 Hence, 由此产生; ~**·'sighted** *adj* having this power. 有预见力的; 千里眼的。~ **'teeth** *n* those which grow after a child's first teeth are out. 永久齿。~ **'wind,** ⇨ **wind²**(3). surpassed by no other. 不次于任何人(事物)。 2 additional; extra: 补助的; 额外的: *You will need a ~ pair of shoes.* 你需要额外一双鞋。 3 ,S~ **'Advent /'Coming,** return of Jesus Christ at the Last Judgement. (最后审判时)基督的再临。~ **'ballot,** a method used in some elections by which, if the winner of the first ballot receives less than half the votes cast, a new ballot is taken, in which only he and the next candidate are voted for. 决选投票; 第二次投票(第一次投票之获胜者不能获得过半数票时, 就须与得票数次多者间, 再举行第二次投票)。~ **'chamber** *n* upper house in a legislature: 议会之上议院; *The House of Lords is the ~ chamber of Parliament in Great Britain.* 贵族院是英国国会之上议院。~ **'nature** *n* acquired tendency that has become instinctive: 第二天性: *Habit is ~ nature.* 习惯成自然。~ **'thoughts,** opinion or resolution reached after reconsideration: 再思; 重新考虑; 重新考虑后的意见或决定: *On ~ thoughts I will accept the offer.* 重新考虑的结果, 我愿意接受那提议(求钱等)。 *I'm having ~ thoughts* (= am not so sure) *about buying that house.* 关于买那栋房子的事我正重新考虑中。 4 of the same kind as one that has gone before; subordinate: 类似的; 附属的: *This fellow seems to think he's a Napoleon!* 这家伙似乎认为他是拿破仑第二! ~**'childhood** *n* old age when accompanied by weakening of the mental powers. 老耄期(伴以心智之衰退)。~**'cousin** *n* child of a first cousin of either of one's parents. 堂 (表) 伯, 姑, 姨, 母等之小孩子。*play ~ fiddle (to sb),* be of only secondary importance (to sb else). 做(某人)之副手; 居于次要地位。 □ *adv* in the ~ place; ~ in order or in importance: 第二(地); 次要地: *The English swimmer came (in) ~.* 那位英国游泳选手得第二。~**·ly** *adv* in the next place; furthermore. 第二; 其次。

sec·ond² /'sekənd; 'sɛkənd/ *n* 1 person or thing that comes next to the first: (人, 事物, 日期等之)第二: *the ~ of May;* 五月二日; *George the S~,* King George II. 国王乔治二世。*get a ~,* get a ~ class in an examination. 获得第二等优良成绩。 2 another person or thing besides the person or thing previously mentioned: (前述者以外的)另一人; 另一物: *You are the ~ to ask me that question.* 你是另一位向我提出那问题的人。 3 (*pl*) goods below the best in quality. (复)次等货。 4 (*pl*) second helping of food. (复)第二份食物。 5 person chosen by the principal in a duel to support him; supporter of a boxer in a boxing-match. 决斗者之助手; 拳击者之帮手。

sec·ond³ /'sekənd; 'sɛkənd/ *n* 1 (indicated by the mark '') 60th part of a minute (of time or of an angle, ⇨ **App 5**): 秒(时间或角度的一分钟或一分的六十分之一, 以 '' 符号表示之; 参看附录五): *winning time 1 minute, 5 ~s;* 优胜者的时间是一分五秒。*1° 6' 10" = one degree, six minutes, and ten ~s.* 1° 6' 10" 即一度六分十秒。~**·hand** *n* extra hand in some watches and clocks recording ~s. 钟表之秒针。 ⇨ also *second-hand* at **second¹**(1). 2 moment; short time: 片刻; 短时: *I shall be ready in a ~ or two/in a few ~s.* 几秒钟内我即可准备妥当。

se·cond⁴ /'sekənd; 'sɛkənd/ *vt* [VP6A] 1 support (esp in a duel or a boxing-match). 支持; 辅助(尤指在决斗或拳赛中)。 2 (of a member of a debating body) rise or speak formally in support of a motion to show that the proposer is not the only person in favour of

it: (指辯論團體的一分子)贊成某提案; 附議: *Mr Smith proposed, and Mr Green ～ed, a vote of thanks to the lecturer.* 史密斯先生提議向演說者鼓掌致謝, 格林先生附議之。 **～er** *n* person who ～s a proposal at a meeting. 開會時贊成某動議的人; 附議者。

se·cond⁵ /'sɪ'kɒnd *US:* 'sekənd; 'sɛkənd/ *vt* [VP 6 A, 15 A] (official GB use, esp mil) take (sb) from his ordinary duty and give him special duty: (英, 官方用語, 尤用於軍中)調動(某人)離其平常的職守而派以特殊任務: *Captain Smith was ～ed for service on the General's staff.* 史密斯上尉奉調擔任將軍的幕僚。 **～·ment** *n* ～ing or being ～ed. 調或被調任特殊任務。

sec·ond·ary /'sekəndrɪ *US:* -derɪ; 'sekən,dɛrɪ/ *adj* coming after, less important than, what is first or chief: 第二的; 從屬的; 次要的: *～ education/schools,* for children over eleven; 中等教育(學校); *a ～ stress,* eg on the first syllable of 'sacrifical' /,sækrɪ'fɪʃl; ,sækrə'fɪʃl/. 次重音(如 sacrificial 之第一音節上的)。 **sec·ond·ar·ily** /-drəlɪ *US:* -,derəlɪ/ *adv*

se·crecy /'siːkrəsɪ; 'sikrəsɪ/ *n* [U] keeping of secrets; ability to keep secrets; habit of keeping secrets; state of being kept secret: 守秘密; 守秘密的能力; 守秘密的習慣; 被保守秘密的狀態; 隱瞞; *rely on sb's ～;* 相信某人不會泄密; *prepare sth in ～,* secretly; 暗中準備某事; *do sth with great ～.* 極祕密地做某事。 *swear/bind sb to ～,* make him promise to keep sth secret. 使某人應允對某事守密。

se·cret /'siːkrɪt; 'sikrɪt/ *adj* **1** (to be) kept from the knowledge or view of others; of which others have no knowledge: 防止他人知悉的; 他人不知的; 祕密的: *a ～ marriage;* 祕密結婚; *keep sth ～ from one's family.* 不把某事告訴家人。 *He escaped through a ～ door.* 他從暗門逃走。 **the ,～ 'service,** government department concerned with espionage and counter-espionage. 政府的情報機構。 **,～ 'agent** *n* member of this department (called a 'spy' if he works for a foreign government and 'secret agent' if he works for one's own government). 情報人員 (如為外國政府工作稱為'間諜', 如為本國政府工作則稱為'情報人員')。 **2** (of places) secluded; quiet. 僻靜的; 幽僻的; 寧靜的。 **3** (of persons) secretive (the more usu word). (指人)有守密之習慣的; 好遮掩的 (secretive 較常用)。 □ *n* **1** [C] sth ～. 祕密。 *keep a ～,* not tell anyone else: 保守機密: *Can you keep a ～?* 你能保守祕密嗎? **in the ～,** among those who are allowed to know it: 參與祕密: *Is your brother in the ～?* 你的兄弟知道這項祕密嗎? *let sb into a/the ～,* share it. 使某人與聞(或參與)某項祕密。 **(be) an open ～,** (of sth which is said to be ～) be (in fact) widely known. 公開的祕密。 **2** [C] hidden cause; explanation, way of doing or getting sth, that is not known to some or most people: 祕訣; 祕傳; 訣竅: *What is the ～ of his success?* 他成功的祕訣是什麼? **3** [U] secrecy: 祕密: *I was told about it in ～.* 我被暗中告以此事。 **4** [C] mystery; sth hard to learn about or understand: 神秘; 奧妙; 難以理解之事: *the ～s of nature.* 自然的奧秘。 **～·ly** *adv*

sec·re·tariat /,sekrə'teərɪæt; ,sɛkrə'tɛrɪət/ *n* staff or office of the Secretary-General of a large organization: 秘書處; 秘書處之全體職員: *get a position on the ～ of UNO in New York.* 在紐約聯合國組織的秘書處獲得一職位。

sec·re·tary /'sekrɪtrɪ *US:* -,rɪterɪ; 'sɛkrə,tɛrɪ/ *n* (*pl* **-ries**) **1** employee in an office, who deals with correspondence, keeps records, makes arrangements and appointments for a particular member of the staff (and often called *private ～*). 書記; 秘書(辦公室中雇來為某一職員處理信函, 保管檔案, 安排業務及約會之人員; 常稱作'私人秘書')。 **2** official who has charge of the correspondence, records, and other business affairs of a society, club or other organization: (會社, 俱樂部或其他組織中)主管信函, 通訊, 記錄及其他事務的職員; 幹事: *honorary ～,* (abbr 略作 *hon sec*) unpaid ～ of a

society, etc which is not conducted for profit. (非以營利為目的之会社等不支薪水的)名譽幹事。 **3** (GB) (英) **S～ of State,** minister in charge of a Government office: (主管政府一部門的)國務大臣的: *the S～ of State for Foreign and Commonwealth Affairs/Home Affairs/Scotland/Defence, etc.* 外相(內政大臣; 蘇格蘭事務大臣; 國防大臣等)。 (US) (美) *S～ of State,* head of the Foreign Affairs Department; 國務卿; *S～ of the Treasury,* head of the Treasury Departmemt. 財政部長。 **Permanent S～,** senior official in the Civil Service. 高級文官。 **,S～'General,** principal executive office of a large organization (eg of UNO). (聯合國等庞大机构之)祕书长。 **sec·re·tar·ial** /,sekrə'teərɪəl; ,sɛkrə'tɛrɪəl/ *adj* of (the work of) secretaries: 书记(之工作)的; 祕书的: *secretarial duties/training/colleges.* 书记工作(训练, 专科学校)。

se·crete /sɪ'kriːt; sɪ'krit/ *vt* [VP 6 A] **1** produce by secretion(1). 分泌。 **2** put or keep in a secret place. 隐匿; 隐藏。 **se·cre·tion** /sɪ'kriːʃn; sɪ'kriʃən/ *n* **1** [U] process by which certain substances in a plant or animal body are separated (from sap, blood, etc) for use, or as waste matter; [C] substance so produced, eg *saliva, bile.* 动物物体内从汁液, 血液等处析出有用物或废物之程序; 分泌; 分泌物(如唾液, 胆汁)。 **2** act of secreting: 隐藏: *the ～ of stolen goods.* 赃物的隐藏。

se·cret·ive /'siːkrətɪv; sɪ'kritɪv/ *adj* having the habit of keeping things secret; tending to hide one's thoughts, feelings, intentions, etc. 有保守秘密之习惯的; 有掩饰自己之思想, 感情, 意欲等之倾向的; 秘而不宣的; 含蓄的。 **～·ly** *adv* **～·ness** *n*

sect /sekt; sekt/ *n* [C] group of people united by (esp religious) beliefs or opinions that differ from those more generally accepted. (信仰或意见迥异于多数人所接受者的)派系; 宗派; (尤指)教派。

sec·tarian /sek'teərɪən; sɛk'tɛrɪən/ *n, adj* (member, supporter) of a sect or sects: 某(些)宗派的(份子, 支持者); ～ *jealousies,* eg between one sect and another; 派系猜忌; ～ *politics,* in which the advantage of a sect is considered more important than the public welfare. 派系政治(某一派系之利益较公共福利视受到重视的)。 **～·ism** /-ɪzəm; -ɪzəm/ *n* [U] tendency to split up into sects, work in the interest of sects, etc. 门户之见; 宗派意识。

sec·tion /'sekʃn; 'sekʃən/ *n* **1** part cut off; slice; one of the parts into which sth may be divided: 断片; 切片; 部分; 片段: *the ～s of an orange.* 橙的各瓣。 **2** one of a number of parts which can be put together to make a structure: (可拼拢成整体的)零件; 各部分: *fit together the ～s of a complete prefabricated building.* 把预制房屋的各部分拼起来。 **3** subdivision of an organized body of persons (the 'Postal S～), or of a piece of writing (often indicated by the '～-mark §, as § 21), or of a town, county, country or community: 机构之次一区分(如 the Postal Section 邮务处); 处; 科; 组(等); (文章等的)节; 项(常以节号§标明之, 如§21); (城镇, 国家或社会之)地区; 区域; 区划; 阶层: */,resɪ'denʃəl/ 'shopping ～s (area* is more usu). 住宅(商业)区 (area 较常用)。 **4** view or representation of sth seen as if cut straight through; thin slice of sth, eg tissue, suitable for examination under a microscope. 截面; 剖面; 断面; (适合于显微镜下观察之)切片。 **～al** /-ʃənl; -ʃənl/ *adj* **1** made or supplied in ～s(2): 由各部分组合而成的; 零件拼拢的: *a ～al fishing-rod;* 可拆卸拼拢的钓鱼竿; *～al furniture.* 可拆卸拼拢的家具。 **2** of a ～ of ～s of a community, etc: 地域的; 区域的; 区划的; 社会之一部分或数部分的; 阶层的: *～al interests,* the different and often conflicting interests of various ～s of a community; 社会各阶层间的且常为相互冲突的利益; *～al jealousies.* 区域或阶层间的猜忌。 **～·al·ism** /-ʃənəlɪzəm; -ʃənlɪzəm/ *n* [U] devotion to ～al interests instead of to those of the community as a whole. 地域或偏狭观念; 地方主义; 小社群意识。

sec·tor /'sektə(r); 'sɛktə/ *n* [C] **1** part of a circle

lying between two straight lines drawn from the centre to the circumference. (数学) 扇形. ⇨ the illus at **circle.** 参看 circle 之插图. **2** one of the areas into which a battle area is divided for the purpose of controlling operations. (为了指挥作战而划分之)战区; 防区. **3** branch (of industry, etc): (工业等的)部门: *the public and private ~s of industry*, those parts publicly owned and those privately owned. 国有工业和私有工业.

sec·u·lar /ˈsekjʊlə(r); ˈsɛkjələ/ *adj* **1** worldly or material, not religious or spiritual: 现世的; 尘世的; 世俗的; 物质的; 非宗教的; 非精神的: ~ *education*; 世俗教育; ~ *art/music*; 非宗教艺术(音乐); *the ~ power*, the State contrasted with the Church. 政府(与教会相对). ⇨ **sacred.** **2** living outside monasteries: 居住于修道院以外的: *the ~ clergy*, parish priests, etc. 教区僧侣. **~·ism** /-ɪzəm; -ɪzəm/ *n* [U] the view that morality and education should not be based on religion 现世主义; 世俗主义(主张伦理与教育不应以宗教为基础). **~·ist** /-ɪst; -ɪst/ *n* believer in, supporter of, ~ism. 现世主义者; 世俗主义者. **~·ize** /-aɪz; -aɪz/ *vt* [VP 6A] make ~: 使现世化; 使世俗化: ~*ize church property/courts*; 使教会财产作俗化(使法院不受教会之支配); *a ~ized Sunday*, eg when professional sporting events are permitted. 世俗化的星期天(如允许职业性运动项目).

se·cure /sɪˈkjʊə(r); sɪˈkjʊr/ *adj* **1** free from anxiety: 无虑的; 安心的: *feel ~ about one's future*. 对于自己的前途觉得安心. **2** certain; guaranteed: 确定的; 可靠的: *Our victory is ~*. 我们的胜利是有把握的. *He has a ~ position in the Civil Service*. 他有稳当的公务员职位. **3** unlikely to involve risk; firm: 无危险性的; 牢固的; *Don't go higher up the cliff unless you find ~ footholds*. 除非你找到稳固的踏脚处, 不要再往悬崖的高处爬了. *Are you sure the doors and windows are ~*? 你确知门窗是关牢的吗? *Is that ladder ~*? 那梯子牢靠吗? **4** ~ *(from, against)*, safe: 安全的: *Are we ~ from interruption/attack, etc*? 我们不受打扰(攻击等)之虞吗? □ *vt* **1** make fast: 使牢固; 紧闭: ~ *all the doors and windows before leaving the house*. 离家前关好所有门窗. **2** [VP 6A, 14] ~ *sth (against/from)*, make certain, firm or safe: 使安全; 使牢固: *By strengthening the embankments they ~d the village against/from floods*. 他们借加强堤防使该村庄免去洪水之患. **3** [VP 6A, 12B, 13B] succeed in getting (sth for which there is a great demand): 获得 (众所需要之物): *Can you ~ me two good seats for the concert?* 你能为我弄到音乐会的两个好座位吗? *She has ~d a good job*. 她已获得一个好工作. ~**·ly** *adv*

Se·curi·cor /sɪˈkjʊərɪkɔː(r); sɪˈkjʊrəkɔr/ *n* (P) commercial organization for the secure transportation of money and other valuables (eg to and from banks, offices), for guarding property, etc: (商标)受雇护送金钱或贵重物品 (如往返银行或办公场所), 保护财产等的商业组织: '~ *van*, one used for this purpose. 护送财物的货车.

se·cur·ity /sɪˈkjʊərɪtɪ; sɪˈkjʊrətɪ/ *n* (*pl* **-ties**) **1** [C, U] (sth that provides) safety, freedom from danger or anxiety: 安全; 无危险; 无忧虑; 提供安全之物; 使免除危险或忧虑之物: *children who lack the ~ of parental care*; 缺乏父母照顾的儿童; *cross the street in ~ at a pedestrian crossing*. 在行人穿越道上安全地过马路. *Is there any ~ from/against H-bombs*? 有防御或抵抗氢弹之物吗? **the Se'curity Council**, the permanent peace-keeping organ of the United Nations (with five permanent and ten elected members). 联合国安全理事会. '~ **police/forces**, those policemen or soldiers whose duty it is to protect important people or places, and to see that secret agents of foreign powers do not operate successfully. 安全部队 (其职责为保护重要人物或场所, 不让外国之间谍得逞). '~ **risk**, a person who, because of his political affiliations, etc may be a danger to the security of the State. 因其政治

背景等而可能危害政府的人. **2** [C, U] sth valuable, eg a life-insurance policy, given as a pledge for the repayment of a loan or the fulfilment of a promise or undertaking: 抵押品; 担保品(如寿险单等). *lend money on ~*; 抵押贷款; *give sth as (a) ~*. 以某物作担保. **3** [C] document, certificate, etc showing ownership of property (esp bonds, stocks and shares): 产权证明; 证券; (尤指)债券; 股票: *government securities*, for money lent to a government. 公债券.

se·dan /sɪˈdæn; sɪˈdæn/ *n* **1** ~ **(-'chair)**, enclosed seat for one person, carried on poles by two men, used in the 17th and 18th cc. 轿(通用于十七、十八世纪). **2** saloon car for four or more persons 轿车.

a sedan-chair

se·date /sɪˈdeɪt; sɪˈdet/ *adj* (of a person, his behaviour) not lively or agitated; composed. (指人, 其行为) 安静的; 肃穆的; 庄重的. ~·**ly** *adv* ~·**ness** *n*

se·da·tion /sɪˈdeɪʃn; sɪˈdeʃən/ *n* [U] treatment by sedatives; condition resulting from this: 施以镇静剂; 镇静状态: *The patient is under ~*. 那病人已服用镇静剂.

seda·tive /ˈsedətɪv; ˈsɛdətɪv/ *n, adj* (medicine, drug) tending to calm the nerves and reduce stress: 定神的; 镇定的; 镇静剂: *After taking a ~ she was able to get to sleep*. 服过镇静剂之后, 她就睡着了. *Tobacco has a ~ effect on some people*. 烟对于某些人有定神的效果. ⇨ *tranquillizer* at **tranquil.**

sed·en·tary /ˈsedntrɪ US: -terɪ; ˈsɛdn̩terɪ/ *adj* (of work) done sitting down (at a desk, etc); (of persons) spending much of their time seated: (指工作) 坐着做的; (指人) 惯坐的; 久坐的: *lead a ~ life*. 过着案牍生活(其工作需要久坐的或劳心的).

sedge /sedʒ; sɛdʒ/ *n* [U] forms of grasslike plant growing in marshes or near wet places. 芦苇; 菅茅. **sedgy** *adj* covered or bordered with ~. 生有芦苇的; 以芦苇为界的; 多菅茅的.

sedi·ment /ˈsedɪmənt; ˈsɛdəmənt/ *n* [U] matter (eg sand, dirt, gravel) that settles to the bottom of a liquid, eg mud left on fields after a river has been in flood over them. 渣; 沉淀物(沙, 垢, 砾等之沉于液体底部者, 如河流泛滥后留于田野之泥土). **sedi·men·tary** /ˌsedɪˈmentrɪ; ˌsɛdəˈmɛntərɪ/ *adj* of the nature of ~; formed from ~; 沉淀性的; 由渣形成的: ~*ary rocks*, eg slate, sandstone, limestone. 水成岩 (如板石, 沙石, 石灰石).

se·di·tion /sɪˈdɪʃn; sɪˈdɪʃən/ *n* [U] words or actions intended to make people rebel against authority, disobey the government, etc: 煽动叛乱的言论或行动: *incitement to ~*. 唆使从事叛乱. **se·di·tious** /sɪˈdɪʃəs; sɪˈdɪʃəs/ *adj* of the nature of ~: 煽动性的; 叛乱性的: *seditious speeches/writings*. 煽动性的演说(著作).

se·duce /sɪˈdjuːs US: -ˈduːs; sɪˈdjus/ *vt* [VP 6A, 14] ~ *sb (from/into sth)*, **1** persuade (sb) to do wrong; tempt (sb) into crime or sin: 引诱(某人)做坏事; 诱使(某人)犯罪: ~ *a man from his duty*; 诱使人舍弃职守; ~*d by the offer of money into betraying one's country*. 因受金钱诱惑而叛国. **2** by charm, knowledge of the world, etc persuade sb less experienced to have

sexual intercourse: 勾引;诱奸: *How many women did Don Juan ~?* 唐璜勾引过多少女子? *Potiphar's wife tried to ~ young Joseph.* 波提乏的妻子试图勾引年轻的约瑟. **se·ducer** n person who ~s, esp (2). 引诱者; (尤指)诱奸者; 好色者.

se·duc·tion /sɪ'dʌkʃn; sɪ'dʌkʃən/ n **1** [U] seducing or being seduced; [C] instance of this. 诱惑; 勾引; 诱奸. **2** sth very attractive and charming; sth likely to lead a person astray (but often with no implication of immorality): 极有诱惑力之物; 易使人误入歧途之物(但通常不含不道德之意): *surrender to the ~s of country life.* 屈服于田园生活的诱惑. **se·duc·tive** /sɪ'dʌktɪv; sɪ'dʌktɪv/ adj alluring; captivating: 引诱的; 有魅力的: *seductive smiles;* 诱人的微笑; *a seductive offer.* 令人心动的提议. **se·duc·tive·ly** adv

sedu·lous /'sedjʊləs US: 'sedʒʊləs; 'sedʒələs/ adj persevering; done with perseverance: 勤勉的; 不屈不挠的; 坚毅地做成的: *He paid her ~ attention,* was persevering in his attempt to please her 他一心一意地讨好她(一直向她献殷勤). **~·ly** adv

see[1] /siː; siː/ vi, vt (pt **saw** /sɔː; sɔ/, pp **seen** /siːn; sin/) (For special uses with *adverbial particles* and *preps,* ⇨ 11 below.) (与副词性小品词及介词连用的特殊用法参看下列第 11 义.) **1** [VP2A, B, C, 4A] (often with *can, could;* not usu in the progressive tenses) have or use the power of sight: 看; 见; 视 (常与 can, could 连用; 通常不用进行式): *If you shut your eyes you can't see.* 闭上眼睛, 你便看不见. *It was getting dark and I couldn't see to read.* 天渐黑了, 我看不见, 不能阅读. *On a clear day we can see (for) miles and miles from this hill-top.* 在晴朗的日子, 我们能从这小山顶看得很远很远. *Move aside, please: I can't see through you!* 请让开——你挡住了我的视线! *He'll never be able to see again,* He has gone blind. 他再也看不见了 (他的眼睛已经瞎了). *seeing is believing,* (prov) What one sees oneself is the most satisfactory evidence. (谚)眼见是实(百闻不如一见). **2** [VP6A, 8, 9, 10, 18A, 19A, 24A] (often with *can, could,* esp when an effort of perception is needed; not in the progressive tenses) be aware of by using the power of sight: 借视力发觉; 看见; 看到(常与 can, could 连用, 尤其在需要作视觉上的努力时; 不用进行时): *Can/Do you see that ship on the horizon?* 你看到(你能看到)地平线上那条船吗? *I looked out but saw nothing.* 我向外张望, 什么也没看到. *I saw him put the key in the lock, turn it and open the door.* 我看到他把钥匙插入锁眼, 转动钥匙, 把门打开. *The suspected man was seen to enter the building.* 那嫌疑犯被人看到进入那房屋. *I saw two men struggling for the knife.* 我看到两个人在抢那把刀. *He was seen running away from the scene of the crime.* 他被人看见从犯罪现场跑开. *Have you ever seen a man hanged?* 你见过绞人处死刑吗? *I saw that the box was empty.* 我看见那盒子是空的. *If you watch carefully you will see how to do it/how I do it/how it is done.* 如果你仔细观察, 你就会看出如何做此事(我如何做此事, 此事是怎样完成的). *be 'seeing things,* have hallucinations, ie see things that are not there or that do not exist, as a drunken man may: 生幻觉(即看见不在或不存在之物, 如醉汉可能发生者): *You're seeing things—there's nobody there!* 你有幻觉——那里根本没有人! *see the back of sb,* get rid of him; see him for the last time: 摆脱某人; 见最后一次: *That fellow's a nuisance; I shall be glad to see the back of him.* 那家伙是个讨厌鬼; 我乐于摆脱他. *see the last of sb/sth,* have done with: see for the last time: 做完; 和…断绝关系; 见最后一次: *I shall be glad to see the last of this job,* get to the end of it. 我真愿意这件工作赶快做完. *see the sights,* visit notable places, etc as a sightseer. 游览名胜; 观光. *see stars,* have dancing lights before the eyes, eg as the result of a blow on the head. 眼冒金星(如头部受打击的结果). *see visions,* be a seer. 做先知; 做卜者. *see one's way (clear) to doing sth,* see how to manage to do it, feel disposed to doing it: 有把握或有意

做某事: *He didn't see his way to lending me the money I needed.* 他没有把握借给我我所需要的钱. **3** [VP6A, 2A] (in the *imper*) look (at): (用于祈使句中)看; 瞧: *See, here he comes!* 看, 他来了! *See page 4.* 请看第四页. **4** [VP6A, 9, 10, 2A] (not in the progressive tenses) understand; learn by search or inquiry or reflection: (不用进行时)(借研究、询问、反省等而)了解; 领会; 明白; 懂: *He didn't see the joke/the point of the story.* 他不明白那笑话的可笑处(故事的寓意). *We saw that the plan was unwise.* 我们看出那计划是不智的. *Do you see what I mean?* 你懂得我的意思吗? *As far as I can see...,* To the best of my understanding.... 就我所能了解的…. *I think I'll be able to help, but I'll have to see,* wait until I know more. 我想我能帮得上忙, 但要等我把事情弄清楚再说. *Go and see if/whether the postman has been yet.* 去看看邮差来没过有. *see for oneself,* find out in order to be convinced or satisfied: 亲自求证; 亲眼去看: *If you don't believe me, go and see for yourself!* 如果你不相信我, 你亲自去察看吧! *not see the use/good/fun/advantage etc of doing sth,* feel doubt about whether it is useful, etc to do it. 怀疑某事的益处(好处, 乐趣, 利益等). *you see,* (used parenthetically) (作插入语用) **(a)** as you no doubt know or understand. 你无疑地明白. **(b)** as I must now tell you or explain to you. 我必须现在告诉你; 我必须现在向你解释. *seeing that,* in view of the fact that; considering. 鉴于…的事实; 照…看来. **5** [VP9] learn from the newspaper or other printed sources: (从报纸或其他印刷物中)阅悉: *I see that the Prime Minister has been in Wales.* 我在报上看到首相已前往威尔士. **6** [VP6A, 22, 24A] have knowledge or experience of; have (sth) presented to one's attention: 经历; 阅历(某事): *This coat of mine has seen hard wear,* ie has been worn for a long time. 我这件外套已穿过很多年了. *He has seen a good deal in his long life.* 他在漫长的一生中阅历甚丰. *I never saw such grief.* 我从未经历过如此的悲伤. *I want to see you happy/settled before I leave,* I don't want to leave until I know that you are happy/settled. 我要确知你快乐(安顿好)才离开. *will never see thirty/forty, etc again,* is already past that age. 年龄已逾三十(四十等). *have seen the day/time when...,* used to call attention to a past state of affairs: 曾经历…的日子(用以引起对过去情境的注意): *He had seen the day when there were no cars on the roads,* was living before there were cars. 他经历过没有汽车的时代. *have seen better days,* have now declined, lost former prosperity, etc. 现已式微; 已失去昔日的繁荣等. *see sb damned/in hell,* used to express an absolute refusal to do what one is asked, etc. 坚决拒绝; 绝不答应. *see service in sth; see (good) service,* ⇨ **service.** **7** [VP15A, 6A] give an interview to; visit; receive a call from: 会见; 访问; 接见: *Can I see you on business?* 我可以和你洽谈公务吗? *You ought to see a doctor about that cough.* 你在咳嗽, 该去看看医生. *She's too ill to see anyone at present.* 她目前病重, 不能会客. *The manager can see you for five minutes.* 经理可以接见你五分钟. Note: The progressive tenses are used for this sense: 注意: 本定义可用进行式: *I'm seeing my solicitor this afternoon.* 今日下午我将与我的律师会面. *I shall be seeing them tomorrow.* 我将于明天和他们见面. *'seeing you/,See you 'soon,* (colloq) used as an equivalent for 'Goodbye!'. (口)再见; 再会. **8** [VP18A, 15A, 24A] allow to; look on without protest or action: 听任; 坐视: *You can't see people starve without trying to help them, can you?* 你不会坐视人们挨饿而不想法子去帮助他们吗? *You wouldn't see me left here all alone?* 你不会把我一个人留在此地吧? **9** [VP9] attend to; take care; make provision: 留神; 注意; 预备: *See that the windows and doors are fastened.* 务必要把门窗关牢. **10** [VP16B, 19A] call up a picture of; imagine: 想起…之情景; 想象: *He saw himself as the saviour of his country.* 他幻想自己为国家的数星. *I can't see myself allowing people to cheat me.* 我无法想象会让人欺骗. **11** (specia[l]

uses with *adverbial particles* and *preps*): (与副词性小品词及介词连用的特殊用法):

see about sth, deal with: 处理(某事); 照料(某事): *He promised to see about the matter.* 他答应处理此事。

see sb about sth, consult sb, take advice (on sth): 和某人商量(某事); 向某人请教(某事): *I must see a builder about these tiles that have fallen from the roof.* 我必须找个建筑商谈谈从屋顶掉下来的这些瓦。

see sb across sth, guide, conduct, help sb across (a road, etc): 指导或协助某人穿越(道路等): *That man's blind—I'd better see him across the street.* 那人是个瞎子—我应该帮助他穿越这条街。

see (sb) around (sth), = **see (sb) over (sth)**. *See you around!* (sl) Goodbye! (俚)再见!

see sb back/home, accompany sb: 护送或陪伴某人回家: *May I see you home?* 我可以送你回家吗? *Tom's had too much to drink—we'd better see him back/home.* 汤姆喝了太多酒——我们最好护送他回家。

see sb off, go to a railway station, an airport, the docks, etc with sb about to start on a journey: (到火车站,机场,码头等处)送(某人): *I was seen off by many of my friends.* 许多朋友来送我。***see sb off sth***, go with him until he is at the door, outside, etc: 送某人到门口或屋外等: *I don't want this fellow here; please see him off the premises*, get rid of him. 我不愿这家伙待在这里; 请把他赶出屋外。

see sb out (of sth), accompany sb until he is out of a building: 送某人到(…的)外面: *My secretary will see you out.* 我的秘书将送你出去。***see sth out***, = **see sth through**.

see over sth, visit and examine or inspect carefully: 查视; 调查: *see over a house that one wishes to buy or rent.* 查看想要购买或租赁的房子。

see (sb) over (sth), show him around (a place). 带(某人)参观(一地方)。

see (sb) round (sth), = **see (sb) over (sth)**.

see through sb/sth, not be deceived by: 看透(某人或某事); 不为…所蒙蔽: *I see through your little game*, am aware of the trick you are trying to play on me. 我看穿了你玩的那套把戏(我知道你要向我耍什么花样)。*We all saw through him*, knew what kind of man he really was. 我们全看透他(是什么样的人)了。**'see-through** *adj* (esp of clothing) that can be seen through; transparent. (尤指衣服)透明的。***see sb through (sth)***, give him support, encouragement, until the end: 帮助(某人)到底: *You'll have a difficult time, but I'll see you safely through.* 你将会遇到困难, 但我将帮助你平安度过。***see sth through***, not give up an undertaking until the end is reached: 贯彻(某事); 坚持到最后: *He said that whatever happened he would see the struggle through.* 他说无论发生什么事, 他决心奋斗到底。

see to sth, attend to sth: 注意; 留心; 照料: *This machine is out of order; get a mechanic to see to it.* 这部机器坏了, 找位技工来检修一下。*Will you see to the arrangements for the next meeting of the committee?* 请你负责安排委员会的下一次会议好吗?

see² /siː; si/ *n* district under a bishop; bishop's position, office, jurisdiction: 主教的辖区; 主教的地位、职位、管辖权: *the See of Canterbury;* 坎特伯雷主教的辖区; *the Holy See/the See of Rome,* the Papacy. 教皇之职位及权威; 罗马教廷。

seed /siːd; sid/ *n* (*pl* **~s** or **~**, unchanged) (复数加 s 或不变) **1** flowering plant's unit of reproduction, from which another plant can grow: 种; 种子(有花植物的繁殖单位): *a packet of ~(s).* 一包种子。⇦ the illus at **flower, fruit.** 参看 **flower, fruit** 之插图。*Sow the ~ in May or June.* 在五月或六月播种。*Its ~s are/Its ~ is very small.* 它的种子很小。**run/go to ~**, stop flowering as ~ is produced; (fig) become careless of one's appearance and clothes. 花谢结子; (喻)变为不留心仪表和衣着; 不修边幅。**'~-bed** *n* bed of fine soil in which to sow **~**. 播种床。**'~-cake** *n* cake containing

~s, eg caraway, as a flavouring. 含有芳香子实(如葛缕子等)的糕饼。**'~-corn** *n* grain kept for **~**. 作种用的谷物; 谷种。**'~-man** /-mən; -mən/ *n* (*pl* **-men**) dealer in **~**s. 种子商。**'~-time** *n* sowing season. 播种期。**2** [U] (old use) offspring: (旧用法)后裔; 子孙: *the ~ of Abraham,* the Hebrews. 亚伯拉罕的后裔(即希伯来人)。**3** cause, origin (*of* a tendency, development, etc): (趋势、发展等的)原由; 根源(与…连用): *sow the ~s of virtue in young children.* 在儿童的心田播下美德的种子。**4** [U] semen. 精液; 胚种。**5** '~-potato *n* potato kept and allowed to sprout before being planted. 留待发芽以供栽植的马铃薯; 马铃薯种。**'~-pearls** *n pl* small pearls. 小粒珍珠。**6** (sport) ~ed player: (运动)种子选手: *England's No. 1 ~* (in a championship). (在锦标赛中之)英国第一号种子选手。⇦ below. 参看下列词语第 4 义。□ *vi, vt* **1** [VP2A] (of a plant) produce ~ when full grown; let ~ fall. (指植物)结实; 生子; 自然播种。**2** [VP6A] sow with ~: 播种于: *a field with wheat;* 在田里种下小麦的种子; *a newly-~ed lawn.* 刚播种过的草地。**3** [VP6A] remove ~ from: 除去…之子: *~ raisins.* 除去葡萄干之子。**4** [VP6A] (esp in tennis) separate those players well tested and known to be stronger from the weaker players (in order to have good matches later in a tournament): (尤指在网球赛中) 抽出种子选手(以使精采比赛排在后头): ~ *ed players.* 种子选手。**'~-less** *adj* having no ~: 无子的; 无核的: *~less raisins.* 无籽葡萄干。**'~-ling** /'siːdlɪŋ; 'sidlɪŋ/ *n* young plant newly grown from a **~**. 刚从种子长出的幼小植物; 幼苗。

seedy /'siːdɪ; 'sidɪ/ *adj* (**-ier, -iest**) **1** full of seed: 多(种)子的: *as ~ as a dried fig.* 象干无花果一般地多子。**2** shabby-looking; in worn clothes: 破旧的; 褴褛的: *a ~ boarding-house;* 破旧的寄宿舍; *a ~-looking person.* 衣着褴褛的人。**3** (colloq) unwell: (口)不适的: *feel ~.* 觉得不舒服。**seed·i·ly** /-ɪlɪ; -əlɪ/ *adv.* **seedi·ness** *n.*

seek /siːk; sik/ *vt, vi* (*pt, pp* **sought** /sɔːt; sɔt/) (formal) (正式用语) **1** [VP6A, 15A] look for; try to find: 寻觅; 找: ~ *shelter from the rain;* 寻找避雨之所; ~ *safety in flight.* 逃难; 避难。*The reason is not far to ~*, is found near at hand, quickly found. 道理很显然。*Are you ~ing a quarrel*, trying to start one? 你在寻衅争吵吗? *He is going to Canada to ~ his fortune*, to try to become rich. 他去加拿大想赚大钱。**2** [VP6A] ask for: 请求; 求: *I will ~ my doctor's advice.* 我将请教医生的意见。**3** [VP7A] try; attempt: 试图; 企图: *They sought to kill him.* 他们企图杀他。**4** [VP3A] ~ *for*, try to win: 试图获得: *unsought-for fame, fame which came without being looked for.* 不谋而得的名声。*(much) sought after,* (much) in demand. 供不应求; 极受欢迎。

seem /siːm; sim/ *vi* [VP4D, E, 2A] have or give the impression or appearance of being or doing; appear to be: 似乎是; 看似; 好象; 似觉; 仿佛: *Things far off ~ (to be) small.* 远处之物看上去小些。*What ~s easy to some people ~s difficult to others.* 某些人觉得容易的事, 别的人可能觉得困难。*There ~ to be no objections to the proposal*, 对这提议似乎没有反对意见。*He ~s to think so.* 他似乎认为如此。*I shall act as ~s best (=as it ~s best to me).* 我将尽力而为。*The book ~s (to be) quite interesting.* 这本书好象很有趣。*The child ~s to be asleep.* 这孩子好象是睡着了。*It ~s that no one knew what had happened.* 似乎没有人知道发生过什么事。*I can't ~ (=am unable) to get out of that bad habit.* 我似乎无法戒除那坏习惯。*It would ~ that…,* (a cautious way of saying 'It ~s that…'). 似乎…(为 'It seems that' 的谨慎说法)。*'I've been out in the rain'—'So it ~s',* ie from your wet clothes it appears that you've been out in the rain. '我刚才淋过雨'—'果然好象淋过雨的样子。' ~ **-ing** *adj* apparent but perhaps not real or genuine: 表面上的; 似乎的; 仿佛的(也许不是实在的或真正的): *In spite of his ~ing friendship he gave me no help.* 尽管他维持表面上的友谊, 他未曾帮助过我。~ **-ing·ly** *adv* in appearance;

apparently. 表面上；外观上。

seem·ly /ˈsiːmlɪ; ˋsimlɪ/ *adj* **(-ier, iest)** (formal) (正式用语) **1** (of behaviour) proper or correct (for the occasion or circumstances): (指行为，在某种场合或环境)适宜的: *It isn't ~ to praise oneself.* 自夸是不适宜的。**2** decent; decorous: 正当的；体面的: *Strip-tease is not a ~ occupation for any girl.* 脱衣舞对于任何女孩子而言，都不是正当的职业。**seem·li·ness** *n*

seen /siːn; sin/ *pp* of **see**[1].

seep /siːp; sip/ *vi* [VP2C] (of liquids) ooze out or through; trickle: (指液体)漏出；渗出: *water ~ing through the roof of the tunnel.* 从隧道顶部渗出的水。**~·age** /ˈsiːpɪdʒ; ˋsipɪdʒ/ *n* [U] slow leaking through. 漏出；渗出；渗流。

seer /sɪə(r); sɪr/ *n* person claiming to see into the future; prophet. 自称能透视未来者；预言家；先知。

seer·sucker /ˈsɪəsʌkə(r); ˋsɪr,sʌkə/ *n* [U] thin fabric with a striped pattern and a crinkled surface: 皱面条纹薄织物: *a ~ tablecloth.* 一条皱面条纹薄织物桌布。

see·saw /ˈsiːsɔː; ˋsi,sɔ/ *n* [C, U] (game played on a) long plank with a person astride each end which can rise and fall alternately; up-and-down or to-and-fro motion: 跷跷板；轩轾戏；上下或往复之运动: *play at ~.* 玩跷跷板。□ *vi* play at ~; move up and down or to and fro; (fig) vacillate: 玩跷跷板；上下或往复运动；(喻)犹疑；踌躇: *~ between two opinions.* 犹疑于两种意见之间。

seethe /siːð; sið/ *vi, vt* **1** [VP2A, 3A] **~ (with),** boil, bubble over; be crowded, agitated (esp fig): 沸腾；起泡；骚动；激昂(尤用于比喻中): *~ with anger;* 大发雷霆; *a country seething with discontent;* 激荡着不满情绪的国家; *streets seething with people.* 挤满人而闹哄哄的街道。**2** [VP6A, 2A] (old use) cook by boiling. (旧用法)煮沸；滚。

seg·ment /ˈsegmənt; ˋsɛgmənt/ *n* [C] **1** part cut off or marked off by a line: 切开的部分；以线划开的部分: *a ~ of a circle.* 弓形。**2** division or section: 区分；节；段；片: *a ~ of an orange.* 一瓣橘子。⇨ the illus at **fruit.** 参看 fruit 之插图。□ *vt, vi* /segˈment; sɛgˋmɛnt/ divide, become divided, into ~s. 分开为若干部分；变为若干部分。**seg·men·ta·tion** /segmenˈteɪʃn; ˌsɛgmənˋteʃən/ *n* division into ~s. 分割；切断。

seg·re·gate /ˈsegrɪgeɪt; ˋsɛgrɪ,get/ *vt* [VP6A] put apart from the rest; isolate: 隔离；分开: *~ the sexes;* 将男女分开; *~ people with infectious diseases.* 隔离传染病患者。**seg·re·ga·tion** /ˌsegrɪˈgeɪʃn; ˌsɛgrɪˋgeʃən/ *n* segregating or being ~d: 隔离；分开: *a policy of racial segregation.* 种族隔离政策。⇨ *integration* at **integrate.**

seign·ior /ˈseɪnjə(r) *US:* ˈsiːnjər; ˋsinjə/ *n* feudal lord; landowner in feudal times. 领主；诸侯；(封建时代之)地主。

seine /seɪn; sen/ *n* [C] large fishing-net which hangs like a curtain, with floats along the top edge and sinkers (weights) along the bottom edge, used to encircle fish, and usu hauled ashore. 拉网；大捕鱼网；拖地大围网(张起时似幕；上缘有浮子，下缘有坠子，用以兜围鱼类，通常拖拉上岸)。□ *vt, vi* fish, catch (fish), with a ~. 以拉网捕(鱼)。

seis·mic /ˈsaɪzmɪk; ˋsaɪzmɪk/ *adj* of earthquakes. 地震的。**seis·mo·graph** /ˈsaɪzməgrɑːf *US:* -græf; ˋsaɪzmə,græf/ *n* instrument which records the strength, duration and distance away of earthquakes. 地震仪(记录地震之强度，持续时间及距离者)。**seis·mol·ogy** /saɪzˈmɒlədʒɪ; saɪzˋmɑlədʒɪ/ *n* [U] science of earthquakes. 地震学。**seis·mol·ogist** /saɪzˈmɒlədʒɪst; saɪzˋmɑlədʒɪst/ *n*

seize /siːz; siz/ *vt, vi* **1** [VP6A, 15A] take possession of (property, etc) by law: 依法律占有或取得(财产等)；扣押；没收；查封: *~ sb's goods for payment of debt.* 扣押某人之货物以偿付债务。**2** [VP6A, 15A] take hold of, suddenly and violently: 攫取；强取；抓住: *~ a thief by the collar.* 抓住贼的衣领。**3** [VP6A, 3A] **~ (on/upon),** see clearly and use: 利用；采用: *~ (upon) an idea/a chance/an opportunity.* 采纳意见(抓住机会；把握良机)。**4** [VP2A, C] **~ (up),** (of moving parts of machinery) become stuck or jammed, eg because of too much heat or friction. (指机器)陷于停顿；停止转动(如因为过热或摩擦太大等)。**seiz·ure** /ˈsiːʒə(r); ˋsiʒə/ *n* **1** [U] act of seizing or taking possession of by force or the authority of the law; [C] instance of this: 依法律占有；强占；没收；查封；其实例: *seizure of contraband by Customs officers.* 海关官员没收违禁品。**2** [C] sudden attack of apoplexy; heart attack. 中风骤发；心脏病发作。

sel·dom /ˈseldəm; ˋsɛldəm/ *adv* (usu placed with the *v*) not often; rarely: (通常置于动词之旁)很少；不常；罕: *I have seen such large apples.* 我很少见到这么大的苹果。*She ~ goes out.* 她不常外出。*She goes out very ~.* 她极少外出。*His wife ~, if ever, has a holiday.* 他的妻子难得有一天休息。*He ~ or never gives his wife a present.* 他可以说从未送过礼物给妻子。

se·lect /sɪˈlekt; səˋlɛkt/ *vt* [VP6A, 15A, 16A] choose (as being the most suitable, etc): 选择；挑选: *~ a book/a Christmas present for a child.* 选择一本书(给孩子的圣诞礼物)。*Who has been ~ed to lead the delegation?* 谁被选为代表团的领队？□ *adj* **1** carefully chosen: 精选的: *~ passages from Milton.* 密尔顿选集。**2** (of a school, society, etc) of or for carefully chosen persons, not for all: (指学校，会社等)选择份子严格的；苛择的；挑剔的: *a ~ club;* 选择会员严格的俱乐部; *shown to a ~ audience,* 向经过挑选的观众公开的。**~ committee,** (in the House of Commons) small committee appointed for a special investigation. (下议院中之)特别委员会(受命作某项特别调查者)。**se·lec·tor** /-tə(r); -tə/ *n* one who, that which, ~s, eg a member of a committee ~ing a national sports team, etc. 选择者(如挑选国家代表队之选拔委员等)；挑选器械；选择器。

se·lec·tion /sɪˈlekʃn; səˋlɛkʃən/ *n* **1** [U] choosing. 选择；挑选；淘汰。**ˈ~ committee,** one appointed to select, eg new members for a sports team. 选拔委员会(如设立以挑选运动员者)。**natural ~,** (Darwin's theory of) the process in nature by which certain plants and animals flourish and multiply while others are less suited to their surroundings and die out. 自然淘汰；天择(依照达尔文的理论，某些动植物能够兴旺与繁殖，而其他较不能适应其环境者灭绝)。**2** [C] collection or group of selected things or examples; number of things from which to select: 精选品集；供选择之物: *~s from 18th-century English poetry.* 十八世纪英国诗选。*That shop has a good ~ of denim jeans.* 那商店有很多牛仔裤可供挑选。

se·lec·tive /sɪˈlektɪv; səˋlɛktɪv/ *adj* having the power to select; characterized by selection. 有选择力的；淘汰的。**~ service,** (US) selection, for compulsory military service, of men with certain requirements, abilities, etc. (美)选募某些有特殊条件或能力的人服义务兵役。**~·ly** *adv* **sel·ec·tiv·ity** /sɪˌlekˈtɪvətɪ; səˌlɛkˋtɪvətɪ/ *n* [U] (esp) power (of a radio) to receive broadcasts from one station without interference from other stations. (尤指收音机之)选择性(即收听一电台时不受其他电台之干扰)。

se·le·nium /sɪˈliːnɪəm; səˋlinɪəm/ *n* non-metallic element (symbol **Se**) whose power to conduct electric current increases with the intensity of the light reaching it. 硒(非金属化学元素，符号为 Se)。**~ cell,** one containing a strip of ~, used in photo-electric devices, eg the exposure meter of a camera. 硒(质)光电管。

self /self; sɛlf/ *n* (*pl* **selves** /selvz; sɛlvz/) **1** [U] person's nature, special qualities; one's own personality: 本性；本质；自身；自己；自我: *one's better/worse ~,* one's nobler nature/base nature; 某人较高尚(低劣)的

本质; *one's former* ~, oneself as one formerly was; 本来面目; 从前的样子; *analysis of the* ~; 自我分析; *the conscious* ~. 自觉. **2** [U] one's own interests or pleasure: 私利; 利己心: *She has no thought of* ~, thinks only of the interests, welfare, etc of others. 她未想到私利. **3** (comm, dated style, or joc) myself, yourself, etc: (商, 过时文体或谑)我自己; 你自己等: *pay to* ~, (on a cheque) pay to the person whose signature appears on it; (支票用语)认票不认人; *a room for* ~ *and wife*. 一个我和太太住的房间. *Let us drink a toast to our noble selves*. 让我们为(高贵的)自己干一杯.

self- /self; self/ *pref* short for *itself, myself, himself, oneself*, etc: 为 itself, myself, himself, oneself 等之略: ~-'taught, taught by oneself; 自学的; ~-'governing colonies, colonies that govern themselves. 自治殖民地. ~-a'basement n [U] humiliation of oneself. 自卑. ~-ab'sorbed adj having one's attention taken up by one's own interests, thoughts, etc; unaware of other person. 专心于自身利益的; 只顾自己的. ~-'acting adj automatic. 自动的. ~-'activating adj (eg of an explosive device) made so as to activate itself without external control. (指爆炸装置等)自动引发的. ~-ad'dressed adj addressed to oneself: 写有回信地址的: *I enclose a stamped* ~-addressed envelope. 我附了一个贴好邮票写有回信地址的信封. ~-ap'pointed adj chosen or declared by oneself; unsanctioned (and perhaps unqualified): 自命的; 自封的: *a* ~-appointed arbiter/expert. 一位自命的调停人(专家). ~-as'sertion n [U] the putting forward of one's own claims in a determined manner; the putting forward of oneself in an effort to be noticed by everyone. 坚持己见; 专断; 自作主张; 爱出风头. ~-as'sertive adj ~-as'surance n [U] confidence in oneself. 自信. ~-as'sured adj ~-'centred adj interested chiefly in oneself and one's own affairs. 自私自利的; 自我中心的. ~-col'lected adj (of persons) having or showing presence of mind and composure; calm. (指人)泰然自若的; 沉静的. ~-'coloured adj of the same colour all over. 单色的; 纯色的. ~-com'mand n [U] power of controlling one's feelings. 自制; 克己. ~-com'placency n [U] state of being too easily pleased with oneself. 自满; 自得. ~-con'fessed adj on one's own confession: 自己承认的; 坦供的: *a* ~-confessed thief. 一个坦供行窃的贼. ~-'confidence n [U] belief in one's own abilities. 自信. ~-'confident adj ~-'conscious adj aware of one's own existence, thoughts and actions; (colloq) shy; embarrassed. 意识到本身之存在, 思想和行为的; 自觉的; (口)害羞的; 忸怩的; 怕难为情的. ~-'consciousness n [U]. ~-con'tained adj **(a)** (of a person) not impulsive or communicative. (指人)不易冲动的; 沉默寡言的. **(b)** (esp of a flat) complete in itself (not sharing the kitchen, bathroom, etc with occupants of other flats) and (usu) with its own private entrance. (尤指公寓)独立门户的(不与他住户共用厨房、浴室等, 且通常有自用的房门). ~-con'trol n [U] control of one's own feelings, behaviour, etc: 自制; 克己: *exercise* ~-control; 运用自制力; *lose one's* ~-control. 失去自制力. ~-de'fence n [U] defence of one's own body, property, rights, etc: 自卫: *kill sb in* ~-defence, while defending oneself against attack; 因自卫杀死某人; *the art of* ~-defence, boxing. 拳术. ~-de'nial n [U] going without things one would like to have in order to help others: 自我克制; 自我牺牲: *practise* ~-denial to help the children. 克制自我牺牲以帮助孩子们. ~-de'nying adj ~-de,termi'nation n [U]. **(a)** (in politics) decision, made by a people having the characteristics of a nation, whether they shall be independent or (continue to) be part of another state: (政治)民族自决—(民族就其自身应成为独立国家, 或继续为其他国家一部分所做之决定): *the right of all peoples to* ~-determination. 所有民族自决的权利. **(b)** the making of one's own decisions; the guidance, by the individual, of his own conduct. 自己

决定; 自己作主. ~-'educated adj educated without (much) help from schools or teachers. 自修的; 自学的. ~-ef'facing adj keeping oneself in the background; not trying to get attention. 谦逊的; 避免出头的. ~-em'ployed adj working, eg as a shopkeeper, a jobbing gardener, without an employer. 非为雇主或不专为某一雇主而工作的(如店主, 作零工的园丁等). ~-e'steem n [U] good opinion of oneself; (sometimes) conceit: 自尊;(有时用作)自负或自大: *injure one's* ~-esteem, lower one's opinion of oneself. 伤害某人的自尊. ~-'evident adj clear without proof or more evidence. 毋待证明的; 自明的. ~-ex,ami'nation n [U, C] examining one's own behaviour, motives, moods, etc. 自省; 自我检讨. ~-ex'planatory adj clear without (further) explanation. 毋须解释的; 不解自明的. ~-'help n [U] use of one's own powers to achieve success, etc. 自助; 自立. ~-im'portant adj pompous; having too high an opinion of oneself. 自夸的; 自大的; 自视过高的. ~-im'portance n [U]. ~-im'posed adj (of a duty, task, etc) imposed on oneself. (任务、工作等)自愿负责的; 自愿承担的. ~-in'dulgent adj giving way too easily to desires for one's own comfort, pleasures, etc. 纵欲的; 放纵自己的. ~-in'dulgence n [U]. ~-'interest n [U] one's own interests and personal advantage. 私利; 利己. ~-'locking adj locking automatically when closed. 关闭时自动锁上的. ~-'made adj having succeeded by one's own efforts, esp after beginning life without money, education or influence. 自力成功的; 白手起家的. ~-o'pinionated adj over-certain that one's own opinions are correct; having strong opinions not firmly based. 固执己见的; 执迷不悟的; 刚愎自用的. ~-'pity n [U] (exaggerated) pity for oneself. (夸张的)自怜; 自悯. ~-pos'sessed adj calm, cool, confident. 沉着的; 冷静的; 有信心的. ~-pos'session n [U] coolness; composure: 冷静; 沉着: *lose/regain one's* ~-possession. 失去(恢复)冷静. ~-,preser'vation n [U] keeping oneself from harm or destruction: 自保; 自卫: *the instinct of* ~-preservation. 自卫的本能. ~-'raising adj (of flour) not needing the addition of baking-powder (when bread, etc is being made). (指面粉)自行发酵的. ~-re'liant adj having or showing confidence in one's own powers, judgement, etc. 依靠自己的; 信赖自己的. ~-re'liance n [U]. ~-re'spect n [U] feeling that one is behaving and thinking in ways that will not cause one to be ashamed of oneself: 自尊; 自重: *lose all* ~-respect. 失去一切自尊. ~-re'specting adj having ~-respect: 自尊的; 自重的: *No* ~-respecting man could agree to do such a thing. 凡是有自尊心的人都不会做这样的事. ~-'righteous adj convinced of one's own goodness and that one is better than others. 自以为正真(较他人公正善良)的. ~-'rule n = ~-government. ~-'sacrifice n [U, C] the giving up of one's own interests and wishes for the sake of other people. 自我牺牲. ~-'sacrificing adj ~-'same adj very same; identical: 同一的; 同样的: *Tom and I reached Paris on the* ~-same day. 汤姆和我在同一天抵达巴黎. ~-'sealing adj (of a fuel tank, pneumatic tyre, etc) having a substance (eg soft rubber) that automatically seals a puncture made in it. (指油箱, 气胎等)有自动封闭孔眼之物质(如软橡胶)的; 自动封闭的. ~-'seeker n person who is too much concerned with gaining advantages for himself. 唯利是图者; 自私自利者. ~-'seeking n, adj ~-'service adj **(a)** (of a canteen, restaurant) one at which persons collect their own food and drink from counters and carry it to tables. (指餐馆, 饭店)自助的. **(b)** (of a shop) one at which customers collect what they want from counters or shelves and pay as they leave. (指商店)自助的. **(c)** (of a garage) one at which customers fill their cars with petrol and then go and pay the charge at a counter. (指加油站)顾客自行加油的. ~-'sown adj (of plants) coming from seed that has dropped from the plant (not sown by a gardener).

(指植物)自然播种的; 自然生长的。 ,~-'starter n device
(usu electric) for starting an engine. 自行起动机(通常
为电动的); 自行开动器。 ,~-'styled adj using a name,
title, etc which one has given oneself and to which one
has no right: 自称的; 自任的; 自封的(自行使用某名字、
头衔等): The ~-styled 'Dr' Smith had never been
awarded a degree of any kind. 那位自称为'博士'的史
密斯先生从未得过任何学位。 ,~-suf'ficient adj (a)
needing no help from others: 自给自足的: The country
has now become ~-sufficient in woollen goods, no longer
has to import them. 这个国家在毛织品方面现在已能自
给自足了。 (b) over-confident. 过于自信的; 傲慢的。
,~-suf'ficiency n [U]. ,~-suf'ficing adj = ~-suffi-
cient: a ~-sufficing economic unit. 自给自足的经济单位。
,~-sup'porting adj (of a person) earning enough
money to keep oneself: (指人)自谋生活的; 自立的: now
that my children are ~-supporting; 既然我的孩子们都能
自立; (of a business, etc) paying its way; not needing
a subsidy. (指商业等)能维持自己的; 不须补助的。 ,~-
'will n [U] wilfulness; determined to do as one wishes
and not be guided by others. 执拗; 固执己见。 ,~-'willed
adj obstinate; refusing advice or guidance. 执拗的;
固执己见的。 ,~-'winding adj (of a watch) winding
itself automatically (from movements of the wrist, etc).
(指表)自动上发条的。

self·ish /'selfiʃ; 'sɛlfɪʃ/ adj chiefly thinking of and
interested in one's own needs and welfare; without
care for others: 自私的; 自利的; 不顾他人的: act from
~ motives. 出于自私的动机而行事。 ~·ly adv ~·ness n

sell /sel; sɛl/ vt, vi (pt, pp **sold** /sould; sold/) **1**
[VP6A, 12A, 13A, 15B] ~ sth (to sb); ~ sb sth, give
in exchange for money: 卖;售;销: ~ fruit; 卖水果; ~
sth by auction; 拍卖某物; ~ sth at a good price; 按高价
卖某物; ~ oranges at five-pence each; 橘子每个卖五便士;
~ a man into slavery. 把一个人卖掉做奴隶。 I'll ~ it to
you for £5. 我愿以五英镑价格把它卖给你。 Will you ~
me your bicycle? 你愿把你的脚踏车卖给我吗? ~ sth off,
~ (a stock of goods) cheaply. 廉售(存货)。 ~ sth out,
(a) ~ part or all of one's share in a business: 脱售(在
某企业中的一部分或全部股份): He sold out his share of
the business and retired. 他脱售他在公司中的股份并且退
休了。 **(b)** ~ all of one's stock of sth: 售出全部存货:
We are sold out of small sizes. 我们小号的货品完全卖光
了。 The book you ask for is sold out, There are no
copies left. 你要的书卖完了。 ~ *(sb) out*, (colloq) be
treacherous; betray sb. (口)不忠; 出卖某人。 '~-out n
(a) event, eg a concert, for which all tickets are sold.
入场券全部售完的音乐会等; 客满的演出。 **(b)** (colloq)
betrayal. (口)出卖; 背叛。 ~ *sb up*, ~ (a person's
goods and property) for payment of debt: 为偿债而出
卖(某人之货物及财产): I went bankrupt and was sold
up. 我宣告破产, 财产被卖掉偿债。 ~ *(sb) short*,
short²(3). **2** [VP6A] keep stocks for sale; be a dealer
in: 备货出售; 做…之买卖: Do you ~ needles? 你卖针吗?
This little shop ~s a wide variety of goods. 这家小店备

有各色货物。 '~-ing price, price to be paid by the
customer; cash price. 零售价格; 售价。 Cf 参较 cost
price. **3** [VP2A, C] (of goods) be sold; find buyers:
(指货物)被卖出; 出售; 有买主: Ice-cream sells best in
summer. 冰淇淋在夏天销路最好。 His new novel is ~ing
well. 他的新小说销售良好。 These articles ~ at 20p
apiece. 这些物品按每件二十便士出售。 Your house ought
to ~ for at least £20000. 你的房子至少要卖二万英镑。
4 [VP6A] cause to be sold: 使卖出: It is not the low
prices but their quality which ~s our goods. 我们的货物
能销出, 非因价廉而因质好。 **5** (fig uses): (比喻用法):
~ one's life dearly, kill or wound a number of one's
attackers before being killed. 予攻击者巨大伤亡后才被
杀死。 '~ oneself, **(a)** present oneself to others in a
convincing way (eg when applying for a job). 自我推
销; 自我吹嘘(如申请工作时)。 **(b)** do sth dishonourable
for money or reward. 出卖自己(为金钱或报酬而做不名
誉的事)。 ~ *the pass*, (prov) do sth that weakens
one's country or side; be a traitor. (谚)做削弱本国或
己方之事; 做叛徒。 **6** (usu passive) cheat; disappoint by
failure to keep an agreement, etc: (通常用被动语态)欺
骗; 因未能守约而使失望: I've been sold! 我被欺骗了!
Sold again! I've been tricked, let down, etc! 又被骗了!
又上当了! **7 be sold on sth**, (colloq) accept it, believe
that it is good, etc: (口)接受某事物; 相信某事物是好的
等: Are the workers sold on the idea of profit-sharing? 工
人们接受分红的主意吗? □ n (colloq, from **6** above)
disappointment: (口, 由上列第 6 义)失望: What a ~!
多令人失望! **hard / soft** ~, aggressive / persuasive
~ing technique. 硬行(说服式)推销(法)。 ~**er** n **1**
person who ~s: 卖卖人; a 'book~er. 书商。 a ~**ers'
market**, (comm) situation when goods are scarce and
money plentiful, so that ~ers are favoured. (商)销售
者市场; 求过于供(货物少而货币多, 故卖方获利厚)。 **2**
sth that is sold. 出售之物。 best-'~er n ⇨ best²(2).

sel·vage, sel·vedge /'selvidʒ; 'sɛlvɪdʒ/ n edge of
cloth woven so that threads do not unravel. 布的织边。

selves /selvz; sɛlvz/ pl of **self**.

sem·an·tic /sɪ'mæntɪk; sə'mæntɪk/ adj relating to
meaning in language; of ~s. 关于语义的; 语义学的。
se·man·tics n (with sing v) branch of linguistics
concerned with studying the meanings of words and
sentences. (用单数动词)语义学(语言学之一分支, 讨论字
和句之含义)。

sema·phore /'semefɔː(r); 'sɛmə,fɔr/ n [U] **1** system
for sending signals by using arms on a post or flags
held in the hands, with various positions for the
letters of the alphabet: 信号; 旗语(利用杆上的支臂或
握于手中的旗帜传送信号的方法, 以不同的位置代表不同
的字母): send a message by ~. 以旗语传送信息。
2 mechanical device with red and green lights on
mechanically moved arms, used for signalling on
railways. (铁路之)信号装置(红绿灯)。 □ vt, vi [VP6A,
2A] send (messages) by ~(1). 以信号或旗语发送(消
息)。

(thin line = left arm; thick line = right arm)

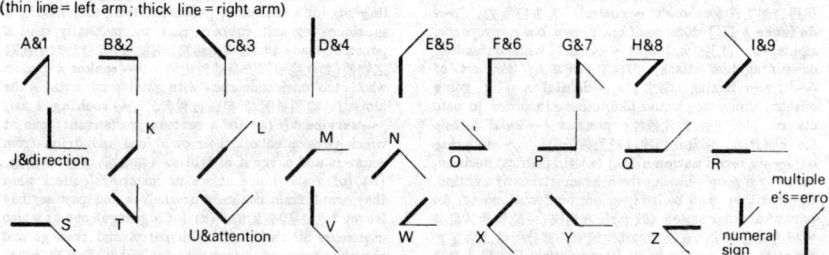

semaphore

sem·blance /'sembləns; 'sɛmbləns/ n [C] likeness; appearance: 相似; 外观: put on a ~ of gaiety. 佯装快乐的样子。

se·men /'si:mən; 'simən/ n [U] fertilizing sperm-bearing fluid of male animals. 精液。 **se·minal** /'semInl; 'sɛmənl/ adj of seed or semen or reproduction; embryonic; (fig) providing a basis for development: 种子的; 精液的; 生殖的; 发生的; 胚胎的; (喻) 能够引发的; 启发性的: seminal ideas. 启发性的念头。

sem·es·ter /sI'mestə(r); sə'mɛstə/ n (esp in Germany and US) each of the two divisions of an academic year. (尤用于德, 美) 一学期; 半学年。 Cf 参较 term in GB. 英国用 term。

semi- /'semI-; 'sɛmə-/ prep **1** half of. …之半。 '~·circle n half a circle. 半圆。 ⇨ the illus at circle 参看 circle 之插图。 ,~·'circular adj having the shape of a half a circle. 半圆的。 '~·breve (US 美 = whole note), the longest written musical note in common use. 全音符。 '~·quaver, half a quaver. 十六分音符。 ⇨ the illus at notation. 参看 notation 之插图。 '~·tone n half a tone in a musical scale, the smallest interval in normal Western music. (音乐) 半音; 半音程 (西方正规音乐中之最小音程)。 **2** on one of two sides. 在两边中之一边。 ,~·de'tached adj (of a house) joined to another on one side only (by one wall in common). (指房屋) 一侧与他屋相连的; 共一墙的。 **3** little better than: 比…稍好: ,~·bar'barian; 半野蛮的(人); ,~·'barbarism. 半野蛮。 **4** (various) (用于各种复合词中) ,~·'colon (US = 'semi·colon) the punctuation mark (;) used in writing and printing, between a comma and a full stop in value. 半支点; 分号 (即) ';' 用于写作及印刷中, 其功能介于逗点与句点之间)。 ⇨ App 9. 参看附录九。 ,~·'conscious adj partly conscious. 半清醒的; 半知觉的。 ,~·'final n match or round that precedes the final (eg in football matches). 半决赛; 准决赛。 ,~·'finalist n player/team, in the ~-finals. 参加准决赛之选手或队。 ,~·of'ficial adj (esp of announcements, etc made to newspaper reporters by officials, with the stipulation that they must not be considered as coming from an official source). 半官方的 (尤指官员对新闻记者所发表的声明等, 约定不能视为来自官方者)。 ,~·'rigid adj (esp of airships) having a rigid keel attached to a flexible gas-bag. (尤指飞艇) 半硬式的。 ,~·'tropical adj of regions near but not in the tropics. 亚热带的。 '~·vowel n (letter representing a) sound with a vowel quality but a consonant function (eg/w/,/j/). 半元音 (有元音的性质而有辅音作用的音, 如英语的/w/, /j/等); 半元音字母。 **5** occurring, published, etc twice in (a year, etc) (bi- 较为 more usu): (一年中中) 出现, 出版等二次的 (bi- 较常用): ,~·'annual; 半年刊的; a ,~·'weekly. 半周刊的。

semi·nal /'semInl; 'sɛmənl/ ⇨ **semen**.

sem·inar /'semInɑ:(r); 'sɛmə,nɑr/ n class of students, etc studying a problem and meeting for discussion with a tutor or professor. 学生为研究某问题而与教师共同讨论之班级; 研习班。

sem·inary /'semInərI US: -nerI; 'sɛmə,nɛrI/ n (pl -ries) **1** Roman Catholic training college for priests. (天主教之) 神学院。 **2** (formerly used as a pretentious name for a) place of education: 养成所; 学校 (昔时用做矫饰之名称): a ~ for young ladies. 女子专门学校。 **semin·ar·ist** /'semInərIst; 'sɛmə,nɛrIst/ n man trained in a ~(1). 神学院之学生。

Sem·ite /'si:maIt; 'sɛmaIt/ n, adj (member) of any of the group of peoples that includes the Hebrews and Arabs and formerly the Phoenicians and Assyrians. 闪族人 (包括希伯来人, 阿拉伯人, 腓尼基人及亚述人); 闪族的; 闪族人的。 **Se·mitic** /sI'mItIk; sə'mItIk/ adj of the ~s or their languages: 闪族的; 闪族语的: a Semitic people. 闪族之一支。

semo·lina /,semə'li:nə; ,sɛmə'linə/ n [U] hard grains of wheat meal, used for pasta, and in milk puddings, etc. 粗粒小麦粉(用于面食, 牛奶布丁等中)。

semp·stress /'sempstrIs; 'sɛmpstrIs/ ⇨ **seamstress**.

sen·ate /'senIt; 'sɛnIt/ n [C] **1** (in ancient Rome) highest council of state. (古罗马之) 元老院。 **2** (in modern times) Upper House (usu the smaller) of the legislative assembly in various countries, eg France, US. (现代之) 上议院; 参议院(如法, 美等国通常在国会中较下议院为小)。 **3** governing council of some universities. (若干大学之) 评议会。 **senator** /'senətə(r); 'sɛnətə/ n member of ~(1, 2). (古罗马之) 元老院议员; (现代之) 上议员; 参议员。 **senatorial** /,senə'tɔ:rIəl; ,sɛnə'tɔrIəl/ adj of a ~ or senator: 元老院的; 上议院的; 参议院的; 元老院议员的; 上议员的; 参议员的: senatorial rank/powers; 上议员之地位(权力); senatorial district, (US) one entitled to elect a senator. (美) 参议员选举区。

send /send; sɛnd/ vt, vi (pt, pp sent) (For special uses with adverbial particles and preps, ⇨ **5** below.). (与副词性小品词及介词连用之特殊用法, 参看下列第 5 义。) **1** [VP 12A, 13A, 6A, 15A] ~ sb/sth; ~ sth to sb, cause sb or sth to go or be carried without going oneself: 送; 寄; 遣; 派送: ~ a telegram, 打电报送电报; ~ a message to sb/~ sb a message. 送消息予某人。 The children were sent to bed. 小孩们都被打发睡觉去了。 John was sent to school with an older child. 约翰跟一个较大的孩子一起去上学。 ⇨ take[1](4). **2** [VP 19 B] use force to cause sb/sth to move sharply or rapidly: 使某人 (某物) 急遽地移动: The earthquake sent the crockery and cutlery crashing to the ground. 地震将杯盘和刀叉震落在地上。 Mind how you go—you nearly sent me flying, ie you nearly knocked me over. 小心点, 你差点把我撞倒。 ~ sb packing/about his business, (colloq) dismiss him at once, without formality: (口) 解雇某人; 要某人立刻卷铺盖: His incompetent typist was sent packing. 他那不称职的打字员被解雇了。 S~ that fellow about his business—he's no use to anybody! 叫那家伙滚蛋——他对任何人都没有用处! ⇨ **bring**. **3** [VP22, 6A] cause to become: 促使; 使变为: This noise is ~ing me crazy. 这吵声快使我发疯。 This music/This gorgeous girl really ~s me, (sl) excites me intensely, rouses me to ecstasy. (俚) 这声音 (这可爱的女郎) 使我觉得飘飘然。 **4** (old use, of God, Providence): (旧用法, 指上帝、天意): Heaven ~ that he arrives safely, may God grant this. 天佑他安全到达。 'S~ her victorious!' (in the British national anthem) May God grant that the Sovereign may be victorious. (英国国歌中)天佑我王胜利。 **5** [VP15 B, 2 C, 3 A] (special uses with adverbial particles and preps): (与副词性小品词及介词连用的特殊用法):

send sb away, dismiss. 解雇。 ~ **away for sth**, order (goods) from a distance, to be delivered by rail, post, etc: 从远处订(货): When we lived in the country, we had to ~ away for many things we needed. 我们住在乡下时, 必须向远处订购我们所需要的许多东西。

send sb down, (esp) expel a student from a university (for misconduct, etc). (尤指) 勒令大学生退学 (因行为不检等); 开除。 ~ **sth down**, cause to fall: 使下降: The good harvest sent the prices down. 丰收使价格下跌。 The storm sent the temperature down. 暴风雨使气温下降。

send for sb/sth (to do sth), ask or order sb/sth to come, for sth to be delivered: 派人去叫(某人); 遣人去拿(某物); 召; 请; 叫: ~ for a doctor/taxi. 延请医生/雇计程车。 We must ~ for a man to repair the TV. 我们必须叫人来修理电视机。 Please keep these things until I ~ for them. 请替我保留这些东西, 等我派人来取。

send sth forth, (formal) produce, issue: (正式用语)生出; 发出: ~ forth leaves. 生叶。

send sth in (for sth, eg a competition, exhibition): 登记或提出 (以参加比赛或展览等): ~ in one's name for a contest; 登记参加比赛; ~ in two oil paintings; 送两幅油画参加展览会; ~ in a report for consideration. 提出一份报告供参考。 ~ **one's name in**, cause one's name to be made known. 通报某人的名字。

send sb off, (more usu *see sb off*) go with sb to the place from which he will start a journey: (see sb off 较常用)送别: *Many of his friends went to the airport to ~ him off.* 很多朋友赶往机场为他送行。他到此产生, *'~-off n: He was given a good ~-off.* 他受到了热烈的送别。 *~ sth off,* dispatch: 发送: *Please see that these parcels are sent off at once.* 请留意把这些包裹立即送出去。

send sth on, (a) ~ it in advance. 预送(某物)。 **(b)** (of letters) readdress and repost: (指信件)转寄: *I asked my wife to ~ all my letters on while I was away from home.* 在我离家时,我请我太太转寄我所有的信件。

send sth out, (a) distribute; give out: 分发;发出: *The sun ~s out light and warmth.* 太阳发出光和热。 **(b)** produce: 生出: *The trees ~ out new leaves in spring.* 树在春天长新叶。

send sb/sth up, tease; parody; show that sb/sth is ridiculous or false. 取笑某人(某事物);滑稽地模仿诗文;暴露某人(某事物)的可笑或不实之处。Hence, 由此产生, *'~-up n* mocking imitation or parody. 讥讽性的模仿或歪改(他人诗文)。 *~ sth up,* cause to rise: 使上升: *The heavy demand for beef sent the price up.* 大量的需要使牛肉价格上升。

sender /'sendə(r); 'sɛndɚ/ *n* person or thing that sends: 送者;发送之人或物: *If lost, return to ~* (eg on a letter). (信件等上之说明)如无法投递,请退还原寄人。

se·nes·cent /sɪ'nesnt; sə'nɛsn̩t/ *adj* showing signs of old age: 显老的: *I may be ~, but I'm not yet senile.* 我可能显老,但我尚未衰老。 **se·nes·cence** /-sns, -sn̩s/ *n* [U].

sen·eschal /'senɪʃl; 'sɛnəʃəl/ *n* (in the Middle Ages) important official (steward or major-domo) in the castle of a noble. (中世纪贵族城堡中的)管家。

se·nile /'si:naɪl; 'sinaɪl/ *adj* suffering from bodily or mental weakness because of old age; caused by old age: 因年老而身心衰弱的;由年老引起的;衰老的;老迈的: ~ *decay.* 年老体衰。 **sen·il·ity** /sɪ'nɪlɪtɪ; sə'nɪlətɪ/ *n* [U] weakness (of body or mind) in old age. 衰老;老衰;龙钟;老糊涂。

sen·ior /'si:nɪə(r); 'sinjɚ/ *adj* (opp of *junior*) (为 junior 之反义词) **1** ~ (*to*), older in years; higher in rank, authority, etc: 年长的;权位等较高的;资深的: *He is ten years ~ to me.* 他比我年长十岁。 *Smith is the ~ partner in* (= the head of) *the firm.* 史密斯是公司的老板。,~ **'citizen,** (euphem for) person over the age of retirement; old age pensioner. (委婉语)超过退休年龄之人;领养老金者。 **2** (after a person's name, esp when a father and his son have the same first name; abbr 略作 **Sen**) (用于人名之后,尤其当父子名字相同时): *John Brown (Sen).* (老)约翰·布朗。 ⇨ **major.** □ *n* **1** ~ person: 年长者;资深者: *He is my ~ by ten years.* 他比我长十岁。 *The ~s* (= members of the ~ class) *defeated the juniors by 3—1.* 高班同学以三比一击败了低班同学。 **2** (US) student in his/her fourth year at high school or college. (美)高中、大学最高年级的学生;大学四年级的学生。 **~·ity** /,si:nɪ'brɒtɪ US: -'ɔːr-; sin'jɔrətɪ/ *n* [U] condition of being ~ (in age, rank, etc): 年长;资深: *Should promotion be through merit or through ~ity?* 升级应该根据功绩还是根据年资? *Remember the precedence due to ~ity.* 记住,优先权应该让给长辈。

senna /'senə; 'sɛnə/ *n* [U] dried leaves of the cassia plant, used as a laxative. 番泻叶(山扁豆之干叶,用作通便剂)。

se·ñor /se'njɔː(r); sen'jɔr/ *n* (*pl* **señores** /se'njɔːreɪz; se'njɔrez/) used of or to a Spanish-speaking man; Mr; sir. (**S~** when preceding a name) 先生; 君(西班牙语系对男子之称呼; 置于人名之前大写 **S**)。 **se·ñora** /se'njɔːrə; sen'jɔrə/ *n* used of or to a Spanish-speaking woman; Mrs; Madam. 太太;夫人;女士(西班牙语系对妇女之称呼)。 **se·ñorita** /,senjɔː'riːtə; ,senje'rite/ *n* used of or to an unmarried woman or girl; Miss. 小姐

(用于未婚女子)。

sen·sa·tion /sen'seɪʃn; sɛn'seʃən/ *n* **1** [C, U] ability to feel; feeling: 感觉: *lose all ~ in one's legs.* 失去腿部的一切知觉; *have a ~ of warmth / dizziness / falling.* 感到温暖(晕眩,下落)。 **2** [C, U] (instance of, sth that causes, a) quick and excited reaction: 感动;激动;引起激动或兴奋之实例: *Our popular newspapers deal largely in ~.* 我们那些受欢迎的报纸多报导令人听闻的新闻。 *The news created a great ~.* 这消息造成了很大的轰动。 **~·al** /-ʃənl; -ʃənl/ *adj* **1** causing a ~(2): 令人激动的; 激起感情的; 轰动的: *a ~al murder.* 轰动一时的谋杀案。 **2** (of newspapers, etc) presenting news in a manner designed to cause ~(2): (指报纸等)耸人听闻的: *a ~al writer / newspaper.* 耸人听闻的作家(报纸)。 **~·ally** /-ʃənlɪ; -ʃənlɪ/ *adv* **~·al·ism** /-ʃənlɪzəm/ *n* [U] the deliberate rousing of ~(2): 故意耸人听闻; 故意危言耸听: *the ~alism of the cinema;* 那部电影的故意耸人听闻; *avoid ~alism during an election campaign.* 在竞选时避免故意危言耸听。 **~·al·ist** /-ʃənlɪst; -ʃənlɪst/ *n*

sense /sens; sɛns/ *n* **1** any one of the special powers of the body by which a person is conscious of things (ie sight, hearing, smell, taste and touch): 官能; 感觉; 知觉(如视觉,听觉,嗅觉,味觉及触觉): *be in the enjoyment of all one's ~s;* 享有一切知觉;五官健全; *have a keen ~ of hearing.* 听觉锐敏。 *'~-organ* n part of the body, eg the ear or eye, concerned in producing sensation. 感觉器官; 感官(如耳朵或眼睛)。 ,**sixth '~,** ⇨ **six.** **2** (*pl*) normal state of mind (as when a person has the five ~s of **1** above): (复)心智健全: *in one's (right) ~s,* sane; 心智健全的; *out of one's ~s,* insane; 心智不健全的; 癫狂的; *frighten sb out of his ~s,* frighten him so that he behaves in an excited way. 把某人吓得惊慌失措; *bring sb to his ~s,* cause him to give up behaving foolishly or wildly. 使醒悟; 使心智恢复健全。 *come to one's ~s,* stop behaving like a fool or madman. 醒悟; 心智恢复健全。 *take leave of one's ~s,* become mad; start behaving irrationally. 发疯; 失常。 **3** (*a / the*) ~ *of,* appreciation or understanding of the value or worth (of): 辨识; 意识: *a ~ of humour;* 幽默感; *my ~ of duty;* 我的责任感; *the moral ~;* 是非感; *a ~ of locality / direction,* ie recognition of places, landmarks, directions, etc. 对于方位(方向)的辨识力。 **4** (*a / the*) ~ *of,* consciousness (of): 意识; 自觉: *have no ~ of shame;* 无羞耻心; *a ~ of one's own importance / responsibility.* 对自己重要性(职责)的觉察。 **5** (*U*) power of judging; judgement; practical wisdom: 判断力; 判断; 见识: *Haven't you ~ enough to come in out of the rain?* 你怎么不避雨呢? *There's a lot of ~ in what he says.* 他说话颇有见识。 *There's no ~ in doing that,* It's pointless. 做那件事情没有道理。 *What's the ~ of doing that?* 做那件事究竟有何道理? *Now you're talking ~.* 你的话颇有道理。 ⇨ also **common ~** at **common¹(2).** **6** [C] meaning: 意义; 意味: *a word with several ~s.* 具有数义的一个词。 *In what ~ are you using the word?* 你用这个词所指的是那一个意义? *The ~ of the word is not clear.* 该词的意义不明确。 *in a ~,* if the statement, etc is taken in a particular way: 某某意义而言: *What you say is true in a ~.* 就某种意义而言, 你说的是实话。 **make ~,** have a meaning that can be understood: 有意义: *What you say doesn't make ~ / makes no ~,* means nothing. 你的话毫无意义。 **make ~ of sth,** find a meaning in it: 懂; 了解其含义: *Can you make ~ of this poem?* 你懂得这首诗的含义吗? *in the strict / literal / figurative / full / best* (= most favourable) */ proper, etc ~,* interpreting (the statement, etc) strictly/literally, etc. 就精确(字面,比喻,全貌,最好,适当)的意义而言。 **7** [U] general feeling or opinion among a number of people: 一般的意见; 舆论: *take the ~ of a public meeting,* ask questions in order to learn the general sentiment or opinion. 提出问题以求了解与会者的一般意见。 □ *vt* [VP6A, 9] feel; be vaguely

aware of; realize: 觉得; 感知; 理会; 了解; 明白: *He ~d that his proposals were unwelcome.* 他觉得他的建议不受欢迎。

sense·less /'senslɪs; 'sɛnslɪs/ *adj* **1** foolish. 愚蠢的: *a ~ idea.* 愚蠢的观念。*What a ~ fellow he is!* 他是多么愚蠢的家伙! **2** unconscious: 无感觉的; 不省人事的: *fall ~ to the ground.* 失去知觉倒在地上。~·**ly** *adv* ~·**ness** *n*

sen·si·bil·ity /ˌsensə'bɪlətɪ; ˌsɛnsə'bɪlətɪ/ *n* (*pl* -**ties**) [U, C] power of feeling; (esp) power of receiving or feeling delicate emotional impressions; such feeling(s): 感觉能力; 感性; (尤指) 敏感性; 情绪上的善感性: *the ~ of a poet.* 诗人之敏感性。*Her sensibilities are easily wounded.* 她的情绪容易受到伤害。

sen·sible /'sensəbl; 'sɛnsəbl/ *adj* **1** having or showing good sense(5); reasonable; practical: 有判断力的; 明智的; 明理的; 切实的: *a ~ woman;* 明理的女子; *~ shoes for mountain climbing;* 适合爬山的鞋子; *~ clothing,* functional, not merely for appearance or ornament; 实用的衣服; *~ ideas.* 明智的观念。*That was ~ of you.* 你那样做很明智。**2** ~ of, (old use) aware of: (旧用法)知道(的); 觉察的: *He is ~ of the danger of his position.* 他发觉处境的危险。**3** (old use) that can be perceived by the senses(1); perceptible (the usu word now): (旧用法)感觉得到的; 显著的(现常用 perceptible): *a ~ fall in the temperature;* 温度显著的下降; *~ phenomena.* 感觉得到的现象。**sen·sibly** /-əblɪ; -əblɪ/ *adv* in a ~ way: 有判断力地; 明智地; 切实地; 感知地; 可感觉地: *sensibly dressed for hot weather.* 穿着适合炎热气候的。

sen·si·tive /'sensɪtɪv; 'sɛnsətɪv/ *adj* ~ (to), **1** quickly or easily receiving impressions: 敏感的; 容易感受的: *The eyes are ~ to light.* 眼睛对光敏感。*A ~ skin is easily hurt by too much sunshine.* 敏感的皮肤晒太阳过多易受伤害。*A ~ nerve in a tooth can cause great pain.* 牙齿中敏感的神经能引起巨痛。**2** easily hurt in the spirit; easily offended: 易受伤害的; 易被冒犯的: *Children are usually ~ to blame.* 小孩子们通常容易因为责备而受到伤害。*An author must not be too ~ to criticism* 作家不宜对批评太敏感。*He is very ~ about his ugly appearance.* 他对自己的丑陋外表十分敏感。**3** (of instruments, and institutions thought of as measuring things) able to record small changes: (指仪器及可作测量物的之机构)能记录小变化的; 灵敏的: *~ thermometers/scales.* 灵敏的温度计 (天平)。*The Stock Exchange is ~ to political disturbances.* 证券交易所对于政治上的不安很敏感。**4** (of photographic film, paper, etc) affected by light. (指摄影软片,感光纸等)易感光的。~·**ly** *adv* **sen·si·tiv·ity** /ˌsensɪ'tɪvətɪ; ˌsɛnsə'tɪvətɪ/ *n* [U] quality, degree, of being ~: 敏感; 敏感性; 敏感度; 灵敏性; 灵敏度: *The dentist gave her an injection to reduce the sensitivity of the nerves.* 牙医师为她注射以减少神经的敏感感度。**sen·si·tize** /'sensɪtaɪz; 'sɛnsə,taɪz/ *vt* [VP 6A] make sensitive; (photo) make (film, paper, etc) ~ to light (for use in photography). 使敏感; 使(软片,感光纸等)易于感光(以供摄影使用)。

sen·sory /'sensərɪ; 'sɛnsərɪ/ *adj* of the senses(1) or sensation: 感觉的; 感官的: *~ organs/nerves.* 感觉器官(神经)。

sen·sual /'senʃʊəl; 'sɛnʃʊəl/ *adj* of, given up to, the pleasures of the senses; self-indulgent in regard to food and drink and sexual enjoyment: 肉欲的; 声色之乐的; 耽于声色饮食的; 淫荡的: *~ enjoyment;* 声色的享受; *a ~ life;* 耽于声色的生活; *~ lips,* giving the impression that a person is ~. 性感的嘴唇。~·**ism** /-ɪzəm; -,ɪzəm/ *n* ~·**ity**. ~·**ist** /-ɪst; -ɪst/ *n* ~ person. 耽于声色之人。~·**ity** /senʃʊ'ælətɪ; ,sɛnʃʊ-'ælətɪ/ *n* [U] love of, indulgence in, ~ pleasures, esp of the body. 耽于声色; 耽于肉欲; 淫荡。

sen·su·ous /'senʃʊəs; 'sɛnʃʊəs/ *adj* affecting, noticed by, appealing to, the senses(1): 影响感觉的; 敏感的; 为感觉所认知的; 诉诸感觉的: *~ music/painting.* 引起美感的音乐(画)。(Note that ~ is free of the sense of

'self-indulgence' in *sensual*). (注意: sensuous 没有 sensual 一词所含示的 '放纵自己' 的意味)。~·**ly** *adv* ~·**ness** *n*

sent /sent; sɛnt/ *pt, pp* of **send.**

sen·tence /'sentəns; 'sɛntəns/ *n* [C] **1** (statement by a judge, etc, of) punishment: (法官等之)判决; 宣判; 刑罚: *pass ~ (on sb),* declare what the punishment is to be; 判(某人的)刑: *under ~ of death.* 被判处死刑。*The ~ of the court was three years' imprisonment.* 法院的判决是三年徒刑。**2** (gram) the largest grammatical unit, consisting of phrases and/or clauses, used to express a statement, question, command, etc. (语法)句; 文句。□ *vt* [VP 6A, 14, 17] state that (sb) is to have a certain punishment: 判决; 宣判: *a thief to six months' imprisonment.* 判处窃贼六个月徒刑。*He had been ~d to pay a fine of £10.* 他被判罚款十英镑。

sen·ten·tious /sen'tenʃəs; sɛn'tɛnʃəs/ *adj* **1** (old use) in the habit of saying or writing things in a short and witty manner. (旧用法)言简意赅的; 简洁精辟的。**2** (mod use) having, putting on, an air of wisdom; dull and moralizing: (现代用法)佯装有智慧的; 沉闷而说教的: *a ~ speaker/speech.* 沉闷而说教的演说者(演讲)。~·**ly** *adv*

sen·ti·ent /'sentʃnt; 'sɛntʃənt/ *adj* having, able to have, feeling; experiencing sensation. 有知觉的; 有感觉的; 感觉到的。

sen·ti·ment /'sentɪmənt; 'sɛntəmənt/ *n* **1** [C] mental feeling, the total of what one thinks and feels on a subject; [U] such feelings collectively as an influence: 感情; 情绪; 情操: *The ~ of pity is made up of the feeling of sympathy and of a desire to help and protect.* 怜悯的情绪是由同情心以及给予帮助和保护的愿望所构成。*A true statesman is animated by lofty ~s.* 真正的政治家是受到高尚情操的激励。*Should reason be guided by ~?* 理智应受感情的支配吗? *What are your ~s towards my sister.* 你对我姐姐(妹妹)的感情如何? **2** [U] (tendency to be moved by) (display of) tender feeling (contrasted with reason): 伤感; 软弱之情感; 多情善感; (过分的)情感: *There's no place for ~ in business.* 做生意不可感情用事。**3** expression of feeling; opinions or point of view: 意见; 观点: *The ambassador explained the ~s of his government on the question.* 大使解释其政府对该问题的观点。

sen·ti·men·tal /ˌsentɪ'mentl; ˌsɛntə'mɛntl/ *adj* **1** having to do with the feelings; emotional: 感情的; 情绪的: *do sth for ~ reasons;* 由于感情上的缘故而做某事; *have a ~ attachment to one's birthplace.* 对某人的诞生地有深厚的情感。*The bracelet had only ~ value,* eg because it belonged to one's mother. 那只手镯仅有情感上的价值。**2** (of things) tending to arouse, expressing (often excessive, inappropriate or false) feelings: (指事物)有引起或表达情感之倾向的; 感伤的; 过于感伤的: *~ music;* 感伤的音乐; *~ novelettes;* 过于感伤的中篇小说; (of persons) having such excessive feelings: (指人)多愁善感的; 感情过于丰富的: *She's far too ~ about her cats.* 她对她的猫过份关爱。~·**ly** /-təlɪ; -tlɪ/ *adv* ~·**ist** *n* person who is ~. 多愁善感者。~·**ity** /ˌsentɪmen-'tælɪtɪ; ˌsɛntəmɛn'tælətɪ/ *n* [U] the quality of being weakly or foolishly ~. 多愁善感; 感伤。~·**ize** /-təlaɪz; -tl,aɪz/ *vt, vi* [VP 6A, 2A] (cause) to become ~(2). (使)溺于感情; (使)感伤。

sen·ti·nel /'sentɪnl; 'sɛntənl/ *n* = sentry (now the usu word): *stand ~ (over),* (liter) keep guard (over). (文)守卫; 放哨。

sen·try /'sentrɪ; 'sɛntrɪ/ *n* (*pl* -**ries**) soldier posted to keep watch and guard. 哨兵; 步哨。'~·**box** *n* hut or cabin for a ~. 哨岗; 哨亭。'~·**go** *n* duty of pacing up and down as a ~: 步哨勤务; 站岗: *be on ~-go.* 放哨。

se·pal /'sepl; 'sɪpl/ *n* (bot) one of the divisions of the calyx of a flower. (植)(花之)萼片。⇨ the illus at **flower.** 参看 flower 之插图。

sep·ar·able /'sepərəbl; 'sɛpərəbl/ *adj* that can be

separated. 可分开的；能区分的。 **sep·ar·ably** /-əblɪ; -əblɪ/ *adv* **sep·ar·abil·ity** /ˌseprəˈbɪlətɪ; ˌsepərəˈbɪlətɪ/ *n*

sep·ar·ate[1] /ˈseprət; ˈseprɪt/ *adj* **1** divided; not joined or united: 分离的；分开的: *Cut it into three ~ parts.* 把它切成三分。 **2** forming a unit which is distinct and which exists apart: 各别的；单独的: *The children sleep in ~ beds,* Each of them has his own bed. 孩子们分别睡在自己的床上。 *Mr Green and his wife are living ~* (= apart) *now.* 格林先生和他的妻子现在分居。 *Keep these ~ from those.* 把这些和那些分开开。 □ *n* (trade use, *pl*) ~ garments which may be worn in a variety of combinations, eg jerseys, blouses and skirts. (商业用语，复)不是成套的女装(如紧身毛衣，衬衫，裙子等)。 ~·**ly** *adv* in a ~ manner: 分离地；各别地: *Tie them up ~ly.* 把它们分别绑起来。

sep·ar·ate[2] /ˈsepəreɪt; ˈsepəˌret/ *vt, vi* **1** [VP6A, 14, 15B] ~ (*from*), make, be, ~ from: 使分离；分开；隔开: *S~ the good ones from the bad.* 使好的和坏的分开。 *England is ~d from France by the Channel.* 英国和法国被英吉利海峡隔开。 ~ *sth (up) into,* divide into: 分开为(几分)；分割成(几段): *The land was ~d (up) into small fields.* 那块地被分割为小块的田地。 **2** [VP2A] (of a number of people) go in different ways: (指一群人)分手；解散: *We talked until midnight and then ~d.* 我们谈到午夜才分手。 **sep·ar·at·ist** /ˈsepərətɪst; ˈsepəˌretɪst/ *n* (opp of *unionist*) member of a group which wants (esp political or ecclesiastical) separation. (为unionist 之反义词)(尤指政治或宗教上之)分离主义者；要求独立者。 **sep·ar·ator** /ˈsepəreɪtə(r); ˈsepəˌretə/ *n* (esp) device for separating cream from milk. 分离器；(尤指)脱脂器(使奶油与奶分离者)。

sep·ar·ation /ˌsepəˈreɪʃn; ˌsepəˈreʃən/ *n* **1** [U] (state of) being separated or separate; act of separating: 分离；分开: *S~ from his friends made him sad.* 与朋友们分离使他伤心。 **judicial ~,** (commonly called 通常称作 *legal ~*) arrangement (ordered by a court of law) which does not end a marriage, but which requires married persons no longer to live together. 经法庭判定的夫妻分居。 ⇨ **divorce**[1](1). **2** [C] instance of, period of, separation: 分离之实例；分离之期间: *after a ~ of five years;* 分离五年以后; *~s of husbands and wives in time of war.* 战时丈夫和妻子的分离。

se·pia /ˈsiːpɪə; ˈsipɪə/ *n* [U] dark brown (ink or paint): 深褐色；深褐色油墨或颜料: *a '~-drawing,* one done in ~. 深褐色的图画。

sep·sis /ˈsepsɪs; ˈsepsɪs/ *n* [U] contamination from a festering wound. 败血症；脓毒病。

Sep·tem·ber /sepˈtembə(r); sɛpˈtɛmbə/ *n* the ninth month of the year. 九月。

sep·tet /sepˈtet; sɛpˈtɛt/ *n* (musical composition for a) group of seven voices or instruments. (音乐)七重奏；七部合奏曲；七部合唱曲。

sep·tic /ˈseptik; ˈsɛptɪk/ *adj* of sepsis; causing, caused by, infection (with disease germs): 腐败的；使腐败的；致使败血的: *~ poisoning.* 败血症。 *A dirty wound may become ~,* caused by bacteria. 脏的伤口可能变为脓毒。 ~ **tank,** one in which sewage is disposed of by bacterial activity. (借细菌作用之)阴沟净化槽；化粪池。

sep·ti·cemia /ˌseptɪˈsiːmɪə; ˌsɛptəˈsimɪə/ *n* blood-poisoning. 败血症；血毒病。

sep·tua·gen·ar·ian /ˌseptjuːədʒɪˈneərɪən US: -tʃuːədʒə-; ˌsɛptjuˌədʒɪˈnɛrɪən/ *n* person 70 to 79 years old. 七十岁至七十九岁之间的人。

Sep·tua·gint /ˈseptjuːədʒɪnt US: -tu-; ˈsɛptuəˌdʒɪnt/ *n* Greek version of the Old Testament and the Apocrypha made about 270 BC. 旧约和伪经之希腊文本(约于纪元前 270 年译成)。

sep·ulchre (US = **sep·ul·cher** /ˈseplkə(r); ˈsɛplkə/ *n* [C] tomb, esp one cut in rock or built of stone. 坟墓；冢(尤指凿石岩石而成或以石块砌成者): **the Holy S~,** that in which Jesus Christ was laid. 圣墓(耶稣之墓)。

whited ~ *n* hypocrite. 伪君子；假冒为善的人。 ⇨ **Matt.** 23:27. 参看马太福音 23 章 27 节。 **sep·ulchral** /sɪˈpʌlkrəl; səˈpʌlkrəl/ *adj* **1** of a ~; of burial. 墓的；埋葬的。 **2** deep and gloomy; suggestive of burial: 深而幽暗的；阴森森的；令人想起埋葬的: *sepulchral looks;* 阴森森的面貌; *in a sepulchral voice.* 阴沉的声音。

se·pul·ture /ˈseplt ʃə(r); ˈsɛpltʃə/ *n* [U] burying; putting in the tomb or grave. 埋葬；埋入墓中。

se·quel /ˈsiːkwəl; ˈsikwəl/ *n* [C] **1** that which follows or arises out of (an earlier happening): (早先事件之)继续；后续；后果；结局: *Famine has often been the ~ of war.* 饥馑常是战争的后果。 *Her action had an unfortunate ~.* 她的行为带来不幸的结局。 **in the ~,** later on; as things developed afterwards. 后来；结果。 **2** story, film, etc with the same character of an earlier one. (故事，影片等的)续集；续篇。

se·quence /ˈsiːkwəns; ˈsikwəns/ *n* [U] succession: [C] connected line of events, ideas, etc: 继续；连续；(事件，观念等之)系列；一连串；次第；顺序；关联: *deal with events in historical ~;* 按历史的次序讨论事件; *the ~ of events,* the order in which they occur: 事件发生之顺序; *a ~ of bad harvests;* 接连的歉收; *a ~ of clubs* (in playing cards), three or more next to each other in value, eg Ace, King, Queen, or 10, 9, 8. (牌戏) 梅花顺子(三张以上的连牌，如爱斯，王，后，或十点，九点，八点)。 ~ **of tenses,** (gram) principles according to which the tenses of subordinate clauses are suited to the tenses of principal clauses. (语法)时态的一致 (附属从句中的动词时态，配合主要从句中的 动词时态之原则)。 **se·quent** /-ənt; -ənt/ *adj* (formal) following in order or time; resulting. (正式用语)继续的；连续的；结果的。 **se·quen·tial** /sɪˈkwenʃl; sɪˈkwɛnʃəl/ *adj* following in order of time or place; following as a result. 按时间或顺序而来的；连续的；继起的；结果的。

se·ques·ter /sɪˈkwestə(r); sɪˈkwɛstə/ *vt* [VP6A] **1** keep (sb) away or apart from other people; withdraw to a quiet place: 使(某人)与他人分离；退隐；隐遁: *oneself from the world;* 隐居; *lead a ~ed life.* 过退隐的生活。 **2** (legal) = sequestrate. **~ed** *adj* (of places) quiet; secluded. (指地方)幽静的；隐僻的。

se·ques·trate /sɪˈkwestreɪt; sɪˈkwɛstret/ *vt* [VP6A] **1** (legal) take temporary possession of (a debtor's property, estate, etc) until debts are paid or other claims met. (法律)假扣押(债务人之财产，地产等)。 **2** confiscate. 查封；没收。 **se·ques·tra·tion** /ˌsiːkweˈstreɪʃn; ˌsɪˌkwɛsˈtreʃən/ *n*

se·quin /ˈsiːkwɪn; ˈsikwɪn/ *n* **1** tiny metal disc of silver, jet, etc sewn on to a dress, etc as an ornament. (衣服等上作饰物用之)小金属圆片。 **2** (hist) gold coin once used in Venice. (史)(昔时威尼斯所用之)金币。

se·quoia /sɪˈkwɔɪə; sɪˈkwɔɪə/ *n* large evergreen coniferous tree of California (the *redwood*) of great height. 美洲杉(红杉，产于美国加州之高大常青树)。

se·ra·glio /seˈrɑːlɪəʊ; sɪˈræljo/ *n* (*pl* ~s /-lɪəʊz, -ljoz/) harem; (hist) Turkish ruler's walled palace with government offices, etc. 闺房；(史)(土耳其之)皇宫；皇城(包括政府机关等)。

ser·aph /ˈserəf; ˈsɛrəf/ *n* (*pl* ~s or ~**im** /-fɪm; -fɪm/)(biblical) one of the highest order of angels. (圣经)六翼天使；炽爱天使(等级最高的天使)。 ⇨ **cherub.** ~**ic** /sɪˈræfɪk; səˈræfɪk/ *adj* angelic; happy and beautiful as a ~. 天使的；似天使般快乐而美丽的。

sere /sɪə(r); sɪr/ = **sear**[2].

ser·en·ade /ˌserəˈneɪd; ˌsɛrəˈned/ *n* (piece of) music (to be) sung or played outdoors at night. 夜曲；小夜曲。 □ *vt* [VP6A] sing or play a ~ to (sb). 为(某人)唱或奏夜曲。

ser·en·dip·ity /ˌserənˈdɪpɪtɪ; ˌsɛrənˈdɪpətɪ/ *n* (talent for) making fortunate and unexpected discoveries by chance. 偶然做成珍宝(之才能)。

ser·ene /sɪˈriːn; səˈrin/ *adj* clear and calm; tranquil: 晴朗的；宁静的: *a ~ sky;* 晴朗的天空; *a ~ look;* 安祥的

神情; *a ~ smile.* 安详的微笑。 **~·ly** *adv* **ser·en·i·ty** /sɪ'renɪtɪ; sə'rɛnətɪ/ *n* [U].

serf /sɜːf; sɝf/ *n* (hist) person who was not allowed to leave the land on which he worked; (fig) person treated almost like a slave; drudge. (史)农奴; (喻)被虐待如奴隶的人; 苦役。 **~·dom** /-dəm; -dəm/ *n* [U] **1** social and economic system in which land was cultivated by ~s. 农奴制(土地由农奴耕种之社会经济制度)。 **2** ~'s condition of life. 农奴之境遇。

serge /sɜːdʒ; sɝdʒ/ *n* [U] hard-wearing woollen cloth: (一种耐穿的)毛哔叽: (attrib) (用作定语) *a blue ~ suit.* 一套蓝色毛哔叽的衣服。

ser·geant /'sɑːdʒənt; 'sɑrdʒənt/ *n* **1** non-commissioned army officer above a corporal and below a ~-major. 士官; 军士; 中士。 **,~-'major** *n* highest grade of non-commissioned army officer. 准尉; 士官长。 **2** police-officer with rank below that of an inspector. 警官; 警佐; 巡佐(等级低于巡官者)。

serial /'sɪərɪəl; 'sɪrɪəl/ *adj* **1** of, in or forming a series: 连续的; 一串的; 排成一系列的: *the ~ number of a banknote or cheque.* 一张纸币或支票的序号码。 **2** (of a story, etc) appearing in parts (in a periodical, on radio, TV, etc): (指故事等)连续的; (在杂志、广播、电视中)连续刊登或播出的: *An exciting new ~ story will begin in our next week's issue.* 一个刺激而新颖的连载故事, 将于下周开始在本刊登出。 □ *n* ~ play, story, etc. 连续剧, 连载小说等。 **~·ly** /-ɪəlɪ; -ɪəlɪ/ *adv* **~·ize** /-aɪz; -ˌaɪz/ *vt* [VP6A] publish or produce in ~ form. 以连续方式出版或制作。

seri·atim /,sɪərɪ'eɪtɪm; ,sɪrɪ'etɪm/ *adv* (Lat) point by point; taking subjects, etc after one another in order: (拉)逐一地; 按顺序地; 连续地: *deal with arguments ~.* 逐一进行辩论。

seri·cul·ture /'serɪkʌltʃə(r); 'serɪˌkʌltʃɚ/ *n* (breeding of silkworms for) the production of silk. 养蚕; 蚕丝业。 **seri·cul·tural** /,serɪ'kʌltʃərəl; ,serɪ'kʌltʃərəl/ *adj* **ser·i·cul·tur·ist** /-tʃərɪst; -tʃərɪst/ *n*

series /'sɪəriːz; 'sɪrɪz/ *n* (*pl* unchanged) number of things, events, etc each of which is related in some way to the others, esp to the one before it: (复数不等)连贯的东西, 事件等; 连续; 系列: *a ~ of stamps/coins,* eg of different values, but issued at one time; 一套邮票(钱币)(例如一次发行之各种不同价值者); *a ~ of brilliant statesmen;* 连续出现的一批卓越政治家; *a ~ of good harvests;* 连年的丰收; *a 'Television ~,* a number of programmes, each complete in itself, linked by cast, theme, etc. 电视影集(每辑为一完整之单元, 但演员和主题则前后连贯)。 **in ~,** in an orderly arrangement; (of the components of an electrical circuit) with the supply of current fed directly through each component. 串联电路的; 成串联的。 ⇨ *in parallel* at *parallel.*

serio·comic /,sɪərɪəʊ'kɒmɪk; ,sɪrɪo'kɑmɪk/ *adj* serious in intention but appearing to be comic (or vice versa); having both serious and comic elements. 表面滑稽而内容严肃的; 表面严肃而实质滑稽的; 亦谐亦庄的。

seri·ous /'sɪərɪəs; 'sɪrɪəs/ *adj* **1** solemn; thoughtful; not given to pleasure-seeking: 严肃的; 庄重的; 深思的; 不喜寻欢作乐的: *a ~ mind/appearance/face;* 严肃的心情(外表, 脸色); *look ~.* 表情严肃的。 **2** important because of possible danger: 严重的; 重大的: *a ~ illness/mistake.* 重病/大错。 *The international situation looks ~.* 国际情势看来相当严重。 **3** in earnest; sincere: 认真的; 真诚的: *a ~ worker/lover.* 工作认真者(真诚的爱人)。 *Please be ~ about your work.* 请用心从事你的工作。 **~·ly** *adv* in a ~ manner: 严肃地;庄重地;严重地;重大地;认真地; 诚恳地: *speak ~ly to sb;* 严肃地对某人说话; *be ~ly ill.* 病得利害。 **~·ness** *n* state of being ~: 严肃; 庄重; 严重; 重大;认真; 真诚: *the ~ness of the country's financial situation.* 该国财政情况严重。 **in all ~ness,** very ~ly; not at all in a light-hearted way: 非常严肃地, 认真地: *I tell you this in all ~ness.* 我十分严重地告诉你这件事。

ser·jeant /'sɑːdʒənt; 'sɑrdʒənt/ *n* **,s~-at-'arms**

official with ceremonial duties or who keeps order in a court, legislature, etc. (担任礼仪勤务或维持法庭, 议会等处之秩序的)卫士; 警卫官。

ser·mon /'sɜːmən; 'sɝmən/ *n* [C] spoken or written address on a religious or moral subject, esp one given from a pulpit in a church; serious talk reproving a person for his faults, etc. (宗教或道德方面, 尤其以写出的)说教; (立于教堂之讲台上所作之)讲道; (因某人犯错等, 对其所作之)训诫。 **~·ize** /-aɪz; -ˌaɪz/ *vt, vi* [VP6A, 2A] preach or talk seriously to: (对…)说教或训诫: *Stop ~izing,* lecturing to me on my faults, etc! 别教训我了!

serous /'sɪərəs; 'sɪrəs/ *adj* of or like serum: 血浆的; 血清的; 如血浆的; 如血清的; 浆液性的。

ser·pent /'sɜːpənt; 'sɝpənt/ *n* snake (which is the more usu word); (fig) sly, treacherous person: 蛇(snake 较常用); (喻)狡诈的人: *the old S~,* the Devil. 魔王; 魔鬼; 恶魔。

ser·pen·tine /'sɜːpəntaɪn US: -tiːn; 'sɝpənˌtin/ *adj* twisting and curving like a snake: 似蛇般弯曲的; 蜿蜒的: *the ~ course of the river.* 蜿蜒的河道。

ser·rated /sɪ'reɪtɪd US: 'sereɪtɪd; 'serɛtɪd/ *adj* having notches on the edge like a saw; having a toothed edge: 边上呈锯齿状的; 有锯齿形边的: *~ leaves.* 有锯齿状边缘的叶子。

ser·ried /'serɪd; 'sɛrɪd/ *adj* (of lines or ranks of persons) close together, shoulder to shoulder: (指人的行列)密集的; 林立的: *in ~ ranks.* 密集排列的。

serum /'sɪərəm; 'sɪrəm/ *n* **1** [U] watery fluid in animal bodies; thin, transparent part of blood. 浆液;血浆。 **2** (dose of) such a fluid taken from the blood of an animal which has been made immune to a disease, used for inoculations. 血清, 一剂血清。

ser·vant /'sɜːvənt; 'sɝvənt/ *n* **1** (**domestic**) ~, person who works in a household for wages, food and lodging: 仆人; 用人: *have a large staff of ~s;* 仆从众多; *engage/dismiss a ~.* 雇请(解雇)用人。 **2** public ~, person who works for the public, eg a police officer, member of the Fire Service. 官吏; 公仆(如警官, 救火队员等)。 **civil** ~, government employee, member of the civil service. 公务员。 *your humble ~,* form sometimes used preceding the signature in an official letter. 在公务信件中有时冠于签名前之敬称。 **3** person devoted to sb or sth: 忠于某人或某事者: *a ~ of Jesus Christ,* eg a Christian priest. 耶稣基督的仆人(如基督教教士)。 **4** sth useful that should be treated as a means but not as an end: 有用之工具: *Fire is a good ~ but a bad master.* 火可造福人类, 也能成为祸首。

serve /sɜːv; sɝv/ *vt, vi* **1** [VP6A, 15A, 2A, C] be a servant to (sb); work for (sb): 做(某人)的仆人; 为(某人)工作; 服务: *She ~d the Ambassador for ten years.* 她为这大使工作了十年之久。 *He ~s as gardener and also as chauffeur.* 他兼为园丁和车夫。 **2** [VP6A, 15A, 2A, B, 3A] perform duties (for): (为…)尽责: *~ one's country,* eg in Parliament; 为人民服务(如在国会等中); *~ a year in the Army.* 在陆军服役一年。 *Can I ~ you in any way,* Is there anything I can do for you? 我能帮你忙吗? *~ sb,* be a member of: 为…的一员: *~ on a committee.* 担任委员。 *~ under sb,* be in the armed forces under the command of: (在军中)为某人的部下; 在某人属下: *My grandfather ~d under Montgomery.* 我祖父是蒙哥马利的部下。 *~ two masters,* (fig) be divided in one's loyalty; or between two opposite principles. 事二主; 左右为难。 **3** [VP6A, 2A, 14, 15B] *~ sth (to sb); ~ sb (with sth); ~ sth (out),* attend to (customers in a shop, etc); supply (with goods and services); place (food, etc) on the table for a meal; give (food, etc) to people at a meal: 侍候 (顾客); 供以(货物及服务); 上(菜等); 开(饭等): *There was no one in the shop to ~ me.* 店铺里没有人招呼我。 *We have to ~d with gas/electricity, etc in this town.* 在这城镇中我们有足够的煤气(电等)。 *Rations were ~d (out) to the*

troops. 口粮已发给各部队。 *Roast pork is often ~d with apple sauce.* 烤肉常和苹果酱一起上: *Dinner is ~d,* is ready. 饭已备好(或已开出)。 S~ *the coffee in the next room, please.* 请在隔壁房间上咖啡。 4 [VP6A, 2A, C, 4A] ~ *sb (for/as sth)*, be satisfactory for a need or purpose: 符合某需要或目的: *This box will ~ for a seat.* 这箱子可用做座椅。 *It isn't very good but it will ~ me.* 它并不很好, 但我正用得着。 *That excuse will not ~ you/That will not ~ you as an excuse,* will not be accepted. 你的那个借口不太合适。 *This accident ~s to show the foolishness of not being prepared.* 这次意外事件可以证明事先不作准备是多么的愚蠢。 ~ *sb's needs/purpose(s),* meet his requirements: 满足某人的需要; 符合某人的要求: *The house will ~ his needs admirably.* 这房子将十分符合他的需要。 *as occasion ~s,* when there is a suitable or convenient occasion or opportunity. 一有适当的时机或机会。 5 [VP15A, B] act towards, treat (sb in a certain way): 对付; 对待: *They have ~d me shamefully,* behaved very badly towards me. 他们待我很坏。 *I hope I shall never be ~d such a trick again,* have such a trick played on me. 我希望以后别再向我要这一套了。 *It ~s him right,* His failure, misfortune, etc is deserved; he does not merit sympathy. 他活该。 6 [VP6A] pass the usual or normal number of years (learning a trade, etc); go through one's term of office: 度过通常或一般的年限(如习艺等); (在任期内)供职: ~ *one's time;* 供职; ~ *one's apprenticeship.* 做学徒。 7 [VP6A] ~ *a sentence; ~ time,* undergo a period of imprisonment. 服刑。 *He has ~d five years of his sentence.* 他已服刑五年。 8 [VP14] ~ *a summons/writ/warrant on sb; ~ sb with a summons/writ/warrant,* (legal) deliver (a summons, etc) to the person named in it. (法律)送达 (传票等)给某人。 9 [VP6A, 2A] (tennis, etc) put the ball into play by striking it to an opponent: (网球等)发球: ~ *a ball;* 发球; ~ *well/badly.* 球发得好(坏)。 10 [VP6A] of a male animal, eg a bull, ram or boar, copulate with. (指雄性动物,如公牛、公羊、公猪等)与…交配。 11 [VP2A, 6A] help a priest at Mass: 在弥撒仪式中充当助祭者: ~ *Mass.* 在弥撒仪式中充当助祭者。 □ *n* (tennis, etc) first stroke; term for striking and putting the ball into play: (网球等)发球; 轮到发球: *Whose ~ is it?* 该谁发球? ~**r** *n* 1 person who ~s, eg one who helps a priest at Mass or ~s at tennis. 服务者; 服役者; 侍者; 送达员; (尤指)弥撒时助祭者; (网球)发球者。 2 tray for dishes; salver. 菜盘; 托盘。 3 utensil used in serving out food: 上某用的器皿: *'salad~rs.* 上生菜用的叉和匙。 **serv·ing** *n* quantity of food (to be) served to one person. 一人份的食物: *This recipe will be enough for four servings.* 这食谱足够四人吃的份量。

ser·vice /'sɜ:vɪs; 'sɝvɪs/ *n* 1 [U] being a servant; position as a servant. 帮佣; 仆人的职位。 *be in/go into/go out to ~,* be employed as a domestic servant. 做用人; 当仆役。 2 [C] department or branch of public work, government employment, etc: 公务部门; 政府机构: *the ,Civil 'S~;* 文职部门; *the ,Diplo-'matic S~;* 外交部门; *the fighting ~s,* the Navy, Army, Air Force; 海陆空军; 战斗军种; ~ *men and women,* members of the fighting ~s. 战斗人员。 *on active ~,* performing duties required by membership of the fighting ~s in time of war. 服现役。 *see ~ in sth,* serve (in the armed forces): (在军中)服役: *He saw ~ in both World Wars.* 他在两次世界大战中都服过役。 *He has seen ~ in many parts of the world.* 他在世界许多地方服过役。 *have seen (good) ~,* have served one well: 有(大的)用途; 帮(大)忙: *These old climbing-boots have seen good ~ on my numerous holidays in the Alps.* 我屡次在阿尔卑斯山度假这双旧登山靴都有很大的用处。 3 [C] sth done to help or benefit another or others: 服务; 贡献; 帮助: *His ~s to the State have been immense.* 他对政府的贡献极大。 *Do you need the ~s of a doctor/lawyer?* 你需要医生(律师)的服务吗? *do sb a ~,* help him: 协助某人; 帮助某人: *She did me a great ~ by*

driving me to the airport. 她驾车送我到机场, 帮了我一个大忙。 4 [U] benefit, use, advantage: 利益; 有用; 好处: *Can I be of ~ to you,* help you in any way? 我能帮得上忙吗? *I am at your ~,* ready to help you. 我随时都可以为你效劳。 *My car is at your ~,* ready for you to use when you want to. 你随时可用我的汽车。 5 [C] system or arrangement that supplies public needs, esp for communications: 公共需要物之供应系统; 公共设施: (尤指)交通设施: a '*bus/'train ~;* 公共汽车(火车)之交通服务; *the 'telephone ~;* 电话设施; *a good 'postal ~.* 良好的邮政。 '~ **road** *n* minor road, off a main road, giving access to houses, etc. (主要道路旁之)辅助道路; 支道; 支线。 6 [C] form of worship and prayer to God: 礼拜式; 崇拜仪式: *three ~s every Sunday;* 每星期日三次礼拜; *attend morning/evening ~;* 参加早(晚)礼拜; '*marriage/'burial ~.* 结婚(葬礼)仪式。 7 [C] complete set of plates, dishes, etc for use at table: 盘、碟等之全套: *a 'tea/'dinner ~ of 30 pieces.* 三十人份的茶具(餐具)。 8 [U] serving of food and drink (in hotels, etc); work done by domestic servants, hotel staff, etc: (旅馆等中之)上菜; 上饮料; 仆役等之服务: *The food is good at this hotel, but the ~ is poor.* 这家旅馆的食物不错, 但侍者的服务很差。 *The waiter added 10 per cent to the bill for ~,* eg to a bill at a restaurant, instead of getting a tip. 那侍者另加了一成服务费。 *Do you make a '~ charge at this hotel,* eg add 10%? 你们这家旅馆要收服务费吗(如另加一成)? '~ **flat** *n* one (usu furnished) of which the rent includes a charge for ~. 房租中包括服务费用之公寓(通常备有家具)。 9 [U] expert help or advice given by manufacturers or their agents after the sale of an article: 厂商之售后服务: *send the car in for ~ every 3000 miles,* eg for greasing, checking of brakes, etc: 每行驶三千英里把汽车送工厂检修(如加润滑油、检查煞车等); (attrib) (用作定语) ~ *department.* 服务部。 '~ **station** *n* petrol station which also offers general servicing facilities. 加油站(附设一般性修护设备者)。 10 (legal) serving of a writ, summons, etc. (法律)传票等之送达。 11 (tennis, etc) act of serving the ball; manner of doing this; person's turn to serve: (网球等之)发球; 发球之方式; 轮到发球: *Her ~ is weak.* 她发球没有力。 *Whose ~ is it?* 该谁发球? □ *vt* [VP6A] maintain or repair (a car, radio, machine, etc) after sale (⇨ 9 above): 售后保养或检修(汽车、收音机、机器等)(参看上列第9义): *have the car ~d regularly.* 定期将汽车送厂检修。 ~**able** /-əbl; -əbl/ *adj* 1 suited for ordinary wear and use; strong and durable: 适于一般用途的; 耐用的: ~*able clothes for school-children.* 适于学童的耐穿衣服。 2 of use; capable of giving good service. 有用的; 能有服务的。

ser·vi·ette /,sɜ:vɪ'et; ,sɝvɪ'et/ *n* [C] table napkin: 餐巾: *I prefer a linen napkin to a paper ~.* 我喜欢亚麻布餐巾而不爱用纸餐巾。

ser·vile /'sɜ:vaɪl US: -vl; 'sɝvl/ *adj* 1 (archaic) of or like a slave. (古)奴隶的; 似奴隶的。 2 lacking in the spirit of independence; ungenerous: 缺乏独立精神的; 卑劣的; ~ *flattery;* 双膝婢膝的谄媚; ~ *to public opinion,* paying excessive attention to it. 过份顺从舆论。 ~**ly** /-aɪllɪ; -lɪ/ *adv* **ser·vil·ity** /sɜ:'vɪlətɪ; sɝ'vɪlətɪ/ *n* [U] : behaviour or attitude. 卑劣的行为或态度。

ser·vi·tor /'sɜ:vɪtə(r); 'sɝvətɚ/ *n* (old use) servant; attendant. (旧用法)仆人; 随员。

ser·vi·tude /'sɜ:vɪtju:d US: -tu:d; 'sɝvə,tjud/ *n* [U] condition of being forced to work for others and having no freedom. 苦役; 奴役; 劳役。 ⇨ **penal**.

servo- /'sɜ:vəʊ; 'sɝvo/ *pref* (of machinery) using a system that automatically controls a larger system: (指机器)有自动控制系统的: ~*motor,* controlling motor in such a system; 伺服电动机; ,~**as'sisted brakes,** eg in a large car; 副煞; 辅力车架 (如大汽车中者); ~'*mechanism,* general name for the controlling system. 伺服机构。

ses·ame /'sesəmɪ; 'sɛsəmɪ/ *n* 1 plant with seeds used

in various ways as food and giving an oil used in salads. 芝麻；胡麻。 2 *Open* ~! magic words used, in one of the Arabian Nights stories, to cause a door to open; hence, easy way of securing access to what is usu inaccessible: (天方夜谭一故事中的)开门咒；(由此产生)通过难关之简易方法: *an open ~ to high society.* 进入上流社会之捷径。

ses·qui·ped·al·ian /ˌseskwɪpɪˈdeɪlɪən ; ˌsɛskwɪpəˈdeⁱlⁱən/ *adj* (of a word) having many syllables; (fig) tedious; long-winded. (指字)多音节的；(喻)令人厌倦的；冗长的。

session /ˈseʃn; ˈsɛʃən/ *n* [C] 1 meeting of a law court, law-making body, etc; time occupied by discussions at such a meeting: (法庭之)开庭；(议会等之)开会；开庭期: *the autumn* ~ (= sitting) *of Parliament;* (英国国会之)秋季会期; *have a long* ~; 开会(会)期甚长; *go into secret* ~. 开秘密会议。 **Court of S~,** supreme civil court of Scotland. 苏格兰高等民事法庭。 **petty ~s,** courts held by magistrates to hear certain offences without a jury. 即决法庭(案件由地方法官审理,而无须成立陪审团即可开庭者)。 2 (Scot and US) university term. (苏,美)大学之学期。 3 single, uninterrupted meeting for other purposes: (为其他目的所举行之)单独而无中断之集会; from that which wins more than half the games in it. (网球等)盘(由数局组成之单位,获胜半数以上者即算获胜全盘)。 9 the act of *re'cording ~,* period of time during which material is recorded (on discs or tapes, eg for broadcasts). 录音时间。

set¹ /set; sɛt/ *n* 1 [C] number of things of the same kind, that belong together because they are similar or complementary to each other: 套；组；副: *a set of golfclubs/the novels of Dickens/ Albanian stamps;* 一套高尔夫球球杆(狄更斯的小说, 阿尔巴尼亚的邮票); *a 'tea-set and 'dinner-set,* (= *service*⁽⁷⁾, the more usu word);一套茶具和餐具(与 service 第 7 义相同, 较常用 service); *a new set of false teeth.* 一副新的假牙。 2 [C] number of persons who associate, or who have similar or identical tastes and interests: 一群同伴；一群志趣相投者: *the 'racing/'literary/'golfing set;* 爱好赛马(文学,高尔夫球)的人士; *the 'smart set,* those who consider themselves leaders in society; 自认为领导社会的一群人; *the 'fast set,* those who gamble, etc; 不务正业之流; *the 'jet set,* rich pleasure-loving people flying from one holiday resort to another. 喜爱游乐的有钱人(乘飞机去各处度假)。 3 radio or television receiving apparatus: 无线电或电视接收机: *an ˌall-'mains set;* 可适用各种电压的收音机; *a transistor set.* 一架晶体管收音机。 4 (not *pl*) direction (of current, wind, etc); tendency (of opinion): (不用复数)(潮流,风等的)方向；(意见的)趋向: *the set of the tide.* 潮水的流向。 5 (not *pl*) position or angle; posture: (不用复数)位置；角度；姿势: *I recognise him by the set of his head/shoulders.* 我从他的头(肩)的姿态认出是他。 6 way in which a garment conforms to the shape of the body: 衣服穿在身上的样子；款式: *I don't like the set of this coat,* the way it fits (or doesn't fit). 我不喜欢这上装的款式。 ⇨ *set²*(14). 7 [U] (poet) sunset: (诗)日落: *at set of sun.* 在日落之际。 8 (tennis, etc) group of games counting as a unit to the side that wins more than half the games in it. (网球等)盘(由数局组成之单位,获胜半数以上者即算获胜全盘)。 9 the act of pointing at game (birds, animals) by a setter. 猎犬之以鼻指示猎物(鸟兽)。⇨ *set²*(15). *make a dead set at,* **(a)** combine to attack vigorously, by argument or ridicule. (以言词等)协力猛烈攻击。 **(b)** (of a person) try to win the attention and affection of (another person to whom one is attracted). (指人)设法获得(所爱慕者)之注意和感情。 10 [C] granite paving stone (as used for road surfaces). (用以铺路面等的)花岗石板。 11 [C] built-up scenery on the stage of a theatre, or in a studio or outdoors for a film: (戏剧、电影中的)布景；场景；外景: *everyone to be on the set by 7am.* 所有的人在上午七时以前到达拍外景的地方。 12 [C] young plant, cutting, bulb, etc ready to be planted: 幼苗；树秧: *get*

the onion sets in. 栽种洋葱的幼苗。 13 badger's burrow. 獾所掘之地洞。 14 setting of the hair: 做头发: *shampoo and set,* £4. 洗头做发, 定价四英镑。⇨ *set²*(9).

set² /set; sɛt/ *vt, vi* (-tt-, *pt, pp* set) (For special uses with *adverbial particles and preps,* ⇨ 19 below.) (与副词性小品词及介词连用之特殊用法, 参看下列第 19 义。) 1 [VP2A] (of the sun, moon, stars) go down below the horizon: (指太阳、月亮、星星)降落于地平线下: *It will be cooler when the sun has set.* 日落之后, 天就会凉爽些。 *His star has set,* (fig) The time of his power, greatness, etc is over. (喻)他的好运已过。 2 [VP14] *set sth to sth,* move or place sth so that it is near to or touching sth else: 移动或放置(某物)致使与他物接近或接触: *set a glass to one's lips/one's lips to a glass.* 将玻璃杯贴近嘴唇(将嘴唇贴近玻璃杯)。 *set the axe to,* cut down (a tree); (fig) start to destroy (sth). 砍倒(树); (喻)着手摧毁(某物)。 *set fire/a match/(a) light to sth,* cause it to begin burning. 将某物开始燃烧。 *set pen to paper,* begin to write. 开始写。 *set one's seal to sth; set the seal on sth,* authorize or confirm it. 批准; 认可。 *set one's shoulder to the wheel,* ⇨ shoulder. 3 [VP22, 16A] cause (sb/sth) to be in, or reach, a specified state or relation. 使(某人或某物)处于或达到某种特殊的状态或关系。 *set sth at defiance/ naught/nought,* ⇨ defiance; nought. *set sth at his ease,* make him feel free from embarrassment, feel comfortable, etc. 使某人安逸;使某人心情放松;使某人舒坦。 *set sb/sth on his/its feet,* **(a)** help him to get to his feet after a fall. 扶某人站起(如跌倒后)。 **(b)** help sb/sth to gain strength, financial stability, etc: 使某人(某事物)获得力量、经济安定等: *Foreign aid set the country on its feet after the war.* 外援使该国战后经济稳定。 *set sth on fire,* (= set fire to sth) cause it to begin burning. 点火燃某物。 *,not/,never ,set the Thames on fire,* not/never do ʌnything wonderful, extraordinary. 不会(决不会)做出惊人之事;不会(决不会)成为杰出的人物;不会(决不会)有很大的出息。 *set sb free/at liberty,* free (prisoners, etc). 释放(囚犯等)。 *set people at loggerheads/variance,* cause them to argue and dispute. 唆使人们争辩;使人们不和。 *set sth in order,* arrange, organize (one's papers, affairs, etc) properly. 整理(个人的文件、事物等)。 *,set one's ('own) 'house in order,* (fig) order one's own affairs, one's own life (before criticizing others). 管好自己的事;自身先站得稳(在批评别人)。 *set sb's mind at ease/ rest; set sb's doubts/fears/mind at rest,* help him to be free from worry, free him from anxiety. 使某人安心;使某人放心。 *set sb's teeth on edge,* jar his nerves: 使某人心神不安: *That noise sets my teeth on edge.* 那吵声使我不安。 *set sb right,* **(a)** correct his errors; put him on the right road. 改正某人的错误;引导某人走向正确的方向。 **(b)** cause him to feel well and fit again. 使某人康复。 *set sth right/to rights,* correct, remedy (faults, grievances). 改正或弥补错误。 *set sb on his way,* (old use) go part of the way with him (when he starts out on foot). (旧用法)陪某人走一段路; 送某人一程(当其徒步出发时)。 *be all set (for sth/to do sth),* be quite ready (for the start of a race, etc). 准备妥当(开始赛跑、赛车等)。 *be set on doing sth,* be determined to do it: 决心做某事: *My Uncle Ernest is set on swimming the English Channel.* 我叔叔欧内斯特决心游过英吉利海峡。 4 [VP19B] cause sb/sth to begin to do sth: 使某人(某物)开始做某事(发生作用): *It's time we set the machinery going,* start operations. 是我们发动机器的时候了。 *What has set the dog barking?* 什么东西使那只狗叫起来? *The news set me thinking.* 那消息使我陷入沉思。 *My jokes set everyone laughing.* 我的笑话使每个人大笑。 *'Blow, bugles, blow, set the wild echoes flying!'* 号角,响起来,让激昂的回声在空中震荡!' 5 [VP6A, 15A] (usu with an *adv* or *adv phrase;* ⇨ 19 below for combinations of *set* and *adverbial particles* with special meanings) put, place, lay, stand: (通常与副词或副词短

语连用;参看下列第 19 义, set 与副词性小品词连用而形成具有特殊意义的短语)置;放;搁;ази: *She set the dishes on the table.* 她把碟子放在桌上。*We set food and drink before the travellers.* 我们把食物和饮料放在旅客面前。*He set the stake in the ground.* 他竖桩于地上。6 [VP6A, 14, 12C] **set (for)**, put forward as (material to be dealt with as a task, a pattern, etc): 提出; 规定(工作, 作业等); 出(题目等): *The teacher set the children a difficult problem*, gave them one to be solved. 教师给孩子们出了一个难题。*I have set myself a difficult task.* 我为自己安排了一件困难的工作。*Who will set the papers for the examination*, draw up the examination questions? 这次考试谁命题? *What books have been set for the Cambridge Certificate next year*, What books are to be studied? 明年剑桥大学检定考试规定念哪些书? Hence, 由此产生, **'set 'book**, book on which examinations are to be given. 考试用书。**set (sb) a (good) example**, offer a good standard for others to follow: 为(某人)树立(好)榜样: *You should give the younger boys a good example.* 你应该为较年幼的男孩子树立良好的榜样。**set the fashion**, start a fashion to be copied by others. 开风气之先。**set the pace**, fix it by leading (in a race, etc); (fig) fix a standard for an activity, style of living, etc: 领先定步调(在赛跑等中); (喻)订下活动、生活方式等之榜样: *The Joneses set the pace and their neighbours try to keep up with them.* 琼斯一家人立下榜样, 他们的邻居都想向他们看齐。**set the stroke**, (rowing) fix the number of strokes per minute. (划船)定下每分钟划桨的次数。7 [VP17A] **set (sb/oneself) to do sth**, give sth to sb/oneself) as a task: 支使、派遣、规定(某人或自己)做某事: *He set the farm labourer to chop wood.* 他派遣农场工人去砍木材。*I set myself to study the problem.* 我决定研究这问题。*I've set myself (= have resolved) to finish the job by the end of May.* 我决心于五月底以前完成那工作。**Set a thief to 'catch a thief**, (prov) 以毒攻毒; 令贼捉贼。8 [VP6A, 15A] (with various grammatical objects, the nn in alphabetical order) (与各种语法上的宾语连用, 其中名词系按字母次序排列) **set one's cap at sb**, ⇨ cap. **set eyes on sb**, see him: 看见某人: *I hope I never set eyes on that fellow again.* 我希望再也不要看到那家伙。**set one's face against sth**, steadfastly oppose sth. 坚决反对。**set one's heart/hopes/mind on sth**, be filled with strong desire for, determination to get; direct one's hopes towards: 亟欲; 决心要得到; 希冀: *The boy has set his heart on becoming an engineer.* 这男孩子下决心要当工程师。**set a price on sth**, declare what it will be sold for. 给某物定价格。**set a price on sb's head**, offer a specified reward to anyone who kills him. 悬赏杀死某人。**set much/great/little/no store by sth**, value sth highly/little/not at all. 非常(极, 不太, 根本不)重视某物。9 [VP6A, 15A] put in a certain state or condition for a particular purpose: 为了某一目的而置于某种状态之下: *set a (broken) bone*, bring the parts together so that they may unite. 接(断)骨。**set a butterfly**, arrange it with wings outspread (in a glass case) as a specimen. 摆蝴蝶(使两翼张开, 置于玻璃盒中, 以作为标本)。**set a clock/watch**, put the hands to the correct time (or, for an alarm clock, to sound at the desired time): 对钟; 对表; 将闹钟等定时: *set one's watch by the time-signal on the radio.* 按收音机之报时信号对表。**set eggs**, place them (to be hatched) under a hen, etc in a nest. 置卵于母鸡窝中等以便(使孵之)。**set one's hair**, arrange it (when damp) so that when it is dry, it is in the required style: (趁湿)做头发: *She's having her hair set for this evening's party.* 她为了今晚的宴会正在做头发。**set a hen**, place it over eggs (to hatch them). 使母鸡孵卵。**set a saw**, sharpen the teeth with a file and put them (alternately) at the right outward angle. 磨锉锯齿并调整其倾角。**set the scene**, describe a place and the people taking part in an activity, eg in a play, novel or sporting event: 描述戏剧、小说或运动项目中的地点及参与活动的人; 形成…的背景或形式: *Our commentator will now set the scene in the stadium.* 我们的播音员现在将描述运动场的情形。*The scene is now set for the tragedy*, Events leading up to the tragedy have taken place and the tragedy will follow. 这出悲剧的背景业已形成。*The scene is now set for a direct confrontation between the major powers.* 列强正面对抗的形势已经形成。**set sail (from/to/for)**, begin a voyage. 启航; 开航。**set the table**, lay it ready with plates, cutlery, etc: 将餐具摆在餐桌上: *She set the table for five people.* 她摆设五人的食具于餐桌上。**set one's teeth**, put, fix, one thing firmly in another: 使(一物)固定于(他物)之中; 镶; 嵌: become determined and inflexible (against some course of action, etc). 咬紧牙关; (喻)决心坚持到底。**set a trap (for sth/sb)**, (a) adjust one to catch a mouse, rat, etc. 设置捕捉机(捕鼠等)。(b) do sth to discover a dishonest person, etc: 设陷阱, 设圈套(以揭发行为不轨之人等): *set a trap to catch a thief/for a boy who cheats.* 设下圈套捉拿扒手(拆穿作弊的男孩)。**set (up) type**, arrang it ready for printing sth. 排铅字。10 [VP6A, 14] **set sth in sth; set sth with sth**, put, fix, one thing firmly in another: 使(一物)固定于(他物)之中; 镶; 嵌: *set a diamond in gold*; 镶钻石于黄金之中; *a crown set with jewels*; 镶有珠宝的皇冠; *a gold ring set with gems*, 镶有宝石的金戒指; *a heavy lathe set (= embedded) in concrete*; 固定在混凝土中的大车床; *glass panes set in lead*, ie strips of lead, as in old lattice windows. 嵌于铅格框中的窗玻璃。*The tops of the walls were set with broken glass*, ie to discourage persons from climbing over them. 墙顶嵌有碎玻璃(以阻人攀越)。*The sky seemed to be set with diamonds*, the stars looked like diamonds. 天空似乎镶嵌了钻石(星星看起来像钻石)。11 [VP2A, C] (of tides, currents) move or flow along; gather force; (fig) show or have a tendency: (指潮水, 潮流, 气流, 思潮)流动; 增加力量; (喻)显出或感到某种倾向: *A strong current sets through the channel.* 一股强大的潮流流过海峡。*Tee current sets in towards the shore.* 潮水上涨, 流向岸边。*The wind sets from the west.* 风自西方吹来。*The tide has set in his favour*, (fig) He is winning public support and approval. (喻)他逐渐赢得公众的支持和赞许。*Public opinion is setting against the proposal.* 舆论反对那提议。12 [VP6A, 14] **set sth (to sth)**, provide with music, usu composed for the purpose: 为…配曲: *set a poem to music*; 为诗歌配曲; *set new words to an old tune.* 为旧曲作新词。13 [VP2A, 2A] (of plants, fruit trees, their blossom) form or develop fruit as the result of fertilization: (指植物, 果树, 其花)结果实: *The apple-blossom hasn't set well this year*, The apples haven't set well this year. 苹果花(树)今年没有结多少果实。*This liquid, if sprayed on the flowers, helps to set the tomatoes.* 这液体洒在花上, 能帮助蕃茄结实。14 [VP2C] (of a garment) adapt itself to the shape of the body; sit (which is the more usu word): (指衣服)适合身材; 合身(sit 较常用): *A well-tailored jacket ought to set well.* 裁制良好的上衣应该合身。*That dress sets rather badly.* 那衣服不甚合身。15 [VP2A, C] (of a sporting dog) stop and stand with the muzzle pointing, to indicate presence of game; (of dancers) take positions facing partners: (指猎犬)站着以口鼻指示猎物所在; (指舞者)面向舞伴: *set to partners.* 面向舞伴。16 [VP6A, 2A] (cause to) become firm, solid, rigid (from a liquid or soft state): (使)凝固; (使)凝结: *Some kinds of concrete set more quickly than others.* 某些种混凝土比其他混凝土凝固得快。*The jelly is/has not set yet.* 冻子尚未结好。*Heat sets eggs and cold sets jellies.* 热使蛋凝结, 冷使冻子凝结。17 [VP6A, 2A] (rare) (cause to) develop into definite lines and shapes, become mature: (罕)(使)发育成形; (使)变成熟: *His body has/is set*, is fully developed. 他的体型已完全发育。*Too much exercise may set a boy's muscles prematurely.* 运动过多可能使男孩子的肌肉过早僵化。*His character has/is set*, is no longer pliant, is already formed. 他的性格已经定型(不会再变)。18 (pp) (a)

unmoving, fixed: 不动的；固定的: *a set smile / look / purpose.* 呆板的微笑(呆滞的表情；确定的目标). **(b)** pre-arranged: 预定的；事先安排的: *at a set time*; 在预定的时间; *set lunches £2.50,* (eg at a restaurant, there being no choice of dishes); 二英镑半的午餐客饭; *a set piece,* a large and elaborate firework set on a platform or scaffold; 固定于平台上或台架上的大型烟火; (attrib) (用作定语) *a set-piece attack,* ie carefully planned in advance. 预先经过周详策划的攻击. **(c)** unchanging: 不变的；固定的: *set in one's ways,* having fixed habits; 有固定生活习惯的; *a man of set opinions,* unable or unwilling to change them. 固执己见的人. **(d)** regular; fixed or planned in advance: 循规的；预先准备好的；预先计划好的: *set phrases;* 现成的词句；套语; *a set speech;* 预先准备好的演说; *set forms of prayers.* 规定的祷告方式. **(e)** *set fair,* (of the weather) fine and with no signs of change. (指天气)稳定的晴天. **19** [VP15A, 2C, 3A] (special uses with *adverbial particles* and *preps*): (与副词性小品词及介词连用的特殊用法):

set about sth, start; take steps towards: 开始；着手: *I must set about my packing,* begin to pack my clothes, etc. 我必须开始收拾行装. *I don't know how to set about this job,* how to make a start on it. 我不知怎样着手这件工作. **set about sb,** (colloq) attack: 攻击: *They set about each other fiercely,* began to exchange blows. 他们凶猛地互殴. **set sth about,** spread (rumours, etc) 散布(谣言等): *Who set (put is more usu) it about that he is resigning?* 谁说他要辞职(put 较常用)?

set sb against sb, cause him to compete with, struggle against, sb. 使某人和某人竞争、对抗. **set one thing against another,** regard it as compensating for, balancing, another. 使某事物和另一事物相抵补、平衡或牵制.

set sth apart / aside, **(a)** put on one side for future use. 拨出；留下将来使用. **(b)** disregard: 不注意；忽视: *Let's set aside my personal feelings.* 让我们撇开个人的情感. **(c)** (legal) reject: (法律)拒绝；驳回; 宣告无效: *set a claim aside.* 驳回一项要求.

set sth back, **(a)** move back: 将......往后移；拨回: *set back the hands of a clock.* 把钟拨慢. *The horse set back its ears.* 这马将其耳朵后仰放平(俗谓马耳向后刷). **(b)** be placed away, at a distance, from: 置于远处；分开放置: *The house is well set back from the road.* 这幢房子和大街有相当的距离. **set sb / sth back,** **(a)** hinder or reverse the progress of: 阻碍；阻止: *All our efforts at reform have been set back.* 我们对改革所做的一切努力均受到了挫折. Hence, 由此产生, **'set-back** *n* (*pl* **setbacks**) check to progress or development: 阻碍; 挫折: *meet with many set-backs;* 遭到许多挫折; *have a set-back in one's career / business.* 在事业(业务)上受到一次挫折. **(b)**(sl) cost:(俚)花费: *That haircut set me back £5.* 理那次发花了我五英镑. **set sb down,** **(a)** put down: 放下；置下: *set down a load.* 卸下背负之物. **(b)** write down on paper. 记载；登记. **set sb down,** (of a vehicle, its driver) allow (a passenger) to get down or out: (指车辆，其驾驶者)让(乘客)下车: *The bus stopped to set down an old lady.* 公共汽车停下让一位老妇人下车. *I'll set you down at the corner of your street.* 我让你在你所住街道的转角处下车. **set sb / oneself down as,** (*put is more usu*) explain or describe as: (put 较常用)把某人(自己)说成或视为: *How should I set myself down in the hotel register—as a journalist or as an author?* 在旅馆的登记簿上，我应如何写下自己的身份——写成记者还是作家呢? *We must set him down as either a criminal or a fool.* 我们该把他视为犯人或傻子. **set sth down to sth,** (*put is more usu*), attribute sth to, say that sth is the result of. (put 较常用)把......归于；认某事物......造成: *set one's success down to hard work.* 将成功归于努力工作.

set forth, begin a journey (*set out* is more usu). 启程; 动身 (set out 较常用). **set sth forth,** (formal) make known; declare: (正式用语)宣布；发表: *set forth one's political views.* 发表政见. *Is this condition set forth (= included) in the agreement?* 这条件载于合约中吗?

set in, **(a)** start and seem likely to continue: 开始: *The rainy season has set in.* 雨季已开始了. *It set in to rain.* 开始下雨了. *Go to your dentist before decay of the teeth sets in.* 在牙齿开始腐蚀以前去看牙医师. **(b)** (of tides, winds; ⇨ **11** above) begin to flow: (指潮汐, 风; 参看上列第 11 义)开始流动: *The tide is setting in,* flowing towards the shore. 潮水正在上涨.

set off, start (a journey, race, etc): 开始(旅程、赛跑等); 出发: *They've set off on a journey round the world.* 他们已出发环球旅行. **set sth off,** **(a)** explode a mine, firework, etc. 使(地雷, 烟火等)爆发; 引爆. **(b)** make more striking by comparison: (用比较的方法)使更加显; 衬托: *Use blue eye-shadow to set off your green eyes.* 用蓝色眼影衬托你的绿眼睛. *This gold frame sets off the painting very well.* 这个金框把画衬托得很美. **(c)** balance; compensate: 平衡; 抵销: *set off gains against losses.* 以利得抵销损失. **(d)** mark off: 分开; 划分: *set off a clause by a comma.* 用逗点把一句分开. **set sb off (doing sth),** cause to start (doing sth): 使开始(做某事): *Don't set him off talking politics or he'll go on all evening.* 别让他开始谈论政治，否则他会谈上整整一个夜晚. **,set 'on,** (formal) go forward; advance to the attack. (正式用语)前进；迎击. **'set on / upon sb,** attack: 攻击某人: *She was set on by a savage dog.* 她被凶犬袭击. **'set on / upon doing sth,** be determined to do it: 决心做某事: *My daughter is set on becoming an airline pilot.* 我女儿决心做客机驾驶员.

set out, begin a journey (venture): 出发; 启程: *They set out at dawn.* 他们在拂晓出发. *He set out with the best intentions.* 抱着最大的希望出发. **set out to do sth,** have sth as an aim or intention: 朝某个目标进行; 为了某个目的而努力: *He set out to break the record for the Channel swim / to make his first million in five years.* 他决心打破渡过英伦海峡的记录(在五年内赚到第一个一百万). **set sth out,** **(a)** declare; make known: 宣布; 发表: *set out one's reasons (for sth).* 陈述(某事)的理由. **(b)** show; put on display: 展示; 陈列: *The women set out their chickens and ducks on the market stalls.* 妇女们把鸡鸭陈列在市场的摊子上. *He sets out his ideas clearly in this essay.* 他在这篇文章中明确地列出他的观点. **(c)** plant out: 散栽; 移植: *Set the young plants out one foot apart.* 把幼苗每隔一英尺栽种一棵.

set sb over sb, put sb in control / command of sb. 使某人控制(指挥)某人.

,set 'to, **(a)** begin doing sth: 开始做某事: *The engineers set to and repaired the bridge.* 工程师们开始修桥. *They were all hungry and at once set to,* began eating. 他们都很饿, 立刻狼吞虎咽地吃起来了. **(b)** (usu *with pl* subject) begin to fight, struggle, quarrel, etc. (通常用复数主语) 开始斗、争执、吵闹等. Hence, 由此产生, **,set-'to** *n* struggle; quarrel. 斗争; 争吵.

set sth up, **(a)** place sth in position: 设立; 建立: *set up a post / statue / memorial.* 设置哨岗(雕像, 纪念碑). **(b)** establish (an institution, business, argument, etc): 建立(机构, 商店); 提出(辩护): *set up a tribunal.* 设立法庭. *What defence did his counsel set up in the trial?* 在审判时他的律师提出什么辩护? Hence, 由此产生, **'set-up** *n* (colloq) arrangement of an organization, group of people, etc: (口)组织; 结构: *What's the set-up here?* How's your business, etc organized? 你的商店(等)的组织如何? **(c)** cause: 造成; 促成: *I wonder what has set up this irritation in my throat / this rash on my face?* 我不知道是什么东西使得我的喉头发炎(脸部出疹)? **(d)** utter loudly: 高声喊出: *set up a yell.* 大声喊叫. **(e)** make ready for printing: 排版: *set up type / a book.* 排字(一本书). **set sb up,** restore after illness: 使康复: *Her holiday in the country has set her up again.* 在乡间度假使她恢复了健康. **set (oneself) up as,** **(a)** go into business as: 从事或经营某种行业, 成为某种行业的人: *He has set (himself) up as a bookseller.* 他已成为书商. **(b)** have pretensions to being: 自称为: *I've never set myself up as a scholar.* 我从来自称为学者. **set sb up**

(as sth), get sb started or established, eg by supplying capital: *set up one's son in business.* 资助他人创业;资助某人创业: 资助自己的儿子做生意。*His father set him up as a bookseller* 他的父亲资助他成为书商。**set up house,** start living in one, eg after being in lodgings. 开始住在自己的房子里。**set up house with sb/together,** (of two persons) begin living together. (指两人)一起生活;同居。**be well set up, (a)** have a body well developed by exercises, etc: 健壮的;健美的: *He has a well set up figure.* 他有健美的身材。*What a well set up young woman!* 多么健美的女郎啊! **(b)** be well provided with: 充分供应: *be well set up with clothes/reading matter.* 有充足的衣服(读物)。

set-square /'set skweə(r); 'sɛtskwɛr/ n [C] triangular plate of wood, plastic, metal, etc with angles of 90°, 60° and 30° (or 90°, 45°, 45°), used for drawing lines at these angles. 三角板。

sett /set; sɛt/ n = set¹(10).

set·tee /se'tiː; sɛ'ti/ n [C] long, soft seat like a sofa, with sides and back, for two or more persons. 有靠背及扶手之长椅(类似沙发,可坐两人或更多的人)。

set·ter /'setə(r); 'sɛtɚ/ n 1 breeds of) long-haired dog trained to stand motionless on scenting game. 一种长毛猎狗。⇨ set¹(9). **2** (in compounds) person who, thing which, sets (various meanings): (用于复合词中)从事 set (包括各义)之人或物: *a 'bone-~;* 接骨者; *a 'type-~.* 排字工人;排字机。

set·ting /'setɪŋ; 'sɛtɪŋ/ n [C] **1** framework in which sth is fixed or fastened: 安置或固定东西之框、架等: *the ~ of a jewel;* 镶嵌珠宝的底座; (by extension) (引申) surroundings, environment: 背景;环境: *a beautiful natural ~ for a play,* eg the grounds of an old castle. 适于演出戏剧之美丽的天然背景(如一古堡之庭园)。**2** music composed for a poem, etc. 为一首诗等所配之音乐。⇨ set²(12). **3** descent of the sun, moon, etc) below the horizon (指太阳、月亮等)落下(地平线)。

settle¹ /'setl; 'sɛtl/ n [C] long, wooden seat with a high back and arms, the seat often being the lid of a chest. 高背长靠椅(座板常为箱盖)。

settle² /'setl; 'sɛtl/ vt, vi (For special uses with *adverbial particles and preps,* ⇨ **10** below.) (与副词性小品词及介词连用之特殊用法参看下列第10义。) **1** [VP2C, 6A] make one's home in (permanently, as a colonist);establish colonists in: 殖民;殖民于: *The Dutch ~d in South Africa.* 荷兰人曾在南非殖民。*By whom was Canada ~d?* 加拿大是由谁殖民的? **2** [VP2C] make one's home in; live in (not as a colonist): 安家;定居: *~ in London/in Canada/in the country.* 定居于伦敦(加拿大,乡下)。**3** [VP2A,3A] *~ (on sth),* come to rest (on), stay for some time (on): 停留;暂时栖息: *The bird ~d on a branch.* 鸟栖止于枝上。*The dust ~d on everything.* 尘土落在每样东西上。*The cold has ~d on my chest.* 风寒使我胸口难受。**4** [VP6A, 15A] cause (sb) to become used to, or comfortable in, a new position or posture (after a period of restless movement or activity): (经过一段不停的运动或活动后)使适应于或适合于新的位置或姿势;使安静;使安息: *The nurse ~d her patient for the night,* made him/her comfortable, gave him/her medicine, etc. 那护士使她的病人安静过夜。*Then the nurse ~d herself in an armchair in the next room.* 然后那护士自己在隔壁房间的扶手椅上坐下来休息。**5** [VP6A, 2C] make or become calm, untroubled, composed: (使)镇定; (使)稳定; (使)平静: *The thunderstorm will perhaps ~ the weather.* 大雷雨可能使天气稳定下来。*We want a period of ~d weather for the harvest.* 我们收获时需要一段稳定的天气。*Wait until the excitement has ~d.* 等兴奋的情绪平静下来(再说或做某事)。*Things are settling into shape,* becoming orderly, normal. 事情逐渐上轨道了。*Have a brandy—it will ~ your nerves.* 喝一点白兰地吧——它会使你镇静下来。**6** [VP6A, 7A, 8, 10] make an agreement about; decide; determine: 了结; 决定: *That ~s the matter.* 事情就这样决定了。*It's time you ~d the dispute/argument.* 该是你们结束争论的时候了。*Nothing*

is ~d yet. 诸事未定。*You ought to ~ your affairs* (eg by making your will) *before you go into hospital for that lung operation.* 在你住院接受肺部手术以前,你应该把诸事料理妥当(如写遗嘱等)。*The lawsuit was ~d amicably/out of court/between the parties,* a decision was reached by the parties themselves (and their lawyers) instead of by the court. 诉讼案已在庭外和解。*What have you ~d to do about it?* 你决定怎样处理这事? *Have they ~d where to go/where they'll spend their holiday?* 他们已决定去什么地方(去什么地方度假)吗? **7** [VP6A,2A, C] pay: 付;偿付: *~ a bill.* 付帐。*Will you ~ for all of us,* pay what is owing for all of us, eg at a restaurant? 你会为我们大家付帐吗(如在餐馆)? **8** [VP6A, 2A] (of dust, etc in the air, particles of solid substances in a liquid, etc) (cause to) sink; (of a liquid) become clear as solid particles sink. (指空气中之尘埃等,液体中之颗粒) (使)沉淀; (使)降落; (指液体)澄清: *We need a shower to ~ the dust.* 我们需要降雨来清除尘埃。*Stir the coffee to ~ the grounds.* 搅动咖啡使其澄清。*The grounds ~d and the coffee was clear.* 渣滓沉没,咖啡澄清。**9** [VP2A, C] (of the ground, the foundation of a building, etc) sink gradually to a lower level: (指地面,地基等)下陷: *The road-bed ~d.* 路基下陷了。*The ship was settling down by the stern,* tending to sink. 船正由尾部逐渐下沉。**10** [VP2C,14,15B, 2A] (special uses with *adverbial particles and preps*): (与副词性小品词及介词连用之特殊用法): **settle down,** sit or lie comfortably (after a period of movement or activity) 安适地坐下或躺下: *He ~d down in his armchair to read a new novel.* 他安闲地坐在扶手椅上阅读一本新的小说。**~ (sb) down,** make or become calm and peaceful: (使)镇定; (使)平静: *Wait until the children have ~d down before you start your lesson.* 等孩子们安静下来你再开始上课。*The chairman tried to ~ the audience down,* get them to stop talking, etc. 主席设法使听众安静。**~ (down) to sth,** overcome distractions, etc and give one's attention to one's work: 避免分心;专心工作: *It's terrible—I can't ~ (down) to anything today,* am too restless to do my work, etc. 真糟糕——我今天无法专心做任何事。**~ down (to sth),** become established (in a new way of life, new work, etc): 立身;安顿于(新的生活方式,新行业等): *~ down well in a new career/job.* 在新的事业(工作)中安顿下来。**~ down to married life; marry and ~ down,** live the regular routine life said to be typical of married persons. 过规律的婚姻生活;结婚而安定下来。**settle for sth,** accept, although not altogether satisfactory: 勉强接受(条件而解决某事): *I had hoped to get £1000 for my old car but had to ~ for £650.* 我原希望我的旧车子能卖一千英镑,结果只卖了六百五十英镑。**settle (sb) in,** (help sb to) move into a new house, flat, job, etc and put things in order: (帮某人)迁入新居,担任新的工作: *We haven't ~d in yet.* 我们尚未迁入新居。*You must come and see our new house when we're/we've ~d in.* 我们迁入新居后,你务必要来看看我们的新房子。**settle sth on/upon sb,** (legal) give sb (property, etc) for use during his/her lifetime: (法律)授与(某人财产): *~ part of one's estate on one's son;* 把部分财产授给儿子; *~ an annuity on a nephew.* 赠予侄儿年金。⇨ **settlement**(2). **~ on/upon sth,** decide to take; choose: 选定;决定;选择: *Which of the recordings have you ~d on?* 你已选定哪一段录音了? *We must ~ on a place to meet.* 我们须选定一个见面的地点。

settle (up) (with sb), pay what one owes to sb: 清偿: *I shall ~ (up) with you at the end of the month.* 我将在月底和你清账。*I've already settled up with the waiter,* paid for our meal. 我已向服务员付清饭钱。*Now to ~ with you!* Now I'll deal with you (according to context, pay, fight with you, get rid of you, etc). 现在跟你算帐! (可指我将付你钱, 和你打架或将你除掉等, 视上下文而定)。*have an ac'count to ~ with sb,* (colloq) have some unpleasant business, a quarrel, etc to discuss. (口)与某人有不欢之事, 争吵等待解决; 跟某人算帐。

settled /'setld ; 'setḷd/ *adj* **1** fixed; unchanging; permanent: 固定的; 不变的; 永久的: ～ *weather*, 稳定的天气; *a man of* ～ *convictions*: 信念坚定之人; ～ *melancholy*. 深深的忧郁. **2** (written on a paid bill) payment is acknowledged. (写于帐单上) 结讫.

settle·ment /'setlmənt; 'setḷmənt/ *n* **1** [U] the act of settling (a dispute, debt, etc): [C] instance of this: 解决; 和解; 清偿; 其实例: *The terms of* ～ *seem just.* 和解的条件似乎还公道. *We hope for a lasting* ～ *of all these troubles.* 我们希望这些纠纷能获得永久的解决. *The strikers have reached a* ～ *with the employers.* 罢工者与雇主已达成协议. *I enclose a cheque in* ～ *of your account.* 我寄上支票一张以清偿你的帐目. **2** [C] (statement of property settled(10) on sb: 财产授与文书; 所授与的财产: *a 'marriage* ～, one made by a man in favour of his wife. 授与妻子的财产. **3** [U] process of settling people in a colony; [C] new colony; group of colonists: 殖民; 新殖民地; 殖民团体; 殖民人群: *empty lands awaiting* ～; 尚待殖民的空旷之地; *Dutch and English* ～*s in North America.* 荷兰人和英国人在北美洲的殖民地; *penal* ～*s in Australia* 澳大利亚的罪犯殖民地. **4**[C] group of persons engaged in social welfare work, eg in a slum district. 从事社会福利工作的团体 (如在贫民区等处).

set·tler /'setlə(r); 'setḷɚ/ *n* colonist; person who has come to live in a newly developing country: 殖民者; 侨居新兴国家者: *Welsh* ～*s in Argentina.* 在阿根廷的威尔士侨民.

seven /'sevn; 'sɛvən/ *n, adj* the number 7. 七(的); 七个(的). ⇨ **App 4.** 参看附录四. **'～·fold** /-fəʊld; -fold/ *adj, adv* ～ times as much or as many; ～ times as great. 七倍的(地). **sev·enth** /'sevnθ; 'sɛvənθ/ *n, adj* 第七(的) *in the /one's* ～*th heaven*, extremely happy. 极端快乐的. **the S～th Day**, Saturday, the Sabbath of the Jews. 一周的第七天(即星期六; 为犹太人之安息日). **sev·enth·ly** *adv* in the 7th place. 第七. **～·teen** /ˌsevnˈtiːn; ˌsɛvənˈtin/ *n, adj* the number 17. 十七(的); 十七个(的). **～·teenth** /-ˈtiːnθ; -ˈtinθ/ *n, adj* 17th; next after 16, one of ～teen parts. 第十七(的); 十七分之一(的). **～·ty** /'sevntɪ; 'sɛvəntɪ/ *n, adj* the number 70. 七十(的); 七十个(的). **the ～·ties** *n pl* 70—79. 七十至七十九. **～·ti·eth** /'sevntɪɪθ; 'sɛvəntɪɪθ/ *n, adj*

sever /'sevə(r); 'sɛvɚ/ *vt, vi* **1** [VP6A, 15A] cut: 切断; 割开: ～ *a rope*; 割断绳子; ～ *the head of a sheep from the body;* 割下羊头; (fig) break off: (喻)断绝; 终止: ～ *one's connections with sb.* 与某人断绝关系. **2** [VP2A] break: 分裂; 断: *The rope* ～*ed under the strain.* 绳子拉得太紧, 绷断了. **～·ance** /'sevərəns; 'sɛvərəns/ *n* [U] severing or being ～ed: 切断; 断绝; 分裂; 断: *the severance of diplomatic relations/of communications.* 外交关系(交通)的断绝.

sev·eral /'sevrəl; 'sɛvrəl/ *adj* **1** three or more; some but not many: 三个或更多的; 几个的; 数个的: *You will need* ～ *more.* 你还需要几个. *I've read it* ～ *times.* 我已经读过好几遍了. **2** (formal) (with *pl nn* only) separate; individual: (正式用语) (仅与复数名词连用)各自的; 个别的: *They went their* ～ *ways.* Each went his own way. 他们各走各的路. □ *some* ～, few; *some*: 几个; 数个: *S～ of us decided to walk home.* 我们之中有几个人决定步行回家. **～·ly** /'sevrəlɪ; 'sɛvrəlɪ/ *adv* separately. 各自地; 个别地.

se·vere /sɪ'vɪə(r); sə'vɪr/ *adj* **1** stern; strict: 严厉的; 严格的: ～ *looks*: 严厉的面容; *be* ～ *with one's children*: 对孩子严厉; *be too* ～ *on a pupil.* 对学生太严格. **2** (of the weather, attacks of disease, etc) rigorous; violent: (指天气, 疾病之发作等)严重的; 剧烈的: *a* ～ *storm*; 强烈的暴风雨; ～ *pain*; 剧痛; *a* ～ *attack of toothache.* 牙痛的剧烈发作. **3** making great demands on skill, ability, patience and other qualities: 非常需要技术、能力、耐心和其他条件的; 艰难的; 激烈的: ～ *competition.* 激烈的竞争. *The pace was too* ～ *to be kept up for long.* 速度太

快, 无法持久. **4**(of style, etc)simple; without ornament. (指文体等) 简朴的; 不事修饰的. **～·ly** *adv* **se·ver·ity** /sɪ'verətɪ; sə'verətɪ/ *n* (*pl* **-ties**) **1** [U] quality of being ～: 严厉; 严格; 剧烈; 激烈: punish sb with severity; 严厉地责罚某人; *acts of severity*; 激烈的行为; *the severity* (== extreme cold) *of the winter in Canada.* 加拿大冬天的严寒. **2** (*pl*) ～ treatment or experiences: (复)严苛的待遇或艰苦的经验: *the severities of the winter campaign.* 冬令出征的艰苦.

sew /səʊ; so/ *vt, vi* (*pt* sewed, *pp* sewn /səʊn; son/ or sewed) [VP6A, 15B, 2A, B, C] work with a needle and thread; fasten with stitches; make (a garment) by stitching: 缝纫; 缝合; 缝(衣服): *sew a button on*; 钉扣子; *sew a dress.* 缝制衣服. *The garment is ,hand-'sewn /sewn by hand.* 这件衣服是手缝的. *She has been sewing all evening.* 她整个晚上都在缝纫. **sew** *sth* **up**, **(a)** join with stitches: 缝拢; 缝接: *The corpse was sewn up in a sack and thrown into the river.* 尸体被装在布袋中缝好后抛入河里. **(b)** (colloq) arrange; complete: (口)安排; 完成: *All the details of the project are sewn up.* 这计划的所有细节均有妥善安排. *The deel is sewn up.* 交易谈妥了. **sewer** /'səʊə(r); 'soɚ/ *n* **sew·ing** *n* [U] work (clothes, etc) being sewn. 缝制物(衣服等). **'sewing-machine** *n* machine for sewing. 缝纫机.

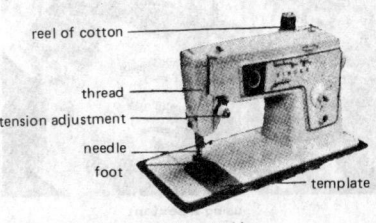

reel of cotton
thread
tension adjustment
needle
foot
template

a sewing-machine

sew·age /'sjuːɪdʒ US: suː-; 'sjuɪdʒ/ *n* [U] foul liquid material, waste organic matter, etc carried off in sewers; the disposal of ～. (下水道中之)污水; 污物; 污水之处理. **'～-farm /works** *nn* place where ～ is treated and disposed of. 污水处理场(厂).

sewer¹ /'sjuːə(r) US: suː-; 'sjuɚ/ *n* [C] underground channel (pipeline, or construction of brick, concrete, etc) to carry off sewage and rain water to centres (sewage-farms) for treatment, or to a natural waterway for disposal. 下水道; 阴沟(地下之管路或砖、混凝土等砌成的水道, 用以将污水及雨水送至污水处理场或排至河川). **'～-gas** *n* bad-smelling gas formed in ～s. 下水道发出的臭气. **'～-rat** *n* brown rat commonly found in ～s. (常见于阴沟的)褐色老鼠. **～·age** /-ɪdʒ; -ɪdʒ/ *n* system of ～s; drains. 污水排除系统; 下水道系统.

sewer² /'səʊə(r); 'soɚ/ *n* ⇨ **sew.**

sewn /səʊn; son/ *pp* of **sew.**

sex /seks; seks/ *n* **1** being male or female: 性; 性别: *What is its sex?* 它的性别是什么? *Help them all, without distinction of race, age or sex.* 帮助他们全体, 不分种族、年龄或性别. **2** males or females as a group. (集合用法)男; 女. **3** [U] differences between males and females; consciousness of these differences: 两性差别; 两性差别意识: *'sex antagonisms.* 异性间的敌对. **4** [U] the activities surrounding, centring on and leading to coitus: 色情: *a film /novel with lots of sex in it*; 充满色情的电影(小说); *the 'sex instinct*; 性的本能; *'sex appeal*, sexual attractiveness. 性感. **5** [U] sexual intercourse: 性交: *have sex with sb.* 与某人性交. □ *vt* [VP6A] determine the sex of. 决定…之性别. **sexed** *part adj* having a (specified) sexual nature: 有某种性欲的: *highly /weakly* ～*ed.* 性欲很强(很弱)的. **sex·less** *adj* neither male nor female; displaying neither masculine nor feminine characteristics. 无性的; 无性别的; 不具性

特征的。**sex-starved** *adj* (colloq) deprived of sexual gratification. (口)性饥渴的；性欲得不到满足的。**sexy** *adj* (-ier, -iest) (colloq) of or about sex; sexually attractive. (口)性的；有关性的；性感的。

sexa·gen·ar·ian /ˌseksədʒɪˈneərɪən ; ˌseksədʒəˈnɛr-ɪən/ *n, adj* (person) between 59 and 70 years of age. 五十九岁至七十岁间的(人)。

sex·ism /ˈseksɪzəm ; ˈsɛksɪzəm/ *n* [U] unfair or unreasonable discrimination between the sexes; unreasonable maintaining of traditional sexual roles (eg that men are strong and women are weak). 性别歧视；男性主义。**sex·ist** /ˈseksɪst ; ˈsɛksɪst/ *adj* of ~: 性别歧视的；男性主义的：*sexist attitudes*; 性别歧视的态度；~ *words*, eg *baby, bird, chick, doll*, used to mean a girl or woman. 用以指女孩或女人的词(如 baby, bird, chick, doll 等)。□ *n* person who displays or approves of ~. 性别歧视者；男性主义者。⇨ **male chauvinist** at **chauvinism**.

sex·tant /ˈsekstənt ; ˈsɛkstənt/ *n* instrument used for measuring the altitude of the sun, etc (in order to determine a ship's position, etc). 六分仪(用以测量太阳等之高度以决定船的位置等的仪器)。

using a sextant

sex·tet, sex·tette /seksˈtet ; sɛksˈtɛt/ *n* [C] (piece of music for) six voices, instruments or players in combination. 六重唱(曲)；六重奏(曲)。

sex·ton /ˈsekstən ; ˈsɛkstən/ *n* man who takes care of a church buildings, digs graves in the churchyard, rings the church bell, etc. 教堂司事(管理教堂，挖掘墓地，敲钟等)。

sex·ual /ˈseksjʊəl ; ˈsɛksjʊəl/ *adj* of sex or the sexes: 性的；两性的：~ *intercourse* = **coitus**. 性交。~**·ity** /ˌseksjʊˈæləti ; ˌsɛksjʊˈælətɪ/ *n* [U] ~ nature or characteristics. 性的特征；性别。

sh (also **ssh, shh**) /ʃ ; ʃ/ *int* be quiet! be silent! 嘘！别作声！别讲话！

shabby /ˈʃæbɪ ; ˈʃæbɪ/ *adj* (-ier, -iest) **1** in bad repair or condition; much worn; poorly dressed: 破旧的；褴褛的；衣着寒酸的：*wearing a ~ overcoat*. 穿着破旧的大衣。*You look rather ~ in those clothes*. 你的衣着使你显得有点寒酸。**,~·genˈteel** *adj* having evidence of former gentility but now ~; trying to keep up appearances. 从前很阔而现在穷酸的；穷要面子的。**2** (of behaviour) mean; unfair: (指行为)卑鄙的；不正当的：*a ~ excuse*; 不正当的借口；*play a ~ trick on sb*. 对某人要卑鄙的手段。**shab·bily** /ˈʃæbɪlɪ ; ˈʃæblɪ/ *adv* **shab·bi·ness** *n*

shack /ʃæk ; ʃæk/ *n* [C] small, roughly built shed, hut or house (usu of wood). 简陋之小屋 (通常为木材架成)。□ *vi* [VP2C] ~ *up (with sb / together)*, (sl) live together. (俚)(与某人)同居。

shackle /ˈʃækl ; ˈʃækl/ *n* [C] one of a pair of iron rings joined by a chain for fastening a prisoner's wrists or ankles; (*pl*) fetters; (fig) sth that prevents freedom of action: (一只)手铐；脚镣；(复)(整副的)镣铐；(喻)束缚物；羁绊物：*the ~s of convention*. 习俗的桎梏。□ *vt* [VP6A] put ~s on; prevent from acting freely. 加镣铐于；束缚羁绊。

shad /ʃæd ; ʃæd/ *n* (*pl* unchanged) large edible fish of the N Atlantic coast of N America. (复数不变)鲥鱼 (北美北大西洋海岸所产之大食用鱼)。

shad·dock /ˈʃædək ; ˈʃædək/ *n* (tropical tree with a) large edible fruit related to the grapefruit; pomelo. 柚子(树)；朱栾(树)。

shade /ʃeɪd ; ʃed/ *n* **1** [U] (with *adj, v* and *art*) comparative darkness caused by the cutting off of direct rays of light; (fig) comparative obscurity: 荫；荫凉；(喻)隐晦：*a temperature of 35°C in the ~*. 在荫凉处温度为三十五摄氏度。*Keep in the ~; it's cooler*. 你就待在荫凉处吧；那儿比较凉爽。*The trees give a pleasant ~*. 树木供给舒畅的荫凉。*put sb / sth in / into the ~*, cause to appear small, unimportant, etc, by contrast: 使(某人或某物)黯然无光；使相形见绌：*You are so clever and good-looking that my poor efforts are put into the ~*. 你是如此的聪明而且才华横溢，以致我的小小成就显得黯然无光。**'~-tree** *n* (esp US) tree planted to give ~. (尤美)遮荫树。**2** [U] darker part(s) of a picture; etc; reproduction of the darker part of a picture: (图画等)之阴暗部分；阴影部分；暗影：*There is not enough light and ~ in your drawing*. 你的图画中明暗不够显明。**3** [C] degree or depth of colour: 色度；颜色之深浅：*dress materials in several ~s of blue*. 数种不同深浅之蓝色的衣料。**4** [C] degree of difference: 差异的程度；细微的差别：*a word with many ~s of meaning*. 其意义有许多差度的一个字。*She is a ~ better today*. 她今天好了一些。**5** sth that shuts out light or lessens its brilliance; 遮光物：*an 'eye-~*; 遮眼物；眼罩；*a 'lamp-~*; 灯罩；*a 'window-~*. 窗帘。⇨ **blind**[3]. (*pl*) (US colloq) sun-glasses. (复)(美口)太阳眼镜。**6** (*pl*; liter) darkness. (复)(文)黑暗：*the ~s of evening*. 夜晚之黑暗。**7** [C] unreal or unsubstantial thing; soul after death. 不实在之物；无实质之物；死后之灵魂。**8** the abode of spirits; the Greek underworld. 亡魂之居所；(希腊神话之)阴间；冥府。□ *vt, vi* **1** [VP6A, 15A] keep direct rays of light from: 遮蔽：*He ~d his eyes with his hands*. 他用手遮眼睛。**2** [VP6A] screen (a light, lamp, etc) to reduce brightness. 遮(光, 灯等)。**3** [VP6A] darken with parallel pencil lines, etc (parts of a drawing, etc), to give the appearance of light and ~. 绘(图画等)之阴影；加线条等于(图画中)。**4** [VP2C] change by degrees: 渐变：*scarlet shading off into pink*; 渐变为淡红之深红；*a colour that ~s from blue into green*. 由蓝渐变为绿的颜色。**shad·ing** *n* **1** [U] use of black, etc to give light and shade to a drawing. (绘画之)描影法；皴法。**2** [C] slight difference or variation. 细微的差别。

shadow /ˈʃædəʊ ; ˈʃædo/ *n* **1** [C] area of shade, dark shape, thrown on the ground, a wall, floor, etc by sth which cuts off the direct rays of light: 影；阴影：*The earth's ~ sometimes falls on the moon*. 地球的阴影有时投落在月球上面。*be afraid of one's own ~*, be very timid. 怕自己的影子(非常胆怯)。*Coming events cast their ~s before them*, give warning of their coming. 未来的事件先有预兆发生。**2** [U] area of shade of indefinite shape or extent: 大小或形状不定的阴影：*Her face was in deep ~*. 她的脸布满阴影。**3** [C] sth unsubstantial or unreal: 无实质之物；不实在之物；幽灵；鬼：*catch at ~s, run after a ~*, try to get hold of sth unreal. 捕捉不实在之物，追逐不实在之物。*He is only the ~ of his former self*, is very thin and weak. 他瘦得不成样子。*worn to a ~*, (of a person) weakened, exhausted. (指人)虚弱得不成人形。**'~-boxing** *n*, sparring against an imaginary opponent (for practice). 与假想对手斗拳；太极拳。**4** (*pl*) partial darkness: (复)部分黑暗；半暗：*the ~s of evening*. 暮色。**5** [C] dark patch or area: 黑斑；乌黑之处：*have ~s under / round the eyes*, such areas thought to be caused by lack of sleep, illness, etc. 有黑眼圈(为缺乏睡眠，疾病等所造成)。**6** (*sing* only) slightest trace: (仅用单数) 微痕：*without / beyond a ~ of (a) doubt*. 无丝毫的怀疑。**7** person's constant attendant or companion. 形影相随的人。**~ cabinet,**

(GB) group formed from the leaders of the Parliamentary Opposition, ie those who might form a new cabinet if there is a change of government after a general election. (英)影子内阁(由国会中反对党的领袖们所组成,一旦该党大选获胜, 即可组成新内阁)。 □ *vt* [VP6A] **1** darken; overspread with ~. 使黯; 遮蔽; 覆以阴影。 **2** keep a secret watch on; follow closely and watch all the movements of sb: 秘密尾随; 跟: *The suspected spy was ~ed by detectives.* 那个有间谍嫌疑的人被侦探们秘密跟踪。 **shadowy** *adj* **1** having ~ or shade; shady(1): 有阴影的; 阴凉的: *cool, ~y woods.* 阴凉的树林。 **2** like a ~; indistinct: 似阴影的; 模糊的: *a ~y outline* 模糊的轮廓。

shady /'ʃeɪdɪ; 'ʃedɪ/ *adj* (**-ier, -iest**) **1** giving shade from sunlight; situated in shade: 遮荫的; 在荫处的: *the ~ side of the street.* 街道背阳的一边。 **2** of doubtful honesty; 可疑的; 有问题的; 靠不住的: *a ~ transaction/financier;* 可疑的交易(靠不住的资本家); *a ~-looking customer,* (colloq) person who appears to be a rogue. (口)形迹可疑的家伙。 *Politics has its ~ side.* 政治有其黑暗面。

shaft /ʃɑːft US: ʃæft; ʃæft/ *n* [C] **1** (long, slender stem of) an arrow or spear: 箭(杆); 矛(柄); (fig) (喻) *~s of envy/ridicule,* expressions of envy, etc. 嫉妒(揶揄)之表情。 **2** long handle of an axe or other tool. 斧柄; 其他器具之长柄。 **3** one of the pair of bars (wooden poles) between which a horse is harnessed to pull a cart, etc. 车辕; 车杠。 **4** main part of a column (between the base and the capital). 柱干; 柱身(柱基与柱头之间的部分)。 ⇨ the illus at **column.** 参看 column 之插图。 **5** long, narrow space, usu vertical, eg for descending into a coalmine, for a lift in a building, or for ventilation. 狭长而通常垂直之空间(如煤矿之竖坑, 建筑物内之升降机井或通风井)。 **6** bar or rod joining parts of a machine, or transmitting power. 机械之轴(用以连接机器之各部分, 或用以传动动力者)。 **7** ray (of light); bolt (of lightning). 光线;(闪电之)闪光。

shag /ʃæg; ʃæg/ *n* [U] coarse kind of cut tobacco. 粗烟丝。

shagged /ʃægd; ʃægd/ *pred adj ~ (out),* (GB sl) very tired. (英俚)筋疲力尽。

shaggy /'ʃægɪ; 'ʃægɪ/ *adj* (**-ier, -iest**) **1** (of hair) rough, coarse and untidy. (指毛发)粗浓杂乱的。 **2** covered with rough coarse hair: 覆有粗浓之毛发的: *~ eyebrows;* 粗眉; *a ~ dog.* 粗毛犬。 *'***dog story,** long joke that is funny because it is so boring and its punchline is so weak. 枯燥平淡的冗长笑话。 **shag·gily** /-ɪlɪ; -ɪlɪ/ *adv* **shag·gi·ness** *n*

shah /ʃɑː; ʃɑ/ *n* (title of a) former ruler of Iran. (昔时)伊朗国王(之称号)。

shake[1] /ʃeɪk; ʃek/ *vt, vi* (*pt* **shook** /ʃʊk; ʃʊk/, *pp* **shaken** /'ʃeɪkən; 'ʃekən/) **1** [VP6A, 15A, B, 2A, C] (cause to) move from side to side, up and down etc: (使)摇动; 摇摆; 挥动; 震动; 抖动: ~ *a rug;* 抖动地毯; ~ *a man by the shoulder;* 摇动某人的肩膀; ~ *the dice* (in a box, etc before throwing them on to a table); (在掷出之前)摇动盒子等中的骰子; ~ *one's head (at sb),* to indicate 'No' or doubt, disapproval, etc; (对某人)摇头(表示'不'或怀疑、不赞成等); ~ *one's finger at sb,* to indicate disapproval or as a warning; 以食指指点着某人(表示不赞同或警告); ~ *one's fist at sb,* to show defiance. 对某人挥拳(表示挑战)。 *His sides were shaking with laughter.* 他捧腹大笑。 *He was shaking with cold.* 他冷得打颤。 *He was shaking in his shoes,* trembling with fear. 他吓得直发抖。 *The earth shook under us,* eg in an earthquake. 地在我们脚下震动(如在地震时)。 ~ **hands (with sb),** ⇨ **hand**[1](1). **2** [VP6A] shock; trouble; weaken: 使震惊; 动摇; 减弱: ~ *sb's faith/courage.* 动摇某人的信心(勇气)。 *They were badly ~n by the news.* 那消息令他们大为震惊。 *The firm's credit has been badly ~n.* 公司的信誉已大大受损。 **3** [VP2A, C] (of sb's voice) tremble; become weak or faltering: (指人的声

音)颤抖; 变弱或结结巴巴: *Her voice shook with emotion.* 她的声音因激动而颤抖。 **shak·ing** /ʃeɪkɪŋ; ʃekɪŋ/ *n* **1** [C] *give sth a good shaking,* shake it well; 使劲地摇动某物; *get a shaking,* be ~n. 被摇动; 受惊。 **shaker** *n* one who, that which, ~s; container in which or from which sth is ~n: 摇动者; 摇荡器; 震荡器; *a 'cocktail~r.* 鸡尾酒调酒器; *a 'flour~r.* 面粉搅拌器; **4** [VP14, 15B] (special uses with *adverbial particles* and *preps*): (与副词性小品词及介词连用之特殊用法):

shake down, (colloq) (口) **(a)** get into harmony, become adjusted to new conditions: 和谐相处; 能适应新的状况: *The new staff are shaking down well.* 新来人员适应良好。 **(b)** lie down for sleep: 躺下睡觉: ~ *down on the beach/floor.* 躺在海滩上(地板上)睡觉。 ~ *sb down,* (US) get money from him by threats, violence, etc. (美)以威胁、暴力等索取金钱; 敲诈; 勒索。 ■ *sb/sth down,* (US) search him/it thoroughly. (美)彻底搜查。 ~ *sth down,* give it a ~-down of). 试航; 试飞。 '**~-down** *n* (colloq) (口) **(a)** temporary or makeshift bed. 临时搭的床铺; 地铺。 **(b)** (US) extortion of money. (美)敲诈; 勒索。 **(c)** (US) thorough search. (美)彻底搜查。 **(d)** final test (eg of a new ship, aircraft): (新船、新飞机等的)试验; 试飞: *a ~-down voyage/flight.* 试航(试飞)。

shake sth from/out of sth, get from/out of by shaking: 把…自…中摇出(下): ~ *a fruit from a tree/out of one's shoe.* 从树上摇下(从鞋里抖出)一片叶子。

shake sb off, free oneself from: 摆脱; 避开: *The thief ran fast and soon shook off his pursuers.* 那个贼跑得很快, 很快就把追逐者摆脱了。 ~ *sth off,* get rid of: 除去: ~ *off a cold/a fit of depression.* 除去风寒(沮丧)。

shake out, (mil) spread; disperse: (军)散开: *The troops were ordered to ~ out when crossing open country.* 军队在穿越旷野时奉命散开。 ~ *sth out,* spread so as to out by shaking: 抖开; 摊开: ~ *out a sail/tablecloth.* 扬帆(铺桌布)。 '**~-out** *n* process or act of making workers redundant: 使劳工过剩的过程或行动; 裁汰: *a new ~-out in the shipbuilding industry.* 造船业再度裁汰。

shake sth up, (a) mix well by shaking: 摇动使均匀: ~ *up a bottle of medicine.* 摇匀一瓶药。 **(b)** restore sth to shape by shaking: 抖动使恢复原状: ~ *up a cushion.* 抖松坐垫。 ~ *sb up,* restore from apathy or lethargy: 使振作; 激励; 鞭策(使某人脱离淡漠、倦怠而无生气的状态): *Some of these managers need shaking up—they're asleep on the job.* 这些经理中有些人需要鞭策——他们在工作时睡着了。 Hence, 由此产生, '**~-up** *n: We need a good ~-up in our firm—the management are completely out of touch with the facts of modern life.* 我们的公司需要大事整顿——管理方面与现代生活实况完全脱了节。

shake[2] /ʃeɪk; ʃek/ *n* [C] **1** shaking or being shaken: 摇动; 震动; 颤抖: *a ~ of the head,* to indicate 'No': 摇头(以表示不同意); *give sth a good ~.* 猛摇某物。 **2** (colloq) moment: (口)片刻: *in two ~s;* 一会儿; *in half a ~,* almost at once. 几乎立刻地。 **3** (*pl*) (复) **no great ~s,** (sl) not very good or efficient. (俚)平凡之物。 **4** '**egg~,** '**milk-~,** etc, glass of milk and egg or milk alone, flavoured and shaken up. 蛋和牛奶之饮料(加香料搅匀);泡沫奶。

Shake·spear·ian /ʃeɪk'spɪərɪən; ʃek'spɪrɪən/ *adj* (in the style of) Shakespeare. 莎士比亚的; 莎士比亚风格的。 ⇨ **App 8.** 参看附录八。

shaky /'ʃeɪkɪ; 'ʃekɪ/ *adj* (**-ier, -iest**) **1** (of a person, his movements, etc) weak; unsteady: (指人, 其动作等)虚弱的; 不稳的; 颤抖的: ~ *hands;* 颤抖的手; *speak in a ~ voice;* 以颤抖的声音说; *be ~ on one's legs;* 两腿站不稳能; *feel very ~.* 感到非常虚弱。 **2** unsafe; unreliable: 不安全的; 不可靠的: *a ~ table.* 摇晃的桌子。 *My French is rather ~,* 我的法文不甚流利。 **shak·ily** /-ɪlɪ; -ɪlɪ/ *adv* **shaki·ness** *n*

shale /ʃeɪl; ʃel/ *n* [U] soft rock that splits easily into layers. 页岩; 泥板岩(易于裂成板片的软岩石)。 '**~-oil** *n* oil obtained from bituminous ~. 页岩油(由沥青质

页岩所提炼之油)。

shall /weak form ʃl ; ʃl; strong form ʃæl; ʃæl/ anom fin (shall not is often shortened to **shan't** US: ʃænt ; ʃænt /; with thou the old form **shalt** /ʃælt; ʃælt /occurred; pt form **should** /ʃʊd; ʃʊd, weak form ʃəd ; ʃəd/; should not is often shortened to **shouldn't** /'ʃʊdnt; 'ʃʊdnt/ (shall not 常简略为 shan't; 与 thou 连用时, 则用古体 shalt; 过去式作 should; should not 常简略为 shouldn't) **1** (used as an aux v to express the future tense, used with the first person, affirm and interr, and second person, interr only. The word will is often used for shall in colloq style. I'll and We'll are used for I / We shall.): (用作助动词以表示未来时,用于第一人称之肯定式及疑问式,于第二人称之疑问式。在口语体中,will 常用来代替 shall): We ~ arrive tomorrow. 我们将于明日到达。S~ we be back in time? 我们将及时回来吗? He said I was not to go, but I certainly ~. 他说我不会去,但我一定前往。(The use of should in place of ~ indicates either future in the past, or a conditional statement, with an if-clause expressed or understood): (以 should 代替 shall 时,或表示过去未来时态,或用于条件叙述或句中,其条件与句或写出或省略): I told him that I should see him the next day. 我对他说过我将于翌日去看他。 I should have bought it if I had had enough money. 如果我有足够的钱,我早已买下它了。**2** (used with the second and third persons to form a future or conditional statement expressing the speaker's will or intention; with stress on ~, should, this expresses obligation or compulsion; without special stress on ~, should, it expresses a promise or a threat): (用于第二及第三人称以构成叙述句或意志或意愿的未来式或条件式; shall, should 重读时,表示义务或强制; shall, should 不重读时,表示允诺或威胁): You say you will not do it, but I say you ~ do it. 你说你不做(它),但我说你必须做。 He says he won't go, but I say he ~. 他说他不去,但我说他会去。 You ~ not catch me so easily next time. 你下次不会那样容易抓到我了。 If you work well, you ~ have higher wages. 如果你工作良好,你可得较高的工资。**3** (used with all persons to form statements or questions expressing the ideas of duty, command, obligation, conditional duty, and (in the neg) prohibition): (用于所有人称以构成叙述句或疑问句,表示责任、命令、义务、假定的责任及(否定式中)禁止等观念): S~ I (= Do you want me to) open the window? 要不要我把窗子打开吗? S~ the boy (= Do you want the boy to) wait? 要让那个男孩子等吗? (Note that Will I / he is not used here, but that 'Would you like us / him to', is the usu equivalent.) (此处不用 Will I (he), 但通常可用 Would you like us (him) to 代替。) I asked the man whether the boy should wait. 我问那人是否要那个男孩子等待。You shan't have it; it's mine! 你不可拿它; 那是我的! You should (= ought to) have been more careful. 你不应该如此粗心大意。He shouldn't (= oughtn't to) do things like that. 他不该做那种事。**4** (used with all persons in clauses expressing purpose, equivalent to may or might, thus forming a subjunctive equivalent): (与所有人称合用,用于表示目的的从句中,相当于 may 或 might, 而构成相当于假设语气之说法): I lent him the book so that he should study the subject. 我借给他那本书,使他可以研究该问题。**5** (used with all persons as a subjunctive equivalent): (与所有人称合用,用作假设语气之同等语): I'm anxious that it ~ /should be done at once. 我急欲使这事立即办妥。 It is surprising that he should be so foolish. 他竟是那么愚笨,实在令人惊讶。**6** (in reported speech) ~, should are used when reporting the first person to other persons (eg He said: 'I ~ do it' —he said he should do it, but will, would are now commoner), or when reporting from other persons to the first person (eg He said to me: 'You will succeed' —he told me that I should succeed). (在间接叙述中) shall, should 用于将第一人称引述为其他人称 (如 He said: 'I ~ do it'—he said he should do it, 但目前 will, would 比较通用), 或将其他人称引述为第一人称(如

He said to me: 'You will succeed'—he told me that I should succeed)。**7** (should is used after how, why, and (occasionally) other interrogative words): (should 用于 how, why, 及 (有时) 其他疑问词的后面): How should I know? 我怎么知道? Why should you / he think that? 你(他)为什么那么想? **8** (should is used to express probability or expectation): (should 用于表示可能或期望): The should be there by now, I think. 我想他们现在应该已经到那里了。**9** (should is used to express what is advisable or desirable): (should 用以表示应该或合理): You should drink your coffee while it's hot. 你应该趁热把咖啡喝掉。You should see the new film that's on at the Odeon. 你该去看在奥狄昂上演的新影片。(also ⇨ **ought**).

shal·lot /ʃəˈlɒt; ʃəˈlɑt/ n sort of small onion with cloves like, but not so strong-tasting as, those of garlic. 冬葱(一种小洋葱,有似蒜之蒜茎,不如蒜之辛辣)。

shal·low /ˈʃæləʊ; ˈʃælo/ adj of little depth: 浅的; 不深的: ~ water; 浅水; a ~ saucer / dish; 浅的茶杯碟(盘子); (fig) not earnest sound or serious: (喻)不认真的; 肤浅的; 浅薄的: a ~ argument; 浅薄的议论; ~ talk. 肤浅的谈话。□ n (often pl) ~ place in a river or in the sea; shoal. (常用复数)河流或海洋中的浅水处; 浅滩。□ vi become ~. 变浅。

sha·lom /ʃæˈlɒm; ʃəˈlom/ int (Hebrew word) (used as a greeting and on parting) Peace! (希伯来字) (用于问候及道别时)平安!

shalt /ʃælt; ʃælt/ ⇨ **shall**.

sham /ʃæm ; ʃæm/ vi, vt (-mm-) [VP2A, D, 6A] pretend to be; simulate: 假装; 佯为: He ~med dead / death. 他装死。He's only ~ming. 他只是假装罢了。□ n 1 person who ~s; sth intended to deceive: 假装者; 伪为者; 骗人之物; 赝品: His love was a mere ~; what he really wanted was her money. 他的爱情是虚假的; 他真正要的是她的钱。He's a ~, an impostor. 他是个骗子。□ [U] pretence: 虚假; 借口: What he says is all ~. 他所说的全是托辞。□ adj false; pretended: 虚假的; 假装的: ~ piety; 佯装虔敬; a ~ battle (as in military training); 演习战; 模拟战; ~-'Tudor, imitating the Tudor style of architecture. 模仿都铎王朝之建筑风格的。

shamble /ˈʃæmbl ; ˈʃæmbl/ vi [VP2A, C] walk unsteadily as if unable to lift the feet properly: 蹒跚而行; 踉跄而行: The old man ~d up to me. 老人蹒跚地向我走来。□ n shambling walk. 蹒跚的步子; 踉跄的步子。

shambles /ˈʃæmblz ; ˈʃæmblz/ n sing (作单数用) **1** (archaic) scene of bloodshed: (古)屠场; 杀人流血之所: The place became a ~. 那地方变成了一个屠场。**2** (colloq) (scene of) muddle or confusion: (口)紊乱(之处); 混乱(的场面): His flat is a complete ~. 他的公寓非常凌乱。He made a ~ of the job. 他把那工作弄得一塌糊涂。

shame /ʃeɪm ; ʃem/ n [U] **1** distressed feeling, loss of self-respect, caused by wrong, dishonourable or foolish behaviour, failure, etc (of oneself, one's family, etc): 羞愧; 羞耻; 耻辱; 惭愧: feel ~ at having told a lie / at failing in an examination; 因说谎(考试失败)而感到羞愧; hang one's head in / for ~. 因羞愧而垂头。To my ~, I must confess that…. 我很惭愧地承认…。'~-faced adj showing ~; looking distressed through ~. 惭愧的; 羞愧的; 羞怯的。Hence, 由此产生, '~-faced·ly /ˈʃeɪmfeɪstlɪ; ˈʃem.festlɪ/ adv '~-making adj (colloq) causing a feeling of ~. (口)引起羞耻感的。**2** capacity for experiencing ~: 羞耻心; 羞耻感: He has no ~ / is quite without ~ / is lost to ~. 他毫无羞耻心。(For) ~! an appeal to sb not to disregard this feeling (used as a reproof to sb who does wrong and does not show ~). 真丢脸! 真可耻! (对做错事而不表示惭愧者之谴责语)。**3** [U] dishonour. 不名誉。bring ~ on sb / oneself, dishonour sb / oneself. 使某人(自己)蒙羞。cry ~ on sb, say that he is disgraceful, ought to be ashamed of himself. 说某人应该自觉可耻。put sb to ~, disgrace him (eg by showing superior qualities). 羞辱某人; 使某

人相形见绌; 使某人黯然失色. *S~ on you!* You should be ashamed of yourself! 真可耻！真丢脸！真不要脸！ **4 a ~,** sth unworthy; sth that causes ~; sth or sb that is wrong or regrettable: 不足取之事物; 引起羞耻之事物; 可耻之事物或人: *What a ~ to deceive the girl!* 欺骗那女孩是多么羞耻的事啊！ *It's a ~ to take the money for doing such easy work.* 做那么容易的工作而拿那么多的钱真难为情. *He's a ~ to his family.* 他是他家的败类. □ *vt* **1** [VP6A] cause ~ to; cause sb to feel ~; bring disgrace on (sb or oneself). 使蒙羞; 使耻辱; 使不名誉: ~ *one's family.* 玷辱门楣. **2** [VP14] ~ *sb into/out of doing sth,* frighten or force (sb to do/not to do sth) by ~: 使(某人)因羞愧而做某事(不做某事): ~ *a man into apologising.* 使一个人因羞愧而道歉. ~**ful** /-fl ; -fʊl/ *adj* causing or bringing ~: 导致羞耻的; 可耻的: ~*ful conduct.* 可耻的行为. ~**.fully** /-fəlɪ; -flɪ/ *adv* ~**.less** *adj* without ~; immodest. 无耻的; 厚颜的. ~**.less.ly** *adv* ~**.less.ness** *n*

sham.my /'ʃæmɪ ; 'ʃæmɪ/ *n* '~**(leather),** ⇨ **chamois**

sham.poo /ʃæm'puː ; ʃæm'pu/ *n* [C, U] (special soap, liquid, powder, etc for a) washing of the hair: 洗发; 洗发用的肥皂、水剂、粉等; 洗发精: *give sb a ~;* 给某人洗头发; *a ~ and set.* 洗头做发. □ *vt* [VP6A] wash (the hair of the head). 洗(头发).

sham.rock /'ʃæmrɒk ; 'ʃæmrɑk/ *n* clover-like plant with (usu) three leaves on each stem (serving as the national emblem of Ireland). 酢浆草 (为爱尔兰的国花).

shandy /'ʃændɪ ; 'ʃændɪ/ *n* [U] mixed drink of beer and ginger-beer or lemonade. 啤酒和姜汁啤酒或柠檬水混合的饮料.

shang.hai /ʃæŋ'haɪ; 'ʃɑŋhaɪ/ *vt* (sl) make (a man) unconscious (with drink or drugs) and then carry him off to be a seaman on an outgoing ship; trick (a person) into an awkward situation. (俚)(以酒或麻醉剂)使(某人)失去知觉而拐带至出航的船上做水手; 骗(某人)入困境.

shank /ʃæŋk ; ʃæŋk/ *n* **1** leg, esp the part between the knee and the ankle; shin-bone. 胫(膝与踝间的部分); 胫骨. *go on ~s's mare/pony,* on one's own legs (not riding a horse, etc). 步行(未骑马或驴等). **2** straight, slender part of an anchor, key, spoon, etc; smooth part of the stem of a screw. 锚、钥、匙等之直而细长的部分; 螺钉体.

shan't /ʃɑːnt *US:* ʃænt; ʃænt/ = shall not.

shan.tung /ʃæn'tʌŋ; ʃæn'tʌŋ/ *n* [U] kind of heavy silk, usu undyed. 山东绸; 茧绸(通常未染色).

shanty[1] /'ʃæntɪ ; 'ʃæntɪ/ *n* [C] (*pl* **-ties**) poorly made hut, shed or cabin. 简陋的小屋. '~**-town** *n* slum area of a town, or on the outskirts of a town, consisting of huts or shanties. 城镇中之简陋房舍区, 贫民区; 有简陋房舍之城郊地区.

shanty[2] (US = **chant(e)y**) /'ʃæntɪ ; 'ʃæntɪ/ *n* (*pl* **-ties**) (often 常作 '**sea ~**) song sung by sailors in rhythm with their movements while working. 水手们随工作的节拍所唱的歌; 船歌.

shape[1] /ʃeɪp ; ʃep/ *n* **1** [C, U] form; total effect produced by the outlines of sth: 外形; 形状; 样子: *There were clouds of different ~s in the sky.* 天空有各种形状的云. *The garden is in the ~ of a square/oblong/crescent.* 那园子是方的(长方/弦月)形的. *What's the ~ of his nose?* 他的鼻子是什么形状呢？ *That hat hasn't much ~/has a queer ~.* 那顶帽子的式样不佳(样子很怪). *get/put sth into ~,* give definite form to; arrange in an orderly way: 定形; 有条理地安排; 整理: *get/put one's ideas into ~.* 整理思绪. *give ~ to,* express (clearly): (清晰地)表达: *He has some difficulty in giving ~ to his ideas.* 他很难清晰地表达他的意见. *knock sth into/out of ~,* put sth into/out of the right ~. 使成形(使变形或走样). *take ~,* become definite in form or outline: 具体化; 成形: *The new building is beginning to take ~.* 这座新的建

筑物开始成形了. *take ~ in,* find expression in: 具体化; 成形; 体现: *His intentions took ~ in action,* were realized in action. 他的意向已付诸行动. *in ~,* in form, outline or appearance: 在形式上; 在外形上: *What a fat fellow! He's like a barrel in ~!* 多胖的家伙！他的体型象只木桶！ *He looks like a devil/monster in human ~.* 他看起来象徒具人形的魔鬼(怪物). **2** sort, description: 种; 类: *I've had no proposals from him in any ~ or form,* none of any sort. 我未得到他任何形式的建议. **3** condition: 情况; 状况: *Her affairs are in good ~,* are satisfactory. 她的事情令人满意. *Ali is in good ~ for his forthcoming fight,* is physically fit. 阿里的身体状况甚佳, 足以应付即将来临的比赛. **4** [C] sth indistinctly seen; vague form; apparition: 看来模糊之物; 模糊的形影; 幽灵: *Two ~s could be discerned in the darkness.* 在黑暗中可以看到两个模糊的形影. *A huge ~ loomed up through the fog.* 一个巨大的影象在雾中隐隐出现. **5** [C] pattern or mould on which sth is given ~, eg a block on which facts are made. 底样; 模; 模型(如帽型等).

shape[2] /ʃeɪp ; ʃep/ *vt, vi* **1** [VP6A, 15A] give a shape or form to: 使具...形状; 塑造; 制作; 筹划: *a pot on a wheel;* 在拉坯转轮上制作陶罐; ~ *clay into an urn,* on a potter's wheel or lathe: (在拉坯转轮或旋盘上)将泥土制成瓮; ~ (= direct) *one's course for home;* 计划回家的路线; (*pp*) (过去分词) ~*d like a pear,* having the shape of a pear. 形状似梨的. **2** [VP2A, C] take shape; give signs of future shape or development: 成形; 形成; 发育; 发展: *Our plans are shaping well,* giving promise of success. 我们的计划进展顺利. *The students are shaping satisfactorily,* making good progress. 学生们发育得很好. ~**.less** *adj* ~**.less.ly** *adv* ~**.less.ness** *n*

shape.ly /'ʃeɪplɪ ; 'ʃeplɪ/ *adj* (**-ier, -iest**) (esp of a person's form, or of limbs) well-formed; having a pleasing shape: (尤指人的体型或肢体)美好的; 匀称的, 有悦人之模样者: *a ~ pair of legs.* 一双匀称的腿.

shard /ʃɑːd ; ʃɑrd/ *n* (old use, but still used by gardeners and archaeologists for a) piece of broken earthenware, eg one placed over the hole in a flower-pot. (旧用法, 但园艺家及考古学家仍习用之)陶器碎片(如覆于花盆洞上者).

share[1] /ʃeər ; ʃɛr/ *n* **1** [C] part or division which sb has in, receives from, or gives to, a stock held by several or many persons, or which he contributes to a fund, expenses, etc: (共有、分得、给付或贡献出的一份): 部份: *Please let me take a ~ in the expenses,* pay sth towards them. 这些费用请让我出一份. *We shall all have a ~ in the profits.* 我们都可以分得一份利润. *go ~s (with sb) (in sth),* divide (profits, costs, etc) with others; become part owner (with others); pay (a part of an expense): 与他人分摊(利润、费用等); (与他人)成为共有者; 付(费用之一份): *Let me go ~s with you in the taxi fare.* 让我和你分摊计程车车费. ~**-cropper** *n* (in some countries, not in GB) tenant farmer who pays a ~ of his crop as rent to the owner of the land. (在英国以外之若干国家中, 以作物之一部分付与地主作为及租的)佃农. **2** [U] part taken or received by sb in an action, undertaking, etc, eg of responsibility, blame: (参与或分担责任、过失等的)部份: *What ~ did he have in their success?* 在他们的成功中他有何贡献？ *You must take your ~ of the blame.* 你必须承受你那一份过失. *You're not taking much ~ in the conversation,* are saying little. 你未积极参与谈话. **3** [C] one of the equal parts into which the capital of a company is divided, entitling the holder of the ~ to a proportion of the profits: 股份; 股(公司资本诸等分之一, 持有者得按一定比率分享红利): *hold 500 ~s in a shipping company;* 在某船公司持有五百股; *£1 ~s are now worth £1.75.* 一英镑的股份现值 1.75 英镑. '**ordinary ~,** on which dividends are paid according to profits after payments on preference ~s. 普通股(于优先股分红后才能分的红利). '**preference ~,** one on which a fixed dividend is guaranteed before payments are made on others. 优先股(较

普通股优先享有定额红利)。**'~ certificate,** document proving ownership of ~s. 股票。**'~·holder** n owner of (business) ~s. 股东。**'~ index** n number used to show how ~ prices have fluctuated, based on prices of ~s selected for this purpose: 股票指数: *The Financial Times ~ index went up/down five points yesterday.* 经济时报的股票指数昨天上升了(下降了)五点。□ *vt, vi* **1** [VP6A, 14, 15B] ~ *sth (out) (among/between),* give a ~ to others; divide and distribute: 分给;分配;分派: ~ *£20 among five men,* eg by giving them £20 each: 将一百英镑分与五人(如每人给二十英镑); ~ *the sweets between you.* 你们两人分这些糖果。Hence, 由此产生, **'~·out** n distribution. 分配;分派。~ *with sb,* give part of it to him: 分给别人;和别人分享;和别人合用: *He would ~ his last pound with me.* 他到了只剩最后一英镑的时候,也会分给我用。**2** [VP6A, 14] ~ *sth (with sb),* have or use (with); have in common: 共有;共用: *He hated having to ~ the hotel bedroom with a stranger.* 他讨厌与陌生人共住这个旅馆房间。**3** [VP6A, 3A] ~ *(in) sth,* have a ~; partake; 分摊;分享;共同负担: *I will ~ (in) the cost with you.* 我将与你分摊费用。*She ~s (in) my troubles as well as (in) my joys.* 她和我苦乐与共。~ *and ~ alike,* have equal ~s with others in the use, enjoyment, expense, etc of sth. 均分;均享,均摊。

share² /ʃeəʳ; ʃɛr/ n blade of a plough. 犁头;犁刀。

shark /ʃɑːk; ʃɑrk/ n **1** sea-fish, some kinds of which are large and dangerous to bathers, etc. 鲨。⇨ the illus at **sea.** 参看 sea 之插图。**'~-skin** n textile fabric with a smooth and shiny surface, used for outer clothing: 鲨皮布(表面光滑发亮的一种织物,用制外衣): *a ~-skin jacket/suit.* 鲨皮布做的短上衣(套装)。**2** swindler; usurer. 骗子;放高利贷者。

sharp /ʃɑːp; ʃɑrp/ *adj* (**-er, -est**) **1** with a fine cutting edge; not blunt: 有利刃的;锋利的: *a ~ knife;* 快刀; with a fine point, able to make holes: 尖锐的: *a ~ pin/needle.* 尖锐的大头针(缝衣针)。**2** well-defined, clear-cut; distinct: 轮廓明显的; 周边清楚的;明晰的: *a ~ outline;* 明晰的轮廓; *a ~ image,* (in photography) one with clear contrasts between light and shade. 明暗对比明显的影像。**3** (of curves, slopes, bends) abrupt; changing direction quickly: (指曲线、斜坡、弯)陡峭的;急转的: *a ~ bend in the road;* 路上的一处急转弯; *a ~ turn to the left;* 向左的急转; **,~-'featured,** (of a person) having angular features. (指人)面部轮廓分明的。**4** (of sounds) shrill; piercing: (指声音)尖锐的; 刺耳的: *a ~ cry of distress.* 痛苦的尖叫声。**5** quickly aware of things; acute: 敏锐的;伶俐的;机警的: ~ *eyes/ears;* 灵敏的眼(耳); *a ~ intelligence;* 聪慧; *a ~ sense of smell;* 敏锐的嗅觉; *keep a ~ lookout,* 注意地守望着; *a ~ child;* 伶俐的小孩; ~ *at arithmetic.* 精于算术。**'~-shooter** n man skilled at shooting with a rifle. placed where accurate shooting (in war) is required. 神枪手;狙击手。Hence, 由此产生, **'~-'eyed** /**-'sighted** /**-'witted** *adjj* **6** (of feelings, taste) producing a physical sensation like cutting or pricking: (指感觉、味道)强烈刺激的;辛辣的;刺骨的;刺耳的: *a ~ pain;* 剧痛; *a ~ flavour;* 辛辣的味道; *a ~ frost.* 严寒。**7** harsh; severe; 尖刻的;苛刻的;厉害的;严厉的: ~ *words;* 尖刻的话; *a ~ rebuke;* 严厉的指责; *a ~ tongue,* of a person who speaks sarcastically, bitterly. 利舌。**8** quick; brisk; lively: 敏捷的;轻快的;活泼的;生气勃勃的: *go for a ~ walk;* 去作轻快的散步; *a ~ struggle/contest.* 有生气的奋斗(竞赛); *That was ~ work,* was finished or done quickly and energetically. 那是一鼓作气完成的工作。**9** quick to take advantage; unscrupulous: 精明的;狡猾的;不择手段的: *a ~ lawyer.* 狡猾的律师。*He was too ~ for me,* He got the better of me by being unscrupulous. 他太不择手段,我对付不了他。~ *practice,* business dealings that are not altogether honest. 诈骗的手段。**10** (music) above the normal pitch; (of a note) raised half a tone in pitch: (音乐)高调的;(指音符)升半音的;要音的: *C=(=C♯).* ⇨ **flat²**(4). ⇨ the illus at **notation.** 参看 notation 之插图。□ *n*

(music) ~ note; the symbol ♯ used to indicate a ~ note. (音乐)升半音音符;升半音记号(♯)。□ *adv* **1** punctually: 准时地: *at seven (o'clock) ~.* 七时整。**2** suddenly; abruptly: 突然地;急剧地: *turn ~ to the left.* 向左急转。**3** (music) above the true pitch: (音乐)升半音: *sing ~.* 升半音唱。**4** *look ~,* waste no time; hurry, 不要浪费时间; 赶快。**5** **'~-set** *adj* hungry. 饥饿的。**~en** /'ʃɑːpən; 'ʃɑrpən/ *vt, vi* [VP6A, 2A] make or become ~: 使尖锐;使急剧;变尖锐;变急剧: ~ *en a pencil.* 削铅笔。*This knife needs ~ening.* 这把刀子需要磨了。*The walk has ~ened my appetite.* 散步增进了我的食欲。**~-ener** /'ʃɑːpənə(r); 'ʃɑrpənə/ *n* sth that ~ens: 使尖锐或急剧之物; 磨具; 削具: *a 'pencil-~ener,* 铅笔刀(刨); *a 'knife-~ener.* 磨刀石(器)。**~er** *n* swindler, esp (**'card-~er**)person who makes a living by cheating at cards. 骗子;(尤指)赌纸牌为生的人(card-sharper)。**~·ly** *adv* in a ~ manner: 锋利地;尖地;明晰地;苛刻地: *a ~ly pointed pencil,* 笔尖尖的铅笔; *a ~ly defined image;* 轮廓分明的影像; ~ly. 严厉地回答。**~·ness** *n*

shat /ʃæt; ʃæt/ *pt, pp* of **shit.**

shat·ter /'ʃætə(r); 'ʃætəʳ/ *vt, vi* [VP6A, 2A] break suddenly and violently into small pieces: 突然而剧烈地破成碎片; 使粉碎;使破灭;损毁: *The explosion ~ed every window in the building.* 那次爆炸把该建筑物的窗户都震碎了。*Our hopes were ~ed.* 我们的希望破灭了。*What a nerve-~ing noise!* eg that of pneumatic drills or jet engines. 这种噪音真会使人神经崩溃!(如气压钻孔机或喷射引擎的声音)。**~·proof, ⇨ proof².**

shave /ʃeiv; ʃev/ *vt, vi* (*pt, pp* **~d** or, chiefly as *adj,* 主要用作形容词词 ~**n** /'ʃeivn; 'ʃevən/) **1** [VP6A, 2A, 15B] ~ *(off),* cut (hair) off the chin, etc with a razor: 剃去下颚等处之(毛发);刮(胡子);剃面;修面: *Do you ~ yourself or go to the barber's?* 你自己修面还是去理发店修面? *He has ~d off his beard.* 他已剃去胡子。*He doesn't ~ every day.* 他并不每天刮脸。**'shaving-brush** *n* brush for spreading lather over the face before shaving. 修面刷(刮脸前用以涂肥皂沫于脸上)。**2** [VP15B] ~ *sth off,* pare off (a thin layer, etc). 刨; 削; 刮去薄薄一层等。**3** [VP6A,15B] pass very close to, almost but not touching: 掠过; (几乎触及而)擦过: *The bus just ~d me by an inch.* 公共汽车从我身边一英寸左右处擦过。**4** ~**n** (*pp* as *adj*),**clean-~n, ,well-'~n,** having been ~d clean, well. 已剃(刮)干净的; 已剃(刮)好的。□ *n* [C] **1** shaving(of the face): 修(面); 薙; 刮: *A sharp razor gives a close ~.* 锋利的剃刀刮得很干净。*How much does a ~ cost?* 修面要多少钱? **2** close approach without touching. 掠过;擦过。(only in) (仅用于) *a close/narrow ~,* narrow escape from injury, danger, etc. 间不容发(逃脱伤害,危险等)。**~r** *n* **1** (electric) ~**r,** razor with an electric motor, operated from the mains or by a battery. 电动刮胡刀。⇨ the illus at **razor.** 参看razor之插图。**2** (joc, dated, usu *young* ~**r**) lad, youngster. 少年;年轻人。**shav·ings** *n pl* thin parings of wood ~**d** off (esp with a plane):薄木片;薄木屑;(尤指)刨花: *The floor of the carpenter's shop was covered with shavings.* 木匠店的地板上满是木屑刨花。

Shav·ian /'ʃeiviən; 'ʃeviən/ *adj, n* (in the manner) (devotee) of G B Shaw, Irish dramatist and critic. 戏剧家萧伯纳的;萧伯纳风格的;萧伯纳之崇拜者;致力于研究萧伯纳者。

shawl /ʃɔːl; ʃɔl/ *n* [C] large (usu square or oblong) piece of material worn about the shoulders or head of a woman, or wrapped round a baby (妇女或婴儿用之)披肩;围巾(通常为方形或长方形)。

she /ʃiː; ʃi/ *pron* (⇨ **her**) **1** female person, etc already referred to or implied: 她: *My sister says she is going for a walk.* 我姐姐(妹妹)说她要出去散步。*This cat's a she, not a he.* 这只猫是雌的,不是雄的。**3** (pref) (前缀) female: 女性; 雌性: *a 'she-goat/-ass, etc.* 雌山羊(驴等)。

sheaf /ʃiːf; ʃif/ *n* (*pl* **sheaves** /ʃiːvz; ʃivz/) **1** bundle of corn, barley, etc stalks tied together after reaping.

(收割后之小麦、大麦等之)束；捆。 **2** bundle of papers, arrows, etc laid lengthwise and tied together. (文件等之)束；扎。

shear /ʃɪə(r); ʃɪr/ vt (pt ~ed, pp shorn /ʃɔːn; ʃɔrn or ~ed) [VP6A] cut the wool off (a sheep with shears; (fig) strip bare of deprive of: (羊)毛；(喻)剥夺； They'll be ~ing (the sheep) next week. 他们将在下星期剪羊毛. shorn of, having lost completely: 完全失去： The gambler came home shorn of his money. 那赌徒回家,钱已输光.

shears /ʃɪəz; ʃɪrz/ n pl (pair of) ~, large cutting instrument shaped like scissors, used for shearing sheep, cutting cloth, etc. (用于剪羊毛、裁布等之)大剪刀；剪切机. ⇨ the illus at **tool**. 参看 tool 之插图.

sheath /ʃiːθ; ʃiθ/ n (pl ~s /ʃiːðz; ʃiðz/) **1** cover for the blade of a weapon or tool: 鞘；套： Put the dagger back in its ~. 把匕首放回鞘中. '~-knife n knife with a fixed blade, that fits into a ~. 刀身固定而插于鞘内的刀子. **2** ~-like cover (of tissue, skin, etc) fitting over part of an animal or plant (eg the 'wing-~ of some insects). 动植物之鞘状包覆物；鞘(如某些昆虫之翅鞘). (protective) ~, contraceptive device used on the penis. (避孕用的)保险套. **3** (attrib; dressmaking) close-fitting: (用作定语,女服裁制)紧身的： a ~ corset/gown. 紧身的束腹(长袍).

sheathe /ʃiːð; ʃið/ vt [VP6A] **1** put into a sheath: 插入鞘： ~ the sword, stop fighting. 休战. **2** protect with a casing or covering: 包覆;包护： a ship's bottom with copper. 以铜板包覆船底. **sheathing** n protective layer of boards, metal plates, etc eg on parts of a building, the underpart of a ship's hull. 屋顶(或墙壁)的内层板;覆板;覆套;船底包板.

sheaves /ʃiːvz; ʃivz/ ⇨ **sheaf**.

she-bang /ʃɪ'bæŋ; ʃə'bæŋ/ n the whole ~, the whole collection of facts or things; the whole situation, organization. 整个的事情；情况;组织.

she-been /ʃɪ'biːn; ʃɪ'bin/ n unlicensed public house (esp in Ireland and S Africa). 无执照的酒馆、客栈(尤指在爱尔兰与南非者).

shed[1] /ʃed; ʃed/ n building, roughly made structure, used for storing things ('tool-~, 'wood-~, 'coal-~, etc), for sheltering animals ('cattle-~), vehicles, etc ('engine-~, 'bicycle-~). 棚;小屋(用于储物者如 tool-shed 工具房, wood-shed 柴房, coal-shed 煤库; 用于安顿牲者如 cattle-shed 畜棚, 用于车辆等者如 engine-shed 机车车库, bicycle-shed 脚踏车棚).

shed[2] /ʃed; ʃed/ vt (pt, pp ~; -dd-) [VP6A] **1** let (leaves, etc) fall; let come off: 脱落(叶等); 褪;流出: Trees ~ their leaves and flowers ~ their petals. 树落叶, 花掉瓣. Some kinds of deer ~ their horns. 有些种鹿脱换鹿角. ~ (one's) blood, (a) be wounded or killed: 受伤或被杀死;流血: ~ one's blood for one's country. 为国家流血. (b) cause the blood of others to flow. 使他人流血. Hence, 由此产生, 'blood-~ n ~ tears, weep. 流泪;哭泣. **2** throw or take off; get rid of: 脱去；摆脱： People in the park began to ~ their clothes as it got hotter and hotter. 天气愈来愈热了, 公园里的人们开始脱去衣服. **3** spread or send out: 散开; 放射: a fire that ~s warmth; 发散温暖的炉火, a woman who ~s happiness around her; 向周遭散佈欢乐的女人, a lamp that ~s a soft light. 发射柔光的灯, ~, light on, (fig) make clear to the mind. (喻)阐明; 弄明白. **4** 'load-~ding, ⇨ load[1](3).

she'd /ʃiːd; ʃid/ = she had; she would.

sheen /ʃiːn; ʃin/ n [U] brightness; shiny quality: 光辉;光泽;光泽: the ~ of silk. 丝绸的光泽. That girl's hair has a ~ like gold. 那女孩的头发有金色的光泽.

sheep /ʃiːp; ʃip/ n (pl unchanged) (复数不变) grass-eating animal kept for its flesh as food (mutton) and its wool. 羊;绵羊. ⇨ the illus at **domestic**. 参看 domestic 之插图. ⇨ **ewe, lamb** and **ram**. separate the ~ from the goats, separate good from bad persons. 分辨善人与

恶人. ⇨ Matt 25: 33. 参看马太福音第 25 章第 33 节. cast/make ~'s eyes at, look at in an amorous but foolish way. 向…眉目传情; 向…愚蠢地送秋波. a wolf in ~'s clothing, a wicked man who pretends to be good. 假装善良的坏人. as well be hanged for a ~ as a lamb, commit a big crime rather than a small one if the punishment is the same. 如果所得处罚相同, 则宁愿犯大罪而舍小恶; 一不做二不休. black '~, ⇨ black(4). '~-dog n dog trained to help a shepherd to look after ~. 牧羊犬. ⇨ the illus at **domestic**. 参看 domestic 之插图. '~-fold n enclosure for ~. 羊栏; 羊舍. '~-run n tract of land (esp in Australia) on which ~ are pastured. (尤指澳大利亚之)大牧羊场. '~-skin n (a) rug of a ~'s skin with the wool on it; garment made of two or more such skins. 两面羊皮; 羊皮所制之衣服; 羊皮袄. (b) leather of ~'s skin used in book-binding, etc. (用于装订书籍等之)羊革. (c) parchment made from such skin; (esp US) diploma written on such parchment. 羊皮纸; (尤美)用羊皮纸书写的文凭; 证书. ~·ish /-ɪʃ; -ɪʃ/ adj **1** awkwardly self-conscious: 腼腆的; 不自在的; 局促不安的: a ~ish-looking boy. 局促不安的男孩. **2** (feeling) foolish or embarrassed by consciousness of a fault. (因意识到犯错而觉得)羞愧的; 困窘的. ~·ish·ly adv ~·ish·ness n

sheer[1] /ʃɪə(r); ʃɪr/ adj **1** complete; thorough; absolute: 全然的; 纯粹的; 绝对的: ~ nonsense; 毫无意义; 一派胡言; a ~ waste of time; 简直是浪费时间; by ~ chance. 完全出于偶然地. **2** (of textiles, etc) finely woven and almost transparent: (指织物等)细织而几乎透明的: stockings of ~ nylon. 透明尼龙丝袜. **3** without a slope; (almost) perpendicular: 无斜坡的; 陡峭的; (近乎)垂直的: a ~ drop of 50 feet; 五十英尺的垂直降落; a ~ rock. 陡峭的山壁. adv straight up or down: 陡峭地; 垂直地: a cliff that rises ~ from the beach. 矗立于海边上之悬崖. He fell 500 feet ~. 他垂直地落下五百英尺.

sheer[2] /ʃɪə(r); ʃɪr/ vi [VP2C] **1** ~ away/off, (esp of a ship) deviate from course. (尤指船)逸出路线; 偏航. **2** ~ off, (colloq) go away (from sb one dislikes, sb by whom one had been offended). (口)避开(不喜欢之人,曾犯其冒犯者).

sheet[1] /ʃiːt; ʃit/ n [C] **1** large rectangular piece of linen or cotton cloth, as used in pairs for sleeping between: 被单;褥单: put clean ~s on the bed. 铺平净的床单在床上. **2** broad, flat piece (of some thin material): 平板; 薄片: a ~ of glass/tin wrapping-paper/note-paper, etc; 一片玻璃/一片马口铁; 一张包装纸; 一张信纸等): ~ copper/iron, etc, rolled or hammered into thin ~s; 铜片(铁片等); ~ music, published in ~s, not in book form. 散页乐谱. The book is in ~s, ie in ~s of paper ready for binding. 这本书尚未装订(准备装订). **3** wide expanse (of water, ice, snow, flame, etc): (水、冰、雪、火等的)一片: The rain came down in ~s, very heavily. 大雨滂沱. '~-lightning n lightning that comes in sheet-like flashes of diffused brightness (not in zigzags, etc). 片状闪电(漫射或散光形式之闪电, 非呈锯齿形者). ~·ing n [U] material used for making ~s(1). 被单布;床单布.

sheet[2] /ʃiːt; ʃit/ n cord fastened at the lower corner of a sail to hold it and control the angle at which it is set. 帆脚索. ⇨ the illus at **sail**. 参看 sail 之插图. '~-anchor n (usu fig) sth on which one depends for security as a final resort when other things have failed. 副锚; (通常作喻)紧急时赖以获得安全之事物; 最后之依恃.

sheik(h) /ʃeɪk US: ʃiːk; ʃik/ n Arab chieftain, head of an Arab village tribe, etc. (阿拉伯的)酋长; 族长. ~·dom /-dəm; -dəm/ n

shekel /'ʃekl; 'ʃekl/ n ancient silver coin used by the Jews: (古犹太人使用之)银币; (复) money, riches. 钱;财富.

shel·drake /'ʃeldreɪk; 'ʃel,drek/ n (kinds of) fish-eating wild duck with brightly coloured feathers. 潦凫; 冠鸭(数种羽色鲜艳捕食鱼类的野鸭).

shelf /ʃelf; ʃɛlf/ n (pl **shelves** /ʃelvz; ʃɛlvz/) **1** flat, rectangular piece of wood, metal, glass or other material, fastened at right angles to a wall or in a cupboard, bookcase, cabinet, etc. 架子; 搁板. **on the ~, (a)** put aside as done with, eg of a person too old to continue working. (指年老不能继续工作之人等)投闲置散的; 搁在一旁的. **(b)** (colloq, of a woman) unmarried and considered as being unlikely to be asked to marry. (口, 指女人)无结婚希望的. **2** ~-like projection of rock on a cliff face, etc (as used by rock-climbers). 悬崖等上突出的岩石; 崖路; 岩棚(如爬岩之人使用者).

shell /ʃel; ʃɛl/ n [C] **1** hard outer covering of bird's eggs, nuts (eg walnuts, coconuts), some seeds (eg peas) and fruits, and of some animals (eg oysters, lobsters, snails) or parts of them. (鸟卵或胡桃、椰子等坚果之)壳; (豌豆等之)荚; (蚝、龙虾、蜗牛等动物之)介壳; 贝壳. ⇨ the illus at **mollusc**. 参看 mollusc 之插图. **go / retire into one's ~; come out of one's ~,** become / cease to be shy, reserved, uncommunicative. 变为(不再)羞怯沉默. **'~-fish** n kinds of molluscs (oysters, etc) and crustaceans (crabs, shrimps, etc) having ~s. 贝(如蚝等); 介壳类(如蟹、虾等). **2** walls, outer structure, of an unfinished building, ship, etc or of one of which the contents have been destroyed (eg by fire): (尚未完工之房屋、船等或内部被大火烧毁坏后之)框架; 骨架; 船体: Only the ~ of the factory was left when the fire had been extinguished. 火扑灭以后这工厂只剩下屋架了. **3** (US 美 = cartridge) metal case filled with explosive, to be fired from a large gun. 炮弹. Cf 参较 cartridge for rifles, shot-guns. 猎枪之 cartridge. ⇨ the illus at **cartridge**. 参看 cartridge 之插图. **'~-proof** adj so thickly or strongly built that a ~ cannot pierce it.防炮弹的. **'~-shock** n nervous or mental disorder caused by the noise and blast of bursting ~s. 炮弹休克; 弹震症(由炮弹之爆炸和震声所引起之精神病). **4** light racing-boat propelled by oarsmen. (竞赛用之)轻舟. □ vt, vi **1** [VP6A] take out of a ~ (1) (cf 参较 US 美 shuck): 去壳; 剥壳: It's as easy as ~ing peas, is very easy. 那就象剥豌豆一般的容易极了. These peas ~ easily, are easily ~ed. 这些豌豆容易剥. **2** [VP6A] fire ~s(3) at: 炮击: ~ the enemy's trenches. 炮击敌人之战壕. **3** ~ out, [VP15B, 2C] (colloq) pay up (money, a required sum): (口)付(款, 所需之数): I shall be expected to ~ out (the money) for the party. 我将要付出这个集会的费用.

shells

she'll /ʃiːl; ʃil/ = she will; she shall.

shel·lac /ʃəˈlæk; ʃəˈlæk/ n [U] resinous substance in the form of thin sheets used in making varnish and (formerly) gramophone records. 虫胶片(用以制造漆漆, 昔时并用以制唱片); 虫胶; 漆; 假漆. □ vt varnish with ~. 涂以虫漆.

shel·ter /ˈʃeltə(r); ˈʃɛltɚ/ n **1** [U] condition of being kept safe, eg from rain, danger: 庇护; 保护; 遮蔽(如使不受雨、危险等之侵害): take ~ from the rain, eg under a tree; 躲雨(如在树下等); get under ~, eg when bombs are dropping during an air raid. 获得掩蔽(如空袭投弹

时). **2** [C] sth that gives safety or protection, esp a hut, etc built to keep off wind and rain: 庇护物; 遮蔽物;(尤指)躲避风雨之处; 庇护所; 避难所: a bus ~, in which people wait for buses; 公共汽车候车亭; a taxi-drivers' ~, one where they wait until called by phone etc; 计程车行; 计程车候客站; an 'air-raid ~. 防空洞(壕). □ vt, vi **1** [VP6A, 14] ~ (from), give ~ to; protect: 庇护; 保护; 掩护: trees that ~ a house from cold winds; 遮蔽房屋使不受寒风侵袭之树木; ~ (=hide, protect) an escaped prisoner; 窝藏逃犯: dig trenches to ~ the men from gunfire; 挖战壕使兵士免受炮火的攻击; ~ sb from blame; 庇护某人不受责骂; ~ed trades, those which (like building and inland transport) are not exposed to foreign competition. 受保护的贸易. **2** [VP2A, C] take ~: 托庇; 隐匿: ~ from the rain; 躲雨; ~ under the trees. 避在树下.

shelve¹ /ʃelv; ʃɛlv/ vt [VP6A] **1** put (books, etc) on a shelf. 置(书等)于架上. **2** (fig, of problems, plans, etc) postpone dealing with; defer consideration of. (喻, 指问题、计划等)搁置; 缓议. **3** cease to employ (a person). 解雇; 辞退.

shelve² /ʃelv; ʃɛlv/ vi [VP2A, C] (of land) slope gently: (指土地)渐次倾斜: The shore ~s down to the sea. 海岸向海渐次倾斜.

shelves /ʃelvz; ʃɛlvz/ pl of shelf.

shep·herd /ˈʃepəd; ˈʃɛpɚd/ n man who takes care of sheep. 牧羊人. **the Good S~,** Jesus Christ. 好牧人(耶稣基督). **~'s pie,** [U] minced meat baked under mashed potatoes. (以捣烂之马铃薯焙成之)肉饀马铃薯饼. **~'s plaid,** small black and white check pattern in cloth. 黑白色棋盘图案花布. □ vt [VP6A, 15A] take care of; guide or direct (people) like sheep: 照看; 似牧羊般引领或指导(人群): The passengers were ~ed across the tarmac to the airliner. 旅客们被引导走过柏油碎石路道上飞机. **~·ess** /ˈʃepəˈdes US: ˈʃɛpɚdes; ˈʃɛpɚdɪs/ n woman ~ (esp as idealized in pastoral poetry). 女牧羊人(尤指牧歌中理想化者).

Shera·ton /ˈʃerətən; ˈʃɛrətṇ/ n [U] 18th-century style of furniture (in GB): (英国)十八世纪之雪里顿式家具; (attrib) (用作定语) ~ chairs. 雪里顿式椅子.

sher·bet /ˈʃɜːbət; ˈʃɝbɪt/ n [C, U] (glass of) cooling drink of sweetened fruit juices, sometimes effervescent (made from powder); (US) water-ice. (一杯)加糖之清凉果汁饮料; (美)冰糕.

sher·iff /ˈʃerɪf; ˈʃɛrɪf/ n **1** (usu 通常作 **High S~**) chief officer of the Crown in counties and certain cities, with legal and ceremonial duties. (郡或若干城市之)担任法律及礼仪职务的主要政府官吏; 行政司法长官. **2** (US) chief law-enforcing officer of a county. (美)一郡执行法律的主要官员; 郡长; 郡警察局长.

sherry /ˈʃeri; ˈʃɛri/ n [U] yellow or brown fortified wine of S Spain; similar kinds of wine from S Africa, Cyprus, etc. 雪利酒(西班牙南部所产加有烈酒之黄色或褐色葡萄酒); (南非, 塞浦路斯等地所产类似的)葡萄酒.

she's /ʃiːz; ʃiz/ = she is; she has.

Shet·land /ˈʃetlənd; ˈʃɛtlənd/ n (also 亦作 **the ~s**) group of islands NNE of Scotland. 设德兰群岛(苏格兰北北东方之群岛). ~ **pony,** small, hardy breed. 设德兰驹(该地所产之耐劳的小马). ~ **wool,** soft, fine kind spun in the S ~s. 设德兰羊毛或毛线.

shew /ʃəʊ; ʃo/ ⇨ **show**.

shib·bol·eth /ˈʃɪbəleθ; ˈʃɪbəlθ/ n [C] **1** custom whose use is regarded as a criterion for distinguishing membership of a group. 作为辨别某一团体份子之标准的习惯. **2** old-fashioned and now generally abandoned custom which was at one time considered to be essential: 过去认为必要而现在一般已抛弃的陈旧习俗: the outworn ~s of the past. 不合时宜的旧习俗.

shied /ʃaɪd; ʃaɪd/ ⇨ **shy²**, **shy³**.

shield /ʃiːld; ʃild/ n [C] **1** piece of armour (metal, leather, wood) carried on the arm, to protect the body when fighting; representation of a ~, eg carved on a

stone gateway, showing a person's coat of arms. 盾(甲胄之一件,金属质、皮质或木质,佩于臂,打仗时用以保护身体);盾形纹徽(如刻于石门框上,显示某人纹章之盾形物)。⇨ **arms.** ⇨ the illus at **armour.** 参看 armour 之插图。**2** (fig) person or thing that protects. (喻)保护之人或物。**3** (in machinery, etc) protective plate or screen; sth designed to keep out dust, wind, etc. (US 美 *wind~* = GB 英 *windscreen.*) (机器等中之)护板;护幕;防尘板;挡风板;遮泥板。□ *vt* [VP6A, 15A] protect; keep safe; save (sb) from punishment or suffering: 保护;防御;使(某人)免于惩罚或痛苦; *~ one's eyes with one's hand;* 用手保护眼睛; *~ a friend from censure.* 使朋友不受责难。

shift[1] /ʃɪft; ʃɪft/ *n* **1** change of place or character; substitution of one thing for another: 位置或性格的改变;变换;更易: *a ~ in emphasis,* placing the emphasis differently. 重点的改变。**2** [C] group of workmen who start work as another group finishes; period for which such a group works: 轮值之一班(在另一班下工时开始工作者);换班;轮值之时间: *on the day/night ~;* 日(夜)班轮值; *an eight-hour ~;* 八小时的轮值时间; *working in ~s.* 轮值工作。**3** dodge, trick, scheme, way of evading a difficulty, of getting sth: (逃避困难,获得某物之)计谋;方策;手段: *resort to dubious ~s in order to get some money.* 使用有问题的手段以期获得一些钱。*As a last desperate ~, he pawned his wife's wedding ring.* 他最后迫不得已只好把妻子的结婚戒指当掉。***make ~ (with sth/to do sth),*** manage or contrive, be able somehow or other: 设法;尽量想办法: *We must make ~ with the money we have.* 我们必须就我们所有的钱设法(维持生活等)。*He must make ~ without help.* 他必须自已想办法。⇨ *make~* at **make**[1]**(29). 4** woman's narrow dress without a waistline; (old use) chemise. 布袋装;(旧用法)连身衬裙。**5 ('gear-)~,** (motoring) mechanism for gear change: (驾车)排挡;排挡杆: *Do you prefer a manual to an automatic gear-~?* 你是不是比较喜欢手排挡而不大喜欢自动排挡呀? **~·less** *adj* without ability to find ways of doing things; unable to get on in life. 没有办事能力的;没有谋生能力的。

shift[2] /ʃɪft; ʃɪft/ *vt, vi* [VP6A, 14, 15A, 2A, C] **1** ***~ sth (from/to),*** change position or direction; transfer: 改变位置或方向;移动;更易: *~ a burden from one shoulder to the other;* 将负担自一肩移至另一肩上; *~ the blame (on) to sb else.* 诿过于他人。*Will you help me to ~ the furniture about/round please?* 请你帮助我移动家具,好吗? *The wind has ~ed to the north.* 风转向北吹。*The cargo has ~ed,* has been shaken out of place by the movement of the ship. 船货已因船身的颠簸而移动了位置。*Don't try to ~ the responsibility on to me.* 不要企图把责任推给我。***~ one's ground,*** take up a new position, approach the subject in a different way, during an argument. 采取新的立场;(辩论中)改变论据。**2** (motoring) change (gears): (驾车)变换(排挡): *~ into second/third gear.* 换成二(三)挡。**3 *~ for oneself,*** manage as best one can (to make a livelihood, get sth done) without help: 自谋生计;自行设法完成某事: *When their father died the children had to ~ for themselves.* 爸爸死后,孩子们只好自谋生活。**shifty** *adj* **(-ier, -iest)** untrustworthy; deceitful; not straightforward: 不可靠的;诡诈的;不正直的: *a ~y customer;* 不可靠的家伙; *~y behaviour;* 不正直的行为; *~y eyes.* 诡诈的眼睛。**~·ily** /-ɪlɪ; -ɪlɪ/ *adv* **~i·ness** *n*

shil·ling /ˈʃɪlɪŋ; ˋʃɪlɪŋ/ *n* **1** (until 1971) British coin with the value of twelve pennies, one-twentieth of a pound. (到1971年止)先令(英国钱币,值十二便士,为一英镑的二十分之一)。⇨ **App 4.** 参看附录四。**2** basic monetary unit of Kenya, Uganda and Tanzania, equal to 100 cents. 肯尼亚、乌干达、坦桑尼亚的基本货币单位,相当于100分。

shilly-shally /ˈʃɪlɪ ʃælɪ; ˋʃɪlɪˌʃælɪ/ *vi* [VP2A] be unable to make up one's mind; be undecided. 犹豫不决;踌躇;逡巡。□ *n* [U] indecision. 犹豫不决;踌躇;逡巡。

shim·mer /ˈʃɪmə(r); ˋʃɪmə/ *vi* [VP2A, C], *n* [U] (shine with a) wavering soft or faint light: 发闪光;闪光: *moonlight ~ing on the lake;* 湖上月光闪烁: *the ~ of pearls.* 珍珠的闪光。

shin /ʃɪn; ʃɪn/ *n* front part of the leg below the knee 外胫。⇨ the illus at **leg.** 参看 leg 之插图。**'~-bone** *n* tibia. 胫骨。⇨ the illus at **skeleton.** 参看 skeleton 之插图。**'~-guard** *n* pad worn on the ~ at football. (踢足球用的)护胫。□ *vi* **(-nn-)** [VP3A] ***~ up,*** climb up (using arms and legs to grip sth): (用手臂和腿攀着某物)往上爬: *~ up a tree.* 爬上一棵树。

shin·dig /ˈʃɪndɪg; ˋʃɪndɪg/ *n* (sl) (俚) **1** lively and noisy party. 狂欢会;舞会;庆祝会。**2** (= *shindy*) brawl. 吵闹;喧嚣;骚动。

shindy /ˈʃɪndɪ; ˋʃɪndɪ/ *n* [C] (*pl* **-dies**) (colloq) brawl; noisy disturbance: (口)吵闹;喧嚣;骚动: *kick up a ~.* 引起一阵骚动。

shine /ʃaɪn; ʃaɪn/ *vi, vt* (*pt, pp* **shone** /ʃɒn *US:* ʃəʊn; ʃon/ but ⇨ **2** below) **1** [VP2A, C] give out or reflect light; be bright (lit or fig); excel in some way: 发光;反射光;照耀(字面或喻);卓越;出众: *The moon is shining.* 月光在照耀。*The sun shone out,* suddenly began to ~ (as clouds moved). 太阳(穿云而出)重新照耀大地。*His face shone with excitement.* 他脸上露出兴奋的神色。*He does not ~ in conversation,* is not a good talker. 他不健谈。*I don't ~ at tennis.* 我不擅长网球。**2** [VP6A] (colloq, and with *pp* ~d) polish (which is more usu); make bright: (口,过去分词作 ~d) 磨光;擦亮(polish 较常用);使发亮;使照耀; *~ shoes.* 擦鞋。*Have you ~d your shoes/the brass?* 你把你的鞋子(那铜器)擦亮了吗? □ *n* **1** (*sing* only) polish; brightness: (仅用单数)刷擦;光亮;光辉: *Give your shoes a good ~.* 把你的鞋好好擦一下。*How can I take the ~ out of the seat of my trousers?* 我怎样才能把裤臀上的亮光去掉? **2** [U] ***come rain or ~,*** whatever the weather may be; (fig) whatever may happen. 不论晴雨;(喻)无论如何。**shiny** *adj* **(-ier, -iest)** polished; rubbed bright: 擦亮的;磨光的: *a shiny coat,* one with the nap rubbed off (so that the surface ~s). 磨去布毛而发光的外衣。

shingle[1] /ˈʃɪŋgl; ˋʃɪŋgl/ *n* [U] small, rounded pebbles on the seashore. 海滨之小圆石。**shin·gly** /ˈʃɪŋglɪ; ˋʃɪŋglɪ/ *adj* of ~: 海滨小圆石的: *I prefer a sandy beach to a shingly beach.* 我宁爱沙滩而不喜欢有小圆石的海滩。

shingle[2] /ˈʃɪŋgl; ˋʃɪŋgl/ *n* [C] **1** small, flat square or oblong piece of wood used (like tiles and slates) on roofs, spires and walls. 盖板;屋顶板;木瓦;墙面板。**2** (US colloq) small, wooden signboard (used by lawyers, dentists, etc): (美口)木质小招牌(律师、牙医等用之): *put up one's ~,* set up for the first time, eg as a doctor. 挂牌;开业(如医师等)。□ *vt* cover (a roof, etc) with ~s: 以屋顶板盖(屋顶等): *a ~d church spire.* 以屋顶板覆盖之教堂尖顶。

shingle[3] /ˈʃɪŋgl; ˋʃɪŋgl/ *vt* [VP6A] cut (a woman's hair) so that it is short at the back but longer at the sides. 将(女发)剪成后短侧长的发式。□ *n* this kind of haircut. 后短侧长的女发式。

shingles /ˈʃɪŋglz; ˋʃɪŋglz/ *n* (with *sing v*) skin disease forming a band of inflamed spots (often round the waist). (用单数动词)带状疱疹(常生于腰际)。

ship[1] /ʃɪp; ʃɪp/ *n* **1** sea-going vessel of considerable size: 海船;舰: *a 'sailing-~;* 帆船; *a 'merchant-~;* 商船; *a 'war~,* etc; 战舰(等); *take ~,* go on board a ~; 上船; *the ~'s company,* the entire crew; 全体船员; *the ~'s articles,* the terms on which seamen are engaged; 雇用船员合同; *the ~'s papers,* the documents showing ownership, nationality, nature of the cargo, etc. 船证;船照(记有船主、国籍、船货之性质等)。⇨ the illus at **barque.** 参看 barque 之插图。***when my '~ comes in/home,*** when I have made my fortune. 等我有钱的时候。***on '~·board,*** on board ~. 在船上。**2** (colloq) spacecraft; (US colloq) aircraft. (口)太空船;(美口)飞机。**3** (compounds) (复合词) **'~('s) biscuit,** hard, coarse biscuit used, in former times, during long voyage. 一种

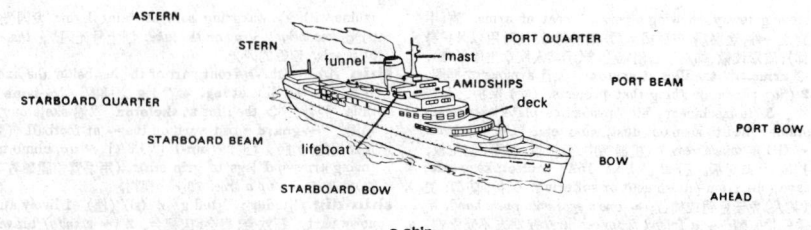

ASTERN · STERN · funnel · mast · PORT QUARTER · AMIDSHIPS · deck · PORT BEAM · STARBOARD QUARTER · PORT BOW · STARBOARD BEAM · lifeboat · BOW · STARBOARD BOW · AHEAD

a ship

粗硬的饼干(昔日远航时所备用者). '~·breaker *n* contractor who buys and breaks up old ~s (for scrap). 收购并拆散废船之承包人(以获取废铁). '~·broker *n* agent of a shipping company who does a ~'s business in port; one who buys, sells and charters ~s; agent for marine insurance. 船舶经纪人; 买、卖和租雇船舶者; 水险掮客. '~·builder *n* one whose business is building ~s. 造船者. Hence, 由此产生, '~·building *n* [U]: *building yard*, ~ yard. 船坞; 造船所. '~·canal *n* canal large enough for sea-going vessels. (可供海船航行的)运河. '~'s-chandler *n* one who deals in equipment for ~s. 船具商. '~·load *n* as much cargo, or as many passengers, as a ~ can carry. 船载量. '~·mate *n* fellow sailor; person belonging to the same ~ as another: 同船水手; 同船同事: *Harry and I were ~mates in 1962.* 一九六二年哈利和我是同船同事. '~·owner *n* person who owns a ~ or ~s, or shares in a shipping company. 船主; 船公司股东. '~·shape *adj* tidy; in good order. 整齐的; 井然有序的. □ *adv* in a ~shape manner. 整齐地; 井然有序地. '~·way *n* sloping structure on which a ~ is built and down which it slides into the water. 造船台; 下水台. '~·wreck *n* [U] loss or destruction of a ~ at sea by storm, collision, etc: 船舶之损失或失事; 船难: *suffer ~ wreck*: 遭受船难; [C] instance of this. 船难之实例. □ *vt* cause to suffer ~wreck; destroy by ~wreck. 使遭船难; 使毁于船难. '~·wright *n* ~builder. 造船者. '~·yard *n* place where ~s are built. 船坞; 造船所.

ship² /ʃɪp; ʃɪp/ *vt, vi* (**-pp-**) 1 [VP6A, 15A, B] put, take, send, in a ship: 装上船; 用船运: ~ *gold to India*: 用船运黄金前往印度; (comm) take, send, by train, road, etc: (商)以火车, 公路等运送: ~ *goods by express train.* 以特快火车运送货物. ~ *off*, send: 送往; 遣去: ~ *off young men to the war.* 送年轻人赴战场. 2 [VP6A] ~ *oars*, take them out of the water into the boat. 把桨自水中取出置于船上. ~ *water*; ~ *a sea*, be flooded by water breaking over the side. 水自舷侧进入船舱. 3 [VP6A, 15A, 2C] engage for service on a ship: 在船上服务;雇用(船员): ~ *a crew for a voyage round the world.* 雇用环航世界的一批水手. *He ~ped* (= took service) *as a steward on an Atlantic liner.* 他在航行大西洋的一艘邮轮上担任服务员. ~·**ment** *n* [U] putting of goods, etc on a ship; [C] quantity of goods ~ped. 装船; 装运; 所装运之货量. ~·**per** *n* person who arranges for goods to be ~ped. 安排装运货物之人. ~·**ping** *n* [U] all the ships of a country, port, etc. (一国、一海港等的)船舶总数. '~·**ping-agent** *n* shipowner's representative at a port. 船主在港口之代理人; 水路运输业者. '~·**ping-office** *n* ~ping-agent's office; office where seamen are engaged. 水路运输业者之事务所; 海员雇用所.

shire /ʃaɪə(r); ʃaɪr/ *n* [C] county (now chiefly used as a suffix in the names of certain counties, and can pronounced /-ʃə(r); -ʃə/): (英国的)郡(现在主要用作某些郡名的后缀, 通常读作 /-ʃər; -ʃə/); *Hampshire*, 汉普郡(在英格兰南部); *Yorkshire.* 约克郡(在英格兰北部). **the ~s**, certain midland counties of England and parts of these well known for foxhunting. 英国中部以 shire 为后缀之各郡; 这些郡以猎狐出名的各地方. '~**horse**, powerful breed of horse used for pulling carts and

wagons. (用于拖车之)大种马.

shirk /ʃɜːk; ʃɝk/ *vt, vi* [VP6A, D, 2A] avoid, try to escape (doing sth, responsibility, duty, etc.) 规避; 躲避(做某事, 尽责任, 义务等): ~ *going to the dentist*: 规避去看牙医; ~ *work/school.* 规避工作 (逃学). *He's ~ing.* 他在躲避. ~·**er** *n*

shirt /ʃɜːt; ʃɝt/ *n* man's loose-fitting garment for the upper part of the body (of cotton, linen, silk, etc) usu worn under a jacket, with long sleeves or ('*sports* ~) half sleeves. 男衬衣; 衬衫(短袖衬衫称作 '*sports* ~). *in one's '~-sleeves*, not wearing a jacket or coat. 未穿外衣. *keep one's ~ on*, (sl) keep one's temper. (俚)不发脾气; 保持冷静. *put one's ~ on* (a horse, etc), bet all one has on. 以所有的钱下注(某马等). '~-**front** *n* usu stiffened and starched breast of a white ~. 白衬衣的前胸 (通常浆硬). '~·**waister** (US 美 '~-**waist**) woman's blouse or dress that buttons down the front. 宽松的女上衣(由正面扣钮扣). ~·**ing** *n* material for making ~s. 衬衣衣料. ~·**y** *adj* (**-ier, -iest**) (sl) ill-tempered. (俚)坏脾气的; 发怒的.

shish kebab /ˌʃɪʃ kəˈbæb US: ˈʃɪʃ kəbæb; ˈʃɪʃkəˌbab/ *n* dish of pieces of meat roasted and served on skewers. 烤肉; 叉烧肉.

shit /ʃɪt; ʃɪt/ (⚠, not in polite use) *n* [U] 1 excrement. 排泄物; 粪便. 2 (sl) hashish (俚)大麻烟. 3 (contemptuous for a) person: (蔑)人: *You big ~!* 你这个大笨蛋! □ *vi* (**-tt-**) (*pt, pp* ~**ted** or **shat** /ʃæt; ʃæt/) [VP2A, 3A] empty the bowels of excrement. 排泄粪便; 大便. ~ *on sb*, (vulg sl) (鄙, 俚) (a) severely scold or find fault with him. 严厉责骂某人; 找某人的碴儿. (b) report on him, esp to the police. (尤指向警方)密告某人. □ *int* ⚠ (vulg) (as an expression of irritation or objection) Bother! Rubbish! (俚) (鄙)(表示愤怒或反对)讨厌! 胡说!

shiver¹ /ˈʃɪvə(r); ˈʃɪvɚ/ *vi* [VP2A, C] tremble, esp from cold or fear: 颤抖(尤指因寒冷或恐惧): ~*ing all over with cold*; 冷得全身颤抖; ~*ing like a leaf.* 象树叶一般地颤抖. □ *n* 1 trembling that cannot be controlled: (无法控制的)颤抖. *The sight sent cold ~s down my back.* 那景象使我的背脊打了一股冷颤. 2 (pl) (复) *get/have/give sb the ~s*, (colloq) get/give sb ~ing movements, a feeling of fear or horror. (口)发抖(使某人颤栗). ~·**y** *adj* inclined to ~; having or causing a feeling of cold, fear, horror. 易颤抖的; 感到或引起寒冷, 害怕, 恐惧的.

shiver² /ˈʃɪvə(r); ˈʃɪvɚ/ *n* (usu *pl*) one of the many small pieces into which sth is broken. (通常用复数)碎片; 破片: *break sth to ~s*; 把某物打碎; *burst into ~s.* 变粉碎. □ *vt, vi* [VP15A, 2C] break into ~s. 打碎; 碎裂.

shoal¹ /ʃəʊl; ʃol/ *n* [C] great number of fish swimming together; great number of (people, things): 鱼群(人, 物之)大群; 大量: *a ~ of herring*, 一群鲱鱼; *swimming in ~s.* 成群地游. □ *vi* (of fish) form ~s. (指鱼)成群; 群集.

shoal² /ʃəʊl; ʃol/ *n* [C] shallow place in the sea, esp where there are sandbanks; (*pl; fig*) hidden dangers. 海洋之水浅处(尤指有沙洲的地方); 浅滩; (复; 喻)隐伏的危险. □ *vi* [VP2A] become shallow(er). 变浅或更浅.

shock¹ /ʃɒk; ʃɑk/ n 1 [C] violent blow or shaking
(eg as caused by a collision or explosion): 冲击; 震动(例
如因相撞或爆炸所引起): the ~ of a fall; 落地的冲击;
earthquake ~s. 地震引起的颤动。'~ absorber n kinds
of device fitted to motor-vehicles, aircraft, etc to lessen
~s and add to the cushioning effects of tyres, springs,
etc. (汽车,飞机等之) 减震器(减少震动并增加轮胎、弹簧
等缓冲效果的器械)。 '~ tactics, use of massed forces to
attack (in war). (作战中)密集袭击法; 突袭战术。 '~
troops, troops specially trained for violent assaults. 突
击部队。 '~·brigade, '~·workers, (esp in USSR) body
of workers engaged in specially arduous work. (尤指苏
联之)担任特别艰巨工作的工人组织; 工人突击队。 ~
wave, region of intensely high air pressure caused by
an atomic explosion or aircraft moving at supersonic
speed. (由原子爆炸或超音速飞机所引起的)空气激流; 冲
击波; 激波。 2 [C] effect caused by the passage of an
electric current through the body: 电震; 电击(电流通
过身体所引起者): If you touch that live wire you'll
get a ~. 如果你接触那条已经通电的电线,你就会遭电
击。 3 [C] sudden and violent disturbance of the
feelings or the nervous system (caused by bad news,
severe injury, etc); [U] condition caused by such a
disturbance: 休克(因坏消息,重伤等引起的情绪或神经系
统之突然而激烈的障害); 休克所引起的状况; 震惊; 激动:
The news of her mother's death was a terrible ~ to her.
她母亲死亡的消息使她极为震惊。 The stock market
quickly recovered from the ~ of the election results. 证
券市场迅速地由选举结果所引起的震动中恢复了常态。 It
gave me quite a ~ to learn that he had married again. 听
说他再婚,我感到很震惊。 He died of ~ following an
operation on the brain. 他死于大脑手术后所发生的休克。
⇨ shell-~ at shell(3). '~ treatment / therapy,
treatment of (esp mental) disorder by using electric
~s or drugs on the nervous system. (电击神经系统或
给予神经系统药物以治疗精神病之)休克疗法。 □ vt
[VP6A] cause ~ to: 使休克; 使震惊; 使惊骇; 使骇异: I was ~ed
at the news of her death. 她死去的消息使我震惊。 He
was ~ed to hear his daughter swearing. 听到女儿赌咒他
甚为震骇。 I'm not easily ~ed, but that book really is
obscene. 我不容易感到震惊,但那本书实在太猥亵。 ~er
n 1 person who ~s: He's a ~er, a
~ingly bad person. 他是个大坏蛋。 2 sth that ~s, eg
a sensational novel; bad specimen of sth. 令人震惊之事
物(如黄色或恐怖小说); 某物的坏品; 坏的事例。 ~·ing
adj 1 very bad or wrong: 极坏的; 大错的: ~ing
behaviour. 极坏的行为。 2 causing ~(3): 令人震惊的;
可怕的: ~ing news, eg of a flood that causes great loss
of life. 令人震惊的消息(如导致重大死亡之水灾等)。 3
(colloq) bad: (口)坏的; 不好的: a ~ing dinner; 不好的
餐食; ~ing handwriting. 不好的书法。 □ adv (colloq,
as an intensive) very: (口,用作强势语)甚; 极: a ~ing
bad cold. 极为严重的感冒。 ~·ing·ly adv 1 badly: 恶
劣地: You're playing ~ingly. 你玩得极不高明。 2
extremely: 极端地: How ~ingly expensive! 太贵了!
shock² /ʃɒk; ʃɑk/ n number of sheaves of grain placed
together and supporting each other in a field to dry
during harvest. 在收获季,若干捆禾谷成堆放置田里,彼
此支撑,以便晒干之)禾束堆。
shock³ /ʃɒk; ʃɑk/ n (usu 通常作 ~ of hair) rough,
untidy mass of hair (on sb's head): (某人头上之)蓬乱
的头发。 '~·headed adj having such hair. 头发蓬乱的。
shod /ʃɒd; ʃɑd/ pt, pp of shoe.
shoddy /'ʃɒdɪ; 'ʃɑdɪ/ n [U] (cloth of poor quality,
made from) fibre from old cloth, etc. 旧布等之纤维; 用
旧布等之纤维再织成的布。 □ adj (-ier, -iest) of poor
quality; made to seem better than it is: 质劣的; 冒充好
货的: ~ cloth; 用旧料之纤维再织成的布; a ~ piece of
work. 劣品。
shoe /ʃuː; ʃu/ n 1 (often 常作 pair of ~s) outer
covering for the foot, esp one which does not reach

above the ankle (⇨ boot): 鞋(尤指鞋面未及足踝者):
put on / take off one's ~s. 穿鞋(脱鞋)。 be in / put
oneself in 'sb's ~s, occupy, imagine oneself to be in,
his position; be in his plight: 处于他人之地位; 居于他人
之处境: I wouldn't be in your ~s for a thousand pounds.
给我一千英镑我也不愿处于你那种地位。 know where
the ~ pinches, understand from one's own experience
all about hardships, etc. 知道困苦等之所在。 2 (compounds) (复合词) '~·black n boy or man who polishes
~s of passers-by. 擦鞋童; 擦鞋匠。 '~·horn n device
with a curved blade for getting the heel easily into a
~. 鞋拔。 '~·lace n cord for fastening the edges of a
shoe's uppers. 鞋带。 '~·leather n leather suitable for
making ~s. 制鞋用的皮革。 '~·maker n person who
makes and / or repairs ~s and boots. 鞋匠。 '~·making
n [U] trade of a ~ maker. 制鞋; 做鞋业。 '~·string n
(US) (美) = ~lace. do sth on a ~string, do sth (eg
start a business) on a very small amount of capital. 以
极少的资本做某事(如创业等)。 '~·tree n thin, flexible,
shaped block for inserting in a shoe to keep its shape.
鞋楦。 3 (horse-) /'hɔːʃʃuː; 'hɔrʃʃu/, metal band
nailed to the hoof of a horse: 蹄铁: His horse cast /
threw a ~, lost one. 他的马掉了一块蹄铁。 4 part of a
brake that presses against the wheel or drum (of a
bicycle, motor-vehicle, etc); any object like a ~ in
appearance or use. 车辆的闸皮; 形状或用途似鞋之物。
□ vt (pt, pp shod /ʃɒd; ʃɑd/) [VP6A] fit with ~s:
穿以鞋; 钉以蹄铁; 配以鞋状物: well shod for wet weather,
having good ~s able to keep out the wet; 穿着防雨良
好之鞋; an iron-shod stick, one with an iron ferrule at
the end. 装有铁包头的手杖。
sho·gun /'ʃəuɡuːn US: -ɡʌn; 'ʃoʊɡʌn/ n (until 1867)
hereditary commander-in-chief of the Japanese army
(1867 年以前)日本陆军世袭统帅; 幕府将军。
shone /ʃɒn US: ʃəun; ʃɒn/ pt, pp of shine.
shoo /ʃuː; ʃu/ int cry used for driving away birds,
etc. (驱赶鸟等的)嘘声。 □ vt (pt, pp ~ed) [VP15B]
~ sth / sb away / off, drive away by making this cry.
以嘘声驱赶某物(某人)。
shook /ʃuk; ʃuk/ pt of shake.
shoot¹ /ʃuːt; ʃut/ n [C] 1 new, young growth on a
plant or bush: (植物或灌木之)芽; 苗; 嫩枝: train the
new ~s of a vine. 整理藤蔓的新枝。 2 = chute(1, 2).
3 party of people shooting for sport; area of land over
which birds, etc are shot: 狩猎队; 狩猎地: rent a ~ for
the season. 租狩猎地以供狩猎季节之用。
shoot² /ʃuːt; ʃut/ vi, vt (pt, pp shot /ʃɒt; ʃɑt/) 1
[VP2C, 15A, B] move, come, go, send, suddenly or
quickly (out, in, up, forth, etc): 突然或迅速地动, 来,
去, 送: The snake's tongue shot out. 蛇舌突然伸出。 The
snake shot its tongue out. 蛇突然伸舌。 Flames were ~ing
up from the burning house. 火焰自燃烧着的房子冒出。
The meteor shot across the sky. 陨星快速地掠过天空。
The horse stumbled and the rider was shot over its head.
马绊脚, 骑者由马头上面跌了下来。 As the car hit the tree
the occupants were shot out. 汽车撞在树上的时候, 车内的
人被掉了出来。 At the half-way mark, Hill shot ahead,
(in a race) came on quickly and passed his competitors.
在赛跑的半途, 希尔突然冲前领先。 They shot angry
glances at us. 他们对我们投以愤怒的眼色。 Rents have
shot up, (= risen suddenly) in the last few months. 在
过去几个月之中, 租金突然上涨了。 Tom is ~ing up fast,
quickly growing tall. 汤姆长高得很快。 She shot an
angry look at him / shot him an angry look. 她对他投以
愤怒的眼光。 ~ a bolt, send a bolt (of a door, etc) into
(or out of) its fastening. 关上或打开(门等)的插销。 ~
one's bolt, make one's last effort. 做最后的努力。 ~
dice, throw dice. 掷骰子。 ~ rubbish, let it slide from
a cart, etc (on to a heap or dump). 从车上等处倾倒垃
圾。 ~ing 'star, meteor which burns up as it passes
into and through the earth's atmosphere. 流星(进入并
穿过大气层时燃烧的陨石)。 2 [VP2A, C] (of plants,

bushes) sprout; send out new twigs or branches from a stem: (用花草, 灌木)发芽; 生枝: *Rose bushes ~ again after being cut back.* 玫瑰丛修剪后会再发新枝。 **3** [VP2A, C] (of pain) pass with a stabbing sensation suddenly and swiftly: (指疼痛)刺痛; 剧痛: *The pain shot up his arm.* 他的臂刺痛。 *I have a ~ing pain in my left leg.* 我的左腿剧痛。 **4** [VP6A] (of boats) move, be moved, rapidly over, through, etc: (指船)迅速通过: ~ *the rapids;* 迅速通过急流; ~ *the bridge,* 随着水流迅速穿过桥下。 **5** [VP6A, 15A, B, 2A, C, 4A] aim and fire with a gun or revolver; aim with a bow and send an arrow at; hit with a shell, bullet, arrow, etc; wound or kill (a person, animal, etc) by doing this: 放(炮); 打(枪); 射(箭); 以炮弹, 子弹, 箭等打击; 射伤; 射杀(人; 动物等): *They were ~ing at a target.* 他们在向目标射击。 *He ~s well.* 他善于射击。 *He shot an arrow from his bow.* 他射出弓上的箭。 *Can you/Does your gun ~ straight?* 你(你的枪)能命中吗? *The soldier was shot* (= executed by ~ing) *for desertion.* 那兵士因逃亡而被枪决。 *The police did not ~ to kill,* They used their weapons only to frighten the people (eg by firing over their heads). 警察鸣枪镇压(非为射杀人而开枪)。 *He's in Africa ~ing lions.* 他在非洲猎狮。 *He neither rides, ~s nor fishes,* does not take part in these sports. 他不骑马, 不射击, 也不钓鱼。 *He fell like a shot rabbit,* like a rabbit that had been shot. 他象被射中的兔子那样摔在地上。 ~ *away,* (more usu 较常用 *fire away*) **(a)** keep on and continue ~ing. 开始不停地射击。 **(b)** (fig) go ahead; begin. (喻)开始。 ~ *sth away,* (more usu 较常用 *fire sth away*) get rid of by ~ing: 射完: ~ *away all one's ammunition* 射完所有的弹药。 ~ *sth down,* bring to the ground by ~ing: 射落; 击落: *The bomber was shot down in flames.* 那轰炸机被击落而燃烧起来。 ~ *sth off,* sever by ~ing: 击掉, 击断; 射断某物: *He had his arm shot off.* 他的臂被击(炮弹)击断。 ~ *a covert/an estate, etc,* ~ the game in it. 在森林(所有地等)打猎。 ~ *a line,* (sl) exaggerate; lie; deceive. (俚)夸大; 说谎; 欺骗。 ~ *one's 'mouth off,* (US sl) talk indiscreetly or wildly. (美俚)轻率地谈话; 瞎吹胡扯。 ~ *a place up,* (US sl) terrorize (a town, district, etc) by going through it and shooting at random, firing at houses, etc. (美俚)盲目放枪使(城镇, 地区等)惊恐。 ~**'ing-box** *n* house used by sportsmen in the ~ing season (eg one on moorlands). 猎舍; 狩猎小屋。 **'~-ing-brake** *n* (former times) large horse-drawn open carriage used by sportsmen (for carrying equipment, game that was shot, etc); (in modern times, occasionally used for) estate car. (昔时)猎人所用之敞篷大马车; (现时偶尔用作)旅行车。 **'~-ing-gallery** *n* place where ~ing at targets is practised with pistols or airguns. 手枪或气枪射击场。 **'~ing-range** *n* ground with butts for rifle practice. 射击场; 靶场。 **'~ing-stick,** stick with a spiked end (to be pushed into the ground) and a handle which unfolds to form a seat. (一端插在地上, 另一端可为座垫的)独脚支撑座椅。 **6** [VP6A, 2A] (cinema) photograph (a scene): (电影)拍摄(一景); 摄影: *a ~ing script,* one to be used while a film is being shot (giving the order in which scenes are photographed, etc). 拍摄剧本(拍电影时所用之剧本, 指示各景如何拍摄等者)。 **7** [VP2A] (football, hockey, etc) (chiefly imper) make a shot at scoring a goal. (足球, 曲棍球等)(主用于祈使)射门。 ~**ing** *n* [U] (esp) (right of) ~ing (game) over an area of land: (尤指)狩猎; 狩猎权: *sell the ~ing on an estate.* 出售所有地之狩猎权。 ⇨ also **6** above. 亦参看上列第6义。

shooter /'ʃuːtə(r)/ 'ʃutə/ *n* (in compounds) shooting implement: (用于复合词中)射具; 枪: *a 'pea-~* 豆子枪(一种玩具); *a ,six-'~,* revolver firing six shots without reloading. 装六发子弹之左轮手枪。

shop /ʃɒp/ /ʃɑp/ **1** (US 美 = *store*) building or part of a building where goods are shown and sold retail: 店铺; 商店: *a butcher's/chemist's ~;* 肉(西药)店; *a*

'fruit-~. 水果店。 **come/go to the wrong ~,** (colloq) to the wrong place/person (for help, information, etc). (口)找错地方或人(求助, 打听消息等)。 ~ **,** be on duty (eg in a small ~): 照顾商店: *Mr Green got a friend to keep ~ for him while he went to his wife's funeral.* 格林先生为妻子出殡时, 找到一位朋友为他看店。 **keep a ~,** be a shopkeeper, own and manage a ~. 做店主; 开店。 **set up ~,** set up in business as a retail trader. 开店; 开业。 **'~-assistant** *n* employee in a ~. 店伙计; 店员。 **'~-bell** *n* bell (on the door of a small ~) which rings when a customer enters, warning the ~-keeper. 店铃(在小商店门上之铃, 顾客进入时鸣响以通知店主)。 **'~-girl/-boy** *n* young ~-assistant. 年轻的女店员(男店员)。 **'~-front** *n* frontage of a ~ with its window display, etc. (商店的)店面(包括橱窗等部分)。 ~ **hours** *n pl* hours during which a ~ is, or may legally be, open for business. 营业时间。 **'~-keeper** *n* owner of (usu a small) ~. (通常为小店之)店主。 **'~-lift** *vi, vt* [VP2A, 6A] steal (sth) from a shop while pretending to be a customer. 佯为顾客而偷窃(货品)。 Hence, 由此产生, **'~-lifter** *n* person who does this; 佯为顾客而偷窃货品之人; **'~-lifting** *n* [U] doing this. 佯为顾客而偷窃。 **'~-soiled/-worn** *adjj* damaged or dirty as the result of being put on view or handled in a ~. 店中摆旧的。 **'~-walker** *n* person who directs customers (in a large ~ or department store) to the right counters, departments, etc. (大商店或百货公司之)接待顾客者; 巡视员。 **'~-'window** *n* window used for the display of wares, etc. 商店橱窗。 **put all one's goods in the ~-window,** (fig) make a display of all one's knowledge, ability, etc and have nothing in reserve (used of a superficial person). (喻)毫不保留地卖弄才学(指肤浅之人)。 **2** [U] one's profession, trade, business, things connected with it. 职业; 本行; 工作; 与职业有关之事。 **talk ~,** talk about one's work, profession, etc with other people who do the same work. 与同行谈论本行。 **shut up ~,** (colloq) stop doing sth (not necessarily connected with buying and selling). (口)停止做某事(并非一定指停止营业)。 **3** *all 'over the* ~, (sl) (fig) **(a)** disordered, scattered in confusion: 零乱地; 纷乱地散置: *My belongings are all over the ~.* 我的东西零乱地散置着。 **(b)** in every direction: 在各处; 在每一方向: *I've looked for it all over the ~.* 我已在各处找过过(它)。 **4** (= *work*) place where manufacturing or repairing is done: 工厂; 修理厂: *an ,engi'neering-~;* 工程厂; *a ma'chine-~;* 机器厂; *the men on the floor,* the workers (contrasted with the management). 工人(与经理部门相对)。 **'~-'steward** *n* member of a local branch committee of a trade union, chosen by his fellow workers to represent them. (代表工会地方分会之工人的)工会代表。 **,closed '~,** system of compulsory membership of trade unions or other professional associations. 必须雇用工会或其他公会会员的制度; 实施此种制度的工厂或公司行号。 □ *vi* (**-pp-**) [VP2A, C] **1** go to ~ to buy things (usu 通常用 *go ~ping*). 购物。 ~ *around,* (colloq) visit various ~s, markets, etc to obtain the best value for one's money, etc. (口)逛商店(寻找物美价廉的东西)。 **2** ~ *on sb,* (sl) inform against, esp to the police. (俚)(尤指向警方)密告某人。 ~**ping** *n* [U] do one's ~ping; 购物; *a '~ping street,* one with many ~s; 商店众多的街道; 闹市; *a '~ping bag/basket,* in which to carry purchases. 购物袋(篮)。 **'~ping centre,** part of a town where there are ~s, markets, etc close together and often where cars are not allowed. 购物中心; (城市中的)商业区。 **'window-~ping** *n* [U] visiting a ~ping centre, street, etc to look at the displays in the ~ windows. 游览商店橱窗。 **'~per** *n* person who is ~ping: 购物的人: *crowds of Christmas ~pers.* 圣诞节大群购物的人。

shore¹ /ʃɔː(r)/ /ʃɔr/ *n* [U, C] stretch of land bordering on the sea or a large body of water: (海或湖的)岸; 滨: *a house on the ~(s) of Lake Geneva;* 在日内瓦湖滨的房

子; *go on* ~ (from a ship). (从船) 上岸.

shore[2] /ʃɔː(r); ʃor/ *n* [C] wooden support set against a wall, tree, etc to keep it up; prop set against the side of a ship while it is being built or repaired out of the water. (支撑墙、树等使之直立, 支撑建造或修理中之船的) 支柱; 撑柱. □ *vt* [VP15B] ~ *sth up*, support, prop up (with a wooden beam, etc). 以支柱支撑.

shore[3] /ʃɔː(r); ʃor/, **shorn** /ʃɔːn; ʃorn/ ⇨ **shear**.

short[1] /ʃɔːt; ʃort/ *adj* (-er, -est) **1** (opp of *long*) measuring little from end to end in space or time; (opp of *tall*) below the average height: (为 *long* 之反义词) 短的; 短暂的; (为 *tall* 之反义词) 矮的: *a* ~ *stick*; 短棍; *a* ~ *way off*, not far away; 不远; *a* ~ *man*; 矮人; ~ *grass*; 短草; *a* ~ *holiday*; 短暂的假期; *a* ~ *time ago*. 不久以前. *You've cut my hair very* ~. 你把我的头发剪得太短了. *She walked with* ~, *quick steps*. 她以小而快的步子走路. *The coat is a little* ~ *in the sleeves*. 这件外衣的袖子略短. *The days are getting* ~*er now that autumn is here*. 秋天到了, 白昼渐短. *a* ~ *ball*, (cricket) not bowled on a correct length. (板球) 投球的距离不够长; 短球. ~ *circuit n* accidental fault in wiring enabling an electric current to flow without going through the resistance of the complete circuit. (电流)短路(电路之意外故障, 电流未能通过全部电路之电阻而流动). ~'**circuit** *vt, vi* cause, make or take a ~ circuit in; cut off current from (sth) in this way; (fig) shorten or simplify (a procedure, etc): (使) 发生短路; 以 短路 切断 (某物) 之电流; (喻)缩短, 简化 (手续等): *The system has* ~-*circuited*. 这个电路系统发生短路了. '~ *cut n* way of getting somewhere, doing sth, etc (thought to be) quicker than the usual or ordinary way: (至某地, 做某事等的) 近路; 捷径: *They took a* ~ *cut across the fields instead of going by the road.* 他们穿越田野抄近路而不走大路. '~ *list, n* list of candidates (for a position, etc) that has been reduced to a small number from which a final selection is to be made. 决选名单(候选人已淘汰至少数, 以待作最后决定所列出的名单). Hence, 由此产生, '~*list vt: the candidates who have been* ~-*listed*, whose names have been put on a ~ list (perhaps for interviews). 已列入决选名单的候选人. ~-'**lived** /'lɪvd *US*: 'laɪvd; 'laɪvd/ *adj* lasting for a ~ time; brief: 持续不久的; 短命的; 短暂的: *a* ~-*lived triumph*. 昙花一现的胜利. ~-'**range**, *adj* (a) (of plans, etc) designed for a limited period of time. (指计划等)短程的, 短时间的. (b) (of missiles, etc) with a comparatively limited range[1](3). (指导弹等)短程的; 射程有限的. *have a* ~ *temper*, be lacking in self-control, so that one quickly or easily becomes angry; 易怒; 脾气急躁; hence, 由此产生, ~-'**tempered** *adj*, ~-'**term** *attrib adj* limited to, due to be repaid in, a ~ period of time: 限于短期的; 须短期内清偿的: ~-*term loans*. 短期贷款. **2** not reaching the usual, stated or required (amount, distance, weight, etc): (总数, 距离, 重量等)不足的; 短少的; 缺少的: *The shopkeeper was fined for giving* ~ *weight/measure*. 那店主因卖东西重量(分量)不足而受罚. *The factory is/ The workmen are on* ~ *time*, working fewer hours per day, or days per week, than usual. 这工厂(工人们)缩短工作时间. *These goods are in* ~ *supply*, The supply is not equal to the demand (*are scarce* is more usu.) ⇨ also **commons**(2). 这些货物来源不充裕 (*are scarce* 较常用). *You've given me* ~ *change*, less than the correct change. 你少找给我零钱了. Hence,由此产生, ~'**change** *vt* cheat (sb) by giving less than the correct change. 少找零钱以欺骗(某人). *be* ~ *of,* (a) not have enough of: 短少; 不足的量: ~ *of money/time*. 缺少钱(时间). (b) be distant from: 有一段距离; 未达到: *The cat broke down when we were still five miles* ~ *of our destination.* 我们距目的地尚有五英里的时候, 车子抛锚了. *little/ nothing* ~ *of*, little/nothing less than: (几乎不, 完全不)少于或亚于: *Our escape was little* ~ *of miraculous*, was almost a miracle. 我们的逃亡几乎是一项奇迹. *make* ~ *work of*, deal with, dispose of, eat or drink,

quickly. 迅速处理、支配、吃或喝. ~ *of breath*, panting, eg after running fast. 喘气; 气促(如快跑后). '~-**coming** *n* (usu *pl*) failure (to reach a required standard, to develop properly, to do one's duty). (通常用复数)缺点; 短处(未能达到所要求的标准, 未充分发展或未尽责). ,~'**drink** *n* [C] (or, colloq □ **a** ~) whisky, gin, etc in comparatively small glasses or small portions at a time (contrasted with a long drink such as a glass of beer). 以小杯饮用的酒(如威士忌、杜松子酒等, 与大杯饮用的酒如啤酒等相对). ,~-'**handed** *adj* having not enough workmen or helpers. 人手不足的; 人手短少的. ,~'**sight** *n* [U] inability to see clearly things that are distant, or (fig) to see into the future. 近视; (喻)无眼光. Hence, 由此产生, ,~-'**sighted** *adj*: *The Government's policy is* ~-*sighted*, does not take into account future needs, developments, etc. 政府的政策是短视的. ,~-'**winded** *adj* easily and quickly becoming breathless after exertion; unable to run for long. 用力后易喘气的; 不能久跑的. **3** (in comm) maturing early; to be paid or met soon: (商)短期的; 即将兑现的: *a* ~ *bill/ paper*; 短期汇票(票据); ~ *date*, early date for maturing of a bill, bond, etc. (兑现票据等的)短期. Hence, 由此产生, ,~-*dated adj* ~'**bond** ~ *one* which that matures within a period of five years. (五年期满的)短期债券. ,~-'**term 'capital**, capital raised for short periods. 短期资本; 短期资金. **4** (of a person) saying very little, or saying much in few words; (of what he says, his manner of speaking) expressed in few words; curt; abrupt: (指人)说话少的; 长话短说的; 说话扼要的; (指其所说之话, 说话的态度) 言简意赅的; 简洁的; 唐突的; 简慢的: *He/His answer was* ~ *and to the point*. 他说话(他的回答)简短切实. *He was very* ~ *with me*. 他对我甚为无礼. *for* ~, as a ~er form; for brevity's sake: 简称; 为简略起见: *Benjamin, called 'Ben' for* ~. 本杰明, 简称为 '本'. *in* ~, in a few words; to sum up briefly (after a long description, etc). 简言之; 总之(在冗长的叙述之后等). *the long and the* ~ *of it*, all that can or need be said. 一切所能说或所需要说的话; 总而言之. **5** (of cake, pastry) easily breaking or crumbling. (指饼, 面点)易碎的; 松脆的. ~'**pastry** *n*; [U] made with much butter or fat. 油酥面点. ~-**bread/cake** *nn* easily crumbled dry cake made with flour, sugar and much butter. (用面粉、糖和大量奶油做成的)脆饼; 酥饼. **6** (of vowels or syllables) taking the less of two usual durations: (指元音或音节)短音的; 非长音的: *the* ~ *vowel in 'pull' and the long vowel in 'pool'*. pull 之短元音和 pool 之长元音. **7** (other compounds and special uses). (其他复合词及特殊用法). '~-**fall** n deficit. 不足之额. '~-**hand** *n* [U] system of rapid writing using special signs; stenography. 速记; 速记术. *by a* ~ *head*, (**a**) (racing) by a distance of less than the length of a horse's head: (赛马) 以短于马首长度之距离: *Fly-by-Night won by a* ~ *head*. '夜莺'以短于一头之差取胜. (**b**) (fig by only a little. (喻)借少量(越过). '~-**horn** *n* [C] name of a breed of cattle with ~ curved horns. 一种短角牛. ~ **leg slip** *n* (cricket)(板球) ⇨ the illus at **cricket**. 参看 cricket 之插图. ~ **wave** *n* (radio telegraphy) one having a wave-length of from 10 to 100 metres. (短波)短波 (波长在 10 至 100 公尺之间). ~-**ly** *adv* **1** soon; in a ~ time: 即刻; 不久: ~*ly after(wards)*; 不久之后; ~*ly before noon*. 中午前不久. *He is* ~*ly to leave for Mexico.* 他即将前往墨西哥. **2** briefly; in a few words. 简略地; 简言之. **3** sharply; curtly: 唐突地; 简慢地: *answer rather* ~*ly*. 颇为无礼地回答. ~-**ness** *n*

short[2] /ʃɔːt; ʃort/ *adv* **1** abruptly; suddenly: 唐突地; 突然: *stop* ~. 突然停止. *bring/pull/take sb up* ~, interrupt or check him abruptly. 唐突地打断某人 (所说的话或所做的事). ~ *of*, leaving out of question; except: 除⋯外; 除去: *They would commit every crime* ~ *of murder*. 除谋杀外, 他们无恶不作. **2** before the natural or expected time. 未到自然的或预定的时间地;

不足地; 缺乏地。 **come / fall ~ of,** be insufficient, inadequate, disappointing (expectations, etc): 不足; 不及; 未达到(期望等): *The box-office receipts fell ~ of the manager's expectations*. 票房收入未达到经理的期望。 **cut sth / sb ~,** (a) interrupt; bring to an end before the usual or natural time: 阻止; 使提早结束: *The chairman had to cut ~ the proceedings*. 主席必须提早结束议程。 (b) make ~(er). 使短; 使简短。 **go ~ (of),** do without; deprive oneself (of): 无需; 使自己不能有: *I don't want you to go ~ (of money, etc) in order to lend me what I need*. 我不要你为了借给我所需要的(如钱等), 而自己感到短缺。 **run ~ (of),** reach the end: 用罄: *Our supplies ran ~*. 我们的给养用罄了。 *We're running ~ of paraffin.* 我们的石蜡快用完了。 **be taken ~,** (colloq) have a sudden motion of the bowels necessitating a hurried visit to the lavatory. (口语)腹泻。 **3 sell ~,** (comm) sell for future delivery (stocks, shares, commodities, etc that one does not own) in the expectation of being able to buy more cheaply before the date agreed upon for delivery. (商)卖空(约定将来交货而卖出证券、股票、商品等, 希望交货前以低价承买进)。 **sell sb ~,** betray, cheat, belittle him. 背叛、欺骗、贬抑他。

short³ /ʃɔːt; ʃɔrt/ *n* (colloq) short circuit, ⇨ **short¹**(1); short drink. (口)(电)短路; 用小杯饮用的酒。 □ *vi, vt* short-circuit. (使)短路; 简化。

short·age /ˈʃɔːtɪdʒ; ˈʃɔrtɪdʒ/ *n* [C, U] (amount of) deficiency; condition of not having enough: 不足; 不足之量; 缺乏; 缺少: *food—s*; 食物缺乏; *a ~ of rice* 米的缺乏; *owing to ~ of staff*; 由于人员的缺乏; *a ~ of 50 tons.* 缺少五十吨。 ⇨ **glut,** *n*

shorten /ˈʃɔːtn; ˈʃɔrtn/ *vt, vi* [VP6A, 2A] make or become shorter: 使短; 变短; 使不足; 变不足; 使松脆; 变松脆: *The days are beginning to ~,* eg in autumn. 白昼开始变短了(如在秋天)。 *The captain ordered his men to ~ sail,* reduce the area of sail spread to the wind. 船长命令船员缩帆。 **~·ing** /ˈʃɔːtnɪŋ; ˈʃɔrtnɪŋ/ *n* [U] fat used for making pastry light and flaky. 用以使面点松脆的油脂。 ⇨ **short¹**(5).

shorts /ʃɔːts; ʃɔrts/ *n pl* (pair of) ~, short trousers extending to or above the knees, (as worn by children, by adults for games, informal wear (on the beach, etc)· (孩童或成人在户外活动时穿着的)短裤。

shot¹ /ʃɒt; ʃɑt/ *n* 1 [C] (sound of the) firing of a gun, etc: (枪, 炮等的)发射; 射击; 枪声; 炮声: *hear ~s in the distance;* 听到远处的枪声; *the first ~s in the campaign,* the start of the attack. 此一战役攻击的开始。 *At each ~ he got nearer to the centre of the target.* 他每射击一发便更接近靶心。 **(do sth) like a ~,** at once; without hesitation. 立刻; 毫不迟疑地(做某事)。 **off like a ~,** off at great speed. 似弹矢般离去; 飞快地离去。 **2** [C] attempt to hit sth, hitting of sth; attempt to do sth, answer a question, etc; throw, stroke, hit, in certain games: (击中某物之)试图; 击中某物; 试为; 试猜; 试答; (某些游戏之)打击; 投射: *Good ~, Sir!* 先生, 您射得真准! *That remark was a ~ at me,* was aimed at me. 那话是针对我说的。 **a ~ in the dark,** a wild or random guess. 瞎猜; 乱猜。 **have a ~ (at sth),** try to do sth: 尝试; 试试看; 设法: *Have a ~ at solving the problem.* 设法解决此问题。 *The striker had a ~ at goal,* tried to score. 击球者试图射门得分。 *Let me have a ~ at it.* 让我试试看。 *He made several lucky ~s at the examination questions.* 他幸运地猜中了数个试题。 **a 'long ~,** an attempt to solve a problem, etc with little evidence, few facts to go on: 猜测; 大胆的企图: *It's a long ~ but I think John must have known about the murder.* 虽然这只是个猜测, 但我认为约翰对这件谋杀案必一定知情。 **,not by a 'long ~,** not even if circumstances were most favourable. 即使在最有利的条件下亦不可。 **3** [C] that which is fired from a gun, esp (formerly stone, later metal) non-explosive projectile for old-fashioned cannon: 弹; 弹丸; 炮弹; (尤指)旧式炮所用之非爆炸性弹丸(从前为石块, 以后为金属物)。 **shell(3);** heavy iron ball

thrown in athletic competition (called the '~-put): (运动竞赛用的)铅球: *putting the ~.* 推铅球。 **4 lead ~,** [U] quantity of tiny balls (or pellets) of lead contained in the cartridge of a sporting gun (instead of a single bullet), used against birds and small animals. (猎枪所用之)散弹。 ⇨ the illus at **cartridge.** 参看 cartridge 之插图。 **~-gun** *n* sporting gun with a smooth bore firing cartridges containing ~. 散弹枪; 猎枪。 **'~-tower** *n* tower in which ~ is made from molten lead poured through a sieve at the top and falling into water. 制弹塔(熔化之铅经由顶部细筛落入水中以制铅丸)。 **5** [C] person who shoots, with reference to his skill: 射手; 枪手(就其技术而言者): *He's a first-class / good / poor, etc ~.* 他是第一流(好, 坏等)的射手。 **6** [C] photograph, or one of a series of photographs, taken with a cinecamera: (电影摄影机所拍的)镜头; 景: *The exterior ~s were taken in Bermuda.* 外景系在百慕大岛拍摄的。 **'long ~,** (opp of *close-up*) taken with a long distance between the camera and the subject. (与 close-up 之反义语)远景; 远镜头。 **7** (esp US) injection from a hypodermic needle (of a drug): (尤美)皮下注射(药物): *have a ~ in the arm.* 在臂上注射。 **have / get / give sb a ~ in the arm, (a)** have / give sb an injection. 在(某人)臂上注射一针。 **(b)** have / give sb / sth that revives or restores, eg the economy. (为某人)注射一剂强心针(使在经济方面复苏)。 **8 a 'big ~,** (sl) an important person, esp a conceited one. (俚)要人; 大人物; 自负之人。

shot² /ʃɒt; ʃɑt/ *n* share of a reckoning or of expense: 应付的费用; 该付的帐: *pay one's ~.* 付帐。

should /ʃʊd; ʃud/ *v* weak form /ʃəd; ʃəd/ *v* ⇨ **shall.**

shoul·der /ˈʃəʊldə(r); ˈʃoldɚ/ *n* **1** that part of the body of a human being or animal where an arm or foreleg is joined to the trunk (⇨ the illus at **trunk**), or where the wing of a bird joins its neck; curve from this point to the neck: 肩(人之臂与躯干相连处, 兽之前肢与躯体相连处, 参看 trunk 之插图, 鸟之翅膀与躯体相连处); 肩部; 肩膀(肩颈间之弯曲部): *This coat is narrow across the ~s.* 这件衣的肩部狭窄。 *He has one ~ a little higher than the other.* 他的一肩比另一肩略高。 **~ to ~,** side by side and touching; (fig) united. 并肩; (喻)协力; 团结。 **give sb the cold ~,** ⇨ **cold¹**(1). **put one's ~ to the wheel,** work energetically at a task. 努力工作。 **stand head and ~s above** (others), be considerably taller (or, fig, mentally or morally better) than. 远高于(他人); (喻, 在智力或道德上)远胜过。 **straight from the ~,** (fig, of criticism, rebukes, etc) frankly put. (喻, 指批评、责难等)率直的; 直陈的。 **'~-blade** *n* either of the flat bone of the upper back, behind and below the neck; shoulder blade. 肩胛骨。 ⇨ the illus at **skeleton.** 参看 skeleton 之插图。 **'~-strap** *n* **(a)** narrow strap on the ~ of a military uniform (with badges of rank, etc). 军人的肩章; 肩徽(附有等级标志)。 **(b)** ribbon which passes over a woman's ~ and supports a garment. (挂在女人肩上用以吊住衣服的)肩带。 **'~-flash** *n* strip of material on the ~ of a military uniform, with a coloured patch as the distinguishing emblem of a division, etc. 军服之肩饰(有彩色之小片用作识别某师等之标帜)。 **2** (*pl*) *shoulders* (之复)背的上部: *give a child a ride on one's ~s;* 让小孩骑在肩膀上; *shift the blame to other ~s,* let others take the blame. 把责任推给别人承担。 **have broad ~s,** be able to bear much weight or (fig) responsibility, 能肩负重担; (喻)可负重任。 **3** ~-like part of a bottle, tool, mountain, etc. (瓶, 器具, 山等的)肩状部分。 **hard ~,** hard surface at the side of a roadway (esp a motorway). (高速公路等靠边的)路肩。 □ *vt* **1** [VP6A] take on the ~s (lit and fig): 肩负(字面及喻): *~ a burden / a task / the responsibility for sth.* 负起重物(工作, 某事之责任)。 *arms,* (mil) move the rifle to an upright position in front of the right ~. (军)使枪口朝上垂直地托于右肩前; 托枪。 **2** [VP15A] push with the ~; make (one's

way) thus: 以肩冲; 挤(路): ~ *people aside:* 用肩膀把人们推开; *be ~ed to one side:* 被挤在一旁; ~ *one's way through a crowd.* 从人丛中挤过。

shout /ʃaʊt/ *n* [C] loud call or cry: 大叫; 呼喊: ~*s of joy;* 欢乐的呼声; *a ~ of alarm.* 惊恐的喊叫。 *They greeted him with ~s of 'Long live the President'.* 他们高呼着'总统万岁'迎接他。 □ *vi, vt* = **(out)**, **1** [VP2A, B, C, 4B, 22] speak or cry out in a loud voice: 大声喊; 呼; 叫: *Don't ~ at me!* 不要对我叫喊! *He ~ed to attract attention.* 他大声叫喊以引起注意。 *He ~ed with pain.* 他痛得大叫。 *He ~ed himself hoarse.* 他叫得嗓子都哑了。 **2** [VP6A, 15A, B, 3A] say in a loud voice: 大声说: ~ *(out) one's orders.* 高声发出命令。 *They ~ed their disapproval,* expressed it by ~ing. 他们喊叫表示反对。 *He ~ed to me/~ed for him.* 他大声喊我来/叫他来。 *'Go back!' he ~ed.* '回去!'他大喊着说。 ~ *sb down,* = to prevent sb from being heard: 大声喊叫而使对方的声音听不见; 大声嚷倒某人: *The crowd ~ed the speaker down.* 群众大声喝倒彩以压制那位演说者的声音。 ~*ing* [U] =~s. 叫; 喊。 *It's all over but/bar the ~ing,* The struggle, fight, etc is over and the praise, cheers, etc will follow. 竞赛(等)已完毕,欢呼声不绝。

shove /ʃʌv/ *vt, vi* [VP6A, 15A, B, 2A, C] (colloq) push (usu heavily): (口)推; 挤; 撞: ~ *a boat into the water.* 把船推进水中。 *Stop shoving!* 别推了! ~ *off,* **(a)** start from the shore in a boat (by pushing the shore, etc). (借推撑岸等而)开船离岸。 **(b)** (sl) leave (a place): (俚)离开(一地方): *I'm sick of this place; let's ~ off.* 我讨厌这地方, 我们离开吧。 □ *n* [C] vigorous push: 用力推; 推开: *Give it a ~.* 推它一下。 ~

'ha'penny /ʃʌv/ 'heɪpnɪ/, /ʃʌv'hepnɪ/ *n* = **shove-board.**

shovel /'ʃʌvl/ ~ /ˈʃʌvl/ *n* spade-like tool, used for moving coal, sand, snow, etc, ⇨ the illus at **tool;** large device used for the same purpose, mechanically operated from a crane in a vehicle. 铲; 锹(用以铲煤、沙、雪等) (参看 tool 之插图); (挖土机之)铲头。 □ *vt* (**-ll-, US -l-**) **1** [VP6A, 15A, B] lift, move, with a ~: 铲起; 铲动: ~ *up coal;* 铲煤; ~ *the snow away from the garden path.* 自园径上铲去雪。 **2** [VP6A, 15A] clear or clean with a ~: 铲干净: ~ *a path through the snow.* 在雪中铲开一条小路。 ~**ful** /-fʊl/ *n* as much as a ~ will hold. 一铲或一锹之量。

shovel-board /'ʃʌvl bɔːd/ ~ /'ʃʌvl,bord/ *n* [U] game in which discs or coins are pushed along a board to a mark. (在板上推小圆片或硬币的)推移板游戏。

show[1] /ʃəʊ/ *n* **1** [U, C] showing (chiefly in): 表示(主要用于): *by (a) ~ of hands,* (voting) by the raising of hands for or against (a proposal). (投票)借举手以赞成或反对(提案)。 **2** [C] collection of things publicly displayed, esp for competition, or as a public entertainment: 展览; 展览会; 竞赛会: *a 'flower/ 'horse/'cattle ~;* 花(马,牛)的展览会; *the 'motor ~,* = exhibition; 汽车展览会; *the Lord Mayor's ~,* a procession through the City of London when a new Lord Mayor is installed; 伦敦市长的就任游行; *a travelling ~,* eg of circus animals. 巡回展(如马戏团之动物等)。 *on ~,* exhibited. 被陈列着; 展览中。 **3** [C] (colloq) natural display: 自然显露: *sth to be shown.* (口)自然景观; 景物: *a fine ~ of blossom in the Kent orchards.* 肯特果园内百花盛开的景观。 **4** [C] (colloq) kind of public entertainment, eg circus, theatre, radio, TV, etc: (口)公众娱乐; 表演(如马戏、戏剧、无线电、电视等): *Have you seen any good ~s lately?* 你最近看过什么好的表演吗? *'~-business,* (colloq) (口): *'~-biz* /-biz/ *n* the public entertainment business. 表演业; 娱乐界。 **5** [C] (colloq) performance (not theatrical, etc): (口)表现: *put up a good ~,* do sth creditably; 表现良好; *a poor ~,* sth done badly. 表现不佳。 *steal the ~,* attract all the attention: 吸引全部注意力; 抢镜头: *Good ~!* used to express approval of sth done well. 精彩! 做得好! **6** [C] (colloq) organization: undertaking; business; something that is happening: (口)组织; 事业; 企业;(正

在发生的)事情: *Who's running this ~,* Who controls or manages it? 谁在主持此业务? *give the (whole) '~-away,* let people know what is being done or planned: 把整个事情泄漏; 走漏消息: *I wish she wouldn't talk and give the ~ away.* 我希望她不会多话而走漏消息。 **7** (sing only; dated colloq use) opportunity of doing sth, defending oneself, etc: (仅用单数; 过时口语用法)(做某事, 为自己辩护等之)机会: *Give the man a fair ~.* 给那人一个公平的机会。 *He had no ~ at all.* 他简直没有机会。 **8** outward appearance; impression: 外观; 印象: *a claim with some ~ of justice;* 看起来相当合理的要求; *with a ~ of reason.* 似乎有理地。 *He didn't offer even a ~ of resistance.* 他甚至未作出抵抗的样子。 **9** [U] pomp; display; ostentation: 炫耀; 夸示; 铺张; 虚饰: *a house furnished for ~,* not comfort. 不为舒适, 只为虚饰而装璜的房子。 *They're fond of ~.* 他们好表弄。 **10** (compounds) (复合词) *'~-boat n* river steam-boat on which theatrical performances were given (esp on the Mississippi, US). 演艺船(尤指在美国密西西比河上者)。 *'~-case n* case with glass sides and (or) top, for showing and protecting articles in a shop, museum, etc; (fig) special exhibition of sth, esp sth new. (店铺, 博物馆等之)玻璃柜橱; 陈列柜;(喻)特展(尤指新产品或新作品)。 *'~-down n* (colloq) full and frank declaration of one's strength, intentions, etc: (口)明白表示自己的力量, 意向等; 摊牌: *call for a ~-down.* ask (opponents, rivals, etc) for such a declaration; 要求(对方, 敌人等)摊牌; *if it comes to a ~-down,* if such a declaration is (or has to be) made. 如果到了摊牌的阶段。 *'~-girl n* girl who sings or dances (or is merely decorative) in a musical play, revue, etc. (在音乐喜剧,时事讽刺剧等中之)歌舞女郎。 *'~-jumping n* display of skill in riding horses over fences, barriers, etc. 骑马跳越围墙、障碍物等之表演。 *'~-man /-mən/ -men/* *n* (pl -men) (a) organizer of public entertainments (esp circuses). 大众娱乐(尤指马戏团)之主持人。 **(b)** person (esp in public life) who uses publicity, etc to attract attention to himself: 自我宣传之人 (尤指从事公务者): *Some politicians are great ~men and very little else.* 有些政客别无所长, 只会做自我宣传。 *'~-man·ship /-mənʃɪp; -mənʃɪp/ n* art of attracting, ability to attract, public attention, eg to what one is trying to sell. 吸引大众注意之技术或能力 (如使注意所售货之物)。 *'~-place n* one that tourists go to see: 可游览之处; 胜地: *old palaces, castles and other ~ places.* 故宫, 古堡及其他胜地。 *'~-room/-window n* one in which goods are kept for display, inspection, etc. 货品陈列室(商店之橱窗)。 *'~y adj* (-ier, -iest) likely to attract attention; (often contemptuous) (too) decorated or ornamented; (too) brightly coloured: 可能吸引注意的; (常含轻蔑意味)(过分) 装饰的; (太)华丽的: *~y flowers,* eg some kinds of dahlia; 艳丽的花 (如某些大丽花); *a ~y dress;* 华服; *the ~y patriotism of persons hoping for titles.* 希冀获得勋位的人所夸示的爱国心。 ~**·ily** /-ɪlɪ; -əlɪ/ *adv* ~**i·ness** *n*

show[2] (archaic **shew**) /ʃəʊ; ʃo/ *vt, vi* (pt ~**ed**, pp ~**n** /ʃəʊn; ʃon/, rarely ~**ed**) **1** [VP6A, 12A, 13A, 15A, 19B, 24A] = *sth (to sb); ~ sb sth,* bring before the sight: 出示; 展示; 上演: *~ your ticket at the barrier.* 你在入口处必须出示门票。 *What films are they ~ing at the local cinema this week?* 本地的电影院本周放映什么影片? *He won several prizes for the roses he ~ed,* exhibited. 他展出的玫瑰获得好几个奖。 *He ~ed me his pictures.* 他把他的照片给我看。 *He has ~n them to all his friends.* 他把它们给所有的朋友看。 *The photograph ~s him sitting/seated at his desk.* 在这张照片里, 他坐在书桌旁边。 **2** [VP6A] allow to be seen: 使显露: *That frock ~s your petticoat,* is too short to cover it. 那件洋装太短, 让你的衬裙露出来了。 *A dark suit will not ~ the dirt.* 黑色的套装不显脏。 *My shoes are ~ing signs of wear.* 我的鞋子已穿旧了。 **3** [VP2A, C] be visible or noticeable: 可看出; 显露: *Your petticoat is ~ing, Jane.* 你的衬裙露出来了, 简。 *Does the mark of

the wound still ~? 伤痕还看得见吗? *The pink of the apple-blossom is beginning to ~.* 苹果花的淡红色已开始出现。*His fear ~ed in his eyes.* 他的眼中露出恐惧。 **4** [VP6A] **~ itself,** be visible: 呈现; 可看出: *His annoyance ~ed itself in his looks.* 他的烦恼在他的表情上可以看出。 **~ oneself,** be present (at a meeting, etc): 出席; 出现 (在会议等中): *Ought we to ~ ourselves at the Evans's party tonight?* 我们应出席今晚伊凡家的宴会吗? **~ one's face,** appear before people: 露脸; 出面: *He's ashamed to ~ his face in the street.* 他羞于在街上露面。 **~ fight,** give signs of being ready to fight. 显出愿战的样子; 表示不妥协。 **~ one's hand/cards,** (fig) make known one's intentions or plans. (喻)表明意图或计划; 摊牌。 **~ a leg,** (colloq) get out of bed. (口)起床。 **~ one's teeth,** (fig) look angry. (喻)发怒。 **have nothing to ~ for it/sth,** have nothing that is evidence of what one has achieved or tried to achieve. 毫无成就可言; 无表现。 **5** [VP6A, 14, 12A, 13A] give; grant: 给; 施与: *~ mercy on sb.* 宽恕某人。*He ~ed me great kindness.* 他对我极为亲切或帮忙。 **6** [VP6A, 25] give evidence or proof of having or being: 表现; 显示: *He ~s no sign of intelligence.* 他表现得一点也不聪明。*She ~ed great courage.* 她表现得很有勇气。*His new book ~s him to be a first-rate novelist.* 他的新书显示他是第一流的小说家。 **7** [VP15A, B] direct; conduct. 引导; 引领。**~ sb in; ~ sb into sth; ~ sb out; ~ sb out of sth,** direct or conduct sb into/out of a place: 引领某人进入(离开)一地方: *Please ~ this gentleman out.* 请送这位先生出去。*We were ~n into the living-room.* 我们被引入起居室。 **~ sb over/around/round sth,** take sb round a place: 带某人参观某处: *The guide ~ed us over the old castle.* 向导带领我们去参观那古堡。 **~ sb the door,** require him to leave and go with him to the door to see that he does so. 要某人离开, 并且陪他走到门口看着他离去。 **~ sb the way,** explain which way to go; (fig) set an example. 指示走那一条路; (喻)示范。 **8** [VP6A, 9, 10, 20, 21, 25] make clear; cause (sb) to understand; prove: 说明; 表明; 证明; 显出: *He ~ed me how to do it/how he had done it.* 他向我说明如何做这事(他如何做这事)。*He ~ed his annoyance/that he was annoyed/how annoyed he was.* 他显得极愤慨。*That ~s how little you know.* 那证明你所知极少。*We have ~n the falsity of the story/that the story is false/the story to be false.* 我们已证明那个不是导不真实。 **9** [VP2C, 15B] **~ sb/sth off,** display (sth) to advantage: 显示(某物)的优点; 使显眼: *a swim-suit that ~s off her figure well,* 能充分显示她美好身材的泳装; *mothers who like to ~ off their daughters,* display their daughter's good looks, abilities, accomplishments, etc. 喜欢宣扬女儿长处的母亲们。**~ off,** make a display of one's wealth, learning, abilities, etc in order to impress people: 炫耀自己的财富, 学识, 能力等; 卖弄: *a man who is always ~ing off.* 老是卖弄的人。Hence, 由此产生, '**~-off** n person who ~s off: 喜爱炫耀、卖弄之人: *He's an irritating ~-off,* is always trying to show his abilities, etc. 他是个讨人嫌的卖弄才华之人。 **~ sb/sth up,** make the truth about (sb or sth dishonest, disreputable, etc) known: 揭露(不诚实, 不名誉等的人或事物)之真相;拆穿: *~ up a fraud/a rogue/an impostor.* 揭发骗局(恶徒, 骗子)。 **~ up, (a)** be conspicuous, easily visible: 显眼; 易见: *Her wrinkles ~ed up in the strong sunlight.* 她的皱纹在强烈的阳光下很显眼。 **(b)** [VP2A] (colloq) put in an appearance; be present (at sth): (口)出现; 出席: *Only three of the people we invited to the party didn't ~ up.* 我们邀请来参加宴会的人只有三人未出席。 **~-ing** n (usu *sing*) (act of) displaying or pointing out; appearance; evidence: (通常用单数)表现; 陈述; 外观; 外表; 形迹: *a firm with a poor financial ~ing,* whose financial accounts do not appear to be good; 财政状况不佳的公司; *on present/past ~ing,* on present/past evidence. 就现在(过去)的迹象。**on one's own ~ing,** by one's own admission. 如某人自己所承认的。

shower /'ʃaʊə(r); 'ʃaʊɚ/ n [C] **1** brief fall of rain,

sleet or hail; sudden sprinkle of water: 一阵雨, 霰或雹; 一阵喷洒: *be caught in a ~;* 被阵雨淋湿; *a ~ of spray.* 一阵喷雾。 **'~(-bath)** n (washing one's body by using a) device by which water comes down in a ~ through a plate with numerous small holes: 淋浴设备; 淋浴: *have a ~(-bath) every morning.* 每天早上淋浴一次。 **2** large number of things arriving together: 大量涌到之事物: *a ~ of blows/stones/blessings/insults;* 一阵打击(石块, 祝福, 侮辱); *sparks falling in a ~/in ~s.* 阵雨似的火花。 **3** (US) party at which presents are given to a woman about to become a bride. (美)送礼前将做新娘者的聚会。 □ vt, vi **1** [VP14] **sth upon sb; ~ sb with sth,** send or give it to him in a ~: 大量地给与: *They ~ed honours upon the hero/~ed the hero with honours.* 他们纷纷向那英雄致敬。*Questions were ~ed upon the new arrival.* 大家纷纷向那新到者提出问题。 **2** [VP2C] fall in a ~: 似阵雨般降落: *Good wishes ~ed (down) upon the bridegroom.* 大家纷纷向新郎祝福。 **~y** adj (of the weather) with frequent ~s. (指天气)多阵雨的。

shown /ʃəʊn; ʃon/ *pp* of **show²**.

shrank /ʃræŋk; ʃræŋk/ *pt* of **shrink.**

shrap·nel /'ʃræpnəl; 'ʃræpnəl/ n [U] fragments of shell or bullets packed inside a shell which is designed to explode and scatter these contents over a wide area: 榴霰弹(含有使弹片及弹头散布于广阔地区之炸药的炮弹或炸弹): *hit by (a piece of) ~.* 被榴霰弹(弹片)击中。

shred /ʃred; ʃred/ n [C] strip or piece scraped, torn or broken off sth; fragment: 碎片; 裂片; 细条: (fig) (喻) *not a ~ of truth in what she says;* 她所说的话无一丝真实性; *not a ~ of evidence against me.* 没有丝毫对我不利的证据。 **tear to ~s,** (lit and fig) destroy: (字面和喻)毁灭; 破坏: *They have torn her reputation to ~s.* 他们已使她身败名裂。 □ vt **(-dd-)** [VP6A] tear or scrape into ~s. 撕成碎片; 裂为细条。

shrew /ʃruː; ʃru/ n **1** bad-tempered, scolding woman. 坏脾气而好骂的妇女; 泼妇; 悍妇。 **2** '**~(-mouse),** small mouse-like animal that feeds on insects. 鼩鼱(似鼠小动物, 以昆虫为食)。 **~·ish** /-ɪʃ; -ɪʃ/ adj scolding; sharp-tongued. 好骂人的; 利舌的; 悍泼的。 **~·ish·ly** adv **~·ish·ness** n

shrewd /ʃruːd; ʃrud/ adj (-er, -est) **1** having, showing, sound judgement and common sense: 明智的; 精明的: *~ businessmen;* 精明的商人; *~ arguments.* 明智的辩论。 **2** astute; discriminating: 狡狯的; 明敏的; 有眼光的: *make a ~ guess,* one likely to be correct; 准确的猜测; *a ~ blow/thrust,* one carefully made and likely to be effective. 有效的一击。 **~·ly** adv **~·ness** n

shriek /ʃriːk; ʃrik/ vi, vt **~ (out),** **1** [VP2A, C] scream shrilly. 尖叫。 **2** [VP6A, 15B] utter in a shrill, screaming voice: 以尖叫声说出: *~ out a warning;* 尖声警告; *~ with laughter.* 尖声大笑。 □ n **1** shrill scream: 尖叫: *~s of girlish laughter;* 女孩的尖锐笑声; *the ~ (= whistle) of a railway engine.* 火车头的尖鸣声。

shrift /ʃrɪft; ʃrɪft/ n [U] (archaic) confession (of sins) to a priest; confession and absolution. (古) 对教士之忏悔; 告解。**give sb/get short ~,** give him/get curt treatment, brief and unwilling attention. 怠慢某人(受到怠慢)。

shrike /ʃraɪk; ʃraɪk/ n (kinds of) bird (also called 亦称作 'butcher-bird') with a strong, hooked bill and the habit of fastening its prey (small birds and insects) on thorns. 伯劳; 百舌鸟(喙弯而坚, 惯于将其捕获之小鸟与昆虫固牢于荆棘上)。

shrill /ʃrɪl; ʃrɪl/ adj (of sounds, voices, etc) sharp; piercing; high-pitched: (指声音, 语音等)尖锐的; 高频率的: *~ cries;* 尖锐的喊叫; *a ~ voice/whistle.* 尖锐的声音(汽笛)。 **~y** /'ʃrɪlɪ; 'ʃrɪlɪ/ adv **~·ness** n

shrimp /ʃrɪmp; ʃrɪmp/ n [C] small marine shellfish used for food, ⇨ the illus at **crustacean.** (hum) very small person. 小虾(参看 crustacean 之插图); (谐)短小

之人。 □ *vi* catch ~s: 捕虾; (usu) (通常作) *go* ~*ing*. 去捕虾。

shrine /ʃraɪn; ʃraɪn/ *n* [C] **1** tomb or casket containing holy relics; altar or chapel of special associations or hallowed by some memory. 藏置圣徒遗骨之墓或小箱; 神龛; 圣祠; 殿堂。 **2** building or place associated with sth or sb deeply respected or venerated: 与深受敬重之某物或某人有关系的建筑物或地方: *a Shinto* ~, *in Japan*. (日本之) 神道庙。 **worship at the** ~ **of Mammon**, give excessive devotion to wealth and money-making. 崇拜财神之庙堂 (即过份追求财富)。 □ *vt* = **enshrine** (the usu word). (enshrine 为常用字)。

shrink /ʃrɪŋk; ʃrɪŋk/ *vi, vt* (*pt* **shrank** /ʃræŋk; ʃræŋk/, or **shrunk** /ʃrʌŋk; ʃrʌŋk/, *pp* **shrunk**, or, as *adj* **shrunken** /ˈʃrʌŋkən; ˈʃrʌŋkən/) **1** [VP6A, 2A] make or become less, smaller (esp of cloth through wetting): (使) 收缩; (使) 绉缩 (尤指布料浸湿后之收缩): *Will this soap* ~ *woollen clothes?* 这种肥皂会使毛织品收缩吗? *Those jeans will* ~ *in the wash.* 那些牛仔裤洗过以后会缩水。 *How your gums have shrunk since your teeth were extracted!* 你的牙齿拔去后, 你的齿龈萎缩了不少啊! **2** [VP2A, C, 3A] ~ (**back**) (**from**), move back, show unwillingness to do sth (from shame, dislike, etc): 退缩; 畏缩 (由于羞耻, 厌恶等): *A shy man* ~*s from meeting strangers.* 羞怯的人怕见生人。 *She shrank back from the horrifying spectacle.* 她看到那可怖的景象就往后退。 '~·**age** /-ɪdʒ; -ɪdʒ/ *n* [U] process of ~ing degree of ~ing: 收缩; 绉缩; 收缩的过程或程度: *Make the pullover a little longer, and allow for* ~*age.* 把这套头毛衣织长一些, 以防收缩。 *The* ~*age in our export trade / in the value of our currency is serious.* 我们的出口贸易 (币值) 严重萎缩。

shrive /ʃraɪv; ʃraɪv/ *vt* (*pt* ~**d** or **shrove** /ʃrəʊv; ʃrov/, *pp* ~**d** or **shriven** /ˈʃrɪvn; ˈʃrɪvn/) [VP6A] (archaic, of a priest) hear the confession of a penitent sinner and absolve him from the spiritual consequences of his sin(s). (古, 指教士) 听忏悔者忏悔而赦其罪。

shrivel /ˈʃrɪvl; ˈʃrɪvl/ *vt, vi* (**-ll-**, US also **-l-**) [VP 6A, 15B, 2A, C] ~ (**up**), (cause to) become dried or curled (through heat, frost, dryness or old age): (使) 枯萎; (使) 卷缩: *The heat* ~*led up the leaves / the leather* 炎热使树叶枯萎 (皮革卷缩)。 *He has a* ~*led face, with the skin wrinkled.* 他有一张满是皱纹的脸。

shriven /ˈʃrɪvn; ˈʃrɪvn/ ⇨ **shrive**.

shroud /ʃraʊd; ʃraʊd/ *n* [C] **1** (also called 亦称 '*winding-sheet*') cloth or sheet (to be) wrapped round a corpse: 尸布; 寿衣: *You'll have no pockets in your* ~. 你死后带不走财产。 **2** sth which covers and hides: 覆盖物; 遮蔽物: *a* ~ *of mist.* 一片浓雾。 **3** (*pl*) ropes supporting a ship's masts, ⇨ the illus at **barque**; ropes linking a parachute and the harness which is strapped to the parachutist. (复) 护桅索; 横桅索 (参看 barque 之插图); (降落伞的) 吊伞索。 □ *vt* [VP6A, 15A] **1** wrap (a corpse) in a ~. 以尸布包裹 (尸体)。 **2** cover; hide: 覆盖; 遮蔽: ~*ed in darkness / mist*. 笼罩在黑暗 (雾) 中; *a crime* ~*ed in mystery*. 一件离奇的罪案。

shrove /ʃrəʊv; ʃrov/ ⇨ **shrive**.

Shrove Tues·day /ˌʃrəʊv ˈtjuːzdɪ US: ˈtuːz-; ˌʃrov-ˈtjuzdɪ/ *n* day before the beginning of Lent, on which, and on preceding days (**Shrove·tide**), it was formerly the custom to be shriven. 四旬斋开始之前一日 (旧俗于是日及前数日 (Shrovetide) 向神父告解可获赦罪)。

shrub /ʃrʌb; ʃrʌb/ *n* [C] plant with woody stem, lower than a tree, and (usu) with several separate stems from the root. 灌木 (较矮木矮, 通常自根部丛生树干)。 ~·**bery** /ˈʃrʌbərɪ; ˈʃrʌbərɪ/ *n* (*pl* **-ries**) place, eg part of a garden, planted with ~s. 灌木栽植地; 灌木丛。

shrug /ʃrʌg; ʃrʌg/ *vt* (**-gg-**) [VP6A, 15B] lift (the shoulders) slightly (to show indifference, doubt, etc). 耸 (肩) (以表示冷淡, 怀疑等)。 ~ **sth off**, dismiss it as not deserving attention, as sth trivial. 对某事物不屑一

顾。 □ *n* [C] such a movement: 耸肩: *with a* ~ *of the shoulders / a* ~ *of despair.* 耸耸肩 (失望地耸耸肩)。

shrunk(en) /ʃrʌŋk; ˈʃrʌŋkən; ʃraŋk; ˈʃraŋkən/ ⇨ **shrink**.

shuck /ʃʌk; ʃʌk/ *n* (US) husk; pod; outer covering; (fig) sth of little value. (美) 壳; 荚; 外皮; (喻) 无价值之物。 **s~s!** *int* (US) (exclamation of disbelief, regret, or irritation). (美) 胡说! 唉! 真无聊 (表示不信, 懊悔或气恼之感叹词)。 □ *vt* [VP6A] remove the ~s from: 剥…之壳, 荚或外皮: ~ *peanuts / maize.* 剥花生壳 (玉米之外皮)。

shud·der /ˈʃʌdə(r); ˈʃʌdə/ *vi* [VP2A, C, 4C] shake convulsively; tremble with fear or disgust: 抽动; 战栗; 因恐惧或厌恶而发抖: ~ *with cold / horror;* 寒冷 (恐怖) 得发抖; ~ *at the sight of blood.* 看见流血便战栗。 *The ship* ~*ed as she struck the rocks.* 船因撞着礁石而摇动。 *He* ~*ed to think of it.* 他一想到它就发抖。 □ *n* [C] uncontrollable shaking: 战栗; 发抖: *a* ~ *passed over her.* 她不由自主地发抖。 *It gives me the* ~*s*, (colloq) terrifies me. (口语) 它使我害怕极了。

shuffle /ˈʃʌfl; ˈʃʌfl/ *vi, vt* [VP2A, C, 6A] walk without raising the feet properly. 曳 (足) 而行。 ~ **one's feet**, slide or drag them on the ground when walking, or when standing or sitting. 曳足 (走、站或坐时, 双足在地上滑或拖)。 **2** [VP6A, 15A, B, 2A] slide or move (playing-cards, etc) one over the other to change their relative positions: 洗 (纸牌等); 弄混; 乱挪: ~ *the dominoes.* 洗骨牌。 *He* ~*d the papers together in a drawer.* 他把文件胡乱地放在抽屉里。 **3** [VP2C, 15B] do sth in a careless way; slip (sth *off, on*) casually: 马虎地做某事; 随便地脱下或穿上 (某物, 与 *off, on* 连用): ~ *through one's work;* 敷衍了事; ~ *one's clothes on / off;* 随便地穿衣 (脱衣); (fig) (喻) ~ *off responsibility upon others*, get rid of it by passing it to others. 把责任推诿给他人。 **4** [VP2A] keep shifting one's position; be unstraightforward; try to avoid giving a certain answer, etc: 闪避; 蒙混; 支吾; 闪烁其辞: *Don't* ~; *give a clear answer.* 不要闪烁其辞, 给一个明确的答复。 □ *n* [C] **1** shuffling movement; shuffling dance: 曳足而行; 曳足跳舞: *soft-shoe '~*, 滑步舞; shuffling of cards: 洗牌: *Give the cards a good* ~. 把这副纸牌好好洗一下。 **2** general change of relative position: 改组; 混合: *a* ~ *of the Cabinet; a Cabinet* ~, giving members different portfolios. 内阁改组。 **3** piece of dishonesty; misleading statement or action. 欺骗之行为; 支吾之辞; 闪避之行为。 **shuf·fler** *n* one who ~s. 曳足而行者; 洗牌者; 做事马虎者; 蒙混者。

shufty /ˈʃʌftɪ; ˈʃʌftɪ/ *n* (GB sl) *take / have a* ~ (*at sth / sb*), have a (quick) look (at it / him). (英俚) (很快地) 瞄一眼。

shun /ʃʌn; ʃʌn/ *vt* (**-nn-**) [VP6A, D] keep away from; avoid: 规避; 避免: ~ *temptation / publicity / society.* 避开诱惑 (避免出风头, 避免交际)。

'shun /ʃʌn; ʃʌn/ *int* (abbr of) **attention(3)** (as a word of command). (口令) 立正! (为 attention (3) 之略)。

shunt /ʃʌnt; ʃʌnt/ *vt, vi* **1** [VP6A, 15A] send (railway wagons, coaches, etc) from one track to another, esp to keep a track clear for important traffic: 使 (铁路之货车, 客车等) 调到另一轨道上以让开重要交通; 使转轨: ~ *a train on to a siding.* 将一列火车调至旁轨。 **2** [VP2A] (of a train) be ~ed to a siding. (指火车) 被转至旁轨。 **3** [VP6A, 15A] (fig, colloq) divert; postpone or evade discussion of (sth): (喻, 口) 转移; 拖延或回避讨论 (某事): *She* ~*ed the conversation on to less morbid topics.* 她把话转向比较不可怕的话题上。 **4** [VP6A, 15A] (fig) lay-aside (a project); leave (sb) unoccupied, or inactive. (喻) 搁置 (计划); 使 (某人) 闲散 或无事可做。 ~**er** *n* (esp) railway employee who ~s wagons, etc. (尤指) 调动货车等于旁轨之铁路工人; 转辙手。

shush /ʃʊʃ; ʃʌʃ/ *vi, vt* **1** = **hush**. **2** = **sh**.

shut /ʃʌt; ʃʌt/ *vt, vi* (*pt, pp* **shut; -tt-**) (For special uses with *adverbial particles* and *preps*, ⇨ **5** below.) (与副

词性小品词、介系连用之特殊用法,见下列第 5 义)。**1** [VP 6A, 15A] move (a door, one's lips, etc) into position to stop an opening: 关;闭(门,唇等): ~ *the doors and windows;* 关闭门窗; ~ *a drawer:* 关抽屉; ~ *one's mouth.* 闭嘴。*He ~ his ears to all appeals for help,* refused to listen to them. 他对于一切求助的呼声都充耳不闻。*He ~ his eyes to* (= deliberately refused to notice) *her faults.* 他对她的过失装做没看见。*Why have you ~ the door upon further negotiations,* refused to consider them? 你为什么要拒绝进一步的谈判呢? *They ~ the door against her / on her / in her face,* refused to receive or admit her. 他们不准她进去(对她予以闭门羹)。**'~-eye** n (colloq) nap; sleep: (口)午睡;睡觉: *It's time for half an hour's ~-eye.* 到了午睡半小时的时候了。**2** [VP2A] become closed; be able to be closed: 关上;闭起;能关闭: *The window ~s easily.* 这窗子容易关闭。*The door won't ~.* 这门关不上。**3** [VP6A] bring the folding parts of (sth) together: 折起;合拢: ~ (= close, the more usu word) *a book / a clasp-knife.* 合拢(close 较常用)书(折刀)。**4** [VP15A] catch or pinch by shutting sth: [因关闭某物而]夹住: ~ *one's fingers / dress, etc in the door,* ie between the door and the doorpost. 把手指(衣服 等)夹在门与门柱之间。**5** [VP2C, 15B] (special uses with *adverbial particles* and *preps*): (与副词性小品词及介系连用之特殊用法):

shut (sth) down, (of a factory, etc) stop working; end activity; close: (指工厂等)停工;关闭: *The workshop has ~ down and the workers are unemployed.* 那工场已关闭,工人失业了。*They've ~ down their factory.* 他们关闭了他们的工厂。Hence, 由此产生, **'~-down** n (temporary or permanent) closing of a factory, etc. [工厂等]暂时或永久之]关闭。

shut sb in, confine or enclose: 监禁;围住: *we're ~ in by hills here,* surrounded by hills which make access difficult and which prevent us from seeing far.我们这里被山丘环绕着(交通阻塞,视野有限)。*They ~ the boy in the cellar,* kept him there as a prisoner. 他们把那男孩囚禁在地客中。

shut sth off, stop the supply or flow of, eg gas, steam, water. 停止供应(煤气,蒸气,水等)。

shut sb / sth out, keep out; exclude; block: 将…关在外面; 排除; 遮住: ~ *out immigrants / competitive goods.* 拒绝移民(竞争性的货物)。*Don't ~ me out,* Don't close the door(s) so that I must stay out. 不要把我关在门外。*These trees ~ out the view.* 这些树遮住了那边的景色。

shut sth up, (a) close and secure all the doors and windows of: 关闭…所有门窗: ~ *up a house before going away for a holiday.* 去度假之前关闭房屋所有的门窗。*It's time to ~ up shop,* close the shop and stop doing business. 是打烊(或停业)的时候了。**(b)** put away for safety: 妥藏: ~ *up one's jewels in the safe.* 将珠宝妥藏在保险箱中。~ **(sb) up,** (colloq) (cause sb to) stop talking: (口)(使)停止谈话;(使)住口: *Tell him to ~ up.* 叫他住口。*Can't you ~ him up?* 你不能叫他住口吗?

shut·ter /'ʃʌtə(r); 'ʃʌtɚ/ n [C] **1** movable cover (wooden panel or iron plate, hinged or separate and detachable) for a window, to keep out light or intruders: 窗板;窗扇;铠窗(窗户之木质或金属质之活动遮板,或以铰链相连,或可自由装卸,用以遮光或防贼): *The shop-front is fitted with rolling ~s.* 那商店的店面装有卷门。**put up the ~s,** stop doing business (for the day, or permanently). 打烊; 歇业。**2** device that opens to admit light through the lens of a camera. (照相机镜头的)光阑;快门。□ vt [VP6A] provide with ~s; put up the ~s of. 为…装窗板或快门]关闭…之窗板或快门。

shuttle /'ʃʌtl; 'ʃʌtl/ n **1** (in a loom) cigar-shaped instrument with two pointed ends by which thread of weft is carried between threads of warp; (in a sewing-machine) sliding holder which carries the lower thread to meet the upper thread to make a stitch. (织布机之)梭(形似雪茄,两端尖,用以使纬线穿织于经线间者);(缝纫机之)滑梭(使底线与面线相合而成一针脚)。**2** (compounds) (复合词) **'~-cock** n round-based cork with feathers in it, struck to and fro across a net in the games of battledore and ~cock and badminton. 羽毛球;键球。⇨ the illus at **badminton.** 参看 badminton 之插图。~ **diplomacy,** diplomatic negotiation requiring the diplomat(s) to travel to and fro between the groups involved. 穿梭外交活动(外交人员需往返于有关团体间以磋商事务者)。'~ **service,** service (of trains, buses, etc) to and fro between places not far apart. (火车,公共汽车等之)短距离的区间车。□ vt, vi [VP6A, 15A, 2C] (cause to) move backwards and forwards, to and fro, like a ~ (使)穿梭般前后活动;(使)往返移动。

shy¹ /ʃaɪ; ʃaɪ/ adj (-er, -est) **1** (of persons) self-conscious and uncomfortable in the presence of others: (of behaviour, etc) showing this: (指人)在别人面前难为情或不自在的; 怕羞的; 害臊的; (指行为等)表现怕羞的: *He's not at all shy with women.* 他与女人们在一起一点也不害臊。*She gave him a shy look / smile.* 她羞怯地做着法的一瞥(笑)。**2** (of animals, birds, fish, etc) easily frightened; unwilling to be seen. (指动物,鸟,鱼等)易被惊走的,不愿被看见的。**3** shy of, chary of; hesitating about: 慎于; 对…踌躇: *They're shy of speaking to one another.* 他们彼此之间很少谈话。*Don't be shy of telling me what you want.* 你需要什么,尽管告诉我好了。**fight shy of,** ⇨ **fight²(1).** **shy·ly** adv **shy·ness** n

shy² /ʃaɪ; ʃaɪ/ vi (pt, pp shied /ʃaɪd; ʃaɪd/) [VP2A, 3A] **shy (at sth),** (of a horse) turn aside from fear or alarm: (指马)惊退。惊跳: *The horse was shying at a white object in the hedge.* 那马看到树篱中有个白色东西就吓得往后退。

shy³ /ʃaɪ; ʃaɪ/ vt (pt, pp shied /ʃaɪd; ʃaɪd/) (colloq) [VP6A, 15A] throw: (口)投; 掷: *shying stones at a bottle.* 向瓶子掷石块。□ n (pl **shies** /ʃaɪz; ʃaɪz/) throw: 投; 掷: *fivepence a shy,* eg throwing balls at coconuts at a fair; 五便士掷一次(如在义卖会中以球掷椰子);(colloq) any kind of attempt: (口)尝试: *have a shy at a task / an examination.* 尝试做某工作(参加考试)。

shy·ster /'ʃaɪstə(r); 'ʃaɪstɚ/ n (US colloq) person without professional honour, esp an unscrupulous lawyer. (美口)无职业道德之人;(尤指)奸猾的律师。

Sia·mese /ˌsaɪə'miːz; ˌsaɪə'miz/ adj of Siam (now 现称作 Thailand). 暹罗的;泰国的。~ **twins,** two persons joined together from birth. 连体双胞胎。~ **(cat),** oriental breed of cat with blue eyes and short-haired coat of cream, fawn or light grey hair. 暹罗猫。□ n (now 现称作 Thai) native of Siam; language of Siam. 暹罗人;泰国人;暹罗语;泰国语。⇨ **App 6.** 参看附录六。

Si·berian /saɪ'bɪərɪən; saɪ'bɪrɪən/ adj, n coming from, Siberia. 西伯利亚的;来自西伯利亚的。

sibi·lant /'sɪbɪlənt; 'sɪblənt/ adj having, making, a whistling kind of sound. 有咝咝声的;发咝咝声的。□ n sound such as one of the six English sounds /s, z, ʃ, ʒ, tʃ, dʒ/. 有咝声的辅音; 咝音(如英语中之 /s, z, ʃ, ʒ, tʃ, dʒ/)。

sib·ling /'sɪblɪŋ; 'sɪblɪŋ/ n one of two or more persons having the same parents; brother or sister. 兄弟(或姐妹)。

sibyl /'sɪbl; 'sɪbl/ n one of several women in ancient times who, it was believed, could see the future and give out messages from the gods; (hence, contemptuous or hum) fortune-teller; prophetess. 古代女预言家; (由此产生, 蔑或谐)算命者;女先知。~ **·line** /'sɪbɪlaɪn; 'sɪbl-ˌin/ adj uttered by, characteristic of, a ~; mysteriously prophetic. 女预言家或算命者所言的;女预言家的;神秘预言的。

sic /sɪk; sɪk/ adv (Lat) thus (placed in brackets to indicate that the preceding word, statement, etc is correctly quoted even though this seems unlikely or is clearly incorrect). (拉)原文如此(置放于括号内,表示前面的字或叙述等,纵有不妥当处,但系照原文引用)。

Si·cil·ian /sɪ'sɪlɪən; sɪ'sɪlɪən/ n, adj (native) of Sicily. 西西里岛的;西西里岛人。

sick /sɪk; sɪk/ adj 1 (pred only) (仅用作表语) be ~, throw up food from the stomach: 翻胃; 反胃; 作呕. feel ~, feel that one is about to do this. 觉得要呕吐; 欲呕. '**air·**'**car·**'**sea·**~ adj vomiting or inclined to vomit because of the motion of a plane/car/ship. 晕机(车, 船)的. Hence, 由此产生, '**air·**'**car·**'**sea·**~**ness** n: I was sea~ on the first day of the voyage. 我在航海的第一天晕船. 2 unwell; ill (in GB ill and unwell are polite usage, in US sick is normal usage): (在英国用 ill 和 unwell 二字较雅; 在美国 sick 为通用字): He's been ~ for six weeks. 他已经病了六周. He's a ~ man. 他是病人. be off ~ (with sth), be away from one's work because of bad health or disease: 因健康不佳或生病而不上班: Kate's off ~ with flu/a bad back. 凯蒂因流行性感冒(背痛)而不上班. fall ~, become ill. 生病. go/report ~, (mil use) report to the doctor for medical treatment (军事用语)到医生处去看病; 挂病号. the ~, (pl) those who are ill. (复)患者. '~**bay** n (a) (Navy) part of a ship for those who are ill. (海军)(船上之) 医务室. (b) medical centre on a university campus, etc. (大学等的)医疗中心. '~**bed** n bed of a sick person. 病床. '~**benefit** n ⇨ **sickness**. '~**berth** n = ~bay(a). '~**headache** n bilious headache. 偏头痛. '~**leave** n [U] permission to be away from duty or work because of illness: 病假: on ~ leave. 在病假中. '~**list** n list of those who are ill (eg in a regiment, on a warship, etc). (团, 军舰等内之)患病者名簿. '~**parade** n (mil) parade of those who are reporting ~. (军)患病士兵排队请假或接受诊疗之行列. '~**pay** n [U] pay to an employee who is absent from work because he is ill 付给生病员工的薪资; 生病补助费. '~**room** n room occupied by, or kept ready for, sb who is ill. 病房. 3 ~ (and tired/to death) of, (colloq) tired of, disgusted with: (口)厌烦; 厌恶: I'm ~ to death, of being blamed for everything that goes wrong. 每件差错都推在我头上, 真把我烦死了. 4 ~ at heart, deeply sad. 深为悲伤. ~ at/about sth, (colloq) unhappy, filled with regret about it: (口)对…感到不快, 遗憾: ~ at failing to pass the examination. 对考试不及格感到遗憾. 5 ~ for, filled with a longing for: 渴望; 恋慕: ~ for home/old happy times. 怀念家乡(旧日欢乐时光). 6 (sl) morbid; perverted: (俚)病态的; 变态的; 反常的: ~ humour/jokes; 下流的诙谐(笑话); a ~ mind. 精神不健全. □ vt ~ sth up, (colloq) vomit; throw up from the stomach. (口)呕吐.

sicken /'sɪkən; 'sɪkən/ vi, vt 1 [VP2A, 3A] ~ (for sth), be in the first stages of (an illness): 染上初期之(疾病); 生病: The child is ~ing for something. 这孩子象是生病了. 2 [VP6A] cause to feel disgusted: 使感到厌恶: Cruelty ~s most of us. 残酷使我们大多数人感到厌恶. Their business methods ~ me. 他们做生意的方法使我感到厌恶. 3 [VP3A, 4C] ~ at sth/to see sth, feel sick to see: 对(看到)…感到厌恶或难过: They ~ed at the sight of so much slaughter/~ed to see so many people slaughtered. 看到那么多人遭受屠杀, 他们感到很难过. 4 ~ of sth, become tired of, disgusted with: 厌倦; 厌烦. He ~ed of trying to bring about reforms. 他对试图改革感到厌恶. ~**ing** /'sɪkənɪŋ; 'sɪkənɪŋ/ adj disgusting: 使人厌恶的: ~ing smells/cruelty. 使人厌恶的气味(残酷). ~**ing·ly** adv

sick·ish /'sɪkɪʃ; 'sɪkɪʃ/ adj somewhat sick or sickening: 有点要呕吐的; 令人作呕或厌恶的; 象是生病的; 有点生病的: feel ~; 觉得有点生病似的; a ~ smell. 令人作呕的气味.

sickle /'sɪkl; 'sɪkl/ n [C] short-handled tool with a curved blade for cutting grass, grain, etc. 镰刀. ⇨ the illus at **tool**. 参看 tool 之插图.

sick·ly /'sɪklɪ; 'sɪklɪ/ adj (-ier, -iest) 1 frequently ill; often in poor health: 多病的; 不健康的: a ~ child. 多病的小孩. 2 having the appearance of sickness or ill health; pale: 有病容的; 不健康的; 苍白的: These plants are/look rather ~. 这些植物看来长得不大好. 3

weak; faint; suggesting unhappiness: 虚弱的; 无力的; 显示不快的: a ~ smile. 苦笑. 4 causing, or likely to cause, a feeling of sickness or distaste: 使人作呕的; 易令人生厌的: a ~ smell/taste; 令人作呕的气味(味道); ~ sentiments. 令人生厌的情感.

sick·ness /'sɪknɪs; 'sɪknɪs/ n 1 [U] illness; ill health: 患病; 不健康: Is there much ~ in the village now? 这村庄现在有许多疾病吗? They were absent because of ~. 他们因病缺席. '~ **benefit**, insurance payment to sb absent from work through illness. 疾病保险给付. 2 [C, U] (an) illness or disease: 病; 疾病: suffering from 'mountain ~/'sea~/'air~. 患高山病(晕船; 晕机). 3 [U] inclination to vomit; vomiting. 作呕; 呕吐.

side[1] /saɪd; saɪd/ n [C] (except **13** below) (下列第 **13** 义为不可数名词) 1 one of the flat or fairly flat surfaces of a solid object: (物体之平或相当平的)面: the 'six ~s of a cube. 立方体的六面. 2 one of the surfaces which is not the top or the bottom: 侧面(物体之面不属于顶或底者): A box has a top, a bottom, and four ~s. 匣子有一顶, 一底和四个侧面. 3 one of the surfaces which is not the top, bottom, front or back: 侧(物体之面不属于顶, 底, 前面或后面者): (attrib) (用作定语) the ~ entrance of the house (contrasted with the front or back entrance). 房子的侧门(与前门或后门相对). 4 (maths) one of the lines bounding a plane figure such as a rectangle or triangle. (数学)边. 5 either of the two surfaces of a thin, flat object or of material such as paper, cloth, anything manufactured in sheets: (纸, 布等平而薄的制品的)面: Write on one ~ of the paper only. 只在纸的一面书写. Which is the right ~ of the cloth, the ~ intended to be seen? 哪一面是这块布的正面? 6 inner or outer surface of sth vertical, sloping, round or curved: (垂直物, 倾斜物, 圆形物或弯曲物的)内面; 外面: the ~ of a mountain; 山坡; put one's socks on the wrong ~ out (= inside out, the usu phrase); 反穿袜子 (inside out 较常用); prehistoric paintings on the ~s (= walls) of a cave. 穴壁上的史前图画. 7 one of the two halves of a person on his left or right, esp from armpit to hip: (身体的)侧边(尤指腋至股之部分); 胁: wounded in the left ~. 左胁受伤. Come and sit by/at my ~. 来坐在我的旁边. by my ~, close together, for mutual support. 并肩坐; 互相支持地. split/burst one's ~s (laughing/with laughter), laugh heartily. 捧腹大笑. Hence, 由此产生, ~**splitting** adj causing hearty laughter. 令人捧腹大笑的. by the ~ of; by one's ~, close to and compared with: 与…在一起比较: She looks small by the ~ of her companion. 她与她的同伴站在一起, 显得娇小. 8 one of the two halves of an animal from foreleg to hindleg, esp as part of a carcass: (尤指宰后之动物由前腿至后腿分开的)半边躯体; 肋肉: a ~ of beef/bacon. 牛肋肉块(腌熏的猪肋肉). 9 part of an object, area, space, etc away from, at a distance from, a real or imaginary central line: 物体, 地区, 空间等与(真或想象的)中心线离开的部分; 面; 方; 边: the left/right/shady/sunny ~ of the street; 街道的左面(右面, 背阳面, 向阳面); the east ~ of the town; 城镇的东区; the debit/credit ~ of an account. 帐簿中的借(贷)方. He crossed to the far/the other ~ of the room. 他走向房间的另一边. on/from all ~s; on/from every ~, in/from all directions; everywhere. 在(从)各方面; 到处. take sb on one ~, take him aside, apart, eg to speak to him in confidence. 带某人到一边(如单独和他讲话). on the right/wrong ~ of (fifty, etc), below/above (50 years of age, etc). 不足(已过)(五十岁等). (do sth) on the ~, (colloq) as a ~line. 作为兼差或副业. ⇨ **sideline** below. 参看下列之 sideline. ~, secretly, discreetly: 秘密地; 谨慎地: He lived with his wife but regularly saw Julia on the ~. 他和妻子住在一起, 但暗地里经常会见朱莉娅. put sth on one ~, (a) put it aside, apart: 将某物置于一边. (b) postpone dealing with it. 延缓处置; 搁置. 10 one of two groups or parties of people who are opposed (in games, politics, war, etc) or who uphold

beliefs, opinions, etc against the other: (比赛的)队; (政治的)党; (敌对的)一方; 集团; 派系: *be on the winning/losing ~*; 属于胜(败)方; faults on both ~s; 咎在双方; *to pick* (= choose) ~s. 选择立场. *Austria has a strong ~*, eg a good football team. 奥地利有一支强劲的代表队(如足球队). *be on sb's ~*, be a supporter of him: 支持某人: *Whose ~ are you on, anyway?* Aren't you supposed to be supporting me? 你到底在支持谁? *Both countries claimed that God was on their ~*, eg in a war. 两国均称上帝站在他们的一方(如在交战时). *let the ~ down*, give an inferior performance and disappoint one's colleagues, team-mates, etc. 表现不佳而使其同事(队友)失望. *take ~s (with)*, support (sb, a party) in a dispute. (争论中)袒护(某人, 某团体). ⇨ side². *off/on ~*, (football, hockey) in a position (for receiving or playing the ball) that is/is not contrary to the rules. (足球, 曲棍球)在不合(合)于规则的位置. **11** aspect or view that is not complete; aspect different from or opposed to other aspects: 不完全的方面或观点; 与其他方面不同或相对的一方面: *look on the dark/bright/gloomy, etc ~ of things/life, etc*; 看事物(生命等)的黑暗面(光明面, 暗淡面等); *study all ~s of a question*; 研究一问题的各方面; *a man with many ~s to his character*. 有多种性格的人. *There are two ~s to the story*, two aspects. 这故事有两个说法. *on the 'high/low, etc ~*, rather high/low, etc: 相当高(低等): *Prices offered for fat cattle were on the high ~*. 购买肥牛所出的价钱相当高. **12** line of descent through a parent: 家系; 血统: *a cousin on my father's ~*. 父系的堂亲. **13** [U] (colloq) behaviour suggesting that one is better than other people; arrogance. (口)妄自尊大; 自负. *have no/be without ~*, make no pretence, assumption, of being superior or important. 不摆架子; 不自负. *put on ~*, claim to be, behave as if one is, superior. 摆架子; 自负. **14** (compounds, etc) (复合词等) '~-arms n pl swords or bayonets, worn at the left ~ by soldiers. (军人佩于左侧的)佩剑; 刺刀; 随身武器. '~-board n table, usu with drawers and cupboards, placed against the wall of a dining-room. 餐具桌(通常有抽屉和食柜, 置于餐室之墙边): 餐具架. '~-burns/-boards n pl ~-whiskers. (蓄于两颊的)侧须. '~-car n small one-wheeled car fastened to the ~ of a motorcycle. (附于机器脚踏车旁之)独轮侧车. '~-chapel n one in the aisle or at one ~ of a church. (教堂走廊或其一侧之)附属礼拜堂. ⇨ the illus at church. 参看 church 之插图. '~-dish n extra dish or course at a meal. (正菜外加的)附加菜; 小菜. '~-drum n small, double-sided drum, (originally hung at the drummer's ~) in a jazz or military band. (爵士乐队或军乐队中早先挂在鼓手身边之)小鼓. '~-effect n secondary or indirect effect, eg an undesirable effect of a drug used for a specific purpose. (药物等之)副作用. '~-face adv in profile: 侧面地: *photograph sb ~-face*. 拍摄某人的侧面照片. '~-glance n look to or from one ~. 斜视; 侧视. '~-issue n question of less importance (in relation to the main one). (与主题有关的)次要问题. '~-light n light from or at the ~; (fig) incidental illumination, eg of a person's character, of a problem, etc. 侧光; 侧灯; (喻)(对某人性格或某一问题等的)偶然启示; 间接说明. '~-line n class of goods sold in addition to the chief class of goods; occupation which is not one's main work. 附带售卖之货品; 副业; 兼职. '~-lines n pl (space immediately outside) lines bounding a football pitch, tennis-court, etc at the ~s. (球场等之)界线; 界线以外之地. *on the ~-lines*, (fig) merely as a spectator, not taking part. (喻)做旁观者; 不参与. '~-long adj, adv (directed) to or from one ~: 横向的(地); 斜向的(地); 侧面的(地): *look ~long at sb*; 斜视某人; *a ~long glance*. 斜视. '~-road n minor road branching off a main road. 叉路; 小道. '~-saddle n woman's saddle, made so that both feet may be on the same ~ of the horse. 偏座鞍; 横鞍; 女鞍. □ adv on a ~-saddle: 偏座地; 在女鞍上: *In*

former times most women used to ride ~-saddle. 从前大多数女子用偏座鞍骑马. '~-show n (a) small show at a fair or exhibition. 附属之表演; 杂耍. (b) activity of small importance in relation to the main activity. 小活动; 附属事件. '~-slip n (a) (motoring) skid. (驾车)横滑; 滑向一边. (b) (flying) movement to one ~ instead of forward. (飞行)侧滑. □ vi (-pp-) make a ~-slip. 横滑; 侧滑. '~-man /-zmən/ n (pl -men /-men/) church helper who shows people to their seats, takes up the collection, etc. (教堂之)助手(带领礼拜者就座, 收集捐款等). '~-step n step taken to one ~ (eg to avoid a blow in boxing). 侧步; 横步(如在拳击中躲开打击等). □ vt, vi (-pp-) [VP6A] avoid (a blow, etc) by stepping to one ~; evade (a question); [VP2A] step to one ~. 走向侧步以避免(打击等); 规避(问题等); 走侧步. '~-stroke n (kinds of) stroke used in swimming in which one ~ is above and the other below the water. 侧泳. '~-track n railway siding; branch road. (铁路之)侧线; 旁轨. □ vt [VP6A] turn (a train) into a siding; (fig) turn (a person) from his purpose; postpone consideration of (a proposal, etc). 将(火车)转入侧线; (喻)转移(某人)的目标; 缓议(提案等). '~-view n view obtained from the ~. 侧景; 侧面图. '~-walk n (chiefly US; GB 英 = pavement) path at the ~ of a street for persons on foot. (主美)人行道. ~-wards /-wədz/, -wədz/, ~-ways /-weiz/ -, wez/ adv to, towards, from, the ~; with the ~ or edge first: 斜着; 斜向一边地; 自一边地; 一边向前地: *look ~ways at sb* 斜视某人; *walk/carry sth ~ways through a narrow opening*; 侧着身子走过(携物经过)狭窄的通道; (attrib) directed to one ~. (用作定语)向旁边的; 倾斜的; '~-whiskers n pl hair on the ~s of the face down to, but excluding, the chin. (蓄于两颊之)侧须; 络腮胡子. ◆ **beard. -sided** /-'saɪdd/ suff having a specified number of ~s: 有(若干)边的: *a 'five-~d figure*. 五边形.

side² /saɪd/ vi [VP3A] ~ *with*, take part, be on the same side (as sb in an argument or quarrel): (在辩论或争论中)参与; 袒护; 支持(某人): *It is safer to ~ with the stronger party*. 参与实力较强的一边比较稳妥.

sid·e·real /saɪ'dɪərɪəl/ sar'dɪrɪəl/ adj of the stars and their measurements: 星的; 恒星的; 以恒星为衡量标准的: ~ *time*, measured by the stars; 恒星时(以恒星的位置作衡量标准的时间); *the ~ year*, 365 days, 6 hours, 10 minutes. 恒星年(即 365 天, 6 小时, 10 分).

sid·ing /'saɪdɪŋ/ 'saɪdɪŋ/ n [C] short railway track to and from which trains may be shunted. (铁路之)侧线; 旁轨(转轨之用).

si·dle /'saɪdl/ 'saɪdl/ vi [VP2C] ~ *along/off; ~ away from/up to sb*, move in a shy or nervous way: 羞怯或不安走近来(走开); 羞怯或不安地离开(走向)某人: *The little girl ~d up to me*. 那小女孩羞怯地走向我.

siege /siːdʒ/ siːdʒ/ n [C, U] (period of) operations of armed forces who surround and blockade a town or fortress in order to capture it: 围困; 围攻; 围城; 围攻期间: *a ~ of 50 days*. 围攻五十天. *Before the ~ ended, the citizens were almost starving*. 在围困结束以前, 市民已濒临饥饿边缘. *lay ~ to (a town, etc)*, surround and blockade it. 围攻(一城等). *raise a ~*, end it by forcing the enemy's forces to withdraw. 解围; 强迫敌人撤围. '~ artillery/guns, big guns used in ~s (too heavy, in former times, for use in the field). 攻城炮.

si·en·na /sɪ'enə/ sɪ'ɛnə/ n [U] kind of earth used as a colouring matter: 浓黄土; 赭土(用作颜料): *burnt ~*, reddish-brown; (经过锻制之)红褐色颜料; 锻赭土; *raw ~*, brownish-yellow. 赭黄颜料.

si·er·ra /sɪ'erə/ sɪ'erə/ n [C] long mountain chain with sharp slopes and edges (esp in Spain and Spanish America). 峰峦起伏之山岭(尤指在西班牙及西班牙语系的美洲国家).

si·es·ta /sɪ'estə/ sɪ'estə/ n [C] period of rest or sleep taken in the early afternoons, as is customary in hot countries. 午睡(气候炎热国家的习惯).

sieve /sɪv ; sɪv/ n [C] utensil with wire network or gauze for separating finer grains, etc from coarse grains, etc or solids from liquids. 筛；漏杓；滤器。 *have a head / memory like a ~*, be incapable of remembering anything. 健忘。 □ vt [VP6A] put through, sift with, a ~. 以筛或漏杓筛滤；滤。

sift /sɪft/ vt, vi 1 [VP6A, 14, 15A, B] ~ *(out) (from)*, put, separate by putting, through a sieve: 筛；筛分；过滤： *the cinders*; 筛煤渣； ~ *(out) ashes from the cinders / the wheat from the chaff.* 自煤渣中筛出灰 (将小麦的壳子筛掉)。 2 [VP6A, 15A] shake through a sieve: 筛撒： ~ *flour;* 筛撒面粉； ~ *sugar on to a cake.* 筛糖在糕饼上。 3 [VP6A] (fig) examine carefully: (喻)详审；细审： ~ *the evidence.* 细审证据。 4 [VP2C] fall, pass, come through, as from a sieve. 筛下；纷落。 ~**er** n small sieve-like utensil, chiefly used in cooking: 小筛(主要用于烹饪)： *a 'flour-~er.* 面粉筛。

sigh /saɪ ; saɪ/ vi, vt 1 [VP2A] take and exhale a deep breath that can be heard (indicating sadness, tiredness, relief, etc); (of the wind) make a sound like ~ing. 叹息；叹气(表示悲哀, 疲倦, 慰藉等)；(指风)发出似叹息之声；哀鸣。 2 [VP3A] ~ *for sth*, feel a longing for: 热望；渴念： ~ *for the good old days to return.* 渴望昔日美好的时光再度出现。 3 [VP6A, 15B] ~ *(out)*, express, utter, with ~s: 以叹息表示；叹息地说出： ~ *out a prayer.* 叹息着说出祷告词。 □ n [C] act of ~ing; sound of ~ing: 叹息；叹息声；叹鸣声： *utter / heave a ~;* 发出一声叹息； *with a ~ of relief.* 带着慰藉的叹息。

sight¹ /saɪt/ saɪt/ n 1 [U] power of seeing: 视力；视觉： *lose one's ~,* become blind; 失明；变盲； *have long / short* or *far / near ~,* be able to see things well only at long / short range; 患远(近)视； *have good / poor ~* (= eyesight). 目力良好(不好)。 *know sb by ~,* know him by appearance only, not as an acquaintance. 和某人面熟(并不相识)。 **second ~,** ⇨ **second¹(1).** 2 [U, but sometimes with *indef art* in *high art*] 有时用不定冠词] seeing or being seen: 见；被见；观见： *Their first ~ of land came after three days at sea.* 他们在海上三天之后才首次看见陆地。 *catch ~ of; have / get a ~ of,* begin to see; succeed in seeing: 发现；看到： *If you ever catch ~ of Ted Clark anywhere, call the police.* 如果你在任何地方看见特德·克拉克, 就去报警。 *keep ~ of; keep sb / sth in ~,* remain near enough to see or watch. 保持在视线之内；照看；监视。 *lose ~ of,* see no longer; fail to pay further attention to; forget about: 再也看不见；忽略；忘记： *I've lost ~ of that bird.* 我不知那鸟的去向。 *We must not lose ~ of the fact that....* 我们切不可忽略…之事实。 *at / on ~,* as soon as (sb or sth) is seen: 一见可(某人, 某物)立即： *play music at ~,* from printed music without previous study or practice; 看谱演奏(未先行研究或练习)； *a draft payable at / a '~ draft,* to be paid at once when presented. 即期汇票。 *The sentry had orders to shoot at / on ~,* as soon as he saw any suspicious person, etc. 哨兵奉令见到可疑的人立即射杀。 *at first ~,* when first seen; without study, examination, etc: 初见；乍看；未加研究, 细察等： *At first ~ the problem seemed insoluble.* 乍看之下这问题似乎无法解决。 *He fell in love with her at first ~.* 他对她一见即钟情。 *at (the) ~ of,* on seeing: 一看见…就： *At ~ of the police officers the men ran off.* 那些人一看到警官的影子就跑了。 *They all laughed at the ~ of old Percy dancing with a girl of sixteen.* 他们看到老珀西与一位十六岁的女郎跳舞, 全都大笑。 3 [U] range of seeing; distance within which seeing is possible: 视域；眼界： *in / within / out of (one's) ~,* (of objects, etc) visible / invisible. (指物体等)看得见(看不见)。 *那火车尚看得见 (尚未消失)。 Victory was not yet in ~.* 胜利尚不可预料。 *in / within / out of ~ of sth,* (of the viewer) where sth can / cannot be seen: (指观看者)能看见(看不见)： *We are not yet out of ~ of land, can still see it.* 我们仍可看见陆地。 *We are now within ~ of the end of this boring task,* can look forward to reaching

the end. 这件令人厌烦的工作不久可望结束。 *come into / go out of ~,* come near enough / go too far away to be visible. 进入(走出)视野。 *keep out of ~,* stay where one cannot be seen. 待在不会被人看见的地方。 *keep out of sb's ~,* stay where he cannot see you. 不要让某人看见。 4 [U] opinion; way of looking at sth: 意见： *Do what is right in your own ~.* 做你认为对的事。 *All men are equal in the ~ of God.* 上帝对所有的人同等看待。 5 [C] sth seen or to be seen, esp sth remarkable; (*pl*) noteworthy buildings, places, features, etc of a place or district: 情景；景象；(尤指)奇观；(复)一地方或地区之值得看的建筑物、胜地、特色等；名胜；风景： *The Grand Canyon is one of the ~s of the world.* 大峡谷是世界名胜之一。 *Our tulips are a wonderful ~ this year / are a ~ to see.* 今年的郁金香(今年)至为可观。 *Come and see the ~s of London.* 来看看伦敦的名胜。 Hence, 由此产生, '~-**seeing** n going about to see places, etc. 观光；游览。 '~-**seer** /-siə(r) ; -,siə/ n person who goes to see the ~s. 观光者。 *a ~ for sore eyes,* person or thing one enjoys seeing; sb or sth very welcome. 乐于看见的人或物；极受欢迎的人或物。 6 *a ~,* (colloq) person or thing that excites ridicule or unfavourable comment: (口)惹起嘲弄或物议的人或事物： *What a ~ she looks in that old dress!* 她穿那件旧衣服看起来多怪里怪气! *What a ~ you are!* 瞧你这副德性! *She 'does look a ~!* 她的样子真怪! 7 [C] (often *pl*) device that helps to aim or observe when using a rifle, telescope, etc: (常用复数)(步枪, 望远镜等帮助瞄准或观察的)瞄准器；照准具；准星；照门： *the ~s of a rifle;* 步枪之准星与照门； aim or observation taken with such a device: (以瞄准器所作的)瞄准： *take a careful ~ before firing;* 发射前仔细瞄准； *take a ~ with a compass / quadrant;* 以罗盘(象限仪)瞄看； *take a ~ at the sun,* eg to determine a ship's position. 观测太阳(以推定船的位置等)。 8 *a ~,* (sl) great quantity: (俚)大量；很多： *It cost him a ~ of money / trouble.* 那花了他一大笔钱(为他招来一大堆麻烦)。 *He's a ~* (adverbial, 作副词用, = very much) *too clever to be caught by the police.* 他非常聪明, 警察抓不到他。 *not by a 'long ~,* not nearly. 差得远；远不如。 ~**ed** *suff* (with *adjj*) having the kind of ~(1) indicated: (与形容词连用)有某种之视力的： *'weak- / 'long- / 'far-~ed.* 视力弱的／眼光远大的(远视的)。

sight² /saɪt/ ; saɪt/ vt [VP6A] 1 get sight of, esp by coming near: 看见(尤指因接近而看见)： *After many months at sea, Columbus ~ed land.* 在海上航行许多月以后, 哥伦布终于看到了陆地。 2 observe (a star, etc) by using sights(7); adjust the sights (7) of (a gun); furnish (a gun, etc) with sights: 观测(星等)；调整(枪炮)的瞄准器；将瞄准器装于(枪, 炮等)： *a '~ing shot,* one to get the range. (为测距及调整瞄准器所作之)试射。 ~**ing** n occasion on which sth is ~ed: 某物被看到之时机；出现： *new ~ings of the Loch Ness monster.* 尼斯湖水怪新近的出现。

sight·less /'saɪtlɪs; 'saɪtlɪs/ *adj* blind. 盲的；无视力的。

sign¹ /saɪn/ saɪn/ n [C] 1 mark, object, symbol, used to represent sth: 记号；符号： *mathematical ~s,* eg +, −, ×, ÷. 数学符号(如 +, −, ×, ÷)。 2 word or words, design, etc, as a public notice, to give a warning, or to direct sb towards sth: 告示；牌示： *'traffic ~s,* eg for a speed limit, a bend in the road. 交通牌示(如说明速度限制, 路弯等)。 '~-**post** n post at or near crossroads with names of places on each road (and often distances). 路标(置于十字路口, 标示地名、距离等)。 □ vt provide with ~posts: 为…设置路标： *The road is well ~posted.* 这条路设有明确的路标。 3 sth that gives evidence, points to the existence or likelihood of sth: 迹象；征兆；痕迹： *the ~s of suffering on his face.* 他脸上的痛苦的痕迹。 *Are dark clouds a ~ of rain?* 乌云是天雨的征兆吗? *Violence is a ~ of weakness or fear, not a ~ of strength or confidence.* 暴力是懦弱或恐惧的表象, 不是力量或信心的表征。 ~ **and counter~,** secret sentences, etc by which friends can be distinguished

from enemies or from those who do not share a secret. 口令; 隐语; 黑话。 **4** movement of the hand, head, etc used with or instead of words; signal: 手、头等的示意动作; 手势; 信号: *a '~-language,* eg one used by deaf and dumb persons; 手语(聋哑者等所用之语言); *the ~ of the cross,* a movement with the hand outlining a cross, as a blessing, or with a prayer. (祝福或祈祷时)用手画十字。 **5 '~(-board),** device (often painted on a board) displayed by traders and shopkeepers *('shop-~),* and by inns *('inn-~),* to advertise their business: 招牌; 店招(商店, 旅社等用以招揽生意者, 如: 'shop-~, 'inn-~): *at the ~ of the Red Lion,* at the inn of this name. 在红狮旅社。 **'~-painter** *n* person who paints ~boards. 制作招牌者。

sign² /saɪn; saɪn/ *vt, vi* **1** [VP6A, 15B, 2A, 2C] write one's name on (a letter, document, etc) to show that one is the writer or that one accepts or agrees with the contents: 签字于(信, 文件等): *~ a letter/a Will and Testament/a cheque;* 签字于信件(遗嘱, 支票); *~ one's name,* write it for this purpose. 签名。 *Please ~ on the dotted line.* 请在虚线上签名。 ***~ sth away,*** give up (rights, property, etc) by ~ing one's name. 签字让渡(权利, 财产等)。 ***~ (sb) in/out,*** write one's/sb's name as a record of arrival/departure. 登记(自己或某人的)姓名以示到达(离去)。 ⇨ *clock in/out* at **clock¹(2).** ***~ on,*** (colloq) (of an unemployed worker) become formally registered for money on social security, ⇨ **social(2).** (口)(指失业工人)正式登记领社会救济金。 ***~ on/up,*** (of a worker, etc), ~ an agreement about employment: (指工人等)签约受雇: *The seaman ~ed on for a voyage to Valparaiso and back.* 那水手签约受雇作一次来往瓦尔帕莱索之航行。 ***~ sb on/up,*** (of an employer, etc) ~ an agreement about employment: (指雇主等)签约雇用: *The firm ~ed on fifty more workers last week.* 该公司上周签约增雇了五十名工人。 *The manager,* is of a football team, *has ~ed up some new players.* (足球队之) 经理已签约雇用几名新的球员。 ***~ sth over (to sb),*** confirm the sale of sth (to sb) by ~ing legal papers. 签字转让某物(与某人)。 **2** [VP3A, 6A, 16A] ***~ (to/for) sb (to do sth),*** make known (to sb) an order or request by making signs(4): 做手势; 做信号: *The policeman ~ed (for) them to stop.* 警察做手势叫他们停住。 *He ~ed to me to be quiet.* 他做手势要我安静。 **3** [VP2C] ***~ on/off,*** (radio) indicate the beginning/end of a broadcast, eg by means of a few bars of a tune or by other sound effects. (无线电)以曲调或音响表示广播开始(结束)。 ⇨ **signature(2).**

sig·nal¹ /'sɪgnəl; 'sɪgnḷ/ *n* [C] **1** (making of a) movement, (showing of a) light, (sending of a) message, device used, to give a warning, an order or information, esp to sb at a distance; order, warning, etc. conveyed in this way: 信号; 暗号; 打信号等; 借信号所发出的命令, 警告等: *'traffic ~s,* for cars, etc in the streets; 交通信号; *'hand ~s,* made with the hand by the driver of a motor-vehicle to show which way it will turn, etc; 汽车驾驶者的手势(如表示转弯等); *give the ~ for an attack.* 发出进攻的信号。 *A red light is usually a ~ of danger.* 红灯通常是危险的信号。 *A train must not pass a ~ that is at danger.* 火车切不可闯危险号志。 **'~-box** *n* building on a railway from which ~s and movements of trains are controlled. (铁路上之)信号所。 **'~·man** /-mən; -,mæn/ *n* (*pl* **-men**) person who operates ~s on a railway; man who sends and receives ~s (in the army and navy). (铁路之)信号手; (陆海军之)信号兵。 **'~ gun** *n* one fired as a ~ in case of distress, eg on a wrecked ship. (危难时, 如遭船难, 所用之)信号枪; 号炮。 **2** event which is the immediate cause of general activity, etc: (一般活动等之)直接原因; 导火线: *The arrival of the President was the ~ for an outburst of cheering.* 总统的到达引起一阵欢呼。 **3** electronic impulse in radio, TV, etc; sound or TV image, transmitted or received: 讯号; 电台、电视发送或接收之声音或影像: *an area with a poor/excellent TV signal.* 影像不清(极佳)之地区。 □ *vt, vi* (**-ll-,** US, **-l-**) [VP6A, 9, 17, 2A, C] make a ~ or ~s to; send by ~; make use of ~(s): 向…发信号; 以信号报知; 用信号: *~ a message:* 以信号发送消息; *~ (to) the commanding officer (that...);* 向指挥官发信号 (报告…); *~ (to) the waiter to bring the menu;* 作手势要侍者拿菜单; *~ that one is about to turn left.* 作手势表示将向左转。 *Sailors ~ with flags by day and with lights at night.* 水手们白日用旗, 夜晚用灯, 发信号。 **~·ler** (US=**~er**) /'sɪgnələ(r); 'sɪgnələ/ *n* person who ~s, esp a soldier (cf Navy, 参较海军用语, **'~·man**) specially trained in sending and receiving messages. 信号员; (尤指)信号兵。

sig·nal² /'sɪgnəl; 'sɪgnḷ/ *attrib adj* remarkable; outstanding: 显著的; 非常的: *a ~ victory/success/achievement.* 重大的胜利(成功, 成就)。 **~ly** /-nəlɪ; -nḷɪ/ *adv* in a ~ manner: 显著地; 非常地: *fail ~ly.* 大败。

sig·nal·ize /'sɪgnəlaɪz; 'sɪgnə,laɪz/ *vt* [VP6A] make (an event) noteworthy or conspicuous. 使(事件)著名; 使显著。

sig·na·tory /'sɪgnətrɪ *US:* -tɔ:rɪ; 'sɪgnə,torɪ/ *n* [C] (*pl* **-ries**) (person, country, etc) that has signed an agreement: 签约者; 签约国: *the signatories to the Treaty;* 签约之各国; (attrib) (用作定语) *the ~ powers.* 签约诸强国。

sig·na·ture /'sɪgnətʃə(r); 'sɪgnətʃə/ *n* [C] **1** person's name signed by himself: 签字: *put one's ~ to a letter;* 签名于信件; *send letters in to the manager for ~,* for him to sign. 把信送给经理签字。 **2 '~ tune,** tune (a few bars of a piece of music) identifying a broadcasting station or a particular programme or performer. 信号调; 信号曲(某一广播节目或表演者启播前的数小节音乐)。 **'key ~,** (music) indication of a (change of) key. (音乐)调号。

sig·net /'sɪgnɪt; 'sɪgnɪt/ *n* [C] private seal used with or instead of a signature. 私章; 图章。 **'~-ring,** finger ring with a ~ set in it. 图章戒指。 **Writer to the S~,** Scottish law officer. (苏格兰之)律师; (苏格兰最高法院的)司法官。

sig·nifi·cance /sɪg'nɪfɪkəns; sɪg'nɪfəkəns/ *n* [U] meaning; importance: 意义; 意味; 重要; 重大: *understand the ~ of a remark;* 了解某句话的意义; *a matter/speech of great/little ~;* 重大的(无关紧要的)事(演讲); *a look of deep ~.* 含意深刻的一瞥。

sig·nifi·cant /sɪg'nɪfɪkənt; sɪg'nɪfəkənt/ *adj* ***~ (of),*** having a special or suggestive meaning; important: 有特殊意义的; 有含义的; 重要的; 重大的: *a ~ speech.* 意味深长的演说。 *Few things are more ~ of a man's interests than the books on his shelves.* 一个人书架上的书籍最能显示这个人的兴趣。 **~·ly** *adv*

sig·nifi·ca·tion /,sɪgnɪfɪ'keɪʃn; sɪg,nɪfə'keʃən/ *n* [C] (intended) meaning (of a word, etc). (字等的)意义; 含义。

sig·nifi·cat·ive /sɪg'nɪfɪkətɪv *US:* -keɪtɪv; sɪg'nɪfə,ketɪv/ *adj* ***~ (of),*** offering evidence (of). 提供证据的; 有意义的。

sig·nify /'sɪgnɪfaɪ; 'sɪgnə,faɪ/ *vt, vi* (*pt, pp* **-fied**) **1** [VP6A, 9, 15A] make known (one's views, intentions, purpose, etc); be a sign of; mean: 表示(个人的见解, 意向, 目的等); 为…之表征; 意味: *He signified his agreement/that he agreed by nodding.* 他点头表示同意。 *His wife signified her approval.* 他的妻子表示赞成。 *Do dark clouds ~ rain?* 乌云表示有雨吗? *What does this phrase ~?* 这短语的意义是什么? **2** [VP2A, C] matter; be of importance: 有关系; 有重要性: *It doesn't ~.* 那无关重要。 *It signifies much/little.* 那甚为重要(不大重要)。

si·gnor /'si:njɔ:(r); 'sinjɔr/, **si·gnora** /sɪ'njɔ:rə; sin'jɔrə/, **si·gnor·ina** /,sɪnjɔ:'ri:nə; ,sinjə'rinə/ *nn* **S~,** titles used of or to Italians corresponding to Mr, Mrs and Miss or (with a small *s*) Sir, Madam and young lady. (大写 S, 意大利人称呼)先生; 太太; 小姐; (小写 s)大人; 夫人; 少女。

Sikh /siːk; sik/ *n* member of a monotheistic Hindu sect founded in the 16th c in the Punjab. (印度北方的)锡克教徒。

si·lage /ˈsaɪlɪdʒ; ˋsaɪlɪdʒ/ *n* [U] green fodder stored in a silo or pit without drying (to feed cattle in winter). 保藏于粮秣库或坑中之新鲜饲料(以备冬季饲牛用)。

si·lence /ˈsaɪləns; ˋsaɪləns/ *n* [U] **1** condition of being quiet or silent; absence of sound: 寂静; 无声: *the ~ of night/of the grave.* 夜(墓地)的寂静。 **2** condition of not speaking, answering (questions, spoken or written), or making comments, etc; (with *indef art*) period (of saying nothing): 沉默; (与不定冠词连用)沉默的一段时间: *Your ~ on recent events surprises me.* 你对于近来发生的事情保持沉默令我惊奇。*There was a short ~ and then uproar broke out.* 沉默片刻之后又喧嚣起来了。 ***S~ gives consent,*** (prov) If nothing is said in answer to a proposal or suggestion we may suppose that it is agreed to. (谚)沉默即表示同意。 ***reduce sb to ~,*** (esp) refute his arguments so that he has to stop talking. (尤指)(反驳其论点)使无话可说。 ***in ~,*** silently: 沉默地; 无声地: *listen to sb in ~.* 默默地听某人说话。*We should not pass over this disgraceful affair in ~,* We ought to protest, etc. 我们不应对这件可耻的事保持缄默。□ *vt* [VP6A] make (sb or sth) silent; cause to be quiet(er): 使(某人或某物)沉默; 使哑口无言; 使(较)安静: *~ a baby's crying;* 使婴儿停止哭叫; *~ one's critics/the enemy's guns.* 使批评者哑口无言(压制敌人炮火)。 **si·lencer** *n* device that reduces the noise made by the exhaust of a petrol engine, the report of a gun, etc. (汽油引擎, 枪, 炮等之)消音器; 减音器; 遏声器。

si·lent /ˈsaɪlənt; ˋsaɪlənt/ *adj* **1** making no or little sound; still; not accompanied by any sound: 声音极小的; 寂静的; 无声的: *a ~ prayer;* 默祷; *with ~ footsteps;* 脚步轻悄地; *the ~ running of a Rolls Royce car;* 劳斯莱斯汽车跑起来声音非常小; *a ~ film,* without a sound track. 无声电影; 默片。 **2** saying little or nothing; giving no answer, views, etc: 沉默的; 寡言的: *Do you know when to keep ~,* say nothing, keep a secret? 你知道在什么时候该保持沉默吗? *You'd better be ~ about what happened.* 你对于所发生的事最好不开口。*Her husband is the strong, ~ type.* 她丈夫是个坚定、沉默型的人。 **ˈ~ partner,** (US) (美) = sleeping partner. ⇨ **sleep²(1).** **3** written but not pronounced: 写出而不发音的: *a ~ letter, eg b in doubt, w in wrong.* 不发音的字母(如 doubt 中之 b, wrong 中之 w)。 **~·ly** *adv*

sil·hou·ette /ˌsɪluːˈet; ˌsɪluˋɛt/ *n* picture in solid black showing only the outline; outline of sb or sth seen against a light background: 黑色轮廓像; 黑色半面画像; 侧影; 轮廓; 剪影: *see sth in ~.* 看见某物的轮廓。□ *vt* (usu passive) show, exhibit, in ~: (通常用被动语态)现出…之轮廓: *~d against the eastern sky at dawn.* 破晓时东方天际映出的轮廓。⇨ the illus at **hansom.** 参看 hansom 之插图。

sil·ica /ˈsɪlɪkə; ˋsɪlɪkə/ *n* [U] silicon dioxide **(SiO_2)**, occurring as ~ sand (used in glass-making) and in quartz, and as the principal constituent of sandstone and other rocks. 硅石; 硅氧; 二氧化硅(SiO_2, 天然者为硅沙, 用以制玻璃, 存于石英中, 并为沙岩及其他岩石之主要成分)。

sili·cate /ˈsɪlɪkeɪt; ˋsɪlɪˌket/ *n* [U] one of a great number of compounds containing silica: 硅酸盐: *~ of soda.* 硅酸苏打。

sili·con /ˈsɪlɪkən; ˋsɪlɪkən/ *n* [U] non-metallic element (symbol **Si**) found combined with oxygen in quartz, sandstone, etc. 硅(Si)(非金属元素, 以氧化物之形式见于石英、沙岩等中)。 **ˌ~ ˈchip** *n* chip made of ~, used to make an integrated circuit. (用以制造集成电路之)硅片。⇨ **integrate(1).**

sili·cone /ˈsɪlɪkəʊn; ˋsɪlɪkon/ *n* [U] (kinds of) complex organic compounds of silicon used in paints, varnish and lubricants. 硅酮; 矽酮(用于油漆, 假漆及滑润剂中的(数种)复合有机化合物)。

sili·co·sis /ˌsɪlɪˈkəʊsɪs; ˌsɪlɪˋkosɪs/ *n* [U] disease caused by breathing in quartz dust (eg in a coalmine). 矽肺; 石末沉着病(因吸进石英尘所产生之病, 如在煤矿中者)。

silk /sɪlk; sɪlk/ *n* **1** [U] fine, soft thread from the cocoons of certain insects; material made from this; (attrib) made of this: 丝; 丝织品; 绸; (用作定语)丝制的; 绸做的: *raw ~;* 生丝; *~ stockings,* 丝袜; *a ~ shirt* 丝制衬衫。 **ˈ~·screen (printing),** method of printing by forcing the colour(s) through a stencil of ~ or other finely woven material. 绢印(印制法)。 **ˈ~·worm** *n* caterpillar that spins ~ to form a cocoon. 蚕。 **2** *(pl)* garments of ~: (复)绸衣: *dressed in ~s and satins,* wearing rich clothes. 穿着锦衣华服。 **3** [C] (in England) Queen's/King's Counsel (abbr 略作 **QC,KC**). (英)敕选律师; 高等律师。⇨ **counsel¹(3).** ***take ~,*** become a QC/KC. 做敕选律师。

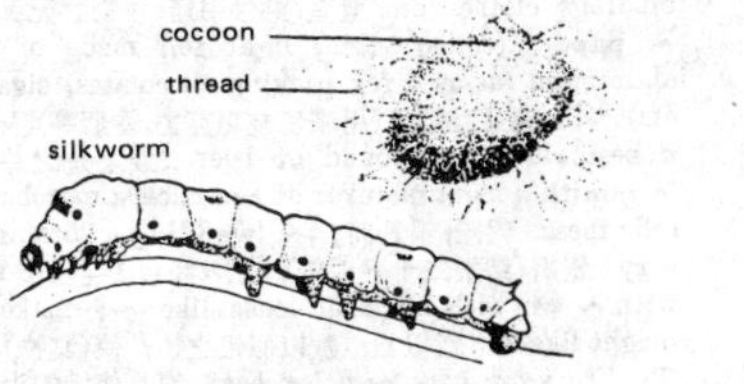

a silkworm

silken /ˈsɪlkən; ˋsɪlkən/ *adj* **1** soft and smooth soft and shining: 柔软光滑的; 柔和而有光泽的: *a ~ voice;* 柔和的声音; *~ hair.* 柔软光滑的头发。 **2** (old use, or liter) made of silk: (旧用法, 文)丝织的; 绸制的: *~ dresses.* 绸衣。

silky /ˈsɪlkɪ; ˋsɪlkɪ/ *adj* **(-ier, -iest)** soft, shiny, smooth, like silk: 象丝一般柔软, 光亮, 光滑的: *a ~* (= suave) *manner;* 温和的态度; *a ~ voice.* 柔和的声音。 **silki·ness** *n*

sill /sɪl; sɪl/ *n* [C] flat shelf or block of wood or stone at the base of a window (= **ˈwindow-sill**) or (rarely) of a doorway. 窗台; (罕)门槛。⇨ the illus at **window.** 参看 window 之插图。

sil·la·bub (US = **syll-**) /ˈsɪləbʌb; ˋsɪləˌbʌb/ *n* [C, U] soft, sweet dish of food made of cream or milk mixed with wine into curd, etc. 乳酒冻(一种用奶油或牛奶加葡萄酒制成之冻状甜食)。

silly /ˈsɪlɪ; ˋsɪlɪ/ *adj* **(-ier, -iest)** foolish; weak-minded: 愚蠢的; 低能的; 无智慧的: *say ~ things;* 说蠢话; *a ~ little boy.* 傻小男孩。*Don't be ~!* 别傻! *How ~ of you to do that!* 你做那事多笨啊! □ *n* (*pl* **-lies**) (chiefly used to or by children) ~ person. (主要用于指小孩或由小孩所用)傻人; 笨伯。 **sil·li·ness** *n*

silo /ˈsaɪləʊ; ˋsaɪlo/ *n* (*pl* **~s** /-ləʊz; -loz/) [C] air-tight structure (either a tall cylindrical tower or a pit) in which green food *(silage)* is stored for farm animals. 贮藏新鲜饲料之密室(圆柱型高塔或地下坑); 粮秣室。

silt /sɪlt; sɪlt/ *n* [U] sand, mud, etc carried by moving water (and left at the mouth of a river, in a harbour, etc). 淤沙; 淤泥; 泥滓(由流动之水带至河口, 港中等处者)。□ *vt, vi* [VP2C, 15B] **~ *(sth)* up,** (cause to) become stopped with ~: (使)为淤泥充塞: *The harbour has ~ed up.* 这海港已为淤泥充塞。*The sand has ~ed up the mouth of the river.* 泥沙充塞了河口。

sil·van /ˈsɪlvən; ˋsɪlvən/ = **sylvan.**

sil·ver /ˈsɪlvə(r); ˋsɪlvɚ/ *n* [U] **1** shining white precious metal (symbol **Ag**) used for ornaments, coins, utensils, etc: 银(Ag)(光亮之白色贵重金属, 用于制装饰品、硬币、器皿等): *ˈtable ~,* spoons, forks, etc. 银餐具。 **~ plate,** metal articles coated with ~. 镀银之金属器具。 ***be born with a ~ ˈspoon in one's mouth,*** be born into

a wealthy family. 生来有钱;生于有钱人家。 **2** ~ coins: 银币: £20 *in notes and £5 in* ~; 二十英镑'纸币和五英镑 银币; *a handful of* ~; 一把银币。 **3** a *collection*, to which ~ coins are to be given. 银币募捐。 *Have you any* ~ *on you?* 你身上带有银币(钱)吗? **3** ~ vessels, dishes, articles, eg candlesticks, trays: 银器; 银币; 银具(如烛 台,盘等): *have all one's* ~ *taken by burglars;* 所有银器 全被窃贼偷走; *sell one's* ~ *to pay the mortgage interest.* 出售银器以偿付抵押贷款之利息。 **4** (attrib) the colour of ~: (用作定语)银色: *the* ~ *moon;* 银色的月亮; (of sounds) soft and clear: (指声音)清越的; 清亮的: *He has a* ~ *tongue/is* ‚~-*tongued,* is eloquent. 他能言善辩。 ~ **grey,** lustrous grey. 银灰色的。 **the** ~ **screen,** cinema; cinema screen. 电影; 银幕。 **5** (in art and literature) second best: (艺术及文学之)第二等; 次好的: *the* ~ *age,* ⇨ **golden(2).** **6** (compounds) (复合词) ‚~ '**birch** *n* common white birch with ~-coloured bark. 白桦树(其皮为银白色)。 '~-**fish** *n* (kinds of) small wingless insect that damages book bindings, clothes, etc. 蠹鱼(蛀蚀书籍,衣物之无翼小虫)。 ~ **paper,** (colloq) thin, light foil made of tin or aluminium (as used for packing chocolates, cigarettes, etc). (口)锡(铝)箔纸(用来包装巧克力,香烟等)。'~-**side** *n* best side of a round of beef. 最上头之牛腿肉。 '~-**smith** *n* manufacturer of ~ articles; merchant who sells these. 银匠;银器商。‚~ '**wedding** *n* 25th anniversary. 银婚(结婚二十五周年)。 □ *vt, vi* **1** [VP6A] coat with ~ or with sth that looks like ~; make (sth) bright like ~: 镀以银; 敷以似银之物; 使(某物)光亮如 银: *The years have* ~*ed her hair.* 岁月使她的头发变白 了。 **2** [VP2A] become white or ~ colour: 变白; 变银 色: *Her hair had* ~*ed.* 她的头发白了。 ~**y** *adj* like ~: 似银的。 *the* ~*y notes of a temple bell.* 清越的寺院钟声。

sil·vern /'sɪlvən ; 'sɪlvən/ *adj* (archaic) silver: (古) 银的; 似银的: *Speech is* ~ *but silence is golden,* it is better to be silent than to speak. 说话为银, 沉默是金。

sim·ian /'sɪmɪən ; 'sɪmɪən/ *adj, n* (of, like, a) monkey or ape. 猴或猿(的);似猴或猿的。

simi·lar /'sɪmələ(r) ; 'sɪmələ/ *adj* ~ **(to),** like; of the same sort: 类似的;同样的: *My wife and I have* ~ *tastes in music.* 我的妻子和我在音乐方面有相似的爱好。 *Gold is* ~ *in colour to brass.* 金和黄铜的颜色相似。 ~**·ly** *adv* /‚sɪmə'lærətɪ ‚sɪmə'lærɪtɪ/ *n* (*pl* -**ties**) [U] likeness; state of being ~; [C] point or respect in which there is likeness: 类似;相似;相似之点: *points of* ~*ity between the two men.* 二人相似之点。 *Are there any* ~*ities between China and Japan?* 中国和日本有任何相似 之点吗?

sim·ile /'sɪmɪlɪ ; 'sɪmə‚lɪ/ *n* [C, U] (use of) comparison of one thing to another, eg 'He is as brave as a lion,' 'Childhood is like a swiftly passing dream': 直喻; 明喻; 直喻或明喻之使用(例如:'他勇猛如狮,' '童年象一 场疾逝的梦')。 *He uses interesting* ~*s.* 他惯用有趣的直 喻。 *His style is rich in* ~. 他的文体颇多明喻。

sim·ili·tude /sɪ'mɪlɪtjuːd US: -tuːd ; sə'mɪlə‚tjud/ *n* **1** [U] (formal) resemblance (in general details but not in everything). (正式用语)类似; 相似。 **2** [C] comparison; simile: 比喻; 直喻: *talk in* ~*s.* 说话引用 比喻。

sim·mer /'sɪmə(r) ; 'sɪmə/ *vi, vt* **1** [VP2A, B, 6A, 15A] be, keep (sth), almost at boiling-point: 煨;煨;慢 煮: *Let the soup* ~ *for a few minutes.* 让那汤再煨几分 钟。 *S*~ *the stew for an hour.* 把那菜用慢火炖一小时。 **2** [VP2C] be filled with (anger, etc), which is only just kept under control: 内心充满; 按捺着(怒气等): *with rage/laughter/annoyance.* 按捺着怒气(很想笑; 心 里感到很厌烦)。 ~ **down,** (fig) become calm (after being angry or excited). (喻)变冷静; 安静下来(在发怒 或激动之后)。 □ *n* (*sing* only) (仅用单数) **keep sth at a** ~/**on the** ~, ~**ing** 将食物保持在将沸未沸的状态。

sim·ony /'sɪmənɪ ; 'saɪmənɪ/ *n* [U] (hist) offence of accepting or offering money for a position in the

---

Church. (史)买卖圣职罪。

si·moom /sɪ'muːm ; sɪ'mum/, **si·moon** /sɪ'muːn; sɪ'mun/ *n* hot, dry, dust-laden wind blowing in a straight track in the Sahara and the deserts of Arabia. 撒哈拉及阿拉伯沙漠地区所刮的干燥而带有尘沙的 热风; 西蒙风。

sim·per /'sɪmpə(r) ; 'sɪmpə/ *vi* [VP2A], *n* (give a) silly, self-conscious smile. (作)痴笑; 假笑。 ~**·ing·ly** /'sɪmprɪŋlɪ; 'sɪmpərŋlɪ/ *adv*

simple /'sɪmpl ; 'sɪmpl/ *adj* (**-r, -st**) **1** unmixed; not divided into parts; having only a small number of parts: 单纯的; 单一的; 简单的; 简易的: *a* ~ *substance;* 单纯的 物质; *a* ~ *machine;* 简单的机器; *a* ~ *sentence,* one without subordinate clauses. 简单句。 ~ **interest,** on capital only, not on accumulated interest. 单利(只对本 金而不对其累积之利息所生者)。 ⇨ **compound**[1](3). **2** plain; not much decorated or ornamented: 朴实的; 无甚 装饰的: ~ *food/cooking;* 简单的食物(烹饪); *a* ~ *style of architecture;* 朴实的建筑风格; *the* ~ *life,* a way of living without luxuries, servants or artificial pastimes, or in the country, contrasted with cities. 简朴的生活(如 乡居生活等)。 **3** not highly developed: 未充分发展的: ~ *forms of life.* 未充分发展的生命形态。 **4** easily done or understood; not causing trouble: 易做的; 易懂的; 不 会引起困难的: *written in* ~ *English;* 以简单英文写出; *a* ~ *task.* 易做的工作。 **5** innocent; straight-forward: 天真的; 率直的; 老实的: *behave in a pleasant and* ~ *way,* 举止可爱而率真; *as* ~ *as a child;* 象小孩一样天真的; ~ *folk.* 老实人。'~-'**hearted** *adj* frank. 坦白的; 率直 的。~'**·minded** *adj* **(a)** frank; unsophisticated. 率真 的; 不世故的。 **(b)** feeble-minded. 低能的。 **6** inexperienced; easily deceived: 无经验的; 易受欺的: *Are you* ~ *enough to believe everything your newspapers tell you?* 你会蠢到相信报纸告诉你的每一件事吗? *I'm not so* ~ *as to suppose you like me.* 我不至于笨到以为你喜欢我。*She's a* ~ *soul,* innocent of guile. 她是个没有心眼的人。 **7** with nothing added; absolute: 纯然的; 绝对的: *a* ~ *fact.* 纯粹的事实。 *pure and* ~, (colloq) absolute(ly), unquestionably: (口)绝对地; 无疑地: *It's a case of kill or be killed, pure and* ~. 这无疑是个人杀人或被杀的问题。□ *n* [C] (old use) herb used medicinally. (旧用法)草药。

sim·ply /'sɪmplɪ ; 'sɪmplɪ/ *adv* **1** in a ~ (2) manner: 朴素地; 朴实地; 无甚装饰地: *live simply;* 过朴实的生活; *dress simply;* 衣着朴素; *simply dressed.* 衣着朴素。 **2** completely, absolutely: 完全地; 绝对地: *His pronunciation is simply terrible,* is very bad indeed. 他的发音实在 糟透了。 *She looks simply lovely.* 她看起来十分可爱。 **3** only; merely; nothing more nor less than: 仅; 只; 恰好 地: *This drink consists simply of fresh oranges.* 这饮料 仅含新鲜柑汁。 *You must believe me simply on my word,* with nothing more than my assertion, without proof or evidence. 你必须完全相信我的话。 *It is simply a matter of working hard.* 此事只须努力做去。

simple·ton /'sɪmpltən ; 'sɪmpltən/ *n* foolish, weak-minded person, esp one who is easily deceived. 傻瓜; 笨 蛋; (尤指)容易受骗的人。

sim·plic·ity /sɪm'plɪsətɪ ; sɪm'plɪsətɪ/ *n* [U] the state of being simple: 简单; 简易; 朴素; 朴实; 率真: *the* ~ *of the problem;* 该问题的单纯性; *speak with* ~ 平实 地说话。 *be* ~ *itself,* (colloq) be extremely easy. (口) 极其容易。

sim·plify /'sɪmplɪfaɪ ; 'sɪmplə‚faɪ/ *vt* (*pt, pp* -**fied**) [VP6A] make simple; make easy to do or understand: 使单纯; 使易做; 使易懂; 简化: *a simplified reader/text.* 简易读本(教本)。 *That will* ~ *my task.* 那将简化我的工 作。 **sim·pli·fi·ca·tion** /‚sɪmplɪfɪ'keɪʃn ; ‚sɪmpləfə- 'keʃən/ *n* [U] act or process of ~*ing;* 简化; [C] instance of ~*ing;* sth simplified. 单纯化; 简化; 简化之实例; 简化 之物。

simu·lac·rum /‚sɪmju'leɪkrəm ; ‚sɪmjə'lekrəm/ *n* (*pl* -**cra** /-krə ; -krə/) sth made in the likeness of a person or object; shadowy likeness that deceives. 像; 类

像；伪物；幻影．

simu·late /'sɪmjʊleɪt ; `sɪmjə,let/ *vt* [VP6A] **1** pretend to be; pretend to have or feel: 假装；伪装；伴为：*~d innocence/enthusiasm.* 假装的天真（热心）．**2** counterfeit: 伪造；仿造；模仿: *insects that ~ dead leaves.* 伪装枯叶的昆虫．**simu·la·tion** /,sɪmjʊ'leɪʃn；,sɪmjə'leʃən/ *n* [U] pretence; imitation. 假装；伪为；模仿；拟态．**simu·la·tor** /-tə(r)；-tə/ *n* (esp) apparatus designed to provide (for testing purposes) conditions (eg non-gravity, for simulating weightlessness) like those which are encountered in real operations. (尤指做试验用的)摹拟仪器(如摹拟失重之试验).

sim·ul·ta·neous US: ,saɪm-；,saɪml-'teɪnɪəs／ *adj* ~ (with), happening or done at the same time as. 同时发生的；同时做出的；同时的．**~·ly** *adv* **~·ness, sim·ul·ta·ne·ity** /,sɪmltə'niːəti US: ,saɪmltə'nɪeɪti／ *nn*

sin /sɪn ; sɪn/ *n* [U] **1** breaking of God's laws: behaviour that is against the principles of morality, ⇨ **crime;** [C] instance of this; immoral act such as telling a lie, stealing, murder: 对上帝律法之违背；(宗教上的)罪；违背道德原则之行为；此种罪行之实例；不道德行为(如说谎,偷窃,谋杀): *confess one's sins to a priest;* 向教士告解；*ask for one's sins to be forgiven.* 请求赦罪．**live in sin,** (dated or hum use) live together as if married (过时或诙谐用语)过同居生活．**original sin,** proneness to commit sin which, some Christians believe, is part of mankind's nature. 原罪(犯罪之倾向, 某些基督教徒认为此乃凡人类本性的一部分)．**deadly mortal sin,** one that is fatal to salvation of the soul. 严重的罪恶；使灵魂不得超度的罪．*the seven deadly sins,* pride, covetousness, lust, anger, gluttony, envy, sloth. 七大罪(骄傲, 贪婪, 色欲, 愤怒, 贪食, 妒嫉, 怠惰)．**2** [C] (colloq) offence against convention; sth considered contrary to common sense: (口)违背习惯；不合情理之事；过失: *It's a sin for the children so much homework.* 给小孩如此多的家庭作业有悖情理．*It's a sin to stay indoors on such a fine day.* 这样好的天气留在屋里实在罪过．□ *vi* (-nn-) [VP2A, 3A] **sin (against),** commit sin; do wrong: 犯罪；违过: *We are all liable to sin.* 我们都易于犯罪．*Is it sinning against society to have a very large family?* 生很多孩子是违反社会的吗？**sin·ful** /-fl; -fəl/ *adj* wrong; wicked. 有过的；邪恶的．**sin·ful·ness** *n* **sin·less** *adj* free from sin; innocent. 无罪的；无辜的．**sin·less·ness** *n* **sin·ner** /'sɪnə(r); 'sɪnɚ/ *n* person who has sinned. 犯罪者；犯过者．

since /sɪns ; sɪns/ *adv* **1** (with the perfect tenses) after a date, event, etc in the past; before the present time; between some time in the past and the present time, or the time referred to: (与完成时连用)在过去的某一日期,事件等以后；在现在以前；在过去的某一时间与现在或所提及的时间之间: *The town was/had been destroyed by an earthquake ten years ago/earlier and has/had been rebuilt.* 这小城在十年前为地震所毁, 后来曾予以重建．他在一九七0年离家, 以后即无音讯．*ever ~,* throughout the whole of a period of time referred to and up to the present: 从那时到现在；此后一直: *He went to Turkey in 1956 and has lived there ever ~.* 他在一九五六年前往土耳其, 此后一直住在那里．**2** (with the simple tenses) ago (which is the usu word): (与简单时连用)以前(ago 较常用): *He did it many years ~.* 他在许多年以前做该事．*How long ~ is/was it?* 那是多久以前的事？□ *prep* (with the perfect tenses in the main clause) after; during a period of time after: (与主句中的完成式连用)自…以后；自从: *S~ last seeing you I have been ill.* 上次看到你以后我一直生病．*I have not seen him ~ her marriage.* 她自结婚后未曾回过家．□ *conj* **1** (with the perfect tenses in the main clause) from the past time when: (与主句中的完成式连用)自…以后；从…以来: *Where have you been ~ I last saw you?* 自上次见面以后, 你到哪里去了？(with the simple present tense in

the main clause): (与主句中之简单现在时连用): *How long is it ~ you were in London?* 你在伦敦多久了？*It is just a week ~ we arrived here.* 我们到达此地刚好一星期．**2** seeing that; as: 既然；因为: *S~ we've no money, we can't buy it.* 因为我们没钱, 我们买不起(它)．

sin·cere /sɪn'sɪə(r); sɪn'sɪr/ *adj* **1** (of feelings, behaviour) genuine; not pretended: (指感情, 行为)真实的; 诚挚的: *It is my ~ belief that....* 我确信…．*Are they ~ in their wish to disarm?* 他们真的想裁军吗？**2** (of persons) straightforward; not in the habit of expressing feelings that are pretended. (指人)真率的；不矫情的．**~·ly** *adv* in a ~ manner: 真实地: *Yours ~ly,* commonly used before a signature at the end of a letter to a friend or acquaintance. 一般用于致友人信札末尾签名前的套语．**sin·cer·ity** /sɪn'serəti; sɪn'serətɪ/ *n* [U] the quality of being ~; honesty: 真实；诚挚；诚实: *speaking in all sincerity,* very ~ly and honestly. 极其诚恳地谈话．

sin·ecure /'saɪnɪkjʊə(r) ; 'saɪnɪ,kjʊr/ *n* [C] position for which one receives credit or payment but which does not entail work or responsibility. 领干俸的职位；闲差事．

sine die /,saɪnɪ 'daɪiː ; 'saɪnɪ'daɪ·i／ *adv* (Lat) without a date fixed: (拉)无确定日期地；无限期地: *adjourn a meeting ~,* indefinitely. 无限期休会．

sine qua non /,saɪneɪ kwɑː 'nəʊn ; 'saɪnɪkwe'nɑn/ *n* (Lat) condition or qualification that cannot be done without; essential condition. (拉)必须条件(或资格)．

sinew /'sɪnjuː; 'sɪnju/ *n* [C] **1** tendon (strong cord) joining a muscle to a bone. 腱(连接骨与肉的强韧素状组织)．**2** (pl) muscles; energy; physical strength; (fig) means of acquiring strength: (复)肌肉；精力；体力；(喻)获得力量的方法: *the ~s of war,* money (with which to buy supplies). 军费．**sin·ewy** *adj* tough; having strong ~s: 坚韧的；强壮的: *~y arms;* 强壮的手臂; (fig) vigorous; having or showing nervous strength. (喻)精力充沛的；强有力的．

sing /sɪŋ ; sɪŋ/ *vi, vt* (*pt* **sang** /sæŋ ; sæŋ/, *pp* **sung** /sʌŋ; sʌŋ/) **1** [VP2A, C, 3A, 6A, 12B, 13B, 15A] make musical sounds with the voice, utter words one after the other to a tune: 唱；歌唱: *She ~s well.* 她很会唱歌．*He was ~ing a Malay song.* 他在唱一首马来亚歌．*He was ~ing to the guitar/to a piano accompaniment.* 他正和着吉他(由钢琴伴奏)唱歌．*She sang the baby to sleep.* 唱得不合调子．*You're ~ing out of tune.* 你唱走调了．*Will you ~ me a song/~ a song for me?* 唱一支歌给我听好吗？*~ another tune,* behave or speak in a different way, eg with less confidence or presumption. 改变态度；变谦恭．*~ small,* (colloq) speak or behave humbly (after being reproved, etc). (口)(在受责等后)言行变谦逊．**2** [VP2A, C] make a humming, buzzing or ringing sound: 发嗡嗡声；发营营声；发鸣叫声: *The kettle was ~ing (away) on the cooker.* 水壶在炉子上发嗡鸣的叫声．*My ears are ~ing,* are affected with buzzing sounds. 我的耳朵在鸣响．**3** [VP6A, 3A] **~ (of)** sth, (liter) celebrate in verse: (文)歌颂；吟咏: *~ (of) sb's exploits.* 歌颂某人的勋业．*~ sb's praises,* praise him with enthusiasm. 衷心赞美某人；歌颂某人．**4** **~ out (for),** shout (for). 大声叫；喊叫．**~ sth out,** shout sth: 大声叫；大叫: *~ out an order.* 喊出命令．**~ up,** with more force, ~ more loudly: 更用力唱；更大声唱: *S~ up, girls, and let's hear you.* 唱大声一点, 女孩子们, 让我们听清楚．**~·er** *n* person who does this in public. 歌者；歌手．**~·ing** *n* (esp) art of the ~er: 歌唱；(尤指)歌唱者的技巧: *teach ~ing;* 教唱歌；*my ~ing-master;* 我的歌唱老师；*take ~ing lessons.* 上歌唱的课程；学歌唱．**~·able** /-əbl; -əbl/ *adj* that can be sung: 可歌唱的；可吟咏的: *Some of this modern music is not ~able.* 这种现代音乐有的不能歌唱．

singe /sɪndʒ ; sɪndʒ/ *vt, vi* (*pres part* **singeing**) **1** [VP6A] burn off the tips or ends (esp of hair, as may

be done at the hair-dresser's): 烧焦尖端(尤指头发, 如在理发店中所做者); 燎: *have one's hair cut and ~d.* 剪烫头发。 **2** [VP6A] blacken the surface of by burning; burn slightly: 烧黑…之表面; 微烧: *If the iron is too hot you'll ~ that nightdress.* 如果熨斗过热, 你会把睡衣烫焦。 *She was busy ~ing the poultry,* burning the downy feathers off the birds (after they had been killed). 她正忙于烧去(杀死之)家禽的细毛。 **3** [VP2A] become ~d or scorched. 烧焦; 烫焦。 □ *n* slight burn or scorch (on cloth, etc). (布等上面的)轻微的烧灼。

single /'sɪŋgl; 'sɪŋgl/ *adj* **1** one only; one and no more: 唯一的; 单一的; 一个的: *a ~ cherry hanging from the tree.* 树上唯一的一颗樱桃。 **in ~ file,** (moving, standing) one behind the other in a line. (行进, 站立)一路纵队。 **,~-'breasted** *adj* (of a coat) having only one row of buttons down the front. (指外衣)单排钮的。 **~ 'combat,** fight with weapons, one man against another man. 一人对一人的作战。 **,~-'handed** *adj, adv* done by one person without help from others. 独自的(地); 独力的(地)。 **,~-'minded** *adj* having, intent on, only one purpose. 赤诚的; 一心一意的; 专诚的。 **~ -stick** *n* [C, U] (fencing with a) stick about the length of a sword. 剑状木棍; 木剑; 使用木剑之剑术。 **~ ticket** *n* ticket for a journey to a place, not there and back. 单程票。 Cf 参较 US 美 *one-way* ticket. **~ track** *n* (on a railway) one line only, with traffic in one direction only at one time. (铁路)单线。 **2** not married: 未婚的; 独身的: ~ *men and women;* 未婚男女; *remain ~;* 仍然单身; *the ~ state/life,* that of an unmarried person. 独身状态(生活)。 **3** for the use of, used for, done by, one person: 适于一人的; 一人用的; 一人做的: *a ~ bed;* 单人床; *reserve* (at a hotel) *two ~ rooms and one double room.* (在旅社)预定两间单人房间和一间双人房。 **4** (bot) having only one set of petals. ⇨ **double**(5): (植物)单瓣的: *a ~ tulip.* 单瓣之郁金香。 □ *n* [C] **1** (tennis and golf) game with one person on each side: (网球, 高尔夫球)单打: *play a ~;* 玩单打球赛; *the men's/women's ~s at Wimbledon;* 温布顿网球锦标赛之男子(女子)单打; (cricket) hit for which one run is scored: (板球)一分打: *run a quick ~;* 打击后快跑得一分; (baseball) base hit. (棒球)一垒打。 **2** (short for a) ~ ticket: 单程票(为single ticket 之略): *two second-class ~s to Leeds.* 两张前往里兹之二等单程票。 □ *vt* [VP15B] ~ *sb/sth out,* select from others (for special attention, etc): 挑选; 拣选: *Why have you ~d out this incident for criticism?* 为什么单挑这件事批评呀? **sing-ly** /'sɪŋglɪ; 'sɪŋglɪ/ *adv* one by one; by oneself. 一个个地; 个别地; 独自地; 单独地。 **~-ness** *n* [U] quality of being ~. 单一; 独特; 独自; 专一。 **~ness of purpose,** complete devotion to one purpose only. 一心一意; 专心致志。

sin-glet /'sɪŋglɪt; 'sɪŋglɪt/ *n* (GB) sleeveless garment worn for games or under a shirt; vest. (英)无袖之运动衫或汗衫; 背心。

single-ton /'sɪŋgltən; 'sɪŋgltən/ *n* [C] (in card games) single card of any suit held in one hand (of 13 cards): (纸牌戏)一手牌中某一花色独有的一张牌: *a ~ in hearts.* 一张红心孤牌。

sing-song /'sɪŋsɒŋ; 'sɪŋ,sɔŋ/ *n* **1** meeting of friends to sing songs together; impromptu vocal concert: (朋友们聚在一起的)歌唱会; 即席歌唱会: *have a ~ round the camp fire.* 围绕着营火举行歌唱会。 **2 in a ~,** (of a voice) in 'a rising and falling way: in a monotonous rhythm: (指声音)忽高忽低地; 节奏单调地; (attrib) (用作定语) *in a ~ voice/manner.* 声音单调地(态度呆板地)。

sin-gu-lar /'sɪŋgjʊlə(r); 'sɪŋgjələ/ *adj* **1** (liter) uncommon; strange: (文)异常的; 奇特的: *Isn't it unwise to make yourself so ~ in your dress,* to be so unconventional? 你这样奇装异服不是不智吗? **2** (formal) outstanding: (正式用语)非凡的; 卓越的: *a man of ~ courage and honesty.* 异常勇敢和诚实的人。 **3** (gram) of the form used in speaking or writing of one person

or thing. (语法)单数的。 □ *n* the ~ number: (语法)单数; 单数式: *What is the ~ of children?* 'children' 的单数是什么? **~·ly** *adv* outstandingly; strangely; peculiarly. 非凡地; 奇特地; 特殊地。 **~·ity** /,sɪŋgjʊ'lærɪtɪ; ,sɪŋgjə-'lærətɪ/ *n* (*pl* -ties) [U] strangeness; [C] sth unusual or strange. 奇异; 特异; 非凡或奇特之事物。 **~·ize** /-aɪz; -aɪz/ *vt* make ~ (1). 使异形。

Sin·ha·lese, Sin·gha·lese /,sɪnhə'liːz, ,sɪŋhə'liːz; ,sɪnhə'liz, ,sɪŋgə'liz/ *adj* of the larger of the communities in Sri Lanka and their language. 锡兰族的; 锡兰语的。 ⇨ **Tamil.** □ *n* member, language, of this community. 锡兰族人, 锡兰语。

sin·is·ter /'sɪnɪstə(r); 'sɪnɪstə/ *adj* **1** suggesting evil or the likelihood of coming misfortune: 不吉祥的; 凶兆的: *a ~ beginning.* 不吉祥的开始。 **2** showing ill will: 显示恶意的; 凶恶的; 阴险的: *a ~ face;* 凶恶的脸(上); *looks.* 阴险的神情。 **3** (in heraldry) on the left side of the shield (regarded from the bearer's point of view). (纹章)在盾之左方的(由持者之观点认定之)。 **bar ~,** mark on a shield showing illegitimate descent. 盾牌上表示庶出之记号。

sink[1] /sɪŋk; sɪŋk/ *n* [C] **1** fixed basin (of stone, porcelain, steel, etc) with a drain for taking off water, usu under water taps in a kitchen or scullery, used for washing dishes, cleaning vegetables, etc: 洗涤槽(为石, 瓷, 钢等做成之固定盆槽, 有排水管, 通常置于厨房之水龙头下面, 用于洗涤碗碟、蔬菜等): *She complains that she spends half her life at the kitchen ~,* seldom gets away from dull domestic work. 她埋怨做了半辈子的家务。 **2** cesspool. 污水池; 污水坑; 粪坑。 **3** (fig) place where evil people and evil practices collect: (喻)坏人恶事滋生之地; 藏污纳垢之所: *That part of the town is a ~ of iniquity.* 小城的那一区是罪恶的渊薮。

sink[2] /sɪŋk; sɪŋk/ *vi, vt* (*pt* **sank** /sæŋk; sæŋk/, *pp* **sunk** /sʌŋk; sʌŋk/, and, as *adj,* **sunken** /'sʌŋkən; 'sʌŋkən/) **1** [VP2A, C] go down, esp below the horizon or the surface of water or other liquid or a soft substance, eg mud: 沉下; 沉落(尤指低于地平面或水等之面): *The sun was ~ing in the west.* 太阳正在西方沉落。 *Wood does not ~ in water,* it floats. 木在水中不沉, 它漂浮着。 *The ship sank,* went to the bottom. 那船沉了。 **~ or swim,** phrase used of running great risks when the alternatives are complete loss or failure and safety or success. 成败全凭自己; 无论成败; 不管好歹。 **2** [VP2A, C] slope downwards; become lower or weaker: 倾斜; 下陷; 变低; 变弱: *The foundations have sunk.* 地基已下陷。 *The ground ~s to the sea.* 陆地向海倾斜。 *The soldier sank to the ground badly wounded.* 这兵士重伤倒地。 (fig) (喻) *His heart sank at the thought of failure.* 他一想到失败就觉得沮丧。 **3** [VP6A, 15A] make by digging: 掘; 挖; 凿; 掘井; 掘水井; place (sth) in a hole made by digging: 掘洞插入(某物); 埋入: ~ *a post one foot deep in the ground.* 将一根柱子埋在地里一英尺深。 **4** [VP2C, 3A] ~ *in; ~ into sth,* (of liquids, and, fig) go down deep: (指液体, 喻)沁渗; 渗入: *The rain sank into the dry ground.* 雨水沁进干地。 *Let this warning ~ into your mind.* 把这个警告铭记于心。 *The lesson hasn't sunk in,* (fig) has not been learnt or fully understood. 这一课还不十分了解。 **5** [VP2C, 3A] ~ *in; ~ into/to sth,* come to a lower state or state (physical or moral): 陷入; 降低(物质的或精神的): ~ *into a deep sleep;* 陷入沉睡中; ~ *into vice;* 堕入恶习; ~ *into insignificance;* 变得不足道; ~ *in the estimation of one's friends.* 朋友们对他的评价降低。 *He was sunk in thought/despair.* 他陷入沉思(失望)。 *He is ~ing fast,* will soon die. 他快要死了。 *The old man has sunken cheeks.* 这老人脸颊凹陷。 *His cheeks have sunk in.* 他的脸颊凹陷。 *His voice sank to a whisper.* 他的声音降低成耳语。 **6** [VP6A, 15A] cause or allow to ~: 使沉; 使低落: ~ *a ship.* 沉船。 *He sank* (= lowered) *his voice to a whisper.* 他把声音降低为耳语。 *Let us ~ our differences* (= put them out of our thoughts, forget them), *and*

work together. 让我们摒弃歧见，一起工作吧。**7** [VP6A, 14] ~ *(in)*, invest (money), esp so that it is not easy to withdraw it: 投(资)(尤指不易收回者): *He has sunk half his fortune in a new business undertaking.* 他已把一半财产投资于一新的企业中。 ~·**able** /-əbl /-əbl/ *adj* that can be sunk. 可沉的; 会低落的。

sinker /'sɪŋkə(r)/ ; 'sɪŋkɚ/ *n* [C] (esp) lead weight attached to a fishing line or net to keep it under the water. (尤指装于钓丝或网使之沉入水中之)铅锤。 **hook, line and** ~, ⇨ **hook**(1).

sink·ing /'sɪŋkɪŋ/ ; 'sɪŋkɪŋ/ *n* (gerund) (esp) (动名词) (尤用于) *a* '~ *feeling*, feeling in the stomach caused by fear or hunger. 由恐惧或饥饿在胃中造成的感觉; 无力气;虚弱。 '~-*fund n* money from revenue put aside by a government, business company, etc for gradual repayment of a debt. (政府, 公司等拨出的)偿债基金。

Sinn Fein /ˌʃɪn 'feɪn/ ; 'ʃɪn'feɪn/ *n* political movement and organization founded in Ireland in 1905 for independent republican government. (以争取独立为目的于一九〇五年成立的)爱尔兰新芬党。

Si·nol·ogy /saɪ'nɒlədʒɪ/ ; saɪ'nɑlədʒɪ/ *n* [U] knowledge, study, of the Chinese language and culture. 汉学(关于中国语言, 文化等之知识与研究)。 **Si·nol·ogist** /-dʒɪst/ ; -dʒɪst/ *n* expert in ~. 汉学家。

sinu·ous /'sɪnjuəs/ ; 'sɪnjuəs/ *adj* winding; full of curves and twists. 弯曲的; 蜿蜒的。 **sinu·os·ity** /ˌsɪnju-'bsətɪ/ ; ˌsɪnju'ɑsətɪ/ *n* (pl -ties) [U] being ~, [C] curve or twist. 弯曲; 蜿蜒; 弯曲处; 曲折。

sinus /'saɪnəs/ ; 'saɪnəs/ *n* (pl ~es) [C] hollow in a bone, esp one of several air-filled cavities in the bones of the skull, communicating with the nostrils. 窦(骨骼中之孔穴, 尤指脑骨中充有空气的数穴之一, 与鼻相通者)。 ~·**itis** /saɪnə'saɪtɪs/ ; ˌsaɪnə'saɪtɪs/ *n* [U] inflammation of a ~. 窦炎。 ⇨ the illus at **skeleton**. 参看 skeleton 之插图。

Sioux /suː/ ; suː/ *n* member of a N American Indian tribe. 苏族(北美印地安人的一族); 苏族印第安人。

sip /sɪp/ ; sɪp/ *vt, vi* (-pp-) [VP6A, 15B, 2A] drink, taking a very small quantity at a time: 呷; 呷; 细饮: *sip (up) one's coffee.* 呷饮咖啡。 □ *n* [C] (quantity taken in a) sipping: 呷; 一呷之量: *drink brandy in sips, not gulps.* 细品白兰地酒, 不是牛饮。

si·phon /'saɪfən/ ; 'saɪfən/ *n* [C] **1** bent or curved tube, pipe, etc so arranged (like an inverted U) that liquid will flow up through it and then down. 弯管; 虹吸管。 **2** bottle from which soda-water can be forced out by the pressure of gas in it. 虹吸瓶; 压力瓶。 □ *vt, vi* [VP15B] ~ *sth off/out*, draw (liquid) out or off through or as if through a ~: 用虹吸管或类似装置抽出 (液体): *Who has* ~*ed off all the petrol from the tank of my car?* 谁把我汽车油箱里的汽油抽光了？

sir /sɜː(r)/ ; sɜː/ *n* **1** polite form used in addressing a man to whom one wishes to show respect: 先生; 君; 阁下; 足下(对人表示敬意的礼貌称呼): *Yes, sir.* 是的, 先生。 *Dinner is served, sir.* 先生, 饭已备好。 *Sir, it is my duty to inform you that....* 先生, 我必须通知您…。 **2 Sir**, used at the beginning of a formal letter: 用于正式信函之开头: *Dear Sir/Sirs.* 先生台鉴(执事诸君台鉴)。 **3 Sir** /sɜː/ ; sɜː/, title used before the first name of a knight or baronet: 冠于爵士或准男爵的名之前: *Sir 'Edward;* 爱德华爵士; *Sir John 'Jackson.* 约翰·杰克逊爵士。

sir·dar /'sɜːdɑː(r)/ ; sə'dɑr/ *n* (in some Asian countries) officer or leader of high, esp military, rank. (某些亚洲国家中的)首领; 司令官。

sire /'saɪə(r)/ ; saɪr/ *n* **1** (old use) father or male ancestor. (旧用法)父; 男性祖先。 **2** (old use) title of respect used when addressing a king or emperor. (旧用法)陛下(对国王或皇帝的敬称)。 **3** male parent of an animal: 动物之雄亲; 父兽: *race-horses with pedigree* ~*s.* 有雄豪血统记录之比赛用的马。 □ *vt* [VP6A] (esp of horses) be the ~ of: (尤指马)为…之雄亲: *a Derby*

winner ~*d by Pegasus.* 属于'裴佳沙斯'种的赛马会优胜马。

si·ren /'saɪərən/ ; 'saɪrən/ *n* **1** (Gk myth) one of a number of winged women whose songs charmed sailors and caused their destruction; (hence) woman who attracts and is dangerous to men. (希神)海妖(为有翅膀的女人, 其曼妙歌声蛊惑水手而使彼等毁灭); (由此产生)引诱男人而对其有害的女子。 **2** ship's whistle for sending warnings and signals; device for producing a loud shrill noise (as a warning, etc): 船上的号笛(用以发出警报及信号); 警报器(用作警号等): *an 'air-raid~.* 空袭警报器; *an ambulance/a fire-engine racing along with its* ~*s wailing.* 一辆救护车(救火车)响着警报器鸣驰而过。

sir·loin /'sɜːlɔɪn/ ; 'sɜːlɔɪn/ *n* [C, U] best part of loin of beef. 最好的牛腰肉。

sir·occo /sɪ'rɒkəʊ/ ; sə'rako/ *n* (pl ~**s** /-kəʊz; -koz/) [C] hot, moist wind reaching Italy from Africa. (由非洲吹到意大利之)潮湿热风。

sir·rah /'sɪrə/ ; 'sɪrə/ *n* (contemptuous; archaic) sir. (蔑; 古)先生。

sirup /'sɪrəp/ ; 'sɪrəp/ = syrup.

si·sal /'saɪsl/ ; 'saɪsl/ *n* [U] plant (⇨ **agave**) with fleshy leaves which provide strong fibre used for making rope. 西沙尔麻(适于制绳用): ~ *grass/fibre/rope.* 西沙尔麻草(纤维, 绳)。

sissy /'sɪsɪ/ ; 'sɪsɪ/ *n* (colloq; derog) effeminate or cowardly person. (口; 贬)柔弱或怯懦的人。 **sis·si·fied** /'sɪsɪfaɪd; 'sɪsɪ,faɪd/ *adj* effeminate or cowardly. 女人似的; 女人气的; 柔弱的; 怯懦的。

sis·ter /'sɪstə(r)/ ; 'sɪstɚ/ *n* **1** daughter of the same parents as oneself or another person: 姐; 妹; 姐妹: *my/your/his* ~. 我(你,他)的姐姐(妹妹)。 '**half-**~ *n* related by one parent only. 异父或异母; 异母姐妹。 ⇨ also *step-* at *step-.* '~-**in-law** *n* (pl ~**s-in-law**) ~ one's wife or husband; wife of one's brother. 夫或妻之姐妹; 姑; 姨; 兄或弟之妻; 嫂; 弟妇。 **2** person who behaves towards one as a ~ does: 亲如姐妹之人: *She was like a* ~ *to him.* 她对他亲如姐姐。 **3** (GB) senior hospital nurse. (英)(医院里的)资深护士。 **4** member of certain religious orders; nun: 修女; 尼姑: *S~s of Mercy*, a nursing sisterhood. 慈光修女会。 **5** (attrib) of the same design or type: (用作定语)同样款式的, 同型的: ~ *ships/organisations.* 姐妹舰(团体)。 ~·**ly** *adj* of or like a ~: 姐妹的; 姐妹般的: ~*ly love;* 姐妹般的爱; *a* ~*ly kiss.* 姐妹般的亲吻。 ~·**hood** /-hʊd ; -,hʊd/ *n* [C] society of women who devote themselves to charitable works, nursing, etc or live together in a religious order. 妇女团体(从事慈善事业, 护理等); 修女会。

sit /sɪt/ ; sɪt/ *vi, vt* (pt, pp **sat** /sæt; sæt/, **-tt-**) (For special uses with *adverbial particles* and *preps,* ⇨**8** below.) (与副词性小品词及介词连用的特殊用法,参看下列第 8 义。) **1** [VP2A, C] take or be in a position in which the body is upright and supported by the buttocks (resting on the ground or on a seat): 坐(在地上或座位上): *sit on a chair/on the floor/in an armchair/at a table or desk/on a horse, etc.* 坐在椅子上(地板上, 扶手椅中, 桌子或书桌前, 马上)。 *The child is not big enough to sit at table yet.* 那孩子尚小, 不能上桌进食。 *sit to an artist,* have one's portrait painted by him (while sitting). 坐着由画家画像。 *sit (for) an examination,* take one. 参加考试。 *sit for one's portrait,* have one's portrait painted while sitting before an artist. 坐着由人画像。 *sit tight,* **(a)** remain firmly in one's place, esp in the saddle. 坐稳; (尤指)坐稳在马鞍上。 **(b)** (colloq) stick firmly to one's purpose, opinions, etc. (口)坚持目标, 意见等。 *sit for (a borough, etc),* represent it in Parliament. 在国会代表(某自治市镇等)。 Hence, 由此产生, *sitting member,* the candidate (at a general election) who held the seat before the dissolution of Parliament. 竞选连任的国会议员。 **2** [VP6A] cause to sit; place in a sitting position: 使坐; 安置于坐着的姿势: *He lifted the child and sat* (=

seated) *her at a little table;* 他抱起小孩，把她安置在小桌前；*(reflex):* (反身式)：*Sit yourself down,* be seated. 请坐。 **3** [VP2A] (of Parliament, a law court, a committee, etc) hold meetings: (指国会，法庭，委员会等)开会；开庭：*The House of Commons was still sitting at 3am.* 下议院在清晨三点钟仍在开会。**4** [VP6A] keep one's seat on (a horse, etc)：骑；乘(马等)：*She sits her horse well.* 她善于骑马。*He couldn't sit his mule.* 他不会骑自己的骡子。 **5** [VP2A, C] (of birds) perch: (指鸟)栖：*sitting on a branch.* 栖息于枝上。**ˌsitting ˈduck,** an easy target or victim. 容易击中之目标；容易受骗之人。**ˌsitting ˈtenant,** one who is actually in occupation (of a house, flat, etc, contrasted with a prospective tenant)：(房舍、公寓等之)现住租用人(与未来租用人相对)：*greedy owners who want to get rid of sitting tenants and then charge higher rates to new tenants.* 想赶走现住租用人而以较高的租金把房子租给新租户之贪婪房东。**6** [VP2A] (of domestic fowls) remain on the nest in order to hatch eggs: (指家禽)孵卵：*That hen wants to sit.* 那母鸡要孵卵。 **7** [VP2C] (of clothes) suit, fit, hang: (指衣服)合身；适合；穿起来：*That dress sits well/loosely, etc on her.* 那衣服她穿起来很合适(宽松等)。*The coat sits badly across the shoulders.* 那外衣肩部不合适。*His new dignity sits well on him,* (fig) suits him well. (喻)他的新的显赫地位很适合他。**8** [VP2C, 3A, 15B] (special uses with *adverbial particles* and *preps*)：(与副词性小品词及介词连用的特殊用法)：

sit back, **(a)** settle oneself comfortably back, eg in a chair. 舒适地倚坐在椅子上等。**(b)** (fig) take one's ease (after strenuous activity, etc); take no action. (喻)宽舒地休息(在紧张活动等之后)；不采取行动；观望。

sit down, take a seat: 坐下：*Please sit down, all of you.* 请大家都坐下。 **ˌsit-down ˈstrike,** strike by workers who refuse to leave the factory, etc until their demands are considered or satisfied. 静坐罢工；怠留罢工(工人拒绝离开厂房等，直到要求被接受或获得满意答复为止)。***sit down under (insults, etc),*** suffer without protest or complaint. 未抗议或无怨言地忍受(凌辱等)。

sit in, (of workers, students, etc) demonstrate by occupying a building (or part of it) and staying there until their grievances are considered or until they themselves are ejected: (指工人、学生等)静坐示威(占据一建筑物或建筑物之一部分，直到他们的抱怨被重视或直到他们被赶走为止)：*There are reports of students sitting in at several universities.* 据报导有学生在几所大学里静坐示威。 Hence, 由此产生，**ˈsit-in** *n* such a demonstration. 静坐示威。***sit in on sth,*** attend (a discussion, etc) as an observer, not as a participant. 列席(讨论会等)。

sit on/upon sth, **(a)** (of a person) be a member of (a jury, committee, etc). (指人)做陪审员，委员等。 **(b)** (colloq) neglect to deal with: (口)疏于处理；忽略：*They've been sitting on my application for a month.* 他们把我的申请搁置一个月了。***sit on/upon sth,*** (of a jury, etc) inquire into, investigate (a case). (指陪审团等)调查；审查。***sit on/upon sb,*** (colloq) repress; snub: (口)压制；冷落：*That impudent fellow needs to be sat on.* 那厚脸皮的家伙需要压制一下。

sit out, sit outdoors: 坐在户外：*It's hot indoors— let's sit out in the garden, shall we?* 室内很热，我们到外面花园坐坐，好吗？ ***sit sth out,*** **(a)** stay to the end of (a performance, etc)：留在(表演等)现场直到结束的时候：*sit out a boring play.* 看完一场乏味的戏。**(b)** take no part in (esp a particular dance)：不参加(尤指某一支舞)：*I think I'll sit out the next dance.* 我不想跳下一支舞。

sit up, not go to bed (until later than the usual time): (超过通常的就寝时间)不睡：*I shall be late getting back, so please don't sit up for me.* 我将晚归，请不要不睡觉等我。*The nurse sat up with her patient all night.* 那护士整夜不睡照顾她的病人。*Ought children to sit up late looking at TV programmes?* 孩子们看电视而晚睡应该吗？***sit (sb) up,*** (cause to) take an upright position after lying flat or sitting badly: (使)在躺平或坐姿不正以后坐起；坐正：*The patient is well enough to sit up in bed now.* 那病人现在已能在床上坐起来了。*Just sit me up a little,* help me to sit up. 帮我坐直一些。***sit up straight!*** Don't lean back! Don't sprawl! 坐直！不要向后倚！不要伸开着手脚坐！***make sb sit up (and take notice),*** (colloq) alarm or frighten him; rouse him from lethargy to activity. (口)惊吓某人；促使活动。

si·tar /sɪˈtɑː(r); sɪˋtɑr/ *n* Hindu stringed musical instrument. 一种印度弦乐器。⇨ the illus at **string.** 参看 string 之插图。

site /saɪt; saɪt/ *n* [C] place where sth was, is, or is to be: 位置；场所：*built on the ~ of an old fort;* 建筑于古堡的旧址上；*a ~ for a new school;* 建一新学校的地点；*deliver materials to a ˈbuilding ~.* 把建筑材料送至工地。□ *vt* [VP6A] locate; place: 设置；定场所：*Where have they decided to ~ the new factory?* 他们决定把新工厂设置在何处？

sit·ter /ˈsɪtə(r); ˋsɪtɚ/ *n* **1** person who is sitting for a portrait. 坐供画像者。**2** hen that sits(6)：孵卵的母鸡：*a good/poor ~.* 善(不善)于孵卵的母鸡。 **3** bird or animal that is sitting and therefore easy to shoot; (hence) easy shot; sth easily done. 栖息的禽兽(易于猎杀)；(由此产生)容易的一击；易做的事。 **4** ⇨ *baby-~* at **baby.**

sit·ting /ˈsɪtɪŋ; ˋsɪtɪŋ/ *n* **1** time during which a court of law, Parliament, etc is ~ continuously: 开庭，开会等的期间；庭期；会期：*during a long ~.* 在冗长的庭(会)期中。 **2** period of time during which one is engaged continuously in a particular occupation: 连续从事某一工作的期间：*finish reading a book at one ~.* 一口气把书读完。 **3** act of ~ for a portrait: 坐着供人画像：*The artist wants you to give him six ~s,* sit for him six times. 那画家要你坐着供他画像六次。 **4** occasion of ~ (for a meal, etc)：就座(进食等)：*In the dining-room of this hotel 100 people can be served at one ~,* ie at the same time, together. 这旅馆的餐厅，可供一百人同时进餐。**5** collection of eggs on which a hen sits. 孵卵数。**6** **ˈ~-room** *n* room for general use (contrasted with a dining-room, bedroom, etc). 起居室(别于饭厅，寝室等)。

situ·ated /ˈsɪtʃʊeɪtɪd; ˋsɪtʃʊˌetɪd/ *pred adj* **1** (of a town, building, etc) placed: (指城镇，建筑物等)位于…的；坐落在…的：*The village is ~ in a valley.* 这村庄位于一山谷中。 **2** (of a person) in (certain) circumstances: (指人)处于(某种)境地的：*Having six children and no income, the widow was badly ~.* 这寡妇有六个孩子又没有收入，处境不好。*I'm awkwardly ~ just now,* in difficult circumstances. 我目前处境困难。

situ·ation /ˌsɪtʃʊˈeɪʃn; ˌsɪtʃʊˋeʃən/ *n* [C] **1** position (of a town, building, etc). (城镇，建筑物等之)位置；场所。 **2** condition, state of affairs, esp at a certain time: 状况；事态；情势(尤指在某一时间者)：*be in an embarrassing ~.* 处于尴尬的境地。 **3** work, employment: 工作；职业：*S~s vacant, S~s wanted,* headings of newspaper notices of employment offered and asked for; 事求人，人求事(报纸之人事广告栏标题)；*be in/out of a ~,* be employed/unemployed. 有工作(失业)。

six /sɪks; sɪks/ *n, adj* the number 6, ⇨ **App 4.** 六；六个；六的；六个的(参看附录四)。***(It is) six of one and half a dozen of the other,*** There is very little difference between the one and the other. 半斤八两；差不多。***in sixes,*** in groups of six at a time. 六个六个地。***at sixes and sevens,*** in confusion. 乱七八糟；杂乱地。**ˌsix-ˈfooter** *n* (colloq) person six feet in height; thing six feet long. (口)身高六英尺之人；六英尺长的东西。**ˈsix·pence** *n* **(a)** former GB coin worth (formerly) six pennies *(6d),* or (since 1971) $2^1/_2$p. (英国昔时之)六便士硬币(原值六便士，自1971年后值$2^1/_2$便士)。 **(b)** the sum of six pennies, either *6p* or *6d.* 六便士之额(略作 6p 或 6d)。⇨ **App 4.** 参看附录四。**ˈsix·penny** *adj* costing *6d* or *6p.* 值六便士的。 **six-shooter** *n* revolver with six chambers. 六发左轮手枪。 **ˈsix·fold** /-fəʊld; -ˋfold/

adj, adv six times as much or as many; six times as great. 六倍的(地); 六重的(地). **six·teen** /ˈsɪkˈstiːn; ˌsɪksˈtin/ *n, adj* the number 16. 十六; 十六个; 十六的的. **six·teenth** /ˈsɪkˈstiːnθ; ˌsɪksˈtinθ/ *n, adj* **sixth** /sɪksθ; sɪksθ/ *n, adj* **sixth form**, *n* (in secondary schools, GB) form (= class) for pupils being prepared for A-level examinations. (英国的中等学校的六年级(为参加 A 级考试之学生的级次). ⇨ **level**² (3). '**sixth-former** *n* pupil in this form. (英国中等学校之)六年级学生。 **,sixth 'sense**, power to be aware of things independently of the five senses; intuition. 第六感; 直觉。 **sixthly** *adv* **six·ti·eth** /ˈsɪkstɪɪθ; ˈsɪkstɪθ/ *n, adj,* **sixty** /ˈsɪkstɪ; ˈsɪkstɪ/ *n, adj* the number 60. 六十; 六十的。 **the sixties** *n pl* 60-69. 六十至六十九。

size¹ /saɪz; saɪz/ *n* **1** [U] degree of largeness or smallness: 大小; 尺寸: *a building of vast* ~; 甚大的建筑物: *about the* ~ *of* (= about as large as) *a duck's egg*; 大小大约如鸭蛋; *of some* ~, fairly large. 相当大的. *They're both of a* ~, are the same ~. 它们大小一样. *That's about the* ~ *of it*, (colloq) That's a fair account of the affair, situation, etc. (口)其真相大致如此. **2** [C] one of the standard and (usu) numbered classes in which articles of clothing, etc are made: (衣着等之)号; 码: *a* ~ *fifteen collar*; 十五号领; *trousers three* ~s *too large*; 大了三号的裤子; *a* ~ *of gloves* 各种号码的手套. *I take* ~ *nine shoes*. 我穿九号的鞋子. □ *vt* **1** [VP6A] arrange in ~s or according to ~. 按大小排列. **2** [VP15B] ~ *sb/sth up*, (colloq) form a judgement or opinion of. (口) 判断, 品评. -**sized** /-saɪzd; -saɪzd/ *suff* (in compounds) having a certain ~: (用于复合词中)有…大小的; …号的: *medium-sized*. 中号的; '**siz(e)·able** /-əbl; -əbl/ *adj* fairly large. 颇大的; 相当大的。

size² /saɪz; saɪz/ *n* [U] sticky substance used to glaze textiles, paper, plaster, etc. 胶水; 浆糊(用以使纺织品, 纸, 灰泥, 石膏等变光滑). □ *vt* [VP6A] stiffen or treat with ~. 以胶水或浆糊使挺实; 上胶于; 上浆于。

sizzle /ˈsɪzl; ˈsɪzl/ *vi* [VP2A], *n* (colloq) (make the) hissing sound as of sth cooking in fat: (口)发嘶嘶声; 嘶声(如油炸食物时之声音): *sausages sizzling in the pan*; 在锅中发嘶嘶声的香肠; (fig) (喻) *a sizzling hot day*. 灼热的一天。

skate¹ /skeɪt; sket/ *n* ('ice-)~, one of a pair of sharp-edged steel blades to be fastened to a boot for moving smoothly over ice. 溜冰鞋. ⇨ the illus at **hockey**. 参看 hockey 之插图。 ⇨ also *roller-* ~s *at* **roller** (2). □ *vi* [VP2A, C] move on ~s: 溜冰: ~ *over/round a difficulty/a delicate problem*, make only passing and cautious references to. 谨慎而约略地提及某困难(微妙的问题). ~ *on thin ice*, talk about a subject that needs great tact. 谈论一个必须谨慎处理的题目. '~·**board** *n* narrow board for standing on, about 50cm long, mounted front and back on two pairs of roller-skate wheels, used in sport over a smooth surface (eg for racing, demonstrating skill). 滑板(约五十公分长之窄板, 板下前后端各装有一对滑轮, 于平滑表面上做溜冰竞赛、表演等). '~·**boarder** *n* person using a ~board. 溜滑板者. '~·**boarding** *n* [U] sport of using a ~board. 溜滑板运动. '**skat·ing** *n* sport of using ~s. 溜冰; 滑冰. '**skat·ing-rink** *n* specially prepared surface for skating. 溜冰场. ~*r n* person who ~s. 溜冰者。

skate² /skeɪt; sket/ *n* large, flat, long-tailed seafish, valued as food. 鳐鱼; 虹鱼(大而扁平之长尾海鱼, 为珍贵食品)。

ske·daddle /skɪˈdædl; skɪˈdædl/ *vi* [VP2A] (GB, colloq, usu imper) run away. (英, 口, 通常用于祈使句中)跑开; 逃窜。

skeet /skiːt; skit/ *n* (kind of) clay-pigeon shooting. 陶土盘飞靶射击(之一种). ⇨ **pigeon** (2)。

skein /skeɪn; sken/ *n* [C] length of silk or wool yarn or thread coiled loosely into a bundle. (丝, 毛线或线之)

– skate
blade

ice-skating

一束; 一绞。

skel·eton /ˈskelɪtn; ˈskelətn/ *n* [C] **1** bony framework of an animal body; bones of an animal body in the same relative positions as in life; hard framework of woody fibre containing a vegetable body: (动物之)骨骼; 骨架; (植物之)木质纤维结构: *He looks like a living* ~. 他看来象具苗骨架. *reduced to a* ~, (of an animal, a human being) very thin as the result of hunger, illness, etc. (指动物, 人)因饥饿, 疾病等而皮包骨. *the* ~ *in the cupboard, the family* ~, sth of which a family is ashamed and which it tries to keep secret. 家丑. **2** framework of a building, organization, plan, theory, etc; outline to which details are to be added: (建筑物, 组织, 计划, 理论等之)骨架; 基干; 纲要: *the steel* ~ *of a new building*. 新建筑物之钢梁. **3** (attrib) (用作定语) '~ *key*, one that will open a number of different locks. 万能钥匙. **a** ~ *staff/crew/service, etc*, one reduced to the smallest possible number needed for maintenance. 基干作业人员(照料或处理业务所需之最少人数)。

skep /skep; skεp/ *n* (kinds of) wicker basket; straw or wicker bee-hive. 柳条篮子; 稻草或柳条做成的蜂房。

skep·tic /ˈskeptɪk; ˈskεptɪk/ ⇨ **sceptic**。

sketch /sketʃ; skεtʃ/ *n* **1** rough, quickly made drawing: 略图; 素描; 速写: *make a* ~ *of a face/place* 作一面孔(一地方)之速写. '~·**book**/-**block** *nn* book or pad of sheets of drawing-paper for making ~es on. 素描簿. '~·**map** *n* one with outlines but little detail. 略图. **2** short account or description; rough draft or general outline, without details: 简短的记载或描述; 概略; 大纲: *He gave me a* ~ *of his plans for the expedition.* 他对我略述其远征的计划. **3** short, humorous play or piece of writing. 诙谐之短剧或短文。 □ *vt, vi* **1** [VP6A] make a ~ of; [VP15B] ~ *sth out*, give a rough plan of; indicate without detail: 草绘; 草拟: ~ *out proposals for a new road.* 草拟开辟新路的计划. **2** [VP2A] practise the art of making ~es: 绘略图; 作素描: *My sister often goes into the country to* ~. 我的姐姐(妹妹)常去乡下写生。 ~*er n* person who ~es (2). 绘略图者; 作素描者. **sketchy** *adj* (-**ier**, -**iest**) **1** done roughly and without detail or care. 简略的; 概要的; 随便的. **2** incomplete: 不完全的; 不足的: *He has a rather* ~*y knowledge of geography.* 他对于地理仅有些概略的知识. ~·**ily** /-ɪlɪ; -əlɪ/ *adv* ~·**i·ness** *n*

skew /skjuː; skju/ *adj* twisted or turned to one side; not straight. 歪的; 斜的; 不直的. '~-**eyed** *adj* (colloq) squinting. (口)斜视的. *on the* ~, (colloq) ~. (口)歪斜着。

skewer /ˈskjuə(r); ˈskjuɚ/ *n* pointed stick of wood or metal for holding meat together while cooking. (烤肉时串肉用的)串肉签; 烤肉叉. □ *vt* [VP6A] fasten with, or as with, a ~. (用串肉签等)串起。

ski /skiː; ski/ *n* (*pl* **skis**) one of a pair of long, narrow strips of wood, strapped under the feet for moving over snow: 滑雪屐: *a pair of skis*; 一付滑雪屐; *bind on one's skis*. 缚在滑雪屐上。 '**ski-bob** *n* bicycle frame fitted with skis in place of wheels. 滑雪脚踏车. '**ski-jump** *n*

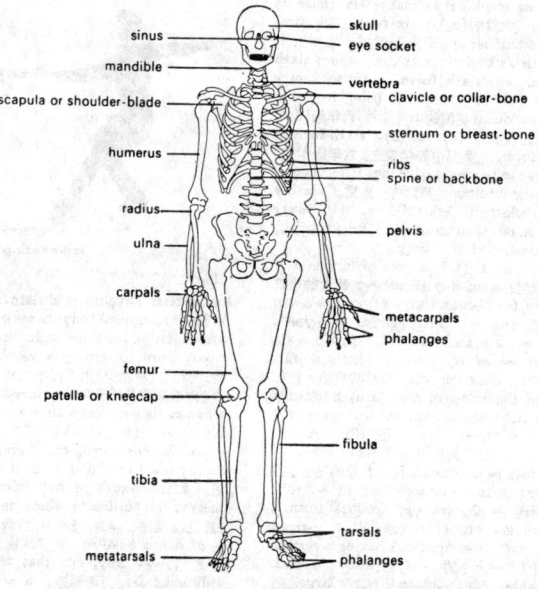

sinus
mandible
scapula or shoulder-blade
humerus
radius
ulna
carpals
femur
patella or kneecap
tibia
metatarsals

skull
eye socket
vertebra
clavicle or collar-bone
sternum or breast-bone
ribs
spine or backbone
pelvis
metacarpals
phalanges
fibula
tarsals
phalanges

the human skeleton

jump made after getting up speed on a downward slope. 滑雪跳跃(下坡高速时所作之跳跃)。 **'ski-lift** *n* ropeway for carrying skiers up a mountain side. 运送滑雪者上山坡之吊索设备。 **'ski-plane** *n* aircraft fitted with skis instead of wheels, to enable it to land on an expanse of snow. 雪上飞机(以滑雪履代替起降轮之飞机, 适于雪地降落)。 □ *vi* (*pt, pp* **ski'd**, *pres part* **skiing**) move over snow on ski(s): 滑雪: *go skiing in Switzerland;* 到瑞士去滑雪; *go in for skiing.* 喜好滑雪。 **skier** /'ski:ə(r); 'skiə/ *n* person using ski(s). 滑雪者。

skiing

skid /skɪd; skɪd/ *n* [C] **1** piece of wood or metal fixed under the wheel of a cart, etc to prevent it from turning, and in this way check the speed when going downhill. 制轮器; 煞车。 **2** log, plank, etc used to make a track over which heavy objects may be dragged or rolled. (使重物等在上面容易滑动的)滑材; 枕木。 **row** /rəu; ro/ *n* (US) slum area where vagrants live. (美)流浪者者落脚之贫民区。 **3** slipping movement, often sideways, of the wheels of a car, etc on a slippery or icy road, or caused by excessive speed while turning a corner: (在光滑或结冻之道路上, 或因速度过高在转弯时所引起的)车轮之打滑: *How would you get out of/correct a ~?* 车轮打滑时你如何控制你的车子? **'~-pan** *n* surface specially prepared to cause ~s, used for

practice in controlling vehicles which ~. 练习控制车辆打滑的特制路面。 *put the ~s under sb,* (sl) do sth to make him hurry. (俚)催促某人。 □ *vi* (**-dd-**) [VP2A] (of a car, etc) move or slip sideways, etc; have a ~(3). (指汽车等)滑向一侧; 打滑。

skies /skaɪz; skaɪz/ *pl of* **sky.**

skiff /skɪf; skɪf/ *n* small, light boat, esp one rowed or sculled by a single person: 小艇; 轻舟(尤指单人所划者)。

skiffle /'skɪfl; 'skɪfəl/ *n* [U] (1950's) mixture of jazz and folksong, with improvised instruments and a singer who usu has a guitar or a banjo. (二十世纪五十年代的)爵士民谣。 **'~-group,** group of such players. 爵士民谣团。

skil·ful (US = **skill·ful**) /'skɪlfl; 'skɪlfəl/ *adj* having or showing skill: 有技巧的; 巧妙的; 熟练的: *He's not very ~ with his chopsticks / at using chopsticks.* 他用筷子不大熟练。 **~ly** /-fəl; -fəl/ *adv*

skill /skɪl; skɪl/ *n* [U] ability to do sth expertly and well; [C] particular kind of ~: 技能; 熟巧; 某种技能; 技艺: *Is learning a foreign language a question of learning new ~s, or a question of acquiring new knowledge?* 学习外国语是学习一种技能, 还是获取新知呢? **~ed** *adj* **1** trained; experienced; having ~: 有训练的; 有经验的; 熟练的: *~ed workmen;* 有经验的工人; *~ed in doing sth.* 做某事熟练。 **2** needing ~: 需要技能的: *~ed work.* 需要技能的工作。

skil·let /'skɪlɪt; 'skɪlɪt/ *n* **1** small metal cooking-pot with a long handle and (usu) feet. 长柄煮锅(通常有支脚, 一般有三足)。 **2** (US) frying-pan. (美)平底锅; 煎锅。

skilly /'skɪlɪ; 'skɪlɪ/ *n* [U] thin broth or soup (usu oatmeal and water flavoured with meat). 薄羹(通常为燕麦加水汤); 稀粥。

skim /skɪm; skɪm/ *vt, vi* (**-mm-**) **1** [VP6A, 15B, 14] *~ (off) (from),* remove floating matter from (the surface of a liquid): 撇去(液体表面)之漂浮物: *~ milk;* 撇去牛乳之乳皮; remove (cream, scum, etc) from the surface of a liquid: 自液体表面撇取(油脂、浮渣等):

the cream from the milk; 自牛奶中撇取奶油; ~ off the fat from the soup. 把菜汤的油脂撇去。 '~med-milk n milk from which the cream has been ~med. 脱脂牛奶。 2 [VP2C, 3A, 6A, 15A] move lightly over (a surface), not touching, or only lightly or occasionally touching (it): (使)轻轻掠过(某表面); 轻轻擦过: The swallows were ~ming (over) the water / ~med along the ground. 燕子掠过水面(地面)。 3 [VP6A, 3A] ~ (through) sth, read quickly, noting only the chief points: 略读; 快读: ~ (through) a newspaper / catalogue, etc. 略读报纸(目录等)。 '~·mer n 1 utensil with a perforated bowl for ~ming liquids. 撇取浮物的用具; 撇渣器。 2 long-winged water-bird. 撇水鸟(一种长翼海鸟)。

skimp /skɪmp; skɪmp/ vt, vi [VP6A, 2A] supply. use, less than enough of what is needed: 吝于供给或使用; 吝啬; 节俭: ~ the butter when making cakes / the material when making a dress. 做饼时省下奶油(做衣服时省布料)。 They are so poor that they have to ~. 他们很穷, 所以必须撙节。 **skimpy** adj (-ier, -iest) 1 giving, using, less than enough. 不充分给予的; 吝于使用的; 节俭的。 2 (of a dress, etc) made with insufficient material; too small; too tight. (指衣服等)材料不足做成的; 太小的; 太窄的。 ~·ily /-ɪlɪ; -əlɪ/ adv: a ~ily made dress. 做得太小的衣服。

skin /skɪn; skɪn/ n 1 [U] elastic substance forming the outer covering of the body of a person or animal: (人或动物之)皮; 皮肤: We all got wet to the ~, thoroughly wet (eg in heavy rain). 我们全都浑身淋湿了。 ~ and bone, very thin: 瘦成皮包骨: He's only ~ and bone. 他瘦成皮包骨。 by the ~ of one's teeth, by a narrow margin; narrowly. 好不容易; 侥幸。 get under one's ~, (fig) annoy, irritate, anger one; infatuate one. (喻)激怒; 使迷恋。 get sb under one's skin, be infatuated with him. 迷恋某人。 have a thin / thick ~, (fig) be sensitive / insensitive; be easily / not easily hurt by unkindness, criticism, rebuke, etc. (喻)脸皮薄(厚); 敏感(不敏感); 容易(不易)因冷待、批评、责骂等而受伤害。 Hence, 由此产生, ,thin-/,thick-' ~ned adj save one's ~, avoid being hurt, etc: escape safely. 免受损伤; 安然逃脱。 ,~-'deep adj (of beauty, feelings, etc) only on the surface; not deep or lasting. (指美、感情等)肤浅的; 皮相的; 不深刻的; 不持久的。 '~-diving n form of sport in which a person dives into and swims under the water without a diving-suit, with goggles to protect the eyes and a snorkel or aqualung to help breathing. 轻装潜水(不穿潜水衣, 以潜水面罩保护眼睛, 以呼吸管或水肺帮助呼吸)。 '~-flint n miser. 吝啬者。 '~ game n fraudulent gambling game; swindle. 骗局; 诈骗。 '~-graft n surgical process of grafting ~ from one part of a person's body (or from another person's body) on to a part which has been damaged, eg by burning. 皮肤移植(把自身某处或他人之皮肤移植于伤患之处的外科手术)。 'skin-head n (GB, early 1970's) young gangster with closely-cut hair. (英, 二十世纪七十年代早期)留平头的不良少年。 ,~-'tight, (of a garment) fitting closely to the body. (指服装)贴身的; 合身的。 2 [C] animal ~ with or without the hair or fur; hide; pelt: 兽皮; 毛皮; 皮革; 生皮: 'rabbit-~s. 兔皮。 3 [C] vessel for storing or carrying liquid, made of the whole ~ of an animal: 装液体用之皮囊(用整块之兽皮制成者): 'wine-~s. 酒囊。 4 [C, U] outer covering of a fruit, or plant: 果皮; 植物之外皮: slip on a ba'nana ~; 踩上香蕉皮而滑倒; 'grape ~ s. 葡萄皮; ⇒ the illus at fruit. 参看 fruit之插图。 Cf 参较 peel for potatoes, apples, etc; the bark of a tree. 马铃薯、苹果等之皮用 peel; 树皮用 bark。 5 thin layer that forms on boiled milk: 结于煮沸牛奶上之薄层; 奶皮: the ~ on milk pudding. 牛奶布丁上之奶皮。 □ vt, vi (-nn-) 1 [VP6A] take the ~ off: 剥皮; 去皮; 去壳: ~ a rabbit. 剥兔皮。 keep one's 'eyes ~ned, (colloq) be alert, watchful. (口)留心; 警戒。 2 [VP6A, 14] (colloq) swindle; fleece: 欺骗; 诈诈: He was ~ned of all his money by confidence tricksters. 他所

有的钱都被专骗老实人的骗子骗去了。 3 [VP2C] ~ over, become covered with ~: 为皮所覆盖; 生皮; 长皮: The wound ~ned over. 伤处长皮了。 ~·ny adj (-ier, -iest) with little flesh; (colloq) mean; miserly. 无肉的; 瘦削的; (口)小气的; 吝啬的。 ⇨ skinflint above. 参看上列之 skinflint。

skint /skɪnt; skɪnt/ adj (GB sl) without money; penniless. (英俚)一文不名的; 囊空如洗的。

skip[1] /skɪp; skɪp/ vi, vt (-pp-) 1 [VP2A, C] jump lightly and quickly: 轻快地跳; 跳跃: ~ over an obstacle / over a brook / out of the way of a bus. 跳过障碍物(跳过小河/闪开公共汽车)。 The lambs were ~ping about in the fields, jumping about, gambolling. 小羊在田里蹦来跳去。 2 [VP2A] jump over a rope which is turned over the head and under the feet as one jumps. 跳绳。 '~ping-rope n length of rope (usu with two wooden handles) used in the children's game of ~ping. 跳绳游戏所用之绳。 3 [VP2C] go from one place (or, fig, subject) to another quickly or casually: 匆匆地或随兴所至地由一地到另一地; (喻)随兴所至东谈西谈: ~ over / across to Paris for the weekend. 匆匆前往巴黎度周末。 He ~ped (= left) without saying anything to any of us. 他匆匆离开, 未对我们任何人说什么。 He ~ped from one subject to another. 他随便地从一个话题跳到另一个话题。 4 [VP6A, 2A] make omissions, go from one part (of a book, etc) to another without reading, paying attention, etc: 漏看(书等之)某部分; 略过; 遗漏: He ~ped the dull parts of the book. 他把这书的枯燥部分略过不读。 We'll ~ the next chapter. 我们将略过下一章。 Do you read without ~ping? 你读书不跳着读吗? □ n [C] ~ping movement: 跳; 跳跃; 漏读; 略过; 遗漏: a hop, a ~ and a jump. 三级跳远。

skip[2] /skɪp; skɪp/ n cage or bucket in which men or materials are raised and lowered in mines and quarries; large metal container for carrying away builders' refuse, etc. (矿坑及采石场中载人或物上下之笼形或桶形)吊桶; (用以运走工地废料等之)大铁箱; 箕斗。

skip·per /'skɪpə(r); 'skɪpɚ/ n captain, esp of a small merchant ship or fishing-boat; (colloq) captain of a team in games such as baseball and cricket. 船长(尤指小商船或渔船者); (口)(足球、板球等之)球队队长。

skirl /skɜːl; skɝl/ n shrill, piercing sound: 尖锐声: the ~ of the bagpipes. 风笛之尖锐声。

skir·mish /'skɜːmɪʃ; 'skɝmɪʃ/ n [C] (often unpremeditated) fight between small parts of armies or fleets; (hence) short argument or contest of wit, etc. 陆上或海上之小战; 冲突(通常为遭遇战); (由此产生)小争论; 短暂的斗智。 □ vi [VP2A, C] engage in a ~. 小战; 小争论。 ~·er n one who ~es, esp a member of a force sent out from the main body of troops to hide its movements, or to learn about the movement of the enemy. 参与小战者; (尤指)散兵; 侦察(派出以掩护本队或探知敌情者)。

skirt /skɜːt; skɝt/ n 1 woman's garment that hangs from the waist. 女裙。 2 part of a dress or other garment (eg a long coat or shirt) that hangs below the waist. 衣服之下身(如长外套或衬衣的下部); 下摆。 3 (pl) (= outskirts) border; extreme parts: (复)边界; 边缘; 极端的部分: on the ~s of the town. 在城郊。 □ vt, vi [VP6A, 2C] be on, pass along, the edge of: 位于…之边缘; 沿…之边缘而行: Our road ~ed the forest. 我们的路位于森林的边缘。 Our path ~ed along the moor. 我们的小径沿松鸡场猎场蜿蜒。 ~ round sth, be indirect about it; avoid direct reference to it: 不直接处理某事; 避免提及某事: He ~ed round the subject of his family. 他谈论有关他家庭的问题。 '~-ing-board n strip or line of boards fixed round the walls of a room close to the floor. 踢脚板; 壁脚板。

skit /skɪt; skɪt/ n [C] short piece of humorous writing, short play, mimicking and making fun of sth or sb: (模拟斯取笑某人或某事物之)幽默之短文或短剧: a ~ on Wagner / on 'Macbeth'. 讽刺华格纳('麦克白'剧本)的短文。

skit·tish /'skɪtɪʃ ; 'skɪtɪʃ/ *adj* (of horses) excitable; lively; difficult to control; (of a person) lively and coquettish, fond of flirting, etc. (指马)易惊恐的; 活泼的; 难控制的; (指人)轻浮的; 喜调情的。 ~·**ly** *adv* ~·**ness** *n*

skittle /'skɪtl ; n (*pl* ~**s**, with *sing v*) (复数 skittles 用单数动词) game in which a ball is bowled along an alley ('~-**alley**) with the purpose of knocking down a number of bottle-shaped pieces of wood (called ~**s** or '~-**pins**). 九柱戏; 撞柱戏(以球沿球道 ~-alley 撞击若干个瓶状木柱 ~s 或 ~-pins 的游戏)。 ⇨ **ninepins, tenpins. (all) beer and ~s,** amusement; fun: 娱乐; 嬉戏: *Life is not all beer and ~s.* 人生非仅游乐而已。□ *vt* [VP15B] ~ **out,** (cricket) dismiss easily: (板球)轻易地使遭封杀出局: *The whole side was ~d out for 100 runs.* 满 100 分时, 全队出局。

skivvy /'skɪvɪ ; 'skɪvɪ/ *n* (*pl* -**vies**) (GB *sl*) (*pej*) servant who is required to do all sorts of work. (英俚, 蔑)仆人; 佣人。

skua /'skjuːə ; 'skjuə/ *n* large kind of seagull. 贼鸥 (一种大海鸥)。

skulk /skʌlk ; skʌlk/ *vi* [VP2A, C] hide, move secretly, through cowardice, or to avoid work or duty, or with an evil purpose. 藏匿; 潜伏; 潜行(因胆小, 或逃避工作责任, 或心怀不轨)。 ~**er** *n* 隐藏的人; 潜行者; 潜伏者。

skull /skʌl ; skʌl/ *n* bony framework of the head. 脑壳; 头盖骨。 ⇨ the illus at **skeleton.** 参看 skeleton 之插图。 **have a thick ~,** be stupid. 笨头笨脑。 **,~ and 'cross-bones,** picture of a ~ and two thigh-bones crossed below it (as an emblem of death or danger, and formerly used on a flag by pirates). 骷髅画(为死亡或危险之象征; 昔时海盗用作旗帜)。 '~-**cap** *n* close-fitting (often velvet) cap worn indoors by old or bald men, by Popes and cardinals. 室内便帽(常用天鹅绒制成, 老人, 秃头者, 教皇及红衣主教等戴之)。 -**skulled** *suff* (with *adj* prefixed): (用形容词作前缀): *,thick-'~ed,* having a thick ~. 笨头笨脑的。

skull·dug·gery /skʌl'dʌgərɪ;skʌl'dʌgərɪ/ *n* (*colloq*) clever deception; trickery. (口)诈骗; 诡计; 奸计。

skunk /skʌŋk ; skʌŋk/ *n* **1** small, bush-tailed N American animal able to send out a strong, unpleasant smell as a defence when attacked; [U] its fur. 臭鼬 (北美洲产, 体小, 尾毛厚, 遇敌放出恶臭以自卫); 臭鼬毛皮。 **2** detestable or contemptible person. 可恶的人; 卑鄙的人。

sky /skaɪ; skaɪ/ *n* (*pl* skies /skaɪz ; skaɪz/) **1** (usu **the sky; a sky** when modified by an *adj*, often *pl* in the same sense) the space we look up to from the earth, where we see the sun, moon and stars: (通常以形容词修饰时, 可以定冠词或不定冠词连用; 复数义同义)天; 天空: *under the open sky,* out of doors; 在户外; *a clear, blue sky;* 晴朗蔚蓝的天空; *a starry sky / (the) starry skies.* 多星辰的天空。 *praise/extol/laud sb to the skies,* praise him very highly. 极力称赞某人。 **,sky·'blue** *adj* *n* (of) the bright blue colour of the sky on a cloudless day. 天蓝色的; 天蓝色。 **,sky·'high** *adv* so as to reach the sky; as high as the sky: 高入云霄地; 极高地: *When the bomb exploded, the bridge was blown sky-high.* 炸弹爆炸时, 那桥被炸裂飞散得极高。 '**sky·lark** *n* small bird that sings as it flies up into the sky. 云雀(高飞时鸣唱之小鸟)。 □ *vi* = lark². '**sky·light** *n* window in a sloping roof. 天窗。 '**sky·line** *n* outline of hills, buildings, etc, defined against the sky: 山, 建筑物等以天空为背景所映出的轮廓: *the skyline of New York.* 纽约市高大建筑的空中轮廓。 '**sky pilot** *n* (*sl*) parson (esp, among sailors, a chaplain on a warship). (俚)牧师(尤指军舰上的随军牧师)。 '**sky-rocket** *vi* (of prices) soar; go up steeply. (指物价)上升; 猛涨。 '**sky·scraper** *n* very tall building. 摩天楼。 '**sky-writing** *n* [U] (making of) smoke-trails forming legible words in the sky (by aircraft for advertising purposes). (飞机放烟书写的)空中文字; (做)

空中广告。 **2** (often *pl*) climate: (常用复数)天气; 气候: *the sunny skies of southern Italy.* 意大利南部之晴朗的天候。 □ *vt* hit (eg a ball) high up. 将(球等)击向空中。 **sky·ward(s)** /'skaɪwəd(z) ; 'skaɪwəd(z)/ *adj, adv* toward(s) the sky; upward(s). 向天空; 向上。

skyscrapers

slab /slæb ; slæb/ *n* thick flat (usu square or rectangular) piece of stone, wood or other solid substance. 板; 片(石、木或其他硬物的厚块, 通常为方形或矩形): *paved with ~s of stone:* 以石板铺成的; *a ~ of cheese / cooking chocolate;* 一块干酪(烹调用的巧克力); *a mortuary ~.* 停尸板。

slack¹ /slæk ; slæk/ *adj* **1** giving little care or attention to one's work; having or showing little energy: 疏忽职守的; 懈怠的; 无气力的: *Don't get ~ at your work.* 不要懈怠你的工作。 *She feels ~* (= lacking in energy) *this morning.* 她今晨感觉没有气力。 **2** dull; inactive; with not much work to be done or business being done: 呆滞的; 萧条的; 不景气的: *Trade / Business is ~ this week.* 这周的贸易(营业)不景气。 *There is only a ~ demand for S African mining shares.* 南非的矿业股票滞销。 **3** loose, not tight; loose on: 松弛的; 不紧的: *a ~ rope.* 松弛的绳。 *keep a ~ rein on sth,* control sth negligently; (fig) govern carelessly. 粗心大意地管理; (喻)懒散地治理。 **4** slow-moving; sluggish: 缓慢的; 迟滞的: *periods of ~ water,* when the tide is neither ebbing nor flowing. 平潮期间(潮水不涨不退之时)。 □ *vi* [VP2A, C] **1** ~ **(off),** be lazy or careless in one's work: 懈怠; 疏忽职守: *Don't ~ off in your studies.* 不要荒废你的学业。 **2** ~ **up,** reduce speed: 减速: *S~ up before you reach the crossroads.* 快到交叉路时减速。 **3** ~ **off / away,** make loose (a rope, etc). 放松(绳等)。 ~**er** *n* (colloq) lazy person; person who avoids his proper share of work. (口)懒惰者; 规避职责者。 ~·**ly** *adv* ~·**ness** *n*

slack² /slæk ; slæk/ *n* **1 the ~,** that part of a rope, etc that hangs loosely. 绳等松弛的部分。 **take up the ~,** pull a rope so that it is taut; (fig) regulate industry so that it is active and productive. 拉紧绳子; (喻)整顿工业(使其增产)。 **2** (*pl*) loose-fitting trousers, not part of a suit, eg as informal wear for men or women. (复)宽松的裤子(如男女平时所穿者)。 **3** [U] coal dust. 煤屑; 煤渣。

slacken /'slækən ; 'slækən/ *vt, vi* [VP6A, 2A] **1** make or become slower, less active, etc: 使缓慢; 变缓慢; 使迟滞; 变为不景气: ~ *speed.* 减缓速度。 *The ship's speed ~ed.* 船速减缓。 *The gale is ~ing a little.* 暴风减弱了一点。 **2** make or become loose(r): 使松弛; 变松弛: ~ *the reins.* 放松缰绳。 *S~ away / off!* eg as an order to loosen ropes. 放开! 放松! (如吩咐放松绳等)。

slag /slæg ; slæg/ *n* [U] waste matter remaining when metal has been extracted from ore. 矿渣; 熔渣。 '~-**heap** *n* hill of ~ (dumped from a mine). 熔渣堆(矿坑倒出者)。

slain /sleɪn ; slen/ *pp* of **slay.**

slake /sleɪk ; slek/ *vt* [VP6A] **1** satisfy or make less strong (thirst, desire for revenge). 满足或缓和(口渴, 报复之心)。 **2** change the chemical nature of (lime) by adding water. (加水)使(生石灰)熟化; 消和(生石灰)。 ⇨ **calcium.**

sla·lom /'slɑːləm ; 'slɑləm/ *n* ski-race along a zigzag

course marked out by poles with flags. 弯道滑雪比赛。

slam /slæm ; slæm/ *vt, vi* (**-mm-**) **1** [VP6A, 15A, B, 22] ~ **(to)**, shut violently and noisily: 使劲关; 砰然关闭: *the door (to);* ~ *the window shut/* 使劲关上窗子; ~ *the door in sb's face.* 当某人之面将门砰然关闭。 **2** [VP2A, C] ~ **(to)**, be shut violently: 砰然关起: *The door* ~*med (to).* 门砰然关起来。 **3** [VP 15A, B] put, throw or knock with force: 砰然放下; 猛力投掷或敲击: *She* ~*med the box down on the table.* 她将匣子砰然摔在桌上。 *The batsman* ~*med the ball into the grand-stand.* 击球员把球击入了大看台。 □ *n* **1** noise of sth being ~med: 砰然声; *the* ~ *of a car door.* 关车门时的砰然声。 **2** (in whist, bridge) **a grand** ~, taking of 13 tricks. (惠斯特纸牌戏, 桥牌戏) 大满贯 (赢十三磴牌)。 **a small** ~, taking of 12 tricks. 小满贯 (赢十二磴牌)。

slan·der /'slɑːndər/ *US:* 'slæn-; 'slændɚ/ *n* [C, U] (offence of making a) false statement that damages a person's reputation: 诽谤; 诋毁; 诽谤罪: *bring a* ~ *action against sb,* charge him with ~ in a court of law. 以诽谤罪控告某人。 □ *vt* [VP6A] utter ~ about (sb). 诽谤; 诋毁 (某人)。 ~**er** *n* ~**ous** /-əs ; -əs/ *adj* uttering or containing ~. 诽谤的; 造谣中伤的。

slang /slæŋ; slæŋ/ *n* [U] (abbr *sl* used in this dictionary) words, phrases, meanings of words, etc commonly used in talk among friends or colleagues, but not suitable for good writing or formal occasions, esp the kind used by and typical of only one class of persons: (本词典用 sl 为其略语) 俚语 (一般用于朋友或同事间之谈话, 但不适于好的写作或正式场合的字词); (尤指)某一阶层人士的惯用语: *army* ~; 军队俚语; *prison* ~; 狱中俚语; (attrib) (用作定语) ~ *words and expressions.* 俚语的字词和说法。 *The use of out-of-date* ~ *is sometimes a feature of foreigners' English.* 使用过时的俚语是外国人所用英文的特色。 ⇨ **colloquial.** □ *vt* [VP6A] use violent language to; abuse: 对...讲粗话; 谩骂: *Stop* ~*ing me.* 别骂我。 **a** ~*'ing match,* a long exchange of insults and accusations. 长期的彼此攻讦或辱骂。 ~**y** *adj* (**-ier, -iest**) using, in the nature of, ~. 用俚语的; 俚语性的。 ~**·ily** /-ɪlɪ; -əlɪ/ *adv* ~**i·ness** *n*

slant /slɑːnt *US:* slænt; slænt/ *vi, vt* **1** [VP2A, C, 6A] slope: (使)倾斜; 歪向: *His handwriting* ~*s from right to left.* 他写的字从右往左斜。 **2** [VP6A] ~ *the news,* present it so that it is seen from, and supports, a particular point of view, eg of the writer's newspaper or government. 从某一观点或立场 (如报社或政府) 发布或报导新闻。 □ *n* **1** [C] slope. 倾斜; 斜面。 **on a/the** ~, in a sloping position. 倾斜着。 **2** [colloq] point of view (sometimes prejudiced or biased) when considering sth: (口)考虑某事时的观点 (有时是偏见或成见): 看法: *get a new* ~ *on the political situation.* 获知对政治形势的新观点。 ~**·ing·ly, ~·wise** /-waɪz; -waɪz/ *advv* in a ~ing position or direction. 倾斜地; 歪斜地。

slap /slæp; slæp/ *vt* (**-pp-**) **1** [VP6A 15A] strike with the palm of the hand; smack: 掌击; 掴; 拍: *She* ~*ped his face/* ~*ped him on the face.* 她打他一个耳光。 *I don't like being* ~*ped on the back as a greeting.* 我不喜欢在我被拍一下当做招呼。 **2** [VP15B] ~ *sth down,* put sth down with a ~ping noise: 拍的一声放下某物: *He* ~*ped the book down on the table.* 他拍的一声把书摔在桌上。 □ *n* [C] quick blow with the palm of the hand or with sth flat. 以手掌或扁平物快速的击; 掴; 拍。 *get/give sb a* ~ *in the face,* (fig) a rebuff or snub. (喻)严拒; 奚落。 □ *adv* straight; directly; full: 一直地; 直接地; 充分地: *The car ran* ~ *into the wall.* 那汽车与墙撞个正着。 ~**'-bang** *adv* violently; headlong. 猛烈地; 卤莽地。 ~**'-dash** *adj, adv* carelessly; impetuously: 粗心的(地), 卤莽的(地); 猛烈的(地); 草率的(地): *a* ~*dash worker;* 粗心的工人; *do one's work* ~*dash/in a* ~*dash manner.* 草率地做工作。 ~**'-happy** *adj* (colloq) impetuous; carefree. (口)鲁莽的; 无忧无虑的。 ~**'-stick** *n* [U] low comedy of the roughest kind; fun arising from violence: 打打闹闹的滑稽剧; 动作激烈的笑闹: (attrib) (用作定语) ~*stick comedy.*

粗俗喜剧; 闹剧。 '~*-up* *adj* (sl) first-class; extremely good: (俚)第一流的; 极好的; 上等的: *be treated to a* ~*up dinner at a* ~*up restaurant.* 在上等的餐馆接受款待吃了一顿上等的大餐。

slash /slæʃ; slæʃ/ *vt, vi* **1** [VP6A, 2C] make a cut or cuts in or at sth with sweeping strokes; strike with a whip: 挥砍; 挥斩; 切伤; 鞭打: *His face had been* ~*ed with a razor-blade.* 他的脸被刀片割伤了。 *Don't* ~ *your horse in that cruel way.* 不要那么残忍地鞭打你的马。 *He* ~*ed at the tall weeds with his stick.* 他用手杖挥击高高的野草。 **2** [VP6A] condemn vigorously and outspokenly: 严苛而直言地谴责; 酷评: *a* ~*ing attack on the government's policy:* 对政府政策之猛烈的攻击; *a new book/play,* criticize it adversely, 严苛地批评新书 (剧本)。 **3** [VP6A] (colloq) cut, reduce drastically: (口)削减; 大幅减少: ~ *prices/taxes/salaries.* 大大地减低价格(税金, 薪水)。 **4**(usu passive) make long, narrow gashes in (for ornament, etc): (通常用被动语态)开长缝; 开叉(以为装饰等): ~*ed sleeves,* the lining or other material being seen through the ~es. 开叉的衣袖。 □ *n* **1** act of ~ing; long cut or gash. 挥砍; 鞭打; 谴责; 削减; 伤痕; 长缝; 叉。 **2** (vulg sl) act of urinating. (鄙俚)小便; 撒尿。

slat /slæt; slæt/ *n* long, thin, narrow piece of wood, metal or plastic material, eg as in Venetian blinds or louvred doors: (木, 金属或塑胶等之)薄的细狭长条; 条板(如百叶板或羽板)。 ~**·ted** *adj* made with, having, ~. 装有条板的; 有条板的。

slate /sleɪt; sleɪt/ *n* **1** [U] kind of blue-grey stone that splits easily into thin, flat layers; [C] one of these layers, square or oblong, used for roofs: 板石; 粘板岩; 石板; 石板瓦: *hit on the head by a falling* ~; 被落下的一块石片打在头上; *a* ~*-covered roof:* 石板瓦覆盖的房顶; '~*-coloured,* blue-grey; 灰蓝色的; *a '* ~ *quarry.* 采板石场。 **2** [C] sheet of ~ in a wooden frame for writing on (as formerly used by school-children). 石板(昔时学童书写用)。 *a clean* ~, (fig) a good record: (喻)好的记录: *start with a clean* ~, (fig) make a new start with past errors, enmities, etc, forgotten. (喻)改过自新; 重新开始; 弃嫌宿好。'~*-club* *n* (GB) club collecting small weekly contributions of money, usu saved until Christmas, when the total is distributed to members. (英)每周缴出少数钱的互助会 (通常储存到圣诞节, 全部用来分配于会员)。 ~*-'pencil* *n* thin rod of soft ~, used for writing on ~s (2). 石笔(细而软之板石, 用于书写石板者)。 □ *vt* **1** [VP6A] cover (a roof etc) with ~s. 以石板瓦盖(屋顶等)。 **2** (US, colloq) propose (sb) for an office, a position, etc: (美口)提名 (某人) 担任公职、职务等: (newspaper headline) (报纸标题) *Green* ~*d for the Presidency.* 格林被提名为总统候选人。 **3** [VP6A] (colloq) criticize severely (esp in a newspaper notice of a book, play, etc). (口)酷评 (尤指在报纸中对书籍、戏剧等的评述)。 **slaty** *adj* of or like ~; containing ~: 板石的; 似板石的; 含石石的; *slaty coal.* 含板石成分的煤。 **slat·ing** *n* adverse criticism: 批评; 酷评: *give sb a sound slating.* 痛责某人。

slat·tern /'slætən/ *US:* 'slætɚn/ *n* dirty, untidily dressed woman. 衣着不整洁的女人。 ~**·ly** *adj* (of women) dirty and untidy. (指女人)不整洁的。 ~**·li·ness** *n*

slaugh·ter /'slɔːtə(r); 'slɔtɚ/ *n* [U] **1** killing of animals (esp for food). 屠宰(尤指为食物)。 '~*-house* *n* place where animals are butchered for food. 屠宰场。 **2** killing of many people at once; massacre: 屠杀; 杀戮: *the* ~ *on the roads,* the killing of people in road accidents. 路上车祸造成的死亡。 □ *vt* [VP6A] kill (animals, people) in large numbers. 屠杀(动物、人); 杀戮; 屠宰。 ~**er** *n*

Slav /slɑːv; slɑv/ *n* member of a race spread over most of Eastern Europe, including Russians, Czechs, Poles, Bulgarians, etc. 斯拉夫族人(包括俄国人、捷克人、波兰人、保加利亚人等)。 □ *adj* of the ~s. 斯拉夫人的。

slave /sleɪv; sleɪv/ *n* **1** person who is the property of another and bound to serve him. 奴隶。 '~*-driver* *n*

overseer of ~s at work; person who makes those who are under him work very hard. 双工监督; 迫使下属工作过度的人。**'~ ship** n ship used in the ~-trade. 双隶贸易船。**'~ States** n pl southern States of N America in which there was slavery before the Civil War. 南北战争以前美国南方蓄奴各州。**'~-trade**/**-traffic** n capturing, transportation, buying and selling, of ~s. 双隶买卖。**2** person compelled to work very hard for someone else: 被双役之人; 苦工; 双工: You mustn't make a ~ of your au pair girl. 你不可把照午以工作交换食宿的女孩当做你的双隶。**3** sb completely in the power of, under the control of, an impulse, habit, etc: 完全受冲动、习惯等控制之人: ~s of fashion, eg persons who feel compelled to dress in the latest fashions; 拎命赶时髦的人们; a ~ to duty/passion/convention/drink. 被职务(热情, 习俗, 杯中物)所控制的人。□ vi [VP2A, B, C, 3A] ~ (away) (at sth), work hard: 努力工作; 作苦工: Poor Jane! She's been slaving away (= cooking) over a hot stove for three hours! 可怜的简! 她已在热火炉旁边辛苦工作(烹饪)三个小时了! ~r n '~-trader; ~ ship. 贩卖双隶者; 双隶贸易船。**slav·ery** /'sleɪvərɪ; 'slevərɪ/ n [U] **1** condition of being a ~: 双隶状态; 双役: sold into ~ry. 被卖为双役。**2** custom of having ~s: 双隶制度: men who worked for the abolition of ~ry. 为废除双隶制度奋斗的人们。**3** hard or badly paid work. 苦役; 低酬工作。**slav·ish** /'sleɪvɪʃ; 'slevɪʃ/ adj lacking in independence or originality; abject (2): 双隶性的; 缺乏独立或创作性的; 卑鄙的; 卑躬的: a slavish imitation, an exact copy showing no originality. 抄袭; 毫无创造性的仿品。**slav·ish·ly** adv

slaver /'slæv(r); 'slævə/ vi [VP2A, 3A] ~ (over) let spit run from the mouth(because of hunger): (因饥饿而)流涎; 垂涎: ~ing over a plate of spaghetti; 垂涎于一盘意大利面条; (fig) (喻) ~ing over a travel brochure. 兴奋或渴望地看着旅游样册。□ n [U] spit; saliva. 吐沫; 口水。also ⟹ slaver at slave.

slavey /'sleɪvɪ; 'slevɪ/ n (pl -veys) (sl) young servant. (俚)年轻的仆人。

Slav·onic /slə'vɒnɪk; slə'vɑnɪk/ adj of the Slavs or their languages. 斯拉夫族的; 斯拉夫语的。

slaw /slɔː; slɔ/ n [U] (often 通常作 'cole-~) sliced cabbage, raw or cooked, served with a dressing. (生或熟的)甘蓝菜丝(菜肴之一, 食时加酱汁等佐料)。

slay /sleɪ; sle/ vt (pt **slew** /sluː; slu/, pp slain /sleɪn; slen/) [VP6A] (liter, or rhet) kill, murder. (文,修辞)杀; 谋杀。~er n (journalism) murderer. (新闻)谋杀者; 凶手。

sleazy /'sliːzɪ; 'slezɪ/ adj (-ier, -iest) (colloq) uncared-for, dirty, untidy: (口)没人照顾的; 肮脏的; 不整齐的: a ~ hotel/appearance. 肮脏的旅社(外貌)。

sled /sled; slɛd/ n = sledge.

sledge[1] /sledʒ; slɛdʒ/ n vehicle with runners (long, narrow strips of wood or metal) instead of wheels, used on snow, larger types being pulled by horses or dogs and smaller types being used in sport for travelling downhill at speed. 雪橇 (以木质或金属质长条代轮之交通工具, 用于雪地, 大型者以马或狗曳之, 小型者用于沿斜坡迅速滑行以为游戏)。□ vi, vt (-dd-) travel or carry by ~: 乘雪橇旅行; 以雪橇运送: go sledging. 乘雪橇去。

sledge[2] /sledʒ; slɛdʒ/ n '~(-hammer), heavy hammer with a long handle, used for driving posts into the ground, and by blacksmiths. (铁匠用的)大锤。

sleek /sliːk; slik/ adj (of hair, an animal's fur, etc) soft, smooth and glossy; (of a person) having such hair. (指毛发、动物之毛皮等)柔滑而发亮的; (指人)有柔软而发亮之毛皮的。as ~ as a cat, (fig) having smooth manners (perhaps over-anxious to please). (喻) 像猫一般地圆滑诙谐的。□ vt [VP6A] make ~: 使柔软发亮, 使光滑: ~ a cat's fur. 使猫的毛皮光滑。~·ly adv ~·ness n

sleep[1] /sliːp; slip/ n [U] condition of the body and mind such as recurs regularly every night, in which the eyes are closed and the muscles, nervous system, etc

are relaxed: 睡眠: How many hours' ~ do you need? 你需要几小时的睡眠? He didn't get much ~. 他睡得不多。Do you ever talk in your ~? 你睡觉时说梦话吗? **get to ~,** manage to fall asleep, succeed in passing into the condition of ~: 睡着; 入眠: I couldn't get to ~ last night. 我昨夜睡不着。**go to ~,** fall asleep. 睡着。**have one's ~ out,** continue ~ing until one wakes up naturally: 睡足而自行醒来: Don't wake her up—let her have her ~ out. 别叫醒她—让她睡足而自己醒。**put sb to ~,** cause him to fall asleep. 使某人入睡。**put (a pet animal) to ~,** (euphem) deliberately kill it (because of illness, etc). (委婉语)故意杀死(生病等的心爱动物)。**2 a ~,** period of ~: 睡眠时间: have a short/good/restful, etc ~; 有一个短时间(良好, 安静等)的睡眠; a ~ of three hours. 三小时的睡眠。**'~-walker** n person who walks while asleep. 梦游者; 患梦游症者。~·less adj without ~: 缺乏睡眠的; 失眠的: pass a ~less night. 一夜无眠。~·less·ly adv ~·less·ness n

sleep[2] /sliːp; slip/ vi, vt (pp, pt **slept** /slept; slɛpt/) **1** [VP2A, B, C] rest in the condition of ~, be or fall asleep: 睡; 睡着: We go to bed to ~. 我们上床睡觉。He's well/badly. 他睡得好(不好)。She slept (for) eight hours. 她睡了八小时。~ like a top/log, ~ very soundly. 熟睡。~ round the clock; ~ the clock round, ~ for twelve hours continuously. 连续睡十二小时。**2** [VP6A] provide beds for: 供给床位; 供给住宿: This hotel ~s 300 guests. 这旅馆可供三百名客人住宿。~·ing (in compounds) (复合词) **'~·ing-bag** n warmly lined and water proof bag in which to ~ when out of doors (eg on holiday) or in a tent. 睡袋(在户外或露营时用之, 有暖和的衬料和衬垫物, 并防水)。**'~·ing-car** n railway coach fitted with beds or berths. (铁路的)卧车。**'~·ing-draught**/**-pill** n one that contains a drug to help sb ~. 安眠剂(药丸)。**~·ing partner** n (US 美 = silent partner) person who provides a share of the capital of a business but does not share in the management. 不参与实际业务的股东; 隐名合伙人。**'~·ing-sickness** n [U] disease caused by the tsetse-fly; it results in weakening of the mental powers and (usu) death. 睡眠症; 昏睡病(采采蝇所引起之一种疾病; 会导致患者心智减弱, 而且通常会造成死亡)。~er n **1** person who ~s: (with adj) (与形容词连用) a heavy/light ~er, one whom it is hard/easy to wake up; 沉(浅)睡者; a good/bad ~er. 易熟睡(不能熟睡)者。**2** (US 美 = tie) heavy beam of wood (or similarly shaped piece of other material) on a railway track, etc supporting the rails. (铁路轨道之)枕木。**3** (bed or berth in a) ~ing-car on a train. (火车之)卧车; 卧铺。**3** [VP2C, 15B, 3A] (with adverbial particles and preps): (与副词性小品词及介词连用):

sleep around, (colloq) be promiscuous. (口)乱交; 杂交。

sleep in/**out,** ~ at/outside one's place of employment: 在(不在)工作场所住宿: Does the housekeeper ~ in? 管家在他的雇主处住宿吗?

sleep sth off, recover from sth by ~ing: 借睡眠而消除: ~ off a bad headache/a hangover. 借睡眠消除头痛(宿醉)。

sleep on, continue to sleep: 继续睡: Don't wake him up—let him ~ on for another hour. 别叫醒他—让他继续睡一小时。~ on sth, (often ~ over it), leave the answer, solution, to a problem etc to the next day. 把(问题等)留待第二天解决。

sleep through sth, not be woken up by (a noise, the alarm-clock, etc). 不被(噪音、闹钟等)吵醒。

sleep with sb, (euphem for) have sexual intercourse with. (委婉语)与人性交。

sleepy /'sliːpɪ; 'slipɪ/ adj (-ier, -iest) **1** needing, ready for, sleep: 要睡的; 欲睡的; 困的: feel/look ~. 觉得(显来)欲睡。**'~-head** n (esp as a form of address to sb) ~ or inattentive person. 贪睡者; 玩忽者(尤用于称呼某人)。**2** (of places, etc) quiet; inactive; (指地方等)静寂的; 不活跃的: a ~ little village. 静寂的小村。**3** (of some kinds of fruit) over-ripe: (指某些水果)太熟的: ~ pears/

bananas, soft and brown inside. 过熟的梨子(香蕉)。

sleep·i·ly /-ɪlɪ; -əlɪ/ *adv* **sleepi·ness** *n*

sleet /sliːt; slit/ *n* [U] falling snow or hail mixed with rain: 雨雪; 霙; 冰珠; 雨雹; 霰: *squalls of* ~. 带雨雪冰雹的狂风。 □ *vi* [VP2A] *It was* ~*ing*, S~ *was falling.* 下雨雪; 降雹。 **sleety** *adj*

sleeve /sliːv; sliv/ *n* **1** part of a garment that covers all or part of the arm: 袖; 衣袖: *roll up the* ~*s of one's shirt/one's 'shirt-*~*s.* 卷起衬衫的袖子。 **have sth up one's** ~, have an idea, plan, etc which one keeps secret for future use. 怀藏有用的计策等。 **laugh up one's** ~, be secretly amused. 窃喜。 **roll up one's** ~*s*, prepare to work or fight. 准备工作或打架。 **wear one's heart on one's** ~, allow one's feelings (of love for sb) to be seen; fail to show proper reserve. 流露真情; 表示爱慕; 未能作适当之保留。 **2** stiff envelope for a disc of recorded sound, often with notes on the composer, player(s), etc. 唱片之封套(常印有作曲者, 演奏者等之说明)。 **3** windsock. 风向袋; 套筒风标。 ⇨ wind¹(8). **-sleeved** *suff*: *'short / 'loose-*~*d.* 短(宽)袖的。 ~**·less** *adj* without ~s. 无袖的。

sleigh /sleɪ; sle/ *n* sledge, esp one drawn by a horse: 雪车; 雪橇(尤指马拖者): *go for a* ~*-ride/a ride in a* ~. 乘雪车(橇)。 '~**-bell** *n* one of several small tinkling bells commonly attached to a ~ or to the harness of the horse pulling the ~. 雪橇铃(常于雪橇或拖雪橇之马上的小铃)。 □ *vi*, *vt* [VP2A, 6A] travel in a ~; carry (goods) by ~. 乘雪车(橇)旅行; 以雪车(橇)搬运(货物)。

sleight /slaɪt; slaɪt/ *n* (usu in) (通常用于) ~ *of hand*, great skill in using the hand(s) in performing tricks, juggling, etc. (变戏法等中的)手法巧妙; 花招; 精于手上把戏。

slen·der /'slendə(r); 'slɛndə/ *adj* **1** small in width or circumference compared with height or length: 细长的; 纤细的: ~ *fingers;* 细长的手指; *a* ~ *waist;* 纤腰; 细腰; *a wineglass with a* ~ *stem.* 细腰酒杯; 高脚杯。 **2** (of persons) slim; not stout: (指人)纤巧的; 轻盈的: *a* ~ *girl, slight and graceful;* 纤巧的女郎; *a woman with a* ~ *figure.* 身材苗条的女子。 **3** slight; scanty; inadequate: 微薄的; 不足的; 不充分的: *a* ~ *income;* 微薄的收入; ~ *means/hopes.* 微少的资产(渺茫的希望)。 ~**·ly** *adv* ~**·ness** *n* ~**·ize** /-aɪz; -aɪz/ *vt*, *vi* [VP6A, 2A] (US) make, cause to appear, become, ~(2). (美)使显得(变得)苗条。

slept /slept; slɛpt/ *pt*, *pp* of **sleep**.

sleuth /sluːθ; sluθ/ *n* (colloq) detective. (口)侦探。 '~**-hound** *n* bloodhound; dog that follows a scent. 警犬; 探犬; 嗅迹猎犬。

slew¹ /sluː; slu/ *pt* of **slay**.

slew² (US = **slue**) /sluː; slu/ *vi*, *vt* [VP2C, 15B] ~ *(sth) round*, force or turn round in a new direction: 使或迫使(某物)转向新方向; 转向: *The crane* ~*ed round.* 吊车转向了。 *The driver* ~*ed his crane round.* 驾驶员转动吊车。

slice /slaɪs; slaɪs/ *n* [C] **1** thin, wide, flat piece cut off sth, esp bread or meat: 薄片; 片(尤指面包或肉类): ~*s of cold beef between* ~*s of bread make good sandwiches.* 冷牛肉片夹在面包片间即为上好的三明治。 **2** part, share: 部分; 份儿: *a* ~ *of good luck.* 一份好运气。 *Smith took too large a* ~ *of the credit for our success.* 对于我们的成功, 史密斯所获得的称赞超过了他的贡献。 **3** utensil with a wide, flat blade for cutting, serving or lifting (eg cooked fish, fried eggs). (切片、上菜或挑起用的)切刀; 餐刀; 锅铲。 **4** (in games such as golf) bad stroke that causes the ball to go spinning off in a direction different from that desired, ie to the right of a right-handed player. (高尔夫球等)右曲球; 斜击。 □ *vt*, *vi* **1** [VP6A, 15A, B, 22, 3A] cut into ~s: 切成~: *slice into/through a cake;* 切蛋糕; ~ *(up) a loaf.* 把一条面包切片。 S~ *the beef thin.* 把牛肉切成薄片。 *The butcher* ~*d off a thick steak.* 屠夫切下厚厚的一片肉。 **2** [VP6A] (golf): (高尔夫球): ~ *the ball*, strike with a ~(4). 曲打球; 斜击球; 击成右曲球。

slick /slɪk; slɪk/ *adj* (colloq) (口) **1** smooth; slippery: 平滑的; 滑溜的: *The roads were* ~ *with wet mud.* (那些)道路泥泞滑溜。 **2** carried through smoothly and efficiently, perhaps with some trickery: 圆滑而有效完成的; 巧妙完成的; 做得漂亮而有技巧的: *a business deal;* 一笔漂亮的生意; (of a person) doing things in a ~ way: (指人)有手段的; 有技巧的; 熟练的; 伶俐的: *a* ~ *salesman.* 一个伶俐的推销员或售货员。 □ *n* [C] *'oil* ~, film of thick oil covering an area of the sea, etc (eg from an oil-tanker after a collision). 水上浮油(如从撞沉的油船流出浮于海面等者)。 □ *adv* directly, completely: 直接地; 完全地: *hit a man* ~ *on the jaw.* 正好打在一个人的下颚上。 ~**er** *n* (US colloq) (美口) **1** long, loose, waterproof coat. (长而宽松的)雨衣。 **2** ~ *person*, ~(2 above): 骗子; (大都市的)老滑头; 老油条(参看上列第2义): *city* ~*ers.* 都市里的老油条、骗徒等。

slide¹ /slaɪd; slaɪd/ *n* **1** act of sliding(1); smooth stretch of ice, hard snow, etc on which to slide: 滑; 滑行; (冰、硬雪等的)滑面: *Have a* ~ *on the ice.* 在冰上滑行。 **2** smooth slope down which persons or things can slide (eg for felled timber down a mountain slope, or a wooden or metal slope made for children to play on). 滑道; 滑坡; 滑梯(如运送木材下山或儿童游戏所用者)。 **3** picture, diagram, etc on photographic film .(and usu mounted in a frame); (formerly) such a picture on a glass plate, to be slid into a 'projector and shown on a screen. 幻灯片。 **4** glass plate on which is placed sth to be examined under a microscope. (显微镜的)承物玻璃片。 **5** part of a machine, etc that slides (eg the U-shaped part of a trombone). (机器等的)滑动机件(如大喇叭上的 U 型部分)。 **6** ('land) ~, ⇨ land¹(6). **7** ('hair) ~, ⇨ hair (2).

slide² /slaɪd; slaɪd/ *vi*, *vt* (*pt*, *pp* slid /slɪd; slɪd/) **1** [VP2A, C, 6A, 15A] (cause to) move smoothly over, slip along, a polished surface: (使)在光滑表面上滑动或滑行: *children sliding on the ice.* 溜冰的孩子们。 *The book slid* (= slipped, which is more usu) *off my knee.* 书从我膝盖上滑落了 (slipped 比 slid 常用)。 *Let's down this grassy slope.* 咱们顺着这草坡滑下去吧。 *The drawers of this desk* ~ *in and out easily.* 这张书桌的抽屉拉出推进都很容易。 S~ *the drawer into its place.* 把抽屉推进去。 ~ *over sth*, pass over (a delicate subject, etc) quickly; barely touch upon it. 轻轻带过某事; 轻触(某一棘手问题等)即过; 点到为止。 *let things* ~, not trouble about them, be negligent. 听其自然。 **2** [VP3A] ~ *into*, pass gradually, without being fully aware, into (a condition, etc): 不知不觉地逐渐陷入(某种情况等): ~ *into dishonesty / bad habits.* 逐渐变得不诚实(慢慢染上坏习惯)。 **3** [VP2C, 6A, 15A] (cause to) move quickly, or so as to avoid observation: (使)快速行动; 溜进; 潜行: *The thief slid behind the curtains.* 窃贼溜到帷幕后面。 *She slid a coin into his hand.* 她很快把一枚硬币塞进他的手里。 **4** (compounds) (复合词) '~**-rule** *n* device of two rulers with logarithmic scales, one of which ~s in a groove, used for rapid calculations. 计算尺; 滑尺。 **slid·ing door** *n* one that is pulled across an opening (instead of turning on hinges). 拉门。 **slid·ing scale** *n* scale by which one thing, eg wages, goes up or down in relation to changes in sth else, eg the cost of living. 滑准法 (某一事项之高低计算随另一事项而改变的计算法; 如薪金随生活费用之变化而决定其标准)。 **slid·ing seat** *n* seat on runners, esp in a racing boat, to lengthen the stroke of the rower or sculler. 滑座(装在滑板上的座位, 尤指赛艇上可借以延伸桨手之划动者)。

slight¹ /slaɪt; slaɪt/ *adj* (-er, -est) **1** slim; slender; frail-looking: 细长的; 苗条的; 瘦小的; 脆弱的: *a* ~ *figure;* 苗条的身材; *supported by a* ~ *framework.* 由脆弱的骨架支撑的。 **2** small; not serious or important: 微小的; 轻微的; 不重要的: *a* ~ *error;* 小错; 小差误; *a* ~ *headache;* 轻微的头痛; *do sth without the* ~*est difficulty*, with no difficulty at all. 毫无困难地做某事。 *She takes*

offence at the ~est thing, is very easily offended. 他动不动就生气。 *not in the ~est*, not at all: 毫不；一点也不: *You didn't embarrass me in the ~est.* 你一点也没有使我为难。 **~·ly** *adv* **1** slenderly: 细长地；苗条地: *a ~ly built boy.* 瘦长的男孩。 **2** to a ~ degree; somewhat: 些许；稍稍: *The patient is ~ly better today.* 病人今天稍稍好一点。 *I know her ~ly.* 我略知道她些。 **~·ness** *n*

slight[2] /slaɪt/ *vt* [VP6A] treat without proper respect or courtesy; neglect in a marked manner: 慢待；轻视；藐视；不礼遇: *She felt ~ed because no one spoke to her.* 她感到受轻视，因为没有人跟她谈话。 □ *n* [C] marked failure to show respect or courtesy: 慢待；轻视；藐视: *put a ~ on sb;* 慢待某人； *suffer ~s.* 受到慢待。 **~·ing·ly** *adv*

slim /slɪm/ *adj* (**-mer, -mest**) **1** slender: 苗条的；细长的；纤细的: *a ~-waisted girl.* 细腰女郎。 **2** (colloq) small; insufficient: (口)细小的; 微少的; 不足的: *~ hopes/chances of success;* 成功的希望(机会)不大; *condemned upon the ~mest (of) evidence.* 根据微不足道的证据被判罪。 □ *vi* (**-mm-**) eat less, diet, take exercise, etc with the object of reducing one's weight and becoming ~ (1): 借少吃、进规定饮食、运动等以减轻体重而变苗条: *~ming exercises.* 减肥运动; 健美运动。 **~·ly** *adv* **~·ness** *n*

slime /slaɪm/ *n* [U] **1** soft, nasty, thick, sticky mud. 烂泥；泥泞。 **2** sticky substance from snails, etc: (蜗牛等的)粘液: *a trail of ~.* 一道(蜗牛等的)粘液痕。 **slimy** /'slaɪmɪ/ *adj* (**-ier, -iest**) of, like, covered with, ~; hard to hold because slippery with ~; (fig)disgustingly dishonest, meek, flattering, obsequious, etc: 泥泞(般)的;粘滑而难以捉摸的; (喻)奸诈的;过于温顺的;谄媚的;卑躬屈节的: *a slimy(-tongued) coward.* 油腔滑调的懦夫。

sling[1] /slɪŋ/ *n* [C] **1** band of material, length of rope, chain, etc looped round an object, eg a barrel, a broken arm, to support or lift it. 吊带；(用以悬吊断臂的)吊带；(用以悬吊圆桶等物件的)吊索。 **2** strip of leather used (held in the hand in a loop) to throw stones to a distance. 投石器；抛；投。 □ *vt* (*pt, pp* **slung** /slʌŋ/) **1** [VP6A, 15A, B] throw with force: 用力投掷: *naughty boys ~ing stones at street lamps.* 向路灯投掷石块的顽皮男孩们。 **~ one's hook**, (sl) go away: (俚)走开；滚蛋: *Tell him to ~ his hook.* 叫他滚蛋。 **~ mud at sb**, (fig) abuse him. (喻)诋毁某人。 **~ sb out**, throw sb out; expel him by force. 撵走某人；驱逐某人。 **2** [VP6A, 15A, B] support (sth) so that it can swing, be lifted, etc: 悬挂: *~ a hammock between two tree-trunks;* 在两树中间悬一吊床; *~ (up) a barrel;* 悬吊(起)一只大桶; *with his rifle slung over his shoulder.* 他的步枪挂在肩上。 **~er** /'slɪŋə(r)/; 'slɪŋə/ *n* person armed with a ~ (2). 携带或使用投石器的人。

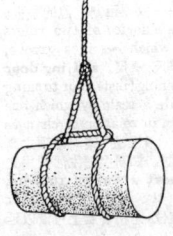

slings

sling[2] /slɪŋ/; slɪŋ / *n* drink made of gin, rum, etc sweetened with fruit juices(esp lime). 用杜松子酒,朗姆酒等加酸橙或其他果汁调制而成的一种饮料。

slink /slɪŋk/; slɪŋk/ *vi* (*pt, pp* **slunk** /slʌŋk/; slʌŋk/) [VP2C] go or move (*off, away, in, out, by*) in a secret, guilty or sneaking manner. 潜行；溜走；潜逃(于 off,

away, in, out, by 等连用)。

slip[1] /slɪp/; *n* [C] **1** act of slipping; false step; slight error caused by carelessness or inattention: 滑；溜；失足；失误；小疏忽: *make a ~.* 失误；犯小错。 *a ~ of the tongue/pen*, error in speaking/writing. 口(笔)误。 *give sb the ~; give the ~ to sb*, escape from, get away from (one's pursuers, etc). 躲开、避开或逃离(追踪者等)。 *There's many a ~ 'twixt (the) cup and (the) lip*, (prov)Something may easily go wrong before a plan is fully carried out. (谚)事情往往会功败垂成。 **2** ('pillow-~) loose cover for a pillow; loose sleeveless garment worn under a dress; ('gym-~) girl's garment for gymnastic exercises. 枕套；女用衬裙；女子运动装。 **3** narrow strip of paper; printer's proof on such a strip. 纸条；(印刷)长条校样。 **4** cutting (short length of stem) taken from a plant for planting or grafting (to grow a new plant, etc). (种植用的)接枝；插枝。 **5** young, slender person: 瘦弱的年轻人: *a (mere) ~ of a boy/girl*, a slim boy/girl. 瘦削的男孩(女孩)。 **6** (usu *pl*; 通常用复数; also 亦作 **~·way**) sloping way (of stone or timber) down to the water, on which ships are built, or pulled up out of the water for repairs: 修造船只的坡道；船台: *The ship is still on the ~s.* 该船仍在建造(或修理)中。 **7** (*pl*) (more usu 较常用 *wings*) parts of the stage of a theatre from which the scenery is pushed on, and where actors stand before going on to the stage: (复)舞台侧翼 (上布景或演员出场前停留处): *watch a performance from the ~s.* 从舞台侧翼看表演。 **8** (cricket) one of the fielders: (板球)三柱门守球员背后的守球员: *first/second/leg ~;* 第一(第二,左后)守球员; (*pl*) part of the ground where these fielders stand. (复)上述守球员的守球区。 ⇨ the illus at **cricket**. 参看 cricket 之插图。 **9** [U] semi-fluid clay for coating earthenware or making patterns on it. (涂于陶器外表或用以涂绘图样的)泥釉。

slip[2] /slɪp/; slɪp/ *vi, vt* (**-pp-**) **1** [VP2A, C] lose one's balance; fall or almost fall as the result of this: 失足；滑；滑倒: *He ~ped on the icy road and broke his leg.* 他在结冰的路面上滑倒而跌断了腿。 **2** [VP2A, C] go or move quietly or quickly, esp without attracting attention: 匆匆行动或悄悄移动; 潜行: *She ~ped away/out/past without being seen.* 她悄悄溜走(溜出去,溜过去),没人看见。 *The years ~ped by.* 岁月在不知不觉中逝去。 **3** [VP2A, C] move, get away, escape, fall, by being difficult to hold, or by not being held firmly: (由于很难抓住或未抓紧而)滑落；滑脱；掉: *The fish ~ped out of my hand.* 鱼从我手中滑落。 *The blanket ~ped off the bed.* 毯子从床上滑落。 *The knife ~ped and cut my hand.* 刀子滑动割破了我的手。 *let sth ~*, **(a)** allow sth to fall from one's hands, escape, or be neglected: 放手;放开;放过；错过: *Don't let the opportunity ~.* 不要坐失良机。 **(b)** accidentally reveal (a secret, etc): 无意中透露(秘密等): *let ~ a secret.* 无意中泄露秘密。 **~ through one's fingers**, (lit or fig) fail to grasp, keep a hold on. (字面或喻)未掌握住; 未抓住。 **4** [VP15A, B, 2C] put, pull on or push off, with a quick, easy movement: 迅速俐落地放置、穿上或脱去: *~ a coat on/off;* 迅速穿上(脱下)上装; *~ into/out of a dress;* 迅速穿起(脱去)衣服; *~ a coin into the waiter's hand.* 把一枚硬币很快地塞进侍者的手中。 **5** [VP2C] (of small mistakes, etc) be allowed to enter, esp by carelessness: (指小错误等由于粗心而)发生: *errors that have ~ped into the text;* 发生在原文里的错误; *make a small error.* 犯小错。 **~ up**, (colloq) make a mistake. (口)犯错。 Hence, 由此产生, **'~-up** *n* [C] mistake. 错误。 **6** [VP2C] move smoothly and effortlessly; go with a gliding motion: 滑动；滑行: *The ship ~ped through the water.* 那条船在水上滑行。 **7** [VP6A] get free from; let go from restraint: 放开;释放: *~ greyhounds from the leash;* 松开皮带释放灵缇; *~ anchor*, detach a ship from the anchor; 起锚; 开航; (of a cow) (指母牛) *~ her calf*, give birth to it prematurely; 早产小牛; *~ a stitch*, (knitting) move a

stitch from one needle to the other without knitting it. (针织)滑漏一针。 *The dog ~ped its collar*, got out of it. 那狗溜脱了颈圈。 *The point ~ped my attention.* 这一点我疏忽了。 *~ one's mind*, (of a name, address, message, etc) be forgotten (because one is in a hurry, busy, etc). (指姓名、住址、信息等) 被忘记(因匆忙、忙碌等)。 **8** (compounds) (复合词) '**~-carriage**/**-coach** *nn* one at the end of a train which can be detached without stopping the train. (火车的) 末节车厢(不必停车可将之与列车分离)。 '**~-cover** *n* detachable cover for a piece of furniture. 家具套。 ⇨ **2** above. 参看上列第 2 义。 '**~-knot** *n* **(a)** knot which slips along the cord round which it is made to tighten or loosen the cord. (绳索的) 滑结。 **(b)** knot which can be undone by a pull. 活结。 ⇨ the illus at **knot**. 参看 knot 之插图。 '**~-on**/**over** *n* shoe or garment to be slipped easily on or over sth. (便于穿脱的) 套头外衣; 套鞋。 '**~-road** *n* road for joining or leaving a motorway (US 美 = *access-road*); minor or local by-pass road. (与快车道相接的) 侧道; 又道。 '**~-stream** *n* stream of air from the propeller or jet engine of an aircraft. (由飞机的螺旋桨或喷射引擎造成的) 后向气流; 滑流。

slip·per /'slɪpə(r); 'slɪpɚ/ *n* (often 常作 *pair of ~s*) loose-fitting light shoe worn in the house. 拖鞋; 便鞋。 **~ed** *adj* wearing ~s. 穿拖鞋的。

slip·pery /'slɪpərɪ; 'slɪpərɪ/ *adj* (**-ier, -iest**) **1** (of a surface) smooth, wet, polished, etc so that it is difficult to hold, to stand on, or to move on: (指表面) 光滑的; 湿滑的: *~ roads*; 湿滑的路; *~ under foot*; 脚下滑溜的; (fig) (of a subject) needing care: (喻) (指问题) 需要小心的: *We're on ~ ground when dealing with this subject.* 我们处理这个问题时需要小心。 *be on a ~ slope*, (fig) on a course of action which may lead to failure or disgrace. (喻)采取可能招致失败或耻辱的行动。 **2** (fig, of persons) unreliable; unscrupulous: (喻, 指人) 不可靠的; 滑头的; 无耻的: *a ~ customer*, a rogue. 无赖。 *He's as ~ as an eel*, is untrustworthy, difficult to manage. 他非常狡猾。 **slip·peri·ness** *n*

slippy /'slɪpɪ; 'slɪpɪ/ *adj* (colloq) (口) **1** slippery. 滑的; 不可靠的; 狡滑的。 **2** (dated) quick: (过时用语)快: *Be ~ about it!* 快点(做)! *Look ~!* 赶快!

slip·shod /'slɪpʃɒd; 'slɪp,ʃɑd/ *adj* slovenly; careless: 懒散的; 随便的; 散漫的; 粗心的: *a ~ piece of work*; 潦草的作品; *a ~ style*. 散漫的风格。

slit /slɪt; slɪt/ *n* [C] long, narrow cut, tear or opening: 狭长的切口; 裂缝; 裂口: *the ~ of a letterbox* (through which letters are put); 信箱的投信口; *eyes like ~s.* 细长的眼睛; 眯缝眼。 □ *vt, vi* (*pt, pp* **slit; -tt-**) **1** [VP6A, 15A, 22] make a ~ in; open (by cutting): 在…上开口; 切开: *~ a man's throat*; 切割一男人的喉咙(杀死一男人); *~ an envelope open*; 拆开信封; *~ cloth into strips*/*a sheet of leather into thongs.* 把布撕成细条(把一张皮革分割成条)。 **2** [VP2A, C] be cut or torn lengthwise: 被纵切(割或撕): *The shirt has ~ down the back.* 那衬衣的背部被由上而下撕破了。

slither /'slɪðə(r); 'slɪðɚ/ *vi* [VP2A, C] slide or slip unsteadily: 颤簸地滑动或滑行: *~ down an ice-covered slope.* 颤簸地滑下结冰的斜坡。 **~y** *adj* slippery. 滑的; 滑溜的。

sliver /'slɪvə(r); 'slɪvɚ/ *n* [C] small, thin strip of wood; splinter; thin piece pared off a large piece: 小而薄的木条; 小木片; (大块上削下来的)薄片; 碎片: *a ~ of cheese.* 一片干酪。 □ *vt, vi* [VP6A, 2A] break off as a ~; break into ~s; splinter. 把…切成薄片; 把…裂成碎片; 碎裂; 分裂。

slob /slɒb; slɑb/ *n* (sl) unpleasantly dirty or rude person. (俚)肮脏或粗鲁的人。

slob·ber /'slɒbə(r); 'slɑbɚ/ *vi, vt* **1** [VP2A, 3A] let saliva run from the mouth (as a baby does). 淌口水; (如婴儿般)流涎。 *~ over sb*, show excessive and maudlin love or admiration for (eg by giving wet kisses). 露骨或粗俗地向某人表达恋情或仰慕(如吮吻爱

恋或仰慕的对象)。 **2** [VP6A] make wet with saliva: 以口涎弄湿: *The baby has ~ed its bib.* 那婴儿的口水弄湿了自己的围兜。 □ *n* [U] saliva running from the mouth; mauldin talk, etc. 口水; 涎; 涕泗纵横的谈话等。

sloe /sləʊ; slo/ *n* [C] small, bluish-black, very bitter wild plum, fruit of the blackthorn; the blackthorn bush. 野李; 野李树。 *~'gin* *n* liqueur made from ~s steeped in gin. (用野李泡在杜松子酒中制成的)野李酒。

slog /slɒg; slɑg/ *vi, vt* (**-gg-**) [VP6A, 2C, 3A] *~ (at)*, hit hard and wildly, esp in boxing and cricket; walk or work hard and steadily: 猛击(尤指拳击及板球赛时); 辛苦而坚定地工作或步行: *~ (at) the ball*; 猛击球; *~ing away at one's work*; 孜孜地工作; *~ing along the road.* 沿途艰涉前进。 *~·ger* *n* person who ~s, eg at cricket; hard worker. 猛击者(如板球赛时); 孜孜工作者。

slo·gan /'sləʊgən; 'slogən/ *n* [C] striking and easily remembered phrase used to advertise sth, or to make clear the aim(s) of a group, organization, campaign, etc: 标语; 口号(显明易记的辞句, 用以宣传某物或表示某一组织或运动等之目标者): *political ~s.* 政治口号。

sloop /slu:p; slup/ *n* small one-masted sailing-ship with fore-and-aft rig. (纵帆装置的)单桅帆船。

slop¹ /slɒp; slɑp/ *vi, vt* (**-pp-**) **1** [VP2A, C] (of liquids) spill over the edge: (指液体)溢出; 泼出: *The tea ~ped (over) into the saucer.* 茶溢出流入茶托中。 **2** *~ over sb*, = slobber over sb. **3** [VP6A, 15A] cause to spill: 使溢出或泼出: *~ beer over the counter of a pub*; 使啤酒溢出流到酒吧的柜台上; 泼酒。 *~ milk.* 溅出牛奶。 **4** *~ out*, empty ~s(1). 倒污水; 倒马桶。 **5** [VP6A, 15A] make a mess with: 以…弄污; 溅污: *~ paint all over the floor.* 使地板上到处溅了油漆。 **6** [VP2C] splash: 溅着水行进: *Why do some children love ~ping about in puddles?* 为什么有些孩子喜欢在水坑里溅着水走来走去呢? □ *n* *~s*, **1** dirty waste water from the kitchen or from bedrooms (where there are no basins with running water and drains), urine, excrement (in pails, as in a prison cell). (厨房或卧房的)污水; (马桶里的)尿便(如牢房中者)。 '**~-basin** *n* basin into which dregs from teacups are emptied at table. 残茶盆(盛茶杯中的残渣者)。 '**~-pail** *n* one into which bedroom ~s are removed. 污水桶; 马桶。 **2** liquid food, eg milk, soup, esp for people who are ill; swill (for pigs). 流质食物(如牛奶、汤等, 尤指供病人食用者); (喂猪的)残食。

slop² /slɒp; slɑp/ *n* (esp as supplied to sailors in the Navy, usu *pl*) cheap, ready-made clothing; bedding. (通常用复数)廉价的成衣; 寝具(尤指海军发给水兵者)。 '**~-shop** *n* shop where ~s are sold. 廉价成衣店。

slope /sləʊp; slop/ *n* **1** [C, U] slanting line; position or direction at an angle, less than 90°, to the earth's surface or to another flat surface: 斜线; 倾斜; 坡度: *the ~ of a roof*; 屋顶的斜度; *a slight*/*steep ~*; 轻微的(急陡的)倾斜; *a ~ up*/*down*; 向上(向下)的倾斜; *a hill with a ~ of 1 in 5.* 有五分之一坡度的小山。 **2** area of rising or falling ground: 倾斜面; 斜坡: '*mountain ~s*; 山坡; '*ski ~s.* 滑雪斜坡。 **3** position of a (soldier with his) rifle on the shoulder: (士兵的)托枪姿势: *with his rifle at the ~.* 托着枪。 □ *vi, vt* **1** [VP2A, C] have a ~; slant: 有斜度; 倾斜: *Our garden ~s (down) to the river.* 我们的花园向河倾斜。 *Does your handwriting ~ forward or backward?* 你的书法是向前斜还是向后斜? **2** [VP6A] cause to ~. 使倾斜; 使成斜度。 *~ arms*, (mil) place and hold the rifle in a sloping position on the left shoulder. (军)托枪。 **3** [VP2C] (colloq) (口) *~ off*, (also 亦作 *do a ~*), go off or away (to evade sb, or escape doing sth). 走开; 逃开(避开某人或逃避做某事)。 **slop·ing·ly** *adv*

sloppy /'slɒpɪ; 'slɑpɪ/ *adj* (**-ier, -iest**) **1** wet or dirty with rain, etc; full of puddles; (of a table, etc) wet with slops: 为雨水等弄湿或弄污的; 泥泞的; 多水坑的; (指桌子等)为残食弄湿的: *The melting snow made the roads ~.* 融雪使道路泥泞。 **2**(of food) consisting of slops. (指食物)流质的。 ⇨ **slop¹***n*(2). **3**(colloq) unsystematic; not done

with care and thoroughness: (口)无系统的; 做得马虎而不彻底的; 草率的: *a ~ piece of work.* 一件草率的制品。 **4** (colloq) foolishly sentimental; weakly emotional: 过分多愁的; 感情脆弱的; 容易感伤的: *~ sentiment;* 多愁善感; *~ talk about girlfriends and boyfriends.* 有关交女友和交男友的伤心话。 **slop·pily** /-ɪlɪ/ *adv* in a manner: 污混地; 泥泞地; 草率地; 草率地; 感伤地: *sloppily (= carelessly) dressed.* 衣着随便的。 **slop·pi·ness** *n*

slosh /slɒʃ; slɑʃ/ *vt, vi* **1** [VP6A, 15A] (sl) hit: (俚)打; 击: *~ sb on the chin.* 打某人的下颌。 **2** [VP2C] *~ about,* flounder about in slush or mud. 在泥雪中或烂泥中挣扎着前行或移动。 **3** [VP15B] *~ sth about,* throw water or other liquid or semi-liquid substance about. 溅泼水或其他液体或半液体。 **~ed** *adj* (sl) drunk. (俚)酒醉的。

slot /slɒt; slɑt/ *n* [C] **1** narrow opening through which sth is to be put; slit for a coin in a machine ('**~-machine** or *vending-machine*) that automatically delivers sth, eg tickets, cigarettes, packets of sweets. (容物出入的)狭缝; 长孔; 口; (自动售货机上的)投币孔(自动售货机称为 '**~-machine** or vending-machine). **2** slit, groove or channel into which sth fits or along which sth slides. 沟; 槽; 槽沟。 **3** (colloq) right or suitable place for sth (in a broadcast programme, scheme, etc): (口)(广播节目、设计、计划等中的)适当位置: *find a ~ for a talk on bee-keeping.* 设法安排一个以养蜂为题的演讲。 □ *vt* (-tt-) [VP6A, 15B] provide with ~s; make a ~ or ~s in: 在…上开长孔; 开槽于; 安插; 安插: *~ a song recital into a radio programme;* 在广播节目中安插一个独唱项目; *~ 30000 graduates a year into jobs,* find jobs for them. 为一年三万大学毕业生安排工作。

sloth /sloʊθ; sloθ/ *n* **1** [U] laziness; idleness. 懒散; 怠惰。 **2** [C] S American mammal which lives in the branches of trees and moves very slowly. 树懒(南美洲的哺乳动物, 栖于树枝, 行动缓慢)。 **~·ful** /-fl; -fəl/ *adj* inactive; lazy. 不活泼的; 怠惰的。

slouch /slaʊtʃ; slaʊtʃ/ *vi* [VP2A, C] stand, sit or move, in a lazy, tired way: 没精打采地站、坐或行动: *louts who ~ about at street corners all day.* 整天在街角闲荡的坦汉。 □ *n* ~ing attitude or way of walking: 没精打采的态度或姿态: *walk with a ~.* 没精打采地走。 *~·'hat* n soft hat with a turned-down brim. 垂边帽。 **~·ing·ly** *adv*

slough[1] /slaʊ; slaʊ/ in *US topography:* slu:; slu/ *n* [C] swamp; marsh. 沼地; 沼泽。

slough[2] /slʌf; slʌf/ *n* [C] cast-off skin of a snake; any dead part of an animal dropped off at regular periods. 蛇的蜕皮; 脱壳; 动物体上按时脱落的部分。 □ *vt, vi* [VP6A, 15B, 2A] *~ (off),* put, come or throw off: 蜕去; 脱除; 弃去: *~ (off) bad habits;* 抛弃坏习惯; *a snake that has ~ed its skin.* 已蜕皮的蛇。

sloven /'slʌvn; 'slʌvən/ *n* person who is untidy, dirty, careless or slipshod in his appearance, dress, habits, etc. 邋遢的人; 不修边幅的人; 仪表、穿着、习惯等方面不整洁、草率、懒散的人。 **~·ly** *adj* of or like a ~: 邋遢的; 不修边幅的; 不整洁的; 潦草的: *a ~ly appearance;* 不整洁的仪容; *~ in his dress.* 衣着邋遢的。 **~·li·ness** *n*

slow[1] /sloʊ; slo/ *adj* (-er, -est) **1** not quick; taking a long time: 慢; 缓慢的; 迟缓的; 费时的: *a ~ runner;* 跑得慢的人; *a ~ train,* eg one that stops at all or almost all stations, contrasted with an express train; 慢车(如每站或几乎每站都停的火车, 与快车相对); *a ~ journey.* 费时的旅程。 **2** at less than the usual rate or speed. 未达常速的; 速度缓慢的。 *a ~ march,* eg at a military funeral. 缓慢行进 (如军队的送葬行列)。 *in ~ motion,* (of a cinema film) with the number of exposures per second greatly increased (so that when the film is shown at normal rate the action appears to be ~); (指电影片高速拍摄后, 以常速播放所映出之)慢动作的; 由此产生, *a ~-motion film.* 慢动作电影。 **3** not quick to learn; dull: 迟钝的; 笨的: *a ~ child;* 迟钝的小孩; *~ in*

acting immediately; acting only after a time: 不立刻起作用的; 反应迟的: *~ poison.* 慢性毒药。 *'He is ~ to anger /~ to make up his mind /~ of speech /~ at accounts /not ~ to defend himself.* 他不轻易发怒(不容易下决心、嘴钝, 不精于算帐, 敏于自卫)。 '*~·coach* n person who is ~ in action, or who is dull, or who has out-of-date ideas. 行动迟钝的人; 笨伯; 思想陈腐的人。 **4** (usu *pred;* of watches and clocks) showing a time behind the correct time (eg 1.55 when it is 2.00) (用作表语, 指钟表)慢的; 较正确时刻落后的(如正确时间为两点, 而钟面上为一点五十五分): *That clock is five minutes ~.* 那(座)钟慢五分钟。 **5** not sufficiently interesting or lively: 不太有趣味的; 不太精采的; 不太有生气的: *We thought the party was rather ~.* 我们觉得那次舞会不太精采。 **6** (of a surface) of such a nature that what moves over it (esp a ball) tends to do so at a reduced speed: (指表面)能减低(尤指球的)速度的: *a ~ running track /cricket pitch /billiard table.* 能减速度的跑道(板球两三柱门间的球道, 撞球台)。 **~·ly** *adv* in a manner: 缓慢地: *walk /speak /learn ~ly.* 缓慢地走(说话, 学习)。 *He ~ly opened the door.* 他慢慢地打开门。 *S~ly the door opened.* 那门慢慢地开了。 ⇨ **slow**[2] below. 参看下列 slow[2]。 **~·ness** *n*

slow[2] /sloʊ; slo/ *adv* (-er, -est) (Note that *slowly* may precede the finite *v* as in 'He slowly walked up the path', or follow, as in 'He walked slowly up the path', or have front position, as in 'Slowly he walked up the path', whereas *~* follows the *v*, except when used with *how*, or in participial compounds as in **2** below.) (注意: slowly 可用于限定动词之前, 如 'He slowly walked up the path', 或用于限定动词之后, 如 'He walked slowly up the path', 或置于句首, 如 'Slowly he walked up the path', 而 slow 除与 how 连用外, 只可用于动词之后, 或用于如第 2 义中所举的分词复合词中。) **1** at a low speed; slowly: 低速地; 缓慢地: *Tell the driver to go ~er.* 告诉司机开慢一点。 *How ~ /How slowly the time passes!* 时间过得多慢啊! *S~ astern!* (a command to go astern slowly). 缓慢退后! (口令或命令)。 *go ~,* **(a)** (of workers in a factory, etc) work slowly as a protest, or in order to get attention to demands, etc. (指工厂里的工人等)怠工(以示抗议或使提出之要求等受到注意)。 Hence, 由此产生, *go·'slow* n 怠工。 **(b)** be less active: 减少活动: *You ought to go ~ until you feel really well again.* 你在完全康复以前应该减少活动。 **2** (compounds) (复合词) *~·'going /·'moving /·'spoken,* going / moving / speaking slowly. 进行缓慢的(活动缓慢的; 说话缓慢的)。

slow[3] /sloʊ; slo/ *vi, vt* [VP2C, 15B] *~ (sth) up /down,* (cause to) go at a slower speed: (使)缓行; (使)减速: *S~ up /down before you reach the crossroads.* 到达十字路口前你要减速。 *You should ~ up a bit (= stop working so hard) if you want to avoid a breakdown.* 如果你不想把身体累坏了, 你应该减少一点工作。 *All this conversation ~s down the action of the play.* 所有这些对话使剧情缓慢。 '*~-down* n (esp) intentional decrease of industrial production by labour or management. 降低生产(尤指劳工或资方特意安排者)。

slow-worm /sloʊ wɜːm; 'slo,wɜm/ *n* small, limbless non-poisonous reptile. 蛇蜥蜴(一种无腿、无毒的小爬行动物)。

sludge /slʌdʒ; slʌdʒ/ *n* [U] **1** thick, greasy mud; slush. 烂泥; 泥泞的雪。 **2** sewage. 污水; 下水道中的污物。 **3** thick, dirty oil or grease. 浓厚的污油或油垢。

slue /sluː; slu/ ⇨ **slew**[2].

slug[1] /slʌɡ; slʌɡ/ *n* slow-moving creature like a snail but without a shell, a garden pest destructive to seedlings and plants. 黑蛞蝓(一种行动缓慢, 似蜗牛而无壳的园艺害虫, 危害幼苗及植物)。 ⇨ the illus at **mollusc**. 参看 mollusc 之插图。

slug[2] /slʌɡ; slʌɡ/ *n* **1** bullet of irregular shape. 形状不规则的子弹。 **2** strip of metal with a line of type along one edge. (印刷用的)嵌条。

slug[3] /slʌɡ; slʌɡ/ *vt, vi* (-gg-) (US) (美) = **slog.**

slug·gard /'slʌgəd; 'slʌgɚd/ n lazy, slow-moving person. 懒惰而行动迟缓的人; 懒汉。

slug·gish /'slʌgɪʃ; 'slʌgɪʃ/ adj inactive; slow-moving: 不活泼的; 行动迟缓的: a ~ river / pulse / liver. 流动缓慢的河 (跳动缓慢的脉搏; 功能减弱的肝脏)。 ~·ly adv ~·ness n

sluice /sluːs; slus/ n [C] 1 '~(-gate / -valve), apparatus, contrivance, for regulating the level of water by controlling the flow into or out of (a canal, lake, etc): 水门; 水闸: open the ~-gates of the reservoir. 放开水库的水闸。 2 '~(-way), artificial water channel, eg one made by gold-miners for rinsing gold from sand and dirt. 人工水道; 水槽 (洗矿槽 (如金矿工人以水洗金砂者)。 3 flow of water above, through or below a floodgate. 经闸门上面, 下面或闸门的水流; 壩水。 □ vt, vi 1 [VP6A] send a stream of water over; wash with a stream of water: 放水流过; 冲洗: ~ ore, to separate it from gravel, etc. 冲洗矿砂 (使之与砂砾等分开)。 2[VP6A, 15B] ~ (out), wash or flood with water from a ~. 引水道或水槽的水冲洗或灌溉。 3 [VP3A] ~ out, (of water) rush out as from a ~. (指水)流出; 奔流。

slum /slʌm; slʌm/ n 1 court, alley or street of small, badly-built, dirty, crowded houses: 房屋肮脏而拥挤的巷弄或街道; 陋巷: live in a ~. 居于陋巷。 2 the ~s, part(s) of a town where there are such houses. 贫民区; 贫民窟。 ~ clearance, the demolishing of ~s and the rehousing of the people living in them. 消除贫民窟运动 (重新安置贫民居住户的努力)。 □ vi (-mm-) 1 visit the ~s to give charitable aid to the people in them. 访问贫民窟而给予慈善救济。 2 (colloq) live very cheaply. (口) 过贫民窟般的生活。 '~my adj of ~s: 贫民窟的: a ~my part of the town. 城市里的贫民窟。

slum·ber /'slʌmbə(r); 'slʌmbɚ/ vi, vt (liter and rhet) (文学与修辞) 1 [VP2A] sleep, esp sleep peacefully or comfortably. 睡眠; (尤指)安祥而舒服地睡眠。 2 [VP15B] pass (time) in ~: 以睡眠度过(时间): ~ away a hot afternoon. 以睡觉打发掉一个炎热的下午。 □ n (often pl) sleep: (常作复数)睡眠: fall into a troubled ~; 进入不安宁的睡眠; disturb sb's ~(s). 扰乱某人的睡眠; 扰人清梦。 ~er n one who ~s. 睡眠者。 ~·ous /-əs; -əs /adj sleepy. 想睡的; 不活泼的。

slump /slʌmp; slʌmp/ vi 1 [VP2A, C] drop or fall heavily: 沉重地落下或倒下; 重陷: Tired from his walk, he ~ed into a chair. 他走累了, 一屁股坐在一张椅子上。 The bullet entered his chest and he ~ed down to the floor. 子弹打进他的胸膛, 于是他重重地倒在地板上。 2 [VP2A] (of prices, trade, business activity) fall steeply or suddenly. (指价格、贸易、商业活动)突然下落, 下跌或下降; 暴跌。 □ n [C] general drop in prices, trade activity, etc; business depression. (物价、商业活动等的)普遍下降或跌落; 商业萧条; 不景气。

slung /slʌŋ; slʌŋ/ pt, pp of **sling**.

slunk /slʌŋk; slʌŋk/ pt, pp of **slink**.

slur /slɜː(r); slɚ/ vt, vi (-rr-) 1 [VP6A] join (sounds, letters, words) so that they are indistinct; (music) sing or play legato. 连接(声音、字母、字)使之不清楚; 含糊地读或写; (音乐)圆滑唱; 圆滑奏。 2 [VP3A] ~ over sth, deal quickly with in an attempt to conceal: 意图掩饰或隐匿而匆匆处理; 略过; 忽视: He ~red over the dead man's faults and spoke chiefly of his virtues. 他对死者的过失轻轻带过, 主要讲述他的美德。 □ n 1 [C] reproach; suggestion of wrongdoing: 责备; 微词; 对过失的讽示: cast a ~ on sb's reputation. 损毁某人的名誉; keep one's reputation free from ~. 保持美誉(免受责备)。 2 [C] act of ~ring sounds. 含糊语音。 3 [C] (music) the mark ⌒ or ⌣ used to show that two or more notes are to be sung to one syllable or performed legato. (音乐)连结线; 圆滑线 (表示两个以上的音符唱做一个音节或圆滑演奏的符号, 即 ⌒ 或 ⌣。 记于同度音符者称连接线, 记于不同度音符者称圆滑线)。 ⇨ the illus at notation. 参看 notation 之插图。

slurry /'slʌrɪ; 'slɝɪ/ n [U] thin semi-liquid mixture of cement, clay, mud, etc. 水泥、粘土、泥浆等的半流体稀薄混合物。

slush /slʌʃ; slʌʃ/ n [U] soft, melting snow; soft mud; (fig) foolish sentiment. 半融之雪; 烂泥; (喻)痴情; 愚痴情怀。 '~ fund n (comm) fund of money used by a business company for the purpose of bribing public officials, etc. (商)用以行贿官员等的钱。 ~y adj

slut /slʌt; slʌt/ n slovenly woman; slattern. 邋遢女子; 懒女人。 ~·tish /-ɪʃ; -ɪʃ/ adj

sly /slaɪ; slaɪ/ adj(-er, -est) 1 deceitful; keeping or doing things secretly; seeming to have, suggesting, secret knowledge: 狡诈的; 诡诈的; 暗中进行的; 似有或暗示有秘闻的: a sly dog, secretive person. 做事隐秘的人。 on the sly, secretly. 秘密地; 暗中地。 2 playful; mischievous. 好玩的; 顽皮的; 淘气的。 sly·ly adv sly·ness n

smack[1] /smæk; smæk/ n [C] 1 (sound of a) blow given with the open hand on sth with a flat surface; sound of the lips parted suddenly or of a whip: 掌掴; 掌掴声; 咂唇声; 拍击声: with a ~ of the lips, this sound (suggesting enjoyment of food or drink): 咂着嘴唇(表示对食物或饮料的满足); give sb a ~ on the lips, a loud kiss. 给某人一个响吻。 I heard the ~ (= crack) of a whip. 我听到鞭子的噼啪声。 2 slap, blow: 拍击; 打击: give the ball a hard ~, hit it hard (eg in cricket). 用力击球(如板球)。 get a ~ in the eye, (colloq) experience a setback; suffer a sharp disappointment. (口) 遭受挫折; 感到很大的失望。 have a ~ at sth, (colloq) have a try to do it. (口)试做某事。 □ vt [VP6A] 1 strike with the open hand: 掌掴; 拍击: ~ a naughty child. 掌掴淘气的孩子。 2 ~ one's lips, part the lips with a ~ing sound to show pleasure (at food or drink, or in anticipation of other sensual pleasures). 咂唇作响(表示对饮食感到满意, 或预期其他肉体上的乐趣)。 □ adv in a sudden and violent way: 急剧而猛烈地: run ~ into a brick wall; 猛然撞在砖墙上; hit sb ~ in the eye. 猛然打在某人的眼部。 ~·er n (colloq) (口) 1 loud kiss. 响吻。 2 pound (£) or dollar. 英镑或美元。 □ ~·ing n act or occasion of hitting with the palm of the hand: 用巴掌打; 掌掴: The child needs a good ~ing. 这孩子该好好打一顿。

smack[2] /smæk; smæk/ n small sailing-boat for fishing. 小渔舟; 捕鱼小帆船。

smack[3] /smæk; smæk/ vi [VP3A], n ~ of, (have a) slight flavour or suggestion (of): 微带某味; 微含某意; 滋味; 气味; 意味: opinions that ~s of heresy; 带有异端意味的意见; medicine that ~s of sulphur; 带硫磺气味的药; have a ~ of obstinacy in one's character. 某人性格有点顽强。

small /smɔːl; smɔl/ adj (-er, -est) (opp of big or large; also ⇨ **little**) (为 big 或 large 之反义词) 1 not large in degree, size, etc: 小的; 少的: a ~ town / room / audience / sum of money, etc; 小镇 (小房间; 人数少的听众; 小额的钱等); a ~ pony, 小马, Cf 参较 a nice little pony, 漂亮的小马, 'little' being preferred when there are emotive implications: 有感情成分时, 宜用 'little'; ~ children, 小孩们, Cf 参较 charming / nice / naughty, etc little children. 可爱的 (漂亮的、顽皮的等)小孩们。 2 not doing things on a large scale: 小规模的: ~ farmers / business men / shopkeepers. 小农 (小本商人, 小店东)。 3 unimportant, trifling. 不重要的; 琐细的。 be thankful for ~ mercies, for trifling pieces of good fortune. 对小的恩惠或幸运要表示感激。 '~ talk, conversation about everyday and unimportant social matters. 闲谈; 闲聊。 4 (attrib only) (仅用作定语) a ~ eater, person who eats ~ quantities of food. 食量小的人。 5 morally mean; ungenerous: 卑鄙的; 卑劣的; 气量狭小的; 吝啬的: Only a ~ man / a man with a ~ mind would behave so badly. 只有卑鄙的 (小心眼的)人行为才会这样恶劣。 Hence, 由此产生, ,~'minded adj 气量小的; 心地狭小的。 6 of low social position; humble: 社会地位低的; 卑微的: great and ~, all classes of people. 社会各阶层。 7 in a ~

way, modestly, unpretentiously: 适度地;谦恭地;小范围地: *He has contributed to scientific progress in a ～ way.* 他于对科学的进展小有贡献。*They live in quite a ～ way,* simply and without social ambitions. 他们过着朴实的生活。**8** little or no: 些微的; 几无的: *have ～ cause for gratitude.* 几无可感激的原因。*He failed, and ～ wonder,* It is not surprising. 他失败了,如众所料。**9** (compounds and special uses) (复合词及特殊用法) '～-**arms** *n pl* weapons light enough to be carried in the hand by a single soldier, eg rifles, revolvers. 轻武器(可由一士兵单独携带者,如步枪、左轮等)。 **～ change** *n* (a) coins of ～ denominations: 小额硬币: *Can you give me ～ change for this note?* 你能不能把这张钞票兑成小额的硬币? (b) (fig) trivial remarks; light conversation. (喻)无关重要的话; 轻松的谈话。 **'～ fry** *n* ⇨ **fry²**. '～-**holding** *n* (in GB) piece of land under fifty acres in extent let or sold to sb for cultivation. (英)小片耕地(五十英亩以下者)。'～-**holder** *n* person owning or renting a ～holding. (拥有或租有小片耕地的)小农。 **the ～ hours** *n pl* ⇨**hour**(1). **～ letters** *n pl* not capitals. 小写字母。 '～-**pox** *n* [U] serious contagious disease which leaves permanent scars on the skin. 天花(传染病的一种)。 '～-**time** *adj* (colloq) of minor importance; third-rate. (口)不重要的; 三等的; 劣等的。 **the still, ～ voice,** the voice of conscience. 良心的低呼。 **on the '～ side,** somewhat too small. 略嫌小;太小了一点。 **look/feel ～,** be humiliated. 自惭形秽; 感到羞愧。 □ *adv* **sing ～,** ⇨ **sing** (1). □ *n* **the ～ of,** the slenderest part of: 最纤细部分: *the ～ of the back.* 后腰 (背部的最细处)。**～s,**

(colloq) ～ articles of clothing(for laundering). (口)内衣裤。**～ness** *n*

smarmy /'smɑːmɪ; 'smɑrmɪ/ *adj* (GB, colloq) ingratiating; trying to win favour by flattery, etc. (英,口)迎合的; 逢迎的; 巴结的。

smart¹ /smɑːt; smɑrt/ *adj* (**-er, -est**) **1** bright; new-looking; clean; well-dressed: 鲜明的; 新奇的; 整洁的; 衣冠楚楚的: *a ～ hat/suit/car.* 别致的帽子(套装,汽车)。*You look very ～.* 你看起来很帅。*Go and make yourself ～ before we call on the Joneses.* 我们去拜访琼斯家以前,你先去打扮整齐。 **2** fashionable; conspicuous in society: 时髦的; 社会上特出的; 有名气的: *the '～ set.* 时髦的一群; 社会名流。**3** clever; skilful; having a good, quick brain; showing ingenuity: 聪敏的; 有技巧的; 机灵的; 精明的; 有创造力的: *a ～ student/officer;* 一个聪敏的学生(干练的军官); *a ～ retort/saying;* 巧妙的反驳(说法); *～ dealing,* clever and intelligent, but perhaps dishonest. 巧妙的手段 (但可能是狡猾的)。 **4** quick; brisk: 轻快的;敏捷的: *go for a ～ walk;* 做一次轻快的散步; *start out at a ～ pace.* 以轻快的步子起程。 **Look ～!** Hurry!赶快!赶紧! **5** severe: 厉害的; 剧烈的: *～ punishment;* 严厉的处罚; *a ～ rebuke;* 严厉的呵斥; *a ～ box on the ear.* 重重的一记耳光。**～ly** *adv* **～ness** *n* **～en** /'smɑːtn; 'smɑrtn/ *vt, vi* [VP6A, 15B, 2C] **～en (oneself)(up),** make or become ～(1, 4): (使)变得漂亮,整洁等; (使)变得活泼,敏捷等: *～en oneself up to receive visitors.* 打扮整洁以便迎客。*She has ～ened up since I met her last.* 我上次见到她以后,她变得活泼了。

smart² /smɑːt; smɑrt/ *vt* [VP2A, C, 3A] feel or

BADGER
Lc 91cm

RABBIT
Lc 40cm

BEAVER
Lc 73cm

MONGOOSE
Lc 45cm

MOLE
Lc 12cm

ARMADILLO
Lc 76cm

FOX
Lc 104cm

OTTER
Lc 76cm

BAT
Lc 5cm

RAT
Lc 20cm

SQUIRREL
Lc 25cm

GUINEA-PIG
Lc 17cm

DUCKBILLED PLATYPUS
Lc 51cm

KOALA
Lc 60cm

HEDGEHOG
Lc 17cm

small wild animals

cause a sharp pain (of body or mind): 感到或引起(身体或心灵方面的)剧痛: The smoke made my eyes ~. 烟使我的眼睛感到剧痛。He was ~ing under an injustice / under his father's rebukes. 他因受冤屈(挨父亲斥责)而深感痛苦: She was ~ing with vexation. 她因有事烦恼而痛苦。~ for, suffer the consequences of, be paid out for: 因…而吃苦头，受罪等；因…而付出代价: You'll make you ~ for this impudence. 你这次对他的失礼他必将给你颜色看。□ n [U] sharp pain, bodily or mental: (身体或心灵方面的)剧痛: The ~ of his wound kept him awake. 他伤口的剧痛使他无法入睡。

smash /smæʃ; smæʃ/ vt, vi **1** [VP6A, 15A, B, 22, 2A, C] break, be broken, violently into small pieces: (被)打破; (被)打碎; (被)捣烂: ~ a window. 打破一扇窗户。The drunken man ~ed up all the furniture. 那醉汉捣毁了所有的家具。The firemen ~ed in / down the doors. 消防人员破门而入。Don't ~ the door open; I have a key! 不要把门撞开; 我有钥匙! '~-and-'grab raid, one in which a thief ~es a shop-window, eg a jeweller's, and grabs valuables from behind it. 破窗行窃(窃贼打破珠宝店等之橱窗，窃走贵重物品)。**2** [VP2A, C] rush, force a way, violently (into, through, etc): 猛冲; 猛然碰撞: The car ~ed into a wall. 汽车撞到了墙。**3** [VP6A] deal a heavy blow to; defeat: 痛击; 重击; 打败: give sb a ~ing blow; ~ the enemy: 击败敌人; ~ a record, (in sport, etc) set up a far better record. (运动等)大破纪录; 远胜旧记录; 创造新记录。**4** [VP6A] (tennis) hit (a ball) downwards over the net with a hard, overhand stroke. (网球)杀(球); 扣(球)。**5** [VP 2A] (of a business firm) go bankrupt. (指商行)破产。□ n [C] **1** ~ing; breaking to pieces. 打碎; 捣裂; 破产。'~(-up), violent collision: 猛烈碰撞: The teapot fell with an awful ~. 茶壶摔下来打得粉碎。He fell and hit his head an awful ~ on the kerbstone. 头部猛撞在马路边石上。There has been a terrible ~(-up) on the railway. 曾经发生一次可怕的火车相撞(事件)。When the banks failed, many businesses were ruined in the ~ that followed. 银行一倒闭,许多商行连带地破产了。go ~, be ruined 破产; 毁灭; 垮台。**2** (tennis) stroke in which the ball is brought swiftly down. (网球)扣球; 杀球; 高压球。**3** a ~ hit, (colloq) sth (esp a new play, song, film, etc) which is at once very successful. (口) 轰动一时之事物); 风行一时之事物(尤指新剧, 新歌, 新影片等)。□ adv with a ~: 破碎地; 猛烈碰撞地; 打得粉碎地等: go / run ~ into a wall. 撞到墙上。~er n (sl) (俚) (a) violent blow. 重击。(b) sth or sb considered to be remarkably fine, attractive, etc. 非常出色的人或物; 非常有吸引力的人或物。~ing adj (sl) remarkably fine, attractive, etc (俚) 非常出色的人或物: John Travolta's ~ing! 约翰·特拉沃尔塔真迷死人了!

smat·ter·ing /'smætərɪŋ; 'smætərɪŋ/ n (usu 通常作 a ~ (of)) slight knowledge (of a subject). 一知半解; 浅薄的知识。

smear /smɪə(r); smɪr/ vt, vi **1** [VP14] ~ sth on / over / with, cover or mark with sth oily or sticky; spread (sth oily, etc) on: 覆以或沾以油质或黏性物; 敷(油质物等)于; 涂,搽,抹油质物: ~ one's hands with grease; 双手涂以油脂; ~ grease on the kerbstone. 把油脂涂双手; hands ~ed with blood. 染有血迹的双手。**2** [VP6A] make dirty, greasy marks on; (fig) defame or sully (sb's reputation), 沾以污迹或油迹; 弄脏; 使污; (喻)中伤, 玷辱, 诽谤(某人的名誉)。a '~(ing) campaign, one that aims at damaging sb's reputation (by spreading rumours, etc). 企图毁人名誉的有计划活动(如借散布谣言等)。**3** [VP6A] blot; obscure the outline of: 抹掉; 涂去; 使模糊: ~ a word. 涂掉一个字。**4** [VP2A] become ~ed. 弄脏; 涂污; 玷污。□ n [C] stain; mark made by ~ing: 污迹; 污迹斑迹: a ~ of paint. 油漆的污迹; ~s of blood on the wall. 墙上的血迹。'~-word n word suitable for ~ing (sb's reputation). 足以中伤或毁人名誉的字眼。

smell[1] / smel; smel / n **1** [U] that one of the five senses which is special to the nose: 嗅觉: Taste and ~ are closely connected. 味觉和嗅觉关系密切。S~ is more acute in dogs than in men. 狗的嗅觉比人灵敏。**2** [C, U] that which is noticed by means of the nose; quality that affects this sense: 气味; 引起嗅觉的特质: What a nice / horrible / unusual ~! 多么好闻(难闻, 不寻常)的气味! There's a ~ of cooking. 有一股食物的香味。S~ like ~ of thyme. 我喜欢麝香草的气味。**3** [C] (without an adj) bad or unpleasant quality that affects the nose: (不加形容词)臭味; 难闻的气味: What a ~! 多难闻的气味! **4** [C] (usu 通常作 a ~) act of breathing in through the nose to get the ~(2) of sth: 嗅; 闻: Have / Take a ~ of this egg and tell me whether it's bad. 闻一闻这个蛋,告诉我是不是坏的。

smell[2] /smel; smel/ vt, vi (pt, pp **smelt** /smelt; smelt/) **1** [VP6A, 19A] (not in the progressive tenses; often with can, could) be aware of through the sense of smell: (不用进行时; 常与 can, could 连用) 嗅出; 闻到; 经由嗅觉察觉: Can / Do you ~ anything unusual? 你有没有闻到(一股)特别的气味? The camels smelt the water a mile off. 骆驼嗅出一英里外有水。I can ~ something burning. 我闻到有烧焦的气味。~ a rat, ⇨ rat. **2** [VP 6A, 15B, 2A, C] (with progressive tenses possible) use one's sense of smell in order to learn sth; inhale the odour of: (可用进行时) 嗅; 吸入…的气味: S~ this and tell me what it is. 闻闻这东西,告诉我是什么。The dog was ~ing (at) the lamp-post. 那只狗正在闻那根(路)灯柱。~ round / about, go from place to place, try to get information (lit and fig). (字面及喻) 到处用鼻子闻以察知某事; 到处打听消息。~ sth out, discover, hunt out, by means of the sense of smell or (fig) by intuition. 以嗅觉发现或察知; (喻)借直觉以发现或察知。**3** [VP2A] (not in the progressive tenses) have the sense of smell: (不用进行时)有嗅觉: Do / Can fishes ~? 鱼类有嗅觉吗? **4** [VP2A, D, 3A] ~ (of sth), give out or recall the smell (of): 发出或显出(…所显示的)气味; 有…的气味; 含有或令人想起…的气味: The flowers ~ sweet. 这些花气味芬芳。The dinner ~s good. 这饭菜闻起来真香。The lamb ~s of garlic. 这羔羊(肉)有大蒜味。Your breath ~s of brandy. 你的呼吸带有白兰地酒味。(Note that if there is no adj, the suggestion is usu sth unpleasant): (注意: 如无形容词修饰,通常指气味不好的东西): Fish soon ~s in summer if it is not kept on ice. 鱼在夏天如果不加冷冻很快就臭了。His breath ~s. 他的呼吸有臭味。~ of the lamp, (of work) seem to have been composed late at night, with much hard work. (指作品)似乎是熬夜下工夫写成的。'~·ing-salts n pl sharp-smelling substances to be sniffed as a cure for faintness, etc; sal volatile. 嗅盐 (治疗昏晕等症者)。'~·ing-bottle n one containing ~ing-salts. 嗅盐瓶。**smelly** adj (-ier, -iest) (colloq) having a bad ~. (口)有臭味的; 不好闻的。

smelt[1] /smelt; smelt/ vt [VP6A] melt (ore); separate (metal) from ore by doing this: 熔解(矿石); 熔矿以提炼(金属): a copper-~ing works. 炼铜(工)厂。

smelt[2] /smelt; smelt/ n small fish valued as food. 香鱼; 沙钻鱼; 胡瓜鱼(一种主要供食用的小鱼)。

smelt[3] pp, pt of **smell[2]**.

smi·lax /'smaɪlæks; 'smaɪlæks/ n [U] kind of plant with trailing vines much used in decoration. 牛尾菜; 圆形菝葜(其茎蔓多用于装饰)。

smile /smaɪl; smaɪl/ n [C] pleased, happy, amused or other expression on the face, with (usu a parting of the lips and) loosening of the face muscles: 微笑; 笑脸(愉快、高兴、欢喜等的面部表情): There was a pleasant / ironical / amused, etc ~ on her face. 她露出了悦人的(讽刺的, 高兴的等) 微笑。He was all ~s, looked very happy. 他满脸笑容 (看起来非常高兴)。His face was wreathed in ~s. 他满脸堆笑容。□ vi, vt **1** [VP2A, B, 4B, 3A] ~ (at / on / upon), give a ~ or ~s; show pleasure, amusement, sympathy, contempt, irony, etc

by this means: 微笑; 以微笑表现愉快、兴趣、同情、轻视、讽制等: He never ~s. 他从不露笑脸。What/who are you smiling at? 你在笑什么(谁)? Fortune has not always ~d upon (= favoured) me. 幸运之神并不一直向我微笑(垂青于我)。He ~d to see her so happy. 看到她这么高兴, 他笑了。2 [VP6B] express by means of a ~: 以微笑表示: Father ~s his approval. 父亲以微笑表示许可。She ~s her thanks. 她以微笑表示感谢。3 [VP6B] give the kind of ~ indicated: 发出某种微笑: ~ a bitter ~. 苦笑。**smil·ing·ly** adv with a ~ or ~s. 带微笑地; 微笑着。

smirch /smɜːtʃ; smɝtʃ/ vt [VP6A] make dirty; (fig) dishonour. 使污; 弄脏; (喻)污辱; 玷污。□ n [C] (fig) blot or stain. (喻)污点; 瑕疵。

smirk /smɜːk; smɝk/ vi [VP2A], n (give a) silly, self-satisfied smile. 傻笑; 得意地笑。

smite /smaɪt; smaɪt/ vt, vi (pt **smote** /sməʊt; smot/, pp **smitten** /ˈsmɪtn; ˈsmɪtn/) (archaic, or, in mod use, hum or liter) (古; 或现代用法中, 谐或文) 1 [VP6A] strike; hit hard: 痛击; 重击: He smote the ball into the grandstand. 他把球打过了看台。His conscience smote him, he was conscience-stricken. 他的良心受到谴责。He was smitten with remorse/smitten with that pretty girl. 他悔恨交加(那个漂亮女孩子令他神魂颠倒)。2 [VP6A] defeat utterly: 彻底击败: God will ~ our enemies. 上帝将击溃我们的敌人。3 [VP2A, C] strike; come forcibly: 打; 击; 侵袭: A strange sound smote upon our ears. 一怪声音直入我的耳畔。

smith /smɪθ; smɪθ/ n worker in iron or other metals: 铁匠; 冶工; 锻工: 'black'~. 铁匠。⇨ **black, gold, silver, tin. smithy** /ˈsmɪðɪ; ˈsmɪθɪ/ n black ~'s workshop. 铁匠店。

smith·er·eens /ˌsmɪðəˈriːnz; ˌsmɪðəˈrinz/ n pl small fragments: 碎片; 碎屑: smash sth to/into ~. 将某物打得粉碎。

smit·ten /ˈsmɪtn; ˈsmɪtn/ pp of **smite**.

smock /smɒk; smɑk/ n loose garment (with smocking on it) like an overall. (有蜂窝形褶饰, 式样类似工作服的)罩衫; 罩衣。~**·ing** n [U] kind of ornamentation on a garment made by gathering the cloth tightly with stitches. (衣服上)蜂窝形褶饰。

smog /smɒg; smɑg/ n [U] mixture of fog and smoke. 烟雾(雾的混合物)。

smoke¹ /sməʊk; smok/ n 1 [U] visible vapour with particles of carbon, etc coming from a burning substance: 烟(燃物所生的含炭粒雾气气): ~ pouring from factory chimneys: 工厂烟囱冒出的烟; ,ciga'rette/ci'gar ~. 香烟(雪茄)的烟。**end up in** ~, come to, end in, nothing. 烟消云散; 转眼成空; 化为乌有。**go up in** ~, be burnt up; (fig) be without result, leave nothing solid or worth while behind. 被烧光; (喻)无结果; 未留下实在或有价值之物。**There is no** ~ **without fire**, (prov) ⇨ **fire¹(1)**. '~**-bomb** n one that sends out clouds of ~ (used to conceal military operations, etc). 烟幕弹(用以掩护军事行动等者)。'~**-cured/-dried** adj (of ham, certain kinds of fish, etc) dried and cured in wood ~. (指火腿, 某些种类的鱼等)烟熏的。'~**-screen** n clouds of ~ made to hide military or naval operations; (fig) explanation, etc designed to mislead people about one's real intentions, etc. 烟幕(掩护军事行动者); (喻)掩饰作用的解释等(使入发生错觉以掩饰真正意图)。'~**-stack** n (a) outlet for ~ and steam from a steamship(and, US, from a steam locomotive). 轮船的烟囱; (美国)指火车的烟囱。(b) tall chimney. 高大的烟囱。2 [C] act of smoking tobacco: 吸烟: stop working and have a ~. 停止工作吸一口烟; (colloq) cigar or cigarette: (口)雪茄; 香烟: pass the ~s round. 传递香烟。~**·less** adj 1 that burns without ~: 燃烧而无烟的: ~less fuel. 无烟燃料。2 free from ~: 不发烟的; 无烟的: a ~less zone, where ~ is prohibited. 禁烟区; 无烟区; the ~less atmosphere of the countryside. 乡间不含烟的清新空气。**smoky** adj (**-ier, -iest**) 1 giving out much ~; full of ~: 发烟多

的; 充满烟的: smoky chimneys/fires: 冒烟的烟囱(火); the smoky atmosphere of an industrial town. 工业城市多烟的空气。2 like ~ in smell, taste or appearance. 气息, 味道或外观似烟的。

smoke² /sməʊk; smok/ vi, vt 1 [VP2A] give out smoke, or sth thought to resemble smoke, eg visible vapour or steam: 冒烟; 冒气; 起烟雾: a smoking volcano. 冒烟的火山。That oil-lamp ~s badly. 那盏油灯冒烟冒得很厉害。2 [VP2A] (of a fire or fireplace) send out smoke into the room (instead of up the chimney): (指火或壁炉)烟熏入屋内(未由烟囱冒出): This fireplace ~s badly. 这壁炉冒烟熏得厉害。3 [VP2A, 6A] draw in and let out the smoke of burning tobacco or other substance: 抽烟: ~ a pipe/cigar, etc. 抽烟斗(雪茄等)。Do you ~? 你抽不抽烟? If you ~ opium, give it up. 如果你吸鸦片, 就戒掉吧。4 [VP22] bring (oneself) into a specific state by smoking tobacco, etc: 因抽烟而(使自己)入于某种状态: He ~d himself sick. 他因吸烟而致病。5 [VP2A, C] (of pipes, cigars, etc. with passive force): (指烟斗,雪茄等,含被动意义): This pipe ~s well, is satisfactory when ~d. 这烟斗抽起来很够味。A good cigar will ~(= can be ~d) for at least half an hour. 一根好的雪茄至少可抽半小时。6 [VP6A] dry and preserve (meat, fish) with smoke (from wood fires): 用烟熏制(肉, 鱼): ~d ham/salmon. 熏制的火腿(鲑)。7 [VP6A] stain, darken, dry, with smoke: 熏污; 熏黄; 熏黑; 熏干: a ~d ceiling; 熏黄的天花板; a sheet of ~d glass, eg through which to look at the sun. 一片熏黑的玻璃片 (可用以观看太阳等)。8 [VP6A, 15B] send smoke on to (plants, insects): 以烟熏(植物,昆虫): ~ the plants in a greenhouse, to kill insects. 以烟熏温室植物, 以杀死害虫。~ **sth out**, force to leave by smoking: 因烟熏出: ~ out snakes from a hole. 熏出洞中的蛇。**smok·ing** n [U] (gerund, in compounds)(动名词,用于复合词中)'**smoking-carriage /-car/-compartment** nn one for smokers on a railway train. (火车上的)吸烟车厢。'**smoking-mixture** n blend of tobaccos for smoking in pipes. (烟斗用的)混合烟草。'**smoking-room** n room (in a hotel, etc) where smoking is permitted. (旅馆等处的)吸烟室。**smoker** n 1 person who habitually ~s tobacco. 吸烟者; 爱君子。2 smoking-carriage on a train. (火车上的)吸烟车厢。

smol·der /ˈsməʊldə(r); ˈsmoldɚ/ ⇨ **smoulder**.

smooth¹ /smuːð; smuð/ adj (**-er, -est**) 1 having a surface like that of glass; free from roughness or (fig) difficulty: 平滑的; 平静的; 光滑如镜的; (喻)无困难的; 顺利的: ~ paper/skin; 光滑的纸(皮肤); a ~ road; 平坦的路; a ~ sheet of ice; 一片光滑的冰; ~ to the touch; 摸起来光滑的; a ~ sea, calm, free from waves; 平静的海; make things ~ for sb, (fig) remove difficulties for him. (喻)为某人除去困难。The way is now ~, is no longer difficult. 前路现在已无阻碍; 困难清除了。**take the rough with the ~**, take (both the good and the bad things of life) as they come. 逆来顺受。'~**-bore** adj (of a gun) having no rifling in the barrel. (指枪炮)滑膛的; 无膛线(或来复线)的。'**smooth-faced** adj (fig) friendly but hypocritical. (喻)假友善的; 作友善状的; 虚伪的。2 (of movement) free from shaking, bumping, etc: (指开动中)不摇晃的; 不颠簸的; 平稳的: a ~ ride in a good car; 坐一部好汽车所作的一次平稳行驶; a ~ flight in a jet airliner; 乘喷气客机所作的一次平稳航行; a ~ crossing, eg by sea from England to France. 一次平稳的横渡(如从英国渡海到法国)。3 (of a liquid mixture) free from lumps; well beaten or mixed: (指液体混合物)无颗粒的; 匀和的; 搅拌得好的: a ~ paste. 没有疙瘩的糊。4 free from harshness of sound or taste; flowing easily: 无刺耳声音的, 无涩味的; 悦耳的; 柔和的; 醇美的; 圆润的; 流畅的: ~ verse; 流畅的诗句; a ~ wine; 柔和的酒; ~ claret/whisky. 味醇的红葡萄酒(威士忌)。5 (of a person, his manner) flattering, polite, unruffled, conciliatory: (指人,举止及行为)奉承的; 有礼貌的; 温顺的; 屈修好的: a ~ temper; 温和的脾气; ~ manners; 奉承的态度; a ~ face, often used to suggest hypocrisy. 温和有礼的面孔

（常暗示虚伪）；Hence, 由此产生，~-'faced／-'spoken／
-'tongued adjj (all having a suggestion of insincerity).
（均暗示不诚实）. ~·ly adv in a ~ manner: 平滑地；光
滑地；平静地；平稳地. a ~ly running engine. 运转平稳的引擎.
Things are not going very ~ly, There are troubles,
obstacles, interruptions, etc. 事情进行得不太顺利.
~·ness n

smooth² ／smuːð; smuð／ vt, vi 1 [VP6A, 15B] ~
sth (down／out／away／over), make smooth: 使光滑；
使平滑；使顺利；使平静: ~ down one's dress; 拉平衣
服；~ away／over obstacles／difficulties／perplexities,
etc, get rid of them. 清除障碍(困难, 困惑等). ~ sb's
path, (fig) make progress easier. (喻) 清除或铺平某人
的道路；扫除前途的障碍. 2 [VP2C] become smooth or
quiet: 变光滑；变平滑；变平静: The sea has ~ed down.
海上已风平浪静. 3(compounds) (复合词) '~·ing-iron n
(iron is the usu word)flat-iron used (heated) to ~ linen,
clothes, etc. (通常用 iron) 烫斗；熨斗. '~·ing-plane n
small plane for finishing the planing of wood. 小刨子
(用以修整刨平木料者). □ n act of ~ing: 使光滑、平
滑、平静等:give one's hair a ~. 梳理一下头发.

smor·gas·bord ／'smɔːgəsbɔːd; 'smɔrgəs,bɔrd／ n [U]
(Swedish) meal with a variety of dishes served from a
buffet. (瑞典式)精美自助餐(备有各式精美菜肴).

smote ／smǝut; smot／ pt of smite.

smother ／'smʌðǝ(r); 'smʌðǝ／ vt 1 [VP6A] cause the
death of, by stopping the breath of or by keeping air,
from; kill by suffocation. 使窒息；闷死. 2 [VP6A] put
out(a fire); keep(a fire) down(so that it burns slowly)
by covering with ashes, sand. etc. 熄(火)；覆以灰、沙等
而使(火)慢燃. 3 [VP14] ~ sth／sb with sth, cover,
wrap up, overwhelm with: 覆盖；掩蔽；掩没；压上: ~ a
grave with flowers／a child with kisses／one's wife with
kindness; 以花覆盖坟墓(接二连三地吻小孩; 体贴殷叨妻
子不知所措)；to 花覆盖坟墓(接二连三地吻小孩; 体贴殷叨妻
全身沾满来往汽车所扬起的尘土. 4 [VP6A, 15B]
suppress; hold back: 遏止；压制: ~ a yawn／one's
anger／feelings of resentment; 抑制呵欠(愤怒,憎恨)；~
up a scandal, try to conceal it. 掩饰丑闻. □n(usu a ~)
cloud of dust, smoke, steam, spray, etc. 尘、烟、水气等
造成的烟雾.

smoul·der (US= smol·) ／'smǝuldǝ(r); 'smoldǝ／ vi
[VP2A, C] burn slowly without flame; (fig, of feelings,
etc) exist or operate unseen, undetected, suppressed,
etc: 无火焰地闷燃；(喻, 指感情等)潜伏；酝酿: ~ing
discontent／hatred／rebellion. 酝酿着的不满(憎恨, 反
叛). □ n [U] ~ing burning: 闷烧；不发火焰的燃烧:
The ~ became a blaze. 闷火变成了烈焰.

smudge ／smʌdʒ; smʌdʒ／ n [C] 1 dirty mark;blotted
or blurred mark: 污点；污迹；斑痕: You've got a ~ on
your cheek. 你的脸颊上有一块污渍. Wash your hands or
you'll make a ~ on the writing-paper. 把手洗干净,否则
你会弄脏写字纸. 2 (chiefly US) outdoor fire with thick
smoke made to keep away insects. (主美) 户外熏虫用的
浓烟. □ vt, vi 1 [VP6A] make a ~ or ~s on; make
a ~ on (when writing a letter or word). 弄污; (书写时)
弄脏. 2 [VP2A] (of ink, paint, etc) become blurred
or smeared. (指墨水,油漆等)变模糊或污成一片: Ink ~s
easily. 墨水很容易污濡.

smug ／smʌg; smʌg／ adj (-gg-) self-satisfied; having,
showing, a character that is satisfied although without
ambition, imagination, broadmindedness: 自满的；自鸣
得意的；沾沾自喜的: a ~ smile; 自鸣得意的微笑；a life
of ~ respectability; 沾沾自喜的市侩生活；~ optimism;
自鸣得意的乐观；~ rich men. 自满的有钱人. ~·ly adv
~·ness n

smuggle ／'smʌgl; 'smʌgl／ vt [VP6A, 14, 15A, B]
1 get (goods) secretly and illegally (into, out of, a
country, through the customs, across a frontier): 走私；
偷运 (货物进出某国, 通过某国海关等): ~ Swiss
watches into England. 偷运瑞士表进入英国. 2 take (sth
or sb) secretly and in defiance of rules and regulations:

偷带(某物或某人): ~ a letter into a prison. 偷带信件进
监狱. smug·gler ／'smʌglǝ(r); 'smʌglǝ／ n

smut ／smʌt; smʌt／ n 1 [C] (mark or stain made by
a) bit of soot, dirt, etc. 一点点煤烟、煤灰、油烟、尘垢等；
污物；积烟；污处；污点；污迹. 2 [U] disease of corn
(wheat, etc) that causes the ears to turn black. (谷物
的)黑穗病. 3 [U] (colloq) indecent or obscene words,
stories: (口)淫词；秽语；淫秽的故事: Don't talk ~. 不
要说脏话. □ vt (-tt-) [VP6A] mark with ~s(1). 弄
污；弄脏；使黑. □ vi ~ty adj (-ier, -iest) 1 dirty with ~s.
给烟灰等弄脏的；熏黑的. 2 containing ~(3): 含淫词的；
猥亵的: ~ty stories. 猥亵的故事. ~·tily ／-ɪlɪ; -ɪlɪ／
adv ~·ti·ness n

snack ／snæk; snæk／ n light usu hurriedly eaten meal.
小吃；快餐. '~-bar／-counter nn bar／counter where
~s may be eaten. 小吃店；快餐柜.

snaffle¹ ／'snæfl; 'snæfl／ n '~-(bit)horse's bit without
a curb. 轻勒(无勒索的轻马衔).

snaffle² ／'snæfl; 'snæfl／ vt [VP6A] (GB sl) take
without permission; pinch(4). (英俚)偷;窃; 不告而取.

snag ／snæg; snæg／ n [C] 1 rough or sharp object, root
of a tree, hidden rock, which may be a source of danger.
(可造成危险的)不平、尖锐、粗糙等之物；树根；暗礁.
2 (colloq) hidden, unknown or unexpected difficulty or
obstacle: (口)隐伏或突发的困难或障碍: strike／come
upon a ~. 遭遇阻碍或困难. There's a ~ in it somewhere.
其中某处有障碍.

snail ／snell;snel／ n kinds of small, soft animal, most of
them with a spiral shell. 蜗牛. ⇨ the illus at mollusc.
参看 mollusc 之插图. at a '~'s pace, very slowly. 非
常缓慢;像蜗牛般行进.

snake ／sneik; snek／ n kinds of long, legless, crawling
reptile, some of which are poisonous; (fig) (often ~ in
the grass) treacherous person who pretends to be a
friend. 蛇; (喻)(常作~ in the grass) 阴险而佯为友善的
人. see ~s, have hallucinations. 发生错觉或幻觉. '~-
charmer n person who can control ~s with music. 弄
蛇者(可借音乐控制蛇者). □ vi [VP2C] move in twists
and glides: 蜿蜒; 蛇行; 曲折滑行: The road ~s through
the mountains. 那条路蜿蜒穿越群山. snaky adj move in
like a ~; (fig)venomous, ungrateful, treacherous. 蛇的;
象蛇的; (喻)恶毒的; 狡诈的; 阴险的.

snap ／snæp; snæp／ vt, vi (-pp-) 1 [VP6A, 15B, 2A,
3A] ~ (at) (sth), (try to) snatch with the teeth: 咬;
猛然咬; 猛地咬住: The dog ~ped at my leg. 那条狗咬我
的腿. The fish ~ped at the bait. 鱼吃饵. They ~ped at
the offer, (fig) offered eagerly to accept it. (喻)他们迫
不及待地接受该提议. ~ sth up, buy eagerly: 急切地
买;抢购: The cheapest articles were quickly ~ped up. 最
便宜的东西很快地被抢购一空. 2 [VP6A, 14, 15A, B,
22, 2A, C] break with a sharp crack; open or close
with, make, a sudden, sharp sound; say (sth), speak,
sharply: 发咯裂声而折断; 啪的一声关闭或打开; 发咯声;
厉声地说话或说出(某事): He stretched the rubber band
till it ~ped. 他拉长橡皮筋; 直至拉断了. The rope
~ped. 绳子突然断了. He ~ped down the lid of the box.
他咔哒一声关上箱子的盖. He ~ped his whip. 他挥鞭作
响. Her whip ~ped down on the pony's back. 她的鞭子
抽在小马背上发出清脆的声音. The sergeant ~ped out
his orders. 那士官厉声地发布命令. ~ at sb, speak to
sb sharply: 向某人厉声说话: I'm sorry I ~ped at you just
now. 我很抱歉刚才对你厉声说话. ~ one's finger at
sb／in sb's face, make a cracking noise by flicking a
finger audibly against the thumb(usu to show contempt):
向某人或当某人面弹指(通常表示轻蔑). ~ sb's 'nose／
'head off, speak angrily to; interrupt rudely or
impatiently. 向某人怒气地说话; 无礼或不耐烦地打断某
人的话. 3 [VP6A] take a ~shot (⇨ 8 below) of. 拍—
的快照(参看下列第8义). 4 (sl) ~ 'to it, start moving,
get going, quickly. (俚)快速地开动、移动或进行. ~ 'out
of it, get out of a mood, habit, etc. 突然改变心情、习惯
等. □ n 1 [C] act or sound of ~ping: 咬; 猛咬; 折断;

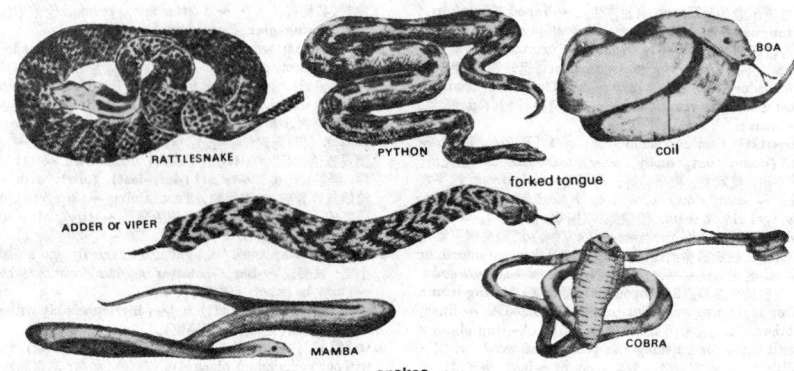

RATTLESNAKE

PYTHON

BOA

coil

forked tongue

ADDER or VIPER

MAMBA

COBRA

snakes

折断声；脆裂声: *The dog made an unsuccessful ~ at the meat.* 那条狗企图咬而未咬到那块肉。 *The lid shut with a ~.* 盖子啪哒一声关上了。 *The oar broke with a ~.* 桨啪哒一声折断了。 *S~ went the oar.* (adverbial use) It broke with a ~ping noise. (作副词用) 桨啪哒一声断了。 **2** [C] **cold ~**, sudden, short period of cold weather. 突然而短暂的寒冷天气。 **3** [U] (colloq) energy, dash, vigour, liveliness: (口) 精力；冲力；活力；生气: *Put some ~ into it.* 用一点劲。 ⇨ **snappy** below. 参看下列之 snappy. **4** [C] kinds of small, crisp cake: 小脆饼: (usu in compounds) (通常用于复合词中) 'ginger~s. 姜脆饼。 **5** [C] (usu in compounds) (通常用于复合词中) catch, device for fastening things, closed by pressing. 钩；扣 (借压力而关闭者)。 '~-**fasteners** (also 亦作 press-stud) fastening device used on dresses, gloves, etc. 暗扣；按扣。 ~**shot** ⇨ 8 below. 参看下列第 8 义。 **7**(attrib) done quickly and with little or no warning: (用作定语) 急就的；突然的；仓卒的: *a ~ election*; 仓卒的选举; *take a ~ vote*; 举行临时表决; *a ~ division*, in the House of Commons. (在下议院中) 匆匆分组表决。 **8**(compounds, etc) (复合词等) '~-**dragon** n [C] (=antirrhinum) kinds of plant with flowers that are like bags and can be made to open (like lips) when pressed. 金鱼草(开袋状花, 可压之使开, 形似嘴唇)。 '~-**shot** n quickly taken photograph with a hand camera by an amateur: 快照；快相 (通常为业余摄影师用手提照相机所拍摄)。 ~**py** adj (**-ier, -iest**) bright; lively: 聪明的；活泼的；生动的: *Make it ~py! Look ~py!* (sl) Be quick about it! (俚) 爽快一点! 干脆一点! ~**pish** /-ɪʃ, -ɪʃ/ adj inclined to ~, to be ill-tempered or irritable. 爱咬人的；脾气大的。 ~**pish·ly** adv ~**pish·ness** n

snare /sneə(r); snɛr/ n [C] **1** trap, esp one with a noose, for catching small animals and birds. 罗网；陷阱 (尤指有套索, 用以捕捉小动物及鸟类者)。 **2** (fig)sth that tempts one to expose oneself to defeat, disgrace, loss, etc: (喻)(诱人失败、丢脸、损失等之)圈套: *His promises are a ~ and a delusion.* 他的诺言是一种圈套, 也是欺骗。 **3**string of gut stretched across the bottom of side-drum to produce a sharp, rattling sound. 边鼓之响弦。 '~-**drum** n side-drum with ~s attached. 响弦鼓。 □ vt [VP6A] catch in a ~: 用罗网或陷阱捕捉: *~ a rabbit.* 用陷阱捕捉兔子。

snarl[1] /snɑ:l; snɑrl/ vi, vt [VP2A, 3A, 6A] ~ **(at)**, (of dogs) show the teeth and growl (at): (of persons) speak in a harsh voice. (指狗) 嗥叫；猛嚼；(指人) 咆哮，厉声地说。 □ n act or sound of ~ing: 嗥叫；咆哮；嗥叫声；咆哮声: *answer with a ~.* 咆哮着回答。

snarl[2] /snɑ:l; snɑrl/ n tangle;confused state: 缠结；纠结；混乱: *the traffic ~s in a big town.* 大城市交通混乱的情形。 □ vt, vi [VP6A, 15B, 2A, C, 3A] ~ **(up)**, (cause to) become jammed: (使) 变得拥塞或挤在一起:

The traffic (was) ~ed up. 交通拥塞了。 Hence, 由此产生, '~-**up** n = traffic jam. ⇨ **traffic.**

snatch /snætʃ; snætʃ/ vt, vi [VP6A, 2A, 15A, B] **1** put out the hand suddenly and take: 突然伸手拿取；抢；夺；攫取: *He ~ed the letter from me /~ed the letter out of my hand.* 他从我这里(从我手上)抢去了那封信。 *It's rude to ~.* 抢取是鲁莽行为。 *He ~ed at* (ie tried to seize) *the letter but was not quick enough.* 他想抢走那封信, 但动作不够快。 *He ~ed up his gun and fired.* 他突然拿起枪来射击。 **2** get quickly or when a chance occurs: 迅速获得；趁机获取: ~ *an hour's sleep /a meal*; 抓住机会睡一小时觉 (吃一顿饭); ~ *a kiss.* 偷吻。 □ n [C] **1** act of ~ing; sudden attempt to get sth by stretching out the hand: 抢；攫；夺；突然伸手拿取: *make a ~ at sth*; 攫取某物; (attrib)(用作定语) *a ~ decision,* one that is ~ed(2). 迅速决定；突下决心；趁势决定。 **2** short outburst or period: 片刻；短暂；片段；一阵: *short ~es of music*; 片段的音乐; *overhear ~es of conversation*; 偶然听到片段的谈话; *work in ~es,* not continuously, 断断续续地工作。 ~**er** n

snaz·zy /'snæzɪ; 'snæzɪ/ adj (sl) smart; fine. (俚)漂亮的;美好的。

sneak /sni:k; snik/ vi, vt **1** [VP2A, 3A] go quietly and furtively (*in, out, away, back, past,* etc). 潜行；偷偷走(与 in, out, away, back, past 等连用)。 **2** [VP2A] ~ **(on sb)**, (school sl) go to the teacher and tell him about the faults, wrongdoing, etc of another. (学校俚语)(向老师)告密;打小报告。 **3** [VP6A] (sl) steal. (俚)偷窃。 □ n **1** (sl) cowardly, treacherous person. (俚)怯儒鬼祟的人。 '~-**thief** n petty thief; person who steals things from open doors and windows. (顺手牵羊的)小偷；从开着的门窗偷东西的人。 **2.** (school sl) boy or girl who ~s(2). (学校俚语)向老师告密的男生或女生。 ~·**ing** adj furtive: 鬼鬼祟祟的；偷偷摸摸的；诡秘的: *have a ~ing respect /sympathy, etc for sb,* respect, etc which is not shown openly: 私下(非公开地)对某人怀有敬意(表示同情等): *a ~ing suspicion,* a vague, puzzling one. 令人困扰而扯不清的嫌疑。 ~·**ing·ly** adv **sneaky** adj = ~ing. ~·**ers** n pl (chiefly US) (also 亦作 *a pair of ~ers*) rubber-soled canvas shoes; plimsolls. (主美)胶底帆布鞋;软底鞋。

sneer /snɪə(r); snɪr/ vi [VP2A, 3A] ~ **(at)**, show contempt by means of a derisive smile; utter contemptuous words: 嘲笑；讥诮；说轻蔑话: ~ *at religion.* 嘲笑宗教。 □ n derisive look, smile, word or utterance: 讥诮的表情、微笑、字或言词: *You should ignore their ~s at your efforts.* 你应当不理会他们对你努力所作的冷笑。 ~·**ing·ly** adv

sneeze /sni:z; sniz/ n [C] sudden, uncontrollable outburst of air through the nose and mouth: 喷嚏: *Coughs and ~s spread diseases.* 咳嗽和喷嚏会传播疾病。

□ *vi* [VP2A] make a ~: 打喷嚏: *Use a handkerchief when you* ~. 打喷嚏的时候, 用手帕遮住。 **not to be** ~**d at**, (colloq) not to be despised; passable: (口)不可轻视; 过得去; 还可以: *A prize of £50 in the lottery is not to be* ~*d at.* 五十英镑的彩券奖金不可小看。

snick /snɪk/ *vt, vi, n* 1 (make a) small cut in sth. 细划痕; 细割痕; 作细划痕或割痕(于某物)。 2 (cricket) (make a) slight deflection of the ball with the bat: (板球)削(球) (以球棒擦触投出之球, 使之略微偏向); 削球: ~ *a ball through the slips.* 削球使滚过左后或右后防区。

snicker /'snɪkər/; 'snɪkɚ/ *vi, n* whinny; snigger. (指马)嘶叫; 嘶叫声; 暗笑; 窃笑。

snide /snaɪd/ snaɪd/ *adj* sneering; slyly critical: 轻视的; 嘲笑的; 讥讽的: ~ *remarks.* 讥讽话。

sniff /snɪf/ snɪf/ *vi, vt* 1 [VP2A] draw air in through the nose so that there is a sound: 以鼻吸气而带声音: *They all had colds and were* ~*ing and sneezing.* 他们都伤风了, 呼吸有声音而且打喷嚏。 2 [VP2A, 3A] ~ (*at*), ~ (1) to show disapproval or contempt: 嗤之以鼻 (表示轻视或不赞成): *The offer (eg to buy a good car for £4000) is not to be* ~*ed at.* 出价还算过得去(如出价四千英镑买一辆好的轿车)。 3 [VP2A, 3A, 6A, 15B] ~ (*at*) *sth;* ~ *sth up*, draw in through the nose as one breathes: 用鼻子吸入; 用鼻子闻; 嗅: ~ *the sea-air;* 吸入海上的空气; ~ (*at*) *a rose;* 闻玫瑰花; *a preparation (eg for catarrh) to be* ~*ed up through the nostrils.* 由鼻孔吸入的药物(如治疗鼻粘膜炎的药物)。 *The dog was* ~*ing (at) the lamp-post.* 那只狗正在嗅路灯柱。 □ *n* [C] act or sound of ~ing; breath (of air, etc): 以鼻吸气(声); 呼吸; 嗅; 闻: *get a* ~ *of sea air.* 吸一口海上的空气。 *One* ~ *of this stuff is enough to kill you.* 此物闻一闻即足以致命。 ~**y** *adj* (colloq) (口) 1 contemptuous. 藐视的; 轻视的。 2 (of sth that should have no smell) ill smelling. (指本该无气味的东西)臭的; 难闻的。

sniffle /'snɪfl/; 'snɪfl/ *vi* = **snuffle.**

snif·ter /'snɪftə(r)/; 'snɪftɚ/ *n* (dated sl) small portion of strong alcoholic drink. (过时俚语)一小份烈酒; 一小杯烈酒。

snig·ger /'snɪɡə(r)/; 'snɪɡɚ/ *n* [C] half-suppressed laugh (esp at sth improper, or in a cynical manner). 窃笑; 暗笑(尤指笑某事物不适当, 或笑里带讥讽)。 □ *vi* [VP2A, C] ~ (*at/over*), laugh in this way. 暗笑; 窃笑。

snip /snɪp/ snɪp/ *vt, vi* (-pp-) [VP6A, 15B, 3A] ~ (*at*) *sth;* ~ *sth off*, cut with scissors or shears, esp in short, quick strokes: 剪; 剪断; 剪去(尤指快速而张开角度小地剪动): ~ *off the ends of sth;* 剪去某物的末端; ~ *a hole in sth;* 在某物上剪一个洞; ~ *cloth/paper.* 剪布(纸)。 □ *n* 1 cut made by ~ping; 剪; 剪断; 剪开下之物。 2 (colloq) profitable bargain: (口)获利的交易; 赚钱的交易; 合算的交易: *Only 50p! It's a* ~*!* 才五十便士! 真合算! ~**ping** *n* small piece of material ~ped off a larger piece. 从大片物料剪下来的小片。

snipe[1] /snaɪp/ snaɪp/ *n* (*pl* unchanged) (复数不变) bird which frequents marshes with a long bill. 鹬; 沙雏鸟。 ⇨ the illus at **water**. 参看 water 之插图。

snipe[2] /snaɪp/ snaɪp/ *vi, vt* [VP2A, 3A] ~ (*at*), fire shots (at) from a hiding-place, usu at long range; [VP 6A] kill or hit thus. 伏击; 狙击(通常指长距离); 借伏击或狙击射杀或命中。 **sniper** *n* person who ~s. 狙击手; 狙击兵。

snip·pet /'snɪpɪt/; 'snɪpɪt/ *n* small piece cut off; (*pl*) bits (of information, news, etc). 切下的小片; 断片; 碎片; (复)(消息、新闻等的)片段。

snitch /snɪtʃ/; snɪtʃ/ *vt, vi* 1 [VP6A] (sl) steal (usu sth of little or no value). (俚)偷(通常指价值很小或无价值之物)。 2 [VP2A, 3A] ~ (*on sb*), sneak, inform (on sb). 告密; 告发(某人)。

snivel /'snɪvl/ 'snɪvl/ *vi* (GB -ll-; US -l-) [VP2A] cry from pretended grief, sorrow or fear; complain in a miserable, whining way: 假哭; 哭泣; 哭诉; 抽泣的抱怨: *a harassed woman with six* ~*ling children.* 带着六个哭哭

啼啼的孩子的苦命女人。 ~·**ler** (US = ~·**er**) *n* person who ~s. 假哭者; 哭诉者。

snob /snɒb/; snɑb/ *n* person who pays too much respect to social position or wealth, or who despises persons who are of lower social position: 谄上欺下之人; 势利之人: *'~ appeal*, power to attract the interest of ~s. 财势(引起势利之人兴趣的力量)。 ~·**bish** /-ɪʃ; -ɪʃ/ *adj* of or like a ~. 谄上欺下的; 势利的。 ~·**bish·ly** *adv* ~·**bish·ness**, ~·**bery** /'snɒbərɪ; 'snɑbərɪ/ *nn* [U] state, quality, of being ~bish; (*pl*) ~bish acts or utterances. 谄上欺下; 势利; (复)势利的言行。

snood /snuːd/ snud/ *n* ornamental net worn by a woman to keep her hair in position. (女子的)束发网。

snook /snuːk/ snuk/ *n* (only in) (仅用于) *cock a* ~ (*at sb*)*,* (lit or fig) show impudent contempt by placing the thumb to the nose and spreading out the fingers towards him (字面或喻)以拇指指着鼻尖并以其余四指向对方张扬摇动以表示轻蔑。

snooker /'snuːkə(r)/; 'snukɚ/ *n* game (a variety of *pool*) played with 15 red balls and six balls of other colours on a billiard-table. 落袋撞球游戏(为 pool 之一种, 使用 15 个红色球, 及 6 个他色球)。 *be* ~*ed*, (colloq) be placed in a difficult position. (口)处困境。

snoop /snuːp/ snup/ *vi* [VP2A, C, 3A] (colloq) (口) ~ (*about/around*), search, examine (eg to find error, the breaking of rules, etc) in a secretive way. 窥察(以找出过失、违规等); 窥探。 ~ *into*, pry into matters one is not properly concerned with. 窥视或探听(与己无关的事)。 ~**er** *n* person who ~s. 窥察者; 管闲事者; 包打听。

snooty /'snuːtɪ; 'snutɪ/ *adj* (**-ier, -iest**) (colloq) supercilious; snobbish. (口)自大的; 目中无人的。 **snoot·ily** /-ɪlɪ; -əlɪ/ *adv*

snooze /snuːz; snuz/ *vi* [VP2A], *n* (sl) (take a) short sleep (esp in the daytime): (俚)小睡(尤指在日间): *have a* ~ *after lunch.* 午饭后小睡。

snore /snɔː(r); snor/ *vi* breathe roughly and noisily while sleeping: 打鼾; 发鼾声: *Does my snoring bother you?* 我打鼾会搅扰你吗? □ *n* sound of snoring: 打鼾声: *His* ~*s woke me up.* 他的鼾声把我吵醒了。 **snorer** *n* person who ~s. 打鼾者。

snor·kel, schnor·kel /'snɔːkl; 'ʃn-; 'snɔrkl/ *n* tube that enables a submarine to take in air while submerged; device for enabling a swimmer to take in air while under water. (潜水艇用的)呼吸管; 通气管; (潜水者用的)通气装置或呼吸装置。 ⇨ the illus at **frog**. 参看 frog 之插图。

snort /snɔːt; snort/ *vi, vt* 1 [VP2A, C] force air violently out through the nose; do this to show impatience, contempt, etc: 自鼻喷气作声; 嗤之以鼻; 喷鼻息以表示不耐烦、轻视等: ~ *with rage (at sb or sth);* (对某人或某事)愤怒地哼之以鼻; (colloq) indicate amusement with a burst of loud laughter. (口)突然大笑表示欢娱。 2 [VP6A, 15B] express by ~ing: 喷鼻息以表示; 哼然表示: ~ *defiance at sb;* 对某人喷鼻息以表示不服; ~ *out a reply.* 哼鼻作答(喷鼻息作答)。 *'Never!' he* ~*ed.* 他哼了一声说, '决不!' □ *n* 1 act or sound of ~ing: 哼鼻或喷鼻息的动作或声音; 哼鼻; 哼鼻声: *give a* ~ *of contempt.* 作轻蔑的哼鼻之插图。 2 snorkel (of a submarine). (潜水艇的)通气管。 ~**y** *adj* (colloq) ill-tempered. (口)坏脾气的; 脾气不好的。 ~**er** *n* (colloq) 1 sb or sth that is violent or outstanding in some way: (在某方面)特别激烈或突出的人或事物: *This problem is a real* ~*er*, very difficult. 这问题确是非常棘手。 2 strong gale. 强风; 暴风。

snot /snɒt; snɑt/ *n* [U] (vulg) mucus of the nose. (鄙)鼻涕。 ~**ty** *adj* (vulg) (鄙) 1 running with, wet with, ~. 流鼻涕的; 鼻涕弄湿的。 2 (~**-nosed**), (sl) superior; snooty. 目空一切的; 傲慢的: *You* ~*-nosed little bastard!* 你这个目中无人的小杂种!

snout /snaʊt; snaʊt/ *n* nose (and sometimes the mouth or jaws) of an animal (esp a pig); pointed front of sth, thought to be like a ~. 动物(尤指猪)的鼻子或口口部; 猪嘴; (某物之)猪嘴形前端; 状似猪嘴的装置。 ⇨ the illus

at **domestic, fish.** 参看 domestic, fish 之插图。

snow[1] /snəʊ; sno/ n 1 [U] frozen vapour falling from the sky in soft, white flakes; mass of such flakes on the ground, etc: 雪; 雪片; 雪花; (地面上等处的)积雪: a heavy fall of ~; 下大雪; roads deep in ~; 积雪深的道路; (pl) falls or accumulation of ~. (复)积雪; 降雪. 2 (compounds) (复合词) '~·ball n (a) mass of pressed into a hard ball for throwing in play. (团雪而成的)雪球 (用以投掷以为游戏). (b) sth that increases quickly in size as it moves forward. 象滚雪球般快速增大的事物。○ vt, vi (a) throw ~balls (at). (向…)掷雪球. (b) grow quickly in size, importance, etc: (在体积、重要性等方面)快速增加: Opposition to the war ~balled. 反战的情绪迅速增长。'~·berry n garden shrub with white berries. 一种结白色浆果的园艺灌木。'~·blind adj (temporarily) unable to see because the eyes are tired by the glare of the sun on ~. 雪盲(眼睛受雪地反射的阳光刺激而暂时失明)的。Hence, 由此产生, '~·blind·ness n '~·bound adj unable to travel because of heavy falls of ~. 被大雪阻阻的; 被大雪封闭的。'~·capped/-clad/-covered adjj covered with ~: 为雪所覆盖的: ~-capped mountains; 覆盖着雪的山; ~-covered roofs. 覆盖着雪的屋顶。'~·drift n bank of ~ heaped up by the wind: (为风吹成的)雪堆: The train ran into a ~drift. 火车开进了雪堆。'~·drop n bulb plant with small white flowers at the end of winter or in early spring. 雪花(一种绿茎植物,残冬或初春时开小白花)。⇨ the illus at flower. 参看 flower 之插图。'~·fall n [C] amount of ~ that falls on one occasion or in a period of time, eg one winter, one year. 降雪; (一次或某一时期的)降雪量: heavy ~s in high mountains. 雪原; 雪野(面积广大的常年积雪,如高山上者)。'~·flake n one of the feather-like collections of small crystals in which ~ falls. 雪片; 雪花。'~·line n level (in feet or metres) above which ~ lies permanently at any place: 雪线(以英尺或米丈量,在此一水平线之上积雪终年不溶): climb above the ~-line. 攀越雪线。'~·man /-mæn; -,mæn/ n (pl -men) figure of a man made of ~ by children for amusement. (儿童以雪堆成的)雪人。'~-plough (US 美 ~-plow) n device for pushing ~ from roads and railways. 除雪机; 雪犁 (用以清除道路及铁轨上之积雪者)。'~-shoes n pl frames with leather straps for walking on deep ~ without sinking in. 雪鞋 (以革条穿于木框等上制成,可在积雪处行走而不致下陷)。'~·storm n heavy fall of ~, esp when accompanied by strong wind. 大雪; (尤指伴有暴风雪之)暴风雪。'~·white adj pure, bright white in colour. 雪白的; 纯白的。'~·y adj (-ier, -iest) 1 covered with ~: 被雪所覆盖的: ~y roofs. 被雪覆盖的屋顶。2 characterized by ~: 下雪的; 雪花纷飞的: ~y weather. 下雪的天气。3 as white or fresh as newly fallen ~: (象刚下的雪那样)洁白清新的: a ~y tablecloth. 洁白的桌布。

snow[2] /snəʊ; sno/ vi, vt 1 [VP2A, B] (of snow) come down from the sky: (指雪) 降雪; 落下: It ~ed all day. 整天下雪。2 [VP2C] ~ in, come in large numbers or quantities: 大量拥到; 似雪片般飞来: Gifts and messages ~ed in on her birthday. 她生日那天, 礼物和函电象雪片般涌来。3 be ~ed 'in/'up, be prevented by heavy snow from going out. 被大雪困阻。be ~ed 'under (with), (fig) be overwhelmed: (喻)被压倒; 累倒: ~ed under with work/with invitations to dinner parties. 为工作(宴会的邀请)累倒。

snub[1] /snʌb; snʌb/ vt (-bb-) [VP6A] treat (esp a younger or less senior person) with cold behaviour or contempt; reject (an offer) in this way: 慢待或冷落(尤指年龄较幼或地位较低者); 冷淡地或轻蔑地拒绝(建议、要求等): get ~bed by a civil servant. 被一位公务员所慢待。○ n [C] ~bing words or behaviour: 慢待; 冷落; 慢待或冷落的言词: suffer a ~. 受冷落。

snub[2] /snʌb; snʌb/ adj (only in) (仅用于) a ~ nose, short, stumpy, turned up: 狮鼻(短粗而上翻者); hence, 由此产生, '~-nosed adj

snuff[1] /snʌf; snʌf/ n [U] powdered tobacco to be taken up into the nose by sniffing: 鼻烟(粉末状烟草, 伸从鼻孔吸入者): take a pinch of ~. 吸一撮鼻烟。up to ~, (colloq) (口) (a) shrewd; not childishly innocent. 精明的; 老练的。(b) in normal health. 健康正常的。'~·box n box for ~. 鼻烟盒。'~·coloured adj, n (of) dark yellowish-brown. 鼻烟色(的); 黄褐色(的)。

snuff[2] /snʌf; snʌf/ vi, vt, n = sniff.

snuff[3] /snʌf; snʌf/ vt, vi 1 [VP6A, 15B] cut or pinch off the burnt black end of the wick of (a candle). 剪(烛)花。~ sth out, (lit or fig) put out, extinguish (the light of a candle): (字面或喻)熄灭(烛光); 清灭: His hopes were nearly ~ed out. 他的希望几乎破灭了。2 [VP2C] ~ out, (sl) die. (俚)死亡。'~·ers n pl scissors or small bit of box to catch the burnt wick of candles when they are ~ed. 烛花用的剪刀。

snuffle /'snʌfl; 'snʌfl/ vi [VP2A] make sniffing sounds; breathe noisily (as when the nose is partly stopped up while one has catarrh). 抽鼻子; 发声地呼吸 (如鼻子半塞时)。○ n act or sound of snuffling: 抽鼻子; 发声呼吸; 鼻塞声; 鼻音: speak in/with a ~, nasally. 语语带鼻音。

snug /snʌg; snʌg/ adj (-gg-) 1 sheltered from wind and cold; warm and comfortable: 不受风寒侵袭的; 温暖而舒适的: ~ and cosy by the fireside. 在火炉旁边温暖而舒适的; ~ in bed; 舒适的在床上; a ~ woollen vest. 温暖的毛背心。2 neat and tidy; rightly or conveniently placed or arranged: 整洁的; 安排适当的: a ~ cabin, on a ship. 整洁的船舱。3 good enough for modest needs: 可满足此需要的: a ~ little income. 可维持适度生活的微薄收入。4 closely fitting: 紧贴的; 紧身的: a ~ jacket; 紧身的上衣; (as an adv) (用作副词) a ~-fitting coat. 合身的上装。○ n = snuggery. '~·ly adv '~·ness n

snug·gery /'snʌgərɪ; 'snʌgərɪ/ n (pl -ries) snug place, esp a private room planned for comfort. 温暖而舒适的地方; (尤指)舒适的私人房间。

snuggle /'snʌgl; 'snʌgl/ vi, vt 1 [VP2C] ~ (up) (to sb), lie or get (close to sb) for warmth, comfort or affection: 挨近; 靠近(某人)(使获得温暖或温情): The child ~d up to its mother/~d into its mother's arms. 那孩子贴在母亲身边(贴在母亲怀里)。The children ~d (together) in bed. 那些孩子在床上挤偎住一起。She ~d down in bed, made herself comfortable. 她舒舒服服地蜷在被窝里。2 [VP14] ~ sb to sb, draw close (to one): 拉近; 紧抱; 拥近: She ~d the child close to her. 她把孩子拉近自己。

so[1] /səʊ; so/ adv of degree 程度副词 so such an extent. 至某种程度。1 (in the pattern: 用于句型: not+so+adj/adv+as): It is not so big as I thought it would be. 那东西不如我想象的大。We didn't expect him to stay so long, (as, in fact, he did stay). 我们未料到他会停留那么久。He was not so much angry as disappointed. 他的失望甚于恼怒。2 (in the pattern: 用于句型: so+adj+as+to+inf): Would you be so kind as to help me, ie will you please help me? 请帮帮忙好吗? He is not so stupid as to do that. 他不至于蠢到做那种事。3 (in the pattern: 用于句型: so+adj/adv+that): He was so ill that he had to send for a doctor. 他病得不轻, 我们必须为他请医生。There were so many that we didn't know where to put them all. 数量太多了, 我们不知道什么地方去放得下。He was so angry that he couldn't speak. 他非常愤怒, 竟至说不出话来。(Colloq: 口: He couldn't speak, he was so angry). 他非常愤怒, 竟至说不出话来。4 (If the adj modifies a sing n, the indef art is placed between the adj and the n. It is often better to use such): (形容词修饰单数名词时, 不定冠词应放在形容词与名词之间。such 常较为佳): He is not so clever a boy (= such a clever boy) as his brother. 他不如他哥哥(弟弟)聪明。5 (used, colloq style, with exclamatory emphasis for very. 用于口语用法中代替 very, 具有感叹和加强语气的作用。'Ever so 为口语): I'm 'so glad to see you! 我真高兴见到你! It was 'so kind of you! 你真好! There was 'so much to do! 有这么多事情

要做! *That's 'ever so much better!* 那再好也没有了! **6** (in phrases) (用于短语中) **'so far,** up to this／that time, point or extent: 至此(那)时; 至此(那)点; 到此(那)程度或范围: *Now that we've come so far, we may as well go all the way.* 我们既然已经走到这里，干脆就走完全程。*Everything is in order so far.* 迄今诸事顺遂。**so 'far as,** to the extent or degree that: 至某种限度或程度: *So far as I know／as I'm concerned ...* 就我所知(就我而言)…。**So far, so 'good,** Up to this point all is satisfactory. 到现在为止，一切都很好。**so 'far from,** instead of; quite contrary to: 决不是; 绝非: *So far from being a help, he was a hindrance.* 他不但帮不上忙，反而碍事。**so 'long as,** on condition that; provided that: 设或; 假如; 只要; *You may borrow the book so long as you keep it clean.* 你可以借这本书，只要你将它保持干净。**'so much／many,** an unspecified quantity／number: 这么多(表示未明确指出的分量或数目): *So much butter, so much sugar, so many eggs,....* 这么多的奶油，这么多的糖，这么多的鸡蛋，…。*Twelve dinners, at so much a head.* 来十二份客饭，每客这个价钱。*not so 'much as:* 甚至不; 与其…不如: *He didn't so much as* (= didn't even) *ask me to sit down.* 他甚至没有请我坐。*He is not so much unintelligent as uneducated,* ie he lacks education, not intelligence. 他缺乏的是教育，并非聪明才智。⇨ **much**[1]. **'so much** (nonsense, etc) all, merely: 不过; 全是(无稽之谈等): *What you have written is so much nonsense.* 你写的这些全是无稽之谈。**'so much for,** that is all that need be said, done, etc, about: 有关…要说的或要做的就尽在于此: *So much for the first stage of our journey.* 我们旅行的第一个阶段到此为止。**,so much 'so that,** to such an extent that: 到如此程度以致: *He is rich — so much so that he does not know what he is worth.* 他很富有——富有到连自己都不知道究竟有多少钱。

so[2] /sʊɔ; soʊ/ *adv of manner* 表方式的副词 **1** in this／that way; thus: 这样; 那样; 以这(那)种方式: *So, and so only, can it be done.* 这样做，并且只有这样做，才做得成。*Stand just so.* 就这样站着。*As X was* (= That is how) *I became a sailor.* 那就是我变成水手的来由。*As X is to Y, so Y is to Z.* Y 跟 Z 的关系犹如 X 跟 Y 的关系。*As you treat me, so I shall treat you.* 你怎么对待我，我就怎么对待你。**2** (in phrases) (用于短语中) **'so-called,** called or named thus but perhaps wrongly or doubtfully: 所谓的; 号称的: *Your so-called friends won't help you in your troubles.* 你那些所谓的朋友在你遇到困难时不会帮助你。**'so that, (a)** in order that: 为的是; 以便: *Speak clearly, so that they may understand you.* 讲清楚一点，好让他们听懂。**(b)** with the result that: 因此; 结果是; 以致: *Nothing more was heard of him, so that 'people thought that he was dead.* 未再听到他的消息，因此人们以为他死了。**'so ... that, (a)** with the intent that: 意图; 有意要: *We have so arranged matters that one of us is always on duty.* 我们已经安排好，我们之间总有一个人当班。**(b)** with the result that; in a way that: 因此; 结果是; 以致: *It so happened that I couldn't attend the meeting.* 事情发生的那样巧，以致我无法参加那次会议。**'so as to do sth,** in order to; in such a way that: 为了; 以便; 以致: *Don't let your television blare so as to disturb your neighbours.* 不要把你的电视机的声音开得太大，以致打扰邻居。*I will have everything ready so as not to keep you waiting.* 我会把一切准备就绪，使你不用等候。⇨ **as**[2](15). **3** (used as a substitute for a word, phrase or situation): (用以代替单词，短语或某种情况): *I told you so!* That is what I told you! 我告诉过你会这样的! *I could scarcely believe it, but it was so,* ie that was the state of affairs, etc. 我简直无法相信，但的确是这样。*So I believe／hope／suppose, etc.* 我相信(希望，以为等)如此。**4** (used to express agreement, in the pattern 用以表示同意，其句型为: so+pron+aux v): *A: 'It was cold yesterday.' B: 'So it was.'* 甲: '昨天很冷。'乙: '的确很冷。'*A: 'Tomorrow will be Friday.' B: 'So it will.'* 甲: '明天是礼拜五。'乙: '不错，是礼拜五。'*A: 'We have all worked hard.' B: 'So we have.'* 甲: '我们大家都辛苦。'乙: '的确都很辛苦。'

5 (used meaning 'also' in the pattern: 作 also 解，其句型为: so+aux v+(pro)n): *You are young and so am I,* ie I also am young. 你(们)年轻，我也年轻。*Tom speaks French and so does his brother.* 汤姆会讲法语，他哥哥(弟弟)也会。*A: 'I went to the cinema yesterday.' B: 'Oh, did you? So did I.'* 甲: '昨天我去看电影了。'乙: '噢，是吗? 我也去了。'**6** (various uses) (其他用法) *so* (unstressed), about: (不重读)大约: *He must be forty or so,* about forty years old. 他一定有四十来岁了。*It will be warmer in another month or so,* about a month from now. 大约再过一个月(天)就会暖和一点了。**and 'so on (and 'so forth),** and other things of the same kind; et cetera. 等等; 诸如此类。*just so,* **(a)** used to express agreement (用以表示同意) 正是如此; 一点不错。**(b)** neat and tidy 整齐清洁: *Eric likes everything to be just so.* 埃里克喜欢每样东西都整齐清洁。**'so to say／speak,** used as an apology for an unusual use of a word or phrase, an exaggeration, etc. 可以说; 打个比方说(表示勉强将某一词，短语，夸张语等作不寻常用法)。⇨ this entry below. 参看下列 so-so 条。**'so-and-so** /ˈsʊɔ ən sʊɔ; ˈsoən,so/ (*pl* **so-and-so's**) (colloq) (口) **(a)** person or thing not wanting to be named: 某某; 某人; 某事物(指无须说出姓名或名称者): *Don't worry about what old so-and-so says.* 某某老先生说的话不要放在心上。**(b)** (derog) unpleasant person. (贬) 讨厌的人。

so[3] /sʊɔ; soʊ/ *conj* **1** therefore; that is why: 因此; 所以: *The shops were closed so I couldn't buy anything.* 商店都打烊了，所以我什么也买不到。*She asked me to go, so I went.* 她要我去，所以我去了。*They cost a lot of money, so use them carefully.* 这些东西花不少钱，所以要小心使用。**2** (exclamatory) (惊叹用法) *So you're back again!* 你又回来了! *So you've lost your job, have you?* 那么你失业了，是不是? *So you're not coming!* 这么说，你不来了! *So there you are!* 情况就是如此!

so[4],**soh** /sʊɔ; soʊ/ *sol* /sɒl; sɑl/ *n* fifth note in the musical octave. 任何大音阶之第五音。

soak /sʊk; sok/ *vt, vi* **1** [VP2A] become wet through by being in liquid or by absorbing liquid: 浸湿; 泡: *The clothes are ~ing in soapy water.* 衣服在肥皂水里泡着。**2** [VP6A, 14] ~ **sth** (*in sth*), cause sth to absorb as much liquid as possible: 使某物尽量吸收液体; 使浸透; 使濡湿: *~ dirty clothes in water／bread in milk.* 把脏衣服泡在水里(把面包泡在牛奶里)。*S~ the cloth in the dye for one hour.* 把布放进颜料里泡一个钟头。**3** [VP15A, B] ~ **sth up,** absorb; take in (liquid): 吸收; 吸入(液体): *Blotting-paper ~s up ink.* 吸墨纸吸收墨水。~ **oneself in sth,** (fig) absorb: (喻) 沉醉; 沉湎: ~ *oneself in the atmosphere of a place.* 沉湎于某一个地方的气氛中。**4** [VP6A, 15B] ~ (*of rain, etc*) (指雨等) ~ **sb** (*through*), make him very wet: 淋湿; 湿透: *We all got ~ed (through).* 我们都淋得湿透了。**be ~ed to the skin,** get wet right through one's clothes. 全身湿透。**5** [VP3A] ~ **through sth,** penetrate; enter and pass through: 浸入; 透过; 渗透: *The rain had ~ed through the roof／his overcoat.* 雨水已经透过屋顶(透过他的大衣)。**6** [VP6A] (sl) extract money from by charging or taxing very heavily: (俚)向…榨取金钱或征收重税: *Are you in favour of ~ing the rich?* 你赞成向富人课重税吗? **7** [VP2A] (colloq) drink alcohol excessively (and habitually). (口) 狂饮; 酗酒。□ *n* **1** act of ~ing: 浸; 泡; 渍: *Give the sheets a good ~.* 把被单好好地浸一浸。*in ~,* being ~ed: 在浸泡中; 泡着: *The sheets are in ~.* 被单在浸泡中。**2** (sl, 俚, usu 通常作 **old ~**) person greatly addicted to alcoholic drink. 酒鬼; 酒徒。~ **er** *n* **1** (colloq) heavy fall of rain: (口) 大雨: *What a ~er!* 好大的雨! **2** drunkard. 醉汉; 酒徒。

soap /sʊp; sop/ *n* [U] substance made of fat or oil and an alkali, used for washing and cleaning: 肥皂: *a bar／cake of ~;* 一条(一块)肥皂; *'~-flakes,* 肥皂片; *'~-powder;* 肥皂粉; *use plenty of ~ and water.* 用大量的肥皂和水。**'soft ~,** ⇨ **soft**(15). *'~-box n* improvised stand for an orator (in a street, park, etc): (街头、公园

等处的) 临时演说台; 肥皂箱演说台: ~-**box oratory**, of the kind heard from demagogues. 肥皂箱演说(政客们的煽动性演说). '~-**bubble** n filmy ball of ~y water with changing colours, full or air. 肥皂泡. ~-**opera** n (US) radio or TV serial drama dealing with domestic problems, etc in a sentimental or melodramatic way. (美)(无线电广播或电视) 连续剧 (以伤感或闹剧的方式处理家庭问题等). '~-**suds** n pl frothy lather of ~ and water. (含肥皂和水的)肥皂泡沫. □ vt 1 [VP6A, 15B] apply ~ to; rub with ~: 涂肥皂于; 用肥皂擦: ~ oneself down. 用肥皂擦洗身子. 2 [VP6A] (colloq) flatter; try to please. (口)讨好; 谄媚. ~y adj (-ier, -iest) 1 of or like ~: 肥皂的; 似肥皂的: This bread has a ~y taste. 这面包有肥皂味. 2(fig)over-anxious to please: (喻)过分想讨好的; 谄媚的; 圆滑的: He has a ~y voice/manner. 他有一种谄媚的声音(态度).

soar /sɔː(r)/ sor/ vi [VP2A, C] fly or go up high in the air; hover in the air without flapping of wings; rise: 高飞; 翱翔; 高耸; 升高: ~ like an eagle; 象老鹰一般翱翔; a ~ing flight, eg in a sailplane: 翱翔飞行(如乘滑翔机); a cathedral nave that ~s up to the vaulted roof; 高耸至拱顶的大教堂正厅; the ~ing spire of Salisbury cathedral. 索尔兹伯里大教堂的高耸尖顶. Prices ~ed when war broke out. 战争爆发时,物价飞涨.

sob /sɒb/ sab/ vi, vi(-**bb-**) 1 [VP2A, C] draw in the breath sharply and irregularly from sorrow or pain, esp while crying; [VP15A, B]: 呜咽; 啜泣; 欷歔: She sobbed her heart out, sobbed bitterly. 她哭得痛不欲生. She sobbed herself to sleep. 她哭泣着入睡了. 2[VP15B] **sob sth out**, tell while doing this: 呜咽地说; 哭诉: She sobbed out the story of her son's death in a traffic accident. 她呜咽着叙说她儿子死于车祸的经过. □ n [C] act or sound of sobbing: 呜咽(声); 啜泣(声); 欷歔(声): The child's sobs gradually died down. 那孩子的啜泣渐趋沉寂. '**sob-stuff** n [U] (colloq) the sort of writing, film, etc which is full of pathos and sentiment. (口)充满伤感情绪的文章、电影等. **sob·bing·ly** adv

so·ber /ˈsəʊbə(r)/ ˈsobə/ adj 1 self-controlled; temperate; serious in thought, etc; calm: 自制的; 适度的; 冷静的; 镇定的; 认真的; 严肃的: be in ~ earnest; 严肃认真的; make a ~ estimate of what is possible; 对可能的情况作冷静的估计; exercise a ~ judgement; 作冷静的判断; be ~-minded, serious; 认真的; 严肃的; ~ colours, not bright; 素色; in ~ fact, in fact (contrasted with what is fancied or imagined). 事实上(与空想或想象相对). '~-**sides** n (dated colloq) serious and sedate person. (过时口语)严肃而正经的人. 2 avoiding drunkenness; not drunk: 未醉的; 清醒的: Does he ever go to bed ~? 他有清醒着就寝的时候吗? □ vt, vi [VP6A, 15B, 2C] 1 ~ (**sb**) **down**, make or become (1): 使或变自制、严肃、镇定: The bad news ~ed all of us. 那坏消息使我们全都变严肃了. I wish those noisy children would ~ down, become less excited, etc. 我希望那些闹哄哄的孩子们静下来. 2 ~ (**sb**) **up**, make or become (2): 使或变清醒; 使不醉: Put him to bed until he ~s up. 送他上床去待他清醒过来. Throw a pail of water over him—that'll ~ him up. 浇他一桶水——这会使他清醒过来. ~·**ly** adv

so·bri·ety /səˈbraɪətɪ/ /səˈbraɪətɪ/ n [U] quality or condition of being sober (1, 2). 清醒; 自制; 严肃; 镇定.

so·bri·quet /ˈsəʊbrɪkeɪ/ /ˈsobrɪˌke/ n [C] nickname. 绰号; 浑名.

soc·cer /ˈsɒkə(r)/ /ˈsɑkɚ/ n [U] (colloq) (as used by those who play Rugby football for) association football. (口)(Rugby football 球员所指的)英式足球.

so·ciable /ˈsəʊʃəbl/ /ˈsoʃəbl/ adj fond of the company of others; friendly; showing friendliness. 好与人交往; 好交际的; 友善的; 表示友善的. **so·ciably** /-əblɪ/ /-əblɪ/ adv **so·cia·bil·ity** /ˌsəʊʃəˈbɪlətɪ/ /ˌsoʃəˈbɪlətɪ/ n [U].

so·cial /ˈsəʊʃl/ /ˈsoʃəl/ adj 1(of animals, etc) living in groups, not separately: (指动物等) 群居的; 营社会生活的: ~ ants/wasps. 群居的蚂蚁(黄蜂). Man is

a ~ animal. 人是群居的动物. 2 of people living in communities; of relations between persons and communities: 群居之人的; 社区的; 人与社区间之关系的: ~ customs/reforms/welfare. 社会习俗,福利). ,S~ 'Democrat, (in politics) person who wishes society to move, by peaceful, democratic changes, to a system of socialism. (政治)社会民主主义者,社会民主党员. se'curity, government provisions for helping people who are unemployed, ill, disabled, etc: 社会救济; 社会福利(政府对失业,生病,残疾等的人所作的救济): The family is on ~ security, receiving such help. 这个家庭领社会救济金. (the) ,~ 'services n pl organized government service providing help and advice (eg in matters of health, housing, mental illness, law-breaking) to people who are in need or trouble. 社会服务(政府对人民之协助, 如解决健康、房屋、精神病、违法等问题). '~-**work** n [U] the profession of those who work in the ~ services. 社会服务. '~ **worker** n person who works in the ~ services. 社会服务者. 3 of in society: 社会的; 社会上的: one's ~ equals, persons of the same class as oneself in society; 同一阶层者; 社会地位相当的人; ~ advancement, improvement of one's position in society; 个人社会地位的提高; ~ climbers, persons trying to obtain ~ advancement. 谋求提高社会地位者. 4 for companionship: 社交的; 交谊的: a '~ club; 联谊会; spend a ~ evening, in the company of friends. 与友人度过一个晚上. 5 = sociable. □ n ~ gathering, party, organized by a club. (某团体的)交谊会; 联欢会. ~·**ly** /-ʃəlɪ/ /-ʃəlɪ/ adv

so·cial·ism /ˈsəʊʃəlɪzəm/ /ˈsoʃəlˌɪzəm/ n [U] 社会义. **so·cial·ist** n supporter of, believer in ~. 社会主义者. □ adj of, tending towards, ~: 社会主义的; 趋向社会主义的: a Socialist Party, political party which advocates and works for ~. 社会党. **so·cial·ize** /-aɪz/ /-aɪz/ vt [VP6A] make social(1) or socialist; govern on socialist principles. 使社会主义化; 以社会主义的原则治理. **socialized medicine**, (US) the provision of free medical services by the Government. (美) 社会医疗 (政府提供的免费医疗). **so·cial·iz·ation** /ˌsəʊʃəlaɪˈzeɪʃn US: -lɪˈz-/ /ˌsoʃəlɪˈzeɪʃən/ n

so·cial·ite /ˈsəʊʃəlaɪt/ /ˈsoʃəˌlaɪt/ n (colloq) person prominent in fashionable society. (口)上流社会人士; 名流; 闻人.

so·ciety /səˈsaɪətɪ/ /səˈsaɪətɪ/ n(pl -**ties**) 1 [U] social way of living; customs, etc of a civilized community; system whereby people live together in organized communities: 群体生活; 文明社会的习俗; 社会体制: a danger to ~, person, idea, etc that endangers the bodily or moral welfare of a community: 社会之患 (危害社会人群身心福利的人、观念等); pests of ~, persons who prey on the community and contribute nothing to its welfare. 社会的害虫. 2 [C] social community: 社会: modern industrial societies; 近代工业社会; certain grouping of humanity, eg Western Christendom, the people of Islam. 人类集团 (如西方基督教世界, 伊斯兰教教徒). 3 [U] company; companionship: 友伴;友谊; 交际: spend an evening in the ~ of one's friends. 和朋友们聚会度过一个晚上. 4 [U] people of fashion or distinction in a place, district, country, etc; the upper classes: (一个地方、地区、国家等的)社会名流;上流社会(人士): leaders of ~; 社会的领袖; high(ie the most wealthy, influential, etc) ~; 上流社会人士(有钱有势者); the customs of polite ~; 上流社会的习俗;(attrib)(用作定语)a '~ man/woman; 上流社会的男子(女士); ~ weddings, of fashionable persons; 名流们的婚礼; ~ gossip/news, as printed in newspapers, etc. 上流社会的琐闻(新闻). 5 [C] organization of persons formed with a purpose; club; association: (为某种目的组成的)会;社;团体;协会: the school de'bating ~; 学校里的辩论社; a co'operative ~; 合作社; the S~ of Friends. 教友会(基督教一支派).

socio- /ˌsəʊsɪəʊ-; /ˌsosɪo/ pref of society or sociology.

表示'社会'或'社会学'。

so·ci·ol·ogy /ˌsəʊsɪˈɒlədʒɪ; ˌsoʃɪˈɑlədʒɪ/ n [U] science of the nature and growth of society and social behaviour. 社会学(研究社会本质, 社会发展及社会行为之学科)。 **so·ci·ol·ogist** /-dʒɪst; -dʒɪst/ n student of, expert in ~. 社会学家; 社会学者。 **so·cio·logi·cal** /ˌsəʊsɪəˈlɒdʒɪkl; ˌsoʃɪəˈlɑdʒɪkl/ adj of ~. 社会学的。 **so·cio·logi·cally** /-klɪ; -klɪ/ adv

sock /sɒk; sɑk/ n 1 (often 常作 **pair of ~s**) short stocking not reaching the knee. 短袜。 **pull one's ~s up,** (colloq) improve oneself, one's performance. (口)改进自己; 改进自己的成绩。 **put a ~ in it,** (sl) be quiet; stop speaking. (俚)安静; 停止说话。 2 loose sole used inside a shoe. (鞋子里面的)活动衬垫。 ⇨ **wind~ at wind¹(8).**

sock² /sɒk; sɑk/ n (sl) blow given with the fist or sth thrown: (俚)用拳头或投掷物的打击; 拳击; 掷击: Give him a ~ on the jaw! Hit him hard! 在(他)下颚上猛击一拳!(用力揍他!) □ vt [VP6A, 15A] (sl) give (sb) such a blow: (俚)用拳头或投掷物打(某人); 拳打; 掷击: S~ him on the jaw! 在下颚上给他一拳! S~ a brick at him! 丢砖头砸他! S~ it to him! 丢(那东西)过去打他! □ adv (sl) squarely: (俚)正对地; 不偏不倚地: (hit sb) ~ in the eye. (打)在(某人的)眼睛上。

socket /ˈsɒkɪt; ˈsɑkɪt/ n natural or artificial hollow into which sth fits or in which sth turns: 承物凹处; 承口; 插座; 窝; 孔: the 'eye-~; 眼窝; a ~ for an electric light bulb/a candle. 电灯泡座(蜡烛承座)。

So·cratic /səˈkrætɪk US: soʊ-; soˈkrætɪk/ adj characteristic of Socrates, the Greek philosopher. (希腊哲学家)苏格拉底的; 有苏格拉底特色的。 **the ~ method,** examining an idea, theory, etc by question and answer between two or more people. 苏格拉底法; 问答法; 对话法。

sod¹ /sɒd; sɑd/ n [U] upper layer of grassland including the grass with its roots and earth; 草地; 草皮; 草泥; square or oblong piece of this pared off; turf. 草地; 草皮; 草泥。

sod² /sɒd; sɑd/ n ⚠ (vulgar term of abuse, used in annoyance and sudden anger): (俚)用于气愤或突然发怒时之粗鄙的骂人语)畜生: You sod! 你这畜生! □ vi ⚠ **Sod it!** Damn(it)! (俚)畜生! 他妈的! **Sod off!** Go away! 滚开! **sod·ding** attrib adj ⚠ (used as an intensive) (俚)(用以加强语气) What a sodding mess! 真他妈的乱七八糟!

soda /ˈsəʊdə; ˈsodə/ n [U] common chemical substance used in soap-making; glass manufacture, etc: 苏打; 碳酸钠(用以制肥皂、玻璃等): 'washing-~(sodium carbonate, **Na₂CO₃**), used for softening water, etc(洗涤用苏打(用以使水软化等); 'baking-~(sodium bicarbonate, **NaHCO₃**), used in cooking, 烹调用苏打; 小苏打。 '~-**biscuit**/-**cracker** n biscuit from dough containing baking-~ and sour milk. 苏打饼干(用苏打调用苏打及酸奶者)。 '~-**fountain** n counter, bar, from which ~-water, ices, etc are served. 苏打泉(供应汽水、冰等的柜台)。 '~-**pop** (US colloq) soft drink of ~-water, flavoured sometimes with ice-cream. (美口)苏打冷饮(一种汽水, 有时加冰淇淋以增味)。 '~-**water** n water charged with carbon dioxide gas to make it bubble. 苏打水; 汽水。

sod·den /ˈsɒdn; ˈsɑdn/ adj 1 soaked through: 浸透的; 泡透的; 水渍的: clothes ~ with rain. 为雨水浸透的衣服。 2 (of bread, etc) heavy and doughlike; moist or sticky because undercooked. (指面包等)没发好而似面团的;(因未烘熟而)粘湿的。 3(often 常作 'drink-~) stupid through too much drinking of alcoholic liquor. (因嗜酒而变成)迟钝的; 痴呆的。

so·dium /ˈsəʊdɪəm; ˈsodɪəm/ n [U] silver-white metal (symbol **Na**) occurring naturally only in compounds: 钠(银白色金属, 符号为 Na, 自然界仅存其化合物); ~ chloride, (**NaCl**) common salt. 氯化钠; 食盐(分子式为 NaCl)。 ⇨ **soda.**

sod·omy /ˈsɒdəmɪ; ˈsɑdəmɪ/ n [U] anal sexual intercourse, esp between males. (尤指男性)鸡奸; 兽奸; 同性态。 **sod·om·ite** /ˈsɒdəmaɪt; ˈsɑdəmˌaɪt/ n person

practising ~. 鸡奸者; 兽奸者; 同性恋者。

so·ever /səʊˈevə(r); soˈevə/ suff (formal, used with relative pronouns, adv and adj) any kind or sort of: (正式用语, 与关系代词, 副词及形容词连用)任何种类; 任何程度; 无论: 'how ~, 无论如何; 'who ~, 无论是谁, 'what ~. 无论是什么。

sofa /ˈsəʊfə; ˈsofə/ n long seat with raised ends and back, on which several persons can sit or one person can lie. 沙发。

soft /sɒft US: sɔ:ft; sɔft/ adj 1 (opp of hard) (为 hard 之反义词) changing shape easily when pressed not resisting pressure: 软的; 柔软的: ~ soil/ground/mud. 软土(地, 泥)。 Warm butter is ~. 温热的奶油是软的。 She likes a ~ pillow and a hard mattress. 她喜欢软的枕头, 硬的床垫。 a ~ landing, (eg of a spacecraft on the moon) one that avoids damage or destruction. 徐缓的着陆(如太空船降落月球表面的着陆, 以避免损坏或破坏)。 Hence, 由此产生, ~-**land** vi land in this way. 徐缓(或缓慢)着陆。 2 (of surfaces) smooth and delicate: (指表面)软滑的; 细嫩的; 细软的: as ~ as velvet; 象天鹅绒一般细软的; ~ fur; 软滑的毛皮; ~ furnishings, curtains, hangings, etc; 软滑的室内陈设(帷幔、帘幕等); ~ goods, textiles. 纺织品。 3 (of light, colours) opp of glaring; restful to the eyes: (指光, 颜色)不刺目的; 柔和的: lampshades that give a ~ light. 使光线柔和的灯罩。 4 (of sounds) subdued; not loud: (指声音)轻柔的; 放低的: ~ music; 轻柔的音乐; ~ murmurs/whispers; 低声的呢喃(耳语); in a ~ voice. 轻声地。 5 (of outlines) indistinct. (指轮廓)不明显的。 6 (of answers, words, etc) mild; gentle; intended to please: (指答语, 话等)温和的; 文雅的; 悦人的: a ~ answer; 温和的回答; have a ~ tongue. 讲话温文的。 7 (of the air, weather) mild: (指空气, 气候)温和的; 宜人的: a ~ breeze/wind; 和风; ~ weather. 温和的气候。 8 (of water) free from mineral salts and therefore good for washing: (指水)软性的; 不含矿盐的(宜于洗涤): as ~ as rainwater. 雨水一般不含矿盐的。 9 (of certain sounds) not a plosive: (指某些语音)软音的: C is ~ in 'city' and hard in 'cat'. 在 city 中, C 为软音; 在 cat 中, C 为硬音。 G is ~ in 'gin' and hard in 'get'. 在 gin 中, G 为软音; 在 get 中, G 为硬音。 10 easy: 容易的; 轻松的: (指空气, 气候) have a ~ job, (sl) an easy, well-paid job; business deal with easily earned money. (俚)担任轻松而待遇优厚的工作(好差使); 做一笔容易赚钱的买卖。 11 feeble; lacking in strength and determination: 软弱的; 意志不坚的: muscles that have got ~ through lack of exercise; 因缺乏运动而变得松软的肌肉; a ~ generation, eg of young people 柔弱的一代(例如年轻人)。 12 sympathetic; considerate: 有同情心的; 心软的; 体谅的: have a ~ heart. 有一副软心肠。 **have a ~ spot for sb,** a liking or fondness for him. 偏爱某人。 13 (colloq) feeble-minded: (口)痴愚的; 疯癫的: He's not as ~ as he looks. 他并不象他的外貌那样痴愚。 He's gone ~. 他变得疯疯癫癫。 Jack is ~ (= sentimentally silly) about Anne. 杰克痴恋着安妮。 14 (various uses; compounds) (其他用法; 复合词), ~ '**boiled** adj (of eggs) boiled so that the egg is ~. (指蛋)煮得半熟的。 ~ '**coal** n coal that burns with yellow, smoky flames. 烟煤; 软煤。 ~ '**currency** n one that is not convertible to gold, or into certain other currencies which are more in demand. 软性货币(不能兑换为黄金或某些其他更为人所需要之货币者)。 ,~ **drink** n [C] cold, sweet and non-alcoholic drink, eg fruit juice (often charged with gas). 软饮料(不含酒精的冷饮, 如果汁或带果汁味的汽水等)。 '~ **drug** n [C] drug (eg marijuana) that is mildly habit-forming (as opposed to a hard drug, eg heroin, which is addictive). 软性毒品; 软性麻醉药(如大麻烟, 毒瘾较缓和, 与毒瘾剧烈的海洛英等硬性毒品相对)。 ~-'**footed** adj (of a person) moving with quiet, gentle steps. (指人)步履轻盈的。 ,~-'**headed** adj idiotic; foolish. 笨的; 愚蠢的。 ,~-'**hearted** adj sympathetic; kind. 软心肠的; 有同情心的;

仁慈的。 **~ option** *n* alternative which is thought to involve little work. 比较轻松的选择；比较容易做的工作。 **,~·'palate** *n* back part of the roof of the mouth. 软颚 (口腔的后上部)。 **,~·'pedal** *vi*, *vt* play (music, the piano) with the ~ pedal down; (fig) make (a statement, etc) less definite or confident. 减弱音量演奏(音乐,钢琴);(喻)使(陈述等)变得较不肯定或较不明确。 **'~ soap** *n* semi-liquid soap made with potash; (fig) flattery. 软皂 (含钾碱的半流质肥皂)；(喻)谄媚。 **'~soap** *vt* flatter. 谄媚。 **,~·'solder** *n* kinds of solder used for easily fusible metal. 软焊料；软焊锡。 **,~·'solder** *vt* solder with these soft kinds. 以软焊料焊接。 **,~·'spoken** *adj* having a gentle voice; saying pleasant, friendly things. 声音柔和的；讲话动听的。 **'~·ware** *n* data, programmes, etc not forming parts of a computer but used for its operation. 软件；软体；软品(电脑作业系统,包括资料,计算程式等,不包括计算机之机件)。 ⇨ **hardware** at **hard¹**(9). **,~·'witted** *adj* foolish. 愚蠢的。 **'~-wood** *n* [C, U] (kinds of) easily sawn wood such as pine and other coniferous trees. 软木料；软材(如针叶树材)。 **-ish** /-ɪʃ; -ˌɪʃ/ *adj* somewhat ~. 略软的。 **~·ly** *adv* in a ~ manner: 软地；柔软地；轻轻地： *tread/speak ~ly.* 轻轻地走(温和或说话)。 *She ~ly pressed his hand.* 她轻握他的手。 **~·ness** /'~·n **~y** *n* stupid person; feeble person. 愚蠢的人；软弱的人。

sof·ten /'sɒfn US: 'sɔːfn; 'sɔfən/ *vt*, *vi* [VP6A, 2A] make or become soft: (使)变软；(使)变温和、柔和、软弱： *curtains that ~ the light;* 使光线柔和的窗帘； *people who are ~ed by luxurious living.* 由于生活奢侈而变得意志消沉的人们。 **~ sb up,** weaken (enemy positions) by shelling, bombing, etc; make (persons) unable or less able to resist (attack, salesmanship, etc). 借轰击、轰炸等减弱敌人的防卫力；说服某人或使某人不再顽强抗拒(批评、推销等)。 **~er** *n* [C] sth used to ~, esp a chemical substance (or apparatus using this) for ~ing hard water. 软化剂；软水剂；硬水软化器。

soggy /'sɒgɪ; 'sɑgɪ/ *adj* (-ier, -iest) (esp of ground) heavy with water. (尤指地面)湿润的；湿透的。 **sog·gi·ness** *n*

soh /səʊ; so/ *n* ⇨ **so⁴**.

Soho /'səʊhəʊ; 'soho/ *n* district in the West End of London noted for its foreign restaurants, food shops and night clubs. 苏和区(伦敦西区之一地区,以其外国餐馆、食品及夜总会出名)。

soi·gné /'swɑːnjeɪ US: swɑːˈnjeɪ, swɑˈnje/ *adj* (F) (fem 阴性作 **-née**) (of a person's way of dressing, etc) carefully finished or arranged, with attention to detail. (法)(指衣着等)非常考究的。

soil /sɔɪl; sɔɪl/ *n* [C, U] **1** ground; earth, esp the upper layer of earth in which plants, trees, etc grow: 土地；土壤；地表层(植物、树木等生长之处)： *good/ poor/alluvial/sandy, etc ~;* 沃(瘠,冲积,砂质等)土； *clay ~s.* 粘土。 **'~-pipe** *n* pipe from a water-closet pan to the drains. 排粪管(自抽水马桶至下水道的管道)。 **2** *one's native ~,* one's native country; 故国；故土； *a man of the ~,* one who works on the land (and is devoted to it). 农民；热爱农作的人。 □ *vt*, *vi* **1** [VP6A] make dirty: 弄脏；弄污： *~ed linen/underwear, etc,* that has been used and is to be laundered. (用过待洗的)衣服(内衣等)。 *He refused to ~ his hands, refused to do dirty work.* 他不肯弄脏手(不做肮脏工作)。 **2** [VP2A, C] admit of being ~ed: 可被弄脏；容易弄脏； 易于变污： *material that ~s easily,* is easily ~ed. 容易脏的料子。

soi·rée /'swɑːreɪ US: swɑːˈreɪ, swɑ're/ *n* social gathering in the evening, esp for music, conversation, etc, and often to help the aims of a society(5). (音乐,聊天等)晚会(往往用以促成社团预定的目标)。

so·journ /'sɒdʒɜːn US: səʊ'dʒɜːn; so'dʒɜːn/ *vi* [VP 2C], *n* (liter) (make a) stay (*with* sb, *at* or *in*) for a time. (文)逗留；寄居(与 with sb, at 或 in 连用)。 **~er** *n*

sol /sɒl; sɑl/ *n* ⇨ **so⁴**.

Sol /sɒl; sɑl/ *n* (hum) (often 常作 *old Sol*) the sun. (谐)太阳。

sol·ace /'sɒlɪs; 'sɑlɪs/ *n* [C, U] (that which gives) comfort or relief (when one is in trouble or pain): (苦难或痛苦时的)慰藉；安慰；安慰物；慰藉物： *The invalid found ~ in music.* 那病人从音乐中获得安慰。 □ *vt* [VP6A, 15A] give ~ to: 安慰；慰藉： *The unhappy man ~d himself with whisky.* 那忧伤的人以威士忌酒洗愁。

so·lar /'səʊlə(r); 'solɚ/ *adj* of the sun. 太阳的；与太阳有关的。 **a ~ cell,** device (as used in satellites) which converts the energy of sunlight into electric energy. 太阳电池(转太阳光为电能的设计,如用于人造卫星的)。 **the '~ system,** the sun and the planets which revolve round it. 太阳系(太阳与绕行的诸行星)。 **~ 'plexus** /'pleksəs; 'plɛksəs/ network of nerves at the pit of the stomach. 腹腔神经丛(在心窝处)。 **the ~ year,** time occupied by the earth to complete one revolution round the sun, about 365 days, 5 hours, 48 minutes and 46 seconds. 太阳年(地球绕太阳一周所需的时间,为365天5时48分46秒)。

so·larium /səʊ'leərɪəm; so'lɛrɪəm/ *n* (*pl* **-ria** /-rɪə; -rɪə/) place enclosed with glass for enjoyment of the sun's rays, esp one for the medical use of sunlight. 日光浴室(享受日光的玻璃房间,尤指供医疗用者)。

sold /səʊld; sold/ *pt, pp* of **sell**.

sol·der /'sɒldə(r) US: 'sɒdər; 'sadɚ/ *n* [U] easily melted alloy used, when melted, to join harder metals, wires, etc. 焊料(焊接较坚硬金属、金属线等的易熔合金)。 □ *vt* [VP6A, 15A, B] join with ~. 焊接。 **'~ing-iron** *n* tool used for this work. 烙铁；焊铁(焊接用的工具)。

sol·dier /'səʊldʒə(r); 'soldʒɚ/ *n* member of an army: (陆军)军人；士兵： *three ~s, two sailors and one civilian.* 三个(陆军)士兵,两个海员及一个平民。 *The children were playing at ~s.* 孩子们在扮演军人。 **private ~,** one who is not a commissioned or non-commissioned officer. 士兵；兵。 **~ of fortune,** man who will take service under any State or person who will hire him; mercenary. 雇佣兵(价价替任何国家或个人作战的军人)。 □ *vi* [VP 2A] serve as a ~: 当兵；(主要用于)从军。 **~ on/ enjoy ~ing;** 从军； *be tired of ~ing.* 厌倦或马生涯。 **~ on,** continue bravely with one's work, etc in the face of difficulties. (遭遇困难而)勇敢地继续工作。 **~·ly,** **'~-like** *adj* like a ~; smart; brave. 似军人的；英俊的；帅的；勇敢的。 **~y** *n* (*sing* only, *collective n*) ~s of a specified character: (仅用单数形,为集合名词)某种军人； 军队： *the undisciplined ~y;* 不守纪律的军队； *brutal, licentious ~y.* 残暴放肆的军队。

sole¹ /səʊl; sol/ *n* flat sea-fish with a delicate flavour. 鲽(一种扁平的海水鱼,味美)。

sole² /səʊl; sol/ *n* under surface of a human foot, or of a sock, shoe, etc, other than the heel. (人足、袜等的)底部；脚掌；鞋底；袜底。 □ *vt* [VP6A] put a ~ on (a shoe, etc): 上(鞋等的)底；配底于(鞋等)： *send a pair of shoes to be ~d and heeled.* 送一双鞋去换底和补后跟。 **-soled** *suff* (with *n* or *adj* prefixed) (加于名词或形容词之后)*rubber-~d boots;* 橡皮底的靴子； *thin-~d shoes.* 薄底鞋。

sole³ /səʊl; sol/ *adj* **1** one and only; single: 唯一的；独一的；仅有的： *the ~ cause of the accident.* 失事的唯一原因。 **2** restricted to one person, company, etc: (某人或某公司等)专用的；独占的： *We have the ~ right of selling the article.* 我们有独家出售该物的权利。 **~·ly** *adv* alone; only: 单独；仅仅；唯一： *~ly responsible;* 单独负责的； *~ly because of you.* 仅仅为了你。

sol·ecism /'sɒlɪsɪzəm; 'salə,sɪzəm/ *n* [C] error in the use of language; offence against good manners; mistake in etiquette. 使用语言错误；语法错误；举止不当；失礼。

sol·emn /'sɒləm; 'saləm/ *adj* **1** performed with

religious or other ceremony; causing deep thought or respect: 以宗教或其他仪式举行的; 令人深思或崇敬的; 神圣的; 合仪式的; 庄严的: a ～ silence as the coffin was carried out of the church; 棺材抬出教堂时一种肃穆的沉寂; a ～ duty; 庄严的职责; ～ music; 肃穆的音乐; a ～ oath, grave and important. 庄严的誓言. **2** serious-looking; grave: 表情严肃的; 沉重的: ～ faces; 阴沉的面孔; look as ～ as a judge. 显得象法官殷的严肃。**～·ly** adv →**ness** n

sol·em·nity /səˈlemnəti; səˈlɛmnətɪ/ n (pl **-ties**) **1** [U] seriousness; gravity. 庄重; 严肃. **2** [U] (but also pl) solemn ceremony: (但可用复数形)庄严的仪式: The Queen was crowned with all ∼/with all the proper solemnities. 女王在极为庄严的仪式中加冕(女王在适当的仪式中加冕)。

sol·em·nize /ˈsɒləmnaɪz; ˈsɑləmˌnaɪz/ vt [VP6A] perform (a religious ceremony, esp a wedding) with the usual rites; make solemn. 举行(宗教仪式); 举行(宗教婚礼); 使庄重; 使严肃. **sol·em·niz·ation** /ˌsɒləmnaɪˈzeɪʃn US: -nɪˈz-; ˌsɑləmnɪˈzeʃən/ n [U].

sol-fa /ˌsɒlˈfɑː; US: ˌsəʊl; ˌsolˈfɑ/ n = tonic ～, ⇨ tonic.

sol·icit /səˈlɪsɪt; səˈlɪsɪt/ vt, vi **1** [VP6A, 14] ～ sb (for sth), ask (for) earnestly; make requests (for): 请求; 乞求: Both the candidates ～ed (me for) my vote. 两位候选人都向我拉票. The tradesmen are all ～ing us for our custom, asking us to deal with them. 那些商人都向我们拉生意. **2** [VP6A, 2A] (of a prostitute) make an immoral sexual offer (to), esp in a public place: (指妓女)在公开场所作出(指): I was openly ～ed at Piccadilly Circus. 我在皮卡迪利广场遇到妓女公开向我兜揽生意. **sol·ici·ta·tion** /səˌlɪsɪˈteɪʃn; səˌlɪsəˈteʃən/ n [U] →ing; [C] instance or occasion of this. 恳求; 恳请; [C] 恳求; (妓女之)拉客.

sol·ici·tor /səˈlɪsɪtə(r); səˈlɪsətə/ n **1** (GB) lawyer who prepares legal documents, eg wills, sale of land or buildings, advises clients on legal matters, and speaks on their behalf in lower courts. (英)律师. ⇨ **advocate**, **attorney**, **barrister**. So,licitor-'General, one of the principal law officers in the British Government, advising on legal matters. 英国政府中之主要法律官员之一(为法律事务的顾问); 副检查长。**2** (US) person who solicits trade, support, etc; canvasser (eg for votes). (美)招揽生意, 恳求支持等的人; 游说者(如拉票者)。

sol·ici·tous /səˈlɪsɪtəs; səˈlɪsətəs/ adj ～ (for/about sth/sb); ～ (to do sth), anxious, concerned about (sb's welfare, etc) or to help/serve sb: 焦虑的; 悬虑的; 热心的; 切望(助人等)的; 渴望(某人福利等)的: ～ to please; 渴望让人喜欢; ～ for her comfort. 关心她的安适。**～·ly** adv **sol·ici·tude** /səˈlɪsɪtjuːd US: -tuːd; səˈlɪsəˌtjud/ n [U] being ～; concern or anxiety: 焦虑; 悬虑; 切望; 关心: my deep solicitude for your welfare. 我深深关心你的福利。

solid /ˈsɒlɪd; ˈsɑlɪd/ adj **1** not in the form of a liquid or gas: 固体的; 非液体或气体的: ～ fuels, eg coal, wood; 固体燃料; ～-fuelled rockets. 固体燃料火箭. When water freezes and becomes ～, we call it ice. 水冻结变成固体时, 我们称之为冰. **～-state** adj (of electronic devices) totally transistorized, ie without valves: (指电子装置)全晶体的: a ～-state amplifier. 全晶体扩大器. **2** compact; substantial; heavy: 致密的; 结实的; 丰富的; 难消化的: a man with good ～ flesh on him; 一个肌肉结实的男人; ～ food, not slops. 食物(不是流质的). **3** without holes or spaces; not hollow: 实心的; 无孔的; 无空隙的: a ～ sphere. 实心球. **4** of strong or firm material or construction; able to support weight or resist pressure: 坚固的; 可支持重物的; 可抵抗压力的: ～ buildings/furniture; 坚固的建筑物(家具); build on ～ foundations; 在坚实的地基上建筑; a man of ～ build; 体格结实的人; on ～ ground; 在坚实的地面上; steps cut in the ～ rock. 在坚石上凿出的台阶. **5** that can be depended on: 可靠的; 可依赖的: ～ arguments;

理由充分的论点; a ～ (= financially sound) business firm; 信用可靠的商家; a man of ～ character. 性格稳定的人. **6** alike all through; of the same substance throughout: 纯的; 全部为同一物质的; 全部一样的: made of ～ gold. 纯金制成. **7** unanimous; undivided: 一致的; 不分歧的: We are ～ for peace. 我们一致拥护和平. The miners are ～ on this issue. 矿工们对此一争端立场一致. There was a ～ vote in favour of the proposal. 该提案获全体一致通过. **8** continuous; without a break: 继续不断的; 无间断的: wait for a ～ hour; 整整等了一个小时; sleep ten ～ hours/ten hours ～. 连续睡了十小时. **9** (maths) having length, breadth and thickness: (数学)立体的; 立方体的: a ～ figure, eg a cube; 立体图形(立立方体); ～ geometry, of ～, not plane, figure. 立体几何。□ n [C] **1** body or substance which is ～, not a liquid or a gas. 固体. **2** (geom) figure of three dimensions. (几何)立体(图)形。**～·ly** adv **sol·id·ity** /səˈlɪdəti; səˈlɪdətɪ/, **～·ness** nn [U] quality of being ～: 固体性; 可靠性; 坚固; 致密: the ～ity of a building/ argument, etc. 建筑物的坚固(论点之可靠性)。

soli·dar·ity /ˌsɒlɪˈdærəti; ˌsɑləˈdærətɪ/ n [U] unity resulting from common interests or feelings: (因共同利益或感情所产生的)团结; 一致: national ～ in the face of danger. 面临危难时全国团结一致。

sol·id·ify /səˈlɪdɪfaɪ; səˈlɪdəˌfaɪ/ vt, vi (pt, pp -**fied**) [VP6A, 2A] make or become solid, hard or firm. (使)变凝固; (使)变凝结; (使)变一致。**sol·idi·fi·ca·tion** /səˌlɪdɪfɪˈkeɪʃn; səˌlɪdəfəˈkeʃən/ n

sol·il·oquy /səˈlɪləkwɪ; səˈlɪləkwɪ/ n (pl -**quies**) [C, U] (instance of) speaking one's thoughts aloud; (in drama) speech in which a character speaks his thoughts without addressing a listener. 自言自语; (戏剧)独白. **sol·il·oquize** /səˈlɪləkwaɪz; səˈlɪləˌkwaɪz/ vi [VP2A] talk to oneself; think aloud. 自言自语; 独语; 独白。

sol·ip·sism /ˈsɒlɪpsɪzəm; ˈsɑlɪpˌsɪzm/ n (metaphysics) theory that one can have knowledge only of the self. (形而上学)唯我论(人的知识止于认识自己的理论)。

soli·taire /ˌsɒlɪˈteə(r); ˈsɑləˌter/ n **1** (ornament such as an earring having a) single gem or jewel. 独粒宝石; 镶嵌独粒宝石的饰物(如耳环). **2** (also called 亦称 patience) kinds of card-game for one player. 单人纸牌戏.

soli·tary /ˈsɒlɪtrɪ US: -terɪ; ˈsɑləˌterɪ/ adj **1** (living) alone; without companions; lonely: 独居的; 无伴的; 孤独的: a ～ life; 独居的生活; a ～ walk. 独自散步. **～ confinement**, prison punishment by which a person is isolated in a separate cell. 隔离拘禁(监狱的一种惩罚). in ～, in ～ confinement. 受隔离拘禁. **2** only one: 只有一个的; 唯一的: not a ～ instance of sth, not even one instance of it. 一个例子都没有. **3** seldom visited: 人迹罕到的; 偏僻的: a ～ valley. 人迹罕到的山谷. **soli·tar·ily** /ˈsɒlɪtrəlɪ US: ˌsɒlɪˈteəlɪ; ˈsɑləˌterəlɪ/ adv

soli·tude /ˈsɒlɪtjuːd US: -tuːd; ˈsɑləˌtjud/ n **1** [U] being without companions; solitary state: 独居; 孤独; 单独: live in ～; 独居; not fond of ～. 不喜孤独. **2** [C] lonely place: 人迹罕到之处; 荒僻的地方: spend six months in the ～s of the Antarctic. 在人迹罕到的南极待了六个月.

solo /ˈsəʊləʊ; ˈsolo/ n (pl -**s** /-ləʊz; -loz/) **1** piece of music (to be) performed by one person: 独奏曲; 独唱曲: a violin/piano ～. 小提琴(钢琴)独奏曲. **2** any performance by one person: 任何单独表演; 单独作业; 单独执行任务: (as adv) (作副词用) fly ～; 单独飞行; (attrib) (用作定语) his first ～ flight. 他的首次单独飞行. **3** [U] kind of whist in which one player opposes others. 一种惠斯特纸牌戏(由一人对抗其余的人). **'～·ist** /-ɪst; -ɪst/ n person who gives a ～(1). 独奏者; 独奏者.

So·lon /ˈsəʊlɒn; ˈsolən/ n (the name of an Athenian lawgiver, hence) wise legislator. (梭伦, 古雅典立法者之名, 由此产生)贤明的立法者。

sol·stice /'sɒlstɪs; 'sɑlstɪs/ n [C] either time (*summer* ~, about 21 June; *winter* ~, about 22 Dec) at which the sun is farthest N or S of the equator. 至(指冬至或夏至(太阳离赤道南北最远之时), 北半球夏至约在六月二十一日; 冬至约在十二月二十二日)。

sol·uble /'sɒljʊbl; 'sɑljəbl/ *adj* **1** ~ (*in*), that can be dissolved. 可溶解的。 **2** (= solvable) that can be solved or explained. 可解决的; 可解释的。 **solu·bil·ity** /ˌsɒljʊ'bɪlətɪ; ˌsɑljə'bɪlətɪ/ n

sol·ution /sə'lu:ʃn; sə'ljuʃən/ n **1** [C] ~ (*to/for/of*), answer (to a question, etc); way of dealing with a difficulty: (问题的)解答; (困难的)解决方法或方式: *Recourse to arms is not the best ~ to a quarrel between two countries.* 诉诸武力不是两国间解决争端的最好办法。 *Might economy be the ~ to/for/of your financial troubles?* 节约能解决你财务方面的困难吗? **2** [U] process of finding an answer or explanation: 寻求解答或解释的过程或途径: *problems that defy ~, cannot be solved.* 无法解决的问题。 **3** [U] process of dissolving a solid or a gas in liquid: 溶解; 溶解过程: *the ~ of sugar in tea.* 糖在茶中溶解。 **4** [C, U] liquid that results from this process: 溶液: *a ~ of salt in water.* 盐水; 盐的水溶液。

solve /sɒlv; sɑlv/ *vt* [VP6A] find the answer to (a problem, etc): 解答(问题等): ~ *a crossword puzzle/an equation;* 解答纵横字谜(方程式); find a way out of a difficulty, etc: 解决(困难等): *Help me to ~ my financial troubles.* 帮助我解决我的经济困难。 **solv·able** /-əbl; -əbl/ *adj* that can be ~d or explained. 可解决的; 可解释的。

sol·vent /'sɒlvənt; 'sɑlvənt/ *adj* **1** of the power of dissolving or forming a solution: 溶解力的: *the ~ action of water.* 水的溶解作用。 **2** having money enough to meet one's debts. 能偿还债务的。 □ n [C] substance (usu a liquid) able to dissolve another substance (usu specified): 溶剂; 溶媒(通常为一液体): *grease* ~, eg petrol. 油脂溶剂(如汽油)。 **sol·vency** /-nsɪ; -nsɪ/ [U] being ~(2). 有偿债力。

so·matic /səʊ'mætɪk; soʊ'mætɪk/ *adj* of the body. 身体的。

sombre (US = **som·ber**) /'sɒmbə(r); 'sɑmbɚ/ *adj* dark-coloured; gloomy; dismal: 暗色的; 忧郁的; 阴沉的; 惨淡的: *a ~ January day;* 正月某一个阴沉的日子; ~ *clothes;* 暗色的衣服; *a ~ picture of the future of mankind.* 人类未来的惨淡写照(或远景)。 ~**·ly** *adv* ~**·ness** n

som·brero /sɒm'breərəʊ; sɑm'brero/ n (*pl* ~s /-rəʊz; -roz/) broad-brimmed hat (as worn in Latin American countries). (拉丁美洲等国人所戴的)阔边帽。

some¹ /sʌm; sʌm; *weak form* səm; səm, *used only in the adjectival sense of* 'consisting of an undefined amount or number of' 只用于形容词, 表示某一不确定的数量/ *adj* **1** (used in affirm sentences; usually replaced by *any* in interr and neg sentences, in conditional clauses, and in sentences where doubt or negation is implied. *S~* and *any* are used with material *nn* to indicate an amount or quantity that is either unknown or not given, with abstract *nn* to indicate a certain degree, and with *pl* common *nn* to indicate a certain number (three or more). *S~* and *any* are *pl* equivalents of the numeral article *a/an* (⇨ *a²*), of numeral *one*, and the *indef pron* 'one'): (用于肯定句中; 在间句与否定句中, 条件从句中, 及含示怀疑或否定的句中, 通常用 *any* 代替。 *Some* 及 *any* 与物质名词连用时, 表示未知或未指明的总额或分量, 与抽象名词连用时, 表示某种程度, 与复数普通名词连用时, 表示某一数目(三个或三个以上)。 *Some* 及 *any* 系数词冠词 *a/an*, 数字 *one*, 以及不定代词 *one* 的复数用语): *Please give me ~ milk.* 请给我一些牛奶。 Cf 参较 *Have you any sugar?* 你有没有糖? *We haven't any tea.* 我们没有茶了。 *There are ~ children outside.* 外面有几个小孩。 Cf 参较 *There is a child outside.* 外面有一个小孩。 *They haven't any children.* 他

们没有小孩。 *Are there any stamps in that drawer?* 那个抽屉里有邮票吗? *I wonder whether Mr Black has any flowers in his garden.* 我不知道布莱克先生的花园里有没有花。 *I doubt whether there are any flowers in Mr Green's garden.* 我怀疑格林先生的花园里有没有花。 *I don't like a garden without any flowers in it.* 我不喜欢没有花的花园。 *There are scarcely/hardly any flowers in this garden.* 这个花园里很少(简直没有)花。 *S~* (= *S~* people) *say that* .... 有些人说.... 。 **2** (*S~* is used in sentences that are interr in form if the speaker expects, or wishes to suggest, an affirm answer): (如果问话者期待或希望对方作件肯定答复时, some 亦用于问句中): *Aren't there ~ stamps in that drawer?* 那抽屉里不是有几张邮票吗? Cf 参较 *There are ~ stamps in that drawer, aren't there?* 那抽屉里有几张邮票吗? *Didn't he give you ~ money?* 他不是给了你一些钱吗? Cf 参较 *He gave you ~ money, didn't he?* 他给了你一些钱, 不是吗? (*S~* is used in sentences that are interr in form if these sentences are really invitations or requests: 如果问句实际上表示邀请或请求时, some 亦用于问句中: *Please have ~ cake.* 请用一点糕饼。 *Will you please buy me ~ stamps when you go out?* 你出去的时候请替我买几张邮票好不好? Cf 参较 *Please buy me ~ stamps.* 请替我买几张邮票)。 **3** (After *if*, introducing a supposition, either *some* or *any* may be used): (在 If 引导的假设从句之后, some 及 any 皆可用): *If we had ~/any money, we could buy it.* 如果我们有钱, 我们就能买(它)了。 *If we find ~/any, we'll share them with you.* 如果我们找得到一些, 我们会分给你。 **4** (*S~* and *any* are used with *more*): (Some 与 any 可与 more 连用): *Give me ~ more /sə 'mɔː(r); sə'mɔr/.* 再给我一些。 *Do you want any more?* 你还要(一些)吗? *I haven't any more.* 我再没有了。 *Won't you have ~ more?* 你不再要一些吗?(不再来一点吗?) **5** (*S~* (always 总是读作 /sʌm; sʌm/) is often contrasted with *the rest, other*(s), and *all*): (Some 常与 the rest, other(s) 及 all 相对): *S~ children learn languages easily (and others with difficulty).* 有些小孩子学习语言很容易(不过有些则很困难)。 *All work is not dull;* ~ *work is pleasant.* 工作不全是枯燥的; 有些工作满有趣的。 **6** (*S~* (always 总是读作 /sʌm; sʌm/) is used before *sing* common *nn* to indicate that the person, place, object, etc is unknown, or when the speaker does not wish to be specific. The words *or other* are often added): (Some 用于单数普通名词前, 表示该人, 地, 物等不详或不欲指明。 作此用时, 后常接 or other 两字): *He's living at ~ place in East Africa.* 他(目前)住在东非某地。 *I've read that story before in ~ book or other.* 我在一本书中读过那个故事。 *S~ man at the door is asking to see you.* 门口有一个人要见你。 **7** (*S~* (always stressed) is used with *nn* meaning 'a considerable quantity or number of'): (Some 可与名词连用表示'相当大的数量', 唯须重读): *I shall be away for ~ 'time,* a fairly long time. 我将离开相当长的一段时间。 *Mr Green spoke at ~ (= considerable) length.* 格林先生滔滔不绝地说了好一阵子。 *We went ~ (= several) miles out of our way.* 我们岔出正路好几英里。 *The railway station is at ~ distance (= quite a long way) from the village.* 火车站离村子相当远。 **8** (*S~* (always stressed) is also used with *nn* meaning 'to a certain extent or degree'): (Some 亦可与名词连用, 表示'到达某种范围或程度', 须重读): *That is ~ help* (ie It helps to a certain extent) *towards understanding the problem.* 那对于了解该问题确有一些帮助。 □ *adv* (*S~* (always 总是读作 /sʌm; sʌm/) is used adverbially, meaning *about* or *approximately*, before numbers): (Some 可作副词用, 作'大约或相近'解, 用在数字之前): *That was ~ twenty years ago.* 那大约二十年前的事。 *There were ~ fifteen people there.* 那里大约有十五个人。 ~**· few,** ⇨ **few(3).**

some² /sʌm; sʌm/ *pron* (*S~* as a *pron* is used in the same ways as ~, *adj*, (1, 2 and 3). *S~ of* and *any of*

are equivalent to *a few of*, *a little of*, *part of*): (some 作代词用时，与作形容词用的 1, 2, 3 义的用法相同。Some of 及 any of 与 a few of, a little of, part of 相等）: *S~ of these books are useful.* 这些书中有几本颇为有用。*I don't want any of these* (*books*). 这些(书)我一本也不需要。*I don't want any of this* (*paper*). 这东西(这种纸)我一点也不需要。*I agree with ~ of what you say.* 你说的话我部分同意。*Scotland has ~ of the finest scenery in the world.* 苏格兰有几处全世界最美丽的风景。

some·body /'sʌmbədɪ; 'sʌm,bɑdɪ/, **some·one** /'sʌm-wʌn; 'sʌm,wʌn/ *pron* **1** (replaced by *anybody* in *interr*, *neg*, etc sentences) some person: 某人(在否定句，问句中用 anybody 代替): *There's ~ at the door.* 门口有一个人。*Is there anyone at home?* 家里有人吗? *That must be ~ from the Department of Education.* 那一定是教育部某人士。**2** (often with the *indef art*; also in the *pl*) a person of some importance: (常与不定冠词连用; 并有复数形)重要人物; 有份量的人: *If you had studied harder at college you might have become* (*a*) *~.* 你当初上大学时如果多用点功，说不定已经变成重要人物了。*He's nobody in town but I suppose he's a ~ in his own village.* 他在这城里默默无闻，不过我想在他村子里他是一位颇有份量的人物。

some·how /'sʌmhaʊ; 'sʌm,haʊ/ *adv* **1** in some way (or other): by one means or another: 以某种方法或方式; 借某种手段; 设法地: *We must find money for the rent ~* (*or other*). 我们总会找法找钱付房租。*We shall get there ~.* 我们总会有办法到那里的。**2** for some (vague) reason (or other): 为某种理由; 说不上什么理由;反正: *She never liked me, ~.* 她反正总不太喜欢过我。*S~ I don't trust that man.* 说不出什么道理，我就是不相信那个人。

some·one /'sʌmwʌn; 'sʌm,wʌn/ *n* = **somebody.**

some·place /'sʌmpleɪs; 'sʌmples/ *adv* (US colloq) somewhere: (美口)某处: *I've left my bag ~.* 我把我的提包忘在某处了。*He lives ~ between Baltimore and Washington.* 他住在巴尔的摩与华盛顿之间的某个地方。*Let's go ~ else.* 我们到别处去吧。

som·er·sault /'sʌməsɔːlt; 'sʌmə,sɔlt/ *n* [C] leap or fall in which one turns heels over head before landing on one's feet: 筋斗: *turn/throw a ~.* 翻筋斗。□ *vi* [VP2A] turn a ~. 翻筋斗。

some·thing /'sʌmθɪŋ; 'sʌmθɪŋ/ *pron* **1** (replaced by *anything* in *interr*, *neg*, etc sentences) something, object, event, etc (of an indefinite nature): (未明的)某事; 某物(在否定句与问句中，用 anything 代替): *There's ~ on the floor.* 地板上有一样东西。*Is there anything in that box?* 那盒子里有东西吗? *I want ~ to eat.* 我想吃东西。*There's ~* (= some truth, some point) *in what he says.* 他说的有点道理。*It's ~* (= some satisfaction, some comfort to have home again without an accident. 平平安安地回到家里颇值得安慰。*He is ~* (= has some position or other) *in the Department of the Environment.* 他在环境卫生部颇有地位。**2 or ~**, (colloq) indicates absence of precise information: 用以表示不十分肯定: *Mr Green is a shopkeeper or ~*, is engaged in trade of some kind. 格林先生大概是商店老板之类的人物。*I hear he has broken an arm and has broken a limb, etc.* 我听说他折断了手臂什么的。*He struck a match too near the petrol tank or ~*, did something equally foolish and dangerous. 他在太靠近汽油桶的地方擦火柴或做出同等愚蠢及危险的事情。**3 ~ of**, used to indicate an indefinite degree: 用以表示不确定的程度: *The soldier found himself ~ of a hero* (= was greeted as a hero to some extent) *when he returned to his village.* 那士兵回到家乡，受到人们对那种英雄般看待。*He's ~ of a liar*, (= is not wholly truthful), *don't you think?* 他说话不大靠得住佳，你不觉得吗? *I'm ~ of a carpenter*, I have some ability as a carpenter. 我懂一点木工。□ *adv ~ like*, (a) rather like; having some resemblance to: 颇似; 有一点象: *The airship was shaped ~ like a cigar.* 那飞船的外型有点象

一支雪茄。(b) approximately: 近乎; 大约; 约: *He left ~ like ten thousand*, ie died leaving about £10 000. 他遗留下大约一万英镑(的财产)。(c) (colloq) *Now that's ~ like it*, (used to denote satisfaction). (口)那倒满好(用以表示满意)。

some·time /'sʌmtaɪm; 'sʌm,taɪm/ *adv* **1** at some time: 于某时; 在某一时间: *I saw him ~ in May.* 我在五月里见过他。*It was ~ last summer.* 去年夏天的某个时候。*I will speak to him about it ~.* 我会找个时间跟你说此事。*I hope you will come ~ soon.* 我希望你不久能抽空前来。(Do not confuse with *some time* meaning 'for some period of time', as in: 不要与意为'一段时间'的 some time 混淆，如: I have been waiting some time 我已等了一些时候了。) **2** (also as *adj*) (亦用作形容词) former(ly): 以前; 从前: *The Rev Thomas Atkins, ~ priest of this parish*; 托马斯·阿特金斯牧师，本教区从前的牧师; *Mr Snuffle, ~ fellow of Trinity College.* 斯诺佛先生，三一学院的前校务委员。

some·times /'sʌmtaɪmz; 'sʌm,taɪmz/ *adv* at some times; now and then; from time to time: 有时; 不时; 往往; 间或: *I ~ have letters from him.* 我不时接到他的信。*I have ~ had letters from him.* 我不时接到他的来信。*S~ we go to the cinema and at other times we go for a walk.* 我们有时去看电影，有时去散步。(When ~ is used in a contrasting statement, or when it is repeated, it may follow the *v*): (用于对照的句子中，或重复使用时，可接在动词后): *She likes ~ the one and the other.* 她有时喜欢这个，有时喜欢那个。*He says the one thing and at other times the exact opposite.* 他有时这么说，有时却说得完全相反。

some·way /'sʌmweɪ; 'sʌm,we/ *adv* (US colloq) (美口) = **somehow.**

some·what /'sʌmwɒt; US: -hwɒt; 'sʌm,hwɑt/ *adv* **1** rather; in some degree: 颇为; 稍稍; 有几分: *I was ~ surprised/disappointed*, etc. 我略感吃惊(失望等)。*He answered ~ hastily.* 他回答得略嫌草率。*I've given ~ late, I'm afraid.* 恐怕我们到得晚了一点。**2 ~ of**, rather: 颇为; 稍稍; 有一点: *He was ~ of a liar.* 他讲话有点不诚实。*I found it ~ of a difficulty.* 我发现这事有些困难。

some·where /'sʌmweə(r); US: -hweər; 'sʌm,hwɛr/ *adv* (in *interr*, *neg*, etc sentences replaced by *anywhere*) in, at, to, some place: (在问句，否定句等中用 anywhere 代替)在某处; 到某处: *It must be ~ near here.*(它)一定在附近某处。*Is it anywhere near here?* (它)就在附近吗? *I didn't go anywhere yesterday.* 昨天我那里都没有去。*He lost it ~ between his office and the station.* 他在办公室与车站之间的路上遗失了那件东西。*You will find the text ~ in the Bible.* 你可以在圣经里(某处)找到该原文。

som·nam·bu·lism /sɒm'næmbjʊlɪzəm; sɑm'næm-bjə,lɪzəm/ *n* [U] sleep-walking. 梦游; 梦行; 梦游病。**som·nam·bu·list** /-ɪst; -ɪst/ *n* sleep-walker. 梦游者; 患梦游症者。

som·nol·ent /'sɒmnələnt; 'sɑmnələnt/ *adj* sleepy; almost asleep; causing sleep. 思睡的; 欲睡的; 快睡着的; 催眠的; 致睡的。**~·ly** *adv* **som·nol·ence** /-əns; -əns/ *n* [U] sleepiness. 欲睡; 熟睡; 思睡。

son /sʌn; sʌn/ *n* **1** male child of a parent. 儿子。*the Son of God; the Son of Man*, Jesus Christ. 耶稣基督。*the sons of men*, mankind. 人类。**'son-in-law** (*pl* **'sons-in-law**) husband of one's daughter. 女婿。**2** (used as a form of address, eg by an older man to a young man, a priest to a penitent): 作为称呼语，如年长者对年幼者，神父对忏悔者): *my son.* 我的孩子。**3 ~ of**, person having the qualities, etc indicated: 具有指明之性质等的人: *sons of freedom*, those who have inherited freedom from their ancestors; 自由的儿女(由其祖先继承自由的人们); *a son of the soil*, one whose father worked on the land and who follows his father's occupation. (继承父业的)农民。

so·nar /'səʊnɑː(r); 'sɑnɑr/ *n* device or system for detecting and locating objects submerged in water by

means of reflected sound waves. 声纳(借声波反射作用，探测水面下物体位置的仪器)。

so·na·ta /sə'nɑːtə; sə'nɑtə/ n (pl ~s /-təz; -təz/) musical composition for one instrument (eg the piano), or two (eg piano and violin), normally with three or four movements. 奏鸣曲(供一种乐器如钢琴，或两种乐器,如钢琴及小提琴,演奏的乐曲,通常有三或四个乐章)。

song /sɒŋ US: sɔːŋ; sɔŋ/ n 1 [U] singing; music for the voice: 歌唱；声乐：burst into ~, (突然)歌唱；唱； the ~ (= musical cry) of the birds. 鸟的鸣啭。'~·**bird** n bird (eg blackbird, thrush) noted for its ~. 鸣禽；鸣鸟(如山鸟、画眉等)。2 [U] poetry; verse: 诗；韵文：renowned in ~. 以诗著称。3 [C] short poem or number of verses set to music and intended to be sung: 歌词；歌曲：a marching ~; 进行曲；popular ~s. 流行歌曲。'~·**book** n collection of ~s (with both words and music). 歌集；歌本。**buy sth for a ~/an old ~; go for a ~,** buy sth/be sold for a small amount. 贱价买入；贱价卖出。**nothing to make a ~ and dance about,** (colloq) of little or no importance. (口)区区的；不重要的。**a ~ and dance,** (colloq) fuss. (口)无谓的纷扰。~·**ster** /-stə(r); -stɚ/ n singer; ~bird. 歌唱者；歌手；鸣禽。~·**stress** /-strɪs; -strɪs/ n female singer. 女歌唱家；女歌手。

sonic /'sɒnɪk; 'sɑnɪk/ adj relating to sound, sound-waves or the speed of sound: 声音的；音波的；音速的：a ~ bang/boom, noise made when an aircraft exceeds the speed of sound: 音爆(飞机超过音速时所发的声音)：the ~ barrier, ⇨ sound barrier at **sound²**(3). 音障。⇨ **super~, ultra~.**

son·net /'sɒnɪt; 'sɑnɪt/ n kind of poem containing 14 lines, each of 10 syllables, and with a formal pattern of rhymes. 十四行诗(每行十个音节,具严整的押韵格式)。~·**eer** /ˌsɒnɪ'ɪə(r); ˌsɑnə'tɪr/ n (usu derog) writer of ~s. (通常含贬义)十四行诗作者。

sonny /'sʌnɪ; 'sʌnɪ/ n (pl -**nies**) familiar form of address to a young boy. 孩子；宝宝(对小男孩的亲密称呼)。

son·or·ous /sə'nɔːrəs; sə'nɔrəs/ adj 1 having a full, deep sound: 发宏亮声音的；响亮的：a ~ voice; 宏亮的声音；the ~ note of the temple bell. 寺庙的宏亮钟声。2 (of language, words, etc) impressive; imposing: 语言、文字等)造成深刻印象的；醒目的；堂皇的：~ titles; 醒目的标题；a ~ style of writing. 庄严的文体。~·**ly** adv son·or·ity /sə'nɒrətɪ US: -'nɔːr-; sə'nɔrətɪ/ n

sonsy /'sɒnsɪ; 'sɑnsɪ/ adj (Scot) (苏) a lass, a plump, merry, cheerful girl. 一个丰满、愉快、高兴的女孩子。

soon /suːn; sun/ adv 1 not long after the present time or the time in question; in a short time. (S~ may occupy mid-position with the v, or, esp if modified by too, very or quite, end-position): 不久；即刻。(soon可置于动词前后,如为 too, very 或 quite 修饰时,多置于句末)：We shall ~ be home. 我们不久就到家了。We shall be home quite ~ now. 现在我们很快就会到家。He'll be here very ~. 他很快就会到达(此地)。It will ~ be five years since we came to live in London. 自从我们搬到伦敦来住,转瞬就快五年了。~ after, a short time after: 在…之后不久：He arrived ~ after three. 三点钟过后不久他就到了。(The opposite of ~ after is a little before.) (soon after 的相对语是 a little before。) 2 early: 早；快：How ~ can you be ready? 你最快在什么时候可以准备好? Must you leave so ~? 你一定要这么早就离去吗? We reached the station half an hour too ~. 我们早半小时到达车站。He will be here ~ than you expect. 他会比你所期待的时间早到。3 as/so ~ as, at the moment that; when; not later than: 一…就；当；不迟于；于某一时刻：He started as ~ as he received the news. 他一听到消息就立刻动身了。I'll tell him the news as ~ as I see him. 我一见到他就立刻告诉他这个消息。We didn't arrive so/as ~ as we had hoped. 我们未能象我们希望的那么早到达。**no ~er ... than,** immediately

when or after: 一…就；刚…就：He had no ~er/No ~er had he arrived home than he was asked to start on another journey. 他刚到家就被要求去作另一次旅行。No ~er said than done, ie done immediately. 说了就做。4 (in double comparative constructions): (用于复式比较结构中)：The ~er you begin the ~er you'll finish. 你开始得早，就会愈早结束。The ~er the better. 愈快愈好。~**er or later,** one day whether ~ or (much) later. 迟早；早晚。5 (suggesting comparison) (含示比较意) (just) as ~ ... (as), with equal readiness or willingness ... (as): 同样愿意；无轩轾之分：I would (just) as ~ stay at home as go for a walk. 我待在家里散步我都一样愿意，出去散步也好。~**er than,** rather than: 宁可…而不：He would ~er resign than take part in such dishonest business deals. 他宁可辞职，也不愿意参与这种不诚实的买卖。S~er than marry that man, she would earn her living as a waitress. 她不肯嫁给那人，宁愿做女侍维持生活。as ~ as not, (most) willingly: (很)愿意；同乐意，乐乐意过：I'd go there as ~ as not. 我很乐意去彼处。

soot /sut; sut/ n [U] black powder in smoke, or left by smoke on surfaces: 黑烟灰；煤烟；黑灰；油烟：sweep the ~ out of the chimney. 扫除烟囱的烟灰。~**y** adj black with ~; black like ~. 因有煤灰、烟灰等而黑的；黑如烟灰色的。□ vt cover with ~. 覆以黑烟灰等。

sooth /suːθ; suθ/ n (archaic) truth. (古)事实；真相。in ~, truly. 事实上。'~·**sayer** /-seɪə(r); -seɚ/ n fortune-teller. 算命先生；占卜者。

soothe /suːð; suð/ vt [VP6A] 1 make (a person, his nerves, passions) quiet or calm: 使(某人,其神经,其激情)平静；安慰；抚慰；使镇静：a crying baby; 抚慰哭叫的婴儿。~ sb's anger; 使人息怒；a soothing voice. 安抚的语气。2 make (pains, aches) less sharp or severe: 使(痛苦,疼痛)缓和或减轻：an aching tooth; 减轻牙疼；a soothing lotion for the skin, eg against sunburn. 润肤剂(如防日晒者)。**sooth·ing·ly** adv

sop /sɒp; sɑp/ n [C] 1 piece of bread, etc soaked in milk, soup, etc. (泡在牛奶、汤等中的)面包片等。2 a sop to sb, sth offered to prevent trouble or to give temporary satisfaction: 贿赂：(throw) a sop to Cerberus, (do) sth to pacify or bribe a trouble some person. 贿赂；收买某人；向某人行贿。□ vt (-pp-) [VP6A, 15B] soak (bread, etc in broth, etc). 浸泡(面包等于汤等中)。sop sth up, take up liquid, etc: 吸取液体等：Sop up the water with this towel. 用这条毛巾把水吸干。**sop·ping** adj soaking (wet): 浸湿的；泡透的：sopping (wet) clothes. 湿淋淋的衣服。

soph·ism /'sɒfɪzəm; 'sɑfɪzəm/ n [C, U] false reasoning or argument, intended to deceive. 诡辩；诡辩之词。

soph·ist /'sɒfɪst; 'sɑfɪst/ n person who uses clever but misleading arguments. 诡辩者。

soph·is·ti·cated /sə'fɪstɪkeɪtɪd; sə'fɪstɪˌketɪd/ adj 1 having learnt the ways of the world and having lost natural simplicity; showing this: 世故的；老练的；失去天真的：a ~ girl; 世故的女孩子；a girl with ~ tastes. 趣味及爱好显得很世故的女孩子。2 complex; with the latest improvements and refinements: 复杂的；最新而且最进步的：~ modern weapons; 复杂的近代武器；~ devices used in spacecraft. 太空船的最新设备。3 (of mental activity) refined; complex; subtle: (指心灵活动)精细的；复杂的；高深的；奥妙的：a ~ discussion/argument. 高深的讨论(议论)。**soph·is·ti·ca·tion** /səˌfɪstɪ'keɪʃn; səˌfɪstɪ'keʃən/ n

soph·is·try /'sɒfɪstrɪ; 'sɑfɪstrɪ/ n (pl -**tries**) [U] use of sophisms; [C] instance of this. 诡辩(的使用); 诡辩术；诡辩事例。

sopho·more /'sɒfəmɔː(r); 'sɑfmˌɔr/ n (US) person in his second year at a four-year college. (美)大学二年级学生。

sop·or·ific /ˌsɒpə'rɪfɪk; ˌsɑpə'rɪfɪk/ n, adj (substance, drink, etc) producing sleep. 催眠的；催眠剂。

sop·ping /'sɒpɪŋ; 'sɑpɪŋ/ adj ⇨ sop.

soppy /'sɒpɪ; 'sɑpɪ/ adj (-ier, -iest) 1 very wet. 非常湿的; 浸透的。 2 (colloq) foolishly sentimental. (口)过于感情用事的; 过于伤感的。

so·prano /sə'prɑːnəʊ; -'præn-; sə'præno/ n (pl ~s /-nəʊz; -noz/), adj (person having the) highest singing voice of women and girls and boys. (女子、女孩及男孩声乐的)最高音(的); 女高音(的); 唱女高音或最高音者; 能唱女高音或最高音者。

sorbet /'sɔːbət; 'sɔbət/ n = **sherbet**.

sor·cerer /'sɔːsərə(r); 'sɔrsərə/ n man who practises magic with the help of evil spirits. 男巫; 术士; 魔法师。 **sor·cer·ess** /'sɔːsərɪs; 'sɔrsərɪs/ n woman ~. 女巫; 术士; 女魔法师。 **sor·cery** /'sɔːsərɪ; 'sɔrsərɪ/ n (pl -ries) [U] witchcraft; (pl) evil acts done by a ~. 巫术;(复)术士行的法术或魔法。

sor·did /'sɔːdɪd; 'sɔrdɪd/ adj 1 (of conditions) wretched; shabby; comfortless: (指状况)破烂的; 污秽的; 肮脏的; 不舒服的: a ~ slum; 破烂肮脏的贫民窟; living in ~ poverty. 生活于贫苦中。 2 (of persons, behaviour, etc) contemptible; prompted by self-interest or meanness: (指人、行为等)卑鄙的; 自私的; 下贱的: ~ motives. 卑鄙的动机。 ~·ly adv ~·ness n

sore /sɔː(r); sɔr/ adj 1 (of a part of the body) tender and painful; hurting when touched or used: (指身体的某部)敏感而疼的; 碰到或用到就痛的; 疼痛的: a ~ knee/throat. 膝(喉咙)痛。 **like a bear with a ~ head**, ill tempered, grumpy. 脾气大的; 拗性的。 **a sight for ~ eyes**, sb or sth welcome, pleasant. 受欢迎的、令人愉快的人或物。 2 filled with sorrow; sad: 充满哀伤的; 伤心的: a ~ heart. 哀伤的心。 3 causing sorrow or annoyance. 使人或引起哀伤或烦恼的。 **a ~ point/subject**, one that hurts the feelings when talked about. 使人伤心之处(话题)。 4 irritated; aggrieved: 恼怒的; 受冤抑的: feel ~ about not being invited to the party. 因未被邀请参加舞会而恼怒。 5 (old use; also adverbial) grievous(ly); severe(ly): (旧用法; 亦作副词用)严重的(地); 剧烈的(地): in ~ distress; 极为痛苦的; in ~ need of help; 极端需要帮助。 a ~ oppressed. 深受压迫的。 □ n [C] 1 ~ place on the body (where the skin or flesh is injured): (身上的)痛处; 伤处; 疮; 溃疡: treat/bandage/heal a ~. 治疗(用绷带包扎, 治愈)伤处。 2 (fig) ~ subject; painful memory: (喻)伤心的话题; 痛苦的回忆: Let's not recall old ~s. 我们不要再提那些伤心的往事了。 ~·ly adv 1 severely: 严重地; 剧烈地: ~ly tempted/afflicted. 深受诱惑(折磨)。 2 greatly: 非常; 很: More financial help is ~ly needed. 迫切需要更多的经济支援。 ~·ness n

sor·ghum /'sɔːgəm; 'sɔrgəm/ n [U] kinds of millet. 蜀黍; 高粱。

sor·or·ity /sə'rɒrɪtɪ US: -'rɔːr-; sə'rɔrɪtɪ/ n (pl -ties) (US) women's social club in a college or university. (美)(大学中的)女生联谊会。

sor·rel¹ /'sɒrəl US: 'sɔːrəl; 'sɔrəl/ n kinds of herb with sour-tasting leaves used in cooking. (植)酸木(叶含酸浆的植物,用于烹调)。

sor·rel² /'sɒrəl US: 'sɔːrəl; 'sɔrəl/ adj, n (of a) reddish-brown colour; horse of this colour. 红褐色(的); 栗色(的); 栗色马。

sor·row /'sɒrəʊ; 'sɑro/ n [C, U] (cause of) grief or sadness; regret: 悲哀; 悲伤; 悔恨; 其原由: express ~ for having done wrong; 因做错事而悔恨; to my great ~; 使我感到非常悲哀; to the ~ of all who were present; 使所有在场的人感到悲哀; in ~ and in joy, when we are sad and when we are happy. 在悲哀时及喜悦时。 His ~s had turned his hair white. 哀伤使他的头发变白。 **more in ~ than in anger**, with more regret than anger for what was done, etc. (对做过的事等)懊悔多于愤怒。 **the Man of S~s**, Jesus. 耶稣。 □ vi [VP2A, 3A] ~ (at/for/over), feel ~ (at/for/over sth): (为…)感到悲哀、悲伤、悔恨等: ~ing over her child's death. 为她孩子的死感到悲伤。 ~·ful /-fl; -fəl/ adj feeling, showing, causing, ~. 感到、显示、引起悲

哀(悲伤、悔恨等)的; 可悲的; 悔恨的。 ~·fully /-fəlɪ; -fəlɪ/ adv

sorry /'sɒrɪ; 'sɔrɪ/ adj 1 (pred only) feeling regret or sadness: (仅用作表语)感到遗憾或悲伤的; 惋惜的; 抱歉的: We're ~ to hear of your father's death. 听到令尊逝世, 我们甚为难过。 I should be ~ for you to think/if you were to think that I dislike you. 如果你认为我不喜欢你, 我会感到遗憾。 I was ~ to hear that you thought I disliked you. 我听说你认为我不喜欢你, 我实在感到遗憾。 **be/feel ~ (about/for sth)**, feel regret or repentance: 感到遗憾或懊悔: Aren't you ~ for/about what you've done? 你对你所做的事情不感到遗憾吗? If you'll say you're ~ (= that you repent), we'll forget the incident. 如果你对你懊悔, 我们就不再计较这件事。 **be/feel ~ for sb, (a)** feel sympathy: (对某人)表同情: I feel ~ for anyone who has to drive in weather like this. 我对于在这种天气还必须驾车的(任何)人表示同情。 **(b)** feel pity or mild contempt: 表怜悯或轻蔑的轻视: I'm ~ for you, but you've been rather foolish, haven't you? 我很替你难过, 不过你颇为不智, 不是吗? If he doesn't realise that he must make sacrifices, I'm ~ for him. 如果他不明白他必须有所牺牲, 那我觉得他实在可怜。 2 (used to express mild regret or an apology): (用以表示适度的遗憾或道歉): 'Can you lend me a pound?'— '(I'm) S~, but I can't.' '你能借给一英镑吗?'—'抱歉, 我无能为力。' ⇨ **excuse²**(3), **pardon**(2). 3 (attrib) (用作定语)(-ier, -iest) pitiful: 可怜的: in a ~ state; 处于可怜的状况; worthless; shabby: 无价值的; 不体面的: a ~ excuse. 理由不充足的借口。

sort¹ /sɔːt; sɔrt/ n [C] 1 group or class of persons or things which are alike in some way: (人或物的)类; 群; 品等: Pop music is the ~ she likes most. 流行音乐是她最喜欢的音乐。 What ~ of people does he think we are? 他认为我们是哪一类的人? We can't approve of this ~ of thing/these ~ of things/things of this ~. 我们不能赞同这类的事。 **of a ~; of ~s**, used (colloq) to suggest that what is referred to does not fully deserve the name: (口)用以暗示名实不全相符的事物: They served coffee of a ~/coffee of ~s/a ~ of coffee. 他们供应勉强称得上是咖啡的饮料。 ~ **of**, (colloq) rather; to some extent: (口)颇为; 有几分; 到某种程度: I sort of thought ~ had a vague idea that would happen. 我总有点觉得这事会发生。 ⇨ **kind of** at **kind²**(2). 2 **after a ~; in a ~**, to a certain extent. 到达某种程度; 有几分; 有些。 3 **a good ~**, (esp) a person who is likable, who has good qualities. (尤指)可爱的人; 有良好品质的人。 4 **out of ~s**, (colloq) feeling unwell, out of spirits. (口)不适; 精神不佳。

sort² /sɔːt; sɔrt/ vt, vi 1 [VP6A, 15B] ~ **sth (out)**, arrange in groups; separate things of one sort from things of other sorts: 分类; 整理; 归类; 划分: The boy was ~ing/~ing out/over the foreign stamps he had collected. 那男孩在整理他所搜集的外国邮票。 We must ~ out the good apples from the bad. 我们必须把好的苹果与坏的分开。 ~ **sth out**, (colloq) put in good order; solve: (口)整理好; 解决: I'll leave you to ~ that out, find a solution. 我将把该问题交给你解决。 Let's leave that pair to ~ themselves out, clear up their problems, misunderstandings, etc. 我们让那一对(夫妇等)自行解决他们之间的问题吧。 2 ~ **well/ill with**, (liter) be in/out of harmony with: (文)配得上(配不上); 与…相符(不相符): His heroic death ~ed well with his character. 他那种英雄式的死法正合他的个性。 ~·**er** n (esp) post-office worker who ~s letters. 分类者; 整理者; (尤指)邮局中的信件归类者。

sor·tie /'sɔːtiː; 'sɔrti/ n [C] 1 attack made by besieged soldiers on their besiegers. (被围攻之士兵对围攻者的)突围; 出击; 突击; 反击。 2 flight made by one aircraft during military operations: (作战时一架飞机的)出勤次: The four planes each made two ~s yesterday. 那四架飞机昨天各出动两架次。

SOS /ˌes əʊ 'es; 'es,o'es/ n [C] 1 message for help

(sent by radio, etc) from a ship, aircraft, etc when in danger. Cf 参较 *mayday call.*(船、飞机等遇险时经由无线电等发出的)求救信号; 求救电码。 **2** urgent call for help, eg a broadcast to find relatives of a person seriously ill. 紧急求救呼吁(如广播找寻重病者的亲属等)。

so-so /ˌsəʊ ˈsəʊ; ˌsoˌso/ *pred adj, adv* (colloq) not very good: (口)还好; 马马虎虎; 勉勉强强: *'How are you feeling today?'—'Oh, only so-so'.* '你今天觉得如何?'——'哦, 马马虎虎。'

sot /sɒt; sɑt/ *n* habitual drunkard, esp one whose mind has become dulled. 经常喝醉酒的人; 酒鬼(尤指心智已变迟钝者)。 **sot·tish** /ˈsɒtɪʃ; ˈsɑtɪʃ/ *adj* habitually drinking too much and, for this reason, dull or stupid. 经常饮酒过多(因而变愚钝的);滥饮酒的。 **sot·tish·ly** *adv* **sot·tish·ness** *n*

sotto voce /ˌsɒtəʊ ˈvəʊtʃɪ; ˈsɑtoˈvotʃi/ *adv* (I) in a low voice, aside. (意)低声地; 轻声地; 旁白地。

sou /suː; su/ *n* former French coin of low value; (fig) very small amount of money: 苏(法国昔时一种低值硬币); (喻)极少量金钱: *He hasn't a sou,* is penniless. 他一文不名。

sou·brette /suːˈbret; suˈbrɛt/ *n* maidservant (usu pert, coquettish, fond of intrigue) in a comedy for the theatre; actress taking such a part. (舞台剧中)喜剧里的女佣(通常孟浪、卖俏而喜弄诡谋);扮此角色的女演员。

sou·bri·quet /ˈsuːbrɪkeɪ; ˈsubrɪˌke/ *n* = **sobriquet.**

souf·flé /ˈsuːfleɪ *US:* suːˈfleɪ; suˈfle/ *n* [C] (F) dish of eggs, milk, etc beaten to a froth, flavoured (with cheese, etc) and baked. (法)蛋奶酥(蛋、奶等搅成泡沫状, 以乳酪等调味, 焙制而成的食物)。

sough /sʌf *US:* saʊ; sʌf/ *vi* [VP2A], *n* (make a) murmuring or whispering sound (as of wind in trees). (发)飒飒声; (发)飕飕声(如树间风声)。

sought /sɔːt; sɔt/ *pt, pp* of **seek.**

soul /səʊl; sol/ *n* [C] **1** non-material part of a person, believed to exist for ever: 灵魂(人之非物质部分), 被相信永远存在者: *believe in the immortality of the ~;* 相信灵魂不朽: *commend one's ~ to God,* (when at the point of death). (弥留时)把灵魂付托给上帝。 *He eats hardly enough to keep body and ~ together,* to keep him alive. 他吃的份量简直不够维持其生命。 *She has a ~ above material pleasures.* 她有一个超越物质享受的灵魂。 **2** (often without *indef art*) emotional, moral and intellectual energy: (常不加不定冠词)感情、精神及智力; 心力; 精神; 魄力: *This music has no soul.* 这音乐缺乏力量。 *He is a man without a soul,* is unfeeling, selfish. 他是个寡情自私的人。 *He put his heart and ~ into the work.* 他把精神心力全部贯注在工作上。 **3** *the life and ~ of the party, etc,* (person looked upon as the) liveliest person present at the party, etc. (某团体等中的)核心人物;主脑。 **4** person regarded as the pattern or personification of some virtue or quality: 典型; 化身: *He is the ~ of honour / discretion.* 他是荣誉(谨慎)的典型。 **5** spirit of a dead person: 幽灵; 死者的灵魂: *ˌAll 'S~s' Day,* 2 Nov. 万灵节(十一月二日)。 **6** person: 人: *There wasn't a ~ to be seen,* No one was in sight. 连一个人也看不见。 *The ship sank with 200 ~s.* 那船载着二百人沉没了。 **7** (expressing familiarity, pity, etc according to context): (依上下文, 表示熟悉、亲爱、怜悯等): *He's a cheery ~,* a cheerful man. 他是一个活泼愉快的人。 *Be a good ~ and lend me a dollar.* 做做好事借给我一块钱吧。 *She's lost all her money, poor ~.* 她损失了全部的钱, 可怜的人。 **8** (US colloq) all those qualities that enable a person to be in harmony with himself and others, used esp by Afro-Americans and expressed through their music and dancing. (美口)谐和力(使自己保持谐和以及与他人保持谐和的一切特质, 尤指美国黑人所使用, 并表现在他们的音乐及舞蹈中者)。 **brother / sister,** fellow Afro-American; person who thinks and feels in the same way as oneself. 美国黑人; 与自己想法和感觉相同的人。 '**~ music,** modern Afro-American popular blues music with strong rhythm for dancing. 美国黑人音乐(指其近代流行的布鲁斯舞曲)。 **9** (compounds) (复合词) '**~-destroying** *adj* killing the ~ or spirit: 毁灭灵魂的: *~-destroying work.* 损人神志的作品。 '**~-stirring** *adj* exciting, etc. 振奋的; 鼓舞的; 提神的。 **~ful** /-fl; -fl/ *adj* having, affecting, showing, deep feeling: 热情的; 深情的: *~ful eyes / music / glances.* 热情的眼睛(音乐、瞥视)。 **~fully** /-fəlɪ; -flɪ/ *adv* **~·less** *adj* without higher or deeper feelings. 无灵魂的;无情的;肤浅的。 **~·less·ly** *adv*

sound¹ /saʊnd; saʊnd/ *adj* **1** healthy; in good condition; not hurt, injured or decayed: 健全的; 完好的; 未受损伤的;未腐败的: *~ fruit / teeth;* 完好的水果(牙齿); *have a ~ constitution.* 有健全的体格。 *a ~ mind in a ~ body,* good mental and physical health. 身心健康。 *~ in wind and limb* (colloq) physically fit. (口)体格健全的。 **2** dependable; based on reason; prudent: 可靠的;有理由的;慎重的: *a ~ argument / policy;* 可靠的论据(明智的政策); *~ advice;* 睿智的忠告; *a ~ business firm.* 信誉昭著的商家。 *Is he ~ on national defence?* Are his views, etc reasonable, well-founded? 他的国防见解正确吗? **3** capable, careful: 有能力的; 小心的; 稳健的: *a ~ tennis player.* 稳健的网球员。 **4** thorough; complete: 彻底的; 完全的: *have a ~ sleep,* a deep and peaceful sleep; 酣睡; *be a ~ sleeper;* 是酣睡者; *give sb a ~ thrashing.* 痛殴某人。 □ *adv be / fall ~ asleep,* be / become deeply and peacefully asleep. 酣睡。 **~·ly** *adv* in a manner; thoroughly: 健全地; 完好地; 可靠地; 慎重地; 稳健地; 彻底地: *a ~ly based argument,* 基础健全的论据; *sleep ~ly;* 酣睡; *be ~ly beaten at tennis.* 在网球赛中被彻底击败。 **~·ness** *n*

sound² /saʊnd; saʊnd/ *n* [C, U] **1** that which is or can be heard: 声音; 音响: *within ~ of the guns,* near enough to hear them; 在可闻枪炮声范围内; *'vowel ~s,* eg /uː, ʌ, ə/ and 'consonant ~s, eg /p, b, ʃ, ʒ/. 元音(如 /uː, ʌ, ə/)和辅音(如 /p, b, ʃ, ʒ/)。 *We heard the ~ of voices.* 我们听到人声。 **2** (*sing* only) mental impression produced by sth stated (or read): (仅用单数)叙述或阅读的事物所产生的印象: *The news has a sinister ~,* seems to be sinister. 这新闻似乎不吉祥。 *I don't like the ~ of it.* 这东西听起来叫我不喜欢。 **3** (compounds, etc) (复合词等),*~* '**archives** *n pl* recordings on disc or magnetic tape of broadcasts considered to deserve being kept for future use: 录音档案; 音响档案(广播录音带等), 被认为有保存价值者): *the BBC ~ archives.* 英国广播公司的音响档案。 '**~ barrier** *n* point at which an aircraft's speed equals that of sound; 音障(飞机达到音速产生音爆的时刻)。 *break the ~ barrier,* exceed the speed of sound. 超越音速。 '**~-box** *n* part of an old-fashioned gramophone containing a diaphragm and into which the needle that moves over a record is fixed (corresponding to the pick-up of an electrical reproducer). (旧式留声机的)唱头(相当于电唱机的拾音器)。 '**~ effects** *n pl* sounds (recorded on discs, magnetic tape, film, etc) for use in broadcasts, in making films, etc or produced when needed (in a studio, etc). 音响效果(录于唱片、录音带、软片等上的声音, 用于广播、电影制作等中)。 '**~film** *n* cinema film with dialogue, music, etc recorded on it. 有声影片。 '**~-proof** *adj* constructed so that ~(s) cannot pass through or into: 隔音的; 防音的: *a ~-proof studio.* 有隔音设备的工作室。 Hence, 由此产生, '**~-proof,** *vt* [VP6A] make ~proof. 使隔音; 给…隔音。 '**~-recording,** (contrasted with *video-recording*) sth recorded in ~ only. 录音(与 video-recording 相对)。 '**~-track** *n* (music, etc on a) track or band at the side of a cinema film which has the recording ~. 音带;音道(有声电影片边上的录音部分);音带上所录之音乐等。 '**~-wave** *n* vibrations made in the air or other medium by which ~ is carried. 音波;声波。 **~·less** *adj* **~·less·ly** *adv*

sound³ /saʊnd; saʊnd/ *vt, vi* **1** [VP6A] produce sound from; make (sth) produce sound: 使响; 使(某物)

发声: ~ *a trumpet*. 吹喇叭. **2** [VP6A] utter: 发出: ~ *a note of alarm/danger*. 放警报(发出危险讯号). **3** [VP6A] pronounce: 发…的音; 读…的音: *Don't ~ the 'h' in 'hour' or the 'b' in 'dumb'*. hour 中的 h 或 dumb 中的 b 不要发音. **4** [VP6A] give notice of: 通知; 发布: ~ *the alarm*, eg by ringing a bell; 发布警报(如借鼓钟); ~ *the retreat*, by blowing a bugle. 吹撤退号. **5** [VP2A] give forth sound: 发声; 作响: *The trumpet ~ed*. 喇叭响了. *This black key* (eg on the piano) *won't ~*, No sound is produced when the key is struck. 这黑键(如钢琴上者)按下去不会响. **6** [VP6A] test, examine (the wheels of a railway carriage, etc by striking them, a person's lungs by tapping the chest). 听验(火车之轮等); 击验; 听诊(人之肺); 敲诊. **7** [VP2C, D] give an impression when heard (often fig): 听起来; 似乎(常作比喻用法): *How sweet the music ~s!* 这音乐听起来多悦耳! *It ~s to me as if there's a tap running somewhere*, I think I can hear water running from a tap. 我好象听到某处水龙头的流水声. *His explanation ~s all right*, seems reasonable enough. 他的解释听起来似乎有道理. *Her excuse ~s very hollow*, is unconvincing. 她借口难以令人心服. 理由虚假而难令人心服. **8** '~·ing-board *n* canopy placed over a platform to direct the ~ of the speaker's voice towards his listeners; thin plate of wood on a musical instrument, for magnifying its ~; (fig) way of causing an opinion, plan, etc to be widely heard. (装在讲台等上面,使声音送至听众的)响板; 共鸣板; 乐器上扩大音响的薄板; (喻)宣传品, 计划等的方法.

sound⁴ /saʊnd/ *n*; saʊnd/ *vt, vi* **1** [VP6A, 2A] test the depth of (the sea, etc) by letting down a weighted line (called a '~*ing-line* or ~*ing apparatus*); find the depth of water in a ship's hold (with a '~*ing-rod*); get records of temperature, pressure, etc in the upper atmosphere) (by sending up instruments in a '~*ing-balloon*). 以测深索(sounding-line 或 sounding apparatus) 测量(海等)的深度; 以测深杆(sounding-rod) 探测船舱内的水深; 借升空探测气球中的仪器以获得(上层大气层之)温度,压力等的记录. **2** [VP6A, 15A, B] ~ *sb (out) (about/on sth)*, try (esp cautiously or in a reserved manner) to learn sb's views, sentiments etc: (尤指小心或含蓄地)试探他人的观点、意见等: *I will ~ the manager about/on the question of holidays*. 我将就假日问题试探经理的意见. *Have you ~ed him out yet*, tried to learn his views? 你已探听出他的看法吗? ~·**ings** *n pl* **1** measurements obtained by ~ing(1). (以测深索等测出的)水之深度; (借升空气球记录下来的)上层气流的温度,压力等. **2** reactions obtained by ~ing(2). 试探或调查他人意见等所得的反应. **3** place or area near enough to the shore to make it possible to ~(1): 近岸可测水深之处或区域: *We are in ~ings/have come into ~ings*. 我们在浅水处(接近海岸了).

sound⁵ /saʊnd/ saʊnd/ *n* [C] narrow passage of water joining two larger areas of water; strait. 海峡; 水峡.

soup¹ /suːp/ sup/ *n* [U] liquid food made by cooking meat, vegetables, etc in water: 汤; 羹: *chicken/pea/tomato ~*. 鸡(豌豆,番茄)汤. *in the ~*, (colloq) in trouble. (口)在困难中. '~·**kitchen** *n* public establishment for supplying ~ to persons who are poor, or after a calamity such as an earthquake or flood. (救济贫苦者, 或在灾后所设立的)施汤所; 施粥场.

soup² /suːp/ sup/ *vt* [VP15B] ~ *sth up*, (sl) fit a motor-vehicle, its engine) with a supercharger (to increase the power output, and so its speed): (俚)以增压器装在(机动车, 其引擎)上(俾加大其马力, 增加其速度): *a ~ed-up car*. 装有增压器的轿车.

soup·çon /'suːpsɔːn US: suːp'sõ/ sup'sõ/ *n* (F) (usu 通常作 *a ~ of*) small amount; trace: (法)少量; 少许: *a ~ of garlic in the salad/of malice in his remarks*. 色拉中的蒜味(他的言词中的恶意).

sour /saʊə(r)/ saʊr/ *adj* **1** having a sharp taste (like that of vinegar, a lemon or an unripe plum, apple,

etc). 酸的; 有酸味的. ~ *grapes* ⇨ grape. **2** having a taste of fermentation: 有发酵味道的; 酸腐的: ~ *milk*; 酸奶; *a ~ smell*, ie of sth that has fermented. 酸腐气味. **3** (fig) bad-tempered; sharp-tongued: (喻)坏脾气的; 乖戾的; 说话尖刻的: *made ~ by disappointments*. 因失望而变得乖戾. *What a ~ face she has!* 她的脸色多难看! □ *vt, vi* [VP6A, 2A] turn or become ~ (lit, fig): (使)变酸; (使)变乖戾(字面,喻): *The hot weather has ~ed the milk*. 炎热的天气使牛奶变酸了. *Her personality has ~ed*. 她的性情变得乖戾了. *The old man has been ~ed by poverty*. 那老人因贫困而变得乖戾了. ~·**ly** *adv* ~·**ness** *n*

source /sɔːs/ sors/ *n* [C] **1** starting-point of a river: 河的源头; 水源: *the ~s of the Nile*. 尼罗河的发源地. *Where does the Rhine have its ~?* 莱茵河发源于何处? **2** place from which sth comes or is got: 来源; 出处: *The news comes from a reliable ~*. 这消息出自可靠的来源. *Is that well the ~ of infection for these cases of typhoid?* 那口井是 传染这些伤寒病例的来源吗? **3** (*pl*) original documents, etc serving as material for a study, eg of sb's life, a period of history: (复)原始资料; 原始文件等: (attrib) (用作定语) ~ *materials*. 原始资料.

souse /saʊs/ saʊs/ *vt* [VP6A] **1** throw into water; throw water on. 投入水中; 泼水于…上. **2** put (fish, etc) into salted water, vinegar, etc to preserve it: 把(鱼等)放进盐水, 醋等中以腌藏; 腌渍: ~d *herrings*. 腌青鱼. ~d *(pp)* (sl) drunk. (俚)酒醉的.

sou·tane /suːˈtɑːn/ suːˈtɑn/ *n* (F) (in the RC Church) priest's cassock. (法)(天主教)教师的法衣.

south /saʊθ/ saʊθ/ *n* **1** ⇨ the illus at **compass**. (参看 compass 之插图) one of the four cardinal points of the compass, on the right of a person facing the sunrise; part of any place, country, etc lying farther in this direction than other parts: 南; 南方; 南部: *the ~ of London/England*. 伦敦(英格兰)南部. *Mexico is to the ~ of the US*. 墨西哥在美国南方. **2** (attrib) situated in, living in, pertaining to, coming from, the ~: (用作定语)位于、住在、有关、来自南方的: *S~ Wales*; 南威尔士; *S~ America*; 南美洲; *the S~ Pacific*; 南太平洋; *a room with a ~ aspect*, with windows facing ~; 南面有窗的房间; *grow roses on a ~ wall*; 在南面的墙上种蔷薇; *the S~ Pole*. 南极. □ *adv* to or towards the ~: 在或向南方: *The ship was sailing due ~*. 那船向正南方航行. ,~·'east, ,~·'west (abbr 略作 **SE, SW**), *nn, adjj, advv* (sometimes, esp naut, 有时作, 尤用于航海, **sou·'east** /,saʊ'iːst/ ,saʊ'ist/, **sou·'west** /,saʊ'west/ ,saʊ'west/) (regions) midway between ~ and east, ~ and west. (向)东南方(的); (向)西南方(的). ,~·~·'east, ,~·~·'west (abbr 略作 **SSE, SSW**) *nn, adjj, advv* (sometimes, esp naut, 有时作, 尤用于航海, **sou·'sou·'east**, **sou·'sou·'west**) (regions) midway between ~ and ~east, ~west. 南南东方(的); (向)南南西方(的). ,~·'**easter** *n* [C] strong wind blowing from the ~east. 东南(强)风. ,~·'**easter·ly** *adj* (of wind) from the ~east; (of direction) towards the ~east. (指风)来自东南的; (指方向)向东南方的. ,~·'**wester, sou·'wester** /,saʊ'westə(r)/ ,saʊ'westɚ/ *n* (a) strong ~west wind. 西南(强)风. (b) (always 总是作 *sou'wester*) waterproof (usu oilskin) hat with a wide flap at the back to protect the neck. 护防水帽(通常为油布制成, 后沿宽平, 以护后颈). ,~·'**wester·ly** *adj* (of wind) from the ~west; (of direction) towards the ~west. (指风)来自西南方的; (指方向)向西南方的. ,~·'**eastern** /-'iːstən/ -'istən/ *adj* of, from, situated in, the ~east. 来自、位于、有关东南方的. ,~·'**western** /-'westən/ -'westən/ *adj* of, from, situated in the ~west. 来自、位于、有关西南方的. ~·**ward(s)** /'saʊθwədz/ 'saʊθwɚdz/ *adv* towards the ~. 向南方.

south·er·ly /'sʌðəlɪ/ 'sʌðɚlɪ/ *adj, adv* **1** (of winds) blowing from the south. (指风)吹自南方. **2** towards the south: 朝向南方: *The plane flew off in a ~ direction*.

那飞机向南方飞去。

south·ern /'sʌðən; 'sʌðən/ adj in or of the south: 南方的; 在南方的; 有关南方的: *Europe*; 南欧; *the S~ States of the USA.* 美国南方各州。**~er** n person from the ~ part of the country, esp from the S~ States (US). 南方人; 南部人; (尤指)美国南方各州的人。**'~·most** /-məust; -,most/ adj farthest south. 极南的。

sou·venir /,su:və'nɪə(r) US: 'su:vəniər; ,suvə'nɪr/ n [C] sth taken, bought or received as a gift, and kept as a reminder of a person, place or event. 纪念物; 纪念品; 有纪念意义的礼物。

sou'wester /,sau'westə(r); ,sau'westə/ ⇨ south(2).

sov·er·eign /'sɒvrɪn; 'sɑvrɪn/ adj 1 (of power) highest; without limit; (of a nation, state, ruler) having ~ power: (指权力)最高的; 无上的; 无限的; (指国家、政府、统治者)有至高无上权力的; 有主权的: *become a ~ state,* fully self-governing and independent in foreign affairs. 变为主权国(独立自主的国家)。2 excellent; effective: 极好的; 有效的: *Is there a ~ remedy for cancer?* 治疗癌症有好的方法吗? □ n 1 ~ ruler; eg a king, queen or emperor. 最高统治者(如国王、女王、皇帝)。2 British gold coin not now in circulation (face value one pound). 英国金币(面值一英镑, 现已不通用)。**~·ty** /'sɒvrəntɪ; 'sɑvrəntɪ/ n [U] ~ power. 主权; 君权; 统治权; 至高无上的权力。

so·viet /'səuvɪət; 'sɒvɪɪt/ n [C] 苏维埃(意即代表会, 后成为苏联机关的名称): *the S~ Union.* 苏联。**'~·ize** /-aɪz; -,aɪz/ vt convert to the ~ system of government. 苏维埃化(使变为苏维埃体制的政府)。

sow[1] /sau; sau/ n fully grown female pig. (发育成熟的)母猪; 牝猪。⇨ **boar, hog, swine.**

sow[2] /səu; so/ vt, vi (pt sowed, pp sown /səun; son/ or sowed) [VP6A, 15A, 2A] put (seed) on or in the ground or in soil (in pots, seed-boxes, etc); plant (land with seed): 播(种子)于地面或土壤中, 在花盆中, 或种子箱中等; 以种子播于(土地): *sow grass;* 种草; *sow a plot of land with grass;* 播种草种子于一片土地; (fig) (喻) *sow the seeds of hatred.* 散布仇恨种子。*It's too soon to sow yet.* 现在还不到播种的时候。**~er** n one who sows. 播种者。

sox /sɒks; saks/ n pl (trade use) (商业用法) pl of sock.

soy /sɔɪ; sɔɪ/, **soya** /'sɔɪə; 'sɔɪə/ n **'soy(a) bean**, bean grown as food and for the oil obtained from its seeds. 黄豆(作物); 大豆(作物)。**,soy 'sauce**, sauce made by fermenting soy beans in brine. (用黄豆制造的)酱油。

soz·zled /'sɒzld; 'sɑzəld/ adj (GB, sl) very drunk. (英, 俚)烂醉的。

spa /spa:; spa/ n (place where there is a) spring of mineral water having medicinal properties. 有治疗功效的矿泉; 温泉; 有矿泉或温泉之处。

space /speɪs; spes/ n 1 [U] that in which all objects exist and move: 空间; 太空: *The universe exists in ~.* 宇宙存在于太空。*Travel through ~ to other planets interests many people today.* 现在很多人对太空其他行星旅行感到兴趣。**'~·capsule**, **'~·craft**, **'~·helmet**, **'~·rocket**, **'~·ship**, **'~·suit**, **'~·vehicle** nn of the kind needed for travel beyond the earth's atmosphere. (太空旅行所需要的)太空舱; 太空船; 太空帽; 太空火箭; 太空衣; 太空车。⇨ the illus at **capsule**, **rocket**. 参看 capsule, rocket 之插图。**'~·time** n (also known as 'the fourth dimension') fusion of time and the three dimensions of ~, as a concept much used in modern physics and philosophy. 第四度空间(时间与三度空间的结合, 在近代物理及哲学用到甚多的概念)。2 [C, U] interval or distance between two or more objects: (二物或多物之间的)间隔; 距离: *the ~s between printed words;* 印刷文字间的间隔; *separated by a ~ of ten feet;* 隔以十英尺距离; *put as much ~ as possible between the lines;* 尽量拉开行间的距离; *leave a blank ~ for sth*

to be added. 留出空白以便加添某物。**'~·bar** n bar in a typewriter, tapped to make ~s between words. (打字机上的)空间棒(按之即可在字间留出空格)。3 [C, U] area or volume: 面积; 体积: *open ~s,* (esp) land, in or near a town, not built on. 空旷处; (尤指市内或市郊的)空地。*Clear a ~ on the platform for the speakers.* 给演说的人们在台上腾出一块地方。**'~·heater** n heating apparatus (electric, or oil-burning) designed to warm a room by radiation or convection. 空间加热器(用电力或燃油, 借辐射或对流作用, 使房间温暖)。4 [U] limited or unoccupied place or area; room(3): 有限的或未占用的地方或区域; 空位; 空处; 余地: *There isn't enough ~ in this classroom for thirty desks.* 这教室容纳不下三十张书桌。*Have you enough ~ to work in?* 你有够你做事的空间吗? 5 (sing only) period of time: (仅用单数)一段时间; 期间: *a ~ of three years.* 三年的时间。□ vt [VP6A, 15B] ~ **sth (out)**, set out with regular ~s between: (依一定的距离)分隔某物; 隔开: *~ out the posts three feet apart;* 接三英尺的间隔栽放柱子; *~ out the type more;* 字间多留些空白(打字或铅印)字母与字母间隔开一点; ~ (= spread) *out payments* (eg for a house) *over twenty years;* 二十年分期付款(如购屋); *a well~d family,* one in which children are born at planned intervals of time. 计划生育的家庭(子女生育相隔的时间依照计划者)。**'~ed 'out** adj (US sl) drugged; drunk. (美俚)服过麻醉药的; 服过迷幻药的; 喝醉了的。**,single-**, **,double-'spacing** n [U] the arrangement of typed material with single /double ~s between the lines. (打字时行与行间的)单行(双行)空距。

spacious /'speɪʃəs; 'speʃəs/ adj having much space; roomy. 空间多的; 广大的; 宽敞的。**~·ly** adv ~·ness n

spade /speɪd; sped/ n 1 tool for digging. 铲; 锹。⇨ the illus at **tool**. 参看 tool 之插图。**'~·work** n (fig) hard work (to bed) done at the start of an undertaking. (喻)事业等起始的艰苦工作; 起步工作。*call a ~ a ~,* speak plainly. 直言不讳; 坦白地说。2 (one of a) suit of playing-cards: (一张)黑桃牌: *the five of ~s,* 黑桃五(点)(牌面上有五个黑桃图形者)。⇨ the illus at **card**. 参看 card 之插图。□ vt [VP6A, 15B] ~ **sth (up)**, dig (up) with a ~. 以铲或锹挖掘; 铲起。**~·ful** /-ful; -,ful/ n amount that is taken up by a ~. 一铲或一锹(之量)。

spa·ghetti /spə'getɪ; spə'gɛtɪ/ n [U] Italian pasta of narrow long rods, cooked by boiling. 意大利面条。

spake /speɪk; spek/ (old or poet) (旧或诗) pt of **speak**.

spam /spæm; spæm/ n [U] (P) chopped or minced ham, spiced, cooked, sold tinned in the form of a loaf, and usu eaten cold. 斯般(剁碎的火腿, 加香料烹制而成, 以长条形罐头包装, 通常冷食)。

span /spæn; spæn/ n [C] 1 distance between the tips of a person's thumb and little finger when stretched out (esp as a measure = 9 inches). 指距; 一拃(拇指与小指伸开时的距离, 尤用作量度单位, 合九英寸)。2 distance or part between the supports of an arch: 拱架二支柱间的距离或部分; 砌距; 跨度; 架径; 孔; 支点距: *The bridge crosses the river in a single ~.* 这桥只用一个架径跨河。*The arch has a ~ of 60 metres.* 这拱门内宽六十米。3 length in time, from beginning to end: 自始至终的一段时间; 期间: *the ~ of life;* 一生的时间; *for a short ~ of time.* 短短的一段时间。4 (S Africa) pair of horses or mules, yoke of oxen. (南非)双马; 双骡; 共轭牛。5 ~ **roof** n one with two inclined roofs (contrasted with a lean-to roof): 等斜屋顶; 双斜屋顶(与单向倾斜之屋顶相对): *a ~-roof greenhouse.* 等斜(屋)顶温室。□ vt (-nn-) [VP6A] 1 extend across (from side to side): 跨过; 架(从一边至另一边): *The Thames is ~ned by many bridges.* 泰晤士河上架设有许多桥。*His life ~ned almost the whole of the 19th c.* 他的一生几乎跨过整个十九世纪。2 measure by ~s(1). 以指距量; 以拃量。

spangle /'spæŋgl; 'spæŋgl/ n [C] tiny disc of shining metal, esp one of many, as used for ornament on a

dress, etc. 发光的小金属片(尤指衣着等上装饰用者)。 □ vt (esp in pp) (尤用过去分词) cover with, or as with, ~s. 覆以或似覆以发光的小金属片。 **the Star-S~d Banner,** ⇨ **star(2).**

Span·iard /'spænjəd/; 'spænjəd/ n native of Spain. 西班牙人。

span·iel /'spænɪəl; 'spænjəl/ n sorts of dog with short legs, long, silky hair and large, drooping ears. 猥(一种毛长耳垂之犬)。

Span·ish /'spænɪʃ; 'spænɪʃ/ adj of Spain; of the Spaniards, or their language. 西班牙的;西班牙人的;西班牙语的。 ~ **onion,** mild flavoured, yellow-skinned variety. 西班牙洋葱(皮黄, 味较淡)。 **the S~ Main,** (hist) the NE coast of S America and the Caribbean Sea, near this coast. (史)南美洲之东北岸及靠近此海岸的加勒比海。 □ n the ~ language. 西班牙语。

spank /spæŋk; spæŋk/ vt, vi 1 [VP6A] punish (a child) by slapping on the buttocks with the open hand or a slipper, etc. 用巴掌或拖鞋等打(小孩)屁股以为惩罚;拍打;拍击。 2 [VP2C] ~ **(along),** (esp of a horse or a ship) move along at a good pace. (尤指马或船)疾行;快行。 ~ **·ing** n slapping on the buttocks: 打屁股: give a child a ~ing. 打小孩一顿屁股。 □ adj (dated colloq) first-rate; excellent: (过时口语)第一流的; 极好的: have a ~ing time. 玩得很开心; a ~ing (= strong) breeze. 疾风。

span·ner /'spænə(r); 'spænə/ n (US 美 = **wrench**) tool for gripping and turning nuts on screws, bolts, etc. 扳手;扳钳;螺旋钳。 ⇨ the illus at **tool.** 参看 tool 之插图。 **throw a** '~ **in/into the works,** sabotage a scheme, etc. 破坏一项计划等。

spar[1] /spɑː(r); spɑr/ n strong wooden or metal, pole used as a mast, yard, boom, etc. mast; 桁; 帆桅。 ⇨ the illus at **barque.** 参看 barque 之插图。

spar[2] /spɑː(r); spɑr/ vi (-rr-) [VP2A, C] make the motions of attack and defence with the fists (as in boxing); (fig) dispute or argue. 用拳攻击及防御(如拳赛中); 拳斗; (喻)争论; 争辩; 对驳。 '~**·ring-match** n demonstration boxing match; (fig) dispute or argument. 示范或练习性拳赛; (喻)争论; 争辩; 对驳。 '~**·ring-partner** n man with whom a boxer ~s as part of his training. 拳击者训练时的对手; 练拳伴。

spar[3] /spɑː(r); spɑr/ n kinds of non-metallic mineral, easily cleavable. 晶石(各种易劈裂的非金属矿石)。

spare[1] /speə(r); spɛr/ adj 1 additional to what is usually needed or used; in reserve for use when needed; (of time) for leisure; unoccupied; 多余的; 剩余的; 备用的; (指时间)空暇的; 未占用的: I have no/very little ~ time/money, so time/money that I cannot use. 我没有(很少有)空暇(余钱)。 Surely you carry a ~ wheel in the back of your car? 你一定在车子后面带着一个备用的轮胎吧? We have no room/We don't have a ~ room (= extra bedroom, eg for a guest) in our house. 我们家里没有多余的房间(如供客人住者)。 ~ **part,** part to replace a broken or worn-out part of a machine, etc. (机器等的)备用零件。 2 (of persons) thin; lean:(指人)瘦的: a tall, ~ man; 高而瘦的人; a ~ figure; 瘦人; ~ of build. 体态清瘦的。 3 (attrib only) small in quantity: (仅用作定语)少量的; 贫乏的: a ~ meal; 不丰富的一餐; on a ~ diet. 在节食。 '~**'rib,** rib of pork with most of the meat cut off. (猪肉)小排。 □ n [C] ~ part (for a machine, etc). (机器等的)备件。 ~**·ly** adv in a ~ **(2, 3)** manner: 瘦瘠的; 清瘦地; 不丰富地: ~ly built. 体态清瘦的。 ~**·ness** n

spare[2] /speə(r); spɛr/ vt, vi 1 [VP6A, 12A, 13A] refrain from hurting, damaging or destroying; show mercy to: 不伤害; 赦免; 宽宥: ~ sb's life, ~ sb his life, not kill him or have him killed. 饶某人的命; We may meet again if we are ~d, if our lives are ~d by Providence. 如果我们不死, 还会见面的。 He doesn't ~ himself, is severe with himself, does not refrain from

making great demands upon himself (his energies, time, etc). 他律己甚严。 ~ **sb's feelings,** avoid hurting his feelings. 避免伤某人的感情。 **S~ the rod and spoil the child,** (prov) If you refrain from punishing the child, you will spoil its character. (谚)孩子不打不成器。 2 [VP12B, 13B, 6A] ~ **sth (for sb/sth);** ~ **sb sth,** afford to give (time, money, etc) to sb, or for a purpose: 提供(时间、金钱等)给某人或为某种目的; 匀出; 分出; 分让: Can you ~ me a few litres of petrol? 你能匀给我几公升汽油吗? Can you ~ one of them for me? 你能让(其中的)一个给我吗? Can you ~ me a few minutes (of your time)? 我能耽搁你几分钟吗? I can't ~ the time for a holiday at present. 目前我抽不出时间来度假。 We have enough and to ~, more than we need. 我们不但足够而且有余。 3 [VP6A] use in small quantities, expend or use in a saving manner. 小量使用; 爱惜; 节省。 **no expense(s)/pains ~ed,** with no economy in money or effort: 不惜工本(不遗余力); 全力以赴: I'm going to redecorate the house, no expense ~ed. 我将不惜工本重新把房子装修一番。 **spar·ing** adj **sparing of,** economical, frugal, careful (of): 节约的; 俭省的; 小心的; 谨慎的: You should be more sparing of your energy. 你应该多多节省你的精力。 **spar·ing·ly** adv

spark[1] /spɑːk; spɑrk/ n [C] tiny glowing bit thrown off from a burning substance or still present in ashes, etc or produced by striking flint or hard metal and stone together; flash of light produced by the breaking of an electric current; (fig) sign of life, energy, etc; flash of wit: 火星; 火花; (电流切断时产生的)电花; (喻)生命、精力等的标志; 智慧的闪动: The firework burst into a shower of ~s. 那烟火爆发为一阵火花。 He hasn't a ~ of generosity in him. 他一点也不慷慨。 □ vt, vi [VP2A, 15B] give out ~s. 发出火花; 放散火星。 ~ **sth off,** (fig) lead to; be the immediate cause of: (喻)导致; 为...的直接原因: His statement ~ed off a quarrel between them. 他的话引起他们之间一场争吵。 '~**-(·ing)-plug** n device for firing the gas in a petrol engine by means of an electric ~. (内燃机的)火星塞; 火花塞。 ⇨ the illus at **motor.** 参看 motor 之插图。

spark[2] /spɑːk; spɑrk/ n (colloq) gay and elegant person. (口)风度翩翩之人; 愉快而风雅的人。

sparkle /'spɑːkl; 'spɑrkl/ vi [VP2A, C] send out flashes of light: 闪闪发光; 闪耀; 闪烁; 闪亮: ~d in the bright light. 她的钻石在亮光下闪闪发光。 Her eyes ~d with excitement. 她的眼睛由于兴奋而发亮。 □ n spark; glitter. 火花; 火星; 闪光; 闪耀。 **spark·ler** /'spɑːklə(r); 'spɑrklə/ n sth that ~s, eg a kind of firework; (sl, esp among criminals, often pl) diamond. 发闪光物(如喷射的烟火); (俚, 尤用于盗贼间, 常作复数)钻石; 金刚钻。 **spark·ling** /'spɑːklɪŋ; 'spɑrklɪŋ/ adj (esp) (of wines) giving out tiny bubbles of carbonic acid gas when the bottle is opened. (尤指酒类)起泡沫的; 开瓶时冒出碳酸气泡的。 ⇨ **still**[1](2).

spar·row /'spærəʊ; 'spæro/ n small brownish-grey bird common in many parts of the world, esp the 'house~, European kind found around buildings. 麻雀 (尤指家雀, 称 the house-~)。 ⇨ the illus at **bird.** 参看 bird 之插图。

sparse /spɑːs; spɑrs/ adj 1 thinly scattered: 稀少的: a ~ population. 稀少的人口。 2 not dense, thick or crowded: 稀落的; 稀疏的; 不浓密的: a ~ beard. 稀疏的胡须。 ~**·ly** adv: a ~ly furnished room, one with little furniture. 陈设简陋的房间。 ~**·ness, spar·sity** /'spɑːsətɪ; 'spɑrsətɪ/ n [U].

Spar·tan /'spɑːtn; 'spɑrtn/ n, adj (person) caring little for the ordinary comforts of life, unafraid of pain and hardship; (of living conditions) hard because very simple: 刻苦的(人); 不畏痛苦和艰辛的(人); (指生活状况)简朴而刻苦的: live a ~ life; 过简单刻苦的生活; in ~ simplicity. 斯巴达式的简朴。

spasm /'spæzəm; 'spæzəm/ n [C] 1 sudden and involuntary tightening of a muscle or muscles: 痉挛;

抽筋: *asthma* ~*s*. 喘哮性痉挛。 **2** sudden, convulsive movement: 突然颤动的动作; 突发的一阵; 痉挛性动作: *in a* ~ *of pain/excitement/grief*: 在一阵痛苦(兴奋,忧伤)中; *a* ~ *of coughing*. 一阵咳嗽。 **3** sudden burst of energy: (精力或能量的)一阵发作或突然爆发。

spas·mod·ic /spæz'mɒdɪk; spæz'mɑdɪk/ *adj* **1** taking place, done, at irregular intervals. 时作时停的; 断断续续的。 **2** caused by, affected by, spasms: 由痉挛引起的;受痉挛影响的;阵发性的: ~ *asthma*. 痉挛性气喘。 **spas·modi·cally** /-klɪ; -klɪ/ *adv*

spas·tic /'spæstɪk; 'spæstɪk/ *n, adj* (person) suffering from cerebral palsy, physically disabled because of faulty links between the brain and motor nerves, causing spasmodic movements through difficulty in controlling voluntary muscles. 患脑麻痹的(人);痉挛的(人)。

spat¹ /spæt; spæt/ *n* **(a pair of)** ~*s*, cloth cover worn over the upper part of a shoe and round the ankle. 鞋罩(穿于鞋面及踝部的覆盖物)。

spat² /spæt; spæt/ *pt, pp* of **spit**.

spat³ /spæt; spæt/ *vi, vt* **(-tt-)**, *n* (US) (have a) slight quarrel; (give a) light slap (to). (美)口角; 小争吵;轻拍;轻击。

spat⁴ /spæt; spæt/ *n* spawn of oysters. 蚝卵; 牡蛎卵。□ *vi* **(-tt-)** (of oysters) spawn. (指蚝)产卵。

spatch·cock /'spætʃkɒk; 'spætʃ,kɑk/ *n* fowl killed and cooked at once. 杀后立即烹调的鸡。□ *vt* [VP6A, 14] ~ **(in/into)**, (colloq) insert (words): (口)插入(文字): *He* ~*ed into his speech a curious passage about* .... 他在演说中加入一段有关…的奇特的话。

spate /speɪt; spet/ *n* **1** strong current of water at abnormally high level (in a river): (河中之)洪流; 洪水: *After the storm the rivers were all in* ~. 暴风雨过后各河流河水暴涨。 **2** sudden rush of business, etc: 营业等突然涌到: *a* ~ *of orders*: 订单大量涌到; *a* ~ *of new cars on the market*. 市场上大量的新车。

spa·tial /'speɪʃl; 'speʃl/ *adj* of, in relation to, existing in, space. 空间的; 有关空间的; 存在于空间的。~*ly* /-ʃəlɪ; -ʃəlɪ/ *adv*

spat·ter /'spætə(r); 'spætɚ/ *vt, vi* **1** [VP6A, 14] ~ *sth* **(on/over sth)**; ~ *sth* **(with sth)**, splash, scatter, in drips: 溅;洒;泼: ~ *grease on one's clothes/* ~ *one's clothes with grease*. 油脂溅到衣服上。 *As the bus went by it* ~*ed us with mud*. 公共汽车开过时,溅了我们一身泥。 **2** [VP2C] fall or spread out in drops: 呈点滴降落或散开;滴落;纷落;溅开;溅下: *We heard the rain* ~*ing down on the tin roof of the hut*. 我们听到雨滴落在小屋的铁皮屋顶上。□ *n* [C] sprinkling; shower: 溅;洒;泼;滴落;纷落;溅落: *a* ~ *of rain/bullets*. 一阵雨(枪弹)。

spat·ula /'spætjʊlə US: 'spætʃʊlə; 'spætʃələ/ *n* tool with a wide, flat, flexible blade used for mixing or spreading various substances. (混合或涂敷用的)阔扁而有弹性的抹刀;刮铲。

spavin /'spævɪn; 'spævɪn/ *n* [U] disease of horses in which a bony swelling forms at the hock, causing lameness. 马的后脚跟关节内肿; 飞节内肿。 **spav·ined** *adj* affected with ~. 患飞节内肿的。

spawn /spɔːn; spɔn/ *n* [U] **1** eggs of fish and certain water animals, eg frogs. 鱼卵; 鱼子;(蛙等水生动物的)卵;子。⇨ the illus at **amphibian**. 参看 amphibian 之插图。 **2** threadlike matter from which mushrooms and other fungi grow. 菌丝(真菌类植物即由此生长)。□ *vt, vi* [VP6A, 2A] lay or produce in great numbers: 大量产生: *departments which* ~ *committees and sub-committees*. 委员会及附属委员会众多的政府机构。

spay /speɪ; spe/ *vt* [VP6A] remove the ovaries of (a female animal). 割除(雌性动物的)卵巢。

speak /spiːk; spik/ *vi, vt* (*pt* **spoke** /spəʊk; spok/, archaic (古) **spake** /speɪk; spek/, *pp* **spoken** /'spəʊkən; 'spokən/) **1** [VP2A, C] make use of language in an ordinary, not a singing, voice: 说; 说话: *Please* ~ *more slowly*. 请说慢一点。 **2** [VP2B, C, 3A] ~ **(to/**

with sb) (about sth): 与某人谈论某事: *I was* ~*ing to him about plans for the holidays*. 我在同他谈论度假的计划。 ~ *for sb*, **(a)** state the views, wishes, etc of; act as spokesman for. 作某人的发言人; 陈述某人的意见,愿望等。 **(b)** give evidence on behalf of. 代表…证明某事; 证实。 ~ *for oneself*, **(a)** express one's views, etc in one's own way. 以自己的方式说明自己的见解等。 **(b)** (usu 通常作 *S*~ *for yourself!*) not presume to ~ for others. 说出你自己的意见(不要代表旁人发言); ~ *to sb*, admonish: 训诫;训斥;告诫;规劝;说: *Your secretary was late again this morning* ―― *you'd better* ~ *to her about it*. 你的秘书今天早晨又迟到了――你最好说说她。 ~ *to sth*, in confirmation of or in reference to: 证到; 提到; 证明: *Is there anyone here who can* ~ *to his having been at the scene of the crime*, *who can say that he was there*? 这里有人能够证明他曾在犯罪的现场吗? *You must* ~ *to the subject*, not wander away from it. 你(讲话)不可离题。 ~ *of the devil!* said when, just after being spoken about, sb is seen, heard, etc. 刚谈到某人,某人就来了; 说曹操,曹操就到。 *nothing to* ~ *of*, nothing worth mentioning; not much. 无可称述;乏善可陈;不值一谈。 ~ *out/up*, **(a)** ~ loud(er). 大(更大)声说。 **(b)** give one's opinions, etc without hesitation or fear. 毫不迟疑或恐惧地说出自己的意见等。 *be not on* ~*ing terms with sb*, **(a)** not know him well enough to ~ to him. 与某人认识的程度还不到可以谈话的地步。 **(b)** no longer ~ to him because one has quarrelled with him. 因与人交恶而不再与之谈话。 *so to* ~, as one might say; if I may use this expression, etc. 可以说; 可谓。 '~*-ing-trumpet* *n* (now replaced by *hearing-aids*) trumpet-shaped device held to the ear by a deaf person to help him to hear. (现已为 hearing-aids 所取代) 喇叭形助听器。 '~*-ing-tube* *n* tube that carries the voice from one place to another, eg from a ship's bridge to the engine-room. 通话管(如从舰桥通至引擎室者)。 **3** [VP2C, 15A] give evidence (of), convey ideas (not necessarily in words): 说明;证实; 传达概念(不一定用语言): *Actions* ~ *louder than words*. 行动胜于空言。 *The portrait* ~*s/is a* ~*ing likeness*, is excellent, tells us well what the sitter was like. 这人像得非常好(很象本人)。 ~ *volumes for*, be strong evidence of: 极足以证明;为有力证据: *This evidence* ~*s volumes for his honesty*. 这证据足以证明他的诚实。 ~ *well for*, be evidence in favour of. 对…为有利证据。 **4** [VP6A] know or be able to use (a language): 懂或通(某种语言);会使用或会通晓(某种语言): *He* ~*s several languages*. 他通数种语言。 *Is English spoken here?* 此地通用英语吗? **5** [VP2A, B] address an audience; make a speech: 演说;演讲。 *He* ~*s for forty minutes*. 他(演)讲了四十分钟。 *Are you good at* ~*ing in public*? 你擅长当众演说吗? **6** [VP6A] make known; utter: 说明; 说出: ~ *the truth*. 说实话。 ~ *one's mind*, express one's views frankly or bluntly. 坦率表明自己的见解及意见。 **7** (in the pattern, *adv* (in -*ly*) and *pres part*): (用于副词(以 -ly 结尾)加现在分词的句型中): *strictly/roughly/generally, etc* ~*ing*, using the word(s) in a strict/rough/general, etc sense. 严格地(约略地,一般地等)说。 **8** [VP6A] (naut) hail and exchange information with (by flag signals, etc): (航海)(借旗语等)联络;招呼; 交换情报: ~ *a passing ship*. 与经过的船联络。 **9** [VP2A] (of a gun, musical instrument, etc) make sounds. (指枪炮,乐器等)发响声。 **10** '~*-easy* *n* illicit liquor shop (esp in the US during the period of prohibition). 非法卖酒的商店(尤指美国禁酒时期)。 ~*er* *n* **1** person who makes speeches (in the manner indicated): 说话者; 演说者(与形容词连用): *He's a good/poor, etc* ~. 他是一个好的(差劲的等)说话者。 **2** (short for) *loud-*~*er*. 为 loud-~er 之略。 **3** *the S*~*er*, presiding officer of the House of Commons and other legislative assemblies. (英国下议院及其他议会的)议长。 '~*er·ship* /-ʃɪp; -ʃɪp/ *n* office of the S~er; period of office of a S~er. 议长的职位;议长的任期。

spear /spɪə(r); spɪr/ *n* weapon with a metal point on a long shaft, used in hunting, or (formerly) by men fighting on foot. 矛; 枪。□ *vt* [VP6A] pierce, wound, make (a hole) in, with a ~. 用矛刺、戳或伤; 用矛戳 (洞) 于。'~**-head** *n* (usu *fig*) individual or group chosen to lead an attack. (通常为喻) 前锋; 先锋; 领导攻击的个人或部队。□ *vt* act as ~-head for: 为…的先锋: *armoured vehicles that* ~-*head the offensive.* 作为攻击前锋的装甲车辆。

spear·mint /'spɪəmɪnt; 'spɪr,mɪnt/ *n* aromatic variety of mint used for flavouring; chewing-gum flavoured with this. 荷兰薄荷(用于调味); 薄荷口香糖。

spec /spek; spek/ *n* (colloq abbr of) speculation: (口) 为 speculation 之略: *Those mining shares turned out a good* ~, proved profitable. 那些矿产股票结果赚了钱。 **on** ~, as a speculation; as a guess. 推测; 臆测。

special /'speʃl; 'speʃəl/ *adj* 1 of a particular or certain sort; not common, usual or general; of or for a certain person, thing or purpose: 特别的; 特殊的; 专用的; 特设的: *He did it for her as a* ~ *favour.* 他为她做那件事以示特别关切。*What are your* ~ *interests?* 你的特殊兴趣是什么? *Newspapers send* ~ *correspondents to places where important events take place.* 报馆派遣特派员至发生重要事件的地方。*On holidays the railways put on* ~ *trains,* run extra trains for ~ purposes. 假日各线铁路增开加班火车。~ **constable,** man enrolled to help the ordinary police in time of need. 临时警察。 ~ **delivery,** delivery of mail (a letter, package, etc) by a ~ messenger instead of by the usual postal services. 快递; 快信。~ **licence,** licence which allows a marriage to take place at a time or place other than those legally authorized. 特别结婚许可证(准予在非规定的时间或地方举行婚礼)。2 exceptional in amount, degree, etc: 在数量、程度或方面的; 格外的: *Why should we give you* ~ *treatment?* 我们为什么要给你特殊待遇呢? *You've taken no* ~ *trouble with your work for us.* 你为我们工作,并不特别卖力。~ *n* constable, ~ train, ~ edition of a newspaper, etc. 临时警察; 加班火车; (报纸等的)特刊。~**ly** /-ʃəlɪ; -ʃəlɪ/ *adv* particularly: 特别的; 专门的: *I came here* ~*ly* (= on purpose) *to see you.* 我是特意来看你的。~·**ist** /-ʃəlɪst; -ʃəlɪst/ *n* person who is an expert in a ~ branch of work or study, esp medicine: 专家; (尤指医)专家: *an* ~*ist in plastic surgery.* 整形外科专家。

spe·ci·al·ity /,speʃɪ'ælətɪ; ,speʃɪ'ælətɪ/ *n* [C] (*pl* **-ties**) 1 special quality or characteristic of sb or sth. 特质; 特性。2 (also 亦作 **spe·cialty** /'speʃəltɪ; 'speʃəltɪ/ (*pl* **-ties**)) special pursuit, activity, product, operation, etc; thing to which a person (firm, etc) gives special attention or for which a place is well known: 专门研究; 专业; 专长; 特制品; 特产品: *Embroidery is her* ~. 刺绣是她的专长。*Wood-carvings are a* ~ *of this village.* 木器雕刻品是这个村子的特产。

spe·cial·ize /'speʃəlaɪz; 'speʃəl,aɪz/ *vi, vt* 1 [VP 2A, 3A] ~ (*in sth*), be or become a specialist; give special or particular attention to: 成为或变为专家; 专攻; 专门研究: ~ *in oriental history.* 专攻东方史。*After his first degree he wishes to* ~. 获得学士学位以后, 他希望专攻某科。2 (usu *pp*) (通常用过去分词) adapt for a particular purpose: 使适应特殊目的; 使专用于: *a hospital with* ~*d wards,* (cf 参较 *general wards*); 有专科病房的医院; (cf 参较 *general wards*); ~*d knowledge,* (cf 参较 *general knowledge*). 专门知识。 **spe·cial·iz·ation** /,speʃəlaɪ'zeɪʃn US: -lɪ'z-; ,speʃələ'zeʃən/ *n*

spe·cialty /'speʃəltɪ; 'speʃəltɪ/ *n* (*pl* **-ties**) ⇨ speciality (2).

specie /'spiːʃiː; 'spiʃɪ/ *n* [U] (store of, consignment of) money in the form of coins: 硬币; 钱币; 钱币的储备或支付: ~ *payments;* 硬币支付; *payment in* ~. 硬币支付。

spe·cies /'spiːʃiːz; 'spiʃɪz/ *n* (*pl* unchanged) (复数不变) 1 (biol) group having some common characteristics (division of a genus) able to breed with each other but not with other groups: (生物)种(属以下的分类法); 具有共同特质可相互繁殖的类群: *the human* ~, mankind. 人类。□ *n* 2 sort: 种类: *Blackmail is a* ~ *of crime hated by all decent folk.* 恫吓勒索是所有正人君子所憎恨的一种罪行。

spe·ci·fic /spə'sɪfɪk; spɪ'sɪfɪk/ *adj* 1 detailed and precise: 详细而精确的; 明确的: ~ *orders.* 明确的命令。 *What are your* ~ *aims?* 你的明确目标是什么? 2 relating to one particular thing, etc, not general: 特种的; 特殊的; 涉及某特定一个的: *The money is to be used for a* ~ *purpose.* 该款将用于特定的用途。~ **gravity,** mass of any substance relative to that of an equal volume of water. 比重(任何物质的重量与同体积水的重量之比)。 ~ **name,** (biol) distinguishing name of the species. (生物)种名。~ **remedy,** one for a particular disease. 特效药。□ *n* [C] ~ remedy: 特效药: *Quinine is a* ~ *for malaria.* 奎宁是治疟疾的特效药。 **spe·cifi·cally** /-klɪ; -klɪ/ *adv* in a ~ manner; 明确地; 特殊地: *You were* ~*ally warned by your doctor not to eat lobster.* 医生曾特别警告你不可吃龙虾。

spec·ifi·ca·tion /,spesɪfɪ'keɪʃn; ,spesəfə'keʃən/ *n* 1 [U] specifying. 指定; 载明; 详述。2 (often *pl*) details, instructions, etc for the design, materials, of sth to be made or done: (常用复数)做某事物的详细说明; 计划书; 清单; 规格: ~*s for* (*building a*) *a garage;* (建造)车房的详细规格; *the technical* ~*s of a new car.* 一辆新汽车的技术细则。

spec·ify /'spesɪfaɪ; 'spesə,faɪ/ *vt* (*pt, pp* **-fied**) [VP 6A, 9] state or name definitely; include in the specifications: 指定; 载明; 详述; 逐一登记: *The contract specifies red tiles, not slates, for the roof.* 合约载明屋顶用红瓦,而非石板。*The regulations* ~ *that you may use a dictionary in the examination.* 规则指明考试时可用词典。

speci·men /'spesɪmɪn; 'spesəmən/ *n* [C] 1 one as an example of a class: 标本; 范例: ~*s of rocks and ores.* 岩石及矿石的标本。2 part taken to represent the whole: 样品: *a publisher's catalogue with* ~ *pages of books.* 有书籍样张的出版物目录。3 sth to be tested, etc for definite or special purposes: 供特定目的而取的待试验物; 抽样; 取样: *supply a* ~ *of one's urine.* 检送某人的小便取样。4 (colloq) unusual thing or person regarded with contempt or amusement: (口)(含轻视意或出以戏言)怪人; 怪物: *What a queer* ~ (*of humanity*) *he is!* 他是一个多么古怪的人啊!

spe·cious /'spiːʃəs; 'spiʃəs/ *adj* seeming right or true, but not really so: 似是而非的; 华而不实的; 表里不一致的: *a* ~ *argument/person.* 似是而非的论点(表里不一致的人)。~**ly** *adv* ~**ness** *n*

speck /spek; spek/ *n* [C] small spot or particle (of dirt, etc); stain; discoloured spot on fruit (showing rottenness); dot: (泥土等的)微粒; 污点; 斑点; (水果上表示腐烂的)疵伤; 瑕疵: *Do you ever seem to see* ~*s in front of your eyes?* 你曾否感觉眼前面面似可看见许多小点? *The ship was a mere* ~ *on the horizon.* 那条船在地平线仅是一个小黑点。~**ed** *adj* marked with ~s: 有微粒的; 有斑点的; 有疵痕的: ~*ed apples.* 有疵痕的苹果。 ~**·less** *adj*

speckle /'spekl; 'spɛkl/ *n* [C] small mark or spot, esp one of many, distinct in colour, on the skin, feathers, etc. 小点; 斑点(尤指皮肤、羽毛等上颜色不同者)。~**d** *adj* marked with ~s: 有斑点的; 有小点的: ~*d hen;* 有斑点的母鸡; ~*d plumage.* 带斑点的羽毛。

specs /speks; speks/ *n pl* (colloq) spectacles(3). (口)眼镜。

spec·tacle /'spektəkl; 'spɛktəkl/ *n* [C] 1 public display, procession, etc, esp one with ceremony: 公开展示、行列等(尤指有仪式者); 观览(物); 展览(物): *The ceremonial opening of Parliament was a fine* ~. 英国国会的开幕式是一个很壮丽的场面。2 (sing only; sth) sth taking place before the eyes, esp sth fine, remarkable or noteworthy: 景象; 光景; 奇观; 壮观: *The sunrise as seen*

from the top of the mountain was a tremendous ~. 从山顶所见的日出景象,蔚为奇观. *The poor drunken man was a sad* ~. 那可怜的醉汉样子令人悲痛. *Don't draw a* ~ *of yourself*, don't draw attention to yourself by dressing, behaving, etc ridiculously. 不要现眼(衣服及举止等, 不可荒唐可笑而引人注意). **3** ~*s; a pair of* ~*s*, pair of lenses in a frame, resting on the nose and ears, to help the eyesight (or to protect the eyes from bright sunlight) (*glasses* is the more usu name). 眼镜; 护目镜 (glasses 较常用). *see everything through rose-coloured* ~*s*, take a cheerful, optimistic view of things. 对事持乐观看法. ~**d** *adj* wearing ~s. 戴眼镜的.

spec·tac·u·lar /spek'tækjʊlə(r); spɛk'tækjələ/ *adj* making a fine spectacle (1, 2); attracting public attention: 洋洋大观的; 蔚为奇观的; 壮观的; 引人入胜的; 吸引人的: *a* ~ *display of fireworks*. 施放烟火的壮观景象. □ *n* [C] spectacle; ~ show: 奇观; 壮观; 引人入胜的表演: *a Christmas TV* ~. 圣诞节引人入胜的电视演出. ~**ly** *adv*

spec·ta·tor /spek'teɪtə(r) US: 'spekteɪtər; 'spɛkteɪtə/ *n* onlooker (esp at a show or game): 旁观者; (尤指表演或比赛的)观众: (attrib) (用作定语) ~ *sports*, those which draw crowds of ~s, eg football. 观众多的体育活动(如足球).

spectre (US = **spec·ter**) /'spektə(r); 'spɛktə/ *n* [C] ghost; haunting fear of future trouble. 鬼; 幽灵; 对未来困难的忧惧. **spec·tral** /spektrəl; 'spɛktrəl/ *adj* **1** of or like a ~. 鬼的; 幽灵的; 似鬼或幽灵的. **2** of spectra or the spectrum: 光谱的: *spectral colours*. 谱色.

spec·tro·scope /'spektrəskəʊp; 'spɛktrəskop/ *n* instrument for producing and examining the spectra of a ray of light. 分光镜; 分光器. **spec·tro·scopic** /ˌspektrə'skɒpɪk; ˌspɛktrə'skɑpɪk/ *adj* of, by means of, a ~: 分光镜(器)的; 借分光镜(器)的: *spectroscopic analysis*. 借分光镜所作的分析; 分光分析.

spec·trum /'spektrəm; 'spɛktrəm/ *n* (*pl* **-tra** /-trə, -trə/) image of a band of colours (as seen in a rainbow and usu described as red, orange, yellow, green, blue, indigo and violet) formed by a ray of light which has passed through a prism; (fig) wide range or sequence: 光谱(光线通过三棱镜所产生的色带); (喻)广阔的范围,领域或系列: *the whole* ~ *of recent philosophical enquiry*. 新近哲学研究的整个范围.

1 red
2 orange
3 yellow
4 green
5 blue
6 indigo
7 violet

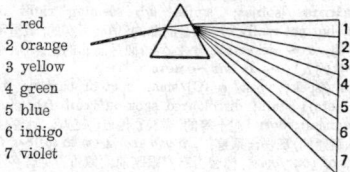

the colours of the spectrum

specu·late /'spekjʊleɪt; 'spɛkjə,let/ *vi* [VP2A, C] **1** consider, form opinions (without having complete knowledge); guess: (无充分知识而)思考并形成意见; 玄想; 臆测; 推测: ~ *about/upon the future of the human race;* 推测人类的将来; ~ *what sort of man one will marry*. 思索何类男子可为结婚对象. **2** buy and sell goods, stocks and shares, etc with risk of loss and hope of profit through changes in their market value: 做投机买卖: ~ *in oil shares/wheat.* 做石油股票(小麦)投机买卖. **specu·la·tor** /-tə(r); -tə/ *n* person who ~s(2). 投机商人.

specu·la·tion /ˌspekjʊ'leɪʃn; ˌspɛkjə'leʃən/ *n* **1** [U] speculating(1); meditation; [C] opinion reached by this means; guess. 玄思; 沉思; 默想; 玄想; 臆测. **2** [U] speculating(2): 做投机买卖: ~ *in rice;* 做稻米投机生意; [C] transaction, business deal, of this kind:

投机买卖; 投机生意: *make some bad* ~*s*; 做数次亏本的投机生意; *buy mining shares as a* ~. 投机买进矿业股票.

specu·lat·ive /'spekjʊleɪtɪv US -leɪtɪv; 'spɛkjə,letɪv/ *adj* **1** concerned with speculation(1): 玄想的; 思索的; 推测的: ~ *philosophy*. 思辨哲学. **2** concerned with speculation(2). 投机的; 投机性的: ~ *purchase of grain;* 投机性购买谷物; ~ *housing*, the building of houses as a speculation(2). 投机性营造房屋. ~**ly** *adv*

sped /sped; spɛd/ *pt, pp* of **speed**.

speech /spiːtʃ; spitʃ/ *n* **1** [U] power, act, manner, of speaking: 语言; 说话; 讲话的能力、方式等: *Man is the only animal that has the faculty of* ~. 人是唯一有语言能力的动物. *Our thoughts are expressed by* ~. 我们的思想是用语言表达的. *They say that* ~ *is silver but silence is golden.* 人们说言语是银, 沉默是金. *His indistinct* ~ *made it impossible to understand him.* 他口齿不清使人无法听懂他的话. ~ *therapy*, remedial treatment for defective speech, eg for stuttering. 语言医疗(矫治语言缺失, 如口吃的医疗). **2** [C] talk or address given in public: 演说; 当众讲话: *make a* ~ *on/about the Common Market to a receptive audience.* 就欧洲共同市场问题向能接受该政策的听众发表演说. '~**day** *n* annual school celebration when ~es and distribution of certificates and prizes. 学校每年的毕业典礼发奖日(发表演说, 并分发证书及奖品). ~**less** *adj* **1** unable to speak, eg because of deep feeling: 说不出话来的(尤指由于情绪激动): ~*less with surprise.* 因惊讶而说不出话来. *Anger left him* ~*less.* 愤怒使他说不出话来. **2** that causes a person to be unable to speak: 使人说不出话来的: ~*less rage.* 使人说不出话来的盛怒. ~**less·ly** *adv* ~**ify** /'spiːtʃɪfaɪ; 'spitʃə,faɪ/ *vi* (*pt, pp* **-fied**) make ~es; talk as if making ~es (usu implying that this is done unnecessarily or badly): 演说; 长篇大论(通常含有无必要或很差劲): *town councillors* ~*ifying at the unveiling of a statue/at a welcome to the Queen.* 在雕像揭幕(欢迎女王)时市议员们发表演说.

speed /spiːd; spid/ *n* **1** [U] swiftness; rapidity of movement. 迅速; (行动)快捷. *More haste, less* ~, (prov) Too much haste may result in delay. (谚)欲速则不达. **2** [C, U] rate of motion or moving: 速度; 速率: ~ *travelling at full/top* ~; 以全(高)速行进; *at a* ~ *of thirty miles an hour.* 以每小时三十英里的速度. *It's dangerous to corner at* ~, to round corners (in a vehicle) at a high ~. 高速转弯是危险的. **3** (sl) amphetamine used as a drug to produce euphoria. (俚)(使人产生舒适感的药物)苯基丙胺; 安非他明; 苯齐特林. **4** (compounds) (复合词) '~**boat** *n* motor-boat designed for high ~s. 快艇. '~**cop** *n* (sl) police motor-cyclist who checks the ~ of motorists. (俚)取缔汽车超速的骑摩托车的警察; 验速警察. '~**indicator** *n* = ~ometer. ⇨ below. 参看下列之 ~ometer. '~**limit** *n* ~ which must not be exceeded, eg in a built-up area. 速度上限. '~ **merchant**, (sl) person who drives a car or motor-bike extremely fast. (俚)速度贩子(以极高速度驾驶汽车或机车者). '~**way** *n* **(a)** track, for fast driving and racing, esp by motor-bikes. 高速道; (尤指)机车赛车道. **(b)** (US) road for fast traffic; expressway. (美)高速公路. □ *vt, vi* (*pt, pp* **sped**) **1** [VP2A, C] move along, go, quickly: 迅速; 急行: *cars* ~*ing past the school.* 快速经过学校的车辆. *He sped down the street.* 他沿街急行. **2** [VP6A, 14] cause to move or go quickly: 使速进; 使急行: ~ *an arrow from the bow.* 拉弓射箭. **3** (archaic) give success to: (古)使成功: *God* ~ *you*, May God make you prosper. 祝你成功(愿上帝使你成功). **4** [VP15B, 2C] (*pt, pp* ~**ed**) ~ (*sth*) *up*, increase the ~ (of): 增加…的速度或速率: *They have* ~*ed up production/the train service.* 他们业已加速生产(增加火车班次). *He* ~*ed the engine up.* 他加快引擎的速率. *The train soon* ~*ed up.* 火车不久就加速前进. Hence, 由此产生, '~**up** *n* ~ing up the rate of

production, etc. 加快; 加速(生产等)。 ~·ing n (of motorists) travelling at an illegal or dangerous ~: (指驾驶者)超速: fined £30 for ~ing. 因超速而罚款三十英镑。 ~·om·eter /spi'dɒmɪtə(r)/ spi'dɒmətə(r) n instrument showing the ~ of a motor-vehicle, etc. (汽车等的)计速表。 ⇨ the illus at **motor**. 参看 motor 之插图。 ~·y adj (-ier, -iest) quick; coming, done, without delay; 快速的; 迅速来临或完成的: wish sb a ~y recovery from illness. 希望某人迅速康复。

a speed-boat

speed·well /'spiːdwel/ 'spidwel/ n kinds of small, wild plant with bright blue flowers. 草本威灵仙属植物(开鲜艳的蓝花)。

spelae·ol·ogy (also **spele-**) /,spiːlɪ'ɒlədʒɪ/ spiːlɪ'ɑl-ədʒɪ/ n [U] the scientific study and exploration of caves. 洞穴学(岩洞的探测及其科学研究)。 **spelae·ol·ogist** (also **spele-**) /-dʒɪst; -dʒɪst/ n expert in, student of, ~. 洞窟学家。

spell[1] /spel; spel/ n [C] 1 words used as a charm, supposed to have magic power: 符咒; 咒语: cast a ~ over sb; 以符咒镇某人; put a ~ on sb; 以符咒镇某人; be under /lay sb under a ~. 被符咒镇住(以符咒镇住某人)。 '~·bound /-baʊnd/ -,baʊnd/ adj with the attention held by, or as by, a ~: 被符咒镇住的; 入迷的: The speaker held his audience ~bound. 那演说者使听众入迷。 '~·binder /-baɪndə(r)/ -,baɪndə/ n speaker who can hold audiences ~bound. 能使听众入迷的演说者。 2 attraction, fascination, exercised by a person, occupation, etc: 吸引力; 迷惑力; 魔力; 魅力: under the ~ of her beauty; 为她的美色所吸引; the mysterious ~ of the music of Delius. 狄里惠斯音乐的神秘魅力。

spell[2] /spel; spel/ n 1 period of time: 一段时间; 时期: a long ~ of warm weather; 一段长时间的暖和天气; a cold ~ in January; 正月里一段寒冷的时期; rest for a (short) ~. 休息一段(短)时间。 2 period of activity or duty, esp one at which two or more persons take turns: 活动时间; 工作时间; (尤指)轮值时间: take ~s at the wheel, eg of two persons making a long journey by car. 轮流开车。 □ vt ~ sb (at sth), take turns with sb: 与某人轮值; 轮替; 轮流: Will you ~ me at rowing the boat? 你愿意同我轮流划船吗？

spell[3] /spel; spel/ vt, vi (pt, pp ~ed /speld; speld/ or **spelt** /spelt; spelt/) 1 [VP6A] name or write the letters of (a word): 拼或拼出(某词)的字母; 拼字; 拼写: How do you ~ your name? 你的名字怎么拼？ '~·ing pronunciation, one suggested by the written form of the word (eg /'nefjuː/; 'nefjuː instead of /'nevjuː; 'nevjuː for nephew). 照拼法发音(如 nephew 一词读成 /'nefjuː/; 'nefjuː/ 而不读成 /'nevjuː; 'nevjuː/)。 2 [VP6A] (of letters) form when put together in a particular order: (指字母)拼作; 拼缀; 拼成: C-A-T ~s cat. C-A-T 拼成 cat (猫)。 3 [VP15B] ~ sth out, (a) make out (words, writing) laboriously, slowly: 费力而缓慢地了解(词或文): It took the boy an hour to ~ out a page of German. 那男孩花了一小时才吃力地读懂一页德文。 (b) make clear and easy to understand; explain in detail: 使清楚易懂; 详细解释: My request seems simple enough—do you want me to ~ it out for you? 我的要求很简单——你要不要我为你详细解释？ 4 [VP6A] have as a consequence: 招致; 带来: Does laziness always ~ failure? 怠惰必会招致失败吗？ 5 [VP2A,

6A] place the letters of words in the correct or accepted order: 拼字; 缀字: These children can't ~. 这些孩子不会拼字。 Why don't you learn to ~ my name (correctly)? 你为什么不学习我的名字的(正确)拼法呢？ ~**er** n person who ~s: 拼字者; 缀字者: a good /poor ~er. 长于(不长于)拼字者。 ~**ing** n [C] way a word is spelt: (词的)拼法; 缀字法: Which is the better ~ing: Tokio or Tokyo? 哪一种拼法较佳: Tokio 还是 Tokyo? Do you use English or American ~ing(s)? 你使用英国拼法还是美国拼法？

spelt[1] ⇨ **spell**[3].

spelt[2] /spelt; spelt/ n [U] kind of wheat giving very fine flour. 一种小麦(可制上好的面粉)。

spend /spend; spend/ vt, vi (pt, pp **spent** /spent; spent/) 1 [VP6A, 14, 2A] ~ money (on sth), pay out (money) for goods, services, etc: 用(钱); 花(钱): ~ all one's money; 用光所有的钱; ~ too much money on clothes; 花在服装上的钱太多; ~ £30 a week. 每周花费三十英镑。 He's always ~ing. 他挥霍成性。 '~·thrift n person who ~s money extravagantly. 挥霍者; 浪费者; 挥金如土的人。 2 [VP6A, 14, 19B] ~ sth (on sth/(in) doing sth), use up; consume: 用尽; 耗尽; 消耗; 使竭尽: ~ a lot of time on a project / (in) explaining a plan; 花费许多时间于一计划(说明一计划); ~ all one's energies. 耗尽所有的精力。 They went on firing until all their ammunition was spent. 他们继续射击, 直到耗尽所有的弹药。 3 [VP6A, 19B] pass: 度过; 消磨: ~ a weekend in London /one's spare time in gardening. 在伦敦度过周末(把空闲消磨在园艺上)。 How do you ~ your leisure? 你如何消磨空暇时间？ ~**er** n person who ~s money (usu in the way shown by the adj): 用钱者; 花钱者 (通常用形容词以示其花钱方式): an extravagant ~er. 挥金如土者。 **spent** (pp as adj) exhausted; used up: 用尽的 (过去分词作形容词用)筋疲力竭的; 耗尽的: a spent runner /swimmer /horse; 筋疲力竭的跑者(游泳者, 马); a spent cartridge /bullet, one that has been fired and is now useless. 打过的子弹(弹头)。

sperm /spɜːm; spɝm/ n [U] fertilizing fluid of a male animal. (雄性动物的)精液。 '~·whale n whale producing spermaceti. 抹香鲸(产鲸脑油)。

sper·ma·ceti /,spɜːmə'setɪ; ,spɝmə'ssti/ n [U] white, waxy, fatty substance contained in solution in the heads of sperm-whales, used for ointments, candles, etc. 鲸脑油(抹香鲸脑部的白色蜡状油脂, 呈溶液状态, 用制油膏、蜡烛等)。

sper·mato·zoon /,spɜːmətə'zəʊən; ,spɝmætə'zoʊn/ n (pl **-zoa** /-'zəʊə; -'zoʊə/) male fertilizing element contained in sperm (fusing with an ovum to produce new offspring). 精虫; 精子(与卵结合, 产生新生的后代)。

spew /spjuː; spju/ vt, vi [VP6A, 15B, 2A] vomit. 呕吐; 吐; 呕。

sphag·num /'sfægnəm; 'sfægnəm/ n (pl ~s) kinds of moss growing in peat and bogs, used in packing and medicinally. 水苔; 水藓(生长于泥炭地及沼泽的苔藓, 用作填料及药用)。

sphere /sfɪə(r); sfɪr/ n 1 solid figure that is entirely round; form of a ball or globe. 球体; 球形。 music of the ~s, (myth) music produced by the movement of heavenly bodies; inaudible to mortals. (神话)星球乐(天体运动发出的乐声, 一般凡人听不到)。 2 globe representing the earth or the sky. 地球仪; 浑天仪。 3 person's interests, activities, surroundings, etc: 个人的兴趣、活动、环境等; 活动范围; 圈子; 方面: a woman who is distinguished in many ~s, eg in literary and artistic circles, in the political world. 一位在多方面杰出的妇女(如在文艺界、政界等)。 Skiing lies outside the ~ of my activities. 滑雪超出了我的活动范围(非我所长)。 4 range, extent: 领域; 范围: a ~ of influence, area over which a country claims certain rights or is recognized as having them. (一国的)势力范围。 **spher·ical** /'sferɪkl; 'sferɪkl/ adj sphere-like; 似球的; ~ . 球形的。 **sphe·roid** /'sfɪərɔɪd; 'sfɪrɔɪd/ n body that is almost spherical. 球状体; 橢形体(几乎呈球状)。

sphinx /sfɪŋks; sfɪŋks/ n stone statue (esp 尤作 **the S~**) in Egypt with a lion's body and a woman's head; person who keeps his thoughts and intentions secret; enigmatic person. (埃及的)斯芬克斯(狮身人首雕像);不露出自己的思想及意愿的人;神秘人物;谜样的人。

a pyramid and the Sphinx

spice /spaɪs; spaɪs/ n 1 [C, U] sorts of substance, eg ginger, nutmeg, cinnamon, cloves, used to flavour food: 香料;调味品(如姜、肉豆蔻、肉桂、丁香等); a dealer in ~ (collective) (总称)香料经销商; mixed ~(s); 混合的香料; too much ~ in the cake. 糕饼中香料太多。 ⇨ **herb.** 2 [U] (and with indef art) (fig) interesting flavour, suggestion, or trace (of): (可与不定冠词连用)(喻)趣味;意味;风味: a story that lacks ~. 缺乏趣味的故事。 She has a ~ of wildness in her character. 她的性格有点放荡不羁。 □ vt [VP6A] add flavour to (sth) with ~, or as with ~: 借香料以增(某物)之味; 为…增添趣味: ~d with humour. 因幽默而增加趣味。 **spicy** adj (-ier, -iest) of, flavoured with, ~, (fig) exciting or interesting because somewhat improper: 香料的;用香料调味的;加有香料的; (喻)迹近猥亵而富于低级趣味的: spicy details of the film star's love life. 该电影明星爱情生活迹近猥亵而富于低级趣味的细节。 **spic·ily** /-ɪlɪ; -ɪlɪ/ adv **spici·ness** n

spick /spɪk; spɪk/ adj (only in) (仅用于) ~ **and span**, bright, clean and tidy. 整齐清洁的;一尘不染的。

spi·der /'spaɪdə(r); 'spaɪdɚ/ n sorts of creature with eight legs, many species of which spin webs for the capture of insects as food. 蜘蛛。 ⇨ the illus at **arachnid.** 参看 arachnid 之插图。 ~**y** adj (esp of handwriting) with long, thin strokes. (尤指书法)笔画细长的。

spied /spaɪd; spaɪd/ pt, pp of **spy.**

spiel /ʃpiːl US: spiːl; spiːl/ vi, vt (sl) talk; say (sth) glibly and at length. (俚)流利而冗长地讲话或讲述(某事); 滔滔不绝地说; 口若悬河地讲述。 □ n long voluble talk (usu intended to persuade sb). 滔滔不绝的谈话(通常意图说服或劝阻某人)。

spigot /'spɪgət; 'spɪgət/ n 1 (usu wooden) plug or peg which can be used to stop the hole of a cask or barrel. (通常为木质)(桶口用的)栓; 塞子。 2 valve for controlling the flow of water or other liquid from a tank, barrel, etc. (控制槽、桶等之水流或其他液体的)活门;龙头。

spike /spaɪk; spaɪk/ n 1 sharp point; pointed piece of metal, eg on iron railings or on running-shoes. 尖端;金属尖头或尖钉(如铁栏杆或跑鞋上者)。 ~ **heel,** (also 亦作 stiletto heel) thin, pointed heel on a (woman's) shoe. (女鞋上)尖而细的高后跟。 2 ear of grain, eg barley; long, pointed cluster of flowers on a single stem: 穗(如大麦穗);穗状花: ~s of lavender. 薰衣草的穗状花。 □ vt [VP6A] 1 put ~s on (shoes, etc): 加尖钉于(鞋等)上: ~d running-shoes. 钉鞋(带尖钉的跑鞋)。 2 pierce or injure with a ~; (of cannon in former times) make useless by driving a ~ into the opening where the powder was fired. 以尖钉刺穿或伤害;(指昔日大炮)把尖钉打入火门使无用。 Hence, 由此产生, ~ **sb's guns,** spoil his plans. 破坏某人的计划。 **spiky** adj (-ier, -iest) having ~s or sharp points; (fig, of persons) difficult to manage because unwilling to yield. 有尖钉或尖端的;(喻,指人)(因不肯屈服而)难驾驭的。

spike·nard /'spaɪknɑːd; 'spaɪknɚd/ n [U] (costly ointment formerly made from a) tall, perennial,

sweet-smelling plant. 甘松(一种高大,有香味的多年生植物);甘松香油(从前用甘松制的一种高香油膏)。

spill[1] /spɪl; spɪl/ vt, vi (pt, pp **spilt** /spɪlt; spɪlt/ or ~**ed**) 1 [VP6A, 2A, C] (of liquid or powder) (allow to) run over the side of the container: (指液体或粉末)溢出;洒出;泼出: Who has spilt/~ed the milk? 谁把牛奶泼出来了? The ink has spilt on the desk. 墨水洒在桌子上了。 ~ **the beans,** ⇨ **bean.** ~ **blood,** be guilty of wounding or killing sb. 伤害某人; 杀死某人; 使某人流血。 2 [VP6A] (of a horse, cart, etc) upset; cause (the rider, passenger, etc) to fall: (指马、马车等)弄翻使(骑者,乘客等)摔下;使跌落: His horse spilt him. 他的马把他摔下来了。 The horse shied and we were all spilt (= thrown out of the cart, etc) into the ditch. 那马惊跳了起来,把我们全都摔入沟中。 □ n fall from a horse, out of a cart, etc: 摔下(自马、马车等上)跌落; 摔下: have a nasty ~. 摔得很重。 '~·**over** n (often attrib) (of population) excess: (常用作定语)(指人口)过剩: new towns for London's ~over (population). 容纳伦敦过剩人口的新市镇。 '~·**way** n passage for surplus water from a reservoir, river, etc. (堰,河等的)放水道;溢洪道。

spill[2] /spɪl; spɪl/ n [C] thin strip of wood, rolled or twisted strip of paper, used to light candles, tobacco in a pipe, etc. (点燃蜡烛,烟斗等用的)木片;纸捻。

spilt /spɪlt; spɪlt/ ⇨ **spill**[1].

spin /spɪn; spɪn/ vt, vi (pt **spun** /spʌn; spʌn/ or **span** /spæn; spæn/, pp **spun**) (-nn-) 1 [VP6A, 14, 2A] ~ (into/from), form (thread) by twisting wool, cotton, silk, etc; draw out and twist (wool, cotton, etc) into threads; make (yarn) from wool etc in this way; engage in the occupation of ~ning thread: 纺(纱);抽绩(毛,棉等)成纱;纺绩;从事纺绩工作: ~ning wool/thread/yarn. 纺绩毛(线,纱)。 ~·**ning jenny** n early kind of machine for ~ning more than one thread at a time. (早期的)多轴纺纱机。 '~·**ning-wheel** n simple household machine for ~ning thread continuously on a spindle turned by a large wheel, usu worked by a treadle. (家庭用的)纺车。 2 [VP6A] form by means

a spinning-wheel

of threads: 以丝或线做成: spiders ~ning their webs; 结网的蜘蛛; silkworms ~ning cocoons. 做茧的蚕。 3 [VP6A, 15B] (fig) produce, compose (a narrative). (喻)编制;杜撰;讲述;撰述(故事)。 ~ **a yarn,** tell a story: 讲故事: The old sailor loves to ~ yarns about his life at sea. 那老水手喜欢讲述他的航海生涯。 ~ **sth out,** make it last as long as possible: 尽量使某物持续; 延长; ~ out the time by talking; 以谈话拖延时间; economize in order to make one's money ~ out until next pay-day. 节省用费以期维持到下一次发薪日。 4 [VP6A] cause (sth) to go round and round: 使(某物)旋转: ~ a top, ⇨ **top**[2]; 抽陀螺; ~ a coin, send it up in the air, revolving as it goes up, to decide sth (by 'heads or tails'). 抛转钱币(以落下后呈现正面或背面以决定某事)。 ~ **the ball,** (in cricket, tennis). 抽球; 旋球(在板球或网球中)。 ,~·**drier** n device that uses centrifugal force to dry what is placed in it (eg laundered clothes). 脱水机(利用离心力旋干洗过之衣服等)。 ,~·**dry** vt (pt, pp **dried**) dry in a ~-drier.

在脱水机中脱除…的水分; 在脱水机中旋干。 **'~-off** *n* incidental benefit or product (from a larger enterprise, or from research for such an enterprise). (从较大企业、或从其研究工作产生的) 附带利益; 副产品。 **5** [VP 2A, C] move round rapidly: 迅速旋转: *The top was ~ning merrily.* 陀螺在轻快地旋转。 *The collision sent the car ~ning across the roadway.* 那辆汽车被撞得转向而横在道路上。 *The blow sent him ~ning to the wall.* 他被重击而晕转到墙边。 *The bicycle was ~ning along (= moving along) at a good speed.* 那辆脚踏车快速疾驰。 **6 spun glass,** glass made into threads (by being spun when heated). 玻璃丝(玻璃加热后抽成丝状者)。 **spun silk,** cheap material of short-fibred and waste silk, often mixed with cotton. 纺绸(由短而零碎的丝织成的便宜料子, 常混有棉纺)。 □ *n* **1** [U] turning or ~ning motion esp as given to the ball in some games, eg cricket, baseball: 旋转(尤指给于板球、网球等者): *The pitcher gave (a) ~ to the ball.* 投手使球旋转。 **2** short ride for pleasure in a motor-car, on a bicycle, etc: 乘汽车、脚踏车等短途的旅行;乘车兜风: *go for/have a ~.* 坐(乘、骑等)车溜溜。 **3** fast ~ning movement of an aircraft during a diving descent: 飞机快速螺旋下降: *get into/out of a ~.* 开始(停止)螺旋下降。 *in a flat ~,* in a panic. 惊慌地。

spin·ach /'spɪnɪdʒ US: -ɪtʃ; 'spɪnɪdʒ/ *n* [U] common garden plant with green leaves, cooked and eaten as a vegetable. 菠菜。

spi·nal /'spaɪnl; 'spaɪnl/ *adj* of or to the spine: 脊椎骨的: *the ~ column,* the backbone; 脊椎骨; *the ~ cord,* nerve-fibres in the spine; 脊髓; *a '~ injury.* 脊椎受伤。

spindle /'spɪndl; 'spɪndl/ *n* **1** (in spinning) thin rod for twisting and winding thread by hand. (纺织)纺锤; 锭子。 ⇨ the illus at **spin.** 参看 spin 之插图。 **2** bar or pin which turns round, or on which sth turns (eg an axle or a shaft). 指轴;心轴。 **'~-legged/-shanked** *adjj* having long, thin legs. 腿细长的。 **'~-shanks** *n* person with such legs. 腿细长的人。 **'~-berry/-tree** *n* small tree with deep-pink berries and hard wood, used for ~s. 卫矛(一种小树, 木质坚硬, 结深桃红色果, 用制纺锤)。 **spin·dly** /'spɪndlɪ; 'spɪndlɪ/ *adj* long and thin; too tall and thin. 细长的; 过于高而细的。

spin·drift /'spɪndrɪft; 'spɪn,drɪft/ *n* [U] foam or spray blown along the surface of the sea. (海面激起的) 浪花。

spine /spaɪn; spaɪn/ *n* **1** backbone. 脊椎骨。 ⇨ the illus at **skeleton.** 参看 skeleton 之插图。 **2** one of the sharp needle-like parts on some plants, eg a cactus, and animals, eg a porcupine. (植物如仙人掌, 动物如豪猪等的)棘状突起;刺;针。 **3** part of a book's cover that is visible when it is in a row on a shelf, usu with the book's title on it. 书脊; 书背。 **~·less** *adj* having no ~(1); (fig) cowardly; timid. 无脊椎骨的;(喻)怯懦的; 优柔寡断的。 **spiny** *adj* (**-ier, -iest**) having ~s(2). 有棘状突起的; 多刺的; 多剌的。

spinet /spɪ'net US: 'spɪnɪt; 'spɪnɪt/ *n* old type of keyboard instrument like a harpsichord. 古钢琴(早期的一种有键乐器, 似大键琴)。 ⇨ the illus at **keyboard.** 参看 keyboard 之插图。

spin·na·ker /'spɪnəkə(r); 'spɪnəkə/ *n* large triangular sail carried on the main-mast of a racing yacht on the side opposite the mainsail when runnig before the wind. (赛艇主桅上的)大三角帆。

spin·ney /'spɪnɪ; 'spɪnɪ/ *n* (*pl* ~**s**) thicket; small wood with thick undergrowth, esp (in England) one used for sheltering game[1]. 杂树林; 小树丛(尤指在英国供猎物栖身者)。

spin·ster /'spɪnstə(r); 'spɪnstə/ *n* (usu official or legal use) unmarried woman; woman who remains single after the conventional age for marrying. (通常为正式或法律用语)未婚女人;老处女。 **~·hood** /-hʊd; -,hʊd/ *n* the state of being a ~. (女子的)独身;未婚。

spi·ral /'spaɪərəl; 'spaɪrəl/ *adj, n* (in the form of an) advancing or ascending continuous curve winding round a central point: 螺旋形(的); 螺线(的): *A snail's shell is ~.* 蜗牛壳是螺旋形的。 *The rocket went up in a ~.* 火箭盘旋着上升。 *A ~ nebula is a group of stars that has the appearance of a ~.* 螺旋星云是成螺旋形状的星群。 ⇨ also **inflationary** at **inflate.** ⇨ the illus at **whorl.** 参看 whorl 之插图。 □ *vi* (**-ll-,** US also **-l-**) [VP2A, C] move in a ~: 呈螺旋状移动; 盘旋移动: *The smoke ~led up.* 烟盘旋上升。 *Prices are still ~ling.* 物价仍在盘旋上涨。

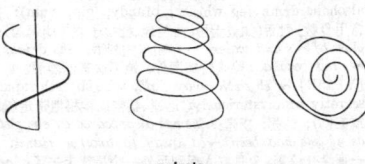

spirals

spire /'spaɪə(r); spaɪr/ *n* pointed structure like a tall cone or pyramid rising above a tower (esp of a church). (尤指教堂的)塔尖; 尖顶。 ⇨ the illus at **church.** 参看 church 之插图。

spirit /'spɪrɪt; 'spɪrɪt/ *n* **1** [C, U] soul; immaterial, intellectual or moral part of man: 心灵; 精神(指个人之心智, 道德或其他超物质的方面): *He was vexed in ~,* inwardly. 他内心气恼。 *I shall be with you in (the) ~, My thoughts will be with you even though I am not with you in the flesh.* 我的心思将与你同在(虽然我是不和你在一起)。 *The ~ is willing but the flesh is weak,* One is willing to do sth, but physically unable to do it. 心有余而力不足;力不从心。 **the Holy S~,** the Third Person of the Trinity. 圣灵(和天父, 耶稣成三位一体)。 **2** the soul thought of as separate from the body; disembodied soul: 灵魂; 亡魂: *the abode of ~s,* where the ~s of the dead are; 灵魂安息处; *believe in ~s;* 相信灵魂; *raise a ~.* 招魂。 **'~-rapper** *n* person who claims to receive messages from the dead by means of raps on a table. 招魂巫师(宣称可借敲桌子而通亡魂)。 **3** [C] sprite; elf; goblin. 幽灵; 妖精; 鬼怪。 **4** [U] life and consciousness not associated with a body; supernatural being: (不与肉体结合的)生命与意识; 神灵: *God is pure ~.* 上帝是纯灵。 **5** [C] (always with an *adj*) person considered from the intellectual, moral or emotional point of view: (恒与形容词连用)人(从智力、道德或情绪的观点而论); 具有某种特质的人: *What a noble/generous, etc ~ he is!* 他是一位多么高贵(慷慨等)的人啊! *He was one of the leading ~s of the Reform Movement.* 他是革新运动领导人物之一。 **moving ~,** person who is the originator and sustainer of an idea, project, etc. 倡导者。 **6** [U] quality of courage, vigour, liveliness: 勇气; 锐气; 元气; 生气: *Put a little more ~ into your work.* 工作要多卖点力。 *You haven't the ~ of a mouse.* 你的胆量还不如老鼠。 **7** (*sing* only) mental or moral attitude: (仅用单数)心理或道德方面的态度; 气度: *in a ~ of mischief.* 以戏谑的态度。 *Whether it was unwise or not depends upon the ~ in which it was done.* 这事之是否不智, 端视做此事所持的态度而定。 **8** [U] real meaning or purpose underlying a law, etc (contrasted with the apparent meaning of the words, etc): 法律等的真谛; 精神(与文字的表面含义相对): *obey the ~, not the letter, of the law.* 遵从法律的真谛, 非拘泥条文词句。 *Have you followed out the ~ of his instructions?* 你已贯彻明行他的指示的本意了吗? **9** (*pl*) state of mind (as being happy, hopeful, etc or the opposite): (复)心境; 心情(如愉快、充满希望或痛苦、失望等): *in high ~s,* cheerful; 高兴的; *in poor/low ~s,* out of ~s, depressed, unhappy. 不高兴的。 *Have a glass of brandy to keep up your ~s.* 喝一杯白兰地来提提

神。 **10** (*sing* only) influence or tendency that rouses or causes development: (仅用单数)引起进展的影响或趋势: *The wind of change is blowing and we cannot resist the ~ of the times.* 要求改变现状的风气正在流行，我们无法抗拒时代的潮流。 **11** [U] industrial alcohol. 火酒；酒精。 '~-**lamp**/-**stove** *n* one in which ~ is burned. 酒精灯 (炉)。 '~-**level** *n* glass tube partly filled with water or alcohol, with a bubble of air which, when centred, shows that a surface is horizontal. 酒精水平仪。 **12** (*pl*) solution in alcohol: (复)酒精溶液: ~*s* of camphor/turpentine; 樟脑油(松节油)；~(*s*) of salt, hydrochloric acid. 氢氯酸；盐酸。 **13** (usu *pl*) strong alcoholic drink (whisky, brandy, gin, rum): (通常用复数)烈酒(如威士忌、白兰地、杜松子酒与朗姆酒): *a glass of ~s and water.* 一杯和水的烈酒。 *She drinks no ~ but vodka.* 除伏特加酒外，她不饮其他烈酒。 □ *vt* [VP15B] ~ *sb*/*sth away*/*off*, take sb/sth rapidly, secretly or mysteriously: 迅速、秘密或神秘地带走(某人或某物)；诱拐；拐骗: *She has disappeared as completely as if she had been ~ed away to another planet.* 她一直没有踪影，象是被人拐到另外一个星球上去了。 ~**ed** /'spɪrɪtɪd/ *adj* **1** full of ~(6); lively; courageous: 有锐气的；有生气的；活泼的；勇敢的: *a ~ed attack*/*defence*/*reply;* 猛烈的攻击(英勇的防御；有力的答复)；*a ~ed horse;* 有生气的马; *a ~ed conversation.* 活泼的谈话。 **2** (in compounds) (用于复合词中)having the kind of spirits(9) indicated: 有…心境的; ,high-/,low-/,poor-'~ed, etc. 高兴的(沮丧的，不快的等)。 ~-**less** *adj* without ~(6); not having or showing energy or courage; depressed. 无精神的；无生命力的；没有勇气的；委靡的。

spir·i·tual /'spɪrɪtʃʊəl; 'spɪrɪtʃʊəl/ *adj* **1** of the spirit(1) or soul(1); of religion, not of material things; of, from, God: 精神的；心灵的；宗教上的；上帝的；神圣的；属灵的: *concerned about sb's ~ welfare.* 关心某人精神上的福利。 **2** of spirits(2); supernatural. 神灵的；超自然的。 **3** caring much for things of the spirit(1). 爱好精神方面的事物的；脱俗的；崇高的。 **4** of the church: 教会的: *lords ~,* (GB) bishops and archbishops in the House of Lords. (英)上议院中有主教及大主教身份的议员。 □ *n* (Negro) ~, religious song as sung by Negroes in the US. (美国黑人等所唱的)黑人圣歌。~**ly** /-tʃʊlɪ; -tʃʊəlɪ/ *adv* ~-**ity** /,spɪrɪtʃʊ'ælɪtɪ; ,spɪrɪtʃʊ-'ælətɪ/ *n* [U] ~ quality; devotion to ~ things. 属于心灵或精神方面的特质；灵性；有宗教信仰、教会、教堂、教士等的事物。

spir·i·tu·al·ism /'spɪrɪtʃʊəlɪzəm; 'spɪrɪtʃʊəl,tzəm/ *n* [U] belief in the possibility of receiving messages from the spirits of the dead; practice of attempting to do this. 灵魂论；招魂术。 **spir·i·tu·al·ist** /-ɪst; -ɪst/ *n* believer in ~. 灵魂论者。 **spir·i·tu·al·is·tic** /,spɪrɪtʃʊə-'lɪstɪk; ,spɪrɪtʃʊə'lɪstɪk/ *adj* of ~ or spiritualists. 灵魂论的；灵魂论者的。

spir·i·tu·al·ize /'spɪrɪtʃʊəlaɪz; 'spɪrɪtʃʊəl,aɪz/ *vt* [VP6A] make pure or spiritual. 使纯净；使精神化；灵化。 **spir·i·tu·al·iz·ation** /,spɪrɪtʃʊəlaɪ'zeɪʃn US: -lɪ'z-; ,spɪrɪtʃʊəl'zeʃən/ *n* [U].

spir·i·tu·ous /'spɪrɪtjʊəs US: -tʃʊəs; 'spɪrɪtʃʊəs/ *adj* (of liquids) containing alcohol: (指液体)含酒精的: ~ *liquors,* distilled liquors such as whisky, not (usu) fermented liquors such as beer. 蒸馏酒(如威士忌、非如啤酒之酿造者)。

spirt /spɜːt; spɝt/ *vi* [VP2C, 2A] *n* = **spurt**.

spit¹ /spɪt; spɪt/ *n* **1** long thin metal spike to which meat, etc is secured for roasting. 烤肉叉；炙叉。 **2** small, narrow point of land running out into a body of water. (伸入水域中的)狭长地嘴；岬。 □ *vt* (-**pp**-) put a ~ through (a chicken, piece of meat, etc); pierce with the point of a sword, spear, etc. 以炙叉穿过(鸡、肉片等);以刀、矛等刺；戳。

spit² /spɪt; spɪt/ *vt, vi* (*pt, pp* **spat** /spæt; spæt/) (-**tt**-) **1** [VP2A, C, 3A] ~ (*at*/*on*/*upon sb*/*sth*),

send liquid (saliva) out from the mouth; do this as a sign of contempt or hatred: 吐口水；吐痰；吐口水以示藐视或憎恨: *If you ~ in a London bus you may be fined £5.* 如果你在伦敦的公共汽车上吐痰，你可能被罚5英镑。 *He spat in the man's face*/*spat at him.* 他向口水在那人的脸上(向他吐口水)。 *The cat spat (= made an angry or hostile ~ting noise) at the dog.* 那只猫向那条狗发出愤怒或表示敌意的呼噜呼噜声。 **2** [VP6A, 15B] ~ *sth (out),* send out from the mouth; (fig) utter angrily or sharply: 从嘴里吐出；(喻)愤怒地或尖刻地说: *The baby spat out the nasty pill.* 那婴儿吐出了那难吃的药丸。 *After the tooth had been extracted the boy spat a lot of blood.* 牙齿拔掉后,那男孩吐出了许多血。 *She spat (out) curses at me.* 她尖刻地咒诅我。 ~ *it out,* (colloq) say what you have to say, quickly. (口)爽爽快快地说出来。 **3** [VP2A, 6A] (of a fire, candle, gun, etc) throw out; make the noise of ~ting: (指火、烛、枪等)发出；发吐吐声；发突突声: *The engine was ~ting.* 引擎在突突地作响。 *The guns were ~ting fire.* 枪炮在不断地发射。 '~-**fire** *n* hot-tempered person. 急躁的人；急性子的人。 **4** [VP2A] (of rain or snow) fall lightly: (指雨或雪)微降: *It's not raining heavily, only ~ting.* 雨下得不大,只是小雨而已。 □ *n* **1** [U] saliva. 唾液；口水。 **2** act of ~ting. 唾吐。 ~ *and polish,* the cleaning and polishing of equipment (by soldiers, etc). (兵士等)装备的擦拭。 **3** *the dead ~ of; the ~ and image of* /,spɪt n 'ɪmɪdʒ; 'spɪtṇ'ɪmɪdʒ/; *the ~ting image of,* exact counterpart or likeness of: 与…完全相同或相似的人或物: *He's the dead ~*/*the ~ting image of his father.* 他象极了他的父亲。 **4** frothy secretion of some insects (seen on plants, etc). (见于植物等上的)某些昆虫之泡沫状分泌物。

spit³ /spɪt; spɪt/ *n* (*pl* ~ or ~**s**) spade's depth: 一铲之深度；一锹之深度: *Dig the patch two ~(s) deep.* 把这块地挖两铲深。

spite /spaɪt; spaɪt/ *n* **1** [U] ill will; desire to cause pain or damage: 恶毒；恶意；使遭受痛苦或损害的意思: *do sth out of*/*from ~.* 出于恶意做某事。 **2** (with *indef art*) grudge: (与不定冠词连用)怨恨: *have a ~ against sb;* 怨恨某人。 *do sth to satisfy a private ~.* 做某事泄私愤。 **3** (*prep phrase*) (介词短语) *in ~ of,* not to be prevented by; notwithstanding: 虽然; 不顾; 尽管…仍: *They went out in ~ of the rain.* 尽管下雨,他们仍然外出。 *In ~ of all his efforts he failed.* 他虽然做了各种努力,仍然失败了。 □ *vt* [VP6A] injure or annoy because of ~: 因怨恨而伤害或搅扰; 向…泄愤; 刁难: *The neighbours let their radio blare every afternoon just to ~ us.* 邻居每天下午故意把收音机的声音开得很大, 以向我们泄愤。 ~-**ful** /-fl; -fəl/ *adj* having, showing, ~. 有恶意的; 怀恨的。 ~-**fully** /-fəlɪ; -fəlɪ/ *adv* ~-**ful-ness** *n*

spittle /'spɪtl; 'spɪtl/ *n* [U] liquid of the mouth; saliva. 口水; 唾液; 痰。

spit·toon /spɪ'tuːn; spɪ'tun/ *n* container to spit into. 痰盂。

spiv /spɪv; spɪv/ *n* (GB sl) person not in regular employment but who makes money by dubious business methods, and who goes about smartly dressed and having a good time. (英俚)靠不正当行业赚钱, 并且讲究衣着经常游手好闲的人。

splash /splæʃ; splæʃ/ *vt, vi* **1** [VP6A, 15B, 14] ~ *sth (about)* (*on*/*over sth*); ~ *sth*/*sb (with sth),* cause (a liquid) to fly about in drops; make (sb or sth) wet: 溅水；泼溅(某人或某物)：~ *water on*/*over the floor;* 泼水在地板上；~ *the floor with water;* 以水泼在地板上；~ *water about.* 四处溅水。 *The children love to ~ water over one another.* 那儿童喜欢彼此往身上泼水。 **2** [VP2A] (of a liquid) fly about and fall in drops: (指液体)飞溅；激溅: *fountains ~ing in the park.* 公园中飞溅的喷泉。 *This tap is a bad one—it ~es.* 这个龙头不好——会溅水。 **3** [VP2C] move, fall, so that there is ~ing: 溅着水行进; 溅着水落下: *We ~ed (our*

way) across the stream/into the lake, etc. 我们溅着水走过溪流(跳入湖中等)。 *Look at that hippo ~ing about in the river.* 看那只在河里溅水的河马。 *The spacecraft ~ed down in the Pacific.* 这太空船降落在太平洋中。 Hence, 由此产生, '**~-down** *n* landing of a spacecraft in the sea. (太空船之)海上溅落。 4 [VP15B] ~ *money/news about,* spend/display it freely, prominently. 挥霍钱财(散布新闻)。 □ *n* [C] 1 (sound, spot, mark, made by) ~ing: 溅; 飞溅; 飞溅声; 噗通声; 溅污的斑点。 污迹: *He jumped into the swimming pool with a* ~. 他噗通一声跳进游泳池中。 *There are some* ~*es of mud on your trousers.* 你的裤子上溅有泥浆。 2 patch of colour: 有颜色的斑点: *Her dog is brown with white* ~*es.* 她的褐毛狗带有白色斑点。 3 (colloq) small quantity of soda-water etc: (口)少量汽水等: *a whisky and* ~. 掺有少量汽水的威士忌酒。 4 *make a* ~, (colloq, fig) attract attention by making a display of (esp) one's wealth. (口, 喻)炫耀(尤指)财富; 摆阔; 摆排场。

splay /spleɪ/ *vt, vi* make opposite sides (of an opening) diverge; cause to slant or slope; (of an opening) be constructed in this way: 使(开口、缺口等)相对两旁斜出; 使成斜面; 使倾斜; (指开口)倾斜: *a ~ed window,* eg one in a very thick wall, so that the opening in the wall is wider on one side than the other. 侧斜窗 (两侧斜出, 即开在厚墙上者, 两面的开口, 一面较另一面宽)。 *The plumber ~ed the end of the pipe before fitting it over the next section.* 水管工人先把管口弄斜, 再接合在下一段管子上。 □ *n* sloping side of a window opening, etc. (窗等)开口的倾面。 □ *adj* (esp of feet) broad, flat and turned outwards. (尤指脚)平蹼外翻的; 成外八字形的。 Hence, 由此产生, '**~-foot** *n* '**~-footed** *adj* having ~ feet. 外八字脚的。

spleen /spliːn/ *n* 1 [C] bodily organ in the abdomen which causes changes in the blood. 脾; 脾脏。 ⇨ the illus at **alimentary**. 参看 alimentary 之插图。 2 [U] lowness of spirits; bad temper: 抑郁; 意气消沉; 坏脾气; 愤怒: *in a fit of* ~; 在发怒; *vent one's* ~ *on* sb. 对某人发脾气。

splen·did /'splendɪd/ *adj* 1 magnificent: 华丽的; 壮丽的; 堂皇的; 辉煌的: *a* ~ *sunset/house/victory.* 灿丽的夕阳(堂皇的房屋; 辉煌的胜利); ~ *jewellery.* 灿烂的珠宝。 2 (colloq) very satisfactory; excellent: (口)极令人满意的; 绝妙的; 极佳的: *a* ~ *dinner/idea.* 极好的餐食(意见)。 ~·**ly** *adv*

splen·dif·er·ous /splen'dɪfərəs/ splen'dɪfərəs/ *adj* (colloq, often hum or ironic) splendid. (口, 常用作诙谐或反语)华丽的; 壮丽的; 堂皇的; 绝妙的; 极佳的。

splen·dour (US = **-dor**) /'splendə(r)/ 'splendə/ *n* 1 [U] magnificence; brightness: 华丽; 壮丽; 光亮: *the* ~ *of stained glass windows.* 彩色玻璃窗之灿丽。 2 (sometimes *pl*) grandeur, glory. (有时用复数)堂皇; 威严; 壮丽。

sple·netic /splɪ'netɪk/ splɪ'netɪk/ *adj* ill-tempered; peevish. 坏脾气的; 乖戾的; 易怒的。

splice /splaɪs/ splaɪs/ *vt* [VP6A] 1 join (two ends of rope) by weaving the strands of one into the strands of the other; join (two pieces of wood, magnetic tape, film) by fastening them at the ends. 绞接(绳头); 叠接(木材、录音带、影片)。 2 *get* ~*d,* (sl) get married. (俚)结婚。 □ *n* joint made by splicing. 编接或叠接的接合处; 连接点; 接头。 ~*r n* device for joining two pieces of paper or magnetic tape, film, etc. 编接器; 叠接器。

splint /splɪnt/ splɪnt/ *n* strip of wood, etc bound to an arm, leg, etc to keep a broken bone in the right position: (绑在臂, 腿等上用以固定骨折之)夹板: *put an arm/a limb in* ~*s.* 以夹板夹住手臂(肢)。

splin·ter /'splɪntə(r)/ 'splɪntə/ *n* sharp-pointed or sharp-edged bit of hard material (wood, metal, glass, etc) split, torn or broken off a larger piece: (木, 金属、玻璃等的)尖片; 碎片; 裂片: *get a* ~ *into one's finger.* 指头上扎了根刺。 *a* '~ *group/party,* (in politics)

group of persons who have broken off from their party. (政治)自原来政党分裂出来的团体。 '**~-proof** *adj* (eg of glass) that will not ~; giving protection against ~s, eg of broken glass, or from a bomb. 防碎裂的; 防裂片的(如防碎玻璃片或弹片)。 □ *vt, vi* [VP2A, C, 6A, 15B] ~ *(off),* break into ~s; come off as a ~. 碎裂; 成碎片; 分裂。 ~·**y** *adj* apt to ~; full of ~s; like ~s. 易碎裂的; 多碎片的; 似碎片的。

split /splɪt/ splɪt/ *vt, vi* (*pt, pp* **split**; **-tt-**) 1 [VP 6A, 14, 2A, C] ~ *(into),* break, cause to break, be broken, into two or more parts, esp from end to end along the line of natural division: 裂开; 劈开; 破裂(尤指沿自然纹理从一端至另一端裂开者); ~*ting logs.* 劈木。 *Some kinds of wood* ~ *easily.* 有些木头易劈开。 *Only a skilled workman can* ~ *slate into layers.* 惟有巧匠才能把板岩劈成石片。 2 [VP2D, 22] ~ *(open),* break open by bursting 爆裂; 撑破; 绷裂; 绽裂: *His coat has* ~ *at the seams.* 他的上衣绽线了。 3 [VP6A, 15A, B, 2A, C] ~ *(up) (into),* (cause to) break into parts; divide: (使)分裂; 分开: ~ *the atom;* 分裂原子; ~ *(up) a compound into its parts.* 分裂某种化合物为诸元素。 *The party* ~ *up into small groups.* 该党分为若干小派系。 *Let's* ~, (mod colloq) leave (a party, etc). (现代口语)咱们走吧(离开一聚会等)。 *Let's* ~ *the cost of the meal,* share it. 我们来分摊餐费。 *Joe and Jenny have* ~ *up,* (of a couple) separated from each other. 乔和珍妮已离异了。 ~ *the difference,* (when making a bargain) compromise (on the price, cost, etc). (讲价钱时)(在价钱、价格等方面)让步; 妥协。 *a* ~*ting headache,* so severe that it feels that one's head may crack. 剧烈或严重的头痛。 ~ *hairs,* make very fine distinctions (in an argument, etc). 在辩论等中(剖析)毫发; 吹毛求疵。 Hence, 由此产生, '**hair-**~*ting adj* ~ *an infinitive,* place an adverb between to and the infinitive, (as in *'to quickly read a book'*). 分离不定式(在 to 与动词之间加入一副词, 如 to quickly read a book)。 ~ *level* (of houses, housing) in which adjoining rooms are in a level midway between successive storeys of other parts. 错层式的(指一房屋或一住处, 其中各邻接房间的地高错落不一)。 *a* ~ *mind/personality,* person who behaves sometimes with one set of actions, emotions, etc, and sometimes with another set; of two natures, etc. 患人格分裂症者。 also ⇨ **schizophrenia; Jekyll and Hyde.** ~ *peas,* dried peas ~ *into halves.* 豌豆瓣。 *a* ~ *ring,* one split along its length, as used for keeping keys on. 钥匙圈。 *a* ~ *second,* a brief instant of time. 刹那; 顷刻。 ~ *one's sides (with laughter),* laugh with movements of the sides. 捧腹(大笑)。 Hence, 由此产生, '**side-**~*ting adj* 4 [VP2A, 3A] ~ *(on sb),* (sl) give away the secret of (usu an accomplice); give information about him (to his disadvantage). (俚)泄露(通常为同犯)的秘密; 告发; 告发。 5 [VP2A] (US sl) leave (a place). (美俚)离开(某地)。 □ *n* [C] 1 splitting; crack or tear made by splitting: 劈开; 劈片; 分裂; 分开; *sew up a* ~ *in a seam.* 把裂开的缝线起来。 2 separation or division resulting from splitting: 分歧; 不和; 内讧: *a* ~ *in the Labour Party.* 劳工党之内讧。 3 (colloq) half-bottle of soda water, etc. (口)半瓶汽水(等)。 4 **the** ~**s,** acrobat's feat of sinking to the floor by extending the legs laterally with the trunk upright: 两腿劈开坐落地上的技艺; 劈叉; 劈八字: *do the* ~*s.* 表演劈叉把式。

splosh /splɒʃ/ splɑʃ/ *vt* = **splash**(4).

splotch /splɒtʃ/ splɑtʃ/, **splodge** /splɒdʒ/ splɑdʒ/ *n* [C] daub or smear (of ink, dirt, etc); irregular patch (of colour, light, etc). (墨水、泥污等的)污痕; 污渍(颜色、光等的)不规则形的一片。

splurge /splɜːdʒ/ splɝdʒ/ *vi, n* (colloq) (make a) noisy display or effort (intended to attract attention); show off. (口)大声夸示; 炫耀; 卖弄。

splut·ter /'splʌtə(r)/ 'splʌtə/ *vi, vt* 1 [VP2A, C] speak quickly and confusedly (from excitement, etc).

(因激动等)急促而杂乱地说。2 [VP6A, 15B] **~ *sth (out),*** say quickly, confusedly, indistinctly: 急促、杂乱、含糊地说出某事: *~ out a few words/a threat.* 急促含糊地说出几个词(威胁)。3 [VP2A] make a series of spitting sounds; sputter(1): 发爆裂声; 作拍拍声: *The swimmers dived and came ~ing to the surface.* 游泳的人们跳入水中, 拍击着水浮出水面。□ *n* [U] ~ing sound. 劈拍声; 爆裂声。

Spode /spəud; spod/ *n* [U] type of English porcelain. 斯泼德(英国的一种瓷器)。

spoil /spɔɪl; spɔɪl/ *vt, vi* (*pt, pp* **~t** or **~ed**) **1** [VP 6A] make useless or unsatisfactory: 使无用或不令人满意; 损坏; 破坏: *fruit ~t by insects;* 被昆虫损坏的水果; *holidays ~t by bad weather;* 为坏天气破坏的假日; *~t ballot papers,* made invalid because the voters have not marked them as required by regulations. 废票(未按规定圈选的无效选票)。*Don't ~ your appetite by eating sweets just before dinner.* 不要在饭前吃糖果以免吃不下饭。'**~-sport** *n* person who does things that interfere with the enjoyment of other people. 扫人兴的人; 煞风景的人。**2** [VP6A] harm the character or temperament of by wrong upbringing or lack of discipline: 宠坏; 溺爱; 姑息: *parents who ~ their children.* 溺爱孩子的父母亲。**3** [VP6A] pay great attention to the comfort and wishes of: 非常注意照应…的安适和愿望; 宠爱: *He likes having a wife who ~s him.* 他喜欢有一位对他非常关心的太太。**4** [VP2A] (of food, etc) become bad, unfit for use: (指食物等)变坏; 腐败: *Some kinds of food soon ~.* 有些食物很容易变坏。**5** ***be ~ing for*** *(a fight,* etc), be eager for. 渴望; 切望(打斗等)。**6** [VP6A, 14] **~ *sb (of sth),*** (old use, or liter; *pt pp* always **~ed**, never **~t**) plunder, rob by force or stealth: (旧用法或文; 过去式及过去分词总是作 ~ed, 不作 ~t) 掠夺; 抢劫; 偷窃: *financiers who ~ed* (= despoiled) *widows of their money.* 掠夺寡妇们钱财的金融家。□ *n* **1** (either [U] or *pl,* not with numerals) stolen goods; plunder: (用单数或复数皆可, 但不与数字连用) 掠夺物; 偷来的东西; 赃物: *The thieves divided up the ~(s).* 贼分赃。**2** *(pl)* profits, profitable positions, gained from political power: (复)(用政治力量获得的)利益; 肥缺: *the ~s of office;* 肥缺; *the '~s system,* (in some countries) system by which positions in the public service (their salaries and other advantages) are given to supporters of the political party which wins power. (某些国家的)政党分赃制(公职委派给获胜政党之支持者的制度)。**3** [U] earth, unwanted material, etc thrown or brought up in excavating, draining, etc. 挖出的泥土等; 弃土。

spoke[1] /spəuk; spok/ *n* **1** any one of the bars or wire rods connecting the hub (centre) of a wheel with the rim (outer edge). 轮辐; 辐条。⇨ the illus at **bicycle.** 参看 bicycle 之插图。***put a '~ in sb's wheel,*** hinder him; prevent him from carrying out his plans. 阻碍某人; 使某人之计不得逞。**2** rung of a ladder. 梯级; 梯磴。

spoke[2]**, spoken** /spəuk, 'spəukən; spok, 'spokən/ *pt* and *pp* of **speak.**

spokes·man /'spəuksmən; 'spoksmən/ *n* (*pl* **-men**) person speaking, chosen to speak, on behalf of a group. 发言人; 代言人。

spo·li·ation /ˌspəulɪ'eɪʃn; ˌspolɪ'eʃən/ *n* [U] plunder, esp of neutral merchant ships by countries at war. (尤指交战国对中立国商船所作的)掠夺; 抢劫。

spon·dee /'spɒndi:; 'spandi/ *n* (prosody) metrical foot of two long or stressed syllables, used in poetry to vary other metres. (韵律学)扬扬格(二长音节或重音节之音步, 在诗歌中用以使其他韵律有变化)。**spon·daic** /spɒn'deɪk; span'de·ɪk/ *adj*

sponge /spʌndʒ; spʌndʒ/ *n* **1** [C] kinds of simple sea animal with light structures of elastic material full of holes and able to absorb water easily; one of these, or sth of similar texture (eg porous rubber), used for washing, cleaning, etc. 海绵; 海绵体; (用于洗濯、清洁等的)海绵或似海绵物。***pass the ~ over,*** wipe out, agree to forget (an offence, etc). 抹消; 同意忘记(嫌隙等); 不念(旧恶)。***throw up/in the ~,*** admit defeat or failure. 承认失败; 认输。**2** piece of absorbent material, eg gauze, used in surgery; mop used in cleaning the bore of a gun, etc. (外科用的)棉球; (清洁炮膛等用的)洗杆; 擦膛刷。**3** '**~-cake** *n* soft, light yellow cake made of eggs, sugar and flour. 软蛋糕; 海绵蛋糕。□ *vt, vi* **1** [VP6A, 15B] **~ *sth (out),*** wash, wipe or clean with a ~: 用海绵等洗涤、擦拭或清除: *~ a wound/a child's face;* 用棉球洗擦伤口(孩子的脸); *~ out a memory,* wipe it out, end it. 抹除记忆。**2** [VP 15B] **~ *sth up,*** take up (liquid) with a ~: 用海绵吸收(液体): *~ up the mess.* 用海绵吸去污水(等)。**3** [VP3A] **~ *on/upon sb,*** (colloq) live at his expense, get money from him, without giving, or intending to give, anything in return: (口)依赖某人生活; 诈取某人钱财: *~ (up) on one's friends;* 依赖朋友为生; [VP6A, 14] **~ *sth (from sb),*** get by sponging: 诈得; 骗取: *~ a dinner;* 骗得一餐饭; *~ a fiver* (= £5) *from an old acquaintance.* 从老友处骗得五英镑。**~r** *n* person who ~s(3). 依赖他人生活者; 诈骗者。**spongy** *adj* **(-ier, -iest)** soft, porous and elastic like a ~: 象海绵的; 柔软、多孔而有弹性的: *spongy, moss-covered land.* 生满苔藓的柔软土地。**spongi·ness** *n*

spon·sor /'spɒnsə(r); 'spansə/ *n* **1** person (eg a godfather) making himself responsible for another. 负责人(如教父等)。**2** person who first puts forward or guarantees a proposal; person, firm, etc paying for a commercial radio or TV programme (usu in return for advertising of products). 发起人; 保证人; 资助人; 赞助人; 赞助广播或电视节目的人或公司行号(通常为其产品做宣传); 广告客户。□ *vt* [VP6A] act as a ~ for. 资助; 赞助。

spon·ta·neous /spɒn'teɪnɪəs; span'tenɪəs/ *adj* done, happening, from natural impulse, not caused or suggested by sth or sb outside: 自然产生的; 自发的; 自动的: *He made a ~ offer of help.* 他自动提供帮助。*Nothing he says is ~—he always thinks carefully before he speaks.* 他从不贸然发言——他总是谨慎思考后才讲话。**~ combustion,** burning caused by chemical changes, etc inside the material, not by the application of fire from outside. 自燃(借自身的化学变化等而燃烧)。**~·ly** *adv* **~·ness, spon·ta·neity** /ˌspɒntə'ni:ətɪ; ˌspantə'niətɪ/ *nn*

spoof /spu:f; spuf/ *vt, n* (sl) hoax; trick; swindle: (俚)愚弄; 欺骗: *You've been ~ed,* You've been hoaxed. 你上当了。

spook /spu:k; spuk/ *n* (hum) ghost. (谐)鬼。**~y** *adj* **(-ier, -iest)** of, suggesting, ~s: 鬼的; 使人想到鬼的: *a ~y* (= haunted) *house.* 鬼屋。

spool /spu:l; spul/ *n* reel (for thread, wire, photographic film, typewriter ribbon, paper or magnetic tape, etc). (缠绕线、铁丝、照相软片、打字机色带、纸、录音带等的)卷轴; 卷盘。⇨ the illus at **tape.** 参看 tape 之插图。

spoon[1] /spu:n; spun/ *n* utensil with a shallow bowl on a handle, used for stirring, serving and taking up food; named according to use, as: 匙; 调羹; 按其用途分为: *des'sert-/'soup-/'table/'tea/'egg-~.* 甜食匙(汤匙, 桌匙, 茶匙, 蛋匙)。***be ˌborn with a ˌsilver '~ in one's mouth,*** ⇨ **silver(1).** '**~·feed** *vt* **(a)** feed (a baby, etc) from a ~. 用羹匙喂(婴儿等)。**(b)** (fig) give (sb) excessive help or teaching: (喻)给予(某人)过分的帮助或教导; 填鸭式地教(不给学生独立思考的机会): *Some teachers ~-feed their pupils.* 有些老师用填鸭式的方法教学生。□ *vt* [VP15B] **~ *sth up/out,*** take with a ~: 以匙取: *~ up one's soup;* 以匙舀汤; *~ out the peas,* serve them. 以匙取食豌豆。'**~·ful** /-ful; -ˌfʊl/ *n* (*pl* **~·fuls**) as much as a ~ can hold. 一匙之量。

spoon[2] /spu:n; spun/ *vi* [VP2A] (dated colloq) behave in a way that shows that one is in love. (过时口

语)做出在恋爱中的举动。

spoon·er·ism /ˈspuːnərɪzəm; ˈspunəˌrɪzəm/ *n* [C] confusion of two or more words by wrong placing of the initial sounds, eg *well-boiled icicle* for *well-oiled bicycle*. 混成 (词的) 始018；首音误置(如把 *well-oiled bicycle* 说成 *well-boiled icicle*)。

spoor /spʊə(r); spʊr/ *n* [C] track or trail of a wild animal, enabling it to be followed. (野兽的) 足迹；嗅迹。

spor·adic /spəˈrædɪk; spoˈrædɪk/ *adj* occurring, seen, only here and there or occasionally: 时有时无的；散见于各处的：~ *raids/firing*. 偶发性的袭击(零星的射击)。 **spor·adi·cally** /-klɪ; -klɪ/ *adv*

spore /spɔː(r); spɔr/ *n* [C] germ, single cell, by which a flowerless plant (eg moss, a fern) reproduces itself. (无花植物如苔藓、羊齿等借以繁殖的)孢子；芽胞。

spor·ran /ˈspɒrən; ˈspɑrən/ *n* pouch, usu fur-covered, worn by Scottish Highlanders in front of the kilt. 苏格兰高地人佩于短裙前的囊袋(通常以毛皮包覆)。 ⇨ the illus at **kilt**. 参看 kilt 之插图。

sport /spɔːt; spɔrt/ *n* 1 [U] amusement, fun: 有趣；娱乐；玩笑；戏谑：*say sth in* ~, not seriously: 戏言；*make* ~ *of sb*, make him appear ridiculous. 开某人玩笑。 2 [U] ⇨ the illus at **base, cricket, football, hockey, rugby, tennis**. activity engaged in, esp outdoors, for amusement and exercise; [C] particular form of such activity: (参看 base, cricket, football, hockey, rugby, tennis 之插图)活动；运动；游戏(尤指户外者)；某种形式的户外活动或运动：*fond of/devoted to* ~; 喜爱(热心于)户外运动；*country* ~s, eg hunting, fishing, shooting, horse-racing: 乡间户外活动(如打猎、钓鱼、射击、赛马)；*athletic* ~s, eg running, jumping; 体育活动 (如赛跑、跳高、跳远)；'~s *coverage/reporting on TV*. 电视之体育新闻报导。 3 (*pl*) meeting for athletic contests: (复)运动会：*the school* ~s; 学校(举行的)运动会；*inter-university* ~s. 大学校际运动会。 4 (compounds, etc) (复合词等) '~s-car *n* small motor-car designed for high speeds. 跑车。'~s-coat/ ~s-jacket, informal jacket. 运动衫。'~s-editor *n* newspaper editor responsible for reports of ~s and games. 报纸的体育版编辑。'~s·man /-mən; -mən/ *n* (*pl* -men) (a) person who takes part in, is fond of, ~. 运动员；爱好运动者。 (b) (also 亦作 ~) person who plays fairly, who is willing to take risks, and is not downhearted if he loses. 有运动精神的人；失败而不气馁的人；输得起的人。 Hence, 由此产生，'~s·man·ship /-ʃɪp; -ʃɪp/ *n* '~s·man·like *adj*. 5 (colloq) (口) = ~sman; agreeable, easy-going person: 有运动道德的人；讨人喜欢的人；平易近人的人：*Come on, be a* ~! 好了，不要再别扭了！ 6 [C] plant or animal that deviates in a striking way from the normal type. 变态的植物或动物。 □ *vi, vt* 1 [VP2C] play about, amuse oneself: 自娱；游戏；嬉戏；玩耍：*seals* ~*ing about in the water*. 在水中嬉戏的海豹。 2 [VP6A] (colloq) have or wear for proud display: (口)夸示地保有、穿、戴等；炫耀：~ *a moustache/a diamond ring/a flower in the buttonhole of one's jacket*. 炫耀胡髭(钻石戒指，上衣扣孔中佩戴的花)。 ~**·ing** *adj* 1 connected with ~, interested in ~. 娱乐的；运动的；对运动有兴趣的。 2 willing to take a risk of losing; involving a risk of losing: 愿冒失败危险的；输得起的，有输赢的；有风险的：*make sb a* ~*ing offer*; 提供某人一个冒险性的建议；*give sb a* ~*ing chance*. 给予某人一赌输赢的机会。 3 ~smanlike: 有运动家风度的：*It's very* ~*ing of you to give me such an advantage*. 你让我占这样的便宜，很有运动员的风度。 ~**·ing·ly** *adv*

sport·ive /ˈspɔːtɪv; ˈspɔrtɪv/ *adj* playful; merry. 嬉戏的；愉快的；开心的。 ~**·ly** *adv* ~**·ness** *n*

spot /spɒt; spɑt/ *n* 1 small (esp round) mark different in colour from what it is on: 小点；(尤指)圆形斑点：*white dress material with red* ~s. 带红色斑点的白色衣料。*Which has* ~s, *the leopard or the tiger?* 豹与虎，哪一个有斑点？ 2 dirty mark or stain: 污点；污迹：~s *of mud on your boots*. 你长靴上的泥污。 3 small,

red mark, blemish, on the skin; pimple: (皮肤上的)红斑；丘疹：*This ointment won't clear your face of* ~s. 这种油膏不会去除你脸上的红斑。 4 (fig) moral blemish: (喻)德性上的污点或瑕疵：*There isn't a* ~ *on her reputation*. 她的名誉上没有污点。 5 drop: 滴；点：*Did you feel a few* ~s *of rain?* 你有没有感觉到下了几滴雨？ 6 particular place or area: 地点；场所：*the (very)* ~ *where he was murdered*. 他被谋杀的(确实)地点。 *TV/radio* ~, place in a TV/radio programme for an item or a commercial advertisement. 电视(无线电广播)节目中某一项目或广告出现的位置。 ⇨ **slot**(3). 7 (phrases) (短语) **a** ~ **check**, a quickly-made investigation, esp one made suddenly and without warning. 临时检查；突击检查。 **a tender** ~, (fig) a subject on which a person's feelings are easily hurt. (喻)易伤某人感情的话题；痛处。 **in a** ~, (colloq) in a difficult situation. (口)处困难境遇。 **knock** ~s **off sb**, easily surpass, do better than, him. 轻易超越或胜过某人。 **on the** ~, (a) at the place where one is needed: 在现场；临现场：*The police were on the* ~ *within a few minutes of hearing about the crime*. 获悉该项犯罪后几分钟，警察即到达现场。 (b) then and there; immediately: 当时当地；即刻；立即；当场：*He fell dead on the* ~. 他当场就死了。*The bullet struck his head and he was killed on the* ~. 子弹打中他的头部，他当时即被打死。 (c) (sl) in trouble. (俚)在困难中。 Cf 参较 'on the carpet'. **the person on the** ~, the man at the place in question (who, presumably, is acquainted with local conditions, happenings, etc and able to deal with them): 熟悉当地情况并能应付事情的人；当地有办法的人；当地有力人士：*Let's leave the decision to the man/the men/the people on the* ~. 让我们把决定权留给当地有办法的人(们)去决定好了。 **put sb on the** ~, (a) place sb in danger or difficulty: 置某人于危境或困境：*You've put me on the* ~. *I can't answer your question*. 这你可把我难住了。我无法回答你的问题。 (b) (of gangsters) decide to kill (eg a rival gangster): (指歹徒)决定杀死(如敌对的歹徒)。 **put one's finger on/find sb's weak** ~, find the point (of character, etc) where he is most open to attack. 找出某人的弱点。 8 (comm) ~ **cash**, payment on delivery of goods. (商)交货付款；现金。 ~ **prices**, prices quoted for such payment. 现价价格。 9 (GB colloq) small quantity of anything: (英口)少量；少许：*I need a* ~ *of brandy*. 我需要一点白兰地。*What about doing a* ~ *of work?* 做一点事怎么样？ *He's having a* ~ *of bother with his brother*, a quarrel. 他同他的哥哥(弟弟)在吵架。 □ *vt, vi* (-tt-) 1 [VP6A, 2A] mark, become marked, with ~s: 加斑点于；弄污；变得有斑点；*a table* ~*ted with ink*; 被墨水弄污的桌子；*material that* ~s *easily*, easily becomes ~ted. 易被弄污的料子。 2 [VP6A] pick out, recognize, see (one person or thing out of many): (从很多人或物中)察出；认出；看出；看见(某一个人或物)：~ *a friend in a crowd*; 在人群中认出一位朋友；~ *the winner in a race*, pick out the winner before the start. 预先指出赛跑的获胜者(看好某人)。 3 [VP2A] (colloq) rain slightly: (口)下小雨：*It's beginning to* ~/*is* ~*ting with rain*. 天开始下起小雨来了。 ~**·ted** *adj* marked with ~s, eg of such animals as the leopard and panther, and of birds with ~s of different colour on their plumage, of textile material with ~s. 有斑点的(如豹、黑豹等动物，羽毛有不同颜色斑点的鸟，以及有斑点的布料等)。 ~**·ted 'fever** *n* form of meningitis; form of typhus. 斑疹热；流行性脑脊髓膜炎；斑疹伤寒。 ~**·less** *adj* free from ~s; clean: 干净的；清洁的；无污点的；无暇疵的：*a* ~*less kitchen/reputation*. 清洁的厨房(无瑕疵的名誉)。 ~**·less·ly** *adv*; ~*lessly* clean. 极为清洁的；一尘不染的。 ~**·ty** *adj* (**-ier, -iest**) 1 marked with ~s (esp on the skin): (尤指皮肤上)有斑点的：*a* ~*ty complexion*; 多雀斑的脸；*windows that are* ~*ty with fly marks*. 有苍蝇污痕的窗户。 2 of varying quality: 品质不一的，不规则的：*a* ~*ty piece of work*, done unevenly. 做得不均匀的工作

(有的地方做得好，有的地方做得坏)。 **~·ter** *n* person who ~s(2), eg '*aircraft-~ter*, person who, eg during a war, looks for and identifies different types of aircraft; '*train-~ter*, (usu) schoolboy who looks for and notes different types of railway-engines. 观察员;侦察员(例如飞机侦察员,如在战时搜寻及辨认敌机机种的人员;火车观察员,通常指注意查火车机车之不同类型的学童)。

spot·light /'spɒtlaɪt; 'spat,laɪt/ *n* [C] (projector or lamp used for sending a) strong light directed on to a particular place or person, eg on the stage of a theatre: 注光; 射光圈(投射于舞台等上某处或某人的强光); 聚光灯(射出注光者): *He likes to be in the/to hold the ~*, (fig) he be the centre of attention. (喻)他喜欢出风头。□ *vt* [VP6A] direct a ~ on to. 投射注光于;把光线集中于;使显著。

spouse /spauz *US:* spaus; spauz/ *n* (legal or archaic) husband or wife. (法律或古)配偶;夫;妻。

spout /spaut; spaut/ *n* [C] **1** pipe or lip through or from which liquid pours, eg for carrying rainwater from a roof, or tea from a teapot. (液体流出或经过的)管道; 管口; 嘴; 喷水孔; 水筧(如茶壶嘴或屋檐下的导水管槽)。 **2** stream of liquid coming out with great force. 喷水;水柱;液柱;涌流。⇨ *water-~* at **water**[1](7). **3** *up the ~*, (sl) (俚) **(a)** in pawn. 在典当中。 **(b)** in difficulties, broken, etc according to context. 处困境; 破产等。 **(c)** pregnant. 怀孕的。□ *vt, vi* **1** [VP2A, C, 6A] *~ (out)*, (of liquid) come or send out with great force: (液体)喷出;涌出;喷出;流出: *water ~ing (out) from a broken water-main*; 从破裂的自来水主管喷出的水; *blood ~ing from a severed artery*; 从切断的动脉涌出的血; *a broken pipe ~ing water*. 喷水的破裂水管。 *The whales were ~ing*, sending up jets of water. 那些鲸鱼正在喷水。 **2** [VP2A, 6A] (colloq) speak, recite (verses, etc) pompously: (口)装腔作势地说话、朗诵(诗等): *~ing unwanted advice*. 装腔作势地说出多余的忠告。

sprain /sprem; spren/ *vt* [VP6A] injure (a joint, eg in the wrist or ankle) by twisting violently so that there is pain and swelling: 扭伤(关节): *~ one's wrist*; 扭伤腕关节; *suffering from a ~ed ankle*. 因踝部扭伤而感到痛苦。□ *n* [C] injury so caused. 扭伤。

sprang /spræŋ; spræŋ/ *pt* of **spring**[3].

sprat /spræt; spræt/ *n* small European sea-fish used as food. 小鲲(欧洲产的食用小海鱼)。

sprawl /sprɔːl; sprɔl/ *vi* [VP2A, C] **1** sit or lie with the arms and legs loosely spread out; fall so that one lies in this way: 伸展手足坐或卧; 手足摊开地倒下: *~ing on the sofa*; 伸开四肢躺在沙发上; *be sent ~ing in the mud*. 被击倒而仰卧在污泥中。 **2** (of plants, handwriting, fig of large towns) spread out loosely and irregularly over much space: (指植物、笔迹,并喻指大城市)蔓生; 蔓延; 散乱地延伸: *suburbs that ~ out into the countryside*. 向乡间散乱延展的市郊。□ *n* [U, C] ~ing position or movement; widespread untidy area, esp of buildings: 四肢伸开躺卧的姿势或动作; 大片杂乱的地区; (尤指)建筑物散乱的大片地区: *London's suburban ~*. 伦敦近郊建筑物散乱的大片地区。

spray[1] /spreɪ; spre/ *n* small branch of a tree or plant, esp a graceful one with leaves and flowers as an ornament; artificial ornament in a similar form: 小枝(尤指有花带叶优美而作装饰者); (人工做的)小枝花饰: *a ~ of diamonds*. 镶有钻石的枝状饰物。

spray[2] /spreɪ; spre/ *n* **1** [U] liquid sent through the air in tiny drops (by the wind, or through an apparatus): (借风力或喷雾器形成的)水雾; 水花; 浪花: '*sea-~*, blown from waves; 海水的浪花; *the ~ of a water-fall*. 瀑布的水花。 **2** [C] (kinds of) liquid preparation, eg a perfume, disinfectant or insecticide, to be applied in the form of ~ through an atomizer or other apparatus. (用作喷雾的其他器具具喷射的)喷体制剂(如香水、消毒剂、杀虫剂等)。 **3** [C] atomizer, etc used for applying such a liquid. 喷雾器。 '*~-gun* *n* apparatus

using pressure to spread cellulose, paint, varnish, etc over surfaces. 喷(漆)枪。□ *vt* [VP6A, 14] *~ sth/sb (with sth); ~ sth (on sth/sb)*, scatter ~ on: 喷液体制剂于; 似喷雾般发射: *~ mosquitoes/fruit-trees*; 喷杀虫剂于蚊虫(果树); *~ the enemy with bullets*. 向敌人扫射。 **~er** *n* **1** person who ~s. 喷洒者; 喷漆者。 **2** apparatus for ~ing. 喷雾器; 喷洒器。

spread /spred; spred/ *vt, vi* (*pt, pp* ~) **1** [VP6A, 14, 15B] *~ sth on/over sth; ~ sth with sth; ~ sth (out)*, extend the surface or width of sth by unfolding or unrolling it; cover (sth) by doing this: 展开; 铺开; 摊开; 铺盖(某物): *~ a cloth on a table/a table with a cloth*; 把桌布铺在桌面上; *~ out a map; ~ (out) one's arms*. 张开两臂。 *The bird ~ its wings*. 鸟展翅。 **2** [VP14] *~ sth on sth; ~ sth with sth*, put (a substance) on a surface and extend its area by flattening, etc; cover (a surface) by doing this: 涂敷; 涂布: *~ butter on bread/a slice of bread with butter*. 涂奶油在(一片)面包上。 **3** [VP6A, 15A, B, 2A, C] (cause to) become more widely extended or distributed: (使)传布;(使)广布;(使)散开;(使)流传: *~ knowledge*. 传播知识。 *Flies ~ disease*. 苍蝇传布疾病。 *The water ~ over the floor*. 水漫布在地板上。 *The rumour quickly ~ through the village*. 这谣言很快就在村子里传开了。 *The fire ~ from the factory to the houses near by*. 火势从工厂延烧至附近的房舍。 *~ oneself*, **(a)** occupy much space, eg by lying with the limbs extended. 伸开四肢躺卧等而占去去很多地方。 **(b)** talk or write at length (on a subject). (就某一问题)滔滔不绝地说或写。 **(c)** let oneself go, eg by being generous in hospitality. 尽力而为; 十分尽力(如殷勤待客)。 **4** [VP2A, B, C] show an extended surface: 伸展; 扩展: *a desert ~ing for hundreds of miles*. 绵延数百英里的沙漠。 **5** [VP6A, 15B] extend in time: (时间)延长; 延长: *a course of studies ~ over three years*; 为时三年的课程; *instalments/payments ~ over twelve months*. 分十二个月偿付的分期付款。 **6** *~·'eagle* *n* figure of an eagle with the legs and wings extended (as seen on coins). 张足展翼的鹰像(像如硬币上者)。□ *vt* (reflex) take up a lying position with arms and legs extended to form a cross: (反身)伸展四肢躺卧: *sunbathers ~eagled on the grass/sands*. 在草地(沙滩)上四肢张开躺卧的日光浴者。 '*~-over* *n* arrangement in an industry by which hours of work are adjusted to special needs. 工作时间按工作需要调整的制度。□ *n* (rarely *pl*) (罕用复数) **1** extent; breadth: 范围; 广度: *the ~ of a bird's wings*. 鸟的展展。 **2** extension; spreading(3): 传播; 散布; 蔓延: *the ~ of disease/knowledge/education*. 疾病的蔓延(知识的传播; 教育的普及)。 **3** (colloq) table ~ with good things to eat and drink: (口)摆满酒佳肴的桌子; 丰盛的酒席: *What a ~!* 多丰盛的酒席呀! **4** sth that is ~(1) (usu in compounds): 铺开之物: (通常用于复合词中): *a 'bed~*, a cover ~ over the bed-clothes. 床单; 被单; 垫单。 *He's developing (a) middle-age ~*, (colloq) is getting big round the waist (as some persons do in middle age). (口)他逐渐发福了(腰围逐渐增大, 象有些中年人那样)。 **5** name used for various kinds of paste (to be) ~ on bread, etc. 涂敷于面包等片的某些酱的名称。 **~er** *n* one who, that which, ~s, eg a '*flame-~er* in an oil-stove; an implement used for ~ing paste, etc on bread. (涂敷者涂敷物等); 涂敷器(涂敷等于面包上者)。

spree /spriː; spri/ *n* lively frolic: 欢闹; 游乐: *have a ~*, have a lively, merry time. 作乐; 兴高采烈。 *be on the ~; go out on a ~*, be having, go out to enjoy, a ~. 在作乐、狂欢; 外出寻乐或狂欢。 *a 'spending/'buying ~*, an occasion of (extravagant or unusual) spending of money. 疯狂挥霍(狂购乱买)。

sprig /sprɪg; sprɪg/ *n* **1** small twig (of a plant or bush) with leaves, etc: 有叶的小枝; 嫩枝: *a ~ of mistletoe for Christmas*. 用作圣诞节装饰用的檞寄生的小

枝。**2** (usu contemptuous) young person. (通常为轻蔑语)少年;青年。**~·ged** *adj* ornamented with designs of ~s: 用小枝或嫩枝图案装饰的: *~ged muslin*. 有小枝图案的薄棉布。

spright·ly /ˈspraɪtlɪ; ˋspraɪtlɪ/ *adj* **(-ier, -iest)** lively; brisk. 活泼的;轻快的。**spright·li·ness** *n*

spring[1] /sprɪŋ; sprɪŋ/ *n* **1** act of springing or jumping up. 跳;跳跃。**2** (place where there is) water coming up from the ground: 泉; 泉水; 有泉水处: *ˈhot-~;* 温泉; *ˈmineral-~;* 矿泉; *a hot-ˈ~ resort;* 有温泉的胜地; (attrib) (用作定语) *~ water*. 泉水。**3** device of twisted, bent or coiled metal or wire which tends to return to its shape or position when pulled or pushed or pressed: 发条; 弹簧; 板弹簧: *the ~s of a motor-car;* 汽车的板弹簧(俗称钢板); *the ~ of a watch*. 表的发条。**ˌ~-ˈbalance** *n* device that measures weight by the tension of a ~. 弹簧秤。**ˈ~-board** *n* board to give a ~ing motion to sb jumping from it. 跳板; 弹板。**ˈ~-gun** *n* one that goes off when a trespasser comes against a wire which is attached to the trigger. 伏击枪(扳机与一金属线相连,线被触及即引发)。**ˌ~-ˈmattress** *n* one containing spiral ~s in a rigid frame. 弹簧床垫。**~ tide** *n* (two words; 此处须分开写; ⇨ *~tide, ~time* at **spring**[2]) tide with the greatest rise or fall, occurring shortly after new and full moon in each month; ⇨ *neap-tide* at **neap.** 每个月新月及满月后的大潮; 子午潮。**4** [U] elastic quality: 弹性; 弹力: *rubber bands that have lost their ~*. 失去弹性的橡皮圈。*The old man's muscles have lost their ~*. 这老人的肌肉已失去了弹性。**5** (often *pl*) cause or origin: (常用复数)起源; 本源; 原由;动机: *the ~s of human conduct*. 人类行为的动机。**~·less** *adj* without ~s(3): 无发条、弹簧(板)等的: *a ~less cart*. 无弹簧的马车。**~y** *adj* **(-ier, -iest)** (of movement or substances) elastic; that springs: (指动作或物质)有弹性的; 有弹力的: *walk with a youthful, ~y step*. 以富有青春活力、有弹性的脚步行走。

spring[2] /sprɪŋ; sprɪŋ/ *n* [U, C] season of the year in which vegetation begins; season between winter and summer (in GB from about 21 March to 22 June): 春; 春季(在英国约自三月二十一日至六月二十二日): *in (the) ~;* 在春天; (attrib) (用作定语) *~ flowers/weather*. 春季的花(天气)。**ˌ~-ˈclean** *vt* clean (a house, a room) thoroughly. 彻底打扫(房子, 房间); 大扫除。Hence, 由此产生, **ˌ~-ˈcleaning** *n*. **ˈ~·like** *adj*: *~like weather*. 和煦如春的天气。**ˈ~·time** (also, poet 诗中亦作 **ˈ~-tide**) *nn* season of ~. 春季。

spring[3] /sprɪŋ; sprɪŋ/ *vi, vt* (*pt* **sprang** /spræŋ; spræŋ/, *pp* **sprung** /sprʌŋ; sprʌŋ/) **1** [VP2C] jump suddenly from the ground; move suddenly (*up, down, out*, etc) from rest, concealment, etc: 跳; 跳跃; 跃出; 突然活动(与 up, down, out 等连用): *He sprang to his feet/sprang out of bed/sprang forward to help me/sprang up from his seat*. 他跳了起来(从床上跳下来,跳过来帮助我,从座位上突然站起来)。*The branch sprang back and hit me in the face*. 那树枝弹回来打在我脸上。**2** [VP2C] **~ *(up)*,** appear; grow up quickly from the ground or from a stem: 出现;发生;萌芽;迅速长出: *A breeze has sprung up*. 吹起了微风。*Weeds were ~ing up everywhere*. 杂草到处丛生。*The wheat is beginning to ~ up*. 小麦正开始茁长。(fig) (喻) *A suspicion/doubt sprang up in her mind*. 她心中起了怀疑。**3** [VP3A] **~ *from*,** arise or come from: 崛起; 来自: *He is sprung from royal blood*, is of royal ancestry. 他是皇室肯裔。*Where have you sprung from*, suddenly and unexpectedly appeared from? 你从哪里跳出来(突然出现)的? **4** [VP 14] **~ *sth on sb*,** bring forward suddenly: 突然提出; 突然带来: *~ a surprise on sb;* 使某人吃一惊; *~ a new theory/proposal on sb*. 突然向某人提出新理论(建议)。**5** [VP6A] cause to operate by means of a mechanism: (借机械作用)使发动; 开动: *~ a mine*, cause it to explode; 使地雷爆炸; *~ a trap*, cause it to go off. 触引(拉动)陷阱(或捕机等)。**6** [VP6A, 2A] (of wood) (cause to) warp, split, crack: (指木材)(使)弯曲; (使)裂开; (使)分裂: *My cricket bat has sprung*. 我的板球拍弯曲了。*I have sprung my tennis racket*. 我把我的网球拍弄弯了。**~ *a leak*,** (of a ship) crack or burst so that water enters. (指船)漏裂; 生漏缝。

spring·bok /ˈsprɪŋbɒk; ˋsprɪŋˌbɑk/ *n* small S African gazelle. 南非洲产的一种小瞪羚。

sprinkle /ˈsprɪŋkl; ˋsprɪŋkl/ *vt* [VP6A, 14] **~ *sth (on/with sth)*,** direct, throw, a shower of (sth) on to (a surface): 撒(某物)于(某物之表面); 洒: *~ water on a dusty path;* 洒水于多尘土的路上; *~ a dusty path with water;* 以水洒于多尘土的路上; *~ the floor with sand*. 把沙撒在地板上。**sprink·ler** /ˈsprɪŋklə(r); ˋsprɪŋklɚ/ *n* (esp) apparatus or device for sprinkling water (eg on to a lawn) or (permanently installed in buildings) for fighting fire. (尤指)洒水器; 洒水车; 洒水装置; (固定在建筑物上的)消防装置。**sprink·ling** *n* small quantity or number here and there: (散布在各处的)微量或少数: *There was a sprinkling of hooligans in the crowd*. 群众之中夹杂有少数的不良少年。

sprint /sprɪnt; sprɪnt/ *vi* [VP2A, C] run a short distance at full speed: 以全速跑短距离: *He ~ed past his competitors just before reaching the tape*. 刚好在到达终点之前,他全速冲刺而超越了他的对手们。□ *n* such a run; (esp) burst of speed at the end of a race. 短距离快跑; 短跑; (尤指)赛跑到达终点前的冲刺。**~er** *n*

sprit /sprɪt; sprɪt/ *n* small spar reaching from a mast to the upper outer corner of a sail. (自桅伸至帆上外角以撑帆的)斜杠。⇨ the illus at **barque.** 参看 barque 之插图。**ˈ~·sail** *n* sail extended by a ~. 斜杠帆。

sprite /spraɪt; spraɪt/ *n* fairy; elf. 妖精; 鬼怪; 精灵。

sprocket /ˈsprɒkɪt; ˋsprɑkɪt/ *n* each of several teeth on a wheel connecting with the links of a chain or holes in a movie film, paper or magnetic tape. 扣连齿(链轮上与链条结合之齿, 或与影片、纸带、磁带旁边小洞结合之齿)。**ˈ~-wheel** *n* such a wheel, eg as on a bicycle. 扣连轮(如脚踏车上者)。

sprout /spraʊt; spraʊt/ *vi, vt* **1** [VP2A, C] **~ *(up)*,** put out leaves; begin to grow: 发芽; 萌芽; 开始生长: *Peter has really ~ed up in the past year*. 彼得过去这一年长高了不少。**2** [VP6A] cause to grow: 使生长; 使发芽: *The continuous wet weather has ~ed the barley*, eg after it has been cut and left in the field. 连续下雨的天气已使大麦发芽了(如收割后仍置于田中者)。**3** [VP6A] develop, produce: 发展; 产生: *When do deer first ~ horns?* 鹿在多大的时候开始生角? *Tom has ~ed a moustache*. 汤姆长胡子了。□ *n* [C] shoot, newly ~ed part, of a plant. 植物的苗、芽等新生部分。⇨ **Brussels ~s.**

spruce[1] /spruːs; sprus/ *adj* neat and smart in dress and appearance. 衣着及外表整洁漂亮的。□ *vt, vi* [VP6A, 15B, 2C] **~ *(sb/oneself) (up)*,** make oneself ~: 打扮; 修饰: *Go and ~ yourself up*. 去打扮打扮。*They were all ~d up for the party*. 他们为参加舞会都打扮得漂漂亮亮。**~·ly** *adv* **~·ness** *n*

spruce[2] /spruːs; sprus/ *n* **~ (fir),** kinds of fir-tree grown in plantations for its wood, used for making paper. 针枞; 云杉。

sprung /sprʌŋ; sprʌŋ/ *pp* of **spring**[3].

spry /spraɪ; spraɪ/ *adj* **(-er, -est)** lively; nimble: 活泼的; 轻快的; 敏捷的: *still ~ at eighty*. 八十岁仍很矫健。***look ~*,** be quick. 轻快; 敏捷。

spud /spʌd; spʌd/ *n* [C] **1** (colloq) potato. (口)马铃薯。**2** short spade with a narrow blade for digging or cutting up weeds. 草铲; 小铲。

spue /spjuː; spju/ *vt, vi* = **spew.**

spume /spjuːm; spjum/ *n* [U] foam; froth. 泡沫。

spun /spʌn; spʌn/ *pp* of **spin.**

spunk /spʌŋk; spʌŋk/ *n* [U] (colloq) courage; mettle; spirit: (口)勇气; 胆量; 精神: *have no ~;* 没有胆子; *a boy with plenty of ~;* 胆量大的男孩; (sl) semen. (俚)精液。**~y** *adj* having ~. 有勇气的; 有胆量的。

spur /spɜː(r); spɚ/ n 1 one of a pair of sharp-toothed wheels, worn on the heels of a rider's boots and used to make the horse go faster. 马刺; 马扎子; 马靴刺. **win one's ~s**, (hist) gain knighthood; (fig) win honour and reputation. (史)获得爵位; (喻)获得荣誉及声名. 2 (fig) sth that urges a person on to greater activity: (喻)激励物; 刺激物; 驱策: the ~ of poverty. 贫困的驱策. **act on the ~ of the moment**, on a sudden impulse. 凭一时的冲动做事. 3 sharp, hard projection on a cock's leg. 公鸡腿上的肉距. ⇨ the illus at **bird**. 4 ridge extending from a mountain or hill. 山的支脉; 横岭. □ vt, vi (-rr-) 1 [VP6A, 15B] ~ **sb/sth (on)**, urge on with, or as with, ~s: 以马刺刺激; 驱策; 激励: It's foolish to ~ on a willing horse. 驱策驯驯的马是愚蠢的. He was ~red on by ambition. 他为野心所驱使. 2 [VP2C] ride fast or hard: 疾驰; 疾驱: The rider ~red on/forward to his destination. 骑者向目的地疾驰而去.

spu·ri·ous /ˈspjʊərɪəs; ˈspjʊrɪəs/ adj false; not genuine: 错误的; 假的; 伪造的: ~ coins/credentials/arguments. 假硬币(伪造的证件/错误的论据). ~**ly** adv ~**ness** n

spurn /spɜːn; spɚn/ vt [VP6A] reject or refuse contemptuously; have nothing to do with (an offer, a person or his advances). 轻蔑地拒绝; 弃绝; 摈斥(提议, 某人, 某人的亲近).

spurt /spɜːt; spɚt/ vi 1 [VP2C, 3A] ~ **(out)(from)**, (of liquids, flame, etc) come out in a sudden burst: (指液体, 火焰等)喷出; 进出; 涌出: Blood ~ed (out) from the wound. 血从伤口喷出. 2 [VP2A] make a sudden, short and violent effort, esp in a race or other contest: 作突然、短暂而剧烈的努力(尤指在赛跑或其他比赛时); 冲刺: The runner ~ed as he approached the winning-post. 那赛跑者在接近终点时全力冲刺. □ n [C] sudden bursting forth; sudden burst of energy: 喷出; 涌出; 精力的奋发: ~s of water/flame/energy; 水的涌出(火焰的喷出; 精力的奋发); a ~ of anger; 一阵怒气; put on a ~ (= increase speed) towards the end of a race. 赛跑接近终点时加快速度.

sput·nik /ˈspʊtnɪk; ˈspʊtnɪk/ n artificial unmanned satellite put into space by means of rocket propulsion (esp the first, launched from the Soviet Union in 1957). (用火箭射入太空的) 人造卫星(尤指一九五七年苏联发射的第一颗人造卫星).

sput·ter /ˈspʌtə(r); ˈspʌtɚ/ vi, vt 1 [VP2A, C] make a series of spitting sounds: 发连续吐唾液声: ~ing 拍声: The sausages were ~ing in the frying-pan. 腊肠在煎锅中拍拍作响. ~ **out**, stop burning after making spitting sounds: 拍拍声后熄灭了: The candle ~ed out. 那支蜡烛发出拍拍声后熄灭了. 2 = **splutter(1, 2)**.

spu·tum /ˈspjuːtəm; ˈspjutəm/ n [U] saliva; matter coughed up from the throat (esp as indicating the nature of an illness). 唾液; 口涎; 痰(尤指显示某种疾病性质者).

spy /spaɪ; spaɪ/ n (pl **spies**) 1 person who tries to get secret information, esp about the military affairs of other countries (called a 'secret agent' if he is employed by one's own government and a 'spy' if he is working for other countries). 间谍(受雇于本国政府者, 称为'特工人员', 为其他国家工作者, 称为'间谍'). 2 person who keeps a secret watch on the movements of others: 侦探; 探员; 秘密侦察他人行动者: police spies, persons employed by the police to watch suspected criminals; 警探(警察雇用以侦察嫌疑犯者); industrial spies, employed to learn trade secrets, etc. 工业间谍(受雇刺探商业秘密等者). □ vi, vt 1 [VP2A, 3A, 15B] ~ **(into/on/upon sth.)** ~ **sth out**, act as a spy on, watch secretly: 作侦探; 侦察; 窥探: spy on the enemy's movements; 侦察敌方行动; spy out the land, 秘密侦察该地; spy into other people's affairs. 窥探他人事务. 2 [VP6A, 19A] observe; see; discover: 观察; 看见; 发现: I spy someone coming up the garden path.

我看到有人从花园小径走过来. You are quick at spying her faults. 你很容易看出她的缺点. **'spy-glass** n small telescope. 小望远镜. **'spy-hole** n peep-hole. 窥视孔.

squab /skwɒb; skwɑb/ n 1 young bird, esp an unfledged pigeon: 雏鸟; (尤指)羽毛未丰的雏鸽: ~ pie, pigeon pie. 鸽肉馅饼. 2 (comm) soft seat or cushion, esp as a seat in a car. (商)软座; 软坐垫(尤指用于轿车中者).

squabble /ˈskwɒbl; ˈskwɑbl/ vi [VP2C] engage in a petty or noisy quarrel: 争吵; 争论; 争论: Tom was squabbling with his sister about who should use the bicycle. 汤姆正同他姐姐(妹妹)争论谁该使用那辆脚踏车. □ n [C] noisy quarrel about sth trivial. (因小事而)大声的口角; 无谓的争吵和争论.

squad /skwɒd; skwɑd/ n small group of persons, eg of soldiers, working or being trained together: 一小群一起工作或受训的人; 小队; 小组; 班: Scotland Yard's flying ~, number of special police cars and men always ready for prompt action, eg on reports of burglaries, etc. 英国伦敦警察厅的机动小组(随时待命行动的人车编组). '~ **car**, (US) police patrol car. (美)警察巡逻车.

squad·ron /ˈskwɒdrən; ˈskwɑdrən/ n 1 sub-unit of a cavalry, armoured or engineer regiment (120–200 men). (由 120 人至 200 人组成的)骑兵队; 装甲连; 工兵连. 2 number of warships or military aircraft forming a unit. (海军)战队; 中队; (空军)中队. **'S~ Leader** n RAF rank, next below Wing Commander. 英国皇家空军少校.

squalid /ˈskwɒlɪd; ˈskwɑlɪd/ adj dirty, mean, uncared for: 污秽的; 卑劣的; 无人照料的: living in ~ conditions/houses. 住在污秽的环境(房屋)中. ~**ly** adv

squall /skwɔːl; skwɔl/ n [C] 1 loud cry of pain or fear (esp from a baby or child). 痛苦或恐惧的高声喊叫(尤指婴儿或孩童所发出的高声). 2 sudden violent wind, often with rain or snow: 狂风; 暴风(常夹有雨或雪者): look out for ~s, (often fig) be on one's guard against danger or trouble. (常作喻)防备危险或困厄. □ vi [VP2A] utter ~s(1): 大声喊叫; 尖叫: ~ing babies. 大声喊叫的婴儿. The boy ~s as soon as he sees the dentist. 那男孩一见到牙医就大声尖叫. ~**y** adj having, marked by, ~s(2): 有狂风的; 有暴风的: a ~y February day. 二月里刮狂风的一天.

squalor /ˈskwɒlə(r); ˈskwɑlɚ/ n [U] squalid state: 污秽; 卑劣: born in ~; 出身卑下的; the ~ of the slums. 贫民窟的污秽状况.

squan·der /ˈskwɒndə(r); ˈskwɑndɚ/ vt [VP6A] waste (time, money). 浪费(时间, 金钱). '~**·mania** /-meɪnɪə; -ˈmenɪə/ n [U] (craze for) extravagant spending of money. 浪费金钱(狂).

square[1] /skweə(r); skwer/ adj 1 having the shape of a square[2](1): 正方形的; 方的: a ~ table. 方桌. **a ~ peg in a round hole**, ⇨ **peg**[1](1). ⇨ **dance/game**, one in which the dancers/players face inwards from four sides. 方块舞(游戏). 2 having or forming (exactly or approx) a right angle: 成直角或近乎直角的; 方的: ~ corners; 方隅; a ~ jaw/chin, with angular, not curved, outlines. 方形下颚(下巴). ~ **brackets** n pl the marks [ ]. 方括弧 ⇨ **bracket(2)**. 3 (of a person) of comparatively broad shape. (指人)体型宽阔的. ~**·'rigged** adj (of a sailing ship) having the principal sails set at right angles to the mast. (指帆船)有横帆装置的. Cf 参较 **fore-and-aft**. ~**·'shouldered** adj with the shoulders at right angles to the neck, not sloping. 方肩的; 肩膀平(不倾斜)的. '~**-toed** adj (of shoes) having a ~ toe-cap; (fig, of persons) formal; prim. (指鞋)平头的; 方头的; (喻, 指人)方方正正的; 拘谨的. ~ **toes** n formal or prim person. 拘谨的人; 老古板. 3 level or parallel (with); balanced; settled: 水平的; 平行的(与 with 连用); 平衡的; 结清的; 结清的: get one's accounts ~, settled. 把帐结清. **be (all) ~**, (a) (golf) have equal scores (高尔夫)积分相等: all ~ at the ninth hole. 在第九洞积分相等. **(b)** with neither person in

debt to the other: 两不欠帐; 两不亏欠: *Let's call it all
~, shall we?* 我们从此两不亏欠, 行吗? **get ~ with sb,**
settle accounts; (fig) have one's revenge on him. 和某
人结帐; (喻)找某人算帐; 找某人报仇. **4** of a number
multiplied by itself: 平方的; 自乘的: *a ~ metre,*
surface area of a ~ which has sides of one metre in
length; 一平方米; *nine ~ cm.* 九平方厘米. *The ~
root of x⁴ is x²/of 9 is 3.* x⁴ 的平方根是 x² (9的平
方根是 3). *A carpet 6 metres ~ has an area of
36 ~ metres.* 六米见方的地毯面积是三十六平方米.
measure, expressed in ~ feet, metres, etc. 平方
积; 面积(用平方英尺、米等表示者). **5** thorough; uncompromising: 彻底的; 不妥协的; 坚决的: *meet with a
~ refusal.* 遭到断然拒绝. **a ~ meal,** one that is
satisfactory because there is plenty of good food. 丰盛
的餐食. **6** fair, honest: 公正的; 诚实的: ~ *dealings,*
in business; (生意)公平交易; *play a ~ game,* in sport.
(运动)公平竞赛. **(get/give sb) a ~ deal,** a fair
bargain, fair treatment, equality of opportunity. (获
得, 给予某人)公平的交易, 公平的待遇, 公平的机会等. **7
~ leg,** ⇨ the illus at **cricket.** 参看 cricket 之插图. □
adv **1** in a ~ (2) manner: 成直角地; 直地: *stand/sit
~;* 真立(坐); *hit a man ~ on the jaw.* 正好打在一个人
的下颚上. **2 fair and ~,** in a ~ (6) manner. 正大光
明地; 公平地; 直直地. **~·ly adv 1** so as to form a right
angle. 成直角地; 成方形地. **2** fairly; honestly: 公正
地; 诚实地: *act ~ly.* 行为正直. **3** directly opposite: 正
对面地: *He faced me ~ly across the table.* 他在桌子那
边正对着我. **~·ness** *n*
square² /skweə(r)/ *n* [C] **1** plane figure with
four equal sides and four right angles, ie 正方形.
⇨ the illus at **quadrilateral.** 参看 quadrilateral 之插
图. **back to ~ one,** (from the use of ~s on board
games, played by throwing dice, and with penalties for
certain numbered ~s) back to the starting-point and
forced to start again. 回到出发点; 被迫重新开始(起源
于掷骰子玩的方块游戏, 方块上带号码, 遇到某些号码则受
罚). **2** anything having the shape of a ~. 方形物. **3**
four-sided open area, eg in a town, used as a garden or
for recreation, or one enclosed by streets and buildings:
(城市等中的)广场, 方场: *listening to the band playing in
the ~.* 聆听广场上乐队的演奏. **'barrack ~** *n* such an
open space in a military barracks. 营房中的广场或操
场. **'~-bashing** (sl) military drill (esp marching, etc).
(俚)军事训练(尤指行军等). **4** buildings and streets
surrounding a ~(3): 广场四周的建筑及街道: *He lives
at No 95 Russell S~.* 他住在罗素广场九十五号. **5**
block of buildings bounded by four streets; distance
along one side of such a block (the word *block* being
more usu, esp US). (四周有街道的)街区; 街区一面的距
离(block 较常用, 尤其在美国). **6** result when a number
or quantity is multiplied by itself: 平方; 自乘; 二次幂:
The ~ of 7 is 49. 7 的平方是 49. *What is the ~ of x²?*
x² 的自乘是什么? **7** L-shaped or (**'T-~**) T-shaped
instrument for drawing or testing right angles. 曲尺;
丁字尺; 矩尺; 直角规. **out of ~,** not at right angles.
不成直角(地); 不正的(地). **8 on the ~,** (fairly),
honestly: 正直的(地); 公平的(地); 诚实的(地): *Can we
trust them to act on the ~?* 我们能信赖他们处事公正吗?
Is their business on the ~? 他们做生意规矩吗? **9** body
of infantry drawn up in a ~ form. 步兵的方阵. **10
'word ~,** number of words arranged so that they read
alike forwards and downwards. 纵横字谜; 字阵游戏
(方格内填入字母, 纵横方向可组合成相同之词). **11** (sl)
person (considered to be) out of touch with new ideas,
styles, etc: (俚)与新的观念、风尚等脱节的人; 老古板; 旧
派人物: *I'm not even a ~, I'm a cube!* I'm rigidly
conventional and old-fashioned. 说我是旧派人物还嫌不
够, 我是旧派中的旧派人物.
square³ /skweə(r)/ *vt, vi* **1** [VP6A] make
square; give a square shape to. 使成方形. **~ the circle,**
attempt sth that is impossible. 尝试做不可能的事; 变圆

为方. **2** [VP6A] cause one line or side to make a right
angle with another: 使成直角; 使垂直: *~ timber,* give
it rectangular edges. 使木材各边成直角. **3** [VP6A]
make straight or level: 使直; 使平: ~ *one's shoulders.*
把肩膀放平; 挺胸. **4** [VP6A] multiply a number by
itself; get the square²(6) of a number: 自乘; 得出某数
的平方: *Three ~d is nine.* 三自乘得 9. x² = x ~d.
x 自乘得 x 平方. **5** [VP6A, 15B] **~ sth off,** mark
(off) in squares. 划分为方形. **6** [VP2C, 14, 15B] ~
(sth) (up) (with sb), settle, balance: 结算: ~
accounts (up) with sb, settle one's debts; (fig) have one's
revenge on sb. 与某人结帐; (喻)找某人算帐; 找某人报
仇. *It's time I ~d up with you.* 我该同你结帐了(我们该结帐了). **7** [VP
6A] bribe; get the (dishonest) co-operation of: 贿赂;
自… 处获得非法合作: *Henry and James had to be ~d
before they would do anything for him.* 亨利和詹姆斯须先
行贿赂才能为他作事. *He has been ~d to hold his tongue.*
他已被收买而保持缄默. **8** [VP14, 3A] ~ (sth) with,
make or be consistent: (使)与…相符; (使)与…一致: *You
should ~ your practice with your principles.* 你应该言行
一致(使你的行为符合你的主张). *It's hard to ~ the statement
if the facts ~d with the theory, but they do not.* 如果事
实与理论相符, 那就好了, 不过并非如此. **9** [VP2C] ~
up to sb, take up the attitude of a boxer (ready to
begin fighting). 对某人摆起拳击手的姿势(准备格斗);对
某人摩拳擦掌.
squash¹ /skwɒʃ/ *vt, vi* **1** [VP6A, 15A, B,
22] crush; press flat or into a small space: 压碎; 压烂;
压扁; 压挤; 压缩: ~ *too many people into a bus.* 把太多
的人挤进一辆公共汽车. *Don't ~ my hat; you'll ~
it flat.* 不要坐在我的帽子上; 你会把它压扁. **2** [VP2A]
become ~ed or pressed out of shape: 被压坏; 被压烂; 被
压扁: *Soft fruits ~ easily.* 柔软的水果容易压烂. **3**
[VP2C] squeeze or crowd: 挤; 挤进去: *Don't all try to
~ into the lift together.* 不要统统挤进电梯里去. *They
~ed through the gate into the football ground.* 他们挤过
大门进入足球场. **4** [VP6A] (colloq) silence (sb) with
a crushing retort; snub: (口)以压服性的反驳使(某人)
缄默; 斥止; 反驳(某人)使哑口无言: *He was/felt completely ~ed.* 他被(他感觉被)完全驳倒了. **5** [VP6A] (colloq) subdue (a rebellion). (口)镇压(反叛). □ *n* (rarely *pl*) (罕用复数) **1** crowd of persons
~ed together: 挤在一起的人群; 杂沓的人群: *There was
a violent ~ at the gate.* 大门口挤满了一群暴民. **2**
(sound of) sth ~ing or being ~ed: 压坏压烂的; (被)
压烂之物; 压坏或压烂的声音: *The ripe tomato hit the
speaker in the face with a ~.* 那个熟番茄叭哒一声打中
了演说者的脸. **3** [C, U] drink (cold, usu bottled) made
from fruit juice: 果汁(冰的, 通常瓶装)饮料; 果汁冷饮:
orange/lemon ~. 橘子(柠檬)水. **4 '~(-rackets),**
game played with rackets and a rubber ball in a walled,
roofed court. 软式网球(用球拍及橡皮球在四周围起并且
有顶的场地上玩的一种球戏). **~·y** *adj* easily ~ed; soft
and wet. 易压烂; 软而湿的.
squash² /skwɒʃ/ *n* (*pl* unchanged) kinds of
gourd, like a pumpkin, eaten as a vegetable. (复数不
变)南瓜; 葫芦.
squat /skwɒt/ *vi, vt* (**-tt-**) **1** [VP2A, C] sit
on one's heels, or on the ground with the legs drawn
up under or close to the body; [VP6A, 15B] put
(oneself) in this position: 蹲踞; 跪坐; 盘坐; 使(自己)蹲
踞、跪坐或盘坐: *The old man ~ted in front of the fire.*
那老人蹲在火(炉)前面. *He ~ted (himself) down.* 他蹲
了下来. **2** [VP2A, C] (of animals) crouch with the
body close to the ground. (指动物)蜷伏. **3** [VP2A,
C] (colloq) sit: (口)坐: *Find somewhere to ~.* 找个地
方坐下. **4** [VP2A] settle on land without permission,
esp publicly owned and unoccupied land (in order
to acquire ownership); occupy empty (usu deserted,
derelict) buildings without authority. 擅自居于未占
用的公地(以期获得所有权);擅自搬进(通常系为人遗弃或

无人居住的)空屋。☐ *adj* short and thick: 矮胖的: *a ~ man;* 矮胖的人; dumpy: 粗短的; 粗矮的: *a ~ teapot*. 粗矮的茶壶。**~·ter** *n* **1** person who ~s(4); (in Australia) sheep-farmer. 擅自定居于未占用的公地者; (在澳大利亚)牧羊农场主。**2** person who takes unauthorized possession of unoccupied premises. 擅自占有无人居住的房屋者。

squaw /skwɔː; skwɔ/ *n* N American Indian woman or wife. 北美印第安人的妇女或妻子。

squawk /skwɔːk; skwɔk/ *vi* [VP2A, C], *n* (chiefly of birds) (utter a) loud, harsh cry, as when hurt or frightened; (colloq) (make a) loud complaint; (sl) betray: (主要指鸟)(发)粗厉的叫声(如受伤或受惊吓时); (口)高声抱怨; 诉苦; (俚)泄露秘密: *The old man ~ed (to the police)*. 那老人(向警察)高声抱怨。**~er** *n*

squeak /skwiːk; skwik/ *n* [C] **1** short, shrill cry, eg made by a mouse, or similar sound, eg from an unoiled hinge. 吱吱声(如鼠叫); 轧轧声(如未涂油的铰链所发者); 短而尖的声音。**2** *a narrow ~*, a narrow escape from danger or failure. 险遭不测; 幸免于难; 险胜。☐ *vi, vt* **1** [VP2A] make a ~: 发吱吱声或轧轧声; 发短而尖锐的声音: *These new shoes ~*. 这双新鞋吱吱作响。**2** [VP6A, 15B] *~ sth (out)*, utter in a ~ing voice: 以尖锐声音说出: *~ out a few frightened words*. 尖锐地说出几个充满恐惧的词。**3** [VP2A, C] (colloq) become an informer. (口)告密。**~er** *n* (colloq) informer. (口)告密者。**~y** *adj* **(-ier, -iest)** ~ing: 发短而尖锐之声的; 吱吱叫的; 作轧轧声的: *a ~y floor;* (走上去)发吱吱声的地板; *in a ~y voice*. 尖声地; 吱吱地。

squeal /skwiːl; skwil/ *n* [C] shrill cry or sound, longer and louder than a squeak, often indicating terror or pain: 吱嘎声; 长而尖锐的叫声(常表示恐惧或痛苦); 号叫: *the ~ of brakes*, eg on lorries. 煞车发出的吱嘎声。☐ *vi, vt* **1** [VP2A, C] make a ~: 发吱嘎声; 发长而尖锐的叫声: *The pigs were ~ing*. 猪在号叫。*He ~ed like a pig*. 他象猪一样地号叫。**2** [VP6A, 15B] utter with a ~; say in a ~ing voice. 尖声地说; 号叫着说。**3** [VP2A, C] (colloq) become an informer. (口)告密; 揭露。**~er** *n* **1** animal that ~s. 号叫的动物; 尖声喊叫的动物。**2** informer. 告密者。

squeam·ish /ˈskwiːmɪʃ; ˋskwimɪʃ/ *adj* **1** having a delicate stomach and easily made sick; feeling sick. 胃敏感而易呕吐的; 想呕吐的; 恶心的。**2** easily disgusted or offended; too modest, scrupulous or proper. 易感厌恶或易生气的; 太讲究规矩的; 太拘谨、谦逊等的。**~·ly** *adv* **~·ness** *n*

squee·gee /ˌskwiːˈdʒiː *US:* ˈskwiːdʒiː; ˋskwidʒi/ *n* implement with a rubber edge, fastened to a long handle, used for pushing water, etc off a smooth surface; similar implement with a short rubber roller for pressing water from photographic prints. (扫去光滑表面上的水等的)橡皮拖把; (压去相片上水分的)橡皮滚子。☐ *vt* [VP6A] use a ~ on. 用此等工具拖擦或辗滚。

squeeze /skwiːz; skwiz/ *vt, vi* **1** [VP6A, 15A, 22] press on from the opposite side or from all sides; change the shape, size, etc of sth by doing this: 压; 挤; 榨; 紧握; 把…压成; 把…挤成: *~ sb's hand;* 紧握某人的手; *~ a sponge;* 挤压海绵; *~ a lemon dry;* 将柠檬榨干; *~ one's fingers*, eg by catching them in a doorway; 手指给夹住了(如夹在门缝); *~ paste into a ball*. 把面团捏成球形。**2** [VP6A, 14, 15A, B] *~ sth (from/out of sth); ~ sth out*, get (water, juice, etc) out of sth by pressing hard: 压出; 榨出(水, 汁等): *~ (the juice out of) a lemon;* 榨柠檬(汁); *~ the water out*. 压出水分。**3** [VP15A, B, 2C] force (sb, oneself) into or through a narrow passage or small space: 推挤(某人, 自己)进入或通过狭窄的过道或狭小的空间; 挤入; 挤过: *~ (one's way) into a crowded bus;* 挤进拥挤的公共汽车; *~ (oneself) through a gap in a hedge;* 由篱笆的缺口挤过去; *~ (one's way) through a crowd*. 从人丛中挤过去。*Can you ~ in?* eg into a crowded lift. 你能挤进去(如拥挤的电梯)吗? **4** [VP15B] *~ sth out of sth/sb*, get by extortion, entreaty, etc: 榨取; 勒索; 敲诈: *~ more money out of the public*, eg by increasing taxes; 榨取大众的金钱(如加税); *blackmailers who ~ the last penny out of their victims*. 榨取受害者最后一分钱的勒索者。**5** [VP2A] yield to pressure: 压缩; 受压变形: *Sponges ~ easily*. 海绵容易压缩。☐ *n* [C] **1** act of squeezing; condition of being ~d; sth obtained by squeezing: 压榨; 紧握; 挤; 被压挤等的状态; 压榨出之物: *give sb a hug and a ~;* 紧抱某人; *a* ˈ*~ bottle*, plastic container that ejects the contents, eg scent, liquid detergent, when ~d. 压挤瓶(受压时即排出所盛装之物, 如香水、液体清洁剂等的塑胶瓶)。*It was a tight ~*, we were ~d tightly, eg in a crowd. 太拥挤了。*Add a ~ of lemon to your drink*. 在你的饮料中加一点柠檬汁吧。⇨ also **credit**[1]**(3)**. **2 close/narrow/tight ~**, narrow escape. 幸免; 勉强逃过。**3** [U] (colloq) policy of high taxation, high interest rates, etc aimed at deflation; [U] money obtained by squeezing(4). (口)(为防止通货膨胀所采取的)高税政策; 高利率政策; 榨取来的钱; 回扣。**~r** *n* one who, that which, ~s, eg a device for squeezing out juice: 压榨者; 压榨器; 压榨等的人或物: *a* ˈ*lemon-~r*. 柠檬压汁器。

squelch /skweltʃ; skwɛltʃ/ *vi, vt* **1** [VP2A, C] make a sucking sound as when feet are lifted from stiff, sticky mud: 发格喳声; 发吮吸声(如脚从粘泥中拔出时): *cows ~ing through the mud*. 格喳着走过泥地的母牛群。*The water ~ed in my boots*. 我靴子里的水发出格喳声。**2** [VP6A] crush; put an end to; force to be silent. 压碎; 压制; 使终止; 使缄默。☐ *n* ~ing sound; act of ~ing. 格喳声; 吮吸声; 压碎; 压制; 使缄默。

squib /skwɪb; skwɪb/ *n* **1** small firework of the kind thrown by hand, one that first hisses and then explodes. 水鸳鸯(一种用手投出的小爆竹, 先发嗤嗤声, 然后再爆炸)。**damp ~**, unsuccessful attempt to do sth impressive. 未成功的引人注意之举; 未达预期效果之事。**2** short satirical attack on sb, spoken or (more usu) written. 简短的讽刺(文)。

squid /skwɪd; skwɪd/ *n* kind of cuttle-fish with ten arms round the mouth (smaller kinds used as bait). 乌贼; 墨鱼; 鱿鱼。⇨ the illus at **mollusc**. 参看 mollusc 之插图。

squiffy /ˈskwɪfɪ; ˋskwɪfɪ/ *adj* (sl) slightly drunk. (俚)微醉的。

squiggle /ˈskwɪgl; ˋskwɪgl/ *n* small twisty line or scrawl: 小的弯曲线或潦草笔画: *Is this ~ supposed to be his signature?* 这个弯弯曲曲的笔画就视为他的签名吗? **squig·gly** /ˈskwɪglɪ; ˋskwɪglɪ/ *adj*

squint /skwɪnt; skwɪnt/ *vi* **1** [VP2A] have eyes that do not turn together but look in different directions at once; be cross-eyed. 斜视。**2** [VP3A] *~ at/through*, look at sideways or with half-shut eyes or through a narrow opening. 瞟; 眯着眼看; 由小孔窥视。☐ *n* **1** ~ing position of the eyeballs: 眼球的斜视位置; 斜视; 瞟: *a man with a ~*. 斜视的人。ˈ**~-eyed** *adj* having a ~; cross-eyed; (fig) malignant; disapproving. 眼睛斜视的; (喻)恶意的; 不赞许的。**2** (colloq) look or glance: (口)瞥; 看: *Let me have a ~ at it*. 让我看一看。

squire /ˈskwaɪə(r); skwaɪr/ *n* **1** (in England) chief landowner in a country parish. (在英国)乡绅(英国乡区的大地主)。**2** (hist) young man who was a knight's attendant until he himself became a knight. (史)武士或骑士的年轻扈从(至他自己变为骑士为止)。**3** (often hum) man who escorts a woman; man who is attentive to women and frequents their company. (常为谐语)妇女的护卫; 护花者; 对妇女殷勤而常与妇女厮混的人。**4** (US) justice of the peace or local judge. (美)治安推事; 地方法官。**5** (GB sl) fellow. (英俚)人; 家伙。☐ *vt* [VP6A, 15A] (of a man) attend upon, escort (a woman). (指男子)随从, 护卫(妇女)。ˈ**~·ar·chy** /-ɑːkɪ; -ˌɑrkɪ/ *n* (*pl* **-chies**) (in England) great landowners (before 1832); these men as a class. (在英国)(一八三二

年以前的)大地主; 大地主阶级。

squirm /skwɜːm; skwɝm/ vi [VP2A, C] twist the body, wriggle (from discomfort, shame or embarrassment). 蠕动; 扭动身体; 局促不安(由于不舒服、羞耻或困窘)。□ n ~ing movement. 蠕动; 扭曲。

squir·rel /ˈskwɪrəl; ˈskwɝəl/ n (kinds of) small, tree-climbing, bushy-tailed animal with red or grey fur. 松鼠。⇨ the illus at **small**. 参看 small 之插图。

squirt /skwɜːt; skwɝt/ vt, vi [VP6A, 15A, B, 2A, C] (of liquid, powder) force out, be forced out, in a thin stream or jet: (指液体, 粉末)迸出; 喷出: ~ soda-water into a glass. 把汽水倒在玻璃杯中。The water ~ed all over me. 水喷了我一身。□ n 1 thin stream or jet (of liquid, powder, etc). (液体、粉末等的)喷射; 喷射的液体或粉末。2 sth from which liquid, etc can be ~ed, eg a syringe, as a child's toy. 喷射液体等的器具; 注射器; 喷射器; (儿童玩的)水枪。3 (colloq, as a term of abuse) insignificant but self-assertive person. (口语, 用作骂人话)夜郎自大的人。

stab /stæb; stæb/ vt, vi (-bb-) 1 [VP6A, 15A, 3A] ~ (at), pierce or wound with a sharp-pointed weapon or instrument; push (a knife, etc) into (sb); aim a blow (at sb) with such a weapon. 以尖形刺或刺伤; 用(刀等)刺入(某人身体); 用尖锐武器刺向(某人)。截; 扎: ~ a man in the back; 背后冷枪某人之背; 背后向某人又。~ sb to the heart. 刺某人之心脏; 使某人极为伤心。His conscience ~bed (at) him, (fig) caused him to feel regret. (喻)良心刺痛(使他感到懊悔)。2 [VP2A] produce a sensation of being ~bed: 产生刺痛: ~bing pains in the back. 背部刺痛。□ n [C] 1 ~bing blow; pain inflicted by this. 刺; 截; 扎; 刺痛; 伤痛; 剧痛。a ~ in the back, (fig) a treacherous attack, eg on sb's reputation. (喻)背后中伤; 暗箭伤人。2 (colloq) try, attempt (= colloq 'go' or 'shot'): (口)试作; 试图(与口语中的 go 或 shot 同): Let me have a ~ at it, try to do it. 让我试试(试做此事)。~·ber n

stable¹ /ˈsteɪbl; ˈstebl/ adj firm; not likely to move or change: 坚固的, 稳定的, 安定的; 不动摇的: What we need is a ~ Government. 我们所需要的是一个稳定的政府。He needs a ~ job. 他需要一份安定的工作。**sta·bil·ity** /stəˈbɪlətɪ; stəˈbɪlətɪ/ n [U] quality of being ~. 坚固性; 稳定性; 安定; 不动摇。**sta·bil·ize** /ˈsteɪbəlaɪz; ˈstebl,aɪz/ vt [VP6A] make ~: 使坚固、稳定、不动摇: stabilise prices and wages. 稳定物价与工资。**sta·bi·lizer** n person or thing that stabilizes (esp) device to keep a ship or aircraft steady, free from rolling or pitching. 有稳定力的人或物; 安定剂; (尤指); (使船或飞机稳定的)稳定装置; 平衡器; 安定面。**sta·bil·iz·ation** /ˌsteɪbəlaɪˈzeɪʃn; US: -lɪˈz-; ˌstebləˈzeʃən/ n making or becoming ~. 使成变稳定。安定等。

stable² /ˈsteɪbl; ˈstebl/ n building in which horses are lodged and fed; number of horses (esp race-horses) belonging to one particular owner and kept in one set of ~s. 厩; 马房; (尤指赛马用的马)一位主人所拥有并养在一同马房中的马群。'~-boy /'~-man nn boy /man employed in a ~. 马童; 马夫。'~-companion /'~-mate n horse of the same ~; (fig) member of same group. 厩伴(同厩中的马); (喻)伙伴; 同伙。□ vt put, keep, in a ~: 置于马房; 养于马房: Where did you ~ your horse? 你的马养在哪个马房里? **stab·ling** /ˈsteɪblɪŋ; ˈsteblɪŋ/ n [U] accommodation for horses: 马房设备: The house has stabling for 20 horses. 这幢房子有容纳二十匹马的马房设备。

stac·cato /stəˈkɑːtəʊ; stəˈkɑto/ adj, adv (musical direction) (to be played) with each successive note clear and detached. (乐谱说明)(应奏成)断音的(地); 以断奏。v. 断唱。

stack /stæk; stæk/ n [C] 1 circular or rectangular pile of hay, straw, grain, etc usu with a sloping, thatched top, for storage in the open. 堆(干草、麦秸、谷物等的圆形或长方形堆, 通常有覆盖的斜顶, 以便于户外贮存)。2 group of rifles arranged in the form of a pyramid; pile or heap (of books, papers, wood, etc); (colloq) large amount: 架起的枪; 堆置的书、报、木材等; (口)大量: I have ~s of work waiting to be done. 我有很多工作要做。3 (brickwork or stonework enclosing a) number of chimneys. 烟囱群(结在一起的许多烟囱); 烟囱群的砖、石围砌。⇨ smoke-~ at **smoke¹**(1). 4 rack with shelves for books (in a library or bookshop). (图书馆或书店中的)书架; 书库。5 number of aircraft circling at different heights while waiting for instructions to land. 在不同高度盘旋等待指示降落的诸飞机。□ vt 1 [VP6A, 15B] ~ (up), make into a ~ or ~s; pile up: 使成堆; 堆起: ~ hay /wood. 堆置干草(木材)。~ up the dishes on the draining-board. 把碗盘放在滴水板上。2 (US) arrange (playing-cards) unfairly. (美)洗牌作弊。**have the cards ~ed a'gainst one**, be at a great disadvantage. 洗牌作弊使对某人不利。3 [VP6A] arrange aircraft in a ~(5). 指示(诸飞机)在不同高度盘旋等待降落。

sta·dium /ˈsteɪdɪəm; ˈstedɪəm/ n (pl ~s) enclosed area of land for games, athletic competitions, etc, usu with stands for spectators: (通常有看台的)体育场; 运动场: build a new ~ for the Olympic Games. 为奥运会建造新的运动场。

an Olympic stadium

staff /stɑːf US: stæf; stæf/ n 1 strong stick used as a support when walking or climbing, or as a weapon; (now usu fig): (用作身体支持物, 或用作武器的)棍; 杖; 棒; (现通常作比喻用法): the ~ of life, bread. 面包。He is the ~ of my old age. eg a son who supports his old father. 他是我老年的依恃(如奉养老父的儿子)。2 such a ~ as a sign of office or authority: 权杖; 权标: a pastoral ~, eg an ornamental one carried by or before a bishop, etc. 牧杖(主教等所携或持于主教之前的饰杖)。3 pole serving as a support: 竿; 支杖: a 'flag~. 旗竿。4 group of assistants working together under a manager or head: (辅佐首长的)全体职员; (某一首脑下面的)全体工作人员: the headmaster and his ~, ie the teachers; 校长及全体教师; 'office-~; 办公人员; be on the ~, 为正式职员。A large ~ (collective n, sing v) of advisers has been employed for the President. 总统已任用许多顾问(staff 为集合名词, 用单数动词)。The school ~ (= Members of the ~, pl v) are expected to supervise school meals. 学校的教职员应监督学校的膳食(staff 视为复数, 用复数动词)。'~-office, personnel office. 人事室。⇨ **personnel**. 5 group of senior army officers engaged in planning and organization: (军)参谋; 幕僚; 参谋部: the General S~; 参谋本部; (attrib) (用作定语) '~ officers. 参谋; 参谋军官。6 (music) (pl **staves** /steɪvz; stevz/) set of five parallel lines on or between which notes are placed to indicate their pitch. (音乐)五线谱。⇨ the illus at **notation**. 参看 notation 之插图。□ vt [VP6A] provide with, act as, a ~(4): 供以人员; 预备职员或幕僚; 充当职员或幕僚: ~ a new school; 预备一个新学校的人员; a well-~ed hotel /hospital; 人员充足的旅馆(医院); an under-~ed office. 人员不足的机关。

stag /stæg; stæg/ n 1 male deer. 牡鹿。'~-party n (colloq) party for men only (eg one for a man about to get married). (口)雄鹿会(只有男子参加的聚会, 如为某一即将结婚的男子所举行者)。2 person who buys

newly issued stocks and shares hoping that prices will rise and enable him to sell at a profit. 购买新发行的股票及证券，希望涨价后卖出获利者。

stage /steɪdʒ; stedʒ/ n 1 (in a theatre) raised platform or structure of boards on which the actors appear. (戏院的)舞台。2 **the ~**, theatrical work; the profession of acting in theatres. 戏剧工作；剧业；剧坛。'**be/go on the ~**, be/become an actor or actress. 当演员。'**~-craft** n [U] skill or experience in writing or directing plays. 编剧及导演的技巧或经验。'**~ direction** n printed direction in a play to actors about their positions, movements, etc. 舞台指导(剧本中有关演员位置、动作等的说明)。'**~ door** n entrance at the back of a theatre, used by actors and workmen. 舞台后门(戏院的后门，供演员及工作人员使用)。'**~ fright** n [U] nervousness felt when facing an audience. 怯场(面对观众或听众时所感到的紧张)。'**~ 'manager** n person who superintends the production of a play, supervises the rehearsals, etc. 舞台监督。'**~-struck** adj having a strong desire to become an actor or actress. 渴望做演员的。'**~'whisper** n whisper that is meant to be overheard. 存心叫人听见的私语；舞台低语。3 (fig) scene of action; place where events occur. (喻)(活动的)场所；(事件发生的)现场。4 point, period or step in development: 发展的程度、时期、阶段、步骤等: at an early ~ in our history. 在我们历史发展的早期。The baby has reached the 'talking ~', is learning to talk. 这婴儿已到达学语的阶段。5 any of two or more successive periods on the journey of a rocket vehicle when one part has been jettisoned: 火箭的节；火箭飞行途中依次脱离其环节的步骤: a multi-~ rocket. 多节火箭；能分数次脱离步骤的火箭。6 journey, distance, between two stopping-places along a road or route; such a stopping-place: 一程；一段路；站；驿: travel by easy ~s, for only a short distance at a time. 分段从容旅行。'**~(-coach)** n (hist) horse-drawn public vehicle carrying passengers (and often mail) along a regular route. (史)驿(马)车。'**fare-~** n section along the route of a bus or tram for which there is a fixed fare. (公共汽车或电车)车资固定的路段。7 structure with tiers or shelves, eg for plants. 台架(如花架等)。⇨ also **staging** below, and *landing-~ at landing*. □ vt, vi 1 [VP6A] put on the ~(1); put before the public: 搬上舞台；上演: ~ 'Hamlet'; 上演'哈姆雷特'; (fig) arrange to take place dramatically. (喻)使(某事)戏剧性地发生。~ a '**come-back**, come back (to a sport, eg to the boxing ring) from retirement or after having failed. 东山再起(如已退休或被击败的拳击手重返擂坛)。2 [VP2C] ~ well/badly, (of a drama) be well/badly suited for the theatre. (指剧本)适于(不适于)上演。

stager /'steɪdʒə(r); 'stedʒɚ/ n (only in) (仅用于) an old ~, a person of long experience; an old hand. 经验丰富的人；老手。⇨ hand¹(6).

stag·fla·tion /ˌstæɡˈfleɪʃn; ˌstæɡˈfleʃən/ n [U] (fin) (word formed from stagnation+inflation) monetary inflation without growth of industrial production. (财政)(为stagnation和inflation二词所形成)停滞性通货膨胀。

stag·ger /'stæɡə(r); 'stæɡɚ/ vi, vt 1 [VP2A, C] walk or move unsteadily (from weakness, a heavy burden, drunkenness, etc): 蹒跚；摇摆(因衰弱、负重、酒醉等): The man ~ed along/to his feet/across the room/from side to side of the road. 那人摇摇晃晃地走(摇摆地站起来，蹒跚地走过房间，摇晃着横过道路)。2 [VP6A] (of a blow or shock) cause to walk or move unsteadily; (of news, etc) shock deeply; cause worry or confusion to: 给以打击或震惊；使踉跄；使震惊；(指新闻等)使惊愕；使对…担心或不知所措: receive a ~ing blow. 受到使人摇晃晃的打击。I was ~ed to hear/on hearing/when I heard that the group's leader was. 听到谁是那个团体的领导人时，我感到十分震惊。3 [VP6A] arrange (times of events) so that they do not all occur

together: 错开(事情的时间): ~ office hours, so that employees are not all using buses, trains, etc, at the same time; 错开办公时间; ~ the annual holidays. 错开年假。□ n 1 (sing) ~ing movement. (单数)蹒跚；摇摆。2 the ~s, giddiness; nervous disease of cattle and horses, marked by ~ing. 家畜晕倒病；蹒跚病。~er n

stag·ing /'steɪdʒɪŋ; 'stedʒɪŋ/ n 1 [C, U] stage(6); (platform or working area on) scaffolding for men on constructional work, eg building. 脚手架；台架；鹰架；架；工作架。2 [U] (method of) presenting a play on the stage of a theatre. (戏剧的)演出；导演术。

stag·nant /'stæɡnənt; 'stæɡnənt/ adj 1 (of water) without current or tide; still and stale. (指水)不流动的；停滞的；静止的: water lying ~ in ponds and ditches. 池塘和沟渠中的死水。2 (fig) unchanging; inactive: (喻)不变化的；不活泼的；不景气的: Business was ~ last week. 上周生意萧条。**stag·nancy** /-nənsɪ; -nənsɪ/ n [U].

stag·nate /stæɡ'neɪt US: 'stæɡneɪt; 'stæɡnet/ vi [VP2A] be stagnant; (fig) be or become dull or sluggish through disuse, inactivity, etc. 不流动；静止；(喻)变呆钝；不活泼；不景气。**stag·na·tion** /stæɡ'neɪʃn; stæɡ'neʃən/ n [U].

stagy /'steɪdʒɪ; 'stedʒɪ/ adj theatrical in style, manner or appearance. 戏剧性的；具戏剧效果的；夸大做作的。**stag·ily** /-ɪlɪ; -əlɪ/ adv **stagi·ness** n

staid /steɪd; sted/ adj (of persons, their appearance, behaviour, etc) conservative, quiet and serious. (指人，其外表、行为等)保守的；沉静而严肃的。~·**ly** adv ~·**ness** n

stain /steɪn; sten/ vt, vi 1 [VP6A] (of liquids, other substances) change the colour of; make coloured patches or dirty marks on: (指液体，其他物质)改变…的颜色；染污；玷污: fingers ~ed with nicotine; 为尼古丁染黄的手指; blood—ed hands; 血污的手; a tablecloth ~ed with gravy; 沾有肉汁的桌布; (fig) (喻) a guilt—ed reputation. 为罪名玷污的声誉。2 [VP6A, 22] colour (wood, fabrics, etc) with a substance that penetrates the material: 着色于(木材、布等)；染色: He ~ed the wood brown. 他把木材染为褐色。The scientist ~ed his specimen before examining it under the microscope. 那位科学家先把抽样染色，再置于显微镜下检视。~ed glass, glass made by mixing into it transparent colours during the process of manufacture: 着色玻璃；彩色玻璃: ~ed glass windows in a church. 教堂里的彩色玻璃窗。3 [VP2A] (of material) become discoloured or soiled: (指布料等)褪色；变色；变脏: Does this material ~ easily? 这料子容易褪色(弄脏)吗? □ n 1 [U] liquid used for ~ing wood, etc. (染木材等的)着色剂；染料。2 [C] ~ed place; dirty mark or patch of colour: 染污之处；污点: 'ink—/'blood—s; 墨水(血)的污渍; (fig) (喻) a ~ on one's reputation; 名誉上的污点; without a ~ on your character. 无污点的无瑕疵的清白的。~·**less** adj 1 without a ~: 无污点的；无瑕疵的；清白的: a ~less reputation. 清白的名誉。2 (esp of a kind of steel alloy) that resists rust and corrosion: (指某一种合金钢)不锈的；抗锈的: ~less steel cutlery. 不锈钢刀。

stair /steə(r); ster/ n [C] (any one of a) series of fixed steps leading from one floor of a building to another. 楼梯；梯级。⇨ downstairs, upstairs. The child was sitting on the bottom ~. 那孩子正坐在楼梯最下面的一级。She always runs up/down the ~s. 她总是跑着上(下)楼。I passed her on the ~s. 我在楼梯上遇见她。**below ~s**, in the basement of a house (in large houses, formerly the part used by servants): 在一幢房屋的地下室(昔为仆人住处): Their affairs were being discussed below ~s, by the servants. 他们的事情正在仆人之间谈论着。a **flight** of ~s, a set of ~s in a continuous line, or from one landing, eg halfway between two floors, to another. (两楼梯间或两拐弯高度间，成一直行的)一段楼梯。at the **foot/head** of the ~s, at the bottom/top of a flight of ~s. 在一段楼梯的底部(顶端)。'~-**carpet** n strip of carpet for laying

on ~s. 梯毯(条状地毯,铺于梯阶上)。 '~-rod n rod for keeping a ~-carpet in the angle between two steps. 梯毯夹条(压在二梯级转角处,以固定梯毯)。 '~-case n series of ~s (often with banisters) inside a building: *Many old Edinburgh houses have spiral ~cases*, ie winding round a central pillar. 爱丁堡的许多古老房屋有螺旋梯。 '~-way n = ~case.

stake /sterk; stek/ n [C] 1 strong, pointed length of wood or metal (to be) driven into the ground as a post (eg for a fence) or as a support for sth, eg plants, young trees. 桩;杙;柱。 2 post, as used in olden times, to which a person was tied before being burnt to death as a punishment (for heresy): (昔时的)火刑柱(处死宗教异端者): *condemned to the ~*; 被判处火刑; *suffer at the ~*. 在火刑柱上受苦。 *go to the ~*, be burned at the ~; (fig) suffer the consequences of an ill-advised action. 被处以火刑; (喻)因行为卤莽而受苦。 3 sum of money risked on the unknown result of a future event, eg a horse-race; interest or concern (in sth); sum of money invested in an enterprise: 赌注;赌金;利害关系;关心;投于某一企业的金额;投资: *He has a ~ in the country*, is concerned in its welfare, is interested in its prosperity, etc (eg because he is a landowner). 他关心农村的情形(例如因为他是地主)。 *at ~*, to be won or lost; risked, depending, upon the result of sth: 得失攸关;濒胜败关头;处危险境地: (fig) (喻) *His reputation / His life itself was at ~*. 他面临身败名裂的危险(他有生命危险)。 '~-holder n person with whom ~s are deposited until the result is known. 赌金保管者。 4 (pl) money to be contended for, esp in a horse-race; such a race: (复)(尤指赛马的)奖金;(有奖金的)赛马: *the trial ~s at Newmarket*. 新市赛马的预赛。 □ vt 1 [VP6A] support with a ~: 以桩或杙支撑: ~ *newly planted trees*. 以桩支撑新栽的树。 2 [VP6A, 15B] ~ *sth (out/off)*, mark (an area) with ~s: 以桩区分或界分(地区): ~ *out a claim* (to land in a new country, etc; also fig). 用桩标出地权界限(亦作比喻用法)。 3 [VP6A, 14] ~ *sth on sth*, risk (money, one's hopes, etc): 赌;以(金钱,希望等)下注: ~ *£5 on the favourite*, eg in a horse-race. 以五英镑下注于被看好的马。 *I'd ~ my all / my life on it*, am very confident about it. 我愿意拿我的一切(性命)打赌(我极有把握)。

stal·ac·tite /'stæləktaɪt US: stə'læk-; stə'læktaɪt/ n [C] pencil-shaped or cone-shaped formation of lime hanging from the roof of a cave as water drips from it. 钟乳石(洞穴顶部因滴水作用而形成的铅笔形或圆锥状的石灰石)。 **stal·ag·mite** /'stæləgmaɪt US: stə'læg-; stə'lægmaɪt/ n [C] similarly shaped growth mounting upwards from the floor of a cave as water containing lime drips from the roof. 石笋(含石灰质的水,自洞穴顶部滴下时,在地面上所形成的笋状直立物)。

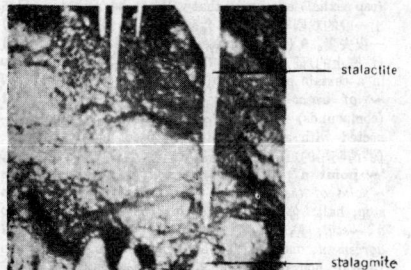

stalactite

stalagmite

stale /steɪl; stel/ adj 1 (of food) dry and unappetizing because not fresh: (指食物)因不新鲜而干瘪无味的;陈旧的: ~ *bread*. 陈面包。 2 uninteresting because heard before: 因以前曾听到过而感到无趣味的;老的;陈旧的;陈腐的;拾人牙慧的: ~ *news / jokes*. 旧新闻(老笑话)。

3 (of athletes, pianists, etc) no longer able to perform really well because of too much playing, training, practice, etc: (指运动员、钢琴家等)因过劳而表现不佳的;疲惫的: ~. 变为疲惫。 □ vi [VP2A] become ~: 变陈旧; 变疲惫; *Are there any kinds of pleasure that never ~?* 有没有永不会让人感到乏味的娱乐呢? ~·ness n

stale·mate /'steɪlmeɪt; 'stel,met/ n [C, U] 1 position of the pieces in chess from which no further move is possible. (国际象棋)无法继续; 僵局; 和棋。 2 (fig) any stage of a dispute at which further action by either side seems to be impossible. (喻)(争执的)僵持; 僵局。 □ vt [VP6A] (chess) reduce a player to a ~. (国际象棋)使棋手受困; (喻)使停顿; bring to a standstill. (国际象棋)使棋手受困; (喻)使停顿。

stalk[1] /stɔːk; stok/ n [C] non-woody part of a plant that supports a flower or flowers, a leaf or leaves, or a fruit or fruits; stem. (植物的)柄; 梗; 秆(支持花、叶、果实的非木质部分)。

stalk[2] /stɔːk; stok/ vt, vi 1 [VP2C, 6A] walk with slow, stiff strides, esp in a proud, self-important or grim way: 高视阔步; 大踏步走; ~ *out of the room*; 大踏步走出房间; ~ *along (the road)*. 高视阔步(地沿路前进)。 *Famine ~ed (through) the land*. 饥馑遍及全境。 2 [VP6A] move quietly and cautiously towards (wild animals, etc) in order to get near: 潜近; 偷偷接近(动物等): ~ *deer*. 潜近鹿。 '~·ing-horse n horse behind which a hunter hides; (more usu, fig) pretext; means of hiding one's real intentions. 其后有猎人掩藏的马; (较常用作喻)托词; 口实; 烟幕。 ~·er n person who ~s animals: 用潜近法猎动物的人: a 'deer-~er. 用潜近法捕鹿者。

stall /stɔːl; stɔl/ n 1 compartment for one animal in a stable or cattle shed. 畜舍中的一间或一栏; 厩。 '~-fed adj kept and fattened in a ~, not in the fields. 在厩中饲养的。 2 small, open-fronted shop; table, etc used by a trader in a market, on a street, in a railway-station, etc: 摊; 售货台; 货品陈列台: a 'book-/ 'flower-/ 'coffee-~. 书(花, 咖啡)摊。 3 (usu pl) (not US) seat in the part of a theatre nearest to the stage. (通常用复数)(不用于美国)院院中的正厅前排座位; 最近舞台的座位。 4 fixed seat in a church (usu enclosed at sides and back, often in carved wood) for the special use of a clergyman (usu in the choir or chancel): (教堂中)圣职或牧师的座位(常以雕花的木材制成, 两侧及背后皆围起, 通常置于合唱团席位或高坛上): *canon's / dean's ~*. 牧师(地方主教)的座位。 5 ('finger-)~, = 'finger-. 6 condition of an aircraft when its speed has decreased to the point at which it no longer answers to the controls. (飞机之)失速(飞机速度减低到无法控制的程度)。 □ vt, vi 1 [VP6A] place or keep (an animal) in a ~(1), esp for fattening: 置(动物)于畜舍中饲肥; 关(动物)于厩中: ~ed oxen. 关着养肥的牛。 2 [VP2A] (eg of an internal combustion engine) fail to keep going through insufficient power or speed; [VP2A, 6A] (of a driver) cause an engine to stop from such a cause. (指内燃机等)力量或速度不够而停止转动; 发生故障; (指司机)减低引擎速力而停止转动。 3 [VP6A, 2A] (of an aircraft) cause to be, become, out of control through loss of speed. (指飞机)(使)失速而无法控制。 4 [VP2A] avoid giving a clear answer to a question (in order to get more time): 避免给予明确的答复(以拖延时间); 不作正面答复: ~ *for time*; 避免正面答复以拖延时间; ~ *off creditors*. 敷衍债主。 *Quit ~ing!* 不要规避! (不要拖延时间!)

stal·lion /'stæliən; 'stæljən/ n uncastrated fully grown male horse, esp one used for breeding. 长成的(未阉)公马; (尤指)种马。

stal·wart /'stɔːlwət; 'stɔlwət/ adj tall and muscular; solidly built; firm and resolved: 高大而结实的; 强壮的; 坚决的: ~ *supporters*. 坚决的支持者。 □ n loyal supporter of a political party, etc. (政党等的)忠实拥护者。

sta·men /'steɪmən; 'stemən/ n male part of a flower,

bearing pollen. (花的)雄蕊(产生花粉部分)。⇨ the illus at **flower.** 参看 flower 之插图。

stam·ina /'stæmɪnə; `stæmənə/ *n* [U] vigour, energy, enabling a person or animal to work hard for a long time, to survive a serious illness, exposure, etc; (fig) mental toughness; moral strength. (使人或动物能做长久辛苦工作,挨过重病等的)体力; 精力; 活力; 道德力; (喻)精神上的耐力; 心理上的坚忍力。

stam·mer /'stæmə(r); `stæmɚ/ *vi, vt* **1** [VP2A] speak haltingly with a tendency to repeat rapidly the same sound or syllable, as in 'G-g-give me that b-b-book'. 口吃; 结结巴巴地说。**2** [VP6A, 15B] **~ *sth (out),*** say sth in this confused or halting way: 结结巴巴地说出某事: *~ out a request.* 结结巴巴地请求某事。□ *n* (tendency to) ~ing talk. 口吃; 结巴说话; 口吃的倾向。**~er** *n* person who ~s. 口吃者。**~·ing·ly** *adv*

stamp[1] /stæmp; stæmp/ *vt, vi* **1** [VP6A, 3A, 2C, 22, 15B] put (one's foot) down with force (on sth): 跺(脚); 顿足; 用力踏或踩: *~ one's foot;* 跺脚; *~ the ground;* 用力踏地; *~ on a spider;* 踩一只蜘蛛; move (about, etc) doing this: 来回地跺脚;重步走: *~ about/out of the room;* 在屋里来回跺脚(跺着脚走出屋子); *~ upstairs;* 在楼上跺脚; flatten by doing this: 踏平; 踩扁: *~ the soil flat.* 把土地踏平。**~ *sth out,*** crush, destroy, end: 扑灭; 踏灭; 毁掉; 镇服: *~ out a fire in the grass/a rebellion/an epidemic disease.* 扑灭草地上的火(叛变,传染病)。**'~·ing-ground** *n* **(a)** place where specified animals, eg elephants, may usually be found. 践踏地; 某些兽类(如象)常出没之地。**(b)** place where specified people often gather: 某类人士常聚集之地: *Soho, the ~ing-ground in London of those who enjoy exotic food and entertainment.* 苏和区,伦敦喜爱外国食物及娱乐人士聚集之处。**2** [VP6A, 14] **~ *sth (on/with sth),*** print (a design, lettering, the date, etc) on paper, cloth or other surface: 印(图案、字、日期等)于纸、布或其他表面上;压印: *~ one's name and address on an envelope/~ an envelope with one's name and address;* 印姓名及地址于信封上; *a manufacturer's goods ~ed with his trademark.* 印有商标的制成品。*The library assistant forgot to ~ my library books,* ~ the date on which they were taken out (or should be returned). 图书馆助理员忘了在我借的书上盖日期(何时借出或何时应归还)。**3** [VP6A] put a postage ~ on (a letter, etc), an insurance ~ on (a card): 贴邮票于(信等); 贴保险印花于(卡片): *I enclose a ~ed and addressed envelope for your reply.* 兹附上贴有邮票及写有地址的回邮信封一个。*Your insurance card is insufficiently ~ed.* 你的保险卡片未贴足印花。**4** [VP6A, 15B] **~ *sth (out),*** give shape to sth (eg pieces of metal) with a die or cutter. 用铸模或刻刀等赋予某物(如金属片)以形状; 造形。**5** [VP6A, 15A] (fig uses) impress: (比喻用法)给予印象; 铭刻; 刻记: *He ~ed his authority/personality on the game,* eg of a great footballer. 他的权威(人格)已经铭刻在这项运动上了(如指一位伟大的足球运动员)。[VP16B] mark out: 标出; 显示出; 表示出: *These actions ~ him as a man of high principles.* 这些行为显示出他是个很有节操的人。

stamp[2] /stæmp; stæmp/ *n* **1** act of stamping with the foot: 踏; 跺; 踩; 顿足: *a ~ of impatience.* 因不耐烦而跺脚。**2** that with which a mark or design is made on a surface: 印章; 图章: *a rubber ~,* one on which a design, words, etc are cut (used for printing dates, signatures, addresses, etc). 橡皮图章。**3** design, word(s), etc made by stamping on a surface. 印记; 图记。**4 ('postage-)~,** piece of printed paper (usu with perforated edges) stuck on letters, etc to show the postage, insurance dues, etc paid, or the duty paid on legal documents. 邮票; 印花。**'~-album** *n* one in which a collector of postage-~s keeps his specimens. 邮票簿; 集邮簿。**'~-collector** *n* person who collects ~s. 集邮者; 集邮家。**'~-dealer** *n* person who buys and sells ~s for collectors. 邮票商(为集邮者买卖邮票者)。**'~-duty** *n* tax imposed on certain kinds of legal documents. 印花税。**5** (usu *sing*) characteristic mark or quality: (通常用单数)表征; 标记; 特点; 特质: *He bears the ~ of genius.* 他具有天才的特质。*Her face bears the ~ of suffering.* 她面露痛苦。**6** (usu *sing*) kind; class: (通常用单数)种; 类: *men of that ~.* 那类的人(们)。

stam·pede /stæm'pi:d; stæm`pid/ *n* [C] sudden rush of frightened people or animals. (受惊吓的人或动物的)惊逃; 奔逃; 奔窜; 溃散。□ *vi, vt* **1** [VP2A, 6A] take part in a ~; cause to do this. (使)惊逃; (使)奔逃; (使)奔窜; (使)溃散。**2** [VP14] **~ *sb into sth/doing sth,*** hustle or frighten sb into rash action: 怂恿、催促或恐吓某人致轻率做某事: *Don't be ~d into buying the house.* 不要受怂恿而轻率买那幢房子。

stance /stæns; stæns/ *n* (golf, cricket) position taken for a stroke; pose; person's (intellectual, moral, etc) attitude. (高尔夫,板球)击球(时的)姿势; 看法; (一个人所持的)观点。

stanch /stɑ:ntʃ *US:* stæntʃ; stæntʃ/ = **staunch**[1].

stan·chion /'stænʃən *US:* 'stæntʃ-; `stænʃən/ *n* upright post for supporting sth (eg bars for confining cattle in stalls). 直立的支柱(如关牛于厩中的栅等)。

stand[1] /stænd; stænd/ *n* **1** stopping of motion or progress: 停止;停顿: *come/be brought to a ~* (or, more usu 或,较常用 *~still*), stop, be stopped. 陷于停顿。**2 *make a ~,*** be ready to resist or fight: 准备抵抗或格斗;准备奋斗: *make a ~ against the enemy;* 抵抗敌人; *make a ~ for one's principles.* 为某人的原则奋斗。**3** position taken up: 立场; 立脚地; 位置: *He took his ~ near the window.* 他站在窗旁。***take one's ~,*** declare one's position, opinion, etc. 宣布立场、意见等; 表明态度。*I take my ~ upon sound precedents,* use these to support my claim, etc. 我采取的立场系基于有力的先例。**4** small article of furniture, support, etc on or in which things may be placed: 置物台; 架: *a 'music-/'hat-/um'brella-~.* 乐谱(帽,伞)架。⇨ also *hand~* at **hand**[1]**(16)**, *ink~* at **ink,** *wash-~* at **wash-.** **5** structure from which things are sold; 售货台; 摊: *a 'news~;* 报摊; area, structure(s), for the exhibition of goods, etc: 陈列货物的区域或建筑; 摊位: *the British ~ at the Hanover Fair.* 汉诺威博览会中的英国摊位。**6** place where vehicles may stand in line in a street, etc while waiting for passengers: (车辆等的)停留地; 候客站: *a 'cab-~;* 出租马车站; 出租汽车站; *a ~ for six taxis.* 容六辆计程车的候客站。**7** structure, usu sloping, where people may stand or sit to watch races, sports-meetings, etc: 看台: *open ~s;* 露天看台; *the 'grand~.* 大看台; 级级升高或有顶盖的看台。**8** halt made by a theatrical company when touring the country. (旅行剧团所作的)停留; 上演站; 演出地。***ˌone-night '~,*** theatrical performance on one evening only; (fig) an (esp sexual) encounter that will not be repeated. 只演出一晚的戏剧等; (喻)(不会重复发生的)短暂聚会; (尤指)一夜夫妻。**9** (US) witness-box (in a law court): (美)(法庭上的)证人席: *take the ~.* 做证。**10** growing crop in a certain area: (一地区之)正在成长的作物: *a good ~ of wheat/timber.* 生长茂盛的小麦(林木)。**11** (compounds) (复合词) **'~-pipe** *n* vertical pipe (connected with a water-main and used as a hydrant). (供消防用的)直立水管(与总管连接,供救火车等取水者)。**'~·point** *n* point of view: 立场; 见解; 观点: *from the ~point of the consumer.* 从顾客的立场言。**'~·still** *n* stop; halt: 停顿; 停止: *be at/come to/bring sth to a ~still;* 陷于停顿; (attrib) (用作定语) *a ~still agreement,* one that agrees to no change, eg in wage rates or hours of work. 不变动的协议(如维持原来的工资或工作时间,不加变动)。

stand[2] /stænd; stænd/ *vi, vt* (*pt, pp* **stood** /stʊd; stʊd/) (For special uses with *adverbial particles* and *preps,* ⇨ **10** below.) (与副词性小品词及介词连用的特殊用法,参看下列第 10 义。) **1** [VP2A, B, C, 4A] have, take, keep, an upright position; balance, support, the body

on the feet: 站; 立; 站住; 站定; 站稳; 起立: *He was too weak to* ~. 他太虚弱，不能站立。*A chair will not* ~ *on two legs.* 一把椅子只用两条腿着地是站不稳的。*We had to* ~ *all the way back in the bus.* 我们在回程的公共汽车上不得不站着。*S~ing room only,* all seats are occupied, eg in a bus or cinema. 仅有站位了(座位卖光了，如公共汽车或电影院里)。*His hair stood on end,* ie with terror. 他的毛发竖立(感到恐怖)。*He* ~*s six foot two,* is of this height when ~ing. 他站着时身高六英尺二英寸。*Don't* ~ *there arguing about it.* 不要站在那儿争论此事。*He stood looking over my shoulder.* 他站起来从我的肩头望过去。*S~ still while I take your photograph.* 我为你拍照的时候，站着不要动。*S~ and deliver!* (command given by a highwayman) Stop and give me your valuables, etc! 站住,把值钱的东西交出来! (拦路的强盗所发的口令)。2[VP2A, C, 4A] ~ (*up*), rise to the feet: 站立; 站起来: *S~ up, please.* 请站起来。*Everyone stood (up) when the Queen entered.* 女王进来时大家都站起来。*We stood (up) to see better.* 我们站了起来，以便看得清楚些。3 [VP2A, C] remain without change: 持续; 维持不变; 原样继续: *Let the words* ~, don't alter them or take them out. 不要改变动这些字。*The agreement must* ~, cannot be altered or cancelled. 这合约必须维持原状。*The house has stood two hundred years and will* ~ *another century.* 这房子已有二百年之久,还可以再维持一百年。~ *firm / fast,* not give way, retreat, change one's views, etc. 坚定; 不退让; 不撤退; 不改变意见等。4 [VP2C] be in a certain condition or situation: 处于某种状况或情形: *The emergency services* ~ (= are) *ready to help if called on.* 紧急救难处一获得通知随时可以驰援。*The matter* ~ *thus,* this is the state of affairs. 事情就是这样的; 事实就是这样。*As affairs now* ~ ..., As they are at present .... 其现况是…。*He* ~ (= is) *in need of help.* 他正处于需要帮助的情况。*Who* ~ (= is) *first on the list?* 名单上谁的名字列在首位? *Will you* ~ (= be) *godmother to the child?* 你愿意做那孩子的教母吗? *He stood convicted of treachery.* 他被判犯有叛逆罪。*I* ~ *corrected,* accept the correction of my views, etc. 我愿接受指正。*He* ~*s alone among his colleagues,* None of them equals him in ability, etc. 他在同事间鹤立鸡群。~ *clear (of sth),* move away: 站开; 避开; 移开: *S~ clear of the gates,* eg as a warning when they are about to be closed. 离开闸门(如将关闭时的警语)。~ *easy / at ease,* ⇨ easy, ease. 5 [VP2C] have a certain place; be situated: 位于; 在某处: *These dishes* ~ *on the top shelf.* 这些碗盘是放在顶架上的。*A tall poplar tree once stood there.* 该处曾有一棵高大的白杨树。*The house* ~*s on the hill.* 那幢房子位于小山上。*Where does Tom* ~ *in class,* What is his position (in order of ability, etc)? 汤姆在班上的名次如何? 6 [VP 15A] cause to be placed in an upright position: 使直立; 竖起: *S~ the ladder against the wall.* 把梯子靠着墙放。*S~ the bottle on the table.* 把瓶子竖立在桌子上。*S~ the empty barrels on the floor.* 把空桶竖着放在地板上。*Don't* ~ *this tin of petrol near the fire.* 不要把这罐汽油放在火旁边。*The traitor was stood up against the wall and shot.* 那叛逆犯奉令靠墙站立接受枪决。7 [VP6A, C] endure; bear: 忍耐; 忍受: *He can't* ~ *hot weather.* 他不能忍受炎热的天气。*She says she will* ~ *no nonsense,* not put up with foolish behaviour. 她说她不能容忍愚蠢的行为。*I can't* ~ *that woman,* strongly dislike her. 我不能忍受那女人(深恶她)。*She can't* ~ *being kept waiting.* 她不能忍受久等。~ *one's ground,* maintain one's position, eg in an argument. 坚守阵地(如作战时); 坚持立场; (喻)固执己见。~ (*one's*) *trial,* be tried (in a court of law). (在法庭上)受审。8 [VP6A, 12A] ~ *sb sth,* provide at one's expense: 付账; 供给; 供应: ~ *sb a good dinner;* 供应某人一顿好饭; ~ *drinks all round,* pay for drinks for everyone. 为每个人购应购买的饮料付账。*Will he* ~ *us champagne?* 他会供应我们香槟酒吗? ~ *treat,* pay the costs of entertaining sb or others. 请客; 作东。9

(phrases) (短语) ~ *a (good / poor, etc) chance,* (of success, etc) have a (good / poor, etc) prospect (of success, etc). (指成功等)有(很大、很小等)成功等的机会。~ *sb in good stead,* ⇨ stead. ~ *on ceremony,* ⇨ ceremony. *It* ~*s to reason that,* ⇨ reason[1](3). ~ *to win / gain / lose sth,* be in a position where one is likely to win, etc: 很可能会赢(获利, 输或亏损): *What do we* ~ *to gain by the agreement?* 依照合约我们可能得到何种利益? 10 [VP2C, 3A, 15B] (special uses with *adverbial particles* and *preps*): (与副词性小品词及介词连用的特殊用法):

stand aside, (a) be inactive, do nothing: 不活跃; 不活动; 不做事: *He's a man who never* ~*s aside when there's something that needs doing.* 有事需要做时,他从不会避开做。(b) move to one side: 站开; 站在一边: ~ *aside to let someone pass.* 站开让人通过。(c) withdraw one's name (as a candidate): 撤消名字(如候选人); 退出竞选: ~ *aside in favour of a better man.* 让贤。

stand at, be at a certain level (on a scale, etc): (在尺度、等级、程度等上)处于某一程度、位置、水准、阶段等: *The appeal fund* ~ *at £10 000.* 救助基金为数一万英镑。*The temperature stood at 30°C.* 气温为 30 摄氏度。

stand back, (a) move back: 离开; 向后站: *The policeman ordered us to* ~ *back.* 警察命令我们向后退。(b) be situated away from: 离开; 隔开; 隔有距离: *The house* ~*s back from the road.* 那房子不在路边。

stand by, (a) be a bystander; look on without doing anything: 袖手旁观: *How can you* ~ *by and see such cruelty?* 你怎能对这样残酷的行为袖手旁观呢? (b) be ready for action; remain: 准备行动; 待机: *The troops are* ~*ing by.* 部队随时待命行动。~ *by sb,* support, side with, sb; show oneself to be a good friend: 援助、支持某人; 向某人表示支持: *I'll* ~ *by you whatever happens.* 无论发生什么事,我都会支持你。~ *by sth,* be faithful to (a promise, one's word, etc). 信守(承诺、诺言等); 遵守。Hence, 由此产生, '~*by,* state of readiness: 待机; 准备就绪: *The troops are on 24-hour* ~*by,* ready to move at 24 hours' notice. 部队处于二十四小时待命状态。(b) sb or sth that one may depend upon: 可信赖或依靠的人或物; 备用的人或物: (attrib) (用作定语) *a* ~*by generator,* one for use in an emergency, eg for use when electric current from the mains is cut off. 备用发电机。*Aspirin is a good* ~*by for headaches.* 阿斯匹林是必备的头痛良药。

stand down, retire from a witness-box or similar position; (of a candidate) withdraw (in favour of sb else). 离开证人席; (指候选人)退出竞选(以支持他人)。

stand for sth, (a) represent; 代替: *PO* ~*s for Post Office or postal order.* PO 两个字母代表 Post Office (邮局)或 postal order (邮政汇票)。*I condemn fascism and all it* ~*s for.* 我谴责法西斯主义及其所代表的一切。(b) support, contend for: 赞同; 支持; 拥护: ~ *for racial tolerance.* 支持种族平等自由。(c) (GB) be a candidate for: (英)为候选人: ~ *for Parliament.* 为国会议员候选人。(d) (colloq; ⇨ 8 above) tolerate: (口语;参看上列第 8 义)容忍: *She says she's not going to* ~ *for her own children disobeying her.* 她说她不容许自己的孩子不服从她。

stand in (with sb), take a share in: 参加; 分担; 分摊一份: *Let me* ~ *in with you if it's expensive.* 如果花钱很多,让我分摊一份。~ *in (for sb),* take the place of, eg a principal actor or actress until filming begins. 代替(某人)(如影片开拍前代替男女主角)。Hence, 由此产生, '~*in* person who does this. 替身。

stand off, remain at a distance; move away. 远离; 离开; 避开。~ *sb off,* dispense with the services of, eg workers, temporarily. 暂时解雇(如工人)。~*·'off·ish* adj reserved; cold and distant in behaviour. 冷淡的; 矜持的。Hence, 由此产生, ,~*·'off·ish·ly* adv ~*·'off·ish·ness n*

stand out, (a) be easily seen above or among others: 显著; 杰出: *Does your work* ~ *out from that of others,*

Is it obviously better? 你的工作比别人的突出吗？⇨ **outstanding**. **~ out a mile**, be extremely obvious. 极为明显。**(b)** continue to resist: 继续抵抗: *The troops stood out against the enemy until their ammunition was exhausted.* 这支军队继续抵抗敌人，直至弹药用尽。

stand over, be postponed: 延缓; 延后; 展期: *Let the matter ~ over until the next meeting.* 这件事等下次开会再讨论吧。**~ over sb**, supervise, watch closely: 监督; 监视: *Unless I ~ over him he makes all sorts of foolish mistakes.* 如果我不监督他，他就会犯各种错误。

stand to, (mil) take up positions to resist possible attack: (军)各就岗位以成备敌意; 警戒: *The company (was) stood to for half an hour.* 该连(奉命)警戒防守半小时。Hence, 由此产生, '**~-to** n army signal to be on the alert. 军队警戒讯号。

stand up, ⇨ 2 above. 参看上列第 2 义。'**~-up** adj **(a)** (of collars) upright (opp of turn-down). (指衣领) 直立 (与 turn-down 之反义 reel)。**(b)** (of a meal) eaten while ~ing: (指餐食) 站着吃的: *a ~-up buffet*. 立食餐馆。**(c)** (of a fight) violent and hard-hitting. (指打斗) 猛烈跟毒的。**~ sb up**, (colloq) not keep a rendezvous with him: (口) 爽约; 不守约; 不赴约: *First she agreed to come out with me, then she stood me up.* 起初她答应同我一起出去，后来她爽约了。**~ up for sb**, support; take the part of; defend. 支持某人; 维护某人; 袒护某人。**~ up to sb**, defend oneself with courage against him. 勇敢地对抗某人。**~ up to sth**, (of materials) remain in good condition after long or hard use, etc: (指物料) 耐久; 耐用; 经得起: *metals that ~ up well to high temperatures*. 耐高热金属。

stand (well) with sb, be on (good) terms with, be (well) thought of: 与某人相处(甚佳); 得某人(好)评: *How do you ~ with your boss?* 你同你的上司相处如何? *He ~s well with his bank manager* (and may, therefore, get an overdraft without difficulty). 他在他的银行经理那里信用良好(透支少一点钱，可能不会有困难)。

stan·dard /'stændəd; 'stændəd/ n **1** distinctive flag, esp one to which loyalty is given or asked: 旗; 旗帜; 旗标(尤指拥有或要求效忠的标志): *the royal ~*, eg as flown to show that the Queen is in residence. 王室旗帜(如悬出以示女王驻跸状)。*raise the ~ of revolt*, (fig) begin a struggle and call for support. (喻)揭竿而起。'**~-bearer** n person who carries a ~; (fig) prominent leader in a cause. 掌旗者; (喻)卓越的领导者。**2** (often attrib) sth used as a test or measure for weights, lengths, qualities or for the required degree of excellence: (常用作定语)标准; 基准; 模范; 水准; 规范: *the ~ yard/pound, etc*: 标准码(磅等); ~ *weights and measures*. 标准度量衡; *the ~ of height required for recruits to the police force*; 招募警察人员所需要的身高标准; *set a high ~ for candidates in an examination*. 为参加考试人员规定一项高的录取标准; *conform to the ~s of society*, live and behave as society expects: (生活)合于社会的标准; *a high ~ of living*, one with plenty of material comforts, etc; 高的生活水准; *a high moral ~*; 崇高的道德标准; ~ *authors*, accepted as good. 够水准的作家。**be up to/below ~**, be equal to/not so good as, what is normal, required, etc: 达(未达)到标准: *Their work is not up to ~.* 他们的工作未达到标准。**~ time**, time officially adopted for a country or part of it. 标准时间。**3** (former) grade of classification in primary schools (now usu *class*): (昔)小学的年级(现通常用 class): *boys in 8~ One*. 小学一年级的男生。**4** **monetary ~**, proportion of weight of fine metal and alloy in gold and silver coin. 金银币中之纯金银与合金的比例; (货币的)法定纯分; 纯度标准。**the 'gold ~**, system by which the value of money is based on that of gold. 金本位制。*abandon/go off the gold ~*, abandon such a system. 放弃金本位制。**5** (often attrib) upright support; pole or column; vertical water- or gas-pipe. (常用作定语)直立的支物架; 支柱; 垂直的水管或煤气管。'**~ lamp**, lamp on a tall support with its base on the floor. 落地灯。**6** tree or shrub that has been grafted on an upright stem (contrasted with climbing plant): 接枝于直干的树或灌木(与矮丛或攀缘植物相对)。~ *roses*. 接枝在直立树干上的玫瑰。

stan·dard·ize /'stændədaɪz; 'stændəd,aɪz/ vt [VP 6A] make of one size, shape, quality, etc according to fixed standards: 使合乎规格; 使标准化: *The parts of motor-vehicles are usually ~d*. 机动车辆的零件通常都是标准化的。*S~d products are usually cheaper than hand-made articles*. 标准化的产品通常比手工制品便宜。**stan·dard·iz·ation** /,stændədaɪ'zeɪʃn US: -dɪ'z-; ,stændədə'zeɪʃən/ n [U] standardizing; making regular: 标准化; *the problem of the standardization of the use of hyphens in compounds*. 统一复合词中连字符号使用法的问题。

stand·ing /'stændɪŋ; 'stændɪŋ/ n **1** [U] duration: 持续; 期间: *a debt/dispute of long ~*. 长期债务(纠纷)。**2** [C, U] position or reputation; (if there is no *adj*) established position: 身份; 地位; 名誉; (不加形容词)美名; 令誉; 好名誉: *men of (high) ~*, 地位高的人; 名望高的人; *a member in full ~*. 正式会员。**□** adj **1** established and permanent; ready for use: 永久的; 固定的; 持续的; 备用的; 常备的: *a ~ army*; 常备军; *a ~ committee*, a permanent one that meets regularly; 常务(常设)委员会; *a ~ order for newspapers and periodicals*, to be delivered regularly; 长期订阅报纸及杂志; *a ~ order to a bank*, customer's order for payments that recur regularly, eg rent, rates; 客户对银行之长期委托(由银行从存款代为支付固定开销，如房租，水电等); *a ~ joke*, sth that regularly causes amusement. 经常引人发笑的笑料; 笑柄。**~ orders**, (pl) rules and regulations which remain in force until repealed by the proper authorities. (复)常规; 常法。**2** ~ *corn*, not yet cut (harvested). 尚未收割之谷物。**~ jump**, made without a preliminary run. 立定跳高或跳远。

stank /stæŋk; stæŋk/ pt of **stink**.

stanza /'stænzə; 'stænzə/ n (*pl* ~s) [C] group of rhymed lines forming a division in some forms of poem. (诗的)节。

staple[1] /'steɪpl; 'stepl/ n U-shaped metal bar with pointed ends hammered or pressed into a surface, to hold sth, eg flexible wire for electric current, in position; hoop-shaped bar hammered into wood, etc to take the point of a hook, or the hasp of a padlock, ⇨ the illus at **padlock**; piece of wire for fastening sheets of paper together (as in some periodicals). U 形钉(固定某物于表面所使用者，如固定电线); 锁扣环(参看 padlock 之插图); U 形钉; 订书钉。[VP6A] fasten or fit with a ~. 以 U 形钉或订书钉固定或钉住; 以 U 形环或锁扣环套住。'**sta·pling-machine** n one used for fastening sheets of paper together with ~s. 订书机。**sta·pler** /'steɪplə(r); 'steplə/ n small hand-operated device for fastening papers together. (用手操作的)小订书机。

staple[2] /'steɪpl; 'stepl/ n **1** [C] chief sort of article or goods produced or traded in: 主要产品或商品; 土产; 名产: *Cotton is one of the ~s of Egypt*. 棉花是埃及主要产品之一。**2** chief material or element (of sth): (事物的)主要原料; 主要成分; 主要因素: *The weather forms the ~ of their conversation*. 天气是他们的主要话题。**3** [U] fibre of cotton, wool, etc (as determining its quality): (棉、羊毛等的)纤维(可借以决定其质地者): *cotton of short/long ~*; 短(细等)纤维棉花; *long~ cotton*. 长纤维棉花。**4** (attrib) forming the ~(2): (用作定语)构成主要原料、成分、因素等的; 主要的: *Is coffee still the ~ product of Brazil?* 咖啡仍然是巴西主要产物吗? *Rice is the ~ food in many Asian countries*. 米是许多亚洲国家的主食。

star /stɑː(r); star/ n **1** any one of the bodies seen in the sky at night as distant points of light. (晚上天空中见到的)星。**fixed ~** n one which is not a planet. 恒星。**shooting ~** n ⇨ **shoot**[2](1). '**~-fish** n ~-shaped

sea-animal. 海星；海盘车(星状海生动物). ⇨ the illus at **sea**. 参看 sea 之插图. **'~·light** n [U] light from the ~s: walk home by ~light; 在星光下步行回家; (attrib) (用作定语) a ~light night. 星光照耀之夜. **'~-lit** adj lighted by the ~s: 星光照耀的景色. a ~lit scene. 星光照耀的景色. **2** figure or design with points round it, suggesting a ~ by its shape; an asterick (*): 星标；星符；星状物: a five-~ hotel, given five ~s (in guide-books, etc) to show its grading; 五星(标)旅馆(旅行指南等上赋以五个星标,以示其等级); badge of rank (worn by officers on the shoulder-strap). (军官肩带上表示等级的)星标；军阶标志. **see** ~s, seem to see flashes of lights, eg as the result of a blow in the eye(s). (眼睛)冒金星；目眩(如眼睛被击后所感觉者). **the ,S~-Spangled 'Banner, (a)** the national flag of the US. 美国国旗. **(b)** the national anthem of the US. 美国国歌. **the S~s and Stripes** n sing the national flag of the US. 美国国旗. **3** planet or heavenly body regarded as influencing a person's fortune, etc: (被视为影响个人命运等的)星宿: born under a lucky ~. 生有福星照命. What do the ~s foretell? 星象预示什么? You may thank your lucky ~s you were not killed in that accident. 你多亏有福星高照, 在那次意外事故中没有丧生. **'~-gazer** n (hum) astrologer or astronomer. (谑)占星家；天文家. **4** person famous as a singer, actor, actress, etc: (歌唱,演戏等的)明星；高手；名家: the ~s of stage and screen; 舞台及影视明星；'film ~s; 电影明星; an all-~ cast, in which leading players are all ~s; 主角均为大明星的演员阵容; the ~ turn, the principal item in an entertainment or performance. 余兴或表演中的主要节目. □ vi, vt (-rr-) **1** [VP6A] mark or decorate with, or as with, a ~ or ~s, eg an asterisk to direct attention to sth: 以星标或星状物标示或装饰；点缀；加星号以引起注意: a lawn ~red with daisies. 点缀着雏菊的草坪. **2** [VP3A, 14] ~ (sb) in, be a ~(4) (in a play, film, etc); present (sb) as a ~(4): (在一部戏剧,电影等中)演出；主演；使(某人)担任主角或主演: She is to ~ to be ~red in a new film. 她将主演一部新片(在一部新片中担任主角). **'~·dom** /-dəm/ /-dɔm/ n status of being a ~(4). 明星或主角的身份、地位等. **'~·let** /-lɪt/ /-lɪt/ n young actress on the way to ~dom. 未成名的年轻女演员；准明星. **'~·less** adj with no ~s to be seen: 看不见星的；无星的: a ~less sky/night. 无星的天空(夜晚). **~ry** /'stɑːrɪ/ /'stɑrɪ/ adj lighted by, shining like, ~s: 星光照耀的；闪烁如星的: a ~ry night; 星空之夜; ~ry eyes. 闪闪发光的眼睛；明眸. **'~ry-'eyed** adj (colloq) visionary but impractical: (口) 不切实际的；幻想的: ~ry-eyed reformers. 不切实际的改革者.

star·board /'stɑːbəd/ /'stɑrˌbɔrd/ n right side of a ship or aircraft from the point of view of a person looking forward. ⇨ **port**: (船的)右舷, (飞机的)右侧(边): alter course to ~; 转向右(舷)航; on the ~ bow. 在船首右舷. ⇨ the illus at **ship**. 参看 ship 之插图. □ vt turn to ~: 把…转向右舷: ~ the helm, turn the helm to ~. 将舵转向右边.

starch /stɑːtʃ/ /stɑrtʃ/ n [U] **1** white, tasteless, carbohydrate food substance, plentiful in potatoes, grain, etc. 淀粉. **2** this substance prepared in powdered form and used for stiffening cotton clothes, etc; (fig) stiffness of manner; formality. (浆硬棉布等用的)浆粉；(喻)拘谨；古板；生硬. □ vt [VP6A] make, eg shirt collars, stiff with ~; 浆(衬衫领等); (in pp) (喻,用过去分词) a ~ed manner. 古板的态度. **~y** adj of or like ~; containing ~: 淀粉的；似淀粉的；含淀粉的: ~y foods. 含淀粉的食物.

stare /steə(r)/ /ster/ vi, vt **1** [VP2A, B, C, 3A] ~ (at), look fixedly; (of eyes) be wide open: 凝视；盯着看；(指眼)睁大；张大: Do you like being ~d at? 你喜欢被人注视吗? She was staring into the distance. 她凝视着远方. They all ~d with astonishment. 他们都惊异地张大眼睛. He gazed at the scene with staring eyes. 他张

大眼睛注视那景象. **make sb ~,** surprise him. 使某人惊愕. **2** [VP15B] ~ sb **out (of countenance),** ~ until he becomes nervous, etc. 盯得某人难为情；把某人盯得局促不安. ~ **sb out/down,** ~ at him longer than he is able to ~ at you. (在互盯的场合)把某人盯下去(你盯他的时间长于他盯你的时间);盯某人一眼. ~ **one in the face, (a)** ~ at sb's face. 注视某人的面孔. **(b)** be right in front of one: 就在面前；就在眼前: The book I was looking for was staring me in the face. 我找的书就在我的面前. Defeat was staring them in the face, was clearly inevitable. 他们的失败就在眼前. □ n 凝视. **staring look:** 凝视；注视；瞪；盯: give sb a rude ~; 鲁莽地盯某人一眼；with a ~ of horror/astonishment; 心怀恐怖(惊愕)的凝视；with a vacant ~, suggesting an empty mind; 茫然凝视者；with a glassy ~, suggesting indifference. 带着漠不关心的眼神. **star·ing** adj (of colours, etc) too bright or conspicuous: (指色彩等)过于鲜艳的；太显眼的: His tie was a staring red. 他的领带是大红色的. □ adv (only in) (仅用于) **stark staring mad,** completely mad. 完全疯狂的.

stark /stɑːk/ /stɑrk/ adj **1** stiff, esp in death. (尤指死亡后)僵硬的. **2** complete; downright: 完全的；纯然的: ~ madness/folly. 简直疯狂(愚蠢). □ adv completely: 完全地: ~ naked. 全裸的. **~ers** /'stɑː-kəz/ /'stɑrkəz/ pred adj (GB sl) completely naked. (英俚)完全赤裸的.

star·ling /'stɑːlɪŋ/ /'stɑrlɪŋ/ n common bird (with black, brown-spotted plumage) which nest near buildings and is a good mimic. 欧椋鸟；燕八哥(一种常见之鸟, 羽毛黑色而有褐色斑点, 筑巢于建筑物附近, 善模仿).

starry /'stɑːrɪ/ /'stɑrɪ/ ⇨ **star.**

start[1] /stɑːt/ /stɑrt/ n **1** [C] beginning of a journey, activity, etc: 启程；动身；开始；着手: make an early ~; 动身(开始)早; the ~ of a race; 赛跑的起始; after several false ~s; 数次错误的起步以后; from ~ to finish. 自始至终. **2** [U, C] (no pl) amount of time or distance by which one person starts in front of competitors; advantageous position: (无复数形)先跑权；先跑的时间或距离；优势地位: The small boys were given a ~ of ten yards. 小男孩们获得先跑十码的优先权. They didn't give me much/any ~. 他们未给我很多(任何)优先. He got the ~ of (= gained an advantage over) his rivals. 他较他的对手们占优势. He got a good ~ (= a position of advantage) in life/business. 他在人生(商业)中得天独厚. **a ,head** ~ n (lit or fig) advantageous position: (字面或喻)优势: give sb/have/get a head ~ (over sb). 让某人(比某人)占优势. **3** [C] sudden movement of surprise, fear, etc: (惊愕、恐惧等的)惊起；突动: He sat up with a ~. 他一惊而坐起. The news gave me a ~, surprised me. 这消息使我吃惊. **by fits and ~s,** ⇨ **fit**[3](3).

start[2] /stɑːt/ /stɑrt/ vi, vt (Note: begin may replace start only as in **2** below) (注意: begin 仅在第 2 义中可代替 start) **1** [VP2A, C] ~ (out), leave; set out: 出发；启程；动身: We must ~ (out) early. 我们必须早些动身. We ~ed at six. 我们在六时出发. At last the bus ~ed. 公共汽车终于启程了. **2** [VP6A, D, 7A] begin: 开始；着手: ~ work. 着手工作. It ~ed raining. 开始下雨了. It's ~ing to rain. 开始下雨了. Have you ~ed working yet? 你开始工作了吗? **3** [VP6A, 3A] ~ (on) sth, make a beginning: 创始；启始: ~ (on) one's journey home. 启程回家. Have you ~ed on your next book yet, begun to read (or write) it? 你已经开始(读或写)下一本书了吗? **4** [VP2A, C] ~ (up), make a sudden movement (from pain, surprise, fear, etc) or change of position; jump: (因痛苦、惊讶、恐惧等)惊起；惊跳: He ~ed up from his seat. 他从座位上惊跳起来. He ~ed at the sound of my voice. 他听到我的声音吓了一跳. **5** [VP2C] move, rise, spring, suddenly: 突然活动、升起、跳起、跃起: Tears ~ed to her eyes, suddenly came to her eyes. 她的眼睛里突然涌出了泪水. His eyes nearly ~ed out of his head, suddenly opened wide (in

surprise, etc). 他的眼睛突然睁得很大 (因惊愕等)。 **6** [VP2A, C, 6A] (of timbers) (cause to) spring out of position; make or become loose: (指梁木或栋木) (使)歪; (使)弯翘; (使)脱离定位; (使)变松: *The ship has ~ed at the seams.* 船的接缝处已经松了。 *The planks have ~ed.* 厚板已经弯翘了。 *The damp has ~ed the timbers.* 潮湿已使梁木弯翘了。 **7** [VP6A, 15A, 19B] set going; originate, bring into existence; cause or enable to begin: 发动; 引起; 使产生; 使开始: *This news ~ed me thinking.* 这消息引起我的思绪。 *The smoke ~ed her coughing.* 这烟使她咳嗽。 *He decided to ~ a newspaper.* 他决定创办一份报纸。 *A rich uncle ~ed him in business,* helped him, eg by supplying capital. 一位有钱的叔父帮助他创办事业 (如提供资金)。 *She has ~ed a baby,* (colloq) become pregnant. 口)她怀孕了。**8**[VP2C,15B] (with *adverbial particles*) (与副词性小品词连用) **~ back,** begin to return: 开始回程; 赋归: *It's time we ~ed back.* 我们该回去了。 **~ in (on sth/to do sth),** (colloq) begin to do it: (口)开始做某事; 着手: *Poor Jane! She's ~ed in on a huge pile of ironing.* 可怜的简! 她着手烫那一大堆衣服了。 **~ off,** begin to move: 开始活动: *The horse ~ed off at a steady trot.* 那马以稳健的快步出发。 **~ out (to do sth),** (colloq) begin; take the first steps: (口)开始; 起始; 动工: *~ out to write a novel.* 开始写一部小说。 **~ up, (a)** rise suddenly; jump. 惊起; 惊跳。 ⇨ **4** above. 参看上列第4义。 **(b)** come into existence suddenly or unexpectedly: 突然出现; 崛起: *Many difficulties have ~ed up.* 突然出现了很多困难。 **~ sth up,** put (an engine, etc) in motion: 发动(引擎等): *We couldn't ~ up the car.* 我们无法发动那部汽车。 **9 to ~ with, (a)** in the first place: 第一; 首先: *To ~ with, we haven't enough money, and secondly we haven't enough time.* 第一, 我们没有足够的钱; 第二, 我们也没有足够的时间。 **(b)** at the beginning: 起初; 起始: *We had only six members to ~ with.* 开始的时候我们只有六个会员。 **10 '~·ing-gate** n barrier where horses ~ a race, raised when the time comes for them to ~. (赛马时的)起跑门, 起赛栅门。 '**~·ing-point** n place at which a start is made. (赛跑的)起点。'**~·ing-post** n place from which competitors ~ in a race. (赛跑的)起跑点, 起赛点。'**~·ing-prices** n pl (in horseracing) the odds just before the start of a race. (赛马)临赛赌价; 起赛价(开赛前一刻的胜算比例)。 **~er** n **1** person, horse, etc that takes part in a race: 参加赛跑的人、马等: *There were only five ~ers in the last race.* 上次的赛跑仅有五人参加。 **2** person who gives the signal for a race to start: 赛跑中的起赛发令员。 **under ~er's orders,** (of horses, athletes, etc lined up for a race) awaiting the starter's order or signal to ~ the race. (指参加赛跑排成一列的马、运动员等)等待起赛的口令或讯号。 **3** device for causing an engine to ~ working; ignition. (引擎中的)启动装置; 引燃物或装置。 ⇨ *self-~er* at *self-*. **4** (colloq) first course of a meal. (口)餐食的第一道食物或菜。 **for ~ers,** (sl) = to ~ with, ⇨ **9** above. (俚)第一; 首先; 起初(参看上列第9义)。

startle /'staːtl; 'startl/ vt [VP6A, 15A] give a shock of surprise to; cause to move or jump: 使惊愕; 使吃惊; 惊吓; 惊动; 惊跳: *~d out of one's sleep,* 从睡梦中惊起; *~d out of one's wits,* suffered a sudden great shock. 惊呆了。 *She was ~d to see him looking so ill.* 看到他病到这种程度, 使她大为吃惊。 *What startling news!* 多令人震惊的消息!

starve /staːv; starv/ vi, vt **1** [VP6A, 15A, 2A, C, 3A] (cause to) suffer or die from hunger: (使)饿; (使)饿死。 *~ to death.* 饿死。 *The proud man said he would ~ rather than beg for food.* 那个骄傲的人说他宁愿挨饿也不愿讨饭。 *They tried to ~ the army into surrender/~ them out,* force them to surrender by preventing them from getting supplies of food. 他们试图使守军因饥饿而投降。 **be ~d of ~, for,** (fig) long for, be in great need of: (喻)渴望; 急需; 迫切需要: *The motherless children were ~d of/were starving for affection.* 这些没

有母亲的孩子们渴望母爱。 **2** (colloq) feel very hungry: (口)感觉很饿: *What's for dinner?—I'm starving!* 晚餐吃什么? ——肚子饿死了! **star·va·tion** /staːˈveɪʃn; starˈveʃən/ n [U] suffering or death caused by lack of food: 饥饿; 饿死: *die of starvation,* 饿死; *starvation wages,* too low to buy adequate supplies of food; 饥饿工资(低到不能维持生活者); *be on a starvation diet,* a diet that is inadequate for health. 吃不足维持健康的饮食。 **~·ling** /'staːvlɪŋ; 'starvlɪŋ/ n starving or ill-fed person or animal. 挨饿或营养不足的人或动物。

stash /stæʃ; stæʃ/ vt [VP15B] **~ sth away,** (sl) put it safely; hide it. (俚)存放; 藏起。

state¹ /steɪt; stet/ n **1** (sing only) condition in which sth or sb is (in circumstances, appearance, mind, health, etc): (仅用单数)(人或物在环境、外观、心情、健康等方面的)状态; 情况; 情形: *The house was in a dirty ~.* 那房子很脏。 *These buildings are in a bad ~ of repair,* need to be repaired. 这些房屋极须修葺。 *She's in a poor ~ of health.* 她的健康欠佳。 *What a ~ he's in!* How anxious, dirty, untidy, etc he is, according to context. 他竟然成了这个样子! (不安、肮脏、不修边幅等, 根据上下文决定)。 *Now don't get into a ~,* (colloq) Don't get excited or anxious! (口)不要激动或担心! **~ of play,** **(a)** (cricket) score. (板球)分数。 **(b)** (fig) how parties in dispute stand in relation to one another (as likely to win or lose). (喻)争论双方的相对处境(如可能获胜或失败)。 **2** (often 常作 **S~**) organized political community with its apparatus of government; territory in which this exists; such a community forming part of a federal republic: 国家; 领土; (构成联邦共和国的)州; 邦: *Railways in Great Britain belong to the S~.* 大不列颠的铁路是属于国家的。 *How many S~s are there in the United States of America?* 美国有多少州? *The President's 'Message to the Union' is not addressed to individual S~s but to the Union as a whole/to the nation.* 总统的'国情咨文'不是向个别的州, 而是向整个联邦(国家)发表的。 **the (United) S~s** (also 亦作 **the US**), (colloq) the United States of America (the USA). (口)美国。 **Head of S~,** ⇨ **head¹**(12). ⇨ also *police*, *totalitarian* at *police, totalitarian*. **3** (attrib) of, for, concerned with, the S~(2): (用作定语)国家的; 领土的; 州的; 有关国家的; 公的: *S~ documents/records/archives,* 公文(官方记录、档案); *S~ forests,* belonging to the S~, not privately owned; 国有森林; *bring industries under S~ control;* 使工业由国家管制; *S~ socialism,* policy of ~ control of industry etc. 国家社会主义。 **the 'S~ Department,** (US) Government Ministry of Foreign Affairs. (美)国务院。 **~'s 'evidence,** (US) evidence for the state in criminal cases. (美)(刑事案件中的)政府(检查官)提出的证据。 Cf 参较 *King's/Queen's evidence* in GB. **'S~·house,** building in which a S~ Legislature sits. 州(邦)议事厅或议会大厦。 **S~ 'Legislature,** representative law-making assembly of a ~ within a federation, eg that of the S~ of Madras in India. 州或邦议会(如印度Madras 邦议会)。 Cf 参较 the *National Assembly* for the whole of India. (印度全国的)国民大会。 **S~(s')** '**rights,** (US) all rights which are not delegated to the Federal Government in Washington. (美)州权(各州保有而未交付联邦政府的权利)。 **4** [U] civil government: 政府; 民治政府: *Church and S~,* 教会与政府; 政教; *S~ schools,* contrasted with Church schools. 政府办的学校(与教会学校相对)。 **5** [U] rank; dignity: 地位; 尊严; 荣耀: *persons in every ~* 各阶层人士。 *He lived in a style befitting his* (high or low) ~. 他过着适合他身份的生活方式。 **6** [U] pomp; ceremonial formality: 盛况; 隆重的仪式: *The Queen was in her robes of ~.* 女王穿着御礼服。 *in ~,* with ceremonial formality: 以隆重的仪式: *The President was driven in ~ through the streets of Washington.* 总统在隆重的仪礼下乘车穿过华府市街。 **7** (attrib) of or for ceremony and formality: (用作定语)仪礼的; 仪式的; 礼仪用的:

the ~ coach, eg as used by the Queen on ceremonial occasions; 礼车; 贵宾车; 御辇; *the ~ apartments at the palace;* 王宫中的大厅; *a ~ call,* (colloq) formal visit. (口) 正式的访问; 官式拜会. **8** *lie in ~,* (of a dead person) be placed on view in a public place before burial. (指死人埋葬前)置于公共场所供人凭吊. **9** '~·**room** n private cabin (or sleeping-compartment) on a ship (and, in US, in a railway-carriage). (轮船的)特别客舱; 睡舱; (美国火车上的)特别包厢; 卧室. ~·**ly** adj (-ier, -iest) impressive; dignified; 威严的; 庄严的; 堂皇的; 高贵的: *a ~ly dowager;* 仅态高贵的富婆; *the ~ly homes of England,* those of the nobility, etc; 英国贵族等的富丽堂皇的家庭; *with ~ly grace.* 庄重文雅地. ~·**li·ness** n '~·**craft** n [U] = ~smanship. ⇨ below. 参看下列之 statesmanship. ~·**less** adj (of a person) not recognized as a citizen or national of any country: (指人)无国籍的: *~less persons,* eg some political refugees. 无国籍的人如某些政治难民).

state² /steɪt/ vt [VP6A, 9] express in words, esp carefully, fully and clearly: 说; 陈述(尤指仔细、详尽而明确地): ~ *one's views.* 陈述己见解. *I have seen it ~d that ....,* 我曾经见过有人这么说……. *He ~d positively that he had never seen the accused man.* 他肯定地说他从未见过被告. ~·**d** adj made known; announced: 说出的; 宣布的; 陈述的: *at ~d times/intervals.* 在明示的时间(间隔). ~·**ment** n **1** [U] expression in words: 陈述; 叙述: *Clearness of ~ment is more important than beauty of language.* 叙述清楚较用词优美更重要. **2** [C] stating of facts, views, a problem, etc; report: (事实、见解、问题等的)供述; 说明; 声明; 报告: *issue a ~ment;* 发表声明; *a 'bank ~ment;* 银行报告; 银行结单; *make a ~ment (in court),* give a formal account in a law court setting out the cause of a legal action or its defence. 在法庭上)供述. *My bank sends me monthly ~ments of the state of my bank account.* 银行按月寄给我各款帐目.

states·man /'steɪtsmən; 'stetsmən/ n (pl **-men**) person taking an important part in the management of State affairs; disinterested political leader. 政府高级要员; 政治家. '~·**like** adj gifted with, showing, wisdom and a broad-minded outlook on public affairs. 有政治家风度的(在政治上具有智与远见的). ~·**ship** /-ʃɪp; -ʃɪp/ n [U] skill and wisdom in managing public affairs. 治国之才; 政治家的才能、智慧、技巧等.

static /'stætɪk; 'stætɪk/ adj at rest; in a state of balance: 静止的; 静态的; 平衡状态的: ~ *water,* not flowing (eg water in a tank, needing to be pumped); 静止的水 (如储水池中需要抽出的水); ~ *electricity,* as accumulated on an insulated body. 静电. **statics** n [U] (pl with sing v) (复数形式作单数用) **1** branch of knowledge dealing with bodies remaining at rest or with forces which balance one another. 静力学(研究静态物体或平衡力). ⇨ **dynamic. 2** (radio, TV) atmospherics. (无线电, 电视)静电干扰; 天电.

sta·tion /'steɪʃn; 'steʃən/ n **1** place, building, etc where a service is organized and provided: (提供某种服务的)站; 所, 台等: *a 'bus/po'lice/'broadcasting/'radar/'fire~.* 公共汽车站(警察派出所; 广播电台; 雷达站; 消防队). **2** [U] position, or relative position, to be taken up or maintained by sb/sth: (人或物所采取、占据或保持的)地位; 位置; 相对或相关的位置; *One of the cruisers was out of ~,* not in its correct position relative to other ships. 有一艘巡洋舰未在其编队位置. **3** stopping-place for railway trains; the buildings, offices, etc, connected with it: 火车站; 火车站的建筑物、办公室等: *a 'goods ~,* one for merchandise. 货站. '~·**master** n man in charge of a railway ~. (铁路的)站长. **4** social position, rank: 社会地位、身份等;职位: *people in all ~s of life.* 社会各阶层人士. **5** (Australia) (usu extensive) sheep or cattle ranch. (澳大利亚)(通常指大的)牧场; 牧羊或牛)场. **6** military or naval base; those living there. 陆 (海)军基地; 驻扎基地人员. **7** S~s

of the Cross, fourteen crosses, usu with images telling the story of the sufferings and death of Jesus, for religious devotions, set up in a church or along a path. (置于教堂中或道路旁供人膜拜之) 十四幅耶稣受难像. **8** '~·**wagon** n (US) estate car. (美) 旅行轿车. ⇨ **estate(5).** □ vt [VP6A, 15A] put (sb, oneself, a military or naval force, etc) at or in a certain place: 安置; 配置; 置(某人、自己、一支军队等)于某处: *The detective ~ed himself among the bushes,* hid there. 那侦探藏身于矮丛中.

sta·tion·ary /'steɪʃənrɪ US: -nerɪ; 'steʃən,ɛrɪ/ adj **1** not intended to be moved from place to place: 固定的; 定置的; 非移动的: *a ~ crane/engine.* 固定式起重机 (发动机). ⇨ **mobile(1). 2** not moving or changing: 不活动的; 不变动的; *remain ~;* 保持不变动; *collide with a ~ van.* 与一停着的货车相撞.

sta·tioner /'steɪʃnə(r); 'steʃənɚ/ n dealer in ~y. 文具商. ~·**y** /'steɪʃnrɪ US: -nerɪ; 'steʃən,ɛrɪ/ n [U] writing materials, etc. 文具. **Her Majesty's/the 'S~y Office** (abbr 略作 **HMSO**), government department which publishes and distributes government papers, books, etc. (英)政府文书部(出版及发行政府文件及书籍等的部门).

stat·is·tics /stə'tɪstɪks; stə'tɪstɪks/ n **1** (with pl v) collection of information shown in numbers: (用复数动词)统计; 统计数字: *S~ suggest that the population of this country will be doubled in ten years' time.* 统计显示本国人口十年后将增加一倍. **vital ~,** ⇨ **vital. 2** (with sing v) the science of ~. (用单数动词)统计学. **stat·is·ti·cal** /stə'tɪstɪkl; stə'tɪstɪkl/ adj of ~; 统计的; 统计学的: *statistical tables/experts.* 统计图表(专家). **stat·is·ti·cally** /-klɪ; -klɪ/ adv **stat·is·ti·cian** /,stætɪ'stɪʃn; ,stætəs'tɪʃən/ n person who is expert in ~. 统计专家; 统计学家.

statu·ary /'stætʃʊərɪ US: -ʊerɪ; 'stætʃʊ,ɛrɪ/ adj of or for statues: 雕像的; 雕塑的; 雕塑用的: ~ *marble.* 雕塑用的大理石. □ n [U] sculpture; statues. 雕塑; 雕像.

statue /'stætʃuː; 'stætʃʊ/ n figure of a person, animal, etc in wood, stone, bronze, etc, usu of life size or more than life size. 雕像; 塑像; 铸像(木、石、铜等制成, 通常与活物体积相等, 或大于活物). ⇨ the illus at **discus.** 参看 discus 之插图. **statu·ette** /,stætʃʊ'et; ,stætʃʊ'et/ n small ~. 小雕像; 小塑像. **statu·esque** /,stætʃʊ'esk; ,stætʃʊ'esk/ adj like a ~ in having clear-cut outlines, in being motionless, etc. 宛若雕像的;似雕像的.

stat·ure /'stætʃə(r); 'stætʃɚ/ n [U] (person's) natural bodily height: (人的)身高; 身长; 身材: *short of ~;* 身材短的; (fig) mental or moral quality; calibre. (喻)气质; 器量; 才干.

status /'steɪtəs; 'stetəs/ n [U] person's legal, social or professional position in relation to others: (人的)地位; 身分: *have no official ~,* no official rank, eg in the Civil Service. 未任公职; 无公职身分. *Many young people desire ~* (= an established social position) *and security.* 许多年轻人希冀社会地位与生活保障. '~ **symbol,** sth which the ownership of is thought to be evidence of social rank, wealth, etc, eg a better car than one's neighbours, a yacht, a colour TV. 身分标志; 身分表征 (被视为可代表其社会地位、财富等者, 如华丽轿车、游艇、彩色电视机等).

status quo /,steɪtəs 'kwəʊ; 'stetəs'kwo/ (Lat) social situation as it is now: (拉)社会现状: *conservatives who defend the ~.* 为社会现状辩护的保守人士. ⇨ **'ante** /'æntɪ; 'æntɪ/, social situation as it was before a recent change. 社会原状; 新近变动之前的社会状况.

stat·ute /'stætʃuːt; 'stætʃʊt/ n [C] (written) law passed by Parliament or other law-making body. 成文法; 法规; 条例. '~ **law** n all the ~s (contrasted with case-law and common law). 成文法 (与 case-law 及 common law 相对). ⇨ **case¹(2), common¹(1).** '~·**book** n book(s) containing the ~ law. 成文法典; 法规全

书。 **statu·tory** /ˈstætʃʊtrɪ *US:* -tɔːrɪ; ˈstætʃʊˌtorɪ/ *adj* fixed, done, required, by ~: 法定的; 依法完成的; 依照法规的: *statutory control of prices and incomes.* 物价与工资的法定管制。

staunch¹ /stɔːntʃ; stɔntʃ/ (*US* also **stanch** /stɑːntʃ *US:* stæntʃ; stæntʃ/) *vt* [VP6A] stop the flow of (esp blood); check the flow of blood from (a wound): 制止(尤指血的)流动; 止住(伤口)出血: ~ *blood / a wound.* 止血(止住一伤口流血)。

staunch² /stɔːntʃ; stɔntʃ/ *adj* (of a friend, supporter, etc) trustworthy; loyal; firm. (指朋友、支持者等)可信赖的; 忠实的; 坚定的。 ~·**ly** *adv* ~·**ness** *n*

stave¹ /steɪv; stev/ *n* **1** one of the curved pieces of wood used for the side of a barrel or tub. 桶板; 桶材(用作桶边的弧形木材)。 **2** (music) (音乐) = **staff**(6). 谱表。 **3** stanza; verse. 诗节; 诗句。

stave² /steɪv; stev/ *vt*, *vi* (*pt*, *pp* ~**d** or **stove** /stəʊv; stov/) **1** [VP15B] ~ *sth in*, break, smash, make a hole in: 打破; 砸破; 击穿; 凿孔于: *The side of the yacht was ~d in by the collision.* 该游艇的舷侧被撞穿了。 [VP3A] ~ *in*, become or get broken or smashed: 被打破; 被砸破; 被击穿: *The boat stove in when it struck the rocks.* 该船触礁时被撞穿了。 **2** [VP15B] ~ *sth off*, keep off, delay (danger, disaster, bankruptcy, etc). 避开; 延缓(危险, 灾难, 破产等)。

stay¹ /steɪ; ste/ *vi*, *vt* **1** [VP2A, B, C, 4A] be, remain, continuously in a place or condition (for a long or short time, permanently or temporarily, as specified by the context): 停留; 逗留; 待在或保持某种情况或位置(长期或短期, 永久或暂时, 由上下文指明): ~ *in the house / at home / in bed*; 待在房子里(家里, 床上)。 ~ (= stay) *at a hotel / with friends.* 住在旅馆里(朋友家里)。 *I'm too busy to ~ if I can't ~,* 我太忙, 不能再待了(我必须走了)。 *I can only ~ a few minutes.* 我只能待几分钟。 *I ~ed to see what would happen.* 我留下来看进一步的发展。 *Why don't you ~ with us* (as a guest) *when you next visit Oxford?* 你下次到牛津来, 住在我们这里好吗? *Jenny's ~ing in Dublin* (eg at a hotel, or with friends) *for a few weeks, but she now lives / is living* (= has her home) *in Belfast.* 珍妮目前在都柏林暂住几个星期, 但她的家是在贝尔法斯特。 ~ *for (an event / meal);* ~ *to (a meal),* remain for it: 为(某件事或一餐饭)而留下; 留下来(吃饭): *Won't you ~ for / to supper?* 你不留下来吃晚饭吗? ~ *in,* (a) not go outdoors: 不出门; 待在家里: *The doctor advised me to ~ in for a few days.* 医生劝我在家里待几天。 (b) remain in school after hours: 放学后留在学校: *The teacher made the boy ~ in and do his exercises again.* 老师命令男生留在学校重做他的练习。 ~ *out,* (a) remain outdoors: 待在外面; 待在户外: *Tell the children they mustn't ~ out after dark.* 告诉孩子们天黑以后不可待在外面。 (b) remain on strike: 继续罢工: *The miners ~ed out for several weeks.* 矿工们罢工达数周之久。 ~ *up,* not go to bed: 不就寝; 熬夜: *I'll ~ up reading until midnight.* 我读书一直读到午夜才睡。 *I'll be late home, but please don't ~ up for me.* 我要晚一点才能回家; 请你别等我的门。 *be ˌhere to ~; have ˌcome to ~,* (colloq) be permanent: (口)持久; 继续流行; 变成根深蒂固: *I hope that the principle of equality of opportunity for men and women has come to ~ to ~.* 我希望男女机会平等的原则能持久。 **come to ~ (with sb),** (of a person) visit sb (ie temporarily); start to live with sb (ie permanently): 到某人处小住; 开始与某人长住: *Sue is coming to ~ for a week next month.* 休下月来住一个星期。 *Since my wife's mother came to ~ with us last year, the TV has been on more or less continuously.* 自从去年我的岳母来与我们同住, 电视几乎没有停过。 '~-**at-home** *n* person who seldom goes anywhere; unadventurous person. 甚少离家外出的人; 不喜出远门的人。 **2** [VP2C] continue in a certain state: 继续保持某种状态; 维持; 保持: ~ *single*, not marry. 不结婚; 保持单身。 *That fellow never ~s sober for long,* frequently gets drunk. 那家伙经常烂醉(难得清醒)。 ~ *put,* (colloq) remain where placed: (口)待在原处; 停留在原处: *I wish this earring would ~ put instead of falling out every time.* 我希望这个耳环箍紧, 不要老是掉下来。 **3** [VP6A] stop, delay, postpone, check: 停止; 延缓; 延后; 制止: ~ *the progress of a disease;* 防止疾病恶化; ~ *one's hand,* refrain from doing sth: 住手(抑制不做某事); ~ (= delay) *judgement / proceedings.* 迟迟不作评断(拖延诉讼程序)。 **4** [VP2A, 6A] be able to continue (work, etc); show endurance: 能够继续(工作等); 显示耐力: *The horse lacks '~ing power.* 这马缺乏耐力。 ~ *the course,* be able to continue to the end of the race, (fig) the struggle, etc. 跑完全程; (喻)坚持到底。 **5** (usu in imper; archaic or lit) pause: (通常用于祈使句中; 古或古而别) 停下; 停下: *S~! or ~!* (= Stop!) *You've forgotten your overcoat!* 一等下! 你忘了你的大衣! **6** [VP6A] satisfy for a time: 暂时满足; 满足一时: *have a sandwich to ~ one's hunger.* 吃一块三明治压饥。 □ *n* **1** period of ~*ing;* visit: 停留; 逗留; 做客: *make a short ~ in Karachi;* 在卡拉奇作短暂停留; *a fortnight's ~ with my rich uncle.* 到我那有钱的叔父家做客两星期。 **2** (legal) delay; postponement. (法律)延误; 延缓; 延后; 中止。 ~ *of execution,* order that a court judgement need not be carried out for the time being. 延缓执行(某一法庭裁决)。 ~**er** *n* person or animal able to ~(4): 有耐力的人或动物: *The horse that won the race is a good ~er.* 获胜的那匹马是一匹很有耐力的马。

stay² /steɪ; ste/ *n* [C] **1** rope or wire supporting a mast, pole, etc. (支持桅, 杆等的)绳索或钢丝。 ⇨ the illus at **barque**. 参看 barque 之插图。 **2** (fig) support: (喻)支持物; 倚靠: *the ~ of his old age,* person who helped him, eg by giving him a home, looking after him. 他老年时的倚靠(如供他住处、照顾他等之人)。 **3** *(pl)* (old-fashioned name for) kind of corset reinforced with strips of stiff material (bone or plastic). (复)(旧称)有硬物支撑的束腹。 □ *vt* [VP6A, 15B] ~ (*up*), support by means of a wire, rope or prop. (以绳索, 钢丝或支撑物)支撑; 支持。

stead /sted; sted/ *n* [U] *in sb's ~,* in his place; instead of him. 代替某人。 **stand sb in good ~,** be useful or helpful to him in time of need: 在需要时对某人有助益: *My anorak has stood me in good ~ this winter.* 我这件带兜帽的夹克今年冬天对我很有用。

stead·fast /ˈstedfɑːst *US:* -fæst; ˈstɛd,fæst/ *adj* firm and unchanging; keeping firm (*to*): 坚定的; 不变的; 不移的: *a ~ gaze;* 凝视; ~ *in adversity,* 处变不惊; *be ~ to one's principles.* 坚守自己的原则。 ~·**ly** *adv* ~·**ness** *n*

steady /ˈstedɪ; ˈstɛdɪ/ *adj* (**-ier, -iest**) **1** firmly fixed or supported; balanced; not likely to fall over: 坚固的; 牢靠的; 平衡的; 不动摇的: *make a table ~,* eg by repairing a leg; 使桌子站稳(如修复一只桌腿); *on a foundation;* 在稳固的基础上; *not very ~ on one's legs,* eg of sb after a long illness. 步履不太稳(如长期病后)。 **2** regular in movement, speed, direction, etc: (动作、速度, 方向等)规律的、稳定的: *a ~ wind / speed / rate of progress / improvement.* 稳定的风(速度, 进度, 进步)。 **3** regular in behaviour, habits, etc: (行为、习惯等)规则的; 稳健的; 可靠的: *a ~ young man;* 稳健的年轻人; *a ~ worker.* 可靠的工作者。 **4** constant, unchanging: 持续的; 不变的: *a ~ faith / purpose.* 不变的信仰(目标)。 **5** (in exclamations) (用于惊叹句中) *Keep her ~!* (naut) Keep the ship on the same course unchanged. (航海)航向不变! *S~ (on)!* (colloq, used as a warning) Control yourself! (口)(用作警告)镇定! 别急! 留心! □ *adv* = steadily. **go ~,** (colloq) go about regularly with sb of the opposite sex, though not being engaged to marry: (口)与异性固定交往(虽尚未论婚嫁): *Are Tony and Jane going ~?* 托尼同简已经是情侣了吗? *n* (sl) regular boy-friend or girl-friend. (俚)固定的异性朋友; 固定的情人。 □ *vt, vi* [VP6A, 2A] make or become ~; keep ~: 使或变得牢靠、稳固等; 保持坚固、稳

定等: ~ a boat/table-leg; 使船(桌子腿)稳定; ~ oneself by holding on to the rail, eg on the deck of a ship that is rolling. 扶住栏杆使自己站稳(如在颠簸的船甲板上)。 Prices are ~ing. 物价渐趋稳定。 **stead·ily** /'stedɪlɪ; 'stɛdəlɪ/ adv in a ~ manner: 坚固地; 稳定地; 不变地; 稳健地: work steadily. 规律地工作。 His health is getting steadily worse. 他的健康每况愈下。 **steadi-ness** n

steak /steɪk; stek/ n [U, C] (thick slice of) meat or fish for (usu) frying or grilling: (供煎、烤等的)肉; 鱼; 肉片; 鱼片; 肉排: fillet/rump ~; 菲力牛排(大腿部肉排); two tuna ~s. 两片金枪鱼排。

steal /stiːl; stil/ vt, vi (pt **stole** /stəʊl; stol/, pp **stolen** /'stəʊlən; 'stolən/) **1** [VP6A, 14, 2A] ~ sth **(from sb)**, take (sb else's property) secretly, without right, unlawfully: 偷; 窃取(他人财物): Someone has stolen my watch. 有人把我的表偷走了。 I have had my watch stolen. 我的表被人偷走了。 Cf 参较 I have been robbed of my watch. 我的表被人抢走了。 It is wrong to ~. 偷东西是不法的行为。 **2** [VP6A, 15A] obtain by surprise or a trick: 出其不意地取得; 以诡计获得: ~ a kiss from sb; 偷吻某人; ~ a glance at sb in the mirror. 在镜中偷瞥某人。 ~ a march on sb, do sth before him and so gain an advantage. 占先; (偷偷地)抢先某人。 **3** [VP2C] move, come, go (in, out, away, etc) secretly and quietly: 偷偷地移动; 潜行; 隐秘而悄悄地移动: He stole into the room. 他偷偷溜进房间。 A tear stole down her cheek. 一颗泪珠在她的面颊上悄悄地滚下。 The morning light was ~ing through the shutters. 晨光悄悄地穿过了百叶窗。

stealth /stelθ; stɛlθ/ n [U] (only used in) (仅用于) **by** ~, secretly and quietly: 偷偷地; 秘密地: enter a house by ~. 潜入一房屋。 **~·y** adj (-ier, -iest) doing things, done, quietly and secretly: 秘密做成的; 秘密进行的; 秘密做成的: ~y footsteps. 潜行的脚步。 **~·ily** /-ɪlɪ; -əlɪ/ adv

steam /stiːm; stim/ n [U] **1** gas or vapour into which boiling water changes; power obtained from ~: 蒸汽; 水气; 蒸汽产生的动力: ~-covered windows; 布满水气的窗子; a building heated by ~. 借蒸汽取暖的建筑物。 The ship was able to proceed under her own ~, using her own engines and not needing to be towed. 那条船可借其本身的蒸汽动力前进(无须拖船曳进)。 **Full ahead!** order to go forward at full speed. (命令)全速前进! **get up/raise** ~, provide ~ at a higher pressure in the boilers, etc: 提高或增加(锅炉等里的)蒸汽压力: The stokers got up ~. 司炉增加了蒸汽的压力。 **2** (fig uses; colloq) energy. (比喻用法; 口语)能力; 精力。 **get up** ~, collect one's energy. 振作; 奋发; 激动; 发怒。 **let off** ~, release surplus energy or emotion; become less excited. 发泄过剩的精力或激动的情绪; 变得不太激动。 **run out of** ~, become exhausted: 变得筋疲力竭; 耗尽: Is there a danger of the housing programme running out of ~, losing its impetus? 住宅兴建计划有半途而废的危险吗? **under one's own** ~, without help from others. 凭一己之力; 不靠别人的帮助。 **3** (compounds) (复合词) **'~·boat** n vessel propelled by ~. 汽船。 **~·'boiler** n vessel in which ~ is generated (to work an engine). 蒸汽锅炉。 ~ **brake/hammer/whistle/winch, etc** nn worked by ~. 蒸汽煞车(汽锤、汽笛、汽绞盘等)。 **~·'coal** n coal used for heating in ~-boilers. 汽锅用煤。 **'~·engine** n locomotive or stationary engine worked or driven by pressure of ~. 蒸汽机。 **~·'heat** n heat given out by ~ from radiators, pipes, etc. 汽热。 □ vt: ~-heated buildings, kept warm by ~-heat 借蒸汽取暖的建筑物。 **'~·radio** n (sl) sound broadcasting (contrasted with TV). (英俚)声音广播; 无线电广播(为电视之对)。 **'~·roller** n heavy, slow-moving locomotive with wide wheels used in roadmaking. 蒸汽压路机; 汽辗。 □ vt [VP6A] crush as with a ~-roller: (似用蒸汽压路机般)压平; 粉碎: ~-roller all opposition. 粉碎一切反对

(力量。) **'~·ship** n ship driven by ~. 汽船; 轮船。 □ vi, vt **1** [VP2A, C] give out ~ or vapour: 蒸发; 冒蒸汽: ~ing hot coffee. 冒汽的热咖啡。 The kettle was ~ing (away) on the stove. 水壶在炉子上冒汽。 **2** [VP 2C] move, work, etc under (or as if under) the power of ~: 借(或似借)蒸汽力量行驶、运转等: a ship ~ing up the Red Sea; 航行于红海的船; ~ at ten knots. 以每小时十海里的速度航行。 The train ~ed into the station. 火车驶入车站。 **3** [VP6A, 22] cook, soften, clean, by the use of ~: 蒸; 蒸软; 用蒸汽清除或清洗: ~ fish; 蒸鱼; ~ open an envelope, use steam to soften the gum on the flap. 用蒸汽(软化封口的胶而)开启信封。 **~ up**, become misty with condensed ~: 因凝结的蒸汽而变得模糊不清: The windows ~ed up. 窗户蒙上一层蒸汽。 **be/get (all) ~ed up**, (colloq) become excited and perhaps violent: (口)变得激动、兴奋、愤怒等: Now don't get all ~ed up over nothing! 不要无缘无故地发脾气嘛! **~er** n **1** ~ship. 轮船; 汽船。 **2** vessel in which food is cooked by being ~ed. 蒸煮器; 蒸笼。 **~·y** adj of, like, full of, ~: 蒸汽的; 象蒸汽的; 充满蒸汽的: ~y windows; 水气朦胧的窗子; the ~y heat of the rainy season in the tropics. 热带雨季潮湿的闷热。

steed /stiːd; stid/ n (liter or hum) horse. (文或谐)马。

steel /stiːl; stil/ n [U] **1** strong, hard alloy of iron and carbon, used for knives, tools, machinery, etc. 钢(铁与碳结合成的合金)。 ~ **band** n (as, orig, in Trinidad) band of musicians who use empty oil drums as percussion instruments. (起源于特立尼达岛)钢鼓乐队(利用空油桶作打击乐器所组成的乐队)。 **'~·clad** adj covered with ~ armour. 装甲的; 裹甲胄的。 **~·'plated** adj covered with ~ plates; armoured. 装甲的; 覆以钢板的。 ~ **wool**, fine ~ shavings (used for scouring and polishing). 钢丝绒(用以擦亮或磨光物件)。 **'~·works** n pl (often with sing v) factory where ~ is made. (常用单数动词)炼钢厂。 **2** ~ **weapon**, eg a sword, contrasted with a firearm: 钢制武器(如刀剑, 与firearm相对): an enemy worthy of one's ~, (rhet or fig) one who will fight well. (修辞或喻)劲敌; 强敌。 **cold** ~, cold¹(1). □ vt [VP6A, 15A, 16A] harden: 使坚硬: ~ oneself/one's heart (against pity/to do sth). 硬起心肠(狠起心来)(不停以同情, 做某事)。 **~·y** adj like ~ in hardness, polish, brightness, etc. 坚硬、光亮等如钢的。

a steel band

steel·yard /'stiːljɑːd; 'stɪljəd/ n balance(1) with an arm in two parts, the longer side being graduated for a weight which slides along it. 秤; 提秤。

steen·bok /'stiːnbɒk; 'stin‚bak/ n kind of small S African antelope. (南非洲产的)小羚羊。

steep¹ /stiːp; stip/ adj (-er, -est) **1** (of a slope) rising or falling sharply: (指斜坡)陡峭的; 险峻的: a ~ gradient/path/descent; 陡峭的倾斜度/路/坡; a ~ roof, with a ~ pitch. 陡峭的屋顶。 **2** (colloq, of a demand) unreasonable; excessive: (口语, 指一项要求)不合理的; 过分的: It's a bit ~ that I should pay for all

of you! 要我为你们全体付帐，有点过份吧! *£ 10 for this dictionary — isn't that a bit ~?* 这本词典索价十英镑 — 是不是贵了一点? *That story's rather ~,* difficult to believe, exaggerated. 那故事不甚合情理。 **~·ly** adv **~·ness** n **~en** /'stiːpən; 'stipən/ vt, vi [VP6A, 2A] make or become ~ or ~er. (使)变为陡峭或更陡峭; (使)变得险峻或更险峻。 '**~·ish** /-ɪʃ; -ɪʃ/ adj rather ~. 颇为陡峭的; 有点险峻的。

steep² /stiːp; stip/ vt, vi [VP6A, 14, 2A] ~ sth *(in sth)*, **1** soak or bathe in liquid: 浸; 渍; 濡湿: ~ *onions in vinegar,* to pickle them. 腌泡洋葱于醋中。 **2** (fig) pervade with; get a thorough knowledge of: (喻) 沉湎; 充满; 精通: *~ed in ignorance/prejudice:* 充满无知(偏见): *a scholar ~ed in the literature of ancient Greece and Rome.* 精通古希腊罗马文学的学者。

steeple /'stiːpl; 'stipl/ n high tower with a spire, rising above the roof of a church. (教堂的)尖阁或尖塔。 ⇨ the illus at **church**. 参看 church 之插图。 '**~·chase** n cross-country horse-race or race on foot with obstacles such as fences, hedges and ditches. 越野障碍赛马; 越野障碍赛跑。 ⇨ *flat racing* at **flat²(1)**. '**~·jack** n man who climbs ~s, tall chimney-stacks, etc to do repairs. 高空作业工人(如装修教堂尖塔、高烟囱等之人)。

steer¹ /stɪə(r); stɪr/ n young (usu castrated) male of an animal of the ox family, raised for beef. 牡犊(通常阉过, 饲供食用)。 ⇨ **bull¹(1)**, **bullock, heifer, ox.**

steer² /stɪə(r); stɪr/ vt, vi [VP6A, 2A, C] direct the course of (a boat, ship, car, etc): 驾驶(舟、船、汽车等): ~ *north;* 向北行驶; ~ *by the stars;* 借星(的位置)辨别方向行驶; (with passive force): (含被动义): *a ship that ~s (= is ~ed) well/easily/badly.* 好(容易, 不好)驾驶的船。 ~ *clear of,* (fig) avoid. (喻)避开。 '**~·ing-gear** n [U] (of a ship) rudder and the mechanism controlling it. (指船)舵及操舵装置。 '**~·ing-wheel** n **(a)** (on a ship) wheel turned to control for rudder. (船上的)舵轮。 **(b)** (on a motor-vehicle) wheel for ~ing (mounted on the '**~·ing-column**). (汽车上的)方向盘;驾驶盘。 ⇨ the illus at **motor**. 参看 motor 之插图。 **~s·man** /-mən; -mən/ n (pl **-men**) person who ~s a vessel. (掌)舵手。

steer·age /'stɪərɪdʒ; 'stɪrɪdʒ/ n [U, C] (sing only, or attrib) **1** act or effect of steering. 驾驶; 操舵。 **2** that part of a ship nearest the rudder; this section formerly used for providing for passengers travelling at the lowest fares. 船尾近舵的部分; 统舱(票价最低的客舱)。 '**~·way** n forward progress needed by a vessel to enable her to be controlled by the helm. 舵效速率(使舵发生功效的最低速度)。

stele /'stiːliː; 'stiliː/ n (also 亦作 **stela** /'stiːlə; 'stilə/ pl **stelae** /-liː; -li/) (Gk archaeology) upright slab or pillar, usu with a sculptured design or inscription. (希腊考古学)石碑; 石柱(通常刻有题字或图案)。

stel·lar /'stelə(r); 'stelə/ adj of stars: 星的: ~ *light.* 星光。

stem¹ /stem; stɛm/ n **1** part of a plant coming up from the roots; part of a leaf, flower or fruit that joins it to the main stalk or twig. (植物的)茎; 干; 叶柄; 花梗; 果柄。 ⇨ the illus at **flower**. 参看 flower 之插图。 **~med** suff (with adjj) (与形容词连用) *,long-'~med, ,short-'~med, ,thick-'~med,* having long, short, thick, ~s. 长茎(干, 柄, 梗等)的, 短茎(干, 柄, 梗等)的, 粗茎(干, 柄, 梗等)的。 **2** ~-shaped part, eg the slender part of a wineglass, between the base and the bowl, the part of a tobacco pipe between the mouthpiece and the bowl. 茎状部分; 杯(子)的脚、烟斗杆等。 **3** root or main part of a noun or verb from which other words are made by additions (esp inflectional endings) (名词或动词的)词干(可衍生其他词的主体部分)。 **4** main upright timber at the bow of a ship. 船首; 船头; 船首材; 船首柱。 *from ~ to stern,* throughout the whole length of a ship. 从船首到船尾。 □ vi **(-mm-)** [VP3A] ~ *from,* arise from; have as origin. 发生; 源于; 来自。

stems

stem² /stem; stɛm/ vt **(-mm-)** [VP6A] **1** check, stop, dam up (a stream, a flow of liquid, etc). 阻止; 遏制; 堵住(河流, 水流等)。 **2** make headway against the resistance of: 逆···而行; 逆···而上; 对抗; 抗拒: ~ *the tide/current;* 逆潮(流)而上; (fig) (喻) ~ *the tide of popular indignation.* 遏止众人公愤。

stench /stentʃ; stɛntʃ/ n [C] horrid smell. 恶臭; 臭气。

sten·cil /'stensl; 'stɛnsl/ n [C] thin sheet of metal, cardboard, waxed paper, etc with letters or designs cut through it; lettering, design, etc printed by inking paper, etc through a stencil: 模板; 型板(有雕空之文字或图案的金属板, 厚纸板, 蜡纸等); (在钢板上书写的)蜡纸; (模板, 用蜡纸印出的)文字或图案等: *cut a ~,* eg by typing without the ribbon on a waxed sheet. 刻蜡纸;打字于蜡纸上。 □ vt **(-ll-,** US also **-l-)** [VP6A] produce (a pattern, wording, etc) by using a ~. 用模板, 蜡纸等印刷(文字, 花样等)。

Sten gun /'sten gʌn; 'stɛn gʌn/ n small kind of machine-gun, usu fired from the hip. 斯顿机枪(一种冲锋枪)。

sten·ogra·phy /stə'nɒɡrəfɪ; stə'nɑɡrəfɪ/ n (US) shorthand. (美)速记; 速记法。 **sten·ogra·pher** /-fə(r); -fə/ n (US) writer of shorthand (GB 英 = shorthand-'typist). (美)速记员。

sten·torian /sten'tɔːrɪən; stɛn'tɔrɪən/ adj (of a voice) loud and strong. (指人声)宏亮的; 响亮的。

step¹ /step; stɛp/ vi, vt **(-pp-) 1** [VP2C] move the foot, or one foot after the other (forward, or in the direction indicated): 走; 举步; 踏步; 行走: ~ *across a stream;* 走过小溪; ~ *into a boat,* 踏进船中; ~ *on to/ off the platform;* 走上(下)讲台; ~ *across to a neighbour's,* cross (the road) to his house. 越过马路到邻居家去。 ~ *this way,* (polite invitation to) follow sb somewhere, eg into a room. (客套话)请往这边走; 请随我来(如进入某房间)。 ~ *on the gas;* ~ *on it,* **(a)** (gas = gasoline) press down the accelerator pedal of a motor vehicle to increase speed. 踏汽车等的加速器加快速度; 踩油门。 **(b)** (sl) hurry. (俚)赶紧; 赶快。 '**~·ping-stone** n **(a)** one of a number of flat stones placed in a shallow stream, so that it can be crossed with dry feet. (浅河中的)踏脚石。 **(b)** (fig) means of attaining sth: (喻)达成目标的手段; 进身之阶: *a first ~ping-stone to success.* 成功的第一步。 '**~·ins** n pl (colloq) woman's undergarment or shoes, put on by being ~ped into. (口)由脚下套上的女用衬裙、衬裤等;不系带的鞋子。 **2** [VP2C, 15B] (uses with adverbial particles): (与副词性小品词连用的用法):

step aside, **(a)** move to one side. 走到一边; 站开。 **(b)** (fig) allow sb else to take one's place. (喻)让位子给别人。

step down, (fig) resign (to make way for sb else). (喻)辞职; 让贤。

step in, (fig) intervene (either to help or hinder): (喻)(为帮助或阻止而)介入; 干预; 干涉: *If the police hadn't ~ped in during the demonstration there would have been a violent struggle.* 示威时若不是警察介入, 早就引起激烈的打斗了。

step sth off/out, measure by taking steps: (以脚)步测(量): ~ *out a distance of ten metres.* 步测十米距离。

step out, **(a)** walk faster, walk briskly. 快步行进; 轻

快走 地. **(b)** (colloq) have a gay time, a busy social life. (口) 过欢乐而繁忙的社交生活; 寻欢作乐.

step sth up, **(a)** (naut) fix (the foot of a mast) in its socket. (航海) 插(桅脚)于桅座中. **(b)** increase: 增加; 促进: ~ *up production*; 促进生产; ~ *up the doses (of medicine)*; 增加(药)的剂量; ~ *up the campaign*, put more effort into it. 加强这项运动.

step² /step; stɛp/ *n* 1 act of stepping once; distance covered by doing this: 步; 一步的距离: *He was walking with slow* ~*s*. 他慢步行走. *The water was deeper at every* ~. 每走一步水就更深. *We must retrace our* ~*s*, go back. 我们必须折回(循原路回去). *It's only a few* ~*s farther*. 那只有几步远了. *We have made a long* ~ (fig, much progress) *towards success*. (喻)我们已向成功迈进一大步. *watch one's* ~, be careful or cautious. 谨慎; 小心. ~ *by* ~, gradually; by degrees. 逐渐地; 一步一步地. '**one-**~, '**two-**~ *nn* names of dances. (舞名)单步舞, 双步舞. 2 ('**foot**~), sound made by somebody walking; way of walking (as seen or heard): 脚步声; 步态; 步调: *We heard (foot)*~*s outside*. 我们听到外面有脚步声. *That's Lucy—I recognize her* ~. 那是露西——我听得出她的脚步声. 3 *be*/*get in*/*out of* ~ (*with*), **(a)** put/not put the right foot to the ground at the same time as others (in walking, marching, dancing). (走路、齐步行进、跳舞等)(与…)合(不合)步调; (与…)步调一致(不一致). **(b)** conform/not conform with other members of a group: 与(一团体中的其他分子)谐调(不谐调): *He's out of* ~ *with the rest of us*. 他同我们大家不谐调. *keep* ~ (*with*), walk or march in ~ (with). (与…)步调一致地行走或行进. *break* ~, get out of ~. 走乱步伐. 4 one action in a series of actions with a view to effecting a purpose: 步骤; 措施: *take* ~*s to prevent the spread of influenza*; 采取步骤阻止流行性感冒蔓延; *a false* ~, a mistaken action. 错误的步骤(或措施). *What's the next* ~, What are we to do next? 下一步该怎么办? *That would be a rash* ~ *to take*. 那将是轻率的措施. 5 place for the foot when going from one level to another: 台阶; 梯级; 踏脚; *Mind the* ~*s when you go down into the cellar*. 走下地下室时当心梯级. *They had to cut* ~*s in the ice as they climbed*. 他们往上爬时, 必须在冰上凿出踏脚处. *The child was sitting on the bottom* ~. 那孩子坐在最底下的台阶上. ~*s, a pair of* ~*s, a* '~*-ladder nn* portable folding ladder with ~*s*, not rungs and usu a small platform at the top. 折梯; 四脚梯. 6 grade, rank; promotion: 官阶的一级; 等级; 升迁: *When do you get your next* ~ *up?* When will you be promoted? 你何时晋级(升迁)?

a step-ladder

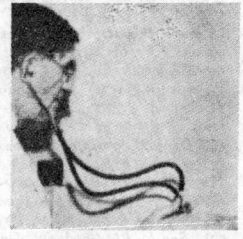

a stethoscope

step- /step; stɛp/ *pref* (used to show a relationship not by blood but by a later marriage) (用以表示非血亲关系, 而系由再婚产生的家庭关系) '~**·child**/·son **·daughter** *nn* child of an earlier marriage of one's wife or husband. 与前妻或前夫所生的孩子(儿子, 女儿); 晚子; 晚女. '~**·brother**/·**sister** *nn* child of an earlier marriage of one's stepfather or stepmother. 异父(母)兄弟(姊妹); 隔山兄弟(姊妹). '~**·father**/·**mother**/

·**parent** *nn* one's parent's later husband or wife. 继父(继母); 继父(继母).

steppe /step; stɛp/ *n* [C] level, grassy treeless plain, esp in SE Europe and central Asia. (尤指东南欧及中亚的)无树大平原; 大草原. ⇨ **pampas, prairie, savanna, veld.**

stereo /'steriəu; 'stɛrɪo/ *n* (abbr of ~*phonic*) ~phonic record-player, apparatus, sound, etc. (为 ~phonic 之略)立体声电唱机、音响装置、音响等.

stereo·phonic /,steriə'fɒnɪk; ,stɛrɪə'fɑnɪk/ *adj* (of broadcast and recorded sound, using two separately placed loudspeakers) giving the effect of naturally distributed sound; (of apparatus) designed for recording or reproducing sound in this way: (指用两个分开放置的扩音器放出的广播及录音)立体声的; (指仪器)录制或发出立体音响的. ~ *a recording*. 立体声录音.

stereo·scope /'steriəskəup; 'stɛrɪə,skop/ *n* [C] apparatus by which two photographs of sth, taken from slightly different angles, are seen as if united and with the effect of depth and solidity. 立体镜(以此镜观看两张角度稍异的照片可产生立体感). **stereo·scopic** /,steriə'skɒpɪk; ,stɛrɪə'skɑpɪk/ *adj* of, by means of, a ~. 立体镜的; 借助立体镜的.

stereo·type /'steriətaɪp; 'stɛrɪə,taɪp/ *n* [C, U] 1 (process of printing from a) printing-plate cast from a mould of a piece of printing set in movable type. 铅版印刷术; (浇制而成的印刷用)铅版. 2 fixed, formalized or standardized (and therefore perhaps false) phrase, idea, belief. 定型的语句、观念或信仰. □ *vt* [VP6A] 1 make ~ of; print by the use of ~s. 浇制…的铅版; 用铅版印刷. 2 (fig) (of phrases, ideas, etc) fix in form; use and repeat without thought or change: (喻)(指语句、观念等)使成固定形式; 反复因袭: ~*d greetings*, eg 'Good morning', 'How d'you do?' 已成固定形式的问候语(如'早安,' '你好'!).

ster·ile /'sterail *US*: 'sterəl; 'stɛrɪl/ *adj* 1 not producing, not able to produce, seeds or offspring. 不结果实的; 不能生育的. 2 (of land) barren. (指土地)不毛的; 贫瘠的. 3 (fig) having no result; producing nothing: (喻)无结果的; 无效果的: *a* ~ *discussion*. 无结果的讨论. 4 free from living germs. 无细菌的. **ste·ril·ity** /ste'rɪləti; stɛ'rɪlətɪ/ *n* [U] being ~. 不结果实; 不能生育; 不毛; 无结果; 无细菌. **ster·il·ize** /'sterəlaɪz; 'stɛrə,laɪz/ *vt* [VP6A] make ~. 使不生产; 使无结果; 消毒; 杀菌: *The surgeon carefully sterilized his instruments*. 外科医生小心清毒他的器械. **ster·il·iz·ation** /,sterəlaɪ'zeɪʃn *US*: -lɪ'z-; ,stɛrələ'zeʃən/ *n* [U].

ster·ling /'stɜːlɪŋ; 'stɝlɪŋ/ *adj* 1 (abbr 略作 **stg**) (of gold and silver) of standard value or purity: 指金银)标准成分的: *plates of* ~ *gold*. 由标准成分之黄金制成的器皿. 2 (fig) of solid worth; genuine: (喻)货真价实的; 可靠的; 真正的: ~ *sense*/*qualities*. 可靠的感觉(性质). □ *n* British money: 英国货币: *the pound* ~ (= £); 英镑; *payable in* ~. 可按英国货币支付的. **the** '~ **area**, group of countries which keep their reserves in British ~ currency and between which money can be transferred freely. 英镑地区(用英镑作准备金的各国).

stern¹ /stɜːn; stɝn/ *adj* (-er, -est) 1 demanding and enforcing obedience: 严苛的; 严格的: *a* ~ *taskmaster*. 严苛的监工. 2 severe; strict: 严厉的; 严肃的: *a* ~ *face*; 严肃的面孔; ~ *looks*; 严厉的表情; ~ *treatment*/*rebukes*. 严厉的对待(叱责). ~**·ly** *adv* ~**·ness** *n*

stern² /stɜːn; stɝn/ *n* [C] rear end of a ship or boat: 船尾: *move out of dock* ~ *foremost*. 船尾向前倒退出船坞. ⇨ the illus at **ship**. 参看 ship 之插图. ~**·'wheeler** *n* steamer with a larger paddle-wheel at the ~. (指装在船尾)明轮船; 船尾装蹼轮的船.

ster·num /'stɜːnəm; 'stɝnəm/ *n* (anat) narrow bone in the front of the chest (also called 亦称作 *'breast-bone'*) connecting the collar-bone and the top seven

pairs of ribs. (解剖)胸骨(胸前的狭骨, 连接锁骨与最上面的七对肋骨). ⇨ the illus at **skeleton**. 参看 skeleton 之插图.

ster·tor·ous /'stɜːtərəs; 'stɝtərəs/ adj (of breathing or a person breathing) making a loud snoring sound. (指呼吸或呼吸的人)发鼾声的; 打鼾的. **~·ly** adv

stet /stet; stɛt/ vi (Lat) direction to a printer, etc to disregard a correction in a MS or proof. (拉)(校对用语, 给予印刷工人等之指示)不改; 不删; 保持原样.

stetho·scope /'steθəskəʊp; 'stɛθə,skop/ n instrument used by doctors for listening to the beating of the heart, sounds of breathing, etc. (医生用的)听诊器. ⇨ the illus at **step²**. 参看 step² 之插图.

stet·son /'stetsn; 'stɛtsn/ n man's hat with a high crown and a wide brim. (男用)高顶阔边帽.

steve·dore /'stiːvədɔː(r); 'stivə,dor/ n man whose work is loading and unloading ships. (码头的)装卸工人.

stew /stjuː; US: stuː; stju/ vt, vi [VP6A, 15A, 2A, C] cook, be cooked, in water or juice, slowly in a closed dish, pan, etc: 用文火煮; 燉; 焖: ~ed chicken/ fruit; 燉鸡(水果); '~ing pears, suitable for ~ing but not for eating uncooked. 煮食梨(只宜燉食, 不宜生食者). **let sb**, **~ in his own 'juice**, do nothing to help him (when he is in trouble for which he is himself responsible). 让某人自食其果或自作自受. **~ in one's own 'juice**, suffer from trouble of one's own making. 自食其果; 自作自受. **let sb ~**, let him continue suffering from the consequences of his own stupidity without offering help or sympathy. 让某人自食其果. □ n 1 [C, U] (dish of) ~ed meat, etc: 燉肉; 燉煮的菜肴: have mutton ~ for supper; 晚餐吃燉羊肉; prepare a ~. 做一道燉的菜. **2 be in/get into a ~ (about sth)**, (口)(对某事)忧虑、敏感、激动等. **stewed** adj (sl) intoxicated. (俚)醉的; 酒醉的.

stew·ard /stjʊəd US: 'stuː-; 'stjuwɚd/ n 1 man who arranges for the supply of food, etc in a club, college, etc. (俱乐部、大学等处的)膳务员. **2** man who attends to the needs of passengers in a ship or airliner: (轮船或飞机上的)服务员: the 'baggage/'cabin/'deck, etc ~. 负责行李(客舱, 甲板等上)的侍者. **3** man responsible for organizing details of a dance, race-meeting, public meeting, show, etc: (舞会、赛马会、公共集会、表演等的)筹备人: ~s of the Jockey Club. 赛马俱乐部的筹备人. The hecklers were thrown out by the ~s. 诘难者被夸备人撵出去了. **4** man who manages another's property (esp a large house or estate). (管理他人财产, 尤指大厦或大地产的)管家; 管理人. **5 shop ~**, ⇨ shop(3). **~·ess** /stjʊə'des US: 'stuːərdɪs; 'stjuwɚdɪs/ n woman ~ (esp 2 above). 女管家; (尤指)轮船或飞机上的女服务员; 女侍者; 空中小姐. **~·ship** /-ʃɪp; -ʃɪp/ n rank and duties of a ~(4); period of office. 管家的职位及其职责; 管家的任期.

stick¹ /stɪk; stɪk/ n 1 thin branch broken, cut or fallen, from a bush, tree, etc: (折断, 砍下或掉下的)小树枝; 柴枝: gather dry ~s to make a fire; 拾干柴枝生火; cut ~s to support the peas in the garden. 砍些小树枝以支撑豆的豌豆. **2** such a branch cut to a convenient length, piece of cane cut, shaped, etc for a special purpose: (为某种用途砍成大小、长短适用的)杖; 棍; 棒: The old man cannot walk without a ~. 那老年人没有手杖不能走路. We have only a few ~s of furniture, only a few very roughly made articles of furniture of the simplest kind. 我们只有几件极简陋的家具. **give sb the ~**, beat him with a cane, as punishment; (fig) punish him. 用杖打某人; (喻)惩罚某人. **get hold of the ,wrong end of the '~**, be confused; misunderstand things completely. 弄混; 迷惘; 困惑; 完全弄错. **the big ~**, (fig) threat of the use of force, eg in relationships between countries: (喻)巨棒(政策)(如两国之间以武力为要挟): a policy of the big ~. 巨棒政策. **hockey ~**,

⇨ **hockey**. **3** slender, rod-shaped piece (of chalk, sealing-wax, charcoal, dynamite, celery, etc). 棒状物(如粉笔、封蜡、木炭、炸药、芹菜等). **4** (colloq) person, esp one who is dull, stiff and reserved: 呆板、固执、拘谨的人; 呆头呆脑的人; 木头人: He's a dull/dry old ~. 他是个乏味的老家伙. **5 the ~s**, (colloq) the backwoods; rural areas far from cities. 森林地带; 远离城市的乡村地区. **out in the ~s**, away from the centre of things. 远离热闹、纷扰或繁华之地. □ vt (pt, pp ~ed) (VP6A) support with ~s(1): support a ~. Have you ~ed your peas yet? 你已用树枝把豌豆撑好了吗?

stick² /stɪk; stɪk/ vt, vi (pt, pp stuck /stʌk; stʌk/) (For special uses with adverbial particles and preps, ⇨ 7 below.) (与副词性小品词及介词连用的特殊用法, 参看下列第 7 义.) **1** [VP6A, 15A, B] **~ sth (in)**, push (sth pointed) (into, through, etc): 以(尖物)插入, 刺, 戳, 贯穿等: S~ the fork into the potato/S~ it in. 把叉子插入马铃薯(把它插进去). The cushion was stuck full of pins. 针垫上插满了针. **~ a pig**, (in sport) kill one with a spear. (打猎)用矛刺杀野猪. **2** [VP2C] (of sth pointed) be, remain, in a position by the point: (尖锐物)扎在某处; 尖端停在某处; 刺入: The needle stuck in my finger. 针扎进我的手指. I found a nail ~ing in the tyre. 我发现一根钉子刺进车胎里. **3** [VP15A, B, 2A, C] (cause to) be or become joined or fastened with, or as with, paste, glue or other substance: (用或似用粘性物质)使或变得粘附; 粘合; 附着: ~ a stamp on a letter/a placard on a hoarding. 贴邮票于信上(在栅墙上张贴布告). These stamps have stuck (together). 这些邮票粘在一起了. **be/get stuck with sb/sth**, (colloq) be/become permanently involved with him/it; be/become unable to escape from him/it: (口)与某人(某事物)纠缠不清; 无法摆脱某人(某事物): It looks as if I'm stuck with the job of clearing up this mess. 我好象非要收拾这个烂摊子不可了. **'~·ing-plaster** n [U] plaster for ~ing on and protecting a cut, injury, etc. (保护伤口等用的)橡皮膏; 胶布. **4** [VP15A] (colloq) put (in some position or place), esp quickly or carelessly: (口)插, 放置; (尤指)乱塞: He stuck his pen behind his ear/his hands in his pockets/the papers in a drawer. 他把笔随手塞在耳后(把手插进口袋, 把文件胡乱塞进抽屉). **5** [VP2A, C] (also in the passive) (亦用被动语态) **~ (in)**, be or become fixed (in); fail to work properly: 陷住; 卡住; 不能转动; 动弹不得: The key stuck in the lock, could not be turned or withdrawn. 钥匙在锁中卡住了不能转动了. The bus (was) stuck in the mud. 公共汽车陷在泥里开不动了. Don't get stuck in the bog. 不要陷进泥沼中. The door has stuck, eg as the result of being newly painted. 门打不开了(关不上了)(如由于刚抽漆过). **~ in one's throat**, (of a proposal, etc) be difficult to accept; (of words) be difficult to utter (because of unwillingness, etc). (指建议等)难以接受; (指言词)难以启齿(由于不愿意等). **'~-in-the-mud** attrib adj resistant to change: 顽固的; 不进步的; 守旧的: ~-in-the-mud ideas. 守旧的观念. □ n person of this kind: 守旧分子; 顽固分子: My grandfather is an old ~-in-the-mud. 我的祖父是个老顽固. **6** [VP6A] (colloq) bear; endure: (口)忍耐; 忍受: How can you ~ that fellow? 你怎么忍受得了那个家伙? I can't ~ it any longer. 我无法再忍受了. S~ it, ⇨ out below. 参看下列第 7 义中的 ~ it out. S~ to it! (used as a cry of encouragement meaning 'Bear the conditions bravely', etc.) (用作鼓励语)勇敢地坚持下去! **7** [VP2C, 3A, 15B] (special uses with adverbial particles and preps): (与副词性小品词及介词连用的特殊用法):

stick around, (sl) (of a person) stay in or near a place: (俚)(指人)(在某处或附近)徘徊; 逗留: S~ around; we may need you. 不要走远; 我们可能需要你.

stick at sth, (a) ~ stop short of, hesitate at: 迟疑; 犹豫; 顾虑: Don't ~ at trifles. 不要为小事伤脑筋. He ~s at nothing, allows no feelings of doubt, no scruples, to

stop him. 他毫无顾忌。**(b)** keep on with sth: 继续做某事; *He ~s at his work ten hours a day.* 他继续每天工作十小时。

stick sth down, **(a)** (colloq) put down: (口) 放下: *S~ it down anywhere you like.* 把它放在你认为合适的地方。**(b)** (colloq) write down. (口) 写下。**(c)** fasten with paste, etc: 粘住: *~ down (the flap of) an envelope.* 把信封(的口盖)粘起。

stick on sth, remain on: 停留在: *Can you ~ on a horse?* 你能骑在马背上吗? *~ sth on,* fasten to with paste, etc: 把某物粘上: *~ on a label.* 粘上标签。Hence, 由此产生, *'~-on* attrib *adj:* ~-on *labels* (as contrasted with *tie-on* labels) 粘贴上的标签(以别于系上的标签)。*~ it on,* (sl) make very high charges: (俚) 索高价: *The hotel keepers ~ it on during the (busy) season.* 旅馆老板在旺季索取高价。

stick (sth) out, (cause to) project, stand out: (使) 突出; 伸出; 显眼: *with his chest stuck out; a rude boy ~ing his tongue out at his sister.* 一个向他姐姐(妹妹)伸舌头的粗鲁的男孩。*Don't ~ your head out of the car window.* 不要把头伸出车窗。*~ it out,* (colloq) endure hardship, etc until the end. (口) 忍耐到底。⇨ **6** above. 参看上列第6义。*~ one's neck out,* ⇨ neck(1). *~ out for sth,* refuse to give way until one gets (sth demanded): 坚索某物, 坚持要求某事(不达目的不罢休): *They're ~ing out for higher wages.* 他们坚持要求较高的工资。

stick to sb/sth, **(a)** be faithful to (one's ideals, a friend, etc); remain determined: 忠于(自己的理想, 朋友等); 坚持; 坚定于一resolution. 坚持决定。**(b)** continue at: 继续; 维持: *~ to a task until it is finished;* 继续一项任务直到完成为止。*~ to a timetable,* make no changes in what has been agreed. 不改动原时间表。*~ to one's guns,* ⇨ gun(1).

stick together, (colloq) (of persons) remain loyal or friendly to one another. (口)(指人)彼此忠诚友善; 共患难;同甘苦。

stick up, be upright, project upwards: 直立; 竖立: *The branch was ~ing up out of the water.* 树枝直直露出水面。*~ sb/sth up,* (sl) threaten to shoot sb in order to rob him/it: (俚) 威吓要开枪以便抢劫; 威逼劫掠; 持枪抢劫: *~ up a bank.* 持枪抢劫银行。Hence, 由此产生, *'~-up n. ~ your 'hands up;* *'em 'up,* raise your hands (so that resistance is not intended). 把手举起来(以示不抵抗)。*~ up for sb/oneself/sth,* defend, support: 维护; 支持; 辩护: *~ up for one's friends.* 为朋友辩护。

stick with sb/sth, remain loyal to, to continue to support: 忠于;继续支持: *~ with a friend/an ideal.* 忠于朋友(理想)。

sticker /'stɪkə(r); 'stɪkɚ/ *n* **1** one who, or that which, sticks, eg a persevering person. 坚持者; 固守者; 粘贴者; 尖物; 芒刺。⇨ **stick²(7).** **2** adhesive label to be stuck on sth. 粘贴的标签。

stick·ler /'stɪklə(r); 'stɪklɚ/ *n* ~ *for sth,* person who insists upon the importance of sth (eg accuracy, discipline, formality, etc). 坚持某事(如精确、纪律、形式等)重要的人;拘泥某事的人;不能权变的人。

sticky /'stɪkɪ; 'stɪkɪ/ *adj* (-ier, -iest) **1** that sticks or tends to stick to anything that touches it: 粘的;粘性的: *~ fingers/toffee;* 粘糊糊的手指(太妃糖); *a ~ road,* eg deep in wet mud. 泥泞的路。*a ~ wicket,* (cricket) soft wet area which makes batting difficult. (板球)湿软三柱门区(击球困难)。*be on a ~ wicket,* (fig) in a situation that is difficult to deal with. (喻)处困境;遇到难以处理的情况。**2** (sl) unpleasant; difficult: (俚)不愉快的; 困难的。*have a ~ time.* 遭遇困难。**come to a ~ end,** die in an unpleasant and painful way. 凄惨而痛苦地死去。**3** (colloq) making, likely to make, objections, be unhelpful, etc: 好异议的; 很可能反对的; 不肯帮忙的; 难同意的: *The bank manager was about letting her have an overdraft.* 那银行的经理不同意

她透支。**stick·ily** /-ɪlɪ; -əlɪ/ *adv* stick**i·ness** *n*

stiff /stɪf; stɪf/ *adj* **1** not easily bent or changed in shape: 不易弯曲的; 坚硬的; 僵硬的; 硬的: *a ~* (ie starched) *collar:* (浆过的)硬领; *a sheet of ~ cardboard,* 一块硬纸板; *have a ~ leg/back,* not easily bent; 腿(背)僵直的; *feel ~ after a long walk,* have ~ muscles and joints; 走长路后感觉肢体发僵; *lying ~ in death.* 死后僵硬地躺着。**keep a ~ upper lip,** show firmness of character (by not complaining when in pain or trouble). 咬紧牙根(遇痛苦或困难而不抱怨以示刚毅坚强)。*~-'necked adj* obstinate. 顽固的; 倔强的。**2** hard to stir, work, move, etc: 不灵活的; 难于移动的: *stir the flour and milk to a ~ paste;* 把面粉及牛奶搅成浓糊; hard to do; difficult: 难做的; 困难的: *a ~ climb/examination.* 困难的攀登(的考试)。*The book is ~ reading.* 这书很不容易懂。**3** (of manners, behaviour) formal, unfriendly, haughty: (指态度、行为)拘谨的; 呆板的;不友善的; 冷淡的; 傲慢的: *get a ~ reception;* 受到冷淡的接待; *be rather ~ with one's neighbours;* 对邻居相当冷淡; *give sb a ~ bow.* 向某人生硬地一鞠躬。**4** great in degree: 强劲的; 强劲的; 猛的: *a ~* (= strong) *breeze;* 强劲的风; *a ~* (= high) *price;* 高昂的价格; *a ~ glass of rum/a ~ drink,* strong in alcoholic content. 一杯强烈的朗姆酒(含酒精成分高的酒)。□ *adv* thoroughly; to the point of exhaustion: 彻底地; 极度地: *It bored me ~,* bored me very much. 烦死我了。*She was scared ~,* very badly scared. 她吓坏了。□ *n* (sl) (俚) **1** corpse. 尸体。**2** (sl) fool. (俚)傻瓜。**~·ly** *adv* **~·ness** *n* **~en** /'stɪfn; 'stɪfən/ *vt, vi* [VP6A, 2A] make or become ~. 使或变得坚硬、强烈等。**~·en·ing** /'stɪfnɪŋ; 'stɪfənɪŋ/ *n* [U] material used to ~en a substance or object. 加硬材料(使某一物质或物体变硬的材料)。**~·ener** /'stɪfnə(r); 'stɪfnɚ/ *n* sth used to ~en. 使坚硬之物;使硬烈之物。

stifle /'staɪfl; 'staɪfl/ *vt, vi* **1** [VP6A, 2A] give or have the feeling breathing is difficult: 使或感到窒息; 使或感到呼吸困难: *They were ~d by the heat.* 他们热得透不过气来。*The heat was stifling.* 热得令人透不过气来。*The smoke filled the building and almost ~d the firemen.* 建筑物里满是烟,几乎使救火员窒息。**2** [VP 6A] suppress; put down; keep back: 镇压; 扑平; 阻遏; 抑止: *~ a rebellion;* 扑平叛乱; *~ a yawn/a cry/one's laughter.* 抑止呵欠(哭叫,笑)。

stigma /'stɪgmə; 'stɪgmə/ *n* [C] **1** (*pl* *-mas* /-məz; -məz/) (fig) mark of shame or disgrace: (喻)污名; 耻辱; 瑕疵: *the ~ of illegitimacy.* 私生子的耻辱。**2** (*pl* *~ta* /-tə; -tə/) marks resembling those made by the nails on the body of Jesus at his crucifixion, said to have appeared on the body of St Francis of Assisi and others. 与耶稣受难的钉痕相似的记号(据说曾在圣弗朗西斯及其他人身上出现过)。**3** (*pl* *~s*) that part of the pistil of a flower which receives the pollen. 花的柱头(接受花粉部分)。⇨ the illus at **flower.** 参看 flower 之插图。

stig·ma·tize /'stɪgmətaɪz; 'stɪgmə,taɪz/ *vt* [VP16B] describe (sb) scornfully (as): 轻蔑地把(某人)描绘为; 诬蔑; 非难: *be ~d as a coward and a liar.* 被指为懦夫及说谎者。

stile /staɪl; staɪl/ *n* arrangement of steps or rungs to enable persons on foot to get over or through a fence, hedge, wall, etc but keeping cattle out. (能让行人爬越篱笆、围栏、围墙等,但能阻止畜类进入的)踏级; 阶梯。⇨ turnstile at **turn²(6). help a lame dog over a ~,** ⇨ dog¹(2).

sti·letto /stɪ'letəʊ; stɪ'lɛto/ *n* (*pl* *~s,* *~es* /-təʊz; -toz/) **small dagger with a narrow tapering blade.** 小剑; 匕首。*~ heel,* (on a woman's shoes) high, thin and (usu) made of metal. (女鞋的)高而细的后跟(通常为金属制成)。

still¹ /stɪl; stɪl/ *adj, adv* **1** without movement or sound; quiet: 不动的(地); 静止的(地); 寂静的(地); 无声的(地): *Please keep/stay ~ while I take your photograph.* 我为

你拍照的时候请不要动。*How ~ everything is!* (一切)多么安静啊! *the ~ small voice*, the voice of conscience. 良心的呼唤。 '~-**life** n [U] representation of non-living things (eg fruit, flowers, etc) in painting; [C] (*pl* ~-**lifes**) painting of this kind. (绘画中的)静物(如水果、花等);静物画。 '~-**birth** n child or foetus dead at birth. 死胎; 死产。 ⇨ *live-birth* at **live**[1](4). '~-**born** *adj* (of a child) dead at birth. (指小孩)死产的。 **2** (of wines) not sparkling; not containing gas. (指酒)不起泡的; 不含气体的。 □ n **1** [U] (poet) deep silence: (诗)寂静; 万籁俱寂: *in the ~ of the night.* 在万籁俱寂的深夜。 **2** [C] ordinary photograph selected from, and contrasted with, a cinema film: (自电影片中选出而与活动影片相对而言的)剧照: *~s from a new film,* eg as used for advertising in the press. 新影片的剧照(如用以登在报上做广告者)。 □ *vt* [VP6A] cause to be ~ or at rest; make calm. 使静止; 使安静; 使平静。 ~**y** *adj* (poet) calm; quiet. (诗)平静的; 安静的; 寂静的。 ~·**ness** n

still[2] /stɪl; stɪl/ *adv* **1** (usu mid position, but may occur after a direct object) even to this or that time: (通常置于动词前后,但可置于直接宾语之后)仍; 尚; 还: *He is ~ busy.* 他仍然很忙。 *He ~ hopes/is ~ hoping for a letter from her.* 他仍希望收到她的信。 *Will he ~ be here when I get back?* 我回来的时候,他还会在这里吗? *In spite of his faults she ~ loved him/loved him ~.* 尽管他有缺点,她仍旧爱他。 Cf *still* and *yet*: 比较 *still* 与 *yet* 的用法: *Is your brother here yet, Has he arrived?* 你哥哥(弟弟)到了吗? *Is your brother ~ here, Hasn't he left?* 你哥哥(弟弟)还在这里吗? **2** (with a comp) even; yet; in a greater degree: (与比较级连用)更; 愈: *Tom is tall but Mary is ~ taller/taller ~.* 汤姆很高,但是玛丽更高。 *That would be better ~/be ~ better.* 那就更好了。 **3** nevertheless; admitting that: 然而; 可是; 依然: *He has treated you badly; ~, he's your brother and you ought to help him.* 他待你不好; 但他总是你的兄弟,你仍旧应该帮助他。

still[3] /stɪl; stɪl/ n [C] apparatus for making liquors (brandy, whisky, etc) by distilling. (蒸馏酒类,如白兰地、威士忌等,用的)蒸馏器。 '~-**room** n house-keeper's storeroom in a large house. 大宅中管家的储藏室。

stilt /stɪlt; stɪlt/ n (often used 常作 (**pair of**) ~s) one of a pair of poles, each with a support for the foot at some distance from the bottom, used to raise the user from the ground: 高跷: *walk on* ~s. 踩高跷。

stilted /'stɪltɪd; 'stɪltɪd/ *adj* (of liter style, talk, behaviour, etc) stiff and unnatural; too formal. (指文体、谈话、举止等)生硬的;不自然的;太呆板的。 ~·**ly** *adv*

Stil·ton /'stɪltən; 'stɪltn/ n rich, white, creamy cheese with a green-blue mould in it. 斯提尔顿干酪(一种有墨绿色霉纹之白色多脂膏状干酪)。

stimu·lant /'stɪmjʊlənt; 'stɪmjələnt/ n [C] drink (eg coffee, brandy), drug, etc that increases bodily or mental activity; sth that spurs one on (eg praise, hope of gain). 兴奋剂;刺激物(如咖啡、白兰地、药物等);激励;鼓舞(如称赞、获利的希望等)。

stimu·late /'stɪmjʊleɪt; 'stɪmjəˌlet/ *vt* [VP6A, 14, 17] ~ *sb* (**to** *sth*/**to do** *sth*), excite; rouse; quicken thought or feeling: 刺激;激励;鼓舞;促进思想或感觉: ~ *sb to further efforts;* 激励某人进一步努力; ~ *sb to make greater efforts.* 激励某人作更大的努力。 **stimu·lat·ing** *adj*

stimu·lus /'stɪmjʊləs; 'stɪmjələs/ n (*pl* -**li** /-laɪ; -laɪ/) [C] sth that stimulates: 刺激物;激励(物);鼓励(物): *work harder under the ~ of praise;* 受到称赞后更加努力工作; *a ~ to further exertions.* 促使进一步努力的激励。

sting[1] /stɪŋ; stɪŋ/ n **1** [C] sharp, often poisonous, pointed organ of some insects (eg bees, wasps, gnats): (蜜蜂、黄蜂、蚋等的)尖而常带毒性的器官;刺;螫针: *The ~ of a scorpion is in its tail.* 蝎子的毒刺在其尾部。 '~-**ray** n broad, flat, tropical fish which can cause

severe wounds with its sharp spines. 魟;黄貂鱼(一种扁而宽的热带鱼,其尖锐的棘状突起可致重创)。 **2** hairs projecting from the surface of the leaf of a plant (esp a '~*ing-nettle*), which causes pain to the fingers, etc when touched. (植物,尤指荨麻,叶上突起的)刺毛(能刺痛手指等)。 **3** [C] sharp pain caused by the ~ of an insect or by nettles, etc; place of a wound made by a ~: (昆虫的刺、荨麻的刺毛等造成的)刺痛;刺伤;刺伤之处: *Her face was covered with a ~.* 她的脸上布满被刺的伤痕。 *Have you any ointment to put on these ~s?* 你有什么涂擦这些刺伤的药膏吗? **4** [C, U] any sharp pain of body or mind: (身心方面的)剧痛;刺痛: *the ~ of a whip/the northeast wind/hunger/remorse.* 鞭打(东北风;饥饿,懊悔)的刺痛。 *His service* (in tennis) *has no ~ in it,* is weak. 他(打网球时)发的球没有劲。

sting[2] /stɪŋ; stɪŋ/ *vt, vi* (*pt, pp* **stung** /stʌŋ; stʌŋ/) **1** [VP6A, 2A] prick or wound with a sting or as with a sting; have the power to ~: 刺;螫;刺伤;螫伤;有刺痛或刺伤力: *A hornet stung me on the cheek.* 一只大黄蜂在我脸上蜇了一下。 *The blows of the cane stung the boy's fingers.* 藤条的鞭打使那男孩的手指感到刺痛。 *Not all nettles ~.* 并非所有的荨麻都会刺人。 **2** [VP6A, 14, 15A] ~ *sb* (**to**/**into** *sth*/**doing** *sth*), cause sharp pain to; anger: 造成剧痛;刺痛;刺伤;激怒: *He was stung by his enemy's insults.* 他被敌人的侮辱激怒了。 *Anger stung* (= roused) *him to action/into fighting.* 愤怒使他采取行动/跟人打起来)。 **3** [VP2A] (of parts of the body) feel sharp pain: (指身体器官)感到剧痛: *His fingers were still ~ing from the caning he had had.* 他的手指接连被鞭打后仍旧感到刺痛。 **4** ~ *sb* (**for** *sth*), (colloq) charge him an excessive price (for sth); swindle sb: (口)向某人索过高的价钱;敲某人竹杠;骗某人钱: *He was stung for £5,* had to pay this sum. 他被敲了五英镑。 *How much did they ~ you for?* 他们敲了你多少钱? ~**er** n (esp) smart, painful blow. (尤指)刺痛的打击。 ~·**less** *adj* having no ~. 无螫刺、刺毛等的。

stingy /'stɪndʒɪ; 'stɪndʒɪ/ *adj* (-**ier**, -**iest**) spending, using or giving unwillingly; niggardly; miserly: 吝啬的;小气的;不大方的: *Don't be so ~ with the sugar!* 不要那么吝惜糖! **stin·gily** /-dʒɪlɪ; -dʒəlɪ/ *adv* **stin·gi·ness** n

stink /stɪŋk; stɪŋk/ *vi, vt* (*pt* **stank** /stæŋk; stæŋk/ or 或 **stunk** /stʌŋk; stʌŋk/, *pp* **stunk**) **1** [VP2A, 3A] ~ (**of** *sth*), have a horrid and offensive smell: 有臭味;发臭: *That fish ~s.* 那鱼发臭了。 *Her breath stank of garlic.* 她的呼吸带有大蒜味。 *cry ~ing fish,* condemn one's own goods, etc. 非难自己的货物等;自败己事。 **2** [VP15B] ~ *sb/sth out,* (**a**) drive out by means of sth evil-smelling: 以臭物驱逐; 以难闻之物逐出: ~ *out a fox,* eg by sending smoke into its hole. 熏出狐狸(如将烟送入狐狸洞中)。 (**b**) fill a place with ~s: 以难闻的气味充塞某处: *You'll ~ the place out with your cheap cigars!* 这地方会被你的劣质雪茄烟味所熏臭! □ n [C] horrid smell. 臭味;难闻的气味。 *raise/kick up a ~* (**about** *sth*), (colloq) cause trouble or annoyance, eg by complaining. (口)惹麻烦;惹烦恼(如发牢骚而引起)。 ~**er** n (sl) (俚) **1** letter intended to convey strong disapproval, reproach, etc. 表达强烈反对、谴责等的信函;意人讨厌的信。 **2** person who arouses strong dislike. 令人讨厌的人。 **3** (colloq) sth difficult: (口)困难之事;难题: *The biology paper* (ie in an examination) *was a ~er.* 生物考卷很难答。

stint /stɪnt; stɪnt/ *vt, vi* [VP6A, 14] ~ *sb* (**of** *sth*), restrict (sb) to a small allowance: 限制(某人)的花费;紧缩;吝惜: *She ~ed herself of food in order to let the children have enough.* 她节省自己的食物好让孩子们吃饱。 *Don't ~ the food.* 不要舍不得吃。 □ n **1** (usu 通常作) *without ~,* without limit, ungrudgingly: 不加限制地;不遗余力地。 **2** [C] fixed or allotted amount of (work): 定量的(工作);指定的分量: *do one's daily ~.* 做某人每天指定(或定量)的工作。

sti·pend /'staɪpend; 'staɪpɛnd/ n [C] (esp clergy-man's) salary. (尤指神职人员的)薪水; 薪给. **sti·pen-di·ary** /staɪ'pendɪərɪ US: -dɪɛrɪ; staɪ'pendɪˌɛrɪ/ adj receiving a ~, not working without pay: 受薪的; 支取薪金的; 非义务工作的: a ~iary magistrate, paid magistrate in a large town (appointed by the Home Secretary) dealing with police court cases. (大城市的)受薪治安推事(内政部长委派,受理违警案件者). □ n (pl -ries) ~iary magistrate. (大城市的)受薪治安推事.

stipple /'stɪpl; 'stɪpl/ vt (of) engrave or paint with dots instead of lines. 点画; 点描(不用线条).

stipu·late /'stɪpjuleɪt; 'stɪpjəˌlet/ vt, vi 1 [VP6A, 9] state, put forward, as a necessary condition: 规定; 约定: It was ~d that the goods should be delivered within three days. 经约定该项货物须在三日内送交. 2 [VP3A] ~ for sth, insist upon (as part of an agreement): ~ for the best materials to be used. 坚持以使用最好的材料为条件. **stipu·la·tion** /ˌstɪpju'leɪʃn; ˌstɪpjə'leʃən/ n [C] sth ~d; condition: 规定; 约定; 条款; 条件: on the stipulation that . . . 按规定….

stir /stɜː(r); stɜ/ vi, vt (-rr-) 1 [VP6A, 2A, C] be moving; cause to move: 动; 移动; 使动: Not a leaf was ~ring, There was no wind to move the leaves. 没有一片树叶在动(一点儿风都没有). A breeze ~red the leaves. 微风吹动树叶. Nobody was ~ring in the house, Everyone was resting. 屋子里没有人在走动(都在休息). She is not ~ring yet / has not ~red yet, is still in bed. 她尚未起床. You had better ~ yourself, get busy, be active. 你最好找点事做(活动活动). I haven't ~red out all morning, haven't left the house. 我整个上午未出过门. not ~ an eyelid, remain unmoved, showing no alarm or concern. 不动声色(未显示惊慌或关心). not ~ a finger, make no effort to do things; give no help. 一事不做; 一点都不帮忙; 袖手旁观. ~ one's stumps, (colloq) make haste, walk faster. (口)赶忙; 赶紧; 快走. 2 [VP6A, 15B] ~ sth (up), move a spoon, etc round and round in liquid, etc in order to mix it thoroughly: 搅和; 拌匀: ~ one's tea; 搅动茶; ~ the porridge; 搅动麦片粥; ~ milk into a cake mixture. 把牛奶和做蛋糕的混合物搅在一起. ~ the fire, use the poker in it. 拨火(使旺). 3 [VP6A, 14, 15B] ~ sb to sth; ~ sth (up), excite: 使激动; 惹起: The story ~red the boy's imagination. 那故事引起那男孩的幻想. Discontented men ~red the crew to mutiny / ~ed up trouble among the crew. 心怀不满的人鼓动船员叛变(在船员间制造纠纷). He wants ~ring up, needs to be roused from lethargy. 他需要激励. ~ the blood, rouse to excitement or enthusiasm. 激起兴奋或热忱. 4 [VP 2A, C] to move (about); 动起; 被激起: Pity ~red in his heart. 他的怜悯心被激起了. □ n (usu take a ~) commotion; excitement: 骚动; 激动: The news caused quite a ~ in the village. 这项消息在村子里引起相当大的骚动. '~·ring adj exciting: 激动的; 刺激的; 令人兴奋的: ~ring tales of adventure; 刺激的冒险故事; live in ~ring times. 生活于表表烈烈的时代. '~·ring·ly adv

stir·rup[1] /'stɪrəp; 'stɜəp/ n [C] foot-rest, hanging down from a saddle, for the rider of a horse. (马鞍上垂下的)马镫. ⇨ the illus at harness. 参看 harness 之插图. '~·cup n drink (of wine, etc) offered to sb mounted on a horse ready for departure. 献给上马欲行者的酒; 钱别酒.

stir·rup[2] /'stɪrəp; 'stɜəp/ n (anat) bone in the ear. (解剖)镫骨. ⇨ the illus at ear. 参看 ear 之插图.

stitch /stɪtʃ; stɪtʃ/ n 1 [C] (in sewing) the passing of a needle and thread in and out of cloth, etc; (in knitting) one complete turn of the wool, etc over the needle. (缝纫)缝; 一缝; 一针; (编织)一针. 2 the thread, etc seen between two consecutive holes made by a needle; result of a single movement with a threaded needle, knitting-needle, etc: 针脚: make long / neat, etc ~es; 缝长(平整等)针脚; put a few ~es in a garment; 在一件衣服上缝几针;

drop a ~, allow a loop to slip off the end of a knitting-needle; (编织时)漏织一针; 漏脱一针; put ~es into / take ~es out of a wound. 缝合伤口(拆去伤口的缝线). have not a ~ on, (colloq) be naked. 口)一丝不挂; 赤裸. A ~ in time saves nine, (prov) A small piece of work done now may save a lot of work later. (谚)及时一针省九针(及时行事, 则事半功倍). 3 (in compounds) particular kind of ~: (用于复合词中)某种针法或编织法: a 'button-hole ~; 钮孔的缝法; a 'chain~, etc. 链形缝法等. 4 (sing only) sharp pain in the side (as caused sometimes by running too soon after a meal). (仅用单数)胁部剧痛(如有时饭后立刻跑步所引起者). □ vt, vi [VP6A, 15A, B, 2A, C] sew; put ~es in or on. 缝合; 缝纫.

stoat /stəʊt; stot/ n small furry animal larger than a rat; weasel; ermine (in its summer coat of brown). 白鼬; 银鼠(尤指夏季毛为棕褐色者).

stock[1] /stɒk; stɑk/ n 1 [C, U] store or goods available for sale, distribution or use, esp goods kept by a trader or shopkeeper. (尤指商人所保有的)储积品; 存货; 现货. (be) in / out of ~, be available / not available: 有(无)现货或存货: The book is in / out of ~. 该书有(无)存货. Have you any linen sheets in ~? 你有没有亚麻布被单存货? 存货. (现)货清单. '~-list n list of goods, etc available. '~-room n room in which ~ is kept. 贮藏室. take ~, examine and make a list of goods in ~; 盘点存货; 清点存货; Hence, 由此产生, '~-taking n: 盘(点)存(货): The annual ~-taking starts tomorrow, eg in a draper's shop. 每年一度的盘存明天开始(如布店). take ~ of sth / sb, (fig) review (a situation); estimate (sb's abilities, etc). (喻)估计(形势); 估计(某人的能力等); 鉴定. '~-in-'trade n [U] everything needed for a trade or occupation. 生财; 营业或职业需要的全部用具. 2 (attrib used, from 1 above) usually kept in ~ (and therefore usually obtainable): (用作定语, 来自上面第1义)通常备有的; 通常可得的: ~ sizes in hats; 常备的帽子尺码; commonly or regularly used; hackneyed: 通常或经常使用的; 平常的; 陈腐的: ~ arguments / comparisons; 陈腐的论点(比较); ~ questions / answers. 常遇见的问题/回答. She's tired of her husband's ~ jokes. 她已听厌了她丈夫所说的那些陈腐的俏皮话. ~ company, company of actors who have a ~ (or repertoire) of plays which they perform. 备妥若干随时可上演的剧目的剧团. 3 [C, U] supply of anything: 贮存备用的任何事物; 贮积; 储蓄: a good ~ of information; 见闻丰富; 备有大量之煤 coal and coke for the winter. 购进煤炭和焦炭以备过冬. '~-piling n purchase (esp by a Government) of ~s of raw materials or goods not easily available from local sources (eg tin, rubber, needed in war). 物资贮备(尤指政府购进原料或当地不易获得之物资, 如战时所需之锡、橡胶等). 4 [U] (live-), farm animals. 家畜. fat ~, ~ fit for slaughter as food: (适于屠宰供食用的)肥家畜: fat-~ prices. 肥家畜的价格. '~-breeder / farmer n farmer who breeds or raises cattle. 畜牧业者. '~-car n (US) railway truck for carrying cattle. (美)运输家畜的火车厢. '~-car racing n racing of ordinary models of motor-cars as sold generally. 普通型式(非跑车)的汽车竞赛. '~-yard n enclosure where cattle are kept temporarily, eg at a market, or before being slaughtered. 临时关家畜的围栏(如市场上或屠宰场上者). 5 [C, U] money lent to a government in return for interest; shares in the capital of a business company: 公债; 股票: have £5000 in the ~s; 有五千英镑公债券; invest one's money in (a) safe ~. 投资于可靠的股票. '~-broker n man whose business is the buying and selling of ~(s). 证券经纪人. '~ exchange n place where ~s and shares are publicly bought and sold. 证券交易所. '~-holder n (chiefly US) shareholder. (主美)股东. '~-jobber n member of a ~ exchange from whom a ~broker buys and to whom he sells. 股票批发商(与证券经纪人做买卖者). '~-list

publication with current prices of ~s(5) and shares. 证券行情表. **6** [U] line of ancestry: 家系; 世系; 血统; 祖先: *a woman of Irish ~/of Puritan/farming, etc ~*. 一位有爱尔兰血统(有清教徒世系, 出身务农等)的女子. **7** ~*s and stones*, lifeless things. 木石; 无生命之物. '~*still* adj motionless. 静止的; 不动的. '**laughing-~**, target or object of ridicule. 笑柄; 嘲笑的对象. **8** [U] raw material ready for manufacture: 原料; 材料: *'paper ~*, eg rags, etc to be made into paper. 造纸原料. **9** [U] liquid in which bones, etc have been stewed; juices of meat and vegetables, used for making soup, gravy, etc. (骨头等炖成的)原汤; (做汤等用的)肉汁; 菜汁; 汤料. '~**cube** *n* cube of dehydrated ~. (经过脱水之)粒状浓汤. '~**fish** *n* fish (esp cod) split open and dried in the air without salt, a staple food in some countries. (鳕)鱼干(剖开除去内脏, 风干, 不用盐, 为某些国家之主要食物). '~**pot** *n* one in which ~ (9) is made or stored. 汤锅. **10** [C] base, support, or handle of an instrument, tool, etc: (仪器、器具等的)基部; 支撑; 把手: *the ~ of a rifle/plough/whip;* 步枪枪托(犁柄, 鞭子的把手); *the ~ of an anchor,* the crossbar. 锚杆. *lock, ~ and barrel,* (fig) completely. (喻)完全地; 整个地. **11** [C] lower part of a tree trunk. 树干的下部; 根茎. **12** [C] growing plant into which a graft is inserted. (插入接木的)台木. **13** (pl) framework supporting a ship while it is being built or repaired. (复)造船台; 修船架. *on the ~s,* under construction; in preparation. 在建造中; 在准备中; 在筹划中. **14** (pl) wooden framework with holes for the feet in which wrongdoers were formerly locked in a sitting position. (复)足枷; 足械(昔日的刑具). **15** [C] wide band of stiff linen worn around the neck by men in former times (like the modern tie). (昔日男子颈间围的)硬领(如同现代男人结领带). **16** sort of garden plant with single or double brightly coloured sweet-smelling flowers. 紫罗兰花(园艺植物之一种).

stock² /stɒk; stak/ *vt* [VP6A, 14] ~ *(with),* supply or equip with; have a stock of; keep in stock: 供应; 备置; 采办; 贮存: ~ *a shop with goods;* 供应商店货物; *well ~ed with the latest fashions.* 充分备有最新式样. *Do you ~ raincoats?* 你有雨衣存货吗? *He has a memory well ~ed with facts.* 他记得许多事实. ~**ist** /-ɪst; -ɪst/ *n* one who ~s (certain goods) for sale. 采办货物的商人.

stock·ade /stɒˈkeɪd; stakˈed/ *n* [C] line or wall of upright stakes, built as a defence. (作防御工事用的)围栅; 围桩. □ *vt* (usu *pp*) defend with a ~. (通常用过去分词)用围桩防御.

stock·in·ette /ˌstɒkɪˈnet; ˌstakɪnˈɛt/ *n* [U] elastic machine-made knitted fabric (esp as used for underclothing). (一种机器织成的)松紧内衣料.

stock·ing /ˈstɒkɪŋ; ˈstakɪŋ/ *n* [C] (often 常作 (**pair of**) ~**s**) tight-fitting covering of nylon, silk, cotton, wool, etc for the foot and leg, reaching to or above the knee. 长(统)袜. *in one's ~ feet,* wearing ~s or socks but not shoes. 穿袜而未穿鞋的. ⇨ **tights**.

stocky /ˈstɒkɪ; ˈstakɪ/ *adj* (**-ier, -iest**) (of persons, animals, plants) short, strong and stout. (指人、动植物)短粗而结实的; 矮而壮的. **stock·ily** *adv* in a ~ manner: 短粗而结实地; 矮而壮地: *a stockily built man.* 身材矮而结实的人.

stodge /stɒdʒ; stadʒ/ *n* [U] (sl) heavy and solid food. (俚)油腻而且难消化的食物. **stodgy** /ˈstɒdʒɪ; ˈstadʒɪ/ *adj* **1** (of food) heavy and solid: (指食物)油腻而且难消化的: *a stodgy meal.* 一顿油腻而且难消化的餐食. **2** (of books, etc) written in a heavy, uninteresting way (overweighted with facts, details, etc); (of persons) having a heavy personality; dull and unenterprising. (指书等)冗长无趣的(如事实、细节等过多的); (指人)头脑又笨的; 迟钝的; 无事业心的.

stoep /stup; stup/ *n* (S Africa) terraced veranda; porch or steps outside the front entrance of a house.

(南非)台式的走廊; 房屋正门外的门廊或台阶.

stoic /ˈstəʊɪk; ˈstoɪk/ *n* person who has great self-control, who bears pain and discomfort without complaint. 忍受痛苦而不适而不抱怨者; 坚忍不拔者. **sto·ical** /-kl; -kl/ *adj* of or like a ~. 高度自制的; 坚忍的. **sto·ically** /-klɪ; -klɪ/ *adv* **sto·icism** /ˈstəʊɪsɪzəm; ˈstoʊɪsɪzəm/ *n* [U] patient and uncomplaining endurance of suffering, etc. 坚忍的精神或操守.

stoke /stəʊk; stok/ *vt, vi* [VP6A, 15B, 2A, C] ~ *(sth) (up),* put (coal, etc) on the fire of (an engine, furnace, etc); attend to a furnace: 加(煤炭等)于(火车头、火炉等的)火上; 加~上; 司炉: ~ *(up) the furnace,* 添煤炭于炉; ~ *(up) twice a day.* 一天加煤两次. '~**hole/~hold** *nn* place where a ship's furnaces are ~d. (轮船上的)火舱; 锅炉室. ~**r** *n* workman who ~s a furnace, etc; mechanical device for feeding a furnace with fuel. 司炉; 照管火炉的工人; 加煤机; 加燃料机.

stole¹ /stəʊl; stol/ *n* **1** strip of silk or other material worn (round the neck with the ends hanging down in front) by priests of some Christian Churches during services. (某些基督教会之教士在宗教仪式中所佩的)圣带. ⇨ the illus at **vestment**. 参看 vestment 之插图. **2** woman's wrap worn over the shoulders. 妇女的披肩.

stole², **stolen** *pt, pp* of **steal**.

stolid /ˈstɒlɪd; ˈstalɪd/ *adj* not easily excited; slow to show the feelings. 不易激动的; 不动声色的; 神经麻木的; 呆头呆脑的. ~**ly** *adv* ~**ness,** **sto·lid·ity** /stɒˈlɪdətɪ; stɑˈlɪdətɪ/ *nn* [U].

stom·ach /ˈstʌmək; ˈstʌmək/ *n* **1** [C] bag-like part of the alimentary canal into which food passes to be digested: 胃: *It is unwise to swim on a full ~/to work on an empty ~.* 吃饱了游泳(枵腹工作)是不智的. ⇨ the illus at **alimentary**. 参看 alimentary 之插图. '~**ache** *n* pain in the ~ or the bowels. 胃痛; 肚子痛;腹痛. '~**pump** *n* pump with a flexible tube, inserted into the ~ through the mouth (for use, eg in a case of poisoning). 胃唧筒(经口腔伸入胃中, 为医疗用具). **2** [U] appetite. 胃口; 食欲; 爱好; 兴趣. *have no ~ for sth,* be disinclined to do or agree with sth, (because one disapproves of it): 对某事没有胃口(不感兴趣); 对某事不表赞同: *have no ~ for bull-fighting.* 对斗牛不感兴趣(不表赞同). □ *vt* [VP6A] (usu neg or interr) endure; put up with: (通常用于否定句与问句中)忍受; 容忍: *How could you ~ the violence in that film?* 你怎么能够忍受那部电影里的暴力呢?

stomp /stɒmp; stamp/ *vi* [VP2C] ~ *about,* stamp, tread, heavily. 用力地踏踩、踩、踩踏. □ *n* (jazz music for a) dance with a heavy beat. 重步舞; 重步舞(爵士)乐.

stone /stəʊn; ston/ *n* **1** [U] (often attrib 常作定语) solid mineral matter which is not metallic; rock (often with a defining word as prefix, as '*sand~, 'lime~*): (常用作定语)石; 岩石(常以一限定性质之词作为前缀, 如 sand~, lime~): *a wall made of ~;* 石砌的墙; ~ *walls/buildings;* 石墙(石屋); ~ *jars,* made of '~*ware,* ⇨ below; 粗陶罐(参看下列之 ~ware); *have a heart of ~,* (fig) be hard-hearted. (喻)铁石心肠; 硬心肠. **the 'S~ Age,** period of culture when weapons and tools were made of ~ (before the use of metals was known). 石器时代(人类使用金属以前的时期). '~**blind/~cold/~dead/~deaf/~sober** *adjj* completely blind, etc. 全盲的(冷透的; 完全死的; 完全聋的; 完全清醒的). '~**breaker** *n* person who breaks up ~, eg for road-making; machine for crushing ~. 打碎石块的人或机器; 碎石工人; 碎石机. '~**mason** *n* man who cuts, prepares and builds with ~. 石匠; 石工. '~**pit** *n* quarry for ~. 采石场; 石坑. '~**wall** *vt* (cricket) be excessively cautious when batting so that runs come slowly; (fig) (in Parliament) obstruct progress by making long speeches, etc. (板球)过度小心地打(使得分缓慢); (喻)(英国国会)借冗长演说等延宕议事. Hence,

由此产生。 **~-'walling** n, **~-'waller** n person given to this. 过度小心的击球员; (借演说等) 阻碍议事者。 **'~-ware** n [U] pottery made from clay and flint. 粗陶器, 石器。 **~-work** n [U] masonry; part(s) of a building made of ~. 石砌工;石造物;建筑物的石造部分。 **2** [C] piece of ~(1) of any shape, usu broken off: 石块; 碎石: *a road covered with* ~s. 碎石路; *a fall of* ~s *down a hillside*. 石块从山坡落下。 *leave no ~ unturned (to do sth)*, try every possible means (to do it). 千方百计; 想尽办法(做某事). *throw* ~s *at*, (fig) attack the character of: (喻)攻击…的品格: *Those who live in glass houses should not throw* ~s, (prov) 自己有缺点不应挑剔别人. *within a '~'s throw (of)*, very close (to). 很接近; 一掷之遥; 在短距离内。 **3** [C] (**precious**), jewel. 宝石;玉。 **4** [C] piece of a definite shape, for a special purpose (usu in compounds): 有确定形状,作特殊用途的石块,(通常用于复合词中): a '*grave*~, ⇨ **grave²**; 墓碑; '*stepping-*~s, ⇨ **step¹**; 踏脚石; '*tomb*~s, ⇨ **tomb**; 墓碑; '*mill*~s, ⇨ **mill¹**. 磨石。 **5** [C] sth round and hard like a ~, esp (a) the hard shell and nut or seed of such fruits as the apricot, peach, plum and cherry. (杏、桃、李及樱桃等的)硬壳;核。 ⇨ the illus at **fruit**. 参看 fruit 之插图。 **'~-fruit** n fruits of this kind. 核果。 **(b)** (usu compound fn '**hail**'. ~) small frozen drop of rain: 雹; 霰: *hail with* ~s *as big as peas*. 雹大如豌豆。 **(c)** small hard object that has formed in the bladder or kidney: 结石; 胆结石; 肾结石; 膀胱结石: *have an operation for* ~. 开刀取出结石。 '**gall**·~, **gall·stone**(1). **6** (not US; pl unchanged) unit of weight, 14 lb: 呎(重量单位,等于十四磅): *two* ~ *of flour*. 面粉二呎。 □ vt **1** [VP6A, 15A] throw ~s at: 向…投石头; 以石掷向: *Christian martyrs who were* ~d *to death*. 被石块击毙的基督教殉道者。 **2** [VP6A] take the ~s(5a) out of (fruit): 去(水果)之硬核; ~d *dates*. 去核的枣。 **~·less** adj (esp of ~-fruit, ⇨ **5(a)** above) without ~s. (尤指)无核的(参看上列第 5 义 (a))。 **stoned** adj (colloq) under the influence of (usu) soft drugs; very drunk. (口) 在(通常为)软性毒品支配之下的; 吸食大麻等后身不由己的; 烂醉的。

stony /'stəʊnɪ; ˈstonɪ/ adj (**-ier, -iest**) **1** having many stones: 多石的; ~ *soil/ground*; 石质土壤(多石之地); covered with stones: 覆有石块或碎石的; *a* ~ *path/ road*. 碎石小径(道路)。 **2** hard, cold and unsympathetic: 冷酷无情的: *a* ~ *heart*; 铁石心肠; '~·*hearted*; 铁石心肠的; *a* ~ *stare*; 冷冷的凝视; ~· *politeness*. 冷淡的礼貌。 **3** (sl) (俚) ~ (-'**broke**), completely without money; penniless. 一文不名的; 手无分文的。 **ston·ily** /-ɪlɪ; -əlɪ/ adv in a ~ (2) manner: 冷酷无情地; 铁石心肠地: *stonily polite*. 冷淡有礼的。

stood /stʊd; stʊd/ pt, pp of **stand²**.

stooge /stuːdʒ; studʒ/ n person who, in variety entertainment, is made fun of by a comedian; (colloq) person used as an assistant (to perform unpleasant jobs or duties that may incur blame, punishment, etc). 在杂要中为滑稽演员取笑的人; 笑把儿; 丑角助手; (口) 替身; 替罪者(执行不愉快或可能受到惩罚、指责等之任务者)。 □ vi ~ *for sb*, act as a ~. 做丑角助手; 做替身。

stool /stuːl; stul/ n **1** seat without a back or arms, usu for one person: 凳子(通常供一人坐): *sitting on* ~s *at the bar drinking beer*; 坐在酒馆凳子上喝啤酒; *a pi'ano*·~. 钢琴凳。 *fall between two* ~s, lose an opportunity through hesitating between two courses of action. 两头落空(在两种行动间犹豫不决而失去机会)。 **2** ('**foot**)~, low support on which to rest the feet. 脚凳(放脚的矮凳)。 **3** [U] (med) solid excrement: (医)粪便: *send a specimen of one's* ~s *to the doctor*, eg to be tested for amoebic infection. 送粪便抽样给医生检查。 **4** '~·**pigeon** n pigeon used as a decoy; (fig) person acting as a decoy, eg one employed by the police to trap a criminal. 媒鸽; 囮鸽; (喻)囮子(如警察雇用诱捕罪犯之人)。

stoop¹ /stuːp; stup/ vi, vt **1** [VP2A, C, 4A, 6A] bend the body forwards and downwards; bend the neck so that the head is forward and down: 屈身; 弯腰; 俯首; 低头: ~*ing with old age*; 因年老而弯腰; ~ *to pick sth up*; 俯身拾物; ~ *one's head to get into a car*. 俯首进入轿车。 **2** [VP3A] ~ *to sth*, (fig) lower oneself morally: (喻)降格;卑屈;堕落而做出愚蠢行为(而行诈欺): *He's a man who would* ~ *to anything*, who has no moral scruples. 他是一个没原则(没节操)的人。 □ n (usu *sing*) ~*ing* position of the body: (通常作单数)屈身; 伛偻: *walk with a* ~, as when very old or ill. 伛偻而行(如年老或生病时)。

stoop² /stuːp; stup/ n (in N America) porch or unroofed platform or set of steps at the entrance to a house. (北美)房屋入口处的门阶; 无顶之平台; 门廊; 台阶。 ⇨ **stoep**.

stop¹ /stɒp; stɑp/ n [C] **1** stopping or being stopped: 停止; 中止: *The train came to a* ~. 火车突然停了下来。 *This train goes from London to Leeds with only two* ~s. 这列火车从伦敦至里兹仅停两站。 *put a* ~ *to sth; bring sth to a* ~, cause it to ~ or end: 停止某事; 结束某事; 制止某事: *I'll put a* ~ *to this nonsense*. 我要制止这种胡闹的事情。 *Traffic was brought to a complete* ~. 交通完全停顿了。 **2** place at which buses, trams, etc stop regularly or (*re'quest*) when requested to do so: 公共汽车、电车等的车站; 招呼站(有人招呼时停车, 称 request ~): *Where's the nearest 'bus-*~? 离此最近的公共汽车站在哪里? **3** (music) key or lever (eg in a flute) for regulating pitch; row of pipes (in an organ) providing tones of one quality; knob or lever working such a row of pipes. (音乐)音栓。 ⇨ the illus at **church, key**. 参看 church, key 之插图。 *pull out all the* ~s, (fig) appeal to all the emotions; make a great effort. (喻)竭尽所能; 全力以赴。 **4** mark of punctuation, esp *full* ~ (.). 标点符号; (尤指)句点(.)。 □ **App 9**. 参看附录九。 **5** (in a camera) device for regulating the size of the aperture through which light reaches the lens. (照相机的)光圈快门。 **6** (in phonetics) consonant produced by the sudden release of air which has been held back (eg /p, b, k, g, t, d/). (语音学)塞音(如 /p, b, k, g, t, d/)。 **7** device that stops the movement of sth at a fixed point, eg a peg of wood to prevent an ill-fitting window from rattling. 塞子; 制子; 阻塞物(如防止窗户被风吹动时发出声响的木栓等)。 **8** (compounds) (复合词) **'~-cock** n valve inserted in a pipe by which the flow of liquid or gas through the pipe can be regulated: (水管或煤气管上的)阀门;管制阀;制栓;开关旋塞: *A water-pipe has burst—where's the* ~*cock?* 一条水管爆裂了——制水栓在哪里? '**~-gap** n temporary substitute. 临时代替的人或物。 '**~-press** n [U] (not US) latest news inserted in a newspaper already on the printing machines. (不用于美国) 报纸付印中临时加插的最新消息。 '**~-watch** n watch with a hand that can be started and stopped when desired, used to time events such as races to a fraction of a second. (赛跑等用的)跑表; 停表; 计秒表。 '**~-page** /'stɒpɪdʒ; 'stɑpɪdʒ/ n [C] **1** condition of being stopped up, ⇨ **stop²(6)**; obstruction. 被阻塞的状况; 阻碍。 **2** stopping (7): 停止; 扣留; 截断; 拒绝给予: ~*page of leave/pay*, (esp in the armed forces, eg as a form of punishment). 假期(薪饷)的停止(尤指军中作为一种惩罚等者)。 **3** interruption of work in a factory, etc as the result of strike action). (工厂等因罢工等而造成的)停工。 '**~·per** n object which fits into and closes an opening, esp the mouth of a bottle or pipe; (US) plug(1). 塞子; 瓶塞; 管塞。 ⇨ the illus at **decanter**. 参看 decanter 之插图。 *put a* ~*per/the* ~*pers on (sth)*, (fig) bring it to

an end; suppress it. (喻)停止或结束(某物);阻止或压制(某事物)。

stop[2] /stɒp/ *vt, vi* (**-pp-**) **1** [VP6A] put an end to the movement or progress of (a person, thing, activity, etc): 停止(人、物、活动等)的动作或进展: ~ *a car/a train/a runaway horse.* 停住汽车、火车、脱缰之马。*The earthquake* ~*ped all the clocks.* 地震使所有的钟都停了。**2** [VP6A, C, 14] ~ *sb (from) (doing sth),* prevent; hinder: 阻止某人(做某事);妨碍;制止: *What can* ~ *our going* ~ *us from going if we want to go?* 如果我们要去,什么能阻止我们(使我们不能成行)呢? *Can't* ~ *the child (from) getting into mischief?* 你不能制止那孩子恶作剧吗? *He will certainly go──there's no one to* ~ *him.* 他一定会去──没有人能阻止他。**3** [VP6A, C] leave off; discontinue (doing sth): 中止(做某事);停止: ~ *work.* 停止工作。~*ped talking.* 我们中止谈话。*Why doesn't he* ~ *beating his wife?* 他为什么不停止打他的妻子? *S~ it!* (imper) ~ doing that (sth disliked or disapproved of). (祈使)停止!不要做了! **4** [VP2A, 3A, 4A] ~ *(at),* break off; discontinue: 中断;停下来: *The rain has* ~*ped.* 雨已停了。*The clock/His heart has* ~*ped.* 钟已停了(他的心脏不再跳动了)。*It has* ~*ped raining.* 雨已停止。*We* ~*ped to have a rest.* 我们停下来休息一下。*We* ~*ped (in order) to talk.* 我们停下来以便谈话。Cf 参较 *We* ~*ped talking.* 我们停止了谈话。**5** [VP2A, 3A, 4A] ~ *(at),* come to rest; halt: 停下;停住;止住: *The train* ~*ped.* 火车停下了。*Does this train* ~ *at Crewe?* 这列火车在克鲁停吗? ~ *dead,* ~ *suddenly.* 突然停止。~ *short at sth,* limit one's actions, etc: 限制在某方面的行动等;停就某事: *Will our neighbours* ~ *short at war?* 我们的邻国会停止战争吗? **6** [VP6A, 15A, B] ~ *sth (up),* fill or close (a hole, opening, etc): 堵塞;填塞;阻塞(洞,口等): ~ *a leak in a pipe;* 塞住管子的漏洞; ~ *up a mouse-hole;* 堵塞老鼠洞; *have a tooth* ~*ped,* have a cavity filled; 填补牙洞; ~ *one's ears,* (fig) refuse to listen; 阻不听; ~ *the way,* prevent progress. 阻碍发展。**7** [VP6A, 14] cut off; keep back or refuse to give (sth normally supplied): 截断;扣留;拒绝给予(通常供应之物): ~ *(payment of) a cheque,* order the bank not to cash it; 止付支票(通知银行不予兑现); ~ *sb's wages.* 扣发某人薪水。*The bank has* ~*ped payment,* is unable to meet its obligations. 该银行已无力支付。~ *sth out of sth,* deduct sth from (wages, salary, etc). 从(工资/薪金等)中扣除某款项。**8** [VP2A, B, (colloq) stay: (口)停留;待在;逗留;住: ~ *at home.* 待在家里。*Are you* ~*ping at this hotel?* 你住在这家旅社吗? ~ *off (at/in),* break a journey for a short period: 中途稍作停留: ~ *off at a store to buy sth.* 半路上在一家商店购物。~ *off/over (at/in),* break a journey for a stay: 中途在某处停留或小住: ~ *off overnight in Edinburgh.* 中途在艾丁堡停留过夜。

~-over *n* [C] break in a journey; place where one does this; (attrib): 中途停留;中途停留之处;(用作定语): '~*-over ticket,* one that permits a journey to be broken in this way. 准许中途下车(下机、下船等)的票。~ *up (late),* stay up, not go to bed until late. 熬夜;迟睡。**9** (music) produce desired note(s) by pressing fingers on strings (eg of a violin), or over holes (eg in a flute). (音乐)按弦;按孔(以发出所要的声音)。**~·ping** *n* filling for a dental cavity. 补牙洞之填补物。⇨ **6** above. 参看上列第6义。

stor·age /'stɔ:rɪdʒ; 'stɔrɪdʒ/ *n* [U] (space used for, money paid for) the storing of goods: (货物的)贮存;贮藏;贮藏所;仓库;仓库费;贮藏费用;栈租;栈费: *put one's furniture in* ~, 把家具存起来; *keep fish in cold* ~; 冷藏鱼; (attrib) (用作定语): '~ *tanks,* eg for oil; 贮存槽(如贮油槽); '~ *heater,* electric radiator which stores heat (accumulated during off-peak periods). 储热电暖炉(可在非高峰用电时贮存热能者)。

store /stɔ:(r); stɔr/ *n* **1** [C] quantity or supply of sth kept for use as needed: 贮藏;贮积;储备;储蓄: *lay in*

~*s of coal for the winter;* 贮藏煤以备过冬; *have a good* ~ *of provisions in the house.* 家里贮存有丰富的食物。**2** [U] *in* ~, (a) kept ready for use; for future use: 准备着;备用的; 供给来用的: *That's a treat in* ~, *a pleasure still to come.* 那是往后还会再有的乐事。(b) destined (for); coming to: 必将发生的; 就要来到的; 注定的: *Who knows what the future has in* ~ *for us?* 谁知道我们将来注定会如何? **3** (pl) goods, etc of a particular kind, or for a special purpose: (复)(某一种类或作特殊用途的)货物;物品: *naval and military* ~*s;* 海陆军的军需品; *marine* ~*s* (but note: ,*marine-*'~ *dealer*). 船舶用品(注意: ,*marine-*~ *dealer* 船舶用品商)。**4** [C] '~(**-house**), place where goods are kept; warehouse: 仓库;栈房: *The book is a* ~*-house of information.* 那本书是知识的宝库。'~*-room* n one in which household supplies are kept. 贮藏室。**5** [C] (chiefly US but ⇨ **6** below) shop: (主美,但参看下列第6义)商店: *a* '*clothing* ~; 服装店; ~ *clothes,* 成衣(非定做或量身裁制者)。**6** (pl) shop selling many varieties of goods: (复)百货店: *the big department* ~*s of London;* 伦敦的大百货公司; *the ,Army and ,Navy S~s;* 陆军及海军的百货店; *a general* ~*s,* (esp) village shop selling a variety of goods. (尤指)乡村的百货店;杂货店。⇨ also *chain-*~ at **chain**(4). **7** [U] *set great/little/no/not much* ~ *by,* consider of great/little, etc value or importance. 重视(忽视);不重视;不太重视)。□ *vt* [VP6A, 15B] ~ *sth (up),* **1** collect and keep for future use: *Do all squirrels* ~ *up food for the winter?* 是不是所有的松鼠都为冬季储备食物? **2** put (furniture, etc) in a warehouse, etc, for safe keeping. 把(家具等)寄存某货栈等以妥善保存。**3** furnish, equip, supply: 供给;供应;装备: *a mind well* ~*d with facts.* 见闻广博的人。

storey (US = **story**) /'stɔ:rɪ; 'stɔrɪ/ *n* (pl ~s, (US) **-ries**) floor or level in a building: 建筑物的一层: *a house of two* ~*s,* with rooms on the ground floor and one floor upstairs. 二层楼的房屋。**-storeyed** (US = **stor·ied**) /-'stɔ:rɪd; -'stɔrɪd/ *adj* having the number of ~s indicated by the prefixed number: 有若干层楼的(数字加于其前): *a six-*~*ed building.* 六层楼的建筑。

stor·ied /'stɔ:rɪd; 'stɔrɪd/ *adj* (liter) made famous in legend or stories: (文)在传说中或故事中有名的: *the* ~ *Rhine.* 历史上有名的莱茵河。

stork /stɔ:k; stɔrk/ *n* large, long-legged, usu white wading-bird (some of which build their nests on the tops of high buildings): 鹳(长腿大涉禽,通常为白色,有些筑巢于高楼顶部)。⇨ the illus at **water.** 参看 water 之插图。

storm /stɔ:m; stɔrm/ *n* **1** [C] occasion of violent weather conditions: 风暴;暴风雨;暴风雪;狂风暴雨;狂暴天气: *a* '*thunder-/'wind-/'rain-/'dust-/'sand-*~; 雷雨(风暴);暴雨;尘暴;大风沙; *cross the Channel in a* ~. 在暴风雨中渡过英吉利海峡。*The forecast says there will be* ~*s.* 气象报告说将有暴风雨。*a* ~ *in a teacup,* much excitement about sth trivial. 大惊小怪。'~-*beaten* adj damaged by ~s. 被暴风雨摧毁的。'~-*bound* adj unable to continue a journey, voyage, etc, unable to go out, because of ~s. 旅途、行程等为暴风雨所阻的。'~-*centre* n centre of a ~ or (fig) of a disturbance or trouble. 风暴中心; (喻)纷扰或骚乱的中心。'~-*cloud* n heavy rain-cloud accompanying, or showing the likelihood of, a ~. 暴风云(伴随或预示暴风雨的密云)。'~-*cone* /-*signal* n one hoisted as a warning of high wind. 风暴球(风暴信号)。'~-*lantern* n one for use outdoors, made so that the light is well protected from wind. 防风灯。'~-*proof* adj able to resist ~s. 防风暴的;抗风暴的。'~-*tossed* adj damaged or blown about by ~s. 被暴风雨损坏的; 在暴风雨中飘摇的。**2** violent outburst of feeling: 情感的猛烈发作: *a* ~ *of protests/cheering/applause/abuse.* (热烈的)欢呼; 热烈的喝彩; 严厉的斥责。*bring a* ~ *about one's ears,* do or say sth that rouses strong

opposition, indignation, etc. 做或说某事而引起强烈反对、愤慨等。 **3** *take by* ~, capture by a violent and sudden attack. 袭取;强夺;攻占。 **~-troops** *n pl* troops trained for violent attacks. 突击队。 **~-trooper** *n* one of these. 突击队员。 □ *vi, vt* **1** [VP2A, 3A] ~ *(at)*, give violent expression to anger; shout angrily. 狂怒; 咆哮。 **2** [VP15A, B, 2C] force (a way) into a building, etc; [VP6A] capture (a place) by sudden and violent attack: 强入建筑物等;闯入;突击(某地);夺取;攻占: The men ~ed *(their way) into the fort /*~*ed the fort*. 士兵们猛攻后进入(袭取了)那座堡垒。 **~-y** *adj* **(-ier, -iest) 1** marked by strong wind, heavy rain or snow or hail: 有暴风雨的;有暴风雪(雹)的: *a* ~*y weather /* 暴风雨的天气; *a* ~*y night / crossing*. 暴风雨之夜(暴风雨中横渡)。 **2** marked by strong feelings of indignation, anger, etc: 感情激烈的;狂怒的;愤怒的: *a* ~*y discussion / meeting*; 激烈的讨论(会议); ~*y scenes during the debate*. 辩论时的激烈情景。 **~·ily** /ɪlɪ; -əlɪ/ *adv*

story[1] /'stɔːrɪ; 'stɔrɪ/ *n* [C] (*pl* **-ries**) **1** account of past events: 事迹;轶事;史话: *the* ~ *of Columbus*; 哥伦布的事迹; *stories of ancient Greece*. 古希腊史话。 **2** account of imaginary events: 小说;故事;传奇: *a 'ghost* ~; 鬼故事; *a children's* '~*-book*; 一本儿童故事书: *a* ~*-book ending*, a happy one (as in most stories for children). 愉快的结局。 *The* ~ *goes that* ..., People are saying that .... 传说…;据闻…。 '~*-teller n* person who tells stories. 讲故事者。 **3** (journalism) any descriptive article in a newspaper; an event, situation, etc suitable for such an article. (新闻)(报纸上的)报导;记事;记述;适合报导的事件、情况等。 **4** untrue statement: 谎言;假话: *Don't tell stories, Tom*. 汤姆,不要扯谎。

story[2] /'stɔːrɪ; 'stɔrɪ/ *n* ⇨ **storey**.

stoup /stuːp; stup/ *n* **1** (old use) drinking-vessel; flagon. (旧用法)酒杯; (有把手的)酒瓶。 **2** stone basin for holy water on the wall of a church or near the porch. (宗教)圣水钵。

stout /staʊt; staʊt/ *adj* **1** strong, thick, not easily broken or worn out: 粗壮的;坚固的;结实的: ~ *shoes for mountain-climbing*. 爬山用的坚固的鞋子。 **2** determined and brave: 坚决的;勇敢的;刚毅的: *offer a* ~ *resistance to the enemy*; 对敌人作顽强的抵抗; *a* ~ *fellow*; 刚毅的人; *a* ~ *heart*. 勇敢。 Hence, 由此产生, '~-'**hearted** *adj* courageous. 勇敢的;有勇气的。 **3** (of a person) rather fat; tending to fatness: 肥(胖)相当肥的;要发胖的;有发胖趋势的: *She's growing too* ~ *to walk far*. 她胖起来了,不能走远路。 □ *n* [U] strongest kind of brown beer. 最烈的黑啤酒。 '~·ly *adv* ~·**ness** *n*

stove[1] /stəʊv; stov/ *n* [U] closed apparatus burning wood, coal, gas, oil or other fuel, used for warming rooms, cooking, etc. 火炉;火炉;暖炉。 '~-**pipe** *n* pipe for carrying off smoke from a ~. 烟囱;烟筒。

stove[2] /stəʊv; stov/ ⇨ **stave**[2].

stow /stəʊ; sto/ *vt* [VP6A, 15A, B] ~ *sth (away);* ~ *sth into / with sth*, pack, esp carefully and closely: 装;载;堆置;包装(尤指小心而紧密地): ~ *cargo in a ship's holds*; 装货物于船舱中; ~ *things away in the attic*; 把东西堆置在阁楼上; ~ *clothes into a trunk /* ~ *a trunk with clothes*. 把衣服装在衣箱中。 '~-**away** *n* person who hides himself in a ship or aircraft (at least until after it starts) in order to make a journey without paying. 偷乘者;藏匿于轮船或飞机中以期免费搭乘者。

straddle /'strædl; 'strædl/ *vt, vi* **1** [VP6A] sit or stand across (sth) with the legs widely separated: 跨; 骑;叉腿坐或站于(某物)上: ~ *a ditch / a horse / a fence*. 跨在沟(座位,马,栅栏)上。 **2** [VP2A] stand with the legs wide apart. 叉腿站立;跨立。

strafe /strɑːf *US*: streɪf; streɪf/ *vt* [VP6A] (口) **1** bombard. 轰击;炮轰。 **2** punish; scold. 处罚;斥责。

straggle /'strægl; 'strægl/ *vi* [VP2A, C] **1** grow, spread, in an irregular or untidy manner: 蔓延;蔓生; 散漫: *a straggling village*; 房舍散漫的村落; *vines straggling over the fences*. 蔓生于篱笆上的蔓藤。 **2** drop behind while on the march; stray from the main body. 落伍;落后;掉队。 **strag·gler** /'stræglə(r); 'stræglɚ/ *n* person who ~s(2). 落伍者;掉队者。 **strag·gly** /'stræglɪ; 'stræglɪ/ *adj* straggling. 蔓延的;散漫的;落伍的。

straight[1] /streɪt; stret/ *adj* **1** without a bend or curve; extending in one direction only: 直的;呈直线的;向一个方向延伸的: *a* ~ *line / road*; 直线(直路); ~ *hair*, with no curls in it. 直直的头发。 **2** parallel to (sth else, esp the horizon); level: 与(他物,尤指地平线)平行的;水平的: *The picture* ~. 把这幅画放正。 *Is my hat on* ~? 我的帽子(戴得)正不正? **3** in good order; tidy: 井然有序的;整齐的: *put a room* ~. 把房间收拾整齐。 *put sth* ~, make it tidy: 把某地弄整齐: *Please put your desk* ~ *before you leave the office*. 离开办公室前,请把你的办公桌整理好。 *put the record* ~, give an accurate account of events, etc. 正确记载事件等。 **4** (of a person, his behaviour, etc) honest, frank, upright: (指人,其行为等)诚实的;坦白的;正直的: *give a* ~ *answer to a question*, answer frankly; 坦白回答某问题; *keep* ~, avoid wrongdoing, live as a good citizen. 安分守己;奉公守法。 *He is perfectly* ~ *in all his dealings*. 他在所有的交易中绝对诚实。 *His wife will keep him* ~ (= help him to live honestly) *when he is released from prison*. 他出狱后,他的妻子将帮助他改过自新。 ⇨ **straight**[2](4). **5** (colloq) (of a person) conventional; heterosexual. (口)(指人)守习俗的;异性恋的。 **6** (phrases) (短语) **a** ~ *fight*, (in politics) one in which there are only two candidates. (政治)只有两人参加的竞选。 **a** ~ *play*, an ordinary drama (contrasted with variety). 普通的戏剧(与'杂要'相对)。 **a** ~ *tip*, (eg about the likely winner of a race, an investment in shares), one (said to come) from a direct and reliable source. 可靠情报(如有关可能获胜的马,对股票的投资等)。忍住不笑;板起面孔。 *vote the* ~ *ticket*, ⇨ *ticket*(3). **7** (of alcoholic drinks) neat, ie without added (soda-)water, etc: (指酒类)纯的;未加水或汽水等的: *Two* ~ *whiskies, please*. 请来两杯不加水威士忌。 □ *n* [C] (colloq) conventional or heterosexual person. (口)守习俗或异性恋的人。 ~*en* /'streɪtn; 'stretn/ *vt, vi* ~*en (out / up)*, [VP6A, 15B, 2A, C] make or become ~: (使)变直; (使)变平正; (使)变整洁: ~*en a piece of wire / one's tie / one's skirt*. 把铁丝(领带,裙子)拉直。 ~**ness** *n*

straight[2] /streɪt; stret/ *adv* **1** directly; not in a curve or at an angle: 直地;笔直地: *The smoke rose* ~ *up*. 烟笔直地上升。 *Keep* ~ *on*. 一直往前走。 *Look* ~ *ahead*. 向前直视。 *The drunken man couldn't walk* ~. 那醉汉无法向前直走。 *Can you shoot* ~, aim accurately? 你能瞄准得很正吗? **2** by a direct route; without turning aside; without delay: 由直路;不拐弯;不延误;直接地: *Come* ~ *home*. 直接回家去。 *He went* ~ *to Rome without staying in Paris*. 他直接前往罗马,未在巴黎停留。 *He went* ~ *from school into the navy*. 他一毕业就加入海军。 *come* ~ *to the point*, make a prompt and clear statement of what is meant, wanted, etc. 直截了当地说;开门见山地说。 **3** ~ *away / off*, immediately. 立即;马上。 ~ *out*, without hesitation or deliberation: 未犹豫地;直言地: *I told him* ~ *out that I thought he was mistaken*. 我老实告诉他,我认为他错了。 **4** *go* ~, (fig) live an honest life (esp after having been dishonest). (喻)正直地生活;(尤指)改过自新;弃邪归正。

straight[3] /streɪt; stret/ *n* (usu 通常作 *the* ~) condition of being straight; straight part of sth, esp the final part of a track or race-course, near the winning-post: 直;平直;(事物的)平直部分;(尤指)跑道接近终点的)直线跑道: *The two horses were together as they*

entered the final ~. 这两匹马同时进入最后的直线跑道。

straight·for·ward /ˌstreɪtˈfɔːwəd; ˌstretˈforwəd/ *adj* **1** honest; without evasion: 诚实的; 坦白的: *a* ~ *explanation.* 坦率的解释。 **2** easy to understand or do: 易懂的; 易做的: *written in* ~ *language;* 用浅易文字写成的; *a* ~ *problem in algebra.* 一道容易的代数题。 ~·**ly** *adv*

straight·way /ˈstreɪtweɪ; ˈstretˌwe/ *adv* (archaic) at once; immediately. (古)立即; 马上。

strain[1] /streɪn; stren/ *n* **1** [C, U] condition of being stretched; force exerted: 拉紧; 扯紧; 紧张; 加力; 拉力; 应变: *The rope broke under the* ~. 绳子被拉断了。 *Engineers calculate the* ~*s and stresses of a bridge.* 工程师们计算桥梁的应变和应力。 *What is the breaking* ~ *of this cable, the* ~ *that will break it?* 这铁缆的断裂应变变如何? **2** [C, U] sth that tests and strains one's powers; severe demand on one's strength, etc: 考验能力之事物; 需要用劲、使力、费神等之事物: *the* ~ *of sleepless nights.* 连夜不眠的辛劳。 *The payment of the lawyer's bills was a great* ~ *on my resources.* 支付律师费是我经济上一项很大的负担。 *Do you suffer from the* ~ *of modern life?* 现代生活使你感到紧张吗? *He has been under severe* ~. 他一直处于极度紧张的状态。 **3** [U] exhaustion; fatigue: 劳累; 竭尽; 疲惫: *suffering from mental/nervous* ~. 精神(神经)疲劳过度。 **4** [C] sprain; injury caused by twisting a joint, etc. 扭筋; 脱臼; 扭伤关节等。 **5** [poet; usu *pl*] music, song, verse (of the kind indicated): (诗; 通常用复数)(某种指明的)音乐; 歌; 诗: *the* ~*s of an organ;* 风琴奏出的音乐; *the martial* ~*s of the band of the Royal Marines.* 皇家海军陆战队乐队奏出的军乐。 **6** [C] manner of speaking or writing: 谈话或书写的方式; 语调; 笔调; 风格: *in a lofty/cheerful/dismal* ~; 以高傲(愉快,忧郁)的语调; *and much more in the same* ~, 与同样调子说了许多其他的事。 **7** tendency in a person's character: 性格的倾向; 气质; 性情: *There is a* ~ *of insanity in the family/of mysticism in her.* 一家人都有疯癫的倾向(她有神秘的气质)。 **8** breed (of animals, insects, etc); line of descent: (动物、昆虫等的)种; 血统: ~*s of mosquitoes that are resistant to DDT;* 对 DDT 有抗力的各种蚊虫; *a spaniel of good* ~. 一只有优良血统的长毛垂耳小狗。

strain[2] /streɪn; stren/ *vt, vi* **1** [VP6A, 15A, 3A] stretch tightly by pulling *(at):* 拉紧; 扯紧; 张紧: ~ *a rope to breaking-point;* 把绳子拉紧到快断的地步; *a dog* ~*ing at its lead.* 一条使劲拖拽皮带的狗。 **2** [VP6A, 16A] make the greatest possible use of; exert one's powers: 尽量利用; 竭尽全力: ~ *every nerve (to do sth),* do one's utmost; 竭尽全力(做某事): ~ *one's ears/voice,* look/listen/speak to the best of one's power. 全神贯注地看看(聚精会神地听),声嘶力竭地说)。 ⇨ **3** below. 参看下列第 3 义。 **3** [VP6A] injure or weaken by ~ing(2): 因过分用力而损伤; 耗损; 耗竭: ~ *a muscle;* 因过分用力而使肌肉受损伤; ~ *one's heart,* injure it by over-exertion; 因过劳而损伤心脏; ~ *one's eyes,* by using them too much, or on small print, in poor light, etc; 耗损目力(因过度使用、看小字、光线不佳等); ~ *one's voice,* by speaking or singing too long or too loudly. 嗓子变哑(因说话太多,或唱得太久或太大声等)。 **4** [VP2A, 3A] ~ *(at/on),* make an intense effort: 努力; 奋力: *The wrestlers* ~*ed and struggled.* 摔角者奋力扭斗。 *We* ~*ed at the oars.* 我们用力划桨。 ~ *after effects,* make exaggerated efforts to get effects: 为求效果而矫揉造作: *There is no* ~*ing after effects in this writer's work.* 这位作家的作品不矫揉造作。 **5** [VP6A1] (fig) stretch the meaning of; force beyond a limit or what is right: (喻)曲解; 歪曲; 滥用: ~ *the belief/credulity of one's listeners,* ask too much of it; 过分利用听众的信心(轻信); ~ *one's authority/rights,* apply them in a way that is beyond what is allowable or reasonable; 滥用权威(权利): ~ *the meaning of a word.* 曲解一词的意义。 **6** [VP15A] (liter) hold tightly;

squeeze: (文)紧握; 紧抱: *She* ~*ed the boy to her bosom.* 她把那男孩紧搂在怀中。 **7** [VP6A, 15B] ~ *(off/out),* pass (liquid) through a cloth, or a network of fine wire, etc; separate solid matter in this way: 滤(某种液体); 过滤: ~ *the soup;* 滤汤; ~ *off the water from the vegetables.* 滤去青菜中的水。 **8** ~ *at sth,* be too scrupulous or hesitant about accepting sth. 对某事过度顾忌或迟疑。 **9** ~*ed (pp)* (esp of feelings and behaviour) forced; unnatural; as if forced: (尤指感情及行为)勉强的;不自然的;似出于被迫的: ~*ed cordiality;* 不自然的热诚; *a* ~*ed laugh.* 勉强的笑。 ~*ed relations,* marked by loss of patience, irritability, risk of quarrelling: (彼此间)紧张的关系(彼此失去耐心, 易怒, 隐伏争吵危机等)。 ~*er n* sieve or other device by means of which solid matter is separated from liquid: 滤器; 滤网: *a 'tea-* ~, for keeping back tea-leaves when tea is poured out from a teapot. 滤茶具; 滤茶器。

strait[1] /streɪt; stret/ *adj* (old use) narrow (现用法) 狭窄的 (rare except in: 罕用,仅见于: ~ *gate,* 窄门, ⇨ **Matt 7: 14.** 参看新约马太福音第 7 章第 14 节)。 '~-**jacket,** long-sleeved jacket used to bind the arms of a mentally ill person to the body and prevent him from struggling; (用以拘束疯人的)拘束衣(袖特长,可将其手臂与身体缚起,以防其挣扎); (喻)阻止生长或发展之事物; 约束; 束缚。 ~-'**laced** *adj* severely virtuous; having a strict attitude towards moral questions; puritanical. (在道德和行为方面)极端拘谨的。 ~·**en** /ˈstreɪtn̩; ˈstretn̩/ *vt* (usu in *pp*) (通常用过去分词) *in* ~*ed circumstances,* in poverty. 在穷困中。

strait[2] /streɪt; stret/ *n* **1** narrow passage of water connecting two seas or two large bodies of water (*pl* or *sing* with proper names): 海峡; 峡 (与专有名词连用时,用复数或单数皆可): *the S~s of Gibraltar;* 直布罗陀海峡; *the Magellan S~.* 麦哲伦海峡。 **2** (usu *pl*) trouble; difficulty: (通常用复数)困难; 窘迫: *be in financial* ~*s;* 经济困难; *in great* ~*s,* in a state of great difficulty. 在极度困难中。

strand[1] /strænd; strænd/ *n* (poet or rhet) sandy shore of a lake, sea or river. (诗或修辞)湖、海或河的沙岸; 滨; 矶。 □ *vi, vt* **1** [VP6A, 2A] (of a ship) (cause to) run aground. (指船)(使)搁浅。 **2** *be (left)* ~*ed,* (of a person) be left without means of transport, in a difficult position, without money or friends: (指人)陷于无交通工具的情况; 难以行动; 陷入困境; 处于无钱或无友的境地; 束手无策: *be* ~*ed in a foreign country.* 在异国陷入困境。

strand[2] /strænd; strænd/ *n* [C] **1** any of the threads, hairs, wires, etc twisted together into a rope or cable, or in a textile material; tress of hiar. (线、毛发、铁丝等绞成绳或缆等的)一股; 缕; 条; 一束发。 **2** (fig) line of development (in a story, etc): (喻)(故事等)发展的线索; 情节: *May I pick up one* ~ *in that narrative?* 我可以先谈该故事的某一情节吗?

strange /streɪndʒ; strendʒ/ *adj* (-r, -st) **1** not previously known, seen, felt or heard of; (by this reason) surprising: 前所未知、未见、未觉察或未听说过的; 奇怪的; 奇异的; 奇妙的; 奇特的: *hear a* ~ *noise;* 听到一奇异的声音; *in a* ~ *land.* 在陌生之地。 ~ *to say* (= unusual) *clothes you're wearing!* 你穿的衣服真新奇啊! *Truth is* ~ *than fiction.* 实际人生比虚构的故事还离奇。 *She says she feels* ~, not in her usual condition, perhaps rather dizzy, etc. 她说她觉得不大舒服。 ~ *to say ...,* It is surprising that .... 说来奇怪…。 **2** (pred) (用作表语) ~ *to sth,* fresh or unaccustomed to: 对…感到陌生或不习惯的: *The village boy was* ~ *to city life.* 那村童不惯于城市生活。 *He is still* ~ *to the work,* has not yet learnt his new job. 他对这项工作仍很生疏。 ~·**ly** *adv* ~·**ness** *n*

stran·ger /ˈstreɪndʒə(r); ˈstrendʒə/ *n* person one does not know; person in a place or with a company that he does not know: 陌生人; 异国人; 异乡人; 外地人。 *The dog always barks at* ~*s.* 这只狗总向陌生人吠叫。 *You're*

quite a **~**, (colloq) It's a long time since we met. (口) 你真是稀客(很久不见了；久违). I am a **~** in this town, do not know my way about. 这城市我很陌生(我不认得此地的路). He is no **~** to misfortune, (fig) has had experience of it. (喻)他饱经不幸.

strangle /'stræŋgl; 'stræŋgl/ vt [VP6A] kill by squeezing the throat of; hinder the breathing of: 扼杀；勒死；绞死；使窒息；阻塞…的呼吸: This stiff collar is strangling me, is so tight that it squeezes my neck. 这硬领扼住了我的颈子. '**~·hold** n (usu fig) deadly grip: (通常作喻)致命的紧扼；压制；束缚: The new tariffs have put a **~hold** on our trade with them. 这项新关税增加了我们同他们贸易上的束缚. **stran·gu·la·tion** /ˌstræŋgju'leɪʃn; ˌstræŋgjə'leʃən/ n [U] strangling or being **~**d. 扼杀；勒死；绞死；窒息.

strap /stræp; stræp/ n strip of leather or other flexible material (often with a buckle) to fasten things together or to keep sth (eg a wrist-watch) in place. 带；皮带；吊带(通常有扣,用于束绑或使某物位置固定). '**~-hanger** n standing passenger in a bus, train, etc who holds on to a **~** with a loop (hanging from the roof) when all the seats are occupied. (公共汽车、火车等上拉着吊带的)站客. □ vt (**-pp-**) 1 [VP6A, 15B] **~ sth (on/up)**, fasten or hold in place with a **~**: 用带捆扎,用带束起或固定: **~** on a wrist-watch; 带上手表; **~** up a suitcase, using **~**s and buckles. 扣紧手提箱(扣上皮带的扣环). 2 [VP6A] beat with a **~**. 用带抽打. '**~·ping** adj big, tall, healthy-looking: 高大健壮的；魁伟的: a **~ping** girl. 高大健壮的女孩.

strata /'strɑːtə US: 'streɪtə; 'stretə/ pl of **stratum**. stratum 之复数.

strat·agem /'strætədʒəm; 'strætədʒəm/ n [C, U] (use of a) trick or device to deceive sb (esp the enemy in war). 计谋；诡计(尤指战时用以诱骗敌人者).

stra·tegic /strə'tiːdʒɪk; strə'tidʒɪk/, **stra·tegi·cal** /-kl; -kl/ adj of, by, serving the purpose of, strategy: 战略的；借战略的；合于战略的: a **~** retreat; 战略性撤退; a **~** link in a line of defence; 防线上的一个战略环节; **~** bombing, eg of industrial areas and communications; 战略性轰炸(如轰炸工业区或通讯设施); **~** materials, those essential for war. 战略物资. **stra·tegi·cally** /-klɪ; -klɪ/ adv **stra·tegics** n [U] science or art of strategy. 兵学；兵法；军事学.

strat·egy /'strætədʒɪ; 'strætədʒɪ/ n [U] the art of planning operations in war, esp of the movements of armies and navies into favourable positions for fighting; skill in managing any affair. 战略；军略；策略；谋略. ⇨ **tactic**(2). **strat·egist** /-dʒɪst; -dʒɪst/ n person skilled in strategy. 战略家；谋略家.

strat·ify /'strætɪfaɪ; 'strætəˌfaɪ/ vt, vi (pt, pp **-fied**) 1 [VP6A] arrange in strata: 使成层；层叠；按层排列: stratified rock. 成层岩. English society is highly stratified. 英国社会层次分明. 2 [VP2A] form into strata. 形成层次. **strat·ifi·ca·tion** /ˌstrætɪfɪ'keɪʃn; ˌstrætəfɪ'keʃən/ n arrangement in strata. 成层；层叠；层化.

stratified rock

strato·sphere /'strætəsfɪə(r); 'strætəˌsfɪr/ n layer of atmospheric air between about 10 and 60 km above

the earth's surface. 平流层；同温层(距地球表面约10至60公里之间的大气层).

stra·tum /'strɑːtəm US: 'streɪtəm; 'stretəm/ n (pl **-ta** /-tə; -tə/) horizontal layer of rock, etc in the earth's crust; social class or division: (地壳的)岩层；地层; (社会的)阶层: Students in Britain come from various strata in society. 英国的学生来自社会各阶层.

straw /strɔː; strɔ/ n 1 [U] dry cut stalks of wheat, barley, rice and other grains, as material for making hats, mats, etc or bedding for cattle, or thatching roofs, etc: 稻草；麦秸(用以制帽、席等,或用以做家畜的垫草,或用来盖屋顶等): a **~** mattress, one stuffed with **~**. 草垫. **make bricks without ~**, make sth without all the necessary materials. 作无米之炊. ⇨ **Exod 5**: 7. 参看旧约'出埃及记'第5章第7节. a man of **~**, imaginary person, easily overcome, set up as an opponent. 稻草人(容易击败的假想对手). '**~·board** n [U] coarse cardboard made of **~** pulp. 马粪纸；草纸板. '**~-coloured** adj pale yellow. 淡黄色的；草黄色的. 2 [C] single stalk or piece of **~**: thin tube of other material for sucking up liquid: (稻草或麦秸的)茎管; (吸取液体的)吸管: suck lemonade through a **~**. 用吸管吸柠檬水. **catch at a ~; clutch at ~s**, try any expedient, however useless (like a drowning man clutching at a **~**). 尝试最没有用的方法(正如溺水的人连一根草都要抓). **not care a ~**, not at all. 毫不介意. **not worth a ~**, worth nothing. 一文不值；毫无价值. a **~ in the wind**, a slight hint that shows which way things may develop; 事态动向的征兆; hence, 由此产生, **a ~ vote**, attempt to discover public opinion on a topic of current interest by an unofficial poll (eg as made by a newspaper). 民意调查(报馆等就当前重要问题所作的非正式投票). **the last ~**, an addition to a task, burden, etc, that makes it intolerable. 突破容忍(耐力等)极限的一桩事、工作、压力等. □ vt spread **~** on; cover with **~**. 铺草于…之上；覆以草.

straw·berry /'strɔːbrɪ US: -berɪ; 'strɔˌbɛrɪ/ n (pl **-ries**) [C] (perennial, low-growing plant having) juicy red fruit with tiny yellow seeds on its surface, eaten raw and in jam. 草莓树；草莓(多年生矮小植物,结红色浆果,生食或制果酱). ⇨ the illus at **fruit**. 参看 fruit 之插图. '**~ mark**, reddish birthmark on the skin. (皮肤上的)红色胎记；莓状痣(一种先天性血管瘤).

stray /streɪ; stre/ vi (pt, pp **~ed**) [VP2A, C] wander from the right path, from one's companions, etc; lose one's way: 走失；迷路；离题: Don't **~** from the point. 不要离题. □ n 1 animal or person (esp a child) that has **~ed**: 迷失的动物或人; (尤指)迷失的小孩. **waifs and ~s**, homeless children. 无家可归的孩童. 2 (attrib) having **~ed**: (用作定语)迷失了的: **~** cats and dogs; 迷失的猫和狗; killed by a **~** bullet, killed by chance, not purposely; 被流弹射杀; occasional; seen or happening occasionally: 偶然的；偶见的；偶尔发生的: The streets were empty except for a few **~** taxis. 除了偶尔可以看到几辆计程车外,街上没有人迹.

streak /striːk; strik/ n [C] 1 long, thin, usu irregular line or band: 线条；条纹；条痕；脉；层(通常呈不规则形): **~**s of lean and fat, eg in meat; 瘦肉和肥肉相间的肉层; like a **~** of lightning, very fast. 似一道闪电般(快速)地. 2 trace or touch (of): 些微；少许: There's a **~** of vanity/cruelty in his character. 他的性格有点虚浮(残酷). 3 brief period: 短时间；一阵: The gambler had a **~** of good luck, won for a time. 那赌徒有过一阵好运(赢过一阵). **hit a winning ~**, have a series of successes (in gambling, etc). 接连获胜或成功(如在赌博中). □ vt, vi 1 [VP6A, 15A] mark with **~**s: 加线条或条纹于: white marble **~**ed with brown. 有褐色条纹的白色大理石. 2 [VP2C] (colloq) move very fast (like a **~**). (口)疾动；飞跑(似闪电般): The children **~**ed off as fast as they could. 孩子们拔腿飞跑. '**~·y** adj (**-ier**, **-iest**) marked with,

having, ~s: 有条纹的; 有线条的; 有层脉的: ~y bacon, with ~s of fat and lean in it. 五花腌肉(肥瘦相间者)。

stream /striːm; strim/ n 1 river or brook; current. 河, 川, 溪; 水流。 **go up**/**down** ~, move up/down the river. 逆流而上(顺流而下)。 **go with the** ~, (fig) do or think as the majority of people do, be carried along by the course of events. (喻)顺应潮流; 跟着大多数人去做或去想。 2 steady flow (of liquid, persons, things. etc): (液体、人、物等的)不断流出: a ~ of blood/curses. 一股血(一连串的咒诅)。 S~s of people were coming out of the railway station. 人潮从火车站涌出。 ~ **of consciousness**, continuous conscious experience of an individual; (in literature) technique of writing novels to indicate this, eg as in James Joyce's Ulysses. 意识流(连续的意识经验); (文学)意识流小说写作技巧(如乔伊斯玛写的"尤利塞斯")。 3 (education) (division of a) class of children in age groups according to ability and intelligence: (教育)(英)同一年级学生根据能力及智力编成的小组; 智力分组: bright boys and girls in the 'A-stream. A组的聪慧男孩和女孩。 □ vi, vt 1 [VP2A, C] flow freely; move continuously and smoothly in one direction: 未受阻碍地流动; 任意地流; 连续而流畅地向一个方向移动: Sweat was ~ing down his face. 他脸上汗水直流。 His face was ~ing with sweat. 他满脸都是汗水。 2 [VP2C] float or wave (in the wind): (在风中)飘扬; 招展: The flag/Her long hair ~ed in the wind. 旗帜(她的长发)在风中飘动。 3 [VP6A] place (children) in ~s(3). 按能力及年级将(孩童)分组。 ~**er** n long narrow flag; long narrow ribbon of paper. 狭而长的旗; 旗幡; 狭长的纸带。 ~**er headline**, (US) (美) = banner headline, ⇨ **banner.** 2 column of light shooting out in the aurora. 从极光射出的光柱; 流光。 '~**let** /-lɪt; -lɪt/ n small ~ or brook. 小溪; 小河。

stream·line /'striːmlaɪn; 'strim,laɪn/ vt make more efficient (by simplifying, getting rid of, wasteful methods, etc): 使更为有效(借简化或废除不经济的方法等); 提高效率: ~ production, eg in a factory. 提高生产效率(如工厂中)。 '~**d** adj 1 having a shape that offers least resistance to the flow of air, water, etc: 流线型的: ~d cars. 流线型轿车。 2 having nothing likely to impede progress: 无阻碍的; 有效率的: ~d controls/methods. 高效率管理(方法)。

street /striːt; strit/ n town or village road with houses on one side or both: 街; 街道: meet a friend in the ~, 在街上遇见一位朋友; cross the ~; 穿越街道; a '~-map/plan of York. 约克城的市街图(计划)。 Cf 参较 a road-map of Yorkshire. 约克郡的道路图。 '~-**car** n (esp US) tram-car. (尤美)电车; 街车。 ~ **door** n door which opens (directly) on to the ~. (If there is a garden front door is preferred). 临街大门。(前有庭园时, 以称 front door 为宜。) **the man in the** ~, typical citizen. 典型公民; 一般人。 **not in the same** (**as**), not nearly so good (as). 难以和……相比; 不如……那样好。 ~**s ahead of**, (colloq) far ahead of. (口)远在前面。 (**right**) **up one's** ~, (colloq) within one's area of knowledge, interests, etc. (口)在自己的知识、兴趣等范围内。 **go on the** ~**s**, earn one's living by prostitution. 以卖淫为生; 当妓女。 '~-**girl**, '~-**walker** nn prostitute. 妓女。

strength /streŋθ; streŋθ/ n [U] 1 quality of being strong: 强壮; 强度; 强壮的性质; 力量; 力气: a man/horse of great ~; 强壮的人(马); the ~ of a rope, its ability to resist strain; 绳子的强度(耐拉力); the ~ of our army; 我们军队的力量; get back one's health and ~ after an illness. 病后恢复健康及体力。 She hasn't the ~/hasn't ~ enough to walk upstairs. 她没有力气走上楼。 How is the ~ of alcoholic liquors measured? 烈酒的浓度是怎样测定的? **on the** ~ **of**, encouraged by, relying upon: 受……的鼓励; 依恃; 凭借: I employed the boy on the ~ of your recommendation. 由于你的推荐我雇用那男孩。 2 that which helps to make sb or sth strong: 使某人或某物坚强之事物; 支持物; 依恃物: God

is our ~. 我们依赖上帝。 3 power measured by numbers of persons present or persons who can be used: 实力; 兵力; 人力; 可供使用的人员: The enemy were in (great) ~, Their numbers were great. 敌人的人马众多。 The police force is 500 below ~, needs 500 more men. 警察的人数尚需五百。 **bring sth**/**be up to** ~, reach/be the required number: 使达到(达到)所需员数字: We must bring the police force up to ~. 我们必需使警察达到所需员额。 ~**en** /'streŋθn; 'streŋθən/ vt, vi [VP6A, 2A] make or become strong(er). 使或变得强壮、坚强、更强壮、更坚强等; 加强; 强化。

strenu·ous /'strenjuəs; 'strɛnjuəs/ adj using or needing great effort; energetic: 费力的; 须全力以赴的; 奋发的; 精力充沛的: ~ work; 吃力的工作; ~ workers; 辛苦的工作者; make ~ efforts; 大大地努力; lead a ~ life. 过奋斗的生活。 ~**ly** adv ~**ness** n

strep·to·coc·cus /ˌstreptəˈkɒkəs; ˌstrɛptəˈkakəs/ n (pl -**cocci** /-ˈkɒkaɪ; -ˈkɑksaɪ/) any of a group of bacteria which causes serious infections and illnesses. (导致多种严重疾病的)链球菌属。

strep·to·my·cin /ˌstreptəʊˈmaɪsɪn; ˌstrɛptəˈmaɪsɪn/ n antibiotic medical preparation. 链霉素(一种抗生素)。

stress /stres; strɛs/ n 1 [U] pressure; condition causing hardship, disquiet, etc: 压力; 压迫; 引起困难、忧虑、不宁等的情况: times of ~, of trouble and danger; 危难之际; 非常时期: driven into harbour by ~ of weather; 因恶劣天气而进入港内; under the ~ of poverty/fear/excitement. 在贫困(恐惧、激动)的压力下。 2 [U] (also with indef art) weight or force: (亦可与不定冠词连用)重要: a school that lays (a) ~ on foreign languages. 注重外国语的学校。 3 [C, U] (result of) extra force, used in speaking, on a particular word or syllable: 重读; 重音: In 'strategic' the ~ is on the second syllable '重音符号'. 一词的重音在第二个音节。 S~ and rhythm are important in speaking English. 讲英语时重音及节奏都很重要。 You must learn where to place the ~es. 你必须学习何处放置重读。 '~-**mark** n mark (eg '(principal or main ~) and ˌ(secondary ~) as used in this dictionary) that indicates the ~ on a syllable. 重音符号(表示某一音节须重读的符号, 如本词典用的 ' 及 ˌ 两个符号)。 4 [C; U] (in mechanics) tension; force exerted between two bodies that touch, or between two parts of one body. (机械)拉力; 应力。 □ vt [VP6A] put ~ on: 重读; 着重; 强调: He ~ed the point that …. 他强调这一点。

stretch /stretʃ; strɛtʃ/ vt, vi 1 [VP6A, 15A, B, 16A, 22] make wider, longer or tighter, by pulling; be or become wider, etc when pulled: 伸展; 张开; 拉长; 拉紧; 扩大。 ~ a rope tight; 把绳子拉紧; ~ a rope across a path; 拉绳横越道路; ~ a pair of gloves/shoes, eg to make them fit better; 撑开手套(鞋子); ~ one's neck, eg to see over the heads of people in a crowd; 伸长脖子(如在人丛中从旁人头上看着过去); ~ one's arms/legs/oneself/one's muscles, extend the limbs, etc and thus tighten the muscles; 伸臂(伸腿; 伸展身体; 伸展肌肉); ~ out one's arm for a book. 伸出手臂去拿一本书。 ~ **one's legs**, exercise oneself by walking as a relief from sitting or lying. 散步; 走动以舒展身体。 2 ~ (**oneself**) **out** (**on**), lie on at full length: 直躺: They were ~ed out on the lawn. 他们(被打倒)直躺在草地上。 He ~ed himself out on the beach. 他直躺在海滩上。 3 [VP6A] make (a word, law, etc) include or cover more than is strictly right; exert beyond what is right: 不当地引申(词义、法律等); 滥用; 曲解: ~ the law/one's principles/a point in sb's favour. 曲解法律(原则, 某一点等以利某人); strain to the utmost: 尽力地使用、努力、拉扯等: ~ one's powers, work very hard or too hard. 非常或过度努力地工作。 **be fully ~ed**, working to the utmost of one's powers. 竭尽所能; 全力以赴。 4 [VP2A, B, C] extend: 延伸; 绵亘: forests ~ing for hundreds of miles. 绵亘数百英里的森林; a road ~ing away across the desert. 穿

越沙漠的道路。□ n [C] **1** act of ~ing or being ~ed: 伸展；张开；拉长；拉紧；扩大；滥用；曲解: *by a ~ of language/the law/one's principles.* 滥用语言(法律,某人的原则)。⇨ **3** above. 参看上列第3义。*The cat woke and gave a ~.* 那只猫醒过来伸伸懒腰。*He got up with a ~ and a yawn.* 他站起来伸伸懒腰,打个呵欠。**by 'any/'no ~ of the imagination,** however much one may try to imagine sth. 无论怎么推想。**at full ~,** fully ~ed(3): 尽力而为: *The factory was/The workers were at full ~.* 工厂全力生产(工人们全力工作)。**2** unbroken or continuous period of time or extent of country, etc: 连续的期间；绵亘的乡野；伸延的空间: *a beautiful ~ of wooded country,* 一大片美丽而有林木的乡野；(sl) (俚) *do a two-year ~ in prison.* 坐牢两年。**at a ~,** continuously: 连续不断地: *Can you work for six hours at a ~?* 你能连续工作六小时吗? **3** straight side of a track or course (for racing). (跑道的)直线部分；直边。**~er** n **1** framework of poles, canvas, etc for carrying a sick, injured or wounded person. (抬伤患用的)担架；异床。**'~er-bearer** n person who helps to carry a ~er. 抬担架者。**'~er-party** n number of persons with ~ers (to carry an injured or wounded person). 担架队。**2** device for ~ing things (eg gloves, shoes). (撑物用的)撑具；撑架；伸张器。

strew /struː; struː/ vt (pt ~**ed**, pp ~**ed** or **strewn** /struːn; struːn/) [VP6A, 14] ~ *sth (on/over sth);* ~ *sth with sth,* scatter (sth) over a surface; (partly) cover (a surface) (with sth scattered): 撒(某物)于表面上;(以撒布之物)遮蔽(某一表面的)全部或一部；散播；点缀: ~ *flowers over a path;* 散花于路上; ~ *a path with flowers.* 以花撒在路上。

strewth /struːθ; struːθ/ = **struth.**

stri·ated /straɪˈeɪtɪd US: ˈstraɪeɪtɪd; ˈstraɪeɪtɪd/ adj striped; furrowed. 有条纹的；有沟纹的。

stricken /ˈstrɪkən; ˈstrɪkən/ adj (pp of **strike;** used pred) (strike 的过去分词;用作表语) affected or overcome: 受害的；染患的；被压服的: '*grief-/'panic-/'terror-,* overcome by grief/panic/terror; 非常悲伤的(非常惊慌的；吓坏了的); ~ *with fever/malaria/cancer;* 发烧(染疟疾；得癌症); '*cancer-~.* 患癌症的。~ *in years,* (archaic) old and feeble. (古)老而衰弱的。

strict /strɪkt; strɪkt/ adj (-**er,** -**est**) **1** stern; demanding obedience or exact observance. 严厉的；严格的: *a ~ father;* 严父; ~ *discipline;* 严格的纪律; *be ~ with one's children;* 对子女严格; *keep a ~ hand over the children;* 严格管教子女; *a ~ rule against smoking,* eg at a petrol station. 禁止吸烟的严格规定(如在加油站)。**2** clearly and exactly defined; precisely limited: 明确的；严密的；精确的: *tell sb sth in ~est confidence;* 极秘密地将某事告诉某人; *in the ~ sense of the word;* 就某词精确的意义而言; *the ~ truth.* 千真万确的事。~**ly** adv in a ~ manner: 严厉地；严格地；明确地；严密地: *Smoking is ~ly prohibited.* 严禁吸烟。~**ness** n

stric·ture /ˈstrɪktʃə(r); ˈstrɪktʃə/ n [C] **1** (often pl) severe criticism or blame: (常用复数)严厉的批评或责难: *pass ~s on sb.* 严厉地批评某人。**2** (med) contraction of a tube-like part of the body, causing a diseased condition. (医)狭窄(身体上管道收缩,造成生理异常)。

stride /straɪd; straɪd/ vi, vt (pt **strode** /strəʊd; strod/, pp (rare) **stridden** /ˈstrɪdn; ˈstrɪdn/) **1** [VP2C] walk with long steps: 大步行走: ~ *along the road;* 沿路大步行走; ~ *off/away.* 大步走开。**2** ~ *over/across sth,* pass over in one long step: 跨过或跨越某物: ~ *over a ditch.* 跨过小沟。**3** [VP6A] = **bestride.** □ n [C] (distance covered in) one long step: 大步；阔步;一大步的距离;跨幅: *walk with vigorous ~s.* 有力地大步行走。**make great ~s,** make good and rapid progress. 大有进步；突飞猛进。**take sth in one's ~,** do it without special effort. 轻易地做某事。

stri·dent /ˈstraɪdnt; ˈstraɪdnt/ adj (of sound) loud and harsh; shrill: (指声音)粗嘎的；尖锐的: *the ~ notes*

of the cicadas. 蝉的尖锐鸣声。~**·ly** adv

stridu·late /ˈstrɪdjʊleɪt US: ˈstrɪdʒʊleɪt; ˈstrɪdʒəˌlet/ vi [VP2A] make shrill grating sounds (esp of insects such as crickets). 发尖锐的摩擦声(尤指昆虫如蟋蟀所发)。**stridu·la·tion** /ˌstrɪdjʊˈleɪʃn US: -dʒ-; ˌstrɪdʒəˈleʃən/ n

strife /straɪf; straɪf/ n [U] quarrelling; state of conflict: 争吵；倾轧；敌对；冲突: *industrial ~* (between workers and employers). 工人与雇主间的冲突。

strike¹ /straɪk; straɪk/ n **1** act of striking(5): 罢工: *the numerous ~s in the coalmines;* 煤矿区的无数次罢工; *a ~ of bus-drivers;* 公共汽车司机的罢工; (attrib) (用作定语) *take ~ action.* 采取罢工行动。*be/go on ~; be/come/go out on ~,* be engaged in, start, a ~. 从事罢工；开始罢工。**a general ~,** by workers in all or most trades, etc; (各行业)总罢工；全面罢工 ⇨ **hunger, lightning, sympathetic, unofficial.** '~**-bound** adj unable to function because of a ~: 因罢工而停顿的: *The docks were ~-bound for a week.* 码头因罢工而瘫痪一周。'~**-breaker** n worker brought in or come in to take the place of a striker. 代替罢工者工作的人；破坏罢工者。~ **fund** n special fund to supplement ~-pay. 罢工准备金；罢工基金。'~**-leader** n worker or official who leads a ~. 罢工领袖。'~**-pay** n money paid to strikers from trade-union funds (during a ~ officially recognized by a union). (工会给予罢工者的)罢工津贴。**2** act of striking (oil, etc) in the earth. (油田等的)发现。**lucky ~,** fortunate discovery. 幸运的发现。**3** sudden attack by aircraft. 飞机的出击。

strike² /straɪk; straɪk/ vt, vi (pt, pp **struck** /strʌk; strʌk/) (also ⇨ **stricken,** above) (亦参看上列之 stricken) (For special uses with *adverbial particles* and *preps,* ⇨ 17 below.) (与副词性小品词及介词连用的特殊用法。参看下列第17义。) **1** [VP6A, 12C, 14, 2A, C, 3A] hit; give a blow or blows to; aim a blow *at:* 打；击；敲；向~打击: *He struck me on the chin* (note use of *def art*). 他打在我的下巴上(注意须用定冠词)。*He struck the table with a heavy blow.* 他重重地拍了一下桌子。*He struck his knee with his hand/struck his hand on his knee.* 他以手拍击膝头。*He seized a stick and struck at me.* 他抓起一根棍子向我打来。*Who struck the first blow,* started the fight? 谁先出手打人? *The ship struck a rock.* 该船触礁了。*That tree was struck by lightning.* 那棵树被闪电击中了。~ *at the root of sth,* attack trouble, evil, etc at its source. 斩草除根；除恶务尽；彻底根绝。*S~ while the iron is hot,* (prov) Act promptly while action is likely to get results. (谚)打铁趁热。*a* '~/'**striking force,** military force ready to attack at short notice. 打击部队(可随时待命出击者)。**within 'striking distance,** near enough to reach or attack easily. 在易达到或攻击范围内。**2** [VP6A, 2A] produce (a light) by striking or scraping: 擦或擦而产生(光亮): ~ *sparks from a flint;* 自燧石打出火花; ~ *a match,* cause it to burst into flame by scraping it on a surface; 擦燃火柴; ~ *a light,* produce one in this way. 擦(打)出光光。*These matches are damp—they won't ~.* 这些火柴潮湿了,擦不燃。**3** [VP6A] come upon, discover (by mining, drilling, etc): (借开矿、钻探等而)发现；找到: *to ~ gold.* 发现黄金。~ *oil,* **(a)** discover oil by drilling. 借钻探而发现石油。**(b)** (fig) have good fortune; find a means of getting rich. (喻)交到好运；发横财；发现致富的方法。~ *it rich,* win wealth suddenly. 突然致富。**4** [VP6A, 2A] (cause to) sound: (使)发声: (使)鸣; (使)响: ~ *a chord on the piano.* 弹一下钢琴。*This clock ~s the hours.* 这钟每小时报时一次。*The clock has just struck (four).* 这钟刚敲过(四下)。*The/His hour has struck,* (fig) the critical moment has come or gone. (喻)(他的)紧要关头到了(已过)。~ *a note of,* give an impression (of the kind indicated): 给予某种(指明的)感觉,造成某种效果: *The President struck a note of warning against over-optimism.* 总统的话有警惕大家勿过分乐观的作用。**5** [VP2A, 3A] ~ *(for/*

against), (of workers, etc) stop working for an employer (in order to get more pay, shorter hours, better conditions, etc or as a protest against sth): (指工人等)罢工: ～ *for higher pay/against bad working conditions.* 为要求增加工资(抗议恶劣工作环境)而罢工。 ⇨ **strike¹(1).** **6** [VP6A, 16A] have an effect upon the mind: 给予…感觉; 在心灵上产生某种效果; 造成某种印象: *How does the idea/suggestion ～ you?* 你对于那个主意(建议)看法如何? *The plan ～s me as ridiculous.* 我觉得那项计划很可笑。 *What struck me* (= The impression I had) *was that he was not telling the truth.* 就我的看法,他讲的不是真话。 *An idea suddenly struck me,* came to me, with an immediate response. 我突然想到一个主意(忽起心生一计)。 **7** [VP16B, or 2D with object and *as* omitted or 2D 省略宾语或 as] have an effect on the body or mind: 对身体或心灵产生某种效果; 使身体或心灵感觉到: *The room ～s you as warm and comfortable when you enter.* 那房间你一进去就会感到温暖与舒适。 *The prison cell struck cold and damp,* was felt as cold and damp by anyone entering it. 那牢房使人觉得阴冷而潮湿。 **8** [VP6A] produce by stamping or punching: 铸造; 压制: ～ *a coin/medal/medallion.* 铸造钱币(纪念章,奖章)。 **9** [VP6A] achieve, arrive at, by reckoning or weighing: 借计算或衡量而达到; 计算出; 衡量出: ～ *an average;* 算出平均数值; ～ *a balance between anarchy and authoritarian rule/between licence and repression.* 在无政府主义与独裁统治之间(放纵与压抑之间)找出中道。 ～ *a bargain (with sb),* reach one by agreement; conclude one. (与某人)达成交易; 订定买卖合同。 **10** [VP6A] come upon; find: 碰遇, 遇见; 发现: ～ *the track/the right path.* 发现踪迹(正确的路径)。 **11** [VP2A, CJ] ～ *(off/out),* set out, go (in a certain direction): 出发; 行进; (向某一方向)走: *We struck (off)* (= turned and went) *into the woods.* 我们转入林中。 *The boys struck (out) across the fields.* 那些男孩走过田野。 *The explorers struck out* (= started, set out) *at dawn.* 那些探险的人天一亮就出发了。 **12** [VP22] cause (sb) to be, suddenly and as if by a single stroke: 使(某人)突然成为, 以单独突然变作: *be struck blind/dumb/silent.* 突然瞎了(哑了, 沉默下来)。 **13** [VP14] ～ *fear/terror/alarm into sb,* fill, afflict, with fear, etc: 使某人心起恐惧(畏惧; 警戒): *Attila struck terror into the people of eastern Europe.* 匈奴王阿提拉曾令东欧人民胆寒。 *The bombing attack struck fear into their hearts.* 轰炸使他们心惊肉跳。 **14** [VP6A] lower or take down (sails, tents). 落下; 取下; 扯下(帆); 撤除(帐篷)。 ～ *one's flag,* lower it (as a signal that one surrenders a ship, fortress, etc to the enemy). 下旗(交出船、堡垒等, 向敌人投降的表征)。 *～ tents/camp,* pack up tents, etc. 拆扎帐篷等; 拔营。 **15** [VP6A] ～ *a cutting,* take a cutting from a plant and insert in soil to ～ root. 插枝(把插条种在泥土里)。 ～ *root,* put out roots. 扎根; 生根。 **16** [VP6A] hold or put the body in a certain way to indicate sth: 把身体摆成某种姿态; 采取; 装出; 摆出: ～ *an attitude of defiance;* 摆出一付藐视人的态度; ～ *a pose.* 采取某种姿势。 **17** [VP2C, 3A, 15B] (special uses with *adverbial particles and preps*): (与副词性小品词及介词连用的特殊用法):

strike sb down, (formal) hit him so that he falls to the ground; (of a disease, etc) attack him: (正式用语)把某人打倒在地上; (指疾病等)侵袭某人: *He was struck down in the prime of life,* eg of sb who was assassinated. 他正值盛年即被打倒(如遭暗杀)。

strike sth off, **(a)** cut off with a blow, eg of an axe. 将某物砍掉或切除等(如用斧头)。 **(b)** print: 印刷: ～ *off 1000 copies of a book.* 将一本书印一千本。 ～ *sth off (sth),* remove: 删除: ～ *sb's name off a list.* 将某人的名字从名单上删除。 *The doctor's name was struck off the Medical Register,* was cancelled, eg because of professional misconduct. 那医师的名字已从医师录上删除(如因职业上的过失)。

strike on/upon sth, get or find suddenly or unexpectedly: 突然得到或发现: ～ *on an idea/a plan.* 突然想起一个主意(计划)。

strike out, **(a)** use the arms and legs vigorously in swimming: (以手臂和腿)用力游: ～ *out for the shore.* 用力游向岸边。 **(b)** aim vigorous blows: 用力打击: *He lost his temper and struck out wildly.* 他大发脾气, 疯狂地出手打人。 **(c)** follow a new or independent path, a new form of activity: 独树一帜; 创新格局; 采取新的行为方式: ～ *out on one's own/in a new direction.* 自谋生计(另求发展)。 ～ *sth out through,* cross out, put a line or lines through: 删除; 划去; 涂去: ～ *out a word/name/item.* 删掉一字(一个名字, 一个项目)。

strike (sth) up, begin to play: 开始演奏等: *The band struck up* (a tune). 乐队开始演奏(一曲)。 ～ *up sth (with sb),* begin (perhaps casually) a friendship or acquaintance: 开始(也许是偶然地)(与某人)结交或认识: *The two boys quickly struck up a friendship.* 那两个男孩子很快就熟悉起来了。 *She struck up an acquaintance with a fellow passenger during the cruise.* 那次(乘船)旅行她结交了一位同船的旅客。

strik·er /ˈstraɪkə(r); ˈstraɪkɚ/ *n* **1** worker who strikes(5). 罢工者。 **2** (football) player in an attacking position. (足球)前锋(在攻击位置的球员)。

strik·ing /ˈstraɪkɪŋ; ˈstraɪkɪŋ/ *adj* **1** attracting attention; arousing great interest. 引人注意的; 引起很大兴趣的。 **2** that strikes(4): 鸣响的: *a ～ clock.* 自鸣钟。 ～·**ly** *adv* in a ～ manner: 显著地; 引人注意地: *a ～ly beautiful woman.* 美貌惊人的女子。

string¹ /strɪŋ; strɪŋ/ *n* **1** [C, U] (piece or length of) fine cord for tying things, keeping things in place, etc; narrow strip of other material used for the same purposes: 细绳; 带子; 一段带子或细绳; 一根细绳或带子: *a ball of ～;* 一团细绳; *a piece of ～;* 一根细绳; ～ *and brown paper for a parcel.* 包裹用的细绳和牛皮纸。 *tied to one's mother's/wife's apron-～s,* ⇨ **apron.** 系在母亲(太太)围裙的带子上; 受母亲(太太)操纵而不能独立。 (US) **'shoe ～,** ⇨ **lace(2).** (美)鞋带。 **2** [C] ～ *bow~,* ⇨ **bow¹(1).** 弓弦。 *have two ～s to one's bow,* have an alternative means of achieving one's purpose. 某人的弓有两根弓弦; 有两套达到目标的方法。 *the first/second ～,* the first/the alternative person or thing relied upon for achieving one's purpose. 第一(第二)弦; 赖以完成某项任务的第一(第二)个人或物。 **3** [C] tightly stretched length of cord, gut or wire, eg in a violin or guitar, for producing musical sounds. (紧绷在小提琴、吉他等上, 用以发出乐音的)琴弦。 *keep harping on one ～/on the same ～,* keep talking or writing on one subject. 继续不断弹一根(同一根)弦; 继续谈或写同一个题目。 **the ～s,** the instruments of the violin family in an orchestra. (管弦乐队中的)弦乐器。 *～ 'orchestra/'band n* one composed of ～ed instruments only. 弦乐队(团)。 *～ quar'tet n* (music for a) quartet of four ～ed instruments. 弦乐四重奏; 弦乐四重奏曲。 **4** [C] ～ used for causing puppets to move. 木偶上的线。 ⇨ the illus at **puppet.** 参看 puppet 之插图。 *have sb on a ～,* have him under one's control. 置某人于控制之下。 *pull ～s,* exert a (hidden) influence: 运用(暗中的)影响力: *pull ～s to get sb a job/to have sb dismissed.* 运用影响力给某人找一工作(让某人被解职)。 *pull the ～s,* control events, or the actions of other people (as if they were puppets on ～s). 操纵事件或他人行动。 *no ～s (attached); without ～s,* (colloq; of help, esp of money, eg given by one country to another) without conditions about how the help is to be used. (口语) 指一国对他国等的援助, 尤指金钱)不附带条件的; 受援者不受限制的。 **5** [C] series of things threaded on a ～: 穿在细绳上的一串东西; 一串: *a ～ of beads/pearls/onions;* 一串珠子(珍珠, 洋葱); number of things in, or as in, a line: 一系列之物; 连续

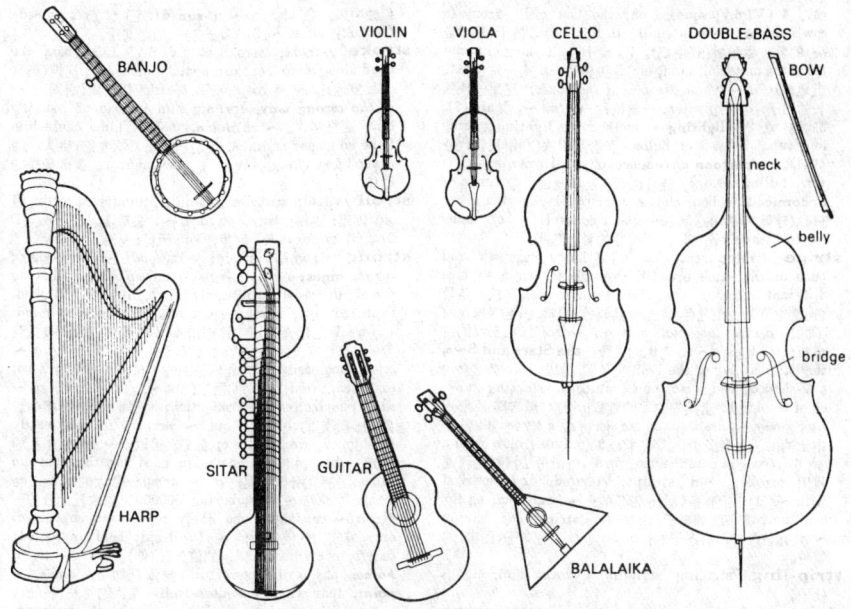

BANJO

VIOLIN   VIOLA   CELLO   DOUBLE-BASS

BOW

neck

belly

bridge

SITAR   GUITAR

HARP

BALALAIKA

stringed instruments

的事物: *a ~ of abuses / curses / lies;* 一连串的咒骂(咒诅,谎言); *a ~ of horses,* number of horses kept for racing. (属于同一主人或马房的)一列准备要参加比赛的马。 ⇨ **stud²**. **6** tough fibre or ~-like substance. 韧纤维;似细绳物质;筋。 ~ **bean,** kind of bean of which the pod is used as a vegetable. 菜豆(豆荚可作蔬菜)。 '**heart~s,** ⇨ **heart(7).** 深挚的情爱。 ~**y** *adj* (**-ier, -iest**) like ~; having tough fibres: 似带、绳等的;有韧纤维的:~*y meat,* tough. 多筋的肉。

string² /strɪŋ; strɪŋ/ *vt, vi* (*pt, pp* **strung** /strʌŋ; strʌŋ/) **1** [VP6A] put a string or strings on (a bow, violin, tennis racket, etc). 装弦于(弓,小提琴,网球拍等);上弦。 ~**ed instrument** *n* musical instrument with ~s(3). 弦乐器。 **2** (*pp*) **strung (up),** (of a person, his senses, nerves) made tense, ready, excited, etc: (指人,其感觉,神经)紧张的;警觉的;准备好了的;兴奋的;抖擞的: *The athlete was strung up before the important race.* 那运动员在重要赛跑前紧张而振奋。 **highly strung,** very nervous or tense. 很紧张的。 **3** [VP6A] put (pearls, etc) on a string. 串(珍珠等)于细绳上。 **4** [VP15A, B] ~ **(up),** tie or hang on a string, etc: 绑或悬于绳等上: ~ *up lanterns among the trees / lamps across a street.* 在林木间悬挂灯笼(横越街道挂灯)。 **5** [VP2C, 15B] (special uses with *adverbial particles*): (与副词性小品词连用的特殊用法):

string sb along, deliberately mislead him into the belief that he will benefit, etc: 骗人;故意使人误信将获得利益等; 吊胃口; *He doesn't intend to marry the girl—he's just ~ing her along.* 他并不想同那女孩子结婚——吊吊她罢了。 ~ **along with sb,** maintain a relationship with sb for as long as it suits one, without making genuine commitments. 与某人虚与委蛇(以达利用的目的)。

string out, be, become, spread out at intervals in a line. 成串地相续展开;间隔着散列;间歇地呈现。 ~ **sth out,** cause this to happen: 使成串地或间歇性地发生;使间隔着散开: *horses strung out towards the end of a long*

race. 长途赛马接近终点时间隔着散开的马。

string sb up, (sl) put him to death by hanging. (俚)吊死或绞死某人。 ~ **4** above. 参看上列第4义。

strin·gent /'strɪndʒənt; 'strɪndʒənt/ *adj* **1** (of rules) strict, severe; that must be obeyed: (指规则)严格的;必须遵守的; 严峻的: *a ~ rule against smoking.* 禁止吸烟的严格规定。 **2** (of the money-market) tight; difficult to operate because of scarcity of money. (指金融市场)银根紧的; 周转困难的。 ~·**ly** *adv* **strin·gency** /-nsɪ, -nsɪ/ *n*

strip /strɪp; strɪp/ *vt, vi* (**-pp-**) **1** [VP2A, C, 6A, 14, 15B, 22] ~ **(off);** ~ *sth/sb* **(off);** ~ *sth* (**from** / **off** *sth*); ~ *sth/sb* (**of** *sth*), take off (coverings, clothes, parts, etc): 脱去;剥去;除去(遮蔽物、衣服、某部分等): ~ *a machine,* dismantle it; 拆卸(拆开)一机器; ~ *paint from a surface* / ~ *a surface of paint,* remove the paint; 除去漆面; ~ *the bark off a tree* / ~ *a tree of its bark.* 剥去树皮。 *The bandits ~ped him naked* / ~*ped him of his clothes.* 强盗们剥光了他的衣服。 *They ~ped the house of all its furnishings.* 他们搬走了房子里的一切设备。 *They ~ped,* / ~*ped off,* / ~*ed off their clothes, and jumped into the lake.* 他们脱下衣服跳入湖中。 ~ *sth* **down,** (eg of an engine) remove detachable parts (for overhaul, etc). (如指引擎)分解或拆卸(以便仔细检查等)。 '~·**tease,** '~·**show** *nn* dance, cabaret or theatrical entertainment in which a woman takes off her garments one by one. 脱衣舞。 Hence, 由此产生, ~·**er** *n* woman who does this. 脱衣舞女。 ~·'**poker** *n* game of poker in which the loser of each hand must take off one garment. 脱衣扑克戏(输一局就得脱下一件衣服的游戏)。 **2** [VP14] ~ *sb* **of** *sth,* deprive him of property, etc: 剥夺某人之财产等: ~ *a man of his possessions / titles, etc.* 剥夺某人之财产(头衔等)。 **3** [VP6A] tear parts from: 拆散; 拆散: ~ *a gear / screw,* tear the cogs / thread from it (by misuse, etc). (因使用不当而)损坏齿轮的齿(螺钉之螺

线). **4** [VP6A] squeeze out the last milk from (a cow's udder); obtain (milk) in this way. 挤干(母牛乳头)的乳; 尽量挤出(牛奶). □ *n* [C] **1** long narrow piece (of material, land, etc): 狭长的一块或一片(材料、土地等): *a ~ of garden behind the house*; 屋后一块狭长的园子; *a ~ of paper*; 一条纸片; *an 'air~*, ⇨ **air¹(7)**. 临时机场. '*~-lighting* *n* method of lighting, using long tubes instead of bulbs. 光管照明法(利用长管代替灯泡). '*~ cartoon* *n* sequence of small drawings in a row, telling a story. 连环图画; 连环漫画. ⇨ *comic ~* at **comic**. **2** (colloq) clothes worn by players in a team: (口)(球队等穿的)队服: *the colourful ~ of many football teams*. 许多足球队所穿的彩色队服.

stripe /straɪp; straɪp/ *n* [C] **1** long, narrow band (usu of the same breadth throughout) on a surface different in colour, material, texture, etc: 条纹; 条带 (通常宽度从头至尾保持一致,其颜色、质料、织地等与底面不同): *a white table-cloth with red ~s*; 有红色条纹的白桌布; *the tiger's ~s*. 老虎的斑纹. **the Stars and S~s**, the national flag of the US. 星条旗; 美国国旗. **2** (often a V-shaped) badge worn on a uniform, showing rank, eg of a soldier: 士兵等的军阶臂章; 袖章(通常作 V 形): *How many ~s are there on the sleeve of a sergeant?* 陆军中士的袖子上有多少 V 字条纹? **3** (old use) blow with a whip (*stroke* is now the usu word). (旧用法)鞭打(现通常用 *stroke*). *~d* /straɪpt; 'straɪpɪd/ *adj* marked with ~s(1): 带有条纹的; 带条的: *~d material*, eg for clothing. 有条纹的料子(如衣料). **stripy** *adj* having ~s: 有条纹的; 有条子的: *a stripy tie.* 有条子(图案)的领带.

strip·ling /'strɪplɪŋ; 'strɪplɪŋ/ *n* youth. 青年; 年轻小伙子.

strive /straɪv; straɪv/ *vi* (*pt* **strove** /strəʊv; strov/, *pp* **striven** /'strɪvn; 'strɪvən/) **1** [VP2A, 3A] *~ (with / against sth/sb)*, struggle. 与某事或某人奋斗; 抗争; 搏斗. **2** [VP3A, 4A] *~ for sth/to do sth*, make great efforts. 奋力; 奋勉; 努力. *~r* *n* person who tries hard. 努力者; 奋勉者.

strobe /strəʊb; strob/ *n, adj* *~* **(light),** (light) that goes on and off very fast. 急速闪动的(光).

strode /strəʊd; strod/ *pt* of **stride**.

stroke¹ /strəʊk; strok/ *n* [C] **1** (act of striking or dealing a) blow: 打击; 一击: *kill a man with one ~ of a sword*; 挥剑一击而杀死某人; *the ~ of a hammer*; 锤的敲击; *20 ~s of the lash*. 鞭打二十下. **2** one of a series of regularly repeated movements, esp as a way of swimming or rowing: 一连串有规律的反复动作之一; (尤指)(游泳或划船时的)一划、一动: *swimming with a slow ~*; 慢划着游泳法; *'breast-/'back-~*; 俯泳(仰泳); *a fast/slow ~* (in rowing). (划船)快划(慢划). **3** (in a rowing crew) oarsman nearest the boat's stern who sets the rate of striking the oars. (划船)浆手(最近船尾者,为主要划手,指挥并决定划船的速度). ⇨ the illus at **eight**; 参看 eight 之插图; ⇨ **bow³(2).** **4** single movement of the upper part of the body and arm(s), esp in games, eg cricket, golf. 身体上部及手臂的活动; (尤指)(板球、高尔夫等的)一击、一挥. **5** single effort; result of this: 一次努力; 一次努力的结果: *That was a good ~ of business.* 那是一笔好买卖. *I haven't done a ~ of work today.* 今天我还未动手工作. *What a ~ of luck!* What a piece of good fortune! 多幸运啊! 真走运! 真是运气! *at a/one ~*, with one effort and immediately. 一举; 一气; 一鼓作气. *put sb off his ~*, ⇨ *put off* at **put²(11).** **6** (mark made by a) single movement of a pen or brush: 一笔; 笔画: *with one ~ of the pen*; 用笔一挥; *thin/thick ~s.* 细(粗)笔画. **7** sound made by a bell striking the hours: (报时的)钟声;鸣(钟)声;敲击声: *on the ~ of three*, at three o'clock. 钟鸣三响; 三时正. *He was here on the ~,* punctually at the time appointed. 他准时到达. **8** sudden attack of illness in the brain, with loss of feeling, power to move, etc: 中风: *a paralytic ~.* 瘫

痪性中风. ⇨ also *sun~* at **sun(4).** □ *vt* [VP6A] act as ~(3) to. 充当…的尾桨手.

stroke² /strəʊk; strok/ *vt* [VP6A, 15B] pass the hand along a surface, usu again and again: 抚摸(通常为反复地): *~ a cat/one's beard.* 抚摸猫(胡须). *~ sb the wrong way*, irritate him instead of soothing him. 激怒某人. *~ sb down*, mollify him, cause him to be no longer irritated. 安抚某人; 劝人息怒;哄人. □ *n* act of stroking; stroking movement. 抚摸; 抚摸的动作.

stroll /strəʊl; strol/ *n* [C] quiet, unhurried walk: 漫步; 闲逛; 遨游: *have/go for a ~.* 去散步. □ *vi* [VP2A, C] go for a ~. 散步; 漫步; 闲逛; 遨游. *~er n*

strong /strɒŋ *US:* strɔŋ; strɔŋ/ *adj* (*-nger* /-ŋɡə(r); -ŋɡɚ/, *-ngest* /-ŋɡɪst; -ŋɡɪst/) **1** (opp of *weak*) having power to resist; not easily hurt, injured, broken, captured, etc; having great power of body or mind: (为 weak 之反义词)有抵抗力的; 不易受伤、折断、被捕获或擒的; 身心方面强有力的; 强大的; 坚固的: *a ~ stick*, not easily broken; 坚固的手杖; *a ~ fort*, not easily captured; 坚固的堡垒; *a ~ wind*; 强风; *a ~ will/imagination*; 坚强的意志(丰富的想象力); 坚定的决心; *have ~ nerves*, be not easily frightened, worried, etc; 沉着; 勇敢; *~ eyes*, 眼利的目光; *feel quite ~ again*, in good health after an illness; 感到身体康复; *a ~ army*; 强大的军队; *an army 500000*, numbering 500000; 为数五十万的军队; *a ~ candidate*, one likely to be well supported, etc; 有实力的候选人; *~ (= deeply held or rooted) beliefs/convictions.* 坚定的信念(信仰). *as ~ as a horse*, physically powerful. 身体壮如马. *one's ~ point*, that which one does well. 某人的特长(长处). '*~-arm*, (of methods, tactics, etc) violent; bullying. (指方法、策略等)暴烈的; 用暴力的; 蛮横的; 威吓的. '*~-box* *n* one that is ~ly built for keeping valuables. 保险箱; 铁柜. '*~-hold* /-həʊld; -hold/ *n* **(a)** fort. 要塞; 堡垒. **(b)** (fig) place where a cause or idea has support: (喻)某种运动或观念被强力支持的地方; 根据地; 大本营: *a ~hold of Protestantism.* 新教的大本营. '*~-minded* /-'maɪndɪd; -'maɪndɪd/ *adj* having a mind that is capable and vigorous. 心智坚强的; 有雄心的; 果断的. '*~-room* *n* one built with thick walls and (usu) a heavy steel door (eg in a bank) for storing valuables. (收藏珍贵物品的)保险库. **2** having a large proportion of the flavouring element, etc: 浓烈的: *~ tea/coffee*; 浓茶(咖啡); *a ~ whisky*, whisky with very little water, etc. 猛烈的威士忌酒. **3** having a considerable effect on the mind or senses: (对心灵或感觉)有强烈效果的: *the ~ light of the tropics*; 热带的强光; *a ~ smell of gas*; 瓦斯的强烈气味; *~ bacon/butter/cheese/onions.* 味浓的熏肉(奶油、乳酪、洋葱). *His breath is rather ~*, is ill-smelling. 他的呼吸带臭味. '*~ language* *n* forcible expressions, esp words that are blasphemous or abusive. 激烈话; (尤指)骂人话. **4** '*~ drink*, containing alcohol, eg gin, rum. 烈性饮料(含酒精者,如杜松子酒及朗姆酒). ⇨ *soft drink* at **soft(9).** **5** (*adverbial use*) (作副词用) *going ~*, (colloq) continuing (the race, activity, etc) vigorously; continuing in good health: (口)使劲地继续(赛跑、活动等); 保持健康: *aged 90 and still going ~*. 年届九十而仍身强体壮. *come/go it (rather/a bit) ~*, (colloq) go to greater lengths than is right; exaggerate somewhat. (口)做得过分; 有几分夸张. **6** *~ verb*, one that forms the past tense by a vowel change (eg *sing, sang*), not by adding *-d, -ed* or *-t.* 以元音变化构成过去式的动词(如 sing, sang, 而非加 -d、-ed 或 -t). **7** (comm; of prices) rising steadily: (商; 指物价)坚挺的; 稳定上升的: *Prices/Markets are ~.* 价格(行情)坚挺. **8** '*~ form*, (of the pronunciation of some words) form occurring in a prominent (and therefore stressed) position: (指某些单词的发音)强式(处于须重读的位置): *The ~ form of 'and' is /ænd/.* and 的强式发音

/ænd/. ⇨ **weak(5)**. ~**ly** adv in a ~ manner: 坚持
地;坚决地;强烈地;极力地: I ~ly advise you to go. 我
极力劝你去。I ~ly feel/I feel ~ly that you've made
the wrong decision, I am ~ly convinced that .... 我深
信你所做的决定是错误的。

stron·tium /'strɒntɪəm US: -nʃɪəm; 'strɑnʃɪəm/ n
[U] soft silver-white metallic element (symbol **Sr**).
锶(一种柔软的银白色金属元素，符号 Sr)。~ **90** n [U]
variety of ~ that is a component of the fall-out from
nuclear explosions. 锶 90(为核爆炸后辐射尘中的成分
之一)。

strop /strɒp; strɑp/ n leather strap for sharpening
razors, esp as used by barbers. 磨剃刀用的皮条; 革砥
(理发师等使用者)。□ vt (**-pp-**) [VP6A] sharpen on
a ~. 在革砥上磨利。

strophe /'strəʊfɪ; 'strofɪ/ n [C] (lines of verse
recited during a) movement of the chorus in ancient
Greek drama; one section of a lyric poem. 古希腊戏剧
中唱歌队的舞动; 舞动时所吟唱的诗句; (合唱歌的)一节;
(抒情诗的)一段。

stroppy /'strɒpɪ; 'strɑpɪ/ adj (GB sl) (of a person)
bad-tempered; difficult to deal with. (英俚)(指人)脾气
坏的;难对付的。

strove /strəʊv; strov/ pt of **strive**.

struck /strʌk; strʌk/ pt, pp of **strike**[2].

struc·ture /'strʌktʃə(r); 'strʌktʃə/ n 1 [U] way in
which sth is put together, organized, etc: 结构; 构造;
建造法: the ~ of the human body; 人体的构造;
molecular ~; 分子的结构; sentence ~. 句子的结构。**2**
[C] building; any complex whole; framework or
essential parts of a building: 建筑物; 构造物; 建筑物的
构架或主要部分: The Parthenon was a magnificent
marble ~. 巴台农神殿是雄伟的大理石建筑物。**struc-
tural** /'strʌktʃərəl; 'strʌktʃərəl/ adj of a ~, esp the
framework: 构造的; 结构的; (尤指)构架的: structural
alterations to a building, eg combining two rooms into
one; 房屋结构上的改变(如把两房并为一房); structural
steel, ie bars, beams, girders, for use in building. 建
筑用钢材。**struc·tur·ally** /-ərəlɪ; -ərəlɪ/ adv: The
building is structurally sound. 这建筑物在结构上很
牢固。

stru·del /'struːdl; 'strudl/ n kind of tart made of
fruit, etc rolled up in puff pastry and baked: 水果卷
(水果馅饼的一种，卷起后烘焙而成): a slice of apple ~.
一片苹果卷。

struggle /'strʌgl; 'strʌgl/ vi [VP2A, B, 3A, 4A]
~ (**against**/**with**), fight, make great efforts: 抗争;
奋斗;努力;挣扎;搏斗: ~ against difficulties; 与困难搏
斗; ~ for influence/power. 争权力(权力)。The thief
~d in the policeman's arms/~d to get free. 那贼在警
察的手臂中挣扎(挣扎着要脱逃)。□ n [C] struggling;
contest: 挣扎;奋斗;努力;挣扎;搏斗: the ~ for
freedom; 为自由奋斗; not surrender without a ~. 未经
奋战不投降。

strum /strʌm; strʌm/ vi, vt (**-mm-**) [VP2A, B, C,
3A, 6A] ~ (**on**), play music, play (on a musical
instrument) carelessly or monotonously (and esp
without skill): 胡乱弹奏音乐; 漫不经心(无指无技巧)
地弹奏(乐器): ~ (on) the banjo; 乱弹五弦琴; ~ a
tune on the piano. 在钢琴上胡乱弹奏一曲。□ n sound
of ~ming: 胡乱弹奏的声音: the ~ of a guitar. 一阵错
落的吉他声。

strum·pet /'strʌmpɪt; 'strʌmpɪt/ n (archaic) prostitute. (古)娼妓。

strung /strʌŋ; strʌŋ/ pt, pp of **string**[2].

strut[1] /strʌt; strʌt/ n [C] piece of wood or metal
inserted in a framework and intended to strengthen it
by bearing weight or resisting pressure in the direction
of its length. (构架的)支柱;支杆;撑子;抗压构件。

strut[2] /strʌt; strʌt/ vi (**-tt-**) [VP2A, C] walk (about,
along, in, out, into a room, etc) in a stiff, self-satisfied
way. 趾高气扬地走; 高视阔步。□ n such a way of

walking. 高视阔步; 趾高气扬的行走。

strych·nine /'strɪknɪn; 'strɪknɪn/ n [U] strong
poison (used in very small doses to stimulate the
nerves). 马钱子碱; 番木鳖碱(一种烈性毒剂，以极微之
量，可用作刺激神经)。

stub /stʌb; stʌb/ n [C] **1** short remaining end of a
pencil, cigarette or similar object: (铅笔、香烟或类似
物的)残余部分; 残段; 铅笔头; 烟蒂; 残根: The dog has
only a ~ of a tail, a very short one. 那只狗只有一小截
短尾巴。**2** counterfoil: 票根; 存根: the ~s of a cheque-
book. 支票簿的存根。□ vt (**-bb-**) **1** [VP6A] ~ one's
toe, strike it against sth. 碰到脚趾。**2** [VP15B] ~
sth out, extinguish (esp a cigarette) by pressing it
against sth hard. 捻熄某物(尤指香烟)。

stubble /'stʌbl; 'stʌbl/ n [U] ends of grain plants
left in the ground after harvest; sth suggesting this,
eg a short stiff growth of beard: (稻等割下后遗留的)
茬; 残株; 残梗; 似此之物(如短须): three days' ~ on his
chin. 三四天未刮过的短须。**stub·bly** /'stʌblɪ;
'stʌblɪ/ adj of or like ~: (似)残株的; (似)残梗的: a
stubbly beard. 短须。

stub·born /'stʌbən; 'stʌbən/ adj obstinate; determined; difficult to deal with: 顽固的; 固执的; 坚定的; 坚
决的; 难应付的; 难处理的: ~ soil, difficult to plough,
etc; 坚硬的土壤(难犁等); ~ illness. 难治的病。as
~ as a mule, extremely obstinate. 非常顽强的; 象骡子
般顽强的。~**·ly** adv ~**·ness** n

stubby /'stʌbɪ; 'stʌbɪ/ adj (**-ier, -iest**) short and
thick: 短而粗的: ~ fingers. 短而粗的手指。

stucco /'stʌkəʊ; 'stʌko/ n (pl ~**s**, ~**es** -kəʊz; -koz/)
[C, U] (kinds of) plaster or cement used for covering
and decorating ceilings or wall surfaces. (涂天花板或墙
壁用的)灰泥。□ vt (pt, pp ~**ed**; ~**ing**) coat with
~. 用灰泥涂。

stuck /stʌk; stʌk/ pt, pp of **stick**[2].

stuck-up /ˌstʌk 'ʌp; 'stʌk'ʌp/ adj (colloq) conceited;
insolently refusing to be companionable. (口)自大的;
傲慢的; 倨傲不群的; 自以为了不起的。

stud[1] /stʌd; stʌd/ n **1** small two-headed button-like
device put through button-holes to fasten a collar,
shirt-front, etc. (穿过钮孔以固定衣领、胸口等的)饰钮;
袖扣; 领扣。**2** large-headed nail or knob, usu one of
many, on the surface of sth (eg a gate or shield), as
ornament or protection. (钉于门、盾等上，作为装饰或保
护用的)饰钉。大头钉。**re'flector** ~, (colloq 口语 cat's
eye) used on roads to mark out lanes (and reflecting
light from headlamps at night). 反光钉(钉在路面上标
示车道，且能在夜间反射车辆前灯的灯光)。□ vt (**-dd-**)
(usu pp) (通常用过去分词)~**ded with**, having (sth)
set in or scattered on the surface: 满布; 散布: a crown
~ded with jewels; 饰满珠宝的王冠; a sea ~ded with
islands/the sails of yachts. 散布着小岛(游艇之帆)的
海面。

stud[2] /stʌd; stʌd/ n number of horses kept by one
owner for a special purpose (esp breeding or racing).
(属于同一主人的)马群; (尤指为繁殖或赛马而饲养的一
群)种马; 赛马。'~**-book** n register of the pedigrees of
horses. 马种系谱; 马的血统记录簿。'~**-farm** n place
where horses are bred. 种马农场。'~**-mare** n mare
kept for breeding purposes. 母种马; 雌性种马。

stu·dent /'stjuːdnt US: 'stuː-; 'stjudnt/ n **1** (GB)
(undergraduate or postgraduate) person who is studying
at a college, polytechnic or university: (英)大学生; 工
艺学院的学生; 研究生: medical ~s; 医科学生; (US
also) boy or girl attending school. (美亦指)中学生; 小
学生。**2** anyone who studies or who is devoted to the
acquisition of knowledge: 学者; 研究学问工作者: a ~
of bird-life/nature/theology. 研究鸟类生活(大自然、神
学)的学者。

stu·dio /'stjuːdɪəʊ US: 'stuː-; 'stjudɪˌo/ n (pl ~**s**
/-dɪəʊz; -dɪˌoz/) **1** well-lit workroom of a painter,
sculptor, photographer, etc. 画室; 雕塑室; 照相室; 工作

室;技术室。 ~ **couch,** couch that can be used as a bed. 沙发床;可作床用的躺椅。 **2** room or hall where cinema films are acted and photographed; (pl) all the ~s of a cinema company, with the office buildings, etc. (制作电影的)摄影棚;(复)(电影公司的)摄影场;制片厂。 **3** room from which radio or TV programmes are regularly broadcast or in which recordings are made. (无线电或电视节目的)播放室;广播室;录制室;工作室。 **audience,** audience in a ~, to provide applause, laughter, etc. 现场观众(听)众(提供掌声、笑声等效果者)。

stu·di·ous /'stju:dɪəs US: 'stu:-; 'stjudɪəs/ adj **1** having or showing the habit of learning. 好学的;用功的;勤学的。 **2** painstaking; deliberate. 费力的;用心的;小心的;故意的: with ~ politeness. 谨慎有礼地。 **~·ly** adv ~·**ness** n

study¹ /'stʌdɪ; 'stʌdɪ/ n (pl **-dies**) **1** [U and in pl 并可用复数] devotion of time and thought to getting knowledge of, or to a close examination of, a subject, esp from books: 研究;研习; fond of ~; 喜读书; give all one's leisure time to ~; 空暇时间全部用来读书; make a ~ of the country's foreign trade. 研究该国的对外贸易。 My studies show that .... 我的研究显示…。 **2** [C] sth that attracts investigation; that which is (to be) investigated: 学科;研究或待研究的对象或课题: scientific studies. 科学方面的学科。 The proper ~ of mankind is man. 研究人类的适当课题就是人。 His face was a ~, was well worth observing closely. 他的脸孔很值得去仔细观察。 **3** be in a brown ~, musing, unaware of people, happenings, etc near one. 出神;沉思;冥想。 **4** room used by sb (eg in his home) for reading, writing, etc: 书房: You will find Mr Green in the/his ~. 你在(他)书房里可找到格林先生的。 **5** sketch etc made for practice or experiment; piece of music played as a technical exercise. (为练习或实验而作的)习作;试作;(音乐的)练习曲。 **6** [U] (old use) earnest effort. (旧用法)认真的努力。

study² /'stʌdɪ; 'stʌdɪ/ vt, vi (pt, pp **-died**) **1** [VP6A, 8, 15A, 2A, B, 4A] give time and attention to learning or discovering sth: 学习;研究;求学: ~ medicine. 研究医学。 He was ~ing for the medical profession/~ing to be a doctor. 他在读医科。 **2** [VP6A] examine carefully: 仔细察看、核阅、检查等: ~ the map. 细阅地图。 **3** [VP6A, 4A] give care and consideration to: 留心; 顾及; 考虑到: ~ the wishes of one's friends/only one's own interests. 考虑到朋友的愿望(只顾到自己的利益)。 **4** (pp) **studied,** intentional, deliberate: 有意的; 故意的: a studied insult. 故意的侮辱。

stuff¹ /stʌf; stʌf/ n **1** [C, U] material or substance of which sth is made or which may be used for some purpose (often fig); [U] material of which the name is uncertain, unknown or unimportant; material of (a certain) quality: 材料;原料;质料;资料;素材(常作喻);名称不知道、不确定或不重要的物质; 有某种性质的物质: We're short of 'green/'garden ~, vegetables. 我们缺乏蔬菜。 He is not the ~ heroes are made of, is not likely to be a hero, to act heroically. 他不是做英雄的材料(不太可能成为英雄)。 Do you call this ~ beer? 你把这东西叫做啤酒吗? We must find out what ~ he is made of, what sort of man he is, what his character is. 我们必须弄清楚他是个什么样的人。 S~ and nonsense! That's foolish talk! 胡扯! 胡说八道! **2** (sl uses) (俚语用法) That's the ~ to give 'em, That's how to treat them, etc. 对待他们就要这样。 Do your ~, Show what you can do, etc. 显显你的本领;露一手。 know one's ~, be expert in what one claims to be able to do, etc. 精通本行。 **3** [U] (old use) woollen cloth: (旧用法)毛织品;毛料: a ~ gown. 毛料长袍。

stuff² /stʌf; stʌf/ vt **1** [VP6A, 14, 15B] ~ sth with/into sth; ~ sth up, fill tightly with; press tightly into sth: 以某物塞满、塞紧或填塞某物; 以某物塞入或装进某物: ~ a bag with feathers, 将一只袋子装满羽

毛; ~ feathers into a bag; 把羽毛塞入袋中; ~ oneself with food, overeat; 暴食; 吃得太饱; a head ~ed with facts/silly romantic ideas; 满脑子事实(天真的想法); ~ (up) one's ears with cotton-wool; 以棉花塞住耳朵; ~ up a hole. 塞洞。 My nose is ~ed up, full of mucus (as when one has a cold). 我的鼻子塞住了(如感冒时)。 a ~ed shirt, (colloq) a pretentious or pompous person. (口)摆架子的人; 神气十足的人。 **2** [VP6A, 14] ~ (with), (colloq) make (sb) believe what is not true: (口)使(某人)误信; 诓骗(某人): He's ~ing you with silly ideas. 他想用鬼主意欺骗你。 **3** [VP6A, 14] put chopped up and specially flavoured food into (a bird, etc) before cooking it: 烹煮前用剁碎的或加味的食物填入(禽等): a ~ed turkey; 加填料的火鸡; ~ed veal. 加填料的小牛肉。 **4** [VP6A] fill the empty carcass of (a bird, an animal, etc) with enough material to restore it to its original shape, eg for exhibition in a museum: 填塞除却内脏的(鸟、兽等)的躯体以做成标本: a ~ed tiger/owl. 做成标本的老虎(枭)。 **5** [VP2A, 6A] overeat: 暴食; 过食: When will that boy stop ~ing (himself)? 那男孩何时才会不暴食呢? **6** ~ it/sth, (sl) do what one likes with it: (俚)随意处理: If you don't like it you can ~ it, will just have to put up with it/do what you like with it. 你如果不喜欢(它),你只有忍耐(随意处理)。 **7** △ (vulg sl) have sexual intercourse (with a woman). (讳)(鄙俚)与(女人)性交。 ~ing n [U] material for ~ing, eg cushions, birds, 填料;填塞物, ⇨ **3**, **4** above. 参看上列第 3, 4 义。 knock the '~ing out of sb, (a) take away his conceit or self-confidence. 挫某人的傲气或锐气。 (b) (of an illness, etc) weaken; make tired. (指疾病等)使弱; 使疲惫; 使疲倦。

stuffy /'stʌfɪ; 'stʌfɪ/ adj (**-ier, -iest**) **1** (of a room) badly ventilated. (指房间)气闷的, 通风不良的。 **2** (colloq) sulky; ill-tempered. (口)不高兴的; 愠怒的。 **3** (colloq, of a person) easily shocked or offended. (口, 指人)易吃惊的; 易得罪的。 **4** dull; formal. 不活泼的; 拘谨的; 呆板的。 **stuff·ily** /-ɪlɪ; -əlɪ/ adv **stuffi·ness** n

stul·tify /'stʌltɪfaɪ; 'stʌltə,faɪ/ vt (pt, pp **-fied**) [VP6A] cause to seem foolish or to be useless; reduce to absurdity: 使显得愚蠢或无用; 使…变成荒谬: ~ efforts to reach agreement. 使达成协议的努力归费心机。 **stul·ti·fi·ca·tion** /ˌstʌltɪfɪ'keɪʃn; ˌstʌltəfə'keʃən/ n

stumble /'stʌmbl; 'stʌmbl/ vi [VP2A, C, 3A] **1** strike the foot against sth and almost fall: 脚碰撞某物而几乎跌倒; 绊跌: ~ over the root of a tree. 为树根绊倒。 The child ~d and fell. 那孩子绊倒了。 ~ across/upon sth, find unexpectedly or by accident. 偶然发现某物。 'stumbling-block n obstacle; sth that causes difficulty or hesitation. 阻碍; 造成困难或引起迟疑之物。 **2** ~ about/along/around, move or walk in an unsteady way. 蹒跚而行; 行动不稳。 **3** speak in a hesitating way, with pauses and mistakes: 断续而有错误地说话; 结结巴巴地说: ~ over one's words; 结结巴巴地说话; ~ through a recitation. 断续而有错误地背诵。 □ n act of stumbling. 绊跌; 结巴。

stump /stʌmp; stʌmp/ n [C] **1** part of a tree remaining in the ground when the trunk has fallen or has been cut down. (树倒下或被砍断后留下的)树桩; 残干; 残体; 根株。 ~ oratory/speeches, political speeches to persuade or rouse the audience. (为说服或争取选票所做的)政治演说。 on the ~, (colloq) engaged in political speech-making, agitation, etc. (口)从事政治演说、煽动等。 **2** anything remaining after the main part has been cut or broken off or has worn off, eg an amputated limb, a worn-down tooth, the useless end of a pencil, cigar, etc; (hum) leg. 残余部分(如剁断的肢体,磨损的牙齿,铅笔头,烟蒂等); (谐)腿; 脚。 stir one's ~s, (colloq) move quickly. (口)急行; 快速行动。 **3** (cricket) one of the three upright pieces of wood at which the ball is bowled: (板球)三柱门的柱: send the

middle ~ *flying*. 撞倒三柱门的中柱. *draw* ~*s*, end play. 结束比赛. ⇨ the illus at *cricket*. 参看 cricket 之插图. □ *vi, vt* 1 [VP2C] walk *(along, about, etc)* with stiff, heavy movements. (以僵直而沉重的步伐行走 (与 along, about 等连用). 2 [VP6A] (colloq) be too hard for; leave at a loss: (口)难倒; 使困惑: *All the examination candidates were ~ed by the second question.* 全体考生都被第二个问题难倒了. 3 [VP6A] go about (a district, the country) making ~ speeches. 在(某地区、全国各处)作巡回政治演说. ⇨ the *n*, 1 above. 参看上列名词第 1 义. 4 [VP6A] (cricket) end the innings of (a batsman) by touching the ~s with the ball while he is out of his crease. (板球)以球触三柱门之柱而封杀跑分的击球员. ⇨ *crease(2)*. 5 [VP15B, 2C] ~ *money up*, (sl) pay or give a sum of money; produce (a sum of money): (俚)付出所需要之款; 拿出(一笔钱): *Mr Green has had to ~ up (£50) for his son's debts.* 格林先生必须为其子偿还(五十英镑)债务. ~*er* *n* (colloq) question that ~*s(2)*; difficult or embarrassing question. (口)难题; 令人困惑的问题.

stump·y /'stʌmpɪ; 'stʌmpɪ/ *adj* (-ier, -iest) short and thick: 短而粗的: *a little man;* 矮胖的人; *a umbrella.* 短而粗的伞.

stun /stʌn; stʌn/ *vt* (-nn-) [VP6A] 1 make unconscious by a blow, esp one on the head; knock senseless: 打击而使失去知觉; (尤指)打击头部使失知觉; 击晕: *The blow ~ned me.* 那一击把我击晕了. 2 shock; confuse the mind of: 使震惊; 使发楞; 使目眩口呆: *He was ~ned by the news of his father's death.* 获悉父亲逝世的消息他目瞪口呆. ~·*ning* *adj* (colloq) splendid; ravishing: (口)出色的; 令人喜悦的; 销魂的: *What a ~ning figure!* 多美的身段呀! ~·*ning·ly* *adv* ~·*ner* *n* (colloq) delightful, attractive person, object, etc. (口)漂亮的人、物等.

stung /stʌŋ; stʌŋ/ *pt, pp* of *sting*[2].

stunk /stʌŋk; stʌŋk/ *pp* of *stink*.

stunt[1] /stʌnt; stʌnt/ *n* [C] (colloq) sth done to attract attention: (口)吸引起人注意之事; 噱头; 特技表演: *advertising ~s*, eg sky-writing by an aircraft; 广告噱头(如飞机在天空作烟幕文字等); ~ *flying*, aerobatics. 特技飞行. *That's a good ~*, a clever idea (for getting publicity, etc). 那是(打出名的)好主意. '~ *man*, person employed to perform ~s (involving risk, etc) as a stand-in for an actor in films, etc. (电影等中临时雇用代替演员表演特技之)替身.

stunt[2] /stʌnt; stʌnt/ *vt* [VP6A] check the growth or development of: 阻碍…的生长或发展: *~ed trees;* 做盆景的矮小树; *a ~ed mind.* 未获充分发展的心智.

stu·pefy /'stjuːpɪfaɪ US: 'stuː-; 'stjupə,faɪ/ *vt* (*pt, pp* -fied) [VP6A] make clear thought impossible: 使昏乱; 使茫然; 使糊涂; 使懵懂: *stupefied with drink/amazement.* 醉得迷迷糊糊(惊得目瞪口呆). *He was stupefied by what happened.* 他所发生之事茅糊涂了. **stu·pe·fac·tion** /ˌstjuːpɪ'fækʃn US: ˌstuː-; ˌstjupə-'fækʃən/ *n* [U] state of being stupefied. 昏迷; 昏乱; 茫然; 错乱; 糊涂.

stu·pen·dous /stjuː'pendəs US: stuː-; stjuː'pɛndəs/ *adj* tremendous; amazing (in size, degree): (在体积、程度方面)巨大的; 惊人的: *a ~ error/achievement.* 大错(惊人的成就). *What a ~ folly!* 实在荒唐到极点! ~·*ly* *adv*

stu·pid /'stjuːpɪd US: 'stuː-; 'stjupɪd/ *adj* 1 slow-thinking; foolish: 鲁钝的; 愚蠢的: *Don't be ~ enough to believe that.* 不要傻到相信那种事. 2 in a state of stupor. 昏迷的; 昏乱的; 不省人事的. □ *n* (colloq) person: (口)蠢材; 愚人; 笨伯: *I was only teasing, ~!* 我只不过是开开玩笑, 傻瓜! ~·*ly* *adv* ~·*ity* /stjuː-'pɪdətɪ US: stuː'pɪdətɪ/ *n* [U] being ~; [C] (*pl* -ties) ~ act, utterance, etc. 鲁钝; 愚行; 傻话等.

stu·por /'stjuːpə(r) US: 'stuː-; 'stjupɚ/ *n* [C, U] almost unconscious condition caused by shock, drugs, alcohol, etc: (震惊、药物、酒等所造成的)昏迷; 恍惚; 不省人事: *in a drunken ~.* 烂醉如泥.

sturdy /'stɜːdɪ; 'stɝdɪ/ *adj* (-ier, -iest) strong and solid; vigorous: 坚实的; 强健的; 有力的; 不屈的: *~ children;* 健壮的孩子们; *offer a ~ resistance;* 作坚强抵抗; *~ common sense.* 丰富的常识. **stur·dily** /-lɪ; -ɪlɪ/ *adv: a sturdily built bicycle.* 构造结实的脚踏车. **stur·di·ness** *adv*

stur·geon /'stɜːdʒən; 'stɝdʒən/ *n* kinds of large fish valued as food, from which caviare is obtained. 鲟鱼; 鳇鱼; 鲟鲛(其卵可制鱼子酱).

stut·ter /'stʌtə(r); 'stʌtɚ/ *vi, vt n* = stammer. 结巴; 口吃而言. ~·*er* *n* person who ~s. 口吃者; 结巴者. ~·*ing·ly* *adv*

sty[1] /staɪ; staɪ/ *n* (*pl* sties) pigsty. 猪圈; 猪栏. ⇨ *pig(1)*.

sty[2] (also **stye**) /staɪ; staɪ/ *n* (*pl* sties, styes) inflamed swelling on the edge of the eyelid. (医)睑腺炎; 麦粒肿.

Styg·ian /'stɪdʒɪən; 'stɪdʒɪən/ *adj* (as) of the River Styx or Hades (the lower world in Gk myth): 希腊神话中之冥府的; 阴间之 Styx 河的; 如冥府的; 如 Styx 河的; hence, 由此产生; dark; gloomy. 黑暗的; 阴郁的.

style /staɪl; staɪl/ *n* 1 [C, U] manner of writing or speaking (contrasted with the subject matter); manner of doing anything, esp when it is characteristic of an artist or of a period of art: 写作或说话的方式(与题材相对); 做某事的方式; 文体; (尤指)某一艺术家或某一时期艺术的特殊风格: *written in an irritating ~.* 以令人不快的文体写成. *The ~ in this book is more attractive than the matter.* 此书的文体胜过其内容. *What do you know about the Norman/decorated/perpendicular, etc ~s of English architecture?* 你对英国诺曼式(十三至十四世纪英国哥德式, 十四至十六世纪英国哥德式)的建筑知道多少? 2 [C, U] quality that marks out sth done or made as superior, fashionable or distinctive: 卓越; 时髦; 气派; 特殊; 格调: *living in a ~ beyond his means,* in a way that he cannot afford. 过着打肿脸充胖子的生活. *Did they live in European ~ when they were in Japan?* 他们在日本的时候是过欧洲式的生活吗? *in ~*, in a grand or elegant way: 富丽堂皇; 高雅脱俗: *do things in ~,* not in a commonplace way; 做事不落俗套; *live in (grand) ~,* with servants, luxuries, etc; 生活阔绰(拥有大批仆役、奢侈品等); *drive up in ~,* eg in a very fine car, not a taxi. 开着豪华轿车来. 3 [C, U] fashion in dress, etc: 衣服等的时式; 样式; 款式; 时尚: *the latest ~s in trousers/in hair-dressing.* 最新的裤子式样(发式). 4 [C] general appearance, form or design; kind or sort: 一般的外表、形式、图案或设计; 种; 类: *made in all sizes and ~s;* 各种尺码及种类制造的; *this ~, £18.50.* 这种的, 18 英镑半. 5 [C] right title (to be) used when addressing sb: 称呼; 称谓; 尊称: *Has he any right to assume the ~ of Colonel?* 他有资格称上校吗? 6 [C] implement used in ancient times for scratching letters on wax-covered surfaces. (古代在蜡板上书写所用的)尖笔; 铁笔. 7 [C] (bot) part of the seed-producing part of a flower. (植)植物的花柱(产种的部分). ⇨ the illus at *flower*. 参看 flower 之插图. □ *vt* [VP6A] 1 describe by a specified ~(5): 称呼; 命名: *Should he be ~d 'Right Honourable' or 'Mister'?* 应该称他为 '阁下' 还是 '先生'? 2 design: 设计: *new cars ~d by the Italian experts;* 意大利专家设计的新型汽车; *an electric cooker brilliantly re-~d,* redesigned. 重新设计的精美电锅. **styl·ish** /-ɪʃ; -ɪʃ/ *adj* having ~(2, 3); fashionable: 有气派的; 时髦的; 漂亮的: *stylish clothes.* 时髦的衣服. **styl·ish·ly** *adv:* stylishly dressed. 穿着入时的. **styl·ish·ness** *n*

sty·list /'staɪlɪst; 'staɪlɪst/ *n* 1 person, esp a writer, who achieves a good or original literary style. (尤指)文体漂亮或独具一格的作家; 讲究文体者; 文体家. 2 (comm, etc) person who is concerned with the styles of decorating, clothes, etc: (商等)设计新款式、花样等的人. *a 'hair-~*, a hairdresser. 发式(发型)家; 美容师.

sty·lis·tic /star'lıstık; star'lıstık/ *adj* of style in writing. 文体的。**sty·lis·ti·cally** /-klı; -klı/ *adv*

sty·lize /'starlaız; 'starlaız/ *vt* represent or treat (art forms, etc) in a particular style. 以某种特殊的式样处理或代表(艺术形式等);使因袭某派风格;使合于某种风格。

sty·lus /'starlas; 'starlas/ *n* (*pl* ~es /-ləsız; -ləsız/) sharp point (made of diamond or sapphire) used to cut the groove of a gramophone record, or to reproduce sound by following this groove. (金钢钻或刚石制成的)电唱机的唱针。

sty·mie /'starmı; 'starmı/ *n* (in golf) situation on the green when an opponent's ball is between one's own ball and the hole; (fig, colloq) check; obstruction. (高尔夫球)球场上对手的球介于自己的球与球洞之间的位置;自己的球在球场上处于困境;(喻,口)阻碍;妨碍。□ *vt* [VP6A] put (one's opponent or his ball, or oneself) in this difficulty; (fig) check; obstruct. 使(对手,对手的球或自己)处此困境;(喻)阻碍;妨碍。

styp·tic /'stıptık; 'stıptık/ *n, adj* (substance) checking the flow of blood; 止血的; 止血剂; 止血药: *a ~ pencil*, stick of this (eg as used on a cut made while shaving). 止血(药)笔(止血剂制成的药笔,如用于刮脸时刮破之处)。

Styx /stıks; stıks/ *n* (Gk myth) river that encircles Hades, where the spirits of the dead exist. (希神)冥河(围绕于死者灵魂生存之冥府)。 *cross the ~,* die. 过冥河;死。

sua·sion /'sweıʒn; 'sweʒən/ *n* [U] (formal) persuasion. (正式用语)劝说; 劝告。 *moral ~,* persuasion based on moral grounds, not force. 道义上的劝告(晓以义理而非借武力者)。

suave /swɑːv; swɑv/ *adj* smooth and gracious (but possibly insincere) in manner. 态度娴雅(但可能是不真诚)的;和蔼的。 *~·ly adv* **suav·ity** /-ətı; -ətı/ *n* [U] quality of being ~; *(pl)* instances of being ~; ~ utterances, etc. 娴雅; 和蔼; 娴雅和蔼的实例,言谈,举止等。

sub¹ /sʌb; sʌb/ *n* (colloq, abbr of) (口,为下列各词之略) 1 submarine. 潜水艇。 2 subscription. 订阅。 3 sub-lieutenant. 海军中尉。 4 sub-editor. 副编辑;副主笔。

sub² /sʌb; sʌb/ *vi, vt* 1 [VP2A, 3A] *~ (for sb),* (colloq) act as a substitute (for him). (口)代理; 代替。 2 [VP6A] (colloq abbr of) subedit. 为 subedit 之略。

sub- /sʌb; sʌb/ *pref* ⇨ App 3. 参看附录三。

sub·al·tern /'sʌbltən US: sə'bɔːltən; səb'ɔltən/ *n* (GB) (formerly) commissioned army officer of lower rank than a captain. (英)(昔时)陆军中少尉。

sub·atomic /ˌsʌbə'tɒmık; ˌsʌbə'tɑmık/ *adj* of, relating to, any of the particles smaller than an atom. 小于原子之质点的;与小于原子之质点有关的。

sub·com·mit·tee /'sʌb kəmıtı; 'sʌbkəˌmıtı/ *n* committee formed from members of a main committee. (由大委员会中的委员组成的)小组委员会;附属委员会。

sub·con·scious /ˌsʌb'kɒnʃəs; sʌb'kɑnʃəs/ *adj* of one's mental activities of which one is not (wholly) aware; 潜意识的; 下意识的: *the ~ self.* 潜意识的自我。 □ *n* **the ~,** ~ thoughts, desires, impulses, etc collectively. 潜意识;下意识(潜意识的思想、欲望、冲动等的总称)。 *~·ly adv* **~·ness** *n*

sub·con·ti·nent /ˌsʌb'kɒntınənt; sʌb'kɑntənənt/ *n* mass of land large enough to be regarded as a separate continent but forming part of a larger mass: 次大陆; 次洲: *India is often called the S~.* 印度常被称为次大陆。

sub·con·tract /ˌsʌb'kɒntrækt; sʌb'kɑntrækt/ *n* contract which is for carrying out a previous contract or a part of it. 附属契约; 分契; 转订的契约(为执行先前订立之契约或其一部分所订的契约)。 □ *vt, vi* /ˌsʌbkən-'trækt US: -'kɒntrækt; ˌsʌbkən'trækt/ [VP6A, 2A] give or accept a ~. 订立附属契约,分契或转包契约。

~or /ˌsʌbkən'træktə(r) US: 'kɒntræk-; ˌsʌbkən'træktə/ *n* person who accepts a ~. 接受此种契约者; 承约人。

sub·cu·taneous /ˌsʌbkju:'teınıəs; ˌsʌbkju'teınıəs/ *adj* under the skin: 皮下的: *~ parasites,* living under the skin; 皮下寄生虫; *a ~ injection.* 皮下注射。

sub·di·vide /ˌsʌbdı'vaıd; ˌsʌbdə'vaıd/ *vt, vi* [VP 6A, 2A] divide into further divisions. 再分; 细分。 **sub·di·vi·sion** /ˌsʌbdı'vıʒn; ˌsʌbdə'vıʒən/ *n* [U] subdividing; [C] sth produced by subdividing. 再分; 细分;再分后之各部分或事物。

sub·due /səb'dju; US: -'duː; səb'dju/ *vt* [VP6A] 1 overcome; bring under control: 征服; 克服; 压制: *~ the tropical jungle/one's passions.* 征服热带森林(压制激情)。 2 make quieter, softer, gentler: 使较为安静、柔和、温顺; 缓和; 减弱: (esp *pp*) (尤用其过去分词) *~d voices/lights;* 降低的声音(减弱的光线); *a tone of ~d satisfaction in his voice.* 他声音中略带满足的语气。

sub·edit /ˌsʌb'edıt; sʌb'edıt/ *vt* act as an assistant editor of (a newspaper, etc). 作(报纸等的)助理编辑或副编辑。 **sub·edi·tor** /-'tə(r); -tə/ *n* 助理编辑; 副编辑。

sub·fusc /'sʌbfʌsk; sʌb'fʌsk/ *adj* rather dark in colour; (口, colloq) unimpressive. 黑黝黝的; 带黑色的; (喻,口)不显眼的; 予人印象不深的。

sub·head·ing /'sʌbhedıŋ; 'sʌbˌhedıŋ/ *n* [C] words showing the contents of part of an article, etc eg in a newspaper. (报纸等上的)小标题; 副标题; 细目。

sub·hu·man /ˌsʌb'hjuːmən; sʌb'hjumən/ *adj* less than human; more like an animal than a human being. 低于人类的; 更象动物的。

sub·ject¹ /'sʌbdʒıkt; 'sʌbdʒıkt/ *adj* 1 under foreign government, not independent: 由他国统治的; 未独立的; 藩属的: *a ~ province;* 属地; *~ peoples.* 属民。 2 *be ~ to,* owe obedience (to): 应服从的; 受制于…的: *We are ~ to the law of the land.* 我们受当地法律的约束。 3 *~ to,* having a tendency (to); prone to: 有…倾向的; 易罹; 易受; 常有: *Are you ~ to colds?* 你易患感冒吗? *The trains are ~ to delays when there is fog.* 有雾的天气火车常会误点。 4 *~ to, (adj, adv)* conditionally: 以…为条件; 听候…; 须经…: *The plan is ~ to confirmation.* 本计划须经批准。 *The arrangement is made ~ to your approval.* 这项安排须须经你赞同方能成立。 *~ to contract,* (legal) conditional upon the signing of a contract. (法律)有待合约之签订; 须经签约。 *~ to prior sale,* conditional upon no sale having been made before a further offer is made, before the date of the auction, etc. 须循先售原则(如果在更高出价出现之前,或拍卖期限前未售出)。

sub·ject² /'sʌbdʒıkt; 'sʌbdʒıkt/ *n* 1 any member of a State except the supreme ruler: 人民; 庶民; 臣民: *British ~s;* 英国国民; *French by birth and a British ~ by marriage.* 出生是法国人,因结婚而成为英国国民。 ⇨ *citizen,* (usu preferred in republics). (共和国多用 citizen)。 2 sth (to be) talked or written about or studied: 题目; 主题; 科目; 学科: *an interesting ~ of conversation;* 有趣的话题; *a ~ for an essay;* 文章的题目; *the ~ of a poem/picture.* 诗(画)的主题。 *change the ~,* talk about sth different. 改变话题。 *on the ~ of,* concerning, dealing with: 关于; 论及: *While we are on the ~ of money, may I ask when you will repay that loan?* 我们既谈到钱,我可不可以问一问你何时偿还那笔贷款? '*~ matter n* [U] the content of a book, speech, etc (contrasted with style). 书或演讲的)主题; 主旨; 题材(与 style 相对)。 3 person, animal or thing (to be) treated or dealt with, to be made to undergo or experience sth: (待)处理或讨论的对象(指人、动物或事物); 被实验者: *a ~ for experiment/dissection.* 实验(解剖)的对象。 4 *~ for sth,* circumstance, etc that gives cause for it: 做…的理由、场合或情况: *a ~ for pity/ridicule/congratulation.* 叫人同情(受人揶揄;值得恭贺)的原因。 5 person with the tendencies (usu undesirable) specified: 有某种(疾病或其他不正常)倾向的人: *a hysterical ~.* 有歇斯底里倾向的人。 6 (gram) (contrasted

with **predicate**¹ word(s) in a sentence about which sth is predicated; (contrasted with **object**¹(4)) *n* or *n* equivalent which carries out the action of a *v*, and which must agree(6) with the *v*, *eg* book in 'There was a book lying on the table' and *they* in 'Did they come early?' (语法)主语(与 predicate 及 object 相对)(如 There was a book lying on the table 中之 book, 及 Did they come early? 中之 they)。 **7** (music) theme on which a composition (or one of its movements) is based. (音乐)主题;主旨;主旋律.

sub·ject³ /'sɒbdʒekt; səb'dʒekt/ *vt* [VP14] ~ **to, 1** bring, get (a country, nation, person) under control: 征服(国家,民族,人);使隶属;使服从: *Ancient Rome ~ed most of Europe to her rule.* 古罗马征服了大半个欧洲. **2** cause to undergo or experience; expose: 使遭受;使经历;使蒙受;使有…之险: ~ *oneself/one's friends to criticism/ridicule;* 使自己(朋友)遭受批评(嘲笑); ~ *a man to torture.* 使人受折磨. *As a test the metal was ~ed to great heat.* 该金属曾置于高温下试验. **sub·jec·tion** /səb'dʒekʃn; səb'dʒekʃn/ *n* [U] ~ing or being ~ed: 征服;隶属;服从: *The ~ion of the rebels took several months.* 该叛乱历时数月始始平. *The people lived in a state of ~ion/were kept/held in ~ion for half a century.* 那个民族被统治达半世纪之久.

sub·jec·tive /səb'dʒektɪv; səb'dʒektɪv/ *adj* **1** (of ideas, feelings, etc) existing in the mind, not produced by things outside the mind; not objective: (指观念、感情等)主观的;存在于心中而非由外在事物产生的;非客观的: *Did he really see a ghost or was it only a ~ impression?* 他真的见到了鬼,抑或仅仅是主观的感觉? **2** (of art and artists, writing, etc) giving the personal or individual point of view or feeling (opp to realistic art, writing, etc). (指艺术及艺术家、写作等)表现个人的观点或感觉的;主观的(与写实艺术、作品等相反). **3** (gram) of the subject. (语法)主语的. ~**ly** *adv* in a ~ manner: 主观上;主观地: *An examination paper in arithmetic can be marked objectively, but a literary essay can be marked only ~ly,* ie on the personal impression of the examiner. 算术试卷可以客观评分,但是一篇文章却只能凭阅卷者的主观印象评分. **sub·jec·tiv·ity** /ˌsʌbdʒek'tɪvətɪ; ˌsʌbdʒek'tɪvətɪ/ *n* [U].

sub·join /ˌsʌb'dʒɔɪn; səb'dʒɔɪn/ *vt* [VP6A] (formal) add at the end: (正式用语)补述;增补;添加: ~ *a postscript to a letter.* 信后加一附记.

sub judice /ˌsʌb'dʒuː'dɪsɪ; səb'dʒudɪsɪ/ (Lat) under judicial consideration, not yet decided (and for this reason, in GB, not (by law) to be commented upon). (拉丁)在审理中; 尚未判决(因此,在英国,(依法)不得置评).

sub·ju·gate /'sʌbdʒugeɪt; 'sʌbdʒə,get/ *vt* [VP6A] subdue, conquer. 压服;征服;抑制. **sub·ju·ga·tion** /ˌsʌbdʒu'geɪʃn; ˌsʌbdʒə'geʃən/ *n* [U].

sub·junc·tive /səb'dʒʌŋktɪv; səb'dʒʌŋktɪv/ *adj* (gram) expressing a condition, hypothesis, possibility, etc. (语法)假设(虚拟)语气的. □ *n* [U, C] the ~ mood; form of a verb in this mood. 假设(虚拟)语气;假设(虚拟)语气的动词形式.

sub·lease /ˌsʌb'liːs; 'sʌb,lis/ *vt, vi* [VP6A, 2A] lease to another person (a house, land, etc which one has oneself leased); sublet. 转租;分租(房屋、土地等). □ *n* lease of this kind. 转租;分租.

sub·let /ˌsʌb'let; sʌb'let/ *vt, vi* (-tt-) [VP6A, 2A] **1** rent to sb else (a room, house, etc of which one is a tenant). 转租或分租(房间、房屋等)给他人. **2** give part of (a contract, *eg* for building a factory) to sb else. 转包或分包(建工厂等的合约)给他人.

sub·lieu·ten·ant /ˌsʌblef'tenənt US: -luː't-; ˌsʌblu-'tɛnənt/ *n* naval officer with rank next below that of a lieutenant. 海军中尉.

sub·li·mate /'sʌblɪmeɪt; 'sʌblə,met/ *vt* [VP6A] **1** (chem) convert from a solid state to vapour by heat and allow to solidify again (in order to purify it). (化

学)使升华(加热使由固体变为气体,再凝为固体,俾使之净化). **2** (psych) unconsciously change (emotions and activities arising from the instincts) into higher or more desirable channels. (心理学)不自觉地(将本能的情绪及活动)导入比较高尚或理想的途径;使(本能)升华;使高尚. □ *n, adj* (substance) refined by being ~d. 升华的(物质);净化的(物质);精华. **sub·li·ma·tion** /ˌsʌblɪ'meɪʃn; ˌsʌblə'meʃən/ *n*

sub·lime /sə'blaɪm; sə'blaɪm/ *adj* **1** of the greatest and highest sort; causing wonder or reverence: 至大至高的;庄严的;伟大的;令人惊异或崇敬的;卓越的: ~ *scenery/heroism/self-sacrifice.* 壮丽的景色(令人崇敬的英勇行为;伟大的自我牺牲). **2** extreme; astounding (as of a person who does not fear the consequences): 极;最;令人震惊的(如指不顾后果的人): *What conceit/impudence/indifference!* 多么令人吃惊的自负(厚颜,冷漠)! □ *n* the ~, that which fills one with awe or reverence. 令人敬畏或崇敬的事物;卓绝. **(go) from the ~ to the ridiculous,** (pass) from what is beautiful, noble, etc to what is trivial, inferior, absurd, etc: 煞风景(从原本美好、高贵等的事物变成平凡、低劣、荒谬等的事物): *To find a snack bar at the top of Mount Olympus would be to go from the ~ to the ridiculous.* 在奥林匹斯山顶发现一个小吃店,真是煞风景. ~**ly** *adv* in a ~ manner: 伟大地;卓越地;崇高地;令人惊异地;异常地: *He was ~ly unconscious (= completely ignorant) of how foolish he looked.* 他根本不知道他的样子有多愚蠢. **sub·lim·ity** /sə'blɪmətɪ; sə'blɪmətɪ/ *n* [U and in *pl* 并用复数: -**ties**] ~ quality or qualities: 伟大性;崇高性;卓越性;异常性: *the sublimity of the Alps;* 阿尔卑斯山的壮丽; *the sublimities of great art.* 伟大艺术的崇高性.

sub·lim·i·nal /ˌsʌb'lɪmɪnl; sʌb'lɪmənl/ *adj* below the threshold of consciousness; of which one is not consciously aware: 下意识的;潜意识的: ~ *advertising,* as when an advertisement is projected on to a cinema or TV screen for a fraction of a second and is noted only by the subconscious mind. 潜意识广告(如电影院的银幕或电视上放映的瞬间广告,观众只在潜意识中留下印象).

sub·mar·ine /ˌsʌbmə'riːn US: 'sʌbmərɪn; 'sʌbmə-,rin/ *adj* existing, designed for use, under the surface of the sea: 海生的;海中的;存在于海面下的;为海面下使用而设计的: ~ *plant life;* 海生植物; *a ~ cable.* 海底电缆. □ *n* ship which can be submerged to operate under water. 潜水艇;潜水舰. **sub·mari·ner** /sʌb-'mærɪnə(r); ˌsʌbmə'rinə/ *n* member of a ~'s crew. 潜水艇上的工作人员.

a submarine

sub·merge /səb'mɜːdʒ; səb'mɜdʒ/ *vt, vi* **1** [VP6A] put under water; cover with a liquid. 置于水中;置于液体中;浸于水或液体中;淹没. **2** [VP2A] sink out of sight; (of a submarine) go down under the surface. 沉没;(指潜水艇)潜入水中;潜航. **sub·merged** *adj* under the surface of the sea, etc: 在海面等下的;在水面下的;被水等淹没的: ~*d rocks;* 暗礁;水面下的岩石; *a wreck that is ~d at high tide.* 高潮时被水淹没的难船. **sub·merg·ence** /səb'mɜːdʒəns; səb'mɜdʒəns/, **sub·mer·sion** /səb'mɜːʃn US: -ʒn; səb'mɜʃən/ *nn* [U] submerging or being ~d. (被)浸没;(被)没入液体中. **sub·mers·ible** /səb'mɜːsəbl; səb'mɜsəbl/ *adj* capable of submerging. 有潜入水中能力的;可潜的.

sub·mission /səb'mɪʃn; səb'mɪʃən/ *n* **1** [U] act of submitting; acceptance of another's power or authority:

归顺; 投降; 降服: *The rebels made their ~ to the army.* 叛徒们向军队投降。 *The enemy were starved into ~,* compelled to submit by hunger. 敌人因饥饿而被迫投降。 **2** [U] obedience; humility: 服从; 忠顺; 谦逊: *with all due ~,* with profound respect. 必恭必敬地。 **3** [C, U] (legal) theory, opinion, etc submitted to a judge or jury: (法律)向法官或陪审团提出的意见、理论等: *My ~ is that .../In my ~, ...* I submit(3) that .... 我认为…; 据我的看法…; 兹提出意见如下…。

sub·mis·ive /səbˈmɪsɪv; səbˈmɪsɪv/ *adj* yielding to the control or authority of another: 归顺的; 降服的; 服从的: *~ to advice.* 顺从忠告。 *Marian is not a ~ wife.* 玛丽安不是一位顺服的妻子。 ⬩**·ly** *adv* ⬩**·ness** *n*

sub·mit /səbˈmɪt; səbˈmɪt/ *vt, vi* (-**tt-**) **1** [VP6A, 14] *~ oneself to sb/sth,* put (oneself) under the control of another: 使(自己)受他人控制; 服从; 屈服于: *~ oneself to discipline.* 服从纪律。 *Should a wife ~ herself to her husband?* 妻子应顺从她的丈夫吗? **2** [VP 14] *~ sb to sth,* cause him to endure it: 使某人忍受某事: *~ a prisoner to torture/interrogation.* 使一囚犯受刑(受审讯)。 **3** [VP6A, 14] *~ sth (to sb/sth),* put forward for opinion, discussion, decision, etc: 提出某事物(供评断, 讨论, 决定等): *~ plans/proposals, etc to a city council;* 向市议会提出计划(建议等); *~ proofs of identity.* 提出鉴定证明。 **4** [VP9] (legal) suggest, argue: (法律)建议; 主张; 声辩: *Counsel ~ted that there was no case against his client.* 辩护人辩称没有一条指控可加罪于他的当事人。 **5** [VP3A] *~ to sb/sth,* surrender; give in; abstain from resistance: 投降; 顺从; 屈服: *~ to the enemy/ill treatment/separation from one's family.* 屈服于敌人(甘受虐待; 忍痛与家庭分离)。

sub·nor·mal /ˌsʌbˈnɔːml; ˌsʌbˈnɔrml/ *adj* below normal: 正常以下的; 低于正常的: *~ temperatures.* 低于正常的温度; less than normal: 未达正常的; 逊常的: *a child of ~ intelligence.* 智力低于常人的儿童。 □ *n* person of ~ intelligence. 智力低于常人之人。

sub·or·bital /ˌsʌbˈɔːbɪtl; sʌbˈɔrbɪtl/ *adj* of less duration or distance than one orbit. 少于绕轨道一圈的距离或时间的。

sub·or·di·nate /səˈbɔːdɪnət US: -dənət; səˈbɔrdn̩ɪt/ *adj* **1** *~ (to),* junior in rank or position; less important: 下级的, 次要的; 局次要地位的: *in a ~ position.* 居次要地位。 **2** *~ clause,* (gram) dependent clause; clause which, introduced by a conjunction, serves as a *noun, adj* or *adv.* (语法)从属句(以连接词引导而用作名词、形容词或副词者)。 ⇨ **co-ordinate.** □ *n* person in a ~ position; person working under another. 居次位者; 属下; 属僚。 □ *vt* /səˈbɔːdɪneɪt US: -dəneɪt; səˈbɔrdn̩et/ [VP6A, 14] *~ sth (to),* treat as ~; make ~ (to). 当作 ~; 使居下位或次要地位。 **subordinating conjunction,** (gram) one that introduces a ~ clause, eg *because, if, as.* (语法)从属连接词(如 because, if, as)。 **sub·or·di·na·tion** /səˌbɔːdɪˈneɪʃn US: -dənˈeɪʃn; səˌbɔrdn̩ˈeʃən/ *n* subordinating or being ~. 下位; 次要; 附属。 **sub·or·di·na·tive** /səˈbɔːdɪnətɪv US: -dənˈetɪv; səˈbɔrdn̩etɪv/ *adj* subordinating. 附属的; 从属的。

sub·orn /səˈbɔːn; səˈbɔrn/ *vt* [VP6A] induce (a person) by bribery or other means to commit perjury or other unlawful act. 以贿赂或其他方法使(人)伪证或为其他不法行为。 **sub·or·na·tion** /ˌsʌbɔːˈneɪʃn; ˌsʌbɔrˈneʃən/ *n* [U].

sub·poena /səˈpiːnə; səˈpinə/ *n* (*pl* ~**s**) [C] (legal) written order requiring a person to appear in a law court. (法律)传票。 □ *vt* (*pt, pp* **-naed**) [VP6A] summon with a ~: 以传票传唤; 传审; 票传: *be ~ed as a witness.* 被传唤作证人。

sub rosa /ˌsʌb ˈrəʊzə; sʌbˈrozə/ (Lat) (of communications, etc) in strict confidence. (拉丁)(指联络、通信等)极端秘密地。

sub·scribe /səbˈskraɪb; səbˈskraɪb/ *vi, vt* **1** [VP2A,

3A, 6A, 14] *~ (sth) (to/for),* (agree to) pay (a sum of money) in common with other persons (to a cause, for sth): 认捐; 应募; 认股(与……共用, 后接缘由或为……用途, 后接某事物): *He ~s liberally to charities.* 他慷慨地捐助慈善事业。 *He ~ed £5 to the flood relief fund.* 他认捐五英镑作为水灾救济基金。 *How many shares did you ~ for in the new company?* 那新公司你认了多少股份? **2** [VP3A] *~ to sth,* (a) agree to take (a newspaper, periodical, etc) regularly for a specified time. 订阅(报纸、杂志)等。 (b) agree with, share (an opinion, view, etc). 同意或赞成(某项意见、观点等)。 *~ for a book,* agree before it is published to buy a copy or copies. 预约某书。 **3** [VP6A] (formal) write (one's name, etc) at the foot of a document: (正式用语)签于文件后; 签署: *~ one's name to a petition.* 签名于请愿书。 □ *~r* *n* person who ~s (esp to funds, newspapers): 捐助者; 订购者; 赞同者; 签署者;(尤指)捐助基金或订阅报纸者。 **sub·scrip·tion** /səbˈskrɪpʃn; səbˈskrɪpʃən/ *n* **1** [U] subscribing or being ~d: 捐助; 订阅; 签署: *The monument was erected by public subscription.* 该纪念碑是由各界捐款建立的。 **2** [C] sum of money ~d (for charity, for receiving a newspaper, magazine, etc), or paid for membership of a club: 慈善捐款; 捐助金; (报纸杂志等的)订阅费; 预约金; (俱乐部会员的)会费。 **sub·scription concert,** one whose seats are all paid for in advance. (座位全部预先订妥的)预约式音乐会。

sub·se·quent /ˈsʌbsɪkwənt; ˈsʌbsɪˌkwent/ *adj* *~ (to),* later; following: 后来的; 随后的; 继起的: *~ events;* 接着发生的事件。 *~ to this event.* 在此事以后。 ⬩**·ly** *adv* afterwards. 此后; 接着。

sub·serve /səbˈsɜːv; səbˈsɝv/ *vt* [VP6A] serve as a means in helping or promoting (an end, a purpose). 助于(某一目标或目的); 促进(某一目标或目的)。

sub·ser·vi·ent /səbˈsɜːvɪənt; səbˈsɝvɪənt/ *adj* *~ to,* **1** giving too much respect to: 过分悚悚的; 阿谀的; 卑屈的; 奉承的: *~ shopkeepers.* 奉承顾客的店主。 **2** useful as a means to a purpose; subordinate or subject to. 有助于某项目的的; 有用的; 辅助的; 隶属的。 ⬩**·ly** *adv* **sub·ser·vi·ence** /-əns; -əns/ *n* [U].

sub·side /səbˈsaɪd; səbˈsaɪd/ *vi* [VP2A] **1** (of flood water) sink to a lower or to the normal level. (指洪水)降落; 退去。 **2** (of land) sink, eg because of mining operations. (指土地)下沉; 凹陷(如因采矿等)。 **3** (of buildings) settle lower down in the ground, eg because of a clay subsoil that shrinks in a dry season. (指建筑物)下陷(如因下层的粘土在干旱季节时收缩所致)。 **4** (of winds, passions, etc) become quiet(er) after being violent: (指风, 激情等)(暴烈后)归于平静; 平息; 减弱: *The storm began to ~.* 暴风雨渐渐平息了。 **5** (hum) (of a person) go down slowly: (谑)(指人)慢慢下坐: *~ into a chair.* 在一张椅子上慢慢地坐下来。 **sub·sid·ence** /ˈsʌbsaɪdns; səbˈsaɪdn̩s/ *n* [C, U] act or process of subsiding (2, 3); instance of this. 降落; 下沉; 凹陷。

sub·sidi·ary /səbˈsɪdɪərɪ US: -dɪeri; səbˈsɪdɪˌɛri/ *adj* *~ (to),* serving as a help or support but not of first importance: 辅助的; 帮助的; 次要的; 附属的: *a ~ company,* one that is controlled by a larger one. 子公司; 附属公司。 □ *n* (*pl* **-ries**) ~ company or thing or person. 附属公司; 辅助物; 协助者; 助手。

sub·sidy /ˈsʌbsədɪ; ˈsʌbsədi/ *n* [C] (*pl* **-dies**) money granted, esp by a government or society, to an industry or other cause needing help, or to a ally in war, or (eg *food subsidies*) to keep prices at a desired level. 补助金(尤指政府或社团补助某项工业或某项运动, 补助战时盟国, 协助稳定物价等者); 资助金; 奖助金。 **sub·si·dize** /ˈsʌbsɪdaɪz; ˈsʌbsəˌdaɪz/ *vt* [VP6A] give a ~ to. 受资助于; 资助; 奖助: *subsidized industries.* 受资助的工业。 **sub·si·diz·ation** /ˌsʌbsɪdaɪˈzeɪʃn US: -dɪˈz-; -dɪˈze-/ *n* [U].

sub·sist /səbˈsɪst; səbˈsɪst/ *vi* [VP2A, 3A] *~ (on),* exist; be kept in existence on: 生存; 存在; 维持生活;

赖(…)为生。 ~ *on a vegetable diet* / *on charity*. 靠素食(施舍)维持生活。 **sub·sis·tence** /-təns; -təns/ *n* [U] existence; means of existing: 生存; 存在; 生计; 维生之道。 *a ~ence wage*, one that is only just enough to enable a worker to exist; 维持生活的工资; *my means of ~ence*, how I make a living; 我的生计; '*~ence crops*, those grown for consumption (contrasted with '*cash crops*, those sold for money): 消费作物(为自用种植者,与种米卖钱的 cash crops 相对); *on a '~ence level*, on a standard of living only just adequate for remaining alive. 过仅足以糊口的生活。

sub·soil /'sʌbsɔɪl; 'sʌb,sɔɪl/ *n* [U] layer of soil that lies immediately beneath the surface layer. (表层之下的)亚壤土; 下层土; 底土。

sub·sonic /,sʌb'sɒnɪk; ,sʌb'sɑnɪk/ *adj* (of speed) less than that of sound; (of aircraft) flying at ~ speed. (指速度)低于音速的; (指飞机)以低于音速飞行的。 ⇨ **supersonic.**

sub·stance /'sʌbstəns; 'sʌbstəns/ *n* **1** [C, U] (particular kind of) matter: 物质; 物; 特殊种类的物质; *Water, ice and snow are not different ~s; they are the same ~ in different forms.* 水, 冰及雪并非不同种类的物质, 它们系不同形式的同一物质。 **2** [U] most important part, chief or real meaning, of sth: 实质; 实体; 要义; 主旨; 真义: *an argument of little ~; the ~ of a speech.* 讲词的主旨。 *I agree in ~ with what you say, but differ on some small points.* 我大体上同意你所说的话, 不过某些小地方上有不同意见的点。 **3** [U] firmness; solidity: 牢固; 坚实: *This material has some ~, is fairly solid or strong.* 这种料子相当结实。 **4** [U] money; property: 钱; 财产; 资产: *a man of ~*, eg a property owner; 有资产者; *waste one's ~*, spend one's money unwisely. 浪费金钱。

sub·stan·dard /,sʌb'stændəd; ,sʌb'stændəd/ *adj* below average standard. 低于标准的; 不够标准的; 一般标准之下的。

sub·stan·tial /səb'stænʃl; səb'stænʃəl/ *adj* **1** solidly or strongly built or made. 构造牢固的; 坚实的。 **2** large; considerable: 大的; 相当可观的: *a ~ meal* / *improvement* / *loan.* 丰盛的餐食(相当大的进步; 大笔贷款)。 **3** possessing considerable property; well-to-do: 拥有相当财产的; 富有的: *a ~ business firm*; 殷实的商号; *~ farmers.* 富有的农民。 **4** essential; virtual: 实际上的; 大体上的; 实质的: *We are in ~ agreement.* 我们大体上意见相同。 **5** real; having physical existence: 真实的; 实在的; 有实体的: *Was what you saw something ~ or only a ghost?* 你见到的是真实在在的东西, 还是仅仅是鬼影? *~ly* /-ʃəlɪ; -ʃəlɪ/ *adv*: *Your efforts contributed ~ly* (= considerably) *to our success.* 你的努力对于我们的成功有重大贡献。

sub·stan·ti·ate /səb'stænʃɪeɪt; səb'stænʃɪ,et/ *vt* [VP6A] give facts to support (a claim, statement, charge, etc). 列举事实以支持(某一主张、陈述、指控等)。 **sub·stan·ti·ation** /səb,stænʃɪ'eɪʃn; səb,stænʃɪ'eʃən/ *n*

sub·stan·ti·val /,sʌbstən'taɪvl; ,sʌbstən'taɪvl/ *adj* (gram) of the nature of a substantive: (语法)实体词的; 名词的; 有名词之性质的: *a ~ clause*, a clause functioning as a noun. 名词从句。

sub·stan·tive /'sʌbstəntɪv; 'sʌbstəntɪv/ *adj* having an independent existence; real; actual: 独立存在的; 真正的; 实际的: *Almost all of Great Britain's colonies now have the status of ~ nations.* 几乎所有英国的殖民地现在都变成了独立的国家。 **a ~ motion,** (in a debate) an amendment which, having been carried, becomes the subject of further discussion. (在国会等辩论中的)正式动议(修正意见经采纳后成为进一步之讨论主题者)。 *~* /səb'stæntɪv/ *rank,* (GB) permanent rank (in the army, etc). (英)(陆军等的)永久军阶。 □ *n* (gram) noun. (语法)名词。

sub·sta·tion /'sʌbsteɪʃn; 'sʌb,steʃən/ *n* branch or subordinate station, eg for the distribution of electric current. 支局; 分局; 分所; 分站; 变电所。

sub·sti·tute /'sʌbstɪtjuːt US: -tuːt; 'sʌbstə,tjut/ *n* person or thing taking the place of, acting for or serving for another: 代理人; 代替者; 代用品; 代用物: *Is chicory a satisfactory ~ for coffee?* 菊苣是一种令人满意的咖啡代用品吗? *S~s for rubber can be made from petroleum.* 石油中可制出橡胶的代用品。 □ *vt, vi* [VP 6A, 14, 3A] *~* (*sth/sb*) (*for*), put, use or serve as a ~: 代替; 替换; 代用: *~ margarine for butter.* 以人造奶油代替奶油。 *Mr X ~d for the teacher who was in hospital.* 某先生代生病住院的那位老师。 **sub·sti·tu·tion** /,sʌbstɪ'tjuːʃn US: -'tuː-; ,sʌbstə'tjuʃən/ *n* [U]

sub·stra·tum /'sʌbstrɑːtəm US: -streɪt-; 'sʌb,stretəm/ *n* (*pl* **-ta** /-tə; -tə/) **1** level lying below another: 下面的一层; 下层: *a ~ of rock.* 下层岩石。 **2** foundation: 基础; 根基: *The story has a ~ of truth*, is based upon facts (though perhaps at first sight seeming false). 这个故事有事实为根据(虽然乍看或似荒诞不经)。

sub·struc·ture /'sʌbstrʌktʃə(r); 'sʌb'strʌktʃə/ *n* foundation; supporting part. 基础; 根柢; 根基; 支撑结构; 下层结构。 ⇨ **superstructure.**

sub·sume /səb'sjuːm US: -'suːm; səb'sum/ *vt* [VP 6A, 14] *~* (*under*), include (an example, etc) under a rule or in a particular class. 把(某一事例等)纳入某一规则或归入某一种类。

sub·tend /səb'tend; səb'tɛnd/ *vt* (geom) (of a chord, the side of a triangle) be exactly opposite to (an arc or angle). (几何)(指弦,三角形之边)正对(弧或角)。

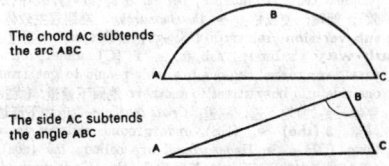

The chord AC subtends the arc ABC

The side AC subtends the angle ABC

sub·ter·fuge /'sʌbtəfjuːdʒ; 'sʌbtə,fjudʒ/ *n* [C] trick, excuse, esp one used to evade trouble or sth unpleasant; [U] trickery. 诡计; 遁辞(尤指用以逃避困难或不愉快之事者); 诡诈; 欺骗。

sub·ter·ranean /,sʌbtə'reɪnɪən; ,sʌbtə'renɪən/ *adj* underground: 地下的: *a ~ passage*; 地下通道; *~ fires.* 地下火。

sub·title /'sʌbtaɪtl; 'sʌb,taɪtl/ *n* secondary title (of a book); translation of the dialogue of a foreign language film, printed on the film. (书的)副标题; 小标题; (印在外国语发音电影片上的)对话译文; 以日翻译。

subtle /'sʌtl; 'sʌtl/ *adj* **1** difficult to perceive or describe because fine or delicate: 因细微、精巧或微妙而难于觉察或描述的; 精巧的; 巧妙的: *a ~ charm/flavour*; 难以形容的魅力(味道); *~ humour*; 巧妙的幽默; *a ~ distinction.* 细微的差别。 **2** ingenious; complex: 机敏的; 灵巧的; 错综复杂的: *a ~ argument/design.* 巧妙的议论(设计)。 **3** quick and clever at seeing or making delicate differences; sensitive: 敏锐的; 敏锐的; 明察秋毫的; 敏感的: *a ~ observer/critic.* 敏锐的观察者(批评家)。 **sub·tly** /'sʌtlɪ; 'sʌtlɪ/ *adv* **~ty** /'sʌtltɪ; 'sʌtltɪ/ *n* (*pl* **-ties**) [U] the quality of being ~; [C] (*pl*) distinction, etc. 微妙; 灵巧; 错综; 明敏; 细微的差别等。

sub·topia /sʌb'təʊpɪə; sʌb'topɪə/ *n* [U] (part of the country where there is a) monotonous urban sprawl of standardized buildings, etc; (result of such a) tendency to urbanize the country. 乡村都市化; 都市化的乡村(如采取单调一致的都市建筑等); 乡村都市化的趋势; 此一趋势所产生的结果。

sub·tract /səb'trækt; səb'trækt/ *vt* [VP6A, 14] *~* (*from*), take (a number, quantity) away from (another number, etc): 自(他数等中)减除(某数或量); 减去; 扣除: *~ 6 from 9*; 九减六; *6 ~ed from 9 gives 3*, ie 9-6=3. 九减六得三。 **sub·trac·tion** /səb'trækʃn;

səb'trækʃən/ n [U] the process of ~ing; [C] instance of this: 减法; 减去; 扣除; 减除的实例: *Two from five is a simple ~ion.* 五减二是简单的减法。

sub·tropi·cal /ˌsʌb'trɒpɪkl/ *adj* bordering on the tropics; nearly tropical; of ~ areas: 亚热带的; 近热带的; 亚热带地区的: *a ~ climate;* 亚热带气候; *~ plants.* 亚热带植物。

sub·urb /'sʌbɜːb; 'sʌbɚb/ n [C] outlying residential district of a town or city. 市郊; 城郊; 郊区。**the ~s,** all these districts collectively. 郊区总称。**sub·ur·ban** /sə'bɜːbən; sə'bɝbən/ *adj* **1** of or in a ~: 市郊的; 城郊的; (在)郊区的: *~an shops.* 郊区的商店。**2** (derog) having the good qualities of neither town nor country people; narrow in interests and outlook. (贬) 既无城市人又无乡下人之优点的; 偏狭的; 偏见的; 井底之蛙的。**sub·ur·bia** /sə'bɜːbɪə; sə'bɝbɪə/ n [U] (usu derog) (kind of life lived by, characteristic outlook of, people in) ~s (collectively). (通常作贬)郊外; 郊区居民的生活及其见识, 兴趣及见识偏狭。

sub·ven·tion /səb'venʃn; səb'venʃən/ n subsidy; grant of money in aid. 补助金; 津贴。

sub·vers·ive /səb'vɜːsɪv; səb'vɝsɪv/ *adj* tending to subvert: 颠覆的; 促使灭亡的; 有推翻之倾向的; 破坏性的: *speeches that are ~ of peace and order;* 破坏治安的演说; *~ propaganda.* 颠覆性的宣传。

sub·vert /sʌb'vɜːt; səb'vɝt/ *vt* [VP6A] destroy, overthrow (religion, a government) by weakening people's trust, confidence, belief: 推翻(政府); 破坏(宗教); 颠覆; 使灭亡: *~ the monarchy.* 推翻君主政体。**sub·ver·sion** /səb'vɜːʃn *US:* -ʒn; səb'vɝʃən/ n [U].

sub·way /'sʌbweɪ; 'sʌbˌwe/ n **1** [C] underground passage or tunnel, eg one to enable people to get from one side of a busy street to another: 地面下通道; (尤指穿越马路的)地下道; 隧道: *Cross by the ~.* 走地下道过马路。**2** (the) ~, (US) underground railway in a town (GB = *the Underground* or, colloq, *the tube*): (美)(城市中的)地下火车(英国称为 the Underground, 口语称为 the tube): *take the ~;* 乘地下火车; *travel by ~.* 乘地下火车旅行。

suc·ceed /sək'siːd; sək'sid/ *vi, vt* **1** [VP2A, 3A] *(in),* do what one is trying to do; gain one's purpose: 成功; 完成; 遂行: *~ in life;* 发达; *~ in (passing) an examination.* 考试及格(通过考试)。*The attack ~ed.* 这次袭击成功了。**2** [VP6A, 16B] come next after and take the place of: 继任; 继续: *Who ~ed Churchill as Prime Minister?* 继邱吉尔出任首相的是谁? **3** [VP2A, 3A] ~ *(to),* inherit; have (a title, position, etc) on the death of sb: 继承; 承袭(爵位, 地位等): *~ to an estate.* 承袭产业。*On George VI's death, Elizabeth II ~ed (to the throne).* 乔治六世死后, 伊利莎白二世继位(继承王位)。

suc·cess /sək'ses; sək'sɛs/ n **1** [U] succeeding; the gaining of what is aimed at: 成功; 成就: *meet with ~.* 获得成功。*Nothing succeeds like ~,* (prov) S~ in one case is likely to be followed by ~ in other cases. (谚)一事如意, 事事顺利。**2** [U] good fortune; prosperity: 好运; 发达; 兴旺: *have great ~ in life.* 交大运; 获得大成功。**3** [C] sb or sth that succeeds; example of succeeding: 成功的人或事物; 成功的例子: *The plan was a great ~.* 这项计划极为成功。*He has had three ~es and one failure,* eg of a dramatist. 他曾获得三次成功, 一次失败(如指剧作家)。*The army has had several ~es (= victories) recently.* 军队最近曾获得数次胜利。**~·ful** /-fl; -fəl/ *adj* having ~: 成功的; 得到成功的; ~ful candidates 成功的候选人; ~ in everything. 事事成功。**~·fully** /-fəlɪ; -fəlɪ/ *adv*

suc·ces·sion /sək'seʃn; sək'sɛʃən/ n **1** [U] the coming of one thing after another in time or order: 继续; 连续: *the ~ of the seasons.* 四季的接续。*in ~,* one after the other: 连续地; 接续地: *five wet days in ~.* 连续五天的雨天。**2** [C] number of things in ~: 连续的若干事物: *a ~ of wet days/defeats.* 连续的雨天(失败)。**3** [U]

(right of) succeeding to a title, the throne, property, etc; person having this right: 继承; 继承权; 有继承权的人: *Who is first in ~ to the throne?* 谁是王位第一继承人? **the Apostolic S~,** the unbroken passing of spiritual authority through the bishops from the Apostles of Jesus, and through the Popes from St Peter. 使徒大统(自耶稣十二门徒历经主教, 以及由圣彼得经教皇传继的信仰大统)。**'~ duty,** tax on inherited property. 遗产税; 继承税。

suc·cess·ive /sək'sesɪv/ *adj* coming one after the other in an uninterrupted sequence: 继续的; 连续的: *The school team won five ~ games.* 校队连续赢得五场比赛的胜利。Cf 参较 *five games in succession,* and *five games running.* 连续的五场比赛。**~·ly** *adv*

suc·cessor /sək'sesə(r); sək'sɛsɚ/ n sb or sth that succeeds another: (指人或物)后继者; 继承者; 继任者: *the ~ to the throne;* 王位继承人; *appoint a ~ to a headmaster.* 任命校长继任人。

suc·cinct /sək'sɪŋkt; sək'sɪŋkt/ *adj* expressed briefly and clearly; terse. 简明的; 扼要的; 简洁的。**~·ly** *adv* **~·ness** n

suc·cour (US = **-cor**) /'sʌkə(r); 'sʌkɚ/ n [U] (liter) help given in time of need. (文)及时的援助; 需要时的救助; 援助。□ *vt* [VP6A] give help to (sb in danger or difficulty). 援助(处于危险或困难中的人); 救助。

suc·cu·bus /'sʌkjʊbəs; 'sʌkjəbəs/ n female demon supposed to have sexual intercourse with a sleeping man. 妖精(传说中和熟睡的男子性交的女妖)。⇨ **incubus.**

suc·cu·lent /'sʌkjʊlənt; 'sʌkjələnt/ *adj* **1** (of fruit and meat) juicy; tasting good: (指水果及肉类)多汁液的; 味道好的; 好吃的: *a ~ steak.* 好吃的牛排。**2** (of stems, leaves) thick and fleshy; (of plants) having ~ stems and leaves. (指茎、叶)厚而肥的; 多肉质的; (指植物)有肥厚之茎和叶的。□ n [C] ~ plant, eg a cactus. 茎叶肥厚的植物(如仙人掌)。**suc·cu·lence** /-əns; -əns/ n [U].

suc·cumb /sə'kʌm; sə'kʌm/ *vi* [VP2A, 3A] ~ *(to),* yield (to temptation, flattery, etc); die: 屈服于(诱惑、谄媚等); 死: *~ to one's injuries.* 受伤而死。

such /sʌtʃ; sʌtʃ/ *adj* (no comp or superl; not placed between the *indef* art and its n; note, in the examples, the place of *such* after *no, some, many, all*). (无比较级和最高级; 不置于不定冠词与名词之间; 注意例句中的 such 置于 no, some, many, all 之后)。**1** of the same kind or degree (as): 同类的; 同等的; 这样的; 如此的: *~ word (as that);* (象那样的)这样一个词; *~ words (as those);* (象那些)同类的词; *no ~ words (as those);* 没有(象那些)同类的词, 无此类词; *poets ~ as Keats and Shelley;* 象济慈和雪莱这样的诗人; *~ poets as Keats and Shelley;* 象济慈和雪莱这样的诗人; *~ people as these;* 象这一类的人们; *people ~ as these;* 象这一类的人们; *on ~ an occasion as this; on an occasion ~ as this;* 在这样的场合; *Harrison, or some ~ name.* 哈里森, 或和这个差不多的名字。*Some ~ plan was in his mind.* 他心里有过这样的计划。*All ~ possibilities must be considered.* 所有这样的可能性都须加以考虑。*I have met many ~ people.* 我曾遇到过许多这样的人。*I've never heard of ~ a thing!* 我从未听说过这样的事! *I hope I never have ~ an experience again.* 我希望(我)永远不再有这种经验了。**2** ~ *as it is,* used to suggest that sth is of poor quality, of little value, etc: 用于表示某物品质不佳, 无甚价值等: *You can use my bicycle, ~ as it is.* 你可以用我的脚踏车, 只是不太好骑。**~ as to** + *inf,* of a degree or kind that would or might: 至…的程度和种类; 致: *Your stupidity is ~ as to fill me with despair.* 你愚蠢得叫我十分失望。*His illness is not ~ as to cause anxiety.* 他的病况尚不足忧虑。**3** ~ *that; ~ … that:* 如此…(…)竟致: *His behaviour was ~ that everyone disliked him.* 他的行为使人人都嫌恶他。*S~ was the force of the explosion/The force of the*

explosion was ~ that all the windows were broken. 爆炸的力量大到把全部的窗户都震破了。**4** (Cf the positions of ~ and so in these examples): (参较以下诸例中 such 及 so 的位置): *Don't be in ~ a hurry,* in so much of a hurry, in so great a hurry. 不要这样匆忙。*I haven't had ~ an enjoyable evening* (= so enjoyable an evening) *for months.* 数月来我未度过象这样愉快的一晚。**5** (intensive, esp in exclamatory sentences): (用作加强语气, 尤用于感叹句中): *It was ~ a long time ago!* 那是很久以前的事了! *You gave me ~ a fright!* 你吓死我了! *We've had ~ a good time!* 我们这一段时间过得多愉快啊! Cf 参较 What a fright you gave me! What a good time we've had! **6** (pred use) this, that, these, those (as already stated, etc): (用作表语)这(些); 那(些)(表示已陈述者等): *S~ is not my intention.* 我的意图不是这样。*S~ were his words.* 他是这么说的。*S~ was her reward.* 这就是她的报酬。*S~ is life!* Life is like that, life is as these circumstances show it to be! 人生就是这样! (人生就象那样, 象这些情况所显示者!) □ *pron ~* person(s) or thing(s); that/those: 象这样的人(们)或(诸)事物; 那(些): *I may have hurt her feelings but ~* (= that) *was certainly not my intention.* 我可能已伤害了她的感情, 但是我的确不是故意的。*He is a brilliant scholar and is everywhere recognized as ~,* as a brilliant scholar. 他是一位有才华的学者, 而且是各地的人都有这样的看法。*Down with anarchists and all ~,* all persons of that kind! 打倒无政府主义者及其所有的同路人! *as ~,* properly so called; in every way: 确切而言; 完全地: *I didn't have a nervous breakdown as ~, it was more a reaction to overwork.* 我不是真的得了神经崩溃, 那只是工作过度的反应。*~ as,* those that: 诸如: *I haven't many specimens but I will send you ~ as I have.* 我没多少样本, 但我将全部送给你。*~-like adj* (colloq) of the same kind; similar: (口)同类的, 同样的; 相似的: *I have no time for concerts, theatres, cinemas and ~like.* 我没有时间赴音乐会、看戏、看电影及诸如此类的消遣。

suck /sʌk; sʌk/ *vt, vi* **1** [VP6A, 15A, B] *~ (in/out/up/through,* etc) *(from/out of,* etc), draw (liquid) into the mouth by the use of the lip muscles: 用嘴吸(液体); 吸: *~ the juice from an orange;* 吸橘子的汁; *~ poison out of a wound;* 吸出伤口的毒液; (fig) (喻) *~ in knowledge.* 吸收知识。**2** [VP6A, 22] draw liquid or (fig) knowledge, information, etc from: 自⋯吸取液体; (喻)自⋯吸取知识、消息等: *a baby ~ing its mother's breast.* 正在吸食母乳的婴儿。Cf 参较 The mother was nursing her baby at the breast. 母亲把她的婴儿抱在怀里哺乳。*She ~ed the orange dry.* 她把橘子吸干了。*~ sb's brains,* = *pick* (now the usu word) sb's brains. 剽窃或获取某人的思想 (pick 现为常用)。*'~-ing-pig n* young pig still taking its mother's milk. 乳猪; 小猪。**3** [VP6A] hold (sth) in the mouth and lick, roll about, squeeze, etc with the tongue: 含(物)在口中以舌舐之、转动、压挤等; 吮; 舐: *~ a toffee.* 吮食太妃糖。*The child still ~s its thumb.* 这孩子还会吮吸他的大拇指。**4** [VP2C] perform the action of ~ing: 吸; 啜; 吮; 舐; 咂: *The baby was ~ing away at the empty feeding-bottle.* 那婴儿继续吮吸那只空奶瓶。*The old man was ~ing at his pipe.* 那老人在吸他的烟斗。**5** [VP6A, 15B] *~ sth (up),* absorb: 吸收: *plants that ~ up moisture from the soil.* 从土壤中吸收水份的植物。**6** [VP15A, B] (of a whirlpool, etc) engulf, pull in: (指漩涡等)吞噬; 拉进; 卷入: *The canoe was ~ed (down) into the whirlpool.* 那独木舟被卷进了漩涡。**7** [VP2C] *~ up (to),* (sl) try to please by flattery, offers of service, etc. (俚)谄媚; 拍马屁; 巴结。□ *n* act or process of ~ing: 吸; 吮; 咂; 舐; 卷入: *have/take a ~ at a lollipop.* 吮食棒棒糖。*give ~ to,* allow (a baby) to ~ at the breast (but nurse and suckle are more usu). 让(婴儿)吸奶(但 nurse 及 suckle 较常用)。

sucker /'sʌkə(r); 'sʌkɚ/ *n* **1** [VP6A] one who, that which, sucks. 吸吮者(指人或物)。**2** organ in some animals enabling them to rest on a surface by suction. (动物的)

吸盘; 吸管。**3** rubber device, eg a concave rubber disc, that adheres by suction to a surface (and can be used to cause articles to adhere in this way). 橡皮吸子(如凹入的橡皮圆盘, 可借吸力附着于平面上, 并可借此固着物件)。**4** unwanted shoot (new growth) coming up from the roots of a tree, shrub, etc. (植物的)旁枝; 吸根(从树或灌木等的根部生出者)。**5** (colloq) person foolish enough to be deceived by unscrupulous tricksters, advertisements, etc. (口)被无耻骗徒、广告等所欺骗的人。

suckle /'sʌkl; 'sʌkl/ *vt* [VP6A] feed with milk from the breast or udder. 哺乳; 喂奶。**suck·ling** /'sʌklɪŋ; 'sʌklɪŋ/ *n* baby or young animal still being ~d. (仍在哺乳的)婴儿或幼兽。*babes and sucklings,* innocent children. 无知的孩子。⇨ **mouth[1]**.

suc·tion /'sʌkʃn; 'sʌkʃən/ *n* [U] **1** action of sucking; removal of air, liquid, etc from a vessel or cavity so as to produce a partial vacuum and enable air-pressure from outside to force in liquid or dust: 吸; 吸收; 吸力; 吸入; 吸除: *Some pumps and all vacuum-cleaners work by ~.* 有些唧筒和所有的真空吸尘器都是借吸力发生作用的。**2** similar process, eg in a rubber disc with a concave surface, a fly's foot, causing two surfaces to be held together: 吸; 吸引; 相吸(如橡皮吸子、苍蝇脚等, 借吸力使两平面相结合)。

sud·den /'sʌdn; 'sʌdn/ *adj* happening, coming, done, unexpectedly, quickly, without warning: 忽然; 突然; 出乎意料的; 快速的; 急速的: *a ~ shower;* 骤雨; *a ~ turn in the road.* 路上的急转弯。□ *n* (only in) (仅用于) *all of a ~,* unexpectedly. 忽然地; 突然地; 出乎意料地。*~·ly adv ~·ness n*

suds /sʌdz; sʌdz/ *n pl* froth, mass of tiny bubbles, on soapy water. 肥皂水上的泡沫。

sue /sju:; su/ *vt, vi sue (for),* **1** [VP6A, 14] make a legal claim against: 起诉; 控告: *sue a person for damages,* for money in compensation for loss or injury. 控告某人要求损害赔偿。**2** [VP14, 3A] beg; ask: 乞; 请求: *sue (the enemy) for peace;* (向敌人)谋求和平; *suing for mercy;* 求饶; *sue for a divorce,* in a law court. (在法庭)要求离婚。

suede /sweɪd; swed/ *n* [U] kind of soft leather made from the skin of goats, with the flesh surface rubbed into a soft nap: 小山羊皮; 软羔皮(带肉的一面磨擦成细软的绒毛): (attrib) (用作定语) *~ shoes/gloves.* 软羔皮鞋(手套)。

suet /'su:ɪt; 'suɪt/ *n* [U] hard fat round the kidneys of sheep and oxen, used in cooking. (牛羊腰子上的)硬脂肪; 板油(烹调用)。*~y adj* like, containing, ~. 似板油的(含有板油的)。

suf·fer /'sʌfə(r); 'sʌfɚ/ *vi, vt* **1** [VP2A, 3A] *~ (from),* feel or have pain, loss, etc: 感觉苦痛; 遭受; 受到; 受损失; 患疾病: *~ from* (= often have) *headaches;* 时常头痛; *~ing from loss of memory.* 患遗忘症。*His business ~ed while he was ill,* His business did not do well. 在他患病期间他的生意不大好。*You will* (= be punished) *one day for your insolence!* 你总有一天会因为你的无礼而受到惩罚! **2** [VP6A] experience, undergo (sth unpleasant). 经历,遭受(不愉快之事): *~ pain/defeat/adversity;* 遭受痛苦(失败, 不幸); *~ death,* lose one's life, eg as a condemned criminal or as a martyr. 丧生(如被处死或殉道)。**3** [VP17] allow, permit (which are the more usu words). 容许; 准许(allow, permit 较常用)。**4** [VP6A] tolerate; put up with: 忍受; 忍耐; 忍住: *How can you ~ such insolence!* 你怎能忍受这样的侮辱呢? *~ fools gladly,* be patient with foolish people. 忍耐地与笨人相处。*~er* /'sʌfərə(r); 'sʌfərɚ/ *n* person who ~s: 受苦者; 受害者; 患病者。*~·able* /'sʌfərəbl; 'sʌfrəbl/ *adj* bearable. 可忍受的; 可容许的; 可堪的。*~·ing* /'sʌfərɪŋ; 'sʌfrɪŋ/ *n* **1** [U] pain of body or mind: 身体或心灵的痛苦; 苦难: *How much ~ing is there in the world?* 世界上有多少苦难? **2** (pl) feelings of pain, unhappiness, etc; (复)痛苦、不幸等的感觉; 苦

恼;折磨: *They laughed at the prisoner's ～ings.* 他们嘲笑这囚犯所受的折磨。

suf·fer·ance /'sʌfərəns; 'sʌfrəns/ *n* [U] **on ～**, with permissions implied by the absence of objection: 默许; 宽许; 容许; 容忍: *He's here on ～*, allowed to be here but not wanted. 他是被容许留在此地(并非人家需要他)。

suf·fice /sə'faɪs; sə'faɪs/ *vi, vt* 1 [VP2A, 3A] **～ (for)**, be enough (which is more usu): 足够 (enough 较常用): *Will £10 ～ for the trip?* 这趟旅行十英镑够用吗? *Your word will ～,* I am content to accept your promise. 你的承诺就够了。*S～ it to say that ...* (= It ～s to say), I will content myself by saying that .... 只须说…就够了。2 [VP6A] meet the needs of: 足敷…之需用; 使满足: *One meal a day won't ～ a growing boy.* 一天一顿饭不够一个正在发育中的男孩子的需要。

suf·fi·cient /sə'fɪʃnt; sə'fɪʃənt/ *adj* enough: 足够的; 充分的: *Is £10 ～ for the expenses of your journey?* 十英镑够你在路上花费吗? *Have we ～ food for ten people?* 我们有够十个人吃的食物吗? **～·ly** *adv* **suf·fi·ciency** /-nsɪ; -nsɪ/ *n* (usu 通常作 *a sufficiency of sth*) ～ quantity: 足够的分量; 充足: *a sufficiency of fuel for the winter.* 足够过冬的燃料。

suf·fix /'sʌfɪks; 'sʌfɪks/ *n* (abbr *suff* used in this dictionary) letter(s), sound(s) or syllable(s) added at the end of a word to make another word, eg *y* added to *rust* to make *rusty*, or as an inflexion, eg *-en* in *oxen*. (本词典略作 suff) 后缀(即加于一词之后的字母、声音或音节, 以构成另一词, 如 y 加于 rust 后构成 rusty; 或构成词尾变化, 如 oxen 中的 -en)。⇨ **prefix** and **App 3.** 参看 prefix 及附录三。

suf·fo·cate /'sʌfəkeɪt; 'sʌfə,ket/ *vt, vi* 1 [VP6A, 2A, C] cause or have difficulty in breathing: (使)窒息; (使)呼吸困难: *The fumes almost ～d me.* 浓烟几乎使我窒息。*He was suffocating with rage.* 他因发怒而呼吸困难。2 [VP6A] kill, choke, by making breathing impossible. 把…闷死。 **suf·fo·ca·tion** /,sʌfə'keɪʃn; ,sʌfə'keʃən/ *n*

suf·fra·gan /'sʌfrəgən; 'sʌfrəgən/ *n* ～ **bishop**, **bishop** ～, bishop who is consecrated to help the bishop of a see by managing part of the diocese. (宗教的)副主教; 副监督。

suf·frage /'sʌfrɪdʒ; 'sʌfrɪdʒ/ *n* 1 [C] (formal) vote; consent expressed by voting. (正式用语)投票; 投票同意。2 [U] franchise; right of voting in political elections: 选举权; 投票权: *When was the ～ extended to all women in Great Britain?* 英国何时选举权扩及全体妇女? *Is there universal ～ in your country,* Have all adults the right to vote? 贵国有普遍的选举权吗(所有的成人都有投票权吗)? **suf·fra·gette** /,sʌfrə'dʒet; ,sʌfrə'dʒet/ *n* woman who, in the early part of the 20th c, agitated for women's ～ in GB. 女权运动者(特指二十世纪初, 为英国妇女争取选举权的女子)。

suf·fuse /sə'fjuːz; sə'fjuz/ *vt* [VP6A] (esp of colours, tears) spread slowly over the surface of: (尤指颜色、眼泪)渐渐布满; 充盈: *eyes ～d with tears;* 泪汪汪的眼睛; *the evening sky ～d with crimson.* 映满深红色的傍晚天空。 **suf·fu·sion** /sə'fjuːʒn; sə'fjuʒən/ *n* [U].

sugar /'ʃʊgə(r); 'ʃʊgɚ/ *n* [U] sweet substance obtained from the juices of various plants, esp ('**cane-～**) from '**～-cane** and ('**beet-～**) from '**～-beet**, used in cooking and for sweetening tea, coffee, etc. 糖(尤指用甘蔗制成的蔗糖以及用甜菜制成的甜菜糖)。 **'～-coated** *adj* coated with ～: 涂有糖的; 有糖衣的: *～-coated pills* 糖衣药丸; (fig) superficially attractive: (喻)表面可受动人的: *～-coated promises.* 甜而诱人的诺言。 '**～-daddy** *n* (colloq) rich, usu elderly, man who is generous to a young woman in return for sexual favours or friendship. 糖老爹; 老监生(通常指有钱的老汉, 肯在年轻女子身上花大钱, 以换取性方面的享受或友情)。 **loaf** *n* hard lump of ～ in the form of a cone, as sold

in former times. (昔时售卖的)圆椎形硬糖块。 '**～-lump** *n* small cube of ～, used to sweeten a cup of tea, coffee, etc. 方糖。 '**～-refinery** *n* establishment where raw ～ is refined. 炼糖厂; 制糖厂。 '**～-tongs** *n pl* small tongs for taking lumps (cubes) of ～ at table. (桌上用的)方糖钳子; 夹糖钳。□ *vt* [VP6A] sweeten or mix with ～. 加糖使甜; 混以糖。⇨ **pill(1). sugary** *adj* tasting of ～; (fig) too sweet: 甜的; (喻)甜美的; 太甜的; 阿谀的: *～y compliments/music.* 阿谀的恭维(甜美的音乐)。

sug·gest /sə'dʒest US: səg'dʒe-; səg'dʒest/ *vt* 1 [VP 6A, C, 9, 10, 14] ～ **sth (to sb)**; ～ **(to sb) that ...**; ～ **doing sth**, propose; put forward for consideration, as a possibility: 提出; 提议; 建议: *I ～ed a visit.* 我提议去参观。*I ～ed going home/that we should go home.* 我提议(我们)回家。*I ～ we go to the theatre.* 我建议我们去看戏。*What did you ～ to the manager?* 你向经理作何建议? *Can you ～ where I could park my car?* 你能建议我在何处停车吗? 2 [VP6A] bring (an idea, possibility, etc) into the mind: 使想起(主意、念头、可能性等); 使联想; 提醒; 暗示; 讽示: *Your wheezing breathing ～s asthma or bronchitis,* causes me to think that these are what you may be suffering from. 你的哮喘显示你可能患气喘病或支气管炎。3 [VP14] (reflex) come into the mind: (反身)想起; 浮现心头: *An idea ～s itself to me,* has occurred to me. 我想到一个主意。 **～·ible** /-əbl; -əbl/ *adj* that can be influenced by ～ion; that can be ～ed. 能被暗示影响的; 可暗示的; 可提议的。 **sug·ges·tion** /sə'dʒestʃən US: səg'dʒ-; səg'dʒestʃən/ *n* 1 [U] ～ing: 提议; 建议: *at the ～ion of my brother;* 由于我哥哥(弟弟)的建议; *on your ～ion.* 照你的建议。 *S～ion is often more effective than persuasion.* 建议常比劝说有效。2 [C] idea, plan, etc that is ～ed: 所提出或建议的主意、观念、计划等: *These ～ions didn't appeal to me.* 我对这些计划毫无兴趣。3 [C] slight indication: 微示; 含意; 略含; 稍带有: *He speaks English with a ～ion of a French accent.* 他讲起英语来稍稍带有法国口音。4 [U] process of bringing an idea into the mind through association with other ideas. 联想; 联想作用; 暗示。 **hypnotic ～ion**, putting ideas or impulses into the mind of a person who is hypnotized. 催眠暗示(把观念或冲动灌输于受催眠者的心中)。 **sug·ges·tive** /sə'dʒestɪv US: səg'dʒ-; səg'dʒestɪv/ *adj* 1 tending to bring ideas, etc into the mind: 提醒的; 暗示的; 引起联想的: *～ive remarks.* 暗示的话。2 tending to ～ sth improper or indecent: 猥亵的: *～ive jokes.* 猥亵的笑话。 **sug·ges·tive·ly** *adv*

sui·cide /'sjuːɪsaɪd; 'sjuə,saɪd/ *n* 1 [U] self-murder: 自杀; **commit ～**; 自杀; [C] instance of this: 自杀实例: *three ～s last week;* 上周的三起自杀事件; [C] person who commits ～. 自杀者。2 [U] action destructive to one's interests or welfare: 自毁; 给自己带来伤害或损失的行为: *political ～,* that makes continuance in office, etc, impossible; 政治自杀; 自毁政治前程; *economic ～,* eg adoption of policies that ruin the country's economy. 经济自杀(如施行导致国家经济破产的政策)。 **sui·cidal** /,sjuːɪ'saɪdl; ,suə'saɪdl/ *adj* of ～; very harmful to one's own interests: 自杀的; 自毁的; 自取灭亡的: *a man with suicidal tendencies;* 有自杀倾向的人; *a suicidal policy.* 自杀政策。

suit /suːt; sjut/ *n* 1 [C] set of articles of outer clothing of the same material: (外套衣服等的)一套, 一副: *a ～ of armour,* 一副甲胄; *a man's ～,* jacket (waistcoat) and trousers; 男子的成套衣服(包括外套、背心和裤子): *a woman's ～,* coat and skirt; 女子套装(包括上衣和裙子); *a 'trouser-～,* woman's ～ of jacket and trousers; 长裤套装(包括外套及裤子的女装); *a two-/three-piece ～,* of two/three garments; 二(三)件式套装: *a 'dress-～,* a man's formal evening ～. 男子的晚礼服。 '**～-case** *n* portable flat-sided case for clothes, used when travelling. 手提衣箱; 小提箱。2 [C] (formal) request made to a superior, esp to a ruler: (正式用语)(对上级, 尤指对统治者的)请求; 恳求:

grant sb's ~; 接受某人的请求; *press one's* ~, beg persistently. 坚决恳求。 **3** [C] (liter or old use) asking a woman's hand in marriage: (文或旧用法)求婚: *plead/press one's* ~ *with a young woman*. 向年轻女子求婚。 **4** (**'law**) ~, case in a law court; prosecution of a claim: 诉讼; 控告; 法律案件: *bring a* ~ *against sb;* 控告某人; *be a party in a* ~; 为诉讼当事人; *a criminal/civil* ~. 刑事(民事)案件。 **5** [C] any of the four sets of cards (*spades, hearts, diamonds, clubs*) used in many card games. (若干纸牌戏中)同花色(黑桃, 红心, 方块, 梅花)的一组牌。 ⇨ the illus at **card**. 参看 card 之插图。 *a long* ~, many cards of one ~, eg ace, king, 10, 8, 6; one player's hand. 一手同花牌(多张同花色的牌, 如么点, 老 K, 十, 八, 六等): 一位玩牌者手中所有的牌。 *follow* ~, (**a**) play a card of the ~ that has been led. 跟牌。 (**b**) (fig) do what sb else has done. (喻)学样; 萧规曹随。 **~·ing** *n* (shop term for) material for clothing: (商店用语)衣料; 套装料: *gentlemen's* ~*ings,* material for men's suits. 男子套装衣料。

suit[2] /suːt; sjut/ *vt, vi* **1** [VP6A, 2A] satisfy; meet the needs of; be convenient to or right for: 使满意; 适合…的要求; 适应; 对…方便: *The seven o'clock trcin will* ~ *us very well*. 七点钟那一班火车对我们很合适。 *Does the climate* ~ *you/your health?* 这气候对你(你的健康)适合吗? *Will Thursday* ~ (*you*), be convenient? 星期四(对你)方便吗? ~ *oneself,* do what one chooses to do; act according to one's own wishes. 由自己作主; 我行我素。 ~ *sb down to the ground,* ~ him very well. 非常适合某人。 **2** [VP6B] (esp of articles of dress, styles of dressing the hair, etc) look well; be appropriate for: (尤指衣服, 发式等)相配; 合式; 适合; 恰当: *Does this skirt* ~ *me?* 这裙子我穿起来好看吗? *That colour does not* ~ *your complexion*. 那颜色不适合你的肤色。 *It doesn't* ~ *you to have your hair cut short*. 你不适合剪短发。 **3** ~ *sth to,* make fit or appropriate: 使相配; 使适合: ~ *the punishment to the crime;* 使惩罚与罪相称; ~ *one's style to one's audience*. 使演讲方式适合听众。 ~ *the action to the word,* carry out the promise (threat, etc) at once. 言行合一; 实践诺言(威胁等); 随说随做。 **4** (*pp*) *be* ~*ed* (*to/for*), be fitted, have the right qualities: 适合于; 有资格: *Is Western democracy* ~*ed to/for the nations of Asia and Africa?* 西方的民主政治适合亚洲与非洲的国家吗? *That man is not* ~*ed for teaching/to be a teacher*. 那人不适于教书(当老师)。 *Jack and his wife seem well* ~*ed to one another,* likely to be and remain on good terms. 杰克和他的妻子似乎很相配。

suit·able /'suːtəbl; 'sjutəbl/ *adj* right for the purpose or occasion: 适合的; 适宜的; 恰当的: *clothes* ~ *for cold weather;* 适于寒冷天气穿的衣服; *a* ~ *place for a picnic;* 适合于野餐的地方; *a* ~ *case for* (medical, psychiatric, etc) *treatment*. 适于(药物, 心理等)治疗的病例。 **suit·ably** /-əblɪ; -əblɪ/ *adv* **suit·abil·ity** /ˌsuːtə'bɪlətɪ; ˌsutə'bɪlətɪ/ *n* **~·ness** *n*

suite /swiːt; swit/ *n* [C] **1** group of personal attendants of an important person (eg a ruler): 随从人, 如统治者的一群随员; 一班扈从。 **2** complete set of matching articles of furniture: 一套家具: *a dining-room* ~, ie a table, chairs, a sideboard; 一套饭厅用的家具; *a lounge/bedroom* ~. 一套客厅(卧房)用的家具。 **3** complete set of rooms (eg in a hotel, a bedroom, a sitting-room and a bathroom). 套房(如旅馆中, 包括一间卧房, 一间起居室及一间浴室)。 **4** complete set of objects that belong together: 一套东西; 一组物品: *a computer suite,* all the machinery needed to run a computer. 一套电脑用具。 **5** (music) orchestral composition made up of three or more related parts. (音乐)组曲(多部管弦乐曲)。

suitor /'suːtə(r); 'sjutə/ *n* **1** person bringing a lawsuit. 起诉者; 控告者; 原告。 ⇨ **suit**[1](4). **2** man courting a woman. 向女子求婚者。 ⇨ **suit**[1](3).

sulfa (US) = **sulpha**. ⇨ **sulphonamides**.

sul·fate (US) = **sulphate**.
sul·fide (US) = **sulphide**.
sul·fona·mides (US) = **sulphonamides**.
sul·fur, sul·fur·ic, sul·fur·ous, etc (US) = **sulphur, sulphuric, sulphurous, etc**.

sulk /sʌlk; sʌlk/ *vi* [VP2A, C] be in a bad temper and show this by refusing to talk. 愠怒; 生气而不讲话; 生闷气。 **the** ~**s** *n pl* condition of ~ing: 愠怒; 生闷气: *be in the* ~*s;* 在生闷气; 在发脾气; *have (a fit of) the* ~*s*. 发(一阵)脾气; 生(一阵)闷气。 **~y** *adj* (**-ier, -iest**) having a tendency to ~; unsociable: 愠怒的; 郁郁不乐的; 不高兴的; 不友善的: *as* ~*y as a bear;* 愠怒的; 象熊一般愠怒的; *be/get* ~*y with sb about a trifle*. 与某人有小争执而郁郁不乐。 **~·ily** /-ɪlɪ; -ɪlɪ/ *adv* **~·i·ness** *n*

sulky /'sʌlkɪ; 'sʌlkɪ/ *n* (*pl* **-kies**) light two-wheeled carriage for one person, drawn by one horse. 苏克马车 (单人乘坐的两轮轻便马车, 由一匹马拖曳)。

sul·len /'sʌlən; 'sʌlɪn/ *adj* **1** silently bad-tempered; unforgiving: 愠怒的; 郁郁不乐的; 愁眉不展的; 不宽恕的: ~ *looks*. 怒容。 **2** dark and gloomy; dismal: 阴暗的; 阴沉的; 悲哀的: *a* ~ *sky*. 阴沉的天空。 **~·ly** *adv* **~·ness** *n*

sully /'sʌlɪ; 'sʌlɪ/ *vt* (*pt, pp* **-lied**) [VP6A] (usu fig) stain or discredit: (通常作喻)染污; 玷污; 毁损: ~ *sb's reputation*. 毁损某人名誉。

sulpha (US = **sulfa**) /'sʌlfə; 'sʌlfə/ *n* ⇨ **sulphona·mides**.

sul·phate (US = **sulfate**) /'sʌlfeɪt; 'sʌlfet/ *n* [C, U] salt of sulphuric acid. 硫酸盐; 硫酸化合物: ~ *of copper/copper* ~, chemical (**CuSO₄**) used in water to kill algae and fungi; 硫酸铜; 胆矾; ~ *of magnesium,* Epsom salts. 硫酸镁; 泻盐。

sul·phide (US = **sulfide**) /'sʌlfaɪd; 'sʌlfaɪd/ *n* [C, U] compound of sulphur and another element: 硫化物: *hydrogen* ~, (**H₂S**) sulphuretted hydrogen, a gas with a smell like that of rotten eggs. 硫化氢。

sul·phona·mides (US = **sul·fo-**) /sʌl'fɒnəmaɪdz; sʌl'fɑnəmaɪdz/ *n pl* group of drugs (synthetic chemical compounds, also called the '*sulpha drugs*') acting as anti-bacterial agents. 磺胺类药剂(有抗菌功效, 亦称 the sulpha drugs)。

sul·phur (US = **sul·fur**) /'sʌlfə(r); 'sʌlfə/ *n* light-yellow non-metallic element (symbol **S**) that burns with a bright flame and a strong smell, used in medicine and industry. 硫; 硫磺(淡黄色非金属元素, 符号为 S, 燃之发强光及恶臭, 用于医药及工业)。 **~·etted** /'sʌlfjʊretɪd; 'sʌlfjʊretɪd/ *adj* having ~ in combination: 含硫的; 硫化的: ~*etted hydrogen,* (**H₂S**). 硫化氢。 **sul·phu·reous** (US = **sul·fu-**) /sʌl'fjʊərɪəs; sʌl'fjʊrɪəs/ *adj* of, like, containing ~. 硫(磺)的; 似硫(磺)的; 含硫(磺)的。 **sul·phu·ric** (US = **sul·fu-**) /sʌl'fjʊərɪk; sʌl'fjʊrɪk/ *adj* ~ **ic acid,** oily, colourless, very strong acid (**H₂SO₄**) important in many industries. 硫酸。 **~·ous** /-əs; -əs/ *adj* of, containing, ~. 硫(磺)的; 含硫(磺)的。

sul·tan /'sʌltən; 'sʌltn/ *n* Muslim ruler, esp of the former Ottoman Empire. 苏丹; 伊斯兰教国的君主; (尤指昔日的)奥托曼帝国的皇帝。 **~·ate** /'sʌltənɪt; 'sʌltnɪt/ *n* position, period of rule of, a ~; territory ruled by a ~. 伊斯兰教国君主的地位, 统治期; 其所统治的领土。 **sul·tana** /sʌl'taːnə *US:* -ænə; sʌl'tænə/ *n* wife, mother, sister or daughter of a ~. 苏丹的妻子, 母亲, 姐妹或女儿; 伊斯兰教国王室女眷。 **sul·tana** /sʌl'taːnə *US:* -ænə; sʌl'tænə/ *n* [C] kind of small seedless raisin used in puddings and cakes. 一种无籽的小葡萄干(用于布丁及糕饼中)。

sul·try /'sʌltrɪ; 'sʌltrɪ/ *adj* (**-ier, -iest**) (of the atmosphere, the weather) hot and oppressive; (of a person's temper) passionate. (指大气, 天气)闷热的; 酷热的; (指人的性情)热情的; 急躁的。 **sul·trily** /-trəlɪ; -trɪlɪ/ *adv* **sul·tri·ness** *n*

sum /sʌm; sʌm/ n 1 (also 亦作 **sum total**) total obtained by adding together items, numbers or amounts. 总数; 总计; 和. 2 problem in arithmetic: 算术题目: *good at sums; 长于算术; do a sum in one's head.* 心算. 3 amount of money: 金额; 钱数: *win a large sum at the Casino.* 在赌场赢一大笔钱; *save a nice little sum out of one's wages each week.* 从每周工资中节省一笔可观的数目. 4 *in sum,* in a few words. 简言之. □ *vt, vi* (-mm-) [VP15B, 2C] **sum** (*sb/sth*) **up,** (a) give the total of. 总计; 合计. (b) express briefly (the chief points of what has been said): 总结; 概括前言; 总括起来; 归纳: *The judge summed up the evidence).* 法官做一总结(归纳证词). (c) form a judgement or opinion of: …形成判断或意见: *He summed up the situation at a glance,* realized it at once. 他一眼就认清了当时的情况. *She quickly summed him up,* judged his character, etc. 她很快就对他的人品下评语. ,**summing-'up** n (pl **summings-up**) judge's review of evidence, arguments, etc, in a law-case. (讼案中法官对证据、辩论等的)总结; 扼要叙述.

su·mac(h) /'ʃuːmæk; 'ʃu:mæk/ n (kinds of) shrub or small tree, the dried leaves being used in tanning and dyeing. 漆树属植物; 盐肤木(其叶干后可用于制革或作染料).

sum·mary /'sʌmərɪ; 'sʌmərɪ/ adj 1 brief; giving the chief points only: 简短的; 简明的; 扼要的: *a ~ account.* 简要的说明. 2 done or given without delay or attention to small matters: 即决的; 即时的; 当场的; 立刻的: *~ justice/punishment/methods.* 即时裁决(当场的惩罚); 直接快速的方法. □ n (pl **-ries**) brief account giving the chief points. 摘要; 概略. **sum·mar·ily** /'sʌmərəlɪ; US: -'merəlɪ/ adv **sum·mar·ize** /'sʌməraɪz; 'sʌmə,raɪz/ vt [VP6A] be or make a ~ of. 摘要; 概述.

sum·mat /'sʌmət; 'sʌmət/ n (sl and dial) something. (俚及方)某事(物).

sum·ma·tion /sə'meɪʃn; sʌm'eʃən/ n 1 addition. 加; 加法. 2 summing up. 总计; 总和; 总结.

sum·mer /'sʌmə(r); 'sʌmə/ n [U, C] (in countries outside the tropics) the warmest season of the year, May or June to August in the northern hemisphere: (在热带地区以外的国家)夏; 夏季(在北半球指五或六月至八月): *in (the) ~;* 在夏季; *in the ~ of 1999;* 在一九九九年的夏天; *this/next/last ~;* 今(明, 去)夏; (attrib) (用作定语) *~ weather;* 夏季的天气; *the ~ holidays;* 暑假; *a ~ cottage/house,* for use during the ~; 夏季别墅; *a girl of ten ~s,* (liter) ten years of age. (文)一个十岁的女孩子. *It's been an unusually hot ~.* 那是个特别酷热的夏天. '~**-house** n shelter with seats in a garden, park, etc. 凉亭. '~ **school** n course of lectures, often at a university, during the vacation. 暑期班; 暑期学校(通常指大学暑假期间所开的课程). '~-**time** n the season of ~. 夏季. '~ **time** n time as recognized in some countries where clocks are put forward one hour so that darkness falls an hour later, giving long light evenings during the ~ months. 夏令时间; 日光节约时间. ⇨ *daylight saving* at **daylight. Indian ~,** ⇨ **Indian(3).** □ vi [VP2C] spend the ~: 过夏天; 避暑; 度夏天: *~ at the seaside/in the mountains.* 在海边(山中)避暑. **~y** adj characteristic of, suitable for, ~: 夏天的; 有夏天特征的; 适于夏季的: *a ~y dress.* 夏天的衣服.

sum·mit /'sʌmɪt; 'sʌmɪt/ n [C] highest point; top: 最高点; 顶点; 绝顶: *reach the ~,* of a mountain; 到达山顶; (fig) (喻) *the ~ of his ambition/power;* 他的野心(权力)的极致; *talks at the ~.* 高峰会谈. □ '~ **talk/meeting,** discussion between heads of States. (各国政府首长间的)高峰会谈(会议).

sum·mon /'sʌmən; 'sʌmən/ vt 1 [VP6A, 14, 17] *~ sb (to sth/to do sth),* demand the presence of; call or send for: 召唤; 传唤; 召集: *~ shareholders to a general meeting;* 召集股东大会; *~ sb to appear as a*

witness, eg in a law court. 传唤某人出席作证(如法庭上). *The debtor was ~ed,* ie to appear in a law court. 债务人被传(出庭). *The Queen has ~ed Parliament,* ordered members to assemble. 女王召集国会. 2 [VP 15B] *~ sth up,* gather together; call up: 集聚; 聚集; 征集: *~ up one's courage/energy/nerve for a task/to do sth.* 鼓起勇气(精力)做一件工作(做某事).

sum·mons /'sʌmənz; 'sʌmənz/ n (pl **~es**) [C] 1 order to appear before a judge or magistrate; document with such an order: 传唤; 传票: *issue a ~.* 发出传票. *The ~ was served by a bailiff.* 该传票由法警递送. 2 command to do sth or appear somewhere: 召唤; 命令. □ vt [VP6A] serve a ~(1) on. 以传票送达.

sump /sʌmp; sʌmp/ n 1 inner casing of a petrol engine containing lubricating oil. (汽油内燃机中装有润滑油的)润滑油槽. 2 hole or low area into which waste liquid drains. 污水坑; 排水坑.

sump·ter /'sʌmptə(r); 'sʌmptə/ n (old use) (often 常作 *'~-horse,* '~-*mule*) horse or mule for carrying burdens; pack-animal. (旧用法)驮马; 驮骡; 驮兽.

sump·tu·ary /'sʌmptjuərɪ US: -tʃuərɪ; 'sʌmptʃu,ɛrɪ/ adj (attrib only) (of laws) controlling or limiting private expenditure of money (on what is considered extravagant, etc). (只用作定语)(指法律)规定或限制私人花费的, 控制私人费用的(对于奢侈等项的花费予以限制).

sump·tu·ous /'sʌmptʃuəs; 'sʌmptʃuəs/ adj magnificent; costly-looking: 华丽的; 奢多的; 豪华的: *a ~ feast;* 豪华的宴会; *~ clothes.* 华服. **~·ly** adv **~·ness** n

sun /sʌn; sʌn/ n 1 (the) **sun,** the heavenly body from which the earth gets warmth and light. 日; 太阳. ⇨ the illus at **planet.** 参看 planet 之插图. *rise with the sun,* get up at dawn. 黎明即起; 早起. *the midnight sun,* the sun as seen in the arctic and antarctic regions. 午夜太阳(在两极地区所见者). 2 (the) **sun,** light and warmth from the sun: 阳光; 日光: *sit in the sun;* 坐在阳光下; *have the sun in one's eyes;* 阳光照在眼中; *draw the curtains to shut out/let in the sun.* 拉窗帘遮蔽(放进)阳光. *under the sun,* (anywhere) in the world: 太阳之下; 在世界上(任何地方): *the best wine under the sun.* 世界上最好的酒. *give sb/have a place in the sun,* (fig) space and conditions favourable to development. (喻)处顺境(给予某人有利的发展空间及环境). 3 [C] any fixed star: 任何恒星: *There are many suns larger than ours.* (宇宙间)有许多恒星比我们的太阳还要大. 4 (compounds) (复合词) '**sun·baked** adj made hard by the heat of the sun: 太阳晒干的: *sunbaked fields.* 太阳晒干的田地. '**sun·bathe** vi expose one's body to sunlight, eg to give a pale skin a tan. 作日光浴. ⇨ *sunburn* below. 参看下列之 sunburn. '**sun·beam** n ray of sunshine; (colloq) cheerful and happy person (esp a child). 日光; 阳光; (口)愉快的人(尤指小孩). '**sun·blind** n window shade, esp an awning outside a window. 遮阳; (尤指窗外的)遮篷; 篷盖. '**sun·bonnet/-hat** nn hat or (usu linen) bonnet made so as to shade the face and neck from the sun. 遮阳帽; 太阳帽. '**sun·burn** n [C, U] (place where there is a) darkening of the skin caused by the sun, or reddening and blistering caused by too much exposure to the sun. 晒黑; 晒黑处; 晒斑; 日炙; 晒斑或晒痛(处). '**sun·burnt, 'sun·burned** adjj having sunburn. 晒黑的; 日炙的; 有晒斑的. '**sun·burst** n sudden burst of sunlight (through broken clouds). (云缝中)突现的阳光. '**sun·dial** n device that shows the time by the shadow of a rod or plate on a scaled dial. 日规; 日晷(仪). '**sun·down** n [U] sunset. 日落; 日没. '**sun·downer** n (a) (in Australia) tramp who habitually arrives (at a sheep farm, etc) at nightfall. (澳大利亚)常到牧场等处傍晚的徒步旅客. (b) (colloq) drink (usu of sth alcoholic) at sundown. (口) 傍晚的饮料(通常为酒类). '**sun·drenched** adj exposed to great light and heat from the sun: 饱受日光照射的;

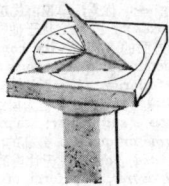

a sundial

晒透了的: *sun-drenched beaches along the Riviera.* 里维埃拉阳光普照的海滩。 **'sun-dried** *adj* (of fruit, etc) dried naturally, by the sun, not by artificial heat. (指水果等)太阳晒干的。 **'sun-fish** *n* large fish almost spherical in shape. 翻车鱼(一种几乎球形的大鱼)。 **'sun-flower** *n* tall garden plant with large golden-rayed flowers. 向日葵。 ⇨ the illus at **flower.** 参看 flower 之插图。 **'sun-glasses** *n pl* glasses of dark-coloured glass to protect the eyes from bright sunshine. 太阳眼镜。 **'sun-god** *n* sun worshipped as a god. 日神; 太阳神。 **'sun-helmet** *n* hat specially made to protect the head from the sun in the tropics. (热带用的)太阳盔; 遮阳盔。 **'sun-lamp** *n* lamp that gives out ultra-violet rays with effects like those of the sun, used for artificial sun-bathing. 太阳灯(可产生紫外线, 用于人工日光浴)。 **'sun-light** *n* [U] the light of the sun. 日光; 阳光。 **'sun-lit** *adj* lighted by the sun: 阳光照耀的; 被阳光照射的: *a sunlit landscape.* 阳光照耀下的景色。 **'sun-lounge,** or, less usu 或, **'sun-parlour/-porch** *nn* made with glass sides and so situated as to admit much sunlight. 日光浴室(廊)(四面以玻璃为屏, 以容大量阳光)。 **'sun-ray** *n* ultra-violet ray used on the body: (用于人体的)紫外光线;太阳光线: (attrib) (用作定语) *'sun-ray treatment.* 日光疗法; 紫外线疗法。 **'sun-rise** *n* [U] (time) of the sun's rising: 日出;日出的时刻; 黎明: *start at sunrise.* 拂晓动身。 **'sun-roof** (or, less usu 或, **'sunshine-roof**) *n* panel on the roof of a saloon car which slides back to admit sunshine. (某种轿车的)活动顶(可拉开让光射入者)。 **'sunset** /-set; -sɛt/ *n* [U] (time of) the sun's setting. 日落; 日落时刻; 傍晚。 **'sun-shade** *n* parasol (like an umbrella) to keep off the sun; awning of a shop window. 遮阳伞; 商店橱窗的遮阳篷。 **'sun-shine** *n* [U] light of the sun. 日光; 阳光。 **'sun-spot** *n* (astron) dark patch on the sun at times, often causing electrical disturbances and interfering with radio communications; (colloq) place that has a sunny climate (eg for holidays). (天文)太阳黑子; 日斑(不时出现在太阳上的黑斑, 常引起电的扰乱, 干扰无线电通讯); (口)阳光充足的地方(如假日去处)。 **'sun-stroke** *n* [U] illness caused by too much exposure to the sun, esp on the head. 日射病; 中暍; 中暑。 **'sun-tan** *n* [U, C] browning of the skin from exposure to sunlight: (因晒太阳而)皮肤变黑; 晒黑; 晒红: *'suntan lotion/oil.* 防晒剂(油)。 **'sun-trap** *n* warm sunny place (sheltered from wind). 日光窝(避风而多阳光的暖和处)。 **'sun-up** *n* [U] (colloq) sunrise. (口)日出; 日出时刻; 黎明。 **'sun-worship** *n* [U] worship of the sun as a deity; (colloq) fondness for sun-bathing. 太阳崇拜(把太阳看作神); (口)爱好日光浴。 □ *vt* (**-nn-**) [VP6A] put in, expose (*oneself*) to, the rays of the sun: 曝; 晒: *The cat was sunning itself on the path.* 那只猫在小径上晒太阳。 **sun-less** *adj* receiving little or no sunlight; without sun; dark: 晒不到太阳的; 无太阳的; 黑暗的: *a sunless day/room.* 阴暗的日子; 阴暗的房间。 **sunny** *adj* (**-ier, -iest**) **1** bright with sunlight: 阳光充足的; 晴朗的: *a sunny room; sunny days.* 晴朗的日子。 *,sunny-side 'up,* (US) (of an egg) fried on one side only. (美)(指蛋)只煎一面的。 **2** cheerful: 欢乐的; 愉快的: *a sunny smile/disposition/welcome.* 愉快的微笑(性情,欢迎)。 **sun-nily** /-ɪlɪ; -ɪlɪ/ *adv*

sun-dae /'sʌndeɪ US: -dɪ:; 'sʌndɪ/ *n* portion of ice-cream with crushed fruit, fruit-juice, nuts, etc. 圣代(加有压碎的水果、果汁、坚果等的冰淇淋)。

Sun-day /'sʌndɪ; 'sʌndɪ/ *n* the first day of the week, a day of rest and worship among Christians. 星期日; 礼拜日; 日曜日(一周的首日,基督徒的休息及崇拜日)。 *one's ~ clothes/best,* (colloq, joc) one's best clothes, not used for working in. (口,谑)最好的衣服(非工作时穿着的衣服)。 *'~ school,* one (in a church, etc) attended by children on ~s for religious teaching. 主日学(校)(教堂等中所设, 于星期日授儿童宗教课程者)。 *a month of ~s,* a long period of time. 很长的一段时间; 长久。

sun-der /'sʌndə(r); 'sʌndə/ *vt* (old use, or liter) [VP6A] keep apart; sever. (旧用法或文)分开; 隔离; 断绝。 □ *n* (only in) (仅用于) *in ~,* = asunder. 分开; 离开; 隔离; 折断。

sun-dries /'sʌndrɪz; 'sʌndrɪz/ *n pl* various small items not separately named. 杂物; 杂货; 杂项; 杂事。

sun-dry /'sʌndrɪ; 'sʌndrɪ/ *adj* various: 不同的; 各种的; 多方面的: *on ~ occasions.* 在各种不同的时机。 *all and ~,* (colloq) everyone; everything. (口)人人; 每人;所有的人; 一切事物。

sung /sʌŋ; sʌŋ/ *pp* of **sing.**

sunk /sʌŋk; sʌŋk/ *pp* of **sink**[2].

sunk-en /'sʌŋkən; 'sʌŋkən/ *pp* of **sink**[2] esp (**5**).

sunny /'sʌnɪ; 'sʌnɪ/ *adj* ⇨ **sun.**

sup[1] /sʌp; sʌp/ *vi, vt* (**-pp-**) [VP2A, C, 6A, 15B] *sup (up),* (esp Scot and N Eng) drink in small amounts; take (liquid) into the mouth a little at a time: (尤用于苏格兰及英格兰北部)啜饮; 啜; 每次一点点地饮(液体): *Sup (up) your broth.* 喝(你的)肉汤。 □ *n* small quantity of (liquid): (液体的)少量; 一饮; 一啜: *a sup of ale.* 少量的麦酒(或淡啤酒)。 *I've had neither bite nor sup* (=neither food nor drink) *for six hours.* 我已六小时未进饮食。

sup[2] /sʌp; sʌp/ *vi* (**-pp-**) [VP3A] *sup on/off,* (rare) eat (on, off): (罕)sup on bread and cheese. 吃面包及乳酪。 *He that sups with the devil must have a long spoon,* (prov) Caution is needed in dealings with someone of doubtful character. (谚)与恶人打交道须特别提防。

super /'su:pə(r); 'su:pə/ *n* (colloq) (口) = supernumerary; superintendent (of police). 冗员; 额外人员; (警察)局长。 □ *adj* (colloq) excellent; splendid. (口)杰出的;特佳的; 上等的。

super-abun-dant /,su:pərə'bʌndənt, ,su:pərə'bʌndənt/ *adj* very abundant; more than enough. 极多的;过剩的;多余的。 **super-abun-dance** /-əns, -əns/ *n*

super-an-nu-ate /,su:pər'ænjueɪt, ,su:pə'ænju,et/ *vt* **1** [VP6A] give a pension to (an employee) when he is old or unable to work; dismiss (an employee) because of age or weakness. 发给(老弱员工)退休金; 令(老弱员工)退休。 **2** (*pp,* **~d,** as *adj*) too old for work or use; (colloq) old-fashioned or out of date. (过去分词,作形容词用)老朽的; 老而无用的;(口)老式的; 陈旧的; 过时的。 **super-an-nu-ation** /,su:pər,ænju'eɪʃn; ,su:pə,ænju-'eʃən/ *n*

su-perb /su:'pɜ:b; su'pɝb/ *adj* magnificent; first class. 宏伟的; 壮丽的; 华美的; 头等的。 **~-ly** *adv*

super-cargo /'su:pəka:gəʊ; ,su:pə'kargo/ *n* (*pl* **~es** /-gəʊz; -goz/) person on a merchant ship who manages the sale of the cargo, etc. (商船上的)营运主管。

super-charger /'su:pətʃa:dʒə(r); ,su:pə'tʃardʒə/ *n* device used in an internal-combustion engine to force extra oxygen into the cylinders. (内燃机的)增压器(将额外的氧气压入气缸中者)。 **'super-charged** *adj* fitted with a ~. 装有增压器的。

super-cili-ous /,su:pə'sɪlɪəs, ,su:pə'sɪlɪəs/ *adj* showing contemptuous indifference: 傲慢的;目空一切的;自大的; 不屑一顾的: *nose high in the air, looking like a ~ camel.* 仰脸朝天,活像一只傲慢的骆驼。 **~-ly** *adv* **~-ness** *n*

super·ego /'suːpəregəʊ US: -iːgəʊ; ,supɚ'igo/ n [U] (the) ~, (psych) the part of the mind that responds to conscience and morality. (心理)超我(个人自我结构中反应良心和道德规范的部分). ⇨ **ego, id.**

super·ero·gation /,suːpəˌerəʊ'geɪʃn; ,supɚ,ɛrə'geʃən/ n [U] the doing of more than is required or expected: 额外工作; 职务以外的工作; a work of ~. 一件功德; 余功.

super·fat·ted /,suːpə'fætɪd; ,supɚ'fætɪd/ adj (chiefly of soap) containing a larger than usual proportion of fat. (主要指肥皂)含脂肪过多的.

super·fi·cial /,suːpə'fɪʃl; ,supɚ'fɪʃəl/ adj 1 of or on the surface only: 表面的; 表皮的; 在表面上的; 在表皮上的: a ~ wound; 表皮的伤; a ~ area. 面积. 2 not thorough or profound: 肤浅的; 浅薄的: a ~ book; 立论肤浅的书; have only a ~ knowledge of a subject; 对某一学科略知皮毛; a ~ mind. 浅薄的心智. ~**ly** /-ʃəl; -ʃəlɪ/ adv ~**ity** /ˌsuːpəˌfɪʃɪ'ælətɪ; ˌsupɚˌfɪʃɪ'ælətɪ/ n [U].

super·fi·cies /ˌsuːpə'fɪʃiːz; ˌsupɚ'fɪʃɪˌiz/ n (pl unchanged) (复数不变) 1 surface; surface area. 表面; 表面积. 2 outward appearance. 外表; 外观.

super·fine /'suːpəfaɪn; ˌsupɚ'faɪn/ adj 1 unusually fine in quality. 极精致的; 最佳品质的; 最上品的. 2 unnecessarily refined or subtle: 过分精细的; 过于微妙的: a ~ distinction. 过细的区别.

super·flu·ous /suːpə'fluəs; su'pɝfluəs/ adj more than is needed or wanted. 累赘的; 过多的; 多余的; 不必要的. ~**ly** adv **super·flu·ity** /ˌsuːpə'fluːətɪ; ˌsupɚ-'fluətɪ/ n (pl -ties) [C, U] (an amount that is) more than is needed: 累赘; 多余; 过剩; 过量: have a ~ fluity of good things. 拥有过多的好东西.

super·hu·man /ˌsuːpə'hjuːmən; ˌsupɚ'hjumən/ adj exceeding ordinary human power, size, knowledge, etc: 超乎常人之力量,体积,尺寸,智识等的; 超人的: by a ~ effort; 借一种超乎常人的努力; an apparition of ~ size. 超乎常人体积的鬼魂.

super·im·pose /ˌsuːpərɪm'pəʊz; ˌsupɚɪm'poz/ vt [VP6A, 14] put (one thing) on top of sth else: 置(一物)于他物之上; 添加; 附加; 重叠: a map of Great Britain ~d on a map of Texas, 叠于德克萨斯州地图上的大不列颠地图(以示相对大小). 在德克萨斯州地图上的大不列颠地图(以示相对大小).

super·in·tend /ˌsuːpərɪn'tend; ˌsjupərɪn'tend/ vt, vi [VP6A, 2A] manage; watch and direct (work, etc). 管理; 监督(工作等). ~**ence** /-əns; -əns/ n [U] ~**ing**: 管理; 监督: under the personal ~ence of the manager. 在经理的亲自监督之下. ~**ent** /-ənt; -ənt/ n person who ~s; manager; police officer above a chief inspector in rank. 管理者; 监督者; 经理; 警察局长.

su·perior /suːˈpɪərɪə(r); sə'pɪrɪə/ adj 1 better than the average: 优良的; 卓越的; 超出一般水准的: ~ cloth; 上等布; a girl of ~ intelligence; 智力高的女孩子; ~ grades of coffee. 上等咖啡. 2 greater in number: 数目较大的; 较多的: The enemy attacked with ~ forces/were ~ in numbers. 敌人以优势兵力进攻(敌人在人数上占优势). 3 ~ to, (a) better than: 优于; 胜过: This cloth is ~ to that. 这一种布比那一种好. (b) higher in rank or position than. 级别或地位高于. (c) not influenced by; not giving way to: 不受…的影响; 不屈服于: ~ to flattery; 不为谄媚所动; rise (= be) ~ to temptation. 不为诱惑所影响. 4 priggish; supercilious: 傲慢的; 自负的; 自大的: 'I never apologize,' he said, with a ~ air. '我从不向人道歉,'他傲慢地说. □ n 1 person of higher rank, authority, etc than another, or who is better, etc than another (in sth): 长官; 上司; 长者; 长辈; 在某方向优于他人者: my ~s in rank/in expertise. 级别高于我的人(专门技术或知识优于我的人). Napoleon had no ~ as a general. 拿破仑之为将, 无出其右者. 2 (in titles) head of a religious community: (用于称号中)修道院院长: the Father S~, eg an abbot; 男修道院院长; the Mother S~, eg an abbess. 女修道院院长. ~**ity** /suːˌpɪərɪ'ɒrətɪ US: -'ɔːr-; səˌpɪrɪ'ɔrətɪ/ n [U]

state of being ~: 优秀; 卓越; 优越: the ~ity of one thing to another; 一物之优于他物; his ~ity in talent. 他才能方面的卓越. '~**ity complex,** (pop use) aggressive or domineering attitude as a defence against a feeling of inferiority. (流行用法)自尊情结(以侵犯性或高压式的作为掩饰自卑的一种行为模式).

su·per·la·tive /suː'pɜːlətɪv; sə'pɝlətɪv/ adj 1 of the highest degree or quality: 最高的; 无上的: a wine of ~ bouquet and flavour. 具有上等醇的酒. 2 (gram) (语法) the ~ degree, the form of an adj or adv expressing the highest degree, eg best, worst, slowest, most foolishly. 最高级(表示最高程度的形容词或副词形式,如 best, worst, slowest, most foolishly 等). □ n ~ form of an adj or adv. 形容词或副词的最高级形式. **speak in ~s,** use language expressing extreme opinions and feelings; exaggerate. 夸大; 夸张; 讲话不离'最'字.

super·man /'suːpəmæn; 'supɚˌmæn/ n (pl -men) man having more than ordinary human powers and abilities, eg as imagined by sb writing about the future of mankind. 具有超乎常人力量及能力的人; 超人(如描写人类未来的作家所想像者).

super·mar·ket /'suːpəmaːkɪt; 'supɚˌmarkɪt/ n large self-service store selling food, household goods, etc. 超级市场.

su·per·nal /suː'pɜːnl; su'pɝnl/ adj (liter) heavenly; divine: (文)天上的; 超凡的; 神圣的: ~ loveliness. 超凡的美妙.

super·natu·ral /ˌsuːpə'nætʃrəl; ˌsupɚ'nætʃrəl/ adj spiritual; of that which is not controlled or explained by physical laws: 神奇的; 不可思议的; 超自然的: ~ beings, eg angels and devils. 超自然的生物(如天使及魔鬼). **the ~,** ~ agencies, phenomena, etc. 超自然的作用,现象等. ~**ly** /-'nætʃrəlɪ; -'nætʃrəlɪ/ adv

super·nor·mal /ˌsuːpə'nɔːml; ˌsupɚ'nɔrml/ adj beyond what is normal. 异常的; 非凡的; 超出正常的.

super·nu·mer·ary /ˌsuːpə'njuːmərərɪ US: -'nuːmə-rerɪ; ˌsupɚ'njuməˌrɛrɪ/ n (pl -ries), adj (person or thing) in excess of the normal number; (esp) person engaged for odd jobs; actor who has only a small part, eg in crowd scenes. 额外的; 多余的; 额外或多余的人或物; (尤指)杂工; 小工; 小配角; 临时演员.

super·scrip·tion /ˌsuːpə'skrɪpʃn; ˌsupɚ'skrɪpʃən/ n [C] word(s) written at the top of or outside sth, eg the address on the envelope of a letter. 写于某物顶端或外面的文字(如写在信封上的地址).

super·sede /ˌsuːpə'siːd; ˌsupɚ'sid/ vt [VP6A] take the place of; put or use sb or sth in the place of: 代替; 取代: Motorways have ~d ordinary roads for long-distance travel. 在长途旅行方面, 高速公路已取代了一般的道路. **super·session** /ˌsuːpə'seʃn; ˌsupɚ'sɛʃən/ n

super·sonic /ˌsuːpə'sɒnɪk; ˌsupɚ'sɑnɪk/ adj (of speeds) greater than that of sound; (of aircraft) able to fly at ~ speed. (指速度)超音速的; 超声速的; (指飞机)能够作超音速飞行的.

super·sti·tion /ˌsuːpə'stɪʃn; ˌsupɚ'stɪʃən/ n [C, U] (idea, practice, etc founded on) unreasoning belief in magic, witchcraft, etc; irrational fear of what is unknown or mysterious: 迷信; 迷信的观念; 迷信的习俗(盲从魔术,巫术等所形成的观念或作为); 对未知,陌生或神秘事物的本能恐惧: sunk in ignorance and ~. 沉溺于无知与迷信中. **super·sti·tious** /ˌsuːpə'stɪʃəs; ˌsjupɚ'stɪʃəs/ adj of, showing, resulting from, ~; believing in ~s: 迷信的; 显示或由迷信而生的; 相信迷信事物的: superstitious beliefs/ideas/people. 迷信的说法(观念,人们). **super·sti·tious·ly** adv

super·struc·ture /'suːpəstrʌktʃə(r); 'supɚˌstrʌktʃɚ/ n structure built on the top of sth else; parts of a ship above the main deck. 上层构造; 上层建筑物; 船只主甲板上面的部分.

super·tax /'suːpətæks; 'supɚˌtæks/ n [C, U] tax on, or the taxation of, incomes (additional to income tax) above a certain level. 附加所得税; 特别附加税.

super·vene /ˌsuːpəˈviːn; ˌsupɚˈvin/ vi [VP2A] (formal) come or happen as a change from or interruption of (a condition or process). (正式用语)附带发生; 并发; 横生枝节; 节外生枝.

super·vise /ˈsuːpəvaɪz; ˌsupɚˈvaɪz/ vt, vi [VP6A, 2A] watch and direct (work, workers, an organization). 监督(工作、工人、组织); 管理; 指导. **super·vi·sor** /-zə(r); -zɚ/ n person who ~s. 监督者; 管理者; 指导者. **super·vi·sion** /ˌsuːpəˈvɪʒn; ˌsjupɚˈvɪʒən/ n supervising: 监督; 管理; 指导: under the supervision of, ~d by. 在…监督(指导)之下. **super·vis·ory** /ˌsuːpəˈvaɪzərɪ; ˌsupɚˈvaɪzɚɪ/ adj supervisory duties. 监督的职责.

su·pine /ˈsuːpaɪn US: suˈpaɪn; suˈpaɪn/ adj 1 lying flat on the back, face upwards. 仰卧的; 仰着的. ⇨ prone(1). 2 inactive; slow to act; indolent. 不活泼的; 怠惰的; 迟缓的; 因循的; 没精打采的. ~·ly adv

sup·per /ˈsʌpə(r); ˈsʌpɚ/ n [C, U] last meal of the day, when this is less large or less formal than a **dinner**: 晚餐: have cold meat for ~; 晚餐吃冷肉; eat very little ~; 晚饭吃得很少; have a good ~; 吃一顿好吃的晚饭; late ~s after the theatre. 看戏后吃吃的延迟的晚餐. ~·less adj without ~: 无晚餐的; 未吃晚餐的: go to bed ~less. 未吃晚餐就上床.

sup·plant /səˈplɑːnt US: -ˈplænt; səˈplænt/ vt [VP6A] 1 take the place of (sth): 代替; 取代: Trams in London have been ~ed by buses. 伦敦的公共汽车已经取代了电车. 2 take the place of (sb), esp after getting him out of office: 取代(某人); (尤指)排挤而取代(某人): The Prime Minister was ~ed by his rival. 首相已被其对手用计排挤掉. She has been ~ed in his affections by another woman. 另外一个女人夺走了他对她的爱. ~er n person who ~s another. 取代者; 排挤他人者.

supple /ˈsʌpl; ˈsʌpl/ adj easily bent or bending; not stiff: 易弯曲的; 柔软的; 灵活的: the ~ limbs of a child; 小孩子的柔软四肢; a ~ mind, quick to respond to ideas. 反应灵敏的心智. ~·ness n

supple·ment /ˈsʌplɪmənt; ˈsʌpləmənt/ n [C] 1 sth added later to improve or complete, eg a dictionary. 补遗; (词典等的)补编. 2 extra and separate addition to a newspaper or other periodical: (报纸或杂志的)增刊; 附刊: The Times Literary S~; 泰晤士报的书评周刊; the Observer colour ~. 观察报的彩色增刊. □ vt /ˈsʌplɪment; ˈsʌpləˌment/ [VP6A, 15A] make an addition or additions to: 增补; 补充: ~ one's ordinary income by writing books. 著书以增加平常的收入.

supple·men·tary /ˌsʌplɪˈmentrɪ; ˌsʌpləˈmentrɪ/ adj 1 additional; extra: 增补的; 补充的; 附加的: ~ estimates, eg for additional expenditure; 追加预算; ~ benefit, (in GB) extra money granted by the State to people in need. (在英国)政府对有困难的人民的额外津贴. 2 (of an angle) making with another a total of 180°. (指角度)补角的.

sup·pli·ant /ˈsʌplɪənt; ˈsʌplɪənt/ n, adj (formal) (person) asking humbly for sth: (正式用法)哀求者; 恳求者; 恳求的: 哀求的: kneel as a ~ at the altar, ie praying to God; 跪在神坛前恳求(向上帝祈祷); in a ~ attitude. 态度恳切地.

sup·pli·cate /ˈsʌplɪkeɪt; ˈsʌplɪˌket/ vt, vi [VP6A, 14, 17, 2C] (formal and liter) make a humble petition to sb: (正式用语及文)恳求; 吁请: ~ sb to help; 恳求某人帮助; ~ sb's protection; 恳请某人保护; ~ for pardon. 恳求原谅. **sup·pli·cant** /ˈsʌplɪkənt; ˈsʌplɪkənt/ n person who ~s; suppliant. 恳求者; 吁请者. **sup·pli·ca·tion** /ˌsʌplɪˈkeɪʃn; ˌsʌplɪˈkeʃən/ n [C, U] humble prayer. 祈求; 祈祷.

supply /səˈplaɪ; səˈplaɪ/ vt (pt, pp **-lied**) [VP6A, 14] ~ sth to sb; ~ sb with sth, 1 give or provide (sth needed or asked for): 供给; 供应(所需要或所请求的): ~ gas / electricity to domestic consumers; 供应瓦斯(电)给住户; ~ consumers with gas, etc. 以瓦斯等供应

消费者. 2 meet (a need): 满足(需要): Should the government ~ the need for more houses, (help to) provide them (eg by building them, or giving subsidies or making loans)? 政府应该满足(人们)对更多房屋的需要吗? □ n 1 [U] ~ing; [C] (pl **-lies**) that which is supplied; stock or amount of sth which is obtainable: 供给; 供应; 供给之物; 现货; 现货贮存量: Have you a good ~ of reading matter for the train journey, plenty of books, magazines, etc? 你有供火车旅行的许多读物吗? We shall be receiving new supplies of shoes next week, (eg of a shop) new stocks. (如指商店)我们将于下周收到鞋子的新货. ~ and demand, quantities available and quantities asked for (thought of as regulating prices): 供给和需要; 供与求(被认为系以系统规律价的因素). in short ~, scarce (which is the more usu word). 稀少的; 缺乏的 (scarce 一词较常用). 2 supplies, (esp) stores necessary for some public need, eg the armed forces; (尤指)公众必需品(如军需品); 生活必需品: 'medical supplies. 医疗用品. 3 be / go on ~, work as a temporary substitute, eg for a teacher or clergyman: 临时代人工作; 作临时替工; (attrib) (用作定语) a ' ~ teacher. 代课教员. 4 supplies, (GB) grant of money by Parliament for the cost of government. (英)国会对政府的开支所做之拨款. S~ Day, (in the House of Commons) day on which approval of the Estimates (of expenditure) is asked for. (下议院中)请求批准预算日. 5 supplies, allowance of money to a person; 个人的津贴; 零用金: Tom's father cut off the supplies. 汤姆的父亲停发零用金. **sup·plier** n person or firm ~ing goods, etc. 供应货物等的人或商店; 供应商.

sup·port /səˈpɔːt; səˈpɔrt/ vt [VP6A] 1 bear the weight of; hold up or keep in place: 支持; 支撑; 扶持: Is this bridge strong enough to ~ heavy lorries? 这座桥经得起重卡车通行吗? He hurt his ankle, so he had to be ~ed home, someone had to help him to walk home. 他伤了足踝, 因此不得不让人搀着回家. 2 strengthen; help (sb or sth) to continue: 加强; 使有力; 拥护; 支援; 帮助(某人或某事物)持续: a claim / a political party; 支持一项要求(某一政党); ~ a football team, eg by regularly watching it play: 支持一足球队(例如经常观其赛球); ~ing troops, held in reserve to help those who are fighting; 支援部队; a hospital ~ed by voluntary contributions; 由捐款维持开支的医院; a theory that is not ~ed by the facts; 无事实为根据的理论; an accusation not ~ed by proofs; 无证据的指控; a ' ~ing actor, one who takes a part secondary to that of the leading actor; 配角; a ' ~ing film, secondary to the main feature film. (电影的)副片; 短片. 3 provide for (financially, etc): 维持; 供养: He has a large family to ~. 他要养一大家人. 4 endure: 忍受; 忍耐: I can't ~ your jealousy any longer. 我无法再忍受你的嫉妒了. □ n 1 [U] ~ing or being ~ed: 支持; 支撑; 扶持; 拥护; 帮助; 维持; 赡养: This bridge needs more ~. 这座桥需要加强支柱. I hope to have your ~ in the election. 我希望在选举中得到你的支持. The proposal obtained no / little / not much ~. 这项建议未获得(鲜款, 略款)支持. Mr X spoke in ~ of the motion. 某先生发言支持该项动议. The divorced wife claimed ~ (ie a regular financial contribution) for her children from her ex-husband, but he was found to be without visible means of ~, with no apparent resources (money, work) on which to live. 那离婚的妻子为其子女向前夫索取赡养费, 但他并无可察见的资财或收入. in ~, (of troops) in reserve, ready to give ~. (指部队)预备的; 支援的. (be) in ~ of / sth, (be) ~ing him / it. 支援某人(某事物). 2 [C] sb or sth that ~s: 支持的人或物; 支援者; 支撑物; 赞助者; 赡养者; 赞助金; 赡养金: Dick is the chief ~ of the family, earns the money for the family. 迪克是这一家的主要赡养者. 'price ~s, (US) subsidies, eg paid by the government to farmers. (美)价格补助金; 价格津贴(如政府给予农民者). ~·able /-əbl; -əbl/ adj that can be ~ed; endurable. 可维持的; 可赡养的; 可忍受的.

~**er** n person or device that ~s. 支持者; 支援者; 支持器械或设备。 ~·**ive** adj ~ing; giving help, encouragement. 支持的; 支援的; 拥护的; 帮助的; 鼓励的。

sup·pose /sə'pəʊz; sə'poz/ vt **1** [VP9, 6A, 25] let it be thought that; take it as a fact that: 认定; 假定: Let us ~ (that) the news is true. 让我们假定这消息是真实的。 S~ the world were flat. 假定地球是扁平的。 Everyone is ~d to know the rules, It is assumed, taken for granted, that we all know the rules. 大家都该知道这些规则。 I don't ~ for one/a minute that ..., I don't believe that .... 我压根儿不相信……。 **2** [VP9, 6A, 25] guess; think; imagine; 猜想; 猜想; 想像: What do you ~ he wanted? 你想他需要什么? All her neighbours ~d her to be/~d that she was a widow. 她的邻人们都以为她是一个寡妇。 You'll be there, I ~. 我想你会去的。 'Will he come?'—'Yes, I ~ so'/'No, I ~ not'/'No, I don't ~ so'. '他会来吗?'——'是的, 我想他会'('不, 我想他不会'; '不, 我认为他不会来')。 I ~ you want to borrow money again! 我猜你又要借钱了! **3** [VP6A] (forming an imper, or used to make a suggestion or proposal): (构成祈使句, 或用以做成一项建议或提议): S~ we go (= Let's go) for a swim. (我提议)我们去游泳吧。 **4** [VP6A] require as a condition; imply: 须以…为条件; 必须有; 意味着: Creation ~s a creator. 创造必须先有创造者。 **5** be ~d to, (a) be expected or required to (by customs, duty, etc): 被期望或要求; 应该: Is he ~d to clean the outside of the windows or only the inside? 他应该把窗户外面擦干净, 还是只擦窗户里面就可以呢? (b) (colloq) (in the neg) not be allowed to: (口)用于否定句中)不被许可: We're not ~d to play football on Sundays. 我们在礼拜天不许踢足球。 **sup·pos·ing** conj if: 假如; 倘若: Supposing it rains, what shall you do? 如果下起雨来, 你怎么办呢? ~**d** adj accepted as being so: 被信以为真的; 假定的; 推测的: his ~d generosity. 他那种被信以为真的慷慨。 The ~d beggar was really a police officer in disguise. 原来是乔装的警官。 **sup·pos·ed·ly** /-idli; -idli/ adv according to what is/was ~d. 臆测上; 想像上; 恐怕; 大概。

sup·po·si·tion /ˌsʌpə'zɪʃn; ˌsʌpə'zɪʃən/ n **1** [U] supposing: 想像; 臆测; 推断; 假设: This newspaper article is based on ~, on what the writer supposes to be the case, not on fact. 报上这篇文章是根据想像写的, 并非事实。 We mustn't condemn him on mere ~. 我们不可全凭臆测而指责他。 **2** [C] sth supposed; guess: 被假定之事物; 臆测; 推想: Our ~s were fully confirmed. 我们所假定的全都证实了。 on this ~; on the ~ that ..., supposing that this is the case. 假如这样; 假使。

sup·posi·tory /sə'pɒzɪtrɪ US: -tɔːri; sə'pazə,tɔri/ n (pl -ries) medical preparation (in a soluble capsule) inserted into the rectum or vagina and left to dissolve. 塞药; 坐药; 栓剂(如装于可溶胶囊中的药剂, 插入直肠或阴道中, 让其溶解)。

sup·press /sə'pres; sə'prɛs/ vt [VP6A] **1** put an end to the activity or existence of: 镇压; 平定; 制止: ~ a rising/the slave trade. 镇压叛乱(制止奴隶贩卖)。 **2** prevent from being known or seen: 抑制; 扣留; 查禁; 隐瞒: ~ the truth/a yawn/one's feelings; 隐匿真相(抑制呵欠; 压抑感情); ~ a newspaper, prevent its publication. 查禁一家报纸。 ~**ion** /sə'preʃn; sə'prɛʃən/ n ~ing: 镇压; 平定; 压止; 抑制; 扣留; 查禁; 隐瞒: a policy of ~ion, eg of ~ing movements for independence or for freedom. 高压政策。 ~**ive** adj tending to ~; designed to ~. 镇压性的; 为镇压而设计的; 平定的; 抑制的; 隐瞒的。 ~**or** /-sə(r); -sɚ/ n sth that ~es; (esp) a device fitted to electric apparatus to prevent interference with radio and television reception: 镇压的事物; (尤指)干扰遏止器(装于电器上, 以防止干扰无线电及电视之接收的装置); fit a ~ to an electric motor. 在电动机(马达)上装置一干扰遏止器。

sup·pu·rate /'sʌpjʊreɪt; 'sʌpjə,ret/ vi [VP2A] (formal) form pus, fester. (正式用语)生脓; 化脓; 酿脓。

sup·pu·ra·tion /ˌsʌpjʊ'reɪʃn; ˌsʌpjə'reʃən/ n

supra /'suːprə; 'suprə/ adv (Lat; formal) above; earlier on (in a book, etc): (拉; 正式用语)在上; (书本中)在前; See ~, p 21, See p 21 earlier on in this book. 请参阅本书的前文第二十一页。

supra·na·tional /ˌsuːprə'næʃnəl; ˌsuprə'næʃənl/ adj above nations or states: 超国家的; 在国家之上的: a ~ authority, one that might be created for world government. 一个超国家的政权。

su·preme /suː'priːm; sə'prim/ adj **1** highest in degree or rank or authority: 级别, 地位或权力最高的; 至高的; 无上的: the S~ Commander; 最高统帅; the S~ Court, highest in one of the States of the US or in the whole of the US: (美国各洲的或全美国的)最高法院; the S~ Soviet, the legislature of the USSR: 最高苏维埃(苏联的立法机构); the S~ Being, God. 上帝。 **2** most important; greatest: 最重要的; 最大的: make the ~ sacrifice, lay down one's life (eg in war). 作最大的牺牲(如战争中捐躯)。 ~·**ly** adv in a ~ manner: 至高地; 无上地; 最重要地; 最大地: ~ly happy. 极快乐的。 **su·prem·acy** /suː'preməsɪ; sə'prɛməsɪ/ n [U] supremacy over, being ~ over; highest authority: 至高; 至上; 最高的权威: His supremacy was unchallenged. 他那种至高无上的权威无人置疑。

sur·charge /'sɜːtʃɑːdʒ; 'sɝ,tʃɑrdʒ/ n **1** payment demanded in addition to the usual charge, eg as a penalty for a letter with insufficient postage paid on it: 额外的索价; 额外的偿付(如邮资不足的罚款)。 **2** excessive or additional load. 过大的负担; 额外负荷; 超载。 **3** mark overprinted on a postage-stamp changing its value. 邮票上的变值印记。 □ vt **1** [VP6A] overload. 使负担过重; 使装载过多。 **2** [VP6A, 15A] demand a ~(1) on or in. 向…额外索价; 对…处以附加罚款。

surd /sɜːd; sɝd/ n (math) quantity, esp a root (√), that cannot be expressed in finite terms of ordinary numbers or quantities. (数学)不尽根数。

sure /ʃʊə(r); ʃʊr/ adj (-r, -st) **1** (pred only) (仅用作表语) free from doubt; having confidence; knowing and believing; having, seeming to have, good reason for belief: 一定的; 必定的; 有信心的; 无疑的; 确知的; 确信的; 有理由相信的: I think he's coming, but I'm not quite ~. 我想他会来的, 但我不太敢确定。 You're ~ of (= certain to receive) a welcome. 你一定会受到欢迎。 I'm not ~ whether I have a copy/where I left my copy/when I lost it. 我不能确定我是不是有一本(我把我那一本遗留在什么地方; 我何时遗失了它)。 I'm not ~ why he wants it. 我不太知道他何以需要它。 be/feel ~ (about sth), have no doubts (about): 有把握; 确信: I think the answer's right, but I'm not ~ (about it). 我想这答案是对的, 但是我(对它)没有把握。 Smith's a good man for the job, but I'm not so ~ about Robinson. 史密斯是这项工作的恰当人选, 但是罗宾逊能不能胜任, 我就没有这么大的把握了。 be/feel ~ of sth/that ..., have confidence: 确信某事(确定…): Are you ~ of your facts? 你确信你所说的都是真的吗? Can we be ~ of his honesty/that he's honest? 我们能确定他是诚实的吗? be/feel ~ of oneself, have self-confidence. 有自信心。 be ~ to do sth; (colloq) (口) be ~ and do sth, don't fail to: 务必; 一定要: Be ~ to write and give me all the news. 务必写信告诉我所有的消息。 to be ~, it is admitted, granted: 诚然; 确然; 的确: She's not pretty, to be ~, but she's very intelligent. 诚然, 她并不漂亮, 但是她却非常聪明。 Well, to be ~! 唉呀, 真的呀! make ~ that .../of sth, (a) feel ~: 确信; 感到确定无疑: I made ~ he would be here. 我确信他会来这里。 (b) satisfy oneself; do what is necessary in order to feel ~ to get sth, etc: 使自己满足或弄明白; 确保; 做必要之事以获得某一物; 得到某物等: I think there's a train at 5.15, but you'd better make ~, eg by looking up trains in a timetable. 我想五点一刻有一班火车, 但是你最好去查一查。 There aren't many seats left for this concert; you'd better make ~ of one/make ~ that you get one today. 这音乐会剩下的座位不多了; 你最好今天订

妥一个位子。**2** (attrib and pred) proved or tested; reliable; trustworthy: (用作定语及表语)经过证实有效、妥当、无害、无误等; 可靠的; 稳妥的; 靠得住的: *no ~ remedy for colds*; 没有一定能治好伤风的药物; **~ proof;** 确切无疑的证据; *send a letter by a ~ hand/a ~ messenger.* 经由可靠的人(专差)送信。 **,~-'footed** *adj* not likely to stumble or slip. 脚步稳的; 踏实的; 无失误之虞的。 □ *adv* **1 ~ enough,** certainly, in fact: 确实地; 事实上: *I said it would happen, and ~ enough it did happen.* 我说(它)会发生, 而确实发生了了。 **for ~,** (usu colloq) certainly. (通常为口语用法)的确; 确实地。 **2 as ~ as,** as certain as: 如…一样切切: *as ~ as fate;* 千真万确; *as ~ as my name's Bob.* 的确。 **3** (colloq, esp US) certainly; 的确。 (口,尤美)确实地; 的确: *It ~ was cold.* 确实很冷。 **~'ness** *n*

sure·ly /'ʃʊəlɪ; 'ʃʊrlɪ/ *adv* **1** (usu placed with the *v*) with certainty: (通常与动词连用)确实地; 无误地; 必然地: *He will ~ fail.* 他必然会失败。 *He was working slowly but ~.* 他(那时)工作得很慢, 但很确实。 **2** (placed either with the subject, usu preceding it, or at the end of the sentence, often indicating either confidence or incredulity) if experience or probability can be trusted. (与主语连用, 通常置于主语前, 或放在一句的末尾, 常用以表示信心或疑) 如果照经验或常理推断(进展): *S~ this wet weather won't last much longer!* 这种下雨的天气必定不会再继续很久! *You didn't want to hurt his feelings, ~!* 不用说, 你无意伤他的感情! *S~ I've met you before somewhere.* 我一定走什么地方遇见过你。 **3** (esp US) (in answers) certainly; undoubtedly: (尤美)(在答话中)当然; 无疑地: *'Would you be willing to help?'—'S~!'* (Certainly is more usu in GB usage.) '你愿意帮忙吗?'——'当然(愿意)!'(英国多用 certainly。)

surety /'ʃʊərətɪ US: 'ʃʊrtɪ; 'ʃʊrətɪ/ *n* (*pl* **-ties**) [C, U] (sth given as a) guarantee; person who makes himself responsible for the conduct or debt(s) of another person: 担保; 担保品; 保证人; *stand ~ for sb.* 做某人的保证人。

surf /sɜːf; sɜrf/ *n* [U] waves breaking in white foam on the seashore, or against rocks or reefs. 拍岸之浪; 击岸碎浪; 海滨的激浪; 海边澎湃之浪。 **'~·ing, '~-riding** *nn* sport in which one balances oneself on a long narrow board while being carried along by heavy ~. 冲浪运动; 冲浪。 **'~-board** *n* board used for this sport. (冲浪运动用的)冲浪板。 **'~-boat** *n* boat specially built for use in ~. 碎浪艇 (能冲过海滨碎浪的特别建造的小艇)。

surfing

sur·face /'sɜːfɪs; 'sɜrfɪs/ *n* [C] **1** the outside of any object, etc; any of the sides of an object: (任何物体的)表面; 物体的任何一面: *Glass has a smooth ~.* 玻璃有光滑的表面。 *A cube has six ~s.* 立方体有六面。 **2** top of a liquid, or body of water, eg the sea: 液面; (尤指海等之)水面: *The submarine rose to the ~.* 那艘潜艇升至水面上来了。 *Most people consider ~ vessels (= ordinary ships) to be more vulnerable than submarines.* 大多数人认为水面上的船只较潜水艇易遭受攻击。 **'~ mail,** mail sent by vehicles or ships moving on the earth's ~: 水陆邮件(由车或船运送者): *S~ mail is cheaper than airmail.* 水陆邮件比航空邮件便宜。 **,~-to-'air,** (of missiles, etc) fired or launched from the ground or from ships, and aimed at aircraft. (指导弹

等)地对空的。 **4** outward appearance; what is seen or learnt from a quick view or consideration: 外表; 外观; 皮相; 皮毛: *You must not look only at the ~ of things.* 你不可只看事物的表面现象。 *His faults are all on the ~. When you get below the ~, you find that he is warm-hearted and considerate.* 他的缺点都是表面上的。当你深一层观察时, 你就会发现他是既热心而又体贴的人。 **5** (attrib) of the ~ only: (用作定语)表面的; 肤浅的: *~ politeness;* 表面上的礼貌; *~ impressions,* received quickly or casually, with no depth of thought, observation, etc; 肤浅的印象; *'~ noise,* eg from a gramophone record, made by the stylus. 表面杂音(如唱片由唱针磨擦而生者)。 □ *vt, vi* **1** bring to a ~ to: 装以面; 使成平面: *a road with gravel/tarmac.* 以砂砾(柏油和砂砾)加铺路面。 **2** [VP6A, 2A] (of a submarine, skin-diver, etc) (cause to) come to the ~. (指潜水艇, 潜水者等)(使)升至水面。

sur·feit /'sɜːfɪt; 'sɜrfɪt/ *n* (usu 通常作 *a ~ (of)*) too much of anything, esp food and drink: 过量; 过度; (尤指)过食; 过饮; *have a ~ of curry while in Madras;* 在马德拉斯的时候吃了太多咖喱; feeling of discomfort resulting from a ~. 饮食过量带来的不适感; 食伤; 食滞。 □ *vt* [VP6A, 14] **~ sb/oneself (with),** (cause to) take too much of anything: (使)取用过度; (使)饮食过量: *~ oneself with fruit;* 吃过多的水果; *be ~ed with pleasure.* 作乐过度。

surge /sɜːdʒ; sɜrdʒ/ *vi* [VP2C] move forward, roll on, in or like waves: (在波浪中或象波浪般)滚流; 起伏; 汹涌; 澎湃; *The floods ~d over the valley.* 洪水在山谷中滚滚流动。 *The crowds ~d out of the sports stadium.* 观众从运动场涌出。 *Anger ~d (up) within him.* 怒气在他内心汹涌澎湃。 □ *n* [C] forward or upward movement; onrush: 滚流; 起伏; 汹涌; 澎湃; 奔流; *the ~ of the sea;* 海浪汹涌; *a ~ of anger/pity.* 一阵怒气(怜悯)。

sur·geon /'sɜːdʒən; 'sɜrdʒən/ *n* **1** doctor who performs operations. 外科医生。 **dental ~** *n* dentist qualified in surgery. 口腔外科医生。 **'house ~** *n* one of the staff of a hospital. 驻院外科医生。 **2** medical officer in the navy: 海军军医; **'~-com'mander.** (海军) 军医中校。

sur·gery /'sɜːdʒərɪ; 'sɜrdʒərɪ/ *n* (*pl* **-ries**) **1** [U] the science and practice of treating injuries and disease by manual and instrumental operations: 外科; 外科手术: *qualified in both ~ and medicine.* 内外科皆合格的。 **2** [C] (GB) doctor's or dentist's room where patients come to consult him: (英)(医师或牙医的)诊疗室; 诊疗室: *~ hours, 4 pm to 6 pm;* 应诊时间, 下午四时至六时; *political ~,* (colloq) where constituents can consult their member of Parliament. (口)政治应诊室(国会议员接见其选民处)。

sur·gi·cal /'sɜːdʒɪkl; 'sɜrdʒɪkl/ *adj* of, by, for, surgery: 外科的; 外科手术的; 外科用的: *~ treatment;* 外科治疗; *~ instruments;* 外科器具; *a ~ boot,* one specially designed to fit a deformed foot. 为治疗畸形足所设计的鞋子。 **~·ly** /-klɪ; -klɪ/ *adv*

sur·ly /'sɜːlɪ; 'sɜrlɪ/ *adj* (**-ier, -iest**) bad-tempered and unfriendly. 乖戾的; 粗暴的; 不友善的。 **sur·lily** /-ɪlɪ; -ɪlɪ/ *adv* **sur·li·ness** *n*

sur·mise /sə'maɪz; sə'maɪz/ *vt, vi* [VP6A, 9, 2A] (formal) guess, conjecture: (正式用语)测测; 臆度: *She ~d as much.* 她如此猜测。 □ */sɜː'maɪz/; sə'maɪz/ n* [C] guess: 猜测; 臆度: *You were right in your ~.* 你猜对了。

sur·mount /sə'maʊnt; sə'maʊnt/ *vt* **1** [VP6A] overcome (difficulties); get over (obstacles). 克服(困难); 越过(障碍)。 **2** (passive) (被动语态) *be ~ed by/with,* have on or over the top: 在顶端; 冠于…之上: *a spire ~ed by a weather-vane.* 顶上装有风标的尖塔。 **~·able** /-əbl; -əbl/ *adj* that can be overcome or conquered. 可克服的; 可超过的。

sur·name /'sɜːneɪm; 'sɜrˌnem/ *n* [C] person's hereditary family name: 姓; 氏: *Smith is a very common*

English ~. 史密斯是一个很普通的英国姓。 ⇨ *given name* at **give**[1](11), *Christian name* at **Christian,** and **forename.**

sur·pass /sə'pɑːs US: -'pæs; sɚ'pæs/ *vt* [VP6A, 15A] do or be better than; exceed; excel: 超越; 凌驾; 胜过: ~ *sb in strength/speed/skill.* 在气力(速度, 技术)方面胜过某人。 *The beauty of the scenery ~ed my expectations.* 该处风景之秀丽超出我的预料。 ~**ing** *adj* matchless: 卓越的; 无与伦比的: *of ~ing beauty.* 美貌超群的。 ~**ing·ly** *adv* in a way that is not ~ed: 卓越地; 超绝地; 无与伦比地: ~*ingly ugly.* 极丑的。

sur·plice /'sɜːplɪs; 'sɚplɪs/ *n* loose-fitting (usu white) gown with wide sleeves worn by (some) priests (over a cassock) during church services. (某些教士于教堂礼拜时所穿的)白法衣 (罩于袈裟外的长袍)。 ⇨ the illus at **vestment.** 参看 vestment 之插图。 **sur·pliced** *adj* wearing a ~. 穿白法衣的。

sur·plus /'sɜːpləs; 'sɚpləs/ *n* **1** [C] amount (of money) that remains after needs have been supplied; excess of receipts over expenditure; ⇨ **deficit;** amount (of anything) in excess of requirements: 余款; 盈余; (指任何事物)剩余; 过剩: *Brazil had a ~ of coffee last year.* 巴西去年咖啡供过于求。 **2** (attrib) exceeding what is needed or used: (用作定语)剩余的; 过剩的: ~ *labour,* workers for whom there are no jobs; 剩余劳力 (过剩劳工); *a sale of ~ stock;* 出售剩余的存货; ~ *population,* in excess of what is thought desirable, or for which there is not enough food, employment, etc; 过剩人口; '~ *store,* (GB) shop where ~ items (eg military clothing) are sold. (英)(出售军服等之)剩余物品店。

sur·prise /sə'praɪz; sɚ'praɪz/ *n* **1** [C, U] (feeling caused by) sth sudden or unexpected: 惊骇; 惊愕; 惊奇; 突然或意外之事物: *His failure did not cause much ~/ was not a great ~.* 他的失败未引起很大的惊奇(并非很意外之事)。 *What a ~!* 多令人吃惊的事! *To my ~/ To the ~ of everyone, his plan succeeded.* 使我(大家)惊奇的是他的计划竟然成功了。 *We have some ~s in store for you.* 我们还有一些出乎你意料的话(礼物)奉告(奉赠)。 *He looked up in ~.* 他吃惊地向上看。 **take sb by ~,** catch him unprepared, at a time when he is not expecting to be seen, etc. 冷不防地使某人吓一跳; (出乎某人意料地)撞见、捉到某人等。 **take a fort/town, etc by ~,** capture it by making an unexpected attack. 奇袭攻占某堡垒(城镇等)。 **2** (attrib) unexpected: made, done, etc, without warning: (用作定语)出乎意料的; 出其不意的; 突然的; 奇袭的: *a ~ visit/attack.* 突然的访问(奇袭)。 □ *vt* **1** [VP6A] give a feeling of ~ to: 使惊骇; 使惊愕; 使惊奇: *You ~ me!* 你真令人一跳! *She was more ~d than frightened.* 她惊讶的程度超过了害怕。 **2 be ~d,** experience ~: 感到吃惊、惊奇、惊愕等: *We were ~d at the news/~d to hear the news.* 我们听到那项消息感到震惊。 *I'm ~d (to learn that) he didn't come.* 他居然没有来,我感到很意外。 *We were ~d at finding the house empty.* 我们发现房子是空的,感到很意外。 *It's nothing to be ~d about/at.* 这事不值得大惊小怪。 *I shouldn't be ~d if it rained this afternoon,* It seems to me likely that it will rain. 如果今天下午下雨,我不会感到意外。 **3** [VP6A] come upon suddenly, without previous warning; take by ~: 不期而遇; 撞见; 奇袭: *the enemy,* attack them when they are off their guard; 奇袭敌人; ~ *a burglar in the act of breaking into a house.* 撞见正要潜入某住宅的窃贼。 **4 ~ sb into doing sth,** hurry him into doing sth, eg by making a sudden challenge. 冷不防地促使某人做某事(如突然向某人挑战)。 **sur·pris·ing** *adj* causing ~. 令人吃惊的; 奇异的。 **sur·pris·ing·ly** *adv* **sur·prised** *adj* showing or feeling ~. 惊愕的; 惊奇的; 吃惊的。 **sur·pris·ed·ly** /-ɪdlɪ; -ɪdlɪ/ *adv* in a ~d manner. 惊愕地; 惊奇地; 吃惊地。

sur·real·ism /sə'rɪəlɪzəm; sə'rɪəl,ɪzm/ *n* [U] 20th-century movement in art and literature that aims at

expressing what there is in the subconscious mind (so that a painting may depict a number of unrelated objects as seen in a dream). 超现实主义; 超写实主义(廿世纪的文学及艺术潮流,其目的在呈现潜意识中的事物,如,一张画所呈现的可能是如梦中所见,许多互不关连的景象)。 **sur·real·ist** /-ɪst; -ɪst/ *n* artist, writer, etc of this movement. 超写实或超现实主义者(指艺术家、作家等)。 **sur·real·is·tic** /ˌsəriː'lɪstɪk; sə,riəl'ɪstɪk/ *adj* of ~; fantastic. 超写实或超现实主义的;幻想的。

sur·ren·der /sə'rendə(r); sə'rendɚ/ *vt, vi* **1** [VP6A, 14, 2A] ~ **(to),** give up (oneself, a ship, a town, etc) (to the enemy, the police, etc): 放弃(船, 城市等); (向敌人, 警察等)投降; 投案; 自首: *We shall never ~.* 我们永不投降。 *We advised the hijackers to ~ (themselves) to the police.* 我们劝那些劫持者向警察投案。 **2** [VP6A] yield up under pressure or from necessity; abandon possession of: 抛弃; 舍弃; 让与: *We shall never ~ our liberty.* 我们永不会舍弃自由。 *He ~ed his insurance policy,* gave up his rights under the policy in return for a lump sum of money (called the ~ *value* of the policy). 他退出保险,获得一笔退保金(surrender value)。 **3** [VP14] ~ **(oneself) to,** yield or give way to (a habit, emotion, influence, etc): 屈服于(习惯、感情、影响等); 任由(习惯等)摆布: *He ~ed (himself) to despair and committed suicide.* 他感到绝望而自杀了。 □ *n* ~ing or being ~ed: 屈服; 投降; 放弃; 让与: *demand the ~ of a town/of all firearms:* 要求一个城市投降(交出所有武器); ~ *value,* ⇨ 2 above. (保险)解约金; 退保金额 (参看上列第2义)。 *No ~!* Let us not ~! 绝不投降!

sur·rep·ti·tious /ˌsʌrəp'tɪʃəs; ,sɚəp'tɪʃəs/ *adj* (of actions) done secretly or stealthily. (指动作)偷偷摸摸的; 暗中进行的。 ~**ly** *adv*

sur·ro·gate /'sʌrəgeɪt; 'sɚə,get/ *n* deputy, esp of a bishop. (尤指主教的)代理者; 替身。 ⇨ **suffragan.**

sur·round /sə'raund; sə'raund/ *vt* [VP6A] be, go, all round, shut in on all sides: 包围; 环绕: *a house ~ed with trees.* 四周为树木所环绕的房子。 *We are ~ed with/by dangers.* 我们(现在)的处境危机四伏。 *The troops were ~ed,* had enemy forces all round them. 部队被(敌人)包围了。 □ *n* floor between the walls and the carpet; its covering: 地毯四周与墙之间的地板; 其覆盖物: *a linoleum ~.* 铺在地毯四周的油布。 ~**ing** *adj* which is around about: 周围的; 环绕的: *York and the ~ing countryside.* 约克城及其近郊。 ~**ings** *n pl* everything around and about a place; conditions that may affect a person: 周围的事物; 环境: *living in pleasant ~ings.* 生活于舒适的环境中。 *You don't see animals in their natural ~ings at a zoo.* 你在动物园里看不到生活在自然环境中的动物。

sur·tax /'sɜːtæks; 'sɚ,tæks/ *n* [C, U] (levying of) additional tax on personal incomes beyond a certain level. 附加税(对超过某一标准之个人收入所课者); 附加税的征收。 □ *vt* impose ~ on. 课以附加税。

sur·veil·lance /sɜː'veɪləns; sɚ'veləns/ *n* [U] close watch kept on persons suspected of wrongdoing, etc: (对嫌疑犯等的)监视; 盯梢: *under police ~.* 受警察监视。

sur·vey /sə'veɪ; sɚ've/ *vt* [VP6A] **1** take a general view of: 眺望; 纵览: ~ *the countryside from the top of a hill.* 从山顶眺望乡区。 **2** examine the general condition of: 通盘考虑; 审度; 衡量一般情况: *The Prime Minister, in his speech at the Guildhall, ~ed the international situation.* 首相在伦敦市政厅大会堂所作的演说中,评述了国际形势。 **3** measure and map out the position, size, boundaries, etc of (an area of land, a country, coast, etc): 测量; 查勘(地区、国家、海岸等): ~ *a parish/a railway.* 测量某一教区(一条铁路)。 **4** examine the condition of (a building, etc): 检查(房屋等)的状况, 鉴定: *Have the house ~ed before you offer to buy it.* 在你出价买那房子之前,先找人鉴定一下。 ~**ing** *n* [U] the work of ~ing (3, 4): 测量; 查勘; 检查; 鉴定: *'land-~ing;* 土地查勘; *a '~ing ship,* used for ~ing coasts;

海岸测量船; instruction in the principles of making surveys(3). 测量术;测量学. □ *n* /'sɜːveɪ/, 'sɜːve/ [C] **1** general view; 概观; 审视; 考察. 考察: *make a general ~ of the situation / subject.* 对形势（问题）作通盘考虑. **2** piece of land-surveying;map or record of this: 土地测量;测量图;测量记录: *an aerial ~ of East Africa,* made by photography from aircraft; 东非的航空测量(图); *the ordnance ~ of Great Britain,* ⇨ **ordnance.** 英国官方土地测量;其所制的地图. **~or** /-ə/;vɜː/veɪə(r)/ *n* **1** person who ~s(3) land, etc. 测量员(测量土地等者). **2** person who ~s and values buildings, etc. 房屋等的鉴定人. **3** official inspector: 检查人员或官员;视查人员或官员: *~or of weights and measures.* 度量衡的检查官员; *the ~or of highways.* 公路视查员. **quantity ~or,** ⇨ **quantity.** 估料师;积算师.

sur·vival /sə'vaɪvl; sə'vaɪvḷ/ *n* **1** [U] state of continuing to live or exist; surviving: 继续生存或存在;生存;生存: *~ after death,* the spirit after the death of the body; 死后灵魂的存在; *the ~ of the fittest,* the continuing existence of those animals and plants which are best adapted to their surroundings, etc; 适者生存(指动植物之最能适应其环境者以继续生存,否则淘汰); (attrib) (用作定语) *a '~ kit,* package of necessities for a person after a disaster, etc (eg at sea). 救生背囊(装有维持生命的必需品,供遭逢灾变者,如遭海难者,使用). **2** [C] person, custom, belief, etc that has survived but is looked upon as belonging to past times. 残存的人、风俗、信仰等; 遗风; 残存物; 过时代的人.

sur·vive /sə'vaɪv; sə'vaɪv/ *vt, vi* [VP6A, 2A] continue to live or exist; live or exist longer than; remain alive after: 残存;继续生存;经历…后仍然活着;生命较…长久: *survive an earthquake / shipwreck;* 遭遇地震(沉船)后幸存; *those who ~d.* 残存者. *The old lady has ~d all her children.* 那位老妇人的子女都先她而去世了. *I hope I shall never ~ my usefulness,* continue to live (or to hold a position) after I have ceased to be useful. 我希望在我生之年永远不要变成废物. **sur·vivor** /-ə(r); -və/ *n* person who has ~d: 残存者; 生还者; 生存者: *send help to the survivors of the earthquake.* 对地震生还者于以救助.

sus·cep·tible /sə'septəbl; sə'septəbḷ/ *adj* **1** easily influenced by feelings; impressionable: 易受情感影响的;易动感情的;多情的: *a girl with a ~ nature;* 易动感情的女郎; *a young man,* one who easily falls in love. 多情的年轻人. **2** ~ *to,* sensitive to; easily affected by: 易感的; 敏感的; 易受…感动的: *~ to flattery / kind treatment;* 易为谄媚(礼遇)所动的; *~ to pain.* 对痛苦敏感的. **3** ~ *of,* (formal) capable of, that can receive or be given: (正式用语)能…的;容许…的: *Is your statement ~ of proof?* 你的陈述可加以证明吗? **sus·cep·ti·bil·ity** /sə,septə'bɪlɪti; sə,septə'bɪlɪti/ *n* (*pl* -ties) **1** [U] sensitiveness: 易感性; 敏感性; 感受性: *~ to hay fever / hypnotic influences.* 对花粉热(催眠)的敏感性. **2** (*pl*) sensitive points of a person's nature: (复)(一个人性格上的)敏感处; 感情: *We must avoid wounding their susceptibilities,* not say or do anything that might hurt their feelings. 我们必须避免伤害他们的感情.

sus·pect /sə'spekt; sə'spekt/ *vt* **1** [VP6A, 9, 25] have an idea or feeling (concerning the possibility or likelihood of sth): 猜想; 疑有; 觉得会; 有点感觉到: *He ~ed an ambush.* 他猜有伏兵. *She has more intelligence than we ~ed her to possess.* 她的智慧比我们所猜想的要高. *I ~ (that) he's a liar* (less usu 较不常用 *~ him to be a liar*). 我料想他是一个说谎者. **2** [VP6A] feel doubt about: 怀疑; 觉得可疑: *~ the truth of an account.* 怀疑一项报告的真实性. **3** [VP6A, 14] ~ *sb* (*of sth*), have a feeling that sb may be guilty (of): 怀疑某人有…罪: *He is ~ed of telling lies.* 别人怀疑他说谎. □ *n* /'sʌspekt; 'sʌspekt/ person ~ed of wrongdoing, disloyalty, etc: 有嫌疑的人; 嫌疑犯: *Are*

political ~s kept under police observation in your country? 贵国的政治嫌疑犯受警察监视吗? □ *pred adj* /'sʌspekt; 'sʌspekt/ of doubtful character; possibly false; 有可疑性质的; 可疑的; 被怀疑的: *His statements are ~.* 他的陈述可疑.

sus·pend /sə'spend; sə'spend/ *vt* **1** [VP6A, 14] ~ *sth (from),* hang up (from): 悬挂; 吊起: *lamps ~ed from the ceiling.* 悬挂在天花板上的灯. **2** (passive) (被动语态) (of solid particles, in the air or other fluid medium) be or remain in place: (指空气中或其他流体中的固体微粒)悬浮: *dust / smoke ~ed in the still air.* 悬浮在静止空气中的尘埃(烟). **3** [VP6A] stop for a time; delay; keep in an undecided state for a time: 暂停; 延缓; 悬而不决: ~ *payment,* stop payment (eg when bankrupt); 暂停支付(如破产时); ~ *a rule,* 中止一项规则; ~ *judgement,* postpone giving one; 延缓判决; (of a person) *in a state of ~ed animation,* alive but unconscious, (fig, joc; of institutions, committees, etc) temporarily inactive. (指人)不省人事; (喻、谐; 指制度、委员会等)暂时停止活动的. *He was fined £50 with a ~ed sentence / ~ed execution of sentence,* the payment of the fine being not required for a time, ie while he continues to observe the law. 他被判罚款50镑, 暂缓缴纳(只要他继续守法, 可暂时不缴罚款). **4** [VP6A] announce that (sb) cannot be allowed to perform his duties, enjoy privileges, etc for a time: 使停职; 暂停权利: ~ *a (professional) football player,* eg because of repeated breaches of the rules. 暂停一位(职业)足球员的比赛权.

sus·pender /sə'spendə(r); sə'spendə/ *n* (*pair of*) ~s, **1** (GB) garter. (英)束袜带. '~ **belt,** light garment worn round the waist, with clasps for keeping up women's stockings. 吊袜带(妇女系于腰际,附有吊袜子的扣钩). **2** (US) pair of straps (*braces* in GB) worn over the shoulders to keep up trousers. (美)吊裤带; 背带(英国称作 braces).

sus·pense /sə'spens; sə'spens/ *n* [U] uncertainty, anxiety (about news, events, decisions, etc): 不确定(指新闻,事件,决定等)悬而未决;不确定;悬疑;焦虑: *We waited in great ~ for the doctor's opinion.* 我们非常焦急地等候医生的意见. **keep sb in ~,** delay telling him what he is eager to know: 使某人悬念或挂虑: *They've kept me in ~ for five days already.* 他们已使我挂虑五天了.

sus·pen·sion /sə'spenʃn; sə'spenʃən/ *n* [U] suspending or being suspended: 悬挂; 悬浮; 暂停; 延缓; 停职; 悬而未决: *the ~ of a member of Parliament,* eg for abuse of Parliamentary privileges; 暂停某一国会议员的职权(如因滥用国会特权等); ⇨ **suspend(4)**; *the ~ of a motor-vehicle,* the means by which it is supported on its axles (springs, shock absorbers, etc). 汽车等的缓冲装置(弹簧,避震器等). '~ **bridge,** bridge suspended on or by means of steel cables supported from towers. 吊桥. ⇨ the illus at **bridge.** 参看 bridge 之插图.

sus·pi·cion /sə'spɪʃn; sə'spɪʃən/ *n* **1** [C, U] feeling that a person has when he suspects; suspecting or being suspected; feeling that sth is wrong: 猜疑; 怀疑; 嫌疑; 疑心: *I have a ~ that he is dishonest.* 我怀疑他不诚实. *I resent your ~s about my motives.* 我讨厌你怀疑我的动机. *He was looked upon with ~.* 他被人猜疑. *He was arrested on (the) ~ of having stolen the money.* 他因有偷那笔钱的嫌疑而被捕. *His behaviour aroused no ~.* 他的行为未引起怀疑. *Don't lay yourself open to ~.* 不要招惹嫌疑. *Don't let ~ fall on you / Don't fall under ~.* 不要使自己受到怀疑. *above ~,* of such good reputation that ~ is out of the question. (名誉极好而)无可怀疑. **2** *a ~ (of),* slight taste or suggestion: 些微; 一点点: 稍含某意味: *There was a ~ of sadness in her voice / of garlic in the stew.* 她的声音有一点悲怆意味(那道炖菜有一点大蒜味道).

sus·pi·cious /sə'spɪʃəs; sə'spɪʃəs/ *adj* having, showing or causing suspicion: 怀疑的; 表示怀疑的; 引起怀疑

的; 可疑的: *The affair looks ~ to me.* 这事在我看来可疑。 *He's a ~ character,* There is reason to suspect that he is dishonest, etc. 他是一个品性不太可靠的人物 (不诚实的)。 *(be/become/feel) ~ about/of sb/sth,* have suspicions about: 对某人(某物)感到怀疑: *The policeman became increasingly ~ of his movements.* 那警察对他的行动日益怀疑。 **~·ly** *adv*

suss /sʌs/ sʌs/ *vt* [VP15B] *~ sth out,* (colloq) (口) **1** discover. 发现。 **2** reconnoitre. 侦察。

sus·tain /səˈsteɪn/ səˈsten/ *vt* [VP6A] **1** keep from falling or sinking: 支撑; 承住; 承受得起: *Will this light shelf ~ (the weight of) all these books?* 这个轻便的书架承受得住所有这些书的(重量)吗? **2** (enable to) keep up, maintain: (使能)维持; 支持: *~ing food, that gives strength:* 维持体力的食物; *~ an argument/attempt:* 支持一项议论(一项尝试); *~ a note,* continue to sing or play the note without faltering: 继续(唱或奏)某一音符; *make a ~ed effort.* 作不断的努力。 **3** suffer; undergo: 蒙受; 遭受: *~ a defeat.* 遭受失败。 *The pilot ~ed severe injuries when his plane crashed.* 飞机坠毁时驾驶员受到重伤。 **4** (legal) uphold; give a decision in favour of: (法律)确认; 准许: *The court ~ed his claim/~ed him in his claim.* 法庭准许他的要求。

sus·ten·ance /ˈsʌstɪnəns/ ˈsʌstenəns/ *n* [U] (nourishing quality of) food or drink; nourishment: 食物; 饮料; 营养: *There's more ~ in cocoa than in tea.* 可可比茶富有营养。

sut·tee /ˈsʌtiː/ sʌˈti/ *n* Hindu widow who cremated herself on the funeral pyre of her husband; practice (now illegal) of doing this. 印度昔时随同丈夫火葬的寡妇; 寡妇殉夫的习俗(现已非法)。

su·ture /ˈsuːtʃə(r)/ ˈsutʃə/ *n* seam formed in sewing up a wound; thread used for this. (伤口的)缝合; (缝合伤口所用的)缝线。

su·ze·rain /ˈsuːzəreɪn US: -rɪn/ ˈsuzərɪn/ *n* State or ruler in relation to a country over which it or he has some control or authority; (formerly) feudal overlord. 宗主国; 宗主; (昔日的)封建大君主。 **~·ty** /ˈsuːzərəntɪ; ˈsuzərɪntɪ/ *n*: 宗主权: *under the ~ty of.* 在…保护之下; 在…宗主权下。

svelte /svelt/ svelt/ *adj* (F) (of a person) slender and graceful. (法)(指人)苗条而优雅的; 婀娜袅袅的。

swab /swɒb/ swab/ *n* **1** mop or pad for cleaning, eg floors, decks. (擦地板、甲板等的)拖把; 擦帚。 **2** sponge, bit of absorbent material, for medical use, eg taking a specimen from the throat for testing infection; specimen (eg of mucus) so taken: 医疗用的海绵、具吸收性物质等; 拭子; 药签(用拭子取供检验的)的拭样(如喉粘膜等): *take ~s from children suspected of having diphtheria.* 从疑似患有白喉的小孩(喉中)取拭样供检验。 □ *vt* (-bb-) [VP6A, 15B] clean with a ~: (以拖把等)擦净; 擦洗; *~ down the decks;* 用拖把擦洗甲板; *~ up water that has been upset on the floor.* 用擦帚把打翻在地板上的水拖干。

swaddle /ˈswɒdl/ ˈswɑdl/ *vt* [VP6A] bind (a baby) with long narrow strips of cloth (as was formerly the custom). 用襁褓包裹(婴儿)(如昔日风俗所为); 绑裹。 **'swaddling-clothes,** the strips of cloth used: 襁褓: *still in his swaddling-clothes,* (fig) still not free from restraining influences. (喻)仍在襁褓中; 仍受束缚或支配。

swag /swæg/ swæg/ *n* [U] **1** (sl) stolen goods; things obtained dishonestly. (俚) 赃物; 不正当所得物。 **2** (Australia) bundle of personal belongings carried by a vagrant. (澳大利亚)流浪汉随身携带的捆扎物。

swag·ger /ˈswægə(r)/ ˈswægə/ *vi* [VP2A, C] walk or behave in a self-important or self-satisfied manner. 自大地或自我满足地行走或举止; 装模作样; 摆架子。 □ *n* ~ing walk or way of behaving: 装模作样; 摆架子: *with a ~.* 装模作样地。 □ *adj* (sl) very chic. (俚)非常时髦的; 非常别致的。 **~er** *n*

swain /sweɪn/ swen/ *n* (poet or archaic) young rustic

man (esp regarded as a lover): (诗或古)年轻的乡下人 (尤指被当作情郎者): *lasses and their ~s.* 女孩子和她们的情郎; (joc) lover. (谑)爱人。

swal·low¹ /ˈswɒləʊ/ ˈswɑlo/ *n* kinds of small, swiftly-flying insect-eating bird with a forked tail, which migrates to warm countries, eg to England every summer, and is associated with the beginning of summer. 燕子(体小、飞行迅速、食昆虫的小鸟, 尾部分叉, 徙栖温暖处, 如每年迁徙至英格兰, 故在英国燕子使人联想到初夏)。 ⇨ the illus at **bird.** 参看 bird 之插图。 *One ~ doesn't make a summer,* (prov) It is unwise to form a judgement on the basis of a single instance. (谚)一燕不成夏 (仅凭一个事例即下判断是不智的)。 **'~-dive** *n* dive with the arms outspread till close to the water. 燕子式跳水(跳起时两手分开, 近水时合拢)。 **'~-tailed** *adj* (of butterflies, birds) with a deeply forked tail; (of a man's coat) with long tails (as of an evening dress coat). (指蝴蝶、鸟类)尾巴分叉长的; (指男服)燕尾形式的(如晚礼服)。

swal·low² /ˈswɒləʊ/ ˈswɑlo/ *vt, vi* [VP6A, 15B, 2C] **1** *~ (up),* cause or allow to go down the throat: 吞; 咽: *~ one's food,* eat it quickly: 吞咽食物(很快地吃); work the muscles of the throat as when *~ing* sth (to give relief to some kind of emotion): 吞咽肌活动喉部肌肉; 忍气吞声: *He ~ed hard,* eg as if *~ing* an insult; 他强忍下去(如似将侮辱吞下); ⇨ **3** below. 参看下列第 3 义。 **2** *~ (up),* take in; exhaust; cause to disappear; use up: 吞没; 耗尽; 使消失; 用罄: *earnings that were ~ed up by lawyers' bills.* 被律师费用耗尽的收入。 *The earth seemed to ~ them up,* They suddenly disappeared. 地球好像把他们吞没了(他们突然不见了)。 *The aircraft was ~ed (up) in the clouds.* 飞机没入云中。 **3** (fig uses) (比喻用法) accept an insult/affront, accept it meekly: 忍受侮辱(无礼); *~ sth whole,* believe it without argument; doubt: 囫囵吞枣(轻易相信某事物); *~ one's words,* take them back, express regret for them; 取消前言; *~ a story,* believe it too easily; 轻信一个故事; *~ the bait,* (of a person) accept a proposal, an offer etc made to tempt one to do sth. (指人)上当; 上钩。 □ *n* act of *~ing;* amount *~ed* at one time 吞; 咽; 一吞之量。

swam /swæm/ swæm/ *pt* of **swim.**

swami /ˈswɑːmɪ/ ˈswɑmɪ/ *n* Hindu religious teacher; (loosely) mystic, yogi. 印度教的教师; (非严格用法)神秘主义者; 瑜伽信徒。

swamp /swɒmp/ swɑmp/ *n* [C, U] (area of) soft wet land; marsh. 湿地; 沼地; 沼泽; 沼泽区。 □ *vt* **1** [VP6A] flood, soak, with water: 淹水; 淹没; 浸在水中; 使覆水而沉没: *A big wave ~ed the boat.* 一个巨浪淹没了那只小舟。 *Everything in the boat was ~ed.* 船上的东西都浸水了。 **2** [VP14] *~ with,* (fig) overwhelm: (喻)使困窘; 应接不暇; 使忙得不可开交: *We are ~ed with work.* 我们被工作压得透不过气来。 *The firm is ~ed with orders,* ie for their goods. 大量订单使那家商行应接不暇。 **~y** *adj* (-ier, -iest).

swan /swɒn/ swɑn/ *n* large, graceful, long-necked (usu white) water-bird. 天鹅(通常为白色)。 ⇨ the illus at **water.** 参看 water 之插图。 **'~-dive** *n,* (US) (美) = swallow-dive. **'~-song** *n* (from the old belief that a swan sang sweetly when about to die) last performance, appearance, work before death of a poet, musician, etc. 天鹅之歌; (即)诗人、音乐家等的最后演出、出现或其最后的作品(此典来自古老的传说, 谓天鹅将死时, 发悦耳的鸣声); 绝笔; 临终作品等。 **'~'s-down** *n* [U] **(a)** soft underfeathers of *~s.* 天鹅的软绒毛。 **(b)** kind of thick cotton cloth with a soft nap on one side. 一种单面有绒毛的厚棉布; 棉法兰绒; 天鹅绒布。 □ *vi* (-nn-) [VP2C] (colloq) (口) *~ off/around, etc,* move, go in a leisured, often aimless manner, esp of a privileged person or one who need not work: 优闲地走动; 优哉游哉地闲逛; 优游度日(尤指拥有特权者, 或无须工作者): *I suppose you're ~ning off to Paris for the*

weekend. 我想你周末要到巴黎去优游一番。*The boys are* ∼*ing around Austria on a mountaineering holiday.* 在登山假日里那些男孩在奥地利四处漫游。

swank /swæŋk; swæŋk/ *vi* [VP2A, C] (colloq) swagger; behave or talk in a boastful way; show off. (口) 装模作样; 摆架子; 炫耀。□ *n* [U] ∼ing behaviour; 装模作样; 摆架子; 炫耀: *wear a gold wristwatch just for* ∼; 仅为炫耀而戴金手表; (口) person who ∼s. 装模作样的人; 炫耀者。∼**y** *adj* smart; characteristic of a person who ∼s: 时髦的; 炫耀的; 装模作样的: *a* ∼*y sports car*; 时髦的跑车; *Jill and her* ∼*y friends.* 吉尔和她那些时髦的朋友们。

swap /swɒp; swɑp/ *vt, vi* (-pp-) = swop.

sward /swɔːd; swɔrd/ *n* [U] (liter) turf. (文)草土; 草地。

swarm¹ /swɔːm; swɔrm/ *n* [C] colony, large number, of insects, birds, etc moving about together: (昆虫,鸟等)的大群: *a* ∼ *of ants/locusts*; 一大群蚂蚁(蝗虫); *a* ∼ *of bees*, cluster of honeybees when migrating with a queen bee to establish a new colony; 分封时的蜂群(随一蜂王迁徙建立新巢者); ∼*s of children in the parks.* 在公园里的一群孩子们。□ *vi* 1 [VP2A] (of bees) move or go in large numbers round a queen bee for emigration to a new colony. (指蜜蜂)随蜂王迁徙建立新巢; 分封。2 [VP3A] *be* ∼*ing with*; ∼ *with*, (of places) be overrun or crowded: (指地方)充满; 拥挤: *The beaches were* ∼*ing with bathers.* 海滩上挤满了作海水浴的人们。*The stables* ∼*ed with flies.* 马厩里到处都是苍蝇。3 [VP2C] be present in large numbers; move in a ∼: 群集; 蜂拥而进: *When the rain started the crowd* ∼*ed back into the hotel.* 雨一开始下, 人群即拥回旅社。*Beggars* ∼*ed round the rich tourists.* 乞丐成群地围在有钱的观光客的四周。

swarm² /swɔːm; swɔrm/ *vt* [VP6A, 15B] ∼ *(up)* climb by clinging with the arms and legs. 抱着…往上爬; 用手臂及腿攀住…往上爬。

swarthy /ˈswɔːðɪ; ˈswɔrðɪ/ *adj* having a dark complexion. 黑皮肤的; 黝黑的。

swash·buck·ler /ˈswɒʃbʌklə(r); ˈswɑʃˌbʌklɚ/ *n* bully; boastful fellow who behaves recklessly. 暴徒; 欺凌弱小者; 轻率而浮夸之徒。**swash·buck·ling** /ˈswɒʃbʌklɪŋ; ˈswɑʃˌbʌklɪŋ/ *adj* reckless and boastful. 轻率而浮夸的。□ *n* [U] behaviour of a ∼. 虚张声势; 轻率而浮夸。

swas·tika /ˈswɒstɪkə; ˈswɑstɪkə/ *n* [C] kind of cross emblematic of the sun, good fortune or Nazism. (相似物为象征太阳、好运等的标志)卍字; (德国纳粹主义的)卐字。

swat /swɒt; swɑt/ *vt* (-tt-) slap with a flat object: (用平物)拍打: *a* ∼ *fly.* 拍打苍蝇。□ *n* 1 slap of this kind: 拍打; 拍击: *Give that fly a* ∼. 给那只苍蝇一拍。2 flexible device on a handle for ∼ting (flies, etc): 用来拍打之物; 苍蝇拍: *a* '*fly-*∼ (also 亦作 '*fly-swatter*). 苍蝇拍。

swath /swɔːθ; swɑθ/, **swathe** /sweɪð; sweð/ *n* 1 ridge of grass, wheat, barley, etc lying after being cut. 刈下的一行草、小麦、大麦等。2 space left clear after one passage of a mower. 一刈的面积; 刈幅。

swathe¹ /sweɪð; sweð/ *vt* [VP6A, 15A] wrap or bind up: 包裹; 卷; 绑: *He came out of hospital with his leg still* ∼*d in bandages.* 他离出了医院, 腿仍裹在绷带中。□ *n* bandage; wrapping. 绷带; 包布。

swathe² /sweɪð; sweð/ *n* ⇨ **swath**.

sway /sweɪ; swe/ *vi, vt* 1 [VP2A, C, 6A, 15A] (cause to) move, first to one side and then to the other; swing: (使)摇摆; (使)摆动: *The branches of the trees were* ∼*ing in the wind.* 树枝在风中摇曳。*Do you sway your hips when you walk?* 你走路时摆动臀部吗? 2 [VP6A] control or influence; govern the direction of: 控制; 影响; 支配: ∼*ed by his feelings*; 受他感情的支配; *a speech that* ∼*ed the voters.* 一篇影响选民决定的演说。□ *n* [U] 1 ∼ing movement. 摇摆; 摆动。2 rule or

control: 统治; 支配: *the peoples who were under the* ∼ *of Rome*, were ruled by Rome (in ancient times). (古代)被罗马帝国统治的诸民族。

swear /sweə(r); swɛr/ *vt, vi* (*pt* swore /swɔː(r); swor/, *pp* sworn /swɔːn; sworn/) 1 [VP6A, 7A, 9] say solemnly or emphatically: 郑重地说; 强调; 发誓: *He swore to tell the truth/swore that he would tell the truth.* 他发誓要说实话。*I could have sworn that there was somebody in the next room,* I felt certain of this. 我敢说(当时)隔壁房间里有人。2 [VP6A, 15A, B] take an oath; cause (sb) to take an oath. 宣誓; 使(某人)宣誓或立誓。∼ *sb in,* cause him to take the oath of office. 使某人宣誓就职。∼ *sb to secrecy,* make him ∼ to keep sth secret. 使某人誓守秘密。∼ *a witness,* administer the oath to him. 使证人宣誓。**sworn enemies,** enemies who can never be reconciled. 不共戴天的仇敌。**sworn friends/brothers,** very close friends. 莫逆之交(结拜兄弟)。3 [VP3A] ∼ *by sth,* (a) appeal to as a witness or witnesses: 对…发誓: ∼ *by all the gods that ...;* 对诸神发誓(请诸神明见); ∼ *by all that one holds dear.* 在所有亲人面前发誓。(b) (colloq) use and have great confidence in: (口)使用并深信; 极其信赖: *He* ∼ *by quinine for malaria.* 他深信奎宁可以治好疟疾。∼ *off sth,* (colloq) declare that one will give up, stop using: (口)立誓弃绝或停止用: *He swore off smoking when the doctors said it caused lung cancer.* 医生们说吸烟能引起肺癌时,他立誓戒烟。∼ *to sth,* say emphatically: 强调地说: 断然地说: *He swore to having paid for the goods,* said emphatically that he had done so (when accused of not having done so). 他断然地说已经付清货款。*I think I've met that man somewhere but I wouldn't* ∼ *to it,* am not very confident of having met him. 我想我曾在什么地方见过那个人, 但是我不太敢确定。4 [VP3A, 14] make an affirmation after having taken an oath: 立誓后确定; 起誓证实: ∼ *an accusation/a charge against sb;* 立誓指控某人; **sworn evidence/statements.** 立誓指证(陈述)。5 [VP2A, 15B, C, 3A, 22] ∼ *(at sb),* use obscene etc words to insult, or for emphasis (⇨ section on stylistic values in **introduction**): 咒骂; 诅骂(参看序文中的'文体标准'): *The foreman swore at his workers.* 工头咒骂工人。*He gave vent to his anger by* ∼*ing loudly.* 他高声咒骂以发泄他的愤怒。*He swore himself hoarse,* continued ∼*ing until he was hoarse.* 他一直到嗓子哑哑才停止了咒骂。'∼-**word** *n* word used in ∼*ing.* 诅咒; 骂人话; 亵渎之语。∼**er** *n* person who ∼s. 咒骂者; 诅骂者。

sweat /swet; swet/ *n* 1 [U] moisture that is given off by the body through the skin: 汗: *wipe the* ∼ *off one's brow.* 揩去额上的汗。'∼-**band** *n* (a) band of absorbent material inside a hat. (帽子里的)吸汗箍; 汗圈。(b) cloth tied round the forehead, wrist, etc to absorb ∼. (绕在前额、手腕等处的)吸汗带。'∼-**shirt** *n* cotton sweater with sleeves, worn esp by athletes before and after exercise. 长袖棉线衫(尤指运动员所穿者)。2 *a* ∼, condition of a person or animal (esp a horse) when covered with ∼: 发汗; 出汗; 满身汗: *be in a* ∼. 满身大汗。*They say that a good* ∼ *will cure a cold.* 人们说好好发一身汗可以治愈感冒。*be in a cold* ∼, in a state of fear or anxiety. 发冷汗; 冒冷汗; 处于恐惧或焦虑状态。*all of a* ∼, (colloq) wet with ∼; (口) anxious or frightened. (口)汗湿的; (喻)焦虑的; 害怕的。3 (colloq, *sing* only) hard work: (口,仅用单数)苦工; 辛苦工作: *This job is a frightful* ∼. 这工作极为辛苦。4 [C] *an old* ∼, (sl) soldier with many years' service; (by extension) person with many years' experience of his job. (俚)老兵; (引申义)老手; 有多年经验的工作者。5 [U] moisture on the surface of anything, eg condensation on an inner wall. (任何东西表面上的)水气, 水珠或湿气(如内壁上凝聚者)。□ *vt, vi* 1 [VP2A] give out ∼ (1, 5): 出汗; 结成水珠; 发出水气或湿气: *The long hot climb made him* ∼. 长距离的激烈攀登使他出汗。2 [VP6A, 15B] give out (sth that comes out of

a surface). 使发出; 使渗出; 使从表面发出. ~ *blood*, (fig) work like a slave. (喻)像奴隶般地工作. ~ *out a cold*, get rid of it by ~ing. 发汗医治感冒. 3 [VP6A] (cause to) ~ 出汗; 使出汗: *The doctor* ~ed *his patient*. 医生使他的病人出汗. *Don't* ~ *your horse*. 不要使马流汗. 4 [VP6A, 2A, C] (cause to) work hard: (使)辛苦工作; (使)努力工作: ~ *one's workers*. 使工人们辛苦工作. ~ed *goods*, produced by ~ed labour. 廉价劳工的产品. ~ed *labour*, the labour of underpaid workers. 工资低微的劳工; 廉价劳工. '~-*shop* n workshop where ~ed labour is used. 雇用廉价劳工的工厂. ~y *adj* (-ier, -iest) 1 damp with ~: 汗湿的; 多汗的: ~y *underwear*. 汗湿的内衣. 2 causing one to ~: 使出汗的; 费力的: ~y *work*. 费力的工作.

sweater /'swetə(r); 'swɛtə/ n knitted garment usu of thick wool with long sleeves, worn by athletes before or after exercise; similar woolly garment (not necessarily thick or heavy) worn for warmth. 厚运动衫; 毛线衫; 卫生衣. ⇨ **jersey, jumper, pullover.**

swede /swi:d; swid/ n kind of turnip. 芸薹; 瑞典芜菁.

sweep¹ /swi:p; swip/ n 1 '~ (-*up*/-*out*), act of sweeping with, or as with, a broom, etc: 扫; 扫除; 打扫: *Give the room a good* ~. 把这房间好好打扫一下. *Let's have a thorough* ~-*up*/*out*. 让我们来一次大扫除. *make a clean* ~ (*of sth*), get rid of (what is unwanted) completely: 清除; 清扫; 全部去掉: *They made a clean* ~ *of their old furniture and replaced it with brand new pieces*. 他们把旧家具全部丢掉, 换成全新的. *In forming his new Cabinet the Prime Minister has made a clean* ~. 首相组织新内阁时, 撤掉全部旧阁员. 2 sweeping movement: 扫动; 挥动; 打扫的动作: *with a* ~ *of his arm/scythe*. 他的手臂(镰刀)挥了一挥. 3 space covered by a sweeping movement; range of such a movement: 一挥所及的空间; 一挥的距离或范围: *The knight killed everyone who came within the* ~ *of his sword*. 那武士杀死了他的刀刃所及的每一个人. 4 long unbroken stretch, eg curved, on a road, river, coast, etc or of sloping land: (路、河、海岸等的)弯曲部分; 绵亘的区域; 一片地区: *a fine* ~ *of country*. 一片美丽的乡野. 5 steady uninterrupted flow: 稳定不断的流动: *the* ~ *of the tide*. 潮的流动. 6 ('**chimney-**)~, man whose work is sweeping soot from chimneys. 清扫烟囱者; 烟囱清扫夫. 7 long oar worked by a rower who stands, for steering or moving a boat, eg a sailing-boat when there is no wind. (立划桨手所操作的)长桨; 大桡. 8 long pole mounted as a lever for raising a bucket from a well. 自井中提起水桶用的长杠杆. 9 '~(·**stake**), form of gambling on horse-races, the money staked by all those who take part being divided among those who have drawn numbered tickets for the winners (usu the first three). 赛马的赌金独得制(通常由押注前三名赛马的胜利者分之).

sweep² /swi:p; swip/ *vt, vi* (*pt, pp* **swept** /swept; swɛpt/) 1 [VP6A, 15A, B, 22, 2A] ~ *sth* (*from sth*); ~ *sth* (*free*) *of sth*; ~ *sth up*/*away*, etc, clear (dust, dirt, etc) away with, or as with, a brush or broom; clean by doing this: 扫除(尘、土等); 清扫; 清除; 打扫: ~ *the dust from the carpets*; 清除地毯上的尘土; ~ *the carpets/the floor/the yard*; 打扫(地毯、地板、院子); ~ *the chimney (free of soot)*; 扫除烟囱的(煤灰); ~ *up dead leaves from the garden paths*; 扫除园中小径的枯叶; ~ *up the crumbs*; 清扫屑屑; ~ *the crumbs under the carpet/into a corner/into a dustpan*. 清扫地毯下面的碎屑(把碎屑扫到角落里, 扫进畚箕). 2 [VP6A, 15A, B] clean or clear away as with a broom; push away: 似用扫帚清扫; 扫荡; 清理; 推开; 冲掉: ~ *the seas of pirates*. 扫荡海盗. *The current swept the logs along*. 水流冲走了木材. *The wind swept my hat off/the clouds away*. 风吹掉了我的帽子(吹散了云). *Many bridges were swept away by the floods*. 很多桥梁被洪水冲断了. *We were almost swept off our feet by the waves*. 我们几乎被浪冲倒了. ~ *all before one*, have complete

uninterrupted success. 所向披靡; 大获全胜. ~ *the board*, (a) win all the money on the table when gambling. 横扫台面(赌博时)赢去台面上所有的钱. (b) win all the prizes; have every possible success. 囊括所有奖品; 大获全胜. *be swept off one's feet*, (fig) be overcome by feeling, filled with enthusiasm, eg an audience by a great singer. (喻)被弄得神魂颠倒; 变得如醉如痴(如听众之被某一伟大歌唱家所感动). ,**swept-'back** *adj* (a) (of aircraft wings) attached so that they are at an acute angle to the axis of the aircraft. (指飞机翼)与飞机轴线呈锐角安装的; 后掠翼的. (b) (of hair) arranged so that it is combed or brushed away from the face. (指发)梳向后方的. 3 [VP2C, 6A] pass over or along, esp so as to overcome obstacles; move quickly over or with a rush: 冲过; 扫过; 掠过; 疾驰; 驰过: *A huge wave swept over the deck*. 巨浪掠过甲板. *A blizzard swept the country*. 大风雪横扫全国. *The big tanks swept over the enemy's trenches*. 大型战车冲过敌人的战壕. *The wind swept along the street*. 风吹过街道. 4 [VP2C] move in a dignified or stately manner; go majestically: 威风凛凛地行走; 昂然走进: *She swept out of the room*. 她昂然走出房间. *The big car swept up the drive to the entrance of the palace*. 那辆大型轿车威风凛凛地驶进车道抵达皇宫大门. 5 [VP2C] extend in an unbroken line, curve or expanse: 绵亘; 伸展; 延展: *The road* ~s *round the lake*. 这条路环湖延伸. *The coast* ~s *northwards in a wide curve*. 海岸向北方呈大弧形展开. 6 [VP6A] pass over (as if) to examine or survey: (似)扫视; 环视; 周览: *The searchlights swept the sky*. 探照灯扫索天空. *Her eyes swept the room*. 她的眼睛扫视整个房间. 7 [VP6A] move along lightly and quickly: 轻快地移动; 拂; 轻掠过: *His fingers swept the keys of the piano*. 他的手指在钢琴键盘上轻快地移动. *Her dress swept the ground*. 她的衣服在地面拖曳. 8 [VP12A] make (a bow, curtsey) with a ~ing movement: 匆匆或草草地鞠躬或行礼: *She swept him a curtsey*. 她向他匆匆行一屈膝礼. ~**er** n 1 person or thing that ~s: 扫除之人或物: '*street* ~*ers*; 清洁工; *a* '*carpet*-~*er*. 地毯清扫器. 2 (football) defender who covers the backs, tackling any opponent who passes them. (橄榄球)后卫(防守球门附近区域、阻止对方球员带球进入该区者). ~**ing** *adj* far-reaching; taking in very much: 范围广大的; 包括很广的; 概括的: ~*ing changes/reforms*; 彻底的改变(改革); *a* ~*ing statement/generalization*, with no limitations or exceptions; 概括的叙述(说法); *a* ~*ing* (=complete) *victory*; 全胜; ~*ing* (= very great) *reductions in prices*, eg at a sale. 大减价. ~**ing·ly** *adv* ~**ings** *n pl* dust, rubbish, scraps, etc, collected by ~ing: 扫集物; 扫拢的尘屑; 垃圾; 废物堆: *a heap of* '*street* ~*ings*. 一堆街头垃圾.

sweet /swi:t; swit/ *adj* 1 (opp of *sour*) tasting like sugar or honey: (为 sour 之反义词)甜的; 甜的: *Do you like your tea* ~? 你喜欢你的茶加糖吗? *It tastes* ~, has a ~ taste. 这东西味道是甜的. *have a* ~ *tooth*, like things that taste ~. 爱吃甜食. ~ *wine*, wine with a ~ or fruity flavour (contrasted with *dry* wine). 甜酒(带甜味或水果味道者, 与 dry wine 相对). 2 fresh and pure: 新鲜而纯净的: ~ *milk*; 鲜奶; *keep a room clean and* ~; 保持房间的清新; ~ *breath*; 清新的呼吸; ~ *water*, fit to drink (contrasted with brackish water, etc). 净水; 清水; 饮用水(与带咸味的水等相对). 3 having a fragrant smell, like roses: 芬芳的; 芳香的: *The garden is* ~ *with thyme*. 园子里有麝香草的芬芳气味. *Don't the roses smell* ~! 多芳香的玫瑰花! ,~'*scented adj* having a ~ smell. 芳香的; 芬芳的. 4 pleasant or attractive: 可爱的; 漂亮的; 有吸引力的: *a* ~ *face*; 讨人喜欢的脸; *a* ~ *voice*; 悦耳的声音; *a* ~ *singer*, sb having a ~ voice; 声音悦耳的歌唱家; *a* ~ *little girl*; 漂亮的小女孩; *a* ~ *temper*; 温和的性情; ,~-'*tempered adj*. *It was* ~ *to hear people praise me so much*. 真高兴听到人们这样称赞我. *What a* ~ *little poodle you have*! 你这只小狮子狗真可爱! *Isn't the baby* ~! 多可爱

的娃娃! **5** (phrases) (短语) *at one's own ~ will,* as and when one pleases, with no one to give orders or advice. 随己喜欢; 任某人自便。*be ~ on (sb),* (colloq) very fond of, in love with. (口)非常喜欢或爱上(某人)。 **6** (compounds) (复合词) '**~-bread** *n* pancreas of a calf or lamb used as food. (小牛或小羊的)胰; 胰脏(供食用者)。'**~-briar /-'brier** *n* wild rose with ~-scented leaves and single pink flowers. 野蔷薇(叶芳香, 开淡红色单瓣花)。'**~-heart** *n* either of a pair of lovers: 爱人; 情人; 恋人: *David and his ~heart.* 大卫和他的爱人。'**~-meat** *n* piece of ~-tasting food (usu made of sugar or chocolate); fruit preserved in sugar. 糖果(通常用糖或巧克力做成); 甜品; 蜜饯。 '**pea** *n* garden plant (an annual) with brightly-coloured, ~-scented flowers. 麝香豌豆; 香豌豆(一年生园艺植物, 花芳香而色艳)。 '**~ potato** *n* tropical climbing plant with thick edible roots, cooked as a vegetable. 红薯; 甘薯。 '**~ 'william** *n* garden plant with flowers in close clusters, often parti-coloured. 美洲石竹(园艺植物, 花丛集, 色常斑驳)。□ *n* [C] **1** (US 美 = *candy*) small piece of ~-tasting food (eg boiled flavoured sugar, chocolate, etc). 糖果; 甜食(糖, 巧克力等)。 **2** (US 美 = *dessert*) dish of ~ food (eg a pudding, tart, jelly, trifle, etc) as one of the courses of a meal. (In GB *dessert* usu means a course of fresh fruit, nuts, etc.) 饭后甜食(布丁, 馅饼, 果子冻、蛋糕等, 包括于正餐的一道食品)。 (在英国, dessert 通常指餐末上的新鲜水果, 坚果等)。 **3** (*pl*) delights; pleasures: (复)快乐; 欢乐: *taste the ~s of success;* 尝到成功的乐趣; *enjoy the ~s of life while one is young.* 年轻时享受人生的欢乐。 **4** (as a form of address) darling? (称呼语)亲爱的: *Yes, my ~.* 是的, 我亲爱的。'**~·ly** *adv* '**~·ness** *n* '**~·ish** /-ɪʃ; -ɪʃ/ *adv* rather ~. 略甜的; 有点可爱的。 '**~en** /'switn; 'switn/ *vt, vi* [VP6A, 2A] make or become ~. 使成变甜; 使或变甜; 使或变可受等。 ⇨ **pill(1)**. **~·en·ing** /'switnɪŋ; 'switnɪŋ/ *n* [C, U] that which ~ens; sth ~ used in cooking, etc. 使甜之物; 用于烹调等的甜东西。

swell /swel; swel/ *vi, vt* (*pt* **~ed** /sweld; sweld/, *pp* **swollen** /'swəʊlən; 'swoʊlən/, rarely **~ed**) [VP6A, 14, 15B, 2A, C] *~ (up) (with),* (cause to) become greater in volume, thickness or force: (使)增大, 增厚或增强; 膨胀; 肿起: *Wood often ~s when wet.* 木材浸湿后常会膨胀。 *The river was swollen with melted snow.* 河水因融雪而上涨。 *His face began to ~ up,* eg from toothache. 他的脸孔开始肿起(如因牙痛)。 *He / His heart was ~ing with pride.* 他骄傲自大。 *The boy's eyes were swollen up with tears.* 那男孩的眼里充满了泪水。 *These small items help to ~ the total.* 这些小项目使总额增加了。 *have / suffer from a swollen head,* be conceited. 自负; 自大。 Hence, 由此产生, **,swollen-'headed** *adj* **2** [VP2A, C, 6A, 15B] *~ (out),* have, cause to have, a curved surface: (使)隆起; 鼓胀; (使)有弧形表面: *The sails ~ed out in the wind.* 船帆迎风鼓起。 *The wind ~ed the sails.* 风使船帆鼓胀。 □ *n* **1** gradual increase in the volume of sound: 音量逐渐增加: *the ~ of an organ.* 风琴声音渐响。 **2** (*sing only*) slow rise and fall of the sea's surface after a storm (with large but unbroken waves); (仅用单数)暴风雨后海上的滚滚大浪; 潮涌: *There was a heavy ~ after the storm.* 暴风雨后海有滚滚的大浪。 **3** (US colloq) smartly dressed person; person of distinction or ability: (美口)衣着入时的人; 优秀人士; 有才能的人: *What a ~ you look in that new suit!* 你穿起那套新衣多帅! *come the heavy ~ over sb,* (sl) try to appear great and important and in this way impress him. (俚)图示显贵以打动某人。 □ *adj* (US colloq) (美口) **1** smart, fashionable: 漂亮的; 时髦的: *Who are your ~ friends?* 你那些时髦的朋友是谁? *He took her to a ~ dinner party.* 他请了她去参加一个讲究的餐会。 **2** excellent; first-rate: 极好的; 第一流的: *He's a ~ tennis player.* 他是第一流的网球手。 '**~·ing** *n* [U, C] swollen place

on the body, eg the result of a knock or blow or toothache. 身体上的肿处(如因碰撞, 打击或因牙痛所致)。 **2** increase in size. 增大; 加大; 胀大; 膨胀。

swel·ter /'sweltə(r); 'swɛltɚ/ *vi* [VP2A] be uncomfortably warm; suffer from the heat: 酷热; 热得发昏; 中暑: *a ~ing hot day.* 酷热的一天。

swept /swept; swɛpt/ *pt, pp* of **sweep**[2].

swerve /swɜːv; swɝv/ *vi, vt* [VP2A, C, 4A, 6A] (cause to) change direction suddenly: (使)突然转向: *The car ~d to avoid knocking the boy down.* 那辆车突然转向, 以免撞着那男孩。 *Don't ~ from your purpose.* 不要突然改变你的目标。 □ *n* [C] swerving movement; (esp) turn or curve of a ball in the air. 突然转向; 逸出常轨; (尤指)球在空中的转动或弧线。

swift[1] /swift; swift/ *adj* (**-er, -est**) quick; fast; prompt: 快的; 迅速的; 敏捷的: *~ of foot;* (liter) able to run fast; (文)能跑得快的; *a ~ revenge;* 迅速的报复; *~ to anger,* (formal) quickly becoming angry. (正式用语)易于发怒的。 **~·ly** *adv* **~·ness** *n*

swift[2] /swift; swift/ *n* sorts of small insect-eating bird with long wings, similar to a swallow. (褐)雨燕(食虫小鸟, 翼长, 似燕)。 ⇨ the illus at **bird.** 参看 bird 之插图。

swig /swig; swig/ *vt, vi* (**-gg-**) [VP6A, 15B, 2A, C] *~ (down/off),* (colloq) take drinks of: (口)饮; 大口喝: *~ging beer;* 饮啤酒; *~ off a glass of rum.* 饮完一杯朗姆酒。 □ *n* long drink: 长饮; 痛饮; 牛饮: *take a ~ at a bottle of beer,* have a drink direct from the bottle. 拿着整瓶啤酒猛喝。

swill /swil; swil/ *vt, vi* **1** [VP6A, 15B] *~ sth (out),* rinse; wash by pouring liquid into, over or through: 涮; 冲洗; 冲涮: *~ out a dirty tub.* 冲洗脏盆子。 **2** [VP6A] (colloq) drink greedily: 贪饮; 大喝: *The workmen were ~ing tea when they ought to have been working.* 工人们在应该工作的时候大喝其茶。 □ *n* **1** [C] rinsing: 涮洗; 冲洗: *Give the bucket a good ~ out.* 把那只桶好好冲洗一下。 **2** [U] waste food, mostly liquid, eg as given to pigs. 残食; 泔脚; 潲水(如用以喂猪)。

swim /swim; swim/ *vi, vt* (*pt* **swam** /swæm; swæm/, *pp* **swum** /swʌm; swʌm/) (**-mm-**) **1** [VP2A, B, C] move the body through water by using arms, legs, fins, the tail, etc: 游泳; 游水: *Fishes ~.* 鱼游水。 *We swam all afternoon.* 我们游泳游了一个下午。 *Let's go ~ming.* 咱们去游泳吧。 *We swam across the river.* 他游过了那条河。 *When the boat sank they had to ~ for it,* save themselves by ~ming. 小船下沉的时候, 他们必须游水逃生。 *~ with the tide / the stream,* do as the majority do (taking the easiest course). 顺应潮流。 '**~·ming-bath /-pool** *n* indoor or outdoor, large or small, pool for ~ming in. (室内或室外的, 大的或小的)游泳池。 '**~·ming costume, '~·suit** *nn* garment worn for ~ming. 游泳衣; 泳装。 '**~·ming-trunks** *n pl* garment worn by boys and men for ~ming. (男用)游泳裤。 **2** [VP6A] cross by ~ming: 游过; 游泳横渡; 从一边游到另一边: *~ the English Channel;* 游过英吉利海峡; take part in (a race) in this way; compete with (sb) in this way: 参加(游泳比赛); 与(某人)作游泳比赛: *~ a race;* 参加游泳比赛; *~ two lengths of the pool;* 在游泳池中来回游了一趟; cause (an animal) to ~: 使(动物)游泳: *~ one's horse across a river.* 使马游过河。 **3** [VP3A] *~ with; ~ in/on,* be covered or overflowing (with); be (as if) floating (in or on): 弥漫; 盈溢; 漂浮; 浸: 泡: *eyes ~ming with tears;* 泪珠盈眶的眼睛; *meat ~ming in gravy;* 浸泡在浓汁中的肉; *strawberries ~ming in cream.* 浸泡在乳酪中的草莓。 **4** [VP2A] seem to be moving round and round; have a dizzy feeling: 似在转动; 晕眩; 眼花: *The room swam before his eyes.* 他感觉房子在他眼前转动。 *His head swam.* 他感到晕眩。 □ *n* **1** act or period of ~ming: 游泳; 游泳的期间: *have / go for a ~.* 去游泳。 **2** *the ~,* main current of affairs. 潮流; 时势。 *be in / out of the ~,* be / not be

taking part in, aware of, current affairs. 合乎(不合)时代潮流。 ~·**mer** n person who ~s. 游泳者。 ~·**mingly** adv easily and without trouble: 容易地; 顺利地: *We're getting along ~mingly*, 我们进展顺利。 *Everything went ~mingly, without obstruction or delay of any kind.* 一切进行顺利。

swindle /'swɪndl; 'swɪndl̩/ vt, vi [VP6A, 14] ~ **sth out of sb**; ~ **sb out of sth**, cheat; get (money, etc out of sb) by cheating: 行骗; 欺骗(钱财等): ~ *money out of sb*; 诈取某人钱财; ~ *sb out of his money*. 诈取某人钱财。 *Some people are easily ~d.* 有些人容易受欺诈。 □ n [C] piece of swindling; sth sold, etc that is less valuable than it is described to be: 行骗; 欺骗; 骗人的假货; 名实不符的货色: *This new radio set is a ~, the quality of the sound is bad.* 这种新的收音机是骗人的玩艺儿。 **swin·dler** /'swɪndlə(r); 'swɪndlə/ n person who ~s. 行骗者; 欺骗者; 诈欺者。

swine /swaɪn; swaɪn/ n (pl unchanged) (复数不变) 1 (old use, or liter) pig. (旧用法或文)猪。 '~·**herd** n man who (formerly) looked after ~ (when they were out in the woods, etc). (昔时的)牧猪人。 2 △ (abusive, derog) disgusting person. (讽)(骂人话,贬)猪猡; 下流胚子; 贱人。 **swin·ish** /-ɪʃ; -ɪʃ/ adj beastly and disgusting: 像猪一样的; 讨厌的; 卑贱的。

swing /swɪŋ; swɪŋ/ vi, vt (pt, pp **swung** /swʌŋ; swʌŋ/) 1 [VP2A, B, C, 6A, 15A, B, 22] (of sth having one end or one side fixed and the other free) move, cause to move, forwards and backwards or in a curve: (指一端固定,他端活动之物)(使)摇摆; (使)摆动: *His arms swung as he walked.* 他走路的时候摆动手臂。 *He was ~ing his arms.* 他在摆动手臂。 *The door swung shut/swung to.* 门关上了。 *The big ape swung (itself) from branch to branch.* 那只大猿猴在树枝间荡来荡去。 ~ *for sb/sth*, (colloq) be hanged (for murder): 绞死; (因谋杀而)被处绞刑。 **no room to** ~ *a cat in*, (of an enclosure) very small; having very little space for movement: (指范围)非常狭小; 很少活动余地。 ~ **the lead**, ⇨ lead¹(3). 2 [VP6A, C] walk or run with a free easy movement (the arms ~ing freely): (手臂自由摆动地)轻快地走或跑: *The soldiers advanced at a ~ing trot.* 士兵们以轻快的步伐前进。 3 [VP2A] dance to or play ~ music; (sl) be lively, gay and up-to-date. 演奏摇摆乐; (配合此乐而)跳摇摆舞; (俚)显得活泼,快活和时髦。 4 [VP2C, 15A, B] turn, cause to turn, in a curve: (使)旋转; (使)回转; 回旋: *He swung* (= turned quickly) *round and faced his accusers.* 他迅速地转身,面对指控他的人们。 *The car swung round the corner.* 那辆汽车在街角转弯。 □ n 1 ~ing movement: 摇摆; 摆动; 旋转; the ~ *of the pendulum.* 钟摆的摆动。 2 strong rhythm. 强烈的节奏; 韵律; 旋律。 **in full** ~, active; in full operation. 活跃的; 全力进行中。 **go with a** ~, **(a)** (of music, poetry) have a good rhythm. (指音乐, 诗歌)有节奏地; 节奏分明地。 **(b)** (fig) (of an entertainment, event, etc) proceed smoothly, without delays, etc. (喻)(指表演, 事件等)顺利进行(未延缓等)。 ~ **(music)**, (1930's) orchestral jazz, usu played by big bands. 摇摆乐(一种二十世纪三十年代的爵士乐, 通常由大乐队演奏)。 3 [C] seat held by ropes or chains for ~ing on; act, period, of ~ing on such a seat. 秋千; 打秋千; 打秋千的时间。 ~·**ing** adj (sl) lively; gay; up-to-date; enjoyable. (俚)活泼的; 欢乐的; 时髦的; 令人快乐的。

swinge /swɪndʒ; swɪndʒ/ vt (archaic) strike hard. (古)猛打; 重击。 ~·**ing** part adj huge; very forcible: 巨大的; 非常有力的: ~*ing damages*, eg awarded by a judge in a law suit: 巨额的损害赔偿金(如诉讼中经法官判处者): ~*ing taxation*. 巨额的课税。

swipe /swaɪp; swaɪp/ vt (colloq) (口) 1 [VP6A, 15A, 3A] hit hard: 重击; 猛打: *The batsman ~d the ball into the grandstand.* 击球员把球打进了大看台。 *He ~d at the ball and missed it.* 他向球猛击, 但未打中。 2 [VP6A] (colloq, usu hum) steal. (口, 通常作诙谐语)偷; 窃。 □

n swinging blow: 重打; 猛击: *have/take a ~ at the ball.* 向球猛击。

swirl /swɜːl; swɝl/ vi, vt [VP2C, 15B] (of water, air, etc) (cause to) move or flow at varying speeds, with twists and turns: (指水, 空气等)(使)涡旋而动; (使)起涡流: *dust ~ing about the streets*; 在街道上涡旋的尘土; carry (sth) *off*, *away*, in this way. 使(某物)涡旋而去; 把(某物)打着旋带走。 □ n 1 ~ing movement; (指涡旋的动作)涡旋; 涡流; 涡流: *a ~ of dust.* 一阵涡旋的尘土。 2 (US) twist or curl: (美)扭曲; 卷曲: *a hat with a ~ of lace round it.* 有一匝花边围绕的帽子。

swish /swɪʃ; swɪʃ/ vt, vi 1 [VP6A, 15B] ~ **sth (off)**, move (sth) through the air with a hissing or brushing sound; cut (sth off) in this way: 发飕飕声地挥动(某物); 飕飕地挥动; 瑟瑟地或飕飕地弄断(某物): *The horse ~ed its tail.* 那匹马瑟瑟地挥动尾巴。 *He ~ed his whip/~ed off the tops of the thistles with his whip.* 他飕飕地挥动鞭子(用鞭子抽断前丛的顶部)。 2 [VP2A] make, move with, a sound like that of sth moving through the air: 作瑟瑟声; 飕飕地响; 瑟瑟地动: *Her long silk dress ~ed as she came in.* 她进来的时候, 她穿的丝质长服瑟瑟作响。 □ n sound of, sound suggesting, sth being ~ed; (挥动某物时的)瑟瑟声, 飕飕声; 咻咻声: *We heard the ~ of a cane.* 我们听到一根手杖的抽打声。 □ adj (colloq) smart; expensive and fashionable: (口)豪华的; 时髦的; 价钱很贵的: *a ~ restaurant.* 豪华而气派的餐厅。

switch /swɪtʃ; swɪtʃ/ n [C] 1 device for making and breaking a connection at railway points (to allow trains to go from one track to another): (铁路的)转辙器; 闸。 '~·**man** /-mən; -mən/ n (pl -**men**) man in charge of railway ~es. (铁路的)转辙员; 扳道工人。 2 device for making and breaking an electric circuit: (电路的)开关: *a two-way* ~, one of a pair that can be used for turning electric current on or off from two points (eg at the bottom and the top of a staircase). 两线开关; 双路开关(可在两处接通或关闭电流的装置, 如楼梯上下皆可开关者)。 '~·**board** n panel with numerous ~es,

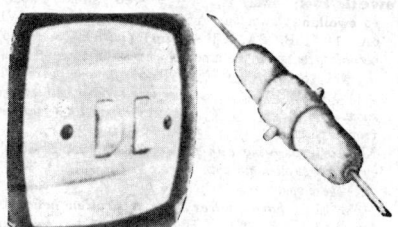

switches

esp for making connections by telephone or operating electric circuits. 电键板; 交换机; (尤指)电话总机; 配电板(或盘)。 3 thin twig or easily bent shoot cut from a tree, eg as used for urging a horse on. (从树上砍下的)枝条; 软枝; 嫩枝(如用于策马)。 4 bunch of false hair used by a woman to make her hair appear thicker or longer. (女人的)假发。 5 '~·**back** n (a) ~*back* (*railway*), one that twists and turns up and down steep slopes, esp the kind seen in amusement parks (US 美 = roller-coaster). 在陡斜坡上回旋升降的铁道(尤指游乐场之云霄飞车)。 (b) ~*back* (*road*), road with numerous ups and downs. 多斜坡的道路; S 形斜坡路。 6 transfer; change-over: 调换; 调匀; 改变: *a ~ from glass bottles to plastic cartons.* 把玻璃瓶换成塑料盒。 □ vt, vi 1 [VP15B] ~ *sth on*/*off*, use a ~(2) to turn (electric current) on/off: 接通或切断(电流); 打开或关闭: ~ *the light*/*radio*, etc on. 打开电灯(收音机等)。 *Don't* ~ *off yet, please.* 请暂且不要关闭。 2 ~ *sb on*, (sl, esp pp) cause sb to feel happy, excited;

(俚，尤用过去分词形式) 使某人感到快乐或兴奋: *That music really ~es me on!* 那音乐的确使我入迷! *He's really ~ed on!* 他真的被迷住了! **3** [VP6A, 15B] move (a train, tram, etc) on to another track: 使(火车，电车等)转辙: *~ a train into a siding.* 使火车转辙至傍轨。 **4** [VP6A, 15A] *~ (to); ~ (over to)*, shift; change: 转变; 改变: *~ the conversation (to a less embarrassing subject);* 改变谈话内容(谈论较不尴尬的话题)。 *~ over to modern methods.* 改采现代方法。 **5** [VP6A] whip or flick with a *~*(3). 以枝条鞭打。 **6** [VP6A, 15A] swing (sth) round suddenly; snatch suddenly: 突然摆动(某物); 甩动; 突然抢夺: *The cow ~ed (more usu swished) her tail.* 那只母牛摆动尾巴(较常用 swished)。 *He ~ed it out of my hand.* 他一下子从我手中(把它)抢了过去。

swivel /ˈswɪvl; ˈswɪvl/ *n* ring and pivot or ring with a linked hook to a chain joining two parts so that one can turn round without turning the other: 转镮; 转臂; 旋转轴承; 铰口镮: *a 'swivel-chain/-hook,* provided with a *~;* (装有转镮的)转动链(转动钩); *a 'swivel-chair/-gun,* one that can rotate on a pivot. 转动的转椅(转动枪炮)。 □ *vt, vi* (-ll-, US also -l-) [VP6A, 15B, 2A, C] turn on or as on a *~:* (在或似在旋轴上)转动; 回旋: *He ~ed round in his chair ~ed his chair round to see who had come in.* 他把所坐椅子转过来看看进来的是谁。

swiz /swɪz; swɪz/ *n* (sl) bitter disappointment; fraud. (俚)深切的失望; 欺骗。

swizzle /ˈswɪzl; ˈswɪzl/ *n* (colloq) (kinds of) mixed alcoholic drink served in a tall glass. (口)用高脚杯盛的鸡尾酒; 瑞器鸡尾酒。 *'swizzle-stick n* glass rod for stirring such a drink. 瑞器鸡尾酒棒。

swob /swɒb; swɑb/ *n, vt* (-bb-) = swab.

swol·len /ˈswəʊlən; ˈswolən/ *pp* of swell, esp as *adj:* 为 swell 的过去分词, 尤用作形容词: *a ~ ankle.* 肿踝。

swoon /swuːn; swun/ *vi* (archaic) (in *vi* [VP2A] faint. 昏晕; 晕倒; 晕过去。 □ *n* fainting fit. 晕厥; 晕倒。

swoop /swuːp; swup/ *vi, vt* 1 [VP2A, C] *~ (down) (on),* come down on with a rush: 猝然下降; 猝然攻击: *The eagle ~ed down on its prey.* 那只老鹰猝然飞下攫掠其猎食物。 *The soldiers ~ed down on the bandits,* attacked them suddenly. 兵士们突袭土匪。 **2** [VP15B] *~ sth up,* grab, snatch it. 攫取某物。 □ *n ~ing* movement; sudden attempt to snatch and carry off sth. 猝然攫取; 猛扑; 突袭。 *at one (fell) ~,* in one sudden swift attack or movement. 一举; 一下子; 突袭地。

swop (also **swap**) /swɒp; swɑp/ *vt, vi* (-pp-) [VP 6A, 15A, 2A] (colloq) exchange by barter: (口)交换; 物物交换: *~ foreign stamps;* 交换外国邮票; *~ yarns,* tell one another stories (of adventure, etc). 互相诉说(奇遇、历险等)故事。 *~ places with sb,* exchange seats. 与某人交换座位。 *Don't ~ horses in mid-stream,* (prov) if changes are needed, make them before the crisis is reached. (谚)过河中途莫换马(莫在危急时作更易)。 □ *n* exchange by barter: 交换; 物物交换: *I think your hat would suit me—shall we try a ~?* 我想你的帽子我戴很合适—我们交换一下好吗?

sword /sɔːd; sord/ *n* long steel blade fixed in a hilt, used as a weapon, or worn by army officers, etc as part of a uniform or as court dress. 剑; 刀。 *cross ~s with sb,* (fig) dispute with him. (喻)与…争论。 *draw/ sheathe the ~,* (rhet) begin/end a war. (修辞)开战 (停战)。 *put to the ~,* (rhet) kill. (修辞)杀死。 *at the point of the ~,* under threat of violence. 在暴力威胁下。 *'~-cane/-stick n ~* blade enclosed in a hollow walking-stick. 内藏刀的手杖。 *'~-cut n* (scar left by a) wound given with a *~-edge.* 刀(剑)伤; 刀(剑)伤疤。 *'~-dance n* dance over *~s* laid on the ground, or one in which *~s* are waved or clashed. 刀剑舞(穿行刀剑之间，或挥动刀剑); (挥)剑舞。 *'~-fish n* large sea-fish with a *~-like* upper jaw. 箭鱼; 旗鱼

(为一种大海鱼,有剑状长上颚)。 ⇨ the illus at **sea.** 参看 sea 之插图。 *'~-play n* [U] fencing; (fig) repartee; lively arguing. 剑术; 舞剑; (喻)巧答; 激辩。 *'~s·man* /-zmən; -zmən/ *n* (*pl* **-men**) man skilled in the use of a *~* (usu with *adj*): 精于剑术者; 击剑家; 剑客(通常与形容词连用): *a good ~sman.* 优秀的击剑家。 *'~s·man·ship* /-mənʃɪp; -mən‚ʃɪp/ *n*

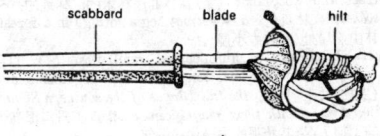

a sword

swore, sworn ⇨ swear.

swot /swɒt; swɑt/ *vi, vt* (-tt-) [VP2A, C, 3A, 15B] (not US) (不用于美国) *~ (for sth),* study hard (for an examination, etc). 苦读; 用功(为应付考试等); 临阵磨枪地研读。 *~ sth up,* work hard at; revise: 辛苦工作;用功;温习: *~ up one's geometry.* 用功习几何。 □ *n* **1** person who *~s.* 苦读者;用功者;临阵磨枪的学生。 **2** hard work: 辛苦的工作: *What a ~!* 多吃力的工作!

swum /swʌm; swʌm/ *pp* of swim.

swung /swʌŋ; swʌŋ/ *pt, pp* of swing.

syb·ar·ite /ˈsɪbəraɪt; ˈsɪbə‚raɪt/ *n* person who is devoted to comfort and luxury. 耽于奢侈逸乐的人; 淫逸之徒。 *syb·ar·itic* /‚sɪbəˈrɪtɪk; ‚sɪbəˈrɪtɪk/ *adj* luxurious; characteristic of a *~.* 爱奢侈的; 好享乐的。

syca·more /ˈsɪkəmɔː(r); ˈsɪkə‚mor/ *n* **1** [C] large tree valued for its wood (in GB a kind of maple-tree; in US a kind of plane-tree, also called a 'buttonwood'; in Egypt and Syria a kind of fig-tree). 木材贵重的大树 (在英国为一种大枫树; 在美国为扁桃木; 在埃及和叙利亚, 为无花果树)。 **2** [U] valuable hard wood of the *~.* 上述大树的珍贵木材。

syco·phant /ˈsɪkəfænt; ˈsɪkəfənt/ *n* person who tries to win favour by flattering rich or powerful people. 阿谀者; 奉承有钱有势者; 趋炎附势者。 *~ic* /‚sɪkəˈfæntɪk; ‚sɪkəˈfæntɪk/ *adj*

syl·lable /ˈsɪləbl; ˈsɪləbl/ *n* minimum rhythmic unit of spoken language, consisting of a vowel or sustained consonant, often preceded or followed by unsustained consonant(s); similar unit of written language: 音节(由一个元音或持续辅音构成, 常伴以非持续辅音): *'Arithmetic' is a word of four ~s.* arithmetic 一词有四个音节。 *-syl·labled adj* having a stated number of *~s:* 有…个音节的: *'Sycophant' is a three-~d word.* sycophant 是一个三音节词。 **syl·la·bary** /ˈsɪləbərɪ US: -berɪ; ˈsɪlə‚berɪ/ *n* [C] (*pl* **-ries**) list of characters (eg in Japanese) representing *~s.* 音节表; 词音表; (日文的)假名表。 **syl·labic** /sɪˈlæbɪk; sɪˈlæbɪk/ *adj* (**a**) of or in *~s.* 音节的; 拼音的。 (**b**) (of consonant) making a *~.* (指辅音)自成音节的。 **syl·labi·cate** /sɪˈlæbɪkeɪt; sɪˈlæbɪ‚ket/, **syl·labify** /sɪˈlæbɪfaɪ; sɪˈlæbə‚faɪ/ *vt* (*pt, pp* **-fied**), **syl·la·bize** /ˈsɪləbaɪz; ˈsɪlə‚baɪz/ *vt* divide into *~s.* 分成音节。 **syl·labi·ca·tion** /sɪ‚læbɪˈkeɪʃn; sɪ‚læbɪˈkeʃn/, **syl·labi·fi·ca·tion** /sɪ‚læbɪfɪˈkeɪʃn; sɪ‚læbəfəˈkeʃn/ *nn* (system of) division into *~s.* 分成音节; 音节划分法。

syl·la·bus /ˈsɪləbəs; ˈsɪləbəs/ *n* (*pl* **-es** /-bəsɪz/-bəsɪz/ or 或 **-bi** /-baɪ; -‚baɪ/) outline or summary of a course of studies; programme of school studies. 课程摘要; 教学大纲; 课程进度表。

syl·lo·gism /ˈsɪlədʒɪzəm; ˈsɪlə‚dʒɪzəm/ *n* [C] reaching a conclusion from two statements, eg: 三段论法(从两个前提得出结论的推理), eg: *All men must die; I am a man; therefore I must die.* 凡人必定会死; 我是人; 所以我必定会死。 ⇨ premise(2). **syl·lo·gis·tic** /‚sɪlə-ˈdʒɪstɪk; ‚sɪlə‚dʒɪstɪk/ *adj* in the form or nature of a

~. 三段论法的; 推论式的; 演绎的。

sylph /sɪlf/ *n* one of a class of female nature spirits believed to inhabit the air (cf *nymph*, spirit of the woods, etc); (hence) slender, graceful girl or woman. 风精(据说住在空中的女精灵)(参较 *nymph*, 山林等的精灵); (由此产生)优雅苗条的女郎或女子。'~-**like** *adj* slender and graceful. 苗条而优雅的; 窈窕的。

syl·van, sil·van /'sɪlvən/ *adj* (liter) of trees and woodland: (文)森林的; 林木的; 林地的: ~ *scenes*; 森林景色; *a* ~ *retreat*, eg a cottage in a forest. 林中隐居处(如林中小屋)。

sym·bio·sis /ˌsɪmbɪ'əʊsɪs; ˌsɪmbaɪ'osɪs/ *n* [U] (biol) harmonic association of different organisms, etc: (生物)共生; 共栖: *the tall Dingas of the southern Sudan, living in* ~ *with their magnificent cattle.* 苏丹南部高大的丁卡人, 与其壮观的牛马住在一起。

sym·bol /'sɪmbl; 'sɪmbl̩/ *n* [C] sign, mark, object, etc looked upon as representing sth: 符号; 象征; 代表物: *mathematical* ~*s*, eg ×, ÷, +, −; 数学符号(如 ×, ÷, +, −); *phonetic* ~*s*. 注音符号; 音标。*Red is a symbol of danger.* 红色是危险的象征。*The Cross is the* ~ *of Christianity.* 十字架是基督教的象征。~**ic** /sɪm-'bɒlɪk; sɪm'bɑlɪk/, ~**i·cal** /-kl; -kl̩/ *adjj* of, using, used as, a ~. 符号的; 象征的; 用符号的; 用作符号的。~**i·cally** /-klɪ; -klɪ/ *adv* ~**ize** /'sɪmbəlaɪz; 'sɪmbl̩ˌaɪz/ *vt* [VP6A] be a ~ of; make use of a ~ or ~s for. 象征; 为...的符号; 以符号表示。~**iz·ation** /ˌsɪmbəlaɪ'zeɪʃn US: -lɪ'z-; ˌsɪmbl̩ə'zeʃən/ *n* ~**ism** /'sɪmbəlɪzəm; 'sɪmbl̩ˌɪzəm/ *n* **1** [U] representation of ideas by the use of ~s; literary and artistic movement (late 19th c) that used artistic invention to express sensually ideas, emotions, abstractions in place of realism. 用符号代表概念; 象征主义(十九世纪晚期兴起的文学及艺术潮流, 提倡借巧构的具体意象, 表达思想、感情、意念等, 以取代先前流行的写实风格)。**2** [C] system of ~s used to represent a particular group of ideas. (代表某系列概念的)符号系统; 意象体系。

sym·me·try /'sɪmɪtrɪ; 'sɪmɪtrɪ/ *n* [U] (beauty resulting from the) right correspondence of parts; quality of harmony or balance (in size, design, etc) between parts: 对称; 匀称; 调和; 对称美: *The bump on the left side of her forehead spoilt the* ~ *of her face.* 她前额左方肿起的一块, 破坏了她脸部的对称美。**sym·met·ric** /sɪ'metrɪk; sɪ'mɛtrɪk/, **sym·met·ri·cal** /-kl; -kl̩/ *adjj* having (usu two) exactly similar parts on either side of a dividing line. 有对称美的; 对称的; 匀称的; 调和的; (指图案)对称的。**sym·met·ri·cally** /-klɪ; -klɪ/ *adv*

sym·path·etic /ˌsɪmpə'θetɪk; ˌsɪmpə'θɛtɪk/ *adj* having or showing sympathy; caused by sympathy: 有同情心的; 表示同情的; 由同情心引起的; 同感的: ~ *looks/words*; 显示同情的表情(话); *a* ~ *face/heart*; 显示同情的面孔(心); *a* ~ *audience*; 起共鸣的观众(听众); *be/feel* ~ *to/towards sb.* 对某人表同情。~ *strike n* strike¹(1) by workers purely to show support for other workers who are on strike. 同情罢工(为表示支持其他罢工之工人所作的罢工)。**sym·path·eti·cally** /-klɪ; -klɪ/ *adv*

sym·path·ize /'sɪmpəθaɪz; 'sɪmpəˌθaɪz/ *vi* [VP2A, 3A] ~ **(with)**, feel or express sympathy (with): 同情; 同感: ~ *with sb in his afflictions.* 同情某人的困苦。*Tom's parents do not* ~ *with his ambition to become an actor,* do not give him their approval and encouragement. 汤姆的双亲不赞同他当演员的志愿。**sym·path·izer** *n* person who ~s, eg one who supports a cause or political party. 同情者; 赞同者(如支持某种主义或政党者)。

sym·pathy /'sɪmpəθɪ; 'sɪmpəθɪ/ *n* (*pl* **-thies**) **1** [U] (capacity for) sharing the feelings of others, feeling pity and tenderness: 同情; 怜悯; 同感; 赞同; 同情心: *send sb a letter of* ~; 寄给某人一封慰问信; *feel* ~ *for sb;* 对某人表同情; *have no* ~ *with sb's foolish opinions.* 不赞同某人愚蠢的意见。*I have some* ~ *with their views,* share them to some extent. 我对于他们的意见略有同感。*in* ~ *with,* agreeing with, approving of: 同意; 赞同: *We are all in* ~ *with your proposals.* 我们全都赞同你的提议。*Will the bus workers strike in* ~ *with* (= to show their ~ for) *the railway workers?* 公共汽车工人会同情铁路工人而罢工吗? **2** (*pl* in a few usages): (若干用法中用复数): *a man of wide sympathies,* with a great capacity for fellow-feeling. 极富同情心的人。*You have my sympathies,* my feelings of ~. 我非常同情你。*My sympathies are with the miners in this dispute,* I'm on their side. 在这项争议中, 我同情矿工的立场。

sym·phony /'sɪmfənɪ; 'sɪmfənɪ/ *n* [C] (*pl* **-nies**) (long and large-scale) musical composition in (usu) three or four parts (called *movements*) for (usu a large) orchestra. 交响乐; 交响曲(通常有三或四个乐章, 由管弦乐队演奏)。**sym·phonic** /sɪm'fɒnɪk; sɪm'fɑnɪk/ *adj* of, having the character of, a ~. 交响乐的; 有交响乐特点的。

sym·po·sium /sɪm'pəʊzɪəm; sɪm'pozɪəm/ *n* (*pl* ~**s** or 或 **-sia** /-zɪə; -zɪə/) collection of essays, etc (eg forming a book) by several persons on a problem or subject; conference for discussion of a subject. (对某一问题的)诸家论丛; 专题论文集; (为某一问题所召开的)专题研讨会。

symp·tom /'sɪmptəm; 'sɪmptəm/ *n* **1** change in the body's condition that indicates illness: 症候; 症状: *A persistent cough may be a* ~ *of tuberculosis.* 持续的咳嗽可能是肺结核的症候。**2** sign of the existence of sth: (事物存在的)表征; 征兆; 征候: *The Government must not ignore these* ~*s* of discontent among their own supporters. 政府切不可忽视其支持者间所表现出的这些不满征候。**symp·to·matic** /ˌsɪmptə'mætɪk; ˌsɪmptə'mætɪk/ *adj* serving as a ~: 症状的; 征兆的: 表征的: *A headache may be* ~*atic of brain fever.* 头痛可能是脑膜炎的症状。**symp·to·mati·cally** /-klɪ; -klɪ/ *adv*

syna·gogue /'sɪnəgɒg; 'sɪnəˌgɔg/ *n* [C] (building used for an) assembly of Jews for religious teaching and worship. 犹太教教堂; 犹太教徒的聚会。

inside a synagogue

syn·chro·flash /ˌsɪŋkrəʊ'flæʃ; 'sɪŋkrəˌflæʃ/ *n* (usu attrib) device for simultaneous flashlight and opening of the shutter of a camera: (通常用作定语)闪光灯与照相机快门同时起作用的同步装置: ~ *photography/attachments for a camera.* 快门和闪光同步照相术(照相机上的快门和闪光同步装备)。

syn·chro·mesh /'sɪŋkrəʊmeʃ; 'sɪŋkrəˌmɛʃ/ *n* system of gear-changing (esp in motor-vehicles) so that the parts revolve at the same speed and so change smoothly. 同步齿轮系(尤指汽车中的齿轮变速装置, 可使变速平稳顺利)。

syn·chron·ize /'sɪŋkrənaɪz; 'sɪŋkrəˌnaɪz/ *vt, vi* [VP6A, 2A] (cause to) happen at the same time, agree in time, speeds, etc: (使)同时发生; 时间一致; 同速进行: ~ *the sound-track of a film with the movements seen;* 使电影的音带配合动作; ~ *all the clocks in a building.* 把一座建筑物内所有时钟校准。**syn·chron·iz·ation** /ˌsɪŋkrənaɪ'zeɪʃn US: -nɪ'z-; ˌsɪŋkrənɪ'zeʃən/ *n*

syn·chro·tron /'sɪŋkrəʊtrɒn; 'sɪŋkrə,trɑn/ *n* apparatus for accelerating electrons. 同步加速器(使电子加速的器械)。

syn·co·pate / 'sɪŋkəpeɪt; 'sɪŋkə,pet / *vt* [VP6A] (music) change the rhythm of; displace the normal beats or accents of, eg as in some jazz. (音乐)改变…的節律; 不守或改置…的正常节奏或重拍子; 切分(如某些爵士乐中)。 **syn·co·pa·tion** /ˌsɪŋkə'peɪʃn; ˌsɪŋkə'peʃən/ *n*

syn·cope /'sɪŋkəpɪ; 'sɪŋkəpɪ/ *n* (med term for) fainting; brief loss of consciousness from fall of blood-pressure. (医学名称)晕厥; 因血压降低而失去知觉。

syn·dic /'sɪndɪk; 'sɪndɪk/ *n* member of a committee (for business purposes) of a university or other organization. (大学或其他机构的)委员会的委员。

syn·di·cal·ism /'sɪndɪkəlɪzəm; 'sɪndɪkḷ,ɪzəm/ *n* [U] theory that political power should be in the hands of trade unions and that these unions should own and manage the industries in which their members work. 工团主义(认为政权应操在工会手中,而且工会应拥有并管理其会员所从事的工业)。 **syn·di·cal·ist** /-ɪst; -ɪst/ *n* supporter of ~. 工团主义者。

syn·di·cate /'sɪndɪkɪt; 'sɪndɪkɪt/ *n* **1** business association that supplies articles, cartoons, etc to periodicals. 资料供应社(以稿件、文章、漫画等供给报章杂志的机构); 报业辛迪加。 **2** combination of commercial firms associated to forward a common interest. 企业的联合组织; 辛迪加。 □ *vt* /'sɪndɪkeɪt; 'sɪndɪ,ket/ [VP6A] publish (articles, strip-cartoons, etc) in numerous periodicals through a ~ (1). 经由报业辛迪加加在多个刊物发表(文章、连环漫画等)。 **syn·di·ca·tion** /ˌsɪndɪ'keɪʃn; ˌsɪndɪ'keʃən/ *n*

syn·drome /'sɪndrəʊm; 'sɪndrom/ *n* (med) number of symptoms which collectively indicate an often abnormal condition of the body or mind; (fig) particular combination of a person's actions, opinions, etc that can be expected to occur together. (医)症候簇; 症状群; 综合病症; 复征; (喻)(个人)经常同时出现的行动, 言论等。

synod /'sɪnɒd; 'sɪnəd/ *n* [C] meeting of church officers to discuss and decide questions of policy, government, teaching, etc. (讨论和决定政策、管理、教义等问题的)宗教会议。

syn·onym /'sɪnənɪm; 'sɪnə,nɪm/ *n* word with the same meaning as another in the same language but often with different implications and associations. 同义词, **syn·ony·mous** /sɪ'nɒnɪməs; sɪ'nɑnəməs/ *adj*

syn·op·sis /sɪ'nɒpsɪs; sɪ'nɑpsɪs/ *n* (*pl* -opses /-siːz; -siz/) summary or outline (of a book, play, etc). (书、剧本等的)大纲; 要略。 **syn·op·tic** /sɪ'nɒptɪk; sɪ'nɑptɪk/ *adj* giving a ~: 提示大纲的; 要略的: the synoptic Gospels, those of Matthew, Mark and Luke (similar in contents, order, etc). 对观福音书(指马太、马可及路加三福音书)。 **syn·op·ti·cal·ly** /-klɪ; -klɪ/ *adv*

syn·tax /'sɪntæks; 'sɪntæks/ *n* [U] (gram) (rules for) sentence-building. (语法)造句; 造句法。 **syn·tac·tic** /sɪn'tæktɪk; sɪn'tæktɪk/ *adj* of ~. 造句(法)的。 **syn·tac·ti·cal·ly** /-klɪ; -klɪ/ *adv*

syn·thesis /'sɪnθɪsɪs; 'sɪnθəsɪs/ *n* (*pl* -theses /-siːz; -,siz/) [C, U] combination of separate parts, elements, substances, etc into a whole or into a system; that which results from this process: 综合; 合成; 由合成法制成之物: produce rubber from petroleum by ~. 借合成法从石油制造橡皮。 **syn·thesize** /'sɪnθəsaɪz; 'sɪnθə,saɪz/ *vt* [VP6A] produce a whole by this process: 由合成法制造: synthesize diamonds/rubber. 用合成法制钻石(橡

皮)。 **syn·thetic** /sɪn'θetɪk; sɪn'θetɪk/ *adj* **1** produced by ~: 借合成法产生的; 人工制造的: synthetic rubber, artificially made. 人造橡皮。 **2** pertaining to ~: 综合的; 综合性的: synthetic chemistry. 合成化学。 **3** (of a language) containing, tending to form, many compound words: (指语言)含有许多复合词的; 有形成许多复合词之趋势的; 综合性的: German is a synthetic language. 德语是一种复合式的语言。 **syn·theti·cally** /-klɪ; -klɪ/ *adv*. ⇨ **analysis**.

syph·ilis /'sɪfɪlɪs; 'sɪflɪs/ *n* [U] infectious venereal disease. 梅毒(一种传染的性病)。 **syphi·litic** /ˌsɪfɪ'lɪtɪk; ˌsɪfə'lɪtɪk/ *adj* pertaining to, suffering from, ~. 梅毒的; 患梅毒的。 □ *n* person affected with ~. 梅毒患者。

syphon *n* = **siphon**.

syr·inga /sɪ'rɪŋgə; sə'rɪŋgə/ *n* shrub with strong-scented white flowers (popularly called the mock-orange); botanical name of the lilac genus. 山梅花; 紫丁香花(开白花,香味浓郁,一般通称为 mock-orange); 紫丁香属。

syr·inge /sɪ'rɪndʒ; 'sɪrɪndʒ/ *n* kinds of device for drawing in liquid by suction and forcing it out again in a fine stream, used for washing out wounds, injecting liquids into the body, in spraying plants, etc: 注射器; 注水器; 洗涤器; 灌肠器; 喷水器: a hypodermic ~; 皮下注射器; a garden ~. 浇花木用的喷水器。 □ *vt* [VP 6A, 15B] clean, inject liquid into, with a ~; apply (liquid) with a ~. 灌洗; 注射。

needle

a hypodermic syringe

syrup /'sɪrəp; 'sɪrəp/ *n* [U] thick sweet liquid made from sugar-cane juice or by boiling sugar with water: 糖浆: pineapple tinned in ~; 浸于糖浆的罐装凤梨; 'cough ~, ~ with medicine in it to relieve a cough; 治咳糖浆(掺和咳嗽药水制成者); fruit ~, ~ flavoured with fruit juices. 果汁糖浆(以果汁增味者)。 **~y** *adj* of or like ~; (fig, eg of music) too sweet. 糖浆的; 似糖浆的; (喻,指音乐等)太甜腻的。

sys·tem /'sɪstəm; 'sɪstəm/ *n* **1** group of things or parts working together in a regular relation: 系统: the 'nervous ~; 神经系统; the di'gestive ~; 消化系统; a 'railway ~. 铁路系统。 The poison has passed into his ~, his body as a whole. 毒药已进入他的全身。 Too much alcohol is bad for the ~. 喝酒太多有害身体。 **2** ordered set of ideas, theories, principles, etc: (思想、理论、原则等的)体系; 体制; 制度; 方式; 方法: a ~ of philosophy; 哲学体系; a ~ of government; 政府体制; 政体; a good ~ of teaching languages; 教授语言的良好方法; '~-building /'~-built houses, built of prefabricated sections, put together on the site. 系统建筑(系统建筑的房屋); 预筑(预筑房屋)。 **3** [U] orderliness: 秩序; 规律: You mustn't expect good results if you work without ~. 如果你工作不讲究先后秩序,你休想有好的结果。 **~·atic** /ˌsɪstə'mætɪk; ˌsɪstə'mætɪk/ *adj* methodical; based on a ~: 有方法的; 有系统的; 有体系的; 基于制度、系统等的; 按照这式的: a ~atic attempt. 有计划的行为。 **~·ati·cally** /-klɪ; -klɪ/ *adv* **~·atize** /'sɪstəmətaɪz; 'sɪstəmə,taɪz/ *vt* [VP6A] arrange according to a ~; make into a ~. 系统化; 体系化; 做成制度。 **~·ati·za·tion** /ˌsɪstəmətaɪ'zeɪʃn US: -tɪ'z-; ˌsɪstəmtɪ'zeʃən/ *n*

T t

T,t /tiː; ti/ (*pl* **T's t's** /tiːz; tiz/) the twentieth letter of the English alphabet; used before names of various objects shaped like the letter T: 英文字母的第二十个字母: T 形(物); 丁字形(物): *a 'T-bandage*; 丁字形绷带; *a 'T-shirt*, short-sleeved, close-fitting, collarless and buttonless usu cotton shirt worn informally; 短袖汗衫; 圆领衫; 运动衫(短袖,紧身,无领,无扣,通常为棉质,非正式场合着用); *a 'T-square*, ⇨ square²(7). *to a T*, ⇨ tee.

ta /taː/; taː/ *int* (colloq) thank you. (口)谢谢你.

tab /tæb/; tæb/ *n* **1** small piece or strip of cloth, etc fixed to a garment, etc as a badge or distinguishing mark or (as a loop) for hanging up a coat, etc; binding at the end of a shoelace, etc. (钉于衣服等上用作记号、标志或挂环的)垂片; 飘带; 垂圈; 悬垂牌; 鞋带等的护头. **2** (colloq) account; check. (口)帐目; 直帐. *keep a tab / tabs on sth / sb*, keep an account of, keep under observation: 记录…的帐目; 看顾; 监视: *keep a tab on the expenses*. 记录各笔费用的帐目.

tab·ard /'tæbəd; 'tæbəd/ *n* (hist) short, sleeveless outer garment (worn eg by a knight over his armour, or by a herald). (史)(武士穿在铠甲外面的)无袖短外套; 传令官制服.

tabby /'tæbɪ; 'tæbɪ/ *n* (*pl* **-bies**) '~(-cat), cat with grey or brown stripes. 虎斑猫.

tab·er·na·cle /'tæbənækl; 'tæbə͵nækl/ *n* **1** (in the Bible) **the T~**, the portable structure used by the Israelites as a sanctuary during their wanderings before they settled in Palestine. (经)圣幕(以色列人定居巴勒斯坦以前所使用的移动式神殿). **2** (eccles) receptacle for a pyx. (教会)圣体容器. **3** place of worship, eg a Baptist Church or Mormon temple. 教堂; 礼拜堂; 会堂(如浸信会或摩门教者).

table /'teɪbl; 'tebl/ *n* **1** piece of furniture consisting of a flat top with (usu four) supports (called legs): 桌; 台; 几: *a 'dining-~*; 餐桌; *a 'kitchen-~*; 厨房用桌; *a 'billiard-~*. 撞球台. *at ~*, having a meal: 用餐(用饭): *They were at ~ when we called*. 我们往访时,他们正在吃饭. '~**-cloth** *n* one (to be) spread on a ~. 桌布; 台布. '~**-knife** *n* steel knife for use at ~. 餐刀. '~**-lifting** / **-rapping** / **-turning** *nn* lifting / rapping, etc of a ~, apparently without physical exertion, occurring while people sit at a ~ during a spiritualistic seance. (行降神术时)桌子的灵动(桌子升起、敲击、转动等,似未加外力者). '~**-linen** *n* [U] ~**-cloths**, napkins, etc. 桌布、餐巾等. '~**-mat** *n* one to be placed under a hot dish on a ~. 碗盘垫. '~**-spoon** *n* large spoon for serving food at ~ from a dish, etc. 餐匙; 大调羹. '~**-spoon·ful** *n* as much as a ~spoon holds. 一餐匙(之量). '~**-talk** *n* conversation during a meal. 餐桌; 进餐时的谈话. '~ **tennis** *n* game (sometimes called *ping-pong*) played with bats and balls, similar to tennis, on a ~. 桌球; 乒乓球. '~**-ware** *n* [U] dishes, silver, cutlery, etc used for meals. 餐具. **2** (*sing* only) people seated at a ~: (仅用单数)同席的人; 坐在一桌的人: *a ~ of card-players*; 一桌玩牌的人; *King Arthur and his Round T~*, his knights; 亚瑟王及其圆桌武士; *jokes that amused the whole ~*. 使举座欢悦的笑话. **3** (*sing* only) food provided at ~: (仅用单数)餐食; 伙食: *He keeps a good ~*, provides good meals. 他讲究餐食. **4** '~(-**land**), plateau; extensive area of high, level land. 高原; 台地. **5** list, orderly arrangement, of facts, information, etc (usu in columns): 表; 一览表; 目录: *a ~ of contents*, summary of what a book contains; 目次; 目录; *multiplication ~s*; 乘法表; 九九表; *a railway 'time-~*. 火车时刻表. **6** (phrases) (口语) *lay sth on*

the ~, (in Parliament) postpone (a measure, report, etc) indefinitely. (国会中)搁置一项法案、报告等. *turn the ~s on sb*, gain a position of superiority after having been defeated or in a position of inferiority. 从劣势转为优势; 扭转形势. **7** [C] (in the Bible) flat slab of stone, wood, etc; tablet(1); what is written or inscribed on such a ~: (圣经)石板; 木板; 平板; 刻写于此种平板上的文字: *the ~s of the law*, the ten commandments given to Moses by God. 摩西十诫. □ *vt* [VP6A] **1** submit for discussion: 提出讨论: ~ *a motion / Bill / amendment*. 提出动议(议案; 修正案). ~ **6** above. 参看上列第 6 义. **2** (esp US) postpone (a proposal, etc) indefinitely. (尤美)搁置(提议等). **3** put in the form of a ~(5). 列表.

tab·leau /'tæbləʊ; 'tæblo/ *n* (*pl* ~**x** /-ləʊz; -loz/) (often 常作 ~ **vivant** /'viːvɑːn US: viːˈvɑːn; vi'vɑn/) representation by living persons of a picture or scene, without words or action, esp on a stage or platform; dramatic situation suddenly brought about. 活人造景(以活人扮演的静态画面,尤指在舞台或讲台上者); (突然发生的)戏剧性场面.

table d'hôte /͵tɑːblˈdəʊt; ͵tɑːblˈdot/ *adj*, *adv* (F) (of a restaurant meal) at an inclusive fixed price: (法)(指餐馆饮食)客饭式的; 和英方式: *a ~ lunch*. 一顿客饭式的午餐. ⇨ **à la carte**.

tab·let /'tæblɪt; 'tæblɪt/ *n* **1** flat surface with words cut or written on it, eg one fixed to a wall in memory of sth or sb. 碑; 匾额(如固定于墙壁以纪念某事或某人者). **2** number of sheets of writing-paper fastened together along one edge. 拍纸簿. **3** lump of hard soap; small flattened pellet of compressed medicine: 硬肥皂块; 药片; 锭剂: *two ~s of aspirin*; 两片阿斯匹林; flat, hard sweet: 硬糖片: *throat ~s*, to be sucked to relieve a cough, sore throat, etc. (治喉咙、喉痛等的)喉片. **4** (hist) flat sheet of wood, stone, etc for cutting words on (eg as used in ancient Rome). (史)书板(供刻字的木板,石板等,如古罗马所使用者).

tab·loid /'tæblɔɪd; 'tæblɔɪd/ *n* small size newspaper with many pictures, strip cartoons, etc and with its news presented in simplified form: 小(型)报(有大量图片、连环图画等,并以简明扼要的方式报导新闻者): (attrib) (用作定语) ~ *journalism*. 小型报纸; 小报业.

ta·boo /təˈbuː; US: tæˈbuː; təˈbu/ *n* **1** [C, U] (among some peoples) something which religion or custom regards as forbidden, not to be touched, spoken of, etc: (某些民族的)禁忌; 忌讳: *That tree is under (a) ~*. 那棵树禁止接近(不可亵渎等). **2** [C] general 'agreement not to discuss sth, do sth. 避讳; 忌讳. □ *adj* under ~: 禁忌的; 避讳的: *Questions and problems that were once ~ are now discussed openly*. 过去曾经列为禁忌的许多问题现在可以公开讨论了. *Unkind gossip ought to be ~*. 不厚道的闲话应该避讳. '~ **words**, those which convention avoids or prohibits (eg most of those marked △ in this dictionary). 忌讳语(为社会习俗所避免或禁止者,如本词典标有 △ 者大多属此类语). □ *vt* [VP6A] forbid, esp on moral or religious grounds. 禁止; 禁用(尤指基于道德或宗教立场).

ta·bor /'teɪbə(r); 'tebə/ *n* small drum, esp one used to accompany a pipe or fife. 小鼓(尤指用以伴奏无键短笛者).

tabu·lar /'tæbjʊlə(r); 'tæbjəlɚ/ *adj* arranged or displayed in tables(5): 列成表的: *a report in ~ form*. 列表式报告.

tabu·late /'tæbjʊleɪt; 'tæbjə͵let/ *vt* [VP6A] arrange (facts, figures, etc) in tables(5), in lists or columns. 将(事实、数字等)列成表. **tabu·la·tor** /-tə(r); -tɚ/ *n*

machine, device, that ~s. 制电机(仪). **tabu·la·tion** /ˌtæbjuˈleɪʃn; ˌtæbjʊˈleʃən/ *n*

tacho·graph /ˈtækəɡrɑːf; ˈtækəˌɡræf/ *n* device that records the speed and duration of a journey in a motor-vehicle. (汽车之)速度计.

tacit /ˈtæsɪt; ˈtæsɪt/ *adj* unspoken; understood without being put into words: 沉默的,心照不宣的: ~ *consent* / *agreement*. 默许(默契). ~·**ly** *adv*

taci·turn /ˈtæsɪtɜːn; ˈtæsəˌtɜn/ *adj* (in the habit of) saying very little. 沉默寡言的. ~·**ly** *adv* **taci·tur·nity** /ˌtæsɪˈtɜːnɪtɪ; ˌtæsəˈtɜnɪtɪ/ *n* [U].

tack /tæk; tæk/ *n* **1** small, flat-headed nail (eg as used for securing some kinds of carpet or linoleum to the floor): 大头钉;平头钉 (如用于将地毯或油布等钉于地板上者): 'tin-~, of iron coated with tin; 镀锡平头钉; 'thumb-~ (US) (美) = drawing-pin. **2** long, loose stitch used in fastening pieces of cloth together loosely or temporarily. 假缝;粗缝. **3** sailing-ship's direction as fixed by the direction of the wind and the position of the sails: (依风向及帆之位置而定)航行方向: *on the port/starboard* ~, with the wind on the port/starboard side. 风在船的左(右)方. **on the right/wrong** ~, (fig) following a wise/unwise course of action. (喻)方针正确(错误). **4** [U] (**hard**) ~, hard ship's biscuits. 硬饼干. □ *vt, vi* **1** [VP6A, 15A, B] fasten with ~s(1): 以平头钉钉固定: ~ *down the carpet.* 把地毯钉起来. **2** [VP6A, 15A, B] fasten with ~s(2): 假缝;粗缝: ~ *a ribbon on to a hat;* 在帽子上加缎一条饰带; ~ *down a fold;* 粗缝衣褶; (fig) (喻) ~ *an appeal for money on to a speech,* add one. 在说话中加添要钱的请求. **3** [VP2A, C] sail in a zigzag course; make a ~ or ~s(3). 作Z字形航行; 蛇航; 迎风; 抢风转向; ~*ing about;* 抢风转向; ~ *to port.* 左舷抢风.

tackle /ˈtækl; ˈtækl/ *n* **1** [C, U] set of ropes and pulleys for working a ship's sails, or for lifting weights, etc. (操纵船帆, 或吊起重物等用的)滑车; 滑车辘轳; 复滑车. ⇨ the illus at **pulley**. 参看 pulley 之插图. **2** [U] equipment, apparatus, for doing sth: 用具; 器械: 'fishing ~, a rod, line, hooks, etc. 钓(鱼)具. **3** [C] act of seizing and bringing down an opponent with the ball (in Rugby and American-style football). (橄榄球及美式足球中的)擒抱(即抱住带球跑的对方球员). □ *vt, vi* **1** [VP6A, 14] deal with, attack (a problem, a piece of work): 处理; 解决; 应付(问题,工作): *I don't know how to* ~ *this problem,* how to start on it. 我不知道如何着手处理此一问题. ~ *sb about/over sth,* speak to sb frankly (about a matter). 坦白地向某人谈(某事). **2** [VP6A, 2A] seize, lay hold of, sb, eg a thief, a player who, in Rugby, has the ball: 捉住(贼等); 擒抱 (橄榄球中带球跑的对方球员): *He* ~s *fearlessly.* 他无所畏惧地紧抱住对方.

tacky /ˈtækɪ; ˈtækɪ/ *adj* sticky; not yet dry: 粘的; 未干的: *The paint/varnish is still* ~. 油漆(亮光漆)还没有干了. **2** (US) (美) = **tatty.**

tact /tækt; tækt/ *n* [U] (use of) skill and understanding shown by sb who handles people and situations successfully and without causing offence: (运用)机智; 老练; 圆通; 圆滑: *great* ~ *in dealing with people.* 在与人交往上显得圆滑(极为圆通). ~·**ful** /-fl; -fəl/ *adj* having or showing ~. 机智的; 老练的; 圆通的; 圆滑的. ~·**fully** /-fəlɪ; -fəlɪ/ *adv* ~·**less** *adj* lacking ~. 缺乏机智的; 不圆滑的. ~·**less·ly** *adv* ~·**less·ness** *n*

tac·tic /ˈtæktɪk; ˈtæktɪk/ *n* **1** expedient; means of achieving an object. 权谋; 权变; 达成目标的方法. **2** (*pl* often with *sing v*) art of placing or moving fighting forces for or during battle. (复数,常与单数动词连用)战术; 兵法. ⇨ **strategy.** (fig) plan(s) or method(s) for carrying out a policy: (喻)实现政策的计划或方法; 策略: *win by surprise* ~s; 出奇制胜; *These* ~s *are unlikely to help you.* 这些方法对你未必有帮助. **tac·ti·cal** /-kl; -kl/ *adj* of ~s: 战术的; 兵法的; 策略的. ~*al*

exercises; 战术演习; *a* ~*al error.* 战术上的错误. ⇨ **strategic.** **tac·ti·cally** /-klɪ; -klɪ/ *adv* **tac·ti·cian** /tækˈtɪʃn; tækˈtɪʃən/ *n* expert in ~s. 战术家; 兵法家.

tac·tile /ˈtæktaɪl US: -təl; ˈtæktl/ *adj* of, experienced by, the sense of touch: 触觉的; 触知的; 可感触到的: *a* ~ *organ/reflex.* 触觉器官(反射).

tad·pole /ˈtædpəʊl; ˈtædˌpol/ *n* form of a frog or toad from the time it leaves the egg to the time when it takes its adult form. 蝌蚪. ⇨ the illus at **amphibian.** 参看 amphibian 之插图.

taf·feta /ˈtæfɪtə; ˈtæfɪtə/ *n* [U] thin, shiny, rather stiff silk material: similar material of linen, rayon, etc. 一种光亮而质硬的薄绸; 波纹绸; 与波纹绸相似的亚麻布,人造丝等.

taff·rail /ˈtæfreɪl; ˈtæfˌrel/ *n* rail round a ship's stern. 船尾栏杆.

Taffy /ˈtæfɪ; ˈtæfɪ/ *n* (colloq) Welshman. (口)威尔士人.

taffy /ˈtæfɪ; ˈtæfɪ/ *n* **1** (US) toffee. (美)太妃糖. **2** insincere flattery. 谄媚.

tag /tæɡ; tæɡ/ *n* **1** metal or plastic point at the end of a shoe-lace, string, etc. 鞋带、绳子等末端的金属或塑胶头. **2** label (eg for showing prices, addresses) fastened to or stuck into sth. 附签; 标签(如标示价格、地址者). **3** phrase or sentence often quoted: 常被引用的短语或句子: *Latin tags.* 常被引用的拉丁文句. **4** any loose or ragged end. 任何松散或不完整的末端. '**question tags,** (gram) phrases such as *isn't it? won't you? are there?* added to statements. (语法)附加问句(附加于叙述句后的短问句). **5** [U] game in which one child chases and tries to touch another. 小孩子玩的捉人游戏. □ *vt, vi* (-**gg-**) **1** [VP6A] fasten a tag(2) to. 附以签条; 加标签于. **2** [VP14] *tag sth on (to),* fasten, attach. 附加某物于…上; 系某物于…上. **3** [VP2C] *tag along/behind/after,* follow closely: 尾随; 紧随: *children tagging after their mother.* 紧跟在母亲后面的孩子们. *Tag along with us* (= Come with us) if you like. 你如果喜欢,就跟着我们走吧. **4** [VP15A,B] join: 连接; 结合: *tag old articles together to make a book.* 把旧文章凑成一本书.

tail /teɪl; tel/ *n* **1** movable part (from the end of the backbone) at the end of the body of a bird, animal, fish or reptile: (鸟、兽、鱼或爬虫的)尾; 尾巴: *Dogs wag their* ~s *when they are pleased.* 狗在高兴时会摆动尾巴. *turn* ~, run away. 逃走. ~*s up,* (of persons) in good spirits. (指人)心情好; 兴致勃勃. **2** ⇨ the illus at **aircraft.** 参看 aircraft 之插图. sth like a ~ in position: 尾状物; 似尾之部; 尾部: *the* ~ *of a kite/comet/air-craft/cart/procession.* 纸鸢(彗星,飞机,马车,行列)的尾部; (attrib) (用作定语) *a* ~ *(= following) wind.* 顺风; 后面吹来的风. '~-**board** *n* board, usu on hinges, forming the back part of a cart or truck. (马车或汽车的)尾板(通常用铰链相连接). ~-'**coat,** ~ *s n,* man's evening coat, long, divided and tapered at the back. 燕尾服. ~-'**end** *n* (usu 通常作 *the* ~**-end (of)**) final part: 末端; 尾端; 结尾: *at the* ~**-end of** *the procession.* 在行列的末尾. '~-**gate** *n* door or flap at the rear of a motor-vehicle which can be opened for loading and unloading. (汽车的)尾门(可供上下或装卸用者). '~-**light** *n* light at the end of a train, tram or other vehicle. 尾灯(装于火车、电车等之尾部者). '~-**piece** *n* (a) (in a book, etc) decoration printed in the blank space at the end of a chapter, etc. (印在书等章节后的空白处的)补白图案. (b) sth added to the end of sth. 附加之物. '~-**spin** *n* spiral dive of an aircraft in which the ~ makes wider circles than the front. (飞机的)尾旋下降(尾部较头部旋转的圆形大). *the* ~ *of the eye,* the outer corner: *watching me from the* ~ *of his eye.* 他从眼角斜视我. **3** ~*s,* side of a coin opposite to that in which there is the head of sb. 硬币的背面或反面 (与人头相对的一面). ⇨ **head¹(3). 4** ~*s,* (colloq) ~-coat: (口)燕尾服: *Am I to wear a dinner-jacket or* ~*s?*

我该穿常礼服还是燕尾服? **5** (colloq) sb employed to follow and watch sb, eg a suspected criminal: (口)尾随的侦探: *put a ~ on sb.* 派侦探尾随某人。 □ *vt, vi* **1** [VP3A] *~ after sb,* follow close behind. 尾随某人。 **2** [VP6A] *~ a person,* follow him closely, eg because he is suspected to be a criminal. 跟踪某人(例如因他有罪嫌)。 **3** [VP2C] *~ off* / *away,* **(a)** become smaller in number, size, etc. 变小; 变少。 **(b)** (of remarks, etc) end in a hesitating or inconclusive way. (指谈话等)迟疑或不得要领地结束。 **(c)** fall behind or away in a scattered line. 落伍; 零零落落地掉在后面。 **-tailed** /-teɪld; -teld/ *adj* (in compounds) (用于复合词) *long-* ~*ed, short-* ~*ed,* having a long / short ~. 长尾的; 短尾的。 **~·less** *adj* having no ~: *a* ~*less cat* 一只无尾猫。

tailor /'teɪlə(r); 'telɚ/ *n* maker of (esp outer) garments: 成衣匠; 裁缝(尤指缝制外衣者): *go to the* ~*'s to be measured for a suit / an overcoat.* 去裁缝店量身做一套衣服(一件大衣)。 ,~*'·made adj* made by a ~, with special attention to exact fit; (fig) appropriate, well-suited: 定制的; 定做的; 合身的; (喻)适当的; 合适的: *He seems* ~*-made for the job.* 他好象很适合这项工作。 □ *vt* **1** [VP6A] cut out and sew: 裁制; 缝制: *a well-* ~*ed suit.* 裁制得好的一套衣服。 **2** [VP15A] adapt: 适应; 适合: ~*ed for a special purpose* / *to a particular audience.* 适合一项特殊目的(特定的听众)。

taint /teɪnt; tent/ *n* [C, U] trace of some bad quality, decay or infection: 品质恶劣、腐败或污染的迹象; 污点; 耻辱: *There was a* ~ *of insanity in the family.* 这个家族的(成员)有癫狂的迹象。 *Is the meat free from* ~? 这肉是好的(新鲜的)吗? □ *vt, vi* [VP6A, 2A] make or become infected: 使感染; 受污染; 使腐败; 变坏: ~*ed meat.* 腐肉。 ~*·less adj* without ~; pure. 未污染的; 未腐败的; 纯洁的; 无污的。

take¹ /teɪk; tek/ *vt, vi* (*pt* **took** /tuk; tuk/, *pp* **taken** /'teɪkən; 'tekən/) (For uses with a large number of *nn,* ⇨ **15** below. For special uses with *adverbial particles* and *preps* ⇨ **16** below.) (与诸多名词的连用法,参看下列第15义。与副词性小品词及介词连用的特殊用法,参看下列第16义。) **1** [VP6A, 15A] get or lay hold of with the hand(s) or any other part of the body, eg the arms, teeth or with an instrument (Cf *let go of* or *release,* as opposite in meaning): 握; 攫; 执; 抱(参较反义词 let go of 或 release): ~ *sb's hand;* 握住某人的手; ~ *sth on one's back;* 背负某物; ~ *a man by the throat;* 扼住某人的咽喉; ~ *sb in one's arms,* put one's arms round him, embrace him; 拥抱某人; ~ *sth up* (= pick it up) *with one's fingers* / *with a pair of tongs;* 用手指(钳子)拾起或夹起某物; ~ *a person's arm,* put, rest, one's hand on his arm, eg to support him or be supported by him. 挽住某人的臂(例如扶着他,或被他扶着)。 ~ *hold of sth,* grasp or seize it. 抓住或捉住某物。 **2** [VP6A, 15A, 2A] capture; catch (sb or sth) by surprise or pursuit; win (in a contest, etc): 捕捉; 袭取; 占领; 获得; (竞赛等中)获胜: ~ *a town* / *a fortress,* in war; 夺取一城市(堡垒); ~ *500 prisoners;* 俘获五百名俘虏; *be* ~*n prisoner* / *captive,* be caught and be made a prisoner. 被俘。 *The rabbit was* ~*n in a trap.* 那兔子被捕兔机捉住了。 *the major's bull took* (= was awarded) *the first prize at the agricultural show.* 少校的公牛在农业展览会上获得首奖。 *How many tricks did you* ~, ie win, eg at a card game such as whist or bridge? 你们得了多少墩牌(如在惠斯特或桥牌戏中)? *Be careful not to* ~ *cold,* become ill with a cold (catch cold is more usu). 小心不要着凉(catch cold 较常用)。 *sb's fancy,* please, delight: 使高兴; 使愉快: *The new dance has really taken the public's fancy.* 这种新的舞蹈深为大家所喜爱。 ~ *sb at a disadvantage,* be approached, attacked, etc when unready, in an unfavourable situation, etc. 乘人不备; 乘人之危。 *be* ~*n ill,* (passive only) become ill, catch an illness. (只用被动语态)患病; 罹疾。 ~ *sb unawares* / *by surprise,*

approach or discover sb doing sth when he is unaware of one's presence, that one sees him, etc. 在某人不知有人在场,不知有人看到等时接近某人或发现某人做某事; 冷不防出现; 突然接近; 撞见某人做某事。 **3** [VP6A] use; use or borrow without permission; steal; avail oneself of: 使用; 不经同意擅自利用或借用; 偷窃; 盗取; 擅自利用: *Someone has* ~ *my hat,* ie by mistake. 有人把我的帽子拿走了(无意中拿错了)。 *Who has* ~ *my bicycle,* borrowed or stolen it? 谁把我的脚踏车拿走了(借用或偷去)? *He's whatever he can lay his hands on.* 他取用他能拿到手的东西。 **4** [VP6A, 15A, B, 12A, 13A, 19B] carry (sth), accompany (sb), away, from a place: 携带; 拿走某物; 伴随某人: ~ *letters to the post;* 把信付邮; ~ *the luggage upstairs;* 把行李搬上楼; ~ *a friend home in one's car;* 用汽车送朋友回家; ~ *the dog out for a walk;* 带狗出去散步; ~ *one's wife to the cinema;* 带太太去看电影; ~ *the children swimming* / *for a swim.* 带孩子们去游泳。 *Please* ~ *these things in* / *out* / *away* / *back* / *home, etc.* 请把这些东西拿进去(拿出去,拿开,拿回来,拿回家等)。 *Shall I* ~ *your message to her* / ~ *her your message?* 要我把你的信带给她吗? *T* ~ *her some flowers.* 带一些花给她。 *He took me a new way to the coast,* by a route that was new to me. 他带我走一条新路去海滨。 ,~*-home wages* / *pay,* (colloq) net sum after deduction of compulsory national insurance contribution, income tax, etc. (口)(扣除各项捐税后的)净薪; 实领工资。 **5** [VP6A, 15A] get; have; eat or drink; allow oneself: 得到; 享有; 吃; 喝; 享受: ~ *a holiday* / *a walk* / *a bath* / *a quick look round* / *a deep breath;* 休假(散步; 沐浴; 迅速向四周望一眼; 作深呼吸); ~ *a chair* / *a seat,* sit down; 坐下; 就座; ~ *medical* / *legal advice,* get the advice of a doctor / lawyer; 听取医生(律师)的意见; ~ *driving lessons;* 学习驾驶; ~ (= hire) *a taxi;* 雇计程车; ~ (= rent) *a cottage at the seaside for the holidays.* 在海边租一幢别墅度假; *Let's go into the garden and* ~ *the air,* have some fresh air. 咱们到园子里去透透气。 *Will you* ~ *tea or coffee?* 你要喝茶还是要喝咖啡? *I'll* ~ (= buy) *2 lb of your Kenya coffee.* 我要向你买两磅肯尼亚咖啡。 *Why don't you* ~ *a wife,* (old use) marry? (旧用法)你为什么不娶妻? *You should* ~ *a partner into the business* / ~ *your brother into the business.* 你应该找一个人合伙经营这生意(找你兄弟合伙经营)。 **6** [VP6A, 15A, 16A, B] accept; receive: 接受; 领受; 收到: *Will you* ~ *£1500 for the car,* sell it for this sum? 你愿以一千五百镑的价钱出售该车吗? *This small cafe* ~*s £500 a week,* This is the total of the receipts. 这家小饮食店每周做五百镑的生意。 ⇨ **takings** below. 参看下列之 takings. (From the C of E marriage service) (来自英国教会婚礼仪式) *Do you* ~ *this man to be your lawful wedded husband?* 你接受此人为合法婚姻的丈夫吗? *You must* ~ *us as you find us,* not expect exceptional treatment, consideration, etc (while you are with us). 你不可对我们另有期望(我们对你的态度或待遇,就是你所见到的这样)。 *He will* ~ *no nonsense,* will not allow any. 他不允许胡闹。 *I'm not taking any more of your insults,* I refuse to listen to them. 我不再听你这些无礼的话了。 ~ *one's chance,* **(a)** trust to one's luck; accept whatever may come or happen! 碰运气; 接受可能发生之事: *She'll have to* ~ *her chance with the other applicants for the job.* 她必须碰自己的运气与其他的求职者竞争那份工作。 **(b)** attempt sth though aware of the possibility of failing. 明知可能失败而从事某事。 ~ *a chance (on sth),* accept the possibility of not getting sth: 做做看; 冒险试做(某事); 接受失败的可能性: *I'm ready to* ~ *a chance on finding him at home,* he will call hoping to find him there. 我准备到他家去看看他,希望他在家。 ~ *it from me;* ~ *my word for it,* believe me when I say: 听我信我; 我保证; 我这话你可以相信: *T* ~ *it from me,* there'll be some big changes made in the coming year. 我保证未来这一年会发生若干重大的变化。 *be able to* ~ *it; can* ~ *it,* be able to endure suffering, punishment, attack, etc without

showing weakness, readiness to admit defeat, etc. 能忍
受痛苦、惩罚、攻击等; 挺得住; 挨得过; 受得了。**7** [VP6A]
subscribe to; receive and pay for regularly: 订阅; 订
购; 定: *Which newspapers do you ~?* 你订阅哪些报纸?
8 [VP6A, 15A, B] **~ (down),** make a record of: 记
录; 记下: *~ notes of a lecture;* 作听讲笔记; *~ sth
down in shorthand;* 用速记记下某事; *~ a letter,* from
dictation; (根据口述)写下一封信; *~ (down) a broadcast
on tape,* ie using a tape-recorder; 用录音机录下一段广
播; *~ a photograph.* 拍照片。 [VP2A] *He does not ~
well,* It is difficult to ~ good photographs of him. 他
不上相(不容易拍摄到他的好看的照片)。**9** [VP2B, 6B,
15A] need, require: 需要; 花费: *The work took four
hours.* 这项工作花了四小时。*These things ~ time.* 这些
事情需要花时间去做。*How long will this job ~ you/
How long will you ~ over this job?* 你做这事要花多久的
时间? *The wound took a long time to heal.* 这伤口过了很
久才痊愈。*~ one's time (over sth),* **(a)** not hurry;
use as much time as one needs: 不匆忙; 不急; 慢慢来; 用
时不限制: *Take your time over the job, and do it well.*
这工作慢慢做做, 把它做好。**(b)** (ironic) use more time
than is reasonable: (反语)浪费时间; 拖延; 磨洋工: *The
workmen are certainly taking their time over the job.* 工
人们显然在那里拖延工作的时间。*It ~s 'two to make a
quarrel,* (prov) suggesting that both parties to a
quarrel are at fault. (谚)一个巴掌拍不响, 两个人才吵
得起来(含示双方皆有错)。*~ a lot of doing,* need much
effort, skill, etc. 费事; 费力; 需要努力、技巧等。**10**
[VP14, 25] **~ sb/sth for ...; ~ sb/sth to be ...,**
suppose; conclude; infer; consider: 假定; 推断; 推定; 以
为: *I took you to be an honest man.* 我以为你是个诚
诚实。*Do you ~ me for a fool?* 你以为我是傻瓜吗?
*Even the experts took the painting for a genuine
Rembrandt.* 甚至专家们也把那幅画认定是仑布兰特的真
品。**~ it (from sb) that ...,** assume: 认为; 假定; 想象:
I ~ it that we are to come early. 我认为我们应该早点
来。*You may ~ it from me that ...,* be confident
because I tell you .... 你可以相信我所说的(...)。**~ sb/
sth for granted,** ⇨ grant v(2). **11** [VP6A] find out
(by inquiry, measurement, etc.): (借询问、测量等)找
出; 量出; 测出: *The doctor took my temperature.* 医生量
我的体温。*Has the tailor ~n your measurements for
that new suit?* 裁缝已为你量做那套新衣吗? *Did the
police ~ your name and address?* 警察问过了你的姓名及
住址吗? **12** [VP22, 16B] treat or regard in a
specified way: (用某种指明的方式)处理; 对待: **~ it/
things easy,** not work too hard or too fast; 不赶做; 不赶
工; 不过劳或过快。**~ things coolly/calmly,** not get
excited; 处之泰然; 不激动。**~ sth ill/amiss,** resent it.
对某事表示不高兴。*I should ~ it kindly* (= be grateful
to you) *if ....* 我应该感谢你, 如果...。*Don't ~ it so
seriously,* Don't treat the matter with such seriousness.
不要把这事看得如此严重。**~ sth as+pp,** assume it to
be: 认为某事业...: *~ an apology as given / an
objection as answered.* 作已道歉(答复一异议)。**~
sth as read,** agree that it is unnecessary to read it, eg
the minutes of the previous meeting. 认为不必读(上次
会议记录等)。*~ (it) as read (that ...),* assume that,
assume that ...: 认为...; 以为...: *We can ~ (it) as read
that an apology was given.* 我们可认为业已道歉。**13**
[VP6A] accept responsibility for: 负起...的责任; 履
行: *~ evening service,* (at church) conduct it; (在教堂)
主持晚间礼拜; *~ a class,* be in charge, give the class
its lesson, etc. 授课; 教课; *The smallpox injection did
not ~,* did not become popular; 乔治·格林的第二部小
说不畅销。have the required effect: 奏效; 显示要的反
应; 生预期效果: *That smallpox injection did not ~.* 那
次种的牛痘没有效果。*The dye doesn't ~ in cold water,*
is ineffective. 那染料在冷水中不起染作用。**15** (with *nn*)
(For other examples, ⇨ the *n* entries.)
(其他例句参看各名词) **~ account of sth,** (= ~ sth into

account), ⇨ **account**[1](7). **~ advantage of sb/sth,**
⇨ **advantage.** **~ aim,** ⇨ **aim**[1](2). **~ the biscuit/
the cake,** ⇨ **biscuit, cake.** **~ care,** ⇨ **care**[1](2). **~
a chair,** ⇨ **5** above. 参看上列第 5 义。**~ a/one's
chance,** ⇨ **6** above. 参看上列第 6 义。**~ charge (of),**
⇨ **charge**[1](9). **~ courage,** ⇨ **courage.** **~ a degree,**
obtain a degree(5). 获得学位。**~ (a) delight/an
interest/(a) pleasure/(a) pride in sth,** be, show
that one is, delighted/interested, etc in it. 对某事感到
高兴(兴趣, 愉快, 骄傲)。**~ a dislike to sb,** ⇨ **dislike.**
~ effect, ⇨ **effect**(1). **~ an examination,** be tested
on one's knowledge or ability. 应试; 参加考试。**~
exception to,** ⇨ **exception**(3). *not/never take one's
eyes off,* ⇨ **16** below. 参看下列第 16 义。**~ a fancy
to;** **~ the fancy of,** ⇨ **fancy**[1](3). **~ fright (at sth),**
become frightened. (对某事)感到惊慌。**~ a gamble
(on sth),** do sth knowing it is risky. 冒险做(某事)。
~ a hand at, ⇨ **hand**[1](13). **~ sb in hand,** accept
responsibility for him (esp to improve his behaviour).
负责照顾某人(尤指改进其行为)。**~ (fresh) heart;
sth to heart,** ⇨ **heart**(2). **~ heed,** pay attention. 注
意。**~ a/the hint,** ⇨ **hint.** **~ (one's) leave (of sb),**
⇨ **leave**[2](3). **~ the liberty of; ~ liberties with,**
⇨ **liberty**(2). **~ a liking to,** become fond of. 喜欢。
~ the measure of sb, ⇨ **measure**[1](1). **~ one's/sb's
mind off (sth),** ⇨ **mind**[1](2). **~ no notice (of),** ⇨
notice(3). **~ an oath,** ⇨ **oath**(1). **~ objection to,**
⇨ **objection**(1). **~ offence (at sth),** ⇨ **offence**(2).
~ the opportunity of doing/to do sth, recognize a
favourable moment and act. 趁机或抓住机会做某事。
~ (holy) orders, become a priest, etc. 出任圣职(当僧侣
等)。**~ (great) pains (over sth/to do sth),** ⇨ **pains.**
~ part (in), ⇨ **part**[1](4). **~ place; ~ the place of,**
⇨ **place**[1](10). **~ the path of; ~ risks,** ⇨ **risk**(1).
~ a seat, ⇨ **5** above. 参看上列第 5 义。**~ silk,** ⇨
silk(3). **~ stock,** ⇨ **stock**[1](1). **~ one's time (over
sth),** ⇨ **9** above. 参看上列第 9 义。**~ the trouble (over
sth); ~ the trouble to do sth,** ⇨ **trouble,** *n*(3). **~
umbrage to,** ⇨ **umbrage.** **~ my word for it,** ⇨ **12**
above. 参看上列第 6 义。**16** [VP3A, 2C, 15B, 14]
(special uses with *adverbial particles* and *preps*): (与副
词性小品词及介词连用的特殊用法):

be taken aback, ⇨ **aback.**

take after sb, resemble (esp a parent or relation) in
features or character: (在长相或性格方面)象某人(尤指
象父母亲或某一亲属): *Your daughter does not ~ after
you in any way.* 你的女儿没有一个地方象你。

take sth apart, separate sth (machinery, etc) into its
(component) parts. 把某物(机器等)分解为其组成部分;
拆散; 拆开。

take (away) from, lessen, weaken, diminish: 减少; 减
弱; 减小; 降低: *That foolish indiscretion took away from
his public image.* 那次愚蠢的轻率行为损坏了他的形像。
*These faults to some extent ~ (away) from his credit as
a biographer.* 身为传记作家, 这些缺点多多少少降低他的信
誉。**~ sth/sb away (from sb/sth),** remove: 拿去;
消除; 移动; 使离开; 使退出。不可取走(如图书馆里的书)。*The
child was ~n away from school,* not allowed to attend.
那孩子被勒令退学。*What ~s you away so early,* Why
are you leaving so early? 你为什么这么早就要走?
'*Sandwiches to ~ away'* (eg as a sign outside a shop, =
'... to be ~n away'), Sandwiches may be bought here
and eaten elsewhere. '可带走食用的三明治'; '三明治外
卖'(例如商店外面之标示)。Hence, 由此产生, '**~-away**
attrib to be ~n away: 可带走的; 外卖的: *~-away
hamburgers;* 外卖牛肉饼; *a ~-away restaurant,* one
that sells food that may be ~n away. 外卖餐馆。

take sth back, **(a)** retreat or withdraw (what one has
said) as an admission of error, as an apology, etc: 撤
销; 收回(所说的话, 以承认错误或道歉等): *I ~ back
what I said.* 我收回我所说的话。**(b)** agree to receive

back: 同意拿回; 取回: *Shopkeepers will not usually ~ back goods after they have been paid for.* 店主人通常不收回已付过钱的货物。 **~ sb back (to),** carry or conduct to an earlier period: 使某人回想或追忆: *These stories took him back to his childhood days,* (fig) brought them back to his mind. (喻)这些故事使他回想到童年时代。

take sth down, (a) write down: 记录: *The reporters' took down the speech.* 记者们记录演讲词。 **(b)** lower; get by lifting down from (a shelf, etc): 降下; 降低; 从(架上等)取下: *~ down a book from the top shelf;* 从上面的架上取下一本书; *~ down the curtains/pictures from the walls,* 落幕(从墙上取下图书); *~ down a mast.* 降下桅杆。 **(c)** dismantle; pull down; get into separate parts: 拆毁; 拆除; 拆开: *~ down a crane/the scaffolding round a building;* 拆除重机(房屋四周的脚手架); *~ down a partition.* 拆掉隔板。 **~ sb down a peg (or two),** humble; lower the pride of: 挫某人的傲气; 贬抑: *That fellow needs to be ~n down a peg.* 那家伙需要挫挫他的傲气。

take from, ⇨ take *(away) from* above. 参看上列之 take (away) from.

take sth in, (a) receive (work) to be done in one's own house for payment: 承揽(工作)在自己家中做: *The poor widow earns money by taking in washing/sewing.* 那贫苦的寡妇靠在家里替人洗(缝)衣服度日。 **(b)** (⇨ **7** above) pay for and receive regularly: (参看上列第 7 义)订阅; 订购: *~ in journals/periodicals.* 订阅杂志(期刊)。 **(c)** reduce the state, area length or width of (a garment, sail, etc): 减小(衣服、帆等)的尺码、面积、长度或宽度; 改小; 缩小; 卷起; 叠起: *This dress needs to be ~n in* (= made smaller) *at the waist.* 这件女装腰部需要改小。 *Orders were given to ~ in sail.* 已发布了收帆的命令。 *~ up the slack* ⇨ slack²(1). **(d)** comprise; include, eg in one's journey or route: 包含; 包括(如包括在某人的行程中): *a motor-coach tour that ~s in six European capitals.* 行程包括欧洲六个国家首都在内的乘坐游览车的观光旅行。 **(e)** take (territory, common land, etc) into one's possession; (re)claim: 取得(领土、公有地等); 开垦; 填筑: *A good deal of Romney Marsh has ~n in from the sea by monks.* 洛木尼沼地有很大一部分系由僧侣们填海而成。 **(f)** understand; absorb; digest mentally: 了解; 吸收; 领会: *They listened to my lecture, but how much did they ~ in, I wonder?* 他们听了我的课, 但是我不知道他们领会了多少? *We need more time to ~ in the situation,* form a correct idea of it. 我们需要多一点时间来了解当前的情况。 **(g)** see at a glance; see at once: 一眼看清; 同时看到: *She took in every detail of the other woman's clothes.* 她一眼就看到了另一位女士衣服的每一个细微处。 *He took in the scene at a glance.* 他看了一眼那(地方)的景色。 **(h)** listen to, watch, with excitement: 激动地听或看: *The children took in the whole spectacle open-mouthed.* 孩子们张着嘴惊奇地注视整个的精采表演。 **~ sb in,** (a) receive, admit: 接待; 收容: *make a living by taking in guests/lodgers.* 靠接待客人(寄宿者)维持生活。 *~ a traveller in for the night.* 接待旅客住宿。 **(b)** deceive; get the better of by a trick: 欺骗; 诈骗: *Don't let yourself be ~n in by these politicians.* 不要(使你自己)受这些政客的欺骗。 *He was badly ~n in when he bought that second-hand car.* 他购买那辆旧汽车时, 大大地受骗了。

take sth into account, ⇨ account(7). *~ a person into one's confidence,* ⇨ confidence(1). *~ sth into one's head,* ⇨ head¹(19).

take off, (a) make a start in jumping. 起跳。 **(b)** (of an aircraft) leave the ground and rise: (指飞机)起飞: *The plane took off despite the fog.* 那架飞机不顾大雾而起飞。 Hence, 由此产生, **'~-off n** (a) (also *jump-off,* esp in show jumping) place at which the feet leave the ground in jumping. (亦作 jump-off, 尤指超越障碍骑术表演中)(脚离地面的)起跳处; 起跳点。 **(b)** (of aircraft) leaving the ground and rising: (指飞机)起飞: *a smooth ~-off.* 平稳的起飞。 ⇨ *touch-down* at touch²(11).

sth off, (a) remove: 除去; 脱掉: *~ off one's shirt.* 脱掉衬衫。 *Why don't you ~* (= shave) *off that silly little moustache?* 你为什么不剃掉那无聊的小胡子呢? *The surgeon took off* (= amputated) *his leg.* 外科医生切去了他的腿。 *~ one's hat off to sb,* ⇨ hat. **(b)** withdraw (from service): 撤消(…的服务): *The 7 am express to Bristol will be ~n off next month,* will not run. 上午七时开往布里斯尔的快车将于下月停驶。 *~ sth off (sth),* (a) lift and move to another position: 移动; 移位: *T~ your hand off my shoulder.* 把你的手从我肩膀上拿开。 **(b)** deduct: 减去; 减少: *~ 50p off the price.* 减价五十便士。 *~ sb off,* (a) conduct; lead away somewhere: 引导; 带走; 引开: *He was ~n off to prison.* 他被送进监狱。 *She took me off to see her garden.* 她引导我去看她的花园。 *~ sb off sth,* remove him from: 使某人离开某处: *The crew were ~n off* (rescued from) *the wrecked ship by the lifeboat.* 船员们被救生艇救离了难船。 **(b)** ridicule by imitation; mimic; burlesque: 借学样取笑: *Alice is clever at taking off the headmistress.* 艾丽丝善于模仿女校长的样子以取笑她。 Hence, 由此产生, **'~-off n** caricature; burlesque imitation of sb's behaviour: (对某人行为等的)滑稽的模仿: *a good ~-off of the Prime Minister.* 学首相的样子而模仿得惟妙惟肖的动作。 *not/never ~ one's eyes off sth/sb,* look at constantly: 不停地注视某物或某人; 盯着看: *He never took his eyes off his small daughter while she was swimming in the sea.* 当他的小女儿在海里游泳时, 他一直注视着她。 *~ one's mind off (sth),* ⇨ mind¹(2).

take on, (a) (colloq) become excited or agitated; make a fuss: (口)激动; 激昂; 作无谓纷扰: *She took on something dreadful when I said she'd told a pack of lies.* 当我告诉她她撒了很多流言时, 她激动得可怕。 **(b)** (colloq) become popular; have a vogue: (口)受欢迎; 流行: *We introduced a new sports car last year but it never took on.* 去年我们引进一种新型跑车, 但未受欢迎。 *~ sth on,* (a) undertake; charge oneself with: 从事; 担任: *an extra work/heavy responsibilities.* 承担额外工作(重责)。 *You've ~n on too much.* 你承担的工作太多了。 **(b)** assume; put on (a quality, appearance): 装出; 表现(某种性质, 外表): *The chameleon can ~ on the colours of its background.* 变色蜥蜴可现出与背景相同的颜色。 *~ sb on,* (a) accept as an opponent: 接受某人作为对手; 接受挑战: *~ sb on at golf/billiards;* 与某人比赛高尔夫球(撞球); *ready to ~ on all comers,* play against, fight, anyone who accepts a challenge. 准备迎战所有接受挑战者。 **(b)** engage; 雇用: *~ on twenty more workers.* 再雇用二十名工人。 **(c)** (of a train, etc) allow to enter: (指火车等)许可进入: *The bus stopped to ~ on some children.* 那公共汽车停下来载一些小孩子。 **(d)** (of trains, etc) carry too far, past the destination: (指火车等)使过站; 送送过远: *I fell asleep in the train and was ~n on to York.* 我在火车上睡着了, 一直被带到约克。

take sth out, extract; remove: 除去; 拔去; 剪除: *have one's appendix/a tooth ~n out.* 切除盲肠(拔牙)。 *How can I ~ out* (= remove) *these inkstains from my blouse?* 我怎样才能把我罩衫上这些墨水污迹除去呢? **(b)** obtain; procure (sth issued): 获得; 领得(颁发之文件/summons/a patent.* 领到保险单(驾驶执照, 传票, 专利证书)。 *~ sb out,* (a) conduct; accompany: 带某人外出; 引领; 伴随: *~ the children out for a walk;* 带孩子们出去散步; *~ one's wife out for dinner,* ie at a restaurant. 带太太出去(在馆子里)吃饭。 **(b)** (in bridge): (桥牌戏中): *~ one's partner out,* make a higher bid (than that which he has made). 叫牌高于搭档。 *~ it out in sth,* accept as recompense or compensation: 接受某物作为赔偿或补偿: *The innkeeper couldn't pay me the £10 he owed me but let me ~ it out in drinks and cigars.* 小旅店老板无力偿还欠我的十镑, 但是他让我拿酒及雪茄作为抵偿。 *~ it out of sb,* leave him weak and exhausted: 使某人衰弱; 使某人筋疲力竭: *His recent illness/All that hard work has ~n it out of him.* 他最近的一场病(所有

那些繁重的工作)已耗尽他的体力。~ *it out on sb*, vent
one's anger, disappointment, etc on (usu) sb else: 向
某人发泄怒气、失望等: *He came home angry at losing his
job and took it out on his wife.* 他回到家里因为失去工作
而生气,并把一肚子的怒气发泄到他妻子身上。

take sb over (to), carry from one place to another: 从
一地送某人至另一地: *Mr White took me over to the
island in his launch.* 怀特先生用他的汽艇载我至该岛。

~ sth over (from sb), assume control of; succeed to
the management or ownership of (a business, etc): 接
管; 接收(商店等): *Was it in 1948 that the Government
took over the railways in Great Britain,* nationalized
them? 英国政府接管铁路(将铁路收为国有)是在一九四八
年吗? *When Mr Green retired his son took over the
business from him.* 格林先生退休后, 由他儿子接管他的
生意。Hence, 由此产生, '**~·over** n change of control
of a firm or company, eg after another has made a
successful bid to buy its stock: (公司或商店的)接收; 接
管(控制权的出价)制控权(如因他人购得其股票): *a '~over bid.* 取
得控制权的出价。**~ over (from sb),** accept duties,
responsibilities, etc: (从某人)接收职务、责任等; 接任:
*The new Chancellor took over (ie from his predecessor)
yesterday.* 新校长昨天(从他的前任)接事。

take to sth, (a) adopt as a practice or hobby, as a
means of livelihood; get into a habit: 采纳某事(作为习
惯或嗜好,或作为谋生的方法); 从事; 养成; 沉湎于: ~ *to
gardening when one retires;* 退休后从事园艺; ~ *to
drink(ing),* get into the habit of taking alcoholic liquor;
嗜酒; 沉湎于酒: ~ *to the road,* become a tramp (or, in
former times a high wayman); (of a circus, etc) go on
tour from town to town giving shows. 沦为流浪汉; (指
昔时)沦为强盗; (指马戏班等)到各处巡回演出。**(b)** take
refuge in; use a means of escape: 逃入; 利用…作为
逃亡工具: ~ *to flight,* run away; 逃走; ~ *to the
woods/the jungle/the heather,* go to the woods, etc, to
avoid capture. 逃入林中(丛林,石南林)。*The crew took
to the boats when the torpedo struck the ship.* 鱼雷击中
那船时, 船员们乘救生艇逃生。⇨ *to one's heels,* ⇨
heel¹(1). **~ to sth/sb,** conceive a liking for: 对某事
物或某人产生好感; 喜欢: *Has the baby ~n to its new
nursemaid?* 那婴儿喜欢新来的保姆吗? *That boy will
never ~ to cricket.* 那个男孩子永远不会喜欢板球。

take sth up, (a) lift up; raise: 拿起; 举起; 抬起; 收起:
~ *up one's pen/book/gun;* 拿起笔(书,枪); ~ *up a
carpet.* 收起地毯。**(b)** (of trains, taxis, etc) more usu
较常用 **~ on)** stop to allow (passengers) to enter.
(指火车、计程车等)停下来接纳(旅客)。**(c)** absorb (a
liquid): 吸收(液体): *Blotting-paper ~s up ink.* 吸墨
纸吸吸墨水。**(d)** dissolve (solids): 溶解(固体): *How
much water is needed to ~ up a pound of salt?* 溶解一
磅食盐需要多少水? **(e)** interest oneself in; engage in
(sth) (as a hobby, business, etc): 对…有兴趣; 从事(某
事)(作为嗜好、事业等): ~ *up photography/market
gardening.* 从事摄影(蔬菜种植)。**(f)** pursue further;
begin afresh (sth left off, sth being done by sb else): 继续;
重新开始(停顿之事,他人所开始之事): *Harry took up the
tale at the point where John had left off.* 哈利接着约翰
停止的地方继续讲那个故事。**(g)** occupy (time, space): *How
使占据(时间,空间); 占用: *This table ~s up too much space.*
这张桌子占地方太大。*My time is fully ~n up with
writing.* 我的时间全都花在写作上了。**(h)** (comm)advance
money (on a mortgage); accept (a Bill of Exchange);
subscribe for (shares, etc) at the time of issue. (商)
(按抵押)垫款; 承兑(汇票)认购(股份等)。**(i)**
catch the end of and make secure: 抓住…的末端使住
牢固; 使稳定: ~ *up a dropped stitch.* 系牢一处脱线的针
脚。'**~·up spool** on a cine projector, tape-recorder,
etc) spool on to which film, tape, etc is wound from the
spool having the film, tape, etc that is being used. (电
影放映机,录音机等上的)收带卷轴(将一卷轴上
收卷使用中之影片或录音带者)。~ **sth up (with sb),**
speak or write (to him) about it; (口头或书面向某人)

提出某事: *I will ~ the matter up with the Ministry,*
eg by asking for information, or by making a protest.
我将向政府提出此事(如要求说明或提出抗议)。~ **sb up,**
make a protégé of; help: 保护; 帮助: *The young soprano
was ~n up by the famous conductor,* He encouraged and
helped her in her career. 那位年轻的女高音得到那位名
指挥家的照顾。~ **sb 'up on sth,** accept from him his
offer, challenge, bet, etc: 接受某人的提议, 挑战, 打赌
等: *Why don't you take Jim up on his offer to lend you
£50?* 吉姆要借给你五十镑,你为何不接受? 你为何不接受~ **up
with sb/sth,** be much interested in: 对某人或某事物深
感兴趣: *He seems to be very much ~n up with that tall
Swedish girl.* 他似乎对那位高个子瑞典女郎特别感兴趣。
~ **sb up sharp/short,** interrupt and correct (a
speaker): 打断并改正(说话者): *He took me up short
when I suggested that ~.* 当我建议~时,他打断了我的
话。~ **up one's residence at,** (formal) proceed to
occupy: (正式用语)定居于; 迁入: *The new ambassador
has ~n up his residence in* (in the Embassy). 新任大使已
经进入(大使馆)定居。

take sth upon/on oneself, assume responsibility;
undertake: 承担责任; 揽事: *You mustn't ~ upon
yourself the right to make decisions.* 你不可擅权而自
做主张。

take² /teik; tek/ n 1 amount (of money) taken. 取得
或获得的金钱数额。**2** (film industry) scene that has
been or is to be photographed. (电影制片)已拍摄或待拍
摄的景; 镜头。**3** act of taking. 拿取的动作; 取; 拿。

taker /'teikə(r); 'tekə/ n one who, that which, takes,
esp one who takes a bet: 拿取的人或物; 接受者; (尤指)
接受打赌者: *There were no ~s,* no one willing to take
bets. 没有人愿意接受打赌。

tak·ing /'teikiŋ; 'tekiŋ/ adj attractive; captivating.
动人的; 迷人的。□ n (pl) money taken in business;
receipts. (复)营业所得; 收入。

talc /tælk; tælk/ n [U] soft, smooth mineral that can
be split into thin transparent plates. 云母; 滑石。'~
powder n perfumed powder to rub on the body, made
from ~. (滑石制成的)扑粉; 滑石粉; 爽身粉。

tal·cum /'tælkəm; 'tælkəm/ n '~ **powder,** = talc
powder.

tale /teil; tel/ n [C] **1** story: 故事: '*fairy-~s;* 神仙
故事; 童话; ~*s of adventure.* 冒险故事。*It tells its own
~,* explains itself, requires no comment or explanation.
显而易见; 无须说明。**2** report; account. 报告; 记述; 传
闻。*tell ~s,* tell sth about another person that he
wishes to be kept secret, eg his wrongdoing. 搬弄是非;
讲坏话; 揭人短处。Hence, 由此产生, '**~·bearer**/
-teller nn person who tells ~s. 搬弄是非者。

tal·ent /'tælənt; 'tælənt/ n **1** [C, U] (particular
kind of) natural power to do sth well: (某种的)天才; 才
干; 才能; 智能: *a man of great ~,* 有大才干的人; local
~, (usu amateur) musicians, actors, etc of a district;
地方上的人才(通常指当地业余的音乐家、演员等); *a '~
scout,* (colloq) person who watches out for persons of
~ for films, the theatre, sports, etc: (口)星探; 球探
(发掘适于做演员、球员等的人); *have a ~ for music/
not much ~ for painting;* 有音乐天才(不大有绘画天才);
an exhibition of local ~, of works, eg paintings, by
people of a district or locality. 当地人士作品展(如画展
等)。**2** [C] measure of weight, unit of money, used in
ancient times among the Greeks, Romans, Assyrians,
etc. (古希腊、罗马、亚述等国的)一种重量及货币单位;
泰伦。~*ed adj* having ~; gifted: 有才能的; 有才干的; 有
天才的: *a ~ed musician.* 天才音乐家。

tal·is·man /'tælizmən US: -ism-; 'tælismən/ n [C]
(pl ~s) sth that is thought to bring good luck, eg a
trinket or ring. 被认为可带来好运之物(如小装饰物或戒
指); 辟邪物。

talk¹ /tɔːk; tɔk/ n **1** [C] talking; conversation;
discussion: 谈话; 商议; 讨论: *I've had several ~s with
the headmaster about my boy.* 我已与校长就我的男孩作

过谈次谈话。*There's too much* ~ (= ~*ing*) *and not enough work being done.* 说得太多而做得太少。**2** [C] informal speech: 非正式的演讲: *give a* ~ *to the Women's Institute on one's travels in Asia.* 就一位赴亚洲旅行的妇女曾发表非正式演讲。**3** (phrases) (短语) **the** ~ **of the town**, sth or sb everyone is ~ing about. 为大家谈论的人或事物; 街头巷尾的话题。**be all** ~, said of sb who ~s a lot but does not get results. 只会说空话(指某人会说不会做)。**'small** ~, conversation on everyday but not important topics. 闲话; 闲谈; 杂谈。

talk² /tɔːk; tɔk/ *vi, vt* (*pt, pp* ~**ed**) **1** [VP2A, B, C, 3A, 15B] ~ **(to/with sb) (about/of sth)**, say things; speak to give information; discuss sth, etc: 讲话; 谈话; 讨论: *He was* ~*ing to* (less often 较少用 *with*) *a friend.* 他在和一个朋友谈话。*What are they* ~*ing about* (less often 较少用 *of*)? 他们在谈什么? *We* ~*ed all afternoon/for two hours.* 我们整整谈了一个下午(两个钟头)。*Were they* ~*ing in Spanish or in Portuguese?* 他们讲的是西班牙语还是葡萄牙语? **be/get oneself** ~**ed about**, (in some contexts) be made the subject of gossip: (在某些上下文中) 成为闲谈的话题; 成为话柄: *You'll get yourself* ~*ed about if you go on being so foolish.* 如果你继续这样的愚行, 你会成为旁人的话柄。~ **at sb**, speak to sb without paying attention to his replies: 指桑骂人; 指桑骂槐: *I don't like people who* ~ *at me instead of with me.* 我不喜欢人们含沙射影地对我讲话, 而不直接跟我讲话。~ **away**, continue ~ing: 继续谈话: *They were still* ~*ing away at midnight.* 他们谈到半夜还没有停止。~ **back (to sb)**, (often 常作 *answer back*) reply defiantly. (对某人)反唇相讥; 回嘴。~ **big**, brag; boast. 吹牛; 说大话。~ **sb down**, silence him by talking loudly at him. 高声压倒某人。~ **down an aircraft**, ~ by radio to the pilot while he is about to make a landing, giving him instructions, etc. (借无线电)指示飞机降落。~ **down to sb**, in a way that suggests that the speaker is superior, eg by using condescendingly simple words, etc: 自觉高人一等对某人谈话; 以含示优于对方的方式说话: *It's unwise for a lecturer to* ~ *down to his audience.* 演说者自觉高人一等地向听众发表演讲是不智的。~ing **of**, while on the subject of: 说到; 讲到; 谈到: *T*~*ing of travel, have you been to Munich yet?* 谈到旅行, 你去过慕尼黑吗? ~ **sth over**, discuss it. 讨论某事。~ **round sth**, ~ about a subject without reaching the point or a conclusion. 不得要领地或无结论地谈论某事; 兜圈子地谈论某事。~ **to sb**, (colloq) scold; chide. (口)训诫; 斥责; 数说。Hence, 由此产生, **'~ing-to** n scolding: 斥责; 训诫: *The teacher gave the lazy boy a good* ~*ing-to!* 老师把那个懒惰的男孩好好训斥了一顿。**2** [VP2A] have the power of speech: 有说话的能力: *Can the baby* ~ *yet?* 这娃娃会说话了吗? **3** [VP6A] be able to use (a language): 会使用(一种语言); 会讲(某种语言): ~ *English/Spanish.* 说英语(西班牙语)。**4** [VP6A] discuss 讨论; 蹉商: ~ *business,* ~ *shop,* 谈正经事, 讲本行的话, ⇨ **shop(2).** ~ed *music all evening.* 我们整晚都在谈论音乐。**'~ing-point**, topic likely to cause discussion; argument likely to persuade or convince sb. 话题; 有说服力的论据。**5** [VP6A] express in words; 借语言表示: ~ *sense/nonsense/treason.* 讲得有道理; 讲得不道理; 言谈中有叛国之意。**6** [VP14, 22] bring into a certain condition by ~ing: 借谈话而使陷入某一状况; 以言语使: ~ *oneself hoarse,* ~ *until one is hoarse.* 讲话讲到声音嘶哑。~ **sb into/out of doing sth**, persuade sb to do/not to do sth: 说服某人做(不做)某事: *She* ~*ed her husband into having a holiday in France.* 她说服丈夫去法国度假。*He* ~*ed his wife out of buying a new car.* 他说服他太太不要买辆新车。~ **sb over/round**, persuade sb to agree to or to accept sth: 说服某人同意或接受某事物: *We* ~*ed them over to our way of thinking.* 我们说服他们接受我们的想法。**7** [VP2A] (various uses): (各种用法): *Don't do anything indiscreet—you know how people* ~, gossip. 行为不要

太随便——你知道, 别人会说闲话的。*Has the accused man* ~*ed yet*, given under coercion, eg under coercion or threats? 被告招供了吗? *Some parrots can* ~, imitate the sounds of human speech. 有些鹦鹉会学人语。~**a-tive** /'tɔːkətɪv, 'tɔkətɪv/ *adj* fond of ~ing. 多话的; 喜欢谈话的; 多嘴的。~**er** n 1 (esp with an *adj*) person who ~s: 说话者 (尤与形容词连用): *a good/poor, etc* ~*er.* 健谈的(不善于讲话等)的人。*What a* ~*er that woman is!* How fond she is of ~ing! 那女人真喜欢讲话呀! **2** person who ~s a lot but does not get results: 空谈者: *He's a mere* ~*er.* 他只会讲空话。

talkie /'tɔːkɪ; 'tɔkɪ/ n [C] (dated colloq term for a) cinema film with spoken dialogue (used when these were a novelty). (过时口语)有声影片(初期尚感新奇时之用语)。**the** ~**s**, (colloq) cinema films with spoken dialogue. (口)有声电影。

tall /tɔːl; tɔl/ *adj* (-er, -est) **1** (of persons) of more than average height; (of objects such as a ship's mast, a flagpole, a church spire, a tree whose height is greater than its width, but not of mountains) higher than the average or than surrounding objects: (指人)高的; (指桅杆、旗杆、教堂尖塔、树等高而细之物, 但不指山)超过一般高度的; 高于周围事物的: *She is* ~*er than her sister.* 她比她姐姐(妹妹)高。*She wears high heels to make herself look* ~*er.* 她穿高跟鞋使自己看起来高一些。*That yacht has a very* ~ *mast.* 那游艇有一根非常高的桅杆。**'~-boy** (GB; US 美 = *highboy*) n bedroom chest of drawers 5 or 6 ft high. (英)(卧室用的)高衣柜(约五、六英尺高)。**2** of a specified height: 有某种(指明的)高度的: *Tom is six foot* ~. 汤姆身高六英尺。**3** (colloq) excessive, exorbitant. (口)过分的; 越轨的; 过度的。**a** ~ **order**, an unreasonable request; a task difficult to perform. 过分的要求; 难完成的任务。**a** ~ **story**, one that it is difficult to believe. 难以相信的故事。~**ish** /-ɪʃ; -ɪʃ/ *adj* rather ~. 颇高的; 高高的; 略高的。

tal·low /'tæləʊ; 'tælo/ n [U] hard (esp animal) fat used for making candles, etc. (用于制蜡烛等的)硬脂肪; 脂; (尤指)兽脂。

tally /'tælɪ; 'tælɪ/ n [C] (*pl* -lies) **1** score; reckoning: 分数; 计算: *keep the* ~. 记分数。**2** ticket, label, etc used for identification. 用以核对的票据、标签等。**'~-clerk** n clerk who checks cargo, etc eg at the docks. 货物核对员(如码头等处者)。**'~-man** /-mæn; -men/ n (*pl* -men) person who sells goods and collects weekly payments. 赊卖人; 赊卖者(每周收款一次)。□ *vi* (*pt, pp* -lied) [VP2A, 3A] ~ **(with)**, (of stories, amounts, etc) correspond; agree: (指叙事、故事、数量等)符合; 吻合: *The two lists do not* ~. 这两张单子不相符。*Does your list* ~ *with mine?* 你的单子与我的符合吗? *The stories of the two men tallied.* 这两个人话一致。

tally-ho /ˌtælɪ 'həʊ; ˌtælɪ'ho/ *int* huntsman's cry on catching sight of the fox. 唷(猎人发现狐狸时的喊声)。

Tal·mud /'tælmʊd US: 'tɑːl-; 'tælməd/ n compendium of Jewish law and teaching. 犹太法典。

talon /'tælən; 'tælən/ n claw of a bird of prey, eg an eagle. 猛禽(如鹰)的爪。

talus /'teɪləs; 'teləs/ n (geol) sloping mass of fragments at the foot of a cliff or precipice. (地质)崖锥(悬崖脚下的斜坡状碎石堆)。

ta·male /tə'mɑːlɪ; tə'mɑlɪ/ n Mexican dish of chopped meat, red peppers, etc steamed in corn (= maize) husks. 特马利(一种墨西哥食物, 将碎肉、辣椒等包在玉蜀黍外壳中蒸熟而成)。

tam·a·rind /'tæmərɪnd; 'tæmə,rɪnd/ n (edible fruit of a) tropical tree. 罗望子(一种热带植物); 罗望子的果实(可食)。

tam·a·risk /'tæmərɪsk; 'tæmə,rɪsk/ n [C] evergreen shrub with feathery branches, often planted in sandy soil near the sea. 柽柳(一种枝条轻柔的常绿灌木, 常栽于近海沙土中, 又名赤杨、三春柳等)。

tam·bour /'tæmbʊə(r); 'tæmbʊr/ n rolling front for a TV set or the top of a writing-desk, made of narrow

strips of wood glued to canvas. (多根细木条粘在帆布上制成的)电视机的拉门;书桌的活动桌面。

tam·bour·ine /ˌtæmbəˈriːn; ˌtæmbəˈrin/ *n* small, shallow drum with metal discs in the rim, played by striking with the knuckles and shaking it at the same time. 铃鼓(四周有金属圆片,边击边摇,使发鼓声及铃铃声)。 ⇨ the illus at **percussion**. 参看 percussion 之插图。

tame /teɪm; tem/ *adj* (**-r, -st**) **1** (of animals) brought under control and/or accustomed to living with human beings; not wild or fierce: (指动物)驯服的;养鴟了的;不野的: a ~ monkey. 驯服的猴子。 *The deer in the park are very* ~. 公园里的鹿非常驯服。 **2** (of a person) spiritless; submissive; docile: (指人)无精打采的; 顺从的;温顺的: *Her husband is a* ~ *little man*. 她的丈夫是一位个子矮小的好丈夫。 **3** dull; 沉闷的;乏味的: a ~ *baseball match*. 不精采的棒球赛。 *The story/film, etc has a* ~ *ending*. 这故事(电影等)结尾很沉闷。 □ *vt* [VP6A] make ~: 使驯服; 使顺从: ~ *a lion*. 驯服狮子。 **tam·er** *n* (usu in compounds) person who ~s: (通常用于复合词中)训养者; 驯兽师: *a 'lion-~r*. 驯狮者。 **tam·able, -able** /-əbl; -əbl/ *adj* that can be ~d, converted from a savage state. 可改变其野性的。 ~**·ly** *adv* ~**·ness** *n*

Tam·many /ˈtæmənɪ; ˈtæmənɪ/ *n* **(Hall)**, central organization of the Democratic Party in New York City; (attrib) of its politics, members, etc. 坦慕尼协会(美国民主党在纽约市的中心组织);(用作定语)其政策、会员等的。

tam-o'-shan·ter /ˌtæm ə ˈʃæntə(r); ˌtæməˈʃæntə/, **tammy** /ˈtæmɪ; ˈtæmɪ/ *nn* round, woollen or cloth cap fitting closely to the forehead. 一种圆帽(用呢或布制成,紧覆于前额)。

tamp /tæmp; tæmp/ *vt* [VP15B] ~ *sth down*, tap or drive down by repeated light blows: 借连续的轻击而敲下; 捣固; 舂牢: *He* ~ed *down the tobacco in his pipe*. 他把烟丝轻按几下使紧塞在烟斗里。

tam·per /ˈtæmpə(r); ˈtæmpə/ *vi* [VP3A] ~ *with*, meddle or interfere with; make unauthorized changes in: 干预;干涉;乱弄;擅自改变;未经授权而改动: *Someone has been* ~ing *with the lock/the seal of this letter*. 有人乱动了这把锁(这信上的封蜡)。

tan /tæn; tæn/ *n, adj* yellowish brown; brown colour of sunburnt skin: 黄褐色(的);晒黑的皮肤颜色(的): *tan leather shoes/gloves*; 黄褐色的皮鞋(手套); *get a good tan* (on one's skin). (皮肤)晒得很黑。 □ *vt, vi* (**-nn-**) [VP6A, 2A] **1** (of an animal's skin) make, be made, into leather (by treatment with tannic acid, etc). (指动物皮)制成革; 被制成革; 硝皮; 鞣。 *tan sb's hide*, (sl) give him a good beating. (俚)痛打某人。 **2** make or become brown with sunburn: 晒成褐色: *return from the holidays with a tanned face*. 休假回来面孔晒得很黑。 *Some people tan quickly*. 有些人易于晒黑。 **tan·ner** *n* workman who tans skins. 制革工人; 硝皮匠。 **tan·nery** /ˈtænərɪ; ˈtænərɪ/ *n* (*pl* **-ries**) place where skins are tanned. 制革厂;硝皮厂。

tan·dem /ˈtændəm; ˈtændəm/ *n* bicycle made for two persons to ride on, one behind the other, with pedals for both. 前后双座脚踏车(有两副脚板者)。 □ *adv* (*in*) ~, (of horses in harness or two persons on a ~ bicycle) one behind the other; (指上了挽具的马,或骑在双座脚踏车上的两人)一前一后地; 纵列地: *drive/ride in* ~. 纵列地驾车(骑车)。

tang /tæŋ; tæŋ/ *n* sharp taste or flavour; that is characteristic of sth: 强烈的味道或气味; (尤指)某物的特有气味或风味: *the salt* ~ *of the sea air*. 海上空气中的强烈盐味。 **tangy** *adj*: *a* ~*y aroma/sauce*. 味道浓烈的香味(酱油)。

tan·gent /ˈtændʒənt; ˈtændʒənt/ *n* straight line touching but not cutting a curve. 切线; 正切; 正切线。 ⇨ the illus at **circle**. 参看 circle 之插图。 *go/fly off at a* ~, (fig) change suddenly from one line of thought,

action, etc to another. (喻)突然改变思想、行动等。

tan·ger·ine /ˌtændʒəˈriːn US: ˈtændʒəriːn; ˈtændʒəˌrin/ *n* [C] small, sweet-scented, loose-skinned orange. 红桔。

tan·gible /ˈtændʒəbl; ˈtændʒəbl/ *adj* **1** that can be perceived by touch. 可触知的。 **2** clear and definite; real: 确切的; 真实的; 明确的: ~ *proof*; 明确的证据; *the* ~ *assets*, eg of a business company, its buildings, machinery, etc but not its goodwill. 有形资产(如指公司的建筑物、机器等,但不包括商誉)。 **tan·gibly** /-əblɪ; -əblɪ/ *adv* **tan·gi·bil·ity** /ˌtændʒəˈbɪlətɪ; ˌtændʒəˈbɪlətɪ/ *n*

tangle[1] /ˈtæŋgl; ˈtæŋgl/ *n* [C] **1** confused mass (of string, hair, etc): (绳子、毛发等的)纠结; 缠结; 乱槽槽的一团; 乱作一团的纠结障碍; 刷刚狗毛。 *The kitten has made a* ~ *of my ball of wool*. 那小猫把我的毛线球弄得一团槽。 **2** confused state: 混乱的状态: *The traffic was in a frightful* ~. 交通混乱得可怕。 □ *vt, vi* **1** [VP6A, 15B, 2A, C] make or become confused, disordered: 使或变得混乱; 使或变得纠结; ~*d hair*. 蓬乱的头发。 **2** [VP3A] ~ *with sb*, (colloq) be/become involved in a fight or quarrel with: (口)与某人吵嘴或打架;与某人纠缠: *I shouldn't* ~ *with Peter—he's bigger than you*. 我不该与彼得纠缠——他比你块头大。

tangle[2] /ˈtæŋgl; ˈtæŋgl/ *n* [U] (kinds of) seaweed with long leathery fronds. (数种)长叶海带;昆布;海带。

tango /ˈtæŋgəʊ; ˈtæŋgo/ *n* (*pl* ~**s** /-gəʊz; -goz/) (music for a) S American dance with strongly marked rhythm. (南美的)探戈舞;探戈舞曲。

tank /tæŋk; tæŋk/ *n* **1** (usu large) container for liquid or gas: (通常指大型的)液体或气体的大容器; 大桶、箱、槽等; *the 'petrol-~ of a car*; 汽车的油箱; a *'rain-water* ~, eg for storing rain-water from roofs; 雨水槽(如储存屋顶雨水者); *a ship's* ~*s*, the compartments into which the double hull is divided, to contain fuel-oil, fresh water, etc. 船的储油(水)舱。 **'~-car**, large (usu cylindrical) ~ for carrying petroleum, etc by rail. (铁路运送石油等的)油(槽)车。 **2** (in India, Pakistan, etc) large, artificial (usu rectangular) pool for storing water. (印度、巴基斯坦等处的)人工大水池(通常为长方形)。 **3** armoured fighting vehicle with guns, moving on caterpillar tracks, 坦克车; 战车。 **'~ trap**, deep ditch or other obstruction built to hinder or stop the advance of ~s. 战车陷阱。 □ *vt* ~ *sth up*, fill up the ~ of a vehicle, etc. 把车辆等的油箱加满。 *be/get* ~*ed up*, (sl) be/get drunk. (俚)喝醉。 ~*er* *n* ship or aircraft with ~s for carrying petroleum as freight; heavy road vehicle with a large cylindrical ~ for carrying oil, milk or other liquid in bulk. (运送石油的)油轮; 运油机(陆上运送油、奶或其他液体的)水车; 油车等。

a tank

tank·ard /ˈtæŋkəd; ˈtæŋkəd/ *n* large drinking mug, esp one for beer. 大杯; (尤指)大啤酒杯。

tan·ner[1] /ˈtænə(r); ˈtænə/ *n* (sl) former British silver coin, value sixpence (6 d, = 2 1/2 p). (俚)英国昔时银币名(面值为六便士,改制后合 2 1/2 便士)。

tan·ner[2] /ˈtænə(r); ˈtænə/ **tan·nery**, ⇨ **tan**.

tan·nic /ˈtænɪk; ˈtænɪk/ *adj* ~ **acid**, = **tannin**.

tan·nin /ˈtænɪn; ˈtænɪn/ *n* [U] acid obtained chiefly

from the bark of oak and other trees, and used in preparing leather, dyeing, the manufacture of ink, etc. 鞣酸; 单宁酸(由橡树等树皮提取的一种酸, 用于硝皮, 染色, 制造墨水等).

tan·noy /ˈtænɔɪ; ˈtænɔɪ/ n (P) type of loudspeaker or loudspeaker system, eg as used for public-address systems. (商标)坦诺扩音器; 坦诺扩音器系统(如用于公众演说).

tansy /ˈtænzɪ; ˈtænzɪ/ n herb with yellow flowers and bitter leaves, used in medicine and cooking. 艾菊(草本植物,开黄花,叶味苦,用于医药及烹调).

tan·ta·lize /ˈtæntəlaɪz; ˈtæntḷˌaɪz/ vt [VP6A] raise hopes that cannot (yet) be realized; keep just out of reach of sth that sb desires: 引起(尚)无法实现的希望,使某人对想获得之事物可望而不可及; 挑逗; 逗惹: a tantalizing smell of food. 引起人食欲的食物香味.

tan·ta·mount /ˈtæntəmaʊnt; ˈtæntəˌmaʊnt/ adj ~ to, equal in effect to: 效果等于; 相等于: The Queen's request was ~ to a command. 女王的要求等于命令.

tan·trum /ˈtæntrəm; ˈtæntrəm/ n [C] fit of bad temper or anger: 发脾气; 阵怒: He's in one of his ~s again. 他又在发脾气了.

tap¹ /tæp; tæp/ n 1 device for controlling the flow of liquid or gas from a pipe, barrel, etc. (Cf valve for controlling flow through a pipe; of faucet, the usu word in the US): (控制液体流出的)龙头; 活嘴(参较 valve, 控制液体在管内流动的装置; 参较 faucet, 美国通用之词): turn the tap on/off. 打开(关闭)龙头. Don't leave the taps running, ie turn them off. 别让龙头关上. on tap, (of beer, etc) in a barrel with a tap, ready to be drawn off: (hence, fig) available when needed. (指啤酒等)随时可自装有活嘴的桶中放出; (由此产生, 喻)现成的; 需要时即可获得的. 'tap-room n (in an inn, etc) room in which barrels are stored and cheaper drinks sold. (旅馆等中的)酒室;酒吧间. 'tap·root n chief descending root of a plant, tree, etc (going straight down for moisture). (植物的)直根;主根(向下直伸吸收水份者). 2 plug used to close the opening of a cask. (桶口的)栓; 塞子. □ vt (-pp-) [VP6A, 14, 15B] tap (off) sth (from sth), 1 draw out liquid through the tap of a (barrel): 从(桶)的龙头或开口取出液体: tap a cask of cider; 打开桶的活塞取苹果酒; tap (off) cider from a cask; 打开活塞从桶里汲取苹果酒. cut (the bark of a tree) and get (the sap, etc): 切开(树皮)并汲取(树液等): tap rubber-trees; 切开像胶树(的树皮)汲取树液; tap sugar-maples, eg in Canada. 在糖枫树上凿孔以汲取树液(如在加拿大). 2 extract or obtain (sth from sb or sth): 引出; 获取(自某人或某物得到某物): tap a man for money/information; 图自某人获得金钱(消息); tap a telephone/wire/line, make a connection so as to intercept messages. 私接电话线以窃听消息. My phone is being tapped. 我的电话现在有人窃听. 3 furnish (a cask, etc) with a tap. 在(桶等)上装龙头或塞子.

tap² /tæp; tæp/ n [C] 1 quick, light blow: 轻快的敲击; 轻拍; 轻叩; a ~ on the window/at the door. 敲窗(门). 'tap-dancing n stage-dancing with rhythmical tapping of the foot, toe or heel. 踢踏舞. 2 taps, (US armed forces) last signal of the day (by drum or bugle) for lights to be put out. (美军)熄灯鼓; 熄灯号. □ vt, vi (-pp-) [VP6A, 15A, 2A, C] give a tap or taps (to): 轻敲; 轻拍; 轻踏; 轻击: tap a man on the shoulder; 轻拍一个人的肩膀; tap at/on the door; 敲门; tap one's foot on the floor impatiently. 不耐烦地用脚敲击地板.

tape /teɪp; teɪp/ n [C, U] 1 (piece, length of) narrow strip of material used for tying up parcels, etc or in dressmaking: (用以捆扎包裹等, 或用于制作女服的)带子; 线带: three yards of linen ~; 三码亚麻带; do up the ~s of an apron into neat bows. 把围裙上的带子打成漂亮的蝴蝶结. '~-measure n length of ~ or strip of thin, flexible metal or of strengthened cloth graduated for measuring things with. 卷尺; 皮尺. '~-worm n

kinds of many-jointed, long, flat worm that lives during its adult stage as a parasite in the intestines of man and other animals. 条虫. 2 ('ticker-)~, narrow strip of paper on which telegraph instruments automatically print news, etc. 电报的收报纸带. '~ insulating ~, strip of sticky cloth used for insulating electrical connections, etc. (使电话接头绝缘的)绝缘包带; 胶带. magnetic ~, strip of a plastic material magnetized to record sound or vision. 录音带; 录影带. red ~, ⇨ red, adj(3). '~ deck, ~ recorder (without amplifiers or speakers) as a component in a hi-fi system. (高度传真系统中的)录音座(但无扬声器). '~-recorder n apparatus for recording sound on, and playing sound back from, this kind of ~. 录音机. 3 length of ~ stretched between the winningposts on a race-track: (拉在跑道终点的)终点线: breast the ~, reach and pass this ~. 抵达终点; 冲过终点. □ vt [VP6A] 1 fasten, tie together, with ~. 以带系、捆、扎. 2 record (sound) on magnetic ~. 录(音). 3 (colloq) have sth/sb ~d, understand it/him thoroughly. (口)彻底了解某事物(某人).

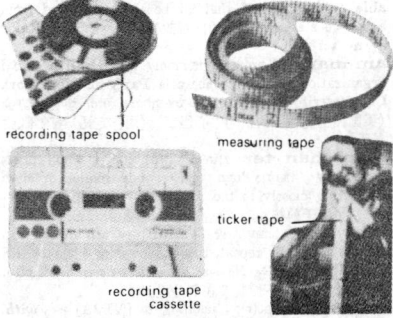

recording tape spool measuring tape

ticker tape

recording tape cassette

tapes

taper¹ /ˈteɪpə(r); ˈtepɚ/ n [C] length of thread with a covering of wax, burnt to give a light; very slender candle. 蜡(烛)心; 小蜡烛.

taper² /ˈteɪpə(r); ˈtepɚ/ vt, vi [VP6A, 15B, 2A, C] make or become gradually narrower towards one end: (使)逐渐向一端尖削; 渐尖: One end ~s/is ~ed off to a point. 一端逐渐变细成一尖头.

tap·es·try /ˈtæpɪstrɪ; ˈtæpɪstrɪ/ n (pl -ries) [C, U] (piece of) cloth into which threads of coloured wool are woven by hand to make designs and pictures, used for covering walls and furniture. (一块)绣帷; 缀锦; 挂帷; 挂毯. tap·es·tried adj hung, decorated, with ~: 挂有绣帷或挂毯的; 以绣帷或挂毯装饰的: tapestried walls. 挂有绣帷的墙.

tapi·oca /ˌtæpɪˈəʊkə; ˌtæpɪˈokə/ n [U] starchy food (in the form of hard, white grains) from the root of the cassava plant. 木薯淀粉; 树葛粉; 珍粉(一种淀粉质食料, 自木薯根中提取, 呈坚硬白粒状).

ta·pir /ˈteɪpə(r); ˈtepɚ/ n pig-like animal of Central and S America with a long, flexible nose. (产于中南美洲的)貘.

taps /tæps; tæps/ ⇨ tap²(2).

tap·ster /ˈtæpstə(r); ˈtæpstɚ/ n person employed to draw and serve beer, spirits. etc. 酒保. ⇨ tap-room at tap¹(1).

tar¹ /tɑː(r); tɑr/ n [U] black substance, hard when cold, thick and sticky when warm, obtained from coal, etc used to preserve timber (eg in fences and posts), in making roads, etc. 焦油; 柏油; 木焦油; 沥青(用以保护木材; 筑路等). tarmacadam = tarmac. □ vt (-rr-) [VP6A] cover with tar. 铺以柏油; 以柏油覆盖. tar and feather sb, put tar on him and then cover with

feathers as a punishment. 将某人涂以柏油然后覆以羽毛 (作为一种处罚)。 ***tarred with the same brush,*** having the same faults. 具有相同的缺点。

tar² /tɑ:(r)/; tɑr/ n (**Jack**) **tar,** (dated colloq) sailor. (过时口语)水手；水兵。

tara·diddle /'tærədɪdl US: 'tærə'dɪdl; 'tærə,dɪdl/ n (colloq) untruth; fib. (口)虚言；谎话。

tar·an·tella /ˌtærən'telə; ˌtærən'tɛlə/, **tar·an·telle** /-'tel; -'tɛl/ nn [C] (music for a) rapid, whirling Italian dance for two persons. 塔兰台拉舞(意大利的一种快速旋动的二人舞)；塔兰台拉舞曲。

ta·ran·tula /tə'ræntjulə US: -tʃulə; tə'ræntʃələ/ n large, hairy, poisonous spider of S Europe; other kinds of spider. (南欧产的)一种大而带毛的毒蜘蛛；袋蜘蛛类。

tar·boosh /tɑ:'bu:ʃ; tɑr'buʃ/ n brimless felt cap like a fez, worn by some Muslim men. (有些伊斯兰教徒戴的)无沿毡帽。

tardy /'tɑ:dɪ; 'tɑrdɪ/ adj (**-ier, -iest**) **1** slow; slow-moving; coming or done late: 缓慢的；缓缓移动的；迟来的；迟做的: ~ *progress/repentance;* 缓慢的进步(为时已晚的忏悔); ~ *in offering help.* 帮助提供得太慢。 **2** (US) late: (美)迟的；晚的: *be ~ for school.* 上学迟到。 **tar·dily** /-ɪlɪ; -ɪlɪ/ adv **tar·di·ness** n.

tare¹ /teə(r); tɛr/ n (Biblical; usu pl) weed growing among corn. (圣经;通常用复数)稗子；莠草。

tare² /teə(r); tɛr/ n allowance made to a purchaser for the weight of the vehicle carrying the commodity he has brought or for the weight of the container in which the commodity is packed, in cases where the commodity is weighed together with the vehicle or container; weight of a motor-vehicle, etc without fuel. 皮重；包装重量(货物与搬运工具或包装容器同时过秤时,在商品重量上对购买者所作的折让);(汽车等除去燃料的)车身重；净重；空重。

tar·get /'tɑ:gɪt; 'tɑrgɪt/ n **1** sth to be aimed at in shooting-practice; any object aimed at. 标的;靶;鹄。 ⇨ the illus at **archery.** 参看 archery 之插图。 **2** thing, plan, etc against which criticism is directed: 被批评的事物、计划等; 批评目标: *This book will be the ~ of bitter criticism.* 这本书将受到严厉的批评。 **3** objective (set for savings, production, etc); total which it is desired to reach. (储蓄,生产等的)目标;欲达到的总数。

tar·iff /'tærɪf; 'tærɪf/ n [C] **1** list of fixed charges, esp for meals, rooms, etc at a hotel; price-list. 价目表(尤指旅馆的餐金、房间等的)。 **2** list of taxes on goods imported or (less often) exported; tax on a particular class of imported goods: 进出口货物(较少指出口货物)课税表;某一类货物进口税或关税: *raise ~ walls against foreign goods.* (try to) exclude them by means of import taxes; 建立关税壁垒以抵制舶来品; ~ *reform,* movement (esp in GB, 19th century) to get rid of inequalities in ~s. 关税改革(尤指十九世纪英国所推行者)。

tar·mac /'tɑ:mæk; 'tɑrmæk/ n [U] mixture of tar and gravel, used for the surfaces of paths, roads, aircraft runways, etc. 柏油碎石(用以铺道路,飞机跑道等)。

tarn /tɑ:n; tɑrn/ n small mountain lake. 山中的小湖。

tar·nish /'tɑ:nɪʃ; 'tɑrnɪʃ/ vi, vt [VP6A, 2A] (of metal surfaces) lose, cause the loss of, brightness: (尤指金属表面)失去光泽或使失去光泽: *The damp atmosphere has ~ed the gilt.* 潮湿的空气已使镀金表面失去光泽。 *Chromium does not ~ easily.* 铬不易失去光泽。 *His reputation is ~ed.* 他的名誉受到玷污了。 □ n dullness; loss of polish. 暗晦;失去光彩。

taro /'tɑ:rəʊ; 'tɑro/ n (pl ~**s** -rəʊz; -roz/) kinds of tropical plant with a starchy root used as food, esp in the Pacific islands. 芋;芋头(热带植物,根富淀粉,用作食品,尤产于太平洋诸岛)。

tar·pau·lin /tɑ:'pɔ:lɪn; tɑr'pɔlɪn/ n (1) [U] (sheet or cover of) canvas made waterproof, esp by being tarred: (一块)防水帆布;柏油防水帆布;防水帆布罩;雨布(罩): *cover the goods on the lorry with a ~.* 用防水帆布

遮盖卡车上的货物。

tar·pon /'tɑ:pɒn US: -pən; 'tɑrpɑn/ n large fish found in the warmer parts of the Atlantic Ocean. (产于大西洋温暖区域的)海鲢。

tarra·diddle n = taradiddle.

tar·ra·gon /'tærəgən US: -gɒn; 'tærə,gɑn/ n [U] herb with sharp-tasting leaves, used in salads and for flavouring vinegar (~ *vinegar*). 龙蒿(草木植物,叶有辛辣味,用于做色拉,并用于增醋味,用此增强的醋称为 ~ vinegar)。

tarry¹ /'tɑ:rɪ; 'tɑrɪ/ adj covered, sticky, with tar. 涂有柏油的;因涂有柏油而粘粘的。

tarry² /'tærɪ; 'tærɪ/ vi (archaic or liter) (古或文) [VP2A, B, C] **1** stay, remain, lodge: 停留; 逗留;住: ~ *a few days at/in a place;* 在某处小住几天; ~ *(behind) for sb.* 等待某人。 **2** be slow in coming, going, appearing. 担搁;迟延。

tar·sal /'tɑ:sl; 'tɑrsl/ adj (anat) of the bones in the ankle. (解剖)跗骨的。 □ n (anat) bone in the ankle. (解剖)跗骨。 ⇨ the illus at **skeleton.** 参看 skeleton 之插图。

tar·sus /'tɑ:səs; 'tɑrsəs/ n (pl **tarsi** -saɪ; -saɪ/) (anat) collection of seven small bones in the ankle. (解剖)跗;跗骨(由七块小骨聚合而成)。

tart¹ /tɑ:t; tɑrt/ adj acid, sharp in taste; (fig) sharp: 酸的;辛辣的;(喻)尖酸的;尖刻的: ~ *fruit;* 酸的果子; *a ~ flavour;* 酸味; ~ *humour;* 尖酸的诙谐; *a ~ manner/disposition.* 尖刻的态度(性情)。 ~**·ly** adv ~**·ness** n.

tart² /tɑ:t; tɑrt/ n **1** fruit pie. 水果馅饼。 **2** circle of pastry cooked with fruit or jam on it. (上面有水果或果酱的)小圆饼。

tart³ /tɑ:t; tɑrt/ n (derog sl) prostitute. (贬,俚)妓女。 □ vt [VP15B] ~ *sth/sb up,* (colloq) make gaudy; add superficial attractions to; smarten. (口)使某物或某人变得俗丽;增加外表的吸引力;使漂亮。

tar·tan /'tɑ:tn; 'tɑrtn/ n [U] Scottish woollen fabric woven with coloured crossing stripes; [C] particular pattern of ~, eg of a Scottish clan. 苏格兰格子呢;有某种图案的格子呢(如苏格兰某一氏族者)。 ⇨ the illus at **kilt.** 参看 kilt 之插图。

tar·tar¹ /'tɑ:tə(r); 'tɑrtə/ n [U] **1** chalk-like substance deposited on the teeth. 齿垢;齿石;牙砂。 **2** substance deposited on the sides of casks from fermented wine. (由于盛发酵的酒而积附于酒桶侧的)酒石。 **cream of ~,** purified form of this, used with baking soda to make baking powder. 酸性酒石;酒石酸氢钾(与小苏打合制发酵粉)。 ~**ic** /tɑ:'tærɪk; tɑr'tærɪk/ **acid,** acid of ~, found in the juice of grapes, oranges, etc (used in making baking powder, etc). 酒石酸(含于葡萄汁、桔汁等中的一种酸,用制发酵粉等)。

tar·tar² /'tɑ:tə(r); 'tɑrtə/ n rough, violent, troublesome person. 粗暴而难处的人; 慓悍的人。 *catch a ~,* have to deal with a person of this kind, esp one who is more than one's match. 遭遇顽强对手;碰到强敌。

tar·tar³ /'tɑ:tə(r); 'tɑrtə/ n ~ **sauce,** cold mayonnaise with chopped onions, herbs, gherkins, pickles, etc. 塔塔(辣)酱油(冷蛋黄酱加碎洋葱、香料、小黄瓜及泡菜等合制而成)。

task /tɑ:sk US: tæsk; tæsk/ n [C] piece of (esp hard) work (to be) done: 任务;工作;作业;课业等(尤指困难者): *set a boy a ~.* 分派男孩一项工作。 *She finds housekeeping an irksome ~.* 她发现操持家务是一项令人厌烦的工作。 *take sb to ~ (about/for sth),* scold him: 斥责或责备某人: *take sb to ~ for arriving late.* 责备某人之迟到。 '~**force** n specially organized unit (of warships, etc) for a special purpose. 特遣部队; 特遣舰队。 (**hard**) '~**master/-mistress** nn (strict) overseer. (严厉的)男(女)监工。 □ vt [VP6A] (of a ~) put a strain on: 使负担: *Mathematics ~s that boy's brain.* 数学使那男孩大感吃力。

tas·sel /'tæsl; 'tæsl/ n bunch of threads, etc tied

together at one end and hanging (from a flag, hat, etc) as an ornament. (旗、帽等垂下的)缨;缨;流苏. ⇨ the illus at **kilt**. 参看 kilt 之插图. **~·led** (US = **~ed**) *adj* having a ~. 有缨的;有流苏的.

taste[1] /teɪst; test/ *n* **1 the ~**, sense by which flavour is known: 味觉: *sweet/sour to the ~*. 尝起来是甜(酸)的. '**~ bud** *n* group of cells in the tongue for this sense. 味蕾(舌上的味觉细胞). ⇨ the illus at **mouth**. 参看 mouth 之插图. **2** [C, U] quality of a substance made known by this sense, eg by putting some on the tongue: (某物的)味; 味道: *Sugar has a sweet ~*. 糖有甜味. *I don't like the ~ of this mixture*. 我不喜欢这混合物的味道. *This medicine has no/very little/not much/a queer ~*. 这药没有 (很少, 不大有, 有一股怪)味道. *leave a bad/nasty '~ in the mouth*, (lit or fig) be followed by a feeling of dislike or disgust. (字面或喻)留下一种嫌恶的感觉. **3** (usu 通常作 *a ~ (of)*) small quantity (of sth to eat or drink, or fig): 小量; 少量; 一口(指饮食或作比喻用法): *Won't you have a ~ of this cake/wine?* 你不尝一点这糕饼(酒)吗? *Give him a ~ of the whip*, enough to be a sample of what it feels like to be whipped. 让他尝鞭子的滋味. **4** [C, U] **~ (for)**, liking or preference for: 爱好; 嗜好: *He has a ~ for French cigarettes*. 他喜欢法国香烟. *She has expensive ~s in clothes*. 她爱好昂贵重的衣服. *There's no accounting for ~s*, We cannot explain why different people like different things. 嗜好是无法解释的(各人有不同的嗜好, 无法解释). *Abstract art is not to his ~/not to the ~ of everyone*. 抽象艺术不合他的口味(并非人人喜爱). **5** [U] ability to enjoy beauty. esp in art and literature; ability to form judgements about these; ability to behave in the most appropriate and pleasing way: (尤指对艺术及文学的)审美力; 鉴赏力; 欣赏力; 判断力; 举止适度宜人: *She has excellent ~ in dress/dresses in perfect ~*. 她对衣着有极好的鉴赏力(她穿着极佳). *It would be bad ~ to refuse their invitation*. 拒绝他们的邀请是不礼貌的. **(be) in good/bad/poor/excellent, etc ~**, (be, be done, etc) showing this ability well/badly, etc. 有良好的(坏的,差的,极佳的)审美力或风度. **(be) in the best/worst of ~**, (be, be done, etc) showing this ability in the best/worst way. 鉴赏力或风度极佳的(极差的). **~·ful** /-fl; -fəl/ *adj* showing good ~(5). 有良好审美力、鉴赏力等的; 举止高雅的. **~·fully** /-fəlɪ; -fəlɪ/ *adv* in a ~ful manner: 有良好审美力、鉴赏力等地; 举止高雅地: *~fully decorated with flowers*. 用花装饰得雅致的. **~·less** *adj* **1** (of food) having no ~ or flavour. (指食物)无味的. **2** without ~(5); in bad ~(5). 无鉴赏力、审美力等的; 举止庸俗的. **~·less·ly** *adv* **tasty** *adj* (**-ier, -iest**) having a pleasant flavour; pleasing to the ~. 味美的; 可口的. **tast·ily** /-ɪlɪ; -ɪlɪ/ *adv*

taste[2] /teɪst; test/ *vt, vi* **1** [VP6A, 2A] (not in the progressive tenses; often with *can, could*) be aware of the taste of sth: (不用进行时; 常与 can, could 连用)认出或辨别出某物的味道; 尝出; 品尝: *Can you ~ anything strange in this soup?* 你尝得出这汤里有什么怪味道吗? *If you have a bad cold you cannot ~ (anything)*. 如果你患重感冒, 你尝不出(任何东西的)味道. **2** [VP3A, 2D] **~ (of)**, have a particular taste or flavour: 有某种特殊的味道: *~ sour/bitter/sweet*. 有酸(苦,甜)味. *It ~s too much of garlic/spice*. 这东西大蒜(香料)的味道太重. **3** [VP6A] test the ~ of: 尝…的味道; 试…的味道: *The cook ~d the soup to see whether he had put enough salt in it*. 厨师尝汤的味道, 看看盐放的够不够. **4** [VP6A] (fig) experience: (喻)体验; 领略: *~ happiness/the joys of freedom*. 领略幸福(自由的快乐). **~ of**, (liter) know; experience. (文)知道; 经验. **~r** *n* person who is employed to judge teas, wines, etc by ~: 受雇品尝茶、酒等以鉴定其品质的人; 品尝员: *A wine-~r doesn't swallow what he ~s*. 尝酒员才不吞下所品尝的酒.

tat[1] /tæt; tæt/ *vi, vt* (**-tt-**) do tatting; make by tatting. 梭织; 用梭织法编织.

tat[2] /tæt; tæt/ *n* [U] quality of being tatty; tatty person or thing. 不整洁; 邋遢; 不整洁的人或物.

tat[2] /tæt; tæt/ *n* ⇨ **tit**[2].

ta ta /ˌtæ 'tɑ:; ˈtɑ,tɑ/ *int* (baby language) goodbye. (儿语)再会.

tat·ter /ˈtætə(r); ˈtætɚ/ *n* (usu *pl*) rag; piece of cloth, paper, etc torn off or hanging loosely from sth: (通常用复数)破布; 褴褛; (撕下或悬垂的)纸片、布片等: *in ~s*, in rags or torn strips; 破烂; 褴褛: *tear sb's reputation to ~s*, (fig) destroy it. (喻)破坏某人名誉. **~ed** *adj* ragged. 破烂的; 褴褛的. **~·de·ma·lion** /ˌtætədɪ-ˈmeɪliən; ˌtætədɪˈmeljən/ *n* sb dressed in ~s. 衣衫褴褛的人.

tat·ting /ˈtætɪŋ; ˈtætɪŋ/ *n* [U] (art or process of making a) kind of handmade knotted lace-work used for trimming. 梭织; 梭织法; 梭织的花边.

tattle /ˈtætl; ˈtætl/ *vi, vt* [VP2A] chatter, gossip, prattle. 闲谈; 聊天; 空谈. □ *n* [U] idle talk. 闲谈; 聊天; 空谈. **~·tler** /ˈtætlə(r); ˈtætlɚ/ *n* person who ~s. 闲谈者; 聊天者; 空谈者.

tat·too[1] /təˈtu: US: tæˈtu:; tæˈtu/ *n* (*pl* **~s**) **1** (sing only) beating of drum(s) to call soldiers back to quarters; hour at which a ~ is sounded: (仅用单数)归营鼓; 击归营鼓的时刻: *beat/sound the ~*. 击(鸣)归营鼓. **2** [C] continuous tapping: 连续的轻击: *He was beating a ~ on the table with his fingers*. 他用手指在桌上连续轻击. **3** [C] public entertainment, usu at night (often 常作 *torchlight ~*) with music and marching, by soldiers. 军队的游行(通常在夜晚, 配以音乐行进).

tat·too[2] /təˈtu: US: tæˈtu:; tæˈtu/ *vt* [VP6A] mark (sb's skin) with a permanent picture or pattern by pricking it and putting in dyes or stains; put (a picture or pattern) on the skin thus: 文刺(某人的皮肤); 刺染(图案)于皮肤上; 文身: *The sailor had a ship ~ed on his arm*. 那水手在手臂上刺着一只船. □ *n* [C] (*pl* **~s**) picture or pattern of this kind. 文身; 刺花; 黥墨.

tatty /ˈtætɪ; ˈtætɪ/ *adj* (**-ier, -iest**) (sl) untidy and shabby looking; tawdry. (俚)样子不整洁的; 邋遢的; 俗丽的. **tat·tily** /-ɪlɪ; -ɪlɪ/ *adv*

taught /tɔːt; tɔt/ *pt, pp* of **teach**.

taunt /tɔːnt; tɔnt/ *n* [C] remark intended to hurt sb's feelings; contemptuous reproach: 辱骂; 讥笑: *endure the ~s of a successful rival*. 忍受一位成功敌手的辱骂. □ *vt* [VP6A, 14] **~ sb (with sth)**, attack (sb) with ~s: 辱骂; 讥笑: *They ~ed the boy with cowardice/with being a coward*. 他们讥笑那男孩胆怯(是懦夫). **~·ing·ly** *adv*

Taurus /ˈtɔːrəs; ˈtɔrəs/ *n* (astrol) second sign of the zodiac. (天文)黄道第二宫; 金牛宫; 金牛座. ⇨ the illus at **zodiac**. 参看 zodiac 之插图.

taut /tɔːt; tɔt/ *adj* (of ropes, wires, etc) tightly stretched; (of muscles and fig) of nerves) tense. (指绳索、金属线等) 拉紧的; (指肌肉, 喻)指神经)紧张的. **~·ly** *adv* **~·ness** *n*

taut·ol·ogy /tɔːˈtɒlədʒɪ; ˌtɔˈtɑlədʒɪ/ *n* [U] the saying of the same thing again in different ways without making one's meaning clearer or more forceful; needless repetition; (U) (*pl* **-gies**) instance of this. 同义反复; 无谓的重复; 赘言. **tauto·logi·cal** /ˌtɔːtəˈlɒdʒɪkl; ˌtɔtə-ˈlɑdʒɪkl/ *adj*

tav·ern /ˈtævən; ˈtævɚn/ *n* (archaic or liter) inn or public house. (古或文)客栈; 旅店; 酒店.

taw·dry /ˈtɔːdrɪ; ˈtɔdrɪ/ *adj* (**-ier, -iest**) showy; brightly coloured or decorated, but cheap or in bad taste: 俗丽的; 鲜丽而廉价的; 庸俗的: *~ jewellery/dresses*. 俗丽的珠宝(衣服). **taw·drily** /-əlɪ; -ɪlɪ/ *adv* **taw·dri·ness** *n*

tawny /ˈtɔːnɪ; ˈtɔnɪ/ *adj* brownish yellow. 黄褐色的; 茶色的.

tawse /tɔːz; tɔz/ *n* [C] (Scot) leather strap for punishing children. (苏)打孩子用的皮鞭.

tax /tæks; tæks/ *n* **1** [C, U] (sum of) money (to be)

paid by citizens (according to income, value of purchases, etc) to the government for public purposes: 税; 税额: *state/local taxes;* 国(地方)税; *levy a tax on sth;* 课某物之税; *direct taxes,* ie on income; 直接税(即所得税); *indirect taxes,* eg paid when one buys goods. 间接税(如货物税). *How much income tax did you pay last year?* 去年你缴了多少所得税? *He paid £50 in taxes.* 他付了税金五十镑. '**tax-collector** n official who collects taxes. 税务员;收税员. '**tax-payer** n person who pays taxes. 纳税人. ,**tax-'free** *adj* **(a)** not subject to taxation. 免税的. **(b)** (of dividends or interest) on which tax has been deducted before distribution. (指股利或利息)已先行扣缴税金的. **2** *a tax on,* sth that is a burden or strain: 负担;重负. *a tax on one's strength/ health/patience.* 对某人体力(健康,耐心)的一项负担. □ *vt* **1** [VP6A] put a tax(1) on; require (a person) to pay a tax: 课税于;抽税;征税: *tax luxuries/incomes/ rich and poor alike.* 课征奢侈品税(课征所得税;贫富同样课税). **2** [VP6A] be a tax(2) on: 为…的负担或重负; 使负重荷: *tax a person's patience,* eg by asking him many silly questions. 使某人不胜其烦(如提出许多愚蠢的问题). **3** [VP14] *tax sb with sth,* accuse him of it: 指控;责备: *tax sb with neglect of/with having neglected his work.* 责备某人疏忽职守. **4** (legal) examine and decide, eg costs of a lawsuit. (法律)判定; 评定(如诉讼费用). **tax-able** /-əbl; -əbl/ *adj* capable of being taxed. 可课以税的;应课税的. **tax-abil-ity** /,tæksə'bɪlətɪ; ,tæksə'bɪrətɪ/ n **tax-ation** /tæk'seɪʃn; tæk'eʃən/ n [U] (system of) raising money by taxes; taxes (to be) paid: 课税;税制;征税;税: *reduce taxation;* 减税; *grumble at high taxation.* 抱怨重税.

taxi /'tæksɪ; 'tæksɪ/ n (pl ~s) (also 亦作 '~-cab, usu abbr to 通常略作 cab, esp in US 尤用于美国) motor-car, esp one with a ~meter, which may be hired for journeys. 出租汽车;计程车. '~-meter n (usu abbr to 通常略作 meter) device which automatically records the fare during a journey in a ~. 计程表;计程器;计价表. '~ rank, place where ~s wait to be hired. 计程车候客处. □ *vi, vt* [VP2C, 15A] (of an aircraft) (cause to) move on wheels along the ground (or on floats, etc on the surface of water): (指飞机)(使)在地面或水面滑行: *The plane ~ed/was taxiing along the runway.* 飞机在跑道上滑行.

taxi-dermy /'tæksɪdɜːmɪ; 'tæksə,dɝmɪ/ n [U] art of preparing and stuffing the skins of animals, birds and fish so that they look as they did when living. (动物标本的)剥制术. **taxi-der-mist** /-ɪst; -ɪst/ n person who practises ~. 剥制动物标本的人;标本剥制家.

tax-on-omy /tæk'sɒnəmɪ; tæks'ɑnəmɪ/ n [U, C] (principles of) classification. 分类;分类学.

tea /tiː; ti/ n **1** [U] (dried leaves of an) evergreen shrub of eastern Asia, Africa, etc; drink made by pouring boiling water on these leaves: 茶叶;茶树;(泡成的)茶; *a pound of tea;* 一磅茶叶; *Ceylon/China, etc tea;* 锡兰(中国等)茶; *a cup of tea;* 一杯茶; *make (the) tea,* prepare it. 泡茶;沏茶. *not my cup of tea,* (fig) not the sort of thing I like. (喻)不是我所喜欢的事物. '**tea-bag** n small porous bag holding enough tea-leaves for use in a teacup or teapot. 茶袋(装有少量茶叶的有孔小袋,置茶杯或茶壶中用之). '**tea-break** n (in an office, factory, etc) short period when work is stopped for tea drinking. 喝茶时间(办公室、工厂等处,让工作人员喝茶的短暂休息时间). '**tea-caddy** n (pl -dies) air-tight box in which to keep a supply of tea for daily use. 茶罐;茶筒. '**tea-cake** n small, flat, sweetened cake, usu eaten hot with butter at tea. 茶饼(扁平的甜饼,通常在饮茶时趁热加奶油食之). '**tea-chest** n large wooden box in which tea is packed for export. 茶箱(装运茶叶出口的大木箱). '**tea-cloth** n **(a)** cloth to be spread on a tea-table or tea-tray. 茶几布;茶盘布. **(b)** tea-towel. 擦拭茶具用的抹布. '**tea-cosy** n cover for keeping the contents of a teapot warm. 茶壶保温罩;茶壶暖罩. '**tea-cup** n cup in

which tea is served. 茶杯. *a storm in a teacup,* a lot of fuss about sth trivial. 因小事而引起的风波; 小题大做。 '**tea-garden** n **(a)** garden in which tea and other refreshments are served to the public. 露天茶馆. **(b)** tea plantation. 茶圃;茶园. '**tea-house** n (in Japan and China) restaurant where tea is served. (日本及中国等处的)茶馆. '**tea-kettle** n one in which water is boiled for making tea. (烧水沏茶的)茶壶;开水壶. '**tea-leaf** n (usu pl; -leaves) one of the leaves in a teapot after tea has been made, or left in a teacup after drinking: (茶壶里或茶杯中泡开的)茶叶或茶叶渣: *tell sb's fortune from the tea-leaves in her cup.* 借察看她杯中的茶叶渣为其算命. '**tea-party** n social gathering for afternoon tea. 茶会(下午举行的社交集会). '**tea-pot** n vessel in which tea is made. (沏茶的)茶壶. '**tea-room** n restaurant in which tea and light refreshments may be obtained. 茶室(贩卖茶及点心处). '**tea-service/-set** n set of cups, saucers, plates, with a teapot, milk-jug, etc. 一套茶具. '**tea-spoon** n small spoon for stirring tea. (搅茶用的)茶匙. '**tea-spoon-ful** /-ful; -ful/ n as much as a teaspoon can hold. 一茶匙之量. '**tea-strainer** n device for keeping back tea-leaves when pouring tea into a cup. 滤茶网;滤茶器. '**tea-table** n (usu small) table at which tea is served: (通常为小的)茶几;茶桌: (attrib) (用作定语) '**tea-table** conversation. 茶话. '**tea-things** n pl (colloq) tea-set as needed for a meal: (口)茶具: *put the tea-things on the table.* 把茶具放在桌上. '**tea-time** n [U] time at which tea is usu taken in the afternoon. 喝(下午)茶时间. '**tea-towel** n cloth for drying washed crockery, cutlery, etc. 擦干陶器,餐具等的抹布. '**tea-tray** n one on which a tea-set is used or carried. 茶盘. '**tea-trolley** n tea-wagon. (有脚轮的)茶具台. '**tea-urn** n urn in which water is boiled for making tea in quantity, eg in a café. (泡大量茶用的)大型茶壶. '**tea-wagon** n small table on wheels, used for serving tea. (有脚轮的)茶具台. **2** [C, U] occasion (in the late afternoon) at which tea is drunk: 下午茶; 午后茶点: *We have tea at/Tea is at half-past four.* 我们在四点半喝下午茶. *They were having/at tea when I called.* 我去访时他们在喝下午茶. *The waitress has served twenty teas since four o'clock.* 这位女侍四点钟起已供应了二十份下午茶. **high tea,** meal taken between lunch and supper if a dinner is not taken in the evening (usu a more substantial meal than afternoon tea as taken by people who have dinner in the evening). 大下午茶(正餐不在晚上的人们,于下午五六点钟所进食的简便小餐,较一般下午茶丰盛).

teach /tiːtʃ; titʃ/ vt, vi (pt, pp **taught** /tɔːt; tɔt/) [VP6A, 11, 12A, 13A, 17, 20, 21, 2A, B, C] give instruction to (sb); cause (sb) to know or be able to do sth; give to sb (knowledge, skill, etc); give lessons (at school, etc); do this for a living: 教(某人); 使(某人)知道做某事; 教授(知识、技能等);(在学校等)授课;教书维持生活: ~ *children;* 教小孩子们; ~ *French/ history, etc;* 教授法文(历史等); ~ *a child (how) to swim.* 教小孩(如何)游泳. *He has taught his dog to perform some clever tricks.* 他已经训练他的狗玩几样灵巧的把戏. *Who taught you German?* 谁教你德文? *She is ~ing the piano to several of the village children.* 她教几个村子里的儿童弹钢琴. *He ~es for a living.* 他以教书为生. *He has taught four hours already this morning.* 今天早上他已经上了四小时的课. *I'll ~ you (not) to …,* (colloq, used as a threat) I'll show the risk or penalty of … . (口,用作威吓语)你如果(如果不)…我可要教训你. '*~-in* n (colloq) discussion of a subject of topical interest (as held in a college, with students, staff and other speakers). (口)时事问题讨论(如大学中由学生、教师及其他演讲者所举行的讨论). *~-able* /-əbl; -əbl/ *adj* that can be taught. 可教的;肯学的. *~er* n person who ~es. 教师;老师;教员. *~ing* n **1** [U] work of a ~er: 教师的工作;教导;教授: *earn a living by ~ing.* 靠教书维持生活. **2** [U, C] that which is taught: 所教的

东西; 教训; 教义; 训示: the ~ing(s) of Buddha. 佛陀的教训.

teak /tiːk/ tik/ n tall, evergreen tree of India, Burma, Malaysia, etc; [U] its hard wood, used for making furniture, in shipbuilding, etc. (印度、缅甸、马来西亚等地的)柚木树; 其坚硬木材; 柚木(用于制造家具、船等).

teal /tiːl/ tiːl/ n (pl unchanged) kinds of small wild duck living on rivers and lakes. (复数不变)小野鸭; 小凫.

team /tiːm/ tim/ n [C] **1** two or more oxen, horses, etc pulling a cart, plough, etc together. (共同拉车、拉犁等的)一组牛、马等; 联畜. **2** number of persons playing together and forming one side in some games, eg football, cricket, hockey, and in some sports, eg relay races; group of people working together: 运动比赛的队(如足球、板球、曲棍球及接力赛跑等); 在一起工作的队、组等: the players in my ~, my fellow players. 我队的选手. '~-work n [U] combined effort; organized co-operation: 协力工作; 同队工作; 有组织的合作: succeed by means of good ~-work. 借良好的协力合作而成功。□ spirit, spirit in which each member of a ~ thinks of the success, etc of the ~ and not of personal advantage, glory, etc. 团队精神; 合作精神。□ vi [VP2C] ~ up (with sb), (colloq) make an effort in co-operation (with); work together (with). (口)(与…)协力从事; (与…)合作。□ '~-ster /'tiːmstə(r)/ 'timstə/ n driver of a ~ of animals; (US) truck-driver. 驾驭联畜者; (美)卡车司机.

tear¹ /tɪə(r)/ tir/ n [C] drop of salty water coming from the eye: 泪; 泪水; 泪珠: Her eyes filled with ~s. 她的眼睛里充满了泪水。The sad story moved us to ~s, made us cry. 这个悲惨故事使我们感动得流泪。The girl burst into ~s, ~s began to flow from her eyes. 那女孩子哭起来了。They all laughed till ~s came. 他们全都笑出眼泪来了。Molly was teasing the cat, eg by pulling its tail. 莫利在逗弄猫. **2** [VP6A, 15B] pick up into separate fibres; fluff up the surface of (cloth, etc) by doing this: 梳理; 使(布等)的表面起毛: ~ flax/wool. 梳绒亚麻(羊毛)。□ n person who is fond of teasing others: 好揶揄他人者; 嘲弄者; 逗弄者: What a ~ she is! 她真好揶揄别人! ~r n **1** person who often ~s or who is fond of teasing. 好揶揄他人者; 嘲弄者. **2** (colloq) difficult question or task; puzzling problem. (口)困难的问题或工作; 令人困惑的难题。teas·ing·ly adv in a teasing manner; in order to ~. 揶揄地; 嘲弄地.

tea·sel, tea·zel, teazle /'tiːzl/ 'tizl/ n (kinds of plant with) large prickly flower with hooked points (used formerly for teasing cloth, etc). 起绒草; 起绒草的球花(昔时用来使布等表面起绒毛).

teat /tiːt/ tit/ n nipple. 奶嘴; 乳头; 奶头。➪ the illus at domestic. 参看 domestic 之插图.

tec /tek/ tek/ n (sl abbr for) detective. (俚)侦探(为detective 之略).

tech /tek/ tek/ n (colloq abbr for) technical college. (口)工(艺)学院; 工艺学校(为 technical college 之略).

tech·ni·cal /'teknɪkl/ 'teknɪkl/ adj **1** of, connected with, the execution of a work of art (as contrasted with general considerations of the form of the work): 技术上的; 技巧方面的: ~ difficulties; 技术上的困难: a pianist who has ~ skill but not much feeling. 有专门技巧而无太多感情的钢琴家. **2** of, connected with, a particular art, craft, science, etc: 专门的; 工艺的; 有关工业技术的: ~ terms/training. 专门术语(训练)。□ college, (former name for a) polytechnic. 工艺学院(为polytechnic 之旧称)。~·ly /-klɪ/ adv ~·ity /,teknɪ'kælətɪ/ ,tɛknɪ'kælətɪ/ n (pl -ties) ~(2) word, phrase, point, etc: 专门用词、用语、细节等: The two architects were discussing building ~ities. 这两位建筑师在讨论建筑上的专门问题。The judge explained the legal ~ities of the case to the jury. 法官向陪审员解释该案件涉及法律上的有关名点.

tech·ni·cian /tek'nɪʃn/ tɛk'nɪʃən/ n expert in the technique(s) of a particular art, etc; highly skilled craftsman or mechanic. (精通某一专门技艺的)技术人员; 专门技师; 巧匠.

Tech·ni·color /'teknɪkʌlə(r)/ 'tɛknɪˌkʌlɚ/ n (P) process of colour photography used for cinema films. (商标)电影片的彩色印片法.

tech·nique /tek'niːk/ tɛk'nik/ n **1** [U] technical(1) or mechanical skill in music, painting, etc. (音乐、绘画等的)技巧; 技术. **2** [C] method of doing sth expertly; method of artistic expression in music, painting, etc. 熟练的方法; 工艺法; (音乐、绘画等的)表现法.

tech·noc·racy /tek'nɒkrəsɪ/ tɛk'nɑkrəsɪ/ n [C, U] (pl -cies) (state where there is) organization and management of a country's industrial resources by technical experts. 技术管理(一国之工业资源由技术专家加以组织及管理); 行技术管理的政府. tech·no·crat

tear² /teə(r)/ teɪr/ vt, vi (pt tore /tɔː(r)/ tor/, pp torn /tɔːn/ torn/) **1** [VP6A, 15A, B, 22, 3A] pull sharply apart or to pieces; make (a rent in sth), damage, by pulling sharply: 撕; 撕扯; 撕裂; 扯破: ~ a sheet of paper in two/~ it to pieces/to bits; 把一张纸撕成两半(把它撕成小片、小块); ~ sth up, ~ it into small pieces; 把某物撕碎; ~ one's dress on a nail; 在钉子上挂破了衣服; ~ a hole in one's jacket; 上衣撕破一个洞; wearing old and torn clothes; 穿着又旧又破的衣服; ~ (= hurt, injure, cause to bleed) one's hand on a nail. 在钉子上戳伤了手。He tore (= pulled violently) at the wrapping of the parcel. 他用力撕包裹的包装纸。He tore (= pulled at) his hair with rage. 他愤怒地扯扯头发。He tore the parcel open. 他把包裹撕开. **2** [VP6A, 15A, B] cause (sth) to be out of place (down, off, away, etc) by pulling sharply: 撕下(某物); 撕掉; 扯去(与 down, off, away 等连用): ~ a page out of a book/a notice down from a notice-board/a leaf from a calendar. 撕下一页书(布告牌上的布告, 日历); ~ oneself away (from), leave; stop doing sth: 离开; 停止做某事: She could scarcely ~ herself away from the scene, make up her mind to leave. 她几乎舍不得离去。He could not ~ himself away from his book, couldn't put it down. 他放不下他那本书. **3** [VP6A] (usu passive) destroy the peace of: (通常用被动语态)破坏…的安宁; 扰乱; a country torn by civil war; 因内战而动乱不安的国家; a heart torn by grief. 忧伤的心。torn between, painfully distracted by having to choose between (conflicting demands, wishes, etc). (在相互抵触的愿望、要求等之间)作痛苦的抉择. **4** [VP2A] become torn: 撕碎; 撕裂; 撕破: This material ~s easily. 这料子容易撕破。As I pulled the sheet out of the typewriter it tore. 我把那张纸从打字机上拉出来的时候拉破了. **5** [VP2C] go in excitement or at great speed: 激动地或急速地奔跑; 急奔; 冲: The children tore out of the school gates/were ~ing about in the playground. 孩子们冲出校门(在运动场上奔跑)。He tore down the hill. 他奔跑下山。'~·away adj, n (colloq) impetuous (person). 冲动的(人); 鲁莽的(人)。□ n [C] torn place in sth, eg cloth, paper. 破处; 裂缝(如布、纸上的).

tear³ /tɪə(r)/ tir/ n [C] drop of salty water coming from the eye: 泪; 泪水; 泪珠: Her eyes filled with ~s. 她的眼睛里充满了泪水。The sad story moved us to ~s, made us cry. 这个悲惨故事使我们感动得流泪。The girl burst into ~s, ~s began to flow from her eyes. 那女孩子哭起来了。They all laughed till ~s came. 他们全都笑出眼泪来了。'~-drop n single ~. 泪珠。'~-gas n [U] gas that causes severe watering of the eyes: 催泪性毒气; 催泪瓦斯: '~-gas bombs, as used by the police to disperse a mob of demonstrators, unruly crowds, etc. 催泪弹。~·ful /-fl/ fl/ adj crying; wet with ~s: 哭泣的; 眼泪汪汪的; 为泪水所湿的: a ~ful face; 哭湿的脸; ~ful looks. 含泪的表情。~·fully /-fəlɪ/ -flɪ/ adv ~·less adj without ~s, not weeping: 无泪的; 未哭泣的: The mother stared at her dead baby in a ~less grief, grief that was too deep for ~s. 母亲带着欲哭无泪的深切悲哀凝视着她那死去的婴儿.

/'teknəkræt; 'teknə,kræt/ n supporter, member, of a ～. 支持、拥护技术管理者；行技术管理的政府中的一员。

tech·nol·o·gy /tek'nɒlədʒɪ; tɛk'nɑlədʒi/ n [U] study, mastery and utilization of manufacturing and industrial methods; systematic application of knowledge to practical tasks in industry: 工艺学；工业技术；工艺: the ～ of computers／printing／plastics, etc. 电脑(印刷、塑胶等)之工业技术。**tech·nol·o·gist** /-dʒɪst; -dʒɪst/ n expert in, student of, ～. 工艺专家；工艺学家；工学家。**tech·no·logi·cal** /,teknə'lɒdʒɪkl; ,tɛknə'lɑdʒɪkl/ adj of ～: 工艺(学)的；工学的; technological advances／problems. 工艺的进步(问题)。

techy /'tetʃɪ; 'tɛtʃi/ = tetchy.

teddy bear /'tedɪ beə(r); 'tɛdɪ bɛr/ n child's toy bear stuffed with soft material. 儿童的玩具熊。

Teddy boy /'tedɪ bɔɪ; 'tɛdɪ bɔɪ/, (also colloq 俗亦作 **Ted** /ted; tɛd/) n (GB) teenager (in the 1950's and early 1960's), who expressed opposition to authority by engaging in vicious gang fights and wore clothes like those worn during the reign of Edward VII (1901——1910). (英)(二十世纪五十年代及二十世纪六十年代早期)不良少年；太保(穿着爱德华七世时代(一九○一至一九一○)的衣服，行为泼纵，反抗权威)。

Te Deum /tiː 'diːəm; tɪ'dɪəm/ n (music for a) Latin hymn beginning Te Deum laudamus (meaning 'We praise you, God'), sung at morning service and on special occasions of thanksgiving. 感恩赞美诗(拉丁文赞美诗，开头为 Te Deum laudamus '我们赞美你，上帝'，于早祷及特殊感恩场合唱之)；此种赞美诗的乐曲。

tedi·ous /'tiːdɪəs; 'tidɪəs/ adj tiresome; wearying; uninteresting: 沉闷的；厌烦的；乏味的: a ～ lecture(r); 沉闷的演说(者); ～ work. 乏味的工作。**～·ly** adv **～·ness** n **te·dium** /'tiːdɪəm; 'tidɪəm/ n [U] ～ness; monotony; boredom. 沉闷；单调；乏味。

tee /tiː; ti/ n 1 (golf) place from which a player starts in playing a hole; small pile of sand, or specially shaped piece of wood, plastic, etc, on which the ball is placed before the player drives used instead of such a pile of sand. (高尔夫)开球处；球座(发球时放置球的小沙堆等；用以代替此种沙堆者之小块木材或塑胶等)。'**tee-shirt** n = T-shirt, ⇨ **T.** 2 mark aimed at in certain games, such as quoits. 套圈或掷环游戏的目标。**to a tee／T**, perfectly; exactly. 完美地；正确地。□ vt, vi 1 [VP 2C, 15B] tee (the ball) up, put (the ball) on a tee(1). 置(高尔夫球)于球座上。2 [VP2A] tee off, drive from a tee. 自球座击球。

teem¹ /tiːm; tim/ vi 1 [VP2C] be present in large numbers: 大量出现；有很多: Fish ～ in this river. 这条河中鱼很多。2 [VP3A] ～ with, have in great numbers: 有很多；充满；富于: The lakeside ～ed with gnats and mosquitoes. 湖滨充满蚊蚋。His head is ～ing with bright ideas. 他的脑子里有很多聪明的主意。

teem² /tiːm; tim/ vi [VP2A, C, 3A] ～ (down) (with), (of rain, etc) fall heavily; pour: (指雨等)倾盆暴降: It was ～ing with rain／a ～ing wet day. 大雨倾盆(下大雨的日子)。The rain was ～ing down. 大雨倾盆。

teens /tiːnz; tinz/ n pl the ages of 13 to 19. 十三至十九的年龄: girls in their ～, between the ages of 13 and 19 inclusive. 少女，十三至十九岁的女孩子。She's still in／not yet out of her ～, is under 20. 她还不到二十岁。

teen·age /'tiːneɪdʒ; 'tinɪdʒ/ adj of or for a teenager: 青少年的: teenage fashions／problems. 青少年的风尚(问题)。**teen·ager** /'tiːneɪdʒə(r); 'tin,edʒɚ/ n boy or girl in his or her ～; (loosely) young person up to 21 or 22 years of age: 青少年(十三至十九岁的少年男女)；(不严格地指)十三至二十一或二十二的年轻人: a club for teenagers. 青少年俱乐部。

teeny /'tiːnɪ; 'tini/ adj = tiny.

teeny·bop·per /'tiːnɪbɒpə(r); 'tinɪbɑpɚ/ n young, fashion-conscious teenager. 赶时髦的青少年。

tee·ter /'tiːtə(r); 'titɚ/ vi [VP2C] stand or walk unsteadily: 摇摆地或不稳地站立或步行: ～ing on the

edge of disaster. 在灾难边缘摇摇欲坠。

teeth /tiːθ; tiθ/ pl of tooth.

teethe /tiːð; tið/ vi [VP2A] (used only in progressive tenses, and as gerund and pres part) (of a baby) be getting its first teeth. (仅用于进行时中，并用作动名词及现在分词)(指婴儿)生牙；出牙齿；长牙。'**teething troubles**, discomfort, slight illnesses, etc of a baby while its first teeth are coming through; (fig) troubles which may occur during the early stages of an enterprise. 婴儿长牙时的不舒适；(喻)创业初期所遭遇的困难。

tee·total /tiː'təʊtl; US: 'tiːtoʊtl; ti'totl/ adj not drinking, opposed to the drinking of, alcoholic liquor. 不饮酒的；戒酒的；反对饮酒的。**～·ler** (US also **～·er**) /-tlə(r); -tlɚ/ n person who abstains completely from alcoholic liquor. 完全不饮酒者；滴酒不沾者。

tee·totum /tiː'təʊtəm; ti'totəm/ n top spun with the fingers, esp a four-sided one with letters on it. 手转陀螺；捻转儿(尤指四面形，其上有字母者)。

teg /teg; tɛg/ n sheep in its second year. 两岁的绵羊。

tegu·ment /'tegjʊmənt; 'tɛgjəmənt/ n [C] (more usu 较常用 integument) natural covering of (part of) an animal body, eg a turtle's shell. (动物身上天生的)外被；覆皮；壳(如海龟的壳)。

tele·cast /'telɪkɑːst US: -kæst; 'tɛlə,kæst / n, vt broadcast by television. 用电视播送；电视播放。

tele·com·muni·ca·tions /,telɪkə,mjuːnɪ'keɪʃnz; ,tɛləkə,mjunə'keʃənz/ n pl communications by cable, telegraph, telephone, radio or TV. 电讯(借海底电缆、电报、电话、无线电或电视所作的通讯)。

tele·gram /'telɪgræm; 'tɛlə,græm /n [C] message sent by telegraphy. 电报；电信。

tele·graph /'telɪgrɑːf US: -græf; 'tɛlə,græf/ n means of, apparatus for, sending messages by the use of electric current along wires or by wireless. 电报；电报机。'**～-post／-pole** nn post supporting ～ wire(s). 电线杆。'**～-line／-wire** nn wire along which messages (including telephone messages) travel. 电线；电线线路。**bush ～** n sending of messages over long distances by smoke signals, beating of drums, etc. 丛林传信(借烟火讯号、擂鼓等辗转传信至远方的方法)。□ vi, vt[VP6A, 12A, 13A, 11, 2A] send (news, etc) by ～: 以电报传达(消息等): He ～ed (to) his brother. 他打电报给他的哥哥(弟弟)。(Note: send a telegram and send a cable are commoner than the use of the v.) (注意: send a telegram 及 send a cable 较 telegraph 的动词用法更为普遍。) **tel·egra·pher** /tɪ'legrəfə(r); tə'lɛgrəfɚ/ n skilled operator whose work is to send and receive messages by ～. 电报员；报务员。**～·ic** /,telɪ'græfɪk; ,tɛlə'græfɪk/ adj sent by, suitable for, connected with, the ～: 电报的；由电报发送的；适于电报的；有关电报的; a ～ic address, abbreviated address or brief registered address, for use in telegrams. 电报挂号。**～·i·cally** /-klɪ; -klɪ/ adv **tel·egra·phese** /,telɪgrə'fiːz; ,tɛlɪgrə'fiz/ n [U] style of language used in telegrams (with unessential words omitted). (省略非必要字句的)电报文体。**tel·egra·phist** /tɪ'legrəfɪst; tə'lɛgrəfɪst/ n ～er. **tel·egra·phy** /tɪ'legrəfɪ; tə'lɛgrəfi/ n [U] art, science, process, of sending and receiving messages by ～, of constructing ～ic apparatus, etc. 电报术；电报术；电报收发过程；电报机装置术、过程等。

te·lem·etry /tɪ'lemɪtrɪ; tə'lɛmɪtrɪ/ n [U] automatic transmission and measurement of data from a distance, usu by radio. 遥测术(由无线电等自动发射及测量远方之资料)。

tele·ol·ogy /,telɪ'ɒlədʒɪ; ,tɛlɪ'ɑlədʒɪ/ n theory, teaching, belief, that events and developments are due to the purpose or design that they are serving (as opposed to the mechanistic theory of the universe, ⇨ **mechanisitic**. (哲学上的)宇宙目的论(认为事件的发生及演变，都有其目的理论、教训或信仰，与宇宙机械论相反)。**teleo·logi·cal** /,telɪə'lɒdʒɪkl; ,tɛlɪə'lɑdʒɪkl/ adj

tele·ol·ogist /ˌtelɪˈɒlədʒɪst; ˌtɛlɪˈɑlədʒɪst/ n believer in ~. 宇宙目的论者。

tel·epa·thy /tɪˈlepəθɪ; təˈlɛpəθɪ/ n [U] 1 transference of thoughts or ideas from one mind to another without the normal use of the senses. 心灵感应;传心术;两心灵通(不使用一般的官能,而思想意念等可在二人心中相互传递)。 2 (colloq) ability to be immediately aware of the thoughts and feelings of others. (口)解心(能)力 (对旁人的思想及感情能够立即了解的能力)。 **tele·pathic** /ˌtelɪˈpæθɪk; ˌtɛləˈpæθɪk/ adj **tel·epa·thist** /tɪˈlepəθɪst; təˈlɛpəθɪst/ n person who studies or believes in ~ or who claims to have telepathic powers. 研究或信仰心灵感应者;自称通灵术者。

tele·phone /ˈtelɪfəʊn; ˈtɛləˌfon/ (usu abbr phone in colloq speech) (谈话中常略作 phone) n [U] means, system, of transmitting the human voice by electric current, through wires (usu called telegraph wires, not ~ wires) supported by poles (usu called telegraph poles, not ~ posts), or by radio (radio~); [C] apparatus (with receiver and mouthpiece) for this purpose: 电话 (通常经由电线杆 telegraph poles 所支持的电线 telegraph wires 或无线电传达);电话机: You're wanted on the phone. 你有电话(请你来接你的电话)。 Mr Green is on the phone just now, is using the ~. 格林先生正在打电话。 Will you answer the phone, please, pick up the receiver and answer. 请接电话。 '~ booth, (also 亦作 'phone-booth 或 'call-box) small enclosure with a coin-operated public ~. 公用电话亭。 '~ directory, (also 亦作 'phone-book) list of names with numbers and addresses. 电话簿。 '~ exchange, place where ~ connections are made. 电话局;电话交换所;总机。 □ vt, vi [VP6A, 9, 12A, 13A, 11, 2A, 4A] send (a message to sb) by ~: 以电话传送(信息给某人): I'll phone you tomorrow. 我明天会打电话给你。 He phoned (through) to say that.... 他来电话上说…。 It's Mary's birthday today—we must phone her a greetings telegram, send her a greeting ('Happy Birthday') by asking for such a telegram to be sent (and usu received by ~). 今天是玛丽的生日——我们必须发一通电话贺电给她(要求电信局发'生日快乐'的贺电,而通常是从电话上收到该贺电)。 **tel·eph·ony** /tɪˈlefənɪ; təˈlefənɪ/ n [U] method, process, of sending and receiving messages by ~. 电话术;电话学;电话机的收发过程。 **tel·ephon·ist** /tɪˈlefənɪst; təˈlefənɪst/ n operator in a ~ exchange. (电话交换或总机的)接线生;接员。

tele·photo /ˌtelɪˈfəʊtəʊ; ˈtɛləˌfoto/ n 1 ~ lens, = telescopic lens. (摄影机的)望远镜头。 2 (colloq abbr of) ~graph. (口)为 telephotograph 之略。 ~·graph /-ˌgrɑːf US: -ˌgræf; -ˌgræf/ n 1 photograph made with a ~ lens. 用望远镜头摄得的相片。 2 picture transmitted and received by ~graphy. 传真相片。 **tele·pho·tography** /ˌtelɪfəˈtɒɡrəfɪ; ˌtɛləfoˈtɑɡrəfɪ/ n [U] 1 process of photographing distant objects, etc using a ~ lens. (用望远镜头)望远摄影术。 2 process of transmitting and receiving charts, pictures, etc over a distance. 远距离传真术。

tele·prin·ter /ˈtelɪprɪntə(r); ˈtɛlɪˌprɪntɚ/ n telegraph instrument for sending messages (typed by an operator at the sending end), which are retyped automatically and almost simultaneously by machine at the other end. 打字电报机(报务员在发报处打字发送消息,在收报处立即自动重新打出)。

tele·promp·ter /ˈtelɪprɒmptə(r); ˈtɛlɪˌprɑmptɚ/ n TV device by which a speaker can read in front of him an enlargement of his script, so that he seems to speak spontaneously. 电视提词器(可将讲话者的原稿逐行放大显出,故讲话者虽在读预先准备的讲稿,而在观众看来,似在当场自由发挥)。

tele·scope /ˈtelɪskəʊp; ˈtɛləˌskop/ n tube-like instrument with lenses for making distant objects appear nearer and larger. 望远镜。 **radio ~**, ⇨ radio·. □ vt, vi [VP6A, 2A] make or become shorter by means of

or in the manner of sections that slide one within the other: 把一部分套进、滑进或缩进另一部分而使之变短: 嵌进;叠缩: When the trains collided, the first two cars of one of the trains ~d/were ~d. 火车相撞时,其中一列火车的前两节车厢叠缩在一起了。 **tele·scopic** /ˌtelɪˈskɒpɪk; ˌtɛləˈskɑpɪk/ adj 1 of, containing, able to be seen with, a ~: 望远镜的;包括望远镜的;可用望远镜见到的: a telescopic lens, extra lens attached to a camera to enable distant objects and scenes to be photographed (and now often called a telephoto lens); (照相机的)望远镜头 (现常称为 telephoto lens); a telescopic sight, (on a rifle, to magnify the target); (来复枪上的)望远照门; 望远瞄准器; a telescopic view of the moon, seen through a ~. 从望远镜中所见到的月亮。 2 having sections which slide one within the other: 嵌进的;叠缩的;套入的: a telescopic aerial, eg as part of a portable radio receiver. 伸缩式天线(如手提无线电收音机上者)。

tele·type·writer /ˌtelɪˈtaɪpraɪtə(r); ˌtɛleˈtaɪpˌraɪtɚ/ n (US) (美) = teleprinter.

tele·vi·sion /ˈtelɪvɪʒn; ˈtɛləˌvɪʒən/ n 1 [U] (abbr 略作 TV, or colloq (口) telly /ˈtelɪ; ˈtɛlɪ/) process of transmitting a view of events, plays, etc (while these are taking place, or from films or tapes on which a record has been made) by radio to a distant ~ receiving set with synchronized sound: 电视: Did you see the boat race on (the) ~? 你看了电视上的赛船(节目)吗? 2 [C] ~ (set), apparatus for receiving and showing this transmission. 电视机。 **tele·vise** /ˈtelɪvaɪz; ˈtɛləˌvaɪz/ vt [VP6A] send views of by ~: 用电视播送或播出: The Olympic Games were televised. 奥林匹克运动会的实况曾由电视播出。

telex /ˈteleks; ˈtɛlɛks/ n system of communication using teleprinters. 使用打字电报机的传送系统;打字电报;交换电报。

tel·fer /ˈtelfə(r); ˈtɛlfɚ/ = telpher.

tell /tel; tɛl/ vt, vi (pt, pp told /təʊld; told/) 1 [VP6A, 13A, 12A, 11, 20, 21] ~ sth (to sb), ~ sb sth, make known (in spoken or written words); give information concerning or a description of: (用语言或文字)告知;告诉;讲述: He told the news to everybody in the village. 他把这项消息告诉了村子里每一个人。 I told him my name. 我把我的名字告诉了他。 T~ me where you live. 把你的住址告诉我。 I can't ~ you how happy I am, can't find words that are adequate. 我无法告诉你我是多么的快乐。 He told me (that) he was coming. 他告诉我他要来。 So I've been told, I've already been told that. 有人告诉过我了。 If he asks, ~ him. 如果他问起,就告诉他。 Don't ~ me it's too late! (used to express surprise or alarm) 别说太晚吧!(用以表惊讶或惊恐)。 I'll ~ you what.... used meaning 'Here's a suggestion, idea, etc that may help'. 我讲给你听(意谓'我有一项建议、主意等,可能有帮助')。 I ~ (= assure) you, he's thoroughly dishonest! 我敢说,他一点也不诚实! I told you so, I warned you that this would happen, etc and now you see that I'm right: 我早跟你说过吧(我以前警告过你会如何如何,现在你知道我对了吧): Things have gone wrong but please don't say 'I told you so!' 事情弄糟了,但请不要讲'我早跟你说过吧'! You're ~ing 'me! I fully agree with you. 我完全同意你哪! T~ me another! I don't believe you. 我才不相信哩! ~ the world, (colloq) ~ everybody: (口)告诉每一个人: We all know you're clever, but do you have to ~ the world, be so emphatic about it? 我们都知道你很聪明,不过你有必要告诉每一个人吗(或:你有必要特别强调这一点吗)? 2 [VP6A, 13A, 12A, 15A] utter; express with words: 讲;述;说: ~ a lie; 说谎; ~ the children a tale/story. 讲故事给小孩听。 'When in doubt, ~ the truth', said Mark Twain. '没有把握的时候,要照实说', 马克•吐温说。 ~ the tale, (colloq) ~ a pitiful story in order to get sympathy, etc. 讲诉悲惨故事事以博取同情等。 ~ tales about/on sb, make known sb's secrets, misconduct, etc in a malicious way. 讲某人坏话;搬弄是

非。~·**tale** /'teltel/; `tɛl,tel/ *n* person who ~s about another's private affairs, makes known a secret, etc; circumstances, etc that reveal a person's thoughts, activities, etc (often attrib): 谈论旁人私事者; 泄露秘密者; 显露某人思想, 活动等的环境、景况等(常用作定语): *a ~tale blush*; 泄露底蕴的脸红; *the ~tale cigarette ash on the carpet*, that made known the fact that someone had been smoking a cigarette. 地毯上的香烟灰 (显示曾有人吸过香烟)。 **3** [VP17] order; direct: 吩咐; 命令: *Do what I ~ you.* 你必须遵照命令行事。 *You must do what you're told.* 你必须遵照命令行事。 *T~ him to wait.* 叫他等一等。 *He was told to start at once.* 命他立即出发。 **4** [VP6A, 14] (esp with *can/could/be able to*) ~ *sb/sth* (*from sb/sth*), know apart; distinguish: (尤与 can, could, be able to 连用) 区别: *Can you ~ Tom from his twin brother?* 汤姆和他的孪生兄弟, 你能分辨谁是谁吗? *They look exactly the same—how can you ~ which is which?* 他们看起来完全一样—你怎么认得出哪个是哪个呢? **5** [VP6A, 8, 10, 2A] learn by observation; make out; become aware (of sth): 借观察而认知; 弄明白; 察觉 (某事物): *How do you ~ which of these buttons to press?* 你怎么知道要按这些电钮中的哪一个? ~ *the time*, (be able to) read (or say) the time from a clock, etc: (能够) 看钟表等: (能够) 看懂钟表上的时间: *Can Mary ~ the time yet?* 玛丽现在看得懂 (钟表上的) 时间了吗? *Can you ~ me what time it is?* 你能告诉我现在的时刻吗? *You can never ~; You never can ~*, you can never be sure, because appearances are often deceptive. 谁也不知道; 谁也说不准 (譬如外表常常靠不住)。 *there is/was, etc no ~ing*, it is impossible or difficult to know: 不可能知道; 很难知道: *There's no ~ing what may happen/ where she's going/what he's doing, etc*. 不可能 (很难) 知道会发生什么事 (她到哪里去了, 他在干什么等)。 **6** [VP6A, 15B] (old use) count. (旧用法) 计算; 数。 ~ *one's beads*, say one's prayers (counting beads on a rosary). 念经; 数念珠; 念祷词。 ~ *sb off* (*for sth/to do sth*), (a) count one by one and give orders: 一个一个地点派工作; 逐一派定任务: *Ten men were told off for special duty/ to clean the latrines.* 十个人被点派从事特殊任务 (去打扫厕所)。 (b) (colloq) give a list of sb's misdoings; scold him: (口) 数说某人的坏行为; 斥责; 责骂: *That fellow needs to be told off.* 那家伙该骂一顿。 *She told the typist off for making so many careless mistakes.* 她因为打字员犯了很多的错误而把她说了一顿。 **7** [VP2A, 3A] ~ (*on/upon sb*), have a marked effect on; influence the result of: 奏效; 对…产生显著效果; 影响…的结果: *All this hard work is ~ing on him*, is affecting his health. 所有这些辛苦的工作都对他的健康有影响。 *Every blow ~s*. 每一击都击中了。 ~*ing adj* effective; impressive: 有效的; 有力的; 显著的: *a ~ing speech/argument/blow*. 有力的演说 (论据, 打击)。 ~·**ing·ly** *adv* **8** [VP2A, 3A] ~ (*on sb*), (colloq) reveal a secret; inform against: (口) 泄露秘密; 告发 (某人): *John told on his sister.* 约翰打他姐姐 (妹妹) 的小报告。 ⇨ *tale-bearer* at **tale(2)**. *You promised not to ~ and now you've done so!* 你答应过不泄露秘密, 而你现在已经泄露了!

tel·ler /'telə(r)/; `tɛlɚ/ *n* **1** person who receives, and pays out, money over a bank counter. (银行的) 出纳员。 **2** man who counts votes, eg in the House of Commons. (投票时的) 计票员 (如下议院中者)。

telly /'telɪ/; `tɛlɪ/ *n* (colloq abbr for) television. (口) 为 television 之略。

tel·pher /'telfə(r)/; `tɛlfɚ/ *n* conveyance for goods, suspended from overhead wire cables, usu driven by electricity; transportation system of this kind, eg for rock from a quarry. 索道输送; 索道车; 索道运输工具; 索车; 缆车系统。

Tel·star /'telstɑ:(r)/; `tɛl,star/ *n* (P) communications satellite used (commercially) for the transmission of telephone messages and TV. (商标) 通信 (讯) 卫星; 电讯卫星。

te·mer·ity /tɪ'merətɪ/; təˈmɛrətɪ/ *n* [U] rashness. 凶莽; 孟浪。

tem·per¹ /'tempə(r)/; `tɛmpɚ/ *n* **1** condition of the mind and emotions: 心情; 脾气; 性情; 气质: *in a good ~*, calm and pleasant; 心情好的; *in a bad ~*, angry, impatient, etc. 心情坏的 (愤怒、不耐等)。 *get/fly into a ~*, become angry. 发怒。 *keep/lose one's ~*, keep/ fail to keep one's ~ under control. 忍住 (发) 脾气。 *out of ~* (*with*), angry (with). (对…) 发脾气。 **tem·pered** /'tempəd/; `tɛmpɚd/ *adj* (in compounds) (用于复合词中) having or showing a certain kind of ~: 有某种心情的; 显示某种气质的: *a good-/sweet-/fiery-/hot-, etc 'ed man.* 脾气好 (柔和, 急、躁等) 的人。 **-tem·pered·ly** *adv* (in compounds) (用于复合词中) *good-~edly.* 好脾气地。 **2** [U] degree of hardness, toughness, elasticity, of a substance, esp of steel. (尤指钢等物质的) 硬度、韧度、弹性; 回火度。

tem·per² /'tempə(r)/; `tɛmpɚ/ *vt, vi* **1** [VP6A] give the required temper(2) (to (eg steel) by heating and cooling; bring (eg clay) to the required condition by moistening, mixing, kneading, etc. 锻炼 (钢等); 炼至所需要的硬度; 捏和 (粘土等); [VP2A] come to the required condition as the result of treatment. 经处理后成为所需要的硬度。 **2** [VP6A, 15A] soften or modify; mitigate: 使软化; 调剂; 缓和: ~ *justice with mercy*, be merciful when giving a just punishment. 恩威并施; 执法公正而仁慈。

tem·pera /'tempərə/; `tɛmpərə/ *n* [U] = distemper, esp as used in fresco painting. 色胶 (尤指用于壁画中者)。

tem·pera·ment /'temprəmənt/; `tɛmprəmənt/ *n* **1** [C, U] person's disposition or nature, esp as this affects his way of thinking, feeling and behaving: 气质; 性情 (尤指影响人的思想、感情及行为者): *a girl with a nervous/an artistic ~*. 带有神经质 (艺术家气质) 的女孩子。 *The two brothers have entirely different ~s*. 这两兄弟的性情完全不同。 *Success often depends on ~*. 成功常视一个人的性情而定。 **2** [U] (without an *adj*) kind of disposition that is easily excited, passionate, not easily controlled or restrained, eg as in some actresses and opera singers. (不与形容词连用) (某些女演员及歌剧演唱家等之) 易激动; 易怒; 急躁。 **tem·pera·men·tal** /,temprə'mentl/; ,tɛmpərə'mɛntl/ *adj* **1** caused by ~: 由气质引起的; 本质的: *a ~al dislike for study.* 本性不喜读书。 **2** subject to quickly changing moods: 神经质的; 喜怒无常的; 心情变化快的: *a ~al tennis player*, one whose playing changes according to his mood. 球技不稳定的网球员 (球技随心情而改变)。 **tem·pera·men·tally** /-təlɪ/; -tl̩ɪ/ *adv*

tem·per·ance /'tempərəns/; `tɛmprəns/ *n* [U] **1** moderation, self-control, in speech, behaviour and (esp) in the use of alcoholic drinks. (言词、行为上的) 节制; 自制; 克己; (尤指) 节酒; 节饮。 **2** total abstinence from alcoholic drinks: 禁酒: (attrib) (用作定语) *a '~ society*, one for the restriction or abolition of the use of alcoholic drinks. 禁酒会。

tem·per·ate /'tempərət/; `tɛmprɪt/ *adj* **1** showing, behaving, with temperance(1): 有节制的; 适度的: *Be more ~ in your language, please.* 言词上请节制一点。 **2** (of climate, parts of the world) free from extremes of heat and cold: (指气候, 世界上某些地区) 温和的: *the north '~ zone*, between the Tropic of Cancer and the arctic zone. 北温带。 ~·**ly** *adv* ~·**ness** *n*

tem·pera·ture /'temprətʃə(r)/ US: `tempərtʃʊr/; `tɛmprətʃɚ/ *n* [C, U] degree of heat and cold: 温度; 冷热; 体温: *In Hawaii there is no extremes of ~*. 在夏威夷没有特别冷或特别热的气温。 *The nurse took the ~s of all the patients*, measured their body ~s with a thermometer. 那位护士为所有的病人量体温。 *have/run a ~*, have a fever. 发热。

tem·pest /'tempɪst/; `tɛmpɪst/ *n* [C] violent storm; (fig) violent agitation: 暴风雨; 风暴; (喻) 骚乱; 风潮; 骚

动; 大激动: *A ~ of laughter swept through the crowd.* 群众爆发出一阵大笑. '**~-swept**/**-tossed** *adj* (liter) swept, etc by ~s. (文)遭暴风雨袭击的; 风暴横扫的。

tem·pes·tu·ous /tem'pestʃuəs; tɛm'pɛstʃʊəs/ *adj* (of the weather and fig) violent; stormy: (指天气, 亦作比喻用法)剧烈的; 骚乱的; 有暴风雨的: *in a ~uous mood;* 心情极为激动的; *a ~uous political meeting.* 骚动的政治集会。

tem·plate, tem·plet / 'templɪt; 'templɪt / *n* pattern or gauge (usu a thin board or metal plate) used as a guide in cutting or drilling metal, wood, etc. (切割或钻穿金属、木材等用的)样板; 模板; 型板。

temple¹ /'templ; 'templ/ *n* **1** building used for the worship of a god (esp ancient Greek, Roman, Egyptian and modern Hindu, Buddhist, etc.). *in*; 寺; 神殿(尤指古代希腊、罗马、埃及和近代印度教及佛教等者)。 **2** (applied occasionally to a) place of Christian worship (*church* and *chapel* being the usn words): (偶尔用以指)教堂; 礼拜堂 (*church* 与 *chapel* 较为通用): *a Mormon ~.* 摩门教堂。 **3** any of the three successive religious centres of the Jews in ancient Jerusalem. 古代耶路撒冷犹太人连续建立的三个宗教中心之任一。 **4 the Inner**/**Middle T~,** two Inns of Court in London. 伦敦的内(中)殿法学协会。 ⇨ **inn(2).**

a Hindu temple

temple² /'templ; 'templ/ *n* flat part of either side of the forehead. (前额两侧的)太阳穴; 颞; 颞颥。 ⇨ the illus at **head.** 参看插图之插图。

tem·plet /'templɪt; 'templɪt/ *n* ⇨ **template.**

tempo /'tempəu; 'tempo/ *n* (*pl* ~**s** or, 或, in music, **tempi** /-pi:; -pi/) (I) (意) **1** rate of movement or activity: 动作或活动的速率; 进度; 进行或发展的速度: *the tiring ~ of city life.* 叫人疲于奔命的都市生活。 *This long strike has upset the ~ of production.* 这次的长期罢工已经破坏了生产进度。 **2** speed at which music is (to be) played. (音乐的)速度; 拍子; 缓急。

tem·poral /'temperəl; 'tempərəl/ *adj* **1** of, existing in, time: 时(间)的; 时间上的; 暂时的: (gram) (语法) ~ *conjunctions,* eg *when, while.* 表示时间的连接词(如 when, while)。 **2** of earthly human life; of this physical life only, not spiritual: 尘世生活的; 世俗的; 现世的; 非精神生活的: *the ~ power of the Pope,* ie as head of the Vatican State; 教宗的世俗权力(即作为教廷领袖); *the lords ~ (=* the peers of the realm) *and the lords spiritual (=* the bishops). 上议院中的贵族议员及主教议员。 ~**·ity** /,tempə'rælɪtɪ; ,tempə'rælətɪ/ *n* (usu *pl;* -ties) secular possessions: (通常用复数)世俗的财产; 俗利: *the temporalities of the Church.* 教会的财产。 ~**ty** /'temperəltɪ/ *n* laity. 俗人。

tem·por·ary /'tempreri US: -pəreri; 'tempə,rɛrɪ/ *adj* lasting for, designed to be used for, a short time only: 暂时的; 临时的; ~ *employment;* 临时工作; *a ~ bridge.* 临时桥。 **tem·por·ar·ily** /'temprerəlɪ US: ,tempə'rerəlɪ; 'tempə,rɛrəlɪ/ *adv* **tem·por·ari·ness** *n*

tem·por·ize /'tempəraɪz; 'tempə,raɪz/ *vi* [VP2A] delay making a decision, giving an answer, stating one's purpose, etc; act so as gain time: 稽延作决定、作答复、陈述自己的目的等; 敷衍; 拖延以争取时间: *a temporizing politician*/*answer.* 八面玲珑的政客(敷衍的答复)。

tempt /tempt; tempt/ *vt* [VP6A, 17, 14] ~ *(to sth*/*into doing sth),* **1** (try to) persuade (sb) to do sth wrong or foolish: 劝诱(某人)做坏事或蠢事; 勾引: *Nothing could ~ him to such a course of action*/*to take such a step.* 没有什么事情能够诱使他那样做(采取这样的步骤)。 *He was ~ed into making a false step,* doing sth unwise. 他被引诱做了一件蠢事。 **2** attract (sb) to have or do sth: 诱使(某人)保有或做出某事; 诱导; 导致: *The warm weather ~ed us to go for a swim.* 暖和的天气诱使我们去游泳。 *She ~ed the child to have a little more soup.* 她诱使那孩子多喝一点汤。 *What a ~ing (=* attractive) *offer!* 多吸引人的提议(出价等)! **3** (old use, biblical) test. (旧用法, 圣经用法)考验; 试验。 ~ *Providence,* take a risk. 冒险。 ~**·ing·ly** *adv* ~**er** *n* person who ~s; 劝诱者; 诱惑者; (esp) (尤指) **the T~er,** Satan, the Devil. 撒旦; 魔鬼。 **temp·tress** /'temptrɪs; 'temptrɪs/ *n* woman who ~s. 女引诱者; 诱惑者等。

temp·ta·tion /temp'teʃn; temp'teʃən/ *n* **1** [U] tempting or being tempted: (被)劝诱; (被)诱惑: *the ~ of easy profits;* 赚钱容易的诱惑; *yield*/*give way to ~;* 屈服于诱惑; *put ~ in sb's way.* 诱惑某人。 **2** [C] that which tempts or attracts: 诱惑物; 有吸引力之物: *The sight of the purse on the table was a strong ~ to the poor child.* 桌上那个钱包对那贫苦的孩子是一个很大的诱惑。 *Clever advertisements are ~s to spend money.* 巧妙的广告诱使人花钱。

ten /ten; tɛn/ *n, adj* the number 10. 十; 拾。 ⇨ **App 5.** 参看附录五。 *ten to one,* very probably: 十之八九; 非常可能地: *Ten to one he will arrive late.* 十之八九他会迟到。 **tenth** /tenθ; tɛnθ/ *n, adj* the next after the 9th; one of 10 equal parts. 第十(的); 十分之一(的)。 **tenth·ly** *adv* '**ten·fold** *adv* ten times as many or much. 十倍地。 '**ten·pence** *n* (GB decimal coin with the) value of ten pennies. (英国十进制硬币)十便士(的价值)。

ten·able /'tenəbl; 'tɛnəbl/ *adj* **1** that can be defended successfully: 可防守的; 守得住的; 可维护或防护的: *His theory is hardly ~.* 他的理论很难站得住。 **2** (of an office or position) that can be held (*by sb for a time*): (指职务或职位)可保有的; 可维持的(*由 by 处有一个时间连用*): *The lectureship is ~ for a period of three years.* 该讲师的职位为期三年。 **ten·abil·ity** /,tenə'bɪlətɪ; ,tɛnə'bɪlətɪ/ *n*

ten·acious /tɪ'neɪʃəs; tɪ'neʃəs/ *adj* holding tightly, refusing to let go: 抓紧的; 不放松的; 紧握的: *a ~ memory;* 很强的记忆力; ~ *of our rights.* 坚决维护我们的权利。 ~**·ly** *adv* ~**·ness** *n* **ten·ac·ity** /tɪ'næsɪtɪ; tɪ'næsətɪ/ *n*

ten·ant /'tenənt; 'tɛnənt/ *n* person who pays rent for the use of land, a building, a room, etc: 佃户; 房客; 租户: *evict ~s for non-payment of rent;* 赶出未付房租的房客; ~ *farmers,* who cultivate farms which they do not own. 佃农。 □ *vt* (usu passive) occupy as a ~: (通常用被动语态)租赁; 租佃: *houses ~ed by railway workers.* 铁路工人租赁的房屋。 **ten·ancy** /-ənsɪ; -ənsɪ/ *n* **1** [U] use of land, etc as a ~: 租赁; 租佃: *during his tenancy of the farm.* 在他租用该农场期间。 **2** [C] length of time during which a ~ uses land, etc: 租赁或租用期间: *hold a life tenancy of a house.* 终生租用某房屋。 **ten·an·try** /'tenəntrɪ; 'tɛnəntrɪ/ *n* (collective *sing*) all the ~s occupying land and houses on one estate. (集合单数)某一地产的全体佃户及租户。

tench /tentʃ; tɛntʃ/ *n* edible European freshwater fish; carp. 欧洲产可食淡水鲤鱼。

tend¹ /tend; tɛnd/ *vt* [VP6A] watch over; attend to: 照料; 照管: *shepherds ~ing their flocks;* 照料其羊群的牧羊人; (esp US) (尤美) ~ *the store,* serve customers.

招呼顾客; 照看店铺.

tend² / tend; tɛnd/ *vi* [VP2C, 4A] be inclined to move; have a direction: 倾向; 有某种趋势; 趋于: *Prices are ~ing upwards.* 物价正在上涨. *He ~s to pitch the ball too high.* 他常把球 掷得过高. *He ~s towards atheism.* 他倾向于无神论. **ten·dency** /'tendənsɪ; 'tɛndənsɪ/ *n* [C] (*pl -cies*) turning or inclination, leaning: 倾向; 趋势: *Business is showing a ~ency to improve.* 业务有改进的趋势. *There was a strong upward ~ency in oil shares yesterday*, prices ~ed upwards. 石油股票昨天有强烈上涨的趋势.

ten·den·tious / ten'denʃəs; tɛn'dɛnʃəs/ *adj* (of a speech, a piece of writing, etc) having an underlying purpose, aimed at helping a cause; not impartial: (指演说,文章等)有目的的; 宣传性的; 非持平之论的: *Countries at war often send out ~ reports*, reports designed to show their cause in a favourable light, win sympathy, etc. 交战国常发出宣传性的报导. **~·ly** *adv* **~·ness** *n*

ten·der¹ /'tendər; 'tɛndə/ *adj* **1** delicate; easily hurt or damaged; quickly feeling pain: 脆弱的; 纤弱的; 敏感的; 易伤的; 易损坏的; 触及易疼痛的: *~ blossoms*, eg easily hurt by frosts; 娇嫩的花; *touch sb on a ~ spot*, one that hurts when touched; 碰到某人的痛处; *a ~ subject*, (fig) one that has to be dealt with carefully to avoid hurting people's feelings; (喻)敏感的问题(需要小心处理以免伤人感情者); *a person of ~ age/years*, young and immature; 年幼而未成熟的人; *have a ~ conscience*; 容易感到良心不安; *a ~ heart*, easily moved to pity, 软心肠, hence, 由此产生, ~*·'hearted adj* '~*·foot n* (*pl -foots*) new-comer to the sort of country where there is rough living, hardship, etc. 新来到艰苦生活环境的人; 生手. **2** (of meat) easily chewed; not tough: (指肉)嫩的; 易咀嚼的; 柔软的: *a ~ steak*. 嫩牛排. '~*·loin n* [U] ~ part of the loin of beef or pork; undercut of sirloin. 牛或猪的腰部嫩肉; 嫩腰肉. **3** kind, loving: 温和的; 仁慈的: *~ looks*; 温和的表情; *~ care*; 悉心的照顾; *~ parents*; 仁慈的双亲; *bid sb a ~ farewell*. 与某人亲切地道别. **~·ly** *adv* **~·ness** *n*

ten·der² /'tendər; 'tɛndə/ *n* **1** person who looks ofter, watches over, sth: 照管者; 照料者; 照看者: *a ma'chine-~*; 机器工人; *a 'bar~*, ⇨ bar¹(13). 酒保; 酒馆侍者. **2** small ship attending a larger one, to carry stores, put on or take off passengers, etc. 大船的勤务船(运送必需品, 接运旅客等); 供应船. **3** wagon for fuel and water behind a steam locomotive. (蒸汽火车头后面的)煤水车.

ten·der³ /'tendər; 'tɛndə/ *vt, vi* **1** [VP6A, 12A, 13A] offer; present: 提出; 提供; 贡献: *~ money in payment of a debt.* 提出金钱偿还债务. *He ~ed his resignation to the Prime Minister/his services to the Government.* 他向首相提出辞呈(为政府效力). **2** [VP2A, 3A] *~ (for)*, make an offer (to carry out work, supply goods, etc) at a stated price: 投标: *~ for the construction of a new motorway.* 投标承建一条新的高速公路. □ *n* [C] **1** statement of the price at which one offers to supply goods or services, or to do sth: 投标: *invite ~s for a new bridge*; 新桥工程招标; *put in/make/send in a ~ for sth*; 参加某项投标; *accept the lowest ~*. 接受最低价格的投标. **2** legal ~, form of money which must, by law, be accepted in payment of a debt: 偿还债务时必须接受的合法钱币; 法偿; 合法货币; *Are 'copper coins legal ~ for a sum in excess of £10?* 超过十镑的数目可以用铜币偿付吗?

ten·don /'tendən; 'tɛndən/ *n* [C] tough, thick cord that joins muscle to bone; sinew. 腱.

ten·dril /'tendrəl; 'tɛndrɪl/ *n* [C] thread-like part of a plant, eg a vine, that twists round any nearby support. 植物的卷须. ⇨ the illus at ivy. 参看 ivy 的插图.

ten·ement /'tenəmənt; 'tɛnəmənt/ *n* [C] **1** '~(-house), large building with apartments for the use of many families at low rents. 廉租公寓(多家合住, 租金

便宜的大房屋). **2** (legal) any dwelling-house; any kind of permanent property. (法律)住宅; 不动产.

tenet /'tenɪt; 'tɛnɪt/ *n* [C] principle; belief; doctrine. 主义; 信条; 教理; 教条.

ten·ner /'tenər; 'tɛnə/ *n* (colloq) ten pounds in GB money; ten-pound note. (口)十英镑; 十镑的纸币.

ten·nis /'tenɪs; 'tɛnɪs/ *n* [U] game for two or four players who hit a ball backwards and forwards across a net. 网球. '~-court *n* marked area on which ~ is played. 网球场. ~-'elbow *n* inflammation of the elbow caused by playing ~. 网球员肘病(因打网球而引起的肘部发炎).

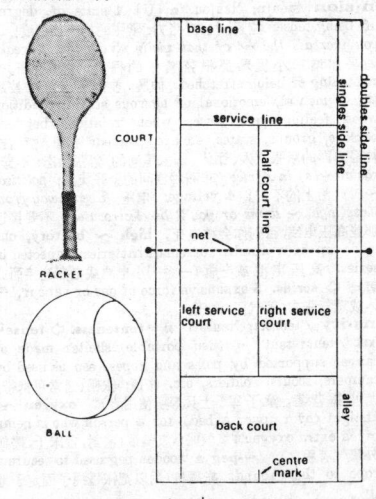

tennis

tenon /'tenən; 'tɛnən/ *n* end of a piece of wood shaped to go into a mortise to make a joint. 榫; 榫头.

tenor¹ /'tenər; 'tɛnə/ *n* (usu 通常作 the ~ (of)) general routine or direction (of one's life): (生活的)常规或方向: *interrupt sb's even ~*, 扰乱了某人生活中的常规; general meaning, thread, drift (of a speech, etc): (演讲等的)要旨; 条理; 大意(与 of 连用): *She knew enough Spanish to get the ~ of what was being said.* 她懂得的西班牙语足以了解对方谈话的大意.

tenor² /'tenər; 'tɛnə/ *n* **1** (music for, singer with, the) highest normal adult male voice: 男高音; 次中音; 适于男高音或次中音的乐曲; 男高音或次中音歌手或歌唱家: (attrib) (用作定语) ~ *voice*; 男高音; 次中音: *the ~ part*. (乐谱中的) 男高音或次中音部. **2** (of instruments) with a range about that of the ~ voice: (指乐器)音域相当于男高音或次中音的: *a ~ horn/saxophone*. 次中音喇叭(萨克管).

ten·pin /'tenpɪn; 'tɛn.pɪn/ *n* **1** (*pl* with *sing* v) game like *ninepins* with ten skittles instead of nine. (复数与单数动词连用)十柱戏(与 ninepins 相似, 但用十柱); 十柱保龄球. **2** pin used. 十柱戏中所用之柱. **3** (attrib) (用作定语) ~ *bowling*. 十柱保龄球.

tense¹ /tens; tɛns/ *adj* (lit or fig) tightly stretched; strained to stiffness: (字面或喻) 拉紧的; 紧张的: ~ *nerves*; 紧张的神经; *faces ~ with anxiety*; 因焦急而显得紧张的面孔; *a moment of ~ excitement*. 极度激动的一刻. *We were ~ with expectancy*, Our nerves were ~, keyed up. 我们因期待而神经紧张起来. *There was a ~ atmosphere*, People had a feeling of nervous strain and an attitude of expectancy. 人们紧张地期待着. □ *vt, vi* [VP6A, 2A] make or become ~; stiffen: 拉紧; 使紧张; 变紧; 变紧张; *He ~d his muscles for the effort.* 他紧绷

着肌肉使动。 **be/get ~d up**, feel nervous strain: 感到神经紧张: *He's always ~d up before a game /an exam.* 他在比赛(考试)前总会感到神经紧张。 ~ **·ly** *adv* ~ **·ness** *n*

tense² /tens; tɛns/ *n* (gram) verb from that shows time: (语法)动词的时态: *the present/past, etc* ~. 现在(过去等)时态。

ten·sile /'tensail US: 'tensl; 'tɛnsl/ *adj* **1** of tension. 拉紧的; 紧张的: *measure the '~ strength of wire,* eg to find the load it will support without breaking. 测量金属线的抗张强度。 **2** capable of being stretched. 可延展的; 可伸长的; 可伸延的。

ten·sion /'tenʃn; 'tɛnʃən/ *n* [U] **1** state of, degree of, being tense: 拉紧; 拉力; 张力; 紧张的状态或程度: *If you increase the ~ of that violin string it will break.* 如果你增加小提琴那根弦紧张的程度, 它就会断。 **2** stretching or being stretched. 伸展; 被伸展; 延伸; 被延伸。 **3** mental, emotional or nervous strain; condition when feelings are tense, when relations between persons, groups, states, etc are strained: 心理、情绪或神经方面的紧张: (人、团体、国家等间的)紧张状态; 不安: *racial ~(s) in Africa;* 非洲种族间的紧张状态; *political ~.* 政治上的不安。 **4** voltage: 电压: *Keep away from those high ~ wires or you'll be electrocuted.* 不要接近那些高压电线, 否则你会被电死。 **high ~ battery**, one made up of a number of small batteries connected in series. 高压电池或电瓶(一系列小电池或电瓶连接而成者)。 ⇨ **series**. **5** expansive force of gas or vapour. 气体或蒸气张力; 蒸气压; 汽压。

tens·ity /'tensəti; 'tɛnsəti/ *n* =**tenseness**. ⇨ **tense¹**.

tent /tent; tɛnt/ *n* (usu portable) shelter made of canvas supported by poles and ropes, esp as used by campers, scouts, soldiers, etc. 帐篷; 帐棚(通常可携带, 尤指露营者、童子军、士兵等所使用者)。 '**oxygen** ~, airtight cover (over a bed) for a person who is being given extra oxygen. 氧气帐; 氧气罩(密封, 置床上, 需额外吸氧气者用)。 '~**-peg** *n* wooden peg used to secure a rope to the ground. 帐篷桩(用以把帐篷绳子固定于地上)。

ten·tacle /'tentəkl; 'tɛntək/ *n* [C] long, slender, flexible, snake-like, boneless growth on the head or round the mouth of certain animals used for touching, feeling, holding, moving, etc. (动物的)触须; 触角; 触手。 ⇨ the illus at **mollusc**. 参看 mollusc 之插图。

ten·ta·tive /'tentətɪv; 'tɛntətɪv/ *adj* made or done as a trial, to see the effect: 试验性质的; 尝试的; 暂时的: *only a ~ suggestion;* 仅系试验性质的建议; *come to a ~ conclusion;* 获致暂时的结论; *make a ~ offer.* 作尝试性的出价(建议)。 ~**·ly** *adv*

ten·ter·hooks /'tentəhuks; 'tɛntə,huks/ *n pl* (only in) (仅用于) **on ~**, in a state of anxious suspense. 忧虑不安; 如坐针毡。

tenth /tenθ; tɛnθ/ *n, adj* ⇨ **ten**.

tenu·ous /'tenjuəs; 'tɛnjuəs/ *adj* thin; slender: 薄的; 细的: *the ~ web of a spider;* 纤细的蜘蛛网; (of distinctions) subtle. (指区别)细微的; 微妙的。 **ten·uity** /tɪ'nju:ɪtɪ US: te'nu:-; tɛ'nuətɪ/ *n*

ten·ure /'tenjuə(r) US: -jər; 'tɛnjə/ *n* [C, U] (period, time, condition of) holding (eg political office) or using (land): (官职、职位等的)保有; 保有期间或状态; (土地之)使用; 使用期间或状态: *The farmers want security of ~,* to be secure in their tenancies. 农民们希望土地使用权有保障。 *The ~ of office of the President is four years.* 总统的任期是四年。

tepee /'ti:pi:; 'tipɪ/ *n* cone-shaped tent of skins or bark of the American Indians; wigwam. (美洲印第安人的)兽皮或树皮帐篷。

tepid /'tepɪd; 'tɛpɪd/ *adj* lukewarm (lit and fig). 微温的; 不大热心的(字面及喻)。 ~**·ly** *adv* ~**·ness** *n* ~**·ity** /te'pɪdətɪ; tɪ'pɪdətɪ/ *n*

ter·cen·ten·ary /ˌtɜ:sen'ti:nərɪ US: tɜ:'sentənerɪ; ˌtɝsɛn'tɛnərɪ/, **ter·cen·ten·nial** /ˌtɜ:sen'tenɪəl;

ˌtɜsɛn'tɛnɪəl/ *nn* 300th anniversary: 三百周年纪念: (attrib) (用作定语) ~ *celebrations.* 三百周年庆典。

ter·gi·ver·sate /'tɜ:dʒɪvəseɪt; 'tɝdʒɪvə,set/ *vi* (formal) make a complete change in one's opinions, principles, etc; make conflicting statements. (正式用语)完全改变自己的见解、原则等; 作矛盾的陈述; 支吾; 搪塞; 变节。 **ter·gi·ver·sa·tion** /ˌtɜ:dʒɪvə'seɪʃn; ˌtɝdʒɪvə-'seʃən/ *n*

term /tɜ:m; tɝm/ *n* [C] **1** fixed or limited period of time: 期限; 期间: *a long ~ of imprisonment;* 长期监禁; *during his ~ of office as President.* 在其总统任期内。 **2** (of schools, universities, etc) one of the periods (usu three or four) into which the academic year is divided: (指学校, 大学等)学期(通常一学年分为三或四学期); 季: *the summer ~;* 夏季学期; 夏季班; *end-of-~ examinations;* 期考; *during '~(-time).* 在学期当中。 **3** (legal) period during which a Court holds session. (法律)法庭的开庭期。 **4** (*pl*) conditions offered or agreed to: (复)(提出的或同意的)条件: *enquire about ~s (ie prices) for a stay at a hotel;* 询问住旅馆的价钱; ~*s of surrender,* eg offered to a defeated enemy; 投降条件(如向战败的敌人提出者); ~*s of reference.* ⇨ **reference(1)**. **come to ~s/make ~s (with sb)**, reach an agreement (with him). (与某人)达成协议。 **come to ~s with sth**, accept, become resigned to it: 接受或容忍某事物: *come to ~s with a difficult situation.* 逆来顺受。 **do sth on one's own ~s/sb else's ~s**, on conditions that one/sb else decides: 照自己(旁人)的意思或决定做某事: *If he agrees to help, it will be on his own ~s.* 如果他答应帮忙, 那是他自己的意思。 **5** (*pl*) relations. (复)关系; 交谊。 **be on good/friendly/bad ~s (with sb)**, be friendly, etc (with him): (与某人)关系良好(友善, 恶劣): *I didn't know you and she were on such good ~s,* were such good friends. 我并不知道你同她是非常要好的朋友。 **on equal ~s**, as equals. 伯仲之间; 不相上下; 相匹敌。 **not be on 'speaking ~s with sb**, ⇨ **speak(2)**. **6** word(s) used to express an idea, esp a specialized concept: 名词; 术语; 表示特殊化概念的用词: *technical/scientific/legal ~s.* 专门(科学, 法律)术语。 *In box-office ~s* (as expressed in financial, or box-office receipts) *the film was a failure.* 从票房记录看, 这部影片是失败的。 **7** (*pl*) mode of expression: (复)措辞; 说法: *He referred to your work in ~s of high praise/in flattering ~s.* 他对你的工作大加赞扬(奉承)。 *How dare you speak of her in such abusive ~s?* 你怎么敢用这种恶言骂她? *a contradiction in ~s,* a statement that contradicts itself. 自相矛盾的陈述。 **8** (maths) part of an expression joined to the rest by + or −: (数学)项: *The expression a² + 2ab + b² has three ~s.* a² + 2ab + b² 这一个式子有三项。 □ *vt* [VP23] name; apply a ~ to: 把…称做: *He has no right to ~ himself a professor.* 他无权自称为教授。

ter·ma·gant /'tɜ:məgənt; 'tɝməgænt/ *n* noisy, quarrelsome woman; shrew. 好争吵的女子; 泼妇; 悍妇。

ter·min·able /'tɜ:mɪnəbl; 'tɝmɪnəbl/ *adj* that may be terminated. 可终止的; 有期限的。

ter·min·al /'tɜ:mɪnl; 'tɝmɪnl/ *adj* **1** of, taking place, each term (1, 2, 3): 每期的; 每学期的; 按期举行的: ~ *examinations/accounts.* 学期考试(按期结账)。 **2** of, forming, the point or place at the end: 末期的; 末端的; 终点的; 尽头的: ~ *cancer,* not curable; ending in death; 末期癌症(无法救治者, 必死无疑); *the '~ ward,* (in a hospital) for persons who cannot be cured and must soon die. (医院里的)垂死病房; 弥留病房。 □ *n* **1** end of a railway line, bus line, etc; centre (in a town) used by passengers departing for, or arriving from, an airport: (铁路之)终点; 终点站; (城市的)航空集散站(往来飞机场之旅客的集散中心)。 *the ,West ,London 'Air T~.* 伦敦西区的航空集散站。 **2** point of connection in an electric circuit: (电路的)接头: *the ~s of a battery.* 电池的接头。 **ter·min·ally** *adv*

ter·min·ate /'tɜ:mɪneɪt; 'tɝmə,net/ *vt, vi* [VP6A, 2A, 15A] (formal) bring to an end; come to an end:

(正式用语)终止；终结；结束：~ *sb's contract*: 终止某人的合约；~ *a pregnancy*. 堕胎。

ter·mi·na·tion /ˌtɜːmɪˈneɪʃn; ˌtɝməˈneʃən/ *n* **1** [C, U] ending: 终止；结束；结局；结尾: *the ~ of a contract*; 合约的终止；~ *of pregnancy*, abortion. 堕胎。 **2** [C] final syllable or letter of a word (as in inflexion or derivation). 词的末一音节或末一字母；词尾(如见于词尾变化或派生词中者)。

ter·mi·nol·ogy /ˌtɜːmɪˈnɒlədʒɪ; ˌtɝməˈnɑlədʒɪ/ *n* [C, U] (*pl* -**gies**) (science of the) proper use of terms (6); terms used in a science or art: 术语学；术语用法；专门名词；术语：*problems of terminology*; 专门术语的问题；*medical /grammatical ~*. 医学(语法)术语。 **ter·mi·no·logi·cal** /ˌtɜːmɪnəˈlɒdʒɪkl; ˌtɝmɪnəˈlɑdʒɪkl/ *adj* of ~: 专门术语的；术语的：*a terminological inexactitude*, (hum) an untruth. (谐)谎话。

ter·mi·nus /ˈtɜːmɪnəs; ˈtɝmənəs/ *n* [C] (*pl* -**es** /-nəsɪz; -nəsɪz/) station at the end of a railway line; end of a tram, bus or air route. (铁路的)终点站;(电车、公共汽车或航线的)终点。

ter·mite /ˈtɜːmaɪt; ˈtɝmaɪt/ *n* insect (popularly but wrongly called *white ant*), found chiefly in tropical areas, very destructive to timber, textiles, etc and which makes large hills of hard earth. 蟹(一般人误称为 white ant, 主要产于热带地区, 对木材、纺织品等极具破坏力, 以硬土营垤)。 ⇨ the illus at **insect**. 参看 insect 之插图。

tern /tɜːn; tɝn/ *n* sea-bird like a gull, but usu smaller and swifter in flight. 燕鸥(较海鸥小, 飞行较快)。

Terp·si·chorean /ˌtɜːpsɪkəˈrɪən; ˌtɝpsɪkəˈrɪən/ *adj* of dancing: 舞蹈的：*the ~ art*. 舞蹈艺术。

ter·race /ˈterəs; ˈterɪs/ *n* **1** level(led) area of ground with a vertical or sloping front or side; a series of these, separated by sloping banks, rising one above the other, eg as a method of irrigation on a hillside. (边缘呈垂直或斜坡状的)平坦地区;台地;梯田;梯状地段。 **2** flight of wide, shallow steps (eg for spectators at a sporting event such as a football match, or on the banks of the Ganges at Benares, used by bathers). 宽广而浅的阶梯(如球场上观众坐的梯座, 或贝拿勒斯印度恒河堤岸上供沐浴者使用的梯级)。 **3** continuous row of houses in one block (often as part of a postal address): 一排房屋(常作为通信地址的一部分);巷;坊;里;台街: *6 Olympic T~, Glasgow*. 格拉斯哥市奥林匹克台街六号。 **4** (US) porch, paved area, adjacent to a house, used as an outdoor living area. (美)走廊;(连接房屋的)露台;阳台;平台(用作户外活动场所)。 □ *vt* [VP6A] (usu *pp*) form into ~s; make ~s in: (通常用过去分词)使成梯形地;筑梯形地于：*a ~d lawn*; 梯形草坪；*~d houses*, (long line of) houses joined together, sometimes with an alley in the rear for access to the backyards. 成排的房屋(有时后面有巷弄可通后院)。

irrigation terraces

terra-cotta /ˌterə ˈkɒtə; ˈterəˈkɑtə/ *n* [U] hard, reddish-brown pottery (used for vases, small statues, ornamental building material, etc): 混合陶器；赤陶(用作花瓶、小雕像、建筑的饰物等): (attrib) (作形容词) *a ~ vase*; 赤陶花瓶; the colour reddishbrown. 赤褐色;土红色。

terra firma /ˌterə ˈfɜːmə; ˈterəˈfɝmə/ *n* [U] (Lat) dry land, solid land (contrasted with water): (拉)陆地;大地(与 water 相对): *glad to be on ~ again*. 很高兴又

踏上陆地。

ter·rain /teˈreɪn *US*: tə-; teˈren/ *n* stretch of land, esp with regard to its natural features: 地形；地貌；地势;地带: *difficult ~ for heavy armoured vehicles*. 重装甲车辆难以行走的地形。

terra in·cog·nita /ˌterə ɪnˈkɒɡnɪtə; ˌterəɪnˈkɑɡnɪtə/ *n* (Lat) unknown territory, eg on maps of unexplored areas. (拉)未知地域(如地图上未勘探之区域)。

ter·ra·pin /ˈterəpɪn; ˈterəpɪn/ *n* kinds of freshwater tortoise and turtle of N America: (北美产的)淡水龟;泥龟;鳖;甲鱼: (esp) (尤指) *the diamond-back ~*, valued as food. 菱纹背泥龟(为珍贵食品)。

ter·res·trial /tɪˈrestrɪəl; təˈrestrɪəl/ *adj* **1** of, on, living on, the earth or land: 陆地的; 陆栖的; 长于陆地的: *the ~ parts of the world*. 地球的陆地部分。 **2** of the earth (opposed to *celestial*): 地球的; 世界的; 现世的(与 celestial 之反义词): *a ~ globe*, representing the earth. 地球仪。

ter·rible /ˈterəbl; ˈterəbl/ *adj* **1** causing great fear or horror: 可怕的; 可怖的; 令人恐惧的: *a ~ war / accident*. 意外灾难。 *He died in ~ agony*. 他在可怕的痛苦中死去。 **2** causing great discomfort; extreme: 使人感到极度不舒服的; 极端的: *The heat is ~ in Baghdad during the summer*. 巴格达在夏季炎热异常。 **3**(colloq) extremely bad: (口)极坏的: *My room was in a ~ state of disorder*. 我的房间凌乱不堪。 *What ~ food they gave us*! 他们供给我们的食物多糟啊! **ter·ribly** /-əblɪ; -əblɪ/ *adv* (colloq) extremely: (口)极端地; 非常地: *How terribly boring he is*! 他是多么令人讨厌!

ter·rier /ˈterɪə(r); ˈterɪɚ/ *n* kinds of small and active dog, esp the kind that digs into burrows to pursue its prey. 㹴(数种活泼的小狗, 尤指进入地穴追赶其猎物者)。 ⇨ the illus at **dog**. 参看 dog 之插图。

ter·rific /təˈrɪfɪk; təˈrɪfɪk/ *adj* **1** causing fear; terrible. 可怕的; 令人恐怖的。 **2**(colloq) very great; extreme: (口)非常大的; 极端的: *driving at a ~ pace*. 以极高的速度驾驶。 **ter·rifi·cally** /-klɪ; -klɪ/ *adv* (colloq) extremely. (口)极度地。

ter·rify /ˈterɪfaɪ; ˈterɪfaɪ/ *vt* (*pt, pp* -**fied**) [VP6A, 15A] fill with fear: 使恐怖; 惊吓: *The child was terrified of being left alone in the house*. 那孩子因为一个人留在家里而害怕。 *She was terrified out of her wits*. 她吓得魂不附体。 *What a ~ing experience*! 多可怕的一次经验!

ter·ri·torial /ˌterɪˈtɔːrɪəl; ˌterəˈtorɪəl/ *adj* **1** of land, esp land forming a division of a country: 领土的; 土地的: ~ *possessions*; 领地; *have ~ claims against a State*, claim part of its territory. 对某国提出领土要求。 **~ waters**, the sea near a country's coast, over which special rights are claimed, eg for fishing. 领海。 **2** T~, of any of the US Territories: 美国之领地的: *T~ laws*. 美国领地的法律。 **3** (GB) (often 常作 *T~*) of the force of mostly non-professional soldiers organized for the defence of Great Britain and trained in their spare time: (英)本土防卫队的; 国防义勇军的: *the T~ Army*. 国防义勇军。 □ *n* member of the T~ Army. 国防义勇军兵士。

ter·ri·tory /ˈterɪtrɪ *US*: -tɔːrɪ; ˈterəˌtorɪ/ *n* (*pl* -**ries**) **1** [C, U] (area of) land, esp land under one ruler or Government: 领土: *Turkish ~ in Europe*. 土耳其在欧洲的领土。 **2** [C] land or district; (large) extent of such land, etc: 土地; 地方; 区域; 此等土地的范围; 领域: *This salesman travels over a large ~*. 这位推销员旅行推销很大一个区域。 *How much ~ does he travel over*? 他旅行的地方有多大? *Mating blackbirds will defend their ~ (= the area which they regard as belonging to themselves) against intruders*. 山鸟交配时不容许入侵者侵犯它们(视为己有)的领域。 **3** (US) district not admitted as a State but having its own law-making body: (美)属地; 地方(尚未成为一州, 但有其立法机构): *Until 1959 Hawaii was a T~, not a State*. 在一九五九年之前, 夏威夷是一个属地, 不是一个州。

ter·ror /ˈterə(r); ˈterɚ/ *n* **1** [U] great fear: 恐怖; 惊

骇: *run away in* ~; 惊慌地跑开; *be in* ~ *of one's life*, fear that one will lose one's life. 恐惧自己有生命的危险。*strike* ~ *into sb*, fill him with ~. 使某人恐惧。Hence, 由此产生, **'~-struck**, **'~-stricken** adj struck, filled, with ~. 惊惧的; 害怕的; 恐惧的。**2** [C] instance of great fear; sth or sb that causes great fear: 恐怖的实例; 令人恐怖的人或事物: *have a* ~ *of fire*. 害怕火。*This added to our* ~*s*. 这增加了我们的恐惧。**3** [C] (colloq) troublesome person: (口) 讨厌的人: *This child is a perfect* ~, *a great nuisance*. 这孩子讨厌透了。**~·ism** /-ɪzəm/; -,ɪzəm/ n use of violence and intimidation, esp for political purposes. 恐怖手段; 恐怖主义(尤指为达到政治目的者)。**~·ist** /-ɪst; -ɪst/ n supporter of, participant in, ~ism. 支持或参与恐怖主义者; 恐怖分子。**~·ize** /-aɪz; -,aɪz/ vt [VP6A] fill with ~ by threats or acts of violence. 借威胁或暴行使充满恐怖; 恐吓。

terse /tɜːs; tɜːs/ adj (of speech, style, speakers) brief and to the point; concise. (指言词、文体、说话者)简明切题的; 精简的。**~·ly** adv · **~·ness** n

ter·tian /'tɜːʃn; 'tɜːʃən/ adj (of fever) marked by paroxysms which occur every other day. (指疾病)隔日发作的; 间日的。

ter·ti·ary /'tɜːʃərɪ US: -ʃɪerɪ; 'tɜːʃɪ,ɛrɪ/ adj third in rank, order, occurrence, importance: 第三位的; 第三等的; 第三级的; 第三的: *the T~ period*, (geol) the third period in the formation of rocks; (地质)岩石形成的第三纪。~ *burns*/*syphilis*, a severe stage. 三级灼伤(三期梅毒)。

tery·lene /'terəliːn; 'tɛrə,lin/ n [U] (GB)(P) (fabric made from) kinds of man-made fibre. (英)(商标)人造纤维; 人造纤维布料; 台丽龙。

tes·sel·lated /'tesəleɪtɪd; 'tɛsl,etɪd/ adj formed of small, flat pieces of stone of various colours (as used in mosaic): 以不同颜色的小石块(如镶嵌细工所用者)做成的; 嵌装图案的: *a* ~ *pavement*. 嵌装图案的人行道。

test /test; tɛst/ n [C] (often attrib) examination or trial (of sth) to find its quality, value, composition, etc; trial or examination (of sb, his powers, knowledge, skill, etc): (常用作定语)测验; 试验; 考验: *methods that have stood the* ~ *of time*; 禁得起时间考验的方法; *an endurance* ~, eg for a new aero-engine; 耐力试验(如测验新的飞机引擎); *a 'blood* ~, eg at a hospital, for infection, etc. 验血。*a* ~ *in arithmetic*; 算术测验; *an in'telligence* ~. 智力测验。*put sth to the* ~, submit it to conditions, etc, that will show its qualities, etc. 使某物接受考验。*a* **'** ~ *bore*, hole bored into the ground or sea-bed to learn whether there is mineral ore, oil, etc: (探测矿藏、石油等, 在地面或海床所作的)钻(探)孔: ~ *bores in the North Sea*. 北海钻(探)孔。*a* **'** ~ *case*, (in law) one that shows the principle involved (even though it may not be important in itself). (法律)判例案件; 判决先例。**'** ~ *drive* n drive in a car one thinks of buying, to judge its qualities, worth, etc. 试车(驾驶欲购之车, 以判定其性质、价值等)。Hence, 由此产生, **'~-drive** vt. *a* **'driving** ~, an examination of one's ability to drive a car in the way required by law. 驾驶考试。**'** ~ *match* n one of the matches in any of the cricket or Rugby tours arranged between certain countries. (板球或橄榄球的)国际锦标赛。**'** ~ *pilot* n one who flies newly built aircraft to try their qualities, performance, etc. (新飞机的)试飞员。**'~-tube** n slender glass tube, closed at one end, used in chemical ~s and experiments. 试管。**'~-tube baby**, baby whose early development took place in a laboratory (after artificial insemination) and is later implanted in the womb. 试管婴儿(人工受精后, 先在实验室中培育, 再移入子宫者)。□ vt [VP6A, 15A] put to the ~; examine: 试验; 考验; 检验: *have one's eyesight* ~*ed*; 检验视力; ~ *ore for gold*; 化验矿石中黄金的成分; *a well*-~*ed remedy*. 经试验有效的医疗法。*The long climb* ~*ed* (= was a ~ of) *our powers of endurance*. 那次长距离的爬山考验了我们的持久力。

tes·ta·ment /'testəmənt; 'tɛstəmənt/ n **1** [C] (often 常作 *last Will and T~*) statement in writing saying how sb wishes his property to be distributed after his death. 遗嘱。**2 Old T~, New T~**, the two main divisions of the Bible. 旧约(圣经), 新约(圣经)。⇨ App 10. 参看附录十。**tes·ta·men·tary** /,testə'mentrɪ; ,tɛstə-'mɛntərɪ/ adj of, connected with, given in, a ~ (1). 遗嘱的; 关于遗嘱的; 遗嘱中写明的。

tes·tate /'testeɪt; 'tɛstet/ n, adj (person) who has made a testament (and died leaving it in force). 立有遗嘱的(人); 死后留有有效遗嘱的(人)。**tes·ta·tor** /te-'steɪtə(r) US: 'testeɪtər; 'tɛstetɚ/ n man who has made a testament. 立有遗嘱的男子; **tes·ta·trix** /te'steɪtrɪks; tɛs'tetrɪks/ n woman testator. 立有遗嘱的女子。

tes·ticle /'testɪkl; 'tɛstɪkl/ n each of the two glands of the male sex organ that secrete spermatozoa. 睾丸。

tes·tify /'testɪfaɪ; 'tɛstə,faɪ/ vt, vi (pt, pp -**fied**) [VP2A, 3A, 9] ~ *that...*; ~ *to sth*; ~ *against*/*in favour of sb*, bear witness, give evidence: 提供证据: *He testified under oath that he had not been at the scene of the crime*. 他发誓作证他当时并不在犯罪现场。*The teacher testified to the boy's ability*. 教师为那男孩的能力作证。*Two witnesses will* ~ *against her and three will* ~ *on her behalf*. 两位证人将作不利于她的证明, 另三位将作有利于她的证明。**2** [VP6A] serve as evidence of: 成为…的证据; 证明: *Her tears testified her grief*. 她的眼泪证明了她的忧伤。

tes·ti·mo·nial /,testɪ'məʊnɪəl; ,tɛstə'monɪəl/ n **1** written statement testifying to a person's merits, abilities, qualifications, etc as sent with an application for a position. (优点、能力、资格等的)推荐书; 证明书。**2** sth given to sb to show appreciation of services, usu sth subscribed for by several or many colleagues. 褒扬状; 感谢状; 谢礼; 纪念品(通常系同事或同僚间集资赠与某人者)。

tes·ti·mony /'testɪmənɪ US: -məʊnɪ; 'tɛstə,monɪ/ n [U] **1** declaration, esp in a law court, testifying that sth is true: 证言; 证词(尤指在法庭上所作者): *The witness's* ~ *is false*. 那证人的证言不实。*Several men were called in to bear* ~ *to what the police officer said*. 数人被传入为警官所说的话作证。**2** declarations; statements: 宣言; 陈述: *According to the* ~ *of the medical profession, the health of the nation is improving*. 根据医学界的陈述, 国民的健康在进步中。

tes·tis /'testɪs; 'tɛstɪs/ n (pl -**tes** /-tiːz; -tiz /) = **testicle**.

testy /'testɪ; 'tɛstɪ/ adj (-**ier**, -**iest**) quickly or easily annoyed; impatient. 易被激怒的; 性子急的; 暴躁的。**tes·tily** /-ɪlɪ; -əlɪ/ adv **tes·ti·ness** n

teta·nus /'tetənəs; 'tɛtŋəs/ n [U] disease marked by stiffening and tightening of some or all of the muscles which are normally under conscious control: 破伤风(平时可随意控制的肌肉, 部分或全部变为强直的疾病): ~ *of the lower jaw* (colloq called 口语称 *lockjaw*). 下颚破伤风; 咀嚼肌痉挛。

tetchy /'tetʃɪ; 'tɛtʃɪ/ adj (-**ier**, -**iest**) peevish; irritable. 易怒的; 暴躁的。**tetch·ily** /-ɪlɪ; -əlɪ/ adv **tetchi·ness** n

tête-à-tête /,teɪt ɑː 'teɪt; 'tetə'tet/ n private meeting between two persons; their talk: 两人间的秘密聚会; 两人间的面谈或密谈; 促膝谈心: *have a* ~ *with sb*; 与某人密谈; *have a* ~ *talk*. (与某人)密谈。□ adv in a ~: 两人在一起私下地; 两人间秘密地: *He dined* ~ *with the Prime Minister*. 他单独与首相共餐。

tether /'teðə(r); 'tɛðɚ/ n rope or chain by which an animal is fastened while grazing. (拴牲畜的)系绳; 系链。*at the end of one's* ~, (fig) at the end of one's powers, resources, endurance, etc. (喻)用尽某人的体能、智能、忍耐力等; 智穷技竭; 筋疲力尽; 忍无可忍。□ vt [VP6A, 15A] fasten with a ~: 以系绳或系链拴: *He* ~*ed his horse to the fence*. 他把马拴在篱笆上。

Teu·ton /'tjuːtən US: 'tuːtn; 'tjutŋ/ n member of

any of the Teutonic nations. 条顿人。 **~ic** /tjuː'tɒnɪk US: tuː-; ˌtjuˈtɑnɪk/ *adj* of the Germanic (ie Anglo-Saxon, Dutch, German and Scandinavian) peoples. (包括盎格鲁撒克逊人、荷兰人、日耳曼人及斯塔的纳维亚人之)条顿民族的。

text /tekst; tɛkst/ *n* 1[U] main body of a book or printed page (contrasted with notes, diagrams, illustrations, etc): (书或印刷物的) 正文: 本文 (与 notes, diagrams, illustrations 等相对): *too much ~ and not enough pictures.* 正文太多而插图不够。2 [C] original words of an author, apart from anything else in a book: (作者的) 原文: *a corrupt ~,* one that, perhaps because of mistakes in copying, is no longer in its original form. 与原作有出入的原文。3 [C] short passage, sentence, esp of Scripture, as the subject of a sermon or discussion. (讲道或讨论的) 主题文字: *a favourite ~.* 常用经文。4 ~(**·book**) /'teksbʊk; 'tɛkst,bʊk/) book giving instruction in a branch of learning: 教科书: *an algebra ~ book.* 代数教科书。**tex·tual** /'tekstʃuəl; 'tɛkstʃʊəl/ *adj* of, in, a ~: 正文的; 本文的; 原文的; 在正文、原文等中的: *~ual errors;* 原文的错误; *~ual criticism.* 原文校勘。

tex·tile /'tekstaɪl; 'tɛkstl/ *attrib adj* of the making of cloth: 纺织的; 织物的: *~ processes;* 纺织的过程; *the ~ industry;* 纺织工业; woven; suitable for weaving: 织成的; 适于纺织的: *~ fabrics/materials.* 纺织品(纺织原料)。□ *n* [C] ~ material. 纺织品; 织物; 纺织原料。

tex·ture /'tekstʃ(r); 'tɛkstʃɚ/ *n* [C, U] 1 the arrangement of the threads in a textile fabric: (织物的) 质地; 织质: *cloth with a loose/close ~.* 质地稀松(紧密)的布。2 arrangement of the parts that make up sth: 构造; 结构; 纹理: *the ~ of a mineral.* 矿物的构造。3 tissue: 组织; 纹理: *a skin of fine/coarse ~.* 细(粗)皮肤。**~d** *pp* (in compounds): (用于复合词中): *ˌcoarse-/ˌthin-'~d.* 质地、纹理粗(薄)的。

thal·ido·mide /θə'lɪdəmaɪd; θə'lɪdə‚maɪd/ *n* [U] (P) sedative drug which caused some women to give birth to deformed babies (esp with undeveloped limbs). (商标)反应停; 撒利豆迈(一种镇痛剂, 某些妇女服用此药会生产畸形婴儿, 特别是四肢发育不全)。

than /ðən; ðən; *rarely heard strong form:* ðæn; ðæn/ *conj* 1 (introducing the second part of a comparison): 比(后面接比较的第二部分): *John is taller ~ his brother.* 约翰比他哥哥(弟弟)高。*I have never met anyone more stupid ~ you.* 我从未碰到过比你更笨的人。**different than,** ⇨ **different.** 2 (with a *transitive v* the form of a *pron* after *than* depends upon the sense of the complete sentence. Note the words in parenthesis in these examples): (与及物动词连用时; than 后的代词形式视全句文意而定。注意下列诸例句括号内的词): *I know you better ~ he (does),* ie ~ he knows you. 我比他更了解你。*I know you better ~ him,* ie ~ I know him. 我了解你胜过我了解他。*I like her no better ~ he (does),* ie ~ he likes her. 我和他喜欢她的程度相等。*I like her no better ~ him,* ie ~ I like her. 我喜欢她和他的程度相等。3 (with an *intransitive v* the *pron* after *than* is often in the object form, in both colloquial and written English, even though the subject form is required by formal grammar. This is esp so when the *pron* is followed by *all*): (与不及物动词连用时, 无论是在口语或是文章中, than 后面的代词常用宾格形式, 尽管正式的语法要求使用主格。而代词后接有 all 时, 该代词尤其采用宾格): *He is several years older ~ me/~ I am.* 他比我大几岁。*He can run faster ~ me/~ I can.* 他跑得比我快。*He is wiser ~ us all.* 他比我们都聪明。4 (in phrases) (用于短语中) *no other ~,* (used as an equivalent to a construction with an emphatic *pron*): 就是(是indf正等于emphatic的代词结构): *It was no other ~ my old friend Jones,* ie it was Jones himself. 就是我的老友琼斯。*nothing else ~,* only, entire(ly): 仅仅; 完全地; 完全地; 全然: *His failure was due to nothing else ~* (= was entirely due to) *his own carelessness.* 他的失败完全由于他自己的疏忽所致。*What he told you was*

nothing else ~ nonsense, was complete nonsense. 他告诉你的全是无稽之谈。*rather ~,* ⇨ **rather**(1). *sooner ~,* ⇨ **soon**(3, 5).

thane /θeɪn; θeɪn/ *n* (hist) man who gave military service in return for land. (史)借纳兵役而取得土地的大乡绅。

thank /θæŋk; θæŋk/ *vt* ~ *sb (for sth),* 1 [VP6A, 14] express gratitude to: 谢; 感谢; 道谢: *~ a person for his help.* 感谢某人帮忙。*There's no need to ~ me.* 无须向我道谢。*'T~ you,* the usual formula for 'I ~ you.' 谢谢你。*'No, '~ you,* formula used to decline an offer (Note that the 'No' is essential; *'T~ you'* is used for acceptance and may mean 'Yes, please.') (不(必)了, 谢谢你(用于婉拒一项提议)。(注意: 'No' 字是必要的; 如无 no, 即变为接受该提议, 其含义可能就是 '好的, 麻烦你了')。[VP11] *T~ Heaven (that) you've come.* 感谢老天, 你可来了。*T~ God she's safe.* 感谢上帝, 她安然无恙。2 [VP14, 17] (in peremptory request, future tense): (用于表示强制的要求, 用将来时): *I'll ~ you for that book,* please give it to me. 请把那本书给我。*I'll ~ you to be a little more polite/to mind your own business.* 请你客气一点 (请你别管闲事)。□ *n* (now only in *pl* except in *~-offering* and with suffixes as below): (现仅用复数形, 唯 *~-offering* 一词及下列诸例中与后缀连用的情形, 仍用单数形): (expression of) gratitude: 谢意; 谢忱; 感谢的表示: *give ~s to God;* 感谢上帝; *T~s/No, ~s,* colloq formulas of gratitude/refusal. 谢谢(不必了, 谢谢)。*~s to,* as the result of; owing to: 由于; 因为: *T~s to your help we were successful.* 由于你的帮助, 我们成功了。*small ~s to,* used ironically: 一点也不感谢(反语用法): *We were successful, but small ~s to you,* you gave us no help. 我们成功了, 但并不感谢你(你未帮我们忙)。*'~-offering n* offering made, eg to a charity, a religious organization, as an expression of gratitude. 感恩捐献。*~s-'giving n* (a) expression of gratitude, esp to God; prayer in thankfulness for mercies: 感恩; 感恩祈祷。(b)(US) (also 亦作 *T~s-'giving Day*) day set apart each year for giving ~s to God (usu the fourth Thursday in November). (美)感恩节(通常为十一月的第四个星期四)。**~ful** /-fl; -fəl/ *adj* grateful: 感谢的; 感激的; 欣慰的: *Be ~ful for small mercies.* 虽小恩亦要感激。*You should be ~ful to have/that you have escaped with minor injuries.* 你应该为你仅受轻伤而脱险感到欣慰。**~fully** /-fəlɪ; -fəlɪ/ *adv* **~·ful·ness** *n* **~·less** *adj* not feeling or expressing gratitude; (of actions) not arousing gratitude or winning appreciation: 不感谢的; 不领情的; 忘恩的; (指行为) 徒劳的; 不令人感谢的: *a ~less task,* one which brings no ~s, appreciation or reward 徒劳的工作。

that¹ /ðæt; ðæt (*no weak form*)/ (*pl* **those** /ðəuz; ðoz/) *adj, pron* (contrasted with *this, these.* ~/*those* and *this/these* are used to make a person or thing specific. *this/these* are used when the person or thing is near to the speaker.) (与 this, these 相对。that, those 与 this, these 均特指某(些)人或物, this, these 指与说话人较近者。) 1 *Look at ~ man/those men there.* 看那个人(那些人)。*What's ~ over there?* 那边那个是什么? *What are those?* 那些是什么? *What was ~ noise?* 那是什么响声? *What noise was ~?* 那是什么响声? *Is ~ you, Mary?* 是你吗, 玛丽? *Are those children yours?* 那些孩子是你(们)的吗? *Is ~ what you really think?* 你真的那样想吗? *T~'s what he told me.* 那就是他告诉我的(话)。*This book is much better ~ those.* 这本书比那本好得多。*These are much better than those.* 这些远比那些好。*Life was easier in those days/at ~ time,* then, during that period. 那时(在那个时间), 谋生比较容易。*So ~'s ~!* (formula used to indicate finality, the end of a discussion, an argument, etc). 就这样了! 就这样决定了! (用于表示定局, 表示讨论、辩论等的终结。) 2 (as antecedent to a *rel pron,* expressed or omitted): (用作关系代词的先行词, 明示或省略): *All those (that) I saw were old.* 我见到的那些统统是旧的。*Those who do not*

wish to ~go need not go. 凡是不愿意去的人就不必去。*It's a different kind of car from* ~ (= kind of car) (which) *I am used to.* 这种汽车同我用习惯的那一种不一样。*Throw away all those* (which are) *unfit for use.* 把那些不合用的统统扔掉。*Those* (= People who were) *present at the ceremony were…*. 出席典礼的那些人是…。*There are those who say* (= some people who say)…. 有人说…。**3** (with a *pl n*, considered as a collective *sing*): (与复数名词连用，视为集合单数): *What about* ~ *five pounds you borrowed from me last month?* 你上个月向我借的那五镑何时归还? *When do you intend to repay* ~ *sum of five pounds?* 你打算何时还我那五镑? **4** (*That* and a possessive cannot be used together. Note the construction used when ~ and a possessive are both needed): (that 和可与所有格连用时，注意需要同时使用 that 与所有格时的句型结构): *I don't like* ~ *new secretary of his.* 我不喜欢他那位新来的秘书。*Well, how's* ~ *bad leg of yours getting on?* 唔, 你那条疼痛的腿复元的情况如何? □ *adv* (colloq) to such a degree; so: (口)达到这样的程度; 如许: *I can't walk* ~ *far,* = as far as ~. 我可走不了那么远。*I've done only* ~ *much,* ie as much as is shown, indicated, etc. 我就做了那么多。*It's about* ~ *high,* ie as high as ~. 它大约有那么高。*I was* ~ (= so) *angry I could have hit him,* ie I wanted to hit him. 我那时气得简直想揍他。*It isn't all* ~ *cold,* eg not so cold that a fire/overcoat, etc is needed. 还没有冷到那种程度(如还没有冷到生火、穿大衣等的程度)。

that² /*usual form*: ðət; ðət; *strong form*: ðæt; ðæt/ *conj* **1** (introducing *n* clauses, but often omitted): (引导名词性从句, 但常被省略): *She said* ~ *she would come.* 她说她要来的。*It so happens* ~ *I know the man.* 碰巧我认识那个人。*The trouble is* ~ *we are short of money.* 困难就在于我们缺钱。*I will see to it* ~ *everything is ready.* 我会注意把一切准备妥当的。**2** *so* ~; *in order* ~, (introducing clauses of purpose): 俾; 以便; 为了(引导表示目的的从句): *Bring it nearer* (*so*) ~ *I may see it better.* (把它)拿近一点, 好让我看清楚些。*I will give up my claim so* ~/*in order* ~ *you may have the property.* 我愿意放弃我的要求权, 俾使你获得那份财产。**3** (introducing clauses of result): (引导表示结果的从句): *His behaviour was such* ~/*was so bad* ~ *we all refused to receive him in our homes.* 他行为不检, 我们全都拒绝在家里招待他。**4** (introducing clauses of condition): (引导表示条件的从句): *supposing* ~…; *on condition* ~…. 设若…; 假使…; on condition ~…. 设若…。**5** (introducing clauses of reason or cause): (引导表示理由或原因的从句): **not(4)**, and *now, conj.* **6** (rhet) in exclamations: (修辞)用于感叹句中: *Oh,* ~ *I could be with you again!* How I wish…! 啊, 我真希望能够再同你在一起! *Oh,* ~ *I should live to see my own son sent to prison as a thief!* How sad it is ~…! 我竟然(活着)亲眼看到我的儿子作贼而被抓去坐牢(多令人伤心呀)!

that³ /*usual form*: ðət; ðət; *strong form*: ðæt; ðæt/ *rel pron* (*pl* unchanged; used in defining or restrictive clauses; not preceded by a pause or a comma; often preferred to *which* for things; often preferred to *whom* and often used in place of *who*) (复数不变; 用于限定从句中; 前面不停顿亦不加逗点; 指物时较 which 常用; 较 whom 常用, 并常代替 who) **1** (as the subject of the *v* in a clause): (在从句中作动词的主语): *The letter* ~ *came this morning is from my father.* 今天早晨收到的那封信是我父亲寄来的。*Those dogs* ~ *attacked your sheep ought to be shot.* 攻击你羊群的那些狗该射杀。*The man* ~ (*who* is preferred) *sold you that camera is a rogue.* 卖照相机给你的那个人是个流氓(本句中 who 较 that 为佳)。*The man* ~ (*who* is preferred) *cycled past you is nearly ninety.* 骑脚踏车从你旁边经过的那个人快要九十岁了(本句中 who 较 that 为佳)。**2** (Although *who* is usually preferred to *that*, *that* is preferred to *who* after superlatives, *only, all, any*, and *it is* or *it was*): (虽然 who 通常较 that 佳, 惟在最高级形容词后, 在 only, all, any 后, 以及在 it is 或 it was 后时, that 较 who 为佳):

Newton was one of the greatest men ~ *ever lived.* 牛顿是世上最伟大的人物之一。*He's the cleverest man* ~ *I ever met.* 他是我所遇到的人当中最聪明的了。*You're the only person* ~ *can help me.* 你是唯一能帮我忙的人。*Anyone* ~ *wants to succeed must work hard.* 任何人要想获得成功就必须勤奋工作。*It's you* ~ *I want to speak to, not Paul.* 我要跟你说话, 不是跟保罗。**3** (as the object of the *v* in the clause; *whom* is to be avoided; the *pron* is often omitted): (在从句中作动词的宾语; whom 避免用; 代词 that 常省略): *The watch* (~) *you gave me is working perfectly.* 你给我的那个表走得好极了。*Is this the best* (~) *you can do?* 你最多只能做到这样吗? *The girl* (~) *you met yesterday wants to see you again.* 你昨天遇到的那个女孩想再见你。*All the people* (~) *I invited have agreed to come.* 所有经我邀请的人都同意来。**4** (after an expression of time. Cf *when, rel adv*): (用于表时间的用语之后。参较关系副词 when): *the year* (~) *my father died;* 我父亲过世的那一年; *the week* (~) *we went camping.* 我们去露营的那个礼拜。**5** (as the object of a *prep; whom* is to be avoided; *that* is often omitted, and the *prep* follows the *v*): (用作介词的宾语; whom 避免用; that 常省略, 介词接在动词后): *The photographs* (~) *you were looking at were taken by my brother.* 你看的那些相片是我哥哥(弟弟)拍的。*The man* (~) *I was talking to had just arrived from Canada.* 和我谈话的那个人刚从加拿大来。*Where's the man* (~) *you borrowed it from?* 你向他借这东西的那个人在哪里?

thatch /θætʃ; θætʃ/ *n* [U] (roof covering of) dried straw, reeds, etc; (colloq) thick hair of the head. 茅草(千的稻草、芦苇等); 茅草(屋)顶; (口)厚密的头发。□ *vt* [VP6A] cover (a roof, etc) with ~. 以茅草盖(屋顶等)。

thaw /θɔ:; θɔ/ *vi, vt* [VP6A, 15B, 2A, C] ~ (*out*), **1** *It is* ~*ing,* The temperature has risen above freezing-point (so that snow and ice begin to melt). 天解冻了(冰雪开始融化了)。**2** (cause anything frozen to) become liquid or soft again: (使)融化; 融解: ~ *out the radiator,* (of a car); 使(汽车)冷却器的冰化除; *leave frozen food to* ~ *before cooking it.* 让冰冻食物在烹调前先行退冰。**3** (of persons, their behaviour) (cause to) become less formal, more friendly: (指人, 其行为)(使)变得较不拘礼, 较友善: *A good dinner he began to* ~. 吃这一餐美好的饭, 他开始变得友善了。*A bottle of wine helped to* ~ (*out*) *our guests.* 我们的客人喝过一瓶酒之后不再那么拘束了。□ *n* (usu *sing*) (state of the weather causing) ~*ing:* (通常用单数)融化; 融解; 解冻的天气: *Let's go skating before the* ~/*a* ~ *sets in.* 我们趁着还未解冻去溜冰吧。

the /*before consonants*: ðə; ðə; *before vowels*: ðɪ; ðɪ; *strong form*: ðiː; ði/ *def art* **1** (used as a less specific form of *this, these, that, those,* applied to person(s), thing(s), event(s), etc already referred to or, being discussed. Note the changes from the *indef art* to the *def art* in these sentences): (э this, these, that, those 的较不明确的形式, 用以指已提过的或正在讨论中的人、物、事等。注意下列诸句中从不定冠词变为定冠词的用法): *An old man and an old woman once lived in a small hut by a river near a forest. One day the old man left the hut and went into the forest to gather wood. The old woman went to the river to wash clothes.* 从前有一位老人及一位老妇住在河畔靠近森林的一座小茅屋里。有一天那位老人离开茅屋, 进入森林去采薪。那位老妇则河边去洗衣服。**2** (used when who or what is referred to is quite obvious): (用于所指的人或物十分明显的情况): *Please take these letters to the post office,* ie the post office near by, the post office of this district. 请把这些信拿到邮局去(指附近的或本区的邮局)。*Please close the window,* ie the window that is open. 请把窗户关起来(指开着的那个窗户)。*Shall we have a walk by* ~ *river?* eg in London, the River Thames. 咱们到河边去散散步好不好?(如在伦敦, 指的是泰晤士河。)**3** (used with a *n* when it stands for sth unique): (与代表独一无二事物的名词连用): *the*

sun; 太阳; *the* (*moon*) 月亮; *the year 1939*: 一九三九年; *the universe*. 宇宙. **4** (used with *nn* such as *sea, sky,wind* (as in **2** above) when there is no *adj*): (与无形容词修饰的名词如 sea, sky, wind 等词连用, 用法如上列第 2 义): *The sea was calm*. 海上风平浪静. *There's an aeroplane in the sky*. 天上有一架飞机. *Isn't the wind strong!* 多强的风啊! Note that the use of an *adj* to describe the sea, wind, etc may make the use of the *indef art* possible: 注意: 这些词如有形容词修饰, 亦可能用不定冠词: *There was a calm sea* (cf 参较 *The sea was calm*) *when I crossed from Dover to Calais*. 我从多佛渡海至加来时, 海上风平浪静. *What a stormy-looking sky!* 好一个阴沉的天空, 象是暴风雨要来了! *There was a cold wind* (cf 参较 *The wind was cold*) 刮起了一阵冷风. **5** (used with a *n* if it is modified by a phrase or clause that makes it unique): (如某名词为短语或从句所修饰因而具有独特性质时, 则与该名词连用): *the back of the house*; 房屋的后部; *the left side of the road*; 路的左侧; (In many phrases the *def art* is or may be omitted: (在许多短语中, 定冠词须省去或可以省去: *from beginning to end*; 自始至终; *from* (*the*) *top to* (*the*) *bottom*; 从顶端到底部; *in* (*the*) *future*. 在未来.) **6** (used with the superl): (与最高级连用): *the best way to get there*; 去那里最佳的方法; *the tallest of the five men*; 五人中的最高者; *the most interesting book I have ever read*. 我读过的最有趣的书. (The *def art* is not needed in the predicate after the *v* '*be*' when the superl is used without a *n*: 接在 be 动词后面的最高级形容词不与名词连用时无需定冠词: *It is wisest* (= The wisest plan is) *to avoid the centre of the town*. 避开市中心是最聪明的(最聪明的计划). When most means 'very', the *def art* is not used: 作 'very' 解的 most 之前, 不加定冠词: *The story was most exciting*. 这故事非常动人. *This is a most useful reference book*. 这是一本极有用的参考书.) most²(3). **7** used before the 用于下列各专有名词之前 **(a)** names of seas and oceans: 海洋的名称: *the Mediterranean, the Red Sea*; 地中海, 红海; *the Atlantic* (*Ocean*), *the Indian Ocean*. 大西洋, 印度洋. **(b)** names of rivers and canals: 河流及运河的名称: *the Nile*; 尼罗河; *the river Thames*; 泰晤士河; *the Suez Canal*. 苏伊士运河. **(c)** *pl* geographical names: 复数地理名称: *the Alps*; 阿尔卑斯山; *the Philippines*; 菲律宾群岛; *the West Indies*; 西印度群岛; *the Netherlands*. 荷兰. **(d)** in a few geographical names: 在少数几个地名中: *the Sudan*; 苏丹; *the Sahara*. 撒哈拉. **8** (used with *adjj* and participles to denote all members of a class): (与形容词及分词连用, 表示一类的全体分子): *the rich, the young, and the beautiful*; 富人、年轻人及美丽的人; *the dead, the dying, and the wounded*, eg after a battle. 死者、垂死者及伤者. **9 the** + *adj*, (equivalent to an abstract *n*): (与形容词连用, 相当于抽象名词): *the sublime*, sublimity. 崇高. **10** (used formerly with names of diseases, now usually ommitted except with colloq or sl *pl*): (昔与病名连用, 现在除口语或俚语的复数外, 通常不加定冠词): *She's got the creeps/the fidgets/the blues*. 她感到战栗(不安, 沮丧). Survivals of the older use: 我存的旧用法: *The child has* (*the*) *measles*. 那孩子患麻疹. **11** Note: 注意(乐器名称前面加 the): *to play the piano/the violin/the banjo, etc*, 弹钢琴(拉小提琴); 弹班卓琴等), but (with names of games): 但是 (游戏名称前面不加 the): *to play tennis/football/cards/chess/billiards. etc*. 打网球(踢足球; 玩牌; 下棋; 打弹子等). **12** (used with a *sing common n* to denote the whole class, eg of animals or plants): (与单数普通名词连用表示全类, 如指动物或植物): *Is it true that the owl cannot see well in daylight?* 猫头鹰白天看不清楚是真的吗? (In colloq style, the use of the *pl*, without the *def art*, is more usu: 口语中, 不加定冠词的复数形式更为通用: *Is it true that owls cannot...?*). **13** (used in a similar way with names of inventions. In this case the use of the *def art* with the *sing n* is usu in both liter and colloq styles): (与发明物连用, 用法同上. 唯定冠词与单数名词连用的用法, 在 '文学及口语文体中皆通用): *We don't know who invented*

the wheel. 我们不知道轮子是谁发明的。 *The telephone is a most useful invention*. 电话是一项极有用的发明。 **14** (used with *nn* expressing a unit): (与名词连用表示一单位): *This car does thirty miles to the gallon*, ie to each gallon of petrol. 这部汽车每加仑汽油跑三十英里。 *These apples are small; there are seven or eight to the kilo*, ie to each kilo. 这些苹果很小; 一公斤有七、八个。 *I get paid by the hour*, ie I earn so much for each hour's work. 我是按小时计酬的。 □ *adv* by so much; by that amount; (used before an *adj* or *adv* in the comparative degree to indicate that two things increase or decrease in a parallel way, or that one increases in a degree equal to that by which another decreases): 达此程度; 至该数额; 愈; 更; (用于形容词或副词的比较级前, 表示二物同样增加或减少, 或一方增加的程度相当于另一方减少的程度): *The more he gets the more he wants*. 他得到的愈多, 想要的愈多。 *The more he reads the less he understands*. 他愈读愈读不懂。

the·atre (US = **the·ater**) /ˈθiːətə(r)/; /ˈθiːətə/ *n* **1** building or arena (*open-air ~*) for the performance of plays, for dramatic spectacles, etc: 剧院; 剧场; 露天剧场 (称 open-air *~*): *go to the ~ to see a Shakespeare play*. 去戏院看莎士比亚的戏。 '~ **·goer** *n* person who frequently goes to *~*s. 常看戏者; 戏院常客; 戏迷。 **2** hall or room with seats in rows rising one behind another for lectures, scientific demonstrations, etc. (供演讲、科学示范等用的) 有阶梯式座位的讲堂或会场。 '**operating ~**, room (in a hospital, etc) where surgical operations are performed. (医院等处的)手术室; 手术示范室。 **3** scene of important events: 重大事件发生的场所; 现场: *Belgium has often been a ~ of war*. 比利时常常成为战场。 **4** [U] dramatic literature or art; the writing and acting of plays, esp when connected with one author, country, period, etc: 戏剧; 戏剧文学或艺术; 剧本的写作及演出(尤指关于某一作家、国家、时代等者): *a book about the Greek ~*. 讨论希腊戏剧的书。 *Do Henry James's plays make good ~*, are they satisfactory when presented on the stage? 亨利·詹姆士的剧本演出的效果好吗? **the·atri·cal** /θiˈætrɪkl/ *adj* of or for the *~*: 戏院的; 剧场的; 戏剧的; 适于演出的: *theatrical scenery/performances*; 舞台布景(戏剧演出); *a 'the'atrical company*, of actors. 剧团; 戏班。 **2** (of behaviour, manner, way of speaking, persons, etc) designed for effect; showy, not natural. (指行为、样子, 说话方式, 人等)为产生某种效果而设计的; 炫耀的; 夸张的; 做作的; 戏剧性的。 □ *n* (usu *pl*) (usu amateur) dramatic performance. (通常用复数)(通常指业余的)戏剧演出; 票戏。 **the·atri·cally** /-klɪ; -klɪ/ *adv*

thee /ðiː/; /ði/ *pron*, ⇨ **thou**.

theft /θeft; θeft/ *n* [C, U] (the act of, an instance of) stealing. 偷; 行窃; 偷窃的事例。

their /ˈðeə(r); ˈðer/ *adj* of them: 他(她, 它)们的: *They have lost ~ dog*. 他们的狗丢了。 *They have a house of ~ own*. 他们自己有一幢房子。 *~·s* /ðeəz; ðerz/ *pron* of them: 他们的: *That dog is ~s, not ours*. 那只狗是他们的, 不是我们的。 *It's a habit of ~s*, one of *~* habits. 那是他们(们)的习惯。

the·ism /ˈθiːɪzəm; ˈθiːɪzəm/ *n* [U] belief in the existence of a revealed God, creator and ruler of the universe. 一神论; 有神论。 ⇨ **deism**. **the·ist** /ˈθiːɪst; ˈθiːɪst/ *n* believer in *~*. 一神论信徒。 **the·is·tic** /θiːˈɪstɪk; θiːˈɪstɪk/, **the·is·ti·cal** /-kl; -kl/ *adjj*

them /ðem; ðem; *strong form*: ðem; ðem / *pron*, ⇨ **they**.

them·atic /θɪˈmætɪk; θɪˈmætɪk/ *adj* (music) of a theme(3) or themes. (音乐)主题的; 主题曲的。

theme /θiːm; θim/ *n* [C] **1** topic; subject of a talk or a piece of writing. 题; (谈话或写作的)题目。 **2** (esp US) (subject set for a) student's essay. (尤美)学生的作文; 作文题。 **3** (music) short melody which is repeated expanded, etc eg in a sonata or symphony. (音乐)主题; 主题曲; 主旋律(如奏鸣曲或交响曲中者)。 '~ **song**, one

that is often repeated in a musical play, film, etc. (音乐剧、电影等中的)主题歌.

them·selves /ðəmˈselvz; ðəmˈsɛlvz/ *pron* **1** (reflex): (反身式); *They hurt* ~. 他们弄伤了自己. *They kept some for* ~. 他们为自己保存了一些. *They did the work by* ~, *without help.* 他们靠自己做那项工作. *They were by* ~ (= alone, without company) *when I called.* 我往访他们时他们没有客人. **2** (emphat): (加重语气): *They* ~ *have often made that mistake.* 他们自己也常犯那项错误.

then /ðen; ðɛn/ *adv* **1** at the time (past or future): (指过去或未来时间了)当时; 那时: *We were living in Wales* ~. 那时我们住在威尔士. *I was still unmarried* ~. 当时我还没有结婚. (*every) now and* ~, ⇨ **now(1)**. ~ *and there; there and* ~, ⇨ **there¹(5)**. **2** (used to modify a *n*): (用以修饰名词): *the* ~ *Lord Mayor*, the Lord Mayor at that time. 当时的市长. **3** (used after a *prep*): (用于介词后): *from* ~ (= from that time) *onwards*; 自那时以后; *until* ~; 直至那时; *since* ~. 自那时以来. **4** next; after that; afterwards: 其后; 然后; 以后: *We'll have fish first, and* ~ *roast chicken.* 我们将先吃鱼, 然后吃烤鸡. *We had a week in Rome and* ~ *went to Naples.* 我们在罗马住了一星期, 然后往那不勒斯. **5** (usu at the beginning or end of a sentence) in that case; that being so: (通常置于句首或句尾)那么; 因此; 既然这样: *A: 'It isn't here.'* —*B: 'It must be in the next room,* ~.' 甲: '(它)不在这里.' —乙: '那么, 一定在隔壁房间.' *You say you don't want to call a doctor.* —*T~ what do you want to do?* 你说你不想请医生. ——那么你想怎么办? **6** furthermore; and also: 并且; 还; 而且: *T~ there's Mrs Green*—*she must be invited to the wedding.* 还有格林太太——必须请她来参加婚礼. *And* ~, *you must remember....* 而且, 你必须记得.... **7** '*Now* ~', used to call attention, or to express a warning, make a protest, etc: 用以引起注意, 或表示警告、抗议等: *Now* ~, *who's smoking?* 喂, 谁在抽烟?

thence /ðens; ðɛns/ *adv* (formal) from there; for that reason. (正式用语)由彼处; 因为那个缘故; 因而. ~·**forth** /ˌðensˈfɔːθ; ˌðɛnsˈforˈθ/, ~·**for·ward** /ˌðensˈfɔːwəd; ˌðɛnsˈforwəd/ *advv* from that time onwards. 从那时以后; 从那时起.

the·oc·ra·cy /θɪˈɒkrəsɪ; θiˈɑkrəsɪ/ *n* [C, U] (*pl* -cies) (country with a) system of government in which the laws of the State are believed to be the laws of God; (hence) government by priests or a priestly class. 神权政治; 神治国家; (由此产生)僧侣政治; 僧侣统治. **theo·crat·ic** /ˌθɪəˈkrætɪk; ˌθiəˈkrætɪk/ *adj*

the·odo·lite /θɪˈɒdəlaɪt; θiˈɑdl̩ˌaɪt/ *n* instrument used by surveyors for measuring horizontal and vertical angles. 经纬仪(测量水平及垂直角度者).

the·ol·ogy /θɪˈɒlədʒɪ; θiˈɑlədʒɪ/ *n* **1** [U] formal study of the nature of God and of the foundations of religious belief. 神学; 宗教学; 宗教信仰学. **2** [C] theological system or interpretation: 宗教信仰制度或解说: *rival theologies*; 敌对的宗教信仰制度或解释; *a/the* ~ *of sex.* 宗教上对于性的解说. **theo·lo·gian** /ˌθɪəˈləʊdʒən; ˌθiəˈlodʒən/ *n* expert in or student of ~. 神学者; 神学家. **theo·logi·cal** /ˌθɪəˈlɒdʒɪkl; ˌθiəˈlɑdʒɪkl̩/ *adj* **theo·logi·cally** /-klɪ; -klɪ/ *adv*

the·orem /ˈθɪərəm; ˈθiərəm/ *n* **1** statement which logical reasoning shows to be true. 定理; 可借推理证明的命题. **2** (maths) statement for which a reasoned proof is required. (数学)定理.

the·or·etic, the·or·eti·cal /ˌθɪəˈretɪk, -ɪkl; ˌθiəˈrɛtɪk, -kl̩/ *adjj* based on theory, not on practice or experience. 理论上的; 理论上的; 推理的; 非基于实用或经验的. **the·or·eti·cally** /-klɪ; -klɪ/ *adv*

the·ory /ˈθɪərɪ; ˈθiərɪ/ *n* (*pl* -ries) **1** [C, U] (explanation of the) general principles of an art or science (contrasted with practice): 学理; 原理; 理论(与 practice 相对): *Naval officers must understand both the* ~ *and practice of navigation.* 海军军官对于航海术的理论与实

践皆须了解. *Your plan is excellent in* ~, *but would it succeed in practice?* 你的计划在理论上甚佳, 但是实行起来会成功吗? **2** [C] reasoned supposition put forward to explain facts or events: 学说; 论说: *Darwin's* ~ *of evolution.* 达尔文的进化论. **3** [C] sth conjectured, not necessarily based on reasoning: 意见; 推测; 臆说; 说法(未必基于推理): *He has a* ~ *that wearing hats makes men bald.* 他有一种说法, 认为戴帽子会使人秃顶. *In* ~, *three things could happen*, There are three possibilities. 推测起来, 有三种可能性. **the·or·ist** /ˈθɪərɪst; ˈθiə,rɪst/ *n* person who forms theories. 理论家. **the·or·ize** /ˈθɪəraɪz; ˈθiəˌraɪz/ *vi* [VP2A, 3A] ~ (*about sth*), form theories. 建立理论; 理论化.

the·os·ophy /θɪˈɒsəfɪ; θiˈɑsəfɪ/ *n* [U] any of several systems of philosophy which aim at a direct knowledge of God by means of spiritual ecstasy and contemplation. 通神学; 通神论(认为可借精神上的忘我及冥思达到直接认识神的哲学体系). **the·os·oph·ist** /-fɪst; -fɪst/ *n* believer in ~. 通神论者; 信通神论者. **theo·sophi·cal** /ˌθɪəˈsɒfɪkl; ˌθiəˈsɑfɪkl̩/ *adj*

thera·peutic, thera·peut·i·cal /ˌθerəˈpjuːtɪk, -ɪkl; ˌθɛrəˈpjutɪk, -kl̩/ *adj* connected with the art of healing, the cure of disease: 治疗学的; 治疗术的; 关于治病的: *take* ~ *baths at a spa.* 在一处矿泉沐浴治疗病. **thera·peutic(s)** /ˌθerəˈpjuːtɪk(s); ˌθɛrəˈpjutɪk(s)/ *n* (usu with *sing v*) branch of medicine concerned with curing disease. (通常用单数动词)治疗学.

ther·apy /ˈθerəpɪ; ˈθɛrəpɪ/ *n* [U] curative treatment, esp of a kind indicated by a preceding word: 治疗; 疗法(尤用于前面有词标明的某种治疗法): *radio-*~, treatment by x-rays; 放射(线)疗法; *psycho-*~, treatment by psychoanalytic methods; 心理疗法; *occupational* ~, treatment by means of work that exercises certain muscles. 职业治疗法(借可使某些肌肉运动的工作以治疗的方法). **thera·pist** /ˈθerəpɪst; ˈθɛrəpɪst/ *n* specialist in ~. 精于某种疗法的专家; (尤指)物理治疗家; 精神治疗家.

there¹ /ðeə(r); ðɛr/ *adv of place and direction* (contrasted with *here*) 表示地方及方向的副词(与 here 相对) **1** in, at or to, that place: 在那里; 在彼处; 往那里; 向彼处: *We shall soon be* ~. 我们很快就会到那里去. *We're nearly* ~, have nearly arrived. 我们快到了. *Put the box* ~, *in that corner.* 把盒子放在那里, 那个角落里. *I've never been to Rome but I hope to go* ~ *next year.* 我还没有去过罗马, 但是我希望明年去那里. **2** (front position, in exclamatory style; always stressed, and not to be confused with *there + be/appear/seem*, etc, dealt with at **there²** below; ⇨ **here(2)**; used with inversion of subject and *v* if the subject is a *n*, but not if the subject is a *pers pron*): (置于句首, 具感叹词性质; 总是重读, 不可与 there² 所不提到之 there+be, appear seem 等形式混淆; 主语为名词时, 须与动词巅倒位置, 主语为人称代词时, 位置不对换): *T~ goes the last bus!* 最后一班公共汽车开走了! *T~ it goes!* (它)走了! (去了!) *T~ come the rest of the party!* 该组(队等)其余的人到了! *T~ they come!* 他们来了! **3** (used to call attention; always stressed): (用以引起注意; 总是重读): *T~'s the bell ringing for church.* 听, 做礼拜的钟声响了. *T~'s a fine stroke!* (used to give praise or encouragement.) 做得好! (用于赞美或鼓励.) *You have only to turn the switch and* ~ *you are,* ie you get the desired result. 你只要转动开关就行了(就可达到目的). *T~'s a fine, ripe pear for you!* 瞧, 给你一只又大, 熟的梨! *T~'s a fine, ripe pear this is!* 瞧, 你这个梨多漂亮, 多成熟! *T~'s gratitude for you!* Note how grateful he, she, etc is! (used either sincerely or ironically). 你看, 他(她等)对你是多么的感激! (真诚的或讽刺的用法皆可.) **4** at, in connection with, that point (in an action, story, argument, etc): (行动, 故事, 辩论等)在那一点; 有关那一点: *Don't stop* ~! 不要停在那儿! *T~* (ie on that point) *I disagree with you.* 在那一点上, 我不同意你的意见. *T~ you are mistaken.* 这一点你错了. *T~ comes the difficulty.* 关于这一点, 困难来了.

5 (in phrases): (用于短语中): **all ~**, ⇨ **all²(1)**. **here and ~**, ⇨ **here(5)**. **~ and back**, to a place and back again: 往返; 来回: *Can I go ~ and back in one day?* 我一天能够来回吗? **over ~**, (indicating a place farther than is indicated by **~** alone): (指较单独用 there 为远的地方)在那里: *I live here, Mr Green lives* **~**, *and Mr Brown lives over* **~**, *on the other side of the river.* 我住在这里, 格林先生住在那样, 布朗先生住得更远些, 在河对岸. **then and ~; ~ and then**, at that time and place. 当场立即; 当时当地. Cf 参较 *here and now.* **6** (in colloq style only, after a *n* or *pron*, for emphasis): (仅用于口语文体中, 接在名词或代词后, 用以加重语气): *Hi! You* **~!** 嗨! *That woman* **~** *is eating a lot!* 那女人吃得好多! **7** (used after *preps* and *advv*): (用于介词及副词之后): *Put them in/under/near, etc* **~**. 把它们放在那里面(那下面, 靠近那里等). *Pass along* **~**, *please!* (used to request people to move along in a crowded street, bus, etc). 请往前走!(用于请求拥挤在街道上, 公共汽车上等的人群向前移动).

there² /*usual form:* ðə(r); ðə; *strong form:* ðeə(r); ðer/ *adv* (used to introduce a sentence in which the *v* (esp *'be*') normally precedes its subject, which is usu indef, ⇨ [VP1, 2A, 4E]) (用以引导一个句子, 其动词, 尤其是 be 动词, 经常置于主语前, 主语通常是不确定的): **1** (with the *v* '*be*'): (与动词 be 连用): *T~'s a man at the door.* 门口有一个人. Cf 参较 *The man is at the door.* 那个人就在门口. *T~ can be no doubt about it.* 此事无可怀疑. *I don't want* **~** *to be any misunderstanding.* 我不想有任何误会存在. *T~'s no stopping him*, It is impossible to stop him. 阻止他是不可能的. **2** (with other *vv*, esp *seem* and *appear*): (与其他动词连用, 特别是 seem 及 appear): *T~ seems (to be) no doubt about it.* 此事似乎无可怀疑. *T~ appeared to be no one who could answer our inquiries.* 好象没有人能答复我们的询问. *T~ comes a time when....* 有这么一个时期….

there³ /ðeə(r); ðer/ *int* (always stressed) (总是重读) **1** (used, chiefly to children, to soothe or comfort): (用于抚慰或安慰, 主要对象为小孩): *T~! T~! Never mind, you'll soon feel better.* 好啦! 好啦! 不要紧, 很快你就会感到舒服一点. **2** (used to suggest that the speaker was right in sth, or to indicate triumph, dismay, etc according to the context): (用以暗示说话者是对的, 或用以表示胜利, 沮丧等, 依上下文而定): *T~, now! What did I tell you*, You now see that I was right! 你瞧! 我怎么跟你说的?(你现在知道我对了吧!) *T~! You've woken the baby!* 哎呀! 你把小孩吵醒了!

there·about(s) /'ðeərəbaut(s); ,ðer'baʊt(s)/ *adv* (usu preceded by *or*) near that place, number, quantity, degree, etc (表接近某地方, 数目, 数量, 程度等) 大约; 左右; 附近: *in Eye or* **~**, 在瑞埃附近; £5/15 lb/3 o'clock or **~**. 五英镑(十五磅, 三点钟)左右.

there·after /ðeə'ɑ:ftə(r) US: -'æf-; ðer'æftə/ *adv* (formal) afterwards. (正式用语)此后; 其后.

there·by /ðeə'bai; ðer'bai/ *adv* (formal) by that means; in that connection. (正式用语)借以; 从而; 由此; 在那一点上; 在那一方面.

there·fore /'ðeəfɔ:(r); 'ðer,fɔr/ *adv* for that reason. 为了那种理由; 为此; 因此.

there·in /ðeər'in; ðer'ɪn/ *adv* (formal) in that place; in that respect; in that particular. (正式用语)在那地方; 在那里; 在那方面; 在那一点上.

there·in·after /,ðeərɪn'ɑ:ftə(r) US: -'æf-; ,ðerɪn-'æftə/ *adv* (chiefly legal) in that part which follows. (主要为法律用语)在下文.

there·of /ðeər'ɒv; ðer'ʌv/ *adv* (formal) of that; from that source. (正式用语)由是; 由此; 从那个来源; 其.

there·to /ðeə'tu:; ðer'tu/ *adv* (formal) to that; in addition to that. (正式用语)至该处; 到那里; 其外; 此外; 更.

there·under /ðeər'ʌndə(r); ðer'ʌndə/ *adv* (formal) under that. (正式用语)在其下.

there·upon /,ðeərə'pɒn; ,ðerə'pɑn/ *adv* (formal) then; as the result of that. (正式用语)随后; 立即; 于是; 因此.

there·withal /'ðeəwɪðɔ:l; ,ðerwɪð'ɔl/ *adv* (archaic) in addition; besides. (古)此外; 除此而外.

therm /θɜ:m; θɜm/ *n* [C] (100000 GB thermal units as a) unit of heat as used for measuring the consumption of gas (coal-gas or natural gas). 撒姆(热量单位, 用以计算瓦斯消耗量, 相等于十万个英国热量单位).

ther·mal /'θɜ:ml; 'θɜml/ *adj* of heat: 热的; 热量的: **~ springs**, of warm or hot water; 温泉; the '**~ barrier**, barrier to the use of high speeds (in flying) caused by increased friction of the air on the surfaces of the aircraft; 热障碍(由空气与飞机表面所产生的对高速飞行的障碍); a , '**power station**, one using heat (from coal, oil) (contrasted with a hydro-electric power station). 火力发电厂(以煤或油为燃料, 以别于水力发电厂). **~ capacity**, (phys) number of units of heat needed to raise the temperature of a body by one degree. (物理)热容量. **~ unit**, (phys) unit of measure of heat. (物理)热量单位. **British ~ unit**, (abbr 略作 **BTU**), amount of heat needed to raise 1 lb of water by 1°F. 英国热量单位(使一磅水之温度增加华氏一度所需之热量). □ *n* rising current of warm air (as needed by a glider to gain height). 热气流(热空气的上升气流, 如滑翔机上升时所需要者).

ther·mi·onic /,θɜ:mɪ'ɒnɪk; ,θɜmɪ'ɑnɪk/ *adj* of that branch of physics that deals with the emission of electrons at high temperatures. 热离子学的. **~ valve** (US 美 = **~ tube**) *n* system of electrodes arranged in a glass or metal envelope exhausted of air. 热离子管.

thermo- /'θɜ:məʊ; 'θɜmo/ (in compounds) (用于复合词中) of heat. 热的. ,**~·dy'nam·ics** *n pl* [U] (usu with *sing v*) science of the relations between heat and mechanical work. (通常与单数动词连用)热力学. ,**~'nu·clear** *adj* (eg of weapons) of, using, the high temperatures released in nuclear fission: (指武器等)热核的: the **~**-*nuclear bomb*, the hydrogen bomb. 氢弹; 热核弹. ,**~'plastic** *n*, *adj* (substance) which can at any time be made plastic by the application of heat. 受热即变软及可塑的; 热熔的; 热塑或热熔物质; 热熔塑胶. ,**~'setting** *adj* (of plastics) becoming permanently hard after being heated and shaped. (指塑胶)加热成形后即硬化的. '**~·stat** /'θɜ:məstæt; 'θɜmə,stæt/ *n* [C] device for automatically regulating temperature (eg in central heating, refrigerators, airconditioning). 恒温器(自动调节并可保持一定温度者, 如中央暖气系统、电冰箱及空气调节系统中者). **~·static** /,θɜ:mə'stætɪk; ,θɜrmə-'stætɪk/ *adj* of a **~**stat: 恒温器的: **~**static control. 恒温器的控制.

ther·mom·eter /θə'mɒmɪtə(r); θə'mɑmətə/ *n* instrument for measuring temperature. 温度计; 寒暑表. ⇨ **App 5**. 参看附录五.

ther·mos /'θɜ:məs; 'θɜməs/ *n* (also 亦作 '**~ flask**) (P) vacuum flask. (商标)热水瓶. ⇨ **vacuum**.

the·sau·rus /θɪ'sɔ:rəs; θɪ'sɔrəs/ *n* (*pl* **~es** /-rəsɪz; -rəsɪz/) dictionary of words and phrases grouped together according to similarities in their meanings. 同义语词汇; 同义语词典.

these /ðiːz; ðiz/ ⇨ **this**.

the·sis /'θiːsɪs; 'θisɪs/ *n* (*pl* theses /'θiːsiːz; 'θisiz/) statement or theory (to be) put forward and supported by arguments, esp a lengthy written essay submitted (as part of the requirements) for a university degree. 论题; 论文; (尤指)毕业论文; 学位论文.

Thes·pian /'θespɪən; 'θespɪən/ *adj* (liter) connected with the drama. (文)戏剧的; 有关戏剧的. □ *n* actor or actress. 演员.

thews /θjuːz; θjuz/ *n pl* (liter) muscles: (文)肌肉: **~ and sinews**, bodily strength. 体力.

they /ðeɪ; ðe/ *pers pron* (subject form, *pl*, of *he, she, it*): (主格形式, 为 he, she, it 的复数): *T~* (= People in general) *say that the government will have to resign.* 据说内阁势将辞职。*What a lot of questions ~* (= those in authority) *ask in this tax form!* 这张税务调查表上问的问题好多啊! **them** /ðəm; ðəm; *strong form:* ðem; ðem/ *pers pron* (object form of *they*): (they 的宾格形式): *Give them to me.* 把它们给我。*It was very kind of them,* They were very kind. 他们很客气。

they're /ðeə(r); ðer/ = they are.

thick /θɪk; θɪk/ *adj* (**-er, -est**) **1** (opp of *thin*) of relatively great or a specified measurement in diameter, from one side to the other, or from the front to the back: (为 thin 的反义词)厚的; 粗的: *a ~ slice of bread;* 厚厚的一片面包; *a ~ line;* 一条粗线; *ice three inches ~;* 三英寸厚的冰; *~ print,* of lines. 粗体字。'~-'skinned *adj* (fig) not sensitive to reproach or insults. (喻)脸皮厚的; 对责备或侮辱感觉迟钝的。**2** having a large number of units close together; 稠密的; 密集的: *~ hair;* 浓密的头发; *a ~ forest;* 丛林; *in the ~est part of the crowd.* 在人丛最密集的部分。*The corn was ~ in the fields.* 田里的麦子长得很茂盛。'~-'set *adj* **(a)** having a short, stout body; solidly built. 矮而壮的; 结实的。**(b)** (of a hedge) with bushes, etc closely planted. (指树篱)密植矮树等的; 繁密的。**3** *~ with,* abounding or packed with: 充满…的; 填满…的: *The air was ~ with dust/snow.* 空气中充满了尘埃(雪花)。**4** (of liquids) semisolid: (指液体)稠的; 浓厚的: *~ soup;* 浓汤; (of vapour, the atmosphere) not clear; dense: (指烟雾,大气)不清明的; 浓密的: *a ~ fog.* 浓雾。**5** (of voices) obstructed, eg because one has a cold. (指声音)阻塞的, 重浊的(如因伤风所致)。**6** (colloq) stupid; dull. (口)愚笨的; 迟钝的。'~-'headed *adj* stupid. 愚笨的。**7** (colloq) intimate: (口)亲密的: *John is very ~ with Anne now.* 约翰现在和安妮很亲近。*as ~ as thieves,* very friendly. 非常亲密。**8** (various colloq uses) (各种口语用法) *a bit ~; rather ~,* beyond what is reasonable or endurable: 不太合理的; 令人受不了的: *Three weeks of heavy rain is a bit ~,* 一连下了三星期的大雨,真叫人受不了。*give sb a ~ ear,* give him a blow that causes his ear to swell. 打肿某人的耳朵。*lay it on ~,* (sl) be profuse, esp in paying compliments. (俚)过分 (尤指过分恭维)。□ *n* [U] **1** most crowded part; part where there is greatest activity: 最拥挤的部分; 活动最多的部分: *in the ~ of the fight.* 在酣战中。*We were in the ~ of it.* 我们正积极参与此事。*through ~ and thin,* under any kind of conditions, good or bad. 在任何情况下; 不计甘苦。**2** part of anything; 事物的浓厚部分; 事物的粗大浓密部分: *the ~ of the thumb.* 拇指最粗部分。**3** ~ *ly adv* in a manner: 浓密地; 稠密地: *cut the bread/spread the butter ~ly.* 厚厚地切面包(抹奶油)。*~en* /'θɪkən; 'θɪkən/ *vi, vt* make or become ~: (使)变厚; (使)变浓; (使)变密集: *~en the gravy.* 使肉汁浓厚。*The plot ~ens,* becomes more complex. 情节变复杂了。'~-*en·ing* /'θɪkənɪŋ; 'θɪkənɪŋ/ *n* [U] material or substance used to ~en sth; process of becoming ~(er) or making sth ~(er). 浓化剂; 浓化或加厚的过程。~-*ness n* **1** [U] quality or degree of being ~: 厚; 浓; 厚度; 浓度: *four centimetres in ~ness;* 厚四厘米; *a ~ness of four centimetres.* 四厘米的厚度。**2** [C] layer: 层; 张: *two ~nesses of cotton-wool and two ~nesses of felt.* 一层棉花及两层毛毡。

thicket /'θɪkɪt; 'θɪkɪt/ *n* [C] mass of trees, shrubs, undergrowth, growing thickly together. 灌木丛。

thief /θiːf; θif/ *n* (*pl* **thieves** /θiːvz; θivz/) person who steals, esp secretly and without violence. 贼; 小偷; 窃贼。⇨ *bandit, burglar, robber at rob.* **thieve** /θiːv; θiv/ *vi, vt* [VP2A] be a ~; [VP6A] steal (sth). 做贼; 当小偷; 偷窃(东西)。**thiev·ery** /'θiːvəri; 'θivəri/ *n*

theft. 偷窃。**thiev·ish** /-ɪʃ; -ɪʃ/ *adj* having the habit of stealing; thief-like. 有偷窃习惯的; 象贼的。**thievish·ly** *adv*

thigh /θaɪ; θaɪ/ *n* [C] **1** part of the human leg between the knee and the hip. 股; 大腿 (人腿自膝至臀的部分)。⇨ the illus at **leg**. 参看 leg 之插图。'~-**bone** *n* bone of this part of the leg; femur. 股骨; 大腿骨。**2** corresponding part of the hind legs of other animals. 其他动物之后腿的相当部分; 股。

thimble /'θɪmbl; 'θɪmbl/ *n* cap (of metal, etc) used to protect the end of the finger when pushing a needle through cloth, etc. 顶针; 针箍; 嵌环。~-**ful**/-ful; -ful/ *n* (colloq) sip, very small quantity (of a liquid). (口)(液体的)微量; 一啜。

thin /θɪn; θɪn/ *adj* (**-ner, -nest**) **1** (opp of *thick*) having opposite surfaces close together; of small diameter: (为 thick 的反义词)薄的; 细的: *a ~ slice of bread;* 一片薄面包; *a ~ sheet of paper;* 一张薄纸; *~ boards;* 薄板; *a ~ piece of string;* 一根细绳; *a ~ stroke,* of the pen, etc. (钢笔等的)细的笔画。'~-'skinned *adj* (fig) sensitive to criticism; easily offended. (喻)脸皮薄的; 对批评敏感的; 容易受罪的。**2** lacking density: 稀薄的; *a ~ mist.* 薄雾。*~ air,* invisibility; nothingness: 看不见; 不存在; 虚无: *He seemed to vanish into ~ air,* disappear mysteriously without leaving a trace. 他好象消失在虚无中了。**3** (opp of *fat*) having not much flesh: (为 fat 的反义词)瘦的: *rather ~ in the face.* 脸孔瘦瘦的。*Your illness has left you very ~.* 你的病使你消瘦了。**4** not full or closely packed: 稀疏的; 寥寥的: *a ~ audience,* with more seats empty than occupied. 寥寥可数的观众。*'Your hair's getting rather ~ on top, sir',* said the barber. 理发师说, '先生, 您头顶上的头发有点稀疏了'。**5** (of liquids) lacking substance; watery: (指液体)稀薄的; 淡的: *~ beer/wine,* lacking body; weak. 淡啤酒(葡萄酒)。**6** lacking in some important ingredient; poor: 缺乏某些重要成分的; 贫乏的; 浅薄的; 浅显的: *~ humour;* 肤浅的谐谑; *a ~ excuse,* not very convincing; 不能令人信服的托辞; *a ~ disguise,* easily seen through; 易为人识破的伪装; *a ~ story,* one that contains nothing very exciting; one that does not convince (as an excuse, etc). 乏味的故事; 不能自圆其说的借口等。**7** (colloq) (口) *have a ~ time,* an uncomfortable, distasteful one. 过得很不舒服, 很不愉快。□ *adv* so as to be ~: 稀薄地; 稀疏地; 淡地: *You've spread the butter very thin.* 你奶油涂得太薄了。□ *vt, vi* (**-nn-**) [VP6A, 15B, 2A, C] make or become ~. (使)变薄; (使)变细; (使)变度; (使)变稀疏; (使)变贫乏。*~ (down),* make (a liquid) less dense: (使)(液体)变稀: *~ down paint with turpentine.* 加松节油使油漆变稀。*~ (out),* make or become less dense, or fewer in number: (使)变为稀疏; (使)减少: *War and disease had ~ned (out) the population.* 战争和疾病已使人口减少。*He ~ned out the seedlings,* pulled up some of them to allow the others to grow better. 他拔掉一些幼苗使变稀疏(好让别的幼苗长得更好)。*We had better wait until the fog ~s out.* 我们最好等到雾变薄一点。*At last the crowd/traffic ~ned out.* 人群(车辆)终于变得稀少了。~·*ly adv* in a ~ manner: 薄地; 细地; 疏地; 稀疏地: *Sow the seed ~ly.* 把种子撒稀一点。~·*ness* /'θɪnnɪs; 'θɪnnɪs/ *n*

thine /ðaɪn; ðaɪn/ ⇨ **thy**.

thing /θɪŋ; θɪŋ/ *n* **1** any material object: 东西; 物: *What are those ~s on the table?* 桌上的那些东西是什么? *There wasn't a ~* (= nothing) *to eat.* 没有东西可吃。*She's too fond of sweet ~s,* sweet kinds of food. 她太爱吃甜食了。**2** (*pl*) belongings; articles of which the nature is clear (or thought to be clear) from the context: (复)财物; 物件; 用品(其性质可由上下文判明者): *Bring your swimming ~s* (= your swimming-suit, towel, etc) *with you.* 带着你的游泳用品。*Have you packed your ~s* (= clothes, etc) *for the journey?* 旅行用的衣物都收拾好了吗? *Put your ~s* (= coat, hat, etc) *on and let's leave.* 把你的衣帽等穿戴起来让我们离开这

里。**3** subject: 题目; 主题: *There's another ~* (=something *else*) *I want to ask you about.* 还有一件事我想和你问你。**4** that which is non-material: 非物质的事物: *He values ~s of the mind more than ~s of the body.* 他对于心灵方面的事物看得比肉体方面的事物重。**be 'seeing ~s,** have hallucinations. 产生幻觉。**5** circumstance; event; course of action: 情况; 事件; 行为: *That only makes ~s* (= the situation) *worse.* 那会使情况更糟。*You take ~s* (= happenings) *too seriously.* 你把事情看得太严重了。*I must think ~s over,* consider what has happened, what has to be done, etc. 我必须把情势考虑一下。*What's the next ~ to do,* What must be done next? 下一步该做什么? *It's just one of those ~s,* sth that can't be helped, explained, remedied, etc (according to context). 那真是没有法子的事(指无可奈何, 无法解释, 无法挽救的事等, 根据上下文而定)。*~s* (= The state of affairs) *are getting worse and worse.* 事态愈来愈糟了。*Well, of all ~s!* (expressing surprise, indignation, etc, at what has been done, suggested, etc). 呀, 居然如此! (对所做、所建议等的事情表示惊讶、愤慨等)。**for 'one ~,** used to introduce a reason: 一则; 首先(用以举出一项理由): *For one ~, I haven't any money; for another....* 一则, 我没有钱; 再则, …。**Taking one ~ with another,** considering various circumstances, etc. 考虑各种情况; 考虑各方面的情形。**6** (used of a person or an animal, expressing an emotion of some kind): (用以指人或动物, 显露某种情绪): *She's a sweet little ~ / a dear old ~.* 她是一个可爱的小东西(一位亲切的老太太)。*Poor ~, he's been ill all winter.* 可怜的人, 他已经病了整个冬天。**7 the ~,** just what will be best in the circumstances: 最适合的事物; 最好的事物: *A holiday in the mountains will be the best ~ for you.* 上山去度假对你来说最好不过了。*That's not the ~ to do,* is unsuitable, inappropriate. 那是不宜做的事。*He always says the right / wrong ~,* makes the most suitable / unsuitable remark or comment. 他说话总是很得体(不适当)。*quite the ~,* fashionable. 时髦的。**8** (phrases) (短语) *the ,~ 'is,* the question to be considered is: 目前的问题是; 目前要考虑的是; 最要紧的是: *The ~ is, can we get there in time?* 目前的问题是, 我们能否及时赶到那里? *The ~ is* (= The most important factor is) *to make your views quite clear to everyone.* 现在最要紧的是把你的观点向每一个人解释清楚。*first ~,* before anything else; early: 第一件事; 最先; 早: *I'll do it first ~ tomorrow morning.* 明天一早我便做这件事。*first ~s first,* ⇨ first[2](1). *the ,general / ,common / ,usual ~,* the common practice. 常例; 惯例。*a near ~,* a narrow escape (from an accident, missing a train, etc). 好险的事; 侥幸的事(如幸免于难, 险些未赶上火车等)。*an understood ~,* sth that has been / is accepted. 已被接受或认可之事。*do one's (own) ~,* (colloq) do sth which one does well, or which one feels an urge to do; act without inhibition. (口)做得心应手之事; 做渴望做之事; 为所欲为。*have a ~ about,* (colloq) be obsessed by. (口)被…迷住; 被…困扰; 对…感到厌恶。**9** (*pl* with an *adj* following) all that can be so described: (复数, 后接形容词)…的事物; 文物; 该形容词所描述的事物总称: *~s Japanese,* Japanese customs, art, etc. 日本的文物。**10** (legal) (法律) *~s personal / real,* personal / real property. 动产(不动产)。

thing·um·my /ˈθɪŋəmɪ; ˈθɪŋəmɪ/, **thing·u·ma·bob** /ˈθɪŋəməbɒb; ˈθɪŋəməˌbɑb/, **thing·u·ma·jig** /ˈθɪŋəmədʒɪg; ˈθɪŋəməˌdʒɪg/ *nn* (colloq) person or thing whose name one forgets or is not known (used in the same way as *what's-his-name, what d'you call it*). (口)某人或某物(指其名为人忘记或不详的人或事物, 用法与 what's-his-name, what d'you call it 相同)。

think[1] /θɪŋk/ *vi, vt* (*pt, pp* **thought** /θɔːt; θɔt/) (For special uses with *adverbial particles and preps,* ⇨ **8** below.) (与副词性小品词及介词连用的特殊用法, 参看下列第 8 义。) **1** [VP2A, B, C, 6A, 8] (with cognate object) use, exercise, the mind in order to form opinions, come to conclusions: (与同源宾语连用)思索; 考虑; 想:

Are animals able to ~? 动物能思考吗? *You should ~* (= not be hasty) *before doing that.* 做那事之前你应该考虑考虑。*Do you ~ in English when you speak English, or translate mentally?* 你讲英语时是用英语构思, 还是经过心里的翻译过程? *Let me ~ a moment,* Give me time before I answer. 让我先想一下。*He may not say much but he ~s a lot.* 他也许不大讲话, 但是他想得很多。*~ aloud,* utter one's thoughts as they occur. 自言自语。**'~-tank** *n* group or organization that provides advice, ideas, solutions to problems, etc. 提供意见、解决问题之方法等的团体或组织; 智囊团。**2** [VP9, 25] consider; be of the opinion: 以为; 认为: *Do you ~ it will rain?* 你认为会下雨吗? *Yes, I ~ so.* 是的, 我认为会。*No, I don't ~ so.* 不, 我认为不会。*It's going to rain, I ~.* 我看快要下雨了。*I ~* (*that*) *you're very brave.* 我认为你很勇敢。*Do you ~ it likely / that it is likely?* 你认为这事可能吗? *I thought I heard a scream.* 我认为我听到一声尖叫。*They had been thought* (*to be*) *lost.* 大家都以为他们迷路了。*It will be better, don't you ~, to start early.* 早一点动身比较好, 你说是吧。*~ fit.* 认为适当。⇨ fit[1](2). **3** [VP10] (neg with *can / could*) imagine, form a conception of: (用于否定句, 与 can 或 could 连用)构想; 想象; 形成概念: *I can't ~ what you mean.* 我想象不出你的意思是什么。*I can't ~ where she has gone off to / how she did it / why she left.* 我想不出她逃往何处(她怎么做的, 她为什么离开)。*You can't ~ how glad I am to see you.* 你无法想象我是多么高兴见到你。**4** [VP9] have a half-formed intention: 有意; 打算: *I ~ I'll go for a swim.* 我想去游泳。**5** [VP10] reflect: 反省; 思维; 细想: *She was ~ing* (*to herself*) *how cold the room was.* 她在想那房间真冷。**6** [VP7A, 9] expect, intend: 预料; 企图: *I never thought that I'd see you here!* 我从未料到会在这里见到你! *Who would have thought to see you here!* 谁会想到在这里看到你你! *I thought as much,* That is what I expected or suspected. 我也这样想。**7** [VP22] bring into a mental condition by ~ing: 因思而导致某种心理状态; 想到某种地步: *Stop worrying or you'll ~ yourself sick!* 别着急, 否则你会急出病来的! **8** [VP3A, 15B] (special uses with *adverbial particles* and *preps*): (与副词性小品词及介词连用的特殊用法):

think about sth, (a) examine, consider (esp a plan, idea, to see whether it is desirable, practicable, etc): 考虑; 慎思; 审查(尤指计划、观念, 看它是否相宜、可行等): *She was ~ing about emigrating to Canada.* 她在考虑移居加拿大。*Please ~ about the proposal and let me have your views tomorrow.* 请考虑那项建议, 明天把你的看法告诉我。**(b)** recall; reflect upon: 想起; 回想; 回顾: *She was ~ing about her childhood days.* 她在回想她的童年时期。

think of sth, (a) consider; take into account: 考虑; 计及; 思索: *We have a hundred and one things to ~ of before we can decide.* 在我们做决定前, 我们有许许多多的事情待考虑。*You ~ of everything!* 你全都想到了! **(b)** consider, contemplate (without reaching a decision or taking action): 有意; 想; 打算; 盘算(未做成决定亦未采取实际行动): *We're ~ing of emigrating to Canada.* 我们打算移民到加拿大。*I did ~ of visiting him, but I've changed my mind.* 我确曾想去拜访他, 不过我已改变了主意。**(c)** imagine: 想象: *Just ~ of the cost / danger!* 想想那笔费用(那危险)吧! *To ~ of his not knowing anything about it!* Isn't it surprising? 想想他对此事竟一无所知(宁非怪事)! **(d)** have, entertain, the idea of (often with *could, would, should,* and *not* or *never,* with *dream* as a possible substitute for *think*): 有…的看法; 持…的念头(常与 could, would, should, 以及 not, never 连用, dream 可代替 think): *Surrender was not to be thought of.* 投降不列入考虑。*I couldn't ~ of such a thing.* 我不可能有这种想法。*He would never ~ of letting his daughter marry a fellow like you.* 他从未想到让他的女儿嫁给象你这样的人。**(e)** call to mind; recall: 记忆; 记起: *I can't ~ of his name at the moment.* 我一时想不起他的名字。**(f)** put forward; suggest: 提出; 建议: *Who first*

thought of the idea? 谁先提出那个主意的? *Can you ~ of a good place for a weekend holiday?* 你能提出一个周末度假的好去处吗? ⇨ **highly/well/not much/little, etc of sb/sth,** (not in the progressive tenses) have a high/good/poor, etc opinion of: (不用进行时)对某人或某事物持评价甚高(评价高, 评价不太高, 评价甚低等): *His work is highly thought of by the critics.* 批评家对他的作品评价甚高。*He ~s the world of her,* ~s she's wonderful, loves her dearly. 他对她十分倾心。~ **nothing of sth/doing sth,** consider (doing) it to be insignificant or unremarkable: 轻视; 看不起; 不把…当一回事: *Barbara ~s nothing of walking 20 miles a day.* 巴巴拉并不把每天走二十英里路当一回事。~ **nothing of it,** (formal) Don't mention it, ⇨ **mention.** (正式用语)不必客气。~ **better of sb,** have a higher opinion of (than to...): 看重某人(不至于做…); 对某人持较…高的看法: *I had always thought better of you than to suppose you could be so unkind.* 我过去一直认为你不至于会那样残忍。~ **better of sth,** reconsider and give up: 重新考虑并放弃: *What a foolish idea! I hope you'll ~ better of it.* 多么愚蠢的想法! 我希望你重新考虑一下(把它放弃)吧。**think sth out,** consider carefully and make a plan for: 想出; 想通; 熟思: *It seems to be a well-thought out scheme.* 那似乎是一项考虑周详的计划。*That wants ~ing out,* needs careful consideration. 那事需要仔细考虑。

think sth over, reflect upon, consider further (before reaching a decision, etc): 仔细想; 作进一步考虑; 审慎思考: *Please ~ over what I've said.* 请仔细考虑我说的话。*I'd like more time to ~ things over.* 我希望多一点时间把事情做进一步的考虑。

think sth up, devise, conceive, invent (a scheme, etc): 想出; 想到; 设计出(一项计划等): *There's no knowing what he'll ~ up next.* 一回他会想出什么花样。

think² /θɪŋk/ θɪŋk/ *n* (colloq) occasion of, need for, thinking: (口)思索; 思考; 考虑: *If that's what he wants, he's got another ~ coming,* will need to think again. 如果那就是他想要的, 他需要再考虑一下。

think·able /ˈθɪŋkəbl/ ˈθɪŋkəbl/ *adj* conceivable: 可想象的: *It's not ~* (more usu 较常用 *It's un~*) *that....* 不可想象的是…。

thinker /ˈθɪŋkə(r)/ ˈθɪŋkə/ *n* person who thinks (usu with an *adj*): 思考者; 思想家 (通常与形容词连用): *a great/shallow ~.* 伟大的(肤浅的)思想家。

think·ing /ˈθɪŋkɪŋ/ ˈθɪŋkɪŋ/ *adj* thoughtful; intelligent: 有思考力的; 肯思考的: *the ~ public;* 有思想力的人们; 思想界; 有心人士; *all ~ people.* 凡是有思想的人们。□ *n* thought; reasoning: 思想; 思考: *do some hard ~,* think deeply. 深思; 沉思。*You are of my way of ~,* You think as I do. 你和我的想法一样。*He is, to my (way of) ~* (ie in my opinion), *the best living novelist.* 依我看来, 他是当代最优秀的小说家。*Can I bring you round to my way of ~,* get you to think as I do, agree with me? 我能使你同意我的想法吗? **put one's '~cap on,** (colloq) think about a problem, etc. (口)好好思考; 认真思考。

third /θɜːd/ θɜrd/ *adj, n* (abbr 略作 **3rd**) next after the second (in place, time, order, importance, etc); one of the three equal divisions of a whole: 第三(的); 三分之一(的): *the ~ month of the year,* ie March; 三月; *on the ~ of April;* 四月三号; *on the ~ floor* (US 美 = fourth floor); 在四楼; *every ~ day;* 每三天; 每隔两天; *the ~ largest city in France;* 法国的第三大城; *Edward the T~,* Edward III, *the ~ king of this name;* 爱德华三世; *one-~ of a litre.* 三分之一升。~ **degree,** prolonged or hard questioning, use of torture (as used by the police in some countries to get confessions or information). (某些国家的警察为获得口供或情报所用的)疲劳讯问; 刑讯; 逼供。**a/the ~ party,** another person besides the two principal people. 第三者。~**party insurance,** of a person other than the person insured, which the insurance company undertakes to meet. 第三者责任保险(对受保人以外的第三者有承诺的)。

保险)。~ **rail,** conductor rail, carrying electric current. 带电的第三轨。~**·rate** *adj* of poor quality. 三流的; 三等的; 劣质的。~**·rater** *n* person who is ~-rate. 三流人物; 差劲的人。**the T~ World,** 第三世界。~**·ly** *adv*

thirst /θɜːst/ θɜrst/ *n* [U, and with *indef art* as in examples] (不可数名词, 但如例句所示, 可与不定冠词连用) **1** feeling caused by a desire or need to drink; suffering caused by this: 渴; 口渴: *The horse satisfied its ~ at the river.* 那马在河里饮水解渴。*This kind of work gives me a ~.* 这种工作使我感到口渴。*They lost their way in the desert and died of ~.* 他们在沙漠中迷路而渴死了。**2** (fig) strong desire (*for,* or, liter and biblical, *after*): (喻)热望; 渴望(与 *for* 连用; 文学及圣经, 与 *after* 连用): *a ~ for knowledge;* 求知欲; *satisfy one's ~ for adventure.* 满足冒险的热望。□ *vi* [VP2A, 3A] *~ (for),* have ~; be eager (for): 口渴; 渴望; 热望: *~ for* (liter and biblical, *after*) (文学及圣经, 与 *after* 连用) *revenge.* 渴望复仇。~**·y** *adj* (**-ier, -iest**) having or causing ~: 渴的; 使人口渴的: *be/feel ~y.* 口渴。*Some kinds of food make one ~y.* 有些种类的食物吃了使人口渴。*Tennis is a ~y game on a hot day.* 热天打网球是一种令人口渴的运动。*The fields are ~y for rain.* 田地亟旱需要雨水。~**·ily** /-ɪlɪ; -əlɪ/ *adv*

thir·teen /ˌθɜːˈtiːn; θɜrˈtin/ *adj, n* the number 13. 十三(的); 十三个。 ⇨ **App 4.** 参看附录四。**thir·teenth** /ˌθɜːˈtiːnθ; θɜrˈtinθ/ *adj, n* next after the twelfth; one of ~ equal parts. 第十三(的); 十三分之一(的)。

thirty /ˈθɜːtɪ; ˈθɜrtɪ/ *adj, n* the number 30. 三十(的); 三十个。 ⇨ **App 4.** 参看附录四。**the thirties,** 30—39. 三十至三十九之间; 三十年代。**thir·ti·eth** /ˈθɜːtɪəθ; ˈθɜrtɪəθ/ *adj, n* next after the 29th; one of ~ equal parts. 第三十(的); 三十分之一(的)。

this /ðɪs; ðɪs/ (*pl* **these** /ðiːz; ðiz/) *adj, pron* (contrasted with *that, those.* ~ /*these* and *that*/*those* are used to make a person or thing specific. ~/*these* are used when the person or thing is near in space or time to the speaker.) (与 *that, those* 相对。this 与 these 和 that, those 均用以特指人或物。this 和 these 用来指在空间或时间上距说话者较近者。) **1** *Look at ~ box/these boxes here.* 看这里的这个(这些)盒子。*What's ~ over here?* 这个是什么? *What are these?* 这些是什么? *Are these books yours?* 这些书是你的吗? *Are these your children?* 这些孩子是你的吗? *Is ~ what you want?* 这就是你要的吗? *T~ (one) is larger than that.* 这个比那个大。*These are better than those.* 这些比那些好。*Do it like ~,* ie in ~ way, as shown here, etc. 像这样去做。*Life is difficult these days, nowadays.* 目前谋生不容易了。*He will be here ~ Thursday,* Thursday of ~ week. 他将于这个星期四来此。*What's all ~?* (colloq) What's the trouble? What's happening? (口)这是怎么一回事? 怎么了? (有什么麻烦? 或, 发生了何事?) **2** (*T~* and a possessive cannot be used together. Note the construction used when ~ and a possessive are both needed): (this 与所有格不能连在一起用。注意下列例句中 this 与所有格同时使用的结构): *T~ car of yours needs a thorough overhaul.* 你的这部汽车需要彻底检修。*These new shoes of mine are painfully tight.* 我的这双新鞋太紧, 夹得脚疼。**3** (in narrative) a certain: (故事中)某一个: *Then ~ funny little man came up to me.* 然后一个有趣的小矮子向我走过来。*We all ended up at ~ pub.* 我们统统到一家酒馆(痛饮)。□ *adv* (colloq) to ~ degree; so: (口)到此程度; 如此: *It's about ~ high.* (它)大约有这么高。*Now that we have come ~ far* (=as far as ~)... 我们既然已经走了这么远…。*Can you spare me ~ much* (=as much as ~)? 你能不能匀给我这么多? *I know ~ much* (=what I am about to state), *that his story is exaggerated.* 就我所知, 他的故事过分夸大了。

thistle /ˈθɪsl; ˈθɪsl/ *n* [C] (sorts of) wild plant with prickly leaves and yellow, white or purple flowers. 蓟(野生植物, 叶带刺, 开黄, 白或紫色花)。~**·down** *n* [U] fluff of ~ flowers, carrying the seed. 蓟花的冠毛(带有种子)。

thither /'ðiðə(r) US: 'θiðər; 'θiðə/ *adv* (old use) to that place; in that direction. (旧用法)到彼处；向彼方。 **hither and ~**, here and there; in all directions. 到处；向各方。

tho' /ðəu; ðo/ *adv, conj* (informal spelling of) **though**. 为 though 之非正式拼法。

thole /θəul; θol/ *n* (also 亦作 **'~-pin**) pin or peg in the gunwale of a boat to keep an oar secure; one of two pins between which an oar is held. 桅座；桨座；桨架。➪ **rowlock**.

thong /θɒŋ US: θɔːŋ; θɔŋ/ *n* narrow strip of leather, eg as a fastening, the lash of a whip. 狭长的皮带(如用以系物或用作鞭打)。

tho·rax /'θɔːræks; 'θɔræks/ *n* **1** part of an animal's body between the neck and the belly, eg in a man, the chest. 动物的胸；(人的)胸部。 **2** middle of the three main sections of an insect (bearing the legs and wings). 昆虫身体三主节的中间一节。➪ the illus at **insect**. 参看 insect 之插图。

thorn /θɔːn; θɔrn/ *n* **1** [C] sharp-pointed growth on the stem of a plant. (植物之)刺；棘。➪ the illus at **flower**. 参看 flower 之插图。 **a ~ in one's flesh/side**, (fig) constant source of annoyance. (喻)经常苦恼的原因；不断使人烦恼的事物；芒刺在背。 **2** [C, U] (usu in compounds) kinds of shrub or tree with ~s. (通常用于复合词中)荆棘；有刺的树：*'haw~;* 山楂; *'black~.* 黑刺李。 **~·y** *adj* (**-ier, -iest**) **1** having ~s. 有刺的；多刺的。 **2** (fig) full of trouble and difficulty; causing argument. (喻)麻烦多的；困难多的；棘手的；引起争论的：*a ~y problem/subject.* 棘手的问题(题目)。

thor·ough /'θʌrə US: -rəu/ *adj* complete in every way; not forgetting or overlooking anything; detailed: 完全的；彻底的；周到的；详细的；充分的：*a ~ worker.* 彻底的工作者；*receive ~ instruction in English;* 接受完善的英语训练；*give a room a ~ cleaning;* 把房间彻底打扫一番；*be ~ in one's work.* 工作认真。 **'~-going** *adj* ~; complete; uncompromising. 彻底的；完全的；十足的；不妥协的：*a ~-going revision.* 彻底的校订。 **~·ly** *adv* **~·ness** *n*

thor·ough·bred /'θʌrəbred; 'θrə,brɛd/ *n, adj* (animal, esp a horse, also fig, person) of pure breed; high-spirited; thoroughly trained. 纯种的；纯种的动物(尤指马)；(喻)精神奕奕的(人)；经过严格训练的(人)。

thor·ough·fare /'θʌrəfeə(r); 'θrə,fɛr/ *n* [C] road or street, esp one much used by traffic and open at both ends: 通衢；大街；大街：*The Strand is one of London's busiest ~s.* 斯特兰德大街是伦敦最热闹的要衢之一。*No ~*, (as a sign) Not open to the public; no way through. (用告示)禁止通行。

those /ðəuz; ðoz/ *pl* of **that**.

thou /ðau; ðau/ *pron* (archaic) you (*sing*). (古) 你。 **thee** /ðiː; ði/ *pron* object form of ~. 你(thou 的宾格形式)

though /ðəu; ðo/ *conj* **1** (also 亦作 **al·~** /'ɔːl'ðəu; ɔl-'ðo/) in spite of the fact that; notwithstanding the fact that: 虽然；虽则。 *Al~ it was so cold, he went out without an overcoat.* 天气虽然很冷，他没有穿大衣就出去了。(cf 参较 *but:* It was very cold, but he.... 天很冷，但是他…。) *T~ they are so poor, they have enough to eat.* 他们虽然很穷，食物还是够吃的。*He passed the examination al~ he had been prevented by illness from studying.* 虽然他一直生病无法念书，他还是考及格了。 **2** (also 亦作 **al·~** and **even ~**) even if: 即使；纵然：*strange ~ it may appear/al~ it may appear strange,* even if it appears strange. 即使看来有点奇怪(虽似奇怪)。*He will never be dishonest even ~ he (should) be reduced to poverty.* 即使他沦为贫困，他也决不会不诚实。 **3** *adv,* (liter) what does it matter if: (文)即使…又有什么关系：*What ~ the way be long,* .... 即使路途遥遥远又有何妨…。 **4** *as ~,* ≃ *as ~/as if* as at **as²(11)**. **5** (also 亦作) and yet; all the same: (引导独立叙述)可是；然而；不过：*He will probably agree,*

~ you never know, and yet one can never be certain. 他很可能会同意，不过谁也不知道。*I'll try to come, ~ I don't think I shall manage it.* 我会尽量来，不过我看来不一定能来。□ *adv* (used absolutely, in the sense **5** above) however: (用于独立叙述中,同上面第 5 义)可是；然而；不过；*He will probably agree; you never know, ~.* 他很可能同意；不过没有人知道。*He said he would come; he didn't, ~.* 他说他会来；不过他没有来。

thought¹ /θɔːt; θɔt/ *pt, pp* of **think¹**.

thought² /θɔːt; θɔt/ *n* **1** [U] (power, process of) thinking: 思索；思考；思考力；思考的过程：*He spends hours in ~.* 他通常思考好几个小时。*He was lost/deep in ~,* thinking so deeply as to be unaware of his surroundings, etc. 他陷于沉思中。 **2** [U] way of thinking characteristic of a particular period, class, nation, etc: (某一时期、阶层、国家等的)思想；思潮：*Greek/working-class/scientific/modern ~.* 希腊(工人阶级、科学, 现代)思想。 **3** [U] ~ (*for*), care, consideration: 悬念；顾虑；关怀；考虑：*after serious ~.* 认真考虑后。 *He often acts without ~.* 他常常鲁莽行事。*The nurse was full of ~ for her patient.* 那护士非常关怀她的病人。**take ~ for,** be concerned about. 顾虑到；对…悬念。 **4** [C, U] idea, opinion, intention, formed by thinking: (由思考形成的)观念；概念；意见；意向；企图：*His speech was full of striking ~s.* 他的演讲充满了不平凡的见解。*Please write and let me have your ~s on the matter.* 请写信让我知道你对此事的意见。*That boy hasn't a ~ in his head.* 那男孩不用脑筋(自己没有主见)。*He keeps his ~s to himself,* does not tell anyone what he thinks. 他不对别人吐露心事。*She says she can read my ~s.* 她说她能看出我的意向。*He had no ~ (= intention) of hurting your feelings.* 他无意伤你的感情。*You must give up all ~ of marrying Tom.* 你必须完全放弃与汤姆结婚的念头。*I had some ~ of going* (= had half intended to go) *to Spain this summer.* 今年夏天我曾经打算到西班牙去。**on ~,second ~s,** after further consideration. 再思之后；经过进一步考虑。**~-reader** *n* person who claims to know people's ~s. 自称了解旁人思想者；读心术者。**~-transference,** telepathy. 心灵感应。 **5** *a ~,* a little: 些微；稍稍；一点：*You should be a ~ more considerate of other people.* 你应该多体谅旁人一点。 **~·ful** /-fl; -fəl/ *adj* **1** full of ~; showing ~: 深思的；思索的表情。 **2** considerate; thinking of, showing ~ (3) for, the needs of others: 体谅的；体贴的；关切的；考虑到旁人需要的：*a ~ful friend.* 关心旁人的朋友。*It was ~ful of you to warn me of your arrival.* 你来之前先通知我，真是考虑得很周到。**~·fully** /-fəlɪ; -fəlɪ/ *adv* **~·ful·ness** *n* **~·less** *adj* **1** careless; unthinking: 欠思虑的；粗心的；疏忽的；不注意的：*Young people are often ~less for the future.* 年轻人常常没想到未来。 **2** selfish; inconsiderate (of others): 自私的；不顾及别人的(与of连用)：*a ~less action.* 自私的行为。**~·less·ly** *adv* **~·less·ness** *n*

thou·sand /'θauzṇd; 'θauzṇd/ *adj, n* the number 1000, ➪ **App 4**; (loosely, exaggerated style) a great number: 千(的)；千个(的)(参看附录四)；(非严格地, 夸张用法)大数目；成千上万：*A ~ thanks for your kindness.* 多谢你的盛情。*He made a ~ and one excuses.* 他的借口多极了。*a ~ to 'one (chance),* remote (possibility): 极小的(可能性)；渺茫的(机会)。*one in a ~,* a rare exception. 稀有的例外；千里挑一；极优秀的人物。**~th** /'θauzṇθ; 'θauzṇdθ/ *adj, n* **~fold** /-fəuld; -'fold/ *adj, adv* a ~ times (as much or many). 千倍的(地)。

thrall /θrɔːl; θrɔl/ *n* [C, U] (condition of being a) slave: 奴隶；为奴的状况；(fig) (喻) *He is (in) ~ to his passions.* 他是感情的奴隶(顺情欲的)。**thral·dom** /-dəm; -dəm/ *n* [U] slavery. 奴役；奴役的身分。

thrash /θræʃ; θræʃ/ *vt, vi* **1** [VP6A] beat with a stick, whip, etc: 鞭打；笞打；棒打：*Stop ~ing that donkey, you cruel boy!* 不要打那驴子，你这残忍的孩子！*He ~ed the boy soundly,* gave him a thorough beating. 他痛打那男孩。*He threatened to ~ the life out of me.* 他

威吓着要打死我。**2** [VP6A] (colloq) defeat (a team, etc) in a contest. (口)竞赛中击败(一队等); 胜过。**3**[VP 15B] ~ *sth out*, (colloq) (口) **(a)** clear up (a problem, etc) by discussion. 借讨论而澄清或解决(一问题等)。**(b)** arrive at (the truth, a solution, etc) by discussion. 借讨论获致 (真相, 解决等)。**4** [VP6A, 15A, 2C] (cause to) toss, move violently: (使) 颠簸; (使) 剧烈移动: *The whale ~ed the water with its tail.* 那条鲸鱼用尾巴猛烈地扑水。*The swimmer ~ed about in the water.* 那游泳者在水中用力地游动。*The gale made the branches of the trees ~ against the windows.* 强风吹得树枝猛击窗户。**5**=**thresh**. ~**·ing** *n* [C] (esp) beating: (尤指)鞭打; 笞打: *give sb/ get a good ~ing*; 痛打某人(挨痛打); defeat, eg in games. (在比赛中)被击败; 失败。

thread /θred; θrɛd/ *n* 1 [C, U] (length of) spun cotton, silk, flax, wool, etc esp for use in sewing and weaving: (一段)线; 细丝; 纤维(尤指用于缝纫及纺织者): *a reel of silk ~*; 一卷丝线; *a needle and ~*; 针线; *gold ~*, ~ with gold wire wound round it. 金线。*hang by a ~*, (fig)be in a dangerous or precarious state. (喻)千钧一发; 势如累卵; 处境危险。**2** sth very thin, suggesting a ~: 线状物: *A ~ of light came through the keyhole.* 从钥匙孔射出来一线光亮。**3** chain or line (connecting parts of a story, etc): (连接故事等各部分的)线索; 脉络: *lose the ~ of one's argument*; 失去议论的线索; *gather up the ~s of a story*, bring parts of it together and relate them to one another; 综合一个故事的脉络; *pick up/resume the ~s*, continue (after an interruption). (打断后)接续下去。**4** spiral ridge round a screw or bolt. 螺纹。⇨ the illus at **bolt**. 参看 bolt 之插图。□ *vt* 1 [VP6A] pass a ~ through the eye of (a needle); put (beads, pearls, etc) on a ~; make (a chain of beads, etc) thus: 穿线于(针)孔; 以线穿起(珠子、珍珠等); 以线穿成(珠链等); ~ *a film*, put it in place (eg in a cine-projector, ready for showing it on a screen). 装妥影片(以待放映等)。**2** [VP15A] ~ *one's way through*, find, pick, one's way (through a crowd, streets, etc). 挤过(人群等); 穿过(街道等)。**3** (of hair) streak: (指头发)杂有…的发丝: *black hair ~ed with silver*, with streaks of silver hair in it. 杂有银丝的黑发。~·**bare** /-beə(r); -ˌbɛr/ *adj* 1 (of cloth) worn thin; shabby: (指布)磨薄的; 褴褛的: *a ~bare coat*. 褴褛的上衣。**2**(fig) much used and therefore uninteresting or valueless; hackneyed: (喻)陈腐的; 无趣的; 用旧的: ~*bare jokes/arguments*. 陈旧的笑话(议论)。~·**like** *adj* resembling a ~; long and slender. 象线的; 细长的。

threat /θret; θrɛt/ *n* [C] 1 statement of an intention to punish or hurt sb, esp if he does not do as one wishes: 恐吓; 威胁: *utter a* ~ *(against sb)*; 威吓(某人); *carry out a* ~; 采取恐吓; *be under the* ~ *of expulsion*, eg from a university. 受到开除的威胁; 有被开除之虞。**2** *a/ the* ~ *(to sb/sth) (of sth)*, sign or warning of coming trouble, danger, etc: 恶兆; 坏兆头; 不祥之兆: *the* ~ *to the country's economy of inflation.* 该国通货膨胀之危机。*There was a* ~ *of rain in the dark sky.* 天空黑云密布有下雨的朕兆。

threaten /θretn; θrɛtn̩/ *vt, vi* 1 [VP6A, 14, 17] ~ *sth*; ~ *sb (with sth)*; ~ *to do sth*, announce sth, using a threat; be a threat of sth to sb; use a threat (of sth) against sb: 恐吓; 威胁; 威胁着要; 扬言要: ~ *an employee with dismissal*; 用开革威胁一位雇员; ~ *an enemy*; 恐吓敌人; ~ *to murder sb.* 扬言要谋杀某人。*They ~ed revenge.* 他们扬言要报复。*The race was ~ed with extinction*, It seemed possible that all people of this race would die. 有种族有灭绝之虞。**2** [VP6A, 2A] give warning of: 预示; 有…朕兆: *The clouds ~ed rain.* 这乌云预示有雨。*It ~s to rain.* 天有下雨之势。**3** [VP2A] seem likely to occur or come: 似有发生或来临的可能; 将发生; 可能来临: *Knowing that danger ~ed, the sentry kept an extra careful watch.* 因为知道随时有危险发生, 那岗哨特别注意戒备。~·**ing·ly** *adv*

three /θriː; θri/ *adj, n* the number 3, ⇨ **App 4**: 三(的); 三

个(的)(参看附录四): *a* ~*-act play*, one with ~ acts. 三幕剧。~·'**cornered** *adj* triangular: 三角形的: *a* ~*-cornered contest/fight*, with ~ contestants or competitors, eg in a Parliamentary election. 三角竞争(战斗)(有三个角逐者参加者, 如竞争下议院席位)。⇨ *straight fight* at **straight**[1](5). ~'**D**, (abbr for) ~*-dimensional.* 为 ~*-dimensional* 之略。⇨ below. 参看下列之 ~*-dimensional*。~·'**decker** *n* **(a)** old type of sailing-ship with ~ decks. (旧式的)三层甲板的帆船或军舰。**(b)** kind of sandwich with ~ layers of bread and two layers of filling. 三层三明治(有三层面包, 两层夹物)。**(c)** novel in ~ volumes (common in the 18th and 19th cc). 三部头小说(十八九世纪间甚为流行)。~·**di'mensional** *adj* (abbr 略作 **3-D**) having, or appearing to have, ~ dimensions (length, breadth and depth); stereoscopic. 三度空间 (长、宽、高) 的; 具有或有三度空间的; 立体的。~·'**figure** *adj* (of numbers) between 100 and 999 (inclusive). (指数字)三位数字 (100 与 999 之间者)。~·'**pence** /'θriːpens; 'θrɪpens/ *n, sing of* ~*pence*. 三便士额。~·**penny** /'θriːpeni; 'θrɪˌpeni/ *adj* costing or worth ~ pence: 价值三便士的: *a* ~*penny stamp*. 三便士的邮票。~·'**lane** *adj* (of a roadway) marked for ~ lanes of traffic. (指车道)三线车道的。~·'**legged** /-'legid; -'legid/ *adj* **(a)** having ~ legs: 三条腿的: *a* ~*-legged stool*. 三条腿的凳子。**(b)** (of a race) one in which the competitors run in pairs, the right leg of one runner being tied to the left leg of the other. (指赛跑)两人三脚赛跑(两人为一组, 中间的两腿绑在一起)。~·'**piece** *adj* consisting of ~ pieces: 三件式的: *a* ~*-piece suit*, set of ~ garments (a man's jacket, waistcoat and trousers, or a woman's skirt/trousers and blouse); 三件头的衣服(男服包括上下装及背心, 女服包括上装、裙或裤、及衬衫); *a* ~*-piece suite*, set of ~ pieces of furniture (usu a sofa and two armchairs). 三件式的家俱(通常为一个长沙发, 两个小沙发)。~·'**ply** *adj* **(a)** (of wool, thread) having ~ strands. (指毛线、线)三股的。**(b)** (of wood) having ~ layers glued together. (指木材)三层粘合的; 三层的。~·'**quarter** *n* (Rugby football) person who plays between the half-back and the full-back. (橄榄球)中卫。⇨ the illus at **Rugby.** 参看 Rugby 之插图。□ *adj* (of a portrait) down to the hips. (指画像)半身像。Cf 参较 *a full-length portrait* at **full**(7). ~·**score** *adj, n* sixty. 六十(的)。~·'**some** /-səm; -səm/ *n* group of, or game played by, ~ persons. 三人之一组; 三人一组之游戏或竞技。~·'**storey(ed)** *adj* (of a building) having ~ storeys. (指建筑)有三层的; 三层的。~·'**wheeled** *adj* having ~ wheels. 有三个轮子的; 三轮的。

thren·ody /'θrenədi; 'θrɛnədi/ *n* (*pl* -**dies**) song of lamentation; funeral song. 挽歌; 哀歌。

thresh /θreʃ; θrɛʃ/ *vt, vi* [VP6A, 15A, 2A] beat the grain out of (wheat, etc); beat wheat etc for this purpose: 打(麦等); 打谷: ~ *corn by hand* 用手打谷。*Have the farmers started* ~*ing yst?* 农民们已开始打谷了吗? '~·**ing-floor** *n* part on which grain is ~ed out. 打谷场。'~·**ing-machine** *n* one for ~ing grain. 打谷机。~·**er** *n* 1 ~ing-machine, person who ~es. 打谷机; 打谷者。**2** large shark with a long tail. 长尾鲨鱼; 长尾鲛。

thresh·old /'θreʃhəʊld; 'θrɛʃold/ *n* [C] 1 stone or plank under an outside doorway; part of an entrance over which one must step: 门槛; 门口: *cross the* ~, enter. 跨越门槛; 进入。**2**(fig)entrance, start, beginning: (喻)入口; 开始; 开始: *He was on the* ~ *of his career*. 他的事业刚刚开始。*We are at the* ~ *of an era of peace.* 我们是处于和平时代的开端。**3** (physiol, psych) limit: (生理、心理)最低限度, point at which a sensation is felt as pain; 痛阈; *above/below the* ~ *of consciousness*, above/below the limit at which we are aware of things. 在意识阈之上(下); 有意识作用(下意识)的。**subliminal.**

threw /θruː; θru/ *pt of* **throw**[1].

thrice /θraɪs; θraɪs/ *adv* (rarely used) three times. (罕用)三倍地；三度地。

thrift /θrɪft; θrɪft/ *n* [U] care, economy, in the use of money or goods. 节俭；俭约。**~y** *adj* (**-ier, -iest**) **1** economical; using ~. 节俭的；俭约的。**2** (US) thriving; prosperous. (美)旺盛的；繁荣的。**~·ily** /-ɪlɪ; -ɪlɪ/ *adv* **~·less** *adj* wasteful. 不节俭的；浪费的；奢侈的。**~·less·ly** *adv* **~·less·ness** *n*

thrill /θrɪl; θrɪl/ *n* (experience causing an) excited feeling passing like a wave along the nerves: 激动；震颤；震颤感；令人震颤的经验：*a ~ of joy/pleasure/horror*. 一阵高兴(愉快,恐怖)。*It gave her quite a ~ to shake hands with the Princess*. 同公主握手使她至感兴奋。*This film will give you the ~ of a lifetime*, excite you as you have never been excited before. 这部电影将会带给你前所未有的刺激。□ *vt, vi* **1** [VP6A] cause a ~ or ~s in: 使震颤；使激动；使生震颤感：*The film ~ed the audience*. 那部电影带给观众很大的刺激。She were ~ed with horror/joy. 我们恐惧(喜悦)极了。**2** [VP2A, C] feel a ~ or ~s: 感到震颤或激动：*We ~ed at the good news*. 我们听到那项好消息感到很兴奋。*She ~ed with delight when the handsome footballer kissed her*. 当那位英俊的足球员亲吻她的时候,她高兴得颤抖。*There was a ~ing finish to the race*. 最后一段赛程非常紧张刺激。**~er** *n* novel, play or film in which excitement and emotional appeal are the essential elements. 惊险、动人、恐怖、刺激等的小说、戏剧或电影。

thrive /θraɪv; θraɪv/ *vi* (*pt* **~d** or (archaic) 或(古) **throve** /θrəʊv; θrov/, *pp* **~d** or (archaic) 或(古) **thriven** /'θrɪvn; 'θrɪvən/) [VP2A, 3A] **~ (on sth)**, prosper; succeed; grow strong and healthy: 兴盛；成功；长得健壮：*A business cannot ~ without good management*. 管理不善的企业是不可能兴盛。*Children ~ on good food*. 儿童要吃得好才能长得健壮。*He has a thriving business*. 他的生意兴旺。

thro' /θruː; θru/ (informal spelling of) **through**. 为 through 的非正式拼法。

throat /θrəʊt; θrot/ *n* **1** front part of the neck: 喉头；*grip sb by the ~*; 抓住某人的喉头；*cut one's ~*, eg intending to commit suicide or (fig) destroy one's own opportunities. 割喉咙(如企图自杀)；(喻)自取灭亡；自毁前程；毁坏自己的机会。⇔ the illus at **head**. 参看 head 之插图。'**cut-~** *attrib adj* (**a**) (of a razor) having a long movable blade set into the handle, ⇔ the illus at **razor**. (指剃刀)有活动长刀和把手的 (参看 razor 之插图)。(**b**) (of competition, etc) intense and ruthless. (指竞争等)剧烈而无情的；残酷的。**2** passage in the neck through which food passes to the stomach and air to the lungs: 咽喉；喉咙；*A bone has stuck in my ~*. 有一根骨头梗在我的喉咙。*force/thrust sth down sb's ~*, (fig) try to make sb accept one's views, beliefs, etc. (喻)勉强旁人接受自己的意见、信仰等。*stick in one's ~*, (fig) not be readily acceptable. 梗在喉头；(喻)不能立刻接受。**-~ed** in compounds: 用于复合词中：*a red-~ed bird*. 红脖子鸟。**~y** *adj* (**-ier, -iest**) uttered deep in the ~: 喉音的,发自喉咙深处的：*a ~y voice*, guttural. 喉音；低沉重浊的声音。

throb /θrɒb; θrɑb/ *vi* (**-bb-**) [VP2A, C] (of the heart, pulse, etc) beat, esp beat more rapidly than usual: (指心脏、脉搏等)跳动；悸动(尤指跳动较平常快)：*His head ~bed*, He had a bad headache. 他头痛得很厉害。*His wound ~bed with pain*. 他的伤口阵阵地疼痛。*Her heart was ~bing with excitement*. 她的心因兴奋而跳得很快。□ *n* [C] ~bing or vibration: 跳动；悸动；震颤；~*s of joy/pleasure*; 一阵阵的高兴(愉快)；*the ~ of distant gun-fire*. 远处阵阵的炮声。**~·bing** *adj* that ~s: 跳动的；悸动的；*the ~bing (sound of) machinery*. 机器的震颤(声)。

throe /θrəʊ; θro/ *n* **~s**, sharp pains, esp of childbirth. 剧痛；(尤指)分娩时的阵痛。*in the ~s of sth/of doing sth*, (colloq) struggling with the task of it/doing it: (口)辛苦做某事；苦干；*in the ~s of an examination/*

of packing one's luggage. 为考试(包捆行李)而辛苦。

throm·bo·sis /θrɒm'bəʊsɪs; θrɑm'bosɪs/ *n* [U] clot of blood in a blood-vessel or in the heart. (血管或心脏的)栓塞；血栓形成。

throne /θrəʊn; θron/ *n* [C] **1** ceremonial chair or seat of a king, queen, bishop, etc. (国王、女王、主教等的)宝座；御座。**2 the ~**, royal authority: 王权；王位；帝位：*come to the ~*, become king/queen; 登王位；即位；*united in loyalty to the T~*, to the Sovereign. 团结一致效忠帝王。

throng /θrɒŋ *US*: θrɔːŋ; θrɔŋ/ *n* crowd. 群；群众。□ *vt, vi* [VP6A, 4A, 2C] crowd: 挤；群集：*The railway stations were ~ed with people going away for their holidays*. 火车站挤满了外出度假的人们。*People ~ed to see the new play*. 人们蜂拥着去观赏那出新戏。

throstle /'θrɒsl; 'θrɑsl/ *n* song-thrush. 善鸣的画眉鸟。

throttle /'θrɒtl; 'θrɑtl/ *vt, vi* **1** [VP6A] seize (sb) by the throat and stop his breathing; choke; strangle: 扼(某人)的喉头；勒死；使窒息；绞死：~ *the nightwatchman and then rob the bank*. 勒死守夜者然后抢劫银行。*The tyrant ~d freedom in his country*. 那个暴君在他的国家内压制自由。**2** [VP6A, 15B, 2C] ~ **(back/down)**, control the flow of steam, petrol vapour, etc in an engine; lessen the speed of (an engine) by doing this. 控制引擎或机车的蒸气汽油油等；调整节气阀以减低(引擎)的速度；节流。□ *n* '**~(-valve)**' valve controlling the flow of steam, petrol vapour, etc in an engine: 节气阀；节流阀；*open out the ~*; 打开节气阀；*close the ~*; 关闭节气阀；*with the ~ full open*. 全速地。

through /θruː; θru/ ⇔ the *v* entries: 参看各动词；specimens only here 以下仅举范例) **1** from end to end, beginning to end, side to side: 自一端至另一端；贯穿地；自始至终：*They wouldn't let us ~*, eg pass ~ the gate. 他们不让我们过去(如通过大门等)。*Did your brother ~*, eg the examination? 你的哥哥(弟弟)通过(考试等)了吗？*He slept the whole night ~*, all night. 他睡了一个通宵。*His trousers are ~* (= have holes or rents in them) *at the knees*. 他的裤子膝头已破了。*Read the book ~ carefully*. 把这本书仔细通读。*all ~*, all the time (while sth was happening, etc): (当某事发生之际)始终；一直；老是：*I knew all ~ that he was lying*. 我完全知道他在说谎。**2** to the very end. 到最后。*be ~ (with)*, (**a**) finish (with): 结束；做好；完成。*When will you be ~ with your work?* 你什么时候可以做完你的工作？(**b**) (colloq) have had enough of: (口)对…已经厌烦：*I'm ~ with this job; I must find something more interesting*. 我厌烦这项工作；我必须找一份更有趣味的工作做。*go ~ with*, continue until it is finished or completed. 贯彻某事；继续做完某事；完成某事。*see sth ~*, be present at, help in, a series of events, etc until the end. 将某事做到底；参与或协助做彻某事。*~ and ~*, in all parts; completely: 完全地；彻底地：*He's a reliable man ~ and ~*. 他是一个完全可靠的人。*You're wet ~/~ and ~*, Your clothes are thoroughly wet. 你全身湿透了。**3** all the way to: 全程地；直达地：*This train goes ~ to Paris*, There is no need to change trains. 这列火车直达巴黎(无须换车)。*Book your tickets/luggage ~ to Vienna*. 订购直达维也纳的车票(把你的行李托运至维也纳)。**4** (telephoning) (电话)(**a**) (GB) connected: (英)接通：*I will put you ~ to the manager*, connect you. 我将把你的电话接到经理那里。*You're ~*, Your telephone connection has been made. 你的电话接通了。(**b**) (US) finished; not wishing to continue the call. (美)讲完了；不打算继续讲话。**5** (used, in the sense of **3** above, to modify *nn*): (用以修饰名词,其意义上与上面第 **3** 义同)：*a ~ train to Paris*; 直达巴黎的直达火车；~ *tickets/passengers/fares*; 直达车的车票(乘客、车费)；~ *traffic*, road traffic which is going ~ a place (contrasted with local traffic). 直达车(与区间车相对)。'~**put** /-pʊt;-pʊt/ *n* [U, C] output; amount of material put ~ a process. 生产量；生产总额。'~**way**

n ~ express way. 高速公路. ⇨ **express**¹(2).

through² (US in informal writing also 在美国非正式写作中亦作 **thru**) /θru:; θru/ *prep* **1** (of places) from end to end or side to side of; entering at one side, on one surface, etc and coming out at the other: (指地方) 从一端至另一端; 从一边至另一边; 穿过; 经过; 经过: *Two of the jockeys were ~n in the second race.* 两位骑师在第二次赛马时被摔了下来. **(b)** (of a wrestler) force (an opponent) to the floor. (指摔交者)摔倒(对手). **(c)** (of a snake) cast (its skin). (指蛇)蜕(皮). **(d)** (of animals) bring forth (young). (指动物)生产(幼仔). **5** [VP6A] (of dice) ~ on to the table (after shaking them in sth); get by doing this: (指骰子)掷出; 掷得: ~ *three sixes.* 掷得三个六点. **6**[VP6A] twist (silk) into threads. 搓(丝)成线. **7** [VP6A] shape (pottery) on a potter's wheel. 在拉坯轮车上制成(陶器). **8** [VP6A] (colloq) disturb; distress; distract: (口)惊扰; 使苦恼; 使分心: *The news of her death really threw me.* 她去世的消息真使我难过. **9** (sl) (俚) ~ *a party,* give a party. 举行宴会、酒会等. ~ *a fit,* have a fit. 大惊; 大怒; 突然发作等. ⇨ **fit³**(2). **10** ~ *sth open (to),* [VP22] **(a)** make (eg a competition) open to all persons. 公开举行(竞赛等). **(b)** allow the general public to enter (eg gardens which are usually closed). 开放(如通常关闭的花园). **11** [VP6A] (with *nn,* to which cross-references are given): (与名词连用, 参看各名词): ~ *cold water on sth,* ⇨ **water**¹(1). ~ *doubt upon,* ⇨ **doubt**¹. ~ *dust in sb's eyes,* ⇨ **dust**¹(1). ~ *down the gauntlet,* ⇨ **gauntlet**¹(1). ~ *light on,* ⇨ **light³**(5). ~ *a sop to Cerberus,* ⇨ **sop.** ~ *one's weight about,* ⇨ **weight.** **12** [VP15B, 14, 2C] (special uses with *adverbial particles* and *preps*): (与副词性小品词及介词连用的特殊用法):

through² (US in informal writing also 在美国非正式写作中亦作 **thru**) /saw:/ ~ *prep* **1** (of places) from end to end or side to side of; entering at one side, on one surface, etc and coming out at the other: (指地方) 从一端至另一端; 从一边至另一边; 穿过; 经过: *The River Thames flows ~ London.* 泰晤士河流经伦敦. *The burglar came in ~ the window.* 夜贼是从窗户进来的. *The road goes ~ the forest.* 该路穿越那森林. *There is a path ~ the fields.* 有一条小路穿过田野. *She passed a comb/her fingers ~ her hair.* 她用梳子(用她的手指)拢梳她的头发. *He was looking ~ a telescope.* 他从望远镜里观望. *One can see ~ glass.* 人能从玻璃看过去. **2** (fig uses; 比喻用法; ⇨ the *v* entries; 参看各该词目; specimens only here 下列仅系范例): *He went ~/has come ~* (= experienced) *many hardships.* 他经历过许多艰辛. *He soon got/went ~* (= got to the end of, spent the whole of) *his fortune.* 他很快就花光了他的财产. *We must go ~* (= examine) *the accounts.* 我们必须查阅帐目. *He got ~* (= passed) *the examination.* 他通过了考试. *He saw ~* (= was not deceived by) *the trick.* 他查看了那项诡计(未受骗). **3** (of time) from beginning to end of: (指时间)从头至尾; 自始至终: *He won't live ~ the night,* He will die before morning. 他活不过今晚了. *The children are too young to sit ~ a long concert.* 孩子们太小, 不能坐着听完冗长的音乐会. **4** (US) up to and including: (美)一直到并包括: *We'll be in London from Tuesday ~ Saturday.* 从星期二至星期六, 我们将在伦敦. **5** (indicating the agency, means or cause): (表示作用、方法、工具或原因): *I learnt of the position ~ a newspaper advertisement.* 我从报上一则广告获知这一职位. *The accident happened ~ no fault of yours.* 这意外事件的发生, 并非由于你的过失. *We lost ourselves ~ not knowing the way.* 我们因为不认识路而迷失了. *It was all ~ you* (= It was your fault) *that we were late.* 我们之所以迟到, 完全要怪你. **6** without stopping for: 不停: *Don't drive ~ a red light.* 不要驾车闯过红灯.

through·out /θru:'aut; θru'aut/ *adv* right through; in every part; in all ways or respects: 一直; 全部; 各处; 各方面: *The coat is lined with fur ~.* 那外套全部用毛皮做衬里. *The woodwork in the house was rotten ~.* 那幢房子的木结构部分整个腐烂了. □ *prep* all or right through; from end to end of: 遍及, 在整个期间; 从一端至另一端: ~ *the country;* 遍及全国; 整个国家; ~ *the length and breadth of the land;* 遍及该土地; ~ *the war.* 在整个战争期间.

throve /θrəuv; θrov/ ⇨ **thrive.**

throw¹ /θrəu; θro/ *vt, vi* (*pt* **threw** /θru:; θru/, *pp* **thrown** /θrəun; θron/) (For special uses with *adverbial particles* and *preps,* ⇨ **12** below) (与副词性小品词及介词连用的特殊用法, 参看下列第 12 义) **1** [VP2A, 6A, 15A, B, 12A, 13A] cause (sth) to go through the air, usu with force, by a movement of the arm or by mechanical means: 投; 抛; 掷; 扔: *He ~s well.* 他掷得很好. *He can ~ a hundred yards.* 他能掷一百码远. *Don't ~ stones at my dog!* 不要向我的狗投石子! *He threw the ball to his sister.* 他把球抛给他的姊姊(妹妹). *Please ~ me that towel.* 请把那条毛巾丢给我. *He threw the ball up and caught it.* 他把球抛起再把它接住. *He seized the man and threw him to the ground.* 他抓住那人并把他摔在地上. *The drunken man was thrown out.* 那醉汉被推出门外. *He threw an angry look at me/me an angry look.* 他对我怒目而视. **2** [VP15A, B] put (articles of clothing) (*on, off, over,* etc) quickly or carelessly: 匆忙或粗心地穿、脱、披(衣物等): ~ *off one's clothes/disguise;* 匆促脱去衣服(卸下伪装); ~ *a scarf over one's shoulders.* 匆忙把围巾披在肩上. **3** [VP15A, B] move (one's arms, legs, etc) (*out, up, down, about*) violently: 用力或猛烈地移动(臂、腿等): ~ *one's chest out;* 用力挺起胸膛; ~ *up one's arms;* 用力举手; ~ *one's head back.* 把头用力向后仰. *You'll never learn to swim properly while you*

~ your legs and arms about so wildly. 你这样猛烈地划动腿和臂, 永远不会把游泳学好.

throw sth about, scatter: 撒布; 乱掷: *Don't ~ waste paper about in the park.* 不要在公园乱掷纸屑. *He's ~ing his money about,* (fig) spending it recklessly. (喻)他在胡乱花钱.

throw oneself at, **(a)** rush violently at. 冲向; 向~突进. **(b)** force one's attentions on; behave without restraint in an effort to win the love of. 全力争取~的爱、友谊或恩爱; 博取~的欢心; 勾引.

throw sth away, **(a)** lose by foolishness or neglect: 因愚蠢或疏忽而失去; 抛却; 丢掉: ~ *away an advantage.* 失去优势. *My advice was ~ n away upon him,* wasted. 我对他的忠告是白费了. **(b)** (of words spoken by actors, broadcasters, etc) utter in a casual way, with conscious under-emphasis. (指演员、广播员等所说的话)有意不予强调; 轻轻带过; 点到即止. Hence, 由此产生, '~·**away** *n* sth that may be ~n away (eg a printed handbill); sth of small value, discarded after use: 可予抛弃之物(如广告单); 价值小而且用过即可丢弃之物: (attrib) (用作定语) *a ~away ballpen;* 用完即可抛弃的原子笔; *a ~away line,* sth spoken casually, without emphasis. 可轻轻带过的话(随便说出, 无须加重).

throw back, show characteristics of, revert to, a remote ancestor. 显示出远祖的特征; 返回祖先型态; 呈返祖现象. Hence, 由此产生, '~·**back** *n* (example of) reversion to an ancestral type. 祖型重现; 返祖现象; 其实例. ~ *sb back on/upon sth,* (often passive) force sb to go back to (because nothing else is available): (常用被动语态)迫使重新依靠(某事物); 迫使反求(某事): *After this failure to get help we were ~n back upon our own resources.* 经过这一次求助失败以后, 我们被迫依赖自己的力量.

throw oneself down, lie down at full length. 全身伸展地躺下; 倒下.

throw sth in, **(a)** supply sth extra, without an addition to the price: 额外赠送: *You can have the piano for £60, with the stool ~n in.* 你可以用六十镑购买那架钢琴, 坐凳奉送. **(b)** put in (a remark, etc) casually. 偶尔插进(话等); 插嘴说. **(c)** (football) ~ the ball in after it has gone out of play. (足球)球出界后把球扔进. Hence, 由此产生, '~·**in** *n in one's hand,* give up an attempt to do sth; confess one's inability to do sth. 放弃尝试; 承认无能为力; 承认不能做某事. ~ *in one's lot with sb,* 承

decide to share his fortunes. 与某人同进退；与某人祸福与共。 ~ *in the towel*/*sponge*, (colloq) (from boxing) admit defeat. (口)(来自拳击)承认失败。

throw oneself into sth, begin to work vigorously at. 投身于；开始积极从事。

throw *sb*/*sth* **off**, manage to get rid of; become free from: 摆脱某人或某事；除去: ~ *off a cold*/*a troublesome acquaintance*/*one's pursuers*. 伤风痊愈(摆脱一位讨厌的熟人；摆脱追逐者)。 ~ *sth off*, produce or compose, easily, as if without effort: 轻易做出；轻易作出: ~ *off a few lines of verse*. 即席写成数行诗句。

throw oneself on/**upon** *sb*/*sth*, place one's reliance on: 仰赖于；信赖；委身于: ~ *oneself* (*up*)*on the mercy of one's captors*/*the court*/*the judge*. 任凭捕捉者(法庭、法官)的处置。

throw sth out, (a) utter (esp casually): 说出；(尤指无意间)吐露: ~ *out a hint*/*suggestion*; 作暗示(提出建议)； ~ *out a challenge*. 出言挑战。 **(b)** reject (a Bill in Parliament, etc). 否决(国会议案等)。 **(c)** build as an extension: 增建；加盖: ~ *out a new wing*, eg to a hospital or other large building. 增建一幢边房或厢房。 ~ *sb out,* **(a)** (cricket, of a fielder) get (a batsman) out by ~*ing* the ball and hitting the wicket. (板球，指外场员)投球击中三柱门而使(击球员)出场。 **(b)** disconcert or distract (sb whose attention is concentrated on sth) so that he makes an error, has to stop, etc: 使(某人)分心；扰乱(某人): *Keep quiet for a while or you'll* ~ *me out in my calculations*. 安静一会儿，否则我就无法专心计算了。

throw sb over, desert; abandon: 放弃；舍弃: ~ *over an old friend*/*one's girlfriend*. 遗弃一位老朋友(女朋友)。

throw sth together, assemble hastily: 仓促地集成: *That last textbook of his seems to have been* ~*n together,* written or compiled carelessly and hurriedly. 他写的最后一册教科书似乎是仓促间草草编成的。 ~ *people together,* bring together: 集合；集拢: *Chance had* ~*n us together at a skiing resort.* 机缘使我们在一个滑雪胜地相遇。

throw sth up, (a) vomit (food). 吐出(食物)；呕。 **(b)** resign from: 辞去: ~ *up one's job*. 辞职。 ~ *sth up,* bring it to notice: 使某物被人看到: *A search through his pockets threw up a very strange collection of objects.* 搜查他的口袋发现一些十分奇怪的东西。 ~ *up one's hands (in horror)*, express horror by doing this. 吓得举起双手。

throw² /θrəu; θro/ *n* [C] throwing; distance to which sth is or may be thrown: 投；掷；抛；投掷的距离；a well-aimed ~, eg cricket, to get a batsman out; 一次准确投掷(如板球，使击球员出局的一次投球)；a ~ of the dice; 骰子的一掷；a ~ *record* ~ *with the hammer* (as a competition in athletic sports). (运动会中)链球创记录的一掷。 *within a 'stone's* ~ *(of)*, quite near (to). 近在咫尺；在投石可及的距离内。

thru /θruː; θru/ (US informal spelling for) **through**. (美)为 through 的非正式拼法。

thrum /θrʌm; θrʌm/ *vt, vi* (**-mm-**) [VP6A, 3A] ~ **(on)** *sth*, play monotonously or idly on (a stringed instrument): 漫弹或单调地弹(弦乐器)；弹弄: ~ (*on*) *a guitar*, ⇨ **strum;** 弹奏吉他; tap or drum idly with the fingers: 以手指轻敲或轻击: ~ *on the table*. 以手指轻敲桌子。

thrush¹ /θrʌʃ; θrʌʃ/ *n* [C] sorts of song-bird, esp the kind called '*song*-~, or *throstle*. 鸫；画眉鸟(尤指善鸣的一种，称作 song-~ 或 throstle)。

thrush² /θrʌʃ; θrʌʃ/ *n* internal inflammatory disease. 鹅口疮；雪口症。

thrust /θrʌst; θrʌst/ *vt, vi* (*pt, pp* ~) [VP6A, 15A, B, 2A, C] push suddenly or violently; make a forward stroke with a sword, etc: 力推；插；刺；戳: *He* ~ *his hands into his pockets*/*a dagger into his enemy's heart*. 他把双手插入衣袋内 (把短剑刺入敌人的心脏中)。 *We had to* ~ *our way through the crowd*. 我们不得不挤过人群。 *They* ~ *themselves forward*/*past*/*into the bus.* 他

们用力向前挤(挤过去，挤进公共汽车)。 *Some people have greatness* ~ *upon them,* ie obtain renown without their own effort. 有些人的成名是时势造成的。 *He has* ~ *himself into a well-paid position,* obtained one by ruthless methods. 他不择手段取得一个待遇优厚的工作。 □ *n* 1 [C] act of ~*ing*; (in war) strong attempt to push forward into the enemy's positions; (in debate, etc) attack in words; hostile remark aimed at sb. 推；挤；刺；戳；(作战时之)挺进；突袭；(辩论等时之)口头攻击；抨击；讽刺。 2 [U] stress or pressure on a neighbouring part of a structure (eg an arch); force directed forward in a jet-engine as a reaction to the ejection rearward of gases. (拱等)向邻接部分的推压(力量)；(喷射引擎的)推进力；推力。 ~*er* *n* (esp) person who ~s himself forward (to win an advantage, etc). (尤指)争先恐后(自我推进的)者；钻营者；强求名利者。

thud /θʌd; θʌd/ *n* dull sound as of a blow on sth soft: 重击声；砰击声；重击软物声: *The bullet entered his brain and he fell with a* ~ *to the carpet.* 子弹射进他的脑部，他砰然倒在地毯上。 □ *vi* (**-dd-**)[VP2C] strike, fall, with a ~: 砰然打击或落下；重击: *Bullets* ~*ded into the sandbags behind which we were sheltering.* 子弹砰砰地射进掩护我们的沙袋内。

thug /θʌg; θʌg/ *n* violent criminal; murderous ruffian. 凶残的罪犯；嗜杀的恶棍。 ~*gery* *n* [U].

thumb /θʌm; θʌm/ *n* short, thick finger set apart from the other four. 拇指。 ⇨ the illus at **arm.** 参看 arm 之插图。 (*one's fingers*) *be all* ~*s; have ten* ~*s,* be very clumsy. 十分笨拙；笨手笨脚。 *rule of* ~, method or procedure based on experience and practice. 根据经验的作法；经验得来的办法。 *under sb's* ~, under his influence and control. 在某人的影响或支配之下。 ~*-up*/*down,* (phrase signifying success/failure). (表示成功或失败的用语)。 ~*-nail sketch,* portrait on a small scale; hasty word-picture. 小型图像；速写；简略描述。 '~*-screw* *n* **(a)** (also 亦作 '~*-nut*) one that can be turned easily with the ~ and a finger. 翼形螺钉；翼形螺母。 **(b)** old instrument of torture which squeezed the ~s. 拇指夹(昔时的刑具)。 '~*-stall* *n* sheath to cover an injured ~. 指套(保护受伤拇指者)。 '~*-tack* *n* (US) drawing-pin. (美)图钉。 □ *vt* 1 [VP6A] turn over (pages, etc); make dirty by doing this: 翻动(书页等)；以拇指翻动而弄脏: ~ *a dictionary*; 翻动词典(的书页)；a well-~*ed book*. 常被翻阅的书。 2 ~ *a lift*, ask for (and get) a free ride in a motor-vehicle (by signalling to the driver). 向驾车者翘拇指要求(并获准)搭便车。 ⇨ **hitch-hike.** ~ *one's nose at sb,* cock a snook at him. 把拇指放在鼻子上向某人张翘其余四指以表示轻蔑。 ⇨ **snook.**

thump /θʌmp; θʌmp/ *vt, vi* [VP6A, 15A, 22, 2A, C, 3A] strike heavily, esp with the fists; deliver heavy blows: 重击(尤指用拳)；给予重击: *He* ~*ed* (*on*) *the door.* 他重击门。 *She* ~*ed the cushion flat.* 她把垫子捶平。 *His heart was* ~*ing with excitement.* 他激动得心砰砰跳。 *The two boys began to* ~ *one another.* 那两个男孩开始用拳头互殴。 *He was* ~*ing the keys of the piano*/~*ing out a tune on the piano,* playing noisily. 他用力弹钢琴(用力拍钢琴上弹奏一曲)。 □ *n* [C] noise of, or as of, a heavy blow (esp one given with the fist): 重击(尤指用拳者)；重击声；砰然声: *I dislike being given a friendly* ~ *on the back.* 我讨厌别人友善却很重的拍打我的背。 *The baby fell out of its cot with a* ~. 那娃娃砰然一声从小床上跌落。 ~*-ing* *adj* (colloq) of great size. (口)尺码巨的。 □ *adv* (colloq) extremely: (口)极度地；极端地: *What a* ~*ing great lie!* 好大的一个谎言！

thun·der /θʌndə(r); θʌndɚ/ *n* 1 [U] noise which usu follows a flash of lightning: 雷；雷声: *a loud crash*/*a long roll of* ~. 雷声大作(隆隆)。 *There's* ~ *in the air,* T~ seems likely. 好象要打雷了。 *We haven't had much* ~ *this summer.* 今年夏天我们未听到很多雷声。 ~*-bolt* *n* flash of lightning with a crash of ~; (fig) unexpected and terrible event. 雷电；霹雳；(喻)突然而又可怕的事

件。'~‧clap n crash of ~; sth that comes like ~; sudden, terrible event, bad news, etc. 雷声；霹雳；来势如霹雳的事物；突然、可怕的事件，坏消息等。'~‧storm n storm of ~ and lightning, usu with heavy rain. (通常为大的)雷雨。'~‧struck adj (pred; fig) amazed. (用作表语；喻)惊呆的；惊愕的。2 [U, C] loud noise like or suggesting ~; 似雷的声响; the ~ of the guns; 大炮的隆隆声; ~s of applause. 如雷的掌声。steal sb's ~, spoil his attempt to be impressive by anticipating him. 抢先使用别人的方法或观点；掠人之美。□ vi, vt 1 [VP2A, C] (impersonal): (无人称): It was ~ing and lightening. 其时雷电交加。2 [VP2C] make a noise like ~: 发出如雷之声: Someone was ~ing at the door, beating at it. 有人在猛烈地敲门。The train ~ed through the station. 火车隆隆地驶过车站。The juggernauts ~ed past. 巨型运输车隆隆地驶过。3 [VP2C, 3A, 15B] ~ (out) (against), speak in a loud voice, attack violently in words: 大声地说话；以言词猛烈攻击: The reformers ~ed against gambling. 社会改革者大声疾呼反对赌博。How dare you ~ out your orders at me? 你怎敢对我大声地发号施令？~er n (esp) (尤指) the T~er, one of the names of the god Jupiter. 朱庇特的名字之一。~‧ing adj, adv = thumping: He was in a ~ing (= violent) rage. 他大发雷霆。~‧ous/-əs; -əs/adj making a noise like, sounding like, ~: 喧声如雷的；轰隆如雷的; ~ous applause. 雷声雷动。~‧y /-dərɪ; -dərɪ/ adj (of weather) giving signs of ~. (指天气)预示要打雷的；象要打雷的。

thu‧rible /'θjʊərəbl US: 'θjʊər-; 'θjʊrəbl/ n = censer.

Thurs‧day /'θɜːzdɪ; 'θɝzdɪ/ n fifth day of the week. 星期四；礼拜四；木曜日。

thus /ðʌs; ðʌs/ adv in this way; so: 象这样；如此；~ far, to this point. 至此；迄今。

thwack /θwæk; θwæk/ vt, n = whack.

thwart¹ /θwɔːt; θwɔrt/ n seat across a rowing-boat for an oarsman. (划艇上桨手的)坐板。

thwart² /θwɔːt; θwɔrt/ vt [VP6A] obstruct, frustrate: 阻挠；挫折；妨碍；反对: ~ sb's plans; 阻挠某人的计划; be ~ed in one's ambitions/aims. 自己的企图(目标)受到挫折。

thy /ðaɪ; ðaɪ/ adj (archaic) your. (古)你的。thine /ðaɪn; ðaɪn/ adj (archaic) (before a vowel sound) your. (古)(用于元音前)你的。□ pron yours. 你的。thy‧self /ðaɪ'self; ðaɪ'sɛlf/ reflex, emph pron (archaic) yourself. (古)你自己。

thyme /taɪm; taɪm/ n [U] kinds of herb with fragrant aromatic leaves, growing wild and in gardens, used in cookery. 百里香(叶芳香，野生或培植，用于烹饪)。

thy‧roid /'θaɪrɔɪd; 'θaɪrɔɪd/ n ~ (gland), gland in the front part of the neck, producing a substance which affects the body's growth and activity. 甲状腺(位于颈之前部，其分泌物能影响身体的发育及活动)。⇨ the illus at head. 参看 head 之插图。

ti /tiː; ti/ n seventh note in the musical octave. 全音阶的第七音。

ti‧ara /tɪ'ɑːrə; taɪ'ɛrə/ n [C] 1 coronet for a woman. 女人的冠状头饰；女人的冠冕。2 triple crown worn by the Pope. 罗马教皇的三重冠。

tibia /'tɪbɪə; 'tɪbɪə/ n (pl ~e /-bɪiː; -bɪɪ/) (anat) shin-bone; inner and thicker of the two bones between the knee and the foot. (解剖)胫骨；胫节。⇨ the illus at skeleton. 参看 skeleton 之插图。

tic /tɪk; tɪk/ n involuntary, spasmodic twitching of the muscles (esp of the face). 肌肉抽搐；(尤指)面肌抽搐。

tick¹ /tɪk; tɪk/ n [C] 1 light, regularly repeated sound, esp of a clock or watch. 滴答声(尤指钟或表的)。,~-'tock n ~ing sound (of a clock, etc). (钟等的)滴答声。2 (colloq) moment: (口)片刻; 刹那: I'll be with you in two ~s. 一会儿我就来陪你。Half a ~! Just a moment! 马上就好! 3 small mark (often ✓) put against names, figures, etc in a list or to show that sth is

correct. 核对记号；勾号(通常作✓形，注于表册中的名称、数字等旁边，或表示某事物为正确者)。4 '~-tack n system of signalling (a kind of hand semaphore) used by bookmakers' assistants on race-courses. (赛马场上赌业者之助手所用的)手势信号。□ vi, vt 1 [VP2A, C] (of a clock, etc) make ~s(1): (指钟等)作滴答声; The child put the watch to its ear and listened to it ~ing. 那孩子把表放近耳旁，听它的滴答声。The taxi's meter was ~ing away. 计程车的计程表在滴答的跳动。What makes sb/sth ~, (colloq) What makes him/it function, act, behave, etc in the way he/it does? (口)什么使得某人(某事物)成为这个样子呢？2 [VP15B] ~ away, (of a clock): ~ away the minutes, mark their passing with ~s(1). 滴答地响，表示时间一分一分地过去。3 [VP2C] ~ over, (of an internal-combustion engine) operate slowly with gears disconnected (and the vehicle stationary). (指内燃机)(未接合连动装置地)空档慢转。4 [VP6A, 15B] ~ sth (off), put a ~(3) against: 画勾号于…旁边; ~ a name/the items on a list. 画勾号于名字(清单上各项目)旁边。~ sb off, (colloq) rebuke, scold him: (口)指责或叱责某人; get ~ed off; 受责骂; give sb a good ~ing-'off. 痛责某人。

tick² /tɪk; tɪk/ n small spider-like parasite that fastens itself on the skin, eg of dogs, and sucks blood. 扁虱(似蜘蛛的小寄生虫，附于狗等的皮肤上，并吸取其血液)。⇨ the illus at arachnid. 参看 arachnid 之插图。

tick³ /tɪk; tɪk/ n 1 [C] outside cover of stout striped linen for a mattress, bolster or pillow. (褥、垫或枕头的)坚固而有条纹的亚麻布外套；套袋。2 [U] (also 亦作 ~‧ing) material used for ~s. (用以做套袋的)坚固而有条纹的亚麻布。

tick⁴ /tɪk; tɪk/ n [U] (colloq) credit(1): (口)信用；赊欠: buy goods on ~; 赊帐购物; get ~. 赊帐。

ticker /'tɪkə(r); 'tɪkɚ/ n [C] 1 telegraphic machine which automatically prints news (eg stock market prices) on paper tape (called '~-tape): 自动收报机(将资讯自动印在'现字纸条'上者); (尤指)股票行情的自动指示器: get a ~-tape reception, eg in New York City, of a visiting celebrity in a procession through the streets, be welcomed with streamers of ~-tape thrown from office windows, etc. 受到盛大欢迎(如纽约市自办公室窗户等抛出彩色纸带，以欢迎通过街道的贵客等)。⇨ the illus at tape. 参看 tape 之插图。2 (colloq) watch. (口)表。3 (sl) heart: (俚)心；心脏: a dicky ~, a weak heart. 心脏衰弱。

ticket /'tɪkɪt; 'tɪkɪt/ n [C] 1 written or printed piece of card or paper giving the holder the right to travel in a train, bus, ship, etc or to a seat in a cinema, concert hall, etc: 票；车票；入场券: Do you want a single or a return ~ (US 美 = one-way or round-trip ~)? 你要单程票还是来回票？Admission by ~ only, (as a notice outside a hall, etc). 凭票入场。'~-collector n person who collects ~s (esp railway ~s). 收票员(尤指火车票收票员)。2 piece of card or paper, label, attached to sth and giving information, eg about the price, size of clothing, etc. 标签(附于某物上，标明价格、尺码等者)。3 (US) list of candidates to be voted on, belonging to one political party: (美)(某一政党提出的)候选人名单: vote the straight ~, cast the ballot on strict party lines. 严格地根据政党路线投票；投票给本党提名的候选人。4 printed notice of an offence against traffic regulations (eg a parking offence): 交通违章通知单；罚款单: get a ~. 接到违章通知单。5 the ~, (dated sl) the proper thing to do. (过时俚语)适当的事情；该做之事；对的事情。6 ~ of leave, (archaic) parole. (古)(犯人的)假释许可状。7 certificate stating the qualifications of a pilot, a ship's mate, etc. (飞行员、船上的大副等的)资格证明书。□ vt [VP6A] put a ~(2) on; mark with a ~. 加标签于；标明。

tick‧ing /'tɪkɪŋ; 'tɪkɪŋ/ n ⇨ tick³.

tickle /'tɪkl; 'tɪkl/ vt, vi 1 [VP6A, 2A] excite the nerves of the skin by touching lightly, esp at sensitive

parts, often so as to cause laughter: 轻触以刺激表皮神经; 胳肢; 搔痒: ～ *sb in the ribs.* 胳肢某人的肋骨。 *The rough blanket ～s (me).* 粗毯使我的皮肤发痒。 **2** [VP 6A] please (one's sense of humour, etc): 满足 (某人的幽默感等): *The story ～d her fancy.* 那故事讨她喜欢。 *I was ～d to death / ～d pink* (colloq, very amused and delighted) *at the news.* 我听到那消息高兴死了。 *They ～d his vanity by praising his work to the skies.* 他们极力赞扬他的工作以满足他的虚荣心。 **3** [VP2A, 6A] have, feel, cause, an itching or tingling sensation: (使)感觉酥痒: *Pepper ～s if it gets into the nose.* 胡椒进入鼻孔会使人有酥痒的感觉。 *My nose ～s.* 我的鼻子发痒。 *It ～d my nose.* 那东西使我的鼻子发痒。 **tick·ler** /ˈtɪklə(r)； ˈtɪklɚ/ *n* (colloq) 难题; 棘手之事。 **tick·lish** /ˈtɪklɪʃ； ˈtɪklɪʃ/ *adj* **1** (of a person) easily made to laugh or wriggle when ～d. (指人)怕痒的; 易痒的。 **2** (of a problem, piece of work, etc) needing delicate care or attention: (指问题、工作等)需小心处理的; 棘手的: *a ticklish question;* 棘手的问题; *in a ticklish situation.* 处于需要小心应付的情况中。

ti·dal /ˈtaɪdl； ˈtaɪdl/ *adj* of a tide or tides: 潮的; 潮水的; 有潮的: *a ～ river / estuary / harbour,* in which the tide rises and falls. 感潮河道(感潮河口; 潮港)。 '～ **wave** *n* great ocean wave, often destructive of life and property, eg one that is (thought to be) caused by an earthquake; (fig) great wave of popular feeling (enthusiasm, indignation, etc). 潮波; 海啸; (喻)公众情绪(如热情、愤怒等)的浪潮; 激动的民心。

tid·bit /ˈtɪdbɪt； ˈtɪd,bɪt/ *n* (US) = **titbit.**

tid·dler /ˈtɪdlə(r)； ˈtɪdlɚ/ *n* (colloq) (口) **1** very small fish. 非常小的鱼。 **2** young small child. 婴儿。

tid·dley /ˈtɪdlɪ； ˈtɪdlɪ/ *adj* (colloq) (口) **1** small; negligible. 很小的; 微不足道的。 **2** tipsy; slightly drunk. 有醉意的; 微醉的。

tid·dly·winks /ˈtɪdlɪwɪŋks； ˈtɪdlɪ,wɪŋks/ *n*[U] game in which players try to make small discs or counters jump into a tray or cup in the centre of a table by pressing them on the edge with a larger disc. 提得利温 (一种以大圆片用力压小圆片或筹码的边缘, 使之跳入桌子中央大盘或杯中的游戏)。

tide /taɪd； taɪd/ *n* **1** [C, U] regular rise and fall in the level of the sea, caused by the attraction of the moon: 潮; 潮汐: *at high/low ～;* 在高(低)潮; *washed up by the ～(s);* 被潮水冲击的; *spring (= maximum) and neap (= minimum) ～s.* 大潮和小潮。 '～·**mark** *n* highest point reached by a ～ on a beach. 高潮标(潮水达到的最高点)。 '～·**way** *n* channel in which a ～ runs; ebb or flow in such a channel. 潮路; 潮流。 **2** [C] flow or tendency (of public opinion, feeling, etc): (舆论、公众情绪等的)潮流; 趋势: *We must not ignore the rising ～ of public discontent.* 我们切不可忽视大众不满情绪的不断增涨。 *The Socialists hoped for a turn of the ～,* that public opinion might turn in their favour. 社会党人士希望舆论转变为对他们有利。 **3** (old use) season (旧用法)时; 季(now only in compounds, as 现仅用于复合词中, 如 'Easter～, 复活节季节, 'even～, 日暮; 'Whitsun～ 圣灵降临周)。 □ *vt* [VP14, 15B] ～ *sb over (sth),* get over; help him to get through or survive (a period of difficulty, etc): 帮助某人度过(困难时期等): *He sold his car to ～ himself over his period of unemployment,* to provide money for his needs. 他卖掉汽车以度过失业的困难。 *She needs more coal to ～ her over the winter.* 她需要更多的煤炭度过严冬。 *Will £5 ～ you over until you get your wages?* 五英镑钱能帮助你维持到你领薪水的时候吗?

tid·ings /ˈtaɪdɪŋz； ˈtaɪdɪŋz/ *n pl* (archaic) news: (古) 消息; 音信。 *Have you heard the glad ～?* 你听到过那令人愉快的消息吗?

tidy /ˈtaɪdɪ； ˈtaɪdɪ/ *adj* (**-ier, -iest**) **1** arranged neatly and in order; having the habit of placing and keeping everything in its right place: 安排得或排列得整齐的; 整洁的; 爱整齐的; 有整洁习惯的: *a ～ room/desk;* 整洁的房间(书桌); *a ～ boy;* 整洁的男孩; *a ～ habits.* 整洁的

习惯。 **2** (colloq) considerable; fairly large (esp of money): (口)相当大的; 可观的(尤指钱): *a ～ sum of money;* 一笔巨款; *cost a ～ penny,* quite a lot of money. 值相当多的钱。 □ *n* (*pl* **-dies**) receptacle for odds and ends: 盛零星物件的容器: *a 'hair-～,* eg on a dressing-table for hair from a hair-brush; 盛屑屑的容器; *a 'sink-～,* for bits of kitchen waste. 厨房洗涤槽的残渣过滤器。 □ *vt, vi* [VP6A, 15B, 2A, C] ～ *(up),* make ～: 使整齐; 使整洁: *I must ～ myself,* make myself look ～: 我得梳理一下。 *You'd better ～ (the room) before the guests arrive.* 客人们到达前, 你最好先整理一下(房间)。 **ti·di·ly** /ˈtaɪdɪlɪ； ˈtaɪdɪlɪ/ *adv* **ti·di·ness** *n*

tie[1] /taɪ； taɪ/ *n* [C] **1** sth used for fastening; rod or beam holding parts of a structure together; (US) railway sleeper, ⇨ **sleeper(2)** at **sleep**[2]; (fig) sth that holds people together: 用以系捆之物; 带; 结; 构成结构物各部分的系材; 系杆; 系条; (美)铁路枕木; 轨枕; (喻)使人结合在一起的关系: *the ties of friendship;* 朋友关系; *family ties;* 家族关系; *ties of blood.* 血缘。 **2** sth that takes up one's attention and limits one's freedom of action: 使某人劳神并限制其行动自由的事物; 束缚: *Mothers often find their small children a tie.* 做母亲的常觉得小孩子是一种束缚。 **3** equal score in a game, etc: (比赛等)得分相同; 不分胜负; 平手: *The game ended in a tie, 2—2.* 这场比赛不分胜负, 二比二。 *The tie will be played off (= will be replayed) on Saturday.* 星期六将加赛一场以定胜负。 **4** (music) curved line joining two notes of the same pitch that are to be played or sung as one. (音乐)连结线。 ⇨ the illus at **notation.** 参看 notation 之插图。 **5** = **necktie.**

tie[2] /taɪ； taɪ/ *vt, vi* (*pres p* **tying,** *pt, pp* **tied**) **1**[VP6A, 15A, B] fasten or bind (with string, rope, wire, etc) (用带、绳、铁丝等)系; 结; 缚; 绑; 扎; 捆; 拴: *tie a man's feet together;* 将某人两脚绑在一起; *tie up a parcel;* 捆包裹; *tie a branch down;* 将树枝绑成垂枝; *tie a dog to the street railings.* 将狗拴在街旁的栏杆上。 *tie sb down,* restrict sb's freedom: 限制某人自由; 束缚某人: *He's not in a hurry to get married; he doesn't want to get tied down.* 他还不急于结婚, 因为他不想受束缚。 *Young children do tie a woman down, don't they?* 小孩子的确使一个女人受到束缚, 对不对? *tie sb down to sth,* restrict sb to (the terms of a contract, etc). 置某人于(契约条款等)约束之下。 *tie oneself down to sth,* accept limits to one's freedom of action. 使自己接受某事物的约束。 *tie (sth) in with sth,* link, be linked with: 连系; 与…连系; 与…关联: *Doesn't this tie in with what we were told last week?* Aren't the two things linked, connected? 这件事与我们上周所听到的那件事不是有关联吗? *tie sth up,* **(a)** invest (capital) so that it is not easily available, eg because of legal restrictions. 使(资金)专作某种用途; 冻结(资金)。 **(b)** ensure that (property, eg land, buildings) can be used, sold, etc only under certain (usu legal) conditions. 确保(某财产, 如土地或房屋)只有在某些(通常为法律的)条件下始得使用、出售等; 冻结(财产)。 *be/get tied up (with sth/sb),* **(a)** be, get, involved (with sth/sb) so that one has no time for other things: 为(某人或某事)缠住而无暇顾及其他: *I'm afraid I can't help you now—I'm too tied up with other things.* 恐怕我现在不能帮你的忙——旁的事情把我缠得太紧了。 **(b)** be, become, linked with: 与…结合; 与…相连系; 与…关联: *Isn't this company tied up with Vickers-Armstrong?* 这家公司不是Vickers-Armstrong 的关系企业吗? Hence, 由此产生, **'tie-up** *n* link; merger; partnership. 连系; 合并; 合伙。 **tied house,** (GB) public house controlled by a particular brewery. (英)(专销某一酒厂产品的)特约酒店。 ⇨ *free house* at **free**[1](3). **2** [VP6A, 15B] **tie (sth on),** fasten by means of the strings, etc of: 系上或系牢: *tie an apron (on);* 系上围裙; *tie on a label.* 系上标签。 Hence, 由此产生, **'tie-on,** *attrib adj: a tie-on label.* 系上标签的标签。 **3** [VP6A, 15A] arrange (a ribbon, etc) in the form of a bow or knot: 系结(丝带等): *tie one's shoelaces;*

系鞋带; *tie a ribbon*/*scarf*; 系丝带(围巾); *tie the ribbon in(to) a bow.* 把丝带打成蝴蝶结。4 [VP6A, 15A] make by tying: 系作; 打(结): *tie a knot in a piece of string.* 在一条细绳上打结。5 [VP2A] be fastened: 结起; 打结: *Does this sash tie in front or at the back?* 这条腰带是在前面还是在后面打结? 6 [VP2A, 3A] **tie (with) (for),** (of players, teams, candidates in a competitive examination) make the same score (as); equal in points, marks, etc: (指选手、队、应试者)得分(与…)相同; 不分胜负: *The two teams tied.* 两队赛成平手。*They tied for first place (in the examination).* 他们(在考试中)并列第一名。*We tied with Arsenal in the last game.* 上一次比赛我们和阿森纳队得分相同。

tier /tɪə(r); tɪr/ n row (esp of seats), shelf, etc esp one of a number parallel to and rising one above another, eg in a theatre or stadium: (阶梯式的)一排; 一层; 一列; (尤指)(戏院, 体育馆等中的)一排座位: *a first*/*second box,* in a theatre. (戏院中)第一(二)排的一个包厢。

tiff /tɪf; tɪf/ n slight quarrel (between friends or acquaintances): (朋友或熟人间的)小争执: *Alice has had a ~ with her boyfriend.* 艾丽丝和她的男朋友发生了小争执。

ti·ger /ˈtaɪɡə(r); ˈtaɪɡɚ/ n large, fierce animal of the cat family, yellow-skinned with black stripes, found in Asia. 虎; 老虎(产于亚洲)。⇨ the illus at cat. 参看 cat 之插图。'**~-lily** n garden lily with orange flowers spotted with black or purple. 虎皮百合; 卷丹; 萱草。**~-ish** /-ɪʃ; -ɪʃ/ adj like, cruel as a ~. 似虎的; 虎一般残忍的。**ti·gress** /ˈtaɪɡrɪs; ˈtaɪɡrɪs/ n female ~. 母老虎; 雌虎。

tight /taɪt; taɪt/ adj (-er, -est) 1 fastened, fixed, fitting, held, closely: 紧的: *a ~ knot.* 系得很紧的结。*I can't get the cork out of the bottle—It's too ~.* 我无法把瓶塞拔出来—太紧了。*The drawer is so ~ that I can't open it.* 这抽屉太紧了, 我打不开。*These shoes are so ~ that they hurt.* 这双鞋太紧, 挤脚。**,~-'lipped** adj keeping the lips firmly together; saying little or nothing; (fig) grim-looking. 紧闭嘴唇的; 寡言的; 沉默的; (喻)表情冷酷的; 样子狠忍的。2 closely or firmly put together in a small space: 塞紧的; 坚固的; 密集的: *a ~ joint;* 紧密的接头; (esp in compounds) made so that sth cannot get out or in: (尤用于复合词中)不漏的; 不透的: *'water-*/*'air- ~.* 不漏水(不透气)的。3 packed so as to occupy the smallest possible space or to get in as much as possible: 装满的; 装紧的: *Make sure that the bags are filled*/*packed ~.* 务必确实把那些袋子装满(塞满)。4 (colloq) having had too much alcoholic drink: (口)喝酒太多的; 醉的: *He gets ~ every pay-day.* 他每逢发薪的日子都会喝得烂醉。5 fully stretched: 绷紧的; 张紧的: *a ~ rope.* 绷紧的绳子。'**~-rope** n one on which acrobats perform feats. (卖艺者表演特技用的)绷索。6 produced by pressure; causing difficulty. 由压力或压迫产生的; 紧迫的; 引起困难的。**in a ~ corner**/**spot,** (usu fig) in a difficult or dangerous situation. (通常作喻)处于困境或危境。**~ schedule,** one that it is difficult to keep to. 非常紧迫的日程。**~ squeeze,** condition of being uncomfortably crowded: 挤得水泄不通; 十分拥挤: *We got everyone into the bus, but it was a ~ squeeze.* 我们让每一个人都搭上了那辆汽车, 不过拥挤得很厉害。7 (of money) not easily obtainable, eg on loan from banks: (指钱)难得到的; 银根紧的: *Money is ~.* 银根很紧。*The money-market is ~,* It is possible to borrow money only by paying a high rate of interest. 金融市场银根很紧。8 **,~-'fisted,** stingy; miserly. 吝啬的; 小气的。**,~-'laced** adj = straitlaced. ⇨ strait¹. '**~-wad** /-wɒd; -ˌwɑd/ n (sl) stingy person. (俚)小气鬼; 吝啬者。□ adv **~ly:** *squeeze*/*hold sth ~* 紧紧地抓住(握住)某物。**sit ~,** ⇨ sit(1). (Note that ~ adv is not used before a pp; **~ly** must be used in this position: *packed ~,* but *~ly packed*). (请注意: 分词之前不用 tight 做副词, 必须用 ~ly, 例如 packed ~, 但 ~ly packed)。**~·ly** adv in a ~ manner: 紧紧地; 密密地: *squeeze*/*hold sth ~ly;*

紧紧地压榨(执握)某物; *~ly packed together;* 紧密地包扎在一起; *~ly sealed.* 密封的。**~·ness** n **~en** /ˈtaɪtn; ˈtaɪtn/ vt, vi [VP6A, 15B, 2A, C] make or become ~er: (使)变紧; (使)变得更紧; (使)变得更紧: 旋紧螺钉; *~en the ropes of the tent.* 拉紧帐篷的绳子。*It needs ~ening up.* (它)需要再拉紧一点。**~en one's belt,** go without food (when there is little or none available); become frugal. 挨饿; 束紧腰带(食物不足或无食物时); 节食。

tights /taɪts; taɪts/ n pl 1 close-fitting garment covering the hips, legs and feet, as worn by girls and women. (妇女穿的)紧身下装; 裤袜(等)。2 skintight garment covering the legs and body, worn by acrobats, ballet-dancers, etc. (表演特技者, 跳芭蕾舞者等穿的)紧身衣。

tike /taɪk; taɪk/ n = tyke.

tilde n 1 /ˈtɪldə; ˈtɪldə/ the mark placed over Spanish n when it is pronounced ny /nj; nj/ (as in cañon). 颚音符(即~, 西班牙语中的 n 读作 ny 时, 加在上面的符号, 如 cañon)。2 /tɪld; tɪld/ the mark (~) as used in this dictionary to indicate the use of a headword in an entry. 代词号; 波浪号(即~, 在本词典中代表每一条的词目)。

tile /taɪl; taɪl/ n (usu square or oblong) plate of baked clay for covering roofs, walls, etc, often, eg Dutch, Italian and Portuguese ~s, painted with designs or pictures. 瓦; 瓷砖(通常为方形或长方形, 用以盖屋顶、贴墙壁等, 荷兰、意大利、葡萄牙等国所用者常绘有图案或图书)。**be (out) on the ~s,** (sl) be merry-making. (俚)作乐; 行乐。**have a '~** (more usu 较常用 screw) **loose,** (sl) be rather mad. (俚)有点发疯。□ vt [VP6A] cover (a roof, etc) with ~s. 用瓦覆盖(屋顶等)。

till¹ /tɪl; tɪl/ (also 亦作 **until** /ʌnˈtɪl; ənˈtɪl/) (until) is more formal than *till*; *until* is preferred when its clause or phrase comes first)(until 较 till 正式; 由其引导的短语或从句置于句首时, 多用 until) conj up to the time when: 直到…之时; 在…以后: *Go straight on until you come to the post-office and then turn left.* 一直向前走到邮局再向左转。*Let's wait ~ the rain stops.* 让我们等到雨停。*Until you told me, I had heard nothing of what happened.* 一直到你告诉我, 我才知道发生了什么事。*She won't go away ~ you promise to help her.* 在你答应帮助她之前, 她不会走的。□ prep up to (the time when): 直到…之时; 直至; 迄: *I shall wait ~ ten o'clock*/*next Monday, etc.* 我将要等到十点钟(下周一等)。*Goodbye ~ tomorrow.* 明天见。*Until now I knew*/*Until then I had known nothing about it.* 直到现在(直到那时)我才知道这件事。*He works from morning ~ night, day after day.* 他从早到晚都在工作, 日复一日。*He lived at home until soon after his father's death.* 他一直住在家里, 到他父亲死后不久才离开。

till² /tɪl; tɪl/ n money-drawer, eg in a cash-register: (店铺中的)钱柜; 盛钱抽屉: *The boy was caught with his hand in the ~,* caught stealing. 那男孩从钱柜里偷钱时当场被捉住。

till³ /tɪl; tɪl/ vt [VP6A] cultivate (land). 耕(地)。**~age** /ˈtɪlɪdʒ; ˈtɪlɪdʒ/ n [U] act or process of ~ing; ~ed land. 耕种; 耕作; 耕作的过程; 耕过的田地。**~er** n person who ~s. 耕者; 农民。

tiller /ˈtɪlə(r); ˈtɪlɚ/ n lever (like a long handle) used to turn the rudder of a small boat. (小船的)舵柄。⇨ the illus at sail. 参看 sail 之插图。

tilt /tɪlt; tɪlt/ vt, vi 1 [VP6A, 15A, B, 2A, C] (cause to) come into a sloping position (as by lifting one end); tip: (使)倾斜; (使)倾侧: *Don't ~ the table.* 不要使桌子倾斜。*T~ the barrel (up) to empty it.* 把大桶倾侧, 倒空里面的东西。*T~ed over (and over) and the plates slid off it to the floor.* 桌子倾斜了, 碗盘滑落到地板上。2 [VP2A, 3A] **~ (at),** (hist, of men on horseback) ride (at another) with a lance; (fig) attack in speech or writing: (史, 指骑士)骑车马上用长矛刺(另一骑士); (喻)以言词或文字攻击; 抨击: *The reformer ~ed at the tax and property*

laws. 该社会改革者抨击税法和财产法。 **～ at windmills,** fight imaginary enemies (from the story of Don Quixote). 攻击想象中的敌人 (由堂·吉诃德的故事而来); 无的放矢。 **2** act of ～ing with a lance: 马上以长矛刺; 马上比武: *have a ～ at sb,* (fig) attack him (in a friendly way) in a debate, etc. (喻)(在辩论等中以友善的方式)攻击某人。 **(at) full ～,** at great speed; with great force: 高速地; 用力地: *The boy ran full ～ into me.* 那男孩猛然间和我撞来。 **～-yard** *n* place where ～ing was practised in former times. (昔时的)马上比武场。

tilth /tɪlθ; tɪlθ/ *n* depth of soil affected by cultivation; tilled land: 耕作深度; 耕地: *rake a seedbed to a good ～,* until there is a depth of fine, crumbly soil. 把苗床耙成适耕的深度。

tim·ber /'tɪmbə(r); 'tɪmbɚ/ *n* **1** [U] wood prepared for use in building, etc: (建筑等用的)木材; 木料: *～ merchants;* 木材商; *a '～-yard,* place where ～ is stored, bought and sold, etc; 贮材场; 木材场: *dressed ～,* sawn, shaped and planed ready for use. 修整材(可立即使用者)。 **2** [U] growing trees (sometimes *standing ～*) thought of as containing wood suitable for building, carpentry, etc: 树林; 森林; 木材林(被认为含有建筑、木工等用之木材者,有时作 standing ～): *cut down*／*fell ～;* 伐木(取材); *put a hundred acres of land under ～,* plant with trees for ～. 种植一百英亩的木材林。 *The fire destroyed thousands of acres of ～.* 大火摧毁了数千英亩的木材林。 **3** [C] large piece of shaped wood, beam, forming a support (eg in a roof or a ship): 栋木; 梁木 (如建筑屋顶或船只所用者)。 **4** [U] (in fox-hunting) wooden fences and gates. (猎狐)木造障碍物; 围篱与门。 **～ed** /'tɪmbəd; 'tɪmbɚd/ *adj* (of buildings) made of ～ or with a framework of ～. (指建筑物)木造的; 木质架构的。

timbre /'tæmbrə US: 'tɪmbər; 'tɪmbɚ/ *n* characteristic quality of sound produced by a particular voice or instrument. 音色; 音质; 音品。

tim·brel /'tɪmbrəl; 'tɪmbrəl/ *n* tambourine. 铃鼓; 手鼓。

time¹ /taɪm; taɪm/ *n* **1** [U] all the days of the past, present and future: 时; 时间(指过去、现在、将来全部的日子): *past, present and future ～.* 过去、现在及将来的时间。 *The world exists in space and ～.* 世界存在于空间与时间中。 **2** [U] the passing of all the days, months and years, taken as a whole (sometimes personified as *(old) Father T～*): 时间的度过; 光阴的流逝; 时间流逝(有时予以拟人化,称为'时间老人'): *T～ will show who is right.* 时间会证明谁是对的。 *T～ waits for no man,* (prov). (谚)时间不等人; 时不我与; 时不我饶人。 **3** [U] (also 为作 *a + adj + ～*) portion or measure of ～: 一段时间; 一部分时间: *Six o'clock is a point of ～; six hours is a period of ～.* 六点钟是时间的一点; 六小时是一段时间。 *What a (long) ～ you've been!* 你花费相当(长)的时间了! *I had a most unpleasant ～ at the dentist's.* 我在牙医那里经历了一段很不愉快的时间。 *That will take ～,* cannot be done soon or quickly. 那要花费相当的时间(才能做成)。 *I have no*／*not much ～ for sport.* 我没有(没有太多)时间做户外运动。 *We have no ～ to lose,* We must hurry. 我们不能耽误时间了(必须赶紧)。 *He spent a lot of ～ (in) getting ready.* 他花了很多时间做准备。 *Take your ～ over it,* Don't hurry. 慢慢来,不要急。 *We were pressed for ～,* had not enough ～, were forced to hurry. 我们的时间甚为急迫。 *behind ～,* **(a)** late: 迟; 晚: *The train is ten minutes behind ～.* 火车误点十分钟。 **(b)** behindhand: 落后; 拖欠: *He's always behind ～ with his payments.* 他总不能按时付款。 *for the ～ being,* ➪ be³(4). *on ～,* up to ～, not late, punctual(ly): 按时; 准时: *The train is*／*came in on ～.* 火车准时(到达)。 *in 'no ～,* very soon; very quickly. 立即; 很快地。 *(from*／*since) ～ immemorial; (from*／*since) ～ out of mind,* for a period of ～ longer than any one can remember. (从)远古时代(起); (从)人们不复记忆的时

代(起)。 *gain ～,* obtain extra ～ by making excuses, deliberately using slow methods, etc. 拖延时间。 *all the ～,* **(a)** during the whole of the ～ in question: (在某时间内内)一直: *I looked all over the house for that letter, and it was in my pocket all the ～,* while I was searching. 我在屋里到处找那封信, 而它却一直在我的口袋里。 **(b)** at all times; first and last: 始终; 从头到尾; 自始至终: *He's a business man all the ～,* has no other interests in life. 自始至终他就是一个生意人。 *'half the ～,* **(a)** half of the ～ available: 一半的时间: *He did the work in four hours; I could have done it in half the ～,* in two hours. 他花了四小时才做完那工作, 我花一半的时间(两小时)就能做好。 **(b)** for long periods of ～; (loosely) very often; nearly always: 长时间地;(非严格用法)常常; 几乎总是: *He says he works hard, but he's day-dreaming half the ～.* 他说他工作很努力, 但他大部分时间都在做白日梦。 **4** [U] point of ～ stated in hours and minutes of the day: (以当日的小时和分说明的)时刻: *What ～ is it?* 几点钟了? *What is the ～?* 几点钟了? *The child can now tell the ～.* 那孩子会看得懂钟(表)了。 **5** [U] ～ measured in units (years, months, hours, etc): 以(年、月、小时等)单位量出的时间: *The winner's ～ was 11 seconds.* 获胜者使用的时间共十一秒。 *He ran the mile in record ～,* a period of ～ shorter than that of any previous runner. 他跑一英里的时间已打破以往的记录。 *keep good*／*bad ～,* (of a clock or watch) show the hour correctly／incorrectly. (指钟表)走得准确(不准确)。 *the ～ of day,* the hour as shown by a clock. (钟表上的)时刻。 *pass the ～ of day (with...),* exchange a greeting, say 'Good morning!', etc. 相互问候或请安(如说'早安'等)。 **6** [U] point or period of ～ associated with, or available or suitable for, a certain even⁺ purpose, etc: 时机; 时期; 时候; 机会: *at the ～ you're speaking of;* 在你所说的时间; *by the ～ we reached home;* 在我们到家的时候; *last ～ I was there;* 我上次在那儿的时候; *every ～ I looked at her.* 每次我看她的时候。 *It is 'lunch-～.* 是午餐的时间了。 *There is a ～ for everything.* 凡事必有其时。 *Now's your ～ (= opportunity).* (现在)你的机会来了。 *It's ～ I was going*／*for me to go,* I ought to leave now. 我(现在)该走了。 *It's ～ somebody taught you to behave yourself.* (现在)该有人教导你如何待人接物了。 *I must bide my ～,* be patient, wait for a suitable ～. 我必须等待时机了。 *T～ is up,* The allowed for something is ended. 时间到了。 *(work, etc) against ～,* with the greatest speed (because only a limited amount of ～ is available). 以最快速度; 全力(工作等); 加紧(赶工等)。 *at the same ～,* **(a)** together: 同时; 一齐: *to laugh and cry at the same ～.* (同时)又哭又笑。 **(b)** notwithstanding; nevertheless: 可是; 然而: *He's slightly mad; at the same ～, he's one of the kindest men I know.* 他有一点疯狂, 然而他是我所认识的最和善的人之一。 *at ～s; from ～ to ～,* occasionally; now and then. 间或; 偶尔。 *at 'all ～s,* always. 总是; 始终; 经常。 *at 'your*／*'his, etc ～ of life,* at your／his, etc age. 在你(他等)这样的年纪。 *in ～,* **(a)** not late; early enough: 及时; 还早: *We were in ～ for the train*／*to catch the train.* 我们赶上了火车。 *We arrived in good ～,* with ～ to spare. 我们到得很早。 **(b)** sooner or later; after the passing of an indefinite period of ～: 早晚; 终久; 经过一段(不确定的)时间以后; 将来: *You will learn how to do it in ～.* 你将来会学到怎样来做这件事。 *in the nick of ～,* ➪ nick¹(2). *near her ～,* (of a woman) soon to give birth to a child. (指妇女)临盆; 分娩期近。 *do ～,* (colloq) undergo a period of imprisonment. (口)服刑。 *serve one's ～,* **(a)** work as an apprentice for an agreed number of years: 当学徒; 做(若干年)学徒: *The boy has served half his ～.* 这男孩做学徒的期限已经过去大半。 **(b)** = do ～, ➪ above. 参看上列之 do ～。 *My*／*His, etc ～ is drawing near,* I am／He is, etc near a ～ of crisis, of some important happening, etc (according to the context). 我(他等)面临危急关头(决定性时刻等, 视上下文而定)。 **7** [C] (Cf 参较 *twice*) occasion: 次数; 次;

回: *this/that/next/another* ~; 这(那,下一,另一)回; *the* ~ *before last*; 上上一次; *for the first/last* ~. 第一(最后一)回. *He failed five* ~s. 他失败过五次. *I've told you a dozen* ~s, (= very often, repeatedly) *not to do that*. 我已经一再告诉你不要那样做. **at 'one**, during a period of past ~, known but not mentioned: 过去有一段时间: *At one* ~ *I used to go mountain-climbing every summer*. 过去有一段时间我每年夏天去爬山. **at other** ~s, on other occasions. 在其他时候; 又有时. ~ *and again;* ~s *without number*, again and again; repeatedly. 一再; 屡屡. **'many a** ~; 'many ~s, often; on many occasions. 时常; 多次; 屡屡. **one/two, etc at a** ~, one/two, etc on each occasion; separately: 一次(两个等)地; 各别地. *Hand them to me two at a* ~. 把那些东西拿给我, 一次两个. **8** (*pl*) used to indicate multiplication (but note that *twice* is used instead of *two* ~s): (复)倍; 乘(注意: twice 用以表示二倍): *Three* ~s *five is/are fifteen*, $3 \times 5 = 15$. 三乘五得十五. *Yours is ten* ~s *the size of mine/ten* ~s *as large as mine*. 你的(那东西)是我的十倍大. **9** [C] (often *pl*) period of ~, more or less definite, associated with certain events, circumstances, persons, etc: (常用复数) 时代; 时期: *in 'Stuart* ~s, when the Stuart kings ruled; 在斯图亚特王朝时代; *in the* ~(*s*) *of the Stuarts*; 在斯图亚特诸王治理时期; *in 'ancient/prehis'toric* ~s. 在古代(史前期). *Mr Curtis was the manager in 'my* ~, *when I was working there*. 我在那里工作时期, 柯蒂斯先生是经理. *The house is old but it will last my* ~, will serve me for the rest of my life. 这房子旧了, 不过在我有生之年尚可住. **10** [C] (often *pl*) the conditions of life, the circumstances, etc of a period characterized by certain qualities, etc: (常用复数)某一时期的生活状况,环境等(有某些特色者): *We lived through terrible* ~s *during the war years*. 打仗的那几年我们过得很惨. *T*~s *are good/bad*, (often meaning that it is easy/difficult to make a living). 年头好(坏)(常表示谋生容易, 困难等). **ahead of one's** ~; **born before one's** ~, having ideas too much in advance of, too enlightened for, the period in which one lives. 超出时代前, 具有不容于当世的前进或开明的思想. **(even) at the 'best of** ~s, even when conditions are good: 即使情况良好; 在状况最好的时候; *He's an irritating fellow even at the best of* ~s. 即使在好的时候, 他也是一个令人讨厌的家伙. **behind the** ~s, antiquated; having out-of-date ideas, etc. 过时的; 落伍的; 思想等陈旧的. **have a good** ~, enjoy oneself. 自得其乐; 玩(等)得很痛快. **have the** ~ **of one's life**, (colloq) experience a period of exceptional happiness or enjoyment. (口)度过一段非常欢乐或愉快的时间. **11** [U] **Greenwich/local/summer/standard** ~, 格林威治(当地, 夏令, 标准)时间. ⇨ these words. 参看各词. **12** [U] (music) style of rhythm depending upon the number of beats in the successive bars of a piece of music: (音乐)拍子; 'common ~, two or four beats in a bar; 普通拍子(每一小节二拍或四拍); *'waltz* ~, three or six beats in a bar; 华尔兹拍子(一小节三或六拍); also, the rate (or *tempo*) at which a piece of music is to be played. 演奏(乐曲的)速度. **in/out of** ~, in/not in accordance with the ~ of the music. 合(不合)节拍. **in double-quick** ~, very quickly. 非常快. **beat** ~, show the ~ (*tempo*, etc) by movements made with the hand or a stick (*baton*). (用手或指挥棒)打拍子. **keep** ~, sing or dance in ~. 按节拍唱歌或跳舞. **13** (compounds) (复合词) '~-**ball** *n* one which slides down a staff (at an observatory to show a fixed ~, usu noon or 1 pm). (升降于气象台杆子上的)报时球(所报的时刻通常为中午或下午一时). '~-**bomb** *n* designed to explode at some ~ after being dropped, placed in position, etc. 定时炸弹. '~-**card/-sheet** *n* one for a record of workmen's hours of work. 工作时间记录卡(纸). '~-**expired** *adj* (of soldiers and sailors) having completed the period of service. (指兵士和水手)已服役期满的. '~-**exposure** *n* exposure of a photographic

film for a ~ longer than half a second. 照相底片超过半秒钟的曝光. '~-**fuse** *n* one that has been made to burn for a given ~, eg to explode a bomb. 定时信管. '~-**honoured** (US = -**honored**) *adj* respected because of its antiquity. 因年代久远而受尊敬的; 由来已久的. '~-**keeper** *n* **(a)** one who, or that which, records the ~ spent by workers at their work. 工作时间记录员或记录器. **(b)** (of a watch, etc) one that keeps ~ well, etc: (走得准或不准的)时计: *a good/bad* ~*keeper*. 走得准(不准)的时计. '~-**lag** *n* interval of ~ between two connected phenomena or events (eg between a flash of lightning and the thunder, or between a decision to do sth and its accomplishment). 时滞(两个相关联现象或事件所间隔的时间, 如闪电与打雷之间或决心做某事与其完成之间者). '~-**limit** *n* limited period of ~; last moment of this: 时限; 时限的最后片刻: *set a* ~*limit for the completion of a job*. 为某项工作的完成规定期限. '~-**piece** *n* clock. 钟; 表; 时计. '~-**saving** *adj* serving to save ~: 节约时间的; a ~*saving idea*. 省时的办法(主意). '~-**server** *n* one who acts, not according to principles, but according to self-interest, esp one who is always trying to please powerful people. 趋炎附势者; 以一己的利益为行事准则者. '~-**serving** *adj* behaving as a ~server: 趋炎附势的; 谋私利的; ~*serving politicians*. 趋炎附势的政客. '~-**signal** *n* signal (eg a series of pips) indicating the ~. 报时信号. '~-**slip** *n* = *time warp*. '~-**switch** *n* switch set to operate at a desired ~ (eg to turn a heating system on or off). 定时开关(如暖气系统上者). '~-**table** *n* list showing the days or hours at which events will take place, work will be done, trains etc will depart. 时间表; 时刻表. '~-**warp** *n* (in science fiction) breaking of past or future ~ into present ~. (科幻小说)将过去或将来时间变成现在时间. '~-**work** *n* [U] work (esp manual work) paid for by the hour or day (contrasted with *piece-work*). 计时工作(尤指手工, 与 piece-work 相对). ~-**less** *adj* (liter) unending; not to be thought of as having duration. (文)无限的; 永久的; 超时间的.

time[2] /taɪm; taɪm/ *vt* **1** [VP6A, 15A] choose the time or moment for; arrange the time of: 选择…的时机; 安排…的时间; 使之适宜: *He* ~*d his journey so that he arrived before dark*. 他把旅程的时间做了适当的安排, 因此在天黑前就到了. *The remark was well/ill* ~*d*, made at a suitable/an unsuitable moment. 这话正合(不合)时宜. **2** [VP6A] measure the time taken by or for (a race, runner, an action or event). 记录(赛跑、跑者、行动或事件)的时间; 计算…的时间. **3** [VP6A] regulate; 调整; 校准: ~ *one's steps* (in dancing) *to the music*; 调整舞步使配合音乐; ~ *the speed of a machine*. 调整机器的速度. **tim·ing** *n* [U] act of determining or regulating the (order of) occurrence of an action, event, etc to achieve the desired results: 定时; 调整时间: *a 'timing device*; 定时设计; (theatre) speed of dialogue/cues, etc: (戏剧)对白(尾白、表演等)的速度: *The timing in last night's performance was excellent*. 昨晚的演出, 时间控制得非常好.

time·ly /'taɪmlɪ; 'taɪmlɪ/ *adj* (-ier, -iest) occurring at just the right time; opportune. 适时发生的; 合时宜的. **time·li·ness** *n* [U].

timid /'tɪmɪd; 'tɪmɪd/ *adj* easily frightened; shy: 胆怯的; 羞怯的: *That fellow is as* ~ *as a rabbit*. 那家伙胆小如兔. ~·**ly** *adv* ~·**ity** /tɪ'mɪdɪtɪ; tɪ'mɪdətɪ/, ~·**ness** *nn* [U].

tim·or·ous /'tɪmərəs; 'tɪmərəs/ *adj* (liter) timid. (文)胆怯的; 羞怯的. ~·**ly** *adv*

tim·othy /'tɪməθɪ; 'tɪməθɪ/ *n* [U] ~ (**grass**), grass grown as fodder for cattle. (喂牛之)筒状长穗牧草.

tim·pani /'tɪmpənɪ; 'tɪmpə,ni/ *n pl* set of kettledrums (eg of an orchestra). (音乐)一组定音鼓(如交响乐团者). ⇨ the illus at **percussion**. 参看 percussion 之插图. **tim·pan·ist** /'tɪmpənɪst; 'tɪmpənɪst/ *n* player of

a kettledrum. 定音鼓手。

tin /tɪn; tɪn/ n **1** [U] soft, white metal (symbol **Sn**) used in alloys and for coating iron sheets. 锡(符号 Sn, 用于合金中, 并用于镀铁皮)。 **'tin·foil** n [U] tin in the form of foil (thin pliable sheets), used for wrapping and packing. 锡箔(用于包装)。 *(little) tin god,* (colloq) sth or sb mistakenly given great veneration or worship. (俚)受到不应得的过份崇敬的人或物。 ～ **hat,** (sl) steel helmet (as worn by soldiers in modern times). (俚)钢盔。 **'tin-plate** n [U] sheet iron coated with tin (used in the canning industry). 洋铁皮; 马口铁; 白铁皮。 **'tin·smith** n worker in tin-plate. 洋铁匠。 **'tin-tack** n short nail of tinned iron. 包铁钉; 镀锡钉。 **2** [C] tin-plated container for food, etc esp one made so as to be air-tight (US 美 = *can*): 洋铁罐(尤指作罐头用而且可密封者); 听: *a tin of sardines/oil.* 一罐沙丁鱼(油)。 (Cf 参较 *a can of beer* 一罐啤酒)。 **'tin-opener** n device for opening tins. 开罐器。 □ vt (-nn-) [VP6A] **1** put a coating of tin on. 镀锡; 包以锡。 **2** pack (food, etc) in tins.(2) (US 美 = *can*): 装(食物等)于罐中: *tinned peaches* 罐装桃子。 **tinny** adj of or like tin (eg in sound): 锡的; 似锡的; 叮玲声的: *a tinny piano.* 发叮玲声的钢琴。

tinc·ture /'tɪŋktʃə(r)/ n **1** medical substance dissolved in alcohol: 溶解在酒精中的药物; 酊剂: ～ *of iodine/quinine.* 碘酒(奎宁酊剂)。 **2** *a ～ (of),* slight flavour or suggestion (of). 些微的味道或迹象。 □ vt give a ～(2) (of sth) to: 使带味道、气息、意味于: *teachings ～d with heresy.* 微带异端意味的教义。

tin·der /'tɪndə(r)/ n [U] material (eg dry, scorched linen, etc) that easily catches fire from a spark. 火绒; 导火线(与火花接触即易着火之物)。 **'～-box** n box containing ～, flint and steel (as used in former times for kindling fire). 火绒箱(内装火绒、燧石及钢片, 昔时用以引火)。

tine /taɪn; taɪn/ n point, prong (eg of a fork, harrow, etc); branch of a deer's antler. (叉、耙等的)叉齿; 尖端; 鹿角的分叉。 ⇨ the illus at **large**. 参看 large 之插图。 **-～d** /-taɪnd; -taɪnd/ suff (in compounds) having the number or kind of ～s indicated: (用于复合词中)有若干或某种叉齿的: *a three-～d hayfork.* 三叉干草耙。

ting /tɪŋ; tɪŋ/ n, vt, vi n (cause to make, make, a) clear, ringing sound. 叮玲声; (使)发叮玲声。

tinge /tɪndʒ; tɪndʒ/ vt [VP6A, 14] ～ *sth (with),* **1** colour slightly (with red, etc). 微染(红色等)。 **2** (esp in pp) affect slightly: (尤用过去分词)微沾; 微感染; 含: *admiration ～d with envy.* 含有妒意的赞美。 □ n slight colouring or mixture (of): 微染; 意味; 些微气息(与 of 连用): *There was a ～ of sadness in her voice/of irony in his remark.* 她的声音中略带哀伤(他的话中略带讥讽)的意味。

tingle /'tɪŋgl; 'tɪŋgl/ vi [VP2A, C] have a pricking or stinging feeling in the skin; (fig) be stirred: 皮肤有刺痛的感觉; (喻)被激动; 兴奋: *His cheek ～d from the slap she had given him.* 他的脸上因挨了她一巴掌而有刺痛的感觉。 *His fingers ～d with the cold.* 他的手指冻得有刺痛感。 *The children were tingling with excitement.* 孩子们大为兴奋。 □ n tingling feeling: 刺痛之感; *have a ～ in one's finger-tips.* 指尖有刺痛感。

tin·ker /'tɪŋkə(r); 'tɪŋkɚ/ n **1** worker with metal who travels from place to place and repairs kettles, pans, etc. 补锅匠; 修理锅盘等的流动匠人。 *not care a ～'s cuss/damn,* not care in the least. 毫不介意。 **2** ～ing: 笨拙的修补或修理; 不内行的做: *have an hour's ～ at the radio set,* try to mend it. 笨拙地修理收音机一小时。 □ vi [VP2A, C, 3A] ～ *(at/with),* work in an amateurish or inexpert way (at): 不内行地、笨拙地或不熟练地做或修理: ～ *(away) at a broken machine.* 笨拙地修理一架坏机器。 *Please don't ～ with my car engine.* 请不要乱弄我的汽车引擎。

tinkle /'tɪŋkl; 'tɪŋkl/ vi, vt [VP2A, C, 6A] (cause) make a succession of light, ringing sounds, eg of a small bell. (使)发叮珰声; (使)发叮玲声。 □ n (sing)

such sounds: (单)叮玲声; 叮珰声: *the ～ of a bell/of falling glass/of ice being stirred round in a glass.* 铃(玻璃落地, 冰块在杯中搅动)的叮珰声。

tinny /'tɪnɪ; 'tɪnɪ/ adj ⇨ **tin.**

tin pan alley /ˌtɪn pæn 'ælɪ; ˌtɪn pæn 'ælɪ/ n composers, players and publishers of popular music (as a group). 丁班巷; 丁班胡同(原为地名, 转用作流行音乐的作曲家、演奏者及出版商的总称)。

tin·sel /'tɪnsl; 'tɪnsl/ n [U] **1** glittering metallic substance made in sheets, strips and threads, used for ornament: 装饰用的光亮金属片、金属条或金属线: *trim a Christmas tree/a dress with ～.* 以光亮金属片等装饰圣诞树(衣物)。 **2** superficial, cheap, showy brilliance. 表面的光亮; 庸俗而华丽的光彩。 ～**ly** /-səlɪ; -səlɪ/ adv trimmed with, suggesting, ～. 以或似以光亮金属物装饰的。 □ vt (-ll-, US also -l-) trim with ～. 以光亮金属物装饰。

tint /tɪnt; tɪnt/ n (esp pale or delicate) shade or variety of colour: 色度; 颜色的浓淡; (尤指)淡色: ～*s of green in the sky at dawn;* 黎明时天空中浓淡不同的绿色; *an artist who excels at 'flesh-～s.* 长于使用肉色的艺术家。 □ vt [VP6A, 22] give a ～ to; put a ～ on; tinge. 着色于; 加色度于···上; 微染。

tin·tin·nabu·la·tion /ˌtɪntɪnˌæbjʊ'leɪʃn; ˌtɪntɪ,næ-bjə'leʃən/ n [U] tinkling of bells. 铃声; 叮玲声。

tiny /'taɪnɪ; 'taɪnɪ/ adj (-ier, -iest) very small. 甚小的; 微小的。

tip¹ /tɪp; tɪp/ n [C] **1** pointed or thin end of sth: 尖; 尖端: *the tip of one's fingers/one's fingertips;* 手指尖端; *the tip of one's nose;* 鼻尖; *asparagus tips.* 芦笋尖。 *The bird measured 12 inches from tip to tip,* from the tip of one wing to the tip of the other. 那鸟两翼张开两翼端的距离为十二英寸。 *(have sth) on the tip of one's tongue,* (be) just going to say (it). 话到嘴边; 即将要说某话。 **'tip·top** adj, adv (dated colloq) first-rate: (口语)第一流的(地): *a tip-top hotel/dinner.* 第一流的旅馆(餐食)。 *You've done tip-top.* 你做得好极了。 **2** small piece put at the end of sth: 装在末端的小物: *cigarettes with filter-tips.* 末端有滤嘴的香烟。 □ vt (-pp-) supply with a tip(2): 装以尖头: *filter-tipped cigarettes.* 装有滤嘴的香烟。

tip² /tɪp; tɪp/ vt, vi (-pp-) **1** [VP6A, 15A, B, 2A, C] *tip (sth) (up),* (cause) to rise, lean or tilt on one side or at one end: (使)倾斜; (使)翻倒: *The table tipped up.* 那桌子翻倒了。 *Tip the barrel up and empty it.* 把那桶倒空。 *tip sth (over),* (cause) to overbalance or overturn: (使)翻倒; 翻覆: *Careful! You'll tip the canoe over.* 当心! 你会把小船弄翻。 *tip the scale (at),* **(a)** be just enough to cause one scale or pan (of a balance) to go lower than the other; (fig) be the deciding factor (for or against). 刚可使天平倾斜; (喻)成为决定因素。 **(b)** weigh: 称量; 秤: *He tipped the scale at 140 lb.* 他体重一百四十磅。 **tip-up seat,** seat with a hinge, eg the kind used in cinemas, etc to allow people to pass freely. (戏院等处的)翻椅(一端有绞链, 可翻起伸便利人们通行者)。 **2** [VP6A, 15A, B] *tip sth (out); tip sth (out of sth) (into sth),* empty (the contents of sth) out/out of/into: 把(盛装物)倒出或倒入: *No rubbish to be tipped (out) here,* a warning put up in open spaces. 此处不准倾倒垃圾。 *She tipped the slops out of the bucket into the sink.* 她把脏水从桶里倒进洗涤槽中。 *He was tipped out of the cart into the ditch.* 他从马车上翻落到沟里。 *Which is better, to incinerate the rubbish from our towns or to tip it into disused quarries?* 我们城里的垃圾予以焚化, 或是倒进废弃的采石坑, 哪一种方法好? □ n (not US) place where rubbish may be tipped(2): (不用于美国)垃圾堆置场: *the municipal 'refuse tip;* 市区垃圾堆置场; hill of waste material from a coalmine, etc (colloq) untidy place: 煤矿区等的废物堆; (口)不雅观处; 脏乱处: *They live in a tip.* 他们住在陋巷里。

tip³ /tɪp; tɪp/ vt (-pp-) **1** [VP6A] touch or strike lightly: 轻触; 轻打; 轻敲: *His bat just tipped the ball.* 他

的球棒仅仅擦到球。 **,tip-and-'run** adj (of a raid by robbers, etc) in which there is a brief attack followed by a quick escape. (指强盗的抢掠等)抢了就逃的; 拿了就跑的。 **2** [VP6A, 12C] give a tip to (1, 2 below): 赏给小费; 给予劝告; 供以情报: *tip the porter 50p.* 赏给脚夫五十便士。 **tip sb off,** (colloq) give him a warning or a hint. (口)给予某人警告或暗示。 Hence, 由此产生, **'tip-off** n hint or warning: 警告; 暗示: *give the police a tip-off.* 给予警方警告或暗示。 **tip sb the wink,** (colloq) give him special information; warn him secretly. (口)予某人特别情报; 暗中警告某人。 **tip the winner,** name the winner (usu of a horse-race) before the event takes place. 事先指出(通常为赛马的)获胜者。 □ n [C] **1** gift of money to a porter, waiter, taxi-driver, etc for personal services: 小费; 赏钱: *leave a 50p tip,* eg at a restaurant. 留五十便士小费(如在餐馆中)。 **2** piece of advice on how to do sth, esp information about the probable winner of a horse-race, on the future value of shares (on the Stock Exchange, etc): 劝告; (尤指有关赛马的)可能获胜者, 或未来的证券价值的)情报; 特别消息; 秘密提示: *a tip for the Derby.* 德比大赛马的一项情报。 *If you take my tip* (=follow my advice) *you'll make a lot of money.* 你如果采纳我的意见, 你会赚大钱。 **3** light blow; tap. 轻击; 轻拍。

tip·pet /'tɪpɪt; 'tɪpɪt/ n (archaic) scarf or long fur worn by a woman round the neck and shoulders with the ends hanging down to the waist in front; similar article of dress worn by judges, clergy, etc. (古)妇女的肩巾(垂至腰前者); (法官、僧侣等所着的)披肩。 ⇨ the illus at **vestment.** 参看 vestment 之插图。

tipple /'tɪpl; 'tɪpl/ vi, vt **1** [VP2A] be in the habit of drinking alcoholic liquor. 酗酒。 惯于饮烈酒。 **2** [VP6A] drink (wine, spirits, etc). 饮(葡萄酒、烈酒等)。 □ n [U] alcoholic drink; (hum) any kind of drink: 烈酒; (谐)饮料: *John's favourite ~ is lager; mine is sherry.* 约翰喜欢淡啤酒; 我喜欢雪利(酒)。 **tip·pler** n

tip·staff /'tɪpstɑːf US: -stæf; 'tɪp,stæf/ n sheriff's officer. 法警; 警吏。

tip·ster /'tɪpstə(r); 'tɪpstɚ/ n person who gives tips about races. 提供赛马情报者; 泄露内情者。 ⇨ tip³(2).

tipsy /'tɪpsɪ; 'tɪpsɪ/ adj (colloq) slightly drunk. (口)微醉的。

tip·toe /'tɪptəʊ; 'tɪp,to/ adv on ~, on the tips of the toes: 踮着脚; *be/wait on ~ with excitement.* 兴奋地翘首企望(等待)。 □ vi [VP2A, C] walk quietly on ~: 踮着脚走: *She ~d to the bedside of the sleeping child.* 她踮着脚走到酣睡孩子的床边。

ti·rade /taɪ'reɪd; 'taɪred/ n long, angry or scolding speech. 长篇的激烈演说; 冗长的指摘性演说。

tire¹ /'taɪə(r); taɪr/ n (US) (美)=**tyre.**

tire² /'taɪə(r); taɪr/ vt, vi [VP6A, 15B, 2A, 3A] ~ (sb) (out), make or become weary, or in need of rest, or uninterested: (使)疲倦; (使)厌倦: *The long walk ~d the child/~d him out/made him ~d.* 长距离的步行使那孩子(使他)疲倦了。 *The long lecture ~d the audience.* 冗长的演说使听众厌倦了。 *She never ~s of talking about her clever son.* 谈到她儿子的聪明伶俐, 她从不会感到厌倦。 **be ~d of,** have had enough of, be exhausted with: 对…感到厌烦; 厌倦: *I'm ~d of boiled eggs,* I have had too many of them, or too often. 我吃厌了煮蛋。 **~d** /taɪəd; taɪrd/ adj weary in body or mind: (身体或精神)疲倦的; 疲乏的: *He was a ~d man when he got back from the long climb.* 长途爬山回来, 他感到疲倦了。 **~d out,** completely exhausted. 筋疲力竭的。 **~d·ness** n **~·less** adj **1** not easily ~d: 不易疲倦的: *a ~less worker.* 不倦的工作者。 **2** ceaseless; continuing a long time: 不停的; 持续长时间的: *~less energy.* 持久的精力。 **~·less·ly** adv **~·some** /-səm; -səm/ adj troublesome; tedious. 令人厌倦的; 讨人厌的。 **tir·ing** adj making a ~d: 令人疲倦的; 使人疲倦的: *a tiring journey/argument.* 令人疲倦的旅行(令人厌倦的议论)。

tiro, tyro /'taɪərəʊ; 'taɪro/ n (pl ~s /-rəʊz; -roz/)

beginner; person with little experience. 新手; 缺乏经验者。

tis·sue /'tɪʃuː; 'tɪʃʊ/ n **1** [C, U] (any kind of) woven fabric. (任何种类的)织物。 **2** [C, U] mass of cells and cell-products in an animal body: (动物的)组织: *muscular/connective ~.* 肌肉(结缔)组织。 **3** '~ **paper,** thin, soft paper for wrapping things, protecting delicate articles, etc: (包装、保护精致物品等用的)薄纸; 棉纸: '**toilet ~,** soft paper for use in the WC; 卫生纸; '**face/facial ~,** for use in wiping off lip-stick, face-cream, etc. 面纸; 化妆纸(用于揩去口红, 面霜等)。 **4** [C] (fig) web or network; series: (喻)网状物; 一连串: *a ~ of lies.* 一套谎言。

tit¹ /tɪt; tɪt/ n kinds of small bird: (数种)小鸟: *titmouse;* 小山雀; *titlark;* 云雀类的小鸣禽; *tomtit;* 山雀类; *long-tailed tit,* etc. 长尾山雀等。 ⇨ the illus at **bird.** 参看 bird 之插图。

tit² /tɪt; tɪt/ n (only in) (仅用于) **tit for tat,** blow in return for blow; (fig) equal retaliation. 还击; (喻)以牙还牙; 一报还一报。

tit³ /tɪt; tɪt/ n △ (vulg sl) teat; nipple; woman's breast. (伟)(鄙俚)奶头; 乳头; 妇女的乳房。

ti·tan /'taɪtn; 'taɪtən/ n **1** T~, (Gk myth) one of a family of giants who once ruled the world. (希神)泰坦(曾经统治世界的巨人家族中的一员)。 **2** person of superhuman size, strength, intellect, etc. 具有超人体积、力量、体力、智慧等出众的人; 巨人; 杰出之士。 **~·ic** /taɪ'tænɪk; taɪ'tænɪk/ adj immense. 巨大的; 极有力的。

tit·bit /'tɪtbɪt; 'tɪt,bɪt/ n [C] choice and attractive bit (of food, news, gossip, etc). 精美而有吸引力的少量(食物、消息、漫谈等); 珍品; 珍闻。

tithe /taɪð; taɪð/ n [C] **1** (hist) tenth part of farm produce given for the support of (Church of England) parish priests. (史)(用以维持英国国教的)农产品什一税。 '**~·barn** n barn in which ~s were stored. 储放什一税农产品的仓房。 **2** (rhet) tenth part. (修辞)十分之一; 小部分。

tit·il·late /'tɪtɪleɪt; 'tɪtl,et/ vt [VP6A] stimulate or excite pleasantly. 刺激使感到愉快; 使爽快; 使高兴。 **tit·il·la·tion** /,tɪtɪ'leɪʃn; ,tɪtl'eʃən/ n

titi·vate (also **tit·ti·**) /'tɪtɪveɪt; 'tɪtɪvet/ vt, vi [VP6A, 2A] (colloq) adorn; make smart: (口)装饰; 打扮; 使漂亮: *She was titivating (herself) before the mirror.* 她在镜前打扮(自己)。

tit·lark /'tɪtlɑːk; 'tɪt,lɑrk/ n ⇨ **tit¹.**

title /'taɪtl; 'taɪtl/ n **1** [C] name of a book, poem, picture, etc. (书籍、诗歌、图画等的)名称; 题目; 标题。 '**~·page** n page at the front of a book giving the ~, the author's name, etc. 书名页。 '**~·role** n part in a play that gives the play its name: 剧名角色(以该剧中人之名为剧名者): *a performance of 'Othello' with Olivier in the ~role,* with Olivier as Othello. 演出奥赛罗, 由奥利维尔担任奥赛罗这一角色。 **2** [C] word used to show a person's rank, occupation, status, etc, eg Lord, Prince, Professor, Dr. 称号; 头衔(如勋爵、王子、教授、博士等)。 **3** [C, U] ~ **to sth/to do sth,** (legal) right or claim, esp right to the possession of a position, property: (法律)权益; 权利(尤指对某地位或财产所保有的权利): *What ~ has he to the throne?* 他有何种权利继承王位? *Has he any ~ to the land?* 他有权保有该土地吗? '**~·deed** n document proving a ~ to property. 所有权状; 地契; 房契。 **4** '**credit ~s,** (or 或 credits), names of persons (eg script-writers, producers, camera men) responsible for a cinema film or TV production, shown at the beginning or end of the film, etc. 电影或电视制作者的名单(如编剧、制片人、摄影等)。 **~d** /'taɪtld; 'taɪt-ld/ adj having a ~ of nobility: 有爵位的; 有贵族头衔的: *a ~d lady,* eg a duchess. 命妇(如女公爵)。

tit·mouse /'tɪtmaʊs; 'tɪt,maʊs/ n (pl **-mice** /-maɪs; -,maɪs/) ⇨ **tit¹.**

tit·ter /'tɪtə(r); 'tɪtɚ/ vi [VP2A], n (give a) silly, half-suppressed little laugh. 傻笑; 窃笑。

tittle /'tɪtl; 'tɪtl/ n **not one jot or ~**, not a particle; not even a very little bit. 没有一点; 根本没有。

tittle-tattle /'tɪtl tætl; 'tɪtl,tætl/ n, vi gossip. 闲谈; 聊天。

titu·lar /'tɪtjʊlə(r) US: -tʃʊ-; 'tɪtʃələ/ adj **1** held by virtue of a title(3): 有权持有或保有的: ~ possessions. 有权保有的财产。 **2** existing in name but not having authority or duties: 有名无实的, 名义上的: the ~ ruler; 名义上的统治者; ~ sovereignty. 有名无实的统治权。

tizzy /'tɪzɪ; 'tɪzɪ/ n **be in a ~**, (colloq) in a nervous state. (口)处于紧张状态; 处于激动状态。

T-junction /'ti: dʒʌŋkʃn; 'ti dʒʌŋkʃən/ n one where two roads, wires, pipes, etc meet to form a **T**. 丁字形结合; 丁字形结合处或结合点。

TNT /ˌti: en 'ti:; 'ti,ɛn'ti/ n (= trinitrotoluene) powerful explosive. 黄色炸药。

to[1] /usual form before consonants: tə; tə; before vowels: tʊ or tu:; tʊ or tu; strong form or finally: tu:; tu/ prep **1** in the direction of; towards: 向; 对; 朝…方向: walk to work; 步行上班; go to the pub; 到酒馆去; fall to the ground; 落向地面; off to London; 到伦敦去; point to sth; 指向某物; hold sth (up) to the light; 把物举向光亮处; on the way to the station; 在前往车站途中; twenty miles to Dover; 距多佛二十英里; sitting with his feet to the fire; 他的脚朝着火坐着; turn to the right; 转向右方; going from town to town/place to place, etc. 一城走向另一城(一地走向另一地等)。 Scotland is to the north of England. 苏格兰在英格兰以北。 **2** (fig uses) towards (a condition, quality, etc); to reach the state of: 比喻用法)趋于; 倾向(某种情况、性质等); 至某种状态: a tendency to laziness/fat, to be lazy/fat; 懒惰(发胖)的倾向; all to no purpose, without any, or a satisfactory, results; 毫无结果; stir sb to action; 鼓励某人行动; bring/move/reduce sb to tears. 使某人(感动)落泪。 The mother sang her baby to sleep, sang until the baby slept. 母亲唱歌直到那婴儿睡着。 He tore the letter to pieces, eg in anger. 他把那封信撕碎(如在愤怒时)。 Don't start moving until the traffic lights change from red to green. 交通灯由红变绿时再开始走。 **3** (introducing the indirect object, as in VP13A): (引导间接宾语, 用法见 VP13A): To whom did you give it? 你(把它)给谁了? Who did you give it to? 你(把它)给谁了? The man I gave it to has left. 我把它交给他的那个人已经离开了。 **4** as far as: 至; 到; 达; 给: from beginning to end; 自始至终; from first to last; 从头到尾; faithful to the end/last; 忠实到底; fight to the last gasp; 战斗至最后一口气; wet to the skin; 湿透, 浑身淋透; to the marrow; 冷彻骨髓; count (up) to ten; 数到十; shades of colour from red to violet; 从红到紫的各种色度; push sb to violent action. 迫使某人采激烈行动。 **5** before: 在…之前: a quarter to six; 五点三刻; ten to two. 一点五十。 ⇨ past. **6** until: 直至; 到: from Saturday to Monday; 从礼拜六到礼拜一; from morning to night. 从早到晚。 I didn't stay to the end of the meeting. 我未待到会议结束。 He was conscious to the last. 他到最后仍很清醒。 **7** (indicating comparison, ratio, reference): (表示比较, 比率, 参照): He's quite rich now, compared to what he used to be. 同他过去比起来, 他现在很富了。 It's nothing to what it might be. 比起可能的结局, 这算不了什么。 I prefer walking to climbing. 我喜欢步行胜过爬山。 We won by six goals to three. 我们以六比三获胜。 The picture is true to life/nature. 那幅画画得逼真。 This is inferior/superior to that. 这个不如(胜过)那个。 Draw it to scale. 按比例画(它)。 **8** against; touching: 紧靠; 接触: dance cheek to cheek; 脸贴脸跳舞; march shoulder to shoulder. 肩并肩行进。 **9** for; of; 为; 属于: the key to the door; 这个门的钥匙; a secretary to the managing director; 总经理的秘书; the words to a tune; 一致的音谱; be/hear/say etc sth to one's/sb's advantage/liking, etc. (听到, 说出)对自己(某人)有利(自己(某人)爱听等)的话。 **10** forming; making: 形成; 构成: 100p to the pound/100c to the dollar, ie £1 = 100p/$1 = 100c. 一英镑有一百便士(一元有一百分)。 **11** in honour of: 向…表敬意: drink (a health) to sb; 举杯向某人致敬(祝某人健康); erect a monument to (the memory of) the soldiers who died in the war. 为阵亡将士立纪念碑。 ⇨ health(4); monument(1). **12** (when comparing two amounts; when quoting a rate) for each; per: (比较两个数量或谈及比率时)每一: petrol consumption of 30 miles to the gallon; 每加仑汽油可驶三十英里; a tax of 10p to the pound. 每镑抽十便士的税。 ⇨ per; rate[1](1). **13** causing: 使: To my surprise/annoyance/delight/sorrow, etc, the Liberals were defeated in the election, 真懊恼, To my shame, I completely forgot our date, I am ashamed that I forgot it. 真懊恼, 我竟然把我们的约会忘得干干净净。 **14** (used with verbs of perception like seem, appear, feel, look, smell, sound, etc) in the judgement of; according to: 与seem, appear, feel, look, smell, sound 等表示感觉的动词连用)据…的判断; 根据: It feels/looks/smells/sounds, etc to me like velvet/gold/ammonia/crying, etc. 摸起来像天鹅绒(看起来像金子; 闻起来像阿摩尼亚; 听起来像是在哭等)。

to[2] /usual form before consonants: tə; tə; before vowels and strong form: tu:; tu/ particle, marking the infinitive, used immediately before the v(作不定式的符号, 直接用于动词前) **1** (⇨ VP7A, 17; used after many vv but not after can, do, may, must, shall, will 用于许多动词之后, 但不用于 can, do, may, must, shall, will 之后): He wants to go. 他想去。 He wants me to go. 他要我去。 **2** (with adverbial functions of purpose, result, outcome): (具有副词功能, 表示目的、结果、结局): They came (in order) to help me. 他们来为(为要)帮助我。 He lived to be ninety. 他活到九十岁。 We make our goods to last, ie so that they will last. 我们的货物造得经久耐用。 **3** (limiting the meanings of adjj and advv): (限制形容词及副词的意义): I'm ready to help. 我愿意帮忙。 The book is easy to understand. 这本书易懂。 He's old enough to go to school. 他已届学龄。 She's too young to marry. 她年纪太轻, 还不能结婚。 This coffee's too hot to drink, to be drunk. 这咖啡太热, 还不能喝。 **4** (indicating a subsequent fact; 表示后继事实; ⇨ VP4B): The good old days have passed away, and will never return. 美好的往日已成过去, 永不会再来了。 He awoke to find himself (= and found himself) in a strange room. 他醒过来发现自己在一个陌生的房间中。 **5** (with an adjectival function): (具有形容词的功能): John was the first to arrive, who arrived first. 约翰第一个到。 **6** (used with an inf as an): (与不定式合成的代词用): It is wrong to steal. 偷窃是不对的。 To err is human, to forgive divine. 犯错是人之常情, 宽恕是超凡的。 **7** (as a substitute for the inf): (代替不定式): We didn't want to go but we had to. 我们本不想去, 但是不去不行。 I intended to go, but forgot to. 我打算要去, 但是忘了去。 He often does things you wouldn't expect him to. 他常会做出你意料不到的事。

to[3] /tu:; tu (no weak form)/ adv **1** to or in the usual or required position, esp to a closed or almost closed position: 到或者在通常或被要求的位置; (尤指)达到密闭或几乎密闭的位置: Push the door 'to. 把门关上。 Leave the door 'to, almost closed. 让门就那样虚掩着好了。 **2** to and fro, ⇨ fro. **3** bring 'to; come 'to; fall 'to, ⇨ bring(6); come(15); fall[2](14).

toad /təʊd; tod/ n rough-skinned, frog-like animal that lives on land except when breeding. 蟾蜍; 癞虾蟆。 ⇨ the illus at **amphibian**. 参看 amphibian 之插图。 **,~-in-the-'hole** n sausages baked in batter. 面拖腊肠(一种将腊肠裹上面糊烘成之食物)。 **'~-stool** n kinds of umbrella-shaped fungus, some of them poisonous. 菌蕈; 毒蕈。 ⇨ the illus at **fungi**. 参看 fungi 之插图。

toady /'təʊdɪ; 'todɪ/ n obsequious flatterer. 谄媚者; 拍马屁者。 □ vi [VP2A, 3A] ~ (to sb), flatter in the hope of advantage or gain: 奉承; 谄媚: ~ to the boss. 对上司谄媚。

toast[1] /təʊst; tost/ n [U] (slice of) bread made brown

and crisp by heating at a fire, etc: 烤面包；烤面包片；吐司: *a poached egg on* ~; 烤面包加一个荷包蛋; *two slices of buttered* ~. 两片涂奶油的烤面包。'~·rack *n* for holding slices of ~. 吐司架；烤面包架。□ *vt, vi* [VP6A, 2A] **1** make or become brown and crisp by heating. 烤；烘。'~·ing-fork *n* fork with a long handle used for holding bread in front of a fire. 吐司叉；烤面包叉。**2** warm (oneself, one's toes, etc) before a fire. 烘暖(自己、脚趾等)。~**er** *n* device (usu electric) for ~ing bread. 烤面包机(通常是用电的)。

toast[2] /təust/ *vt* [VP6A] wish happiness, success, etc to (sb or sth) while raising a full drinking-glass: 敬酒；举杯祝颂(某人或某事物)快乐、成功等: ~ *the bride and bridegroom.* 举杯祝颂新娘和新郎。~ *n* [C] act of ~ing; person, etc ~ed: 敬酒；举杯祝颂；被敬酒的人等: *propose a* ~ *to the bridesmaids;* 提议向女傧相敬酒; *drink a* ~; 敬酒; *the* ~; 干杯; *respond/reply to the* ~, eg of the speeches made after a wedding to and by the bride and bridegroom. 答谢敬酒(例如，婚礼后向新娘新郎或由新娘新郎所作的演说)。'~**-master** *n* person who announces the ~s at a banquet at which there are distinguished guests. (宴会上的)祝酒人；宴会主人。

to·bac·co /tə'bækəu; tə'bæko/ *n* [U] (plant having) leaves which are dried, cured and used for smoking (in pipes, cigars, cigarettes) or as snuff; (*pl*, for kinds of ~ leaf): 烟草；烟叶；(复数指各种烟叶): *This is a mixture of the best* ~s. 这是由各种最好的烟叶配制成的。~**·nist** /tə'bækənist; tə'bækənist/ *n* dealer in ~. 烟草商。

to·bog·gan /tə'bɒgən; tə'bɑgən/ *n* long, narrow sledge, curved up in front, used for going downhill on snow. 长滑橇(前端向上弯曲，用以在积雪的山坡上往下滑)。□ *vi* [VP2A, C] go down a snow- or ice-covered slope on a ~. 乘滑橇滑下。

tobogganing

toby-jug /'təubi dʒʌg; 'tobi dʒʌg/ *n* drinking-mug shaped like a man, wearing a three-cornered hat. 人形(酒)杯。

toc·cata /tə'kɑːtə; tə'kɑtə/ *n* (music) composition for a keyboard instrument (organ, piano, etc) in a free style, designed to show the performer's technique. (音乐)触技曲。

toc·sin /'tɒksɪn; 'tɑksɪn/ *n* [C] (bell rung to give a) signal of alarm (now usu fig). 警钟；警铃；警声；警报(现通常作喻)。

to·day /tə'deɪ; tə'de/ *adv, n* [U] **1** (on) this day: 今天；本日: *T* ~ *is Sunday.* 今天是礼拜天。*Have you seen* ~*'s newspaper?* 你看过今天的报纸吗? *We're leaving* ~ *week/a week* ~, in one week's time. 我们将于下周今天(七天后)离开。**2** (at) this present age or period: 当今；现代；当世: *the writers/the young people of* ~. 现代的作家(年青的一代)。

toddle /'tɒdl; 'tɑdl/ *vi* [VP2A, C] walk with short, uncertain steps as a baby does; (colloq) walk: 婴儿般摇摇摆摆地走路；以短而不稳定的步伐行走; (口语) 走: ~ *off/round to see a friend.* 走去看朋友。**tod·dler** /'tɒdlə(r); 'tɑdlə/ *n* baby who can ~. 初学走路的婴儿。

toddy /'tɒdɪ; 'tɑdɪ/ *n* (*pl* **-dies**) **1** [C, U] (drink of) alcoholic spirits (esp whisky) and hot water. 加热的

烈酒；掺水威士忌。**2** [U] fresh or fermented sap of some kinds of palm-trees. 某些棕榈树的汁液(新鲜或经发酵)。

to-do /tə'duː; tʊ'du/ *n* ado; fuss; commotion: 骚乱；纷扰；喧闹: *What a* ~! What a lot of excitement and talk! 多吵闹啊!

toe /təu; to/ *n* **1** each of the five divisions of the front part of the foot; similar part of an animal's foot: 脚趾；动物的脚趾: *turn one's toes in/out,* ie in walking. (走路时)脚尖朝内(外)。⇨ the illus at **leg**. 参看 leg 之插图。*tread/step on sb's toes,* (fig) offend his feelings or prejudices. 踩(踏)在某人脚趾上；(喻)伤某人感情；触怒某人。*from top to toe,* from head to foot, completely. 从头到脚；完全。*on one's toes,* (fig) alert, ready for action. (喻)警觉的；准备行动的。'**toe-cap** *n* outer covering of the toe of a shoe or boot. 鞋或靴尖的饰包；靴头；靴头。'**toe-hold** *n* small, insecure foothold (eg when climbing a cliff). 不稳的小立足点；踏脚处(如攀爬时)。'**toe-nail** *n* nail of the toe of a human being. 脚趾甲。**2** part of a sock, shoe, etc covering the toes. 袜、鞋等的趾部。□ *vt* [VP6A] touch, reach, with the toes. 以趾触；足趾伸及。*toe the line,* (a) stand with a toe on the starting-line ready for a race. (赛跑时)准备起跑。(b) (fig) obey orders given to one as a member of a group or party. (喻)服从团体或党的命令。

toff /tɒf; tɔf/ *n* (dated GB sl) well-dressed or distinguished-looking person. (过时英俚)衣着讲究的人；仪表出众的人。

toffee /'tɒfɪ US: 'tɔːfɪ; 'tɔfɪ/ *n* (*pl* ~**s**) (US = *taffy* /'tæfɪ; 'tæfɪ/) [C, U] (piece of) hard, sticky sweet made by boiling sugar, butter, etc. (一块)太妃糖。

tog /tɒg; tag/ *vt* (**-gg-**) [VP15B] *tog oneself up/out (in),* (colloq) put on smart clothes. (口)穿起漂亮衣服。*togs n pl* (colloq) clothes: (口)衣服: *put on one's best togs.* 穿起最漂亮的衣服。

toga /'təugə; 'togə/ *n* loose flowing outer garment worn by men in ancient Rome. (古罗马男子所着的)宽松外袍；托加袍。

to·gether /tə'geðə(r); tə'gɛðə/ *adv* **1** in company: 在一起；共同地: *They went for a walk* ~. 他们一起去散步。*We are working* ~. 我们在一起工作。~ *with,* as well as; in addition to; and also: 和；加之；连同: *These new facts,* ~ *with the evidence you have already heard, prove the prisoner's innocence.* 这些新的事实，连同你已听到的证据，证明在押被告是无辜的。**2** so as to be in the same place, to be in contact, to be united: 致使在同一地方，有接触，结合合；在一起: *Tie the ends* ~. 把末端结起来。*He nailed the boards* ~ *and made a crate.* 他把木板钉起来，做成一个板条箱。*Stand the two boys* ~ *and see who is taller.* 让这两个男孩站在一起比比看谁高。*The leader called his men* ~. 首领召集他的部属。*be* ~; *get sth/it* ~, (sl) (cause) to be organised, be organised, be organised, under control. (俚)(使)有组织；在控制之下。*put your/ our, etc heads* ~, consult with each other (to find a solution to sth, make plans, etc). 你们(咱们等)商量一下(以解决某事，做成计划等)。**3** at the same time: 同时: *All his troubles seemed to come* ~. 他的一切麻烦似乎同时来临。**4** without interruption; in continuous succession: 无间断地；连续地: *They sat talking for hours* ~. 他们坐着聊天一连好几个钟头。*He has been away from school for weeks* ~ *through illness.* 他因病已连续数周未去上学。~**·ness** *n* [U] comradeship; feeling of unity. 同志关系；友谊；团结一致。

toggle /'tɒgl; 'tagl/ *n* short piece of wood (like a peg) (to be) put through a loop (to fasten two things together, eg as used instead of a button on a coat). 挂索栓；套索钉（用以套索眼的短木栓，俾使两物连系在一起者）。

togs /tɒgz; tagz/ *n pl* ⇨ **tog**.

toil /tɔɪl; tɔɪl/ *vi* [VP2A, B, C, 3A, 4A] ~ *(at),* work long or hard (at a task); move with difficulty and trouble: 辛劳；辛苦工作；艰难地行动；跋涉: ~ *at one's*

studies; 苦读; ～ *up a steep hill.* 吃力地爬上陡峭的山。 □ *n* [U, C] labour; hard work: 辛劳; 辛苦工作: *after long* ～. 长时间辛苦工作之后。 ～**er** *n* hard worker. 辛劳者; 辛苦工作的人。

toilet /'tɔɪlɪt; 'tɔɪlɪt/ *n* 1 process of dressing, cleaning, arranging the hair, face, body, etc: 化妆; 梳妆; 打扮: *She spent only a few minutes on her* ～. 她只花了几分钟打扮一下。 2 (attrib) (用作定语) a '～ *set,* '～ *articles,* such things as a hair-brush, comb, hand-mirror, etc. 一套梳妆用具; 梳妆用具(发刷、梳子、手镜等)。 '～**-powder** *n* [U] talc. 扑粉; 爽身粉。 '～**-table** *n* dressing-table (with a mirror or mirrors). 梳妆台。 3 water-closet. 盥洗室; 厕所。 '～**-paper** *n* for use in a water-closet. 卫生纸; 手纸。 '～**-roll** *n* roll of ～-paper. 一卷卫生纸。

toils /tɔɪlz; tɔɪlz/ *n pl* nets; snares: 罗网; 陷阱; 圈套: (usu *fig*) (通常作喻) *caught in the* ～ *of the law.* 落入法网。

To·kay /təʊ'keɪ; to'ke/ *n* [U] kind of sweet, rich Hungarian wine. 投喀酒 (一种甜而醇的匈牙利葡萄酒)。

to·ken /'təʊkən; 'tokən/ *n* [C] 1 sign, evidence, guarantee or mark: 表征; 表号; 证据; 保证; 象征; 记号: *A white flag is used as a* ～ *of surrender.* 白旗是用作投降的信号。 *I am giving you this jewel as a* ～ *of my esteem/affection.* 我送给你这珠宝以表示我对你的敬意(挚情)。 *in* ～ *of,* as evidence of. 作为…的证据; 表示。 '**book**/'**record**/'**gift**'～, receipt (usu on an attractive card) for payment of money, exchangeable for a book/ record, etc of the value stated. 书券(唱片券; 礼券)(可换取券面所载金额同值的书, 唱片等)。 2 (attrib) serving as a preliminary or small-scale substitute: (用作定语) 象征性的; 用作初期或小规模之代表的: *The enemy offered only a* ～ *resistance,* did not resist seriously. 敌人仅仅作了象征性的抵抗。 '～ **money,** coins of low intrinsic value, but exchangeable for money of standard value. 代币(实值较低而可兑换标准价值之钱币者)。 ～ **payment,** payment of a small part of what is owed, made to show that the debt is recognized. 象征性的偿付(偿付小部分欠款, 作为承认该债务的象征)。 ～ **strike,** for a few hours only (as a warning that a long strike may follow). 象征性罢工(仅罢工数小时, 以警告将有可能发动长时间罢工)。 ～ **vote,** Parliamentary vote of money for government purposes, it being understood that a larger sum may be taken without further discussion or voting. 议会象征性的拨款(表示政府可支付较大金额的款项, 不必再行讨论或表决)。

told /təʊld; told/ *pt, pp of* **tell**.

tol·er·ate /'tɒləreɪt; 'tɑlə,ret/ *vt* [VP6A, C] 1 allow or endure without protest: 容许: *I won't* ～ *your selfishness/your doing that.* 我不能容许你那么自私(你做那件事)。 2 endure the society of: 容忍; 忍受: *How can you* ～ *that pompous idiot?* 你怎么能容忍那个自大的糊涂虫呢? **tol·er·able** /'tɒlərəbl; 'tɑlərəbl/ *adj* that can be ～d: fairly good: 可容忍的; 尚可的; 还好的: *tolerable food;* 尚佳的伙食; *in tolerable health.* 健康还好的。 **tol·er·ably** /-əblɪ; -əblɪ/ *adv* in a tolerable manner or degree: 可容忍地; 可忍受地; 尚可地; 相当地; *feel tolerably (= fairly) certain about sth.* 对某事觉得相当有把握。 **tol·er·ance** /'tɒlərəns; 'tɑlərəns/ *n* [U] quality of tolerating opinions, beliefs, customs, behaviour, etc different from one's own: 容忍; 宽容: *religious/racial tolerance.* 宗教(种族)上的容忍。 **tol·er·ant** /-rənt; -rənt/ *adj* having or showing tolerance: 容忍的; 宽容的: *Mr X is not very tolerant of criticism/ contradiction,* does not endure it easily. 某先生不大能容忍批评(反驳)。 **tol·er·ant·ly** *adv* **tol·er·ation** /ˌtɒlə-'reɪʃn; ˌtɑlə'reʃən/ *n* [U] tolerance. 容忍; 宽容。

toll[1] /təʊl; tol/ *n* [C] 1 payment required for the use of a road, bridge, harbour, etc. (使用道路、桥梁、海港等的)通行税或费; 过桥费; 过路费; 港税。 '～**-bar**/**-gate** *n* bar/gate across a road at which a ～ is payable. (征收过路费的)卡门; 征收卡; 关闸。 '～**-house** *n* house for

the man in charge of a ～-bar. (过路费等的)征收所。 2 (fig) sth paid, lost or suffered: (喻)付出、失去或损失之物; 代价; 牺牲: *the* ～ *of the roads,* deaths and injuries from traffic accidents. 交通事故的伤亡人数。 *The war took a heavy* ～ *of the nation's manhood.* 战争攫取了该国许多男子的生命。 3 '～ **call** *n* telephone call for which the rates are higher than for local calls. 长途电话(比当地电话费高者)。

toll[2] /təʊl; tol/ *vt, vi* [VP6A, 2A] (cause to) ring with slow, regular strokes: (指钟)(使)缓慢而有规律地鸣钟; 鸣钟; 敲钟: *The funeral bell* ～*ed solemnly.* 丧钟肃穆地鸣响。 *Whose death is being* ～*ed?* 在为谁敲丧钟? □ *n* (*sing only*) ～ing stroke, of a bell. (仅用单数)鸣钟; 敲钟; 钟声。

toma·hawk /'tɒməhɔːk; 'tɑmə,hɔk/ *n* light axe used as a tool and a weapon by N American Indians. (北美印第安人用作工具和武器的)轻斧; 战斧; 钺。 □ *vt* strike with a ～. 用轻(战)斧挥砍或杀。

tom·ato /tə'mɑːtəʊ US: tə'meɪtəʊ; tə'meto/ *n* (*pl* ～**es** /-təʊz; -toz/) [C] (plant with) soft, juicy, red or yellow fruit usu eaten with meat, in salads, and in sauces: 西红柿; 番茄: (attrib) (用作定语) ～ *juice.* 番茄汁。 ⇨ the illus at **vegetable.** 参见 vegetable 之插图。

tomb /tuːm; tum/ *n* place dug in the ground, cut out of rock, etc for a dead body, esp one with a monument over it. 坟; 墓。 '～**-stone** *n* stone set up over a ～. 墓碑。

tom·bola /tɒm'bəʊlə; 'tɑmbolə/ *n* [C] (*pl* ～**s**) (now usu called 现通常称作 *bingo*) kind of lottery with sums of money or small fancy articles as prizes. 唐伯拉(以钱或小的装饰品作为奖品)。

tom·boy /'tɒmbɔɪ; 'tɑm,bɔɪ/ *n* girl who likes rough, noisy games and play. 野丫头; 顽皮的女孩子。

tom·cat /'tɒmkæt; 'tɑm,kæt/ *n* male cat. 雄猫。

tome /təʊm; tom/ *n* large, heavy book. 大部头书; 大本书。

tom·fool /ˌtɒm'fuːl; 'tɑm'ful/ *n* stupid person; (attrib) stupid: 笨伯; 愚人; (用作定语)愚蠢的: *a* ～ *speech.* 愚蠢的谈话(演说)。 ～**·ery** /-ərɪ; -ərɪ/ *n* [U] senseless behaviour; [C] (*pl* **-ries**) stupid joke. 愚蠢的举止;愚蠢的笑话。

tommy-gun /'tɒmɪ gʌn; 'tɑmɪ gʌn/ *n* submachine-gun (light kind that can be carried and used by one man). 汤姆逊冲锋枪。

tommy-rot /ˌtɒmɪ'rɒt; 'tɑmɪ,rɑt/ *n* (colloq) utter foolishness: (口)极愚; 荒唐: *You're talking* ～. 你在胡扯。 *That's all* ～. 荒唐之至。

to·mor·row /tə'mɒrəʊ; tə'mɔro/ *adv, n* [U] (on) the day after today: 明天; 在明天: *If today is Monday,* ～ *will be Tuesday and the day after* ～ *will be Wednesday.* 如果今天是星期一, 明天就是星期二, 后天就是星期三。 *Don't wait until* ～. 不要等到明天。 *Where will he be* ～ *morning/afternoon/evening/night?* 明天早上(下午, 晚上, 夜里)他会在哪儿呢? *The announcement will appear in* ～*'s newspapers.* 这项宣布将刊在明天的报纸上。 *What will the men and women of* ～ (= of the next few years) *think of us?* 未来的男女会对我们作何看法呢? ～ *week,* eight days hence. 八天后(下周明日)。

tom·tit /ˌtɒm'tɪt; 'tɑm,tɪt/ *n* kind of small bird. 山雀类。 ⇨ **tit**[1].

tom·tom /'tɒmtɒm; 'tɑm,tɑm/ *n* (kind of) African or Asian drum, esp a long and narrow kind, beaten with the hands. 唐唐鼓(见于非洲及印度等处, 用手击之)。

ton /tʌn; tʌn/ *n* 1 measure of weight (2 240 lb in GB, 2 000 lb in the US). 吨(英国为 2 240 磅, 美国为 2 000 磅)。 **metric ton, = tonne.** ⇨ **App 5.** 参看附录五。 2 measure of the internal capacity (100 cu ft) or carrying capacity (40 cu ft) of a ship. 船的吨位(船的登记吨位, 为 100 立方英尺; 或指船的载运或容积吨位, 为 40 立方英尺)。 3 (colloq) large weight, quantity or number: (口)

沉重；大量；众多：*He has tons of money.* 他有很多钱。**4 the ton,** (sl) speed of 100 mph：(俚)一百英里时速：*Can your motor-bike do the ton?* 你的机车每小时能跑 100 英里吗？□ *vi* [VP2C] **ton up,** drive a (motor-cycle) for sport at a high speed. 高速骑(机车)出游；飞车兜风。

to·nal /ˈtəʊnl; ˈtonl/ *adj* of tone or tones; of ~ity. 声音的；音调的；调性的。~·**ity** /təʊˈnælətɪ; toˈnæləti/ *n* (*pl* -**ties**) (music) character of a melody, depending upon the scale in which it is written, the key in which it is developed, etc. (音乐)音调，调性(旋律的性质，视该曲调所用的音阶，调子的演变等而定)

tone[1] /təʊn; ton/ *n* **1** [C] sound, esp with reference to its quality, pitch, duration, feeling, etc: 声音；音调；音质；语调；语气：*the sweet ~(s) of a violin;* 小提琴的优美声音；*speak in an angry / entreating ~.* 以愤怒(恳求)的语气说话。*The doctor's ~ was serious.* 医生的语气很严肃。**,** ~-**deaf** *adj* unable to distinguish between differences of pitch. 不能辨别不同音高的；音痴的。**'~- poem** *n* musical composition for an orchestra, illustrating a poetic idea, legend, etc. 音诗(管弦乐队演奏的乐曲，表现一种诗的意境、传说等者)。**2** [C] the pitch aspect of a (usu stressed) syllable; rise, fall, etc of the pitch of the voice in speaking: 音节(通常指重音节)的高低或抑扬；语调的高低或抑扬：*In 'Are you ill?' there is usu a rising ~ on 'ill'; in 'He's ill', there is usu a falling ~ on 'ill'.* 在 Are you ill？一句中，ill 一词的音调通常上扬；在 He's ill 一句中，ill 一词的音调通常下降。**3** (*sing* only) general spirit, character, morale, of a community, etc: (仅用单数)社会等的风气、特性、风纪等：*The ~ of the country is buoyant.* 该国的风气活泼。*The next speaker gave a serious / flippant ~ to the discussion.* 下一位发言者为这场讨论加添了一些严肃(不正经)的气氛。*There was a ~ of quiet elegance in the room,* The furnishings, etc gave this impression. 房间中有一种静谧的高雅气氛。**4** [C] shade (of colour); degree (of light): 色调；色度；光度：*a carpet in ~s of brown;* 有深浅不同褐色之地毯；*a picture in warm ~s,* in shades suggesting warmth. 有温暖色调的照片。**5** (music) any one of the five larger intervals between one note and the next which, together with two semi-~s, make up an octave. (音乐)全音。**6** [U] proper and normal condition of (parts of) the body: 身体(各器官)的健康状态：*good muscular ~;* 肌肉结实；*recover mental ~.* 恢复心理健康。**-toned** *adj* having a particular kind of ~(1): 有某种声音，音调，语气等的：*silver-~d trumpets.* 声音清脆的喇叭。~**·less** *adj* lacking colour, spirit, etc; dull: 无风格的；单调的；沉闷的：*answer in a ~less voice.* 以单调的声音回答。~**·less·ly** *adv*

tone[2] /təʊn; ton/ *vt, vi* **1** [VP6A] give a particular tone of sound or colour to. 加以某种调音或色调。**2** [VP15B, 2C] ~ (*sth*) **down,** make or become less intense: 缓和；减轻：*The excitement ~d down.* 兴奋的情绪降低了。*The artist ~d down the cruder colours in his painting.* 那位画家使他画中刺眼的色彩变得柔和些。*You'd better ~ down some of the offensive statements in your article.* 你最好把你文章里的攻击性词句说得含蓄一点。~ (*sth*) **up,** make or become more vigorous, intenser, brighter, etc: 提高；加强；强化：*Exercise ~s up the muscles.* 运动使肌肉结实。**3** ~ **in** (**with**), (esp of colours) be in harmony: (尤指颜色)(与…)调和；相配：*These curtains ~ in well with your rugs.* 这些帘幕的色调与你的地毯配合得很好。

tongs /tɒŋz; tɔŋz/ *n pl* (**pair of**), one of various kinds of usu hinged tool for taking up and holding sth: 钳；夹具：*'sugar ~;* 糖夹子；*'coal ~,* 火钳；煤炭夹子；*'ice ~.* 冰块夹子。*be / go at it hammer and ~,* ⇨ **hammer**(1).

tongue / tʌŋ; tʌŋ/ *n* **1** [C] movable organ in the mouth, used in talking, tasting, licking, etc: 舌；舌头：*The doctor asked me to put out my ~.* 医生要我伸出舌头。*Don't put your ~ out at me, you cheeky girl!* 不要向我伸舌头，你这没规矩的丫头！⇨ the illus at **mouth,**

snake. 参看 mouth, snake 之插图。**have sth on the tip of one's ~,** ⇨ **tip**[1](1). **find one's ~,** become able to speak again (after being too shy to do so). (在羞怯得说不出话之后)开口说话；恢复说话能力。**have / say sth with / speak with one's ~ in one's cheek,** say sth that one does not intend to be taken seriously. 无诚意地说话；非认真地说话。Hence, 由此产生，**'~-in-'cheek** *adj, adv:* ~-*in-cheek remarks;* 无诚意的话；*speak ~-in-cheek.* 非认真地说。**have lost one's ~,** be too shy to speak. 羞怯得说不出话来。**have a ready ~,** be fluent, quick to answer questions, etc. 口齿伶俐；能言善道；口才好。**hold one's ~,** be silent, saying nothing. 缄默；不开口。**keep a civil ~ in one's head,** not be rude. 言语谨慎措辞；谈吐温雅。**'~-tied** *adj* silent; unable or unwilling to speak through shyness, fear, etc. 沉默的；(因羞怯、恐惧等而)张口结舌的；说不出话的。**'~-twister** *n* word or succession of words difficult to utter quickly and correctly. 绕口令。**2** [C] language: 语言：*one's mother ~,* one's native language: 本国话；母语；*the German ~.* 德国话。**3** [C, U] animal's ~ as an article of food: (用作食物的)动物的舌头；舌肉：*boil an 'ox-~;* 煮牛舌；*ham and ~ sandwiches.* 火腿和舌肉的三明治。**4** sth like a ~ in shape or function, eg the clapper of a bell, the strip of leather under the laces of a shoe, a jet of flame (which licks things), a long promontory *(a ~ of land)*. 舌状物(如铃舌、鞋舌、火舌、狭长的海角等)。**~d** *adj* (in compounds) having a ~ of the kind indicated: (用于复合词中)有某种舌的；说话…的：*a sharp-~d woman.* 言词锋利的女人。

tonic /ˈtɒnɪk; ˈtɑnɪk/ *n, adj* **1** (sth, eg medicine) giving strength or energy: 滋补品(如药物)；给予力量或精力的；滋补的；激励的：*the ~ quality of sea air;* 海上空气使人振奋的特性；*get a bottle of ~ from the doctor.* 从医生处拿到一瓶补剂。*Praise can be a fine ~.* 称赞可成为一种良好的鼓励。*The good news acted as a ~ on us all,* cheered us up. 那好消息使我们大家感到振奋。**~ (water),** bottled, carbonated water with quinine: (通常为瓶装)奎宁水：*a gin and ~* (as a drink). 奎宁杜松子酒(用作饮料)。**2** (music) keynote. (音乐)主音。**~·sol-fa** /ˌsɒlˈfɑ; ˌsolˈfa/ *n* (in teaching singing) method of showing musical notes by syllables, eg *sol, fa, do.* 首调唱法(以字音，如 sol, fa, do, 表示音符的歌曲教唱法)。⇨ **do**[5].

to·night /təˈnaɪt; təˈnaɪt/ *adv, n* [U] (on) the night of today: (在)今晚；今夜：*last night, ~, and tomorrow night;* 昨晚，今晚和明晚；*after ~;* 今夜以后；~'s *radio news.* 今晚的新闻广播。

ton·nage /ˈtʌnɪdʒ; ˈtʌnɪdʒ/ *n* **1** internal cubic capacity of a ship (1 ton = 100 cu ft). 船的登记吨位 (每吨为 100 立方英尺)。**2** cargo-carrying capacity of a ship stated in tons (of 40 cu ft). 船的货运或容积吨位(每吨为 40 立方英尺)。**3** total ~(1) of a country's merchant shipping. (一国商船的)总吨位(指登记吨位)。**4** charge per ton on cargo, etc for transport. 每吨货物的运费；吨税。

tonne /tʌn; tʌn/ *n* metric ton, = 1 000 kilograms. 公吨(1 000 公斤)。⇨ **App 5.** 参看附录五。

ton·sil /ˈtɒnsl; ˈtɑnsl/ *n* either of two small oval masses of tissue at the sides of the throat, near the root of the tongue: 扁桃腺：*have one's ~s out,* have them removed by a surgeon. 割除扁桃腺。⇨ the illus at **head.** 参看 head 之插图。**~·litis** /ˌtɒnsɪˈlaɪtɪs; ˌtɑnslˈaɪtɪs/ *n* [U] inflammation of the ~s. 扁桃腺炎。

ton·sorial /tɒnˈsɔːrɪəl; tɑnˈsorɪəl/ *adj* (often hum, 常为诙谐语, eg 如 *the ~ art* 理发技艺) of a hairdresser and his work. 理发师的；理发的。

ton·sure /ˈtɒnʃə(r); ˈtɑnʃər/ *n* shaving of the top of the head of a person about to become a monk or priest; part of the head that has been shaved in this way. 做僧侣时头顶的剃光；削发；(僧侣的)光秃圆顶。□ *vt* give the ~ to. 为…削发。

ton·tine /ˈtɒntiːn; ˈtɑntin/ *n* annuity shared by

subscribers to a loan, the shares increasing as the subscribers die, till the last subscriber gets all that is left. 联合养老保险法(参加者共享一笔基金,有人死亡时,生者即增加其份额,最后仅存者,获该基金之全部余额)。

too /tu:; tu/ *adv* **1** also; as well, in addition (usu in end position but placed immediately after the word it modifies if there is a risk of ambiguity): 也; 又; 加之(通常置于句末, 若有意义含糊之虞时, 则紧放在所修饰之词后): *I, too, have been to Paris,* eg I, as well as he, you, etc. 我也去过巴黎(如谓不只他、你等去过)。*I've been to Paris, too,* eg to Paris as well as to Rome, Milan, etc. 我还去过巴黎(如谓不只去过罗马、米兰等)。*She plays the piano, and sings, too,* plays the piano and also sings. 她会弹钢琴, 也会唱歌。*Sally, too,* (= Sally, as well as Mary, etc) *plays the piano.* 莎莉也会弹钢琴(意谓不只玛丽等会)。(Cf the construction in negative sentences: 参较否定结构: *I know the answer, too.* 我也知道那答案。Neg: 否定: *I don't know the answer, either.* 我也不知道那答案。) **2** moreover; nevertheless: 而; 此外; 而且: *There was frost last night, and in May too!* 昨晚降霜了, 而竟在五月! **3** (*adv of degree,* modifying *adjj* and *advv*) in a higher degree than is allowable, required, etc: (表程度的副词, 修饰形容词及副词)过于; 太: *We've had too much rain lately.* 近来这里的雨下得太多了。*You're driving too fast for safety.* 你开车太快了, 恐不安全。*These shoes are much too small for me.* 这双鞋我穿太小了。*It's too hot for work/too hot to work.* 天太热无法工作。*It's too difficult a task for me.* 这工作对我来说是太难了。*That's too small a box/That box is too small to hold all these things.* 那盒子太小, 装不下所有这些东西。(Note that *too* is used to modify a participle that is adjectival, but that with a participle that is purely verbal, *too much* is preferred in formal style. 注意: too 用以修饰作形容词用的分词, 如该分词纯为动词性质, 正式文体中, 宜用 too much。Cf: 参较: *He was too tired to go any farther.* 他太疲倦不能再往前走了。*I hope you were not too (much) disturbed by all the noise we made.* 我希望我们的闹声不致打扰你太厉害。*I'm not too (much) bothered by his criticisms.* 我未因他的批评而感到太大的困扰。) **4** (phrases) (短语) ***carry sth/go too far,*** ⇨ **far²(2).** ***all too soon/quickly, etc,*** sooner, more quickly, etc than is desired: 太早(太快等): *The holidays ended all too soon.* 假期结束得太早了。***none too soon, etc,*** not at all too soon, etc: 一点也不早等: *We were none too early for the train,* We caught the train with very little time to spare. 我们刚好赶上火车。***one too many,*** ⇨ **many(1).** ***have one too many,*** take more than one can drink and remain sober. 饮酒过量。***be too much for,*** ⇨ **much¹.** ***only too*** (+ *adj*), ⇨ **only²(2).**

took /tuk; tʊk/ *pt* of **take¹.**

tool /tu:l; tul/ *n* **1** instrument held in the hand(s) and used by workmen, eg gardeners and carpenters. 工具; 用具; 器具。**ma,chine '~** *n* ⇨ **machine. 2** person used by another for dishonest purposes: 受人利用做不正当活动者; 为人利用的工具; 走狗; 傀儡: *He was a mere ~ in the hands of the dictator.* 他只是那独裁者手中的工具而已。□ *vt, vi* **1** [VP6A] ornament (the edges of a book-cover) with designs pressed on with a heated ~. 压印图案于(书籍封面的边缘)。**2** [VP2C] **~ *up,*** provide a factory with machine-~s (eg as needed for a particular kind of work). 以工作母机装备某一工厂。

toot /tu:t; tut/ *n* [C] short, sharp warning sound from a horn, whistle, trumpet, etc. (号角、笛、喇叭等)短而尖锐的鸣声; (示警之)嘟嘟声。□ *vi, vt* [VP2A, 6A] (cause to) give out a ~ or ~s. (使)发嘟嘟声。

tooth /tu:θ; tuθ/ *n* (*pl* **teeth** /ti:θ; tiθ/) **1** each of the hard, white, bone-like structures rooted in the gums, used for biting and chewing: 牙; 齿: *have a ~ out* (US 美 = *have a ~ pulled*), ie by a dentist; 拔一颗牙; *have all one's own teeth/a fine set of artificial teeth.* 有一嘴好牙(一副好的假牙)。⇨ the illus at **mouth.** 参看 mouth 之插图。***armed to the teeth,*** completely and elaborately armed. 全副武装。***cast sth in a person's teeth,*** reproach him with it. 以某事责备某人。***escape by the skin of one's teeth,*** have a narrow escape. 仅以身免; 幸免于难。***fight ~ and nail,*** fiercely, with a great effort. 猛烈打斗、作战等。***get one's teeth into sth,*** attack (a job) vigorously. 奋力工作。***have a sweet ~,*** be fond of sweet food. 喜吃甜食。***lie in one's teeth/throat,*** lie shamelessly. 无耻地说谎。***long in the ~,*** (originally of horses, because gums recede with age) old. 上年纪; 年纪大(原指马, 因马年纪大则齿龈向后收缩)。***show one's teeth,*** take up a threatening attitude. 恐吓; 作威胁姿态。***in the teeth of,*** against the full force of; in opposition to. 抵抗…的全力; 对抗。**(a/the) '~-ache** *n* pain in a ~ or teeth. 牙痛。**'~·brush** *n* one for cleaning the teeth. 牙刷。⇨ the illus at **brush.** 参看 brush 之插图。**'~·paste/·powder** *n* [U] for cleaning the teeth. 牙膏(牙粉)。**'~·pick** *n* short, pointed piece of wood, etc, for removing bits of food from between the teeth. 牙签。**2 ~**-like part, esp of a comb, saw or rake. (尤指梳子、锯或耙的)齿状部分。⇨ the illus at **gear.** 参看 gear 之插图。**,fine-'~ comb,** one with fine teeth set closely together. 细齿梳; 篦子。***go over/through sth with a ,fine-'~ comb,*** examine it closely and thoroughly. 密切而彻底地调查某事。**3** (*pl,* colloq) effective force: (复, 口)有效的力量: *When will the new legislation be given some teeth,* be made effective? 新的立法何时生效? **~ed** /tu:θt; tuθt/ (attrib) having teeth (eg of the kind named): (用作定语)有某种(名称之)齿的: *a saw-~ed wheel.* 锯齿轮。**~·less** *adj* without teeth. 无牙的; 无齿的。**~·some** /-səm; -səm/ *adj* (liter) (of food) pleasant to the taste. (文)(指食物)美味的; 可口的。

tootle /'tu:tl; 'tutl̩/ *vi, n* toot softly or continuously, as on a flute. (发)柔和或连续的嘟嘟声(如横笛所发者)。

top¹ /tɒp; tap/ *n* (usu 通常作 ***the top (of)***) **1** highest part or point: 顶; 巅; 上端; 上部: *at the top of the hill;* 在山顶; *the hilltop;* 山顶; *at the top of the page;* 在书页上端; *line 5 from the top.* 从上面数下来第五行。***on top,*** above: 在上边: *The green book is at the bottom of the pile and the red one is on top.* 绿皮书在那一堆的底下, 红皮书在上边。***on (the) top of,*** **(a)** over, resting on: 在…之上: *Put the red book on (the) top of the others.* 把红皮书放在其他书的上面。**(b)** in addition to: 加之; 除…外: *He borrowed £50 from me for the journey and then, on top of that, asked me if he could borrow my car.* 他向我借五十英镑作旅费, 除此而外, 还向我借汽车。***from top to bottom,*** completely. 完全地; 全部地。***from top to toe,*** from head to foot. 从头到脚。***blow one's top,*** (colloq) explode in rage. (口)异常恼怒; 气炸了。***off the top of one's head,*** (of sth said) without careful thought or preparation. (指说出的话)未经仔细考虑或准备的。**2** upper surface, eg of a table: (桌子等的)上表面; 上边: *polish the top of a table/the table top;* 擦亮桌面; *put the luggage on the top of the car.* 把行李放在汽车顶上。***go over the top,*** (mil) go over the front of a trench to attack the enemy; (fig) act quickly after a period of doubt or hesitation. (军)爬出战壕攻击敌人; (喻)(经过一阵迟疑或犹豫后)迅速行动。***on top of the world,*** (colloq) extremely happy, satisfied with everything: (口)极为愉快; 万事如意; 样样满足; 诸事顺逐: *I'm feeling on top of the world today!* 今天我真觉得万事如意。**3** highest rank, foremost (or most important) place: 最高等级; 最前面或最重要的位置: *He came out at the top of the list,* eg of examination results. 他名列前茅(例如指考试的结果)。*Our host placed us at the top* (= the upper end) *of the table,* the part for honoured guests. 我们的主人安置我们坐在首席上。***come to the top,*** (fig) win fame, success, etc. (喻)成名、成功等。***reach/be at the top of the ladder/tree,*** the highest position in a profession, career, etc. 达到(居于)职业、事业等的最高地位; 达到(处于)颠峰。**4** utmost height or degree. 最高度; 最高级。***shout at the top of one's voice,***

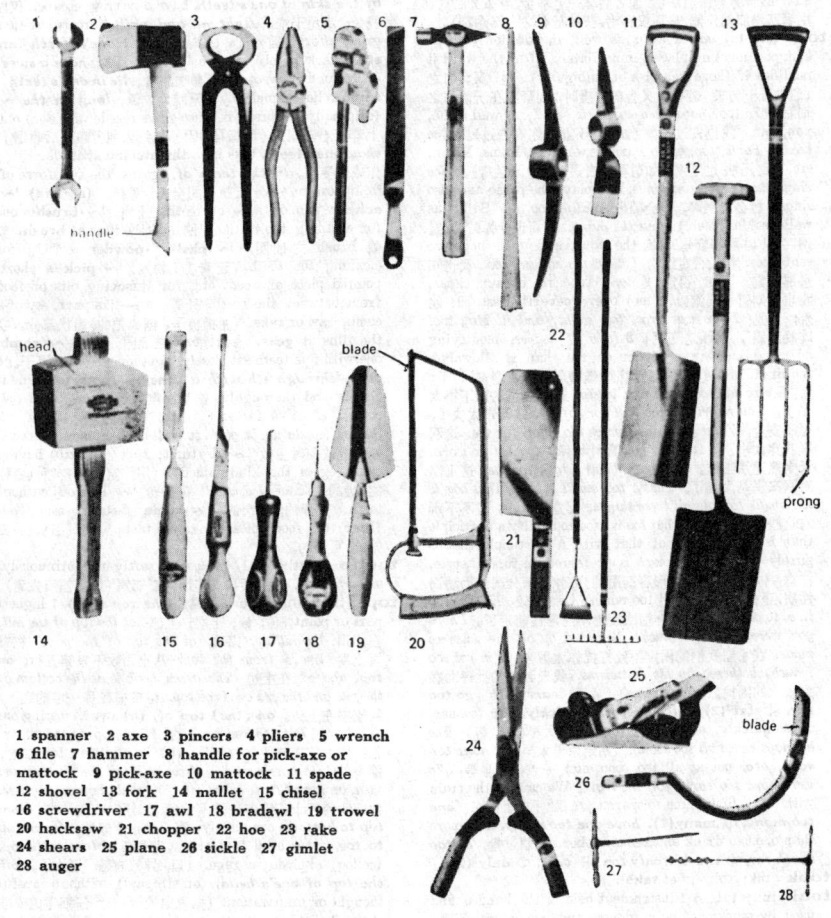

1 spanner 2 axe 3 pincers 4 pliers 5 wrench
6 file 7 hammer 8 handle for pick-axe or
mattock 9 pick-axe 10 mattock 11 spade
12 shovel 13 fork 14 mallet 15 chisel
16 screwdriver 17 awl 18 bradawl 19 trowel
20 hacksaw 21 chopper 22 hoe 23 rake
24 shears 25 plane 26 sickle 27 gimlet
28 auger

tools and implements

⇨ **voice**, *n*(3); **to the top of one's bent**, ⇨ **bent**[1]. **5** (motoring) (驾车) **in top**, in top (the highest) gear: 以高速挡; 全速地: *What will the car do in top?* 这车高速行驶的情况如何? **6** (often *pl*) leaves, etc of a plant grown chiefly for its roots: (常用复数) 根菜植物的叶子等: *'turnip tops.* 芜菁的叶子。 **7 the big top**, very large circus tent. 马戏团的大帐篷。 **8** (attrib, and in compounds) highest in position or degree: (用作定语, 并用于复合词中) 地位或程度最高的; 最大的: *on the top shelf;* 在最高一层架子上; *at top speed;* 全速地; 以全速; *in top gear;* (驾车) 全速; 以高速挡; *the top right-hand corner;* 右上角; *charge top prices.* 讨高价。 **'top-boot** *n* boot with a high top, usu reaching to just below the knee. 长筒(及膝)马靴。 **'top-coat** *n* overcoat. 大衣; 外套。 **be top dog**, (sl) victor, master. 〈俚〉优胜者; 主人。 ⇨ **underdog**. **,top 'drawer** *n* the highest social class: 社会最高阶层; 上流社会: *She's out of the top drawer / is very top drawer.* 她出身上流社会。 **,top-'dress** *vt* apply

(manure, etc) to the surface of (ground) instead of ploughing or digging it in; 施(肥料等)于地面; 施追肥; 施顶肥; Hence, 由此产生, **,top-'dressing** *n*: 追肥; 顶肥; *give a field a top-dressing of lime.* 在田地上施石灰。 **,top-'flight / -'notch** *attrib adjj* (colloq) first-rate; best possible: (口)第一流的; 最好的: *top-flight French authors.* 法国的第一流作家。 **,top-'gallant** *adj, n* mast, sail, etc immediately above the topmast and topsail. 上桅(帆); 上桅(帆)的。 ⇨ the illus at **barque.** 参看 barque 之插图。 **,top 'hat** *n* tall silk hat. 高顶丝质礼帽。 **,top-'heavy** *adj* over-weighted at the top so as to be in danger of falling. 上部过重的; 头重脚轻的; 不稳的。 **,top-'hole** *adj* (dated sl) excellent; first-rate. (过时俚语)最优的; 第一流的。 **'top-knot** *n* knot of hair, bunch of feathers, etc on the top of the head. 冠毛; 顶髻; 头饰。 **'top-mast** *n* upper mast (clamped to the mainmast). 中桅(夹于主桅上)。 **'top-most** / -məʊst; -,məʊst / *adj* highest. 最高的; 最上的。 **,top 'people**, those at the top

of their profession, holding the highest positions, etc: (某一行业的)顶尖人物; 高阶层人士: *Not all top people read 'The Times'.* 并非所有上层人物阅读 '泰晤士报'。 ,top·'ranking *adj* of the highest rank. 最高等级的。 'top·sail *n* square sail next above the lowest. 中桅帆。 ⇨ the illus at **barque.** 参看 barque 之插图。,top 'secret, most secret. 绝对机密的。 **top·less** *adj* (of a woman's garment) leaving the breasts bare: (指女装)上空的; 露出胸部的: *a topless dress/swimsuit:* 上空装(上空游泳衣); (of a woman) wearing such a garment: (指女子)穿着上空装的: *topless waitresses in California.* 加州穿上空装的女侍。

top² /tɒp; tɑp/ *vt* (**-pp-**) [VP6A] **1** provide a top for; be a top for; be a top to: 加以顶; 作为…之顶端: *a church topped by/with a steeple.* 顶部有尖阁的礼拜堂。**2** reach the top of; be at the top of: 达于…之顶峰; 居于…的最高位: *When we topped the hill we had a fine view.* 当我们爬到山顶时，看到了优美的景色。**3** *top (sth) up,* fill up (a partly empty container): 装满(部分尚空的容器): *top up a car battery,* add distilled water to raise the level to what is normal; 把汽车电瓶里的蒸馏水加满足; *top up with oil,* add lubricating oil; 加润滑油; *top up a drink,* refill a partly emptied glass. 加满(原来未满的)杯中的酒去饮料。*top (sth) out,* mark the completion of a tall building (a tower block, etc) with drinks, speeches, etc: 借举杯、演讲等以庆祝某一高耸建筑物的落成: *a ,topping-'out ceremony.* 高大建筑落成典礼。**4** surpass; be taller or higher than: 超越; 高过; 胜过: *Our exports have just topped the £80 000 000 mark.* 我们的出口贸易刚刚超过八千万镑。*to 'top it all,* to crown all, add the last (and surprising, etc) touch; 最妙的是; 增添最后(而令人惊异等)的一笔。**5** cut the tops off: 截去顶端: *lift and top beets/turnips,* take them from the ground and cut off the leaves; 拔起甜菜(芜菁)并去其叶; *top and tail gooseberries,* remove the ends from the berries. 除去醋栗的末梢。

top³ /tɒp; tɑp/ *n* toy that spins and balances on a point, set in motion by hand, or by winding round it a string which is pulled away, and (in some cases) kept in motion by being whipped. 陀螺(一种玩具)。*sleep like a top,* soundly. 睡得很熟。

to·paz /'təʊpæz; 'tɔpæz/ *n* [U] transparent yellow mineral; [C] gem cut from this. 黄玉矿; 黄玉; 黄晶。

tope /təʊp; top/ *vi, vt* [VP2A, 6A] (dated) drink (alcoholic liquors) to excess; drink habitually. (过时用语)饮(酒)过量; 经常饮酒。**toper** *n* person who ~s. 酒鬼;过量或经常饮酒者。

topi /'təʊpi US: təʊ'pi:; təʊ'pi/ *n* sun-helmet. 遮阳盔; 兜帽。

topi·ary /'təʊpɪərɪ US: -ɪerɪ; 'təpɪ,ɛrɪ/ *n* [U], *adj* (concerned with) the clipping of shrubs, eg yew, into ornamental shapes, eg birds, animals: 修剪灌木(使成装饰形式的,如将紫杉修剪作鸟兽形); 修剪灌木的: *the ~ art;* 灌木修剪术; *a ~ garden.* 修剪过的花园。

topic /'tɒpɪk; 'tɑpɪk/ *n* subject for discussion. 论题; 话题; 题目。**topi·cal** /-kl; -kl/ *adj* of present interest; of ~s of the day: 与目前有关的; 时事问题的: *a ~al 'news film,* of current events. 时事影片。**topi·cally** /-klɪ; -klɪ/ *adv*

top·ogra·phy /tə'pɒgrəfɪ; tə'pagrəfɪ/ *n* [U] (description of the) features, eg rivers, valleys, roads, of a place or district. 地形; 地志; 地形学。**topo·graphi·cal** /ˌtɒpə'græfɪkl; ˌtapə'græfɪkl/ *adj* **topo·graphi·cally** /-klɪ; -klɪ/ *adv*

top·per /'tɒpə(r); 'tɑpə/ *n* (colloq) top hat. (口)高帽; 礼帽。

top·ping /'tɒpɪŋ; 'tɑpɪŋ/ *adj* (colloq) excellent. (口)第一流的; 最优的。**~·ly** *adv*

topple /'tɒpl; 'tɑpl/ *vi, vt* [VP2A, C, 6A, 15B] (cause to) be unsteady and overturn: (使)摇摇欲坠; (使)倾覆; 倒下: *The chimney ~d and fell.* 烟囱倾倒了。

The pile of books ~d over/down. 那一堆书倒了。*The dictator was ~d from power.* 那独裁者被推翻了。

tops /tɒps; tɑps/ *n pl* (usu 通常作 the tops) (colloq) the very best. (口)最佳者; 最好者。

topsy-turvy /ˌtɒpsɪ 'tɜːvɪ; ˌtɑpsɪ'tɜvɪ/ *adj, adv* (colloq) in confusion; upside down: (口)混乱的(地); 颠倒的(地): *The whole world is/has turned ~.* 整个世界是混乱的(已混乱)。**~·dom** /-dəm; -dəm/ *n* condition of being ~. 混乱; 颠倒。

toque /təʊk; tok/ *n* (woman's) small, brimless, close-fitting hat. (妇女的)小圆帽; 无边女帽。

tor /tɔː(r); tɔr/ *n* small hill, rocky peak (esp in place-names on Dartmoor, S W England): 冈; 岩山(尤用于英格兰西南部达特木的地名中): *Hay Tor.* 赫冈。

torch /tɔːtʃ; tɔrtʃ/ *n* **1** piece of wood, twisted flax, etc treated with oil, soaked in tallow, etc for carrying or using as a flaming light; (fig) sth that gives enlightenment: 火炬; 火把; (喻)启发之物: *the ~ of learning;* 学问之光; *hand on the ~,* keep knowledge, etc alive. 使知识等继续不衰; 传薪火。*carry a ~ for sb,* have (esp unrequited) love for him. 爱上某人; (尤指)单恋(某人)。**'~·light** *n* [U] light of a ~ or ~es: 火炬光: *a ~light procession/tattoo,* one in which lighted ~es are used. 火炬游行。**'~-race** *n* (in ancient Greece) performance of runners who handed lighted ~es to others in relays. (古希腊)火炬接力赛跑。**'~-singer** *n* woman who sings sentimental love-songs. 唱感伤恋歌的女歌手。**2** (GB) electric hand-light (US 美=*flashlight*); (US) blow-lamp (for welding, etc). (英)手电筒; (美)(焊接等用的)吹灯。

tore /tɔː(r); tɔr/ *pt of* tear².

tor·ea·dor /'tɒrɪədɔː(r) US: 'tɔr:-; 'tɔrɪə,dɔr/ *n* Spanish bullfighter (usu mounted on a horse). 西班牙的斗牛士(通常指骑马者)。

tor·ment /'tɔːment; 'tɔrment/ *n* [C, U] (sth that causes) severe bodily or mental pain or suffering: (身体或心灵的)剧烈的痛苦或烦恼; 痛苦或烦恼之因: *be in ~;* 受苦; 受折磨; *suffer ~(s) from an aching tooth;* 忍受牙痛折磨; *the ~s of jealousy.* 嫉妒的苦恼。*What a little ~ that child is!* (because it worries, asks constant questions, etc). 那孩子多烦人啊! □ *vt* /tɔː'ment; tɔr'ment/ [VP6A, 15A] cause severe suffering to; annoy: 使受剧烈痛苦; 使烦恼; 折磨: *~ed with neuralgia/hunger/mosquitoes.* 为神经痛(饥饿、蚊子)所苦。*Stop ~ing your father by asking silly questions.* 别再同一些愚蠢的问题折磨你父亲了。**tor·men·tor** /tɔː'mentə(r); tɔr'mentə/ *n sb* or sth that ~s. 使痛苦的人或物; 造成苦恼的人或物; 折磨者。

torn /tɔːn; tɔrn/ *pp of* tear².

tor·nado /tɔː'neɪdəʊ; tɔr'nedo/ *n* (*pl* ~es /-dəʊz; -doz/) violent and destructive whirlwind. 龙卷风; 陆龙卷。

tor·pedo /tɔː'piːdəʊ; tɔr'pido/ *n* (*pl* ~es /-dəʊz; -doz/) cigar-shaped self-propelling shell filled with explosives, aimed at ships (from surface ships, submarines and aircraft), and launched to travel below the surface of the sea. 鱼雷。**'~-boat** *n* small, fast warship from which ~es are fired. 鱼雷艇。**'~-tube** *n* tube from which ~es are discharged. 鱼雷发射管。□ *vt* [VP6A] attack or destroy with a ~ or ~es; (fig) attack (a policy, institution, etc) and make it ineffective: 以鱼雷袭击或摧毁; (喻)破坏(某项政策, 某一制度等): *Who ~ed the Disarmament Conference?* 谁破坏裁军会议?

tor·pid /'tɔːpɪd; 'tɔrpɪd/ *adj* **1** dull and slow; inactive. 呆钝的; 不活泼的。**2** (of animals that hibernate) not moving or feeling. (指冬眠动物)蛰伏的。**~·ly** *adv* ~·ness, ~·ity /tɔː'pɪdətɪ; tɔr'pɪdətɪ/ *nn* [U] ~ condition. 呆钝; 不活泼; 蛰伏。

tor·por /'tɔːpə(r); 'tɔrpə/ *n* [U, C] torpid condition. 呆钝; 不活泼; 蛰伏。

torque /tɔːk; tɔrk/ *n* **1** [C] necklace, collar or arm-

band of twisted metal, as worn by the ancient Britons and Gauls. (古 不列顛人及高卢人佩用的)捻扭的金属项圈、领圈或臂圈。**2** [U] twisting force causing rotation, eg as exerted on a ship's propeller shaft. 扭(力)矩; 转(力)矩(如施于船的螺旋浆轴者)。

tor·rent /'tɒrənt US: 'tɔːr-; 'tɔrənt/ n [C] **1** violent, rushing stream of liquid (esp water): (尤指水的)急流; 湍流: mountain ~s; 山洪; ~s of rain; 雨水的急遽下降; 大雨如注; rain falling in ~. 倾盆大雨。**2** (fig) violent outpouring: (喻)爆发; 迸发; 连续不断: a ~ of words/abuse/insults. 连续不断的话(漫骂、凌辱)。 **tor·ren·tial** /tə'renʃəl/ adj of, like, caused by, a ~: 急流的; 湍流的; 似急流的; 由急流形成的: ~ial rain. 暴雨。

tor·rid /'tɒrɪd US: 'tɔːr-; 'tɔrɪd/ adj (of the weather, a country) very hot; tropical: (指天气、国家)很热的; 热带的: the '~ zone, part of the earth's surface between the tropics(1). 热带。 **~·ity** n [U] extreme heat. 酷热; 炎热。

tor·sion /'tɔːʃn; 'tɔrʃən/ n [U] act or process of twisting; state of being twisted. 扭; 捻; 扭转; 被扭的状态。

torso /'tɔːsəʊ; 'tɔrso/ n (pl ~s) (statue of a) human body without head, arms and legs. (无头和四肢的)躯干雕像; 人体的躯干。

tort /tɔːt; tɔrt/ n (legal) private or civil wrong for which the wronged person may get redress in a law court. (法律)民事过失; 侵权行为(受害者可在法庭上获得损害赔偿)。

tor·tilla /tɔː'tiːjə; tɔr'tija/ n pancake omelette (Mexican style). 托厄亚(墨西哥式薄玉米煎饼)。

tor·toise /'tɔːtəs; 'tɔrtəs/ n slow-moving, four-legged land (and fresh-water) varieties of turtle with a hard shell. 龟; 陆龟。 ⇔ the illus at **reptile**. 参看 reptile 之插图。 **'~-shell** n [U] outer shell, esp the kind with yellow and brown markings, of some sea-turtles. 海龟甲; (尤指有黄色和褐色斑点之)玳瑁壳。

tor·tu·ous /'tɔːtʃʊəs; 'tɔrtʃʊəs/ adj full of twists and bends: 弯曲的; 多扭曲的: a ~ path; 弯曲的小路; (fig) not straightforward; devious: (喻)不正直的; 不正当的; 拐弯抹角的: a ~ argument/policy/politician. 拐弯抹角的议论(不正当的政策; 不正直的政客)。 **~·ly** adv

tor·ture /'tɔːtʃə(r); 'tɔrtʃə/ vt [VP6A, 16A] cause severe suffering to: 使受剧烈痛苦; 折磨: ~ a man to make him confess sth; 对某人施刑使招认某事; 拷问; 刑求; ~d with anxiety. 为烦恼所苦。 □ n **1** [U] torturing; infliction of severe bodily or mental suffering: 折磨; 拷问; 对身心的折磨: put a man to the ~, 对某人施(刑)(esp to get a confession or to make him supply information): 折磨某人; (尤指)拷问; 刑求; instruments of ~. 刑具。 **2** [C, U] pain so inflicted or suffered; method of torturing: (折磨或刑求所造成的)痛苦; 折磨或拷问的方法: suffer ~ from toothache; 因牙痛而受折磨; the ~s of the damned, ie in Hell. 地狱中永劫不复的灵魂所受的痛苦。 **tor·turer** n

Tory /'tɔːrɪ; 'tɔrɪ/ n (pl -ries) = **Conservative**.

tosh /tɒʃ; taʃ/ n (sl) nonsense. 胡言乱语; 瞎扯。

toss /tɒs US: tɔs; tɔs/ vt, vi **1** [VP6A, 12A, 13A, 15B] throw up into or through the air; jerk: 投; 掷; 抛: a ball to sb; 投球给某人; ~ sth aside/away. 把某物丢在一边(丢开)。 The horse ~ed its rider, caused the rider to fall to the ground. 那马把骑者摔落(地上)。 He ~ed the beggar a coin/~ed a coin to the beggar. 他丢给那乞丐一个铜板。 The horse ~ed its head. 那马抬起头。 She ~ed her head back, ie with a suggestion of contempt, indifference, etc. 她把头往上一扬(表示轻视、冷漠等)。 He was ~ed by the bull. 他被那只公牛抵抛在地上。 **(up) a coin; ~ (sb) for sth; ~ up**, send a coin spinning up in the air and guess which side will be on top when it falls; use this method to decide sth (with sb): 掷铜板(以猜其正反面); (与某人)掷铜板以作决定: Who's to pay for the drinks? Let's ~ up/Let's ~ for

it. 谁来付饮料的钱呢? 让我们掷铜板决定吧。 **'~-up** n such ~ing of a coin; (hence) sth about which there is doubt: 掷钱币; (由此产生)有疑问的事: It's a ~up whether he will get here in time. 他是否能及时来此地, 尚有疑问。 **2** [VP2C, 6A, 15A, B] (cause to) move restlessly from side to side or up and down: (使)摇荡; (使)摇摆; 颠簸: The ship (was) ~ed about on the stormy sea. 那条船在汹涌的海上颠簸不定。 The sick child ~ed about in its sleep all night. 病童整夜在睡眠中辗转反侧。 The branches were ~ing in the wind. 树枝在风中摇曳。 **~ sth off, (a)** drink sth straight down. 一饮而尽。 **(b)** produce sth quickly and without much thought or effort: 迅速地写成报纸文章。 ~ off a newspaper article. 迅速地写成报纸文章。 □ n [C] **1** ~ing movement: 投; 掷; 抛; 摇荡: a contemptuous ~ of the head; 轻蔑地把头一扬; take a ~, (esp) be thrown from the back of a horse. 跌下; (尤指)从马背上摔下。 **2** win/lose the ~**, guess correctly/incorrectly when a coin is ~ed up (esp at the beginning of a game): 掷钱币猜中(猜错); 掷赢(输)(尤指比赛开始时)。

tot¹ /tɒt; tat/ n **1** (often 常作 **tiny tot**) very small child. 小孩; 小娃娃。 **2** (colloq) small glass of liquor. (口)小杯的酒; 少量的酒。

tot² /tɒt; tat/ vt, vi (-tt-) [VP15B, 2C] (colloq) add up: (口)加; 总计: expenses totting up to £5; 合计五英镑的费用; tot up a column of figures. 把一行数字加起来。

to·tal /'təʊtl; 'totl/ adj complete; entire: 完全的; 全部的; 全体的: ~ silence; 寂静无声; be in ~ ignorance of sth. 全然不知某事。 What are your ~ debts? 你的全部债务有多少? There was a ~ eclipse of the sun. 有一次日全蚀。 **~ war**, war in which all the resources of a country (manpower, industry, etc) are involved. 总体战。 □ n [C] amount: 总数; 总额: Our expenses reached a ~ of £20. 我们的花费总计达二十英镑。 What does the ~ come to? 总数若干? □ vt, vi (-ll-, US also -l-) [VP6A, 2C] find the ~ of; reach the ~; amount to: 总计; 共计; 总数达: The visitors to the exhibition ~led 15 000. 展览会的参观者达一万五千人。 It ~s up to £16. 总计十六英镑。 **~·ly** /'təʊtəlɪ; 'totlɪ/ adv completely: 完全地; 全部地: ~ly blind. 全盲的。 **~·ity** /təʊ'tælətɪ; to'tæləti/ n entirety; (esp) period during which an eclipse is ~. 全体; 全部; (尤指)(日、月)全蚀的时间。

to·tali·tar·ian /,təʊtælɪ'teərɪən; ,to,tælə'tɛrɪən/ adj of a political system in which only one political party and no rival loyalties are permitted: 极权主义的: a ~ State, eg Germany under Hitler. 极权国家(如希特勒统治下的德国)。 **~·ism** /-ɪzəm; -,ɪzəm/ n

to·tal·iz·ator /'təʊtəlaɪzeɪtə(r) US: -lɪz-; 'totlə,zetɔ/ n machine for registering bets (eg on horses) with a view to dividing the total amount among those who bet on the winners. (赛马等的)赌金计算机。

tote¹ /'təʊt; tot/ n (colloq abbr of) **totalizator**. (口) 为 totalizator 之略。

tote² /təʊt; tot/ vt [VP6A] (sl) carry (esp a gun) (俚)携带; 荷(尤指枪): He ~s a six-shooter. 他带着一支六发左轮手枪。

to·tem /'təʊtəm; 'totəm/ n [C] natural object, esp an animal, considered, esp by N American Indians, to have a close connection with a family group. 图腾(北美印第安人等认为与其家族有密切关系的自然物, 尤指动物)。 **'~-pole** n one on which is carved or painted a series of ~s. 图腾柱(刻有或绘有一系列图腾者)。

tot·ter /'tɒtə(r); 'tatə/ vi [VP2A, C] **1** walk with weak, unsteady steps; get up unsteadily: 以软弱而不稳定的步子走路; 不稳地起立; 蹒跚: The wounded man ~ed to his feet. 伤者不稳地站了起来。 **2** be almost falling; seem to be about to collapse: 摇摇欲坠; 行将倒塌: The tall chimney-stack ~ed and then fell. 那座高烟囱摇摇晃晃, 然后倒了下来。 **~·y** adj unsteady; insecure. 不稳的; 摇动的; 蹒跚的。

tou·can /'tu:kæn; 'tukæn/ n kinds of tropical American bird with brightly coloured feathers and an immense beak. 鸚鵡; 巨嘴鳥(產于美洲熱帶, 有彩色鮮艷的羽毛及巨喙)。 ⇨ the illus at **rare**. 參看 rare 之插圖。

touch¹ /tʌtʃ; tʌtʃ/ n **1** [C] act or fact of touching: 觸; 接觸: I felt a ~ on my arm. 我覺得臂上有人摸了一下。 Even the slightest ~ will break a soap-bubble. 即使最輕微的一觸也會弄破一個肥皂泡。 at a ~, if touched, however lightly. 一觸即; 一碰就。 **2** [U] (sense giving) feeling by touching: 觸覺; 觸感: soft/rough to the ~, when touched; 摸起來柔軟(粗糙); the cold ~ of marble. 觸摸大理石的冰冷感覺。 '~-stone n sth used as a test or standard (of purity, etc); criterion. 試金石; (批評、判斷等的)標準; 準則。 **3** [C] stroke made with a brush, pen, etc: (刷、筆等的)一揮; 一筆; 一畫; 一觸; 筆劃; 筆法; 筆致: add a few finishing ~es (to a drawing or any piece of work); 添加最後的幾筆; give a horse a ~ of the spurs. 以馬刺驅策馬。 **4** [C] a ~ (of), slight quantity, trace: 少許; 微量: a ~ of frost in the air; 空氣中少許的霜; have a ~ of the sun, slight sunstroke; 輕微中暑; a ~ of irony/bitterness in his remarks; 他話中諷刺(怨恨)的意味; have a ~ (= a slight attack) of rheumatism. 害輕微的風濕症。 **5** [C] style or manner of touching the keys, strings, etc of a musical instrument, etc of workmanship (in art): 彈奏法; 觸鍵法;(藝術作品的)風格; 特征: the ~ of a master, expert style, eg in painting; 大師手法或風格; a sculpture with a bold ~; 作風豪邁的雕刻作品; have a light ~, eg on a piano, a typewriter; 以輕觸法(彈鋼琴、打字等); the (eg) 'Nelson ~, the bold way of dealing with a situation characteristic of (eg) Nelson. 納爾遜(等)的作風;處事大膽的作風。 '~-type vi [VP2A] type without looking at the typewriter keyboard (because familiar with it). 觸打(不看打字機鍵盤, 憑熟練的指法打字)。 **6** [U] communication. 聯系。 in/out of ~ (with), in /not in regular communication (with); having/not having information about: 與…有(無)聯系; 有(無)…的消息: keep in ~ with old friends; 與老友保持聯系; be out of ~ with the political situation. 對政局生疏。 lose ~ (with), be out of ~ with: (與…)失去聯系: If we correspond regularly we shan't lose ~. 如果我們經常通信, 我們就不會失去聯系。 **7** (football and Rugby) part of the pitch outside the side-lines: (足球, 橄欖球)邊線區域: The ball is in/out of ~. 球在(已出)邊線區。 '~-line n side line of the field of play. (足球場, 橄欖球場的)邊線。 ⇨ goal-line at **goal**; ⇨ the illus at **football, Rugby.** 參看 football, Rugby 之插圖。 **8** a near ~, a narrow escape. 九死一生; 幸免于難。 '~-and-'go adj (colloq) risky; of uncertain result: (口)危險的; 結果不定的; 無把握的: It was ~-and-go whether the doctor would arrive in time. 醫生能否及時到達并無把握。 It was ~-and-go with the sick man, uncertain whether he would live. 那病人情況危篤。 **9** a soft/easy ~, (sl) sb from whom one can beg or borrow easily. (俚)好講話的人; 好好先生。 ⇨ ~ sb for sth, at **touch²(11).**

touch² /tʌtʃ; tʌtʃ/ vt, vi (For special uses with adverbial particles and preps, see ⇨ 11 below.) (與副詞性小品詞及介詞連用的特殊用法, 參看下列第 11 義。) **1** [VP6A, 15A, B, 2A](cause to) be in contact with; be separated from at one or more points by no space or object; bring a part of the body (esp the hand) into contact with: (使)接觸; 碰及; 觸摸: One of the branches is ~ing the water. 有一根樹枝碰到了水面。 The two farms ~ (each other), have, in part, a common boundary. 這兩塊農田(彼此)相毗鄰。 Can you ~ (= reach with your hand) the top of the door? 你能夠得到門頂嗎? The mountains seemed to ~ the clouds. 群山似乎觸及雲霄。 Visitors (eg in a museum) are requested not to ~ the exhibits. 游客請勿觸摸陳列品。 He ~ed me on the arm/shoulder, eg to attract my attention. 他碰我的臂(肩)(如促我注意)。 I merely ~ed the eggs together and they cracked. 我只不過

把這些蛋放在一起, 它們就破了。 The thermometer ~ed 35°C yesterday. 昨天氣溫高達三十五攝氏度。 ~ bottom, (a) reach the bottom: 到達底部: The water isn't deep here; I can just ~ bottom, ie with my feet. 這里的水不深, 我能觸到底。 (b) (fig) reach the lowest point of misfortune, depravity, etc. (喻)到達極度不幸、墮落等。 ~ wood, sth made of wood in the belief that one will avert ill luck: 摸觸木制物以避邪霉運或不幸; 觸木辟邪: I've never been in a road accident—~ wood. 我從未出過車禍——觸木辟邪(一面說一面觸摸木制物以避開霉運)。 **2** [VP6A] apply a slight or gentle force to: 輕觸; 輕輕地施力于: He ~ed the bell, rang it by pressing the button. 他輕輕按鈴。 He ~ed the keys of the piano. 他輕觸鋼琴鍵。 **3** [VP6A] (usu in neg) compare with; be equal to: (通常用于否定句中)匹敵; 及得上; No one can ~ him as an actor of tragic roles. 作為一個悲劇角色的演員, 沒有人及得上他。 There's nothing to ~ mountain air for giving you an appetite. 沒有東西及得上山間清新的空氣更能促進你的食欲了。 **4** [VP6A] (usu neg) take (food, drink): (通常用于否定句中)吃; 喝: He hasn't ~ed food for two days. 他兩天未吃東西了。 **5** [VP6A] affect (a person or his feelings); concern: 感動(某人或其情緒); 關心: The sad story ~ed us/our hearts. 那悲慘的故事令我們感動。 We were all ~ed with remorse/pity when we heard what had happened. 當我們聽到所發生的事故時, 我們的內心感到懊悔 (憐憫)。 **6** [VP6A] have to do with: 關涉; 涉及; 論及; 談及: What you say does not ~ the point at issue. 你所說的未涉及討論的主題。 The question ~es your interests closely. 該問題與你的利益有密切關系。 **7** [VP6A] injure slightly: 微傷; 微損: The apple-blossom was ~ed by the frost. 蘋果的花瓣受霜害。 The valuable paintings were not ~ed by the fire. 那些名畫未遭火災波及。 **8** (pp ~ed) (colloq) slightly mad or deranged: (口)微瘋的; 精神有點錯亂的: He seems to be a bit ~ed. 他似乎有點精神錯亂。 **9** [VP 6A,15A] rouse painful or angry feeling in; wound: 引起痛苦或憤怒; 傷害: You've ~ed his self-esteem. 你損傷了他的自尊。 You've ~ed him on a tender place (lit or fig); 你觸及他的痛處(字面或喻); ~ him to the ~ quick (n). **10** [VP6A] deal with; cope with; get a result from: 應付; 善處; 從…得到結果: Nothing I have used will ~ (= get rid of) these grease spots. 我用過的東西, 沒有一樣能除去這些油漬。 She couldn't ~ (= even begin to answer) the first two questions in the biology paper, ie in an examination. 她無法答出生物學試卷上的頭兩個問題。 **11** [VP3A, 2C, 15B] (special uses with adverbial particles and preps): (與副詞性小品詞及介詞連用的特殊用法):

touch at, (of a ship) call at: (指船)停靠: Our steamer ~ed at Naples. 我們的輪船會在那不勒斯停靠。

touch down, (a) (Rugby) ~ the ball on the ground behind the opponent's goal line. (橄欖球)底線得分; 挽球在對方球門線後以球觸地。 **(b)** (of aircraft) come down to land; alight. (指飛機)落地; 降落。 Hence, 由此產生, '~down n

touch sb for sth, (sl) get money from (by begging): (俚)(借乞求)從…得到錢: He ~ed me for a fiver (ie £5). 他乞求五英鎊。

touch sth off, discharge (a cannon, etc); (fig) cause to start: 發射(炮等);(喻)觸發; 引起: The arrest of the men's leaders ~ed off a riot. 逮捕那些人的首領觸發了一場暴動。

touch on/upon sth, treat (a subject) briefly. 簡略地論述(某題目)。

touch sth up, make small changes in (a picture, a piece of writing, etc) to improve it, give the finishing touches, etc. 修飾(圖畫、文章)。

touch·able /'tʌtʃəbl; 'tʌtʃəbl/ adj that may be touched. 可觸的; 可觸知的; 可被感動的。

touch·ing /'tʌtʃɪŋ; 'tʌtʃɪŋ/ adj pathetic; arousing pity or sympathy. 感傷的; 悲慘的; 引起憐憫或同情的。 □ prep concerning. 關于。 ~·ly adv

touchy /'tʌtʃɪ; 'tʌtʃɪ/ adj (-ier, -iest) easily or

quickly offended. 易怒的; 暴躁的. **touch·ily** /-ɪlɪ; -ɪlɪ/ *adv* **touchi·ness** *n*

tough /tʌf; tʌf/ *adj* (**-er, -est**) **1** (of meat) hard to cut or get one's teeth into. (指肉)坚韧的; 咬不动的. **2** not easily cut, broken or worn out: 强韧的; 不易切开、打破或磨损的: *as ~ as leather*. 坚韧如皮革. *T~ rubber is needed for tyres*. 强韧橡皮为制轮胎所需. **3** strong; able to endure hardships: 强壮的; 坚强的; 能耐劳苦的: *~ soldiers*. 能耐劳苦的军人. **4** (of persons) rough and violent: (指人)粗暴的; 凶恶的: *a ~ criminal*. 凶恶的罪犯. *~* **customer,** (colloq) person likely to cause trouble, unlikely to submit to control or discipline. (口)爱惹祸的人; 惹是生非者; 难驾驭者. **5** stubborn; unyielding. 偏强的; 固执的. *be/get ~ (with sb)*: (对某人)强硬: *The employers got ~ with/adopted a get-policy towards their workers*. 雇主们对他们的工人毫不让步(采取严峻措施). **6** hard to carry out; difficult: 难以执行的; 困难的: *a ~ job/problem*. 棘手的工作(问题). **7** *~ luck*, (colloq) bad luck. (口)坏运气; 霉运. □ *n* (also 亦作 **~ie** /'tʌfɪ; 'tʌfɪ/) (colloq) (= **~y**) (4) person. (口)粗暴的人; 凶恶的人. **~·ly** *adv* **~·ness** *n* **~·en** /'tʌfn; 'tʌfn/ *vt, vi* make or become *~.* (使)变坚韧; (使)变强壮; (使)变偏强.

tou·pee /'tuːpeɪ US: tuːˈpeɪ; tuˈpe/ *n* patch of false hair worn to cover a bald spot; small wig. (遮覆秃处的)一撮假发; 小顶假发.

tour /tʊə(r); tʊr/ *n* **1** journey out and home again during which several or many places are visited: 旅行; 漫游; 周游: *a round-the-world ~*; 环球旅行; *a coach ~ of France*; 乘坐长途汽车的法国旅行; *conducted ~s*, made by a group conducted by a guide. 导游旅行(有导游的团体旅行). **2** brief visit to or through: 短暂访问; 参观: *a ~ of the palace/house*. 参观皇宫(房舍). **3** period of duty (at a military or naval station overseas); interval between passage-paid home leaves (⇨ **leave²** (1)) in service abroad: (在海外陆海军基地的)任职期间; 海外服务期间: *a ~ of three years as a lecturer in the University of Ibadan*. 在伊巴丹大学担任讲师的三年海外服务期间. **4** round of (official) visits to institutions, units, etc: (至机构, 单位的)视察: *The Director leaves tomorrow on a ~ of overseas branches*. 董事长明天离此视察海外分支机构. **5** number of visits to places made by a theatrical company, etc. 剧团等赴各地之一连串访问; 巡回演出. *on ~*, visiting in this way: 巡回演出: *be/go on ~*; 作巡回演出; *take a company on ~ to perform three of Shakespeare's plays*. 率领剧团巡回演出三部莎士比亚戏剧. □ *vt, vi* [VP6A, 2A, C] make a *~* (of): (作…)旅行; 游历; 巡回; 漫游: *~ Mexico*. 漫游墨西哥. *They are ~ing in Spain*. 他们正在西班牙游历. *The play will ~ the provinces in the autumn*. 该剧将于秋天在各地巡回演出. *~·ing* *n, adj*: *a ~ing car*, one suitable for *~ing*; 游览车; *a ~ing party*. 旅行团. *~·ist* /-ɪst; -ɪst/ *n* **1** person making a *~* for pleasure: 旅行者; 游历者; 观光客: *London is full of ~ists in summer*. 伦敦在夏季有很多观光客. **2** (attrib) of or for *~s*: (用作定语)旅行的; 观光的: *a '~ist agency*; 旅行社; *a '~ist ticket*, one issued on special terms, eg at a lower price; 游览票(按特殊条件, 如低价, 所发售者); *'~ class*, (on liners, airliners) second class. (船、飞机上的)二等舱(座); 经济舱(座). *~·ism* /'tʊərɪzəm; 'tʊr,ɪzəm/ *n* [U] organized *~ing*: 游览; 观光; 观光事业: *Some countries obtain large sums of foreign exchange from ~ism*, from the money brought in by *~ists*. 有些国家靠观光事业赚取大量外汇.

tour de force /ˌtʊə də ˈfɔːs; ˌturdə'fɔrs/ *n* (F) feat of strength or skill. (法)力技; 技技; 绝技.

tour·na·ment /'tɔːnəmənt US: 'tɜːn-; 'tɜnəmənt/ *n* [C] **1** series of contests of skill between a number of players: 锦标赛; 比赛; 竞赛: *a 'tennis ~/chess ~*. 网球(国际象棋)比赛. **2** (in the Middle Ages) contest between knights on horseback, armed with blunted weapons. (中世纪之)武士的马上比武; 马上比武大会.

tour·ney /'tʊənɪ; 'tɜnɪ/ *n* = **tournament**(2).

tour·ni·quet /'tʊənɪkeɪ US: 'tɜːnɪkɪt; 'tʊrnɪ,kɛt/ *n* device for stopping a flow of blood through an artery by twisting sth tightly around a limb. 止血带; 压脉器.

tousle /'taʊzl; 'taʊzl/ *vt* [VP6A] put (esp the hair) into disorder by pulling it about, rubbing it, etc; make untidy: 弄乱(尤指头发); 使零乱: *a girl with ~d hair*. 蓬发女孩.

tout /taʊt; taʊt/ *n* person who worries others to buy sth, use his services, etc, esp one who sells information about race-horses; 招徕顾客者; 兜售物品者; (尤指)出售赛马情报者: *a 'ticket ~*, eg selling tickets for a major football match at a greatly inflated price. 售黄牛票者; 售票黄牛. □ *vi* [VP2A, 3A] *~ (for)*, act as a *~*: 招徕; 出售赛马情报: *There were men outside the railway station ~ing for the hotels*. 火车站外有人为旅馆招徕顾客.

tout en·sem·ble /ˌtuːt ɒn'sɒmbl; ˌtu,tä'säbl/ *n* (F) sth viewed as a whole; its general effect. (法)整体; 整体观念; 整体效果; 粗麻屑(用制绳索).

tow¹ /təʊ; to/ *vt* [VP6A, 15A, B] pull along by a rope or chain: 拖; 曳: *tow a damaged ship into port*; 将损坏的船拖进港; *tow a broken-down car to the nearest garage*. 将抛锚汽车拖至最近的修车厂. **'tow(ing)-line/-rope** *nn* one used in towing. 拖绳; 曳缆. **'tow(ing)-path** *n* path along the bank of a river or canal for use in towing, eg by horses pulling canal boats. (河或运河沿岸的)曳船路; 纤路. □ *n* [C, U] towing or being towed: 拖; 被拖; 曳: *have/give a boat in tow*. 拖一艘船. *Can we give you a tow?* 我们能帮你拖一下吗? *The lorry was on tow*. 那货车被拖曳前进. *He usually has his family in tow*, (colloq) has them with him. (口)他通常带着家人在一起.

tow² /təʊ; to/ *n* [U] coarse and broken fibres of flax, hemp, etc (for spinning or making rope). 粗麻屑(用制绳索).

to·ward(s) /tə'wɔːd(z) US: tɔːrd(z); tord(z)/ *prep* **1** approaching; in the direction of: 向; 对; 趋; 朝…的方向: *walking ~ the sea*; 向着海走去; *sit with one's back turned ~ the window*; 背向窗子坐下; *drifting ~ war*; 盲目地走向战争; *first steps ~ the abolition of armaments*. 走向废除军备的最初步骤. **2** as regards; in relation to: 对于; 关于: *Are his feelings ~ us friendly?* 他对我们友善吗? *What will the Government's attitude be ~ the plan?* 政府对于该项计划抱何态度? **3** for the purpose of (helping): 为了(帮助): *We must save money ~ the children's education*. 我们必须为了孩子的教育而存钱. **4** (of time) near: 将(指时间)接近: *~ the end of the century*; 将近该世纪的末尾; *~ evening*. 傍晚; 黄昏.

towel /'taʊəl; 'taʊəl/ *n* [C] piece of cloth or absorbent paper for drying or wiping sth wet (eg one's hands or body): 毛巾; 手巾; 抹布; 擦拭纸; 纸巾: *a 'bath-~*; 浴巾; *a 'roller-~*, an endless one on a revolving bar. 卷式毛巾; 环状毛巾(纸巾). **'~-rack/-horse** *nn* wooden frame for hanging *~s* on. (木制)毛巾架. **'~-rail** *n* (usu metal) rail for a *~* (eg near a wash-basin). (通常为金属的)毛巾杆. *throw in the ~*, ⇨ **throw¹**(12). □ *vt* (**-ll-,** US **-l-**) dry or rub oneself) with a *~*. 以毛巾擦干或擦搓(自己). **~·ling** (US = **~·ing**) *n* [U] material for *~s*. 毛巾料.

tower /'taʊə(r); 'taʊə/ *n* **1** tall, usu equal-sided (esp square) or circular building, either standing alone (eg as a fort, the *T~ of London*) or forming part of a church, castle or other large building (eg a college). 塔; 高楼(或为独立建筑物, 如堡垒, 伦敦塔, 或为构成教堂、城堡或大建筑物之一部分). ⇨ the illus at **church**. 参看church之插图. **2** (fig) (喻) *a ~ of strength,* a person who can be relied upon for protection, strength or comfort in time of trouble. 可依赖的人; 干城. **'water-~,** *n* that supports a large tank for the storage and distribution of water at high pressure. 水塔. **'~-block** *n* high block of flats or offices. 高楼区; 连幢高楼.

☐ *vi* [VP2C] rise to a great height, be very tall, esp in relation to the height of the surroundings: 高耸; 超越(尤指与周围的高度相比较而言): *the skyscrapers that* ∼ *over New York.* 高耸于纽约市的摩天大楼。∼ *above sb*, (fig, of eminent persons) greatly exceed in ability, in intellectual or moral qualities: (喻, 指杰出人士)在能力、智慧或道德方面超出或高于: *a man who* ∼*s above his contemporaries.* 超出其同时代的人。∼*·ing* *adj* (esp): (尤指): *in a* ∼*ing rage*, violently angry. 暴怒的。

town /taun/; taun/ *n* **1** centre of population larger than a village, smaller than, or not created, a city (and often used in contrast to *country*): 镇; 城镇; 市镇(大于村而尚未成为市, 常用做 country 的相对词): *Would you rather live in a* ∼ *or in the country?* 你愿意住在城里还是乡下? (In GB the word ∼ is used much more frequently than *city*, even when the place actually is a city, the word *city* being used chiefly in connection with local government affairs.) (在英国, town 远比 city 常用, 即使该地实际上为城市, 亦用 town 字, 一词主要用于地方政府事务方面。) ⇨ **city**(1). *be / go out on the* ∼, be / go out to enjoy the entertainment facilities of a ∼: 去城里取乐。*paint the* ∼ *red*, ⇨ **red**(1). **2** (attrib) (用作定语) ∼ **centre**, area around which public buildings, eg the town hall, the public library, are grouped. 市镇中心(如市政厅、图书馆等公共建筑集中地)。∼ **clerk**, official who keeps ∼ or city records. 镇执事; 镇书记(掌管案卷)。∼ **council**, governing body of a ∼. 镇(议)会。∼ **councillor**, member of a ∼ council. 镇议会会员; 镇会评议员。'∼*-gas* *n* manufactured gas for domestic and industrial use. 煤气; 自来瓦斯(将煤加热而制成, 供家庭及工业之用)。∼ **hall**, building with offices of local government and usu a hall for public events (meetings, concerts, etc). 市政厅; 镇公所; 市镇集会所。'∼ **house**, house in ∼, belonging to sb who also has a house in the country. 市内宅邸(属于在乡间另有住宅者)。∼ **planning**, preparation of plans for the regulated growth and improvement of ∼s. 都市计划。**3** (preceded by a *prep*, and without the *def* or *indef art*) the business, shopping, etc part of a ∼ (contrasted with the suburbs, etc): (前加介词, 不加冠词)市镇商业区; 闹市; 市中心区(与市郊等相对): *go to* ∼ *to do some shopping.* 到市区购物。*He's in* ∼ *today.* 他今天上街去了。*I'm going down* ∼ *this afternoon.* 我今天下午要到市区去。⇨ **downtown**. *go to* ∼, (sl) act, behave, without inhibitions, eg by spending lavishly, having a spree. (俚)放浪形骸; 举止无节制(如挥霍无度, 狂欢作乐等)。**4** (without the *def* or *indef art*) the chief city or ∼ in the neighbourhood (esp, in England, London): (不加冠词)附近的主要城市(在英格兰, 尤指伦敦): *He is spending the weekend in* ∼. 他正在伦敦度周末。*He went up to* ∼ *from Leeds.* 他从里兹前往伦敦。*Mr Green is not in* ∼*/is out of* ∼. 格林先生不在城里。*man about* ∼, fashionable man who spends much time amusing himself. 把很多时间花在享乐上的时髦人士; 花花公子。**5** *the* ∼, the people of a ∼: 市民; 全镇镇民; 市镇居民: *The whole* ∼ *was talking about it.* 全镇的人都在谈论此事。*the talk of the* ∼, ⇨ **talk**¹(3). **6 the** ∼, ∼s in general: 市镇通称: *Farm workers are leaving the country in order to get better paid work in the* ∼. 农场工人离开乡间, 为要在城市中获得待遇较好的工作。**7** '∼*'s·folk* *n pl* **(a)** (with *def art*) the people of the ∼ referred to. (与定冠词连用)市民; 全镇镇民。**(b)** (without *def art*) people who live in ∼s. (不加定冠词)住在镇里的人们。'∼*s·people* *n pl* = ∼sfolk. '∼*s·man* /-zmən; -zmən/ *n* (*pl* **-men**) **(a)** man who lives in a ∼. 住在镇里的人。**(b)** (often 常作 *fellow*-'∼*sman*) person who lives in one's own ∼. 本城居民; 同城市民。

tow·nee /tau'ni/; tau'ni/ *n* (derog) person who lives in a town and is ignorant of rural things. (贬)不谙农事的城市居民; 五谷不分的城里人。

town·ship /'taunʃip; 'taunʃip/ *n* **1** (US, Canada) subdivision of a county having certain powers of

government; district six miles square in US surveys of land. (美国, 加拿大)镇区(为郡下面的行政区划, 享有若干行政权); (美国土地测量)六英里见方的地区。**2** (S Africa) area, suburb, for houses, etc, of non-Europeans. (南非)非欧洲人居住的地或郊区。**3** (Australia) site laid out for a town. (澳大利亚)都市计划地区; 都市预留地。

tox·aemia (also **tox·emia**) /tɒk'si:mɪə; taks'imiə/ *n* [U] blood-poisoning. 血中毒症; 毒血症。

toxic /'tɒksɪk; 'taksɪk/ *adj* of, caused by, a toxin; poisonous. 毒的; 中毒的; 有毒的; 毒素的。∼*·ity* /tɒk-'sɪsətɪ; taks'ɪsəti/ *n* [U] quality or degree of being ∼: 毒性; 毒力: *study the* ∼*ity of insecticides.* 研究杀虫剂的毒性。**toxi·col·ogy** /,tɒksɪ'kɒlədʒɪ; ,taksɪ'kɑlədʒi/ *n* [U] branch of medical science dealing with the nature and effects of poisons. 毒理学; 毒物学(医学一分支)。**toxi·col·ogist** /-dʒɪst; -dʒɪst/ *n* student of, expert in, toxicology. 毒物学家; 理理学家。

toxin /'tɒksɪn; 'taksɪn/ *n* [C] poisonous substance, esp one formed by bacteria in plants and animals and causing a particular disease. 毒素(尤指细菌在动植物中所形成, 而引起某种疾病者)。

toy /tɔɪ; tɔɪ/ *n* **1** child's plaything; small thing meant for amusement rather than for serious use. 玩具。**2** (attrib) (用作定语) *toy dog/spaniel, etc*, small kinds kept as pets; (供玩赏的)小狗(长耳狗等); *toy soldier*, one made as a toy(1). 玩具士兵。'**toy·shop** *n* shop where toys are sold. 玩具店。☐ *vi* [VP3A] *toy with sth*, **1** amuse oneself (with); think not very seriously about: (以……)自娱; 不太认真地考虑: *He toyed with the idea of buying a yacht.* 他考虑买一艘游艇, 但不太认真。**2** handle carelessly or absent-mindedly: 玩弄; 不小心或心不在焉地要弄: *toying with a pencil.* 要弄铅笔。

trace¹ /treɪs; tres/ *n* **1** [U, C] mark, sign, etc showing that sb or sth has been present, that sth has existed or happened: 踪迹; 痕迹; 形迹: ∼*s of an ancient civilization.* 古代文明的遗迹。*The police were unable to find any* ∼ *of the thief.* 警察找不出那窃贼的任何踪迹。*We've lost all* ∼ *of them*, don't know where they are. 我们不知道他们现在何处。**2** [C] very small amount: 微量; 少许: *The postmortem showed* ∼ *of arsenic in the intestines.* 验尸显示肠内留有微量的砒霜。'∼ **element**, element of which a ∼ is necessary for the development of animal or plant life and without which growth is poor (eg manganese in the soil, for wheat and oats). 微量元素(此种元素之少量为动植物生长所必需, 如栽种小麦及燕麦时土壤中之锰)。

trace² /treɪs; tres/ *vt, vi* **1** [VP6A, 15B] ∼ *sth (out)*, draw, sketch, the course, outline, etc, of: 画出……的轮廓、路线、过程等; 描绘出; 标出: ∼ *out the site of an old castle*; 标出一古城堡的所在地; ∼ *(out) one's route on a map*; 在地图上画出某人行经的路线; (fig) (喻) ∼ *out a policy*, give its outlines. 厘订政策大纲。**2** [VP6A] copy (sth), eg by drawing on transparent paper the lines, etc on (a map, design, etc) placed underneath. 描摹。**3** [VP6A] write slowly and with difficulty: 缓慢而困难地书写: *He* ∼*d the words laboriously.* 他很费力地写了那几个字。**4** [VP6A, 15A, B, 2C] follow or discover (sb or sth) by observing marks, tracks, bits of evidence, etc: 追踪; 追溯; 探索: *The criminal was* ∼*d to Glasgow.* 那罪犯被追踪至格拉斯哥。*I cannot* ∼ (= cannot find, do not think I received) *any letter from you dated 1st June.* 我找不到(或想不出曾收到)你六月一日寄来的信。∼ *(sth/sb) back (to sth)*, **(a)** find the origin of by going back in time: 追究; 追溯; 回溯; 溯自: *He* ∼*s his descent back to an old Norman family.* 他的血统可追溯至一个古老的诺尔曼家族。*His fear of dogs* ∼*s back/can be traced to a childhood experience.* 他对狗的恐惧溯自他孩童时代的一次经验。**(b)** find the origin of by going back through evidence: (借证据而)找出根源; 源自; 来自: *The rumour was* ∼*d back to a journalist.* It was discovered that he had started it. 那项谣言来自一个新闻记者。**5** [VP6A] discover the

position, size, etc of (sth) from its remains: 由遗迹发现(某物)之位置、大小等; 探寻出: *Archaeologists have ~d many Roman roads in Britain.* 考古学家已在英国发现许多古罗马的道路。 **~·able** /-əbl; -əbl/ *adj* capable of being ~d (*to*). 可描摹的; 可追踪的; 可探寻的。 **~r** *n* **1** person who ~s(2). 描摹者。 **2** (often 常作 '*~r bullet / shell*) projectile whose course is made visible by a line of flame or smoke left behind it. 曳光弹。 '**~r element**, radioactive element which, when introduced into sth, can be ~d by the use of a Geiger counter. 放射示踪元素; 放射显迹剂(导入某物时, 可用盖氏计数器追踪). **trac·ing** *n* reproduction of (a map, design, etc) made by tracing(2). (地图、图案等的)复制; 摹绘。 '**tracing-paper** *n* [U] strong transparent paper on which tracings are made. (透明)摹图纸.

trace³ /treɪs; tres/ *n* [C] either of the leather straps, ropes, etc by which a wagon, carriage, cart, etc is pulled by a horse. (马车的)挽绳; 挽缰。 ⇨ the illus at **harness.** 参看 harness 之插图。 **kick over the ~s**, (fig) become undisciplined; refuse to accept control. (喻)变得不守纪律; 不受管束。

tracery /'treɪsərɪ; 'tresərɪ/ *n* [C, U] (*pl* **-ries**) ornamental arrangement of designs (eg as made by frost on glass, or of stonework in a church window); decorative pattern. 装饰的图案; 花纹(如玻璃上由霜结成者, 或教堂窗子上的石细工); 装饰花样。 ⇨ the illus at **window.** 参看 window 之插图。

tra·chea /trə'kɪə US: 'treɪkɪə; 'trekɪə /-kiː; -'ki·i/ (anat) windpipe. (解剖)气管。 ⇨ the illus at **respiratory.** 参看 respiratory 之插图。

tra·choma /trə'kəʊmə; trə'komə/ *n* [U] contagious eye disease causing inflammation of the inner surfaces of the eyelids. 沙眼; 颗粒性结膜炎。

track /træk; træk/ *n* [C] **1** line or series of marks left by a vehicle, person, animal, etc in passing along; path or rough road made by persons /animals: (车辆、行人、动物等经过后留下的)踪迹; 足迹; 痕迹; (人或动物)踏成的路或小径: *~s in the snow*, eg footprints; 雪上的踪迹(如足印); *follow the ~s left by a bear*; 跟踪熊的踪迹; *sheep~s across the moor*: 由羊群践出的越过荒野的小径; *a ~ through the forest.* 穿越森林的小路。 **be on sb's ~** /**on the ~ of sb**, be in pursuit of: 追踪: *The police are on the ~ of the thief.* 警察在追这踪那窃贼。 *I'm on his ~.* 我在追他。 **cover up one's ~s**, conceal one's movements or activities. 掩饰自己的行动或活动; 隐藏行踪。 **go off** /**keep to the beaten ~, ⇨ beaten. have a ,one-~ 'mind**, habitually follow the same line of thought; give all one's attention to one topic. 习惯性地循相同的思想路线; 固执于某种想法; 把全部注意力集中于一项问题上。 **keep** /**lose ~ of sb** /**sth**, keep in /lose touch with; follow /fail to follow the course or development of: 与…保持(失去)接触; 跟上(跟不上)…的进度或发展: *read the newspapers to keep ~ of current events.* 阅读报纸俾熟悉时事。 **make ~s**, (colloq) depart (usu in a hurry) (口)离开(通常为匆忙地): 跑开。 **make ~s for**, (colloq) go towards: (口)走向: *It's time we made ~s for home.* 是我们回家的时候了。 **in one's ~s**, (sl) where one stands, there and then: (俚)就在那里; 当场; 立即: *He fell dead in his ~s.* 他当场死去。 **off the ~**, (fig) away from the subject; following a wrong line of action. (喻)离题; 离谱; 出轨; 误入歧途。 **2** course; line taken by sth (whether marked or not): 进度; 路径; 某事物所采取的路线(标明或未标明者): *the ~ of a storm* /*comet* /*spacecraft.* 风暴(彗星, 太空船)的路线。 **3** set of rails for trains, etc: (火车等的)轨道; 辙: *single* /*double ~*, one pair /two pairs of rails. 单轨(双轨). *The train left the ~*, was derailed. 火车出轨了。 **on** /**from the wrong side of the ~s**, (US) from the part of a town that is socially inferior, the part lived in by poor people. (美)从(来自)低层社会; 出身贫寒。 **4** path prepared for racing (eg made of cinders, clinkers, etc): 跑道(如用煤渣、熔渣等铺成者): *a 'motor-racing*

'*cycling* /'*running ~*; 汽车比赛(单车比赛, 赛跑)的车道; (*attrib*) (用作定语) '*~-racing*; 径赛; '*~ events*, eg running races, contrasted with field events such as jumping, throwing the discus. 径赛项目(如赛跑)与田赛项目, 如跳高、跳远、掷铁饼等相对)。 ⇨ **suit** *n* loose-fitting warm suit worn by an athlete while not taking part in ~ events. 田径装(运动员在比赛时所着的宽松保暖装)。 **5** endless belt used instead of wheels on some tractors, military tanks, etc. (曳引车、战车等的)轮带; 履带。 □ *vt, vi* [VP6A, 15A, B] follow the ~ of. 追踪; 尾随: *~ an animal to its den.* 追踪动物至其窝穴。 '*~·ing station* *n* one which, by radar or radio, maintains constant contact with space-vehicles, etc. 追踪站(籍雷达或无线电与太空船等保持接触者)。 **~ sb** /**sth down**, find by searching: 追踪、搜索等而发现: *~ down a bear* /*a reference.* 搜寻出入熊(找到一项参考资料)。 **~ out**, trace (the course or development of sth) by examining ~s. 借研究踪迹、痕迹等而找到(某事物的进程或发展情形)。 **2** (cinema, TV) move a camera (mounted on a mobile platform) while taking a long shot (called *a* '*~ing shot*). (电影, 电视)摄取远距离镜头 a ~ing shot 时)转动或移动架于活动平台上的摄影机; 追踪摄影。 '**~ed** *adj* having ~s(5): 有轮带的; 有履带的: *~ed vehicles.* 履带车。 **~er** *n* person, esp a hunter, who ~s wild animals. 追踪野兽者; (尤指)猎人。 '**~er dog**, dog used in pursuing persons escaping from justice. (追踪逃犯的)追踪犬; 搜索犬。 '**~·less** *adj* having no ~s(1): 无踪的; 人迹未到的: *~less forests.* 无路的森林。

tract¹ /trækt; trækt/ *n* **1** stretch or area (of forest, farmland, etc): (森林、农地等的)广阔的地面; 区域: *the wide ~s of desert in N Africa.* 北非一片片的广大沙漠。 **2** system of related parts in an animal body: 动物身体上相关器官的系统; 道; 径; 束; 管; 域: *the di'gestive* /*re'spiratory ~s.* 消化(呼吸)道。

tract² /trækt; trækt/ *n* short printed essay on sth, esp a moral or religious subject. 小册子; 短文(尤指以道德或宗教为题材者)。

tract·able /'træktəbl; 'træktəbl/ *adj* easily controlled or guided. 易驾驶的; 易于引导的。 **trac·ta·bil·ity** /,træktə'bɪlətɪ; ,træktə'bɪlətɪ/ *n*.

trac·tion /'trækʃn; 'trækʃən/ *n* [U] (power used in) pulling or drawing sth over a surface: 拖; 曳; 牵引; 牵(引)力: *electric* /*steam ~*. 电力(蒸气力)牵引。 '**~-engine** *n* engine used for pulling heavy loads. (牵引重物的)牵引机.

trac·tor /'træktə(r); 'træktə/n powerful motor-vehicle used for pulling agricultural machinery (ploughs, drills, etc), or other heavy equipment. 拖拉机; 曳引机(用于拖引农业机械, 或其他笨重装备者)。 ⇨ the illus at **plough.** 参看 plough 之插图。

trad /træd; træd/ *n* [U] (colloq abbr of) traditional; (esp) jazz of the 1920's and 1930's played by a small group with simple rhythms and much improvisation. (口)为 traditional 之略; (尤指)一九二〇年代及一九三〇年代的传统爵士乐。

trade¹ /treɪd; tred/ *n* **1** [U] buying and selling of goods; exchange of goods for money or other goods; [C] particular branch of this: 买卖; 交易; 贸易; 商业; 某一行业: *Great Britain does a lot of ~ with some countries and not much with others.* 大不列颠与某些国家交易甚多, 与另一些国家则交易甚少。 *T~ was good last year.* 去年贸易良好。 *He's in the 'cotton* /*furniture* /*book, etc ~.* 他做棉花(家具, 书籍等)生意。 ,**stock-in-~**, ⇨ **stock**¹(1). **the ~**, (colloq) those engaged in the manufacture and sale of a certain commodity. (口)商人; 制造商。 '**~·mark** *n* design, special name, etc used to distinguish a manufacturer's goods from others; (fig) distinguishing characteristics: 商标; (喻)明显的特征: *He leaves his ~mark on all his undertakings.* 他做每件事情都会留下他那明显的特征。 '**~ name** *n* name given by manufacturers to a proprietary article. 商品名称; 专利品名称。 '**~ price** *n* the price charged by a

manufacturer or wholesaler to a retailer. 同业卖价; 批发价格。 ,~(s)-'union n organized association of workers in a ~ or group of ~s, formed to protect their interests, improve their conditions, etc. 工会; 职工协会。 ,~'unionism n [U] this system of association. 工会制度; 工会主义。 ,~'unionist n member of a ~union. 工会会员。 T~s Union Congress, (abbr 略作 TUC) association of British ~ unions. (英国的)工会联合会; 工会联盟; 全国总工会。 ,~-wind n strong wind blowing always towards the equator from the SE and NE. 信风; 贸易风(由东南或东北方向赤道吹来的强风)。 the T~s, these winds. 东南及东北信风。 **2** occupation; way of making a living, esp a handicraft: 职业; 谋生之道; (尤指)手艺: He's a weaver/mason/carpenter/tailor by ~. 他是织工(石匠, 木匠, 裁缝)。 Shoemaking is a useful ~. 制鞋是一种有用的手艺。 The college teaches many useful ~s. 该学院传授许多有用的手艺。 '~s-folk, '~s-people nn persons engaged in ~; shopkeepers (and their families). 商人; 开店者(及其家属)。 '~s-man /-zmən; -zmən/ u (pl -men) shopkeeper. 开店者;店主。

trade² /treɪd; tred/ vi, vt **1** [VP2A, C, 3A] ~ (in) (with), engage in trade(1); buy and sell: 做生意; 从事贸易; 买卖: ~ in furs and skins; 做皮货生意; ships that ~ between London and ports in the Mediterranean. 往来于伦敦与地中海各港口的贸易船。 Britain ~s with many European countries. 英国与很多欧洲国家贸易。 'trading estate, (usu large) planned industrial area rented to manufacturers. 计划工业区(租给厂商使用,通常为大工业区)。 'trading stamp, (= gift coupon) coupon given to customers with purchases, exchangeable for various articles or cash. (购物时附带的)赠券(可换取他物或现金)。 **2** [VP14] ~ sth for sth, exchange; barter: 交换; 交易; 易物: The boy ~d his knife for a cricket bat. 那男孩用他的刀子换了一个板球棒。 **3** [VP15B] ~ sth in, hand over (a used article) in part payment for a new purchase: 以(同类旧品)折价购物: He ~d in his old car for a new model. 他以旧车折价添钱买了一部新型汽车。 Hence, the verb ~ in 产生, '~-in n [C] sth sold in this way. 用作折价之旧物品。 **4** [VP3A] ~ on/upon, take a wrong advantage of, use, in order to get sth for oneself: 利用…以图私利; 滥用: ~ upon sb's sympathy; 滥用某人的同情; ~ upon one's past reputation. 利用过去的名誉。 **5** (US) shop: (美)购物; 买东西: Which stores do you ~ at, do your shopping? 你平常到哪几家商店去买东西? ~r n merchant. 商人; 贸易者。

tra·di·tion /trə'dɪʃn; trə'dɪʃən/ n [U] (handing down from generation to generation of) opinions, beliefs, customs, etc; [C] opinion, belief, custom, etc handed down: 传统; 因袭; 意见、信仰、风俗等的世代相传; 传统的意见、信仰、风俗等; 惯例; 传说: The stories of Robin Hood are based mainly on ~(s). 罗宾汉的故事主要是根据传说而来的。 It is a ~ in that family for the eldest son to enter the army and for the second son to become a lawyer. 那个家庭的传统是长子从军, 次子当律师。 ~al /-ʃənl; -ʃənl/ adj ~·ally /-ʃənlɪ; -ʃənlɪ/ adv ~·al·ism /-ʃənlɪzəm; -ʃənlˌɪzəm/ n (excessive) respect for ~, esp in religious matters. 传统主义; 过分墨守传统; 过分尊重传统(尤指对宗教事务)。 ~·al·ist /-ʃənlɪst; -ʃənlɪst/ n person who attaches great importance to ~. 传统主义者; 守旧分子。

tra·duce /trə'dʒuːs US: -'duːs; trə'djus/ vt [VP6A] (formal) slander. (正式用语)诽谤; 中伤。 tra·ducer n slanderer. 诋毁者; 中伤者。

traf·fic /'træfɪk; 'træfɪk/ n [U] **1** (movement of) people and vehicles along roads and streets, or aircraft in the sky: 交通; 运输; 通行; 往来于街道上的行人与车辆或天空中的飞机; 交通量: There was a lot of/not much ~ on the roads yesterday. 昨天道路上的行人车辆很多(不多)。 T~ in large towns is controlled by ~ lights. 大城市的交通由交通灯管制。 The ~ control tower at an airport uses radar screens. 机场上的航行管制塔使用雷达

幕。 '~ circle, (US) (美) = roundabout. '~ indicator = trafficator. ⇨ the illus at motor. 参看 motor 之插图。 '~ jam, condition in which many road vehicles are prevented from moving forward. 交通拥塞。 '~ light(s), mechanical signal controlling road ~ (esp at junctions) by coloured lights (red, amber, green). 交通指挥灯; 红绿灯。 '~ warden, ⇨ warden. **2** transport business done by road, rail, ship, air, etc. (公路、铁路、轮船、飞机等的)运输业: 违法买卖: 违法行业: the ~ in liquor; 非法卖酒; illegal drug ~. 非法贩毒。 □ vi (-ck-) [VP3A] ~ in sth (with sb), trade: (与某人)做生意; 从事贸易: ~ in hides (with…). (与…)做皮货生意。 ~ker n (usu in a bad sense) trader: (通常指坏的或不法的)商人; 贩子: a 'drug ~ker. 毒品贩子; 鸦片商。

traf·fi·ca·tor /'træfɪkeɪtə(r); 'træfɪˌketɚ/ n device (usu a flickering amber light) used on a motor-vehicle to indicate the direction in which the vehicle is about to turn. (汽车的)方向灯; 方向指示器。

tra·gedy /'trædʒədɪ; 'trædʒədɪ/ n (pl -dies) **1** [C] play for the theatre, cinema, TV, of a serious or solemn kind, with a sad ending; [U] branch of the drama with this kind of play. 悲剧(严肃而结局悲惨的舞台剧、电影或电视剧); 悲剧(戏剧中的一个部门)。 **2** [C, U] very sad event, action, experience, etc, in real life. 实际生活中的极为悲惨的事件、行为、经历等; 惨剧。 tra·gedian /trə'dʒiːdɪən; trə'dʒidɪən/ n writer of, actor in, ~. 悲剧作家或演员。 tra·gedi·enne /trə,dʒiːdɪ'en; trə,dʒidɪ'ɛn/ n actress in ~. 悲剧女演员。

tra·gic /'trædʒɪk; 'trædʒɪk/ adj of tragedy: 悲剧的; 悲惨的: a ~ actor/event. 悲剧演员(悲惨事件)。 tragi·cally /-klɪ; -klɪ/ adv

tragi-com·edy /,trædʒɪ'kɒmədɪ; ,trædʒɪ'kɑmədɪ/ n (pl -dies) drama, event, that is a mixture of tragedy and comedy. 悲喜剧; 悲喜事件。 ,tragi-'comic/-'kɒmɪk; -'kɑmɪk/ adj

trail /treɪl; trel/ n [C] **1** line, mark or series of marks, drawn or left behind by sb or sth that has passed by: 踪迹; 痕迹: a ~ of smoke, (from a railway steam-engine) (火车头冒出的)一道烟; 'vapour ~s, as left in the sky by high-flying aircraft; 蒸气尾迹(如高空飞行的飞机在天空中留下者); a ~ of destruction, eg left by a violent storm. 破坏的痕迹(如暴风雨留下者)。 The wounded tiger left a ~ of blood. 那受伤的老虎留下了一条血迹。 **2** track or scent followed in hunting. 打猎的嗅迹; 臭迹。 hot on the ~ (of), (lit or fig) close behind. (字面或喻)紧跟在后。 **3** path through rough country. 小径; 崎岖小道。 blaze a ~, ⇨ blaze³. □ vt, vi **1** [VP6A, 15A, B, 2A, C] pull, be pulled, along; drag; draw: 拖; 拉; 曳: The child was ~ing a toy cart. 那孩子拖着一辆玩具车。 Her long skirt was ~ing along/on the floor. 她的长裙拖在地板上。 **2** [VP6A, 15A] follow the ~ of: 追踪; 尾随: ~ a wild animal/a criminal. 追踪野兽(罪犯)。 **3** [VP2C] (of plants) grow over or along the ground, etc: (植物)蔓生; 蔓延; 长在地面: roses ~ing over the walls. 蔓延于墙壁上的玫瑰; (of persons) walk wearily: (指人)没精打采地走; 慢行; 拖着步子走: The wounded soldiers ~ed past us. 伤兵们拖着步子走在我们身边。 The tired children ~ed along behind their father. 疲倦的孩子们没精打采地跟在他们父亲的后面。 ~er n **1** transport-vehicle hauled by a tractor or truck; van or caravan drawn by a motor-vehicle (used for living in when parked). 拖车; 挂车; (汽车拖着的)活动住宅。 **2** ~ing plant. 蔓生植物。 **3** series of short extracts from a cinema or TV film to advertise it in advance. (电影或电视的)预告片。

train¹ /treɪn; tren/ n **1** [C] (locomotive and) number of railway coaches, wagons, etc joined together: 火车(包括机车); 列车: 'passenger/'goods/'freight ~s; 客车(货车; 货车。 The 1.15 am ~ is very ~; 乘这差一点十五分的火车进城; travel by ~; 乘火车旅行; get into/out of a ~; 上(下)火车; get on/off a ~; 上(下)火车;

have lunch on the ~. 在火车上进午餐。 *The* ~ *is in/is waiting,* is at the station. 火车现在停在车站。 *He missed/just caught his* ~. 他错过(刚好赶上)火车。 '~ **ferry,** for carrying ~s over water (eg from England to France). 火车渡轮(载火车渡过水面者)。 '~ **man** /-mən; -mən/ *n* (*pl* -**men**) (US) member of the crew operating a ~. (美)列车乘务员。 **2** number of persons, animals, carriages, etc, moving in a line: 成纵队行进的若干人,动物,车辆等;队列: *a* ~ *of camels;* 骆驼队; *the 'baggage* ~; 辎重队(驮辎重的一队牲畜、车辆等); *persons in the king's* ~, in his retinue of attendants. 国王的侍从。 **3** series or chain: 连续;连环: *A knock at the door interrupted my* ~ *of thought.* 敲门声打断了我的思绪。 *What an unlucky* ~ *of events!* 多么不幸的一连串事件! *War often brings disease in its* ~. 战争常带来疾病。 **4** part of a long dress or robe that trails on the ground behind the wearer. 长袍拖曳在地上的部分; 拖裙。 '~-**bearer** *n* attendant who holds up, or helps to hold up, such a ~. 牵衣裙的人。 **5** line of gunpowder leading to a place where material has been placed for an explosion (eg in a mine), to be lit at a safe distance. 导火线(连于爆炸物,以便在安全距离点燃)。 *in* ~, in readiness; being prepared. 准备妥当。

train² /treɪn; tren/ *vt, vi* **1** [VP6A, 14, 17, 2C, 3A] ~ (*for*), give teaching and practice to (eg a child, a soldier, an animal) in order to bring to a desired standard of behaviour, efficiency or physical condition: 教养;教育;训练;锻炼: ~ *children to be good citizens;* 教养小孩使成为良好公民; ~ *a horse for a race/performing seals for a circus.* 训练马参加比赛(海豹在马戏团表演)。 *Very little escapes his* ~*ed eye.* 很少东西能逃过他那老练的眼睛。 *He was* ~*ed for the law/to be a lawyer.* 他受过政律师的训练。 *There is a shortage of* ~*ed nurses.* 缺乏受过正规训练的护士。 *They are* ~*ing for the boat-race.* 他们在接受训练备划船比赛。 **2** [VP6A, 15A] cause to grow in a required direction: 使朝某方向生长;整枝;修剪: ~ *roses against/over a wall.* 使玫瑰靠(覆)墙生长。 **3** [VP6A, 14] ~ *sth on/upon sth,* point, aim: 指向; 瞄准: ~ *a gun upon the enemy's positions.* 把大炮瞄准敌人的阵地。 ~**ee** / treɪ'niː; tren'i/ *n* person undergoing some form of (usu industrial) ~ing. 受训者;(通常指接受工艺训练的)练习生。 ~**er** *n* **1** person who ~s(esp athletes horses for races, animals for the circus, etc). 训练者;(尤指)训练运动员的教练;驯马师;驯兽师。 **2** aircraft used for ~ing pilots. 教练机。 ~**ing** *n* [U] ~ing or being ~ed. 教养;教育;训练。 *in/out of* ~*ing,* in /not in good physical condition (eg for athletic contests). 身体状况良好(不好);身体锻炼得好(不好)。 *go into* ~*ing,* oneself. 训练自己;开始练习。 '~-*ing*-**college** *n* college for ~ing people for a trade, profession, etc. 专科学校;职业学校。 '~-*ing*-**ship** *n* one for ~ing boys in seamanship. (海员)训练船。

traipse / treɪps; treps/ *vi* [VP2A, B, C] (colloq) walk wearily: (口)疲累地走: ~ *round the shops buying food for the family.* 在各商店疲乏地走来走去, 购买家用的食物。

trait / treɪt; tret/ *n* [C] distinguishing quality or characteristic: 显著的特质, 特性或特点: *Two* ~*s in the American character are generosity and energy.* 美国人性格中的两大特点是慷慨和干劲十足。

trai·tor /'treɪtə(r); 'tretɚ/ *n* (*to*), person who betrays a friend, is disloyal to a cause, his country, etc. 出卖朋友者; 背叛主义者; 卖国贼; 奸逆; 叛逆。 *turn* ~, become a ~. 变为奸逆。 ~·**ous** /-əs; -əs/ *adj* treacherous or like a ~: 背叛的;不忠的;奸逆的;似奸逆的: ~*ous conduct.* 背叛的行为。 ~·**ous·ly** *adv* **trai·tress** /'treɪtrɪs; 'tretrɪs/ *n* woman ~. 女叛徒; 女叛逆。

tra·jec·tory /trə'dʒektərɪ; trə'dʒɛktɚɪ/ *n* (*pl* -**ries**) curved path of a projectile (eg a bullet, missile). 抛射物(如子弹,导弹)的弧形行程; 弹道; 射道; 轨线; 轨道。

tram / træm; træm/ *n* **1** (also 亦作 '~-**car** or 'trolley-**bus**) electric car used for public transport, running on

rails along public streets (US 美 ='street-car or 'trolley-car). 电车。 '~-**line** *n* line of rails for ~s; route served by ~s. 电车道; 电车所行驶的路线。 **2** four-wheeled car used in coalmines. 煤矿坑中所用的四轮车; 煤车。

tram·mel /'træml; 'træml/ *vt* (-**ll-**; US **-l-**)[VP6A] hamper; make progress difficult. 阻碍; 妨害。 □ *n pl* ~**s,** sth that ~s. 障碍物; 束缚物; 妨碍物。 *the ~s of routine / etiquette/superstition.* 例行手续(礼仪,迷信)的束缚。

tramp /træmp; træmp/ *vi, vt* **1** [VP2A, C] walk with heavy steps: 重步行走; 踩; 踏; He ~ed up and down the platform waiting for the train. 他漫步沉重地在月台上走来走去, 等候火车。 **2** [VP2A, B, C, 6A] walk through or over (esp for a long distance): 步行; 行走过或穿越(尤指长距离): ~ *through the mountains of Wales;* 徒步穿越威尔士山区; ~ *over the moors.* 走过荒野。 *They* ~*ed (for) miles and miles/~ed all day.* 他们行行重行行(竟日步行)。 *He enjoys* ~*ing the hills.* 他喜欢在山间徜徉。 □ *n* **1** *the* ~ *of,* sound of heavy footsteps: 重脚步声: *I heard the* ~ *of marching soldiers.* 我听到兵士们行进的重步声。 **2** long walk: 长途步行; 徒步旅行: *go for a* ~ *in the country.* 在乡间作徒步旅行。 **3** person (usu homeless) who goes from place to place and does no regular work: (无固定工作的)飘泊者(通常为无家者); 流浪汉; 游民: *There's a* ~ *at the door begging for food.* 有一个流浪汉在门口乞食。 **4** '~ (-**steamer**), cargo boat which goes to any port(s) where cargo can be picked up. 航线不定的货船; 不定期货船。

trample /'træmpl; 'træmpl/ *vt, vi* **1** [VP6A, 15B] ~ *sth* (*down*), tread heavily on with the feet; crush under the feet: 用力践踏; 踩坏; 踏碎; 践踏坏: *The children have* ~*d* (*down*) *the flowers /* ~*d the grass down.* 孩子们把花践踏坏(把草践踏坏)了。 *You wouldn't like to be* ~*d to death by elephants.* 你不会愿意被象群踩死。 **2** [VP3A] ~ *on,* tread heavily on: 践踏; 重步践过: ~ *on sb's toes/feelings.* 踩到某人的脚趾(伤害某人的情感)。 **3** [VP2C] ~ *about,* walk about heavily. 重步行走。 □ *n* sound, act, of trampling. 践踏; 踩踏; 践踏声。

tram·po·line /'træmpəliːn; 'træmpəlin/ *n* [C] sheet of strong canvas on a spring frame, used by gymnasts for acrobatic leaps. (体操表演用的)弹簧床(弹簧框架上覆以牢固帆布,用作表演花式弹跳技巧者)。

trance / trɑːns US: træns; træns/ *n* **1** sleep-like condition: 出神; 恍惚: *be in/fall/go into a* ~. 精神恍惚。 **2** abnormal, dreamy state; hypnotic state: 昏睡状态; 催眠状态: *send sb into a* ~. 使某人进入催眠状态。

tran·quil /'trænkwɪl; 'trænkwɪl/ *adj* calm; quiet: 安静的; 平静的; 宁静的; 安谧的: *a* ~ *life in the country.* 乡间宁静的生活。 ~·**ly** /-wɪl; -wɪl/ *adv* ~·**lity** (US also ~·**ity**) /træŋ'kwɪlətɪ; træn'kwɪlətɪ/ *n* [U] ~ state. 安静的; 宁静; 平静; 宁谧。 ~·**lize** (US also ~·**ize**) /-aɪz; -aɪz/ *vt* [VP6A] make ~ (esp by means of a drug). 使安静(尤指用药物); 使平静; 镇定。 ~·**li·zer** (US also ~·**izer**) *n* drug that ~lizes; sedative. 镇静剂。

trans·act /træn'zækt; træns'ækt/ *vt* [VP6A, 14] ~ *sth* (*with sb*), conduct, carry through (business, etc with sb). 办理; 处理(事务等)。

trans·ac·tion /træn'zækʃn; træns'ækʃən/ *n* **1** [U] *the* ~ *of,* transacting. 办理; 处理; 执行: *the* ~ *of business.* 处理事务。 **2** [C] piece of business: 事项; 交易: *cash* ~*s;* 现金交易; *the bank's* ~*s in stocks and shares.* 银行的股票业务。 **3** (*pl*) (records of the) proceedings of (esp a learned society, eg its meetings, lectures): (复)(学术团体等的)会议; 会报; 议事录; 记录: *the* ~*s of the Kent Archaeological Society.* 肯特考古学会的记录。

trans·al·pine / træn'zælpaɪn; træns'ælpɪn /, *adj* (person living) beyond the Alps (esp as viewed from Italy). (尤指自意大利方面言)阿尔卑斯山彼方的; 阿尔卑斯山彼方的居民。

trans·at·lan·tic /ˌtrænzət'læntɪk; ˌtrænsət'læntɪk/

adj beyond the Atlantic; crossing the Atlantic: 大西洋
彼岸的; 横越大西洋的: *a ~ voyage/flight*; 横渡大西洋
的航行(飞行); concerning (countries on) both sides of
the Atlantic: 涉及大西洋两岸(之国家)的: *a ~ treaty/
trade agreement*. 大西洋两岸国家的条约(贸易协定)。

tran·scend /træn'send; træn'sɛnd/ *vt* [VP6A] go
or be beyond or outside the range of (human experience,
reason, belief, powers of description, etc). 超出; 超越
(人类的经验, 理性, 信念, 描写力等)。

tran·scen·dent /træn'sendənt; træn'sɛndənt/ *adj*
surpassing; excelling: 超出的; 超越的; 超凡的; 卓越的:
a man of ~ genius. 才华出众之士。 **tran·scen·dence**
/-dəns/; **tran·scen·dency** /-dənsɪ/ *nn*

tran·scen·den·tal /ˌtrænsen'dentl; ˌtrænsɛn'dɛntl/
adj 1 not based on experience or reason; going beyond
human knowledge; that cannot be discovered or
understood by practical experience; known by intuition.
先验的; 直觉的; 超出人类知识的; 不能借实际经验去发现
或了解的。⇨ **empirical** 2 (colloq) vague; not clear
to ordinary minds. (口)含糊的; 暧昧的; 一般人不懂的。
~ly /-təlɪ; -tl̩ɪ/ *adv* **~ism** /-təlɪzəm; -tl̩ɪzəm/ *n*
[U] ~ philosophy; doctrine that knowledge may be
obtained by a study of the mental processes, apart from
experience. 先验哲学; 认为不必依赖经验, 仅研究心智活
动即可获得知识的学说。**~ist**/-təlɪst; -tl̩ɪst/n believer
in ~ism. 先验论者; 先验哲学的信奉者。

trans·con·ti·nen·tal /ˌtrænzkɒntɪ'nentl; ˌtrænz
kɑntə'nɛntl/ *adj* crossing a continent: 横越大陆的; 贯穿
大陆的: *a ~ railway*. 横越大陆的铁道。

tran·scribe /træn'skraɪb; træn'skraɪb/ *vt* [VP6A]
copy in writing, esp write (sth) in full from shorthand
notes. 转录; 抄写; 誊写; (尤指)译写出速记符号所代表的
全文。**tran·script** /'trænskrɪpt; 'trænskrɪpt/ *n* [C]
sth ~d. 抄本; 誊本; 副本。 **tran·scrip·tion** /træn
'skrɪpʃn; træn'skrɪpʃən/ *n* 1 (U) transcribing: 抄写;
誊写; 速记符号的翻译: *errors in transcription*. 抄写的错
误。2 [C] sth ~d, esp into a special form of writing:
抄本; 誊本; (尤指)以某种特别书写方式改写之物: *phonetic
transcriptions*. 用发音符号注出的词句; 音标。3
(broadcast made from a) recording (on a disc or tape):
录音; 灌片; 录音广播: *the BBC transcription service*. 英
国广播公司的录音(广播)业务。

tran·sept /'trænsept; 'trænsɛpt/ *n* [C] (archit)
(either end of the) transverse part of a cross-shaped
church: (建筑)十字形教堂的左右翼部; 袖廊: *the
north/south of the cathedral*. 大教堂(或主教座堂)的
北(南)袖廊。⇨ the illus at **church**. 参看 church 之
插图。

trans·fer[1] /'trænsfə(r); 'trænsfɚ/ *n* [C, U] (instance
of) transferring; document that transfers sth or sb;
drawing, plan, etc transferred from one surface to
another; ticket that allows a passenger to continue his
journey on another bus, etc. 迁移; 移徙; 让渡; 转印; 转
接; 换车; 转业; 调任; 让渡证书; 转印的图书、图表等; 换车
票。'~ fee, sum paid for a ~ (esp of a professional
footballer to another club). 转移费(尤指职业足球员转
移至另一俱乐部时所付者)。

trans·fer[2] /træns'fə:(r); træns'fɚ/ *vt, vi* (-rr-) [VP6
A, 14, 3A] ~ *(sb/sth) (from) (to)*, 1 change
position, move: 迁移; 移动; 调动; 转移。*The head office has
been ~red from York to London*. 总部已由约克迁移至伦
敦。*He has been ~red from the Manchester branch to the
London branch*. 他已由曼彻斯特分公司(或办事处)调往
伦敦分公司(或办事处)。*The dog has ~red its affection
to its new master*. 那狗已把它的感情转移给新主人。2
hand over the possession of (property, etc to): 让渡(财
产等): ~ *rights to sb*. 让渡权利给某人。3 convey (a
drawing, design, pattern, etc) from one surface to
another (eg from a wooden surface to convas). 转写; 摹
写; 转印(图书、设计、图案等)(如从木质表面转至帆布上)。
4 change from one train, bus, etc to another; move
from one occupation, position, etc to another: 换车、换

船等、转业、转学等; 调任、调职等: *He has ~red from the
warehouse to the accounts office*. 他已由仓库调至会计室
服务。~**able** /-əbl; -əbl/ *adj* that can be ~red: 可迁
移的; 可转印的; 可让渡的; 可转印的: ~**able accounts**, of
money that may be ~red from one currency to another.
*Railway tickets are not ~*able. 火车票不能换车使用。~**abil·ity** /ˌtrænsˌfɜ:rə'bɪlɪtɪ; ˌtrænsfɚ'bɪlətɪ/ *n* [U]. ~**ence** /'trænsfərəns
US: træns'fɜ:rəns; træns'fɜrəns/ *n* act or being
~red, esp from one job to another. 迁移; 转移; 让渡;
转印; 换车; 转业; (尤指)调任。

trans·fig·ure /træns'fɪgə(r) US: -gjər; træns'fɪgjɚ/
vt [VP6A] change the shape and appearance of, esp so
as to make glorious, exalted or idealized. 使变形; 使改
观。/ˌtrænsfɪgə'reɪʃn US: -gjə'r-; ˌtrænsfɪgjə'reʃən/ *n* [U,
C] change of this sort, esp **the Transfiguration**, that
of Jesus, as described in the Bible. 变形; 改观; (大指)耶
稣的改变形象。⇨ Matt 17. 参看马太福音第 17 章。

trans·fix /træns'fɪks; træns'fɪks/ *vt* [VP6A] 1 pierce
through; 刺穿; 戳穿: ~*a leopard with a spear*. 以矛刺穿
一豹。2 cause (sb) to be unable to move, speak, think,
etc; paralyse the faculties of: 使(某人)不能活动、说
话、思想等; 使麻木: *He stood ~ed with fear/horror/
amazement*. 他因害怕(恐怖, 惊愕)而站着发呆。

trans·form /træns'fɔ:m; træns'fɔrm/ *vt* [VP6A,
14] ~ *sth (into sth)*, change the shape, appearance,
quality or nature of: 改变…的形式, 外观, 品质或性质;
转变某事物至另一事物: *Success and wealth ~ed his
character*. 成功和财富改变了他的性格。*A steam-engine
~s heat into energy*. 蒸气机把热变成能。*A caterpillar is
~ed into a butterfly*. 一只毛虫变成了蝴蝶。~**able** /-əbl;
-əbl/ *adj* that can be ~ed. 可变形的; 可变化的。**trans·form·ation** /ˌtrænsfə'meɪʃn; ˌtrænsfɚ'meʃən/ *n* [U]
~ing or being ~ed; [C] instance of this: 变形; 变化; 变
质; 转变; instance of this: *His character has undergone a
~ation since his brain operation*. 自从他动过脑部手术以
后, 他的性格已经改变了。~**er** *n* sb or sth that ~s, esp
apparatus that increases or decreases the voltage of
an electric power supply. 促使改变的人或物; (尤指)变
压器。

trans·fuse /træns'fju:z; træns'fjuz/ *vt* [VP6A]
transfer (sth, esp the blood of one person to another).
移注; 灌输; (尤指)输(血)。**trans·fusion** /træns'fju:ʒn;
træns'fjuʒən/ *n* [U] act or process of transfusing; [C]
instance of this: 移注; 灌输; 输血; 其实例: *The injured
man was given a 'blood transfusion*. 受伤者输过一次血。

trans·gress /træns'gres; træns'grɛs/ *vt, vi* 1 [VP6
A] go beyond (a limit or bound): 逾越(某一限度或范
围): ~ *the bounds of decency*. 逾越轨范; 不守礼法。2
[VP6A] break (a law, treaty, agreement). 违犯(法律,
条约, 协议)。3 [VP2A] sin; offend against a moral
principle. 道德犯罪; 违背道德规范。**trans·gress·ion**
/træns'greʃn; træns'grɛʃən/ *n* [U] ~ing; [C] instance
of this; sin. 逾越; 违犯; 犯规; 其实例; 道德犯罪。~**or**
/-sə(r); -sɚ/ *n* person who ~es; sinner. 违规者; 罪人。

tran·si·ent /'trænzɪənt US: 'trænʃənt; 'trænʃənt/ *adj*
lasting for a short time only; brief: 短暂的; 倏忽的; 仅
持续片刻的: ~ *happiness*; 片刻欢乐; *a ~ success*. 一时的
成功。□ *n* (US) guest (in a hotel, boarding-house, etc)
who is not a permanent resident. (美)(旅馆、寄宿舍
等的)暂时寄居的人; 过客。**tran·si·ence** /-əns; -əns/,
tran·si·ency /-nsɪ; -nsɪ/ *nn*

tran·sis·tor /træn'zɪstə(r); træn'zɪstɚ/ *n* [C] 1
small electronic device, often used in place of a
thermionic valve, used in radio sets, hearing aids and
other kinds of electronic apparatus: 晶体管(小型电子
装置, 常用以代替真空管, 用于收音机、助听器及其他电子
仪器中): (attrib) *a portable ~ set*. 一架手
提晶体管收音机。2 ~ set; ~ radio. 晶体管收音机。~**ized** /-aɪzd; -aɪzd/ *adj* fitted with ~s instead of valves:
装有晶体管的: *a ~ized computer*. 晶体管计算机。

tran·sit /'trænsɪt; 'trænsɪt/ n [U] **1** conveying or being conveyed, across, over or through: 通过; 经过; 搬运; 运送: *goods lost/delayed in ~*, while being carried from one place to another. 搬运中遗失(延误)的货物。'~camp, one for the use of persons (eg refugees, soldiers) who are in ~ from one place to another. 过境者(如难民、士兵等)所用的营地。'~ visa, visa allowing passage through (but not a stay in) a country. 过境签证(允许在某一国家过境,但不许停留)。**2** apparent passage of a heavenly body, eg a planet, across the disc of another one, eg of Venus across the sun. 凌日; 中天(某一天体, 如一行星, 经过另一天体圆面的现象, 例如金星经过太阳圆面)。

tran·si·tion /træn'zɪʃn; træn'zɪʃən/ n [C, U] changing, change, from one condition or set of circumstances to another: 转移; 变化; 变迁; 过渡; 经过: *the period of ~ in Africa*, eg when colonial countries there were becoming self-governing states. 非洲国家的过渡时期(如那里的殖民地变为自治国的时期)。*Adolescence is the ~ period/the period of ~ between childhood and adulthood.* 青春期是童年与成年之间的过渡时期。*The frequent ~s from cold to warm weather this spring have caused much illness.* 今年春天的天气时冷时热, 引起了许多疾病。~al /-ʃənl; -ʃənl/ adj ~ally /-ʃənlɪ; -ʃənlɪ/ adv

tran·si·tive /'trænsɪtɪv; 'trænsətɪv/ adj (gram) (of a verb) taking a direct object. (语法)(指动词)及物的。~ly adv

tran·si·tory /'trænsɪtrɪ US: -tɔːrɪ; 'trænsə,tɔrɪ/ adj transient. 短暂的; 倏忽的; 片刻的。

trans·late /trænz'leɪt; træns'let/ vt, vi [VP6A, 14, 2A] **1** ~ sth (from) (into), give the meaning of (sth said or written) in another language: 翻译; 移译: ~ *an English book into French*; 将一本英文书译成法文; ~*d from (the) Italian.* 由意大利文译成的。*The poems don't ~ well.* 这些诗不容易翻译得好。**2** remove (a bishop) to a different see; (in the Bible) take to heaven without death. 调动(主教)至另一教区; (圣经)使肉身不死而升天。**trans·lat·able** /-əbl; -əbl/ adj **trans·la·tor** /-tə(r); -tə/ n person who ~s (esp sth written). 翻译者(尤指笔译者)。Cf 参较 *interpreter* for sth spoken. 指"口译者"。**trans·la·tion** /-'leɪʃn; -'leʃən/ n [U] translating: 翻译; errors in translation; 翻译的错误; [C] sth ~d: 翻译品; 译文: *make/do a translation into French.* 译成法文。

trans·lit·er·ate /,trænz'lɪtəreɪt; træns'lɪtə,ret/ vt [VP6A, 14] ~ sth (into...), write (a word, passage) in the characters of a different language or system: 将(一词、一节)改用另一种语言或系统的单词或符号写出; 字译; 音译; 拼写: ~ *Greek into Roman letters;* 把希腊文拼写为罗马字母; ~ *English words into phonetic symbols.* 把英文词以音标写出。**trans·lit·er·ation** /,trænzlɪtə'reɪʃn; træns,lɪtə'reʃən/ n [C, U] transliterating; sth ~d. 字译; 音译; 拼写; 字译、音译或拼写出的文字。

trans·lu·cent /trænz'luːsnt; træns'lusn̩t/ adj allowing light to pass through but not transparent (as ordinary glass is): 半透明的: *Frosted glass is ~.* 毛玻璃是半透明的。**trans·lu·cence** /-sns; -sn̩s/, **trans·lu·cency** /-snsɪ; -sn̩sɪ/ nn

trans·mi·gra·tion /,trænzmaɪ'greɪʃn; ,trænsmaɪ'greʃən/ n [U] migration; 移居; 移民; (esp) (尤指)~ *of the soul,* the passing of the soul at death into another body. 死后灵魂的转生; 转世。

trans·mission /trænz'mɪʃn; træns'mɪʃən/ n **1** [U] transmitting or being transmitted: 传送; 传达; 传播; 遗传; 传导; 传递: *the ~ of news/disease/a radio or TV programme.* 消息的传达(疾病的传播;无线电或电视节目的播送)。**2** [C] clutch, gears and drive which transmit power from the engine to (usu) the rear axle of a motor-vehicle). (汽车等的)传动系统。

trans·mit /trænz'mɪt; træns'mɪt/ vt (-tt-) [VP6A, 14] ~ sth (to), **1** pass or hand on; send on: 传送; 传达; 传播; 遗传: ~ *a message by radio;* 由无线电传送讯息; ~ *a disease.* 传播疾病。*Parents ~ some of their*

characteristics to their children. 父母把一些特质遗传给子女。**2** allow through or along: 传导: *Iron ~s heat.* 铁传热。~**ter** n sb or sth that ~s, esp (part of a) telegraph or radio apparatus for sending out signals, messages, music, etc. 传送者; 传达者; (尤指)发报机; 发送器; 传达器。

trans·mog·rify /trænz'mɒgrɪfaɪ; træns'mɑgrə,faɪ/ vt (pt, pp -fied) [VP6A] cause to change completely in appearance or character, esp in a magical or surprising way. 使形象或性质完全转变; 使变形; 使变性(尤指借魔法或以令人吃惊的方式)。**trans·mog·ri·fi·ca·tion** /,trænzmɒgrɪfɪ'keɪʃn; træns,mɑgrəfɪ'keʃən/ n

trans·mute /trænz'mjuːt; træns'mjut/ vt [VP6A, 14] ~ sth (into), change the shape, nature or substance of: 改变...的形状、性质或原料: *We cannot ~ base metals into gold.* 我们不能把贱金属变为黄金。**trans·mut·able** /-əbl; -əbl/ adj that can be ~d. 可改变的; 可变化的。**trans·mu·ta·tion** /,trænzmju:'teɪʃn; ,trænsmju'teʃən/ n

trans·oceanic /,trænz,əʊʃɪ'ænɪk; ,trænsoʃɪ'ænɪk/ adj beyond or crossing an ocean: 在海洋彼岸的; 横越海洋的: *the ~ migrations of birds.* 鸟类的越洋迁徙。

trans·om /'trænsəm; 'trænsəm/ n horizontal bar of wood over the top of a door or window. (门、窗上的)横楣。'~(-window), hinged window over a door or other window; (US) fanlight. (门、窗上面的)顶窗; 腰窗; (美)门上的扇形窗; 气窗。

trans·par·ent /træns'pærənt; træns'pɛrənt/ adj **1** allowing light to pass through so that objects (or at least their outlines) behind can be distinctly seen: 透明的: ~ *window-panes,* 透明的窗玻璃; ~ *silk.* 透明的绸子。⊳ *translucent.* **2** about which there can be no mistake or doubt: 显而易见的; 显然的; 无疑的: *a ~ lie;* 显然的谎话; *a man of ~ honesty.* 显而易见的老实人。**3** clear; easily understood: 明晰的; 易了解的: *a ~ style of writing.* 明晰的文体。~**ly** adv **trans·par·ence** /-rəns; -rəns/ n [U] state of being ~. 透明; 透明性; 透明度。**trans·par·ency** /-rənsɪ; -rənsɪ/ n (pl -cies) **1** [U] = transparence. **2** [C] diagram, picture, etc (usu in a frame) on photographic film, made visible by light behind it (so that it may be projected on to a screen). 幻灯片(其上有图表、图书等之透明软片, 可放映在银幕上)。

tran·spire /træn'spaɪə(r); træn'spaɪr/ vi, vt **1** [VP2A] (of an event, a secret) become public; come to be known: (指事件、秘密)泄露; 公开; 为人所知: *It ~d that the President had spent the weekend golfing.* 据报总统打高尔夫球度过周末。**2** [VP2A] (colloq) happen. (口)发生。**3** [VP6A] (of the body, plants) give off, pass off (moisture, vapour). (指身体、植物)散发; 排出(湿气、蒸气)。**tran·spi·ra·tion** /,trænspə'reɪʃn; ,trænspə'reʃən/ n transpiring(3): loss of water vapour, eg from the surface of leaves. 散发; 蒸发(如自叶表面)。

trans·plant /træns'plɑːnt US: -'plænt; træns'plænt/ vt, vi **1** [VP6A, 2A] take up (plants, etc) with their roots and plant in another place: 移植; 移栽: ~ *young cabbage plants.* 移植甘蓝幼苗。*Some seedlings do not ~ well.* 有些幼苗不适于移植。**2** transfer (tissue, or an organ, eg a heart or kidney) from one body to another. 移植(组织或器官, 如心或肾)。**3** [VP6A] (fig, of people) move from one place to another. (喻, 指人)使迁徙; 使迁移。□ n /'trænsplɑːnt US: -plænt; 'trænsplænt/ instance of ~ing(2): (组织或器官的)移植: *a kidney ~.* 肾脏移植(换肾)。**trans·plan·ta·tion** /,trænsplɑːn'teɪʃn US: -plæn-; ,trænsplæn'teʃən/ n

trans·po·lar /,trænz'pəʊlə(r); træns'polə/ adj across the polar regions: 横越极区的: ~ *flights from London to Tokyo.* 从伦敦至东京横越(北)极区的飞行。

trans·port[1] /'trænspɔːt; 'trænspɔrt/ n **1** [U] conveying or being conveyed; means of conveyance: 输送; 运输; 运输工具: ~ *of troops by air;* 空运军队; *road ~;* 道路运输; *water-borne ~,* by ship. 水路运输。*My car is being repaired so I am without ~/without means of ~ at present.* 我的汽车正在修理, 因此我现在是没有交通工具。

2 (attrib) of or for carrying, conveying: (用作定语)输送的;运输的: London's ~ *system;* 伦敦的运输系统; ~ *charges.* 运输费用。'~ **café,** one used by long-distance lorry drivers, etc. 运输餐馆(长途货车司机等所用者)。**3** [C] (**'troop-**)~, ship or aircraft for carrying troops and supplies. (运送部队及补给品的)运输船;运输机。**4** (often *pl*) (常用复数) *in a ~/in ~s of,* (liter) filled with, carried away by, strong feelings of (delight, rage, etc). (文)满怀(喜悦、愤怒等)强烈情绪而不能自制; (喜)不自胜;(怒)不可遏。

trans·port² /træn'spɔːt; træns'pɔrt/ *vt* [VP6A, 15 A] carry (goods, persons) from one place to another: ~ *goods by lorry.* 用卡车运货。**2** [VP6A, 15A] (hist) send (a criminal) to a distant colony as a punishment: (史)放逐(罪犯);流放;处以流刑: ~*ed to Australia.* 被放逐到澳大利亚。**3** *be ~ed with,* (liter) be overcome with, carried away by (strong emotion): (文)为(强烈情绪)所激动;心荡神移;失去自制力: *On hearing of the victory, the nation was ~ed with joy.* 听到胜利的消息,举国欢腾。~**·able** /-əbl; -əbl/ *adj* that can be ~ed or conveyed. 可运输的;应处以流刑的; 应放逐的。**trans·por·ta·tion** /ˌtrænspɔː'teɪʃn; ˌtrænspər'teɪʃən/ *n* [U] ~ing or being ~ed: 运送;运输; 放逐;流刑: *The criminal was sentenced to ~ation for life.* 那罪犯被判处终身放逐。

trans·porter /træn'spɔːtə(r); træns'pɔrtər/ *n* person or thing that transports, eg a travelling crane, or a long vehicle for carrying motor-vehicles from a factory, or a conveyor belt. 输送者;运送者;运送的装置或机械 (如移动式起重机, 汽车运送车或输送带)。'~**-bridge,** bridge with a movable deck or car used to convey passengers and goods from one end to the other. 输送桥(以移动的平台或汽车, 送送人或货往返于两岸)。

trans·pose /træn'spəʊz; træns'poz/ *vt* [VP6A, 14] **1** cause (two or more things) to change places. 改换(两件或三件以上事物)的位置;换置;换位。**2** (music) put into another key. (音乐)变调;移调。**trans·po·si·tion** /ˌtrænspə'zɪʃn; ˌtrænspə'zɪʃən/ *n* [C, U] transposing; or being ~d. 转换;换置;换位;移调。

trans·sexual /trænz'sekʃʊəl; trænz'sɛkʃʊəl/ *n* (psych) person who belongs physically to one sex, but who feels psychologically that he belongs to the other sex; person who has had a surgical operation, medical treatment, etc, to modify his sexual organs, etc, so that he physically resembles the other sex. (心理)心理上认为自己属于异性者;(经外科手术等)变性者。

trans·ship /træn'ʃɪp; træns'ʃɪp/ *vt* (**-pp-**) [VP6A] transfer from one ship or conveyance to another. 使换船;使换运输工具。~**·ment** *n*

tran·sub·stan·ti·ation /ˌtrænsəbˌstænʃɪ'eɪʃn; ˌtrænsəbˌstænʃɪ'eʃən/ *n* (RC Church) doctrine that the bread and wine in the Eucharist are changed into the body and blood of Christ. (天主教)化体说(领圣餐时面包和酒即转变为基督的身体和血的说法)。

trans·verse /'trænzvɜːs; træns'vɝs/ *adj* lying or placed across: 横亘的;横放的;横断的;横向的: *a ~ engine,* one placed parallel, instead of at right angles, to the axles of a car. 横向引擎(与车轴平行装置者)。~**·ly** *adv*

trans·vest·ism /trænz'vestɪzəm; trænz'vɛstɪzəm/ *n* [U] (psych) practice of dressing in clothing of the other sex. (心理)易装狂(喜穿着异性服装的变态行为)。**trans·ves·tite** /-taɪt; -taɪt/ *n* person who practises ~. 易装狂者。

trap /træp; træp/ *n* **1** device for catching animals, etc: 捕捉机;陷阱: *a 'fly~;* 捕蝇器; *a 'mouse~;* 捕鼠机; *caught in a ~;* 掉入陷阱; (fig) plan for deceiving sb; trick or device to make sb say or do sth he does not wish to do or say: (喻)诡计;圈套: *The employer set a ~ for the man by putting marked money in the till.* 雇主把有记号的钱放入钱柜中作为圈套, 来诱捕那个人。*Our soldiers pretended to run away and the enemy, in pursuing them, fell into a ~.* 我们的士兵假装逃跑, 敌人追赶他们,

遂陷入圈套。**2** U-shaped or other section of a drain-pipe which retains liquid and so prevents return flow of sewer gas (eg under the pan of a lavatory). 排水管之弯头而能阻止下水道的臭气倒流的)存水弯; U 形口弯;凝气弯。**3** light, two-wheeled vehicle pulled by a horse or pony. 轻便二轮马车。**4** ~, ~('door), hinged door or opening in roof, ceiling, floor or the stage of a theatre. (屋顶、天花板、地板或戏院舞台上的)活门。**5** (sl) mouth: (俚)口;嘴: *Shut your ~!* 住嘴! **6** device (eg a box) from which an animal or object can be released, eg greyhounds at the start of a race, or clay pigeons, balls, etc. 释放器(如赛狗时放出狗的箱子, 或练习射击时, 放出活靶的装置等)。~**-shooting,** the sport of shooting at clay pigeons or balls released by springs into the air. 活靶射击(射击弹入空中之活靶或球者)。□ *vt* [VP6A, 15A] take in a ~; capture by a trick. 设陷阱捕捉;诱捕;使落入圈套。~**·per** *n* person who ~s animals, esp fur-bearing animals. (设陷阱)诱捕野兽(尤指有毛皮的兽类)者。

tra·peze /trə'piːz US: træ-; træ'piz/ *n* horizontal bar or rod supported by two ropes, used by acrobats and for gymnastic exercise. (特技表演者所用, 并用作健身练习的)高秋千。

tra·pezium /trə'piːzɪəm; trə'pizɪəm/ *n* (*pl* ~s) (geom) (GB) four-sided figure having only two sides parallel; (US) = **trapezoid.** (几何)(英)梯形; (美)不规则四边形 (= trapezoid)。⇨ the illus at **quadrilateral.** 参看 quadrilateral 之插图。

trap·ezoid /'træpɪzɔɪd; 'træpəˌzɔɪd/ *n* (geom) (GB) four-sided figure having no sides parallel; (US) = **trapezium.** (几何)(英)不规则四边形; (美)梯形 (= trapezium)。⇨ **parallelogram.** ⇨ the illus at **quadrilateral.** 参看 quadrilateral 之插图。

trap·pings /'træpɪŋz; 'træpɪŋz/ *n pl* (fig) ornaments or decorations, esp as a sign of public office: (喻)装饰物;装饰品(尤指作为官职之标帜者): *He had all the ~ of high office but very little power.* 他有大官的一切排场, 但权力却很小。

Trap·pist /'træpɪst; 'træpɪst/ *n* member of an order of monks noted for refraining from speaking and for other austerities. 特拉比斯特会的修道士(以禁言及他种严肃戒律者称)苦修会修道士。

trash /træʃ; træʃ/ *n* [U] **1** worthless material or writing. 无价值之物;无聊作品。**2**(US) rubbish; refuse: (美)垃圾;废物;残屑: *a '~-can* (GB 英 = dustbin). 垃圾箱。~**·y** *adj* worthless: 无价值的;无用的: ~ *y novels.* 无价值的小说。

trauma /'trɔːmə US: 'traʊmə; 'trɔmə/ *n* (*pl* ~s /-məz; -məz/)(med) diseased condition of the body produced by a wound or injury; (psych) emotional shock, often leading to neurosis. (医)(身体上的)外伤;创伤;损伤;(心理)精神创伤(常导致神经机能病)。**trau·matic** /trɔː'mætɪk US: traʊ-; trɔ'mætɪk/ *adj* of a wound or injury; of or for the treatment of a wound or injury; (of an experience) distressing and unforgettable. 外伤的;创伤的; 治疗外伤的; (指经验)痛苦而难忘的。

tra·vail /'træveɪl US: trə'veɪl; trə'vel/ *n* [U] **1** (liter) laborious effort. (文)辛劳; 劳苦。**2** (archaic) pains of childbirth. (古)分娩的阵痛。

travel /'trævl; 'trævl/ *vi, vt* (**-ll-;** US **-l-**) **1** [VP2A, B, C, 4A, 6A] make a (esp long) journey or journeys: 旅行; 游历, (尤指)作长途旅行: *go ~ling;* 旅行; ~ *round the world;* 环球旅行; ~*(for) thousands of miles;* 旅行数千英里; ~*(for) three months;* 旅行三个月; ~ *(over) the whole world.* 游遍世界各地。**2** [VP3A] ~ *(in sth) (for sb),* go from place to place as a salesman: 外出推销; 巡回生意;到各处推销: *He ~s in cotton goods.* 他到各处推销棉织品。*He ~s* (ie as a salesman) *for a London publisher.* 他为一家伦敦出版商巡回生意。**3** [VP2A, B, C] move; go: 移动; 行进: *Light ~s faster than sound.* 光比声行进的速度(快)。*Cars are assembled as they ~ from one part of a workshop to another.* 汽车系移送至工

厂各部门逐渐装配完成的。 **4** [VP2C] pass from point to point: 依次经过; 遍历: *The general's eyes ～led over the enemy's positions.* 将军的眼睛扫视敌人的阵地。*Her mind ～led over recent events.* 她把新近发生的事件思索了一遍。 **～·ling,** (US=**～·ing**) *n* [U] (esp attrib) (尤用作定语): '～*ling expenses;* 旅费; *a* '～*ling bag ⁄ dress,* used or designed for ～ling. 旅行袋(服装)。 **～·ling fellowship** *n* grant of money for educational ～ing. (为教育旅行所发的)旅行补助金。 □ *n* **1** [U] ～ling: 旅行; 游历: *T～ was slow and dangerous in olden days.* 从前旅行费时而且危险。 *He is fond of ～.* 他喜欢游历。 **'～ agent** *n* person who makes arrangements for ～ing, by selling tickets, reserving accommodation, etc. 旅游代理商; 旅游捐客(代客人买票、安排膳宿等)。 Hence, 由此产生, **～ agency ⁄bureau** *n* ! **～ sickness** *n* [U] nausea caused by the motion of ～ling. 晕车, 晕船或晕机。 **2** (in compounds) (用于复合词中) '～**-soiled ⁄ -stained ⁄ -worn,** soiled, etc, by ～. 风尘仆仆的(旅行中弄脏的; 因旅行而疲倦的)。 **3** (*pl*) journeys, esp abroad: (复)(尤指海外的)游历: *write a book about one's ～s.* 写游记。 **4** extent of the movement of a mechanical part, eg the shuttle of a loom. (机件的)行程; 冲程; 活动范围(如织布机的行程)。 **～·led.** (US = **～ed**) *adj* **1** having made many long journeys: 曾作多次长途旅行的; 富于旅行经验的: *a ～led man.* 富于旅行经验的人。 **2** used by people who ～: 旅客用的: *a much ～led part of the country.* 该国经常有旅客往来的地方。 **～·ler,** (US=**er**) /'trævlər; 'trævlə/ *n* **1** person on a journey. 旅客; 游客; 游历者。 **'～ler's cheque** (US ! **～er's check**), *n* one issued by a bank, tourist agency, etc, for the convenience of ～lers. 旅行支票(为旅客方便由银行、旅行社等所发行者)。 **2** (often *pron* **commercial** ～*ler*) ～ling salesman. 旅行推销员。 **trav·elogue** (also 亦作 **-log**) /'trævəlɒg US: -lɔ:g; 'trævl,ɔg/ *n* film or lecture describing ～s. 描写游历的演讲或电影; 游记影片或演说。

tra·verse /'trævɜːs US: trə'vɜːs; 'trævəs/ *vt* [VP 6A] travel across; pass over: 走过; 经过; 横越: *Search-lights ～d the sky.* 探照灯扫过天空。 *The railway ～s hun-dreds of miles of desert.* 这条铁路贯穿数百英里的沙漠。 □ *n* [C] **1** (mountaineering) sideways movement across the face of a precipice, steep slope of ice, etc from one point where ascent or descent is possible to another; place where this is necessary. (爬山) Z 字形爬登; Z 字形爬登处。 **2** change of direction in a trench to prevent the enemy from firing along it. 战壕的折曲; Z 形战壕(俾防止敌人沿壕射击均勿射击向)。

trav·esty /'trævəsti; 'trævɪstɪ/ *n* [C] (*pl* **-ties**) parody; imitation or description (of sth) that is, often on purpose, unlike and inferior to the real thing: 歪曲; 曲解; 丑化; 拙劣的模仿或描述(常为故意地): *His trial was a ～ of justice.* 他的审判是对法律正义的歪曲。 □ *vt* (*pt, pp* **-tied**) /VP6A] make or be a ～ of: 歪曲; 丑化: *～ a person's style of writing.* 拙劣地模仿某人的文体。

trawl /trɔːl; trɔl/ *n* [C] **1** '～**(-net)**, large wide-mouthed net to be dragged along the sea-bottom. (海上渔船用的)拖网。 **2** (US) (美) '～ **line** (also 亦作 **setline**), long sea-fishing line to which are attached many short lines with hooks. 捕鱼鱼的排钩。 □ *vi, vt* [VP2A] fish with a ～; [VP6A] drag along the sea-bottom: 用拖网或排钩捕鱼; 沿海底拖: ～ *a net.* 拖网。 **～·er** *n* boat, fisherman, that ～s. 以拖网或排钩捕鱼的船或渔民; 拖网船; 拖拉船; 拖捞渔民。

tray /treɪ; tre/ *n* flat piece of wood, metal, etc with raised edges, for holding light articles, eg a '*pen*-～, or carrying things, eg a '*tea*-～; container on a writing-desk for papers, etc. 盘; 碟(装小物件者, 如 a '*pen*-～ 笔盘, 或承托东西者, 如 a tea-～ 茶盘); 书桌上的公文盘。 **in-** / **out-tray,** for papers, letters, etc coming in ⁄ ready to go out. 待办(发文)盘。

treach·er·ous /'tretʃərəs; 'tretʃərəs/ *adj* **1** false or disloyal (to a friend, cause, etc). (对朋友、主义等)虚伪

a trawler

的; 不忠的; 叛逆的; 奸诈的。 **2** deceptive; not to be relied upon: 不可信的; 靠不住的: ～ *weather.* 靠不住的天气。 *The ice is ～,* appears to be strong but may break. 这冰可能会破(虽然看起来很厚实)。 *My memory is ～.* 我的记忆靠不住。 **～·ly** *adv* **treach·ery** /'tretʃərɪ; 'tretʃərɪ/ *n* (*pl* **-ries**) [U] being ～; (*pl*) ～ acts. 不忠; 叛逆; (复)奸诈行为; 叛逆行为。

treacle /'triːkl; 'trɪkl/ *n* [U] thick, sticky, dark liquid produced while sugar is being refined (US 美 = **molasses**). 糖蜜; 糖浆。 **treacly** /'triːklɪ; 'trɪklɪ/ *adj* like ～; thick and sweet; (fig) excessively sweet: 似糖浆的; 浓而甜的; (喻)过分亲热的: *treacly sentiments.* 过分亲热的感情。

tread /tred; tred/ *vi, vt* (*pt* **trod** /trɒd; trad/, *pp* **trodden** /'trɒdn; 'tradn/ or **trod**) **1** [VP2C, 3A] ～ **(on sth),** walk, put the foot or feet down (on): 走; 踩; 践踏: ～ *on sb's toes.* 踩在某人的足趾上。 *Don't ～ on the flower beds.* 勿践踏花坛。 *She trod lightly so as not to wake the baby.* 她轻轻地走, 以免惊醒孩子。 ～ **on air,** be light-hearted and gay, transported with joy. 得意洋洋; 欢天喜地。 ～ **on sb's corns ⁄ toes,** (fig) offend him. (喻)触忤某人。 ～ **on sb's heels,** (lit or fig) follow closely after. (字面或喻)紧随…之后。 **2** [VP6A, 15A, B] ～ **(out ⁄ down),** stamp or crush; push (down, etc) with the feet: 踩碎; 踩灭; 踩出; 踩紧: ～ *out a fire in the grass;* 踩灭草中的火; ～ *grapes,* when making wine; (制酒时)踩碎葡萄; ～ *(out) the juice from grapes;* 踩出葡萄汁; ～ *(down) the earth round the roots.* 把根部四周的泥土踩紧。 **3** [VP6A] make by walking: 踏成; 踩出; 借步行而做成: *The cattle had trodden a path to the pond.* 牛群踏出一条通往池塘的小径。 **4** [VP6A] walk along: 沿…走; 行走于; 步行在: (fig) (喻) ～ *a dangerous path,* follow a risky course of action; 采取冒险行动; ～ *the boards,* (rhet) be an actor; (修辞)作演员; ～ *a measure,* (archaic) dance. (古)跳舞。 ～ *water,* keep oneself afloat in deep water by moving the feet up and down (as if working the pedals of a bicycle). 踩水(在深水中使足上下动而不使身体下沉, 动作象踩脚踏车般)。 □ *n* **1** way or sound of walking: 踏; 踩; 步法; 步态; 足音: *with a heavy ⁄ loud ～.* 脚步沉重(大声)地。 **2** part of a step or stair on which the foot is placed. 踏面; 踏板(台阶或梯级的踏脚部分)。 **'～-mill** *n* appliance or apparatus for producing circular motion by the movements of a person or animal walking on the steps (or treads) of a wheel or a sloping endless belt (eg the kind formerly used in prisons as a punishment); (fig) monotonous routine. (借人力或兽力的)踏轮; (昔时用以惩治囚犯等的)踏车; (喻)单调的例行工作。**3** grooved part of a tyre which touches the ground: 轮胎的接地部分; 胎面: *Good ～s minimize the risk of skidding.* 良好的胎面可将滑动的危险减至最低限度。 ⇨ **retread.**

treadle /'tredl; 'tredl/ *n* pedal or lever that drives a machine, eg a lathe or sewing-machine, worked by pressure of the foot or feet. (车床、缝纫机等的)踏板。 □ *vi* [VP2A] work a ～. 用脚踏机械的踏板。

trea·son /'triːzn; 'trizn/ *n* [U] treachery to, betrayal of, one's country or ruler; disloyalty; betrayal

of trust. 叛国; 叛逆; 不忠; 背信。 ~·ous /ˈtriːzənəs; ˈtrizṇəs/, ~·ably /ˈtriːzṇəbl; ˈtrizṇəblɪ/ adj; ~·ably /-əblɪ; -əblɪ/ adv

treas·ure /ˈtreʒə(r); ˈtrɛʒɚ/ n 1 [C, U] (store of) gold and silver, jewels, etc; wealth: 金银; 珠宝; 财宝; 宝物; 财货; 财富: The pirates buried their ~. 海盗埋藏他们的宝物。 '~·house n building where ~ is stored. 宝库; 宝藏室。 '~·trove n [U] ~ found hidden in the earth and of unknown ownership. 埋于地下的无主宝藏。 2 highly valued object or person: 极受珍爱的物或人: The National Gallery has many priceless 'art ~s. 国家画廊有许多无价的艺术珍藏。 She says her new secretary is a perfect ~. 她说她新用的秘书非常理想。 My ~! (as a term of endearment). 我的宝贝! (亲密语)。 □ vt 1 [VP6A, 15B] ~ sth (up), store for future use: 储藏; 珍藏: ~ memories of one's holiday in Thailand; 珍惜在泰国度假的回忆; ~ sth up in one's memory. 铭记某事。 2 [VP6A] value highly: 重视; 珍惜: ~ sb's friendship. 珍惜某人的友谊。 He ~s the watch his father gave him. 他珍爱他父亲送给他的那只表。 ~r /ˈtreʒərə(r); ˈtrɛʒɚrɚ/ n person in charge of money, etc belonging to a club or society. 掌管俱乐部或社团之钱财者; 财务; 会计; 出纳。

treas·ury /ˈtreʒərɪ; ˈtrɛʒɚrɪ/ n (pl -ries) 1 the T~, (in GB) department of State controlling public revenue. (英国的)财政部。 First Lord of the T~, the Prime Minister. 首相。 the 'T~ Board/Lords of the T~, officers in charge of public revenue (usu the Prime Minister, the Chancellor of the Exchequer, and three others). 财政委员会(通常由首相、财政大臣及另外三人组成)。 the 'T~ Bench, bench in the House of Commons occupied by members of the Cabinet. (英国下议院的)内阁阁员席。 ~ bill, (GB) bill of exchange issued by the T~ to raise money for temporary needs. (英)国库债券(临时需款时, 由英国财政部所发行者)。 '~ note, currency note issued by the US T~; (formerly) currency note issued by the British T~ (now replaced by Bank of England notes). 国库券(美国财政部所发行者; 昔英国财政部所发行者, 现为英格兰银行发行之纸币所代替)。 2 place where funds are kept; funds of a society, organization, etc: 经费存放处; 金库; 班基; 机关等的经费; 基金: The ~ of our tennis club is almost empty. 我们网球俱乐部的基金几乎用光了。 3 person, book, etc looked upon as containing valuable information or as a valued source: 被视为宝库的人、书等: This dictionary is a ~ of information. 这部词典是知识的宝库。

treat /triːt; trit/ vt, vi [VP15A, 16B] ~ (as), act or behave towards: 对待; 看待: He ~s his wife badly. 他对待太太不好。 Don't ~ me as (if I were) a child. 不要把我当作小孩子看待。 You must ~ them with more consideration. 你必须多体谅他们一点。 2 [VP16B] ~ as, consider: 视为; 以为: We had better ~ it as a joke, instead of taking it seriously. 我们最好把它当作笑话(不必认真)。 3 [VP6A] discuss; deal with: 讨论; 探讨: The lecturer ~ed his subject thoroughly. 那演讲者对讲题阐释得很透彻。 The problem has been ~ed by numerous experts. 这问题已由很多专家探讨过了。 4 [VP3A] ~ of, (formal) be about: (正式用语)论述; 论及: The essay/lecture/book ~s of the progress of cancer research. 这篇文章(这演讲, 这本书)论述癌症研究的进展情形。 5 [VP6A] give medical or surgical care to: 治疗: Which doctors are ~ing her for her illness? 哪几位医生在为她诊治?How would you ~ a case of rheumatism/~ sb ill with influenza? 你怎样治疗风湿症(治疗流行性感冒患者)? 6 [VP6A] put (a substance) through a process (in manufacture, etc): (在制造等过程中)处理(某物): ~ a substance with acid/wood with creosote. 以酸处理某物(以杂酚油处理木材)。 7 [VP6A, 14] ~ sb/oneself (to sth), supply (food, drink, entertainment, etc) at one's own expense (to): (以食物、饮料、娱乐等)宴飨; 款待; 招待: ~ one's friends to oysters and champagne. 请朋友享用蚝及香槟酒。 I shall ~ myself to a good weekend holiday. 我要好好地度个周末。 It's my turn to ~ us

today. 今天该我请客。 8 [VP3A] ~ with sb, discuss or arrange with him: 谈判; 磋商。 ~ with the enemy for peace. 与敌人谈和。 If we are to ~ with you, it must be on equal terms. 如果我们同你谈判必须基于平等的条件。 □ n 1 [C] sth that gives pleasure, esp sth not often enjoyed or sth that comes unexpectedly: 予人愉悦的事物;乐事(尤指不常享用或突如其来者): What a ~ to get into the peace and quiet of the country! 居住在宁静的乡间真是一件乐事! It's a great ~ for her to go to the ballet. 去欣赏芭蕾舞对她来说真是一大乐事。 2 act of ~ing (7): 宴飨; 款待; 招待: This is to be my ~, I'm going to pay. 这次我请客。 stand ~, (colloq) bear the expense of the entertainment. 作东道。

treat·ise /ˈtriːtiz US: -tis; ˈtritɪs/ n ~ (on/upon), book, etc that deals systematically with one subject: 论文;论说: a ~ on racial prejudice. 一篇有关种族偏见的论文。

treat·ment /ˈtriːtmənt; ˈtritmənt/ n [C, U] (particular way of) treating sb or sth; what is done to obtain a desired result: 对待; 待遇; 处置; 处理; 治疗; 处理或对待人或物的特别方法: Is the ~ of political prisoners fair in your country? 在贵国对政治犯的处置公平吗? He soon recovered under the doctor's ~. 他在医生治疗下很快就康复了。 That dog has suffered from cruel ~. 那只狗受到残酷的待遇。He has tried many ~s for skin diseases. 他已试过许多治疗皮肤病的方法。 They are trying a new ~ for cancer. 他们正在试验一种治疗癌症的新方法。 She is still under ~ in hospital. 她仍在住院接受治疗。

treaty /ˈtriːtɪ; ˈtritɪ/ n (pl -ties) 1 [C] formal agreement made and signed between nations: (国与国间缔结的)条约: a 'peace ~; 和约; commercial ~ of commerce (with). (与…)缔结商约。 '~ port, one that a country is bound by ~ to keep open for foreign trade. (根据条约开放的)商港; 通商口岸。 2 [U] agreement or negotiation between persons: (人与人间的)协商; 协议; 谈判: be in ~ with sb for…; 与某人谈判…; sell a house by private ~, instead of by public auction or other method. 私下协议售卖房屋(非经由公开拍卖或其他方法)。

treble¹ /ˈtrebl; ˈtrɛbl/ adj, n three times as much or many (as): 三倍(的); 三重(的): He earns ~ my salary. 他赚的薪水是我的三倍。,~ 'chance, method of competing in football pools. 三重机会(一种赌足球比赛的方法)。 □ vt, vi [VP6A, 2A] make or become ~: (使)增为三倍: He has ~d his earnings/His earnings have ~d during the last few years. 在过去的数年间他的收入已增为三倍。

treble² /ˈtrebl; ˈtrɛbl/ n (boy's voice with, instrument that takes, the) highest part in a piece of music. (乐曲的)最高音部; 唱最高音部的童声; 演奏最高音部的乐器。 ~ clef, ➪ clef, and the illus at notation. 参看 clef 与 notation 之插图。

tree /triː; tri/ n 1 perennial plant with a single self-supporting trunk of wood with (usu) no branches for some distance above the ground: 树; 树木; 乔木: cut down ~s for timber. 伐树取材。 ~ bush, shrub. at the top of the ~, at the top of one's profession. 居某行业的最高地位。 up a ('gum-)~, (colloq) cornered; in a position from which escape is difficult. (口)进退维谷; 处于困境。 family ~, diagram or list showing or giving family descent. 家系图; 系谱; 家谱。 '~-fern n fern that grows to the size of a tree. 树蕨; 桫椤(高大如树的蕨类植物); 巨大羊齿类植物。 2 piece of wood, metal, etc for a special purpose: (用于特殊目的的)木材; 木块; 金属块: a 'boot-/'shoe-~, for keeping a boot or shoe in shape while not being worn: 鞋(靴)撑; 鞋(靴)型; an 'axle-~, connecting two opposite wheels. 轴木; 轴木; 心杆。 □ vt [VP6A] cause to take refuge up a ~: 使逃躲上树: The hunter was ~d by the bear. 猎人被熊赶上了树。 The dog ~d the cat. 狗赶猫上树。 ~·less adj without ~s: 无树木的; the ~less plains of Argentina. 阿根廷的无树大平原。

tre·foil /ˈtrefɔɪl; ˈtrifɔɪl/ n kinds of three-leaved

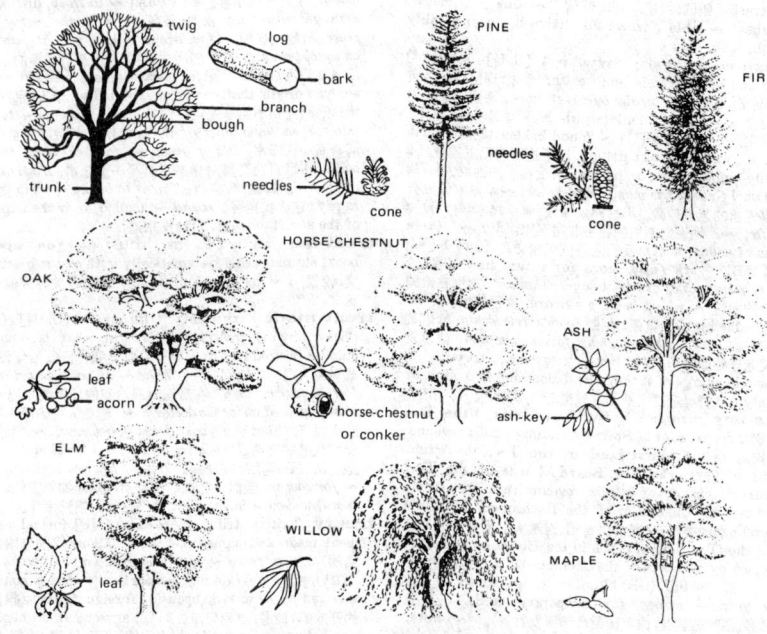

trees

plant, eg clover; ornament or design like a three-fold leaf, eg as in stonework. 车轴草; 三叶植物; 三叶型装饰或花样(如石器上者)。

trek /trek; trɛk/ *vi* (**-kk-**) [VP2A, B, C] make a long, hard journey. 作艰辛的长途旅行。 □ *n* long, hard journey. 艰辛的长途旅行。

trel·lis /'trelɪs; 'trɛlɪs/ *n* light upright structure of strips of wood, etc esp as used for supporting climbing plants. 格子架; 格子棚(尤指用以支撑蔓生植物者)。 □ *vt* [VP6A] furnish with, support on, a ~, 为…装设格子架; 以格子架支撑。

trem·ble /'trembl; 'trɛmbl/ *vi* [VP2A, B, C, 4B] **1** shake involuntarily (as from fear, anger, cold, physical weakness, etc): 战栗; 震颤; 发抖(因恐惧、愤怒、寒冷、体弱等): *His voice* ~*d with anger.* 他的声音因愤怒而发抖。 *We were trembling with cold/excitement.* 我们因寒冷(兴奋)而颤抖。 **2** move to and fro: 摇动; 摆动; 颤动: *The bridge* ~*d as the heavy lorry crossed it.* 那座桥因重卡车通过而颤动。 *The ground* ~*d under our feet.* 地面在我们脚下颤动。 **3** be in a state of agitation: 担心; 担忧; 不安: *I* ~ *to think what has happened to him,* am deeply worried. 我一想到他的遭遇就替他担心。 *She* ~*d for his safety.* 她担忧他的安全。 **in fear and trembling,** in a state of frightened anxiety. 提心吊胆地。 □ *n* shudder; uncontrollable shaking: 战栗; 震颤; 身不由己的颤动: *There was a* ~ (more usu 较常用 a *tremor*) *in his voice.* 他的声音有一点发抖。 *He was all of a* ~, (colloq) was trembling all over. (口)他全身发抖。

tre·men·dous /trɪ'mendəs; trɪ'mɛndəs/ *adj* **1** very great; enormous; powerful: 极大的; 巨大的; 极有力的: *a* ~ *explosion:* 威力极大的爆炸; *travelling at a* ~ *speed.* 高速行进。 **2** (colloq) extraordinary: (口)异常的; 非常的: *He's a* ~ *eater/talker, talks to an extraordinary degree;* 他的食量惊人(他是一个非常健谈的人); splendid, first-rate: 极好的; 第一流的: *a* ~ *concert/performance/meal.* 极佳的音乐会(表演/餐食)。 ~**ly** *adv*

trem·olo /'tremələu; 'trɛmə,lo/ *n* (*pl* ~**s** /-ləuz/) (music) trembling or vibrating effect in singing, or in the playing of a bowed musical instrument. (音乐)(歌唱或有弓弦乐器的)颤音。

tremor /'tremə(r); 'trɛmɚ/ *n* [C] **1** shaking or trembling: 颤抖; 战栗; 颤动: *the* ~ *of a leaf,* eg in a breeze; 树叶的颤动(如在微风中); '*earth* ~*s,* as during an earthquake. 地面的颤动(如地震时)。 **2** thrill: 激动; 兴奋: *A* ~ *of fear went through the audience when the assassin fired at the President.* 刺客对着总统开枪时,观众感到一阵惊恐。

tremu·lous /'tremjuləs; 'trɛmjələs/ *adj* **1** trembling: 战栗的; 震颤的; 抖动的: *in a* ~ *voice,* 声音颤抖地; *with a* ~ *hand.* 手颤动地。 **2** timid; nervous. 胆怯的; 紧张的。 ~**ly** *adv*

trench /trentʃ; trɛntʃ/ *n* [C] ditch dug in the ground, eg for the draining of water, for a latrine, as a protection for soldiers against the enemy's fire: 沟; 沟渠; 壕沟; 战壕: *dig* ~*es for irrigation;* 挖掘灌溉用的沟渠; ~ *warfare,* fought in and from ~es; 堑壕战(据壕的作战); *a'* ~*-coat,* soldier's waterproof coat. 战壕衣(士兵穿的防水衣)。 □ *vt* [VP6A] surround with a ~; fortify with a ~ or ~es; make ~es in: 以沟围绕; 筑壕以防御; 挖壕沟于: ~ *a field,* for draining. 在田地上挖沟(以排水)。

trench·ant /'trentʃənt; 'trɛntʃənt/ *adj* (of language) vigorous; incisive: (指言词)有力的; 犀利的: ~ *wit,* 犀利的言词; *a* ~ *speech.* 有力的演讲。 ~**ly** *adv* **trench·ancy** /-ənsɪ; -ənsɪ/ *n*

trencher /'trentʃə(r); 'trɛntʃɚ/ *n* (hist) large wooden plate on which food was formerly served or carved. (用以端菜或切菜的)大木盘。 '~**-man** /-mən; -mən/ *n* (*pl* **-men**) *a good/poor* ~*man,* person who usu eats a lot/a little. 食量大(小)的人。

trend /trend; trɛnd/ *n* [C] general direction; tendency: 朝向; 趋势; 倾向: *The* ~ *of the coastline is to the*

south. 海岸线向南延伸. *Is the ~ of modern thought away from materialism?* 现代思潮有摆脱物质主义的倾向吗? *The ~ of prices is still upwards.* 物价仍有上涨趋势. **set the ~,** start a style, etc which others follow. 开风气之先. Hence, 由此产生, **'~-setter,** **'~-setting** *nn.* **-y** *adj* **(-ier, -iest)** (sl, often derog) showing, following, the latest ~s of fashion, etc. (俚, 常为贬抑语)最时髦的; 赶时髦的. □ *vi* [VP2C] have a certain ~: 向; 倾向: *The road ~s towards the west.* 这条路通向西方.

tre·pan /trɪˈpæn; trɪˈpæn/ *vt* (**-nn-**), *n* **1** = **trephine**. **2** bore for drilling a mine shaft. 钻掘矿坑.

tre·phine /trɪˈfiːn; trɪˈfaɪn/ *vt* [VP6A] (med) make a small hole in (sb's skull). (医)以环锯在(头盖上)开圆洞; 环钻. □ *n* cylindrical saw used for this. (此种手术用的)环锯.

trepi·da·tion /ˌtrepɪˈdeɪʃn; ˌtrɛpəˈdeʃən/ *n* [U] alarm; excited state of mind. 惊恐; 惶恐; 激动.

tres·pass /ˈtrespəs; ˈtrɛspəs/ *vi* **1** [VP2A, 3A] ~ (**on/upon**), go on to privately owned land without right or permission: 未经许可进入私地; 非法侵入: ~ *upon sb's (private) property.* 非法侵入某人的(私有)土地. *No ~ing!* (a sign put up on privately owned land as a warning). 不准入内! (作告示). **2** [VP3A] ~ **on/upon**, encroach upon, make too much use of: 侵夺; 侵犯: ~ *upon sb's time/hospitality/privacy.* 占用某人的时间(即扰某人; 打扰某人的清静). **3** [VP2A, 3A] ~ (**against**), (archaic) do wrong; sin: (古)违规; 犯罪: *'as we forgive them that ~ against us.'* '如同我们原谅那些冒犯了我们的人.' □ *n* **1** [U] ~ing(1); [C] instance of this. 非法入侵; 其实例. **2** [C] (old use, and biblical) sin; wrong: (旧用法, 圣经)罪; 过失; 罪过: *'Forgive us our ~es.'* '赦免我们的罪.' **'~er** *n* person who ~es(1): 非法入侵者: *T~ers will be prosecuted.* 非法入侵者将依法究办.

tress /tres; trɛs/ *n* (poet or liter) (诗或文) **1** (*pl*) hair (esp of a woman's or girl's head): (复)头发(尤指女人或女孩者): *her beautiful golden ~es.* 她的美丽金发. **2** plait or braid of hair. 辫子; 发辫.

trestle /ˈtresl; ˈtrɛsl/ *n* horizontal beam of wood with two diverging legs at each end, used in pairs to support planks, a table top, a workman's bench, etc. 叉架; 支架(横木两端支以人字支脚而成, 成对使用, 以支撑桌面、工作台等). **~·'bridge** *n* bridge supported by a framework of timber or steel. 支架桥; 架柱桥; 构脚桥. ⇨ the illus at **bridge.** 参看 bridge 之插图. **,~·'table** *n* one made by laying planks on ~s. 台架, 支架台.

trews /truːz; truz/ *n pl* close-fitting tartan trousers. 格子花呢制成的紧身裤.

tri- /traɪ-; traɪ-/ *pref* three. 三. ⇨ **App 3.** 参看附录三.

triad /ˈtraɪæd; ˈtraɪæd/ *n* group or set of three closely related persons or things. 三人或三物组成的一组; 三个之一组.

trial /ˈtraɪəl; ˈtraɪəl/ *n* **1** [U] testing, trying, proving; [C] instance of this: 试验; 考验; 证明; 其实例: *give sb a ~,* use it to learn about its qualities, value, etc; 试验某物; *give a new worker a ~,* give him a chance to show his skill; 试用新工人; *have a ~ of strength with sb,* a contest to learn who is stronger. 与某人较量气力. *We shall put the machine to further ~,* test it further. 我们将进一步试验这部机器. *The ship performed well during her ~s.* 那艘船在试航时情况良好. **on ~,** (a) for the purpose of testing: 试验性的; 试用的: *Take the machine on ~ and then, if you like it, buy it.* 请试用这部机器, 如果你喜欢再买. **(b)** when tested: 在试验时; 被试用时之际: *The new clerk was found on ~ to be incompetent.* 那新来的职员在试用时(被)发现不合格. ~ **and error,** method of solving a problem by making tests until error is eliminated. 尝试错误法; 反复试验法(解决问题的一种方法, 借多次试验逐渐消除错误). **2** (attrib) for the purpose of testing: (作定语)试验性的; 试用的: *a ~ flight,* eg of a new aircraft; (如新新出厂的飞机)试飞; *a ~ trip/voyage;* 试验性的旅行(试航); *a ~ order,*

eg for goods that are to be tested. 试用货品清单. **3** [C, U] examination in a law court before a judge (or judge and jury): 审讯; 受审; 审判: *The judge conducted four ~s in one day.* 那法官在一天之内主持了四次审判. *The ~ lasted a week.* 那案审讯持续了一个星期. **be/go on ~ (for sth),** be tried in a court of law (for an offence). (在法庭上)(为某项罪名而)受审讯; 受审判. **bring sb to ~; bring sb up for ~; put sb on ~,** cause him to be tried in a court of law. 使某人受审. **stand (one's) ~,** be tried. 受审讯. **4** [C] sth or sb troublesome or annoying, esp thought of as a test of one's patience: 讨厌的人或事物(尤指被认为考验着人的忍耐力者); 磨难: *That child is ~ to his parents.* 那个小孩对他的父母来说是个麻烦. *Life is full of little ~s.* 人生充满了小磨难. **~s and tribulations,** irritations and troubles. 烦恼; 忧患.

tri·angle /ˈtraɪæŋgl; ˈtraɪˌæŋgl/ *n* **1** plane figure with three straight sides; any three points not in a straight line. 三角形; 不在一直线上的任意三点. **2** musical instrument made of a steel rod in the shape of a ~, struck with another steel rod. (音乐)三角铃(一种由钢条弯曲成三角形的敲击乐器, 用另一根钢杆敲击之). ⇨ the illus at **percussion.** 参看 percussion 之插图. **3** group of three. 三个的组或群. **the eternal ~,** the situation existing when two persons are both in love with a third. (两人同时爱上第三者的)三角恋爱. **tri·angu·lar** /traɪˈæŋgjʊlə(r); traɪˈæŋgjələr/ *adj* **1** in the shape of a ~. 三角形的. **2** in which there are three persons, etc: 三人之间的; 三者的: *a triangular contest in an election,* with three candidates. 有三位候选人的竞选.

tribal /ˈtraɪbl; ˈtraɪbl/ *adj* of a tribe or tribes: 种族的; 部落的; 部族的; 族类的; 伙众的: ~ *loyalties;* 对部族的效忠; ~ *dances.* 部族舞蹈. **~·ism** /ˈtraɪblɪzəm; ˈtraɪblɪzm/ *n*

tribe /traɪb; traɪb/ *n* **1** racial group, esp one united by language and customs, living as a community under one or more chiefs: 种族; 部落; 部族: *the Indian ~s of America;* 美洲的印第安部落; *the twelve ~s of ancient Israel.* 古代以色列人的十二支族. **2** (bot, zool) group of plants or animals, usu ranking between a genus and an order. (植物、动物)族; 类. **3** (usu contemptuous) group of persons, etc of one profession: (通常为轻蔑语)同一行业或职业的众人; 侪辈; 伙党: *the ~ of politicians.* 政客之辈. **'~s·man** /-zmən; -zmən/ *n* (*pl* **-men**) member of a ~(1). 部族的一分子; 种族或部落的一员.

tribu·la·tion /ˌtrɪbjuˈleɪʃn; ˌtrɪbjəˈleʃən/ *n* [C, U] (cause of) trouble, grief: 苦难; 忧患; 苦难或忧患的原由: *The war was a time of ~ for all of us.* 那次战争对我们大家来说是一段苦难的时期. *He bore his ~s bravely.* 他勇敢地承受困苦. ⇨ **trial(4).**

tri·bu·nal /traɪˈbjuːnl; trɪˈbjunl/ *n* [C] place of judgement; board of officials or judges appointed for special duty, eg to hear appeals against high rents, for exemption from military service: 法庭; 裁判所; 审理团(被派审理特殊案件的官吏或法官, 如受理反对高地租、或免除兵役之诉愿等): (fig) (喻) *the ~ of public opinion.* 舆论的裁决.

tri·bune¹ /ˈtrɪbjuːn; ˈtrɪbjun/ *n* **1** official chosen by the common people of ancient Rome to protect their interests. (古罗马由民众选出的)护民官. **2** (later use) popular leader; demagogue. (后来用法)公众支持的首领; 民众领袖.

tri·bune² /ˈtrɪbjuːn; ˈtrɪbjun/ *n* raised platform for speakers addressing an assembly (eg that used in the French National Assembly). 讲坛(如法国国民议会中所用者).

tribu·tary /ˈtrɪbjutrɪ US: -terɪ; ˈtrɪbjəˌtɛrɪ/ *adj* **1** (of a state, ruler, etc) paying tribute(1) to another. (指国家、统治者等)纳贡的; 进贡的. **2** (of a river) flowing into another. (指河川)支流的. □ *n* (*pl* **-ries**) ~ state, ruler, river, etc. 纳贡的国家; 纳贡的君主或统治者; 河川的支流.

trib·ute /ˈtrɪbjuːt; ˈtrɪbjut/ n [C, U] **1** (usu regular) payment which one government or ruler exacts from another: 贡; 贡金; 贡物(通常为定期的); *Many conquered nations had to pay ~ to the rulers of ancient Rome.* 许多被征服的国家必须向古罗马的统治者纳贡。*lay sb under ~*, force payment of ~ from. 强使某人进贡。**2** sth done, said or given to show respect or admiration: 表示尊敬或赞美的行为、言辞或东西: *By erecting this statue we have paid (a) ~ to the memory of the founder of our college.* 我们树立这座雕像, 借以对本学院已故的创办人表示敬意。*The actress received numerous floral ~s,* bunches of flowers. 那女演员接受许多献花。

trice¹ /traɪs; traɪs/ n *in a ~,* in an instant. 顷刻; 立即; 立刻。

trice² /traɪs; traɪs/ vt [VP15B] *~ sth up,* (naut) haul up and secure *(a sail, the boom)* in place with rope. (航海)拉起并用绳索绑住(帆, 帆杆)。

trick /trɪk; trɪk/ n [C] **1** sth done in order to deceive, to outwit or outdo, sb; sth done to make a person appear ridiculous: 诡计; 计谋; 欺诈手段: *The wearing of white clothes is a common ~ of soldiers fighting in snow-covered country.* 在积雪的地区作战时, 穿着白衣服是士兵们惯用的计策。*He got the money from me by a ~.* 他从我这里诈取到那笔钱。*the ~s of the trade,* ways of attracting customers, gaining advantages over rivals, etc. 生意经; 商业技巧、花招等。**2** mischievous act, practical joke: 顽皮的行为; 恶作剧: *The children are always up to amusing ~s.* 孩子们总喜欢调皮捣蛋寻开心。*That was an unfair ~.* 那是个过分的恶作剧。*play a ~ on sb,* ⇨ play²(3). *dirty ~,* a contemptible action. 卑劣行为。**3** feat of skill or dexterity: 技巧; 技艺; 妙诀戏法; 把戏; *conjuring ~s.* 变戏法。*Does your dog know any ~s?* 你的狗会变把戏吗？*Are you clever at card ~s?* 你擅长用纸牌变戏法吗？*do the ~,* (sl) accomplish one's purpose: (俚)达到目的: *One more turn of the screwdriver should do the ~,* fasten the screw securely. 再把那(螺丝)起子转一圈就行了(就把那螺丝转紧了)。*a ~ worth two of that,* (colloq) a better way of doing it (than yours). (口)(比你的方法)更好的方法。*(soon) get/learn the ~ of it,* learn the knack (which is the more usu word) of doing it, managing it, etc. (很快就)学会(做或处理某事等的)诀窍(较常用 knack)。**4** strange or characteristic habit, mannerism, etc: 特异的习惯、风格等; 奇癖: *He has a ~ of pulling his left ear when he is thinking out a problem.* 当他思索某一问题时, 他有拉左耳的习惯。**5** (cards played in) one round (of bridge, etc): (桥牌等的)一圈; 一墩; 一圈所打的牌; 一墩牌; *take/win a ~,* win one round. 得一墩牌。**6** (naut) period of duty at the helm, usu two hours:(航海)舵手的轮值时间(通常为两小时): *take one's ~ at the wheel.* 当值掌舵。▢ vt **1** [VP6A, 14] *~ sb (into/out of sth),* deceive; swindle: 欺; 骗: *You've been ~ed.* 你受骗了。*He ~ed the poor girl out of her money/~ed her into marrying him by pretending that he was rich.* 他骗去了那可怜女孩的钱(他假装有钱而骗她与他结婚)。**2** [VP15B] *~ sb/sth out/up,* decorate, dress, ornament. 修饰; 打扮; 装璜。*~·ery* /-ərɪ; -ərɪ/ n [U] deception; cheating. 欺骗; 欺诈; 诡计。*~·ster* /-stə(r); -stə/ n person who makes a practice of ~ing people; swindler. 有骗人习惯者; 骗子。*~·y* adj *(-ier, -iest)* **1** (of persons and their actions) deceptive: (指人及其行为)奸诈的; 狡猾的: *a ~y politician.* 狡猾的政客。**2** (of work, etc) requiring skill; full of hidden or unexpected difficulties: (指工作等)需要技巧的; 多困难的; 不易处理的: *a ~y problem/job.* 困难的问题(工作)。

trickle /ˈtrɪkl; ˈtrɪkl/ vi, vt [VP2A, C, 15A] (cause to) flow in drops or in a thin stream: (使)滴流; 细流: *Blood ~d from the wound.* 血从伤口缓缓地流出。*The tears ~d down her cheeks.* 泪水从她的面颊上缓缓地滴下来。*He was trickling oil into the bearings of the machine.* 他正在把润滑油徐徐地注入机器的轴承。*People began to ~ out of the bar as midnight approached.* 午夜时人们一个个慢慢地走出酒吧。▢ n weak or thin flow: 滴流; 细

流: *The stream had shrunk to a mere ~.* 那条溪已干涸到只有细微的流水了。*'~ charger,* device for the slow continuous charging of an accumulator (from the mains). 涓流充电器(一种使蓄电池缓慢持续充电的装置)。

tri·col·our (US = **-color**) /ˈtraɪkələ(r) US: ˈtraɪkʌlər; ˈtraɪˌkʌlə/ n flag of three colours in stripes of the same width, esp, the **T~**, the French national flag of blue, white and red stripes. 三色旗(三种颜色宽度均等者); (尤指 the T~)法国国旗。

tri·cycle /ˈtraɪsɪkl; ˈtraɪsɪkl/ n three-wheeled bicycle 三轮脚踏车。

tri·dent /ˈtraɪdnt; ˈtraɪdṇt/ n spear with three points (as carried by Neptune); this as a symbol of sea-power. 三叉戟(如海神 Neptune 所持者); 海权的标帜。

tried /traɪd; traɪd/ ⇨ try¹.

tri·en·nial /traɪˈenɪəl; traɪˈɛnɪəl/ n, adj (sth) lasting for, happening or done every, three years. 延续三年的; 每三年发生或完成的; 延续三年的事物; 每三年有一次的事物; 三年生植物; 三周年纪念。

trier /ˈtraɪə(r); ˈtraɪə/ n ⇨ try¹.

trifle /ˈtraɪfl; ˈtraɪfl/ n **1** thing, event, etc of little value or importance: 无价值或不重要的东西、事件等; 琐事; 小事; 琐物: *It's silly to quarrel over ~s.* 为小事争吵是愚蠢的。*The merest ~ upsets that man, He easily gets out of temper,* etc. 一点点小事就会使那人发脾气。*not stick at ~s,* not allow small things to interfere with one's plans, etc. 不让小事扰自己的计划等。**2** small amount of money: 少量的钱: *It cost me only a ~.* 我只花了很少的钱。*3 a ~, (adv)* somewhat, a little: 稍微; 有点: *This dress is a ~ too short.* 这衣服稍嫌短了一点。*Isn't the meat a ~ tough?* 这肉不是稍稍硬了一点吗？**4** [C, U] sweet dish made of cream, white of eggs, cake, jam, etc: 一种用奶油、蛋白、糕饼、果酱等制成的甜食; 蛋糕; 松糕: *make a ~;* 做蛋糕; *eat too much ~.* 吃太多的甜食。▢ vi, vt 1[VP3A] *~ with,* play idly with, behave lightly or insincerely towards: 玩弄; 戏弄; 忽视: *He's not a man to be ~d with,* He must be given serious attention. 他不是一个可以轻慢的人。*It's wrong of you to ~ with the girl's affections,* make her think that you love her when you don't. 你玩弄那女孩的感情是不对的。*Don't ~ with your food: either eat it or leave it.* 不要玩你的食物: 要么就把它吃掉, 要么就把它剩下。**2** [VP15B] *~ sth away,* fritter away (which is more usu): 浪费; 虚掷(较常用 fritter away): *~ away one's time/energies/money.* 浪费时间(精力, 金钱)。**tri·fling** /ˈtraɪflɪŋ; ˈtraɪflɪŋ/ adj unimportant: 不重要的; 微小的: *a trifling error;* 小错误; *of trifling value.* 价值小的。*It's no trifling matter,* is serious. 这不是无关重要的事(这事很要紧)。**tri·fler** /ˈtraɪflə(r); ˈtraɪflə/ n person who ~s. 玩弄者; 戏弄者; 浪费者。

trig·ger /ˈtrɪgə(r); ˈtrɪgə/ n lever for releasing a spring, esp of a firearm. (释放弹簧的)扳机; 触发器; (尤指枪上的)扳机。*be quick on the ~,* quick to shoot. 射击迅速的。*have one's finger on the ~,* (fig) be in full control, esp of military operations. (喻)完全控制(尤指军事行动)。*'~-happy* adj (sl) ready to use violence, eg by shooting, at slight provocation. (俚)动不动就动武的; 动辄开枪的。▢ vt [VP15B] *~ sth off,* be the immediate cause of (sth serious or violent): 为(某严重或激烈事件)的直接原因; 引发; 引起: *Who/What ~ed off the rebellion?* 是谁(什么原因)触发了这次叛变？

trig·on·om·etry /ˌtrɪgəˈnɒmətrɪ; ˌtrɪgəˈnɑmətrɪ/ n [U] branch of mathematics that deals with the relations between the sides and angles of triangles. 三角学。

tri·lat·eral /ˌtraɪˈlætərəl; traɪˈlætərəl/ adj three-sided: 三边的; 三方面的: *a ~ agreement/treaty.* 三边协定(条约)。

trilby /ˈtrɪlbɪ; ˈtrɪlbɪ/ n *(pl -bies)* *~ (hat),* (man's) soft felt hat. (男子的)软呢帽。

trill /trɪl; trɪl/ n [C] quavering sound; shaky or vibrating sound made by the voice or as in bird song.

抖颤声;(鸟叫般的)颤声. **2** (music) quick alternation of two notes a tone or a semitone apart. (音乐)颤音;震音. **3** speech sound (eg Spanish *rr*) uttered with a ~. 颤动语音(如西班牙语中的 rr 音). □ *vi, vt* [VP6A, 2A, C] sing or play (a musical note) with a ~; pronounce with a ~: 以颤音唱或奏(一音符);以颤音发音: *The canary was ~ing away in its cage.* 那只金丝雀在笼子里(颤声)鸣叫. *Can you ~ the sound 'rr' as in Spanish?* 你能发西班牙语'rr'那样的颤音吗?

tril·lion /ˈtrɪljən; ˈtrɪljən/ *n, adj* (GB) million million million; (US) million million. (英)百万兆(即百万个百万的百万);(美)兆(即百万个百万). ⇨ **App 4.** 参看附录四.

tril·ogy /ˈtrɪlədʒɪ; ˈtrɪlədʒɪ/ *n* [C] (*pl* **-gies**) group of three plays, novels, operas, etc to be performed, read, etc in succession, each complete in itself but having a common subject. (戏剧、小说、歌剧等的)三部曲(各自独立完整,而有共同的主题).

trim /trɪm; trɪm/ *adj* (**-mmer, -mmest**) in good order; neat and tidy: 整齐的;整洁的: *a* ~ *ship/cabin*, 整洁的船(舱); *a* ~ *little garden*. 整洁的小花园. □ *n* [U] ~ state; readiness; fitness: 整齐;齐备;准备;适当: *Everything was in good/proper* ~. 一切都已准备就绪. *The crew is in/out of* ~ *for the boat-race.* 划船选手已(还没有)准备好划船比赛. *We must get into* (*good*) ~ *for the sports meeting.* 我们必须好好准备这次运动会. □ *vt, vi* (**-mm-**) **1** [VP6A, 15A, 22] make ~, esp by taking or cutting away uneven, irregular or unwanted parts: 使整齐;整饰(尤指借除去或切除不整齐、不规则或不需要的部分): ~ *one's beard/the wick of a lamp.* 修胡子(剪灯心). **2** [VP6A, 14] ~ *sth* (*with sth*), decorate or ornament (a hat, dress, etc): 装饰(帽、衣等): *a hat ~med with fur*; 饰有毛皮的帽子; ~ *a dress with lace.* 以花边装饰衣服. **3** [VP6A] make (a boat, ship, aircraft) evenly balanced by arranging the position of the cargo, passengers, etc; set (sails) to suit the wind. 安排货物、旅客等的位置使(船、轮船、飞机)平衡;调整(船帆)以适应风向. **4** [VP2A] hold a middle course in politics; change one's views, policy, etc in an effort to win popular approval: 采取中间政治路线;改变见解、政策等以博取大众赞许;见风转舵;骑墙: *a politician who is always ~ming.* 总是采取骑墙态度的政客. ~**·mer** *n* person or thing that ~s. 整修者;整修的人或物;骑墙者;剪切器具. ~**·ming** *n* [U, C] sth used for ~ming(2): 装饰物: *lace ~ming(s).* 装饰用的花边. ~**·ly** *adv*

tri·maran /ˈtraɪməræn; ˈtraɪməræn/ *n* boat with three parallel hulls. 三体船(三船身并列者). ⇨ **catamaran.**

tri·nitro·tolu·ene /ˌtraɪˌnaɪtrəʊˈtɒljuːiːn; traɪˌnaɪtrəˈtɑljuˌin/ *n* [U] (usu 通常作 **TNT** /ˌtiː en ˈtiː; ˌti ɛn ˈti/) powerful explosive. 黄色炸药;三硝基甲苯(一种猛烈炸药).

trin·ity /ˈtrɪnɪtɪ; ˈtrɪnətɪ/ *n* group of three. 三个的一组或一群。 **the T~,** (in Christian teaching) union of three persons, Father, Son and Holy Spirit, in one God. (基督教)三位一体(圣父、圣子、圣灵合为一神之谓). **T~ House,** British institution which licenses pilots of ships, maintains lighthouses, marks wrecks, etc. (英国的)领港公会(主持领港员的考试,管理灯塔,标示船难等). **,T~ 'Sunday,** Sunday after Pentecost. 三一节(圣灵降临节后第一个礼拜天).

trin·ket /ˈtrɪŋkɪt; ˈtrɪŋkɪt/ *n* ornament or jewel of small value; small fancy article. 价值微小的饰物或珠宝;小装饰品;琐物.

trio /ˈtriːəʊ; ˈtrio/ *n* (*pl* ~**s**) group of three; (musical composition for) three singers or players. 三个之一组;(音乐)三人合唱团;三人合奏团;三重唱(奏).

trip /trɪp; trɪp/ *vi, vt* (**-pp-**) **1** [VP2A, C] walk, run or dance with quick, light steps: 以轻快的脚步走、跑或跳舞: *She came ~ping down the garden path.* 她轻快地沿着花园小径跑过来. **2** [VP2A, C, 3A, 15B] ~ (*over*) (*sth*), catch one's foot, etc in an obstacle and stumble: 绊在某物上而跌跤;失足;颠踬: *He ~ped over the root of a tree.* 他被树根绊倒. ~ (*sb*) (*up*), (cause to) stumble or make a false step: (使某人)绊倒或失足: *He ~ped up and nearly fell.* 他失足而几乎跌倒. *The wrestler ~ped (up) his opponent.* 那摔角者把对手摔倒. *That lawyer is always trying to ~ the witness up*, (fig) trying to make him contradict himself, be inaccurate, etc. (喻)那律师总是想使证人自相矛盾. **3** [VP2A, C] ~ (*out*), (sl) have a ~ (3 below). (俚)(因服用迷幻药而)陷入幻觉;进入迷幻状态. **4** (archaic) (古) ~ *a measure*, dance with quick light steps. 以轻快步子跳舞. □ *n* [C] **1** journey, esp a pleasure excursion: 旅行;(尤指)远足: *a ~ to the seaside*, 去海滨远足; *a weekend* ~; 周末旅行; *a holiday/honeymoon ~ to Venice.* 往威尼斯的假日(蜜月)旅行. **2** fall or stumble; (fig) fault or error: 颠踬;绊倒;失足; (喻)错误;过失: *a* ~ *of the tongue* (*slip* is more usu). 失言(此语中较常用 slip). '~ *wire* *n* wire stretched along the ground, working a trap when an animal, etc trips against it. 陷井的绊索(动物触及进入陷阱). **3** (sl) experience, esp one resulting from taking a hallucinatory drug. (俚)(服迷幻药后产生的)迷幻感觉;幻觉经验. ~**·per** *n* person making a (usu short) excursion for pleasure: (通常为短程的)旅行者;远足者: *weekend ~pers.* 周末的旅行者. ~**·ping** *adj* light and quick. 轻快的. ~**·ping·ly** *adv*

tri·par·tite /ˌtraɪˈpɑːtaɪt; traɪˈpɑrtaɪt/ *adj* **1** in which three parties have a share: 三者间的;三方面缔结的: *a ~ agreement*; 三方面缔结的合约; ~ *talks, discussion(s) between three (groups) of people.* 三者(三个团体)间的协谈. **2** having three parts. 有三部分的.

tripe /traɪp; traɪp/ *n* [U] **1** part of the wall of the stomach of an ox or cow used as food: (供食用的)牛肚: *a dish of stewed ~ and onions.* 一道卤洋葱牛肚. **2** (sl) worthless talk, writing, ideas etc: (俚)无价值的谈话、写作、主意等: *Stop talking ~!* 别胡扯了!

triple /ˈtrɪpl; ˈtrɪpl/ *adj* made up of three (parts or parties): 三部分合成的;三重的; 三方面的: *the T~ Alliance*, one of several military alliances (in European history) between three countries; 三国联盟(指欧洲史的数次军事联盟之任一); ~ *time*, (music) of 3 beats to the bar; (音乐)三拍子; *the ~ crown*, the Pope's tiara. (罗马教宗的)三重皇冠. □ *vt, vi* [VP6A, 2A] make, become, be, three times as much or many: (使)成为三倍: *He ~d his income.* 他使他的收入增至三倍. *His income ~d.* 他的收入增至三倍.

trip·let /ˈtrɪplɪt; ˈtrɪplɪt/ *n* **1** (*pl*) three children born at one birth: (复)三胞胎;同胎所生的三个孩子: *One of the ~s is ill.* 三胞胎中有一个病了. **2** set of three. 三个所组成的一组.

trip·lex /ˈtrɪpleks; ˈtrɪpleks/ *adj* triple; threefold. 三倍的;三重的. ~ (**glass**), (P) strong glass (as used in motor-cars, etc) made of a sheet of plastic material between two sheets of glass. (商标)三夹安全玻璃(汽车上所用者,系两层玻璃中间夹一层塑胶而成).

trip·li·cate /ˈtrɪplɪkɪt; ˈtrɪplɪkɪt/ *adj* of which three copies are made. 一式三份的. □ *n in* ~, consisting of three like things, esp documents: (尤指文件)一式三份的(地): *drawn up in* ~, consisting of one original and two copies. 写成一式三份(原本一份及副本两份)的. □ *vt* /ˈtrɪplɪkeɪt; ˈtrɪpləˌket/ [VP6A] make in ~. 将…作成一式三份.

tri·pod /ˈtraɪpɒd; ˈtraɪpɑd/ *n* three-legged support, eg for a camera; stool table, etc, resting on three legs. (摄影机等使用的)三脚架;三脚凳;三脚桌等.

tri·pos /ˈtraɪpɒs; ˈtraɪpɑs/ *n* examination for an honours degree at Cambridge University: (剑桥大学的)荣誉学位考试: *the History/Classics, etc* ~. 历史学(古典文学等)荣誉学位考试.

trip·per /ˈtrɪpə(r); ˈtrɪpɚ/ *n* ⇨ **trip.**

trip·tych /ˈtrɪptɪk; ˈtrɪptɪk/ *n* picture or carving on three (usu hinged) panels fixed side by side, eg of religious subjects in a Christian church. 三幅相联的图

画或雕刻(通常用铰链结合,如教堂中的宗教画)。

tri·reme /'traɪriːm; 'traɪrim/ n ancient (esp Greek) warship with three tiers of oars on each side. 古代(尤指希腊)有三层桨座的战船。

tri·sect /traɪ'sekt; traɪ'sɛkt/ vt [VP6A] divide (a line, an angle, etc) into three (esp equal) parts. 分(线、角等)成三部分; (尤指)三等分。

trite /traɪt; traɪt/ adj (of remarks, ideas, opinions) commonplace; not new. (指评语、观念、意见)平凡的;陈腐的。 ~·ly adv ~·ness n

tri·umph /'traɪʌmf; 'traɪəmf/ n 1 [C, U] (joy or satisfaction at a) success or victory: 成功;胜利; (获胜的喜悦); 狂喜; 得意扬扬: return home in ~, 凯旋归来; shouts of ~, 一阵阵胜利的欢呼声; score a resounding ~ over one's enemies; 击败敌人而获得一次轰动的胜利; recount all one's ~s. 细述所有得意事件。 2 [C] (in ancient Rome) procession and ceremony in honour of a victorious general. (古罗马向打胜仗之将军祝贺的)凯旋式。 □ vi [VP2A, 3A] ~ (over), (over), show joy because of success: 获胜;成功;击败;因成功而欣喜;得意: over opposition/adversity, overcome it; 克服阻碍(艰苦); ~ over a defeated enemy. 击败敌人而奏凯。 **tri·um·phal** /traɪ'ʌmfl; traɪ'ʌmfl/ adj of, for, a ~; expressing ~: 成功的;胜利的;凯旋的;庆祝胜利的;表现欣喜的: erect a ~al arch, one built to commemorate a victory. 建筑一座凯旋门。 **tri·um·phant** /traɪ'ʌmfnt; traɪ'ʌmfənt/ adj (rejoicing at) having ~ed. 成功的;获胜的;得意扬扬的。 **tri·um·phant·ly** adv

tri·um·vir /traɪ'ʌmvə(r); traɪ'ʌmvɚ/ n (in ancient Rome) each of three men holding an office jointly. (古罗马的)三执政之一。 **tri·um·vir·ate** /traɪ'ʌmvɪrət; traɪ'ʌmvərɪt/ n set of ~s. 三头政治;三人政治;三人小组。

tri·une /'traɪjuːn; 'traɪjun/ adj three in one: 三位一体的;三合一的:the ~ Godhead, the Trinity. 三位一体的神。

trivet /'trɪvɪt; 'trɪvɪt/ n (usu three-legged or three-footed) stand or support for a pot or kettle on or by a fire; iron bracket to be hooked on to the bars of a fire-grate. (搁在火上支承烹煮器皿的)台架;三脚架;挂于炉格的托架。 as right as a ~, in good condition or health; in satisfactory circumstances. 情况或健康良好;在令人满意的环境。

trivia /'trɪvɪə; 'trɪvɪə/ n pl trivial, unimportant things. 琐事;不重要的事。

triv·ial /'trɪvɪəl; 'trɪvɪəl/ adj 1 of small value or importance: 无价值的;不重要的;琐屑的: a ~ offence; 小过失; a ~ loss; 轻微损失; raise ~ objections against a proposal. 对某建议提出毫无价值的反对。 2 commonplace; humdrum: 平凡的; 无聊的; 没有趣味的: the ~ round, the ordinary course of everyday events, duties, etc. 平凡的日常事务。 3 (of a person) trifling; lacking seriousness; superficial: (指人)轻浮的;不严肃的;浅薄的: Don't marry that ~ young man. 切勿与那轻浮的年轻人结婚。 ~·ly /-ɪəlɪ; -ɪəlɪ/ adv ~·ity /ˌtrɪvɪ'ælətɪ; ˌtrɪvɪ'ælətɪ/ n [U] state of being ~; [C] (pl -ties) ~ idea, event, etc: 琐屑; 平凡; 轻浮; 平凡的观念、事件等: talk/write ~ ities. 谈论(论述)琐屑之事。 ~·ize /-aɪz; -aɪz/ vt [VP6A] make ~. 使无足轻重;使平凡。

tro·chee /'trəʊkiː; 'troki/ n (prosody) metrical foot of one stressed and one unstressed syllable (—ˇ), (诗体)扬抑格(由一重音节及一轻音节构成的音步), as in: 如: 'Life is/'but an/'empty/'dream. 人生不过一场幻梦。 **tro·chaic** /trəʊ'keɪɪk; tro'ke·ɪk/ adj

trod, trod·den /trɒd; trɒdn; trɑd; 'trɑdn̩/ pt, pp of **tread**.

trog·lo·dyte /'trɒglədaɪt; 'trɑglə͵daɪt/ n cave-dweller in ancient times. 古代的穴居者。

troika /'trɔɪkə; 'trɔɪkə/ n [C] 1 small Russian carriage drawn by a team of three horses abreast. 俄式三马并曳的小马车。 2 group of three persons (esp political leaders). 三人集团; (尤指)三头政治。

Tro·jan /'trəʊdʒən; 'trodʒən/ n, adj (inhabitant) of ancient Troy: 古代特洛伊城的; 特洛伊人: the ~ war, between the Greeks and the Trojans, as described by Homer. 特洛伊战争(古希腊人与特洛伊人的战争,荷马曾作诗叙述其事)。 work like a ~, work very hard. 勤奋地工作。 ~ horse, (fig) sb or sth, introduced from outside, that causes the downfall of an enemy from within. (喻)渗入敌人内部而使其毁灭的人或物。

troll¹ /trəʊl; trol/ n (in Scandinavian myth) supernatural being, a giant or, in later tales, a mischievous but friendly dwarf. (北欧神话)巨神/(后期神话中的)顽皮而友善的小精灵或侏儒。

troll² /trəʊl; trol/ vt, vi [VP2A, C] fish with rod and line by pulling bait through the water behind a boat: 在船后拉饵钓鱼; 拖钓: ~ for pike. 拖钓梭鱼。

trol·ley /'trɒlɪ; 'trɑlɪ/ n (pl ~s) 1 two- or four-wheeled handcart. (二轮或四轮的)手推车。 2 small, low truck running on rails, eg one worked by a handlever, used by workers on a railway. 铁轨上行驶的查道车;台车;压车。 3 (often 常作 'tea-~) small table on castors (small wheels) used for serving food. (装有小脚轮,送食物用的)活动食台; 活动茶台。 4 small contact-wheel between a tram and an overhead cable. (电车与架空电线接触的)触轮。 5 '~-(bus), (US) (美) '~-(-car), = **tram**.

trol·lop /'trɒləp; 'trɑləp/ n (colloq) slut; prostitute. (口)邋遢女人; 妓女。

trom·bone /trɒm'bəʊn; 'trɑmbon/ n large brass musical instrument with a sliding tube. 长号; 伸缩喇叭; 长喇叭。 ⇨ the illus at **brass**. 参看 brass 之插图。 **trom·bon·ist** /trɒm'bəʊnɪst; 'trɑmbonɪst/ n ~ player. 吹奏长号。

troop /truːp; trup/ n [C] 1 company of persons or animals, esp when moving: 人或动物的群(尤指移动中者): a ~ of schoolchildren; 一群学童; a ~ of antelope(s). 一群羚羊。 2 (pl) soldiers: (复)军队;部队: find billets for the ~s. 为部队找寻住宿地。 ~ trooper below. 参看下列之 trooper。 '~-carrier n ship or large aircraft for transporting ~s. 运兵船;运兵机。 '~-ship n ship for transporting ~s. 运兵船。 3 unit of cavalry, armoured vehicles or artillery (under the command of a lieutenant). 骑兵队或连; 装甲骑兵队或连(指挥官为中尉)。 4 company of boy scouts. 童子军队。 □ vi, vi [VP2C] (with pl subject) come or go together in a group: (用复数主语)结队; 群集; 成群而行: children ~ing out of school. 结队离开学校的学童。 2 ~ the colour, (GB, mil) carry the colour (flag) through the ranks of a regiment. (英,军)行军旗敬礼分列式(持军旗穿过部队行列)。 ~ing the colour, such a ceremony (esp as on the Sovereign's birthday). 军旗敬礼分列式(尤指君主生日所举行者)。 ~er n 1 soldier in a cavalry or armoured regiment. 骑兵;坦克兵。 2 (US) member of state police force (now using a motor-vehicle). (美)州警察(从前骑马,现在驾摩托车或警车)。 swear like a ~er, swear fluently. 不住地骂诅。

trope /trəʊp; trop/ n figurative use of a word (as of tread in 'The years like great black oxen tread the world'). 借喻; 转义(如 'The years like great black oxen tread the world' 一句中的 tread 即为借喻)。

trophy /'trəʊfɪ; 'trofɪ/ n [C] (pl -phies) 1 sth kept in memory of a victory or success (eg in hunting, sport, etc). 战利品; 胜利纪念品(如狩猎、运动等)。 2 prize, eg for winning a tournament: 奖品(如赢得比赛者): 'tennis trophies. 网球赛的奖品。

tropic /'trɒpɪk; 'trɑpɪk/ n 1 line of latitude 23°27' north (T~ of Cancer) or south (T~ of Capricorn) of the equator. 回归线(北回归线称 T~ of Cancer, 南回归线称 T~ of Capricorn)。 2 the ~s, the parts of the world between these two latitudes. 热带;热带地方。 **tropi·cal** /-kl; -kl/ adj of, or as of, the ~s: 热带的; (似)热带地方的: a ~al climate; 热带气候; a ~al fruits. 热带水果。 **tropi·cally** /-klɪ; -klɪ/ adv

trot /trɒt; trɑt/ vi, vt (-tt-) 1 [VP2A, B, C] (of horses, etc) go at a pace faster than a walk but not so fast as a gallop. (指马等)疾走;快步走。2 [VP2A, C] run with short steps; (colloq, hum) go (at an ordinary speed): 小跑;(口, 谐)(以普通速度)走: *Well, I must ~ting off home.* 唔, 我必须回家了。*You ~ along!* Go away! 走开! 3 [VP15B] ~ *sth out*, (colloq) produce; bring out: (口)提示;举以示人: ~ *out one's knowledge,* eg to get admiration. 夸示学识。4 [VP15A, B] cause to ~; (with *off*): *make;* 使或快步走;使快步走: ~ *a person off his legs,* take him round, eg sight-seeing, until he is exhausted; 领人走得筋疲力尽; ~ *sb round,* take him round with one (eg shopping). 带着某人以某事(如购物)。□ n (sing only) (仅用单数) 1 ~ting pace: 疾走;快步; 小跑: *go at a steady ~.* 一路以快步行进。on the ~, (sl) one after the other: (俚)一个接一个: *five whiskies on the ~.* 一连 五杯威士忌。be on the ~; keep sb on the ~, (a) (colloq) busy on one's feet, moving from one task to another: (口)奔波;奔走;忙碌;席不暇暖: *I've been (kept) on the ~ all morning and I'm exhausted.* 我忙了一个上 午, 现在疲惫不堪。(b) (sl) be running away (esp from prison or the police) (俚)逃脱(尤指从监狱或警察)。be on the ~, (US 美 = have the ~s), (colloq) have diarrhoea. (口)泻肚子。2 period of ~ting: 疾走、步行或 小跑的一段时间: *go for a ~.* 去小跑一阵。~ter n 1 horse bred and trained to ~. 快步马; 受过疾行训练的 马。2 (usu pl) pig's or sheep's foot as food. (通常用复数)(作食物用的)猪蹄或羊蹄。

troth /trəʊθ US: trɔ:θ; trɔθ/ n [U] (archaic) (古) *plight one's ~,* pledge one's word; (esp) promise to marry. 盟誓(尤指答应结婚)。

trou·ba·dour /'tru:bədɔ:(r); 'trubə,dɔr/ n travel- ling poet and singer in France and Italy, 11th to 13th cc. (十一至十三世纪在法国及意大利的)吟游诗人; 游唱 诗人。

trouble /'trʌbl; 'trʌbl/ vt, vi 1 [VP6A] cause worry, discomfort, anxiety or inconvenience to: 使忧虑、不适、 苦恼或不方便: *be ~d by bad news;* 为坏消息烦恼; ~d *with a nasty cough.* 为顽咳所苦。*What ~s me is that…* 使我苦恼的是…。2 [VP17, 14] ~ *sb to do sth,* put sb to the inconvenience of doing sth. 麻烦某 人做某事。(a) (with *may*/*might,* a polite request): (与 may, might 连用, 表示客气的请求): *May I ~ you to pass the salt, please.* 麻烦您把盐递给我好吗? *May I ~ you for a match?* 请给我一支火柴好吗? (b) (with *I'll, I must,* a sarcastic or ironic request): (与 I'll, I must 连 用, 表示讽刺性质的请求): *I'll ~ you to be quiet.* 拜托拜 托, 安静一点。*I must ~ you to remember your manners.* 我必须请你规矩一点。3 [VP2A, C, 4A] (esp in neg and in terr) bother or inconvenience oneself: (尤用于否 定句及问句中)麻烦自己;费神;费心: *Don't ~ to meet me at the station.* 不必劳驾来车站接我了。*Don't ~ about that.* 不必为那事烦心。*Oh, don't ~, thanks.* 啊, 不要麻 烦了, 谢谢。*Why should I ~ to explain?* 我为什么要费事 解释呢? 4 [VP6A] agitate; disturb: 激动;扰乱: (esp *pp*) (尤用过去分词)为苦恼的表情; ~d *expression;* 忧愁的表情; ~d *looks.* 苦恼的表情。*fish in ~d waters,* try to gain an advantage from a confused state of affairs. 混水摸鱼。 □ n 1 [C, U] worry; anxiety; discomfort; unhappiness; difficulty; possible punishment: 忧虑; 苦恼; 不适; 不幸; 困难; 可能的处罚: *Her heart was full of ~.* 她内心充满 了烦恼。*She's always making ~ for her friends.* 她总是 给她的朋友们带来麻烦。*He has been through much ~(*/ *has had many ~).* 他已度过许多困难(已遭遇到许多困 难)。*He has a lot of family/domestic ~.* 他有许多 家务上的麻烦。*His ~s are over now* (sometimes said of a person who dies). 他的烦恼现在过去了(有时用以指死去 的人)。*The ~ is that…,* The difficulty is that…。困难 的是…。*What's the ~ now?* 现在)发生了什么不幸事件? *in ~,* suffering, or likely to suffer, misfortune, anxiety, etc, eg because one has done wrong. 处于不幸、烦恼等苦境中(如因做错

某事). '*ask*/'*look for ~,* (colloq) behave in such a way that ~ is likely: (口)自寻烦恼/自找苦吃; 自找麻 烦: *It's asking for ~ to experiment with drugs.* 随便试用 药品乃是自找麻烦。get into ~, do sth that will bring unhappiness, punishment, etc. 陷入困境; 因做某事而将 招致不幸, 处罚等。get sb into ~, (a) cause sb to be in ~. 使某人陷入困境。(b) (sl) make (an unmarried woman) pregnant. (俚)使(未婚女子)怀孕。2 [C] (sing only) sb or sth that causes ~(1): (仅作单数)引起忧虑、 苦恼、不适、不幸或困难等的人或事物: *I don't want to be any ~* (= nuisance) *to you.* 我不想老你讨厌。*Some dishes are very enjoyable to eat but a great ~ to prepare.* 有些菜很好吃, 但是很难于很麻烦。*I find it a great ~ to get up at 6 am.* 我觉得早上六点钟起床是一件苦事。3 [U] care; attention; (extra) work; inconvenience: 小心; 注意; (额外的)工作; 烦劳; 不方便: *Did the work give you much ~?* 那工作给你添了许多麻烦吗? *I don't like putting you to* (= causing you) *so much ~.* 我不愿意为你添那 么多麻烦。*Thank you for all the ~ you've taken to help my son.* 多谢你尽心帮助我儿子。*It will be no ~,* will not inconvenience me. 那不费事(不会给我添麻烦)。4 [C, U] political or social unrest: (政治或社会的)不安; 纷争; 扰乱。'*Labour ~s* (eg strikes) *cost the country enormous sums last year.* 劳工纠纷(如罢工)去年使国家 耗损了巨额金钱。*They've been having a lot of ~s in Southern Africa recently.* 非洲南部最近一直扰攘不安。5 [C, U] illness: 疾病; '*liver ~,* 肝病; '*mental ~,* 精神病; '*children's ~s.* 儿童的疾病。3 (compounds) (复合词) '*~-maker,* person who stirs up discontent (eg in industry). 是非人物; 挑拨是非者; 鼓动不满情绪者(例如 在工业上)。'*~-shooter,* person employed in conciliating and arbitrating between parties in conflict (eg in industry), or in detecting and correcting faults (esp in machinery). 调解人; 调停人(如工业上的); (机器的)修理 人或矫正人。'*~some* /-səm, -səm/ adj causing ~: 使 人苦恼或烦劳的; 困难的; 麻烦的: *a ~some child*/*head- ache*/*problem.* 使人苦恼的孩子(头痛, 问题)。'*Her cough is very ~some today.* 她今天咳嗽得很厉害。'*~ spot,* place where ~(4) often occurs. 常发生纷争的地方; 是非之地。 **troub·lous** /-əs; -əs/ adj (liter) disturbed; unsettled: (文)动乱不安的; 纷扰的: *live in troublous times.* 生于动 乱时代。

trough /trɒf US: trɔ:f; trɔf/ n 1 long, open (usu shallow) box for animals to feed or drink from. (喂动 物用的)食槽; 水槽。2 long open box in which a baker kneads dough for bread. (面包师用的)揉面槽; 和面槽。3 (in the sea, etc) long hollow between two waves. (海洋 等之)波谷; 两海浪间的凹处。4 (met) region of lower atmospheric pressure between two regions of higher pressure. (气象)槽(两个高气压地区间的低压带)。

trounce /traʊns; traʊns/ vt [VP6A] beat; thrash; defeat; reprimand: 打; 鞭打; 击败; 痛惩: *Her team was ~d on Saturday.* 我队在星期六惨遭击败。 **trounc·ing** n beating; reprimand: 痛打; 严责: *give sb a good trouncing.* 痛打(责)某人。

troupe /tru:p; trup/ n company, esp of actors or of members of a circus. 班;队;团(尤指演员或马戏团员 所组成者)。~r n member of a theatrical ~: (戏 剧、马戏团等的)团员:演员: *He's a good ~r,* a loyal, hard-working and uncomplaining colleague 他是个忠 心耿耿、任劳任怨的好同事。

trouser /'traʊzə(r); 'traʊzə/ n 1 (*pair of*) ~s, two- legged outer garment, reaching from the waist to the ankles. 裤子。⇨ **shorts, slack²**. 2 (attrib) of or for ~s: (用作定语)裤子的; 裤子之用的; 用在裤子上的: '*~ buttons*/*pockets.* 裤扣(袋)。

trous·seau /'tru:səʊ; 'truso/ n (pl ~s or ~x /-səʊz -soz/) outfit of clothing, etc, for a bride. 嫁妆; 妆奁。

trout /traʊt; traʊt/ n (pl unchanged) freshwater fish valued as food and for the sport of catching it (with rod and line). (复数不变)鳟鱼。

trove /trəʊv; trov/ n ⇨ **treasure(1)**.

trowel /'trəʊəl; 'traʊəl/ n 1 flat-bladed tool for spreading mortar on bricks or stone, plaster on walls, etc. (用以涂抹灰泥于砖石或墙上的)镘刀;抹子;抹刀。2 hand-tool with a curved blade for lifting plants, etc. (移植树木等用的)小铲子。⇨ the illus at **tool**. 参看 tool 之插图。

troy /trɔɪ; trɔɪ/ n [U] British system of weights, used for gold and silver, in which one pound = 12 ounces: (英国的)金衡;金衡制(每金衡英磅等于十二英两): *This spoon weighs 4 oz* ~. 此匙重四金衡英两。⇨ **App 5.** 参看附录五。

tru·ant /'truːənt; 'truənt/ n 1 child who stays away from school without good reason. 逃学的学童。*play* ~, stay away thus. 逃课;逃学;旷课。2 (attrib) (of persons, their conduct, thoughts, etc) wandering; idle; shirking (duty, etc). (用作定语)(指人,其行为、思想等)游荡的;怠惰的;规避(责任等)的。**tru·ancy** /-ənsɪ; -ənsɪ/ n (pl **-cies**) [U] playing ~; [C] instance of this. 逃学;旷课;其实例。

truce /truːs; trus/ n [C] (agreement for the) stopping of fighting for a time (eg to take away the wounded). 休战;停战(如运走伤兵等);休战协定。

truck[1] /trʌk; trʌk/ n 1 (GB) open railway wagon for heavy goods. (英)(铁路上运笨重货物的)敞篷货车。2 (US) lorry. (美)货车;卡车。3 porter's two-wheeled barrow (for moving heavy objects). (搬运工人的)两轮手车(用以搬运重物者)。

truck[2] /trʌk; trʌk/ n [U] 1 barter; exchange. 买卖;交易。*have no* ~ *with*, have no dealings with. 不与~来往;不与~打交道。2 '**garden**-~, (US) fresh garden produce (vegetables, fruit) grown for the markets. (美)新鲜蔬菜水果(为出售而种植者)。3 ~ **(system)**, (hist) payment of wages in goods instead of money. (史)以实物偿付工资的(制度)。

truckle[1] /'trʌkl; 'trʌkl/ vi [VP3A] ~ *to*, submit in a timid or cowardly way: 屈从;胆小或懦弱地顺从: *This country will never ~ to bullies.* 这个国家绝不会向恃强凌弱者低头。

truckle[2] /'trʌkl; 'trʌkl/ n '~-**bed**, low, wheeled bed that can be pushed under another when not in use. 有脚轮的矮床(不用时可推入另一床下)。

trucu·lent /'trʌkjʊlənt; 'trʌkjələnt/ adj looking for, desiring, a fight; aggressive. 寻衅的;找碴儿的;爱打架的;好攻击的。~·**ly** adv **trucu·lence** /-ləns; -ləns/, **trucu·lency** /-ənsɪ; -ənsɪ/ nn

trudge /trʌdʒ; trʌdʒ/ vi [VP2A, B, C] walk wearily or heavily: 疲累或沉重地走;跋涉: *trudging through the deep snow.* 在深雪中跋涉。*He ~d 20 miles.* 他艰苦地走了二十英里。□ n long tiring walk. 跋涉;长途疲累的步行。

true /truː; tru/ adj **(-r, -st)** 1 in accordance or agreement with fact: 合于事实的;确实的: *Is it ~ that you are going to Rome?* 你真的要去罗马吗? *Is the news* ~? 这消息确实吗? *come* ~, (of a hope, dream) really happen, become fact. (指希望,梦想)实现;达到。2 ~ **(to)**, loyal, faithful: 忠诚的;忠实的: *be ~ to one's word/promise*, do what one has promised to do. 重然诺;守信。,~-'**blue** n, adj (person who is) of uncompromising principles, firmly loyal. 坚持原则的(人);忠于主义的(人);坚贞的(人);忠心耿耿的(人)。~-'**hearted** adj loyal. 忠实的;诚实的。'~-**love** n one who loves truly/is truly loved. 爱人(真正爱人或被人所爱者)。3 in accordance with reason or received standards; genuine; rightly so named: 合于道理或一般标准的;真正的;名副其实的: *T~ friendship should last for ever.* (真实的)友谊(应)永恒不渝。*The frog is not a ~ reptile.* 青蛙不是真正的爬虫。*Who was the ~ heir to the throne?* 谁是真正的王位继承人? 4 ~ *to type*, accurately conforming to its type or class: 与原型或原种子完全相同的: *Plants grown from seed are not always ~ to type.* 从种子长出来的植物并不总是与原型相同。5 accurately fitted or placed: 安装确实的;装置得妥当的: *Is the wheel/post ~?* 那轮

子(柱子)装妥了吗? **6** exact; accurate: 精确的;切实的;正确的: *a ~ copy of a document*; 一项文件的正确抄本;*a ~ pair of scales.* 精确的天平。□ n (only in) (仅用于) *out of ~*, not in its exact or accurate position: 不在其正确或确实的位置;脱离定位: *The axle/beam/door is out of ~.* 轴(梁、门)的位置不正了。□ adv (with certain vv) truly: (与某些动词连用)真实地;正确地: *aim* ~. 正确地瞄准;*breed* ~ (4); 育出纯种;*tell me* ~. 老实告诉我。□ vt [VP15B] ~ *sth up*, make, adjust so as to be ~ (5):使安装、调整得确实;配准;校正。~ *up a wheel*. 把车轮装妥当。

truffle /'trʌfl; 'trʌfl/ n kind of fungus that grows underground, used for flavouring savoury food dishes, pâté, etc. 松露;麦蕈;块菌(一种地下菌,用于调制美味肴馔及小面饼等)。

tru·ism /'truːɪzəm; 'truɪzəm/ n [C] statement that is obviously true and need not have been made: 显然真实而没有必要说出的话;自明之理;不提自明的事实: *It's a ~ to say that your body was once much smaller than it is now.* 说你的身体过去曾比现在小得多,乃是不提自明的事实。

truly /'truːlɪ; 'trulɪ/ adv 1 truthfully: 真实地;诚实地;*speak* ~. 说实话。2 sincerely: 诚恳地;笃实地;*felt ~ grateful.* 我诚实地感激。*Yours* ~ (used at the close of a letter, before the signature). (用于信札末尾签名前的套语)。3 genuinely; certainly: 真正地;确定地: *a ~ beautiful picture*; 一幅真正美丽的图画;*a ~ brave action.* 真正勇敢的行为。

trump[1] /trʌmp; trʌmp/ n [C] 1 (in card games such as whist, bridge) each card of a suit that has been declared as having higher value than the other three suits: (牌戏,如惠斯特,桥牌)王牌;将牌: *Hearts are* ~s. 红心是王牌。⇨ **declare**(1). *play one's ~ card*, (fig) make use of one's most valuable resource, means of gaining one's ends (esp after trying other means). (喻)使用最后手段;使出杀手锏;拿出王牌;使出最厉害的一招。*turn up* ~s, (colloq) (口)**(a)** have a better result than was expected. 结果较预期为佳。**(b)** have a stroke of good luck. 走好运。2 (colloq) excellent fellow; person who is full of resource, is generous, etc. (口)才俊;杰出之士;好人;有智谋、性情慷慨等的人。□ vt, vi 1 [VP6A, 2A] play a ~ card (on): 出王牌;以王牌取胜: ~ *the ace of clubs*. 出梅花爱司牌。2 [VP15B] (usu passive) (通常用被动语态) ~ *sth up*, invent (an excuse, a false story, etc) in order to deceive sb: 捏造(借口,虚假故事等): *He was arrested on a ~ed-up charge.* 他以诬告罪被捕。

trump[2] /trʌmp; trʌmp/ n (liter) (sound made by a) trumpet. (文)喇叭;喇叭声。*the last ~; the ~ of doom*, the trumpet call which will, some people believe, be sounded on the Last Day, the day when everyone will be judged by God. 世界末日的号角。

trump·ery /'trʌmpərɪ; 'trʌmpərɪ/ adj showy but of little value: 华丽而无甚价值的;俗丽的: ~ *ornaments*. 俗丽的饰物。

trum·pet /'trʌmpɪt; 'trʌmpɪt/ n 1 musical wind instrument of brass. 喇叭;号。⇨ the illus at **brass**. 参看 brass 之插图。*blow one's own* ~, (fig) praise oneself. (喻)自吹自擂。2 sound (as) of a ~. 喇叭声;似喇叭声。3 sth suggesting a ~ in shape or use (eg the corona of a daffodil). 形状或功用似喇叭之物(如水仙花的花冠)。□ vt, vi 1 [VP6A, 15B] proclaim, make known; celebrate: 宣布;鼓吹;庆祝: ~ *(forth) sb's heroic deeds.* 宣扬某人的英勇事迹。2 [VP2A, C] (esp of an elephant) make loud sounds. (尤指象)高声吼叫。~**er** n person who plays a ~. 喇叭手;号手。

trun·cate US: '**trʌŋkeɪt**; 'trʌŋket/ vt [VP6A] shorten by cutting the tip, top or end from: 切掉…的头或末端;截短;修短: *a ~d cone/pyramid.* 截锥(截角锥)。

trun·cheon /'trʌntʃən; 'trʌntʃən/ n short thick club (esp one used by the police). 粗短之棍;(尤指)警棍。

trundle /'trʌndl; 'trʌndl/ vt, vi [VP6A, 15A, B, 2C] (esp of sth heavy or awkward in shape) move or roll: (尤指内形笨重之物)移动; 推动; 滚动: The porter ~d his barrow along the platform. 搬运工人在月台上推动手推车. The child was trundling a hoop along the sidewalk. 那孩子沿人行道在滚动铁环. '~ bed, (US)(美) = truckle bed. (可推至其他床下面的)有脚轮矮床.

trunk /trʌŋk; trʌŋk/ n [C] **1** main stem of a tree (contrasted with the branches). 树干(与树枝相对). ➪ the illus at **tree**. 参看 tree 之插图. **2** body without head, arms or legs; main part of any structure. 躯干(头、臂、腿除外的部分); 任何结构的主体部分. **3** large box with a hinged lid, for clothes, etc while travelling. (旅行用的)大衣箱. **4** long nose of an elephant. 象鼻. ➪ the illus at **large**. 参看 large 之插图. **5** (pl)(复) ~ shorts. **6** (US)(美) = boot(2) of a car. 汽车尾部的贮物箱; 车尾箱. **7** (attrib)(用作定语) '~-call n telephone call to a distant place, with charges according to distance. (按距离计费的)长途电话; 长途通话; 长途呼叫. '~-line n **(a)** main line of a railway. 铁路的干线. **(b)** long-distance telephone line. 长途电话线. '~-road n main road. 干道; 干线道路.

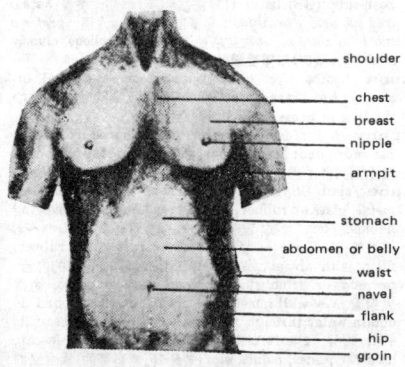

— shoulder
— chest
— breast
— nipple
— armpit
— stomach
— abdomen or belly
— waist
— navel
— flank
— hip
— groin

the trunk

truss /trʌs; trʌs/ n [C] **1** (GB) bundle (of hay, straw). (英)(干草, 稻草的)捆; 束. **2** framework supporting a roof, bridge, etc. (支持屋顶,桥等的)构架; 桁架. **3** padded belt worn by a person suffering from hernia. 疝带; 突造带(患疝气病者所围的有衬垫的带子). □ vt [VP6A, 15B] ~ sth (up), **1** tie or fasten up: 捆; 系: ~ hay; 捆干草; ~ up a chicken, pin the wings to the body before boiling or roasting it. (烹煮前)把鸡翅膀申紧在鸡身上. The policemen ~ed up the struggling criminal with rope, tied his arms to his sides. 警察用绳子把挣扎的罪犯捆起. **2** support (a roof, bridge, etc) with a ~ or ~es(2). 以构架或桁架支持(屋顶,桥梁等).

trust¹ /trʌst; trʌst/ n **1** [U] ~ (in), confidence, strong belief, in the goodness, strength, reliability of sth or sb: 信赖; 信任; 信靠: put one's ~ in God. 信靠上帝. A child usually has perfect ~ in its mother. 小孩通常完全信赖母亲. She hasn't place much ~ in his promises. 她不大信任他的诺言. on ~, **(a)** without proof; without close examination: 不加证明地; 不作深究地; 凭信任地: You'll have to take my statement on ~. 你必须信任我的话. **(b)** on credit. 以赊欠方式. **2** [U] responsibility: 责任; 职责: a position of great ~. 责任重大的职位. **3** [U] (legal) property held and managed by one or more persons (trustees) for the benefit of another or others; [U] the legal relation between the trustee(s) and the property; the obligation assumed by the trustee(s): (法律)受委托保管的财产; 信托财产; 信托物(由受托人为他人利益保管和经营的财产); 信托; 托管; 受托人的义

By his will he created ~s for his children. 他在遗嘱里为孩子们建立了信托财产. This property is not mine; it is a ~. 这财产不是我的,是信托财产. I am holding the property in ~ for my nephew. 我受托为我的侄子管理财产. '~-money, '~ fund nn money held in ~. 委托金; 信管金. **4** [C] association of business firms for the achievement of various objects, eg reducing competition, maintenance of prices. 企业联合; 托拉斯(为了减轻竞争, 维持价格等而组成者). **5** 'brains ~, ➪ brain. ~·ful /-fəl/, -fʊl/, adj ready to have ~ in others; not suspicious. 易于相信他人的; 信任的; 不疑的. ~·fully /-fəlɪ; -fʊlɪ/, ~·ing·ly advv '~·worthy adj worthy of ~; dependable. 值得信赖的; 可靠的; 可靠的. '~·worthi·ness n ~y adj (archaic or hum) ~worthy: (古或谑)值得信赖的; 可信任的; 可靠的; a ~y sword /bicycle. 可靠的剑(脚踏车).

trust² /trʌst; trʌst/ vt, vi **1** [VP6A] have trust(1) in; believe in the honesty and reliability of: 信赖; 信任: He's not the sort of man to be ~ed /not a man I would ~. 他不是一个可靠的人(不是我可以信赖的人). Can you ~ his account of what happened? 你能相信他对发生的事情所作的报告吗? **2** [VP3A] ~ in sb, have confidence in; believe that he will act for the best: 信仰; 对…有信心: ~ in God. 信上帝. ~ to sth, have reliance on: 依赖; 依靠: Don't ~ to chance. 不要依靠机会. You ~ to your memory too much. 你过分依赖你的记忆了. **3** [VP14] ~ sth to sb, = entrust (the more usu word). 委托; 托付(entrust 较常用). **4** [VP15A, B, 17] allow (sb) to do sth, have sth, go somewhere, etc without anxiety, knowing that he will act sensibly, etc: 对(某人)放心; 信任: Can I ~ you to get the money safely to the bank? 我能信任你将这笔钱安全存入银行吗? He may be ~ed to do the work well. 他或许可以信得过做好那项工作. We can't ~ that boy out of our sight. 那男孩一离开我们的视线, 我们就不放心. It's unwise to ~ small children out of doors in a big town, eg because of traffic dangers. 在大城市中听任小孩在外面玩是不智的(例如因有交通事故的危险). Should boys of 16 be ~ed with high-powered motor-bikes? 十六岁的男孩子应该听任其驾驭马力大的摩托车吗? **5** [VP6A] allow credit to a customer: 赊卖: I wonder whether the newsagent will ~ me; I need some cigarettes and I've no money on me. 我不知道报纸经销商会不会让我赊账; 我需要几支香烟, 而我没有带钱. **6** [VP7A, 9] earnestly hope: 热望; 切望: I ~ you're in good health. 我希望你身体安康. You're quite well, I ~. 我希望你身体很好. (comm)(商)We ~ to receive a cheque from you in settlement of this account. 我们盼望收到你的支票以清理这笔帐.

trustee /trʌ'sti:; -'sti/ n person who has charge of property in trust(3) or of the business affairs of an institution. 受托人; 被信托的人; 受托管理财产或业务的人. the **Public T~**, state official who executes wills and trusts when asked to do so. 公设信托人(得到请求时处理遗嘱及信托财产的政府官员). ~·ship /-ʃɪp; -ʃɪp/ n position of a trustee; (esp) responsibility for the administration of a territory, granted to a country by the United Nations Organization: 受托人的职位; (尤指)联合国的托管(委托某一国家管理某一领土): '~ship territories, eg the Cameroons from 1947 until 1960. 联合国委托管理的领土(如 1947 至 1960 年的喀麦隆).

truth /tru:θ; truθ/ n (pl ~s /tru:ðz; truðz/) **1** [U] quality or state of being true: 确实; 真实性: There's no ~ /not a word of ~ in what he says. 他说的话毫不确实(他说的没有一句实话). ~ moment of ~, time of crisis, test, or revelation. 紧要关头; 考验时刻; 顿悟之际. **2** [U] that which is true: 真实; 真相; 事实: tell the ~. 说实话. to tell the ~, ..., (formula used when making a confession): (作坦白陈述时所用的套语): To tell the ~, I forgot all about your request. 说实话, 我把你要求的事情忘得干干净净. in ~, (liter) truly, really. (文)真实地; 实际上. **3** [C] fact, belief, etc accepted as true: 真理; 真义: the ~s of religion /science. 宗教的真义(科学的真

理)。~**·ful** /-fl; fəl/ *adj* **1** (of persons) in the habit of telling the ~. (指人)惯于说实话的;诚实的。**2** (of statements) true. (指陈述)真实的。~**·fully** /-fəlɪ; -fəlɪ/ *adv* ~**·ful·ness** *n*

try[1] /traɪ; traɪ/ *vi, vt* (*pt, pp* **tried**) **1** [VP2A, B, 7 A] (Note that, in colloq style, *try to + inf* is often replaced by *try and + inf*, esp in the imperative, and *don't try to* and *didn't try to* are often replaced by *don't try and* and *didn't try and*) make an attempt: (注意: try to + inf 在口语中常改用 try and + inf, 尤其在祈使句中更常见; 否定形式 don't try to 与 didn't try to 常改作 don't try and 与 didn't try and)试做; 勉力而为: *I don't think I can do it, but I'll try.* 我不以为我能做该事, 但是我要试试看。*I've tried till I'm tired.* 我一直做累了才停下来的。*He's trying his hardest,* using his utmost efforts. 他现在正全力用力。*Try to get here early.* 请尽量早一点来。*Try to/Try and behave better.* 规矩一点(不要乱来)。*He didn't try to do it.* 他未做尝试(他未试做该事)。*Don't try and swim across the river.* 不要尝试游过那河。**2** [VP3A] **try for sth,** make an attempt to get or win (esp a position): 试图得到; 争取(尤指职位): *try for a scholarship/a position in the Civil Service.* 争取奖学金(文官职位)。**3** [VP6A, B, C, 10] use sth, do sth, as an experiment or test, to see whether it is satisfactory: 试验; 试用或试做以观其结果: *Have you tried sleeping on your back as a cure for snoring?* 你试过仰睡以防止打鼾的办法吗? *Won't you try* (=buy and use) *this new kind of detergent?* 请试购用这种新的清洁剂。*Try how far you can jump/whether you can jump across this stream.* 试试看你能跳多远(你是否跳得过这条小河)。*Try knocking at the back door if nobody hears you at the front door.* 如果前门没有人应门, 去敲后门试试看。*Please try me for the job, let me do it as an experiment.* 请让我试试那工作。⇨ **trial**(1). [VP15B] **try sth on, (a)** put on (a garment, show, etc) to see whether it fits, looks well, etc: 试(衣服等): *I want to try the shoes on before I buy them.* 我要在购买前试穿鞋子。**(b)** (colloq) make a bold or impudent attempt to discover whether sth will be tolerated: (口)作大胆或厚颜的尝试以发现某事是否被容忍; 试探: *It's no use your trying it/your games/your tricks on with me.* 你对我耍这一套是没有用的(我不吃这一套)。Hence, 由此产生, '**try-on** *n* (colloq) an attempt of this sort. (口)试探; 试探。[VP15B] **try sth out,** use it, experiment with it, in order to test it: 借使用、实验以考验某事物; 实际试验某事物: *The idea seems good but it needs to be tried out.* 这构想似乎不错, 但是需要实际考验。'**try-out** *n* preliminary test of ability, qualification, etc, eg of an athlete. (运动员等的)预选; 预赛; (能力、资格等的)初步鉴定。*try one's hand at sth,* ⇨ **hand**[1](5). **4** [VP6A, 15A] inquire into (a case) in a court of law: (法庭上)审判; 审问(案件): *He was tried and found guilty.* 他经过审判并被判决有罪。*He will be tried for murder.* 他将以杀人罪受审。*Which judge will try the case?* 哪一位法官将要审讯这个案子? ⇨ **trial**(3). **5** [VP 6A] put a strain on; cause to be tired, exhausted, out of patience, etc: 考验; 过度使用而损伤; 使疲劳、竭尽、失去耐性等: *Small print tries the eyes.* 小字体伤眼睛。*Don't try his patience too much.* 不要太过分而使他受不了。*His courage was severely tried.* 他的勇气受到了严厉的考验。 **tried** *adj* that has been tested; reliable: 经过试验的; 可信赖的: *a tried friend/remedy.* 可靠的朋友(验方)。'**trier** *n* person who tries hard, who always does his best. 勤劳者; 努力工作者; 尽力工作者。**try·ing** *adj* (⇨ **5** above) distressing; putting a strain on, eg the temper, one's patience: (参看上列第 5 义)使人痛苦的; 难堪的; 考验(脾气、耐性等)的: *a trying person to deal with;* 不易相处的人; *have a trying day,* one during which one's temper, patience, etc are tried; 经历难捱的一天; *work that is trying to the eyes.* 费眼力的工作。

try[2] /traɪ; traɪ/ *n* **1** attempt: 尝试; 试验; 努力: *Let me have a try at it.* 这事让我试试看。*He had three tries and failed each time.* 他尝试了三回, 每回都失败了。**2**(Rugby)

touching down the ball behind the opponents' goal-line (with a score of three points). (橄榄球)在对方球门线后以球触地(获三分); 三分触地法。

tryst /trɪst; trɪst/ *n* (archaic) (time and place for, agreement to have, a) meeting, esp between lovers: (古)约会(尤指爱人间的幽会); 约会的时间及地点; 会晤的约定: *keep/break ~ (with sb).* 赴(不赴)(与某人的)约会。

Tsar /zɑː(r); tsɑr/, **Tsa·rina** /zɑːˈriːnə; tsɑˈrinə/ *nn* = **Czar, Czarina.**

tsetse /ˈtsetsɪ; ˈtsɛtsɪ/ *n* **~(-fly)** blood-sucking fly (in tropical Africa) carrying and transmitting (often fatal) disease to men and animals. (热带非洲的)吸血蝇; 采采蝇(引起并传播人或动物之疾病, 常可致死)。 ⇨ the illus at **insect.** 参看 insect 之插图。

T-shirt /ˈtiːʃɜːt; ˈtiˌʃɝt/ *n* ⇨ **T, t.**

T-square /ˈtiː skweə(r); ˈtiˌskwɛr/ *n* ⇨ **square**[2](7).

tub /tʌb; tʌb/ *n* **1** large open vessel, usu round, made of wood, zinc, etc used for washing clothes, holding liquids, growing plants in, etc: 桶; 盆: *a rain-water tub.* 盛雨水的桶。'**tub-thumper** *n* mob orator. 煽惑群情的演说家。**2** (also dryw作 '**tub-ful**) as much as a tub holds: 一桶或一盆之量: *a tub of water.* 一桶水。**3** (colloq) bath-tub; (GB) bath: (口)浴缸; (英)淋浴; 洗澡: *have a cold tub before breakfast;* 早餐前洗一个冷水澡; *prefer a tub to a shower.* 喜欢盆浴胜过淋浴。**4** (colloq) clumsy slow boat. (口)笨重缓慢的船。

tuba /ˈtjuːbə US: ˈtuː-; ˈtjubə/ *n* large musical instrument of brass, of low pitch. 低音大喇叭; 低音号。⇨ the illus at **brass.** 参看 brass 之插图。

tubby /ˈtʌbɪ; ˈtʌbɪ/ *adj* (**-ier, -iest**) shaped like a tub; fat and round: 桶或盆状的; 胖而圆的: *a tubby little man.* 矮小而圆胖的男子。

tube /tjuːb US: tuːb; tjub/ *n* **1** long hollow cylinder of metal, glass or rubber, esp for holding or conveying liquids, etc: (金属, 玻璃或橡皮制的)管; 筒: '*boiler ~s;* 锅炉管; the '*inner ~ of a bicycle/car tyre,* of rubber, filled with air at pressure; 脚踏车(汽车)轮胎的内胎; *tor'pedo ~s,* from which torpedoes are launched. 鱼雷发射管。'**~-well** *n* metal ~ placed in the ground to obtain water through perforations in the ~ near its end. 管井。**2** soft metal container with a screw-cap, used for pastes, paints, etc: (装牙膏、颜料等的)软金属筒管; *a ~ of toothpaste.* 一管牙膏。**3** [U, C] (in London) underground railway: (在伦敦)地下铁道: *travel in to work by ~ every morning;* 每天早晨乘地下火车到伦敦上班; *take a/the ~ to Oxford Circus.* 乘地下火车至牛津广场。**4** (US) thermionic valve as used in electronic apparatus; large ~ with a screen (*cathode ray ~,* ⇨ cathode) as used in a television set. (美)真空管; 电视机的显像管。**5** hollow ~-shaped organ in the body: (身体内)管状器官: *the bronchial ~s.* 支气管等。**tub·ing** *n* [U] material in the form of a ~: 管子材料; 管材: *five feet of rubber/copper tubing.* 五英尺橡皮(铜)管。**tu·bu·lar** /ˈtjuːbjʊlə(r) US: ˈtuː-; ˈtjubjələ/ *adj* **1** having the shape of a ~: 管状的: *a tubular bridge,* a bridge in the shape of a ~ through which a railway, etc passes. 涵梁桥(铁路等穿过其中的管道)。**2** having, consisting of, ~s or tubing: 有管的; 管式的; 由管或管材构成的: *a tubular boiler,* in which water or steam is heated as it passes through many ~s; 管式锅炉(水或蒸汽经过诸管时受热); *tubular furniture,* with parts made of metal tubing; 管架家具(零件由金属管制成者); *tubular scaffolding.* 管材鹰架。**~·less** *adj* having no inner ~: 无内胎的; 无内管的: '*~less tyres.* 无内胎的轮胎。

tu·ber /ˈtjuːbə(r) US: ˈtuː-; ˈtjubə/ *n* [C] enlarged part of an underground stem with buds from which new plants will grow, eg a potato, Jerusalem artichoke, yam, etc. 块茎; 球根(如马铃薯、菊芋、薯蓣等)。

tu·ber·cu·lo·sis /tjuːˌbɜːkjʊˈləʊsɪs US: tuː-; tjuˌbɝkjəˈlosɪs/ *n* [U] (common abbr 通常略作 **TB**/ˌtiː ˈbiː; ˌti ˈbi/, ˌti'bi/) wasting disease affecting various parts of the body's tissues, esp the lungs: 结核病; (尤指)肺结核; 肺

痨: pulmonary ~, consumption. 肺结核; 肺痨。 **tu·ber·cu·lous** /tjuːˈbəːkjuləs US: tuː-; tjəˈbəːkjələs/, **tu·ber·cu·lar** /tjuːˈbəːkjulə(r) US: tuː-; tjəˈbəːkjələ/ adjj of, affected by, ~. 结核病的; 肺结核的; 感染结核病的。

tub·ing, tu·bu·lar ⇨ tube.

tuck /tʌk; tʌk/ n 1 [C] flat, stitched fold of material in a garment, for shortening or for ornament: (衣服的)褶; 裥; 襞: make/put in/take out a ~ in a dress/the sleeve of a shirt. 在女服(衬衫袖)上打褶(加褶,去褶)。 2 [U] (GB, sl) food, esp the cakes, pastry, etc that children enjoy. (英, 俚)食物; (尤指儿童喜吃的)糕饼、点心等。 '~-shop n shop (esp at a school) where ~ is sold. (尤指学校里的)点心店; 糖果店。 □ vt, vi 1 [VP15A, B] draw together into a small space; put or push into a desired or convenient position: 缩拢; 卷折; 叠起; 打褶缩; 塞在或放在所要的或方便的地方: ~ one's shirt in, put the bottom of it inside one's trousers, etc. 将衬衣底部塞入裤内。 She ~ed the ends of her hair into her bathing-cap. 她把头发的末端塞进游泳帽中。 He sat with his legs ~ed up under him. 他盘坐着。 The bird ~ed its head under its wing. 那鸟把头缩藏在翼下。 The map is ~ed away in a pocket at the end of the book. 那地图藏在该书后面的小袋中。She ~ed the child up in bed, pulled the bed-clothes up round the child and under the mattress. 她为那孩子盖好被子并且把被子的边缘塞在垫褥下面。She took off her shoes, ~ed up (= rolled or turned up) her skirt, and waded across the stream. 她脱去鞋子, 卷起裙子, 涉过小河。 2 [VP2C, 3A] ~ in, eat heartily 大吃; 尽情地吃。 ~ into sth, eat it heartily: 大吃; 尽情地吃: He ~ed into the cold ham. 他大吃冷火腿。 '~·'in n full meal: 饱餐; 丰宴: The boys had a good ~-in. 男孩子们享受了一顿盛宴。

tucker /ˈtʌkə(r); ˈtʌkə/ n piece of lace, linen, etc, worn (in the 17th and 18th cc) to cover a woman's neck and shoulders. (十七, 十八世纪时, 女人围于颈部及肩上的)领边; 饰纱。 one's best bib and ~, (colloq) one's best or finest clothes. (口)个人最讲究或最漂亮的衣服。

Tues·day /ˈtjuːzdɪ US: ˈtuː-; ˈtjuzdɪ/ n third day of the week, next after Monday. 星期二; 礼拜二; 火曜日。

tuft /tʌft; tʌft/ n bunch of feathers, hair, grass, etc growing or held together at the base. (生长或固着于底部的)一束羽毛、发须、草等; 一丛; 一卷; 一簇。 ~ed adj having ~s; growing in a ~ or ~s. 有簇羽、发等的; 成簇生的。

tug /tʌg; tʌg/ vt, vi (-gg-) [VP6A, 15A, B, 2A, C, 3A] tug (at), pull hard or violently; pull hard (at): 用力拉; 拖曳: The child was tugging her toy cart round the garden/tugging it along behind. 那孩子绕着花园拖曳她的玩具车(拖曳着的玩具车在后面)。 We tugged so hard that the rope broke. 我们用力拖曳, 以致绳子断了。 The kitten was tugging at my shoe-lace. 那小猫在拉曳我的鞋带。 □ n 1 sudden hard pull: 突然而用力的拉; 拉扯; 拖曳: The naughty boy gave his sister's hair a tug. 那顽皮的男孩用力拉了一下他姐姐(妹妹)的头发。 I felt a tug at my sleeve. 我觉得有人拉了一下我的袖子。 Parting from his family was a tug (at his heart-strings), It was difficult to leave them. 与家人离别使他难过。 tug of war, contest in which two teams pull against each other on a rope. 拔河比赛。 2 'tug(-boat), small powerful boat for towing ships, etc. 拖船。

a tug-boat

tu·ition /tjuːˈɪʃn US: tuː-; tjuˈɪʃən/ n [U] (fee for) teaching: 教学; 讲授; 学费: have private ~ in mathematics. 私下请人教数学。

tu·lip /ˈtjuːlɪp US: ˈtuː-; ˈtjuləp/ n bulb plant with, in spring, a large bell-shaped or cup-shaped flower on a tall stem. 郁金香; 山慈姑。

tulle /tjuːl US: tuːl; tjul/ n [U] soft, fine, silk net-like material for veils and dresses. 软薄的绸纱(作妇女面纱和衣服)。

tumble /ˈtʌmbl; ˈtʌmbl/ vi, vt 1 [VP2A, C] fall, esp quickly or violently: 跌倒; 跌落 (尤指快速或猛烈地): ~ down the stairs/off a horse or bicycle/out of a window/over the roots of a tree. 从楼梯跌下(从马或脚踏车上跌下; 从窗子摔落; 为树根绊倒)。 The baby is just learning to walk and he's always tumbling over. 那婴儿正在学步, 所以常常跌倒。 2 [VP2A, C] move up and down, to and fro, in a restless or disorderly way: 滚动; 辗转; 不安地或紊乱地行动: The puppies were tumbling about on the floor. 小狗在地板上打滚。The sick man tossed and ~d in his bed: 那病人在床上辗转反侧。 I was so tired that I threw my clothes off and ~d into bed. 我疲倦得把衣服一脱就上床睡觉了。 3 [VP2O] be in a weak state (as if ready to fall): 衰弱; 弱不禁风 (似将随时倾倒): The old barn is tumbling to pieces. 那陈旧的谷仓似将倾颓。 '~-down attrib adj dilapidated; likely to collapse: 破烂的; 似要坍塌的; 可能倒塌的: What a ~-down old house you live in! 你住的房子多破旧啊! 4 [VP15A, B] cause to fall; upset: 使跌倒; 使跌落; 使倾覆: The accident ~d us all out of the bus. 那车祸把我们从公共汽车里全掉了出来。 5 [VP6A] put into a state of disorder: 使紊乱; 弄乱; 搅乱: ~ one's bed-clothes/sb's hair or clothes. 弄乱床单被褥(某人的头发或衣服)。 6 [VP3A] ~ to sth, (colloq) grasp, realize (an idea, etc): (口)领悟; 了解(观念等): At last he ~d to what I was hinting at. 他终于明白了我暗示给他的意思。 □ n 1 [C] fall: 跌倒; 摔落: have a nasty ~. 重重地跌了一跤。 2 confused state: 混乱(状态): Things were all in a ~. 局势很混乱。 '~-weed n (US) plant which grows in desert areas and, when withered, breaks off and is rolled about by the wind. (美)野苋(长于沙漠地区), 枯干后断茎, 随风滚动的)。

tum·bler /ˈtʌmblə(r); ˈtʌmblə/ n 1 flat-bottomed drinking-glass without a handle or stem, ⇨ goblet. (无柄或脚的)平底玻璃杯。 2 part of the mechanism of a lock which must be turned by a key before the lock will open. 锁的制栓 (用钥匙拨动才能使锁开启的部分)。 3 kind of pigeon that turns over in flight. 翻头鸽(飞翔时会向后翻滚)。 4 acrobat. 特技表演者。

tum·brel, tum·bril /ˈtʌmbrəl; ˈtʌmbrəl/ n (hist) cart, esp the kind that carried prisoners to the guillotine during the French Revolution. (史)车; (尤指)(法国大革命期间载运囚犯至断头台的)囚车。

tu·mes·cent /tjuːˈmesnt US: tuː-; tjuˈmesnt/ adj swelling; swollen. 肿起的; 肿胀的。 **tu·mes·cence**/-sns; -sns/ n

tu·mid /ˈtjuːmɪd US: ˈtuː-; ˈtjumɪd/ adj (of parts of the body) swollen; (fig, of a style of writing, etc) bombastic. (指身体的部分)肿起的; (喻, 指某种文体等)浮夸的。 ~·ity /tjuːˈmɪdɪtɪ US: tuː-; tjuˈmɪdɪtɪ/ n

tummy /ˈtʌmɪ; ˈtʌmɪ/ n (pl -mies) (colloq) stomach; belly. (口)胃; 肚子。

tu·mour (US = **tu·mor**) /ˈtjuːmə(r) US: ˈtuː-; ˈtjumə/ n diseased growth in some part of the body. 肿; 肿块; 瘤。

tu·mult /ˈtjuːmʌlt US: ˈtuː-; ˈtjumʌlt/ n [C, U] 1 uproar; disturbance: 喧嚣; 扰乱; 纷扰: the ~ of battle. 战斗的喧嚣。 2 confused and excited state of mind: (心境的)烦乱; 激昂; 激动(地): in a ~, 激动的。 when the ~ within him had subsided. 当他内心的激动消灭的时候。

tu·mul·tu·ous /tjuːˈmʌltʃuəs US: tuː-; tjuˈmʌltʃuəs/ adj disorderly; noisy and violent: 骚乱的; 扰动的; 喧嚣而猛烈的: a ~ welcome. 喧嚣热烈的欢迎。 ~·ly adv

tu·mu·lus /ˈtjuːmjuləs US: ˈtuː-; ˈtjumjələs/ n (pl -li

/-laɪ/, -laɪ/) mound of earth over a (usu ancient) grave. 冢；墓 (通常为古墓之隆起部分)。

tun /tʌn/ tʌn/ n large cask for beer, wine, etc; measure of capacity (252 gallons). (装啤酒，葡萄酒等的) 大酒桶；大桶 (容量单位，等于 252 加仑)。

tuna /ˈtjuːnə US: ˈtuːnə/ ˈtuːnə/ ˈtuːnə/ n (pl ~ or ~s) = tunny.

tun·dra /ˈtʌndrə/ ˈtʌndrə/ n [U, C] wide, treeless plain of the arctic regions, marshy in summer and frozen hard in winter. 冻土地带；苔原 (北极地区不生树木的辽阔地带，夏季湿软，冬季冻结)。

tune /tjuːn US: tuːn/ tjun/ n 1 [C] succession of notes forming a melody (of a song, hymn, etc): (歌，赞美诗等的) 曲；调子：whistle a popular ~; 以口哨吹流行的曲子；~s that are easy to remember. 容易记忆的曲子。 2 [U] quality of having a well-marked melody: 具有某一显明旋律的性质：Some of this modern music has very little ~ in it. 这种现代音乐的旋律不太明显。 3 [U] in/out of ~, at/not at the correct pitch: 音高正确 (不正确)，和调 (不和调)：sing/play in ~. 唱 (奏) 得合调。 The piano is out of ~. 这钢琴走音调不正确。 The piano and the violin are not in ~. 这钢琴和小提琴的调子不谐和。 4 [U] (fig) harmony; harmonious adjustment: (喻) 和合；调和；谐和；协调：be in/out of ~ with one's surroundings/companions. 与环境 (密友们) 协调 (不协调)。 5 (fig uses) (比喻用法) change one's ~; sing another ~, change one's way of speaking, behaviour, etc, or one's attitude to others (eg from insolence to respect). 改变一己的论调、行为等，或改变对人的态度 (如前倨后恭)。 to the ~ of, (colloq) to the amount of (usu with the suggestion that the sum is high or exorbitant): (口) 总数高达 (通常含示总额甚大或过度)：He was fined (eg for a motoring offence) to the ~ of £30. 他被罚款 (例如因驾车违警) 高达三十英镑。 □ vt, vi 1 [VP6A] adjust the strings, etc of a musical instrument to the right pitch: 调整 (乐器) 的弦等使合调；调准：~ a guitar. 调整吉他弦。 [VP2C] ~ up, (of a player or players in an orchestra) a musical instrument: (如指管弦乐队的演奏者) 调整乐器；调弦；调音：The orchestra were tuning up when we entered the concert-hall. 当我们进入音乐厅时，管弦乐队正在调音。 'tuning-fork n small steel instrument, which produces a musical note of fixed pitch when struck. 音叉。 2 [VP2C] ~ in (to), (a) adjust the controls of a radio to a particular frequency /station: 调整收音机至某一频率或电台；校准频率或波长；拨收台：~ in to the B B C World Service. 收听英国广播公司对全球的播音。 You're not properly ~d in. 你没有把收音机校准。 (b) (fig) be aware of what other people are thinking, etc: (喻) 知道或发觉别人有所说的话或表现的情绪等：He's not very well ~d in to his surroundings. 他不太了解他周围的环境。 3 [VP6A] adjust or adapt the engine of a motor-vehicle so that it gives its best, or a special, performance. 调整汽车等的引擎使产生最佳或特定效能。 ~r n 1 (in compounds) person who ~s musical instruments: (用于复合词中) 调整乐器音调的人；调音师：a 'piano-tuner. 钢琴调音师。 2 part of a radio etc which receives the signals. (收音机等的) 调谐器。 ▷ amplifier at amplify, loud-speaker at loud(1). ~ful /-fl; -fʊl/ adj having a pleasing ~; melodious. 有悦耳音调的；谐美的。 ~fully /fəlɪ; -fʊlɪ/ adj ~ful·ness n

tung-oil /ˈtʌŋ ɔɪl; ˈtʌŋ ɔɪl/ n [U] oil (from a tree) used chiefly in varnishing woodwork. 桐油。

tung·sten /ˈtʌŋstən/ ˈtʌŋstən/ n [U] grey metal (symbol **W**) used in making steel and the filaments of electric light bulbs. 钨 (符号 W，用以制合金钢及电灯之丝)。

tu·nic /ˈtjuːnɪk US: ˈtuː-; ˈtjunɪk/ n 1 close-fitting jacket as worn by policemen, soldiers, etc. (警察、军人等所着的) 紧身上衣。 2 loose blouse or coat for a woman or girl, gathered at the waist with a belt, and reaching down to, or below, the hips. (妇女所着垂至臀部或低于

臀部的) 束腰外衣。 3 loose, short-sleeved or sleeveless outer garment reaching to the knees, as worn by ancient Greeks and Romans. (古希腊、罗马人所着，长及膝部的) 短袖或无袖宽大外袍。

tun·nel /ˈtʌnl; ˈtʌnl/ n underground passage (esp through a hill or mountain, for a road, railway, etc); underwater passage (eg the proposed Channel ~ between England and France). 地下通道；(尤指) (道路，铁路等穿越山岭或海底的) 隧道 (如拟议中穿过英伦海峡的海底隧道)。 □ vi, vt (-ll-, US also -l-) [VP2A, C, 3A, 6A] ~ (into through), dig a ~ (into/through) sth; dig a ~ or ~s through (sth). 在…掘地道；开隧道穿过。

tunny /ˈtʌnɪ; ˈtʌnɪ/ n (pl -nies or unchanged 或不变) large sea-fish. used as food, and valued for the sport of catching it. 鲔；金枪鱼 (一种大海鱼，可捕之为食或作为消遣)。

tup /tʌp; tʌp/ n male sheep; ram. 公绵羊；(未阉过的) 公羊。

tup·pence /ˈtʌpəns; ˈtʌpəns/ n (colloq) two pence. (口) 两便士。 **tup·penny** /ˈtʌpənɪ; ˈtʌpənɪ/ adj costing ~; (fig) of trifling value. 值两便士的；(喻) 价值小的；微不足道的。

tu quo·que /ˌtjuː ˈkwəʊkwə US: ˌtuː ˈkwəʊkweɪ; tjuˈkwokwɪ/ n (Lat) (phrase used as a retort) So are you! So did you! (拉) (用于回嘴或反唇相讥) 你也是！彼此彼此！

tur·ban /ˈtɜːbən; ˈtɜːbən/ n 1 headdress made by winding a length of cloth round the head (as worn in some Asian and African countries). (某些亚洲及非洲国家的人民所缠的) 头巾；包头巾。 2 close-fitting hat resembling a ~. (类似头巾之) 小帽。 ~ed adj wearing a ~: 戴头巾的；戴小帽的：a ~ed Sikh. 戴头巾的印度锡克教徒。

tur·bid /ˈtɜːbɪd; ˈtɜːbɪd/ adj 1 (of liquids) thick; muddy; not clear: (指液体) 浓厚的；混浊的：~ waters/rivers. 混浊的矿泉 (河流)。 2 (fig) disordered; confused: (喻) 混乱的；紊乱的：a ~ imagination; 紊乱的想象；~ thoughts. 杂乱的思绪。 ~ness, ~·ity /tɜːˈbɪdətɪ; tɜˈbɪdətɪ/ n

tur·bine /ˈtɜːbaɪn; ˈtɜːbaɪn/ n engine or motor whose driving-wheel is turned by a current of water, steam or air. 涡轮机 (主动轮由水流、蒸汽或空气所推动的引擎)；透平机；水轮机；汽轮机。 ▷ the illus at air. 参看 air 之插图。

tur·bo·jet /ˌtɜːbəʊˈdʒet; ˈtɜːboˌdʒet/ n (aircraft with a) turbine engine that delivers its power in the form of a jet of hot gases (no propellers being needed on the aircraft). 涡轮喷气引擎；涡轮喷气飞机 (无需螺旋桨)。

tur·bo·prop /ˌtɜːbəʊˈprɒp; ˈtɜːboˌprɑp/ n (aircraft with a) turbine engine that uses its power, from hot gases, to turn a propeller. 涡轮螺旋桨引擎；涡轮螺旋桨飞机。

tur·bot /ˈtɜːbət; ˈtɜːbət/ n (pl unchanged) large, flat sea-fish valued as food. (复数不变) 大菱鲆；大比目鱼 (一种扁平的大海鱼，可作珍贵食品)。

tur·bu·lent /ˈtɜːbjʊlənt; ˈtɜːbjələnt/ adj violent; disorderly; uncontrolled: 狂烈的；混乱的；无秩序的：~ waves/passions; 汹涌的波浪 (激动的情绪)；a ~ mob. 一群暴徒。 ~·ly adv tur·bu·lence /-ləns; -ləns/ n

turd /tɜːd; tɜːd/ n [U, C] (sl) (ball or lump of) excrement: (俚) 粪块；屎球；屎：sheep ~s. 羊粪。

tu·reen /tjʊˈriːn US: tuː-; tuˈrin/ n deep dish with a lid, from which soup, vegetables, etc are served at table (盛汤、菜等的) 有盖汤碗。

turf /tɜːf; tɜːf/ n 1 [U] soil-surface with grass-roots growing in it: 草皮；草皮；草根土：strip the ~ off a field; 除去田中的草根；make a lawn by laying ~ (instead of sowing grass-seed). 铺草根土 (代替撒草种) 以做成草皮。 the ~, the race-course; the occupation of profession of horse-racing. 跑马场；赛马业。 '~ accountant, ~ commission agent, bookmaker. ▷ book[1](8). 赛马业者。 2 (pl ~s or 或 turves /tɜːvz; tɜvz/) piece of ~ cut out; (in Ireland) (piece of) peat. 草皮；草皮块；

(爱尔兰)泥煤(块); 泥煤(块)。 □ *vt* 1 [VP6A] cover or lay (a piece of land) with ~. 以草泥覆盖(一片土地); 铺草皮。 2 [VP15B] ~ *out*, (GB sl) throw out. (英俚)赶出; 抛出。

tur·gid /'tɜːdʒɪd; 'tɝdʒɪd/ *adj* 1 swollen; bloated. 因病肿胀的; 浮肿的。 2 (of language) pompous; full of high-sounding words. (指语言)虚饰的; 多浮夸用语的。 ~·**ly** *adv*/ ~·**ity**/ tɜː'dʒɪdetɪ; tɝ'dʒɪdetɪ/ *n*

Turk /tɜːk; tɝk/ *n* native or inhabitant of Turkey. 土耳其人或其居民。

tur·key /'tɜːkɪ; 'tɝkɪ/ *n* (*pl* ~s) 1 [C] large bird valued as food; [U] its flesh; ⇨ the illus at fowl. 吐绶鸡; 火鸡(参看 fowl 之插图); 火鸡肉。 2 (US sl) a flop. (美俚)失败的作品(戏剧、电影、作品等)。 *cold* ~, (a) sudden withdrawal from, or hangover after taking, narcotics. 突然(而完全地)戒毒; 吸毒后的残留不适。 (b) frank, determined statement of truth (usu about sth unpleasant). 实话实说(通常指说出令人不快之事)。 *talk* ~, (US sl) talk frankly and bluntly. (美俚)直率地讲; 直截了当地说; 开门见山地讲。

Tur·kish /'tɜːkɪʃ; 'tɝkɪʃ/ *n, adj* (language) of Turkey or the Turks. 土耳其语; 土耳其的; 土耳其人的。 ~ *bath*, of hot air or steam, followed by a shower and massage. 土耳其浴; 蒸汽浴。 ~ *delight*, sweetmeat of jelly-like substance covered with powdered sugar. 软糖; 橡皮糖。 ~ *towel*, one made of rough absorbent cloth. (富吸水性的)粗面毛巾。

tur·meric /'tɜːmerɪk; 'tɝmerɪk/ *n* [U] (E Indian plant with a) root which is used, in powdered form, as a colouring substance and a flavouring (esp in making curries). 郁金(东印度植物, 其根磨成粉, 可作染料及调味料, 尤用于制咖喱粉); 郁金粉)。

tur·moil /'tɜːmɔɪl; 'tɝmɔɪl/ *n* [C, U] (instance of) trouble, agitation, disturbance: 骚动; 混乱; 扰乱; 其实: *The town was in a* ~ *during the elections.* 该城在选举期间陷入一片混乱。

turn[1] /tɜːn; tɝn/ *n* 1 act of turning; turning movement: 旋转; 转动; *a few* ~s *of the handle*, 把手的数次转动; *a* ~ *of Fortune's wheel*, a change of fortune. 机运的转变。 ~ *of the century*, the time when a new century (2) starts. 新世纪开始时(一世纪末与下一世纪初)。 *on the* ~, about to change: 即将改变; 正要改变: *The milk is on the* ~, about to turn sour. 牛奶快要酸了。 *The tide is on the* ~. 潮水快要涨(退)了。 *done to a* ~, (from the use of a ~spit) cooked just enough, neither underdone nor overdone. (来自从前用狗转动烤肉叉之方法)(指食物)烹煮得恰到好处; 火候到家。 2 change of direction: 转变方向; 弯; *sudden* ~s *in the road.* 路上的急弯。 *at every* ~, (fig) very frequently: (喻)经常地; 不时地: *I've been coming across old friends at every* ~ *during this reunion.* 在这次团聚中, 我经常遇见老友。 *He was frustrated at every* ~, every time he tried to achieve his aim. 他每次都遭遇挫折。 3 change in condition: 改变情况; 转机; 变化: *The sick man / My affairs took a* ~ *for the better /worse.* 病人(我的事情)转好(坏)了。 *His illness took a favourable* ~. 他的病情有了良好的转机。 4 occasion or opportunity for doing sth, esp in one's proper order among others: (轮流做某事的)时机; 机会; 次序: *It's your* ~ *to read now, John.* 约翰, 现在轮到你们读了。 *Wait (until it is) your* ~. 等着轮到你吧。 *My* ~ *will come* (sometimes meaning 'I shall have my time of success, triumph, revenge, etc', according to context). 总会轮到我(有时意谓'我总有出头、胜利、报复等的一天')。 *(do sth)* ~ *and* ~ *about*, (of two or more persons) first one and then the other(s); alternately (指两人或多人)轮流地(做某事); 交替地。 *by* ~s, (of persons, groups, actions) in rotation; one after the other: (指人, 团体, 行为)轮流地; 轮替地; 依次地: *She went hot and cold by* ~s. 她一阵发热一阵发冷。 *They laughed and cried by* ~s. 他们一会儿笑一会儿哭。 *in* ~, (of two persons) = ~ and ~ about; (of more than two persons) in succession: (指两人)轮流地; (指三人以上)一个接一个

地; 接连地; 依次: *The boys were summoned in* ~ *to see the examiner.* 男孩子们依次被召入会见考试官。 *out of* ~, before or after the permitted time: 在规定时间之前或后; 不按顺序地: *You mustn't speak out of (your)* ~, 轮到你的时候, 不可发言。 *take* ~s *(at sth); take* ~s *about*, do it in ~: 轮流做某事: *Mary and Helen took* ~s *at sitting up with their sick mother*, Mary sat up first, Helen next, and so on. 玛丽和海伦轮流熬夜陪伴她们生病的母亲。 5 action regarded as affecting sb. 被认为具有影响力的举动或行为。 *One good* ~ *deserves another*, (prov) Help, kind service, etc should be repaid. (谚)施惠者应受惠(好心应有好报)。 *do sb a good / bad* ~, be/not be helpful. (对某人)有恩惠或帮助(有损害)。 6 natural tendency: 自然的趋势; 倾向; 癖性: *a boy with a mechanical* ~, interested in, clever at, mechanical things. 爱好机械的男孩子。 *He has a gloomy* ~ *of mind.* 他有忧郁的癖性。 7 purpose; special need. 目的; 特殊需要。 *serve one's* ~, meet one's requirements: 适合自己的需要: *I think this book will serve my* ~. 我想这本书将会适合我的需要。 8 short period of activity: 短时间的活动: *I'll take a few* ~s *(* = have a walk*) round the deck before I go to bed.* 睡觉前我将在甲板上散一会儿步。 *I'll take a* ~ *at the oars now if you want a rest.* 如果你需要休息, 我来划一会儿桨。 9 short performance on the stage (esp of a variety theatre, or similar entertainment for sound or TV broadcasts), eg a song, dance, juggling feat, display of skill. 短时间的综艺节目(尤指杂耍戏院, 或无线电、电视广播中出现的娱乐节目, 如歌、舞、戏法、特技)。 *star* ~, most popular ~. 最受欢迎的综艺节目。 10 (colloq) nervous shock: (口)震惊; 吃惊: *The news gave me quite a* ~. 这消息使我大吃一惊。

turn[2] /tɜːn; tɝn/ *vt, vi* (For uses with *adverbial particles and preps*, ⇨ 7 below.) (与副词性小品词及介词连用的用法, 参看下列第 7 义)1 [VP6A, 15A, B, 2A, C, 4A] (cause to) move round a point; (cause to) move so as to face in a different direction: (使)旋转; (使)转动; 翻转: *The earth* ~s *round the sun*. 地球绕日运行。 *The wheels of the car were* ~ing *slowly*. 汽车的轮子在缓缓地转动。 *What* ~s *the wheels?* 什么力量使车轮转动? *He* ~ed *away from me*. 他避开我。 *He* ~ed *his back on me*, ⇨ *back*[1](1). 他转过身去不理我。 *He* ~ed *his back to the wall.* 他把背转向墙。 *He* ~ed *his head (round) and looked back.* 他转头往后看。 *He* ~ed *to look at me.* 他转过(身)来看着我。 *He* ~ed *(to the) felt.* 他向左边转。 *It's time we* ~ed *and went back home.* 我们(现在)应该折返回家去了。 *He was idly* ~ing *the pages of a magazine.* 他在无聊地翻(看)一本杂志。 *The car* ~ed *(round) the corner.* 汽车转过街角。 *Be careful how you* ~ *that corner.* 转那个(街)角要格外当心。 *The mere thought of food* ~ed *his stomach*, upset his stomach, made him feel ill. 一想到食物就使他作呕。 *His stomach* ~ed *at the sight of food.* (当时)他一看到食物就觉得想吐。 *When does the tide* ~, begin to flow in/out? 潮水何时涨(退)? *This tap* ~s *easily.* 这个水龙头转动起来很容易。 *It's easy to* ~ *this tap.* 转动这个水龙头容易得很。 *Nothing will ever* ~ *him from (*=cause him to change*) his purpose.* 什么也不能使他改变他的目标。 ~ *one's mind / thoughts / attention to sth*, direct one's mind, etc to: 把自己的心智(思想, 注意力)灌注在某事物上: *Please* ~ *your attention to something more important.* 请把注意力灌在较重要的事情上。 ~ *one's hand to sth*, (be able to) undertake (a task, etc): (能够)从事或担任(一项工作等): *He can* ~ *his hand to most jobs about the house*, can deal with them. 家里的事情大多数他都能做。 ~ *sth to account*, ⇨ *account*[1](3). ~ *a deaf ear to sth*, refuse to listen to: 不听; 拒绝听: *They* ~ed *a deaf ear to my request for help.* 他们对我的求助置若罔闻。 ~ *sb's flank*; ~ *the flank of sb*, pass round an enemy's position so as to attack it in the flank or rear; (fig) outwit him; defeat him in debate, etc. 由侧面迂回包抄敌人; (喻)机智上胜过某人; 在辩论等中击败某人。 ~ *the corner*, (fig use)

(比喻用法) ⇨ **corner**(1), ~ **the scale**(s), ⇨ **scale³**(1). **2** [VP6A, 14, 15A, B, 2A, C, 3A] ~ **(sth) (into sth)**, (cause to) change in nature, quality, condition, etc: (使)改变性质，品质，状况等: *Frost ~s water into ice*. 严寒使水结成冰。(使)变: *The cold weather has ~ed the milk, made it sour*. 这次热的天气使牛奶变酸了。*His hair has ~ed grey*. 他头发花白了。*Anxiety ~ed his hair white*. 焦虑使他的头发发白了（他的头发花白了）。*The leaves are beginning to ~*, change colour (as in autumn). 树上的叶子开始改变颜色了（如在秋天）。*Could you ~ this piece of prose into verse/this passage into Greek?* 你能把这篇散文改写成韵文(把这段文字翻译成希腊文)吗？*He has ~ed traitor*, become a traitor. 他变成了叛徒。*He's a politician ~ed poet*, who has become a poet. 他由从政者变成了诗人。*T~ the dog loose*, let it go free, eg by releasing it from a chain. 把那只狗放开。~ **sb's brain**, upset him mentally. 使某人精神恍惚或错乱。~ **sb's head**, unsettle him, make him vain: 使某人狂妄；使某人自负: *The excessive praise the young actor received ~ed his head*. 那年轻(男)演员所受到的过分赞誉使他狂妄起来了。**3** [VP6A] reach and pass: 到达并超过: *He has ~ed* (= reach the age of) *fifty*. 他已届知命之年。*It has just ~ed two*, is just after two o'clock. 现在刚过两点钟。**4** [VP6A] shape (sth, wood or metal) on a lathe, etc: 在车床等上车(某物，木质或金属): ~ *brass*; 在车床上车铜器; *a machine-~ed cigarette-case*; 机械雕花的香烟盒; *a bowl on a potter's wheel*; 在拉坯轮车上车一陶碗; (fig) give a graceful form to: (喻)赋与优美的形式: ~ *an epigram / a compliment*; 作隽语(动听的恭维话); *a well-~ed phrase /sentence*; 措辞巧妙的话(句子); *a well-~ed ankle*; 外型美好的足踝; (with passive force): (含被动义): *wood /metal that ~s* (= can be ~ed) *easily*. 容易加工的木材(金属)。**5** [VP6A] remake (a garment) so that the inner surface becomes the outer surface: 翻面改做(衣服): *I'll have this old overcoat ~ed*. 我(要)要把这件旧大衣翻一翻。~ **one's coat**, ⇨ **coat**(1). '~**coat** n person who deserts one party to join another, esp to win profit, advantage, safety, etc. 脱党者; 变节者(尤指为获得利益、好处、安全等)。**6** (compounds) (复合词) '~**cock** n person employed to ~ water on or off (at the mains). (总水管的)水龙头开关员。'~**key** n keeper of the keys in a prison; jailer. (监狱的)看守; 狱卒。'~**pike** n (hist) gate kept closed across a road and opened on payment of a toll; (US) toll road for fast traffic. (史)收路税关卡; (美)收费高速公路。'~**spit** n (hist) dog or servant who turned the spit on which meat, etc used to be roasted. (史)(往昔烤肉时转动肉叉的)转叉狗; 转叉仆。'~**stile** n revolving gate that admits, lets out, one person at a time. (一次只能容许一人出入的)旋转栅门。'~**table** n flat circular platform, eg one on which gramophone discs are played, or on which a railway locomotive is turned round. 圆形转盘(如唱机转盘); 圆形转台(如铁路机车的调向台)。**7** [VP14, 15B, 2C, 3A] (special uses with *adverbial particles* and *preps*): (与副词性小品词和介词连用的特殊用法): **turn (sb) about**, (cause to) ~ to one side or in a different direction: (使)转向; 回头; 转向一边: *About ~!* (as a military command, in drills, etc). 向后转! (军队操练等时的口令。)

turn sb adrift, send sb away without help or support: 逐出某人(使漂泊无依); 使某人流浪: *He ~ed his son adrift in the world*, sent him away from home and refused to help him. 他将其子逐出家门。

turn (sb) against sb, (cause to) become hostile to: (使)对…变为敌对; 采取敌对态度; 反抗: *She ~ed against her old friend*. 她反叛她的老友。*He tried to ~ the child against his mother*. 他试图使孩子反抗他的母亲。

turn (sb) aside (from), (more usu 较常作 ~ *away*) (cause to) ~ to one side or in a different direction (使)转变方向; (使)转向一边; (使)避开。

turn (sb) away, (cause to) ~ in a different direction so as not to face sb/sth; refuse to look at, welcome, help, admit(to a place): (使)转脸而不面对某人或某物; 拒绝看, 欢迎, 帮助; 让人进入某地: *She ~ed away in disgust*. 她憎恶地把脸转开。*He ~ed away a beggar*. 他逐出一名乞丐。*We had to ~ away hundreds of people*, eg from a stadium, because all seats were sold. 我们不得不谢绝数以百计的观众(如球场的票已全部卖光)。

turn (sb/sth) back, (cause to) return the way one has come: (使)从原路回去; 折回; 逐回; 赶回去: *It's getting dark—we'd better ~ back*. 天快黑了——我们最好回去吧。*We were/Our car was ~ed back at the frontier*. 我们(我们的车)在边界上被赶了回去。

turn (sth) down, (a) (cause to) fold down: (使)折起; 翻下: ~ *down one's coat collar*; 把衣领翻下; *a ~down collar*; 翻领; ~ *down the bed-clothes*. 折起床单。(b) reduce (the flame or brilliance of a gas- or oil-lamp, stove, etc) by ~ing a wheel or tap: 转小或扭小(煤气灯或油灯、炉火等): ~ *down the lamps*. 扭小灯光。(c) place (a playing-card) on the table face downwards. (纸牌)面向下; 翻扣(纸牌)在桌上。~ **sb/sth down**, refuse to consider (an offer, a proposal, or the person who makes it): 拒绝; 摒斥(提议、建议、作建议的人等): *He tried to join the army but was ~ed down because of poor health*. 他想从军，但因身体不好而遭到拒绝。*He asked Jane to marry him but she ~ed him down/ ~ed down his proposal*. 他要简娜给他，但她拒绝了他(拒绝了他的求婚)。

turn in, (colloq) go to bed. (口)就寝。~ **in on oneself/itself**, withdraw from contact with others; become a recluse; (of a country) become isolationist. 隐居(不与他人接触); 做隐士; (指国家)变为孤立主义者。~ **sb in**, (colloq) surrender sb to the police. (口)把某人交给警察; 向警方交出某人。~ **(sth) in**, (cause to) fold or slant inwards: (使)向内弯: *His toes ~ in*. 他的足趾内弯。*He ~ed his toes in*. 他使足趾内曲。~ **sth in**, (colloq) give back to those in authority: (口)归还当局: *You must ~ in your equipment* (eg uniform) *before you leave*. 你离开军队时，必须缴回装备(如制服)。

turn (sth) inside out, (cause to) become inside out: (使)翻转; 将里面翻作外面: *The wind ~ed my old umbrella inside out*. 风把我的伞吹得翻过去了。*He ~ed his pockets inside out in search of his keys*. 他把口袋翻出来找他的钥匙。

turn off, change direction; leave (one road) for another: 改变方向; 离开(一条路)而走上另一条路; 转弯; 分歧: *Is this where we ~ off/where our road ~s off for Hull?* 这里就是我们要转往赫尔(我们的路转向赫尔)的地方吗？~ **sth off**, stop the flow of (liquid, gas, current) by ~ing a tap, switch or other control: 借转动龙头、开关或其他控制器而停止(液体、瓦斯、电流等)的流动; 关上; 关闭: ~ *off the water/lights/radio/TV*. 关掉自来水(电灯、收音机、电视)。~ **(sb) off**, (sl) (cause sb to) lose interest, desire, etc: (俚)(使某人)失去兴趣、欲望等; 对人失去兴致: *He/This music really ~s me off!* 他(这音乐)真使我扫兴！Hence, 由此产生, '~**off** n sth/sb that causes this. 令人扫兴的人或事物。

turn sth on, start the flow of (liquid, gas, current) by ~ing a tap, switch, etc: 借转动龙头、开关等而使(液体、瓦斯、电流等)流动; 开启; 打开; 开启: *T~ the lights/radio on*. 开灯(开收音机)。*She's fond of ~ing on the charm*, (fig) using her charm to influence people. (喻)她喜欢利用她的姿色去影响别人。~ **(sb) on**, (sl) (cause sb to) have great pleasure or excitement: (俚)(使某人)感到极大的愉快或激动: (使)高兴或兴奋: *Some girls ~ on easily*. 有些女孩子很容易激动。*What kind of music ~s you on?* 哪一种音乐特别使你感到兴奋？*Some drugs ~ you on very quickly*, quickly change your mental or emotional state. 有些药物很快就会使你兴奋。Hence, 由此产生, '~**on** n sth/sb that causes this. 使人激动与兴奋的人或事物。~ **on sth**, depend on: 依赖;

视…而定定;以…为转移: *The success of a picnic usually ~s on the weather.* 一次野餐的成功通常要靠天气。 **~ on sb,** become hostile or attack: 变为与…敌对;攻击: *The dog ~ed on me and bit me in the leg.* 那狗向我扑击并且咬伤了我的腿。

turn out (well, etc), prove to be; be in the end: 证明为;结果: *Everything ~ed out well/satisfactory.* 结果一切都很好(令人满意)。 *The day ~ed out wet.* 那天竟然下雨了。 *As it ~ed out...,* As it happened in the end.... 结果(终于)…;后来演变成…。 **~ (sth) out,** (cause to) point outwards scholars. (使)向外: *His toes ~ out.* 他的足趾外翻。 *He ~ed his toes out.* 他使足趾外曲。 **~ sth out, (a)** extinguish by ~ing a tap, switch, etc: 关掉; 灭掉: *Please ~ out the lights/gas-fire before you go to bed.* 请在就寝前关掉电灯(煤气炉)。 **(b)** empty (a drawer, one's pockets, a room, etc) when looking for sth, when cleaning sth: 倒空或腾空(抽屉,口袋,房间等,如寻物或清理时);彻底清除或清理: *~ out all the drawers in one's desk;* 彻底清理书桌所有的抽屉; *~ out the attic,* to get rid of unwanted articles, etc. 彻底清理阁楼(丢弃不需要的东西等)。 **~ sth/sb out,** produce, esp manufactured goods: 制造;生产(如工业制品): *Our new factory is ~ing out large quantities of goods.* 我们的新工厂正在生产大量的货物。 *The school has ~ed out some first-rate scholars.* 该校已造就出若干位第一流的学者。 **~ (sb) out, (a)** (cause him to) assemble for some event, or for duty: (使某人)为某事件或某职责而集合;出动: *The whole village ~ed out to welcome the princess.* 全村的人都出来欢迎公主。 *Not many men ~ed out for duty.* 没有许多人出动。 **(b)** (colloq) (cause sb to) get out of bed. (口)(使某人)起床。 **~ sb out (of/from sth),** expel by force, threats, etc: (以强迫、威胁等方式)驱逐;迫使放弃: *~ sb out of his job/chair;* 迫使某人放弃他的工作(讲座); *~ out a tenant (= from his house) for not paying the rent.* 因不付租金而逐出房客。 **~ed out,** (of a person, equipment, etc) dressed, equipped: (指人,装备等)穿着的; 有…装备的: *a well-~ed out young man.* 衣着良好的年轻人。 *She was beautifully ~ed out,* elegantly dressed. 她装束得很美丽。 Hence, 由此产生, **'~-out** n **(a)** persons who have ~ed out (assembled): 群集的人们; 一批出勤者: *There was a good ~-out at the meeting.* 出席会议者十分踊跃。 **(b)** occasion when one ~s out (empties, etc) a drawer, etc: 清理;清除: *The drawers in my desk are full of old papers—it's time I had a good ~-out.* 我书桌的抽屉里塞满了旧文件——我该彻底整理一下了。 **(c)** equipment; way in which sth is equipped; clothes and accessories worn together: 装备;装备的方式;装束;穿着打扮(包括衣服及配件): *a smart/sloppy ~-out.* 漂亮(草率)的装扮。 **(d)** output (the more usu word) of manufactured goods, etc. 产额;生产量(较常用)。

turn (sb/sth) over, (cause to) fall over, upset; change the position of: (使)跌落; (使)打翻;翻转;倒转;翻身: *The car (was) ~ed right over,* completely upset. 那辆汽车来了个大翻身。 *He ~ed over in bed.* 他在床上翻身。 *The nurse ~ed the old man over and gave him an injection in the left buttock.* 那护士把那位老人翻过去,在他的左臀上打了一针。 **~ sth over,** do business to the amount of: 营业额达于: *His business ~s over £500 a week.* 他的商店每周的营业额为五百英镑。 **~ sth over in one's mind,** think about sth (before making a decision). 思考某事;熟思; (做决定前)再三考虑。 **~ sth/sb over (to sb),** give the control or conduct of sth/sb to: 移交;交付;让渡;转϶: *I've ~ed over the management of my affairs to my brother.* 我已经把我的事务交给我的哥哥(弟弟)处理。 *He's ~ed over his business to his successors.* 他已经把他的事业移交给他的继承人了。 *The thief was ~ed (= handed) over to the police.* 那窃贼已被逮交警察。 Hence, 由此产生, **'~-over** n **(a)** amount of money ~ed over in business within a period of time or for a particular transaction:(某一期间或某一笔买卖的)营业额;销货金额: *a profit of £1000 on a ~over of £10 000;* 做一万镑的生意

获利一千英镑; *sell goods at low prices hoping for a quick ~over,* quick sales and quick replacement of stock. 低价售货以期周转迅速。 **(b)** rate of renewal: 更换率; 换新率: *There is a higher ~over of the labour force in unskilled trades than in skilled trades,* unskilled workers leave and are replaced more quickly. 非技术行业比技术行业的人事变动率高。 **(c)** tart made by folding over half of a circular piece of pastry over the other half, with jam, meat, etc inside. 卷酥; 半圆卷饼。

turn (sth/sb) round, (cause to) face another way, be in another direction: (使)面对另一方向; 转向; 采取新方向: *T~ round and let me see your profile.* 转过去, 让我看看你的侧面。 *T~ your chair round to the fire.* 把你的椅子转向火。 Hence, 由此产生, **'~-round** n (esp of a ship or aircraft) process of getting it ready for the return voyage or flight. (尤指船或飞机)回航的准备过程或手续(如进港、卸货、装货、离港等);装卸: *a ~round of 24 hours in Southampton,* esp for an Atlantic liner. 在南安普敦作二十四小时的装卸停留(如一艘大西洋客轮)。

turn to, get busy: 开始工作;动手做事: *The design staff ~ed to and produced a set of drawings in twenty-four hours.* 制图人员着手工作并在二十四小时内制成了一套图样。 **~ to sb,** go or apply to: 求助于: *The child ~ed to its mother for comfort.* 那孩子向母亲求安慰。 *She has nobody to ~ to.* 她无人可求助。

turn up, (a) make one's appearance; arrive: 出现; 出席;到达: *He promised to come, but hasn't ~ed up yet.* 他答应来,但尚未到。 *My boss hasn't ~ed up this morning—I hope she isn't ill.* 我的老板今天早晨还没有来——我希望她没有生病。 **(b)** be found, esp by chance: 被发现(尤指偶然地): *The book you've lost may ~ up one of these days.* 你遗失的那本书也许这几天会找到。 **(c)** (of an opportunity, etc) happen; present itself: (指机会等)发生;出现: *He's still waiting for something* (eg a job, a piece of good luck) *to ~ up.* 他仍在期待机会出现。 **~ (sth) up, (a)** (cause to) slope upwards: (使)向上倾斜: *~ (= roll) up one's shirt sleeves.* 卷起衬衣袖子。 **(b)** expose; make visible: 暴露; 使可见: *The share of a plough ~s up the soil.* 犁头将土翻起。 *The ploughman ~ed up some buried treasure/an old skull.* 那农民用犁翻起了若干埋藏的财宝(一个古老的头盖骨)。 **~ sb up,** (colloq) cause to vomit; disgust: (口) 使作呕; 使厌恶: *The stink from the slaughter-house ~ed me up.* 屠宰场的恶臭使我作呕。 **~ up one's nose at sth,** (fig) express a superior and critical attitude towards: (喻)轻视; 瞧不起;对…持优越及批评态度: *She ~ed up her nose at the suggestion.* 她对这项建议显出不屑一顾的样子。 **'~-up n (a)** turned fold at the bottom of a trouser-leg: (裤脚的)卷边。 **(b)** **~-up (for the book),** surprising and unexpected event: 出人意料的惊人事件; 突发事件: *Fancy seeing you after all these years. What a ~-up for the book!* 没料到过了这许多年(在这里)见到你, 真是做梦也想不到!

turn upon, ⇨ **~ on** above, (= attack). 参看上列之 **~ on** 。

turn·er /ˈtɜːnə(r), ˈtɜːnɚ/ n person who works a lathe. 车床工人;旋匠。 ⇨ **turn²(4)**.

turn·ing /ˈtɜːnɪŋ, ˈtɜːnɪŋ/ n place where a road turns, esp where one road branches off from another: (路的)转弯处; (尤指)岔路口: *Take the first ~ on/to the right.* 在第一个拐弯处向右转。 **'~-point** n (fig) point in place, time, development, etc which is critical: (喻)转捩点;重大关键;转机: *reach a ~-point in history/in one's life.* 到达历史上(生命中)的重大关键。 *There was a ~-point in the negotiations yesterday.* 昨天的商谈有了转机。

tur·nip /ˈtɜːnɪp, ˈtɜːnɪp/ n [C] (plant with a) large round root used as a vegetable and as food for cattle, 萝卜;芜菁。

tur·pen·tine /ˈtɜːpəntaɪn, ˈtɜːpəntaɪn/ n [U] oil obtained from certain trees, used as a solvent in mixing paint and varnish, and in medicine. 粗松脂; 松油; 松节油(用作溶剂以调油漆,并用于药物中)。

tur·pi·tude /'tɜ:prtjuːd *US:* -tuːd ; 'tɝpə,tjud/ *n*
[U] (formal) wickedness; depravity. (正式用语)邪
恶;卑鄙。

turps /tɜ:ps; tɝps/ *n* [U] (colloq abbr for) turpentine.
(口)松脂;松节油(为 turpentine 之略)。

tur·quoise /'tɜ:kwɔɪz; 'tɝkwɔɪz/ *n* [C] (colour of a)
greenish-blue precious stone. 绿松石;土耳其玉;蓝绿色;
青绿色。

tur·ret /'tʌrɪt; 'tɝɪt/ *n* **1** small tower, esp at a corner
of a building or defensive wall. (建筑物或城墙的)小塔;
角楼。 **2** steel structure protecting gunners, often made
so as to revolve with the gun(s): 炮塔(通常可连同炮旋
转): *a warship armed with twin-gun ~s.*一艘装备着双联
炮塔炮的军舰。

turtle¹ /'tɜ:tl; 'tɝtl/ *n* sea-animal with a soft body
protected by a hard shell like that of a tortoise. 海龟;
甲鱼;海鳖。 ⇨ the illus at **reptile**. 参看 reptile 之插图。
turn ~, (of a ship) turn upside down; capsize. (指船)
翻船;倾覆。 '**~-neck(ed)** *adj* (of a garment, esp a
sweater) having a high, circular, close-fitting collar.
(指衣服,尤指毛线衫)有高而紧的圆领的;高领的。

turtle² /'tɜ:tl; 'tɝtl/ *n* (usu) (通常作) '**~-dove**, kinds
of dove, esp a wild kind noted for its soft cooing, and
its affection for its mate and young. 斑鸠;雉鸠。

turves /tɜ:vz; tɝvz/ *n pl* ⇨ **turf**.

tusk /tʌsk; tʌsk/ *n* long-pointed tooth, esp one coming
out from the closed mouth, as in the elephant, walrus
or wild boar. (象,海象或野猪等的)长牙。 ⇨ the illus
at **large, sea**. 参看 large, sea 之插图。

tussle /'tʌsl; 'tʌsl/ *n, vi* [VP2A, 3A] **~** (**with**);
(colloq) (have a) hard struggle or fight. (口)剧烈的争
斗;作剧烈的打斗;扭打。

tus·sock /'tʌsək; 'tʌsək/*n* clump or hillock of growing
grass. (生长中的)草丛;簇。

tut /tʌt; tʌt/ , **tut-tut** /,tʌt 'tʌt; 'tʌt 'tʌt/ *int* used to
express impatience, contempt, rebuke. 嘘! 啧!不要讲
了!(用以表示不耐烦、轻蔑、责难。) □ *vt* (**-tt-**) [VP6A]
express impatience, etc by using this word: (用此词)
对…表示不耐烦等: *He tut-tutted the idea.* 他对那主意表
示轻蔑。

tu·te·lage /'tjuːtɪlɪdʒ *US:* 'tuː-; 'tutlɪdʒ/ *n* [U]
(formal) guardianship: (正式用语)保护;监护;教导: *a
child in ~;* 受监护的孩子; (period of) being under ~.
受保护;受监护;受教导;保护期;监护期;教导期。

tu·te·lary /'tjuːtɪləri *US:* 'tuːtəlɛri; 'tutl,ɛri/ *adj*
(formal) serving as a guardian or protector; of a
guardian: (正式用语)保护的;守护的; 监护的;保护者的;
守护者的;监护人的: **~** *authority.* 监护人的权威。

tu·tor /'tjuːtə(r) *US:* 'tuː-; 'tutɚ/*n* **1** private teacher, esp
one who instructs a single pupil or a very small class,
sometimes one who lives with the family of his pupil(s).
家庭教师;私人教师。 **2** (GB) university teacher who
guides the studies of a number of students. (英)大学的
指导教师;导师。 □ *vt* [VP6A, 15A, 16A] **1** teach as a
~. (以家庭教师或大学导师身份而)教导学生;指导学生。
2 train, exercise restraint over: 熏陶; 养成; 管制: ~
one's passions; ~ oneself to be patient. 培养耐
心。 **~ial** /tjuː'tɔːrɪəl *US:* tuː-; tu'tɔrɪəl/ *adj* of a tutor or
his duties: 家庭教师的;大学导师的;其职责的: *~ial
classes.* (导师)的个别指导课。 □ *n* period of instruction
given by a college ~: 大学导师的指导期间; 个别指导时
间: *attend a ~ial.* 上导师指导课。

tutti-frutti /,tuːtɪ 'fruːtɪ; 'tutɪ'frutɪ/ *n* (portion of)
ice-cream with chopped nuts and various fruits. 什锦水
果冰淇淋。一份什锦水果冰淇淋。

tutu /'tuːtuː; 'tutu/ *n* short skirt with many layers of
stiffened fabric worn by women dancers in classical
ballet. 突突裙(芭蕾舞女演员所穿的硬布料制的短裙)。

tux·edo /tʌk'siːdəʊ; tʌk'sido/ *n* (*pl* **~s** /-dəʊz; -doz/)
(US) dinner-jacket. (美)(男子在晚间正式场合所穿的)
黑色礼服。

twaddle /'twɒdl; 'twɑdl/ *n* [U] foolish talk. 愚蠢的

话。 □ *vi* [VP2A] talk or write ~: 说或写愚蠢的话。
Stop twaddling! 别再说蠢话!

twain /twein; twen/ *n* (archaic) two. (古)两;二。

twang /twæŋ; twæŋ/ *n* **1** sound of a tight string or
wire being pulled and released: 绷紧的弦或金属丝被拉
扯及放开时发出的声音;弦声: *the ~ of a guitar.* 吉他的
弦声。 **2** harsh, nasal tone of voice: 刺耳的鼻音或鼻声:
speak with a ~. 说话带鼻音。 □ *vt, vi* [VP6A, 2A]
(cause to) make this kind of sound: (使)发弦声;(使)发
刺耳鼻音: *The bow ~ed and the arrow whistled through
the air.* 弓响的一声,箭嗖嗖地破空而过。 *He was ~ing a
banjo.* 他在弹班卓琴。

'twas /twɒz; twɑz; *weak form:* twəz; twəz/(archaic or
poet) (古或诗) = it was.

tweak /twiːk; twik/ *vt* [VP6A] pinch and twist: 拧;
扭。 *Wouldn't you like to ~ that rude fellow's nose /
ears?* 你不想拧那个无礼的家伙的鼻子(耳朵)吗? □ *n* act
of ~ing. 扭;拧。

twee /twiː; twi/ *adj* affectedly or inappropriately
dainty or quaint. 漂亮但矫饰的;妖艳的。

tweed /twiːd; twid/ *n* **1** [U] (often attrib) thick,
soft, woollen cloth, usu woven of mixed colours: (常作
定语用法)花呢(厚而软的毛呢, 通常由杂色织成): *a ~
hat / coat.* 花呢帽(上衣)。 **2** (*pl*) (suit of) clothes made
of ~: (复)(一套)花呢制的衣服: *dressed in Scottish
~s.* 穿苏格兰花呢装。

'tween /twiːn; twin/ *adv, prep* (archaic or poet) between, (古或诗)在…之间;当中, esp (尤用于) '**~-decks**,
between decks. 在二甲板之间。

tweet /twiːt; twit/ *n, vi* (of a bird) chirp. (指鸟)啾啾
声;嘲啾而鸣。

tweeter /'twiːtə(r); 'twitɚ/ *n* loudspeaker for reproducing high notes. 高频扬声器(用以播出高声调者)。 ⇨
woofer.

tweez·ers /'twiːzəz; 'twizɚz/ *n pl* (*pair of*) **~**, tiny
pair of tongs for picking up or pulling out very small
things, eg hairs from the eyebrows. 镊子; 小钳子(用以
拾取或拔出细小物者)。

twelfth /twelfθ; twelfθ/ *adj, n* next after the 11th;
one of twelve equal parts. 第十二; 第十二的; 十二分之
一; 十二分之一的。 **~ man**, (in cricket) reserve player.
(板球)候补队员。 '**T~-night**, eve of the festival of
Epiphany, celebrated with festivities. 主显节前夕(以祝
典庆祝)。

twelve /twelv; twelv/ *adj, n* the number 12. 十二; 十二
的。 ⇨ **App 4** 参看附录四。 **the T~,** the apostles of
Jesus. 耶稣的十二门徒。 '**~-month** *n* (archaic) year.
(古)年;十二个月。

twenty /'twentɪ; 'twentɪ/ *adj, n* the number 20. 二十;
二十的。 ⇨ **App 4.** 参看附录四。 **the twenties,** 20-29.
二十至二十九;二十年代。 **twen·ti·eth** /'twentɪθ; 'twen-
tɪθ/ *adj, n* next after the 19th; one of 20 equal parts.
第二十; 第二十的; 二十分之一; 二十分之一的。

'twere /twɜː(r); twɝ/ (archaic or poet) (古或诗) =
it were (= *it would be*).

twerp /twɜːp; twɝp/ *n* (sl) contemptible or insignificant person. (俚)可鄙的人;无足轻重的人。

twice /twaɪs; twaɪs/ *adv* two times: 两倍;两次: *~ as
much / as many.* 两倍之多。 *I've been there once or ~.*
我去过那儿一两回。 *He's ~ the man he was, ~ as well,
strong, confident, capable, etc.* 他现在比以前强两倍。
think '~ about doing sth, hesitate, think carefully,
before deciding to do it. 三思而行; 仔细考虑(做)某事。
a ,~-told 'tale, a well-known one. 人所皆知的故事。

twiddle /'twɪdl; 'twɪdl/ *vt, vi* **1** [VP6A] twist or
turn idly or aimlessly. 旋弄; 捻弄。 *~ one's thumbs.* 旋
弄大拇指; 闲着没事做。 **2** [VP3A] **~ with sth,** play
idly. 玩弄; 抚弄。 *~ with one's hair / a ring on one's
finger.* 抚弄头发(手指上的戒指)。 □ *n* slight twist
or turn. 旋弄; 捻弄; 小卷; 小弯。 **twid·dly** /'twɪdlɪ;
'twɪdlɪ/*adj* having a ~. 有小卷或小弯的。

twig¹ /twɪg; twɪg/ *n* [C] small shoot on or at the end

of a branch (bush, plant). 小枝; 嫩枝。 ⇨ the illus at **tree**. 参看 tree 之插图。 **~gy** adj having many ~s: 多小枝或嫩枝的: support plants with ~gy sticks. 用多小枝的柴枝支撑植物。

twig² /twɪg; twɪg/ vt, vi (**-gg-**) [VP6A, 2A] (GB colloq) observe; notice; understand: (英口) 观察到; 注意到; 了解; 懂: I soon ~ged what he was up to, saw the trick he was trying to play. 我很快就看穿了他想要什么把戏。

twi·light /'twaɪlaɪt; 'twaɪˌlaɪt/ n [U] **1** faint half-light before sunrise or after sunset: (日出前或日落后的) 微明; 曙光; 薄暮: go for a walk in the ~. 在黄昏散步。 **2** (fig) remote period about which little is known: (喻) 遥远而鲜为人所知的时代: in the ~ of history. 在远古时代。 **twi·lit** /'twaɪlɪt; 'twaɪˌlɪt/ adj dimly lit. 微明的; 昏暗的。

twill /twɪl; twɪl/ n [U] strong cotton cloth woven so that fine diagonal lines or ribs appear on the surface. 斜纹布。 **~ed** adj (of cloth) woven in this way. (指布) 斜纹的。

'twill /twɪl; twɪl/ (archaic or poet) (古或诗) = it will.

twin /twɪn; twɪn/ n **1** either of two children born together of the same mother: 双胞胎之一: one of the ~s; 双胞胎之一: (attrib) (用作定语) ~ brothers. 孪生兄弟。 **2** (usu attrib) completely like, closely associated with, another: (通常用作定语) 完全相似的; 关系密切的: a ship with ~ propellers, two identical propellers, 双螺旋桨轮船; ~ beds, two identical single beds; 两张完全一样的单人床; a '~-set, woman's jumper and long sleeved cardigan of the same colour and style. (颜色与式样相同、配在一起穿的) 女用套头毛衣及长袖毛线外套。 □ vt [VP6A, 14] ~ (with), join closely together; couple; pair. 密切结合; 匹配; 成对。 ⇨ **twinned**.

twine /twaɪn; twaɪn/ n [U] thin strings made by twisting two or more yarns together. 细绳; 合股线。 □ vt, vi [VP15A, B, 2A, C] twist; wind: 编结; 缠绕; 捻: ~ flowers into a garland; 把花编成花环; vines that ~ round a tree. 缠绕树的藤枝。 She ~d her arms round my neck. 她用双臂围绕着我的脖子。

twinge /twɪndʒ; twɪndʒ/ n [C] sudden, sharp pain: 剧痛; 刺痛: a ~ of toothache/rheumatism/conscience. 一阵牙痛 (风湿痛, 良心的谴责)。

twinkle /'twɪŋkl; 'twɪŋkl/ vi [2A, C] **1** shine with a light that gleams unsteadily: 闪烁; 闪耀: stars that ~ in the sky. 天上闪烁的星辰。 **2** (of eyes) sparkle; (of eyelids, feet in dancing, etc) move rapidly up and down, to and fro: (指眼睛) 闪亮; (指眼睑, 跳舞时之双足等) 迅速移动, 闪动: 眨眼: Her eyes ~ with amusement/mischief. 她的眼睛闪耀着欢愉 (淘气) 的神情。 □ n **1** [U] twinkling light: 闪烁; 闪光: the ~ of the stars/of a distant light. 星辰 (远处灯火) 的闪光。 **2** sparkle; rapid twitching: 闪亮; 闪动; 抽动; 急动: There was a mischievous ~ in her eyes. 她眼睛里闪耀着淘气的眼神。

twink·ling /'twɪŋklɪŋ; 'twɪŋklɪŋ/ n (sing only) (仅用单数) in the twinkling of an eye, in an instant. 转瞬间; 顷刻。

twinned /twɪnd; twɪnd/ attrib adj ~ (with), paired (with): 结成一对的: a town in England ~ with a town in France, (for cultural, educational, etc exchanges) 英国某城市与法国某城市结为姐妹市 (为文化、教育等交流)。

twirl /twɜːl; twɝl/ vt, vi [VP6A, 15B, 16A, 2A, C] **1** (cause to) turn round and round quickly: (使) 迅速旋转; 快速地转动: She ~ed the mop to get the water out of it. 她迅速地转动拖把, 把它拧干。 He sat ~ing his thumbs. 他坐着无聊地转动他的拇指。 **2** curl; twist: 卷曲; 扭: He ~ed his moustache (up). 他捻起他的胡子。 □ n rapid circular motion. 快速的旋转; 扭曲。

twist /twɪst; twɪst/ vt, vi **1** wind or turn (a number of threads, strands, etc) one around the other: 搓; 捻; 绞 (若干条线或若干股等): ~ pieces of

straw into a rope. 把稻草搓成绳子。 She ~ed the girls' hair round her fingers to make it curl. 她把那女孩的头发卷在她手指上使之卷曲。 **2** [VP6A] make (a rope, a garland, etc) by doing this. 编; 织 (绳索、花环等)。 **3** [VP6A, 15A, B, 16A] turn, esp by the use of force; turn the two ends of (sth) in opposite directions; turn one end of (sth): 转动 (尤指用力地); 以相反的方向转动 (某物) 的两端; 转动 (某物) 的一端; 拧; 扭: ~ (more usu 较常用 wring) a wet cloth, to squeeze out the water; 拧干一块湿布; ~ the cap of a fountain-pen/a tube of toothpaste. 转开钢笔帽 (牙膏盖)。 If you use too much force, you'll ~ the key, bend it out of shape. 如果你太用力, 你会把钥匙拧弯。 His features were ~ed (= distorted) with pain. 他的面容因痛苦而扭曲。 He fell and ~ed his ankle. 他摔下来, 扭伤了足踝。 She ~ed her head round as she reversed the car into the garage. 她转头向后把车倒进车房里。 ~ sth off, break off by ~ing: 拧断; 扭断: ~ off the end of a piece of wire. 拧断一根铁丝的末端。 ~ sb's arm, (a) force it round to cause pain. 扭某人的臂使之痛苦。 (b) (fig, colloq) put (friendly or unfriendly) pressure on him to do sth. (喻, 口) 对某人威迫利诱; 对某人施加压力使他做某事。 ~ sb round one's little finger, (colloq) get him to do what one wants him to do. (口) 任意指使某人; 对某人颐指气使。 **4** [VP6A, 15A] force (sb's words) out of their true meaning: 曲解 (某人的话): The police tried to ~ his words into a confession of guilt. 警察试图把他的话曲解为招供。 **5** [VP6A, 15A, 22A, C] give a spiral form to (a rod, column, etc); receive, have, move or grow in, a spiral form: 使 (杆、柱等) 成螺旋形; 作螺旋形; 呈螺旋状移动或生长: ~ed columns, as in architecture. (建筑物等的) 螺旋形柱; 卷柱。 **6** [VP2A, C] turn and curve in different directions; change position or direction: 盘旋; 曲折; 迂回: The road ~ed and turns up the side of the mountain. 这条路沿着山坡弯来弯去。 The thief ~ed out of the policeman's grip and ran off. 那贼挣脱警察的手逃跑了。 The injured man ~ed about in pain. 受伤者痛苦地挣扎着。 **7** [VP6A, 2A] (of a ball, esp in billiards) (cause to) take a curved path while spinning. (指球, 尤指桌球) (使) 旋转时取一曲线行进。 **8** [VP2A] dance the ~, ⇨ **6** below. 跳扭扭舞 (参看下列第 6 义)。 □ n **1** ~ing or being ~ed: 搓; 捻; 绞; 编; 织; 拧; 扭; 弯曲; 曲折: The bully gave the little boy's arm a ~. 那恶汉把小男孩的手臂扭了一下。 Give the rope a few more ~s. 把那绳子再搓几下。 There are numerous ~s in the road over the pass. 那条路越过隘口有无数弯道。 **2** sth made by ~ing: 搓捻而成之物; 扭卷而成之物: a rope full of ~s (= kinks, coils); 一根满是扭结的绳子; a ~ of paper, a paper packet with screwed-up ends. 将末端拧紧而成的纸袋。 **3** [C, U] thread, yarn, rope, etc made by ~ing together two or more strands, esp certain kinds of silk thread and cotton yarn; coarse tobacco made by ~ing dried leaves into a roll. 线; 索; 绳; (尤指) 丝线; 棉纱线; 烟草卷。 **4** motion given to a ball to make it take a curved path. (使球成曲线前进的) 扭转; 曲球。 **5** peculiar tendency of mind or character: (心境或性格的) 失常; 偏差; 癖: He has a criminal ~ in him. 他有犯罪癖。 **6** the ~, dance (popular in the 1960's) in which ~ing of the arms and hips. 扭摆舞; 扭扭舞 (盛行于二十世纪六十年代, 跳时扭动臂部及臀部)。 ~er n **1** (colloq) dishonest person. (口) 不诚实的人; 说谎话的人。 **2** difficult task, problem, etc: 困难的事情、问题等: a 'tongue-~er, word or phrase difficult to pronounce. 绕口令。 ~y adj (-ier, -iest) **1** having many ~s: 扭曲的; 卷曲的; 多弯曲的: a ~y road. 弯弯曲曲的道路。 **2** not straightforward: 不正直的; 歪曲事实的: a ~y politician. 不正直的政客。

twit¹ /twɪt; twɪt/ vt (**-tt-**) [VP6A, 14] tease sb (usu in jest) (with or about sth): 嘲笑; 挖苦; 揶揄 (某人): ~ a man about the state he was in after a drinking bout. 嘲笑某人狂饮后的狼狈相。

twit² /twɪt; twɪt/ n (sl) contemptible fool, idiot. (俚)

twitch /twɪtʃ; twɪtʃ/ n [C] **1** sudden, quick, usu uncontrollable movement of a muscle; tic. 抽搐; 抽动; 痉挛. **2** sudden quick pull: 急拉; 急扯: *I felt a ~ at my sleeve.* 我觉得有人拉了一下我的袖子. □ *vi, vt* **1** [VP2A, C, 6A] (cause to) move in a ~(1): (使)抽搐; 抽动; 痉挛: *The dog's nose ~ed as it passed the butcher's shop.* 那狗经过肉店时, 鼻子在抽动. *His face ~ed with terror.* 他的面孔因恐惧而抽动. *The horse ~ed its ears.* 那马抽动耳朵. **2** [VP15A, B] jerk; give a ~(2): 急拉; 急扯: *The wind ~ed the paper out of my hand.* 风吹走了我手中的纸.

twit·ter /'twɪtə(r); 'twɪtɚ/ *vi* [VP2A, C] (of birds) chirp; make a succession of soft short sounds: (of persons) talk rapidly through excitement, nervousness, etc. (指鸟)啭鸣: 啭; (指人)喊喊喳喳地说话: *~ing* chirping: 鸟啭: *the ~ of sparrows.* 麻雀的叫声. **2** (of persons) (colloq, esp in) (指人)(口, 尤用于) *(all) of a ~,* in an excited state. 兴奋地; 紧张地.

twixt /twɪkst; twɪkst/ *prep* (archaic or poet) (古或诗) = betwixt.

two /tu:; tu/ *n, adj* **1** the number 2. 二; 两个. ⇨ **App 4.** 参看附录四. *break/cut sth in two,* into two parts. 分裂(切割)某物为二. *put two and two together,* infer sth from what one sees, hears, learns, etc. 根据所见, 所闻, 所知等推断某事物. *by twos and threes,* two or three at a time. 三三两两地; (一次)两个三个地. *Two can play (at) 'that game,* used as a threat of retaliation. 那把戏可是彼此都可玩的啊(此语系在一人吃亏后的威胁话, 意谓你这样做, 我也可以照样报复). **2** (compounds) (复合词), **two-'edged** *adj* (of a sword) having a cutting edge on each side; (fig, of an argument, etc) having two possible (and contrary) meanings. (指刀剑)双锋的; 有两刃的; (喻论据等)有正反两意义的. **two-'faced** *adj* (fig) insincere. (喻)两面的; 虚伪的. **'two·fold** *adj, adv* double, doubly. 二倍; 二重. **two-'handed** *adj* (of a sword) needing two hands to use it: (of a saw, etc) to be used by two persons, one at each end. (指刀剑)需要双手运用的; (指锯等)需要两人使用的. **'two-pence** /'tʌpəns *US:* 'tu:pens; 'tʌpəns/ *n* sum of two pence. 两便士金额. **'two·penny** /'tʌpənɪ *US:* 'tu:penɪ; 'tu,penɪ/ *adj* costing two pence. 值两便士的. **,twopenny 'piece,** GB coin worth two pence. (英)两便士硬币. **,two·penny-'half·penny** /,tʌpnɪ 'heɪpnɪ *US:* ,tu:penɪ 'hæfpenɪ; 'tʌpənɪ'hepənɪ/ *adj* (colloq) almost worthless. (口)几乎无价值的; 微不足道的. **'two-a-penny** *adj* easy to obtain; cheap; almost worthless. 易得的; 便宜的; 几乎无价值的. **,two-'piece** *n* set of garments of similar or matching material, eg skirt and jacket, trousers and jacket; bra and briefs (for swimming); 两件式的成套衣服(裙和上衣或相似或相配的两件衣服, 如裙子及上衣, 裤子及上装); (女子的)两件式泳装(奶罩及短裤); (attrib) (用作定语) *a two-piece suit* 二件式套装. **'two-ply** *adj* of two strands or thicknesses. 双股的; 两层(厚)的: *two-ply wool/wood.* 双股毛线(双层木料). **,two-'seater** *n* car, aircraft, etc with seats for two persons. 双座汽车、飞机等. **'two-timing** *adj* (sl) deceitful; engaged in double-crossing. (俚)欺骗的; 不忠实的; 从事欺骗勾当的. **,two-'way** *attrib adj* **(a)** (of a switch) allowing current to be switched on or off from either of two points. (指开关)双向的; 两路的. **(b)** (of a road or street) in which traffic may move in both directions. (指路或街)双向的; 对向交通的. Cf. *one-way street.* **(c)** (of radio equipment, etc) for both sending and receiving. (指无线电装备等)收发两用的.

twould /twud; twʊd/ (archaic or poet) (古或诗) = it would.

ty·coon /taɪ'ku:n; taɪ'kun/ *n* (colloq) wealthy and powerful business man or industrialist: (口)大实业家; 大亨: *'oil ~s.* 石油界的大亨们.

ty·ing /'taɪŋ; 'taɪŋ/ *pres p* of **tie²**.

tyke, tike /taɪk; taɪk/ *n* cur, (as a term of abuse) low fellow. 劣犬; 野狗; (骂人话)坏蛋; 下三滥; 小子.

tym·pa·num /'tɪmpənəm; 'tɪmpənəm/ *n* (pl ~s or -na /-nə; -nə/) (anat) (解剖) **1** eardrum. 耳鼓; 鼓膜. **2** middle ear 中耳; 鼓室. ⇨ **middle;** ⇨ the illus at **ear,** 参看 ear 之插图.

type¹ /taɪp; taɪp/ *n* **1** [C] person, thing, event, etc considered as an example of a class or group: 典型; 模范; 表率(被视为可代表一类或一群的人、物、事等): *Abraham Lincoln was a fine ~ of the American patriot.* 林肯是美国爱国者的良好典范. **2** [C] class or group considered to have common characteristics: 型; 型式; 样式; 类型: *men of this ~.* 这一类型的人们. *Her beauty is of the Italian ~.* 她的美是意大利型的. *They claim to make good Burgundy ~ wine/wine of the Burgundy ~ in Australia.* 他们声言在澳大利亚酿造出良好的勃艮地型红葡萄酒. *true to ~,* representative of that ~: 代表其类型的: *A cowardly bulldog is not true to ~.* 一只胆小的牧牛犬不足以代表其类型. **3** [U] letters, etc cast in blocks of (usu) metal, for use in printing; any fount of these: [C] one of these blocks: 印刷用的活字; 一套字体; 一个活字或铅字: *The printers are short of ~/cast(ing) ~s.* 印刷厂缺乏铅字(某些铅字). *Wooden ~ is/wooden ~s are sometimes used for printing posters.* 木刻的活字有时用来印制海报. *The material is now in ~,* has been set ready for printing. 该资料现正付印中. *The examples in this dictionary are in italic ~.* 本词典中的例句用斜体字排印. **2** (compounds) (复合词) '**~·face** *n* style of type (3). 铅字之字体. ⇨ **face¹ (3).** '**~·script** *n* typewritten copy (prepared for printing, etc). 用打字机打出的文稿或原稿; 打字稿. '**~·setter** *n* worker or machine that sets ~ for printing. 排字工人; 排字机. '**~·writer** *n* machine with which one prints letters on paper, using the fingers on a keyboard. 打字机. '**~·written** *adj* written using a ~writer: 用打字机打出的: *a ~written message.* 用打字机打出的讯息.

type² /taɪp; taɪp/ *vt, vi* **1** [VP6A, 2A] use a typewriter; write with a typewriter: 打字; 用打字机打出: *~ a letter.* (用打字机)打信. *She ~s well.* 她打字打得很好. **2** [VP6A] determine the type(2) of sth: 确定或决定某物的型式或种类: *~ a virus;* 确定一种病毒的类型; *~ a person's blood.* 确定一个人的血型. **typ·ist** /'taɪpɪst; 'taɪpɪst/ *n* person who ~s. 打字员.

type·cast /'taɪpkɑ:st *US:* -kæst; 'taɪpt,kæst/ *vt* (pt, pp unchanged) (过去式及过去分词不变) [VP6A] (theatre) cast (a person) for a part which he/she has the reputation of doing well or which seems to fit his/her own personality. (戏剧)分派(某人)角色(使之担任最拿手或是最适合其性格的角色).

ty·phoid /'taɪfɔɪd; 'taɪfɔɪd/ *n* [U] ~ **(fever),** infectious disease which attacks the intestines, caused by bacteria taken into the body with food or drink. 伤寒; 肠热病.

ty·phoon /taɪ'fu:n; taɪ'fun/ *n* [C] violent hurricane of the kind that occurs in the western Pacific. 台风(西太平洋发生的飓风).

ty·phus /'taɪfəs; 'taɪfəs/ *n* [U] infectious disease marked by fever, great weakness and the appearance of purple spots on the body. 斑疹伤寒.

typi·cal /'tɪpɪkl; 'tɪpɪkl/ *adj* ~ **(of),** serving as a type; representative or characteristic. 代表性的; 典型的; 象征性的. **~·ly** /-klɪ; -klɪ/ *adv*

typ·ify /'tɪpɪfaɪ; 'tɪpə,faɪ/ *vt* (pt, pp **-fied**) [VP6A] be a symbol of; be representative of. 作为…的象征; 代表.

typ·ist /'taɪpɪst; 'taɪpɪst/ *n* ⇨ **type².**

ty·pogra·phy /taɪ'pɒgrəfɪ; taɪ'pɑgrəfɪ/ *n* [U] art or style of printing. 印刷术; 印刷式样. **ty·pogra·pher** /taɪ'pɒgrəfə(r); taɪ'pɑgrəfɚ/ *n* person skilled in ~. 印刷工人; 排字工人. **ty·po·graphic** /,taɪpə'ɡræfɪk; ,taɪpə'græfɪk/ *adj* **ty·po·graphi·cally** /-klɪ; -klɪ/ *adv*

ty·ran·ni·cal /tɪˈrænɪkl; tɪˈrænɪkl/ adj of or like a tyrant; acting like a tyrant; obtaining obedience by force or threats. 暴君的; 似暴君的; 暴虐的; 专横的; 残暴统治的。

tyr·an·nize /ˈtɪrənaɪz; ˈtɪrəˌnaɪz/ vi, vt [VP6A,3A] ~ (over), rule cruelly and unjustly: 暴虐统治; 虐待; 压制: ~ over the weak. 欺压弱小。 He ~s his family 他虐待其家人。

tyr·an·ny /ˈtɪrənɪ; ˈtɪrənɪ/ n (pl **-nies**) 1 [U] cruel or unjust use of power; [C] instance of this; tyrannical act. 残暴; 专横; 暴虐; 其实例; 暴行。 2 [C, U] (instance of, country with, the) kind of government existing when a ruler with complete power, esp when this power has been obtained by force and is used unjustly: 暴政;

其实例; 施行暴政的国家: live under a ~. 在暴政下生活。

tyr·an·ous /ˈtɪrənəs; ˈtɪrənəs/ adj = **tyrannical**.

ty·rant /ˈtaɪərənt; ˈtaɪrənt/ n cruel or unjust ruler. esp one who has obtained complete power by force. 暴君;暴虐统治者(尤指用武力获得全部权力者)。

tyre (US = **tire**) /ˈtaɪə(r); taɪr/ n band of solid or inflated rubber on the rim of a wheel, esp (pneumatic ~) the kind on bicycle and motor-car wheels. 轮箍; 轮胎; 车胎; (尤指脚踏车及汽车车轮上的)气胎。 ⇨ the illus at **bicycle, motor.** 参看 bicycle, motor 之插图。

tyro /ˈtaɪərəʊ; ˈtaɪro/ n = **tiro.**

tzar /zɑː; tsɑr/ , **tza·rina** /zɑːˈriːnə; tsɑˈrinə/ nn = **czar, czarina.**

U u

U, u /juː; ju/ the 21st letter of the English alphabet. 英文字母的第二十一个字母。 '**U-boat** n German submarine. 德国潜水艇。 '**U-turn,** one of 180° (by a car, etc): (汽车等) 一百八十度的转弯; 向后转; 回转: No U-turns! (as a traffic notice in towns, on motorways). 禁止回转(用于城市中或高速公路上的交通牌示)。

ubi·qui·tous /juːˈbɪkwɪtəs; juˈbɪkwətəs/ adj (formal) present everywhere or in several places at the same time. (正式用语)无所不在的; 遍在的; 在数处同时出现的。 **ubi·quity** /juːˈbɪkwɪtɪ; juˈbɪkwətɪ/ n [U] quality of being ~. 到处存在; 遍在。

ud·der /ˈʌdə(r); ˈʌdɚ/ n bag of a cow, goat or other animal, from which milk comes, esp a large one with two or more teats. 牛、羊或其他动物的乳房(尤指乳头不只一个者)。 ⇨ the illus at **domestic.** 参看 domestic 之插图。

ugh /This usu suggests a sound like ɜː: made with the lips either spread or rounded very strongly and one's facial expression showing disgust 此词通常含示一种类似 ɜː; ɚ 的声音, 发此音时, 或撇着嘴唇, 或用力撮起嘴唇发出, 同时面部现出厌恶的表情/ int used to indicate disgust. (用以表示厌恶)啊!呸!

ugly /ˈʌglɪ; ˈʌglɪ/ adj (**-ier, -iest**) 1 unpleasant to look at; hideous: 难看的; 丑陋的: ~ children/furniture/surroundings. 难看的儿童(家具、环境)。 2 threatening; unpleasant: 险恶的; 阴沉的; 不祥的: ~ly 令人厌恶的: The sky looks ~, suggests bad weather. 天色阴沉。 The news in today's newspapers is ~, suggests unpleasant possibilities, eg, of war. 今天报上的消息不妙(意味着有不祥事件发生, 如战争)。 ~ **customer,** (colloq) dangerous person; person difficult to deal with. (口)危险人物; 很难对付的人。 **ug·lify** /ˈʌglɪfaɪ; ˈʌglɪˌfaɪ/ vt (pt pp **-fied**) make ~. 使变得丑陋; 弄得难看。 **ug·li·ness** n ~.

ukase /juːˈkeɪs; ˈjukes/ n (hist) edict of the Czarist Russian government; arbitrary order. (史)帝俄沙皇政府的敕令; 谕旨; 专横的命令。

uku·lele /ˌjuːkəˈleɪlɪ; ˌjukəˈleli/ n Hawaiian four-stringed guitar. 尤克里里琴(一种类似吉他的夏威夷四弦琴)。

ul·cer /ˈʌlsə(r); ˈʌlsɚ/ n open sore forming poisonous matter (on the outside or inside surface of the body); (fig) corrupting influence or condition. (身体内部或外部表面形成的)溃疡; (喻)令人腐化的影响或情况。 ~**ous** /-əs; -əs/ adj ~ -ert; -et/ vi, vt[VP6A, 2A] form, convert or be converted into, an ~. 生溃疡; 形成溃疡; 使生溃疡; 被弄成溃烂。 ~ · **ation** /ˌʌlsəˈreɪʃn; ˌʌlsəˈreʃən/ n.

ulna /ˈʌlnə; ˈʌlnə/ n (pl ~**e** /-niː; -ni/) (anat) inner of the two bones of the forearm. (解剖)(前臂的)尺骨。 ⇨ the illus at **skeleton.** 参看 skeleton 之插图。

ul·ster /ˈʌlstə(r); ˈʌlstɚ/ n long, loose, belted overcoat. 阿斯特大衣(一种长而宽松并系带的大衣)。

ul·terior /ʌlˈtɪərɪə(r); ʌlˈtɪrɪɚ/ adj situated beyond; beyond what is first seen or said. 在那一边的; 超出最初所见或所说之范围的; 未揭露的; 隐秘的。 ~ **motive,** motive other than what is expressed or admitted. 隐秘或未显露的动机。

ul·ti·mate /ˈʌltɪmət; ˈʌltəmɪt/ adj last, furthest, basic: 最后的; 最远的; 终极的; 根本的; 主要的: ~ principles/truths; 基本原理(真理); the ~ cause, beyond which no other cause is known or can be found; 终极原因; 第一因; 第一原理; the ~ deterrent (used of nuclear weapons). 终极或最后的威慑力量 (用指核武器)。 ~ **·ly** adv finally; in the end. 最后; 终极地。

ul·ti·ma·tum /ˌʌltɪˈmeɪtəm; ˌʌltəˈmetəm/ n (pl ~**s, -ta** /-tə; -tə/) [C] final statement of conditions to be accepted without discussion, eg one sent to a foreign government and threatening war if the conditions are not accepted. 最后通牒; 哀的美敦书。

ul·timo /ˈʌltɪməʊ; ˈʌltəˌmo/ adj (abbr 略作 **ult**) (formerly used in business letters) of the month before the current month: (往昔用于商业信函中)上月份的: Thank you for your letter of the 10th ult. 谢谢你上月十日的来函。

ultra- /ˈʌltrə; ˈʌltrə/ pref beyond. 超过; 在…那边。 ⇨ **App 3.** 参看附录三。

ultra·mar·ine /ˌʌltrəməˈriːn; ˌʌltrəməˈrin/ adj, n brilliant pure blue (colour). 绀青的; 群青的; 绀青色; 群青色。

ultra·mon·tane /ˌʌltrəmɒnˈteɪn; ˌʌltrəˈmɑntɛn/ adj (RC Church) favouring the absolute authority of the Pope in matters of faith and discipline. (天主教)(在信仰及教规方面)赞成教皇有绝对权力的。

ultra·sonic /ˌʌltrəˈsɒnɪk; ˌʌltrəˈsɑnɪk/ adj relating to sound waves beyond the range of normal human audibility. (指声波)超出人类正常听力范围的; 超声的。

ultra·vio·let /ˌʌltrəˈvaɪələt; ˌʌltrəˈvaɪəlɪt/ adj of the invisible part of the spectrum beyond the violet. 光谱之紫色外方看不见之部分的; 紫外的; 紫外线的。 ~ **rays,** invisible rays (in sunlight, light from mercury-vapour lamps, etc) which have an effect upon the skin, curing certain skin diseases, forming vitamins, etc. 紫外线。

ultra vires /ˌʌltrə ˈvaɪəriːz; ˌʌltrəˈvaɪriz/ adj, adv (Lat) beyond the powers or authority granted by law. (拉)超过法律所赋予之权力的(地); 逾越权限的(地); 越权的(地)。

ulu·late /ˈjuːljʊleɪt US: ˈʌl-; ˈjuljəˌlet/ vi [VP2A] howl; wail loudly. 嗥; 吠; 大声哭。 **ulu·la·tion** /ˌjuːljʊˈleɪʃn US: ˈʌl-; ˌjuljəˈleʃən/ n.

um·ber /ˈʌmbə(r); ˈʌmbɚ/ adj, n yellowish-green (colouring substance). 赭色的; 赭土(颜料)。 **burnt** ~ reddish-brown. 煅赭土(颜料)。

um·bili·cal /ʌmˈbɪlɪkl; ʌmˈbɪlɪkl/ adj ~ **cord,** cord

connecting a foetus at the navel with the placenta. (连结胎儿与胎盘的)脐带。 ⇨ the illus at **reproduce.** 参看 reproduce 之插图。

um·brage /ˈʌmbrɪdʒ; ˈʌmbrɪdʒ/ n [U] **give/take ~ (at sth)**, cause the feeling/feel that one has been treated unfairly or without proper respect. 感觉未受到公正待遇或未受尊敬; 愤怒; 埋怨; 不快。

um·brella /ʌmˈbrelə; ʌmˈbrɛlə/ n 1 folding frame (with a stick and handle), covered with cotton, silk, etc used to shelter the person holding it from rain; (in some countries) such a device, used as a symbol of rank. 伞; 雨伞; (某些国家用以代表社会阶层的)伞形物。 ⇨ **parasol;** ⇨ **sunshade** at **sun (4).** 2 (fig) screen of fighter aircraft, eg flying over bombers to protect them against enemy aircraft. (喻)由战斗机构成的掩护幕; 伞幕。 3 protection; patronage: 庇护; 保护: *under the ~ of the UNO.* 在联合国组织的庇护下。

um·laut /ˈʊmlaʊt; ˈʊmlaʊt/ n (in Germanic languages) vowel change shown by two dots over the vowel (as in the German plurals *Männer,* of *Mann,* and *Füsse,* of *Fuss*). (日耳曼语系中的)元音变化(在元音上加两点表示之, 如德语 Mann 的复数形 Männer, Fuss 的复数形 Füsse)。

um·pire /ˈʌmpaɪə(r); ˈʌmpaɪr/ n person chosen to act as a judge in a dispute, to see that the rules are obeyed in cricket, baseball, tennis, netball and other games. 仲裁人; 公断人; (板球、棒球、网球、落网球及他种比赛的)裁判员。 Cf 参较 *referee* for football and boxing. 足球及拳击之裁判员称作 referee. □ vt, vi [VP6A, 2A] act as ~: 仲裁; 裁判; 担任仲裁者或裁判员: *~ a cricket match.* 担任板球赛裁判。

ump·teen /ˈʌmptiːn; ˈʌmpˈtin/ adj (sl) many. (俚) 许多的。 **~th** /-θ; ˈʌmptɪnθ; ˈʌmpˈtinθ/ adj: *for the ~th time,* for I don't know how many times. 无数次。

'un /ən; ən/ pron (colloq) one: (口)(一个)人或东西: *He's a good 'un,* a good fellow. 他是一个好人。 *That's a good 'un,* a good specimen, joke, etc. 那是一个好的样品、有趣的笑话等。

un- /ʌn; ʌn/ pref (⇨ **App 3;** 参看附录三; specimens only here 此处所举者仅为范例)。 **1** (before *adjj* and *advv*) not: (用于形容词和副词前)不; 非; 未: *uncertain-(ly),* 不确定的(地); *unwilling(ly).* 不愿意的(地)。 **2** (before *vv*) do the opposite of, reverse the action of, what is indicated by the *v*: (用于动词前)做出与该动词所表示之动作相反的行为: *unscrew;* 扭松螺丝; *unroll;* 展开; *undress;* 脱去衣服; *unlock.* 开锁。 **3** (before *nn*) indicating absence of: (用于名词前)无; 不: *uncertainty;* 不确定; *unwillingness.* 不愿意。

un·abashed /ˌʌnəˈbæʃt; ˌʌnəˈbæʃt/ adj not abashed, embarrassed or awed. 不脸红的; 不难为情的; 满不在乎的。

un·abated /ˌʌnəˈbeɪtɪd; ˌʌnəˈbetɪd/ adj (of a storm, etc) (continuing) as strong, violent, etc as before. (指风暴等)未减弱的; 猛烈如前的。

un·able /ʌnˈeɪbl; ʌnˈebl/ adj (pred only) (仅用作表语) *~ to do sth,* not able to do it. 不能做某事。

un·accom·pan·ied /ˌʌnəˈkʌmpənɪd; ˌʌnəˈkʌmpənɪd/ adj 1 without a companion: 无伴的: *~ luggage,* sent separately, the owner not travelling with it. 无人伴行而单独交运的行李。 **2** (music) performed without an accompaniment. (音乐)无伴奏的。

un·ac·count·able /ˌʌnəˈkaʊntəbl; ˌʌnəˈkaʊntəbl/ adj in a way that cannot be accounted for or explained. 不能说明的; 无法解释的。 **un·ac·count·ably** /-əblɪ; -əblɪ/ adv

un·ac·cus·tomed /ˌʌnəˈkʌstəmd; ˌʌnəˈkʌstəmd/ adj 1 *~ to,* not accustomed to: 不习惯的; 不适应的: *~ as I am to speaking in public.* 象我这样不惯于作公开演说的。 **2** not usual; strange: 不寻常的; 奇异的: *his ~ silence.* 他那罕有的沉默。

un·ad·vised /ˌʌnədˈvaɪzd; ˌʌnədˈvaɪzd/ adj without advice; (esp) not discreet or wise; rash. 未经磋商的;

(尤指)不明智的; 卤莽的; 轻率的。 **~·ly** /ˌʌnədˈvaɪzɪdlɪ; ˌʌnədˈvaɪzɪdlɪ/ adv rashly. 卤莽地; 轻率地。

un·af·fec·ted /ˌʌnəˈfektɪd; ˌʌnəˈfɛktɪd/ adj 1 free from affectation; sincere. 不矫揉造作的; 自然的; 真心的。 **2 ~ by,** not affected by. 未受…影响的; 未被…感化的。

un·alien·able /ʌnˈeɪlɪənəbl; ʌnˈeljənəbl/ adj that cannot be taken away or separated: 不能转让的; 不能让渡的: *~ rights.* 不能转让的权利。

un·al·loyed /ˌʌnəˈlɔɪd; ˌʌnəˈlɔɪd/ adj pure; unmixed: 纯粹的; 完全的: *~ joy.* 真正的快乐。

un·al·ter·ably /ʌnˈɔːltərəblɪ; ʌnˈɔltərəblɪ/ adv in a way that cannot be changed. 不可改变地。

unani·mous /juːˈnænɪməs; juˈnænəməs/ adj in, showing, complete agreement: 全体一致的; 无异议的: *The country is ~ in support of the Government's policy.* 举国一致支持政府的政策。 *He was elected by a ~ vote.* 他获得全部选票而当选。 *The proposal was accepted with ~ approval.* 该项建议经全体一致的同意而通过。 **~·ly** adv **una·nim·ity** /ˌjuːnəˈnɪmətɪ; ˌjunəˈnɪmətɪ/ n [U] complete agreement or unity. 全体同意或一致; 无异议。

un·an·nounced /ˌʌnəˈnaʊnst; ˌʌnəˈnaʊnst/ adj without having been announced: 未告知的; 未经宣布的; 未通知的: *He walked into the room ~,* no one having told the persons there who he was, that he had arrived. 他未先通报而走入房间。

un·an·swer·able /ʌnˈɑːnsərəbl US: -ˈæn-; ʌnˈænsərəbl/ adj (esp) against which no good argument can possibly be brought: 无法回答的; (尤指)无可辩驳的: *His case is ~.* 他的案子无法申辩。

un·an·swered /ʌnˈɑːnsəd US: -ˈæn-; ʌnˈænsəd/ adj not replied to: 无回答的; 无答复的: *~ letters;* 未回复的信件; not returned: 无回报的: *~ love.* 单恋。

un·ap·proach·able /ˌʌnəˈprəʊtʃəbl; ˌʌnəˈprotʃəbl/ adj (esp, of a person) difficult to approach (because too stiff or formal): (尤指人)(因为太呆板或拘谨而)难接近的: *The new manager is an ~ sort of man.* 新任经理是一位不易接近的人。

un·armed /ˌʌnˈɑːmd; ʌnˈɑrmd/ adj without weapons or means of defence. 未武装的; 徒手的; 无武器的。

un·asked /ˌʌnˈɑːskt US: -ˈæs-; ʌnˈæskt/ adj *~ (for),* not asked (for), requested, or invited: 未经要求的; 未经邀请的: *She's always ready to help and often does so ~.* 她总是乐于帮助旁人, 而且常常是出于主动。 *Many of the contributions to the relief fund were ~ for.* 救济金的捐献, 有许多是未经要求而主动捐出的。

un·as·sum·ing /ˌʌnəˈsjuːmɪŋ US: -ˈsuː-; ˌʌnəˈsumɪŋ/ adj not pushing oneself forward; not drawing attention to oneself; modest. 不爱出风头的; 不爱表现的; 谦逊的。 **~·ly** adv

un·at·tached /ˌʌnəˈtætʃt; ˌʌnəˈtætʃt/ adj 1 not connected or associated with a particular person, group, organization, etc; independent. 不与某人、团体、组织等相关联的; 独立的。 **2** not married or engaged to be married. 未结婚的; 未订婚的。

un·at·tended /ˌʌnəˈtendɪd; ˌʌnəˈtɛndɪd/ adj 1 without attendants or escort. 没有随员的; 没有同伴的。 **2** not attended to; with no one to give care or attention to: 没人管的; 没人照顾的: *Would you leave small children at home ~ while you went to the cinema?* 你(们)去看电影时, 会把小孩子留在家里无人照料?

un·avail·ing /ˌʌnəˈveɪlɪŋ; ˌʌnəˈvelɪŋ/ adj without effort or success. 无效的; 无益的; 无用的。

un·avoid·able /ˌʌnəˈvɔɪdəbl; ˌʌnəˈvɔɪdəbl/ adj that cannot be avoided. 不可避免的; 不得已的。 **un·avoid·ably** /-əblɪ; -əblɪ/ adv: *He was unavoidably absent.* 他不得已而缺课(席)。

un·aware /ˌʌnəˈweə(r); ˌʌnəˈwɛr/ adj (pred) (用作表语) *~ of sth/that...,* not knowing; not aware: 不知道的; 未觉察的: *He was ~ of my presence/that I was present.* 他不知道我在场。 **~s** /-ˈweəz; -ˈwɛrz/ adv 1 by surprise; unexpectedly. 意外地; 突如其来地; 未料到

地。**take sb ~s,** surprise him. (由于突然出现而)令某人惊讶。**2** without being aware; unconsciously: 不知不觉地;无意地: *She probably dropped the parcel ~s.* 她很可能无意间丢掉了那包裹。

un·backed /ˌʌn'bækt; ʌn'bækt/ adj **1** (of a proposal, etc) not supported. (指提议等)不受支持的。**2** (of a horse in a race) having no bets placed on it. (指赛马中的马)无人下注的。

un·bal·anced /ˌʌn'bælənst; ʌn'bælənst/ adj (esp of a person, the mind) disordered; not sane or normal. (尤指人,其心智)不正常的;不健全之;错乱的。

un·bar /ˌʌn'bɑː(r); ʌn'bɑr/ vt (**-rr-**) remove bars from (a gate, etc); (fig) throw open: 移去(门等)上的横木; 拔去门闩; 打开; (喻)开放: ~ *all the professions to women.* 开放所有的职业给妇女。

un·bear·able /ˌʌn'beərəbl; ʌn'bɛrəbl/ adj that cannot be borne or tolerated: 不能忍受的; 忍无可忍的; 难堪的: *I find his rudeness ~.* 我觉得他的无礼难以忍受。**un·bear·ably** /-əblɪ; -əblɪ/ adv in a way that cannot be endured: 不能忍受地; 无法忍耐地: *unbearably hot/rude.* 热(粗野)得叫人受不了。

un·beaten /ˌʌn'biːtn; ʌn'bitn/ adj (esp) not having been beaten, defeated or surpassed: (尤指)未被打破、击败或胜过的: *an ~ record for the 1000 metres race;* 未被打破的一千米赛跑记录; *an ~ team.* 常胜队。

un·be·com·ing /ˌʌnbɪ'kʌmɪŋ; ˌʌnbɪ'kʌmɪŋ/ adj **1** not suited (to the wearer): (对于穿戴者)不称身的; 不合身的: *an ~ dress.* 不合身的衣服。**2** ~ *to/for,* not appropriate or befitting. 不适当的; 不相配的。**~·ly** adv

un·be·known /ˌʌnbɪ'nəʊn; ˌʌnbɪ'non/, **un·beknownst** /-nst; -nst/ adj, adv (colloq) not known (to), without the knowledge of: (口)…为…所不认识的(地); 不为人知的(地): *He did it ~st to me,* without my being aware of it. 他瞒着我干那事。

un·be·lief /ˌʌnbɪ'liːf; ˌʌnbɪ'lif/ n [U] (esp) lack of belief, state of not believing, in God, religion, etc. (尤指)不信上帝; 不信宗教。**un·be·liev·able** adj **1** not believable. 难以相信的。**2** (colloq) very surprising. (口)非常惊人的。**un·be·liev·ably** adv **un·be·liev·ing** adj not believing; doubting. 不信的; 怀疑的。**un·be·liev·ing·ly** adv

un·bend /ˌʌn'bend; ʌn'bend/ vi, vt (pt, pp **unbent** /-'bent; -'bent/ or **-ed**) **1** [VP2A] behave in a way free from strain, formality; become relaxed: 不拘泥; 变得平易近人; 变得缓和: *In the classroom the teacher maintains discipline but after class he ~s.* 教师在课堂上很严厉,但下课后就变得平易近人了。**2** [VP6A] relax: 松弛: ~ *one's mind.* 使心情松弛。**~·ing** adj (esp) firm in purpose, in not changing decisions, etc: (尤指)坚持目标的;不改变决定、主张等的: *maintain an ~ing attitude,* make no concessions, etc. 采取坚定不移的态度。

un·biassed (also **-biased**) /ˌʌn'baɪəst; ʌn'baɪəst/ adj not biassed; impartial. 没有偏见的, 不偏不倚的; 公正的。

un·bid·den /ˌʌn'bɪdn; ʌn'bɪdn/ adj (formal) uninvited; not requested or ordered. (正式用语)未受邀请的; 未被要求的; 未受到指使或命令的。

un·bind /ˌʌn'baɪnd; ʌn'baɪnd/ vt (pt, pp **-bound** /-'baʊnd; -'baʊnd/) [VP6A] free from fastenings, bindings, etc. 释开; 拆散; 解开。

un·blush·ing /ˌʌn'blʌʃɪŋ; ʌn'blʌʃɪŋ/ adj (esp) shameless; not bashful: (尤指)无羞耻心的; 不知耻的: *the ~ corruption of some politicians.* 若干政客恬不知耻的腐败。

un·born /ˌʌn'bɔːn; ʌn'bɔrn/ adj not yet born; future: 尚未出生的; 未来的: ~ *generations.* 未来的世代; 后代。

un·bosom /ˌʌn'buzəm; ʌn'buzəm/ vt [VP6A, 14] ~ *oneself (to sb),* tell, reveal (one's sorrows, etc). 告知;表白;说出;倾诉(自己的忧愁等)。

un·bounded /ˌʌn'baʊndɪd; ʌn'baʊndɪd/ adj boundless; without limits: 无限制的; 无际的; 极大的: ~ *ambition.* 极大的野心。

un·bowed /ˌʌn'baʊd; ʌn'baʊd/ adj not bowed or bent; not conquered or subdued: 不弯曲的; 不屈服的: *His head is bloody but ~.* 他的头是血淋淋的, 但他没有低头。

un·bridled /ˌʌn'braɪdld; ʌn'braɪdld/ adj (esp, fig) not controlled: (尤指,喻)放纵的; 放肆的: ~ *insolence/passions;* 放肆的侮辱(放纵的情欲); *an ~ tongue.* 饶舌。

un·bro·ken /ˌʌn'brəʊkən; ʌn'brokən/ adj (esp) **1** (eg of a horse) not tamed or subdued. (指马等)未养驯的; 不驯服的。**2** not interrupted: 未受阻碍的: *six hours of ~ sleep.* 六小时不间断的睡眠。**3** (of records, etc) not beaten or surpassed. (指记录等)未被打破的; 未被超过的。

un·buckle /ˌʌn'bʌkl; ʌn'bʌkl/ vt [VP6A] loosen, undo, the buckle(s) of. 松开或解开…的扣子或带扣。

un·bur·den /ˌʌn'bɜːdn; ʌn'bɜrdn/ vt [VP6A, 15A] ~ *oneself/sth (of sth),* relieve of worry, anxiety, etc: 释负; 解除负担: ~ *one's heart/conscience,* eg by talking about one's troubles, making a confession; 解除心情(良心)上的负担(如借诉苦、告解); ~ *oneself to a friend,* find relief by speaking to him about one's feelings, etc; 对朋友叙说隐衷; ~ *oneself of a secret,* tell it to sb. 把秘密告知某人。

un·but·toned /ˌʌn'bʌtnd; ʌn'bʌtnd/ adj with the buttons not fastened; (fig) relaxed; (feeling) free from formality. 解开钮扣的; (喻)松弛的; 不(觉得)拘束的。

un·called-for /ˌʌn'kɔːld ,fɔː(r); ʌn'kɔld,fɔr/ adj neither desirable nor necessary: 不必要的; 没有理由的; 不应当的: *insults.* 没道理的侮慢。*Such comments are ~.* 这评论是多余的。

un·canny /ˌʌn'kænɪ; ʌn'kænɪ/ adj unnatural, mysterious; weird: 离奇的; 怪异的; 神秘的: *an ~ noise;* 神秘的声响; ~ *shapes in the darkness.* 黑暗中呈现的怪异形象。**un·can·nily** /-ɪlɪ; -ɪlɪ/ adv

un·cared-for /ˌʌn'keəd fɔː(r); ʌn'kɛrd,fɔr/ adj not looked after; neglected: 没人照顾的; 被忽略的: ~ *children;* 没有人照顾的孩子们; *an ~ garden.* 荒废的花园。

un·ceas·ing /ˌʌn'siːsɪŋ; ʌn'sisɪŋ/ adj incessant; going on all the time. 不断的; 继续的; 始终不停的。**~·ly** adv

un·cer·e·mo·ni·ous /ˌʌnˌserɪ'məʊnɪəs; ˌʌnsɛrə'monɪəs/ adj (esp) informal; lacking in courtesy. (尤指)随便的; 不拘礼的; 没有礼貌的; 不客气的。**~·ly** adv **~·ness** n

un·cer·tain /ˌʌn'sɜːtn; ʌn'sɜrtn/ adj **1** changeable; not reliable: 变化的; 不可靠的; 靠不住的: ~ *weather;* 变化无常的天气; *a man with an ~ temper.* 喜怒无常的人。**2** not certainly knowing or known: 不确知的; 不明的; 不为人确知的: *be/feel ~ (about) what to do next;* 不确知下一步如何做; ~ *of/about/as to one's plans for the future;* 不确知未来的计划; *a woman of ~ age,* one whose age cannot be guessed. 无法断定其年龄的女子。**~·ly** adv **~·ty/**-tntɪ; -tntɪ/ n (pl **-ties**) **1** [U] state of being ~. 变化无常; 不可靠; 不确知。**2** [C] sth which is ~: 不确定的事物: *the uncertainties of adequate reward in the profession of an actor.* 演员这一行的报酬时高时低。

un·chari·table /ˌʌn'tʃærɪtəbl; ʌn'tʃærətəbl/ adj (esp) severe or harsh (in making judgements of the conduct of others): (尤指)(在评判他人行为时)严厉的; 苛刻的: *offer an ~ explanation of/put an ~ interpretation on sb's actions.* 对某人的行为作严厉的解释。

un·charted /ˌʌn'tʃɑːtɪd; ʌn'tʃɑrtɪd/ adj **1** not marked on a map or chart: 图上未标明的: *an ~ island.* 地图上没有标明的岛屿。**2** (lit or fig) not explored and mapped: (字面或喻)未经探测并绘制成图的: *an ~ sea;* 未经探勘和绘图的海; ~ *emotions.* 未经探测的情绪。

un·checked /ˌʌn'tʃekt; ʌn'tʃekt/ adj not checked or restrained: 未被遏止的; 未受抑制的: *an ~ advance;* 未受制止的进犯; ~ *anger.* 未受制止的愤怒。

un·chris·tian /ˌʌn'krɪstʃən; ʌn'krɪstʃən/ adj **1** not Christian; contrary to Christian principles. 不是基督徒

的;非基督教的;反基督教教义的。**2** (colloq) inconvenient and unreasonable: (口)不方便的;不合理的: *Why do you call on me at this ~ hour?* (eg at 5am). 你为什么在这个时候(例如凌晨五时)来看我呢?

un·civil /ˌʌn'sɪvl; ˌʌn'sɪvl/ *adj* (esp) impolite. (尤指)不礼貌的;不客气的;失礼的。

un·claimed /ˌʌn'kleɪmd; ˌʌn'klemd/ *adj* that has not been claimed: 无人认领的: *~ letters/parcels* (at the post-office, a lost property office, etc). 没有人认领的信件(包裹)。

uncle /'ʌŋkl; 'ʌŋkl/ *n* brother of one's father or mother; husband of one's aunt: 伯父;叔父;舅父;姑丈;姨丈: *my ~ Charlie.* 我的伯父(叔父等)查理。**U~ Sam,** personification of the US. 山姆大叔(美国的拟人称)。**U~ Tom,** ⚠ (US, derog) black person who is very friendly to white people. (讳)(美,贬)汤姆叔叔(对白人非常友善的黑人)。**Dutch U~,** ⇨ **Dutch (2).**

un·clean /ˌʌn'kliːn; ˌʌn'klin/ *adj* (esp, Jewish law) ceremonially impure, eg the pig. (尤用于犹太法律)在礼仪上不洁净的(例如猪)。

un·clouded /ˌʌn'klaʊdɪd; ˌʌn'klaʊdɪd/ *adj* (esp fig) bright; serene: (尤用作喻)晴朗的;平静的: *a lift of ~ happiness.* 平静幸福的生活。Cf 参较 *cloudless,* as in a *cloudless sky.*

unco /'ʌŋkəʊ; 'ʌŋko/ (Scot) (苏) *adj* strange; unusual: 古怪的;奇异的;不寻常的: *an ~ sight.* 奇观。□ *adv* remarkably: 显著地;非常地: (esp)(尤指) *the ~ good,* religious people who are rigid in their views and behaviour. 看法及行为均极严谨的教徒。

un·col·oured(US=**-colored**) /ˌʌn'kʌləd; ˌʌn'kʌləd/ *adj* (esp fig) not exaggerated or heightened in description: (尤用作喻)未夸张的; 未加渲染的: *an ~ description of events.* 对事件不加渲染的叙述。

un·come-at-able /ˌʌnkʌm'ætəbl; ˌʌnkʌm'ætəbl/ *adj* (colloq) not easy to get to; not accessible. (口)难得到的;难接近的。

un·com·fort·able/ ʌn'kʌmftəbl US: ʌn'kʌmfətəbl/ *adj* not comfortable; uneasy: 不舒适的;不安的: *an ~ chair/feeling.* 不舒适的椅子(不安的感觉)。

un·com·mit·ted /ˌʌnkə'mɪtɪd; ˌʌnkə'mɪtɪd/ *adj ~ (to),* not committed or bound (to a course of action, etc); free, independent: 不负义务的; 不受(某行动等)限制的; 自由的, 独立的: *the ~ countries,* those not allied to or bound to either of the power blocs of the modern world. 不结盟国家。

un·com·mon /ˌʌn'kɒmən; ˌʌn'kɑmən/ *adj* unusual; remarkable: 不普通的;非寻常的;不凡的; 显著的。**~·ly** *adv* (esp) remarkably: (尤指)显著地; 极: *an ~ly intelligent child.* 极聪明的儿童。

un·com·pro·mis·ing /ˌʌn'kɒmprəmaɪzɪŋ; ʌn'kɑmprə,maɪzɪŋ/ *adj* not ready to make any compromise; unyielding; firm: 不妥协的; 不让步的; 坚定的: *a ~ member of the Tory party.* 一个不妥协的保守党党员。

un·con·cern /ˌʌnkən'sɜːn; ˌʌnkən'sɚn/ *n* [U] lack of care or interest. 冷漠;不关心;不感兴趣。

un·con·cerned /ˌʌnkən'sɜːnd; ˌʌnkən'sɚnd/ *adj* **1** *~ in sth,* not involved in. 没有关系的;不相干的;未牵入的。**~ with sth/sb,** not (emotionally) concerned with. (对某事或某人)无感情牵连的。**2** free from anxiety; untroubled; uninterested. 无忧愁的;漠不关心的;不感兴趣的。**un·con·cern·ed·ly** /-'sɜːnɪdlɪ; -'sɝnɪdlɪ/ *adv*

un·con·di·tional /ˌʌnkən'dɪʃənl; ˌʌnkən'dɪʃənl/ *adj* absolute; not subject to conditions: 绝对的;无条件的: *The victors demanded ~ surrender.* 胜利者要求无条件投降。**~·ly** /-ʃənlɪ; -ʃənlɪ/ *adv*

un·con·di·tioned /ˌʌnkən'dɪʃnd; ˌʌnkən'dɪʃnd/ *adj* not subject to conditions; 无条件的: (psych)(心理) *~ reflex,* instinctive response to a stimulus. 非制约反射;无条件反射(对刺激的本能反应)。

un·con·scion·able /ˌʌn'kɒnʃənəbl; ʌn'kɑnʃənəbl/ *adj* unreasonable; not guided by conscience; excessive: 不合理的; 没良心的; 过分的: *You take an ~ time*

dressing. 你花在化妆上的时间太多了。

un·con·scious /ˌʌn'kɒnʃəs; ʌn'kɑnʃəs/ *adj* not conscious (all senses): 失去知觉的; 无意识的;不能察觉的; 无意的: *~ humour,* not intended as humour by the speaker or writer; 无意中的幽默; *be ~ of having done wrong.* 不知道做错。□ *n* **the ~** (psych) that part of one's mental activity of which one is unaware, but which can be detected and understood through the skilled analysis of dreams, behaviour, etc. (心理)下意识(自己觉察不到的心智活动,但可从梦与行为等的巧妙分析,探知其存在并了解其性质)。**~·ly** *adv* **~·ness** *n*

un·con·sid·ered /ˌʌnkən'sɪdəd; ˌʌnkən'sɪdəd/ *adj* **1** (of words, remarks) spoken, made, etc without proper consideration or reflection. (指文字,言词)未加熟虑而说出、写出等的。**2** disregarded (as if of little value or worth). 未受到理会的;被忽视的。

un·con·ven·tional /ˌʌnkən'venʃənl; ˌʌnkən'venʃənl/ *adj* not usual or ordinary; not bound by the customs of society: 不寻常的; 不依惯例的; 不从习俗的: *an ~ dress/person/way of life.* 不从习俗的衣服(人,生活方式)。

un·con·vinc·ing /ˌʌnkən'vɪnsɪŋ; ˌʌnkən'vɪnsɪŋ/ *adj* not seeming true, right, or real: 不足以令人相信的; 不令人信服的: *an ~ explanation/attempt/disguise.* 不足以令人相信的解释(企图、伪装)。

un·cork /ˌʌn'kɔːk; ʌn'kɔrk/ *vt* [VP6A] draw the cork from (a bottle). 拔去(瓶)上的塞子; 开(瓶)口。

un·couple /ˌʌn'kʌpl; ʌn'kʌpl/ *vt* [VP6A] unfasten: 解开: *~ hounds from the leash/a locomotive from a train.* 解开猎狗的系带(使火车的机车与列车分离)。

un·couth /ˌʌn'kuːθ; ʌn'kuθ/ *adj* (of persons, their behaviour) rough, awkward, not cultured. (指人, 其行为)粗鲁的; 笨拙的; 无教养的。**~·ly** *adv* **~·ness** *n*

un·cover /ˌʌn'kʌvə(r); ʌn'kʌvə/ *vt, vi* **1** [VP6A] remove a cover or covering from; (fig) disclose; make known: 移去…的覆盖物; (喻)揭露; 宣布: *The police have ~ed a plot against the President.* 警方已破获了一件谋害总统的阴谋。**2** [VP6A] (mil) expose to attack: (军)暴露; 除去掩护: *By a sudden movement we ~ed the enemy's right flank.* 我们采取突然的行动攻击敌人的右翼。**3** [VP2A] (archaic) take off one's hat or cap. (古)脱帽。

un·crossed /ˌʌn'krɒst US: -'krɔːst; ʌn'krɔst/ *adj* (esp, of a cheque) not crossed. (尤指支票)未划线的。⇨ **cross²(2).**

un·crowned /ˌʌn'kraʊnd; ʌn'kraʊnd/ *adj* **1** (of a king, etc) not yet crowned. (指国王等)尚未加冕的; 尚未举行加冕礼的。**2** having the power but not the title or name of a king, etc. 有国王等的权力而无名位的;有实权而无名的。

unc·tion /'ʌŋkʃn; 'ʌŋkʃən/ *n* [U] **1** act of anointing with oil, esp as a religious rite. 涂油; (尤指)宗教的涂油式。**Extreme U~,** the anointing of a dying person by a priest (of the Orthodox and Roman Catholic Churches). (东正教及天主教)僧侣为垂死者所行的涂油式。**2** (pretended, insincere) earnestness, smoothness in speech or manner: 虚情假意; 油腔滑调: *She related the scandal with a great deal of ~;* 她添油加醋地叙述那件丑闻; flattery. 谄媚。

unc·tu·ous /'ʌŋktjʊəs; 'ʌŋktʃʊəs/ *adj* (insincerely) earnest, smooth in speech or manner; flattering: 虚假意的;油腔滑调的;谄媚的: *~ tones/assurances.* 虚假的语调(承诺)。**~·ly** *adv*

un·cut /ˌʌn'kʌt; ʌn'kʌt/ *adj* (of a book) with the outer folds of the pages not trimmed or cut; (of a book, film, etc) not abridged or censored. (指书)边没切齐的; 书页未割开的; (指书, 电影等)未被删节的; 未被判掉的。

un·dated /ˌʌn'deɪtɪd; ʌn'detɪd/ *adj* not having a date: 无日期的;未注明年月日的: *an ~ cheque;* 未注日期的支票; *~ stocks,* with no specified date for redemption. 无定期债券(未明确规定贴现日期者)。

un·daunted /ˌʌn'dɔːntɪd ; ʌn'dɒntɪd/ *adj* not daunted; fearless. 大无畏的; 勇敢的; 不惧怕的.

un·de·ceive /ˌʌndɪ'siːv/ *vt* [VP6A] cause to be no longer deceived or in error. 使不再受欺骗; 使不犯错误; 使醒悟.

un·de·cided /ˌʌndɪ'saɪdɪd ; ˌʌndɪ'saɪdɪd/ *adj* not decided; not yet having made up one's mind: 未被决定的; 尚未作决定的: *She was ~ whether to go to a concert or the cinema.* 她还没有决定是去听音乐会还是去看电影.

un·de·clared /ˌʌndɪ'kleəd ; ˌʌndɪ'klεrd/ *adj* 1 (of goods liable to customs duty) not declared or shown to the customs officers. (指应缴纳关税的货物)未向税务人员申报的; 未报关的. 2 not announced or made known: 未(被)宣布的; 未公之于世的: *~ war.* 不宣而战的战争.

un·de·fended /ˌʌndɪ'fendɪd ; ˌʌndɪ'fεndɪd/ *adj* (esp of a lawsuit) in which no defence is offered. (尤指诉讼)未提答辩或抗辩的.

un·de·mon·stra·tive /ˌʌndɪ'mɒnstrətɪv ; ˌʌndɪ-'mɑnstrətɪv/ *adj* reserved; not in the habit of showing feelings of affection, interest, etc. 含蓄的; 不惯于表露喜爱、好恶等.

un·de·ni·able /ˌʌndɪ'naɪəbl ; ˌʌndɪ'naɪəbl/ *adj* that cannot be denied; undoubtedly true: 无可否认的; 确实的: *~ worth/value.* 确有价值的. **un·de·ni·ably** /-əblɪ; -əblɪ/ *adv*

un·de·nomi·na·tional /ˌʌndɪˌnɒmɪ'neɪʃənl , ˌʌndɪ-ˌnɑmə'neʃənl/ *adj* not associated with any particular religious sect: 不属于任何宗教派系的; 非教派的: *~ education/schools.* 非教会教育(学校).

un·der¹ /'ʌndə(r); 'ʌndə/ *adv* 1 in or to a lower place, position, etc: 在下; 在下位; 往下面: *The ship went ~,* sank. 那条船下沉了. *Can you stay ~ (= ~ the water) for two minutes?* 你能在水面下停留两分钟吗? **down ~,** (used in GB, colloq) (in/to) Australia and New Zealand. (用于英国, 口)在(往)澳大利亚及新西兰. 2 (used to modify *nn*) subordinate; lower in rank, etc: (用以修饰名词)从属的; 从下的; 在下面的; 级别等较低的: '*secretary.* 次长; (美)副部长; 副国务卿; (尤指)政务次长.

un·der² /'ʌndə(r); 'ʌndə/ *prep* 1 in or to a position lower than: (位置)低于; 在…之下: *The cat was ~ the table.* 猫在桌子下面. *It is shady ~ the trees.* 在树下是荫凉的. *There's nothing new ~ the sun,* (谚)太阳底下无新事. *We passed ~ several bridges.* 我们从几座桥下面通过. *The soldiers were standing ~ (= at the foot of) the castle wall.* 士兵们站在城堡的墙脚下. *The village nestles ~ (= at the foot of) the hill.* 那村庄坐落在山脚下. 2 in and covered by: 被…遮蔽着; 在…的包裹中: *The part of an iceberg ~ the water is much larger than the part above the water.* 冰山在水面下的部分远大于水面上的部分. *He hid his face ~ the bedclothes.* 他把脸藏在被子中. *Her hair came out from ~ her hat.* 她的头发从帽子下面露了出来. 3 less than; lower (in rank) than: 少于; 在级别或地位上低于: *children ~* (opp 反义词: *over/above*) *fourteen years of age;* 十四岁以下的儿童; *books for the ~-'tens* (opp 反义词: *over-tens*), children under ten; 适于十岁以下儿童的书; *incomes ~* (opp 反义词: *over/above*) *£3000;* 不到三千英镑的收入; *run a hundred metres in ~ the seconds;* 不到十秒钟跑完一百米; *~ half an acre;* 不到半英亩; *no one ~* (opp 反义词: *above/over*) *(the rank of) a captain;* 没有人低于上尉(的军阶); *speak ~ one's breath,* in a whisper. 低声说话; 悄悄讲. *~ age,* ⇨ **age. 4** (indicating various conditions): (表示各种情况): *road ~ repair,* being repaired; 在修理中的道路; *~ discussion,* being discussed; 在讨论中; *fifty acres ~* (= planted with) *wheat;* 五十英亩的小麦田; *~ sentence of* (= sentenced to) *death;* 被判处死刑; *living ~ an assumed name;* 隐姓埋名度日; *England ~ the Stuarts,* during the times of the Stuart kings and queens; 在斯图亚特王朝统治下的英国; *be ~ the impression that...,* have the idea or belief that.... 以为; 相信…; *The book is listed ~ biology,* within that classification. 该书列入

生物学的类别下. **5** weighed down by (lit and fig): 被…重压(字面及喻): *marching ~ a heavy load;* 载负着重物行进; *sink ~ a load of grief (taxation, etc).* 因悲伤(重税等)的负担而倒下去.

under- /'ʌndə(r); 'ʌndə/ *pref* ⇨ **App 3.** 参看附录三.

under·act /ˌʌndər'ækt , ˌʌndə'ækt/ *vt, vi* [VP6A, 2A] act with too little spirit, energy, emphasis, etc: 表演不够实力; 表演不够精彩: *~ the part of Hamlet.* 没演出哈姆雷特这个角色的特色. *The star overacted; the other players ~ed.* 主角演得太过火, 而其他演员却不太实力.

under·arm /'ʌndərɑːm; 'ʌndəɑrm/ *adj, adv* (cricket, tennis) with the hand kept below the level of the elbow: (板球, 网球)低手的(地): *~ bowling;* 低手式投球; *bowl/serve ~.* 投(发)低手球.

under·belly /'ʌndəbelɪ; 'ʌndəˌbεlɪ/ *n* (*pl* **-lies**) under surface of an animal's body, eg as a cut of meat, esp pork. 动物身体的下腹部(如一块下腹肉, 尤指猪肉).

under·bid /ˌʌndə'bɪd ; ˌʌndə'bɪd/ *vt* (*pt, pp* unchanged) ⇨ **bid¹(1). 1** make a lower bid than (sb else). 出价低于(他人); 出价较低. **2** (card games, bridge) bid less on (a hand of cards) than its strength warrants. (纸牌, 桥牌)叫(牌)低于手上的牌力.

under·brush /'ʌndəbrʌʃ ; 'ʌndəˌbrʌʃ/ *n* [U] = **undergrowth** (which is more usu 此词较常用).

under·car·riage /'ʌndəkærɪdʒ ; 'ʌndəˌkærɪdʒ/ *n* landing gear of an aircraft. 飞机的起落架. ⇨ illus at **air.** 参看 air 之插图.

under·charge /ˌʌndə'tʃɑːdʒ; ˌʌndə'tʃɑrdʒ/ *vt* [VP 6A] charge too little for (sth) or to (sb). 少讨(某物)的价钱; 对(某人)少讨某物的价钱. □ *n* /'ʌndətʃɑːdʒ; 'ʌndəˌtʃɑrdʒ/ charge that is too low or small. 太低或太少的价格.

under·clothes /'ʌndəkləʊðz ; 'ʌndəˌkloðz/ *n pl* clothing worn under a shirt, dress, etc next to the skin. 内衣裤; 贴身内衣. **under·cloth·ing** /'ʌndə-kləʊðɪŋ; 'ʌndəˌkloðɪŋ/ *n* [U] = **~.**

under·cover /ˌʌndə'kʌvə(r); ˌʌndə'kʌvə/ *adj* secret; surreptitious: 秘密的; 暗中从事的: *an ~ agent,* person who associates with suspected criminals, etc to get evidence against them, or who acts as a spy, eg during a war; 密探; 间谍; *~ payments,* eg made in order to bribe sb. 暗中所付的款(如用以行贿).

under·cur·rent /'ʌndəkʌrənt ; 'ʌndəˌkɜrənt/ *n* [U] current of water flowing beneath the surface; (fig) tendency (of thought or feeling) lying below what is apparent: 潜流; 底流; 暗流; (喻)(思想或感情的)暗潮; 潜势: *an ~ of opposition/melancholy,* 一般反对的暗潮(内心的伤感情怀).

under·cut¹ /'ʌndəkʌt ; 'ʌndəˌkʌt/ *n* [U] meat cut from the underside of sirloin. 牛腰的下脊肉.

under·cut² /ˌʌndə'kʌt ; ˌʌndə'kʌt/ *vt* (*pt, pp* unchanged, **-tt-**) [VP6A] (comm) offer (goods, services) at a lower price than competitors. (商)减低(货物, 服务)的价格; 索价低于竞争者.

under·de·vel·oped /ˌʌndədɪ'veləpt , ˌʌndədɪ'vεləpt/ *adj* not yet fully developed: 发育尚不充分的; 未充分发展的; 未完全开发的: *~ muscles/countries.* 发育不充分的肌肉(低度开发国家).

under·dog /'ʌndədɒɡ *US:* -dɔːɡ; 'ʌndə'dɔɡ/ *n* (often 常作 **the ~**) poor and helpless person who usu gets the worst of an encounter, a struggle, etc: 在竞赛、打斗等中居于劣势的人; 失败者; 受压迫者: *plead for the ~,* for sb who is oppressed. 为受压迫者说明.

under·done /ˌʌndə'dʌn ; 'ʌndə'dʌn/ *adj* (esp of meat) not completely cooked throughout. (尤指肉)未完全熟的.

under·esti·mate /ˌʌndər'estɪmeɪt ; 'ʌndə'εstə,met/ *vt* [VP6A] form too low an estimate of: 低估; 对…作过低的评价: *~ the enemy's strength.* 低估敌人的兵力. □ *n* /-mət; -mɪt/ [C] estimate which is too low. 低估; 评价过低.

under·ex·pose /ˌʌndərɪkˈspəʊz ; ˌʌndərɪkˈspoz/ vt [VP6A] (photo) expose (a plate or film) for too short a time. (摄影)使(底片)感光不足. **under·ex·posure** /-ˈspəʊʒə(r); -ˈspoʒə/ n

under·fed /ˌʌndəˈfed; ˌʌndəˈfɛd/ adj having had too little food. 吃得太少的; 没吃饱的.

under·floor /ˌʌndəˈflɔː(r); ˌʌndəˈflor/ adj (of systems for heating buildings) with the source of heat placed under the floor(s): (指房屋的暖气系统) 热源装置于地板下面的; ~ heating. 热源置于地板下的暖气系统.

under·foot /ˌʌndəˈfʊt; ˌʌndəˈfʊt/ adv under one's feet; on the ground: 在脚下面; 在地上: It is very hard ~, eg when the ground is frozen hard. 地面很硬(如地面冻结时).

under·gar·ment /ˈʌndəgɑːmənt; ˈʌndəˌgɑrmənt/ n [C] article of underclothing. 内衣.

under·go /ˌʌndəˈgəʊ; ˌʌndəˈgo/ vt (pt -went /-ˈwent/, pp -gone /-ˈgɒn US -ˈgɔn/ -ˈgon/) (pt, pp) experience; pass through: 经验; 经历; 遭受: The explorers had to ~ much suffering. 探险的人们不得不忍受很多困苦. The new aircraft underwent its tests well. 这架新飞机经试验后令人满意.

under·grad·uate /ˌʌndəˈgrædʒʊət; ˌʌndəˈgrædʒʊɪt/ n university student working for a bachelor's degree: 大学生; 大学肄业生: (attrib) (用作定语) '~ work/studies. 大学生的课业(学业); in his '~ days. 在他的大学时代.

under·ground /ˈʌndəgraʊnd; ˈʌndəˌgraʊnd/ attrib adj 1 under the surface of the ground: 在地面下的; 地下的: London's ~ railways; 伦敦的地下铁路; ~ passages/caves. 地下通道(洞穴). 2 (fig) secret, esp of a secret political movement or one for resisting enemy forces in occupation of another country: (喻)秘密的(尤指有关秘密的政治活动或反抗敌人占领军的秘密活动的): ~ workers. 地下工作者. □ adv (in the senses of the adj): (用作形容词各义): He went ~ (= into hiding) when he heard the police were after him. 他听到警察要抓他就躲藏起来了. □ n (the) ~, (in the senses of the adj): (用作形容词各义): travel in London by ~, ie the ~ railway (US = subway); 乘地下火车游伦敦; a member of the French ~, the secret resistance movement during World War Two. (第二次世界大战期间)法国地下抗敌组织的一名工作人员.

under·growth /ˈʌndəgrəʊθ; ˈʌndəˌgroθ/ n [U] shrubs, bushes, low trees, growing among taller trees. 下层林丛(生长于较高大林木下的灌木、小树丛或矮树).

under·hand /ˈʌndəhænd; ˈʌndəˌhænd/ adj, adv secret(ly); deceitful(ly); sly(ly): 秘密的(地); 欺骗的(地); 狡诈的(地); 玩弄阴谋的: play an ~ game; 玩弄诡谋; ~ methods; 卑鄙手段; behave in an ~ way. 举止狡诈. ~ed adj = ~.

under·hung /ˌʌndəˈhʌŋ; ˌʌndəˈhʌŋ/ adj (attrib) (of the lower jaw) projecting beyond the upper jaw. (用作定语) (指下颌) 比上颌突出的.

under·lay /ˈʌndəleɪ; ˈʌndəˌle/ n [U] material (felt, rubber, etc) laid under a carpet or mattress (to preserve its condition). (放在地毯或床垫下面的)衬垫 (如毛毡或橡皮等,以保持其良好状态).

under·lie /ˌʌndəˈlaɪ; ˌʌndəˈlaɪ/ vt [VP6A] 1 be or lie under. 位于…之下. 2 form the basis of (a theory, conduct, behaviour, doctrine): 成为(理论、行为、举止、主义)的基础: the underlying reason/fault/guilt. 根本的原因(根本的毛病; 内心的愧疚).

under·line /ˌʌndəˈlaɪn; ˌʌndəˈlaɪn/ vt [VP6A] draw a line under (a word, etc); (fig) emphasize. 画线于(字等)的下面; (喻)强调; 加强. □ n /ˈʌndəlaɪn; ˈʌndəˌlaɪn/ line drawn under a word or words. (画在字下面的)底线.

under·ling /ˈʌndəlɪŋ; ˈʌndəlɪŋ/ n (usu contemptuous) person in an unimportant position under another or others. (通常含轻蔑意)职位低的人; 下属.

under·manned /ˌʌndəˈmænd ; ˌʌndəˈmænd/ adj (of a ship, factory, etc) having not enough men to do all the work that needs to be done. (指船上、工厂等)人员不足的.

under·men·tioned /ˌʌndəˈmenʃnd ; ˈʌndəˈmenʃənd/ adj mentioned below or later (in an article, etc). (在文章等中)下面提到的; 下述的; 下记的.

under·mine /ˌʌndəˈmaɪn; ˌʌndəˈmaɪn/ vt [VP6A] 1 make a hollow or tunnel under; weaken at the base: 在…之下掘洞与地道; 使从基础损坏: cliffs ~d by the sea. 被海浪冲坏底部的悬崖. 2 weaken gradually: 逐渐削弱或损坏: His health was ~d by drink. 他的健康由于饮酒而逐渐损坏. The President's enemies are spreading rumours to ~ his authority. 总统的敌人在散布谣言, 以逐渐破坏他的威信.

under·neath /ˌʌndəˈniːθ; ˌʌndəˈniθ/ adv, prep beneath; below; at or to a lower place. 在…的下面; 在…之下; 在下位; 向下位.

under·nour·ished /ˌʌndəˈnʌrɪʃt; ˌʌndəˈnɜɪʃt/ adj not provided with sufficient food for good health and normal growth. 营养不良的. **under·nour·ish·ment** n

under·pants /ˈʌndəpænts; ˈʌndəˌpænts/ n pl short undergarment worn by men and boys over the loins. (男人或男孩穿的)内裤. ⇨ **panties.**

under·pass /ˈʌndəpɑːs US: -pæs; ˈʌndəˌpæs/ n [C] section of a road that goes under another road or railway. 地下穿越道(为某道路的一段, 自另一条道路或铁路下穿过). ⇨ **overpass, flyover.**

under·pay /ˌʌndəˈpeɪ; ˌʌndəˈpe/ vt (pt, pp -paid /-ˈpeɪd; -ˈped/) [VP6A] pay (workmen, etc) inadequately. 付给(工人等)太低的工资. ~·ment n

under·pin /ˌʌndəˈpɪn; ˌʌndəˈpɪn/ vt (-nn-) place a support of masonry, etc under (a wall, etc); (fig) support, form the basis for (a case, an argument, etc). 在(墙等)下面加置基础; (喻)支持; 为(某一立场、论据等)立基础.

under·popu·lated /ˌʌndəˈpɒpjʊleɪtɪd; ˈʌndəˈpɑpjəˌletɪd/ adj (of a country or area) having a small population in view of its size or natural resources. (指一国家或地区)人口稀少的.

under·privi·leged /ˌʌndəˈprɪvɪlɪdʒd; ˈʌndəˈprɪvəlɪdʒd/ adj not having had the educational and social advantages enjoyed by more fortunate people, social classes, nations, etc. 没有地位的; 下层社会的; 贫困的.

under·pro·duc·tion /ˌʌndəprəˈdʌkʃn; ˈʌndəprəˈdʌkʃən/ n [U] production of goods in insufficient quantity or below full capacity. 生产不足; 生产能力未全部发挥.

under·quote /ˌʌndəˈkwəʊt; ˌʌndəˈkwot/ vt [VP6A] quote lower prices for goods than (others). 开价较(他人)低; 开价低于.

under·rate /ˌʌndəˈreɪt; ˌʌndəˈret/ vt [VP6A] place too low a value or estimate on: 低估; 估计过低: ~ an opponent, fail to realize his abilities, strength, etc. 低估对手的能力、力量等.

under·score /ˌʌndəˈskɔː(r); ˌʌndəˈskor/ vt [VP6A] = **underline.**

under·sec·retary /ˌʌndəˈsekrətrɪ US: -terɪ ; ˌʌndəˈsɛkrəˌtɛrɪ/ n (pl -ries) assistant secretary, esp (Parliamentary U~) member of the Civil Service and head of a Government Department. 次长; (美)副部长; 副国务卿; (尤指)政务次官.

under·sell /ˌʌndəˈsel; ˌʌndəˈsɛl/ vt (pt, pp -sold /-ˈsəʊld; -ˈsold/) [VP6A] sell (goods) at a lower price than (competitors). 较(竞争者)廉价出售货物.

under·sexed /ˌʌndəˈsekst; ˌʌndəˈsɛkst/ adj having less sexual desire or potency than normal. 性欲或性机能较常人低的; 性欲很弱的.

under·shoot /ˌʌndəˈʃuːt; ˌʌndəˈʃut/ vt (pt, pp -shot /-ˈʃɒt; -ˈʃɑt/) (of an aircraft) (指飞机) ~ the runway, land short of it. 进场太低; 未抵跑道即已着陆. ⇨ **overshoot.**

under·side /ˈʌndəsaɪd; ˈʌndəˌsaɪd/ n side that is underneath. 下侧; 底面.

under·sign /ˌʌndəˈsaɪn; ˌʌndəˈsaɪn/ vt [VP6A] sign (a letter, etc) at the foot of: 签名于(信函等)的下方: *We, the ~d,* We whose signatures appear below. 我们, 文件下方署名者.

under·sized /ˌʌndəˈsaɪzd; ˈʌndəˈsaɪzd/ adj of less than the usual size; stunted or dwarfish. 较一般尺寸小的; 发育不全的; 矮小的.

under·slung /ˌʌndəˈslʌŋ; ˈʌndəˈslʌŋ/ adj (in a vehicle) having springs attached to the axles from below. (指车辆)弹簧与轴的下方相连接的; 车身置于车轴下面之弹簧上的.

under·staffed /ˌʌndəˈstɑːft US: -stæft; ˌʌndəˈstæft/ adj having too small a staff: 职员过少的; 工作人员太少的; 人手不足的: *The school / hospital is badly ~.* 这所学校(医院)人手不足的现象很严重. ⇨ **undermanned.**

under·stand /ˌʌndəˈstænd; ˌʌndəˈstænd/ vt, vi (pt, pp **-stood** /-ˈstʊd; -ˈstʊd/) 1 [VP6A, C, 8, 10, 19C, 2A] know the meaning, nature, explanation, of (sth): 懂; 了解; 领会; 知道(某事物)的意义、性质、解释: *~ French / figures / a problem.* 懂得法语(计算, 某一问题). *He didn't ~ me / what I said.* 他不懂我的话. *You don't ~ me* (= realize) *what a difficult position I'm in.* 你不了解我处境是如何艰苦. *A good teacher must ~ children.* 一位优秀教师必须了解儿童. *I cannot ~ his robbing his friend / why he robbed his friend.* 我不明白他为何抢劫他的朋友. *It is easy to ~ his anger / why he was angry.* 他发怒的原因(他何以发怒)不难了解. **make oneself understood,** make one's meaning clear: 使自己的意思被人明白; 说清楚自己的意思: *Can he make himself understood in Russian?* 他能用俄语把他的意思表达清楚吗? **(Now), ~ me,** phrase often used to preface a warning or threat. (喂), 听清楚; 听着(常用于警告或威胁之前). **~ one another,** (of two persons, parties) be clearly aware of one another's views, feelings, intentions: (指二人, 两方)互相了解; 彼此了解对方的观点、感情、意图等: *The employers and workers have not reached an agreement yet, but at least they ~ one another,* 雇主与工人之间尚未达成协议, 不过至少彼此已臻相互了解. 2 [VP9, 17] learn (from information received); infer; take for granted: 闻悉; 推断; 以为; 相信; 视为当然: *I ~ that you are now married.* 我听说你现在已结婚了. *Am I to ~ that you refuse?* 我可以认为是你拒绝吗? *I understood him to say that he would co-operate.* 我推断他会说他愿意合作. **give sb to ~ (that...),** cause sb to believe or have the idea (that): 告诉某人; 通知; 使某人相信或认为: *We were given to ~ that free accommodation would be supplied.* 我们得到通知, 住宿将免费供应. 3 [VP6A] supply (a word or phrase) mentally: 不言明; 能意会而无需说出(某词或短语): *In the sentence 'He is taller than I', the verb 'am' is to be understood after 'I'.* 在 He is taller than I 这句话中, I 后面省去了动词 am. **~·able** /-əbl; -əbl/ adj that can be understood: 可被了解的; 能领会的: *His reluctance to agree is ~able.* 他之不愿意同意是可以理解的. **~·ably** /-əblɪ; -əblɪ/ adv: *He is ~ably furious.* 他大怒是可以理解的. **~ing** adj (good at) ~ing or realizing other persons' feelings or points of view; having or showing insight: (擅长)了解他人的情绪或观点的; 有理解力的; 颖悟的; 聪明的: *with an ~ing smile.* 带着会心的微笑. *Please be ~ing; do not punish the child.* 请体谅一点; 不要处罚那孩子. □ n 1 [U] power of clear thought. 理解力; 悟性; 了解. 2 [U] capacity for sympathizing, seeing from another's point of view, etc. 同情心; 同感; 体谅. 3 (often **an ~ing,** but rarely pl) agreement; realization of another's views or feelings towards oneself: (常作 an ~ing, 但罕用复数) 协议; 协定; 谅解: *reach / come to an ~ing with sb.* 与某人达成协议(谅解). **on this ~ing,** on this condition. 在此条件之下. **on the ~ing that...,** on condition that...: 以…为条件; 如果….

under·state /ˌʌndəˈsteɪt; ˌʌndəˈstet/ vt [VP6A] fail to state fully or adequately; express in excessively

restrained language: 未充分或完整地陈述; 以比较谨慎或简略的语句表达; 少报; 少说: *They exaggerated the enemy's losses and ~d their own.* 他们夸大敌人的损失, 而把自己的损失轻描淡写地带过. *She ~d her age on the census form.* 她在户口调查表上少报她的年龄. **~·ment** /ˈʌndəsteɪtmənt; ˈʌndəˌstetmənt/ n [U] understating; [C] statement that expresses an idea, etc, too weakly: 不充分的陈述; 保守或简略的陈述; 少报; 少说: *To say that the boy is rather clever is an ~ment,* eg of a boy who is brilliant. 说这男孩颇为聪明是一种保守的说法(如指一个非常聪明的男孩言).

under·stock /ˌʌndəˈstɒk; ˌʌndəˈstak/ vt [VP6A] equip with less stock than is desirable: 未充分供以存货; 未充分供以牲畜: *Is the farm ~ed,* Could it support more animals, etc than it now has? 这农场还能饲养更多的牲畜吗?

under·study /ˈʌndəstʌdɪ; ˈʌndəˌstʌdɪ/ n (pl **-dies**) person learning to, able to, take the place of another (esp an actor). 候补人员; (尤指)候补演员. □ vt (pt, pp **-died**) [VP6A] study (a part in a play) for this purpose; act as ~ to (an actor): 研习(剧中的角色)以为候补演员; 充当(某一演员)的候补演员: *He is ~ing Macbeth / ~ing the leading actor in the play.* 他正在研习麦克佩斯一角以备临时做替角(目前是该剧主角的候补演员).

under·take /ˌʌndəˈteɪk; ˌʌndəˈtek/ vt (pt **-took** /-ˈtʊk; -ˈtʊk/, pp **-taken** /-ˈteɪkən; -ˈtekən/) 1 [VP6A, 7A] **~ (to do) sth,** make oneself responsible for; agree (to do sth): 担任; 承揽; 答应; 约定(做某事): *Gladstone undertook the premiership when he was 72 years old.* 格拉德斯通在他八十二岁时担任首相职务. *He undertook to finish the job by Friday.* 他答应在星期五以前完成那工作. 2 [VP6A] start (a piece of work). 着手; 开始(某项工作). 3 [VP7A, 9] affirm; promise: 确定; 许诺; 担保: *I can't ~ that you will make a profit.* 我不能担保你会赚钱. **under·tak·ing** /ˌʌndəˈteɪkɪŋ; ˌʌndəˈtekɪŋ/ n [C] 1 work that one has ~n to do; task or enterprise. 所承担的工作; 事业; 企业. 2 promise; guarantee. 承诺; 保证.

under·taker /ˈʌndəteɪkə(r); ˈʌndəˌtekə/ n one whose business is to prepare the dead for burial or cremation and manage funerals (US 美 = **mortician.** 承办殡葬者; 殡仪员. **under·tak·ing** /ˈʌndəteɪkɪŋ; ˈʌndəˌtekɪŋ/ n [U] the business of an ~. 殡葬事宜; 丧葬事宜.

under-the-counter /ˌʌndə ðə ˈkaʊntə(r); ˌʌndəðəˈkaʊntə/ adj ⇨ **counter¹.**

under·tone /ˈʌndətəʊn; ˈʌndəˌton/ n [C] 1 low, quiet, tone: 低调; 低音: *talk in ~s,* with subdued voices. 低声谈话. 2 underlying quality: 潜伏的感情或意思: *an ~ of discontent / hostility / sadness.* 潜伏的不满(敌意, 悲哀). 3 thin or subdued colour. 淡色; 底彩.

under·took /ˌʌndəˈtʊk; ˌʌndəˈtʊk/ pt of **undertake.**

under·tow /ˈʌndətəʊ; ˈʌndəˌto/ n (current caused by the) backward flow of a wave breaking on a beach: (波浪冲击岸边后退回去的)回流; 退波: *The swimmer was caught in an ~ and carried out to sea.* 那游泳者陷入回流而被卷出海.

under·value /ˌʌndəˈvæljuː; ˌʌndəˈvælju/ vt [VP6A] value at less than the true worth. 低估…的价值. **under·valu·ation** /ˌʌndəˌvæljuˈeɪʃn; ˌʌndəˌvæljuˈeʃən/ n

under·water /ˈʌndəwɔːtə(r); ˈʌndəˌwɔtə/ adj below the surface of the water: 水面下的; 水中的: *~ swimming,* eg with a snorkel. 潜水游泳(如带有呼吸管).

under·wear /ˈʌndəweə(r); ˈʌndəˌwer/ n [U] underclothing. 内衣.

under·weight /ˈʌndəweɪt; ˈʌndəˌwet/ n [U] weight less than what is usual or legal. 未达标准之重量; 不足之重量. □ adj below the weight that is usual or legal: 重量未达标准的; 重量不足的: *an ~ boy.* 体重未达标准的男孩. *These onions are ~ / are ten ounces ~.* 这些洋葱重量不足(重量差半盎

斯）。⇨ **overweight.**

under·went /ˌʌndə'went; ˌʌndɚ'wɛnt/ pt of **undergo.**

under·whelm /ˌʌndə'welm US: -'hwelm; -'hwɛlm/ vt [VP6A] (colloq, facet) fail to cause enthusiasm, interest, excitement in: (口, 玩笑语)未能引起…之热情、兴趣或兴奋: to ~ an audience; 未能引起观众的热情、兴趣或兴奋; an ~ing argument/speech/performance. 不动人的辩论(演说、表演)。

under·world /'ʌndəwɜːld; 'ʌndɚ,wɝld/ n 1 (in Gk myths, etc) place of the departed spirits of the dead. (希神等)下界; 地狱。 2 part of society that lives by vice and crime. 下流社会; 黑社会。

under·write /ˌʌndə'raɪt; ˌʌndɚ'raɪt/ vt (pt **-wrote** /-'rəʊt; -'rot/, pp **-written** /-'rɪtn; -'rɪtn/) [VP6A] undertake to bear all or part of possible loss of (by signing an agreement about insurance, esp of ships); engage to buy all the newly issued stock in (a company) not bought by the public. (借签名于保险船只等的合约而)负责保险; 承保全部或部分损失; 认购(公司)尚未出售的新股票; 包销。 **'under-writer** n one who ~s policies of (esp marine) insurance: 保险业者;保险商; (尤指)海上保险商; an ~r at Lloya's 英国劳埃德公司的保险业者。

un·de·served /ˌʌndɪ'zɜːvd; ˌʌndɪ'zɝvd/ adj not fair or just: 不公平的; 不当的; 不应得的: an ~ punishment/reward. 不公平的惩罚(报酬)。

un·de·signed /ˌʌndɪ'zaɪnd; ˌʌndɪ'zaɪnd/ adj (esp) not premeditated or done on purpose; not foreseen. (尤指)非故意的; 非预谋的; 偶然的。

un·de·sir·able /ˌʌndɪ'zaɪərəbl; ˌʌndɪ'zaɪrəbl/ adj objectionable; (esp of persons) of a kind not to be welcomed in society. 令人不快的; 不理想的; (尤指人)不受欢迎的; 讨厌的。 □ n ~ person. 讨厌的人。

un·de·terred /ˌʌndɪ'tɜːd; ˌʌndɪ'tɝd/ adj not deterred or discouraged: 未受阻的; 未受挫折的: ~ by the weather/by failure. 未为天气所阻碍的(未因失败而气馁的)。

un·de·vel·oped /ˌʌndɪ'veləpt; ˌʌndɪ'vɛləpt/ adj not developed: 未发展的; 未发达的; 未开发的: ~ land, not yet used (for agriculture, industry, building, etc). 未开发的土地(尚未用于农、工、建筑等方面者)。

un·did /ʌn'dɪd; ʌn'dɪd/ pt of **undo.**

un·dies /'ʌndɪz; 'ʌndɪz/ n pl (colloq) underclothes. (口)内衣。

un·dig·nified /ʌn'dɪgnɪfaɪd; ʌn'dɪgnə,faɪd/ adj not showing proper dignity; clumsy. 不庄重的; 样子不好看的。

un·dis·charged /ˌʌndɪs'tʃɑːdʒd; ˌʌndɪs'tʃɑrdʒd/ adj (of a cargo) not unloaded; (of a debt) not paid; (esp, of a bankrupt person or firm) not relieved of a further liability to pay money still owing to creditors. (指船货)未卸下的; 未起货的; (指债务)未偿付的; 未还清的; (尤指已破产的个人或公司)所欠债务将来仍须偿付的; 未解除偿债义务的。 ⇨ **discharge²(5).**

undo /ʌn'duː; ʌn'du/ vt (pt undid /ʌn'dɪd; ʌn'dɪd/, pp undone /ʌn'dʌn; ʌn'dʌn/) [VP6A] 1 untie, unfasten, loosen (knots, buttons, etc): 解开; 松开(结、钮扣等): My shoe-lace has come undone. 我的鞋带松开了。 2 destroy the result of; bring back the state of affairs that existed before: 破坏…的结果; 恢复…的原状: He has undone the good work of his predecessor. 他已毁弃了他前任者的良好成就。 What is done cannot be undone. 覆水难收。 ~ing n (cause of) ruin: 毁灭; 毁灭的原因: Drink was his ~ing. 酗酒是他失败的原因。 He went to the money-lenders, to his complete ~ing. 他向高利贷者借贷, 以致完全毁了。 **un·done** pred adj 1 not done; not finished: 未做的; 未做完的: leave one's work undone. 留下工作未做完。 We have left undone those things which we ought to have done. 我们没做完那些该完成的工作。 2 (archaic) (of a person) ruined. (古)(指人)破产的。

un·dock /ʌn'dɒk; ʌn'dɑk/ vt, vi [VP6A, 2A] uncouple (a module, etc) from a spacecraft: 使(太空舱等)与太空船分离: The astronauts had some difficulty in

~ing the lunar module. 太空人在使登月小艇与太空船分离时, 遭遇到一些麻烦。

un·dom·es·ti·cated /ˌʌndə'mestɪkeɪtɪd; ˌʌndə'mɛstɪˌketɪd/ adj not trained or interested in household, affairs. 对家务无训练或无兴趣的; 不谙家事的。

un·doubted /ʌn'daʊtɪd; ʌn'daʊtɪd/ adj certain; accepted as true: 确定的; 无疑的: There is an ~ improvement in the patient's condition. 病人的情况有明显的进步。~·ly adv

un·dreamed /ʌn'driːmd; ʌn'drimd/, **un·dreamt** /ʌn'dremt; ʌn'drɛmpt/ adjj (usu) (通常作) ~-of, not thought of; not imagined: 梦想不到的; 想像不到的: earn ~-of wealth; 赚到梦想不到的财富; ~-of beauties. 意想不到的美女。

un·dress /ʌn'dres; ʌn'drɛs/ vt, vi 1 [VP6A] remove the clothes of: 除去或脱去…的衣服: Jane ~ed her doll. 简脱去她那洋娃娃的衣服。 2 [VP2A] take off one's clothes: 脱去自己的衣服; 宽衣; 卸装: ~ and get into bed. 宽衣就寝。 □ n [U] 1 uniform for ordinary (non-ceremonial) occasions. 便服; 军便服。 2 state of being partly or not dressed. 半裸; 全裸。

un·due /ˌʌn'djuː US: -'duː; ʌn'dju/ adj improper; more than is right: 不适当的; 过度的; 过分的: with ~ haste; 过分匆忙地; exercise an ~ influence upon sb. 对某人施展不当的影响力。 **un·duly** /ˌʌn'djuːli US: -'duːli; ʌn'djulɪ/ adv in an ~ manner: 不适当地; 过度地; 过分地: unduly pessimistic. 过度悲观的。

un·du·late /'ʌndjulert US: -dʒə-; 'ʌndʒə,let/ vi [VP2A, C] (of surfaces) have a wave-like motion or look: (指表面)波动; 起伏; 呈波浪形: a field of wheat undulating in the breeze; 在微风中起伏的麦田; undulating land, that rises and falls in gentle slopes. 波状地; 起伏地。 **un·du·la·tion** /ˌʌndju'leɪʃn US: -dʒə-; ˌʌndʒə'leʃən/ n [U] wave-like motion or form; [C] one of a number of wave-like curves or slopes. 波动; 波形; 起伏; 波状的弯曲或斜坡。

un·dy·ing /ʌn'daɪɪŋ; ʌn'daɪɪŋ/ adj everlasting; never-ending: 不朽的; 永恒的: ~ love/hatred/fame. 不朽的爱(永久的恨); 不朽的名誉。

un·earned /ʌn'ɜːnd; ʌn'ɝnd/ adj 1 not gained by work or service: 不劳而获的: ~ income, eg from investments, or land or property that is inherited; 不劳而获的收入; 不劳所得; ~ increment, increase in the value of property, eg houses, land, not due to the owner's expenditure or efforts, eg because of a rise in the value of land. 自然增值(房、地等财产非因所有者的投资或努力, 而其价值有所增加之谓)。 2 not deserved: 不应得的: ~ praise. 不应得的赞美。

un·earth /ʌn'ɜːθ; ʌn'ɝθ/ vt [VP6A] discover and bring to light: 发掘; 发现: ~ new facts about the life of Shakespeare; 发现有关莎士比亚生平的新事实; ~ a buried treasure. 发掘埋在地下的宝藏。 The dog has ~ed some bones. 那狗掘出了几根骨头。

un·earth·ly /ʌn'ɜːθlɪ; ʌn'ɝθlɪ/ adj 1 supernatural 超自然的; 非尘世的。 2 mysterious; ghostly; frightening: 神秘的; 鬼怪的; 可怕的: ~ screams. 可怕的尖叫。 3 (colloq) unreasonable: 不合理的: Why do you wake me up at this ~ hour? 你为什么在这个时候叫醒我?

un·easy /ʌn'iːzɪ; ʌn'izɪ/ adj not easy in body or mind; troubled or anxious: 身体或心境不舒适的; 不安的; 焦虑的: have an ~ conscience; 良心不安; be ~ in one's mind about the future; 悬虑未来; pass an ~ night, sleep badly. 过不安稳的一夜。 We grew ~ at their absence. 他们离开甚久, 我们渐感不安。 **un·eas·ily** /ʌn'iːzɪlɪ; ʌn'izɪlɪ/ adv **un·easi·ness, un·ease** /ʌn'iːz; ʌn'iz/ nn

un·eaten /ʌn'iːtn; ʌn'itn/ adj (of a meal) left out but left unused. (指食物, 餐食)摆出而未吃的。

un·edu·cated /ʌn'edʒukeɪtɪd; ʌn'edʒə,ketɪd/ adj not educated; suggesting lack of education (or the kind of education or social background considered desirable): 未受教育的; 缺乏适当教育的; 缺乏教养的: He has an ~ mind/voice. 他的思想(说话的方式)缺乏教养。

un·em·ploy·able /ˌʌnɪmˈplɔɪəbl; ˌʌnɪmˈplɔɪəbl/ *adj* that cannot be employed. 不能被雇用的；不能使用的。

un·em·ployed /ˌʌnɪmˈplɔɪd; ˌʌnɪmˈplɔɪd/ *adj* not being used: 未在使用中的；未用的：~ *capital*; 游资; not working, not able to get work: 无工作的；失业的: ~ *men*. 无工作的人们。**the ~**, those for whom there is no work or who are temporarily without work. 失业者。

un·em·ploy·ment /ˌʌnɪmˈplɔɪmənt; ˌʌnɪmˈplɔɪmənt/ *n* [U] **1** state of being unemployed: 失业；无工作: *U~ is a serious social evil*. 失业是社会的一大弊害。**2** amount of unused labour: 失业人数: *There is more ~ now than there was six months ago*. 现在失业的人比六个月以前多。**3** (attrib) (用作定语): ~ *insurance*; 失业保险; ~ *pay/benefit*, money paid from insurance funds to a worker who cannot get employment. 失业津贴(救济金)。

un·end·ing /ʌnˈendɪŋ; ʌnˈɛndɪŋ/ *adj* everlasting; unceasing; (colloq) frequently repeated: 永远的；不断的; (口)经常被重复的: *She's tired of your ~ grumbles*. 她厌倦了你那无休止的抱怨。~·**ly** *adv*

un·en·dur·able /ˌʌnɪnˈdjʊərəbl; ˌʌnɪnˈdjʊrəbl/ *adj* not able to be endured: 不能忍受的；无法忍耐的: ~ *pain/injustice*. 不能忍受的痛苦(冤枉)。

un·en·light·ened /ˌʌnɪnˈlaɪtnd; ˌʌnɪnˈlaɪtnd/ *adj* uneducated; not well-informed; (in some contexts) prejudiced or superstitious. 未受或缺乏教育的；见闻不广的; (在某些上下文中可解释为)偏心的，迷信的，闭塞的。

un·equal /ʌnˈiːkwəl; ʌnˈikwəl/ *adj* ~ (**to** *sth*), **1** not equal. 不相等的。**2** (esp of work such as writing) not of the same quality throughout; variable. (尤指写作)品质不均匀的；前后不一致的；不一律的。**3** not strong, clever, etc enough: 不胜任的；不够强壮、聪明等的: *I feel ~ to the task*. 我对这项工作感到无法胜任。~**ly** /-kwəlɪ; -kwəlɪ/ *adv*

un·equalled /ʌnˈiːkwəld; ʌnˈikwəld/ *adj* unmatched; unrivalled. 无与伦比的；无敌手的；无双的；极好的。

un·equivo·cal /ˌʌnɪˈkwɪvəkl; ˌʌnɪˈkwɪvəkl/ *adj* clear; having one only possible meaning. 清楚的；不含混的；只有一种可能的含义的。

un·err·ing /ʌnˈɜːrɪŋ; ʌnˈɝɪŋ/ *adj* accurate: 正确的；无错误的；准确的: *an ~ aim*; 瞄得很准确地射击; *strike an ~ blow*. 不偏不倚地一击。~·**ly** *adv*

un·ex·ampled /ˌʌnɪɡˈzɑːmpld US: -ˈzæm-; ˌʌnɪɡˈzæmpld/ *adj* of which there is no other exampke that can be compared with it: 无可比拟的；无前例的: *the ~ heroism of our soldiers*. 我们士兵无可比拟的英勇。

un·ex·cep·tion·able /ˌʌnɪkˈsepʃənəbl; ˌʌnɪkˈsɛpʃənəbl/ *adj* beyond criticism; altogether admirable. 无可非难的；极好的；完美的。

un·ex·pected /ˌʌnɪkˈspektɪd; ˌʌnɪkˈspɛktɪd/ *adj* not expected: 意外的；未料到的: ~ *guests/questions/results*. 不速之客(未料到的问题；未料到的结果)。

un·fail·ing /ʌnˈfeɪlɪŋ; ʌnˈfelɪŋ/ *adj* never coming to an end; meeting one's expectations at all times: 无止境的；始终符合期望的；可靠的: *his ~ good humour/patience*; 他那始终如一的好脾气(耐性); ~ *friend*. 忠实可靠的朋友。~·**ly** *adv* at all times: 始终；永远；永久: *~ly courteous*. 始终有礼貌的。

un·fair /ˌʌnˈfeə(r); ˌʌnˈfɛr/ *adj* not right or fair, unjust: 不正当的；不公平的；不公正的: ~ *treatment/competition*. 不公平的待遇(竞争)。~·**ly** *adv* ~·**ness** *n*

un·faith·ful /ˌʌnˈfeɪθfl; ʌnˈfeθfl/ *adj* not true to one's duty, a promise, etc; (esp) not faithful to marriage vows: 不忠实的；不诚实的; (尤指)不贞洁的；有外遇的: *Her husband is ~ to her*. 她的丈夫对她不忠实。~·**ly** /-fəlɪ; -fəlɪ/ *adv* ~·**ness** *n*

un·fal·ter·ing /ʌnˈfɔːltərɪŋ; ʌnˈfɔltərɪŋ/ *adj* not wavering or hesitating: 不踌躇的；坚决的；坚定的: *with ~ steps/courage*. 脚步坚定地(以坚定不移的勇气)。~·**ly** *adv*

un·fam·il·iar /ˌʌnfəˈmɪliə(r); ˌʌnfəˈmɪljə/ *adj* **1** **(to)**, not well known: 不深知的；生疏的: *That face is not ~ to me*, I feel that I know it, have seen it before. 那面孔我并不生疏(似曾相识)。**2** ~ **with**, not acquainted with: 不熟悉的；不熟识的: *He is still ~ with this district*. 这一地区他仍旧不熟悉。

un·fath·om·able /ʌnˈfæðəməbl; ʌnˈfæðəməbl/ *adj* so deep that the bottom cannot be reached; (fig) too strange or difficult to be understood. 深不可测的; (喻)难以了解的；深奥的。**un·fath·omed** /ʌnˈfæðəmd; ʌnˈfæðəmd/ *adj* (of a person's character) not understood; (of a crime, etc) not solved; (of ocean depths, etc) not measured. (指人的个性)不了解的; (指一项犯罪等)未定案的; 未侦破的; (指海深等)未测定的。

un·feel·ing /ʌnˈfiːlɪŋ; ʌnˈfilɪŋ/ *adj* **1** hard-hearted; unsympathetic. 我酷的；无情的。**2** not able to feel. 无感觉的。~·**ly** *adv*

un·feigned /ʌnˈfeɪnd; ʌnˈfɛnd/ *adj* not pretended; genuine (which is more usu with genuine); sincere: 不虚伪的；真实的；诚心的: *He showed ~ satisfaction at his son's success*. 他对他儿子的成功表现出真正的满足。~·**ly** *adv* openly and sincerely. 开诚地；诚心地。

un·fit /ˌʌnˈfɪt; ʌnˈfɪt/ *adj* ~ **(for** *sth***/to do** *sth***)**, not fit or suitable: 不适当的；不胜任的；不合适的: *He is ~ for business*/~ *to be a doctor*. 他不适合经商(当医生)。*This road is ~ for heavy traffic*. 这条路不能负荷频繁的交通。*He was rejected* (eg for military service) *as medically ~*. 他因健康不合格而遭淘汰(如服兵役)。□ *vt* (-**tt**-) [VP14] ~ *sb for sth*, make ~ (which is more usu): 使不适合；使不相宜；使不能胜任(较常用 make ~): *A bad attack of lumbago ~ted him for work in the garden*. 因腰部风湿痛发作得很厉害，他无法做园子里的工作。

un·flag·ging /ʌnˈflæɡɪŋ; ʌnˈflæɡɪŋ/ *adj* not showing signs of weariness; uninterrupted: 毫无倦容的；不减弱的；不松懈的；未间断的: *work with ~ energy*. 精力充沛地。

un·flap·pable /ʌnˈflæpəbl; ʌnˈflæpəbl/ *adj* (colloq) unlikely to get into a flap; never upset in a crisis. 不易惊慌失措的；临危不乱的；从容不迫的。⇨ **flap**[1](4).

un·fledged /ʌnˈfledʒd; ʌnˈflɛdʒd/ *adj* (of a bird) not yet able to fly; (fig, of a person) immature; inexperienced. (指鸟)还不会飞的; 羽毛未丰的; (喻, 指人)未成熟的；无经验的。

un·flinch·ing /ʌnˈflɪntʃɪŋ; ʌnˈflɪntʃɪŋ/ *adj* fearless; resolute. 无畏惧的；坚定的。

un·fold /ʌnˈfəʊld; ʌnˈfold/ *vt, vi* [VP6A, 2A, C] **1** (of sth folded) open out: (指折叠的东西)展开; 展开: ~ *a newspaper/a prospectus*. 展开报纸(计划书)。**2** reveal, make known; become known or visible: 显露; 表露; 显现; 呈现: *as the story ~s* (*itself*). 随故事所显现。*She ~ed to him her plans for the future*. 她向他表露她未来的计划。*The landscape ~ed before us*. 景色显现在我们面前。

un·for·get·table /ˌʌnfəˈɡetəbl; ˌʌnfɚˈɡɛtəbl/ *adj* that cannot be forgotten: 不能忘记的；永远记得的: *an ~ experience*. 永远忘不了的一次经验。

un·for·tu·nate /ʌnˈfɔːtʃunət; ʌnˈfɔrtʃənɪt/ *adj* unlucky: 不幸运的；倒霉的: *an ~ expedition*; 一次运气不佳的探险; regrettable: 令人遗憾的；可惜的: *an ~ remark/lack of good manners*. 失言(失礼)。~·**ly** *adv*: *You're wrong, ~ly*. 抱歉，你错了。*U~ly for you, you're wrong*. 为你遗憾的是，你错了。

un·founded /ʌnˈfaʊndɪd; ʌnˈfaʊndɪd/ *adj* without foundation: 无根据的；无稽的: ~ *rumours*. 无稽的谣言。

un·fre·quented /ˌʌnfrɪˈkwentɪd; ˌʌnfrɪˈkwɛntɪd/ *adj* seldom visited. 冷落的；罕有人访问的；人迹罕到的。

un·friend·ly /ˌʌnˈfrendlɪ; ʌnˈfrɛndlɪ/ *adj* not friendly; unfavourable. 不友善的；有敌意的；不相宜的；不利的。

un·frock /ˌʌnˈfrɒk; ʌnˈfrɑk/ *vt* [VP6A] (of a priest guilty of bad conduct) dismiss from the priesthood. (指

行为不检的僧侣)解除僧职。

un·fruit·ful /ʌn'fruːtfl; ʌn'frutfəl/ adj not bearing fruit; without results or success. 不结果实的; 无结果的; 不成功的; 徒然的。

un·furl /ʌn'fɜːl; ʌn'fəl/ vt, vi [VP6A, 2A] roll out; spread out: 展开; 张开; 铺开。~ the sails. 扬帆。

un·fur·nished /ʌn'fɜːnɪʃt; ʌn'fɝnɪʃt/ adj (esp) without furniture: (尤指)无家具的; 无陈设的: rooms / a house to let ~. 无家具的房间(房屋)招租。

un·gain·ly /ʌn'ɡeɪnlɪ; ʌn'ɡenlɪ/ adj clumsy; awkward; ungraceful. 笨拙的; 难看的; 不雅的。

un·gen·er·ous /ʌn'dʒenərəs; ʌn'dʒɛnərəs/ adj not generous; unkind. 不慷慨的; 气量小的; 胸襟狭窄的。

un-get-at-able /ˌʌnɡet'ætəbl; ˌʌnɡet'ætəbl/ adj un-come-at-able.

un·god·ly /ʌn'ɡɒdlɪ; ʌn'ɡɑdlɪ/ adj 1 not religious; not giving reverence to God; sinful. 不敬神的; 不虔诚的; 罪孽的。2 (colloq) annoying; shocking. 令人讨厌的; 惊人的; 可怕的。3 (colloq) unreasonable. (口)不合理的: Why did you phone me at this ~ hour? 你为什么在这个时候打电话给我呢?

un·gov·ern·able /ʌn'ɡʌvənəbl; ʌn'ɡʌvənəbl/ adj that cannot be controlled: 不能控制的; 难驾驭的: ~ passions; 难控制的热情; a man with an ~ temper. 不能控制脾气的人。

un·grate·ful /ʌn'ɡreɪtfl; ʌn'ɡretfəl/ adj 1 not showing gratitude. 不感恩的; 不领情的; 忘恩负义的。2 (of a task) not pleasant or agreeable. (指工作)讨厌的; 令人不快的。

un·guarded /ˌʌn'ɡɑːdɪd; ʌn'ɡɑrdɪd/ adj (esp of a person and what he says) careless; indiscreet: (尤指人及其所说的话)不小心的; 不谨慎的: In an ~ moment, he gave away most important secrets. 一不留神, 他泄露了非常重要的秘密。

un·guent /'ʌnɡwənt; 'ʌnɡwənt/ n [C, U] any soft substance used as an ointment (eg for soothing skin injuries) or for lubrication. 药膏; 软膏; 润滑油。

un·hal·lowed /ʌn'hæləʊd; ʌn'hæləd/ adj 1 not made holy: 未奉为神圣的; 亵渎神明的: ~ ground, not consecrated by the Church. 葬在未经教会奉献的土地上。2 wicked; impious: 邪恶的; 不恭敬的: with ~ joy. 带着邪恶的喜悦。

un·hand /ʌn'hænd; ʌn'hænd/ vt [VP6A] (archaic) let go; take the hands off. (古)放开; 松手。

un·happy /ʌn'hæpɪ; ʌn'hæpɪ/ adj (-ier, -iest) 1 not happy. 不高兴的; 不愉快的。2 not suitable or tactful: 不适合的; 不适当的: an ~ comment. 不适当的评论。

un·healthy /ʌn'helθɪ; ʌn'helθɪ/ adj harmful to bodily or mental health; (colloq) dangerous. 对身心有害的; 不卫生的;不利于健康的; (口)危险的。

un·heard /ʌn'hɜːd; ʌn'hɝd/ adj not heard; not allowed a hearing. 未听见的; 听不到的; 未予审理的; 不允审判的。go ~, (a) not be heard. 未审理; 未加审判。(b) have no-one willing to listen to it: 无人愿意听: Her request for help went ~. 她求助的呼吁无人理会。**un·heard-of** /ʌn'hɜːd ɒv; ʌn'hɝd‚ʌv/ adj extraordinary; without an earlier example. 不寻常的; 空前的; 前所未闻的。

un·hinge /ʌn'hɪndʒ; ʌn'hɪndʒ/ vt [VP6A] take (a door, gate, etc) from the hinge(s); cause (sb's mind, brain) to lose off its balance: 从枢纽拿下(门, 门扉等); (某人的精神, 头脑)失常: His mind is ~d, He is mentally ill. 他的精神失常。

un·holy /ʌn'həʊlɪ; ʌn'holɪ/ adj 1 wicked; sinful. 邪恶的; 有罪的。2 (colloq) unreasonable. (口)不合理的。

un·hook /ʌn'hʊk; ʌn'huk/ vt [VP6A] undo the hooks of (a dress, etc); release from a hook. 松开或解开(衣服等)上的钩扣; 从钩上取下或放下。

un·hoped-for /ʌn'həʊpt fɔː(r); ʌn'hopt‚fɔr/ adj unexpected: 未料到的; 意外的: an ~ piece of good fortune. 意外的好运。

un·horse /ʌn'hɔːs; ʌn'hɔrs/ vt [VP6A] throw from

a horse's back; cause to fall from a horse. 自马背上抛下; 使从马背上摔下。

uni·corn /'juːnɪkɔːn; 'junɪˌkɔrn/ n (in old stories) horse-like animal with one long horn; (heraldry) representation of this with a lion's tail. (古老故事中似马的)独角兽; (纹章)(带有狮尾的)独角兽标记。

un·iden·ti·fied /ˌʌnaɪ'dentɪfaɪd; ˌʌnaɪˌdentɪˌfaɪd/ adj which cannot be identified: 不能指证的; 无从辨识的; 来路不明的: The dead man is still ~. 死者身份仍未查明。~ flying object, (abbr 略作 UFO /ˌjuː ef 'əʊ; ‚ju ef 'o/ or /'juːfəʊ; 'jufo/) ⇨ flying saucer at flying.

uni·form /'juːnɪfɔːm; 'junəˌfɔrm/ adj the same; not varying in form, quality, etc: 相同的; 一律的; 形式、性质等无变化的: sticks of ~ length; 长度一致的棍子; to be kept at a ~ temperature. 保持于恒温。□ n [C, U] (style of) dress worn by all members of an organization, eg the police, the armed forces: 制服; 军服; 制服或军服的款式: the blue ~(s) of the police; 警察的蓝色制服; the khaki ~(s) of the army. 卡其布军服。in ~, wearing such dress: 穿制服或军服: He looks handsome in ~. 他穿制服显得很英俊。~ed adj wearing ~: 穿着制服或军服的: the ~ed branch of the police, contrasted with those who wear plain clothes, eg detectives. 警察编制之着制服组(以别于着便衣组, 如便衣警探)。~·ly adv ~·ity /ˌjuːnɪ'fɔːmətɪ; ‚junə'fɔrmətɪ/ n [U] condition; condition of being the same throughout. 同一; 一律; 一致。

unify /'juːnɪfaɪ; 'junəˌfaɪ/ vt (pt, pp -fied) [VP6A] 1 form into one; unite. 使合一; 统一; 结合。2 make uniform. 使一致。**uni·fi·ca·tion** /ˌjuːnɪfɪ'keɪʃn; ‚junəfə'keʃən/ n ~ing or being unified: 统一; 一致; 单一化: work for the unification of Europe. 致力于欧洲的统一。

uni·lat·eral /ˌjuːnɪ'lætərəl; ‚junɪ'lætərəl/ adj of, on, affecting, done by, one side or party only: 单方面的; 片面的; 单方面做的; 只影响一方的: a ~ declaration of independence, (abbr 略作 UDI) 单方宣告独立; ~ repudiation of a treaty, by one of the parties that signed it, without the consent of the other party or parties .单方面废除条约。~·ly /-rəlɪ; -rəlɪ/ adv

un·im·peach·able /ˌʌnɪm'piːtʃəbl; ‚ʌnɪm'pitʃəbl/ adj that cannot be questioned or doubted: 不可指责的; 无可怀疑的; 可靠的: ~ honesty; 无可怀疑的诚实; news from an ~ source. 来源可靠的消息。

un·in·formed /ˌʌnɪn'fɔːmd; ‚ʌnɪn'fɔrmd/ adj (esp) not having, made without, adequate information: (尤指)无充分认识或情报的; 无充分知识(而做成)的: ~ criticism. 无知的批评。

un·in·hib·ited /ˌʌnɪn'hɪbɪtɪd; ‚ʌnɪn'hɪbətɪd/ adj without inhibitions; free from the social and moral restraints usual among conventional people. 无限制的; 不拘束的; 不拘形式的。

un·in·spired /ˌʌnɪn'spaɪəd; ‚ʌnɪn'spaɪrd/ adj without inspiration; dull: 无灵感的; 乏味的; 无趣味的: an ~ lecture/lecturer. 枯燥的演讲(者)。

un·in·ter·ested /ʌn'ɪntrəstɪd; ʌn'ɪntərɪstɪd/ adj ~ (in), having, showing no interest. 无兴趣的; 不感兴趣的; 不开心的。

union /'juːnɪən; 'junjən/ n 1 [U] uniting or being united; joining or being joined; [C] instance of this: 联合; 合并; 其实例: the ~ of the three towns into one; 三市镇合而为一; the Universal Postal U~, of countries for the purpose of interchanging mail services to mutual advantage: 万国邮政协会; the U~ of Soviet Socialist Republics (abbr 略作 USSR). 苏维埃社会主义共和国联邦; 苏联。the U~, (a) of England and Scotland (in 1707). (1707 年)英格兰和苏格兰的合并。(b) the United States of America: 美利坚合众国; 美国: the President's address to the ~, to all US citizens. (美国)总统对全民的演讲。the U~ Jack, the British flag. 英国国旗。⇨ the illus at flag. 参看 flag 之插图。2 [U] state of being in agreement or harmony: 一致; 和

谐: *live in perfect ~;* 十分和睦地生活; [C] instance of this: 一致或和谐的实例: *a happy ~,* eg *a happy marriage.* 美满的结合(如愉快的婚姻). **3** [C] association formed by the uniting of persons, groups, etc, 同盟; 协会, esp 尤指 **trade-~,** ⇨ **trade**¹(1). **4** (old use; GB) workhouse built by two or more parishes for administration of the poor laws. (旧用法; 英)救贫院; 贫民所. **5 the U~,** general society at some universities, etc. (某些大学等的)学生会. **6** [C] coupling for connecting rods or pipes. (机械)管接; 管套节. **7 ~ suit.** (US) combinations(4). (美)连裤内衣. **~·ist** /-ɪst; -ɪst/ *n* [C] **1** member of a trade ~; supporter of trade ~s. 工会的会员; 支持工会者. **2 U~·ist, (a)** (GB politics) person who, before the Irish Free State was established, opposed the granting of independence to Ireland. (英国政治)(爱尔兰自由邦成立前)反对爱尔兰独立者. **(b)** supporter of the Federal Government of the US during the Civil War; opponent of secession. (美国内战期间)联邦主义者; 反对分裂者; 支持联邦政府者.

unique /juːˈniːk; juˈnik/ *adj* having no like or equal; being the only one of its sort. 唯一的; 独特的; 无与伦比的. **~·ly** *adv* **~·ness** *n*

uni·sex /ˈjuːnɪseks; ˈjunɪseks/ *adj* (of clothes, etc) of a style designed for both sexes. (指衣服等)不分性别的; 男女皆可穿的.

uni·son /ˈjuːnɪsn; ˈjunəsn/ *n* [U] *(in)* ~, (in) concord or agreement: 和谐; 一致: *sing in ~,* all singing the same notes, not harmonizing; 齐唱; 同声合唱; *act in ~ (with others).* (与他人)一致行动.

unit /ˈjuːnɪt; ˈjunɪt/ *n* [C] **1** single person, thing or group regarded as complete in itself: 一人、一物、一个; 整体; 组织单位; 部队单位: (mil) (军) *an armoured ~;* 装甲兵单位; 装甲部队; *~s of the US Sixth Fleet.* 美国第六舰队各单位. *The family is often taken as the ~ of society.* 家庭常被视为社会的基本单位. **2** quantity or amount used as a standard of measurement: 用作计算标准的数或量; 单位: *The metre is a ~ of length.* 米是长度单位. *The monetary ~ of Great Britain is the pound.* 英国的货币单位是英镑. **3** smallest whole number; the number 1. 最小的整数; 一. **4** (compounds) (复合词) **'kitchen ~,** article of kitchen equipment, eg a sink, draining board, with cupboards, that can be fitted with others of similar design and appearance along a wall. 厨房的成套用具. **~ 'furniture,** article of furniture of similar design, materials, etc, to be used together. 成套家具. **'~ trust,** trust(3) that invests in a large number and wide variety of stocks and issues certificates (called 称作~s) on which dividends are payable. 投资信托(受托机构将资金投资于多种股市并发行凭证, 信托者凭证分红).

Uni·tar·ian /ˌjuːnɪˈteərɪən; ˌjunəˈterɪən/ *n* member of a Christian church that rejects the doctrine of the Trinity and believes that God is one person. 唯一神教派(基督教的一支派, 反对三位一体说, 认为上帝系单一体)的教徒. □ *adj* of the ~s. 唯一神教派的. *the U~ Church.* 唯一神教派教会. **~·ism** /-ɪzəm; -ɪzəm/ *n*

unite /juːˈnaɪt; juˈnaɪt/ *vt, vi* **1** [VP6A, 2A] make or become one; join: (使)联合; 结合; 团结; 团结: *~ one country to another;* 使一国与另一国结合; *the common interests that ~ our two countries,* that bring them together. 使我们两国团结一致的共同利益. *England and Scotland ~d in 1707.* 英格兰与苏格兰于一七○七年合并. **2** [VP2A, 3A, 4A] *~ (in sth/to do sth),* act or work together: 协力; 一致行动: *Let us ~ in fighting/~ to fight poverty and disease.* 让我们协力以共同克服贫穷和疾病. **~d** *adj* **1** joined in spirit, by love and sympathy: 一致的和同情的精神上结合的; 和睦的: *a ~ family.* 和睦的家庭. **2** resulting from association for a common purpose: 为共同目标相结合而产生的; 一致的: *make a ~d effort.* 作出一致的努力; *present a ~d front to the enemy;* 对敌人成立联合阵线以对抗敌人; *the U~d Nations* 联合国. **3** joined politically: 在政治上联合的: *the U~d Kingdom;* 联合王

国; *the U~d States of Mexico.* 墨西哥合众国. **~d·ly** *adv*

unity /ˈjuːnətɪ; ˈjunətɪ/ *n* (*pl* **-ties**) **1** [C, U] the state of being united; (an) arrangement of parts to form a complete whole: 联合; 结合; 单一; 独一; 统一; 协调: *The figure on the left spoils the ~ of the painting.* 左边那个人像破坏了那幅画的整体性. **the dramatic unities; the unities of place, time and action,** (drama) the use of the same scene throughout, the limitation of the duration of the play to one day, or the time taken to act it, and the use of one single plot, with nothing irrelevant to that plot. (戏剧)三一律; 地点、时间和情节的一致. **2** [U] harmony, agreement (of aims, feelings, etc): (目标, 感情等的)和谐; 一致: *in ~ with others;* 与他人一致地; *live together in ~;* 和睦地住在一起; *political ~.* 政治上的统一. *National ~ is essential in time of war.* 举国团结在战时是必要的.

uni·ver·sal /ˌjuːnɪˈvɜːsl; ˌjunəˈvɝsl/ *adj* of, belonging to, done by all; affecting all: 普遍的; 一般的; 全体的; 属于全体的; 全体做的; 影响全体的: *War causes ~ misery.* 战争引起普遍的苦难. *Television provides ~ entertainment.* 电视提供了大众化的娱乐. **a ~ joint,** one that permits the turning of connected parts in all directions. 万向接头. **a ~ rule,** one with no exceptions. 普遍(适用)的法则. **~ suffrage,** suffrage extending to all members of a community. 普选权; 全民参政权. **~ time,** ⇨ **Greenwich. ~·ly** /-səlɪ; -slɪ/ *adv.* **~·ity** /ˌjuːnɪvɜːˈsælətɪ; ˌjunəvɝˈsælətɪ/ *n* [U].

uni·verse /ˈjuːnɪvɜːs; ˈjunəˌvɝs/ *n* **1 the U~,** everything that exists everywhere; all the galaxies, stars, planets, their satellites, etc; the whole creation and the Creator. 天地万物; 万有; 宇宙; 造物主与其所造之物; 世界. **2** [C] system of galaxies: 恒星系; 星辰系: *a new telescope that may reveal new ~s.* 一座可能显现新恒星系的新型望远镜.

uni·ver·sity /ˌjuːnɪˈvɜːsɪtɪ; ˌjunəˈvɝsətɪ/ *n* (*pl* **-ties**) (colleges, buildings, etc of an) institution for the promotion and dissemination of advanced learning, conferring degrees and engaging in academic research; members of such an institution collectively: 大学(通指用法)大学的全体组成分子; (attrib) (用作定语) *a ~ student/lecturer;* 大学生(大学讲师); *the ~ chess team.* 大学国际象棋队.

un·kempt /ˌʌnˈkempt; ˌʌnˈkɛmpt/ *adj* untidy; (esp of the hair) uncombed. 不整洁的; (尤指头发)未梳理的; 蓬乱的.

un·kind /ˌʌnˈkaɪnd; ˌʌnˈkaɪnd/ *adj* lacking in, not showing, kindness: 不和善的; 不客气的; 不礼貌的; 不厚道的: *an ~ remark.* 不客气的话. **~·ly** *adv* in an unkind manner: 不客气地; 不礼貌地: *Don't take it ~ly if...,* *Don't think I intend to be ~ if....* 不要认为我无情, 如果….

un·know·ing /ˌʌnˈnəʊɪŋ; ˌʌnˈnoɪŋ/ *adj* not knowing; unaware. 不知道的; 无知的; 没有发觉的. **~·ly** *adv* in ignorance; unawares. 不知道地; 未发觉地.

un·known /ˌʌnˈnəʊn; ˌʌnˈnon/ *adj* not known or identified: 不为人知道的; 未认明的; 不详的; 无名的: *the tomb of the ~ warrior,* of an ~ soldier (in Westminster Abbey) buried there in memory of those killed in World Wars I and II; 无名战士墓(在威斯敏斯特教堂, 以纪念两次大战中之阵亡将士); *an ~ quantity,* of which the value, etc is not known. 未知量.

un·learn /ˌʌnˈlɜːn; ˌʌnˈlɝn/ *vt* [VP6A] get rid of (ideas, habits, etc); learn to give up (sth one has previously learnt). 扫除(观念、习惯等); 忘却(从前所学的).

un·leash /ˌʌnˈliːʃ; ˌʌnˈliʃ/ *vt* [VP6A] let go from a leash 解开皮带以释放: ~ *a dog;* 放开一条狗; (fig) release set into action: (喻)发泄; 发动; 实行: ~ *one's fury;* 勃然大怒; ~ *a new atomic weapon.* 施行一新原子武器.

un·leav·ened /ˌʌnˈlevnd; ˌʌnˈlɛvənd/ *adj* (of bread) made without yeast. (指面包)未用酵粉做成的; 不经发酵的.

un·less /ən'les; ən'lɛs/ *conj* if not; except when: 若不、除非；如果…不；除非在…的时候：*You will fail ~ you work harder.* 你若不更加努力，你就会失败。*U~ bad weather stops me, I go for a walk every day.* 除非受阻于坏天气，我每天都出去散步。

un·let·tered /ʌn'letəd; ʌn'lɛtəd/ *adj.* uneducated; unable to read. 未受教育的；目不识丁的；文盲的。

un·like /ˌʌn'laɪk; ʌn'laɪk/ *pred adj prep* not like; different from: 不同；不象；与…有别；*His new novel is ~ all his previous ones.* 他的新小说与他以前的小说不同。*My son is ~ me in every respect.* 我的儿子没有一处象我。

un·like·ly /ʌn'laɪklɪ; ʌn'laɪklɪ/ *adj* not likely to happen or be true: 不太可能发生的；靠不住的：*an ~ event/ hypothesis.* 不太可能的事情(靠不住的假设)。

un·load /ʌn'ləʊd; ʌn'lod/ *vt, vi* 1 [VP6A, 2A] remove a load from: 从…卸下货物：*~ a ship;* 卸下船上之货；remove (cargo) from: 卸下(货)：*~ cargo.* 卸货。*The ship is ~ing.* 该船正在卸货。2 [VP6A, 14] ~ (on to), (colloq) get rid of (sth not wanted): (口)除去(不需要之物)；摆脱…的负担：*She ~ed her old car/her mother-in-law on to me.* 她将旧汽车脱手(婆婆的负担推给我)。

un·looked-for /ʌn'lʊkt fɔ:(r); ʌn'lʊkt,for/ *adj* unexpected; for which one is not prepared. 意外的；没有料到的；没有防备的。

un·loose /ʌn'lu:s; ʌn'lus/ *vt* [VP6A] let loose; make free. 放开；放松；释放。

un·man /ʌn'mæn; ʌn'mæn/ *vt* (-nn-) [VP6A] weaken the courage and self-control of: 削弱…的勇气和自制：*The news of his friend's death ~ned him for a while.* 他朋友逝世的消息使他悲伤了一阵子。

un·man·ly /ʌn'mænlɪ; ʌn'mænlɪ/ *adj* 1 weak; cowardly. 软弱的；懦弱的。2 effeminate. 无丈夫气概的；带女人气的。

un·manned /ˌʌn'mænd; ʌn'mænd/ *adj* having no crew; 没有人员的；缺乏人员的：*~ aircraft with remote control;* 一架遥控的无人飞机；*send an ~ spacecraft to Mars.* 发射无人太空船至火星。

un·man·nered /ʌn'mænəd; ʌn'mænəd/, **unman·ner·ly** /ʌn'mænəlɪ; ʌn'mænəlɪ/ *adj* discourteous; having bad manners. 不礼貌的；粗鲁的；失礼的。

un·mask /ʌn'mɑ:sk US: -'mæsk; ʌn'mæsk/ *vt, vi* 1 [VP6A, 2A] remove a mask (from): 揭去(…的)假面具或伪装：*The revellers ~ed at midnight,* took off their masks. 狂欢者在午夜揭下了面具。2 [VP6A] show the true character or intentions of: 展示…的真正性格或意向；暴露；揭发；揭穿：*~ a traitor/hypocrite;* 揭穿卖国贼(伪君子)的假面具；*~ treachery/hypocrisy.* 揭发叛逆(虚伪)。

un·match·able /ʌn'mætʃəbl; ˌʌn'mætʃəbl/ *adj* that cannot be matched or equalled. 不能匹敌的；无法相比的。**un·matched** /ʌn'mætʃt; ʌn'mætʃt/ *adj* without an equal. 无匹敌的。

un·men·tion·able /ʌn'menʃənəbl; ʌn'mɛnʃənəbl/ *adj* so bad, shocking, etc that it may not be spoken of. 不堪出口的；不宜出口的；说出来会令人难堪的。

un·mind·ful /ʌn'maɪndfl; ʌn'maɪndfəl/ *adj ~(of)*, forgetful; oblivious; heedless. 忘记的；不留心的；不注意的；漫不经心的：*~ of the time/the need to hurry.* 未注意到时间的消逝(情况的急迫)。

un·mis·tak·able /ˌʌnmɪ'steɪkəbl; ˌʌnmə'stekəbl/ *adj* clear; about which no mistake or doubt is possible: 明显的；不会错的；无容置疑的：*Are black clouds an ~ sign of rain?* 乌云是下雨的明显征兆吗？ **un·mis·tak·ably** /-əblɪ; -əblɪ/ *adv*

un·miti·gated /ʌn'mɪtɪgeɪtɪd; ʌn'mɪtə,getɪd/ *adj* complete; absolute: 完全的；绝然的；绝对的：*an ~ disaster;* 十足的大灾难；*an ~ evil,* sth which has no accompanying advantages whatever. 一件彻头彻尾的歹事。

un·moved /ʌn'mu:vd; ʌn'muvd/ *adj* (esp) not moved in feelings; undisturbed; indifferent: (尤指)不动

心的；不动情的；坚决的；冷淡的：*He remained ~ by her entreaties for pity.* 他未因她恳求怜悯而动心。

un·natu·ral /ʌn'nætʃrəl; ʌn'nætʃərəl/ *adj* not natural or normal: 不自然的；反常的：*A mother who is cruel to her children is ~.* 对子女残酷的母亲是反常的。*~·ly adv: He expected, not ~ly, that his father would help him.* 他理所当然地期望他父亲会帮助他。

un·nec·ess·ary /ʌn'nesəsrɪ US: -serɪ; ʌn'nɛsə,sɛrɪ/ *adj* not necessary; superfluous. 不需要的；无必要的；多余的；累赘的。**un·nec·ess·ar·ily** /ʌn'nesəsrəlɪ; ˌʌn'nɛsə,sɛrəlɪ/ *adv* in an ~ manner. 无必要地；不需要地；多余地。

un·nerve /ʌn'nɜ:v; ʌn'nɝv/ *vt* [VP6A] cause to lose self-control, power of decision, courage. 使失去自制，决断，勇气。

un·not·iced /ʌn'nəʊtɪst; ʌn'notɪst/ *adj* not observed or noticed: 未被注意的；未顾及的：*The event passed ~.* 那件事被忽略过去了。*Are you going to let the insult pass ~?* 你对那番侮辱就这样不了了之吗？

un·num·bered /ʌn'nʌmbəd; ʌn'nʌmbəd/ *adj* 1 more than can be counted. 不可胜数的；数不清的。2 having no number(s): 无数字的；没编号的：*~ tickets/ seats,* eg at a concert-hall. 未编号的票(席次)。

un·ob·tru·sive /ˌʌnəb'tru:sɪv; ˌʌnəb'trusɪv/ *adj* not too obvious or easily noticeable; discreet. 不太显著的；不太容易注意到的；不冒失的；谨慎的。

un·of·fi·cial /ˌʌnə'fɪʃl; ˌʌnə'fɪʃəl/ *adj* not official: 非官方的；非正式的：*an ~ strike,* not authorized by the union; 非工会认可的罢工；*~ news,* not officially confirmed. 未经官方证实的消息。

un·or·tho·dox /ʌn'ɔ:θədɒks; ʌn'ɔrθə,dɑks/ *adj* not in accordance with what is orthodox, conventional, traditional: 非正统的；非传统的：*~ teaching methods.* 非正统的教学方法。

un·pack /ˌʌn'pæk; ʌn'pæk/ *vt, vi* [VP6A, 2A] take out (things packed): (由某包装)取出(东西)：*~ one's clothes;* (开箱等)取出衣服；take things out of: 开启包裹，行囊等：*~ a suitcase.* 开启衣箱。

un·par·al·leled /ʌn'pærəleld; ʌn'pærə,lɛld/ *adj* having no parallel or equal; matchless: 无比的；无双的；空前的：*an ~ achievement/disaster.* 空前的成就(灾难)。

un·par·lia·men·tary /ˌʌnˌpɑ:lə'mentrɪ; ˌʌnparlə'mɛntərɪ/ *adj* (of language, conduct) not suitable (because abusive, disorderly) for Parliament. (指语言，行为)不适于议会的(因为侮慢、不守秩序)。

un·placed /ʌn'pleɪst; ʌn'plest/ *adj* (esp) not one of the first three in a race or competition. (尤指)(在比赛中)未获得前三名的。

un·play·able /ʌn'pleɪəbl; ʌn'pleəbl/ *adj* (of a ball, in games) that cannot be played; (of ground) not fit to be played on. (指球，在比赛等中)打不着的；很难打的；(指场地)不适于比赛的。

un·pleas·ant /ʌn'pleznt; ʌn'plɛzn̩t/ *adj* disagreeable. 不愉快的；不中意的。*~·ness n* [U] ~ or disagreeable feeling; bad feeling (between persons); [C] quarrel, disagreement: 不愉快的；(人与人之间)的恶感；不和；争执：*a slight ~ness.* 小争执。

un·prac·tised /ʌn'præktɪst; ʌn'præktɪst/ *adj* having little experience, inexpert; unskilled. 无经验的；不熟练的；不内行的。

un·prece·dented /ʌn'presɪdentɪd; ʌn'prɛsə,dɛntɪd/ *adj* without precedent; never done or known before. 无前例的；空前的。*~·ly adv*

un·preju·diced /ʌn'predʒudɪst; ʌn'predʒədɪst/ *adj* free from prejudice. 无偏见的；公平的。

un·pre·ten·tious /ˌʌnprɪ'tenʃəs; ˌʌnprɪ'tɛnʃəs/ *adj* modest; not trying to seem important. 谦虚的；不自大的；不骄傲的。

un·prin·cipled /ʌn'prɪnsəpld; ʌn'prɪnsəpl̩d/ *adj* without moral principles; unscrupulous; dishonest. 无道德原则的；无节操的；无耻的；不正直的。

un·print·able /ʌn'prɪntəbl; ʌn'prɪntəbl/ *adj* too

rude or indecent to be printed. 粗鄙或猥亵不宜印出的。

un·pro·fessional /ˌʌnprəˈfeʃnəl ; ˌʌnprəˈfeʃənl/ adj (esp of conduct) contrary to the rules or customs of a profession. (尤指行为)违反职业惯例或习俗的;不合行规的。

un·prompted /ˌʌnˈprɒmptɪd ; ʌnˈprɑmptɪd/ adj (of an answer, action) spontaneous; not said, done, etc as the result of a hint, suggestion, etc. (指回答、行为)主动的;未受到提示、暗示等的。

un·pro·vided /ˌʌnprəˈvaɪdɪd ; ˌʌnprəˈvaɪdɪd/ adj 1 ～ for, without provision having been made for: 未预先准备好的;无供给的;无所给养的: The widow was left ～ for, No means of support had been left for her on her husband's death. 这寡妇自丈夫死后, 生活无着落。2 ～ with, not provided with: 无…设备的: schools ～ with books and equipment. 无图书及其他设备的学校。

un·pro·voked /ˌʌnprəˈvəʊkt ; ˌʌnprəˈvokt / adj without provocation: 未经挑衅的;无刺激之原因的;无端的: ～ aggression/attacks. 无端侵犯(攻击)。

un·put·down·able /ˌʌnpʊtˈdaʊnəbl ; ˌʌnpʊtˈdaʊnəbl/ adj (colloq) (of a book, etc) so interesting that the reader cannot put it down until he has finished it. (口)(指书籍等)太有趣味而不忍释手的。

un·quali·fied /ˌʌnˈkwɒlɪfaɪd ; ʌnˈkwɑlə·faɪd/ adj 1 not limited or restricted; absolute: 无限制的; 无条件的;绝对的: ～ praise; 赞不绝口;极力称赞; an ～ denial. 完全否认。2 ～ as sth/to do sth, not qualified: 不合格的; 无资格(做某事)的: ～ to speak on the subject. 无资格就此一题目发表意见。

un·ques·tion·able /ʌnˈkwestʃənəbl ; ʌnˈkwestʃənəbl/ adj beyond doubt; certain. 无疑的, 确定的。**un·ques·tion·ably** /-əblɪ; -əblɪ/ adv

un·ques·tioned /ˌʌnˈkwestʃənd ; ʌnˈkwestʃənd/ adj not questioned or disputed: 未受到质问或质疑的: I cannot let your statement pass ～, I must dispute its truth. 我不能毫无疑问地接受你的声明(我必须对它的真实性表示怀疑)。

un·ques·tion·ing /ʌnˈkwestʃənɪŋ ; ʌnˈkwestʃənɪŋ/ adj (esp) given, done, without question or protest: (尤指)不质问的; 不质疑的; 无异议的: ～ obedience. 无异议的遵从。

un·quiet /ʌnˈkwaɪət ; ʌnˈkwaɪət/ adj (formal) restless; uneasy; disturbed: (正式用语)不安的; 不平静的; 纷乱的: live in ～ times. 生于乱世。

un·quote /ʌnˈkwəʊt ; ʌnˈkwot/ (v, imper only 仅用祈使语气) (in a telegram, a telephoned message, etc) end the quotation; close the inverted commas: (在电报,以电话发出的电文等中)结束引语:引号止于此;引号终止: The rebel leader said (quote) 'We shall never surrender' (unquote). 叛军领袖说(引号开始)'我们决不投降'(引号终止)。

un·ravel /ʌnˈrævl ; ʌnˈrævl/ vt, vi (-ll-; US -l-) [VP6A, 2A] 1 separate the threads of; pull or become separate: 解开…的线; 拆开: The cuff of my jersey has ～led. 我的毛衫上装袖口松绽了。The baby ～led the knitting that its mother left on the chair. 那婴儿弄散了她母亲放在椅子上的编织物。2 make clear; solve: 使明白; 阐明; 解决: ～ a mystery/plot. 揭开一秘密(阴谋)。

un·real /ʌnˈrɪəl ; ʌnˈrɪəl/ adj imaginary; illusory. 不真实的;空想的;虚幻的。

un·reas·on·able /ˌʌnˈriːznəbl ; ʌnˈriznəbl/ adj not governed by reason; immoderate; excessive: 不合理的; 无理性的; 无节制的; 过分的: make ～ demands. 做过分的要求。

un·reas·on·ing /ˌʌnˈriːzənɪŋ ; ʌnˈrizənɪŋ/ adj not using or guided by reason. 不使用理性或推理的; 非由理性引导的;没道理的。

un·re·lent·ing /ˌʌnrɪˈlentɪŋ ; ˌʌnrɪˈlentɪŋ/ adj not becoming less in intensity, etc: 强度等未减弱的: ～ pressure/attacks. 未减弱的压力(攻击)。⇨ relentless at relent.

un·re·li·able /ˌʌnrɪˈlaɪəbl ; ˌʌnrɪˈlaɪəbl/ adj that

cannot be relied on; untrustworthy. 不能依赖的; 靠不住的;不能相信的。

un·re·lieved /ˌʌnrɪˈliːvd ; ˌʌnrɪˈlivd/ adj (esp) without anything to vary monotony: (尤指)单调而无变化的: a plain black dress ～ by a touch of colour or trimming of any kind; 没有一点彩色或装饰的单调黑色女装; ～ boredom/tedium. 单调而无变化的厌烦(沉闷)。

un·re·mit·ting /ˌʌnrɪˈmɪtɪŋ ; ˌʌnrɪˈmɪtɪŋ/ adj unceasing: 不停止的;不间断的: ～ care/efforts. 不断的注意(努力)。The doctor was ～ in his attention to the case. 医生毫不松懈地注意那病例。

un·re·quit·ed /ˌʌnrɪˈkwaɪtɪd ; ˌʌnrɪˈkwaɪtɪd/ adj not returned or rewarded: 无报答的; 无报酬的: ～ love/service. 单恋(无报酬的服务)。

un·re·serv·ed·ly /ˌʌnrɪˈzɜːvɪdlɪ ; ˌʌnrɪˈzɜvɪdlɪ/ adv without reservation or restriction; openly: 无保留地;无限制地;坦白地: speak ～; 坦白地说; trust sb ～. 完全信任其人。

un·rest /ʌnˈrest ; ʌnˈrest/ n [U] (esp) disturbed condition(s): (尤指)纷乱的状态; 不安; 不稳: social ～, eg because of widespread unemployment or poverty; 社会的不安(如因普遍失业或贫穷); political ～. 政治的不安。

un·re·strained /ˌʌnrɪˈstreɪnd ; ˌʌnrɪˈstrend/ adj not checked or held in. 无节制的; 无拘束的; 放纵的。

un·re·strict·ed /ˌʌnrɪˈstrɪktɪd ; ˌʌnrɪˈstrɪktɪd/ adj without restriction(s): (esp of a road) not having a speed limit for traffic. 无限制的; (尤指道路)无速度限制的。

un·ri·valled (US = -ri·valed) /ʌnˈraɪvld ; ʌnˈraɪvld/ adj having no rival (in courage, etc); unequalled: (在勇气等方面)无对手的(与 in 连用); 无双的; 无匹敌的; 无与伦比的: an ～ reputation. 极佳的声誉。

un·roll /ʌnˈrəʊl ; ʌnˈrol/ vt, vi [VP6A, 2A] roll out; open out by rolling: 展开; (将成卷之物)打开: ～ a carpet/map. 展开一地毯(地图)。My sleeping-bag has ～ed. 我的睡袋已经打开。

un·ruffled /ʌnˈrʌfld ; ʌnˈrʌfld/ adj calm; not upset or agitated: 平静的; 镇定的; 从容不迫的; 沉着的: He remained ～ by all these criticisms. 受到这些批评他仍能保持镇静。

un·ruly /ʌnˈruːlɪ ; ʌnˈrulɪ/ adj (-ier, -iest) not easily controlled; disorderly: 难控制的;难驾驭的; 蛮横的; 任性的; 不守规矩的: an ～ child. 任性的小孩。

un·said /ʌnˈsed ; ʌnˈsɛd/ adj not expressed: 未说明的; 未讲出的: Some things are better left ～. 有些事情还是不说出来好。

un·sa·voury (US = -sa·vory) /ʌnˈseɪvərɪ ; ʌnˈsevərɪ/ adj (esp) nasty; disgusting: (尤指)不好的; 令人厌恶的: ～ stories/scandals; 令人厌恶的故事(丑闻); a man with an ～ reputation. 声名狼藉的人。

un·say /ˌʌnˈseɪ ; ʌnˈse/ vt (pt, pp **-said** /- sed; -'sɛd/) [VP6A] (liter) take back (sth that has been said); retract (which is the usu word): (文)取消(前言); 撤回(retract 较常用)。

un·scathed /ʌnˈskeɪðd ; ʌnˈskeðd/ adj unharmed; unhurt. 未受损伤的;未遭伤害的。

un·scramble /ˌʌnˈskræmbl ; ʌnˈskræmbl/ vt (of a scrambled message) restore to a form that can be understood. (指杂乱片段的消息、情报等)修整为可了解的形式。

un·scripted /ˌʌnˈskrɪptɪd ; ʌnˈskrɪptɪd/ adj (eg of a broadcast talk or discussion) not read from a prepared script. (如指广播谈话或讨论)无底稿的; 不是宣读讲稿的;当场讲出的。

un·scru·pu·lous /ʌnˈskruːpjʊləs ; ʌnˈskrupjələs/ adj not guided by conscience; not held back (from doing wrong) by scruples. 无耻的; 没有操守的; 不受良心节制的。～ly adv

un·seas·oned /ˌʌnˈsiːznd ; ʌnˈsiznd/ adj (of wood) not matured; (of food) not flavoured with seasoning. (指木材)未熟的; 未长成的; (指食物)没有调味的; 未加作料的。

un·seat /ˌʌn'siːt; ʌn'sit/ vt [VP6A] **1** remove from office: 免职；罢免；罢黜: *Mr Fowell was ~ed at the General Election*, lost his seat in the House of Commons. 鲍威尔先生在大选中落选了(失去了下议院席位)。**2** throw from a horse: 使落马；使从马上摔下: *Several riders were ~ed at the water-jump*, eg in a steeplechase. 有几位骑士在跃过障碍时摔了下来(例如在障碍赛马中)。

un·seem·ly /ˌʌn'siːmlɪ; ʌn'simlɪ/ adj (of behaviour, etc) not suitable or proper. (指行为等)不相宜的；不适当的。

un·seen /ˌʌn'siːn; ʌn'sin/ adj not seen; invisible. 未被看见的；看不见的。□ n **1** the ~, the spiritual world. 精神世界。**2** [C] passage to be translated, without preparation, from a foreign language into one's own language: 未经准备而要从外国语译为本国语的一段文字；需要即席翻译的文字: *German ~s*. 需要即席翻译的几段德文。

un·settle /ˌʌn'setl; ʌn'sɛtl/ vt [VP6A] make troubled, anxious or uncertain: 使不安、担心或不确定；扰乱: *~d weather*, uncertain, changeable weather. 不稳定而多变的天气。

un·sex /ˌʌn'seks; ʌn'sɛks/ vt [VP6A] deprive of the attributes of one's sex. 使失去性别的特征。**~ed** adj not separated according to sex. 尚未分出性别的。

un·sight·ly /ˌʌn'saɪtlɪ; ʌn'saɪtlɪ/ adj displeasing to the eye: 难看的；不雅观的: *~ advertisements in the countryside*. 乡间不雅观的广告。**un·sight·li·ness** n

un·skilled /ˌʌn'skɪld; ʌn'skɪld/ adj (of work) not needing special skill; (of workers) not having special skill or special training. (指工作)不需特别技巧的；粗笨的;(指工人)无特别技巧的；未受特殊训练的。

un·soph·is·ti·cat·ed /ˌʌnsə'fɪstɪkeɪtɪd; ˌʌnsə'fɪstɪˌketɪd/ adj naive; inexperienced; simple: 天真的；纯朴的；没心眼儿的；无经验的；单纯的: *~ children/techniques*. 天真的儿童(简单的技巧)。

un·sound /ˌʌn'saʊnd; ʌn'saʊnd/ adj not in good condition; unsatisfactory: 不健全的；不佳的；不能令人满意的；不坚固的: *an ~ argument*. 没有根据的论据。*The structure/building is ~*. 那建筑物(房屋)不坚固。*of ~ mind*, unbalanced in mind; mentally disordered. 精神不健全的；精神错乱的。

un·spar·ing /ˌʌn'speərɪŋ; ʌn'spɛrɪŋ/ adj liberal; holding nothing back: 慷慨的；不吝惜的: *be ~ in one's efforts; 不遗余力; ~ of praise*. 大加赞赏。

un·speak·able /ˌʌn'spiːkəbl; ʌn'spikəbl/ adj that cannot be expressed or described in words: 不能以言语表达的；无法形容的: *~ joy/wickedness*; 无法形容的快乐(邪恶); (colloq) very unpleasant: (口)令人很不愉快的: *~ behaviour*. 令人讨厌的行为。**un·speak·ably** adv

un·spot·ted /ˌʌn'spɒtɪd; ʌn'spɑtɪd/ adj (of reputation) without stain; pure. (指名誉)无瑕疵的；清白的。

un·strung /ˌʌn'strʌŋ; ʌn'strʌŋ/ adj (esp) with little or no control over the nerves, mind or emotions. (尤指)失去自制力的；不能抑制的。

un·stuck /ˌʌn'stʌk; ʌn'stʌk/ adj not stuck or fastened: 未粘牢的；未系住的；未贴紧的: *The flap of the envelope has come ~*. 这信封的封口松开了。**come (badly) ~**, (colloq) be unsuccessful; fail to work according to plan: (口)未成功的；未照计划进行的；不灵光的: *Our plan has come ~*. 我们的计划未成功。

un·stud·ied /ˌʌn'stʌdɪd; ʌn'stʌdɪd/ adj (of behaviour) natural; not aimed at impressing other persons. (指行为)自然的；非着眼于使他人有深刻印象的；不矫揉造作的。

un·sung /ˌʌn'sʌŋ; ʌn'sʌŋ/ adj not celebrated (in poetry or song): 未(在诗或歌中)被赞颂的: *an ~ hero*. 未被人歌颂的英雄。

un·swerv·ing /ˌʌn'swɜːvɪŋ; ʌn'swɝvɪŋ/ adj (esp of aims, purposes) not changing; straight: (尤指目标、目的)不改变的；坚定的: *~ loyalty/devotion*; 不变的忠诚(奉献); *pursue an ~ course*. 采取某一坚定的方针。**~·ly** adv

un·syl·labic /ˌʌnsɪ'læbɪk; ˌʌnsɪ'læbɪk/ adj **1** not syllabic. 非音节的。**2** (of a consonant) not making a syllable, eg in the word little /'lɪtl; 'lɪtl/ the first /l/ is unsyllabic and the second is syllabic. (指辅音)不构成音节的(如 little 中的第一个 /l/ 不成音节，第二个 /l/ 成音节)。

un·think·able /ˌʌn'θɪŋkəbl; ʌn'θɪŋkəbl/ adj such as one cannot have any real idea of or belief; not to be considered: 难以想象的；难以置信的;不加以考虑的；不可能的: *It's ~ that he should resign now*. 他现在要辞职令人难以想象。

un·think·ing /ˌʌn'θɪŋkɪŋ; ʌn'θɪŋkɪŋ/ adj thoughtless; done, said, etc without thought of the effect: 无思想的；轻率的；未加思考的: *in an ~ moment*. 一时轻率。**~·ly** adv

un·thought-of /ˌʌn'θɔːt ɒv; ʌn'θɔtˌɑv/ adj quite unexpected; not imagined. 完全未料到的；出乎意外的；想像不到的。

un·tidy /ˌʌn'taɪdɪ; ʌn'taɪdɪ/ adj (**-ier, -iest**) (of a room, desk, etc) in disorder: (of a person) slovenly; not neat. (指房间，书桌等)零乱的；不整齐的;(指人)邋遢的；不整洁的。**un·tidi·ly** adv

un·til /ən'tɪl; ən'tɪl/ prep, conj ⟹ **till**.

un·time·ly /ˌʌn'taɪmlɪ; ʌn'taɪmlɪ/ adj occurring at a wrong or unsuitable time, or too soon: 不合时宜的；过早的: *an ~ remark*. 不合时宜的话。*He came to an ~ end*, died before he had completed his life's work. 他赍志而亡。

un·tir·ing /ˌʌn'taɪərɪŋ; ʌn'taɪrɪŋ/ adj **1** continuing to work without getting tired: 继续工作而不疲倦的: *She seems to be ~*. 她似乎不知疲倦。**2** continuing as if never causing tiredness: 坚持不懈的；不屈不挠的: *his ~ efforts*. 他那坚持不懈的努力。

unto /'ʌntu; 'ʌntu/ prep (archaic) (古) = to (prep).

un·told /ˌʌn'təʊld; ʌn'told/ adj (esp) too many or too much to be counted, measured, etc: (尤指)不能计数的；数不清的；无数的；太多的: *a man of ~ wealth*. 财富数不清的人。

un·touch·able /ˌʌn'tʌtʃəbl; ʌn'tʌtʃəbl/ n, adj (member) of the lowest caste in India. 贱民(印度最低社会阶层的成员)(的)。

un·to·ward /ˌʌntə'wɔːd; US: ʌn'tɔːrd; ʌn'tord/ adj (formal) unfavourable; unfortunate; inconvenient: (正式用语)不利的；不幸的；困难重重的: *There were no ~ incidents*. 并无不吉利事件。

un·truth /ˌʌn'truːθ; ʌn'truθ/ n [U] lack of truth; [C] (pl ~s /-'truːðz; -'truðz/) untrue statement; lie 虚伪；不真实；虚言；谎话。**~·ful** /-fl; -fəl/ adj **~·fully** /-fəlɪ; -fəlɪ/ adv

un·tu·tored /ˌʌn'tjuːtəd; US: -'tuː-; ʌn'tutəd/ adj untaught; ignorant. 未受教育的；无知的。

un·used[1] /ˌʌn'juːzd; ʌn'juzd/ adj not made use of; not put to use; never having been used. 未使用的；未利用的;从未使用过的。

un·used[2] /ˌʌn'juːst; ʌn'just/ adj **~ to**, not accustomed to: 不习惯的；不惯的: *The children are ~ to city life*. 孩子们过不惯城市生活。

un·usual /ˌʌn'juːʒl; ʌn'juʒʊəl/ adj not usual; strange; remarkable: 不寻常的；奇异的；罕有的；独特的: *clothes/opinions*; 奇异的衣服(意见); *a nose of ~ size*. 罕有的大鼻子。**~·ly** /-ʒlɪ; ʌn'juʒʊəlɪ/ adv: *~ly small/large/late/early*. 非常小(大、晚、早)。

un·ut·ter·able /ˌʌn'ʌtərəbl; ʌn'ʌtərəbl/ adj unspeakable. 说不出的；无法形容的；非语言所能表达的。

un·var·nished /ˌʌn'vɑːnɪʃt; ʌn'vɑrnɪʃt/ adj (esp of accounts, descriptions) plain; straightforward: (尤指说明，描述)未加渲染的实情；率直的；直言无讳的: *the ~ truth*; 未加渲染的实情; *give an ~ account of what happened*. 照实记述所发生之事。

un·veil /ˌʌn'veɪl; ʌn'vel/ vt, vi **1** [VP6A, 2A] remove a veil from; remove one's veil. 除去…的面纱或面罩；除去面罩。**2** [VP6A] disclose; reveal; (trade

use) show publicly for the first time: 揭示；揭露；(交易用语)首次公开；首次展示: *Several new models were ～ed yesterday at the Motor Show.* 昨天的汽车展示会上公开了数种新型汽车。

un·voiced /ˌʌn'vɔɪst; ʌn'vɔɪst/ *adj* (of thoughts, etc) not expressed or uttered. (指思想等)未明说的；未表明的；未讲出来的。

un·wieldy /ʌn'wiːldɪ; ʌn'wildɪ/ *adj* awkward to move or control because of shape, size or weight. (因形状、大小或重量等而)不易移动或控制的；庞大的；笨重的。 **un·wieldi·ness** *n*

un·wind /ˌʌn'waɪnd; ʌn'waɪnd/ *vt, vi* (*pt, pp* **-wound** /-'waʊnd; -'waʊnd/) 1 [VP6A, 2A] wind off (what has been wound up); become unwound. 解开，展开(缠或卷在一起之物)；旋开；转开。 2 [VP2A] (colloq) relax after a period of tension, exhausting work, etc. (经过一段紧张时期、吃力的工作之后)放松自己；轻松一下。 ⇨ **wind**³(6).

un·wit·ting /ʌn'wɪtɪŋ; ʌn'wɪtɪŋ/ *adj* unknowing; unaware; unintentional. 不知情的；无心的；非故意的。 **～·ly** *adv*: *If I hurt your feelings it was ～ly.* 如果我伤了你的感情，那不是故意的。

un·writ·ten /ˌʌn'rɪtn; ʌn'rɪtn̩/ *adj* not written down: 未写下的；不成文的；口传的: *the ～ songs of the countryfolk,* folksongs not to be found in writing or print. 乡民口传的歌谣。 **an ～ law,** one based on custom or tradition, but not precisely stated anywhere. 不成文法。

un·zip /ˌʌn'zɪp; ʌn'zɪp/ *vt* (**-pp-**) unfasten or open by pulling a zip fastener: 拉开…的拉链: *～ a handbag.* 拉开拉链以打开手提包。

up /ʌp; ʌp/ *adv part* (contrasted with *down*. ⇨ the *v* entries for combinations with *up.* Specimen entries only here.) (与 down 相对，参看 up 连用的动词诸条。下面所列，仅系范例) **1** to or in an erect or vertical position (esp as suggesting readiness for activity): 趋向于或处于直立的姿势或位置(尤指含有准备活动的意思): *He's already up,* out of bed. 他已起床。 *I was up late* (= did not go to bed until late) *last night.* 我昨夜很晚才就寝。 *She was up all night with a sick child.* 她陪伴着生病的孩子彻夜未眠。 *It's time to get up,* out of bed. 是起床的时候了。 *He got up* (= stood up) *to ask a question.* 他站起来发问。 *He jumped up* (ie to his feet) *from his chair.* 他从椅子上跳了起来。 *Up with you!* Get up! Stand up! 起来!(起床!起立!) *Up with them!* Put, bring, etc them up! 把它们真立起来! *Parliament is up,* no longer sitting, no longer in session. 国会闭会了。 *His blood was up,* His passions were roused. 他发脾气了。 **What's up,** (colloq) What's going on, happening? (口)什么事?发生什么事了？ *There's something up,* Sth unusual is happening, being planned, etc. 不寻常的事即将发生。 **up and about,** out of bed and active (esp of a person recently ill). (尤指最近生过病的人)已起床活动。 **2** to or in a high(er) place, position, degree, etc: 往或居于高或较高的地方、位置、程度等: *Lift your head up.* 抬起头来。 *Pull your socks up.* 振作起来。 *The tide's up,* in. 潮水上涨了。 *He lives three floors up.* 他住在往上第三层。 *Prices are still going up,* rising. 物价仍在上涨。 *He's well up in Greek,* has made good progress. 他的希腊文大有进步。 **3** to a place of importance; (in England) to London; to a place in or to the north: 至重要之处或地方；(在英国)至伦敦或至北部或北方之地: *He has gone up to London for the day.* 他今天上伦敦去了。 *He lives up in the Lake District.* 他住在北部的大湖区。 *We're going up to Edinburgh.* 我们要去爱丁堡。 *The case was brought up before the High Court.* 那案件已呈请高等法院审理。 **4** (used vaguely, in a way similar to the use of *down, round, over, across*) to the place in question, or in which the speaker is, was, will be: (笼统用法，与 down, round, over, across 的用法相似)至所指定的地方，至讲话者所在之处: *He came up (to me) and asked the time.* 他走过来(走到我前面)询问时间。 *She went straight*

up to the door. 她一直走到门口。 **5** (with *vv* to indicate completeness, finality): (与动词连用，表示完全，彻底，终结): *The stream has dried up,* has become completely dry. 溪水全干了。 *We've eaten everything up.* 我们把每一样食物都吃光了。 *Time's up,* The allowed time is ended. 时间到了。 *When is your leave up?* When must you return to duty? 你的假期何时届满? *Tear it up.* 把它撕碎。 *Lock/Tie/Fasten/Chain/Nail it up,* Make it fast, secure, safe, etc by locking, tying, etc. 把它锁好(绑好，固定好，用链子拴好，用钉子钉好)。 **6** (with *vv* to indicate an increase in intensity, etc): (与动词连用，表示强度等的增加): *Speak/Sing up!* (ie with more force). 说(唱)大声一些! *Her spirits went up,* rose. 她的兴致提起来了。 *Blow the fire up.* 把火吹大一些。 **7** (attrib uses with *nn*): (用作定语，属名词前): *the 'up train* (to London); (开往伦敦的)上行火车; *the 'up line/platform* (used by up trains); 上行线(上行火车使用的月台); *an 'up stroke,* eg of the pen when writing the letter 1. 向上的笔画(如写 1 时)。 **8 up against sth,** faced with (difficulties, obstacles, etc). 面临(困难，阻碍等)。 **be up before sb,** appear in court (before a magistrate, etc): 上法庭(接受法官等审判): *He was up before the magistrate for being drunk while driving a car.* 他因酒醉驾车而被法庭传讯。 **up and down, (a)** backwards and forwards; to and fro: 前后地；往返地；来回地: *walking up and down the station platform.* 在车站月台上来回地走。 **(b)** so as to rise and fall: 上下地; 起伏地: *The float bobbed up and down on the water.* 漂浮物在水面上下浮动。 Hence, 由此产生, **ups and downs,** (usu fig) alternations of good and bad fortune. (通常作比喻用法)好运与坏运的交替; 盛衰; 浮沉。 **on the up (and up),** (colloq) steadily improving; becoming more successful. (口)愈来愈好; 越来越成功。 **up for sth, (a)** being tried for (an offence, etc): (以某项罪行等)受审: *up for exceeding the speed limit.* 因(驾车)超速而受审。 **(b)** being considered for; on offer: 考虑中; 出售; 出售: *The contract is up for renewal.* 该合约正考虑换新。 *The house is up for auction/sale.* 该房屋在拍卖(出售)。 **be well up in/on sth,** be well informed about; be expert in: 熟知; 对…内行; 对…有充分知识: *He's well up on electronic music.* 他对电子音乐很内行。 **up to sth, (a)** occupied or busy with: 忙于; 从事于; 正在做: *What's he up to?* 他在忙什么呢? *He's up to no good.* 他在做坏事。 *What tricks has she been up to, playing?* 她一直在玩什么把戏? **(b)** equal to: 胜任; 能作; 及得上: *I don't feel up to going to work today.* 我今天身体不适不能去工作。 *This new book of Hugh Fleetwood's isn't up to his last,* is not as good. 休·弗利特伍德的这本新书不及他的前一本。 *He's not up to his work/to the job,* not good enough for the job. 他不能胜任他的工作(这份工作)。 **(c)** as far as: 直到: *up to now/then;* 直到现在(那时); *count from one up to twenty.* 从一数到二十。 **up to sb,** required, looked upon as necessary, from him: 应由某人…; 视为某人的职责: *It's up to us* (= It is our duty) *to give them all the help we can.* 我们理应竭尽所能给予他们协助。 **all up (with sb),** ⇨ **all²**(1). **,up-and-'coming,** (of a person) making good progress, likely to succeed, in his profession, career, etc: (指人)在其职业、事业等方面有长足进步的; 很可能成功的; 进取的: *an up-and-coming young MP.* 一位有进取心的年轻国会议员。 □ *prep* (in the senses of the *adv*): (具有副词的各种意义): *climb up a mountain;* 爬山; *walk up the stairs;* 上楼梯; *sail up* (towards the source of) *a river;* 向河的上游航行; *travel up country,* away from the coast; 到内陆旅行; *walk up* (= along) *the road.* 沿大路而行。 □ *vi, vt* (**-pp-**) [VP2A, 6A] **1** (humor or colloq use only) rouse oneself; get or jump up: (仅作诙谐或口语用法)奋起; 起立; 跳起: *She upped and threw the teapot at him.* 她跳起来将茶壶向他掷去。 **2** (colloq) increase: (口)增加: *up the price;* 加价; *up an offer.* 提高出价。

up- /ʌp-; ʌp-/ *pref* in an upward direction. 向上。

up-beat /'ʌp biːt; 'ʌpˌbit/ *n* (music) unaccented beat,

esp at the end of a bar (eg when the conductor's hand is raised). (音乐)上拍; 弱拍(尤指一小节末尾的一拍).

up·braid /ʌp'breɪd; ʌp'bred/ *vt* [VP6A, 14] ~ *sb (for doing sth/with sth)*, scold, reproach. 谴责; 叱责 (某人).

up·bring·ing /'ʌpbrɪŋɪŋ; 'ʌp,brɪŋɪŋ/ *n* [U] training and education during childhood: 儿童期的训练和教育; 幼年的教养: *His ~ explains a lot about his attitude towards authority/women.* 他幼年的教养充分说明他对权威(妇女)的态度.

up·coun·try /ʌp'kʌntrɪ; 'ʌp'kʌntrɪ/ *adj, adv* (esp in a large thinly populated country) towards the interior; inland: (尤指地广人稀的地区)向内地(的); 在内地(的): ~ *districts*; 内陆区域; *travel ~.* 在内地旅行.

up·date /ʌp'deɪt; 'ʌp'det/ *vt* [VP6A] bring up-to-date; modernize: 使…现代化; 使…合时代: ~ *a dictionary/textbook.* 修订词典(教科书).

up·grade /ʌp'greɪd; 'ʌpgred/ *vt* [VP6A] raise to a higher grade. 提高…之等级. □ *n* /'ʌpgreɪd; 'ʌp,gred/ (esp) (尤用于) *on the ~*, improving; making progress. 有进步; 有进展.

up·heaval /ʌp'hiːvl; ʌp'hivl/ *n* [C] great and sudden change: 巨大而突然的变化; 巨变; 骚变: *a volcanic ~*; 火山突然爆发; *political/social ~s.* 政治(社会)的大变动.

up·held /ʌp'held; ʌp'hɛld/ *pt, pp* of **uphold**.

up·hill /ʌp'hɪl; 'ʌp'hɪl/ *adj* sloping upward; ascending: 上坡的; 向上的: *an ~ road;* 上坡路; (fig) difficult; needing effort. (喻)困难的; 费力的: *an ~ task,* very difficult one. 极艰巨的工作. □ *adv* up a slope: 上坡: *walk ~.* 爬坡; 走上坡.

up·hold /ʌp'həʊld; ʌp'hold/ *vt* (*pt, pp* upheld /-'held; -'hɛld/) [VP6A] 1 support or approve (a person, his conduct, a practice, etc): 支持; 赞成(某人,其行为,某习俗等): *I cannot ~ such conduct.* 我不能赞成这种行为. 2 confirm (a decision, a verdict). 证实; 确定(一项决定, 判决).

up·hol·ster /ʌp'həʊlstə(r); ʌp'holstɚ/ *vt* [VP6A] provide (seats, etc) with padding springs, covering material, etc; provide (a room) with carpets, curtains, cushioned seats, etc: 为(椅子等)加装垫子,弹簧,面子等; 为(房间)装设地毯,帘幕,座垫等; 装潢: ~ *a settee in tapestry;* 为长椅椅背上花毯的面子; ~ed *in/with velvet.* 以天鹅绒装设的. ~**er** *n* person whose trade is to ~. 室内装潢商; 室内装潢匠. ~**y** /-stərɪ; -stərɪ/ *n* [U] (materials used in, business of) ~ing. 室内装潢; 室内装潢品; 室内装潢业.

up·keep /'ʌpkiːp; 'ʌp,kip/ *n* [U] (cost of) keeping sth in good order and repair: 保养; 维护费; 保养费: *£450 for rent and ~*, eg of a house. 租金及维护费四百五十镑(如指房屋). *The ~ of this large garden is more than I can afford.* 这个大花园的维护费非我所能负担.

up·land /'ʌplənd; 'ʌplənd/ *n* (often *pl*) higher part(s) of a region or country (not necessarily mountainous): (常用复数)高地(并不一定是山); (attrib) (用作定语) *an ~ region.* 高地区域.

up·lift /ʌp'lɪft; ʌp'lɪft/ *vt* [VP6A] (fig) raise (spiritually or emotionally): (喻)(精神或情绪方面)提高; 振奋: *His soul was ~ed by the music.* 那种音乐使他的精神振奋起来了. □ *n* /'ʌplɪft; 'ʌp,lɪft/[U] socially or mentally elevating influence; moral inspiration. 社会或精神方面有激发或振奋作用的影响力; 道德的鼓舞.

up·most /'ʌpməʊst; 'ʌp,most/ *adj* = **uppermost**.

upon /ə'pɒn; ə'pɑn/ *prep* (formal) (正式用语) = **on²(1-7)** (which is more usual). *Upon* is the only normal form in) (通常多用 on. 在下例中 upon 为唯一正规的形式): ~ *my word;* 的确; *once ~ a time.* 从前.

up·per /'ʌpə(r); 'ʌpɚ/ *adj* (contrasted with *lower*) higher in place; situated above: (与 lower 相对)位置较高的; 在上的: *the ~ lip;* 上唇; *the ~ rooms;* one of the ~ *rooms.* 楼上的一个房间. ~ *case,* ⇨ **case²(2).** ~ *class,* ⇨ **class(3). the ~ crust,** (colloq) the highest social class. (口)社会的最高阶层; 上流社会; 贵族. **the ~ storey,** (fig, colloq) the brain: (喻,口)头脑: *wrong in the ~ storey,* mentally disordered. 精神错乱. **have/ get the ~ hand (of),** have/get the advantage or control (over). 胜过; (比…)占优势; 占(…的)上风. **the U~ House,** (in Parliament) the House of Lords. (国会)上议院. ~**-cut** *n* (boxing) a blow delivered upwards with the arm bent inside an opponent's guard. (拳击)上击拳(曲臂向上出击对方的防御部位). □ *n* part of a shoe or boot over the sole. 鞋面或靴面; 鞋帮. **be (down) on one's ~s,** be at the end of one's financial resources. 穷困不堪. '~**·most** /-məʊst; -,most/ *adj* highest; predominant: 最高的; 最主要的: *Thoughts of the holidays were ~most in their minds.* 他们心中最主要的念头是假日. □ *adv* on, to, at, the top or surface: 最上地; 至上地; 在或至表面: *It's not always wise to say whatever comes ~most,* whatever comes to the top of one's thoughts. 想到什么就说什么并不一定是明智的.

up·pish /'ʌpɪʃ; 'ʌpɪʃ/ *adj* (colloq) self-assertive, conceited: (口)盛气凌人的; 自大的: *Don't get ~ with me!* 不要对我盛气凌人! *Don't be too ~ about it!* 对此事不要太骄傲! ~**·ly** *adv* ~**·ness** *n*

up·pity /'ʌpətɪ; 'ʌpətɪ/ *adj* (colloq) uppish. (口)盛气凌人的; 自大的.

up·right /'ʌpraɪt; 'ʌp,raɪt/ *adj* 1 erect; placed vertically (at an angle of 90° to the ground): 直立的; 垂直的(与地面成九十度): *an ~ post;* 直立的柱子; *stand/hold oneself ~;* 笔直地站立; *set a post ~.* 把柱子竖直. ~ **piano,** with the strings vertical, not horizontal, as in a grand piano. 竖式钢琴(琴弦直立者). 2 honourable; straightforward in behaviour: 正直的; 老实的; 规矩的: *an ~ man/judge;* 正直的人(法官); *be ~ in one's business dealings.* 规矩矩地做生意. ~ *support in a structure;* ~ *post.* (结构中的)直立支撑物; 直柱. ~**·ly** *adv* ~**·ness** *n* [U].

up·ris·ing /'ʌpraɪzɪŋ; 'ʌp,raɪzɪŋ/ *n* [C] revolt; rebellion. 叛乱; 叛变; 起义.

up·roar /'ʌprɔː(r); 'ʌp,ror/ *n* [U, C] (*sing* only) (仅用单数) (outburst of) noise and excitement; tumult: 喧嚣; 骚动; 鼓噪; 爆出喧嚣声. *The meeting ended in (an) ~.* 会议在一阵喧嚣中结束. ~**·i·ous** /ʌp'rɔːrɪəs; ʌp'rorɪəs/ *adj* noisy, esp with loud laughter and great good humour: 喧嚣的; 骚动的; 鼓噪的; 闹哄哄的; (尤指)哄然大笑的: *We were given an ~ious welcome.* 我们受到热烈的欢迎. *They burst into ~ious laughter.* 他们哄然大笑. ~**·i·ous·ly** *adv*

up·root /ʌp'ruːt; ʌp'rut/ *vt* [VP6A] pull up by the roots: 连根拔起; 根除: 根拔: *The gale ~ed numerous trees.* 大风将很多树连根拔起. *After he had lived in New York for fifteen years his firm ~ed him and sent him to Chicago.* 他在纽约住了十五年后,他的公司调派他去芝加哥.

up·set /ʌp'set; ʌp'sɛt/ *vt, vi* (*pt, pp* upset) (-tt-) 1 [VP6A, 2A] tip over; overturn: 打翻; 弄翻; 倾覆: *Don't ~ the boat.* 不要把船弄翻了. *The boat ~.* 船倾覆了. *The cat has ~ its saucer of milk.* 那只猫弄翻了它的牛奶碟子. 2 [VP6A] trouble; cause (sb or sth) to be disturbed: 扰乱; 使(某人或某物)不安: ~ *the enemy's plans;* 破坏敌人的计划; ~ *one's stomach by eating too much rich food.* 吃太多油腻食物而使胃不舒服. *The sight of physical suffering ~s her.* 肉体受苦的景象使她不安. *She is easily ~ emotionally.* 她的心绪容易烦乱. □ *n* /'ʌpset; 'ʌp,sɛt/ [C] 1 ~ting or being ~: 翻倒; 倾覆; 扰乱; 不安: *have a 'stomach ~.* 胃不舒服. *She's had a terrible ~,* eg an emotional shock. 她情绪上受了大震撼. *You can imagine what an ~ we have had with the decorators and upholsterers in the house all week.* 室内设计师和装潢工人在我们家整整忙了一个礼拜,我们受到的扰乱可想而知. 2 (sport) unexpected result. (运动)出乎意料的败北.

up·shot /'ʌpʃɒt; 'ʌp,ʃɑt/ *n* **the ~ (of sth),** outcome,

result: 结果; 结局: *What will be the ~ of it all?* 其结局将如何呢?

up·side-down /ˌʌpsaɪd ˈdaʊn; ˌʌpˌsaɪdˈdaʊn/ *adv* with the upper side underneath or at the bottom; (fig) in disorder: 倒转地; 倒置地; (喻)混乱地: *The boy pretended he could read, but he was holding the book ~.* 那男孩假装在阅读, 但是他握着那本书倒着拿书. *The house was turned ~ by the burglars,* Everything was left in disorder. 那房屋被窃贼翻得乱七八糟.

up·stage /ˌʌpˈsteɪdʒ; ˈʌpˈsteɪdʒ/ *adj* (colloq) uppish; uppity. (口)高傲的; 自负的. □ *adv* (theatre) towards the back of the stage. (戏剧)向舞台后部地. □ *vt* [VP6A] divert attention from sb else to oneself; put at a disadvantage. 把(某人)所受到的注意引向自己; 抢(某人)的锋头; 抢占(某人)的光彩; 使处于不利情况.

up·stairs /ˌʌpˈsteəz; ˈʌpˈsterz/ *adv* 1 to or on a higher floor: 向楼上; 在楼上: *go/walk ~.* 上楼. 2 (attrib) belonging to, situated on, an upper floor: (用作定语)属于楼上的; 在楼上的: *an ~ room.* 楼上的房间.

up·stand·ing /ˌʌpˈstændɪŋ; ˈʌpˈstændɪŋ/ *adj* standing erect; strong and healthy: 直立的; 强健的: *fine ~ children.* 健康的孩子们.

up·start /ˈʌpstɑːt; ˈʌpˌstɑːrt/ *n, adj* (person) who has suddenly risen to wealth, power or higher social position, esp one whose behaviour causes resentment: 暴富者; 骤贵者; 暴发户(尤指其行为招致反感者); 暴富的; 骤贵的: *~ officials in government offices.* 政府机构中突然发迹的官员们.

up·stream /ˌʌpˈstriːm; ˈʌpˈstrim/ *adv* up a river; against the stream or current. 往上游地; 逆流地.

up·surge /ˈʌpsɜːdʒ; ˈʌpˌsɜːdʒ/ *n* surging up (of emotion): (情绪的)激起; 汹涌: *an ~ of anger/ indignation.* 勃然发怒(愤怒).

up·take /ˈʌpteɪk; ˈʌpˌtek/ *n quick/slow on the ~,* (colloq) quick/slow to understand (sth said or hinted at). (口)敏(钝)于了解(所说或所暗示的事物); 领悟很快(慢).

up·tight /ˌʌpˈtaɪt; ˈʌpˈtaɪt/ *adj ~ (about),* (sl) (俚) 1 extremely tense; nervous: 极度紧张的; 神经质的; 情绪不自然的: *~ about an interview/examination.* 对于会见(考试)显得神经紧张. 2 uneasy; prejudiced; hostile; fearful. 不安的; 有偏见的; 敌意的; 害怕的.

up-to-date /ˌʌp tə ˈdeɪt; ˈʌptəˈdet/ *adj* modern; fashionable: 近代的; 时髦的: *~ clothes/ideas/books.* 时髦的衣服(新思想、新书).

up·town /ˌʌpˈtaʊn; ˈʌpˈtaʊn/ *adj, adv* (US) to or in the upper (the residential or non-business, non-commercial) part (of a town): (美)向或在上城区(即住宅区或非商业区): *~ New York;* 纽约的住宅区; *go ~.* 往上城区(住宅区).

up·turn /ˈʌptɜːn; ˈʌpˌtɜːn/ *n* upward turn; change for the better: 向上翻转的; 向上转; 情况好转: *an ~ in business/employment/production.* 营业(就业, 生产)情况好转.

up·ward /ˈʌpwəd; ˈʌpwəd/ *adj* moving or directed up: 上升的; 向上的: *the ~ trend of prices;* 物价上升的趋势; *an ~ glance.* 向上的一瞥. *~ (social) mob·il·ity,* ~ movement of sb from one class(3) to another. 社会地位之升高. □ *adv ~(s),* towards a higher place, level, etc: 向上地; 上升地: *The boat was on the beach, bottom ~s,* turned upside-down. 那船搁置在海滩上, 船底朝天. *Is our civilization moving ~?* 我们的文明还在继续上升吗? *~s of,* more than: 多于; 超过: *~s of a hundred people.* 超过一百人.

ura·nium /juˈreɪnɪəm; juˈreɪnɪəm/ *n* [U] heavy white metal (symbol **U**) with radioactive properties, a source of atomic energy. 铀(白色重金属, 符号U, 具放射性, 为原子能之来源).

Ura·nus /ˈjuəreɪnəs; ˈjurənəs/ *n* (astron) planet seventh in order from the sun. (天文)天王星(太阳系中的第七个行星). ⇨ the illus at **planet.** 参看 planet 之插图.

ur·ban /ˈɜːbən; ˈɜːbən/ *adj* of or in a town: 都市的; 在都市的: *the overcrowded ~ areas of England;* 英格兰过度拥挤的都市区; *~ guerrillas.* 城市游击队, ⇨ **guerrilla.** *~·ize* /-aɪz; -ˌaɪz/ *vt* [VP6A] change from a rural to an ~ character. 使都市化. *~·iz·ation* /ˌɜːbənaɪˈzeɪʃn US: -nɪˈz-; ˌɜːbənɪˈzeʃən/ *n* [U].

ur·bane /ɜːˈbeɪn; ɜˈben/ *adj* polite; polished in manners; elegant. 有礼貌的; 态度温文的; 文雅的. *~·ly adv* **ur·ban·ity** /ɜːˈbænətɪ; ɜˈbænətɪ/ *n* [U] refinement; politeness: (pl, *-ties)* courteous manners. 温文; 有礼; (复)礼貌(有礼貌的)态度.

ur·chin /ˈɜːtʃɪn; ˈɜːtʃɪn/ *n* mischievous small child; (often derog) poor destitute child. 顽童; 恶作剧的小孩; 贫苦无依的孩子.

Urdu /ˈuəduː; ˈurduː/ *adj, n* (of) one of the official languages of Pakistan. 乌尔都语(巴基斯坦法定语言之一); 乌尔都语的.

urge /ɜːdʒ; ɜːdʒ/ *vt* 1 [VP6A, 15B] *~ sb/sth (on/onward/forward),* push or drive on: 驱策; 推进: *With whip and spur he ~d his horse onward.* 他以马鞭及马刺策马前进. *The foreman ~d his workmen on.* 工头督促工人努力工作. 2 [VP6A, D, 9, 14, 17, 19C] *~ sb (to sth),* request earnestly; try to persuade; strongly recommend: 力请; 力劝; 敦促: *The salesman ~d me to buy a new car.* 那推销商向我大力推销一部新的汽车. *Agitators ~d the peasants to revolt/to revolution.* 煽动者怂恿农民反抗(革命). *He ~d leaving/our leaving/ that we should leave/us to leave.* 他极力主张离去(我们离去). 3 [VP6A, 14] *~ sth (on/upon sb),* press it (on him) with requests and arguments: 力陈; 力言: *He ~d on his pupils the importance of hard work.* 他向学生们力言用功的重要. *He ~d his youth/the fact that he was young.* 他强调他是年轻的. □ *n* [U, C] strong desire: 强烈的欲望: *He has/feels an ~/no ~ to travel.* 他很想(不太想)去旅行.

ur·gent /ˈɜːdʒənt; ˈɜːdʒənt/ *adj* 1 needing prompt decision or action: 需要立即决定或行动的; 急迫的: *An SOS is an ~ message.* SOS 是紧急呼救信号. *It is most ~ that the patient should get to hospital.* 那病人应该立即送医院. *The earthquake victims are in ~ need of medical supplies.* 地震灾民迫切需要医疗品. 2 (of a person, his voice, etc) showing that sth is ~; persistent in making a demand. (指人, 其声音等)表示某事物是急迫的; 坚持要求项要求的. *~·ly adv* **ur·gency** /ˈɜːdʒənsɪ; -dʒənsɪ/ *n* [U] need for, importance of, haste or prompt action: 紧急; 急迫: *a matter of great urgency.* 极为紧急的事件.

uric /ˈjuərɪk; ˈjurɪk/ *adj* of **urine.** 尿的.

urine /ˈjuərɪn; ˈjurɪn/ *n* [U] waste liquid which collects in the bladder and is discharged from the body. 尿. **uri·nal** /ˈjuərɪnl; ˈjurənl/ *n* 1 ('bed urinal') vessel into which ~ may be discharged (by sb ill in bed). 尿壶; (病人在床上使用的)便溺器. 2 (public 'urinal) place for the convenience of men who need to discharge ~. 小便所; (男人用的)公共小便处. **uri·nate** /ˈjuərɪneɪt; ˈjurəˌnet/ *vi* discharge ~. 排尿; 小便. **uri·nary** /ˈjuərɪnrɪ US: -nerɪ; ˈjurəˌnerɪ/ *adj* of ~: 尿的: *a urinary infection.* 尿毒.

urn /ɜːn; ɜːrn/ *n* 1 vase, usu with stem and base, esp as used for holding the ashes of a person whose body has been cremated. 瓮; (尤指)骨灰缸. 2 large metal container in which a drink such at tea or coffee is made or kept hot, eg in cafés and canteens. (烹茶或保温用的)金属质的)大茶壶; 大咖啡壶.

us /weak form: əs; əs; strong form: ʌs; ʌs/ *pron* object form of **we.** 为 we 的宾格形式.

usage /ˈjuːzɪdʒ US: ˈjuːs-; ˈjusɪdʒ/ *n* 1 [U] way of using sth; treatment: 对待: *Machines soon wear out under rough ~.* 机器如果使用不小心, 很快就会用坏. 2 [C, U] body of conventions governing the use of a language (esp those aspects not governed by grammatical rules): 语言的惯用法(尤指超出语法规则者): *a guide to English grammar and ~.* 英语语法及用

urns

法指南。 *Do you have difficulty in learning the finer points of ~?* 你在学习(语言)较为精微细致的用法上有困难吗? *Such ~s are not characteristic of educated speakers.* 这种用法并非有教养人士所惯用。 **3** [C, U] agreed codes of behaviour: 习俗; 惯例: *Industrialization and urbanization influence social ~(s).* 工业化及都市化影响社会习俗。

use[1] /juːs; jus/ *n* **1** [U] using or being used; condition of being used: 用; 使用; 利用; 使用状况: *the use of electricity for lighting;* 利用电力照明; *learn the use of tools;* 学习使用工具; *a room for the use of women only;* 妇女专用的房间; *for use only in case of fire;* 限火警时使用; 限用于消防; *bought for use, not for ornament.* 买来使用, 非为装饰。 **in use,** being used. 在使用中。 **out of use,** not being, no longer, used. (目前)不使用; 不再使用。 **come into use,** begin to be used: 开始被使用: *When did the word 'transistor' come into common use?* 晶体管一词何时开始被普遍使用? **go/fall out of use,** be no longer used: 被废弃; 不再被使用: *The custom has gone out of use.* 那风俗已被废弃。 **make (good/the best) use of,** use (well/in the best way): (好好地, 尽量地)利用: *You must make good use of any opportunities you have of practising English.* 你该好好地利用所有的机会练习英语。 **2** [C, U] purpose for which sth or sb is or may be employed; work that sth or sb is able to do: (某事物或某人的)用途; 用处; 效用; 功能: *a tool with many uses;* 有多种用途的工具; *find a use for sth;* 设法利用某物; *put sth to (a) good use;* 善为利用某物; *have no further use for sth.* 不再需要某物。 *I have no use for* (fig, dislike, have no patience with) *people who are always grumbling.* 我讨厌那些总是发牢骚的人。 **3** [U] value; advantage: 价值; 效用; 益处: *Is this of any use to you?* 这东西对你有什么益处吗? *It's no use your pretending/no use for you to pretend that you didn't know the rules.* 假装不懂规则对你无益。 *There isn't much use for that sort of thing nowadays.* 那种东西在当前没有多大价值了。 **4** [U] power of using: 使用的能力: *lose the use of one's legs,* become a cripple, unable to walk. 失去使用腿的能力; 变瘸; 不能行走。 **5** [U] right to use: 使用权: *give a friend the use of one's bike.* 让朋友使用自己的脚踏车。 **6** [U] usage; familiarity through continued practice: 惯用; 习惯; 习例: *In these cases use is the best guide.* 在这些事件中, 惯例是最好的指针。
use·ful /ˈjuːsfl; ˈjusfəl/ *adj* **1** helpful; producing good results: 有帮助的; 有效的; 有用的: *A spade is a useful tool.* 铲子是有用的工具。 **2** (colloq) capable, efficient: (口)能干的; 有效率的: *He's a useful member of the team.* 他是该队的一员猛将。 **use·fully** /-fəlɪ; -fəlɪ/ *adv* **use·ful·ness** *n* **use·less** *adj* **1** of no use; worthless: 无用的; 无价值的; 无(什)益的: *A car is useless without petrol.* 汽车如无汽油就没有用了。 **2** without result; ineffectual: 无结果的; 无效的: *It's useless to argue with them.* 同他们争辩论是不会有结果的。 **use·less·ly** *adv* **use·less·ness** *n*

use[2] /juːz; juz/ *vt* (*pt, pp* **used** /juːzd; juzd/) **1** [VP6A, 16A, 14] **use (for),** employ for a purpose: 用;

使用; 利用: *You use your legs when you walk.* 你走路时用腿。 *You use a knife to cut bread.* 你用刀切面包。 *A hammer is used for driving in nails.* 锤是用来敲钉子的。 *When persuasion failed they used force.* 劝说无效时, 他们就使用武力了。 *May I use* (= quote) *your name as a reference,* eg in an application for a post. 我可以把你(的名字)列为我的证明人吗? (如列在求职申请单上?) **2** [VP6A, 15B] **use sth (up),** consume: 消耗; 用(尽): *How much coal did we use last winter?* 去年冬天我们用了多少煤? *He has ~d up all his strength.* 他已耗尽了他的体力。 **3** [VP15A] behave towards: 对待: *Use others as you would like them to use you.* 你希望别人如何对待你, 你就该如何对待别人。 *He thinks himself ill used,* considers that he is badly treated. 他认为自己受到了虐待。 **used** /juːzd; juzd/ *adj* no longer new: 用旧了的: *used cars,* cars offered for sale after they have been used and are no longer in new condition. (出售的)旧汽车。 **us·able** /ˈjuːzəbl; ˈjuzəbl/ *adj* that can be used, that is fit to be used. 可被使用的; 适宜使用的。 **user** *n* sb or sth that uses: 使用者(指人或物): *There are more telephone users in the USA than in any other country.* 美国使用电话的人数多于任何其他国家。

used[1] /juːst; just/ *anom fin* (neg 否定式为 **used not;** **usedn't/usen't** /ˈjuːsnt; ˈjusn̩t/; (colloq) (口) **didn't use**) *~ to* + *inf,* (indicating a constant or frequent practice in the past): (~ to + 不定式表示过去经常的习惯): *That's where I ~ to live when I was a child.* 那是我幼年的住处。*Life isn't so easy here as it ~ to be.* 如今在此地谋生已经不像往日那么容易了。*You ~ to smoke a pipe, use(d)n't you* (or *didn't you*)? 你过去是抽烟斗的, 是不是? *Didn't you use to smoke a pipe?* 你过去不是抽烟斗吗? **there ~ to be,** (indicating the existence of sth in the past): (表示过去某事物的存在): *There ~ to be some trees in this field, use(d)n't there/didn't there?* 这片地上以前有几棵树, 不是吗?

used[2] /juːst; just/ *adj ~ to,* accustomed to: 习于; 惯于; 适应于: *He's quite ~ to hard work/working hard.* 他颇习惯于辛苦工作。*I'm not ~ to being spoken to in that rude way.* 我不惯于别人对我那样粗鲁地讲话。*You will soon be ~ to it.* 你很快就会适应(它)。

usher /ˈʌʃə(r); ˈʌʃə/ *n* **1** person who shows people to their seats in theatres, cinemas, etc. (戏院, 电影院等的)招待员; 引座员。 **2** doorkeeper in a law court, etc. (法院等处的)门房; 司阍。 □ *vt* **1** [VP15B, 14] lead, conduct: 引导; 招待: *The girl ~ed me to my seat* (in a cinema). (电影院中)引座小姐引我至我的座位上。 **2** [VP15B] ~ *sth in,* herald, announce: 预报; 预示; 宣布: *The change of government ~ed in a period of prosperity.* 政府的变动预示一个繁荣时期的来临。 **~ette** /ˌʌʃəˈret; ˌʌʃəˈɛt/ *n* girl or woman ~ (1). (戏院, 电影院等处的)女引座员; 女服务员。

usual /ˈjuːʒl; ˈjuʒʊəl/ *adj* such as commonly happens; customary: 通常的; 寻常的; 平素的; 通例的: *Tea is considered to be the ~ drink of British people.* 茶被认为是英国人的日常饮料。 *He arrived later than ~.* 他到得比平常晚。 *As is ~ with many picnickers, they left a lot of litter behind them.* 象许多野餐者一样, 他们留下了大堆的垃圾。*When the accident happened, the ~ crowd quickly gathered.* 那意外事件发生时, 照例围观的人群很快地聚拢来了。 **as ~,** as is ~: 如平常: *You're late, as ~.* 你象平常一样迟到了。 *The meeting was, as ~, badly attended.* 那次会议象平常一样参加的人不多。 **~ly** /ˈjuːʒəlɪ; ˈjuʒʊəlɪ/ *adv* in the way that is ~: 通常地; 通例地: *What do you do on Sundays?* 你星期天通常做什么呢? *He's ~ly early.* 他通常早到。

usurer /ˈjuːʒərə(r); ˈjuʒərə/ *n* person whose business is usury. 放高利贷者。

usurp /juːˈzɜːp; juˈzʌp/ *vt* [VP6A] wrongfully take (sb's power, authority, position): 霸占; 篡夺; 僭取(某人的权力、权威、地位): *~ the throne.* 篡夺王位。 **~er** *n* person who does this. 篡夺者; 僭取者; 霸占者。 **usur·pa·tion** /ˌjuːzɜːˈpeɪʃn; ˌjuzəˈpeʃən/ *n* [C, U] (instance

usury /'juːʒərɪ; 'juʒərɪ/ n [U] (practice of) lending money, esp at a rate of interest considered to be too high; such high interest. (放)高利贷; 高利. **usuri·ous** /juːˈʒjʊərɪəs US: -ʒʊ-; juˈʒʊrɪəs/ adj of ~: (放)高利贷的; 高利的: a usurious transaction; 一笔高利贷; a usurious rate of interest. 高利利率.

uten·sil /juːˈtensl; juˈtensl/ n instrument, tool, etc esp for use in the house: 器皿; 器具; (尤指)家庭用具: 'household ~s, eg pots, pans, brushes; 家庭用具(如壶、锅、刷子); 'writing ~s, eg paper, pens, ink. 书写用具(如纸、笔、墨水).

uterus /'juːtərəs; 'jutərəs/ n (anat) womb. (解剖)子宫. ⇨ the illus at reproduce. 参看 reproduce 之插图. **uter·ine** /-ɪn; -tərɪn/ adj of the ~. 子宫的.

utili·tar·ian /juːˌtɪlɪˈteərɪən; ˌjutɪləˈtɛrɪən/ adj 1 characterized by usefulness rather than by beauty, truth, goodness. 以实用为主的; 功利的; 以实用、美、善、美为目的的. 2 of the U~s and their ideas. 功利主义者的; 功利主义者的观念的. □ n U~, supporter of ~ism. 功利主义者. ~·ism /-ɪzəm; -ɪzəm/ n [U] political and moral theory that the best rule of life is to aim at 'the greatest happiness of the greatest number', actions being considered right or wrong according as they help or hinder the achievement of this aim. (政治及道德上的)功利主义(认为生活最好的准则旨在增进'绝大多数人最大的幸福', 并以此为衡量行为的标准).

util·ity /juːˈtɪlətɪ; juˈtɪlətɪ/ n (pl -ties) 1 [U] quality of being useful: 有用; 实用; 效用: (attrib) (用作定语) '~ van/truck, one that can be used for various purposes. 可作多种用途的篷车(货车). 2 [C] (public) ~, public service such as the supply of water, electricity, gas, or a bus or railway service. 公共事业(指自来水, 电, 瓦斯, 公共汽车, 铁路等).

util·ize /'juːtɪlaɪz US: -təlaɪz; 'jutl̩ˌaɪz/ vt [VP6A] make use of; find a use for. 利用; 使有用; 化为有用. **util·iz·able** /-əbl; -əbl/ adj that can be ~d or put to a useful purpose. 有用的;可利用的. **util·iz·ation** /ˌjuːtɪlaɪ-ˈzeɪʃn US: -təlɪ'z-; ˌjutl̩ə'zeʃən/ n [U] utilizing or being ~d. 利用; 被利用.

ut·most /'ʌtməʊst; 'ʌtˌmost/ adj most extreme; greatest: 极度的; 极端的; 最大的: in the ~ danger. 处于极端危险中; of the ~ importance; 极为重要; with the ~ care. 极为当心. □ n one's/the ~, the most that is possible: 极限; 竭尽所能: do one's ~; 竭尽全力; exert/enjoy oneself to the ~. 尽力而为(尽情享受). That is tine ~ I can do. 那是我所能做到的极限.

Uto·pia /juːˈtəʊpɪə; juˈtopɪə/ n [C] imaginary perfect social and political system. 乌托邦; 理想国. **Uto·pian** /-pɪən; -pɪən/ adj (also ~ u-) attractive and desirable but impracticable: 乌托邦的; 理想而不切合实际的; 空中楼阁的: a ~n scheme for giving all old people a pension of £100 a week. 计划给予所有老年人每周一百英镑养老金的一项不切实际的构想.

ut·ter[1] /'ʌtə(r); 'ʌtə/ adj complete; total: 完全的; 全然的: ~ darkness; 漆黑; 全然黑暗; an ~ slander. 十足的诽谤. She's an ~ stranger to me. 我根本不认识她. ~·ly adv 1 completely. 完全地. 2 to the depths of one's being: 极致; 彻底; 透顶: She ~ly detests him. 她对他憎恶透顶.

ut·ter[2] /'ʌtə(r); 'ʌtə/ vt [VP6A] 1 make (a sound or sounds) with the mouth: 以口发出(声音): ~ a sigh/a cry of pain. 叹息(发出痛苦的喊叫). 2 say: 说; 讲: the last words he ~ed. 他临终之言. 3 put (false money, etc) into circulation. 流通; 使用(假钞票等). ~·ance /'ʌtərəns; 'ʌtərəns/ n 1(sing only) way of speaking: (仅用单数)说法; 语调; 发音: a clear/defective/very rapid ~ance. 清晰(有缺陷, 很快)的语调. 2 [C] sth said; spoken word or words. 所说的话; 言词. 3 [U] ~ing: 说; 讲; 表达: give ~ance to (one's feelings, etc), express in words. 以言词表达(感情等).

ut·ter·most /'ʌtəməʊst; 'ʌtəˌmost/ adj, n = utmost. 最远的; 最大的; 极度的; 最大限度: the ~ ends of the earth. 天涯海角.

uvula /'juːvjʊlə; 'juvjələ/ n (anat) small piece of fleshy matter hanging from the back of the roof of the mouth. (解剖)悬雍垂; 小舌. ⇨ the illus at mouth. 参看 mouth 之插图. **uvu·lar** /-lə(r); -lə/ adj of the ~. 悬雍垂的; 小舌的.

ux·ori·ous /ʌkˈsɔːrɪəs; ʌkˈsɔrɪəs/ adj excessively fond of one's wife. 过度宠爱妻子的;对妻子言听计从的. ~·ly adv ~·ness n

V v

V,v /viː; vi/ n (pl V's, v's) 1 the 22nd letter of the English alphabet; symbol for the Roman numeral 5. 英文字母的第二十二个字母; 罗马数字的五. ⇨ App 4. 参看附录四. 2 V-shaped thing: V 形物: the V sign, sign made by the hand with the palm outwards and the first and second fingers spread to form a V (for victory). 胜利手势(以食指和中指伸出作 V 形, 表示胜利). V 1, 2 /ˌviː ˈwʌn, ˈtuː; ˌvi ˈwʌn, ˈtu/, flying bomb. V 1, 2 型飞弹. ⇨ doodlebug.

vac /væk; væk/ n (colloq, abbr of vacation (= holidays). (口)假日 (为 vacation 之略).

va·cancy /'veɪkənsɪ; 'vekənsɪ/ n (pl -cies) 1 [U] condition of being empty or unoccupied. 空; 未占用. 2 [U, C] unoccupied space; blank: 空处; 空白; 空间: look over the edge of a cliff into ~. 由悬崖边缘望入空际. 3 [U] lack of ideas or intelligence; lack of concentration. 头脑空虚; 茫然若失; 失神. 4 [C] position in business, etc for which sb is needed: 空缺: good vacancies for typists and clerks. 待遇不错的打字员和职员的空缺.

va·cant /'veɪkənt; 'vekənt/ adj 1 empty: 空的: gaze into ~ space. 凝视浩瀚空际. 2 not occupied by anyone: 未被占用的: a ~ room, eg in a hotel; (旅馆等的)空房间; apply for a ~ position, eg in an office. 申请(如某机构中的)空缺职位. ~ possession, phrase used in advertisements of houses, etc declaring that the buyer can enter into immediate occupation. 空产可立即迁入(卖房子等的广告用语). 3 (of time) not filled with any activity; leisured. (指时间)未安排活动的; 空档的; 空闲的. 4 (of the mind) unoccupied with thought; (of the eyes) showing no signs of thought or interest: (指心智)空虚的; (指眼睛)茫然的: with ~ looks; 带着茫然的神情; a ~ stare/expression. 茫然的凝视(表情). ~·ly adv

va·cate /vəˈkeɪt US: 'veɪkeɪt; 'veket/ vt [VP6A] 1 give up living in: 搬出; 迁出: ~ a house/rented rooms. 迁出房屋(所租的公寓). 2 leave unoccupied: 空出; 腾出: ~ one's seat. 空出自己的座位. 3 (formal) give up possession or use of. (正式用语)放弃.

va·ca·tion /vəˈkeɪʃn US: veɪ; veˈkeʃən/ n 1 [U] (formal) vacating: (正式用语)放弃; 空出; 迁出: His ~ of a good position in the Civil Service was unwise 他放弃政府机构的一个好职位诚属不智. 2 [C] weeks during which universities and law courts stop work: (大学的)假期; (法庭的)休庭期: the long ~; 长假; the summer ~; 暑假; the Christmas ~. 圣诞假期. 3 [C] (esp US) holiday (2); any time or period of rest and freedom from work. (尤美)假日; 休息日; 休假. on ~, on holiday. 度假. □ vi [VP3A] ~ at/in, (US) spend a holiday: (美)在…度假: ~ing in Florida. 在佛罗里达州度假. ~·ist /-ʃənɪst; -ʃənɪst/ n (US) person

on ~ (3). (美)度假者。

vac·ci·nate /'væksɪneɪt US: -səneɪt; 'væksn̩,et/ vt [VP6A, 14/ ~ sb (against sth), protect (sb) (against a disease) by injecting vaccine. 为(某人)种痘, 接种疫苗; 打预防针 (以预防某种疾病)。 **vac·ci·na·tion** /,væksɪ'neɪʃn, ,væksn̩'eʃən/ n [C, U] (instance of) vaccinating or being ~d. 种痘; 接种疫苗; 其实例。

vac·cine /'væksiːn US: væk'siːn; 'væksin/ n [C, U] substance injected into the bloodstream, used to protect persons from a disease by causing them to have a slight, but not dangerous, form of the disease. 疫苗; 痘苗。

vac·il·late /'væsɪleɪt; 'væsl̩,et/ vi [VP2A, 3A] (between), waver; hesitate; be uncertain (in opinion, etc): (在意见等方面)犹豫; 迟疑; 踌躇: ~ between hope and fear. 既抱着希望又感到恐惧。 **vac·il·la·tion** /,væsɪ'leɪʃn, ,væsl̩'eʃən/ n [C, U] (instance of) vacillating. 犹豫; 迟疑; 其实例。

vacu·ous /'vækjʊəs; 'vækjʊəs/ adj showing or suggesting absence of thought or intelligence: 没有思想的; 没有头脑的; 空虚的; 愚蠢的; 茫然的: a ~ expression/stare/remark/laugh. 茫然的表情(茫然的凝视; 空洞的话; 傻笑)。 ~·ly adv vacu·ity /və'kjuːətɪ; væ'kjuətɪ/ n (pl -ties) state of being ~; (pl) ~ remarks, acts, etc. (思想或智力的)贫乏; 空虚; 愚蠢; 茫然; (复)空洞的话; 愚蠢的行为等。

vac·uum /'vækjʊəm; 'vækjʊəm/ n (pl ~s or, in science, 或在科学用语中作, -ua /-jʊə; -jʊə/) space completely empty of substance or gas(es); space in a container from which the air has been pumped out. 真空; 真空状态。 '~ **cleaner**, apparatus which takes up dust, dirt, etc by suction. 真空吸尘器。 '~ **flask/bottle**, one having a ~ between its inner and outer walls, keeping the contents at an unchanging temperature. 热水瓶; 保温瓶。 ⇨ **thermos.** '~ **pump**, (a) pump to create a partial ~ in a vessel. 抽气唧筒; 真空唧筒。 (b) pump in which a partial ~ is used to raise water. 真空式抽水机。 '~ **tube/valve**, sealed glass tube with an almost perfect ~ in it, for observing the passage of an electric charge. 真空管。

vade-mecum /,veɪdɪ 'miːkəm; 'vedɪ'mikəm/ n [C] small handbook which can be carried about and used for reference. (随身携带以供参考的)便览; 手册。

vaga·bond /'vægəbɒnd; 'vægə,bɑnd/ adj having no fixed living-place; habitually wandering: 无固定住所的; 游荡的: live a ~ life. 过游荡生活。 □ ~ Gypsies. 流浪的吉卜赛人。 □ n ~ person; tramp. 漂泊者; 流浪者。

va·gary /'veɪgərɪ; və'ɡɛrɪ/ n [C] (pl -ries) strange, unusual act or idea, esp one for which there seems to be no good reason: 怪异的行为或观念(尤指似乎无良好理由者): 异想天开: the vagaries of fashion/of human emotions. 时尚(人类感情)所表现出的怪异。

va·gina /və'dʒaɪnə; və'dʒaɪnə/ n (anat) passage (in a female mammal) from the external genital organs to the womb (colloq 'birth canal'). (解剖)阴道(口语称 birth canal 产道)。戾。 ⇨ the illus at **reproduce.** 参看 reproduce 之插图。 **vag·inal** /'vædʒaɪnl; və'dʒaɪnl/ adj

va·grant /'veɪgrənt; 'veɡrənt/ adj leading a wandering life: 生活无定居的; 过流浪生活的: ~ tribes/musicians; 生活无定居的部落(各处游荡的音乐师); wandering: 漂泊的; 游荡的; 飘忽不定的: lead a ~ life; 过流浪生活; ~ thoughts. 飘忽不定的思想。 □ n person; vagabond or tramp. 漂泊者; 流浪者; 游民。 **va·grancy** /-rənsɪ; -rənsɪ/ n [U] being a ~. 漂泊; 流浪; 游荡。

vague /veɪg; veɡ/ adj (-r, -st) 1 not clear or distinct: 不清楚的; 模糊的; 含混的: ~ outlines; 模糊的轮廓; ~ demands; 含糊的要求。 I haven't the ~st idea what they want. 我丝毫不知道他们需要什么。 2 (of persons, their looks, behaviour) uncertain, suggesting uncertainty (about needs, intentions, etc). (指人、其表情、行为)含糊

的; 茫然的; (有关需要、意向等)不确知的。 ~·ly adv ~·ness n

vain /veɪn; ven/ adj (-er, -est) 1 without use, value, meaning or result: 无益的; 无效的; 徒然的; 无结果的: a ~ attempt; 徒劳的尝试; ~ hopes/promises. 无结果的希望(许诺)。 **2 in ~, (a)** without the desired result: 无效地; 无结果地; 徒然: try in ~ to do sth. 试图做某事而无结果。 All our work was in ~. 我们的一切工作均归徒然。 **(b)** without due reverence, honour or respect: 随便地; 冒渎地; 不尊敬地: take the name of God in ~, use the word 'God' irreverently; 妄用或滥用上帝之名; take a person's name in ~, use it lightly, disrespectfully. 不尊敬地使用一个人的名字。 **3** having too high an opinion of one's looks, abilities, etc; conceited: (对自己的容貌、能力等)自视过高的; 自负的: He's as ~ as a peacock. 他极其自负。 She's ~ of her beauty. 她自负貌美。 ~·**'glory** n extreme vanity or pride in oneself 极度的自负或自鸣; 虚荣。 ~·**'glorious** adj full of ~glory; conceited and boastful. 虚荣心强的; 自满而浮夸的。 ~·ly adv **1** in ~. 无效地; 无结果地。 **2** in a conceited manner. 自负地。

val·ance, val·ence /'væləns; 'vælɛns/ n short curtain or frill, round the frame or the canopy of a bedstead, above a window, or under a shelf. (床架四周, 窗子上方或架子下方的)短帷幔; 挂布。

vale /veɪl; vel/ n (liter except in place-names) valley (文, 不用于地名)谷。

val·edic·tion /,vælɪ'dɪkʃn; ,vælə'dɪkʃən/ n [C] (words used in) saying farewell. 告别; 告别辞。

val·edic·tory /,vælɪ'dɪktərɪ; ,vælə'dɪktərɪ/ adj relating to, in the nature of, a farewell: 告别的; 辞别性的: a ~ speech. 告别演说。

val·ence[1] /'væləns; 'vɛləns/ n **1** [U] (chem) capacity of an atom to combine with, or to be replaced by, another atom. (化学)原子价(原子与其他原子相结合或由其他原子所代替的能力)。 **2** [C] (US) (美) = **valency.**

val·ence[2] /'væləns; 'væl'əns/ n ⇨ **valance.**

val·ency /'veɪlənsɪ; 'vɛlənsɪ/ n (pl -cies) (chem) unit of **valence**[1]: (化学)原子价之单位: Carbon has 4 valencies. 碳是四价。

val·en·tine /'væləntaɪn; 'vælən,taɪn/ n (letter, card, etc, usu anonymous, sent on St V~'s Day, 14 Feb, to a) sweetheart. 在二月十四日圣瓦伦丁节寄给情人的信或卡片等(寄发者通常匿名); 情人。

val·erian /və'lɪərɪən; və'lɪrɪən/ n [U] kinds of small perennial plant with strong-smelling pink or white flowers; root of this used medically. 缬草; 缬草根(作药用)。

valet /'vælɪt; 'vælɪt/ n manservant who looks after his master's clothes; employee in a hotel with similar duties. 专司主人衣服的男仆; 旅馆中洗烫衣服的人。 □ vt [VP6A] act as ~ to: 为…管理衣服; 替(某旅馆)洗烫衣服: The hotel has a good ~ing service. 那旅馆有良好的洗烫衣服的服务。

val·etu·di·nar·ian /,vælɪtjuːdɪ'neərɪən US: -tuːd-; ,vælə,tjudn'ɛrɪən/ adj (formal) of poor health; unduly troubled about, almost wholly occupied with, the state of one's health. (正式用语)有病的; 健康不佳的; 过份为自己的健康担忧的。 □ n ~ person. 健康不佳者; 过份为自己的健康担忧者。

val·iant /'vælɪənt; 'væljənt/ adj brave. 勇敢的; 豪勇的。 ~·ly adv

valid /'vælɪd; 'vælɪd/ adj **1** (legal) effective because made or done with the correct formalities: (法律)有效的: a ~ claim/marriage. 有效的要求(婚姻)。 **2** (of contracts, etc) having force in law: (指合约等)法律有效的, 有法律效力的: ~ for three months; 三个月内有效; a ticket ~ for one single journey between London and Dover. 伦敦与多佛间的单程有效票。 **3** (of arguments, reasons, etc) well based; sound: (指论据、理由等)有充分根据的; 正当的; 健全的: raise ~ objections to a scheme. 对

某一计划提出有力的反对。 ~·**ly** adv ~·**ity** /vəˈlɪdɪtɪ; vəˈlɪdətɪ/ n [U] state of being ~. 有效; 效力; 正确。
vali·date /ˈvælɪdeɪt; ˈvæləˌdet/ vt [VP6A] make ~; 使有效; 使有法律效力; 使有充分根据: ~ate a claim. 使一要求生效。

va·lise /vəˈliːz US: vəˈliːs; vəˈlis/ n small leather bag for clothes, etc during a journey; soldier's kitbag. (装衣服等的)皮制小旅行袋; 兵士的背囊。

val·ley /ˈvælɪ; ˈvælɪ/ n (pl -leys) stretch of land between hills or mountains, often with a river flowing through it. 谷; 山谷(通常有河流穿过); 溪谷; 河谷。 ⇨ the illus at **mountain**. 参看 mountain 之插图。

val·our (US = **valor**) /ˈvælə(r); ˈvælɚ/ n [U] bravery, esp in war. 勇敢; (尤指在战争中)英勇; 勇武。 **val·or·ous** /ˈvælərəs; ˈvælərəs/ adj brave. 勇敢的; 英勇的。

valu·able /ˈvæljʊəbl; ˈvæljʊəbl/ adj of great value, worth or use: 有很大价值的; 贵重的; 很有用的: a ~ discovery. 有价值的发现。 □ n (usu pl) sth of much value, eg articles of gold, jewels. (通常用复数)贵重物品(如黄金、珠宝等)。

valu·ation /ˌvæljʊˈeɪʃn; ˌvæljʊˈeʃən/ n [U] process of deciding the value of sth or sb; [C] the value that is decided upon: 评价; 估价; 估定的价格; 价值: The surveyors arrived at widely different ~s. 鉴定人作了截然不同的估价。 It is unwise to accept a person at his own ~, the opinion which he has of himself. 相信一个人对他自己的评价是不智的。

value /ˈvæljuː; ˈvælju/ n **1** [U] quality of being useful or desirable: 有用性; 重要性; 价值: the ~ of walking as an exercise. 步行的运动价值。 **2** [U] worth of sth when compared with sth else: 某物与他物比较时的价值; 某物的相对价值: This book will be of great/little/some/no ~ to him in his studies. 这本书对于他的研究(与其他书比起来)有很大(很小、一些、没有)价值。 **3** [C, U] worth of sth in terms of money or other goods for which it can be exchanged: 交换价值; 交易价值; 购买价值; 价格: Is the ~ of the American dollar likely to decline? 美金价格可能会下降吗? Does this volume give you good ~ for your money? 这本书值得你所花的钱吗? The property is going down in ~ all the time. 那地产一直在落价。 Market ~s rose sharply last week. 市场价格上周涨得很凶。 ~ added tax, (abbr 略作 **VAT**) tax on the rise in ~ of a product at each stage of manufacture and marketing. 增值税; 增值税。 **4** [U] what sth is considered to be worth (contrasted with the price obtainable): 价值(与该物的卖价(索价)相对): I've been offered £500 for my old car but its ~ is much higher. 有人出价五百英镑,但是它的价值远高于此数。 **5** [C, U] **(a)** (in music) full time indicated by a note: (音乐)音符所表示的音长: Give the note its full ~. 把这一音符的音长充分唱足。 **(b)** (in painting) relation of light and shade. (绘画)明暗的关系。 **(c)** (in language) meaning; effect: (语言)意义; 意旨; 效果: use a word with all its poetic ~. 充分发挥一个词的诗意。 **(d)** (pl) standards: (复)标准: moral/artistic ~s. 道德(艺术)标准。 ~·**less** adj without ~; worthless. 无价值的; 无用的。 □ vt [VP6A, 15A, 16B] **1** estimate the money ~ of: 估…的价格; 定…价: He ~d the house for me at £20000. 那幢房子他替我估价两万英镑。 **2** regard highly; have a high opinion of: 尊重; 重视: ~ sb's advice. 尊重某人的劝告。 Do you ~ her as a secretary? 你重视她的秘书才干吗? ~**r** n person whose profession is to estimate the money ~ of property, land, etc. 职业估价者。

valve /vælv; vælv/ n **1** (sorts of) mechanical device for controlling the flow of air, liquid, gas or electrons in one direction only: (控制空气、液体、瓦斯或电子使之单向流动的)制阀; 活门; 活瓣; 汽门: the inlet/outlet ~s of a petrol or steam engine; 汽油发动机或蒸汽机的进气(排气)门; the ~ of a bicycle tyre. 脚踏车轮胎的气瓣。 ⇨ the illus at **bicycle**. 参看 bicycle 之插图。 **2** structure

in the heart or in a blood-vessel allowing the blood to flow in one direction only. (心脏或血管的)瓣膜。 **3** (**'radio**) ~, thermionic ~ used in a radio (US 美 = tube). 真空管。 ⇨ **thermionic**. **4** device in musical wind instruments, eg a cornet, for changing the pitch by changing the length of the column of air. (管乐器, 如短号,用以改变音调的)栓塞。 **val·vu·lar** /ˈvælvjʊlə(r); ˈvælvjələ/ adj of the ~s of the heart or blood-vessels: (心脏或血管的)瓣膜的: valvular disease of the heart. 心脏瓣膜病。

va·moose /vəˈmuːs; væˈmus/ vi (US sl) go away quickly. (美俚)匆匆离去; 跑开。

vamp[1] /væmp; væmp/ n upper front part of a boot or shoe. 靴或鞋前端的鞋面; 鞋面皮。 □ vt, vi **1** [VP 6A, 15B] repair (a boot or shoe) by putting a new ~ on. 换修(靴或鞋)的鞋面。 ~ **up**, (fig) make sth from odds and ends: (喻)以零星材料凑成某物: ~ up some lectures out of old notes. 利用旧稿材料拼写成几篇演讲。 **2** [VP6A, 2A] make up (a tune) for a song; improvise a musical accompaniment to a song or dance. 谱(曲); 即席为某歌或舞伴奏或作伴奏曲。

vamp[2] /væmp; væmp/ n seductive woman who uses her attractions to exploit men. 以美色利用男子或榨取男子金钱的妇人。

vam·pire /ˈvæmpaɪə(r); ˈvæmpaɪr/ n **1** (in stories) reanimated corpse that leaves its grave at night and sucks the blood of sleeping persons; ruthless ill-disposed person who preys on others. (故事中的)夜间离开扒坟墓并吸取睡觉者的血); 剥削他人的恶汉; 吸血者。 **2** '~ (**bat**), sorts of blood-sucking bat. 吸血蝙蝠。

van[1] /væn; væn/ n **1** covered or roofed motor-vehicle for carrying and delivering goods: (有盖的)货车: the 'baker's van; 装载面包的货车; a 'furniture van. 搬运家具的货车。 **2** (GB) roofed railway carriage for goods: (英)有顶盖的铁路货车厢: the 'luggage van. 行李车。

van[2] /væn; væn/ n **1** front or leading part of an army or fleet in battle. (作战时军队或舰队的)前锋; 前卫; 先头部队; 先驱。 **2** = **vanguard**.

Van·dal /ˈvændl; ˈvændl/ n one of a Germanic tribe that overran Gaul, Spain and N Africa in the 4th and 5th cc and sacked Rome in 455 AD. 汪达尔人(日耳曼一部族,约第四、五世纪时,横扫高卢、西班牙及北非,并于纪元 455 年攻掠罗马)。 ⇨ **Goth**.

van·dal /ˈvændl; ˈvændl/ n person who wilfully destroys works of art or public and private property, spoils the beauties of nature, etc. 故意破坏艺术品、天然美景等的人; 艺术品或公私财产等的破坏者。 ~·**ism** /-dəlɪzəm; -dlˌɪzəm/ n [U] behaviour characteristic of ~s. 艺术品或公私财产等的破坏行为。 ~·**ize** /-dəlaɪz; -dlˌaɪz/ vt [VP6A] wilfully destroy or spoil (as above). 故意破坏艺术品或公私财产等。

vane /veɪn; ven/ n **1** arrow or pointer on the top of a building, turned by the wind so as to show its direction. 风向标; 风信旗。 **2** blade of a propeller, sail of a windmill, or other flat surface acted on by wind or water. (螺旋桨、风车、水轮等的)叶; 翼。

van·guard /ˈvænɡɑːd; ˈvænˌɡɑrd/ n **1** advance party of an army, etc as a guard against surprise attack. (军队以防突袭之)先锋; 先头部队。 **2** those persons who lead a procession or (fig) a movement: (行列之)领队; (喻)(运动之)领导人; 先驱: in the ~ of scientific progress. 在领导科学进步的人物中。

va·nilla /vəˈnɪlə; vəˈnɪlə/ n **1** [C] (pods or beans of) plant with sweet-smelling flowers. 香草; 香草荚。 **2** [U] flavouring substance from ~ beans or synthetic product used for it: (自香草荚中提出或由人工合成的)香精: ~ custard; 香草乳蛋糕; two ~ ices. 两份香草冰淇淋。

van·ish /ˈvænɪʃ; ˈvænɪʃ/ vi [VP2A] suddenly disappear; fade away gradually; go out of existence: 突然不见; 逐渐消散; 消灭: Your prospects of success have ~ed. 你成功的希望已经消失了。 The thief ran into the crowd and ~ed from sight. 那贼跑进入群中

不见了。 **~ into thin air**, disappear suddenly and completely. 突然完全消失; 突然不见。 '**~·ing cream**, cosmetic cream quickly absorbed into the skin. 粉底霜 (一种涂后很快即为皮肤所吸收的面霜)。 '**~·ing point**, (in perspective) point at which all parallel lines in the same plane appear to meet. (透视法)没影点(同一平面上所有平行线似乎相会合的那一点)。

van·ity /'vænətɪ; 'vænətɪ/ *n* (*pl* -**ties**) **1** [U] conceit; having too high an opinion of one's looks, abilities, etc: 自负; 自大; 虚夸; 虚荣心: *do sth out of ~;* 出于虚荣心而做某事; *tickle sb's ~*, do or say sth that pleases his conceit; 迎合某人的虚荣心(说或做某事以满足其虚荣心); *injured ~*, resentment caused by some slight or humiliation. 受到伤害的虚荣心。 '**~ bag/case**, bag or case carried by the owner for a small mirror, cosmetics, etc. (随身携带的)小梳妆袋(盒)。 **2** [U] worthlessness; quality of being unsatisfying, without true value: 无价值; 空虚; 无真实价值因而不能令人满足的性质: *the ~ of pleasure;* 欢乐的空虚; [C] vain, worthless thing or act. 空虚而无价值的东西或行为。

van·quish /'væŋkwɪʃ; 'vænkwɪʃ/ *vt* [VP6A] (liter) conquer. (文)征服; 克服。

van·tage /'vɑːntɪdʒ *US:* 'væn-; 'væntɪdʒ/ *n* **1** advantage: 优势; 好机会; 有利之点: '**~-ground**; 有利地形; *point of ~*. 有利地位。 '**~-point** (lit or fig) place from which one has a (good) view of sth (advantageous) position. (字面或喻)(良好的)观望地方; 有利地势; 地利。 ⇨ **coign**. **2** (in tennis) first point scored after deuce. (网球)平手后获得的第一分。

vapid /'væpɪd; 'væpɪd/ *adj* dull; uninteresting: 乏味的; 索然的; 无趣味的: ~ *conversation;* 乏味的谈话; *the ~ utterances of the clergy*. 教士的索然无味的言词。 **~·ly** *adv* **~·ness** *n* **va·pid·ity** /væ'pɪdətɪ; və'pɪdətɪ/ *n* [U] state of being ~; (*pl*, -**ties**) ~ remarks. 索然乏味; 乏味的话语。

va·por·ize /'veɪpəraɪz; 'vepə,raɪz/ *vt, vi* [VP6A, 2A] convert into, become, vapour. (使)化为蒸汽; 蒸发。 **va·por·iz·ation** /veɪpəraɪ'zeɪʃn *US:* -rɪ'z-; ,vepərə'zeʃən/ *n*

va·por·ous /'veɪpərəs; 'vepəs/ *adj* **1** full of, like, vapour. 多蒸汽的; 似蒸汽的。 **2** (fig) full of idle fancies; unsubstantial. (喻)多妄想的; 无实质内容的。

va·pour (*US* = **va·por**) /'veɪpə(r); 'vepə/ *n* **1** [U] steam; mist; gaseous form to which certain substances may be reduced by heat: 汽; 雾; 烟雾; 蒸汽; *water ~*. 水(蒸)汽。 '**~-bath** (enclosed space or apparatus for a) bath in ~ or steam. 蒸汽浴; 蒸汽浴室或设备。 '**~ trails**, ⇨ **trail**(1). **2** [C] unsubstantial thing; sth imagined: 无实质之物; 空想的事物; 幻想的事物: *the ~s of a disordered mind*. 精神错乱者的幻象。 **3 the ~s**, (archaic) melancholy. (古)忧郁。

vari·able /'veərɪəbl; 'veərɪəbl/ *adj* varying; changeable: 变化的; 可变的; 易变的: ~ *winds;* 方向不定的风; ~ *standards;* 可变易的标准; ~ *costs*, (accounting) costs that go up or down according to the quantity of goods produced. (会计)可变成本(随产量之多少升降者)。 *His mood/temper is ~*. 他的心情(脾气)变化无常。 □ *n* ([C]) ~ thing or quantity; factor which may vary, eg in an experiment. 可变物; 可变量; (实验等中之)变量; 变数; 变项。 **vari·ably** /-əblɪ; -əblɪ/ *adv* **~·ness** *n* **vari·bil·ity** /ˌveərɪ'bɪlətɪ; ,veərɪ'bɪlətɪ/ *n* [U] quality of being ~; tendency to vary. 变化性; 变化的倾向; 易变。

vari·ance /'veərɪəns; 'veərɪəns/ *n* [U] **at ~ (with)**, in disagreement; having a difference of opinion: (与…) 不和; 意见不同; 龃龉: *The two sisters have been at ~ for years*. 这两姐妹不和睦已有若干年了。 *We are at ~ among ourselves/at ~ with the others*. 我们彼此(与他人)不和。

vari·ant /'veərɪənt; 'veərɪənt/ *adj* different or alternative: 不同的; 变异的; 替换的: ~ *spellings of a word* (eg 'tire' and 'tyre'). 一词的不同拼法(如 tire 和

tyre)。 □ *n* ~ form (eg of spelling). 替换的形式(如指拼词法)。

vari·ation /veərɪ'eɪʃn; ,veərɪ'eʃən/ *n* **1** [C, U] (degree of) varying or being variant: 异量; 异差; 变异的程度: ~*s(s) of pressure/temperature;* 压力(温度)的异差; ~*s in public opinion*. 舆论的变异。 **2** [C] (music) simple melody repeated in a different (and usu more complicated) form: (音乐)变奏曲; 变奏: ~*s on a theme by Mozart*. 莫扎特所作某一曲子的变奏。 **3** [U] (biol) change in bodily structure or form caused by new conditions, environment, etc; [C] instance of such change. (生物)变种; 变异; 变种的实例。

vari·col·oured (*US* = **-col·ored**) /'veərɪˌkʌləd; 'verɪ,kʌləd/ *adj* of various colours. 杂色的; 五颜六色的。

vari·cose /'værɪkəʊs; 'værɪ,kos/ *adj* (esp in) (尤用于) ~ **vein**, vein that has become permanently swollen or enlarged. (永久性)静脉肿大或曲张。

var·ied /'veərɪd; 'verɪd/ *adj* **1** of different sorts diverse: 各种不同的; 各式各样的: ~ *opinions;* 各种不同的意见; *the ~ scenes of life*. 生活中各式各样的情景。 **2** full of changes or variety: 多变化的: *a ~ career*. 多变化的生涯。

varie·gated /'veərɪgeɪtɪd; 'verɪ,getɪd/ *adj* marked irregularly with differently coloured patches: 杂色的; 斑驳的: *The leaves of geraniums/The flowers of pansies are often ~*. 天竺葵的叶(紫罗兰的花)常是杂色的。 **varie·ga·tion** /ˌveərɪ'geɪʃn; ,verɪ'geʃən/ *n*

var·iety /və'raɪətɪ; və'raɪətɪ/ *n* (*pl* -**ties**) **1** [U] quality of not being the same, or not being the same at all times: 变化性; 多变性; 多样性; 多变: *a life full of ~*. 变化多端的生活。 *We demanded more ~ in our food*. 我们要求我们的伙食多一点变化。 **2** (*sing* only) number or range of different things: (仅用单数)若干不同的事物; 种种: *for a ~ of reasons;* 由于种种原因; *a large ~ of patterns to choose from*. 可供选择的种类繁多的花样。 **3** [C] (biol) subdivision of a species. (生物)变种; 种类。 **4** [C] kind or sort which differs from others of the larger group of which it is a part: 异种; 异类; 同类中的分支: *rare varieties of early postage stamps*. 早期邮票中的珍品。 *There are now several varieties of spaniel*. 长耳狗现在有好些不同种类。 **5** [U] kind cf entertainment consisting of singing, dancing, acrobatic. feats, short plays, etc as given in music-halls (GB), some nightclubs and hotels, and for broadcasting: 杂耍(包括歌、舞、特技表演、短剧等): *a ~ en-tertainment;* 杂耍(综艺)表演; *a ~ theatre;* 杂耍(综艺)剧场; '*~ artists*. 杂耍(综艺)演员。 (*US* 美 = **vaudeville**).

vari·form /'veərɪfɔːm *US:* 'vær-; 'verɪ,fɔrm/ *adj* of various forms. 形形色色的; 形式繁多的。

vari·orum /ˌveərɪ'ɔːrəm; ,verɪ'orəm/ *adj* (only in) (仅用于) ~ **edition**, edition, eg of a Shakespeare play, with the notes of various commentators. 集注本 (如莎士比亚剧本的集注本)。

vari·ous /'veərɪəs; 'verɪəs/ *adj* (usu attrib) different; of a number of different sorts: (通常用作定语)不同的; 种种的; 各式各样的: *for ~ reasons;* 为了种种的理由; *at ~ times;* 在不同的时代; *a criminal who is known to the police under ~ names*. 警方认得其许多化名的罪犯。 **~·ly** *adv*

var·let /'vɑːlɪt; 'vɑrlɪt/ *n* (archaic) rascal. (古)无赖; 流氓。

var·nish /'vɑːnɪʃ; 'vɑrnɪʃ/ *n* [C, U] (particular kind of) (liquid used to give a) hard, shiny, transparent coating on the surface of sth, esp woodwork or metalwork; (fig) false or deceiving appearance: 假漆; 光漆; 亮漆; 凡立水(尤指用于木器或金属器上者); (喻)虚饰; 文饰; 粉饰: *scratch the ~ on a table*; 刮坏桌子上的亮漆; *a ~ of good manners;* 虚饰的礼貌; '*nail-~*, for finger-nails. 指甲漆。 □ *vt* [VP6A] put a coating of ~ on: 涂亮漆或凡立水于…上; 上光: *a piece of furniture/an oil-painting*. 上光于一件家具(一幅油画)。

Some women ∼ their toe-nails. 有些女人在脚趾甲上涂指甲油。

vars·ity /'vɑːsətɪ; 'vɑrsətɪ/ n (pl **-ties**) (colloq) university. (口) 大学。

vary /'veərɪ; 'verɪ/ vi, vt (pt, pp **-ried**) [VP2A, 6A] be, become, cause to become, different: 不同; 改变; 使不同; 使有变化: *∼ing prices;* 变动的物价; *prices that ∼ with the season.* 随季节而变动的物价。 *They ∼ in weight from 3 lb to 5 lb.* 这些东西的重量从三磅到五磅不等。 *You should ∼ your diet.* 你应该改变饮食全。

vas·cu·lar /'væskjulə(r); 'væskjələ/ adj of, made up of, containing, vessels or ducts through which blood, lymph or sap flows: 脉管的; 血管的; 导管的; 脉管形成的; 含有脉管的: *∼ tissue.* 脉管组织。

vase /vɑːz US: veɪs; ves/ n [C] vessel of glass, pottery, etc for holding cut flowers, or as an ornament. 花瓶; 饰瓶。

vases

va·sec·tomy /və'sektəmɪ; væs'ɛktəmɪ/ n (pl **-mies**) simple surgical operation to make a man sterile. (男性的) 输精管切除术 (一种简单的绝育手术); 男性结扎术。

vas·eline /'væsəliːn; 'væsl,in/ n [U] (P) yellowish substance, petroleum jelly, almost without taste or smell, used as an ointment or lubricant. (商标) 矿脂; 凡士林。

vas·sal /'væsl; 'væsl/ n (hist) person who held land in return for which he vowed to give military service to the owner of the land; feudal tenant; (fig) humble dependant: (史) 家臣; 封臣; (喻) 谦恭的从属者; 下属: (attrib) (用作定语) *a ∼ state,* one subject to another. 属国。 **'∼·age** /-səlɪdʒ; -slɪdʒ/ n [U] state of being a ∼; servitude. 家臣的地位; 从属; 隶属; 服从; 附属。

vast /vɑːst US: væst; væst/ adj immense; extensive: 巨大的; 广袤的: *∼ sums of money;* 巨额金钱; *a ∼ expanse of desert.* 一片广大的沙漠。 *∼·ly* adv *∼·ness* n

vat /væt; væt/ n tank or great vessel for holding liquids, esp in distilling, brewing dyeing and tanning. 大桶; 大缸 (尤指供蒸馏、酿造、染色及鞣皮用者)。

Vati·can /'vætɪkən; 'vætɪkən/ n **the ∼**, the residence in Rome of the Pope; centre of Papal government. 梵蒂冈 (罗马教皇的驻在地); 教廷; 教廷政府所在地。

vaude·ville /'vɔːdəvɪl; 'vodə,vɪl/ n [U] (US) (美) = **variety(5)**.

vault¹ /vɔːlt; vɔlt/ n **1** arched roof; series of arches forming a roof. 拱形圆屋顶; 穹窿。 ⇨ the illus at **crypt**. 参看 crypt 之插图。 **2** underground room or cellar (with or without an arched roof) as a place of storage ('wine-∼s), or for burials (eg under a church, or in a cemetery), or for safe-keeping of valuables: 窖; 地下室 (用作贮存物品之处, 如 wine-∼s 酒窖, 或作埋葬所, 如教堂或墓地的地窖, 或用以存放贵重物品): *keep one's jewels in the ∼ at the bank.* 把珠宝存放在银行地窖中。 **3** ∼-like covering: 穹窿状覆盖物: (poet) (诗) *the ∼ of heaven,* the sky. 苍穹; 天空。 **∼ed** adj built with, having, a ∼ or ∼s; in the form of a ∼: 有拱形圆屋顶的; 穹窿状的: *a ∼ roof/chamber.* 拱形屋顶 (的屋宇或教堂)。

vault² /vɔːlt; vɔlt/ vi, vt [VP2A, B, C, 6A] jump in a single movement, with the hand(s) resting on sth,

or with the help of a pole: 以手撑物跳跃 (过); 撑竿跳跃 (过): *∼ (over) a fence.* 跳过篱墙。 *The jockey ∼ed into the saddle.* 骑士一跃而跨坐鞍上。 **'∼·ing-horse** n apparatus for practice in ∼ing. (练习跳跃用的) 木马。 □ n jump made in this way. 撑物跳跃; 撑竿跳。 **∼·er** n person who ∼s. 撑物 (竿) 跳者。

vaunt /vɔːnt; vɔnt/ vi, vt, n (liter) boast. (文) 吹牛; 夸张。 **∼·er** n **∼·ing·ly** adv

veal /viːl; vil/ n [U] flesh of a calf as food. (供食用的) 小牛肉。

veer /vɪə(r); vɪr/ vi [VP2A, C] (esp of the wind, fig of opinion, talk) change direction: (尤指风, 喻指意见或谈话) 改变方向; 转向; 转变: *The wind ∼ed round to the north.* 风改向北吹了。

veg·etable /'vedʒtəbl; 'vedʒtəbl/ adj of, from, relating to, plants or plant life: 植物的; 由植物得来的; 关于植物的; 蔬菜的: *the ∼ kingdom;* 植物界; *∼ oils.* 植物油。 □ n [C] plant, esp of the sort used for food, eg potatoes, cabbages, beans, onions, carrots, etc. 植物; (尤指) 蔬菜 (如马铃薯、卷心菜、豆类、洋葱、胡萝卜等)。

vag·etar·ian /,vedʒɪ'teərɪən; ,vedʒə'terɪən/ n person who, for humane or religious reasons or for his health's sake, eats no meat: 蔬食者; 素食者: (attrib) (用作定语) *a ∼ diet;* 素菜; *∼ principles.* 素食戒条 (规则)。

veg·etate /'vedʒɪteɪt; 'vedʒə,tet/ vi [VP2A] live as plants do, without mental effort or intellectual interests; lead a dull life with little activity or interest. 象植物般生活 (不运用心智, 缺乏智力方面的兴趣); 过枯燥而少活动或趣味的生活。

veg·eta·tion /,vedʒɪ'teɪʃn; ,vedʒə'teʃən/ n [U] plants generally and collectively: (泛指一般的) 植物; 草木: *the luxuriant ∼ a the tropical forests;* 热带森林中茂盛的草木; *a desert landscape with no sign of ∼ anywhere.* 寸草不生的沙漠景观。

ve·he·ment /'viːəmənt; 'viəmənt/ adj **1** (of feelings) strong, eager; (of persons, their speech, behaviour, etc) filled with, showing, strong or eager feeling: (指感情) 强烈的; 热切的; (指人, 其言词, 其行为等) 充满或显示强烈或热切情绪的: *a man of ∼ character;* 热情的人; *∼ desires/passions.* 强烈的欲望 (情欲)。 **2** violent: 猛烈的: *a ∼ wind.* 强风。 **∼·ly** adv **ve·he·mence** /mens; -məns/ n

ve·hicle /'viːɪkl; 'viɪkl/ n [C] **1** any conveyance (usu wheeled, eg a cart, lorry, motor-car, but also a sledge) for goods or passengers on land. 陆上之工具; 车辆 (包括雪橇)。 Cf 参较 craft for water, space. 指水上及空中交通工具。 **2** means by which thought, feeling, etc can be conveyed: 传达思想; 掩饰感情的工具; 媒介物: *Art may be used as a ∼ for/of propaganda.* 艺术可用作宣传的工具。 **ve·hicu·lar** /vɪ'hɪkjulə(r); vɪ'hɪkjələ/ adj related to, consisting of, conveyed by, ∼s: 车辆的; 陆上交通工具的; 媒介物的: *The road is closed to vehicular traffic.* 此路不准车辆通行。

veil /veɪl; vel/ n [C] **1** covering of fine net or other material to protect or hide a woman's face, or as part of a headdress: (妇女的) 面纱; 面罩: *She raised/dropped/lowered her ∼.* 她揭起 (拉下, 放下) 面罩。 **take the ∼,** become a nun. 当修女。 **2** (fig) sth that hides or disguises: (喻) 遮蔽物; 掩饰物; 假托; 口实: *a ∼ of mist;* 一层雾; *commit murder under the ∼ of patriotism,* do so under the pretence of patriotism. 假爱国之名而谋杀。 *draw a ∼ over sth,* be discreet or secretive about: 隐晦或隐藏某事; 对某事警戒或谨慎: *Let us draw a ∼ over what followed.* 后来的事情我们不必提了。 □ vt [VP6A] put a ∼ over; (fig) conceal: 以面纱遮掩; (喻) 隐藏: *Some Muslim women are ∼ed.* 有些穆斯林妇女戴面罩。 *He could not ∼ his distrust.* 他不能掩饰他的疑惑。 **∼·ing** n [U] light material used for making ∼; such material used as a ∼. (做面罩用的) 薄纱; 面纱。

vein /veɪn; ven/ n **1** blood-vessel along which blood flows from all parts of the body to the heart. 静脉 (血

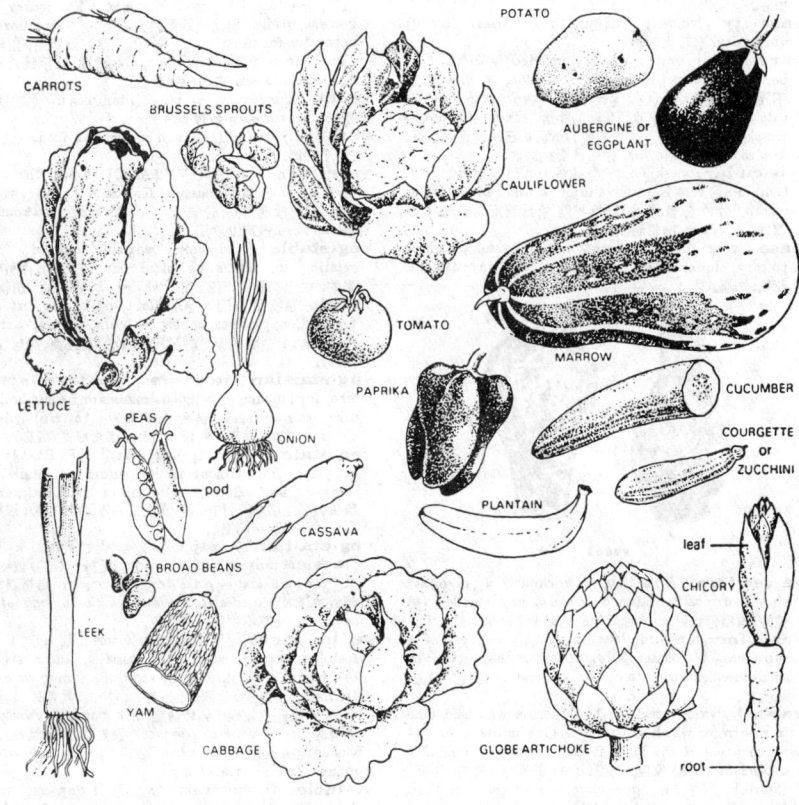

CARROTS

BRUSSELS SPROUTS

POTATO

AUBERGINE or EGGPLANT

CAULIFLOWER

TOMATO

MARROW

CUCUMBER

COURGETTE or ZUCCHINI

LETTUCE

PAPRIKA

PEAS

pod

ONION

PLANTAIN

leaf

CHICORY

CASSAVA

BROAD BEANS

LEEK

YAM

CABBAGE

GLOBE ARTICHOKE

root

vegetables

液从身体各部流回心脏的血管）。 ⇨ the illus at **respiratory**. 参看 respiratory 之插图。 ⇨ **artery**(1). **2** one of the ~-like lines in some leaves or in the wings of some insects; a coloured line or streak in some kinds of stone, eg marble; 叶脉；(昆虫的)翅脉；(大理石等的有色)纹理；(fig): (喻): *There is a ~ of melancholy in his character.* 他的性格中带有少许忧郁的气质。 **3** crack or fissure in rock, filled with mineral or ore; lode or seam: 矿脉；岩脉；*a ~ of gold.* 金矿脉。 **4** mood; train of thought: 心情；心绪；心思；意向: *in a merry/melancholic/imaginative ~.* 心情愉快的(忧郁的，充满想象的)。 *He writes humorous songs when he is in the (right) ~.* 他心情好的时候会写一些幽默歌曲。 **~ed** /veɪnd/ vend/ adj having, marked with, ~s: 有静脉,叶脉,翅脉,纹理或矿脉的; *~ed marble.* 有纹理的大理石。

veld /velt; vɛlt/ n [U] flat, treeless grassland of the S African plateau. (南非高原上的)草原。 ⇨ **pampas, prairie, savannah, steppe.**

vel·lum /'veləm; 'vɛləm/ n [U] parchment. 皮纸。

vel·oci·pede /vɪ'lɒsɪpiːd; vəˈlɑsəˌpid/ n early kind of bicycle with pedals on the front wheel; (US) child's tricycle. 早期脚踏车(踏板在前轮者)；(美) 儿童三轮脚踏车。

vel·oc·ity /vɪ'lɒsɪtɪ; vəˈlɑsətɪ/ n [U] **1** speed; quickness. 迅速；快。 **2** rate of motion: 速率；速度: *at the ~ of sound;* 以声音的速度；*'muzzle ~,* the speed of

a bullet as it leaves the muzzle of a gun. (弹丸离开枪口或炮口时的)初速。

ve·lour /vəˈlʊə(r); vəˈlʊr/ n [U] fabric like velvet or felt. 丝绒。

vel·vet /'velvɪt; 'vɛlvɪt/ n [U] cloth with a thick soft nap (⇨ **nap²**) on one side: 天鹅绒; (attrib) (用作定语) *a ~ frock;* 一件天鹅绒女长服; *a ~ tread,* (fig) soft and quiet. (喻)轻悄的脚步。 *an iron hand in a ~ glove,* ruthlessness concealed by good manners, soft speech, etc. 笑里藏刀；外柔内刚。 **·een** /velvɪ'tiːn; ˌvɛlvəˈtin/ n [U] cheap type of ~. 劣质天鹅绒；假天鹅绒。 **~y** adj smooth and soft like ~. 光滑柔软似天鹅绒的。

ve·nal /'viːnl; 'vinl/ adj **1** (of persons) ready to do sth dishonest (eg using influence or position) for money: (指人) 为金钱而做坏事的；贪赃枉法的；贪污的: *~ judges/politicians.* 贪污的法官(政客)。 **2** (of conduct) influenced by, done for, (possible) payment: (指行为) 受贿赂影响的；为金钱而做的: *~ practices.* 受贿的恶习。 **~ly** /-nəlɪ; -nlɪ/ adv **·ity** /vɪ'nælətɪ; viˈnælətɪ/ n quality of being ~. 贪赃枉法；贪污；受贿。

vend /vend; vɛnd/ vt [VP6A] (chiefly legal) sell; offer for sale (esp small wares). (主要为法律用语)贩卖；售卖(尤指小商品)。 **'~ing machine,** coin-operated slot machine for the sale of small articles, eg cigarettes and food. 自动贩卖机(贩卖香烟、食品等小物品)。

~ee /ˌvenˈdiː; ˌvɛnˈdi/ n person to whom sth is sold.; 买主; 买方。 **~er, ~or** /-ə(r); -də(r)/ n seller: 卖主; 卖方: 'newsvendor, seller of newspapers. 报贩。

ven·detta /venˈdetə; vɛnˈdɛtə/ n hereditary feud between families in which members of each family commit murders in revenge for previous murders. 家族间的宿怨; 仇杀; 血仇。

ve·neer /vəˈnɪə(r); vəˈnɪr/ n 1 [C, U] (thin layer of) fine quality wood glued to the surface of cheaper wood (for furniture, etc). 粘在廉价木材上的上等木材; 此种上等木材薄板 (如家具等上者)。 2 (fig) surface appearance (of politeness, etc) covering the true nature: (喻)遮掩真情的外表; 虚饰: a ~ of Western civilization. 西方文明的外表。 □ vt [VP6A] put a ~ on: 以上等木材薄板粘于⋯上: ~ a deal desk with walnut. 以胡桃木薄板粘于枞木书桌的表面上。

ven·er·able /ˈvenərəbl; ˈvɛnərəbl/ adj 1 deserving respect because of age, character, associations, etc: 年岁、品格、交往关系等方面值得尊敬的; 令人肃然起敬的: a ~ scholar; 可敬的学者; the ~ ruins of the abbey. 古老的大寺院的遗迹。 2 (Church of England) title of an archdeacon; (Church of Rome) title of a person in process of being canonized. (英国国教)副主教的尊称; (天主教)被列入圣者之人的头衔。

ven·er·ate /ˈvenəreɪt; ˈvɛnəˌret/ vt [VP6A] regard with deep respect: 对⋯深怀敬意; 崇敬: They ~ the old man's memory. 他们对那老人怀着崇敬的追念。 **ven·er·ation** /ˌvenəˈreɪʃn; ˌvɛnəˈreʃən/ n

ve·nereal /vəˈnɪərɪəl; vəˈnɪrɪəl/ adj, communicated by, sexual contact: 性交的; 交媾的; 因性交而感染的: ~ diseases, (abbr 略作 **VD**). 性病; 花柳病。

Ve·ne·tian /vəˈniːʃn; vəˈniʃən/ adj of Venice. 威尼斯的。 ~ **blind**, window screen made of many horizontal strips (slats of wood or plastic material) that can be adjusted to let in light and air as desired. 百叶窗。

ven·geance /ˈvendʒəns; ˈvɛndʒəns/ n [U] 1 revenge; the return of injury for injury: 报仇; 复仇; 以牙还牙: seek ~ upon sb (for an injury), (因遭某伤害而)向某人报复; take ~ on an enemy. 向敌人复仇。 2 **with a ~**, (colloq) thoroughly; to a greater degree than is normal, expected or desired: (口)彻底地; 强烈地; 极端地; 过分地: The rain came down with a ~. 雨下得很大。

venge·ful /ˈvendʒfl; ˈvɛndʒfəl/ adj showing a desire for revenge; vindictive. 显示复仇心的; 报仇心切的; 报复的。

ve·nial /ˈviːnɪəl; ˈvinɪəl/ adj (of a sin, error, fault) excusable; not serious. (指罪、错误、过失)可宽恕的; 轻微的。

ven·ison /ˈvenɪzn; ˈvɛnəzn/ n [U] deer meat. 鹿肉。

venom /ˈvenəm; ˈvɛnəm/ n [U] poisonous fluid of certain snakes; (fig) hate; spite. (某些蛇的)毒液; (喻)怨恨; 恶意。 **~ed** /ˈvenəmd; ˈvɛnəmd/ adj (fig) full of malice or hate: (喻)充满恶意或怨恨的: ~ed remarks. 恶言。 **~ous** /ˈvenəməs; ˈvɛnəməs/ adj deadly; spiteful: 致命的; 恶毒的: ~ous snakes/criticism. 致命的毒蛇(恶毒的批评)。 **~ous·ly** adv

ve·nous /ˈviːnəs; ˈvinəs/ adj 1 of the veins: 静脉的: ~ blood, (contrasted with arterial blood). 静脉血(与动脉血相对)。 2 (bot) having veins: (植物)多叶脉的: a ~ leaf. 有脉的叶子。

vent /vent; vɛnt/ n 1 hole serving as an inlet or outlet for air, gas, liquid, etc, eg a hole in the top of a barrel, for air to enter as liquid is drawn out. 孔; 口; 通风孔(如大桶顶上的通孔, 液体抽出时, 供空气进入)。 '~-hole n hole for escape of air, smoke, etc. 出气口(孔); 出烟孔(口)。 2 (trade use) slit in the back of a coat or jacket. (商业用语)上衣背部的叉口。 3 means of escape: 逃避或逃脱的出路; 原口: The floods found a ~ through the dykes. 洪水从堤上的一处漏洞溢流。 4 (sing only) outlet for one's feelings. (仅用单数)感情的出口。 发泄; 吐露。 **give ~ to**, (fig) give free expression to: (喻)(无禁忌或拘束地)发出; 发泄; 吐露: He gave ~ to

his feelings in an impassioned speech. 在一篇激动的演说中, 他无顾忌地吐露心声。 □ vt [VP6A, 14] ~ **sth on sb/sth**, find or provide an outlet for: 发泄; 出气: He ~ed his ill-temper upon his long-suffering wife. 他把怒气向他长久受苦的妻子发泄。

ven·ti·late /ˈventɪleɪt US: -leɪt; ˈvɛntl̩ˌet/ vt [VP 6A] 1 cause air to move freely through: 使空气流通; 使通风: ~ a room/the galleries of a coalmine. 使房间(煤矿坑道)通风。 2 (fig) make (a question, a grievance) widely known and cause it to be discussed. (喻)宣泄; 公开; 引起公开讨论(某问题, 苦况)。 **ven·ti·la·tor** /ˈventɪleɪtə(r) US: -təl-; ˈvɛntl̩ˌetə/ n device for ventilating. 通风设备。 **ven·ti·la·tion** /ˌventɪˈleɪʃn US: -təlˈeɪʃn; ˌvɛntl̩ˈeʃən/ n [U] ventilating or being ~: 通风; 流通空气: the ventilation shaft of a coalmine. 煤矿的通风竖坑道。

ven·tricle /ˈventrɪkl; ˈvɛntrɪkl/ n cavity in the body; hollow part of an organ, esp of the heart. (体内的)穴; 腔; 室; (尤指)心室。 ⇨ the illus at **respiratory**. 参看 respiratory 之插图。

ven·tril·oquism /venˈtrɪləkwɪzm; vɛnˈtrɪlə̩kwɪzəm/ n [U] art of producing voice-sounds so that they seem to come from a person or place at a distance from the speaker. 口技(使语音听起来非发自说话者, 而似发自他人或他处的技术)。 **ven·tril·oquist** /-kwɪst/ n person skilled in ~. 擅长口技者; 口技表演者。

ven·ture /ˈventʃə(r); ˈvɛntʃə/ n [C, U] undertaking in which there is risk. 冒险; 冒险事业。 □ vt,vi 1 [VP 6A, 15A, 16A, 3A] ~ **(on)**, take the risk of, expose to, danger or loss: 冒险; 使⋯可能遭受危险或损失: ~ one's life to save sb from drowning; 冒生命危险拯救某人使免淹死; ~ too near the edge of a cliff; 冒险地过分接近崖的边缘; ~ on a dangerous journey. 大胆地从事危险的旅行。 **Nothing ~, nothing gain/win/have**, (prov) One cannot expect to achieve anything if one risks nothing. (谚)不入虎穴, 焉得虎子(不敢冒险者将一事无成)。 2 [VP6A, 7A] go so far as, presume, dare: 敢; 敢于; 胆敢; 竟敢: to (put forward) an opinion; 敢于陈述一项意见; ~ a guess. 大胆地猜测。 I ~ to disagree/to suggest that.... 我冒昧地不同意(建议)⋯。 '**V~ Scout**, senior Scout. 年长的童子军。 '**~·some** /-səm; -səm/ adj 1 (of persons) ready to take risks; daring. (指人)好冒险的; 大胆的。 2 (of acts, behaviour) involving danger; risky. (指动作, 行为)有危险的; 危险的。 **ven·tur·ous** /ˈventʃərəs; ˈvɛntʃərəs/ adj = **adventurous**.

venue /ˈvenjuː; ˈvenju/ n rendezvous; meeting-place; (sport) place fixed for a contest or match. 集合地点; 会场; (运动)竞赛场; 比赛地点。

Venus /ˈviːnəs; ˈvinəs/ n 1 (Roman myth) goddess of love and beauty. (罗神)维纳斯(爱和美的女神)。 2 (astron) planet second in order from the sun. (天文)金星; 太白星(环绕太阳的第二颗行星)。 ⇨ the illus at **planet**. 参看 planet 之插图。

ver·acious /vəˈreɪʃəs; vəˈreʃəs/ adj (formal) true; truthful. (正式用语)真实的; 可靠的; 诚实的。 **~·ly** adv **ver·ac·ity** /vəˈræsətɪ; vəˈræsətɪ/ n [U] truth; truthfulness. 真实; 可靠。

ve·ran·da(h) /vəˈrændə; vəˈrændə/ n roofed and floored open space along the side(s) of a house, sports pavilion, etc (US often called 美常作 porch). 走廊; 游廊; 阳台。

verb /vɜːb; vɝb/ n word or phrase indicating what sb or sth does, what state sb or sth is in, what is becoming of sth or sb. 动词; 动词短语。

ver·bal /ˈvɜːbl; ˈvɝbl/ adj 1 of or in words: 言辞的; 词句的: a ~ error; 用词的错误; have a good ~ memory, be able to remember the exact words of a statement, etc. 对文句有好记性。 2 spoken, not written; 口头的: a ~ statement/explanation. 口头的叙述(解释)。 3 word for word, literal: 逐字的; 照字面的: a ~ translation. 直译。 4 of verbs: 动词的: a ~ noun (eg

swimming in the sentence 'Swimming is a good exercise'). 动名词 (如 'Swimming is a good exercise' 中的 swimming)。 ~**ly** /'vɜːbəlɪ; 'vɜbl̩ɪ/ *adv* in spoken words, not in writing. 口头上。

ver·bal·ize /'vɜːbəlaɪz; 'vɜbl̩aɪz/ *vt* put into words. 用言辞表达。

ver·ba·tim /vɜː'beɪtɪm; vɚ'betɪm/ *adv, adj* word for word, exactly as spoken or written: 逐字地(的); 完全照字面地(的): *report a speech* ~; 逐字地报导一项演说; *a* ~ *report*. 逐字报告。

ver·bena /vɜː'biːnə; vɚ'binə/ *n* kinds of herbaceous plant of which garden varieties have flowers of many colours. 马鞭草。

ver·bi·age /'vɜːbɪɪdʒ; 'vɜbɪɪdʒ/ *n* [U] (use of) unnecessary words for the expression of an idea, etc: 冗词; 赘语; 使用冗词赘语: *The speaker lost himself in* ~. 那演讲者废话连篇。

ver·bose /vɜː'bəus; vɚ'bos/ *adj* using, containing, more words than are needed: 用字过多的; 冗赘的: *a* ~ *speech/speaker/style*. 冗长的演讲(冗赘的演讲者/冗赘的文体)。 ~·**ly** *adv* ~·**ness, ver·bos·ity** /vɜː'bɒsətɪ; vɚ'basətɪ/ *nn* [U] state or quality of being ~. 冗长; 冗赘。

ver·dant /'vɜːdnt; 'vɜdn̩t/ *adj* **1** (liter) (esp of grass, vegetation, fields) fresh and green: (文) (尤指草, 植物, 田野)青葱的; 新绿的: ~ *lawns*. 新绿的草地。 **2** (fig) inexperienced; unsophisticated. (喻)无经验的; 不老练的。 **ver·dancy** /-dnsɪ; -dn̩sɪ/ *n*

ver·dict /'vɜːdɪkt; 'vɜdɪkt/ *n* [C] **1** decision reached by a jury on a question of fact in a law case: 陪审团的裁决; 判决: *The jury brought in* (= announced) *a* ~ *of guilty/ not guilty*. 陪审团判决有(无)罪。 **open** ~, ⇨ **open¹(6).** **2** decision or opinion given after testing, examining, or experiencing sth: (对某事物的)决定; 判断; 论断; 意见: *the* ~ *of the electors*. 选举人的决定。 *The popular* ~ (= The opinion of people in general) *was that is served him right*. 公众的意见认为他罪有应得。

ver·di·gris /'vɜːdɪgrɪs; 'vɜdɪˌgrɪs/ *n* [U] green substance formed on copper, brass and bronze surfaces (as rust is formed on iron surfaces). 铜绿; 铜绿。

ver·dure /'vɜːdʒə(r); 'vɜdʒɚ/ *n* [U] (liter) (fresh green colour of) growing vegetation. (文)生长中的草木; 新绿色; 青葱色: *the* ~ *of (the trees in) spring*. 春天(树木)的青葱。

Verey /'verɪ; 'verɪ/ *adj* '~ *light*, ⇨ **Very.**

verge /vɜːdʒ; vɜdʒ/ *n* **1** [C] edge; border (eg strip of ground at the side of a road, grass edge of a lawn). 边; 缘; 边际; 外缘。 **2** *be on the* ~ *of; bring* (*sb*) *to the* ~ *of*, very close to, on the border of: 濒于; 使(某人)濒临: *The country is on the* ~ *of disaster*. 该国濒于火难。 *She was brought to the* ~ *of bursting into tears*. 她я弄得几乎要哭出来了。 ⇨ *vi* [VP3A] ~ *on/upon*, approach closely, border upon: 濒临; 接近: *verge on bankruptcy*. 濒于破产。 *Such ideas* ~ *on foolhardiness*. 这种念头近于蛮勇。

verger /'vɜːdʒə(r); 'vɜdʒɚ/ *n* **1** (C of E) official with various duties (eg showing people to their seats). (英国国教)教堂的司事; 堂守(如领人入座者)。 **2** officer who carries a staff before a bishop in a cathedral, a vice-chancellor in a university, etc. (为大教堂的主教, 大学的副校长等)持权杖者。

ver·ify /'verɪfaɪ; 'verəˌfaɪ/ *vt* (*pt, pp* -**fied**) [VP 6A] **1** test the truth or accuracy of: 鉴定; 查对; 核对: ~ *a report/statement*; 核对一项报告(陈述)的真实性; ~ *the figures/details of a report*. 核对一项报告中的数字(细节)。 **2** (of an event, etc) show the truth of; bear out: (指事件等)证实; 证明: *Subsequent events verified my suspicions*. 后来发生的事件证实了我的猜疑。 **veri·fi·able** /'verɪfaɪəbl; 'verəˌfaɪəbl/ *adj* that can be verified. 可证明的; 能鉴定的。 **veri·fi·ca·tion** /ˌverɪfɪ'keɪʃn; ˌverɪfɪ'keʃən/ *n* ~ing or being verified; proof or evidence. 鉴定; 证实; 证据。

ver·ily /'verəlɪ; 'verəlɪ/ *adv* (archaic) really; truly. (古)真实地; 真正地; 确然地。

veri·si·mili·tude /ˌverɪsɪ'mɪlɪtjuːd; US: -tuːd/ /ˌverəsə'mɪləˌtjud/ *n* [U] appearance, semblance, of truth; [C] sth that seems to be true. 逼真; 逼真的事物。

veri·table /'verɪtəbl; 'verətəbl/ *adj* real; rightly named. 真正的; 名符其实的。

ver·ity /'verətɪ; 'verətɪ/ *n* (*pl* -**ties**) **1** [U] (old use) truth (*of* a statement, etc). (旧用法)(陈述等的)真实; 确实。 **2** [C] sth that really exists; true statement. 实物; 实存事物; 真实的陈述: *the eternal verities*, fundamental moral principles; laws of God. 基本的道德准则; 上帝的律法。

ver·mi·celli /ˌvɜːmɪ'selɪ; ˌvɜməˈsɛlɪ/ *n* [U] paste of white flour made into long slender threads, like spaghetti but much thinner. 细面条; 线面。

ver·mi·form /'vɜːmɪfɔːm; 'vɜməˌfɔrm/ *adj* worm-like in shape: 蠕虫形的: *the* ~ *appendix*. 蚓突; 阑尾。 ⇨ the illus at **alimentary.** 参看 alimentary 之插图。

ver·mil·ion /və'mɪljən; vɚ'mɪljən/ *adj, n* bright red (colour). 朱红; 朱红色; 朱红的。

ver·min /'vɜːmɪn; 'vɜmɪn/ *n* [U] (with *pl v*, but not with numerals) (用复数动词, 但不与数词连用) **1** wild animals (eg rats, weasels, foxes) harmful to plants, birds and other animals. 害兽(如鼠, 鼬, 狐)。 **2** parasitic insects (eg lice) sometimes found on the bodies of human beings and other animals. 寄生虫; 害虫(如虱)。 **3** human beings who are harmful to society; persons who prey on others. 社会上的蟊贼; 歹徒。 ~·**ous** /-əs; -əs/ *adj* **1** infested with fleas, lice, etc: 长有虱子, 虱等的: ~*ous children*. 长有虱子的孩子(们)。 **2** caused by insect ~: 由害虫引起的: ~*ous diseases*. 由害虫引起的疾病。

ver·mouth /'vɜːməθ; *US*: vɚ'muːθ; 'vɚmuθ/ *n* [U] fortified white wine flavoured with herbs, drunk as an aperitif (often in cocktails). 苦艾酒(作为开胃酒饮用, 常放于鸡尾酒中)。

ver·nacu·lar /və'nækjulə(r); vɚ'nækjəlɚ/ *adj* (of a word, a language) of the country in question: (指文字, 语言)该国的; 本国的; 土语的: *the* ~ *newspapers in India*, those in the various languages (except English) of India; 印度诸语(英语除外)的报纸; *a* ~ *poet*, one who uses a ~ language. 方言诗人。 ⇨ *n* [U] language or dialect of a country or district. 方言; 土语: *the* ~*s of the USA*. 美国的方言。

ver·nal /'vɜːnl; 'vɜnl̩/ *adj* (liter) of, in, as in, the season of spring. (文)春季的; 在春季的; 如在春季的。 **the** ~ **equinox**, about 21st March. 春分(约在三月廿一日)。

ve·ron·ica /və'rɒnɪkə; vɚ'rɑnɪkə/ *n* kinds of herb or shrub with blue, purple, pink or white flowers. 婆婆纳属植物; 水苦荬; 葳灵仙属。

ver·ruca /ve'ruːkə; vɛ'rukə/ *n* small, hard growth on the skin (usu on the bottom of the feet); wart. 疣(通常生于足底); 瘤肿。

ver·sa·tile /'vɜːsətaɪl; *US*: -tl; 'vɜsətl̩/ *adj* interested in and clever at many different things; having various uses: 多才多艺的; 多方面的; 有多种功用的: *a* ~ *inventor*; 多方面的发明家; *a* ~ *mind*; 多才多艺的人; *a* ~ *tool*. 多种功用的工具。 **ver·sa·til·ity** /ˌvɜːsə'tɪlətɪ; ˌvɜsə'tɪlətɪ/ *n*

verse /vɜːs; vɜs/ *n* **1** [U] (form of) writing arranged in lines, each conforming to a pattern of accented and unaccented syllables: 诗; 韵文; 诗体: *prose and* ~; 散文和韵文; *written in* ~; 以诗体写成的; *a* ~ *translation of Homer's 'Odyssey'*. 荷马《奥德赛》的诗体翻译; *blank* ~, without rhymes at the end of the lines. 无韵诗。 **2** [C] group of lines of this kind forming a unit in a rhyme scheme: 诗节: *a poem/hymn of five* ~*s*. 一首有五节的诗(赞美诗)。 **3** [C] one line of (a) ~ with a definite number of feet or accented syllables: (有一定

音步或重音节的)一行诗: *quote a few ~s from Tennyson*. 引用英国诗人坦尼森的几行诗。 **4** one of the short numbered divisions of a chapter in the Bible. (圣经的)节。 **give chapter and ~ (for sth),** supply the exact reference (for a statement, an authority one quotes, reports, etc). 注明所引用的章节; 说明⋯的出处。

versed /vɜːst; ˈvɜːst/ *adj* **~ in,** skilled or experienced in: *well ~ in mathematics / the arts.* 精通数学(文史)。 ⇨ *conversant with* at **conversant.**

ver·si·fy /ˈvɜːsɪfaɪ; ˈvɜːsəˌfaɪ/ *vt, vi (pt, pp* **-fied)** [VP 6 A] put into verse: *~ an old legend;* 将一古老的传说用韵文写出; [VP 2 A] write verses. 作诗。 **ver·si·fier** *n* maker of verses. 改写散文为韵文的作者; 诗人。 **ver·si·fi·ca·tion** /ˌvɜːsɪfɪˈkeɪʃn; ˌvɜːsəfəˈkeɪʃn/ *n* [U] art of *~*ing; style in which verse is written; metre. 作诗法; 诗体; 韵律。

ver·sion /ˈvɜːʃn *US:* -ʒn; ˈvɜːʒən/ *n* [C] **1** account of an event, etc from the point of view of one person: (由个别观点对事件等所作的)叙述; 说法; 看法: *There were contradictory ~s of what happened / of what the Prime Minister said.* 对于所发生的事(首相所说的话)有相互矛盾的说法。 **2** translation into another language: 翻译; 译本。 *a new ~ of the Bible.* 圣经的新译本。

verso /ˈvɜːsəʊ; ˈvɜːso/ *n (pl ~s, /-səʊz; -soz/)* any left-hand page of a book (opp of *recto*); reverse side of a medal or coin. 书籍左方的书页 (为 recto 之反义词) 奖章、勋章、硬币等的反面。

ver·sus /ˈvɜːsəs; ˈvɜːsəs/ *prep* (Lat) (in law and sport; often shortened to **v** or **vs** in print) against: (拉) 〈法律和运动用语〉; 印刷时常略作 **v** 或 **vs〉** 对; 对抗; (legal) (法律) *Robinson v Brown;* 鲁宾逊对布朗案; (cricket) (板球) *Kent vs Surrey.* 肯特对萨里(的比赛)。

ver·te·bra /ˈvɜːtɪbrə; ˈvɜːtəbrə/ *n (pl ~e /-briː; -ˌbriː/)* any one of the segments of the backbone. 脊骨的一节; 脊椎骨。 ⇨ the illus at skeleton. 参看 skeleton 之插图。 **ver·te·brate** /ˈvɜːtɪbreɪt; ˈvɜːtəˌbreɪt/ *n, adj* (animal, bird, etc) having a backbone. (动物, 鸟等) 有脊椎骨的; 脊椎动物。

ver·tex /ˈvɜːteks; ˈvɜːteks/ *n (pl* **vertices** /-tɪsiːz/ -təˌsiz/) highest point; top; point of a triangle, cone, etc opposite the base. 最高点; 顶点; (三角形, 圆锥体与底相对的)顶。

ver·ti·cal /ˈvɜːtɪkl; ˈvɜːtɪkl/ *adj* (of a line or plane) at a right angle to the earth's surface or to another line or plane: (指线或平面)垂直的; 直立的: *a ~ cliff;* 陡直的峭壁; *a ~ take-off aircraft,* one that can rise *~*ly, not needing a runway. 垂直起飞的飞机。 ⇨ **horizontal.** □ *n* ~ line: 垂直线: *out of the ~,* not *~* 不垂直的。 **~ly** /-klɪ; -klɪ/ *adv*

ver·tices /ˈvɜːtɪsiːz; ˈvɜːtəˌsiz/ *n pl* ⇨ **vertex.**

ver·tigo /ˈvɜːtɪgəʊ; ˈvɜːtɪˌgo/ *n* [U] (formal) dizziness. (正式用语)眩晕; 头晕。 **ver·tigin·ous** /vɜːˈtɪdʒɪnəs; vɜːˈtɪdʒənəs/ *adj* of, causing, ~. 眩晕的; 令人眩晕的。

verve /vɜːv; vɜːv/ *n* [U] enthusiasm, spirit, vigour. 热情; 精神; 活力。

very[1] /ˈverɪ; ˈverɪ/ *attrib adj* **1** itself and no other; truly such: 同一的; 真正的; 恰好的: *This is the ~ thing I want!* 这正是我所需要的东西! *At that ~ moment the phone rang.* 恰在那个时候电话铃响了。 *You're the ~ man I want to see.* 你就是我想要见的人。 **2** extreme: 极端的: *at the ~ end / beginning.* 在结束(开始)之际。 **3** (equivalent to an emphatic or intensive *pron* ending in *-self* or *-selves*): (相当于以 -self 或 -selves 为后缀的加强语气的代词): *He knows our ~ thoughts,* ie our thoughts themselves, even our innermost thoughts. 他深知我们的想法。 *The ~ idea of being sent abroad* (ie the idea alone, quite apart from the reality) *delighted him.* 单是想到可能被派往国外就使他觉得高兴。

very[2] /ˈverɪ; ˈverɪ/ *adv* **1** (used intensively with *advv*, *adjj* and *part adjj*): (与副词、形容词及分词形容词连用, 以加强语气): *~ quickly / carefully / soon, etc;* 十分快速(当心, 早等); *~ much / little;* 很多(少); *~ amusing /*

interesting, *etc;* 很好玩(有趣等); *~ small / cold / useful, etc.* 很小(冷, 有用等)。 (Note that when the *pp* is part of a passive *v* phrase, *much,* or *very much* is preferred; when the *pp* is the complement of *be, seem, feel, ~* is used): (注意: 过去分词为被动语态动词短语的一部分时, 宜用 much 或 very much; 过去分词为 be, seem, feel 的补语时, 用 very): *I wasn't much surprised at the news.* 我对那消息不太惊讶。 *He wasn't much interested in the news.* 他对那消息并不太感兴趣。 Cf 参较 *He was / seemed ~ interested.* 他(似乎)很感兴趣。 **2** **well,** often used to indicate agreement or assent (often after persuasion or argument, or in obedience to a command, request, etc): 好; 很好 (常用来表示同意或赞成, 多用于劝告或辩论之后, 或对命令、请求等的服从): *V~ well, doctor, I'll give up smoking.* 好的, 医生, 我就戒烟好了。 *Oh, ~ well, if you insist.* 哦, 好罢, 如果你坚持的话。 **2** (with a *superl,* or *own*) in the highest possible degree: (与最高级的词或 own 连用)极度地; 极点地; 完全地: *the ~ best quality;* 最好的品质; 最好的 *first to arrive;* 最先到达者; *six o'clock at the ~ latest.* 最迟六点钟。 *You can keep this for your ~ own.* 你可以保有这个东西做为你自己的。

Very, Verey /ˈverɪ; ˈverɪ/ *adj* **~ light,** (P) coloured signal flare fired from a '~ *pistol,* eg as a signal of distress from a ship. (商标)威利信号闪光弹(从'威利枪'中射出的彩色曳光弹, 如用作船的遇难信号)。

ves·icle /ˈvesɪkl; ˈvesɪkl/ *n* (anat) small cavity, cyst or swelling. (解剖)泡; 胞; 囊。 **ves·icu·lar** /vəˈsɪkjʊlə; vəˈsɪkjələ/ *adj* of *~s;* 胞的; 胞状的; 囊状的: *vesicular disease.* 胞状疾病。

ves·pers /ˈvespəz; ˈvespəz/ *n pl* church service in the evening; evensong. (英国国教之)晚间礼拜; 晚间聚会。

vessel /ˈvesl; ˈvesl/ *n* [C] **1** hollow receptacle, esp for a liquid, eg a cask, tub, bucket, bowl, bottle, cup. 容器; 器皿(尤指盛液体者, 如桶、盆、吊桶、碗、瓶、杯)。 **2** ship or large boat. 船; 舰。 **3** ⇨ *blood-~* at **blood[1]**(7)。

vest[1] /vest; vest/ *n* [C] **1** (GB) garment worn under a shirt, blouse, etc next to the skin. (英)汗衫(贴身穿者)。 **2** (trade use in GB; ordinary use in US) short, sleeveless garment worn by men under a jacket (*waistcoat* being the usual name in GB): (英国为商业用法; 美国为一般用法) 马甲; 背心(英国一般用语为 waistcoat): *coat, ~ and trousers;* 上装, 背心和裤子; *a ~pocket* (ie very small) *camera.* 超小型摄影机(可放在背心口袋中者)。

vest[2] /vest; vest/ *vt, vi* **1** [VP 14] *~ sth in sb; ~ sb with sth,* furnish or give as a fixed right: 给与; 授与某人某种权利: *~ a man with authority / rights in an estate.* 授与某人权力(产权)。 *In some countries authority is said to be ~ed in the people,* ie the people possess final authority on matters of government, etc. 在某些国家, 最高决定权是归于人民的。 *In the United States, Congress is ~ed with the power to declare war.* 在美国, 国会有宣战的权力。 **have a ~ed interest in sth,** be likely to gain or lose from it, or be affected in some way by it. 对某事物保有既得的利益。 **~ed interests, rights,** (eg in trade or manufacture) which are by law securely in the possession of a person or a group of persons. (贸易或制造业等依法保有之)既得利益(权利)。 **2** [VP 3 A] *~ in,* (of property, etc) be *~*ed in: (指财产等)归属: *power / authority that ~s in the Crown.* 属于王室的权力(职权)。 **3** [VP 6 A] (poet or eccles) clothe. (诗或教会)使穿衣服。

ves·tal /ˈvestl; ˈvestl/ *n* ~ **(virgin),** one of the maidens dedicated to the service of the goddess Vesta in ancient Rome, vowed to chastity. 古罗马终身侍奉女灶神的女尼之一 (须誓守贞洁)。 □ *adj* (liter) pure; chaste. (文)纯洁的; 贞洁的。

ves·ti·bule /ˈvestɪbjuːl; ˈvestəˌbjul/ *n* **1** lobby or entrance hall to a building (eg where hats and coats may be left). 前厅; 门厅; 玄关(可置放衣帽等的地方)。

2 porch of a church. 教堂的门廊。 **3** (US) enclosed space at the end of a railway coach. (美)(火车车厢末端的)连廊。

ves·tige /ˈvestɪdʒ; ˈvɛstɪdʒ/ *n* [C] **1** trace or sign; small remaining bit of evidence of what once existed: 痕迹; 形迹; 遗迹: *Not a ~ of the abbey remains.* 那修道院的遗迹荡然无存了。 *There is not a ~ of truth in the report.* 这项报导没有一点真实性。 **2** (anat) organ, or part of one, which is a survival of sth that once existed: (解剖)退化器官; 已退化器官的遗迹: *A human being has the ~ of a tail.* 人类仍有尾巴的痕迹。 **ves·tigial** /veˈstɪdʒɪəl; vesˈtɪdʒɪəl/ *adj* remaining as a ~. 尚留有痕迹的; 退化的。

vest·ment /ˈvestmənt; ˈvɛstmənt/ *n* garment, esp one worn by a priest in church; ceremonial robe. 衣服; (尤指)法衣; 圣衣; 礼服。

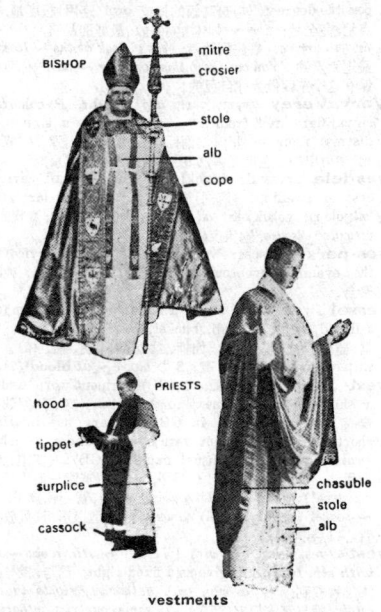

BISHOP
mitre
crosier
stole
alb
cope

PRIESTS
hood
tippet
surplice
cassock
chasuble
stole
cassock

vestments

ves·try /ˈvestrɪ; ˈvɛstrɪ/ *n* (*pl* **-tries**) **1** part of a church where vestments are kept and where the clergy and members of the choir vest themselves. (教堂的)法衣室(放置法衣并供神职人员及唱诗班更衣处)。 ⇨ the illus at church. 参看 church 之插图。 **2** room in a nonconformist church used for Sunday School, prayer meetings, business meetings, etc. (非英国国教的)教堂附属室(用作主日学教室, 祈祷聚会室, 及聚务会议室等)。 **3** (Anglican Church) (council of) ratepayers of a parish, or their representatives, assembled to discuss parish business. (英国国教)教区会(教区纳税人或其代表集会以讨论教区事务者); 教区委员会 (由教区纳税人或其代表组成)。 **'~·man** /-mən; -mən/ *n* (*pl* **-men**) member of a ~. 教区会会员; 教区委员。

ves·ture /ˈvestʃə(r); ˈvɛstʃɚ/ *n* [U] (poet) clothing. (诗)衣服; 衣着。 □ *vt* clothe. 使穿衣服; 覆盖。

vet /vet; vɛt/ *n* (colloq abbr for) veterinary surgeon. (口)兽医(为 veterinary surgeon 之略)。 □ *vt* (**-tt-**) [VP6A] (colloq) (口) **1** give (sb) a medical examination. 诊疗(某人)。 **2** (GB) examine closely and critically, eg sb's past record, qualifications, etc: (英)严格审查(如某人过去的记录、资格等): *He must be thoroughly vetted*

before he's given the job. 他必须经过严格审查才能得到该项工作。

vetch /vetʃ; vɛtʃ/ *n* kinds of plant of the bean family used, wild or cultivated, as fodder for cattle. 大巢菜; 野豌豆(用作牲畜饲料)。

vet·eran /ˈvetərən; ˈvɛtərən/ *n* **1** person who has had much or long experience, esp as a soldier: 老手; 老练者; (尤指)老兵: *~s of two World Wars;* 经历两次大战的老兵; (attrib) (用作定语) *a ~ teacher;* 资深的教师; (of cars) of the years before 1916: (指汽车) 1916 年前的: *a ~ Rolls Royce.* 一部 1916 年前的劳斯莱斯车。 **2** (US) any ex-service man. (美)退伍军人。 **'V~s Day,** 11th November, commemorating the armistice (1918) in World War I. 退伍军人节(十一月十一日, 为第一次大战停战日)。

vet·erin·ary /ˈvetrɪnrɪ US: ˈvetərɪnerɪ; ˈvɛtrəˌnɛrɪ/ *adj* (abbr 略作 **vet** /vet; vɛt/) of or concerned with the diseases of (esp farm and domestic) animals: 兽疾的; 有关家畜之疾病的: *a ~ surgeon/college.* 兽医(学院)。

veto /ˈviːtəu; ˈvito/ *n* (*pl* ~es) constitutional right of a sovereign, president, legislative assembly or other body, or a member of the United Nations Security Council, to reject or forbid sth; statement that rejects or prohibits sth: (国王、总统、议会、或联合国安理会常任理事国的)否决权; 否决; 否决某事物的陈述: *exercise the ~;* 行使否决权; *put a ~ on sth,* forbid it. 否决或禁止某事物。 □ *vt* [VP6A] put a ~ on: 否决; 禁止: *The police ~ed the demonstration that the students wanted.* 警察禁止学生们所要举行的示威。 *John's parents ~ed his plan to buy a motor-cycle.* 约翰的双亲否决了他购买摩托车的计划。

vex /veks; vɛks/ *vt* [VP6A] **1** annoy; distress; trouble: 使恼怒; 使苦恼; 烦扰: *His silly chatter would vex a saint.* 他那喋喋不休的无聊话连圣人也会被惹恼。 *She was vexed that I didn't help her.* 她因为我未帮忙她而生气。 *He was vexed at his failure.* 他因失败而苦恼。 *a vexed question,* a difficult problem that causes much discussion. 争论不休的难题; 议论纷纷的问题。 **2** (poet, rhet) put (the sea) into commotion: (诗、修辞)使(海)激涌: *vexed by storms.* 因风暴而汹涌澎湃的。 **vex·ation** /vekˈseɪʃn; veksˈeʃən/ *n* [U] state of being vexed; [C] sth that vexes; 恼怒; 苦恼; 烦扰; 令人恼怒等的事物: *the little vexations of life;* 生活中的小烦恼; *constant vexations from our neighbours.* 我们邻居的经常烦扰。 **vex·atious** /vekˈseɪʃəs; veksˈeʃəs/ *adj* annoying: 令人烦恼的; 困扰的: *vexatious rules and regulations.* 苛细的规章和条例。

via /ˈvaɪə; ˈvaɪə/ *prep* (Lat) by way of: (拉)经由: *travel from London to Paris via Dover.* 从伦敦经由多佛至巴黎。

vi·able /ˈvaɪəbl; ˈvaɪəbl/ *adj* able to exist; capable of developing and surviving without outside help: 能生存的; 能生长发育的; 行得通的: *Is the newly created State ~?* 这个新国家能生存下去吗? **vi·abil·ity** /ˌvaɪəˈbɪlətɪ; ˌvaɪəˈbɪlətɪ/ *n*

vi·aduct /ˈvaɪədʌkt; ˈvaɪəˌdʌkt/ *n* long bridge (usu with many spans or arches) carrying a road or railway across a valley or dip in the ground. (跨越山谷或下陷地段的)高架桥(通常为多孔桥)。

vial /ˈvaɪəl; ˈvaɪəl/ *n* small bottle, esp for liquid medicine. 小瓶; 小药水瓶。

via media /ˌvaɪə ˈmiːdɪə; ˌvaɪə ˈmɪdɪə/ (Lat) middle course between extremes. (拉)(介于两极端的)中间路线; 中庸之道。

vibes /vaɪbz; vaɪbz/ *n pl* **1** (colloq abbr for) vibra·phone. (口)钟琴; 外布拉风(为 vibraphone 之略)。 **2** (sl) atmosphere(3). (俚)气氛。

vi·brant /ˈvaɪbrənt; ˈvaɪbrənt/ *adj* thrilling; vibrating: 震动的; 震颤的: *the ~ notes of a cello/an electric guitar.* 低音提琴(电吉他)的震颤音调。

vi·bra·phone /ˈvaɪbrəfəun; ˈvaɪbrəˌfon/ *n* (music)

instrument like a xylophone but with metal bars and tone sustained by electronic resonators. (音乐)钟琴；外布拉风.

vi·brate /vaɪˈbreɪt US: ˈvaɪbreɪt; ˈvaɪbret/ *vi, vt* **1** [VP2A, 6A] (cause to) move rapidly and continuously backwards and forwards: (使)快速摆动；摇动；震动；颤动: *The house ~s whenever a heavy lorry passes.* 每有大货车经过时，该屋都会颤动. **2** [VP2A, C] (of stretched strings, the voice) throb; quiver: (指绷紧的弦, 声音)震颤；颤动；颤抖: *The strings of a piano ~ when the keys are struck.* 钢琴的琴键受击时，琴弦就会震颤. *His voice ~d with passion.* 他的声音因激动而颤抖. **vi·brator** /-tə(r); -tɚ/ *n* device that ~s. 震动器.

vi·bra·tion /vaɪˈbreɪʃn; vaɪˈbreʃən/ *n* **1** [U] vibrating movement: 摆动；摇动；震动；颤动: *The ship's engines even at full speed cause very little ~.* 全速时引起的震动也甚微. **2** [C] single movement to and fro when equilibrium has been disturbed: 来回一次振动: *20 ~s per second.* 每秒钟振动二十次.

vi·brato /vɪˈbrɑːtəʊ; vɪˈbrɑto/ *n* (music) throbbing or tremulous effect in singing and the playing of stringed and wind instruments with minute and rapid variations in pitch. (音乐)颤音；振音(唱出或管弦乐器所奏出的快速颤动声音).

vicar /ˈvɪkə(r); ˈvɪkɚ/ *n* **1** (C of E) clergyman in charge of a parish, the tithes of which were partly or wholly payable to another person or body (eg a college) for whom or for which he ~ acts. (英国国教)教区牧师(教区的什一收入, 部分或全部交付其所代表的人或团体). ⇨ **rector**. **2** (RC Church) deputy; representative: (天主教)代理；代表: *the ~ of Christ,* (sometimes used of) the Pope: (有时指)教皇；*cardinal ~,* Pope's delegate acting as the bishop of the diocese of Rome. 罗马教区主教. **~·age** /ˈvɪkərɪdʒ; ˈvɪkərɪdʒ/ *n* ~'s residence. 教区牧师的住宅.

vi·cari·ous /vɪˈkeərɪəs US: vaɪˈk-; vaɪˈkɛrɪəs/ *adj* **1** done, undergone, by one person for another or others: 为别人所做的；代别人遭受的: *the ~ sufferings of Jesus;* 耶稣代人类所受的苦；*a ~ ruler;* 代理的统治者；*feel a ~ pleasure/satisfaction,* eg when sth is done for you or which is sth you would like to do. 感到一种替代性的愉快(满足)(如当他人完成一件为你而做或你愿意做的事情时). **2** deputed; delegated: 代理的；授权的: *~ authority.* 代理权；受托而获得的职权. **~·ly** *adv*

vice¹ /vaɪs; vaɪs/ *n* [C, U] **1** (any particular kind of) evil conduct or indulgence in depraving practices: 恶；邪恶；恶行；不道德的行为: *Gluttony is just as much a ~ as drunkenness.* 饕餮之为恶，不正于酗酒. **2** (in a horse) bad habit (eg kicking) which makes control difficult: (马)使人难驾驭的坏习惯(如踢人)；坏毛病: *He said the horse was free from ~/had no ~.* 他说那匹马没有坏毛病.

vice² (US = **vise**) /vaɪs; vaɪs/ *n* [C] apparatus with strong jaws in which things can be held tightly while being worked upon: 虎钳；钳床: *as firm as a ~,* immovable. 无法移动的；象虎头钳般夹得很紧的.

a vice

vice³ /vaɪs; vaɪs/ *n* (colloq abbr for) vice-president, vice-captain, etc. (口)副总统；副队长等(为 vice-president, vice-captain 等之略).

vice⁴ /vaɪs; vaɪs/ *prep* (Lat) (formal) in place of: (口)(正式用语)代替；取代: *Mr Smith has been appointed chief accountant ~ Mr Brown, who has retired.* 史密斯先生被任命为会计主任, 以接替已退休的布朗先生.

vice- *pref* ⇨ App 3. 参看附录三.

viceroy /ˈvaɪsrɔɪ; ˈvaɪsrɔɪ/ *n* (eg formerly in India) person governing as the deputy of a sovereign. (如昔时印度的)副王；总督. **vice·reine** /vaɪsˈreɪn US: ˈvaɪsreɪn; ˈvaɪsren/ *n* ~'s wife. 副王妃；总督夫人. **vice·regal** /vaɪsˈriːgl; vaɪsˈrigl/ *adj* of a ~. 副王的；总督的.

vice versa /ˌvaɪsɪ ˈvɜːsə; ˈvaɪsɪˈvɝsə/ *adv* (Lat) the other way round; with the terms or conditions reversed: (拉)反过来；反之亦然；逆之亦真: *We gossip about them and ~,* they gossip about us. 我们谈论他们, 他们也谈论我们.

vi·cin·ity /vɪˈsɪnətɪ; vəˈsɪnətɪ/ *n* (*pl* -ties) **1** [U] nearness; closeness of relationship: 近；接近；密切的关系: *in close ~ to the church.* 与教会有密切的关系. **2** [C] neighbourhood: 附近；近处；邻近地区: *the northern vicinities of the capital.* 首都北方的附近地区. *There isn't a good school in the ~.* 附近没有好学校.

vi·cious /ˈvɪʃəs; ˈvɪʃəs/ *adj* **1** of vice¹; given up to vice¹: 恶的；邪恶的；恶行的；为恶的: *~ practices/habits;* 恶习；*a ~ life,* given or done with evil intent: 刻毒的；有恶意的: *a ~ kick/look.* 含有恶意的一踢(一看). **3** (of a horse) having bad habits such as biting, kicking, bolting: (指马)有恶习(如咬人、踢人、逃脱)的；坏脾的. **4** having faults, corrupt: 有缺点的；有错误的；不正确的；谬误的: *a ~ argument.* 谬误的论据. *~ circle,* state of affairs in which a cause produces an effect which itself produces the original cause, eg War breeds hate, and hate leads to war again. 恶性循环(如战争产生仇恨, 仇恨又导致战争). *~ spiral,* continuous rise in one thing (eg prices) caused by a continuous rise in sth else (eg wages). 循环盘旋上升(如工资不断的增加, 造成物价不断的上升). **~·ly** *adv* **~·ness** *n*

vi·ciss·itude /vɪˈsɪsɪtjuːd US: -tuːd; vəˈsɪsəˌtjud/ *n* [C] change, esp in sb's fortunes: 变迁；变化；(尤指个人的)盛衰；荣枯；成败: *His life was marked by ~s,* eg changes from wealth to poverty, success to failure. 他的一生饱经沧桑.

vic·tim /ˈvɪktɪm; ˈvɪktɪm/ *n* **1** living creature killed and offered as a religious sacrifice. 牺牲(为祭神而宰杀的动物). **2** person, animal, etc suffering injury, pain, loss, etc because of circumstances, an event, the ill-will of sb, etc: 牺牲者；受害或遭难的人、动物等: *He is the ~ of his brother's anger/of his own foolishness.* 他为他哥(弟弟)发怒的对象(他因自己的愚昧而自食其果). *A fund was opened to help the ~s of the earthquake.* 设立一专款救助地震的灾民. *Thousands were ~s of the plague in the Middle Ages.* 中世纪时无数的人死于瘟疫. **~·ize** /-aɪz; -ˌaɪz/ *vt* [VP6A] make a ~ of; single out for ill treatment because of real or alleged misconduct, etc: 使牺牲；使受害；选定(某人)受过, 抵罪等: *Trade union leaders claimed that some of their members had been ~ized,* eg by being dismissed. 工会领袖们宣称他们的部分会员被牺牲了(如遭解雇等). **~iz·ation** /ˌvɪktɪmaɪˈzeɪʃn US: -mɪˈz-; ˌvɪktɪməˈzeɪʃən/ *n*: *The strikers said they would return to work if they were promised that there should be no ~ization,* that none of their leaders (or ringleaders) should be ~ized. 罢工者说他们将恢复工作, 如果当局保证他们之中无人成为代罪羔羊.

vic·tor /ˈvɪktə(r); ˈvɪktɚ/ *n* person who conquers or wins. 胜利者；征服者.

vic·toria /vɪkˈtɔːrɪə; vɪkˈtorɪə/ *n* **~ plum,** juicy, sweet-flavoured plum, changing from green to yellow

and red. 维多利亚李子(甜而多汁, 由绿色转为黄色和红色)。

Vic·tor·ian /vɪkˈtɔːrɪən; vɪkˈtorɪən/ *n, adj* (person) of, living in, the reign of Queen Victoria (1837—1901): 维多利亚女王时代 (1837—1901) 的; 生活于此时代的人; 维多利亚时代的人: ~ *authors/manners/dress.* 维多利亚女王时代的作家(礼仪、服饰)。

vic·tory /ˈvɪktərɪ; ˈvɪktərɪ/ *n* [C, U] (*pl* -ries) (instance, occasion, of) success (in war, a contest, game, etc): (战争、竞争、游戏等中的)胜利; 成功; 胜利的实例; 胜利的时际: *gain/win a ~ over the enemy;* 战胜敌人; *lead the troops to ~.* 率领军队迈向胜利。 **vic·tori·ous** /vɪkˈtɔːrɪəs; vɪkˈtorɪəs/ *adj* having gained the ~; triumphant. 获得胜利的; 战胜的; 凯旋的。 **vic·tori·ous·ly** *adv*

vict·ual /ˈvɪtl; ˈvɪtl/ *vt, vi* (-ll-; US also -l-) **1** [VP6A] supply with provisions (of food): 供以食物; 储备食物: ~ *a ship.* 供给一艘船食物。 **2** [VP2A] take in provisions: 取得食物; 储蓄食物: *The ship ~led at Colombo.* 那艘船在科伦坡装贮食物。 □ *n* (usu *pl*) food and drink; provisions. (通常用复数)食料和饮料; 食物。 ~**·ler** (US also ~**·er**) /ˈvɪtlər; ˈvɪtlə/ *n* trader in ~s. 食物供应商。 **licensed** ~**·ler**, (GB) public house keeper who is licensed to sell food, spirits, beer, etc to be consumed on the premises. (英)领有执照的酒店店主(持照可贩卖饮食、烈酒、啤酒等供顾客在店内食用)。

vi·cuña /vɪˈkjuːnə; vɪˈkjunə/ *US:* -ˈkuːnə; vɪˈkjunə/ *n* animal of the central Andes somewhat like, but much smaller than, a camel, with soft, delicate wool. (产于南美安第斯山中部的)骆马。

vide /ˈvaɪdɪ; ˈvaɪdɪ/ *v* (Lat) (imperative form used in references): (拉)(表示参考时所用的祈使形式)见; 参看。 ~, ˈ*infra*, see below. 见下。 ~, ˈ*supra*, see above. 见上。

vide·licet /vɪˈdiːlɪset; vɪˈdeslet/ *adv* (common abbr 通常略作 **viz**, pronounced 读作 /vɪz; vɪz/ or spoken as 或说作 *namely*) that is to say; namely. 就是说; 即是。

video /ˈvɪdɪəʊ; ˈvɪdɪ,o/ *adj* **1** of television broadcasting (cf 参较 *audio*). 电视的。 ~**tape** recording. 电视录象的。 □ *n* **1** (colloq) ~tape recording machine. (口)录象机。 **2** (US) television. (美)电视。 '~**·tape** *n* [U] magnetic tape used to record television pictures and sound. 录象带。 □ *vt* [VP6A] make a recording on ~tape. 录象。

vie /vaɪ; vaɪ/ *vi* [VP3A] **vie (with sb) (for sth)**, rival or compete: 竞争; 争胜: *The two boys vied with one another for the first place.* 那两个男孩子争第一名。

view¹ /vjuː; vju/ *n* **1** [U] state of seeing or being seen; field of vision: 看或被看; 观察; 视野; 视域; 眼界: *Clouds came down and the hill tops passed from our ~,* could no longer be seen. 云层笼罩了下来, 我们看不见山顶了。 **in ~ of**, considering, taking into account: 鉴于; 由于: *In ~ of the facts, it seems useless to continue.* 由这些事实看来, 史似乎是无益的。 **in full ~ of**, fully seen by: 完全被看到了: *The speaker stood in full ~ of the crowd,* could see them and could be seen by them. 演说者站在群众可以完全看得见的地方。 **on ~**, being shown or exhibited: 陈列着; 展览着: *The latest summer fashions are now on ~ in the big shops.* 最新的夏装款式现在正在大的商店中展示着。 **come into ~**, become visible: (就外界事物言)进入视野; 被看见; 被看到: *As we rounded the bend the lake came into ~.* 我们转过弯, 那湖泊就显现在正在大的我们面前了。 **come in to ~ of**, be able to see: (就本身言)能够看见: *As we rounded the bend, we came in ~ of the lake.* 我们转过弯, 就看见了那湖泊。 **2** [C] (picture, photograph, etc) natural scenery, landscape, etc: 天然景色; 风景; 风景画; 风景相片等: *a house with fine ~s over valleys and mountains;* 面山临谷风景优美的房子; *an album of ~s,* eg photographs. 风景照片(画片)簿。 **3** [C] opportunity to see or inspect sth; occasion when there is such an opportunity: 看到或考察某事物的机会; 此种场合或时际: *a private ~,* eg of paintings, before public exhibition. (正式展览前的)预展。 **4** [C] personal opinion; mental attitude; thought or observation (on a subject): 个人的意见; 对某事的态度; 对某一问题的想法或见解: *She had/expressed strong ~s on the subject of equal pay for men and women.* 在男女同酬这一问题上, 她具有(表现出)坚决的态度。 *Your ~s on the situation are not helpful.* 你对于这一情势的见解于事无补。 *He holds extreme ~s,* eg in politics. 他持极端的态度(如在政治上)。 *He took a poor ~ of my conduct,* regarded it unfavourably. 他对于我的行为不以为然。 **fall in with/meet sb's ~s**, agree with, accept, his ideas, opinions, etc. 同意(接受)某人的观念; 意见等。 **5** aim; intention; purpose. 目标; 意图; 目的。 **with a/the ~ to/of**, with the intention or hope: 打算要; 希望; 为了: *with a ~ to facilitating research;* 为了便利研究; *with the ~ of saving trouble.* 为了省却麻烦。 **6** (compounds) (复合词) '~**·point, point of ~**, ⇨ **point¹(4)**. '~**·finder** device in a camera showing the area, etc that will be photographed through the lens. (照相机上的)取景器(显示摄入镜头之范围者)。

view² /vjuː; vju/ *vt* [VP6A] look at; examine; consider: 看; 观察; 检视; 考虑; 认为: *The subject may be ~ed in various ways.* 这问题可从各方面考虑。 *Has the matter been ~ed from the taxpayers' standpoint?* 这件事可曾以纳税人的立场考虑过? **an order to ~**, written authority to look over a house, etc with the idea of buying it: 允许看想买之物(如房屋)的书面许可: *The house agents gave me an order to ~.* 房屋经纪人给了我一张看房子的书面许可。 ~**·er** /ˈvjuːə(r); ˈvjuə/ *n* (esp) (尤指) **1** person watching a television programme. 电视观众。 **2** device for looking at photographic transparencies. 幻灯机。 ~**·less** *adj* **1** (rhet or poet) invisible. (修辞或诗)看不见的。 **2** (US) without ~s (= opinions). (美)无意见的; 无见解的。

vigil /ˈvɪdʒɪl; ˈvɪdʒəl/ *n* **1** [U] staying awake to keep watch or to pray: 守夜; 彻夜清醒(以守望或祈祷): *keep ~ over a sick child;* 彻夜不眠看顾一病童; (*pl*) instances of this: (复)守夜或彻夜不眠的实例: *tired out by her long ~s.* 她由于长时间的熬夜而疲惫不堪。 **2** eve of a religious festival, esp when observed with prayer and fasting. 宗教节日的前夕(尤指须祈祷及斋戒者)。

vigi·lance /ˈvɪdʒɪləns; ˈvɪdʒələns/ *n* [U] watchfulness; keeping watch: 警备; 警戒; 守夜: *exercise ~.* 警戒; 守夜。 '~ **committee**, (chiefly US) self-appointed group of persons who maintain order in a community where organization is imperfect or has broken down. (主美)保安委员会 (一种在组织不健全的地方自行设立的民间治安团体)。

vigi·lant /ˈvɪdʒɪlənt; ˈvɪdʒələnt/ *adj* watchful; on the look-out for danger of any kind. 警戒的; 警惕的。 ~**·ly** *adv*

vigi·lante /ˌvɪdʒɪˈlæntɪ; ˌvɪdʒəˈlæntɪ/ *n* member of a vigilance committee. (主美)保安委员会的成员。

vi·gnette /viːˈnjet; vɪnˈjet/ *n* [C] **1** ornamental design, esp on the title-page of a book, or at the beginning or end of a chapter. 装饰图案; (尤指)(书籍的书名页上或章节的开始或结束处的)小插图。 **2** picture of a person's head and shoulders with the background gradually shaded off. 半身晕映照片或画像(头与肩的背景渐渐变浅)。 **3** short sketch of a person's character. (描写某人性格的)简介; 短文。

vig·our (US = **vigor**) /ˈvɪgə(r); ˈvɪgɚ/ *n* [U] mental or physical strength; energy; forcefulness (of language): 智力; 体力; 精力; 活力; (语言中的)力量。 **vig·or·ous** /ˈvɪgərəs; ˈvɪgərəs/ *adj* strong; energetic. 强壮的; 有力的; 精力充沛的。 **vig·or·ous·ly** *adv*

Vik·ing /ˈvaɪkɪŋ; ˈvaɪkɪŋ/ *n* any of the Scandinavian sea-rovers who raided the coasts of Europe during the 8th, 9th and 10th cc. (八至十世纪间掠夺欧洲海岸的)北欧海盗; 威金人。

vile /vaɪl; vaɪl/ adj (**-r, -st**) **1** shameful and disgusting: 可耻的; 卑鄙的; 令人厌恶的: ~ habits/language; 令人厌恶的习惯(语言); the ~ practice of bribery. 可耻的贿赂恶习。 **2** (colloq) bad: (口)坏的: ~ weather. 坏天气。 **3** (old use) valueless: (旧用法)无价值的: this ~ body, ie contrasted with the soul or spirit. 这不足道的躯体(与灵魂或精神相对而言)。 ~·ly /vaɪlɪ; ˈvaɪlɪ/ adv ~·ness n

vil·ify /ˈvɪlɪfaɪ; ˈvɪləˌfaɪ/ vt (pt, pp **-fied**) [VP6A] slander; say evil things about (sb). 诽谤; 中伤(某人)。 vil·ifi·ca·tion /ˌvɪlɪfɪˈkeɪʃn; ˌvɪləfəˈkeʃən/ n

villa /ˈvɪlə; ˈvɪlə/ n **1** (in GB) (usu as part of the address) detached or semi-detached house or esp one on the outskirts of a town: (在英国)(通常写作住址的一部分)别庄; 庄宅; 别业(尤指在城郊者): No 13 Laburnum Villas. 庐舍别庄十三号。 **2** country house with a large garden, esp in S Europe. (尤指在欧洲南部的)乡间别墅。

vil·lage /ˈvɪlɪdʒ; ˈvɪlɪdʒ/ n **1** place smaller than a town, where there are houses and shops, and usu a church and school: 村庄; 乡村: (attrib) (用作定语) the ~ post-office. 乡村邮局。 **villager** /ˈvɪlɪdʒə(r); ˈvɪlɪdʒə/ n person who lives in a ~. 村民; 村人; 乡村居民。

vil·lain /ˈvɪlən; ˈvɪlən/ n **1** wrongdoer; wicked person. 恶徒; 坏人。 **2** = **villein**. ~·ous /ˈvɪlənəs; ˈvɪlənəs/ adj characteristic of a ~; evil. 有恶徒特性的; 邪恶的。 ~y n (pl **-nies**) [U] evil conduct; (pl) evil acts. 邪恶; (复)恶行; 邪恶行为。

vil·lein /ˈvɪleɪn; ˈvɪlɪn/ n (hist) feudal serf in the Middle Ages. (史)(中世纪的)农奴。 ~·age /ˈvɪlɪnɪdʒ; ˈvɪlənɪdʒ/ n [U] state of being a ~; serfdom. 农奴的状态; 农奴的身份。

vim /vɪm; vɪm/ n [U] (colloq) energy: (口)精力; 活力: feel full of vim. 感到活力充沛。 Put more vim into it! 卖点力做(它)!

vin·ai·grette /ˌvɪnɪˈgret; ˌvɪnəˈgret/ n [U] dressing (for green salads, etc) of vinegar and oil, flavoured with herbs. 酱醋油(由醋及油制成, 并以香料增味, 用于调制凉拌生菜等)。

vin·di·cate /ˈvɪndɪkeɪt; ˈvɪndəˌket/ vt [VP6A] show or prove the truth, justice, validity, etc (of sth that has been attacked or disputed): 证实; 辩明; 辩护; 剖白(已受攻击或曾引起争辩之某事物): ~ a claim/ one's title to a privilege; 辩明一项权利(自己具有某种特权); ~ one's veracity/judgement. 为自己的诚实(判断)辩护。 Events have ~d his judgement/actions. 事情本身已经证实了他的判断(行为)的正确性。 vin·di·ca·tion /ˌvɪndɪˈkeɪʃn; ˌvɪndəˈkeʃən/ n [U] vindicating or being ~d; [C] instance of this: 证实; 辩明; 辩护; 剖白; 其实例: speak in vindication of one's conduct. 为自己的行为辩护。

vin·dic·tive /vɪnˈdɪktɪv; vɪnˈdɪktɪv/ adj unforgiving; having or showing a desire for revenge. 不宽恕的; 有复仇心的; 报复的。 ~·ly adv ~·ness n

vine /vaɪn; vaɪn/ n [C] climbing plant whose fruit is the grape; any plant with slender stems that trails, eg melons, or climbs (eg peas, hops). 葡萄树; 蔓生植物(如甜瓜); 攀缘植物(如豌豆; 蛇麻草); 藤; 蔓。 ~·yard /ˈvɪnjəd; ˈvɪnjəd/ n [C] area of land planted with grape-~s. 葡萄园。 **vin·ery** /ˈvaɪnərɪ; ˈvaɪnərɪ/ n (pl **-ries**) greenhouse for ~s. 栽培葡萄的暖房。

vin·egar /ˈvɪnɪgə(r); ˈvɪnɪgə/ n [U] acid liquor (made from malt, wine, cider, etc) used in flavouring food and for pickling. 醋。 ~y /ˈvɪnɪgərɪ; ˈvɪnɪgərɪ/ adj like ~; (fig) sour-tempered. 似醋的; (喻)尖酸刻薄的。

vino /ˈviːnəʊ; ˈvino/ n (pl **-es** /-nəʊz; -noz/) [U] (colloq) wine. (口)葡萄酒。

vi·nous /ˈvaɪnəs; ˈvaɪnəs/ adj of, like or due to wine. 葡萄酒的; 似葡萄酒的; 由葡萄酒产生的。

vin·tage /ˈvɪntɪdʒ; ˈvɪntɪdʒ/ n **1** (rarely pl) (period or season of) grape harvesting. (罕用复数)葡萄收获; 葡萄收获期或季节: The ~ was later than usual last year. 去年葡萄收获季节较平常略晚。 **2** [C, U] (wine from) grapes of a particular year: 某一年所产的葡萄; 该年葡萄所酿的葡萄酒: of the ~ of 1959; 一九五九年所产的葡萄(酒)酿的酒。 rare old ~s; 名贵的陈年葡萄酒; a ~ year, one in which good wine was made: 酿制好葡萄酒的年份; ~ wines, from ~ years. 上等葡萄酒。 **3** (by extension; attrib) of a period in the past and having a reputation for high quality: (引伸用法; 用作定语)属于过去某一时期而且以品质优良著名的: a ~ car, one built between 1916 and 1930. ⇨ **veteran**; 老式的名贵汽车(造于一九一六至一九三○年之间); sports car more than 30 years old. 车龄超过三十年的跑车。

vint·ner /ˈvɪntnə(r); ˈvɪntnə/ n wine-merchant. 葡萄酒商。

vi·nyl /ˈvaɪnɪl; ˈvaɪnɪl/ n (kinds of) tough, flexible plastic, used for clothing, coverings and binding books. 乙烯基; 维尼龙(数种柔韧而强韧的塑胶产品, 用作衣料; 覆盖物及装订书籍)。

viol /ˈvaɪəl; ˈvaɪəl/ n (usu six-) stringed instrument of the Middle Ages from which the modern violin was developed. 维奥尔(一种中世纪的弦乐器, 通常为六弦, 现代小提琴即由此发展而来)。

vi·ola¹ /vɪˈəʊlə; vɪˈolə/ n tenor violin, of larger size than the ordinary violin. 中提琴(较小提琴大)。 ⇨ the illus at string. 参看 string 之插图。

vi·ola² /ˈvaɪələ; ˈvaɪələ/ n kinds of plant including pansies of one colour only (not variegated) and violets. 堇菜科植物(包括紫罗兰)。

vi·ol·ate /ˈvaɪəleɪt; ˈvaɪəˌlet/ vt [VP6A] **1** break (an oath, a treaty, etc); act contrary to (what one's conscience tells one to do, etc). 违犯(誓言, 条约等); 违背(良心要一个人所做的事等)。 **2** act towards (a sacred place, sb's seclusion, etc) without proper respect: 亵渎; 冒犯; 侵害(神圣的地方, 某人的独处等): ~ sb's privacy. 侵犯某人的私生活。 **3** rape. 强奸。 **vi·ol·ation** /ˌvaɪəˈleɪʃn; ˌvaɪəˈleʃən/ n [U] violating or being ~d: 违犯; 亵渎; 冒犯; 侵害: act in violation of a treaty; 行事违犯某条约; [C] instance of this: 其实例: violations of the rights of the citizens/the right of free speech, etc. 侵犯公民权(言论自由权等)。

vi·ol·ent /ˈvaɪələnt; ˈvaɪələnt/ adj **1** using, showing, accompanied by, great force: 使用暴力的; 显示暴力的; 伴以暴力的; 猛烈的; 强烈的; 激烈的; 凶暴的: a ~ wind/ attack; 暴风(猛攻); ~ blows; 猛烈的打击; ~ passions; 强烈的情欲; in a ~ temper; 在盛怒之下; ~ abuse; 谩骂; a ~ (= extreme) contrast. 明显的对比。 **2** caused by ~ attack: 由猛烈攻击、打击等造成的: meet a ~ death. 横死。 **3** severe: 厉害的; 剧烈的: ~ toothache. 剧烈的牙痛。 ~·ly adv **vi·ol·ence** /-əns; -əns/ n [U] state of being ~; conduct: 猛烈; 强烈; 凶暴; 暴力; 暴行: crimes/acts of violence; 暴力罪行(凶暴的行为); robbery with violence; 暴力抢劫; an outbreak of violence, rioting, etc. 暴动。 **do violence to**, (fig) be a breach of: (喻)违背; 破坏: It would do violence to his principles to eat meat. 吃肉会违背他的原则。

vi·olet /ˈvaɪələt; ˈvaɪəlɪt/ n **1** small wild or garden plant with sweet-smelling flowers. 紫罗兰(野生或栽培)。 **2** [U] bluish-purple colour of wild ~s. 紫罗兰色; 蓝紫色(野生紫罗兰之色)。

vi·olin /ˌvaɪəˈlɪn; ˌvaɪəˈlɪn/ n four-stringed musical instrument played with a bow, ⇨ the illus at string. 小提琴(一种四弦乐器; 参看 string 之插图)。 ~·ist /-ɪst; -ɪst/ n player of a ~. 小提琴手。

vi·per /ˈvaɪpə(r); ˈvaɪpə/ n kinds of poisonous snake of Africa, Asia, and Europe; (fig) spiteful and treacherous person. 蝰(产于非洲、亚洲和欧洲之数种毒蛇); (喻)恶毒之人; 奸诈之人。 **the ~**, the adder (the only poisonous snake in GB). 蝮蛇(英国唯一之毒蛇)。

vir·ago /vɪˈrɑːgəʊ; vəˈrego/ n (pl **-s** or **-es** /-gəuz; -goz/) violent and bad-tempered woman who scolds and shouts. 泼妇; 悍妇。

vir·gin /ˈvɜːdʒɪn; ˈvɝdʒɪn/ n girl or woman (and in

recent use, man) who has not experienced sexual union. 处女; (晚近用法)处男。 **the (Blessed) V~ (Mary),** (abbr 略作 **BVM**), the mother of Jesus Christ. 圣母马利亚。 □ *adj* **1** pure and chaste: 处女的; 童贞的: *the V~ Queen,* Elizabeth I of England. 处子女王(即英国伊利莎白女王一世)。 **the ~ birth,** the doctrine that Jesus was miraculously conceived by the V~ Mary. 童身胎(认为耶稣系由童贞女马利亚神奇地怀孕的说法)。 **2** pure and untouched: 纯洁的; 洁白无瑕疵的; 未被玷污的: *snow.* 白雪。**3**in the original condition; unused: 原始的; 处于原来状态的; 未经使用的: *a ~ forest,* one in its natural state, no trees having been felled, planted, etc; 原始森林; 未采伐过的森林; *~ soil,* soil never before used for crops; (fig) a mind open to receive new ideas. 处女地; 未种植过作物的土地; (喻)易接受新观念的心灵。 **~·ity** /vɔˈdʒɪnɔtɪ; vɔˈdʒɪnɔtɪ/ *n* [U] state of being a ~; ~ condition. 处女的状态; 童贞的或原始的状况。

vir·ginal¹ /ˈvɜːdʒɪnl; ˈvɝdʒɪnl/ *adj,* of, suitable for, a virgin. 处女的; 童贞的; 适于处女的。

vir·ginal² /ˈvɜːdʒɪnl; ˈvɝdʒɪnl/ *n* (often *pl*) square spinet without legs used in the 16th and 17th cc (and also called 亦称作 *the ~s / a pair of ~s*). (常用复数) 古钢琴(十六、十七世纪时所用的方形无腿小键一名维琴娜尔)。

Vir·ginia /vɔˈdʒɪnɪɔ; vɔˈdʒɪnjɔ/ *n* [U] kinds of tobacco produced in the State of V~, US: (美国弗吉尼亚州产的)弗吉尼亚烟叶: *~ cigarettes.* 弗吉尼亚烟叶制成的香烟。 **~ creeper,** ornamental vine grown on walls, with large leaves which turn scarlet in the autumn. 五叶地锦; 美国爬山虎(一名蛇葡萄, 常蔓生于墙上以作装饰, 叶大, 秋天变为猩红色)。

Virgo /ˈvɜːgəʊ; ˈvɝgo/ *n* sixth sign of the zodiac. 处女座; 处女宫(黄道十二宫之第六宫)。 ⇨ the illus at **zodiac.** 参看 zodiac 之插图。

vir·gule /ˈvɜːgjuːl; ˈvɝgjul/ *n* diagonal mark (/), used to separate alternatives (as in *and/or*). 短斜线 (用以表示二者中可任择其一, 如 and/or 表示 and 与 or 可任择其一。

vir·ile /ˈvɪraɪl US: ˈvɪrəl; ˈvɪrəl/ *adj* **1** having or showing strength, energy, manly qualities: 具有或显示力气、活力、男子气概的; 刚健的; 雄纠纠的: *~ eloquence;* 雄辩; *a ~ style (of writing);* 有力的文体; *live to a ~ old age.* 活到老年身体仍然很硬朗。 **2** (of men) sexually potent. (指男人)性机能强的。 **vir·il·ity** /vɪˈrɪlətɪ; vəˈrɪlətɪ/ *n* [U] masculine strength and vigour; sexual power. (指男子)男性的强壮力; 生殖力; 性能力。

vi·rol·ogy /vaɪəˈrɒlədʒɪ; vaɪˈrɑlədʒɪ/ *n* [U] the study of viruses and virus diseases. 滤体学; 滤毒学(研究病毒及病毒疾病者)。

virtu /vɜːˈtuː; vɝˈtu/ *n* (only in) (仅用于) *articles/objects of ~,* art objects interesting because of fine workmanship, antiquity, rarity, etc. 艺术; 古玩; 骨董。

vir·tual /ˈvɜːtʃʊəl; ˈvɝtʃʊəl/ *adj* being in fact, acting as, what is described; in fact; in reality but not accepted openly or in name as such: 事实上的; 实际上的; 实质上的(但未公开或在名义上为人接受)的: *the ~ head of the business;* 商店的实际上的老板; *a ~ defeat/confession.* 实际上的失败(忏悔)。 **~·ly** /-tʃʊəlɪ; -tʃʊəlɪ/ *adv*

vir·tue /ˈvɜːtʃuː; ˈvɝtʃʊ/ *n* **1** [C, U] (any particular kind of) goodness or excellence: 善; 德行; 美德; 好处; 优点: *Patience is a ~.* 忍耐是一种美德。 *Is patriotism always a ~?* 爱国永远是一种美德吗? *Our climate has the ~s of never being too hot or too cold.* 我们这里的气侯有不太热亦不太冷的优点。 **make a ~ of necessity,** do sth pretending it to be an act of ~ when one really does it under compulsion. 以逆来顺受的心情去做迫不得已的事。*V~ is its own reward,* (prov) One should not expect a reward for doing sth that is truly virtuous. (谚)为善不望报; 为善最乐。 **the cardinal ~s,** prudence, fortitude, temperance, justice. (四种)基本美德(审慎、坚毅、克制、公正)。 **the theological ~s,** faith, hope, charity. (基督教的)三德(信、望、爱)。**2** [U] chastity.

贞节; 纯洁。 **3** [U] efficacy; ability to produce a definite result: 效力; 效能: *Have you any faith in the ~ of herbs to heal sickness?* 你对于草药治病的效力有信心吗? **4** [U, C] excellence; advantage: 优点; 长处; 有利处: *The great ~ of the scheme is that it costs very little.* 该项计划的一大优点就是花费很少。 **5** *by/in ~ of,* by reason of; because of: 由于; 因为: *He claimed a pension in ~ of his long military service.* 他以在军中服役多年为由要求发给养老金。**vir·tu·ous** /ˈvɜːtʃʊəs; ˈvɝtʃʊəs/ *adj* having or showing ~. 有品德的; 善良的。**vir·tu·ous·ly** *adv*

vir·tu·oso /ˌvɜːtʃʊˈəʊzəʊ US: -ˈəʊsəʊ; ˌvɝtʃʊˈoso/ *n* (*pl* ~**s** or 或 **-si** /-ziː US: -siː; -si/) person with special knowledge of, or taste for, works of art; person skilled in the methods of an art, esp one who plays a musical instrument with great skill: 艺术品专家或爱好者; (艺术界的)名家; (尤指)大演奏家: (用作定语) *a ~ performer.* 名演奏家。 **vir·tu·os·ity** /ˌvɜːtʃʊˈɒsətɪ; ˌvɝtʃʊˈɑsətɪ/ *n* [U] skill of a ~. 艺术品鉴赏力; (演奏等的)精湛技巧。

viru·lent /ˈvɪrʊlənt; ˈvɪrjələnt/ *adj* (of poison) strong; deadly; (of ill feeling, hatred) bitter; (of words, etc) full of ill feeling; (of diseases, sores) poisonous. (指毒物)剧烈的; 致命的; (指恶感、仇恨)厉害的; 深刻的; (指言词等)恶毒的; 刻毒的; (指疾病, 疮)有毒的; 恶性的。 **~·ly** *adv* **viru·lence** /-ləns; -ləns/ *n*

vi·rus /ˈvaɪərəs; ˈvaɪrəs/ *n* [C] any of various poisonous elements, smaller than bacteria, causing the spread of infectious disease: (造成传染病蔓延的)病毒; 滤过性病原体; 毒素: *the ~ of rabies;* 狂犬病的病毒; ~ *diseases.* 滤过性疾病。

visa /ˈviːzə; ˈvizə/ *n* [C] stamp or signature put on a passport to show that it has been examined and approved by the officials of a foreign country which the owner intends to visit (*'entrance* or *'entry ~*) or leave (*'exit ~*). 签证。 (entrance visa 入境签证, exit visa 出境签证)。 □ *vt* [VP6A] put a ~ on: 签证: *get one's passport ~ed / before going to Poland.* 去波兰前先在护照上办妥签证。

vis·age /ˈvɪzɪdʒ; ˈvɪzɪdʒ/ *n* [C] (liter) face (of a human being). (文)(人的)面貌; 面容。**-vis·aged** /ˈvɪzɪdʒd; ˈvɪzɪdʒd/ *suff* (in compounds) having the kind of ~ indicated: (用于复合词中)有某种面貌的: *gloomy-~d* funeral directors. 面容悲戚的丧葬承办人。

vis-à-vis /ˌviːz ɑː ˈviː US: ˌviːz ə ˈviː; ˌvizəˈvi/ *adv, prep* **1** facing (one another): 和…面对面; 相对: *sit ~ in a train.* 在火车上相对而坐。 **2** (fig) in relation to; compared with. (喻)关于; 与…相较。

vis·cera /ˈvɪsərə; ˈvɪsərə/ *n pl* internal organs of the body, esp the intestines. 内脏; (尤指)肠。 **vis·ceral** /ˈvɪsərəl; ˈvɪsərəl/ *adj* of the ~. 内脏的; 肠子的。

vis·cid /ˈvɪsɪd; ˈvɪsɪd/ *adj* sticky; semi-fluid. 粘的; 粘性的; 半流体的。 **vis·cos·ity** /vɪsˈkɒsətɪ; vɪsˈkasətɪ/ *n* [U] being viscous. 粘; 粘性。

vis·cous /ˈvɪskəs; ˈvɪskəs/ *adj* sticky; semi-fluid. 粘的; 粘性的; 半流体的。

vis·count /ˈvaɪkaʊnt; ˈvaɪkaʊnt/ *n* nobleman higher in rank than a baron, lower than an earl. 子爵(高于男爵而低于伯爵)。 **~·ess** /-ɪs; -ɪs/ *n* wife of a ~; woman who is a ~ in her own right. 子爵夫人; 女子爵。 **~·cy** /-sɪ; -tsɪ/ *n* (*pl* -**cies**) title, rank, dignity, of a ~. 子爵的头衔、地位、尊荣。

vise /vaɪs; vaɪs/ *n* (US) = **vice².**

vis·ible /ˈvɪzəbl; ˈvɪzəbl/ *adj* that can be seen; that is in sight: 可见的; 看得见的: *The eclipse will be ~ to observers in western Europe.* 这次的日(月)蚀西欧的观测者可以见到。**vis·ibly** /-əblɪ; -əblɪ/ *adv* in a ~ manner: 可见地; 看得见地; 显而易见地: *She was visibly annoyed.* 她显然被激怒了。**vis·ibil·ity** /ˌvɪzəˈbɪlətɪ; ˌvɪzəˈbɪlətɪ/ *n* [U] being ~; (esp) condition of the atmosphere for seeing things at a distance: 可见性; (尤指)明视度; 能见度: *The aircraft turned back because of poor visibility.* 由于能见度太低, 飞机折返了。

vi·sion /ˈvɪʒn; ˈvɪʒən/ *n* **1** [U] power of seeing or

imagining, looking ahead, grasping the truth that underlies facts: 视力; 视觉; 想象力; 远见; 洞察力; 观察力: *the field of ~,* all that can be seen from a certain point; 视野; *the ~ of a poet/prophet;* 诗人的想象力(预言家的先见之明); *a man of ~.* 有眼光的人。 **2** [C] sth seen, esp by the mind's eye or the power of imagination, or sth seen during sleep in a trance-like state: 视见之物; 景象; (尤指)幻想; 梦幻; 幻象; 幻影: *the romantic ~s of youth.* 青年人浪漫的幻想。 *Have you ever had ~s of great wealth and success?* 你曾有过发大财成大功的幻想吗?

vi·sion·ary /'vɪʒənrɪ US: -ʒənerɪ; 'vɪʒən,erɪ/ *adj* **1** existing only in a vision or the imagination; unpractical; fanciful: 仅存在于幻想或想象中的; 不切实际的; 空幻的: *~ schemes/scenes/plans.* 幻想中的策略(景象, 计划)。 **2** (of persons) having ~ ideas; dreamy. (指人)爱幻想的; 爱空想的。 □ *n* ~ person. 幻想者; 空想者。

visit /'vɪzɪt; 'vɪzɪt/ *vt, vi* **1** [VP6A] go to see (sb); go to (a place) for a time: 访问; 拜访(某人); 游览; 参观(某地)。 *~ a friend;* 访友。 *~ Rome.* 游罗马。 *His rich relatives seldom ~ him.* 他那些有钱的亲戚很少去拜访他。 [VP2C] (US) stay: (美)停留; 下榻: *~ing in Paris;* 在巴黎停留; *~ing at a new hotel.* 在一家新旅馆下榻。 **2** [VP6A] (chiefly US) go in order to inspect or examine officially: (主美)正式的视察或检查: *Restaurant and hotel kitchens are ~ed regularly by public health inspectors.* 餐馆及旅馆的厨房定期由公共卫生官员检查。 **3** [VP3A] (chiefly US) (主美) *~ with,* pay a ~ to; talk with: 拜访; 与…谈话: *She loves ~ing with her neighbours and having a good gossip.* 她喜欢去邻居家开心地闲话家常。 **4** [VP14] *~ sth on sb,* (biblical use) punish. (圣经用语)惩罚。 *~ the sins of the fathers upon the children,* make the children suffer for their parent's failings. 使儿子因父亲的罪孽而受惩罚。 □ *n* act of ~ing; time of ~ing: 访问; 游览; 访问或游览的时间; pay a ~ to a friend/a patient/a prospective customer; 访友(探望病人,访问可望成为顾客者); go on a ~ to the seaside; 去海滨游玩; a ~ of several hours; 一次数小时的访问; during her first ~ to her husband's parents. 在她第一次探望其翁姑的时候。 *~ing n* [U] paying ~s; making calls on people): 访问; 访晤(人): *~ing hours at a hospital;* 医院里的探病时间; *We are not on ~ing terms,* not sufficiently well acquainted to ~ one another. 我们尚不熟悉; 彼此无往来。 **visi·tor** /'vɪzɪtə(r); 'vɪzɪtɚ/n person who ~s; person who stays at a place: 访问者; 参观者; 宾客: *summer ~ors,* eg at a holiday resort; 夏季的游客(如在度假胜地者); *the ~ors' book,* one in which ~ors sign their names, eg at a hotel or a place of public interest. 来宾签名簿; 旅客或游客登记簿。

visi·tant /'vɪzɪtənt; 'vɪzɪtənt/ *n* **1** (liter) visitor, esp an important or supernatural one. (文)访问者; (尤指)贵宾; (来到人世的)鬼神。 **2** migratory bird: 候鸟: *a rare ~ to these shores.* 到这一带海边的稀见候鸟。

visi·ta·tion /,vɪzɪ'teɪʃn; ,vɪzə'teʃən/ *n* **1** [C] visit, esp one of an official nature or one made by a bishop or priest: 访问; (尤指)巡视; 视察(由主教或教士所作的)访晤: *a ~ of the sick,* made by a clergyman as part of his duties. (教士的)探视病人。 **2** [C] trouble, disaster, looked upon as punishment from God: (视为上帝惩罚的)灾祸; 苦难: *The famine was a ~ of God for their sins.* 那次饥馑被视为上帝对他们犯罪的惩罚。

vi·sor /'vaɪzə; 'vaɪzɚ/ *n* **1** (hist) movable part of a helmet, covering the face. (史)盔的面甲。 ⇨ the illus at **armour.** 参看 armour 之插图。 **2** peak of a cap. 帽舌; 帽檐。 **3** ('sun-) ~, oblong sheet of dark-tinted glass hinged at the top of a windscreen in a car to lessen the glare of bright sunshine. (汽车挡风玻璃上方的)遮阳板。

vista /'vɪstə; 'vɪstə/ *n* [C] **1** long, narrow view: 狭长的景色; 远景: *a ~ of the church spire at the end of an avenue of trees.* 林荫道末端教堂塔尖的景色。 **2** (fig) long series of scenes, events, etc which one can look back on or forward to: (喻)(对一连串情景、事件等之)回顾; 展望: *the ~s of bygone times;* 昔日的一连串追忆; *a discovery that opens up new ~s.* 开拓新的远景的一项发现。

vis·ual /'vɪʒʊəl; 'vɪʒʊəl/ *adj* concerned with, used in, seeing: 看的; 视觉的; 用于看的: *~ images.* 视觉像。 *She has a ~ memory,* is able to remember well things she sees. 她对看过的事物能记得很清楚。 *~ aids,* (used in teaching) eg pictures, film-strips, cinema films. 直观教具(如教学上用的图片、幻灯片及电影片)。 *~ly* /'vɪʒʊəlɪ; 'vɪʒʊəlɪ/ *adv* *~·ize* /-aɪz; -,aɪz/ *vt* [VP6A] bring (sth) as a picture before the mind: 想象; 设想: *I remember meeting the man two years ago but can't ~ize him,* recall what he looked like. 我记得两年前遇见过那个人,但是他的样子我想不起来了。 **vis·ual·iz·ation** /,vɪʒʊəlaɪ'zeɪʃn US: -lɪ'z-, ,vɪʒʊəl'zeʃən/ *n*

vi·tal /'vaɪtl; 'vaɪtl/ *adj* **1** of, connected with, necessary for, living: 生命的; 与生命有关的; 维持生命所必需的: *wounded in a ~ part.* 在要害处受伤。 *the ~ force/principle,* that which is assumed to account for organic life. 生命力; 生机; 活力。 *~ statistics,* (a) relating to the duration of life, and to births, marriages and deaths. 生命统计; 人口动态统计(即有关寿命、出生、婚姻及死亡的统计)。 (b)(colloq) woman's measurements at bust, waist and hips. (口)妇女的三围(胸、腰、臀)数字。 **2** supreme; indispensable: 极度的; 非常的; 不可缺少的: *~ of importance;* 非常重要的; *a ~ necessity.* 极端需要。 *~s n pl* ~ parts of the body, esp the lungs, heart and brain. 身体的重要器官(尤指肺、心和脑); 要害。 *~·ly* /'vaɪtlɪ; 'vaɪtlɪ/ *adv* *~·ism* /-ɪzəm;-,ɪzəm/ *n* [U] belief that there is a controlling force in living things which is distinct from chemical and physical forces (opp of *mechanism*). 生机论(认为生物中有一控制力不同于化学力和物理力)(为 mechanism 之反义词)。 *~·ist* /-ɪst; -ɪst/ *n* person who believes in *~ism.* 生机论者; 持生机论者。

vi·tal·ity /vaɪ'tælɪtɪ; vaɪ'tælɪtɪ/ *n* [U] vital power; capacity to endure and perform functions: 活力; 生命力; 持续力: *Can an artificial language have any ~?* 人造的语言能持久吗?

vi·tal·ize /'vaɪtəlaɪz; 'vaɪtl,aɪz/ *vt* [VP6A] fill with vitality; put vigour into. 赋予生命力; 给予活力。

vit·amin /'vɪtəmɪn US: 'vaɪt-; 'vaɪtəmɪn/ *n* [C] any of a number of organic substances which are present in certain food-stuffs and are essential to the health of man and other animals: 维他命; 维生素: *illnesses* (eg scurvy, rickets) *caused by ~ deficiency;* 因缺乏维生素而引起的疾病(如坏血病,佝偻病); *~ tablets.* 维他命片。

vi·ti·ate /'vɪʃɪeɪt; 'vɪʃɪ,et/ *vt* [VP6A] lower the quality of; weaken or destroy the force of: 降低…的品质; 削弱或破坏…的力量; 污损; 败坏: *~d blood;* 污血; *the ~d air of an overcrowded room.* 过分拥挤之房间内的混浊空气。 *This admission ~s your argument/cliam.* 这项供认减弱了你的论据(权利要求)的力量。

vit·reous /'vɪtrɪəs; 'vɪtrɪəs/ *adj* of or like glass: 玻璃的; 似玻璃的: *~ rocks,* hard and brittle; 坚硬而脆的岩石; *~ enamel,* used instead of porcelain. 搪瓷。

vit·rify /'vɪtrɪfaɪ; 'vɪtrə,faɪ/ *vt, vi* (*pt, pp* **-fied**) [VP6A, 2A] change, be changed, into a glass-like substance. (使)变成玻璃状物质。

vit·riol /'vɪtrɪəl; 'vɪtrɪəl/ *n* [U] sulphuric acid; any of the salts of sulphuric acid: 硫酸; 硫酸盐; 矾: *blue ~,* copper sulphate: 硫酸铜; 胆矾; (fig) sarcasm. (喻)尖酸的讽刺; 尖刻的话; 讥刺。 *~·ic* /,vɪtrɪ'blɪk; ,vɪtrɪ'ɑlɪk/ *adj* (fig, of words, feelings) biting; full of invective: (喻,指言词、感情)尖刻的; 谩骂的: *a ~ic attack on the President;* 对总统的犀利攻击; *~ic remarks.* 尖刻的话。

vit·uper·ate /vɪ'tjuːpəreɪt US: vaɪ'tuː-; vaɪ'tupə,ret/ *vt* [VP6A] abuse in words; curse; revile. 骂; 责骂; 咒骂; 辱骂。 **vit·uper·at·ive** /vɪ'tjuːpərətɪv US: vaɪ-

'tu:pərertɪv/ vaɪ'tjupə,retɪv/ adj abusive. 责骂的; 辱骂的。 **vit·uper·ation** /vɪ,tju:pə'reɪʃn US: vaɪ,tu:-; vaɪˌtupə'reʃən/ n [U] abusive language; severe scolding. 骂人的话; 辱骂。

viva /'vaɪvə; 'vaɪvə/ n (colloq) (口) = viva voce.

vi·vace /viːˈvɑːtʃɪ; vɪ'vatʃɪ/ adv (music) briskly. (音乐) 轻快地; 活泼地。

vi·va·cious /vɪ'veɪʃəs; vaɪ'veʃəs/ adj lively; high-spirited; gay: 活泼的; 快活的; 愉快的; a ~ girl. 活泼的女郎。~·ly adv **vi·vac·ity** /vɪ'væsətɪ, vaɪ'væsætɪ/ n [U].

viva voce /,vaɪvə 'vəʊsɪ; 'vaɪvə'vosɪ/ adj, adv orally. 口头的(地); a ~ examination. 口试。□ n ~ examination or test. 口试。

vivid /'vɪvɪd; 'vɪvɪd/ adj 1 (of colours, etc) intense; bright: (指颜色等)强烈的; 鲜明的; a ~ flash of lightning: 一道耀眼的闪电; ~ green trousers. 翠绿色的长裤。 2 lively; active: 有生气的; 活泼的; a ~ imagination. 活泼的想象。 3 clear and distinct: 清晰的; 生动的; a ~ description of an event: 对一事件的生动描述; have ~ recollections of a holiday in Italy. 对在意大利度假的情景保有清晰的记忆。~·ly adv ~·ness n

vi·vipar·ous /vɪ'vɪpərəs US: vaɪ-; vaɪ'vɪpərəs/ adj having offspring which develop within the mother's body (not from eggs). 胎生的。

vivi·sect /,vɪvɪ'sekt; 'vɪvə,sekt/ vt [VP6A] operate or experiment on (living animals) for scientific research. 活体解剖。(为科学研究而)解剖或实验(活动物)。 **vivi·sec·tion** /,vɪvɪ'sekʃn; ,vɪvə'sekʃən/ n [U] ~ing; [C] instance of this. 活体解剖; 其实例。 **vivi·sec·tion·ist** /-ʃənɪst; -ʃənɪst/ n person who ~s; person who considers vivisection justifiable. 作活体解剖者; 活体解剖论者; 为活体解剖辩护者。

vixen /'vɪksn; 'vɪksn/ n female fox; bad-tempered quarrelsome woman. 雌狐; 牝狐; 悍妇; 泼妇; 刁妇。~·ish /'vɪksənɪʃ; 'vɪksnʃ/ adj scolding; badtempered. 责骂的; 泼辣的; 坏脾气的。

viz /vɪz; vɪz/ (Lat 拉丁 videlicet, usu spoken as 通常说作 namely) that is to say; namely 即是说; 就是。

vi·zier /vɪ'zɪə(r); vɪ'zɪr/ n official of high rank in some Muslim countries, esp the old Turkish empire. (若干伊斯兰教国家的, 尤其是鄂图曼帝国的) 高级官吏; 大官; 大员; 大臣。

vo·cabu·lary /və'kæbjʊlərɪ US: -lerɪ; və'kæbjə,lɛrɪ/ n (pl -ries) 1 total number of words which (with rules for combining them) make up a language: 某一语言所含的全部语词; 语彙总数: No dictionary could list the whole ~ of a language. 没有一本词典能够尽列一种语言的全部语词。 2 [C, U] (range of) words known to, or used by, a person, in a trade, profession, etc: (某人或某行业或某职业等的)用语; 词汇; 语彙: a writer with a large ~. 词汇很广的作家。 3 [C] book containing list of words; list of words used in a book, etc, usu with definitions or translations. 单词集; (书等的)词汇表(通常列有定义或翻译)。

vo·cal /'vəʊkl; 'vokl/ adj of, for, with or using, the voice: 嗓音的; 声音的; 适于嗓音的; 有嗓音的; 使用嗓音的: the ~ chords, ~ **cord(2)**; the ~ organs, the tongue, lips, etc: 发声器官(舌、唇等); ~ music, to be sung: 声乐; 歌乐; a ~ score, musical score, eg of an opera, giving the vocal parts in full. 歌乐总谱。 Anger made the shy girl ~, helped her to express her feelings by speaking. 愤怒使那害着的女孩子开口了。~·ly /'vəʊkəlɪ; 'voklɪ/ adv ~·ist /'vəʊkəlɪst; 'voklɪst/ n singer. 声乐家; 歌唱家。 ⇨ instrumentalist at **instrumental**. ~·ize /-aɪz; -,aɪz/ vt say or sing; voice(2). 说; 唱; 将(某音)发成浊音。

vo·ca·tion /vəʊˈkeɪʃn; voˈkeʃən/ n 1 (sing only) feeling that one is called to (and qualified for) a certain kind of work (esp social or religious): (对某工作的)自己受到召示而且适于做某种工作的)使命感; (大指)天职; 天命; 神召: The nursing of the sick, said Florence Nightingale, is a ~ as well as a profession. 南丁格尔说,

看护病患不仅是一种职业, 更是天职。 2 [U] special aptitude (for): 特殊的才能; 异禀(与 for 连用): He has little ~ for teaching. 他不适于教书。 3 [C] person's trade or profession. 行业; 职业。~al /-ʃənl; -ʃənl/ adj of or for a ~(3): 职业的; 适于职业的: ~al guidance, advice on the choice of a ~. 就业指导; 职业辅导。

voca·tive /'vɒkətɪv; 'vakətɪv/ adj, n (of the) form of a word used when addressing sb: 呼格; 呼格语; 呼格的; 呼格语的: the ~ case. 呼格。 ⇨ **case¹(3)**.

vo·cif·er·ate /və'sɪfəreɪt US: vəʊ-; vo'sɪfə,ret/ vt, vi [VP6A, 2A] say loudly or noisily; shout. 大声说; 呼喊。 **vo·cif·er·ation** /və,sɪfə'reɪʃn US: vəʊ-; vo,sɪfə'reʃən/ n [U] shouting; yelling. 呼喊; 大叫。 **vo·cif·er·ous** /və'sɪfərəs US: vəʊ-; vo'sɪfərəs/ adj noisy; yelling: 嘈杂的; 呼喊的; 大叫的: a vociferous crowd. 嘈杂的群众。

vodka /'vɒdkə; 'vɑdkə/ n [U] strong Russian alcoholic drink distilled from rye and also other vegetable products. 伏特加酒(俄罗斯产的一种烈酒)。

vogue /vəʊg; vog/ n 1 current fashion; sth currently being done or used: 时髦; 流行之物; 流行: Are blue jeans still the ~? 蓝色牛仔裤还流行吗? The ~s of the 18th century seem amusing today. 十八世纪流行的东西在看起来很好笑。 2 popularity; popular use or acceptance: 风行; 普遍; 普遍的使用或接受: Georgette Wheatley's novels had a great ~ ten years ago, but are not read today. 乔吉特·惠特利的小说十年前风行一时, 但是现在已无人阅读了。 be in/come into ~; be/go out of ~, be/become (un)fashionable, (un)popular: 正在(开始)流行; 不再流行: When did pointed shoes come into/go out of ~? 尖头鞋是何时开始(不再)流行的? all the ~, popular everywhere; the latest fashion: 到处受欢迎的; 最新流行品; 最新式样。

voice /vɔɪs; vɔɪs/ n 1 [U] sounds made when speaking or singing: 说话声; 歌唱声; 嗓音: He is not in good ~, not speaking or singing as well as usual. 他现在嗓子不好。 2 [C] power of making such sounds: 发声力: He has lost his ~, cannot speak or sing properly, eg because of a bad cold. 他的嗓子哑了。 3 [C, U] sounds uttered by a person, esp considered in relation to their quality: 人声; 声音(尤指就其音质方面言): in a loud/soft/shrill/rough, etc ~. 大(柔, 尖, 粗)声的声音。 I did not recognize her ~. 我听不出她的声音。 The choir boys have sweet ~s. 唱诗班的男孩声音很美。 They gave ~ to their indignation. 他们以大声说出他们的愤怒。 lift up one's ~, (old use) sing, speak. (旧用法)唱; 说。 shout at the top of one's ~, shout as loudly as one can. 提高嗓门大声喊叫。 with one ~, (liter) unanimously. (文)一致地; 异口同声地。 4 a/some/no, etc ~ in sth, a/some/no, etc right to express an opinion on: 具有(要求)对某事有(有一些, 没有)发言权: I have no ~ in the matter. 我对此事无发言权。 5 [C] anything which may be compared or likened to the human ~ as expressing ideas, feelings, etc: (在表现意念、情感等上)类似或可比拟人类声音之事物: the ~ of Nature; 天籁; the ~s of the night; 夜之声; the ~ of God, conscience. 良知。 6 [U] (in phonetics) sound produced by vibration of the vocal cords, not with breath only, as for vowel sounds and the consonants /b, d, ð, z/, etc. (语音)有声音(由声带颤震而发出的声音,非仅由气息发出者,如元音及辅音 /b, d, ð, z/ 等)。 7 (gram) the contrast between active and passive as shown in the sentences: (语法)动词的(主动或被动)语态: The dog ate the meat and The meat was eaten by the dog. '狗吃肉'为主动语态而'肉被狗吃'则为被动语态。 □ vt [VP6A] 1 put into words: 用话语出来; 表出; 道出; 言述: The spokesman ~d the feelings of the crowd. 那发言人说出了群众的心声。 2 utter (a sound) with ~(6): 把(某音)发成浊音: ~d sounds (eg /d, v, ŋ/). 浊音(如 /d, v, ŋ/)。~d adj (in compounds) having the kind of ~ indicated: (用于复合词中)有某种声音的: rough-~d. 粗声的。 **~·less** adj 1 having no ~; unable to utter words. 无声的;

沉寂的; 哑的。 **2** (of consonants) uttered without ～(6): (指辅音)清(音)的; 不带声的: *The sounds* /p, tʃ, f/ *are ～less.* /p, tʃ, f/ 诸音是清音的。

void /vɔid; vɔrd/ *adj* **1** empty; vacant. 空的; 空虚的。 **2** ～ *of*, without: 没有; 缺乏: *a subject ～ of interest;* 没有趣味的题目; *a proposal ～ of reason.* 没有道理的建议。 **3** *null and ～,* (legal) without force; invalid: (法律)无效的: *The agreement, not having been signed, was null and ～.* 那项合约因未经签字故无效。 □ *n* [C] space: 空处; 空虚; 太空: *There was an aching ～ in his heart,* (fig) a feeling of sadness caused by the loss of someone he had loved. (喻)他心中有悲痛的空虚感(因亲人死亡而引起者)。 □ *vt* [VP6A] (legal) make ～(3). (法律)使无效。

voile /vɔil; vɔɪl/ *n* [U] thin, light dress material. 轻而薄的衣料。

vol·a·tile /ˈvɒlətail US: -tl; ˈvɑlətl/ *adj* **1** (of a liquid) that easily changes into gas or vapour. (指液体)易发散的; 易挥发的。 **2** (of a person, his disposition) lively; changing quickly or easily from one mood or interest to another. (指人, 其性情)快活的; 易变的; 心境或兴趣易转变快速的; 反复无常的。 **vola·til·ity** /ˌvɒləˈtɪlətɪ; ˌvɑləˈtɪlətɪ/ *n*

vol·cano /vɒlˈkeinəu; vɑlˈkeno/ *n* (*pl* **-es** or **-s** /-nəuz; -noz/) hill or mountain with openings(s) (⇨ **crater**) through which gases, lava, etc, come up from below the earth's crust (in *an active ～*), or may come up after an interval (in *a dormant ～*), or have long ceased to come up (in *an extinct ～*). 火山(地壳下的气体、熔岩、灰烬等由火山口 crater 喷出, 如活火山 active ～; 或间歇地喷出, 如休火山 dormant ～; 或久已停止喷出, 如死火山 extinct ～)。 **vol·canic** /vɒlˈkænik; vɑlˈkænɪk/ *adj* of, from, like, a ～. 火山的; 来自火山的; 似火山的。

vole /vəul; vol/ *n* rat-like animal: 野鼠类动物: *a ʼfield-～,* one like a mouse; 田鼠; *a ʼwater-～,* large water-rat. 大河鼠。

vo·li·tion /vəˈliʃn US: vəu-; voˈlɪʃən/ *n* [U] act, power, of using one's own will, of choosing, making a decision, etc: 意志; 决意; 取舍; 意志力: *do sth of one's own ～.* 出于自愿而做某事。 **～al** /-ʃənl; -ʃənl/ *adj*

vol·ley /ˈvɒli; ˈvɑli/ *n* [C] **1** hurling or shooting of a number of missiles (stones, arrows, bullets, etc) together. (石, 箭, 弹丸等的)齐射; 群射; 齐发。 **2** number of oaths, curses, questions, directed at sb, or in quick succession, at sb. (咒詛, 咒骂, 质问等的)齐发; 连发。 **3** (tennis) stroke which returns the ball to the sender before it touches the ground. (网球)飞击; 截击(把对方击来的球在落地之前击回对方)。 **ˌhalf-ʼ～,** return of the ball as soon as it touches the ground. 半飞击; 半截击; 触地击(在球与地接触的瞬间击回对方)。 **ʼ～-ball** *n* game in which players on each side of a high net try to keep a ball in motion by hitting it with their hands back and forth over the net without letting it touch the ground. 排球。 □ *vt, vi* 1 [VP2A, C] (of guns) sound together: (指枪炮)齐响; 齐发: *The guns ～ed on all sides.* 大炮从各方面齐发。 **2** [VP6A, 2A] return a tennis-ball across the net before it touches the ground. 飞击; 截击(网球); 在球落地前击回对方。

volt /vəult; volt/ *n* [C] (abbr 略作 **v**) unit of electrical force; force that would carry one ampere of current against one ohm resistance. (电压单位)伏特。 **～·age** /ˈvəultidʒ; ˈvoltɪdʒ/ *n* electrical force measured in ～s. 电压; 伏特数。

volte-face /ˌvɒlt ˈfɑːs; ˌvɑltˈfas/ *n* complete change; act of turning round to the opposite way of standing or to the opposite way of thinking: 完全改变; (位置或立场或思想等的)彻底转变; 转向: *make a complete ～.* 彻底转变。

vol·uble /ˈvɒljubl; ˈvɑljəbl/ *adj* talking, able to talk, very quickly and easily; (of speech) fluent. 健谈的; 口若悬河的; (指言辞)流利的。 **vol·ubly** /-jubli; -jəblɪ/ *adv* **volu·bil·ity** /ˌvɒljuˈbɪlətɪ; ˌvɑljəˈbɪlətɪ/ *n*

vol·ume /ˈvɒljuːm US: -jəm; ˈvɑljəm/ *n* **1** [C] book, esp one of a set of books; number of sheets, papers, periodicals, etc bound together: 书本; (尤指一套书中的)一部、一卷、一册; (纸页、报纸、杂志等的)合订本: *an encyclopedia in 20 ～s.* 一部有二十册的百科全书。 *speak ～s for,* supply strong evidence of: 充分地证明或显示: *His donations to charity speak ～s for his generosity.* 他对慈善事业的捐助充分地表明他的他慷慨。 **2** [U] amount of space (expressed in cubic metres, etc) occupied by a substance, liquid or gas; cubic contents of a container, etc: 体积 (以立方米等表示者); (容器等的)容量; 容积: *the ～ of a cask;* 大桶的容量; *the ～ of wine in a cask.* 大桶里的酒的体积。 **3** [C] large mass, amount or quantity: 大量; 多量; 大宗: *the ～ of business/work, etc;* 大宗交易(大量的工作等); (esp *pl*) rounded masses of steam or smoke: (尤用复数) 大团的蒸气或烟雾: *V～s of black smoke belched out from the chimneys.* 大量的黑烟从烟囱里冒出。 **4** [U] (of sound) power; sonority: (指声音)响度; 音量: *a voice of great ～.* 音量大的声音。 *Your radio has a ～ control.* 你的收音机有音量控制的装置。

vol·umi·nous /vəˈljuːmɪnəs; vəˈlumənəs/ *adj* **1** (of writing) great in quantity: (指著作)大量的; 长篇的; 大部头的: *a ～ work/history;* 大部头的作品(历史书); (of an author) producing many books. (指作家)多产的; 著作多的。 **2** occupying much space: 体积大的; 宽大的: *a ～ correspondence;* 大堆信函; *～ skirts.* 宽大的裙子。

vol·un·tary /ˈvɒləntrɪ US: -terɪ; ˈvɑlənˌterɪ/ *adj* **1** doing or ready to do things, willingly, without being compelled; (sth) done thus: 自愿的; 自动的; 自动或自愿做成的: *～ work/service;* 志愿的工作(服务); *a ～ statement/confession;* 自动的陈述(自白); *～ workers/helpers.* 志愿工人(帮助者)。 **2** carried on, supported by, ～ work and gifts: 靠自由出捐助或志愿工作维持的: *a ʼ～ school,* one supported by ～ contributions, not by the State, etc. 靠捐助维持的学校。 **3** (of bodily, muscular, movements) controlled by the will (opp of *involuntary*). (指身体的或肌肉的运动)为意志所控制的; 随意的(为 involuntary 之反义词)。 □ *n* [C] (*pl* **-ries**) organ solo, esp one played not as part of a church service. (尤指不属礼拜仪式的)风琴独奏。 **vol·un·tar·ily** /ˈvɒləntrəlɪ US: ˌvɒlənˈterəlɪ; ˈvɑlənˌterɪlɪ/ *adv*

vol·un·teer /ˌvɒlənˈtiə(r); ˌvɑlənˈtɪr/ *n* **1** person who offers to do sth, esp sth unpleasant or dangerous. 志愿者(尤指自愿从事厌烦或危险工作者)。 **2** soldier who is not conscripted: 志愿兵; 义勇兵。 (attrib) (作作定语) *a ～ corps.* 义勇军。 □ *vt, vi* [VP6A, 7A, 2A, 3A] *～ sth/to do sth/for sth,* offer voluntarily; come forward as a ～: 自动提供; 自愿效劳: *He ～ed some information/～ed to get some information.* 他自动提供一些消息(自愿去获取某些资料)。 *How many of them ～ed?* 他们之中有多少人自愿效劳? *He ～ed for the campaign.* 他自愿参加这次战役。

vo·lup·tu·ary /vəˈlʌptjuərɪ US: -uerɪ; vəˈlʌptʃuˌerɪ/ *n* person who gives himself up to luxury and sensual pleasures. 耽于奢华及逸乐的人; 酒色之徒。

vo·lup·tu·ous /vəˈlʌptjuəs; vəˈlʌptʃuəs/ *adj* of, for, arousing, given up to, sensuous or sensual pleasures: 耽于声色享受的; 富于声色的; 激起声色之欲或快感的; 肉感的: *～ music/beauty/thoughts/sensations.* 华丽的音乐(妖艳; 欲念; 声色的刺激)。 **～·ly** *adv* **～·ness** *n*

vo·lute /vəˈljuːt US: vəˈlut; vəˈlut/ *n* spiral scroll, esp as on Ionic and Corinthian capitals. (尤指爱奥尼亚式及科林斯式石柱柱头的)涡形装饰; 螺旋形装饰。 ⇨ the illus at **column**. 参看 column 之插图。 **～d** *adj* decorated with, having, ～s: 涡卷饰的; 有螺旋形饰的: *a ～d sea-shell.* 螺旋形的海贝。

vomit /ˈvɒmit; ˈvɑmɪt/ *vt, vi* **1** [VP6A, 15B, 2A] bring back from the stomach through the mouth; throw

up from the mouth: 呕吐; 吐出: *He* ~*ed everything he had eaten.* 他吐出了所吃的全部食物。 *He was* ~*ing blood.* 他在吐血。 *He began to* ~. 他开始呕吐。 **2** [VP 6A] send out in large quantities: 大量倾出: *factory chimneys* ~*ing smoke.* 大量喷烟的工厂烟囱。 □ *n* [U] food that has been ~ed. 呕出的食物。

voo·doo /'vuːduː; 'vudu/ *n* [U] debased form of religion, made up of sorcery and witchcraft, practised by some people in the West Indies, esp Haiti. 伏都教 (西印度群岛,尤指海地,某些人所崇奉的一种巫术)。

vo·racious /və'reɪʃəs; vɔ'reʃəs/ *adj* very hungry or greedy; desiring much: 非常饥饿的;极为贪心的;贪婪的: *a* ~ *appetite;* 极大的胃口; *a* ~ *reader,* one who reads many books. 求知欲强烈的读者。 ~**ly** *adv* in a ~ manner: 贪婪地;贪得无厌地: *He ate his food* ~*ly.* 他狼吞虎咽咽地吃东西。 **vo·racity** /və'ræsətɪ; vɔ'ræsətɪ/ *n* [U]

vor·tex /'vɔːteks; 'vɔrteks/ *n* (*pl* ~**es** or **vortices** /-tɪsiːz; -tɪˌsiz/) **1** mass of whirling fluid or wind, esp a whirlpool. 水漩; 旋风; (尤指)漩涡。 **2** (fig) whirl of activity; system, pursuit, viewed as sth that tends to absorb things, engross those who engage in it: (喻)忙碌纷乱; 被认为会把事物和参加者卷入的制度或活动: *be drawn into the* ~ *of politics/war;* 被卷入政治(战争)的漩涡; *the* ~ *of social life/pleasure.* 忙碌纷乱的社会活动(游乐)。

vo·tary /'vəʊtərɪ; 'votərɪ/ *n* (*pl* **-ries**) person who gives up his time and energy to sth, esp to religious work and service: 热心者; 爱好者; 支持(尤指宗教工作)者: *a* ~ *of peace/liberation.* 倡导和平(解放运动)者。

vote /vəʊt; vot/ *n* **1** (right to give an) expression of opinion or will by persons for or against sb or sth, esp by ballot or by putting up of hands: 投票(权); 表决(权); 选举(权): *give one's* ~ *to the more handsome candidate.* 投票给容貌比较好看的候选人。 *Do women have the* ~ (ie the franchise) *in your country?* 贵国的妇女有选举权吗? *I'm going to the polling-booth to record/cast my* ~. 我现在去投票所投票。 *Mr X proposed a* ~ *of thanks to the principal speaker,* asked the audience to show, by clapping their hands, that they thanked him. 某先生提议向主讲人鼓掌致谢。 *The Government received a* ~ *of confidence,* a majority of ~s was in its favour, to show confidence in its policies, etc. 政府获得一次信任投票。 *put sth to the* ~, decide it by asking for ~s. 提付表决; 交付表决。 **2** total numbers of ~s (to be) given (eg at a political election): 选票数; 总投票数; 获票总数: *Will the Labour* ~ *increase or decrease at the next election?* 下届选举工党的票数将增加还是减少? **3** money granted, by ~s, for a certain purpose: (为某项用途经投票决定的)拨款; 议决该款额: *the Army* ~. 给陆军的拨款。 □ *vi, vt* **1** [VP3A] ~ *for/against sb/sth,* support/oppose by voting. 投票赞成(反对)某人(某事物)。 ~ *on sth,* express an opinion on sth by voting. 表决某问题; 就某事进行表决。 **2** [VP 6A, 12A, 13A] ~ *sb/sth (for sth),* grant money (to sb): 拨款(给某人); 为某事投款: *a sum of money for Education.* 通过一笔教育经费。 *Parliament* ~*d Charles I £ 100000 for the Army.* 国会拨给查理一世十万镑陆军经费。 **3** [VP15 B] ~ *sth down,* defeat by ~s: 投票否决; 投票拒绝: ~ *down* (= reject) *a proposal.* 投票否决一项提议。 ~ *sth through,* support, approve: 表决通过; 投票同意: ~ *a Bill through.* 投票通过一项法案。 **4** [VP25] (colloq) declare, by general opinion: (口)凭大家意见而宣布; 公认: *The new teacher was* ~*d a pompous bore,* The children gave this as their opinion. 那位新老师被公认是个自大和令人讨厌的家伙。 **5** [VP9] suggest, propose: 提议; 建议: *I* ~ (*that*) *we avoid him in future.* 我建议我们今后躲开他。 ~**r** *n* person who ~s; person who has the right to ~. 投票者; 表决者; 选举者; 有投票、表决、选举权的人。 ~·**less** *adj* having no ~; not having the right to ~. 未得选票的; 无投票权的; 无表决权的; 无选举权的。

vo·tive /'vəʊtɪv; 'votɪv/ *adj* offered or consecrated

in connection with the fulfilment of a vow: 还愿的; 因誓约而奉献的: *There were numerous* ~ *tablets on the walls of the church.* 教堂的墙壁上有无数的还愿铭牌。

vouch /vautʃ; vautʃ/ *vi* ~ *for sb/sth,* be responsible for, express one's confidence in (a person, his honesty, the truth of a statement, etc): 保证; 担保(某人, 其诚实, 某记述等的真实性等): *I am ready to* ~ *for him/for the truth of his story/for his ability to pay.* 我愿替他担保(担保他所言属实, 担保他有能力付款)。

voucher /'vautʃər; 'vautʃə/ *n* receipt or document showing payment of money, correctness of accounts, etc: 收据; 传票; 凭单: *hotel/meal* ~s, (eg as bought from travel agencies) showing that payment has been made in advance. 预付旅馆(餐食)费用的凭单. **'gift** ~, supplied with some articles (eg petrol, cigarettes), to be exchanged for gifts. (商品, 如汽油、香烟等的)附带赠券(可换取赠品数)。 **'luncheon** ~, one supplied by some employers, exchangeable for all or part of a meal (at restaurants which have agreed to accept them). 午餐券(某些雇主发给员工在指定的餐厅用膳者, 全部或部分费用已付)。

vouch·safe /vautʃ'seɪf; vautʃ'sef/ *vt* [VP6A, 7A, 12C] (formal) be kind enough to give (sth), *to do* (sth): (正式用语)惠予(某物); 给; 赐: *He* ~*d* (*me*) *no reply.* 他未予回话。 *He* ~*d to help.* 他惠予协助。

vow /vau; vau/ *n* solemn promise or undertaking: 誓; 誓约; 许愿: *'marriage vows;* 婚誓; *a vow of chastity;* 守贞的誓约; *under a vow of celibacy/silence,* having solemnly undertaken not to marry/speak about sth: 发过誓要独身(保密); *break a vow;* 违反誓约; *perform a vow,* do what one promised. 履行誓言。 □ *vt* **1** [VP6A, 7A, 9] make a vow; promise or declare solemnly: 立誓; 发誓; 许愿: *He vowed to avenge the insult/that he would avenge the insult.* 他发誓要报复那场侮辱。 *She vowed never to speak to him again.* 她发誓永不再同他讲话。 *They were forced to vow obedience.* 他们被迫宣誓服从。 **2** [VP9] (old use) = **avow.** (旧用法)宣布; 宣称; 说出。

vowel /'vauəl; 'vauəl/ *n* sustainable vocal sound made without audible stopping of the breath, or friction in its passage out through the mouth; letter or symbol used to represent such a sound (eg the letters *a, e, i, o, u;* the symbols /iː, ɪ, e, æ, ɑː, ɒ, ɔː, u, ʊ, ʌ, ɜː, ə/). 元音; 母音; 元音的字母或符号(如字母 a, e, i, o, u, 及音标 /iː, ɪ, e, æ, ɑː, ɒ, ɔː, u, ʊ, ʌ, ɜː, ə/)。 ⇨ **diphthong.**

vox /vɒks; vaks/ *n* (Lat) voice. 声音; 声音。 **vox po·puli** /vɒks 'pɒpjʊlaɪ; ˌvaks'papjəlaɪ/, the voice of the people; public opinion. 民众的声音; 舆论。

voy·age /'vɔɪɪdʒ; 'vɔɪ·ɪdʒ/ *n* journey by water, esp a long one in a ship: 航海; 航行(尤指长途者): *a* ~ *from Mombasa to Colombo;* 由蒙巴萨岛至科伦坡的航行; *go on a* ~; 航海去; *on the* ~ *out/home;* (回国)航途中; *on the outward/homeward* ~. 在出(回)航途中。 □ *vi* [VP2A, C] go on a ~: 航行; 航海: ~ *through the South Seas.* 航行穿越南太平洋。 ~**r** /'vɔɪədʒə(r); 'vɔɪ·ɪdʒə/ *n* person who makes a ~ (esp of those who, in former times, explored unknown seas). 航行者; 航海者(尤指昔时探测未知的海洋者)。

voy·eur /vwɑː'jɜː(r); ˌvwɑ'jɜ/ *n* person who gets pleasure from looking at sexual objects or the sexual activities of others, esp in secret. 窥淫狂; 观看(尤指秘密地)色情物或他人性行为获得乐趣和满足者。

vul·can·ite /'vʌlkənaɪt; 'vʌlkənˌaɪt/ *n* [U] hard plastic made from rubber and sulphur. 硬橡皮; 硫化橡皮。 **vul·can·ize** /'vʌlkənaɪz; 'vʌlkənˌaɪz/ *vt* [VP6A] treat (rubber) with sulphur at great heat to harden it. 以高温加硫磺使(橡皮)硬化; 使(橡皮)硫化。 **vul·can·iz·ation** /ˌvʌlkənaɪ'zeɪʃn US: -nɪ'z-; ˌvʌlkənə'zeʃən/ *n*

vul·gar /'vʌlɡə(r); 'vʌlɡə/ *adj* **1** ill mannered; in bad taste: 粗鄙的; 粗俗的: *a* ~ *language/behaviour/ideas;* 粗鄙的语言(行为, 观念); *a* ~ *person;* 粗俗的人; *a* ~ *display of wealth.* 一番庸俗的财富夸耀。 **2** in common

use; generally prevalent: 通俗的; 一般流行的: ~ *errors/superstitions.* 一般的错误(迷信). ~ **fraction,** one written in the usual way (eg ³/₄), contrasted with a decimal fraction (eg 0.75). 普通分数(用普通写法, 如 ³/₄; 与小数, 如 0.75, 相对). **the ~ herd,** (contemptuous) the masses of ordinary people. (蔑)庶民; 一般民众. **the ~ tongue,** the language commonly spoken by the people (formerly, in England, English contrasted with Latin). 本地语; 当地语; 土话(昔时在英国指英语, 与拉丁语相对). ~**ly** *adv* **vul·gar·ian** /ˈvʌlˈɡeərɪən; ˌvʌlˈɡɛrɪən/ *n* ~ person, esp a rich person whose manners and tastes are bad. 粗俗的人; (尤指)粗俗而有钱人. ~**ism** /ˈvʌlɡərɪzəm; ˈvʌlɡəˌrɪzəm/ *n* [C] word, phrase, expression, etc used only by ignorant persons; [U] ~ behaviour. 粗俗的语辞; 粗鄙的话; 粗鄙的行为. ~**ity** /vʌlˈɡærətɪ; vʌlˈɡærətɪ/ *n* (*pl* -**ties**) [U] ~ behaviour; [C] ~ acts, utterances, etc. 粗俗的行为; 粗鄙; (复)粗俗的动作, 言词等. ~**ize** /ˈvʌlɡəraɪz; ˈvʌlɡəˌraɪz/ *vt* [VP6A] make ~. 使粗俗; 使通俗化. ~**iz-ation** /ˌvʌlɡəraɪˈzeɪʃən; US: -rɪˈz-; ˌvʌlɡərəˈzeʃən/ *n* [U].

Vul·gate /ˈvʌlɡeɪt; ˈvʌlɡet/ *n* **the V~,** Latin version of the Bible made in the 4th c. (第四世纪译成的)拉丁文圣经.

vul·ner·able /ˈvʌlnərəbl; ˈvʌlnərəbl/ *adj* that is liable to be damaged; not protected against attack: 易受伤害的; 易受攻击的: *find sb's ~ spot;* 发现某人的弱点; *a position ~ to attack;* 易受攻击的地位; *people who are ~ to criticism.* 易受抨击的人们. **vul·ner·abil·ity** /ˌvʌlnərəˈbɪlətɪ; ˌvʌlnərəˈbɪlətɪ/ *n*

vul·pine /ˈvʌlpaɪn; ˈvʌlpaɪn/ *adj* of, like, a fox; crafty. 狐狸的; 似狐狸的; 狡猾的.

vul·ture /ˈvʌltʃə(r); ˈvʌltʃɚ/ *n* **1** large bird, usu with head and neck almost bare of feathers, that lives on the flesh of dead animals. 兀鹰. ⇨ the illus at **prey.** 参看 prey 之插图. **2** greedy person who profits from the misfortunes of others. (利用他人的不幸而谋取利益的)贪婪者.

vulva /ˈvʌlvə; ˈvʌlvə/ *n* opening of the female genitals. 阴户; 阴门. ⇨ the illus at **reproduce.** 参看 reproduce 之插图.

vy·ing /ˈvaɪɪŋ; ˈvaɪɪŋ/ *pres p* of **vie.**

W w

W, w /ˈdʌblju:; ˈdʌblju/ (*pl* **W's, w's**) the 23rd letter of the English alphabet. 英文字母的第二十三个字母.

wad /wɒd; wɑd/ *n* **1** lump of soft material for keeping things apart or in place, or to stop up a hole. 块块软物; 填料(用以使东西隔离, 固定, 或用以填洞). **2** collection of documents or banknotes folded or rolled together. 一卷或一叠(文件或钞票). □ *vt* (-**dd-**) stuff with a wad; hold in place with a wad; line (a garment, etc) with soft material (usu cotton or wool): (以填料)填塞; 固定; 以软物(棉、毛等)衬填(衣服等): *a wadded jacket/dressing-gown/quilt.* 填有棉或毛的短外套(晨衣, 棉被). **wad·ding** /ˈwɒdɪŋ; ˈwɑdɪŋ/ *n* [U] soft material esp raw cotton or felt, used for packing, lining things, etc. 软物; 填料(尤指用于包装、衬物等的生棉或毛毡).

waddle /ˈwɒdl; ˈwɑdl/ *vi* [VP2A, C] walk with slow steps and a sideways roll, as a duck does: 蹒跚而行; 摇摆而行(脚步缓慢而横摆如鸭子般走路): *The stout old man ~d across the road.* 那胖胖的老人摇摆地横过马路. □ *n* (*sing* only) this kind of walk. (仅用单数)蹒跚; 摇摆的步态.

wade /weɪd; wed/ *vi, vt* [VP2A, C, 6A] **1** walk with an effort (through water, mud or anything that makes progress difficult); walk across (sth) in this way: (从水、泥泞或其他阻碍物中)费力行进; 涉过: *He ~d through the weeds on the bank and then into and across the stream.* 他费力地穿过岸上的杂草, 然后涉过小河. *Can we ~ the brook,* cross it by wading? 我们能涉水走过这小河吗? *The boy ~d* (= read slowly and without interest) *through the dull book.* 那男孩费力地阅读这本枯燥的书. **'wading bird,** long-legged water-bird that ~s (opp to web-footed birds that swim). 涉禽(涉水的长腿水鸟, 与游水的蹼足鸟相对而言). **2** ~ *in,* make a vigorous attack. 作猛烈攻击. ~ *into sth,* attack sth vigorously. 猛烈攻击(某物). ~**r** *n* **1** wading bird (⇨ above). 涉禽(参看上列之 wading bird). **2** (*pl*) waterproof boots reaching the hips, used by anglers when wading in streams. (复)(钓鱼者涉水时穿着的)高统防水靴.

wadi /ˈwɒdɪ; ˈwɑdɪ/ *n* (in the Middle East, Arabia, northern Africa) rocky watercourse dry except after a heavy fall of rain. (中东, 阿拉伯, 北非等处的)多岩石的干涸河床(下大雨除了有水). 河道谷.

wa·fer /ˈweɪfə(r); ˈwefɚ/ *n* **1** thin flat biscuit (eg as eaten with ice-cream). 薄饼干(如连同冰淇淋吃者). **2** small round piece of bread used in Holy Communion.

(领圣体所用的)小圆饼; 圣饼.

waffle¹ /ˈwɒfl; ˈwɑfl/ *n* small cake made of batter baked in a special kind of griddle (*a* '~*-iron*) with two parts hinged together. (用面粉、蛋、牛奶等混合制成的)鸡蛋饼(烘此饼的铁模, 称为 ~*-iron*).

waffle² /ˈwɒfl; ˈwɑfl/ *vi* [VP2A, C] (GB colloq) talk vaguely, unnecessarily, and without much result: (英口)作模糊、不必要、而无结果的谈话; 含糊而言; 说无聊话: *How that man does ~ on!* 那个人怎么那样啰哩不休尽讲一些无聊的话? *What's she waffling about now?* 她现在在瞎说些什么? □ *n* [U] utterance which (even when it sounds impressive) means little or nothing. 动听而无内容的话; 无聊话.

waft /wɒft; US: wæft; wæft/ *vt* [VP6A] carry lightly and smoothly through the air or over water: 使飘浮; 使飘荡; 使飘流: *The scent of the flowers was ~ed to us by the breeze.* 微风送来了花香. □ *n* [C] **1** breath of air, scent, etc. 一阵风; 一阵香气等. **2** waving movement. 摆动; 飘动; 浮动.

wag¹ /wæg; wæg/ *vt, vi* (-**gg-**) [VP6A, 2A, C] (cause to) move from side to side or up and down: (使)摇摆; 摇动; 上下移动: *The dog wagged its tail.* 狗摇尾. *The dog's tail wagged.* 狗尾摆动. *Don't wag your finger at me,* show disapproval in this way. 不要指责我. *The news set tongues/chins/beards wagging,* caused people to talk (esp of sth scandalous). 那则新闻引起人们议论纷纷(尤指关于某项丑闻). **'wag·tail** *n* kinds of small bird with a long tail that wags constantly when the bird is standing. 鹡鸰(站立时其长尾摇动不停的小鸟). □ *n* wagging movement: 摇摆; 摇动: *with a wag of the tail.* 摇摆着尾巴.

wag² /wæg; wæg/ *n* merry person, full of amusing sayings and fond of practical jokes. (好说笑及恶作剧的)诙谐者. **wag·gery** /ˈwæɡərɪ; ˈwæɡərɪ/ *n* (*pl* -**ries**) [U] behaviour or talk of a wag; (*pl*) acts, remarks, etc of a wag. 诙谐; 恶作剧; (复)诙谐话; 诙谐的动作. **wag·gish** /ˈwæɡɪʃ; ˈwæɡɪʃ/ *adj* of or like a wag; done in a joking way. 诙谐的; 滑稽的; 恶作剧的; 谐谑地做出的: *waggish tricks/remarks.* 恶作剧的诡计(滑稽的话). **wag·gish·ly** *adv* **wag·gish·ness** *n*

wage¹ /weɪdʒ; wedʒ/ *n* **1** (now usu *pl* except in certain phrases and when attrib) payment made or received (usu weekly) for work or services: (除用于某些短语中及用作定语外, 现在通常用复数形)工资; 薪给(通常按周计算): *His ~s are £50 a week.* 他的工资每周五十镑. *We*

expect a fair day's ~ for a fair day's work. 我们做好一天的工作，希望能拿到一天应得的工资。*He takes his ~s/his '~-packet home to his wife every Friday.* 每星期五他把薪水（薪水袋）带回家交给妻子。*The postal workers have asked for a '~ increase/rise of £5 a week.* 邮务人员要求周薪提高五镑。⇨ **fee(1), pay¹, salary. living ~,** one which allows a man to live without fear of hunger and hardship. 够维持生活的薪资。**minimum ~,** guaranteed basic level for ~s in an industry or country. 最低工资（某项工业或某一国家所保障的工资最低基准）。'~**-claim** n ~ demanded from the management for workers by their trade union. (工会为工人向经理部门的)工资要求。'~**-earner** n person who works for ~s (contrasted with the salaried classes). 工资劳动者。'~**-freeze,** ⇨ **freeze, n(2). 2** (old use; *pl* in form with *sing v*) reward or requital: (旧用法;用复数形接单数动词)报酬;报偿;代价: *The ~s of sin is death.* 罪恶的代价是死。

wage² /weɪdʒ; wedʒ/ *vt* [VP6A] carry on, engage in (*war, a campaign*). 进行; 从事(战争、战役、运动)。

wa·ger /'weɪdʒə(r); 'wedʒɚ/ *vt, vi* [VP6A, 11, 14, 12C, 2A] bet: 打赌: ~ *£5 on a horse.* 对某一匹马下注五镑。*I'm ready to ~ you a pound that....* 我愿为…同你打赌一镑。□ *n* bet: 赌注: *lay/make a ~;* 下注; *take up* (= accept) *a ~.* 接受打赌。

waggle /'wægl; 'wægl/ *vt, vi* = **wag¹.**

wag·gon (US also **wagon**) /'wægən; 'wægən/ *n* **1** four-wheeled vehicle for carrying goods, pulled by horses or oxen. 四轮运货马(牛)车。⇨ **cart. on the ('water) ~,** (colloq) not drinking alcoholic liquors. (口)不饮酒的。**2** (US 美 = *freight car*) open railway truck (eg for coal). 铁路敞篷货车(如运煤车)。'**station- ~** n (US 美) = estate-car. ~**er** n man in charge of a ~ and its horses. 运货马车夫。

wag·on-lit /,vægɒn 'li:; ,vagõ'li/ *n* (*pl* **wagons-lit** pronunciation unchanged) (复数发音不变) sleeping-car (as on European railways). (欧洲铁路上行驶的)卧车。

wag·tail /'wægteɪl; 'wæg,tel/ *n* ⇨ **wag¹.**

waif /weɪf; wef/ *n* homeless person, esp a child: 无家可归者; (尤指)流浪儿童: ~*s and strays,* homeless and abandoned children. 流浪儿童们。

wail /weɪl; wel/ *vi, vt* [VP2A, B, C, 6A] **1** cry or complain in a loud, usu shrill, voice: (大而通常尖声地)哭; 哭泣; 号哭; 哀泣: ~ *(over) one's misfortunes;* 为不幸而哀泣; *an ambulance racing through the streets with sirens ~ing.* 救护车穿过街道，发出尖锐的呜呜声。*She was ~ing for her lost child.* 她为她死去的孩子哀号。**2** (of the wind) make sounds like a person ~ing. (指风)发哀号声; 发呼啸声。□ *n* ~ing cry; lament: 哭; 哭泣; 哀悼: *the ~s of a newborn child.* 初生婴儿的哭叫声。

wain /weɪn; wen/ *n* (old use, or poet) large farm wagon. (旧用法或诗)(农场上使用的)大马车。**Charles's W~,** the constellation of stars also called the Plough and the Great Bear. 北斗七星。

wain·scot /'weɪnskət; 'wenskət/ *n* wooden panelling (usu on the lower half of the walls of a room). 护壁板 (通常指室内墙壁下半截的木板)。~**ed** *adj* lined with ~: 装以护壁板的: *a ~ed room.* 装有护壁板的房间。

waist /weɪst; west/ *n* **1** part of the body between the ribs and the hips: 腰; 腰部: *wear a sash round the ~;* 在腰际围饰带; *measure 30 inches round the ~.* 腰围(量起来有)三十英寸; *The workmen were stripped to the ~,* 工人们赤膊着上身; *were wearing nothing above the ~.* 上身什么都没有穿。*That man has no ~,* is so stout that he has no narrowing at the ~ as in a normal figure. 那人胖得看不出腰来。⇨ the illus at **trunk.** 参看 trunk 之插图。'~**-band** n band on a garment (eg a skirt) fitting round the ~. 衣服(如裙)的腰带; 束腰带。'~**-deep** *adj, adv* up to the ~: 深及腰部(的): ~*-deep in the water;* 涉水深至腰部的; *wade ~-deep into a stream.* 涉水走入深及腰部的小河。'~**-high** *adj, adv* high enough to reach the ~: 高达腰部(地)(的): *The wheat was ~-high.* 小麦长得高达腰部。

'~**-line** n line round the body at the smallest part of the ~: 腰线; 腰围: *a girl with a neat ~-line.* 腰围纤美的女郎。**2** that part of a garment that goes round the ~: (US 美 '*shirt-~*) garment, or part of a garment, covering the body from the shoulders to the ~. 衣服的腰部; 胸衣(遮覆肩至腰部的); 衣服的上身部分。**3** middle and narrow part: 中间的细狭部分: *the ~ of a ship,* between the forecastle and quarterdeck: 船的中间部分(前后甲板之间); *the ~ of a violin/an hour-glass.* 小提琴(沙漏时计)的腰部。~**-coat** /'weɪskət US: 'weskət; 'wes,kot/ *n* close-fitting sleeveless garment worn under a coat or jacket, buttoned down the front (called *vest* by tailors, and in the US). 背心; 马甲(英国的裁缝及美国称之为 vest)。

wait¹ /weɪt; wet/ *n* **1** act or time of waiting: 等; 等待; 等候的时间: *We had a long ~ for the bus.* 我们等候公共汽车很久。*I don't like these long ~s.* 我不喜欢这种长时间的等候。**2** [U] *lie in ~* (for; (less usu) (较不常作) *lay ~ for,* be in hiding in order to attack; also: 埋伏以待; 伏击: *The highwayman lay in ~ for the stage-coach.* 那强盗等候伏击驿马车。**3** (*pl*) the ~s, persons who go from house to house singing carols at Christmas. (复)圣诞节沿门唱赞美诗者; 报佳音者。

wait² /weɪt; wet/ *vi* **1** [VP2A, B, C, 3A, 4A] ~ *(for),* stay where one is, delay acting, until sb or sth comes or until sth happens: 等; 等候; 期待: *Please ~ a minute.* 请等一会儿。*W~ for me, please.* 请等一等我。*How long have you been ~ing?* 你已经等候多久了？*We are ~ing for the rain to stop.* 我们在等待雨停。*We are ~ing for better weather.* 我们在期待较好的天气。*We ~ed* (in order) *to see what would happen.* 我们等着看会发生什么事情。*They say that everything comes to those who ~.* 人们认为能耐心等候的人自有良机。*keep sb ~ing,* fail to meet him or be ready at the appointed time: 叫人等; 让人等候; 在约定的时间不见某人或未准备妥当: *His wife never keeps him ~ing.* 他的妻子从不让他等候。~ *up (for sb),* stay up, not go to bed. 不睡而熬夜; (为某人)等着不睡。*No ~ing,* warning (indicated by the sign ⊘) that motor-vehicles must not stop at the side of the roadway. 禁止停车(警告机动车辆不得在路边停车, 以⊘表示之)。**2** [VP6A] (= *await*) ~ for; ~ and watch for: 等候; 等待; 守候: *He is ~ing his opportunity.* 他在等候机会。*He always expects me to ~ his convenience,* until it is convenient for him (to do sth). 他总是希望我等到他方便的时候(做某事)。*You must ~ your turn,* ~ until it is your turn. 你必须等到轮到你的时候。**3** [VP6A, 14] ~ *(for),* defer, postpone (a meal): 迟延; 延缓(餐食): *Don't ~ dinner for me.* 不要为我而延缓开饭。**4** [VP3A] ~ *on/upon sb, (a)* act as a servant to, fetch and carry things for: 服侍; 伺候。~ *on sb hand and foot,* attend to his every need: 伺候某人无微不至: *A Japanese wife was formerly expected to ~ upon her husband hand and foot.* 从前日本太太被认为应该无微不至地伺候丈夫。*(b)* (old use) pay a visit to: (旧用法)访问; 拜访: *Our commercial agent will ~ upon you next Monday.* 我们的商务代理将于下周一拜访您。**5** [VP3A] ~ *at/on,* act as a servant at table, serving food, clearing away dishes, etc: 伺候开饭(端菜、清理碗盘等): ~ *at table* (US 美 = ~ *on table*). 伺候开饭。**6** '~**-ing-list,** list of persons who cannot be served, treated, etc now, but who will be served, etc later, if possible: 等候者名单(等待机会接受服务、诊疗等之人的名单): *put sb on a ~ing-list for theatre tickets/an appointment, etc.* 把某人列入申请戏票(某项约会等)的等候名单中。'~**-ing-room** n room in a railway-station, etc used by people who are ~ing for trains; room (eg in a doctor's or dentist's house or office) where people ~ until they can be attended to. 候车室; 候诊室; 等候室。~**er** n man who ~s at table in a restaurant, hotel dining-room, etc. (餐厅、旅馆餐室等的)服务员; 侍者; 应生; 跑堂的。~**-ress** /'weɪtrɪs; 'wetrɪs/ *n* woman ~er. 女服务员; 女侍应生。

waive /weɪv/ *vt* [VP6A] (say that one will) not insist on (a right or claim): 放弃; 不坚持; 声明放弃 (权利或要求); ~ *a privilege/the age-limit.* 放弃特权 (撤弃年龄的限制)。~**r** /ˈweɪvə(r)/ *n* (legal) (written statement) waiving (a right, etc): (法律)放弃; 弃权; 弃权书: *sign a waiver of claims against sb.* 签字于放弃对某人作要求的文件。

wake[1] /weɪk/ *vi, vt* (*pt* **woke** /wəʊk/ wok/ or ~**d**, *pp* **woken** /ˈwəʊkən/ˈwokən/ or ~**d**) **1** [VP2A, C, 4B] ~ (*up*), stop sleeping: 醒。~ *up:* 叫醒。*What time do you usually* ~ (*up*)? 你通常什么时候醒来? *I woke early.* 我醒得早。*Has the baby* ~*d/woken yet?* 那婴儿已醒了吗? *He woke up with a start.* 他一惊而醒。*He woke to find himself in prison.* 他醒来发现自己在监狱中。**2** [VP6A, 15B] ~ *sb (up),* cause to stop sleeping: 打断睡眠; 唤醒; 吵醒: *Don't* ~ *the baby.* 不要弄醒婴儿。*The noise woke me (up).* 那闹声把我吵醒了。*They were making enough noise to* ~ *the dead.* 他们吵闹声大得能把死人吵醒。**3** [VP6A, 15B] ~ *sb (up),* stir up; rouse from inactivity, inattention, etc: 激发; 使奋起; 唤起注意: *He needs someone to* ~ *him up,* stir him from his sloth, stir him to activity. 他需要人激励。*The incident* ~*d memories of his school-days.* 那件事唤起他对学生时代的记忆。**4** [VP6A] disturb with noise; cause to re-echo: 以闹声扰乱; 使再反响; 引起回响: ~ *echoes in a mountain valley.* 在山谷中引起反复回响。**wak·ing** *adj* being awake: 醒的: *in his waking hours,* while awake; 在他醒着的时候; *waking or sleeping,* while awake or asleep. 醒时或睡时。**waken** /ˈweɪkən/ˈwekən/ *vt, vi* [VP6A, 2A] (cause to) ~. (使)醒; 唤醒。~**ful** /-fl ; -fl/ *adj* unable to sleep; with little sleep: 不能入睡的; 睡眠少的: *pass a* ~*ful night.* 一夜未眠。

wake[2] /weɪk/ *n* **1** (usu *pl;* 通常用复数; often 常作 '**W**~s **Week**) annual holiday in N England, esp in the manufacturing towns of Lancashire. (英格兰北部, 尤指兰开夏郡工业都市的)每年一度的假日。**2** (in Ireland) all-night watch by a corpse before burial, with lamentations and drinking of alcoholic liquor. (在爱尔兰)葬体前的守尸; 守夜(彻夜伴守尸旁, 并时作哀歌与饮酒)。

wake[3] /weɪk/ *n* track left by a ship on smooth water, eg as made by propellers. 航迹; 船迹(如推进器在静水上留下者)。**in the** ~ **of,** after; following: 在...之后; 追随; 随着: *Traders came in the* ~ *of the explorers.* 商人们在探险队后接踵而至。

wale /weɪl/ *n* alternative spelling (esp US) of **weal**[2] or **welt**. (尤美)为 weal[2] 或 welt 的另一种拼法。

walk[1] /wɔːk/ wɔk/ *n* [C] **1** journey on foot, esp for pleasure or exercise: 步行; (尤指为游乐或运动所作的)散步: *go for a* ~; 去散步; *have a pleasant* ~ *across the fields.* 做一次越过田野的愉快散步。*The station is a short* ~ *ten minutes* ~ *from my house.* 车站离我家只有几步路(步行十分钟可到)。**2** manner or style of walking: 步态; 步法: *His horse slowed to a* ~, ie after trotting or galloping. 他的马(跑过一阵以后)慢下来改以步行了。*After running for two miles he dropped into a* ~, began to walk. 他跑了两英里以后, 开始步行。*I recognized him at once by his* ~, his way of walking. 从走路的样子我立刻认出是他。**3** path or route for walking: 步道; 人行道; 散步之处: *my favourite* ~*s in the neighbourhood.* 附近我喜欢去散步的地方。**4** ~ *of life,* calling, profession, occupation: 行业; 职业; 身份: *They interviewed people from all* ~*s of life.* 他们会晤了各行各业的人。

walk[2] /wɔːk/ *vi, vt* **1** [VP2A, B, C] (of persons) move by putting forward each foot in turn, not having both feet off the ground at once, ⇨ **run;** (of animals) move at the slowest pace, ⇨ **trot, gallop:** (指人)行走; 步行; (指动物)慢步走: *We* ~ *five miles.* 我们走了五英里。*Shall we ride or* ~? 我们是骑马还是步行? *When old babies when they learn to* ~? 婴儿多大开始学步? *He was* ~*ing up and down the station platform.* 他在火车站的月台上走来走去。'~**about** *n* (a)

(Australian sl, of aborigines in the desert) journey. (澳俚, 指沙漠中的土著)旅行; 游荡。(**b**) (colloq) occasion when a celebrity ~s round meeting people informally. (口)名人或重要人物非正式地在人群中周旋的场合。~ *away from,* beat easily in a contest: 在比赛中轻易胜过: *Smith* ~*ed away from all his competitors,* beat them easily. 史密斯轻易地击败了他所有的对手。Hence, 由此产生, '~**away** *n* easily won contest. 轻易获胜的比赛。(⇨ ~**over** below). (参看下列的 ~over)。~ *away with sth,* win sth easily: 轻易地赢得某物; 轻易地获胜: *Newcombe* ~*ed away with the match.* 纽康姆轻易地赢了那场比赛。~ *off with sth,* (colloq) carry off; take (either on purpose or unintentionally): (口)(故意或无意地)携走; 拿走; 偷走: *Someone has* ~*ed off with my umbrella.* 有人把我的伞拿走了。~ *into,* (sl)(俚)(a) eat heartily of: 开怀地吃; 大吃: ~ *into a meat-pie.* 大吃肉馅饼。(**b**) abuse; scold. 谴责; 斥责。(**c**) (colloq) meet with through inattention: (口)因疏忽或不留心而遭遇: *He just* ~*ed into the ambush.* 他恰好中了埋伏。~ *on,* play a non-speaking part on the stage: 在舞台上扮演不讲话的角色: (attrib) (用作定语) *a* ~*-'on part.* 无台词的角色。~ *out,* (colloq) go on strike: (口)罢工: *The men in this factory* ~*ed out yesterday.* 这工厂的工人昨天罢工。Hence, 由此产生, '~**out** *n* (workers') strike. (工人的)罢工。~ *out on sb,* (sl) abandon or desert him. (俚)遗弃某人。~ *out with sb,* (dated colloq) court; have as a sweetheart. (过时口语)追求某人; 以某人做情人。~ *over sb,* defeat him easily. 轻易击败某人。Hence, 由此产生, '~**over** *n* easy victory; contest in which there is little or no opposition: 轻易获得的胜利; 对手不强的竞赛: *The race was a* ~*over for Jones.* 琼斯轻而易举地赢了这场赛跑。~ *up,* (**a**) invitation to enter (eg as given by men outside a circus). 请进(如请人进去看马戏等)。(**b**) ~ along: 沿...行走: *as I was* ~*ing up Oxford Street.* 当我沿牛津街走的时候。(**c**) ~ upstairs. 走上楼。Hence, 由此产生, a ~*up flat,* one in a building without a lift. 没有电梯的公寓。(**d**) ~ *up (to sb/sth),* approach: 走近; 追近: *A stranger* ~*ed up to me and asked me the time.* 一位陌生人走近我, 问我(当时的)时间。**2** [VP6A, 15A, B] cause to ~: 使步行; 使行走; 使慢步走: *Horses should be* ~*ed for a while after a race.* 马在比赛后应让它作缓步行走。*He* ~*ed his horse up the hill.* 他驱马走上小山。*He put his arm round me and* ~*ed me away/off.* 他用一只臂搂着我, 带我走了。~ *sb off his feet/legs,* tire him out by making him ~ far. 使某人走得筋疲力竭。**3** [VP6A] go over on foot: 步行于; 走过: *I have* ~*ed this district for miles round.* 我走遍了这附近方圆几英里里内的地区。**4** (with various *nn*): (与各词连用): ~ *the boards,* be an actor: 作演员; ~ *the wards,* be a medical student; 习医; 作医学院学生; ~ *the plank,* (of a person captured by pirates in former times) be compelled to ~ blindfolded into the sea along a plank laid over the ship's side; (指昔时被海盗劫获的人)蒙着眼睛被迫走上突出于舷外的木板而终落入海中; ~ *the streets,* be a prostitute (a 'street-~*er*). 做妓女; 为娼。~**er** *n* person who ~s, esp for exercise or enjoyment: 行走者; 步行者; (尤指)散步者。~**·ing** *n* (in compounds) (用于复合词中) '~*ing-shoes,* strong ones for ~ing in; 走路穿的结实鞋子; '~*ing-stick,* stick used in, or carried while, ~ing; 手杖; '~*ing-tour,* holiday spent ~ing from place to place. 假日徒步旅行。

walkie-talkie /ˌwɔːkɪ ˈtɔːkɪ ; ˈwɔkɪˈtɔkɪ/ *n* (colloq) portable two-way radio set. (口)手提式无线电对话机; 步话机。

wall /wɔːl/ wɔl/ *n* **1** continuous, usu vertical, solid structure of stone, brick, concrete, wood, etc forming one of the sides of a building or room, or used to enclose, divide or protect sth (including land): 墙; 壁; 垣: *The castle* ~*s are very thick.* 那城堡的墙很厚。*Hang the picture on that* ~. 把这副画挂在那边的墙上。*Some old towns have* ~*s right round them.* 有些古老的城市周围有城墙。*Dry-stone* ~*s* (ie of stones not fixed in

mortar) *extend across the moors in some parts of England.* 只用石块堆成(无灰泥粘合)的墙,散见于英格兰某些地方的旷野中。*Fruit trees are often trained against garden ~s for protection and warmth.* 果树常经修整,使靠近果园的围墙生长,以利保护和保暖。***with one's back to the ~,*** in a position where retreat or escape is impossible; at bay. 处于无法撤退或逃走的境地; 作困兽斗。***be/go up the ~,*** (sl) be/become furious, distracted. (俚)(变得)狂怒或发狂。***bang/run one's head against a (brick) ~,*** attempt to do sth that is clearly impossible. 试图做显然不可能的事情。***see through a brick ~,*** have wonderful vision or insight. 有眼光; 有深刻的领悟力。**2** (fig) sth suggesting or resembling a ~: (喻)似墙之物: *a ~ of fire;* 一道似墙的火; 火墙; *a mountain ~;* 山壁; *the ~s of the chest,* the enclosing tissue and ribs; 胸壁: *the abdominal ~.* 腹壁。**3** side (contrasted with the centre) of the street: 街道的靠墙部分; 路侧(与路中心相对): (chiefly fig) (主要为比喻用法) ***go to the ~,*** be pushed aside as weak or helpless, get the worst of it in competition. 失败; 败北; 被推在一旁。***push/drive sb to the ~,*** defeat him. 使某人陷入困境; 使某人束手无策; 击败某人。**4** (compounds) (复合词) **'~-flower** *n* **(a)** common garden plant with (usu) brownish-red or orange sweet-smelling flowers. 香罗兰; 墙花(园艺植物,通常开褐红色或橘红色而有香味的花)。**(b)** person who sits out dances because of a lack of partners. 壁花; 因无舞伴仅在一旁作壁上观的人。**'~-painting** *n* [C] painting on a ~, esp a fresco. 墙上的画; (尤指)壁画。**'~-paper** *n* [U] paper, usu with a coloured design, for covering the ~s of rooms. 糊墙纸; 壁纸。□ *vt* **1** (usu *pp*) surround with a ~ or ~s: (通常用过去分词)围以墙; *~ed cities;* 有城墙的城市; *a ~ed garden.* 有围墙的花园。**2** [VP15B] ***~ sth up/off,*** fill or close up with bricks, etc: 以砖等堵塞; 填塞; 隔开: *~ up a window/opening;* 堵塞窗子(开口); *~ off part of a room.* 隔开房间的一部分。

wal·laby /ˈwɒləbɪ; ˈwɑləbɪ/ *n* (*pl* **-bies**) sorts of small kangaroo. 小袋鼠。

wal·lah /ˈwɒlə; ˈwɑlə/ *n* (sl, in India) person employed about or concerned with sth. (俚,在印度)受雇做某事的人; 从事某事的人。

wal·let /ˈwɒlɪt; ˈwɑlɪt/ *n* folding pocket-case, usu leather, for papers, banknotes, etc (US 美 = *pocketbook*). 小夹子; 钱夹; 皮夹。

wall-eyed /ˌwɔːl ˈaɪd; ˈwɔlˌaɪd/ *adj* having eyes that show an abnormal amount of white (eg as caused by a squint). 露出的眼白较一般为多的(如由斜眼所致者); 白星眼的。

wal·lop /ˈwɒləp; ˈwɑləp/ *vt* (sl or hum) beat severely; hit hard. (俚或谐)痛殴; 重击。□ *n* heavy blow; crash: 重击; 击溃; 轰隆声: *Down he went with a ~!* 他轰隆一声摔倒了! **~·ing** *adj* big; thumping: 大的; 极大的: *What a ~ing lie!* 多大的谎言啊! □ *n* defeat: 击溃; 失败: *Our football team got a ~ing.* 我们的足球队大败。

wal·low /ˈwɒləʊ; ˈwɑlo/ *vi* [VP2A, C] roll about (in mud, dirty water, etc): (在泥, 脏水等中)打滚: *pigs ~ing in the mire;* 在泥沼中打滚的猪; (fig) take gross delight in (sth sensual): (喻)沉迷于(声色的享乐): *~ing in sensual pleasures.* 沉迷于声色的享乐。***be '~ing in money,*** (colloq) be very rich. (口)很富有。□ *n* place to which animals (eg buffaloes) go regularly to ~. (水牛等动物经常前往打滚的)泥沼; 水坑。

Wall Street /ˈwɔːl striːt; ˈwɔlˌstrit/ *n* (used for) the American money-market: 华尔街; (指)美国金融市场: *Shares rose sharply on ~ yesterday.* 昨天美国金融市场的股票暴涨。

wal·nut /ˈwɔːlnʌt; ˈwɔlnət/ *n* [C] (tree producing a) nut with an edible in a hard shell; [U] the wood of this tree, used (esp as a veneer) for making furniture. 胡桃; 胡桃树; 胡桃木(用于制家具, 尤用作镶饰家具的薄板)。

wal·rus /ˈwɔːlrəs; ˈwɔlrəs/ *n* large sea-animal of the arctic regions with two long tusks, ⇨ the illus at **sea:** 海象(参看 sea 之插图): *a ~ moustache,* (colloq) one of which the ends come downwards like the tusks of a ~. (口)(末端下垂如海象牙似的)海象胡须。

waltz /wɔːls *US:* wɔːlts; wɔlts/ *n* [C] (music in 3/4 time for a) ballroom dance. 华尔兹舞; 华尔兹舞曲。□ *vi, vt* **1** [VP2A, C] dance a ~: 跳华尔兹舞: *She ~es divinely.* 她的华尔兹舞跳得好极了。***~ in/out/into/out of,*** dance, run or walk (in, out, etc) gaily: 愉快地舞动; 愉快地跑或走: *She ~ed into the room and out again.* 她愉快地走进房间, 又愉快地走了出来。**2** [VP15A] cause to ~: 使跳华尔兹舞: *He ~ed her round the room.* 他引导她在屋里跳华尔兹舞。

wam·pum /ˈwɒmpəm; ˈwɑmpəm/ *n* [U] shells threaded like beads and used as ornaments by N American Indians (and formerly used as money). 贝壳串珠(北美印第安人用作装饰品,昔时并用作钱币)。

wan /wɒn; wɑn/ *adj* **(-nn-)** **1** (of a person, his looks, etc) looking ill, sad, tired, anxious: (指人,其容貌等)有病容,愁容,倦容,忧容等的; 苍白的; 无力的: *a wan smile.* 微弱的一笑。**2** (of light, the sky) pale; not bright. (指光, 天空)淡弱的; 阴暗的。**wan·ly** *adv* **wan·ness** /ˈwɒnnɪs; ˈwɑnnɪs/ *n*

wand /wɒnd; wɑnd/ *n* **1** slender stick or rod as used by a conjurer, fairy or magician; baton(2). (咒法家,仙子,或魔术师用的)杖; 棍; 棒; 魔杖。**2** rod or staff carried as a symbol of authority (eg by an usher, steward or sheriff on ceremonial occasions). 权标(表示职权的官杖, 如仪礼中的引座员、招待员或执法官所用者)。

wan·der /ˈwɒndə(r); ˈwɑndə/ *vi, vt* **1** [VP2A, B, C, 6A] go from place to place without any special purpose or destination: 漫游; 漫步; 漂泊; 徘徊: *~ over the countryside;* 在乡间漫步; *~ up and down the road aimlessly;* 无目的地在路上徘徊; *~ (through/over) the world.* 漫游世界。*Kevin ~ed in to see me this morning,* paid me a casual visit. 凯文今晨顺便来看我。**2** [VP2A, C] leave the right path or direction: 离开正途或正确的方向; 迷失: *Some of the sheep have ~ed away,* are lost. 有些羊走失了。*We ~ed (for) miles and miles in the mist.* 我们在雾中迷失了很多英里的路。**3** [VP2A, C] be absent-minded; allow the thoughts to go from subject to subject: 心不在焉; 胡思乱想: *Don't ~ from the subject/point.* 不要岔离本题(主旨)。*His mind is ~ing* 他心不在焉。*Don't let your thoughts ~.* 不要胡思乱想。*His mind/thoughts ~ed back to his college days.* 他回想到他的大学时代。**~er** *n* person or animal that ~s. 漫游者; 徘徊者; 迷失的人; 走失的动物。**~·ings** *n pl* **1** long travels; journeys: 长途旅行; 漫游: *tell the story of one's ~ings.* 叙述自己的漫游经历。**2** confused speech during illness (esp high fever). (病中, 尤指发高烧时的)胡言乱语; 呓语。

wan·der·lust /ˈwɒndəlʌst; ˈwɑndəˌlʌst/ *n* [U] strong desire to travel. 强烈的旅行欲; 旅行癖; 流浪癖。

wane /weɪn; wen/ *vi* [VP2A] **1** (of the moon) show a decreasing bright area after full moon. (指月亮)亏; 缺; 呈下弦(月)。⇨ **wax²(1).** **2** become less or weaker: 减少; 减弱; 减小; 衰弱: *His strength/influence/reputation is waning.* 他的力量(势力,名声)渐弱了。□ *n* esp 尤用于 ***on the ~,*** process of waning. 减小; 变弱; 衰微。

wangle /ˈwæŋgl; ˈwæŋgl/ *vt* [VP6A] (sl) get, arrange sth, by using improper influence, by trickery, plausible persuasion, etc: (俚)以不正当的影响力、欺诈、巧言等取得或处理某事物: *~ an extra week's holiday.* 不正当地取得一周的额外假期。□ *n* act of wangling: 狡诈行为; 不正当手段: *get sth by a ~.* 借不正当手段获得某物。

wank /wæŋk; wæŋk/ *vi* [VP2A] (GB vulg sl) masturbate. (英鄙俚)手淫。□ *n* [C] instance of masturbation. 手淫。

wanna /ˈwɑnə; ˈwɑnə/ (US sl) (美俚) = want to. ⇨

want²(2).

want¹ /wɒnt US: wɔ:nt/ n 1 [U] lack; scarcity; state of being absent: 缺乏; 稀少; 缺少的状态。 The earthquake victims are suffering for ~ of food and medical supplies. 地震的灾民缺乏食物及药物。 The plants died from ~ of water. 这些植物因缺水而死。 Your work shows ~ of thought/care. 你的工作显示你缺乏思想(不够细心)。 2 [U] need; absence of some necessary thing: 需要; 匮乏: The house is in ~ of repair. 这房子需要修理了。 We may one day be in ~, very poor. 我们也许有一天会很穷。 3 [C] (usu pl) desire for sth as necessary to life, happiness, etc; thing to be desired: (通常用复数)欲望; 欲获得之物: He is a man of few ~s. 他是一个欲望很少的人。 We can supply all your ~s. 我们可以供应你所需要的东西。 The book meets a long-felt ~, sth that has been needed for a long time. 本书满足了人们久已感到的需要。

want² /wɒnt/ vt, vi 1 [VP6A, 17, 19B, 24A] require; be in need of; lack: 要; 需要; 缺乏? You won't be ~ed (= Your services will not be required) this afternoon. 今天下午不需要你做什么了。 These plants are drooping—they ~ water. 这些植物枯萎了——它们需要水。 That man ~s a woman to look after him. 那位男人需要一位女子照顾他。 I don't ~ (= I object to having) anyone meddling in my affairs. 我不要任何人干涉我的事。 Do you ~ (= Would you like to have) this box opened? 你要让这个匣子打开吗? '~-ad n (colloq) (usu short) advertisement (in a newspaper, etc) for sth ~ed, eg a job. (口)(报纸等上通常较短的)征求广告。 2 [VP6A, 7A, 17] wish for; have a desire for ⟹**wish** vi, vt (6); want is used for sth which it is possible to obtain; wish for is used for sth unlikely to be obtained, or obtainable only in exceptional circumstances): 希望; 愿望; 欲得 (参看 wish 动词条第 6 义); want 用于可能获得的事物, wish for 用于不大可能获得, 或仅在例外情况下才能获得的事物): She ~s a holiday. 她想要一个假日。 She ~s to go to Italy. 她想去意大利。 She ~s me to go with her. 她希望我同她一道儿去。 He is ~ed by the police, ie because he is suspected of wrongdoing. 警察在通缉他。 I don't ~ there to be any misunderstanding. 我不想发生任何误会。 3 [VP6A, E, 7A] need, ought (as in the notes to the examples): 需要; 应该(用法见例句的说明): Your hair ~s cutting, needs to be cut. 你的头发该理了。 You ~ (= ought) to see your solicitors about that problem. 那问题你该去请教你的律师。 What that naughty boy ~s (= needs to be given) is a good beating. 那顽皮的男孩子该好好的揍一顿。 That sort of thing ~s some doing, (colloq) needs effort, skill, is not an easy matter. (口)那种事情需要相当的努力与技巧等。 4 [VP2A] (progressive tenses only) (with non-human subject) (仅用于进行时中)(主语须为非人的) be ~ing, be missing or lacking: 缺失; 缺少: A few pages of this book are ~ing. 这本书少了几页。 The infinitive of the verb 'must' is ~ing. 动词 must 无不定式。 be ~ing (in sth), (with human subject): (主语须为人, 而非物)缺乏; 没有: He's ~ing in courtesy, is impolite. 他缺乏礼貌。 be found ~ing: 被发现不合格: He was put to the test and found ~ing, inadequate. 他经过考试后被发现不合格。 He/It was tried and found (to be) ~ing, unequal to a standard or to a need. 他(它)经过试验后被发现不合格。 5 [VP6A] (impers) fall short by: (无人称)缺少; 不够; 差: It ~s one inch of the regulation length, (它)较规定的长度短一英寸。 It ~s half an hour to the appointed time. 距约定的时间还有半小时。 6 [VP2A, 3A] be in want (⟹ **want¹**(3)): 贫乏; 缺少: We mustn't let our soldiers ~ (= suffer poverty or hardship) in their old age. 我们不可使我们的军人在老年时受贫困之苦。 ~ for nothing, have all one needs. 不匮乏; 具所需要的一切。 ~ing prep without; in the absence of: 没有; 无: Without ~ing mutual trust, friendship is impossible. 没有互信便无友谊可言。

wan·ton /'wɒntən US: 'wɔ:n-/ adj 1 (liter)

playful; irresponsible; capricious: (文)嬉戏的; 顽皮的; 不负责的; 反复无常的: a ~ breeze; 变化无常的微风; in a ~ mood. 嬉笑地。 2 unchecked; luxuriant: wild: 未受遏止的; 繁茂的; 野生的: a ~ growth (of weeds, etc): (野草等的)繁茂; 丛生; 茂密; in ~ profusion. 过分丰富地; 浪费地。 3 wilful; serving no useful purpose: 任性的; 胡乱的; 无谓的: ~ destruction/damage; 胡乱的破坏(损坏); a ~ insult. 没道理的侮辱。 4 (archaic) immoral; unchaste: (古)不道德的; 不贞洁的; a ~ woman; 荡妇; lewd, licentious: 放肆的; 放荡的; 淫荡的: ~ thoughts. 淫念。 □ n (archaic) unchaste person. (古)不贞洁的人。 □ vi [VP2A, C] (liter) be ~ in behaviour: (文)嬉戏; 闲荡; 变化无常; 放肆; 淫荡; 漫无目的地行事: the wind ~ing with the leaves. 风舞树叶。 ~·ly adv ~·ness n

war /wɔ:(r); wɔr/ n 1 [C, U] (state created by the use of armed forces between countries or (civil war) rival groups in a nation: 战争; 战争状态; 内战: We have had two world wars in this century. 本世纪我们已经历了两次世界大战。 at war, in a state of war: 处于战争或交战状态: Ruritania and Utopia are at war again. 假里国与乌托邦又交战了。 carry the war into the enemy's camp, attack (instead of being satisfied to defend). 向敌人进攻(不以防御为满足)。 declare war (on), announce that a state of war exists (with another state). (向某一国)宣战。 go to war (against), start fighting. 启战端; 和…开战。 have been in the wars, (used colloq or hum) have suffered injury (eg as the result of an accident). (口或谐)受到创伤(如遇到车祸等)。 make/wage war on, engage in fighting against. 和…开战; 从事战争。 2 (compounds) (复合词) 'war-baby n (pl -babies) illegitimate child with a soldier as father and attributable to conditions during a war. 战时私生子(父为军人, 系由战时状态所致)。 'war-bride n bride of a soldier during a war. 战时新娘(新郎为战时军人)。 'war-cloud(s) n state of affairs that seems to threaten war 战云, 将引起战争的局势。 'war-cry n (pl -cries) word or cry shouted as a signal in battle; catch-word (eg used by a political party) in any kind of contest. 作战时的呐喊; (政党竞选等时所用的)口号; 标语。 'war-dance n one by tribal warriors before going into battle, to celebrate a victory, or (in peace) to represent fighting. (蛮族战士于出发作战前, 庆祝胜利, 或在平时扮演打仗的)战舞。 'war-god n god (eg Mars) worshipped as giving victory in war. 战神(如 Mars)。 'war·head n (of a torpedo, shell, etc) explosive head (contrasted with a dummy charge as used in practice, etc). (指鱼雷、炮弹等的)弹头; 实弹弹头(与演习时用的空包弹相对而言)。 'war-horse n (rhet) horse used in battle; charger; (fig) veteran soldier, politician, etc. (修辞)战马; 军马; (喻)老兵; 资深政客等。 'war-lord n (rhet) great military leader, esp a Chinese general in the period of civil wars, early 20th c. (修辞)大将军; (尤指)(二十世纪初中国内战时期的)军阀。 'war·monger n person who advocates or stirs up war. 战争贩子(鼓动战争者)。 'War Office, (formerly in GB) State department in charge of the Army, under the Secretary of State of War. (昔英国的)陆军部。 (Now named 现称做 Ministry of Defence) 'war-paint n [U] (a) paint put on the body before battle by some primitive people; (fig) full, ceremonial dress: 蛮人出战前涂于身上的颜料; (喻)盛装; 礼服: The General was in full war-paint. 那位将军穿着大礼服。 (b) (sl) make-up (cosmetics). (俚)化妆品。 'war-path n (only in) (仅用于) on the war-path, ready for, engaged in, a fight or quarrel. 准备作战或争吵; 正在作战或争吵。 'war·ship n ship for use in war. 战舰; 军舰。 'war-torn adj exhausted by, worn out in, war. 疲于战争的; 为战争所耗尽的; 饱经战祸的。 'war-widow n woman whose husband has been killed in war. 战时寡妇(丈夫死于战争中)。 3 [U]science or art of fighting using weapons, etc: 军事学; 兵学; 兵法: trained for war; 受过作战训练的; the art of war, strategy and tactics. 战略及战术。 4 (fig) any kind of struggle or

conflict: (喻)任何种类的斗争; 冲突; 不和: *the war against disease;* 对疾病的作战; *the wars of the elements,* storms, natural calamities; 天灾(暴风雨等); *a war of nerves/words.* 神经战(笔战). □ *vi* (**-rr-**) fight; make war: 战斗; 作战: *warring for supremacy;* 为争夺霸权而战; *warring (= rival) creeds/ideologies:* 对立的信念(意识). '**war·fare** /'wɔ:feə(r); 'wɔr,fɛr/ *n* [U] making war; condition of being at war; fighting: 作战; 战争状态; 交战: *the horrors of modern warfare.* 近代战争的恐怖. **war·like** /'wɔ:laɪk; 'wɔr,laɪk/ *adj* ready for, suggesting, war: 准备作战的; 表示战争的: *warlike preparations;* 军备; 战备; fond of war: 好战的: *a cruel, warlike people.* 残忍好战的民族. **war·time** /'wɔ:taɪm; 'wɔr,taɪm/ *n* [U] time when there is war: 战时: *in wartime;* 在战时; (attrib) (用作定语) *wartime regulations/rationing.* 战时条例(配给).

warble /'wɔ:bl; 'wɔrbl/ *vi, vt* [VP2A, C, 6A] (esp of birds) sing, esp with a gentle trilling note: (尤指鸟类)鸣; 唱; (尤指)柔和颤动地啭鸣: *larks warbling high up in the sky;* 在高空鸣叫的云雀; *a blackbird warbling from a branch.* 在枝头歌唱的画眉鸟. □ *n* warbling; bird's song. 啭唱; 鸣啭; 鸟叫. **war·bler** /'wɔ:blə(r); 'wɔrblə/ *n* (kinds of) bird that ~s. (各种的)鸣禽.

ward /wɔ:d; wɔrd/ *n* **1** *keep watch and* ~, guard and protect. 守卫; 监护. **2** [U] state of being in custody or under the control of a guardian: 受监护的状态: *a child in* ~; 在监护下的孩子; [C] person under the guardianship of an older person or of law authorities. 被监护人; 受监护人. **3** division of a local government area, each division being represented by one Councillor. 地方政府的区划: (由一议员代表的)选举区. **4** division of, separate room in, a building, esp a prison or a hospital: 建筑物内的分区或房间; (尤指)监房; 病房: *the fever/isolation/children's* ~. 热病(隔离, 儿童)病房; **5** notch in a key; corresponding part in a lock. 钥匙的缺刻; 锁中相对钥匙的部分. □ *vt* [VP15B] ~ *sth off,* keep away, avoid: 躲开; 避免: ~ *off a blow/ danger.* 躲开打击(危险).

war·den /'wɔ:dn; 'wɔrdn/ *n* **1** person having control or authority: 有管辖权或控制权的人; 看守人; 监护人: *the* ~ *of a youth hostel.* 青年招待所的管理人. '**air-raid** ~, (during World War II in GB) member of a civilian organization with various duties during air-raids. (二次大战时英国的)民防队员. '**traffic** ~, (eg in London) person responsible for controlling the parking of cars in streets, squares, etc at parking meters. (伦敦等地的)计时停车处的管理人. **2** (old use except in a few cases) title of certain governors or presidents: (除少数用法外, 为旧用法) 某些总督、州长、校长等的称谓: *the W*~ *of Merton College, Oxford.* 牛津大学慰顿学院的院长. **3** (US)(美) = **warder**.

war·der /'wɔ:də(r); 'wɔrdə/ *n* (GB) man acting as guard in a prison; jailer. (英)典狱官; 狱史. **war·dress** /'wɔ:drɪs; 'wɔrdrɪs/ *n* woman ~. 女狱吏; 女看守.

ward·robe /'wɔ:drəub; 'wɔrd,rob/ *n* **1** cupboard (*built-in-*~) or movable cupboard-like piece of furniture with pegs, shelves, etc for a person's clothes. 衣柜; 衣橱; 衣室. **2** stock of clothes: 衣服; 行头(总称): *My* ~ *needs to be renewed,* I must buy some new clothes. 我需要添购一些新衣服了. **3** stock of costumes of a theatrical company. (某一剧团的)剧装.

ward·room /'wɔ:drum US: -ru:m ; 'wɔrd,rum/ *n* living and eating quarters for commissioned officers in a warship except the commanding officer. (军舰上)舰长以外的军官的起居室及餐厅.

ware[1] /weə(r); wɛr/ *n* **1** (in compounds) manufactured goods: (用于复合词中)制造品; 加工品: '*silver-*~; 银器; '*iron-*~; 铁器; '*hard-*~; 金属器皿. **2** (*pl*) articles offered for sale: (复)货物; 商品: *advertise one's* ~*s.* 推销某人的货物. ~·**house** /'weəhaus; 'wɛr,haus/ *n* building for storing goods before distribution to retailers; storehouse for furniture (on behalf of owners). 仓库; 货栈; 家具店

ware[2] /weə(r); wɛr/ *vt* [VP6A] (in imper) look out for; be cautious about; beware of: (用于祈使句中)留心; 小心; 注意: *W*~ *wire!* (warning to riders in a fox-hunt that there is barbed wire on a fence, etc). 留心铁丝网! (猎狐时向骑者警告篱笆等上有倒钩铁丝).

war·fare /'wɔ:feə(r); 'wɔr,fɛr/ ⇨ **war**.
war·ily, wari·ness ⇨ **wary**.
warm[1] /wɔ:m; wɔrm/ *adj* (**-er, -est**) **1** having a fairly high degree of heat (between *cool* and *hot*); (of clothing) serving to keep the body ~: 暖的; 温暖的(介于冷与热之间); (指衣服)保暖的: *Come and get* ~ *by the fire.* 来炉火旁取暖. *It was* ~, *but not hot, yesterday.* 昨天暖和而不炎热. *Put your* ~*est clothes on before you go out in the snow.* 下雪天外出前要穿起你最暖和的衣服. *Red, yellow and orange are called* ~ *colours.* 红、黄、橙三色被称为暖色. ~ *work,* (**a**) work or activity that makes one ~. 使人暖和的工作或活动. (**b**) strenuous or dangerous activity or occupation. 吃力或危险的活动或职业. *make things* ~ *for sb,* make things unpleasant, make trouble for him; punish him. 困扰某人; 为某人找麻烦; 惩罚某人. ~ *blood,* that of mammals and birds (ranging from 36°C—42°C). 温血(哺乳类及鸟类的体温, 自摄氏 36° 至 42°). Hence, 由此产生, ,~·'**blooded** *adj* (**a**) having ~ blood; not cold-blooded like snakes, etc. 温血的; 非冷血(冷血动物)的. (**b**) having feelings and passions that are easily roused. 热情的; 易激动的. ~ **front**, ⇨ **front**(7). **2** enthusiastic, hearty; 热心的; 热诚的; *give sb a* ~ *welcome;* 热烈欢迎某人; *a* ~ *friend/supporter.* 热心的朋友(支持者). **3** sympathetic; affectionate: 同情的; 热情的: *He has a* ~ *heart.* 他具有同情心. Hence, 由此产生, ,~·'**hearted** *adj* kind and sympathetic. 亲切而易同情心的. **4** (of scent in hunting) fresh; recently made and easily followed by the hounds; (in children's games, when an object is hidden and searched for) close to the object: (指猎物的气味)新鲜的; 新近发出而易被猎犬跟踪的; (在儿童游戏中, 寻找某隐藏物时)接近目标的: *You're getting* ~, near to what is being sought. 你快找到了. ~·**ly** *adv* in a ~ manner: 温暖地; 亲切地; 热烈地: ~*ly dressed;* 穿得暖和的: *thank sb* ~*ly.* 热烈地感谢某人. **warmth** /wɔ:mθ; wɔrmθ/ *n* [U] state of being ~: 温暖; 亲切; 热烈: *He was pleased with the* ~*th of his welcome.* 他因受到热烈欢迎而高兴. *He answered with a* ~*th,* with some emotion (of pleasure, resentment, etc, according to context). 他激动地(愉快、憎恨等, 视上下文而定之)回答.

warm[2] /wɔ:m; wɔrm/ *vt, vi* [VP6A, 15B, 2A, C] ~ (*sth*)(*up*), make or become warm or warmer: 使暖; 变暖; (使)感到亲切或激动: ~ *oneself/one's hands by the fire.* 烤火取暖(使手温暖). *Please* ~ (*up*) *this milk.* 把这牛奶热一热. *The milk is* ~*ing* (*up*) *on the stove.* 牛奶正在炉子上热着. *He* ~*ed up* (= became more animated, enthusiastic) *as he went on with his speech.* 他愈讲愈起劲. ~ *to one's work/task, etc,* become more interested; like it more. 对工作等开始发生兴趣; 对工作等更为喜欢. '~-ing-pan *n* (hist) round metal pan with a lid and a long handle, holding hot coals and used for ~ing the inside of a bed before it was occupied. (史)长柄暖床器. ~·**er** *n* (usu in compounds) sth which ~s. (通常用于复合词中)温暖器; 保暖装置.

warn /wɔ:n; wɔrn/ *vt* [VP6A, 14, 11, 15, 17] give (sb) notice of possible danger or unpleasant consequences; inform in advance of what may happen: 警告; 警戒; 预告; 预先通知: *He was* ~*ed of the danger.* 他已得到危险的警告. ~ *them not to go skating on such thin ice.* 我们警告他们不要在这样薄的冰上溜冰. *You've been* ~*ed.* 你已受到警告了. *He* ~*ed me that there were pickpockets in the crowd/*~*ed me against pickpockets.* 他提醒我人丛中有扒手(谨防扒手). ~ *sb off,* give him notice that he must go or stay away, eg from private property. 通知某人离开或勿近. ~·**ing**

adj that ～s 警告的; 预告的: *He gave me a ～ing look*. 他向我使了一个警告的眼色. *They fired some ～ing shots*. 他们发射了几枪示警。□ **n 1** [C] that which ～s or serves to ～: 警告或用以警告之物; 警号; 警戒; 预兆; 殷鉴: *He paid no attention to my ～ings*. 他不重视我的警告. *Let this be a ～ing to you*, Let this accident, misfortune, etc teach you to be careful in future. 让此事做为你的殷鉴. *There were gale ～ings to shipping along the coast*. 有强风警报要求沿海航行船只注意. **2** [U] action of ～ing; state of being ～ed: 警告或预告; 受警告的状态: *You should take ～ing (= be ～ed) from what happened to me*. 你应该把我的遭遇作为殷鉴. *The speaker sounded a note of ～ing*, spoke of possible danger. 讲话的人透露警告之意 (提到可能的危险). *The enemy attacked our ～ing*. 敌人突然来袭。

warp¹ /wɔːp; wɔrp/ *vt, vi* [VP6A, 2A] (cause to) become bent or twisted from the usual or natural shape: (使)弯翘; 变歪; 歪曲. *The hot sun ～ed the boards*. 灼热的太阳把木板晒得弯翘了. *His judgement/disposition is ～ed*, biased because of possible advantage for himself. 他的判断(处置)不公平(可能与其切身利益有关而产生偏见)。□ *n* [C] twisted or bent condition in timber, etc, caused by uneven shrinking or expansion. (木材等的)弯翘; 翘曲(由不均匀的胀缩所致)。

warp² /wɔːp; wɔrp/ *n* **the ～**, the threads over and under which other threads (the *weft* or *woof*) are passed when cloth is woven on a loom. (布的)经; 经纱; 经线。

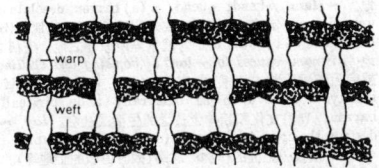

war·rant /ˈwɒrənt US: ˈwɔːr-; ˈwɔrənt/ *n* **1** [U] justification or authority: 正当; 正当的理由; 根据; 权威: *He had no ～ for saying so/for what he did*. 他那样说(做)毫无理由。 **2** [C] written order giving official authority for sth: 令状; 授权状; 委任状: *a ～ to arrest a suspected criminal*. 逮捕嫌疑犯的令状或拘票. *The 'death-～ has been signed*. 死刑执行令已签字了. *A ～ is out for his arrest/against him*. 逮捕他的拘票已发出了. *Here are the ～s for your dividends*, ie on shares. 这是你的股利券. **3** [C] certificate appointing a man as a ～ officer. 准尉委任状. **'～ officer** *n* highest grade of non-commissioned officer in the army, air force, (GB) marines, (US) navy. (陆军,空军,英国海军陆战队,美国海军之)准尉. □ *vt* **1** [VP6A] be a ～ (1) for: 证明…是正当; 保证; 有权力: *Nothing can ～ such insolence*. 这等无礼毫无道理. *His interference was certainly not ～ed*. 他显然无权干预. **2** [VP6A, 9, 25] guarantee (the more usu word); (colloq) assure: 保证(guarantee 较常用); 担保; (口)确定; 包准: *This material is ～ed (to be) pure silk*. 这料子保证是纯丝的. *I'll ～ him an honest and reliable man*. 我保证他是个诚实可靠的人. *I can't ～ it to be/～ that it is genuine*. 我不能担保那是真货. *He'll be back, I ～ (= assure) you, when the money's paid out*. 这笔钱一付, 我保证他会回来. **war·ran·tee** /ˌwɒrənˈtiː US: ˌwɔːr-; ˌwɔrənˈti/ *n* person to whom a warranty is made. 被保证人. **war·ran·tor** /ˈwɒrəntɔː(r) US: ˈwɔːr-; ˈwɔrəntɔr/ *n* person who makes a warranty. 保证人. **war·ranty** /ˈwɒrənti US: ˈwɔːr-; ˈwɔrənti/ *n* [C] (*pl* -ties) authority; (written or printed) guarantee (eg to repair or replace defective goods): 权威; 根据; (写出或印出的)担保; 保证(如修理或掉换有缺点的货物): 保单: *What ～y have you for doing this*? 你凭什么做这

件事? *Can you give me a ～y of quality for these goods*? 你能给我一张这些货物的品质保单吗? *The car is still under ～y*. 这车你仍在保用期间。

war·ren /ˈwɒrən US: ˈwɔːrən; ˈwɔrən/ *n* [C] area of land in which there are many burrows in which rabbits live and breed; (fig) (usu over-populated) building or district in which it is difficult to find one's way about: 养兔场; (喻)(通常指)过分拥挤而易迷路的建筑或地区; *lose oneself in a ～ of narrow streets*. 在纵横交错的狭窄街道间迷了路。

war·rior /ˈwɒrɪə(r) US: ˈwɔːr-; ˈwɔrɪə/ *n* (liter, rhet) soldier; fighter: (文,修辞)兵士; 战士; 勇士: (attrib)(用作定语) *a ～ race*. 骁勇的民族。

wart /wɔːt; wɔrt/ *n* small, hard, dry growth on the skin; similar growth on a plant. 疣; 瘊; 瘤肿; 树疣; 树瘤. **'～hog** *n* kinds of African pig with two large tusks and ～-like growths on the face. (非洲产的)疣猪。

wary /ˈweərɪ; ˈwɛrɪ/ *adj* (**-ier, -iest**) cautious; in the habit of looking out for possible danger or trouble: 小心的; 警惕的; 惯于留神可能的危险或困难的: *be ～ of giving offence/of strangers*; 提防冒犯他人(当心陌生人); *keep a ～ eye on sb*; 密切注意某人; *a ～ old fox*. 机警的老狐. **war·ily** /-əlɪ; -əlɪ/ *adv* **wari·ness** *n*

was /weak form: wəz; wəz/ *weak form*; /strong form: wɒz US: wɑz; wɑz, wʌz/ ⇨ **be¹**

wash¹ /wɒʃ US: wɔːʃ; waʃ/ *n* **1** (*sing* only, usu with *indef* art) act of washing; being washed: (仅用单数, 通常与不定冠词连用)洗; 洗涤: *Will you give the car a ～/a ,～·down, please*. 请把车子洗(冲洗)一下. **have a ～ and brush up**, wash oneself and make oneself tidy. 盥洗; 梳洗; 整容. **2** (*sing* only) clothing, sheets, etc to be washed or being washed; place (laundry) where they are being washed: (仅用单数)洗濯物; 洗濯处; 洗衣店: *She has a large ～ this week*. 这里期她有很多衣物要洗. *She was hanging out the ～*. 她正在晾衣服. *All my shirts are at the ～*. 我所有的衬衫都在洗衣店. *When does the ～ come back from the laundry*? 送洗的衣服何时取回? **3 the ～ (of)**, movement or flow of water; sound made by moving water: 水的流动; 水流声; 冲击声; *the ～ of the waves*; 浪的冲击; *the ～ made by a steamer's propeller(s)*. 汽船的推进器发出的击水声. **4** [U] thin, weak or inferior liquid: 稀薄或浓度不足的液体: *This soup is a mere ～*, is too watery, has no flavour or substance. 这汤实在太稀了. **5** [U] kitchen liquid with waste food (eg vegetable peelings and scraps) to be given to pigs: 厨房的残汁; 馊水. **6** (usu in compounds, ⇨ under the first part) liquid prepared for a special purpose: (通常用于复合词中,参看各该词的第一部分)特别调制的液体: *'white-～*, for putting on walls; (刷墙的)石灰水; *'mouth-～*, for disinfecting the mouth; (消毒用的)漱口剂; *'eye-～*. 洗眼水。

wash² /wɒʃ US: wɔːʃ; waʃ/ *vt, vi* **1** [VP6A, 15B, 2A] make clean with or in water or other liquid: 洗; 清洗; 洗去: ～ *one's hands/clothes*. 洗手(衣). *W～ them clean*. 把它们洗干净. *Go and ～ yourself*. 去洗澡. *I must ～ before dinner*. 饭前我必须洗手. *He never ～es* (ie ～es himself) *in cold water*. 他从不用冷水洗澡. **one's hands of sth/sb**, say one is no longer responsible for. 宣布对某事(某人)不再负责; 从…撒手; 断绝…的关系. ⇨ *one's dirty linen in public*, ⇨ **linen**. ～ **sth down**, clean by ～ing, esp by using a stream or jet of water (eg from a hose): 洗清; (尤指)冲洗; 冲净: ～ *down a car/the decks of a ship*. 冲洗汽车(船上的甲板). ～ **sth away/off/out**, remove by ～ing: 洗去; 洗掉: ～ *dirty marks off a wall*. 把墙上的污迹洗掉; ～ *out blood stains*. 洗去血渍. **be/look/feel ～ed out**, (fig, colloq) pale and tired; exhausted. (喻,口)苍白而疲倦的; 筋疲力竭的. ～ **up, (a)** (GB) ～ dishes, cutlery, etc, after a meal. (英)餐后洗碗盘,刀叉等. **(b)** (US) ～ one's face and hands. (美)洗脸洗手. ～ **sth up**, (GB) ～ dishes, cutlery, etc after a meal: (英)餐后洗碗碟,刀叉等: ～ *up the dinner things*. 洗餐具. Hence, 由

此产生，ˌ~·ing-'up n [U]. (Note: up indicates that a number of dishes, etc are to be ~ed. For a single article up is not used: Please ~ this plate.) (注意: up 意谓要洗的碗盘有若干件，如只有一件，不用 up, 如: Please ~ this plate. 请把这盘子洗一洗。) (all) ~ed up, (colloq) ruined; failed. (口)(全部)毁灭; 失败; 完蛋. 2 [VP2A] (of materials) be capable of being ~ed without damage or loss of colour: (指物料或布料)耐洗; 不褪色: Does this material ~ well? 这料子耐洗吗? That argument/excuse will not ~, (fig) will not bear examination, is weak. (喻)那项论据(借口)站不住脚. 3 [VP6A] (of a sea or a river) flow past or against: (指海或河)流过; 冲击; 拍打: The sea ~es the base of the cliffs. 海水冲击崖壁的底部. 4 [VP15B] (of moving liquid) carry away, on or in a specified direction: (指流动的液体)冲去; 卷走: He was ~ed overboard by a huge wave. 他被一个巨浪从船上卷入海中. All this timber has been ~ed up (ie carried up on to the beach) by the waves. 这些木料都被海浪冲到岸上来的. The cliffs are being gradually ~ed away by the sea. 悬崖正逐渐被海水冲损. ~ sth down (with), swallow (liquid) with: 连同 …吞下(某种液体): My lunch was bread and cheese ~ed down with beer. 我的中餐是面包和乳酪，用啤酒帮助咽下去. ~ed out, (a) (of games such as cricket, of horse-races, etc) made impossible, cancelled, by heavy rain or flooding. (指游戏如板球, 指赛马等)因大雨或淹水而停止或取消. (b) (of roads, etc) made impassable by heavy rain, floods, etc. (指路等)因大雨、淹水等而不通. 5 [VP6A, 15A] scoop out: 挖; 冲出: The water had ~ed a channel in the sand. 水在沙中冲出了一条沟. 6 [VP2C] go flowing, sweeping or splashing (along, out, in, into, over, etc): 流过; 冲去; 冲刷; 溅泼(与 along, out, in, into, over 等连用): We heard the waves ~ing against the sides of our boat. 我们听到波浪冲向我们的船舷. Huge waves ~ed over the deck. 巨浪溅泼在甲板上. ~·able /-əbl/, -əbl/ adj that can be ~ed without being spoiled. 可洗的; 耐洗的.

wash- /wɒʃ US: wɔːʃ; wɑʃ/ (in compounds; often used as a substitute for washing). (用于复合词中; 常用以代替 washing). '~-basin n basin for holding water in which to wash one's face and hands. 洗脸盆; 洗脸盆. '~-board n board with ridges on it, on which clothes are washed (at home). 洗衣板; 搓板. '~-bowl n (US) (美) = basin. '~-cloth n (US) (美) = face-cloth. '~-day n day on which clothes were washed (at home). 洗涤日; 洗衣日. '~-hand-basin n = ~-basin. '~-drawing n one made with a brush in a black or neutral water-colour. 淡彩画. '~-hand-stand n = ~-stand. '~-house n room or out-building equipped for washing. 洗衣间; 洗衣房. '~-leather n [C, U] (piece of) chamois leather, used for cleaning and polishing windows and other surfaces. 擦秧皮(擦拭窗户及其他表面的小羊皮). '~-out n (a) place in a railway or road where a flood or heavy rain has carried away earth, rock, etc and interrupted communications. (因洪水或大雨冲去泥土、碎石等，而阻碍交通的)铁路或道路的冲垮处; 冲塌缺口. (b) (colloq) useless or unsuccessful person; complete failure or fiasco. (口)无用或失败的人; 大败. '~-room n (US) lavatory (esp in a public building, etc). (美)厕所(尤指公共场所者). '~-stand n (now old-fashioned, except in houses where there is no piped supply of water to bathrooms or bedrooms) piece of furniture with a basin, jug, etc for washing in a bedroom. (除尚无自来水接入浴室或卧房的建筑外，现为旧用法)(卧室用)面盆架; 盥洗台. '~-tub n large wooden tub in which to wash clothes. 洗涤盆; 洗衣盆.

washer /'wɒʃə(r) US: 'wɔː-; 'wɑʃə/ n 1 machine for washing clothes, or ('dish-~) dishes. 洗衣机; 洗碗机; 洗灌机. 2 '~-woman, laundress. 洗衣妇. 3 small flat ring of metal, plastic, rubber or leather for making a joint or screw tight. (使接头或螺丝密合的)垫圈; 皮圈. ⇨ the illus at **bolt**. 参看 bolt 之插图.

wash·ing /'wɒʃɪŋ US: 'wɔː-; 'wɑʃɪŋ/ n [U] 1 washing or being washed. 洗; 洗涤; 洗濯. 2 clothes being washed or to be washed: (正在洗或待洗的)衣物: hang out the ~ on the line to dry. 把洗好的衣服晾在绳子上. '~-day n = wash-day, ⇨ **wash-**. '~-machine n power driven machine for washing clothes. 洗衣机. '~ soda n sodium carbonate, used, dissolved in water, for washing clothes or dishes. 洗涤用的碳酸钠; 洗涤碱. ˌ~·'up n ⇨ wash at **wash²(1)**.

washy /'wɒʃɪ US: 'wɔː-; 'wɑʃɪ/ adj (of liquids) thin, watery; (of colours) faded-looking; pale; (of feeling, style) lacking in vigour. (指液体)稀薄的; 水多的; (指色彩)淡的; 浅的; (指感情, 文体)软弱的; 无生气的.

wasp /wɒsp US: wɔːsp; wɑsp/ n kinds of flying insect of which the common kind has a narrow waist, black and yellow stripes and a powerful sting in the tail. 黄蜂; 胡蜂. ⇨ the illus at **insect**. 参看 insect 之插图. ˌ~·'waisted adj slender at the waist. 蜂腰的; 细腰的. ~·ish /-ɪʃ/, -ɪʃ/ adj irritable; ill tempered; sharp in making retorts. 暴躁的; 易怒的; 坏脾气的; 尖刻的.

was·sail /'wɒseɪl; 'wɑsl/ n (archaic) time of drinking and merry-making; spiced ale or other liquor drunk at such a time. (古)饮宴取乐之时; 饮宴时所用的加香料的麦酒或其他酒.

wast·age /'weɪstɪdʒ; 'westɪdʒ/ n [U] amount wasted; loss by waste. 消耗量; 损耗.

waste /weɪst; west/ adj 1 (of land) that is not or cannot be used; no longer of use; barren: (指土地)未或无法利用的; 废弃的; 荒芜的: ~ land, not occupied or used for any purpose. (未作任何利用的)荒芜地; 未利用地. '~-land n /-lænd; -lænd/ n (a) barren, desolate or unused land. 荒芜、人迹罕至或未利用的土地; 荒地. (b) land ravaged by war, etc: 为战争等所破坏之地; 疮痍之地: Vietnam reduced to ~land by bombing and shelling. 越南因轰炸及炮击而变成疮痍之地. (c) (fig) life, society, looked upon as culturally and spiritually barren. (喻)文化和精神上贫乏的生活或社会. □ lay ~, destroy the crops in, ravage (eg territory occupied in war). 损毁…上面的作物; 蹂躏(战时占领的土地等). 2 useless; thrown away because not wanted: 无用的; 抛弃的; 废弃的: ~·paper, 废纸; ~ products, unwanted after a manufacturing process. 制造过程剩下的无用副产品. 废物. □ vt, vi 1 [VP6A, 14, 2A] ~ sth (on sth), make no use of; use without a good purpose; use more of (sth) than is necessary: 未用; 浪费; 徒耗: ~ one's time and money on paying bribes; 将时间和金钱浪费于贿赂; ~ one's words/breath, talk without making any impression (on sb). 徒费唇舌. All his efforts were ~d, had no result. 他的全部努力都白费了. W~ not, want not, (prov) If you do not ~ your money, etc you are unlikely to be in need. (谚)不浪费则不虞匮乏. 2 [VP6A] make (land) waste; ravage. 使(土地)荒芜; 损毁; 蹂躏. 3 [VP6A, 2A, C] (cause to) lose strength by degrees: (使)逐渐失去力量; 耗损; 衰弱: He's wasting away. 他渐渐消瘦了. Consumption is a wasting disease. 肺痨是一种耗损体力的疾病. His body was ~d by long illness. 他的身体因久病而衰弱了. 4 [VP2A] be ~d: 被浪费或耗损: Turn that tap off—the water is wasting. 把那水龙头关起来，水给浪费了. □ n 1 [U] wasting or being ~d: 浪费; 徒耗: There's too much ~ in this house. 这一家人太浪费了. It's a ~ of time to wait any longer. 再等下去是白费时间了. What a ~ of energy! 这么浪费精力! go/run to ~, be ~d: 被浪费; 未被利用: What a pity to see all that water running to ~! eg instead of being used for generating electric current. 眼看着那些水白白浪费掉，多可惜啊! (如果用来发电等). 2 [U] ~ material; refuse. 废物; 废料. '~-basket (US) (美), '~-paper-basket (GB) (英) nn basket or other container for scraps of paper, etc. 字纸篓. '~-pipe n pipe for carrying off used or superfluous water. 排水管. 3 [U] area of ~ land: 荒地; 原野; 沙漠: the ~s of the Sahara. 撒哈拉沙漠; dreary scene: 凄凉的景色; a

~ *of waters.* 一片汪洋的凄凉景色。 **~r** *n* (colloq)
wastrel. (口)无用的人;饭桶;浪子;浪费者。 **~·ful** /-fl;
-fəl/ *adj* causing ~; using more than is needed: 使无用
的; 浪费的: ~*ful habits/processes;* 浪费的习惯(方法);
~*ful expenditure.* 浪费的开支。 **~·fully** /-fəlɪ; -fəlɪ/
adv

wast·rel /'weɪstrəl ; 'westrəl/ *n* good-for-nothing
person; wasteful person. 废人;饭桶;浪费者。

watch¹ /wɒtʃ; watʃ/ *n* **1** [U] act of watching, esp to
see that all is well. 看; 注意; 警戒; 监视; 守望。 *be on
the ~ (for),* be watching for (sth or sb, or esp
possible danger). 看守着; 提防着; 监视着(某人或某物,
尤指可能的危险)。 *keep ~ (on/over),* look out for
danger, etc. 注意危险等。 **'~·dog** *n* dog kept to protect
property, esp a house; (fig) sb or sth that protects. 警
犬;守望犬;(尤指)看家狗;(喻)保护的人或物。 **'~·tower**
n high tower from which to keep ~, eg in a forest, to
look for forest fires, or a fortified observation post. 守
望台; 了望台; 更楼。 **2** *the ~,* (hist) body of men
employed to go through the streets and protect people
and their property, esp at night: (史)看守者;守夜者;更
夫: *the constables of the ~;* 守夜的警官; *call out the ~.*
召喊守夜者。 **3** (in ships) period of duty (4 or 2 hours)
for part of the crew (船上的)轮值; 轮班时间(四或二小
时) *the first ~,* 8pm to midnight: 头班; 首班(夜晚八
时至午夜); *the middle ~,* midnight to 4 am; 中班(午
夜至凌晨四时); *the 'dog-~es,* 4 pm to 6 pm or 6pm to
8pm 暮更(下午四至六时或六至八时的轮班); either of
the halves into which a ship's crew is divided for
purposes of duty (called *the starboard* and *port ~es*
from the positions of the men's bunks in former times).
(船员轮值分为两班)二轮班船员之任何一班(昔时依船员
之床位而分,称右舷班及左舷班)。 *on ~,* on duty in this
way. 当班;值班;轮值。 *keep ~,* be on ~. 值班;守望。 **4**
(old use) period of wakefulness in the night: (旧用法)
夜里睡不着的时刻: *in the ~es of the night,* while one
lies awake. 躺在床上睡不着的时候。 **'~ night service,**
church service at midnight, New Year's Eve. (教堂在
除夕举行的)守岁礼拜;除夕午夜礼拜。 **~·ful** /-fl; -fəl/
adj on the ~; wide-awake. 注意的; 警戒的; 警醒的。 **~·
fully** /-fəlɪ; -fəlɪ/ *adv* **~·ful·ness** *n* **~·man** /-mən ;
-mən/ *n* (*pl* **-men**) **1** (hist) member of the ~(2). (史)
守夜者;更夫。 **2** man employed to guard a building (eg
a bank, block of offices, factory) against thieves, esp at
night. (尤指雇来在夜间看守银行、办公厅、工厂等建筑物,
以防盗窃的)警卫。 **~·word** /-wɜːd ; -,wɜd/ *n* **1**
password. 口令。 **2** slogan. 口号;标语。

watch² /wɒtʃ; watʃ/ *vt, vi* **1** [VP2A, B, C, 3A, 4A,
6A, 8, 10, 15A, 18A, 19A] look at; keep the eyes on:
看; 注视; 注意; 警戒; *W~ me carefully.* 仔细看看我。
W~ what I do and how I do it. 注意看我做什么及如何
做。 *We sat there ~ing the cricket.* 我们坐在那里看板球
赛。 *Are you going to play or only ~?* 你将参加(比赛)或
只当观众? *He ~ed to see (= ~ed in order to see) what
would happen.* 他注意看会发生什么事情。 *I ~ed her cross
the street,* looked at and saw this action from start to
finish. 我看着她走过街道(指留意其过街的整个过程和其
同一举一动)。 *I sat ~ing the shadows creep across the
floor,* looked at and saw this happening (but not
necessarily from start to finish). 我坐着, 观看阴影在地
板上缓缓移动(不一定从开始看到结束)。 *My solicitor is
~ing the case for me/holds a ~ing brief for me,* is
present in court during the case to protect my interests.
我的律师正替我照料这个案子(为我到法庭旁听,留意案情
发展)。 *~ one's step,* **(a)** be careful not to fall or
stumble. 小心走路; 留意不跌倒或摔跤。 **(b)** be careful
not to make an error, let sb win an advantage, etc, eg
in negotiations. 留意不犯错; 不让旁人占便宜(如在谈判
中)。 *~ one's time,* (more usu *bide*) wait for the right
time. (bide 较常用)等待时机。 *~ the time,* keep your
eye on the time (eg to avoid being late for sth). 注意时
间(俾不致耽误某事物)。 *~ (out) (for sth),* look out

for: 注意; 监视; 当心(某事): *There's a policeman ~ing
outside,* ie for anything suspicious. 有一位警察在外面监
视。 *The doctor told her to ~ out* (= be on the look-
out) *for symptoms of measles.* 医生告诉她当心麻疹的病
征。 *~ out,* be on one's guard. 警戒; 提防; 警惕。 *~
(over) sth,* guard; protect: 照料; 照看; 保护: *Will you
~ (over) my clothes while I have a swim?* 我去游泳时,你
替我照看衣服好吗? **2** [VP2A] (old use) remain awake:
(旧用法)不睡; 守夜: *~ all night at the bedside of a sick
child.* 彻夜在病童床边看护。 **~er** *n* person who ~es. 看
者;注视者;守夜者;监视者。

watch³ /wɒtʃ; watʃ/ *n* small timepiece that can be
carried in the pocket or worn on the wrist (of 参较
clock): 表;挂表;手表: *What time is it by your ~?* 你的
表几点钟了? *What does your ~ say?* 你的表几点钟? **'~-
glass** *n* disc covering the face of a ~. 表面玻璃。
'~-guard/-chain *n* strap or chain for securing a ~ to
the clothing. 挂表带; 挂表链。 **'~-key** *n* separate key
for winding a ~. 上表的钥匙。 **'~-maker** *n* person who
makes or repairs ~es. 钟表制造人;修表匠。

water¹ /'wɔːtə(r); 'wɔtɚ/ *n* **1** [U] liquid (**H₂O**) as in
rivers, lakes, seas and oceans: 水 (H_2O): *W~ is
changed into steam by heat and into ice by cold.* 水加热则
变为蒸汽,冷却则结为冰。 *Fish live in (the) ~.* 鱼生活在
水中。 *by ~,* by boat, ship, barge, etc. 由水路; 乘船。
in deep ~(s), experiencing or undergoing difficulty or
misfortune. 遭遇困难或不幸。 *in smooth ~,* making
smooth or easy progress. 进展顺利地。 *on the ~,* in a
boat, etc. 在船(等)上。 *under ~,* flooded: 被水淹的:
The fields were under ~ after the heavy rain. 大雨后
田地均为水所淹。 *be in/get into hot ~,* have/get into
trouble (esp because of foolish behaviour, etc). 陷于困
境(尤指因愚蠢行为等所致)。 *cast/throw one's bread
upon the ~(s),* do a good action without requiring
reward, although later some unexpected return may
come. 不求报酬做善事; 积阴德。 *drink the ~s,* go to a
spa where there are mineral ~s and drink them for
one's health. 至矿泉处饮矿泉水(以维护健康)。 *go through
fire and ~ (for sb/sth),* undergo severe hardship and
trials. (为某人或某事)赴汤蹈火;历经千辛万苦。 *hold
~,* (of a theory, etc) be sound when tested. (指理论等)
有道理; 站得住脚; 说得通。 *keep one's head above ~,*
avoid (esp financial) troubles or misfortunes. 尽力避免
(尤指财务上的)亏欠或损失;不举债。 *make ~,* **(a)** pass
urine from the bladder. 小便; 撒尿。 **(b)** (of a ship)
have a leak, (指船)漏水。 *spend money, etc like ~,*
extravagantly. 挥霍无度; 挥金如土。 *throw cold ~ on*
(a plan, etc), discourage (it). (为一项计划等)泼冷水。
tread ~, ⇨ **tread,** *vi, vi*(4). *like a fish out of ~,*
feeling uncomfortable, behaving awkwardly, because of
unaccustomed surroundings, an unfamiliar situation,
etc. 如出水之鱼; 因处生疏环境而感觉不自在或尴尬。
Still ~s run deep, (prov) Beneath a quiet manner
there may be depths of emotion, knowledge, cunning,
etc. (谚)静水流深; 沉着的举止可能蕴涵深厚的感情、知
识、谋略等。 *written in ~,* (of a name, reputation, etc)
soon forgotten; transient. (指声名等)昙花一现的; 转瞬
即逝的。 *~ on the brain/knee, etc,* morbid accumulation of fluid. 水脑(膝水节等水肿)。 *the ~s of
forgetfulness,* oblivion. 忘却; 湮灭。 **'table/'mineral
~s,** with a mineral ingredient, bottled for use at table.
(餐桌上用的瓶装)矿泉水。 **'back~,** ⇨ **back⁴(3).** **2**
[U] the state of the tide: 潮位; 潮: *at high/low ~;* 在
高(低)潮时; *high/low ~ mark.* 高(低)水位标。 *in low
~,* (fig) short of money. (喻)缺钱。 **3** (*pl*) seas as
indicated by a preceding word: (复)(由前面的词说明之)
海; 海域: *in Korean ~s,* on the seas near Korea; 在朝
鲜附近的海面; *a ship for service in Home ~s,* on the
seas near the country to which the ship belongs. 航行近
海的船。 *a large ~,* (*usu pl*) mass of ~: (通常用复数)一块
大片的水; 洪水: *the ('head-)~s of the Nile,* the lake
from which it flows. 尼罗河的河源。 *The ~s of the lak*

flow out over a large waterfall. 湖水流经一处大瀑布直泻而下. **5** [U] solution of a substance in ~: 溶液: *'lavender-~; 'rose-~, etc.* 玫瑰香水等. **6 of the first ~,** of the finest quality: 最佳品质的; 第一等货色的: *a diamond of the first ~.* 最佳品质的钻石. **7** (in compounds) (用于复合词中) **'~·bird** *n* kinds of bird that swim or wade in (esp fresh) ~. 水鸟; 水禽(尤指栖于淡水中者). **'~·biscuit** *n* thin, hard biscuit made of flour and ~, usu eaten with butter and cheese. 一种薄而硬的饼干(以面粉和水制成, 通常加奶油及干酪食用). **'~·blister** *n* blister on the skin containing a colourless liquid, not blood. (皮肤上的)水疱. **'~·borne** *adj* **(a)** (of goods) carried by ~. (指货物)由水路运送的. **(b)** (of diseases) passed on by the use of contaminated drinking-~. (指疾病)由饮水传染的. **'~·bottle** *n* **(a)** glass container for ~ at table or in a bedroom. 玻璃水瓶. **(b)** metal flask (US 美 = *canteen*) for use by a soldier, scout, etc. (兵士、童军等使用的)水壶. **'~·buffalo** *n* the common domestic buffalo of India, Indonesia, etc. 水牛. ⇨ the illus at **domestic.** 参看 domestic 之插图. **'~·butt,** ⇨ **butt¹(2). '~·cannon,** high-pressure hose, for forcing a jet of ~, eg to disperse rioters. 水炮(喷射高压水流的管道, 如用以驱散暴乱人群者). **'~·cart** *n* cart with a tank for ~, either for sale or for sprinkling on dusty roads, etc. 运水车. **~·chute** *n* sloping channel leading to ~, down which

boats, toboggans, etc slide, eg at a fun fair. (乐园等中供人驾小舟、长橇等自高处滑到水面之)滑槽. **'~·closet** *n* (common abbr 通常略作 **WC**) small room with a pan in which matter evacuated from the bowels may be flushed down a drain-pipe by ~ from a cistern. (有抽水设备的)厕所. **'~·colour** (US = **-color**) *n* **(a)** (*pl*) paints (to be) mixed with ~, not oil. (复)水彩; 水彩颜料. **(b)** picture painted with ~-colours. 水彩画. **(c)** (*pl* or *sing*) the art of painting such pictures. (复数或单数)水彩画法. **'~·course** *n* (channel of a) brook or stream. 河; 溪; 水道; 河床. **'~·cress** *n* [U] creeping plant that grows in running ~, with hot-tasting leaves used in salads. 水芥子(生于流动水中的攀爬植物, 叶有辣味, 用于生菜食品). **'~ diviner,** ⇨ **diviner. '~·fall** *n* [C] fall of ~, esp where a river falls over rocks or a cliff. 瀑布. **'~·finder** *n* dowser, ⇨ **dowsing.** 探寻地下水脉或矿脉者. **'~·fowl** *n* (collective *pl*) ~birds, esp those that swim, considered as suitable for shooting by sportsmen. (集合复数)水鸟; 水禽(尤指能游泳, 被认为适于猎杀者). **'~·front** *n* land at the ~'s edge, esp the part of a town facing the sea, the harbour, a lake, etc. (尤指都市靠近海、海港、湖等的)滨水区; 海边; 江边; 湖滨(等). **'~·glass** *n* [U] thick liquid used for coating eggs to keep them in good condition. 水玻璃(用以涂在蛋上以保持其新鲜). **'~ hen** *n* = *moorhen,* ⇨ **moor¹. '~·hole** *n* shallow depression in which ~ collects (esp

FLAMINGO

PELICAN

BITTERN

CREST

GUILLEMOT

PETREL

CRANE

MOORHEN

SANDPIPER

GULL

waterbirds and seabirds

in the bed of a river otherwise dry, and to which animals go to drink). 水洞(尤指河床干涸时之低洼积水部分, 为动物饮水处)。'**~-ice** *n* [C] frozen ~ with sugar and fruit-juices or other flavouring. 冰糕(由糖、果汁或其他调味品凝冻而成)。'**~-jacket** *n* case filled with ~ and fitted over part of a machine which is to be kept cool. (附装于机器某部分而有散热作用的)水套; 冷却筒管。'**~ jump** *n* obstacle (in show-jumping, steeplechases) of a ditch or water, usu with a fence, over which horses jump. (障碍赛马中, 马需要跃过的)水障碍(沟渠或水滩等)。'**~-level** *n* surface of ~ in a reservoir or other body of ~, esp as a datum for measurement. 水平面; 水准。'**~-lily** *n* kinds of plant with broad, flat leaves floating on the surface of the ~, and white, blue or yellow flowers. 睡莲。'**~-line** *n* line along which the surface of the ~ touches a ship's side: 船的吃水线; 水线: *the load ~-line*, when the ship is loaded, 船装载后的水线; 载货水线; *the light ~-line*, when the ship is empty of cargo. 船未载货时的水线; 未载货水线。'**~-logged** /-lɒgd US: -lɔːgd/; -lɒgd/ *adj* **(a)** (of wood) so saturated with ~ that it will barely float. (指木材)吸饱水的(几乎浮不起)。**(b)** (of a ship) so full of ~ that it will barely float. (指船)漏水严重的; 进水太多几乎浮不起的。**(c)** (of land) thoroughly soaked with ~. (指土地)被水浸透了的; 泥泞的。'**~-main** *n* main pipe in a system of ~-supply. 自来水的

主管。'**~-man** /-mən; -mən/ *n* (*pl* **-men**) boatman; man who manages a boat for hire; ferryman. 船夫; 舟子; 渡船夫。'**~-mark** *n* **1** manufacturer's design in some kinds of paper, seen when the paper is held against light. 纸上的水印; 透明花纹(迎光时可见)。**2** mark which shows how high ~ (eg the tide, a river) has risen or how low it has fallen. (潮水, 河道等处的)水位标; 水量标。'**~-melon** *n* large, smooth-skinned melon with juicy pink or red flesh; trailing plant bearing such melons. 西瓜; 西瓜籐。'**~-mill** *n* mill whose machinery is turned by ~-power. 水车; 水磨。'**~-nymph** *n* nymph associated with a river, lake, etc. 水中女仙; 水精; 水仙。'**~-polo** *n* [U] game played by two teams of swimmers who try to throw a ball into a goal. 水球。'**~-power** *n* [U] power obtained from flowing or falling ~, used to drive machinery or generate electric current. 水力(用以推动机器或发电)。'**~-proof** *adj* which does not let ~ through: 不透水的; 防水的: *~proof material.* 防水料子; 防水布。□ *n* ~proof coat; raincoat. 雨衣; 防水装。□ *vt* make ~proof 使防水; 使不透水。'**~-rat /~-vole** *n* rat-like animal frequenting ~. 河鼠。'**~-rate** *n* (GB) charge made (usu quarterly) for the use of ~ from a public ~-supply. (英)自来水费(通常按季计算)。'**~-shed** *n* line of high land separating river systems; (fig) dividing line between events which take different courses. 分水

PUFFIN

CURLEW

PENGUIN

HERON

ALBATROSS

GREBE

SNIPE

SWAN

STORK

CORMORANT

线；分水界；(喻)事件的分界线(许多事件间各事件个别发展的基点)。'**~·side** n margin of the sea, a river, lake, etc: (海、河、湖等的)水滨；水边: go for a stroll along the ~side. 沿水滨散步。'**~·skiing** n the sport of skiing on ~ while being towed at speed by a fast motorboat. 滑水运动(由汽艇以高速拖着在水上滑行)。'**~·skin** n skin bag for carrying ~. (携水用的)革制水袋。'**~·softener** n device or substance for removing the causes of hardness in ~. (除去硬水中矿物质的)软水剂；软水装置。'**~·spaniel** n kind of spaniel that can be trained to swim out and bring back ~fowl, etc shot down by sportsmen. 水犬(一种长毛垂耳狗，经过训练能游水取回射落水面之水鸟等)。'**~·spout** n (a) pipe or spout from which ~ is discharged, eg rainwater from a roof. 排水管；排水槽；排水口(如用以排除屋顶之雨水)。(b)whirlwind over the sea which draws up a whirling mass of ~ so as to look like a funnel-shaped column of ~ going up to the clouds. (海上龙卷风旋起的)旋水柱；海龙卷。'**~·supply** n system of providing and storing ~, amount of ~ stored, for a district, town, building, etc. 给水系统；供水；自来水；自来水储存量。'**~·table** n level below which the ground is saturated with ~: 地下水位: The ~table has been lowered by drought. 干旱已使地下水位降低了。'**~·tight** adj 1 made, fastened, etc so that ~ cannot get in or out: 不透水的；防水的；水密的；不漏水的: ~tight boots/joints/compartments in a ship. 不透水靴(水密接合；水密小船室)。2 (fig, of an agreement, etc) drawn up so that there can be no escape from any of the provisions; leaving no possibility of misunderstanding. (喻,指协定等)无漏洞的；严谨的；无误解之可能的。'**~·tower** n one which supports a large tank which secures pressure for distributing a ~supply. 自来水塔。'**~·waggon** (US = -wagon) n = ~cart: on the ~waggon, ⇨ waggon(1). '**~·way** n navigable channel (eg a canal, channel up a river where the ~ is deep enough for ships) 航路；航道；水路。'**~·wheel** n one turned by a flow of ~, used to work machinery. (借水流之力旋转以推动机器的)水轮。'**~·wings** n pl floats worn on the shoulders by a person learning to swim. (学习游泳者套在双肩上的)浮水圈。'**~·works** n (with sing or pl v) (用单数或复数动词) 1 system of reservoirs, pumping stations, ~-mains, etc for supplying ~. 自来水厂。2 ornamental fountains. (装饰性质的)人工喷泉。3 (colloq) (working of the) bladder: (口)膀胱(的功能): Are your ~works all right? Can you pass urine normally? 你的膀胱功能正常吗？(你排尿正常吗?) 4 (colloq) tears: (口)眼泪: turn on the ~works, shed tears. 满眼泪；哭泣。'**~·worn** adj (of rocks, etc) made smooth by the action of ~. (指岩石等)水蚀的(因水的作用被磨得平滑的)。

water² /'wɔ:tə(r); 'wɔtə/ vt, vi 1 [VP6A] put water on; sprinkle with water: 浇以水；洒以水: ~ the lawn/the plants/the streets. 洒水于草地(花木、街道)上。'**~·ing-can** /'wɔ:tərɪŋ kæn; 'wɔtərɪŋ ˌkæn/ n container with a long spout, used for ~ing plants. 喷壶；浇水器。'**~·ing-cart** /'wɔ:tərɪŋ kɑ:t; 'wɔtərɪŋ ˌkɑrt/ n one with a tank and a sprinkler for ~ing roads (to settle the dust, clean them). 洒水车。2 [VP6A] give water to: 供以水；给以饮水: ~ the horses. 饮马。3 [VP2A] (of the eyes or mouth) fill with water; have much liquid: (指眼或嘴)出水；多水；充满水: The smoke made my eyes ~. 烟使我的眼睛流泪。The smell from the kitchen made my mouth ~, aroused my appetite 厨房里来的香味使我垂涎。Hence, 由此产生, '**mouth-~ing** adj highly appetizing. 令人垂涎三尺的；极能引起食欲的。4 [VP 15B] ~ sth down, add water to: 加水于；冲淡: This whisky has been ~ed (down). 这威士忌已正加水(冲淡了)。The story has been ~ed down, (fig) weakened, eg by making details less vivid. (喻)这故事的生动性已被减弱了。5 [VP6A] (fin) increase (a company's debt or nominal capital) by issuing new shares without increasing the assets. (财政)借发行新股票以增加(公司

债或名义资本)；名义增资。6 ~ed (pp as adj) supplied with water: (过去分词作形容词用)被供以水的: a country ~ed by numerous rivers. 河川交错的国家。~ed silk, manufactured so that there are wavy markings on the surface. (面上有波纹的) 纹绸。7 ~·ing-place /'wɔ:tərɪŋ pleɪs; 'wɔtərɪŋ ˌpleɪs/ n (a) water-hole; place to which animals go to drink. 水洞；动物饮水处。(b) spa. 有矿泉处或温泉之处。(c) seaside resort. 海滨游憩处。

Wat·er·loo /ˌwɔ:tə'lu:; ˌwɔtə'lu/ n meet one's ~, be finally and crushingly defeated in a contest (esp after a period of success). 最后遭遇惨败(尤指经过一段成功之后)。

wat·ery /'wɔ:tərɪ; 'wɔtərɪ/ adj (-ier, -iest) 1 of or like water; (esp of cooked vegetables) containing, cooked in, too much water: 水的；似水的；(尤指煮好的蔬菜)水的；加水太多的: ~ soup/cabbage. 稀薄的汤(加水太多的包心菜)。2 (of colour) pale. (指颜色)淡的。3(of the eyes or lips) running with, covered with, water. (指眼睛或嘴唇)流着口水的；泪汪汪的。4 suggesting that there will be rain: 有雨意的；有下雨征兆的: a ~ moon/sky. 有雨意的月亮(天空)。

watt /wɔt; wɑt/ n unit of electrical power: 瓦特；瓦(电功率单位): a 60 ~ light-bulb. 六十瓦的灯泡。**wat·tage** /'wɔtɪdʒ; 'wɑtɪdʒ/ n [U] amount of electrical power expressed in ~s. (电)瓦特数；瓦数。

wattle¹ /'wɔtl; 'wɑtl/ n 1 structure of sticks or twigs woven over and under thicker upright twigs, used for fences, walls, etc. 编条(用作篱笆、墙壁等)；柳栅。~ and 'daub, this structure covered with clay, for walls and roofs. 夹条墙壁或屋顶(由编条外面涂灰泥而成)。2 kinds of Australian acacia supplying such twigs, with golden flowers adopted as the national emblem. 澳大利亚产金合欢树(其枝可作编条，花呈金色，为澳国徽)。

wattle² /'wɔtl; 'wɑtl/ n red flesh hanging down from the head or throat of a bird, esp a turkey. (禽类，尤指火鸡的)肉垂。⇨ the illus at **fowl**. 参看 fowl 之插图。

wave /weɪv; wev/ n, vt, vi 1 [VP2A, 3A] ~ (at/to in), (of a fixed object, eg a hand, flag, branch) move regularly to and fro, up and down: (指固定物体,如手、旗、树枝等)波动，飘扬；挥舞: flags/branches waving in the wind. 迎风飘动的旗帜(树枝)。Bill ~ed at me, is his hand, eg as a signal. 比尔向我挥手(示意)。Bill ~ed to me, ie his hand, eg as a greeting in meeting or parting. 比尔向我挥手致意(如相遇或分离时)。2 [VP 6A, 15A, 12A, 13A] cause (sth) to move in this way (eg to make a signal or request, to give a greeting, etc): 使波动、飘扬或挥舞(如作手势、打招呼等): ~ one's hand at sb; 向某人挥手; ~ one's umbrella/a flag. 挥动雨伞(旗帜)。She ~d (me) a greeting. 她向我挥手致意。She ~d goodbye to us. 她向我们挥手告别。3 [VP 15B, 16A] cause (sb) to move in a certain direction by waving: 借挥舞动作使(某人)向某方向移动: The officer ~d his men on/~d them to advance. 那军官指挥其士兵(他们)前进。He ~d us away. 他挥手叫我们走开。~ sth aside, (fig) dismiss: (喻)不予受理；不予考虑: My objections were ~d aside. 我的反对意见未受重视。4 [VP2A] (of a line or surface, of hair) be in a series of curves (~~): (指线条或表面,指头发)卷曲；呈波纹状(~~): Her hair ~s beautifully. 她的头发卷曲得很漂亮。5 [VP6A] cause to be in a series of curves: 使卷曲；使有波纹: She's had her hair ~d. 她已把她的头发烫卷了。~ perm. □ n [C] 1 long ridge of water, esp on the sea, between two hollows (or troughs, furrows); such a ridge curling over and breaking on the shore. 波浪；海浪；(指)海浪；(拍击岸边的)冲浪；碎浪。the ~s, (poet) the sea. (诗)海浪。in ~s, in successive lines like sea-~s: 似海浪波接踵而至地: a ~ after ~. 一波接一波地: The enemy attacked in ~s. 步兵一波接一波地攻击。2 act of waving(1) the hand; waving movement: 挥手；挥动；波动;起伏: with a ~ of his hand, eg as a signal. 挥动一下手(如作为信号)。3 curve like a ~ of the sea: (似海浪般)弯曲；波纹: the ~s in a girl's hair. 一女郎卷发上的

波纹。 *She has a natural ~ in her hair.* 她的头发自然卷曲。 **4** steady increase and spread: 持续的增加及扩散; 高潮: *a ~ of enthusiasm/indignation;* 热情(愤怒)的高潮; *a 'crime ~;* 接踵而来的犯罪事件; *a 'heat ~,* a period of weather with temperatures much higher than usual and over a large area. 热浪(一段特别炎热的时期, 气温比平常高很多, 且波及一广大地区)。 **5** ~-like motion by which heat, sound, light, radio, magnetism, etc is spread or carried. (热, 声, 光, 无线电, 磁等的)波状运动; 波。**'~-length** *n* distance between the highest point (the crest) of one ~ and that of the next (esp with reference to radio telegraphy). (尤指无线电的)波长。 **long/medium/short ~,** used in radio broadcasting: (广播用的)长(中, 短)波: *a short-~ transmitter.* 短波发射机。 **wavy** *adj* (-ier, -iest) having ~-like curves: 有波状曲线的; 波形的: *a wavy line;* 波形线: *wavy hair.* 卷发。

wa·ver /'weɪvə(r) ; 'wevə/ *vi* [VP2A, C] **1** move uncertainly or unsteadily: 摆动; 摇曳: *~ing shadows/flames.* 摇曳的阴影(火陷)。 **2** be or become unsteady; begin to give way: 动摇; 开始退让: *His courage ~ed.* 他的勇气动摇了。 *He ~ed in his resolution.* 他犹豫不定。 *The line of troops ~ed and then broke.* 战线开始动摇, 继而崩溃。 **3** hesitate: 踌躇; 迟疑: *~ between two opinions.* 迟疑于两种看法之间。 **~er** *n* person who ~s. 动摇者; 迟疑者。

wax¹ /wæks ; wæks/ *n* [U] soft yellow substance produced by bees ('beeswax') and used for making honeycomb cells; kinds of substance similar to beeswax (eg as obtained from petroleum); such material bleached and purified, used for making candles, for modelling, etc: 蜂蜡(亦称 beeswax); 蜡状物(如得自石油者); 蜡(经用过漂白及净化之蜡状物, 用以制蜡烛、塑像等): (attrib) (用作定语) *a wax candle;* 蜡烛: *a wax doll,* one with the head made of wax; 蜡玩偶; *'paraffin wax;* 石蜡; *'cobblers'-wax,* kind of resin used on thread; 鞋线蜡; *'ear-wax,* substance secreted in the ears. 耳垢。 **'wax-chandler** *n* maker or seller of candles. 蜡烛制造商或贩卖者。 **'wax·peper** *n* paper that is waterproofed with a layer of wax. 防渗的蜡纸。 **'wax·work** *n* object modelled in wax, esp the form of a human being with face and hands in wax, coloured and clothed to look like life and to be exhibited: 蜡制品; 蜡人; (attrib) *go to see the waxworks at Madame Tussaud's,* a place in London famous for waxworks. 去伦敦参观图梭夫人蜡像馆的蜡像。 **'sealing-wax,** ⇨ **seal** *vt* (1). □ *vt* [VP6A] cover, polish or treat with wax: 以蜡涂敷、擦拭或处理: *wax furniture/a wooden floor/linoleum.* 在家具(木地板, 油地毡)上打蜡。 **waxen** /'wæksn; 'wæksn/ *adj* 1 (old use; now usu *wax*) made of wax. (旧用法; 现通常用 wax) 蜡制的。 **2** like wax: 似蜡的: *a waxen complexion.* 蜡黄的面色。 **waxy** *adj* like wax; having a smooth, pale surface; like wax in texture: 似蜡的; 有光滑而淡色之表面的; 结构或质地似蜡的: *waxy potatoes.* 似蜡的马铃薯。

wax² /wæks; wæks/ *vi* [VP2A] (esp of the moon, contrasted with *wane*) show a larger bright area. (尤指月亮, 与 wane 相对)渐满; 变圆。 **2** [VP2D] (old use) become: (旧用法)变为: *wax merry/lyrical/eloquent.* 变得快乐(有诗意, 能言善谈)。

wax³ /wæks; wæks/ *n* (sl) fit of anger: (俚)震怒; 发怒: *be in/get into/put sb into a wax.* 发怒(震怒; 使某人发怒)。 **waxy** *adj* angry. 愤怒的。

way¹ /weɪ; we/ *n* **1** road, street, path, etc: 路; 街; 径; 道路; 通路: (in compounds) (用于复合词中) *'highway;* 公路; *'railway;* 铁路; *'byway;* 小路; *a way across the fields;* 一条横越田野的路; *a covered* (= roofed) *way;* 一条有遮顶的路; *the Appian Way,* a Roman road in Italy. 艾匹亚斯路(意大利古罗马时期兴建的一条道路)。 **'clear ~,** ⇨ **clear¹**(5). There's no way through. 无路可通。 *My friend lives across/over the way,* on the other side of the street (or road). 我的朋友住在过街那边。 **pave the way for,** prepare for, prepare people to

accept (reforms, etc). 为…做准备工作; 使人民准备接受(改革等)。 **the Way of the Cross,** a series of paintings, carvings, etc (usu in or near a church) illustrating the progress of Jesus to Calvary. 苦路(说明耶稣至髑髅地的一系列图画、雕刻等, 通常展列于教堂内或其附近)。 **2** route, road (to be) used (*from one place to another*): 路线: (从一地至他地的)路途(与 from…to… 连用): *Which is the best/right/quickest/shortest, etc way there/from A to B?* 哪条路是到该地(由甲地至乙地)最好(正确、最快, 最近等)的路? *Can you find your way home?* 你认得你回家的路吗? *We lost the way/our way in the dark.* 我们在黑夜中迷失了归途。 *Which is the way in/out?* 哪条是进入(出去)的路? *The longest/farthest way round/about is the nearest way home,* (prov) Short cuts are often delusive. (谚)最远的路才是捷径; 抄小路常常吃不讨。 *We'd better stop and ask someone the way.* 我们最好停下来向人问问路。 *He made/pushed/fought/felt his way out/back, etc.* 他退出(挤, 冲, 摸索着走)出去的路。 *We had to pick our way along the muddy path.* 我们必须在泥泞的小径上谨慎前行。 **go one's way(s),** depart. 动身; 出发。 **go out of one's way (to do sth),** make a special effort: 特意(花心血, 时间等)(做某事); 故意(做某事): *He went out of his way to be rude to me/to help me.* 他故意对我粗鲁(特意帮助我)。 **lead the way,** go in front as leader; show by example how sth may be done. 带路; 带头; 示范。 **make one's 'way in life,** succeed. 发迹; 成功。 **make the best of one's way,** go as fast as one can. 尽量快走。 **make one's way (to/towards),** go. (向…)走去。 **pay one's way,** (a) keep out of debt. 量入为出; 不举债。 (b) pay one's share of expenses instead of letting others pay. 付自己的费用; 自掏腰包。 **the parting of the ways,** (fig) the time when an important decision must be made as to future plans, etc. (喻)对未来的计划等须做重要决定的时刻。 **by way of,** via; using a route through: 由; 经过: *He came by way of Dover.* 他经山多佛来此。 ⇨ also **14** below. 亦参看下列第 14 义。 **out of the way,** exceptional, uncommon: 奇特的; 不寻常的: *He has done nothing out of the way yet.* 他尚未做出不寻常的事。 **out-of-the-'way,** (attrib use) remote: (用作定语)遥远的; 荒僻的: *an out-of-the-way place/corner.* 偏僻的地方(角落)。 **3 by the way, (a)** during a journey. 在途中; 顺路。 **(b)** (fig) incidentally; in passing (often used to introduce a remark not connected with the subject of conversation). (喻)顺便说; 却说(常用以引入与当时话题无关的插语)。 **on the/one's way,** being engaged in going or coming: 在路上; 在途中: *They're still on the way.* 他们尚在途中。 *I'll buy some on the/my way home.* 我将在回家的途中购买一些。 *He's on the way to success.* 他正在向成功的路上。 *She's got another child on the way,* (colloq) is pregnant again. (口)她又怀孕了。 **on the way out,** (fig; colloq) about to become out of date, out of fashion. (喻; 口)行将变得过时或陈旧; 快要不流行。 **4** [C] method or plan; course of action: 方法; 方式; 行动方针: *the right/wrong/best, etc way to do/of doing a thing.* 做某事的正确(错误, 最好等)的方法。 *Is this the way to do it/the way you do it?* 这就是做(你做)那件事的方法吗? *Do it (in) your own way if you don't like my way.* 如果你不喜欢我的方法, 按照你自己的方法做吧。 *The work must be finished (in) one way or another.* 这工作必须设法做好。 **Where there's a way, there's a way,** (prov) If we want to do sth, we will find a method of doing it. (谚)有志者事竟成。 **ways and means,** methods, esp of providing money. (筹措款项的)方法。 **have/get one's own way,** get/do what one wants. 为所欲为; 随心所欲。 **go/take one's own way,** act independently, esp contrary to the advice of others. 独断独行; 我行我素(尤指所为与他人所进言者相反)。 **5** (*sing* only) distance between two points; distance (to be) traversed: (仅用单数)距离; 路程: *It's a long way off/a long way from here.* 那地方距此很远。 *The roots go a long way down.* 这些根入地很深。 *Your work is still a long way off perfection,* is far from being perfect. 你的工作距

离理想还远得很。*Your work this week is better by a long way,* much better. 你这个礼拜的工作好多了。*This will go a long way* (= will be very helpful) *in overcoming the difficulty.* 这将很有助于克服困难。**6** [C] direction: 方向: *He went this/that/the other way.* 他向这(那,另一)边走。*Look this way, please.* 请向这边看。*He couldn't look my way,* towards me. 他不可能朝我这方向看。*Such opportunities never come/fall my way,* come to me. 这样的好机会总不会落到我身上。*You've got your hat on the wrong way,* eg back to front. 你的帽子戴反了。*He's in a fair way to succeed,* is making progress in the right direction. 他正朝着成功的路前进(很有成功的希望)。*put sb in the way of (doing) sth,* help him to make a start: 帮助某人开始做某事: *A kind friend put him in the way of earning a living.* 一位好心的朋友助他走上自立的道路。**7** (colloq; *sing* only; not stressed) neighbourhood: (口; 仅用单数; 不重读)附近; 邻近: *He lives somewhere Lincoln way,* near Lincoln. 他住在林肯市附近。*The crops are looking very well our way,* in our part of the country. 我们这一带农作物长得很不错。**8** [U] advance in some direction; progress (esp of a ship or boat): (向某方向之)行进; (尤指船之)前进。*be under way; have way 'on,* (of a ship) be moving through the water. (指船)在航行中。*gather/lose way,* gain/lose speed: 增加(减低)速度: *The boat slowly gathered way.* 船在逐渐增加速度。*get under way,* start to move forward. 开始前进。*give way,* (of oarsmen) row hard. (指桨手)努力划。Also ⇨ **give¹(10)**. *make way,* (lit or fig) advance. (字面或喻)前进; 进行。**9** [U] space for forward movement, for passing ahead; freedom to go forward: 向前进的空间; 向前进的自由: *Don't stand in the way.* 不要挡住路。*Tell that boy not to get in the way.* 叫那男孩不要挡住路。*Tell him to stand out of the/my way.* 叫他让开。*Clear the way!* 让路! *be/put sth out of harm's way,* in a safe place. 在(置某物在)安全处。*get sth out of the way,* settle it, dispose of it. 解决某事; 除去某事物。*give way (to sth/sb),* ⇨ **give¹(10)**. *make way (for),* allow space or a free passage: (为⋯)让路: *All traffic has to make way for a fire-engine.* 行人车辆皆应给救火车让路。*put sb out of the way,* put him in prison, kill him (secretly), or otherwise get rid of him. 拘禁某人; 暗杀或干掉某人; 除去某人。*put sb in the way of sth,* give him the opportunity of securing, eg a good bargain. 给某人获得⋯的机会。*see one's way (clear) to doing sth,* see how to do it; (esp) feel justified in doing it: 知道如何做某事; (尤指)觉得该做某事; 有充分理由做某事: *I don't see my way clear to helping you.* 我不知道怎样帮助你。*I don't see my way clear to recommending you for the job.* 我不知道该不该推荐你去做那工作。*right of way,* ⇨ **right²(2)**. **10** [C] custom; manner of behaving; personal peculiarity: 习俗; 态度; 作风; 癖性: *the good old ways;* 良好的古老习俗; *English/Chinese, etc ways of life/living;* 英国人(中国人等)的生活方式; *the way of the world,* what appears to be justified by custom. 世风; 世道常情。*It's not his way to be mean,* Meanness is not in his nature. 卑下不是他的本性。*It's disgraceful the way he drinks,* His habit of (excessive) drinking is disgraceful. 他那种纵饮的习惯真不象话。*I don't like the way* (= manner in which) *he looks at me.* 我不喜欢他那样看我。*Don't take offence—it's only his way,* a manner of behaving that has no special significance. 不要生气——他就是那个样子。*to 'my way of thinking,* in my opinion. 我认为。*the way,* (colloq; adverbial use) as; in the manner that: (口; 作副词用)象; 一如: *He doesn't do it the way I do.* 他做那事的方法和我不一样。*he/she has a way with him/her,* he/she is persuasive. 他(她)有说服力(讲起话来有一套)。*mend one's ways,* improve one's manners, behaviour, etc. 改善自己的举止、行为、方式等。**11** [C] respect; point or detail: 方面; 细节; 点: *He's a clever man in some ways.* 他在某些方面很聪明。*Can I help you in any way?* 我能够帮任何忙吗? *He is in no way* (= not

at all) *to blame.* 他决不该受责备。*They are in no way similar.* 他们根本不相似。*The work was well done in one way,* to a limited extent but not on the whole. 那工作在某方面做得很好(整个看来就不然)。*He's an amusing man in his (own) way.* 他是一个很有趣的人。*What have we in the way of food,* What food is there (eg in the house, for the next meal, etc)? 我们有些什么吃的呢? *no way,* (sl) in no way; not at all. (俚)一点也不; 不行; 决不。**12** [C] condition, state, degree: 情形; 状态; 程度: *Things are in a bad way.* 情势很糟。*She was in a terrible way,* much agitated. 她异常激动。*'any way,* in either case; in any case or event. 在任何情况下; 两种情况无论哪一种。*each way/both ways,* (in backing horses) to win, to get a place in the first three. (赌赛马)获胜; 获前三名之一。*in the 'family way,* (colloq) pregnant. (口)怀孕。*in a big/small way,* on a big/small scale: 大(小)规模地: *live in a small way,* simply, without ostentation: 过着吃俭用的生活: *a printer in a small way;* 小本经营的印刷商; *advertise in a big way.* 大(规模)地作广告。*have it both ways,* choose first one and then the other of alternatives in order to suit one's convenience, argument. etc. 左右逢源; 脚踏双踹; 见风转舵(二者间先选其一, 再选另一, 以配合自己的方便、论据等)。**13** ordinary course: 平常途径; 一般方法: *do sth in the way of business.* 按一般做生意的方法。**14** *by way of,* (a) as a substitute for or as a kind of: 作为; 当作; 代替: *say sth by way of apology/introduction.* 说一点作为道歉(介绍)的话。(b) for the purpose of, with the intention of: 为了; 意在: *make inquiries by way of learning the facts of case.* 为了获知该案的真相而调查。(c) in the course of: 在⋯之中: *by way of business.* 在营业中。⇨ also **2** above. 亦参看上列第 2 义。**15** (pl) structure of heavy timber on which a ship is built and down which it slides when launched. (复)造船架; (新船的)下水台。⇨ **slipway** at **slip¹(6)**. **16** (compounds) (复合词) **'way-bill** n list of goods being conveyed by a carrier, with instructions about their destinations, etc. 运货单(载明运送地点等者)。**'way-farer** /-feərə(r); -ˌferər/ n (liter) traveller, esp on foot. (文)旅人; (尤指)徒步旅行者。**'way·faring** /-feərɪŋ; -ˌferɪŋ/ adj travelling: 旅行的; 徒步旅行的: *a wayfaring man.* (徒步)旅行者。**'way·side** n side of a road: 路旁; 道旁: (attrib) (用作定语) *wayside flowers.* 路旁的花。

way² /weɪ; we/ adv far; by a long way¹(5): 远; 远离: *The discussion wandered way off the point.* 该项讨论远离了主题。*Bill finished way ahead of me in the 100 metres sprint.* 比尔在百米赛跑中远比我先到达终点。*The wage-claim is way above what the firm can afford.* 这项工资要求远非该公司所能负担。**way·'out** adj (colloq) strange; eccentric: (口)奇异的; 古怪的: *way-out clothes/ideas.* 奇装异服(古怪的想法)。

way·lay /ˌweɪˈleɪ; ˌweˈle/ vt (pt, pp **-laid** /-'leɪd; -'led/) [VP6A] (wait somewhere to) attack, rob (sb); accost (sb) unexpectedly (usu with a request): (在某处等待以)袭击; 抢劫(某人); 伏击; (在路上等候以)拦住(某人)而向其搭讪或招呼: *He was waylaid by bandits.* 他遭到盗匪的伏击。*He waylaid me with a request for a loan.* 他(在路上)拦住我向我借钱。

way·ward /'weɪwəd; 'wewəd/ adj self-willed; not easily controlled or guided: 任性的; 刚愎的; 不易管束的; 不听教导的: *a ~ child;* 顽童; *a child with a ~ disposition.* 性情倔强的小孩。

we /wiː; wi/ pron **1** used by a speaker or writer referring to himself and another or others (with object form *us*). 我们(宾格作 us)。**2** used by a King, Pope, etc in proclamations instead of *I,* and by the writer of an unsigned article in a newspaper, etc. 朕(帝王、教皇等在告示中之自称); 报章杂志文章中不署名时之自称谓。

weak /wiːk; wik/ adj (**-er, -est**) **1** (opp of *strong*) lacking in strength; easily broken; unable to resist hard wear or use, attack, etc: (为 strong 的反义词)弱的; 虚弱的; 脆弱的; 易破的; 不耐用的; 不能抵抗攻击等的: *too*

~ *to walk*: 太虚弱不能走动; ~ *in the legs*: 两腿软弱无力; *a table with* ~ *legs*: 摇摇晃晃的桌子; *a* ~ *defence*: 脆弱的防御工事; *a* ~ *team*: 弱队; *the* ~ *points of an argument/plan*. 论据(计划)的弱点。 **,**~**-'kneed** *adj* (fig) lacking determination; ~ in character. (喻)无决心的; 优柔寡断的。 **2** (of the senses, etc) below the usual standard: (指感官等)不够标准的; (more usu 较常用 *poor*) *sight and hearing*; 视力及听力不佳; *a* ~ *heart*. 衰弱的心脏。 Hence, 由此产生, ~**-eyed** 视力不佳的; ~**-headed** 低能的; ~**-minded** 懦弱的; 优柔寡断的; ~**-sighted**. 视力不佳的。 **3** (of mixed liquids or solutions) watery; having little of some substance in relation to the water, etc: (指混合的饮料或溶液)多水的; 淡的: ~ *tea/beer*; 淡茶(啤酒); *a* ~ *solution*. 稀薄的溶液。 **4** not good; not efficient: 不精的; 不擅长的: ~ *in spelling/arithmetic/biology*. 不擅长拼字(算术,生物学)。 **5** (gram) (语法) ~ *verb*, one inflected by additions to the stem, not by vowel change (as *walk, walked*, contrasted with *run, ran* and *come, came*). 弱动词;规则动词(词形变化借助 ed 或 t 等形成,如 walk, walked; 而非经由改变原词的元音,如 run, ran 及 come, came)。 ~ *form* (of the pronunciation of some common words), form occurring in an unstressed position, usu by the use of a different vowel sound or by the absence of a vowel sound or consonant (eg /ən/ or /n/n/ for /ænd/, ænd/ *and*, as in *bread and butter* /,bred n 'bʌtə(r)/; 'bredn'bʌtə/). (指某些常见词的读音)弱式读法(用于不重读的场合,通常不读原元音,或借元音及辅音,如 bread and butter 中的 and, 读作 /ən/ 或 /n/)。 ~**en** /'wiːkən/ 'wiːkən/ *vt, vi* [VP6A, 2A] make or become ~(er). 使弱; 变弱。 ~**-ling** *n* person or animal. 孱弱的人或动物; ~**-ly** *adv* in a ~ manner. 弱地; 虚弱地; 脆弱地。 □ *adj* delicate in health; not robust: 身体虚弱的; 不强壮的: *a* ~*ly child*. 虚弱的小孩。 ~**-ness** *n* **1** [U] state of being ~; 弱; 虚弱; 脆弱: *the* ~*ness of old age*; 老年的虚弱; *the* ~*ness of a country's defences*. 一国的脆弱国防。 **2** [C] fault or defect of character: 性格的缺点; 弱点: *We all have our little* ~*nesses*. 我们都有一些小缺点。 **3** *have a* ~*ness for*, a special or foolish liking for: 特别喜欢…; 喜好…的: *He has a* ~*ness for fish and chips/fast cars*. 他特别喜欢吃油炸的鱼和马铃薯条(开快车)。

weal[1] /wiːl; wil/ *n* [U] (liter) well-being (chiefly in): (文)幸福; 福利(主要用于): ~ *and woe*, good and bad fortune; 祸福; *for the public/general* ~, the welfare of all. 为公益。

weal[2] /wiːl; wil/ *n* [C] mark on the skin made by a blow from a stick, whip, etc. 皮肤上的伤痕、条痕、杖痕、鞭痕等。

weald /wiːld; wild/ *n* (GB) stretch of open country, formerly forest: (英)原野; 旷野; 昔日的森林地带: *the* ~ *of Kent*. 肯特原野。

wealth /welθ; welθ/ *n* **1** [U] (possession of a) great amount of property, money, etc; riches: 大量财产(的拥有); 财富: *a man of* ~; 富人; *acquire great* ~. 获得巨大财富。 **2** *a/the* ~ *of*, great amount or number of: 多量; 大量; 丰富; 大数目: *a book with a* ~ *of illustrations*; 一本有大量插图的画; *the* ~ *of phrases and sentences to illustrate meanings in this dictionary*. 本词典阐明词义的大量短语及例句。 ~**y** *adj* (**-ier, -iest**) having ~(1); rich. 拥有大量财富的; 富有的。 ~**-ily** /-ɪlɪ; -əlɪ/ *adv*

wean /wiːn; win/ *vt* **1** [VP6A] accustom (a baby, a young animal) to food other than its mother's milk. 使(婴儿,幼小动物)断奶。 **2** [VP14] ~ *sb from sth*, cause (sb) to turn away (from a habit, companions, etc). 使某人戒绝或断绝某事(如革除习惯,与人断绝来往等)。

weapon /'wepən; 'wɛpən/ *n* sth designed for, or used in, fighting or struggling (eg swords, guns, fists, a strike by workmen): 武器; 兵器(如刀、枪、拳、工人的罢工): *Whether a gun is a* ~ *of offence or of defence depends upon which end of it you are at*. 枪是攻击武器还是防御武器,端视你的目的而定。 ~**-less** *adj* without ~s.

没有武器的。

wear[1] /weə(r); wɛr/ *n* [U] **1** wearing or being worn; use as clothing: 穿; 着; 佩; 戴: *a suit for everyday* ~; 一套日常穿的衣服; *a coat that has been in constant* ~. 一件经常穿的上装。 *This carpet will stand any amount of hard* ~. 这地毯极其耐用。 *This coat is beginning to look the worse for* ~, shows signs of having been worn for a long time, so that it is no longer in a good or useful condition. 这件上装看起来快破旧了。 **2** damage or loss of quality from use: 用损; 耗损; 磨损: *These shoes are showing (signs of)* ~. 这双鞋子快穿坏了。 ~ *and tear*, damage, loss in value, from normal use. 损耗。 **3** capacity to endure: 耐久性; 耐用性: *There's not much left in these shoes*, They cannot be worn much longer. 这双鞋子穿不久了。 **4** (chiefly in compounds or in terms used by tradesmen) things to wear: (主要用于复合词或商业用语中)穿的东西; 衣着: *'under*~; 内衣; *'foot*~; 鞋袜; *'ladies'/'men's* ~; 女(男)装; *a shop that specializes in 'children's* ~. 专卖童装的商店。

wear[2] /weə(r); wɛr/ *vt, vi* (*pt* wore /wɔː(r); wor/, *pp* worn /wɔːn; worn/) **1** [VP6A, 22, 15B] have on the body, carry on one's person or on some part of it; (of looks) have on the face: 穿; 着; 戴; 佩; (指面貌)带着; 呈现: *He was* ~*ing a hat/spectacles/a beard/heavy shoes/a ring on his finger/a troubled look*. 他戴着一顶帽子(戴着一副眼镜, 蓄着胡子, 穿着笨重的鞋子, 手指上戴着戒指, 面带忧容)。 *This is a style that is much worn now*, that is in fashion now. 这是时下流行的款式。 *She never* ~*s green*, ie green clothes. 她从不穿绿色的衣服。 *She used to* ~ *her hair long*, used to have long hair. 她从前留着长发。 *The house wore* (= had) *a neglected look*. 那房子有一种无人照管的样子。 ~ *the crown*, (a) be a monarch. 做国君; 做皇帝。 (b) be a martyr. 做殉道者。 **2** [VP2C, D, 22, 15A, B] (cause to) become less useful or be in a certain condition, by being used: (使)磨损; (使)变旧; 用坏: *I have worn my socks into holes*. 我的袜子已磨出洞来了。 *This material has worn thin*. 这料子已磨薄了。 *The stones were worn by the constant flow of water*. 经常不断的水流将石头冲蚀了。 *This old overcoat is much worn*, is much the worse for wear. 这件旧大衣已穿得破旧不堪。 ~ *away*, become impaired, thin, weak, as the result of constant use: 磨损; 磨去; 磨减: *The inscription on the stone had worn away*, the words were difficult to read. 刻在石头上的文字已磨损得难以辨认了。 ~ *sth away*, consume or impair sth by constant use, etc: 磨损某物: *The footsteps of thousands of visitors had worn away the steps*. 经过万千游客长时间的践踏, 台阶磨损了。 ~ *down*, become gradually smaller, thinner, weaker, etc: 磨损; 耗损; 磨小; 磨薄; 磨弱等: *The heels of these shoes are* ~*ing down*. 这双鞋子的鞋跟已(渐)磨坏了。 ~ *sth down*, cause to ~ down. 使磨损; 使磨小、磨薄、磨弱。 ~ *sb/ sth down*, weaken by constant attack, nervous strain, etc: 借经常攻击、骚扰等而使某人或某物衰弱: *These noisy children do* ~ *me down!* 这些吵闹的孩子们真把我烦死了! *We wore down the enemy's resistance*. 我们不断攻击敌人而耗弱其抵抗力。 ~ *off*, pass away: 消逝; 消失; 消灭: *The novelty will soon* ~ *off*. 这种新鲜感很快就会消逝。 ~ *sth off*, cause to pass away by degrees; be rubbed off by friction: 使磨损; 使逐渐消失或消灭; 磨掉; 磨去: ~ *the nap off a piece of velvet*. 磨掉一块天鹅绒的绒毛。 ~ *(sth) out*, (cause to) become useless; threadbare, exhausted: 使(某物)变得无用、陈旧、枯竭; 用坏; 穿破; 耗尽: *Cheap shoes soon* ~ *out*. 便宜的鞋子不耐穿。 *My shoes are worn out*. 我的鞋子穿坏了。 *His patience had/was at last worn out*. 他最后终于忍耐不住了。 *He has worn out* (= outstayed) *his welcome*. 他待得太久, 以致不受欢迎了。 ~ *sb out*, exhaust, tire out: 使某人筋疲力竭; 使某人疲惫困乏: *I'm worn out by all this hard work*. 这繁重的工作使我疲惫不堪。 *That fellow* ~*s me out with his silly chatter*. 那家伙喋喋不休, 简直把我烦死了。 Hence, 由此产生, **,worn-'out** *attrib adj*: *a*

wornout coat. 破旧上衣。 **3** [VP6A] make (a hole, groove, etc) in by rubbing or attrition: 由摩擦而造成(洞、沟等): *~ holes in a rug*/*one's socks*. 地毯(短袜)磨破出现洞。 *In time a path was worn across the field*. 时间一久，这块田地上踏出一条小径。 **4** [VP2B, 2A, C] endure continued use; remain in a certain condition: 耐用；耐久: *Good leather will ~ for years.* 好的皮革可以耐用多年。 *This cloth has worn well*/*badly*. 这种布很耐穿(不耐穿)。 *Old Mr Smith is ~ing well*, still looks well in spite of his advanced age. 史密斯老先生不显老。 **5** [VP2C] ~ *on*/*away, etc*, (of time) go slowly or tediously; pass gradually: (指时间)缓慢或沉闷地挨过; 逐渐过去: *as the evening wore on*; 当夜晚缓缓缓度过的时候; *as winter wore away*; 当冬季慢慢地过去; *as his life wore towards its close*. 当他的生命渐趋结束的时候。 ~**er** *n* person who is ~ing sth. 穿戴者; 穿某种衣服者; 佩带某物者。 ~**able** /-əbl; -əbl/ *adj* that can be, or is fit to be, worn. 可穿着的; 可佩带的; 耐磨的。 ~**ing** *adj* tiring: 令人疲倦的; 使人厌烦的: *a ~ing day.* 令人困乏的一天。

weary /'wɪərɪ; 'wɪrɪ/ *adj* (**-ier, -iest**) **1** tired: 疲惫的; 劳累的: ~ *in body and mind*; 身心疲劳; *feel ~*; 感到疲倦; *be ~ of someone's constant grumbling*. 对某人经常的抱怨感到厌倦。 **2** causing tiredness: 令人疲倦的; 令人厌烦的: *a ~ journey*/*wait*; 令人厌倦的旅程(等待); *after walking ten ~ miles*. 步行的令人困乏的十英里以后。 **3** showing tiredness: 显示疲倦的: *a ~ sigh*. 一声疲倦的叹息。 □ *vt, vi* [VP6A, 14, 2A, 3A] ~ *sb (with sth)*; ~ *of sth*, make or become ~: (使)疲倦; (使)厌烦: ~ *sb with requests*; 不住的请求使某人厌烦; *~ of living all alone*; 厌烦独居; *wearied with marching and climbing*. 因行进和爬山而感到疲倦。 **wear·ily** /-əlɪ ;-ɪlɪ/ *adv* **weari·ness** *n* **weari·some** /'wɪərɪsəm; 'wɪrɪsəm/ *adj* tiring; long and dull. 令人疲倦的; 冗长而沉闷的。

wea·sel /'wiːzl; 'wizl/ *n* small, fierce animal with red-brown fur, living on rats, rabbits, birds' eggs, etc. 鼬鼠; 黄鼠狼。

weather[1] /'weðə(r); 'weðæ/ *n* **1** [U] conditions over a particular area and at a specific time with reference to sunshine, temperature, wind, rain, etc. (⇨ **climate**, used with reference to a long period of time, eg a season): 天气; 气象(参看 climate, 指一季等长时期的天气状况): *He stays indoors in wet ~*. 下雨天他常待在家里。 *She goes out in all ~s* (*pl* here = all kinds of ~). 无论天气如何，她都要外出。 *Many crops depend on the ~*. 许多农作物都依靠天气。 *be*/*feel under the ~*, (colloq) ill. (口)不适; 生病。 *keep a*/*one's ~ eye open*, be on the alert; be on the look-out (for trouble, etc). 警戒; 注意(困难、麻烦等)。 *make good*/*bad ~*, (used by sailors) meet with good/bad. (水手用语)遇到好(坏)天气。 *make heavy ~ of sth*, find it (unnecessarily) troublesome, difficult. 小题大作。 *under stress of ~*, because of storms, etc. 因受恶劣天气(暴风雨等)的影响。 **2** (compounds) (复合词) '~**-beaten** *adj* bearing marks or signs which come from exposure to the sun, wind, rain, etc: 饱经日晒、风吹、雨打等的; 饱经风霜的: *a ~-beaten face*. 饱经风霜的脸。 '~**-boarding**/**-boards** *n* horizontal boards each of which overlaps the one below to cause rain to run off and so keep the wall, etc, from becoming damp. 护墙板; 封檐板。 '~**-bound** *adj* unable to make or continue a journey because of bad ~. 为风雨所阻的; 因天气恶劣无法成行或继续旅程的。 '~**-bureau** *n* office where the ~ is studied and where ~ forecasts are made; meteorological office. 气象局; 气象所。 '~**-chart**/**-map** *n* diagram showing details of the ~ over a wide area. 气象图; 天候图。 '~**-cock** *n* ~-vane in the shape of a cock. 风标; 风信标; 风信鸡。 **forecast** *n* ⇨ forecast. '~**-glass** *n* barometer. 晴雨计; 气压计。 '~**-man** /-mæn; -mæn/ *n* (*pl* -**men**) (colloq) man who reports and forecasts the ~. (口)气象员; 预报天气者。 '~**-proof** *adj* able to stand exposure to the ~, to keep out rain, wind, snow, etc. 不受气候影响的; 防风

雨日晒的; 抗风化的。 '~**-ship** *n* one stationed at sea to make observations of the ~. 气象船。 '~**-statoin** *n* one where the ~ is observed. 气象站; 测候站。 '~**-vane** *n* = **vane**(1).

weather[2] /'weðə(r); 'weðæ/ *vt, vi* **1** [VP6A] come through successfully; survive: 平安度过; 捱过: ~ *a storm*; 平安度过暴风雨; ~ *a crisis*. 度过一危机。 **2** [VP6A] sail to the windward of: 航至…的上风: ~ *an island*. 航行至一个岛的上风。 **3** [VP6A] expose to the weather: 晾干; 风干; 暴露: ~ *wood*, leave it in the open air until it is properly shrunk and ready for use. 风干木材。 ⇨ **season**, *vt, vi*(1). **4** [VP6A, 2A] discolour, be discoloured, (cause to) become worn by the weather: 褪色; 被褪色; (使)因天气而变磨损; 风化; 侵蚀: *rocks ~ed by wind and water*; 受风雨侵蚀的岩石; ~*ed limestone.* 风化的石灰石。

weave /wiːv; wiv/ *vt, vi* (*pt* **wove** /wəuv; wov/, *pp* **woven** /'wəuvn; 'wovən/) **1** [VP6A, 15A, B, 2A] ~ *sth (up) into sth*; ~ *sth (from sth)*, make (by hand or by machine) (threads) into cloth, etc; make (cloth, etc) from threads; work at a loom: 织(纱、线)成布等; 以纱、线织成(布等); 纺织; ~ *cotton yarn into cloth*; 把纱纺织成布; ~ *threads together*; 把纱、线织起来; *woven from*/*of silk*; 用丝织成的; make (garlands, baskets, etc) by a similar process: 编制(花环、篮等): ~ *flowers into a wreath*; 把花编成花圈; ~ *a garland of flowers*. 编花环。 **2** [VP6A, 15A] (fig) put together, compose (a story, romance, etc): (喻)编撰; 撰作(故事、传奇小说等): ~ *a story round an incident*; 以某一事件为中心编撰一个故事; ~ *a plot*. 编排一个情节。 *get weaving (on sth)*, (sl) make an energetic start (on a task, etc). (俚)大力开始(一项任务等); 干劲十足地开始(一项事业等)。 **3** [VP2C] twist and turn: 迂回; 盘旋; 曲折: *The driver was weaving (his way) through the traffic.* 驾车者在行人和车辆中迂回前进。 *The road ~s through the valleys*. 那条路曲折地通过山谷。 □ *n* style of weaving: 编法; 织法; 编织型式: *a loose*/*tight*/*coarse*/*plain, etc ~*. 松(紧、粗、平等)的编织。 ~**r** *n* person whose trade is weaving cloth at a loom. 织者; 织工。 ~**r-bird** *n* tropical bird that makes its nest by tightly weaving together leaves, grass, twigs, etc. 一种织巢鸟(产于热带)。

web /web; wɛb/ *n* [C] **1** network (usu fig): 网; 网状组织(通常为比喻用法): *a web of lies*/*deceit*/*intrigue*. 谎话连篇(谎话连篇，一套阴谋诡计)。 **2** sth made of threads by a spider or other spinning creature: (蜘蛛等结的)网; *a spider's web*. 蜘蛛网。 ⇨ **cobweb**. ⇨ the illus at **arachnid**. 参看 arachnid 之插图。 **3** skin joining the toes of some waterbird, eg ducks, geese, bats and some water-animals (eg frogs): (鸭、鹅等水禽, 蝙蝠, 以及蛙等水生动物的)蹼; 掌皮; 翼手。 Hence, 由此产生, ,**web-'footed**/-'toed *adj* **webbed** *adj* having the toes joined by webs. 蹼足的; 有蹼皮的; 翼手的。 ⇨ the illus at **fowl**. 参看 fowl 之插图。

web·bing /'webɪŋ; 'wɛbɪŋ/ *n* [U] strong fabric (usu coarse woven) used in belts, upholstery, binding the edges of rugs, etc. (用作系带, 室内装饰品, 镶地毯之边等的)坚韧的带状织物。

wed /wed; wɛd/ *vt, vi* (*pt, pp* **wedded** or **wed**) [VP 6A, 14, 2A] **1** (journalism) marry. (新闻学)结婚; 娶。 **2** (liter) unite: (文)结合; 合并: *simplicity wed to beauty*. 兼具简朴和美丽。 *wedded to*, devoted to; unable to give up: 专注于; 不能放弃; 固执: *He is wedded to his own opinions and nothing can change him*. 他固执己见, 什么也不能使他改变。

we'd /wiːd; wid/ = we had; we would.

wed·ding /'wedɪŋ; 'wɛdɪŋ/ *n* marriage ceremony (and festivities connected with it): 婚礼; 婚庆: *invite one's friends to one's ~*; 邀朋友参加其婚礼; *a ~ dress*. 结婚礼服。 '~ **breakfast** *n* meal for the bride and bridegroom, their relatives, friends, etc between the ceremony and departure for the honeymoon. 喜宴(在婚

礼后蜜月旅行前举行）。'~-cake n cake distributed to guests and sent in small portions to absent friends. 结婚蛋糕；喜饼(分送客人及缺席朋友)。'~-ring n ring placed on the bride's (and in some cases the groom's) finger and worn by her/him afterwards. 结婚戒指。 **silver/golden/diamond** ~, 25th/50th/60th (or 75th) anniversary of a ~, 银(金，钻石)婚纪念；结婚廿五(五十，六十或七十五)周年。

wedge /wedʒ; wɛdʒ/ n 1 V-shaped piece of wood or metal, used to split wood or rock (by being hammered), to widen an opening, or to keep two things separate. 劈；楔；V 形木片或金属片。**the thin end of the ~**, (fig) a small change or demand likely to lead to big changes or demands. (喻)可能引起重大后果的小事；可能导致重大变化的小变化；可能引发重大需求的小需求。 2 sth shaped like or used like a ~: 形状或用途似楔之物：a ~ of cake, eg cut from a large round cake; 一块楔形糕饼；seats arranged in a ~, so as to form a triangle. 排列成楔形的座位。 □ vt [VP6A, 15A, 22] fix tightly (as) with a ~, keep in place with a ~: 以楔(等)使之牢固；楔住；嵌；插；挤：~ packing into a crack; 把填料楔入裂缝中；a door open, by placing a ~ under it. 在门下置楔，使之敞开。I was so tightly ~d between two fat women that it was difficult for me to get up and leave the bus. 我被两个肥胖女人紧紧地挤在中间，以致要站起来下公共汽车都很困难。

wed·lock /'wedlɒk; 'wɛdlɑk/ n [U] (legal) condition of being married: (法律)结婚的状态；婚姻；结婚生活：born in lawful ~, born of married parents; 婚生的；嫡出的；born out of ~, illegitimate. 私生的；庶出的。

Wed·nes·day /'wenzdɪ; 'wɛnzdɪ/ n fourth day of the week. 星期三；礼拜三；水曜日。

wee[1] /wiː; wi/ adj very small: 很小的；微小的：just a wee drop of brandy in my coffee. 我的咖啡中的一滴掺白兰地酒。a wee bit, (adverbial) a little: (作副词用)少许；些许；有一点。She's a wee bit jealous. 她有点妒嫉。**the wee folk**, little people. 小仙人(总称)；仙人们。**the wee hours**, (US) the hours after midnight. (美)午夜后的一、二、三点钟。 □ n (Scot) bide a wee, stay for a short time. (苏)待一会儿。

wee[2], **wee-wee** /'wiː wiː; 'wi wi/ n (used by or to small children) urine: (儿语;对小孩所说的话)小便；撒尿：do a wee-wee. 撒尿。 □ vi urinate. 小便;撒尿。

weed /wiːd; wid/ n [U] 1 wild plant growing where it is not wanted (eg in a garden, or in a field of wheat): (园子、麦田等中的)杂草；莠草；野草：My garden is running to ~s, is overgrown with ~s. 我的园子里长满了杂草。'~-killer n substance used to kill ~s. 除莠剂；除莠剂。 2 (fig) thin, tall, weak-looking person or horse. (喻)高而瘦弱的人或马；瘦高个子。 3 (dated sl) cigar; cigarette; tobacco; (modern sl) marijuana. (过时俚语)雪茄；香烟;烟草；(现代俚语)大麻烟。 □ vt, vi 1 [VP6A, 2A] take ~s out of (the ground): 除去(地面)的杂草：~ the garden; 除去园子里的杂草；be busy ~ing. 忙于除草。 2 [VP15B] ~ sth/sb out, sort or thin out; remove or get rid of (what is unwanted, or of lower value than the rest): 挑出；拣出；除去；淘汰(不需要者或价值较低者)：~ out the herd, get rid of the inferior animals. 淘汰劣等牲口。**weedy** adj (-ier, -iest) 1 full of, overgrown with, ~s. 多杂草的；长满杂草的。 2(sl) tall, thin and weak: (俚)高而瘦弱的：a ~y young man. 高而瘦弱的青年男子。

weeds /wiːdz; widz/ n pl widow's ~, black clothes as formerly worn by a widow for mourning. (昔时的)寡妇的丧服。

week /wiːk; wik/ n 1 any period of seven days; (esp) seven days from Saturday midnight to Saturday midnight 周；星期(尤指自星期六午夜至次一个星期六午夜的七日)：this/last/next ~, 本(上、下)周；this day ~, one week from today; 自今日起一周；this Monday ~, one week from Monday next; 自下一个星期一起 算一周后；for the last/next six ~s; 在过去(未来)的六周内；a six weeks' holiday; 六周的假日；tomorrow ~, eight days from today; 一周后的明天(八天后)；yesterday ~, eight days ago; 一周前的昨天(八天前)；three ~s ago yesterday, twenty-two days ago; 三周前的昨天(二十二天前)；the working ~, (usu) Monday to Friday or Saturday. 工作周(通常指星期一至星期五或至星期六)。What day of the ~ is it? 今天是星期几? Cf 参较 What's the date? 今天是几号? ~ in, ~ out, for ~s in succession. 一周又一周；接连许多星期。 ,~-'end n Saturday and Sunday (as a period of rest or holiday): 周末(指星期六和星期日，为休息或度假期间)：a ~end visit to the country; 周末的乡间旅行；spend the ~end with friends. 和朋友们在一起度周末。 □ vi spend a ~end: 度周末。I'm ~ending at Brighton. 我在布赖顿度周末。 ,~-'ender n person spending the ~end away from home. 外出度周末的人。long ~-'end n ~end, together with Friday or Monday as a public holiday. 长周末(自星期五开始的周末，或延长至星期一的周末)。 2 the working days of the ~. (一周中的)工作日；工作周。'~-day /-deɪ; -,de/ n any day except Sunday: 周日；工作日；除星期天外的任何一天：I'm always busy on ~days. 我在周日总是很忙。(attrib) (用作定语) There are only ~day trains from this station. 本站仅工作日有火车开出(周末停驶)。 ~-ly adj, adv (happening) once a ~, every ~; of the ~: 每周(发生)一次；每周;每周的；a ~ly wage of £50; 周薪五十英镑；~ly visits. 每周一次的访问。 □ n periodical published once a ~. 周刊；周报。

weeny /'wiːnɪ; 'wini/ adj (-ier, -iest) (often 常作 ,teeny-'~)(colloq) tiny. (口)极小的；微小的。

weep /wiːp; wip/ vi, vt (pt, pp wept /wept; wɛpt/) [VP2A, B, C, 4B, 3A, 6A] (liter) cry; let tears fall from the eyes: (文)哭泣；流泪：~ for joy; 喜极而泣；~ over one's misfortunes. 为某人的不幸而哭泣。She wept to see him in such a terrible state. 看到他处于那种困境，她哭了。She wept over her sad fate. 她为自己悲惨的命运而哀哭。 ~-ing adj (of trees, eg the birch and willow) having drooping branches. (指树,尤指桦树和柳树)垂枝的。

wee·vil /'wiːvl; 'wivl/ n small beetle with a hard shell, feeding on and infesting stores of grain, nuts and other seeds. 象鼻虫；蛄螬。 ⇨ boll.

weft /weft; wɛft/ n the ~, cross-threads taken over and under the warp in weaving. 纬；纬线。 ⇨ the illus at warp. 参见 warp 之插图。

weigh /weɪ; we/ vt, vi 1 [VP6A] measure (by means of a scale, balance, etc) how heavy sth is: 称…的重量；估量；称：He ~ed himself on the scales. 他在体重器上称体重。He ~ed the stone (= estimated how heavy it was) in his hands. 他用手估量这块石头的重量。~ sth out, distribute in definite quantities; take a definite quantity of: 照定量分配；从…中取出一定的数量：She ~ed out flour, sugar and butter for a cake. 她称取面粉、糖和奶油，要做一块糕饼。~ (oneself) in, (of a jockey, boxer, etc) be ~ed before a race or contest. (指骑师、拳击师等)比赛前量体重。~ in (with), produce (arguments, facts, etc) triumphantly; bring (them) to bear on a discussion. 成功地提出(议论、事实等)；把(议论、事实等)运用于讨论。'~-bridge n weigh-machine with a platform on to which vehicles, etc can be driven to be ~ed. (车辆可开上去过磅的)地磅;台秤。'~-ing-machine n machine for ~ing objects that are too large for a simple balance or scale. 称量机；衡器。 2 [VP2B] show a certain measure when put on a scale, etc: 重(若干)：~ 10 kilos/a ton of something, etc. 重十公斤(重一吨,无重量等)。How much do you ~, How heavy are you? 你的体重是多少? 3 [VP2C] (of a machine, etc) be capable of taking, designed to take, objects up to a specified weight: (指机器等)可处理重达若干的物体：This machine will ~ up to 5 tons. 这机器可处理重达五吨的物体。 4 [VP6A, 14, 15B] ~ sth (with/against sth), compare the importance, value, etc of (one thing and another): 权衡；考量；对比；比较(一物与他物)的重要

性或价值: ~ one plan against another. 评估一计划与另一计划的优劣。 ~ sth (up), consider carefully; assess: 仔细估量; 慎重考虑: ~ (up) the consequences of an action: 评估某一行动的后果; 斟酌字句; ~ the pros and cons. 权衡赞成与反对的理由。 5 [VP15B, 3A] ~ sth down, pull or bring down; depress: 把某物压下; 使某物沉下; 压低: The fruit ~ed the branches down. 果实使树枝下坠。 ~ sb down, depress; make tired, troubled, etc: 使某人闷闷不乐; 使某人困乏、担心、悬虑等: ~ed down with sorrow/cares/anxieties. 因忧愁(担心、焦虑)而闷闷不乐。 ~ on sb/sth, cause concern, anxiety (because of importance, seriousness): 重压; (因为重要、严重等而)使关心、焦虑: The problem/responsibility ~s heavily on him/on his mind. 那个难题(那项责任)沉重地压在他的身上(心上)。 ~ with sb, influence: 影响某人: evidence that did not ~ with the judges; 不为法官所重视的证据; the point that ~s with me. 对我有重大关系之处。 6 ~ anchor, raise the anchor and start a voyage. 起锚; 启航。

weight /weɪt; wet/ n 1 [U] gravitational force with which a body tends towards the centre of the earth. 重力。 2 [U] how heavy a thing is; this expressed in some scale (eg tons, kilogrammes) as measured on a scale, weighing-machine, etc (⇨ App 5): (物体的)重量; 分量(如吨, 公斤)(参看附录五): Are bananas sold by ~ or at so much a piece? 香蕉是论重量卖呢, 还是论个卖? That man is twice my ~. 那人的体重是我的两倍。 My ~ is 70 kilos. 我的体重是七十公斤。 The two boys are (of) the same ~. 那两个男孩体重相等。 He is your superior both in size and in ~. 他的块头和体重都超过你。 under/over ~, weighing too little/too much. 过轻(过重); 不到(超过)分量。 pull one's ~, ⇨ pull²(2). put on ~, (of a person) become heavier. (指人)体重增加; 长胖。 throw one's ~ about, (colloq) be domineering or conceited; try to bully people. (口)仗势欺人; 滥用权势。 3 a (the ~ (of), load to be supported: 负担; 重累; 重担: The pillars have a great ~ to bear/have to support the ~ of the roof. 这些柱子须承受重大的压力(须承受屋顶的重量)。 That's a great ~ off my mind. 那真释去了我心头的一大重负。 He has a great ~ of responsibility. 他肩负着重大的责任。 4 [U] (degree of) importance or influence: 重要; 势力; 影响力; 重要或影响力的程度: arguments of great ~; 有力的论据; considerations that had great ~ with me. 对我有重大影响的因素。 carry ~, be important or influential: 具重要性; 具影响力: a man/an opinion that carries ~. 有影响力的人物(意见)。 5 [C] piece of metal of known ~ used in scales for weighing objects: 称锤; 砝码; 秤铊: an ounce/100 grammes/2 lb, etc ~; 一英两(一百克, 两磅等)的砝码; heavy object for various purposes: 作各种用途的重物: a clock worked by ~s; 利用摆走动的钟; keep papers down with a ~ ('paper-~). 用文镇(纸压)把纸压住。 The doctor said he must not lift ~s. 医生说他切不可举重物。 '~-lifting n gymnastic feat of lifting great ~s. 举重(体操项目之一)。 6 [U] system of units, scale or notation, for expressing ~: 计重法; 衡制: troy/avoirdupois ~. 金(常)衡。 □ vt 1 [VP6A] put a ~ or ~s(5) on; add ~ to; make heavy: 放锤或砝码于…之上; 加重; 使重: ~ a walking-stick with lead, eg to make it useful as a weapon. 加铅于手杖, 使之重量增加(俾用作武器等)。 Circumstances are ~ed in his favour, (fig) give him an extra advantage. (喻)情况对他尤其有利。 2 ~ sb down, burden with: 使负重担: He was ~ed down with packages. 他拿着过多的包裹。 3 [VP6A] treat (a fabric) with a mineral substance to make it seem stronger: 用矿物质处理(织物)使之显得更结实: ~ed silk. 以矿物质处理过的绸布。 ~·less adj having no ~, eg because of absence of gravity. 无重量的; 失重的(例如因为没有地心引力)。 ~·less·ness n: 无重状态; 失重状态: become accustomed to ~lessness in a spacecraft. 习惯于太空船里的失重状态。 ~·y adj (-ier, -iest) 1 of great

~; burdensome. 重的; 烦重的; 累人的。 2 influential; important: 有影响力的; 重要的: ~y considerations/arguments. 重要的因素(论据)。 ~·ily /-ɪlɪ; -əlɪ/ adv ~·i·ness n

weir /wɪə(r); wɪr/ n [C] wall or barrier across a river to control the flow of water; fence of stakes or broken branches in a stream as a trap for catching fish. 堰(拦河建筑之墙或似墙物, 用以控制水流); 鱼梁(溪流中以桩或断枝构成的栅栏, 用以捕鱼)。

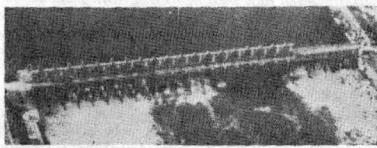

a weir

weird /wɪəd; wɪrd/ adj 1 unnatural; unearthly; mysterious: 不自然的; 怪诞的; 非人世所有的; 神秘的: ~ shrieks from the darkness of the ruined castle. 从我破城堡的黑暗处传来的怪诞尖叫声。 2 (colloq) strange; difficult to understand or explain: (口)奇异的; 难以了解或解释的: What ~ shoes women sometimes wear! 女人穿的鞋子有时多么怪模怪样呀! ~·ie /'wɪədɪ; 'wɪrdɪ/, ~o /'wɪədəʊ; 'wɪrdo/ nn (sl) eccentric person, esp one who is very unconventional in behaviour, dress and appearance. (俚)古怪的人(尤指行为、服饰、模样非常不合习俗者)。 ~·ly adv ~·ness n

wel·come /'welkəm; 'welkəm/ adj 1 received with giving, pleasure: 受欢迎的; 令人愉快的: a ~ visitor/rest; 受欢迎的访客(休息); ~ news; 佳音; 可喜的消息; make a friend ~, show him that his coming is ~. 使朋友觉得受欢迎。 A loan would be very ~ to me just now. 现在如果谁肯借我钱, 我会很高兴。 2 ~ to do sth/to sth; (a) freely permitted: 可随意做某事; 可随意取用某物: You are ~ to borrow my bicycle. 欢迎你借用我的自行车。 You are ~ to the use of my car. 你可以随意借用我的车。 Anyone is ~ to my share, may have it. 欢迎任何人用我这一份。 (b) (ironic) permitted to have sth burdensome or unwanted: (反语)欢迎做(某项烦事); 欢迎享(入所不愿之物): If anyone thinks he can do this job any better, he's ~ to it/~ to try! I'll gladly let him do it. 如果有人认为这件事他可以做得更好一点, 他不妨来做做看(欢迎他试一试)。 (c) absolved of the need to express thanks: 不必表示感谢的: You are ~ to it (usu shortened to) (通常略作) You're ~, = Don't mention it. 别客气。 3 (as an interjection) (用作感叹词) W~ home! 欢迎归来! W~ to England! 欢迎到英国来! (欢迎莅临英国!) □ n [C] greeting, response by word or action, when sb arrives, when an offer is received, etc: 欢迎; 接待; 款待: They gave us/We received a warm/cold/enthusiastic, etc ~. 他们给予我们(我们受到)热烈(冷淡、热诚)的欢迎。 The heartiest of ~s awaited us. 最热烈的欢迎在等待着我们。 □ vt [VP6A, 15A] show pleasure or satisfaction at sth, at the arrival of sb or sth; greet (in the manner indicated): 欢迎; (以某种态度)接受: ~ a friend to one's home; 欢迎朋友到家中; ~ a suggestion warmly/coldly. 热烈地(冷淡地)接受一项建议。

weld /weld; weld/ vt, vi 1 [VP6A, 15A, B] join (pieces of metal) by hammering or pressure (usu when the metal is softened by heat) or fusing by the use of an oxy-acetylene flame or an electric arc; make by doing this: 熔接; 焊接; 锻接: ~ the pieces of a broken axle; 焊接断了的车轴; ~ parts together; 把部件熔接在一起; (fig) (喻) arguments that are closely ~ed. 严谨的论据。 ⇨ the illus at **oxy-acetylene**. 参看 oxy-acetylene 之插图。 2 [VP2A] (of iron, etc) be capable of being ~ed: (指铁等)能熔接: Some metals ~ better than others. 有些金属比其他金属容易焊接。 □ n ~ed joint.

焊接点; 熔接的接头。 ~**er** n workman who ~s. 熔焊工人。

wel·fare /'welfeə(r); 'welfɛr/ n [U] **1** condition of having good health, comfortable living and working conditions, etc: 平安; 安宁; 福祉; 福利; 幸福: *work for the ~ of the nation;* 为谋求国家的福利而工作; *be concerned about sb's ~;* 关心某人的幸福; *child/infant ~.* 儿童(婴儿)的福利; **the W~ State,** name applied to a country with State-financed social services, eg health, insurance, pensions. 福利国家(以政府财政举办卫生、保险、养老金等社会服务的国家)。 **2** (US) social security. (美)社会安全; 社会保障。 ~ **work(er),** (US) social work(er). (美)(社会)福利事业(工作者)。

wel·kin /'welkɪn; 'wɛlkɪn/ n (poet) sky: (诗)天空; 苍穹: *make the ~ ring,* make the air re-echo with shouts. 呼喊之声响彻云霄。

well¹ /wel; wɛl/ n **1** shaft, usu lined with brick or stone, for obtaining water from an underground source: 井: *drive/sink a ~.* 开井; 凿井。 ~-**water** n water from a ~. 井水。 **2** hole bored for mineral oil: 油井: *the 'oil—s of Iran.* 伊朗的油井。 **3** (old use, or in place-names) spring or foundation of water; (fig) source. (旧用法, 或用于地名中)泉; 水源; (喻)来源。 '~-**head** n source of a spring or fountain. 泉源; 水源。 **4** deep, enclosed space in a building, often from roof to basement, for a staircase of lift. 升孔(建筑物中深而封闭的空间, 通常自屋顶至底层, 以安设楼梯或电梯)。 **5** (GB) railed space for barristers, etc in a law court. (英)(法庭上有围栏的)律师席。 **6** '~-**deck** n space on the main deck of a ship, enclosed by bulwarks and higher decks. 井形甲板(主甲板上由舷墙及较高甲板围成的部分)。 □ vi [VP2C] ~ **out** (*from/of*), flow, like water from a ~: 涌出; 喷出; 流出: *The blood was ~ing out (from the wound).* 血(从伤口)涌出。 ~ **over,** overflow. 溢洪; 泛滥。 ~ **up (in),** rise, like water in a ~: 涌升; 涌出; 涌现: *Tears ~ed up in her eyes.* 眼泪从她的眼中涌出。 *Their anger ~ed up.* 他们怒火上升。

well² /wel; wɛl/ (comp **better,** superl **best**) adv **1** in a good, right or satisfactory manner (placed after the v, and after the direct object if the v is transitive): 好; 对; 满意地(置于动词后, 如果是及物动词, 置于直接宾语后): *The children behaved ~.* 孩子们行为良好。 *They are ~-behaved children.* 他们是乖孩子。 *The house is ~ situated.* 那房子地点适中。 *He speaks English ~.* 他的英语说得很好。 *W~ done!* 做得好! *W~ run!* 做得好! *W~ played!* (cries indicating satisfaction, praise, etc). 表演得好! (表示满意、赞美等的喊叫声)。 *I hope everything is going ~* (= satisfactorily) *with you.* 但愿你事事如意。 *Do these two colours go ~ together,* look satisfactory side by side? 这两种颜色调和吗? *Does this colour go ~ with that colour?* 这颜色配得上那颜色吗? **do ~,** succeed; make progress; prosper: 成功; 有进步; 兴旺: *Simon has done ~ at school this term.* 西蒙本学期在学校里成绩很好。 *Peter is doing ~ in Canada.* 彼得在加拿大过得很好。 **be doing ~,** (progressive tenses only) making a good recovery (from illness, etc): (仅用于进行时)(生病等后)复原或恢复情况良好: *Both mother and baby are doing ~.* 母亲与婴儿恢复情况都很好。 **do oneself ~,** provide oneself with good things, esp comforts and luxuries. 生活优裕。 **do ~ by sb,** treat him with generosity. 善待某人。 **do ~ out of,** make a profit from sb or sth. 从(某人或某事物)获得好处或利益。 **wish sb ~,** hope that he has good fortune, success, etc. 祝某人好运; 祝某人成功等。 **2** with praise or approval: 夸奖地; 称赞地: *think/speak ~ of sb.* 重视(称赞)某人。 *It speaks ~ for your teaching that all your pupils passed the examination.* This fact is evidence that your teaching was good. 你教的学生考试都及格了, 这证明你教学优异。 **stand ~ with sb,** be in his favour: 合某人之意: *He stands ~ with his employers,* They like him, think highly of his abilities, etc. 他的雇主们都喜欢他。 **3** fortunately. 幸运地。 **be ,~ 'out of sth,** be out of

an affair without loss, etc: 安然脱免; 未受损失等而摆脱某事: *You are ~ out of it,* may consider yourself fortunate to be out of the affair. 你有幸拥摆脱此事。 *I wish I was ~ out of this business,* that I could free myself from it without misfortune. 我希望我能安然摆脱这事务。 ~ **off, (a)** fortunate: 幸运的: *He doesn't know when he is ~ off,* does not realize how fortunate he is. 他不知道他是多么幸运。 **(b)** wealthy. 富裕的; 有钱的。 ~ '**off for,** provided with: 被充分供以; 充分备有: ~ *off for food/drink/bright ideas.* 有充分的食物(有充分的饮料); 满脑子的巧妙主意。 **come off ~, (a)** (of a person) have good fortune; be lucky. (指人)有好运; 幸运。 **(b)** (of an event) have a satisfactory outcome. (指事件)有满意的结果。 **do ~ to + inf,** used to suggest either good judgement or good luck: 用来表示好的判断或好运: *He did ~ to leave the country before the revolution started.* 他幸好在革命开始前离开了那个国家。 *You would do ~* (= It would be wise for you) *to say nothing about what happened.* 你最好不要提发生了什么事。 *You did ~ to ask my advice.* 你来征询我的意见, 算是你运气。 **4** (mid position) with good reason, justice or likelihood; advisably: (置于句中助动词与动词之间)有理由地; 合理地; 可能地; 适当地: *You may ~ be surprised.* 你可能感到惊讶。 *We might ~ make the experiment.* 我们该做那项实验。 *I couldn't very ~ refuse to help them,* It would have been difficult, unreasonable, etc, to have done so. 我(当时)很难拒绝帮助他们。 *You may quite ~* (= with good reason) *give illness as an excuse.* 你尽可把生病当作借口。 *We may as ~ begin at once.* 我们还是马上开始的好。 *It may ~ be that…,* It is likely or possible that…. 那很可能就是…。 **5** '**may ('just) as ~,** ⇨ **may(4). (a)** with equal reason, advantage, justification, etc: 不如; 等于是; 还是…好: *You might just as ~ say that white is black (as say that…).* 你(说…)等于说白的就是黑的。 *Our holidays were ruined by the weather—we might just as ~ have stayed at home!* 我们的假期被天气糟蹋了; 我们还不如待在家里! *You may as ~ tell me the truth,* ie because if you don't tell me, I shall certainly hear it from others. 你还是把真相告诉我的好。 **be just as ~,** with no loss of advantage, no need for regret: 无何损失; 无须后悔; 不妨: *It's just as ~ I didn't lend him the money.* 我不会后悔没有借钱给他。 **5** (end position) thoroughly; completely: (置于动词之后, 或及物动词的宾语之后)彻底地; 充分地: *Examine the account ~ before you pay it.* 在付款以前仔细检查一下帐目。 *Shake the bottle ~.* 把这个瓶子彻底摇一摇。 **7** to a considerable extent: 至相当的程度; 颇; 甚: *He was leaning ~ back/forward in his chair.* 他坐着身体靠在椅背上(他坐在椅上, 身体前倾着)。 *His name is ~ up in the list,* near the top. 他的名字列在相当前面(靠近顶端)。 *He must be ~ past forty,* ~ *over forty years of age.* 他一定超过四十岁很多了。 *It's ~ worth trying.* 那很值得一试。 '~ **away, (a)** making good progress: 进展良好: *We're ~ away,* have made a good start. 我们已经有了好的开端。 **(b)** (colloq) on the way to being slightly drunk, to becoming hilarious, etc. (口)有点醉意了; 玩闹得快要忘形了。 **be ~ up in/on,** ⇨ **up(8). leave/let ~ alone,** leave it as it is; don't interfere. 保持原来的样子; 维持原状; 不介入; 不干预。 **8 as ~ (as),** in addition to: 除…外: *He gave me money as ~ as advice.* 他除了给我忠告外, 还给我钱。 *He gave me advice, and money as ~.* 他给我忠告, 并给我钱。 *We shall travel by night as ~ as by day,* both by night and by day. 我们将日夜赶路。 *Give me those as ~,* ~ those, too. 把那些也给我。 **9** (with another adv) (与另一副词连用) **pretty ~,** almost: 几乎: *You're pretty ~ the only person who's willing to help.* 你几乎是唯一愿意协助的人。 □ pred adj **1** in good health: 健康的; 安好的: *be/look/feel ~ get ~.* 身体很好, 觉得好, 恢复(康复)。 *I'm quite ~, thank you.* 我很好, 谢谢你。 Cf 参较 *I'm fine, thank you.* **2** in a satisfactory condition: 满意的; 良

好的: *All's ~ that ends ~.* 凡事结局好好, 即全局都好(事业的成败以结局为凭, 不必计较所经历的艰苦)。*We're very ~ where we are.* 我们目前情况甚好。*All is not ~ in the world nowadays.* 当前的世界情势并不令人满意。*It's all very ~...,* formula (used ironically) to indicate discontent, dissatisfaction, disagreement, etc: (反语用法)表示不平, 不满, 不同意等的套语: *It's all very ~ (for you) to suggest a holiday in Italy, but how am I to find the money?* (你)提议去意大利度假的确很好, 但是我如何去筹这笔钱呢? **3** advisable; desirable: 得当的; 适宜的: *It would be ~ to start early.* 最好早点动身。*It would be just as ~ for you to ask your employer's permission.* 你最好征求雇主的同意。**4** lucky; fortunate: 幸运的; 有好运的: *It was ~ for you that nobody saw us.* 没有人看到你, 是你的运气。☐ *int* **1** (expressing astonishment): (表示惊愕): *W~, who would have thought it?* 啊, 谁会想得到是这样呢? *W~,! I should never have guessed it!* 唉呀! 我永远猜不出来! **2** (expressing relief): (表示慰藉): *W~, here we are at last!* 好了, 我们终于到了! **3** (expressing resignation): (表示无可奈何): *W~, it can't be helped.* 唉, 这是没有办法的事。*W~, there's nothing we can do about it.* 唉, 我们无能为力了。**4** (expressing understanding of agreement): (表示了解或同意): *Very ~, then, we'll talk it over again tomorrow.* 很好, 那末明天我们再谈谈吧。**5** (expressing concession): (表示让步): *W~, you may be right.* 好罢, 你也许是对的。**6** (used to resume a story, etc): (用于继续一个故事等): *W~, as I was saying,....* 唔, 当时我谈到,...。*W~, the next day....* 后来, 第二天...。

well- /wel/, wel/ **1** (*pref*), **,~-'being** n [U] welfare; health, happiness and prosperity: 安宁; 健康; 幸福; 福利; 兴盛: *have a sense of ~being,* good bodily health; 觉得健康(快乐); *work for the ~-being of the nation.* 为国家的福利而工作。**,~-'doer** n (archaic) virtuous person. (古)君子, 善人。**,~-'doing** n [U] (archaic) virtuous conduct; good deeds. (古)善行; 好事。**'~-nigh** adv (archaic) almost: (古)几乎; 殆: *It's ~nigh impossible.* 那几乎是不可能的。*He was ~nigh drowned.* 他几乎被淹死。**,~-to-'do** adj wealthy. 富裕的; 富有的。**'~-wisher** n person who wishes well to one, to a cause, etc 祝福者。**2** (compounds with numerous participles and words in -ed, usu hyphened when attrib (before a n), but not hyphened when pred except when the compound has acquired a restricted sense): (与很多分词及加 -ed 的词构成复合词, 作为定语用法(置于名词之前)时, 通常加短连, 作为表语用法时, 除有限定含意外, 不加短连): **,~-ad'vised,** prudent; wise: 审慎的; 明智的: *a ~-advised action.* 审慎的行为。**,~-ap'pointed,** having all the necessary equipment, furniture, etc: 配备或装备齐全的; 设备完善的: *a ~-appointed expedition/hotel/office/suite.* 装备齐全的探险队; 设备完善的旅馆(办公室, 套房)。**,~-'balanced,** sane, sensible. 精神正常的; 意识健全的; 通情达理的。**,~-'born,** of a family with high social position. 出身名门的; 家庭背景好的。**,~-'bred,** of good upbringing. 教养良好的。**,~-con'ducted,** characterized by good organization and control: 品行端正的; 组织良好的; 安排妥当的: *a ~-conducted meeting.* 一次妥为安排的会议。**,~-con'nected,** connected by blood or marriage with families of good social position or to rich or influential people. 与望族或权贵有血亲或姻亲关系的。**,~-dis'posed (towards),** having kind feelings (towards); ready to help. (对...)怀有好意的; 乐于助人的。**,~-'favoured,** (old use) good-looking. (旧法)样子好看的; 貌美的。**,~-'found,** = **~-appointed**。**,~-'founded,** based on facts, having a foundation in fact: 有事实为依据的; 有根据的: *~-founded suspicions.* 有根据的怀疑。**,~-'groomed,** carefully tended; neat; meticulously dressed. 细心照料的; 整洁的; 穿着考究的。**,~-'grounded,** (a) = **~-founded.** (b) having a good training in or knowledge of the groundwork of a subject. 具有某学科之良好基础的; 根底好的。**'~-heeled,** (sl) rich. (俚)有钱的。**,~-in'formed,** (a)

having wide knowledge. 见识广博的; 博识的。**(b)** having access to reliable information: 消息灵通的; 能获得可靠消息的: *in ~-informed quarters.* 消息灵通方面。**,~-in'tentioned,** aimed or aiming (often or usu unsuccessfully) at good results. 出自善意的; 好心的; 指望有好结果的(常常或通常事与愿违, 未产生好的结果)。**,~-'knit,** compact; firmly jointed, not loose-made (esp of a person or his body). (尤指人或其身体)结实的; 强健的; 硬朗的。**,~-'known,** widely known. 出名的; 众所周知的。**,~-'lined,** (of a purse, colloq) full of money. (指钱包, 口)放满钱的。**,~-'marked,** definite; distinct. 清楚的; 明显的。**,~-'meaning,** = **~-intentioned**。**,~-'meant,** done, said, etc, with good intentions. 出于善意的。**,~-'read,** having read much; having a mind well stored with information as the result of wide reading. 读书多的; 博学多闻的; 腹笥宽的。**,~-'rounded,** complete and symmetrical. 完全而对称的。**,~-'set,** = **~-knit**。**,~-'spoken, (a)** speaking well, politely, in refined language. 善于辞令的; 言语谦恭的; 说话漂亮的。**(b)** spoken well. 说得中肯的; 得体的。**,~-'timed,** done, said, at the right or a suitable time. 在正确或适当的时间做出或说出的; 做得或说得恰合时宜的。**,~-'tried,** (of methods, remedies) tested and proved useful. (指方法, 救治法)经过试验而证明有用的。**,~-'turned,** (of a compliment, phrase, verse) gracefully expressed. (指赞语, 短语, 诗句)措辞巧妙的; 说得妙的。**,~-'worn,** much used; (esp) commonplace; trite. 用得太多的; (尤)陈腐的; 平凡的。

we'll /wi:l/, wil/ = we shall; we will.

wel·ling·ton /'welɪŋtən/, 'welɪŋtən/ n (boot), water-proof boot reaching to the knee. 威灵顿长靴(高达膝部的防水靴)。

Welsh /welʃ/, welʃ/ n, adj (the language) of the people of Wales. 威尔士语; 威尔士人的。**~ 'rabbit, 'rarebit,** ⇔ **rarebit.**

welsh /welʃ/, welʃ/ vi [VP3A] **~ on sth/sb, 1** avoid payment of: 赖帐; 逃债: *~ on a debt.* 赖帐。**2** break one's word to: 对...食言: *~ on a friend.* 失信于友人。**~er** n

welt /welt/, welt/ n [C] **1** strip of leather to which the sole and the upper part of a shoe are stitched. (靴底与鞋面接缝之间的)革条。**2** = **weal²**。

Welt·an·schau·ung /'velt,ɑːn'ʃauʊŋ/, 'velt,ɑn-,ʃau·ʊŋ/ n (G) philosophy of life; perception of the world. (德)人生观; 世界观。

wel·ter¹ /'weltə(r)/, 'weltə/ vi [VP2C] roll; wallow; be soaked or steeped (in blood, etc). 滚动; 翻滚; 浸泡(于血等中)。☐ n (sing only) general confusion; disorderly mixture or aimless conflict: (只用单数)混乱; 混杂; 纷争; the ~ of creeds/political beliefs; 各种宗教或政治信仰)的纷争; *a ~ of meaningless verbiage.* 一堆无意义的冗词。

wel·ter² /'weltə(r)/, 'weltə/ adj **'~ race** n race for horses with heavy-weight riders. 重骑师赛马; 重负赛马。**'~-weight** n (esp boxing) boxer weighing 135-147lb/61-66.6kg. (尤指拳击)次中量级的拳击者(体重在 135 至 147 磅, 或 61 至 66.6 公斤之间)。

wen /wen/, wen/ n [C] harmless, usu permanent, tumour on the scalp or other part of the body; (fig) abnormally large or overgrown urban area. (生于头皮或身体其他部分的)良性肿瘤; (通常为永久性的)赘疣; (喻)都市之过分扩大或发展的地区。

wench /wentʃ/, wentʃ/ n (archaic) (古) **1** girl or young woman. 少女; 少妇。**2** prostitute. 妓女。☐ vi [VP2A] associate with prostitutes. 嫖妓。

wend /wend/, wend/ vt (old use, only in) (旧用法, 仅用于) **~ one's way (home),** go, make one's way. 走; 走; 走; 往; 回(家)。

went /went/, went/ pt of **go¹**。

wept /wept/, wept/ pt, pp of **weep**。

were /wɜː(r)/, wɜ/; weak form: wə(r)/, wə/ pt of **be¹**。

we're /wɪə(r)/, wɪr/ = we are.

weren't /wɜːnt/, wɜnt/ = were not.

were·wolf /'wɪəwulf; 'wɪr,wulf/ n (pl **-wolves** /-wulvz; -,wulvz/) (myth) human being turned into a wolf. (神话)变成狼的人; 狼人。

wert /wɜːt; wɜt/ thou ~, (archaic) you were. (古) 你是。

Wes·leyan /'wezlɪən; 'wɛslɪən/ n, adj (member) of the Methodist Church deriving from John Wesley. 美以美教派(起源于约翰·卫斯理的); 美以美教派信徒。

west /west; wɛst/ n 1 the ~, point of the horizon where the sun sets; that part of the world, of a country, etc, in this direction: 西; 西方; 西部: Bristol is in the ~ of England. 布里斯托尔在英格兰的西部。 **the W~, (a)** Europe and the continent of America (contrasted with Asia). 西方; 西洋(指欧洲及美洲大陆, 与亚洲相对)。 **(b)** (world politics) Western Europe and America (contrasted with Eastern Europe, the USSR and China). (国际政治)西方国家; 西方集团(指西欧与美国; 与东欧, 苏联及中国相对)。 **(c)** the part of the US between the Mississippi River and the Pacific Ocean. 美国西部(介于密西西比河与太平洋之间)。 **(d)** ~ern part of any country. 任何国家的西部。 **,~-north-'west, ,~-south-'west,** ⇨ the illus at **compass.** 参看 compass 之插图。 **2** (attrib) coming from the ~: (用作定语)来自西方的: a ~ wind; 西风; towards, at, in the direction of the ~: 向西方的; 在西方的; 西方的: on the ~ coast; 在西海岸; ~ longitude. 西经。 **the W~ End,** part of London with the largest and most fashionable shops, theatres, etc. 伦敦西区(伦敦之最大最时髦的商店, 戏院等的所在地)。 Hence, 由此产生, **,~'end adj:** ~end theatres/department stores. 伦敦西区的戏院(百货公司)。 **the '~country,** part of England ~ of a line from the Isle of Wight to the mouth of the River Severn. 英格兰西部地方(自威特岛至塞文河口连成一直线, 指此线以西的地方)。 Hence, 由此产生, **'~-country adj** of, from, characteristic of the ~ country. (英格兰之)西部地方的; 来自西部地方的; 具有西部地方特征的。 **W~ Central,** (abbr 略作 **WC**) London postal districts. 西中央区(伦敦邮递区之一)。 □ adv towards the ~: 向西; 向西地: sail/travel ~. 向西航行(旅行)。 **go ~,** (sl) be lost, ruined, etc. (俚)归西; 完蛋; 失掉; 失败; 毁灭; 破产等。 **~ of,** farther ~ than. 在…之西。 **'~ward** /-wəd; -wəd/ adj towards the ~: 向西的: in a ~ward direction. 向西方地。 **~ward(s)** /-wəd(z); -wəd(z)/ adv: travel ~ward(s). 向西旅行。

west·er·ly /'westəlɪ; 'wɛstəlɪ/ attrib adj towards the west; (of winds) from the west. 向西的; (指风)来自西方的。 □ adv towards the west. 向西方。

west·ern /'westən; 'wɛstən/ adj of, in, from, characteristic of, the west: 西方的; 在西方的; 来自西方的; 有西方之特征的: **the W~ Hemisphere,** N and S America. 西半球(即南北美洲)。 **the W~ Empire,** that part of the old Roman Empire with Rome as its capital. 西罗马帝国(古罗马帝国分裂后, 以罗马为首都的部分)。 □ n [C] film or novel dealing with life in the ~ part of the US in the times of the wars with the American Indians, or one with cowboys, rustlers, sheriffs, etc. 西部电影或小说(描写美国西部昔日与印第安人作战时代之生活, 或描写西部牛仔、偷牛贼或警官等之生活者)。 **~er** n native of the West, esp of the ~ US. 西方人; 泰西人; (尤指美国的)西部人。 **~·ize** /-aiz; -,aiz/ vt [VP6A] introduce ideas, ways of living, working, etc of the West(b) into. 引进西方的观念、生活方式、活动方式等; 使西化。 **~·iz·ation** /westənai'zeiʃn US: -ni'z-; ,westəni-'zeʃən/ n. 最西的; 极西的。 **~·most** /-məust; -,most/ adj farthest west. 最西的; 极西的。

wet /wet; wɛt/ adj (wetter, wettest) **1** covered or soaked with water or other liquid: 湿的; 潮湿的: wet clothes/roads. 湿衣服(湿路)。 Her cheeks were wet with tears. 她的面颊沾满了泪水。 Did you get wet, eg in the rain? 你淋湿了吗? We got wet to the skin, Our clothes were soaked through. 我们浑身湿透了。 Your coat is wet through, from one side to the other. 你的上装湿透了。

,wet 'blanket, ⇨ blanket(1). **,wet 'dock** n one (that can be) filled with water, able to float a ship. 湿坞(有水的或可进水的船坞)。 **'wet-nurse** n woman employed to suckle another's child. 乳母; 奶妈。 **,wet 'paint,** paint recently applied, not yet dry. 尚未干的油漆。 **2** rainy: 多雨的; 下雨的: wet weather; 雨天; the wettest summer for 20 years. 二十年来最多雨的夏季。 **3** (US) not prohibiting or opposing the sale and use of alcoholic drinks: (美)不禁酒的: a wet State. 不禁酒的州。 **4** (sl, of a person) ineffectual; spiritless. (俚, 指人)无效率的; 没精打采的; 没精神的。 □ n 1 **the wet,** rain: 雨: Come in out of the wet. 进来免得淋雨。 **2** [U] moisture. 湿气; 潮湿; 水分。 □ vt (pt, pp **wetted** or **wet**) (-tt-) [VP6A] make wet: 使湿: The baby has wet(ted) its bed again. 婴儿又尿床了。 **wet one's whistle,** ⇨ whistle, n(3). **wet·ting** n becoming or being made wet: 弄湿; 变湿: get a wetting, eg in heavy rain. 淋湿(如在大雨中)。

wether /'weðə(r); 'wɛðɚ/ n castrated ram. 阉过的公羊; 阉羊。

we've /wiːv; wiv/ = we have.

whack /wæk US: hwæk; hwæk/ vt [VP6A] strike (sb or sth) with a hard blow; thwack. 重击(某人或某物)用力打。 □ n 1 (sound of) a hard blow. 重击; 重击声。 **2** (sl) share: (俚)份: Have you all had a fair ~? 你们都已得到公平的一份了吗? **~ed** adj (colloq) (of a person) worn out; tired. (口)(指人)疲惫的; 困乏的。 **~·ing** n beating: 殴打; 打击: give a naughty child a ~ing. 把顽皮的小孩打一顿。 □ adj (colloq) big of its kind: 特大的; 特大的: a ~ing lie. 大谎言。 □ adv (colloq) very: (口)非常; 甚: a ~ing great lie. 弥天大谎。 **~er** n sth big of its kind. 同类中的大者; 特大物。

whale /weil US: hweil; hwel/ n **1** kinds of large sea-animal some of which are hunted for their oil and flesh (used for pet foods). 鲸。 ⇨ the illus at **sea.** 参看 sea 之插图。 **'~-bone** n thin, horny springy substance from the upper jaw of some kinds of ~. 鲸须(细而有弹性的角质物, 生于数类鲸鱼的上颚)。 **2** (colloq) a '~ of a time,** an exceedingly good time; no end of a good time. (口)非常愉快的时光; 无穷尽的愉快时光。 □ vi [VP2A] hunt ~s: 捕鲸: go whaling; 去捕鲸; the whaling industry. 捕鲸业。 **'whaling-gun** n one used for firing harpoons at ~s. 捕鲸炮。 **~r** /'weilə(r) US: 'hw-; 'hwelɚ/ n man or ship engaged in hunting ~s. 捕鲸人; 捕鲸船。

whang /wæŋ US: hwæŋ; hwæŋ/ vt (colloq) strike heavily and loudly. 砰然重击。 □ n ~ing sound or blow. 重击声; 重击。 □ adv (colloq) exactly; (口)恰好; 正好: hit the target ~ in the centre. 恰好击中靶心。

wharf /woːf US: hwɔːf; hworf/ n (pl **~s** or **wharves** /-vz; -vz/) wooden or stone structure at which ships are moored for (un)loading cargo. 码头; 埠头。 **~·age** /-idʒ; -idʒ/ n [U] (money paid for) accommodation at a ~. 码头设备; 码头费。

what /wɒt US: hwɒt; hwɑt/ adj **1** (interr) asking for a selection from an indefinite number (⇨ **which**): (疑问)什么; 哪一个或哪些个: W~ books have you read on this subject? 你读过哪些有关这方面的书? Tell me ~ books you have read recently. 告诉我, 你近来读过什么书。 W~ time is it? 现在几点钟了? Ask him ~ time it is. 去问问他现在几点钟了。 W~ size/colour/shape, etc do you want? 你要什么尺码(颜色, 形状等)? **2** (exclamatory): (用于感叹句中): W~ a good idea! 多么好的主意! W~ genius you have! 你多么有才气啊! **3** the... that; any... that; as much/many... as: ...的; 任何...的; 所...的: Give me ~ books (= the books, any books, that) you have on the subject. 把你所有关于这方面的书都给我。 W~ little (= The little that) he said on the subject was full of wisdom. 他对该问题所说的几句话充满了智慧。 W~ few friends (= The few friends that) I have here have been very kind to me. 我在这里的几个朋友一直对我很好。 □ pron (interr) ~ thing(s): (疑问)什

么东西；什么：*W~ happened?* 发生了什么事？*Tell me ~ happened.* 告诉我发生了什么事。*W~ is he, W~ is his occupation?* 他是做什么的？ `,~... 'for, for ~ purpose:` 为何；为何目的：*W~ did you do that for,* (colloq) *Why did you do that?* (口)你为什么要做那事？ `,~·'for n` [U] (colloq) punishment: (口)处罚；惩戒：*give sb ~·for.* 处罚某人。 `,~...'like,` (used to ask for a description, for details, etc): (用来要求一番描述，说明细节等)：*W~'s the weather like this morning?* 今天早晨的天气怎么样？*W~'s the new neighbour like?* 新搬来的邻居人怎么样？ `'~ if, ~ will, would, be the result if:` 万⋯⋯怎么办：*W~ if it rains while we are away for a long way from shelter?* 万一天下雨而我们离躲雨的地方又很远怎么办？ `'~ if the rumour is true?` 如果谣言是真的怎么办？ `'~ though,` (liter) → does it matter if: (文)即使⋯又有什么关系：*W~ though we are poor, we still have each other.* 穷算得了什么，只要我们还能彼此相守。 `~ about/of, (a)` → news is there about.... 关于⋯⋯有何消息。 `(b)` → `about³` **(4)**, of (10). `,~ 'of it?` (or, mod colloq) (在现代口语中亦用) `So '~?` (used to admit that sth is true, but questioning the inference (to be) made from it.) 是又怎么样？(用于承认某事是真实的，但质询由此会推论出何种结论)。 `and '~ not,` and other things of the same kind. 等等；诸如此类。 `and/or ~, 'have now,` used to indicate that there are other things: 等等(用来表示还有其他东西等)：*Then there are bills for gas and electricity and ~ have you.* 还有瓦斯及电费等的帐单。 `'~·not n` unnamed thing; piece of furniture with open shelves for small ornaments, odds and ends. 叫不出名字的东西；陈列小装饰品及零碎东西的格架。 `,I know '~,` I have an idea, a suggestion to make.... 我有意见；我建议⋯。 `,I/ I'll tell you '~...,` Here's a suggestion.... 我建议⋯。 `know ,~'s '~,` have common sense; know how to distinguish useful things from useless, good things from bad, etc. 有常识；有判断力等。 `'~·d'you-call-him/-'her/-'it/-'them` etc/ 'wɒt dʒu kɔːl ɪm etc; 'hwɒt dʒu kɔːl ɪm etc/; `'~'s-his/-'her/-'its/-their-name,` used as substitutes for a name that one cannot recall. 某某；某人；某物；某先生；某女士(用以代替记不起来的名字)。 `□ rel pron` that which; the thing(s) which: 兼为先行词的关系代词：*W~ he says is not important.* 他所说的话并不重要。*Do ~ you think is right.* 照你认为对的去做。 *W~ the country needs most is wise leadership.* 国家最需要的是睿智的领导。*When people say that they know ~ they like, they really mean that they like ~ they know,* They like ~ they are familiar with. 当人们说他们知道他们喜欢什么的时候，他们真正的意思是说他们知道的是他们所知道的事物。 *It's a useful book and, ~ is more, not an expensive one.* 这是一本有用的书，而且价钱不贵。 `'~ with... and ('~ with),` between various causes: 一方面因为⋯一方面因为；因⋯和：*W~ with one thing and another,...,* as a result of many things,... 由于种种原因⋯。*W~ with overwork and (~ with) undernourishment he fell ill.* 一方面由于工作过度，一方面由于营养不良，他病倒了。

what·e'er /wɒt'eə(r) US: hw~; hwɑt'eʳ/ (诗) whatever.

what·ever /wɒt'evə(r) US: hw~ ; hwɑt'evə/ adj **1** (emphatic for *what*) of any sort, degree, etc: (what 的强势语)任何种类，程度等的；不论什么：*W~ nonsense the newspapers print, some people always believe it.* 无论报纸上刊登什么荒谬的东西，总会有人相信。*Take ~ measures you consider best.* 采取任何你认为最好的措施。 **2** (placed after a *n* in a negative context, giving emphasis to the negative): (在否定文句中置于名词之后，强调否定语气)：*There can be no doubt ~ about it.* 这事是毫无疑问的。*I have no intention ~* (= not the least intention) *of resigning.* 我毫无辞职的意思。 `□ pron` **1** no matter what: 不论什么；无论如何：*You are certainly right, ~ others may say.* 不论别人怎样评论，确实是对的。 *Keep calm, ~ happens.* 无论发生什么事都要保持冷静。

anything or everything that: 任何⋯的事物；每一⋯的事物：*Do ~ you like.* 做任何你喜欢做的事。*W~ I have is at your service.* 我所有的每一样东西，你都可以任意使用。 **3** or ~, (colloq) (usu at the end of a list of similar *nn* or *adj*) or anything at all: (口)(通常置于一系列类似的名词或形容词之后)或任何东西；诸如此类：*He'd have difficulty in learning any language—Greek, Chinese, or ~.* 他学习任何语言都会遭遇困难——不论是希腊语，汉语，或诸如此类。

what·so·e'er /,wɒtsəʊ'eə(r) US: 'hw~; ,hwɑtsəʊ'eʳ/ (poet for) (诗) **what·so·ever** /,wɒtsəʊ'evə(r) US: 'hw~ ; ,hwɑtsəʊ'evə/ (emphatic for) **whatever.** 为 whatever 的强势语。

wheat /wiːt US: hw~; hwiːt/ n [U] (plant producing) grain from which flour (as used for bread and pastry products) is made: 小麦；小麦粒：*a field of ~.* 小麦田。 → the illus at **cereal.** 参看 cereal 之插图。 `~en` /'wiːtn US: 'hw~; 'hwiːtn/ adj of ~: 小麦的：*~en flour/bread.* 麦粉面包。

wheedle /'wiːdl US: 'hw~; 'hwiːdl/ vt [VP6A, 14] `~ (into/out of),` make oneself pleasant to sb, flatter or coax, to get sth one wants: 谄媚；阿谀(以期获得所需要的东西)；哄；骗；(用甜言蜜语)骗取：*The girl ~d a pound out of her father/~d her father into buying her a bicycle.* 那女孩用甜言蜜语从她父亲那里得到了一英镑(使她父亲为她买了一辆脚踏车)。

wheel /wiːl US: hwiːl; hwiːl/ n **1** circular frame or disc which turns on an axle (as on carts, cars, bicycles, etc and for various purposes in machines): 轮；车轮；机轮。 → the illus at **bicycle.** 参看 bicycle 之插图。 `~s within ~s,` (fig) complicated motives and influences; indirect and secret agencies, all interacting: (喻)错综复杂的动机及影响力；交互作用的间接及隐匿的诸般力量；复杂的情势，局面，结构等。 `put one's shoulder to the ~,` help a cause or undertaking. 帮助推展某项事业、运动或任务；出一把力。 `the man at the ~,` the driver (at the steering- of a car, etc). 驾驶员；舵手。 `~·barrow n` small vehicle with one ~ and two handles for moving small loads. 手推车；独轮手车。 `'~·base n` distance between the axles of a motor-vehicle. (机动车辆的)轴距(即汽车等自前轮轴中点至后轮轴中点的距离)。 `'~·chair n` chair with large ~s for the use of sb unable to walk. (病人等用的)轮椅。 `'~·house n` small enclosed place on a ship (old style sailing-ship, a small riverlaunch, a tug, etc), to shelter the pilot or steersman. (旧式帆船、小型内河汽船、拖船等的)舵手室。 `'~·wright n` man who makes and repairs (new) ~s; 轮匠；车匠。 `~s. 2 potter's ~,` → `potter²;` `'paddle-~,` → `paddle¹(3). 3` [C] motion like that of a ~; motion of a line of men as on a pivoted end, esp as a military movement: 旋转运动；旋转；(尤指军队摒绕时的)方向变换：*a right/left ~.* 向右转(左转)。 `□ vt, vi` **1** [VP6A, 15A, B] push or pull (a vehicle with ~s): 推动；拉动(车子)：*~ a bike up a hill;* 骑脚踏车爬上斜坡；*~ a barrow;* 推动手推车；convey (sb or sth) in a vehicle with ~s: 以车载送：*~ the rubbish out to the dump.* 把垃圾用车运到垃圾场去。 **2** [VP2A, C, 6A, 15B] (cause to) turn in a curve or circle: (使)旋转；回旋：*The sails of the windmill were ~ing round.* 风车的车叶正在旋转。*The seagulls were ~ing in the air above me.* 海鸥正在我的上空盘旋。 `Right/Left ~!` (an order given to a column of men, esp troops, to change their line of route to the right (left)). 向右(左)转走！(队伍，尤指军队，变换方向的口令)。

wheeze /wiːz US: hwiːz; hwiːz/ vi, vt **1** [VP2A, B, C] breathe noisily, esp with a whistling sound in the chest (as when suffering from asthma); (of a pump, etc) make a similar sound. 有响声地呼吸；(尤指)喘息；哮喘；(指唧筒等)发出似喘息的声音。 **2** [VP15B] `~ sth out,` utter with such sounds: 哮喘地说；喘息地发出：*The asthmatic old man ~d out a few words.* 那哮喘的老人喘息地说出几个字。*A barrel-organ was wheezing out an*

old tune. 一架筒风琴正在喝咻喝咻地奏出一首老歌。 □ *n* [C] **1** sound of wheezing. 喘息声；哮喘声。 **2** (dated school sl) trick; bright idea. (过时的学校俚语)诡计；巧妙的主意。 **wheezy** *adj* breathing, speaking, uttered, with ~s: 喘息地呼吸，说话，发声的: *a fat and wheezy old dog;* 一条肥胖喘息的老狗; *a wheezy old pump.* 发喝咻声的旧唧筒。 **wheez·ily** /-ɪlɪ/ -ɪlɪ/ *adv* **wheezi·ness** *n*

whelk /welk *US:* hwelk; hwɛlk/ *n* kinds of marine mollusc (like a snail) with a spiral shell, some used as food. 海螺；蛾螺；油螺(某些可食用)。 ⇨ the illus at **mollusc.** 参看 mollusc 之插图。

whelp /welp *US:* hwelp; hwɛlp/ *n* **1** young dog, lion, tiger, bear, wolf, fox, etc. 幼兽(幼犬,幼狮,幼虎,幼熊,幼狼,幼狐等)。 **2** ill-bred boy or youth. 缺乏教养的男孩或青年。 □ *vi* give birth to ~s(1). 产幼兽。

when /wen *US:* hwen; hwɛn/ *interr adv* **1** at what time; on what occasion: 于何时；于何时代；什么时候: *W~ can you come?* 你什么时候能来? *W~ did that happen?* 那事是何时发生的? *I don't know ~ that happened.* 我不知道那事是何时发生的。 **2** (after a *prep*) what time: (用于介词后)何时；什么时候: *Till ~ can you stay?* 你到什么时候？ *Since ~ has he been missing?* 他从何时起失踪的? □ *rel adv* (with day, time etc as antecedent) at or on which: (以 day, time 这一类词为先行词)在那时；斯时；届时: *Sunday is the day ~ I am least busy.* 星期天是我最不忙的一天。 *There are times ~ joking is not permissible.* 有的时候开玩笑是不许可的。 *It was one of those cold, wet evenings ~ most people stay indoors.* 那是一个寒冷阴雨而人们大都会待在家里的晚上。 □ *conj* **1** at or during the time that: 当…时；在…之际；在…的时候: *It was raining ~ we arrived.* 我们到的时候，正在下雨。 *He waved ~ he saw her.* 当他看到她的时候，他挥手致意。 *W~ speaking French, I often make mistakes.* 我在讲法语的时候，时常出错。 **2** although: 尽管；虽然: *He walks ~ he might take a taxi.* 虽然他可以坐计程车，他还是步行。 **3** since; considering that: 既然；鉴于: *How can I help them to understand ~ they won't listen to me?* 既然他们不愿意听我说说，我怎么能帮助他们了解呢? **4** at or during which time: 届时；在那时；当其时: *The Queen will visit the town in May, ~ she will open the new hospital.* 女王将于五月间访问该城，届时她将主持一所新医院的开幕典礼。

whence /wens *US:* hwens; hwɛns/ *adv* (formal) (正式用语) **1** (in questions) from what place or cause: (用于问句中)从何处；何以；因何；由何: *Do you know ~ she came?* 你知道她是从何处来的吗? *W~ comes it that…,* How is it that…? 怎么会…? **2** (in statements) from which place: (用于叙述句中)从哪地方；从哪处；从哪里: *the land ~ they are come.* 他们来的地方。 **3** to the place from which: 向或到…的地方: *Return ~ you came.* 回到你来的地方去。 **,~so'ever** *adv, conj* from whatever place, cause or origin. 无论从何处；无论由何原因,原由,出处。

when·ever /wen'evə(r) *US:* hw-; hwɛn'ɛvə/ *adv, conj* **1** at whatever time; no matter when: 在任何时候；无论何时: *I'll discuss it with you ~ you like.* 你什么时候高兴，我都愿意同你讨论这件事情。 **2** on any occasion; as often as; every time that: 于任何时间；每逢；每当: *W~ that man says 'To tell the truth', I suspect that he's about to tell a lie.* 每逢那个人说'说实在话'的时候，我都在怀疑他要说谎了。 **3** or ~, (colloq) or at any time: (口)或任何时间；或任何时候: *He might turn up on Monday, or Friday, or ~, and expect to be given a meal.* 他也许星期一，或星期五，或任何时候来，并可望被招待一餐。

where /weə(r) *US:* hweə; hwɛr/ *interr adv* **1** in or to what place or position; in what direction; in what respect: 在何处或何位置；至何处或何位置；在何方向；在何方面: *W~ does he live?* 他住在何处? *I wonder ~ he lives.* 我即知道他住在何处。 *W~ shall we be* (ie What will be our situation) *if another world war breaks out?* 如果另一场世界大战爆发，我们处境如何? **2** (with a *prep*

following the *v*) what place: (与接在动词之后的介词连用)何处；什么地方: *W~ does he come from?* 他是哪里人? *W~ are you going to?* 你到哪里去? *W~ did we get up to,* ie What point did we reach? 我们到达何种地步了? □ *rel adv* **1** (with *place,* etc as antecedent) in or at which: (以 place 等为其先行词)在那里；在该处: *She would like to live in a country ~ it never snows.* 她喜欢住在不下雪的国家。 *That's the place ~ the accident occurred.* 那就是出事的地点。 **2** (with no antecedent) in, at or to the place in which; in the direction in which: (无先行词)在,于, 或至…的地方; 在…方向或方面: *W~ there is no rain, farming is difficult or impossible.* 在不下雨的地方，农业是困难或根本不可能。 *I found my books ~ I had left them.* 我在我原来放的地方找到了我的书。 *That's ~ ~* (ie the point in respect of which), *you are mistaken.* 那就是你错误的地方了。 **,~·a'bouts** *adv* in or near what place; about which: *W~abouts did you find it?* 你在何处找到(它)的? *I wonder ~abouts he put it.* 我不知道他(把它)放在哪里了。 □ **'~·abouts** *n* (with *sing* or *pl v*) place ~ sb or sth is: (与单数或复数动词连用)下落；某人或某物所在之处；行踪: *Her present ~abouts is/are unknown.* 她现在行止不明。 **,~'as** *conj* **1** (esp legal) considering that. (尤作法律用语)鉴于；既然；就…而论。 **2** but in contrast; while on the other hand: 反之；而在另一方面；却；而: *Some people like fatty meat, ~ others hate it.* 有些人喜欢肥肉，而有些人却不喜欢。 **,~'at** *adv* (old use) at or upon which. (旧用法)在那里；对于那个；关于那个。 **,~'by** *adv* by what; by which: 凭什么；凭那；由是: *He devised a plan ~by he might escape.* 他想出了一个可借以逃走的办法。 **'~·fore** *adv* (old use) why. (旧用法)为何；何故。 **the whys and the ~·fores,** the reasons, causes. 理由；原因。 **,~·'in** *adv* (formal) in what; in which; in what respect: (正式用语)在那里面；在其中；在那点上；在那方面；在什么地方: *W~in am I mistaken?* 我错在什么地方? **,~·'of** *adv* (formal) of what; of which. (正式用语)关于什么；关于那个；关于它。 **,~·'on** *adv* (old use) on which; on what. (旧用法)在那上；在那上面；在什么上面。 **,~·so·'ever** *adv* (emphatic for) ~ver. to wherever 的强势语。 **,~·'to** *adv* (old use) to what; to which; to what end (= purpose). (旧用法)向哪里；向那个；为何目的。 **,~·'unto** *adv* (old use) (旧用法) = ~to. 与~to同。 **,~·'upon** *adv* after which; and then. 因此；于是。 **wher·ever** /,weər'evə(r) *US:* ,hw-; hwɛr'evə/ *adv* in, to, at, whatever place; at those places: 在，到，于任何地方；无论何处；在那些…的地方: *Sit ~ver you like.* 随便坐在那里吧。 *He comes from Boula, ~ver that may be,* from a place called Boula, and I have no idea where it is. 他的老家是个叫'布拉'的地方，我不知道这地方在哪里。 **,~·'with** *adv* (old use) with that; with which. (旧用法)用以；用那个。 **'~·withal** /-wɪðɔ:l ; -wɪðɔ,l/ *adv* (old use) (旧用法) = ~with. 与~with同。 □ *n* **the ~·withal,** (colloq) money needed for a purpose: (口)为某项目的而需要的金钱: *I should like to buy a new car but haven't got the ~withal.* 我希望买一部新汽车，但是还没有筹到那笔钱。

wherry /'werɪ *US:* 'hw-; 'hwɛrɪ/ *n* (*pl* **-ries**) light, shallow rowing-boat for carrying passengers and goods on rivers. 摆渡船；舢板；划艇。

whet /wet *US:* hwet; hwɛt/ *vt* (**-tt-**) [VP6A] sharpen (a knife, axe, etc); (fig) sharpen or excite (the appetite, a desire). 磨，磨快(刀,斧等)；(喻)增益；促进；刺激(胃口，欲望)。 **'~·stone** *n* shaped stone used for sharpening tools, eg scythes. 磨刀石；砥石。

whether /'weðə(r) *US:* 'hw-; 'hwɛðə/ *conj* **1** (introducing an indirect question; ⇨ VP10, 21; often replaced by *if* in colloq style except when there is possible confusion with a true conditional clause): (引导间接疑问句；在口语中常为 if 所代替，但可能与真正条件从句混淆时，不可改用 if): *I don't know ~/if she will be able to come.* 我不知道她是否能来。 *I wonder ~/if it's large enough.* 我想知道它是否够大。 (Note that

when there are two indirect questions with *or*, ~ is repeated after *or*): (注意: 二间接问句由 or 相连时, 在 or 之后, whether 再重复一次): *I wonder ~ we shall be in time for the last bus or ~ we shall have to walk home.* 我不知道我们是否赶得上最后一班公共汽车, 还是必须步行回家. (Compare ~ and *if* in these sentences): (比较下列各句中 whether 与 if 的用法): *Send me a telegram letting me know ~ I am to come,* ie saying 'Come' or 'Don't come'. 拍一个电报给我, 告诉我是否要我来. *Send me a telegram if I am to come,* ie only if I am to come, no telegram being needed if I am not to come. 如果要我来, 拍一个电报给我. **2** (introducing an infinitive phrase; ⇨ VP8, 20): *I don't know ~ to accept or refuse.* 我不知道该接受还是该拒绝. *Would you advise me ~ to accept the offer (or not)?* 请教你, 我该不该接受那项提议? **3** (Clauses and infinitive phrases introduced by ~ are used with preparatory *it*): (以 whether 引导的从句及不定式短语, 可与虚词 it 连用): *It's doubtful ~ we shall be able to come.* 我们是否能来, 尚未确定. (Such clauses and phrases may be subjects or complements): (这种从句或短语, 可作为主语或补语): *The question was ~ to take the children to the funeral or to leave them at home.* 问题是该带孩子们去参加葬礼呢, 还是该把他们留在家里. *W~ to pay the price demanded was a question that worried him a long time.* 该不该按照(对方)所要的价钱付款, 是困扰他很久的一个问题. (Such a clause may be the object of a *prep*): (这种从句也可以作介词的宾语): *Everything depends upon ~ we have enough money.* 一切端视我们是否有足够的钱. *I am not interested in ~ you like the plan or not.* 我不在乎你是否喜欢那项计划. (A clause introduced by ~ may be used in apposition to a *n*): (由 whether 引导的从句, 可以用作名词的同位语): *I am in doubt ~ I ought to give this plan my approval.* 我决定不了是否该同意这项计划. *The question ~ we ought to call in a specialist was answered by the family doctor.* 我们是否应该请一位专家来, 这问题由(我们的)家庭医生答复了. ~ **or no, or not.** ~ or not. **(b)** in either case: 总之, 无论如何: *You may rely upon my help,* ~ or no, eg ~ others agree to help, or refuse to help. 无论如何, 你总可以信赖我的帮助(不管旁人是否答应帮忙, 我总会帮助你的). ~ **or not,** (allowing the negative alternative): 是否; 无论是不是; 不管: *W~ or not it rains, I'm giving a party tomorrow.* 不管下雨不下雨, 明天我都要举行宴会. *Tell me ~ or not I should invite Nick and his wife.* 告诉我, 我应不应该邀请尼克夫妇.

whew /hju; ; hwju *or similar sounds roughly breathed out or whistled* 亦可读作类以此音的粗而猛的呼气声或口哨声/ *int* cry used (often in joke) to express consternation, dismay, fatigue or surprise. 哎呀! 唷! (表示恐怖, 沮丧, 疲劳或惊讶的叫声; 有时系出以玩笑态度).

whey /weɪ US: hweɪ ; hwe/ *n* [U] liquid part of sour milk after separation of curds (for cheese). (酸牛奶在提出制干酪的凝乳后的)乳浆; 乳清.

which /wɪtʃ US: hwɪtʃ ; hwɪtʃ/ *interr adj* (asking for selection from two, or from a group, esp from possibilities thought of as limited in number; ⇨ **what**) (要求从二者或一群, 尤指从有限数目的可能性中, 加以选择) **1** *W~ way shall we go—up the hill or along the river bank?* 我们要走哪一条路——是要爬这个斜坡呢, 还是要沿着河岸走? *W~ way (= How) shall we do it?* 我们要怎么做(它)呢? *W~ Jones do you mean—Jones the baker or Jones the postman?* 你说的是哪一位琼斯先生——做面包师的琼斯, 还是做邮差的琼斯? *W~ foreign languages have you studied?* 你已经学过哪几种外国话? *Tell me ~ ones you want.* 告诉我哪几个是你所需要的. **2** (*rel adj*, formal, and rare except after a *prep;* preceded by a comma) and this; and these: (关系形容词, 为正式用语, 除置于介词之外外, 不常使用; 前面须加逗号)而这一个; 而这些个: *I told him to go to a doctor,* ~ *advice he took,* and this advice he took. 我告诉他该去看医生, 这个意见

他采纳了. *Don't call between 1 o'clock and 2 o'clock, at ~ time I am usually having lunch.* 不要在一点至两点之间来访, 我通常在这段时间吃午饭. □ *interr pron* ~ thing(s); ~ person(s): 何物; 何人; 何者; 哪(些)物; 哪(些)人: *W~ is taller, Mike or Steve?* 谁比较高, 是迈克还是史蒂夫? *W~ of the boys is the tallest?* 这些男孩哪一个最高? *W~ of you wish to go with me?* 你们谁要同我一起去? *Tell me ~ of them is better.* 告诉我, 它们当中哪一个比较好. *Please advise me ~ to take.* 请告诉我该选择哪一个. *The twins are so much alike that I never know ~ is ~,* ie I cannot distinguish one from the other. 这一对双胞胎太相象了, 我分辨不出谁是谁. □ *rel pron* (of things only, not of persons; ⇨ **that**) **1** (in defining or restrictive clauses, often replaced by *that;* used with no selective meaning; no pause before the clause and not set off by commas): (用于限定或限制性从句中, 常用 that 取而代之; 不含选择的意义; 在从句之前不停顿, 也不用逗号分开) **(a)** (with the *rel pron* as the subject of the *v* in the clause): (以此关系代词作从句中的动词的主语): *Take the book ~ is lying on that table.* 把桌子上的那本书拿去. *The house ~ is for sale is at the end of the street.* 出售的房子在街的尽头. *The river ~ flows through London is called the Thames.* 流过伦敦的那条河叫做泰晤士河. **(b)** (with the *rel pron* as the object of the *v* in the clause; in spoken English usually suppressed): (以此关系代词作从句中的动词的宾语; 在口语英文中, 通常略去): *Was the book (~) you were reading a novel?* 你(刚才)读的那一本书是小说吗? **2** (with the *rel pron* as the object of a *prep;* when replaced by *that,* the *prep* follows the *v*; if ~ is used, the *prep* should precede): (以此关系代词作介词的宾语; 如换用 that, 介词须置于动词后; 如用 which, 介词该置于 which 前): *The photographs at ~ you were looking / The photographs (that) you were looking at were all taken by my brother.* 你(刚才)看的那些照片, 全是我哥哥(弟弟)拍摄的. *The hotel at ~ we stayed / The hotel we stayed at was both cheap and comfortable.* 我们住的那家旅馆, 既便宜又舒服. *The book to ~ I wanted to refer / The book I wanted to refer to was not in the library.* 我要参考的那本书, 不在图书馆里. *The shop opposite ~ the car is parked is a grocer's.* 对面停着汽车的那家店铺是一家杂货店. **2** (in non-defining or non-restrictive clauses, rare in the spoken language but common in the written language) ~ is not replaceable by *that;* the clause is preceded by a pause and is set off by commas): (用于非限定或非限制性从句中, 在口语中少见, 但在书面语中常见) ~ 不能用 that 代替; 从句前须稍作停顿, 并须用逗号分开) **(a)** (referring to an antecedent *n*): (先行词为名词): *(i)* (with the *rel pron* as the subject of the clause): (以此关系代词为从句的主语): *This house, ~ is to be sold by auction next month, was built about fifty years ago.* 这房子大约是五十年前造的, 下个月要拍卖. *The meeting, ~ was held in the park, was attended by five hundred people.* 那次集会是在公园里举行的, 有五百人参加. *(ii)* (with the *rel pron* as the object of the *v* in the clause): (以此关系代词作从句中动词的宾语): *These apple-trees, ~ I planted three years ago, have not yet borne any fruit.* 这些苹果树是我三年前种的, 现在未结出果实. *This desk, ~ I bought second-hand, is made of oak.* 我买的这张二手货桌子, 是橡木做的. *(iii)* (with the *rel pron* as the object of a *prep*): (以此关系代词作介词的宾语): *His car, for ~ he paid £8000, is a five-seater saloon.* 他花八千英镑买的那汽车, 是一部有五个座位的轿车. *Their house, at ~ I have often stayed, is just outside Dorking.* 他们的房子就在多金市郊外, 我常住在那里. **(b)** (in non-defining clauses that refer to a clause or sentence, not to a *n*): (在非限定从句中, 涉及一个从句或句子, 而非涉及名词): *It was raining hard,* ~ (= and this) *kept us indoors.* 雨下得很大, 把我们困在家里. *He said he had lost the book,* ~ (= but this) *was untrue.* 他说他把那本书遗失了, 但这是不确实的. (The clause may occasionally precede the sentence to ~ it

refers): (这种从句偶而也可能置于它所指涉的句子之前): *Moreover,* ~ *you may hardly believe, the examiners had decided in advance to fail half the candidates!* 还有, 你可能很难相信, 主试人员事先已经决定要淘汰一半应考人!

which·ev·er /wɪtʃ'evə(r) *US:* hwɪtʃ'evə/ *adj, pron* **1** the one which: ⋯的哪一个: *Take* ~ *you like best.* 挑选你最喜欢的那一个。*W*~ *(of you) comes in first will receive a prize.* (你们之中)哪一个最先到, 就可以得到一个奖品。 **2** no matter which: 无论哪个或哪些; 随便哪个或哪些: *W*~ *of the three sisters you choose to marry, you will have a good wife.* 不论你选择的结婚对象是这三姐妹中的哪一位, 你都会娶到一位贤淑的妻子。*Does British foreign policy remain the same,* ~ *party is in power?* 无论哪一个政党执政英国的外交政策都不会改变吗? **,**which·so·'ever, (emphatic for) ~. 为 whichever 的强势语。

whiff /wɪf *US:* hwɪf; hwɪf/ *n* [C] slight puff or breath (*of* sth): (某物的)一阵; 一吹; 一阵 (of 连用): *a* ~ *of fresh air;* 一阵新鲜空气; *the* ~ (= smell) *of a cigar.* 雪茄烟的气味。*The dentist gave her another* ~ *of anaesthetic.* 牙医再给她一剂麻醉剂。*He stopped work to have a few* ~*s,* a short smoke (of a pipe, etc). 他停止工作, 吸几口烟。

Whig /wɪg *US:* hwɪg; hwɪg/ *n* member of a political party in GB which upheld the authority of Parliament (against the sovereign) during the 17th and 18th cc, their place being taken in the 19th c by the Liberals. 英国维新党党员(该党于十七、八世纪时维护国会权力以对抗君主, 在十九世纪时, 其地位为自党所取代)。

while /waɪl *US:* hwaɪl; hwaɪl/ *n* (*sing* only) (period of) time: (仅用单数)时; 时间; 一段(时间): *Where have you been all this* ~? 这一阵子你一直在哪儿? *I haven't seen him for a long* ~ /for this long ~ past. 我已经很久没有见到他了。*We're going away for a* ~. 我们要出门一阵子。*I'll be back in a little* ~, soon. 我很快就会回来。*He was here a short* ~ ago. 他刚才还在这儿。*once in a* ~, occasionally; 偶而; 偶尔: *worth (one's)* ~, worth the time spent in doing it, etc: 值得(花时间做事): *It isn't worth* ~ *going there now,* ie It would be a waste of time to go. 现在去那儿就不值得了。*He will make it worth your* ~, ie will pay or reward you in some way. 他将会酬谢(回报)你的。□ *vt* [VP15B] (only in) (仅用于) ~ *sth away,* pass (the time) in a leisurely way: 消磨(时间); 闲混(时间): ~ *away the time;* 消磨时间; ~ *a few hours away.* 闲混几小时。□ *conj* **1** during the time that; for as long as; at the same time as: 当⋯的时候; 在⋯之时; 和⋯同时: *He fell asleep* ~ (*he was*) *doing his English exercises.* 他在做英文练习的时候睡着了。*W*~ *in London he studied music.* 他在伦敦的时候研究音乐。*W*~ (= As long as) *there is life there is hope.* 只要有生命就有希望。 **2** (implying a contrast) whereas: (含有相对之意)而; 却; 其实; 反之: *Jane was dressed in brown* ~ *Mary was dressed in blue.* 简穿的是咖啡色衣服, 而玛丽穿的是蓝色衣服。 **3** (implying a concession) although: (含有让步之意)虽然: *W*~ *I admit that the problems are difficult, I don't agree that they cannot be solved.* 虽然我承认这些问题很困难, 但我不同意它们不能解决。 **whilst** /waɪlst *US:* hwaɪlst; hwaɪlst/ *conj* = ~.

whim /wɪm *US:* hwɪm; hwɪm/ *n* [C] sudden desire or idea, often sth unusual or unreasonable: 一时的兴致; 突然的念头; 怪念头; 奇想: *only a passing* ~, an idea, a desire, that will soon pass: 只是一时的想法而已; *full of* ~*s.* 充满了怪念头。*His every* ~ *is complied with/ catered for.* 对他(大家)是百依百顺。

whim·per /'wɪmpə(r) *US:* 'hw- ; 'hwɪmpə/ *vi, vt* **1** [VP2A] utter weak, frightened or complaining sounds, eg a baby when ill, a dog when frightened of punishment. 发出虚弱而惊恐或抱怨的声音; 呜咽; 啜泣 (如幼儿生病, 狗怕惩罚时)。 **2** [VP6A] utter in a ~ing voice. 呜咽而言; 抽噎啜泣着。 □ *n* [C] ~ing; low sobbing sound. 呜咽声; 啜泣声。

whimsy, whim·sey /'wɪmzɪ *US:* 'hw- ; 'hwɪmzɪ/ *n* (*pl* **-sies, -seys**) **1** [C] whim; fanciful idea or wish. 一时的兴致; 怪念头; 奇想。 **2** [U] quaintness; odd or fanciful humour. 古怪; 奇癖; 怪脾气。**whim·si·cal** /'wɪmzɪkl *US:* 'hw- ; 'hwɪmzɪkl/ *adj* full of whimsies; quaint. 多古怪念头或奇想的; 古怪的。 **whim·si·cally** /-klɪ ; -klɪ/ *adv* **whim·si·cality** /,wɪmzɪ'kælətɪ *US:* 'hw- ; ,hwɪmzɪ'kælətɪ/ *n* [U] quality of being whimsical; [C] (*pl* **-ties**) caprice; quaint fancy. 古怪; 反复无常; 怪念头。

whin /wɪn *US:* hw-; hwɪn/ *n* [U] = **gorse**.

whine /waɪn *US:* hwaɪn ; hwaɪn/ *n* [C] long complaining cry or high-pitched sound (eg as made by a miserable dog, a siren, a motor or a shell in flight). 长的抱怨声; 哀鸣声; 呜呜声(如痛苦中的狗, 或汽笛, 或汽车, 或飞行中的炮弹等所发的声音)。□ *vi, vt* **1** [VP2A, C, 4A] make such cries; utter complaints, esp about trivial things: 发哀鸣声; 发呜呜声; 作悲鸣; 抱怨(尤指为了无关紧要之事): *The dog was whining outside the door /whining to come into the room.* 那只狗在门外呜呜地叫(呜呜地叫着要进来室内)。*If that child doesn't stop whining, I'll clobber it!* 如果那孩子再不停止哭叫, 我要狠狠地揍他(她)一顿。 **2** [VP6A, 15B] utter with a ~ or ~s: 以哀声说; 抱怨而言; 哀诉: *beggars whining (out) requests for alms.* 乞丐哀声请求施舍的乞丐们。**~r** *n* animal or person that ~s. 发哀声或呜呜声的动物或人; 哀鸣声; 哀诉者。

whinny /'wɪnɪ *US:* 'hw- ; 'hwɪnɪ/ *n* (*pl* **-nies**) gentle neigh. 马嘶声。□ *vi* (*pt, pp* **-nied**) make such a sound. 嘶叫。

whip[1] /wɪp *US:* hwɪp ; hwɪp/ *n* [C] **1** lash (length of cord, strip of leather etc) fastened to a handle, used for urging a horse on, or for punishing. 鞭(用以策马或惩罚)。**have the** ~ **hand (over sb)** have mastery over; be in a position to control. 控制(某人); 居于操纵⋯的地位。'~**cord** *n* [U] **1** tightly twisted cord used for the lashes of whips. 一种耐穿的毛织品; 马裤呢。 **2** kind of hard-wearing worsted fabric. 一种耐穿的毛织品; 马裤呢。 **2** (also 亦作 **,~·per-'in**) (foxhunting) person who controls the hounds. (猎狐)指挥猎犬的人。 **3** organizing secretary of a political party (in GB and US) with authority over its members to maintain discipline and secure attendance at parliamentary debates and divisions(6); such authority; order given by such a secretary to members of his party to attend a debate and vote: (英美国家政党的)组织秘书或政党干事(有维持纪律及要求该党国会议员出席议会及表决之权); 组织秘书或政党干事的权威; 由其发给该党议员要求参加辩论及投票的命令: *take the Liberal* ~. 就任自由党组织秘书。*The* ~*s are off,* Members may vote as they wish. 议员们可以自由投票(直译: 组织秘书不在场)。*a* **,**three-line '~, urgent order of this kind. (组织秘书或政党干事发出的)紧急命令。 **4** preparation of eggs, cream, etc beaten or whipped(2). 搅打鸡蛋、奶油等所制成的食物; 一种餐后甜食。~·**py** *adj* flexible; springy. 易弯曲的; 有弹性的。

whip[2] /wɪp *US:* hwɪp; hwɪp/ *vt, vi* (**-pp-**) **1** [VP6A, 15A, B] strike with a whip; beat or flog: 鞭打; 笞责; 抽打: ~ *a horse/a child;* 抽打马/(小孩); ~ *a top,* ⇨ **top**[3]. *The rain was* ~*ping the windowpanes,* beating against them. 雨点正打击着窗子的玻璃。*The driver* ~*ped the horses on.* 车夫策马前进。 **2** [VP6A] beat (eggs, cream, etc) with a fork or other utensil to mix thoroughly or to make stiff: 搅打(鸡蛋、奶油等): ~*ped cream.* 搅打过的奶油。 **3** [VP6A] (colloq) defeat. (口)击败。 **4** [VP15B, 2O] take, be taken, move, be moved, suddenly: 突然攫取或被攫取; 突然移动或被移动: *He* ~*ped off his coat.* 他迅速地脱去上衣。*He* ~*ped out a knife.* 他突然抽出一把刀。*The thief* ~*ped the jewels off the counter.* 那贼一下子就拿走了柜台上的珠宝。*The thief* ~*ped round the corner and disappeared in the crowd.* 那贼迅速地转过拐角而消失在人丛中。[VP6A] (GB colloq) steal: (英口)偷; 扒窃: *Someone's* ~*ped my*

purse! 有人偷走了我的钱包! **~ *round for money, etc,*** appeal to friends, members of a club, etc for money to buy a gift, etc. 吁请(朋友,俱乐部会员等)捐款。Hence, 由此产生, **'~-round** *n* such an appeal. 捐款呼吁; 募捐。**5** [VP6A] bind (a stick, a rope-end, etc) with a close, tight covering of thread or string; sew (a seam, the edge of a piece of cloth) with stitches that pass over and over. 紧缠线索于(棍、杖、绳端等); 接缝(结口); 包缝(布边)。**~·ping** *n* [C] beating with a whip as a punishment. 鞭笞(作为惩罚)。**'~·ping-boy** *n* (hist) boy educated with a prince and ~ped when the prince deserved punishment; (hence) scapegoat. (史)陪王子读书而代他受罚的少年; (由此产生)代人受罚者。**'~·ping-post** *n* (hist) post to which persons were tied to be ~ped. (史)绑缚受鞭笞者的柱子。**'~·ping-top** *n* = **top**[3].

whip·per-in /ˌwɪpər ˈɪn *US:* ˈhw- ; ˈhwɪpɚˈɪn/ ⇨ **whip**[1]**(2)**.

whip·per-snap·per /ˈwɪpə snæpə(r) *US:* ˈhw- ; ˈhwɪpɚˌsnæpɚ/ *n* young insignificant person who intrudes upon people and behaves as if he were important. 妄自尊大的年轻人; 自以为了不起的青年。

whip·pet /ˈwɪpɪt *US:* ˈhw-; ˈhwɪpɪt/ *n* dog that looks like a small greyhound, used for racing. 一种赛跑用的狗(形似小猎犬)。

whip-poor-will /ˈwɪp pʊə wɪl *US:* ˈhwɪp pər wɪl ; ˌhwɪpɚˈwɪl/ *n* small American bird whose call (made at night or twilight) is imitative of its name. 美国产的一种怪鸱(夜间或晨昏时发鸣声,宛如其名的发音)。

whir /wɜ:(r) *US:* hw-; hwɝ/ = **whirr.**

whirl /wɜ:l *US:* hw- ; hwɝl/ *vt, vi* **1** [VP15A, B, 2C] (cause to) move quickly round and round: (使)回旋; 旋转: *The wind ~ed the dead leaves about.* 风吹得枯叶在四处回旋。*The leaves came ~ing down in the autumn wind.* 树叶在秋风中旋落。*The dancers ~ed round the room.* 舞者绕室旋转。**2** [VP15A, B, 2C] (cause to) move or travel rapidly (*off, away,* etc): (使)急动; 急走(与 off, away 等连用): *The telegraph poles ~ed past us as the train gathered speed.* 火车的速度增加时, 电线杆急速地在我们面前驰过。*Our friends were ~ed away in Jack's sports-car.* 我们的朋友们迅速地被杰克的跑车载走了。**3** [VP2A, C] (of the brain, the senses) seem to go round and round; (of thoughts) be confused: (指脑筋, 知觉)晕眩; (指思绪)纷乱: *His head ~ed.* 他头昏了。□ *n* (*sing* only) (仅用单数) **1** ~ing movement: 回旋; 旋转: *a ~ of dust/of dead leaves.* 尘土飞扬(枯叶纷飞)。*His brain was in a ~,* (fig) a confused state. (喻)他的脑筋昏了。**2** rapid succession of activities, etc: 连续的快速活动, 等: *the ~ of modern life in a big city;* 大都市现代生活的忙碌; *a ~ of social engagements,* eg parties, receptions. 一连串的社交活动(宴会, 招待会等)。**3** (compounds) (复合词) **'~·pool** *n* place where there are ~ing currents (circular eddies) in the sea, etc (usu drawing floating objects towards its centre). (海上等处的)漩涡。**'~·wind** *n* swift circling current of air in a funnel-shaped column. 旋风。***Sow the wind and reap the ~wind,*** (prov) Do wrong and, as a result, bring severe punishment upon oneself. (谚)恶有恶报; 为非做歹终将得到加倍报应。

whirli·gig /ˈwɜ:lɪgɪg *US:* ˈhw-; ˈhwɝlɪˌgɪg/ *n* **1** kinds of spinning top, 陀螺, ⇨ **top**[3]. **2** revolving motion: 旋转; 旋转运动: *the ~ of time,* the changes of fortune that come with time. 时运的变迁。

whirr /wɜ:(r) *US:* hw-; hwɝ/ *n* (*sing* only) sound (as) of a bird's wings moving quickly, or of wheels, etc turning fast: (仅用单数)呼呼声; 飕飕声(如鸟翼迅速鼓动, 或轮子快速旋转的声音): *the ~ of an aircrafts' propellers.* 飞机螺旋桨的呼呼声。□ *vi* [VP2A, C] make such sounds: 作呼呼声; 发飕飕声; *A bird ~ed past.* 一支鸟飕飕地飞过去了。

whisk /wɪsk *US:* hw- ; hwɪsk/ *n* **1** small brush for removing dust (from clothes etc). (刷去衣服等灰尘用的)小刷帚; 掸帚。**('fly-)~,** brush made of hair for flapping flies away. 赶走苍蝇用的毛掸子。**2** device (eg coiled wire) for whipping eggs, cream, etc. 搅拌蛋、奶油等的金属器; 打蛋器。**3** light brushing movement (eg of a horse's tail). 轻扫动作(如马尾之摆拂); 掸; 挥; 拂。□ *vt, vi* **1** [VP15B] **~ *sb/sth off/away,*** brush quickly and lightly: 轻快地扫开或刷去: *~ the flies off.* 赶走苍蝇。**2** [VP6A] move or sweep quickly through the air: 在空中快速活动或扫动; 拂; 掸; 挥: *The cow ~ed her tail.* 母牛拂动她的尾巴。**3** [VP15B] take (sb) quickly and suddenly: 迅速而突然地带走(某人): *They ~ed him off to prison.* 他们突然把他逮捕下狱。*I was ~ed up to the top floor in an express lift.* 我被一架快速电梯很快地送至顶层。**4** [VP6A] = **whip**[2]**(2)**: *~ eggs.* 打蛋。

whisker /ˈwɪskə(r) *US:* ˈhw-; ˈhwɪskɚ/ *n* **1 ~s,** hair allowed to grow on the sides of a man's face. 颊须; 髯; 连鬓胡子。⇨ **beard(1), moustache. 2** one of the long, stiff hairs growing near the mouth of a cat, rat, etc. (猫, 鼠等的)须; 一根须。***cat's ~s,*** (sl) fine thing or person: (俚)美好的事物; 杰出的人: *He thinks he's the cat's ~s,* He thinks highly of himself. 他自视甚高(自以为了不起)。**~ed** *adj* having ~s. 有颊须的; 有髯的。

whis·key /ˈwɪskɪ *US:* ˈhw-; ˈhwɪskɪ/ *n* (*pl* **~s**) US and Irish spelling of **whisky.** 系 whisky 的美国及爱尔兰拼法。

whisky /ˈwɪskɪ *US:* ˈhw-; ˈhwɪskɪ/ *n* (*pl* **-kies**) (GB and Canadian spelling) (英国及加拿大拼法) [C, U] strong alcoholic drink distilled from malted grain (esp barley or rye); drink of this: 威士忌酒; 一份或一客威士忌酒: *Two whiskies, please.* 请来两份威士忌酒。

whis·per /ˈwɪspə(r) *US:* ˈhw- ; ˈhwɪspɚ/ *vi, vt* **1** [VP2A, 3A, 6A, 14, 19] **~ *(to),*** speak, say (sth), using the breath but no vibration of the vocal cords: (声带不振动而)以气音说(某事物); 低语; 耳语; 私语: *~ (a word) to sb;* 对某人低声说(话); *~ (to sb) that.* 低声(对某人)说。**'~·ing-gallery,** gallery in which a sound made at one point may be heard at another far off (owing to acoustic peculiarities). 耳语廊; 低声廊(由于特殊的传音性质, 在此廊之一处所发的声音, 可在远方他处听到)。**2** [VP6A, 15B] tell privately or secretly; (esp) put (a story, slander) into circulation: 私下述说; 秘密告诉; (尤指)散播(故事, 谣言): *The story is being ~ed about the neighbourhood.* 这故事正在附近流传。*It is ~ed that he is heavily in debt.* 据秘密传闻他负债很多。**'~·ing campaign,** systematic attack on sb by passing from person to person malicious statement, etc. 有计划地散布流言以攻击或诽谤某人。**3** [VP2A, C] (of leaves, the wind, etc) make soft sounds; rustle: (指叶, 风等)作低悄声, 发沙沙声; 飒飒地响: *The wind was ~ing in the pines.* 风在松林中飒飒作响。□ *n* **1** ~ing sound or speech: 低悄的声音或话语: *He answered in a ~.* 他低声回答。*They were talking in ~s.* 他们在悄悄地谈话。**2** ~ed remark; sth ~ed secretly; rumour: 耳语; 私语; 传闻: *W~s are going round that the firm is likely to go bankrupt.* 传闻那家公司可能倒闭。**~er** *n*

whist /wɪst *US:* hwɪst ; hwɪst/ *n* card-game like bridge[2] for two pairs of players. 惠斯特(由两对参加者所玩的一种纸牌戏, 类似桥牌)。**'~-drive** *n* series of games played by several sets of partners at different tables, certain players after each round passing to the next table. 数组合伙人在不同的桌上所玩的一连串的纸牌戏(某些参与者在一局终, 转至次一桌)。

whistle /ˈwɪsl *US:* ˈhw- ; ˈhwɪsl/ *n* **1** (usu steady) clear note made by forcing air or steam through a small opening, or made by the wind; tuneful sound made by some kinds of bird (eg the blackbird): (通常为稳定的)口哨声; 口笛声; 汽笛声; 警笛声; 风啸声; (画眉等的)鸟鸣声: *We heard the ~ of a steam-engine.* 我们听到火车头的汽笛声。**'~-stop** *n* (US) short stop (during a journey made by a politician) for electioneering purposes (eg to speak to voters in a rural district):

(美)(从政者旅行期间)为竞选活动(如对乡区选民演讲)所作的短暂停留: (attrib)(用作定语) *a ~stop tour.* 作短暂停留的竞选旅行。**2** instrument for producing such sounds: 口笛; 汽笛; 警笛; 哨子: *the referee's ~;* 裁判的哨子: *a 'steam-~,* sounded by a jet of steam. 汽笛。**3** *wet one's ~,* (sl) have a drink. (俚) 润喉; 喝杯酒。□ *vi, vt* **1** [VP2A, C] make a ~(1) (eg by blowing through the rounded lips or by using a (2): 吹口哨; 吹哨子; 发口笛声: 鸣笛: *The engine/The driver ~d before reaching the level-crossing.* 火车机车(司机)在抵达平交道之前先鸣笛。*The wind ~d through the rigging/up the chimney, etc.* 风呼呼吹过缆索(烟囱等上)。~ *for sth,* wish in vain for: 空想获得; 徒然希望得到: *I owe my butcher £10, but he can ~ for it,* I shan't pay him. 我欠肉商十英镑, 但他休想得到这笔钱。**2** [VP2A, C, 6A] produce a tune in this way: 用口哨吹奏(曲调): ~ *a tune.* 吹出一个曲子。*The boy was whistling (away) merrily.* 那男孩愉快地吹着口哨(离开了)。~ *down the wind,* abandon sth. 放弃某事物。~ *in the dark,* do sth to overcome one's fears. 做某事给自己壮胆。**3** [VP6A, 15B, 16A] ~ *(up),* make a signal (to) by whistling: 用口哨声、笛声、哨声等(向…)作信号: *He ~d his dog back/~d to his dog to come back to him/~d up his dog.* 他用口哨召唤他的狗叫来(召唤他的狗回到他身边)。**4** [VP2A, C] pass swiftly with a whistling sound: 发啸声快速通过或经过: *The bullets/arrows ~d past our ears.* 枪弹(箭)飕飕地从我们耳边飞过。

whit /wɪt US: hwɪt; hwɪt/ *n not a ~; no ~,* not the least, not at all: not a ~; no ~: *There's not a ~ of truth in the statement.* 该项陈述没有一点点真实性。*I don't care a ~.* 我一点也不介意。

Whit /wɪt US: hwɪt; hwɪt/ *n* ⇨ **Whitsun.**

white¹ /waɪt US: hwaɪt; hwaɪt/ *adj* **1** of the colour of fresh snow or common salt: 白的; 白色的; 雪白的: *His hair has turned ~.* 他的头发已变白了。*Her face went ~,* pale. 她的面色变得苍白。~ *bleed (sb/sth)~,* (fig) drain (sb/sth) of wealth, strength, etc. (喻) 耗尽(某人, 某物)的财富, 力量等; 榨尽(某人)的血汗; 用尽(某物)的物力。**2** (special uses, compounds) (特殊用法, 复合词) '~ *alloy,* any of various alloys that are cheap imitations of silver. 假银(类似银的便宜合金)。'~ *ant,* termite. 白蚁; 蠹。'~*·bait n* [U] small fish, the young of several varieties, eaten fried when small (about 2 inches long). 欧洲小鲱鱼; 银鱼(数种鱼类的幼鱼, 长约二英寸, 用油炸食)。'~ *bear,* polar bear. 北极熊。'~*·caps n pl* waves at sea with ~ foam on their crests. 白帽浪(波峰有白色泡沫的海浪)。~ *collar,* used as a symbol of non-manual labour. 白领阶级(指不从事体力劳动者): ~*collar jobs/workers.* 劳心的工作(工作者); 脑力工作(脑力工作者)。⇨ *blue-collared at* blue²(7). ~ *coffee,* with milk added. 加牛奶的咖啡。~ *'elephant,* '*ensign,* '*feather,* ⇨ these nouns. 参看这些名词。~ *flag,* symbol of surrender. 白旗(投降的标帜)。~ *heat,* high temperature at which metals become ~; (fig) intense passion. 白热; 炽热(金属变为白色的高温); (喻)激情; 高度紧张的情绪。Hence, 由此产生, ~*·hot adj.* the 'W~ House, the official residence of the President of the US, in Washington, DC; (hence) US Government (policy). 白宫(美国总统府); (由此产生)美国政府(政策)。~ *lead* a poisonous compound of lead carbonate, used in paints. 白铅(碳酸铅, 有毒, 用于涂料中)。~ *lie,* lie considered to be harmless, esp one told for the sake of being polite: 小谎; 无恶意的谎言; (尤指)不实的客气话: *She tells enough ~ lies to ice a wedding-cake!* 她撒了许多小谎只为了在结婚蛋糕上加一层糖霜! '~*·lipped adj* having ~ lips, esp with fear. (尤指因害怕而)嘴唇发白的。'~*·livered adj* cowardly. 怯懦的; 胆小的。'~ *'magic,* ⇨ magic. '~ *man/woman,* European person. 白种人; 欧洲人。~ *meat,* poultry, veal, pork. 白肉(家禽肉, 小牛肉, 猪肉)。~ *metal,* ~ alloy. 白色合金; 假银。~ *paper,* (GB) report issued by the

Government to give information. (英)白皮书(英国政府的报告书)。~ *sepulchre,* (from Matt 23: 27) person who appears to be righteous but is in fact wicked; hypocrite. 粉饰的坟墓(见新约马太福音23章27节); 伪君子; 假冒为善的人。~ *slave,* ~ girl who is forced to be a prostitute, esp one who is tricked into going to a foreign country by promises of employment: 白奴(指被迫为娼的白种女子, 尤指以工作为饵被骗至外国者); 白种妓女: *the ~-'slave traffic.* 白奴交易(贩卖白种女子为娼的买卖)。'~*·thorn n* hawthorn. 山楂。~ *tie,* ~ bow tie worn with men's full evening dress; (short for) full evening dress: (男性穿着正式晚礼服所用的)白色领结; 男性正式晚礼服(的简称): *Is it dinner jacket or ~ tie?* 那是一般晚礼服还是正式晚礼服? '~*·wash n* [U] mixture of powdered lime or chalk and water, used for coating walls, ceilings, etc; (fig) means used to cover or hide sb's errors, faults, etc. 石灰水; 白粉水; 白涂料(用于粉刷墙壁, 天花板等); (喻)掩饰过失、错误等的方法。□ *vt* put ~wash on (a wall, etc); (fig) try to make (sb, his reputation, etc) appear blameless by covering up his faults, etc. 粉刷(墙壁等); (喻)粉饰(某人, 其名声等)。

white² /waɪt US: hwaɪt ; hwaɪt/ *n* **1** [U] ~ colour: 白; 白色: *dressed in ~.* 穿着白衣。**2** [C] ~ person. 白种人。**3** [C, U] colourless part round the yolk of an egg: 蛋白: *Take the ~s of two eggs.* 吃两个蛋的蛋白。*There's too much ~ of egg in this mixture.* 这混合物中的蛋白太多了。**4** [C] the ~ part of the eyeball: 眼白; 白眼珠: *Don't fire until you see the ~s of their eyes,* until they are very close. 等他们非常接近时再射击。~*·ness n* ~n [U] /waɪtn US: 'hwaɪtn/ *vt, vi* [VP6A, 2A] make or become ~. 使白; 变白; 漂白; 刷白。

White·hall /waɪt'hɔːl US: hw- ; 'hwaɪt'hɔːl/ *n* (street in London where there are) Government offices; (hence) British Government (policy). 白厅(伦敦的一条街道, 为政府机关所在地); 政府机关; (由此产生)英国政府(政策)。

whit·en·ing /'waɪtnɪŋ US: 'hw- ; 'hwaɪtnɪŋ/ *n* [U] = whiting².

whither /'wɪðə(r) US: 'hw- ; 'hwɪðər/ *adv* (old use) to which place; (current use, rhet, or in journalism) what is the likely future of: (旧用法)向何处; 往何处; (现代用法, 修辞或报纸用语)未来可能如何; …的将来可能会怎么样; 什么是…的可能前途: *W~ Ulster?* 阿尔斯特未来可能如何? *W~ the pound sterling?* 英镑的前途可能会怎样? ~*so·'ever adv* (old use) to whatever place; anywhere at all. (旧用法)到或往任何地方; 无论何处。

whit·ing¹ /'waɪtɪŋ US: 'hw- ; 'hwaɪtɪŋ/ *n* (*pl* unchanged) kinds of small sea-fish used as food. (复数不变)鳕类。

whit·ing² /'waɪtɪŋ US: 'hw- ; 'hwaɪtɪŋ/ *n* [U] powdered white chalk used in whitewashing, and for polishing silver, etc. (用于粉刷及擦亮银器等的)白垩粉; 白粉。

whit·low /'wɪtləʊ US: 'hw- ; 'hwɪtloʊ/ *n* small inflamed place on a finger or toe, esp near the nail. 脓性指头炎(尤指在指甲附近的); 指头疽; 瘭疽。

Whit·sun /'wɪtsn US: 'hw- ; 'hwɪtsn/ *n* (also 亦作 ,Whit 'Sunday) 7th Sunday after Easter, the feast of the Pentecost. 圣灵降临节(复活节后第七个星期天)。~*·tide* /-taɪd ; -ˌtaɪd/ *n* ~ and the weekend or the following week. 圣灵降临周(包括圣灵降临节及周末或随后的一周)。

whittle /'wɪtl US: 'hw- ; 'hwɪtl/ *vt, vi* **1** [VP15B, 2C, 3A] ~ *(sth) away,* cut thin slices or strips off, eg wood; (fig) reduce. 削切或削掉(某物, 如木材等); (喻)削减; 逐渐减少: ~ *(away) at sth,* cut at sth in this way: 削; 削切; *He was whittling at a piece of wood.* 他正在削一块木头。~ *sth down,* reduce the size of by cutting away slices, etc; (fig) reduce the amount of: 削小; (喻)削减: *They won't dare to ~ down our salaries.* 他们不敢裁我们的薪。**2** [VP6A, 15A] make or shape by whittling: 削切成; 削削成: *The boy ~d a whip handle from a branch/*

~*d a branch into a whip handle.* 那个男孩把一根树枝削成一个鞭柄.

whiz /wɪz US: hwɪz ; hwɪz/ *vi* [VP2C] (**-zz-**), *n* [U] (make the) sound of sth rushing through the air: 物体掠过空中的声音; 飕飕声; 发放飕声: *The arrows/shells ~zed past.* 箭(炮弹)飕飕地飞过.

whizz-kid /'wɪz kɪd US: 'hw- ; 'hwɪz ,kɪd/ *n* (sl) bright, inventive young person with progressive ideas who achieves rapid success. (俚)出身青年;天才儿童;神童.

who /hu: ; hu/ *interr pron* (used as the subject, and only of persons; object form **whom** /hu:m; hum/) (用作主语,且仅用到j指人;宾格形式为 whom) **1** *Who is that man?* 那个人是谁? *Who are those men?* 那些人是谁? *I wonder who those people are.* 我想知道那些人是谁. *Who broke the window?* 谁把窗子打破了? *Do you know who broke the window?* 你知道窗子是谁打破的吗? *Who do you think he is?* 你认为他是谁? *(know) ,who's 'who,* (know) who people are, what they do, etc. (知道)谁是谁; (知道)谁是有影响力的人物等. **2** (*Whom* is used in formal and literary style, but is usually replaced by *who* in ordinary colloq style): (whom 用于正式的及文学的文体中, 一般通俗文体中常可用 who 代替): *To whom did you give it?* 你把它交给谁了? *Who did you give it to?* 你把它交给谁了? *Who(m) did you see?* 你看到谁了? *Who(m) do you think I met in the post-office this morning?* 你猜今天早晨我在邮局遇到谁了? *I don't know to whom I ought to address the request.* 我不晓得该向谁作此请求. *I don't know who I ought to address the request to.* 我不晓得该向谁作此请求. *Who else did you see?* 你还看见谁了? □ *rel pron* **1** (in difining, or restrictive, clauses) (用于限定从句中;参看有时可代替 who 的 that³): *This is the man who/These are the men who wanted to see you.* 这(这些)就是要见你的那个人(那些人). (After there + to be the *rel pron* 'who' may be omitted: 在 there + to be 之后, 关系代词 who 可省略: *There's somebody (who) wants you on the telephone.* 有人来电话找你. *There was a man (who) called to see you while you were out.* 你出去的时候, 有一个人来看你). **2** (*Whom* is often replaced by *that* except after a *prep*: the *prep* may be placed at the end and *that* used for whom): (whom 常被 that 代替, 但紧接在介词之后, 不可改用 that; 如将介词移至句末, 则可用 that 代替 whom): *That is the man (whom) I met in London last year.* 那就是我去年在伦敦碰见的那个人. *That is the man about whom we were speaking.* 那就是我们刚才在谈论的那个人. *That's the man (that) we were speaking about.* 那就是我们刚才在谈论的那个人. *I know the man (whom) you mean.* 我知道你(的意思)指的是谁. **3** (in non-defining clauses, not replaceable by *that;* clause et off by the use of commas or placed in parentheses): (在非限定从句中, 不可用 that 代替; 从句用逗号分开或置于括号中): *My wife, who has been abroad recently, hopes to see you soon.* 内子刚从海外归来, 她希望很快见到你. *My brother, whom you met the other day, has recently written a book on Indian art.* 前几天你曾遇见家兄(舍弟), 他最近写了一本关于印度艺术的书. *Our new neighbours, to whom I was introduced yesterday, have come here from Yorkshire.* 我们的新邻居是从约克郡搬来的, 昨天我被介绍与他们相识. **4** (independent relative) (独立关系词) *Whom* (= Those whom) *the gods love die young,* Those who are specially favoured by Providence die young. 神所眷爱者常夭折(好人不长寿).

whoa /wəu; hwo/ *int* ⇨ **wo.**

who'd /hu:d; hud/ = who had; who would

who·dun·it /,hu:'dʌnɪt; hu'dʌnɪt/ *n*[sl] (= *who done it*, sl for *who did it*)detective or mystery story. (俚)(= who done it, 在俚语中代替 who did it) 侦探小说; 神秘小说.

who·ever/ hu:'evə(r); hu'evə/ *pron* any person who; the person who: 任何人; 不论谁; …的人. *W~ says that is wrong.* 说那话的人是错误的. *W~ else may object, I*

shall approve. 不管旁人会不会反对, 我是赞成的.

whole /həul; hol/ *adj* **1** not injured or damaged; unbroken: 完整的; 齐全的; 未受伤的; 未损坏的; 未破损的: *You're lucky to escape with a ~ skin.* 你能安然脱险,真是幸运. *There isn't a ~ plate*(=a plate that is not chipped, cracked, broken, etc) *in the house.* 家里竟没有一只完整的盘子. (Because ⇨ (3) means 'all', ~(1) is sometimes placed after the *n.* 因为 whole 的第 3 义作 'all' 解时, whole 作第 1 义解有时可放在名词后面. Cf: 参较 *He swallowed the plum ~,* without chewing it. 他把那个梅子整个吞下去了(未咀嚼). *He ate the ~ loaf,* all of it. 他吃下了一整条面包. *The ox was roasted ~,* without being cut up into joints. 那条公牛是整条烘烤的. *They ate the ~ ox,* all of it. 他们把那条牛吃得光光. *Snakes swallow their victims ~.* 蛇把捕获物整个吞下.) **go the ~ hog,** ⇨ **hog.** **2** entire; complete: 全部;完全. *I waited for a ~ hour.* 我等了整整一个钟头. '~ **food** *n* [U] food that is nutritious and free of artificial substances: (未加人工物质之) 营养食品: (attrib)(用作定语) *a ~ food restaurant/shop.* 营养食品餐厅(商店). ~ **note** *n* [C] (US) semibreve. 全音符. ~ **'number** *n* [C] undivided quantity; integer. 未分割的量; 整数. '~**-meal, ~-'wheat** *nn* [C] flour containing everything in the grain, with nothing extracted. (没有去麸的) 粗面粉; 营养面粉. **3** (attrib only, with a *sing n*) (仅用作定语, 置于单数名词前)**the/one's~,** all that there is of; complete: 所有…的; 全部的: *I want to know the ~ truth about this matter.* 我要知道这件事的全部真相. *The ~ country* (=Everyone in the country)*was anxious for peace.* 全国上下都渴望和平. *I didn't see him the ~ evening.* 我整晚未见到他. *He gave his ~ attention* (= all of his attention) *to the problem.* 他全神贯注在那个问题上. *You haven't eaten the ~ lot* (= all of it, all of them), *have you?* 你尚未全部吃光, 是不是? *do sth with one's ~ heart,* do it with concentrated efforts, undivided attention. 全心全力做某事. Hence, 由此产生, **whole-'hearted(ly),** *adj, adv* **4**(attrib with a *pl n*)not less or fewer than; nothing less than:(用作定语,与在复数名词前)不少于…的; 整整的: *It rained for three ~ days.* 整整下了三天雨. *Give your ~ energies to the task.* 把你全副精力用到那件工作上去. *W~* (= Complete)*regiments surrendered to the enemy.* 整团整团的军队向敌人投降了. **5**(old use;biblical) in good health; well: (旧用法;圣经用词)身体好的; 健康的; 无恙的: (attrib用) *They that are ~ need not a physician.* 健康的人不需要医生. *His hand was made ~.* 他的手被治好了. □ *n* thing that is complete in itself; all that there is of something: 完整事物; 整体; 全部; 全数: *Four quarters make a ~.* 四个四分之一构成全部. *A ~ is greater than any of its parts.* 全量大于分量. *The ~* (= All) *of my money was stolen.* 我的钱都被偷去了. *He spent the ~ of that year in Pakistan.* 他在巴基斯坦度过了那一整年. *Is the land to be divided up or sold as a ~?* 那块土地将予以分割, 还是整个地出售? *on the ~,* taking everything into consideration. 从整体来看; 大体上. *(taken) as a ~,* (considered) all together, not separately. 全部地(加以考虑); 总体上(看来). **wholly** /'həullɪ; 'holɪ/ *adv* completely; entirely: 完全地; 全部地: *Few men are wholly bad.* 很少人是完全坏的. *I wholly agree.* 我完全同意.

whole·sale /'həulseɪl; 'hol,sel /*n* (usu attrib) selling of goods (esp in large quantities) to shopkeepers, for resale to the public. ▷ **retail.** (通常用作定语) 批发; 趸售:*sell by ~*(US 美 *at* ~);批售; 趸售; 批发价格; *a ~ dealer.* 批发商. □ *adj, adv* on the ~ plan;(fig) on a large scale: 批发的(地); 趸售的(地); (喻)大规模的(地): *Our business is ~ only.* 我们只做批发生意. *We buy goods ~.* 我们系大批购货. *Ther's was a ~ slaughter when the police opened fire.* 警察开火造成了大规模屠杀. ~**r** *n* one who sells by ~. 批发商.

Whole·some /'həulsəm; 'holsəm/ *adj* healthy; favourable to the health (bodily or moral); suggesting good

health: 健康的; 有益于(身心)健康的; 显示健康的; 卫生的: ~ *food/exercise/surroundings*; 有益于健康的食物(运动, 环境); *a* ~ *appearance*; 健康的外表; ~ *advice*. 有益的忠言.

who'll /huːl/; hul/ = who will.

whom /huːm; hum/ ⇨ **who.**

whoop /huːp; hup/ *n* [C] **1** loud cry: 大叫; 呼喊; 呐喊: ~*s* of joy. 欢呼. **2** gasping sound heard during a fit of coughing. (咳嗽时的)喘息声; 哮喘声. **'~·ing-cough** *n* [U] children's disease with gasping coughs and long, noisy indrawing of breath. (小儿的)百日咳. □ *vi, vt* utter a loud cry or yell: 高喊; 大叫; 呐喊; 高声说: *to* ~ *with joy.* 欢呼. ~ *it up* /wuːp US: hwʊp; hup/, (sl) have a hilarious time. (俚)欢闹; 狂欢.

whoopee /'wʊpiː; 'hwʊpi/ *n* **make ~,** (sl) take part in noisy rejoicing. (俚)欢闹; 狂欢.

whop /wɒp US: hwɒp; hwɑp/ *vt*(**-pp-**) [VP6A] (sl) beat; defeat. (俚)打败; 击败. ~**·per** *n* anything unusually big, esp a big lie. 特大物; (尤指)漫天大谎. ~**·ping** *adj* very large of its kind: 特大的; 极大的: *a* ~*ping lie.* 大谎. □ *adv* very: 非常; 极: *a* ~*ping big fish.* 非常大的鱼.

who're /'huːə(r); hur/ = who are.

whore /hɔː(r); hor/ *n* △ (derog) prostitute. (讳) (贬) 娼妓.

whorl /wəːl US: hw~; hwɜl/ *n* ring of leaves, petals, etc round a stem of a plant; one turn of a spiral, eg as seen on the shell of a mollusc or on a fingerprint: 轮生体;环生体(环生在植物茎或梗四周的叶或瓣等); 螺纹; 涡旋: *identify a criminal by the* ~*s of his fingerprints.* 由指纹的螺纹辨认罪犯. ~**ed** *adj* having ~; arranged in ~s. 有轮生体或环生体的; 有螺纹的; 有涡旋的; 排列成轮生体或涡旋的.

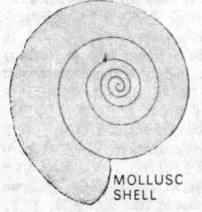

MOLLUSC SHELL

FINGERPRINT

whorls

who's /huːz; huz/ = who is; who has.

whose /huːz; huz/ *poss pron* (⇨ **who**) of whom; of which. 谁的; 何者的. **1** *W*~ *house is that?* 那是谁的房子? *I wonder* ~ *house that is.* 我想知道那是谁的房子. **2** (in rel, defining clause): (用于限定关系从句中): *Is that the man* ~ *house was broken into by burglars last week?* 那就是上星期遭夜贼侵入其住宅的那个人吗? *The boy* ~ *father complained to me is very stupid.* 他父亲向我诉过苦的那个男孩非常愚笨. **3** (*W*~ is sometimes used in place of the usual *of which,* but it is often better to use a different construction, as shown below): (whose 有时用来替代通常所使用的 of which, 但是使用项目外不同的结构常常更好, 见下列例句): *the house* ~ *windows are broken,* the house with the broken windows; 窗子破了的房屋; *that dictionary* ~ */of which the cover has come off,* that dictionary without a cover. 封面脱落的那本词典. **4** (in rel, nondefining clause): (在非限定关系从句中): *Members of the Fire Service,* ~ *work is often dangerous, are paid less than members of the Police Force.* 消防人员的待遇比警员低, 但是他们的工作时常是很危险的. *Mr Hamilton,* ~ *car I borrowed for this journey, is a rich lawyer.* 汉密尔顿先生是一位富有的律师, 我这次旅行就是借用他的汽车.

who·so /'huːsəʊ; 'huso/, **who·so·ever** /ˌhuːsəʊ-'evə(r); ˌhuso'sʌo/ *pron* (old use) (旧用法) = **whoever.**

why /waɪ US: hwaɪ; hwaɪ/ *adv* **1** (interr) for what reason; with what purpose: (疑问副词)何故; 为什么; 有何目的: *Why was he late?* 他为什么迟到? *Do you know why he was late?* 你知道他为什么迟到吗? *Tell me why.* 告诉我为什么. *Why not let her do as she likes?* 为什么不让她想怎么做就怎么做呢? **2** (rel adv): (关系副词): *The reasons why he did it are obscure.* 他做那事的理由还不清楚. *This is (the reason) why I left early.* 这就是我早退的原因. *Why you should always arrive late I don't know.* 我不知道你为什么总是迟到. □ *int* **1** (expressing surprise) (表示惊讶): *Why, it's quite easy! A child could do it!* 啊, 那很容易! 小孩子也会(做它)! **2** (expressing protest): (表示异议或抗议): *Why, What's the harm? is there's no harm in it, is there?* 怎么, 有什么不好吗? □ *n* (*pl* whys) reason or cause. 理由或原因. **the whys and the wherefores,** the reasons, causes. 原由; 理由; 原因.

wick /wɪk; wɪk/ *n* [C, U] (length of) thread through a candle, the top end of which is lit, to burn with a light-giving flame; (strip of) woven material by which oil is drawn up in some cigarette lighters, an oil-lamp or oil-stove to burn: 蜡烛芯; 灯芯; 油头芯(燃烧发光部分); (有些打火机, 油灯, 或油炉的)油绳; 吸油绳: *trim the* ~ *of an oil-lamp.* 修剪油灯的芯子.

wicked /'wɪkɪd; 'wɪkɪd/ *adj* **1** (of a person, his acts) bad; wrong; immoral: (指人, 其行为)坏的; 错的; 不道德的; 缺德的; 邪恶的: *It was* ~ *of you to torment the poor cat.* 你折磨那只可怜的猫真缺德. **2** spiteful; intended to injure: 有恶意的; 意欲加害的: *a* ~ *blow.* 恶意的一击. **3** roguish; mischievous: 淘气的; 恶作剧的: *She gave me a* ~ *look.* 她朝我淘气地看了一眼. ~**·ly** *adv* ~**·ness** *n*

wicker /'wɪkə(r); 'wɪkɚ/ *n* [U] (usu attrib) twigs or canes woven together, usu for baskets and furniture: (通常用作定语)编制篮子及家具的小枝; 枝条; 柔枝; 柳条: *a* ~ *chair.* 柳条椅. **'~·work** *n* [U] things made of ~. 柳条制品.

wicket /'wɪkɪt; 'wɪkɪt/ *n* [C] **1** ~**(-'door/-'gate,** small door or gate, esp one at the side of, or made in, a larger one. 边门; 便门; (尤指大门旁边或大门上的)小门. **2** small opening (eg one with a sliding window) at which tickets are sold. 售票口; 售票处(如有拉窗者). **3** (cricket) either of the two pairs of three stumps (with crosspieces called *bails*) at which the ball is bowled, ⇨ the illus at **cricket**; stretch of grass between two ~s: (板球)三柱though(其横木称作 *bails*) (参看 cricket 之插图); 两个三柱门之间的场地: *take a* ~, act as ~-keeper. 击败一个击球员. *A soft* ~ (= soft ground between ~s) *helps the bowler.* 柔软的板球场有助于投球手. *Surrey were four* ~*s down,* Four or their batsmen were out. 萨里队有四位击球员被判出局了. *We won by six* ~*s,* won with seven of our batsmen not out. 我们因七位击球员未被判出局而获胜. **keep** ~, act as ~-keeper. 防守三柱门. **'~-keeper** *n* player who stands behind the ~ to stop balls not struck by the batsman, to catch batsmen out, etc. 三柱门之守门员; 守门员. **4** (US) croquet hoop. (美) 槌球戏中的弓形小铁门.

wide /waɪd; waɪd/ *adj* (**-r, -st**) **1** measuring much from side to side or in comparison with length; broad: 宽广的; 广阔的: *a* ~ *river;* 宽阔的河; *a road twelve feet* ~. 十二英尺宽的路. **2** of great extent; comprehensive: 广大的; 广泛的; 渊博的: *a man with* ~ *interests,* 兴趣广泛的人; *the* ~ *world;* 广大的世界; *the* ~ *Atlantic;* 广阔的大西洋; *a* ~ *selection of new books.* 类别繁多供选择的新书. **3** fully opened: 张大的; 完全张开的: *She stared at him with* ~ *eyes.* 她睁大了眼睛注视他. *Open your mouth* ~. 张大你的嘴. **4** far from what is aimed at or from a specific point: 远离目标的; 差得远的: *a* ~ *ball,* (in cricket) one judged by the umpire to be out of the batsman's reach. (板球)(裁判员判定的)远球 (击球员不能打中的球). *Your answer was* ~ *of the mark.* 你的回答离题太远了. **5** (sl) shrewdly aware of business chances; unscrupulous. (俚)老奸巨滑

的;不择手段的。 **~ boy,** (sl)such a man. (俚)老奸巨滑的人;不择手段的人。 **~** adv **1** far from the point aimed at: close to/far from the mark: *The arrow fell ~ of the mark.* 那支箭落在距离目标很远的地方。 **2** fully: 完全地; 充分地: *He was ~ awake.* 他完全清醒了。 *The window was ~ open.* 那窗子是大开着的。 **~-a·wake** adj (fig) alert, vigilant: 机警的; 警戒着的: *a ~-awake young woman,* one who realizes what is going on, etc and is not easily deceived. 机警的年轻女子。 **3** over a large area: 广及地; 辽阔地; *travel far and ~.* 到处旅行。 **'~-spread** adj (esp) found, distributed, over a large area. (尤指)广布的; 遍及的; 流传广的。 **~·ly** adv **1** at intervals: 间隔地: *~ly scattered.* 分散地。 Cf 参较 *scattered far and ~.* 分布远而广的。 **2** to a large extent or degree: 达到大范围或程度; 大大地: *~ly different;* 大不相同的; *differing ~ly in opinions.* 意见极不相同。 **3** over a large area: 广泛地; 广及地: *It is ~ly known that....* 很多人知道…。 **~n** /'waɪdn; 'waɪdn/ vt, vi [VP6A, 2A] make or become ~(r): 加宽; 弄宽; 变宽; 扩展: *'road~ning in process.* 正在进行的道路拓宽工程。

wid·geon /'wɪdʒən; 'wɪdʒən/ n kind of wild fresh-water duck 水凫; 赤颈凫(一种淡水野鸭)。

widow /'wɪdəʊ; 'wɪdo/ n woman who has not married again after her husband's death. 寡妇; 孀妇。 **~er** n man who has not married again after his wife's death. 鳏夫。 **widowed** /'wɪdəʊd; 'wɪdod/ adj made into a ~ or ~er: 寡居的; 鳏居的; 丧失配偶的: *~ed by war.* 由于战争而丧失配偶的。 **'~·hood** /-hʊd; -,hʊd/ n state of, time of being, a ~. 孀居; 守寡。

width /wɪtθ; wɪθ/ n [U] **1** [U] quality or state of being wide: 广; 宽; 广阔的性质或状态: *a road of great ~;* 很宽的一条路; (fig)(喻) *~ of mind/intellect/views.* 心胸(悟力,见解)的广阔。 Cf 参较 *broadminded, broad views.* **2** measurement from side to side: 广度; 宽度: *a of 10 metres;* 十米宽; *10 metres in ~.* 宽十米。 **3** [C] piece of material of a certain ~ 有一定宽度的一幅布料: *join two ~s of cloth;* 接合两幅布; *curtain material of various ~s.* 宽度不同的窗帘布。

wield /wi:ld; wild/ vt [VP6A] have and use: 使用;挥舞: *~ an axe;* 挥斧; *~ power/authority/control.* 运用权力(权威;控制)。

wife /waɪf; waɪf/ n (pl **wives** /waɪvz; waɪvz/) married woman, esp in relation to her husband: 妻; 已婚妇女: *Smith and his ~;* 史密斯夫妇; *the baker's ~;* 面包师的妻子; *a club for young wives.* 年轻太太俱乐部。 **old wives' tales,** foolish or superstitious story, usu traditional. 老妇谈; 荒诞故事; 迷信而愚昧的故事。 **~** also *fish~* at **fish**[3], *house~* at **house**[1](7). **'~-like,** **~·ly** adj(of, like, suitable for, a ~: 妻子的; 已婚妇女的; 似妻子的; 适于妻子的: *~ly virtues/duties.* 妇德(妻子的职责)。

wig /wɪg; wɪg/ n head-covering of false hair (as worn to hide baldness, and by actors, barristers and judges, and formerly worn as a fashionable ornament in Europe during the 17th and 18th cc). 假发(秃子,演员, 律师, 法官等所戴者); 在十七、十八世纪时, 欧洲流行戴假发为时髦装饰)。 **~** the illus at **judge.** 参看 judge 之插图。 **wigged** /wɪgd; wɪgd/ adj wearing a wig. 戴假发的。

wig·ging /'wɪgɪŋ; 'wɪgɪŋ/ n (colloq) scolding:(口)骂; 叱责: *get/give sb a good ~.* 挨(给与某人)一顿痛骂。

wiggle /'wɪgl; 'wɪgl/ vt, vi [VP6A, 2A] (cause to) move with quick, short, side-to-side movements: (使)短而快地摆动; 快速扭动: *The baby was wiggling its toes.* 那婴儿正在扭动脚趾。 *Stop wiggling and sit still.* 不要摇摆, 静静地坐着。 **~** n wiggling movement. 快速摆动或摇动。

wight /waɪt; waɪt/ n (archaic) person; human being: (古)人; 家伙: *a luckless ~.* 不幸的家伙。

wig·wam /'wɪgwæm US: -wɑːm; 'wɪgwɑm/ n hut or tent made by fastening skins or mats over a framework of poles, as formerly used by N American Indians. (北美印第安人昔时用木棍作架,蒙以兽皮或草席的)帐篷; 小屋。

wild /waɪld; waɪld/ adj (-er, -est) **1** ⇨ the illus at **cat, large, small.** 参看 cat, large, small 之插图。 (of animals) not tamed or domesticated; living in natural conditions (eg lions, giraffes, wolves); (of plants) growing in natural conditions; not cultivated: (指动物)野的; 野性的; 野居的(如狮,长颈鹿,狼); (指植物)野生的; 非栽植的: *~ flowers;* 野花; *a reserve for the preservation of ~ life,* area where ~ animals, birds, etc are protected and helped to survive; 野生动物保护区; (attrib):(用作定语): *a ~-life sanctuary and plant ~* 保护区, *'~·cat* attrib adj reckless, unsound, impracticable: 莽撞的; 不健全的; 不能实行的: *~cat schemes,* esp in finance and commerce; (尤指在财政及商务方面)不能实行的计划; *a ~cat strike,* unofficial and irresponsible strike (by workers). 未经工会允许的不负责任的罢工。 **'~-fowl** n(esp)birds ordinarily shot or hunted as game, eg ~ ducks and geese, quail, pheasants. (尤指)猎鸟(如野鸭,雁,鹑,雉)。 **~·'goose chase,** foolishly useless enterprise. 荒谬无益的行事; 徒劳无益的追求。 **sow one's ~ oats,** ⇨ oat(1). **2** (of horses, game birds, etc) easily startled; hard to get near: (指马, 猎鸟等) 容易受惊的; 怕人的; 不易接近的: *The deer/pheasants are rather ~.* 鹿(雉) 很容易受惊。 **3** (of persons, tribes, etc) uncivilized; savage. (指人,部族等)未开化的; 野蛮的。 **4** (of scenery, areas of land, etc) desolate; waste; unsettled: (指景色,地区等)荒凉的, 荒芜的; 无人居住的: *~ scenery;* 荒凉的景色; *~, mountainous areas.* 荒芜的山区。 **5** violent; uncontrolled; stormy: 猛烈的; 狂暴的; 暴风雨的: *You'd better stay indoors on a ~ night like this.* 象这样暴风雨的夜晚, 你还是待在家里的好。 *What weather we're having!* 我们遇着多么恶劣的天气! **6** excited; passionate; distracted: 激动的; 激烈的; 狂乱的: *There were sounds of ~ laughter.* 有狂笑的声音。 *He was ~ with anger.* 他狂怒。 *It made her ~* = filled her with anger) *to see such cruelty.* 看到这样残酷的行为, 令她极为愤怒。 *The anxiety drove them almost ~,* mad. 焦虑逼得他们几乎发狂了。 **7 be ~ about sth/sb,** (colloq) have a strong desire for; be madly enthusiastic about: (口)对某事物(某人)极为狂热; 极想做某事; 热中于: *~ about strawberries/Prince Charles.* 极想吃草莓(极崇拜查理王子)。 **8** disorderly; out of control: 紊乱的; 无秩序的; 失去控制的: *a state of ~ confusion;* 混乱的状态; *a room in ~ disorder;* 极为紊乱的房间; *settle down after a ~ youth.* 在一段放荡的青年时期以后安定下来。 **run ~,** be without check, restraint or training: 放肆; 放荡; 失教养: *They allow their children to run ~,* allow them to amuse themselves in any way they like, with no control of any kind. 他们听任孩子们自由放荡。 **'~·fire** n [U] (chiefly in) (主要用于) **spread like ~fire,** (of reports, rumours, etc) very fast. (指传闻,谣言等) 迅速地传播。 **9** reckless; done or said without reflection or consideration: 胡乱的; 卤莽的; 轻率的; 未加考虑而做或说出的: *a ~ guess/scheme;* 胡乱的猜测(轻率的计划); *~ shooting,* without taking aim. 乱射。 **10** (of a playing-card) having any value(as eg a joker): (指纸牌)百搭的(如 joker): *a '~ card.* 一张百搭牌。 **~** adv in a ~ manner: 胡乱地; 卤莽地; 轻率地: *shoot ~.* 乱射。 **~** n pl **the ~s,** uncultivated (and often uninhabited)areas: 荒地; 未开发地区: *the ~s of Africa,* 非洲的荒野; *go out into the ~s.* 进入未开发地区。 **~·ly** adv in a ~ manner: 狂野地; 激动地; 胡乱地; 卤莽地; 轻率地: *rush about ~ly;* 横冲直闯; *talk ~ly,* eg in an exaggerated way: 胡扯; 瞎吹: *a ~ly exaggerated account.* 极度夸张的叙述。 **~·ness** n

wilde·beest /'wɪldɪbiːst; 'wɪlde,bist/ n=gnu. ⇨ the illus at **large.** 参看 large 之插图。

wil·der·ness /'wɪldənɪs; 'wɪldɘnɪs/ n (rarely pl) (罕用复数) **1** wild uncultivated waste land. 荒地; 荒野。 **2** desolate expanse: 茫茫的一大片; 荒凉的一大片: *a ~ of waters.* 一片汪洋。 *From his attic window he looked out over a ~ of roofs.* 从他阁楼的窗子望出去, 他看到一大片屋顶。

wile /waɪl; waɪl /n (usu pl) trick; bit of cunning: (通常用复数)诡计; 奸计: *fall a victim to the ~s of an unscrupulous rogue*; 中了一个无耻恶棍的诡计; *the ~s of the Devil.* 魔鬼的奸计。

wil·ful (US also **will-**) /'wɪlfl; 'wɪlfəl/ *adj* **1** (of a person) obstinate; determined to have one's own way: (指人) 刚愎的; 任性的: *a ~ child.* 任性的孩子。 **2** intentional; for which compulsion, ignorance or accident is no excuse: 故意的; 不能用不得已, 不知, 或巧合作借口的: *~ murder / negligence / waste / disobedience.* 故意的谋杀(疏忽, 浪费, 抗命)。 **~ly** /-fəlɪ; -fəlɪ/ *adv* **~·ness** *n*

will[1] /weak form: l; l; strong form: wɪl; wɪl/ *anom fin* (often shortened to 常略作 **'ll**; *neg* = not or **won't** /wəʊnt; wɒnt/; *pt*, conditional 过去式及条件句 **would** (*after 'I, he, she, we, they*): *weak form:* əd; əd; *elsewhere:* 用于他处: *weak form:* əd; əd; *strong form:* wʊd; wʊd/, *neg* **would not** or **wouldn't** /'wʊdnt; 'wʊdnt/) [VP5] **1** (used as an auxiliary verb of the future tense): (用作表未来时态的助动词): *If today is Monday, tomorrow ~ be Tuesday.* 如果今天是星期一, 明天将是星期二。 *You'll be in time if you hurry.* 如果你快一点就会来得及。 *You won't be in time unless you hurry.* 如果你不赶快, 就来不及了。 (*Would* replaces *~* to show future in the past): (*would* 代替 *will* 表示过去未来): *I wonder whether it ~ be ready.* 我不知道是否会准备好。 *I wondered whether it would be ready.* 我(那时)不知道是不是会准备好。 *You'll be in Oxford this time tomorrow.* 明天这个时候你就到牛津了。 *You would have been in Oxford this time yesterday.* 你本来昨天这个时候就可以到牛津的。 **2** (used with the 1st person (*I, we*) to express willingness, consent, an offer or a promise): (与第一人称 I, we 连用, 表示意愿, 同意, 提议或允许): *All right, I'll come.* 好的, 我去。 *I won't do it again.* 我不会再做那事了。 *We'll pay back the money soon.* 我们很快就会还钱。 (*Would* replaces *~* to show future in the past): (表示过去将来时, 用 *would* 代替 *will*): *I said I would do it.* 我说过我要做那事。 *We said we would help them.* 我们说过我们愿意帮助他们。 **3** (used with the 2nd person in questions, marking polite requests, and often equivalent to *please*): (与第二人称连用, 用在问句中, 用来表示客气的请求, 并且常常相当于 *please* 的用法): *'W~ you (please) come in?'* 请进来好吗? *'Would you (please) come back later?'* 请稍晚回来好吗? *'Pass the salt, would you?'* 递给我盐好吗? *'Would you (please) pass the salt?'* (劳驾) 递给我盐好吗? **4** (used in *affirm* sentences, always with stress (never *'ll* or *'d*), indicating insistence or inevitability): (用于肯定句中, 永远重读, 不可略作 *'ll* 或 *'d*, 表示坚持或不可避免): *He'~ have his own way*, insists on this. 他一意孤行。 *Boys '~ be boys*, *We cannot expect them to behave except as boys naturally behave.* 男孩子总归是男孩子。 *Accidents '~ happen*, They are to be expected from time to time. 意外事件总是会发生的。 *That's just what you 'would say*, what you might be expected to say. 那正是你可能会说的话。 *Of course it 'would rain on the day we chose for a picnic*, We might expect such treatment from Fate. 当然, 我们选定野餐的那天可偏会下雨(我们只好听天由命)。 **5** (used in the neg to indicate refusal): (用于否定句中表示拒绝): *He won't / wouldn't help me.* 他不会帮助我。 *This window won't open*, cannot be opened. 这窗子打不开。 **6** (used to indicate that sth happens from time to time, that sb is in the habit of doing sth, that sth is natural or to be expected): (用于表示某事时常发生, 某人有做某事的习惯, 某事自然会如何或在预料之中): *He'll sit there hour after hour looking at the traffic go by.* 他常常坐在那里看几个钟头, 看着来往的车辆行人。 *Sometimes the boys would play a trick on their teacher.* 有的时候男孩子们会作弄老师。 *Occasionally the machine will go wrong without any apparent cause.* 机器偶而会发生故障而找不出明显的原因。 **7** (used to indicate probability or likelihood): (用于表示可能性): *This'll be the book you're looking for, I think.* 我想, 这本书可能就

是你正在找寻的书。 *She would be about 60 when she died.* 她死时大概是六十岁左右。 *'I want someone to do a lot of typing for me'—'Will / Would I do?'* Am I likely to be suitable for me? '我需要有人为我做许多的打字工作'—'我可以吗?' **8** (*Would* is used with the 2nd and 3rd persons to form conditional statements and questions): (*would* 与第二, 第三人称连用, 形成条件叙述句及问句): *They'd be killed if the car went over the cliff.* 汽车如果翻落悬崖, 他们就送命了。 *They'd have been killed if the car had gone over the cliff.* 当时如果汽车翻落悬崖, 他们就送命了。 *would rather*, ⇨ **rather** (1). **9** (*Would* is used with the 1st person to form conditional statements expressing the speaker's will or intention): (*would* 与第一人称连用, 构成条件叙述句句, 表示说话者的意志或意向): *We would have come if it hadn't rained.* 如果那时没有下雨, 我们就来了。

will[2] /wɪl; wɪl/ *vt* (*pt* **would** /wʊd; wʊd/, no other forms used 其他形式不用) (all old uses) (皆为旧用法) **1** [VP6A] wish: 希望; 希冀: *Let him do what he ~.* 他希望做什么就让他做什么。 *What would you?* 你希望什么呢? **2** [VP9] (the subject *I* is often omitted) used to express wishes: (主语 *I* 常省略)用于表示愿望: *Would (that) it were otherwise!* 要不是这样, 该多好啊! *Would (= I would) to God (that) I had not agreed!* 天啊, 我真希望我当时未同意! *Would that they were safe home again!* 但愿他们还能平安归来! **3** [VP5] choose; desire: 选择; 愿; 想: *the place where he would be.* 他想停留的地方。 *Come whenever you ~* (ie = or wish to come). 你随时想来就来。 (Cf **will**[3] with which **will**[2] is closely connected.) (参较 **will**[3], 该词与 **will**[2] 有密切关系。) **'would-be** *attrib adj* used to indicate what is desired, aspired to, or intended: 用于表示所希求, 所热望或所意欲者: *would-be authors*, persons who aspire to be authors. 热望成为作家的人。

will[3] /wɪl; wɪl/ *vt*, *vi* (*pt*, *pp* **~ed**) **1** [VP6A] make use of one's mental powers in an attempt to do sth or get sth: 立意做某事或获得某物; 意欲; 想要: *We cannot achieve success merely by ~ing it.* 仅仅想要成功, 并不能获得成功。 **2** [VP2A] exercise will-power: 运用意志力: 决意; 决心: *W~ing and wishing are not the same thing.* 决意和愿望并非一回事。 **3** [VP6A, 9] intend unconditionally: 绝对地意欲: *God has ~ed it so.* 上帝已作如此安排。 *God ~s that man should be happy.* 上帝的意旨是要人快乐。 **4** [VP17, 14, 15A] influence, control or compel, by exercising the will: 运用意志力以影响, 控制或驱使: *Can you ~ yourself to keep awake / into keeping awake?* 你能以意志力使自己保持清醒吗? *It would be convenient if we could ~ ourselves across lands and oceans.* 如果我们能够运用意志力驾驭自己越过陆地和海洋, 那就方便多了。 **5** [VP12A, 13A] *~ sth to sb*; *~ sb sth*, leave (property, etc) (to sb) by means of a will and testament: 遗赠(财产等)(给某人): *He ~ed most of his money to charities.* 他把大部分的钱遗赠给慈善机关了。 *I hope my uncle has ~ed me that fine painting.* 我希望我叔叔已立遗嘱把那幅好画遗赠给我。

will[4] /wɪl; wɪl/ *n* **1** the **~**, mental power by which a person can direct his thoughts and actions, and influence those of others: 意志: *the freedom of the ~.* 意志的自由。 **2** [U, C] (*sing only*) (仅用单数) (also 亦作 '**~-power**) control exercised over oneself, one's impulses: 意志力; 自制力; 自我控制: *He has no ~ of his own*, is easily influenced by others. 他没有独立的意志(易受他人左右)。 *W~ can conquer habit.* 意志力可以克服习惯。 *He has a strong / weak ~.* 他的意志力坚强(薄弱)。 *He showed a strength of ~ that overcame all obstacles.* 他表现出坚强的意志力, 克服了所有的障碍。 **-willed**, (in compound *adj*) having the kind of ~ indicated: (用于复合形容词中)有…意志力的: **;strong-'~ed**; 意志坚强的; **,weak-'~ed.** 意志薄弱的。 **3** [U, C] (*sing only*) determination; desire or purpose: (仅用单数) 决心; 意向; 欲望; 目的: *The ~ to live helps a patient to recover.* 求生的欲望有助于病人的康复。 *She has a boundless ~ to*

please, is full of desire to please. 她极力想讨好. **Where there's a ~ there's a way**, (prov) If one has the determination to achieve sth, a way of doing so will be found. (谚) 有志者事竟成. **take the ~ for the deed**, understand and be grateful for the fact that one wants to help, etc although unable to do so. 以意向判断行为为; 事虽未成而仍领其心意. **of one's own free ~**, without being required or compelled: 自愿; 甘心情愿: *I did it of my own free ~*. 我做此事乃出于自愿. **at ~**, whenever and however one pleases: 随意: *You may come and go at ~*. 你可以随意来去. **tenant at ~**, (legal) one who can be required to give up (land, a house, etc). (法律) 可随意令其退租的佃户; 可随意令其迁出的房客. **4 a ~** energy; enthusiasm: 精力; 活力; 热心: *work with a ~*. 努力工作. **5 [U]** (with a *possessive*) desire or determined upon: (与所有格连用) 所意欲或决心要做的事情: *God's ~ be done*. 愿神的旨意能完成. *He has always had his ~* (or, more colloq, *his own way*). 他总是自行其是. *What is your ~* (more usu, *What do you want?*) 你需要什么? **6 good/ill ~**, kind/unkind disposition or feeling: 善/恶意: *feel no ill ~ towards anybody*. 对任何人无恶意. *'Peace on earth and good ~ towards men.'* '愿世界有平安, 以善意待人.' **7 [C]** (also 亦作 *last ~ and testament*), = testament. 遗嘱. ~·**ful** [-fl, -fol/ *adj* (US spelling of) **wilful**. 为 wilful 的美国拼法.

wil·lies /'wɪlɪz; 'wɪlɪz/ *n pl* (sl) feeling of unease or nervousness: (俚) 神经紧张; 心惊肉跳: *This gloomy old house gives me the ~*. 这幢幽暗的老房子使我毛骨悚然.

will·ing /'wɪlɪŋ; 'wɪlɪŋ/ *adj* **1** ready to help, to do what is needed, asked, etc: 愿意按照所需、所求等予以帮助或去做的; 乐意的: *~ workers*. 自愿的工作者. *He's quite ~ to pay the price I ask*. 他愿照我所要的价付钱. **2** done, given, etc readily, without hesitation: 愿意而不犹豫地做成, 给予等的; 甘愿的: *~ obedience*. 甘心情愿的服从. ~·**ly** *adv* ~·**ness** *n* [U].

will-o'-the-wisp /ˌwɪl ə ðə 'wɪsp; ˌwɪləðə'wɪsp/ *n* moving light seen at night over marshy ground; (more usu fig) sth or sb that one pursues unsuccessfully because it or he is difficult to grasp or reach. 沼地的磷火; 鬼火; (通常多作比喻用法) 难于捉摸而令人追逐不到的人或事物.

wil·low /'wɪləʊ; 'wɪlo/ *n* [C] ⇨ the illus at **tree**. 参看 tree 之插图. '~-(tree), kinds of tree and shrub with thin, easily bent branches; [U] twigs of this tree used for weaving into baskets; its wood, used for making cricket bats, etc. 柳; 柳树; 柳枝 (用以编织篮子等); 柳木 (用做板球棒等). '~-**pattern** *n* Chinese design (with a ~-tree, a river, etc) in blue upon white china (seen on plates, etc). 柳景图案 (中国瓷器上的白地蓝花图案). ~·**y** *adj* (of persons) lithe and slender. (指人) 柔软而细长的; 苗条的.

willy-nilly /ˌwɪlɪ 'nɪlɪ; ˌwɪlɪ'nɪlɪ/ *adv* willingly or unwillingly; whether wanted or unwanted. 不管愿意不愿意; 无论需要不需要; 强迫地.

wilt¹ /wɪlt; wɪlt/ *v* (archaic form of **will²**) (为 will² 的古旧形式) *thou ~*, = you will.

wilt² /wɪlt; wɪlt/ *vi, vt* [VP6A, 2A] (of plants, flowers) (cause to) droop, lose freshness; (of persons) become limp. (指植物, 花) (使) 凋谢, 枯萎; (指人) 变为颓丧; 变得衰弱或无生气.

Wil·ton /'wɪltən; 'wɪltn/ *n* kind of carpet. 威尔顿地毯.

wily /'waɪlɪ; 'waɪlɪ/ *adj* (-ier, -iest) full of wiles; cunning: 多智谋的; 狡诈的: *a ~ old fox*. 狡猾的老狐狸.

wimple /'wɪmpl; 'wɪmpl/ *n* linen covering arranged in folds about the head, cheeks, chin and neck, worn by women in the Middle Ages, and still by some nuns. (中世纪妇女所用, 现在有些女尼仍用的) 头巾; 包头围布.

win /wɪn; wɪn/ *vt, vi* (*pt, pp* **won** /wʌn; wʌn/) (**-nn-**) **1** [VP6A, 12B, 13B, 15A, 2A] get by means of hard work, perseverance, struggle, as the result of

competition, gambling, etc; do best (in a fight, etc): 赢获胜; 得到成功; 做得最好: *win a race/a battle/a war/a scholarship/a prize*; 赢得赛跑 (战役, 战争, 奖学金, 奖品); *~ fame and fortune*. 名利双收. *Which side won?* 哪一边赢了? *She has a nature that quickly won her the friendship of her colleagues*. 她具有一种天性, 可以很快地获得同事们的友谊. *He soon won a reputation for himself*. 他很快就成名了. *We've won!* 我们赢了! *He won £5 from me at cards*. 玩纸牌的时候他赢了我十英镑. **win the day/the field**, be victorious. 获胜; 战胜. **win free/clear/out/through**, make one's way through, out, etc; free oneself, get out of a difficult position, etc by effort. 完成; 达成; 挣脱; 摆脱 (困境等). **win hands down**, (colloq) succeed easily. (口) 轻易地成功. '**winning-post** *n* post marking the end of a race. (赛跑的) 终点标志. **2** [VP6A, 15B, 17] *win sb over (to sth)*; (less usu 较不常用) *win sb to do sth*, persuade (sb) by argument; gain the favour of: 说服 (某人) 做某事; 得到…的好感; 把某人争取到: *We won him over to our view*. 我们说服他赞成我们的观点. **3** [VP6A] reach by effort: 借努力而到达: *win the summit/the shore*. 到达山巅 (岸上). *n* [C] success in a game, competition, etc: (游戏, 比赛等中的) 赢; 胜利: *Our team has had five wins this summer*. 我们的球队今年夏天已赢了五场. **win·ner** *n* person, animal, thing, that wins. 获胜的人, 动物, 东西; 获胜者. **win·ning** *adj* **1** that wins: 胜利的; 得胜的: *the winning horse*. 获胜的马. **2** persuasive; gaining confidence and friendship: 动人的; 能获得信任和友谊的: *a winning smile*. 动人的微笑. **winnings** /'wɪnɪŋz; 'wɪnɪŋz/ *n pl* (esp money won in betting, gambling, etc. (尤指在打赌, 赌博等中) 赢来的钱.

wince /wɪns; wɪns/ *vi* [VP2A, C] show bodily or mental pain or distress (by a movement or by loss of composure): (因疼痛或苦恼等而) 畏缩; 退避; 退避: *He~d under the blow/at the insult*. 他因受打击而退避 (因受辱而失常态). *He didn't ~ when the knife shipped and cut his thumb*. 小刀滑过割伤他的拇指时, 他没有闪避. □ *n* wincing movement: 畏缩; 退避; *without a~*. 不畏缩地.

win·cey·ette /ˌwɪnsɪ'et; ˌwɪnsɪ'et/ *n* [U] strong material of wool and cotton, or wool, used for shirts, etc. 一种棉绒布; 绒布 (一种结实的棉毛混纺或纯毛布料用以做衬衫等).

winch /wɪntʃ; wɪntʃ/ *n* windlass; stationary machine for hoisting or pulling. 绞车; (起重或牵引用的) 辘轳. □ *vt* [VP6A, 15B] move by using a ~: 用绞车拉动: *The glider was ~ed off the ground*, pulled along by means of a ~ until it rose into the air: 那滑翔机借绞车拉起而升空. *We can ~ out these big tree roots*, get them out by using a ~. 我们可以借绞车拔出这些巨树的树根.

wind¹ /wɪnd; wɪnd/ *n* **1** [O, U] (often 常作 **the ~**: with *much, little*, etc when the reference is to degree or force; with *indef art* or in *pl* when the reference is to the kind of ~, etc; ⇨ the examples) air in motion as the result of natural forces: 风 (说明风的强度或力量时, 用 much, little 等; 说明风的种类等时, 加不定冠词或用其复数形; 见下面例句): *a north ~*, blowing from the north; 北风; *warm ~s from the south*. 南方吹来的和风. *The ~ blew my hat off*. 风吹落了我的帽子. *He ran like the ~*, very fast. 他跑得象风一般快. *The ~ is rising/falling*, becoming stronger/weaker. 风势在增强 (减弱). *There's no/not much/a lot of ~ today*. 今天无风 (风不大, 风很大). **fling/throw caution/prudence, etc to the ~s**, abandon it, take no thought of it. 不再顾虑; 完全不顾; 不再小心谨慎等. **get/have the ~ up**, (sl) become/be frightened. (俚) 受惊吓; 害怕. **raise the ~**, (sl) obtain the money needed. (俚) 筹款; 获得所需金钱. **put the '~ up sb**, (sl) cause him to feel frightened. (俚) 使某人害怕; 使某人惊吓. **see/find out how the '~ blows**, what people are thinking, what is likely to happen. 看风头; 观望情势. **sail close/near otthe ~**, ⇨ **sail²(1)**. **take the '~ out of sb's sails**,

prevent him from doing or saying sth by doing it or saying it before him; take away his advantage suddenly. 抢先做或说以阻止某人做或说; 先发制人地占某人上风; 突然抢去某人的优势。 *There is / was sth in the ~*, being secretly prepared or plotted. 有什么事快要发生了(目前正在酝酿中)。 **2** (*pl*) the cardinal points: (复)基本方向: *The house stands on a hilltop, exposed to the four ~s of heaven*, ~s from all directions. 该屋位于山顶, 受到四面八方的风吹。 *My papers were blown to the four ~s*, in all directions. 我的文件被吹得到处都是。 **3** [U] breath needed for running or continuous exertion: (跑步或不断用力所需要的)呼吸; 喘息; 气息: *The runner soon lost his ~*, became out of breath. 那跑者很快就喘息不已。 *He stopped to recover / get back his ~*. 他停下来喘一口气。 *get one's second ~*, recover the ability to breathe regularly after a first period of breathlessness; (fig) get new energy for a task. (第一阵喘息后)恢复正常呼吸; (喻)重整旗鼓; 获得新的工作精力。 *sound in ~ and limb*, in excellent physical condition. 健康极佳。 **4** [U] scent carried by the ~ (as indicating where sth is): (显示某物在何处的)气味: *get ~ of*, (fig) hear a rumour of, begin to suspect. (喻)风闻; 开始觉察。 **5** [U] empty words; meaningless or useless talk: 空话; 无聊的或无用的话: *Don't listen to the politicians—they're all ~*. 不要听那些政客们的话——全是空话。 **6** [U] gas formed in the bowels and causing discomfort: (使人不舒服的)肠中的气体: *The baby is suffering from ~*. 那婴儿患肠气症。 *break ~*, expel ~ from the bowels or stomach. 放屁。 **7** the ~, orchestral ~ instruments. 管乐器。 **8** (compounds)复合词) '**~-bag** n(colloq) person who talks a lot but says little important. (口)空谈者; 满口空话的人。 '**~-break** n hedge, fence, line of trees, etc to break the force of the ~ and give protection. 防风篱; 防风墙; 防风林; 防风设备。 '**~-cheater** (US 美 = '**~-breaker**) n close-fitting garment for the upper part of the body, designed to give protection against the ~. 防风的紧身上衣。 '**~-fall** n [C] **1** fruit (eg an apple) blown off a tree by the ~. 风吹落的果实 (如苹果)。 **2** (fig) unexpected piece of good fortune, esp money coming to sb. (喻)意外的好运; (尤指)意外之财。 '**~-flower** n anemone. 银莲花属植物; 白头翁。 '**~-gauge** n instrument for measuring the force of the ~. 风力计; 风速计; 风压计。 '**~ instrument** n musical instrument in which sound is produced by a current of air (eg an organ, a flute, a cornet). 管乐器; 吹奏器 (如风琴, 笛, 短号)。 ⇨ the illus at **brass**. 参看 brass 之插图。 '**~-jammer** n (colloq) merchant sailing-ship. (口)商用帆船。 '**~-mill** n mill worked by the action of the ~ on sails which revolve. 风车。 *fight / tilt at ~mills*, (from the story of Don Quixote) fight imaginary enemies; try to put right imaginary wrongs. (源于堂吉诃德德)同幻想中的敌人作战; 试图改革幻想中的弊端。 '**~-pipe** n passage for air from the throat to the lungs. (由喉至肺的)气管。 ⇨ the illus at **respiratory**. 参看 respiratory 之插图。 '**~-screen** (US 美 = '**~-shield**) n screen of glass in front of a motor-vehicle, etc. 风屏; (汽车等的)挡风玻璃; 挡风屏。 ⇨ the illus at **motor**. 参看 motor 之插图。 '**~-screen-wiper** n ⇨ *wiper* at **wipe**. '**~-sock** n canvas sleeve flown at the top of a pole (eg on an airfield) to show the direction of the

a windmill

~. 风向袋; 风向标 (如飞机场等处者)。 '**~-swept** adj exposed to the ~s; blown bare by strong ~s: 当风的; 被强风吹光的: *a ~swept hillside*. 当风的山坡。 '**~-tunnel** n structure through which air is forced (at controlled speeds) to study its effects on (models of) aircraft, etc. 风洞 (为研究风力对于飞机等的影响而建造的隧道, 风速由人控制)。 '**~-less** adj without ~: 无风的: *a ~less day*. 一个无风的日子。 '**~-ward** /-wəd; -wəd/ n, adj (side) in the direction from which the ~ blows; (side) exposed to the ~: 上风的; 当风的; 上风侧; 上风边; 当风面: *Let's go to ~ward of that tannery* (to avoid the bad smell). 让我们转到制革厂的上风侧去(以躲避臭气)。 **windy** adj (-ier, -iest) **1** with much ~: 多风的: *a ~y day*; 多风的日子; *~y weather*; 多风的天气; *a ~y hilltop*, open to the ~. 当风的山顶。 **2** wordy, ⇨ **5** above. 空谈的; 多废话的(参看上列第 5 义)。 **3** (sl) frightened. (俚)受惊吓的; 害怕的。 **~·ily** /-ɪlɪ; -ɪlɪ/ adv ~·i·ness n

wind² /wɪnd; wɪnd/ vt (from 源自 **wind¹**) (pt, pp ~ed /'wɪndɪd; 'wɪndɪd/) [VP6A] **1** detect the presence of by scent: 嗅出; 闻出: *The hounds ~ed the fox*. 猎大嗅出了狐狸的踪迹。 *The deer ~ed the stalkers*. 那只鹿嗅出了偷偷接近的猎人。 **2** exhaust the wind (3) of; cause to breathe fast: 使喘息; 使呼吸急促: *He was quite ~ed by the long climb / by running to catch the bus*. 他由于长时间的攀爬(跑去赶公共汽车)而呼吸急促。 **3** give an opportunity of recovering the breath to: 使喘口气; 使稍休息: *We stopped to ~ our horses*. 我们停下来使马稍事休息。

wind³ /waɪnd; waɪnd/ vi, vt (pt, pp wound /waʊnd; waʊnd/) **1** [VP2A, B, C, 15A] go, (cause to) move, in a curving, spiral, or twisting manner: 迂回地走; 弯曲前进; (使)蜿蜒; (使)弯曲移动: *The river ~s (its way) to the sea*. 那条河蜿蜒地流入大海。 *We climbed the ~ing* (= spiral) *staircase*. 我们爬上螺旋梯。 *The path ~s up the hillside*. 那条小径沿着山坡蜿蜒而上。 *She wound herself / her way into his affections*, won his affections by her clever ways. 她以聪明的手段赢得了他的感情。 **2** [VP6A, 15A, B] twist (string, wool yarn, etc) into a ball, or round or on to sth: 卷(带, 细绳, 毛线等)成球; 缠绕; 裹: *~ (up) wool into a ball*; 将毛线卷成球; *~ yarn*; 缠绕纱线; *~ thread on to a reel*; 将线缠在线轴上。 *~ in the line*, eg a fishing-line on a reel. 收线(如把钓线卷在轴上)。 *~ sth off*, unwind it. 解开; 放开; 松开。 *sb round one's (little) finger*, make him do whatever one wants him to do. 任意操纵某人; 随意左右或摆布某人。 **3** [VP14, 15A] *~ sth round sb / sth*; *~ sb / sth in sth*, fold or wrap closely; embrace: 包紧; 围裹; 环抱; 裹: *~ a shawl round a baby*; 以围巾裹着婴儿; *~ a baby in a shawl*. 把婴儿裹在围巾里。 *She wound her arms round the child*. 她以双臂环抱那孩子。 '**~ing-sheet** n shroud; sheet (to be) wound round a corpse. 裹尸布。 **4** [VP6A, 15B] *~ sth (up)*, turn (a handle, eg of a windlass); raise (sth) by doing this: 转动(绞盘等的把手); 绞起; 吊起: *~ a handle*; 转动把手; *~ up ore from a mine / a bucket from a well*. 从矿坑中以绞盘吊出矿石 (从井中用辘轳吊出水桶)。 **5** [VP6A, 15B] *~ sth (up)*, tighten the spring of (a watch or clock); raise the weights that operate a clock (to put or keep the watch or clock in motion): 上(钟或表)的弦; 上发条: *If you forget to ~ (up) your watch it will stop—unless it is a self-~ing watch*, ie one that is wound up automatically by movements of the wrist. 如果你忘记上表的弦, 表就会停——除非它是自动(上弦)的表。 **6** *be wound up (to)*, be (emotionally) excited (esp in passive), ⇨ **unwind**. (情绪方面)激动; 紧张; 振奋(用于被动语态中)。 *He was wound up to a high pitch of excitement*. 他极为兴奋。 *Expectation was wound up to a high pitch*. 期待的心情已达到极其紧张的地步。 *She was wound up to a fury*. 她极为愤怒。 **7** [VP2C, 15B] *~ (sth) up*, come or bring to an end: 结束: *It's time for him to ~ up his speech*, come to a conclusion. 现在是他结束演说的时候了。 *He wound*

up by declaring that his efforts would be continued. 他最后宣称他的努力将继续下去。 *They wound up the evening by singing some folksongs.* 他们唱了几支民谣，结束了那个夜晚。 **~ up a business company,** put everything in order before dissolving it. 结束一个公司；解散前清理一个公司。 **~ up one's affairs,** put them in order before bringing them to an end. 结束私务；结束个人事务。 **~ up** (卷表发条等的)一次转动；缠绕；上弦。

wind·lass /'wɪndləs; 'wɪndləs/ n machine for pulling or lifting things (eg water from a well) by means of a rope or chain which is wound round an axle; winch. (起重等用的)绞车；绞盘；辘轳。

win·dow /'wɪndəu; 'wɪndo/ n opening in a wall or roof of a building, the side of a ship, carriage, car, etc to let in light and air: 窗；窗口；窗扉： *look out of the ~.* 从窗口望出去。 '**~·box** n long narrow box fixed to a ~-sill in which to grow plants. 窗槛花箱；窗台花箱(固定在窗前的长而窄的部分，栽花用)。 '**~·dressing** n art of arranging goods attractively in shop-~s; (fig) (art of) making an impressive display of one's work, abilities, qualities, etc. (商店的)橱窗装饰术；橱窗布置；(喻)自我宣传(术)；自我炫耀(术)。 ,~ '**envelope** n one with a transparent part in the front through which an address on the paper inside may be read. 开窗信封(正面部分透明，可看见信纸上收信人的地址)。 '**~-pane** n pane of glass for or in a ~. 窗(子上的)玻璃。 **go** '**~-shopping,** look at goods displayed in shop-~s (for interest, but not necessarily with the idea of buying anything). 浏览商店的橱窗(不一定想买东西)；逛街。 '**~-sill** ⇨ **sill.** *a ~ on the world,* (fig) means of learning about, or coming into contact with, other countries: (喻)了解或接触其他国家的方法、手段、媒介或工具；世界之窗： *The English language is a ~ on the world.* 英语是了解或接触世界的一种工具。

windy /'wɪndɪ; 'wɪndɪ/ ⇨ **wind**[1].

wine /waɪn; waɪn/ n [U] **1** alcoholic drink made from the fermented juice of grapes: 葡萄酒： *a barrel/bottle/glass of ~;* 一桶(瓶，杯)葡萄酒； *French ~(s),* (pl for different kinds of ~). 法国(产的)葡萄酒(复数形表示各种葡萄酒)。 *new ~ in old bottles,* a new principle that is too strong to be held back by old forms. 旧瓶装新酒；旧形式包容不了新内容。 '**~·press** n one in which grapes are pressed (葡萄)压汁器。 '**~·skin** n whole skin of a goat, etc sewn up and used formerly for holding ~. 皮酒袋(整张羊皮等缝制而成，昔时盛酒用)。 **2** fermented drink resembling ~, made from other fruits or plants: 水果酒；酒： *currant/cowslip/palm, etc ~.* 醋栗(樱草，棕榈等)酒。 □ vt (esp) (尤用于) ~ *and dine sb,* entertain at a meal with ~: 以酒宴款待： *We were ~d and dined at the firm's expense.* 公司以酒宴款待我们。

wing /wɪŋ; wɪŋ/ n **1** either of the two organs of a bird by which it flies; one of the similar organs of an insect; one of the surfaces by which an aircraft is supported in the air. (鸟，昆虫，飞机等的)翼；翅。 ⇨ the illus at **air, bird.** 参看 air 与 bird 之插图。 *clip a person's ~s* limit his movements, activities, expenditure, etc. 限制某人的活动、行动、花费等。 *lend/add ~s to,* cause to go fast: 使快走；使加速： *Fear lent him ~s,* made him run off fast. 恐惧使他加快了脚步。 *take (to itself) ~s,* disappear, vanish: 消失；消逝： *As soon as we go on a holiday, our money seems to take ~s.* 每当我们去度假，钱就飞也似地花掉了。 *take sb under one's ~,* take him under one's protection: give him care and guidance. 保护或庇护某人；给予某人照顾与指导。 '**~-nut/-screw,** = thumb-nut. '**~-span/-spread** nn measurement

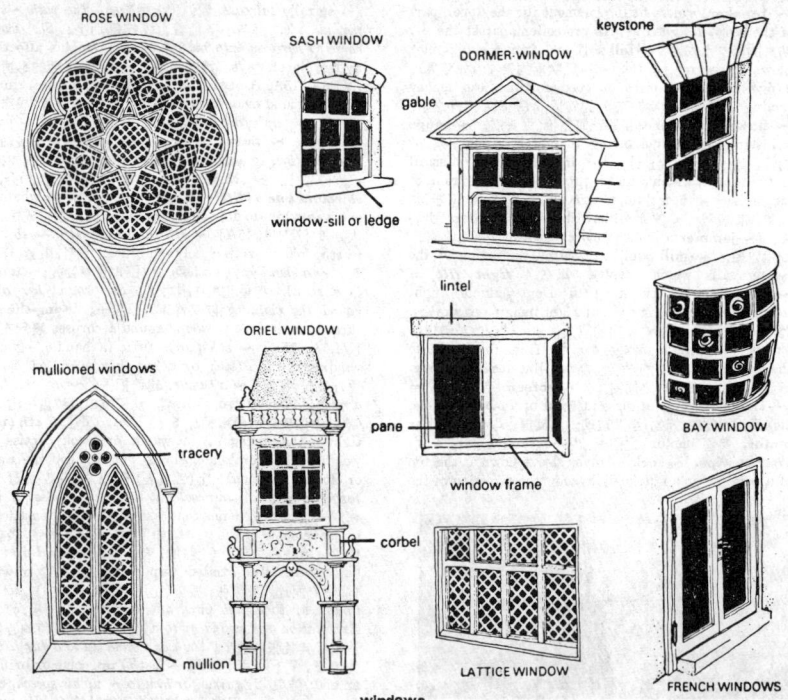

ROSE WINDOW

SASH WINDOW

window-sill or ledge

DORMER·WINDOW

gable

keystone

ORIEL WINDOW

mullioned windows

tracery

corbel

mullion

lintel

pane

window frame

BAY WINDOW

LATTICE WINDOW

FRENCH WINDOWS

windows

across ~s when these are extended. 翼幅; 翼展(两翼张开时的宽度)。 **2** part of an object, building, etc which projects or is extended from one of its sides (eg the part of a motor-vehicle covering a wheel, called a *fender* in US): (物体, 建筑物等的)侧翼; 翼; 厢房; (汽车的)挡泥板(美国称作 fender): *a ~ chair*, an upholstered chair with arms as high as the back; 高边椅(侧边与靠背等高); *add a new ~ to a hospital.* 为医院的一侧增建一一排房屋。 *The north ~ of the house was added 50 years ago.* 那房子北面的厢房是五十年前添建的。 **3** (mil) either of the flanks of an army or fleet; unit placed to guard a flank. (军)(部队、舰队的)翼; 侧翼; 保护侧翼的部队。 **4** those members of a political party holding more extreme views than those of the majority: (政党中的)派别; 翼(所持观点较大多数党员极端): *the radical ~ of the Labour Party.* 工党的激进派。 Hence, 由此产生, **left-/right-'~(er).** 左(右)派(分子)。 **5** unseen areas to the right and left of the stage of a theatre; the scenery there: 舞台的侧面; 舞台的侧景: *We were allowed to watch the performance from the ~s.* 我们获准在舞台的侧面看表演。 **6** flying. 飞行; 飞翔. **on the ~,** in flight; in flying: 在飞行中: *shoot a bird on the ~.* 射击飞行中的鸟。 **take ~,** start flying. 起飞; 飞去。 **7** sth like a ~ in appearance or position, eg certain seeds (esp of the maple and sycamore). 形状或位置似翼之物; (尤指枫树及大枫树的)翼形种子; 翼瓣。 **8** (also 亦作 **~er**) (football, hockey) forward player whose place is either side of the centre. (足球、曲棍球)翼; 边锋(球员)。 ⇨ the illus at **football.** 参看 football 之插图。 **9** (GB; RAF) formation of two or more squadrons; (pl) pilot's badge: (英; 皇家空军)大队; (复)飞行徽章: *get one's ~s.* 获得飞行徽章。 **'~commander,** RAF rank, next below Group Captain. (英国皇家空军的)空军中校。 □ vt, vi **1** [VP6A] give ~s to; lend speed to: 增加…的速度; 加快: (usu fig) (通常作喻) *Fear ~ed his steps.* 恐惧使他加快步子。 **2** [VP2C, 15A] fly; travel on ~s: 飞; 飞行: *The planes ~ed (their way) over the Alps.* 飞机飞越阿尔卑斯山。 **3** [VP6A] wound (a bird) in the ~; (colloq) wound (a person) in the arm. 伤(鸟)之翼; (口)伤(人)之臂。 **~ed** adj having ~s: 有翼的; 有翅膀的: *the ~ed god*, Mercury; (罗马神话中的)信使神; *a ~ed Vistory*, a statue of the goddess of victory with ~s. 有翼的胜利女神雕像。 **~less** adj without ~s. 无翼的; 无翅膀的。 **~er** n person who acts or plays in a position on the ~s. (政党中的)激进分子; 左(右)派(分子); (足球、曲棍球)边锋; 边锋球员。 ⇨ **4** and 8 above. 参看上列第 4 义与第 8 义。

wink /wɪŋk; wɪŋk/ vi, vt **1** [VP2A, 3A, 15B] ~ **(at)**, close and open (one's eyes, or more usu one eye); get rid of (tears) by doing this: 眨眼; 眨单眼; 眨掉 (眼泪): *She ~ed at me*, eg as a sign of secret amusement, or to call my attention to sth, as a private signal of some kind. 她向我眨眼(示意某种私下的喜悦, 或欲引我注意某事物, 或向我打暗号)。 *He ~ed a tear away.* 他眨掉一滴眼泪。 **~ at sth,** purposely avoid seeing; deliberately ignore (a piece of misconduct, a transgression). 有意不看某物; 故意装着不知(一项过失或违犯)。 **2** [VP2A, C] (of a star, light, etc) shine or flash intermittently, at very short intervals: (指星, 光等)闪烁; 闪动; 闪耀: *A lighthouse was ~ing in the far distance.* 一座灯塔正在远处闪烁。 □ n **1** act of ~ing, esp as a signal or hint. 眨眼; (尤指)目语; 眼色。 **tip sb the ~,** (colloq) give him special information; warn him secretly. (口)给某人特别消息, 情报等; 暗中示意某人; 暗中警告某人; 向某人眨眼示意。 **A ~ is as good as a nod,** A hint, etc given by a wink, etc is as effective as a more obvious signal. 眨眼与点头一样有效(同样可达到示意的目的)。 **2** very short time: 瞬息; 极短时间: *I didn't sleep a ~/didn't have a ~ of sleep*, didn't sleep at all. 我未合眼(一点也没有睡)。 **forty ~s,** a short sleep(esp during the day). 小睡; (尤指)白天的小睡。

win·kle /'wɪŋkl; 'wɪŋkl/ n sea snail used as food; periwinkle. 海螺; 蚬介; 玉黍螺。 □ vt [VP15B] ~

sb/sth out, extract, force or pull out (as a ~ is picked or pulled out of its shell with a pin). 拉出; 拔出; 剔出(如用扑把海螺从其壳中挑出来一般)。

win·ner, win·ning ⇨ **win.**

win·now /'wɪnəʊ; 'wɪnoʊ/ vt [VP6A, 14, 15A, B] use a stream of air to separate dry outer coverings from (grain): 吹, 扇(谷物)以除去其糠皮: ~ *wheat*, 簸小麦; 扇小麦; blow (husks, chaff)away from grain in this way: 簸去或吹去(谷壳, 糠皮): ~ *the chaff away/out*, 扇或吹去糠皮; (fig)(喻)~ *truth from falsehood.* 分辨真伪。

win·some /'wɪnsəm; 'wɪnsəm/ adj (of a person, his appearance) attractive; pleasing; bright: (指人, 其外表)有吸引力的; 可爱的; 悦目的; 活泼的; 聪明的: *a ~ smile/manner.* 迷人的微笑(仪态)。 **~·ly** adv ~ **·ness** n

win·ter /'wɪntə(r); 'wɪntə/ n [U, C] season between autumn and spring (Nov or Dec to Feb or March in the northern hemisphere): 冬; 冬季(北半球从十一月或十二月至二月或三月): *many ~s* (liter, 文 = years) *ago;* 多年前; ~ *sports,* eg iceskating, skiing; 冬季运动(如溜冰, 滑雪); ~ *wheat*, planted in the autumn and harvested in the following spring or summer; 冬小麦(秋季下种而于来年春季或夏季收割); ~ *quarters*, (esp) to which troops retired for the ~ (in former times). (尤指昔时军队于冬天驻扎的) 冬营。 **'~ garden,** glassenclosed area with plants, etc eg as the lounge of a hotel. 冬园 (用玻璃围绕而且种有植物的地方, 如旅馆的大厅等)。 □ vi [VP2C] pass the ~: 过冬: ~ *in the south*; 在南方过冬; *the ~ing quarters of wild geese.* 雁的冬季栖息地。 **~y, win·try** /'wɪntrɪ; 'wɪntri/ adj of or like ~; cold: 冬的; 象冬季的; 寒冷的: *a wintry sky/day;* 寒冬的天空(日子); *wintry weather;* 寒冷的天气; (fig) (喻) *a wintry smile/greeting*, one lacking in warmth or liveliness. 冷淡的微笑(招呼)。

wipe /waɪp; waɪp/ vt, vi [VP6A, 15A, B, 22] clean or dry (sth) by rubbing with a cloth, paper, the hands, etc: 擦; 拭; 揩; 揩: ~ *the dishes;* 擦盘子; ~ *one's hands on a towel;* 在毛巾上擦手; ~ *one's face;* 擦脸; ~ *sth dry;* 擦干某物; ~ *one's eyes*, dry the tears. 擦干眼泪。 *Take this handkerchief and ~ your nose, David.* 拿这块手帕揩你的鼻子, 大卫。 ~ *the floor with sb,* ⇨ **floor¹** (1). ~ *the slate clean*, make a new start, with past errors, enmities, etc forgotten. (忘掉过去的错误、仇恨等)重新开始; 勾销往事。 ~ *sth away*, remove (eg tears) by wiping. 擦去 (如眼泪)。 ~ *sth off*, (a) remove by wiping: 擦掉: ~ *off a drawing from the blackboard.* 将黑板上的图画擦掉。 (b) get rid of; cancel; 清除; 清除: ~ *off a debt.* 还清债务。 ~ *sth out*, (a) clean the inside of: 擦洗…的内部: ~ *out a jug*; 擦洗罐子的内部; ~ *out the bath.* 擦拭浴盆。 (b) get rid of; remove: 清除; 除去: ~ *out a disgrace*; 雪耻; ~ *out old scores*, forget old quarrels, etc; 忘掉旧怨; ~ *out an insult* (esp by vengeance). (尤指借报复而)消除侮辱。 (c) destroy completely: 彻底毁灭; 扫灭: *a disease that almost ~d out the population of the island.* 几乎将该岛人口全部消灭的疾病。 ~ *sth up*, take up (liquid, etc) by wiping: 擦净(液体等): ~ *up spilt milk;* 擦干净溅出的牛奶; ~ *up a mess.* 擦净脏污。 □ n act of wiping: 擦; 拭; 揩; 揩: *Give this plate a ~.* 把这只盘子擦一擦。 ~**r** n sth that ~s or is used for wiping: 擦拭物; 擦拭用的东西: *a 'windscreen-wiper*, for wiping rainwater from the windscreen. (汽车挡风玻璃上的)揩拭器; 刮水器; 雨刮。 ⇨ the illus at **motor.** 参看 motor 之插图。

wire /'waɪə(r); waɪr/ n **1** [C, U] (piece or length of) metal drawn out into the form of a thread: (一段)金属线; 金属丝: '*telephone ~(s)*; 电话线; *copper ~*; 铜线; *barbed ~* (⇨ the illus at **barb**), 有刺铁丝 (⇨ 参看 barb 之插图); ~ *rope*, made by twisting strands of ~ together; 金属绳索; 金属缆; 钢缆; ~ *netting*, made by weaving ~ (used for fences, fruit cages, etc). 金属丝网; 铁丝网。 *pull (the)~s*, (fig) use secret or indirect influence to gain one's ends, manage a political party, etc: (喻)暗中操纵; 幕后指挥; hence, 由此产生, '~**puller**

n. live ~, **(a)** ~ charged with electric current. 通电的电线. **(b)** (fig)active, vigorous person. (喻)活泼而有精力的人; 精力充沛的人. '~**cutters** *n pl* tool for cutting ~. 剪断金属丝所用的工具; 钢丝钳. '~**haired** *adj* (esp of a dog) with stiff or wiry hair. (尤指狗)硬毛的. '~ **tapping** *n* [U] tapping of telephones, ⇨ **tap**¹, *vt* (第 2 义.) 电话窃听 (参看 tap¹, vt. 第 2 义.) '~ **wool** *n* [C, U] (pad of) fine ~ for cleaning pots and pans. (清洗锅盘等用的) 金属丝绒 (垫等). '~**worm** *n* kinds of worm-like larva destructive to plants. (对植物有害的)切根虫. 2 [C] (colloq, esp US) telegram: (口, 尤美)电报: *send sb a* ~; 拍电报给某人; *send off a* ~. 拍发电报. *Let me know by* ~ *what time to expect you.* 拍电报告诉我你什么时候到. □ *vt, vi* 1 [VP6A, 15A, B] fasten with ~: 用金属丝捆扎: ~ *two things together;* 用金属丝把二物绑在一起; put ~(s) in or on; put (beads, pearls, etc) on fine ~. 加金属丝于…中; 加金属丝于…上; 用细金属丝穿(珠子、珍珠等). 2 [VP6A] install electrical circuits (in a building, to provide lighting, power, etc): 装置电线于(建筑物中, 以供给电力、照明等): *Has the house been* ~*d for electricity yet?* 这房子已装好电线了吗? 3 [VP 6A] catch, snare (birds, rabbits, etc) with ~. 用铁丝网捕捉, 网住(鸟、兔等). 4 [VP6A, 16A, 12A, 13A, 11, 2C] (colloq, esp US) telegraph: (口, 尤美)拍电报: *He* ~*d (to) his brother to buy oil shares.* 他拍电报给他的哥哥(弟弟)购买石油股票. *He* ~*d me that he would be delayed.* 他拍电报给我, 说他将延期到达. **wir·ing** *n* [U] (esp)system of ~s for electric current. (尤指)电线系统; 布线; 接线. **wiry** *adj* (-ier, -iest) like ~; (of persons) lean and with strong sinews. 似金属丝的; (指人)瘦而结实的.

wire·less /'waɪəlɪs; 'waɪrlɪs/ *adj* without the use of wire(s). 不用电线的; 无线的. □ *n* (dated word for) (过时用语, 指) **1** [U] radio. 无线电. **2** [C] radio set. 收音机.

wis·dom /'wɪzdəm; 'wɪzdəm/ *n* [U] **1** quality of being wise. 智慧; 睿智. '~**-tooth** *n* (*pl* **-teeth**) back tooth, usu coming through after 20 years of age: 智齿(最后面的白齿, 通常在壮年以后长出): *cut one's* ~*-teeth,* reach the age when one has discretion, etc. 到达懂事的年龄; 开始识世故. ⇨ the illus at **mouth**. 参看 mouth 之插图. **2** wise thoughts, sayings, etc: 睿智的思想、言词等: *the* ~ *of the ancients* / *our ancestors.* 古人(我们祖先)的名言、卓识等.

wise¹ /waɪz; waɪz/ *adj* (**-r, -st**) having or showing experience, knowledge, good judgement, prudence, etc: 聪明的; 明智的; 具有或显示经验、知识、良好的判断、审慎等的: ~ *men* / *acts.* 聪明的人 / 聪明的行为. *He was* ~ *enough not to drive when he was feeling ill.* 他很明智, 感觉身体不适的时候便不驾车. *'I don't agree', he said, with a* ~ *shake of the head,* ie suggesting that he was ~. '我不同意', 他说, 颇有见地地摇着头. *It's easy to be* ~ *after the event,* to know, after sth has happened, what one failed to see in advance. 事后聪明是很容易的. **be none the** ~**r,** be no better informed: 仍旧不明白; 照样糊涂: *He came away none the* ~**r,** knowing no more than before. 他离去时仍旧和以前一样的不明白. **be** /**get** ~ **to** *sb* / *sth,* (sl)be / become aware of: (俚)明白; 懂得: *get* ~ *to what's happening* / *to the ways of business men, etc.* 明白现况(商人的成功和作风等). **put** *sb* ~ **to** *sb* / *sth,* inform him of (what is happening, etc). 告诉某人(现况、实情等). '~**-acre** *n* dull and boring person who pretends to be clever. 自作聪明的人; 假聪明人. '~**-crack** *n* (sl) smart, witty saying or remark. (俚)俏皮话; 妙语. □ *vi* make ~cracks. 说俏皮话; 作妙语. **-ly** *adv*

wise² /waɪz; waɪz/ *n* (*sing* only; old use) way, manner. (仅用单数; 旧用法)方法; 方式: *in no* ~; 一点也不; 绝不; *in this* ~. 这样地.

wish /wɪʃ; wɪʃ/ *vt, vi* **1** [VP9] ~ *that...,* (*that* usu omitted; the *that*-clause usu have as an *pt*) have as an unfulfilled desire or a desire that cannot be fulfilled:

(that 通常省去; that 从句中, 通常用过去时)有某种未实现或无法实现的欲望或希望; 但愿: *I* ~ *I knew what is happening.* 我希望我知道现在正在发生什么事. *I* ~ *were rich.* 我希望我很有钱. *I* ~ *I were a bird.* 我希望我是一只鸟. *She* ~*ed she'd stayed at home,* was sorry that she had not stayed at home. 她遗憾当时不在家. 她遗憾当时没有待在家里. **have as a desire:** 切望; 渴望; 希望: *She* ~*ed herself home* (= ~*ed that she was at home*) *again.* 她真希望已经再度回到家里. *They* ~*ed the voyage at an end.* 他们渴望航行告一结束. *He began to* ~ *himself* (= ~ that he was) *out of the affair.* 他开始希望自己未介入那事. **3** [VP22] ~ *sb well* / *ill,* hope that he may have good / ill fortune, etc: 祝某人好运(希望某人倒楣)等: *He* ~*ed me well.* 他祝我好运. *I* ~ *nobody ill.* 我不希望有人遭殃. **4** [VP12A, 13A] say that one hopes for: 颂; 祝: ~ *sb a pleasant journey,* 祝某人旅途快乐; ~ *happiness to all one's friends;* 祝福所有朋友; express as a greeting: 表示某种问候语; 问候; 招呼: ~ *sb good morning* / *goodbye.* 向某人道早安(再见). **5** [VP7A, 17, rarely VP6A with pron] want: (VP6A 与代词连用的用法较少见)想要; 需要: ~ *es to be alone.* 她不想被打扰. *Do you really* ~ *me to go?* 你真的要我去吗? *I* ~ *there to be no misunderstanding on this matter.* 关于这件事我不愿有所误会. *What do you* ~? 你想要什么? *Well, if you* ~ *it,* if that is what you want me to do, etc. 唔, 如果你真要…. **6** [VP3A] ~ *for,* have a desire for, pray for (esp sth unlikely to be obtained or achieved, or sth that can be obtained only by good fortune or in exceptional circumstances): 欲; 愿(尤指不大可能获得或达到的, 或有赖于好运或特殊环境才能获得的某种事物): *She has everything a woman can* ~ *for,* (suggesting unusual good fortune). 女人想要获得的一切, 她都有了 (显示她有不寻常的好运). *How he* ~*ed for an opportunity to go abroad!,* (suggesting small likelihood of getting one). 他多么希望有机会出国啊! (显示这种机会并不大). *The weather was everything they could* ~ *for,* (suggesting unusual good fortune). 他们遇到的天气再好没有了. *What more can you* ~ *for?* 你究竟还想得到什么呢? (Cf 参较: *He would like a glass of cold water,* and *How he* ~*ed for a glass of cold water,* the second sentence suggesting that there was little likelihood of his getting one 第二句话表示他获得一杯冷水的机会很小). **7** [VP2A] express a desire: 表示一种愿望: *Doing is better than* ~*ing.* 行动胜于痴心梦想. '~**-bone** *n* forked bone above the breastbone of a fowl, pulled in two by two persons, the person getting the longer part having the right to the magic fulfilment of any wish. (鸟胸的)叉骨; 如愿骨(两人同时拉扯, 据说后, 扯到长的一段的人, 无论希望什么, 都会神奇地如愿以偿). '~**-ing-cap** *n* (in fairy tales) cap which secures to the wearer the fulfilment of any wish. (神仙故事中)魔帽(戴者随心所欲有求必应). **8** ~ *sb* / *sth on sb,* (colloq) transfer him / it to sb(esp with the idea of getting rid of sb / sth unwanted or disliked): (口) 把某人或某物转交给某人(尤指欲摆脱不需要或不喜欢之人或物); 把某人或某物塞给某人: *I wouldn't* ~ *my mother-in-law on anyone,* suggesting that she is intolerable. 我不会把我丈母娘塞给予人 (意谓其丈母娘叫人受不了). *We had the Jones children* ~*ed on us for the weekend.* 琼斯家的孩子们在周末被塞到我们这儿来. □ *n* **1** [C, U] desire; longing: 欲望; 愿望: *He has no* / *not much* ~ *to go.* 他不 (不大) 想去. *She expressed a* ~ *to be alone.* 她表示愿意独处(不愿有人打扰). *He disregarded his father's* ~*es.* 他不顾他父亲的愿望. *I hope you will grant my* ~. 我希望你答应我的请求. *If* ~*es were horses, beggars might ride,* (prov) If things could be obtained merely by ~ing, poor people would soon be rich. (谚)如果愿望是马, 叫化子都可以乘骑; 如果梦想皆可成事实, 穷人很快就发财了. *The* ~ *is father to the thought,* (prov) We are apt to believe sth because we ~ it were true. (谚)愿望是意念之父; 人们容易相信他们希望相信的事物. **2** [C] that which is ~ed for: 被希冀的事物; 所愿望的事

物: *She got her ~.* 她如愿以偿了。 **~·ful** /-fl; -fəl/ *adj* having or expressing a ~; desiring. 有愿望的;表示愿望的;欲望的。 **~ful thinking**, thinking or believing that sth is true because one ~es it true. 如意的想法或信念;妄想;如意算盘。 **~·fully** /-fəlɪ; -fəlɪ/ *adv*

wishy-washy /'wɪʃɪ wɒʃɪ US: 'wɪʃɪ,wɑʃɪ/ *adj* (of soup, tea, etc) thin; weak; (of talk, persons) lacking in spirit or vigour; sloppy. (指汤、茶等)淡的;稀薄的; (指谈话、人)无力的;软弱的。

wisp /wɪsp; wɪsp/ *n* [C] small bundle, bunch or twist: 小缕;小把;小束;小捆: *a ~ of straw/hay;* 一小捆稻草(秣草) ; *a ~ of hair;* 一绺头发;spiral or ribbon: 螺旋形物;带;条: *a ~ of smoke/steam.* 一缕烟(蒸汽)。 **~·y** *adj* like a ~; slight. 似小束、小绺等的;纤细的;轻微的。

wis·teria /wɪ'stɪərɪə; wɪs'tɪrɪə/ *n* (kinds of)climbing plant with a woody stem and long drooping clusters of pale purple or white flowers and seeds in long pods, often grown on walls or over pergolas. (植)紫藤。

wist·ful /'wɪstfl; 'wɪstfəl/ *adj* sad and longing; having, showing, moved by, a rather unsatisfied and often vague desire: 愁闷而渴望的;具有或显出颇为不满足而带为模糊之欲望的;为此种欲望所激发的: *~ eyes;* 渴望的眼睛; *a ~ expression;* 渴望的表情; *in a ~ mood.* 心情惆怅的。 **~·ly** /-fəlɪ; -fəlɪ/ *adv* in a ~ manner: 愁闷而渴望地: *She looked ~ly at the photographs of herself when she was young and beautiful.* 她若有所思地眺望然看着她自己年轻漂亮时的照片。

wit[1] /wɪt; wɪt/ *n* 1(*sing* or *pl*)intelligence; understanding; quickness of mind: (单数或复数)理智;理解;心智;智力;机智: *He hadn't the wits/hadn't wit enough to realize what to do in the emergency.* 他没有应付紧急事件的才智。 **at one's wit's end**, not knowing what to do or say. 智穷;穷于应付;不知所措。 **out of one's wits**, greatly upset; distracted; mad: 非常不安;精神错乱;发疯: *You'll drive me out of my wits if you go on behaving in this way.* 如果你继续这样胡作非为,你会使我发疯。 **have a ready wit**, be quick to make clever and amusing remarks. 有捷才;口才机敏。 **have/keep one's wits about one**, be quick to see what is happening, alert and ready to act. 警觉;机警。 **live by one's wits**, live by clever, not always honest, methods (as opportunities arise). 靠耍小聪明过日子。 2 [U] clever and humorous expression of ideas; liveliness of spirit: 机智的措词;才智;情趣横溢: *Our teacher/Our teacher's conversation is full of wit.* 我们的老师(我们老师的谈话)很风趣。 *His writings sparkle with wit.* 他的作品闪露着才智。 3 [C] person noted for his wit(2). 有才智者;富于机智的人;才子。 **witty** *adj*(**-ier, -iest**) full of humour: 诙谐的;富趣横生的; *a witty girl/remark.*黠慧风趣的女孩(妙语)。 **wit·tily** /-ɪlɪ; -ɪlɪ/ *adv* **wit·ti·cism** /'wɪtɪsɪzəm; 'wɪtə,sɪzəm/ *n* [C] witty remark. 妙语;隽语;诙谐语。 **wit·less** *adj* stupid. 愚笨的;无机智的。

wit[2] /wɪt; wɪt/ *v* **to wit**, (legal) namely; that is to say. (法律)即;就是。

witch /wɪtʃ; wɪtʃ/ *n* woman said to use magic, esp for evil purpose; (fig) fascinating or bewitching woman. 女巫;巫婆;(喻)迷人的女子。 '**~·craft** *n* [U] sorcery; use of magic. 巫术;魔法。 '**~·doctor** *n* male ~; tribal magician (esp among primitive peoples). 男巫;巫医(尤指原始民族中的)。 '**~·hunt** *n* (fig) searching out and persecution (eg of persons said to be disloyal or untrustworthy). (喻)搜寻迫害 (如政治上不忠或可疑分子等)。 **·ery** /'wɪtʃərɪ; 'wɪtʃərɪ/ *n* [U] 1 ~ craft. 巫术;魔法。 2 fascination; charm. 魅力;诱惑力;蛊惑。 **~·ing** *adj* bewitching: 行巫术的;迷人的;销魂的: *the ~ing hour of night*, the time when ~es are active; midnight. 巫术出动活跃的时刻;午夜。

witch-elm, witch-hazel ⇨ **wych.**

with /wɪð; wɪð/ *prep* **1** (equivalent to constructions with the *v* 'have') having; carrying; characterized by: (相当于带动词 have 的结构)有;带着;有…的特征: *a cup ~ a broken handle;* 把手破损的杯子; *a coat ~ two*

pockets; 有两个口袋的外衣; *a girl ~ blue eyes;* 碧眼女郎; *a baby ~ no clothes on;* 未穿衣服的婴儿; *a woman ~ an angry look in her eyes;* 眼露怒气的妇人; *your permission.* 经你允许。 **~ child** (of a woman 指女人): **~ young** (of an animal 指动物), pregnant. 怀孕的;怀胎的。 **2** (to indicate what is used for filling, covering, etc): (表示填充物、覆盖物等): *Fill the box ~ sand.* 将这个盒子装满沙子。 *The lorry was loaded ~ timber.* 货车装满了木材。 *The sack was stuffed ~ straw.* 袋子里塞满了稻草。 *The hills were covered ~ snow.* 丘陵被雪覆盖了。 **3** (to indicate the means or instrument): (表示方式或工具): *write ~ a pen;* 用笔书写; *take sth ~ both hands;* 用双手取物; *walk ~ a crutch;* 用拐杖走路; *cut sth ~ a knife;* 用刀切割某物; *see sth ~ your own eyes;* 用你的眼睛看某物; *~ the help of your friends;* 借你朋友们的帮助。 *~ your help.* 靠你的帮助。 **4** (to indicate accompaniment or relationship): (表示伴随或关系): *live ~ your parents;* 与你的双亲同住; *go for a walk ~ a friend;* 同一位朋友去散步; *discuss a problem ~ somebody;* 与某人讨论一个问题; *spend the day ~ one's uncle;* 和叔父在一起度过一天; *mix one substance ~ another;* 把一种物质与另一物质混合; *put one thing ~ others.* 把一物与他物放在一起。 *I shall be ~ you in a few minutes.* 我几分钟内(一会儿)就来招呼你。 *Is there anyone ~ you or are you alone?* 有人陪伴你呢,还是你单独一个人? *The general, (together) ~ his staff officers, will inspect the camp.* 那位将军将率同其参谋官们视察营区。 **in ~**, in association ~; mixed up ~; 结交;与…交游;与…交往: *She's in ~ the wrong crowd,* eg of a girl whose companions are criminals. 她结交了一帮不三不四之徒。 **5** (to indicate antagonism, opposition): (表示敌对、反对): *fight/argue/struggle/quarrel, etc ~ sb;* 与某人打架(辩论,竞争,吵架等); *have an argument ~ sb;* 与某人辩论; *in competition ~;* 与…竞争; *a battle ~ savages;* 对抗野蛮人的战斗; *at war ~ the Romans.* 与罗马人作战。 **fall out ~**, ⇨ **fall**[2](14). **have it out ~ sb,** ⇨ **have**[4](9). **6** (to indicate cause) because of; owing to: (表示原因)因为; 由于: *silent ~ shame;* 因羞耻而沉默; *trembling ~ fear/rage;* 因惧(愤怒)而颤抖; *shaking ~ cold;* 冷得发抖; *a face wet ~ tears.* 眼泪湿润的脸。 **7** (to indicate manner): (表示方式或样态): *do sth ~ an effort/~ a light heart/~ one's whole heart/~ joy/~ pleasure;* 努力(心情轻松,全心全意,高高兴兴,甘心情愿)地做某事; *standing ~ his hands in his pockets;* 他站着,双手放在口袋里; *win ~ ease,* easily; 轻易地获胜; *fight ~ courage,* courageously; 英勇地战斗; *a roar/a growl/a shout of triumph;* 大吼(咆哮,欢呼)着; *receive sb ~ open arms.* 热忱地欢迎某人。 **8** in the same way or direction as; at the same time as: 与…同方向或路径; 与…同时: *A tree's shadow moves ~ the sun.* 树影随着太阳移动。 *W~ the approach of sunset it becomes chilly.* 到日落时分,天变冷了。 *Do you rise ~ the sun,* ie at dawn? 你黎明即起吗? **9** (to indicate care, charge or possession): (表示照顾、管理或保有): *Leave the child ~* (= in the care of) *its aunt.* 把小孩留给他的姑姑照管。 *I have no money ~ me.* 我身上没钱。 *The next move is ~ you.* 下一步该你。 *~ you,* ie you must decide. 由你作决定。 **10** in regard to; concerning: 对于;关于: *be patient ~ them;* 对他们有耐性; *sympathize ~ him;* 同情他; *bear/put up ~* (= endure) *sb or sth;* 忍受某人或某事; *have dealings/business ~ sb.* 与某人有交往(商业往来)。 *What do you want ~ me?* 你要我做什么? (你找我干什么?) *What's your business ~ him?* 你和他有什么事? *It's a habit ~ some people.* 这是某些人的习惯。 *We can't do anything/can do nothing ~ him,* cannot influence, control, make use of, him. 我们对他毫无办法(不能影响、控制或利用他)。 *It's holiday time ~ us now.* 对于我们来说现在是假期。 *The first object ~ him* (= His first object) *is always to make a profit.* 他的第一目标永远是赚钱。 *Away ~ him!* Send or take him away! 带他走! *Out ~ you!* Get out! 出去! *Off ~ his head!* 砍掉他的头了! (and many other

exclamatory sentences in the pattern *adv* + ~ + *n*/ *pron* 另有许多感叹句亦属于这类句型,即:副词 + with + 名词或代词). **11** (to indicate separation): (表示分离): *Let us dispense* ~ *ceremony,* ie not be ceremonious. 让 我们免除礼节吧。*I parted* ~ *her at the gate.* 我和她在 大门口分手。*He has broken* ~ *his best friend.* 他已同他 的至友绝交。**12** (to indicate agreement, harmony): (表 示同意,和谐): *He that is not* ~ *me* (= on my side) *is against me.* 不赞成我的人就是反对我。*I'm* ~ *you* (= in agreement or sympathy ~ you) *in what you say.* 我 同意你说的话。*I (dis)agree* ~ *you.* 我同意(不同意)你。 *I can't go along* ~ *you on that question,* can't agree or co-operate with you. 关于那个问题我不能苟和你。*Does this blue go well* ~ *this green?* 这种蓝色和这种绿色相配 吗? *be/get* '~ *it,* (sl) become aware of what is popular and up to date: (俚)知道或懂得最新或最流行的 事物;懂得时髦: (attrib) (用作定语) '~-*it clothes.* 流行 的服装。**13** in spite of; notwithstanding (the possession of): 尽管;纵然(有): *W~ all her faults he still liked her.* 尽管有许多缺点,他还是喜欢她。*He failed* ~ *the best of intentions to win the sympathy of his pupils.* 他虽然费 尽苦心,依然无法获得学生们的赞同。

withal /wɪˈðɔːl; wɪˈðɔl/ *adv* (archaic) in addition. (古) 又,且,加之。

with·draw /wɪðˈdrɔː; wɪðˈdrɔ/ *vt, vi* (*pl* -**drew** /-ˈdruː; -ˈdru/, *pp* -**drawn** /-ˈdrɔːn; -ˈdrɔn/) **1** [VP 6A, 14] ~ *sth/sb (from),* pull or draw back; take out or away: 取回;收回;拿出;拿开: ~ *money from the Bank/dirty banknotes from circulation;* 自银行提款 (收 回肮脏的钞票使不再流通); ~ *a boy from school,* not allow him to attend. 令一男孩退学。*The workers threatened to* ~ *their labour,* to go on strike. 工人们威 胁着要罢工。**2** [VP6A, 2A] take back (a statement, an accusation, an offer): 撤回;撤销(一项陈述、控告、提议): *He refused to* ~ (*the offending expression*), eg after calling sb a liar. 他拒绝道歉(撤回冒犯的话,如称某人为 说谎者)。**3** [VP6A, 14, 2A, C] (cause to) move back or away: (使)撤退;退出;脱离;撤出: ~ *troops from an exposed position;* 把部队撤离无掩蔽的地区; ~ *from society.* 隐遁。*Our troops had to* ~. 我们的部队必须撤 退。(Cf 参较 *The enemy had to retreat.* 敌人不得不退 却。)~**al** /-ˈdrɔːəl; -ˈdrɔəl/ *n* [U] ~ing or being withdrawn; [C] instance of this. 取回;收回;撤回;撤 销;退出;此种实例。'~**al symptom,** physical or mental reaction when steadily deprived of sth to which one is addicted (in order to break the habit). (医) 脱瘾 征状;断除症状(在戒瘾过程中,渐次断除瘾物时,所产生的 身心反应)。~**n** *adj* (of persons, their looks) retiring; unsociable; abstracted. (指人、人的外貌) 孤独的;缄默的; 不喜交际的;孤僻的;出神的;心不在焉的。

withe /wɪθ; wɪθ/, **withy** /ˈwɪðɪ; ˈwɪðɪ/ *nn* [C] tough but easily bent twig or branch, esp of willow or osier used for binding bundles, eg of firewood. 柔枝;(尤指 捆柴等用的)柳枝。

wither /ˈwɪðər; ˈwɪðə/ *vt, vi* **1** [VP6A, 15B, 2A, C] ~ *(sth) up:* ~ *(away),* (cause to) become dry, faded or dead: (使)枯萎;凋谢: *The hot summer* ~*ed* (*up*) *the grass.* 炎热的夏季(阳光)使草枯萎了。*Her hopes* ~*ed* (*away*). 她的希望渐渐凋萎了。**2** [VP6A] cause (sb) to be covered with shame or confusion: 使(某人)感到羞惭 或迷惑: *She* ~*ed him with a scornful look/gave him a* ~*ing look.* 她轻蔑的一瞥使他感到羞惭(她向他投注令他 自惭形秽的一瞥)。~**ing·ly** /ˈwɪðərɪŋlɪ; ˈwɪðərɪŋlɪ/ *adv*

with·ers /ˈwɪðəz; ˈwɪðəz/ *n pl* highest part of the back of a horse, etc between the shoulder-blades (where the strain of the collar is taken). 马肩隆;鬐甲(马等 两肩骨间的隆起部分,为轭的着力处)。 ⇨ the illus at **dog, domestic.** 参看 dog, domestic 之插图。

with·hold /wɪðˈhəʊld; wɪðˈhold/ *vt* (*pt, pp* -**held** /-ˈheld; -ˈheld/) [VP6A, 14] ~ *sth (from),* keep back; refuse to give: 抑制;制止;隐瞒;保留;扣留: *He tried to* ~ *the truth from us.* 他试图隐瞒真相,不让我们

知道。*I shall* ~ *my consent.* 我不会同意。

with·in /wɪˈðɪn; wɪðˈɪn/ *prep* inside; not beyond: 在…之内; 不越出: *remain* ~ *call/reach,* near by; 留在 附近; *live* ~ *one's income,* not spend more than one's income; 量入为出; ~ *an hour,* in less than an hour; 不 到一小时; ~ *a mile of the station.* 距离火车站不到一英 里。□ *adv* (liter) inside, (文)在内;在内部。

with·out /wɪˈðaʊt; wɪðˈaʊt/ *prep* **1** not having; not with; free from; lacking: 没有;无;不: *You can't buy things* ~ *money.* 没有钱买不到东西。*Do you ever travel* ~ *a ticket?* 你曾经无票(搭车、船、飞机等)旅行过 吗? *I once did it* ~ *being caught.* 我试过一次没被抓到。 *The rumour was* ~ *foundation.* 那个谣言毫无根据。*He was working* ~ *any hope of reward.* 他当时工作不希冀酬 劳。*She went out* ~ *a coat.* 她没穿外 衣就出去了。*Please don't leave* ~ *me,* Don't leave until I have joined you. 请等我同来一道去。~ *fail,* certainly. 必定; 无疑; 确然。*do* ~, *do*²(15). ⇨ *doubt,* admittedly; certainly. 无疑; 必定。**2** (before gerunds) (用于动名词前) *He can't speak German* ~ *making mistakes.* He speaks German incorrectly. 他每 说德语必有错误。*Can you make an omelette* ~ *breaking eggs?* 不打破蛋你能煎蛋饼吗? *Can you do it* ~ *his knowing,* so that he will not know? 你能做此事而不让他 知道吗? *He passed* ~ *seeing me,* and did not see me. 他 走过去未看见我。*He passed* ~ *my seeing him,* and I did not see him. 他走过去我没看见。*He left* ~ *so much as saying* (= left and did not even say) *that he was sorry/* ~ *even a thank-you.* 连一句道歉都没说,他就离 开了(连一声谢都没说,他就离开了)。 *go* ~ *saying,* be too obvious, too well known, etc to 'need saying. 不消 说;自不待言。**3** (old use) outside. (旧用法)在…之外。 □ *adv* (liter or old use) outside. (文或旧用法)在外面。

with·stand /wɪðˈstænd; wɪθˈstænd/ *vt* (*pt, pp* -**stood** /-ˈstʊd; -ˈstʊd/) [VP6A] resist; hold out against (pressure, attack): 抵抗; 抗拒; 经得起(压力、攻击): ~ *a siege;* 抵抗围攻; *shoes that will* ~ *hard wear.* 耐穿的 鞋子。

withy /ˈwɪðɪ; ˈwɪðɪ/ *n* (*pl* -**thies**) ⇨ **withe.**

wit·less /ˈwɪtlɪs; ˈwɪtlɪs/ *adj* ⇨ **wit**¹.

wit·ness /ˈwɪtnɪs; ˈwɪtnɪs/ *n* **1** (often 常作 '**eye**~) person who was actually present at an event and should, for this reason, be able to describe it; person who gives evidence under oath in a law court. 目击者; (在法庭上 经过宣誓的)证人。'~-**box** (US also 美亦作 '~-**stand**) *n* enclosure in a law court in which ~es stand while giving evidence. (法庭的)证人席。**2** [U] evidence; testimony; what is said about sb, an event, etc: 证据;证 明; 证言: *give* ~ *on behalf of an accused person at his trial.* 在被告受审时替他作证。*bear* ~ *to sb/sth,* (a) speak in support of, eg sb's character. 作证支持某人 (某事物)(如证明某人的品格)。(b) be evidence of: 为… 的证据; 证明: *The tests bear* ~ *to the quality of this new car.* 这些试验证明了这辆新(汽)车的品质。**3** person who adds his own signature to a document to testify that another person's signature on it is genuine. 连署人; 证 人(在文件上签名以证明他人的签名为亲笔所签者)。**4** *sb* or sth that is a sign or proof of sth: 作为…表征、象征或 证据的某人或某物: *My clothes are a* ~ *to my poverty.* 我穿的衣服证明我是贫穷的。□ *vt, vi* **1** [VP6A] be present at and see: 亲见; 目击: ~ *an accident.* 目睹一 件意外祸事。**2** [VP3A] ~ *to sth/doing sth,* give evidence (in a law court): (在法庭上)作证: ~ *to* (= testify) *to the truth of a statement.* 证明一项陈述的真 实性。*Mr X* ~*ed to having seen the accused near the scene of the crime.* 某先生(当庭)作证说曾看到被告在犯 罪现场附近。**3** [VP6A] be a ~ (3) to the signing of (an agreement, a will, etc): 在(合约、遗嘱等)上签名作 证; 连署: ~ *a signature.* 为一项签名连署。**4** [VP6A] give evidence of; show: 证明; 显示: *Her pale face* ~*ed the agitation she felt.* 她苍白的脸孔显示出她所感到的 激动。

wit·ti·cism /'wɪtɪsɪzəm; 'wɪtə,sɪzm̩/ ⇨ **wit**[1].

wit·ting·ly /'wɪtɪŋlɪ; 'wɪtɪŋlɪ/ adv knowingly; intentionally. 明知地; 故意地; 有意地。

witty /'wɪtɪ; 'wɪtɪ/ adj (-ier, -iest) ⇨ **wit**[1].

wive /waɪv; waɪv/ vi, vt [VP6A, 2A] (archaic) marry. (古)娶; 嫁; 与…结婚。

wives /waɪvz; waɪvz/ pl of **wife**.

wiz·ard /'wɪzəd; 'wɪzəd/ n 1 magician. 术士; 男巫。 2 person with amazing abilities: 有杰出才干的人; 奇才; 能手: a financial ~, person able to make money with amazing ease. 生财有道者。 □ adj (sl) excellent. (俚) 极好的。 **~ry** -drɪ; -drɪ/ n [U] magic (which is more usu). 魔术; 巫术 (magic 较常用)。

wiz·ened /'wɪznd; 'wɪznd/ adj having a dried-up appearance; shrivelled: 外形枯槁的; 皱缩的: an old man; 形容枯槁的老人; an old man with a ~ face; 面孔皱缩的老人; ~ apples. 干瘪的苹果。

wo, whoa /wəʊ; wo/ int (used chiefly to a horse) stop. (主要用于令马停住)喝! 站住!

woad /wəʊd; wod/ n [U] (plant from which is obtained a) kind of blue dye. 大青; 菘蓝; 大青染料。

wobble /'wɒbl; 'wɑbl/ vi, vt [VP2A, C, 6A] (cause to) move unsteadily from side to side; (fig) be uncertain (in opinions, in making decisions, etc): (使)摆动; 摇动; 震颤; (喻)(在意见、主张等方面)游移不定: This table ~s. 这张桌子不稳。 The front wheels of that car ~. 那辆汽车的前轮摆动。 Don't ~ the desk. 不要摇动书桌。 He ~d between two opinions. 他在两个意见之间游移不定。 Her voice sometimes ~s on high notes, Her high notes are not always steady. 她的高音有时不稳。 **wob·bler** /'wɒblə(r); 'wɑblɚ/ n sb or sth that ~s. 摆动、震颤、游移不定的人或物。 **wob·bly** /'wɒblɪ; 'wɑblɪ/ adj not firm or steady; inclined to ~: 不稳定的; 会摇动的; 震颤的: a wobbly chair. 不稳的椅子。 He's still a bit wobbly on his legs after his long illness. 久病之后，他的腿仍然有一点震颤。

woe /wəʊ; wo/ n (chiefly poet; sometimes hum) (主要用于诗歌中; 有时为诙谐用法) 1 [U] sorrow; grief; distress: 悲哀; 悲伤; 疾病以及其他悲哀的故事。 Woe (be) to..., A curse upon.... 愿...受难。 2 (pl) causes of woe; troubles: (复)悲哀的因由; 灾难; 忧患: poverty, illness and other woes. 贫苦, 疾病以及其他悲哀。 **woe·ful** /-fl; -fəl/ adj sorrowful; causing woe; regrettable: 悲哀的; 引起悲哀的; 遗憾的; 不幸的: woeful ignorance. 可悲的无知。 **woe·fully** /-fəlɪ; -fəlɪ/ adv **woe·be·gone** /'wəʊbɪgɒn US: -gɔːn; 'wobɪˌgɔn/ adj dismal(-looking); 显出悲伤的; 忧愁的; 愁眉苦脸的: What woebegone looks! 多么忧愁的神情!

woke, woken ⇨ **wake**[1].

wold /wəʊld; wold/ n [C, U] (area of) open uncultivated country; downs or moor. 荒原; 荒野。

wolf /wʊlf; wʊlf/ n (pl wolves /wʊlvz; wʊlvz/) wild, flesh-eating animal of the dog family, hunting in packs. 狼。 ~ cry /, raise false alarms: 作虚假的警报: You've cried ~ too often (suggesting that genuine cries for help will in future be ignored). 你作虚假的警报次数太多了(意谓以后真有需要请人帮忙时, 就没有人理会了)。 a ~ in sheep's clothing, person who appears friendly but is really an enemy. 披着羊皮的狼; 外貌友善的敌人。 keep the ~ from the door, be able to buy enough food for oneself and one's family. 能够免于饥饿; 勉强可维持生活。 **'~'s-bane** n aconite. 附子; 草乌头。 **'~-cub** n (a) young ~. 小狼。 (b) (former name for) junior Boy Scout (now Cub Scout). 幼童军 (Junior Boy Scout 的旧称, 现称作 Cub Scout)。 **'~-hound** n large dog originally bred for hunting wolves. 猎狼犬。 ~ **whistle** n whistle expressing sexual admiration. 赞美异性容貌、对异性表示爱慕或作挑逗时吹出的口哨。 □ vt [VP6A, 15A] eat quickly and greedily: 狼吞虎咽: ~ (down) one's food. 狼吞虎咽地吃东西。 **~·ish** /-ɪʃ; -ɪʃ/ adj of or like a ~: 狼的; 似狼的: a ~ish appetite. 强烈的食欲。

wol·fram /'wʊlfrəm; 'wʊlfrəm/ n tungsten; tungsten ore. 钨; 钨矿石。

woman /'wʊmən; 'wʊmən/ n (pl women /'wɪmɪn; 'wɪmɪn/) 1 adult female human being: 妇女; 女人: men, women and children; 男人、女人和儿童; a single (= unmarried) ~; 未婚女子; 独身女子; a ~ of the world, one with experience of society, not young and innocent; 深谙世故的女人; (attrib; to be preferred to lady) (用作定语; 比 lady 更为通用) a ~ 'doctor (pl 复数为 women 'doctors); 女医生; a ~ 'driver (pl 复数为 ,women 'drivers); 女驾驶员; a ca'reer-~, with a career; 职业妇女; a 'country-~, who lives and works in the country; 乡下妇女; a 'needle-~, expert at sewing, etc. 善缝纫的妇女; 善女红的妇女。 2 [U] (without article) the female sex. (不加冠词)女性; 女流。 3 [U] feminine character: 女子性格; 女子特质: All the ~ in her rebelled against the treatment she was receiving. 女性的尊严使她反抗所受到的待遇。 **'~-hood** /-hʊd; -ˌhʊd/ n [U] 1 (collective) women in general. (集合用法)女人。 2 the state of being a ~: (女人)成年期; 女人的特性: She had now grown to /reached ~hood. 她现在已经成年了。 **~·ish** /-ɪʃ; -ɪʃ/ adj of, like, for women. 女人的; 象女人的; 为女人的。 **~·ize** /-aɪz; -ˌaɪz/ vi pursue women (esp for casual sexual intercourse). 追求女性; (尤指)玩女人。 **~·izer** n man who does this. 追求女色者; 玩女人者。 **~·kind** n women in general. 女性; 妇女的总称。 **'~·like, ~·ly** adj like a ~. 象女人的。 **womenfolk** /'wɪmɪnfəʊk; 'wɪmɪnˌfok/ n pl women; women of one's family. 妇女; (家中的)女眷。

womb /wuːm; wum/ n (anat) organ in a female mammal in which offspring is carried and nourished while developing before birth: (解剖)子宫; (fig)(喻) It still lies in the ~ of time, is sth which the passage of time will reveal. 那仍在酝酿中(经过一段时间才会见分晓)。 ⇨ the illus at **reproduce**. 参看 reproduce 之插图。

wom·bat /'wɒmbæt; 'wɑmbæt/ n Australian animal (looking like a small bear). the female of which has a pouch for its young. (澳产)袋熊(形似小熊, 雌者生有袋囊, 以携其幼仔)。

won /wʌn; wʌn/ ⇨ **win**.

won·der /'wʌndə(r); 'wʌndɚ/ n 1 [U] feeling caused by sth unusual, surprising or inexplicable; surprise combined with admiration, bewilderment, etc: 惊异; 惊叹; 惊愕; 惊服: They were filled with ~. 他们感到惊奇。 We looked at the conjurer in silent ~. 我们目瞪口呆地看着那魔术师。 no / little /small ~, it is not /hardly surprising: 不(难以, 不太)令人吃惊: No ~ you were so late. 难怪你来得那么迟。 He was taken ill, and no /little ~, considering that he had been overworking for years. 他病了, 以他多年来一直工作过度来看, 实在不足怪。 **'~-land** /-lænd; -ˌlænd/ n 1 fairyland. 仙境; 奇境。 2 country that is remarkable in some way (eg because of abundant natural resources). 在某方面突出的地方(如天然物资丰富)。 **'~-struck** adj overcome with ~. 深感惊异的。 2 [C] thing or event that causes such feeling: 奇物; 奇迹; 奇观; 奇事: Walking on the moon is one of the ~s of our times. 在月球上漫步是现代奇事之一。 signs and ~s, miracles. 奇迹; 奇事。 work ~s, work with remarkable results, perform miracles. 创造奇迹; 做奇事。 a nine days' ~, sth which arouses great interest or admiration for a short time. 轰动一时的事件(很快就会被人忘记)。 for a ~, it is surprising (because unusual, unexpected, etc): 奇怪得很; 令人惊奇; 说也奇怪(由于不寻常、未料到等): For a ~ he paid back the money he had borrowed. 说也奇怪, 他居然还了他所借的钱。 It is a ~ (that), It is surprising that: 奇怪的是; 令人惊奇的是: It's a ~ (that) you didn't lose your way in the dark. 令人惊奇的是你在黑暗中竟未迷路。 What a ~, Haw surprising! 多么令人惊奇! □ vi, vt 1 [VP2A, 3A, B, 4B] ~ (at sth), be filled with ~(1); marvel; feel surprised: 感到惊奇; 惊愕; 惊叹; 惊讶: Can you ~ at it, Isn't it natural, to be expected,

etc? 你能(对它)感到惊奇吗?(那不是很自然,可以预料得到的吗?)*I don't ~ at her refusing to marry him.* 她拒绝和他结婚,我一点也不感到惊异。*It's not to be ~ed at,* is sth one might expect. 那不足为奇。*I ~ (at the fact) (that) he wasn't killed,* am surprised that he wasn't killed. 我感到惊奇他竟未遇难。*I shouldn't ~ if...,* shouldn't be surprised if .... 如果…,我一点也不觉得奇怪。*I'd ~ to hear her voice in the next room.* 我听到她在隔壁房间的声音,觉得很奇怪。**2** [VP2A, 3A] *~ (about sth),* feel curiosity; ask oneself: 觉得好奇; 想要知道; 问自己: *I was ~ing about him.* 我对那事觉得好奇。*I was just ~ing.* 我只不过好奇而已。**3** [VP8, 10] ask oneself: 自忖; 想知道: *I ~ who he is/what he wants/why he is late/whether he will come/whose it is.* 我想知道他是谁(他需要什么,他为什么迟到,他是否会来,那是谁的)。*I was ~ing how to get there quickly/where to spend the weekend, etc.* 我想知道怎么样可以很快地到达那里(在何处度周末等)。 **~ing·ly** /ˈwʌndrɪŋlɪ; ˈwʌndərɪŋlɪ/ *adv* ~. **~·ful** /-fl; -fəl/ *adj* causing ~; surprising; remarkable; admirable: 令人惊奇的; 使人惊服的; 奇妙的; 了不起的; 令人羡慕的: *We've been having ~ful weather recently.* 近来天气非常好。*What a ~ful memory she has!* 她的记忆力多么惊人啊! **~·fully** /-fəlɪ; -fəlɪ/ *adv* ~**·ment** /-mənt; -mənt/ n [U] surprise. 惊异; 惊讶。 **won·drous** /ˈwʌndrəs; ˈwʌndrəs/ *adj* (archaic, or liter) =~ful. (古或文)令人惊奇的; 使人惊服的。 □ *adv* (only with *adjj*) =~fully: (与形容词连用形)令人惊奇地; 使人惊服地: *wondrous kind.* 非常和善的。

wonky /ˈwɒŋkɪ; ˈwɑŋkɪ/ *adj*(GB sl) (英俚) **1** infirm; unreliable: 不稳的; 摇摆的; 靠不住的: *a ~ chair,* one that might break. 一把不牢固的椅子。**2** tottery; in poor health: 虚弱的; 健康不佳的: *She still feels a bit ~ after that attack of flu.* 那次害过流行性感冒以后,她仍旧感到有点虚弱。

wont /wəʊnt US: wɔːnt; wʌnt/ n (archaic or liter) (*sing* only) what sb is accustomed to doing: (古或文) (仅用单数) 习惯; 惯常活动: *He went to bed much earlier than was his ~,* than he usually did. 他(那晚)就寝的时间比平常早了很多。 *use and ~,* established custom. 积习; 世俗。 □ *pred adj be ~ to,* be accustomed to. 习惯于。 **~ed** *attrib adj* customary; usual. 惯例的; 通常的。

won't /wəʊnt; wont/ = will not. ⇨ **will**[1].

woo /wuː; wu/ *vt* (*pt, pp* **wooed**) [VP6A] **1**(old use) try to win (a woman's) hand in marriage; court. (旧用法)向(女子)求婚; 求爱。**2** try to win (fame, fortune, success, sleep). 求取或想要获得(名誉、财富、成功、睡眠)。**3** try to get the support of (voters, customers, businessmen). 求取(选民、顾客、商人)的支持。 **wooer** n one who woos. 求婚者; 求爱者; 寻求名誉、财富、成功、选民的支持等者。

wood /wʊd; wʊd/ n **1** [U] (with *indef art* and *pl* only when meaning kind, sort, variety) hard solid substance of a tree below the bark: (只有表示种类、各色各样等概念时,才可加不定冠词,或用复数形式)木; 木料; 木头; 木柴; 木料: *Tables are usually made of ~.* 桌子通常是木材做的。*Put some more ~ on the fire.* 在火上添加点木柴。*He was chopping ~ for the fire.* 他在劈柴生火。*Teak is a hard (kind of) ~ and pine is a soft (kind of) ~.* 麻栗木是硬材; 松木是软材。(attrib): (用作定语): *floors/pavements,* made of blocks of ~. 木砖地板(人行道)。Cf 参较 **wooden,** used for articles made of ~. 指木制的物件。**2** [C] (often *pl*) area of land covered with growing trees (not as extensive as a forest): (常用复数)树林(不如 forest 范围大): *a ~ of beech (-trees).* 山毛榉林。*a house in the middle of a ~.* 林中一屋; *go for a walk in the ~(s).* 到林中散步。 *out of the ~,* (fig) free from troubles or difficulties: (喻) 脱离麻烦或困难: *We're not yet out of the ~,* still have difficulties to face. 我们尚未脱离困境。 *be unable to see the ~ for the trees,* (fig) be unable to get a clear view of the whole because of too many details: (喻)见树不见林(因

细节过多而看不清全局)。**3** *in/from the ~,* in/from the cask or barrel: 在(从)木桶中: *wine in the ~;* 木桶中的酒; *drawn from the ~.* 从木桶中取出的。**4**(compounds, from 1 above)(复合词,来自上列第 1 义) **~·alcohol** n [U] kind of alcohol distilled from ~ (also called methyl alcohol) used as a fuel and a solvent. 木醇; 甲醇(用作燃料及溶剂,亦称作 methyl alcohol)。 **~·block** n block of ~ from which ~cuts are made. (木刻用的)版木。 **~·cut** n print from a design, picture, etc cut on a block of ~. 木刻; 木刻画; 木版画。 **~·louse** n (*pl* **-lice**) kinds of small, wingless, insect-like creature living in decaying ~, damp soil, etc. 土鳖; 地鳖(数种无翅而似昆虫的小生物,生于朽木、湿地等处)。 **~·pecker** n kinds of bird that clings to the bark of trees and taps or pecks it to find insects. 啄木鸟。 **~·pile** n pile of ~, esp for fuel. 木料堆; (尤指)柴堆。 **~·pulp** n [U] ~ shredded to pulp as the material for making paper. (造纸用的)木浆。 **~·shed** n shed for storing ~ (esp for fuel). 存放木材(尤指柴薪)的小棚。 **~·wind** n musical wind instrument made (originally) of ~. 木管乐器(最初以木材制成,故名)。 **~·work** n [U] **1** things made of ~, esp the ~en parts of a building (eg doors, stairs). 木制品; (尤指)房屋之木造部分(如门、梯)。**2** art of making things of ~; carpentry. 木工手艺; 木工活。 **~·worm** n **1**~=eating larva that bores into ~. 蛀木虫; 蛀船虫。**2** [U] damage caused by ~worm. 蛀木虫或蛀船虫造成的损害。**5**(compounds, from 2 above)(复合词,来自上列第 2 义) **~·bine** n wild honeysuckle. (植)野忍冬。 **~·cock** n (*pl* unchanged) kinds of game bird, brown with a long, straight bill, short legs and tail, found in ~land and valued as food. (复数不变)(动)丘鹬; 山鹬。 **~·craft** n [U] knowledge of forest conditions, skill in finding one's way in ~s and forests, esp as used in hunting, etc. (尤指用于打猎等的)森林知识; 林中识路技巧。 **~·cutter** n man who cuts down trees. 伐木者。 **~·land** /-lənd; -lænd/ n [U] land covered with trees: 林地; 森林; 树林: (attrib)(用作定语) ~land scenery. 林景。 **~·man** /-mən; -mən/ n (*pl* **-men**) forester; ~cutter. 居于森林之人; 看管森林之人; 伐木者。 **~s·man** /-zmən; -zmən/ n (*pl* **-men**) (esp US) (尤美) = ~man. **~ed** *adj* covered with growing trees: 多树木的; 树木繁茂的: ~ed country, abounding in trees. 多树木的地带。 **~en** /ˈwʊdn; ˈwʊdn/ *adj* **1**(attrib) made of ~: (用作定语)木制的: *a ~en leg;* 木腿; *~en walls* (fig, of the old ~en warships, thought of as a defence); 木制干城(喻: 指昔时的木造军舰,被视作防卫屏障); *a ~enhead,* ⇨ **blockhead.** Hence, 由此产生, **~en·headed** *adj* stupid. 木头脑袋的; 愚笨的。**2** stiff, clumsy, awkward (as if made of ~): 生硬的; 愚钝的; 笨拙的(宛如木制的): *a ~en* (= inexpressive) *smile.* 呆板的笑容。*His manners were extremely ~en.* 他的举止极为呆笨。 **~·y** *adj* (**-ier, -iest**) **1**~ed: 多树木的: *a ~y hillside.* 多树木的山坡。**2** of or like ~: 木的; 似木的: *the ~y stems of a plant.* 植物的木茎。

wooer /ˈwuːə(r); ˈwuə/ n ⇨ **woo.**

woof /wuːf; wuf/ n= **weft.**

woofer /ˈwuːfə(r); ˈwufə/ n loudspeaker designed to produce low notes. 低音扬声器; 低音喇叭。

wool /wʊl; wʊl/ n [U] **1** soft hair of sheep, goats and some other animals (eg the llama and alpaca); thread, yarn, cloth, clothing, made from this: 羊毛; 骆马毛; 羊驼毛; 毛线; 绒线; 毛织品; 毛料衣服: *wear ~* (ie clothing made of ~) *next to the skin;* 贴身穿毛料衣服; *the ~ trade;* 羊毛业; *~ merchants;* 羊毛商人; *imports of ~ from Australia;* 从澳大利亚进口羊毛; *knitting~,* ⇨ yarn for knitting. 毛线; 绒线。 *dyed in the ~,* dyed before spinning and weaving; (fig) thorough; complete: 在纺织以前即染色的; 生染的; (喻)彻底的; 道地的; 不可改变的: *a dyed-in-the~ Tory,* person who is strongly convinced that Tory principles, etc are the best. 死硬的英国保守党员。 *much cry and little ~,* much talk with little result; fuss about trifles 说的多做的少; 雷声大雨

点小; 为小事而大惊小怪。 **pull the '～ over sb's eyes,** deceive or trick him. 欺骗或玩弄某人。 **'～-gathering** *adj, n* absent-minded(ness). 心不在焉(的)。 **the '～-sack,** ～-stuffed cushion on which the Lord Chancellor sits in the House of Lords: 英国上议院议长(兼大法官)的席位: *reach the ～sack,* become Lord Chancellor. 膺任上议院议长(兼大法官)。 **2** material similar in appearance or texture to ～; 似羊毛之物; *cotton～,* raw cotton (US 美 = *cotton-batting*). 生棉。 **3** (person's) thick curly hair. (人的)卷曲的厚发。 *lose one's ～,* (colloq) get angry. (口)发怒。 **～len** (US 美 = **～en**) /'wulen/ 'wuln/ *attrib adj* made of ～: 羊毛制的: *～len cloth/blankets;* 呢绒(毛毯); of ～ fabrics: 毛织品的: *～len manufacturers/merchants.* 毛织品制造者(商人)。 **～lens** (US 美 = **～ens**) *n pl* ～len fabrics; cloth, flannel, blankets, etc, made of ～. 毛织品; 毛制的绒布、法兰绒、毯子等。 **～ly** (US also **～y**) /'wuli; 'wuli/ *adj* **(-ier, -iest) 1** covered with, made of, looking like, ～: 覆满羊毛或毛绒等制的; 象羊毛的: *～ly hair;* 卷曲的厚发: *a ～ly coat.* 羊毛制的上装。 **2** (fig, of the mind, ideas, arguments) confused, not clear; not incisive. (喻,指头脑,观念,论点)模糊的; 不清楚的; 不透彻的。 ～*n* (*pl* **-lies**) (colloq) ～len garment, esp a sweater: (口)毛织衣服; (尤指)毛线衫: *Put an extra ～ly on when you go out.* 外出时多加一件毛线衣。

word /wɜːd; wɝd/ *n* **1** [C] sound or combination of sounds (or the written or printed symbols) forming a unit of the grammar or vocabulary of a language: 语; 言; 字; 词; (一种语言的)语法单位或词汇单位: *When we speak we put our thoughts into ～s.* 我们说话时,是用言语表达我们的思想。 *I have no ～s* (or cannot adequately) *express my gratitude.* 我找不到适当的言词来表达我的谢意。 *W～s failed him,* He could not express his thoughts, his emotion, etc in ～s. 他竟吶吶不能言。 *a play on/upon ～s,* a pun. 双关语; 俏皮话。 *be not the ～ for it,* not an adequate or satisfactory description: 非恰当字眼; 不是恰当的或令人满意的措辞: *Warm's not the ～ for it* (ie hot is perhaps a better ～)! '暖和'不是恰当的字眼 ('炎热' 也许更恰当)! *not get a ～ in edgeways,* ⇨ **edgeways. (repeat sth)** ～ *for* ～, exactly, with no changes or omissions. 正确地; 不改变亦不省略地(复述某事)。 **(translate sth)** ～ *for* ～, literally. 逐字地(翻译)。 做字面(翻译); 直译。 Cf 参较 *a free translation.* in *a/one* ～, briefly; to sum up. 简言之; 一句话; 总之。 *by ～ of mouth,* in spoken, not written, ～s. 口头地。 **2** [C] sth said; remark or statement: 所说的话; 谈话; 言词: *He didn't say a ～ about it.* 他对那件事字未提。 *I don't believe a ～ of the story.* 这故事我一点也不相信。 *Mr A will now say a few ～s,* make a few remarks, give a short address. A先生现在要说几句话。 *Don't waste ～s on that fellow,* don't try to persuade, convince, warn, etc him. 不要同那家伙费口舌(不必想劝告、说服、警告他等)。 *eat one's ～s,* admit that one was wrong; take one's ～s back and apologize. 认错; 收回前言并道歉; 认错道歉。 *have a ～ with sb,* speak to him. 同某人说一两句话。 *have ～s* (*with sb*), quarrel: (同某人)口角: *They've had ～s, I hear.* 他们有过争吵, 我听到的。 *have the last ～,* make the final remark in an argument, esp by making a retort to which there is no good answer. 在辩论中作最后的辩驳(尤指说出对方无法回驳的话)。 *put in/say a good ～ (for sb),* speak on his behalf (to support or defend). (为某人)进言或说项。 *suit the action to the ～,* do at once what one has said one will do (eg of a threat). 说了就做; 说做就做 (如威胁)。 *take sb at his ～,* act on the belief that he means what he says. 把某人的话信以为真; 相信某人的话。 *big ～s,* boasting. 大话; 吹牛。 *a ～ as soon as sth has been said.* 说了这话以后(立即…)。 *a ～ in/out of season,* a piece of advice given when it is welcome and helpful/unwelcome and interfering. 合(不合)时宜的忠言。 *the last ～ on (a subject),* statement, etc which includes the latest views and information: 有

关(某问题)的最近的见解及消息: *The last ～ has not yet been said on this subject.* There will be further facts, views, etc. 这问题尚未成定论(尚有进一步的发现、观点等)。 *the last ～ (in sth),* the latest, most up-to-date, etc, in: 为(某事物或某方面)的最近或最新式的产品: *Our coach tours of Scotland are the last ～ in comfort and convenience.* 我们乘长途汽车去苏格兰的旅游,就舒适与方便这点设备而言,是最新式的了。 **3** (*sing,* without *def art*) news; information: (单数,不用定冠词)消息; 音讯: *Please send me ～ of your safe arrival.* 请将您平安到达的消息告诉我。 *Please leave ～ for me at work.* 请在我上班处留言。 *W～ came that I was wanted at home.* 家里传来消息要我回去。 **4** (*sing only,* with a possessive) promise; assurance. (仅用单数, 与所有格连用)诺言; 保证。 *be as good as one's ～,* do what one promises: 守信: *Don't worry—I'm sure he'll be as good as his ～.* 不要担心—我相信他不会食言。 *give sb one's ～ (that...),* promise: 允诺; 答应; 许下诺言: *The goods will arrive on time—I give you my word.* 那批货会准时到达—我向你保证。 *keep/break one's ～,* do/fail to do what one has promised to do. 守(爽)约; 守(失)信。 *take sb's ～ for it,* believe what he says: 相信某人说的话: *I have no proof, but you may take my ～ for it.* 我没有证据,不过你可以相信我的话。 *take sb at his ～,* believe that he is telling the truth, that he will keep a promise. 相信某人的话是真的; 相信某人会信守诺言。 *upon my ～,* **(a)** on my honour, 一定; 的确; 我向你保证是这样。 **(b)** used as an exclamation of surprise. (用作惊讶的呼声)哎呀。 **5** (*sing only*) command; order; spoken signal: (仅用单数)号令; 命令; 口令; 号令: *The officer gave the ～ to fire.* 军官下令射击。 *His ～ is law,* His orders must be obeyed. 他的命令就是法律。 *You must give the ～ before you can pass.* 你必须说出口令才能通过。 ⇨ **password** at **pass**[1] **(10). 6** (in the Christian religion) (基督的) **the W～** (of God); **God's W～, (a)** the Scriptures, esp the Gospel: 圣经; (尤指)福音书: *preach the W～.* 传福音。 **(b)** title of Jesus Christ. 耶稣基督之称谓。 **7** (compounds) (复合词) '**～-book** *n* vocabulary; list of ～s with meanings, etc. 词汇; 单词表; 词典。 '**～-division** *n* [U] dividing of the spelling of a ～, eg at the end of a line on a page. 断字; 断字法(按照音节将某字分开的方法,如在一行的末尾所为)。 '**～-painter** *n* person who can describe vividly in ～s. 擅长以文字作生动描述的人。 '**～-perfect** *adj* knowing, able to repeat, a poem, a part in a play, etc by heart. 熟记或背诵诗歌、台词等的。 '**～-picture** *n* vivid description in ～s. 生动的文字描述。 '**～-splitting** *n* [U] sophistry; making of distinctions of meaning, etc that are subtle. 诡辩; 咬文嚼字; 过细的词义分辨。 □ *vt* [VP6A] express in ～s: 说; 言; 以言辞表达: *a well-～ed letter.* 措辞得当的信。 *The suggestion might be ～ed more politely.* 那项建议的措辞可以更婉转些。 ～**ing** *n* (*sing only*) way in which sth is expressed; choice of ～s to express meaning: (仅用单数)表达法; 语法; 措辞; 用词: *A different ～ing might make the meaning clearer.* 换一个说法可能使意义更为明白。 ～**less** *adj* without ～s; not put into ～s: 无话的; 未明说的: *～less grief.* 无言的悲戚。 **wordy** *adj* (-ier, -iest) using, expressed in, a large number of ～s, esp unnecessary ～s: 多言的; 冗长的; (尤指)废话连篇的; 唠叨的: *a ～y telegram;* 冗长的电报; *～y warfare,* ie argument. 论战。 ～**ily** /-ɪlɪ; -ɪlɪ/ *adv* ～**i-ness** *n*

wore /wɔː(r); wɔr/ *pt* of **wear**[2].

work[1] /wɜːk; wɝk/ *n* **1** [U] use of bodily or mental powers with the purpose of doing or making sth (esp contrasted with play or recreation); use of energy supplied by steam, electric current, etc: 工作; 劳动(尤指与游戏或娱乐相对而言); (由蒸气、电流等供给的)能的使用; 功: *Are you fond of hard ～?* 你喜欢艰苦的工作吗? *The ～ of building the new bridge took six months.* 那座新桥梁的工程费时半载。 *It was the ～ of a moment* (= Only a moment was needed) *to turn the key in the lock and make him a prisoner.* 把门上锁, 将他囚禁, 只需片刻

工夫. *It was very hard ~ getting to the top of the mountain.* 爬到那座山的山顶是一件极为辛苦的事. *This is the ~ of an enemy,* An enemy has done this. 这是敌人干的事. *Machines now do much of the ~ formerly done by man.* 以前由人力做的工作现在大部分用机器来做. **make hard ~ of sth,** make it seem more difficult than it is. 使某事显得更加困难. **make short ~ of sth,** finish it quickly. 匆匆做完某事. **set/get to ~ (on sth/to do sth),** begin; make a start. 开始; 着手工作. **set/go about one's ~,** start doing it: 开始自己的工作: *You're not setting about your ~ in the right way.* 你未以正确的方法开始你的工作. **at ~ (on sth),** busy or occupied with (indicating uncompleted ~, ~ in progress). 在工作; 忙于(未完成的工作, 进展中的工作). **all in the day's ~,** (used to indicate that sth is) normal; what is usual or to be expected. (用于表示某事物是)正常的; 一般的; 合乎常理的. **2** [U] what a person does to earn a living; employment: 谋生所做之工作; 职业; 业务: *What time do you get to (your) ~ every day?* 你每天何时上班? *The men were on their way to ~.* 那些(男)人在上班的途中. *It is difficult to find ~ during a depression.* 经济萧条的时候很难找工作. **at ~,** at one's place of employment: 在工作的地方; 在工作: *He's at ~ now, but he'll be back at six.* 他工作去了, 但他六点钟会回来. **in/out of ~,** having/not having employment: 有(无)职业; 就(失)业: *He has been out of ~ for a year.* 他已经失业一年了. *He'll be glad to be in regular ~ again.* 他将很高兴再从事固定的职业. Hence, 由此产生, (attrib adj) (定语形容词), **out-of-'work.** 失业的. **3** [U] sth to be done, sth connected with a trade or occupation, not necessarily for payment: 待做之事; 工作(不一定与职业有关, 亦不一定为报酬): *I always find plenty of ~ that needs doing in my garden.* 在庭园中我总有许多需要做的事情. *I have some ~ for you to do.* 我有一些事情要你做. **4** [U] things needed or used for ~: 工作时所需用的东西; 工具: *She took her ~ (eg her sewing materials) on to the verandah.* 她把工作所需之物(如缝纫所需的布料和用具)带到走廊上去工作. **'~·bag/·basket/·box** nn bag, etc for holding such things, esp for sewing 工具袋(篮, 匣); (尤指)针线袋(篮, 匣). **5** [U] that which is produced by ~: 制作品; 工艺品: *The ~ of famous silversmiths and sculptors may be seen in museums.* 著名的银匠及雕刻家的制作品可以在博物馆中见到. *What a beautiful piece of ~!* 多么美丽的一件工艺品! *The villagers sell their ~ (eg needlework, wood-carvings, metal articles) to tourists.* 村民把他们的手工艺品(如刺绣, 木雕刻, 金属器具)卖给观光客. ⇨ also compounds such as *stone~, wood~* at **stone(1), wood(4).** **6** [C] product of the intellect or the imagination: 作品; 著作: *the ~s of Shakespeare;* 莎士比亚的著作; *the ~s of Beethoven.* 贝多芬的作品. ⇨ **opus;** *~s of art;* 艺术品; 美术品; *a new ~ (= musical composition) by John Lewis;* 约翰·刘易斯的新作(即新作的乐曲); *a new ~ (= book) on modern art.* 论现代艺术的新著作(即新书). **7** (pl) moving parts of a machine: (复)机器的活动部分; (活动)机件: *the ~s of a clock or watch.* 钟或表的(活动)机件. *There's something wrong with the ~.* 机件出毛病了. **8** (pl, with *sing* or *pl v*) building(s) where industrial or manufacturing processes are carried on: (复数形式, 可用单数或复数动词)工厂; 工场: a '*gas~s,* 煤气厂; an '*iron~s;* 铁工厂; a '*brick~s.* 砖厂. *The 'steel~s was/were closed for the Christmas holidays.* 那家炼钢厂歇工以度圣诞假期. **'~s council/committee,** joint council of representatives of employers and employees to deal with problems of management, labour relations, etc. 工厂委员会 (劳资双方皆有代表的联合会议, 以处理有关管理, 劳工关系等方面的问题). **9 public ~s,** the building of roads, dams, embankments; other engineering operations(by government departments, etc): 公共工程(政府部门等建筑的道路, 水坝, 堤防及其他工程): *the Ministry of Public Building and W~,* (until 1971) government department

(now part of the Department of the Environment) responsible for these operations. (1971 年以前之) 公共工程部(政府机构, 现为'环境部'的一部分). **10** (pl v) (用复数动词) (cf 参较 '*earth~s,* '*out~s*) defensive structures; fortifications: 防御工事; 堡垒: *The ~s were thought to be impregnable.* 那防御工事被认为是无法攻破. **11** (compounds) (复合词) **'~·bench** n table at which a mechanic does his ~. 工匠台; 细工台. **'~·book** n book with outlines of a subject of study, with questions to be answered (in blank spaces, in writing), for notes, etc. (辅助)练习簿; 习题簿; 笔记簿; 记事簿; 工作手册; 业务手册. **'~·day** n day for ~; day which is not a Sunday or a holiday. 工作日; 非星期日或假日. **'~ force** n total number of men working in a particular factory, etc. 某一工厂等的工作总人数; 劳动力. **'~·house** n 1 (GB hist) public institution for homeless people. (英国史)贫民习艺所; 救贫院. **2** (US) place where those who have committed small crimes are confined and made to work. (美)监犯工厂(监禁轻微罪犯并使其工作的所在). **'~·man** /-mən;-mən/ n (pl -**men**) **1** man who earns a living by physical labour or at machines, etc. 工人; 劳工. **2** person who works in a specified way: 以某种方式工作的人: *a skilled/quick, etc ~man.* 熟练(敏捷等)的工作者. **'~man·like** adj characteristic of a good ~man. 象熟练工人的. **'~·man·ship** /-mənʃip; -mənʃip/ n [U] quality as seen in sth made: (成品中显出的)手艺; 技艺; 做工: *articles of poor/excellent ~manship;* 做工拙劣 (极好) 的物品; person's skill in doing ~. 人的工作技巧. **'~·room** n room in which ~ is done. 工作室; 作业室. **'~·shop** n room or building in which things (esp machines) are made or repaired. 工厂; 工场; 修理厂. **'~-shy** adj disinclined to work; lazy. 不愿工作的; 懒惰的. **'~·study** n (pl -**dies**) study of how ~ may be done efficiently and economically (eg by observing the sequence of movements in an operation, time needed, etc). 工作效率的研究(例如观察作业的程序, 所需的时间等). **'~·table** n (esp) table with drawers for sewing materials, etc. (尤指)有抽屉的裁缝台. **~·a·day** /'wɜːkədeɪ; 'wɝkə,de/ adj commonplace; dull: 普通的; 乏味的: *this ~aday world/life.* 这个乏味的世界(生活).

work² /wɜːk; wɝk/ vi, vt (pt, pp **~ed** or **wrought** /rɔːt; rɔt/) (For uses with *adverbial particles* and *preps,* ⇨ 10 below. For uses with *wrought,* ⇨ **wrought**). (与副词性小品词及介词连用的用法, 参看下列第 10 义; wrought 的用法, 参看 wrought 条). **1** [VP2A, B, C, 3A, 4A] do work; engage in physical or mental activity: 工作; 劳动; 劳心; 做事: *He's been ~ing hard all day.* 他整天辛苦地工作了一整天. *These men in this factory ~ 40 hours a week.* 这个工厂里的工人每周工作四十小时. *Most people have to ~ in order to live,* ie to earn a living. 大多数人必须工作以维持生活. *He isn't ~ing now,* eg because unemployed or retired. 他现在不做事(如失业, 退休等). *Have British statesmen always ~ed for peace?* 英国的政治家们一直为和平努力吗? *He's ~ing at (= studying) Physics and Chemistry.* 他正在研习物理学及化学. *Green is ~ing on (= writing) a new novel.* 格林目前正在写一部新小说. *This man ~s in leather,* is a craftsman in leather. 此人是皮匠. *He has always ~ed against (= opposed) reform.* 他一直阻挠改革. **~ to rule,** ⇨ **rule**(1). **~·in** n occasion when workers continue to ~ in a factory to protest against proposed dismissal, closure of the factory, etc. 工作抗议(指工人继续在工厂工作, 以抗议解雇工人, 关闭工厂等计划). **2** [VP2A, C] (of a machine, apparatus, bodily organ, plan, method, etc) do what it is designed to do; have the desired result; function: operate: (机器, 机械, 仪器, 身体器官, 计划, 方法等)运转; 运作; 发挥正常功能; 获得预期结果: *The lift/elevator/bell/telephone is not ~ing.* 电梯 (升降机, 门铃, 电话)坏了. *The gears ~ smoothly.* 齿轮运转灵活. *This machine ~s by electricity.* 这架机器是电力推动的. *My brain doesn't seem to be*

~*ing well today.* 我的脑筋今天好象不太灵活。*Will this new plan/scheme/method* ~? 这项新计划(方案，方法)行得通吗？*The charm* ~*ed.* 那符咒失效了。~ *ed like a charm.* 它非常灵光。**3** [VP6A, 15A] cause to ~; set in motion: 使工作；使活动；使运转： *He* ~*s his wife/himself too hard.* 他使他的妻子(他自己)工作过度了。*Don't* ~ *yourself/your poor wife to death.* 不要让你自己(你那可怜的妻子)过于劳累。*She was* ~*ing the treadle of her sewing-machine.* 她正用脚踩动缝纫机的踏板。*This machine is* ~*ed by steam/electricity.* 这架机器是蒸气(电力)推动的。**4** [VP6A] produce or obtain as the result of effort: 努力做成或获得；完成；造成： ~ *wonders/a cure/harm/mischief.* 造成奇迹(获得痊愈；造成伤害；造成损害)。~ *one's passage,* earn it by ~*ing:* 做工赚取旅费： *He* ~*ed his passage from England to Australia, by* ~*ing on the ship.* 他从英国到澳大利亚时在船上工作以赚取旅费。~ *one's way (through college, etc),* have a paid job, while studying to meet costs: 工读(完成大学学业等)： *He's* ~*ing his way through medical school.* 他以半工半读的方式读医学院。~ *one's will (on sb),* make him do what one wants him to do. 操纵(某人)；使(某人)做自己想要他做的事情。~ *it,* (sl) bring sth about (by scheming, etc): (俚)完成某事；(借阴谋，诡计等)使某事发生： *I'll* ~ *it if I can,* eg by using influence, cajolery, etc. 如果我能够，我会搞出个名堂来。**5** [VP6A] operate; control; be employed in the management of: 经营；管理；控制： ~ *a mine.* 经营一个矿场。*This salesman* ~*s the North Wales area,* travels there as a salesman. 这个推销员在北威尔士地区推销货物。**6** [VP2C, D, 15A, B, 22] (cause to) move into, reach, a new state or position, usu by degrees or with a succession of small movements: (使)逐渐地(或借连续不断的微小活动而)进入或达到一种新的状态或位置；(使)逐渐变动；(使)慢慢移动： *Your shirt has* ~*ed out, has* come out from above the top of your trousers. 你的衬衫跑到裤子外面来了。*One of the screws has* ~*ed loose.* 有一个螺丝钉已经松了。*The rain had* ~*ed through the roof,* had penetrated it slowly. 雨水渐渐渗过屋顶了。*Can you* ~ *the stone into position,* eg when building a stone wall? 你能把这块石头移至适当的位置吗(如建造石墙时)？*The men* ~*ed their way forward.* 那些(男)人奋力向前挤。*Many months later the splinter* ~*ed out of her arm,* came out after travelling through the flesh from the point at which it had entered. 好几个月以后，扎进她手臂的那根刺跑出来了。*The wind has* ~*ed round to the south,* changed direction by degrees. 风已渐渐转向南。**7** [VP6A] make or shape by hammering, kneading, pressure, etc: 借锤、搓、捏、压等而做成或形成；做成；捏成；搓成；压成： ~ *clay,* knead it with water; 捏粘土(使其和水)：~ *dough,* (when making bread). (做面包时)揉面团。⇨ **wrought** for *wrought* iron. **8** [VP2A] ferment; move in an agitated way: 发酵；激动地抽动；颤动： *The yeast began to* ~, to ferment, eg in dough. 酵母开始发酵(如在面团中)。*His face/features began to* ~ *violently,* twitch, stir in a way showing agitation. 他的脸孔(面容)开始剧烈地抽搐(因为感情激动)。**9** [VP6A, 14] make by stitching; embroider: 缝制；刺绣： ~ *a design on a cushion-cover/one's initials on a handkerchief.* 把一个图样绣在垫套上，绣自己的姓名缩写刺绣在手帕上)。**10** [VP 2C, 3A, 14, 15B] (special uses with *adverbial particles* and *preps*): (与副词性小品词及介词连用的特殊用法)：

work away (at sth), continue to ~: 继续工作： *He's been* ~*ing away at this job since breakfast.* 从吃过早饭他就一直做这个工作。

work 'in; ~ into sth, (⇨ 6 above) penetrate; find a way in/into: (参看上列第 6 义)渗透；穿透；进入： *The dust has* ~*ed in everywhere,* eg into a house during a sandstorm. 灰尘无孔不入遍布室内各处(如在一次暴风沙中，房舍遭风沙侵入)。~ *sth in/into,* introduce; find a place for: 引进；插入；加入： *Can't you* ~ *in a few jokes/* ~ *a few jokes into your story?* 你不能插几个笑话进去(插几个笑话到你的故事里)吗？

work sth off, get rid of; dispose of; deal with: 除去；排除；处置： ~ *off arrears of correspondence/superfluous energy/one's excess weight.* 处理积压的信件(发泄过剩的精力；减除过剩体重)。

work on/upon sb/sth, (⇨ 8 above)excite, influence: (参看上列第 8 义)激动;激起；激发；影响： *Will the high figure for unemployment* ~ *on the conscience of the Government?* 庞大的失业数字会使政府的良心不安吗？*The sufferings of the refugees* ~*ed upon our feelings so much that we gave them all the help we could.* 难民们的痛苦令我们如此难过，所以我们给予了他们一切可能的帮助。⇨ **also** 1 above; 亦参看上列第 1 义。~ *on a new novel, etc.* 从事于一部新小说的写作等。

work out, **(a)** be capable of being solved: 可以解决，解答等；可以算出： *This sum/problem will not* ~ *out.* 这一总数(题目)算不出来。**(b)** be, turn out, in the end: 结局；至最后；结果为： *How will things* ~ *out?* 事情将如何变化？*The situation* ~*ed out quite well.* 情况到最后相当不错。*The total* ~*s out at £10.* 金额总计为十英镑。*How much does it* ~ *out at,* What's the total? 总共是多少钱？**(c)** ⇨ 6 above. 参看上列第 6 义。**(d)** exercise, train (for a contest): (为参加竞赛而)练习；训练： *The champion is* ~*ing out in the gym this morning.* 卫冕者今天早晨正在体育馆训练。Hence, 由此产生，'~*-out n* period, form, of training or exercise. 训练或练习的期间或形式。~ *sth out,* **(a)** calculate: 计算；算出： *I've* ~*ed out your share of the expenses at £5.* 我已计算出你该分摊的费用是五镑。**(b)** get results for: 获得结果；解答： *I can't* ~ *out these algebra problems.* 这些代数题目我解不出来。**(c)** devise; invent; develop in detail: 设计；发明；详细制定： *a well-* ~*ed out scheme.* 妥善周详的办法。*They've* ~*ed out a method of sending a spacecraft to Mars.* 他们已经设计出一种发射太空火箭到星的方法。*You must* ~ *out your own salvation,* find a way of saving yourself by your own efforts. 你必须奋力自救。**(d)** solve: 解决；解出： *He was* ~*ing out some coded messages.* 他在译出几则密码电讯。**(e)** (usu passive) exhaust by using, operating, etc: (通常用被动式) 用尽；耗尽： *That silver-mine is now* ~*ed out,* has no more ore. 那银矿已经枯竭了。

work up to sth, advance steadily to a high level: 逐渐而稳定地达到高水准或层面： *The orchestra was* ~*ing up to a crescendo.* 那交响乐团即将演奏到音量渐强的一节。~ *sth up,* **(a)** make by degrees; bring to an efficient or satisfactory condition: 逐渐造成或发展；使达到有效或满意的情况; 拓展： ~ *up a business.* 拓展一家商店。**(b)** excite; stir up: 激动；煽动；鼓动： ~ *up the feelings of an audience.* 煽动听众情绪。~ *sb/oneself up (into),* rouse to a high point (of excitement, etc): 使某人(自己)达到(兴奋等)的最高点；激动；激起；引起： *He* ~*ed himself/everyone up into a frenzy/rage/state of hysteria.* 他(他使每一个人)激动得发狂(狂怒，发疯)。*The audience was really* ~*ed up by this time.* 这时观众已变得非常激动。

work upon sb/sth, ⇨ ~ *on sb/sth* above. 参看上列 work on sb/sth。

work·able /ˈwɜːkəbl; ˈwɝkəbl/ *adj* that can be worked; that will work; practicable: 可使用的；可操作的；可以塑制的；可运转的；可经营的；行得通的；切实际的： *The silver-mine is no longer* ~, it cannot be worked (eg because it is flooded, or because the ore is exhausted). 那银矿已无法采掘了(如为洪水所淹没，或已枯竭)。*Is the proposed scheme* ~, feasible? 那项建议的方案可行吗？

worker /ˈwɜːkə(r); ˈwɝkɚ/ *n* person who works; 工作者；工人； (attrib) (用作定语) ~ *bees* (contrasted with the drones). 工蜂(与雄蜂相对)。

work·ing /ˈwɜːkɪŋ; ˈwɝkɪŋ/ *n* **1** [C] mine, quarry, etc or part of it, which is being, or has been, worked: (正在开采，或已开采过的)矿坑；采矿场等： *The boys went exploring in some disused* ~*s,* eg the shafts of an old tin-mine. 那些男孩子到几个废弃的矿坑中(如旧锡矿的竖坑)去探索。**2** [C] the way sth works, or the result of

this: 运转、活动等的方式或结果; 运转情况; 作用结果: *the ~s of conscience*; 良心的驱策; *the principles that guide the ~s of the human mind.* 指导人类心灵活动的原理原则。 *in ~'order*, able to function properly, do what is required; going smoothly: (工作、营业、机能)正常的; (操作、进行、经营)情况良好的: *put a machine in ~ order.* 使机器操作正常。 **3** (attrib) (in various senses of the *v*): (用作定语) (具有动词诸义): '*~ clothes*, worn while ~; 工作服; *a ~ drawing / plan*, one made as a guide for building, construction, etc. 工作图; 制造图; 建筑蓝图; 施工图。 *The Government has a ~ majority*, one that is sufficient. 政府(在议会中)掌有足够的多数(支持票)。 **breakfast / lunch / dinner**, one at which persons discuss business, etc: 工作早餐(午餐, 正餐)(与餐者于餐席间讨论正事): *The Prime Minister and some of his colleagues had a ~ breakfast to discuss the crisis in the docks.* 首相同他几位同僚共进工作早餐讨论码头危机。 **~ capital**, money needed for carrying on a business, etc. 流动资本; 运用资本; 周转资金; 营运资本。 **~ day**, **(a)** workday (as opposed to a day of rest). 工作日 (与休息日相对)。 **(b)** number of hours worked on a normal day: (一工作日的)工作时数: *a ~ day of eight hours.* 一天工作八小时。 **~ hypothesis**, one formulated for a theory, etc. 运作假设 (为求证或研究某一理论, 学说等所定的假设)。 **~ knowledge**, knowledge that is sufficient for the purpose. 足够的实用知识。 **,~-'out (a)** calculation of results; elaboration of details: 成果统计; 细节的厘定; 计算; 算出; 厘定: *the ~ out of a plan.* 拟定一项计划。 **(b)** execution: 执行: *Don't interfere with them in the ~ out of their scheme.* 在他们执行其方案时, 不要加以干扰。 '**~ party**, (esp) committee appointed to secure efficiency in an industry, or one appointed (eg by a government department) to study and report on a question. (尤指) 为提高某项工业效率, 或为研究及报告某一专题, 而任命的委员会; 专案委员会; 营运委员会。 □ **part** adj engaged in work: 从事工作的: *a hard-~ woman.* 一个勤劳的妇女。 **the ~ class(es)**, those engaged in manual work. 劳工阶级。 Hence, 由此产生, '**~-class** adj of this class: 劳工阶级的: *a ~-class family.* 劳工阶级的家庭。

world /wɜːld/ wɜld/ *n* **1** the ~, the earth, its countries and people: 世界 (地球, 地球上的国家及人民): *the Old W~*, Europe, Asia and Africa: 旧世界(欧、亚、非三洲); *the New W~*, America: 新世界(美洲); *the Roman W~*, that part known to the ancient Romans; 古罗马人(所认为)的世界; *the English-speaking ~*, those parts where English is the mother tongue of the inhabitants; 讲英语的地区; *make a journey round the ~*; 作环球旅行; *to the ~'s end*, to the farthest distance possible. 到天涯海角。 *The whole ~ / All the ~ knows...*, It is widely or generally known.... 世人皆知...。 [C] heavenly body that may resemble our ~: 与地球类似的天体: *Are there any other ~s besides ours?* 宇宙间除地球外, 还有其他类似地球的天体吗? **make a 'noise in the ~**, be widely talked of; become famous. 广为人所谈论; 声名大噪。 **a citizen of the ~**, a cosmopolitan person. 世界公民; 四海为家的人。 *It's a small ~!* (said when meeting someone in an unexpected place). 世界真小 (没想到会在这里遇见你)! **2** (as 1 above; used attrib) affecting, used by, intended for, extending over, the ~: (如上列第 1 义; 用作定语)影响世界的; 世界所用的; 意欲用于世界的; 遍及世界的; 包括世界的: *a ~ language*, one that is or will be used, or is designed for use, in all or most parts of the ~: 世界语: *English is a ~ language now.* 英语现在是一种世界语。 *Esperanto was designed as a ~ language.* 艾斯帕兰多是一种制作出来的世界语。 *Which countries today can be called ~ powers*, countries whose policies, etc affect all parts of the ~? 哪些国家在今天称得上是世界强国呢? *We've had two ~ wars in this century.* 本世纪我们已经经历了两次世界大战。 **the W~ Bank**, international bank established in 1945 for providing loans for development when private capital is not available (officially the *International Bank for Reconstruction and Development*). 世界银行(创设于一九四五年, 提供开发贷款给无法筹集民间资金的国家, 正式名称为'国家重建及开发银行')。 '**~-'wide** adj found in, spread over, all parts of the ~: 遍及全世界的: *~-wide fame.* 享誉全球。 **3** time, state or scene of existence: 生存的时间、状态或景象: *this ~ and the next*, life on earth and existence after death; 今生及来世; *the ~ to come*, existence after death; 来世; *the lower ~*, hell, Hades; 下界; 地狱; 冥府; *bring a child into the ~*, beget one or give birth to one. 生孩子。 '**~-'weary** adj tired of living. 厌世的。 **4** the universe; everything: 宇宙; 万有; 万物: *Is this the best of all possible ~s?* 这是宇宙间最好的世界吗? **in the ~**, at all, in existence: 究竟; 到底; 世界上: *Nothing in the ~ would please me more.* 世界上没有别的比这更使我高兴的了。 *Who in the ~* (= Who ever, Who on earth) *is that strange man?* 那个陌生的人究竟是谁? **for all the ~ like sb / sth**, exactly like: 恰似某人(某物); 与某人(某物)一模一样: *She's for all the ~ like a woman I knew 20 years ago, in looks, behaviour, everything.* 她与我廿年前认识的一个女人一模一样, 外貌、举止, 无论哪一方面。 **be all the ~ to sb**, be everything to: 为某人的一切; 某人所最喜爱: *She's all the ~ to him*, He lives for her alone. 她是他的一切(他仅为她而活)。 **not for the ~**, not on any account: 决不; 无论如何不会: *I wouldn't hurt her feelings for the ~.* 我决不会伤她的感情。 **be / feel on top of the ~**, elated (because of success, good health, etc). (因为成功, 健康等而)得意洋洋的; 兴高采烈的。 **be out of this ~**, (sl) (of sth) be sublime, magnificent. (俚)(指某事物)极佳的; 特别好的; 无与伦比的。 **carry the ~ be'fore one**, have quick and complete success. 获得迅速而完全的成功。 **a ~ of sth**, a great number or quantity of; very much / many: 大量; 许多: *My holiday did me a ~ of good.* 我的假日对我大有益处。 *There was a ~ of meaning in the look she gave him.* 她看他的一眼含意无穷。 *There's often a ~ of difference between promise and achievement.* 承诺与履行诺言之间往往相差甚远。 **think the ~ of sb / sth**, admire him / it. 羡慕某人(某物); 看重某人(某物)。 **5** the material things and occupations of life (contrasted with the spiritual): 物质生活(与精神生活相对)。 **the ~, the flesh, and the devil**, the various temptations that face us. 物质, 肉欲及魔鬼(我们面临的各种引诱)。 **the best of 'both ~s**, the best of what is offered from two different (perhaps conflicting) sources. 两全其美(两不同事物或两相抵触事物的长处兼而有之)。 **forsake / renounce the ~**, devote one's life to spiritual things. 全心追求精神生活; 出家; 遁世。 **6** human affairs; active life: 世事; 世态; 世务: *know / see the ~*, have experience of life; 通达世故; 见过世面; *a man of the ~*, person who has had experience of life, knows the ways of men, is tolerant, etc; 老于世故的人; *take the ~ as one finds it*, adapt oneself to things, not try to reform people, etc. 安于现实; 安于现况。 *How goes the ~ with you*, How are your affairs going? 近况如何? **7** persons, institutions, etc connected with a special social class or special interests: 与某一社会阶层或特殊利益有关系的人, 机构等; 界: *the ~ of sport / art*; 运动(艺术)界; *the 'racing / 'scientific ~*; 赛马(科学)界; all that concerns or belongs to a special sphere: 有关或属于某范围的一切; 领域; 界: *the 'animal / 'mineral / 'vegetable ~*. 动物(矿物, 植物)界。 ⇨ **kingdom** (3). **8** **the ~**, society, its opinions, customs, etc: 社交界; 上流社会; 共见解, 习俗等: *the great ~*, fashionable society. 时髦的上流社会。 *All the ~ and his wife were at the ball*, all those who claim positions in high society. 所有上流社会人士和他们的夫人都参加了该舞会。 *What will the ~ say*, What about public opinion; can we defy it, etc? 人们会怎样说呢(我们能不顾舆论吗...)? '**~-ly** adj **1** material: 物质的: *my ~ly goods*, my property. 我的财产。 **2** temporal; of the affairs of this life (esp the pursuit of pleasure, contrasted with spiritual): 世俗的; 现世的(尤指追求享乐, 与'精神的'相对): '**~ly wisdom**, prudence, etc which enables one to obtain material

gains and advantages. 处世之才; 致富等的本领; 世故. **3**
(also 亦作 ‚~ly·minded) concerned with, interested in,
material things. 耽于利欲的; 汲汲于名利的; 世俗的.
~·li·ness *n*

worm /wɜːm; wɝm/ *n* **1** kinds of small, boneless,
limbless, creeping creature, esp ('**earth**·~) the kind
living in the ground, or the kinds living as parasites in
the intestines, etc of animals. 虫; 蠕虫; (尤指)蚯蚓;
(动物肠等中的)寄生虫. ⇨ the illus at silk. 参看 silk 之
插图. ⇨ *hookworm* at hook(1), *tapeworm* at **tape.** '~-
cast *n* tubular pile of earth pushed up by an earth~ on
the ground. 蚯蚓粪. **the ~ of conscience,** remorse. 良
心的谴责; 悔恨. **2** (in compounds) used as a name for
larvae, insects, etc: (用于复合词中)用作幼虫、昆虫等的
名称: 'silk~; 蚕; 'glow~. 萤火虫. '~-**eaten** *adj* full of
~ holes; (fig) antiquated. 多蛀孔的; (喻)过时
的; 陈旧的. '~-**hole** *n* hole left in wood, fruit, etc
by ~s. (木材,果实等上)虫蛀之孔; 虫孔; 蛀洞. **3** (fig)
insignificant or contemptible person. (喻)小人物; 可鄙
之人; 可怜虫. **Even a ~ will turn,** (prov) There are
limits to patience. (谚)忍耐是有限度的. **4** spiral part
of a screw. 螺纹; 蜗杆(螺丝的螺旋部分). '~-**gear** *n*
arrangement in which a wheel with teeth gears with the
~(4) of a revolving spiral. 蜗轮(联动)装置. □ *vt*
1 [VP15A, B] ~ **oneself/one's way in/into/**
through, move slowly, or by patience, or with
difficulty: 蠕行; 坚忍地或困难地行进: He ~ed himself/
his way through the undergrowth. 他缓慢地穿过灌木丛.
He ~ed himself into favour/into her confidence. 他逐渐
获得宠信(她的信任). ~ **sth out (of sb),** extract (by
persistent questioning, etc): (借不断地询问等)从某人取
得(某物);迫使某人供出(某事): He ~ed the secret out of
me. 他从我这里逐渐探知该项秘密. **2** [VP6A] rid of
parasitic ~s: 除去肠等中的寄生虫; 为…驱虫: I think
we'd better ~ the cat, eg by giving it a powder or pill.
我想我们最好给猫打打虫 (如给它吃一剂药粉或药丸). **~**
~**y** *adj* having many ~s; damaged by ~s; like a ~. 多
虫的;为虫所损坏的;似虫的.

worm·wood /'wɜːmwʊd; 'wɝm,wʊd/ *n* [U] kinds
of perennial plant with a bitter flavour, used in the
preparation of vermouth and absinthe and in medicine;
(fig) bitter mortification and its cause. 苦艾; 茵蔯 (多年
生植物,有苦味,用以调制苦艾酒,并用于医药); (喻)苦恼;
悔恨; 其原由.

worn /wɔːn; wɔrn/ *pp* of **wear**².

worri·some /'wʌrɪsəm; 'wɝɪsəm/ *adj* troublesome;
worrying. 烦恼的; 令人忧虑的.

worry /'wʌrɪ; 'wɝɪ/ *vt, vi (pt, pp* -**ried)** **1** [VP6A,
14, 15A, 17, 22] trouble; give (sb, oneself) no peace
of mind; cause anxiety or discomfort to: 困扰; 使(某人,
自己)不安;使烦恼; 使不适: ~ sb with foolish questions;
用愚蠢的问题困扰某人; ~ oneself sick/be worried sick
about sth, be extremely anxious about it. 为某事愁出病
来;为某事极端烦恼. The noise of the traffic worried her.
交通的嘈杂声使她不安. What's ~ing you? 你在为何事
烦恼? Her child has a bad cough and it rather worries
her. 她的孩子咳嗽得很厉害,这使她很烦恼. I have a bad
tooth that is ~ing me. 我有一颗蛀牙,使我感到不适.
Don't ~ yourself about the children; they're old enough
to take good care of themselves. 别为孩子们担心; 他们已
经大得会照顾自己了. He'll ~ himself to death, kill
himself by ~ing. 他会愁死的. She was always ~ing her
husband for more money/~ing him to give her more
money. 她总是缠着她的丈夫,不断向他要钱. **2** [VP2A,
B, C, 3A] ~(about/over sth), be anxious, uneasy,
troubled: 焦虑; 不安; 烦恼: Don't ~ about trifles. 不要
为小事情烦恼. You have no cause to ~. 你没有理由烦
恼. What's the use of ~ing? 焦虑有什么用? Don't ~
trying to find it—it'll turn up one day. 别急着找它——它
总有一天会出现的. ~ **along,** (colloq) manage to get
along in spite of troubles. (口)不顾困难设法进行; 熬过;
撑持过. **3** [VP6A] (esp of dogs) seize with the teeth

and shake: (尤指狗)衔在口里摇: 咬啮; 撕咬: The dog
was ~ing the rat. 那只狗在撕咬那只老鼠. **4** [VP15B]~
a problem, get it out, attack it again and again until one
solves it. 绞尽脑汁解决问题等. □ *n* (*pl* -**ries**) **1** [U]
condition of being troubled: 困扰; 烦恼; 忧愁: show signs
of ~. 显出忧愁的样子. **2** [C] (usu pl) sth that worries;
cause of anxiety: (通常用复数)令人烦恼的事物; 忧愁的
原因: Is your life full of worries? 你的生活充满了令人
苦恼的事情吗? Money worries and little domestic worries
have made him look old. 由于为钱以及家庭中的琐事发
愁,他显得老了. What a little ~ that child is! 那孩子是
多么烦人的小家伙啊! **wor·ried** *adj* troubled; anxious:
烦恼的; 焦虑的; 担心的: He has a worried look. 他显出焦
虑的神色. ~·**ing** *adj* full of ~; causing ~: 多烦恼的;
令人忧虑的: have a ~ing time. 度过一段烦恼的时间.
~·**ing·ly** *adv*

worse /wɜːs; wɝs/ *adj* (independent comparative; 独
立比较级; ⇨ **bad, worst**) **1** Your work is bad but mine
is much ~. 你的工作很坏,但我的更糟. We couldn't
have had ~ weather for our journey. 这次旅行我们所遇
到的天气再坏不过了. Is there anything ~ than war/a
~ catastrophe than war/a catastrophe ~ than war? 还
有比战争更坏的(灾难)吗? You are making things ~. 你
把事情事情更糟了. He escaped with nothing ~ than a
few scratches. 他安然脱险,仅受到了擦伤. **the ~ for**
wear, badly worn as the result of long wear; (fig)
exhausted: 穿得破旧不堪; (喻)筋疲力尽; 枯萎: He looks
the ~ for wear after only a year as President. 他就任总
统才不过一年,就显得疲惫不堪了. **2** (*pred* only) having
less good health or condition or circumstances: (仅用作
表语)有较差的健康,状况或环境的; 更坏的; 更恶劣的; The
doctor says she is much ~ today. 医生说她的病情今天大
为恶化. I'm glad you don't feel any ~. 我很高兴你没有
觉得更不舒服. **be none the ~ (for sth),** be unharmed
(by it): 未(因…而)受伤害; 安然无恙: He fell into the
river but is none the ~ for it. 他掉入河里,但是并没有什么
样样. □ *adv* (⇨ **badly, worst**) **1** He is behaving ~
than ever. 他的举止更坏了. He has been taken ~, has
become more seriously ill. 他的病势更沉重了. **none**
the ~, not less: 依然; 不差: I like a man none the
~ for being outspoken. 我不因为一个人直言无讳而不喜
欢他. ~ **off,** (⇨ **badly off** at **bad**²; **better off** at
better²(1); **well off** at **well**²(3)) more badly situated;
in ~ circumstances. 情况更坏; 处境更糟; 恶化. **2** (used
to intensify): (用以加强语气) It's raining ~ (= more
heavily) than ever. 雨下得更大了. She hates me ~ (=
more strongly) than before. 她更恨我了. □ *n* [U] ~
things: 更坏的事物: I have ~ to tell. 我有更坏的事情
奉告. The first news was bad, but ~ followed. 最初的消
息很坏,但是接着来的更坏. There has been a change for
the ~ in the patient's condition. 病人的情况更坏化了.
Things seem to be going from bad to ~ nowadays. 目
前的局势似乎愈来愈坏了. ~ *n* /'wɜːsn; 'wɝsn/ *vt, vi*
[VP6A, 2A] make or become ~. 使坏; 变坏; 恶化.

wor·ship /'wɜːʃɪp; 'wɝʃəp/ *n* [U] **1** reverence and
respect paid to God: (对上帝的)崇拜; 礼拜: places of ~,
churches, mosques, synagogues, temples, etc; 教堂, 清真
寺, 犹太教会堂, 佛教庙宇等; 拜神的地方; hours of ~,
times of church etc services; 礼拜时间; 拜神时间; public
~, church etc service(s). 教堂崇拜仪式; 礼拜; 拜神. **2**
admiration and respect shown to or felt for sb or sth:
(对某人或某物的)崇拜; 敬慕; 景仰; 尊敬: the ~ of
success; 仰慕成功; hero ~. 英雄崇拜. She gazed at the
film star with ~ in her eyes. 她注视那电影明星, 眼睛里
充满着仰慕. **3** your/his W~, (GB) title of respect
used to/of a magistrate or mayor: 阁下(对于地方行政
长官或市长的尊称): his W~ the Mayor of Chester. 切斯
特市长阁下. □ *vt, vi* (-**pp**-; US -**p**-) [VP6A, 2A, B]
give ~(1, 2) to: 崇拜; 敬神; 仰慕: ~ God; 崇拜上帝;
attend church service: 参加礼拜; 做礼拜: the church
where she had ~ped for ten years. 她已经在那儿做了十年
礼拜的教堂. ~·**per** (US = ~**er**) *n* ~·**ful** /-fl; -fəl/

adj (in GB titles of respect, eg to Justices of the Peace, aldermen) worthy of respect; honourable. (用于英国对治安推事, 市议员等的尊称中)值得尊敬的; 可敬的。

worst /wɜːst; wɜst/ *adj* (independent superlative; 独立最高级; ⇨ **bad, worse**): *the ~ storm for five years;* 五年来最甚烈的暴风雨; *the ~ dinner I've ever eaten;* 我所吃过的最坏的正餐; *the ~* (= most intense) *frost this winter.* 今年冬天最严烈的霜冻。□ *adv* (independent superlative; 独立最高级; ⇨ **badly, worse**) most badly: 最坏地; 最差地: *Tom played badly, Harry played worse and I played ~.* 汤姆玩得不好, 哈里玩得更坏, 而我玩得最差。□ *n ~* part, state, event, etc: 最坏的部分, 状态, 事件等: *You must be prepared for the ~*, the ~ possible news, outcome, etc. 你必须为最坏的情况作准备 (或你必须作最坏的打算)。 *The ~ of the storm is over.* 暴风雨最猛烈的时候已经过去了。 *She keeps cheerful, even when things are at their ~.* 即使是事情最糟的时候, 她也能保持愉快的心情。 *If the ~ comes to the ~*, If the ~ happens. 如果最坏的事发生。 **get the ~ of it** (in a fight etc), be defeated. (在打斗等中)被打败; 败北。 *The ~ of it is that...*, The most unfortunate part of the affair is that... 最坏的是; 最不幸的是…。 **at (the) ~**, if the ~ happens. 在最坏(最不利)的情况下。 **do your ~ / let him do his ~**, used as expressions of defiance. 你有什么狠处尽管使出来吧(他有什么狠处让他尽管使出来吧) (用作挑战语)。□ *vt* [VP6A] defeat; get the better of: 打败; 击败; 胜过: *He ~ed his enemy.* 他打败了他的敌人。

wor·sted /ˈwʊstɪd; ˈwʊstɪd/ *n* [U] twisted woollen yarn or thread; cloth made from this. 绒线; 毛纱; 绒线或毛纱做成的料子。

worth /wɜːθ; wɜθ/ *pred adj* 1 having a certain value; of value equal to: 值; 相等于…的价值: *I paid only £300 for this used car but it's ~ much more.* 我仅仅花了三百英镑买下这部旧车, 但是它比这种价格值得多的多呢。 *It's not ~ more than two pounds.* 它的价值不会超过两英镑。 *It's not ~ the paper it's printed on.* 它(通常指文章, 小说等)的价值比用来印它的纸张还不如。 ⇨ **(one's) while**, ⇨ **while. for what it is ~**, without any guarantee or promise concerning it: 无任何担保或承诺; 不论真伪: *That's the news I heard — I pass it on to you for what it is ~.* 那是我听来的消息——不管真实与否, 我就原样往后传。 *a ~ 'while adj* that is ~ the time, etc needed: 值得做的: *a ~while experiment.* 一项值得做的实验。 ⇨ **while. 2** possessing; having property to the value of: 拥有的; 有…价值的财产的; *What's the old man ~?* 那个老人有多少财产? *He died ~ a million pounds.* 他死时有一百万英镑财产。 **for all one is ~**, (colloq) with all one's energy; making every effort: 竭(出全力)力; 尽力; 拼命: *He was running for all he was ~.* 他正拼命地跑。 **3 ~** + *verb* in -**ing**, giving a satisfactory or rewarding return for: (后接 -ing 动词)对…有满意的或有代价的回报; 值得: *The book is well ~ reading.* 这本书很值得读。 *It's hardly ~ troubling about.* 这事几乎不值得去麻烦。 *He says life wouldn't be ~ living without friendship.* 他说人生若没有友情便不值得活下去了。□ *n* [U] 1 value; what sb or sth is ~: 价值; 某人或某事物的价值; *books of discoveries, etc of great / little / not much ~;* 极有(极少,不大有)价值的书(发现等); *know a friend's ~.* 认识一位朋友的价值。 2 quantity of sth of a specified value: 值某价额的数量: *a pound's ~ of apples;* 一镑的苹果; *fifty pence ~ of copper coins;* 值半英镑的铜币; *a penny ~ of sweets.* 一便士的糖果。 **~·less** *adj* having no value. 无价值的。 **~·ly** *adv* **~·less·ness** *n*

worthy /ˈwɜːðɪ; ˈwɜðɪ/ *adj* (-ier, -iest) 1 (*of sth / to be sth*), deserving: 值得…的; 应…的; 足以…的: *a cause ~ of support;* 一项值得支持的主张; *behaviour ~ of praise;* 值得称道的行为; *nothing ~ of mention;* 乏善可陈; 没有值得提的事; *a man who is ~ to have a place in the team.* 足以成为该队队员的人。 *He found a ~ enemy / an enemy ~ of his sword*, one brave or strong enough. 他遇到了足以和他匹敌(势均力敌)的敌人。 **2** (often ironic or used with a patronizing effect) having

merit; deserving respect: (常用做反语, 或带有傲慢意味)有价值的; 可敬的: *a ~ gentleman.* 可敬的绅士。 *She says she helps only the ~ poor* (in contrast to those people who, she thinks, are poor through their own laziness, etc). 她说她只帮助那些值得她去帮助的穷人(她不帮助那些她认为是好吃懒做的穷人)。□ *n* 1 person of some distinction (in his own country or during a certain period): (在其本国或某一时代) 杰出的人; 名士: *an Elizabethan ~*, ie during the reign of Queen Elizabeth I. 英国女王伊莎莉白一世时代的杰出人物。 **2** (hum or ironic) person who appears to be distinguished: (谐或反语)似乎了不起的人物; 大人物: *Who's the ~ who has just arrived?* 刚到的那位大人物是谁呀? *Who are the worthies on the platform?* 台上那些大人物是谁呀? **worth·ily** /-ɪlɪ; -ɪlɪ/ *adv* **worthi·ness** *n*

wot /wɒt; wɑt/ *God wot*, (archaic or hum) God knows. (古或谐)天晓得。

wot·cher /ˈwɒtʃə(r); ˈwɑtʃɚ/ *int* (GB sl) (as a greeting) Hello! (英俚)(用作问候语)喂! 哈啰!

would ⇨ **will**[1].

wouldst /wʊdst; wʊdst/ *v* old form used with *thou*: 与 thou 连用的旧形式: *Thou ~*, You would.

wound[1] /wuːnd; wund/ *n* [C] 1 hurt or injury to the living tissue of the body, caused by cutting, shooting, tearing, etc, esp as the result of attack (*injury* being more usu for the result of an accident): 伤; 创伤(指由割切, 射击, 撕扯等, 尤指受攻击所受的伤; 意外事件所受的伤, 通常多用 injury): *a 'knife ~ in the arm;* 臂上的刀伤; *a 'bullet ~.* 子弹伤。 *The dog was licking its ~s*, eg after a fight with another dog. 那只狗在舐他的伤口。 **2** injury to a plant, tree, etc in which the bark is cut or torn. (剥去皮的)草木等的损伤。 **3** pain given to a person's feelings: (加诸感情上的)痛苦: *a ~ to his pride / vanity.* 对于他的自尊心(虚荣心)的伤害。□ *vt* [VP6A] give a ~ to: 伤; 伤害: *Ten soldiers were killed and thirty ~ed.* 十名士兵阵亡; 三十名负伤。Cf 参较 *hurt* or *injured* in an accident. 意外事件负伤, 该用 hurt 或 injured. *He felt ~ed in his honour / affections.* 他觉得他的荣誉(感情)受到了伤害。

wound[2] /waʊnd; waʊnd/ *pt, pp* of **wind**[3].

wove, wo·ven ⇨ **weave**.

wow[1] /waʊ; waʊ/ *n* (sl) tremendous success: (俚)极大的成功; 巨大的成就: *The new play at the National Theatre's a wow.* 在国家剧院上演的新剧获得极大的成功。□ *int* expressing wonder, admiration, etc. (表示惊异, 羡慕等的惊叹声)哇!

wow[2] /waʊ; waʊ/ *n* [C] varieties in the pitch of sound reproduced from a disc or tape, caused by fluctuations in speed (from the motor). (由于马达速度快慢不一, 从唱片或录音带放出来的)不同的音高; 声音的失真; (唱片或录音带放出的)变质音。⇨ **flutter**, *n*(3).

wrack /ræk; ræk/ *n* [U] 1 seaweed thrown up on the shore by the waves (and used for manure, etc). (冲到岸上作肥料等用的)海草。 **2 =** **rack**[4].

wraith /reɪθ; reθ/ *n* apparition of a person seen shortly before or after his death. (人在临终前或死后不久显现的)生魂。

wrangle /ˈræŋgl; ˈræŋgl/ *vi* [VP2A, 3A] **~ (with sb) (about / over sth)**, take part in a noisy or angry argument. 口角; 争吵。□ *n* such an argument. 口角; 争吵。

wrap /ræp; ræp/ *vt, vi* (-**pp**-) 1 [VP6A, 15A, B] **~ (up) (in sth)**, cover or roll up sth: 包; 卷; 缠: *~ a child in a shawl;* 把小孩裹在披巾里面; *~ up sth in tissue paper;* 用薄纸包起某物; *~ oneself in a blanket.* 把自己裹在毯子里。 *The mountain top was ~ped in mist.* 山顶为雾所笼罩。 *You'd better ~ (yourself) up well before you go out*, put on an overcoat, scarf, etc. 你在外出以前最好把衣服穿妥当(穿厚一点)。 *Why does he ~ up his meaning in such obscure language*, Why doesn't he express his meaning clearly? 他为什么不直说呢? **~ sth up**, (sl) complete it: (俚)完成某事: *~ up a business*

deal. 完成一项交易。 **2** [VP14] ~ *sth round sth*, put round; wind or fold round as a covering or protection; pack: 包裹；包装: *W~ plenty of paper round it*. 用很多纸将它包起. *W~ this shawl round your shoulders*. 把这披肩围在你的肩上. **3** *be ~ped up in*, **(a)** be packed or enclosed in; (fig) be concealed in: 被包裹于；被包封于…中; (喻为…所隐蔽；隐藏于: *The affair is ~ped up in mystery*. 这件事隐蔽于神秘之中. **(b)** be deeply interested in: 对…有极大兴趣: *He is ~ped up in his work/studies*. 他对于他的工作(研究)有极大兴趣. **(c)** be deeply devoted to: 专心于；全神贯注于: *She is ~ped up in her children*, devotes all her time, care, attention, etc to them. 她的全部精力花在儿女身上了. □ *n* outer garment or covering (eg a scarf, cloak, fur or rug); outer covering. 外套；罩件(如围巾，披风，皮衣或围毯). (trade uses): *keep sth under* ~s, conceal it. 隐藏某事；保密. *take off the* ~s, place on public view (eg a new model of a car). 公开展示(新型汽车等). ~**per** *n* (尤指) **1** piece of paper (to be) ~ped round a newspaper or other periodical, a book etc (esp for sending by post); cover of loose paper, etc for a book. (尤指邮寄报、杂志等的)包纸；书的封皮；书套. **2** light dressing-gown. 轻便晨衣. ~**ping** *n* **1** [C] sth used for covering or packing: 用于包裹或包装之物: 包装纸、布等: *the* ~*pings of a mummy*. 木乃伊的包裹物. **2** [U] material for covering or packing sth:用于包裹或包装的材料；垫料: *Put plenty of* ~*ping round the cups and saucers when you pack them*. 包装杯碟时，在周围多放些垫料.

wrath /rɒθ US: ræθ; ræθ/ *n* [U] (liter) great anger; indignation. (文)暴怒；愤怒；义愤. ~**·ful** /-fl; -fəl/ *adj* ~**·fully** /-fəlɪ; -fəlɪ/ *adv*

wreak /riːk; rik/ *vt* [VP6A, 14] ~ *sth (on sb)*, (liter) give expression to; give effect to: (文)发泄；遂行；施: ~ *one's fury upon sb*. 对某人发脾气; ~ *havoc/vengeance upon sb*. 对某人加以蹂躏(报复).

wreath /riːθ; riθ/ *n* (*pl* ~s /riːðz; riðz/) **1** flowers or leaves woven or woven together into a circle (worn on the head as a garland, or placed on a coffin, a grave, a memorial to the dead, etc). 花环；花圈；花冠. **2** ring, spiral or curling line (*of* smoke, mist, etc). (烟，雾等的)圈；涡卷(与之连用).

wreathe /riːð; riθ/ *vt*, *vi* **1** [VP6A] (esp in *pp*) cover, encircle: (尤用过去分词形式)遮盖；覆盖；环绕:~d *with flowers*; 覆以花; *hills* ~d *in mist*; 隐蔽于雾中的丘陵; *a face* ~d *in smiles*. 微笑的面孔. **2** [VP14] (reflex) ~ *itself round*, wind: 盘绕；卷缠: *The snake* ~d *itself round the branch*. 那条蛇盘绕在树枝上. **3** [VP14] ~ *sth into*, make. (flowers, etc) (into a wreath). 把(花等)制作成(花环等). **4** [VP2A, C] (of smoke, mist, etc) move in the shape of a wreath. (指烟，雾等) 缭绕；盘旋.

wreck /rek; rɛk/ *n* **1** [U] ruin or destruction, esp of a ship by storms: 破坏；毁灭. (尤指船遭受暴风雨表示所造成的)船难；失事: *save a ship from* ~; 营救遇难船只; (fig)(喻) *the* ~ *of one's hopes/plans*; 希望(计划)的破灭; [C] instance of this: 破灭等的实例；失事；船难: *The storm caused* ~s *all along the coast*. 那次暴风雨沿海岸造成了许多船难. **2** [C] ship that has suffered ~(1): 遭遇暴风雨而失事的船；遇难船: *Robinson Crusoe obtained food and supplies from the* ~. 鲁宾逊·克鲁梭从遇难的船上获得了食物及其他物品. **3** [C] vehicle, building, etc that has been badly damaged or fallen into ruin; person whose health has been destroyed: 遭受严重破坏或完全毁坏的车辆，建筑物等；残骸；废墟；健康受到损坏的人: *The car was a worthless* ~ *after the collision*. 撞车以后，那部车成为毫无价值的破烂了. *He is a mere* ~ *of his former self*. 他已经形销骨立. *If these anxieties continue she will become a nervous* ~. 如果继续为这些事焦虑下去，她将神经衰弱崩溃了. □ *vt* [VP6A] cause the ~ of: 使破坏；使毁灭；使失事: *The ship/train was* ~ed. 那只船(那列火车)失事了. ~**·age**

/'rekɪdʒ; 'rɛkɪdʒ/ *n* [U] ~ed material, fragments: 残骸；残余物；碎片: *The* ~*age of the aircraft was scattered over a wide area*. 那架飞机的残骸散布在一片广大的区域. ~**er** *n* **1** person employed to recover a ~ed ship or its contents. 营救难船或其装载的货物、乘客等的人；救助难船者. **2** (US) person employed to demolish old buildings. 拆除旧建筑者. ⇨ *housebreaker* at **house**[1](7). **3** (hist) person who tried from the shore to bring about shipwreck (eg by showing false lights) in order to plunder the cargo, etc. (史)由于上诱使船只失事而加以劫掠的人;为劫掠而诱使船只失事者.

wren /ren; rɛn/ *n* kinds of small short-winged songbird. 鹪鹩；鹩莺.

wrench /rentʃ; rɛntʃ/ *n* [C] **1** sudden and violent twist or pull: 猛扭；猛拉；突然的扭转: *He gave his ankle a* ~, twisted it by accident. 他扭了脚踝. *He pulled the handle off with a single* ~. 他用力一拉就扭掉了把手. **2** (pain caused by a) sad parting or separation: 别离的痛苦；伤别: *Separation from her children was a terrible* ~. 同她的孩子们分别是一项很大的痛苦. **3** tool for gripping and turning nuts, bolts, etc; spanner. 螺旋钳；扳钳；扳手. ⇨ the illus at **tool**. 参看 tool 之插图. □ *vt* **1** [VP6A, 15A, 22] twist or pull violently: 猛扭；猛拉: ~ *the door open*; 用力把门扭开; ~ *sth from sb*; 从某人处抢夺某物; ~ *sth out of his hand*; 从他手里强夺某物; ~ *a door off its hinges*. 用力扭脱门的铰链. *She* ~ed *herself from the villain's clutches*. 她挣脱了那恶棍的掌握. **2** [VP6A] injure(eg one's ankle) by twisting. 扭伤(足踝等). **3** [VP6A] (fig)distort(facts, the meaning of a sentence, etc). (喻)歪曲；曲解(事实，句义等).

wrest /rest; rɛst/ *vt* **1** [VP14] ~ *sth from/out of*, take (sth) violently away: 夺取(某物)；扭夺: ~ *a knife from sb/~ it out of his hands*. 从某人处(从他手中)夺去一把刀. **2** [VP14] ~ *sth from*, get by effort: 费力取得；努力获致: ~ *a confession of guilt from sb*; 费力取得某人的犯罪自白; ~ *a living from poor farmland*. 靠贫瘠的农田勉强维持生活. **3** twist or pervert (facts, the meaning of sth). 歪曲；曲解(事实，某事物的意义).

wrestle /'resl; 'rɛsl/ *vi* [VP2A, C, 3A] ~ *(with sb)*, struggle with sb (as a sport) and try to throw him to the ground without hitting him: (体育)(与某人)角力；摔角: ~ *with sb*; 和某人摔角; (fig)(喻) ~ *with a problem/a temptation/one's conscience*. 努力解决一个问题(抗拒诱惑；与良心苦斗). □ *n* [C] wrestling match; hard struggle. 角力或摔角比赛；艰苦斗争. **wres·tler** /'reslə(r); 'rɛslə/ *n* person who ~s. 角力者；摔角者；艰苦斗争者.

wretch /retʃ; rɛtʃ/ *n* **1** unfortunate and miserable person. 不幸而可怜的人. **2** contemptible, mean person. 卑鄙的人. **3** (playfully or affectionately) rogue. (戏谑或亲昵语)坏蛋.

wretched /'retʃɪd; 'rɛtʃɪd/ *adj* **1** miserable: 可怜的；不幸的: *lead a* ~ *existence in the slums*; 在贫民窟过可怜的生活; *living in* ~ *poverty*. 过可怜的贫苦生活. *This aching tooth makes me feel* ~. 这一颗痛的牙使我疾苦恼. **2** causing misery: 致使不幸或悲惨的: ~ *houses*. 肮脏破旧的房子. **3** of poor quality; bad: 劣质的，坏的: ~ *weather/food*. 恶劣的天气(食物). **4** (with *nn* implying blame) that causes dismay(because excessive): (与名词连用，含示责难)(由于过度而)致使狼狈或沮丧的: *the* ~ *stupidity of the nation's leaders*. 该国领导人物令人沮丧的愚昧. ~**·ly** *adv* ~**·ness** *n*

wrick, rick /rɪk; rɪk/ *vt* [VP6A] sprain or twist slightly: 稍微扭伤；扭: ~ *one's ankle/a muscle in one's back*. 扭了足踝(背部的肌肉). □ *n* [C] sprain: 扭伤；扭筋: *give one's back a* ~; 扭伤某人的背: *have a* ~ *in the neck*. 脖子扭患.

wriggle /'rɪgl; 'rɪgl/ *vi*, *vt* **1** [VP2A, C, 3A] move with quick, short, twistings; move along in this way: 蠕动；扭动; 蜿蜒行进: ~ *as Jim put it on the fish-hook*. 当吉姆把蚯蚓放在钓鱼钩上的时候，它在蠕动. *Small children* ~ *in their seats when they are bored*. 小孩

子们感到厌烦的时候，就会在座位上扭动。*The eel ~d out of my fingers.* 那条黄鳝从我的指缝间扭动着滑走了。*He ~d out of (= escaped from) the difficulty.* 他千方百计摆脱了困境。*He ~d (his way) through the thick hedge.* 他穿过浓密的树篱蜿蜒行进。*My criticism made him ~, feel uncomfortable.* 我的批评使他很不舒服。**2** [VP6A, 15B, 22] move with a wriggling motion: 蠕动; 扭动; 蜿蜒而行: *~ one's toes;* 扭动足趾; *~ oneself free, get free* (eg from ropes round the body) 挣脱束缚（如从捆在身上的绳子中）; *~ one's way out.* 设法摆脱。 □ *n* wriggling movement. 蠕动; 扭动; 蜿蜒。**wrig·gler** /'rɪɡlə(r); 'rɪɡlɚ/ *n* (esp) larva of a mosquito. (尤指)孑孓。

wright /raɪt; raɪt/ *n* (rare except in compounds) workman, maker. (除见于复合词外, 罕用)工人; 制造者。 ➪ *play~* at **play**[1](5), *ship~* at **ship**[1](3), *wheel~* at **wheel**(1).

wring /rɪŋ; rɪŋ/ *vt* (*pt, pp* **wrung** /rʌŋ; rʌŋ/) **1** [VP6A] twist; squeeze: 拧; 扭; 绞出: *~ a hen's neck,* to kill it; 宰杀一只母鸡; *~ a person's hand,* clasp it warmly. (热情地) 紧握某人的手。 *~ one's hands,* squeeze them together (indicating despair, sorrow, etc). 绞手; 扭手(表示失望, 悲哀等)。**2** [VP15B, 14] *~ sth out;* *~ sth out of / from sth,* twist and squeeze sth tightly; force out (esp water) by doing this: 扭紧; 压紧; 用力绞出(尤指水): *~ out wet clothes;* 绞干湿衣服; *~ out the water from one's swimming-trunks.* 绞出游泳裤的水。*They wrung a confession from her.* (fig) forced her to confess, by persuasion, threats, etc. (喻)他们千方百计逼她招供。 *~ing wet,* (of clothes, etc) so wet that water can be wrung from them. (指衣服等)湿得可以拧出水来。 □ *n* [C] squeeze: 拧; 扭; 绞: *Give it another ~.* 再把它绞一下。 *~er* /'rɪŋə(r); 'rɪŋɚ/ *n* = **mangle**[1].

wrinkle[1] /'rɪŋkl; 'rɪŋkl/ *n* small fold or line in the skin(esp of the kind produced by age)or on the surface of sth: 皱; 皱纹: *She's beginning to get ~s round her eyes.* 她的眼角开始有皱纹了。*Her new dress fits without a ~.* 她的新衣非常合身, 穿起来没一点皱纹也没有。*She ironed out the ~s in her dress.* 她熨平了衣服上的皱纹。□ *vt, vi* [VP6A, 15A, 2A, C] *~ (up),* make, get, have, ~s in: 使皱; 起皱; 有皱纹: *~ up one's forehead,* eg in perplexity; 皱起眉头(如感到困惑时);~*d with age.* 因年老而起皱纹。*The front of this dress ~s.* 这衣服的前襟起皱纹。**wrinkly** /'rɪŋklɪ; 'rɪŋklɪ/ *adj*

wrinkle[2] /'rɪŋkl; 'rɪŋkl/ *n* [C] (colloq) useful hint or suggestion: (口)有用的提示; 好主意; 妙计: *give sb a ~.* 给某人一个好建议。

wrist /rɪst; rɪst/ *n* joint between the hand and the arm: 腕部; 腕关节: *He took me by the ~.* 他握住我的手腕。➪ the illus at **arm**. 参看 arm 之插图。 *'~-band n* band of a shirt-sleeve fitting round the ~. (衬衫的)袖口。 *'~-watch n* one worn on the ~. 手表; 腕表。 *~·let* /'rɪstlɪt; 'rɪstlɪt/ *n* band or ornament for the ~. 腕带; 腕饰。

writ /rɪt; rɪt/ *n* **1** written order issued in the name of a ruler or sb in authority to an official to do or not to do sth: 书面命令; 令状: *a ~ of habeas corpus;* 人身保护令; *a ~ for the arrest of sb.* 拘票; 逮捕某人的令状。**2** Holy W~, the Bible. 圣经。 □ *v* (*pp*) *~ large,* ➪ **write**(6).

write /raɪt; raɪt/ *vi, vt* (*pt* **wrote** /rəʊt; rot/, *pp* **written** /'rɪtn; 'rɪtn̩/) **1** [VP2A, B, C] make letters or other symbols (eg ideographs) on a surface, esp with a pen or pencil on paper: 书写; 写字: *learn to read and ~;* 学习读书和写字; *~ on both sides of the paper* 在纸的两面上书写。*I've been writing (for) three hours.* 我已经写了三个小时了。*Are we to ~ in ink or in pencil?* 我们该用钢笔写, 还是该用铅笔写? **2** [VP6A] put down (on paper) by means of words, etc: (在纸上)写字; 书写; 写下: *~ words / Chinese characters / shorthand;* 写字(写中国字); 速记; *~ one's name;* 写下自己的名字; *~ a cheque / a certificate / an application* (by filling in the spaces with words, figures, etc); 填写支票(证书, 申请

书); *~ (=fill) three sheets.* 填写三张纸。**3** [VP2C, 15B] *~ sth down,* (a) put down (on paper) in words: (在纸上)写下; 记载: *You'd better ~ down the address / it down before you forget it.* 你最好把这地址(它) 写下来, 免得忘了。(b) (more usu 较常用 **mark** down) reduce the nominal value of (stock, goods, etc); reduce in value or price. 减低(资产, 货物)的帐面价值; 减低价值或价格。 *~ sb down as,* describe as: 描写为; 看成: *I'd ~ him down as a fool.* 我要把他描写为一个笨蛋。 *~ in for sth,* apply by letter for. 写信要求; 函购要求。 *~ off (for sth),* order by post: 邮购; 写信订购: *~ off for another dozen bottles of rum.* 邮购另一打瓶装朗姆酒。 *~ sth off,* (a) compose quickly and easily: 迅速而容易地撰述; 容易地写成: *~ off an account of a sports meeting.* 迅速而容易地写成一篇运动会的报导。(b) cancel; recognize that sth is a loss or failure: 取消; 注销; 勾销; 削减: *~ off a debt;* 注销一笔债款; *~ off £500 for depreciation of machinery.* 因机器折旧而削减五百英镑。*He has just written off a new car,* damaged it beyond repair, so that the insurers regard it as a loss. 他刚刚报销了一辆新车(损坏到无法修理, 保险公司视为损失)。Hence, 由此产生, *'~-off n* sth that no longer has any value: 报废物品;不再有任何价值的东西: *The burnt-out airliner was a complete ~-off,* had no value whatever. 被烧毁的班机完全报废了。 *~ sth out,* ~ the whole of; in full: 全部写出; 誊清: *~ out a copy of an agreement;* 誊写一份合约; *~ out a cheque.* 开出一张支票。 *~ sth up,* (a) bring up to date: complete: 补写到最近日期; 整理: *~ up one's diary.* 逐日补写日记。*I must ~ up my notes of the lecture.* 我必须整理演讲的笔记。(b) overstate the value of (assets). 提高(资产)的帐面价值。(c) describe, ~ about, (an event) elaborately: 详细描写; 花心血记述: *The journalist wrote up the wedding for his paper.* 记者为他的报纸详细报导那项婚礼。(d) ~ a description giving praise: 为文赞扬: *A friendly critic wrote up the acting of the leading players.* 一位友善的批评家为文赞扬主角们的演技。Hence, 由此产生, *'~-up n* written account or record of an event. 事件的记述, 说明或记录。**4** [VP6A, 2A] do the work of an author; compose for publication: 写作; 著述: *~ a novel;* 写一部小说; *~ for the newspapers;* 为报纸撰写文章; *make a living by writing.* 以写作为生。**5** [VP2A, B, C, 12A, 13A, 4A] *~ and send a letter (to,* or colloq without *to):* 写信给 (与 to 连用, 在口语中可省去 to): *He promised to ~ to me every week.* 他答应每周写信给我。*He ~s home / ~s to his parents regularly.* 他经常写信回家(给他的双亲)。*He wrote me that he was staying with his brother in York.* 他写信告诉我说, 他正和他哥哥(弟弟)在约克郡小住。*He wrote me an account of his visit.* 他写信向我报导他参观的情形。*I wrote to let them know that I was coming.* 我写信通知他们我就要来了。**6** (usu passive) show clear signs of: (通常用被动语态)显露: *He had trouble / honesty written on his face.* 他的脸上显露他的困难(诚实)。 *written* (also *writ,* archaic form of the *pp*) *large,* easily or clearly recognizable. (亦作 writ large, writ 为古体的过去分词)显而易见; 容易识别。

writer /'raɪtə(r); 'raɪtɚ/ *n* **1** person who writes: 书写者: *the ~ of this letter.* 写这封信的人。 *~'s cramp,* cramp of the muscles in the hand, causing difficulty in writing. 书写痉挛(使人不便书写)。**2** author. 作家; 著者。**3** (GB) clerk in some government offices; naval rating who does office work. (英)某些政府机构中的书记; 海军文书士。

writhe /raɪð; raɪð/ *vi* [VP2A, C] twist or roll about in pain; (fig)suffer mental agony: 因痛苦而折腾; 翻滚; 扭动; (喻)遭受精神痛苦: *~ under insults.* 受侮辱而感到痛苦。

writ·ing /'raɪtɪŋ; 'raɪtɪŋ/ *n* **1** [U] (in the senses of the *v* '*write*'): (与动词 write 的含义同): *busy with his ~;* 忙于写作; *put sth down in ~.* 以书面写下某事。*His ~ (=*'hand~) *is difficult to read.* 他的字迹不易辨认。 *'~-desk n* desk (usu with drawers) for ~ at. 书桌(通常有抽

屈）。'**~-ink** *n* ink for ~ (contrasted with printing-ink). 书写用墨水（与印刷用的油墨相对）。 '**~-paper** *n* [U] (esp) paper cut to the size usual for letters. 写字纸;(尤指)信纸。 **2** (*pl*) literary work: (复)文学作品; 著述: *the ~s of Swift.* 斯威夫特的作品。

writ·ten /'rɪtn; 'rɪtn̩/ ⇨ **write**.

wrong /rɒŋ US: rɔːŋ; rɔŋ/ *adj* (contrasted with *right*) (与 right 相对) **1** not morally right; unjust: 不正当的;不法的;道德不好的: *It is ~ to steal.* 偷窃是不法的。*It was ~ of you / You were ~ to borrow his bicycle without asking his permission.* 你未得他的允许而借用他的脚踏车是不对的。 **2** mistaken; unsuitable; improper: 错误的;不适当的;不合宜的: *He has six ~ answers in his arithmetic.* 他的算术中有六个地方答错。 *Can you prove that I am / that my opinions are ~?* 你能证明我是(我的意见是)错误的吗? *You're doing it the ~ way.* 你正以错误的方法做那事。*We got into the ~ train.* 我们搭错了火车。*We came the ~ way / took a ~ turning.* 我们走错路（转错弯）了。*This is the ~ side of the tablecloth,* not the side intended to be seen. 这是桌布的反面。 **~ side out**, with the ~ side outside. 翻转;反面向外;里面翻向外。 **be caught on the ~ foot,** be caught when one is not ready. 措手不及。 **get out of bed on the ~ side,** said of sb who is in a bad temper early in the day. 一大早就发脾气; 一大早就心绪不好。**get hold of the ~ end of the stick,** have a completely mistaken idea or impression. 想法或印象完全错误。 **in the ~ box,** in an awkward position. 处境尴尬;为难。**on the ~ side of fifty, etc,** over fifty, etc years old. 过了五十岁,等。 **,~-'headed** *adj* perverse and obstinate. 顽固的; 刚愎的。 **,~-'headedly** *adv* **3** out of order; in a bad condition: 失常的; 有毛病的; 状况不佳的: *There's nothing ~ with the engine—perhaps there's no petrol in the tank.* 引擎没有毛病——也许油箱里没有汽油了。*There's something ~ with my digestion.* 我有一点消化不良。*What's ~ with that?* (colloq, as a rhetorical question, meaning 'That's all right, isn't it?') 那有什么不对吗?（口,作为反语问句,意即'那没有什么不对,不是吗?'）□ *adv* (usu end position) not correctly; in a ~ manner: (通常置于句末)不正确地; 不正当地; 错误地;失常地。*guess ~.* 猜错。*You've spelt my name ~.* 把我的名字拼错了。Cf 参较 ~*ly spelt. They told me ~.* 他们告诉我的话是错误的。Cf 参较 ~*ly informed.* **get sth ~,** miscalculate or misunderstand it. 误算或误解某事。**go ~, (a)** take the ~ path or road. 走错路。**(b)** have a bad or poor result; fail: 获致不好的结果; 失败: *All our plans went ~.* 我们所有的计划都失败了。**(c)** (colloq) (of a machine, etc) break down. (口) (指机器,等)出毛病;不对头;坏。□ *n* **1** [U] what is morally ~; [C] ~ action: 道德上的罪; 邪恶; 罪行: *know the difference between right and ~;* 能辨别是非善恶; *do ~, do*

what is ~; sin. 做坏事; 犯罪。*Two ~s don't make a right.* 两个错并不等于对;冤冤相报,永无了时。 '**~-doer** *n* person who does ~. 做坏事者;犯罪行者。 '**~-doing** *n* [U] doing ~; crime; sin. 犯罪;加害;罪恶; (道德上或法律上的)罪。 **2** [U] injustice; unjust treatment; [C] instance of this; unjust action: 不义;不公正的对待;其实例;不义的行为: *suffer ~;* 受冤屈; 受虐待; *do ~ to sb.* 冤屈某人;虐待某人。*You do me ~,* treat me unjustly. 你对我不公正（冤枉我）。*They have done me a great ~.* 他们对我有非常不公正。*She complained of the ~s she had suffered.* 她抱怨所遭受的虐待。 **3** *in the ~,* in the position of being responsible for an error, for having caused a quarrel, etc: 对错误, 对引起争执等应负责任;不对; 不正当; 犯错误: *He admitted that he was in the ~,* that the fault, etc was his. 他承认错在他。*They tried to put me in the ~,* to make it seem that the fault, etc was mine. 他们试图诿过于我。*You are both in the ~,* Each of you is in error. 你们俩都错了。□ *vt* [VP6A] treat unjustly; be unfair to: 虐待; 冤屈;对…不公正: *He ~ed me when he said that I was envious.* 他说我妒忌,是冤枉了我。*His deeply ~ed wife deserves our help and sympathy.* 他那深受虐待的妻子值得我们的帮助和同情。 **~·ful** /-fl; -fəl/ *adj* unjust; unlawful:不正当的;不公正的;不合法的: *~ful dismissal* (from employment). 不合法的解雇。 **~·fully** /-fəlɪ; -fəlɪ/ *adv* **~·ly** *adv* in a ~ manner (used esp before a *pp*): 不正当地; 错误地; 失常地(尤用于过去分词之前): *~ly informed / directed / accused.* 被输入地告知的/被诱入歧途的/被诬告的。

wrote /rəʊt; rot/ ⇨ **write**.

wroth /rəʊθ US: rɔːθ; roθ/ *adj* (pred only; poet, biblical, or in mod use hum) angry; indignant. (仅用于述语中; 诗,圣经体,或现代用法中作诙谐语)愤怒的, 愤慨的; 义愤的。

wrought /rɔːt; rɔt/ *pt, pp* of **work²** **1** beaten into shape: 被打成形的; 敲击成的; 锻的; ~ *iron.* 锻铁; 熟铁。 ⇨ **cast iron** at **cast¹**(3). **2** (archaic or liter) (古或文) *on / upon sb / sth,* excited him / it: 使某人(某物)激动; 刺激某人(某物): *Their sufferings ~ upon our feelings.* 他们所遭受的痛苦使我们情绪激动。 ⇨ **work on / upon sb / sth** at **work²**(10). **,~-'up** *adj* over-excited; extremely agitated. 过度兴奋的; 极度激动的。

wrung /rʌŋ; rʌŋ/ ⇨ **wring**.

wry /raɪ; raɪ/ *adj* (**wrier, wriest**) pulled or twisted out of shape: 扭歪的; 歪斜的: *make a wry face,* usu to show disappointment or disgust: 面孔沮丧; 拉长面孔 (通常表示失望或厌恶); *a wry smile,* a forced smile that indicates disappointment. 苦笑。 **wry·ly** *adv*

wych- (also **wich-, witch-**) /wɪtʃ; wɪtʃ/ *pref* used in names of trees: 用于树名中: '**~-elm,** 欧洲山榆; '**~-hazel.** 山榆;金缕梅。

X x

X, x /eks; ɛks/ *n* (*pl* **X's, x's** /'eksɪz; 'ɛksɪz/) **1** the 24th letter of the English alphabet. 英文字母的第二十四个字母。 **2** symbol for the Roman numeral 10. 罗马数字之十。 ⇨ **App 4.** 参看附录四。 **3** (algebra) first unknown quantity; (fig) factor or influence about which there is uncertainty. (代数)第一个未知数;(喻)未能确定的因素或影响。

xeno·phobia /ˌzenə'fəʊbɪə; ˌzɛnə'fobɪə/ *n* [U] irrational hatred or fear of strangers or foreigners. 陌生恐惧; 生客恐惧(对陌生人或外国人的不合理的憎恨或恐惧)。

Xerox /'zɪərɒks; 'zɪrɑks/ *n, vt* [VP6A] (P) (商标)= photocopy.

Xhosa /'kɔːzə; 'kozə/ *n, adj* (member or language) of the people of *Transkei* /træn'skaɪ; træn'skaɪ/ in Southern Africa. (南非特兰斯凯共和国的)科萨人 (的);

科萨语(的)。

Xmas /'krɪsməs; 'krɪsməs/ *n* (common abbr, in writing, for) Christmas. (书写中常用之略语)Christmas.

X-ray /'eks reɪ; 'ɛks're/ *n* short-wave ray that penetrates solids and makes it possible to see into or through them; photograph taken by this means: 爱克斯光; X光; X光照片: (attrib) (用作定语) *have an X-ray* (*examination*); 照X光(作X光检查); *an X-ray diagnosis.* X光诊断; *X-ray photography.* X光照相术。□ *vt* [VP 6A] examine, treat, photograph, with X-rays. 用X光检查,治疗或照相。

xylo·phone /'zaɪləfəʊn; 'zaɪlə,fon/ *n* musical instrument of parallel wooden bars, graduated in length, which produce different notes when struck with small wooden hammers. 木琴。 ⇨ the illus at **percussion**. 参看 percussion 之插图。

Y y

Y, y /waɪ; waɪ/ n (pl **Y's, y's** /waɪz; waɪz/) the 25th letter of the English alphabet. 英文字母的第二十五个字母。

yacht /jɒt; jɑt/ n 1 light sailing-boat built specially for racing. 竞赛用的轻快小帆船;轻舟;快艇。'~-club n club for ~owners. 快艇俱乐部。'~·man /-smən; -smən/ n (pl -men /-men; -mən/) person who makes a hobby of sailing. 嗜好驾驶快艇者。2 (usu privately-owned, usu motor-driven) vessel kept by a wealthy person for pleasure-cruising. (通常为私有,由发动机推动)游艇。□ vi [VP2A] travel or race in a ~. 乘游艇旅游;作快艇竞赛。~·ing n [U] the art, practice or sport of sailing ~s. 驾驶快艇或游艇的技术、实务或竞技;快(游)艇驾驶;快(游)艇航行。

yah /jɑː; jɑ/ int used to express derision. 呀(用以表示嘲笑)。

ya·hoo /jɑːˈhuː; ˈjɑhu/ n name given by Swift (in *Gulliver's Travels*) to members of a race of inferior human beings with the habits of animals; hence, detestable person with bestial habits. 人形兽;雅虎(Swift 所著 Gulliver's Travels 中的有野兽习性的劣等人);(由此产生)有野兽习性的可恶的人;人面兽心的人。

yak /jæk; jæk/ n long-haired ox, wild or domesticated, of Central Asia. 牦牛;犛牛(产于中亚,毛长,野生或饲养)。

yam /jæm; jæm/ n [C] 1 (edible tuber of) kinds of tropical climbing plant. 山药;薯蓣;其可食块茎。⇨ the illus at **vegetable**. 参看 vegetable 之插图。2 (US)kind of sweet potato. (美)蕃薯;甘薯。

yam·mer /ˈjæmə(r); ˈjæmɚ/ vi (colloq) (口) 1 complain peevishly; whine. 气愤地抱怨;哭诉。2 talk volubly or foolishly. 滔滔不绝地谈或无聊地谈话。

yank /jæŋk; jæŋk/ (colloq) (口) vt [VP6A, 15A, B] give a sudden sharp pull or tug. 用力猛拉;突然拉动:~ out a tooth. 拔出一颗牙。Tom ~ed the bed-clothes off his young brother and told him to get up. 汤姆一把拉开他弟弟的被子,叫他起床。□ n sudden sharp pull. 突然猛拉。

Yank /jæŋk; jæŋk/ n (sl) (abbr of) Yankee. (俚) 为 Yankee 之略。

Yan·kee /ˈjæŋkɪ; ˈjæŋkɪ/ n 1 native of New England (US). (美国的)新英格兰人。2 (in the American Civil War) native of any of the Northern States. (美国南北战争中)北部诸州的人;北方佬。3 (colloq, in GB, Europe) US citizen: (口,用于英国、欧洲)美国公民;美国人:(attrib)(用作定语) ~ inventions. 美国人的发明物。

yap /jæp; jæp/ vi (-pp-) [VP2A] 1 (esp of dogs) utter short, sharp barks. (尤指犬)狂吠;尖声急吠。2 (sl) talk noisily or foolishly. (俚) 哇啦哇啦地讲;瞎谈: Stop yapping! 别再瞎谈了! □ n short, shrill bark. 狂吠;尖声急吠。

yard¹ /jɑːd; jɑrd/ n 1 (usu unroofed) enclosed or partly enclosed space near or round a building or group of buildings, often paved: (通常无顶篷)房屋附近或周围的围地;围院;院子: a 'farm~. 农庄的场院; a 'cattle-~. 家畜的围栏; the school ~, used as a playground; (学校的)运动场;(US) area of land laid out as a garden round a house. (美)庭院;庭园。2(usu in compounds) enclosure for a special purpose: (通常用于复合词中)作专门用途的围地;工作场: the 'railway ~s; 'marshalling ~s, area where trains are made up, where coaches, wagons, etc are stored; 铁路调车场,使运火车集结场; a 'tan-~, where tanning is carried on. 制革场。⇨ also back~ at **back⁴**(3), dock~ at **dock¹**, ship~ at **ship¹**(3), vine~ at **vine**(2). 3 the **Y~,** (colloq abbr for) New Scotland Y~. (口) 为 New Scotland Yard 之略。

yard² /jɑːd; jɑrd/ n 1 (⇨**App 5**) unit of length, 3

feet or 36 inches: (参看附录五)码(长度单位,合三英尺或三十六英寸): Can you still buy cloth by the ~ in Britain? 在英国买布 仍旧用码为单位吗? ~-'measure n rod, tape, etc one ~ long, marked in feet, inches, quarters, etc. 码尺(指直尺,卷尺等)。'~-stick n (fig) standard of comparison. (喻)(用作比较的)标准。2 long, polelike piece of wood fastened to a mast for supporting and spreading a sail. 帆桁。⇨ the illus at **barque**. 参看 barque 之插图。'~-arm n either end of such a ~. 帆桁的一端; 桁端。**man the ~s,** place men along the ~s, stand along the ~s, as a form of salute. 行进(出)港礼。

yarn /jɑːn; jɑrn/ n 1 [U] fibres(esp of wool) which have been spun for knitting, weaving. etc. 纱;线;(尤指)毛线。2 [C] (colloq) story; traveller's tale.(口) 故事;奇谈;旅行者的故事。**spin a ~,** tell a story; make up a story: 讲故事; 编造故事: The beggar spun a long ~ about his misfortunes. 那个乞丐编造了一大篇如何遭遇不幸的故事。□ vi [VP2A, C] tell ~s: 讲故事: We stayed up ~ing until midnight. 我们讲故事一直讲到午夜才睡。

yar·row /ˈjærəʊ; ˈjæro/ n common perennial herb with flat clusters of small flowers. 欧蓍草;西洋蓍草。

yash·mak /ˈjæʃmæk; jaʃˈmɑk/ n veil worn in public by some Muslim women in some countries. (某些国家伊斯兰教妇女在公众场合所戴的)面纱。

yaw /jɔː; jɔ/ vi (of a ship or aircraft) turn unsteadily off the right course. (指船或航空器)偏航;逸出航线。□ n such a turn. 偏航;逸出航线。

yawl /jɔːl; jɔl/ n (naut) (航海) 1 sailing-boat with two masts, the second being a short one near the stern. 纵帆快艇(具有二桅,后桅较低)。2 ship's boat with four or six oars. (有四或六桨的)船载小艇。

yawn /jɔːn; jɔn/ vi [VP2A, C] 1 take (usu involuntarily) a deep breath with the mouth wide open, as when sleepy or bored. 打呵欠。2 be wide open: 张开;裂开: a ~ing fissure. 张开的裂缝。A gulf ~ed at our feet. 一个深坑在我们脚前豁然展开。□ n [C] act of ~ing(1). 打呵欠。

yaws /jɔːz; jɔz/ n pl contagious tropical skin disease. 雅司病;热带莓疮。

ye¹ /jiː; ji/ pron(old form of) you: (you 的古字形)你;你们: Ye fools! 你们这些傻子! How d'ye do /ˌhaʊ djɪˈduː; ˈhaʊdjɪˈdu/? 你好!

ye² /jiː; ji/ def art = **the** (old written form, still seen on signboards over some shops and inns): the 的古书写形 (仍可见于某些商店或旅舍的店招上): Ye Olde Bull and Bush. 布尔及布什老店。

yea /jeɪ; je/ adv, int(archaic) yes. (古)是;然。□ n aye:赞成;赞成者: Yeas and nays, ayes and noes. 赞成者与反对者。

yeah /jeə; je/ adv (sl) yes. (俚)是。

year /jɪə(r) US: jɪər; jɪr/ n 1 time taken by the earth in making one revolution round the sun, about 365¹/₄ days. 太阳年(地球绕行太阳一周所需的时间,约为365¹/₄天)。2 period from 1 January to 31 December (also called 亦称作 the calendar ~): 年; 历年(从一月一日至十二月三十一日): in the ~ 1865; 在一八六五年; last ~; 去年; this ~; 今年; next ~; 明年; the ~ after next; 后年; New Y~'s Day, 1 January. 元旦。~ in ~ out, after ~. 一年一年地;年复一年。all (the) ~ round, at all times of the ~. 一年到头。~ of grace..., ~ of our Lord..., any named ~ after the birth of Jesus: 耶稣纪元;公元: in the ~ of our Lord, 1999. 在公元一九九九年。the ~ dot, (colloq) a very long time ago: (口)很久以前: I've known her since the ~ dot. 我认识她很久很久了。3 any period of 365 consecutive days: 任何相连

的三百六十五天；年；岁；载：*It is just a ~ since I arrived here*. 我到此地恰恰一年了。*He's twenty ~s of age*. 他廿岁了。*He became blind in his twelfth ~*, at the age of 11. 他在十一岁时眼睛瞎了。*~-book* n book issued once a ~ giving information (reports, statistics, etc) esp about trade or commerce. 年鉴。*~-'long adj* continuing for a ~: *a ~-long struggle*. 连续一年的奋斗。**4** period of one ~ associated with sth. 与某事物相关连的一年；…年。*the academic ~*, for schools, colleges and universities (beginning, in GB and US, in the autumn). 学年(英国和美国始于秋季)。*the financial / fiscal ~*, (in GB, for making up accounts, etc from the beginning of April). 财政(会计)年度(英国始于四月)。**5** (*pl*) age; time of life: (复)年龄；年岁：*a boy of ten ~s*; 十岁的男孩；*young for her ~s*, looking young although not young in age; 显得比实际年龄年轻；*reach the ~s of discretion*. 达到懂事的年龄。**~·ly** *adj, adv* (taking place) every ~; once a ~. 每年(的)；每年一次(的)；一年一度(的)。

year·ling /'jə:lɪŋ; 'jɪrlɪŋ/ *n* animal between one and two years old: 一岁至两岁的幼兽: (attrib) (用作定语) *a ~ colt*. 一两岁的小马。

yearn /jə:n; jɝn/ *vi* [VP3A, 4A] ~ *(for sth / to do sth)*, long for with tender feeling, affection, etc: 渴望；思念；怀念；向往: *He ~ed for a sight of the old, familiar faces*. 他渴望一见那些熟悉的老面孔。*He ~ed to return to his native land*. 他渴望返回故乡。**~·ing** *n* strong desire; tender longing. 渴望；思念。**~·ing·ly** *adv*

yeast /ji:st; jist/ *n* [U] substance used in brewing beer, and in the making of bread. 酵母；发酵物。**~y** *adj* frothy like ~. 似酵母般多泡沫的。

yell /jel; jɛl/ *vi, vt* **1** [VP2A, C] utter a loud sharp cry or cries of pain, excitement, etc: 号叫；呼喊: ~ *with fright / laughter*. 惊恐得大声喊叫 (高声大笑)。**2** [VP6A, 15B] ~ *sth (out)*, say in a ~ing voice: 喊出；大声说出；叫着说: ~ *(out) an order / oath*; 大声发布命令(宣誓); ~ *one's defiance*. 大声抗议。□ *n* loud sharp cry: 大喊；号叫: *a ~ of terror*; 恐怖的叫喊; *the college ~*, (US) particular kind of shout or cheer used at a college to encourage a team, etc. (美)大学啦啦队队员的喊声. *They greeted us with ~s of hate*. 他们以愤恨的喊叫声迎接我们。

yel·low /'jeləu; 'jɛlo/ *n, adj* **1** (of) the colour of gold or the yolk of a hen's egg. 黄；黄色；黄色的。~ *fever*, infectious tropical disease causing the skin to turn ~. 黄热病。*'~-flag* n flag coloured ~ displayed by a ship or hospital which is in quarantine. 黄旗(表示船只或医院正在检疫期间者)。*the ~ press*, newspapers which present news in a sensational way. 黄色报刊(以耸人听闻的方式报导新闻者)。**2** (often 常作 *'~-bellied*) (colloq) cowardly: (口)懦弱的;卑怯的: *He has a ~ streak in him*. 他有点胆小。□ *vi, vt* [VP6A, 2A] (cause to) become ~: (使)变黄: *The leaves of the book were ~ed / had ~ed with age*. 书叶因年久而变黄了。*The leaves of the trees are ~ing*. 树上的叶子正变为黄色。**~·ish** /-ɪʃ; -ɪʃ/ *adj* rather ~. 微黄的；带黄色的。**~·ness** *n*

yelp /jelp; jɛlp/ *vi* [VP2A], *n* (utter a) short, sharp cry (of pain, anger, excitement, etc): (发出)(痛苦、愤怒、兴奋等的)叫喊: *The dog ~ed / gave a ~ when I trod on its paw*. 当我踩到那只狗的爪子时, 它发出了嗥叫声。

yen[1] /jen; jɛn/ *n* (*pl* unchanged) unit of currency in Japan. (复数不变)圆(日本的币制单位)。

yen[2] /jen; jɛn/ *n* ~ *(for)*, (colloq) yearning (for sth). (口)热望；渴望。□ *vi* yearn (to do sth). 渴望；热望(接不定式)。

yeo·man /'jəumən; 'joman/ *n* (*pl* -**men**) **1** (hist) working farmer who owned his land (contrasted with tenant farmers and those who own large farms which they did not work themselves). (旧)自耕农(与佃农及地主相对)。~ *service*, long and efficient service; help in time of need. 长期而有效的勤务；紧急时期的援助。**2**

~ *of signals*, (GB) naval petty officer in the branch concerned with signalling by visual means (flags, etc); (US) petty officer with clerical duties. (英)(海军的)信号士官；(美)文书士官。**3** *Y~ of the Guard*, (GB) member of a royal bodyguard with ceremonial duties at the Tower of London, and else-where on special occasions. (英)英国王室的卫士。**4** member of the ~ry. 义勇骑兵。~*ry* /-rɪ; -rɪ/ *n* (hist) (collective for) volunteer cavalry force raised from farmers, etc. (史)义勇骑兵队；志愿骑兵队。

yes /jes; jɛs/ *particle* (contrasted with *no*) expressing agreement, affirmation, consent, etc: (与 *no* 相对) 是；然: '*Can you read this?*' '*Yes*.' '你能读这个吗?' '我能.' Note that *yes* is used in answer to an interrogative-negative if the complete answer is affirmative: 注意: yes 用于答复答案是肯定的否定问句: '*Don't you like it?*' '*Yes*' (= 'Yes, I do like it') '你不喜欢它吗?' '我喜欢.' '*Isn't she beautiful!*' '*Yes, isn't she?*' '她不是很漂亮吗?' '一'是的, 她很漂亮, 不是吗?' '*Waiter!*' '*Yes, sir*.' (='What do you want, sir?') '堂倌!' '一'是的, 先生.' (= '要什么, 先生?') □ *n* [C] affirmation; acceptance: 肯定；接受: *Answer with a plain 'Yes' or 'No'*. 明白回答我是'是'或'不是'('同意'或'不同意')。

yes·ter- /'jestə(r); 'jɛstɚ/ *pref* (on) the day, year, etc before this, chiefly poet except in ~*day* (⇔below): 表示昨日, 去年等义(除下面的 yesterday 外, 主要为诗中用语): *Where are the snows of ~year?* 去年白雪今何在?

yes·ter·day /'jestədɪ; 'jɛstɚdɪ/ *adv, n* (on) the day just past; (on) the day before today: (在)昨天；昨日: *He arrived ~*. 他昨天到了。*Y~ was Sunday*. 昨天是礼拜天。*Where's ~'s (news) paper?* 昨天的报纸在哪里? *Why were you away from work the day before ~?* 前天你为何未上班? *Where were you ~ morning / afternoon / evening?* 昨天早晨(下午, 晚上)你在何处? (Cf 参较 last night.) *She left home ~ week*, eight days ago. 她是上星期的昨天(八天前)离开家的。

yet /jet; jɛt/ *adv* **1** (in neg and conditional contexts and in contexts indicating ignorance or uncertainty; usu in end position, but also immediately after *not*; ⇔ *already*(2)) by this or that time; up to now; up to then: (用于否定及条件的文句中, 并用于表示不知或不确定的文句中；通常用于句末, 亦可紧接在 not 之后)到此时；到那时；至今；至当时: *They are not here yet / not yet here*. 他们还没有到(尚未来此)。*We have had no news from him yet*. 我们还没有接到他的消息。*We have not yet had news from him*. 我们还没有接到他的消息。*At 2 o'clock they had not yet decided how to spend the afternoon*. 到两点钟他们尚未决定如何消磨那个下午。*I wonder whether they have finished the work yet*. 我不知道他们现在是否已做完那件工作。**2** (in interr and neg contexts; ⇔ *already* and *still*) so far; up to this / that time: (用于疑问句及否定句中)到目前为止；至这时；至那时: *Has your brother arrived yet?* 你哥哥(弟弟)到了吗? *Need you go yet?* 你需要去了吗? *We needn't do it just yet*. 此刻我们无须做那事。**3** (in affirm sentences) still: (用于肯定句中): 仍；更；益发: *Be thankful you are yet alive* (*Still* is the more usu word). 你仍然还活着, 真该感谢上苍 (still 比 yet 更常用)。*Go at once while there is yet time*, while it is not too late. 快去吧, 还来得及。*This problem is yet* (= still) *more difficult*. 这个问题益发困难了。*I have yet* (= still) *more exciting news for you*. 我还有令人兴奋的消息告诉你。**4** at some future time; before all is over: 在未来某一时间；迟早；早晚: *The enemy may win yet / may yet win if we relax our efforts*. 如果我们松弛下来, 敌人迟早会获得胜利的。*He may surprise us all yet*. 他总有一天会让我们大家惊奇。**5** *as yet*, up to now / then: 到现在(那时)为止: *As yet we have made no plans for the holidays*. 到目前(那时)为止, 我们还没有计划如何度假。*The scheme has worked well as yet*. 到目前为止, 那项计划进行顺利。*nor yet*, (liter) and not even: (文)甚至也不；而且也不: *The book is not well written—nor yet is it accurate*. 那本书写得不好——而且也不精确。□ *conj*

but at the same time; nevertheless: 然而；可是: *She's vain and foolish, and yet people like her.* 她自负而愚蠢，然而人们喜欢她。*He worked hard, yet he failed.* 他努力工作，可是他失败了。*It is strange, yet (it is) true.* (它)虽然奇怪，却是真实的。*He's a wealthy, yet honest, businessman.* 他是一位富有而又正直的商人。

yeti /'jeti; 'jɛtɪ/ *n* name of a hairy, man-like animal reported to live in the highest part of the Himalayas. 雪人(传说生活在喜马拉雅山最高处,似人而多毛的动物)。

yew /juː; juː/ *n* [C] **'yew(-tree),** evergreen, berry-bearing tree with dark-green leaves, often used for garden hedges; [U] wood of this tree (formerly used for making bows). 紫杉；水松(常用做庭园之树篱)；紫杉木；水松木(昔时用以制弓)。

Yid·dish /'jɪdɪʃ; 'jɪdɪʃ/ *n* [U] international Jewish language, a form of old German with words borrowed from several modern languages, used by Jews in or from Eastern or Central Europe (*note:* the language used in Israel is modern Hebrew). 意地绪语(中欧或东欧的犹太人所使用的国际语,为一种古日耳曼语,并借用数种近代语的字汇。注意: 现在以色列使用的语言为近代希伯来语)。

yield /jiːld; jild/ *vt, vi* **1** [VP6A] give a natural product, a result or profit: 生产；出产；生: *trees that ~ fruit;* 结果的树，*investments ~ing 10 per cent.* 生息百分之十的投资。**2** [VP2A, 3A, 6A, 15A, B] ~ **(to sb/ sth),** give way (to); cease opposition: 让步；屈服；不再反对: *We will never ~ to force.* 我们决不会向暴力屈服。*The disease ~ed to treatment.* 该病经治疗后痊愈 (减轻)了。*He ~ed to temptation.* 他屈服于诱惑之下。~ **(up) sth (to sb),** give up; surrender: 放弃；交出: ~ *a fort;* 放弃要塞。~ *ground to the enemy.* 将阵地放弃给敌人。~ **up the ghost,** (liter or rhet)die. (文或修辞)死。□ *n* [C, U] amount produced: 生产量；获益率；产出率；收益: *a good ~ of wheat.* 小麦的丰收。*What is the ~ per acre?* 每英亩产量若干? *The ~s on his shares have decreased this year,* The dividends are lower. 他的股票今年的红利降低了。~**·ing** *adj* easily giving way or bending; (fig) not obstinate. 易变形的；易弯曲的；(喻)不固执的；让步的；屈从的。~**·ing·ly** *adv*

yip·pee /'jɪpɪ; 'jɪpɪ/ *int* cry of joy or elation. 表示欣鼓舞的欢呼声。

yob /jɒb; jɑb/, **yobo, yobbo** /'jɒbəu; 'jɑbo/ *n*(GB sl) idle, objectionable person. (英俚)游手好闲而令人讨厌的人。

yodel /'jəudl; 'jodl/ *vt, vi* (-ll-; US also l--) sing (a song), utter a musical call, with frequent changes from the normal voice to high falsetto notes, in the manner of Swiss mountaineers. 用真假嗓音常常互换而唱或呼唤(如瑞士高山居民的唱法); 以岳德尔调唱(歌)。□ *n* ~ling song or call. 用此种方式所唱的歌或所作的呼唤; 岳德尔调。~**·ler**(US also ~**·er**) *n* person who ~s. 用岳德尔调唱歌或呼唤者。

yoga /'jəugə; 'jogə/ *n* [U] **1** Hindu system of meditation and self-control intended to produce mystical experience and the union of the individual soul with the universal spirit. 瑜伽；瑜伽术(印度的冥思及自制法,旨在产生神秘经验及天人合一)。**2** system of physical exercises and breathing-control. 瑜伽工夫(一种运动身体及控制呼吸的方法)。**yogi** /'jəugɪ; 'jogɪ/ *n* (*pl* ~s) teacher of, expert in, ~(1). 瑜伽派教师; 精于瑜伽术者。

yo·gurt, yo·ghurt, yo·ghourt /'jɒgət US: 'jəu-gərt; 'jogət/ *n* [U] thick fermented liquor made from milk. (浓厚的)酵母乳; 酸乳酪。

yo-heave-ho /ˌjəu ˈhiːv həu; 'jo'hiv'ho/ *int* cry (formerly) used by sailors when pulling together (eg to raise a sail). 唷嗨嗬(往昔水手们一同扬帆时的喊叫声)。

yoke /jəuk; jok/ *n* **1** shaped piece of wood placed across the necks of oxen pulling a cart, plough, etc. 牛轭；轭。⇨ **harness. 2** (*pl* unchanged) two oxen working together: (复数不变)共同工作的一对牛；共轭牛: *five*

of oxen. 五对共轭牛。**3**(Roman history) arch of three spears (a symbol of the ~ placed on oxen)under which defeated enemies were made to pass; (罗马史)轭门(三只矛做成的拱门，做为轭的象征，战败的敌人被迫从下面穿过)；hence, 由此产生, (fig) (喻) pass/come under the ~, acknowledge and accept defeat; 承认失败; 屈从; *throw off the ~* (of servitude, etc), rebel; refuse to obey; 反抗; 拒绝服从; 摆脱奴役等; *the ~ of a tyrant.* 暴君的奴役。**4** shaped piece of wood to fit a person's shoulders and support a pail at each end. 轭状木扁担。**5** (dress-making) part of a garment fitting round the shoulders and from which the rest hangs; top part of a skirt, fitting the hips. (女服缝制)上衣的抵肩；裙子的腰。□ *vt* [VP6A, 15A] **1** put a ~ on (oxen): 加轭于(牛); 用轭把(牛)连接于: ~ *oxen together;* 用轭连接牛; ~ *oxen to a plough.* 用轭把牛连接于犁。**2** unite: 使结合; 使联合: ~*d to an unwilling partner;* 与一位不情愿的伙伴合作; ~*d in marriage.* 婚姻; 联姻。

yoked oxen

yokel /'jəukl; 'jokl/ *n* simple-minded countryman. 头脑简单的乡下人; 乡下佬; 土包子。

yolk /jəuk; jok/ *n* [C, U] yellow part of an egg: 蛋黄: *Beat up the ~s of three eggs.* 搅匀三个蛋黄。

yon /jɒn; jɑn/ *adj, adv* (archaic or dial) (古或方) = yonder.

yon·der /'jɒndə(r); 'jɑndə/ *adj, adv* (liter) (that is, that can be seen) over there: (文)(在, 见于) 那边 (的); (在,见于)彼处(的); (在,见于)远处的(的): ~ *group of trees.* 远处的树丛。

yore /jɔː(r); jor/ *n* [U] *of ~,* long ago: 很久以前: *in days of ~.* 在很久以前的时代。

you /juː; ju/ *pron* **1** the person(s) addressed: 你; 你们: *You are my friend(s).* 你(们)是我的朋友。*Does he know you?* 他认识你吗? *This is for you* 这是给你的。**2** (colloq; used as an impers pron) one; anyone: (口)用作无人称代词)一个人; 任何人: *It is much easier to cycle with the wind behind you.* 顺着风骑单车容易得多。*You never know,* One can never be certain about things. 事情难以逆料(或: 谁也没法预料)。**3** (preceding a *n*, esp in vocatives): (置于名词前, 尤其用作直接称呼语): *You boys!* 你们男孩子们! *You over there!* 喂, 你们! (in exclamations): (用于惊叹句中): *You bloody fool!* 你这个大傻瓜!

you'd /juːd; jud/ = you had; you would.

you'll /juːl; jul/ = you will.

young /jʌŋ; jʌŋ/ *adj* (-nger, /-ŋgə(r); -ŋgə/, -ngest /-ŋgɪst; -ŋgɪst/) **1** (contrasted with old) not far advanced in life, growth, development, etc; of recent birth or origin: 年轻的(相对 old 而言); 年幼的: *a ~ woman/tree/animal/nation, etc.* 年轻的女人 (幼小的树; 小动物; 新兴国家等)。**2** still near its beginning: 仍然接近开始阶段的: 初期的: *The evening/century is still ~.* 夜还不深(本世纪刚开始不久)。**3** the ~**er,** used before or after a person's name, to distinguish that person from another; contrasted with *elder*): (用于人名前或后,以便和同姓的人区别; 与 elder 相对): *the ~er Pitt;* 小皮特; *Pliny the Y~er.* 小普利尼。*be sb's ~er,* be ~er than him. 较某人年轻。**4** (used before a person's name to distinguish esp a son from his father): (用于人名之前,尤用以分辨父子): *Y~ Jones is always*

ready to help his old parents. 小琼斯时时准备帮助他年老的双亲。 **5** (as a familiar or condescending form of address): (用亲热或屈尊的称呼): *Now listen to me, ~ man/my ~ lady!* 现在听我说，年轻人（我的小姐）！ **6** having little practice or experience (in sth): (对某事物) 不熟练的; 无经验的: *~ in crime.* 无犯罪经验的。 **7 ~ and old,** everyone. 每一个人; 全体。 *~ people;* children: 年轻人; 青年; 孩子们: *books for the ~.* 青少年读物。 □ *n* [U] offspring; *~ ones* (of animals and birds): 后裔; (鸟兽的) 崽; 仔: *The cat fought fiercely to defend its ~, its ~ offspring.* 那只猫拚命打斗以保护其幼仔。 *Some animals quickly desert their ~.* 有些动物很快地就不理它们的幼仔了。 **with~,** (of an animal) pregnant. (指动物) 有孕的。 **~·ish** /ˈjʌŋɪʃ; ˈjʌŋɪʃ/ *adj* fairly ~; somewhat ~. 尚年轻的; 颇幼小的。 **~·ster** /ˈjʌŋstə(r); ˈjʌŋstɚ/ *n* child, youth. 儿童; 少年; 青年。

your /jɔː(r) US: jʊər; jʊr/ *adj* **1** belonging to, relating to, you: 你(们)的; 属于你(们)的: *Show me ~ hands.* 把你两只手伸出来让我看看。 *You'll see the post office on ~ right,* ie ~ right side. 你将会在你的右边看见邮局。 **2** (often indicating polite interest, or disapproval or contempt, or used to suggest that sth is not so good, remarkable, etc as is claimed): (常表示礼貌的关心，或表示不赞成或轻视，或用以示暗某事物不如所说的那么好或那么出色): *So this is what ~ experts said, is it?* 原来这就是你们专家所说的，是吗？ *This is ~ famous English beer, is it?* 这就是你们英国著名的啤酒，是吗？

you're /jʊə(r); jʊr/ =you are.

yours /jɔːz US: jʊərz; jʊrz/ *pred adj, pron* **1** of you: 你的; 你们的: *Is that book ~?* 那本书是你的吗？ *I borrowed a book of ~.* 我向你借过一本书。 **2** (at the end of a letter): (用于信函的结尾处): *~ truly/sincerely/ faithfully.* 信尾套语，相当于中文书信中的'敬启; 敬上'等。

your·self /jɔːˈself US: jʊərˈself; jʊrˈself/ (*pl* **-selves** /-ˈselvz; -ˈselvz/ *reflex pron: Did you hurt ~?* 你弄伤了自己吗？ □ *emphat pron: You ~ said so.* 你自己这样说的。 *You said so ~.* 你自己这样说的。 **(all) by ~, (a)** alone. 独自; 单独。 **(b)** without help. 独力; 靠自己。

youth /juːθ; juθ/ *n* (*pl* ~s /juːðz; juðz/) **1** [U] the state or time of being young: 青春; 青春期; 青少年时代: *the enthusiasm of ~;* 青春时代的热忱; *the friends of one's ~,* 少年时代的朋友; *in ~,* when I was young. 当我年轻时。 **2** [C] young man: 少年; 青年: *As a ~ he showed no promise of becoming a great pianist.* 他在少年时代并未显示出将来会变成一位伟大的钢琴家。 *Half a dozen ~s were standing at the street corner.* 有六个青年站在街角。 **3** [U] (collective *sing,* with *pl v*) young men and women: (集合单数，与复数动词连用)青年男女; 青年们: *the ~ of the nation.* 全国青年; *a ~ hostel,* 青年招待所; *a ~ centre/club,* club(usu provided by a voluntary organization) for the leisure time activities of young people. 青年活动中心 (俱乐部)。 **~·ful** /-fl; -fəl/ *adj* young; having the qualities, etc, of young people: 年少的; 青春的; 有青年之性质等的: *a ~ful appearance.* 青春的外貌。 **~·fully** /-fəlɪ; -fəlɪ/ *adv* **~·ful·ness** *n*

you've /juːv; juv/ =you have.

yowl /jaul; jaʊl/ *vi* howl; wail. 嗥叫; 嗥唬; 恸哭。

yo-yo /ˈjəʊjəʊ; ˈjo.jo/ *n* toy in the shape of a top with a groove for string, the top moving up and down the string by movement of the fingers: 悠悠; 空钟(形似陀螺的玩具，上有沟槽，可使之嵌入细索，以手操纵该索，此玩具即沿索上下移动)。 *The exchange rate is going up and down like a ~.* 外汇的汇率就像悠悠一样忽上忽下。

yule /juːl; jul/ *n* (also 亦作 '**~·tide**) (archaic) Christmas. (古)圣诞节; 圣诞季节。 '**~·log** *n* log of wood burnt on Christmas Eve. 圣诞柴(圣诞前夕焚烧的木柴)。

Z z

Z, z /zed US: ziː; zi/ *n* (*pl* **Z's, z's** /zedz US: ziːz; ziz/) the last letter of the English alphabet. 英文字母的最后一个字母。

zany /ˈzeɪnɪ; ˈzenɪ/ *n* (*pl* **-nies**) half-witted person; foolish joker. 非弱者; 糊涂虫; 愚笨的谐谑者。 □ *adj* foolish; mad. 愚笨的; 荒唐的。

zap /zæp; zæp/ *vt*(**-pp-**) [VP6A] (sl) attack; defeat. (俚)攻击; 打败。

zeal /ziːl; zil/ *n* [U] energy and enthusiasm: 热忱; 热心: *show ~ for a cause;* 显示对某主义热心; *work with great ~.* 非常热心地工作。 **~·ous** /ˈzeləs; ˈzeləs/ *adj* full of, acting with, showing, ~: 热心的; 热忱的; 充满热心的; 热心行事的; 显示热心的: *~ous to please one's employer;* 热心于讨好雇主; *~ous for liberty and freedom.* 热心争取自由。 **~·ous·ly** *adv*

zealot /ˈzelət; ˈzelət/ *n* person who shows great and uncompromising enthusiasm for a religion, a party, a cause, etc; fanatic. 对宗教、党派、主义等极为热心者; 狂热分子。 **~ry** /-trɪ; -trɪ/ *n* [U] .

zebra /ˈziːbrə; ˈzibrə/ *n* horse-like wild animal of Africa, with dark stripes on its body. 斑马。 ⇨ the illus at **large.** 参看 large 之插图。 '**~ 'crossing,** street-crossing marked with broad white stripes, at which pedestrians have priority over traffic. (行人优先通过的)斑马线。 ⇨ **panda.**

zebu /ˈziːbuː; ˈzibju/ *n* domestic animal like an ox, with a hump on its shoulders, used in Asia and E Africa. 瘤牛(似牛家畜，肩上有瘤，亚洲及东非洲用作执兽)。

zee /ziː; zi/ *n*(US) name of the letter z. (美)字母 z。

Zen /zen; zɛn/ *n* [U] form of Buddhism asserting

that enlightenment comes from meditation and intuition, with less dependence upon the scriptures. (佛教的) 禅宗 (强调打坐及专念即可修成正果)。

zen·ith /ˈzenɪθ US: ˈziːnɪθ; ˈzinɪθ/ *n* part of the sky directly overhead; (fig) highest point (of one's fame, fortunes, etc): 天空的正上方部分; 天顶; (喻) (名誉、幸运等的)最高点; 顶点: *at the ~ of his career.* 在他事业的顶点。 □ *adj ~al projection,* map obtained by projecting[2](6). 天顶投影(地图)。 ⇨ **nadir.** ⇨ the illus at **projection.** 参看 projection 之插图。

zephyr /ˈzefə(r); ˈzefɚ/ *n* west wind; (poet) soft, gentle breeze. 西风; (诗)和风; 微风。

zep·pe·lin /ˈzepəlɪn; ˈzepələn/ *n* large dirigible used by the Germans in World War I. 齐柏林飞船(德国人在第一次世界大战中使用的飞船)。

zero /ˈzɪərəʊ; ˈzɪro/ *n* **1** the figure 0; nought. 数字 '零'; 0。 ⇨ App 4(1, note 2). 参看附录四第一项注 2。 **2** the point between the positive (+) and negative (—) on a scale, esp on a thermometer (⇨ App 5): 零点; 零位; (尤指温度计上的)零度 (参看附录五): *The thermometer fell to ~ last night.* 昨天夜里温度计降到了零度。 *It was ten degrees below ~* (eg —10°C or —10°F). 气温是零下十度。 **absolute ~,** ⇨ **absolute** (5). '**~ hour,** (mil) time at which operations are to begin: (军) 行动或攻击开始时刻; 零时: *Z~ hour was 3am.* 攻击开始时刻是凌晨三点钟。 □ *vi* [VP2C] *~ in (on),* (sl) fix attention (on). (俚)集中注意力(于)。

zest /zest; zest/ *n* [U] **1** great interest or pleasure; gusto: 强烈的兴趣; 热心: *He entered into our plans with ~.* 他热心地参加我们的计划。 **2** (often with *indef art*) pleasing or stimulating quality or flavour: (常与不定冠

词连用)可受性; 刺激性; 风味; 兴味: *The possibility of danger gave (a) ~ to the adventure.* 危险的可能性发生增加了那次冒险的刺激性。

zig·zag /'zɪgzæg; 'zɪgzæg/ *n* [C] line or path which turns right and left alternately at sharp (equal or unequal) angles: 锯齿形的线或道路; 之字形: (attrib) (用作定语) *a ~ path up the hillside.* 山坡上的一条曲折小径。口 *adv* in a ~. 成锯齿形地; 曲折地。口 *vi* (-gg-) go in a ~: 曲折地前进: *The drunken man ~ged down the street.* 那个醉鬼歪歪倒倒地沿街走去。

zinc /zɪŋk; zɪŋk/ *n* [U] hard, bluish-white metal (symbol **Zn**) used in alloys and in coating iron sheets and wire to give protection against rust. 锌(金属元素, 化学符号 Zn, 用来制合金, 或镀于铁皮或铁丝外面, 以防止生锈)。

zing /zɪŋ; zɪŋ/ *n* [U] (sl) vigour; energy. (俚)精力; 活力; 生命力。

zin·nia /'zɪnɪə; 'zɪnɪə/ *n* kinds of garden plant with bright-coloured flowers. 百日草; 鱼尾菊(园艺植物)。

Zion /'zaɪən; 'zaɪən/ *n* the Jewish homeland, esp as a symbol of Judaism; Israel. 锡安山(犹太人故乡, 尤指作为犹太人之宗教及其文化的象征); 以色列。 **~·ism** /-ɪzəm; -ɪzəm/ *n* (hist) political movement for the establishment of an independent state for the Jews; (mod use) movement concerned with the development of Israel as a Jewish political and religious State. (史)犹太人复国运动; (现代用法)以色列犹太化运动(使以色列成为犹太人的政治及宗教国家的运动)。 **~·ist** /-ɪst; -ɪst/ *adj, n*

zip /zɪp; zɪp/ *n* **1** sound as of a bullet going through the air, or of the sudden tearing of cloth. 子弹急飞过天空或突然撕裂布帛的)嘶嘶声; 飕飕声; 嘘嘘声; 咻咻声。 **2** (sl) vigour; energy. (俚)精力; 活力; 生命力。口 *vt* (-pp-) [VP6A, 15B, 22] open sth (*zip sth open*) or close sth (*zip sth up*) by means of a zip-fastener: 拉开或拉上(某物上的)拉链: *She zipped her bag open/up.* 她拉开(拉上)她袋子的拉链。 **zip·per, zip-fastener** *nn* device for locking together two toothed metal or plastic edges by means of a sliding tab, used for fastening articles of clothing, bags, etc. 拉链。

zip code /'zɪp kəʊd; 'zɪp,kod/ *n* (US) (美) =**post-code.**

zither /'zɪðə(r); 'zɪθɚ/ *n* musical instrument with many strings on a flat sounding-board, played with a plectrum or the fingers. 齐特琴; 扁琴(在扁平的共鸣盘上有许多琴弦的乐器, 以手指或拨子弹奏)。

zo·diac /'zəʊdɪæk; 'zodɪ,æk/ *n* **1** belt of the heavens extending about 8° on each side of the path followed by the sun and containing the path of the principal planets, divided into 12 equal parts known as the *signs of the ~,* named after 12 groups of stars. 黄道带(天空中太阳行经的路线, 向两侧各延伸 8 度所成的区域, 包括主要行星的运行轨道, 分为十二宫, 称为十二宫 signs of the zodiac, 依十二星群而得名)。 **2** diagram of the ~, used in astrology. 黄道十二宫图(用于占星学中)。

zom·bie /'zɒmbɪ; 'zɑmbɪ/ *n* (colloq) dull, slow, lifeless, mindless person. (口)呆钝、迟缓、无生气、不动脑筋的人; 傻瓜; 呆子。

zone /zəʊn; zon/ *n* **1** belt, band or stripe going round, and distinguished by colour, appearance, etc. 环带; 圈。 **2** one of the five parts into which the earth's surface is divided by imaginary lines parallel to the equator (the *'torrid, N & S 'temperate,* and the *'frigid ~s*). (地球上的)带; 地带(以想像中与赤道平行之线, 分地球为五个地带, 即热带、北温带、南温带、北寒带、南寒带)。 **3** area with particular features, purpose or use: (具有某特征、目的或用途的)地区; 区域: *the war ~;* 战区; *within the ~ of submarine activity,* ie where, during a war, submarines are active; 在潜水艇活动的区域内; *the 'danger ~;* 危险区; *a 'parking ~;* 停车区(场); *smokeless ~s,* (usu urban) areas in which only smokeless fuels may be used (in homes, factories, etc). 无烟区(通常指城市内禁燃发烟燃料的区域)。 **4** (US) particular area in which certain postal, telephone, etc rates are charged. (美)(便于计算邮费、电话费等的)区; 段; 邮区。口 *vt* [VP6A] encircle, mark, with, into, or as with a ~ or ~s; divide into ~s. 用或似用带围起或标示出; 把…分成若干区域。 **zonal** /'zəʊnl; 'zonl/ *adj* relating to, arranged in, ~s. 环带的; 地带的; 划分为区域的; 排列或形成环带的。 **zon·ing** /-ɪŋ; -ɪŋ/ *n* [U] (in planning urban areas) designation of areas for various purposes, eg shopping, residential, industrial. (都市计划中)分区; 区域划分(指定某某地区为商业区、住宅区、工业区等)。

zonked /zɒŋkt; zɑŋkt/ *pred adj* ~ **out,** (US sl) drugged; drunk. (美俚)服过麻醉药的; 喝醉了的。

zoo /zuː; zu/ *n* zoological gardens: 动物园: *take the children to the zoo.* 带孩子们去动物园。

zo·ol·o·gy /zəʊ'blədʒɪ; zo'ɑlədʒɪ/ *n* [U] science of the structure, forms and distribution of animals. 动物学。 **zo·ol·ogi·cal** /,zəʊə'lɒdʒɪkl; ,zoə'lɑdʒɪkl/ *adj* of ~. 动物学的。 **zoological gardens,** park (usu public) in which many kinds of animals are kept for exhibition.

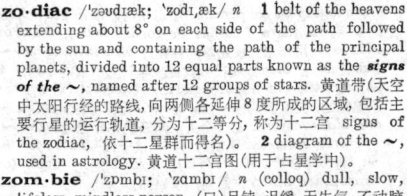

1
Aries (the Ram)
21st March–20th April

2
Taurus (the Bull)
21st April–20th May

3
Gemini (the Twins)
21st May–20th June

4
Cancer (the Crab)
21st June–20th July

5
Leo (the Lion)
21st July–19th/22nd Aug

6
Virgo (the Virgin)
20th/23rd Aug–22nd Sept

7
Libra (the Scales)
23rd Sept–22nd Oct

8
Scorpio (the Scorpion)
23rd Oct–21st Nov

9
Sagittarius (the Archer)
22nd Nov–20th Dec

10
Capricorn (the Goat)
21st Dec–20th Jan

11
Aquarius (the Water Carrier)
21st Jan–19th Feb

12
Pisces (the Fishes)
20th Feb–20th March

the signs of the zodiac

动物园。**zo·ol·ogist**/ zəʊ'ɒlədʒɪst; zoˈɑlədʒɪst/ *n* expert in ~. 动物学家。

zoom /zuːm; zum/ *n* **1** [U] (low, deep humming sound of the) sudden upward flight of an aircraft. 飞机的陡直上升；攒升；攒升时发出的低沉嗡嗡声。**2** ~ **lens,** (on a camera), one with continuously variable focal length. (照相机上) 有连续不同焦距的镜头；可变焦距镜头。⇨ the illus at **camera.** 参看 camera 之插图。□ *vi* [VP2A, C] **2** (of aircraft) move upwards at high speed: (指飞机) 陡直地上升；攒升：(fig, colloq) (喻，口) *Prices* ~*ed,* rose sharply. 物价直线上升了。**2** (of a camera with a ~ lens): (指有可变焦距镜头的照相机)：~ *in/out,* cause the object being photographed to appear nearer/further. 将画面放大 (缩小)；使物体形像变近 (远)。

zo·ophyte /'zəʊəfaɪt; 'zoə,faɪt/ *n* plant-like sea animal (eg a sea anemone, coral). 似植物的海生动物(如海葵、珊瑚虫)。

zoot suit /'zuːt suːt; 'zut ,sut/ *n* one with a knee-length jacket and tight-fitting trousers. 阻特装(一种上衣长达膝部而裤子窄狭的服装)。

zuc·chini /zʊ'kiːnɪ; zʊ'kinɪ/ *n* (*pl* ~*s* or unchanged 复数加 s 或不变) (esp US) (尤美) = **courgette.** ⇨ the illus at **vegetable.** 参看 vegetable 之插图。

Zulu /'zuːluː; 'zulu/ *n, adj* (member or language) of the people of *Kwazulu* / ˌkwaː'zuːluː ; ˌkwɑ'zulu/ (formerly 昔作 *Zululand*) in South Africa. (非洲南部之)祖鲁人(的); 祖鲁语(的)。

APPENDIX 1 IRREGULAR VERBS
附录一 不规则动词表

Note: Full phonetic transcriptions of the irregular past tense and past participle forms are given in the entries on the infinitive forms in the dictionary.

注意: 不规则动词过去式及过去分词的注音, 均列于本词典各该词条的不定式中。

Infinitive 不定式	Past Tense 过去式	Past Participle 过去分词
abide	abode, abided	abode, abided
arise	arose	arisen
awake	awoke	awaked, awoken
be	was	been
bear	bore	borne
beat	beat	beaten
become	became	become
befall	befell	befallen
beget	begot	begotten
begin	began	begun
behold	beheld	beheld
bend	bent	bent
bereave	bereaved, bereft	bereaved, bereft
beseech	besought	besought
beset	beset	beset
bet	bet, betted	bet, betted
betake	betook	betaken
bethink	bethought	bethought
bid	bade, bid	bidden, bid
bind	bound	bound
bite	bit	bitten, bit
bleed	bled	bled
blend	blended, blent	blended, blent
bless	blessed, blest	blessed, blest
blow	blew	blown
break	broke	broken
breed	bred	bred
bring	brought	brought
broadcast	broadcast, broadcasted	broadcast, broadcasted
build	built	built
burn	burnt, burned	burnt, burned
burst	burst	burst
buy	bought	bought
cast	cast	cast
catch	caught	caught
chide	chided, chid	chided, chidden
choose	chose	chosen
cleave	clove, cleft	cloven, cleft
cling	clung	clung
clothe	clothed, clad	clothed, clad
come	came	come
cost	cost	cost
creep	crept	crept
crow	crowed, crew	crowed
cut	cut	cut
dare	dared, durst	dared
deal	dealt	dealt
dig	dug	dug
dive	dived; (US) dove	dived
do	did	done
draw	drew	drawn
dream	dreamt, dreamed	dreamt, dreamed
drink	drank	drunk
drive	drove	driven
dwell	dwelt	dwelt
eat	ate	eaten
fall	fell	fallen
feed	fed	fed
feel	felt	felt

fight	fought	fought
find	found	found
flee	fled	fled
fling	flung	flung
fly	flew	flown
forbear	forbore	forborne
forbid	forbade, forbad	forbidden
forecast	forecast, forecasted	forecast, forecasted
foreknow	foreknew	foreknown
foresee	foresaw	foreseen
foretell	foretold	foretold
forget	forgot	forgotten
forgive	forgave	forgiven
forsake	forsook	forsaken
forswear	forswore	forsworn
freeze	froze	frozen
gainsay	gainsaid	gainsaid
get	got	got; (US) gotten
gild	gilded, gilt	gilded
gird	girded, girt	girded, girt
give	gave	given
go	went	gone
grave	graved	graven, graved
grind	ground	ground
grow	grew	grown
hamstring	hamstringed, hamstrung	hamstringed, hamstrung
hang	hung, hanged	hung, hanged
have	had	had
hear	heard	heard
heave	heaved, hove	heaved, hove
hew	hewed	hewed, hewn
hide	hid	hidden
hit	hit	hit
hold	held	held
hurt	hurt	hurt
inlay	inlaid	inlaid
keep	kept	kept
kneel	knelt	knelt
knit	knitted, knit	knitted, knit
know	knew	known
lade	laded	laden
lay	laid	laid
lead	led	led
lean	leant, leaned	leant, leaned
leap	leapt, leaped	leapt, leaped
learn	learnt, learned	learnt, learned
leave	left	left
lend	lent	lent
let	let	let
lie	lay	lain
light	lit, lighted	lit, lighted
lose	lost	lost
make	made	made
mean	meant	meant
meet	met	met
melt	melted	melted, molten
miscast	miscast	miscast
misdeal	misdealt	misdealt
misgive	misgave	misgiven
mislay	mislaid	mislaid
mislead	misled	misled
misspell	misspelt	misspelt
misspend	misspent	misspent
mistake	mistook	mistaken
misunderstand	misunderstood	misunderstood
mow	mowed	mown; (US) mowed
outbid	outbid	outbid
outdo	outdid	outdone
outgo	outwent	outgone
outgrow	outgrew	outgrown
outride	outrode	outridden
outrun	outran	outrun

outshine	outshone	outshone
overbear	overbore	overborne
overcast	overcast	overcast
overcome	overcame	overcome
overdo	overdid	overdone
overhang	overhung	overhung
overhear	overheard	overheard
overlay	overlaid	overlaid
overleap	overleapt, overleaped	overleapt, overleaped
overlie	overlay	overlain
override	overrode	overridden
overrun	overran	overrun
oversee	oversaw	overseen
overshoot	overshot	overshot
oversleep	overslept	overslept
overtake	overtook	overtaken
overthrow	overthrew	overthrown
partake	partook	partaken
pay	paid	paid
prove	proved	proved, proven
put	put	put
quit	quitted, quit	quitted, quit
read /riːd; rid/	read /red; red/	read /red; red/
rebind	rebound	rebound
rebuild	rebuilt	rebuilt
recast	recast	recast
redo	redid	redone
relay	relaid	relaid
remake	remade	remade
rend	rent	rent
repay	repaid	repaid
rerun	reran	rerun
reset	reset	reset
retell	retold	retold
rewrite	rewrote	rewritten
rid	rid, ridded	rid, ridded
ride	rode	ridden
ring	rang	rung
rise	rose	risen
rive	rived	riven, rived
run	ran	run
saw	sawed	sawn, sawed
say	said	said
see	saw	seen
seek	sought	sought
sell	sold	sold
send	sent	sent
set	set	set
sew	sewed	sewn, sewed
shake	shook	shaken
shave	shaved	shaved, shaven
shear	sheared	sheared, shorn
shed	shed	shed
shine	shone /ʃɒn/; (US) /ʃəʊn; ʃon/	shone /ʃɒn/; (US) /ʃəʊn; ʃon/
shoe	shod	shod
shoot	shot	shot
show	showed	shown, showed
shrink	shrank, shrunk	shrunk, shrunken
shrive	shrove, shrived	shriven, shrived
shut	shut	shut
sing	sang	sung
sink	sank	sunk, sunken
sit	sat	sat
slay	slew	slain
sleep	slept	slept
slide	slid	slid
sling	slung	slung
slink	slunk	slunk
slit	slit	slit
smell	smelt, smelled	smelt, smelled
smite	smote	smitten
sow	sowed	sown, sowed

speak	spoke	spoken
speed	sped, speeded	sped, speeded
spell	spelt, spelled	spelt, spelled
spend	spent	spent
spill	spilt, spilled	spilt, spilled
spin	spun, span	spun
spit	spat	spat
split	split	split
spoil	spoilt, spoiled	spoilt, spoiled
spread	spread	spread
spring	sprang	sprung
stand	stood	stood
stave	staved, stove	staved, stove
steal	stole	stolen
stick	stuck	stuck
sting	stung	stung
stink	stank, stunk	stunk
strew	strewed	strewn, strewed
stride	strode	stridden
strike	struck	struck, stricken
string	strung	strung
strive	strove	striven
swear	swore	sworn
sweep	swept	swept
swell	swelled	swollen, swelled
swim	swam	swum
swing	swung	swung
take	took	taken
teach	taught	taught
tear	tore	torn
tell	told	told
think	thought	thought
thrive	throve, thrived	thriven, thrived
throw	threw	thrown
thrust	thrust	thrust
tread	trod	trodden, trod
unbend	unbent	unbent
unbind	unbound	unbound
underbid	underbid	underbid
undergo	underwent	undergone
understand	understood	understood
undertake	undertook	undertaken
undo	undid	undone
upset	upset	upset
wake	woke, waked	woken, waked
waylay	waylaid	waylaid
wear	wore	worn
weave	wove	woven
weep	wept	wept
win	won	won
wind	wound	wound
withdraw	withdrew	withdrawn
withhold	withheld	withheld
withstand	withstood	withstood
work	worked, wrought	worked, wrought
wring	wrung	wrung
write	wrote	written

Note: This list includes abbreviations that occur in newspapers, timetables, etc. For abbreviations of parts of speech etc used in the text of the dictionary, ➪ the inside covers of this book.

The use of capital or lower case letters indicates the more common usage but some abbreviations can be written in either style. Full points are often used in abbreviations though they are usually omitted in modern style.

Those abbreviations and acronyms that ˌmay be spoken, usually in a colloquial context, are given with phonetic transcriptions or stress marks, e g ˌAG'M is pronounced /ˌeɪ dʒiː 'em; ˌedʒiˈ'em/.

注意：本表所收略语散见于报纸、时间表等。至于本词典正文中所用词类等之略语，请参看封面内页或 liv 页之略语表。大写或小写字母之使用表示比较常见的用法，不过有的略语可写作其中任一种形式。虽然在现代文体中略语通常不用句点，但有的略语常常用有句点。

凡是可以说出来的略语和首字母缩略词（通常见于口语体的上下文中），都加了注音或重音，如 ˌAG'M 读作 /ˌeɪ dʒiː 'em；ˌedʒiˈ'em/。

'A-bomb atomic bomb
'A-level advanced level (examination)
ˌ**A 'A** Alcoholics Anonymous; Automobile Association
ˌ**A A 'A** Amateur Athletics Association; American Automobile Association
ˌ**A 'B** (GB) Able Seaman; (US) Bachelor of Arts
ˌ**A B 'C** Australian Broadcasting Commission
ˌ**a 'c** alternating current
a/c account
acc(t) account
ack(n) acknowledge(d)
ad(vt) advertisement
ˌ**A 'D** *Anno Domini* in the year of the Lord
ˌ**A D 'C** Aide-de-camp
add(r) address
Afr Africa(n)
ˌ**A G 'M** Annual General Meeting
ˌ**A I 'D** (US) Agency for International Development
ˌ**a 'm** *ante meridiem* before noon
ˌ**A M 'A** (US) American Medical Association
amp /æmp/ ampere(s)
anon anonymous
ˌ**A 'P** Associated Press
ˌ**A P 'B** (US) All Points Bulletin (for missing or wanted person)
appro /'æprəʊ; 'æpro/ approval
approx approximately
Apr April
arr arrival; arrives
asap as soon as possible
ASEAN Association of South-East Asian Nations
assoc associate; association
asst assistant
Aug August
ˌ**A 'V** Audio-Visual; Authorised Version (of the Bible)
Av(e) Avenue
ˌ**AWO'L** absent without leave

b born; bowled
ˌ**b & 'b** bed and breakfast
ˌ**B 'A** (GB) Bachelor of Arts; British Airways
Barr Barrister
ˌ**B B 'C** British Broadcasting Corporation
ˌ**B 'C** Before Christ; British Council
ˌ**B 'D** Bachelor of Divinity
bk book
Bldg(s) building(s)
Blvd Boulevard
ˌ**B 'M** British Museum
ˌ**B M 'A** British Medical Association
B Mus /ˌbiː'mʌs; ˌbiˈmʌs/ Bachelor of Music
ˌ**b 'o** body odour; box office

ˌ**Br** Brother
Brig Brigadier
Brit Britain, British
Bro(s) brother(s)
ˌ**B 'S** (US) Bachelor of Science
B Sc /ˌbiːes'siː; ˌbiesˈsi/ (GB) Bachelor of Science
ˌ**B S 'T** British Summer Time
Bt; Bart Baronet
ˌ**B Th 'U** British Thermal Unit
ˌ**B V 'M** *Beata Virgo Maria* Blessed Virgin Mary

C Centigrade; (Roman) 100
c cent(s); century; *circa* about; cubic
ca *circa* about, approximately
ˌ**C 'A** Chartered Accountant
Cantab /'kæntæb; 'kæntæb/ *Cantabrigiensis* of Cambridge University
Capt Captain
CARE /keə(r); kɛr/ (US) Co-operative for American Relief Everywhere
Cath Catholic
ˌ**C B 'C** Canadian Broadcasting Corporation
ˌ**C B 'I** Confederation of British Industry
ˌ**C B 'S** (US) Columbia Broadcasting System
ˌ**c 'c** cubic centimetre(s)
cc *capita* chapters; centuries
ˌ**C 'D** *Corps Diplomatique* Diplomatic Service
Cdr Commander
Cdre Commodore
cert certificate; certified
c 'f *confer* compare
cg centigram
c 'h central heating
ˌ**C 'H** Companion of Honour
ch(ap) chapter
Ch B /ˌsiː eɪlʃ 'biː; ˌsietʃˈbi/ Bachelor of Surgery
ˌ**C 'I** Channel Islands
ˌ**C I 'A** (US) Central Intelligence Agency
ˌ**C I 'D** (GB) Criminal Investigation Department
c i 'f cost, insurance, freight
C-in-'C Commander-in-Chief
cl class; centilitre(s)
cm centimetre(s)
Co (comm) Company
ˌ**C 'O** Commanding Officer
c/o care of
ˌ**C O 'D** Cash on Delivery
ˌ**C of 'E** /ˌsiː əv 'iː; ˌsiəvˈi/ Church of England
ˌ**C O 'I** (GB) Central Office of Information
Col Colonel
Coll College
concl concluded; conclusion

Cons (GB) Conservative (political party)

cont contents; continued

Co-op /'kəʊ ʊp; koʹɑp/ Co-operative (Society)

Corp Corporation

Coy (mil) Company

cp compare

,C 'P Cape Province; Communist Party

Cpl Corporal

,c p 's cycles per second

Cres(c) Crescent

,C 'S Civil Servant; Civil Service

C S 'E (GB) Certificate of Secondary Education

,C S 'T (US) Central Standard Time

cu cubic

cwt hundredweight

D Roman 500

d *denarius* penny; died

D-day day on which a course of action is planned to start; ⇨ **D-day** in the dictionary

,D 'A (US) District Attorney

dbl double

,D 'C (US) District of Columbia

,d 'c direct current

,D 'D Doctor of Divinity

,D D 'T *Dichloro-diphenyl-trichloroethane* insecticide

Dec December

dec deceased

deg degree(s)

Dem Democrat

dep departs; departure; deputy

Dept Department

,D 'G *Dei Gratia* by the grace of God; Director General

diag diagram

diff difference; different

Dip Diploma

Dip Ed /,dɪp 'ed; ,dɪpʹɛd/ Diploma in Education

Dir Director

,D I 'Y do it yourself

,D 'J dinner jacket; disc jockey

D Litt /,diː 'lɪt; ,diʹlɪt/ Doctor of Letters/Literature

DM *Deutschmark* /'dɔɪtʃmɑːk; 'dɔɪtʃmɑrk/ German currency

,D N 'A *deoxyribonucleic acid* basic constituent of the gene

doz dozen

D Phil /,diː 'fɪl; ,diʹfɪl/ Doctor of Philosophy

Dr Debtor; Doctor; Drive (ie small road)

dr dram(s)

D Sc /,diː es 'siː; ,diesʹsi/ Doctor of Science

,D 'T; (the) d ts /,diː 'tiːz; ,diʹtiz/ *delirium tremens* 'trembling delirium' (extreme state of alcoholism)

dupl duplicate

,D 'V *Deo Volente* God being willing

E east

Ed edited by; editor; edition; education; educated

,E D 'P Electronic Data Processing

,E E 'C European Economic Community (the Common Market)

,E E 'G Electro-encephalo-gram/graph

EFTA /'eftə; 'eftə/ European Free Trade Association

,e 'g *exempli gratia* for example, for instance

enc(l) enclosed

ENE east-northeast

Eng Engineer (ing); England; English

,E 'P extended-playing (record)

,E 'R *Elizabeth Regina* Queen Elizabeth

ESE east-southeast

,E S 'P Extra-Sensory Perception

Esq Esquire

,E S 'T (US) Eastern Standard Time

,e t 'a estimated time of arrival

et al /,et 'æl; ,etʹæl/ *et alii* and other people; *et alia* and other things

etc; & c /,et 'setrə; etʹsetərə/ *et cetera* and the rest, and all the others

,e t 'd estimated time of departure

et seq /,et 'sek; ,etʹssk/ *et sequens* and the following

eve evening

excl excluding; exclusive

ext exterior; external

F Fahrenheit; Fellow

f foot; feet; female; feminine

,F 'A Football Association

,F A 'O Food and Agricultural Organisation

,F B 'A Fellow of the British Academy

,F B 'I (US) Federal Bureau of Investigation

,F 'D *Fidei Defensor* Defender of the Faith

Feb February

Fed Federal; Federated; Federation

fem female; feminine

fig figurative; figure

fl fluid; floor

fm fathom(s)

,F 'M Frequency Modulation

,F 'O (GB) Foreign Office

,f o 'b free on board

fol(l) following

for foreign

Fr Father; Franc; France; French

Fri Friday

,F R 'S Fellow of the Royal Society

ft foot; feet

fur furlong(s)

furn furnished

fwd forward

g acceleration due to gravity; gram(s)

gal(l) gallon(s)

GATT /'gæt; gæt/ General Agreement on Tariffs and Trade

,G 'B Great Britain

,G 'C George Cross

,G C 'E (GB) General Certificate of Education

Gdn(s) Garden(s)

Gen General

Ger Germany(y)

,G H 'Q General Headquarters

,G 'I (US) enlisted soldier

Gk Greek

,G L 'C Greater London Council

gm gram(s)

,G 'M General Manager

,G M 'T Greenwich Mean Time

,G N 'P Gross National Product

gov(t) government

Gov Governor

,G 'P General Practitioner (Medical Doctor)

,G P 'O General Post Office

gr grade; grain; gross; group

gt great

h height; hour

ha hectare(s)

,h & 'c hot and cold (water)

'H-bomb Hydrogen bomb

,H 'E high explosive; His/Her Excellency; His Eminence

,H 'F High Frequency

,H 'H His Holiness

,H 'M His/Her Majesty

,H M 'S His/Her Majesty's Ship

,H M S 'O His/Her Majesty's Stationery Office

Hon Honorary; Honourable
hosp hospital
,H 'P Hire Purchase; Horse Power
,H 'Q Headquarters
hr hour(s)
,H R 'H His/Her Royal Highness

I Island; Roman 1
ib; ibid *ibidem* in the same place
,I B 'A (GB) Independent Broadcasting Authority
i/c in charge
,I C B 'M Inter-Continental Ballistic Missile
i 'e *id est* which is to say, in other words
I H 'S *Iesous* (Greek for) Jesus (Christ)
,I L 'O International Labour Organisation
I M 'F International Monetary Fund
in inch(es)
Inc Incorporated
incl including; inclusive
Ind India(n); Independent
inf *infra* below
info /'ɪnfəʊ; 'ɪnfəʊ/ information
infra dig /ˌɪnfrə 'dɪg; ˌɪnfrə'dɪg/ *infra dignitatem* beneath one's social dignity
,I N R 'I *Iesus Nazarenus Rex Iudaeorum* Jesus of Nazareth, King of the Jews
Inst Institute
int interior; internal; international
intro /'ɪntrəʊ; 'ɪntrəʊ/ introduction
I O U I owe you
I 'Q *Intelligence Quotient* comparative measure of intelligence
,I R 'A Irish Republican Army
Ire Ireland
Is Islands
It(al) Italy, Italian
,I T 'V (GB) independent television

Jan January
,J 'C Jesus Christ
Jnr; Jr Junior
,J 'P Justice of the Peace
Jul July
Jun June; Junior

kg kilogram(s)
,K G 'B Intelligence Agency of the USSR
km kilometre(s)
,K 'O knock-out
kw kilowatt(s)

L lake; little; Roman 50; (GB) Liberal (political party)
l left; length; line
,L 'A Legislative Assembly; Los Angeles
Lab (GB) Labour (political party)
lang language
Lat Latin
lat latitude
lb pound(s) (weight)
,l b 'w leg before wicket (cricket term)
Ld Lord
,L E 'A Local Education Authority
,l 'h left hand
Lib (GB) Liberal (political party); Liberation
lit literal(ly); literature; literary
ll lines
LL B /ˌel el 'biː; ˌelel'biː/ Bachelor of Laws
,L M 'T (US) Local Mean Time
loc cit /ˌlɒk 'sɪt; ˌlɑk'ɪt/ *loco citato* in the place mentioned
long longitude
,L 'P long-playing (record)

,L S 'D *lysergic acid diethylamide* drug inducing hallucinations
£ s d /ˌel es 'diː; ˌeles'di/ *librae, solidi, denarii* pounds, shillings, pence (former GB currency system)
,L S 'T (US) Local Standard Time
Lt Lieutenant
Ltd Limited
lux luxury

M Member
m male; married; metre(s); mile(s); million
,M 'A Master of Arts
Maj Major
Mans Mansions
Mar March
masc masculine
math /mæθ; mæθ/ (US) mathematics
maths /mæθs; mæθs/ (GB) mathematics
max maximum
,M 'B Bachelor of Medicine
,M 'C (US) Marine Corps; Master of Ceremonies; (US) Member of Congress; (GB) Military Cross
,M C 'C (GB) Marylebone Cricket Club (the governing body of English cricket)
Mc Megacycle(s)
,M 'D Doctor of Medicine
Med(it) Mediterranean
mg milligram(s)
Mgr Monsignor
,M I '5 (GB) National Security Division of Military Intelligence
min minimum
misc miscellaneous
mkt market
ml mile(s); millilitre(s)
mm millimetre(s)
M 'O Mail Order; Medical Officer; Money Order
mod moderate; modern
mod cons /ˌmɒd 'kɒnz; ˌmɑd'kɑnz/modern conveniences
Mon Monday
,M 'P Member of Parliament (House of Commons); Military Police
,m p 'g miles per gallon
,m p 'h miles per hour
Mr, Mrs, Ms ⇨ dictionary entries
MS(S) manuscript(s)
M Sc /ˌem es 'siː; ˌemes'si/ Master of Science
Mt Mount

N north
NAAFI /'næfɪ; 'næfi/ (GB) Navy, Army and Air Force Institute
nat national; native; natural
NATO /'neɪtəʊ; 'neto/ North Atlantic Treaty Organisation
,N 'B *nota bene* take special note of
,N C 'O Non-Commissioned Officer
NE northeast
,N H 'S (GB) National Health Service
NNE north-northeast
NNW north-northwest
no(s) number(s)
non-U /ˌnɒn 'ju; ˌnɑn'ju/ not upper class; vulgar
Nov November
nr near
,N S P C 'C (GB) National Society for the Prevention of Cruelty to Children
,N 'T New Testament
NW northwest
,N 'Y('C) New York (City)
,N 'Z New Zealand

,**O A 'P**   (GB) old-age pensioner
,**O A 'S**   (US) Organisation of American States
,**O A 'U**   Organisation of African Unity
ob   *obiit* died
Oct October
,**O E C 'D**   Organisation for Economic Co-operation and Development
,**O E 'D**   Oxford English Dictionary
,**O H M 'S**   (GB) On Her/His Majesty's Service
'**O-level**   (GB) Ordinary level (examination)
,**o n 'o**   or nearest offer
op   opus; operation
op cit   /ˌɒp 'sɪt; ˌap'sɪt/ *opere citato* in the work mentioned
O P E C   /'əʊpek; 'opɛk/ Organisation of Petroleum Exporting Countries
opp   opposite
orch   orchestra(l); orchestrated
,**O 'S**   Ordinary Seaman
,**O 'T**   Old Testament
Oxon   /'ɒksn; 'aksn̩/ *Oxoniensis* of Oxford University; Oxfordshire
oz   ounce(s)

P   Parking
p   page; penny, pence; per
,**p 'a**   *per annum* per year
,**P 'A**   Personal Assistant; Press Association; Public Address (System)
para(s)   paragraph(s)
'**P A Y 'E**   pay as you earn
'**P 'C**   (GB) Police Constable; (GB) Privy Councillor; (US) Peace Corps
pd   paid
,**P D S 'A**   People's Dispensary for Sick Animals
,**P 'E**   physical education
PEN   /pen; pɛn/ International Association of Writers
,**P 'G**   Paying Guest
Ph D   /ˌpiːeɪtʃ 'diː; ˌpietʃ'di/ Doctor of Philosophy
Pk   Park
pkt   packet
Pl   Place
,**P 'M**   Prime Minister
,**p 'm**   *post meridiem* after noon; per month
,**P 'O**   Personnel Officer; Petty Officer; Post Office; Postal Order
,**P 'O Box**   Post Office Box
,**P O 'E**   Port of Entry
pop   popular; population
poss   possible; possibly
,**P O 'W**   Prisoner of War
pp   pages
,**p 'p**   *per procurationem* on behalf of (precedes name of person signed for)
,**P P 'S**   *post postscriptum* additional postscript
pr   pair; price
,**P 'R**   Public Relations
Pres   President
,**P R 'O**   Public Records Office; Public Relations Officer
pro   /prəʊ; pro/ professional
pro tem   /ˌprəʊ 'tem; ˌpro'tɛm/ *pro tempore* for the time being; temporarily
Prof   (*informally* /prɒf; praf/) Professor
pron   pronounced; pronunciation
Prot   Protestant
Prov   Province
Ps   Psalm
P 'S   Postscript
'**P S 'T**   (US) Pacific Standard Time
,**pt**   part; payment; pint; point
,**P 'T**   Physical Training
,**P T 'A**   Parent-Teacher Association
Pte   (GB) Private (soldier)

,**P T 'O**   Please turn over
Pty   Proprietary
Pvt   (US) Private (soldier)
,**p 'w**   per week
,**P 'X**   post exchange (US equivalent of NAAFI)

,**Q 'C**   Queen's Counsel
,**Q E 'D**   *quod erat demonstrandum* which had to be proved
qt   quart
,**q 't**   ⇨ **quiet(5)**
Qu   Queen; Question
,**q 'v**   *quod vide* which may be referred to

R   River; Royal
r   radius; right
,**R 'A**   Rear-Admiral; Royal Academy; Royal Academician
RADA   /'rɑːdə; 'radə/ Royal Academy of Dramatic Art
,**R A 'F**   (*also* /rɑːf; ræf/) Royal Air Force
,**R A 'M**   Royal Academy of Music
,**R 'C**   Red Cross; Roman Catholic
,**R C 'M**   Royal College of Music
Rd   Road
rec(d)   received
ref   referee /ref; rɛf/; reference; refer(red)
Rep   Repertory /rep; rɛp/; Representative /rep; rɛp/; Republic (an)
res   residence; resigned; reserved
resp   respectively
ret(d)   retired
rev   revolution
Rev(d)   Reverend
,**r 'h**   right hand
,**R I 'P**   *requiescat/requiescant in pace* may he/they rest in peace
rly   railway
rm   room
,**R 'M**   Royal Marines
,**R 'N**   Royal Navy
,**r p 'm**   revolutions per minute
,**R S 'M**   Regimental Sergeant Major; Royal School of Music
,**R S V 'P**   *répondes s'il vous plaît* please reply
,**R S ,P C 'A**   Royal Society for the Prevention of Cruelty to Animals
rt   right
Rt Hon   Right Honourable
Rt Rev   Right Reverend
,**R (S) 'V**   Revised (Standard) Version (of the Bible)
,**R 'U**   Rugby Union

S   south
s   second(s); shilling(s)
,**S 'A**   South Africa
,**s a 'e**   stamped addressed envelope
SALT   /sɔːlt; sɔlt/ Strategic Arms Limitation Talks
Sat   Saturday
,**S A Y 'E**   save as you earn
sc   *scilicet* namely
s/c   self-contained
Sch   School
sci   science
SE   southeast
sec   second(ary); secretary
Sen   Senate; Senator; Senior
Sept   September
,**S 'F**   Science Fiction
sgd   signed
Sgt   Sergeant
SHAPE   /ʃeɪp; ʃep/ Supreme Headquarters of Allied Powers in Europe
Sn(r)   Senior

Soc Society

Sol Solicitor

sp special; spelling

Sp Spain, Spanish

sp gr specific gravity

Sq Square

Sr Senior; Sister

,S R 'N State Registered Nurse

,S 'S Steamship

SSE south-southeast

SSW south-southwest

St Saint; Street

Sta Station

,S T 'D subscriber trunk dialling (telephone)

Str Strait; Street

sub(s) subscription; substitute

Sun Sunday

Supt Superintendent

SW southwest

T temperature

t time; ton(s)

,T 'B Tuberculosis

Tech /tek; tɛk/ Technical (College)

tel telephone

temp /temp; tɛmp/ temperature; temporary (secretary)

Ter(r) Terrace; Territory

Thurs Thursday

,T K 'O technical knock-out

,T N 'T *Tri-nitro-toluene* explosive

trans translated

treas treasurer

,T 'U Trade Union

,T U 'C (GB) Trades Union Congress

Tues Tuesday

,T 'V television

U Union; Upper; upper class, fashionable, polite, ⇨ **non-U** above

U D 'I unilateral declaration of independence

,U F 'O (*also* /ˈjuːfəu; ˈjufo/) unidentified flying object

U H 'F ultra high frequency

,U 'K United Kingdom

,U 'N United Nations

UNCTAD /ˈʌŋktæd; ˈʌŋktæd/ United Nations Conference on Trade and Development

UNESCO /juːˈneskəu; juˈnɛsko/ United Nations Educational, Scientific and Cultural Organisation

UNICEF /ˈjuːnɪsef; ˈjunɪsɛf/ United Nations Children's Fund

Univ University

UNO /ˈjuːnəu; ˈjuno/ United Nations Organisation

UNRWA /ˈʌnwə; ˈʌnwə/ United Nations Relief and Works Agency

,U P 'I United Press International

,U 'S United States

,U S 'A United States of America; United States Army

,U S A 'F United States Air Force

,U S 'N United States Navy

,U S 'S United States Ship

,U S S 'R Union of Soviet Socialist Republics

V Roman 5; Victory; Volt

v very; verse; versus; *vide* see, refer to

V & A /ˌviː ən ˈeɪ; ˌvien'e/ Victoria and Albert (Museum in London)

vac /væk; væk/ vacation

,V A 'T (*also* /væt; væt/) Value Added Tax, ⇨ **value(3)**

,V 'C Vice Chairman; Vice Chancellor; Vice Consul; Victoria Cross; Vietcong

V 'D Venereal Disease

,V 'E Day Victory in Europe (end of Second World War in Europe: 8. 5. 1945)

Ven Venerable

,V H 'F very high frequency

,V I 'P very important person

viz /vɪz; vɪz/ *videlicet* namely

vol volume

,V 'P(res) Vice-President

vs versus

V 'S (US) Veterinary Surgeon

,V S 'O (GB) Voluntary Service Overseas

W west

w watt(s); week; width; with

WASP /wɒsp; wɑsp/ (US) White Anglo-Saxon Protestant

,w 'c water closet, ⇨ **water¹(7)**

,W C 'C World Council of Churches

,we 'f with effect from

,W H 'O (*also* /huː; hu/) World Health Organisation

,W 'I West Indian; West Indies; Women's Institute

wk week; work

WNW west-northwest

'W 'O Warrant Officer

,w p 'b waste paper basket

,w p 'm words per minute

,W R A 'C Women's Royal Army Corps

,W R A 'F Women's Royal Air Force

,W R N 'S (*also* /renz; rɛnz/) Women's Royal Naval Service

WSW west-southwest

wt weight

X Roman 10; a kiss; an unknown number, thing, name, etc

Xmas Christmas

Y Yen (Japanese currency)

,Y H 'A Youth Hostels Association

,Y M C 'A Young Men's Christian Association

yr year; your

,Y W C 'A Young Women's Christian Association

Note: Many affixes have more than one pronunciation form or stress pattern. This often depends on the form of the word to which it is attached. ⇨ the entries in the dictionary for full phonetic transcriptions of the words given as examples in this appendix.

注意: 很多词缀具有不止一种发音形式或重音型态。这种情形常视视所接的词的形式而定。有关本附录例词的完整音标, 参看本词典各该词目。

a-[1] /eɪ-, ə-, æ-; e-, ɪ-, æ-/ *pref* not, without: 不; 非; 无: *aseptic; atheist.*

a-[2] /ə-; ə-/ *pref* **1** (~ + *n* = *adv*) in: (~ + 名词 = 副词) 在 … 里面: *abed; on, at:* 在 … 上; 在 …: *afield; ashore.* **2** (~ + *v* = *adv*) in the state of, in the process of: (~ + 动词 = 副词) 在 … 状态中; 在 … 过程中: *asleep; ablaze.* **3** (old use) (~ + *gerund* = *adv*) in the act of: (旧用法) (~ + 动名词 = 副词) 正在: *a-running; a-singing.*

ab- /æb-, əb-; æb-, əb-/ *pref* from, away from: 脱离: *absent; abduct.*

-able (also 亦作 **-ible**) /-əbl; -əbl/ *suff* **1** (*n* + ~ = *adj*) showing qualities of: (名词 + ~ = 形容词) 显示 … 性质或特点的: *fashionable; responsible.* **2** (*v* + ~ = *adj*) that can be, fit to be: (动词 + ~ = 形容词) 可被 … 的; 适于 … 的: *eatable; reducible.* **-ably, -ibly** /-əblɪ; -əblɪ/ *adv*

ad- /-əd-, æd-; əd-, æd-/ *pref* to, towards: 向; 往; 朝: *advance; adjoin.*

-ade /-eɪd, -ɑːd; -eɪd, -ɑd/ *suff* (used to form a *n*): (用以构成名词): *blockade; lemonade; façade.*

aer(o)- /eər- etc/; ɛr (ə- etc)/ *pref* of aircraft: 与飞机或飞行有关的: *aerodynamics; aeronaut.*

-age /-ɪdʒ, -ɑːʒ; -ɪdʒ, -ɑʒ/ *suff* (used to form a *n*): (用以构成名词): *breakage; postage; sabotage.*

-al /-l, -əl; -l, -əl/ *suff* **1** (*n* + ~ = *adj*): (名词 + ~ = 形容词): *magical; verbal.* **-ally** /-lɪ, -əlɪ; -lɪ, -əlɪ/ *adv* **2** (*v* + ~ = *n*): (动词 + ~ = 名词): *recital; survival; displayal.*

ambi- /ˈæmbɪ- etc; ˈæmbɪ- etc/ *pref* both, double, two: 双; 双重; 两: *ambiguous; ambidextrous.*

an- /-ən, -n; -ən, -n/ *suff* (*proper n* + ~ = *n* or *adj*, ⇨ **App 6**): (专有名词 + ~ = 名词或形容词, 参看附录六): *Lutheran; Mexican.* ⇨ **-ian** below. 参看下列的 -ian。

-ana ⇨ **-iana**

-ance (also 亦作 **-ence**) /-əns, -ns; -əns, -ns/ *suff* (*v* + ~ = *n*): (动词 + ~ = 名词): *assistance; confidence.*

-ant (also 亦作 **-ent**) /-ənt, -nt; -ənt, -nt/ *suff* **1** (*v* + ~ = *adj*): (动词 + ~ = 形容词): *significant; different.* **2** (*v* + ~ = *n*): (动词 + ~ = 名词): *assistant; deterrent.*

ante- /ˈæntɪ-; ˈæntɪ-/ *pref* in front of: 在前面的: *anteroom;* before, previous to: 在 … 之前的; 先于 … 的: *antenatal.*

anthrop(o)- /ˈænθrəp (ə- etc); ˈænθrəp (ə- etc)/ *pref* of man, of mankind: 人的; 人类的: *anthropoid; anthropology.*

anti- /ˈæntɪ- US: ˈæntaɪ-; ˈæntaɪ-/ *pref* **1** opposed to, against: 反对; 反抗; 对抗: *antisocial; antiseptic.* **2** instead of: 替代; 取代: *anti-hero.*

arch- /ɑːk-, ɑːtʃ-; ɑrk-, ɑrtʃ-/ *pref* first, chief, head: 第一的; 首要的; 为首的: *archetype; archbishop.*

-arian /-eərɪən; -ɛrɪən/ *suff* practiser of: 实行或实践 … 的人: *disciplinarian; vegetarian.*

-ary /-ərɪ, -rɪ US: -erɪ; -ɛrɪ, -ərɪ/ *suff* **1** (used to form an *adj*): (用以构成形容词): *planetary; reactionary.* **2** (*pl* **-aries**) (used to form a *n*): (用以构成名词): *dictionary; functionary.*

astr(o)- /ˈæstr(ə- etc); ˈæstr(ə- etc)/ *pref* of the stars, of outer space: 星球的; 天体的; 太空的: *astronomy; astronaut.*

-ate *suff* **1** /-ət, -ɪt; -ət, -ɪt/ (used to form an *adj*): (用以构成形容词): *affectionate; passionate.*

-ately /-ətlɪ, -ɪtlɪ; -ətlɪ, -ɪtlɪ/ *adv* **2** /-ət, -ɪt; -ət, -ɪt/ (used to form a *n*): (用以构成名词): *directorate; electorate.* **3** /-eɪt; -et/ (used to form a *v*): (用以构成动词): *gyrate; stimulate.* **4** /-eɪt; -et/ (chem) salt formed by the action of an acid on a base: (化学) 酸与盐基化合而成的盐: *phosphate; nitrate*

-ation ⇨ **-tion**

-ative /-ətɪv; -ətɪv/ *suff* (used to form an *adj*, usu from an '-ate' *v*): (用以构成形容词, 通常以 ate 结尾的动词加上本词缀而成): *illustrative; quantitative.* **-atively** /-ətɪvlɪ; -ətɪvlɪ/ *adv*

-ator /-eɪtə(r); -etɚ/ *suff* object or person carrying out the action of an '-ate' *v*: 作用物; 执行者: *percolator; stimulator.*

audio- /ˈɔːdɪəʊ-; ˈɔdɪo-/ *pref* of hearing, of sound: 听觉的; 声音的: *audio-visual; audio-frequency.*

aut(o)- /ˈɔːt(ə- etc); ˈɔt(ə- etc)/ *pref* **1** of oneself: 自己的: *autobiography; autograph.* **2** without help, independent of others: 自动的; 自主的: *automatic; autocrat.*

be- /bɪ-; bɪ-/ *pref* **1** (~ + *v* = *v*) all over, all around, in all directions: (~ + 动词 = 动词) 遍及; 四周; 到处: *bedeck; bespatter.* **2** (~ + *n* or *adj* = *v*) make, become: (~ + 名词或形容词 = 动词) 使成为; 变成 *befriend; belittle.* **3** (~ + *vi* = *vt*): (~ + 不及物动词 = 及物动词): *bemoan; bewail.*

bi- /baɪ-; baɪ-/ *pref* **1** occurring twice in one period: 每 … 二次的(地): *bi-monthly; bi-annual.* **2** occurring once in a period of two: 两 … 一次的(地): *bicentenary; biennial.* **3** having two: 双 … 的; 两 … 的: *bilingual; biped.*

bibli(o)- /ˈbɪblɪ(ə- etc); ˈbɪblɪ(ə- etc)/ *pref* of books: 书籍的: *bibliography; bibliophile.*

bio- /baɪə(ə- etc); baɪ(ə- etc)/ *pref* of life, of living organisms: 生平的; 生活的; 生物的: *biography, biology, biotic.*

by- (also 亦作 **bye-**) /baɪ-; baɪ-/ *pref* of secondary importance, incidental: 次要的; 附带的: *by-election; bye-law; by-product.*

cent(i)- /sent(ɪ- etc); sɛnt(ɪ- etc)/ *pref* a hundred, a hundredth part: 一百的; 百分之一的: *Centigrade; centimetre.*

chron(o)- /ˈkrɒn(ə- etc); ˈkrɑn(ə- etc)/ *pref* of time: 时间的: *chronology; chronometer.*

-cide /-saɪd; -saɪd/ *suff* (used to form a *n*) killing, killer: (用以构成名词)杀害; 消灭; 杀害者; 消灭 … 之物: *suicide; insecticide.*

co- /kəʊ- etc; ko- etc/ *pref* together, jointly, equally: 一起; 共同; 同等: *cohabit; co-operate; co-education.*

con- (also 亦作 **col-, com-, cor-**) /kɒn-, kən-, etc; kɑn-, kən-, etc/ *pref* with, together: 连同; 一起: *conduct; collaborate; combine; correlate.*

contra- /ˈkɒntrə-; ˈkɑntrə-/ *pref* against, opposite to: 反

对;相反;对立: *contraception; contradict.*

-cracy /-krəsɪ; -krəsɪ/ *suff* (*pl* **-cracies**) (used to form a *n*) government or rule by, class characterised by: (用以构成名词)…政体;…政治;…阶级: *democracy; aristocracy.*

-crat /-kræt; -kræt/ *suff* (used to form a *n*) member or supporter of a '-cracy': (用以构成名词)某种政体或政治的支持者;某一阶级的成员: *democrat, aristocrat.*

-cratic /-krætɪk; -krætɪk/ *adj* democratic, aristocratic.

-cy (also 亦作 **-acy**) /-(ə)sɪ; -(ə)sɪ/ *suff* (*pl* **(a)cies**) (used to form a *n*) condition, quality: (用以构成名词)状态;性质: *accuracy; infancy; supremacy.*

-d ⇨ **-ed**

de- /diː-, dɪ-; diː-, dɪ-/ *pref* (used with a *v*) the negative, reverse, opposite of: (与动词连用)…的否定、相对、相反: *depopulate; defrost; defuse.*

demi- /demɪ; demɪ/ *pref* half, partly: 半;部分: *demimonde; demigod.*

di- /daɪ-, dɪ-; daɪ-, dɪ-/ *pref* twice, double: 两倍的;双重的;二的: *dilemma; dioxide.*

dia- /daɪə-; daɪə-/ *pref* through, across: 穿过;横过;通过: *diameter; diagonal; diaphragm.*

dis- /dɪs-; dɪs-/ *pref* (used with a *v*) the negative, reverse, opposite of: (与动词连用)…的否定、相对、相反: *disbelieve; disorder; disagree.*

-dom /-dəm; -dəm/ *suff* (used to form a *n*) (用以构成名词) **1** a condition, state: 状况;状态: *boredom; freedom.* **2** domain: 领域;范围: *kingdom; officialdom.*

-ed (also 亦作 **-d**) /*After* p, k, f, ʃ, f, θ, s *pronounced* -t; *after* t, d *pronounced* -ɪd; *otherwise pronounced* -d. *Exception* 'used', *v* **use²** 在 p, k, f, ʃ, f, θ, s 之后读做 -t; 在 t, d 之后读做 -ɪd; 他处读做 -d。used 的读音例外,参看 use²/ *suff* **1** (used to form *pt* and *pp* of a *v*): (用以构成动词的过去式及过去分词): *laughed; acted; washed.* **2** (*n* + ~ = *adj*) having the characteristics of: (名词 + ~ = 形容词)有…特征的: *diseased; talented; cracked.*

-ee /-iː; -i/ *suff* (*v* + ~ = *n*) (动词 + ~ = 名词) **1** person affected by the action of the *v*: 受…者: *employee; payee.* **2** person acting: 做出…行为的人: *absentee; refugee.* **3** (*n* + ~ = *n*) diminutive (名词 + ~ = 名词) 小型的: *bootee; coatee.*

-eer /-ɪə(r); -ɪr/ *suff* (*n* + ~ = *n*) person concerned with the *n*: (名词 + ~ = 名词)与所述名词有关联的人: *auctioneer; mountaineer.*

electr(o)- /ɪlektr(ə- etc); ɪlektr(ə- etc)/ *pref* concerned with, caused by, electricity: 与电有关的; 由电所引起的: *electrocute; electromagnet.*

en- /ɪn-, en-; ɪn-, en-/ (also 亦作 **em-** /ɪm-, em-; ɪm-, em-/ *pref* **1** (~ + *n* or *adj* = *v*) put in, on: (~ + 名词或动词 = 动词) 置于…中或上: *encase; endanger; emplane.* **2** (~ + *n* or *adj* = *v*) make into, cause to be: (~ + 名词或形容词 = 动词)使变成; 使成为: *enlarge; enrich; empower.*

-en /-ən, -n; -ən, -n/ *suff* **1** (used to form the *pp* of some *vv*): (用以构成某些动词的过去分词): *broken; eaten; hidden.* **2** (*n* + ~ = *adj*) made of: (名词 + ~ = 形容词)用…做成的: *golden; wooden.* **3** (*adj* + ~ = *v*) make, cause to be: (形容词 + ~ = 动词)使变成: *blacken; sadden.*

-ence ⇨ **-ance**

-ent ⇨ **-ant**

equi- /iːkwɪ- etc; ɪkwɪ- etc/ *pref* equal, the same: 相等; 相同: *equidistant; equivalent.*

-er /-ə(r); -ər/ *suff* **1** (*v* + ~ = *n*) person who carries out the action of the *v*: (动词 + ~ = 名词)执行者;实行者: *runner; sleeper.* **2** (*n* + ~ = *n*) practiser of: (名词 + ~ = 名词)从事…的人: *astronomer; philosopher.* **3** (also 亦作 **-r**) (used to form the *comp* of an *adj*): (用以构成形容词的比较级): *stronger; rarer; thinner.* ⇨ also **-ier.**

-ery /-ərɪ, -rɪ; -ərɪ, -ri/ (also 亦作 **-ry** /-rɪ; -rɪ/ *suff* (*pl* **-eries**) (*n* or *v* + ~ = *n*) (名词或动词 + ~ = 名

词) **1** place where an action is carried out: 做某事的地方或场所: *bakery; fishery.* **2** art of, practice of: …术;…法: *cookery; pottery.* **3** state, quality, character: 状态;性质;性格: *rivalry; snobbery.*

-es (also 亦作 **-s**) /-ɪz; -ɪz/ *suff* **1** (used to form *pl* of a *n* ending in /s, z, ʃ, ʒ/): (用以构成以 /s, z, ʃ, ʒ/ 各音结尾的复数): *pieces; judges.* **2** (used to form 3 *rd pers sing pres t* of a *v* ending in /s, z, ʃ, ʒ/): (用以构成以 /s, z, ʃ, ʒ/ 各音结尾的动词之第三人称单数现在式): *washes; urges.*

-ese /-iːz; -iz/ *suff* **1** (*proper n* + ~ = *adj*) of a place or a country: (专有名词 + ~ = 形容词)…地方的;…国家的: *Burmese;* (the *adj* may also be used as a *n* App 6) person or language: (上述的形容词也可作名词用,参看附录六)…地方或国家的人;…地方或国家的语言: *Japanese.* **2** (used to form a *n*) in the (literary) style of: (用以构成名词)…的风格,文体或用语: *journalese.*

-esque /-esk; -esk/ *suff* (*n* + ~ = *adj*) in the manner, style of: (名词 + ~ = 形容词)…样子的; …风格的: *statuesque; picturesque.*

-ess /-ɪs, -es; -ɪs, -es/ *suff* (*n* or *v* + ~ = *n*) female: (名词或动词 + ~ = 名词)女…;雌…;母…: *lioness; actress.*

-est (also 亦作 **-st**) /-ɪst; -ɪst/ *suff* (used to form the *superl* of an *adj* or *adv*): (用以构成形容词或副词的最高级): *fastest; barest; wettest.*

-ette /-et; -et/ *suff* (*n* + ~ = *n*) (名词 + ~ = 名词) **1** diminutive: 小型的: *cigarette; kitchenette.* **2** female: 女性: *usherette; suffragette.* **3** imitation: 仿造物: *flannelette; leatherette.*

ex- *pref* **1** /ɪks-, eks-; ɪgz-, egz/; /ɪks-, eks-, ɪgz-, egz-/ out, out of, from: 向外;脱离;离开: *exclaim; extract.* **2** /eks-; eks-/ former, at one time: 从前的;前任的: *ex-wife; ex-president.*

extra- /ekstrə-; ekstrə-/ *pref* **1** outside, beyond: 在…之外; 超出…范围: *extramarital; extrasensory.* **2** very: 非常;极: *extra-thin.*

-fic /-fɪk; -fɪk/ *suff* (used with a '-fy' *v* to form an *adj*): (用以构成以 fy 结尾的动词之形容词): *horrific; specific.*

-fied /-faɪd; -faɪd/ ⇨ **-fy**

-fold /-fəʊld; -fold/ *suff* (*cardinal numeral* + ~ = *adj*) (基数词 + ~ = 形容词) **1** multiplied by: …倍的: *tenfold; hundredfold.* **2** of (so many) parts: …重的: *twofold.*

fore- /fɔː(r)-; for-/ *pref* before, in front of: 预先; 在前面的: *foretell; foreground.*

-form /-fɔːm; -form/ *suff* (used to form an *adj*) having the shape or character of: (用以构成形容词)具有…形状或特征的: *uniform; cuneiform.*

-ful *suff* **1** /-fl; -fol/ (*n* or *v* + ~ = *adj*) full of, having the quality of: (名词或动词 + ~ = 形容词)充满…的; 具有…性质的: *eventful; peaceful.* **2** /-ful; -fol/ (*n* + ~ = *n*) amount that fills: (名词 + ~ = 名词)充满…的量: *handful; mouthful.*

-gamy /-gəmɪ; -gəmɪ/ *suff* (used to form a *n*) of marriage: (用以构成名词)…的婚姻(制度): *monogamy; polygamy.* **-gamous** /-gəməs; -gəməs/ *adj.*

ge(o)- /dʒiː(ə- etc); dʒiː(ə- etc)/ *pref* (used to form a *n*) of the earth: (用以构成名词)与地球或土地有关的: *geography; geology.*

-gon /-gən; -gən/ *suff* angle, corner: 角;隅: *polygon; pentagon.*

-gram /-græm; -græm/ *suff* (used to form a *n*) sth written down or drawn: (用以构成名词)文字; 图案; 图表: *telegram; monogram; diagram.*

-graph /-grɑːf US: -græf; -græf/ *suff* (used to form a *n*) sth written down, of writing: (用以构成名词)文字; 书写: *autograph; telegraph.* **-graphy** /-grəfɪ; -grəfɪ/ *n:* *calligraphy; orthography.*

hem(o)- (also 亦作 **haem(o)-**) /-hiːmə- etc; hime-, həme-/ *pref* of the blood: 血的: *hemoglobin; hemorrhage.*

heter(o)- /hetər(ə- etc); hstər(ə- etc)/ *pref* the other,

the opposite, different: 其他；相反；不同: *heterogeneous; heterosexual.*

hom(o)- /-hɒm (ə- *etc*) /, həʊm-; hɑm (ə- *etc*) , hom-/ *pref* the same: 相同；同…: *homogeneous; homosexual.*

-hood /-hʊd; -hʊd/ *suff* (*n* + ~ = *n*) status, rank, condition of life: (名词 + ~ = 名词)身分；地位；生活状况: *boyhood; brotherhood.*

hydr(o)- /-haɪdr(ə- *etc*) ; haɪdr(ə- *etc*) / *pref* of water: 水的: *hydrant; hydroelectric.*

hyper- /-haɪpə(r)-; haɪpə-/ *pref* to a large or extreme degree: 非常；过于；极度: *hypercritical; hypersensitive.*

-ial /-ɪəl, -l; -ɪəl, -əl/ *suff* (*n* + ~ = *adj*) characteristic of: (名词 + ~ = 形容词)有…特点的: *dictatorial; palatial*. **-ially** /-ɪəlɪ, -lɪ; -ɪəlɪ, -əlɪ/ *adv*

-ian /-ɪən, -n; -ɪən, -ən/ *suff* **1** (*proper n* + ~ = *n or adj*, ⇨ **App 6**): (专有名词 + ~ = 名词或形容词，参看附录六): *Brazilian; Shakespearian*. **2** (used with an '-ics' *n* to form a *noun n* ending in **-cian** /-ʃn; -ʃən/) specialist in: (用在以 ics 结尾的名词上，以构成由 cian /-ʃn; -ʃən/ 结尾的名词)…专家: *optician; pediatrician.*

-(i)ana /-ɑːnə; -(i)ænə/ *suff* (used with words ending in '-ian' or '-an' to form a *collective n*) collection of facts, objects, etc relating to: (用在以 ian 或 an 结尾的词上，以构成集合名词)与…有关的资料、物件等之总称，…文物: *Victoriana; Africana.*

-ible ⇨ **-able**

-ic /-ɪk; -ɪk/ *suff* (*n* + ~ = *adj*): (名词 + ~ = 形容词): *poetic; romantic*. **-ical** /-ɪkl; -ɪkl/ *adj* **-ically** /-ɪklɪ; -ɪklɪ/ *adv*

-ics /-ɪks; -ɪks/ *suff* (used to form a *n*) science or specific activity: (用以构成名词)学科或某种活动: *physics; politics; athletics.*

-ide /-aɪd; -aɪd/ *suff* (used to form a *n*) (chem) chemical compound: (用以构成名词)(化学)化合物: *chloride; sulphide.*

-ie ⇨ **-y**

-ier ⇨ **-y**

-ies ⇨ **-y**

-(i)fy /-(ɪ)faɪ; -(ə)faɪ/ *suff* (*pt* and *pp* **-(i)fied** /-(ɪ)faɪd; -(ə)faɪd/) (*n or adj*+~=*v*) make into, cause to be, bring to a state of: (名词或形容词+~=动词)使成为；使变成；使进入…状态: *beautify; terrify; solidify.*

in- (also 亦作 **il-, im-, ir-**) /-ɪn-, -ɪl-, -ɪm-, -ɪr-; ɪn-, ɪl-, ɪm-, ɪr-/ *pref* **1** (~+*v*=*v or n*) in, on: (~+动词=动词或名词)在内，上: *intake; imprint*. **2** (~+*adj*=*adj*) not: (~+形容词=形容词)不；无: *infinite; illicit; immoral; irrelevant.*

-ing /-ɪŋ; -ɪŋ/ *suff* (*v*+~=*pres p* and *gerund*): (动词+~=现在分词及动名词): *talking; thinking.*

inter- /-ɪntə(r)-; ɪntə-/ *pref* between, from one to another: 在…之间；从一个到另一个: *international; interplanetary.*

intra- (also 亦作 **intro-**) /-ɪntrə-; ɪntrə-/ *pref* inside: 在内部: *intravenous; intra-uterine; introspection.*

-ise ⇨ **-ize**

-ish /-ɪʃ; -ɪʃ/ *suff* **1** (*national name* + ~ = *adj*, ⇨ **App 6**): (国家名称 + ~ = 形容词，参看附录六): *Irish; Spanish*. **2** (*n* + ~ = *adj*) resembling, in the manner of: (名词 + ~ = 形容词)象…一样的；…似的: *childish; devilish*. **3** (*adj* + ~ = *adj*) somewhat, near to: (形容词 + ~ = 形容词)有点…的；将近…的: *reddish; twentyish.*

-ism /-ɪzəm; -ɪzəm/ *suff* (used to form a *n*) (用以构成名词) **1** showing qualities typical of: …的特质或特点: *Americanism; heroism*. **2** specific doctrine, principle or movement: 学说；主义；教义；原理；运动: *Buddhism; Communism.*

-ist /-ɪst; -ɪst/ *suff* (*n*+~=*n*)(名词+~=名词) **1** agent of an '-ize' *v*: (表示以 ize 结尾的动词之) 实行者；推动者: *dramatist; publicist*. **2** follower, practiser of an '-ism' (表示以 ism 结尾的名词之)信徒；党员；主义者: *industrialist; fascist*. **3** person concerned with a specific activity or thing: 与某种活动或事物有关的人: *tobac-*

conist; motorist.

-ite /-aɪt; -aɪt/ *suff* **1** (*proper n* + ~ = *n*) follower, devotee of a person or organisation: 信奉者(某人或某组织的)追随者；拥护者: *Labourite*. **2** (chem) specific chemical substance: (化学)某种化学物质: *anthracite; dynamite.*

-ities ⇨ **-ity**

-ition ⇨ **-tion**

-itis /-aɪtɪs; -aɪtɪs/ *suff* (med) (used to form a *n*) inflammation of: (医)(用以构成名词)炎症；…炎: *appendicitis; tonsillitis.*

-ity /-ɪtɪ; -ətɪ/ *suff* (*pl* **-ities**) (used with an *adj* to form a *n*): (用在形容词上以构成名词): *crudity; oddity.*

-ive /-ɪv; -ɪv/ *suff* (*v* + ~ = *adj*) having a tendency towards, quality of: (动词 + ~ = 形容词)有…倾向的；有…性质的: *active; constructive.*

-ize (also **-ise**, which is not used in this dictionary, but is equally acceptable) (亦作 -ise，此拼法虽不用于本词典，但同样可接受) /-aɪz; -aɪz/ *suff* (used to form a *v*) (用以构成动词) **1** cause to be, make like, change into: 使成为；使象；使变成: *computerize; dramatize*. **2** act with the qualities of: 以…的特点行事: *criticize; deputize.*

-less /-lɪs; -lɪs/ *suff* (*n* + ~ = *adj*) without: (名词 + ~ = 形容词)没有…的: *treeless; spiritless*. **-lessly** /-lɪslɪ; -lɪslɪ/ *adv* **-lessness** /-lɪsnɪs; -lɪsnɪs/ *n*

-let /-lɪt; -lɪt/ *suff* (*n* + ~ = *n*) diminutive: (名词 + ~ = 名词)小型的: *piglet; booklet.*

-like /-laɪk; -laɪk/ *suff* (*n* + ~ = *adj*) resembling, in the manner of: (名词 + ~ = 形容词)象…的；…般的: *childlike; godlike.*

-ling /-lɪŋ; -lɪŋ/ *suff* **1** (used to form a *n*) diminutive: (用以构成名词)非常小的: *duckling; fledgeling*. **2** (used to form a *n*) person connected with (often used disparagingly): (用以构成名词)与…有关的人(常带贬义): *hireling; underling.*

-logue (US: **-log**) /-lɒg; -lɔːg/ *suff* (used to form a *n*) sth spoken: (用以构成名词)话；谈话: *dialogue; travelogue; monologue.*

-logy /-lədʒɪ; -lədʒɪ/ *suff* (*pl* **-logies**) (used to form a *n*) branch of learning: (用以构成名词)某门学问；…学: *biology; sociology.*

-ly /-lɪ; -lɪ/ *suff* **1** (*n* + ~ = *adj*) having the qualities of: (名词 + ~ = 形容词)具有…性质或特点的: *cowardly; scholarly*. **2** (*n* + ~ = *adj* or *adv*) regular occurrence: (名词 + ~ = 形容词或副词)定期发生；每…一次: *hourly; yearly*. **3** (*adj* + ~ = *adv*) in the manner of the *adj*: (形容词 + ~ = 副词)(以所述形容词的方式)…地: *happily; stupidly.*

macro- /-mækrəʊ-; mækrə-, mækro-/ *pref* relatively large, extending: 比较大的；延长的: *macrocosm; macrobiotic.*

mal- /-mæl; -mæl/ *pref* bad, wrong, not: 坏；差；不良；错误: *maladjusted; malnutrition.*

-man *suff* **1** /-mən; -mən/ (used to form a *n*) dweller in: (用以构成名词)…的居民: *Irishman; countryman*. **2** /-mən, -mæn; -mən, -mæn/ (*n* + ~ = *n*) sb connected by a specific activity to: (名词 + ~ = 名词)与某种活动有关的人: *guardsman; doorman; businessman.*

-mania /-meɪnɪə; -meɪnɪə/ *suff* (used to form a *n*) abnormal behaviour, excessive enthusiasm: (用以构成名词)反常行为；狂热: *kleptomania; bibliomania*. **-maniac** /-meɪnɪæk; -meɪnɪæk/ *sb* affected by a '-mania': 有…狂者: *kleptomaniac.*

matri- /-meɪtrɪ-, mætrɪ-; metrɪ-, mætrə-/ *pref* mother: 母亲: *matriarch; matricide.*

mega- /-medʒɪ; -megə-/ *pref* **1** large: 大: *megalith*. **2** one million: 一百万: *megaton.*

-ment /-mənt; -mənt/ *suff* (*v* + ~ = *n*) result or means of an action: (动词 + ~ = 名词)行为的结果或方式: *development; government*. **-mental** *adj* **-mentally** /-mentlɪ; -mentl(ɪ)/ *adv: governmentally).*

-meter /-mɪtə(r); -mətə/ *suff* (used to form a *n*) a

means of measuring: (用以构成名词)测量用的工具; 计; 表: *speedometer*.

-metre /-mi:tə(r); -mitə/ *suff* (used to form a *n*) a (specified) part of a metre: (用以构成名词)一米的…部分: *centimetre*.

micro- /maɪkr(ə- *etc*); maɪkr(ə- *etc*)/ *pref* **1** relatively small: 比较小的; 微: *microfilm*; *microwave*. **2** of examining or reproducing small quantities: 显微的; 扩大的;放大的: *microscope*; *microphone*.

milli- /mɪlɪ-; mɪlə-/ *pref* a thousandth part of: 千分之一; 毫: *milligram*; *millimetre*.

mis- /mɪs-; mɪs-/ *pref* bad, wrong, not: 不良; 错误; 不: *misconduct*; *misdirect*; *mistrust*.

-monger /-mʌŋgə(r); -mʌŋgə/ *suff* (used to form a *n*) sb who deals in: (用以构成名词)贩卖…的人; 经营…的人: *fishmonger*; *scandalmonger*.

mono- /mɒn(ə- *etc*); mɑn(ə- *etc*)/ *pref* one, a single: 一; 单一: *monosyllable*; *monotone*.

-most /-məʊst; -most/ *suff* (*prep* or *adj* of position + ~ = *superl adj*): (介词或方位形容词 + ~ = 最高级形容词): *inmost*; *outermost*.

multi- /mʌltɪ-; mʌltɪ/ *pref* many: 许多: *multistage*; *multi-coloured*.

neo- /ni:(ə- *etc*); ni:(ə- *etc*)/ *pref* new, revived, later: 新的; 复兴的; 新近的: *neologism*; *neo-classical*.

-ness /-nɪs; -nɪs/ *suff* (*adj* + ~ = *n*) a quality, state, character: (形容词 + ~ = 名词)性质; 状态; 性格: *dryness*; *silliness*.

neur(o)- /njʊər(ə- *etc*) US: nʊə-; njʊr(ə- *etc*)/ *pref* of the nervous system: 神经系统的: *neuralgia*; *neurology*.

non- /nɒn-; nɑn-/ *pref* not: 非; 不: *nonsense*; *nonstop*.

-oid /-ɔɪd; -ɔɪd/ *suff* (used to form an *adj* or *n*) resembling in shape: (用以构成形容词或名词)…状的(东西): *asteroid*; *rhomboid*.

-or /-ə(r), -ɔ:(r); -ə, -ɔr/ *suff* (*v* + ~ = *n*) sb or sth that carries out the action of the *v*: (动词 + ~ = 名词)执行或做出…之人或物: *governor*; *elevator*; *lessor*.

-ories ⇨ **-ory**

ortho- /-ɔ:θ(ə- *etc*); ɔrθ(ə- *etc*)/ *pref* correct, standard: 正确的; 标准的: *orthodox*; *orthopaedic*.

-ory /-ərɪ, -rɪ US: -ɔ:rɪ; -ɔrɪ, -ərɪ/ *suff* (*pl* **-ories**) **1** (used to form a *n*) place where specified activity is carried on: (用以构成名词)从事某种活动的地方: *laboratory*; *observatory*. **2** (used to form an *adj*): (用以构成形容词): *compulsory*; *illusory*.

-osis /-əʊsɪs *etc*; -osɪs *etc*/ *suff* (used to form a *n*) a process, change: (用以构成名词)过程; 变化: *hypnosis*; *metamorphosis*.

-ous /-əs; -əs/ *suff* (*n* + ~ = *adj*) having the qualities of: (名词 + ~ = 形容词)具有…性质的: *poisonous*; *zealous*. **-ously** /-əslɪ; -əslɪ/ *adv* **-ousness** /-əsnɪs; -əsnɪs/ *n*

out- /aʊt-; aʊt-/ *pref* **1** located outside: 在外面的: *outhouse*; *outpost*. **2** surpassing, to a greater extent: 超越; 在…上超过: *outnumber*; *outmanoeuvre*. **3** with the various senses of 'out' as defined in the dictionary: 具有本词典中out各条含义: *outcry*; *outspoken*.

over- /əʊvə(r)-; ovə-/ *pref* **1** across, above: 横越; 在…之上: *overland*; *overhead*. **2** to excess, too much: 过度; 过多: *overcharge*; *overwork*. **3** with the various senses of 'over' as defined in the dictionary: 具有本词典 over条的各种意义: *overthrow*; *overpower*.

pale(o)- (also 亦作 **palae(o)-** /pælɪ(ə- *etc*); pelɪ(ə- *etc*)/ *pref* of ancient times: 古代的: *paleolithic*; *paleontology*.

pan- /pæn-; pæn-/ *pref* all, throughout: 全部; 遍及; 泛: *panchromatic*; *Pan-African*.

patri- /peɪtrɪ-, pætrɪ-; petrɪ-, pætrə-/ *pref* father: 父亲: *patriarch*; *patricide*.

-philia /-fɪlɪə; -fɪlɪə/ *suff* (used to form a *n*) excessive love of: (用以构成名词)对…过度爱好: *Anglophilia*; *bibliophilia*. **-phile** /-faɪl; -faɪl/ *n* lover of: …的爱好者; 亲…的人.

-phobia /-fəʊbɪə; -fobɪə/ *suff* (used to form a *n*) excessive fear of: (用以构成名词)对…过度恐惧: *claustrophobia*; *xenophobia*. **-phobic** *adj* **-phobe** *n* fearer of. 恐惧…的人; 仇视…的人.

-phone /-fəʊn; -fon/ *suff* (used to form a *n*) means of reproducing sound: (用以构成名词)重现声音的工具: *megaphone*; *telephone*. **-phonic** /-fɒnɪk; -fɑnɪk/ *adj* *stereophonic*.

phon(o)- /fəʊn(ə- *etc*); fon(ə- *etc*)/ *pref* of sound: 声音的;语音的: *phonetic*; *phonology*.

photo- /fəʊt(ə- *etc*); fot (ə- *etc*)/ *pref* **1** of light: 光的: *photoelectric*. **2** of photography: 摄影的; 照相的: *photocopy*; *photogenic*.

physi(o)- /fɪzɪ(ə- *etc*); fɪzɪ(ə- *etc*)/ *pref* of the body, of living things: 身体的; 生物的: *physiotherapy*; *physiology*.

poly- /pɒlɪ- *etc*; pɑlɪ- *etc*/ *pref* many: 许多的; 多…的: *polygamy*; *polysyllabic*.

post- /-pəʊst- *etc*; post- *etc*/ *pref* after: 在…之后的: *postscript*; *posthumous*; *postgraduate*.

pre- /pri:- *etc*; pri- *etc*/ *pref* before: 预先; 在…之前: *prefabricate*; *premature*; *prerecorded*.

pro- /prəʊ-; pro-/ *pref* **1** supporting, in favour of: 支持…的; 赞同…的: *pro-Chinese*; *pro-revolutionary*. **2** acting as: 代理…; 临时…: *pro-Vice-Chancellor*.

proto- /prəʊt(ə- *etc*); prot(ə- *etc*)/ *pref* first, original, basic: 最早的; 最先的; 原始的; 基本的: *prototype*; *protoplasm*.

pseud(o)- /sju:d(ə- *etc*) US: su:-; sjud(ə- *etc*)/ *pref* false, fake: 假的;伪造的: *pseudonym*; *pseudointellectual*.

psych(o)- /saɪk(ə- *etc*); saɪk(ə- *etc*)/ *pref* of the mind: 精神的; 心理的: *psychiatry*; *psycho-analysis*.

quasi- /kweɪsaɪ-; kwesaɪ-/ *pref* almost, seemingly: 近乎…的; 似乎是…的: *quasi-serious*; *quasi-explanation*.

re- /ri:- *etc*; ri- *etc*/ *pref* again: 再; 重新: *re-echo*; *reinstate*.

retro- /retr(ə- *etc*); rɛtr(ə- *etc*)/ *pref* backwards, behind: 向过去; 向后: *retrospective*; *retro-rocket*.

-ry ⇨ **-ery**

-s /*After* p, t, k, f, θ, *pronounced* s; *otherwise* z 在 p, t, k, f, θ 音后读做 s; 他处读做 z/ *suff* **1** (used to form the *pl* of a *n*): (用以构成名词的复数) *pots*; *stars*. **2** (used to form 3*rd pers sing pres t* of a *v*): (用以构成动词第三人称单数现在式): *breaks*; *sees*.

-scape /-skeɪp; -skep/ *suff* (*n* + ~ = *n*) a stretch of scenery: (名词 + ~ = 名词)一片景色; …景: *landscape*; *moonscape*.

-scope /-skəʊp; -skop/ *suff* (used to form a *n*) means of observing or showing: (用以构成名词)观察或指示用的工具(或仪器): *microscope*; *stroboscope*.

self- /self-; self-/ *pref* of one's self, alone, independent: 自己;自力;自动;自我;自主: *self-taught*; *self-service*.

semi- /semɪ- US: semaɪ-; semə-/ *pref* half, partially, midway: 一半; 部分地; 在中间: *semicircular*; *semi-detached*; *semi-final*.

-ship /-ʃɪp; -ʃɪp/ *suff* (*n* + ~ = *n*) (名词 + ~ = 名词) **1** state of being, status, office: …的状态、身分、职位或职务: *friendship*; *ownership*; *professorship*. **2** skill, proficiency as: 做为…的技能或熟练: *musicianship*; *scholarship*.

-sion ⇨ **-tion**

soci(o)- /səʊsɪ(ə- *etc*); soʃɪ(ə- *etc*)/ *pref* of society: 社会的: *sociology*; *socio-economic*.

-some /-səm; -səm/ *suff* (used to form an *adj*) likely to, productive of: (用以构成形容词)易于…的; 会引起…的: *quarrelsome*; *meddlesome*.

-sphere /-sfɪə(r); -sfɪr/ *suff* (used to form a *n*) spherical, of a sphere: (用以构成名词)球形的; 球状的: *hemisphere*; *atmosphere*.

-ster /-stə(r); -stə/ *suff* **1** (*n* + ~ = *n*) sb connected with the *n*: (名词 + ~ = 名词)与所述名词有关的人: *songster*; *gangster*. **2** (*adj* + ~ = *n*) sb with the

qualities of the adj: (形容词＋～＝名词)具有所述形
容词的性质的人: youngster.

sub- /sʌb- etc/; sʌb- etc/ pref **1** under: 在…下面的:
subway; subsoil. **2** secondary, lower in rank: 次等; 次
要; 附属: sub-committee; sub-species. **3** not quite: 低
于; 次于; 亚于: subtropical; subnormal. **4** (used with a
v) secondary repetition: (用在动词上)第二次重复; 再:
sublet; subdivide.

super- /suːpə(r)-/; supɚ-/ pref **1** above, over: 在…上面:
superstructure; superimpose. **2** superior to, more than:
超过; 越过: superhuman; supernatural.

sym- (also 亦作 **syn-**) /sɪm-, sɪn- etc; sɪm-, sɪn- etc/ pref
sharing with, together: 共同; 联同: sympathy; synchronize.

-t /-t; -t/ suff (used to form the pt and pp of some vv):
(用以构成某些动词的过去式和过去分词): burnt; lent;
slept.

techn(o)- /tekn(ɒ- etc); tekn(ɑ- etc)/ pref of applied
science: 与应用科学有关的; 与技术有关的: technocracy;
technology.

tele- /telɪ- etc; telə- etc/ pref of linking across distances:
远距离的: telepathy; television.

theo- /θiː(ɒ- etc); θi(ɑ- etc)/ pref of God: 上帝的; 神
的: theocracy; theology.

thermo- /θɜːm(ə- etc); θɜːm(ə- etc)/ pref of heat, of
temperature: 与热有关的; 与温度有关的: thermostat;
thermometer.

-tion /-ʃn; -ʃən/ (also 亦作 **-sion** /-ʃn, -ʒn; -ʃən, -ʒən/;
-ation /-eɪʃn; -eʃən/; **-ition** /-ɪʃn; -ɪʃən/) suff (v +
～＝n): (动词＋～＝名词): relation; confession;
adhesion; hesitation; competition. **-tional** /-ʃənl; -ʃənl/
adj **-tionally** /-ʃənlɪ; -ʃənlɪ/ adv

trans- /trænz- etc; trænz- etc/ pref **1** across: 横越; 横
过: transatlantic; transcontinental. **2** to a changed
state: 转变; 移转: transplant; transform.

tri- /traɪ- etc; traɪ- etc/ pref three: 三; 三个: triangle;
tricolour.

-tude /-tjuːd US: -tuːd; -tjud/ suff (used to form a
n) condition: (用以构成名词)状况; 状态: magnitude;
exactitude.

-ule /-juːl; -jul/ suff (used to form a n) relative
smallness: (用以构成名词)较小; 小: capsule; globule.

ultra- /ʌltrə-; ʌltrə-/ pref beyond, to excess: 在…的那

一边; 超过; 极度: ultraviolet; ultra-liberal.

un- /ʌn-; ʌn-/ pref **1** (used with an adj or n) not: (用
在形容词或名词上)不; 非: unable; untruth. **2** (used
with a v) negative, reverse, opposite of: (用在动词
上)…的否定、还原、相反: uncover; unpack.

under- /ʌndə(r)-; ʌndɚ-/ pref **1** located beneath: 在…
下面的: undercurrent; undergrowth. **2** not enough: 不
足; 过少; 过低: underestimate; undersized. **3** lower in
rank, importance: 低于; 次于; 副: undersecretary;
understudy.

uni- /juːnɪ-; junɪ-/ pref one, the same: 单一; 同一:
uniform; unisex.

up- /ʌp-; ʌp-/ pref to a higher or better state: 向上; 较
高; 较好: uphill; upgrade.

-ure /-juə(r), -jə(r) etc; -jʊr, -jə etc/ suff (used to form
a n) act, process, condition: (用以构成名词)动作; 过
程; 状况: closure; legislature.

vice- /vaɪs-; vaɪs-/ pref who is next in rank to and
may act for another: 次; 副: vice-consul; vice-president.

-ward /-wəd; -wɚd/ suff (used to form an adj or adv)
in the direction of: (用以构成形容词或副词)朝向:
backward; eastward; homeward. **-wards** /-wədz; -wɚdz/
adv

well- /wel-; wel-/ pref (～＋pp of a v＝adj) (～＋动
词的过去分词＝形容词) **1** fortunately: 幸运地: well-
born. **2** properly, thoroughly: 适当地; 完全地: well-
informed; well-worn.

-wise /-waɪz; -waɪz/ suff (n or adj ＋～＝adv) (名词或
形容词＋～＝副词) **1** in the manner of: 以…的方式;
象…一般地: crosswise; crabwise. **2** (colloq) in connection
with: (口) 关于; 在…方面: disciplinewise; accommodationwise.

-worth /-wɜːθ; -wɚθ/ suff (used to form a
n) using the amount of: (用以构成名词)相当于…数目
或价值: poundsworth; daysworth.

-worthy /-wɜːðɪ; -wɜːðɪ/ suff (n ＋～＝adj) deserving
of: (名词＋～＝形容词)值得…的; 应受…的: praise-
worthy; blameworthy. **-worthily** adv

-y¹ (also 亦作 **-ey**) /-ɪ; -ɪ/ suff (n ＋～＝adj): (名词
＋～＝形容词): dusty; bushy; clayey. **-ier** /-ɪə(r);
-ɪɚ/ comp **-iest** /-ɪɪst; -ɪɪst/ superl **-ily** /-ɪlɪ; -ɪlɪ/ adv.

-y² (also 亦作 **-ie**) /-ɪ; -ɪ/ suff (n ＋～＝名词) pet name
or familiar name: (名词＋～＝名词)亲昵或亲密的称
呼: piggy; doggie; daddy.

APPENDIX 4 NUMERICAL EXPRESSIONS
附录四 数字表达法

The following section will give you help in the reading, speaking and writing of numbers and expressions which commonly contain numbers.
本附录就有关数字及通常含有数字的用语之阅读、口说和书写三方面提供如下的资料。

1 Numbers 数字

Note. 'a /ə; ə/ hundred' is a less formal usage than 'one /wʌn; wʌn/ hundred'.
注意: a hundred 的说法不如 one hundred 正式。

CARDINAL 基数	ORDINAL 序数
1 one /wʌn; wʌn/ 一	1st first /fɜːst; fɝst/ 第一
2 two /tuː; tu/ 二	2nd second /'sekənd; 'sekənd/ 第二
3 three /θriː; θri/ 三	3rd third /θɜːd; θɝd/ 第三
4 four /fɔː(r); for/ 四	4th fourth /fɔːθ; forθ/ 第四
5 five /faɪv; faɪv/ 五	5th fifth /fɪfθ; fɪfθ/ 第五
6 six /sɪks; sɪks/ 六	6th sixth /sɪksθ; sɪksθ/ 第六
7 seven /'sevn; 'sɛvən/ 七	7th seventh /'sevnθ; 'sɛvənθ/ 第七
8 eight /eɪt; et/ 八	8th eighth /eɪtθ; etθ/ 第八
9 nine /naɪn; naɪn/ 九	9th ninth /naɪnθ; naɪnθ/ 第九
10 ten /ten; tɛn/ 十	10th tenth /tenθ; tɛnθ/ 第十
11 eleven /ɪ'levn; ɪ'lɛvən/ 十一	11th eleventh /ɪ'levnθ; ɪ'lɛvənθ/ 第十一
12 twelve /twelv; twɛlv/ 十二	12th twelfth /twelfθ; twɛlfθ/ 第十二
13 thirteen /,θɜː'tiːn; θɝ'tin/ 十三	13th thirteenth /,θɜː'tiːnθ; θɝ'tinθ/ 第十三
14 fourteen /,fɔː'tiːn; fɔr'tin/ 十四	14th fourteenth /,fɔː'tiːnθ; fɔr'tinθ/ 第十四
15 fifteen /,fɪf'tiːn; fɪf'tin/ 十五	15th fifteenth /,fɪf'tiːnθ; fɪf'tinθ/ 第十五
16 sixteen /,sɪk'stiːn; sɪks'tin/ 十六	16th sixteenth /,sɪk'stiːnθ; sɪks'tinθ/ 第十六
17 seventeen /,sevn'tiːn; ,sɛvən'tin/ 十七	17th seventeenth /,sevn'tiːnθ; ,sɛvən'tinθ/ 第十七
18 eighteen /,eɪ'tiːn; e'tin/ 十八	18th eighteenth /,eɪ'tiːnθ; e'tinθ/ 第十八
19 nineteen /,naɪn'tiːn; naɪn'tin/ 十九	19th nineteenth /,naɪn'tiːnθ; naɪn'tinθ/ 第十九
20 twenty /'twentɪ; 'twɛntɪ/ 二十	20th twentieth /'twentɪəθ; 'twɛntɪθ/ 第二十
21 twenty-one /,twentɪ'wʌn; 'twɛntɪ'wʌn/ 二十一	21st twenty-first /,twentɪ'fɜːst; 'twɛntɪ'fɝst/ 第二十一
22 twenty-two /,twentɪ'tuː; 'twɛntɪ'tu/ 二十二	22nd twenty-second /,twentɪ'sekənd; 'twɛntɪ'sɛkənd/ 第二十二
23 twenty-three /,twentɪ'θriː; 'twɛntɪ'θri/ 二十三	23rd twenty-third /,twentɪ'θɜːd; 'twɛntɪ'θɝd/ 第二十三
30 thirty /'θɜːtɪ; 'θɝtɪ/ 三十	30th thirtieth /'θɜːtɪəθ; 'θɝtɪθ/ 第三十
38 thirty-eight /,θɜːtɪ'eɪt; 'θɝtɪ'et/ 三十八	38th thirty-eighth /,θɜːtɪ'eɪtθ; 'θɝtɪ'etθ/ 第三十八
40 forty /'fɔːtɪ; 'fɔrtɪ/ 四十	40th fortieth /'fɔːtɪəθ; 'fɔrtɪθ/ 第四十
50 fifty /'fɪftɪ; 'fɪftɪ/ 五十	50th fiftieth /'fɪftɪəθ; 'fɪftɪθ/ 第五十
60 sixty /'sɪkstɪ; 'sɪkstɪ/ 六十	60th sixtieth /'sɪkstɪəθ; 'sɪkstɪθ/ 第六十
70 seventy /'sevntɪ; 'sɛvəntɪ/ 七十	70th seventieth /'sevntɪəθ; 'sɛvəntɪθ/ 第七十
80 eighty /'eɪtɪ; 'etɪ/ 八十	80th eightieth /'eɪtɪəθ; 'etɪθ/ 第八十
90 ninety /'naɪntɪ; 'naɪntɪ/ 九十	90th ninetieth /'naɪntɪəθ; 'naɪntɪθ/ 第九十
100 a /one hundred	100th a /one hundredth
/ə, wʌn 'hʌndrəd; ə, wʌn 'hʌndrəd/ 一百	/ə, wʌn 'hʌndrədθ; ə, wʌn 'hʌndrədθ/ 第一百
1000 a /one thousand	1000th a /one thousandth
/ə, wʌn 'θauznd; ə, wʌn 'θauzn̩d/ 一千	/ə, wʌn 'θauznθ; ə, wʌn 'θauzn̩θ/ 第一千
10 000 ten thousand	10 000th ten thousandth
/,ten 'θauznd; 'tɛn 'θauzn̩d/ 一万	/,ten 'θauznθ; 'tɛn 'θauzn̩θ/ 第一万
100 000 a /one hundred thousand	100 000th a /one hundred thousandth
/ə, wʌn 'hʌndrəd 'θauznd; ə, wʌn 'hʌndrəd 'θauzn̩d/ 十万	/ə, wʌn 'hʌndrəd 'θauznθ; ə, wʌn 'hʌndrəd 'θauzn̩θ/ 第十万
1 000 000 a /one million	1000 000th a /one millionth
/ə, wʌn 'mɪlɪən; ə, wʌn 'mɪljən/ 一百万	/ə, wʌn 'mɪlɪənθ; ə, wʌn 'mɪljənθ/ 第一百万

SOME MORE COMPLEX NUMBERS 比较复杂的数字

101 a /one hundred and one /ə, wʌn ,hʌndrəd n 'wʌn; ə, wʌn 'hʌndrəd n̩ 'wʌn/ 一百零一
152 a /one hundred and fifty-two /ə, wʌn ,hʌndrəd n 'fɪftɪ 'tuː; ə, wʌn 'hʌndrəd n̩ 'fɪftɪ 'tu/ 一百五十二
1001 a /one thousand and one /ə,wʌn ,θauznd ən 'wʌn; ə, wʌn 'θauzn̩d ən 'wʌn/ 一千零一
2325 two thousand, three hundred and twenty-five /,tuː 'θauznd, ,θriː ,hʌndrəd n twentɪ 'faɪv; 'tu 'θauzn̩d 'θr 'hʌndrəd n̩ 'twentɪ 'faɪv/ 二千三百二十五
15 972 fifteen thousand, nine hundred and seventy-two /,fɪftiːn 'θauznd, ,naɪn ,hʌndrəd n ,sevntɪ 'tuː; 'fɪftin 'θauzn̩d, 'naɪn 'hʌndrəd n̩ 'sevntɪ 'tu/ 一万五千九百七十二
234 753 two hundred and thirty-four thousand, seven hundred and fifty-three /,tuː ,hʌndrəd n ,θɜːtɪ ,fɔː 'θauznd,

ˌsevn ˌhʌndrəd n ˌfɪftɪ ˈθriː; ˈtu ˈhʌndrəd ņ ˈθɜtɪ ˈfɔr ˈθauzņd, ˈsevən ˈhʌndrəd ņ ˈfɪftɪ ˈθriː/ 二十三万四千七百五十三

		US 美国	GB and other European countries 英国及其他欧洲国家
1 000 000 000	10⁹	a/one billion /ə, wʌn ˈbɪliən; ə, wʌn ˈbrɪljən/ 十亿	a/one thousand million(s) /ə, wʌn ˈθauznd ˈmɪliən(z); ə, wʌn ˈθauzņd ˈmɪljən(z)/ 十亿
1 000 000 000 000	10¹²	a/one trillion /ə, wʌn ˈtrɪliən; ə, wʌn ˈtrɪljən/ 万亿, 兆	a/one billion /ə, wʌn ˈbɪliən; ə, wʌn ˈbɪljən/ 万亿, 兆
1 000 000 000 000 000	10¹⁵	a/one quadrillion/ə, wʌn kwɒˈdrɪliən; ə, wʌn kwɑˈdrɪljən/ 千万亿, 千兆	a/one thousand billion(s) /ə, wʌn ˈθauznd ˈbrɪliən(z); ə, wʌn ˈθauzņd ˈbrɪljən(z)/ 千万亿, 千兆
1 000 000 000 000 000 000	10¹⁸	a/one quintillion /ə, wʌn kwɪnˈtɪliən; ə, wʌn kwɪnˈtɪljən/ 百亿, 百万兆	a/one trillion /ə, wʌn ˈtrɪliən; ə, wʌn ˈtrɪljən/ 百亿, 百万兆

VULGAR FRACTIONS 分数

¹/₈ an/one eighth /ən, wʌn ˈeɪtθ; ən, wʌn ˈeɪtθ/ 八分之一

¹/₄ a/one quarter /ə, wʌn ˈkwɔːtə(r); ə, wʌn ˈkwɔrtə/ 四分之一

¹/₃ a/one third /ə, wʌn ˈθɜːd; ə, wʌn ˈθɜd/ 三分之一

¹/₂ a/one half /ə, wʌn ˈhɑːf US: ˈhæf; ə, wʌn ˈhæf/ 二分之一

³/₄ three quarters /ˌθriː ˈkwɔːtəz; ˈθri ˈkwɔrtəz/ 四分之三

DECIMAL FRACTIONS 小数

0.125 (nought) point one two five /(ˌnɔːt) pɔɪnt ˌwʌn tuː ˈfaɪv; (ˌnɑt) pɔɪnt ˌwʌn tu ˈfaɪv/ 零点一二五

0.25 (nought) point two five /(ˌnɔːt) pɔɪnt ˌtuː ˈfaɪv; (ˌnɑt) pɔɪnt ˌtu ˈfaɪv/ 零点二五

0.33 (ˌnought) point three /three 零点三三

0.5 (nought) point ˈfive 零点五

0.75 (ˌnought) point ˌseven ˈfive 零点七五

Notes. 注意:

1 In the spoken forms of vulgar fractions, the versions 'and a half/quarter/third' are preferred to 'and one half/quarter/third' whether the measurement is approximate or precise. With more obviously precise fractions like ¹/₈, ¹/₁₆, 'and one eighth/sixteenth' is normal. Complex fractions like 3/462, 20/83 are spoken as 'three over four-six-two; twenty over eighty-three', especially in mathematical expressions, eg 'twenty-two over seven' for 22/7.

用口语表达分数时, and a half/quarter/third 的说法比 and one half/quarter/third 更为人所喜用, 不论所指的数量是近似的或精确的分数。而象 ¹/₈, ¹/₁₆ 这些更清楚而精确的分数, 则常用 and one eighth/sixteenth 的说法。象 3/462, 20/83 复杂的分数, 则分别读做 three over four-six-two 和 twenty over eighty-three, 在数学用语中尤其如此, 例如 22/7 读做 twenty-two over seven。

2 When speaking ordinary numbers we can use 'zero', 'nought' or 'oh' /əʊ; o/ for the number 0; 'zero' is the most common US usage and the most technical or precise form, 'oh' is the least technical or precise. In using decimals, to say 'nought point five' for 0.5 is a more precise usage than 'point five'.

口说一般的数目时, 我们可以用 zero, nought 或 oh 来指数字 0; zero 是最普通的美国用法, 也是最专门或最精确的说法, 而 oh 的说法则是最不专门或是最不精确的。在使用小数时, 0.5 读做 nought point five 比读做 point five 来得精确。

3 In most continental European countries a comma is used in place of the GB/US decimal point. Thus 6.014 is written 6,014 in France. A space is used to separate off the thousands in numbers larger than 9999, eg 10 000 or 875 380. GB/US usage can also have a comma in this place, eg 7,500,000. This comma is replaced by a full point in continental European countries, eg 7.500.000. Thus 23,500.75 (GB/US) will be written 23.500,75 in France.

在大多数欧洲大陆上的国家, 逗号用来替代英美的小数点。在法国 6.014 写做 6,014。在比 9999 大的数目里, 千的倍数皆以间隔隔开, 例如 10 000 或 875 380。在此位置上, 英美的用法也可有逗号, 例如 7,500,000。在欧洲大陆上的国家里, 逗号以句点来替代, 例如 7.500.000。因此 23,500.75 (英美写法) 在法国就写成 23.500,75。

COLLECTIVE NUMBERS 集合数字

6 a half dozen/half a dozen 半打

12 a/one dozen (24 is two dozen *not* two dozens) 一打 (24 写作 two dozen 而非 two dozens)

20 a/one score 二十, 念

144 a/one gross /grəus; gros/ 一罗, 箩; 十二打

three score years and ten (Biblical 圣经用语)=70 years, the traditional average life-span of man. 七十岁 (传统上人之平均寿命)

ROMAN 罗马		ARABIC 阿拉伯	ROMAN 罗马		ARABIC 阿拉伯	ROMAN 罗马	ARABIC 阿拉伯	ROMAN 罗马	ARABIC 阿拉伯
I	i	1	XVI	xvi	16	LX	60	DCC	700
II	ii	2	XVII	xvii	17	LXV	65	DCCC	800
III	iii	3	XVIII	xviii	18	LXX	70	CM	900
IV(IIII)	iv(iiii)	4	XIX	xix	19	LXXX	80	M	1000
V	v	5	XX	xx	20	XC	90	MC	1100
VI	vi	6	XXI	xxi	21	XCII	92	MCD	1400
VII	vii	7	XXV	xxv	25	XCV	95	MDC	1600
VIII	viii	8	XXIX	xxix	29	XCVIII	98	MDCLXVI	1666
IX	ix	9	XXX	xxx	30	IC	99	MDCCCLXXXVIII	1888
X	x	10	XXXI	xxxi	31	C	100		
XI	xi	11	XXXIV	xxxiv	34	CC	200	MDCCCXCIX	1899
XII	xii	12	XXXIX	xxxix	39	CCC	300	MCM	1900
XIII	xiii	13	XL		40	CD	400	MCMLXXVI	1976
XIV	xiv	14	L		50	D	500	MCMLXXXIV	1984
XV	xv	15	LV		55	DC	600	MM	2000

A letter placed after another letter of greater value adds, eg VI=5+1=6. A letter placed before a letter of greater value subtracts, eg IV=5−1=4. A dash placed over a letter multiplies the value by 1000; thus X̄=10 000 and M̄=1000 000. The alternative IIII is seen only on some clock faces (⇨ the illus at **dial**), and iiii is seen only in the preliminary pages of some books.

一个字母置于另一个数值较大的字母之后表示'加', VI=5+1=6。一个字母置于另一个数值较大的字母之前表示'减', 例如 IV=5−1=4。一短横加于一字母上表示'乘上1000'; 因此 X̄=10 000 而 M̄ =1 000 000。IV 的另一写法 'IIII' 只见于某些钟面上(参看 dial 之插图), 而 'iiii' 的写法只见于某些书籍的卷首数页上。

2 Mathematical Expressions 数学用语

Below are some of the more common symbols and expressions used in mathematics, geometry and statistics; in the cases where alternative ways of saying the expressions are given, both are equally common but generally the first is more formal or technical and the second less formal or technical.

下列为在数学、几何及统计学上较常用的一些符号和说法; 凡列有两种可供选择的说法的, 即表示两者同样普遍, 不过通常前者比较正式或专门, 而后者则不太正式或不太专门的说法。

+	plus／and 加(上)		⇨	implies 蕴含; 若…则…
−	minus／take away 减(去)		log.	natural logarithm *or* logarithm to the base e /i; i/ 自然对数(或以 e 为底的对数)
±	plus *or* minus／approximately 正负, 加(上)或减(去); 大约, …左右		√	(square) root 平方根
×	(is) multiplied by／times (*or when giving dimensions*) 或在表示面积、体积时说成)by 乘(以)		³√	cube root 立方根
			x^2	x /eks; ɛks/ squared x 平方
÷	(is) divided by 除以		x^3	x /eks; ɛks/ cubed x 立方
=	is equal to／equals 等于		x^4	x /eks; ɛks/ to the power four／to the fourth **x** 的四次方(或四次幂)
≠	is not equal to／does not equal 不等于		π	pi /paɪ; paɪ/ 圆周率
≃	is approximately equal to (大)约等于		γ	/ɑː(r); ɑr/=radius of circle 半径
≡	is equivalent to／is identical with 全等于		πγ²	pi r squared /ˌpaɪ ɑː ˈskweəd; ˌpaɪ ɑr ˈskwɛrd/ (formula for area of circle) 圆周率乘半径平方(圆面积的公式)
<	is less than 小于			
≮	is not less than 不小于		n!	/en; ɛn/ factorial n 的阶乘
≤	is less than or equal to 小于或等于		∫	the integral of …的积分
>	is more than 大于			
≯	is not more than 不大于		∠	angle 角
≥	is more than or equal to 大于或等于		∟	right angle 直角
%	per cent 百分之…		△	triangle 三角形
∞	infinity 无穷大		∥	is parallel to 平行于
∝	varies as／is proportional to 随…起变化, 与…成比例		⊥	is perpendicular to 垂直于
3:9∷4:12	three is to nine, as four is to twelve, ⇨ proportion(5) 3 比 9 等于 4 比 12		°	degree, ⇨ **degree**(1) 度
			′	minute (of an arc), ⇨ **minute¹**(2); foot *or* feet (unit of length) (弧之)分; 呎, 英尺(长度单位)
∈	is an element of (a set) 属于			
∉	is not an element of (a set) 不属于		″	second (of an arc), ⇨ **second³**(1); inch *or* inches (unit of length) (弧之)秒; 吋, 英寸(长度单位)
∅	*or* { } is an empty set 空集合			
∩	intersection 交, 相交			
∪	union 并集			
⊂	is a subset of 为…的子集			

THE GREEK ALPHABET 希腊字母

Many letters of the Greek alphabet are commonly used in statistics and other branches of mathematics. Here is a complete list of the letters:

希腊字母中有许多常用于统计学及其他种类的数学。以下是完整的希腊字母表:

capitals 大写	small letters 小写	name 名称	capitals 大写	small letters 小写	name 名称
A	α	alpha /ˈælfə; ˈælfə/	Ξ	ξ	xi /ksaɪ; zaɪ/
B	β	beta /ˈbiːtə US: ˈbeɪtə; ˈbeɪtə/	O	o	omicron /əʊˈmaɪkrən US: ˈɒmɪkrən; ˈɑmɪˌkrɑn/
Γ	γ	gamma /ˈgæmə; ˈgæmə/	Π	π	pi /paɪ; paɪ/
Δ	δ	delta /ˈdeltə; ˈdɛltə/	P	ρ	rho /rəʊ; ro/
E	ε	epsilon /epˈsaɪlən US: ˈepsɪlɒn; ˈɛpsəˌlɑn/	Σ	σ, ς	sigma /ˈsɪgmə; ˈsɪgmə/
Z	ζ	zeta /ˈziːtə US: ˈzeɪtə; ˈzetə/	T	τ	tau /taʊ; taʊ/
H	η	eta /ˈiːtə US: ˈeɪtə; ˈetə/	Υ	υ	upsilon /juːpˈsaɪlən US: ˈjuːpsɪlɒn; ˈjupsəˌlɑn/
Θ	θ	theta /ˈθiːtə US: ˈθeɪtə; ˈθetə/			
I	ι	iota /aɪˈəʊtə; aɪˈotə/	Φ	φ	phi /faɪ; faɪ/
K	κ	kappa /ˈkæpə; ˈkæpə/	X	χ	chi /kaɪ; kaɪ/
Λ	λ	lambda /ˈlæmdə; ˈlæmdə/	Ψ	ψ	psi /psaɪ; psaɪ/
M	μ	mu /mjuː; m(j)u/	Ω	ω	omega /ˈəʊmɪgə US: əʊˈmegə; oˈmɛgə/
N	ν	nu /njuː US: nuː; nu/			

3 Computes Numbers　电脑数字

Cheque books, business accounts, etc have long strings of numerals. If such a number has to be read aloud, the numerals are spoken as separate digits (1-9, 0= /əu; o/) grouped rhythmically into pairs. Doubled numerals may be read separately or as eg 'double six'. For example, '05216472' is ,oh ,five/,two ,one/,six ,four/,seven 'two. As mentioned earlier, 0 can also be read as 'zero' (formal) or 'nought' (informal). ⇨ also **binary**.

支票簿、帐簿等上常会有长串的数字。如要大声读出这种数目,则以两个数字 (即 1-9,0 读作 /əu; o/)为一组有节奏地读出。两个相同的数字可分别读出,或读作,如 'double six'。例: '05216472' 读作 ,oh ,five/,two ,one/,six ,four/,seven 'two。如前面所提过的,0 可读作 'zero' (正式)或 'nought' (非正式)。亦参看 binary。

4 Measurements (Inanimate)　量度(指事物)

Traditionally GB and US measurements have been made in inches, feet, yards, miles, etc, but there is now a gradual move towards the metric system of millimetres, metres, kilometres, etc. Examples of both are given below. (For tables of weight, measurement, etc and conversion tables, ⇨ **App 5**.) Even if the move towards metrication is completed in the near future, there will remain a vast amount of literature in which the other units are used.

传统上,英美的测量制度是以英寸、英尺、码、英里等为单位的,但目前逐渐有使用毫米、米、公里等公制单位的趋势。(度量衡表及换算表参看附录五。)即使在最近的将来完全改用公制,依然会留下大量的文献是采用其他的单位。

in	inch(es) 英寸	sq in	square inch(es) 平方英寸	cu in	cubic inch(es) 立方英寸
ft	foot/feet 英尺	sq ft	square foot/feet 平方英尺	cu ft	cubic foot/feet 立方英尺
yd	yard(s) 码	sq yd	square yard(s) 平方码	cu yd	cubic yard(s) 立方码
—	mile(s) 英里	—	square mile(s) 平方英里		
mm	millimetre(s) 毫米	mm²	square millimetre(s) 平方毫米	mm³	cubic millimetre(s) 立方毫米
cm	centimetre(s) 厘米	cm²	square centimetre(s) 平方厘米	cm³, cc	cubic centimetre(s) 立方厘米
m	metre(s) 米	m²	square metre(s) 平方米	m³	cubic metre(s) 立方米
km	kilometre(s) 公里	km²	square kilometre(s) 平方公里		

(⇨ **square¹(4)** for the difference between eg 'four square feet' and 'four feet square')
(像 'four square feet' 与 'four feet square' 之差别,参看 square¹(4))

DISTANCE　距离

London to New York is three thousand, four hundred and forty-one miles. (3 441 miles) 从伦敦到纽约有三千四百四十一英里的距离。

There is a speed limit of thirty miles per an hour. (30 mph) 限制时速为 30 英里。

That ship has a top speed of fifteen knots. (1 knot=1 nautical mile per hour) 该船最高的速度为15节。(1节=每小时1海里)

London to New York is five thousand, five hundred and six kilometres. (5 506 km) 从伦敦到纽约有五千五百零六公里的距离。

There is a speed limit of fifty kilometres per an hour. (50 kph) 限制时速为 50 公里。

HEIGHT/DEPTH　高度/深度

Mount Qomolangma is twenty-nine thousand and twenty-eight feet high. (29 028 ft) 珠穆朗玛峰是两万九千零二十八英尺高。

The airliner is flying at a height/an altitude of twenty thousand feet. (20 000 ft) 该架客机在 (海拔) 二万英尺的高空飞行。

The sea's average depth is twelve thousand feet or two and half miles. (12 000 ft) 该海的平均深度为一万二千英尺或二英里半。

Mount Qomolangma is eight thousand, eight hundred and forty-eight metres high. (8 848 m) 珠穆朗玛峰是八千八百四十八米高。

The airliner is flying at a height/an altitude of six thousand metres. (6 000 m) 该架客机在 (海拔) 六千米的高空飞行。

The sea's average depth is three thousand seven hundred metres. (3 700 m) 该海的平均深度为三千七百米。

DIMENSION　大小

This room is sixteen foot/feet (wide) by twenty-five (foot/feet) (long). (16ft× 25ft or 或 16'×25') 这个房间是十六英尺宽二十五英尺长。

This room is three metres (wide) by eight and half (metres) (long). (3m× 8.5m) 这个房间是三米宽八点五米长。

AREA　面积

We need five thousand square foot/feet of office space. (5 000 sq ft) 我们需要五千平方英尺的空间作办公处所。

Scotland has an area of thirty thousand, four hundred and five square miles. (30 405 sq miles) ⇨ **square¹(4)** 苏格兰的面积为三万零四百零五平方英里。

The house is for sale with ten acres of grounds. 此屋连同十英亩庭园出售。

We need six hundred square metres of office space. (600 sq m) 我们需要六百平方米的空间作办公处所。

Scotland has an area of seventy-six thousand, two hunded and thirty-five square kilometres. (76235 sq km) 苏格兰的面积为七万六千二百三十五平方公里。

The house is for sale with four hectares of grounds. 此屋连同四公顷庭园出售。

VOLUME　容量

You'll need thirty (cubic) feet/foot of sand to mix with the cement. (30 cu ft) ⇨ **cubic** 你需要三十立方英尺的沙与水泥拌合。

You'll need a (cubic) metre of sand to mix with the cement. (1 m³) 你需要一立方米的沙与水泥拌合。

TEMPERATURE　温度

The ordinary GB temperature scale for everyday use has been Fahrenheit. With metrication, the use of Centigrade (which has long been common in scientific usage) is becoming widespread.

英国日常用以量温度的单位向来是华氏。随着公制的使用,摄氏度量法日渐普及 (摄氏度量法早已普遍使用于科学中)。

FAHRENHEIT 华氏

Water freezes at thirty-two degrees Fahrenheit. (32 °F) 水在华氏三十二度时结冰。

CENTIGRADE 摄氏

Water freezes at nought degrees Centigrade. (0°C) 水在摄氏零度时结冰。

Last night we had nine degrees of frost. (23°F) 昨夜温度是冰点下九度(即华氏二十三度)。

It was ninety-five in the shade this morning. (95°F) 今晨在阴处温度为华氏九十五度。

Last night the temperature was five degrees below zero. (−5°C) 昨夜温度是(摄氏)零下五度。

It was thirty-five in the shade this morning. (35°C) 今晨在阴处温度为摄氏三十五度。

ATHLETICS 田径

He holds the record for the fifteen hundred metres (colloq 口 'the metric mile'). (1 500 m)
他保持一千五百米的记录。

She ran for her country in the two hundred metres women's hurdles. (200 m)
她代表她的国家参加两百米女子跳栏赛跑。

Our team was narrowly beaten in the four by four hundred metres relay. (4×400 m)
我们队在一千六百米接力赛跑中以极小之差被击败。

Our captain won the high jump with a jump of two point oh five metres (2.05 m), *and threw the javelin a national record of eighty-three point four four metres* (83.44 m).
我们队长以二点零五米的高度赢得跳高冠军,并以八十三点四四米的成绩刷新掷标枪的全国记录。

SWIMMING 游泳

I swam for Britain in the eight hundred metres freestyle. (800 m)
我代表英国参加八百米自由式泳赛。

She came second in the women's hundred metres back-stroke. (100 m)
她在女子一百米仰泳赛中得第二名。

TENNIS 网球

Smith won the first set six four/by six games to four (6—4). *The scoring in the final game was: fifteen love* (15—0), *fifteen all* (15—15), *thirty fifteen* (30—15), *forty fifteen* (40—15), *forty thirty* (40—30), *deuce* (40—40), *advantage Smith, game to Smith, Smith went on to win the match by three sets to two* (3—2).

史密斯以六比四赢得第一盘。最后一局的得分为十五比零(即一比零),十五比十五(即一比一),三十比十五(即二比一),四十比十五(即三比一),四十比三十(即三比二),(四十比四十)平分,史密斯得分,史密斯赢得此局。史密斯最后以三盘对二盘(即三比二)赢得此次比赛。

ASSOCIATION FOOTBALL (SOCCER) 英式足球

In the first leg the half-time score was one all (1—1). *In the second half only Italy scored and won the match two one/by two goals to one* (2—1). *The full time score in the return match was nil all/a goalless draw/a no goal draw* (0—0), *but Brasil scored two magnificent goals in extra time to win the Cup two nil* (2—0).

初赛上半场的比数是一比一。下半场只有意大利队得分而以二比一赢得此赛。复赛全场的比数是零比零,但巴西队在加赛时踢进两个漂亮的球而得分,以二比零赢得奖杯。

RUGBY FOOTBALL (RUGGER) 橄榄球

Wales beat Scotland sixteen six/by sixteen points to six (16—6). *For Wales, Owen scored two tries* (8 points), *Price converted one* (2 points), *and kicked two penalty goals* (6 points). *Scotland's score came from a penalty* (3 points) *and a dropped goal* (3 points), *both kicked by Frazer.*

威尔士队以十六比六击败苏格兰队。威尔士队中,欧文以两次触地球得八分,普赖斯踢入一球得两分,踢两次罚球得六分。苏格兰队之得分来自一次罚球得三分,一次碰踢得三分,两次皆为弗雷泽所踢。

HORSE-RACING 赛马

The Derby is run over a distance of twelve furlongs/one mile four furlongs/one and a half miles/a mile and a half. (12 fur=1½ miles)
英国大赛马之全程为十二浪(一英里又四浪,一英里半)。(12浪=1½英里)

The favourite in the Grand National was Never Say Die at five to two. (5—2, betting stake; *The odds on Never Say Die were five to two.*)
全英障碍赛马中的热门马是人们以五比二的赌注看好的'甭灰心'。('五比二'为打赌方式,即对'甭灰心'的赔率为赔五赢二)。

5 Measurements (Human) 量度(指人)

HEIGHT, ETC 身高等

i Note that 'tall' not 'high', is used. Feet and inches are used, or metres and centimetres if the metric system is employed.
注意:用 tall 不用 high。用英尺和英寸为单位,如使用公制则以米和厘米为单位。

My wife is five foot/feet six (inches) (tall). (5 ft 6 in/5'6") 我的太太身高五英尺六(英寸)。

My wife is one metre sixty-eight (centimetres) (tall). (1 m 68 cm/1.68 m) 我的太太身高一米六十八(厘米)。

ii Measurements round parts of the body are in inches or centimetres:
量度身体各部的单位用英寸或厘米:

She is 36-24-36. (ie 36 inches round the bust, 24 round the waist, 36 round the hips) 她的三围是36-24-36。(即胸围 36 英寸,腰围 24 英寸,臀围 36 英寸)

She is 91-61-91. (ie 91 centimetres round the bust, 61 round the waist, 91 round the hips) 她的三围是91-61-91。(即胸围 91 厘米,腰围 61 厘米,臀围 91 厘米)

WEIGHT 体重

In GB weight has traditionally been given in stones and pounds, and in the US in pounds only. The metric system uses kilos/kilograms.
在英国,重量的单位传统上用呏与磅,在美国只用磅。公制用公斤。

I weigh twelve stone eleven (pounds)/a hundred and seventynine pounds. (12 st 11 lb/179 lb) 我重十二呏十一磅(一百七十九磅)。

I weigh eighty-one kilos (81 kg). 我重八十一公斤。

AGE 年龄

I have three children. The eldest is nine (years old), the middle one is five and a half and the youngest is four. I'm thirty-three. How old are you?
我有三个孩子。最大的九岁,中间的五岁半,最小的四岁。我三十三岁。你几岁?

6 Time of Day 时刻

Note: When times are quoted, specified precisely or 'read' from a digital clock, the second form given below is more

common.

注意: 报时的时候, 精确报时或根据数字钟说出时, 下列的第二种形式较为常用。

GB 英国		US 美国
7.00	seven o'clock／a m／p m／e'klɒk, ,eɪ'em, ,piː'em; e'klɑk, ,eˈɛm, ,piˈɛm／ (上午, 下午)七点	The system used is similar to that used in GB except that *after* is usual where GB has *past*: 与英国用法类似, 只是英国用 past 之处, 美国通常用 after:
8.15	a quarter past eight／eight fifteen 八点一刻／八点十五分	
9.45	a quarter to ten／nine forty-five 差一刻十点／九点四十五分	5.10 ten after five 五点十分
4.30	half past four／four thirty／(colloq 口) half four 四点半／四点三十分	5.15 a quarter after five 五点一刻
5.10	ten (minutes) past five／five ten 五点十分	9.30 'nine thirty' is more usual than 'half past nine' 'nine thirty' 较 'half past nine' 为常用 九点半／九点三十分
6.25	twenty-five (minutes) past six／six twenty-five 六点二十五分	
6.35	twenty-five (minutes) to seven／six thirty-five 差二十五分七点／六点三十五分	*of* is common where GB has *to*: 英国用 to 之处, 美国常用 of:
9.57	three minutes to ten／nine fifty-seven 差三分十点／九点五十七分	7.45 a quarter of eight 差一刻八点
2.03	three minutes past two／two oh three 两点零三分	7.55 five of eight 差五分八点

TWENTY-FOUR HOUR CLOCK 标示二十四小时之钟

Used originally in military orders etc, but now increasingly used in travel timetables.
原用于军事命令等, 但今于旅行时刻表中渐多使用。

07.00	(,oh) ,seven 'hundred hours 七点(指上午)	=	7.00 a m	19.00	,nineteen 'hundred hours 十九点(即下午七点)	= 7.00 p m
10.30	,ten 'thirty 十点三十分(指上午)	=	10.30 a m	22.50	,twenty-,two 'fifty 二十二点五十分(即下午十点五十分)	= 10.50 p m
12.00	,twelve 'hundred hours 十二点(即正午)	=	midday／noon	23.05	,twenty-,three ,oh 'five 二十三点零五分(即下午十一点零五分)	= 11.05 p m
13.45	,thirteen ,forty-'five 十三点四十五分(即下午一点四十五分)	=	1.45 p m	24.00	,twenty-,four 'hundred hours 二十四点(即午夜)	= midnight
15.15	,fifteen ,fif'teen 十五点十五分(即下午三点十五分)	=	3.15 p m			

7 Dates 日期

2000 BC 读作 'two thousand /ˌbiːˈsiː:; ˌbiˈsi/' 公元前 2000 年	GB 英国
55 BC 读作 'fifty-five /ˌbiːˈsiː:; ˌbiˈsi/' 公元前 55 年	3(rd) January 1985: 1985 年 1 月 3 日, 读作 'the third of January nineteen eighty-five', often abbreviated to 常
AD is usually reserved only for the earlier years:	略作 3 Jan '85 (其余各月略作 Feb, Mar, Apr, May, Jun,
AD 通常只用于较早的年代:	July, Aug, Sept, Oct, Nov, Dec) or to numbers only eg
AD 55 /ˌeɪˈdiː; ˌeˈdi/ fifty-five; but 1066, not AD 1066.	或只以数字表示, 如 3／1／85. Sometimes Roman numbers
公元 55 年写作 AD 55; 但公元 1066 年则不加 AD.	are used for the month, eg 有时用罗马数字表示月份, 如 27
Queen Elizabeth I 1558–1603: 'Queen Elizabeth the	ii 40.
first reigned from fifteen (hundred and) fifty-eight to	US 美国
sixteen (hundred and) three／sixteen oh three.'	May 4, 1985: 1985 年 5 月 4 日, 读作 'May fourth,
'伊丽莎白女王一世 1558–1603' 读作: 伊丽莎白女王一世	nineteen eighty-five.' In numbers only 只以数字表示, 则
在位期间从 1558 年到 1603 年。	为: 5.4.85 (GB 英=4.5.85).

8 Money 钱币

For monetary tables ⇨ Appendix 5 币制表参看附录五		They'll charge you a pound／(sl 俚) a quid membership fee. (£1) 他们 会收你一英镑的会费。	They'll charge you a dollar／(sl 俚) a buck membership fee. ($1) 他们 会收你一元的会费。
GB 英国	US 美国	I was given one (pound) fifty(pence) change. (£1.50) 找了我一英镑五十便士的零 钱。	I was given a dollar fifty／ one fifty／(sl 俚) one and a half bucks change. ($ 1.50) 找了我一块五角钱的 零钱。
I paid a penny／one p for it. (1p) 我付了一便士买的 它。	I bought it for a cent. (1¢) 我花一分钱买的它。		
It's ten pence／ten p a cup. (10p) 一杯十便士。	It's ten cents a cup. (10¢) 一杯十分钱。	The return ticket is thirteen (pounds) twenty-seven (pence). (£13.27) 来 回票是十三英镑二十七便 士。	The return ticket is thirteen (dollars) twenty-seven (cents). ($13.27) 来回票是 十三元二十七分。
The cheapest seats are fifty pence／fifty p each. (50p) 最便宜的座位每个五十便 士。	The cheapest seats are half a dollar／(sl 俚) half a buck each. (50¢) 最便宜的 座位每个半块钱。		

Note: The penny and cent signs (p, ¢) are *never* shown with the pound and dollar signs (£, $) when writing down a sum of money:

eg £6.25 and $6.25 are right

£6.25p and $6.25¢ are wrong

注意: 在写一笔款项时, 便士与分的记号 (p, ¢) '绝不' 与英镑与元的记号 (£, $) 同时标出: 如 £6.25 与 $6.25 是正确的, £6.25p 与 $6.25¢ 是错误的。

9 Telephoning 打电话

Each digit is spoken separately, ie no figure above nine is used. 0 is pronounced /əʊ/; o/. In US usage, 'zero' (and sometimes 'nought') may replace 'oh'. The figures are usually grouped rhythmically in pairs (pairing from the right), though there is a tendency to use rhythmic triplets, especially for six-figure numbers. If the two digits of a pair are the same, it is usually spoken as 'double three' etc. An exception is the GB emergency call 999 which is always ,nine ,nine 'nine.

每个数字分别读出, 亦即大于九的数字不用。0 读成 /əʊ; o/。美国用法中, 0 可读做 zero (有时读成 nought)。所有的数字通常是两个一组(由右至左计算)有节奏地读出, 虽然目前有使用三个为一组读法的趋势, 尤其是具有六个数字的号码。如果一组中两个数字都相同时, 通常读成如 double three 等。例外:英国紧急电话号码 999 总是读作 ,nine ,nine 'nine。

6638 读作 ,double ,six, ,three 'eight

but 但是

3668 读作 ,three ,six, ,six 'eight (or 或 ,three, ,double ,six 'eight)

677 读作 ,six, ,double 'seven

but 但是

667 读作 ,six, ,six 'seven (or 或 ,double ,six, 'seven) In numbers which include a code number, the code is to be separated by a pause:

在包括区域代号的电话号码中, 念区域代号 之后要稍作停顿:

01-629 8495 读作 ,oh 'one ‖ ,six ,two 'nine ‖,eight ,four, ,nine 'five.

10 Chemical Formulae 化学式

In chemical formulae full-size and reduced-size numbers, and capital and lower case letters are not distinguished orally.

在化学式中, 普通写法的数字与缩小的数字, 以及大写字母和小写字母, 口语上均无分别。

NaCl 读作 /,en eɪ si: 'el; ,ɛn e si 'ɛl/
$2H_2 + O_2 = 2H_2O$ 读作 /,tu: eɪtʃ ,tu:‖ plʌs ,əʊ 'tu:‖ ,i:kwəlz ,tu: eɪtʃ tu: 'əʊ; ,tu etʃ ,tu ‖ plʌs ,o,'tu ‖ ,ikwəlz ,tu etʃ tu 'o/

APPENDIX 5 WEIGHTS AND MEASURES
附录五　度量衡表

The Metric System 公制

METRIC 公制	length 长度	GB & US 英美制
10 millimetres (mm) 毫米	=1 centimetre (cm) 厘米	=0.3937 inches (in) 英寸
100 centimetres 厘米	=1 metre (m) 米	=39.37 inches 英寸 or 或 1.094 yards (yd) 码
1000 metres 米	=1 kilometre (km) 公里	=0.62137 miles 英里 or about 或约 5/8 mile 英里

	surface 面积	
100 square metres (m²) 平方米	=1 are (a) 公亩	=0.0247 acres 英亩
100 ares 公亩	=1 hectare (ha) 公顷	=2.471 acres 英亩
100 hectares 公顷	=1 square kilometre (km²) 平方公里	=0.386 square miles 平方英里

	weight 重量	
10 milligrams (mg) 毫克	=1 centigram (cg) 厘克	=0.1543 grains 喱
100 centigrams 厘克	=1 gram (g) 克	=15.4323 grains 喱
1000 grams 克	=1 kilogram (kg) 公斤	=2.2046 pounds 磅
1000 kilograms 公斤	=1 tonne 公吨	=19.684 cwt 英担

	capacity 容量	
1000 millilitres (ml) 毫升	=1 litre (l) 升	=1.75 pints 品脱 (2.101 US pints 美国品脱)
10 litres 升	=1 decalitre (dl) 十升	=2.1997 gallons 加仑 (2.63 US gallons 美国加仑)

Avoirdupois Weight 常衡

GB & US 英美制		METRIC 公制
	1 grain (gr) 喱	= 0.0648 grams (g) 克
437½ grains 谷, 喱	=1 ounce (oz) 啊, 盎斯	=28.35 grams 克
16 drams (dr) 特拉姆, 英钱	=1 ounce 啊, 盎斯	=28.35 grams 克
16 ounces 啊, 盎斯	=1 pound (lb) 磅	= 0.454 kilograms (kg) 公斤
14 pounds 磅	=1 stone 昈	= 6.356 kilograms 公斤
2 stone 昈	=1 quarter 夸特	=12.7 kilograms 公斤
4 quarters 夸特	=1 hundredweight (cwt) 英担	=50.8 kilograms 公斤
112 pounds 磅	=1 cwt 英担	=50.8 kilograms 公斤
100 pounds 磅	=1 short cwt 短担	=45.4 kilograms 公斤
20 cwt 英担	=1 ton 吨	=1016.04 kilograms 公斤
2000 pounds 磅	=1 short ton 短吨	= 0.907 metric tons 公吨
2240 pounds 磅	=1 long ton 长吨	= 1.016 metric tons 公吨

Troy Weight 金衡

system of weights used in England for gold, silver and precious stones
英国金、银及宝石之计量单位

GB & US 英美制		METRIC 公制
24 grains 谷, 喱	=1 pennyweight (dwt) 英钱	= 1.555 grams 克
20 pennyweights 英钱	=1 ounce 啊, 盎斯	= 31.1 grams 克
12 ounces 啊, 盎斯	=1 pound 磅 (5760 grains 喱)	= 0.373 kilograms 公斤

Apothecaries' Weight 药衡

used by pharmacists for mixing their medicines;
they buy and sell drugs by Avoirdupois weight
药剂师配药之计量单位; 买卖药物则用常衡

GB & US 英美制		METRIC 公制
20 grains 谷, 喱	=1 scruple 吩	= 1.296 grams 克

3 scruples 吩	=1 dram 特拉姆, 英钱	= 3.888 grams 克
8 drams 特拉姆, 英钱	=1 ounce 啊, 盎斯	= 31.1035 grams 克
12 ounces 啊, 盎斯	=1 pound 磅	=373.24 grams 克

Linear Measure 长度单位

GB & US 英美制		METRIC 公制
	1 inch (in) 英寸	= 25.3995 millimetres (mm) 毫米
12 inches 英寸	=1 foot (ft) 英尺	= 30.479 centimetres (cm) 厘米
3 feet 英尺	=1 yard (yd) 码	= 0.9144 metres (m) 米
5½ yards 码	=1 rod, pole, or 或 perch 杆	= 5.0292 metres 米
22 yards 码	=1 chain (ch) (测)链	= 20.1168 metres 米
220 yards 码	=1 furlong (fur) 浪	=201.168 metres 米
8 furlongs 浪	=1 mile 英里	= 1.6093 kilometres (km) 公里
1760 yards 码	=1 mile 英里	= 1.6093 kilometres 公里
3 miles 英里	=1 league 里格	= 4.8279 kilometres 公里

Square Measure 面积单位

GB & US 英美制		METRIC 公制
	1 square inch 平方英寸	= 6.4516 sq centimetres 平方厘米
144 sq inches 平方英寸	=1 sq foot 平方英尺	=929.030 sq centimetres 平方厘米
9 sq feet 平方英尺	=1 sq yard 平方码	= 0.836 sq metres 平方米
484 sq yards 平方码	=1 sq chain 平方链	=404.624 sq metres 平方米
4840 sq yards 平方码	=1 acre 英亩	= 0.405 hectares 公顷
40 sq rods 平方杆	=1 rood 路得	= 10.1168 ares 公亩
4 roods 路得	=1 acre 英亩	= 0.405 hectares 公顷
640 acres 英亩	=1 sq mile 平方英里	= 2.599 sq kilometres 平方公里

Cubic Measure 体积单位

GB & US 英美制		METRIC 公制
	1 cubic inch 立方英寸	=16.387 cu centimetres 立方厘米
1728 cu inches 立方英寸	=1 cu foot 立方英尺	= 0.028 cu metres 立方米
27 cu feet 立方英尺	=1 cu yard 立方码	= 0.765 cu metres 立方米

Surveyors' Measure 丈量单位

GB & US 英美制		METRIC 公制
7.92 inches 英寸	=1 link 令	= 20.1168 centimetres 厘米
100 links 令	=1 chain 链	= 20.1168 metres 米
10 chains 链	=1 furlong 浪	=201.168 metres 米
80 chains 链	=1 mile 英里	= 1.6093 kilometres 公里
10 square chains 平方链	=1 acre 英亩	= 0.405 hectares 公顷

Nautical Measure 海程单位

used for measuring the depth and surface distance of seas, rivers, etc

测量海洋、河流等的深度及水面距离所用

GB & US 英美制		METRIC 公制
6 feet 英尺	=1 fathom 噚	= 1.8288 metres 米
608 feet 英尺	=1 cable 锚链	=185.313 metres 米
6080 feet 英尺	=1 sea (or 或 nautical) mile 海里	= 1.852 kilometres 公里
	(1.151 statute miles 法定英里)	
3 sea miles 海里	=1 sea league 海里格	= 5.550 kilometres 公里
60 sea miles 海里	=1 degree 度	
360 degrees 度	=1 circle 圆周	

The speed of one sea mile per hour is called a *knot*

每小时一海里的速率称作一 '节'

Liquid Measure of Capacity 液量单位

	GB 英制	US 美制	METRIC 公制
4 gills 吉尔, 及耳	=1 pint (pt) 品脱	=1.201 pints 品脱	=0.5679 litres 升
2 pints 品脱	=1 quart (qt) 夸脱	=1.201 quarts 夸脱	=1.1359 litres 升
4 quarts 夸脱	=1 gallon (gal) 加仑	=1.201 gallons 加仑	=4.5435 litres 升

Apothecaries' Fluid Measure 液体药量单位

used by pharmacists for measuring medicines
药剂师量药所用

GB & US 英美制		METRIC 公制
60 minims 量滴	=1 fluid dram 液特拉姆	=3.552 millilitres 毫升
8 fluid drams 液特拉姆	=1 fluid ounce 液啊	=2.841 centilitres 厘升
20 fluid ounces 液啊	=1 pint 品脱	=0.568 litres 升
8 pints 品脱	=1 gallon 加仑	=4.546 litres 升

Dry Measure of Capacity 干量单位

		METRIC 公制	
GB & US 英美制		GB 英国	US 美国
	1 gallon 加仑	= 4.5435 litres 升	= 4.404 liters 升
2 gallons 加仑	=1 peck 配克	= 9.0870 litres 升	= 8.810 liters 升
4 pecks 配克	=1 bushel 蒲式耳	= 36.3477 litres 升	= 35.238 liters 升
8 bushels 蒲式耳	=1 quarter 夸特	=290.7816 litres 升	=281.904 liters 升

Circular or Angular Measure 圆弧或角度单位

60 seconds (″) 秒	=1 minute (′) 分	90 degrees 度	=1 quadrant or right angle (L) 象限或直角
60 minutes 分	=1 degree (°) 度	360 degrees 度	=1 circle or circumference 圆(周)

the diameter of a circle = the straight line passing through its centre 圆的直径＝过圆心的直线
the radius of a circle =$^1/_2 \times$ the diameter 圆的半径＝$^1/_2 \times$直径
the circumference of a circle =$^{22}/_7 \times$ the diameter 圆周(长)＝$^{22}/_7 \times$直径

Temperature Equivalents 温度等值

	FAHRENHEIT(F) 华氏	CENTIGRADE(C) 摄氏
Boiling Point 沸点	212°	100°
	194°	90°
	176°	80°
	158°	70°
	140°	60°
	122°	50°
	104°	40°
	86°	30°
	68°	20°
	50°	10°
Freezing Point 冰点	32°	0°
	14°	−10°
	0°	−17.8°
Absolute Zero 绝对零度	−459.67°	−273.15°

To convert Fahrenheit temperature into Centigrade: subtract 32 and multiply by 5/9 (five-ninths).
华氏温度换算成摄氏温度: 减去 32 再乘以 5/9(九分之五)。
To convert Centigrade temperature into Fahrenheit: multiply by 9/5 (nine-fifths) and add 32.
摄氏温度换算成华氏温度: 乘以 9/5(五分之九)再加上32。

Money 钱币

also ⇨ **App 4(8)** 亦参看附录四第八节

GB: £ p (pounds and pence)　英国: £ p (英镑和便士)
100 pence (100 p) 便士=1 pound (£1) 镑

	(amount) （数额）	(coin) （硬币）
¹/₂p	a halfpenny /'heɪpnɪ; 'hepənɪ/, half a penny 半便士	a halfpenny /'heɪpnɪ; 'hepənɪ/ 半便士硬币
1p	a penny, (colloq 口) one p /piː; piˑ/ 一便士	a penny 一便士硬币
2p	twopence /'tʌpəns; 'tʌpəns/, two pence, (colloq 口) two p /piː; piˑ/　两便士	a twopenny /'tʌpnɪ; 'tuˌpɛnɪ/ picce 两便士硬币
5p	five pence /'faɪfpəns; 'faɪˑpɛns/ 五便士	a fivepenny /'faɪfpənɪ; 'faɪvˌpɛnɪ/ piece 五便士硬币
10p	ten pence /'tenpəns; 'tɛnˑpɛns/ 十便士	a tenpenny /'tenpənɪ; 'tɛnˌpɛnɪ/ piece 十便士硬币
50p	fifty pence 五十便士	a fifty pence piece 五十便士硬币
£1	a pound, (sl 俚) a quid 一英镑	(note) （纸币）
£5, £10, £20	five/ten/twenty pounds, (sl 俚) five/ten/ twenty quid　五(十、二十)英镑	a pound note 一英镑面额钞票
£3.82	three pounds eighty-two (pence) 3.82 英镑(即 3 英镑 82 便士)	a five/ten/twenty pound note, (sl 俚) a fiver/ tenner　五(十、二十)英镑面额钞票

US: $¢ (dollars and cents)　美国: $¢: (元和分)
100 cents (100¢) 分=1 dollar ($1) 元

	(amount) （数额）	(coin) （硬币）
1¢	a cent 一分	a penny 一分硬币
5¢	five cents 五分	a nickel 五分硬币
10¢	ten cents 十分	a dime 十分硬币
25¢	twenty-five cents 二十五分	a quarter 二十五分硬币
50¢	half a dollar, (sl 俚) half a buck 五角	a half-dollar 五角硬币
$1	a dollar, (sl 俚) a buck 一元	(note) （纸币）
$5, $10, $20	five/ten/twenty dollars, (sl 俚) five/ten/ twenty bucks　五(十、二十)元	a dollar bill 一元面额钞票
$3.82	three dollars eighty-two (cents) 3.82 元(即 3 元 82 分)	a five/ten/twenty dollar bill 五(十、二十)元面额钞票

Time　时间

60 seconds	=1 minute	4 weeks, or 28 days		=1 lunar month
60 秒	=1 分	4 周或 28 日		=1 太阴月
60 minutes	=1 hour	52 weeks, 1 day; or 13		
60 分	=1 小时	lunar months, 1 day		=1 year
		52 周又 1 日, 或 13 太阴月又1日		=1 年
24 hours	=1 day			
24 小时	=1 日			
7 days	=1 week	365 days, 6 hours		=1 (Julian) year
7 日	=1 周	365 日又 6 小时		=1(凯撒历)年

Number of Days in the Month　日数歌

30 days have September,	四、六、九、十一,
April, June and November;	皆为三十日;
All the rest have 31,	其余三十一,
Excepting February alone,	唯有二月奇,
Which has but 28 days clear	常年二十八,
And 29 in each leap year.	闰年添一日。

Speed　速度

Light travels at 186 300 miles per second, 300 000 kilometres per second.
　　光的速度每秒 186,300 英里, 或 300,000 公里。
Sound travels at 1130 feet per second, 330 metres per second, 770 miles per hour (the 'sound barrier').
　　声音的速度每秒 1,130 英尺, 或 330 米; 每小时则是 770 英里(即 '音障')。

Appendix 6 GEOGRAPHICAL NAMES

附录六 地名

A(a)lborg /'ɔːlbɔːg; 'ɔlborg/ 奥尔堡。
Abadan /ˌɑːbɑːˈdɑːn; ˌabəˈdan/ 阿巴丹。
Aberdeen /ˌæbəˈdiːn; ˌæbəˌdin/ 阿伯丁。
Aberdeenshire /ˌæbəˈdiːnʃə(r); ˌæbəˈdin‚ʃɪr/ 阿伯丁郡。
Abidjan /ˌæbɪˈdʒɑːn; æbɪˈdʒɑn/ 阿比让。
Abilene /ˈæbɪliːn; ˈæbə‚lin/ 阿比林。
Abu Dhabi /ˈæbuːˈðæbɪ; ˌabuˈdæbɪ/ 阿布扎比。
Accra, Akkra /æˈkrɑː; əˈkrɑ/ 阿克拉。
Aconcagua /ˌækɒŋˈkɑːgwə; ˌækənˈkagwə/ 阿空加瓜山。
Acropolis /əˈkrɒpəlɪs; əˈkrɑpəlɪs/ 阿克罗波利斯。
Adana /ˈædənə; ˈadənə/ 阿达纳。
Addis Ababa /ˈædɪsˈæbəbə; ˈædəˈsæbəbə/ 亚的斯亚贝巴。
Adelaide /ˈædəleɪd; ˈædˌled/ 阿德莱德。
Aden /ˈeɪdn; ˈɑdn/ 亚丁。
Adirondacks /ˌædɪˈrɒndæks; ˌædəˈrɑnˌdæks/ 阿迪朗达克山脉。
Adriatic /ˌeɪdrɪˈætɪk; ˌedrɪˈætɪk/ 亚得里亚海。
Aegean /iːˈdʒiːən; ɪˈdʒiən/ 爱琴海。
Aetna=Etna。
Afghanistan /æfˈgænɪstɑːn; æfˈgænəˌstæn/ 阿富汗。
Africa /ˈæfrɪkə; ˈæfrɪkə/ 非洲。
Agra /ˈɑːgrə; ˈɑgrə/ 阿格拉。
Ahaggar /əˈhægə(r); əˈhagə/ 阿哈加尔山脉。
Ajaccio /əˈjætʃɪəʊ; əˈjɑtʃo/ 阿雅克修。
Akkra=Accra。
Akron /ˈækrən; ˈækrən/ 阿克伦。
Alabama /ˌæləˈbæmə; ˌæləˈbæmə/ 亚拉巴马。
Alameda /ˌæləˈmiːdə; ˌæləˈmidə/ 阿拉梅达。
Alaska /əˈlæskə; əˈlæskə/ 阿拉斯加。
Albania /ælˈbeɪnɪə; ælˈbenɪə/ 阿尔巴尼亚。
Albany /ˈɔːlbənɪ; ˈɔlbənɪ/ 奥尔巴尼。
Alberta /ælˈbɜːtə; ælˈbɝtə/ 艾伯塔。
Albuquerque /ˈælbəˌkɜːkɪ; ˈælbəˌkɝkɪ/ 阿尔伯克基。
Aldan /ɑːlˈdɑːn; alˈdɑn/ 阿尔丹河。
Aleutians /əˈluːʃɪənz; əˈluʃənz/ 阿留申群岛。
Alexander /ˌælɪgˈzɑːndə; ˌælɪgˈzændə/ 亚历山大群岛。
Alexandria /ˌælɪgˈzɑːndrɪə; ˌælɪgˈzændrɪə/ 亚历山大。
Algeria /ælˈdʒɪərɪə; ælˈdʒɪrɪə/ 阿尔及利亚。
Algiers /ælˈdʒɪəz; ælˈdʒɪrz/ 阿尔及尔。
Alicante /ˌælɪˈkæntɪ; ˌæləˈkæntɪ/ 阿利坎特。
(Al) Kuwait /ˌæblkuˈweɪt; ˌæblkuˈwet/ 科威特市。
Allahabad /ˌæləhəˈbæd; ˈæləhə‚bæd/ 阿拉哈巴德。
Allegheny /ˌæləˈgeɪnɪ; ˈæləgenɪ/ 1 阿勒格尼河。2 阿勒格尼山脉。
Allentown /ˈælɪntaʊn; ˈælən‚taʊn/ 阿伦敦。
Alma-Ata /ˌælməˈɑːtɑː; ˌɑlmɑˈtɑ/ 阿拉木图。
Almadén /ˌælməˈdeɪn; ˌælmɑˈden/ 阿尔马登。
Alps /ælps; ælps/ 阿尔卑斯山脉。
Alsaca /ˈælsæs; ˈælsæs/ 阿尔萨斯。
Altai /ˈælteɪaɪ; ˈæl‚taɪ/ 阿尔泰山脉。
Amazon /ˈæməzən; ˈæmə‚zɑn/ 亚马孙河。
America /əˈmerɪkə; əˈmɛrəkə/ 1 美洲。2 美国之通称。
Amiens /ˈæmjæŋ; ˈæmɪənz/ 亚眠。
Amman /əˈmɑːn; æˈmɑn/ 安曼。
Amritsar /ʌmˈrɪtsə(r); ʌmˈrɪtsə/ 阿姆利则。
Amsterdam /ˈæmstədæm; ˈæmstə‚dæm/ 阿姆斯特丹。
Amsterdam ship canal 阿姆斯特丹运河。
Amu Darya /ˈɑːmuːˈdɑːrjə; ˌɑmuˈdɑrjə/ 阿姆河。
Anatolia /ˌænəˈtəʊljə; ˌænəˈtolɪə/ 安纳托利亚。
Anchorage /ˈæŋkərɪdʒ; ˈæŋkərɪdʒ/ 安克雷奇。
Ancohuma /ˌæŋkəˈhuːmə; ˌæŋkəˈhumə/ 安科乌马山。
Andalusia /ˌændəˈluːʒɪə; ˌændəˈluʒə/ 安达卢西亚。

Andaman /ˈændəmæn; ˈændəmən/ 1 安达曼群岛。2 安达曼海。
Andes /ˈændiːz; ˈændɪz/ 安第斯山脉。
Andižan (Andizhan) /ˌændɪˈʒæn; ˌændɪˈʒæn/ 安集延。
Andorra /ænˈdɔːrə; ænˈdɔrə/ 1 安道尔。
Andorra la Vella /-ləˈvelə; -ləˈvɛlə/ 安道尔。
Andros /ˈændrɒs; ˈændrəs/ 安德罗斯岛。
Aneto, Pico de /ˈpiːkəʊˈðeɪɑːˈneɪteʊ; ˈpiko‚deəˈneto/ 阿内托峰。
Angara /ˌænˈgærə; ˌɑŋgəˈrɑ/ 安加拉河。
Angkor /ˈæŋˌkɔː(r); æŋˌkor/ 吴哥。
Anglesey, Anglesea /ˈæŋglsɪ; ˈæŋglsɪ/ 安格尔西岛。
Angola /æŋˈgəʊlə; æŋˈgolə/ 安哥拉。
Anguilla /æŋˈgwɪlə; æŋˈgwɪlə/ 安圭拉岛。
Angus /ˈæŋgəs; ˈæŋgəs/ 安格斯。
Anhui /ˈɑːnˈhweɪ; ˈɑnˈhweɪ/ 安徽。
Anjou /ˈɑːŋˈʒuː; ˈɑnˌdʒu/ 昂蒂。
Ankara /ˈæŋkərə; ˈæŋkərə/ 安卡拉。
Annapolis /əˈnæpəlɪs; əˈnæpələs/ 安纳波利斯。
An(n)apurna /ˌænəˈpɜːnə; ˌɑnəˈpʊrnə/ 安纳布尔纳山。
Ann Arbor /ˈænˈɑːbə; æˈnɑrbə/ 安阿伯。
Antananarivo /ˈæntəˌnænəˈriːvəʊ; ˌæntəˌnænəˈrivo/ 安塔那那利佛。
Antarctic /æntˈɑːktɪk; æntˈɑrktɪk/ 南极区;南极地方。
Antarctica /æntˈɑːktɪkə; æntˈɑrktɪkə/ 南极洲。
Antigua /ænˈtiːgə; ænˈtigə/ 安提瓜。
Antigua and Barbuda /ænˈtiːgəənbɑːˈbuːdə; ænˈtigəənbɑrˈbudə/ 安提瓜和巴布达。
Anti-Lebanon /ˈæntɪˈlebənən; ˈæntɪˈlebənən/ 前黎巴嫩山脉。
Antilles /ænˈtɪliːz; ænˈtɪlɪz/ 安的列斯群岛。
Antofagasta /ˌæntəfəˈgɑːstə; ˌæntəfəˈgɑstə/ 安托法加斯塔。
Antrim /ˈæntrɪm; ˈæntrɪm/ 安特里姆。
Antwerp /ˈæntwɜːp; ˈænt‚wɝp/ 安特卫普。
Apennines /ˈæpɪnaɪnz; ˈæpə‚naɪnz/ 亚平宁山脉。
Apia /ˈɑːpiːɑː; əˈpiə/ 阿皮亚。
Apo Mount /ˈɑːpəʊ; ˈɑpo/ 阿波火山。
Appalachian /ˌæpəˈleɪtʃɪən; ˌæpəˈletʃən/ 阿巴拉契亚山脉。
Arabia /əˈreɪbɪə; əˈrebɪə/ 阿拉伯半岛。
Arabian Desert 阿拉伯沙漠。
Arabian Sea 阿拉伯海。
Aragon /ˈærəgən; ˈærə‚gɑn/ 亚拉贡。
Araguaia, Araguaya /ˌærəˈgwaɪə; ˌærəˈgwaɪə/ 阿拉瓜亚河。
Aral Sea /ˈɑːrəl; ˈɛrəl/ 咸海。
Ararat /ˈærəræt; ˈærə‚ræt/ 亚拉腊山。
Archangel /ˈɑːkeɪndʒəl; ˈɑr‚kendʒəl/ 阿尔汉格尔。
Arctic Sea 北极海。
Arden /ˈɑːdn; ˈɑrdn/ 阿尔丁。
Ardennes /ɑːˈden; ɑrˈdɛn/ 阿登。
Arequipa /ˌærɪˈkiːpə; ˌærəˈkipə/ 阿雷基帕。
Argentina /ˌɑːdʒənˈtiːnə; ˌɑrdʒənˈtinə/ 阿根廷。
Argyllshire /ɑːˈgaɪlʃə(r); ɑrˈgaɪlˌʃɪr/ 阿盖尔郡。
Arizona /ˌærɪˈzəʊnə; ˌærəˈzonə/ 亚利桑那。
Arkansas /ˈɑːkənsɔː; ˈɑrkən‚sɔ/ 阿肯色。
Arlington /ˈɑːlɪŋtən; ˈɑrlɪŋtən/ 阿灵顿。
Armagh /ɑːˈmɑː; ɑrˈmɑ/ 阿尔马。
Armenia /ɑːˈmiːnɪə; ɑrˈminɪə/ 亚美尼亚。
Arno /ˈɑːnəʊ; ˈɑrno/ 阿尔诺河。
Arras /ˈærəs; əˈrɑs/ 阿拉斯。
Arthur's Pass /ˈɑːθəz-; ˈɑrθəz-/ 阿瑟山隘。

Ascension /əˈsenʃn; əˈsɛnʃən/ 阿森松岛。

Ashanti /əˈʃæntɪ; əˈʃɛntɪ/ 阿散蒂。

Asia /ˈeɪʃə; ˈeʒə/ 亚洲。

Asia Minor 小亚细亚。

Asmara /æzˈmɑːrə; æzˈmɑrə/ 阿斯马拉。

Assam /ˈæsæm; əˈsæm/ 阿萨姆邦。

Assyria /əˈsɪrɪə; əˈsɪrɪə/ 亚述。

Asunción /ˌɑːsunsiˈon; əˌsunsiˈon/ 亚松森。

Aswân, Ass(o)uan /ˌæsuˈæn; æˈswɑn/ 阿斯旺。

Atbara /ˈætˈbɑːrə; ˈætbərə/ 阿特巴拉河。

Athabasca, Athabaska /ˌæθəˈbæskə; ˌæθəˈbæskə/ 阿萨巴斯卡河。

Athens /ˈæθɪnz; ˈæθɪnz/ 雅典。

Athos /ˈæθɒs; ˈæθˌɑs/ 圣山。

Atlanta /ətˈlæntə; ətˈlæntə/ 亚特兰大。

Atlantic, the /ətˈlæntɪk; ətˈlæntɪk/ 大西洋。

Atlantic City 大西洋城。

Atlas /ˈætləs; ˈætləs/ 阿特拉斯山脉。

Attica /ˈætɪkə; ˈætɪkə/ 阿蒂卡。

Auckland /ˈɔːklənd; ˈɔklənd/ 奥克兰。

Augusta /ɔːˈɡʌstə; əˈɡʌstə/ 奥古斯塔。

Austin /ˈɔːstɪn; ˈɔstɪn/ 奥斯汀。

Australasia /ˌɔːstreɪˈleɪʒɪə; ˌɔstrəˈleʒə/ 澳大拉西亚。

Australia /ɒˈstreɪlɪə; ɔˈstreljə/ 1 大洋洲。2 澳大利亚联邦。

Australian Alps 澳大利亚大山脉。

Austria /ˈɒstrɪə; ˈɔstrɪə/ 奥地利。

Austronesia /ˌɒstrəʊˈniːʒə; ˌɔstrəˈniʒə/ 澳斯特罗尼西亚。

Aux Sources, Mont /ˌməʊn təʊˈsʊəs; ˌmɑntoˈsʊrs/ 苏尔斯山。

Avernus /əˈvɜːnəs; əˈvɚnəs/ 亚维奈斯湖。

Avon /ˈeɪvən; ˈevən/ 1 埃文河。2 埃文郡。

Ayrshire /ˈeəʃə; ˈɛrˌʃɪr/ 埃尔郡。

Ayutthaya /ɑːˈjuːtəjɑː; əˈjutəjə/ 大城(阿育他亚)。

Azerbaijan(Republic) /ˌæzəˌbaɪˈdʒɑːn; ˌæzəˌbarˈdʒɑn/ 阿塞拜疆。

Azores /əˈzɔːz; ˈeˌzɔrz/ 亚速尔群岛。

Azov, Sea of /ˈɑːzɒv; ˈæzɔf/ 亚速海。

Babylon /ˈbæbɪlən; ˈbæbələn/ 巴比伦。

Babylonia /ˌbæbɪˈləʊnɪə; ˌbæbəˈlonɪə/ 巴比伦尼亚。

Back /bæk; bæk/ 巴克河。

Badajoz /ˈbædəhɒz; ˌbadəˈhoz/ 巴达霍斯

Baden /ˈbɑːdn; ˈbɑdn/ 巴登。

Baffin /ˈbæfɪn; ˈbæfɪn/ 巴芬岛。

Bag(h)dad /ˈbæɡdæd; ˈbæɡ,dæd/ 巴格达。

Baguio /ˈbɑːɡɪəʊ; ˈbɑɡɪˈo/ 碧瑶。

Bahamas, the /bəˈhɑːməz; bəˈhaməz/ 巴哈马。

Bahia Blanca /bəˈhiːəˈblɑːŋkə; bə,hiəˈblæŋkə/ 布兰卡港。

Bahrain, Bahrein /bɑːˈreɪn; bɑˈren/ 巴林。

Baikal, Lake /baɪˈkɔːl; barˈkɔl/ 贝加尔湖。

Baku /bɑːˈkuː; bɑˈku/ 巴库。

Balearic /ˌbælɪˈærɪk; ˌbælɪˈɛrɪk/ 巴利阿里群岛。

Bali /ˈbɑːlɪ; ˈbalɪ/ 巴厘岛。

Balikpapan /ˌbɑːlɪkˈpɑː,pɑːn; ˌbɑlɪkˈpapˌɑn/ 巴厘巴板。

Balkan /ˈbɔːlkən; ˈbɔlkən/ 巴尔干半岛。

Balkans, the /ˈbɔːlkənz; ˈbɔlkənz/ 巴尔干半岛诸国。

Balk(h)ash, Lake /ˈbælˈkæʃ; ˈbælˈkæʃ/ 巴尔喀什湖。

Baltic Sea /ˈbɔːltɪk; ˈbɔltɪk/ 波罗的海。

Baltimore /ˈbɔːltɪmɔː(r); ˈbɔltəˌmor/ 巴尔的摩。

Baluchistan /bəˈluːtʃɪstɑːn; bəˌlutʃəˈstæn/ 俾路支。

Bamako /ˈbɑːməkəʊ; ˌbaməˈko/ 巴马科。

Bandar Seri Begawan /ˈbænˈdɑː ˈsɪərɪ bəˈɡɑːwæn; ˌbʌndə ˌserɪ bəˈɡawən/ 斯里巴加湾市。

Ban(d)jarmasin /ˌbænˈdʒɑːˈmɑːsɪn; ˌbændʒəˈmɑsɪn/ 马辰(班贾尔马辛)。

Bandung, Bandoeng /ˈbɑːndʊŋ; ˈbɑnˌdʊŋ/ 万隆。

Banffshire /ˈbænfˈʃə(r); ˈbæmfˌʃɪr/ 班夫郡。

Bangalore /ˌbæŋɡəˈlɔː(r); ˈbæŋɡəˌlor/ 班加罗尔。

Ban(g)ka /ˈbæŋkə; ˈbæŋkə/ 邦加岛

Bangkok /ˈbæŋˈkɒk; ˈbæŋˌkɑk/ 曼谷。

Bangladesh /ˌbæŋɡləˈdeʃ; ˌbɑŋɡləˈdʃ/ 孟加拉人民共和国

Bang(u)i /ˈbɑːŋɡiː; baŋˈɡi/ 班吉。

Bani(y)as /ˈbænɪˈjæs; ˈbænɪˈ(j)æs/ 巴尼亚斯。

Banjul /ˈbændʒuːl; ˈban,dʒul/ 班珠尔。

Barbados /bɑːˈbeɪdɒs; barˈbedos/ 巴巴多斯。

Barbuda /bɑːˈbuːdə; barˈbudə/ 巴布达岛。

Barcelona /ˌbɑːsɪˈləʊnə; ˌbarslˈonə/ 巴塞罗那。

Barisan Mountains /ˌbɑːrɪˈsɑːn-; ˌbarɪˈsɑn-/ 巴里桑山脉。

Baroda /bəˈrəʊdə; bəˈrodə/ 巴罗达。

Barranquilla /ˌbæronˈkiːjə; ˌbæronˈki(j)ə/ 巴兰基亚。

Bartle Frere, Mount /ˈbɑːtlˈfrɪə; ˈbartlˌfrir/ 巴特尔·弗里尔山。

Basel /ˈbɑːzəl; ˈbɑzəl/ 巴塞尔。

Bashi Channel /ˈbɑːˈʃɪ-; ˈbɑʃi-/ 巴士海峡。

Basra /ˈbæzrə; ˈbasrə/ 巴士拉。

Basutoland /bəˈsuːtəʊlænd; bəˈsutəˌlænd/ 巴苏陀兰。

Bataan /bəˈtæn; bəˈtæn/ 巴丹。

Batan /bɑːˈtɑːn; bəˈtan/ 巴坦。

Batangas /bəˈtæŋɡəs; bəˈtæŋɡəs/ 八打雁。

Batavia /bəˈteɪvɪə; bəˈtevɪə/ 巴达维亚。

Bath /bɑːθ; bæθ/ 巴斯。

Bathurst /ˈbæθəːst; ˈbæθəst/ 巴瑟斯特。

Battersea /ˈbætəsɪ; ˈbætəsɪ/ 巴特西。

Batumi /bɑːˈtuːmɪ; bəˈtumɪ/ 巴统。

Bavaria /bəˈveərɪə; bəˈverɪə/ 巴伐利亚。

Bavarian Alps /bəˈveərɪən-; bəˈverɪən-/ 巴伐利亚山脉。

Bear Lake /beə-; bɛr-/ 熊湖。

Beaufort /ˈbəʊfət; ˈbofət/ 波弗特海。

Beaumont /ˈbəʊmɒnt; ˈbo,mant/ 博蒙特。

Bechuanaland /ˌbetʃuˈɑːnəlænd; ˌbetʃ(ə)wanəˌlænd/ 贝专纳。

Bedfordshire /ˈbedfədʃ(ər); ˈbedfəd,ʃɪr/ 贝德福德郡。

Beijing /ˈbeiˈdʒɪŋ; ˈbeiˈdʒɪŋ/ 北京

Beirut, Bayrut /beiˈruːt; beˈrut/ 贝鲁特。

Belém /beˈlem; bəˈlem/ 贝伦。

Belfast /belˈfɑːst; ˈbelˌfæst/ 贝尔法斯特。

Belgium /ˈbeldʒəm; ˈbeldʒəm/ 比利时。

Belgrade /belˈɡreɪd; ˈbelˌɡred/ 贝尔格莱德。

Benares, Banaras /bəˈnɑːrəs; bəˈnarəs/ 贝拿勒斯。

Bengal /benˈɡɔːl; benˈɡɔl/ 孟加拉。

Bengal, Bay of 孟加拉湾。

Benin /beˈniːn; bəˈnin/ 贝宁。

Berchtesgaden /ˈbeəktəsɡɑːdən; ˈberktəsˌɡadən/ 贝希特斯加登。

Bergen /ˈbɜːɡən; ˈbɜrɡən/ 卑尔根。

Bering /ˈbeɪrɪŋ; ˈbɪrɪŋ/ 1 白令海。2 白令海峡。

Berkeley /ˈbɜːklɪ; ˈbɜrklɪ/ 伯克利。

Berkshire /ˈbɑːkʃə(r) US: ˈbɜːrk-; ˈbɜrkˌʃɪr/ 伯克郡

Berlin /bɜːˈlɪn; ˈbɜrlɪn/ 柏林。

Bermuda /bəˈmjuːdə; bəˈmjudə/ 百慕大群岛。

Bern(e) /bɜːn; bɜrn/ 伯尔尼。

Berwickshire /ˈberɪkʃ(ər); ˈberɪkˌʃɪr/ 贝里克郡。

Bessarabia /ˌbesəˈreɪbjə; ˌbesəˈrebɪə/ 比萨拉比亚。

Bethlehem /ˈbeθlɪhem; ˈbeθlɪˌhem/ 伯利恒。

Bhamo /ˈbɑːməʊ; ˈbɑˌmo/ 八莫。

Bhutan /buːˈtɑːn; buˈtæn/ 不丹。

Bialystok /blˈɑːlɪstɔːk; blˈalɪˌstɔk/ 比亚韦斯托克。

Bilbao /bɪlˈbɑːəʊ; bɪlˈbao/ 毕尔巴鄂。

Billiton /bəˈliːˌtɑːn; bəˈli,tan/ 勿里洞岛。

Birkenhead /ˈbɜːkənhed; ˈbɜrkənˌhed/ 伯肯黑德。

Birmingham /ˈbɜːmɪŋəm; ˈbɜrmɪŋˌhæm/ 伯明翰。

Biscay, Bay of /ˈbɪskeɪ; ˈbɪs,ke/ 比斯开湾。

Bismarck /ˈbɪzmɑːk; ˈbɪzmɑrk/ 1 俾斯麦群岛。2 俾斯麦海。

Bismarck Range /ˈbɪzmɑːk-; ˈbɪzmɑrk-/ 俾斯麦山脉。

Bissau /bɪˈsaʊ; bɪsˈaʊ/ 比绍。

Bizerte /bɪˈzɜːtɪ; bəˈzɜtɪ/ 比赛大。

Blackburn /ˈblækbɜːn; ˈblækbən/ 布莱克本。

Blackburn Mount /ˈblækbɜːn; ˈblækbən/ 布莱克本山。

Black Hills 黑山。

Blackpool /ˈblækpuːl; ˈblæk,pul/ 黑潭。

Black Sea 黑海。

Blagoveshchensk /ˌblɑːɡəˈveʃˌtʃensk; ˌblagəˈvɛʃtʃensk/

布拉戈维申斯克。

Blanc, Cape /blæŋk; blæŋk/ 布朗角。

Blanc, Mont /mɔːm'blɑːŋ; mɑnt'blæŋk/ 勃朗峰。

Blanca Peak /'blæŋkə-; 'blæŋkə/ 布兰卡峰。

Bloemfontein /'bluːmfɒnteɪn; 'blumfɑn,ten/ 布隆方丹。

Blue Mts. 兰山山脉。

Bogotá /ˌbəʊgəˈtɑː; ˌbəgə'tɑ/ 波哥大。

Bo Hai /'buːˈhaɪ/ 渤海。

Bokhara /bəʊˈkɑːrə; bo'kɑrə/ 布哈拉。

Bolivia /bəˈlɪvɪə; bə'lɪvɪə/ 玻利维亚。

Bologna /bəˈləʊnjə; bə'lonjə/ 波洛尼亚。

Bolton /'bəʊltn; 'boltən/ 博尔顿。

Bombay /bɒmˈbeɪ; bɑm'be/ 孟买。

Bonin Islands /'bəʊnɪn-; 'bonən-/ 博宁群岛。

Bonn /bɒn; bɑn/ 波恩。

Bordeaux /bɔːˈdəʊ; bor'do/ 波尔多。

Borders /'bɔːdəz; 'bordəz/ 博德斯。

Borneo /'bɔːnɪəʊ; 'bɔrni,o/ 婆罗洲。

Bosporus /'bɒsprəs; 'bɑspərəs/ 博斯普鲁斯海峡。

Boston /'bɒstn; 'bɔstən/ 波士顿。

Botany Bay /'bɒtənɪ; 'bɑtəni/ 博特尼湾。

Bothnia, Gulf of /'bɒθnɪə; 'bɑθnɪə/ 波的尼亚湾。

Botswana /bɒˈtswɑːnə; bɑt'swɑnə/ 博茨瓦纳。

Bougainville /'buːɡənvɪl; 'buɡən,vɪl/ 布干维尔岛。

Boulder /'bəʊldə; 'boldɚ/ 博尔德。

Boulogne /bʊˈləʊn; bu'lon/ 布洛涅。

Bournemouth /'bɔːnməθ; 'bɔrnməθ/ 伯恩茅斯。

Bradford /'brædfəd; 'brædfɚd/ 布拉德福德。

Brandenburg /'brændənbɜːɡ; 'brændən,bɝɡ/ 勃兰登堡。

Brasilia /brəˈzɪːljə; brə'zɪljə/ 巴西利亚。

Bratislava /ˌbrætɪˈslɑːvə; ˌbrætə'slɑvə/ 布拉迪斯拉发。

Brazil /brəˈzɪl; brə'zɪl/ 巴西。

Brazos /'bræzəs; 'bræzəs/ 布拉索斯河。

Brazzaville /'bræzəvɪl; 'brɑːzə,vɪl/ 布拉柴维尔。

Bremen /'breɪmən; 'bremən/ 不来梅。

Breslau /'breslaʊ; 'bres,lau/ 布雷斯劳。

Brest /brest; brest/ 布列斯特。

Bretagne /brəˈtɑːnɪ; brə'tɑn/ 不列塔尼 。

Bridgetown /'brɪdʒtaʊn; 'brɪdʒ,taʊn/ 布里奇顿。

Brighton /'braɪtn; 'braɪtn/ 布赖顿。

Brisbane /'brɪzbən; 'brɪzbən/ 布里斯班。

Bristol /'brɪstl; 'brɪstl/ 布里斯托尔。

Britain /'brɪtn; 'brɪtn/ 不列颠岛。

British Columbia /-kəˈlʌmbɪə; -kə'lʌmbɪə/ 不列颠哥伦比亚。

Brno /'bɜːnəʊ; 'bɝno/ 布尔诺。

Bronx /brɒŋks; brɑŋks/ 布朗克斯。

Brooklyn /'brʊklɪn; 'brʊklɪn/ 布鲁克林。

Brunei /'bruːnaɪ; 'bru,naɪ/ 文莱。

Brunswick /'brʌnzwɪk; 'brʌnzwɪk/ 布伦瑞克。

Brussels /'braslz; 'brʌslz/ 布鲁塞尔。

Bucharest /'bjuːkərest; ˌbjuːkə,rest/ 布加勒斯特。

Buckinghamshire /'bʌkɪŋəmʃə(r); 'bʌkɪŋəm,ʃɪr/ 白金汉郡。

Budapest /ˌbjuːdəˈpest; 'bjudə,pest/ 布达佩斯。

Buenaventura /ˌbwenəˌvenˈtjʊrə; ˌbwɛnə,vɛn'tʊrə/ 布埃纳文图拉。

Buenos Aires /ˌbwenɒs 'aɪərɪz; ˌbwenɪs'særiz/ 布宜诺斯艾利斯。

Buffalo /'bʌfələʊ; 'bʌfə,lo/ 布法罗。

Bug River /buːɡ-; buɡ-/ 布格河。

Bujumbura /ˌbuːdʒəmˈbʊrə; ˌbudʒəm'bʊrə/ 布琼布拉。

Bulgaria /bʌlˈɡeərɪə; bʌl'ɡɛrɪə/ 保加利亚。

Bungay /'bʌŋɡɪ; 'bʌŋɡɪ/ 邦吉。

Burma /'bɜːmə; 'bɝmə/ 缅甸。

Burundi /bʊˈrundɪ; bu'rundi/ 布隆迪。

Bute /bjuːt; bjut/ 比特岛。

Bute(shire) /'bjuːt(ʃə)r); 'bjut(,ʃɪr)/ 比特郡。

Byelorussia /bɪˌeləʊˈrʌʃə; bɪ,elo'rʌʃə/ 白俄罗斯。

Cadiz /'keɪdɪz; 'kedɪz/ 加的斯。

Caernarvonshire /kəˈnɑːvənʃə(r); kə'nɑrvən,ʃɪr/ 卡那封郡。

Cagliari /kæˈljɑːrɪ; 'kɑljəri/ 卡利亚里。

Cairo /'kaɪərəʊ; 'kaɪro/ 开罗。

Caithness /'keɪθnes; 'keθnəs/ 凯思内斯。

Calais /'kæleɪ; 'kæle/ 加来。

Calcutta /kælˈkʌtə; kæl'kʌtə/ 加尔各答。

Calgary /'kælɡərɪ; 'kælɡəri/ 卡尔加里。

Cali /'kɑːlɪ; 'kɑli/ 卡利。

Calicut /'kælɪkət; 'kælɪkət/ 卡利卡特。

California /ˌkælɪˈfɔːnɪə; ˌkælə'fɔrnjə/ 加利福尼亚。

California, Gulf of 加利福尼亚湾。

Callao /kəˈlɑːəʊ; kə'lɑ,o/ 卡亚俄。

Cambridge /'keɪmbrɪdʒ; 'kembrɪdʒ/ 剑桥。

Cambridgeshire /'keɪmbrɪdʒʃə(r); 'kembrɪdʒ,ʃɪr/ 剑桥郡。

Camden /'kæmdən; 'kæmdən/ 卡姆登。

Cameroon /'kæməruːn; ˌkæmə'run/ 喀麦隆山。

Cameroun /ˌkæməˈruːn; kæmə'run/ 喀麦隆。

Campania /kæmˈpeɪnjə; kæm'penjə/ 坎帕尼亚。

Canada /'kænədə; 'kænədə/ 加拿大。

Canadian /kəˈneɪdjən; kə'nedɪən/ 加那丁河。

Canal Zone /kə'næl-; kə'næl-/ 运河区。

Canary Islands /kəˈneərɪ-; kə'nɛrɪ-/ 加那利群岛。

Canaveral, Cape /kəˈnævərəl; kə'nævərəl/ 卡纳维拉尔角。

Canaveral Peninsula 加那维拉尔半岛。

Canberra /'kænbərə; 'kænb(ə)rə/ 坎培拉。

Candia /'kændɪə; 'kændɪə/ 干地亚。

Cannes /kæn; kæn/ 戛纳。

Cantabrian /kænˈteɪbrɪən; kæn'tebrɪən/ 坎塔布连山。

Canterbury /'kæntəbrɪ US: -berɪ; 'kæntə,bɛrɪ/ 坎特伯雷。

Canton /'kæntn; 'kæn,tn/ 坎顿。

Cape Cod 科德角。

Cape Hatteras /-ˈhætərəs; -'hætərəs/ 哈特拉斯角。

Cape Horn 合恩角。

Cape of Good Hope 好望角。

Cape Town, Capetown /'keɪptaʊn; 'kep,taʊn/ 开普敦。

Cape Verde Islands /-vɜːd-; -vɝd-/ 佛得角群岛。

Capri Island /kæ'priː-; kæ'pri-/ 卡普里岛。

Caracas /kəˈrækəs; kə'rækəs/ 加拉加斯。

Cardiff /'kɑːdɪf; 'kɑrdɪf/ 加的夫。

Cardiganshire /'kɑːdɪɡənʃə(r); 'kɑrdɪɡən,ʃɪr/ 卡迪根郡。

Caribbean, the /ˌkærɪˈbiː(ə)n; ˌkærə'biən/ 加勒比海。

Carlow /'kɑːləʊ; 'kɑr,lo/ 卡洛。

Carmarthenshire /kəˈmɑːðnʃə(r); kɑr'mɑrðən,ʃɪr/ 卡马森郡。

Carolina /ˌkærəˈlaɪnə; ˌkærə'laɪnə/ 卡罗林纳。

Caroline /'kærəlaɪn; 'kærə,laɪn/ 加罗林群岛。

Carpathian /kɑːˈpeɪθjən; kɑr'peθɪən/ 喀尔巴阡山脉。

Carstensz /'kɑːstənz; 'kɑrstənz/ 卡斯滕斯峰。

Cartagena /ˌkɑːtəˈdʒiːnə; ˌkɑrtə'dʒinə/ 卡塔赫纳。

Casablanca /ˌkæsəˈblæŋkə; ˌkæsə'blæŋkə/ 卡萨布兰卡。

Cascade Range /kæsˈkeɪd; kæs'ked/ 喀斯喀特山脉。

Caspian, the /'kæspɪən; 'kæspɪən/ 里海。

Castries /'kæstriːz; 'kæs,triz/ 卡斯特里斯。

Catalonia /ˌkætəˈləʊnɪə; ˌkætə'lonɪə/ 加泰罗尼亚。

Catania /kəˈteɪnjə; kə'tenjə/ 卡塔尼亚。

Catskill Mountains /'kætskɪl; 'kæt,skɪl/ 卡茨基尔山。

Caucasia /kɔːˈkeɪzɪə; kɔ'keʒə/ 高加索。

Caucasus /'kɔːkəsəs; 'kokəsəs/ 1 高加索山脉。2 =Caucasia

Cavan /'kævən; 'kævən/ 卡文。

Cavite /kəˈviːtɪ; kə'viti/ 甲米地。

Cayman (islands) /keɪˈmæn; ke'mæn/ 开曼群岛。

Cebu /ˈseɪbuː; se'bu/ 宿务。

Celebes /sɪˈliːbɪz; 'sɛlə,biz/ 西里伯斯岛。

Central /'sentrəl; 'sɛntrəl/ 中区(苏格兰中部)。

Central America 中美洲。

Central Provinces and Benar 中央邦。

Ceuta /'sjuːtə; 'se,utə/ 休达。

Ceylon /sɪˈlɒn; sɪ'lɑn/ 锡兰。

Chad /tʃæd; tʃæd/ 乍得。

Chamonix /'ʃæmənɪ; ʃæmənɪ/ 夏蒙尼。

Champagne /ʃæm'peɪn; ʃæm'pen/ 香槟。

Changchun /'tʃaŋ'tʃun; 'tʃaŋ'tʃun/ 长春。

Chang Jiang /'tʃaːŋ 'dʒaːŋ; 'tʃaŋ 'dʒaŋ/ 长江。

Changsha /'tʃaːŋ'ʃaː; 'tʃaŋ'ʃa/ 长沙。

Channel Islands 海峡群岛。

Charleston /'tʃaːlstən; 'tʃarlstən/ 查尔斯顿。

Charlotte /'ʃaːlət; 'ʃarlət/ 夏洛特。

Chartres /'ʃaːt; ʃart/ 沙特尔。

Chatham /'tʃætəm; 'tʃætəm/ 查塔姆群岛。

Chaud Doc /'tʃʌu'dəuk; 'tʃʌu'dɔk/ 朱笃。

Chautauqua /ʃə'tɔːkwə; ʃə'tɔkwə/ 肖托夸。

Chemnitz /'kemnɪts; 'kemnɪts/ 开姆尼茨。

Chengdu /'tʃʌŋ'du; 'tʃʌŋ'du/ 成都。

Cherrapunji /,tʃerə'pʊndʒɪ; ,tʃerə'pʊndʒɪ/ 切拉朋吉。

Chesapeake Bay /'tʃesəpiːk; 'tʃesə,pik/ 切萨皮克湾。

Cheshire /'tʃeʃɪər; 'tʃeʃə/ 柴郡。

Chester /'tʃestər; 'tʃestə/ 切斯特。

Chesterfield /'tʃestəfiːld; 'tʃestə,fild/ 切斯特菲尔德。

Cheyenne /ʃaɪ'æn; ʃaɪ'æn/ 夏延河。

Chicago /ʃɪ'kaːgəu; ʃə'kago/ 芝加哥。

Chihuahua /tʃɪ'waːwə; tʃə'wawa/ 奇瓦瓦。

Chile /'tʃɪlɪ; 'tʃɪlɪ/ 智利。

Chimborazo /,tʃɪmbə'raːzəu; ,tʃɪmbə'razo/ 钦博拉索山。

China /'tʃaɪnə; 'tʃaɪnə/ 中国。

Chiriquí /,tʃerɪ'kiː; ,tʃɪrɪ'ki/ 奇里基峰。

Chirripó Grande /,tʃerɪ'pəu 'graːndə; ,tʃɪrɪ,po 'grandɪ/ 大奇里波山。

Chita /'tʃiːtaː; tʃɪ'ta/ 赤塔。

Chittagong /'tʃɪtəgaːŋ; 'tʃɪtə,gaŋ/ 吉大港。

Chkalov /'tʃəˈkaːləf; tʃəˈkaləf/ 契卡洛夫。

Chosŏn /'tʃəu'sen; 'tʃo'sen/ 朝鲜。

Christchurch /'kraɪstʃɜːtʃ; 'kraɪs,tʃɜtʃ/ 克赖斯特彻奇 (基督城)。

Christmas Island /'krɪsməs-; 'krɪsməs-/ 圣诞岛。

Chuckchee Sea /'tʃʌktʃɪ; 'tʃʌktʃɪ/ 楚克奇海。

Churchill /'tʃɜːtʃɪl; 'tʃɜ,tʃɪl/ 丘吉尔河。

Chu River /tʃuː-; tʃu-/ 楚河。

Cimarron /'sɪmərəun; 'sɪmə,ran/ 西马伦河。

Cincinnati /,sɪnsɪ'nætɪ; ,sɪnsə'nætɪ/ 辛辛那提。

Ciscaucasia /'sɪskɒ'keɪʒə; ,sɪskɔ'keʒə/ 北高加索

Clare /kleə(r); klɛr/ 克莱尔。

Cleveland /'kliːvlənd; 'klivlənd/ 克利夫兰。

Clifton /'klɪftən; 'klɪftən/ 克里夫顿。

Clwyd /'kluːɪd; 'kluɪd/ 克卢伊德。

Coast Range 海岸山脉。

Coats Island /'kəuts-; kots-/ 科茨岛。

Cocos Islands /'kəukəs-; 'kokəs-/ 科科斯群岛。

Cologne /kə'ləun; kə'lon/ 科伦。

Colombia /kə'lɒmbɪə; kə'lʌmbɪə/ 哥伦比亚。

Colombo /kə'lʌmbəu; kə'lʌmbo/ 科伦坡。

Colorado /,kɒlə'raːdəu; ,kalə'rædo/ 科罗拉多。

Columbia /kə'lʌmbɪə; kə'lʌmbɪə/ 哥伦比亚。

Columbia, Mount 哥伦比亚山。

Columbus /kə'lʌmbəs; kə'lʌmbəs/ 哥伦布。

Como /'kəuməu; 'komo/ 科莫。

Comoro Islands /'kɒmərəu-; 'kamə,ro-/ 科摩罗群岛。

Compiègne /kɒmp'jem; kmpo'jen/ 贡比涅。

Conakry /'kɒnəkrɪ; 'kanəkrɪ/ 科纳克里。

Concepción /,kɒn,sepsi'ɒn; kən,sɛpsi'on/ 康塞普西翁。

Congo, the /'kɒŋgəu; 'kaŋgo/ 1 People's Republic of ~ 刚果人民共和国。2 刚果河。

Connacht /'kɒnɔːt; 'ka,nɔt/ 康诺特。

Connecticut /kə'netɪkət; kə'nɛtɪkət/ 康涅狄格。

Constantine /'kɒnstəntaɪn; 'kanstən,tin/ 君士坦丁。

Constantinople /,kɒnstæntɪ'nəupl; ,kan,stæntə'nopl/ 君士坦丁堡。

Constantsa /kən'staːntsaː; kən'stantsa/ 康斯坦察。

Cook /kuk; kuk/ 库克。

Coolgardie /ku:l'gaːdɪ; kul'gardɪ/ 库尔加迪。

Copenhagen /,kəupn'heɪgn; ,kopən'hegən/ 哥本哈根。

Coral Sea /'kɒrəl-; 'kɔrəl-/ 珊瑚海。

Cordillera Mts. /,kɔːdɪ'ljeərə; ,kɔrdɪ'ljɛrə/ 科迪勒拉山脉。

Cordoba /'kɔːdəubaː; 'kɔrdəbə/ 科尔多瓦。

Corfu /kɔː'fuː; kɔr'fu/ 科孚岛。

Corinth /'kɒrɪnθ; 'kɒrənθ/ 科林斯。

Cork /kɔːk; kɔrk/ 科克。

Corno /'kɔːnə; 'kɔrno/ 科尔诺山。

Cornwall /'kɔːnwɔːl; kɔrn,wɔl/ 康沃尔。

Corrientes /,kɒri'entiːɒz; ,kori'ɛn,tes/ 科连特斯。

Corsica /'kɔːsɪkə; 'kɔrsɪkə/ 科西嘉岛。

Costa Rica /,kɒstə'riːkə; ,kastə'rikə/ 哥斯达黎加。

Côte d'Azur /,kəudə'zuə; ,kodə'zur/ 科特达祖尔。

Cotonou /,kəutə'nuː; ,koto'nu/ 科托努。

Cotopaxi /,kɒtə'pæksɪ; ,kotə'pæksɪ/ 科托帕希山。

Coventry /'kɒvəntrɪ; 'kɒvəntrɪ/ 考文垂。

Cradle Mount /'kreɪdl; 'kredl/ 克雷德尔山。

Cranston /'krænstən; 'krænstən/ 克兰斯顿。

Crefeld /'kreɪfeld; 'kre,fɛlt/ 克雷费尔德。

Crete /kriːt; krit/ 克里特岛。

Crewe /kruː; kru/ 克鲁。

Crimea /kraɪ'mɪə; kraɪ'miə/ 克里米亚。

Croatia /krəu'eɪʃɪə; kro'eʃə/ 克罗地亚。

Cro-Magnon /,krəumə'njaː; ,kromæ'njɔ/ 克鲁麦农。

Crosby /'krɒzbɪ; 'krɔzbɪ/ 克罗斯比。

Croydon /'krɔɪdn; 'krɔɪdn/ 克罗伊登。

Cuba /'kjuːbə; 'kjubə/ 古巴。

Cumberland /'kʌmbələnd; 'kʌmbələnd/ 坎伯兰。

Cumbria /'kʌmbrɪə; 'kʌmbrɪə/ 坎布里亚。

Cumbrian Mountains /'kʌmbrɪən-; 'kʌmbrɪən-/ 坎布连山。

Cyclades /'sɪklədiːz; 'sɪklə,diz/ 基克拉泽斯群岛。

Cyprus /'saɪprəs; 'saɪprəs/ 塞浦路斯。

Cyrenaica /,saɪrə'neɪkə; ,saɪrə'neəkə/ 昔兰尼加。

Czechoslovakia /,tʃekəuslə'vækɪə; ,tʃekəslo'vakɪə/ 捷克斯洛伐克。

Dacca /'dækə; 'dækə/ 达卡。

Dagenham /'dægənəm; 'dægənəm/ 戴根纳姆。

Dahomey /də'həumɪ; də'homɪ/ 达荷美。

Dakar /'dækə(r); 'dæk,ar/ 达喀尔。

Dakota /də'kəutə; də'kotə/ 达科他。

Dallas /'dæləs; 'dæləs/ 达拉斯。

Damascus /də'maːskəs; də'mæskəs/ 大马士革。

Danger Islands /'deɪndʒə-; 'dendʒə-/ 丹杰群岛。

Danube /'dænjuːb; 'dænjub/ 多瑙河。

Danzig /'dæntsɪg; 'dæntsɪg/ 但泽。

Dardanelles, the /,daː'də'nelz; ,dardə'nɛlz/ 达达尼尔海峡。

Dar es Salaam /'daːres sə'laːm; ,dar,ɛs sə'la:m/ 达累斯萨拉姆。

Darien /'dærɪ'en; ,dærɪ'ɛn/ 达连湾。

Darjeeling /daː'dʒiːlɪŋ; dar'dʒilɪŋ/ 大吉岭。

Darling R. /'daːlɪŋ; 'darlɪŋ/ 达令河。

Darlington /'daːlɪŋtən; 'darlɪŋtən/ 达灵顿。

Darmstadt /'daːmstæt; 'darm,stæt/ 达姆施塔特。

Darwin /'daːwɪn; 'darwən/ 达尔文。

Dauphiné Alps /,dəufɪ'neɪ-; ,dofɪ'ne-/ 多芬尼山脉。

Davenport /'dævnpɔːt; 'dævən,port/ 达文波特。

Davis Stait /'deɪvɪs-; 'devəs-/ 戴维斯海峡。

Dawna Range /'dɔːnə-; 'dɔnə-/ 多纳山脉。

Dawson /'dɔːsn; 'dɔsn/ 道森河。

Dayton /'deɪtn; 'detn/ 代顿。

Dead Sea 死海。

Dearborn /'dɪərbɔːn; 'dɪr,bɔrn/ 迪尔本。

Deccan /'dekən; 'dɛkən/ 德干。

Delano Peak /'deləˌnəu-; 'dɛlə,no-/ 德兰诺峰。

Delaware /'deləweər; 'dɛlə,wɛr/ 特拉华。

Delhi /'delɪ; 'dɛlɪ/ 德里。

Delphi /'delfaɪ; 'dɛl,faɪ/ 德尔斐。

Demavend /'deməˌvend; 'demə,vɛnd/ 德马尔德峰。

Denbighshire /'denbɪʃə(r); 'dɛnbɪˌʃɪr/ 登比郡。

Denmark /'denmaːk; 'dɛn,mark/ 丹麦。

Denmark Strait 丹麦海峡。

Denver /'denvə(r); 'dɛnvə/ 丹佛。

Derbyshire /'dɑːbɪʃ(ɪ)ə(r) US: 'dɜːrbɪ-; 'dɑrbɪˌʃɪr/ 德比郡。
Des Moines /dɪ'mɔɪn; dɪ'mɔɪn/ 得梅因。
Detroit /də'trɔɪt; dɪ'trɔɪt/ 底特律。
Devon Island /'devn-; 'devən-/ 得文岛。
Devonport /'devnpɔːt; 'devən,pɔrt/ 德文波特。
Devon(shire) /'devn(ʃə(r)); 'devən(ˌʃɪr)/ 德文郡。
Dhaulagiri /davlə'gɪərɪ; davlə'gɪrɪ/ 道拉吉里峰。
Diamond Peak /'daɪəmənd-; 'daɪəmənd-/ 钻石峰。
Dian Bien Phu /ˌdjen,bjen'fuː; ˌdjen,bjen'fu/ 莫边府。
Dijon /diːʒɔ̃ː; 'diʒən/ 第戎。
District of Columbia /-kə'lʌmbɪə; -kə'lʌmbɪə/ 哥伦比亚特区。
Djibouti /dʒɪ'buːtɪ; dʒə'buti/ 吉布提共和国。
Dnieper /'niːpə(r); 'nipə/ 第聂伯河。
Dniester /'niːstə(r); 'nistə/ 涅斯特河。
Doha /'dəʊhə; 'doha/ 多哈。
Dominica /də'mɪnɪkə; dɑmə'nikə/ 多米尼加。
Dominican Republic /də'mɪnɪkən-; də'mɪnɪkən-/ 多米尼加共和国。
Doncaster /'dɒŋkəstə(r); 'dɑŋkəstə/ 唐克斯特。
Donegal /'dɒnɪgɔːl (in Ireland 爱尔兰读音) ˌdʌnɪ'gɔːl; ˌdɑnɪ'gɔl/ 多尼戈。
Donets /də'nets; də'nɛts/ 顿涅茨河。
Dong Hai /duŋ'hai; 'duŋ'hai/ 东海。
Don River /dɑːn-; dɑn-/ 顿河。
Dongting Hu /'duŋ'tiŋ'huː; 'duŋ'tiŋ'hu/ 洞庭湖。
Dorset(shire) /'dɔːsɪt(ʃə(r)); 'dɔrsɪt(ˌʃɪr)/ 多塞特郡。
Douglas /'dʌgləs; 'dʌgləs/ 道格拉斯。
Douro /'dʊərəʊ; 'doru/ 杜罗河。
Dover /'dəʊvə(r); 'dovə/ 多佛。
Dovrefjell /'dɔːvrə,fjel; 'dovrə,fjel/ 多甫勒高原。
Down /dəʊn; daʊn/ 道恩。
Drakensberg /'draːkənz,bɜːg; 'drakənz,bɜg/ 德拉肯斯山脉。
Dresden /'drezdən; 'drɛzdən/ 德累斯顿。
Duala /duː'ɑːlə; du'alə/ 杜阿拉。
Dublin /'dʌblɪn; 'dʌblɪn/ 都柏林。
Dubrovnik /'dubrɒvnɪk; 'du,brɒvnɪk/ 杜布罗夫尼克。
Dudley /'dʌdlɪ; 'dʌdlɪ/ 德雷德利。
Duff /dʌf; dʌf/ 达夫群岛。
Duluth /dju:'luːθ; də'luθ/ 德卢司。
Dumbarton Oaks /dʌm'baːtn; ˌdʌm'bɑrtn/ 敦巴顿。
Dumbartonshire /dʌm'baːtnʃə(r); ˌdʌm'bɑrtn,ʃɪr/ 丹巴顿郡。
Dumfries and Galloway /dʌm,friːs ən 'gæləweɪ; ˌdʌm,fris ən 'gælə,we/ 邓弗里斯盖洛韦。
Dumfries-shire /dʌm'friːʃ(ə)r; ˌdʌm'fri,ʃɪr/ 敦夫里斯郡。
Dundee /dʌn'diː; ˌdʌn'di/ 邓迪。
Dunedin /dʌ'niːdɪn; dʌ'nidn/ 达尼丁。
Dunkirk /'dʌnkɜːk; 'dʌn,kɜk/ 敦刻尔克。
Durban /'dɜːbən; 'dɜbən/ 德班。
Durham /'dʌrəm; 'dʌrəm/ 达勒姆。
Düsseldorf /'duːsl,dɔːf; 'dusəl,dorf/ 迪塞尔多夫。
Dutch Harbor 荷兰港。
Dvina /də,vɪ'naː; də,vɪ'na/ 德维纳河。
Dvina, Northern 北德维纳河。
Dyfed /'dʌvɪd; 'dʌvɛd/ 德维得。
Ealing /'iːlɪŋ; 'ilɪŋ/ 伊林。
Eastbourne /'iːstbɔːn; 'ist,born/ 伊斯博恩。
Easter Island 复活节岛。
East Ham 东哈姆。
East lothian 东洛锡安。
Eastern Samoa /'iːstən; sə'məʊə/ 东萨摩亚。
Ecuador /'ekwədɔː(r); 'ɛkwə,dɔr/ 厄瓜多尔。
Edinburg /'edn,bɜːg; 'ɛdn,bɜg/ 爱丁堡。
Edinburgh /'ednbrə; 'ɛdn,bɜrə/ 爱丁堡。
Edmonton /'edməntən; 'ɛdməntən/ 埃德蒙顿。
Edward, lake /'edwəd; 'ɛdwəd/ 爱德华湖。
Egypt /'iːdʒɪpt; 'idʒəpt/ 埃及。
Eire /'eərə; 'ɛrə/ 爱尔兰共和国。

Elba /'elbə; 'ɛlbə/ 厄尔巴岛。
Elbe /elb; 'ɛlbə/ 易北河。
Elbert, Mount /'elbət; 'ɛlbət/ 埃尔伯特山。
Elborus /'elbəˈruːz; 'ɛlbə'ruz/ 厄尔布鲁士峰。
Elburz Mts. /el'buəz; el'burz/ 厄尔布尔士山脉。
Eleusis /e'ljuːsɪs; ɪ'lusəs/ 艾留西斯。
Elisabethville /ɪ'lɪzəbəθvɪl; ɪ'lɪzəb(ə)θ,vɪl/ 伊利萨白维尔。
Ellice Islands /'elɪs-; 'ɛlɪs-/ 埃利斯群岛。
El Misti /el'miːstɪ; el'mistɪ/ 米斯提火山。
El Salvador /el'sælvədɔː(r); el'sælvə,dor/ 萨尔瓦多。
Emden /'emdən; 'ɛmdən/ 埃姆登。
Emi Koussi /'emiː'kuːsɪ; ˌemɪ'kusə/ 库西火山。
Emperor Range /'emprə-; 'ɛmprə-/ 帝王山脉。
Enderby land /'endəbɪ-; 'ɛndəbɪ-/ 恩德比地。
England /'ɪŋglənd; 'ɪŋglənd/ 1 英格兰。2 英国之通称。
English Channel 英吉利海峡。
Entebbe /en'tebə; ɛn'tɛbə/ 恩德培。
Ephesus /'efɪsəs; 'ɛfəsəs/ 以弗斯。
Epsom and Ewell /'epsəm ən 'juːəl; ˌɛpsəmən'juəl/ 埃普瑟姆-尤厄尔。
Equatorial Guinea 赤道几内亚。
Erebus, Mount /'erəbəs; 'ɛrəbəs/ 埃里伯斯火山。
Erie /'ɪərɪ; 'ɪrɪ/ 1 伊利湖。2 伊利城。3 伊利运河。
Eritrea /ˌerɪ'treɪə; ˌɛrə'triə/ 厄立特里亚。
Esdraelon, Plain of /ˌezdrɪ'iːlɒn; ˌɛzdrə'ilən/ 厄斯垂伊伦。
Essen /'esn; 'ɛsn/ 埃森。
Essex /'esɪks; 'ɛsɪks/ 埃塞克斯郡。
Estonia, Esthonia /es'təʊnjə; ɛs'tonɪə/ 爱沙尼亚。
Ethiopia /ˌiːθɪ'əʊpɪə; ˌiθɪ'opɪə/ 埃塞俄比亚。
Etna /'etnə; 'ɛtnə/ 埃特纳火山。
Eton /'iːtn; 'itn/ 伊顿。
Euboea /juː'bɪə; ju'bɪə/ 埃维厄岛。
Euphrates /juː'freɪtɪz; ju'fretɪz/ 幼发拉底河。
Eurasia /jʊə'reɪʒə; jʊ'reʒə/ 欧亚大陆。
Europe /'jʊərəp; 'jʊrəp/ 欧罗巴洲。
Evans, Mount /'evənz; 'ɛvənz/ 艾凡山。
Evanston /'evnstən; 'ɛvənstən/ 埃文斯顿。
Everett /'evərɪt; 'ɛvərɪt/ 埃弗里特。
Exeter /'eksɪtə(r); 'ɛksətə/ 埃克塞特。
Eyre, Lake /eə(r); ɛr/ 艾尔湖。
Fanning Island /'fænɪŋ-; 'fænɪŋ-/ 范宁岛。
Federal Republic of Germany /-'dʒɜːmənɪ; -'dʒɜːm(ə)nɪ/ 德意志联邦共和国。
Ferg(h)ana /feə'gɑːnə; fə'gɑnə/ 费尔干纳。
Fermanagh /fə'mænə; fə'mænə/ 弗马纳。
Fernando Po(o) /fə'nændəʊ 'pəʊ; fə,nændo 'po/ 费尔南多波。
Fertile Crescent 肥沃新月地带。
Fife /faɪf; faɪf/ 法夫。
Fifeshire /'faɪf(ə)r; 'faɪf,ʃɪr/ 法夫郡。
Fiji /fiː'dʒiː; 'fidʒɪ/ 斐济。
Finisterre, Cape /ˌfɪnɪs'teə(r); ˌfɪnə'stɜr/ 菲尼斯特雷角。
Finland /'fɪnlənd; 'fɪnlənd/ 芬兰。
Finsteraarhorn /ˌfɪnstər'aːhɔːn; ˌfɪnstə'a,horn/ 芬斯特瓦山。
Flanders /'flaːndəz; 'flændəz/ 佛兰德。
Flattery, Cape /'flætərɪ; 'flætərɪ/ 夫拉特黎角。
Flint(shire) /'flɪnt(ʃə(r)); 'flɪnt(ˌʃɪr)/ 弗林特。
Florence /'flɒrəns; 'florəns/ 佛罗伦萨。
Flores /'flɔːriːz; 'florez/ 弗洛勒斯岛。
Florida /'flɒrɪdə US: 'flɔːr-; 'florədə/ 佛罗里达。
Folkestone /'fəʊkstən; 'fokstən/ 福克斯通。
Foraker, Mount /'fɒrəkə; 'forɪkə/ 福拉克山。
Fort-Lamy /ˌfɔːˌlɑː'miː; ˌforlə'mi/ 拉密堡。
France /frɑːns; fræns/ 法兰西。
Frankfort /'fræŋkfət; 'fræŋkfət/ 法兰克福。
Frankfurt /'fræŋkfət; 'fræŋkfət/ 法兰克福。
Franklin /'fræŋklɪn; 'fræŋklɪn/ 富兰克林。
Fraser /'freɪzə(r); 'frezə/ 弗雷则河。
Freetown /'friːtaʊn; 'fri,taʊn/ 弗里敦。
Freiburg /'fraɪbɜːg; 'fraɪ,burg/ 弗赖堡。

Fremantle /fre'mæntl; frɪ'mæntl/ 弗里曼特尔。
Fresno /'freznəu; 'frezno/ 弗雷斯诺。
Friendly Islands=Tonga Islands
Frisian Islands /'frɪzɪən-; 'frɪʒən-/ 弗里西亚群岛。
Front Range /frʌnt-; frʌnt-/ 弗兰特山脉。
Fuji(yama) /,fuːdʒɪ'jɑːmɑː; ,fudʒɪ'jɑmɑ/ 富士山。
Fujian /,fuː'dʒen; 'fuˈdʒen/ 福建。
Fukuoka /,fuːkuˈəukə; ,fukəˈwokə/ 福冈。
Funafuti /,fuːnəˈfuːti; ,funəˈfuti/ 富纳富提。
Fundy, Bay of /'fʌndɪ; 'fʌndɪ/ 芬迪湾。
Gaberones /,gɑːbəˈrəunəs; ,gɑbəˈronəs/ 加贝罗内斯。
Gabon /gæˈbɒn; gæˈbon/ 加蓬。
Gaborone /,gɑːbəˈrəun; gɑbəˈron/ 哈博罗内。
Galápagos /gəˈlɑːpəgəs; gəˈlɑpəgəs/ 加拉帕戈斯群岛。
Galdhöpiggen /'gɑːlhøːpɪgən; 'gɑlhø,pɪgən/ 加尔赫峰。
Galilee /'gælɪliː; 'gæləˌli/ 加利里。
Galveston /'gælvɪstən; 'gælvəstən/ 加尔维斯敦。
Galway /'gɔːlweɪ; 'gɔl,we/ 戈尔韦。
Gambia /'gæmbɪə; 'gæmbɪə/ 冈比亚。
Gambier /'gæmbɪə(r); 'gæm,bɪr/ 甘比尔群岛。
Ganges /'gændʒiːz; 'gæn,dʒiz/ 恒河。
Gangtok /'gʌŋtɒk; 'gæŋ'tɑk/ 甘托克。
Gansu /'gɑːnˈsuː; 'gɑn'su/ 甘肃。
Garonne /gəˈrɒn; gəˈrɑn/ 加龙河。
Gary /'gerɪ; 'gerɪ/ 加里。
Gascony /'gæskənɪ; 'gæskənɪ/ 卡斯肯尼。
Gasherbrum /'gʌfəbrum; 'gʌfəˌbrum/ 加歇布龙山。
Gateshead /'geɪtshed; 'gets,hed/ 盖茨黑德。
Gdynia /gəˈdɪnɪə; gəˈdɪnɪə/ 格丁尼亚。
Geneva /dʒɪˈniːvə; dʒəˈnivə/ 日内瓦。
Genoa /'dʒenəuə; 'dʒenəwə/ 热那亚。
Georgetown /'dʒɔːdʒtaun; 'dʒɔrdʒˌtaun/ 1 乔治城。2 乔
治教。
Georgia /'dʒɔːdʒə; 'dʒɔrdʒ(j)ə/ 1 佐治亚。2 格鲁吉亚。
Germany /'dʒɜːmənɪ; 'dʒɜˈmənɪ/ 德国。
Ghana /'gɑːnə; 'gɑnə/ 加纳。
Ghats /gɔːts; gɔts/ 加茨山脉。
Ghent /gent; gent/ 根特。
Gibraltar /dʒɪˈbrɔːltə(r); dʒəˈbrɔltə/ 直布罗陀。
Gila /'hiːlə; 'hilə/ 希拉河
Gilbert Islands /'gɪlbət-; 'gɪlbət-/ 吉尔伯特群岛。
Gillingham /'dʒɪlɪŋəm; 'dʒɪlɪŋəm/ 吉灵厄姆。
Gironde /dʒɪˈrɒnd; dʒəˈrand/ 纪龙德湾。
Glamorgan(shire) /gləˈmɔːgən (ʃə(r)); gləˈmorgən(ˌʃɪr)/
格拉摩根。
Glasgow /'glɑːsgəu; 'glæsgo/ 格拉斯哥。
Gloucester /'glɒstə(r); 'glastə/ 格洛斯特。
Gloucestershire /'glɒstəʃə(r); 'glastəˌʃɪr/ 格洛斯特郡。
Gobi, Desert of /'gəubɪ; 'gobɪ/ 戈壁沙漠。
Godavari /gəˈdɑːvərɪ; gəˈdavərɪ/ 戈达瓦里河。
Gold Coast 黄金海岸。
Gorki, Gorky /'gɔːkɪ; 'gɔrkɪ/ 高尔基。
Gosport /'gɒspɔːt; 'gas,port/ 戈斯波特。
Göteborg /,jɜːtəˈbɔːə(jə); ,jɜtəˈbɔrɪ/ 哥德堡。
Gothenburg /'gɒθənbɜːg; 'gɑθən,bɜg/ 哥森堡。
Grampian /'græmpɪən; 'græmpɪən/ 格兰屏。
Grampian Hills /'græmpɪən-; 'græmpɪən-/ 格兰屏山脉。
Granada /grəˈnɑːdə; grəˈnɑdə/ 格拉纳达。
Grand Teton /-'tiːtɒn; -'ti,tɑn/ 大梯顿山。
Granite Peak /'grænɪt-; 'grænɪt-/ 格拉尼特峰。
Grays Peak /greɪz-; grez-/ 格雷斯峰。
Great Bear Lake 大熊湖。
(Great) Britain 1 大不列颠。2 英国之别称。
Great Dividing Range 大分水岭。
Greater Antilles /-æn'tɪliːz; -æn'tɪliz/ 大安的列斯群岛。
Great Slave Lake 大奴湖。
Great Smoky Mountains 大雾山。
Greece /griːs; gris/ 希腊。
Green /griːn; grin/ 格陵河。
Greenland /'griːnlənd; 'grinlənd/ 格陵兰岛。
Greenock /'griːnək; 'grinək/ 格里诺克。

Greenwich /'grɪnɪdʒ; 'grɪnɪdʒ/ 格林威治。
Grenada /grɪ'neɪdə; grəˈnedə/ 格林纳达。
Grenoble /grəˈnəubl; grəˈnobl/ 格勒诺布尔。
Grimsby /'grɪmzbɪ; 'grɪmzbɪ/ 格里姆斯比。
Grossglockner, Gross Glockner /grəus 'glɒːknə; 'grɔs-
'glɑknə/ 大格洛克纳峰。
Grozny /'grɔːznɪ; 'grɔznɪ/ 格洛兹尼。
Guadalupe Mountains /,gwɑːdəː'luːpə-; 'gwɑdə,lup-/
瓜达卢佩山脉。
Guadeloupe /,gwɑːdəˈluːp; 'gwɑdəˌlup/ 瓜德罗普。
Guam /gwɒm; gwam/ 关岛。
Guangdong /,gwɑːŋ'dɒŋ; 'gwɑŋˈdɔŋ/ 广东。
Guangxi /,guɑːŋ'siː; 'guɑŋ'si/ 广西。
Guangzhou /,guɑːŋ'dʒəu; 'guɑŋˈdʒo/ 广州。
Guantánamo /gwɑːn'tɑːnəˌməu; gwɑn'tɑnəˌmo/ 关塔那
摩湾。
Guatemala /,gwɑːtəˈmɑːlə; ,gwɑtəˈmɑlə/ 危地马拉。
Guatemala (City) 危地马拉市。
Guayaquil /,gwɑːjɑːˈkiːl; ,gwaɪəˈkil/ 瓜亚基尔。
Guinea /'gɪnɪ; 'gɪnɪ/ 几内亚。
Guinea-Bissau /,gɪnɪbɪ'sau; ,gɪnɪbɪs'au/ 几内亚比绍。
Guiyang /,guei'jɑː; 'guei'jaŋ/ 贵阳。
Guizhou /'guei'dʒəu; 'guei'dʒo/ 贵州。
Gunong Tahan /'guːnɒŋ 'tɑːhɑːn; ,gunoŋ 'tɑhɑn/ 大汉
山国家公园。
Guyana /gaɪˈænə; gaɪˈænə/ 圭亚那。
Gwent /gwent; gwent/ 格温特。
Gwynedd /'gwɪnəð; gwɪnəð/ 圭内斯。
Haerbin /'hɑːəˈbin; 'hɑə'bin/ 哈尔滨。
Hague, The /heɪg; heg/ 海牙。
Haifa /'haɪfə; 'haɪfə/ 海法。
Haiphong /'haɪˈfɒːŋ; 'haɪˈfɔŋ/ 海防。
Haiti /'heɪtɪ; 'hetɪ/ 海地。
Hakodate /,hækəˈdɑːtɪ; ,hakəˈdatɪ/ 函馆。
Haleakala /,hɑːliː,ɑːkəˈlɑː; ,halɪˌakəˈlɑ/ 哈莱阿卡拉山。
Halifax /'hælɪfæks; 'hælə,fæks/ 哈利法克斯。
Halmstad /'hɑːlmstɑːd; 'halm,stad/ 哈尔姆斯塔德。
Hamburg /'hæmbɜːg; 'hæm,bɜg/ 汉堡。
Hamilton /'hæmɪltən; 'hæmɪltən/ 哈密尔顿。
Hammerfest /'hæməˌfest; 'hæmə,fest/ 哈墨弗斯特。
Hammond /'hæmənd; 'hæmənd/ 哈蒙德。
Hampshire /'hæmpʃə(r); 'hæmp,ʃɪr/ 汉普郡。
Hampstead /'hæmpstɪd; 'hæmpstəd/ 汉普斯特德。
Hangzhow /'hɑːŋ'dʒəu; 'haŋ'dʒo/ 杭州。
Han(n)over /'hænəuvə(r); 'hæn,ovə/ 汉诺威。
Ha Noi /hæ'nɔɪ; hæ'nɪɔɪ/ 河内。
Harney Peak /'hɑːnɪ-; 'hɑrnɪ-/ 哈尼峰。
Hartford /'hɑːtfəd; 'hartfəd/ 哈特福德。
Harvard, Mount /'hɑːvəd; 'harvəd/ 哈佛山。
Harz /hɑːts; harts/ 哈茨山脉。
Hastings /'heɪstɪŋz; 'hestɪŋz/ 黑斯廷斯。
Havana /hə'vænə; hə'vænə/ 哈瓦那。
Hawaii /hə'waɪiː; hə'waɪi/ 夏威夷。
Hawaiian Islands /hə'waɪɪən-; hə'waɪɪən-/ 夏威夷群岛。
Hawke's Bay /'hɔːks'beɪ; 'hɔks'be/ 霍克湾。
Hebei /'hɜː'beɪ; 'hɜˈbeɪ/ 河北。
Hebrides /'hebrɪdiːz; 'hebrə,diz/ 赫布里底群岛。
Hecate Strait /'hekətɪ-; 'hekət-/ 赫卡特海峡。
Heidelberg /'haɪdlbɜːg; 'haɪdl,bɜg/ 海德堡。
Hefei /'hɜːˈfeɪ; 'hɜˈfeɪ/ 合肥。
Heilongjiang /'heɪluŋˈdʒɑːŋ; 'heɪluŋˈdʒaŋ/ 1 黑龙江省。
2 黑龙江。
Helicon /'helɪkən; 'helə,kan/ 赫利孔山。
Helsingör /,helsɪŋˈɜː(r); ,helsɪŋ'ɜː/ 赫尔辛格。
Helsinki /'helsɪŋkɪ; 'hel,sɪŋkɪ/ 赫尔辛基。
Helvetia /hel'viːʃə; hel'viʃə/ 海尔维希亚。
Henan /hɜː'næn; 'hɜˈnæn/ 河南。
Hendon /'hendən; 'hendən/ 亨顿。
Heng Shan /'hʌŋ 'ʃɑːn; 'hʌŋ 'ʃan/ 衡山。
Hereford and Worcester /,herɪfəd n 'wustə(r); ,herəfəd
n 'wustə/ 赫里福德伍斯特。
Herefordshire /'herɪfədʃə(r); 'herəfəd,ʃɪr/ 赫里福德郡。

Hermon, Mount /'hɜ:mən; 'hɝmən/ 赫尔蒙山。
Hertfordshire /'hɑ:(t)fədʃə(r); 'hɑrfəd,ʃɪr/ 赫特福德郡。
Hessen /'hesɪ; 'hesɪ/ 黑森。
Highland /'haɪlənd; 'haɪlənd/ 苏格兰高地。
Himalaya(s), The /ˌhɪmə'leɪə(z); ˌhɪmə'leə(z)/ 喜马拉雅山脉。
Hindustan, Hindostan /ˌhɪndʊ'stæn; ˌhɪndʊ'stæn/ 印度斯坦。
Hiroshima /hi:rəʊ'ʃi:mə; ˌhɪrə'ʃimə/ 广岛。
Hobart /'həʊbɑ:t; 'ho,bɑrt/ 霍巴特。
Hoboken /'həʊ,bəʊkən; 'ho,bokən/ 霍博肯。
Ho Chi Minh City /'həʊ tʃi: ˌmɪn-; 'ho tʃi ˌmɪn-/ 胡志明市。
Hokkaido /hɒ'kaɪdəʊ; hɑ'kaɪdo/ 北海道。
Holland /'hɒlənd; 'hɑlənd/ 荷兰。
Hollywood /'hɒlɪwʊd; 'hɑlɪ,wʊd/ 好莱坞。
Holyoke /'həʊljəʊk; 'hol,jok/ 霍利奥克。
Holy See 教廷。
Honduras /hɒn'djʊərəs; hɑn'd(j)ʊrəs/ 洪都拉斯。
Hong Kong, Hongkong /ˌhɒŋ'kɒŋ; 'hɑŋ,kɑŋ/ 香港。
Honiara /ˌhəʊni:'ɑ:rə; ˌhoni'ɑrə/ 霍尼亚拉。
Honolulu /ˌhɒnə'lu:lu:; ˌhɑnə'lulu/ 檀香山。
Honshu /'hɒnʃu:; 'hɑnʃu/ 本州。
Hood, Mount /hʊd; hʊd/ 胡德峰。
Hornsey /'hɔ:nzɪ; 'hɔrnzɪ/ 霍恩西。
Hua Shan /'huɑ: 'ʃɑ:n; 'huɑ 'ʃɑn/ 华山。
Huai He /'huai 'hɜ:; 'huai 'hɝ/ 淮河。
Huang Hai /'huɑ:ŋ hai; 'huɑŋ hai/ 黄海。
Huang He /'huɑ:ŋ 'hɜ:; 'huɑŋ 'hɝ/ 黄河。
Huascarán /ˌwɑ:skɑ:'rɑ:n; ˌwaskə'rɑn/ 瓦斯卡兰山。
Hubei /'hu:'bei; 'hu'bei /湖北。
Huddersfield /'hʌdəzfi:ld; 'hʌdəz,fild/ 哈德斯菲尔德。
Hudson /'hʌdsn; 'hʌdsn̩/ 哈得孙河。
Hue, Hué /hju:'eɪ; hju'e/ 顺化。
Huhehaote /'hu:hə'hau'tɜ:; 'huhə'haʊ'tɝ/ 呼和浩特。
Huila /'wi:lɑ:; 'wilɑ/ 乌伊拉火山。
Hull /hʌl; hʌl/ 赫尔。
Humberside /'hʌmbəsaɪd; 'hʌmbə,said/ 亨伯赛德。
Hunan /'hu:'nɑ:n; 'hu'nɑn/ 湖南。
Hungary /'hʌŋgərɪ; 'hʌŋg(ə)rɪ/ 匈牙利。
Huntingdon /'hʌntɪŋdən; 'hʌntɪŋdən/ 亨廷顿。
Huntingdonshire /'hʌntɪŋdənʃə(r); 'hʌntɪŋdən,ʃɪr/ 亨廷顿郡。
Huron, Lake /'hjʊərn; 'hjʊrən/ 休伦湖。
Hyderabad /'haɪdrə,bæd; 'haɪdərə,bæd/ 海得拉巴。
Iberia /aɪ'bɪərɪə; aɪ'bɪrɪə/ 伊比利亚半岛。
Iceland /'aɪslənd; 'aɪslənd/ 冰岛。
Ida /'aɪdə; 'aɪdə/ 伊季山。
Idaho /'aɪdəhəʊ; 'aɪdə,ho/ 爱达荷。
Igarka /ɪ'gɑ:kə; ɪ'gɑrkə/ 伊加尔卡。
Illampu /ɪ'jɑ:mpu:; ɪ'jampu/ 伊延普山。
Illinois /ˌɪlə'nɔɪ; ˌɪlə'nɔɪ/ 伊利诺伊。
Incahuasi /ˌi:ŋkɑ:'wɑ:sɪ; ˌɪŋkə'wɑsɪ/ 英加瓦锡山。
Inchon /'ɪn,tʃɒn; 'ɪn,tʃɑn/ 仁川。
India /'ɪndɪə; 'ɪndɪə/ 印度。
Indiana /ˌɪndɪ'ænə; ˌɪndɪ'ænə/ 印第安纳。
Indianapolis /ˌɪndɪə'næpəlɪs; ˌɪndɪə'næp(ə)ləs/ 印第安纳波利斯。
Indian Ocean /'ɪndjən 'əʊʃən; 'ɪndɪən 'oʃən/ 印度洋。
Indochina /'ɪndəʊ'tʃaɪnə; 'ɪndo'tʃaɪnə/ 印度支那半岛。
Indonesia /ˌɪndə'ni:zɪə; ˌɪndə'nɪʒə/ 1 马来群岛。2 印度尼西亚。
Indore /ɪn'dɔ:(r); ɪn'dor/ 印多尔。
Indus /'ɪndəs; 'ɪndəs/ 印度河。
Innsbruck /'ɪnzbrʊk; 'ɪnz,brʊk/ 因斯布鲁克。
Inverness-shire /ˌɪnvə'neʃə(r); ˌɪnvɚ'nɛs,ʃɪr/ 因弗内斯郡。
Iona /aɪ'əʊnə; aɪ'onə/ 爱奥那岛。
Ionia /aɪ'əʊnjə; aɪ'onɪə/ 爱奥尼亚。
Iowa /'aɪəwə; 'aɪəwə/ 衣阿华。
Iowa City 衣阿华城。
Ipoh /'i:pəʊ; 'ipo/ 怡保。
Ipswich /'ɪpswɪtʃ; 'ɪpswɪtʃ/ 伊普斯威奇。
Iran /ɪ'rɑ:n; ɪ'ræn/ 伊朗。
Iraq, Irak/ ɪ'rɑ:k; ɪ'rɑk/ 伊拉克。
Ireland /'aɪələnd; 'aɪrlənd/ 1 爱尔兰岛。2 爱尔兰共和国。
Irish Republic = Eire
Irkutsk /ɜ:'ku:tsk; ɪr'kutsk/ 伊尔库茨克。
Irrawaddy /ˌɪrə'wɒdɪ; ˌɪrə'wadɪ/ 伊洛瓦底江。
Ischia /'ɪskɪə; 'ɪskɪə/ 伊斯其亚岛。
Islamabad /ɪs'lɑ:məbɒ:d; ɪs'lamə,bad/ 伊斯兰堡。
Isle of Wight /ˌaɪl əv 'waɪt; ˌaɪl əv 'waɪt/ 威特岛。
Israel /'ɪzreɪl; 'ɪzrɪəl/ 以色列。
Istanbul /ˌɪstæn'bu:l; ˌɪstəm'bul/ 伊斯坦布尔。
Italy /'ɪtəlɪ; 'ɪtl̩ɪ/ 意大利。
Ivanovo /ɪ'vɑ:nəvə; ɪ'vɑnəvə/ 伊万诺沃。
Ivory Coast 象牙海岸。
Izmir /ɪz'mɪə(r); ɪz'mɪr/ 伊兹密尔。
Iztaccihuatl /ˌi:stɑ:k'si:wɑ:tl; ˌistɑk'si,wɑtl̩/ 伊斯塔西瓦脱山。
Jackson /'dʒæksn; 'dʒæksn̩/ 杰克逊。
Jadotville /ˌʒɑ:ˌdəʊ'vi:l; ˌʒædo'vil/ 雅多维尔。
Jaipur /dʒaɪ'pʊə(r); 'dʒaɪ,pʊr/ 斋浦尔。
Jakarta, Djakarta /dʒə'kɑ:tə; dʒə'kɑrtə/ 雅加达。
Jamaica /dʒə'meɪkə; dʒə'mekə /牙买加。
James /dʒeɪmz; dʒemz/ 詹姆斯河。
Jamshedpur /'dʒɑ:mʃed,pʊə; 'dʒɑm,ʃed,pʊr/ 贾姆谢德布尔。
Japan /dʒə'pæn; dʒə'pæn/ 日本。
Japan, Sea of 日本海。
Japurá /ˌʒɑ:pu:'rɑ:; ˌʒɑpə'rɑ/ 雅普拉河。
Jarvis (或 **Jervis**) **Island** /'dʒɑ:vɪs; 'dʒɑrvəs/ 贾维斯岛。
Jassy /'dʒæsɪ; 'jɑsɪ/ 雅西。
Java /'dʒɑ:və; 'dʒɑvə/ 爪哇。
Jefferson City /'dʒefəsn-; 'dʒɛfəsn̩-/ 杰斐逊城。
Jena /'jeɪnə; 'jenə/ 耶拿。
Jervis Bay /'dʒɑ:vɪs-; 'dʒɑrvəs-/ 查维斯湾
Jesselton /'dʒesltən; 'dʒɛsl̩tən/ 亚庇。
Jiangsu /'dʒɑ:ŋ'su:; 'dʒɑŋ'su/ 江苏。
Jiangxi /'dʒɑ:ŋ'ʃi; 'dʒɑŋ'ʃi/ 江西。
Jibuti = Djibouti.
Jilin /'dʒi:'lin; 'dʒi'lin/ 吉林。
Jinan /'dʒi:'nɑ:n; 'dʒi'nɑn/ 济南。
Jinsen /'dʒɪnsen; 'dʒɪn,sɛn/ 仁川。
Johannesburg /dʒəʊ'hænɪsbɜ:g; dʒo'hænɪs,bɝg/ 约翰内斯堡。
Johore /dʒəʊ'hɔ:(r); dʒə'hor/ 柔佛。
Jönköping /'jɜ:n,tʃɜ:pɪŋ; 'jɝn,tʃɝpɪŋ/ 延雪平。
Jordan /'dʒɔ:dn; 'dʒɔrdn̩/ 约旦。
Julian Alps /'dʒu:ljən-; 'dʒuljən-/ 尤利安山。
Jungfrau /'jʊŋ,fraʊ; 'jʊŋ,fraʊ/ 少女峰。
Juruá /ʒu:'rwɑ:; ʒʊ'rwɑ/ 茹鲁阿河。
Kabul /'kɔ:bl; 'kɑbul/ 喀布尔。
Kalahari Desert /ˌkɑ:lɑ:'hɑ:rɪ-; ˌkælə'hɑrɪ-/ 卡拉哈里沙漠。
Kalgoorlie /kæl'gʊəlɪ; kæl'gʊrlɪ/ 卡尔古利。
Kaliningrad /kə'li:ngræd; kə'linən,græd/ 加里宁格勒。
Kama /'kɑ:mə; 'kɑmə/ 卡马河。
Kamchatka Peninsula /kæm'tʃætkə-; kæm'tʃætkə-/ 堪察加半岛。
Kampala /kɑ:m'pɑ:lə; kɑm'pɑlə/ 坎帕拉。
Kampuchea /kæmpʊ'tʃɪə; ˌkæmpə'tʃɪə/ 柬埔寨。
Kanchenjunga /ˌkʌntʃən'dʒʌŋgə; ˌkæntʃən'dʒʌŋgə/ 干城章嘉峰。
Kansas /'kænzəs; 'kænzəs/ 堪萨斯。
Kaohsiung /'gaʊ'ʃiʊŋ; 'gaʊʃɪ'ʊŋ/ 高雄市。
Karachi /kə'rɑ:tʃɪ; kə'rɑtʃɪ/ 卡拉奇。
Karaganda /ˌkɑ:rɑ:gɑ:n'dɑ:; ˌkɑrəgən'dɑ/ 卡拉干达。
Karakoram Range /ˌkærə'kɔ:rəm-; ˌkærə'korəm-/ 喀拉昆仑山脉。
Kariba /kə'ri:bə; kə'ribə/ 卡里巴水库。
Kashmir /kæʃ'mɪə(r); 'kæʃ,mɪr/ 克什米尔。
Katahdin, Mount /kə'tɑ:dɪn; kə'tɑdn/ 克大定山。

Katanga /kəˈtɑːŋgə; kəˈtɑŋgə/ 加丹加。
Katar = Qatar
Kat(h)mandu, Khatmandu /ˌkɑːtmɑːˈnduː; ˌkæt,mænˈdu/ 加德满都。
Katowice /ˌkɑːtɒˈviːtsæ; ˌkɑtəˈvitsə/ 卡托维兹。
Kawaikini /ˌkɑːwaɪˈkiːnɪ; ˌkɑwaɪˈkini/ 加外基尼山。
Kazak(h)stan /ˌkɑːzɑːkˈstɑːn; kə,zækˈstæn/ 哈萨克。
Kazbek, Kasbek /kʌzˈbjek; kɑzˈbek/ 卡兹别克山。
Kebnekaise /ˌkebnəˈkaɪsə; ˌkebnəˈkaɪsə/ 凯布讷山。
Keelung /ˈkiːluŋ; ˈkiˈluŋ/ 基隆。
Keewatin /kiˈweɪtɪn; kiˈwetɪn/ 基威廷。
Keighley /ˈkiːθlɪ; ˈkiθli/ 基思利。
Kelantan /kəˈlæntən; kəˈlæn,tæn/ 吉兰丹。
Kent /kent; kent/ 肯特。
Kentucky /kenˈtʌkɪ; kenˈtʌki/ 肯塔基。
Kenya /ˈkenjə; ˈkenjə/ 肯尼亚。
Kerch /keətʃ; kertʃ/ 刻赤。
Kerguelen /ˈkɜːgiːlɪn; ˈkɜgələn/ 凯尔盖朗群岛。
Kerintji /kəˈrɪntjɪ; kəˈrɪntʃi/ 克林季山。
Kerry /ˈkerɪ; ˈkeri/ 凯里。
Kew /kjuː; kju/ 克佑。
Key West /ˈkiːˈwest; ˈkiˈwest/ 基韦斯特。
Khabarovsk /kəˈbɑːrəfsk; kəˈbɑrəfsk/ 哈巴罗夫斯克(伯力)。
Kharkov /ˈkɑːkɔːf; ˈkɑr,kɒf/ 哈尔科夫。
Khart(o)um /kɑːˈtuːm; kɑrˈtum/ 喀土穆。
Khyber Pass /ˈkaɪbə-; ˈkaɪbə-/ 开伯尔山口。
Kiel /kiːl; kil/ 基尔。
Kielce /ˈkjeltse; kɪˈeltse/ 凯尔采。
Kiev, Kiyev /ˈkiːev; ˈki,(j)ef/ 基辅。
Kigali /kɪˈgɑːlɪ; kɪˈgɑli/ 基加利。
Kildare /kɪlˈdeə(r); kɪlˈdɛr/ 基尔代尔。
Kilimanjaro /ˌkɪlɪmənˈdʒɑːrəʊ; ˌkɪləmənˈdʒɑro/ 乞力马扎罗山。
Kilkenny /kɪlˈkenɪ; kɪlˈkeni/ 基尔肯尼。
Kimberley /ˈkɪmbəlɪ; ˈkɪmbəli/ 金伯利。
Kinabalu, Kinabulu /ˌkɪnəbəˈluː; ˌkɪnəbəˈlu/ 基纳巴卢。
Kincardineshire /kɪnˈkɑːdɪnʃə(r); kɪnˈkɑrdɪn,ʃɪr/ 金卡丁郡。
Kings Peak /kɪŋz-; kɪŋz-/ 京斯峰。
Kingston /ˈkɪŋstən; ˈkɪŋstən/ 金斯敦。
Kingstown /ˈkɪŋstaʊn; ˈkɪŋ,staʊn/ 金斯敦。
Kinross-shire /kɪnˈrɒʃə(r); kɪnˈrɔ,ʃɪr/ 金罗斯。
Kinshasa /kɪnˈʃɑːsə; kɪnˈʃɑsə/ 金沙萨。
Kintyre /kɪnˈtaɪə(r); kɪnˈtaɪr/ 琴泰半岛。
Kirg(h)iz Republic /kəˈgiːz-; kɪrˈgiz-/ 吉尔吉斯。
Kiribati /ˌkɪərəˈbɑːs; ˈkɪrə,bæs/ 基里巴斯。
Kirkcudbrightshire /kəˈkuːbrɪʃə(r); kəˈkubrɪ,ʃɪr/ 柯尔库布里郡。
Kirkpatrick, Mount /kəkˈpætrɪk; ˌkɜkˈpætrɪk/ 柯克帕特里克峰。
Kirkuk /kɪəˈkuːk; kɪrˈkuk/ 基尔库克。
Kitchener /ˈkɪtʃɪnə(r); ˈkɪtʃ(ə)nə/ 基奇纳。
Kjölen Mts. /ˈtʃɜːlən; ˈtʃɜlən/ 舍伦山脉。
Klondike /ˈklɒndaɪk; ˈklɑn,daɪk/ 克朗代克。
Klyuchevskaya /kljuːˈtʃefskəjə; klɪʊˈtʃefskəjə/ 克留切夫斯克山。
Kobe /ˈkəʊbɪ; ˈkobi/ 神户。
Kokand /kəʊˈkænd; koˈkænd/ 浩罕。
Kola /ˈkəʊlə; ˈkolə/ 科拉半岛。
Kolyma, Kolima /kəʊˈliːmə; kəˈlimə/ 科雷马河。
Komsomolsk /ˈkɒmsəˈmɔːlsk; ˌkɑmsəˈmɔlsk/ 共青城。
Korea /kəˈrɪə; koˈriə/ 朝鲜。
Kosciusko, Mount /ˌkɒsɪˈʌskəʊ; ˌkɑzɪˈʌsko/ 科西阿斯科峰。
Kowait = Kuwait
Kowloon /ˈkaʊˈluːn; ˈkaʊˈlun/ 九龙。
Krasnovodsk /ˈkræsnəvɒdsk; ˌkræsnəˈvɒtsk/ 克拉斯诺夫斯克。
Krasnoyarsk /ˈkræsnəjɑːsk; ˌkræsnəˈjɑrsk/ 克拉斯诺雅茨克。
Kristiansand /ˈkrɪstjənˌsænd; ˈkrɪstjənˌsænd/ 克里斯蒂安桑。

Krivoi (或 **Krivoy**) **Rog** /ˈkrɪvɔɪˈrəʊg; ˌkrɪvɔɪˈrog/ 克里沃罗格。
Krons(h)tadt /ˈkrɒnstæt; kronˌstæt/ 喀琅施塔得。
Kuala Lumpur /ˌkwɑːləˈlʊmpʊə(r); ˌkwɑləˈlʊmpʊr/ 吉隆坡。
Kuching /ˈkuːtʃɪŋ; ˈkutʃɪn/ 古晋。
Kuibyshev, kuybyshev /ˈkwiːbɪʃef; ˈkwibə,ʃəf/ 古比雪夫。
Kunlun /ˈkuənˈluən; ˈkuənˈluən/ 昆仑山脉。
Kunming /ˈkuənˈmɪŋ; ˈkuənˈmɪŋ/ 昆明。
Kursk /kuəsk; kʊrsk/ 库尔斯克。
Kuwait, Kuweit, Kowait /kuˈweit; kəˈwet/ 科威特。
Kuznetsk /kuzˈnetsk; kʊzˈnetsk/ 库兹涅茨克。
Kyoto /ˈkjəʊtəʊ; kiˈoto/ 京都。
Kyushu /ˈkjuːʃuː; kiˈuʃu/ 九州。
Labrador /ˈlæbrədɔː(r); ˈlæbrə,dor/ 拉布拉多。
Labuan /ləˈbuːən; leˈbuən/ 纳闽岛。
Laccadive Islands /ˈlækədaɪv-; ˈlækə,dɪv-/ 拉克代夫群岛。
Lachlan /ˈlæklən; ˈlɑklən/ 拉克伦河。
Ladoga /ˈlɑːdəʊgə; ˈlædəgə/ 拉多加湖。
Lagos /ˈleɪgɒs; ˈle,gɑs/ 拉各斯。
La Guaira /ləˈgwaɪrə; ləˈgwaɪrə/ 拉古纳。
Lahore /ləˈhɔː(r); ləˈhor/ 拉合尔。
Lanarkshire /ˈlænəkʃə(r); ˈlænək,ʃɪr/ 拉纳克郡。
Lancashire /ˈlæŋkəʃə(r); ˈlæŋkə,ʃɪr/ 兰开夏郡。
Langson, Lang Son /ˈlæŋˈsɒn; ˈlæŋˈsɑn/ 谅山。
Lanzhou /ˈlɑːnˈdʒəʊ; ˈlɑnˈdʒəʊ/ 兰州。
Laos /ˈlɑːɒs; laʊs/ 老挝。
Lapland /ˈlæplænd; ˈlæp,lænd/ 拉普兰。
La Plata /ləˈplɑːtə; ləˈplatə/ 拉普拉塔。
Lasa /ˈlɑːsɑː; ˈlɑsɑ/ 拉萨。
La Selle /ləˈsel; ləˈsel/ 拉赛尔山脉。
Lashio /ˈləˈʃəʊ; ˈləˈʃo/ 腊戌。
Las Palmas /læsˈpælməs; ləˈspɑlməs/ 拉斯帕尔马斯。
Lassen Peak, Mount Lassen /ˈlæsn-; ˈlæsn/ 拉孙火山。
Las Vegas /lɑːsˈveɪgəs; lasˈvegəs/ 拉斯韦加斯。
Latakia /ˌlætəˈkiːə; ˌlætəˈkiə/ 拉塔基亚。
Latium /ˈleɪʃəm; ˈleʃəm/ 拉丁姆。
Latvia /ˈlætvɪə; ˈlætvɪə/ 拉脱维亚。
Lausanne /ləʊˈzæn; loˈzan/ 洛桑。
Lawrence /ˈlɒrəns; ˈlɔrəns/ 劳伦斯。
Lebanon /ˈlebənən; ˈlebənən/ 黎巴嫩。
Leeds /liːdz; lidz/ 利兹。
Leghorn /ˈleɡˈhɔːn; ˈlɛg,hɔrn/ 莱戈恩。
(Le) Havre /ləˈhɑːvə(r); ləˈhavə/ 勒阿弗尔。
Leicester /ˈlestə(r); ˈlestə/ 莱斯特。
Leicestershire /ˈlestə(r); ˈlestə,ʃɪr/ 莱斯特郡。
Leinster /ˈlenstə(r); ˈlenstə/ 伦斯特。
Leipzig /ˈlaɪpzɪg; ˈlæɪpsɪg/ 莱比锡。
Leitrim /ˈliːtrɪm; ˈlitrəm/ 利特里姆。
Leix, Laoighis /liːʃ; leɪʃ/ 雷斯。
Lena /ˈliːnə; ˈlinə/ 勒拿河。
Leningrad /ˈleningræd; ˈlenən,græd/ 列宁格勒。
Léopoldville /ˈlɪəpəʊldvɪl; ˈliə,pold,vɪl/ 利奥波德维尔。
Lepontine Alps /lɪˈpɒntaɪn-; lɪˈpɑn,taɪn-/ 利旁廷阿尔卑斯山。
Lesbos /ˈlezbɒs; ˈlez,bas/ 莱斯博斯岛。
Lesotho /ləˈsuːtuː; ləˈsoto/ 莱索托。
Lesser Antilles /-ænˈtɪliːz; -ænˈtɪliz/ 小安的列斯群岛。
Levant /lɪˈvænt; ləˈvænt/ 地中海东部及爱琴海沿岸的国家和岛屿。
Leven, Loch /ˈlɒkˈliːvn; ˈlakˈlivn/ 利文湖。
Lexington /ˈleksɪŋtən; ˈleksɪŋtən/ 列克星敦。
Leyton /ˈleɪtn; ˈletn/ 雷敦。
Liaoning /ˈliaʊˈnɪŋ; ˈliauˈnɪŋ/ 辽宁。
Liberia /laɪˈbɪərɪə; laɪˈbɪrɪə/ 利比里亚。
Libreville /ˈliːbrəvɪl; ˈlibrə,vɪl/ 利伯维尔。
Libya /ˈlɪbɪə; ˈlɪbɪə/ 利比亚。
Lido /ˈliːdəʊ; ˈlido/ 里度。
Liechtenstein /ˈlɪktənstaɪn; ˈlɪktən,staɪn/ 列支敦士登。
Liège /lɪˈeɪʒ; liˈeʒ/ 列日。

Lille /liːl; lil/ 里尔。
Lilongwe /liˈlɔːŋwei; lɪˈlɔŋwe/ 利隆圭。
Lima[1] /ˈliːmə; ˈlimə/ 利马。
Lima[2] /ˈlaɪmə; ˈlaɪmə/ 莱马。
Limerick /ˈlɪmərɪk; ˈlɪm(ə)rɪk/ 利默里克。
Limpopo /lɪmˈpəupəu; lɪmˈpopo/ 林波波河。
Lincolnshire /ˈlɪŋkənʃə(r); ˈlɪŋkənʃ(ə)r; ˈlɪŋkən,ʃɪr/ 林肯郡。
Lingayen Gulf /ˌlɪŋgəˈjen-; ˌlɪŋgəˈjen-/ 林加延。
Lipari Islands /ˈlɪpərɪ-; ˈlɪpəri-/ 利帕里群岛。
Lisbon /ˈlɪzbən; ˈlɪzbən/ 里斯本。
Lithuania /ˌlɪθjuˈeɪnjə; ˌlɪθ(ə)ˈwenɪə/ 立陶宛。
Little Missouri 小密苏里河。
Liverpool /ˈlɪvəpuːl; ˈlivə,pul/ 利物浦。
Locarno /ləuˈkɑːnəu; loˈkɑrno/ 罗迦诺。
Lodz /luːdʒ; ludʒ/ 罗兹。
Logan, Mount /ˈləugən; ˈlogən/ 洛根山。
Loire /ləˈwɑː(r); ləˈwɑr/ 卢瓦尔河。
Lombok /ˈlɑːm,bɑːk; ˈlam,bak/ 龙目岛。
Lomé /ˈləuˈmeɪ; loˈme/ 洛美。
Lomond, Loch /ˈləumənd; ˈlomənd/ 罗蒙德湖。
London /ˈlʌndən; ˈlʌndən/ 伦敦。
Londonderry /ˈlʌndənderɪ; ˈlʌndənˈdɛrɪ/ 伦敦德里。
Longford /ˈlɒŋfəd US: ˈlɔːŋ-; ˈlɒŋfəd/ 朗福德。
Longs Peak /ˈlɒŋz-; ˈlɔŋz-/ 朗斯峰。
Lorain /ləˈreɪn; ləˈren/ 洛雷恩。
Lorne, Firth of /lɔːn; lɔrn/ 罗恩湾。
Lorraine /ləˈreɪn; ləˈren/ 洛林。
Los Angeles /lɒsˈændʒɪliːs; lɔsˈændʒələs/ 洛杉矶。
Lost River Range 迷河山脉。
Lothian /ˈləuðɪən; ˈloðɪən/ 洛锡安。
Louisiana /luːˌiːzɪˈænə; luˌizɪˈænə/ 路易斯安那。
Lourenco Marques /ləˈrensəuˈmɑːk; ləˌrensoˌmɑrˈkɛs/ 洛伦索-马贵斯。
Louth /lauð; lauð/ 劳斯。
Lowell /ˈləuəl; ˈloəl/ 洛厄尔。
Luanda /luːˈɑːndə; luˈɑndə/ 罗安达。
Luang Prabang /luˌɑːŋprəˈbɑːŋ; luˌɑŋprəˈbɑŋ/ 琅勃拉邦。
Lübeck /ˈluːbek; ˈluˌbɛk/ 吕贝克。
Lublin /ˈluːblɪn; ˈlublən/ 卢布林。
Lubumbashi /ˌluːbuːmˈbɑːʃiː; ˌlubumˈbaʃi/ 卢本巴希。
Lucerne /luːˈsɜːn; luˈsɚn/ 卢塞恩。
Lucknow /ˈlʌknau; ˈlʌk,nau/ 勒克脑。
Luleå /ˈluːləˌəu; ˈluləˌo/ 吕勒奥。
Lusaka /luːˈsɑːkə; luˈsɑke/ 卢萨卡。
Luton /ˈluːtn; ˈlutn/ 卢顿。
Luxemb(o)urg /ˈlʌksəmbɜːg; ˈlʌksəm,bɝg/ 卢森堡。
Luzon /luːˈzɒn; luˈzɑn/ 吕宋岛。
Lydia /ˈlɪdɪə; ˈlɪdɪə/ 吕底亚。
Lynn /lɪn; lɪn/ 林恩。
Lyons /ˈlaɪənz; ˈlaɪənz/ 里昂。
Maas /mɑːs; mɑs/ 马斯河。
Macao, Macau /məˈkəu; məˈkəu/ 澳门。
Macassar, Maka(s)sar /məˈkæsə(r); məˈkæsə/ 望加西。
Mackenzie /məˈkenzɪ; məˈkenzɪ/ 马更些。
Madagascar /ˌmædəˈgæskə(r); ˌmædəˈgæskə/ 马达加斯加。
Madeira /məˈdɪərə; məˈdɪrə/ 1 马德拉群岛。2 马代拉河。
Madras /məˈdræs; məˈdræs/ 马德拉斯。
Madrid /məˈdrɪd; məˈdrɪd/ 马德里。
Madura /ˈmædjurə; məˈdurə/ 马都拉岛。
Maebashi, Mayebashi /maɪˈjeˈbaːʃɪ; ˌmaɪeˈbaʃɪ/ 前桥。
Mafeking /ˈmæfɪkɪŋ; ˈmæfəkɪŋ/ 马弗京。
Magdalen /ˈmægdəlɪn; ˈmægdələn/ 马达兰群岛。
Magdalena /ˌmægdəˈleɪnə; ˌmægdəˈlenə/ 马格达莱纳河。
Magdeburg /ˈmægdəbɜːg; ˈmægdə,bɝg/ 马格德堡。
Magellan, Strait of /məˈgelən; məˈdʒelən/ 麦哲伦海峡。
Maggiore, Lake /ˌmædʒɪˈɔːrɪ; məˈdʒorɪ/ 马焦雷湖。
Magnitogorsk /mægˈniːtə,gɒsk; mægˈnɪtə,gɔrsk/ 马格尼托哥尔斯克。

Maidstone /ˈmeɪdstən; ˈmedstən/ 梅德斯通。
Maikop /maɪˈkɒp; maɪˈkɔp/ 迈科普。
Maine /meɪn; men/ 缅因。
Mainz /maɪnts; maɪntbs/ 美因茨。
Majorca /məˈdʒɔːkə; məˈdʒɔrkə/ 马略尔卡岛。
Makalu /ˈmʌkəlu; ˈmʌkə,lu/ 马卡卢峰。
Malabar Coast /ˌmæləˈbɑː-; ˌmæləˌbɑr-/ 马拉巴尔海岸。
Malabo /ˈmɑːlaːbəu; mɑˈlabo/ 马拉博。
Malacca, Malakka /məˈlækə; məˈlækə/ 马六甲。
Malacca, Strait of 马六甲海峡。
Málaga /ˈmæləgə; ˈmæləgə/ 马拉加。
Malagasy Republic /ˌmæləˈgæsɪ-; ˌmæləˈgæsɪ-/ 马拉加西共和国。
Malakka = Malacca
Malawi /məˈlɑːwɪ; məˈlawi/ 马拉维。
Malaya /məˈleɪə; məˈleə/ 马来亚。
Malay Archipelago /məˈleɪ-; məˈle-/ 马来群岛。
Malaysia, (Federation of) /məˈleɪzɪə; məˈleʒ(ɪ)ə/ 马来西亚。
Maldives /ˈmældaɪvz; ˈmɔl,dɪvz/ 马尔代夫。
Male /ˈmɑːleɪ; ˈmalɪ/ 马累。
Mali /ˈmɑːlɪ; ˈmalɪ/ 马里。
Malmö /ˈmælmə; ˈmæl,mə/ 马尔默。
Malta /ˈmɔːltə; ˈmɔltə/ 马耳他。
Man, Isle of /ˈmæn; ˈmæn/ 马恩岛。
Managua /məˈnɑːgwə; məˈnɑgwə/ 马那瓜。
Manama /məˈnæmə; məˈnæmə/ 麦纳麦。
Manaus /məˈnəus; məˈnəus/ 马瑙斯。
Manchester /ˈmæntʃɪstə(r); ˈmæn,tʃestə/ 曼彻斯特。
Mandalay /ˈmændəˈleɪ; ˈmændəˈle/ 瓦城。
Manhattan /mænˈhætn; mænˈhætn/ 1 曼哈顿岛。2 曼哈顿区。
Manila /məˈnɪlə; məˈnɪlə/ 马尼拉。
Manitoba /ˌmænɪˈtəubə; ˌmænɪˈtobə/ 马尼托巴。
Mannheim /ˈmænhaɪm; ˈmænə,haɪm/ 曼海姆。
Mansfield /ˈmænsfiːld; ˈmæns,fild/ 曼斯菲尔德。
Mantua /ˈmæntjuə; ˈmæntʃ(ə)wə/ 曼图亚。
Maputo /məˈpuːtəu; məˈputo/ 马普托。
Maracaibo /ˌmærəˈkaɪbəu; ˌmærəˈkaɪbo/ 马拉开波。
Marañón /ˌmɑːrɑːˈnjɔːn; ˌmɑrəˈnjon/ 马拉尼翁。
Marcus Island /ˈmɑːkəs-; ˈmɑrkəs-/ 马尔库斯岛。
Marcy, Mount /ˈmɑːsɪ; ˈmɑrsɪ/ 马西山。
Mariana Islands /ˌmeərɪˈænə-; ˌmɛrɪˈænə-/ 马里亚纳群岛。
(Marie) Byrd Land /məˌriːˈbɜːd-; məˌriˈbɝd-/ 玛丽·伯德地。
Maritime Territory 沿海州。
Markham, Mount /ˈmɑːkəm; ˈmɑrkəm/ 马坎山。
Marlborough /ˈmɑːlbrə; ˈmɑrl,bərə/ 莫尔伯勒。
Marguesas Islands /mɑːˈkeɪsæs-; mɑrˈkezəz-/ 马克萨斯群岛。
Marsala /mɑːˈsɑːlə; mɑrˈsalə/ 马尔萨拉。
Marseilles /mɑːˈseɪlz; mɑrˈsedz/ 马赛。
Marshall Islands /ˈmɑːʃəl-; ˈmɑrʃəl-/ 马绍尔群岛。
Martha's Vineyard /ˈmɑːθəz-; ˈmɑrθez-/ 马撒葡萄园岛。
Martinique /ˌmɑːtɪˈniːk; ˌmɑrtɪˈik/ 马提尼克岛。
Maryland /ˈmeərɪlənd; ˈmerələnd/ 马里兰。
Maseru /ˈmæzəruː; ˈmæzə,ru/ 马塞卢。
Maskat, Masqat = Muscat
Massachusetts /ˌmæsəˈtʃuːsɪts; ˌmæs(ə)ˈtʃusets/ 马萨诸塞。
Massive, Mount /ˌmæsɪv; ˈmæsɪv/ 马西梧山。
Matterhorn /ˈmætəhɔːn; ˈmætə,hɔrn/ 马特峰。
Mauga Sili /ˈmaugəˈsiːlɪ; ˌmaugəˈsilɪ/ 莫加希里山。
Mauna Kea /ˈmaunə-ˈkeɪə; ˌmaunə-ˈkeə/ 莫纳克亚山。
Mauna Loa /ˈmaunə-ˈləuə; ˌmaunə-ˈloə/ 冒内罗亚火山。
Mauritania /ˌmɒrɪˈteɪnɪə; ˌmɔrəˈtenɪə/ 毛里塔尼亚。
Mauritius /məˈrɪʃəs; məˈrɪʃəs/ 毛里求斯。
Mayo /ˈmeɪəu; ˈmeo/ 梅奥。
Mbabane /mbɑːˈbɑːn; ˌəmbeˈban/ 姆巴巴内。
Mckinley, Mount /məˈkɪnlɪ; məˈkɪnlɪ/ 麦金利山。
M'clure Strait /məˈkluə-; məˈklur-/ 麦克卢尔海峡。
Meath /miːθ; mɪð/ 米斯。

Mecca, Mekka /'mekə; 'mɛkə/ 麦加。
Medina /mə'di:nə; mə'dinə/ 麦地那。
Mediterranean (Sea) /ˌmedɪtə'reɪnjən; ˌmɛdətə'renɪən/ 地中海。
Mekong /'meɪkɒŋ; 'me'kɔŋ/ 湄公河。
Melanesia /ˌmelə'ni:ʒə; ˌmɛlə'niʒə/ 美拉尼西亚。
Melbourne /'melbən; 'mɛlbən/ 墨尔本。
Memphis /'memfɪs; 'mɛmfəs/ 孟菲斯。
Menai Strait /'menaɪ-; 'mɛn,aɪ-/ 麦奈海峡。
Me Nam, Menam /me'na:m; me'nam/ 湄南河。
Mendoza /men'dəʊzə; mɛn'dozə/ 门多萨。
Mercedario /ˌmeəsə'da:rɪəʊ; ˌmɛrsə'dorɪo/ 麻塞达里欧山。
Merionethshire /ˌmerɪ'ɒnɪθ(ə)r; ˌmɛrɪ'anəθ,ʃɪr/ 麦立昂斯夏。
Meroë /'merəʊɪ; 'mɛrə,wɪ/ 梅罗伊。
Merseyside /'mɜːzɪsaɪd; 'mɜzɪ,saɪd/ 默西塞德。
Merthyr Tydfil /'mɜːθə'tɪdvɪl; 'mɜθə 'tɪd,vɪl/ 梅瑟蒂德菲尔。
Meshed /'meʃed; mə'ʃed/ 麦什德。
Mesopotamia /ˌmespə'tæmjə; ˌmɛsə(ə)pə'temɪə/ 美索不达米亚。
Messina /me'si:nə; mə'sinə/ 墨西拿。
Metz /mets; mɛts/ 梅斯。
Mexico /'meksɪkəʊ; 'mɛksɪ,ko/ 墨西哥。
Mexico (City) 墨西哥城。
Mexico, Gulf of 墨西哥湾。
Miami /maɪ'æmɪ; maɪ'æmɪ/ 迈阿密。
Michigan /'mɪʃɪgən; 'mɪʃɪgən/ 密执安。
Micronesia /ˌmaɪkrə'ni:ʒə; ˌmaɪkrə'niʒə/ 密克罗尼西亚。
Middlesex /'mɪdlseks; 'mɪd],sɛks/ 米德尔塞克斯。
Mid Glamorgan 中格拉摩根。
Midlothian /mɪd'ləʊðɪən; mɪd'loðɪən/ 中洛锡安。
Midway /'mɪdweɪ; 'mɪd,we/ 中途岛。
Mieres /'mɪeɪres; mɪ'ɛrəs/ 米耶雷斯。
Milan /mɪ'læn; mə'læn/ 米兰。
Milk /mɪlk; mɪlk/ 密耳克河。
Milwaukee /mɪl'wɔ:kɪ; mɪl'wɔkɪ/ 密尔沃基。
Mindanao /ˌmɪndə'naːəʊ; ˌmɪndə'na,o/ 棉兰老。
Minneapolis /ˌmɪnɪ'æpəlɪs; ˌmɪnɪ'æp(ə)lɪs/ 明尼阿波利斯。
Minnesota /ˌmɪnɪ'səʊtə; ˌmɪnə'sotə/ 明尼苏达。
Minorca /mɪ'nɔ:kə; mə'nɔrkə/ 梅诺卡岛。
Minsk /mɪnsk; mɪnsk/ 明斯克。
Mississippi /ˌmɪsɪ'sɪpɪ; ˌmɪs(ə)'sɪpɪ/ 密西西比。
Missouri /mɪ'zʊərɪ; mə'zurɪ/ 密苏里。
Mitchell, Mount /'mɪtʃl; 'mɪtʃəl/ 米切尔山。
Mobile /'məʊbi:l; mo'bil/ 莫比尔。
Mogadishu /ˌmɒgə'dɪʃu; ˌmagə'dɪʃu/ 摩加迪沙。
Moldavia /mɒl'deɪvjə; mal'devɪə/ 摩尔达维亚。
Molokai /ˌməʊlə'kaɪ; ˌmalə'kaɪ/ 莫洛凯岛。
Molotov /'mɒːlətɔːf; 'malə,tɔf/ 莫洛托夫。
Moluccas /mə'lʌkəz; mə'lʌkəz/ 摩鹿加群岛。
Mombasa /mɒm'bæsə; mam'basə/ 蒙巴萨。
Monaco /'mɒnəkəʊ; 'manə,ko/ 摩纳哥。
Monaghan /'mɒnəhən; 'manəhən/ 莫纳亨。
Mongolia /mɒŋ'gəʊlɪə; maŋ'golɪə/ 蒙古。
Monmouthshire /'mɒnməθ(ə)r; 'manməθ,ʃɪr/ 蒙茅斯郡。
Monrovia /mən'rəʊvɪə; mən'rovɪə/ 蒙罗维亚。
Montana /mɒn'tænə; man'tænə/ 蒙大拿。
Monte Carlo /ˌmɒntɪ'ka:ləʊ; ˌmantɪ'karlo/ 蒙特卡罗。
Montenegro /ˌmɒntɪ'ni:grəʊ; ˌmantə'nigro/ 黑山。
Montevideo /ˌmɒntɪvɪ'deɪəʊ; ˌmantəvə'deo/ 蒙得维的亚。
Montgomeryshire /mənt'gʌmrɪʃə(r); mən(t)'gʌm(ə)rɪ,ʃɪr/ 蒙哥马利郡。
Montmartre /mɔ̃'ma:tə; mɔ̃'martə/ 蒙马特区。
Montpelier /mɒnt'pi:lɪə; mant'pilɪə/ 蒙彼利埃。
Montreal /ˌmɒntrɪ'ɔ:l; ˌmantrɪ'ɔl/ 蒙特利尔。
Montserrat /ˌmɒntsə'ræt; ˌman(t)sə'ræt/ 蒙特塞拉特。
Morava /'mɒrəvə; 'morəvə/ 摩拉瓦。
Morayshire /'mʌrɪʃə(r); 'mʌrɪ,ʃɪr/ 莫里郡。
Morocco /mə'rɒkəʊ; mə'rako/ 摩洛哥。

Moroni /mə'rɒnɪ; mə'ronɪ/ 莫罗尼。
Moscow /'mɒskəʊ; 'masko/ 莫斯科。
Mosul /'məʊsl; 'mosl/ 摩苏尔。
Moulmein /'mul'meɪn; mul'men/ 毛淡棉。
Mozambique /ˌməʊzæm'bi:k; ˌmozəm'bik/ 莫桑比克。
Mulhacén /ˌmu:lɒ'seɪn; ˌmulɑ'sen/ 穆拉森山。
Munich /'mju:nɪk; 'mjunɪk/ 慕尼黑。
Munster /'mʌnstə(r); 'mʌnslə/ 蒙斯特。
Murchison /'mɜ:tʃɪsn; 'mɜtʃəsn/ 默奇森河。
Murmansk /'mɜ:mɑ:nsk; mə'mænsk/ 摩尔曼斯克。
Murray /'mʌrɪ; 'mɜɪ/ 墨累河。
Musala /mu:'sɑ:lɑ:; ˌmusɑ'lɑ/ 穆萨拉峰。
Muscat /'mʌskət; 'mʌs,kæt/ 马斯喀特。
Mycenae /maɪ'si:ni:; maɪ'sini/ 迈锡尼。
Myitkyina /'mjɪtʃi:'nɑ:; mɪtʃɪ'no/ 密支那。
Mytilene /ˌmɪtɪ'li:ni; ˌmɪtl'ini/ 米蒂利尼。
Nagasaki /ˌnægə'sɑ:kɪ; ˌnagə'sakɪ/ 长崎。
Nagoya /nɑ:'gəʊjə; nə'gɔɪə/ 名古屋。
Nagpur /'nɑ:gpʊə(r); nag,pur/ 那格浦尔。
Naha /'nɑːhɑː; 'nɑhɑ/ 那霸。
Nairnshire /'neənʃə(r); 'nɛrn,ʃɪr/ 奈恩郡。
Nairobi /naɪ'rəʊbɪ; naɪ'robɪ/ 内罗毕。
Namibia /nə'mɪbɪə; nə'mɪbɪə/ 纳米比亚。
Nanchang /'nɑːn'tʃɑːŋ; 'nɑn'tʃɑn/ 南昌。
Nancy /'nænsɪ; 'nænsɪ/ 南锡。
Nanda Devi /ˌnʌndə'devi:; ˌnʌndə'devɪ/ 楠达德维山。
Nanga Parbat /ˌnʌŋgə'pɜ:bət; ˌnʌŋgə'pɜbət/ 帕尔巴特山。
Nan Hai /'nɑ:n'haɪ; 'nɑn 'haɪ/ 南海。
Nanjing /'næn'dʒɪŋ; 'næn'dʒɪŋ/ 南京。
Nanning /'næn'nɪŋ; 'næn'nɪŋ/ 南宁。
Nantes /nænts; nænts/ 南特。
Nantucket /næn'tʌkət; næn'tʌkət/ 楠塔基特岛。
Naples /'neɪplz; 'neplz/ 那不勒斯。
Narbada /nɑ:'bʌdə; nə'bʌdə/ 纳巴达河。
Narvik /'nɑːvɪk; 'nɑrvɪk/ 纳尔维克。
Nassau /'næsɔ:; 'næs,ɔ/ 拿骚。
Natal /nə'tæl; nə'tæl/ 纳塔尔。
Nauru /ˌnɑu'ru:; nɑ'uru/ 瑙鲁。
Navarre /nə'vɑ:(r); nə'var/ 那瓦拉。
Nazareth /'næzərɪθ; 'næz(ə)rəθ/ 拿撒勒。
Ndjamena /en'dʒɑ:menə; ɛn'dʒɑmenə/ 恩贾梅纳。
Nebraska /nɪ'bræskə; nə'bræskə/ 内布拉斯加。
Negoiul /ne'gɔɪu:l; nə'gɔɪ,ul/ 内戈尤尔峰。
Negri Sembilan /'negrɪsem'bi:lən; nə,grɪsem'bilən/ 森美兰。
Negro /'neɪgrəʊ; 'negro/ 内格罗河。
Neiges, Piton des /ˌpi:'tɒn deɪ'næʒ; pɪ,tonde 'nɛʒ/ 内日峰。
Nei Menggu /'neɪ 'mʌŋ'gu:; 'ne 'maŋ'gu/ 内蒙古(自治区)。
Neisse /'naɪsə; 'naɪsə/ 奈塞河。
Nelson /'nelsn; 'nɛlsn/ 纳尔逊。
Nepal /nɪ'pɔ:l; nə'pɔl/ 尼泊尔。
Netherlands, The /'neðələndz; 'neðələn(d)z/ 荷兰。
Neva /'neɪvə; 'nivə/ 涅瓦河。
Nevada /nə'vɑ:də US: -'vædə; nə'vædə/ 内华达。
Newark /'nju:ək; 'n(j)uək/ 纽瓦克。
New Britain 新不列颠。
New Brunswick 新不伦瑞克。
New Caledonia /-ˌkælə'dəʊnjə; -ˌkælə'donjə/ 新喀里多尼亚岛。
Newcastle /'nju:ˌka:sl; 'n(j)u,kæsl/ 纽卡斯尔。
New Delhi 新德里。
New England 新英格兰。
Newfoundland /'nju:fənlənd US: 'nu:-; 'n(j)ufənlənd/ 纽芬兰。
New Guinea 新几内亚岛。
New Hampshire /-'hæmpʃə(r); -'hæm(p)ʃə/ 新罕布什尔。
New Haven /-'heɪvn; -'hevn̩/ 纽黑文。
New Jersey /-'dʒɜ:zɪ; -'dʒɜzɪ/ 新泽西。
New Mexico 新墨西哥。
New Orleans /-'ɔ:lɪənz; -'ɔrlɪənz/ 新奥尔良。

New South Wales 新南威尔士。
New York /-'jɔːk; -'jɔrk/ 纽约。
New Zealand 新西兰。
Niagara /naɪˈægərə; neɪˈæg(ə)rə/ 尼加拉河。
Niagara Falls 尼加拉瀑布。
Niamey /ˌnjɑːˈmeɪ; ˌnɪˈɑːmeɪ/ 尼亚美。
Nicaragua /ˌnɪkəˈrægjuə; ˌnɪkəˈrɑgwə/ 尼加拉瓜。
Nice /niːs; nis/ 尼斯。
Nicobar Islands /'nɪkə,bɑː(r)-; 'nɪkə,bɑr-/ 尼科巴群岛。
Nicosia /ˌnɪkəʊˈsiːə; ˌnɪkəˈsiə/ 尼科西亚。
Niger /niːˈʒeə(r); 'naɪdʒə/ 尼日尔。
Nigeria /naɪˈdʒɪərɪə; -'dʒɪrɪə/ 尼日利亚。
Nijmegen, Nimeguen /'naɪˈmeɪgən; neɪ,megən/ 奈梅亨。
Nile /naɪl; naɪl/ 尼罗河。
Ningxia /nɪŋˈʃɑː; 'nɪŋˈʃɑ/ 宁夏。
Nizhni Tagil /ˌnɪʒnɪ təˈgiːl; ˌnɪʒnɪ tə'gɪl/ 下塔吉尔。
Norfolk /'nɔːfək; 'nɔrfək/ 诺福克。
Normandy /'nɔːməndɪ; 'nɔrməndɪ/ 诺曼底。
Norrköping /'nɔːˌtʃɜːpɪŋ; 'nɔrˌtʃɜpɪŋ/ 诺尔雪平。
Northampton /nɔːˈθæmptən; nɔrθ'(h)æmptən/ 北安普顿。
Northampton shire /nɔːˈθæmptənʃə(r); nɔrθ'(h)æmptən-ˌʃɪr/ 北安普顿郡。
North Borneo 北婆罗洲。
North Carolina 北卡罗来纳。
North Dakota 北达科他。
Northern Ireland 北爱尔兰。
Northern Territory 北部地方。
North Platte /-'plæt; -'plæt/ 北普拉特河。
North Sea 北海。
Northumberland /nɔːˈθʌmbələnd; nɔrθ'ʌmbələnd/ 诺森伯兰。
North West Territories 西北地区。
North Yorkshire 北约克郡。
Norton Sound /'nɔːtn-; 'nɔrtn̩-/ 诺顿湾。
Norway /'nɔːweɪ; 'nɔr,we/ 挪威。
Norwegian Sea 挪威海。
Norwich¹ /'nɔrɪdʒ; 'nɑrɪdʒ/ 诺里奇。
Norwich² /'nɔːwɪtʃ; 'nɔrwɪtʃ/ 诺威奇。
Nottingham /'nɒtɪŋəm; 'nɑtɪŋəm/ 诺丁汉。
Nottinghamshire /'nɒtɪŋəmʃə(r); 'nɑtɪŋəmˌʃɪr/ 诺丁汉郡。
Nouakchott /nuˈækʃɒt; nu'ɑkˌʃɑt/ 努瓦克肖特。
Nova Scotia /ˌnəʊvə ˈskəʊʃə; ˌnovə 'skoʃə/ 新斯科舍。
Novosibirsk /ˌnəʊvəsɪˈbɪəsk; ˌnovəsə'bɪrsk/ 新西伯利亚。
Nukualofa /ˌnuːkuəˈlɔːfə; ˌnukəwə'lofə/ 努库阿洛法。
Nuneaton /nʌˈniːtn; nʌˈnitn/ 纳尼顿。
Nyasa, Lake /nɪˈæsə; naɪˈæsə/ 尼亚萨湖。
Nyasaland /'njæsələnd; naɪˈæsəˌlænd/ 尼亚萨兰。
Oahu /əʊˈɑːhuː; əˈwɑhu/ 瓦胡岛。
Oakland /'əʊklənd; 'oklənd/ 奥克兰。
Ob /ɔːb; ɑb/ 鄂毕河。
Oceania /ˌəʊʃɪˈeɪnɪə; ˌoʃɪˈænɪə/ 大洋洲。
Odense /'əʊðənsə; 'odn̩sə/ 欧登塞。
Oder /'əʊdə(r); 'odər/ 奥得河。
Odessa /əʊˈdesə; o'desə/ 敖得萨。
Offaly /'ɒfəlɪ; 'ɔfəlɪ/ 奥法利。
Offenbach /'ɒfənbɑːk; 'ɔfən,bɑk/ 奥芬巴赫。
Ogasawara Islands /ˈɒgɑːsɑː ˈwɑːrɑː-; o,gɑsə'wɑrə-/ 小笠原群岛。
Ohio /əʊˈhaɪəʊ; o'haɪo/ 俄亥俄。
Ojos del Salado /ˌəʊhəʊs ˌdel səˈlɑːdəʊ; 'ohoz,dɛl sə'lɑdo/ 奥霍斯-德尔萨拉多山。
Oka /ʌˈkɑː; o'kɑ/ 奥卡河。
Okhotsk, Sea of /əʊˈkɒtsk; o'kɑtsk/ 鄂霍次克海。
Okinawa /ˌəʊkɪˈnɑːwə; ˌokə'nɑwə/ 冲绳岛。
Oklahoma /ˌəʊkləˈhəʊmə; ˌoklə'homə/ 俄克拉何马。
Oldham /'əʊldəm; 'oldəm/ 奥尔德姆。
Olympic Peninsula 奥林匹克半岛。
Olympus /ə'lɪmpəs; ə'lɪmpəs/ 奥林波斯。
Omaha /'əʊməhɑː; 'omə,hɔ/ 奥马哈。
Oman /əʊˈmɑːn; o'mɑn/ 阿曼。
Omdurman /ˌɒmdəˈmæn; ˌɑmdə'mæn/ 恩图曼。

Omsk /ɒmsk; ɑmsk/ 鄂木斯克。
Onega /əʊˈneɪgə; o'negə/ 奥涅加湖。
Ontario /ɒnˈteərɪəʊ; ɑn'tɛrɪˌo/ 安大略。
Oporto /əʊˈpɔːtəʊ; o'porto/ 奥波尔图。
Öraefajökull /'ɜːˌraɪvɑːˌjəˈkuːtl; ɜˌraɪvəˈjɜˌkjutl/ 厄赖法耶屈德尔。
Oran /ɔːˈrɑːn; ɔˈrɑn/ 奥兰治河。
Oregon /'ɒrɪgən US: 'ɔːr-; 'ɔrɪgən/ 俄勒冈。
Orinoco /ˌɒrɪˈnəʊkəʊ; ˌorə'noko/ 奥里诺科河。
Orissa /ɒˈrɪsə; o'rɪsə/ 奥里萨邦。
Orizaba /ˌɒrɪˈzɑːbə; ˌorə'zɑbə/ 奥里萨巴山。
Orkney /'ɔːknɪ; 'ɔrknɪ/ 奥克尼群岛。
Orléans /'ɔːlɪənz; 'ɔrlɪənz/ 奥尔良。
Orohena, Mount /ˌeʊrəʊˈheɪnə; ˌorə'henə/ 奥罗黑纳山。
Orpington /'ɔːpɪŋtən; 'ɔrpɪŋtən/ 奥尔平顿。
Osage /əʊˈseɪdʒ; o'sedʒ/ 欧塞奇河。
Osaka /'ɔːsəkə; o'sakə/ 大阪。
Oslo /'ɒzləʊ; 'azlo/ 奥斯陆。
Ossa /'ɒsə; 'asə/ 奥萨山。
Ostrava /'ɔːstrəvə; 'ɔstrəvə/ 奥斯特拉发。
Otago /ɒˈtɑːgəʊ; o'tago/ 奥塔戈。
Otranto, Strait of /ɒ'træntəʊ; o'trænto/ 奥特朗托海峡。
Ottawa /'ɒtəwə; 'ɑtəwə/ 渥太华。
Ouachita /'wɒʃɪtɔː; 'waʃə,tɔ/ 沃希托河。
Ouagadougou /ˌwɑːgəˈduːguː; ˌwagə'dugu/ 瓦加杜古。
Oviedo /ˌɒvɪˈeɪdəʊ; ˌovɪˈeðo/ 奥维耶多。
Owen Stanley Range /ˌəʊɪnˈstænlɪ-; ˌoən'stænlɪ-/ 欧文斯坦利山脉。
Oxfordshire /'ɒksfədʃə(r); 'aksfəd,ʃɪr/ 牛津郡。
Pacific, the 太平洋。
Padua /'pædjuə; 'pædʒəwə/ 帕多瓦。
Pakistan /ˌpɑːkɪˈstɑːn; ˌpækɪ'stæn/ 巴基斯坦。
Palau /pɑːˈlaʊ; pa'laʊ/ 帛琉群岛。
Palembang /ˌpɑːləmˈbæŋ; ˌpaləm'baŋ/ 巴邻旁。
Palermo /pəˈlɜːməʊ; pə'lɜːmo/ 巴勒莫。
Palestine /'pæləstaɪn; 'pæləˌstaɪn/ 巴勒斯坦。
Palma (de Mallorca) /'pælmə diː məˈjɔːkə; 'pælmə,de meˈjɔrkə/ 帕尔马。
Palmerston /'pɑːməstn; 'pamˌəstən/ 帕默斯顿岛。
Palmyra Island /pælˈmaɪərə; pæl'maɪrə/ 巴尔米拉岛。
Pamir /pəˈmɪə(r); pə'mɪr/ 帕米尔高原。
Panama /ˌpænəˈmɑː; 'pænəˌmɑ/ 巴拿马。
Panié, Mount /ˌpæˈnjeɪ; ˌpæ'nje/ 帕尼艾山。
Papua /'pæpjuə; 'pæpjəwə/ 巴布亚。
Papua New Guinea 巴布亚新几内亚。
Paraguay /'pærəgwaɪ; 'pærəˌgweɪ/ 巴拉圭。
Paramaribo /ˌpærəˈmærɪbəʊ; ˌpærə'marə,bo/ 帕拉马里博。
Paraná /ˌpɑːrɑːˈnɑː; ˌpærə'na/ 巴拉那河。
Paranaíba /ˌpærəˈnɑːɪˈbə; ˌpærənəˈibə/ 巴拉那依巴河。
Paricutin /ˌpɑːriˈkuːtiːn; pəˈrikə,tin/ 帕里库廷火山。
Paris /'pærɪs; 'pærɪs/ 巴黎。
Parma /'pɑːmə; 'parmə/ 帕尔马。
Parnassus /pɑːˈnæsəs; par'næsəs/ 帕纳塞斯山。
Paros /'peərɒs; 'pɛr,as/ 帕罗斯岛。
Parthia /'pɑːθɪə; 'parθɪə/ 安息。
Patagonia /ˌpætəˈgəʊnjə; ˌpætə'gonjə/ 巴塔哥尼亚高原。
Paterson /'pætəsn; 'pætəsn/ 帕特森。
Patna /'pætnə; 'patnə/ 巴特那。
Pavia /pəˈviːə; pə'viə/ 帕维亚。
Peace /piːs; pis/ 皮斯河。
Pearl Harbor 珍珠港。
Pechenga /'petʃəŋə; 'petʃəngə/ 佩钦加。
Pechora /peˈtʃɔːrə; pə'tʃorə/ 白绍拉河。
Pecos /'peɪkɒs; 'pekəs/ 佩科斯河。
Peebles-shire /'piːblʒə(r); 'pibl̩,ʃɪr/ 皮布尔斯郡。
Peloponnesus, Peloponnesos /ˌpeləpəˈniːsəs; ˌpeləpə'nisəs/ 伯罗奔尼撒半岛。
Pembrokeshire /'pembrʊkʃə(r); 'pɛmbrʊk,ʃɪr/ 彭布罗克郡。
Penang /peˈnæŋ; pə'næŋ/ 槟榔屿。
Penghu /'pəŋˈhuː; pəŋ'hu/ 澎湖。

Pennine Alps /'penaɪn-; ˌpen͵aɪn/ 本宁阿尔卑斯山。

Pennsylvania /ˌpensl'veɪnɪə; ˌpənsəl'venjə/ 宾夕法尼亚。

Perak /'peərə; 'perə/ 霹雳 (吡叻)。

Perlis /'pə:lɪs; 'pə˞lɪs/ 玻璃市。

Perm /pəəm; pɝm/ 彼尔姆。

Persia /'pə:ʃə; 'pɝʒə/ 波斯。

Persian Gulf 波斯湾。

Perth /pə:θ; pɝθ/ 珀斯。

Perthshire /'pə:θʃɪə; 'pɝθˌʃɪr/ 伯斯郡。

Peru /pə'ru:; pə'ru/ 秘鲁。

Pescadores /ˌpeskə'dɔ:rɪz; ˌpeskə'dorɪz/ 澎湖列岛。

Peshawar /pə'ʃɔ:ə(r); pə'ʃɑwə/ 白沙瓦。

Petersburg /'pi:təzbə:g; 'pitə˞ˌbɝg/ 彼得斯堡。

Petsamo /'petsəməu; 'petsəˌmo/ 佩萨莫。

Philadelphia /ˌfɪlə'delfjə; ˌfɪlə'delfjə/ 费城。

Philippines, the /'fɪlɪpi:nz; 'fɪlə͵pinz/ 1 菲律宾群岛。 2 菲律宾共和国。

Phnom Penh, Pnom Penh /'pnɒm'pen; '(p)nɒm'pɛn/ 金边。

Ph(o)enicia /fɪ'nɪʃɪə; fɪ'nɪʃ(ɪ)ə/ 腓尼基。

Phoenix /'fi:nɪks; 'finɪks/ 菲尼克斯。

Pidurutalagala /ˌpɪdəru:tə'lɑ:gələ; ˌpɪdəˌrut'lɑgələ/ 皮杜鲁塔拉格勒山。

Pietermaritzburg /ˌpi:tə'mærɪtsbə:g; ˌpitə'mærɪtsˌbɝg/ 彼得马里茨堡。

Pikes Peak /paɪks-; paɪks-/ 派克斯峰。

Pilcomayo /ˌpɪlkəu'maɪəu; ˌpɪlkə'maɪo/ 皮科马约河。

Pilsen /'pɪlzən; 'pɪlzən/ 比尔森。

Pisa /'pi:zə; 'pizə/ 比萨。

Pittsburg /'pɪtsbə:g; 'pɪts͵bɝg/ 匹次堡。

Pittsburgh /'pɪtsbə:g; 'pɪts͵bɝg/ 匹兹堡。

Plata, Río de la /'ri:əudelə'plɑ:tə; ˌrio͵delə'plɑtə/ 拉普拉塔河。

Ploesti /plɔ:'jeʃt; plɔ'(j)eʃt(ɪ)/ 普洛耶什蒂。

Plymouth /'plɪməθ; 'plɪməθ/ 普利茅斯。

Po /pəu; po/ 波河。

Poitiers /pwɑ:'tjeɪ; pwɑ'tje/ 普瓦捷。

Poland /'pəulənd; 'polənd/ 波兰。

Polynesia /ˌpɒlɪ'ni:zjə; ˌpalɪ'niʒə/ 波利尼西亚。

Pomona /pə'məunə; pə'monə/ 波莫纳。

Pompeii /pɒm'peɪaɪ; pam'pe/ 庞培。

Pondicherry /ˌpɒndɪ'tʃerɪ; ˌpandə'tʃerɪ/ 本地治里。

Poole /pu:l; pul/ 浦耳。

Poona /'pu:nə; 'punə/ 波那。

Popocatepetl /ˌpɒpə͵kætɪ'petl; ˌpopəˌkætə'pɛtl/ 烟峰。

Pori /'pɒ:rɪ; 'porɪ/ 波里。

Porkkala Peninsula /'pɔ:kələ-; 'porkələ-/ 波卡拉半岛。

Port Arthur /-'ɑ:θə(r); -'ɑrθə/ 阿瑟港。

Port Louis /-'lu:ɪs; -'luɪs/ 路易港。

Port Moresby /-'mɔ:zbɪ; -'morzbɪ/ 莫尔斯比港。

Port of Spain, Port-of-Spain 西班牙港。

Porto-Novo /'pɔ:təu 'nəuvəu; 'portə 'novo/ 波多诺伏。

Porto Rico /ˌpɔ:təu 'ri:kəu; ˌportə 'riko/ 见 Puerto Rico。

Port Said /-'saɪd; -sɑ'id/ 塞得港。

Portsmouth /'pɔ:tsməθ; 'portsməθ/ 朴次茅斯。

Portugal /'pɔ:tjugl; 'portʃəgl/ 葡萄牙。

Potomac /pə'təumæk; pə'tomæk/ 波多马克河。

Potosi /pəteu'si:; potə'si/ 波托西。

Potsdam /'pɒtsdæm; 'pats͵dæm/ 波茨坦。

Poyang Hu /'pəu'jæŋ'hu:; 'po'jɑŋ'hu/ 鄱阳湖。

Poznań /'pɔ:znɑ:nje; 'poz͵nænjo/ 波兹南。

Prague /prɑ:g; prɑg/ 布拉格。

Praia /'praɪə; 'praɪə/ 普腊亚。

Preston /'prestən; 'prestən/ 普雷斯顿。

Pretoria /prɪ'tɔ:rɪə; prɪ'torɪə/ 比勒陀利亚。

Prince Edward Island 爱德华王子岛。

Princeton /'prɪnstən; 'prɪnstən/ 普林斯顿。

Providence /'prɒvɪdəns; 'pravədəns/ 普罗维登斯。

Prussia /'prʌʃə; 'prʌʃə/ 普鲁士。

Puerto Rico /'pwɑ:təu 'ri:kəu; pwɝtə 'riko/ 波多黎各。

Pulog /'pu:lɒg; 'pu͵log/ 普洛格山。

Punakha /'punəkə; 'punəkə/ 普那卡。

Punjab, Panjab /pʌn'dʒɑ:b; ˌpʌn'dʒab/ 旁遮普。

Purbeck, Isle of /'pəbek; pə:bek/ 波白克半岛。

Purus /'pu:rus; pə'rus/ 普鲁斯河。

Pusan /'pu:sɑ:n; 'pu͵san/ 釜山。

Pyongyang /'pjɒŋ'jæŋ; pɪ'ɒŋ͵jaŋ/ 平壤。

Pyrenees /ˌpɪrə'ni:z; ˌpɪrə'niz/ 比里牛斯山脉。

Qatar /'kɑtə(r); 'katə/ 卡塔尔。

Qatif, Katif /kɒ'ti:f; kɑ'tif/ 盖提夫。

Qinghai /'tʃɪŋ'hai; 'tʃɪŋ'hai/ 青海。

Qinghai Hu /'tʃɪŋ'hai'hu:; 'tʃɪŋ'hai'hu/ 青海湖。

Quebec /kwɪ'bek; kwɪ'bɛk/ 魁北克。

Queen Alexandra Range /-ˌælɪg'zɑ:ndrə-; -ˌælɪg'zændrə-/ 亚历山德拉皇后山脉。

Queen Maud Mountains /-mɔ:d-; -mɑd-/ 莫德皇后山脉。

Queensland /'kwi:nzlənd; 'kwinz͵lænd/ 昆士兰。

Quincy /'kwɪnsɪ; 'kwɪnsɪ/ 昆西。

Quito /'ki:təu; 'kito/ 基多。

Rabat /rə'bɑt; rə'bɑt/ 拉巴特。

Racine /rə'si:n; rə'sin/ 拉辛。

Radnorshire /'rædnəʃɪə; 'rædnə͵ʃɪr/ 拉德诺郡。

Rainier, Mount /reɪ'nɪə(r); rə'nɪr/ 雷尼尔峰。

Rakaposhi /ˌrɑkə'pɒʃi:; ˌrʌkə'poʃi/ 拉卡波希峰。

Raleigh /'rɔ:lɪ; 'rolɪ/ 罗利。

Rangoon /ræŋ'gu:n; ræŋ'gun/ 仰光。

Rantemario /ˌrɑ:ntə'mɑ:rɪəu; ˌrɑntə'mɑrɪ͵o/ 兰特马里奥山。

Ravenna /rə'venə; rə'vɛnə/ 拉韦纳。

Rawalpindi /ˌrɑ:vəl'pɪndi:; ˌrɑwəl'pɪndɪ/ 拉瓦尔品第。

Red River 红河。

Red Sea 红海。

Regina /rɪ'dʒaɪnə; rɪ'dʒaɪnə/ 里贾纳。

Reims, Rheims /ri:mz; rimz/ 兰斯。

Renfrewshire /'renfruːʃə(r); 'renfru͵ʃɪr/ 伦夫鲁郡。

Reunion /ri:'juːnjən; ri'junjən/ 留尼旺岛。

Reykjavik /'reɪkjɑ͵vɪk; 'rekjə͵vɪk/ 雷克雅未克。

Rhaetian Alps /'ri:ʃɪən-; 'riʃən-/ 里申阿尔卑斯山脉。

Rhine /raɪn; raɪn/ 莱茵河。

Rhode Island /ˌrəud'aɪlənd; rod'aɪlənd/ 罗德岛。

Rhodesia /rəu'di:zjə; ro'diʒə/ 罗得西亚。

Rhodope /'rɒdəpɪ; 'radəpɪ/ 洛多皮山脉。

Rhone /rəun; ron/ 罗讷河。

Richmond /'rɪtʃmənd; 'rɪtʃmənd/ 里士满。

Riga /'ri:gə; 'rigə/ 里加。

Rindjani /rɪn'dʒɑ:nɪ; rɪn'dʒanɪ/ 润亚尼峰。

Rio de Janeiro /'ri:əu də dʒə'nɪərəu; 'rio ˌdə ʒə'nero/ 里约热内卢。

Rio Grande /'ri:əu 'grɑ:ndə; ˌrio 'grændɪ/ 里奥格兰德河。

Riviera /ˌrɪvɪ'eərə; ˌrɪvɪ'ɛrə/ 里维埃拉。

Riyadh /ri:'jɑ:d; ri'jad/ 利雅得。

Roanoke /rəuə'nəuk; roə͵nok/ 罗阿诺克。

Robson, Mount /'rɒbsn; 'rɑbsn/ 洛布森山。

Rochdale /'rɒtʃdeɪl; 'rɒtʃ͵del/ 洛奇代尔。

Rochester /'rɒtʃɪstə(r); 'ratʃəstə/ 罗切斯特。

Rocky Mountains /'rɒkɪ; 'rɑkɪ/ 落基山脉。

Romania /rə'meɪnɪə; rʊ'menɪə/ 罗马尼亚。

Rome /rəum; rom/ 罗马。

Romford /'rɒmfəd; 'ramfəd/ 罗姆福。

Rosa Monte /'rəuzə; 'rozə/ 罗沙峰。

Roscommon /rɒs'kɒmən; ras'kɑmən/ 罗斯康芒。

Roseau /rə'zəu; ro'zo/ 罗佐。

Ross and Cromarty /'rɒs ən 'krɒmətɪ; 'rɔs ən 'krɑmətɪ/ 罗斯和克罗马蒂。

Ross Sea /ˌrɒs-; ros-/ 罗斯海。

Rostov /'rɒstɒv; rə'stɔf/ 罗斯托夫。

Rotherham /'rɒðərəm; 'raðərəm/ 罗瑟勒姆。

Rotterdam /'rɒtədæm; 'ratə͵dæm/ 鹿特丹。

Rouen /'ruːɑːŋ; ruˈɑn/ 卢昂。

Rovaniemi /'roːvɑːnieːmiː; ˈrɔvənˌiemi/ 罗瓦涅米。

Roxburghshire /'rɒksbrəfə(r); ˈraksbeərəˌʃɪr/ 罗克斯巴勒郡。

Ruanda 参看 Rwanda。

Ruapehu /ˌruːəˈpeːhuː; ˌruəˈpehu/ 阿佩胡峰。

Rubicon /'ruːbɪkən; ˈrubɪˌkan/ 卢比肯。

Rudolf, Lake /'ruːdɒlf; ˈru͵dalf/ 鲁道夫湖。

Rugby /'rʌgbɪ; ˈrʌgbɪ/ 拉格比。

Ruhr /ruə(r); rʊr/ 1 鲁尔河。2 鲁尔区。

Russia /'rʌʃə; ˈrʌʃə/ 俄罗斯。

Rutland /'rʌtlənd; ˈrʌtlənd/ 拉特兰。

Rutland(shire) /'rʌtlənd(ʃə(r)); ˈrʌtlənd(ˌʃɪr)/ 拉特兰郡。

Ruwenzori /ˌruːwənˈzɔːrɪ; ˌru(w)ənˈzorɪ/ 鲁文佐里山脉。

Rwanda /ru'ændə; ruˈɑndə/ 卢旺达。

Rye /raɪ; raɪ/ 拉伊。

Ryukyu /riːˈuːkuː; riˈ(j)uk(j)u/ 琉球。

Saarland /'sɑːlænd; ˈsɑrˌlænd/ 萨尔区。

Sabah /'sɑːbə; ˈsɑbə/ 沙巴。

Sabine /sæˈbiːn; səˈbin/ 色宾河。

Sacramento /ˌsækrəˈmentəʊ; ˌsækrəˈmɛnto/ 1 萨克拉门托。2 萨克拉门托河。3 萨克拉门托山脉。

Sahara, the /səˈhɑːrə; səˈhærə/ 撒哈拉。

Saint-Etienne /ˌsæntetˈjen; ˌsæntˈtjɛn/ 圣艾蒂安。

Sakhalin /ˌsɑːkɑːˈliːn; ˈsækəˌlin/ 萨哈林岛(库页岛)。

Salado /sɑːˈlɑːðəʊ; səˈlɑdo/ 萨拉多河。

Salamanca /ˌsæləˈmæŋkə; ˌsæləˈmæŋkə/ 萨拉曼卡。

Salem /'seɪləm; ˈsɛləm/ 塞勒姆。

Salford /'sɔːlfəd; ˈsɔlfəd/ 索尔福德。

Salisbury /'sɔːlzbrɪ; ˈsɔlz͵bɛrɪ/ 索尔兹伯里。

Salonika, Salonica /səˈlɒnɪkə; səˈlɑnɪkə/ 萨洛尼卡(即塞萨洛尼基)。

Salop /'sæləp; ˈsæləp/ 萨洛普。

Salvador /'sælvədɔː(r); ˈsælvəˌdɔr/ 萨尔瓦多。

Salween /'sælwiːn; ˈsælˌwin/ 萨尔温江。

Salzburg /'sæltsbɜːg; ˈsɔlzˌbɜrg/ 萨尔茨堡。

Samaria /səˈmeərɪə; səˈmɛrɪə/ 撒马利亚。

Samarkand /ˌsæməˈkænd; ˈsæməˌkænd/ 撒马尔罕。

Samoa /səˈməʊə; səˈmoə/ 萨摩亚群岛。

Samos /'seɪmɒs; ˈseˌmas/ 萨摩斯岛。

Samothrace /'sæməʊθreɪs; ˈsæməˌθres/ 萨莫色雷斯岛。

San'a, Sanaa /sɑːˈnɑː; ˈsɑnˌɑ/ 萨那。

San Bernardino /ˌsænˌbɜːnəˈdiːnəʊ; ˈsænˌbɜrnəˈdino/ 圣贝纳迪诺山脉。

San Diego /ˌsænˈdɪˈeɪgəʊ; ˌsændɪˈego/ 圣迭戈。

Sanford, Mount /'sænfəd; ˈsænfəd/ 圣福德火山。

San Francisco /ˌsænfrənˈsɪskəʊ; ˌsænfrənˈsɪsko/ 圣弗朗西斯科(或称旧金山)。

San Gorgonio /ˌsængɔːˈgəʊnɪəʊ; ˌsæŋgɔrˈgonɪo/ 桑哥弓尼奥峰。

Sangre de Cristo /ˌsæŋgrɪdeˈkrɪstəʊ; ˌsæŋgrɪdeˈkrɪsto/ 桑格累得克里斯托山脉。

San José /ˌsɑːnhəʊˈseɪ; ˌsæn(h)oˈze/ 圣何塞。

San Juan /ˌsæn ˈhwɑːn; sænˈ(h)wɑn/ 圣胡安。

San Marino /ˌsænməˈriːnəʊ; ˌsænməˈrino/ 圣马力诺。

San Remo /sænˈreɪməʊ; sænˈremo/ 圣雷莫。

San Salvador /ˌsænˈsælvədɔː(r); sænˈsælvəˌdɔr/ 圣萨尔瓦多。

Santa Ana /ˌsæntəˈænə; ˌsæntəˈænə/ 圣安娜。

Santa Isabel /ˌsæntəˈɪzəbel; ˌsæntəˈɪzəˌbɛl/ 圣伊萨贝尔。

Santiago /ˌsæntɪˈɑːgəʊ; ˌsæntɪˈɑgo/ 圣地亚哥。

Santo Domingo /ˌsæntəʊ dəˈmɪŋgəʊ; ˌsæntə dəˈmɪŋgo/ 圣多明各。

Santos /'sæntɒs; ˈsæntəs/ 桑托斯。

São Francisco /ˌsaʊnfrənˈsiːskuː; ˌsaʊnfrənˈsɪsko/ 圣弗朗西斯科河。

São Paulo /ˌsaʊn ˈpaʊləʊ; saʊn ˈpaʊlʊ/ 圣保罗。

São Tomé /ˌsaʊntəˈmeɪ; ˌsaʊntəˈme/ 圣多美。

São Tomé and Principe /ˌsaʊntəˈmeɪ ənd ˈprɪnsəpə; ˌsaʊntəˈme ənd ˈprɪnsəpə/ 圣多美及普林西比人民民主共和国。

Sapporo /səˈpʊərəʊ; ˈsapəˌro/ 札幌。

Saragossa /ˌsærəˈgɒsə; ˌsærəˈgɑsə/ 萨拉戈萨。

Saratoga /ˌsærəˈtəʊgə; ˌsærəˈtogə/ 萨拉托加。

Saratov /sæˈrɑːtəf; səˈrɑtəf/ 萨拉托夫。

Sarawak /səˈrɑːwæk; səˈrɑwɑk/ 沙捞越。

Sardinia /sɑːˈdɪnjə; sɑrˈdɪnjə/ 撒丁。

Sasebo /sɑːˈseɪbəʊ; ˈsɑsəˌbo/ 佐世保。

Saskatchewan /səˈskætʃəwən; sasˈkætʃəwən/ 萨斯喀彻温。

Saudi Arabia /ˌsaʊdɪ-; ˌsaʊdɪ-/ 沙特阿拉伯。

Sawatch Range /səˈwɒtʃ-; səˈwɑtʃ-/ 撒瓦琪山脉。

Saxony /'sæksnɪ; ˈsæksəˌnɪ/ 萨克森。

Scafell Pike /skɔːˈfel paɪk; skoˈfɛl ˌpaɪk/ 斯可斐峰。

Scandinavia /ˌskændɪˈneɪvjə; ˌskændəˈnevjə/ 1 斯堪的那维亚。2 斯堪的那维亚半岛。

Scapa Flow /ˌskæpəˈfləʊ; ˌskæpəˈflo/ 斯卡帕湾。

Schenectady /skɪˈnektədɪ; skəˈnɛktədɪ/ 斯克内克塔迪。

Schiedam /ˌskiːˈdæm; skiˈdæm/ 斯希丹。

Schleswig-Holstein /ˈʃleːzwɪgˈhɒlˌstaɪn; ˈʃlɛzwɪgˈhoʊlstaɪn/ 石勒苏益格－荷尔斯泰因。

Schouten /ˈskaʊtən; ˈskaʊtn/ 实珍群岛。

Schuylkill /ˈskuːlkɪl; ˈskulˌkɪl/ 斯古吉尔河。

Scilly /ˈsɪlɪ; ˈsɪlɪ/ 锡利群岛。

Scotland /ˈskɒtlənd; ˈskatlənd/ 苏格兰。

Scythia /ˈsɪθɪə; ˈsɪθɪə/ 塞西亚。

Seattle /sɪˈætl; sɪˈætl/ 西雅图。

Sedan /sɪˈdæn; sɪˈdæn/ 色当。

Seine /seɪn; sɛn/ 塞纳河。

Selangor /səˈlæŋɔː(r); səˈlæŋə/ 雪兰莪。

Selkirk /ˈselkɑːk; ˈsɛlˌkɔk/ 塞尔扣克山。

Selkirkshire /ˈselkɑːkʃə(r); ˈsɛlkəkˌʃɪr/ 塞尔扣克郡。

Semarang /səˈmɑːrɑːŋ; səˈmɑrˌɑŋ/ 三宝垅。

Senegal /ˌsenɪˈgɔːl; ˌsɛnɪˈgɔl/ 塞内加尔。

Seoul /səʊl; sol/ 汉城。

Serbia /ˈsɜːbjə; ˈsɜbɪə/ 塞尔维亚。

Seville /ˈsevɪl; səˈvɪl/ 塞维尔。

Sèvres /ˈseɪvrə(r); ˈsɛvə/ 塞夫勒。

Seward Peninsula /ˈsiːwəd-; ˈsuəd-/ 西沃德半岛。

Seychelles, (The) /ˈseɪʃelz; seˈʃɛl/ 塞舌尔。

Sham, Jebel /ˈdʒebl ˈʃæm; ˈdʒɛbl ˈʃæm/ 沙姆山。

Shandong /ˈʃænˌtʊŋ; ˈʃanˌtʊŋ/ 山东。

Shanghai /ˈʃæŋˈhaɪ; ˈʃaŋˈhaɪ/ 上海。

Shanxi /ˈʃɑːnˈʃiː; ˈʃanˈʃi/ 山西。

Shanxi /ˈʃɑːnˈʃiː; ˈʃanˈʃi/ 陕西。

Sharon /ˈʃeərɒn; ˈʃɛrən/ 沙伦。

Shasta, Mount /ˈʃæstə; ˈʃæstə/ 沙斯塔山。

Shawnee /ˈʃɔːniː; ʃɔˈni/ 肖尼。

Sheba /ˈʃiːbə; ˈʃibə/ 希巴。

Sheffield /ˈʃefiːld; ˈʃɛfˌild/ 设菲尔德。

Shenyang /ˈʃenˈjɑːŋ; ˈʃɛnˈjaŋ/ 沈阳。

Shetland /ˈʃetlənd; ˈʃɛtlənd/ 设得兰群岛。

Shijiazhuang /ˈʃiˈdʒɑː; dʒuˌaŋ; ˈʃiˈdʒa ˈdʒuaŋ/ 石家庄。

Shikoku /ʃɪˈkəʊkuː; ʃɪˈkoku/ 四国。

Shimonoseki /ˌʃɪməʊnəʊˈseki; ˌʃimənoˈsɛki/ 下关。

Shiraz /ʃɪˈræz; ʃɪˈraz/ 设拉子。

Shkara Tau /ˈʃkɑːrəˈtaʊ; ˌʃəkərəˈtaʊ/ 希卡拉陶山。

Shrewsbury /ˈʃruːzbrɪ; ˈʃruz͵bɛrɪ/ 什鲁斯伯里。

Shropshire /ˈʃrɒpʃə(r); ˈʃrɑpˌʃɪr/ 希罗普郡。

Siam /ˈsaɪæm; saɪˈæm/ 暹罗。

Siberia /saɪˈbɪərɪə; saɪˈbɪrɪə/ 西伯利亚。

Sichuan /ˈsɜː ˈtʃuɑːn; ˈsɜ ˈtʃuɑn/ 四川。

Sicily /ˈsɪsɪlɪ; ˈsɪsɑlɪ/ 西西里岛。

Sidon /ˈsaɪdn; ˈsaɪdn/ 西顿。

Siena, Sienna /sɪˈenə; sɪˈɛnə/ 锡耶纳。

Sierra Leone /sɪˌerə lɪˈəʊn; sɪˌɛrəlɪˈon/ 塞拉利昂。

Sierra Madre Oriental /-ˈmædre ˌɔːrɪˈentl; -ˌmædrɪ ˌɔrɪˌɛnˈtɑl/ 东马德雷山脉。

Sierra Nevada /-nəˈvædə; -nəˈvædə/ 内华达山脉。

Sikkim /ˈsɪkɪm; ˈsɪkəm/ 锡金。

Silesia /saɪˈliːzjə; saɪˈliʒə/ 西里西亚。

Simla /ˈsɪmlə; ˈsɪmlə/ 西姆拉。

Simplon /ˈsɪmplən; ˈsɪmˌplan/ 辛普朗。

Sinai /'saɪnaɪ; 'saɪˌnal/ 西奈半岛。

Singapore /ˌsɪŋgə'pɔː(r); 'sɪŋgə,por/ 新加坡。

Singkep /'sɪŋkep; 'sɪŋˌkɛp/ 辛开普。

Sinuiju /ʃini;ˌdʒu; ʃiniˌdʒu/ 新义州。

Sioux City /suː-; su-/ 苏城。

Skye /skaɪ; skaɪ/ 斯凯岛。

Sligo /'slaɪgəu; 'slaɪgo/ 斯莱戈。

Smethwick /'smeðɪk; 'smeðɪk/ 斯梅西克。

Smoky Hill 烟山河。

Snake 斯内克河。

Society Islands 社会群岛。

Socotra, Sokotra /sə'kəutrə; sə'kotrə/ 索科特拉岛。

Sofia /'səufjə; 'sofɪə/ 索非亚。

Solomon Islands /'sɒləmən-; 'saləmən-/ 所罗门群岛。

Solway Firth /ˌsɒlwə-; 'salwe-/ 索尔威湾。

Somalia /sə'mɑːlɪə; so'malɪə/ 索马里。

Somaliland /sə'mɑːlɪlænd; so'malɪn,lænd/ 索马里兰。

Somali Republic /sə'mɑːlɪ-; so'mali-/ 索马里

Somerset (shire) /'sʌməset (ˌʃə(r)); 'sʌmɔset(ˌʃɪr)/ 萨默塞特。

Somerville /'sʌməvɪl; 'sʌmɔ,vɪl/ 萨莫维尔。

Song Shan /'sun 'ʃɑːn; 'sun 'ʃɑn/ 嵩山。

Sound, the 松德海峡。

South Andaman 安达曼岛。

South Australia 南澳大利亚。

South Carolina 南卡罗来纳。

South Dakota 南达科他。

South Glamorgan 南格拉摩根。

South Yorkshire 南约克郡。

Soviet Union 苏联。

Spain /speɪn; spen/ 西班牙。

Sparta /'spɑːtə; 'spartə/ 斯巴达。

Spitsbergen /'spɪts,bɜːgən; 'spɪts,bɝgən/ 斯匹次卑尔根群岛。

Srilanka /ˌsrɪ'læŋkə; srɪ'lɑŋkə/ 斯里兰卡。

Srinagar /srɪ'nɑːgə/ 斯利那加。

Stafford /'stæfəd; 'stæfəd/ 斯塔福德郡。

Staffordshire /'stæfədʃə(r); 'stæfəd,ʃɪr/ 斯塔福德郡。

Stalingrad /'stɑːlɪŋɡræd; 'stɑlɪnˌɡræd/ 斯大林格勒。

Stalino /'stɑːljɪnə; 'stɑlɪˌno/ 斯大林诺。

Stalin Peak /'stɑːlɪn-; 'stɑlɪn-/ 斯大林峰。

Stalinsk /'stɑːlɪnsk; 'stalɪnsk/ 斯大林斯克。

Stamford /'stæmfəd; 'stæmfəd/ 斯坦福。

Stanley /'stænlɪ; 'stænlɪ/ 1 斯坦利山。 2 斯坦利。

Stassfurt /'ʃtɑːtsfuət; 'stasˌfurt/ 施塔斯富尔特。

Stavanger /stɑ'vɑ:ŋə(r); stə'vɑŋə/ 斯塔万格。

St. Bernard /-'bɜːnəd; -bə'nɑrd/ 圣伯纳山隘。

St. Christopher /-'krɪstəfə(r); -'krɪstəfə/ 圣克里斯托弗。

St. Clair, Lake /-kleə(r); -klɛr/ 圣克莱尔湖。

St. Elias Range /-ɪ'laɪəs-; -ə'laɪəs-/ 圣伊莱亚斯山脉。

Stettin /ʃte'tiːn; ʃtɛ'tin/ 什切青。

Stewart Island /stjuət-; 'stʃuət-/ 斯图尔特岛。

St. George's /-'dʒɔːdʒɪz; -'dʒɔrdʒɪz/ 圣乔治。

St. Gott(h)ard Tunnel /-'ɡɒtəd-; -'ɡɑtəd-/ 圣哥达隧道。

St. Helena /-'helɪnə; -hə'linə/ 圣赫勒拿岛。

Stirlingshire /'stɜːlɪŋʃə(r); 'stɝlɪŋˌʃɪr/ 斯特灵郡。

St. Johns /snt'dʒɒnz; sent'dʒɑnz/ 圣约翰。

St. Lawrence /-'lɒrəns; -'lɔrəns/ 圣劳伦斯河。

St. Lawrence, Gulf of 圣劳伦斯湾。

St. Louis /-'luːɪs; -'luɪs/ 圣路易斯。

St. Lucia /-'luːʃə; -'luʃə/ 圣卢西亚。

Stockholm /'stɒkhəum; 'stak,hom/ 斯德哥尔摩。

Stockport /'stɒkpɔːt; 'stak,port/ 斯托克波特。

Stockton /'stɒktən; 'staktən/ 斯托克顿。

St. Paul /-'pɔːl; -pɔl/ 圣保罗。

St. Petersburg /-'piːtəzbɜːɡ; -'pitəz,bɝɡ/ 圣彼得斯堡。

Strasbourg /'stræzbɜːɡ; 'stras,burɡ/ 斯特拉斯堡。

Stratford-(up)on-Avon /'strætfəd(əp)ɒn'eɪvən; 'strætfəd-(ɒn)ɑn'evən/ 埃文河畔斯特拉特福德。

Strathclyde /stræθ'klaɪd; stræθ'klaɪd/ 斯特拉思克莱德。

Stuttgart /'stutgɑːt; 'stut,gart/ 斯图加特。

St. Vincent and the Grenadines /-'vɪnsənt—, ˌɡrenə-'diːnz; -'vɪnsənt—ˌɡrenə'dinz/ 圣文森特和格林纳达。

Sudan, (The) /suː'dɑːn; su'dæn/ 苏丹。

Sudbury /'sʌdbərɪ; 'sʌd,bɛrɪ/ 萨德伯里。

Sudety /səu'dettɪ; su'detɪ/ 苏台德山脉。

Suez /'suːɪz; su'ɪz/ 1 苏伊士港。2 苏伊士运河。

Suez, Isthmus of 苏伊士地峡。

Suffolk /'sʌfək; 'safək/ 萨福克。

Sulu Archipelago /'suːluː-; 'sulu-/ 苏禄群岛。

Sumat(e)ra /suː'mɑːtrə; su'mɑtrə/ 苏门答腊。

Sunda Isles /'sʌndə-; 'sundə-/ 巽他群岛。

Sunderland /'sʌndələnd; 'sʌndəˌlænd/ 桑德兰。

Sun-moon Lake 日月潭。

Superior, Lake 苏必利尔湖。

Surabaya, Surabaya /sure'bɑːjə; ˌsure'baɪe/ 泗水。

Surat /'suərət; 'suret/ 苏拉特。

Surbiton /'sɜː,bɪtn; 'sɝbɪtn/ 索比顿。

Surinam /ˌsuərɪ'næm; ˌsurɪ'nɑm/ 苏里南。

Surrey /'sʌrɪ; 'sʌrɪ/ 萨里。

Susquehanna /ˌsʌskwe'hænə; ˌsʌskwə'hænə/ 萨斯奎汉纳河。

Sussex /'sʌsɪks; 'sasɪks/ 苏塞克斯。

Sutherland /'sʌðələnd; 'sʌðələnd/ 萨瑟兰。

Sutherland Falls 萨瑟兰瀑布。

Sutlej /'sʌtledʒ; 'sʌtˌledʒ/ 萨特莱杰河。

Suva /'suːvə; 'suvə/ 苏瓦。

Svalbard /'svɑːlbɑː; 'sfalˌbɑr/ 斯瓦尔巴群岛。

Sverdlovsk /svɛ:d'lɒːfsk; sfɛrd'lɔfsk/ 斯维尔德洛夫斯克。

Swaziland /'swɑːzɪlænd; 'swazɪˌlænd/ 斯威士兰。

Sweden /'swiːdn; 'swɪdn/ 瑞典。

Swidon /'swɪndən; 'swɪndən/ 斯温登。

Switzerland /'swɪtsələnd; 'swɪtsələnd/ 瑞士。

Sybaris /'sɪbərɪs; 'sɪbərɪs/ 希巴利斯。

Sydney /'sɪdnɪ; 'sɪdnɪ/ 悉尼。

Syracuse /'saɪərəkjuːz; 'saɪrə,kjus/ 锡拉丘兹。

Syr Darja /'sɪədɑː'jɑː; sɪr'dɑrjə/ 锡尔河。

Syria /'sɪrɪə; 'sɪrɪə/ 叙利亚。

Tabriz /tɑː'briːz; tɑ'briz/ 大布里士。

Tadzhikistan, Tajikistan /tɑ:ˌdʒɪkɪ'stɑ:n; tɑˌdʒɪkɪ'stæn/ 塔吉克。

Taegu /'tæ'gu; tæ'gu/ 大邱。

Tagus /'teɪɡəs; 'teɡəs/ 塔古斯河。

Tahiti /tɑ:'hiːtɪ; tə'hitɪ/ 塔希提。

Taichung /'taɪ'tʃuŋ; 'taɪ'tʃuŋ/ 1 台中市。2 台中县。

Tai Hu /'taɪ 'huː; 'taɪ 'hu/ 太湖。

Tainan /'taɪ'nɑːn; 'taɪ'nɑn/ 1 台南市。2 台南县。

Taipei /'taɪ'peɪ; 'taɪ'pe/ 1 台北市。2 台北县。

Tai Shan /'taɪ 'ʃɑːn; 'taɪ 'ʃɑn/ 泰山。

Taitung /'taɪ'duŋ; 'taɪ'duŋ/ 台东。

Taiwan /taɪ'wɑːn; taɪ'wɑn/ 台湾。

Taiwan Strait 台湾海峡。

Taiyuan /'taɪ'juɑːn; 'taɪ'juɑn/ 太原。

Tallin(n) /'tælɪn; 'tælɪn/ 塔林。

Tamatave /tɑːmɑː'tɑːv; ˌtæmə'tɑv/ 塔马塔夫。

Tampere /'tɑːmpere; 'tæmpə,re/ 坦佩雷。

Tampico /tæm'piːkəu; tæm'piko/ 坦比科。

Tananarive /tɑːnɑːnɑː'riːv; tə'nænə,riv/ 塔那那利佛。

Tanganyika /ˌtæŋgə'nji:kə; ˌtæŋgən'jike/ 坦噶尼喀。

Tangier /tæn'dʒɪə/ 丹吉尔。

Tan-Shui, Tansui /'tɑ:n'suːɪ; 'dɑn'ʃwe/ 淡水。

Tanzania /ˌtænzə'nɪə; ˌtænzə'nɪə/ 坦桑尼亚。

Taranaki /ˌtærə'nɑːkɪ; ˌtærə'nækɪ/ 塔拉纳基。

Taranto /tə'ræntəu; tə'rænto/ 塔兰托。

Tarawa /tə'rɑːwe; tə'rawe/ 塔拉瓦。

Tashkent, Tashkend /tæʃ'kent; tæʃ'kɛnt/ 塔什干。

Tasmania /tæz'meɪnɪə; tæz'menɪə/ 塔斯马尼亚。

Tasman Sea /'tæzmən-; 'tæzmən-/ 塔斯曼海。

Taunton /'tɔːntən; 'tɒntən/ 汤顿。

Taurus /'tɔːrəs; 'tɔrəs/ 托罗斯山脉。

Tayside /'teɪsaɪd; 'teˌsaɪd/ 泰塞德。

Tegucigalpa /təˌɡuːsɪ'ɡælpə; təˌɡusə'ɡælpə / 特古西加

尔巴。

Tehran, Teheran /teˈrɑːn; ˌteəˈræn/ 德黑兰。
Tel Aviv /ˌtelˈviːv; ˌteləˈviv/ 特拉维夫。
Tenerife /ˌtenəˈriːf; ˌtenəˈrif/ 特纳利夫岛。
Tennessee /ˌtenəˈsiː; ˌtenəˈsi/ 田纳西。
Texas /ˈteksəs; ˈteksəs/ 得克萨斯。
Thailand /ˈtaɪlænd; ˈtaɪˌland/ 泰国。
Thames /temz; temz/ 泰晤士河。
Thar Desert /tɑː-; tɑr-/ 塔尔沙漠。
Thebes /θiːbz; θibz/ 底比斯。
Thimbu /ˈθɪmbuː; ˈθɪmbu/ 辛布。
Thousand Islands 千岛群岛。
Thrace /θreɪs; θres/ 色雷斯。
Thule /ˈtuːlɪ; ˈtulɪ/ 图勒。
Thun, Lake of /tuːn; tun/ 土恩湖。
Thuringian Plateau /θjuˈrɪndʒɪən-; θ(j)uˈrɪndʒɪən-/ 绍林吉高原。
Tianjin /ˈtjenˈdʒɪn; ˈtjenˈdʒɪn/ 天津。
Tiber /ˈtaɪbə(r); ˈtaɪbə/ 台伯河。
Tibesti /tɪˈbesti; tɪˈbestɪ/ 提贝斯提高原。
Tiflis /ˈtɪflɪs; ˈtɪflɪs/ 第比利斯。
Tigris /ˈtaɪgrɪs; ˈtaɪgrɪs/ 底格里斯河。
Timor /ˈtiːmɔː(r); ˈtiˌmor/ 帝汶。
Tipperary /ˌtɪpəˈreərɪ; ˌtɪpəˈrɛrɪ/ 蒂珀雷里。
Tirana /tɪˈrɑːnə; tɪˈranə/ 地拉那。
Tisza /ˈtɪsɔ; ˈtɪsˌɔ/ 提萨河。
Tobago /təˈbeɪgəʊ; təˈbego/ 多巴哥岛。
Tobol /təʊˈbɒːl; təˈbol/ 托博尔河。
Tocantins /ˌtəʊkænˈtiːns; ˌtokænˈtinz/ 托坎廷斯河。
Togo /ˈtəʊgəʊ; ˈtogo/ 多哥。
Tokyo /ˈtəʊkɪəʊ; ˈtokɪˌo/ 东京。
Toledo /tɒˈleɪdəʊ; təˈledo/ 托莱多。
Tomsk /tɒmsk; tamsk/ 托木斯克。
Tonga /ˈtɒŋə; ˈtaŋgə/ 汤加王国。
Tonga Islands 汤加群岛。
Tongking /ˈtɒŋˈkɪŋ; ˈtaŋˈkɪŋ/ 东京。
Toronto /təˈrɒntəʊ; təˈranto/ 多伦多。
Torquay /ˈtɔːˈkiː; ˈtɔrˈki/ 托基。
Torres Strait /ˈtɒrɪs-; ˈtɔrɪs-/ 托雷斯海峡。
Toubkal /ˈtuːbkæl; tubˈkal/ 图卜卡勒山。
Toulon /ˈtuːlɒn; tuˈlɑn/ 土伦。
Toulouse /tuːˈluːz; tʊˈluz/ 图卢兹。
Tours /tʊə(r); tʊr/ 图尔。
Trafalgar, Cape /trəˈfælgə(r); trəˈfælgə/ 特拉法尔加角。
Transcaucasia /ˌtrænzkɔːˈkeɪzɪə; ˌtænskɔˈkeʒə/ 外高加索。
Trengganu /treŋˈgɑːnu; treŋˈganu/ 丁加奴。
Trier /ˈtriːə(r); trɪr/ 特里尔。
Trieste /triːˈest; triˈest/ 1 的里雅斯特港。2 的里雅斯特区。
Trinidad /ˈtrɪnɪdæd; ˈtrɪnəˌdæd/ 特立尼达岛。
Trinidad and Tobago 特立尼达和多巴哥共和国。
Tripoli /ˈtrɪpəlɪ; ˈtrɪpəlɪ/ 的黎波里。
Trondheim /ˈtrɒnheɪm; ˈtranˌhem/ 特隆赫姆。
Troy /trɔɪ; trɔɪ/ 特洛伊。
Tsushima Strait /tsuˈʃiːmɑː-; tsuˈʃimə-/ 对马海峡。
Tuapse /tuˈʌpˈsje; tuˌapˈse/ 图阿普谢。
Tucson /ˈtuːsɒn; tuˈsan/ 图森。
Tula /ˈtuːlə; ˈtulə/ 图拉。
Tunis /ˈtjuːnɪs; ˈt(j)unɪs/ 突尼斯。
Tunisia /tjuːˈnɪzɪə; t(j)uˈnɪʒə/ 突尼斯。
Turin /tjuˈrɪn; ˈt(j)ʊrɪn/ 都灵。
Turkey /ˈtɜːkɪ; ˈtɜkɪ/ 土耳其。
Turkmenistan /ˌtɜːkˈmenɪˈstɑːn; ˌtɜkˈmɛnɪˌstæn/ 土库曼。
Turku /ˈtuəkuː; ˈtʊrku/ 图尔库。
Tuscany (Toscana) /ˈtʌskənɪ; ˈtʌskənɪ/ 托斯卡纳。
Tuvalu /tuːˈvɑːluː; tuˈvalu/ 图瓦卢。
Tyler /ˈtaɪlə(r); ˈtaɪlə/ 泰勒。
Tyne and Wear /ˌtaɪn ən ˈwɪə(r); ˌtaɪn ən ˈwɪr/ 泰恩-威尔。
Tynemouth /ˈtaɪnmaʊθ; ˈtaɪnˌmaʊθ/ 泰恩茅斯。
Tyrol, Tirol /ˈtɪrəl; ˈtɪrə/ 蒂罗尔。

Tyrone /tɪˈrəʊn; tɪˈron/ 蒂龙。
Tyrrhenian Sea /tɪˈriːnɪən-; tɪˈrinɪən-/ 第勒尼安海。
Ucayali /ˌuːkaˈjɑːlɪ; ˌukeˈjalɪ/ 乌卡亚利河。
Uganda /juːˈgændə; juˈgændə/ 乌干达。
Ukraine /juːˈkreɪn; juˈkren/ 乌克兰。
Ulan-Ude /ˈuːlɑːn uːˈde; ˌulan ˈuˈde/ 乌兰乌德。
Ulster /ˈʌlstə; ˈʌlstə/ 阿尔斯特。
Umbria /ˈʌmbrɪə; ˈʌmbrɪə/ 翁布里亚。
Union of Soviet Socialist Republics, (The) 苏联。
United Arab Emirates 阿拉伯联合酋长国。
United Kingdom (of Great Britain and Northern Ireland) 大不列颠及北爱尔兰联合王国。
United States (of America) 美利坚合众国；美国。
Upper Volta /-ˈvɒltə; -ˈvaltə/ 上沃尔特。
Ural /ˈjʊərəl; ˈjʊrəl/ 乌拉尔。
Uruguay /ˈjʊərəgwaɪ; ˈ(j)ʊrəˌgwaɪ/ 乌拉圭。
Usumbura /ˌuːsʊmˈbʊrə; ˌusəmˈbʊrə/ 乌松布拉。
Utah /ˈjuːtɑː; ˈjuˌtɔ/ 犹他。
Utica /ˈjuːtɪkə; ˈjutɪkə/ 尤蒂卡。
Utrecht /ˈjuːtrekt; ˈjuˌtrekt/ 乌得勒支。
Uzbekistan /ˌuzbekɪˈstɑːn; ˌuzbekɪˈstæn/ 乌兹别克。
Vaasa /ˈvɑːsɑ; ˈvasə/ 瓦萨。
Vaduz /fɑːˈduːts; vaˈduts/ 瓦杜兹。
Valdai Hills /vælˈdaɪ-; valˈdaɪ-/ 瓦尔代高地。
Valencia /vəˈlenʃɪə; vəˈlɛnʃɪə/ 瓦伦西亚。
Valenciennes /ˌvælænˈsɪen; vəˌlænsɪˈɛnz/ 瓦朗谢讷。
Valladolid /ˌvælæˈdɒˈlɪd; ˌvælædəˈlɪd/ 巴利亚多利德。
Va(l)letta /vəˈletə; vəˈletə/ 瓦莱塔。
Valparaiso /ˌvælpəˈraɪzəʊ; ˌvælpəˈraɪzo/ 瓦尔帕莱索。
Vancouver /vænˈkuːvə(r); vænˈkuvə/ 温哥华。
Vatican City (State) /ˈvætɪkən-; ˈvætɪkən-/ 梵蒂冈。
Vatnajökull /ˈvɑːtnɑːˌjəˈkuːtl; ˈvatnaˌjekutl/ 瓦特纳冰原。
Vaud /vəʊ; vo/ 沃(州)。
Venezuela /ˌvenɪˈzweɪlə; ˌvɛnəˈzwelə/ 委内瑞拉。
Venice /ˈvenɪs; ˈvɛnɪs/ 威尼斯。
Verdun /ˈveədʌn; vɛrˈdʌn/ 凡尔登。
Vermont /vəˈmɒnt; vəˈmant/ 佛蒙特。
Versailles /veəˈsaɪ; vɛˈsaɪ/ 凡尔赛。
Vesuvius /vɪˈsuːvɪəs; vəˈsuvɪəs/ 维苏威火山。
Viborg, Vyborg /ˈviːbɔːg; ˈviˌbɔrg/ 维堡。
Vichy /ˈviːʃiː; ˈviʃɪ/ 维希。
Vicksburg /ˈvɪksbɜːg; ˈvɪksˌbɜg/ 维克斯堡。
Victoria /vɪkˈtɔːrɪə; vɪkˈtorɪə/ 维多利亚。
Victoria, Mount 维多利亚山。
Vienna /vɪˈenə; vɪˈɛnə/ 维也纳。
Vientiane /ˌvjenˈtjɑːn; ˌvjenˈtjan/ 万象。
Vietnam, Viet-Nam /ˌvjetˈnæm; vɪˈetˈnam/ 越南。
Vigo /ˈviːgəʊ; ˈvigo/ 维哥。
Virginia /vəˈdʒɪnɪə; vəˈdʒɪnɪə/ 弗吉尼亚。
Virgin Islands 维尔京群岛。
Vistula /ˈvɪstjʊlə; ˈvɪstʃələ/ 维斯杜拉河。
Vitim /vɪˈtiːm; vɪˈtim/ 维季姆河。
Vitória /vɪˈtʊərɪə; vɪˈtorɪə/ 维多利亚。
Vladivostok /ˌvlædɪˈvɒstɒk; ˌvlædəvəˈstak/ 符拉迪沃斯托克。
Volcano Islands 硫黄列岛。
Volga /ˈvɒlgə; ˈvalgə/ 伏尔加河。
Vorkuta /vɔːˈkuːtə; vɔrˈkutə/ 沃尔库塔。
Vosges /vəʊʒ; voʒ/ 孚日山脉。
Wake /weɪk; wek/ 威克岛。
Wales /weɪlz; welz/ 威尔士。
Walsall /ˈwɔːlsɔːl; ˈwol.sol/ 瓦尔索尔。
Waltham /ˈwɔːltəm; ˈwɔl.θæm/ 沃尔瑟姆。
Wanganui /ˌwɒŋɑːˈnuː; ˌwaŋgəˈnui/ 旺阿努伊。
Warrington /ˈwɒrɪŋtən; ˈwɔrɪŋtən/ 沃灵顿。
Warszawa /ˈwɔːsɔː; ˈwɔr.sɔ/ 华沙。
Warwickshire /ˈwɒrɪkʃə(r) US: ˈwɔːr-; ˈwarɪk.ʃɪr/ 沃里克郡。
Washington /ˈwɒʃɪŋtən; ˈwaʃɪŋtən/ 1 华盛顿州。2 华盛顿。

Waterbury /'wɔːtəbrɪ; 'wɔtø,bɛrɪ/ 沃特伯里。
Waterford /'wɔːtəfəd; 'wɔtøfød/ 沃特福德。
Weimar /'vaɪmaː(r); 'vaɪ,mɑr/ 魏玛。
Welland /'welənd; 'welənd/ 威兰。
Wellesley /'welzlɪ; 'welzlɪ/ 韦尔斯利。
Wellington /'welɪntən; 'welɪntən/ 惠灵顿。
Western Australia 西澳大利亚。
Western Isles 西岛区。
Western Samoa 西萨摩亚。
West Glamorgan 西格拉摩根。
West Indies, (The) /-'ɪndɪz-; -'ɪndɪz/ 西印度群岛。
West Lothian 西洛锡安。
Westmeath /west'miːθ; wɛs(t)'miθ/ 韦斯特米斯。
Westmorland /'westmələnd; 'wɛs(t)mələnd/ 威斯特摩兰。
West Virginia 西弗吉尼亚。
Wexford /'weksfəd; 'wɛksfød/ 韦克斯福德。
Weymouth /'weɪməθ; 'weməθ/ 韦茅斯。
Whales, Bay of 鲸湾。
White 白河。
Whitney, Mount /'hwɪtnɪ; 'hwɪtnɪ/ 惠特尼山。
Wicklow /'wɪkləu; 'wɪklo/ 威克洛。
Wigan /'wɪgən; 'wɪgən/ 威根。
Wigtownshire /'wɪgtənʃə(r); 'wɪgtən,ʃɪr/ 威格敦郡。
Wilmington /'wɪlmɪntən; 'wɪlmɪntən/ 威尔明顿。
Wiltshire /'wɪltʃə(r); 'wɪlt,ʃɪr/ 威尔特郡。
Wimbledon /'wɪmbldən; 'wɪmbḷdən/ 温布尔登。
Winchester /'wɪntʃɪstə(r); 'wɪn,tʃɛstø/ 温切斯特。
Windhoek /'vɪnthuk; 'vɪnt,hʊk/ 温得和克。
Windsor /'wɪnzə(r); 'wɪnzø/ 温莎。
Windward Islands 向风群岛。
Winnipeg /'wɪnɪpeg; 'wɪnə,peg/ 温尼伯。
Wisconsin /wɪs'kɒnsn; wɪs'kansn̩/ 威斯康星。
Witwatersrand /wɪt'wɔːtezrænd; 'wɪt,wɔtøz,rænd/ 威特沃特斯兰德。
Wolverhampton /'wulvə,hæmtən; 'wʊlvø,hæmptən/ 伍尔弗汉普顿。
Worcestershire /'wustəʃə(r); 'wʊstø,ʃɪr/ 伍斯特郡。
Wrath, Cape /rɔːθ; raθ/ 拉斯角。
Wuhan /'wuː'haːn; 'wu'han/ 武汉。
Wulumuqi /uːˈluːmuːtʃi; uˈlumutʃi/ 乌鲁木齐。
Wyoming /waɪˈəumɪŋ; waɪ'omɪŋ/ 怀俄明。
Xian /'ʃiːˈɑːn; 'ʃiˈɑn/ 西安。
Ximalaya /'ʃiˈmaːˈlaːˈjaː; 'ʃimaˈlaˈja/ 喜马拉雅山脉。
Xingu /ʃɪŋˈguː; ʃɪŋ'gu/ 欣古河。

Xining /'ʃiːˈniŋ; 'ʃiˈniŋ/ 西宁。
Xinjiang /'ʃinˈdʒɑːŋ; 'ʃin'dʒaŋ/ 新疆。
Xizhang /'ʃiːˈdzɑːŋ; 'ʃidzaŋ/ 西藏。
Yalta /'jæltə; 'jɔltə/ 雅尔塔。
Yalu /'jaːˈluː; 'jɑ'lu/ 鸭绿江。
Yaoundé, Yaunde /'jaːuːnˈdeɪ; jaʊn'de/ 雅温得。
Yarmouth /'jaːməθ; 'jɑrməθ/ 雅茅斯。
Yaunde=Yaoundé
Yawata /'jaːwaːtɑː; jə'watø/ 八幡。
Yellowstone /'jeləustəun; 'jɛlo,ston/ 1 黄石河。2 黄石公园。
Yemen /'jemən; 'jemən/ ~ Arab Republic 阿拉伯也门共和国。
Yenangyaung /'jeɪnaːnˈdʒaʊŋ; jenan'dʒaʊŋ/ 仁安羌。
Yenisey, Yenise /ˌjenɪˈseɪ; ˌjɛnɪ'seɪ/ 叶尼塞河。
Yinchuan /jin'tʃuaːn; jin'tʃuan/ 银川。
Yokohama /ˌjəukəˈhaːmə; ˌjokə'hamə/ 横滨。
Yokosuka /ˌjəukəˈsukə; jo'kosəkə/ 横须贺。
York /jɔːk; jɔrk/ 约克。
Yorkshire /'jɔːkʃə(r); 'jɔrk,ʃɪr/ 约克郡。
Yuannan /'jüˈnaːn; 'jun'nan/ 云南。
Yucatán /ˌjuːkəˈtaːn; ˌjukə'tæn/ 尤卡坦。
Yugoslavia, Jugoslavia /ˌjuːgəuˈslaːvɪə; ˌjugo'slavɪə/ 南斯拉夫。
Yukon /'juːkɒn; 'ju,kan/ 育空河。
Yukon Territory/ 育空地区。
Zagreb /'zaːgreb; 'zag,rɛb/ 萨格勒布。
Zagros /'zægəs; 'zægrəs/ 扎格罗斯山脉。
Zaire /zaːˈɪə(r); zaˈɪr/ 扎伊尔。
Zama /'zaːmə; 'zamə/ 扎马。
Zambezi, Zambesi /zæmˈbiːzɪ; zæm'bizɪ/ 赞比西河。
Zambia /'zæmbɪə; 'zæmbɪə/ 赞比亚。
Zanzibar /ˌzænzɪˈbaː(r); ˌzænzə,bar/ 桑给巴尔。
Zaporožje /ˌzaːpəˈrɔːʒə; ˌzapə'rɔʒə/ 扎波罗热。
Zealand /'ziːlənd; 'zilənd/ 西兰岛。
Zetland /'zetlənd; 'zɛtlənd/ 昔得兰。
Zhen Zhou /'dʒən 'dʒəu; 'dʒən 'dʒɔu/ 郑州。
Zhu Jiang /'dʒu 'dʒaːŋ; 'dʒu 'dʒaŋ/ 珠江。
Zhumulangmafeng /'dʒuːmuːlɒŋmaː; ˌdʒu'muˈlɒ'ŋ'maˈ/ 珠穆朗玛峰。
Zimbabwe /zɪmˈbaːbwɪ; zɪm'babwɪ/ 津巴布韦。
Zomba /'zɒmbə; 'zɑmbə/ 松巴。
Zugspitze /'tsuːk,ʃpɪtsə; 'tsuk,ʃpɪtsə/ 祖格峰。
Zuider Zee /'zaɪdə 'zeɪ; ˌzaɪdə 'ze/ 须德海。
Zurich /'zjuərɪk; 'zʊrɪk/ 苏黎世。

APPENDIX 7 COMMON FORENAMES

附录七 常见的名字

Note: Pet-names are either shown after the name from which they are formed or listed separately with a note on their origins. Many of the names listed which consist of a single syllable have pet-name forms produced by adding / ɪ / to the pronunciation and -y or -ie to the spelling, and doubling the final consonant if the preceding vowel is short.

注意: 昵称列在自其衍生的名字之后, 或单独列并注明其出处。表内很多单音节的名字都有昵称, 这些昵称是在音标之后加 /ɪ/, ɪ/ 音, 在拼法上加 -y 或 -ie 而构成的, 如果最后一个辅音前面的元音是短元音, 则重复该辅音:

eg 例如: Fred, Freddy /'fredɪ; 'fredɪ/; Hugh, Hughie /'hjuːɪ; 'hjuɪ/;
Liz, Lizzie /'lɪzɪ; 'lɪzɪ/; Rose, Rosie /'rəʊzɪ; 'rozɪ/.

Men 男子名

Abraham /'eɪbrəhæm; 'ebrə,hæm/ 亚伯拉罕
Adam /'ædəm; 'ædəm/ 亚当
Adrian /'eɪdrɪən; 'edrɪən/ 亚德里恩
Alan, Allan, Allen /'ælən; 'ælən/ 艾伦
Albert /'ælbət; 'ælbət/ 艾伯特; **Al** /æl; æl/ 艾尔
Alexander /,ælɪg'zɑːndə(r) US: -'zæn-; ,ælɪg'zændə/ 亚历山大; **Alex** /'ælɪks; 'ælɪks/ 亚历克斯
Alfred /'ælfrɪd; 'ælfrɪd/ 艾尔弗雷德; **Alf** /ælf; ælf/ 艾夫
Andrew /'ændruː; 'ændru/ 安德鲁; **Andy** /'ændɪ; 'ændɪ/ 安迪
Angus /'æŋgəs; 'æŋgəs/ 安格斯
Anthony, Antony /'æntənɪ; 'æntənɪ/ 安东尼
Arnold /'ɑːnld; 'ɑrnld/ 阿诺德
Arthur /'ɑːθə(r); 'ɑrθə/ 亚瑟
Barry /'bærɪ; 'bærɪ/ 巴里
Bartholomew /bɑː'θɒləmjuː; bɑr'θɑlədmju/ 巴塞洛缪; **Bart** /bɑːt; bɑrt/ 巴特
Basil /'bæzl; 'bæzl/ 巴兹尔
Benjamin /'bendʒəmɪn; 'bendʒəmən/ 本杰明; **Ben** /ben; bɛn/ 本
Bernard /'bɜːnəd US: bər'nɑːrd; 'bɜnəd/ 伯纳德; **Bernie** /'bɜːnɪ; 'bɜnɪ/ 伯尼
Bert /bɜːt; bət/ (from 出自 *Albert, Gilbert, Herbert, Hubert*) 伯特
Bill /bɪl; bɪl/ (from 出自 *William*) 比尔
Bob /bɒb; bab/ (from 出自 *Robert*) 鲍勃
Boris /'bɒrɪs US: 'bɔːr-; 'bɔrɪs/ 鲍里斯
Brian, Bryan /'braɪən; 'braɪən/ 布赖恩
Bruce /bruːs; brus/ 布鲁斯
Carl /kɑːl; kɑrl/ 卡尔
Cecil /'sesl US: 'siːsl; 'sɪsl/ 塞西尔
Cedric /'sedrɪk; 'sedrɪk/ 塞德里克
Charles /tʃɑːlz; tʃɑrlz/ 查尔斯; **Chas** /tʃæz; tʃæz/ 查士
Christian /'krɪstʃən; 'krɪstʃən/ 克里斯琴
Christopher /'krɪstəfə(r); 'krɪstəfə/ 克利斯托弗; **Chris** /krɪs; krɪs/ 克里斯
Claud(e) /klɔːd; klɔd/ 克劳德
Clement /'klemənt; 'klemənt/ 克莱门特
Clifford /'klɪfəd; 'klɪfəd/ 克利福德; **Cliff** /klɪf; klɪf/ 克利夫
Clive /klaɪv; klaɪv/ 克莱夫
Colin /'kɒlɪn; 'kɑlɪn/ 科林
Cyril /'sɪrəl; 'sɪrəl/ 西里尔
Daniel /'dænɪəl; 'dænjəl/ 丹尼尔; **Dan** /dæn; dæn/ 丹(恩)
David /'deɪvɪd; 'devɪd/ 大卫; **Dave** /deɪv; dev/ 戴夫
Dean /diːn; din/ 迪恩
Dennis, Denis /'denɪs; 'dɛnɪs/ 丹尼斯
Derek /'derɪk; 'dɛrɪk/ 德里克
Desmond /'dezmənd; 'dɛzmənd/ 德斯蒙德; **Des** /dez; dɛz/ 德兹
Dick /dɪk; dɪk/ (from 出自 *Richard*) 迪克
Dominic /'dɒmɪnɪk; 'damənɪk/ 多明尼克

Donald /'dɒnld; 'dɑnl̩d/ 唐纳德; **Don** /dɒn; dɑn/ 唐
Douglas /'dʌgləs; 'dʌgləs/ 道格拉斯; **Doug** /dʌg; dʌg/ 道格
Duncan /'dʌŋkən; 'dʌŋkən/ 邓肯
Edgar /'edgə(r); 'edgə/ 艾德加
Edmund /'edmənd; 'edmənd/ 艾德蒙
Edward /'edwəd; 'edwəd/ 艾德华; **Ed** /ed; ɛd/ 埃德
Enoch /'iːnɒk; 'inɒk/ 伊诺克
Eric /'erɪk; 'ɛrɪk/ 埃里克
Ernest /'ɜːnɪst; 'ɜrnɪst/ 欧内斯特; **Ernie** /'ɜːnɪ; 'ɜnɪ/ 厄尼
Eugene /juː'dʒiːn; ju'dʒin/ 尤金
Felix /'fiːlɪks; 'filɪks/ 费利克斯
Francis /'frɑːnsɪs US: 'fræn-; 'frænsɪs/ 弗朗西斯
Frank /fræŋk; fræŋk/ 弗兰克
Frederick /'fredrɪk; 'fred(ə)rɪk/ 弗雷德里克; **Fred** /fred; fred/ 弗雷德
Gareth /'gærəθ; 'gærɪθ/ 加雷思
Gary /'gærɪ; 'gærɪ/ 加里
Gavin /'gævɪn; 'gævɪn/ 加文
Gene /dʒiːn; dʒin/ (from 出自 *Eugene*) 吉恩
Geoffrey /'dʒefrɪ; 'dʒefrɪ/ 杰弗里; **Geoff** /dʒef; dʒef/ 杰夫
George /dʒɔːdʒ; dʒɔrdʒ/ 乔治
Gerald /'dʒerəld; 'dʒerəld/ 杰拉尔德; **Gerry** /'gerɪ; 'gerɪ/ 格里
Gerard /'dʒerəd; dʒə'rɑrd/ 杰勒德
Gilbert /'gɪlbət; 'gɪlbət/ 吉尔伯特
Giles /dʒaɪlz; dʒaɪlz/ 贾尔斯
Glen /glen; glɛn/ 格伦
Godfrey /'gɒdfrɪ; 'gɑdfrɪ/ 戈弗雷
Gordon /'gɔːdn; 'gɔrdn/ 戈登
Graham /'greɪəm; 'greəm/ 格雷厄姆
Gregory /'gregərɪ; 'gregərɪ/ 格雷戈里; **Greg** /greg; greg/ 格雷格
Guy /gaɪ; gaɪ/ 盖伊
Harold /'hærəld; 'hærəld/ 哈罗德; **Harry** /'hærɪ; 'hærɪ/ 哈里; **Hal** /hæl; hæl/ 哈尔
Harvey /'hɑːvɪ; 'hɑrvɪ/ 哈维
Henry /'henrɪ; 'henrɪ/ 亨利
Herbert /'hɜːbət; 'hɜbət/ 赫伯特
Hilary /'hɪlərɪ; 'hɪlərɪ/ 希拉里
Horace /'hɒrɪs US: 'hɔːr-; 'hɔrɪs/ 霍勒斯
Howard /'haʊəd; 'haʊəd/ 霍华德
Hubert /'hjuːbət; 'hjubət/ 休伯特
Hugh /hjuː; hju/ 修
Humphrey /'hʌmfrɪ; 'hʌmfrɪ/ 汉弗里
Ian /'iːən; 'iən/ 伊恩
Isaac /'aɪzək; 'aɪzək/ 艾萨克
Ivan /'aɪvən; 'aɪvən/ 艾凡
Ivor /'aɪvə(r); 'aɪvə/ 艾弗
Jack /dʒæk; dʒæk/ (from 出自 *John*) 杰克
Jacob /'dʒeɪkəb; 'dʒekəb/ 雅各布
James /dʒeɪmz; dʒemz/ 詹姆斯
Jason /'dʒeɪsn; 'dʒesn/ 杰森

Jeffrey /ˈdʒefrɪ; ˈdʒɪfrɪ/ 杰弗里; **Jeff** /dʒef; dʒɪf/ 杰夫

Jeremy /ˈdʒerəmɪ; ˈdʒɛrəmɪ/ 哲里米; **Jerry** /ˈdʒerɪ; ˈdʒɛrɪ/ 哲里

Jerome /dʒəˈrəum; dʒəˈrom/ 哲罗姆

Jim /dʒɪm; dʒɪm/ (from 出自 *James*) 吉姆

John /dʒɒn; dʒɑn/ 约翰

Jonathan /ˈdʒɒnəθən; ˈdʒɑnəθən/ 乔纳森

Joseph /ˈdʒəuzɪf; ˈdʒozəf/ 约瑟夫; **Jo, Joe** /dʒəu; dʒo/ 乔

Joshua /ˈdʒɒʃuə; ˈdʒɑʃuə/ 乔舒亚

Julian /ˈdʒuːlɪən; ˈdʒuljən/ 朱里恩

Justin /ˈdʒʌstɪn; ˈdʒʌstɪn/ 贾斯廷

Keith /kiːθ; kiθ/ 基思

Kenneth /ˈkenɪθ; ˈkɛnɪθ/ 肯尼思; **Ken** /ken; kɛn/ 肯

Kevin /ˈkevɪn; ˈkɛvɪn/ 凯文

Laurence, Lawrence /ˈlɒrəns US: ˈlɔːrəns; ˈlɔrəns/ 劳伦斯; **Larry** /ˈlærɪ; ˈlærɪ/ 拉里

Leo /ˈliːəu; ˈlio/ 利欧

Leonard /ˈlenəd; ˈlɛnəd/ 伦纳德; **Len** /len; lɛn/ 莱恩

Leslie /ˈlezlɪ; ˈlɛslɪ/ 莱斯利; **Les** /lez; lɛs/ 勒斯

Lewis /ˈluːɪs; ˈluɪs/ 刘易斯

Lionel /ˈlaɪənl; ˈlaɪənl/ 赖恩内尔

Louis /ˈluːiː US: ˈluːɪs; ˈluɪs/ 路易斯, **Lou** /luː; lu/ 卢

Luke /luːk; luk/ 卢克

Malcolm /ˈmælkəm; ˈmælkəm/ 麦尔肯

Mark /mɑːk; mɑrk/ 马克

Martin /ˈmɑːtɪn US: -tn; ˈmɑrtɪn/ 马丁

Matthew /ˈmæθjuː; ˈmæθju/ 马瑟耳; **Matt** /mæt; mæt/ 马特

Maurice /ˈmɒrɪs US: ˈmɔːr-; ˈmɔrɪs/ 莫里斯

Max /mæks; mæks/ 马克斯

Michael /ˈmaɪkl; ˈmaɪkl/ 迈克尔; 米克; **Mike** /maɪk; maɪk/ 迈克

Miles /maɪlz; maɪlz/ 迈尔斯

Nathaniel /nəˈθænɪəl; nəˈθænjəl/ 纳撒尼尔; **Nat** /næt; næt/ 纳特

Ned /ned; nɛd/ (from 出自 *Edward*) 内德

Neil /niːl; nil/ 尼尔

Neville /ˈnevl; ˈnɛvl/ 内维尔

Nicholas /ˈnɪkələs; ˈnɪk(ə)ləs/ 尼古拉斯; **Nick** /nɪk; nɪk/ 尼克

Nigel /ˈnaɪdʒl; ˈnaɪdʒəl/ 奈哲尔

Noel /ˈnəuəl; ˈnoəl/ 诺埃尔

Norman /ˈnɔːmən; ˈnɔrmən/ 诺曼

Oliver /ˈɒlɪvə(r); ˈɑləvə/ 奥利弗

Oscar /ˈɒskə(r); ˈɔskə/ 奥斯卡

Oswald /ˈɒzwəld; ˈɑzwɔld/ 奥斯瓦尔德

Patrick /ˈpætrɪk; ˈpætrɪk/ 帕特里克; **Pat** /pæt; pæt/ 帕特; **Paddy** /ˈpædɪ; ˈpædɪ/ 珀迪

Paul /pɔːl; pɔl/ 保罗

Percy /ˈpɜːsɪ; ˈpɜsɪ/ 珀西

Peter /ˈpiːtə(r); ˈpitə/ 彼得; **Pete** /piːt; pit/ 皮特

Philip /ˈfɪlɪp; ˈfɪləp/ 菲利普; **Phil** /fɪl; fɪl/ 菲尔

Quentin /ˈkwentɪn US: -tn; ˈkwɛntn/ 昆廷

Ralph /rælf; rælf/ 拉尔夫

Randolph /ˈrændɒlf; ˈrændɑlf/ 伦道夫

Raymond /ˈreɪmənd; ˈremənd/ 雷蒙德; **Ray** /reɪ; re/ 雷

Reginald /ˈredʒɪnld; ˈrɛdʒɪnld/ 雷金纳德; **Reg** /redʒ; rɛdʒ/ 雷吉

Rex /reks; rɛks/ 雷克斯

Richard /ˈrɪtʃəd; ˈrɪtʃəd/ 理查德

Robert /ˈrɒbət; ˈrɑbət/ 罗伯特

Robin /ˈrɒbɪn; ˈrɑbɪn/ 罗宾

Rodney /ˈrɒdnɪ; ˈrɑdnɪ/ 罗德尼; **Rod** /rɒd; rad/ 罗德

Roger /ˈrɒdʒə(r); ˈrɑdʒə/ 罗杰

Ronald /ˈrɒnld; ˈrɑnld/ 罗纳德; **Ron** /rɒn; rɑn/ 罗恩

Roy /rɔɪ; rɔɪ/ 罗伊

Rudolf /ˈruːdɒlf; ˈrudɑlf/ 鲁道夫

Rupert /ˈruːpət; ˈrupət/ 鲁伯特

Samuel /ˈsæmjuəl; ˈsæmjuəl/ 塞缪尔; **Sam** /sæm; sæm/ 萨姆

Sandy /ˈsændɪ; ˈsændɪ/ (from 出自 *Alexander*) 桑迪

Seamus /ˈʃeɪməs; ˈʃeməs/ 谢默斯

Sean /ʃɔːn; ʃɔn/ 肖恩

Sidney /ˈsɪdnɪ; ˈsɪdnɪ/ 锡德尼; **Sid** /sɪd; sɪd/ 锡德

Simon /ˈsaɪmən; ˈsaɪmən/ 西蒙

Stanley /ˈstænlɪ; ˈstænlɪ/ 斯且利; **Stan** /stæn; stæn/ 斯且

Stephen, Steven /ˈstiːvn; ˈstivən/ 斯蒂芬; **Steve** /stiːv; stiv/ 史蒂夫

Stewart, Stuart /ˈstjuːət US: ˈstuː-; ˈst⟨j⟩uət/ 斯图尔特

Ted /ted; tɛd/ (from 出自 *Edward*) 特德

Terence /ˈterəns; ˈtɛrəns/ 特伦斯; **Terry** /ˈterɪ; ˈtɛrɪ/ 特里

Theodore /ˈθiːədɔː(r); ˈθiədor/ 西奥多; **Theo** /ˈθiːəu; ˈθio/ 西奥

Thomas /ˈtɒməs; ˈtɑməs/ 托马斯; **Tom** /tɒm; tam/ 汤姆

Timothy /ˈtɪməθɪ; ˈtɪməθɪ/ 蒂莫西; **Tim** /tɪm; tɪm/ 蒂姆

Toby /ˈtəubɪ; ˈtobɪ/ 托比

Tony /ˈtəunɪ; ˈtonɪ/ (from 出自 *Anthony*) 托尼

Trevor /ˈtrevə(r); ˈtrɛvə/ 特雷弗

Vernon /ˈvɜːnən; ˈvɜnən/ 维он

Victor /ˈvɪktə(r); ˈvɪktə/ 维克多; **Vic** /vɪk; vɪk/ 维克

Vincent /ˈvɪnsnt; ˈvɪnsn̩t/ 文森特

Vivian /ˈvɪvɪən; ˈvɪvɪən/ 维维恩

Walter /ˈwɔːltə(r); ˈwɔltə/ 沃尔特

Wayne /weɪn; wen/ 韦恩

Wilfred /ˈwɪlfrɪd; ˈwɪlfrɪd/ 威(尔)弗雷德

William /ˈwɪlɪəm; ˈwɪljəm/ 威廉; **Will** /wɪl; wɪl/ 威尔

Women 女子名

Ada /ˈeɪdə; ˈedə/ 埃达

Agatha /ˈæɡəθə; ˈæɡəθə/ 阿加莎

Agnes /ˈæɡnɪs; ˈæɡnɪs/ 阿格妮丝; **Aggie** /ˈæɡɪ; ˈæɡɪ/ 艾姬

Alexandra /ˌælɪɡˈzɑːndrə US: -ˈzæn-; ˌælɪɡˈzændrə/ 亚历山德拉

Alice /ˈælɪs; ˈælɪs/ 艾丽斯

Alison /ˈælɪsn; ˈæləsn̩/ 艾丽森

Amanda /əˈmændə; əˈmændə/ 阿曼达

Amy /ˈeɪmɪ; ˈemɪ/ 埃米

Angela /ˈændʒələ; ˈændʒələ/ 安杰拉

Anita /əˈniːtə; əˈnitə/ 阿妮塔

Ann, Anne /æn; æn/ 安

Annabel /ˈænəbel; ˈænəˌbɛl/ 安纳贝尔

Anthea /ˈænθɪə; ænˈθiə/ 安西娅

Audrey /ˈɔːdrɪ; ˈɔdrɪ/ 奥德莉

Barbara /ˈbɑːbrə; ˈbɑrb(ə)rə/ 巴巴拉; **Babs** /bæbz; bæbz/ 巴布丝

Beatrice /ˈbɪətrɪs; ˈbiətrɪs/ 比阿特丽丝

Belinda /bəˈlɪndə; bəˈlɪndə/ 碧琳达

Bella /ˈbelə; ˈbɛlə/ (from 出自 *Isabella*) 贝拉

Beryl /ˈberəl; ˈbɛrəl/ 贝里尔

Bess /bes; bɛs/ (from 出自 *Elizabeth*) 贝丝

Betsy /ˈbetsɪ; ˈbɛtsɪ/ (from 出自 *Elizabeth*) 贝齐

Betty /ˈbetɪ; ˈbɛtɪ/ (from 出自 *Elizabeth*) 贝蒂

Brenda /ˈbrendə; ˈbrɛndə/ 布伦达

Bridget /ˈbrɪdʒɪt; ˈbrɪdʒɪt/ 布里奇特

Carol, Carole /ˈkærəl; ˈkærəl/ 卡罗尔

Caroline /ˈkærəlaɪn; ˈkærəlaɪn/ 卡罗琳

Carolyn /ˈkærəlɪn; ˈkærəlɪn/ 卡罗琳

Catherine /ˈkæθrɪn; ˈkæθ(ə)rɪn/ 凯瑟琳; **Cathy** /ˈkæθɪ; ˈkæθɪ/ 卡西

Cecilia /səˈsiːlɪə; sɪˈsɪljə/ 塞西莉亚

Cecily /ˈsesɪlɪ; ˈsɛsl̩ɪ/ 塞西莉

Celia /ˈsiːlɪə; ˈsiljə/ 西莉亚

Charlotte /ˈʃɑːlət; ˈʃɑrlət/ 夏洛特

Chloe /ˈkləuɪ; ˈkloˑɪ/ 克乐怡

Christina /krɪˈstiːnə; krɪsˈtinə/ 克里斯蒂娜

Christine /ˈkrɪstiːn; krɪsˈtin/ 克里斯婷; **Chris** /krɪs; krɪs/ 克丽斯

Clare /kleə(r); klɛr/ 克莱尔

Constance /ˈkɒnstəns; ˈkɑnstəns/ 康斯坦斯; **Connie** /ˈkɒnɪ; ˈkɑnɪ/ 康妮

Cynthia /ˈsɪnθɪə; ˈsɪnθɪə/ 莘西娅

Daisy /ˈdeɪzɪ; ˈdezɪ/ 戴西

Daphne /ˈdæfnɪ; ˈdæfnɪ/ 达夫妮

Dawn /dɔːn; dɔn/ 唐

Deborah /ˈdebərə; ˈdebərə/ 德博拉; **Debby** /ˈdebɪ; ˈdebɪ/ 德碧

Deirdre /ˈdɪədrɪ; ˈdɪrdrɪ/ 迪尔德莉

Denise /dəˈniːz; dəˈniz/ 丹妮斯

Diana /daɪˈænə; daɪˈænə/ 黛安娜

Dolly /ˈdɒlɪ; ˈdɑlɪ/ (from 出自 Dorothy) 多丽

Dora /ˈdɔːrə; ˈdorə/ 多拉

Doreen /ˈdɔːriːn; ˈdorin/ 多琳

Doris /ˈdɒrɪs US: ˈdɔːr-; ˈdɔrɪs/ 多丽丝

Dorothy /ˈdɒrəθɪ US: ˈdɔːr-; ˈdɔrəθɪ/ 多乐西

Edith /ˈiːdɪθ; ˈidɪθ/ 伊迪丝

Eileen /ˈaɪliːn; aɪˈlin/ 艾琳

Elaine /iˈleɪn; ɪˈlen/ 伊莱恩

Eleanor /ˈelənə(r); ˈelənə/ 埃丽诺

Eliza /ɪˈlaɪzə; ɪˈlaɪzə/ (from 出自 Elizabeth) 伊莱扎

Elizabeth /ɪˈlɪzəbəθ; ɪˈlɪzəbəθ/ 伊丽莎白

Ellen /ˈelən; ˈelən/ 埃伦

Elsie /ˈelsɪ; ˈelsɪ/ (from 出自 Elizabeth) 埃尔西

Emily /ˈeməlɪ; ˈemlɪ/ 埃米丽

Emma /ˈemə; ˈemə/ 埃玛

Erica /ˈerɪkə; ˈerɪkə/ 艾丽嘉

Ethel /ˈeθl; ˈeθəl/ 艾塞尔

Eunice /ˈjuːnɪs; ˈjuːnɪs/ 尤妮斯

Eva /ˈiːvə; ˈivə/ 伊娃

Eve /iːv; iv/ 伊夫

Evelyn /ˈiːvlɪn; ˈɛv(ə)lɪn/ 伊夫琳

Fanny /ˈfænɪ; ˈfænɪ/ (from 出自 Frances) 范妮

Felicity /fəˈlɪsətɪ; fəˈlɪsətɪ/ 菲莉思蒂

Fiona /fɪˈəʊnə; fɪˈonə/ 菲奥纳

Flora /ˈflɔːrə; ˈflorə/ 弗洛拉

Florence /ˈflɒrəns US: ˈflɔːr-; ˈflorəns/ 弗洛伦斯

Frances /ˈfrɑːnsɪs US: ˈfræn-; ˈfrænsɪs/ 法朗西丝

Fran /fræn; fræn/ 法兰

Freda /ˈfriːdə; ˈfridə/ 弗雷达

Geraldine /ˈdʒerəldiːn; ˈdʒerəldˌin/ 杰拉尔丁

Gertrude /ˈgɜːtruːd; ˈgɜtrud/ 格特鲁德; **Gertie** /ˈgɜːtɪ; ˈgɜtɪ/ 葛蒂

Gillian /ˈdʒɪlɪən; ˈdʒɪlɪən/ 吉利恩; **Gill** /dʒɪl; dʒɪl/ 吉尔

Gladys /ˈglædɪs; ˈglædɪs/ 格拉迪斯

Gloria /ˈglɔːrɪə; ˈglorɪə/ 格罗丽亚

Grace /greɪs; gres/ 格雷丝

Gwendoline /ˈgwendəlɪn; ˈgwendlɪn/ 格温德琳; **Gwen** /gwen; gwen/ 格温

Harriet /ˈhærɪət; ˈhærɪət/ 哈丽亚特

Hazel /ˈheɪzl; ˈhezl/ 黑兹尔

Heather /ˈheðə(r); ˈhɛðə/ 希瑟

Helen /ˈhelən; ˈhelən/ 海伦

Hilary /ˈhɪlərɪ; ˈhɪlərɪ/ 希拉里

Hilda /ˈhɪldə; ˈhɪldə/ 希尔达

Ida /ˈaɪdə; ˈaɪdə/ 艾达

Ingrid /ˈɪŋgrɪd; ˈɪŋgrɪd/ 英格里德

Irene /aɪˈriːnɪ US: ˈaɪəriːn; aɪˈrin/ 艾琳

Iris /ˈaɪərɪs; ˈaɪrɪs/ 艾里斯

Isabel, Isobel /ˈɪzəbel; ˈɪzəˌbɛl/ 伊莎贝尔

Isabella /ˌɪzəˈbelə; ˌɪzəˈbelə/ 伊莎贝拉

Ivy /ˈaɪvɪ; ˈaɪvɪ/ 艾维

Jacqueline /ˈdʒækəlɪn; ˈdʒækəlɪn/ 杰桂琳; **Jackie** /ˈdʒækɪ; ˈdʒækɪ/ 杰基

Jane /dʒeɪn; dʒen/ 简

Janet /ˈdʒænɪt; ˈdʒænɪt/ 珍妮特

Janice /ˈdʒænɪs; ˈdʒænɪs/ 贾尼丝

Jean /dʒiːn; dʒin/ 琼

Jennifer /ˈdʒenɪfə(r); ˈdʒɛnəfə/ 珍尼弗; **Jenny** /ˈdʒenɪ; ˈdʒenɪ/ 珍妮

Jessica /ˈdʒesɪkə; ˈdʒesəkə/ 杰西卡; **Jess** /dʒes; dʒes/ 杰斯

Jill /dʒɪl; dʒɪl/ (from 出自 Gillian) 吉尔

Joan /dʒəʊn; dʒon/ 琼

Joanna /dʒəʊˈænə; dʒoˈænə/ 乔安娜

Jocelyn /ˈdʒɒslɪn; ˈdʒɑs(ə)lɪn/ 乔思琳

Josephine /ˈdʒəʊzəfiːn; ˈdʒozəˌfin/ 约瑟芬; **Jo** /dʒəʊ; dʒo/ 乔

Joy /dʒɔɪ; dʒɔɪ/ 乔伊

Joyce /dʒɔɪs; dʒɔɪs/ 乔伊斯

Judith /ˈdʒuːdɪθ; ˈdʒudɪθ/ 朱迪恩; **Judy** /ˈdʒuːdɪ; ˈdʒudɪ/ 朱迪

Julia /ˈdʒuːlɪə; ˈdʒuljə/ 朱丽娅

Julie /ˈdʒuːlɪ; ˈdʒulɪ/ 朱莉

Juliet /ˈdʒuːlɪət; ˈdʒuljət/ 朱丽叶

June /dʒuːn; dʒun/ 琼

Karen /ˈkærən; ˈkærən/ 卡伦

Katherine /ˈkæθrɪn; ˈkæθ(ə)rɪn/ 凯瑟琳; **Kate** /keɪt; ket/ 凯特; **Kathy** /ˈkæθɪ; ˈkæθɪ/ 凯西

Kay /keɪ; ke/ 凯

Kitty /ˈkɪtɪ; ˈkɪtɪ/ (from 出自 Katherine) 基蒂

Laura /ˈlɔːrə; ˈlɔrə/ 劳拉

Lesley /ˈlezlɪ; ˈlɛzlɪ/ 莱斯利

Lilian /ˈlɪlɪən; ˈlɪlɪən/ 丽莲

Lily /ˈlɪlɪ; ˈlɪlɪ/ 莉莉

Linda /ˈlɪndə; ˈlɪndə/ 琳达

Lisa /ˈliːsə; ˈlisə/ 丽莎; **Liza** /ˈlaɪzə; ˈlaɪzə/ (from 出自 Elizabeth) 莱莎

Liz /lɪz; lɪz/ (from 出自 Elizabeth) 利兹

Lois /ˈləʊɪs; ˈlo·ɪs/ 洛伊丝

Lorna /ˈlɔːnə; ˈlɔrnə/ 洛娜

Louise /luːˈiːz; lʊˈiz/ 路易丝

Lucy /ˈluːsɪ; ˈlusɪ/ 露西

Lydia /ˈlɪdɪə; ˈlɪdɪə/ 丽迪亚

Lynn /lɪn; lɪn/ 琳

Mabel /ˈmeɪbl; ˈmebl/ 梅布儿

Madeleine /ˈmædlɪn; ˈmædlɪn/ 马德琳

Madge /mædʒ; mædʒ/ (from 出自 Margaret) 玛奇

Maggie /ˈmægɪ; ˈmægɪ/ (from 出自 Margaret) 玛吉

Mamie /ˈmeɪmɪ; ˈmemɪ/ (from 出自 Mary) 玛米

Mandy /ˈmændɪ; ˈmændɪ/ (from 出自 Amanda) 曼蒂

Margaret /ˈmɑːgrɪt; ˈmɑrg(ə)rɪt/ 玛格丽特

Margery /ˈmɑːdʒərɪ; ˈmɑrdʒərɪ/ 玛杰里; **Margie** /ˈmɑːdʒɪ; ˈmɑrdʒɪ/ 玛吉

Maria /məˈrɪə; məˈrɪə/ 玛丽亚

Marian, Marion /ˈmærɪən; ˈmærɪən/ 玛丽安

Marie /məˈriː, ˈmɑːrɪ; məˈri, ˈmɑrɪ/ 玛丽

Marilyn /ˈmærəlɪn; ˈmærəlɪn/ 玛里琳

Marjorie /ˈmɑːdʒərɪ; ˈmɑrdʒərɪ/ 玛乔里

Marlene /mɑːˈliːn; mɑrˈlin/ 玛琳

Martha /ˈmɑːθə; ˈmɑrθə/ 玛莎

Mary /ˈmeərɪ; ˈmerɪ/ 玛莉

Maud /mɔːd; mɔd/ 莫德

Maureen /ˈmɔːriːn; moˈrin/ 莫琳

Mavis /ˈmeɪvɪs; ˈmevɪs/ 梅维斯

Maxine /ˈmæksiːn; mækˈsin/ 玛可辛

May /meɪ; me/ (from 出自 Mary) 梅

Meg /meg; meg/ (from 出自 Margaret) 梅格

Michelle /mɪˈʃel; mɪˈʃɛl/ 米歇尔

Mildred /ˈmɪldrɪd; ˈmɪldrɪd/ 米尔德里德

Millicent /ˈmɪlɪsnt; ˈmɪləsənt/ 米利森特; **Milly** /ˈmɪlɪ; ˈmɪlɪ/ 米莉

Miranda /mɪˈrændə; məˈrændə/ 米兰达

Miriam /ˈmɪrɪəm; ˈmɪrɪəm/ 米里亚姆

Moira /ˈmɔɪrə; ˈmɔɪrə/ 莫伊拉

Molly /ˈmɒlɪ; ˈmɑlɪ/ (from 出自 Mary) 莫莉

Monica /ˈmɒnɪkə; ˈmɑnɪkə/ 莫妮卡

Muriel /ˈmjʊərɪəl; ˈmjʊrɪəl/ 缪丽尔

Myra /ˈmaɪərə; ˈmaɪrə/ 迈拉

Nancy /ˈnænsɪ; ˈnænsɪ/ 南希

Naomi /'neɪəmɪ; neˈomɪ/ 内奥米
Natalie /'nætəlɪ; 'nætlɪ/ 娜塔莉
Nelly /'nelɪ; 'nelɪ/ (from 出自 *Eleanor* or 或 *Helen*) 内丽
Nora /'nɔːrə; 'norə/ 诺拉
Olive /'ɒlɪv; 'ɑlɪv/ 奥利夫
Olivia /ə'lɪvɪə; oˈlɪvɪə/ 奥利维亚
Pamela /'pæmələ; 'pæmələ/ 帕梅拉; **Pam** /pæm; pæm/ 帕姆
Patience /'peɪʃns; 'peʃəns/ 佩兴斯
Patricia /pə'trɪʃə; pəˈtrɪʃə/ 帕特里夏; **Pat** /pæt; pæt/ 帕特
Paula /'pɔːlə; 'pɔlə/ 葆拉
Pauline /'pɔːliːn; pɔˈlin/ 波琳
Pearl /pɜːl; pɝl/ 珀尔
Peg /peg; peg/ (from 出自 *Margaret*) 佩格
Penelope /pə'neləpɪ; pəˈnɛləpɪ/ 佩内洛普; **Penny** /'penɪ; 'pɛnɪ/ 彭妮
Philippa /'fɪlɪpə; fɪˈlɪpə/ 菲丽帕
Phoebe /'fiːbɪ; 'fibɪ/ 菲比
Phyllis /'fɪlɪs; 'fɪlɪs/ 菲丽丝
Polly /'pɒlɪ; 'pɑlɪ/ 波利
Priscilla /prɪ'sɪlə; prɪˈsɪlə/ 普里西拉
Prudence /'pruːdns; 'prudns/ 普鲁登丝
Rachel /'reɪtʃl; 'retʃəl/ 雷切尔
Rebecca /rə'bekə; rɪˈbɛkə/ 丽贝卡
Rita /'riːtə; 'ritə/ 丽塔
Rosalie /'rəʊzəlɪ; 'rozəlɪ/ 罗茨莉
Rosalind /'rɒzəlɪnd; 'rɑzə(ə)lɪnd/ 罗莎琳德
Rose /rəʊz; roz/ 罗丝
Rosemary /'rəʊzməri US: -meri; 'roz,mɛrɪ/ 罗斯玛莉
Ruth /ruːθ; ruθ/ 鲁斯
Sally /'sælɪ; 'sælɪ/ (from 出自 *Sarah*) 萨莉
Samantha /sə'mænθə; səˈmænθə/ 萨曼莎

Sandra /'sɑːndrə US: 'sæn-; 'sændrə/ 桑德拉
Sarah /'seərə; 'sɛrə/ 萨拉
Sharon /'ʃærən; 'ʃɛrən/ 沙伦
Sheila /'ʃiːlə; 'ʃilə/ 希拉
Shirley /'ʃɜːlɪ; 'ʃɝlɪ/ 雪莉
Sonia /'sɒnɪə; 'sonɪə/ 索妮亚
Sophia /sə'faɪə; soˈfaɪə/ 索菲娅
Sophie /'səʊfɪ; 'sofɪ/ 索菲
Stella /'stelə; 'stɛlə/ 史黛拉
Stephanie /'stefənɪ; 'stɛfənɪ/ 斯蒂法妮
Susan /'suːzn; 'suzn/ 苏珊; **Sue** /suː; su/ 休; **Susie** /'suːzɪ; 'suzɪ/ 苏西
Suzanne /suː'zæn; suˈzæn/ 苏珊娜
Sylvia, Silvia /'sɪlvɪə; 'sɪlvɪə/ 西尔维亚
Teresa, Theresa /tə'riːzə; təˈrisə/ 特里萨; **Tess** /tes; tɛs/ 特丝; **Tessa** /'tesə; 'tɛsə/ 特莎
Tina /'tiːnə; 'tinə/ (from 出自 *Christina*) 婷娜
Tracy /'treɪsɪ; 'tresɪ/ 特雷西
Ursula /'ɜːsjʊlə; 'ɝsjulə/ 欧秀拉
Vanessa /və'nesə; vəˈnɛsə/ 温内莎
Vera /'vɪərə; 'vɪrə/ 维拉
Veronica /və'rɒnɪkə; vəˈrɑnɪkə/ 维伦妮嘉
Victoria /vɪk'tɔːrɪə; vɪkˈtorɪə/ 维多利亚; **Vicky** /'vɪkɪ; 'vɪkɪ/ 维琪
Viola /'vaɪələ; 'vaɪələ/ 维奥拉
Violet /'vaɪələt; 'vaɪələt/ 瓦奥莱特
Virginia /və'dʒɪnɪə; vəˈdʒɪnjə/ 弗吉尼亚
Vivien(ne) /'vɪvɪən; 'vɪvɪən/ 维维恩
Wendy /'wendɪ; 'wɛndɪ/ 温迪
Winifred /'wɪnɪfrɪd; 'wɪnəfrɪd/ 威妮弗雷德; **Winnie** /'wɪnɪ; 'wɪnɪ/ 温妮
Yvonne /ɪ'vɒn; ɪˈvɑn/ 伊冯娜
Zoe /'zəʊɪ; 'zoˑɪ/ 佐伊

APPENDIX 8　THE WORKS OF WILLIAM SHAKESPEARE (1564—1616)
附录八　莎士比亚(1564—1616)的作品

Note: The list below includes the approximate date of composition, full title and common abbreviation; phonetic
transcriptions are provided where necessary.
注意: 下列之表包括作品完成的大约年代, 作品的全名及普通的缩写; 必要时并注有音标。

Plays　剧目

1590—1591	The First Part of King Henry VI (*I Hen VI*) 亨利六世(上)
	The Second Part of King Henry VI (*2 Hen VI*) 亨利六世(中)
	The Third Part of King Henry VI (*3 Hen VI*) 亨利六世(下)
1592—1593	The Tragedy of King Richard III (*Rich III*) 利查三世
	The Comedy of Errors (*Com Err*) 错中错
1593—1594	Titus Andronicus (*Titus A*) /ˌtaɪtəs ænˈdrɒnɪkəs; ˌtaɪtəs ænˈdrɑnɪkəs/ 泰特斯·安庄尼克斯
	The Taming of the Shrew (*Tam Shr*) 驯悍妇
1594—1595	The Two Gentlemen of Verona (*Two Gent*) /vəˈrəʊnə; vəˈronə/ 维洛那二绅士
	Love's Labour's Lost (*Love's L L*) 空爱一场
	Romeo and Juliet (*Rom & Jul*) /ˌrəʊmɪəʊ ən ˈdʒuːljət; ˌromɪo ən ˈdʒuljət/ 罗密欧与朱丽叶
1595—1596	The Tragedy of King Richard II (*Rich II*) 利查二世
	A Midsummer Night's Dream (*Mid N D*) 仲夏夜梦
1596—1597	The Life and Death of King John (*K John*) 约翰王
	The Merchant of Venice (*Mer of Ven*) /ˈvenɪs; ˈvɛnəs/ 威尼斯商人
1597—1598	The First Part of King Henry IV (*I Hen IV*) 亨利四世(上)
	The Second Part of King Henry IV (*2 Hen IV*) 亨利四世(下)
1598—1600	Much Ado about Nothing (*M Ado*) 无事自扰
	As You Like It (*As You L It*) 如愿
	Twelfth Night, or, What You Will (*Tw N*) 第十二夜
	The Life of King Henry V (*Hen V*) 亨利五世
	Julius Caesar (*Jul Caes*) /ˈdʒuːlɪəs ˈsiːzə(r); ˈdʒuljəs ˈsizə/ 朱利阿斯·西撒
1600—1601	Hamlet, Prince of Denmark (*Haml*) /ˈhæmlɪt; ˈhæmlət/ 哈姆雷特
	The Merry Wives of Windsor (*Merry W*) /ˈwɪnzə(r); ˈwɪnzə/ 温莎的风流妇人
1601—1602	Troilus and Cressida (*Tro & Cr*) /ˌtrɒɪləs n ˈkresɪdə; ˌtrɒɪləs n ˈkresədə/ 脱爱勒斯与克莱西达
	All's Well that Ends Well (*All's Well*) 皆大欢喜
1604—1605	Measure for Measure (*Meas for Meas*) 恶有恶报
	Othello, the Moor of Venice (*Oth*) /əˈθeləʊ; əˈθelo/ 奥赛罗
1605—1606	King Lear (*K Lear*) /lɪə(r); lɪr/ 李尔王
	Macbeth (*Macb*) /mækˈbeθ; məkˈbɛθ/ 马克白
1606—1607	Antony and Cleopatra (*Ant & Cleop*) /ˌæntənɪ ən ˌklɪəˈpætrə; ˌæntənɪ ən ˌklɪəˈpætrə/ 安东尼与克利欧佩特拉
1607—1608	Coriolanus (*Cor*) /ˌkɒrɪəˈleɪnəs US: ˌkɔːr-; ˌkɔrɪəˈlenəs/ 考利欧雷诺斯
	Timon of Athens (*Tim of Ath*) /ˌtaɪmən əv ˈæθənz; ˌtaɪmən əv ˈæθənz/ 雅典的泰蒙
1608—1610	Pericles, Prince of Tyre (*Per*) /ˈperɪkliːz; ˈpɛrəˌkliz/ 波里克利斯
	Cymbeline (*Cymb*) /ˈsɪmbəliːn; ˈsɪmbˌlɪn/ 辛伯林
	The Winter's Tale (*Wint T*) 冬天的故事
1611—1612	The Tempest (*Temp*) 暴风雨
1612—1613	The Famous History of the Life of King Henry VIII (*Hen VIII*) 亨利八世

Poems　诗集

(Date given is that of first printing) (年代系根据初版)

1593	Venus and Adonis (*Ven & Ad*) /ˌviːnəs n əˈdəʊnɪs US: əˈdɒnɪs; ˌvinəs n əˈdɑnəs/ 维纳斯与亚东尼斯
1594	The Rape of Lucrece (*Lucr*) /luːˈkriːs; luˈkris/ 路克丽丝的被奸
1601	The Phoenix and the Turtle (*Phoen & T*) 孔雀与海龟
1609	Sonnets (*Sonn*) 十四行诗
1609	A Lover's Complaint (*Lover's Comp*) 情人怨

APPENDIX 9 PUNCTUATION
附录九　标点使用法

Full Stop (US = Period) 句点

Used to mark the end of a sentence: 用以表示一个句子的结束:

Edward walked briskly into the hotel. The receptionist looked at him coldly. 爱德华轻快地步入旅馆。接待员冷淡地望着他。

Also ⇨ **Letters** and **Abbreviations** below. 亦参看下列之'书信'与'略语'。

? Question Mark 问号

1 Used at the end of a *direct question*: 用于'直接问句'之尾:

Who was the first to arrive? 谁是最先到达的?

(*Note*: It is not used at the end of an *indirect question*: 注意: 问号不用于'间接问句'之尾: *He asked who had been the first to arrive.* 他问谁是最先到达的)。

2 Used in parentheses to express doubt: 用于括弧内表示怀疑:

He was born in 1550(?) and died in 1613. 他生于 1550(?)年, 卒于 1613 年。

! Exclamation Mark (US also 美亦称 Exclamation Point) 感叹号

Used at the end of a sentence or remark expressing a high degree of anger, amazement or other strong emotion: 用于句尾或语尾表示高度的愤怒、惊异或其他强烈的感情:

'*What a wonderful surprise!*' *she cried.* '这真是一件令人惊喜的事!' 她大声说。

Get out of here and never come back! 滚出去, 永远不要再回来!

(*Note*: Beware of over-using exclamation marks, or including them where the emotion is only mild.) (注意: 当心不要过度使用感叹号, 或在仅表达平和感情的句中使用)。

, Comma 逗点

1 Used to separate the items in lists of words, phrases or clauses: 用以分开一系列的词、短语或从句:

Red, pink, yellow and white roses filled the huge vases. 那些大花瓶里装满了红的、粉红的、黄的和白的玫瑰花。

If you take your time, stay calm, concentrate and think ahead, you'll pass your driving test. 如果你不着急, 保持镇定, 集中精神注意前面, 你会通过驾驶考试的。

2 Sometimes used after a subordinate adverbial clause or after a phrase which comes before the main clause. It is essential after longer clauses and phrases, and to avoid ambiguity: 有时用于主要从句前面的附属副词从句或短语之后。在较长的从句或短语之后及为了避免意义含糊, 用逗点是必要的:

When the sun is shining brightly above, the world seems a happier place. 当太阳在天空中照耀的时候, 这个世界似乎是一个更快乐的地方。

In the summer of 1984, many trees died. 1984 年的夏季, 许多树木死去了。

3 Used after a non-finite or verbless clause at the beginning of a sentence: 用于句首带非限定动词形式的从句或无动词从句之后:

To get there on time, she left half an hour early. 为了准时到达那里, 她提早半小时离开。

Happy and contented, the cat feel asleep. 又快乐又满足, 那只猫睡着了。

4 Used to separate an introductory or transitional word or phrase (eg *therefore, however, by the way, for instance*) from the rest of the sentence: 用以将一导言的或转变语气的词或短语(如 therefore, however, by the way, for instance)与句中其余部分隔开:

Yes, it certainly had been an eventful day. 是的, 那确实是一个多事之日。

In fact, I don't even know her name. 说实在的, 我甚至不知道她的姓名。

Driving on icy roads can be dangerous and one should, therefore, be very careful. 在覆盖着冰的道路上驾驶有发生危险的可能性, 因此我们应当十分小心。

5 Used before and after any element (eg a dependent clause, a comment) which interrupts the sentence: 用于任何打断一句的部分(例如一附属从句, 评论)之前后:

The fire, although it had been burning for several hours, was still blazing fiercely. 虽然燃烧了好几个小时, 但火势仍很凶猛。

You should, indeed you must, report the matter to the police. 你应该, 说实在的你必须, 把这事向警方报告。

6 Used before and after a non-defining relative clause, or a phrase in apposition, which gives more information about the noun it follows: 用于进一步说明其前之名词的非限制关系从句或同位语之前后:

The Pennine Hills, which have been a favourite with hikers for many years, are situated between Lancashire and

Yorkshire. 奔宁山脉位于兰开夏郡与约克郡之间，许多年来是一个远足者所喜爱的地方。

Queen Elizabeth II, a very popular monarch, celebrated her Silver Jubilee in 1977. 伊丽莎白女王二世为一深受人民爱戴的女王，在 1977 年庆祝她在位二十五周年纪念。

(Note: No commas are used around a relative clause that *defines* the noun it follows: 注意: 在 '限制' 其前之名词的关系从句之前后不用逗点: *The hills that separate Lancashire from Yorkshire are called The Pennines.* 把兰开夏郡和约克郡分开的山峦叫做奔宁山脉）。

7 Sometimes used to separate main clauses linked by a conjunction (eg *and, as, but, for, or*), especially when the first clause is long: 有时用来分隔由一连接词(例如 and, as, but, for, or) 连接的主要从句，尤其当第一个从句过长时:

We had been looking forward to meeting Sarah's husband, but discovered that he was not as pleasant as we had hoped. 我们曾一直盼望能见到莎拉的丈夫，然而却发现他并不象我们所期望的那样讨人喜欢。

Also ⇨ **Conversation** and **Letters** below. 亦参看下列之 '会话' 与 '书信'。

: Colon 冒号

1 (Formal) Used after a main clause where the following statement illustrates or explains the content of that clause. It may be replaced by a semicolon or a full stop: (正式用法)用于一主要从句后，其后的陈述进一步说明该主要从句的含义。冒号可由一分号或句点代替:

The garden hed been neglected for a long time: it was overgrown and full of weeds. 那花园曾长期乏人照料: 里面植物蔓生而且还长满了杂草。

2 Used before a long list, and often introduced by phrases such as: *such as: for example: for instance: in the following examples: as follows:* 用于一长列项目前，并常在 such as: for example: for instance: in the following examples: as follows: 等短语之后:

Your first aid kit should include the following items: cotton wool, lint, antiseptic lotion, sticking plaster, bandages and safety pins. 你的急救工具应包括下列各项: 棉花, 绷带麻布, 消毒药水, 橡皮膏, 绷带和安全别针。

Also ⇨ **Letters** and **Quotations** below. 亦参看下列之 '书信' 及 '引用文'。

; Semicolon 分号

1 (Formal) Used to separate main clauses, not (usually) joined by a conjunction, which are considered so closely connected as to belong to one sentence: (正式用法)用来分隔(通常)没有连接词连接的主要从句，这些主要从句被认为关系密切而属于一个句子:

The sun was setting now; the shadows were long. 太阳正在沉落; 阴影显得很长。

He had never been to Russia before; however, it had always been one of his life-long ambitions. 他以前从未去过俄国; 然而，这一直是他的终生目标之一。

2 Used instead of a comma to separate from each other parts of a sentence that are already separated by commas: 用来代替逗点，分隔业经由逗点分开的句中部分:

There are two facts to consider: first, the weather; second, the expense. 有两项事实要考虑: 第一, 天气; 第二, 费用。

—— Dash 破折号

1 (Colloq) Used instead of a colon or a semicolon to make the writing more vivid or dramatic: (口)用以代替冒号或分号，使写作较生动或动人:

Sirens blared, men shouted, and people crowded in to witness the scene—it was chaos. 号笛响起, 人们在叫喊, 而一大堆人涌进来目睹这景象——那是一团混乱。

So you've been lying to me for years and years—how can I ever trust you again? 既然这些年来你一直在骗我——我怎能再信任你呢?

2 (Colloq) Used singly or in pairs to separate extra information, an after-thought or a comment, in a vivid or dramatic way, from the rest of the sentence: (口)单一或成双使用，将一额外说明，事后想起的解释或评论生动地与句中其余部分隔开:

Schooldays are the happiest days of our lives—or so we are told. 求学时代是我们一生中最幸福的日子——或者据说是如此。

Schooldays—or so we are told—are the happiest days of our lives. 求学时代——或者据说是如此——是我们一生中最幸福的日子。

(Note: In more formal usage, parentheses or commas replace dashes.) (注意: 在较正式用法中，以括弧或逗点代替破折号。)

Also ⇨ **Conversation** below. 亦参看下列之 '会话'。

( ) Parentheses (GB also 英亦称 **Brackets**) 括弧

1 Used to separate extra information, an after-thought or a comment from the rest of the sentence: 用来将一额外说明，事后想起的解释或评论与句中其余部分隔开:

Schooldays (so we are told) are the happiest days of our lives. 求学时代(据说是如此)是我们一生中最幸福的日子。

He said he'd never seen the sea before (but I think he was joking). 他说他以前从未看到过海(不过我想他是在开玩笑)。

2 Used to enclose cross-references: 用以括起表示互相参照之说明:

The abacus (see the picture on page 1) is used for teaching numbers to children.　算盘(参看第一页之插图)是用来教儿童算术的。

' ' Quotation Marks (GB also 英亦称 Inverted Commas) 引号

(*Note*: In GB usage they are usually single: '*Fire!*' In US usage they are usually double: "*Fire!*")　(注意: 英国通常是用单引号: 'Fire!' 美国通常是用双引号: "Fire!")

Used around a slang or technical term when it is in a context in which it is not usually found, or around a word to which the writer wishes to draw particular attention: 用来括起不常出现在上下文中之俚语或专门用语, 或括起作者希望特别引起注意的字:

Next, the clay pot had to be 'fired'.　其次, 土罐必须加以'烘烧'。

He called himself a 'gentleman', but you would never have thought so from the way he behaved.　他自认为是一个'绅士', 但是从他的行为看来, 你绝不会认为他是绅士。

Also ⇨ **Conversation** and **Quotations** below.　亦参看下列之'会话'与'引用文'。

- Hyphen 连字符

(*Note*: It must not be confused with the dash, which separates parts of a sentence. The hyphen is half the length of the dash.)　(注意: 连字符不可与破折号相混, 后者分隔句中的若干部分。连字符的长度为破折号的一半。)

1 Sometimes used to form a compound word from two other words: 有时用以连接两个词形成一复合词:

hard-hearted; 无情的;　*radio-telescope;* 无线电望远镜;　*fork-lift truck.* 又式起重车。

2 Used to form a compound word from a prefix and a proper name: 用以连接一字首和一专有名词而形成一复合词:

pre-Raphaelite; 前拉斐尔派的;　*pro-Soviet;* 亲苏的;　*anti-Nazi.* 反纳粹的。

3 Used to form a compound word from two other words which are separated by a preposition: 用以连接中间加一介词的两个字, 而形成一复合词:

mother-in-law; 岳母;　*mother-to-be;* 孕妇;　*mother-of-pearl;* 真珠母;　*out-of-date.* 过时的。

4 (Esp GB) Sometimes used to separate a prefix ending in a vowel from a word beginning with that same vowel: (尤用于英国)有时用以分隔一字首与一字, 若该字首的末尾字母与该字起首的字母为相同的母音:

co-ordination; 同等;　*re-elect;* 再选;　*pre-eminent.* 超群的。

Also ⇨ **Introduction**: page xvi (*A compound*); page xxii (*How to divide a word*).　亦参看'绪论'第 xvi 页(复合字); 第 xxii 页(怎样断字)。

' Apostrophe 省略号; 所有格符号

1 Used with 's' to indicate the possessive: 与 's' 连用表示所有格:

Singular noun: 单数名词: *the dog's* /dɒgz/ *dog's/ bone.* 狗的骨头。

Singular noun ending in 's': 字尾为 's' 的单数名词: *the princess's* /prɪn'sesɪz/ 'prɪnsɪsɪz/ *smile.* 公主的微笑。

Singular proper noun ending in 's' (two possible forms): 字尾为 's' 的单数专有名词(两种可能的形式): *King Charles's* /'tʃɑːlzɪz/ *crown; King Charles'* /'tʃɑːlzɪz/ 'tʃɑːlzɪz/ *crown.* 查理王的王冠。

Plural noun: 复数名词: *students'* /'stjuːdənts/ 'stjudɪ̩nts/ *books.* 学生们的书。

Irregular plural: 不规则的复数: *men's* /menz/ menz/ *jackets.* 男人的夹克。

2 Used in a *contracted form* to indicate the omission of letters or figures: 用于'缩写式'表示省略字母或数字:

I'm (=I am); *he's* (=he is/has); *they'd* (=they would/had). *In '87* (=1987).

3 Used with 's' to form the plural of a letter, a figure or an abbreviation, when these are used as proper words. In modern usage it is often omitted after a figure or a capital letter: 当某一字母、数字或略语作普通字用时, 与 's' 连用形成复数。在现代用法中, 在一数字或大写字母后, 此号常被省去:

in the 1960's or 或 *in the 1960s.* 在二十世纪六十年代。*MP's* or 或 *MPs.*

He can't pronounce his r's. 他的 r 音发不出来。

4 Used with 's' to form the plural of a word (eg a preposition or a conjunction) that does not usually have a plural: 与 's' 连用形成一个通常没有复数的词(如介词或连接词)之复数:

No if's or but's—just do as I say. 不要'假如'或'但是'——只是照我说的去做。

Abbreviations 略语

1 A full stop may end an abbreviation or a person's initials, although this is becoming less common, especially in GB usage: 在一略语或姓名的起首字母略语后可用句点, 不过这种用法, 尤其是在英国, 越来越不常见:

Mr. R. S. H. Smith or 或 *Mr R S H Smith.*

2 When the abbreviation consists of capitals, it is common GB usage to omit the full stops: 略语由大写字母构成时, 英国的普遍用法是省去句点:

UN WHO BBC

3 The omission of full stops in a lower case abbreviation is less common: 在小写字母构成的略语中省去句点较不

常见:
i. e. p.m. e.g. or 或 *ie pm eg*

4 If the abbreviation includes the last letter of the word, it is usual in GB usage to omit the full stop: 一词之略语如包括该词最后一个字母时,在英国的用法通常是省去句点:
Mr Dr St Rd

5 To form the plural of capital letter abbreviations, add a lower case *'s* or *s*: 大写字母构成的略语,其复数是加一小写的 *'s* 或 *s*:
MP's or 或 *MPs TV's* or 或 *TVs*
Also ⇨ **Appendix 2** *(Abbreviations)*. 亦参看附录二(略语表)。

Conversation 会话

1 A new indented paragraph is begun with each new speaker. 每当换一说话者时,要新起一段,并且第一行应缩进排印或书写。

2 Quotation marks enclose all words and punctuation in direct speech: 直接叙述时,引号将所有的词及标点括进:
'What on earth did you do that for?' he asked. '你做那事究竟是为了什么?'他问道。

3 Introductory words (eg *he said, she cried, they answered*) are separated from the actual words spoken by **commas** if no other punctuation mark (eg question mark, exclamation mark) is used: 如无其他标点(例如问号,感叹号)时,引导的词(例如 he said, she cried, they answered) 与实际说的话之间用逗点分开:
John said, 'That's all I know. 约翰说,'那就是我所知道的一切'。*'That's all I know,' said John.* '那就是我所知道的一切,'约翰说。 *'That,' said John, 'is all I know.'* '那些,'约翰说,'就是我所知道的一切。'*'Why?' asked John.* '为什么?'约翰问道。

4 A comma separates a question tag from the rest of the sentence: 附加问句与句中其余部分之间用逗点分开:
'You knew he'd come, didn't you?' '你知道他会来,是不是?'

5 A mild interjection or the direct use of a name is separated from the rest of the sentence by a comma: 不强烈的感叹语或直呼的姓名与句中其余部分用逗点分开:
'Oh, so that's what he wanted.' '噢,那么那就是他所要的了。'(Cf 参较 *'Oh no! I don't believe you!'* '啊不!我不相信你!')
'Well, Peter, I did my best.' '唔,彼得,我尽了我的力了。'(Cf 参较 *'Peter! Look out!'* '彼得!当心!')

6 Hesitant or interrupted speech can be indicated by dashes: 犹豫或打断的话可用破折号表示:
'Can I—I mean, would you mind if I came too?' '我可以——我是说,我也来你会介意吗?'
'You'll find it in—' were his dying words. '你会发现它在——'他临终时此说。

7 Speech within speech is shown by (GB usage) double quotation marks inside single marks, or (US usage) single quotation marks within double marks: 直接叙述中如再有直接叙述是由单引号中加双引号表示(英国用法),或双引号中加单引号(美国用法):
'When the judge said, "Not guilty," I could have hugged him.' (GB) "当那法官说'无罪'时,我真想拥抱他。'(英)
"When the judge said, 'Not guilty,' I could have hugged him." (US) "当那法官说'无罪'时,我真想拥抱他。"(美)

Letters 书信

1 A business letter is set out as shown below. The punctuation marks are optional. The address of the person who is writing the letter is in the top right-hand corner; the address of the person to whom the letter is being written is in the top left-hand corner, but below the address of the sender: 商业书信的格式如下列所示。其标点符号可用可不用。写信人的地址在右上角;收信人的地址在左上角,但在写信人的地址之下:

> 3 Willow Street,
> Frambleton,
> Suffolk,
> SF5 9PK.
> 6th June, 1984.

Mr D. B. Taylor,
Metalwork Ltd,
Booth Street,
Ormton,
Lancashire.
LC14 3JQ.
Dear Mr Taylor,
Thank you for ...
Yours faithfully/sincerely/(US) truly,
[signature]
Mary Burton.

2 In US usage, a colon is substituted for the comma in the salutation, except informally: 美国用法中,信头之称呼是以冒号代替逗点,但非正式的信函不在此例:
Dear Ms Burton: but 但 *Dear Mary,*

3 In an informal letter, only the address of the sender is necessary, the optional punctuation is more likely to be

omitted, and *Yours sincerely* etc is replaced by a more friendly or personal phrase, eg *Yours, Yours affectionately, With best / warm wishes, With love.* 非正式书信中，仅须写发信人的地址，可以不使用的标点省去的机会更大，而 Yours sincerely 等则由较友好或亲切的短语如 Yours, Yours affectionately, With best / warm wishes, With love 等代替。

Quotations 引用文

1 The quotation is separated from its introduction by a colon and is enclosed by quotation marks: 引用文置于引导语及冒号之后，并由引号括起：
   It was Disraeli who said: 'Little things affect little minds.' 迪斯雷利说过：'小事情会影响小心眼的人。'

2 If a word or phrase is omitted from the quotation, this is indicated by a row of three dots (...): 如果引用文中省略字或短语，用连续三点(…)表示：
   'The condition of man ... is a condition of war of everyone against everyone.' (Thomas Hobbes) '人类的性格…即是你争我夺。'(汤玛斯·霍布士)
   Also ⇨ **Conversation** above. 亦参看上列之'会话'。

APPENDIX 10 THE BOOKS OF THE BIBLE
附录十　圣经目录

The Old Testament　旧约全书

Genesis (Gen) /'dʒenəsɪs; 'dʒɛnəsəs/ 创世记
Exodus (Exod) /'eksədəs; 'ɛksədəs/ 出埃及记
Leviticus (Lev) /lɪ'vɪtɪkəs; lɪ'vɪtɪkəs/ 利未记
Numbers (Num) /'nʌmbəz; 'nʌmbɚz/ 民数记
Deuteronomy (Deut) /ˌdjuːtə'rɒnəmɪ US: ˌduː-; ˌdutə'rɑnəmɪ/ 申命记
Joshua (Josh) /'dʒɒʃuə; 'dʒɑʃuə/ 约书亚记
Judges (Judg) /'dʒʌdʒɪz; 'dʒʌdʒəz/ 士师记
Ruth /ruːθ; ruθ/ 路得记
I Samuel (I Sam) /'sæmjuəl; 'sæmjʊəl/ 撒母耳记上
II Samuel (II Sam) /'sæmjuəl; 'sæmjʊəl/ 撒母耳记下
I Kings (I Kgs) /kɪŋz; kɪŋz/ 列王纪上
II Kings (II Kgs) /kɪŋz; kɪŋz/ 列王纪下
I Chronicles (I Chron) /'krɒnɪklz; 'krɑnɪklz/ 历代志上
II Chronicles (II Chron) /'krɒnɪklz; 'krɑnɪklz/ 历代志下
Ezra /'ezrə; 'ɛzrə/ 以斯拉记
Nehemiah (Neh) /ˌniːə'maɪə; ˌniə'maɪə/ 尼希米记
Esther /'estə(r); 'ɛstɚ/ 以斯帖记
Job /dʒəʊb; dʒob/ 约伯记
Psalms (Ps) /sɑːmz; sɑmz/ 诗篇
Proverbs (Prov) /'prɒvɜːbz; 'prɑvɚbz/ 箴言

Ecclesiastes (Eccles) /ɪˌkliːzɪ'æstiːz; ɪkˌliːzɪ'æstiz/ 传道书
Song of Solomon /ˌsɒŋ əv 'sɒləmən US: ˌsɔːŋ; ˌsɔŋ əv 'sɑləmən/ or 或 Song of Songs (S of S) 雅歌
Isaiah (Isa) /aɪ'zaɪə US: aɪ'zeɪə; aɪ'zeə/ 以赛亚书
Jeremiah (Jer) /ˌdʒerɪ'maɪə; ˌdʒɛrə'maɪə/ 耶利米书
Lamentations (Lam) /ˌlæmən'teɪʃnz; ˌlæmən'teʃənz/ 耶利米哀歌
Ezekiel (Ezek) /ɪ'ziːkɪəl; ɪ'zikɪəl/ 以西结书
Daniel (Dan) /'dænɪəl; 'dænjəl/ 但以理书
Hosea (Hos) /həʊ'zɪːə; ho'zie/ 何西阿书
Joel /'dʒəʊəl; 'dʒoəl/ 约珥书
Amos /'eɪmɒs US: -məs; 'eməs/ 阿摩司书
Obadiah (Obad) /ˌəʊbə'daɪə; ˌobə'daɪə/ 俄巴底亚书
Jonah /'dʒəʊnə; 'dʒonə/ 约拿书
Micah /'maɪkə; 'maɪkə/ 弥迦书
Nahum /'neɪhəm; 'ne(h)əm/ 那鸿书
Habakkuk (Hab) /'hæbəkək US: hə'bækək; hə'bækək/ 哈巴谷书
Zephaniah (Zeph) /ˌzefə'naɪə; ˌzɛfə'naɪə/ 西番雅书
Haggai (Hag) /'hægeɪaɪ US: 'hægaɪ; 'hægɪˌaɪ/ 哈该书
Zechariah (Zech) /ˌzekə'raɪə; ˌzɛkə'raɪə/ 撒迦利亚书
Malachi (Mal) /'mæləkaɪ; 'mælə,kaɪ/ 玛拉基书

The Apocrypha /ə'pɒkrɪfə; ə'pɑkrəfə/　伪经

Tobit /'təʊbɪt; 'tobət/ 透比书
Judith /'dʒuːdɪθ; 'dʒudəθ/ 朱迪丝书
Wisdom /'wɪzdəm; 'wɪzdəm/ 智慧论
Ecclesiasticus /ɪˌkliːzɪ'æstɪkəs; ɪkˌlizɪ'æstɪkəs/ 不经之书

Baruch /'beərək; 'bɛrək/ 巴鲁书
I Maccabees /'mækəbiz; 'mækəbiz/ 麦克比斯前书
II Maccabees /'mækəbiːz; 'mækəbiz/ 麦克比斯后书

The New Testament　新约全书

St Matthew (Matt) /'mæθjuː; 'mæθju/ 马太福音
St Mark /mɑːk; mɑrk/ 马可福音
St Luke /luːk; luk/ 路加福音
St John /dʒɒn; dʒɑn/ 约翰福音
Acts /ækts; ækts/ 使徒行传
Romans (Rom) /'rəʊmənz; 'romənz/ 罗马书
I Corinthians (I Cor) /kə'rɪnθɪənz; kə'rɪnθɪənz/ 哥林多前书
II Corinthians (II Cor) /kə'rɪnθɪənz; kə'rɪnθɪənz/ 哥林多后书
Galatians (Gal) /gə'leɪʃnz; gə'leʃənz/ 加拉太书
Ephesians (Eph) /ɪ'fiːʒnz; ɪ'fiʒənz/ 以弗所书
Philippians (Phil) /fɪ'lɪpɪənz; fə'lɪpɪənz/ 腓立比书
Colossians (Col) /kə'lɒʃnz; kə'lɑʃənz/ 哥罗西书
I Thessalonians (I Thess) /ˌθesə'ləʊnɪənz; ˌθɛsə'lonɪənz/ 帖撒罗尼迦前书

II Thessalonians (II Thess) /ˌθesə'ləʊnɪənz; ˌθɛsə'lonɪənz/ 帖撒罗尼迦后书
I Timothy (I Tim) /'tɪməθɪ; 'tɪməθɪ/ 提摩太前书
II Timothy (II Tim) /'tɪməθɪ; 'tɪməθɪ/ 提摩太后书
Titus (Tit) /'taɪtəs; 'taɪtəs/ 提多书
Philemon (Philem) /fɪ'liːmən; fə'limən/ 腓利门书
Hebrews (Heb) /'hiːbruːz; 'hibruz/ 希伯来书
James (Jas) /dʒeɪmz; dʒemz/ 雅各书
I Peter (I Pet) /'piːtə(r); 'pitə/ 彼得前书
II Peter (II Pet) /'piːtə(r); 'pitə/ 彼得后书
I John /dʒɒn; dʒɑn/ 约翰一书
II John /dʒɒn; dʒɑn/ 约翰二书
III John /dʒɒn; dʒɑn/ 约翰三书
Jude /dʒuːd; dʒud/ 犹大书
Revelation (Rev) /ˌrevə'leɪʃn; ˌrɛvə'leʃən/ or 或 Apocalypse /ə'pɒkəlɪps; ə'pakə,lɪps/ 启示录

Key to the verb patterns 动词类型例释(详见xxxiii-xlviii页)

S=Subject 主语　　*vi*=intransitive verb　不及物动词　　*vt*=transitive verb 及物动词
DO=Direct Object 直接宾词　　IO=Indirect Object 间接宾词

[VP1]　　S+BE+subject complement／adjunct
　　　　　This is a book／where I work.

[VP2A]　S+*vi*
　　　　　The moon rose.

[VP2B]　S+*vi*+(*for*)+adverbial adjunct
　　　　　We walked (for) five miles.

[VP2C]　S+*vi*+adverbial adjunct
　　　　　Go away／Come in.

[VP2D]　S+*vi*+adjective／noun／pronoun
　　　　　She married young.

[VP2E]　S+*vi*+present participle
　　　　　They've gone dancing.

[VP3A]　S+*vi*+preposition+noun／pronoun
　　　　　You can rely on me.

[VP3B]　S+*vi*+(preposition (+*it*))+clause
　　　　　Have you decided (on) what to do next?

[VP4A]　S+*vi*+*to*-infinitive
　　　　　We stopped to rest.

[VP4B]　S+*vi*+*to*-infinitive
　　　　　He awoke to find the house on fire.

[VP4C]　S+*vi*+*to*-infinitive
　　　　　He agreed to come at once.

[VP4D]　S+SEEM／APPEAR+(*to be*)+adjective／noun
　　　　　He seemed (to be) surprised at the news.

[VP4E]　S+SEEM／APPEAR／HAPPEN／CHANCE+*to*-infinitive
　　　　　She appears to have left already.

[VP4F]　S+BE+*to*-infinitive
　　　　　At what time am I to come?

[VP5]　　S+anomalous finite+infinitive
　　　　　You needn't wait.

[VP6A]　S+*vt*+noun／pronoun
　　　　　Everyone likes her.

[VP6B]　S+*vt*+noun／pronoun
　　　　　She has green eyes.

[VP6C]　S+*vt*+gerund
　　　　　She enjoys playing tennis.

[VP6D]　S+*vt*+gerund
　　　　　He began talking about his family

[VP6E]　S+NEED／WANT／BEAR+gerund
　　　　　He needs looking after.

[VP7A]　S+*vt*+(*not*)+*to*-infinitive
　　　　　I forgot to post your letter.

[VP7B]　S+HAVE／OUGHT+(*not*)+*to*-infinitive
　　　　　He often has to work overtime.

[VP8]　　S+*vt*+interrogative pronoun／adverb+*to*-infinitive
　　　　　I couldn't decide what to do next.

[VP9]　　S+*vt*+*that*-clause
　　　　　Do you think (that) it will rain?

[VP10]　S+*vt*+dependent clause／question
　　　　　Does anyone know how it happened?